SENIOR HIGH
CORE COLLECTION

TWENTIETH EDITION

CORE COLLECTION SERIES

FORMERLY
STANDARD CATALOG SERIES

MARIA HUGGER, GENERAL EDITOR

CHILDREN'S CORE COLLECTION
MIDDLE AND JUNIOR HIGH CORE COLLECTION
SENIOR HIGH CORE COLLECTION
PUBLIC LIBRARY CORE COLLECTION: NONFICTION
FICTION CORE COLLECTION
GRAPHIC NOVELS CORE COLLECTION
YOUNG ADULT FICTION CORE COLLECTION

SENIOR HIGH
CORE COLLECTION

TWENTIETH EDITION

EDITED BY

JULIE CORSARO, MLIS

KENDAL SPIRES, MLIS

GABRIELA TOTH, MLIS

AND

MARIA HUGGER, MLIS

H. W. Wilson
A Division of EBSCO Information Services
Ipswich, Massachusetts
2016
GREY HOUSE PUBLISHING

ISBN 978-1-68217-069-4

Abridged Dewey Decimal Classification and Relative Index, Edition 15 is © 2004-2012 OCLC Online Computer Library Center, Inc. Used with Permission. DDC, Dewey, Dewey Decimal Classification, and WebDewey are registered trademarks of OCLC.

Senior High Core Collection, 2016, published by Grey House Publishing, Inc., Amenia, NY, under exclusive license from EBSCO Infomation Systems, Inc.

A catalog record for this title is available from the Library of Congress.

PRINTED IN CANADA

CONTENTS

CONTENTS

PREFACE

SENIOR HIGH CORE COLLECTION is a selective list of books recommended for grades nine through twelve, together with professional aids for librarians and library media specialists. This list is available in full as an EBSCO*host* database, updated weekly. Printed versions are published approximately every two years and contain *Most Highly Recommended* and *Core Collection* books, the top recommended titles in the database. Additional metadata for these titles, plus book reviews and all of the *Supplementary* and *Archival Materials* levels, appear only in the database available via EBSCO. Go to www.ebscohost.com/public/core-collections for more information or for a trial.

What's new in this Edition?

The twentieth edition includes more than 8,600 book titles. There are broad revisions in the areas of computers, math, and the sciences. Special attention was paid to STEM titles. An expanded list of works for the librarian or media specialist includes bibliographies and other resources for the selection and evaluation of materials; library management and programming; library building design; and the use of the Internet in instruction. This volume includes a generous selection of graphic novels, even though a more comprehensive collection of recommended graphic novels can be found in GRAPHIC NOVELS CORE COLLECTION on EBSCO*host*.

History

The first edition of the Collection was published in 1926 as an author-title list, followed by a fuller version in 1928 that also included a subject index and analytical entries. After the appearance of the second edition in 1932 the Collection was published regularly every five years. Initially it was called *Standard Catalog for High School Libraries*, but when *Junior High School Library Catalog* (now *Middle and Junior High Core Collection*) was introduced in 1965, its scope was changed. It became *Senior High School Library Catalog* in the ninth edition, published in 1967. With the seventeenth edition in 2007 the title was changed to *Senior High Core Collection*.

Scope

Like the previous edition, titles that are considered "most highly recommended." These titles constitute a short list of the essential books in a given category or on a given subject. There are often a number of recommended titles on a single subject, such as biographies of Abraham Lincoln, and the Short List designation helps a user who wants only one or two. A star (★) at the start of an entry indicates that a book is a "most highly recommended" title. All books listed are published in the United States, or published in Canada or the United Kingdom and distributed in the United States.

The Core Collection excludes the following: non-English-language materials, with the exception of bilingual materials, dictionaries, and similar items; works of adult fiction other than books originally written for adults but read by young people or books widely used in the curriculum; textbooks; and books about individual computer programs or versions of programs, and other topics that quickly become outdated.

Beginning with the printing of the nineteenth edition, the collection also excludes most works widely known as "classic literature." This was done as an effort to both save space, and to concentrate on recommending titles that are perhaps less well-known. Additionally, extensive conversations with high school librarians indicated that additions of classics to the collection were primarily based on local curricula, not on recommendations from the Core Collection. While some classics remain in the abridged print collection, the removed titles can still be found in the full EBSCO*host* database under the Recommendation Levels "Supplementary Materials" and "Archival."

Preparation

Books included in this edition were selected by experienced librarians representing public library systems and senior high libraries across the United States who also act as a committee of advisors on library policy and trends. The names of participating librarians and their affiliations are listed in the Acknowledgments. EBSCO invites feedback from Core Collections customers at corecollections@ebsco.com.

Organization

The Core Collection is organized into two parts: the Classified Collection; and an Author, Title, and Subject Index.

Part 1. Classified Collection. This is arranged according to the Dewey Decimal Classification. Within classes, arrangement is by main entry, with complete bibliographical and cataloging information given for each book. The classified arrangement, along with the descriptive and critical annotations, provides a useful guide to book selection. Entries include such information as price and ISBN to facilitate acquisitions.

Part 2. Author, Title, and Subject Index. This is a comprehensive key to the Classified List with entries for authors, titles, and subjects.

ACKNOWLEDGMENTS

H. W. Wilson and EBSCO Information Services express special gratitude to the following librarians who both advised the company in editorial matters and assisted in the selection and weeding of titles for this Core Collection:

Advisory Board

James Bobick
Retired, Science & Technology Department
    Head
Carnegie Library of Pittsburgh
Pittsburgh, Pennsylvania

Angela Carstensen
Director of Library & Information Services
Convent of the Sacred Heart
Greenwich, New York

Gail de Vos
Storyteller, Author & Educator
Adjunct Associate Professor
University of Alberta
Edmonton, Alberta, Canada

Laura Harrington
North Andover High School
North Andover, Massachusetts

Pam Spencer Holley
YA Literature Consultant
Hallwood, Virginia

Steven Jablonski
Collection Development Librarian
Skokie Public Library
Skokie, Illinois

Joquetta Johnson
Randallstown High School
Randallstown, Maryland

Angela Leeper
Director of Curriculum Materials Center
University of Richmond
Richmond, Virginia

John Meier
Science Librarian
Penn State University
University Park, Pennsylvania

John Peters
Children's Literature Specialist
Bronx, New York

Mary Rasner
Library Consultant
Melrose, Massachusetts

DIRECTIONS FOR USE OF THE
CORE COLLECTION

USES OF THE COLLECTION

SENIOR HIGH CORE COLLECTION is designed to serve a number of purposes:

As an aid in purchasing. The Core Collection is designed to assist in the selection and ordering of titles. Annotations are provided for each title along with information concerning the publisher, ISBN, price, and availability. Since Part 1, Classified Collection, is arranged according to the Dewey Decimal Classification, the Core Collection may be used to identify parts of the library collection that should be updated or strengthened. In evaluating the suitability of a work each library will want to consider the special character of the school and/or community it serves.

As an aid to the reader's advisor. The work of the reader's advisor is furthered by the information about sequels and companion volumes and the descriptive and critical annotations in the Classified Collection, and by the subject access in the Index.

As an aid in verification of information. For this purpose, full bibliographical data are provided in the Classified Collection. Entries also include recommended subject headings based upon *Sears List of Subject Headings* and a suggested classification derived from the *Abridged Dewey Decimal Classification and Relative Index*. Notes describe editions available, awards, publication history, and other titles in the series.

As an aid in curriculum support. The classified approach, subject indexing, grade levels, and annotations are helpful in identifying materials appropriate for lesson planning and classroom use.

As an aid in collection maintenance. Information about titles available on a subject facilitates decisions to rebind, replace, or discard items. If a book has been deleted from the Core Collection in this edition because it is no longer in print, that deletion is not intended as a sign that the book is no longer valuable or that it should necessarily be weeded from the collection.

As an instructional aid. The Core Collection is useful in courses that deal with literature and book selection for young people.

ORGANIZATION

The Core Collection consists of two parts: a Classified Collection, and an Author, Title, and Subject Index.

Part 1. Classified Collection

The Classified Collection is arranged with nonfiction books first, classified according to the Dewey Decimal Classification in numerical order from 000 to 999. Individual biographies are classed at 92 and precede the 920s (collective biography). Fiction books (Fic) follow the nonfiction. Short story collections (S C) follow fiction. The information supplied for each book includes bibliographic description, suggested subject headings, an annotation, and frequently, an evaluation from a notable source.

An Outline of Classification, which serves as a table of contents for the Classified Collection, is reproduced following this section. It should be noted that many topics can be classified in more than one discipline. If a particular title is not found where it might be expected, the Index should be consulted to determine if it is classified elsewhere.

Within classes, works are arranged alphabetically under main entry, usually the author. Works of individual biography are arranged alphabetically under the biography's subject.

Each listing consists of a full bibliographical description. Prices, which are always subject to change, have been obtained from the publisher, when available, and are as current as possible. Entries include recommended subject headings derived from the *Sears List of Subject Headings,* a suggested classification number from the *Abridged Dewey Decimal Classification and Relative Index,* a brief description of the contents, and, whenever possible, an evaluation from a quoted source. The following is an example of a typical entry and a description of its components:

> **Chbosky, Stephen**
> ★ The **perks** of being a wallflower; [by] Stephen
> Chbosky. Pocket Bks. 1999 213p pa $12
> Grades: 9 10 11 12   **Fic**
> 1. School stories 2. Letters -- Fiction 3. Young
> men -- Social life and customs -- 20th century
> ISBN 0-671-02734-4
>   LC 99-236288
> This novel in letter form is narrated by Charlie,
> a high school freshman. "His favorite aunt passed
> away, and his best friend just committed suicide. The
> girl he loves wants him as a friend; a girl he does not
> love wants him as a lover. His 18-year-old sister is
> pregnant. The LSD he took is not sitting well. And he
> has a math quiz looming. . . . Young adult." (Time)
>   "Charlie, his friends, and family are palpably real.
> . . .This report on his life will engage teen readers for
> years to come." SLJ

The star at the start of the entry indicates this is a "most highly recommended" title. The name of the author, Stephen Chbosky, is given in conformity with *Anglo-American Cataloguing Rules,* 2nd edition, 2002 revision. The title of the book is *The perks of being a wallflower.* The book was published by Pocket Books in 1999.

The book has 213 pages and does not contain illustrations. It is published in paperback, and sells for $12.00. (Prices given were current when the Collection went to press.) The book is recommended for any of the following grade levels: 9 10 11 12.

At the end of the last line of type in the body entry is **Fic** in boldface type. This is the classification number or category derived from the fifteenth edition of the *Abridged Dewey Decimal Classification.* The notation "Fic" implies that the book is a work of fiction.

The numbered terms "1. School stories 2. Letters -- Fiction 3. Young men -- Social life and customs -- 20th century" are recommended subject headings for this book based on *Sears List of Subject Headings.*

The ISBN (International Standard Book Number) is included to facilitate ordering. The Library of Congress control number is provided when available.

Following are three notes supplying additional information about the book. The first is a description of the book's content, in this case, an excerpt from *Time* magazine. The second is a critical note from *School Library Journal.* Such annotations are useful in evaluating books for selection and in determining which of several books on the same subject is best suited for the individual reader. The final note describes special features, such as a bibliography, if applicable. Notes are also made to describe sequels and companion volumes, editions available, awards, and publication history.

Part 2. Author, Title, and Subject Index

The Index is a single alphabetical list of all the books entered in the Core Collection. Each book is entered under author; title (if distinctive); and subject. The classification number, displayed in boldface type, is the key to the location of the main entry for the book in the Classified Collection.

Appropriate added entries are made for joint authors and editors. "See" references are made from forms of names or subjects that are not used as headings. "See also" references are made to related or more specific headings.

The following are examples of Index entries for the book cited above:

Author	**Chbosky, Stephen**	
	The perks of being a wallflower	**Fic**
Title	The **perks** of being a wallflower. Chbosky, S.	**Fic**
Subject	**LETTERS -- FICTION**	
	Chbosky, S. The perks of being a wallflower	**Fic**

Standards Used

Anglo-American Cataloguing Rules, 2nd ed., 2002 revision, 2005 update. Chicago: American Library Association, 2005.

Bristow, Barbara A. and Christi Showman Farrar, eds. *Sears List of Subject Headings*. 21st ed. Ipswich, MA: The H. W. Wilson Company, 2014.

Dewey, Melvil. *Abridged Dewey Decimal Classification and Relative Index*. 15th ed. Edited by Joan S. Mitchell, et al. Dublin, Ohio: OCLC, 2012.

OUTLINE OF CLASSIFICATION

Reproduced below is the Second Summary of the Dewey Decimal Classification.* As Part 1 of this Core Collection is arranged according to this classification, the outline will serve as a table of contents for it. Please note, however, that the inclusion of this outline is not to be considered a substitute for consulting the Dewey Decimal Classification itself.

000	**Computer science, knowledge & systems**		**500**	**Science**
010	Bibliographies		510	Mathematics
020	Library & information sciences		520	Astronomy
030	Encyclopedias & books of facts		530	Physics
040	[Unassigned]		540	Chemistry
050	Magazines, journals & serials		550	Earth sciences & geology
060	Associations, organizations & museums		560	Fossils & prehistoric life
070	News media, journalism & publishing		570	Life sciences; biology
080	Quotations		580	Plants (Botany)
090	Manuscripts & rare books		590	Animals (Zoology)
100	**Philosophy**		**600**	**Technology**
110	Metaphysics		610	Medicine & health
120	Epistemology		620	Engineering
130	Parapsychology & occultism		630	Agriculture
140	Philosophical schools of thought		640	Home & family management
150	Psychology		650	Management & public relations
160	Logic		660	Chemical engineering
170	Ethics		670	Manufacturing
180	Ancient, medieval & eastern philosophy		680	Manufacture for specific uses
190	Modern western philosophy		690	Building & construction
200	**Religion**		**700**	**Arts**
210	Philosophy & theory of religion		710	Landscaping & area planning
220	The Bible		720	Architecture
230	Christianity & Christian theology		730	Sculpture, ceramics & metalwork
240	Christian practice & observance		740	Drawing & decorative arts
250	Christian pastoral practice & religious orders		750	Painting
260	Christian organization, social work & worship		760	Graphic arts
270	History of Christianity		770	Photography & computer art
280	Christian denominations		780	Music
290	Other religions		790	Sports, games & entertainment
300	**Social sciences, sociology & anthropology**		**800**	**Literature, rhetoric & criticism**
310	Statistics		810	American literature in English
320	Political science		820	English & Old English literatures
330	Economics		830	German & related literatures
340	Law		840	French & related literatures
350	Public administration & military science		850	Italian, Romanian & related literatures
360	Social problems & social services		860	Spanish & Portuguese literatures
370	Education		870	Latin & Italian literatures
380	Commerce, communications & transportation		880	Classical & modern Greek literatures
390	Customs, etiquette & folklore		890	Other literatures
400	**Language**		**900**	**History**
410	Linguistics		910	Geography & travel
420	English & Old English languages		920	Biography & genealogy
430	German & related languages		930	History of ancient world (to ca. 499)
440	French & related languages		940	History of Europe
450	Italian, Romanian & related languages		950	History of Asia
460	Spanish & Portuguese languages		960	History of Africa
470	Latin & Italic languages		970	History of North America
480	Classical & modern Greek languages		980	History of South America
490	Other languages		990	History of other areas

* Reproduced from Edition 15 of the Abridged Dewey Decimal Classification and Relative Index, published in 2012, by permission of OCLC Online Computer Library Center, Inc., owner of copyright.

SENIOR HIGH CORE COLLECTION
TWENTIETH EDITION
CLASSIFIED COLLECTION

000   COMPUTER SCIENCE, KNOWLEDGE & SYSTEMS

001.4   Research; statistical methods

Best, Joel

★ **Damned** lies and statistics; untangling numbers from the media, politicians, and activists. University of Calif. Press 2001 190p $19.95

Grades: 9 10 11 12   **001.4**

1. Statistics

ISBN 0-520-21978-3

LC 00-64910

"Invaluable counsel for good citizenship." Booklist

Includes bibliographical references

MacLeod, Don

How to find out anything; from extreme Google searches to scouring government documents, a guide to uncovering anything about everyone and everything. Don MacLeod. 1st ed. Prentice Hall Press 2012 x, 256 p.p (pbk.) $20

Grades: 10 11 12 Adult   **001.4**

1. Research 2. Internet searching 3. Information resources 4. Research -- Methodology 5. Electronic information resources 6. Electronic information resource searching

ISBN 0735204675; 9780735204676

LC 2012010974

In this book, "researcher Don MacLeod explains how to find what you're looking for quickly, efficiently, and accurately--and how to avoid the most common mistakes of the Google Age. . . . [The author] shows you how to unveil nearly anything about anyone. From top CEO's salaries to police records, . . . researching for a term paper or digging up dirt on an ex, the advice in this book arms you with the sleuthing skills to tackle any mystery." (Publisher's note)

Selverstone, Harriet S.

Encouraging and supporting student inquiry; researching controversial issues. Libraries Unlimited 2007 xlix, 238p (Libraries Unlimited professional guides in school librarianship) pa $40

Grades: Adult Professional   **001.4**

1. Research 2. Intellectual freedom 3. High school libraries 4. Bibliographic instruction

ISBN 978-1-59158-496-4; 1-59158-496-5

LC 2007-9266

The author gives "advice for advocating inquiry-based research, especially for hot topics that are most interesting to students. She advises library media specialists on what constitutes controversial topics, how to collaborate with teachers to foster critical thinking, and how to gain administrative support for this kind of program research. . . . The philosophies and ideas presented make this book an ideal purchase to promote and foster collaboration with the school communities in which many of us work." SLJ

Includes bibliographical references

Tufte, Edward R.

The **visual** display of quantitative information; 2nd ed; Graphics Press 2001 197p il $40

Grades: 11 12 Adult   **001.4**

1. Statistics -- Graphic methods

ISBN 0-9613921-4-2

LC 2001-271866

First published 1983

This book focuses "on statistical graphics, charts, tables. Theory and practice in the design of data graphics, 250 illustrations of the best (and a few of the worst) statistical graphics, with . . . analysis of how to display data for precise, effective, quick analysis." Publisher's note

001.9   Controversial knowledge

Clark, Jerome

Unnatural phenomena; a guide to the bizarre wonders of North America. illustrations by John Clark. ABC-CLIO 2005 xxxiv, 369p il $85

Grades: 11 12 Adult   **001.9**

1. Curiosities and wonders

ISBN 1-57607-430-7

LC 2005-11206

"Organized geographically, . . , [this book] explores the history of bizarre natural phenomena in virtually every U.S. state." Publisher's note

Includes bibliographical references

Coleman, Loren

★ **Cryptozoology** A-Z; the encyclopedia of loch monsters, Sasquatch, Chupacabras, and other authentic mysteries of nature. {by} Loren Coleman and Jerome Clark. Simon & Schuster 1999 270p il pa $13

Grades: 11 12 Adult   001.9
1. Reference books 2. Monsters -- Encyclopedias
ISBN 0-684-85602-6

LC 99-31023

Cryptozoology is defined as the study of hidden animals. This encyclopedia "contains nearly two hundred entries, including cryptids (the name given to these unusual beasts), new animal finds, and the explorers and scientists who search for them." Publisher's note

Includes bibliographical references

Grant, John

Debunk it! how to stay sane in a world of misinformation. John Grant. Houghton Mifflin Harcourt 2015 288 p. (paperback) $12.99

Grades: 9 10 11 12   001.9
1. Errors
ISBN 1936976684; 9781936976683

This book, by John Grant, "uses modern, ripped-from-the-headlines examples to clearly explain how to identify bad evidence and poor arguments. He provides a roundup of the rhetorical tricks people use when attempting to pull the wool over our eyes, and even offers advice about how to take these unscrupulous pundits down." (Publisher's note)

"Grant explores the false data, rationales, and conclusions used to exploit misinformation about these topics. At the heart of the book is learning to apply the scientific method and evaluate sources. Although intended for teens, adults would also benefit from this witty, thought-provoking guide." Booklist

Miller, Ron

Is the end of the world near? from crackpot predictions to scientific scenarios. Twenty-First Century Books 2011 120p il

Grades: 6 7 8 9 10   001.9
1. End of the world
ISBN 0-7613-7396-9; 978-0-7613-7396-4

LC 2010051963

"The author devotes most of his presentation to a selective tally of our possible ends, from religious and pseudoscientific predictions (including the supposed Mayan apocalypse 'scheduled' for December 21, 2012) to an array of more feasible pandemics, ecological breakdowns, nuclear conflagrations, supervolcanoes, and other natural catastrophes. . . . He also tucks in references to prominent end-of-days novels and films, and takes his eschatological narrative to the universe-ending 'Big Crunch' before closing on a perversely optimistic note. Capped with generous annotated lists of multimedia resources and illustrated throughout with dramatic photographed or digitally rendered disasters." SLJ

Includes bibliographical references

Sagan, Carl

The **demon**-haunted world; science as a candle in the dark. Random House 1996 457p hardcover o.p. pa $14.95

Grades: 11 12 Adult   001.9
1. Science 2. Parapsychology 3. Unidentified flying objects 4. Hallucinations and illusions
ISBN 0-394-53512-X; 0-345-40946-9 pa

LC 95-34076

Sagan "links today's aliens with yesterday's demons in this lithe, well-supported, sometimes quite wry, and altogether refreshing performance." Booklist

Includes bibliographical references

Shermer, Michael

★ **Why** people believe weird things; pseudoscience, superstition, and other confusions of our time. foreword by Stephen Jay Gould. rev and expanded; Freeman, W.H. 2002 xxvi, 349p il pa $16

Grades: 11 12 Adult   001.9
1. Science 2. Parapsychology 3. Belief and doubt
ISBN 0-8050-7089-3

LC 2002-68784

First published 1997

The author "explores the very human reasons people find otherworldly phenomena, conspiracy theories, and cults so appealing. In . . . [the] chapter, 'Why Smart People Believe in Weird Things' he takes on science luminaries like physicist Frank Tippler and others, who hide their spiritual beliefs behind the trappings of science." Publisher's note

Includes bibliographical references

004 Computer science; computer programming, programs, data; special computer methods

Downing, Douglas

★ **Dictionary** of computer and Internet terms; [by] Douglas A. Downing ... [et al.]; with the assistance of Sharon Covington. 10th ed.; Barron's Educational Series 2009 554p il (Barron's business guides) pa $14.99

Grades: 9 10 11 12 Adult   004
1. Reference books 2. Internet -- Dictionaries 3. Computers -- Dictionaries
ISBN 978-0-7641-4105-8; 0-7641-4105-8

LC 2008-44365

First published 1986 with title: Dictionary of computer terms

The book presents more than 3,200 computer-related terms. Emphasis is placed on information for non-technical home computer users.

Farmer, Lesley S. Johnson

★ **Teen** girls and technology; what's the problem, what's the solution? [by] Lesley Farmer. Teachers College, Columbia University 2008 180p $52; pa $21.95

Grades: Adult Professional   004
1. Information technology 2. Girls -- Education
ISBN 978-0-8077-4876-3; 978-0-8077-4875-6 pa

LC 2007-47698

Provides a framework that teachers, librarians, youth workers, and parents can use to empower girls to succeed in today's technology-rich world.

"Strong emphasis on curriculum and school-related issues makes this most useful for schools, but larger libraries and systems will also want to consider it." SLJ

Includes bibliographical references

Hafner, Katie

★ **Where** wizards stay up late; the origins of the Internet. [by] Katie Hafner and Matthew Lyon. Simon & Schuster 1996 304p il hardcover o.p. pa $16

Grades: 11 12 Adult   **004**
   1. Internet
   ISBN 0-684-81201-0; 0-684-83267-4 pa
                      LC 96-19533

This "book is excellent at enshrining little known but crucial scientist/administrators like Bob Taylor, Larry Roberts and Joseph Licklider, many of whom laid the groundwork for the computer science industry." Publ Wkly

Includes bibliographical references

Saint Amant, Robert

Computing for ordinary mortals; Robert St. Amant; hand drawn illustrations by Stefano Imbert. Oxford University Press 2013 viii, 246 p.p (hardback: alk. paper) $29.95

Grades: 10 11 12   **004**
   1. Problem solving 2. Computer science 3. Computers -- History
   ISBN 0199775303; 9780199775309
                  LC 2012015125

In this book, "computer scientist Robert St. Amant explains" the ideas behind computing technology, "introducing basic computing concepts." He gives "a brief history of the earliest computers, and then he traces two different threads through the fabric of computing. One thread . . . illuminat[es] the architecture of a computer and show[s] how this architecture makes computation efficient. . . . The other thread . . . describ[es] how computers are, in the abstract, machines for solving problems." (Publisher's note)

Includes bibliographical references and index

004.068   Computer science--management

Hollander, Barbara Gottfried

The **next** big thing; developing your digital business idea. Barbara Gottfried Hollander. 1st ed. Rosen Pub. 2013 64 p. col. ill. (Digital entrepreneurship in the age of apps, the web, and mobile devices) (library) $31.95; (paperback) $12.95

Grades: 8 9 10 11 12   **004.068**
   1. Entrepreneurship 2. Internet industry 3. New products 4. Electronic commerce 5. New business enterprises
   ISBN 1448869269; 9781448869268; 9781448869312; 9781448869718
                  LC 2012003029

This book is part of the Digital Entrepreneurship in the Age of Apps, the Web, and Mobile Devices series and focuses on digital businesses. "These how-to titles lead teens through building a digital business. Each volume uses real-world examples from current Internet companies such as Facebook, Twitter, and Netflix to explain the various steps involved in building a website, blog, app, etc." (School Library Journal)

Includes bibliographical references and index.

004.6   Interfacing and communications

Dingwell, Heath

The **truth** about Internet and online predators; Robert N. Golden, general editor, Fred L. Peterson, general editor; Heath Dingwell, principal author. Facts On File 2011 134p il (Truth about series) $35

Grades: 9 10 11 12   **004.6**
   1. Sex crimes 2. Computer crimes 3. Internet and teenagers 4. Internet -- Safety measures
   ISBN 978-0-8160-7648-2; 0-8160-7648-0; 978-1-4381-3628-8 pa; 1-4381-3628-5 pa
                  LC 2010-29296

"While acknowledging the positive aspects of the Internet, this book addresses important safety issues in an A-to-Z format. Topics include blogging, bullies, chat rooms, hate crimes, instant messaging, online predators, phishing and pharming, pornography, privacy, social networking, and more. The information is detailed and easily accessible." SLJ

Includes bibliographical references

Johnson, Doug

★ **Learning** right from wrong in the digital age; an ethics guide for parents, teachers, librarians, and others who care about computer-using young people. Linworth Pub. 2003 122p pa $44.55

Grades: Adult Professional   **004.6**
   1. Internet 2. Cheating (Education) 3. Computers and children
   ISBN 1-586-83131-3
                  LC 2003-43320

"Johnson's '3 P's of Technology Ethics,' Privacy, Property, and a(P)propriate use, are effectively and excitingly addressed through both discussion and instructional scenarios." SLJ

Includes bibliographical references

Mooney, Carla

Online predators. ReferencePoint Press 2011 96p il (Issues in the digital age)

Grades: 7 8 9 10 11 12   **004.6**
   1. Cyberbullying 2. Computer crimes 3. Child sexual abuse 4. Internet -- Safety measures
   ISBN 1-60152-193-6; 978-1-60152-193-4
                  LC 2011020180

"Packed with frightening cases of online attacks by sexual predators, financial predators, and bullies, this detailed, up-to-date, highly readable guide is a warning to young people—and adults—about Internet-based crime and identity theft. . . . Computer-savvy teens will especially welcome the coverage of emerging careers in cybersecurity and forensics. . . . A clean design with color photos and extensive back matter . . . further add to this title's appeal." Booklist

Includes bibliographical references

004.67   Wide-area networks

Nakaya, Andrea C.

Thinking critically; video games and violence. by Andrea C. Nakaya. ReferencePoint Press, Inc.

2014 80 p. color illustrations (Thinking critically) (hardback) $28.95

Grades: 9 10 11 12   **004.67**
1. Video games 2. Violence in popular culture 3. Children and violence 4. Internet and children 5. Internet -- Safety measures
ISBN 1601525907; 9781601525901

LC 2013026248

This juvenile reference book, by Andrea C. Nakaya, "through a narrative-driven pro/con format . . . examines issues related to video games and violence. Topics include: Does Video Game Violence Cause Violent Behavior? How Does Video Game Violence Affect Youth? Are Violent Video Games a Cause of Mass Shootings? and How Should Video Game Violence Be Regulated?" (Publisher's note)

"Likely the topic closest to most students' lives, this issue is strongly and fairly presented on both sides, and this title is particularly thought-provoking. For teachers wishing to use a debate approach to consideration of current political and social issues, the entire series offers useful information and presents an excellent model." Booklist

Includes bibliographical references and index

Video games and violence

Obee, Jennifer

Social networking; the ultimate teen guide. Jenna Obee. Scarecrow Press 2012 258 p.

Grades: 10 11 12 Adult   **004.67**
1. Social networking 2. Internet and teenagers 3. Online social networks
ISBN 0810881209; 9780810881204; 9780810881211

LC 2011049875

This book by Jennifer Obee "helps young adults make the most of their online experience, giving them a complete understanding of social networking while also addressing online safety. . . . Author Jennifer Obee helps teens navigate through the challenging intricacies of social networks, covering such topics as: Facebook . . . Youtube . . . [and] Twitter." The book includes "quotes from teenagers about their favorite sites and personal stories." (Publisher's note)

Includes bibliographical references and index

005.13   Programming languages

Payne, Bryson

Teach your kids to code; a parent-friendly guide to Python programming. by Bryson Payne. No Starch Press 2015 xxvi, 308 p.p color illustraitons (paperback) $29.95

Grades: 6 7 8 9 10 11 12 Adult Professional   **005.13**
1. Python (Computer language) 2. Computer programming 3. Computer programming -- Study and teaching (Elementary) 4. Computer programming -- Study and teaching (Middle school) 5. Python (Computer program language) -- Study and teaching (Elementary) 6. Python (Computer program language) -- Study and teaching (Middle school)
ISBN 9781593276140; 1593276141

LC 2015006794

This book, by Bryson Payne, "is a parent's and teacher's guide to teaching kids basic programming and problem solving using Python, the powerful language used in college courses and by tech companies like Google and IBM. Step-by-step explanations will have kids learning computational thinking right away, while visual and game-oriented examples hold their attention." (Publisher's note)

"The full-color printing includes charming spot illustrations, code-output screenshots, and example codes in a layout and color scheme identical to the Python editor. Sophisticated concepts and serious programming make for an easy, enjoyable game for families." Kirkus

005.35   Programs for mobile computing devices

Gregory, Josh

Apps; from concept to consumer. by Josh Gregory. Children's Press, an imprint of Scholastic Inc. 2015 64 p. illustrations (color) (library binding: alk. paper) $30

Grades: 6 7 8 9 10   **005.35**
1. Computer applications 2. Mobile computing 3. Application software 4. Application software -- Development -- Vocational guidance
ISBN 0531205398; 053121236X; 9780531205396; 9780531212363

LC 2014030460

With this book, by Josh Gregory, part of the "Calling all innovators: A career for you?" series, "[r]eaders will learn how the first mobile apps were created and find out which apps are making the biggest splash today. They will also see how easy it is to get started creating their own apps and what it takes to score the next big hit on the app stores." (Publisher's note)

"Despite a few flaws, [the titles in this series] are recommended for their in-depth descriptions of the histories of different careers." SLJ

Includes bibliographical references and index

005.8   Data security

Earp, Paul W.

Securing library technology; a how-to-do-it manual. [by] Paul W. Earp and Adam Wright. Neal-Schuman Publishers 2009 245p il (How-to-do-it manuals for librarians) pa $65

Grades: Adult Professional   **005.8**
1. Computer security 2. Libraries -- Security measures
ISBN 978-1-55570-639-5

LC 2008-46166

"Have you had your identity stolen? Are all firewalls safe from hackers? What is a hop? What is the difference between a virus and a worm? Can someone listen in on your Voice-Over Internet Protocol service? These are just a few questions answered in this manual, which is full of forms, suggestions, and inventories." Libr Media Connect

Includes glossary and bibliographical references

Harmon, Daniel E.

Careers in Internet security; [by] Daniel E. Harmon. Rosen Pub. 2011 80p il (Careers in computer technology) lib bdg $31.95

Grades: 9 10 11 12 Adult   005.8

1. Internet -- Security measures 2. Internet -- Vocational guidance

ISBN 978-1-4488-13155; 1-4488-1315-8

LC 2010006860

Outlines a variety of different job opportunities in the field of internet security.

"The writing style and language for each book are clear and concise without being too simplistic...This would be good... to incorporate either in the classroom or in a library since it deals with a growing field that is in high demand, and it also discusses job opportunities for individuals as young as high school." VOYA

Includes bibliographical references

Hunter, Nick

Internet safety; Nick Hunter. Heinemann Library 2012 56 p. col. ill.

Grades: 6 7 8 9 10   005.8

1. Internet users 2. Internet -- Safety measures 3. Computer crimes -- Prevention

ISBN 9781432948719; 9781432962050

LC 2010046905

"...Discusses types of crime, cyber bullying, phishing, and scams and viruses, ending with ways to protect yourself. Statistics and websites provide information for both individual research and for educators wishing to lead discussion on the topic... Good choices for student research and debate." SLJ

Includes bibliographical references (p. 54-55) and index

006.3 Artificial intelligence

Baker, Stephen

Final Jeopardy; man vs. machine and the quest to know everything. Houghton Mifflin Harcourt 2011 268p $24

Grades: 11 12 Adult   006.3

1. Database management 2. Artificial intelligence 3. Watson (Computer) 4. Jeopardy (Television program) 5. Natural language processing (Computer science)

ISBN 978-0-547-48316-0; 0-547-48316-3

LC 2010051653

"In February 2011, the world watched as a computer named Watson handily beat the two greatest Jeopardy champions of all time. The contest was reminiscent of when IBM's Deep Blue defeated chess grandmaster Garry Kasparov, but Jeopardy was a much more difficult game for a computer to master. Although Baker . . . reviews the match in his last chapter, his primary focus here is on the compelling story of Watson's creation and education. . . . This is a thought-provoking view of one of IBM's major contributions to the computing field." Libr J

Includes bibliographical references

Henderson, Harry

Artificial intelligence; mirrors for the mind. Chelsea House 2007 190p il (Milestones in discovery and invention) $35

Grades: 7 8 9 10 11 12   006.3

1. Artificial intelligence

ISBN 0-8160-5749-4; 978-0-8160-5749-8

LC 2006-16639

This book includes "portraits of the men and women in the vanguard of this innovative field. Subjects include Alan Turing, who made the connection between mathematical reasoning and computer operations; Allen Newell and Herbert Simon, who created a program that could reason like a human being; Pattie Maes, who developed computerized agents to help people with research and shopping; and Ray Kurzweil, who, besides inventing the flatbed scanner and a reading machine for the blind, has explored relationships between people and computers that may exceed human intelligence." Publisher's note

Includes glossary and bibliographical references

Pearce, Q. L.

Artificial intelligence. Lucent Books 2011 112p il (Technology 360) $33.45

Grades: 7 8 9 10   006.3

1. Robots 2. Artificial intelligence

ISBN 978-1-4205-0384-5; 1-4205-0384-7

LC 2011006362

This offers "clean design with clear explanations of sometimes-complicated scientific subjects. . . . Artificial Intelligence covers the history of how people have tried to teach machines to think and move, concluding with a chapter on the ethics surrounding AI. . . . A strong [title] for report writers and students with a serious interest in technology and its inventions." Booklist

Includes glossary and bibliographical references

006.6 Computer graphics

Hansen, Brad

The dictionary of multimedia; terms & acronyms. 4th ed; Franklin, Beedle & Associates 2005 611p il $50

Grades: 9 10 11 12   006.6

1. Reference books 2. Multimedia -- Dictionaries

ISBN 1-88790-273-2

First published 1997

Contains over 5000 technical and multimedia terms from a multidisciplinary perspective including audio, graphics, video, networking, human factors, and general computing. Copyright issues and international standards are addressed. Includes a basic HTML tutorial and an appendix listing books, software, manuals and periodicals, as well as covering digital video, MIDI and Internet development.

006.7 Multimedia systems

Cooper, Nate

Build your own website; a comic guide to HTML, CSS, and WordPress. Nate Cooper. No Starch Press 2014 250 p. illustrations $19.95

Grades: 7 8 9 10 11 12   **006.7**
1. Web sites -- Design 2. HTML (Document markup language) 3. Web sites -- Design -- Humor 4. Web site development -- Humor
ISBN 1593275226; 9781593275228

LC 2014019597

Author Nate Cooper and illustrator Kim Gee present this "illustrated introduction to the basics of creating a website. Join Kim and her little dog Tofu as she learns HTML, the language of web pages, and CSS, the language used to style web pages, from the Web Guru and Glinda, the Good Witch of CSS." (Publisher's note)

"The comic art engages the readers and gives the broad picture of what the reader will learn from Cooper's text which follows. Best suited for beginning self-learning, it is one of the few books on the topic which entertains as well as educates."

Hussey, Tris

★ **Create** your own blog; [6 easy projects to start blogging like a pro.] Sams Pub. 2010 273p il pa $21.99

Grades: 9 10 11 12 Adult   **006.7**
1. Weblogs
ISBN 978-0-672-33065-0

LC 2009-51118

This guide to starting your own blog includes advice on planning and setting up blogs, as well as on how to create different kinds of blogs including personal blogs, professional blogs, blogs for podcasting, and video blogs.

Kling, Andrew A.

Web 2.0. Lucent Books 2011 128p il map (Technology 360) $33.45

Grades: 7 8 9 10   **006.7**
1. Internet 2. Online social networks
ISBN 978-1-4205-0171-1; 1-4205-0171-2

LC 2010028893

This offers "clean design with clear explanations of sometimes-complicated scientific subjects. . . . The history of the Internet and how people interact with it is the focus in Web 2.0, which discusses groundbreaking sites from Napster to Facebook, with a concluding chapter that tries to foresee the future. . . . A strong [title] for report writers and students with a serious interest in technology and its inventions." Booklist

Includes bibliographical references

Nakaya, Andrea C.

Thinking critically; by Andrea C. Nakaya. ReferencePoint Press, Inc. 2013 80 p. (hardback) $28.95

Grades: 7 8 9 10 11 12   **006.7**
1. Social media 2. Social networking 3. Internet and teenagers 4. Online social networks 5. Internet

-- Safety measures
ISBN 1601525885; 9781601525888

LC 2012043628

This book, by Andrea C. Nakaya, is a "well-researched examination" of social networking. "The first page of each chapter, 'The Debate at a Glance,' offers bullet points that summarize common arguments pro and con. The design is spare, with understated graphics; bright, compelling photos; and text boxes that pull out interesting quotes. Easy-to-read graphs and charts add another layer of visual information." (School Library Journal)

"Diagrams and sidebars support these well-organized models for classroom discourse. First chapters introduce the debates surrounding . . . social networking. . . subsequent chapters present pro and con responses to four key questions. Despite lots of graphic elements, the text-heavy pages may be off-putting. Two pages of facts and a list of related organizations are appended." Horn Book.

Includes bibliographical references and index
Social networking

011 Bibliographies and catalogs

American reference books annual 2014, volume 45; edited by Shannon Graff Hysell. Libraries Unlimited 2014 574 p $155

Grades: Adult Professional   **011**
1. Reference books -- Bibliography 2. Libraries -- Collection development
ISBN 9781610695480
Annual. First published 1970

This book "provides librarians with insightful, critical reviews of all reference resources released in 2013 as well as some from 2012 and 2014. Highlighting both the positive and negative aspects of each resource, users will be able to make informed decisions about which new resources are most appropriate for their collection and their patrons' needs." (Publisher's note)

"Each issue covers the reference book output (including reprints) of the previous year (i.e., the 1970 volume covers 1969 publications). Offers descriptive and evaluative notes (many of them signed by contributors), with references to selected reviews. Limited to titles in English. Classed arrangement; author-subject-title index." Guide to Ref Books. 11th edition

011.6 General bibliographies and catalogs of works for young people and people with disabilities; for specific types of libraries

Barr, Catherine, 1951-

Best books for high school readers; grades 9-12. [by] Catherine Barr and John T. Gillespie. 2nd ed; Libraries Unlimited 2009 1075p $85

Grades: Adult Professional   **011.6**
1. Best books 2. Reference books 3. Teenagers -- Books and reading 4. Young adult literature -- Bibliography
ISBN 978-1-59158-576-3; 1-59158-576-7

LC 2008-50756

First published 1991 by Bowker with title: Best books for senior high readers

"Each title included . . . offers two positive reviews with the exception of some entries in nonfiction series and adult selections suitable for young adults that receive restricted space from journals. All volumes incorporated were in print at the end of October 2008." Voice Youth Advocates

Gillespie, John Thomas, 1928-

Classic teenplots; a booktalk guide to use with readers ages 12-18. [by] John T. Gillespie and Corinne J. Naden. Libraries Unlimited 2006 348p (Children's and young adult literature reference series) $55

Grades: Adult Professional   **011.6**
   1. Book talks 2. Young adult literature 3. Teenagers -- Books and reading
   ISBN 1-59158-312-8

LC 2006017624

"Prefaced by a brief guide to booktalking are one hundred entries for in-print classic titles for teens, taken from the out-of-print Juniorplots and Seniorplots series. Additional titles have been added to round out the eight theme/genre-based sections, which include topics such as Teenage Life and Concerns, Historical Fiction and Other Lands, and Important Nonfiction. . . . This excellent resource offers from sixteen to twenty titles per section." Voice Youth Advocates

Includes bibliographical references

Rosow, La Vergne

Accessing the classics; great reads for adults, teens, and English language learners. Libraries Unlimited 2006 301p pa $40

Grades: Adult Professional   **011.6**
   1. Best books 2. Reading -- Remedial teaching
   ISBN 1-56308-891-6; 978-1-56308-891-9

LC 2005-30838

"The intended audience is wide-ranging and includes anyone who wishes to foster language and literacy skills. Essential reading." Booklist

Includes bibliographical references

Safford, Barbara Ripp

Guide to reference materials for school library media centers; 6th ed; Libraries Unlimited 2010 236p $60

Grades: Adult Professional   **011.6**
   1. Instructional materials centers 2. School libraries -- Catalogs 3. Reference books -- Bibliography
   ISBN 978-1-59158-277-9; 1-59158-277-6

LC 2009-51190

First edition by Christine Gehrt Wynar published 1973 with title: Guide to reference books for school media centers

"This volume has been updated to include web-based reference offerings as well as listings of older sources, provided that their content is still valid. . . . This title profiles resources recommended for use by school librarians for collection management, readers' advisory, teaching, general reference materials, the social sciences and humanities, and science and technology. This volume is an excellent starting point for new school librarians, as well as for those who are building a library from scratch." SLJ

Includes bibliographical references

Silver, Linda R.

Best Jewish books for children and teens; JPS guide. The Jewish Publication Society 2010 325p il pa $20

Grades: Adult Professional   **011.6**
   1. Best books 2. Jewish literature -- Bibliography 3. Children's literature -- Bibliography 4. Young adult literature -- Bibliography
   ISBN 978-0-8276-0903-7

LC 2010-283705

"Chapters are organized by subject and entries within each include a . . . description of the book and author, and Silver's own insights on what makes it worth reading. There are title, subject, author, and illustrator indexes, title-grouping by reading level, and lists of award winners." Publisher's note

Includes bibliographical references

Welch, Rollie James

★ A **core** collection for young adults; 2nd ed; Neal-Schuman Publishers 2011 416p (Teens @ the library series) pa $80

Grades: Adult Professional   **011.6**
   1. Young adult literature 2. Young adults' libraries 3. Teenagers -- Books and reading 4. Young adult literature -- Bibliography
   ISBN 978-1-55570-692-0; 1-55570-692-4

LC 2010-46693

First published 2003 under the authorship of Patrick Jones

Provides information meant to be a practical manual for developing collections that appeal to teens. Includes a guide to more than 100 "Best" lists, tips for maintaining a core collection, and selection tips for major YA genres.

"The book is a wide-reaching resource that introduces literature with appeal to young adults to an audience new to library work with teens." Voice Youth Advocates

Includes bibliographical references

Young Adult Library Services Association

The **official** YALSA awards guidebook; compiled and edited by Tina Frolund for the Young Adult Library Services Association. Neal-Schuman Publishers 2008 171p pa $55

Grades: Adult Professional   **011.6**
   1. Reference books 2. Young adults' libraries 3. Teenagers -- Books and reading 4. Young adult literature -- Awards 5. Young adult literature -- Bibliography
   ISBN 978-1-55570-629-6; 1-55570-629-0

LC 2008-17584

This "volume offers one-stop shopping for an overview of the Alex, Printz, and Edwards awards. In addition to annotated bibliographies of winners and honor books, the title includes acceptance speeches for the Printz and Edwards awards and award interviews from YALSA starwarts Mary Arnold, Michael Cart, and Betty Carter." Bull Cent Child Books

Includes bibliographical references

★ **Outstanding** books for the college bound; titles and programs for a new generation. edited by Angela Carstensen. American Library Association 2011 164p pa $50

Grades: Adult Professional   **011.6**

1. Best books 2. College students

ISBN 978-0-8389-8570-0

LC 2011-11853

First published 1984

This book lists "over 400 books deemed outstanding for the college bound by the Young Adult Library Services Association (YALSA). . . . [It] includes indexes searchable by topic, year, title, and author." Publisher's note

Includes bibliographical references

011.62   Works for young people

Cart, Michael

Cart's top 200 adult books for young adults; two decades in review. Michael Cart. American Library Association 2012 136 p. (paperback) $50

Grades: Adult Professional   **011.62**

1. Best books 2. Young adult literature 3. Best books -- United States 4. Teenagers -- Books and reading -- United States -- Bibliography

ISBN 0838911587; 9780838911587

LC 2012027260

In this book, Michael Cart identifies "exceptional adult books that will satisfy a variety of young adults recreational reading tastes. Drawing on his work as columnist and critic for 'Booklist,' Cart bases his recommendations on the notoriously choosy reading interests of today's older young adults, and his roundup of high-quality titles . . . covers a wide range of genres" and "includes numerous read-alikes and related-titles lists." (Publisher's note)

Includes bibliographical references and index

016   Bibliographies and catalogs of works on specific subjects

Al-Hazza, Tami Craft

Books about the Middle East; selecting and using them with children and adolescents. [by] Tami Craft Al-Hazza and Katherine T. Bucher. Linworth Pub. 2008 168p pa $39.95

Grades: Adult Professional   **016**

1. Reference books 2. Middle East -- Bibliography 3. Children's literature -- Bibliography 4. Young adult literature -- Bibliography

ISBN 978-1-58683-285-8; 1-58683-285-9

LC 2007-40149

"This book examines the body of literature about the diverse groups of people who inhabit the Middle East, and it also explores a variety of ways in which this literature can be used. . . . It fills a huge gap and should not be overlooked. This powerhouse book will be tremendously helpful to media specialists, educators, and public librarians." Voice Youth Advocates

Includes bibliographical references

Cart, Michael

Top 250 LGBTQ books for teens; coming out, being out, and the search for community. Michael Cart and Christine A. Jenkins. Huron Street Press 2015 184 p. illustrations (paperback) $21.95

Grades: Adult Professional   **016**

1. LGBT youth 2. Teenagers -- Books and reading 3. Homosexuality -- Bibliography 4. Sexual orientation -- Bibliography 5. Young adult literature -- Bibliography 6. Homosexuality -- Fiction -- Bibliography 7. Teenagers -- Books and reading -- United States

ISBN 1937589560; 9781937589561

LC 2014031572

This book, by Michael Cart and Christine A. Jenkins, is a "summary of the 250 best books for LGBTQ teens. . . . [They] cover fiction of all kinds, as well as graphic novels and general nonfiction aimed at readers in middle school and high school, and include recent publications as well as classics that continue to be read and enjoyed by 21st-century teens. Information on how to find library programs, services, and additional resources for LGBTQ teens is also provided." (Publisher's note)

"An additional purchase, best used for backlist collection development." SLJ

Includes bibliographical references and index

Crew, Hilary S.

Women engaged in war in literature for youth; a guide to resources for children and young adults. Scarecrow Press 2007 303p (Literature for youth) pa $51

Grades: Adult Professional   **016**

1. Reference books 2. War -- Bibliography 3. Women -- Bibliography 4. Children's literature -- Bibliography 5. Young adult literature -- Bibliography

ISBN 978-0-8108-4929-7; 0-8108-4929-1

LC 2006-101112

"Crew's guide to print and online sources documents women's roles in wars over the centuries and throughout the world, divided by time periods. . . . This is a great addition for libraries looking for a way to move Women's Studies beyond the month of March." SLJ

Includes bibliographical references

Fichtelberg, Susan

Encountering enchantment; a guide to speculative fiction for teens. Libraries Unlimited 2007 328p (Genreflecting advisory series) $48

Grades: Adult Professional   **016**

1. Reference books 2. Fantasy fiction -- Bibliography 3. Science fiction -- Bibliography 4. Young adult literature -- Bibliography

ISBN 1-59158-316-0; 978-1-59158-316-5

LC 2006-33739

"This useful guide should be in every YA collection." SLJ

Includes bibliographical references

Fonseca, Anthony J.

Hooked on horror III; a guide to reading interests. [by] Anthony J. Fonseca and June Michele Pulliam. Libraries Unlimited 2009 xxiii, 515p (Genre-flecting advisory series) $62

Grades: Adult Professional   **016**
1. Horror films 2. Reference books 3. Horror fiction -- Bibliography
ISBN 978-1-59158-540-4

LC 2008-45518

First published 1999 with title: Hooked on horror

This book "provides annotations of horror books published between 2003 and 2008, including collections, anthologies, and series." Voice Youth Advocates

Includes bibliographical references

Frolund, Tina

★ **Genrefied** classics; a guide to reading interests in classical literature. Libraries Unlimited 2007 xxiv, 365p (Genreflecting advisory series) $45

Grades: Adult Professional   **016**
1. Reference books 2. Fiction -- Bibliography
ISBN 1-59158-172-9; 978-1-59158-172-7

LC 2006-33740

"By identifying the genre characteristics of more than 400 classic fiction works, and organizing titles according to these features, this guide helps readers find the type of books they enjoy." Publisher's note

Includes bibliographical references

Gannon, Michael B.

Blood, bedlam, bullets, and badguys; a reader's guide to adventure/suspense fiction. Libraries Unlimited 2004 385p (Genreflecting advisory series) $55

Grades: Adult Professional   **016**
1. Reference books 2. Suspense fiction -- Bibliography 3. Adventure fiction -- Bibliography
ISBN 1-563-08732-4

LC 2003-60527

"Fifteen chapters cover subgenres such as espionage, legal and medical thrillers, sea adventures, and novels with elements of the paranormal. Each chapter begins with a definition of the subgenre and brief discussions of its history and appeal. There is also a very useful list of things to keep in mind when advising a reader." Booklist

Includes bibliographical references

Garcha, Rajinder

The **world** of Islam in literature for youth; a selective annotated bibliography for K-12. [by] Rajinder Garcha, Patricia Yates Russell. Scarecrow Press 2006 xx, 221p (Literature for youth) pa $35

Grades: Adult Professional   **016**
1. Reference books 2. Islam -- Bibliography 3. Children's literature -- Bibliography 4. Young adult literature -- Bibliography
ISBN 978-0-8108-5488-8; 0-8108-5488-0

LC 2005-26645

"This highly useful bibliography fills a conspicuous gap in a much-needed cultural area." Voice Youth Advocates

Includes bibliographical references

Halsall, Jane

Visual media for teens; creating and using a teen-centered film collection. [by] Jane Halsall and R. William Edminster. Libraries Unlimited 2009 xxii, 158p (Libraries Unlimited professional guides for young adult librarians) pa $40

Grades: Adult Professional   **016**
1. Young adults' libraries 2. Libraries and motion pictures 3. Motion pictures -- Catalogs
ISBN 978-1-59158-544-2; 1-59158-544-9

LC 2009-20300

"This is an excellent guide for librarians interested in building a popular film collection to satisfy their teen audiences. It offers professionals an organized look at current films that have young adult appeal and provides analysis of the importance of such a collection." SLJ

Includes filmographies and bibliographical references

Hardy, Lyda Mary

★ **Women** in U.S. history; a resource guide. Libraries Unlimited 2000 344p pa $45

Grades: Adult Professional   **016**
1. Reference books 2. Women -- United States -- History 3. Women -- United States -- Bibliography
ISBN 1-56308-769-3

LC 00-55849

This overview of historical resources includes primary sources as well as biographies, autobiographies and compilations. Best books, Web sites, and videos are included. Subject and author/title indexes are appended.

Includes bibliographical references

Herald, Diana Tixier

Fluent in fantasy; the next generation. [by] Diana Tixier Herald and Bonnie Kunzel. Libraries Unlimited 2008 312p (Genreflecting advisory series) $52

Grades: Adult Professional   **016**
1. Reference books 2. Fantasy fiction -- Bibliography
ISBN 978-1-59158-198-7; 1-59158-198-2

LC 2007-28840

First published 1999

"More than 2,000 titles are arranged by author in 14 thematic chapters, including 'Epic Fantasy,' 'Arthurian Legend,' and 'Time Travel Romance.'... An essential collection development and readers'-advisory tool." Booklist

Includes bibliographical references

★ **Genreflecting**; a guide to popular reading interests. edited by Wayne A. Wiegand. Libraries Unlimited 2013 622 p. (Genreflecting advisory series) (Hardcopy: acid-free paper) $75

Grades: Adult Professional   **016**
1. Reference books 2. Books and reading 3. Reading interests 4. Fiction -- Bibliography 5. Fiction genres -- Bibliography 6. English fiction -- Stories, plots, etc 7. American fiction -- Stories, plots, etc 8. Popular literature -- Stories, plots, etc
ISBN 9781598848403; 1598848402

LC 2012051480

First published 1982 under the authorship of Betty Rosenberg

This book for librarians on popular reading interests features "chapters devoted to each major genre with an overview of the genre's characteristics and appeal elements followed by definitions of popular subgenres, lists of benchmark titles, reader favorites, book-group selections, and resources for further investigation. Parts I and 2 focus on readers'-advisory services in the public library for the novice. . . . The chapters on the genres, found in part 3, are the series' stock-in-trade." (Booklist)

Includes bibliographical references

★ **Teen** genreflecting 3; a guide to reading interests. Libraries Unlimited 2011 xxiv, 377p (Genreflecting advisory series) $48

Grades: Adult Professional   016
    1. Reference books 2. Teenagers -- Books and reading
    3. Young adult literature -- Bibliography
    ISBN 978-1-59158-729-3; 1-59158-729-3
                                                    LC 2010-40791
First published 1997 with title: Teen genreflecting

"The chapters and subchapters provide a brief overview of the topic and are organized by genre, subgenre, or an overall theme. Each entry is annotated and includes a concise subject list, and some entries include a list of read-alikes. Herald also includes books written for children and those for adults that have teen appeal. . . . Herald suggests using this volume to identify read-alikes, to beef up genre collections, and for library staff to familiarize themselves with the literature. . . . A worthy addition to reference or professional-development collection." SLJ

Includes bibliographical references

Hollands, Neil

Read on . . . fantasy fiction; reading lists for every taste. Libraries Unlimited 2007 210p (Read on series) pa $30

Grades: Adult Professional   016
    1. Reference books 2. Fantasy fiction -- Bibliography
    ISBN 978-1-59158-330-1; 1-59158-330-6
                                                    LC 2007-7841
"Librarians who do readers advisory for teens or adults will wonder how they ever got along without this funny, opinionated, wide-angle guide." SLJ

Johnson, Sarah L.

Historical fiction; a guide to the genre. Libraries Unlimited 2005 xxi, 813p (Genreflecting advisory series) $75

Grades: Adult Professional   016
    1. Reference books 2. Historical fiction -- Bibliography
    ISBN 1-59158-129-X
                                                    LC 2005-47483
"Each category, e.g., 'Traditional Historical Novels,' 'Historical Thrillers,' 'Time-Slip Novels,' is subdivided further by world region and historical era. . . . The annotations also indicate benchmarks of the genre, award winners, and titles recommended for young adults and reading groups. . . . This is an excellent resource." Choice

Includes bibliographical references

Historical fiction II; a guide to the genre. Libraries Unlimited 2009 738p (Genreflecting advisory series) $65

Grades: Adult Professional   016
    1. Reference books 2. Historical fiction -- Bibliography
    ISBN 978-1-59158-624-1
                                                    LC 2008-45537
"Johnson has updated her outstanding Historical Fiction: A Guide to the Genre (2005) by covering historical fiction from 2004 through mid-2008 and adding such new features as ISBNs for each book and keyword descriptors after each annotation. . . . This volume continues rather than replaces the earlier work, adding more than 2,700 new titles." Booklist

Includes bibliographical references

Latino literature; edited by Sara E. Martínez; foreword by Connie Van Fleet. Libraries Unlimited 2009 xxii, 364p (Genreflecting advisory series) $60

Grades: Adult Professional   016
    1. Reference books 2. American literature -- Hispanic American authors -- Bibliography
    ISBN 978-1-59158-292-2; 1-59158-292-X
                                                    LC 2009-26355
"The goal [of this book] is to sample broadly from Latino authors in the U.S., Latin America, Portugal, and Spain. Coverage is limited to works available in English that were first published between the years 1995 and 2008. Approximately 750 entries are divided into 9 chapters: 'General Fiction,' 'Historical Fiction,' 'Women's Fiction,' 'Latina Romance and Love Stories,' 'Mysteries and Suspense,' 'Fantastic Fiction,' 'Young Adult Fiction,' 'Life Stories,' and 'Narrative Nonfiction.' Entries include bibliographic information, a plot summary, an excerpt from the book, awards won, key features, subjects, and similar titles. . . . This well-written book is an essential resource for public and high-school libraries, especially if they serve Latino populations." Booklist

Includes bibliographical references

Neumann, Caryn E.

★ **Term** paper resource guide to African American history. Greenwood Press 2009 304p (American mosaic) $65

Grades: 9 10 11 12   016
    1. Report writing 2. Reference books 3. African Americans -- History 4. African Americans -- Bibliography
    ISBN 978-0-313-35501-1
                                                    LC 2008-51972
"These 100 succinct yet detailed guides for planning research on African-American history cover topics from the early slave trade to North America in 1581 to Hurricane Katrina in 2005. Each approximately four-page section opens with a summary of the time period, followed by lists of term-paper suggestions, alternate topics, and annotated citations to primary and secondary materials. Sources include scholarly print works, authoritative Web sites, and quality movies, supporting a variety of learning styles. . . . While supporting

researchers with reliable information, the book clearly puts the direction and depth of research in users' hands." SLJ
Includes bibliographical references

Scales, Pat R.
★ **Books** under fire; a hit list of banned and challenged children's books. Pat Scales. ALA Editions, an imprint of the American Library Association 2015 xvi, 208 p.p illustrations (pbk.) $47
Grades: Adult Professional   **016**
   1. Books -- Censorship 2. Children -- Books and reading -- United States 3. School libraries -- Censorship -- United States 4. Challenged books -- United States -- Bibliography 5. Prohibited books -- United States -- Bibliography 6. Children's literature -- Censorship -- United States
   ISBN 0838911099; 9780838911099
                 LC 2014023945
This book on banned and challenged books, by Pat R. Scales, "covers both children's and young adult books. The main section profiles 34 books (and series such as 'Harry Potter' and 'Captain Underpants') that have recently been challenged for library or curriculum suitability in the US. . . . Each entry includes a . . . synopsis, quotations from some reviews, details of known challenges, awards/accolades, and a 'Further Reading' section." (Choice: Current Reviews for Academic Libraries)
"Like death and taxes, book challenges are always with us, as noted intellectual-freedom advocate Scales implies in her splendid new book about censorship. . . . Books under Fire contains a veritable arsenal of information . . . this one is clearly indispensable and belongs in every library collection." Booklist
   Includes bibliographical references and index

Thomas, Rebecca L.
Popular series fiction for middle school and teen readers; a reading and selection guide. [by] Rebecca L. Thomas and Catherine Barr. 2nd ed; Libraries Unlimited 2009 710p (Children's and young adult literature reference series) $65
Grades: Adult Professional   **016**
   1. Reference books 2. Children's literature -- Bibliography 3. Young adult literature -- Bibliography
   ISBN 978-1-59158-660-9
                 LC 2008-38125
   First published 2005
"The authors have identified nearly 2,200 in-print series . . . (including manga, Cine-Manga, and illustrated novels) that will appeal to readers in grades 6-12. Entries are arranged by the series title and contain author, most recent publisher, grade level, notation for availability of accelerated-reader resources, genre, a descriptive three- to five-sentence annotation, and a list of individual titles in the series, arranged by publication date." Booklist
   Includes bibliographic references

Wadham, Rachel
This is my life; a guide to realistic fiction for teens. [by] Rachel L. Wadham. Libraries Unlimited 2010 431p (Genreflecting advisory series) $55

Grades: Adult Professional   **016**
   1. Teenagers -- Books and reading 2. Young adult literature -- Bibliography
   ISBN 978-1-59158-942-6; 1-59158-942-8
                 LC 2010-24074
This "surveys contemporary realistic fiction for young adults (middle through high school). Wadham . . . annotates some 1,300 titles published for young adults between 1999 and 2009. Arranged by theme, titles represent real-life issues of broad interest (friendship, love, family, work) as well as specific issues faced in 'problem novels' (pregnancy, homelessness, eating disorders, crime and violence, abuse, drugs and alcohol, death, racism). Annotations include plot summaries, availability in audio, awards, grade-level designations, and subject keywords. . . . This is a useful tool for its intended audience of librarians and instructors seeking issue-related fiction." Booklist
   Includes bibliographical references

Welsch, Janice R.
Multicultural films; a reference guide. [by] Janice R. Welsch and J. Q. Adams. Greenwood Press 2005 231p il $49.95
Grades: 11 12 Adult   **016**
   1. Minorities in motion pictures
   ISBN 0-313-31975-8
                 LC 2004-22529
This book "is a collection of synopses and brief analyses of selected American films. . . . It is divided into six sections, each of which covers a particular racial or ethnic group. The groups covered are African Americans, Arab and Middle Eastern Americans, Asian Americans, European Americans, Latino/a Americans, and Native Americans. . . . Each entry examines the way race or ethnicity functions in the film." Ref & User Services Quarterly
   Includes bibliographical references

020   Library and information sciences

★ **Core** technology competencies for librarians and library staff; a LITA guide. Susan M. Thompson, editor. Neal-Schuman Publishers 2009 248p il pa $65
Grades: Adult Professional   **020**
   1. Library education 2. Information technology 3. Technological innovations 4. Librarians -- In-service training
   ISBN 978-1-55570-660-9
                 LC 2008-46174
In this book, "a coterie of experts identify competencies for technology specialists and describe several competency implementation programs. Useful for everyone from the systems librarian to the 'lone information technology librarian.'" Am Libr
   Includes bibliographical references

Lanning, Scott
Concise guide to information literacy; Scott Lanning. Libraries Unlimited 2012 xii, 99 p.p (paperback) $35

Grades: Adult Professional **020**
1. Research 2. Information literacy
ISBN 1598849492; 9781598849493

LC 2011049229

This book "takes the reader through the entire research process, from selecting a topic to evaluating the final project. . . . Topics covered include categories and types of information and how to conduct both print and online searches, how to evaluate information, the research process, and the final project is also included, along with a chapter on utilizing librarians. Charts and graphs help illustrate the research process." (Library Media Connection)

Includes bibliographical references (pages 91-93) and index

What Do I Read Next? A Reader's Guide to Current Genre Fiction. Gale Cengage Learning. Gale / Cengage Learning 2012 738 p. (hardcover) $254

Grades: 11 12 Adult Professional **020**
1. Book selection 2. Books and reading
ISBN 1414461372; 9781414461373

This volume is a book selection guide. It uses similarities in various books to help "readers to independently choose titles of interest published in the last year. Each entry describes a separate book, listing everything readers need to know to make selections. Arranged by author within six genre sections, detailed entries provide" information about the title, publisher, series, and temporal and geographical setting. (Publisher's note)

021.2 Relationships with the community

Gillespie, Kellie M.
Teen volunteer services in libraries. VOYA Books 2004 133p il (VOYA guides) pa $26.95
Grades: Adult Professional **021.2**
1. Libraries 2. Volunteer work
ISBN 0-8108-4837-6

LC 2003-17932

"If you are even considering starting a teen volunteer program, you must read this book. If you already have one in your library, this volume still has much to offer." SLJ
Includes bibliographical references

Librarians as community partners; an outreach handbook. edited by Carol Smallwood. American Library Association 2010 204p pa $55
Grades: Adult Professional **021.2**
1. Cultural programs 2. Libraries and community 3. Libraries -- Public relations
ISBN 978-0-8389-1006-1

LC 2009-20359

"Thirty-seven public, school, and academic librarians here share 'how we did outreach good' and produce a joyful collection. . . . Beyond a bounty of ideas are practical suggestions and examples that can be used for the library to approach organizations, groups, and governmental entities for grant applications. While the creative is foremost, the financial and efficient are also addressed with the essential details of who did what, how it was funded, and the nature

of follow-up. . . . Even the smallest library with a handful of staff could benefit from this book." Libr J
Includes bibliographical references

Squires, Tasha
★ **Library** partnerships; making connections between school and public libraries. Information Today, Inc. 2009 203p pa $39.50
Grades: Adult Professional **021.2**
1. Public libraries 2. School libraries 3. Library cooperation 4. Libraries and schools 5. Libraries and students
ISBN 978-1-57387-362-8; 1-57387-362-4

LC 2008-51647

"Squires's confident advice can get beleaguered librarians through . . . difficulties and into mutually productive partnerships." Voice Youth Advocates
Includes bibliographical references

021.7 Promotion of libraries, archives, information centers

Mahood, Kristine
★ **Booktalking** with teens. Libraries Unlimited 2010 289p (Libraries Unlimited professional guides for young adult librarians) pa $45
Grades: Adult Professional **021.7**
1. Book talks 2. Teenagers -- Books and reading 3. Young adult literature -- Bibliography
ISBN 978-1-59158-714-9; 1-59158-714-X

LC 2009-49893

This "provides advice about preparing, developing, writing, performing and justifying booktalks. . . . Mahood's expertise and enthusiasm are contagious and challenge all of us who work with youth to be as inspiring while sharing books as she is." Booklist
Includes bibliographical references

Phillips, Susan P.
Great displays for your library step by step. McFarland & Co. 2008 234p il pa $45
Grades: Adult Professional **021.7**
1. Libraries -- Exhibitions
ISBN 978-0-7864-3164-9; 0-7864-3164-4

LC 2007-47450

"Phillips' enthusiasm, creativity, and breadth of personal interests are evident throughout this book. . . . This text will inspire readers to locate and showcase the treasures in their own collections." SLJ
Includes bibliographical references

Wolfe, Lisa Ann
★ **Library** public relations, promotions, and communications; a how-to-do-it manual. 2nd ed.; Neal-Schuman Publishers 2005 230p (How-to-do-it manuals for librarians) pa $65
Grades: Adult Professional **021.7**
1. Libraries -- Public relations
ISBN 1-55570-471-9

LC 2004-25944

First published 1997

"The book is divided into two parts—'Planning and Evaluation' and 'Strategies and Methodologies'—with many examples of successful communicating and the impact and changes brought by technology. Ideas on putting together a communications plan, creating clear signage and print products, effectively using a library's Web site, and communicating during a crisis will be helpful for all types of libraries and positions." Booklist

Includes bibliographical references

023   Personnel management (Human resource management)

Allison, Zmuda

Librarians as learning specialists; meeting the learning imperative for the 21st century. [by] Allison Zmuda and Violet H. Harada; foreword by Grant Wiggins. Libraries Unlimited 2008 128p il pa $40

Grades: Adult Professional   **023**

1. School libraries 2. Libraries and schools 3. Duties of librarians 4. Teaching -- Aids and devices 5. School libraries -- Aims and objectives

ISBN 978-1-59158-679-1; 1-59158-679-8

LC 2008-6036

"The book examines the necessity of a mission-centered mindset and changing the role of a library media specialist to a learning specialist. . . . Written for both school administrators and librarians, the well-documented book gives a workable framework for collaboration. The authors make a good case for opening the doors between classroom and library and provide tools for doing so." SLJ

Includes bibliographical references

Giesecke, Joan

Fundamentals of library supervision; [by] Joan Giesecke and Beth McNeil. 2nd ed.; American Library Association 2010 189p il (ALA fundamentals series) pa $55

Grades: Adult Professional   **023**

1. Personnel management 2. Libraries -- Administration

ISBN 978-0-8389-1016-0

LC 2009-28890

First published 2005

"The authors give advice on how to build relationships with bosses, peers, and reports; establish good communication skills; create a healthy work climate; motivate others; and build a team. . . . Each chapter includes a succinct bibliography, allowing the new manager to continue his or her education—especially useful for more complex topics like project management." Libr J

Includes bibliographical references

025   Operations of libraries, archives, information centers

Cohn, John M.

The **complete** library technology planner; a guidebook with sample technology plans and RFPs on CD-ROM. [by] John M. Cohn and Ann L. Kelsey; with a foreword by Keith Michael Fiels. Neal-Schuman Publishers 2010 xxiv, 163p il pa $99.95

Grades: Adult Professional   **025**

1. Information technology 2. Planning, Library 3. Libraries -- Automation 4. Automation of library processes -- Handbooks, manuals, etc.

ISBN 978-1-55570-681-4; 1-55570-681-9

LC 2009-41008

"This book provides a comprehensive wealth of information for libraries in need of creating or updating a technology plan. Whether your goal is to introduce an integrated library system (ILS) or transfer from an existing system to a new one, Cohn and Kelsey make clear the strategic planning process involved and provide the tools needed to create a plan, including how to meet funding requirements, implement the plan, and evaluate its success. The accompanying CD-ROM contains 38 sample technology plans and requests for proposals (RFPs) that have been collected from 32 different libraries." Libr J

Includes bibliographical references

025.04   Information storage and retrieval systems

Berger, Pam

★ **Choosing** Web 2.0 tools for learning and teaching in a digital world; [by] Pam Berger and Sally Trexler; foreword by Joyce Valenza. Libraries Unlimited 2010 221p il map pa $40

Grades: Adult Professional   **025.04**

1. Web 2.0 2. Internet in education 3. Internet searching -- Study and teaching 4. Information literacy -- Study and teaching

ISBN 978-1-59158-706-4; 1-59158-706-9

LC 2009-54069

"This guide offers a plethora of ideas for incorporating digital learning into schools in an accessible and reader-friendly manner." Voice Youth Advocates

Includes glossary and bibliographical references

Harris, Frances Jacobson

I found it on the Internet; coming of age online. 2nd ed.; American Library Association 2010 234p il pa $45

Grades: Adult Professional   **025.04**

1. Internet and teenagers 2. Young adults' libraries 3. Internet -- Social aspects

ISBN 978-0-8389-1066-5

LC 2010-13644

First published 2005

The author offers "advice on how to help young people make good decisions, especially in such thorny areas as music and media sharing; tools for formulating information and communication policies . . . [and] ways of dealing with the problematic issues of hacking, cheating, privacy, harassment, and access to inappropriate content." Publisher's note

Includes bibliographical references

Librarian's guide to online searching; cultivating database skills for research and instruction. Suzanne S. Bell. 4th edition Libraries Unlimitied 2015 xvii, 320 p.p illustrations $55

Grades: Adult Professional   **025.04**
  1. Internet searching 2. Librarians -- Training of
ISBN 161069998X; 9781610699983
                        LC 2014038457

"In its fourth edition, this work still serves as the best how-to on online searching for library degree students and those new to the profession. Bell . . . provides an updated version that includes a more thorough discussion on Google Scholar, and offers fresh discussions on discovery services and video tutorials. . . . Bell discusses the gamut of database basics, starting with database construction, moving to specialized databases by broad subject area and search strategies, and ending with advice on effectively working to engage the audience during instruction." LJ

Includes bibliographical references (pages 299-309) and index

Scheeren, William O.

Technology for the school librarian; theory and practice. Libraries Unlimited 2010 223p il $50

Grades: Adult Professional   **025.04**
  1. School libraries 2. Digital libraries 3. Information technology 4. Libraries -- Special collections
ISBN 978-1-59158-900-6; 1-59158-900-2
                        LC 2009-51922

"This title provides information on the practical aspects of technology in the school library as well as the theoretical framework to spark continued learning. Sharing actual case studies as well as practical tips on technology implentation and terminology, this title will be a valuable resource to any school librarian." Libr Media Connect

Includes bibliographical references

Shaw, Maura D.

Mastering online research; a comprehensive guide to effective and efficient search strategies. [by] Maura Shaw. Writers Digest Books 2007 340p il pa $19.99

Grades: 11 12 Adult   **025.04**
  1. Internet research 2. Internet resources 3. Internet searching 4. Web sites -- Directories
ISBN 978-1-58297-458-3; 1-58297-458-6
                        LC 2007-11286

The author describes "the techniques and tools you need to find information ranging from historical data to medical information to images and videos." Publisher's note

025.042   World Wide Web

Bodden, Valerie

Using the Internet; Valerie Bodden. Creative Education 2012 48 p. (Research for writing) (library) $35.65

Grades: 8 9 10 11 12   **025.042**
  1. Internet resources 2. Internet searching 3. Internet in education 4. Internet research 5. Computer network resources 6. Electronic information resource literacy
ISBN 160818207X; 9781608182077
                        LC 2011040493

This book is part of the Research for Writing series and focuses on using the Internet for research. The titles within the series "explain information such as the difference between qualitative and quantitative data, how to evaluate sources (both in print and online), and the importance of reference librarians." (School Library Journal)

Includes bibliographical references and index.

Devine, Jane

Going beyond Google again; strategies for using and teaching the Invisible Web. Jane Devine and Francine Egger-Sider. Amer Library Assn" "Neal-Schuman, an imprint of the American Library Assn 2013 160 p. illustrations (paperback) $72

Grades: Adult Professional   **025.042**
  1. Internet in education 2. Internet searching -- Study and teaching 3. Invisible Web 4. Database searching 5. Internet searching 6. Invisible Web -- Study and teaching
ISBN 1555708986; 9781555708986
                        LC 2013010867

This book is a follow-up volume to book "Going Beyond Google" by Jane Devine and Francine Egger-Sider, "which placed teaching the Invisible Web into information literacy programs. [This volume] expands on the teaching foundation laid in the first book and continues to document the Invisible Web's existence and evolution, and suggests ways of teaching students to use it." (Publisher's note)

"Chapter summaries and extensive citations make this an attractive choice for students. It should also be of interest to librarians and anyone interested in optimizing their research resources and strategies." LJ

Includes bibliographical references and index

Harris, Frances Jacobson

★ **I** found it on the Internet; coming of age online. Frances Jacobson Harris. 2nd ed. American Library Association 2010 xi, 234 p.p ill. (paperback) $45

Grades: Adult Professional   **025.042**
  1. Internet searching 2. Internet in education 3. Internet and teenagers 4. Young adults' libraries 5. Internet/Social aspects
ISBN 0838910661; 9780838910665
                        LC 2010013644

This book is an "analysis of the fundamental differences in how teens . . . and adults . . . view information and communication. . . . The book opens with a description of the current state of library affairs, wherein information retrieval has become primarily a computerized event and the collision between information technology and communication technology has literally forged a new, merged reality that Harris terms ICT (information community technology)." (School Library Journal)

This is an "analysis of the fundamental differences in how teens (for whom the Internet is a primary language) and adults (who will always be second-language learners) view information and communication." SLJ

Includes bibliographical references and index

025.1 Administration

Casey, Michael E.
Library 2.0; a guide to participatory library service. [by] Michael E. Casey, Laura C. Savastinuk. Information Today, Inc. 2007 xxv, 172p il pa $29.50
Grades: Adult Professional   **025.1**
1. Library services 2. Libraries -- Public relations
ISBN 978-1-57387-297-3; 1-57387-297-0
LC 2007-5247
"This title should be required reading for professional library staffs struggling with change and organizational restructure." Libr Media Connect
Includes bibliographical references

Dresang, Eliza T.
★ **Dynamic** youth services through outcome-based planning and evaluation; foreword by Virginia Walter. American Library Association 2006 155p il pa $42
Grades: Adult Professional   **025.1**
1. Program planning 2. Libraries -- Administration 3. School libraries -- Activity projects 4. Children's library services -- Activity projects 5. Young adults' library services -- Activity projects 6. Libraries -- Services to children -- Activities and projects
ISBN 0-8389-0918-3; 978-0-8389-0918-8
LC 2006-7487
In this "guide, three experts who have conducted extensive research and piloted . . . [an] outcome-based program for youth in the St. Louis Public Library, share their findings and proven strategies." Publisher's note
Includes bibliographical references

Farmer, Lesley S. Johnson
Neal-Schuman technology management handbook for school library media centers; by Lesley S. Johnson Farmer and Marc E. McPhee. Neal-Schuman Publishers 2010 289p il pa $59.95
Grades: Adult Professional   **025.1**
1. School libraries 2. Instructional materials centers
ISBN 978-1-55570-659-3; 1-55570-659-2
LC 2010-9301
"This informative, well-researched text is perfect for those in the early stages of integrating technology into their programs. The first chapter begins with an overview of the impact technology has had on society and defines technology and its role in the library, including past, present, and possible future changes, as well as managerial roles of the librarian. Other chapters examine planning for management, assessing, researching, developing a technology plan, acquiring all types of tech resources, and managing the physical space to accommodate equipment and networking." SLJ
Includes bibliographical references

The frugal librarian; thriving in tough economic times. edited by Carol Smallwood. American Library Association 2011 277p il
Grades: Adult Professional   **025.1**
1. Library finance 2. Libraries and community 3. Libraries -- United States
ISBN 0-8389-1075-0; 978-0-8389-1075-7
LC 2010034317
Includes bibliographical references

Gerding, Stephanie K.
★ **Winning** grants; a how-to-do-it manual for librarians with multimedia tutorials and grant development tools. [by] Pamela H. MacKellar and Stephanie K. Gerding. Neal-Schuman Publishers 2010 xxi, 242p il (How-to-do-it manuals for librarians)
Grades: Adult Professional   **025.1**
1. Fund raising 2. Grants-in-aid
ISBN 978-1-55570-700-2
LC 2010017965
First published 2006 with title: Grants for libraries
"This great all-around resource should be a staple for those just entering the challenging world of grant seeking and for the well-rounded library collection." Libr J
Includes bibliographical references

Harvey, Carl A.
★ **No** school library left behind; leadership, school improvement, and the media specialist. [by] Carl A. Harvey II. Linworth Pub. 2008 106p pa $39.95
Grades: Adult Professional   **025.1**
1. School libraries 2. Instructional materials centers 3. Libraries -- Administration
ISBN 978-1-58683-233-9; 1-58683-233-6
LC 2007-42178
"The content [of this book] constitutes a crash course in school improvement, covering definitions, history, legislation, research, best practices, assessment, profiles of accreditation associations, and most importantly, a strong rationale for why media specialists should lead the way in school improvement efforts. . . . Of major interest to novice and seasoned practitioners, this guide is timely and relevant." Libr Media Connect
Includes bibliographical references

★ **Independent** school libraries; perspectives on excellence. Dorcas Hand, editor. Libraries Unlimited 2010 369p il (Libraries Unlimited professional guides in school librarianship) pa $45
Grades: Adult Professional   **025.1**
1. Private schools 2. School libraries
ISBN 978-1-59158-803-0 pa; 1-59158-803-0 pa; 978-1-59158-812-2 ebook
LC 2010-14567
"Twenty-one essays by prominent independent school librarians both address the current state of independent school librarianship in the United States and offer suggestions for the future. Pieces cover the library's role in the school, statistical comparisons, staffing, advocacy, assessment, technology, information commons, collaboration, college prepara-

tion, programming, traditions, collection development, minors' rights, budgeting, facilities, accreditation, and disaster planning. . . . Librarians from all schools will find a wealth of information here." Voice Youth Advocates

Includes bibliographical references

Johnson, Doug

★ The **indispensable** librarian; surviving and thriving in school libraries in the information age. Doug Johnson; illustrations by Brady Johnson. Linworth, an imprint of ABC-CLIO, LLC 2013 xix, 207 p.p illustrations (pbk.) $40

Grades: Adult Professional   **025.1**

1. Librarians 2. School libraries 3. School librarians -- United States 4. School libraries -- United States -- Administration

ISBN 161069239X; 9781610692397

LC 2012051394

This book, by Doug A. Johnson, "defines and clarifies the role of the school library media specialist in a technologically enhanced school, providing relevant examples and useful advice on a variety of topics; and underscores the importance of strong management skills, especially regarding collaborative planning and communications. The book is written especially for K-12 school librarians, both new and experienced, and is also suitable for pre-service librarians as a textbook." (Publisher's note)

"Johnson offers both theory and practical suggestions on ways to embed [librarians] and [their] jobs into the fabric of a school's culture and curriculum." Lib Med Con

Includes bibliographical references and index

MacDonell, Colleen

★ **Essential** documents for school libraries; 2nd ed.; Linworth 2010 xxiv, 156p il $50

Grades: Adult Professional   **025.1**

1. Libraries -- Administration

ISBN 978-1-58683-400-5

LC 2010-21241

First published 2004

"Each chapter begins with why the documents are needed, followed by practical advice for writing the documents, and examples of how the documents make an effective change in the library media program." Libr Media Connect [review of 2004 edition]

Includes bibliographical references

Martin, Barbara Stein

★ **Fundamentals** of school library media management; a how-to-do-it manual. [by] Barbara Stein Martin and Marco Zannier. Neal-Schuman Publishers 2009 172p il (How-to-do-it manuals for librarians) pa $59.95

Grades: Adult Professional   **025.1**

1. School libraries 2. Instructional materials centers

ISBN 978-1-55570-656-2; 1-55570-656-8

LC 2009-7930

This book "contains useful information to help school librarians manage a myriad of tasks and roles. . . . [The au-

thors] have created a book that is helpful, accessible, and full of down-to-earth, concrete examples." Booklist

Includes bibliographical references

McGhee, Marla W.

★ The **principal's** guide to a powerful library media program; a school library for the 21st century. [by] Marla W. McGhee and Barbara A. Jansen. 2nd ed.; Linworth 2010 xxviii, 149p pa $45

Grades: Adult Professional   **025.1**

1. School libraries 2. Instructional materials centers 3. School superintendents and principals

ISBN 978-1-58683-526-2 pa; 1-58683-526-2 pa; 978-1-58683-527-9 ebook

LC 2010-21243

First published 2005

"With focused and well-organized topics from understanding the research and standards to supporting and sustaining them through collaborative processes, this . . . offers a great deal of concrete information. . . . This book gives administrators a clear idea of what is required in the media center and the role of the librarian as a specialist. . . . An excellent choice for the professional media specialist's or principal's shelf." SLJ

Includes bibliographical references

★ **School** library management; [edited by] Judi Repman and Gail Dickinson. 6th ed.; Linworth Pub. 2007 200p il pa $44.95

Grades: Adult Professional   **025.1**

1. School libraries 2. Libraries -- Administration

ISBN 1-58683-296-4; 978-1-58683-296-4

LC 2006-103468

First published 1987 with title: School library management notebook

"This collection of more than 35 articles written for Library Media Connection from 2003 to 2006 is a virtual treasure trove for library media specialists. . . . The book covers the very practical everyday issues such as scheduling and overdues, and also provides invaluable information on data gathering, facilities planning, professional development, the role of the library in the world of standardized testing, the technological future of libraries, and much more." SLJ

Includes bibliographical references

Tips and other bright ideas for secondary school libraries, volume 3; Sherry York, editor. Linworth Pub. 2006 168p il $36.95

Grades: Adult Professional   **025.1**

1. High school libraries 2. Libraries -- Administration

ISBN 1-58683-210-7; 978-1-58683-210-0

LC 2005-29594

Continues Tips and other bright ideas for school librarians (1991)

"The tips, all from practicing school library media specialists, were collected from Library Media Connection and are categorized into nine sections with a box per section outlining what will be covered. This format is very helpful in locating information quickly and easily. From managing your library and collaborating with teachers to using technology, these tried-and-true tips are well worth the cost of the book." SLJ

Includes bibliographical references

Tips and other bright ideas for secondary school libraries, volume 4; Kate Vande Brake, editor. Linworth 2010 134p pa $35

Grades: Adult Professional   025.1

1. High school libraries 2. Libraries -- Administration

ISBN 978-1-58683-418-0

LC 2010-10428

Continues Tips and other bright ideas for school librarians (1991)

The tips included in this book were taken from Library Media Connection magazine from 2006-2009. The book "is organized into . . . sections that tackle topics such as managing the library, working with students, collaborating with teachers, teaching research skills, building positive public relations, and using technology." Publisher's note

The **whole** library handbook; teen services. edited by Heather Booth and Karen Jensen. ALA Editions, an imprint of the American Library Association 2014 xi, 204 p.p illustrations (alk. paper) $60

Grades: Adult Professional   025.1

1. Young adults' libraries 2. Teenagers -- Books and reading 3. Libraries and teenagers 4. Young adult services librarians 5. Young adults' libraries -- Administration 6. Young adults' libraries -- United States -- Administration

ISBN 0838912249; 9780838912249

LC 2014004303

This book, edited by Heather Booth and Karen Jensen, part of the Whole Library Handbook series from the American Library Association, is "specifically geared towards those who serve young adults, gathering . . . articles and commentary from . . . innovative and successful teen services librarians. Sections focusing on practice, theory, and the philosophical underpinnings of the profession are supported by current research and historical perspectives." (Publisher's note)

"This guide to providing teen services in public libraries is quite comprehensive, earning its place as part of The Whole Library Handbook series." VOYA

Includes bibliographical references and index

025.17 Administration of collections of special materials

★ **No** shelf required; e-books in libraries. edited by Sue Polanka. American Library Association 2011 182p pa $65

Grades: Adult Professional   025.17

1. Electronic books

ISBN 978-0-83891-054-2

LC 2010-14045

"Following a chapter on e-book history are chapters discussing e-books and students' learning; e-books in school, public, and academic libraries; and e-book acquisitions

and management. . . . An essential guide to a topic of high importance." Booklist

Includes bibliographical references

025.2 Acquisitions and collection development

Alabaster, Carol

★ **Developing** an outstanding core collection; a guide for libraries. 2nd ed; American Library Association 2010 191p il pa $60

Grades: Adult Professional   025.2

1. Best books 2. Reference books 3. Libraries -- Collection development 4. Public libraries -- Collection development

ISBN 978-0-8389-1040-5

LC 2009-40342

First published 2002

The author suggests "that the general public needs materials beyond current best-sellers and ready-reference works; that those materials should be high-quality, enduring pieces; and that librarians are the best persons to decide what constitutes appropriate core collections for their communities. . . . [She also] addresses the technological changes that drastically affect reading habits and our ability to satisfy the needs of 'the people's university.' . . . [This book is] required reading for all those charged with the task of adult collection development." Booklist

Includes bibliographical references

Baumbach, Donna

★ **Less** is more; a practical guide to weeding school library collections. American Library Association 2006 194p il pa $32

Grades: Adult Professional   025.2

1. Libraries -- Collection development

ISBN 978-0-8389-0919-5; 0-8389-0919-1

LC 2006-7490

"Chapter one gives an overview for weeding school collections. Chapter two describes common weeding guidelines. Chapter three covers the where and how of the weeding process. Chapter four is the core of the book, covering 70 topics and subject areas or Dewey classifications, giving guidelines for those subjects." Lib Med Con

"This outstanding, easy-to-use guide makes weeding realistic and achievable. . . . This is an indispensable resource for every school library." Booklist

Includes bibliographical references

Brenner, Robin E.

★ **Understanding** manga and anime. Libraries Unlimited 2007 335p il pa $40

Grades: Adult Professional   025.2

1. Anime 2. Manga -- Study and teaching 3. Libraries -- Collection development 4. Libraries -- Special collections -- Graphic novels

ISBN 978-1-59158-332-5; 1-59158-332-2

LC 2007-9773

The author "provides thorough explanations of manga and anime vocabulary, potential censorship issues because of cultural disparities, and typical Manga conventions. . . . No professional collection could possibly be complete without this all-inclusive and exceptional work." *Voice Youth Advocates*

Building and managing e-book collections; a how-to-do-it manual for librarians. edited by Richard Kaplan. Neal-Schuman 2012 xv, 197 p.p (pbk.: alk. paper) $75

Grades: Adult Professional   **025.2**

1. Libraries -- Collection development 2. Libraries and electronic publishing 3. Libraries -- Special Collections -- Electronic books 4. Electronic books

ISBN 1555707769; 9781555707767

LC 2012018143

This book on library collections of e-books, edited by Richard B. Kaplan, focuses on "collection development issues, including the selection process and development policies, the use of approval plans, patron-driven acquisition, and practical solutions for creating your e-book collection policies. Chapters on budgeting and licensing cover ownership versus leasing models . . . on digital rights management, and strategies for success in retention, access, and budgeting." (Publisher's note)

"This title features a wealth of useful information . . . the concepts and issues covered are applicable to all libraries. This book provides a solid snapshot of the current best practices in the world of e-book collecting." CHOICE

Includes bibliographical references and index

Garnar, Martin

★ **Intellectual** Freedom Manual; Trina Magi, Martin Garnar, Office for Intellectual Freedom of the American Library Association. 9th ed. ALA Editions, An imprint of the American Library Association 2015 434 p. $70

Grades: Adult Professional   **025.2**

1. Censorship 2. Library science 3. Intellectual freedom 4. Freedom of information -- United States -- Handbooks, manuals, etc. 5. Libraries -- Censorship -- United States -- Handbooks, manuals, etc.

ISBN 0838912923; 9780838912928

LC 2014037437

First published 1974

This newest edition "is more than just an invaluable compendium of guiding principles and policies. It's also an indispensable resource for day-to-day guidance on maintaining free and equal access to information for all people. Fortifying and emboldening professionals and students from across the library spectrum, this manual includes . . . 34 ALA policy statements and documents [and] explanations of legal points." (Publisher's note)

"All libraries should have a copy of this book to use when writing or revising policies; indispensable." *Libr J*

Includes bibliographical references and index

Graphic novels beyond the basics; insights and issues for libraries. Martha Cornog and Timothy Perper, editors. Libraries Unlimited 2009 xxx, 281p il pa $45

Grades: Adult Professional   **025.2**

1. Graphic novels -- History and criticism 2. Comic books, strips, etc. -- History and criticism 3. Libraries -- Special collections -- Graphic novels

ISBN 978-1-59158-478-0; 1-59158-478-7

LC 2009-16189

Editors Cornog and Perper have collected essays by experts Robin Brenner, Francisca Goldsmith, Trina Robbins, Michael R. Lavin, Gilles Poitras, Lorena O'English, Michael Niederhausen, Erin Byrne, and Cornog herself, all about graphic novels in libraries. Topics covered range from the appeal of superheroes to manga, the appeal of comics to women and girls, anime, independent comics, dealing with challenges to the material, and more. Appendices provide resource information on African American-interest graphic novels, Latino-Interest graphic novels, LGBT-interest graphic novels, religious-themed graphic novels, a bibliography of books about graphic novels in libraries, and online resources.

"Whether you are serious about the genre, interested in the history, or looking for ammunition, this book should be on your shelf. The wealth of knowledge and research that went into these essays is impressive, and reading this book will put you on the road to becoming an expert." *Libr Media Connect*

Includes bibliographical references

Loertscher, David V.

★ **Collection** development using the collection mapping technique; a guide for librarians. [by] David V. Loertscher, Laura H. Wimberley. Hi Willow Research and Pub. 2009 122p il pa $30

Grades: Adult Professional   **025.2**

1. Libraries -- Collection development

ISBN 978-1-933170-43-5

This is "a how-to manual for media specialists to formulate and implement a collection development plan based on a collection map. This book is an excellent resource for every novice or veteran media specialist building a collection for 21st century users." *Libr Media Connect*

Includes bibliographical references

Mayer, Brian

Libraries got game; aligned learning through modern board games. [by] Brian Mayer and Christopher Harris. American Library Association 2010 134p il pa $45

Grades: Adult Professional   **025.2**

1. Board games 2. Libraries -- Special collections

ISBN 978-0-8389-1009-2; 0-8389-1009-2

LC 2009-26839

"This is a valuable resource for K-12 librarians interested in building curriculum-aligned 'designer' game collections. The authors . . . explain how specific games enhance language-arts, social-studies, and math units, and build literacy skills. The two chapters devoted to promoting and justifying the inclusion of games in the library are well documented and a wonderful source to have to convince skeptical administrators. Suggestions for building a core collection, which highlights top recommended games for elementary school, middle school, and high school; a list of game publishers; a list of games discussed; and a glossary of terminology are included." *SLJ*

Includes bibliographical references

Reichman, Henry

★ **Censorship** and selection; issues and answers for schools. 3rd ed; American Library Association 2001 223p pa $37

Grades: Adult Professional   **025.2**

    1. Censorship 2. Academic freedom 3. School libraries
    ISBN 0-8389-0798-9

                              LC 00-67657

    First published 1988

    "Reichman's manual provides sound practical advice on how to handle this complex and emotionally charged subject." Voice Youth Advocates

    Includes bibliographical references

Scales, Pat R.

★ **Protecting** intellectual freedom in your school library; scenarios from the front lines. [by] Pat R. Scales for the Office for Intellectual Freedom. American Library Association 2009 148p (Intellectual freedom front lines) pa $55

Grades: Adult Professional   **025.2**

    1. School libraries 2. Intellectual freedom
    ISBN 978-0-8389-3581-1; 0-8389-3581-8

                           LC 2008-39893

    "Scales uses court opinions, federal and state laws, and ALA documents to offer solutions for responding to infringements. A broad range of potential scenarios—from challenges to materials in both the library and the classroom, the legality of film rating systems, using computerized reading programs as selection tools and labeling books by reading levels, policies for interlibrary loans and reserves to confidentiality of children's and teens' circulation records—are covered. . . . This resource should be in every school library's professional collection." Voice Youth Advocates

    Includes bibliographical references

Singer, Carol A.

Fundamentals of Managing Reference Collections; Carol A. Singer. American Library Association 2012 xii, 167 p.p (pbk.) $60

Grades: Professional   **025.2**

    1. Reference books 2. Libraries -- Special collections 3. Electronic reference services (Libraries) 4. Reference books -- United States 5. Electronic reference sources -- United States 6. Libraries -- Special collections -- Reference sources 7. Collection management (Libraries) -- United States -- Case studies
    ISBN 0838911536; 9780838911532

                           LC 2011044446

    Author Carol A. "Singer's book offers information and insight on best practices for reference collection management, no matter the size, and shows why managing without a plan is a recipe for clutter and confusion." Singer discusses "the importance of collection development policies, and how to effectively involve others in the decision-making process," in addition to "new insights into selecting reference materials" and "strategies for collection maintenance." (Publisher's note)

    Includes bibliographical references and index

Walker, Barbara J.

★ The **librarian's** guide to developing Christian fiction collections for young adults. Neal-Schuman Publishers 2005 200p (The librarian's guides to developing Christian fiction collections) pa $55

Grades: Adult Professional   **025.2**

    1. Reference books 2. Teenagers -- Books and reading 3. Libraries -- Special collections 4. Christian fiction -- Bibliography
    ISBN 1-55570-545-6

                          LC 2005-5112

    The author discusses issues "such as censorship, the legalities in spending tax dollars on Christian novels, and marketing to an underserved clientele. 'Key Book Titles' offers an extensive, annotated bibliography, organized by topic (Apocalyptic, Bible, Contemporary, Fantasy, Historical, Mystery, Romance, Thrillers, Westerns). . . . A thorough, balanced approach." SLJ

    Includes bibliographical references

025.43   General classification systems

★ **Sears** List of Subject Headings; Barbara A. Bristow, editor; Christi Showman Farrar, associate editor. 21st edition Grey House Publishing/H.W. Wilson 2014 946 pp. (hardcover) $165.00

Grades: Adult Professional   **025.43**

    1. Cataloging 2. Library science 3. Subject headings
    ISBN 9781619251908

                          LC 2013498263

    This book, edited by Barbara A. Bristow and Christi Showman Farrar, presents the frameworks for the Sears List of Subject Headings cataloging system. "This resource lists subject headings used by small and medium-sized libraries, with patterns, examples, and notes on usage. The subject headings are listed alphabetically and aligned with the Dewey Decimal Classification system and include a list of canceled and replacement headings, as well as a discussion of the theoretical foundations of the list and the general principles of subject cataloging." (Book News)

025.5   Services for users

Ercegovac, Zorana

Information literacy; search strategies, tools & resources for high school students and college freshmen. 2nd ed.; Linworth Pub. 2008 xxi, 186p pa $44.95

Grades: Adult Professional   **025.5**

    1. Report writing 2. Information literacy 3. Libraries and students
    ISBN 978-1-58683-332-9; 1-58683-332-4

                          LC 2008-1893

    First published 2001

    "This book is a great tool to help . . . [media specialists] build the next generation." Libr Media Connect

    Includes bibliographical references

George, Mary W.

★ The **elements** of library research; what every student needs to know. Princeton University Press 2008 201p il pa $14.95

Grades: 10 11 12 Adult   **025.5**
  1. Research 2. Bibliographic instruction
  ISBN 978-0-691-13857-2
LC 2008-13733

This "is a very useful tool for students struggling to identify a topic for a term paper, and it effectively frames the subsequent information gathering as a challenging but fun treasure hunt." Ref & User Services Quarterly

  Includes bibliographical references

Grassian, Esther S.

Information literacy instruction; theory and practice. [by] Esther S. Grassian and Joan R. Kaplowitz. 2nd ed; Neal-Schuman Publishers 2009 xxvii, 412p pa $75

Grades: Adult Professional   **025.5**
  1. Information literacy 2. Information literacy -- Study and teaching 3. Information retrieval -- Study and teaching 4. Bibliographic instruction -- College and university students
  ISBN 978-155570-666-1; 1-55570-666-5
LC 2009-23647

First published 2001

This "is designed for anyone involved in the creation and management of information literacy programming. Sixteen well-written chapters, organized into five sections, provide both theory and practical applications, with the emphasis on the practical. . . . Several extras appear in the accompanying CD-ROM. . . . A timely, thorough, and endlessly useful must-have title for librarians, teaching librarians, and library schools." Booklist

  Includes bibliographical references

Hernon, Peter

Assessing service quality; satisfying the expectations of library customers. [by] Peter Hernon + Ellen Altman. 2nd ed; American Library Association 2010 206p il pa $65

Grades: Adult Professional   **025.5**
  1. Library services 2. Libraries -- Public relations
  ISBN 978-0-8389-1021-4; 0-8389-1021-1
LC 2009-40332

First published 1998

The authors "concentrate on how to assess service quality and customer satisfaction. Here they suggest . . . ways to think about library services, clarify the distinction between service quality and customer satisfaction, present strategies for developing a customer service plan, identify procedures to measure service quality and satisfaction, and . . . challenge conventional thinking about these powerful principles. . . . Kudos to these authors for providing an essential resource for librarians who understand that folks who walk into their libraries are not patrons but customers." Libr J

  Includes bibliographical references

Kern, M. Kathleen

★ **Virtual** reference best practices; tailoring services to your library. American Library Association 2009 148p il pa $50

Grades: Adult Professional   **025.5**
  1. Reference services (Libraries)
  ISBN 978-0-8389-0975-1
LC 2008-15379

The author "offers advice and assistance for libraries considering VR. . . . Kern's guidebook includes useful forms and exercises for every aspect of the VR process from a market assessment of the library's community served to an evaluation of the service. . . . Even those [libraries] which already offer virtual reference will find assistance and suggestions to improve their services." Voice Youth Advocates

  Includes bibliographical references

Lanning, Scott

Essential reference services for today's school media specialists; [by] Scott Lanning and John Bryner. 2nd ed.; Libraries Unlimited 2010 141p il pa $45

Grades: Adult Professional   **025.5**
  1. School libraries 2. Reference services (Libraries)
  ISBN 978-1-59158-883-2; 1-59158-883-9
LC 2009-39375

"The content focuses on core reference skills, electronic resources, and leadership. The first few chapters discuss information literacy, evaluation of resources, the role of print resources, and the reference interview. These are followed by chapters on the library catalog, electronic resources, and the Web as a reference tool. Finally, there are several chapters dealing with the teacher-librarians' instructional and leadership roles. The authors use a very accessible tone while providing the basics." Booklist

  Includes bibliographical references

Lenburg, Jeff

The **Facts** on File guide to research; 2nd ed; Facts on File 2010 xxxvi, 720p (Facts on File library of language and literature) $50; pa $18.95

Grades: 8 9 10 11 12   **025.5**
  1. Research 2. Information resources
  ISBN 978-0-8160-8121-9; 0-8160-8121-2; 978-0-8160-8122-6 pa; 0-8160-8122-0 pa
LC 2009-48200

First published 2005

This guide includes "lists of thousands of resources and explains general research methods and proper citation of sources. . . . [It features] discussions of Google and other search engines, subject-specific keyword search strategies, a cautionary note about Wikipedia, and . . . more." Publisher's note

  Includes bibliographical references

Saricks, Joyce G.

The **readers'** advisory guide to genre fiction; 2nd ed; American Library Association 2009 352p (ALA readers' advisory series) pa $65

Grades: Adult Professional   **025.5**
  1. Reference services (Libraries) 2. Fiction --

Bibliography
ISBN 978-0-8389-0989-8

LC 2008-51029

First published 2001

"Each section includes three or four specific genres . . . and features a definition and introduction to the genre, the characteristics of the genre's appeal, suggested authors and titles, and other practical information. Well-crafted back matter add to the ease of navigation. This very readable text employs a playful tone that reflects Saricks's love of her work and will inspire readers to use RA techniques in a variety of ways. [This is] a useful tool for both new library employees and established practitioners." Voice Youth Advocates

Includes bibliographical references

Smith, Susan S.

★ **Web**-based instruction; a guide for libraries. [by] Susan Sharpless Smith. 3rd ed.; American Library Association 2010 236p il pa $65

Grades: Adult Professional   **025.5**

1. Bibliographic instruction 2. Library information networks 3. Computer-assisted instruction 4. Web sites -- Design

ISBN 978-0-8389-1056-6; 0-8389-1056-4

LC 2010-6452

First published 2001

This book covers "tools and trends, including current browsers, access methods, hardware, and software. [The author] also supplies tips to secure project funding and provides strategic guidance for all types of libraries." Publisher's note

Includes bibliographical references

Tallman, Julie I.

Making the writing and research connection with the I-search process; a how-to-do-it manual. [by] Julie I. Tallman, Marilyn Z. Joyce. 2nd ed.; Neal-Schuman Publishers 2006 xx, 167p il (How-to-do-it manuals for librarians) pa $55

Grades: Adult Professional   **025.5**

1. Research 2. Report writing 3. Young adults' libraries 4. Bibliographic instruction

ISBN 1-55570-534-0; 978-1-55570-534-3

LC 2005-32473

First published 1997

This volume "covers the I-Search process for middle and high-school students and . . . includes a detailed explanation of I-Search in the context of content units. Although it is useful for the media specialist and teacher who are familiar with I-Search, novices will also find valuable information. . . The accompanying CD-ROM contains all of the figures found in the book (templates, handouts, etc.), which can be reproduced and adapted." Booklist

Includes bibliographical references

Virtual reference on a budget; case studies. editors, Teresa Dalston and Michael Pullin. Linworth Pub. 2008 xx, 191p il pa $39.95

Grades: Adult Professional   **025.5**

1. Reference services (Libraries)

ISBN 1-58683-287-5; 978-1-58683-287-2

LC 2007-25987

"Librarians searching for step-by-step guidance on how to implement virtual reference service will find explicit instructions and many examples in this slim but dense volume. The overview of the history of digital reference provides an excellent introduction to the topic, along with definitions of terms, and also offers detailed case studies from middle school, high school, academic, and deaf community settings." Voice Youth Advocates

Includes bibliographical references

Volkman, John D.

★ **Collaborative** library research projects; inquiry that stimulates the senses. Libraries Unlimited 2008 196p il

Grades: Adult Professional   **025.5**

1. School libraries 2. Bibliographic instruction 3. Instructional materials centers 4. Research and the library 5. School libraries -- Relations with teachers and curriculum 6. Bibliographic instruction -- Elementary and high school students

ISBN 1-59158-623-2; 978-1-59158-623-4

LC 2008-640

"This book provides helpful advice in an area central to the mission of school media specialists everywhere—collaboration with teachers. In clear, jargon-free language, Volkman lays out an argument for using his style of collaborative research units. . . . Units on history, literature, science, and other topics are covered. Planning, preparation, and station construction methods are discussed concisely. . . . Volkman's accessible writing provides a well-thought-out, no-nonsense book that will be useful to the novice or experienced school media specialist." Voice Youth Advocates

Includes bibliographical references

Wichman, Emily T.

Librarian's guide to passive programming; easy and affordable activities for all ages. Emily T. Wichman. Libraries Unlimited Inc. 2012 xvii, 152 p.p ill. (pbk.: acid-free paper) $40

Grades: Adult Professional   **025.5**

1. Librarians 2. Library finance 3. Library services 4. Libraries -- Activity programs -- United States

ISBN 159884895X; 9781598848953; 9781598848960

LC 2011045419

In her book, author Emily T. Wichman discusses library budget cuts, and how "librarians are seeking new ways to stretch their programming dollars and maximize staff resources. Passive programming allows libraries to inexpensively showcase their services while inviting visitors of all ages to enjoy the value that libraries bring to the community." (Publisher's note)

Includes bibliographical references and index.

Woodward, Jeannette A.

★ **What** every librarian should know about electronic privacy. Libraries Unlimited 2007 222p pa $40

Grades: Adult Professional   **025.5**

1. Right of privacy 2. Computer security 3. Internet -- Security measures 4. Libraries -- Security measures

ISBN 978-1-59158-489-6; 1-59158-489-2

LC 2007-13566

"Beginning with a breakdown of the types of library clients and their often blasé attitude toward Internet privacy and security, author Jeannette Woodward then proceeds to use those client types as examples for real-world impact of how privacy could be an issue to librarians. . . . Well written and well researched, this book certainly lives up to its title." Libr Media Connect

Includes bibliographical references

Wyatt, Neal

The **readers'** advisory guide to nonfiction. American Library Association 2007 318p (ALA reader's advisory series) pa $48

Grades: Adult Professional   **025.5**

1. Public libraries 2. Reference services (Libraries)

ISBN 978-0-8389-0936-2; 0-8389-0936-1

LC 2006-102318

Wyatt "focuses on eight popular categories: history, true crime, true adventure, science, memoir, food/cooking, travel, and sports. Within each, she explains the scope, popularity, style, major authors and works, and the subject's position in readers' advisory interviews. Wyatt addresses who is reading nonfiction and why, while providing RAs with the tools and language to incorporate nonfiction into discussions that point readers to what to read next. . . . [This] guide includes nonfiction bibliography, key authors, benchmark books with annotations, and core collections." Publisher's note

Includes bibliographical references

025.7   Physical preparation for storage and use

Schechter, Abraham A.

★ **Basic** book repair methods; illustrated by the author. Libraries Unlimited 1999 102p il pa $37

Grades: Adult Professional   **025.7**

1. Books -- Conservation and restoration

ISBN 1-56308-700-6

LC 98-50950

Photographs accompany step-by-step instructions for common preservation techniques, from the cleaning of pages and their readhesion, to case reattachment and rebacking.

Includes bibliographical references

027   General libraries, archives, information centers

The **whole** library handbook 4; current data, professional advice, and curiosa about libraries and library services. edited by George M. Eberhart.

American Library Association 2006 585p il map $42

Grades: Adult Professional   **027**

1. Library science 2. Library services 3. Libraries -- United States

ISBN 0-8389-0915-9; 978-0-8389-0915-7

LC 2005-33619

First published 1991

This is an "encyclopedic collection of factual data covering all aspects of the library world, together with readable excerpts from recent books and articles on 'librariana.'" Choice

Includes bibliographical references

027.6   Libraries for special groups and organizations

Alire, Camila

★ **Serving** Latino communities; a how-to-do-it manual for librarians. [by] Camila Alire, Jacqueline Ayala. 2nd ed; Neal-Schuman Publishers 2007 229p il (How-to-do-it manuals for librarians) pa $59.95

Grades: Adult Professional   **027.6**

1. Libraries and Hispanic Americans

ISBN 978-1-55570-606-7; 1-55570-606-1

LC 2007-7783

First published 1998

"The information covered helps library staff understand the needs of their library's Latino community; develop successful programs and services; obtain funding for projects and programs; prepare staff to work more effectively with Latinos; establish partnerships with relevant external agencies and organizations; improve collection development; and perform effective outreach and public relations. . . . There are few resources widely available on this topic and none as complete." Libr Media Connect

Includes bibliographical references

Lerch, Maureen T.

Serving homeschooled teens and their parents. Libraries Unlimited 2004 242p (Libraries Unlimited professional guides for young adult librarians) pa $39

Grades: Adult Professional   **027.6**

1. Home schooling 2. Young adults' libraries

ISBN 0-313-32052-7

LC 2004-46518

"After introductory chapters that dispel many myths about homeschooling and delve into adolescent psychology, the two experts give sound advice and great examples for service plan creation, collection development, programming, and promotion of services." Libr Media Connect

Includes bibliographical references

McCook, Kathleen de la Pena

★ **Library** services to youth of Hispanic heritage; Barbara Immroth and Kathleen de la Peña McCook, editors; assisted by Catherine Jasper. McFarland & Co. 2000 197p pa $42.50

Grades: Adult Professional   **027.6**
1. Young adults' libraries 2. Libraries and Hispanic Americans
ISBN 0-7864-0790-5
                                        LC 00-37247

In this "collection of essays, more than 20 experts in the field discuss library programs, collections, planning, and evaluation of services for Hispanic youth." Booklist

Includes bibliographical references

027.62   Libraries for specific age groups

Alessio, Amy J.

A **year** of programs for teens. American Library Association 2007 159p il pa $35
Grades: Adult Professional   **027.62**
1. Young adults' libraries 2. Teenagers -- Books and reading 3. Young adults' library services -- Activity projects
ISBN 0-8389-0903-5; 978-0-8389-0903-4
                                     LC 2006-13758

"Following an overview of the planning component of successful teen programming, this guide is presented as a calendar of ideas for each month of the year. Each month offers three to four programs with the preparation time, the length of the program, the recommended number of teen participants, age range, a shopping list, the setup required, variations or extra activities, and resources. . . . Librarians working with teens will find plenty of fresh ideas here." Booklist

Includes bibliographical references

A **year** of programs for teens 2; [by] Amy J. Alessio and Kimberly A. Patton. American Library Association 2011 pa $45
Grades: Adult Professional   **027.62**
1. Young adults' libraries 2. Teenagers -- Books and reading 3. 3. Young adults' library services -- Activity projects
ISBN 978-0-8389-1051-1; 0-8389-1051-3
                                     LC 2010013661

"The authors offer great suggestions to public and school librarians who either need more ideas or to those who just want to spice up their current routines. The book includes plenty of real-life examples and variety. Part one offers ideas for core programming—those that can be scheduled on a regular basis. The authors give great advice for starting monthly clubs as well as introducing or revamping reading programs. Great book lists and ideas for displays are included, and passive activities like puzzles and quizzes round out this section. The second section lays out a year's worth of possible programming, with multiple options for each month." SLJ

Includes bibliographical references

Braafladt, Keith

Technology and literacy; 21st century library programming for children and teens. by Jennifer Nelson and Keith Braafladt. American Library Association 2012 129 p. (alk. paper) $50.00

Grades: Adult Professional   **027.62**
1. Library services 2. Literacy programs 3. Literature and technology 4. Children's libraries -- Activity programs 5. Scratch (Computer program language) 6. Computer literacy -- Study and teaching 7. Technological literacy -- Study and teaching 8. Young adults' libraries -- Activity programs
ISBN 0838911080; 9780838911082
                                     LC 2011035104

This book by Jennifer Nelson presents a "guide for creating and implementing technology-based programming in public libraries. . . . Beginning chapters explain and present a plan for offering such programs, providing steps on how to execute them. . . . The author explains the value of this type of programming and the process involved with adoption, and covers planning, gathering support from both administration and staff, marketing . . . managing time, etc." (School Library Journal)

Includes bibliographical references and index.

Braun, Linda W.

Risky business; taking and managing risks in library services for teens. [by] Linda W. Braun, Hillias Jack Martin, and Connie Urquhart for the Young Adult Library Services Association. American Library Association 2010 151p
Grades: Adult Professional   **027.62**
1. Young adults' libraries 2. Risk-taking (Psychology) 3. Teenagers -- Books and reading 4. Libraries -- Collection development
ISBN 0-8389-3596-6; 978-0-8389-3596-5
                                     LC 201005995

"This thought-provoking title will pique awareness and present some 'ah ha!' moments. It involves a degree of risk to provide exemplary library services to young adults in terms of collection building, programming, and technology. This book encourages librarians to take the necessary risks and describes factors to consider in different situations. . . . Of particular interest are chapters devoted to developing a mature, appealing, high-interest YA collection. This section alone makes the book a worthwhile addition." SLJ

Includes bibliographical references

Brehm-Heeger, Paula

Serving urban teens. Libraries Unlimited 2008 229p (Libraries Unlimited professional guides for young adult librarians) pa $40
Grades: Adult Professional   **027.62**
1. Young adults' libraries 2. Teenagers -- Books and reading 3. Young adults' library services 4. Public libraries -- Metropolitan areas
ISBN 978-1-59158-377-6; 1-59158-377-2
                                     LC 2007045415

This book "begins with definitions and a brief history of library services to urban teens, followed by a description of issues concerning this special group. The remaining chapters detail every aspect of making positive connections with teens, from training staff—the entire library staff—to making space, developing the collection, designing programs, and developing partnerships within the community. . . . It is not only the mission of libraries but also in their self-interest to capture the minds and hearts of youth while they can.

This book provides the tools to accomplish the job." Voice Youth Advocates

Includes bibliographical references

Burek Pierce, Jennifer

Sex, brains, and video games; a librarian's guide to teens in the twenty-first century. American Library Association 2008 130p pa $35

Grades: Adult Professional   027.62

1. Adolescence 2. Young adults' libraries 3. Teenagers -- United States

ISBN 978-0-8389-0951-5; 0-8389-0951-5

LC 2007-21926

"This guide provides new and reevaluated ideas and insights about the sociological, neurological, emotional, and sexual perspectives of adolescence. The author's purpose is to assist librarians as they try to engage teens through relevant and attractive responses to their recreational, informational, and technological needs and interests. . . . It is filled with a great deal of pertinent and thought-provoking advice and information." SLJ

Includes bibliographical references

Cannon, Tara C.

Cooler than fiction; a planning guide for teen nonfiction booktalks. [by] Jill S. Jarrell and Tara C. Cannon. McFarland & Company, Inc., Publishers 2011 189p il pa $45

Grades: Adult Professional   027.62

1. Book talks 2. Young adults' libraries 3. Teenagers -- Books and reading

ISBN 978-0-7864-4886-9; 0-7864-4886-5

LC 2010040710

"This wonderful professional resource for teen librarians and school media specialists focuses on the art of booktalking with a twist. . . . The authors' take on talking up nonfiction books to teens is refreshing and creative and shows their love of reading and teens. Each title receives a summary, along with extra discussion questions and activities for awesome interactive appeal. Each chapter groups an assortment of nonfiction titles into unique categories like 'Funny, Gross, and Disturbing,' 'Food and Crafts,' 'Knowing Your World,' 'Science,' and 'History.'. . . This book is a much-needed tool for public librarians serving teens, as well as school media specialists, to develop excellent booktalking programs and partnerships while getting more teens to read and fun have doing so. It is a must-have for professional collections in public and school libraries." Voice Youth Advocates

Includes bibliographical references

Coleman, Tina

Teen craft projects 2; Tina Coleman and Peggie Llanes; foreword by Amy Alessio and Katie LaMantia. ALA Editions, an imprint of the American Library Association 2013 xiv, 93 p.p (alk. paper: paperback) $45

Grades: Adult Professional   027.62

1. Handicraft 2. Libraries and teenagers 3. Young adults' libraries -- Activity programs

ISBN 0838911528; 9780838911525

LC 2012041728

This book, by Tina Coleman and Peggie Llanes, features a "selection of innovative ideas. These projects have been chosen especially to engage tweens and teens and have been field-tested by YA librarian Amy Alessio's Teen Corps, students in grades 6 [through] 12 at the Schaumburg Township (IL) Public Library." (Publisher's note)

"The follow-up to The Hipster Librarian's Guide to Teen Craft Projects (2009) features 12 teen-tested activities, such as "No-Sew Organizers" and "Rock Star Jewelry." Going beyond the traditional craft book or blog post, this volume includes library-programming-specific tips for success by discussing difficulty, time expectations, supervision requirements, group-size recommendations, and mess factor...Although the price tag may be hard to swallow for the thriftiest among us, which often lines up with those also considered the "craftiest," the hand-holding may prove invaluable to the DIY-shy and librarians new to the overwhelming realm of teen crafts." (Booklist)

Includes bibliographical references (page 93) and index

Colston, Valerie

Teens go green! tips, techniques, tools, and themes for YA programming. Valerie Colston. Libraries Unlimited 2012 xiii, 142 p.p ill. (acid-free paper) $40

Grades: Adult Professional   027.62

1. School libraries -- Activity projects 2. Environmental education -- Activity projects 3. Libraries and teenagers -- United States 4. Environmental education -- Activity programs -- United States 5. Young adults' libraries -- Activity programs -- United States

ISBN 1591589290; 1591589304; 9781591589297; 9781591589303

LC 2011029006

This book is a reference resource "for librarians or high school teachers looking for low-cost, environmentally themed art projects and programs that teens will relate to and find fun. In Part 1, the author explains the needs for these programs, offers tips for teaching them, and suggests ways to expand teen involvement in the library. Part 2 provides dozens of . . . art project ideas that demonstrate how simple teaching green teen art projects can be." (Publisher's note)

"...A nice resource to have on hand for librarians whose community is ecominded or for those who want affordable programming options to consult." Booklist

Includes bibliographical references and index

De Vos, Gail

Storytelling for young adults; a guide to tales for teens. 2nd ed; Libraries Unlimited 2003 208p $35

Grades: Adult Professional   027.62

1. Storytelling 2. Books and reading 3. School libraries -- Activity projects

ISBN 1-563-08903-3

LC 2003-51648

First published 1991

This is a "collection of recommended stories for young adults . . . Brief synopses of the stories are arranged in themed chapters about the fantastic, laughter, folktales, tales of life, tales of the spirit, and tales of the arts and sciences. A few samples are given in their entirety. Author, theme, and title indexes are included as well as a list of the story collections in which the tales appear . . . The strength of this text is that the author has been storytelling with teens for fifteen years, so the recommended stories have the force of being 'tried and true' with this age group . . . It will be helpful for the beginning storyteller in choosing material, particularly in the school setting, and for educators who are trying to find popular stories for the teen audience." Voice Youth Advocates

Includes bibliographical references

Eagle, MK

★ **Answering** teens' tough questions; a YAL-SA guide. mk Eagle. Neal-Schuman, an imprint of the American Library Association 2012 x, 125 p.p $49.95

Grades: Professional   027.62
1. Librarians 2. Library services 3. Teenagers -- Attitudes 4. Teenagers -- United States -- Attitudes 5. Libraries and teenagers -- United States 6. Young adults' libraries -- United States 7. Teenagers -- Services for -- United States 8. Teenagers -- United States -- Social conditions 9. Young adult services librarians -- United States -- Attitudes
ISBN 1555707947; 9781555707941

LC 2012015104

Author mk Eagle presents a book that "offers any librarian a quick primer on talking with young adults about the tough and often controversial topics of sex, drugs, alcohol, and violence." It provides "quick overviews on the issues themselves as well as tips for navigating these waters with teens. . . . . Chapters include sex, sexuality, homelessness, tattoos and piercings, dating violence, abuse, drugs and alcohol, emotional and mental health, and the juvenile justice system." (Publisher's note)

Includes bibliographical references and index

Edwards, Margaret A.

★ The **fair** garden and the swarm of beasts; the library and the young adult. foreword by Betty Carter for the Young Adult Library Services Association. Centennial ed; American Lib. Assn. 2002 xxxiii, 206p il pa $20

Grades: Adult Professional   027.62
1. Books and reading 2. Young adults' libraries
ISBN 0-8389-3533-8

LC 2002-33276

First published 1969 by Hawthorn Bks.

"This great librarian's blazing devotion to teens and reading makes her book the classic in the field." Voice Youth Advocates

Includes bibliographical references

Flowers, Sarah

Evaluating teen services and programs; Sarah Flowers. Neal-Schuman, an imprint of the American Library Association 2012 xv, 119 p.p (pbk.) $49.95

Grades: Adult Professional   027.62
1. Library services 2. Young adults' libraries 3. Libraries -- United States 4. Libraries and teenagers -- United States 5. Young adults' libraries -- Evaluation

-- United States
ISBN 1555707939; 9781555707934

LC 2012015105

Author Sarah Flowers presents "a guide that provides basic information to help teen/youth services librarians, library directors, library school students studying teen services, and middle/high school librarians examine all aspects of their teen programs and services to determine where improvement is needed. Find out what you need to develop goals and objectives for evaluation, and learn how to collect the data that will give you a realistic picture of your library's strengths and weaknesses." (Publisher's note)

Includes bibliographical references and index

Young adults deserve the best; YALSA's competencies in action. [by] Sarah Flowers for the Young Adult Library Services Association. American Library Association 2011 126p pa $45

Grades: Adult Professional   027.62
1. Librarians 2. Young adults' libraries
ISBN 978-0-8389-3587-3; 0-8389-3587-7

LC 2010-14148

This "guide to the professional competencies developed by the Young Adult Library Services Association of ALA aims to 'outline the skills, the knowledge, and the philosophy that should be a part of the makeup of every librarian who serves teens.' Flowers begins by elaborating on and demonstrating how to execute the YALSA competencies. From there she discusses how to advocate for a teen-services department when none exists. The final section is a compilation of various resources, including the Library Bill of Rights and ALA interpretations of them with regard to labels and rating systems, Internet activity, ethics, and nonprint materials.. . . The information is presented in a clear, concise, and conversational manner, making this resource both easy to navigate and a pleasure to read." SLJ

Includes bibliographical references

Gorman, Michele

★ **Connecting** young adults and libraries; a how-to-do-it manual. [by] Michele Gorman and Tricia Suellentrop. 4th ed; Neal-Schuman Publishers Inc. 2009 xxxiii, 450p il (How-to-do-it manuals for librarians) pa $85

Grades: Adult Professional   027.62
1. Young adults' libraries 2. Teenagers -- Books and reading 3. Young adult literature -- Bibliography
ISBN 978-1-55570-665-4

LC 2009-17657

First published 1992 under the authorship of Patrick Jones

"This useful, comprehensive handbook on how to best serve young adult library patrons is a must-have for any librarian's professional library. . . . All key topics are covered here—customer service (affirming the fact that young adults are our customers), information literacy, collection development, booktalking, outreach, programming, technology, and more. Each chapter is well organized and includes background on the topic, suggestions to improve services, useful ideas, advice, sources, and works cited. . . . [This] is an excellent professional resource." Voice Youth Advocates

Includes bibliographical references

Hardesty, Constance

The **teen**-centered writing club; bringing teens and words together. Libraries Unlimited 2008 174p il (Libraries Unlimited professional guides for young adult librarians) pa $40

Grades: Adult Professional   027.62
   1. Creative writing 2. Young adults' libraries 3. English language -- Composition and exercises
   ISBN 978-1-59158-548-0; 1-59158-548-1
LC 2008-11519

"Hardesty encourages librarians to listen to teens and assist them in their search for identity through the written word. . . . From starting a club and the writing activities to share, to grand finales and how to evaluate the program's effectiveness, the author details all the information needed to create such a club. Particularly useful are chapters on the four roles of facilitators, creating a nonfiction writing club, and how to take your efforts online. Many handouts are included, a boon to any busy librarian. An appendix includes resources for publishing. All this information is laid out in a straightforward, positive manner. An essential resource for planning or presenting writing clubs." SLJ

Includes bibliographical references

Honnold, RoseMary

Get connected; tech programs for teens. [by] RoseMary Honnold for the Young Adult Library Services Association. Neal-Schuman Publishers 2007 149p il pa $65

Grades: Adult Professional   027.62
   1. Internet and teenagers 2. Young adults' libraries 3. Information literacy -- Study and teaching
   ISBN 978-1-55570-613-5; 1-55570-613-4
LC 2007-12847

This book is "divided into three parts: 'Get Connected for Fun'; 'Get Connected for Education'; and 'Get Connected for Teen Advisory Groups.' Topics within each chapter include developing recreation and education-based programs, working with different populations, working with teens and social-networking sites, developing and working with TAGs, and introducing ideas for YALSA's Teen Tech Week. . . . This book is a great resource for starting Library 2.0 to connect with teens, whether you are working on your own, with a technology integrator, or within the community." Libr J

Includes bibliographical references

Jones, Ella W.

Start-to-finish YA programs; hip-hop symposiums, summer reading programs, virtual tours, poetry slams, teen advisory boards, term paper clinics, and more! Neal-Schuman Publishers 2009 217p il pa $75

Grades: Adult Professional   027.62
   1. Cultural programs 2. Young adults' libraries
   ISBN 978-1-55570-601-2; 1-55570-601-0
LC 2008-50853

"Jones's creativity, twenty-five years of experience, and her genuine love for teenagers is obvious in the meticulous and creative programming ideas and materials. This valu-able resource will be appreciated by librarians in public and school settings." Voice Youth Advocates

Includes bibliographical references

Kunzel, Bonnie Lendermon

★ The **teen**-centered book club; readers into leaders. [by] Bonnie Kunzel and Constance Hardesty. Libraries Unlimited 2006 xxi, 211p (Libraries Unlimited professional guides for young adult librarians) pa $40

Grades: Adult Professional   027.62
   1. Young adults' libraries 2. Book clubs (Discussion groups) 3. Teenagers -- Books and reading
   ISBN 1-59158-193-1

"Two experienced youth-services librarians introduce the idea of teen-centered book clubs. . . . In clear prose supported by research, the authors cover every aspect of the program, from assessing the needs of the library and teens to conducting successful meetings to evaluating activities. . . . An excellent reference." SLJ

Includes bibliographical references

Mahood, Kristine

A **passion** for print; promoting reading and books to teens. Libraries Unlimited 2006 239p il (Libraries Unlimited professional guides for young adult librarians) pa $40

Grades: Adult Professional   027.62
   1. Young adults' libraries 2. Teenagers -- Books and reading
   ISBN 1-59158-146-X; 978-1-59158-146-8
LC 2006-3716

"Beginning with research on reading, Mahood moves on to merchandising principles; developing teen collections, spaces, and Web sites; and finally to booktalking, readers' advisory, and events scheduling. The author's enthusiasm and experience, coupled with citing current studies, other professional books, articles, and Web sites, make her suggestions appealing and attainable. She provides everything from lists of YA genres to easy design principles for displays to suggestions for questions to ask for better readers' advisory." Booklist

Martin, Hillias J.

★ **Serving** lesbian, gay, bisexual, transgender, and questioning teens; a how-to-do-it manual for librarians. [by] Hillias J. Martin, Jr., James R. Murdock. Neal-Schuman Publishers 2007 267p bibl (How-to-do-it manuals for librarians) pa $55

Grades: Adult Professional   027.62
   1. Gay men 2. Lesbians 3. Bisexuality 4. Transsexualism 5. Young adults' libraries
   ISBN 978-1-55570-566-4; 1-55570-566-9
LC 2006-39469

"This volume offers abundant useful guidance not only for reaching the target audience, but also for planning and promoting library services to teens in general. . . . The tone is friendly and largely free of jargon. . . . All librarians should turn to this book for pertinent insight on the needs of 5 to 10 percent of the teen population." SLJ

Includes bibliographical references

Miller, Donna P.

★ **Crash** course in teen services. Libraries Unlimited 2008 128p (Crash course) pa $30

Grades: Adult Professional   **027.62**

1. Young adults' libraries

ISBN 978-1-59158-565-7; 1-59158-565-1

LC 2007-32758

"Designed for public librarians new to teen service, the book offers advice on relating to teens and creating teen-friendly space as well as tips on teen-centered reference, collection development, readers' advisory, programming, and 'the three Ps': professional resources, professional development, and public relations." Booklist

Includes bibliographical references

Ott, Valerie A.

Teen programs with punch; a month-by-month guide. Libraries Unlimited 2006 282p il (Libraries Unlimited professional guides for young adult librarians) pa $40

Grades: Adult Professional   **027.62**

1. Young adults' libraries 2. Teenagers -- Books and reading

ISBN 1-59158-293-8

LC 2006012775

"Ott has gathered together less-than-conventional program ideas arranged by month. She provides clear instructions, lists of supplemental materials, promotional ideas, reading lists, costs, and suggested grade levels for each one. For librarians with limited budgets, and who may be pressed for time, there are quick and easy ideas that cost little or no money. . . . Many of the programs are designed to draw underserved populations, such as goths, GLBTQ teens, and vegetarians, into the library. . . . This highly informative guide would make a great addition to any YA librarian's professional collection." SLJ

Includes bibliographical references

Pattee, Amy S.

Developing library collections for today's young adults; Amy S. Pattee. The Scarecrow Press, Inc. 2013 267 p. (cloth) $55

Grades: Adult Professional   **027.62**

1. Multimedia 2. Library services 3. Young adults' libraries 4. Libraries -- Special collections 5. Libraries and teenagers -- United States 6. Multimedia library services -- United States

ISBN 0810887347; 9780810887343

LC 2013018596

This book, by Amy S. Pattee, "features policies that deal expressly with materials that respect the intellectual freedom of young library patrons. It emphasizes the importance of everything from needs assessment to collection development, encouraging librarians to consider informational, recreational, and curricular needs and interests as the library staff select material on behalf of young adults." (Publisher's note)

"The book's greatest asset is that it manages to be extremely specific and thorough without becoming overwhelming." VOYA

Includes bibliographical references and index

Schneider, Elizabeth

Create, relate & pop @ the library; services & programs for teens & tweens. [by] Erin Helmrich and Elizabeth Schneider. Neal-Schuman Publishers 2011 218p il

Grades: Adult Professional   **027.62**

1. Cultural programs 2. Young adults' libraries

ISBN 1-55570-722-X; 978-1-55570-722-4

LC 2011-4986

The authors show "how to capitalize on the latest trends—from TV, movies, and music to indie and niche interests—by incorporating them into compelling, creative programs. . . . The book encompasses both traditional and Web 2.0 participatory programming, offering . . . ideas, program templates, and step-by-step outlines of methods, supplies, and resources."

"This is a handy guide." SLJ

Includes bibliographical references

Teaching Generation M; a handbook for librarians and educators. edited by Vibiana Bowman Cvetkovic and Robert J. Lackie. Neal-Schuman Publishers 2009 368p il pa $85

Grades: Adult Professional   **027.62**

1. Technology 2. Information literacy 3. Internet and teenagers 4. Young adults' libraries

ISBN 978-1-55570-667-8; 1-55570-667-3

LC 2009-17658

"This professional handbook tackles three important topics—who is the millennial generation, what kind of world do millennials live in, and what can we do to teach them? Chapter topics include media literacy, the information search process, Facebook, YouTube, Google, and Wikipedia, gaming, webcomics, mobile technology, cooperative learning, screencasting, and the new generation of research papers. . . . In-text citations make this book more of a resource than a pleasure read, but it is a must-read for non-M-generation librarians new to young adult services and for those new teachers or anyone wanting to understand Web 2.0." Voice Youth Advocates

Includes bibliographical references

Tuccillo, Diane

★ **Library** teen advisory groups; [by] Diane P. Tuccillo. Scarecrow Press 2005 165p il (VOYA guides) pa $29.95

Grades: Adult Professional   **027.62**

1. Volunteer work 2. Young adults' libraries

ISBN 0-8108-4982-8

LC 2004-13873

"A comprehensive how-to guide that covers all the bases from theory to practice to nitty-gritty detail." SLJ

Includes bibliographical references

Teen-centered library service; putting youth participation into practice. [by] Diane P. Tuccillo. Libraries Unlimited 2010 xxii, 259p il (Libraries Unlimited professional guides for young adult librarians) pa $45

Grades: Adult Professional **027.62**
1. School libraries 2. Young adults' libraries
ISBN 978-1-59158-765-1; 1-59158-765-4
LC 2009-45692

This offers "guidelines to YA librarians for getting teens to play a part in their libraries. . . . The book begins with a description of this philosophy and places it into context within the history of YA librarianship. Each chapter then deals with specifics: teen advisory groups, writing and performance ideas, ways to meld teens and technology, ideas for community outreach, ways to combine teen and adult library groups, ideas to involve teens who are only around for limited time, and a chapter on assessing your YA participation. . . . This well-organized title is aimed at public librarians and might also be useful to show administrators how important YA services are to the library as a whole." SLJ
Includes bibliographical references

Urban teens in the library; research and practice. edited by Denise E. Agosto and Sandra Hughes-Hassell. American Library Association 2010 208p bibl il pa $60

Grades: Adult Professional **027.62**
1. Young adults' libraries 2. Teenagers -- Books and reading
ISBN 978-0-8389-1015-3; 0-8389-1015-7
LC 2009-25147

"This work does much to explain who urban teens are and what they need from their libraries. The authors examine the existing research—some of which they have performed—that provides a wealth of data for public and school libraries." SLJ
Includes bibliographical references

Welch, Rollie James

The **guy**-friendly YA library; serving male teens. Libraries Unlimited 2007 xxi, 196p (Libraries Unlimited professional guides for young adult librarians) pa $40

Grades: Adult Professional **027.62**
1. Young adults' libraries 2. Boys -- Books and reading 3. Teenagers -- Books and reading
ISBN 978-1-59158-270-0; 1-59158-270-9
LC 2006-102882

"The first chapter offers key components for quality service for teen males, while the second chapter explains the characteristics and developmental issues of this population. The book emphasizes reading, with three chapters dedicated to male teen reading habits, topics of interest, and detailed genre coverage. . . . The sixth chapter deals with programming and also explains how the establish an effective teen advisory board. . . . The seventh chapter covers school visits and emphasizes the importance of booktalks. The eighth chapter discusses creating a teen area in the library." Booklist
Includes bibliographical references

Young Adult Library Services Association

Excellence in library services to young adults; 5th ed.; Young Adult Library Services Association 2008 144p il pa $30

Grades: Adult Professional **027.62**
1. Young adults' libraries
ISBN 978-0-8389-8457-4; 0-8389-8457-6
LC 2008-22359

First published 1994
This book "highlights 25 of the best programs across the country, providing ideas for replicating and adapting them in school and public libraries." Publisher's note
Includes bibliographical references

027.8 School libraries

Adams, Helen R.
★ **Ensuring** intellectual freedom and access to information in the school library media program. Libraries Unlimited 2008 xxi, 254p il map pa $40

Grades: Adult Professional **027.8**
1. Censorship 2. School libraries 3. Freedom of information
ISBN 978-1-59158-539-8; 1-59158-539-2
LC 2008-16753

This is "an extremely helpful guide for dealing with intellectual-freedom and information-access issues. In chapters geared to school situations and covering topics including selection of resources, the First Amendment, privacy, challenges to resources, the Internet, and access for students with disabilities, Adams offers background on the topic and bulleted lists of strategies for dealing with the issue. . . . This is a book that every school librarian needs to keep handy and share with administrators, colleagues, and parents." Booklist
Includes bibliographical references

Baule, Steven M.
Facilities planning for school library and technology centers; 2nd ed.; Linworth Pub. 2007 134p il pa $39.95

Grades: Adult Professional **027.8**
1. School libraries -- Design and construction 2. Instructional materials centers -- Design and construction
ISBN 978-1-58683-294-0; 1-58683-294-8
LC 2006-34179

First published 1992
The author "provides information on how to put together a planning team; how to perform a needs assessment for the library media center or technology lab; how to create bid documents and specification charts; how to develop time lines; and how to plan to move into the new facility once construction is complete. . . . Anyone who is going to build or renovate a facility will want this book." Booklist
Includes bibliographical references

Bishop, Kay
★ The **collection** program in schools; concepts, practices, and information sources. 4th ed. Libraries Unlimited 2007 xx, 269p il (Library and information science text series) pa $50; $65

Grades: Adult Professional **027.8**
1. School libraries 2. Libraries -- Collection development 3. School libraries -- Collection development 4. Children's literature -- Bibliography of

bibliographies 5. Young adult literature -- Bibliography of bibliographies
ISBN 1-59158-360-8 pa; 1-59158-583-X; 978-1-59158-360-8 pa; 978-1-59158-583-1

LC 2007-9005

First published 1988 under the authorship of Phyllis J. Van Orden

"Media specialists who read this book will be renewed in their quest for excellence in their collections. ... The book covers A-Z: Acquisitions, Evaluation, Ethical Issues, Inventory, Procedure Manual, Selection, Special Groups of Students, Weeding, etc. ... This is a must purchase for every school library media center." Libr Media Connect

Includes bibliographical references

Erikson, Rolf

Designing a school library media center for the future; [by] Rolf Erikson and Carolyn Markuson, 2nd ed; American Library Association 2007 117p il pa $45

Grades: Adult Professional   **027.8**
1. School libraries -- Design and construction 2. Instructional materials centers -- Design and construction
ISBN 978-0-8389-0945-4; 0-8389-0945-0

LC 2006-37644

First published 2000

"The first chapter offers an overview of the various steps involved in any project. Succeeding chapters cover technology planning, space allocations, furniture and placement, lighting and acoustics, ADA requirements, specifications, and bids." Booklist

Includes bibliographical references

Hughes-Hassell, Sandra

★ **School** reform and the school library media specialist; [by] Sandra Hughes-Hassell and Violet H. Harada. Libraries Unlimited 2007 xxiii, 204p il (Principles and practice series) pa $40

Grades: Adult Professional   **027.8**
1. School libraries
ISBN 978-1-59158-427-8; 1-59158-427-2

LC 2007-16437

"This volume covers critical issues impacting school libraries today and offers practical solutions to meet these challenges. Written by leaders in the field such as Pam Berger, Carol Gordon, Barbara Stripling, and Ross Todd, the articles expound on implications of No Child Left Behind legislation, 21st-century literacy requirements, population diversity, and professional growth. ... This volume will empower current and future school librarians as they embrace its guidelines." SLJ

Jones, Jami Biles

★ The **power** of the media specialist to improve academic achievement and strengthen at-risk students; [by] Jami Biles Jones, Alana M. Zambone. Linworth Books 2008 108p il pa $39.95

Grades: Adult Professional   **027.8**
1. School libraries 2. Academic achievement 3.

Instructional materials centers
ISBN 1-58683-229-8; 978-1-58683-229-2

LC 2007-30116

This "volume gives library professionals the information they need to convince the unconvinced of the value of the media center in improving student achievement. Section one provides research results and statistics that identify at-risk students. Section two is devoted to identifying the social and educational approaches that have been proven to help these students. ... This resource is valuable for media specialists ready to make a change to a student-centered library, thus giving all of their students a chance at higher academic and personal achievement." SLJ

Includes bibliographical references

Jurkowski, Odin L.

Technology and the school library; a comprehensive guide for media specialists and other educators. Scarecrow Press 2006 219p pa $45

Grades: Adult Professional   **027.8**
1. Information technology 2. School libraries -- Automation 3. Instructional materials centers -- Automation
ISBN 0-8108-5290-X; 978-0-8108-5290-7

LC 2006-15206

This "manual is a basic primer on school-related technology. The main sections have chapters covering information tools and resources, classroom technologies, technology administration in the school library, and technology training. Each chapter provides a general overview, historical perspective, a detailed set of definitions and explanations, a brief summary of concerns and current research, and a short but carefully chosen list of pertinent Web sites. ... This accessible guide will be of interest to practicing school librarians, educators and school administrators, and library media students." Booklist

Includes bibliographical references

Morris, Betty J.

★ **Administering** the school library media center; 4th ed, rev and expanded; Libraries Unlimited 2004 683p $70; pa $55

Grades: Adult Professional   **027.8**
1. School libraries 2. Instructional materials centers
ISBN 0-313-32261-9; 1-59158-183-4 pa

LC 2004-41797

First published 1973 under the authorship of John T. Gillespie and Diana L. Spirt with title: Creating a school media program

"This volume covers library media center programming, facilities and technologies, student learning, policies and procedures, and library media specialist roles. ... Highlights include budget planning and justification, library media job descriptions, and information on the bid process. The chapter on facilities contains infrequently found information on the psychology of color, URLs for Web sites with floor plans, and guidelines for space planning." Booklist

Stephens, Claire Gatrell

Library 101; a handbook for the school library media specialist. [by] Claire Gatrell Stephens and

Patricia Franklin. Libraries Unlimited 2007 233p il pa $35

Grades: Adult Professional   027.8

1. School libraries 2. Instructional materials centers 3. Procedure manuals 4. Libraries -- Handbooks, manuals, etc.

ISBN 1-59158-324-1; 978-1-59158-324-0

LC 2007-18420

"This handbook provides information for brand-new and inexperienced librarians preparing for a first job in a school library media center. Articles are divided into four subcategories covering day-to-day operations (library organization, circulation policies, media management, scheduling, staffing, and media center arrangement); collaboration with teachers; collection development and management; and equipment." Booklist

Includes bibliographical references

Sykes, Judith A.

Conducting action research to evaluate your school library; Judith Anne Sykes. Libraries Unlimited, an imprint of ABC-CLIO, LLC 2013 118 p. illustrations (hard copy) $40

Grades: Adult Professional   027.8

1. School libraries 2. Librarians -- Rating 3. Educational evaluation 4. School librarians 5. Teacher-librarians 6. Action research in education 7. School libraries -- Evaluation

ISBN 161069077X; 9781610690775

LC 2012051277

In this book, author Judith Anne Sykes "coalesces current expert opinions on the topic of action research in the school library environment and highlighting what other teacher librarians in the field have identified as the pros and cons of using the process. Readers are directed to focus on mitigating the 'cons' through the use of specific working pages and templates and by initially exploring 'five favorite' links." (Publisher's note)

"When budget issues hit, school librarianship can be in danger, and this text provides tools for professionals to evaluate their programs and make necessary changes to stay a vital part of their schools. . . This purchase would be worthwhile for any teacher-librarian interested in evaluating his or her program and taking advantage of Sykes' extensive research and expertise." Booklist

Includes bibliographical references and index

Thomas, Margie J. Klink

★ **Re**-designing the high school library for the forgotten half; the information needs of the non-college bound student. Libraries Unlimited 2008 78p il $45

Grades: Adult Professional   027.8

1. Vocational education 2. High school libraries

ISBN 978-1-59158-476-6; 1-59158-476-0

LC 2008-14019

"This book explores the informational needs of non-college-bound students and addresses how their high school libraries can be restructured to effectively meet these needs. . . . This book will serve as a valuable resource for those

seeking to address the needs of these sometimes-overlooked students." Voice Youth Advocates

Includes bibliographical references

Valenza, Joyce Kasman

★ **Power** tools recharged; 125+ essential forms and presentations for your school library information program. illustrated by Emily Valenza. American Library Association 2004 various paging il pa $55

Grades: Adult Professional   027.8

1. School libraries 2. Libraries -- Public relations

ISBN 0-8389-0880-2

LC 2004-5853

First published 1998 with title: Power tools

This offers a compilation of customizable, reproducible forms and handouts for school library administration and assessment, teaching information literacy, making presentations. Included are such items as templates for a gift book program, letters to parents and faculty members, a checklist of tasks, library equipment sign-out forms, and a reading interest survey.

Includes bibliographical references

Van Deusen, Jean Donham

Enhancing teaching and learning; a leadership guide for school library media specialists. [by] Jean Donham. rev. ed.; Neal-Schuman Publishers 2008 353p il pa $65

Grades: Adult Professional   027.8

1. School libraries 2. Instructional materials centers

ISBN 978-1-55570-647-0; 1-55570-647-9

LC 2008-23321

First published 1998

"This title is well-written, well-researched, and informative. Donham masterfully weaves together current AASL standards and the real world of today's media specialist." Voice Youth Advocates

Includes bibliographical references

Woolls, E. Blanche

The **school** library media manager; [by] Blanche Woolls. 4th ed; Libraries Unlimited 2008 279p il (Library and information science text series) $55; pa $45

Grades: Adult Professional   027.8

1. School libraries 2. Instructional materials centers

ISBN 978-1-59158-648-7; 1-59158-648-8; 978-1-59158-643-2 pa; 1-59158-643-7 pa

LC 2008-18081

First published 1994

Provides information "for teaching the administration of school library media centers. . . . Readers learn how to choose a credential program, how to find the requirements for working in each of the 50 states, what to do when looking for and choosing a job, and how to survive the first week in that new position. . . . Sections also cover: collaborating with teachers, how to write a proposal, and how to accept leadership responsibilities, including the role of a media specialist in the legislative process." Publisher's note

Includes bibliographical references

028 Reading and use of other information media

★ The **CIA** World Factbook 2014; Central Intelligence Agency. W W Norton & Co Inc 2013 960 p. (paperback) $16.95
Grades: 11 12 Adult **028**
1. Almanacs 2. Geopolitics 3. Population -- Statistics
ISBN 1626360731; 9781626360730
This book, updated for 2014, "offers complete and up-to-date information on the world's nations. This . . . guide is packed with detailed information on the politics, populations, military expenditures, and economics of 2014." Included are "detailed maps," "statistics on the population of each country, with details on literacy rates, HIV prevalence, and age structure," and "information on each country's climate and natural hazards." (Publisher's note)

028.1 Reviews

Adamson, Lynda G.
Literature links to world history, K-12; resources to enhance and entice. Libraries Unlimited 2010 684p (Children's and young adult literature reference series) $65
Grades: Adult Professional **028.1**
1. World history -- Bibliography
ISBN 978-1-59158-470-4
LC 2009-46081
"This annotated bibliography might very well become a school librarian's favorite resource when collaborating with history teachers. . . . Entries include fiction, nonfiction, and multimedia. Sections are divided by world regions and sometimes further by time period, with each section subdivided into fiction, history nonfiction, biography, graphic books, DVDs, and compact discs. . . . Adult books for young adults are included. Entries, arranged alphabetically by author, contain bibliographic information, grade levels, descriptive annotations, and awards, where appropriate." Booklist
Includes bibliographical references

★ The **ultimate** teen book guide; editors, Daniel Hahn & Leonie Flynn; associate editor, Susan Reuben. Distributed to the trade by Holtzbrinck Publishers 2008 432p il pa $15.95; $26.95
Grades: Adult Professional **028.1**
1. Teenagers -- Books and reading 2. Young adult literature -- History and criticism
ISBN 0-8027-9731-8 pa; 978-0-8027-9730-8; 0-8027-9730-X; 978-0-8027-9731-5 pa
LC 2007-24238
First published 2006 in the United Kingdom
This "volume includes reviews of more than 700 fiction titles, nonfiction, classics, and graphic novels that will be of interest to young adults. The reviewers/contributors are popular authors, librarians, and teens themselves. . . . It's an excellent source for a variety of book reviews spanning time and genre. Useful for students, librarians, and teachers." SLJ

028.5 Reading and use of other information media by young people

Aronson, Marc
★ **Exploding** the myths; the truth about teenagers and reading. Scarecrow Press 2000 146p (Scarecrow studies in young adult literature) $29.50
Grades: Adult Professional **028.5**
1. Teenagers -- Books and reading
ISBN 0-8108-3904-0
LC 00-61948
Aronson discusses censorship, audience, authenticity, demographics, and YA publishing history. "Whether talking about the graphic novel, poetry, magic realism, or gritty contemporary fiction, he shows that teenagers today are often more open to challenge and diversity in narrative and format than their adult guardians are. What many librarians think is 'popular' is often condescending. Whether you agree with Aronson or not, you'll be caught up in issues that matter. A great starting place for YA literature classes." Booklist

Bartel, Julie
Annotated book lists for every teen reader; the best from the experts at YALSA-BK. [by] Julie Bartel and Pam Spencer Holley for the Young Adult Library Services Association. Neal-Schuman Publishers 2011 270p pa $65
Grades: Adult Professional **028.5**
1. Best books 2. Young adult literature 3. Teenagers -- Books and reading 4. Young adult literature -- Bibliography 5. Young adult literature -- Stories, plots, etc.
ISBN 1-55570-658-4; 978-1-55570-658-6
LC 2010-33312
"Bartel and Holley have scoured the YALSA-BK archives to find more than 1100 books with broad teen readership. While the book's primary purpose is for readers' advisory, the authors also suggest it will be useful in creating displays as well as igniting creativity. . . . The scope is wide ranging with a good mix of standards, classics, and newer titles. With a highly appropriate title, this volume hits the mark." SLJ
Includes bibliographical references

Bodart, Joni Richards
Radical reads 2; working with the newest edgy titles for teens. Scarecrow Press 2010 479p pa $45
Grades: Adult Professional **028.5**
1. Teenagers -- Books and reading 2. Young adult literature -- Bibliography
ISBN 978-0-8108-6908-0; 0-8108-6908-X
LC 2009-25724
Bodart "offers insight into writing book reports and booktalks that secondary school English teachers and library media specialists can share with students. . . . The detailed book entries include citations with suggested reading and interest levels designated by middle school, younger high school, and older high school. Also included are subject areas, character descriptions, a booktalk and booktalk ideas, a list of major themes and ideas, book report ideas, risks, strengths, awards, and full-text reviews. The entries' detail

will be an asset in readers' advisory and a quick resource to check the content and reviews for a title that is being questioned." Voice Youth Advocates

Includes bibliographical references

Booth, Heather

★ **Serving** teens through readers' advisory. American Library Association 2007 159p (ALA readers' advisory series) pa $36

Grades: Adult Professional   **028.5**
1. Young adults' libraries 2. Teenagers -- Books and reading 3. Young adult literature -- Bibliography
ISBN 0-8389-0930-2; 978-0-8389-0930-0

LC 2006-36134

"The first few chapters discuss teen reading habits and why readers' advisory for this group is different and also provide 'tips for the generalist' who may not be an expert in teen fiction. Other chapters cover elements of the readers' advisory interaction . . . and survey the appropriate books. Two unique chapters offer well-thought-out and practical advice on making reading-related homework assignments less painful for staff and students as well as suggestions for providing readers' advisory services to teens through their parents or other adults. . . . [This] is essential reading for all readers' advisors and any library staff who work with teens." Booklist

Includes bibliographical references

Cart, Michael

★ **Young** adult literature: from romance to realism; rev ed.; American Library Association 2010 242p pa $60

Grades: Adult Professional   **028.5**
1. Teenagers -- Books and reading 2. Young adults' literature -- History 3. Young adult literature -- History and criticism
ISBN 978-0-8389-1045-0; 0-8389-1045-9

LC 2010-13674

A revised edition of: From romance to realism: 50 years of growth and change in young adult literature, published 1996 by HarperCollins Pub.

"This updated and expanded second edition of Cart's already lively and comprehensive history of young adult literature (1996) is an essential resource. It is divided into two sections ('That Was Then' and 'This Is Now'), and the author once again discusses the history and current moment to offer a broad and loving overview of the rich literature. . . . Highly accessible and thorough, the text is a staple for any study of the canon." SLJ

Includes bibliographical references

★ **Dear** author; letters of hope. edited by Joan F. Kaywell; with an introduction by Catherine Ryan Hyde. Philomel Books 2007 222p $14.99

Grades: 8 9 10 11 12   **028.5**
1. Authors, American 2. Teenagers -- Books and reading
ISBN 978-0-399-23705-8; 0-399-23705-4

LC 2006-21050

"Chris Lynch, Nancy Garden, and Christopher Paul Curtis and are just a few of the well-known authors who respond to real teens' letters in this powerful compilation.

Not mere fan mail, the selections speak about teens' gravest concerns—bullying, derailed friendships, racism, date rape, incest, illness, divorce, and more—and they describe how the authors' books helped them face the heartaches. . . . For some readers, this dialogue between writers and readers will be inspiring; for those harboring their own wounding secrets, it may be lifesaving." Booklist

Includes bibliographical references

Diamant-Cohen, Betsy

Booktalking bonanza; ten ready-to-use multimedia sessions for the busy librarian. American Library Association 2009 240p il pa $40

Grades: Adult Professional   **028.5**
1. Book talks 2. Books and reading 3. Children's literature
ISBN 978-0-8389-0965-2; 0-8389-0965-5

LC 2008-15371

"This volume is a collection of scripts for multimedia-enriched booktalks. After an introductory chapter that explains the reasoning for this approach, 10 scripts are outlined. Books, music, video, and Web sites are included for each one. The programs are geared toward elementary-aged children, although suggestions for adapting them for a middle or high school audience are included." SLJ

Includes bibliographical references

Fraser, Elizabeth

Reality rules II; a guide to teen nonfiction reading interests. Elizabeth Fraser. Libraries Unlimited 2012 xvii, 230 p.p (Genreflecting advisory series) (cloth) $48

Grades: Adult Professional   **028.5**
1. Best books 2. Teenagers -- Books and reading 3. Young adult literature -- Bibliography 4. Young adult literature -- Stories, plots, etc 5. Teenagers -- Books and reading -- United States
ISBN 1598847902; 9781598847901

LC 2012020232

In this book, Elizabeth Fraser "recommends nonfiction books published after 2007 that will appeal to a wide range of young adults, including reluctant and ESL readers. Sections include 'Adventure,' 'Memoirs and Autobiographies,' 'Biography,' 'Sports,' 'All About You,' and 'The Arts.'" (School Library Journal)

"This is another wonderful research and reference work, a follow-up to Reality Rules I...As a reader's advisory, for collection development, and for helping the classroom teacher get the best resources, this is an excellent and well-researched book for use with the teen reader." (Library Media Connection)

Includes bibliographical references and indexes

Reality rules! a guide to teen nonfiction reading interests. Libraries Unlimited 2008 246p (Genreflecting advisory series)

Grades: Adult Professional   **028.5**
1. Reference books 2. Young adult literature 3. Teenagers -- Books and reading 4. Young adult literature -- Bibliography
ISBN 9781591585633

LC 2007-51063

"This guide focuses on titles created for teens and those with strong teen appeal. The author covers more than 500 titles published since 2000, also including benchmarks and perennial classics." Publisher's note

Includes bibliographical references

Handbook of research on children's and young adult literature; edited by Shelby A. Wolf . . . [et al.] Routledge 2010 555p $295; pa $119.95

Grades: Adult Professional 028.5

1. Children's literature -- History and criticism 2. Young adult literature -- History and criticism

ISBN 978-0-415-96505-7; 0-415-96505-5; 978-0-415-96506-4 pa; 0-415-96506-3 pa; 978-0-203-84354-3 e-book

LC 2010-16339

"The book examines readers, texts, and cultural contexts of children's literature and across the three intersecting disciplines of Education, English, and Library and Information Science, in an effort to model a multidisciplinary approach to children's literature research. Thirty-seven scholarly articles, by figures such as Eliza Dresang, Rudine Sims Bishop, and Roderick McGillis . . . are counterpointed by responses that often provide more personal perspectives, including insights from noted authors such as Lois Lowry, M. T. Anderson, and Markus Zusak." Bull Cent Child Books

Honnold, RoseMary

★ The **teen** reader's advisor. Neal-Schuman Publishers 2006 491p (Teens @ the library series) pa $75

Grades: Adult Professional 028.5

1. Young adults' libraries 2. Teenagers -- Books and reading 3. Young adult literature -- Bibliography

ISBN 1-55570-551-0

LC 2006-12640

"The first part deals with the challenges of working with teens, from developing a rapport and dealing with the more conservative adults in their lives, to marketing a YA collection to its audience. The author's descriptions of the major awards and lists relating to the literature as well as the list of print and online reader's advisory resources are sure to be helpful. Part two consists of subject and genre lists. Each one has at least 10 titles. The annotations are excellent." SLJ

Includes bibliographical references

Jones, Patrick

★ **Connecting** with reluctant teen readers; tips, titles, and tools. [by] Patrick Jones, Maureen L. Hartman, Patricia Taylor. Neal-Schuman Publishers 2006 xxi, 314p $59.95

Grades: Adult Professional 028.5

1. Young adults' libraries 2. Teenagers -- Books and reading 3. Young adult literature -- Bibliography

ISBN 1-55570-571-5; 978-1-55570-571-8

LC 2006-12355

"Well written and well researched, this practical hands-on guide to defining and wooing reluctant readers is a must-read for librarians and teachers who work with adolescents. It is divided into three parts: 'Tips That Work,' 'Titles That Work,' and 'Tools That Work.'" SLJ

Includes bibliographical references

Keane, Nancy J.

101 great, ready-to-use book lists for teens; Nancy J. Keane. Libraries Unlimited, an imprint of ABC-CLIO, LLC 2012 xiv, 263 p.p (paperback) $40; (ebook) $40

Grades: Adult Professional 028.5

1. Book selection 2. Books and reading 3. Young adult literature -- Bibliography 4. High school libraries -- Book lists 5. Young adults' libraries -- Book lists 6. Teenagers -- Books and reading -- United States

ISBN 1610691342; 9781610691345; 9781610691352

LC 2011051428

This book offers a "compilation of YA [Young Adult] materials . . . published prior to August 2011. The book is divided . . . into themed lists such as 'Genres,' 'Readalikes,' and 'Teaching Literary Elements.' The themes . . . include . . . topics such as 'Romance,' 'Autism & Asperger's Syndrome,' 'Different Belief Systems,' and 'Crossing the Border.' Each entry includes the title, author, publisher, publication date, page numbers, an annotation, Lexile level when available, and interest level by grade or age range." (School Library Journal)

"This is a useful resource for new librarians and may also be helpful to seasoned librarians. The emphasis is on books published within the last ten years, but some older titles are included." Lib Med Con

Includes bibliographical references and index

Moore, John Noell

Interpreting young adult literature; literary theory in the secondary classroom. Boynton/Cook Pubs. 1997 202p (Young adult literature series) $27.50

Grades: Adult Professional 028.5

1. Literature -- Philosophy 2. Young adult literature -- History and criticism

ISBN 0-86709-414-1

LC 97-5045

Chapters address "formalism, archetypal criticism, structuralism/semiotics, deconstruction, reader-response, feminism, black aesthetics, and cultural studies. Each of these chapters cover key concepts and basic terms of the theory, introduces and interprets a young adult text from that perspective, and invites readers to join the conversation. The concluding section of each chapter discusses other young adult texts that can be approached from that theory and suggests additional critical studies appropriate for teaching these texts." Publisher's note

Includes bibliographical references

Nilsen, Alleen Pace

★ **Literature** for today's young adults; [by] Alleen Pace Nilsen, Kenneth L. Donelson. 8th ed; Allyn and Bacon/Pearson 2008 xx, 491p il $122.20

Grades: Adult Professional 028.5

1. Books and reading 2. Young adult literature -- History and criticism

ISBN 978-0-205-59323-1; 0-205-59323-2

LC 2008-2625

First published 1980

This is an "introduction to young adult literature framed within a literary, historical, and social context. The authors provide teachers with criteria for evaluating books of all genres, from poetry and nonfiction to mysteries, science fiction, and graphic novels. . . . [It also includes coverage of] issues such as pop culture and mass media." Publisher's note

Includes bibliographical references

Quick and popular reads for teens; edited by Pam Spencer Holley for the Young Adult Library Services Association. American Library Association 2009 228p pa $45

Grades: Adult Professional   **028.5**
1. Teenagers -- Books and reading 2. Young adult literature -- Bibliography 3. Young Adult Library Services Association
ISBN 978-0-8389-3577-4; 0-8389-3577-X

LC 2008-49691

"This practical guide pulls together the Quick Picks for the Reluctant Young Adult Reader lists and the Popular Paperbacks for Young Adults lists created by the Young Adult Library Services Association (YALSA), a division of the American Library Association (ALA) from 1999 to 2008. . . . [The editor] assembles the lists into separate Nonfiction and Fiction categories, with an additional chapter containing Theme-Oriented Booklists that is useful for putting together displays, bookmarks, or readers' advisory. . . . This essential tool for librarians will help them find that popular book to turn a reluctant reader into a teen who appreciates the enjoyment one comes from reading." Voice Youth Advocates

Includes bibliographical references

Schall, Lucy

Genre talks for teens; booktalks and more for every teen reading interest. Libraries Unlimited 2009 309p pa $40

Grades: Adult Professional   **028.5**
1. Book talks 2. Teenagers -- Books and reading
ISBN 978-1-59158-743-9; 1-59158-743-3

LC 2008-54984

"Schall has chosen about 100 books published since 2003 for inclusion in this volume. . . . Each book includes a summary, a booktalk, a read-aloud/reader response sampling, supporting learning activities, and related works. Books are keyed by theme, reading level, and audience. . . . Because of its varied ways to engage readers and its current coverage, the book is a welcome addition." Booklist

Includes bibliographical references

Silvey, Anita

★ **500** great books for teens. Houghton Mifflin Co. 2006 397p $26

Grades: Adult Professional   **028.5**
1. Teenagers -- Books and reading 2. Young adult literature -- Bibliography
ISBN 978-0-618-61296-3; 0-618-61296-3

LC 2006-3350

"Silvey selects and annotates five hundred titles for young adults, arranging them loosely in twenty-one chapters by genre and/or area of interest, from 'Adventure and Survival' to 'War and Conflict.' Each book is coded for either younger (12-14) or older (14-18) teens and gets a couple hundred words or so. . . . The selections are both sturdy and wide-ranging." Horn Book

Includes bibliographical references

Sullivan, Michael

★ **Serving** boys through readers' advisory. American Library Association 2010 152p (ALA readers' advisory series) pa $48

Grades: Adult Professional   **028.5**
1. Children's literature 2. Reference services (Libraries) 3. Boys -- Books and reading 4. Boys
ISBN 978-0-8389-1022-1; 0-8389-1022-X

LC 2009-26841

"This volume was created to give a general direction when helping most boys select books. . . . Sullivan challenges us to throw out our preconceived notions about how to conduct such an interview. Methods of performing indirect readers' advisory with parents and teachers are included. The excellent booktalks for elementary, middle school, and high school boys alone make this a worthwhile purchase." SLJ

Includes bibliographical references

Zbaracki, Matthew D.

Best books for boys; a resource for educators. foreward by Jon Scieszka. Libraries Unlimited 2008 189p il (Children's and young adult literature reference series)

Grades: Adult Professional   **028.5**
1. Best books 2. Children's literature 3. Young adult literature 4. Reading interests 5. Boys -- Books and reading 6. Boys 7. Children's literature -- Book lists 8. Children's literature -- Bibliography 9. Young adult literature -- Bibliography
ISBN 1-59158-599-6; 978-1-59158-599-2

LC 2007-51065

"Good source notes guide readers to additional writings on the topic and speak to the author's significant research in his field. Nicely indexed by author, title, and subject, this [is an] easy-to-navigate resource." Voice Youth Advocates

Includes bibliographical references

028.7   Use of books and other information media as sources of information

Callison, Daniel

★ The **blue** book on information age inquiry, instruction and literacy; [by] Daniel Callison and Leslie Preddy. Libraries Unlimited 2006 643p il pa $45

Grades: Adult Professional   **028.7**
1. Information literacy
ISBN 978-1-59158-325-7; 1-59158-325-X

LC 2006-23645

A revised edition of Key Words, Concepts and Methods for Information Age Instruction, published 2003 by LMS Associates

"Part 1 introduces the concepts of information inquiry, providing foundational documents and exploring search and use models, information literacy, standards, the instructional role of library media specialists, online inquiry learning, and resource management. Part 2 offers concrete examples of inquiry applied to the middle-school student research process and supplies reproducible pages for classroom use. Part 3 discusses and defines 51 key terms. Entries here are several pages in length and include citations and references. Indispensable for all school media specialists, this book will also appeal to other readers, who will be impressed by its well-organized design, thoroughness, and practicality." Booklist

Includes bibliographical references

Smith, Jane Bandy

Teaching & testing information literacy skills; [by] Jane Bandy Smith; Lisa Churchill and Lucy Mason, contributors. Linworth Pub. 2005 xx, 138p il pa $44.95

Grades: Adult Professional   **028.7**

1. School libraries 2. Bibliographic instruction 3. Library information networks

ISBN 1-58683-078-3

    LC 2004-26004

The author "reviews the rise and acceptance of information literacy, traces a continuum from older ideas of isolated library skills to this more inclusive life skill, and presents a frame for curriculum development with five pages of excellent instructional objectives by category and grade level. . . . This powerful book will illuminate the inexperienced and reinvigorate veteran school librarians." SLJ

Includes bibliographical references

Student engagement and information literacy; edited by Craig Gibson. Association of College and Research Libraries 2006 197p pa $27

Grades: Adult Professional   **028.7**

1. Information literacy 2. Libraries and students

ISBN 0-8389-8388-X; 978-0-8389-8388-1

    LC 2006-16956

This book "addresses information literacy in a framework inspired by higher education scholarship and dialogue as it relates to student engagement. Articles are based on what librarians and faculty know about how students learn, how different learning environments affect engagement, and how different groups on campuses can collaborate on student engagement and learning." Publisher's note

Includes bibliographical references

030   General encyclopedic works

Olmstead, Larry

Getting into Guinness; one man's longest, fastest, highest journey inside the world's most famous record book. HarperCollins 2008 293p il $24.95

Grades: 9 10 11 12 Adult   **030**

1. World records 2. Curiosities and wonders 3. Guinness book of world records

ISBN 978-0-06-137348-0; 0-06-137348-6

    LC 2008-29669

"The book is endlessly fascinating, an exploration of what makes ordinary people try to do extraordinary things for no other reason than because no one else has ever done them." Booklist

Includes bibliographical references

★ The **World** Almanac and Book of Facts 2015; edited by Sarah Janssen. Simon & Schuster 2014 1008 p. $13.99

Grades: 6 7 8 9 10 11 12 Adult   **030**

1. Almanacs 2. Geography 3. Popular culture

ISBN 1600571905; 9781600571909

Annual. First published 1868. Publisher varies

"The World Almanac and Book of Facts is America's top-selling reference book of all time, with more than 82 million copies sold. Published annually since 1868, this compendium of information is the authoritative source for all your entertainment, reference, and learning needs. The 2015 edition of The World Almanac [edited by Sarah Janssen] reviews the events of 2014 and will be your go-to source for any questions on any topic." (Publisher's note)

"This is the most comprehensive and well-known of almanacs. . . . Contains a chronology of the year's events, consumer information, historical anniversaries, annual climatological data, and forecasts. Color section has flags and maps. Includes detailed index." N Y Public Libr Book of How & Where to Look It Up

031   General encyclopedic works in specific languages and language families

Canadian Almanac & Directory, 2014; edited by Tannys Williams. Grey House Pub 2013 (hardcover) $384

Grades: 11 12 Adult   **031**

1. Canada 2. Almanacs

ISBN 1619251434; 9781619251434

This book is a reference about Canada. It looks at "cultural, professional and financial institutions, legislative, governmental, judicial and educational organizations." The book offers "access to almost 100,000 names and addresses of contacts throughout the network of Canadian institutions." (Publisher's note)

Guinness world records 2015; by Guinness World Records. St. Martin's Press 2014 255 p. ill. (some col.) $28.95

Grades: 3 4 5 6 7 8 9 10 11 12 Adult   **031**

1. World records 2. World records -- Periodicals 3. Curiosities and wonders -- Periodicals

ISBN 1908843632; 9781908843630

This 2015 edition of the Guinness World Records book "presents thousands of new and updated records. . . . [It] showcases the very best of the most recent world records, with new subjects as diverse as castles, 3D printing, the search for alien life and the latest developments in AI and robotics. Plus, the Flashback features offer a look back at the archives to bring you the best of the classic and iconic records from the past 60 years." (Publisher's note)

The **World** Book Encyclopedia. World Book, Inc 22 v col ill, col maps

Grades: 4 5 6 7 8 9 10 11 12 Adult   **031**

1. Reference books 2. Encyclopedias and dictionaries

New editions published yearly; revised frequently

"A 22-volume, highly illustrated, A-Z general encyclopedia for all ages, featuring sections on how to use World Book, other research aids, pronunciation key, a student guide to better writing, speaking, and research skills, and comprehensive index." (Publisher's note)

031.02 Books of miscellaneous facts

Brahms, William B.

Notable last facts; a compendium of endings, conclusions, terminations and final events throughout history. compiled by William B. Brahms. Reference Desk Press 2005 834p $145

Grades: 11 12 Adult 031.02
1. Reference books 2. Encyclopedias and dictionaries
ISBN 0-9765325-0-6

LC 2005-901194

"This extensive compilation is a groundbreaking core reference work for libraries of all kinds." Choice

Includes bibliographical references

★ **Famous** first facts, international edition; a record of first happenings, discoveries, and inventions in world history. {edited by} Steven Anzovin & Janet Podell. Wilson, H.W. 2000 837p $140

Grades: 11 12 Adult 031.02
1. Reference books 2. Encyclopedias and dictionaries
ISBN 0-8242-0958-3

LC 99-86869

This work "contains more than 5000 firsts from hundreds of countries and ranging in time from 3.5 billion years ago (the age of the oldest continental land discovered) to 2001 (the scheduled date of completion of the first building over 1500 feet tall). . . . {It} groups related entries under broad subject categories (arranged alphabetically) and sub-categories. Within each category or sub-category, entries are arranged chronologically." Publisher's note

Kane, Joseph Nathan

★ **Famous** first facts; a record of first happenings, discoveries, and inventions in American history. [by] Joseph Nathan Kane, Steven Anzovin, & Janet Podell. 7th ed.; H.W. Wilson 2015 1400p il $195

Grades: 5 6 7 8 9 10 11 12 Adult 031.02
1. Reference books 2. Encyclopedias and dictionaries
3. United States -- History -- Dictionaries
ISBN 978-1-61925-468-8

First published 1933. 7th edition of this was published in 2014.

Over 8000 entries cover first occurences in American history, organized into 16 chapters each divided into sections. Sections are alphabetically organized, and individual entries are organized chronologically within each section. Includes five indexes: subject index, index by years, index by days, index to personal names, and geographical index

"Besides serving as an essential ready-reference source, the book is also fun to read out loud to colleagues—when was bubble gum first manufactured in the U.S.? When was the spray can introduced?" Booklist

Knauer, Kelly

Time almanac 2013; Encyclopedia Britannica and Time-Life Books. Time Home Entertainment 2012 864 p. (hardcover) $34.95

Grades: 11 12 Adult 031.02
1. Almanacs 2. Popular culture
ISBN 1618930192; 9781618930194

This almanac from "TIME" magazine and Encyclopedia Britannica "includes global and country statistics, a calendar and holiday list, sports results, a website guide, and information about astronomy and space, health and nutrition, business, economy, personal finance, the internet and more." (Publisher's note)

The **New** York times guide to essential knowledge; a desk reference for the curious mind. Rev. and expanded 2nd ed.; St. Martin's Press 2007 1320p il $35

Grades: 11 12 Adult 031.02
1. Reference books 2. Encyclopedias and dictionaries
ISBN 978-0-312-37659-8; 0-312-37659-6

LC 2007-38724

First published 2004

This book "defines nearly every facet of contemporary life—from arts, grammar, mythology, and culture to science, economics, and geopolitical issues. . . . An essential background reference for almost every subject." Libr J

060.4 Special topics of general organizations

Robert, Henry Martyn

★ **Robert's** Rules of order newly revised. Perseus Pub. 2000 various paging $37.50

Grades: 11 12 Adult 060.4
1. Parliamentary practice
ISBN 0-7382-0384-X; 978-0-7382-0384-3

LC 2004-351757

First published 1876 as Pocket manual of rules of order for deliberate assemblies. Title and publisher vary

"Long the standard compendium of parliamentary law, explaining methods of organizing and conducting the business of societies, conventions, and other assemblies. Includes convenient charts and tables." Ref Sources for Small & Medium-sized Libr. 6th edition

Sturgis, Alice

The **standard** code of parliamentary procedure; original edition by Alice Sturgis. 4th ed; McGraw-Hill 2001 xxiv, 285p pa $14.95

Grades: 11 12 Adult 060.4
1. Parliamentary practice
ISBN 0-07-136513-3

LC 2001-265929

First published 1950

This guide to the rules of parliamentary procedure includes explanations of their purpose and examples of their use. Also considers ways the Internet and other technologies have rewritten rules of meetings.

Includes bibliographical references

Zimmerman, Doris P.

Robert's Rules in plain English. Collins 2005
171p pa $7.95

Grades: 9 10 11 12   **060.4**
1. Parliamentary practice
ISBN 0-06-078779-1; 978-0-06-078779-0
First published 1997
Covers methods of organizing and conducting business
of societies, organizations, governing bodies, and other
types of assemblies.

**070.1   Documentary media, educational media,
news media**

Garner, Joe

We interrupt this broadcast; the events that
stopped our lives--from the Hindenburg explosion
to the Virginia Tech shooting. [foreword by Walter
Cronkite; afterword by Brian Williams; narrated by
Bill Kurtis] 10th anniversary ed.; Sourcebooks MediaFusion 2008 194p il $49.95

Grades: 7 8 9 10 11 12 Adult   **070.1**
1. Disasters 2. Broadcast journalism 3. Television
broadcasting of news
ISBN 978-1-4022-1319-9; 1-4022-1319-0
                                        LC 2008-20015
First published 1998
This book and 3 CD set "documents, in text, audio and
black-and-white photographs, the moments when history,
for better or for worse (though usually for worse), was made
in an instant. . . . In addition to the CDs' reports and sound
bites dramatically introduced and explained . . . each event
gets about four pages of coverage, with an efficient summary
and at least half a dozen photos. . . . These are the kinds of
moments that still shock and amaze. This moving book is 'a
tribute of sorts' to the events that defined eras, the journalists
who reported on them and the media television, radio that
made us all witnesses." Publ Wkly

070.4   Journalism

Foerstel, Herbert N.

From Watergate to Monicagate; ten controversies in modern journalism and media. Greenwood
Press 2001 279p il $60.95

Grades: 11 12 Adult   **070.4**
1. Journalism 2. Mass media
ISBN 0-313-31163-3
                                        LC 00-61698
The author discusses "problems facing the media, such
as mergers that drastically reduce the number of independent
media, government giveaway of the 'digital spectrum,' PR
masquerading as news, the power of lobbyists, CIA agents in
the media, government censorship, paparazzi, and journalistic plagiarism. . . . Chapters cover radio; TV; newspapers;
the Internet; and unlicensed radio stations, which provide
local news coverage that focus on minorities, community

groups, and schools. An excellent book for journalism and
government students and staff." Book Rep
Includes bibliographical references

Freedman, Samuel G.

Letters to a young journalist. Basic Books 2006
184p (Art of mentoring) $22.95

Grades: 11 12 Adult   **070.4**
1. Journalism 2. Vocational guidance
ISBN 0-465-02455-6; 978-0-465-02455-1
                                        LC 2005-37974
The author takes a "look at the practice of American
journalism. He recalls his own achievements and shortcomings over a long career as well as other great and not so great
moments in American journalism. . . . Freedman speaks very
directly and personally, offering encouragement with equal
portions of reality about the state of modern journalism from
corporate influences to the blurring of lines between truth
and propaganda." Booklist
Includes bibliographical references

Kern, Jonathan

Sound reporting; the NPR guide to audio journalism and production. University of Chicago Press
2008 382p $55; pa $20

Grades: 11 12 Adult   **070.4**
1. Broadcast journalism 2. Radio -- Production and
direction
ISBN 978-0-226-43177-2; 0-226-43177-0; 978-0-226-
43178-9 pa; 0-226-43178-9 pa
                                        LC 2008-3994
The author "delineates the values and practices that yield
stellar audio journalism. Comprehensive and lucid, this distinctive handbook explains how sound paints pictures and
how narratives are shaped and paced for the ear instead of
the eye." Booklist

Killed cartoons; casualties from the war on free expression. edited by David Wallis. W.W. Norton &
Co. 2007 282p ill. $15.95

Grades: 11 12 Adult   **070.4**
1. Censorship 2. American wit and humor 3. Comic
books, strips, etc. 4. United States -- Politics and
government -- 2001- 5. American wit and humor,
Pictorial. 6. Censorship -- United States -- Case studies.
7. Editorial cartoons -- United States -- History. 8.
Editorial cartoonists -- United States -- Biography. 9.
Freedom of expression -- United States -- Miscellanea.
10. United States -- Politics and government -- 2001- --
Caricatures and cartoons. 11. United States -- Politics
and government -- 20th century -- Caricatures and
cartoons.
ISBN 9780393329247 (pbk.); 0393329240 (pbk.)
                                        LC 2006033191
This collection of cartoons touches on topics such as former U.S. President George W. "Bush for his 'Bring 'em on!'
speech, . . . pedophile priests, . . . capital punishment, . . .
the disputed 2000 election, or . . . baseball mascots. . . . [The
book includes cartoons], many unpublished, by the likes of
Garry Trudeau, Doug Marlette, Paul Conrad, Mike Luckov-
ich, Matt Davies, and Ted Rall (all Pulitzer Prize winners or
finalists), as well as unearthed editorial illustrations by Nor-

man Rockwell, Edward Sorel, Anita Kunz, Marshall Arisman, and Steve Brodner." (Publisher's note)

Klibanoff, Hank

★ The **race** beat; the press, the civil rights struggle, and the awakening of a nation. Gene Roberts and Hank Klibanoff. Knopf 2006 viii, 518p ill. $30; (pbk.) $17

Grades: 10 11 12 Adult   **070.4**
1. Reporters and reporting 2. Civil rights demonstrations 3. African Americans -- Civil rights 4. United States -- Race relations 5. United States -- Race relations -- Press coverage 6. Civil rights movements -- Press coverage -- United States 7. African Americans -- Civil rights -- History -- 20th century 8. African Americans -- Press coverage -- History -- 20th century
ISBN 0679403817; 9780679403814; 9780679735656
LC 2006045251

Pultizer Prize: History (2007)

This book discusses "reporters who covered the 'race beat' during the volatile desegregation of the South, put[ting] their principles and often their lives on the line." It explores "the role that print and broadcast reporters played in the Movement. . . . Beginning with Gunnar Myrdal's indictment of Southern racial intolerance, 'An American Dilemma' (1944), the authors describe how the white and black presses sought out and presented the stories that enthralled and divided America, from Emmett Till's murder in 1955 to 'Bloody Sunday' at Selma ten years later. The white press replaced the black press as the source of timely civil rights news because Southern political leaders and murderous pro-segregation thugs more often prevented black reporters from covering events." (Library Journal)

Real sports reporting; edited by Abraham Aamidor. Indiana Univ. Press 2003 260p $49.95; pa $19.95

Grades: 11 12 Adult   **070.4**
1. Sports 2. Reporters and reporting
ISBN 0-253-34273-2; 0-253-21616-8 pa
LC 2003-2448

This book "is divided into two sections. The first, 'Beat Coverage,' features articles on writing about various sports: football, hockey, soccer, golf, tennis, baseball; there's even a general article on how to write a sports column. . . . Part two, 'The Rest of the Story,' offers more general advice, with articles on covering high-school and college sports, doing freelance sports writing, and becoming a sports editor. It's a vastly informative book, a real treat for budding journalists and even a few sports fans with an interest in writing." Booklist

★ **Reporting** Vietnam. Library of Am. 1998 2v il maps v1-v2 ea $35; v2 pa $17.95

Grades: 11 12 Adult   **070.4**
1. Vietnam War, 1961-1975 2. Reporters and reporting
ISBN 1-88301-158-2 v1; 1-88301-159-0 v2; 1-88301-190-6 v2 pa
LC 98-12267

"This book will help readers understand better what it was like to live through that tumultuous period of American history." Publ Wkly

Includes bibliographical references

Tobin, James

Reporting America at war; an oral history. compiled by Michelle Ferrari with commentary by James Tobin. Hyperion 2003 241p il $23.95

Grades: 11 12 Adult   **070.4**
1. War 2. Reporters and reporting
ISBN 1-401-30072-3
LC 2003-49966

"Beginning with Edward R. Morrow's live reports during the London blitz and ending with an epilogue on the second war in Iraq, this oral history contains transcripts of interviews with 11 top correspondents. Murrow is one of three deceased reporters included (the others are Martha Gellhorn and Homer Bigart), along with Walter Cronkite, Andy Rooney, Frank Gibney, Malcolm Browne, David Halberstam, Morley Safer, Ward Just, Gloria Emerson, Chris Hedges and Christiane Amanpour. . . . Tobin's introductions and transitional and informational interpolations within the transcripts hold this informative volume together." Publ Wkly

Includes bibliographical references

070.5   Publishing

No shelf required 2; use and management of electronic books. edited by Sue Polanka. American Library Association 2012 xiv, 254 p.p ill. (alk. paper) $65

Grades: Adult Professional   **070.5**
1. Electronic books 2. Library resources 3. Electronic publishing 4. Libraries and electronic publishing 5. Libraries -- Special collections -- Electronic books
ISBN 0838911455; 9780838911457
LC 2011040497

This book "brings together a variety of professionals to share their expertise about e-books with librarians and publishers. Providing forward-thinking ideas while remaining grounded in practical information that can be implemented in all kinds of libraries, the topics explored include an introduction to e-books . . . and an overview of their history and development . . . e-book technology . . . why e-books are good for learning, and how librarians can market them." (Publisher's note)

Includes bibliographical references and index

Todd, Mark

Whatcha mean, what's a zine? the art of making zines and mini comics. [by] Mark Todd + Esther Peal Watson; with contributions by more than 20 creators of Indie-comics and magazines. Houghton Mifflin 2006 110p il pa $12.99

Grades: 7 8 9 10   **070.5**
1. Desktop publishing 2. Comic books, strips, etc. 3. Zines
ISBN 978-0-618-56315-9; 0-618-56315-6
LC 2005-55026

"A zine is a mini-magazine or homemade comic about any topic of the creator's choice, designed for maximum creativity and expression. The authors present a history of self-publishing. . . . Other topics include ideas for zine subjects; copying, binding, and printing tips, including easy-to-understand silk-screening and gocco instruction. . . . Throughout, technical terms are deftly used and advice is dispensed in an accessible, rousing format that includes comics, drawings, and cut-and-paste zine techniques. This well-designed and entertaining resource is sure to find an audience among hip, artistic, and do-it-yourself enthusiasts." SLJ

071 Geographic treatment of journalism and newspapers

Burns, Eric
    Infamous scribblers; the founding fathers and the rowdy beginnings of American journalism. Public Affairs 2006 467p hardcover o.p. pa $15.95
Grades: 11 12 Adult   071
    1. Journalism 2. Newspapers -- United States
    ISBN 978-1-58648-334-0; 1-58648-334-X; 978-1-58648-428-6 pa; 1-58648-428-1 pa
                    LC 2005-53542
"From the sniping feuds among Boston's first papers to sex scandals involving Alexander Hamilton and Thomas Jefferson, the snappy patter gives clear indication of how much Burns . . . relishes telling his story." Publ Wkly
    Includes bibliographical references

The **New** new journalism; conversations with America's best nonfiction writers on their craft. [edited and with an introduction by] Robert S. Boynton. Vintage Books 2005 xxxiv, 456p pa $13.95
Grades: 11 12 Adult   071
    1. Journalism
    ISBN 1-400-03356-X
                    LC 2004-57161
    The author "offers interviews with 19 writers who detail how and why they produce their work. . . . A fascinating book that makes the reader want to go out and get every book the writers have written as well as those mentioned as sources of inspiration." Booklist
    Includes bibliographical references

Written into history; Pulitzer Prize reporting of the twentieth century from the New York times. edited and with an introduction by Anthony Lewis. Times Bks. 2001 xxv, 355p hardcover o.p. pa $17
Grades: 11 12 Adult   071
    1. Journalism 2. Pulitzer Prizes
    ISBN 0-8050-6849-X; 0-8050-7178-4 pa
                    LC 2001-35555
"For anyone interested in recent history or journalism at its best, this book will prove worthwhile." Publ Wkly

080 General collections

Adler, Mortimer J.
    How to think about the great ideas; from the great books of Western civilization. {by} Mortimer J. Adler; edited by Max Weismann. Open Court 2000 xxiv, 530p pa $24.95
Grades: 11 12 Adult   080
    1. Great books of the Western world
    ISBN 0-8126-9412-0
                    LC 99-45251
This volume contains the transcripts of 52 half-hour segments of Adler's 1953-1954 television program The great ideas
    "The book showcases Adler's ideas about all the big categories—truth, beauty, freedom, love, sex, art, justice, rationality, humankind's nature, Darwinism, government." Publ Wkly

Andrews, Robert
    Famous lines; a Columbia dictionary of familiar quotations. Columbia Univ. Press 1997 xxiii, 625p $38.95
Grades: 11 12 Adult   080
    1. Quotations 2. Reference books
    ISBN 0-231-10218-6
                    LC 96-43879
    This work "contains more than 6,000 witticisms, enduring observations, and incendiary statements from all kinds of people from antiquity to yesterday. Besides identifying the source, Andrews . . . provides details of the first publication, specific chapter and scene, and even the character speaking. Besides quotes from Shakespeare and Oscar Wilde, readers will find fascinating quotes from Monty Python, Gloria Steinem, and maybe your favorite author, for example, Agatha Christie. The more than 500 subject headings include homelessness, AIDS, sexual harassment, murder, and war." Booklist
    Includes bibliographical references

081 General collections in specific languages and language families

King, Anita
    Contemporary quotations in black; compiled and edited by Anita King. Greenwood Press 1997 298p il $45
Grades: 11 12 Adult   081
    1. Quotations 2. African Americans -- Quotations
    ISBN 0-313-29122-5
                    LC 96-47431
    "This collection features the words of contemporary African Americans and black Africans. . . . Many of the over 1000 quotations are drawn from magazines and newspaper articles published from 1990 to 1996, and most have never before appeared in anthologies. Those quoted range from journalists and musicians to athletes and physicians. . . . Entries are presented alphabetically by author, quotes are numbered sequentially, and indexing is by author and subject/keyword." Libr J

082   General collections in English

Cordry, Harold V.

The **multicultural** dictionary of proverbs; over 20,000 adages from more than 120 languages, nationalities and ethnic groups. McFarland & Co. 1997 406p hardcover o.p. pa $35

Grades: 11 12 Adult   **082**
1. Proverbs
ISBN 0-7864-0251-2; 0-7864-2262-9 pa

LC 96-33264

"This well-organized multicultural dictionary of proverbs not only illustrates the common insights that different cultures share but also provides a rich resource of wisdom that the casual reader can glean from perusing the proverbs in an entry." Am Ref Books Annu, 1998

★ **Quotations** for all occasions; compiled by Catherine Frank. Columbia Univ. Press 2000 260p $55; pa $18.95

Grades: 11 12 Adult   **082**
1. Quotations
ISBN 0-231-11290-4; 0-231-11291-2 pa

LC 00-24048

This title "organizes its 1500-plus quotes into three sections that cover 150 different occasions. 'Every Year' contains quotes for such annual events as holidays, birthdays, days of the week, and seasons, while 'Occasionally' encompasses quotes for less frequent events, like going back to school, breaking up, quitting smoking, and school reunions. The final section is for 'Once in a Lifetime' experiences, such as turning 16, getting a first car, menopause, and retirement." Libr J

Includes bibliographical references

★ The **Yale** book of quotations; edited by Fred R. Shapiro; foreword by Joseph Epstein. Yale University Press 2006 1104p $50

Grades: 11 12 Adult   **082**
1. Quotations
ISBN 978-0-300-10798-2; 0-300-10798-6

LC 2006-12317

The more than 12,000 "range over literature, history, popular culture, sports, computers, science, politics, law, and the social sciences, and although American quotations are emphasized, the book's scope is global. The authors represented are as diverse as William Shakespeare, John Lennon, Jack Dempsey, both Presidents Bush, J.K. Rowling, Rita Mae Brown, Confucius, Warren Buffet, and Deng Xiaoping. The entries are arranged by author, then chronologically and alphabetically by source title within the same year. A significant effort was made to trace the first published occurrence of a quotation, and whenever possible the wording is taken from the original source. . . . Electronic products such as the Times Digital Archive, JSTOR, Proquest Historical Newspapers and American Periodical Series, LexisNexis, Newspaperarchive.com, Questia, Eighteenth Century Collections Online, and Literature Online were all used." Libr J

100 PHILOSOPHY

100   Philosophy, parapsychology and occultism, psychology

Blackburn, Simon, 1944-

Think: a compelling introduction to philosophy. Oxford Univ. Press 1999 312p $25

Grades: 11 12 Adult   **100**
1. Philosophy
ISBN 0-19-210024-6

LC 00-265266

The author explores such areas as knowledge, mind, free will, identity, God, goodness and justice. "His method is to introduce what other philosophers—primarily Plato, Descartes, Locke, Berkeley, Leibniz, Hume, and Kant—have had to say about these themes. . . . Readers new to the subject could very well be captivated." Libr J

Includes bibliographical references

Phillips, Christopher

Socrates cafe; a fresh taste of philosophy. Norton 2001 232p hardcover o.p. pa $13.95

Grades: 11 12 Adult   **100**
1. Philosophy
ISBN 0-393-04956-6; 0-393-32298-X pa

LC 00-62211

"Former journalist Phillips travels around the country to elicit dialogs, questions, and philosophical investigations from nonacademic participants. Elementary schools, senior-citizen facilities, public coffeehouses, and other well-populated venues provide the backdrops for the discussions he reports in this account of what 'doing philosophy' can and does mean in contemporary culture." Libr J

Includes bibliographical references

The **philosophy** book; [contributors, Will Buckingham ... [et al.]] DK Pub. 2011 352p il $25

Grades: 9 10 11 12   **100**
1. Philosophy
ISBN 978-0-7566-6861-7

LC 2011-280605

"What is the nature of the world? How should I live? Is language really logical? In this accessible guide to the great thinkers, contributors offer the (thoroughly boiled down) perspectives of 107 philosophers on such questions. An introduction defines the discipline, explains its branches, and argues for its continuing relevance. . . . This graphically lively presentation, which also features color reproductions, colorfully framed pull quotes, photos, and a variety of fonts, offers students an overview of the ideas and concepts generated by people who have spent their lives 'wondering about the world.'" SLJ

Includes bibliographical references

Van Lente, Fred

★ **Action** philosophers! Evil Twin Comics 2006 92p il pa $6.95

Grades: 10 11 12   **100**
1. Graphic novels 2. Humorous graphic novels 3.

Philosophy -- Graphic novels
ISBN 0-9778329-0-2; 978-0-9778329-0-3

This book combines a summary of the basic tenets of philosophers Plato, Bodhidharma, Nietzsche, Thomas Jefferson, St. Augustine, Ayn Rand, Sigmund Freud, Carl Jung, and Joseph Campbell with irreverent artistic portrayals. Imagine Plato as a masked wrestler (shouting "Plato smash!"), or Bodhidharma as a kung fu master. The section on Freud frankly discusses and portrays some of his more controversial psychosexual ideas.

103   Dictionaries, encyclopedias, concordances of philosophy

The **Cambridge** dictionary of philosophy; edited by Robert Audi. 2nd ed; Cambridge Univ. Press 1999 xxxv, 1001p il hardcover o.p. pa $32.99
Grades: 11 12 Adult   **103**
1. Reference books 2. Philosophy -- Dictionaries
ISBN 0-521-63136-X; 0-521-63722-8 pa
LC 99-12920
First published 1995

This work contains some 4,400 entries including 50 on major contemporary philosophers. Wide coverage of Western philosophy as well as non-Western and non-European philosophers is included. The rapidly growing fields of philosophy of mind and applied ethics are also covered

★ The **Oxford** companion to philosophy; edited by Ted Honderich. 2nd ed., new ed; Oxford University Press 2005 1056p il $60
Grades: 11 12 Adult   **103**
1. Reference books 2. Philosophy -- Encyclopedias
ISBN 0-19-926479-1
LC 2005-275452
First published 1995

"Including more than 2200 alphabetically arranged entries from nearly 300 contributors, . . . [this book] provides an encyclopedic view of philosophy's past and present, its ideas, disputes (the editor himself contributes an article on unlikely philosophical propositions), and key figures, living and dead. . . . This title makes an excellent companion for standard multivolume subject encyclopedias." SLJ
Includes bibliographical references

109   History and collected biography

Durant, William James
The **story** of philosophy; the lives and opinions of the great philosophers. by Will Durant. [2nd ed]; Simon & Schuster 1933 412p hardcover o.p. pa $15
Grades: 11 12 Adult   **109**
1. Philosophers 2. Philosophy -- History
ISBN 0-671-69500-2; 0-671-20159-X pa
First published 1926

A selective account of western thinkers from Socrates and Kant to Schopenhauer and Dewey.
Includes bibliographical references

King, Peter J.
★ **One** hundred philosophers; the life and work of the world's greatest thinkers. Barron's Educ. Ser. 2004 192p il pa $19.95
Grades: 11 12 Adult   **109**
1. Philosophers
ISBN 0-7641-2791-8
LC 2003-110643

The author "has done a masterful job in presenting the life and work of what he calls 'the world's greatest thinkers.' . . . The concise and clearly written description of the thinker's life and ideas are just what a student or a layperson needs to gather an overview of the thinker's life and intellectual contributions." Am Ref Books Annu, 2005
Includes bibliographical references

Solomon, Robert C.
A **short** history of philosophy; {by} Robert C. Solomon, Kathleen M. Higgins. Oxford Univ. Press 1996 329p hardcover o.p. pa $23.95
Grades: 11 12 Adult   **109**
1. Philosophy -- History
ISBN 0-19-508647-3; 0-19-510196-0 pa
LC 95-12578

"This is a fine overview of the subject that any interested reader will find rewarding." Libr J
Includes bibliographical references

World philosophers and their works; editor, John K. Roth; managing editor, Christina J. Moose; project editor, Rowena Wildin. Salem Press 2000 3v il set $331
Grades: 11 12 Adult   **109**
1. Philosophers
ISBN 0-89356-878-3
LC 99-55143

The editor "presents substantial entries that for 226 philosophers give brief biographies, justify the inclusion of each thinker, list their most important works, analyze their lifework, and locate them within the context of philosophy." Choice
Includes bibliographical references

113   Cosmology (Philosophy of nature)

Lynch, Thomas
★ **Bodies** in motion and at rest; on metaphor and mortality. Norton 2000 275p hardcover o.p. pa $12.95
Grades: 11 12 Adult   **113**
1. Life 2. Death
ISBN 0-393-04927-2; 0-393-32164-9 pa
LC 00-21355

This collection of essays shows how Americans live and how they die. It presents attitude toward death and offers counseling and comforting advice to the bereft.

The author "engages the reader with a mixture of poetic and funerary elements. . . . His voice is rich and generous." N Y Times

Marshall, Peter H.

Nature's web; rethinking our place on earth. [by] Peter Marshall. Paragon House 1994 513p $29.95

Grades: 11 12 Adult   **113**
1. Philosophy of nature
ISBN 1-55778-652-6

LC 93-17233

"This is a wonderful history of 'green' ideas." Choice
Includes bibliographical references

128   Humankind

Beauregard, Mario

Brain wars; the scientific battle over the existence of the mind and the proof that will change the way we live our lives. by Mario Beauregard. HarperOne 2012 250 p. (hardback) $26.99

Grades: 10 11 12 Adult   **128**
1. Brain 2. Consciousness 3. Identity (Psychology) 4. Mind-brain identity theory
ISBN 0062071564; 9780062071569

LC 2012002469

In this book author "Mario Beauregard reveals compelling new evidence set to provoke a major shift in our understanding of the mind-body debate: research showing that the mind and consciousness are transmitted and filtered through the brain--but are not generated by it. Beauregard believes that consciousness is more than simply a physical process that takes place in the brain." (Publisher's note)

Provocative and accessible, this book is ultimately less about hard science and more about the mind-body problem and philosophy of materialistic science. It will be of interest to readers of Andrew Newberg's How God Changes Your Brain." LJ

Includes bibliographical references (p. 217-239) and index

★ The **Oxford** companion to the mind; edited by Richard L. Gregory. 2nd ed; Oxford University Press 2005 1004p il $75

Grades: 11 12 Adult   **128**
1. Reference books 2. Psychology -- Dictionaries
ISBN 0-19-866224-6

LC 2004-275127

First published 1987

This "is one of those texts one wishes for enough hours in the day to read from cover to cover. . . . For those interested in the mind, this is a wonderful reference and a resource for learning more about themselves." Sci Books Films

133.1   Apparitions

Classic American ghost stories; 200 years of ghost lore from the Great Plains, New England, the South, and the Pacific Northwest. edited by Deborah A. Downer. August House 1990 214p $19.95; pa $9.95

Grades: 11 12 Adult   **133.1**
1. Ghosts
ISBN 0-87483-115-6; 0-87483-118-0 pa

LC 90-34782

"Editor Deborah Downer brings together stories from newspapers, journals, and magazines, none of which were written as fictitious. An index references story locations by city and state." Publisher's note

Guiley, Rosemary Ellen

The **encyclopedia** of ghosts and spirits; foreword by Troy Taylor. 3rd ed; Facts on File 2007 564p il $75

Grades: 11 12 Adult   **133.1**
1. Reference books 2. Ghosts -- Encyclopedias
ISBN 978-0-8160-6737-4; 0-8160-6737-6

LC 2006-103302

First published 1992

This work examines famous hauntings, historical personages and happenings, and various legends and myths about ghosts and spirits throughout the world. Recent events, new findings about old myths and updated information on major figures in the field are covered.

"Believers and skeptics alike seeking information on various phenomena will find this book useful." Booklist

Includes bibliographical references

133.109   History, geographic treatment, biography

Nuzum, Eric

Giving up the ghost; a story about friendship, 80s rock, a lost scrap of paper, and what it means to be haunted. Eric Nuzum. Dial Press Trade Paperbacks 2012 305 p.

Grades: 9 10 11 12 Adult   **133.109**
1. Ghosts -- Psychological aspects
ISBN 9780345534682; 9780385342438

LC 2012006290

"A television producer recounts how as a youngster he became convinced he was haunted by the ghost of a little girl, a belief that resulted in a commitment to a psychiatric hospital, until a female friend helps him confront his phobias." Publisher

133.3   Divinatory arts

Levitt, Susan

★ **Teen** feng shui; design your space, design your life. Bindu Books 2003 223p il pa $14.95

Grades: 9 10 11 12   **133.3**
1. Feng shui
ISBN 0-89281-916-2

LC 2003-745

"Feng shui, the Chinese art of placement . . . is explored here with a uniquely young adult perspective, focusing almost solely on a teen's bedroom. . . . Teens with an interest in feng shui, eastern philosophies, or self-improvement will find this book accessible and enjoyable." Voice Youth Advocates

Pickover, Clifford A.
★ **Dreaming** the future; the fantastic story of prediction. Prometheus Bks. 2001 452p $28
Grades: 9 10 11 12   **133.3**
   1. Divination 2. Prophecies 3. Fortune telling
   ISBN 1-573-92895-X
                        LC 00-51838
This work examines various methods of fortune-telling, such as tarot cards, the zodiac, astrology and human sacrifice. Major prophecies by famous soothsayers throughout the history of prediction are explored, including the insight of Nostradamus, Edgar Cayce, Jeanne Dixon and the children of Fatima

"True believers and skeptics alike cannot fail to be won over by Pickover's disarming affection for his subjects . . . this book should delight." Publ Wkly
   Includes bibliographical references

Randi, James
The **mask** of Nostradamus. Scribner 1990 256p il pa $26
Grades: 11 12 Adult   **133.3**
   1. Physicians 2. Prophecies 3. Astrologers 4. Futurologists
   ISBN 0-87975-830-9
                        LC 89-70189
A biographical study of "Michel de Notredame, better known as Nostradamus, the famous 16th-century French physician, astrologer and seer. Commentators claim that Nostradamus's cryptic verses accurately prophesied such events and personalities as Napoleon, Hitler, the French Revolution, the Great Fire of London and the invention of the Montgolfier balloon. Nonsense, argues Randi, and his meticulous readings of key quatrains make a potent case for his contention." Publ Wkly
   Includes bibliographical references

133.4   Demonology and witchcraft

Aronson, Marc
★ **Witch**-hunt: mysteries of the Salem witch trials. Atheneum Bks. for Young Readers 2003 272p il $18.95
Grades: 9 10 11 12   **133.4**
   1. Trials 2. Witchcraft 3. Salem (Mass.) -- History
   ISBN 0-689-84864-1
                     LC 2002-152768
"An eye-opening exploration of what is known to have taken place in Salem in 1692, and of a variety of interpretations that have been perpetuated about the happenings. A dynamic narrative hooks readers into thinking about the mysteries of the past and their continued influence on modern life." SLJ
   Includes bibliographical references

Burns, William E.
Witch hunts in Europe and America; an encyclopedia. Greenwood Press 2003 400p $75
Grades: 9 10 11 12   **133.4**
   1. Trials 2. Persecution 3. Reference books 4. Witchcraft -- Encyclopedias
   ISBN 0-313-32142-6
                     LC 2003-44074
"After an alphabetical list of entries, there's a chronology from 1307 to 1793, indicating the time span of coverage. Topics include witch hunts in various countries, major individual witch hunts and trials, aspects of the witch-hunting process, demonological writers who were both supporters and opponents of witch-hunting, and subsequent interpretations of the witch hunt by historians and others." Libr Media Connect
   Includes bibliographical references and index

Demos, John
★ **Entertaining** Satan; witchcraft and the culture of early New England. [by] John Putnam Demos. Updated ed.; Oxford University Press 2004 543p il map $74; pa $21.95
Grades: 9 10 11 12   **133.4**
   1. Witchcraft 2. New England -- History
   ISBN 0-19-517484-4; 0-19-517483-6 pa
                     LC 2004-54701
First published 1982
"This is not simply a monograph on witchcraft but a major attempt to understand the kind of society and the kind of culture in which witchcraft had a place. To that end Demos employs nearly every conceptual tool available to the historian, including those borrowed from psychology, anthropology, and sociology." N Y Rev Books
   Includes bibliographical references

Goss, K. David
The **Salem** witch trials; a reference guide. Greenwood Press 2007 189p il $55
Grades: 9 10 11 12 Adult   **133.4**
   1. Trials 2. Witchcraft 3. Reference books 4. Salem (Mass.) -- History
   ISBN 978-0-313-32095-8
                     LC 2007-38695
This reference "examines the origins, the accusations, early interpretations, contemporary interpretations, and the impact of the trials. . . . This book also includes a chronology of events, biographies of key figures involved, fifty primary source documents, a glossary of terms, an annotated bibliography, and a thorough index. . . . This book would be a great addition to any library." Libr Media Connect
   Includes bibliographical references

Guiley, Rosemary Ellen
The **encyclopedia** of witches, witchcraft, and Wicca; 3rd ed; Facts On File 2008 436p il $85; pa $24.95

Grades: 11 12 Adult   133.4
1. Reference books 2. Witchcraft -- Encyclopedias
ISBN 978-0-8160-7103-6; 0-8160-7103-9; 978-0-
8160-7104-3 pa; 0-8160-7104-7 pa

LC 2008-8917

First published 1989 with title: The encyclopedia of
witches and witchcraft

"Spanning centuries and continents, the book defines
480 of witchcraft's and wizardry's major historical events,
figures, tools, sites, symbols, and abstract terms. The highly
engaging, alphabetically organized entries run several paragraphs in length and deftly clarify a term's etymology as
well as its spiritual, historical, or spell-making significance."
Libr J

Includes bibliographical references

Kallen, Stuart A.
Witches. Lucent Bks. 2000 112p il (Mystery
library) lib bdg $27.45
Grades: 9 10 11 12   133.4
1. Witchcraft
ISBN 1-56006-688-1

LC 00-8062

The first half of this book "covers the history of witchcraft in Europe and America until the mid-eighteenth century. The second half takes a look at modern witchcraft,
mainly Wicca, explaining rituals and beliefs with an eye toward demystifying Wicca's practice as religion. The author
acknowledges the controversy surrounding witchcraft that
still exists today." Booklist

Includes bibliographical references

Satanism; Allen Gaborro, book editor. Greenhaven
Press 2007 91p (At issue. Religion) lib bdg
$31.80; pa $22.50
Grades: 9 10 11 12   133.4
1. Satanism
ISBN 978-0-7377-2414-1 lib bdg; 0-7377-2414-5 lib
bdg; 978-0-7377-2415-8 pa; 0-7377-2415-3 pa

LC 2006026964

"This is a well-constructed collection of essays on Satanism and its role in modern society. The introduction stays
neutral, and the essays present a broad range of opinion, from
Christian views to secular views and Satanist views." SLJ

Includes bibliographical references

133.5 Astrology

Lewis, James R.
The **astrology** book; the encyclopedia of heavenly influences. 2nd ed; Visible Ink Press 2003
928p il pa $24.95
Grades: 11 12 Adult   133.5
1. Reference books 2. Astrology -- Encyclopedias
ISBN 1-57859-144-9
First published 1994 by Gale Res. with title: The
astrology encyclopedia

"Although aimed at the believer, Lewis' work may be
confidently consulted by the skeptic seeking basic information about astrology." Booklist

Woolfolk, Joanna Martine
★ The **only** astrology book you'll ever need;
New ed., Taylor Trade Pub. pbk. ed. rev. and updated;
Taylor Trade Pub. 2008 534p il pa $19.95
Grades: 9 10 11 12   133.5
1. Astrology
ISBN 978-1-58979-377-4

LC 2001-31798

First published 1982 by Stein and Day

This book features "planetary tables that allow anyone
born between 1900 and 2100 to pinpoint . . . their sun and
moon signs, discover their ascendants, and map out the exact
positions of the planets at the time of their birth. . . . In addition to revealing the planets' influence on romance, health,
and career, . . . [this book] takes a closer look at the inner life
of each sign." Publisher's note

Includes bibliographical references

133.9 Spiritualism

Is there life after death? Rebecca K. O'Connor, book
editor. Greenhaven Press 2005 106p (At issue)
hardcover o.p. pa $22.50
Grades: 9 10 11 12   133.9
1. Future life
ISBN 0-7377-2406-4 lib bdg; 0-7377-2407-2 pa

LC 2004-52399

"Authors in this anthology present both sides of the argument about the afterlife." Publisher's note

Includes bibliographical references

Roach, Mary, 1959-
★ **Spook**; science tackles the afterlife. Norton
2005 311p il
Grades: 11 12 Adult   133.9
1. Future life 2. Religion and science 3. Soul 4. Death
ISBN 0393059626

LC 2005-14450

The author investigates a range of theories and beliefs
about the soul's migration after death.

"Roach perfectly balances her skepticism and her
boundless curiosity with a sincere desire to know. . . . She
is an original who can enliven any subject with wit, keen
reporting and a sly intelligence." Publ Wkly

Includes bibliographical references

141 Idealism and related systems and doctrines

★ The **essential** transcendentalists; edited and in-
troduced by Richard G. Geldard. J.P. Tarcher/
Penguin 2005 265p pa $15.95
Grades: 11 12 Adult   141
1. Transcendentalism
ISBN 1-58542-434-X

LC 2005-44016

This study "is divided into three main sections. . . . The
first is 'Primary Texts,' with selections from the writings of
Sampson Reed, James Marsh, Amos Alcott (father of Louisa
May), and Ralph Waldo Emerson. The second, 'Individual

Voices,' introduces selections from Frederic Hedge, Margaret Fuller, and Henry David Thoreau. The last is 'The Transcendental Heritage,' which features the works of Walt Whitman, Emily Dickinson, Wallace Stevens, Loren Eiseley, and Annie Dillard. This is a highly informed, elegantly written, fascinating story told through commentary, historical overview, and selections from classic works. It belongs in all libraries." Libr J

Includes bibliographical references

150 Psychology

Cohen, Lisa J.
★ The **handy** psychology answer book. Visible Ink Press 2011 502p il pa $21.95
Grades: 11 12 Adult **150**
1. Psychology
ISBN 978-1-57859-223-4; 1-57859-2232
LC 2010-42165

This book covers the fundamentals and history of psychology, plus the practical psychology behind how people deal with money, sex, morality, family, children, aging, addiction, work, and other everyday issues.

"A solid, affordable supplement to introductory psychology texts for readers with a general interest in psychology." Libr J

Includes glossary and bibliographical references

Cordon, Luis A.
★ **Popular** psychology; an encyclopedia. Greenwood Press 2005 274p il $75
Grades: 11 12 Adult **150**
1. Reference books 2. Psychology -- Encyclopedias
ISBN 0-313-32457-3
LC 2004-17426

This book "provides a concise guide for anyone seeking to understand the true scientific nature of psychology." Libr Media Connect

Includes bibliographical references

The **Gale** encyclopedia of psychology; Bonnie R. Strickland, executive editor. 2nd ed; Gale Group 2001 701p il $191.50
Grades: 11 12 Adult **150**
1. Reference books 2. Psychology -- Encyclopedias
ISBN 0-7876-4786-1
LC 00-34736

First published 1996

Coverage includes noteworthy people, movements, theories, and important case studies and experiments. The articles, ranging from 25 to 1,500 words examine such diverse topics as abnormal psychology, bipolar disorder, Sigmund Freud and insomnia

Includes bibliographical references

Reber, Arthur S.
★ The **Penguin** dictionary of psychology; [by] Arthur S. Reber, Rhiannon Allen & Emily S. Reber. 4th ed.; Penguin 2009 xxiii, 904p pa $18

Grades: 9 10 11 12 **150**
1. Reference books 2. Psychology -- Dictionaries
ISBN 978-0-14-103024-1
First published 1985

Contains 17,000 entries on various aspects of psychology, including new developments in neuroscience and social psychology.

150.19 Systems, schools, viewpoints

Freud, Sigmund
The **basic** writings of Sigmund Freud; translated and edited by A.A. Brill. Modern Lib. 1995 973p $24.95
Grades: 11 12 Adult **150.19**
1. Dreams 2. Psychoanalysis
ISBN 0-679-60166-X
LC 95-13411

A reissue of the 1938 edition

Contents: Psychopathology of everyday life; The interpretation of dreams; Three contributions to the theory of sex; Wit and its relations to the unconscious; Totem and taboo; The history of the psychoanalytic movement

Jung, C. G.
The **basic** writings of C. G. Jung; edited with an introduction by Violet Staub de Laszlo. Modern Lib. 1993 xxxiii, 691p $21.95
Grades: 11 12 Adult **150.19**
1. Psychoanalysis
ISBN 0-679-60071-X
LC 93-17801

This is a reissue of the 1959 edition

This volume contains excerpts from Symbols of transformation, On the nature of the psyche, Relations between the ego and the unconscious, Psychological types, Psychology of the transference, and Psychology and religion. It also includes Archetypes of the collective unconscious, Psychological aspects of the mother archetype, On the nature of dreams, On the psychogenesis of schizophrenia, Introduction to the religious and psychological problems of alchemy, and Marriage as a psychological relationship.

Includes bibliographical references

Rogers, Carl R.
A **way** of being. Houghton Mifflin 1980 395p hardcover o.p. pa $15
Grades: 11 12 Adult **150.19**
1. Humanism 2. Psychology
ISBN 0-395-75530-1 pa
LC 80-20275

"This is a book rich in theoretical insights and experiential sharing, and full of invigorating optimism." Libr J

Includes bibliographical references

Skinner, B. F.
About behaviorism. Knopf 1974 256p hardcover o.p. pa $12

Grades: 11 12 Adult   **150.19**
  1. Behaviorism
  ISBN 0-394-71618-3 pa
  The author defines, analyzes and defends the science of
behaviorism with chapters exploring the causes of behavior,
operant behavior, verbal behavior, thinking, causes and reasons, knowledge, emotion and self
  Includes bibliographical references

Thurschwell, Pamela
  ★ **Sigmund** Freud; 2nd ed.; Routledge 2009
162p (Routledge critical thinkers) $95; pa $22.95
Grades: 11 12 Adult   **150.19**
  1. Psychoanalysis 2. Psychoanalysts 3. Writers on
medicine
  ISBN 978-0-415-47368-2; 978-0-415-47369-9 pa
  First published 2000
  "The book contains chapters on early theories, interpretation, sexuality, case histories, maps of the mind, society
and religion, and psychoanalysis's aftermath, including feminist criticism and a remarkable summary of Jacques Lacan's
role." Booklist [review of 2000 edition]
  Includes bibliographical references

152.1   Sensory perception

Herz, Rachel S.
  The **scent** of desire; discovering our enigmatic
sense of smell. [by] Rachel Herz. William Morrow
2007 xxi, 266p $24.95; pa $13.95
Grades: 11 12 Adult   **152.1**
  1. Smell
  ISBN 978-0-06-082537-9; 0-06-082537-5; 978-0-06-
082538-6 pa; 0-06-082538-3 pa
                                       LC 2007-33563
  "This is one of those all-too-rare books that is involving,
well written, and solidly grounded in research." Libr J
  Includes bibliographical references

152.4   Emotions

Chocolate for a teen's heart; unforgettable stories
  for young women about love, hope, and happiness. {compiled by} Kay Allenbaugh. Simon &
  Schuster 2001 219p pa $12
Grades: 9 10 11 12   **152.4**
  1. Girls 2. Teenagers
  ISBN 0-7432-1380-7
                                       LC 2001-20810
  This work presents 55 stories about teen relationships
written by teens and women reminiscing about their teen
years. It relates the happiness of a first romance, conflicts
with parents, and the joys and sorrows of peer relationships.
  "This collection of positive stories should prove refreshing and will be popular with fans of inspirational
tales." Booklist

Fromm, Erich
  The **art** of loving; Centennial ed; Continuum
2000 130p $18.95
Grades: 11 12 Adult   **152.4**
  1. Love
  ISBN 0-8264-1260-2
                                       LC 00-21030
  A reissue of the title first published 1956
  "An astonishingly simple presentation of an abstract
subject." Booklist

Goleman, Daniel
  Emotional intelligence; 10th anniversary ed.;
Bantam Books 2006 xxiv, 358p il $29; pa $18
Grades: 11 12 Adult   **152.4**
  1. Emotions 2. Marriage 3. Medicine 4. Intellect
  5. Parenting 6. Temperament 7. Industrial relations
  8. Emotionally disturbed children 9. Education --
Curricula
  ISBN 978-0-553-80491-1; 0-553-80491-X; 978-0-
553-38371-3 pa; 0-553-38371-X pa
                                       LC 2006-283929
  First published 1995
  The author explains "how to develop our emotional intelligence in ways that can improve our relationships, our
parenting, our classrooms, and our workplaces. Goleman assures us that our temperaments may be determined by neu-
rochemistry, but they can be altered." Booklist
  Includes bibliographical references

Lorenz, Konrad
  On aggression; translated by Marjorie Kerr Wil-
son. Harcourt Brace Jovanovich 1966 306p hard-
cover o.p. pa $13
Grades: 11 12 Adult   **152.4**
  1. Comparative psychology 2. Aggressiveness
(Psychology)
  ISBN 0-15-668741-0 pa
  Original German edition published 1963 in Austria
  The author examines aggression in animals and humans,
noting both the positive and destructive manifestations of
such behavior
  Includes bibliographical references

Ottaviani, Jim
  Wire mothers; Harry Harlow and the science of
love. [by] Jim Ottaviani [and] Dylan Meconis. G. T.
Labs 2007 84p il pa $12.95
Grades: 9 10 11 12 Adult   **152.4**
  1. Psychologists 2. Graphic novels 3. Love -- Graphic
novels
  ISBN 978-0-9788037-1-1; 0-9788037-1-X
                                       LC 2007-900136
  In the 1950s, psychologists warned parents about the
dangers of too much love; in fact, they denied love was anything more than a base instinct based on the need for food.
When scientist Harry Harlow began his experiments on
mother love, was more than just an outsider trying to make
his name. He was also an unhappy man who knew in his
gut the truth about what love, and its absence, meant, and he
set about to prove it. His experiments on monkeys and their

stark results shocked the world. The emotional intensity of his experiments might be overwhelming for younger readers.

"This nonfiction graphic novel retelling psychologist Harry Harlow's famous experiments is as disturbing as it is excellent." Publ Wkly

Includes bibliographical references

Provine, Robert R.

Laughter; a scientific investigation. Viking 2000 258p il $24.95; pa $14

Grades: 11 12 Adult   152.4

1. Laughter

ISBN 0-670-89375-7; 0-14-100225-5 pa

LC 00-38227

"As soon as Provine . . . introduces his groundbreaking, fun-to-read anthropological study of laughter, . . . the full scope of its strangeness and complexity begins to emerge." Booklist

Includes bibliographical references

153.1 Memory and learning

Hudmon, Andrew

Learning and memory. Chelsea House Publishers 2005 136p il (Gray matter) $32.95

Grades: 8 9 10 11 12   153.1

1. Brain 2. Memory 3. Psychology of learning

ISBN 0-7910-8638-0

LC 2005-11699

This "volume provides fascinating insights into various processes involved in how we learn different things in different ways. Particularly enlightening is the section differentiating explicit memory (learning facts) and implicit memory (learning processes) . . . The [book features] colorful historical photos and illustrations, process models, and shaded insets." SLJ

Includes bibliographical references

Schacter, Daniel L.

The **seven** sins of memory; how the mind forgets and remembers. Houghton Mifflin 2001 272p il hardcover o.p.

Grades: 11 12 Adult   153.1

1. Memory 2. Memory disorders 3. Recollection (Psychology)

ISBN 0-618-04019-6; 0-618-21919-6 pa

LC 00-53885

Schacter discusses "the 'different ways in which memory can get us into trouble.' . . . We forget things over time (transience). We often forget where we put our house keys because we were preoccupied with something else (absent-mindedness). We can't remember someone's name (blocking). We mistake an idealized version of our past for a real recollection (misattribution) or claim an 'implanted' memory as our own when it has been suggested by someone else (suggestibility). Our memories are often . . . influenced by our current beliefs (bias). In some cases, we obsessively remember traumatic or painful events that we'd much rather forget (persistence)." (N Y Times Book Rev) Index.

The author discusses "the curious processes of memory by classifying its malfunctions into seven categories: tran-

sience, absent-mindedness, blocking, misattribution, suggestibility, bias, and persistence. Schacter illustrates each of these 'sins' with examples of routine misfortunes common to all." Libr J

Includes bibliographical references

153.4 Thought, thinking, reasoning, intuition, value, judgment

Gladwell, Malcolm

Blink: the power of thinking without thinking. Little, Brown and Co 2005 277p il $25.95

Grades: 11 12 Adult   153.4

1. Intuition 2. Decision making

ISBN 0-316-17232-4

LC 2004-13916

Gladwell "has a dazzling ability to find commonality in disparate fields of study. . . . Each case study is satisfying, and Gladwell imparts his own evident pleasure in delving into a wide range of fields and seeking an underlying truth." Publ Wkly

Includes bibliographical references

153.7 Perceptual processes

Chabris, Christopher

The **invisible** gorilla; and other ways our intuitions deceive us. [by] Christopher Chabris and Daniel Simons. Crown 2010 306p $27; pa $14

Grades: 11 12 Adult   153.7

1. Memory 2. Perception 3. Thought and thinking

ISBN 978-0-307-45965-7; 0-307-45965-9; 978-0-307-45966-4 pa; 0-307-45966-7 pa

LC 2009-45325

The authors "won a 2004 Ig Nobel Prize for their widely reported 'gorilla experiment,' which showed that when people focus on one thing, it's easy to overlook other things—even a woman in a gorilla suit. . . . [In this book,] they explore this habit of 'inattentional blindness' and other common ways in which we distort our perception of reality. Their readable book offers surprising insights into just how clueless we are about how our minds work and how we experience the world." Kirkus

Includes bibliographical references

153.8 Will (Volition)

Bachel, Beverly K.

★ **What** do you really want? how to set a goal and go for it! A guide for teens. Free Spirit 2000 134p il pa $12.95

Grades: 7 8 9 10 11 12   153.8

1. Success 2. Motivation (Psychology)

ISBN 1-57542-085-6

LC 00-57286

The book discusses various ways for teenagers to set goals, build support networks, keep themselves motivated in the process and reap the harvest of their successes

Bachel's "helpful advice is well supported by quotations from teens who have tried some of the techniques, and simple, appealing graphics keep things light. . . . Back matter includes goal-setting resources and some helpful organizations and Web sites." Booklist

153.9　Intelligence and aptitudes

Streznewski, Marylou Kelly

Gifted grownups; the mixed blessings of extraordinary potential. Wiley 1999 292p $24.95

Grades: 11 12 Adult　　**153.9**
1. Genius
ISBN 0-471-29580-9

LC 98-29536

"The book is interesting not only anecdotally, but because it provokes thought about the nature of intelligence and its interactive functioning in our changing society." Readings

Includes bibliographical references

154.6　Sleep phenomena

Lewis, James R.

The **dream** encyclopedia; [by] James R. Lewis and Evelyn Dorothy Oliver. 2nd ed.; Visible Ink Press 2009 xxi, 410p il pa $24.95

Grades: 11 12 Adult　　**154.6**
1. Reference books 2. Dreams -- Encyclopedias
ISBN 978-1-57859-216-6

LC 2009-5132

First published 1995 by Gale Res.

This "reference examines more than 250 dream-related topics, from art to history to science, including how factors such as self-healing, ESP, literature, religion, sex, cognition and memory, and medical conditions can all have an effect on dreams. Dream symbolism and interpretation is examined in historical, cultural, and psychological detail." Publisher's note

Includes bibliographical references

154.7　Hypnotism

Rosen, Marvin

Meditation and hypnosis. Chelsea House Publishers 2005 121p il (Gray matter) $32.95

Grades: 9 10 11 12　　**154.7**
1. Hypnotism 2. Meditation
ISBN 0-7910-8515-5

LC 2005-15848

This book "traces the history of and controversies about manipulating consciousness. Experimentation and medical and psychological applications are discussed in depth, including fascinating subtopics such as brainwashing, dissociation, multiple personalities, and multitasking." SLJ

Includes bibliographical references

155.3　Sex psychology; psychology of people by gender or sex, by sexual orientation

Rosen, Michael J.

Girls vs. guys; surprising differences between the sexes. by Michael J. Rosen. Twenty-First Century Books 2015 72 p. color illustrations (lib. bdg.; alk. paper) $33.27

Grades: 6 7 8 9 10　　**155.3**
1. Gender role 2. Sex differences (Psychology) 3. Gender identity 4. Sex differences
ISBN 1467716103; 9781467716109

LC 2013021833

In this book "author Michael J. Rosen explores the ways in which environment and experience, as well as neurology, physiology, and genetics come together to shape personality and gender behavior - in both expected and unexpected ways." (Publisher's note)

"Approachable format, attractive design, and breezy writing make this look at the science of sex differences both appealing and informative. Rosen highlights current research around varied intriguing topics such as what makes each gender laugh, which is more likely to be struck by lightning, and which sex is more attractive to mosquitoes." Horn Book

Includes bibliographical references and index

155.5　Psychology of young people twelve to twenty

Delisle, Jim

★ The **gifted** teen survival guide; smart, sharp, and ready for (almost) anything. [by] Judy Galbraith & Jim Delisle. Rev. & updated 4th ed; Free Spirit Pub. 2011 261 p. il pa $24.99

Grades: 8 9 10 11 12　　**155.5**
1. Adolescence 2. Examinations 3. College choice 4. Gifted children 5. Parent-child relationship
ISBN 9781575423814

LC 2011020278

Previously published under title: The gifted kids' survival guide: a teen handbook.

This book offers "advice to help . . . [teenagers] understand themselves, relate well with others, and reach their potential in life. Based on . . . surveys of nearly 1,400 gifted teenagers, this [book] . . . is the . . . guide to thriving in a world that doesn't always support or understand high ability. Full of . . . illustrations, surprising facts, . . . [up-to-date] research, revealing quizzes and survey results, step-by-step strategies, inspiring teen quotes and stories, and . . . expert essays, the guide gives readers the tools they need to appreciate their giftedness as an asset and use it to make the most of who they are." (Publisher's note)

Includes bibliographical references and index.

Esherick, Joan

★ **Balancing** act; a teen's guide to managing stress. Mason Crest Publishers 2005 128p il (Science of health) $24.95

Grades: 9 10 11 12   **155.5**
1. Stress (Psychology)
ISBN 1-590-84853-5

LC 2004-10693

The author "describes the body's physical reaction to stress, using words and images that young people can easily understand." SLJ

Includes bibliographical references

Hugel, Bob

I did it without thinking; true stories about impulsive decisions that changed lives. Franklin Watts 2008 112p il (Scholastic choices) lib bdg $27; pa $8.95

Grades: 6 7 8 9 10   **155.5**
1. Decision making 2. Adolescent psychology 3. Risk-taking (Psychology)
ISBN 978-0-531-13868-7 lib bdg; 0-531-13868-2 lib bdg; 978-0-531-20526-6 pa; 0-531-20526-6 pa

LC 2008-690

Teenagers give their stories of impulsive decisions, their reasons for making them, and the consequences—whether good or bad.

This book is "colorful and compact, with . . . an appealing layout. . . . The stories, while not overly preachy, are brief and generally upbeat. . . . [The] book has excellent black-and-white photographs of a diverse array of teens." SLJ

Includes glossary and bibliographical references

Munroe, Erin A.

The **anxiety** workbook for girls. Fairview Press 2010 199p pa $14.95

Grades: 7 8 9 10   **155.5**
1. Anxiety 2. Girls -- Psychology
ISBN 978-1-57749-232-0

LC 2010-6092

The author "explores everything from family problems and body image to sexuality and depression. The book begins with an overview of anxiety, how it manifests, the difference between helpful and harmful anxiety, and a self-assessment quiz which helps the reader pinpoint what situations cause her to be anxious and what kinds of symptoms she typically experiences. Later sections address topics such as peer pressure, relationships, drugs and alcohol, and strategies and treatments for dealing with all of these in addition to more serious problems such as obsessive compulsive disorder and self-mutilation. . . . This engaging workbook will be a helpful source of information and comfort to those who feel the need for it." Voice Youth Advocates

Palmer, Pat

★ **Teen** esteem; a self-direction manual for young adults. [by] Pat Palmer, Melissa Alberti Froehner. 3rd ed; Impact Publishers 2010 115p il pa $11.95

Grades: 9 10 11 12   **155.5**
1. Self-esteem 2. Conduct of life
ISBN 978-1-88623-087-3

LC 2009-23886

First published 1989

Provides guidance on developing self-esteem and the positive attitude necessary to cope with such adoles-cent challenges as peer pressure, substance abuse, and sexual expression.

Includes bibliographical references

Siegel, Daniel J.

Brainstorm; the power and purpose of the teen-age brain. Daniel J. Siegel, M.D. Jeremy P. Tarcher/Penguin 2013 336 p. ill $27.95

Grades: 11 12 Adult   **155.5**
1. Adolescent psychology 2. Brain 3. Cognition in adolescence
ISBN 158542935X; 9781585429356

LC 2013029724

This book, by Daniel J. Siegel, "illuminates how brain development impacts teenagers' behavior and relationships. Drawing on important new research in the field of interpersonal neurobiology, he explores exciting ways in which understanding how the teenage brain functions can help parents make what is in fact an incredibly positive period of growth, change, and experimentation in their children's lives less lonely and distressing on both sides of the generational divide." (Publisher's note)

"Smart advice . . . on providing the most supportive and brain-healthy environment during the tumultuous years of adolescence." Kirkus

Van Wagenen, Maya

★ **Popular**; Vintage wisdom for a modern geek. Maya Van Wagenen. Dutton Juvenile 2014 272 p. illustrations (hardback) $18.99

Grades: 7 8 9 10   **155.5**
1. Popularity 2. Middle schools 3. Autobiographies 4. Teenage girls 5. Self-confidence 6. Life skills -- Humor
ISBN 0525426817; 9780525426813

LC 2014000236

YALSA Award for Excellence in Nonfiction for Young Adults (2015)

This memoir by Maya Van Wagenen tells how "stuck near the bottom of the social ladder at 'pretty much the lowest level of people at school who aren't paid to be here,' Maya has never been popular. But before starting eighth grade, she decides to begin a unique social experiment: spend the school year following a 1950s popularity guide, written by former teen model Betty Cornell." (Publisher's note)

"The clash of eras and cultures is funny—the author wears a girdle, hat, and pearls to class; learns how to apply makeup; improves her posture and poise; and tries a diet. But the best lessons she learns . . . are about how to talk to and understand the people around her." SLJ

155.7   Evolutionary psychology

Burnham, Terry

Mean genes; from sex to money to food, taming our primal instincts. [by] Terry Burnham and Jay Phelan. Penguin Books 2001 263p pa $15

Grades: 11 12 Adult   **155.7**
1. Genetics 2. Psychology
ISBN 978-0-14-200007-6; 0-14-200007-8

LC 2001-32722
First published 2000 by Perseus Bks.
"A delightfully readable presentation of the evolutionary, as distinct from the moralized, appreciation of human nature." Booklist

Ridley, Matt
★ The **agile** gene; how nature turns on nurture.
Perennial 2004 326p pa $13.99
Grades: 11 12 Adult   **155.7**
1. Genetics 2. Nature and nurture
ISBN 978-0-06-000679-2; 0-06-000679-X
First published 2003 with title: Nature via nurture
"In February 2001 it was announced that the human genome contains not 100,000 genes, as originally postulated, but only 30,000. This . . . revision led some scientists to conclude that there are simply not enough human genes to account for all the different ways people behave: we must be made by nurture, not nature. . . . [Ridley argues that] nurture depends on genes, too, and genes need nurture. Genes not only predetermine the broad structure of the brain, they also absorb formative experiences, react to social cues, and even run memory. They are consequences as well as causes of the will." Publisher's note
Includes bibliographical references

155.9   Environmental psychology

De la Bedoyere, Camilla
Balancing work and play. Amicus 2010 46p il (Healthy lifestyles) lib bdg $32.80
Grades: 7 8 9 10 11 12   **155.9**
1. Stress (Psychology)
ISBN 978-1-60753-083-1; 1-60753-083-X
This book is "well-written and satisfyingly informative. . . . [The] magazine-like format includes numerous sidebars, color photos, and charts." SLJ
Includes glossary

Fitzgerald, Helen
The **grieving** teen; a guide for teenagers and their friends. Simon & Schuster 2000 222p pa $12
Grades: 11 12 Adult   **155.9**
1. Bereavement 2. Adolescent psychology
ISBN 0-684-86804-0

LC 00-38746
"Chapters consist of typical questions that young adults may have about grief, followed by a 'What You Can Do' section. The topics covered include such contemporary issues as death from AIDS, post-traumatic stress disorder, and Internet support. Fitzgerald provides many real-life experiences and a true sensitivity to differing religious and cultural practices." Libr J
Includes bibliographical references

Gootman, Marilyn E.
★ **When** a friend dies; a book for teens about grieving & healing. edited by Pamela Espeland. Rev. and updated ed.; Free Spirit Pub. 2005 118p pa $9.95
Grades: 7 8 9 10   **155.9**
1. Death 2. Bereavement
ISBN 1-57542-170-4

LC 2005-447
First published 1994
This offers "information on subjects including: How can I stand the pain? How should I be acting? What is 'normal'? What if I can't handle my grief on my own? and How can I find a counselor or a therapist? Interspersed throughout the book . . . are quotes by teenagers who have experienced grief. . . . Quotes from well-known writers and philosophers give insight into the grieving process and healing." SLJ

Myers, Edward
When will I stop hurting? teens, loss, and grief. illustrations by Kelly Adams. Scarecrow Press 2004 159p il (It happened to me) $34.50
Grades: 7 8 9 10   **155.9**
1. Bereavement 2. Loss (Psychology)
ISBN 0-8108-4921-6

LC 2003-23698
This book "will be extremely helpful for teens struggling to understand their emotions following the loss of a loved one. Grieving is well explained and the individual nature of grief is stressed." Libr Media Connect
Includes bibliographical references

156   Comparative psychology

Waal, Frans de
★ **Our** inner ape; a leading primatologist explains why we are who we are. photographs by the author. Riverhead Books 2005 274p il $24.95
Grades: 11 12 Adult   **156**
1. Human behavior 2. Comparative psychology 3. Primates -- Behavior
ISBN 1-57322-312-3

LC 2005-42768
"Readers might be surprised at how much these apes and their stories resonate with their own lives, and may well be left with an urge to spend a few hours watching primates themselves at the local zoo." Publ Wkly
Includes bibliographical references

158   Applied psychology

Bezdecheck, Bethany
Relationships; 21st-century roles. Rosen Pub. 2010 112p il (A young woman's guide to contemporary issues) lib bdg $31.95

Grades: 7 8 9 10   **158**
1. Family 2. Friendship 3. Interpersonal relations
ISBN 978-1-4358-3540-5; 1-4358-3540-9
LC 2009-12065

"Facts are shared in a conversational tone, creating the sense of a chat with a big sister. . . . [Though] designed for personal reading and browsing, the data provided are accurate and also lend themselves to use in reports. This . . . will be of great interest." SLJ
Includes glossary and bibliographical references

Canfield, Jack
Chicken soup for the teenage soul [I-IV] [by] Jack Canfield, Mark Victor Hansen, Kimberly Kirberger. Health Communications 1997 4v il hardcover o.p. v1 pa $14.95; v2 pa $9.99; v3 pa $14.95; v4 pa $14.95
Grades: 7 8 9 10 11 12   **158**
1. Emotions 2. Interpersonal relations
ISBN 1-55874-468-1 [I]; 1-55874-463-0 [I pa]; 1-55874-615-3 [II]; 1-55874-616-1 [II pa]; 1-55874-761-3 [III]; 0-7573-0233-5 [IV]

These books cover "teenage subjects running the gamut from love, family ties, and self-esteem to developing values and life crises, such as a death in the family. . . . Teenagers not only helped select the poems, stories, and accounts that have been included but also have written some of them . . . with a few contributions by well-known people, including Sandra Cisneros, Helen Keller, and Robert Fulghum. . . . This isn't a religious book, but it is an inspirational and motivational one, sometimes funny, sometimes poignant." Booklist [review of 1997 volume]
Includes bibliographical references

★ **Chicken** soup for the teenage soul's the real deal; school: cliques, classes, clubs, and more. [compiled by] Jack Canfield, Mark Victor Hansen, Deborah Reber. Health Communications 2005 292p pa $12.95
Grades: 7 8 9 10   **158**
1. Emotions 2. Interpersonal relations
ISBN 0-7573-0255-6
LC 2005046051

"The stories included here were submitted by students and are based on their own experiences. Almost every page includes a fun fact, a statistic, or a quiz." SLJ

Fox, Annie
Too stressed to think? a teen guide to staying sane when life makes you crazy. by Annie Fox and Ruth Kirschner; edited by Elizabeth Verdick. Free Spirit Pub. 2005 163p il pa $14.95
Grades: 7 8 9 10   **158**
1. Stress (Psychology)
ISBN 1-57542-173-9
LC 2005018484

"This well-organized, upbeat book discusses what stress is and how it affects the body and brain, talks about tools to reduce and control it, and gives suggestions for recognizing the myriad situations that can trigger stress at home and at school and seeking help when necessary. Best of all, each one of these scenarios includes information on how the situation might be addressed." SLJ
Includes bibliographical references

Goleman, Daniel
Social intelligence; the new science of human relationships. Bantam Books 2006 403p il $28; pa $14
Grades: 9 10 11 12 Adult   **158**
1. Emotions 2. Intellect
ISBN 0-553-80352-2; 978-0-553-80352-5; 0-553-38449-X pa; 978-0-553-38449-9 pa
LC 2006-45971

The author "argues for a new social model of intelligence drawn from the emerging field of social neuroscience. . . . Goleman illuminates new theories about attachment, bonding, and the making and remaking of memory as he examines how our brains are wired for altruism, compassion, concern and rapport." Publ Wkly
Includes bibliographical references

Hong, K. L.
Life freaks me out; and then I deal with it. Search Institute 2005 155p il pa $9.95
Grades: 9 10 11 12   **158**
1. Conduct of life
ISBN 1-57482-856-8; 978-1-57482-856-6
LC 2005-9461

The author "takes readers on a . . . journey of her own teen years (and the years since), offering young people guidance on answering life's big questions: Who am I? What's important to me? What am I called to do on this planet? Each chapter focuses on one important 'truth' the author has gleaned from a variety of sources and life experiences." Publisher's note
Includes bibliographical references

Lavinthal, Andrea
Friend or frenemy? a guide to the friends you need and the ones you don't. [by] Andrea Lavinthal and Jessica Rozler. Harper 2008 xxv, 230p il pa $14.95
Grades: 10 11 12 Adult   **158**
1. Friendship
ISBN 0-06-156203-3; 978-0-06-156203-7

This handbook "takes an honest look at the rules and etiquette of friendship in the digital age. . . . [The authors] discuss everything from becoming a better friend to dealing with 'frenemies' (the backstabbers, users, underminers, etc.) and surviving friendship breakups. . . . Lavinthal and Rozler's guide supplies needed information in an engaging, humorous style." Libr J

170   Ethics (Moral philosophy)

Ethics: opposing viewpoints; Roman Espejo, book editor. Greenhaven Press 2010 224p il (Opposing viewpoints series) $39.70; pa $27.50

Grades: 9 10 11 12   **170**
1. Ethics 2. Bioethics 3. Business ethics
ISBN 978-0-7377-4767-6; 978-0-7377-4768-3 pa
                                    LC 2009-53382

This book "tackles current subjects such as stem cell research and, even more topically, the recent subprime lending debacle. Each topic opens with a general introduction, followed by articles offering different points of view. The first two sections feature opinion pieces on why people should behave ethically and what motivates ethical behavior, while the latter two sections delve into nitty-gritty issues such as cloning, physician-assisted suicide, and business ethics. The articles present a balance of positions, so debaters and researchers are likely to find support for their own viewpoints." SLJ
Includes bibliographical references

Harper, Hill
★ **Letters** to a young brother. Gotham Books 2006 176p $20

Grades: 9 10 11 12   **170**
1. Boys 2. Conduct of life
ISBN 1-59240-200-3; 978-1-59240-200-7
                                    LC 2006-3699

The author "devotes separate chapters to school and work, sex, and life aspirations, tackling such issues as single parenthood, sexually transmitted diseases, the allure of materialism, and the power of words and faith. . . . Although aimed at young black men, this book, with its contemporary language and approach, should have appeal for youth of both sexes and all races." Booklist

The **history** of Western ethics; edited by Brian Duignan. Britannica Educational Pub. 2011 180p il (The Britannica guide to ethics) lib bdg $35

Grades: 9 10 11 12   **170**
1. Ethics
ISBN 978-1-61530-301-4
                                    LC 2010014726

"This history moves chronologically from ancient legal codes to modern questions pertaining to the environment, human rights, and bioethics. Along the way, readers are effectively introduced to monumental thinkers, including Buddha, Confucius, Socrates, Jesus, Machiavelli, Jeremy Bentham, Karl Marx, and Jean-Paul Sartre. . . . [This book] nicely rounds out most philosophy collections." SLJ
Includes bibliographical references

Weinstein, Bruce D.
★ **Is** it still cheating if I don't get caught? [by] Bruce Weinstein; illustrations by Harriet Russell. Roaring Brook 2009 160p il pa $12.95

Grades: 8 9 10 11 12   **170**
1. Ethics
ISBN 978-1-59643-306-9; 1-59643-306-X

"This appealing guide speaks to the ethical dilemmas that all young people experience in their daily lives, and it should prompt considerable conversation and reflection." Kirkus

174   Occupational ethics

Callahan, David
★ The **cheating** culture; why more Americans are doing wrong to get ahead. Harcourt 2004 353p $26; pa $14

Grades: 11 12 Adult   **174**
1. Social ethics 2. Business ethics
ISBN 0-15-101018-8; 0-15-603005-5 pa
                                    LC 2003-15529

"If all business school students could be required to read one book, this should be it." Choice
Includes bibliographical references

Preer, Jean
Library ethics; [by] Jean Preer. Libraries Unlimited 2008 255p il pa $45

Grades: Adult Professional   **174**
1. Ethics 2. Librarians -- Ethics 3. Librarians -- Professional ethics 4. Library science -- Moral and ethical aspects
ISBN 978-1-59158-636-4
                                    LC 2008-21122

"This title takes an inclusive look at why library ethics are needed in the 21st century. This highly practical, substantial, and carefully planned resource is designed to help information professionals figure out their professional values and where they stand when faced with ethical dilemmas. . . . New practitioners entering the field would be wise to use this book as their first professional bible. Those already in the library profession may find this title to be a good refresher." Libr Media Connect
Includes bibliographical references

174.2   Medical and health professions

★ **Biomedical** ethics: opposing viewpoints; Viqi Wagner, book editor. Greenhaven Press 2008 256p (Opposing viewpoints series) lib bdg $38.50; pa $26.75

Grades: 7 8 9 10   **174.2**
1. Cloning 2. Bioethics 3. Medical ethics 4. Stem cell research 5. Genetic engineering 6. Transplantation of organs, tissues, etc. 7. Genetics -- Law and legislation
ISBN 978-0-7377-3737-0 lib bdg; 0-7377-3737-9 lib bdg; 978-0-7377-3738-7 pa; 0-7377-3738-7 pa
                                    LC 2007-34362

Presents opposing viewpoints on biomedical ethics issues such as stem cell research, human cloning, genetic research and engineering, organ transplants and reproductive technologies.
Includes bibliographical references

Boleyn-Fitzgerald, Miriam

Ending and extending life. Facts On File 2010 222p il (Contemporary issues in science) $35

Grades: 9 10 11 12 **174.2**

1. Medical ethics

ISBN 978-0-8160-6205-8; 0-8160-6205-6

LC 2008-30547

"This title covers the medical innovations that have improved the lives of some and have produced questionable ethical decisions in other cases. . . . This series would be an excellent addition to a science collection and would provide high school students and teachers as well, with information on the recent technical and ethical issues in science and technology." Libr Media Connect

Includes glossary and bibliographical references

Caplan, Arthur L.

Smart mice, not-so-smart people; an interesting and amusing guide to bioethics. Rowman & Littlefield 2006 210p $21.95; pa $14.95

Grades: 11 12 Adult **174.2**

1. Medical ethics

ISBN 978-0-7425-4171-9; 0-7425-4171-1; 978-0-7425-4172-6 pa; 0-7425-4172-X pa

LC 2006-14275

The author discusses "issues at the center of the new genetics, cloning in the laboratory and in the media, stem cell research, experiments on human subjects, blood donation and organ transplantation, and healthcare delivery." Publisher's note

★ **Genetic** engineering: opposing viewpoints; David M. Haugen and Susan Musser, book editors. Greenhaven Press 2009 236p il (Opposing viewpoints series) lib bdg $39.70; pa $27.50

Grades: 9 10 11 12 **174.2**

1. Genetic engineering

ISBN 978-0-7377-4368-5 lib bdg; 0-7377-4368-9 lib bdg; 978-0-7377-4367-8 pa; 0-7377-4367-0 pa

LC 2008-35440

A collection of articles explore the social and ethical issues raised by genetic engineering. Governmental and agricultural implications are discussed.

Includes bibliographical references

Lovegrove, Ray

Health; ethical debates in modern medicine. Black Rabbit Books 2008 46p il map (Dilemmas in modern science) lib bdg $34.25

Grades: 7 8 9 10 **174.2**

1. Medical ethics

ISBN 978-1-59920-095-8; 1-59920-095-3

LC 2007-35690

This title is "easy to navigate as evocative photographs, charts, and sidebars help break down complicated arguments into manageable parts for easy digestion." SLJ

Includes glossary and bibliographical references

Merino, Noel

★ **Medical** ethics; Noel Merino, book editor. Greenhaven Press 2010 222p (Current controversies) $39.70; pa $27.50

Grades: 9 10 11 12 **174.2**

1. Medical ethics

ISBN 978-0-7377-4915-1; 0-7377-4915-6; 978-0-7377-4916-8 pa; 0-7377-4916-4 pa

LC 2010015315

Topics discussed in this anthology include organ transplants, government involvement in health care, reproductive technologies, and assisted suicide.

Includes bibliographical references

Morrison, Adrian R.

An **odyssey** with animals; a veterinarian's reflections on the animal rights & welfare debate. Oxford University Press 2009 272p $29.95

Grades: 11 12 Adult **174.2**

1. Animal welfare 2. Animal experimentation 3. Medicine -- Research

ISBN 978-0-19-537444-5

LC 2008-53834

The author "argues that humane animal use in biomedical research is an indispensable tool of medical science, and that efforts to halt such use constitute a grave threat to human health and wellbeing." Publisher's note

Includes bibliographical references

Stem cells: opposing viewpoints; Jacqueline Langwith, book editor. Greenhaven Press 2007 262p il (Opposing viewpoints series) lib bdg $36.20; pa $24.95

Grades: 10 11 12 **174.2**

1. Stem cell research

ISBN 978-0-7377-3648-9 lib bdg; 978-0-7377-3649-6 pa

LC 2007-2991

"This book presents essays, speeches, and articles that offer different opinions on issues related to stem cells. Twenty-eight entries appear under four broad topics: the promise of stem cells to cure diseases, the ethical questions raised by stem cell research, the role of government in that research, and alternatives to the use of embryonic stem cells. Preceding each viewpoint is an introductory summary and a list of three questions that readers are advised to consider as they read. . . . A useful book for students researching stem cell issues for papers or debates." Booklist

Includes bibliographical references

Uschan, Michael V., 1948-

Forty years of medical racism; the Tuskegee experiments. Lucent Books 2005 112p il map (Lucent library of Black history) lib bdg $28.70

Grades: 8 9 10 11 12 **174.2**

1. Syphilis 2. Human experimentation in medicine 3. African Americans -- Health and hygiene

ISBN 1-59018-486-6

This is an account of "the Tuskegee Study of Untreated Syphilis in the Negro Male. . . . Halftone photographs of participants and of the persons who designed, conducted, or criticized the project supplement the text. Informational sidebars provide additional descriptions and photographs of some of the damage done by untreated syphilis." SLJ

Includes bibliographical references

Wittenstein, Vicki Oransky

For the good of mankind? the shameful history of human medical experimentation. Vicki Oransky Wittenstein. Twenty-First Century Books 2014 96 p. (lib. bdg.: alk. paper) $35.93

Grades: 7 8 9 10 11 12   **174.2**
1. Medical ethics 2. Science -- Experiments 3. Human experimentation in medicine -- History 4. Medical sciences -- Research -- Methodology -- History
ISBN 1467706590; 9781467706599

LC 2012043413

In this book, Vicki Oransky Wittenstein "describes many cringe-inducing examples of the ways doctors have exploited the marginalized, powerless and voiceless of society as human guinea pigs over the centuries. . . . Some experiments did lead to important discoveries and breakthroughs, but readers are challenged to consider the costs of violating individual rights for the cause of advancing medical knowledge." (Kirkus Reviews)

Includes bibliographical references (page 89) and index

176   Ethics of sex and reproduction

Cloning; Sylvia Engdahl, book editor. Greenhaven Press 2006 198p il (Contemporary issues companion) lib bdg $39.70

Grades: 9 10 11 12   **176**
1. Cloning
ISBN 0-7377-2771-3; 978-0-7377-2771-5

LC 2005055062

This title discusses public attitudes towards cloning, the cloning of people and animals, and cloning human embryos for research.

Includes bibliographical references

★ **Cloning:** opposing viewpoints; Tamara L. Roleff, book editor. Greenhaven Press 2006 176p il (Opposing viewpoints series) lib bdg $34.95; pa $23.70

Grades: 9 10 11 12   **176**
1. Cloning
ISBN 0-7377-3311-X lib bdg; 0-7377-3312-8 pa

LC 2005-46165

"Scientists, politicians, and seriously ill patients examine the issue of cloning and the issues of whether cloning is ethical, whether cloning research can cure diseases, whether adult or embryonic stem cells should be used in research, and whether cloning should be banned." Publisher's note

Includes bibliographical references

★ The **ethics** of cloning; David M. Haugen, Susan Musser & Kacy Lovelace, book editors.

Greenhaven Press 2009 129p (At issue. Health) $31.80; pa $22.50

Grades: 9 10 11 12   **176**
1. Cloning
ISBN 978-0-7377-4312-8; 0-7377-4312-3; 978-0-7377-4311-1 pa; 0-7377-4311-5 pa

LC 2008054001

An anthology of essays discussing the moral ramifications of human cloning, therapeutic cloning, reproductive cloning, and the cloning of animals.

Includes bibliographical references

Green, Ronald Michael

★ **Babies** by design; the ethics of genetic choice. Yale University Press 2007 279p il hardcover o.p. pa $19

Grades: 11 12 Adult   **176**
1. Medical genetics 2. Genetic engineering 3. Reproductive technology
ISBN 978-0-300-12546-7; 0-300-12546-1; 978-0-300-14308-9 pa; 0-300-14308-7 pa

LC 2007-19927

"By providing examples, contextualizing issues within the framework of stories in popular fiction, and presenting a balanced view of the topics, the author allows the reader to fully explore the issues embedded in the scientific transformation created by the genomic revolution." Sci Books Films

Includes bibliographical references

178   Ethics of consumption

Kerr, Jim

Food; ethical debates on what we eat. Smart Apple Media 2009 46p il map (Dilemmas in modern science) lib bdg $34.25

Grades: 7 8 9 10   **178**
1. Food industry 2. Genetic engineering
ISBN 978-1-59920-094-1; 1-59920-094-5

LC 2007-39651

This title is "easy to navigate as evocative photographs, charts, and sidebars help break down complicated arguments into manageable parts for easy digestion." SLJ

Includes glossary and bibliographical references

179   Other ethical norms

★ **Animal** experimentation: opposing viewpoints; David M. Haugen, book editor. Greenhaven Press 2007 234p il (Opposing viewpoints series) lib bdg $38.50; pa $26.75

Grades: 9 10 11 12   **179**
1. Cloning 2. Genetic engineering 3. Animal experimentation 4. Transplantation of organs, tissues, etc.
ISBN 978-0-7377-3346-4 lib bdg; 0-7377-3346-2 lib bdg; 978-0-7377-3347-1 pa; 0-7377-3347-0 pa

LC 2006-31196

This is an exploration of scientific, religious, and ethical viewpoints on various issues of animal experimentation, including cloning, genetic engineering, and animal donors.

Includes bibliographical references

McCain, John S.

Why courage matters; the way to a braver life. [by] John McCain with Mark Salter. Random House 2004 209p il $16.95

Grades: 11 12 Adult   **179**

1. Courage

ISBN 1-400-06030-3

LC 2003-58626

Senator McCain tells his favorite stories of courage. "In offering anecdotes of individuals whose actions embody the rarity of true courage, his well-drawn examples range from Navajo leaders to Colorado River explorers to Jewish freedom fighter Hannah Senesh and Burmese dissident and Nobel Peace Prize-recipient Aung San Suu Kyi. He reflects on the wellsprings of courage, defining it as conscious self-sacrifice 'for the sake of others or to uphold a virtue,' encompassing actions that may be spurred by honor, outrage, a sense of duty, one's conscience, or moral obligation." SLJ

Phillips, Christopher

Six questions of Socrates; a modern-day journey of discovery through world philosophy. W. W. Norton 2004 320p hardcover o.p. pa $14.95

Grades: 11 12 Adult   **179**

1. Philosophy

ISBN 0-393-05157-9; 0-393-32679-9 pa

LC 2003-18200

The author's "smooth, natural style enables readers to feel that they are part of the discussion at hand, making the book engaging and accessible to those who may have been put off by the formality of traditional works." SLJ

Includes bibliographical references

Ravilious, Kate

Power; ethical debates about resources and the environment. Black Rabbit Books 2009 46p il map (Dilemmas in modern science) lib bdg $29.25

Grades: 7 8 9 10   **179**

1. Conservation of natural resources 2. Natural resources -- Management

ISBN 978-1-59920-096-5; 1-59920-096-1

LC 2007-35691

This title is "easy to navigate as evocative photographs, charts, and sidebars help break down complicated arguments into manageable parts for easy digestion." SLJ

Includes glossary and bibliographical references

Rudy, Kathy

Loving animals; toward a new animal advocacy. University of Minnesota Press 2011 260p $24.95

Grades: 10 11 12 Adult   **179**

1. Animal rights 2. Animal welfare 3. Animal rights activists 4. Animal welfare -- Moral and ethical aspects

ISBN 9780816674688; 081667468X

LC 2011015734

"In her examination of the animal-rights movement, . . . Rudy brings a new concept to the debate about 'animal rights.' In her view, what is missing from the discussion is the role that emotional connections with real animals can play and the value that this sharing of love and life has for both parties involved. . . . Rudy examines the five main ways we interact with the other animals on our planet—as pets, food, captives in zoos, research subjects, and 'clothing'— and argues in each section that it is only through strong connections with individual animals that the broader target of better welfare for all animals can be reached." Booklist

Includes bibliographical references and index.

Sepahban, Lois

Animal testing; life-saving research vs. animal welfare. by Lois Sepahban. First edition Compass Point Books 2015 30 p. (hardcover: alk. paper) $33.32

Grades: 6 7 8 9 10   **179**

1. Animal rights 2. Animal experimentation

ISBN 0756549965; 9780756549961; 9780756550455; 9780756550493

LC 2014026544

This book, by Lois Sepahban, is "like two books in one: Start from one end and learn why some people argue animal testing is needed. Then flip it over and discover why others argue it should be banned. Critical thinking questions help you analyze both perspectives and form your own opinions about the issue." (Publisher's note)

"There's tons of text here, but it's clear and engaging, featuring charts, real-life examples, color photos, and text boxes that supplement the narrative . . . [a] pertinent series for personal or academic use." SLJ

Includes bibliographical references

Yount, Lisa

★ **Animal** rights; Rev ed; Facts On File 2008 332p il (Library in a book) $45

Grades: 9 10 11 12   **179**

1. Animal rights

ISBN 978-0-8160-7130-2; 0-8160-7130-6

LC 2007-27687

First published 2004

This book "provides an overview of the history of the animal rights movement and reactions to it, as well as the issues of animal experimentation, conditions on factory farms, laboratory animals, animals in entertainment, hunting, and the actions of those involved in the animal rights debate." Publisher's note

Includes glossary and bibliographical references

179.7   Respect and disrespect for human life

★ The **Ethics** of abortion; Christine Watkins, book editor. Greenhaven Press 2005 112p (At issue. Social issues) hardcover o.p. pa $19.95

Grades: 9 10 11 12   **179.7**

1. Abortion

ISBN 0-7377-2709-8 lib bdg; 0-7377-2710-1 pa

LC 2005-45119

"Members of the pro-choice and pro-life movements offer conflicting arguments about whether—and in what cases—abortion can be considered ethical." Publisher's note [review of 2000 edition]

Includes bibliographical references

Euthanasia; Sylvia Engdahl, book editor. Greenhaven Press 2006 183p (Contemporary issues companion) $39.70; pa $27.50

Grades: 9 10 11 12   **179.7**

1. Euthanasia

ISBN 0-7377-3251-2; 978-0-7377-3251-1; 0-7377-3252-0 pa; 978-0-7377-3252-8 pa

LC 2006022933

Areas covered include "new technology; medical ethics . . . the legal changes and implications, primarily in Oregon and the Netherlands; and religion and ethics, including the fine line between active and passive euthanasia." Booklist

Includes bibliographical references

Euthanasia: opposing viewpoints; Carrie L. Snyder, book editor. Greenhaven Press 2006 269p il (Opposing viewpoints series) lib bdg $34.95; pa $23.70

Grades: 7 8 9 10   **179.7**

1. Euthanasia

ISBN 0-7377-2933-3 lib bdg; 0-7377-2934-1 pa

LC 2005-55110

"The four chapters explore whether euthanasia is ethical, if it should be legalized, if legalization would lead to involuntary killing, and under what circumstances, if any, doctors should assist in suicide." Booklist [review of 2000 edition]

Includes bibliographical references

Physician-assisted suicide; James H. Ondrey, book editor. Greenhaven Press 2006 101p (At issue. Health) $31.80; pa $22.50

Grades: 9 10 11 12   **179.7**

1. Euthanasia

ISBN 0-7377-3245-8; 978-0-7377-3245-0; 0-7377-3246-6 pa; 978-0-7377-3246-7 pa

LC 2006016760

An anthology of essays discussing "whether or not to legalize physician-assisted suicide. Proponents argue that competent, terminally ill patients should have the right to end their lives when they choose. Opponents contend that legalization of this practice would lead to abuses." Publisher's note

Includes bibliographical references

The **right** to die; Jennifer Dorman, book editor. Greenhaven Press 2010 117p (At issue. Civil liberties) $31.80; pa $22.50

Grades: 9 10 11 12   **179.7**

1. Euthanasia 2. Right to die

ISBN 978-0-7377-4684-6; 0-7377-4684-X; 978-0-7377-4683-9 pa; 0-7377-4683-1 pa

LC 2009048657

A collection of fourteen essays examining both sides of the debate over a person's right to die, addressing top-

ics such as physician-assisted suicide, euthanasia, and legal policies related to the issue.

Includes bibliographical references

Yount, Lisa

★ **Right** to die and euthanasia; rev ed; Facts on File 2007 312p il (Library in a book) $45

Grades: 11 12 Adult   **179.7**

1. Euthanasia 2. Right to die

ISBN 978-0-8160-6275-1

LC 2006-33424

First published 2000 with title: Physician-assisted suicide and euthanasia

This reference source contains an overview of the subjects, a chronology of significant events (including the Terri Schiavo case), biographical information on important figures, a glossary of terms, and an annotated bibliography.

Includes glossary and bibliographical references

180   History, geographic treatment, biography

Price, Joan A.

Ancient and Hellenistic thought. Chelsea House 2008 118p (Understanding philosophy) $35

Grades: 9 10 11 12   **180**

1. Ancient philosophy

ISBN 978-0-7910-8739-8

LC 2007-28320

This book "covers pre-Socratic, Classical, and Hellenistic philosophers and their theories, illuminating some of the first and most enduring answers given about the nature of the world and those who live in it." Publisher's note

Includes glossary and bibliographical references

Van Lente, Fred

Action Philosophers Giant-Size Thing Vol. 2. Evil Twin Comics 2007 94p il $8.95

Grades: 9 10 11 12 Adult   **180**

1. Graphic novels 2. Philosophers -- Graphic novels

ISBN 978-0-9778329-1-0

Karl Marx: The People's Hero! Jacques Derrida: The Deconstructonator! St. Thomas Aquinas: The Scholastic Spastic! Isaac ben-Luria: Rabbi of the Mystic Arts! They're not just great thinkers, ... They also make great comics. This book collects issues #4-6 of the Action Philosophers series, detailing the lives and thoughts of the men above, plus Machiavelli, Sartre, Descartes, Kierkegaard, Wittgenstein. There's just a little bit of strong language in this volume.

181   Eastern philosophy

Creel, Herrlee Glessner

★ **Chinese** thought from Confucius to Mao Tsetung. University of Chicago Press 1953 292p hardcover o.p. pa $15

Grades: 9 10 11 12   **181**

1. Chinese philosophy

ISBN 0-226-12030-9 pa

This history of Chinese philosophy and thought features discussions of: Confucius, Mo Tzu, Menacius, Hsün Tzu, Taoism, Buddhism, and Neo-Confucianism.

Includes bibliographical references

Whitfield, Susan

Philosophy and writing. Sharpe Focus 2009 80p il map (Inside ancient China) $34.95

Grades: 7 8 9 10   181

1. Chinese literature 2. Chinese philosophy 3. China -- Civilization

ISBN 978-0-7656-8168-3; 0-7656-8168-4

LC 2008-31167

"Whitfield covers religion and philosophy [of ancient China] and how they have been passed down using various precursors to books and printing. . . . [This is illustrated with] fine and frequent color photographs and reproductions. Readers will be rewarded . . . with clear, accessible writing, peppered liberally with entertaining stories from history." SLJ

Includes glossary and bibliographical references

184   Platonic philosophy

Hare, R. M.

★ **Plato**. Oxford Univ. Press 1982 82p (Past masters series) hardcover o.p. pa $9.95

Grades: 11 12 Adult   184

1. Authors 2. Philosophers 3. Essayists

ISBN 0-19-287585-X pa

LC 83-159441

The author examines the chief Platonic concepts in their political and intellectual contexts

Includes bibliographical references

Plato

The **selected** dialogues of Plato; the Benjamin Jowett translation. revised, and with an introduction by Hayden Pelliccia. Modern Lib. 2000 xxii, 323p hardcover o.p. pa $14

Grades: 9 10 11 12   184

1. Philosophy

ISBN 0-679-60228-3; 0-375-75840-2 pa

LC 00-30552

This compilation gathers together Plato's most important writings. The topics addressed include: poetic interpretation; cross-examination to arrive at the truth; the nature of rhetoric, psychology and love; and Socrates' art of persuasion in attempting to save his own life

"This {work} is a needed and welcome addition to the translations of the Dialogues. Recommended for all libraries with holdings of the major philosophical writers." Libr J

Includes bibliographical references

185   Aristotelian philosophy

Adler, Mortimer J.

Aristotle for everybody; difficult thought made easy. Macmillan 1978 206p hardcover o.p. pa $13

Grades: 11 12 Adult   185

1. Philosophers 2. Writers on science

ISBN 0-684-83823-0 pa

LC 78-853

Adler traces "in the simplest language and with occasional modern analogues, the logic and growth of Aristotle's basic doctrines." Publ Wkly

Includes bibliographical references

190   Modern western and other noneastern philosophy

Great thinkers of the Western world; edited by Ian P. McGreal. HarperCollins Pubs. 1992 572p $47

Grades: 11 12 Adult   190

1. Science 2. Theology 3. Philosophy

ISBN 0-06-270026-X

LC 91-38362

"This guide to 116 selected authors . . . spans the ancient Greeks to the first half of the twentieth century. . . . The guide is arranged chronologically by the birthdate of the writer. Each entry contains birth and death dates, a list of the author's major ideas, an essay of three to five pages, and a short annotated list of secondary sources. . . . Its readable essays . . . are accessible to the layperson." Booklist

Magee, Bryan

The **story** of philosophy. DK Pub. 1998 240p il hardcover o.p. pa $20

Grades: 11 12 Adult   190

1. Philosophy

ISBN 0-7894-3511-X; 0-7894-7994-X pa

LC 98-3780

"Writing with a clear and lively style, Magee provides an excellent introduction to the topic." SLJ

Includes bibliographical references

Price, Joan A.

Contemporary thought. Chelsea House 2008 160p il (Understanding philosophy) $35

Grades: 9 10 11 12   190

1. Modern philosophy

ISBN 978-0-7910-8792-3

LC 2007-28465

"Framing the evolution of post-Enlightenment philosophy, . . . [this book] begins with a discussion of the British Empiricists and Kant's analysis of the capacity of reason. Biographies and examinations of the Idealists, Materialists, Utilitarians, Individualists, Analytics, Phenomenologists, and Existentialists reveal how philosophers from each of these schools of thought sought to explain the increasingly more secular and industrialized world of the 18th, 19th, and 20th centuries." Publisher's note

Includes glossary and bibliographical references

Medieval and modern philosophy. Chelsea House 2008 136p (Understanding philosophy) $35

Grades: 9 10 11 12   **190**
1. Modern philosophy 2. Medieval philosophy
ISBN 978-0-7910-8740-4

LC 2007-28321

This book "covers the philosophical ideas of the Middle Ages and the Renaissance as well as those of the Protestant Reformation and the age of the Continental Rationalists." Publisher's note

Includes glossary and bibliographical references

★ **Western** philosophy; an illustrated guide. general editor, David Papineau. Oxford University Press 2004 224p il $35

Grades: 9 10 11 12   **190**
1. Philosophy
ISBN 0-19-522143-5

LC 2004-10215

"The lucid writing, with multiple examples and illuminating analogies, will engage readers and provoke them into thought before they know it. . . . This most attractive volume makes its discipline irresistible." SLJ

Includes bibliographical references

191   Philosophy of United States and Canada

Rand, Ayn

The **Ayn** Rand reader; edited by Gary Hull and Leonard Peikoff; introduction by Leonard Peikoff. Plume Bks. 1999 497p pa $16.95

Grades: 9 10 11 12   **191**
1. Capitalists and financiers 2. Objectivism (Philosophy)
ISBN 0-452-28040-0

LC 98-26698

This compilation contains excerpts from all of Rand's novels and serves as an introduction to her basic philosophy expressed in all of her works, fiction as well as non-fiction

193   Philosophy of Germany and Austria

Nietzsche, Friedrich Wilhelm

The **portable** Nietzsche; selected and translated, with an introduction, prefaces, and notes, by Walter Kaufmann. Viking 1954 687p hardcover o.p. pa $17

Grades: 11 12 Adult   **193**
ISBN 0-14-015062-5 pa

Includes the complete texts of Thus spake Zarathustra, Twilight of the idols, The antichrist, and Nietzsche contra Wagner. Selections from other works, notes and letters complete the volume

200   RELIGION

200   Religion

American Academy of Religion

The **HarperCollins** dictionary of religion; general editor, Jonathan Z. Smith; associate editor, William Scott Green; area editors, Jorunn Jacobsen Buckley [et al.]; with the American Academy of Religion. HarperSanFrancisco 1995 154p il maps $47.50

Grades: 11 12 Adult   **200**
1. Reference books 2. Religion -- Dictionaries
ISBN 0-06-067515-2

LC 95-37024

"The 3200-plus articles are written by a team of 327 religion scholars, experts in their respective fields. . . . In addition to the standard alphabetically arranged articles on persons, holy days, rituals, deities, scriptures, etc., there are ten major articles dealing with ancient and modern religious traditions and one on the study of religion." Libr J

Bowker, John

World religions; contributing consultants: David Bowker [et al.] DK Pub. 1997 200p il maps $35; pa $16.95

Grades: 11 12 Adult   **200**
1. Religion 2. Religions
ISBN 0-7894-1439-2; 0-7566-1772-3 pa

LC 96-38277

Each chapter begins with an "introduction and is followed by one-or-two page sections that explain the basic tenets of the faith, symbols, events, people, buildings, works of art, and the differences and similarities to other religions. Hinduism, Buddhism, Judaism, Christianity, and Islam are included as are Jainism, Sikhism, Chinese and Japanese religions, and Native religions." SLJ

World Religions; The Great Faiths Explored & Explained. Dorling Kindersley 2006 216 p. ill. (chiefly col.) $27.95

Grades: 8 9 10 11 12 Adult   **200**
1. Religion 2. Religions 3. Religions -- Handbooks, manuals, etc.
ISBN 9780756617721; 0756617723

LC bl2006011130

This book, by John Bowker, takes a "new approach to understanding different faiths. . . . [It] looks at the beliefs and practices of many different religions, including Christianity, Judaism, Hinduism, Buddhism, Jainism, Sikhism and Islam." (Publisher's note)

"This book is a bold attempt to meld religious information with expressive art and to use the art as a tool for pedagogy. . . . World Religions has generous discussions of the ancient Egyptian, Greek, Roman, Norse, and Celtic religions, topics not even included in the Oxford Dictionary. . . . Ultimately, World Religions is the more commendable publication, though both books are recommended for most libraries." LJ

Breuilly, Elizabeth

★ **Religions** of the world; the illustrated guide to origins, beliefs, traditions & festivals. [by] Elizabeth Breuilly, Joanne O'Brien, Martin Palmer; consultant editor, Martin E. Marty. rev ed; Facts on File 2005 160p il map $29.95
Grades: 7 8 9 10   **200**
1. Religions
ISBN 0-8160-6258-7
LC 2005051101
First published 1997
This "is a valuable resource, covering the beliefs and practices of 10 major religions and lavishly illustrated with color photos, maps, diagrams, and charts." SLJ
Includes bibliographical references

Encyclopedia of religious rites, rituals, and festivals; Frank A. Salamone, editor. Routledge 2004 487p il (Routledge encyclopedias of religion and society) $150
Grades: 11 12 Adult   **200**
1. Reference books 2. Rites and ceremonies 3. Religions -- Encyclopedias
ISBN 0-415-94180-6
LC 2003-20389
"The entries can be understood by readers unfamiliar with the topics covered, but the work is suitable for all levels of scholars." Choice
Includes bibliographical references

★ The **encyclopedia** of world religions; Robert S. Ellwood, general editor; Gregory D. Alles, associate editor. Rev. ed.; Facts on File 2006 514p il map (Facts on File library of religion and mythology) $50
Grades: 7 8 9 10 11 12   **200**
1. Reference books 2. Religions -- Encyclopedias
ISBN 978-0-8160-6141-9; 0-8160-6141-6
LC 2005-56750
First published 1998
This encyclopedia "covers all the major and minor religions of the world, including the religions of the ancient world; the major religions practiced around the world today; religions of contemporary indigenous peoples; definitions of religious symbols and ideas; key leaders and thinkers; and terms and definitions." Publisher's note
Includes bibliographical references

Guiley, Rosemary Ellen

The **encyclopedia** of angels; foreword by Lisa Schwebel. 2nd ed; Facts on File 2004 398p il $75; pa $24.95
Grades: 11 12 Adult   **200**
1. Reference books 2. Angels -- Dictionaries
ISBN 0-8160-5023-6; 0-8160-5024-4 pa
LC 2003-60147
First published 1996
"Guiley's encyclopedia provides researchers with a historical and phenomenological approach to studying angels by examining what folklore, myth, and religion have contributed to research in the field. . . . Brief bibliographies fol-low most of the alphabetically arranged entries, which cover topics such as encounters with angels and the roles of angels in religion, culture, and art." Choice
Includes bibliographical references

★ **Introduction** to the world's major religions; Lee W. Bailey, general editor. Greenwood Press 2006 6v set $325
Grades: 11 12 Adult   **200**
1. Religions
ISBN 0-313-33634-2
LC 2005-30883
"Each volume contains an introduction by the author, time line, and narrative chapters on the history, texts and tenets, branches, practice worldwide (including demographics), rituals and holidays, and major figures. The end matter consists of a glossary, bibliography, and index to the set. . . . The volumes are straightforward and well structured to help locate the answers to most questions asked about beliefs, practices, holidays, and definitions of the major religions people encounter." Booklist
Includes glossary and bibliographical references

Milestone documents of world religions; exploring traditions of faith through primary sources. David M. Fahey, editor in chief. Schlager Group 2010 3v il (Milestone documents) set $325
Grades: 11 12 Adult   **200**
1. Religions 2. Reference books 3. Christianity and other religions
ISBN 978-0-9797758-8-8
This set "comprises 94 documents, ranging from the Pyramid Texts, carved on pyramid walls between 2404 BCE and 2193 BCE, to Calling Humanity, a collection of works by Brazilian spiritual writer José Trigueirinho, published in 2002. The focus is on the five major religious traditions (Buddhism, Christianity, Judaism, Hinduism, and Islam), but documents from other religion-based practices, like Baha'i, Gnosticism, and even atheism and witchcraft, are included as well. Entries are arranged chronologically and include both the primary document and discussion." Booklist
Includes bibliographical references

National Geographic concise history of world religions; an illustrated time line. edited by Tim Cooke. National Geographic 2011 352 p. col. ill. (hardcover) $40.00
Grades: 8 9 10 11 12 Adult   **200**
1. Ethics 2. World history 3. Religious institutions 4. Religions -- Encyclopedias 5. Religion -- History -- Chronology 6. Religions 7. Religion and ethics 8. Religions -- History
ISBN 1426206984; 9781426206986
LC 2011276808
This book "continues the 'Concise History' series with [a] . . . take on major religions and lesser-known faiths of all times and nations." It offers a "global perspective on the history of faith in the Americas, Europe, Asia and Oceania, and Africa and the Middle East. . . . 50 feature essays explore in detail the origins, development and influence of faith." (Publisher's Note)
Includes bibliographical references (p. 343-344)

and index

O'Neal, Michael

    World religions; [by] Michael J. O'Neal and J. Sydney Jones; Neil Schlager and Jayne Weisblatt, editors. UXL/Thomson Gale 2007 6v il map (World religions reference library) set $290

Grades: 7 8 9 10 11 12   **200**

    1. Religions

    ISBN 1-4144-0226-0; 978-1-4144-0226-0

                       LC 2006-12295

    "This set deals with the development and current practice of religions and philosophies. . . . The Almanac volumes surveys 18 religions and philosophies. Biographies contains 50 biographies, and Primary Sources covers 18 sacred writings." Booklist

Philip, Neil

    ★ **Mythology** of the world; [by] Neil A. Philip. Kingfisher 2004 159p il map $24.95

Grades: 9 10 11 12   **200**

    1. Mythology

    ISBN 0-7534-5779-2

                       LC 2003-26801

    The author combines "analysis about mythology and culture, first in general and then about each region of each continent, with brief versions of particular myths, commentary on their origins, and their connections with history, geography, spirituality, and more. . . . Philip's lengthy discussion on myth and society is as fascinating as the particulars of each story." Booklist

Wilkinson, Philip

    ★ **Illustrated** dictionary of religions. DK Pub. 1999 128p hardcover o.p. pa $12.95

Grades: 11 12 Adult   **200**

    1. Reference books 2. Religion -- Dictionaries

    ISBN 0-7894-4711-8; 0-7566-2018-X pa

                       LC 99-30403

    "Following an introductory section that discusses what religion is and what role it plays in society, content is divided into chapters covering the major religious traditions. There are also sections on ancient and primal religions and on new religions. Occultism, the New Age Movement, and the Moonies are mentioned here. . . . Throughout the text, a wealth of illustrations depicts religious practice and artifacts and representations of religion in art." Booklist

Williams, Juan

    ★ **This** far by faith; stories from the African-American religious experience. [by] Juan Williams and Quinton Dixie. Morrow 2003 326p il hardcover o.p. pa $15.95

Grades: 11 12 Adult   **200**

    1. African Americans -- History 2. African Americans -- Religion

    ISBN 0-06-018863-4; 0-06-093424-7 pa

                       LC 2002-71884

    "Brief topical articles and captioned illustrations supplement the main text, creating a balanced, readable, and nu-

anced introduction to the power of faith to sustain the African American community." Libr J

200.9   History, geographic treatment, biography

Armstrong, Karen

    ★ The **battle** for God; fundamentalism in Judaism, Christianity, and Islam. Knopf 2000 442p $29.95; pa $15.95

Grades: 11 12 Adult   **200.9**

    1. Judaism 2. Islamic fundamentalism 3. Christian fundamentalism 4. Religious fundamentalism 5. Israel -- History

    ISBN 0-679-43597-2; 0-345-39169-1 pa

                       LC 99-34022

    This is a "study of fundamentalism among Jews (in Israel), Christians (American Protestants), and Muslims (Sunni Egyptians and Shiite Iranians). Armstrong argues that all strains of fundamentalism, despite their differences, are fearful defenses against modernity. . . . The author is sympathetic to the human need for spiritual meaning, but she points out that the intellectual flaws of fundamentalist beliefs are customarily accompanied by paranoia, anger, and aggression—which, in turn, frequently betray the message of the faith." New Yorker

    Includes bibliographical references

Balmer, Randall Herbert

    Religion in twentieth century America; {by} Randall Balmer. Oxford Univ. Press 2001 142p il (Religion in American life) $28

Grades: 7 8 9 10   **200.9**

    1. United States -- Religion

    ISBN 0-19-511295-4

                       LC 00-60674

    "This title is accessible and reliable, brief and lively, and makes a fine addition to most libraries." SLJ

    Includes bibliographical references

    ★ The **Cambridge** illustrated history of religions; edited by John Bowker. Cambridge Univ. Press 2002 336p il (Cambridge illustrated history) $40

Grades: 11 12 Adult   **200.9**

    1. Religions

    ISBN 0-521-81037-X

                       LC 2001-37866

    "The major religions get thoroughgoing treatment, with short introductions also given to the Zoroastrianism; the religions of Greece, Rome, Egypt, and Mesopotamia; aboriginal religions; and new religious movements. . . . Christianity receives a separate chapter as well as substantial treatment in chapters on Chinese, Korean, and Japanese religions. . . . This volume presents a large amount of information in an engaging way, offering much scholarly insight for the lay reader." Libr J

    Includes bibliographical references

Controversial New Religions; edited by James R. Lewis and Jesper Aa. Petersen. 2nd Edition Oxford University Press 2014 480 p. pa. $35
Grades: 9 10 11 12 Adult   **200.9**
1. Cults 2. Religion
ISBN 9780199315314
     LC 2013049363
"This volume collects papers on those specific New Religious Movements (NRMS) that have generated the most scholarly attention. With few exceptions, these organizations are also the controversial groups that have attracted the attention of the mass media, often because they have been involved in, or accused of, violent or anti-social activities. Among the movements . . . profiled are such groups as the Branch Davidians, Heaven's Gate, Aum Shinrikyo, Solar Temple, Scientology, and Falun Gong." (Publisher's note)

★ **Eastern** religions; origins, beliefs, practices, holy texts, sacred places. general editor, Michael D. Coogan; [contributors] Vasudha Narayanan . . . [et al.] Oxford University Press 2005 552p il $35; pa $19.95
Grades: 11 12 Adult   **200.9**
1. Shinto 2. Taoism 3. Buddhism 4. Hinduism 5. Confucianism 6. East Asia -- Religion 7. South Asia -- Religion
ISBN 0-19-522190-7; 978-0-19-522190-9; 0-19-522191-5 pa; 978-0-19-522191-6 pa
     LC 2004-30376
This is an introduction "to major South Asian and East Asian religious traditions. Four expert authors introduce Hinduism, Buddhism, Taoism, Confucianism, and Shinto. To aid comparison, each article has parallel sections on origins and historical development, aspects of the divine, sacred texts, sacred persons, ethical principles, sacred space, sacred time, death and the afterlife, and society and religion. The clear, crisp prose avoids academic jargon without losing the complexity and richness of the traditions being examined." Libr J
Includes bibliographical references

Encyclopedia of religion in America; edited by Charles H. Lippy, Peter W. Williams. CQ Press 2010 4v il set $600
Grades: 10 11 12 Adult   **200.9**
1. Reference books 2. North America -- Religion -- Encyclopedias
ISBN 978-0-87289-580-5
     LC 2010-18656
"The four volumes encompass a wealth of material, covering many of the denominations and religious movements that have originated or grown in North America, including the United States, Canada, Mexico and Caribbean. Significant coverage is given to Roman Catholicism, the myriad Protestant sects, Islam, Judaism, and Asian religions. Other articles cover topics such as architecture, education, gender roles, missions, music, religious thought, and worship." Voice Youth Advocates
Includes bibliographical references

Friedenthal, Lora
★ **Religions** of Africa; [by] Lora Friedenthal and Dorothy Kavanaugh; [senior consulting editor, Robert I. Rotberg] Mason Crest Publishers 2007 112p il map (Africa: progress & problems) $24.95
Grades: 9 10 11 12   **200.9**
1. Africa -- Religion
ISBN 978-1-59084-958-3; 1-59084-958-2
     LC 2006-31090
This book "covers traditional African beliefs, plus the spread of Christianity and Islam, and how they are practiced today." SLJ
Includes bibliographical references

Gaustad, Edwin Scott
★ **New** historical atlas of religion in America; by Edwin Scott Gaustad and Philip L. Barlow; with the special assistance of Richard W. Dishno. Oxford Univ. Press 2001 xxiii, 435p maps $160
Grades: 11 12 Adult   **200.9**
1. United States -- Religion 2. United States -- Church history
ISBN 0-19-509168-X
     LC 00-30001
First published 1976 with title: Historical atlas of religion in America
"A completely reorganized, updated, and expanded edition of Gaustad's 1962 original work and the 1976 revision, this beautifully illustrated atlas presents a historical narrative of America's rich and diverse religious past. Lively text along with 260 colorful, detailed maps and 200 other graphics provide the histories, migration, developments, and growths of religious communities in the United States." Am Libr

Queen, Edward L.
★ **Encyclopedia** of American religious history; [by] Edward L. Queen II, Stephen R. Prothero, and Gardiner H. Shattuck, Jr.; foreward by Martin E. Marty, editorial adviser; book producer, Marie A. Cantlon. 3rd ed.; Facts On File 2009 3v il (Facts on File library of American history) set $250
Grades: 11 12 Adult   **200.9**
1. Reference books 2. United States -- Religion -- Encyclopedias
ISBN 978-0-8160-6660-5
     LC 2007-52350
First published 1995
This reference source presents over 800 articles examining different religions, religious leaders, events, and other topics that helped shape the history of religion in America. The coverage extends from Puritan America to the moral majority.
Includes bibliographical references

★ **Religion** in America: opposing viewpoints; David Haugen and Susan Musser, book editors. Greenhaven Press 2011 237p il (Opposing viewpoints series) $39.70; pa $27.50

Grades: 8 9 10 11 12　　　　　　　　　**200.9**

1. United States -- Religion

ISBN 978-0-7377-4988-5; 0-7377-4988-1; 978-0-7377-4989-2 pa; 0-7377-4989-X pa

LC 2010016975

This volume explores the topics relating to religion in the United States by presenting varied expert opinions that examine many of the different aspects that comprise these issues.

Includes bibliographical references

201　Specific aspects of religion

Atlas of the world's religions; edited by Ninian Smart and Frederick W. [i.e. M.] Denny; [cartographic editor, Ailsa Heritage; cartography, Advanced Illustration Ltd.] 2nd ed.; Oxford University Press 2007 272p il map $110

Grades: 11 12 Adult　　　　　　　　　**201**

1. Atlases 2. Reference books 3. Religions -- Maps

ISBN 978-0-19-533401-2; 0-19-533401-9

First published 1999

"Beginning with a geographic examination of Palaeolithic religions, the text and maps chart the growth and development of religions throughout history, including the rise and fall of secular alternatives such as New Age belief systems and Marxism. Most of the ten sections are organized by major religion, i.e., the Hindu world, Buddhism, Judaism, Christianity, Islam, and indigenous religions, while the remainder is given to regional treatments of religion. . . . This is an attractive, informative, and practical reference tool that emphasizes the role geography plays in shaping culture and religion." Libr J

Includes bibliographical references

Campbell, Joseph

Creative mythology. Arkana 1991 730p (The masks of God) pa $18

Grades: 11 12 Adult　　　　　　　　　**201**

1. Mythology in literature

ISBN 978-0-14-019440-1; 0-14-019440-1

First published 1968 by Viking

"This volume explores the whole inner story of modern culture since the Dark Ages, treating modern man's unique position as the creator of his own mythology." Publisher's note

Includes bibliographical references

Occidental mythology. Arkana 1991 564p (The masks of God) pa $18

Grades: 11 12 Adult　　　　　　　　　**201**

1. Mythology

ISBN 978-0-14-019441-8; 0-14-019441-X

First published 1964 by Viking

"A systematic . . . comparison of the themes that underlie the art, worship, and literature of the Western world." Publisher's note

Includes bibliographical references

Oriental mythology. Arkana 1991 561p (The masks of God) pa $18

Grades: 11 12 Adult　　　　　　　　　**201**

1. Oriental mythology

ISBN 978-0-14-019442-5; 0-14-019442-8

First published 1962 by Viking

"An exploration of Eastern mythology as it developed into the distinctive religions of Egypt, India, China, and Japan." Publisher's note

Includes bibliographical references

★ The **power** of myth; [by] Joseph Campbell, with Bill Moyers; Betty Sue Flowers, editor. Doubleday 1988 231p il hardcover o.p. pa $29.95

Grades: 11 12 Adult　　　　　　　　　**201**

1. Mythology 2. Religious art 3. Spiritual life

ISBN 0-385-24773-7; 0-385-24774-5

LC 88-4218

This companion to a public television series records conversations between Campbell and Bill Moyers. Campbell reflects on themes and symbols from world religions and mythologies and explores their relevance for his own spiritual journey.

"Campbell is the hero on his own voyage of discovery. This well-bound book on lovely paper with helpful illustrations from art is highly recommended for all libraries." Choice

Primitive mythology. Arkana 1991 504p (The masks of God) pa $18

Grades: 11 12 Adult　　　　　　　　　**201**

1. Mythology

ISBN 978-0-14-019443-2; 0-14-019443-6

First published 1959 by Viking

The author "discusses the primitive roots of mythology, examining them in light of . . . discoveries in archaeology, anthropology, and psychology." Publisher's note

Includes bibliographical references

Davis, Kenneth C.

★ **Don't** know much about mythology; everything you need to know about the greatest stories in human history but never learned. HarperCollins Publishers 2005 545p $26.95; pa $14.95

Grades: 9 10 11 12 Adult　　　　　　　　　**201**

1. Mythology

ISBN 0-06-019460-X; 978-0-06-019460-4; 0-06-093257-0 pa; 978-0-06-093257-2 pa

LC 2005-43341

The author "examines the myths created by societies ranging from Egypt, Greece and Rome to Africa, India and the Americas, proceeding . . . by way of question and answer as he surveys each mythmaking culture. . . . His survey provides a superb starting point for entering the world of mythology." Publ Wkly

Includes bibliographical references

Eliot, Alexander

★ The **universal** myths; heros, gods, tricksters, and others. with contributions by Joseph Campbell and Mircea Eliade. New Am. Lib. 1990 310p pa $15

Grades: 9 10 11 12   **201**

1. Mythology
ISBN 0-452-01027-6

LC 89-38161

First published 1976 by McGraw Hill with title: Myths

This volume provides a "retelling of so-called universal myths, which Eliot and associates have drawn from various cultures worldwide and organized by commonality of theme. . . . It is Eliot's contention that the ubiquity of such myths argues strongly for the essential oneness of humankind. Essays by Joseph Campbell and Mircea Eliade bolster this view." Booklist

Includes bibliographical references

Frazer, James George

The **new** golden bough; a new abridgment of the classic work. edited and with notes and foreword by Theodor H. Gaster. Phillips 1959 xxx, 738p $51.95

Grades: 11 12 Adult   **201**

1. Mythology 2. Religions 3. Superstition
ISBN 0-87599-036-3

"A comparative study of world religions, magic, vegetation and fertility beliefs and rites, kingship, taboos, totemism and the like." New Century Handb of Engl Lit

Includes bibliographical references

Leeming, David Adams

A **dictionary** of creation myths; [by] David Adams Leeming with Margaret Adams Leeming. Oxford University Press 1995 330p il pa $23.95

Grades: 11 12 Adult   **201**

1. Reference books 2. Creation -- Encyclopedias
ISBN 0-19-510275-4

LC 95-39961

First published 1994 by ABC-CLIO with title: Encyclopedia of creation myths

This book "provides access to information on the beliefs (both exotic and ordinary) of ancient civilizations from Sumeria and Babylonia to Egypt, Greece, and ancient Rome, from India and China to Japan and Indonesia, as well as the rich mythological history of Native Americans, the indigenous peoples of Australia, and many other cultures." Publisher's note

Includes bibliographical references

★ The **Oxford** companion to world mythology. Oxford University Press 2006 xxxvii, 469p $65

Grades: 11 12 Adult   **201**

1. Reference books 2. Mythology -- Dictionaries
ISBN 0-19-515669-2

LC 2005-14216

"This volume presents approximately 2,000 concise entries in dictionary format. Leeming, . . . in an attempt to be 'inclusive and reasonably comprehensive,' ranges far outside the Western tradition to cover figures and folklore from Africa, Asia, and the Americas, as well as from the sacred narratives of religions. . . . Approximately 100 black-and-white illustrations, along with a few color plates, provide examples of artistic renderings of various myths. . . . This work should find a place in any general reference collection." Choice

Includes bibliographical references

McIntosh, Kenneth

★ **When** religion & politics mix; how matters of faith influence political policies. by Kenneth McIntosh, M.Div., and Marsha McIntosh. Mason Crest Publishers 2005 112p il (Religion and modern culture) $22.95

Grades: 7 8 9 10   **201**

1. Religion and politics 2. Church and state -- United States
ISBN 1-59084-971-X; 978-1-59084-971-2

LC 2005-3057

This is an "overview of where U.S. voters stand on the relevance of religion in their personal and public lives. The book explores topics such as abortion, same-sex marriage, and stem cell research, and it compares religious views in the U.S. with Canada's more secular perspectives . . . . [The book provides] a lucid perspective on different beliefs within and beyond various religions." Booklist

Includes bibliographical references

Mercatante, Anthony S.

★ The **Facts** on File encyclopedia of world mythology and legend; [by] Anthony S. Mercatante & James R. Dow. 3rd ed; Facts On File 2008 2v il (Facts on File library of religion and mythology) set $150

Grades: 11 12 Adult   **201**

1. Reference books 2. Mythology -- Encyclopedias
ISBN 978-0-8160-7311-5

LC 2007-51965

First published 1988

"Jammed with information and filled with both impressive scholarship and entertaining tidbits . . . it is highly recommended for all libraries." Libr J

Includes bibliographical references

U-X-L encyclopedia of world mythology. UXL 2009 5v il set $314

Grades: 7 8 9 10 11 12   **201**

1. Reference books 2. Mythology -- Encyclopedias
ISBN 978-1-41443-030-0; 1-41443-030-2

LC 2008-12696

"In A-Z format, the set provides more than 300 entries for five content areas: characters, deities, myths, themes, and cultures. . . . The entries generally range from three to four pages. . . . Recommended for middle- and high-school libraries." Booklist

★ **World** mythology; the illustrated guide. Roy Willis, general editor. Oxford University Press 2006 311p il map pa $22.50
Grades: 8 9 10 11 12   **201**
1. Mythology
ISBN 0-19-530752-6; 978-0-19-530752-8
LC 2005-30779
First published 1993 by Holt & Co.

This book describes "the myths of Egypt, the Middle East, India, China, Tibet, Mongolia, Japan, Greece, Rome, the Celtic lands, Northern and Eastern Europe, the Arctic, North and South America, Mesoamerica, Africa, Australia, Oceania, and Southeast Asia." Libr J [review of 1993 edition]

Includes bibliographical references

201.65   Religion and science

Sacks, Jonathan
The **great** partnership; science, religion, and the search for meaning. Jonathan Sacks. Schocken Books 2011 x, 370 p.p $28.95
Grades: 10 11 12 Adult   **201.65**
1. Faith 2. Religion and science
ISBN 0805243011; 9780805243017
LC 2012006601

In this book Jonathan Sacks "argues not only that science and religion are compatible, but that they complement each other--and that the world needs both. . . . [According to Sacks,] Science teaches us where we come from. Religion explains to us why we are here. Science is the search for explanation. Religion is the search for meaning. We need scientific explanation to understand nature. We need meaning to understand human behavior." (Publisher's note)

Includes bibliographical references

203   Public worship and other practices

★ **How** to be a perfect stranger; the essential religious etiquette handbook. edited by Stuart M. Matlins & Arthur J. Magida. 5th ed.; SkyLight Paths Pub. 2011 402p ('Perfect stranger' series) pa $19.99
Grades: 11 12 Adult   **203**
1. Etiquette 2. Rites and ceremonies
ISBN 978-1-59473-294-2
LC 2010-31668
First published 1996-1997 in two volumes by Jewish Lights Pub.

This guide "provides brief overviews of many religions: services, life-cycle events, home celebrations. It explains rituals so that those unfamiliar with them will know what to expect, how to dress, whether to bring a gift, and so on. It also has a glossary, explains various religious calendars, and lists religious festivals." Booklist

★ **Religious** holidays and calendars; edited by Karen Bellenir. 3rd ed; Omnigraphics 2004 424p $84
Grades: 11 12 Adult   **203**
1. Calendars 2. Religious holidays
ISBN 0-7808-0665-4
LC 2004-041500
First published 1993 under the editorship of Aidan A. Kelly, Peter Dresser, and Linda M. Ross

This "handbook provides an overview of the timekeeping and holiday traditions of the world's religions. Part 1 has four chapters that outline the history of calendars. Part 2 covers 24 religious groups in 17 chapters, each surveying the history of the religion, then listing it chronologically and describing the holidays it celebrates. The 28 contributors provide accurate information in readable, double-columned articles, ranging in length from 66 pages on types of Christianity to one on Scientology." Choice

204   Religious experience, life, practice

Chopra, Deepak
★ **Fire** in the heart; a spiritual guide for teens. Simon & Schuster Books for Young Readers 2004 199p $14.95
Grades: 9 10 11 12   **204**
1. Teenagers 2. Spiritual life
ISBN 0-689-86216-4
LC 2003-20174

By recounting his own experiences at age fifteen, Deepak Chopra, a noted Hindu author and physician provides a blueprint for teens who are seeking their own spiritual paths

211   Concepts of God

Seidman, David
What if I'm an atheist? a teenager's guide to exploring a life without religion. David Seidman. Simon Pulse 2015 256 p. maps (hardcover) $19.99
Grades: 9 10 11 12   **211**
1. Atheism 2. Teenagers -- Conduct of life
ISBN 1582704074; 9781582704067; 9781582704074
LC 2014026837

This book, by David Seidman, "offers a thoughtful exploration [aimed at teenagers] of how atheism or the absence of religion can impact your life. From discussing the practical significance of holidays to offering conversation starters and tips, this guide is an invaluable resource about religion, spirituality, and the lack thereof." (Publisher's note)

"Though occasionally disparaging in tone with regard to people who profess some kind of religious faith, overall, Seidman strives for a broad scope and balanced approach that encourages respectful, tolerant discourse. A lengthy list of resources and source notes concludes." Booklist

Includes bibliographical references
What if I am an atheist?

220 Bible

Jacobs, A. J.

The **year** of living biblically; one man's humble quest to follow the Bible as literally as possible. A.J. Jacobs. Simon & Schuster 2007 388p ill. (pbk.) $16; (hbk.) $25

Grades: 11 12 Adult   **220**

1. Bible 2. Authors 3. Religion 4. Humorists 5. Autobiographies 6. Bible -- Criticism
ISBN 9780743291484; 9780743291477; 0743291476
    LC 200709573

It was the author's intent to "follow the more than 800 rules found in the Hebrew Bible" and to chronicle the experience. "Jacobs spends 388 days investigating how a 21st-century New Yorker can live the lifestyle outlined in the Old Testament. Repeatedly, he tries to follow literal meanings only to find that he has misinterpreted the ritual, moral, agricultural, and sacrificial laws. For example, he throws pebbles at a man in Central Park, intending to replicate a stoning, but after consulting with his team of religious advisers discovers that in biblical times, stoning actually meant pushing the victim off a cliff. . . . He concludes that people today practice 'cafeteria religion,' picking and choosing which rules to follow." (Library Journal)

Includes bibliographical references (p. [343]-348) and index.

220.3 Encyclopedias and topical dictionaries

Eerdmans dictionary of the Bible; David Noel Freedman, editor-in-chief; Allen C. Myers, associate editor; Astrid B. Beck, managing editor. Eerdmans 2000 xxxiii, 1425p il maps $45

Grades: 11 12 Adult   **220.3**

1. Reference books 2. Bible (as subject) -- Dictionaries
ISBN 0-8028-2400-5
    LC 00-56124

"Up-to-date, comprehensive, and well written, the EDB is highly recommended." Libr J

Includes bibliographical references

Oxford University Press

★ The **Oxford** companion to the Bible; edited by Bruce M. Metzger, Michael D. Coogan. Oxford Univ. Press 1993 xxi, 874p il map $70

Grades: 8 9 10 11 12 Adult   **220.3**

1. Reference books 2. Bible (as subject) -- Dictionaries
ISBN 0-19-504645-5
    LC 93-19315

"The many contributors read as a veritable who's who among biblical scholars. Although this companion is not meant to be an exhaustive reference, it is a highly reliable guide." Booklist

Vine, W. E.

★ **Strong's** concise concordance and Vine's concise expository dictionary of the Bible. Nelson, T. 1999 2v in 1 $29.99

Grades: 11 12 Adult   **220.3**

1. Reference books 2. Bible -- Concordance
ISBN 0-7852-4254-6
    LC 99-29685

This omnibus volume includes Strong's concise concordance, a version of the original published in 1894

This reference provides definitions, explanations of text, and concordance entries in one reference source.

220.5 Modern versions and translations

★ The **Bible:** Authorized King James Version; with an introduction and notes by Robert Carroll and Stephen Prickett. Oxford University Press 2008 lxxiv, 1039, 248, 445p il map (Oxford world's classics) pa $18.95

Grades: 5 6 7 8 9 10 11 12 Adult   **220.5**

ISBN 978-0-19-953594-1
    LC 2008-273825

This Oxford World's Classics version first published 1997

The authorized or King James Version originally published 1611.

Includes bibliographical references

★ The **Holy** Bible; containing the Old and New Testaments with the Apocryphal/Deuterocanonical books: New Revised Standard Version. Oxford University Press 1989 xxi, 996, 298, 284p map $29.99

Grades: 5 6 7 8 9 10 11 12 Adult   **220.5**

ISBN 0-19-528330-9; 978-0-19-528330-3
    LC 90-222105

"Intended for public reading, congregational worship, private study, instruction, and meditation, it attempts to be as literal as possible while following standard American English usage, avoids colloquialism, and prefers simple, direct terms and phrases." Sheehy. Guide to Ref Books. 10th edition. suppl

The **New** American Bible; translated from the original languages with critical use of all the ancient sources including the revised Psalms and the revised New Testament. authorized by the Board of Trustees of the Confraternity of Christian Doctrine and approved by the Administrative Committee Board of the National Conference of Catholic Bishops and the United States Catholic Conference. Oxford University Press 2006 xxiii, 1514p $39.99

Grades: 8 9 10 11 12 Adult   **220.5**

ISBN 978-0-19-528904-6; 0-19-528904-8
First published 1970 by Kenedy

"Roman Catholic version based on modern English translations; replaces the Douay edition." N Y Public Libr Book of How & Where to Look It Up

★ The **new** Jerusalem Bible; [general editor: Henry Wansbrough] Doubleday 1985 2108p map $45; pa $29.95

Grades: 7 8 9 10 11 12 Adult **220.5**
ISBN 0-385-14264-1; 978-0-385-14264-9; 0-385-24833-4 pa; 978-0-385-24833-4 pa

LC 85-16070

First published in this format 1966 with title: The Jerusalem Bible

"Derives from the French version edited at the Dominican Ecole Biblique de Jerusalem and known as 'La Bible de Jerusalem.' The introductions and notes are 'a direct translation from the French, though revised and brought up to date in some places' but translation of the Biblical text goes back to the original languages." Guide to Ref Books. 11th edition

★ **Seek,** find; the Bible for all people: Contemporary English Version. G.P. Putnam's Sons/American Bible Society 2006 1725p $24.95; pa $15.95

Grades: 11 12 Adult **220.5**
ISBN 0-399-15385-3; 978-0-399-15385-3; 0-399-15397-7 pa; 978-0-399-15397-6 pa

"The CEV was published by the American Bible Society in response to an urgent need for a translation that would reach those many millions who are not reading the Bible. The goal was a serious translation—not a paraphrase—combining historical and scholarly accuracy with contemporary language that everyone can understand." Publisher's note

220.6 Interpretation and criticism (Exegesis)

Manser, Martin H.

Critical companion to the Bible; a literary reference. [by] Martin H. Manser; associate editors, David Barratt, Pieter J. Lalleman, Julius Steinberg. Facts On File, Inc. 2009 488p il (Facts on File library of world literature) $75

Grades: 11 12 Adult **220.6**
1. Bible as literature 2. Bible -- Criticism
ISBN 978-0-8160-7065-7

LC 2008-29257

"This reference provides an excellent introduction to not only just the literary but also the theological studies of the Bible through the ages." Booklist
Includes bibliographical references

220.9 Geography, history, chronology, persons of Bible lands in Bible times

Comfort, Philip Wesley

The **complete** book of who's who in the Bible; [by] Philip Comfort, Walter A. Elwell. Tyndale House Publishers 2004 626p map pa $14.97

Grades: 11 12 Adult **220.9**
1. Reference books 2. Bible -- Biography
ISBN 0-8423-8369-7

LC 2004-20184

This book "provides readers with a complete listing of people in the Bible with descriptions of their lives and accomplishments." Publisher's note
Includes bibliographical references

Currie, Robin

The **letter** and the scroll; what archaeology tells us about the Bible. [by] Robin Currie and Stephen Hyslop. National Geographic 2009 335p il map $40

Grades: 11 12 Adult **220.9**
1. Bible (as subject) -- Antiquities
ISBN 978-1-4262-0514-9

LC 2009-8572

"This gorgeous book . . . . covering the people and events of the Bible, placed into their archaeological context, will delight and inform those who are interested in the Bible from a religious, cultural, or historical perspective. . . . [The book] investigates a variety of topics—such as cities, languages, luxury goods, wars, taxes, writings, and ancient art—through artifacts and archaeological evidence to provide an extensive background for the reader." Libr J
Includes bibliographical references

★ **Oxford** Bible atlas; edited by Adrian Curtis. 4th ed.; Oxford University Press 2007 229p il map $35

Grades: 11 12 Adult **220.9**
1. Reference books 2. Bible -- Geography
ISBN 0-19-100158-9; 978-0-19-100158-1
First published 1962

This atlas includes "81 full-color illustrations as well as 27 maps—e.g., of Jerusalem and the Holy Land, the Middle East and the eastern Mediterranean lands—all with terrain modeling. The text is divided into four main sections: 'The Setting,' 'The Hebrew Bible,' 'The New Testament,' and 'Archaeology in Bible Lands.' . . . [This is] a handsome background resource for Bible study." Libr J
Includes bibliographical references

★ The **Oxford** guide to people & places of the Bible; edited by Bruce M. Metzger, Michael D. Coogan. Oxford Univ. Press 2001 xxii, 374p maps $35

Grades: 11 12 Adult **220.9**
1. Reference books 2. Bible (as subject)
ISBN 0-19-514641-7

LC 00-66900

"This dictionary is a spinoff from The Oxford Companion to the Bible (1993) from which the compilers have extracted the articles about people and places. Many of the more than 300 articles in People and Places are exactly the same as those in the larger Companion, except that the frequent parenthetical references to biblical passages have been deleted. Some articles are extracts from longer articles in the Companion. Articles range in length from a short paragraph, such as the nine lines devoted to Gethsemane, to as many as nine pages (for Jerusalem) or thirteen pages (for Jesus Christ). Longer articles are divided into sections, each with a topical subheading. . . . The bibliography has been updated to include references as recent as 2000." Booklist
Includes bibliographical references

★ The **Oxford** history of the biblical world; edited by Michael D. Coogan. Oxford Univ. Press 1998 643p il maps $60; pa $19.95

Grades: 11 12 Adult **220.9**

1. Ancient civilization 2. Bible -- History of biblical events

ISBN 0-19-508707-0; 0-19-513937-2 pa

LC 98-16042

"Organized chronologically, the essays explore the many cultures of ancient Canaan, Israel, Judea, and Palestine from 10,000 B.C.E. to the rise of Islam in the seventh century C.E. Illustrations, maps, charts, chronologies, and bibliographies enhance the uniformly well-written essays. But the strengths of the work are its currency and breadth of coverage and perspective." Libr J

Includes bibliographical references

Tischler, Nancy M.

Men and women of the Bible; a readers guide. Greenwood Press 2002 267p il $59.95

Grades: 11 12 Adult **220.9**

1. Bible -- Biography

ISBN 0-313-31714-3

LC 2002-75347

This resource provides "information on 100 biblical characters and their cultural significance in Western civilization. . . . Entries are arranged alphabetically from Aaron to Zephaniah, concisely written, and adhere to a uniform pattern. Subjects are listed by name with the addition of etymological information. A synopsis of the relevant biblical story follows, utilizing the King James version of the Bible. . . . The author also includes information on each person as a character in later works, including Western literature, legend, and painting." Booklist

Includes bibliographical references

221 Old Testament (Tanakh)

The **Dead** Sea scrolls Bible; the oldest known Bible. translated for the first time into English [by] Martin Abegg, Jr., Peter Flint, and Eugene Ulrich. HarperSan Francisco 1999 xxii, 649p $39.95; pa $21.95

Grades: 9 10 11 12 **221**

ISBN 0-06-060063-2; 0-06-060064-0 pa

LC 99-26866

This book "presents all 220 of the Dead Sea biblical scrolls, arranged to be read in canonical order." Publisher's note

Includes bibliographical references

222 Historical books of Old Testament

Chittister, Joan

★ The **tent** of Abraham; stories of hope and peace for Jews, Christians, and Muslims. [by] Joan Chittister, Saadi Shakur Chishti, Arthur Waskow;

foreword by Karen Armstrong. Beacon Press 2006 218p $24.95

Grades: 9 10 11 12 **222**

1. Islam 2. Judaism 3. Prophets 4. Christianity 5. Biblical characters

ISBN 0-8070-7728-3; 978-0-8070-7728-3

LC 2006-1274

"Delicate in telling but bold in message, this book encourages every reader to take an inner pilgrimage to understand better others' viewpoints." Libr J

The **contemporary** Torah; a gender-sensitive adaptation of the JPS translation. revising editor, David E.S. Stein; consulting editors, Adele Berlin, Ellen Frankel, and Carol L. Meyers. Jewish Publication Society 2006 xlii, 412p $28

Grades: 8 9 10 11 12 Adult **222**

ISBN 0-8276-0796-2; 978-0-8276-0796-5

LC 2006-40608

A modern adaptation of the Jewish Publication Society's translation of the Torah. "In places where the ancient audience probably would not have construed gender as pertinent to the text's plain sense, the editors changed words into gender-neutral terms; where gender was probably understood to be at stake, they left the text as originally translated, or even introduced gendered language where none existed before. They made these changes regardless of whether words referred to God, angels, or human beings." Publisher's note

Kirsch, Jonathan

Moses; a life. Ballantine Bks. 1998 415p map hardcover o.p. pa $14.95

Grades: 11 12 Adult **222**

1. Prophets 2. Biblical characters

ISBN 0-345-41269-9; 0-345-41270-2 pa

LC 98-25299

The author "distills the vast secondary literature that has grown up around the sparse biblical material on Moses. He draws on the myths, legends, and midrashim of Moses to soften ragged edges left by competing images of him as warrior, magician, shepherd, God's favorite, sorcerer's apprentice, and reluctant prophet." Booklist

Includes bibliographical references

★ The **Torah:** the five books of Moses; a new translation of the Holy Scriptures according to the Masoretic text; first section. Jewish Publication Society 1963 393p $20; pa $15

Grades: 8 9 10 11 12 Adult **222**

ISBN 0-8276-0015-1; 0-8276-0680-X pa

This "translation of Genesis, Exodus, Leviticus, Numbers, and Deuteronomy was prepared . . . to present a version of the Bible that takes into account modern insights and knowledge of ancient times. . . . Of chief value to persons of the Jewish religion but of interest to Bible scholars of any religion." Booklist

225.9   Geography, history, chronology, persons of New Testament lands in New Testament times

Ehrman, Bart D.

Peter, Paul, and Mary Magdalene; the followers of Jesus in history and legend. Oxford University Press 2006 285p il hardcover o.p. pa $15.95

Grades: 11 12 Adult   225.9

1. Saints 2. Apostles 3. Writers on religion
ISBN 0-19-530013-0; 978-0-19-530013-0; 0-19-534350-6 pa; 978-0-19-534350-2 pa

LC 2005-58996

Ehrman "presents three of the best known and most important of Jesus' followers and does so in a way that is uncompromising in its scholarship yet utterly engaging for general readers." Booklist

Includes bibliographical references

230   Christianity

Christianity; edited by Matt Stefon. Britannica Educational Pub. in association with Rosen Educational Services 2012 xvii, 384 p.p ill. (chiefly col.), col. map

Grades: 10 11 12   230

1. Christianity
ISBN 9781615304936

LC 2010046428

This book discusses the history and practice of Christianity. "Although centered around the figure of Jesus of Nazareth, Christianity evolved rapidly, leading to the creation of various sects and traditions that have come to represent different peoples around the world. This . . . tome examines the philosophy, history, dogma, and socio-cultural aspects of a religion that has been found at the heart of both conflict and peace. Sidebars [include] . . . facts and stories that support the main narrative." (Publisher's note)

Includes bibliographical references (p. [369]-371) and index

Encyclopedia of Christianity; edited by John Bowden. Oxford University Press 2005 xli, 1364p il $125

Grades: 11 12 Adult   230

1. Reference books 2. Christianity -- Encyclopedias
ISBN 978-0-19-522393-4; 0-19-522393-4

LC 2005-48801

"This is probably the most comprehensive single-volume encyclopedia of Christianity." Choice

Includes bibliographical references

Guite, Malcolm

What do Christians believe? belonging and belief in modern Christianity. Walker & Co. 2008 125p map pa $9.95

Grades: 9 10 11 12   230

1. Christianity
ISBN 978-0-8027-1640-8; 0-8027-1640-7

First published 2006 in the United Kingdom

Includes bibliograpghical references

"Christianity began as a minor sect within Judaism and has now become one of the major world religions, with nearly two billion adherents spread across every nation on earth. It began with a small group of people who shared the same language, lifestyle, and background, but now embraces many languages and cultures, giving rise to an astounding variety of practices and interpretations." (Publisher's note)

Hale, Rosemary Drage

Christianity. Rosen Pub. 2010 112p il (Understanding religions) lib bdg $31.95

Grades: 7 8 9 10   230

1. Christianity
ISBN 978-1-4358-5621-9; 1-4358-5621-X

LC 2009-10295

This book about Christianity "discusses origins and historical development; aspects of the divine; sacred texts, persons, space, and time; ethical principles; death and the afterlife; and society and religion." SLJ

Includes glossary and bibliographical references

The **Quotable** saint; {compiled by} Rosemary Ellen Guiley. Facts on File 2002 368p $45; pa $16.95

Grades: 9 10 11 12   230

1. Christian life -- Quotations
ISBN 0-8160-4375-2; 0-8160-4376-0 pa

LC 2002-23540

"This book will allow readers, especially neophytes to the topic, to brush elbows with much grand and glorious wisdom." SLJ

Includes bibliographical references

236   Eschatology

Barcella, Laura

The **end**; 50 apocalyptic visions from pop culture that you should know about...before it's too late. Laura Barcella. Zest Books 2012 176 p. $12.99

Grades: 9 10 11 12   236

1. End of the world 2. Popular culture -- United States
ISBN 0982732252; 9780982732250

LC 2011942758

This book presents a "compendium of doomsday scenarios depicted in fiction, film, graphic novels, plays, songs, television series and works of art. . . . The apocalyptic scenarios include alien conquest, bioterrorism, natural catastrophe, nuclear war, superviruses and zombie plagues. . . . Each entry includes a concise synopsis of the work, brief discussion of its impact and influence, photograph or visual outtake, and quotes from or relating to it." (Kirkus Reviews)

"Doomsday buffs will especially enjoy second-guessing Barcella's choices and dissecting her synopses. An amusing, informative look at apocalyptic pop culture." Kirkus

248 Christian experience, practice, life

Lewis, C. S.

The **Screwtape** letters; with, Screwtape proposes a toast. HarperSanFrancisco 2001 209p $22.95; pa $11.95

Grades: 11 12 Adult   **248**

1. Satire 2. Christian life

ISBN 0-06-065289-6; 0-06-065293-4 pa

LC 00-49860

The Screwtape letters first published 1943 by Macmillan; this combined edition first published 1961 by Macmillan

"A popular work on Christian moral and theological problems. . . . It is in the form of a series of letters in which a devil, Screwtape, advises his nephew, Wormwood, on how to deal with his human 'patients.'" Reader's Ency. 4th edition

248.4 Christian life and practice

Campolo, Anthony

★ **Letters** to a young evangelical; the art of mentoring. [by] Tony Campolo. BasicBooks 2007 280p (Art of mentoring) $23

Grades: 9 10 11 12   **248.4**

1. Christian life

ISBN 0-465-00831-3; 978-0-465-00831-5

"In letters to two fictional young evangelicals, Campolo endeavors to challenge and encourage young Christians in much the same way Paul did in his epistles. . . . As Campolo covers such topics as the religious right, fundamentalism, dispensationalism, homosexuality, abortion and Christian-Muslim relations, he admirably steers clear of telling his readers what to think. Rather, he explains his position on the issue at hand, explains the positions of his detractors and leaves his readers to decide for themselves." Publ Wkly

252 Texts of sermons

American sermons; the pilgrims to Martin Luther King, Jr. Library of Am. 1999 939p $40

Grades: 11 12 Adult   **252**

1. Sermons

ISBN 1-88301-165-5

LC 98-34295

"To peruse this work is to become reacquainted with the literary eloquence of our distant and recent past and to observe what has happened to rhetoric itself over the centuries." N Y Times Book Rev

Includes bibliographical references

King, Martin Luther

Strength to love; foreword by Coretta Scott King. Fortress 2010 168p il pa $20

Grades: 11 12 Adult   **252**

1. Sermons

ISBN 978-0-8006-9740-2

First published 1963 by Harper & Row

A collection of sermons addressing social injustice and racism.

Includes bibliographical references

Tutu, Desmond

The **words** of Desmond Tutu; selected by Naomi Tutu. Newmarket Press 2007 111p il (Newmarket 'Words of' series) $15

Grades: 11 12 Adult   **252**

1. Sermons 2. South Africa -- Race relations

ISBN 978-1-55704-719-9

First published 1989

"In this collection of more than 100 excerpts from his most memorable speeches, sermons, and writings, Tutu discusses issues . . . ranging from faith and social responsibility to nuclear disarmament, the Third World, and women in the Church. . . . This volume also contains the full text of the archbishop's acceptance of the Nobel Peace Prize." Publisher's note

Includes bibliographical references

261.5 Christianity and secular disciplines

Grant, Edward

Science and religion, 400 B.C. to A.D. 1550; from Aristotle to Copernicus. Greenwood Press 2004 xxvi, 307p il (Greenwood guides to science and religion) $67.95

Grades: 11 12 Adult   **261.5**

1. Religion and science

ISBN 0-313-32858-7

LC 2004-17429

"With this new book, grounded in five decades of active scholarship, Edward Grant provides a synthetic account of the relationship between science and religion from Greek antiquity to the beginnings of the Scientific Revolution. Intended as an introduction for the general reader, the book successfully argues its central point–namely, that contrary to popular belief today, the medieval Church promoted scientific thought, which in turn profoundly influenced theological understanding. . . . Grant's book, along with the eight primary documents it provides, is an introduction students and teachers will welcome." Journal of the History of Science in Society

Includes bibliographical references

Olson, Richard

Science and religion, 1450-1900; from Copernicus to Darwin. [by] Richard G. Olson. Greenwood Press 2004 292p il (Greenwood guides to science and religion) $65

Grades: 11 12 Adult   **261.5**

1. Religion and science

ISBN 0-313-32694-0

LC 2004-47501

The issues discussed "should be especially helpful to those who are interested in the historical background to current science-religion issues being debated in the United States." Sci Books Films

Includes bibliographical references

270   History, geographic treatment, biography of Christianity; Church history; Christian denominations and sects

Bass, Diana Butler

A **people's** history of Christianity; the other side of the story. HarperOne 2009 353p $25.99

Grades: 10 11 12 Adult   **270**
   1. Church history
   ISBN 978-0-06-144870-6; 0-06-144870-2
                     LC 2008-51764

"What an exciting book. . . . This easily read book encourages Christian activism, inclusivity, and transformed hope that can be lived." Libr J

Includes bibliographical references

270.09   Areas, regions, places in general; biography

McBrien, Richard P.

Lives of the saints; from Mary and Francis of Assisi to John XXIII and Mother Teresa. HarperSanFrancisco 2001 xxiii, 646p il hardcover o.p. pa $19.95

Grades: 11 12 Adult   **270.09**
   1. Christian saints
   ISBN 0-06-123283-1 pa
                     LC 00-53933

"This work goes beyond the Roman Catholic Church's list of saints to include those of the Orthodox, Anglican, and Lutheran churches. Concise and well-researched biographical sketches are arranged by feast days, with access provided by indexes for saints, personal names, and subjects. Complementing the biographies are thoughtful essays on the history of saints, their place in religious history, and canonization; a series of seven tables on feast days, patron saints, iconography, and papal canonization." Libr J

Includes bibliographical references

272   Persecutions in general church history

Perez, Joseph

★ The **Spanish** Inquisition; a history. trans. by Janet Lloyd. Yale University Press 2005 248p $26; pa $17

Grades: 11 12 Adult   **272**
   1. Inquisition 2. Spain -- History
   ISBN 0-300-10790-0; 0-300-11982-8 pa
                     LC 2004-114614

The author "tells the history of the Spanish Inquisition from its medieval beginnings to its nineteenth-century ending. . . . He explores the inner workings of its councils, and shows how its officers, inquisitors, and leaders lived and worked." Univ Press Books for Public and Second Sch Libr, 2006

Includes bibliographical references

280   Denominations and sects of Christian church

Atwood, Craig D.

★ **Handbook** of denominations in the United States; [by] Craig D. Atwood, Frank S. Mead, Samuel S. Hill. 13th ed.; Abingdon Press 2010 416p il $24

Grades: 11 12 Adult   **280**
   1. Sects 2. United States -- Religion
   ISBN 978-1-4267-0048-4; 1-4267-0048-2
                     LC 2010-07092

First published 1951. Periodically revised

"History and present structure of Christian religious bodies in the United States. Reports on doctrines of different churches. Includes bibliography and index." NY Public Libr Book of How & Where to Look It Up

Includes bibliographical references

Brown, Stephen F.

Catholicism & Orthodox Christianity; by Stephen F. Brown and Khaled Anatolios. 3rd ed.; Chelsea House 2009 144p il (World religions) $40

Grades: 7 8 9 10 11 12   **280**
   1. Catholic Church 2. Orthodox Eastern Church
   ISBN 978-1-60413-106-2; 1-60413-106-3
                     LC 2008-43046

First published 2002 by Facts and File

This "traces the roots of [Catholicism and Orthodox Christianity] from the early Christian churches to today. The historical passage of the Catholic and Orthodox faiths is recounted, from the original teachings of Jesus Christ to the separation of the Eastern and Western Churches to recent attempts at reconciliation." Publisher's note

Includes glossary and bibliographical references

Protestantism; 3rd ed.; Chelsea House 2009 144p il map (World religions) $40

Grades: 7 8 9 10 11 12   **280**
   1. Protestantism
   ISBN 978-1-60413-112-3; 1-60413-112-8
                     LC 2008-29659

First published 1991 by Facts on File

This "explores the origins, customs, and history of Protestantism, from its beginnings in the Middle Ages to its role in today's world. Current issues, such as the development of new religious denominations, its stance on abortion, the ordination of gays and women, and the relationship between religion and politics, are explored within the framework of the fundamental moral tenets of the faith." Publisher's note

Includes glossary and bibliographical references

282   Roman Catholic Church

The **Catholic** Church: opposing viewpoints; Noah Berlatsky, book editor. Greenhaven Press 2010

231p il (Opposing viewpoints series) $39.70; pa $27.50

Grades: 9 10 11 12 **282**

1. Catholic Church
ISBN 978-0-7377-5104-8; 978-0-7377-5105-5 pa
LC 2010012406

This anthology discusses topics such as who should be allowed to become priests, homosexuality in the Church, reproductive and sexual issues, and reform within the Church.
Includes bibliographical references

Flinn, Frank K.
★ **Encyclopedia** of Catholicism. Facts on File 2006 xxxi, 670p (Encyclopedia of world religions) $75

Grades: 11 12 Adult **282**

1. Reference books 2. Catholic Church -- Encyclopedias
ISBN 0-8160-5455-X; 978-0-8160-5455-8
LC 2006-9645

This encyclopedia "covers the key people, movements, institutions, practices, and doctrines of Roman Catholicism from its earliest origins." Publisher's note
Includes bibliographical references

New Catholic encyclopedia; prepared by an editorial staff at the Catholic University of America. 2nd ed; Gale Group 2003 15v il maps set $1,981

Grades: 11 12 Adult **282**

1. Reference books 2. Catholic Church -- Encyclopedias
ISBN 978-0-7876-4004-0; 0-7876-4004-2
LC 2002-924

First published 1967 as an update to the Catholic encyclopedia. Kept up-to-date-by yearly supplements

This encyclopedia "covers the history of the eastern churches, the churches of the Protestant Reformation, and other ecclesial communities as well as the Christian roots based in ancient Israel and Judaism. No comprehensive resource on Catholicism can be complete without touching on other world religions as well, including Islam, Buddhism, and Hinduism. This resource provides entries not only on the doctrine, organization, and history of the church, but also on the people, institutions, and social changes that have affected the church over the years. Arranged alphabetically, the entries run in length from half a page to several pages in length. All entries provide the name of the contributor and a bibliography. Cross-references to related articles are located throughout the work. Adding to the usefulness of the set are more than 3,000 black-and-white photographs, maps, and charts that complement the scholarly articles." Am Ref Books Annu, 2003

O'Toole, James M.
The **faithful**; a history of Catholics in America. Belknap Press of Harvard University Press 2008 376p hardcover o.p. pa $17.95

Grades: 11 12 Adult **282**

1. Catholics -- United States 2. United States -- Church history 3. Catholic Church -- United States
ISBN 978-0-674-02818-0; 0-674-02818-X; 978-0-674-03488-4 pa; 0-674-03488-0 pa
LC 2007-38343

"The genial style of writing together with a plentiful amount of fascinating tidbits will keep all but the most jaded expert going." Publ Wkly
Includes bibliographical references

289.3 Latter-Day Saints (Mormons)

Book of Mormon
★ The **Book** of Mormon; another testament of Jesus Christ. [translated by Joseph Smith, Jr.] Doubleday 2004 586p $24.95

Grades: 8 9 10 11 12 Adult **289.3**

1. Mormons 2. Church of Jesus Christ of Latter-day Saints
ISBN 0-385-51316-X
LC 2004-51982

First published 1830

"Based on golden plates which Joseph Smith claimed were revealed to him, and which he unearthed from Cumorah Hill, New York, this book is roughly similar in structure to the Bible. . . . Emphasized are the doctrines of pre-existence, perfection, the afterlife, and Christ's second coming." Haydn. Thesaurus of Book Dig

Brooks, Joanna
The **Book** of Mormon girl; a memoir of an American faith. Joanna Brooks. Free Press 2012 209 p.

Grades: 9 10 11 12 Adult **289.3**

1. Mormons 2. Mormon Church 3. Church of Jesus Christ of Latter-day Saints
ISBN 9781451699685
LC 2012025931

This memoir of Mormon faith and doubt by Joanna Brooks looks at "the comfort of churchly ritual that orders the week and of theological certitude that orders the universe, the once-persecuted minority status, the sense of tribal belonging, [and] the gendered patterns of church and home. . . . Just as resonant is Brooks's journey out of religious fundamentalism and into a young adulthood full of doubts about a faith that suddenly seems prejudiced, myopic and punitive." (Christian Century)

"A thought-provoking, conversation-starting memoir for those interested in Mormonism, feminism, and religion in general." LJ

Bushman, Claudia L.
Mormons in America; [by] Claudia Lauper Bushman and Richard Lyman Bushman. Oxford Univ. Press 1998 142p il (Religion in American life) $28

Grades: 7 8 9 10 **289.3**

1. Mormons 2. Church of Jesus Christ of Latter-day Saints
ISBN 0-19-510677-6
LC 98-18605

Chronicles the history of the Church of Jesus Christ of Latter-Day Saints beginning in America in the early 1800s and continuing to the present day throughout the world

"A solid resource for libraries. Illustrated with historical material and black-and-white photos. Time line and bibliography appended." Booklist

Includes bibliographical references

289.7　Mennonite churches

Hostetler, John A.

★ **Amish** society; 4th ed; Johns Hopkins Univ. Press 1993 435p il maps hardcover o.p. pa $20

Grades: 11 12 Adult　　　　**289.7**

　1. Amish

　ISBN 0-8018-4441-X; 0-8018-4442-8

　　　　　　　　　　LC 92-19304

　First published 1963

This book discusses the sectarian origins of the Amish, immigration history, family and community life, population trends, farming practices, technological innovations, education, medicine and the effects of government regulation.

　Includes bibliographical references

292　Classical religion (Greek and Roman religion)

Beauman, Sally

The **genealogy** of Greek mythology; an illustrated family tree of Greek myth from the first gods to the founders of Rome. [by] Vanessa James. Gotham Books 2003 107p il map $25

Grades: 9 10 11 12　　　　**292**

　1. Reference books　2. Classical mythology

　ISBN 1-592-40013-2

　　　　　　　　　　LC 2004-272120

This "book/chart begins with the earliest surviving account of the creation of the universe from Chaos and quickly covers the children of Gaia, the rise of the Titans, and the triumph of the Olympians. The origins of each of the Olympians, their symbols, and their characters are briefly described. . . . Lists of the gods' children are followed by an index of 3000-plus individuals. When the book is turned over, it opens to a large map of the Aegean Sea, showing the places associated with mythic heroes. This begins the genealogical chart of the mortals who participated in the Trojan War, starting with their immortal ancestors and concluding with their descendants. A map of the Mediterranean Sea shows the routes of the Argonauts, Aeneas, and Odysseus. Lists of Helen's suitors, the 12 labors of Hercules, and more conclude the volume. . . . The appeal here is in the beauty of the more than 125 color photographs of Greek and Roman artwork, the concise biographies, and the elegant ordering of a complex topic." SLJ

Daly, Kathleen N.

Greek and Roman mythology, A to Z; [by] Kathleen N. Daly; revised by Marian Rengel. 3rd ed.; Chelsea House Publishers 2009 162p il (Mythology A to Z) lib bdg $45

Grades: 8 9 10 11 12　　　　**292**

　1. Classical mythology

　ISBN 978-1-60413-412-4; 1-60413-412-7

　　　　　　　　　　LC 2009-8243

　First published 1992 by Facts on File

Alphabetically listed entries identify and explain the characters, events, important places, and other aspects of Greek and Roman mythology

"The format is accessible, making the book useful for school assignments, as well as enjoyable for general reading. Each entry provides a clear definition, and retells the stories associated with the character or place. The broad coverage, ample cross-references, and extensive index enable readers to recognize the many connections and interrelationships between characters and myths." SLJ [review of 1992 edition]

　Includes bibliographical references

Graves, Robert

The **Greek** myths; Combined ed; Penguin Books 1992 782p pa $19.95

Grades: 11 12 Adult　　　　**292**

　1. Classical mythology

　ISBN 0-14-017199-1

　First published 1955

A collection of the author's interpretations of Greek myths based on anthropological and archaeological findings

Hamilton, Edith

★ **Mythology**; illustrated by Steele Savage. Little, Brown 1942 497p il $27.95; pa $13.95

Grades: 8 9 10 11 12 Adult　　　　**292**

　1. Trojan War　2. Norse mythology　3. Gods and goddesses　4. Classical mythology　5. Perseus (Greek mythology)　6. Theseus (Greek mythology)　7. Odysseus (Greek mythology)　8. Argonauts (Greek mythology)　9. Aeneas (Legendary character)　10. Hercules (Legendary character)

　ISBN 0-316-34114-2; 0-316-34151-7 pa

A retelling of Greek, Roman and Norse myths

Mitchell, Adrian, 1941-

Shapeshifters; tales from Ovid's Metamorphoses. retold by Adrian Mitchell; illustrated by Alan Lee. Frances Lincoln Children's 2010 143p il

Grades: 7 8 9 10　　　　**292**

　1. Classical mythology

　ISBN 1-84507-536-6; 978-1-84507-536-1

This is a "marvelous re-creation of myth from Ovid. . . . The language is simple and contemporary, moving from rhyme to free verse to prose and back again. . . . All of these stories explore mystery: the origins of flowers, mountains, lakes. Pygmalion, Persephone, Midas and Arachne all appear here . . . [Lee] makes men and women, gods and beasts, sea, sky and leaf shimmer." Kirkus

★ The **Oxford** dictionary of classical myth and religion; edited by Simon Price and Emily Kearns. Oxford University Press 2003 599p maps $39.95; pa $17.95

Grades: 11 12 Adult　　　　**292**

　1. Reference books　2. Classical mythology --

Dictionaries
ISBN 0-19-280288-7; 0-19-280289-5 pa
LC 2004-298013

"Instead of separating mythology and Judeo-Christian religion into separate references, this work covers all religious life in the ancient Greco-Roman world. The result is a generally accessible and academically current compendium of information on gods and holy beings, religious practices, festivals, sacred sites, myths, authors, and texts of the period. The reader will find not only Athena and Zeus but also Jesus Christ and St. Augustine, Mani and Zoroaster." Libr J

Roman, Luke

Encyclopedia of Greek and Roman mythology; [by] Luke Roman and Monica Roman. Facts On File, Inc. 2009 548p il (Facts on File library of religion and mythology) $75

Grades: 9 10 11 12 Adult   **292**
1. Reference books 2. Classical mythology -- Encyclopedias
ISBN 978-0-8160-7242-2; 0-8160-7242-6
LC 2009-1235

"Although this volume covers some 300 major figures of classical mythology, the focus is on where and how they appeared in the works of Greek and Roman writers. Thus classical writers whose works featured mythological themes are also included. The most notable aspect of the encyclopedia is the extensive treatment of the relevant texts themselves. More than 50 are featured. . . . This is a beneficial resource for anyone wanting to explore the original classical sources of Greek and Roman mythology." Choice
Includes bibliographical references

293 Germanic religion

Daly, Kathleen N.

Norse mythology A to Z; [by] Kathleen N. Daly; revised by Marian Rengel. 3rd ed.; Chelsea House 2009 128p il map (Mythology A to Z) lib bdg $45

Grades: 8 9 10 11 12   **293**
1. Reference books 2. Norse mythology -- Dictionaries
ISBN 978-1-60413-411-7; 1-60413-411-9
LC 2009-13338

First published 1991
Alphabetically listed entries identify and explain the characters, events, and important places of Norse mythology
Includes bibliographical references

294 Religions of Indic origin

Mann, Gurinder Singh

★ **Buddhists,** Hindus, and Sikhs in America; [by] Gurinder Singh Mann, Paul David Numrich & Raymond B. Williams. Oxford University Press 2001 158p il (Religion in American life) hardcover o.p. pa $12.95

Grades: 7 8 9 10   **294**
1. Sikhism 2. Buddhism 3. Hinduism 4. Asian

Americans -- Religion
ISBN 0-19-512442-1; 0-19-533311-X pa
LC 2001-45151

Presents the basic tenets of these three Asian religions and discusses the religious history and experience of their practitioners after immigration to the United States

"Solid information, a large selection of historical and contemporary photographs, interesting readings from primary sources, and accounts from school-age Buddhists, Hindus, and Sikhs combine to make this is a valuable resource." Booklist
Includes bibliographical references

294.3 Buddhism

Eckel, Malcolm David

Buddhism. Rosen Pub. 2010 112p il (Understanding religions) lib bdg $31.95

Grades: 7 8 9 10   **294.3**
1. Buddhism
ISBN 978-1-4358-5619-6; 1-4358-5619-8
LC 2009-10083

Subjects covered in this book include "buddhas and bodhisattvas, Zen meditation, Tantric scriptures, pilgrimage, temples, and festivals and rites." Publisher's note
Includes glossary and bibliographical references

Irons, Edward A.

★ **Encyclopedia** of Buddhism; J. Gordon Melton, series editor. Facts on File 2007 xxxv, 634p il map (Encyclopedia of world religions) $75

Grades: 9 10 11 12 Adult   **294.3**
1. Reference books 2. Buddhism -- Encyclopedias
ISBN 978-0-8160-5459-6
LC 2007-4503

This encyclopedia provides "access to the terms, concepts, personalities, historical events, institutions, and movements that helped shape the history of Buddhism and the way it is practiced today. Although the primary focus of the encyclopedia is clearly on Buddhism in all its forms, it also provides introductions to Daoism, Shinto, Confucianism, and other religious practices in East and Southeast Asia." Publisher's note
Includes bibliographical references

Morris, Tony

★ **What** do Buddhists believe? meaning and mindfulness in Buddhist philosophy. Walker & Co. 2008 96p map pa $9.95

Grades: 9 10 11 12   **294.3**
1. Buddhism
ISBN 978-0-8027-1655-2; 0-8027-1655-5

First published 2006 in the United Kingdom
An introduction to Buddhism discussing its most important beliefs and core practices, its historical role and its growing pervasiveness throughout the modern world.
Includes bibliographical references

Wangu, Madhu Bazaz

Buddhism; 4th ed.; Chelsea House 2009 144p il (World religions) $40

Grades: 7 8 9 10 11 12   **294.3**

1. Buddhism

ISBN 978-1-60413-105-5; 1-60413-105-5

LC 2008-51265

First published 1993 by Facts on File

This "tells the story of Buddhism's origins and its development into three major schools of thought—and presents the particular beliefs and practices of those schools of Buddhism. . . . [This] title explores the concept of the 'socially engaged Buddhist,' the growth and practice of Buddhism in America, and the recent revival of Buddhism in Asia." Publisher's note

Includes glossary and bibliographical references

Winston, Diana

Wide awake: a Buddhist guide for teens. Perigee Bk. 2003 290p pa $13.95

Grades: 7 8 9 10 11 12   **294.3**

1. Buddhism

ISBN 0-399-52897-0

LC 2002-192666

"Switching between anecdotes of her own journey in Buddhism and advice on how teens can apply the Buddha's teachings to their lives, Winston offers a personal and thoughtful introduction to Buddhist thought and practice." Booklist

294.5 Hinduism

Ganeri, Anita

The **Ramayana** and Hinduism. Smart Apple Media 2003 30p il (Sacred texts) $27.10

Grades: 5 6 7 8 9   **294.5**

1. Hinduism

ISBN 1-58340-242-X

LC 2003-42352

Explains the history and practices of the religion of Hinduism, especially as revealed through its sacred book, the Ramayana

Jones, Constance

★ **Encyclopedia** of Hinduism; [by] Constance A. Jones and James D. Ryan; J. Gordon Melton, series editor. Facts on File 2006 xxxvii, 552p il (Facts on File library of religion and mythology) $75

Grades: 9 10 11 12 Adult   **294.5**

1. Reference books 2. Hinduism -- Encyclopedias

ISBN 0-8160-5458-4; 978-0-8160-5458-9

LC 2006-44419

This encyclopedia "focuses on the most significant groups within this religion, noteworthy teachers and their contributions, the religions and cultural movements that enriched its history, and the diaspora of Hindu thought and practice around the world. Two major religious traditions that sprang from Hindu influence, Jainism and Sikhism, also have many entries." Publisher's note

Includes bibliographical references

Mahabharata/Bhagavadgita

★ **Bhagavad** Gita; a new translation. [translated by] Stephen Mitchell. Harmony Bks. 2000 223p hardcover o.p. pa $13.95

Grades: 11 12 Adult   **294.5**

ISBN 0-609-60550-X; 0-609-81034-0 pa

LC 00-28286

"An eighteen-part discussion between the god Krishna, an avatar of Vishnu appearing as a charioteer, and Arjuna, a warrior about to enter battle, on the nature and meaning of life. Sometimes called the New Testament of Hinduism, it is an interpolation in the great Hindu epic the Mahabharata." Reader's Ency. 4th edition

Narayanan, Vasudha

Hinduism. Rosen Pub. 2010 112p il (Understanding religions) lib bdg $31.95

Grades: 7 8 9 10   **294.5**

1. Hinduism

ISBN 978-1-4358-5620-2; 1-4358-5620-I

LC 2009-11026

This book about Hinduism "discusses origins and historical development; aspects of the divine; sacred texts, persons, space, and time; ethical principles; death and the afterlife; and society and religion." SLJ

Includes glossary and bibliographical references

Sivananda Yoga Vedanta Center (London, England)

★ **Yoga** mind & body. DK Pub. 2008 168p il pa $15

Grades: 11 12 Adult   **294.5**

1. Yoga

ISBN 978-0-7566-3674-6

LC 2008-489063

First published 1996

"This guide stresses the five points of exercise, breathing, meditation, diet, and relaxation for improved health and happiness. In addition to basic yoga poses, Yoga Mind & Body provides meditation tools, stress relief exercises, and recipes for healthful nutrition." Publisher's note

Wangu, Madhu Bazaz

Hinduism; 4th ed.; Chelsea House 2009 144p il (World religions) $40

Grades: 7 8 9 10 11 12   **294.5**

1. Hinduism

ISBN 978-1-60413-108-6; 1-60413-108-X

LC 2008-43047

First published 1991 by Facts on File

This describes the history of Hinduism, its customs, beliefs, and rites of passage, the Hindu nationalist movement in India, Hinduism and the interfaith movement, and Hinduism and the environmental movement.

Includes glossary and bibliographical references

294.6 Sikhism

Singh, Nikky-Guninder Kaur

Sikhism; 3rd ed.; Chelsea House 2009 144p il (World religions) $40

Grades: 7 8 9 10 11 12 **294.6**

1. Sikhism

ISBN 978-1-60413-114-7; 1-60413-114-4

LC 2008-29662

First published 1993 by Facts on File

This "describes the basic tenets of Sikhism, examines the recent move toward greater political independence within the Indian nation, and covers issues of cultural adaptation, persecution, and subsequent education now taking place in the West." Publisher's note

Includes glossary and bibliographical references

295 Zoroastrianism (Mazdaism, Parseeism)

Hartz, Paula

Zoroastrianism; by Paula R. Hartz. 3rd ed.; Chelsea House 2009 144p il (World religions) $40

Grades: 7 8 9 10 11 12 **295**

1. Zoroastrianism

ISBN 978-1-60413-116-1; 1-60413-116-0

LC 2008-35811

First published 1999 by Facts on File

This "analyzes how [Zoroastrianism] has a crucial place in religious history and continues to maintain a devoted following today." Publisher's note

Includes glossary and bibliographical references

296 Judaism

Ehrlich, Carl S.

★ **Judaism**. Rosen Pub. 2010 112p il (Understanding religions) lib bdg $31.95

Grades: 7 8 9 10 **296**

1. Judaism

ISBN 978-1-4358-5622-6; 1-4358-5622-8

LC 2009-10055

This "book provides students with an overview of the great religious tradition of Judaism. Readers learn about the covenant with God, the Bible, the Mishnah, and the Talmud. They also read about sects, messianic movements, mysticism, and the Kabbalah. Rabbinical systems of law and custom are covered as are various principles and practices, holy days, and contemporary movements in Judaism." Publisher's note

Includes glossary and bibliographical references

Judaism; history, belief, and practice. edited by Matt Stefon. Britannica Educational Pub. in association with Rosen Educational Services 2012 xix, 366 p.p (The Britannica guide to religion)

Grades: 9 10 11 12 **296**

1. Judaism -- History 2. Judaism -- Doctrines 3.

Judaism -- Customs and practices 4. Judaism

ISBN 9781615304875

LC 2010044168

This "volume in the "Britannica Guide to Religion" series provides an . . . . overview. . . . Beginning with biblical Judaism (from the twentieth to the fourth centuries BCE), the history discusses Hellenistic Judaism under the Greeks and Romans, then Rabbinic Judaism in medieval Europe, up to the modern period, which covers a wide range, including . . . discussion of the Orthodox, Reform, and Conservative movements, Jewish-Christian relations, Zionism, mysticism, and American Judaism. . . . [C]hapters cover Kabbalah, Tzaddiq, Kosher, Haskala, and much more about basic beliefs and practices, the religious year and holidays, medieval and modern leaders, and relations with other religions." (Booklist)

Includes bibliographical references (p. [358]-360) and index

Karesh, Sara E.

★ **Encyclopedia** of Judaism; [by] Sara E. Karesh and Mitchell M. Hurvitz. Facts on File 2006 xxxvi, 602p il (Facts on File library of religion and mythology) $75

Grades: 11 12 Adult **296**

1. Reference books 2. Judaism -- Encyclopedias

ISBN 0-8160-5457-6

LC 2004-26537

This encyclopedia "covers individuals, places, events, theologies, ideologies, organizations, movements, and denominations that span Jewish history. . . . This is a very good one-volume resource that is especially accessible to young adults and non-Jews." Libr J

Includes bibliographical references

Kessler, Edward

★ **What** do Jews believe? the customs and culture of modern Judaism. Walker & Co. 2007 117p il pa $9.95

Grades: 9 10 11 12 **296**

1. Judaism

ISBN 0-8027-1639-3; 978-0-8027-1639-2

First published 2006 in the United Kingdom

The author "explores the variety of ways in which Jews live their lives: religious and secular, Ashkenazi and Sephardi, Jews in Israel and Jews who live in the diaspora. Kessler asks what Judaism means and what it means to be a Jew, and explores the roots of a religion that goes back some four thousand years and was a major influence on the creation and development of both Christianity and Islam." Publisher's note

Morrison, M. A.

Judaism; by Martha A. Morrison and Stephen F. Brown. 4th ed.; Chelsea House 2009 144p il (World religions) $40

Grades: 7 8 9 10 11 12 **296**

1. Judaism

ISBN 978-1-60413-110-9; 1-60413-110-1

LC 2008-29657

First published 1991 by Facts on File under the authorship of Fay Carol Gates

This "presents the basic beliefs of the Jewish religious heritage and highlights the different manners in which these traditions can be upheld. Both Orthodox Judaism and the religious practices and movements within Reformed Judaism, including Reform Judaism, Conservative Judaism, and Reconstructionist Judaism, are explored." Publisher's note

Includes glossary and bibliographical references

The **New** encyclopedia of Judaism; editor-in-chief, Geoffrey Wigoder; coeditors, Fred Skolnik & Shmuel Himelstein. New York Univ. Press 2002 856p il $79.95
Grades: 11 12 Adult   **296**
1. Reference books 2. Judaism -- Dictionaries
ISBN 0-8147-9388-6
LC 2002-16614

First published 1989 with title: The Encyclopedia of Judaism

This reference "seeks to present a balanced picture, offering current thinking among scholars in Reform, Conservative, and Orthodox movements and a roster of contributors hailing from Israel, England, and the United States. While the scholarship is solid, the material is readily accessible to a popular audience, and the work is magnificently illustrated." Libr J

Includes bibliographical references

The **Oxford** dictionary of the Jewish religion; editor in chief, Adele Berlin. 2nd ed. Oxford University Press 2011 xxiv, 934 p.p (hardcover) $195
Grades: 8 9 10 11 12 Adult   **296**
1. Judaism -- Dictionaries 2. Judaism -- Encyclopedias
ISBN 0199730040; 9780199730049; 9780199759279
LC 2010035774

This book, by Maxine Grossman, edited by Adele Berlin, presents an updated, second edition of its original 1997 publication. It "focuses on recent and changing rituals in the Jewish community. . . . Nearly 200 internationally renowned scholars have created a new edition that incorporates updated bibliographies, biographies of 20th-century individuals who have shaped the recent thought and history of Judaism, and an index with alternate spellings of Hebrew terms." (Publisher's note)

Includes bibliographical references and index.

The **student's** encyclopedia of Judaism; editor-in-chief Geoffrey Wigoder; coeditors Fred Skolnik and Shmuel Himelstein; educational editor Barbara Sutnick. New York University Press 2004 390p il map $39.95
Grades: 9 10 11 12   **296**
1. Reference books 2. Judaism -- Encyclopedias
ISBN 0-8147-4275-0
LC 2003-65125

Revised and condensed edition of The new encyclopedia of Judaism, published 2002

Identifies and defines people, places, and terms important to the Jewish faith

"The approximately 1000 entries in this handsome and comprehensive volume describe virtually all aspects of Jewish life and culture, including significant and lesser-known people. The articles are clearly written and abundantly cross-

referenced. . . . There have been a number of recent reference works about Jews and Judaism for this audience, but this encyclopedia stands out. It is a must for any collection supporting the study of religion." SLJ

Includes bibliographical references

297   Islam, Babism, Bahai Faith

Armstrong, Karen
★ **Islam**; a short history. Modern Lib. 2000 xxxiv, 222p maps $19.95; pa $11.95
Grades: 11 12 Adult   **297**
1. Islam
ISBN 0-679-64040-1; 0-8129-6618-X pa
LC 00-25285

This history of the Islamic faith focuses on the religion's attitude toward politics

The author "does an admirable job of presenting Islamic history from an objective, unbiased point of view." Libr J

Includes bibliographical references

★ **Muhammad**; a prophet for our time. Atlas Books/HarperCollins Publishers 2006 249p map (Eminent lives) $21.95; pa $14.95
Grades: 11 12 Adult   **297**
1. Islam 2. Prophets 3. Islamic leaders 4. Writers on religion
ISBN 0-06-059897-2; 978-0-06-059897-6; 0-06-115577-2 pa; 978-0-06-115577-2 pa
LC 2006-45864

First published 1991 in the United Kingdom with subtitle: A Western attempt to understand Islam; Original American edition published 1992 with subtitle: A biography of the prophet

This is a biography of the founder of Islam.

"Readers of these pages cannot escape the genius of Muhammad and his aim for peace and compassion among nations and among Muslims themselves. . . . Recommended for all libraries." Libr J

Includes bibliographical references

Aslan, Reza, 1972-
No god but God; the origins and evolution of Islam. Delacorte Press 2011 166p $16.99; lib bdg $19.99
Grades: 7 8 9 10   **297**
1. Islam -- History
ISBN 0-385-73975-3; 0-385-90805-9 lib bdg; 978-0-385-73975-7; 978-0-385-90805-4 lib bdg
LC 2010020408

Adaptation of: No god but God: the origins, evolution, and future of Islam, published 2006 by Random House for adults

"Packing in a formidable amount of research, legend, and critical analysis, Aslan condenses his adult book of the same name to create a concise introduction to Islam. By breaking up chapters with clear subheadings, maintaining a conversational tone, and incorporating numerous anecdotes that both inform and entertain, Aslan makes 15 centuries of religious history digestible without oversimplifying complex material. . . . This welcome addition to Islamic studies provides a valuable context for reflection about the origins of issues facing Muslims and their neighbors today." Publ Wkly

Campo, Juan Eduardo

★ **Encyclopedia** of Islam; [by] Juan E. Campo. Facts On File 2008 750p il map (Encyclopedia of world religions) $85

Grades: 9 10 11 12 Adult   297

1. Reference books 2. Islam -- Encyclopedias

ISBN 978-0-8160-5454-1; 0-8160-5454-1

LC 2008-5621

"In about 600 A-to-Z entries, this encyclopedic guide explores the terms, concepts, personalities, historical events, and institutions that helped shape the history of this religion and the way it is practiced today." Publisher's note

Includes bibliographical references

Encyclopedia of Islam in the United States; edited by Jocelyne Cesari. Greenwood Press 2007 2v il set $199.95

Grades: 10 11 12 Adult   297

1. Reference books 2. Islam -- Encyclopedias 3. Muslims -- United States -- Encyclopedias

ISBN 978-0-313-33625-6; 0-313-33625-3

LC 2007-16142

This set "takes a refreshing look at Islam and Muslims from a uniquely Muslim American perspective. Hence, it is a valuable reference to both Muslims and non-Muslims alike." Am Ref Books Annu, 2008

Includes bibliographical references

Farah, Caesar E.

★ **Islam**: beliefs and observances; 7th ed; Barron's 2003 500p map pa $14.95

Grades: 9 10 11 12   297

1. Islam

ISBN 0-7641-2226-6

LC 2002-25354

First published 1968

This book traces the historical development of Islam starting with its founder, the prophet Muhammad in the early seventh century A.D. Its rapid spread as a religious, cultural and political force is detailed along with an examination of the Koran and other Islamic beliefs and moral obligations

Includes bibliographical references

Gordon, Matthew

Islam; by Matthew S. Gordon. 4th ed. Chelsea House 2009 144 p. col. ill., map (World religions) (library) $40.00

Grades: 7 8 9 10 11 12   297

1. Islam

ISBN 978-1-60413-109-3; 1-60413-109-8

LC 2008035810

First published 1991 by Facts on File

This describes the founding of Islam and its spread, The Koran, Hadith, and Islamic law, branches of Islam and their basic beliefs, Muslim customs and rituals, the pattern of Islamic life, and the place of Islam in the modern world.

Includes bibliographical references (p. 138-139)

and index.

★ **Understanding** Islam; origins, beliefs, practices, holy texts, sacred places. [by] Matthew S. Gordon. Sterling Pub. Co. 2010 112p pa $9.95

Grades: 8 9 10 11 12 Adult   297

1. Islam

ISBN 978-1-90748-616-6

LC 2010-2376

First published 2001 by Facts on File

This "exploration of Islam's history, beliefs, and practices . . . [addresses] issues such as political Islam, Islam and Israel, and Islamic fundamentalism." Publisher's note

Includes bibliographical references

Hafiz, Dilara

★ The **American** Muslim teenager's handbook; by Dilara Hafiz, Imran Hafiz, and Yasmine Hafiz. [new ed.]; Atheneum Books for Young Readers 2009 168p il pa $11.99

Grades: 7 8 9 10 11 12   297

1. Islam 2. Conduct of life 3. Muslims -- United States 4. Teenagers -- Religious life

ISBN 978-1-4169-8578-5; 1-4169-8578-6

A revised edition of the title first published 2007 by Acacia Pub.

"Casual, colloquial, joking, contemporary, and passionate, this interactive handbook by two Arizona teens and their mom talks about their faith, about what it is like to be both proud Americans and proud Muslims, and about misunderstandings and stereotypes. . . . There are also step-by-step guides on how to pray, how to read the Qur'an, and how to fast at Ramadan. Muslim and non-Muslim teens alike will be caught by the candor, the humor, and the call for interfaith dialogue and tolerance." Booklist

Includes bibliographical references

Hasan, Asma Gull

★ **American** Muslims; the new generation. 2nd edition, with study guide; Continuum 2002 204p pa $19.95

Grades: 9 10 11 12   297

1. Islam 2. Muslims -- United States

ISBN 0-8264-1416-8

LC 2003-270056

First published 2000

This book provides basic information about Islam in America: its major tenets, its various sects and its ethnic groups, including African Americans. In an effort to help Americans overcome anti-Muslim stereotypes the author focuses on Muslim American family values, religious freedom and adaptation of their faith to American culture

"From her perspective as a youthful American Muslim feminist, Hasan provides a fluent evaluation of the Islamic community in the US." Choice {review of 2000 edition}

Includes bibliographical references

Illustrated dictionary of the Muslim world; [editor, Felicity Crowe and others] Marshall Cavendish Reference 2010 192p il (Muslim world) $85.64
Grades: 7 8 9 10   297
1. Reference books 2. Islam -- Dictionaries 3. Islamic civilization -- Dictionaries
ISBN 978-0-7614-7929-1; 0-7614-7929-5
                                             LC 2010008613
Contains hundreds of short entries on Islamic concepts, religious practices, historical events and personalities, geographical places, and fact files of nations with large Muslim populations.

"Attractive trim on the pages, colorful fonts, quality illustrations, and framed (often illustrated) sideboxes create a pleasing layout. Excellent for assignments." SLJ

Includes glossary and bibliographical references

★ **Islam:** opposing viewpoints; David M. Haugen, Susan Musser, and Kacy Lovelace, book editors. Greenhaven Press 2009 215p il (Opposing viewpoints series) lib bdg $38.50; pa $26.75
Grades: 7 8 9 10   297
1. Islam 2. Islamic fundamentalism 3. Terrorism -- Religious aspects
ISBN 978-0-7377-4526-9 lib bdg; 978-0-7377-4527-6 pa
                                             LC 2009-14564
Contributors to this anthology discuss such topics as the conflict between Islamic and western cultures, Islam's relationship to violence, and the treatment of women in Islamic societies.

Includes bibliographical references

Islamic beliefs and practices; edited by Matt Stefon. Britannica Educational Pub., in association with Rosen Educational Services 2010 189 p.
Grades: 9 10 11 12   297
1. Muslims 2. Islam -- Customs and practices 3. Islam -- Doctrines
ISBN 9781615300174
                                             LC 2009038290
This book "focuses on the centrality of Muhammad's life and scripture on Muslim societies. The table of contents advances from the prophet's biography to the Qur'an, the Five Pillars of Islam, and the influence of faith on law, Sufism, and the Sunni and Shi'ite sects. . . . Essentials of socioeconomic history include validation of slaves, polygamy, government, creedal unity, and dynasties. Highlighted passages on the Mahdi and the Ottoman Empire orient readers to critical eras in the rise of Islam as a religious philosophy on a par with Judaism, Hinduism, Confucianism, Zoroastrianism, and Christianity." (VOYA)

Includes bibliographical references (p. 181-182) and index

Islamic beliefs, practices, and cultures. Marshall Cavendish Reference 2010 352p il (Muslim world) lib bdg $114.21
Grades: 7 8 9 10   297
1. Islamic civilization 2. Islam -- Customs and practices
ISBN 978-0-7614-7926-0; 0-7614-7926-0
                                             LC 2010008611

"Attractive trim on the pages, colorful fonts, quality illustrations, and framed (often illustrated) sideboxes create a pleasing layout. Excellent for assignments." SLJ

★ **Islamic** fundamentalism; David M. Haugen, book editor. Greenhaven Press 2008 129p (At issue. Religion) lib bdg $29.95; pa $21.20
Grades: 7 8 9 10   297
1. Islamic fundamentalism 2. Islam -- Relations
ISBN 978-0-7377-3689-2 lib bdg; 978-0-7377-3690-8 pa
                                             LC 2007-29302
Previous edition published 2003 under the editorship of Auriana Ojeda

"After a brief introduction that discusses the various terms used to describe Islamic fundamentalists (such as 'Islamists'), 12 articles from different points of view are presented. . . . Each article includes some fact and some opinion, leaving readers to make up their own minds about the perspectives expressed." SLJ

Includes bibliographical references

Living Islam out loud; American Muslim women speak. edited by Saleemah Abdul-Ghafur. Beacon Press 2005 209p pa $15
Grades: 9 10 11 12   297
1. Muslim women 2. Women in Islam 3. Muslims -- United States
ISBN 0-8070-8383-6 pa
                                             LC 2004-28161
"Themes about negotiating culture, romantic relationships, and faith and spiritual journeys often intersect in the 18 short essays that comprise the book. The majority of writers come from families that immigrated to the United States from the Middle East and Asia, but the book also includes two essays by African-American Muslim women." Sojourners

Modern Muslim societies. Marshall Cavendish Reference 2010 416p il (Muslim world) lib bdg $114.21
Grades: 7 8 9 10   297
1. Islam -- Customs and practices
ISBN 978-0-7614-7927-7; 0-7614-7927-9
                                             LC 2010008612
"Attractive trim on the pages, colorful fonts, quality illustrations, and framed (often illustrated) sideboxes create a pleasing layout. Excellent for assignments." SLJ

★ The **Oxford** history of Islam; {edited by} John Esposito. Oxford Univ. Press 1999 749p il map $49.95
Grades: 11 12 Adult   297
1. Islam
ISBN 0-19-510799-3
                                             LC 99-13219
"Contributors treat, among other things, Muslim history, law, and society; art and architecture; and regional differences. Chapters on the 'Globalization of Islam' and 'Contemporary Islam' are particularly relevant to current events. . . . An ideal one-volume source." Libr J

Includes bibliographical references

Sardar, Ziauddin

What do Muslims believe? the roots and realities of modern Islam. Walker & Co. 2007 140p map pa $9.95

Grades: 9 10 11 12   **297**
1. Islam
ISBN 978-0-8027-1642-2; 0-8027-1642-3

The author discusses "what makes a Muslim; where Muslims come from and who they are today; what, exactly, they believe and how they reflect those beliefs; where Islam is headed; and how you can apply Islam in your life." Publisher's note

Includes bibliographical references

297.09   History, geographic treatment, biography

Allman, Toney

The **rise** of Islam; Toney Allman. Reference-Point Press, Inc. 2015 96 p. (Understanding world history series) (hardback) $28.95

Grades: 7 8 9 10 11 12   **297.09**
1. Islam -- History 2. Islamic civilization 3. Islam -- Origin
ISBN 1601527446; 9781601527448

LC 2014006453

This book, by Toney Allman, part of the "Understanding World History" series, describes how "Islam, as a faith and as a political power, rose to world dominance in an astoundingly brief timespan--little more than one hundred years. From the fascinating events of Muhammad's life to the founding of a vast empire, the rise of Islam is the story of a people, a vibrant culture, and the growth of a civilization." (Publisher's note)

"This latest addition to the Understanding World History series gives a thorough, well-researched background of Islam, from the birth and youth of Muhammad and his call from God to the religion's golden age (750–1258 CE). The introductory time line of important events during the rise of Islam sets the stage for events discussed in the text. . . . Detailed chapter source notes and an extensive list of additional books and websites give young researchers alternate access points to complete their projects on Muhammad or Islam—hot topics that show no signs of cooling down." Booklist

Includes bibliographical references and index

297.1   Islam

★ The **meaning** of the glorious Koran; an explanatory translation by Marmaduke Pickthall; with an introduction by William Montgomery Watt. A.A. Knopf 1992 xxiv, 693p il $22

Grades: 7 8 9 10 11 12 Adult   **297.1**
1. Qur'an
ISBN 0-679-41736-2; 978-0-679-41736-1

LC 92-52928

This translation first published 1930

"The sacred scripture of Islam, regarded by Muslims as the Word of God, and except in sura I.—which is a prayer to

God—and some few passages in which Muhammad or the angels speak in the first person, the speaker throughout is God." Ency Britannica

The **Qur'an**; English translation and parallel Arabic text. translated, with an introduction and notes, by M.A.S. Abdel Haleem. Oxford University Press 2010 xxxix, 624 p.p maps (hardcover) $45

Grades: 7 8 9 10 11 12 Adult   **297.1**
1. Qur'an
ISBN 019957071X; 9780199570713

LC 2010281328

This book, by M. A. S. Abdel Haleem, offers an English translation of the Qur'an with Arab text presented in parallel. "This translation is written in contemporary language . . .', set page-for-page against the most widespread traditional calligraphic Arabic text. . . . Furthermore, Haleem includes notes that explain geographical, historical, and personal allusions as well as an index in which Qur'anic material is arranged into topics for easy reference." (Publisher's note)

"Because the Koran stresses its Arabic nature, devout Muslims believe that only an Arabic version is the actual Koran and insist that its translation cannot be more than an approximate interpretation. . . Yet anyone wishing to understand Islamic civilization and global affairs may find this Koran very useful. . . . Highly recommended." LJ

Includes bibliographical references and index

297.9   Babism and Bahai Faith

Hartz, Paula

Baha'i Faith; 3rd ed.; Chelsea House 2009 144p il (World religions) $40

Grades: 7 8 9 10 11 12   **297.9**
1. Bahai Faith
ISBN 978-1-60413-104-8; 1-60413-104-7

LC 2008043045

First published 2002 by Facts on File

This "explores all aspects of the Baha'i faith, from the original teachings of its founder, Baha'u'llah, to the modern-day communities that exist in 236 countries and territories throughout the world." Publisher's note

Includes glossary and bibliographical references

299   Religions not provided for elsewhere

The **Gnostic** Bible; edited by Willis Barnstone and Marvin Meyer. Rev. ed.; Shambhala 2009 881p pa $29.95

Grades: 11 12 Adult   **299**
1. Gnosticism
ISBN 978-1-59030-631-4; 1-59030-631-7

LC 2008-36431

First published 2003

"The book provides Gnostic texts from their Jewish origins, into early Christianities, on into the medieval world. Though it concentrates on the early Jewish-Christian matrix of early Gnosticism, the collection . . . manifests the breadth and depth of Gnostic variations in neo-Platonist, Manichean, Mandean, Islam, and Cathar movements." Choice

Includes bibliographical references

Green, Miranda J.

The **world** of the Druids. Thames & Hudson 1997 192p il maps hardcover o.p. pa $24.95

Grades: 9 10 11 12   **299**

1. Celts 2. Druids and Druidism

ISBN 0-500-05083-X; 0-500-28571-3 pa

                              LC 96-61291

Published in the United Kingdom with title: Exploring the world of the Druids

"The wide-ranging illustrations from ancient objects to modern ceremonies and modern Druids that are linked with an enthralling text make this a remarkable book." Hist Today

Includes bibliographical references

299.5   Religions of East and Southeast Asian origin

Birrell, Anne

Chinese myths. University of Tex. Press 2000 80p (Legendary past) pa $14.95

Grades: 9 10 11 12   **299.5**

1. Oriental mythology

ISBN 0-292-70879-3

                              LC 00-39296

This book explores the tradition of Chinese myths in the context of world mythology. Topics include: origins and creation myths; myths of the flood; the divine cosmos; gender in myth; metamorphoses; mythic heroes and heroines; and fabled plants and animals

Brennan, J. H.

The **magical** I ching. Llewellyn Publs. 2000 247p pa $14.95

Grades: 9 10 11 12   **299.5**

1. Divination 2. I ching

ISBN 1-567-18087-6

                              LC 00-24132

This work presents the history of the I Ching and explains the magical spiritual technique behind this ancient oracle. It also shows how to develop the symbols used in I Ching by using several different methods and analyzes each of the possible sixty-four hexagrams that form the basis of the oracle

Includes bibliographical references

★ **Confucianism**; Adriane Ruggiero . . . [et al.] Greenhaven Press 2006 239p il map (Religions and religious movements) $36.20

Grades: 9 10 11 12   **299.5**

1. Confucianism

ISBN 0-7377-2567-2; 978-0-7377-2567-4

                         LC 2004-60581

Presents an overview of Confucianism, including its origins in China, an analysis of the major works and ideas of its founder, its influence on Chinese history and society, its spread to other countries, and its status in modern Asia.

"This volume is an excellent comprehensive collection of historical and cultural essays explaining the Confucian beliefs and impact. . . . It is an essential purchase for public and school libraries." Voice Youth Advocates

Includes bibliographical references

Hartz, Paula

Daoism; by Paula R. Hartz. 3rd ed.; Chelsea House 2009 144p il (World religions) $40

Grades: 7 8 9 10 11 12   **299.5**

1. Taoism

ISBN 978-1-60413-115-4; 1-60413-115-2

                          LC 2008-35809

First published 1993 by Facts on File with title: Taoism

This "traces the history of Daoism and explains its basic thoughts, traditions, and practices. It also details the Daoist movement worldwide and how the limitations of consumerism are leading a younger generation to search for their own spiritual harmony." Publisher's note

Includes glossary and bibliographical references

Shinto; by Paula R. Hartz. 3rd ed.; Chelsea House 2009 144p il (World religions) $40

Grades: 7 8 9 10 11 12   **299.5**

1. Shinto

ISBN 978-1-60413-113-0; 1-60413-113-6

                          LC 2008-29661

First published 1997 by Facts on File

This "examines the basic tenets of Shinto, its evolution in response to other religious influences, and how the original Shinto religion—rooted in an agrarian society—survives in contemporary Japan." Publisher's note

Includes glossary and bibliographical references

Hoobler, Dorothy

★ **Confucianism**; by Dorothy and Thomas Hoobler. 3rd ed.; Chelsea House 2009 144p il (World religions) $40

Grades: 7 8 9 10 11 12   **299.5**

1. Confucianism

ISBN 978-1-60413-107-9; 1-60413-107-1

                          LC 2008-29656

First published 1993 with authors' names in reverse order

Examines Confucianism in conjunction with its resurgence in China and the rest of the world. Presents its history, basic beliefs, and evolution in response to historical events in China.

Includes glossary and bibliographical references

Roberts, Jeremy

Chinese mythology A to Z; 2nd ed.; Chelsea House 2009 172p il (Mythology A to Z) lib bdg $45

Grades: 8 9 10 11 12   **299.5**

1. Chinese mythology 2. China -- Religion

ISBN 978-1-60413-436-0; 1-60413-436-4

                          LC 2009-10176

First published 2004

"Coverage includes: Buddhist deities and legendary characters; animal stories, such as the fox legends; important locations, such as shrines and sacred places; [and] allegorical figures, such as the Jade Emperor, the Rain Master, and the Lord of the Granary." Publisher's note

Includes bibliographical references

Japanese mythology A to Z; 2nd ed.; Chelsea House 2009 138p il (Mythology A to Z) lib bdg $45

Grades: 8 9 10 11 12   **299.5**
   1. Japanese mythology 2. Japan -- Religion
   ISBN 978-1-60413-435-3

                        LC 2009-8242

First published 2004

This book about Japanese mythology covers "the early Japanese deities who created the world and the later deities who protect it; Kami, the spirits of all aspects of the living world; animals and mythological creatures; demons and bogeymen; shrines and other sacred places; stories from Kojiki and other historical records of ancient myths; [and] historical emperors, empresses, heroes, and heroines whose deeds live on in legend." Publisher's note

Includes bibliographical references

The **Wisdom** of the Tao; editor, Julian F. Pas. Oneworld Publs. 2000 223p il $15.95

Grades: 9 10 11 12   **299.5**
   1. Taoism
   ISBN 1-85168-232-5
Includes bibliographical references

299.6 Religions originating among Black Africans and people of Black African descent

Galembo, Phyllis
   Vodou; visions and voices of Haiti. Ten Speed Press 2005 xxx, 113p il pa $24.95

Grades: 9 10 11 12   **299.6**
   1. Voodooism 2. Haiti
   ISBN 1-58008-676-4; 978-1-58008-676-9
First published 1998

The book delves into the symbols and spiritual tradition of Voodoo or Vodou. Both the divine and human faces of real Haitian Vodou are presented together with its current practice involving priestesses, zombies, snakes and swamps.

Includes bibliographical references

Lugira, Aloysius Muzzanganda
   African traditional religion; by Aloysius M. Lugira. 3rd ed.; Chelsea House 2009 144p il map (World religions) $40

Grades: 7 8 9 10 11 12   **299.6**
   1. Africa -- Religion
   ISBN 978-1-60413-103-1; 1-60413-103-9

                    LC 2008-51188

First published 1999 by Facts on File with title: African religion

"The African continent is home to more than 6,000 different ethnic and cultural groups, each with its own religious traditions. Yet these many traditions have much in common. . . . [This book] offers a . . . perspective on the beliefs that are a permanent part of Africa's history and future." Publisher's note

Includes glossary and bibliographical references

Lynch, Patricia Ann
   African mythology, A to Z; revised by Jeremy Roberts. 2nd ed.; Chelsea House 2010 xxiv, 149p il map (Mythology A to Z) lib bdg $45

Grades: 8 9 10 11 12   **299.6**
   1. African mythology 2. Africa -- Religion
   ISBN 978-1-60413-415-5; 1-60413-415-1

                  LC 2009-33612

First published 2004

This is a "reference to the deities, places, events, animals, beliefs, and other subjects that appear in the myths of various African peoples." Publisher's note

Includes bibliographical references

299.7 Religions of North American native origin

Gill, Sam D.
   Native American religions; an introduction. 2nd ed.; Wadsworth/Thomson Learning 2005 142p map pa $82.95

Grades: 11 12 Adult   **299.7**
   1. Native Americans -- Religion
   ISBN 0-534-62600-9

                  LC 2004-111567

First published 1982

This "introduction to the religions of Native Americans provides an overview of the latest research and thought in this area. In writing the book, Gill aims to introduce an academically and humanistically useful way of trying to appreciate and understand the complexity and diversity of Native American religions, as well as establish them as a significant field within religious studies. In addition, aspects of European-American history are examined in a search for sources of widespread misunderstandings about the character of Native American religions." Publisher's note

Includes bibliographical references

Hartz, Paula
   Native American religions; [by] Paula R. Hartz. 3rd ed.; Chelsea House 2009 144p il (World religions) $40

Grades: 7 8 9 10 11 12   **299.7**
   1. Native Americans -- Religion
   ISBN 978-1-60413-111-6; 1-60413-111-X

                  LC 2008051197

First published 1997 by Facts on File

This "presents the history of the Native American religions, starting from their roots as tribal religions, and then details the detrimental effects of European colonization, the annihilation of the Native Americans that threatened the religions, and their sudden restoration in the 20th century." Publisher's note

Includes glossary and bibliographical references

300 SOCIAL SCIENCES, SOCIOLOGY & ANTHROPOLOGY

302 Specific topics in sociology and anthropology

Gladwell, Malcolm, 1963-

The **tipping** point; how little things can make a big difference. Malcolm Gladwell. Little, Brown 2000 viii, 279 p $27.99

Grades: 10 11 12 Adult   **302**

1. Causation 2. Social psychology 3. Contagion (Social psychology)

ISBN 0316316962; 9780316316965

LC 99047576

It was the author's intent to demonstrate "that ideas, products, messages and behaviors 'spread just like viruses do.'. . . [Malcolm Gladwell] follows the growth of 'word-of-mouth epidemics' triggered with the help of three pivotal types. These are Connectors, sociable personalities who bring people together; Mavens, who like to pass along knowledge; and Salesmen, adept at persuading the unenlightened. (Paul Revere, for example, was a Maven and a Connector). . . . [The book] offers a smorgasbord of . . . snippets summarizing research on topics such as conversational patterns, infants' crib talk, judging other people's character, cheating habits in schoolchildren, memory sharing among families or couples, and the dehumanizing effects of prisons." (Publishers Weekly)

Includes bibliographical references and index.

Marcovitz, Hal

Teens and volunteerism; Hal Marcovitz. 2nd edition Mason Crest Publishers 2014 112 p. color illustrations (hc) $24.95

Grades: 9 10 11   **302**

1. Volunteer work 2. Teenagers -- United States 3. Teenage volunteers in social service -- United States

ISBN 1422229602; 9781422229606

LC 2013007185

In this book, by Hal Marcovitz, a "recent report showed that each year an estimated 13 million teenagers donate more than 2.4 billion hours of their time to charitable causes, and the Gallup Youth Survey has found that roughly one-third of all teens participate in volunteer work. This volume examines the opportunities young people have for volunteering, and explores the issue of school-mandated community service." (Publisher's note)

Includes bibliographical references and index

302.2 Communication

Biedermann, Hans

★ **Dictionary** of symbolism; cultural icons and the meanings behind them. translated by James Hulbert. Meridan Book 1994 465p il pa $25

Grades: 11 12 Adult   **302.2**

1. Reference books 2. Signs and symbols

ISBN 0-452-01118-3

LC 93-30616

Original German edition, 1989

This dictionary "incorporates symbols that originated in Asia, Africa, Europe and the 'New World'. There are almost 600 entries from mythology, fairy tale, psychology, religion, and sociology, plus historical and legendary figures. With 2000 black-and-white illustrations, the book is highly attractive. The symbols are accompanied by thorough interpretations based on various sources." SLJ

Includes bibliographical references

302.23 Media (Means of communication)

Rowell, Rebecca

Social media; like it or leave it. Rebecca Rowell. Compass Point Books, a Capstone imprint 2015 30 p. (Perspectives flip books: issues) (hardcover: alk. paper) $33.32

Grades: 6 7 8 9 10   **302.23**

1. Internet -- Social aspects 2. Social media

ISBN 0756549949; 9780756549947; 9780756550240; 9780756550479

LC 2014026596

This book, by Rebecca Rowell, is an entry of the "Perspectives flip books: issues" series exploring social media. "Perspectives Flip Books are like two books in one: Start from one end and learn why people are logging off. Then flip it over and discover why others believe responsible social media use can be beneficial. Critical thinking questions help you analyze both perspectives and form your own opinions about the issue." (Publisher's note)

"This cleverly designed Perspectives Flip Book shows the pros and cons of social media . . . students will likely find this book a helpful guide to understanding and safely using this exciting technology." Booklist

Includes bibliographical references

★ **Television:** opposing viewpoints; Margaret Haerens, book editor. Greenhaven Press 2011 213p il (Opposing viewpoints series) $39.70; pa $27.50

Grades: 9 10 11 12   **302.23**

1. Mass media 2. Television broadcasting

ISBN 978-0-7377-5243-4; 978-0-7377-5244-1 pa

LC 2010039232

This anthology of essays discusses reality television, television advertising, television's role in conveying societal values, and government regulations on television broadcasting.

Includes bibliographical references

302.3 Social interaction within groups

Dear bully; seventy authors tell their stories. edited by Carrie Jones and Megan Kelley Hall. Harper-Teen 2011 369p $17.99; pa $9.99

Grades: 7 8 9 10 11 12   **302.3**

1. Bullies

ISBN 978-0-06-206098-3; 0-06-206098-8; 978-0-06-206097-6 pa; 0-06-206097-X pa

LC 2011010166

"In brief, true stories about bullying victims, perpetrators, and bystanders, 70 children's authors look back at what was often the hell of growing up, especially in junior high. . . . This timely collection is an excellent resource, especially for group discussion." Booklist

DiPiazza, Francesca Davis

Friend me! six hundred years of social networking in America. by Francesca Davis DiPiazza. Twenty-First Century Books 2012 112 p.

Grades: 6 7 8 9   **302.3**

1. Social networking -- History 2. Social groups -- United States -- History 3. Community life -- United States -- History 4. United States -- Social life and customs -- History

ISBN 0761358692; 9780761358695

LC 2011021268

This book's title "makes [it] appear to be about the recent phenomena of electronic social networks. However, the subtitle is a clue that the scope includes so much more. The whole of the American history of socializing is covered, beginning with the Iroquois and their method of weaving beads into wampum belts. Early religious groups, colonial coffee-houses, broadsides, secret gatherings of slaves, circuit riders, telegraphs, mail orders, and groups such as the YMCA and NAACP are profiled as examples of social networking. Today's online communities (Facebook, Twitter, blogs, e-mail, etc.) are touched upon with the supposition that face-to-face socializing is still important." (Booklist)

Includes bibliographical references and index

Ellis, Deborah

★ **We** want you to know; kids talk about bullying. Coteau Books 2010 120p il $19.95; pa $15.95

Grades: 5 6 7 8 9 10   **302.3**

1. Bullies

ISBN 978-1-55050-417-0; 1-55050-417-7; 978-1-55050-463-7 pa; 1-55050-463-0

"As part of her work with an anti-bullying campaign in her local Canadian community, Ellis interviewed young people between the ages of 9 and 19 about their experiences. In honest, straightforward prose, she shares their stories, many as targets and some as perpetrators or bystanders. . . . Each story is written from the first-person point of view, some with real names and photos, providing an intimacy and immediacy that are critical with these kinds of issues. Readers will find at least one or two stories they can relate to, and educators should be able to use many of the narratives to jumpstart conversation." SLJ

Includes bibliographical references

Schulman, Nev

In real life; love, lies & identity in the digital age. Nev Schulman. Grand Central Publishing 2014 256 p. illustrations (paperback) $16

Grades: 9 10 11 12 Adult   **302.3**

1. Online social networks 2. Interpersonal relations 3. Internet -- Social aspects

ISBN 1455584290; 9781455584291

LC 2014018244

This book, by Nev Schulman, is a "definitive guide about how to connect with people authentically in today's increasingly digital world. . . . Peppered throughout with Nev's personal stories, this book delves deeply into the complexities of online identity. Nev shows us how our digital lives are affecting our real lives, and provides essential advice about how we should all be living and loving in the era of social media." (Publisher's note)

"Schulman, host of MTV's Catfish: The TV Show and star of the documentary that spawned it, knows a thing or two about "catfish"—people who create one or more false identities online and enter into deceptive relationships. Here he provides an examination and guide to Internet communication that also serves as a Catfish companion piece and even a self-help memoir. . . . This exciting title will be popular among Catfish fans and contains real advice for teens and twentysomethings who will likely relate to the issues he discusses." LJ

Includes bibliographical references

302.34 Social interaction in primary groups

Bazelon, Emily, 1971-

★ **Sticks** and stones; defeating the culture of bullying and rediscovering the power of character and empathy. by Emily Bazelon. Random House 2013 viii, 386 p.p ill. (hardcover) $27

Grades: Adult Professional   **302.34**

1. Bullies 2. Adolescence 3. Social media 4. Bullying 5. Bullying in schools 6. Bullying -- Prevention 7. Bullying in schools -- Prevention

ISBN 0812992806; 9780679644002; 9780812992809

LC 2012022773

This book, by Emily Bazelon, discusses teen culture in the U.S., focusing on bullying. "Being a teenager has never been easy, but in recent years, with the rise of the Internet and social media, it has become exponentially more challenging. . . . Bazelon defines what bullying is and, just as important, what it is not. She explores when intervention is essential and when kids should be given the freedom to fend for themselves. She also dispels persistent myths." (Publisher's note)

"While less prescriptive than other books on the topic, very useful FAQs are included, as are resource lists for readers. Masterfully written, Bazelon's book will increase understanding, awareness, and action." Pub Wkly

Includes bibliographical references and index

Strauss, Susan L.

★ **Sexual** harassment and bullying; a guide to keeping kids safe and holding schools accountable.

Susan L. Strauss. Rowman & Littlefield Publishers 2012 290 p. (cloth: alk. paper) $34.95

Grades: Adult Professional   **302.34**
1. Bullies 2. Social media 3. Sexual harassment 4. Bullying 5. Bullying -- Prevention 6. Sexual harassment in education 7. Sexual harassment -- Prevention
ISBN 1442201622; 9781442201620

LC 2011031731

In this book, "[Susan L.] Strauss draws on her experiences as consultant, former high-school teacher, and parent of a child who was sexually harassed to advise parents, teachers, and other adults on how to protect children" from bullying and harassment. She gives definitions of bullying and harassment, "offers a particular focus on the kind of harassment of gay, bisexual, and transgendered students," and examines "how social media . . . have ramped up bullying and harassment." (Booklist)

Includes bibliographical references and index.

Vicious; true stories by teens about bullying. edited by Hope Vanderberg. Free Spirit Pub. Inc. 2012 167 p. (Real teen voices) (paperback) $11.99

Grades: 6 7 8   **302.34**
1. Bullies 2. Teenagers' writings 3. Bullying -- Case studies 4. Self-esteem in adolescence -- Case studies 5. Aggressiveness in adolescence -- Case studies 6. Interpersonal conflict in adolescence -- Case studies
ISBN 1575424134; 9781575424132

LC 2012015908

This book is a collection of "autobiographical essays" from teenagers involved with the New York-based organization Youth Communication in which they detail "their struggles with bullies, anger about bad home situations and unfair treatment, and pressure to conform or be successful." (School Library Journal)

Includes bibliographical references and index

Whitson, Signe
8 keys to end bullying; strategies for parents & schools. Signe Whitson; foreword by Babette Rothschild. W.W. Norton & Co Inc. 2014 240 p. (8 keys to mental health series) (pbk.) $19.95

Grades: Adult Professional   **302.34**
1. Bullies 2. Classroom management 3. Bullying -- Prevention 4. Aggressiveness in children 5. Bullying in schools -- Prevention
ISBN 0393709280; 9780393709285

LC 2014001241

This book by Signe Whitson discusses how "social media bullying . . . has given the widespread problem a new dimension. While no magic cure-all exists, adults can learn . . . techniques that can make a huge difference in the lives of kids. In 8 core strategies, this book lays them out, from establishing meaningful connections with kids to creating a positive school climate, addressing cyberbullying, building social emotional competence, . . . and much more." (Publisher's note)

"Complete with example scenarios, exercises for readers, and sample responses, the author does a convincing job of helping adults feel empowered to address this important issue." LJ

Includes bibliographical references and index

303.3   Coordination and control

Best, Joel
More damned lies and statistics; how numbers confuse public issues. University of California Press 2004 200p il $19.95

Grades: 9 10 11 12   **303.3**
1. Statistics
ISBN 0-520-23830-3

LC 2003-28076

Companion volume to Damned lies and statistics

"The book is packed with helpful tips for understanding statistics, and it even manages to make a usually dull topic entertaining." Booklist

Includes bibliographical references

Huxley, Aldous
★ **Brave** new world revisited. Harper & Row 1958 147p hardcover o.p. pa $11.95

Grades: 11 12 Adult   **303.3**
1. Culture 2. Propaganda 3. Brainwashing 4. Totalitarianism
ISBN 0-06-089852-6 pa

In response to his 1932 novel Brave new world "Huxley reconsiders his prophecies and fears that some of these may be coming true much sooner than he thought." Oxford Companion to Engl Lit. 5th edition

303.4   Social change

Benjamin, Marina
Rocket dreams; how the space age shaped our vision of a world beyond. Free Press 2003 242p hardcover o.p. pa $14

Grades: 11 12 Adult   **303.4**
1. Astronautics
ISBN 0-7432-3343-3; 0-7432-5534-8 pa

LC 2002-45590

This is "an elegantly written memoir, as the author tells about her youthful fascination with the space program and her travels to places like Arecibo and Roswell, as well as her virtual travels among various computer groups over the last 20 years. Space buffs will appreciate many aspects of her story." Publ Wkly

Includes bibliographical references

Diamond, Jared M.
Guns, germs, and steel; the fates of human societies. [by] Jared Diamond. Norton 2005 518p il map $24.95

Grades: 11 12 Adult   **303.4**
1. Ethnology 2. Food supply 3. Social change 4. Technology and civilization 5. Environmental influence on humans
ISBN 0-393-06131-0; 978-0-393-06131-4

LC 2005-284261

First published 1997

"This book poses a simple but profound question about the distribution of wealth and power in the modern world: 'Why weren't Native Americans, Africans, and Aboriginal

Australians the ones who decimated, subjugated, or exterminated Europeans and Asians?'. . . . To explore the discrepancies in technological and cultural development he looks not at peoples but at places, and at the natural resources available to different indigenous populations since 11,000 B.C. The scope and the explanatory power of this book are astounding." New Yorker [review of 1997 edition]

Includes bibliographical references

★ **Dissent** in America; voices that shaped a nation. [edited by] Ralph F. Young. Pearson Education 2008 792p pa $64.60

Grades: 11 12 Adult   **303.4**

1. United States -- Social conditions -- Sources 2. United States -- Politics and government -- Sources
ISBN 9780205625895

"Divided chronologically, the anthology collects essays, speeches, organizational statements, songs, posters, interviews, broadsides and texts in other media. . . . For readers with something on their minds, 400 years of precedent may be just what they need to stimulate some questions of their own." Publ Wkly

★ The **Radical** reader; a documentary history of the American radical tradition. edited by Timothy Patrick McCarthy and John McMillian; foreword by Eric Foner. New Press 2003 688p $65; lib bdg $21.95

Grades: 11 12 Adult   **303.4**

1. Radicalism
ISBN 1-56584-827-6; 1-56584-682-6 lib bdg
LC 2002-41051

"By bringing many hard-to-find documents under one cover, this anthology will excite readers in discussing why radicals from all walks of life have made progressive ideals meaningful to Americans. Recommended for college, high school, and public libraries." Libr J

Includes bibliographical references

303.48   Causes of change

Drexler, K. Eric

Radical abundance; how a revolution in nanotechnology will change civilization. K. Eric Drexler. PublicAffairs 2013 368 p. illustrations (hardcover: alkaline paper) $28.99

Grades: 11 12 Adult   **303.48**

1. Engineering 2. Nanotechnology 3. Social prediction 4. Technological forecasting 5. Technology and civilization 6. Nanotechnology -- Social aspects
ISBN 1610391136; 9781610391139
LC 2012049031

This book looks at nanotechnology. Twenty-five years ago, K. Eric Drexler "defined nanotechnology as a manufacturing technology using supermicro-scale devices to build products with atomic precision. Unfortunately, the media overhyped nanotechnology's immediate prospects, and interest flagged and funding dried up. Regardless, advances in micromanufacture kept coming," and Drexler discusses them. (Kirkus Reviews)

"An interesting read, not weighed down with overly scientific jargon and not taken over by fantasies of nanobots or grey goo." Choice

Includes bibliographical references and index

Henderson, Harry, 1951-

The **digital** age; by Harry Henderson. ReferencePoint Press 2013 96 p. (Understanding world history series) (hardcover) $27.95

Grades: 9 10 11 12   **303.48**

1. Information society 2. Information technology 3. Information technology -- History
ISBN 160152482X; 9781601524829
LC 2012026168

This book, by Harry Henderson, is part of the publisher's "Understanding World History" series. "The computer and its ability to create online networks has profoundly transformed science, industry, business, and society itself. . . . Our rapidly changing technological landscape raises issues of access, privacy, and security--while challenging our understanding of what it means to be human." (Publisher's note)

Includes bibliographical references and index

303.49   Social forecasts

Kaku, Michio

Physics of the future; how science will shape human destiny and our daily lives by the year 2100. Doubleday 2011 389p il $28.95; ebook $12.99

Grades: 11 12 Adult   **303.49**

1. Science 2. Forecasting 3. Science -- Social aspects 4. Science -- History -- 21st century
ISBN 978-0-385-53080-4; 978-0-385-53081-1 ebook
LC 2010-26569

"The book's lively, user-friendly style should appeal equally to fans of science fiction and popular science." Booklist

Includes bibliographical references

The **way** we will be 50 years from today; 60 of the world's greatest minds share their visions of the next half century. [edited by] Mike Wallace. Thomas Nelson 2008 241p $24.99

Grades: 11 12 Adult   **303.49**

1. Forecasting
ISBN 978-0-8499-0370-0; 0-8499-0370-X
LC 2007-45281

"This collection of essays exploring life in the future is the realization of some of our worst nightmares (water shortages, overpopulation, and nuclear war) but also some hopeful developments: longer and healthier lives, clean energy from the sun and wind. . . . A fascinating look at what may be ahead for human life on the planet." Booklist

Includes bibliographical references

303.6   Conflict and conflict resolution

Gottfried, Ted

The **fight** for peace; a history of antiwar movements in America. 21st Century Bks. 2006 136p il (People's history) $26.60

Grades: 7 8 9 10   **303.6**
1. War 2. Peace 3. Pacifism
ISBN 0-7613-2932-3

"Gottfried starts out by explaining that a group in Connecticut rallied together in 2003 to peacefully protest the war against Iraq. . . . Then the author discusses the antiwar movement during the Civil War and proceeds through history, beginning with the ancient Greek play Lysistrata. . . . The pictures, political cartoons, and quotes are an excellent addition. . . . This is a book that can be read for general interest as well as for reports." SLJ
Includes bibliographical references

Mara, Wil

Civil unrest in the 1960s; riots and their aftermath. Marshall Cavendish Benchmark 2009 127p il (Perspectives on) lib bdg $27.95

Grades: 8 9 10 11 12   **303.6**
1. Riots 2. United States -- Race relations 3. United States -- Social conditions 4. United States -- Politics and government -- 1961-1974
ISBN 978-0-7614-4025-3; 0-7614-4025-9

LC 2008-24673

This book describes "the turbulent decade that bore witness to the Civil Right[s] Movement, the divisive Vietnam War, and various other movements concerning women, gays, and the environment. . . . The potency of [this title] lies in the excellent arrangement of numerous well-chosen sidebars and photos, and fluent, concise prose." SLJ
Includes bibliographical references

★ That **mad** game; growing up in a warzone: an anthology of essays from around the globe. edited by J.L. Powers. Cinco Puntos Press 2012 230 p. (paperback: alk. paper) $16.95

Grades: 10 11 12   **303.6**
1. Refugees 2. Veterans 3. Children and war
ISBN 1935955225; 9781935955221

LC 2012004315

This book, edited by J. L. Powers, asks "What's it like to . . . be a victim of violence or exiled from your homeland, culture, family, and even your own memories? . . . From the cartel-terrorized streets of Juarez . . . to Afghanistan under the Taliban, from Nazi-occupied Holland to the middle-class American home of a Vietnam vet, this collection of personal and narrative essays explores . . . [the] experiences of children and teenagers who came of age during a time of war." (Publisher's note)

Violence in the media; Jodie Lynn Boduch, book editor. Greenhaven Press 2008 183p (History of issues) lib bdg $37.40

Grades: 9 10 11 12   **303.6**
1. Violence 2. Mass media
ISBN 978-0-7377-2875-0; 0-7377-2875-2

LC 2007-939022

An anthology of essays discussing media violence issues throughout history, from ancient Rome to the present.
Includes bibliographical references

Women on war; an international anthology of women's writings from antiquity to the present. edited and with an introduction by Daniela Gioseffi. 2nd ed; Feminist Press 2003 375p $55; pa $19.95

Grades: 11 12 Adult   **303.6**
1. War 2. Peace
ISBN 1-55861-408-7; 1-55861-409-5 pa

LC 2003-42407

First published 1988 by Simon & Schuster
This is a "powerful and important collection." Booklist
Includes bibliographical references

304.2   Human ecology

The **Atlas** of US and Canadian environmental history; edited by Char Miller. Routledge 2003 248p il map $150

Grades: 11 12 Adult   **304.2**
1. Atlases 2. Human ecology 3. Reference books 4. Environmental policy
ISBN 0-415-93781-7

LC 2003-46799

"This resource offers essays written by history scholars on ecological issues for young people. Organized chronologically from 1492 to present times, chapters include two-page treatments of the era's hot topics . . . These controversial topics are explained in a simple, nonbiased way that will appeal to young adults. The statistics offered are frequently enlightening." Voice Youth Advocates
Includes bibliographical references

Carson, Mary Kay

Inside Biosphere 2; earth science under glass. by Mary Kay Carson; with photographs by Tom Uhlman. Houghton Mifflin Harcourt 2015 80 p. color illustrations $18.99

Grades: 7 8 9 10   **304.2**
1. Biosphere 2. Earth sciences 3. Science 4. Human ecology 5. Ecology -- Research 6. Biosphere 2 (Project) 7. Closed ecological systems (Space environment)
ISBN 0544416643; 9780544416642

LC 2014047046

This book by Mary Kay Carson looks at how "in the Arizona desert, scientists conduct studies and experiments aimed to help us better understand our environment and what sort of things are happening to it due to climate change. The location is Biosphere 2, an immense structure that contains a replica ocean, savannah, and rainforest, among other Earth biomes." (Publisher's note)

"Well-chosen, clearly captioned photographs support the text, while flashback boxes inform readers of what came before. For middle and high school readers, an encouraging example of earth scientists working to understand and deal with climate change in new and amazing ways." Kirkus

Inside Biosphere Two

Weisman, Alan

The **world** without us. Thomas Dunne Books/St. Martin's Press 2007 324p il pa $18.00; hc $24.95
Grades: 11 12 Adult 304.2
1. Human influence on nature 2. Material culture 3. Human-plant relationships 4. Human-animal relationships 5. Nature -- Effect of human beings on
ISBN 978-0-312-34729-1; 0312427905; 0-312-34729-4

LC 2007-11565

Weisman speculates on what would become of the Earth if the human population disappeared. Contains index.

"Teasing out the consequences of a simple thought experiment—what would happen if the human species were suddenly extinguished—Weisman has written a sort of pop-science ghost story, in which the whole earth is the haunted house. Among the highlights: with pumps not working, the New York City subways would fill with water within days... . Texas's unattended petrochemical complexes might ignite, scattering hydrogen cyanide to the winds—a 'mini chemical nuclear winter.' After thousands of years, the Chunnel, rubber tires, and more than a billion tons of plastic might remain, but eventually a polymer-eating microbe could evolve, and, with the spectacular return of fish and bird populations, the earth might revert to Eden." New Yorker

"Given the burgeoning human population and the phenomenal reach of our technologies, humankind has literally become a force of nature. We are inadvertently changing the climate; altering, polluting, and eradicating ecosystems . . . what would happen if humankind suddenly vanished? Journalist Weisman . . . traveled the world to consult with experts and visit key sites, and his findings are arresting to say the least. . . . Weisman is a thoroughly engaging and clarion writer fueled by curiosity and determined to cast light rather than spread despair. His superbly well researched and skillfully crafted stop-you-in-your-tracks report stresses the underappreciated fact that humankind's actions create a ripple effect across the web of life." Booklist

Includes bibliographical references

304.6 Population

Peake, Riley

Mapping Census 2010; the geography of American change. Riley Peake. Esri Press 2012 1 atlas (xiv, 90 p.)p (pbk.) $18.95
Grades: Adult 304.6
1. Minorities 2. United States -- Census 3. United States -- Population 4. United States -- Census, 23rd, 2010 -- Maps 5. United States -- Population -- Statistics -- Maps 6. Minorities -- United States -- Population -- Statistics -- Maps
ISBN 1589483197; 9781589483194

LC 2012288678

Author Riley Peake's book "is an atlas of the American people--who we are, and where we are. Using the latest census data and geographic information system (GIS) technology, this atlas examines how our unique population is moving and changing. These large, full-color maps illustrate population density, age, and racial and ethnic composition with clarity." (Publisher's note)

Includes bibliographical references

Perl, Lila

Genocide; stand by or intervene? Marshall Cavendish Benchmark 2010 127p il (Controversy!) lib bdg $25.95
Grades: 8 9 10 11 12 304.6
1. Genocide
ISBN 978-0-7614-4900-3; 0-7614-4900-0

This book is "examines the U.N.'s efforts to define and make the crime of genocide punishable under international law. . . . [It] is suggested for libraries that need updated books covering 21st-century events." SLJ

304.8 Movement of people

This **land** is our land; the history of American immigration. by Linda Barrett Osborne. Abrams Books for Young Readers 2016 124 p. color illustrations (alk. paper) $24.95
Grades: 5 6 7 8 9 10 304.8
1. Immigrants -- United States 2. United States -- Emigration and immigration 3. Immigrants -- United States -- History 4. United States -- Emigration and immigration -- History
ISBN 9781419716607

LC 2015017877

This book, by Linda Barrett Osborne, "explores the history of American immigration from the early colonization of the continent to the contemporary discussions involving undocumented aliens. The so-called American melting pot has a history of exclusion, discrimination, and strife that has resulted in anti-immigration laws, segregation, and, in the case of the Japanese during World War II, unjustified internment." (School Library Journal)

" Well researched, clearly written, and informative, the discussion is particularly useful in offering the broad look at immigration over time, showing how similar arguments and legal restrictions have been used against different groups in different periods. Throughout the book, the perspectives of individual immigrants emerge in paragraphs detailing their personal stories and including quotes. Handsomely designed, the book offers many captioned period illustrations, especially photos. A strong introduction to American immigration." Booklist

Includes bibliographical references and index

305   Groups of people

Azam Zanganeh, Lila

My sister, guard your veil; my brother guard, your eyes; uncensored Iranian voices. Lila Azam Zanganeh, editor. Beacon Press 2006 132p il pa $12

Grades: 11 12 Adult   **305**

1. Women -- Iran 2. Iran -- Social conditions

ISBN 0-8070-0463-4; 978-0-8070-0463-0

LC 2005-27496

This "volume features frank interviews with an array of reputable Iranians intellectuals, artists, and writers, some of whom live in exile. Their compelling personal experiences, views, and opinions answer some persistent questions about the lives of ordinary people in Iran and challenge established myths and stereotypes....This volume opens a window on the irrepressible talents, aspirations, and energy of Iranians both at home and abroad, despite their adverse conditions" MultiCult Rev

Gates, Henry Louis

The **African**-American century; how Black Americans have shaped our country. {by} Henry Louis Gates, Jr. and Cornel West. Free Press 2000 414p il hardcover o.p. pa $16

Grades: 11 12 Adult   **305**

1. African Americans -- Biography 2. African Americans -- Intellectual life

ISBN 0-684-86414-2; 0-684-86415-0 pa

LC 00-63596

"Gates and West have listed and written biographies of their choices of the 100 most important and influential [African Americans] of the . . . twentieth century. In their opinion the subjects that they have selected have made significant impacts and contributions to American society. . . . The entries are arranged by decade and by the person's period of prominence in society, 1900-1909 through 1990-1999. Profiles include Madame C.J. Walker, Langston Hughes, Carter G. Woodson, Paul Robeson, Thurgood Marshall, and Colin Powell." MultiCult Rev

Includes bibliographical references

Reef, Catherine

Working in America. Facts On File 2007 xxviii, 484p il map (American experience) $80

Grades: 11 12 Adult   **305**

1. Labor -- United States

ISBN 978-0-8160-6239-3; 0-8160-6239-0

LC 2006-31191

First published 2000

"Each chapter begins with a . . . narrative that chronicles the experience of workers in the United States—from factory workers, cowboys, seamstresses, and newsboys to truck drivers, migrant farm workers, computer programmers, and genetic engineers. Chronologies of important events follow, along with eyewitness testimonies on the experience of working in a wide range of professions and trades—from Thomas Jefferson, Malcolm X, Samuel Gompers, Charlotte Perkins Gilman, Jesse Jackson, Cesar Chavez, and Jane Addams, as well as a wide range of American workers." Publisher's note

Includes bibliographical references

305.23   Young people

Bradley, Michael J.

The **heart** & soul of the next generation; extraordinary stories of ordinary teens. Harbor Press 2006 232p pa $14.95

Grades: 9 10 11 12   **305.23**

1. Adolescent psychology

ISBN 978-0-936197-53-1; 0-936197-53-6

LC 2005-52704

The author "draws on his 30 years of experience as a teen psychologist to profile 20 adolescents who dealt courageously with pain and suffering. In lively, empathetic prose, he relates cases involving difficult issues indeed, such as the serious illness of a parent, suicide, bullying and abortion. . . . This informed and compassionate look at the courage of teenagers highlights the ability of young people to triumph over adversity." Publ Wkly

Burton, Bonnie

Girls against girls; why we are mean to each other and how we can change. Zest Books 2009 128p il pa $12.95

Grades: 7 8 9 10   **305.23**

1. Bullies 2. Girls -- Psychology

ISBN 978-0-9790173-6-0; 0-9790173-6-X

This guide for teenage girls explains why girls can sometimes be mean to each other, what to do if you are a victim of bullying, and the importance of treating other girls with respect.

This offers "excellent coping techniques. . . . Burton never talks down to her readers, nor does she pull her punches. Readers will respond to the author's clear respect for the painful nature of the problem." Booklist

The **Courage** to be yourself; true stories by teens about cliques, conflicts, and overcoming peer pressure. edited by Al Desetta with Educators for Social Responsibility. Free Spirit Pub. 2005 145p pa $13.95

Grades: 7 8 9 10 11 12   **305.23**

1. Teenagers 2. Conduct of life

ISBN 1-57542-185-2

LC 2005-5173

"There is certainly some value in hearing teens of many ethnicities and orientations speaking plainly about being fat, or being from India in a school full of blond, blue-eyed folk, or being Arab after 9/11." Booklist

Includes bibliographical references

Mangan, Tricia

★ **How** to feel good; 20 things teens can do. by Tricia Mangan. Magination Press 2012 125 p. (pbk.: alk. paper) $12.95

Grades: 8 9 10 11 12   **305.23**

1. Teenagers 2. Life skills 3. Adolescent psychology 4. Teenagers -- Conduct of life 5. Teenagers -- Life skills guides

ISBN 1433810409; 9781433810404

LC 2011020623

This book offers advice to teenagers in areas of psychological health in order "to feel good about . . . [themselves] and . . . [their] abilities. For teens, new relationships and experiences are happening all around them, and can make them feel overwhelmed and stressed. Being confident and secure can seem miles away. . . . [This book] provides interactive exercises and questions to help teens recognize and understand why they feel the way they do and to change hurtful thought patterns and habits. With these 20 . . . . steps, teens can use this book to learn how to be confident and happy with themselves." (Publisher's note)

"With a gentle, firm but never condescending tone . . . clinical psychologist Mangan leads anxious teens through the A's (activating events), B's (beliefs), and C's (consequences) of taking control of spiraling and self-defeating moods." Booklist

My little red book; edited by Rachel Kauder Nalebuff. Twelve Books 2009 225p $14.99
 Grades: 8 9 10 11 12 Adult   **305.23**
 1. Menstruation
 ISBN 978-0-446-54636-2; 0-446-54636-4
         LC 2008-40621
"My Little Red Book is an anthology of stories about first periods, collected from women of all ages from around the world. The accounts range from light-hearted (the editor got hers while water skiing in a yellow bathing suit) to heart-stopping (a first period discovered just as one girl was about to be strip-searched by the Nazis). The contributors include well-known women writers (Meg Cabot, Erica Jong, Gloria Steinem, Cecily von Ziegesar), alongside today's teens. And while the authors differ in race, faith, or cultural background, their stories share a common bond: they are all accessible, deeply honest, and highly informative. Whatever a girl experiences or expects, she'll find stories that speak to her thoughts and feelings." (Publisher's note)

"A rich, welcome collection for readers of various ages and, perhaps surprisingly, more than one gender." Booklist
 Includes bibliographical references

Nazario, Sonia

 ★ **Enrique's** journey; the true story of a boy determined to reunite with his mother. Delacorte Press 2013 288 p. il $16.99
Grades: 11 12 Adult   **305.23**
 1. Unauthorized immigrants 2. Illegal aliens 3. Immigrant children 4. United States -- Immigration and emigration
 ISBN 0385743270; 9780385743273
        LC 200544347
This book tells "the story of Enrique, a teenager from Honduras whom Nazario first wrote about in a Pulitzer Prize-winning newspaper series from which this book springs. . . . Desperately poor, Enrique's mother left Honduras when he was 5 years old, planning to send money back from America and promising to return quickly. Years passed. Enrique was tossed between family members' homes. . . . After more than a decade of waiting for her, Enrique set out for the North." (N Y Times Book Rev)

The author "retraces the travel of immigrants from Central America to El Norte and writes . . . about the trials and tribulations that besiege the journey. Specifically, she focuses on a Honduran boy, Enrique, left behind by his mother,

Lourdes, who fled to the United States, like many Central American women before her, to make enough money to give her children a better life back home and ultimately return to them." Libr J

Robbins, Alexandra

 ★ The **overachievers**; the secret lives of driven kids. Hyperion 2006 439p $24.95; pa $13.95
Grades: 11 12 Adult   **305.23**
 1. Workaholism 2. High school students
 ISBN 1-4013-0201-7; 978-1-4013-0201-6; 1-4013-0902-2 pa; 978-1-4013-0902-2 pa
        LC 2006-41244
The author "follows the lives of students from a Bethesda, Md., high school as they navigate the SAT and college application process. These students are obsessed with success, contending with illness, physical deterioration (senior Julie is losing hair over the pressure to get into Stanford), cheating (students sell a physics project to one another), obsessed parents (Frank's mother manages his time to the point of abuse) and emotional breakdowns. The portraits of the teens are compelling and make for an easy read." Publ Wkly
 Includes bibliographical references

Rookie Yearbook Two; by Tavi Gevinson. Farrar Straus & Giroux 2013 352 p. $29.95
 Grades: 9 10 11 12   **305.23**
 1. Fanzines 2. Teenagers 3. Teenage girls 4. Popular culture
 ISBN 1770461485; 9781770461482
This book, edited by Tavi Gevinson, "anthologizes the best of the online magazine's June 2012-May 2013 offerings. . . . Whether examining standard teen fare such as 'The Complete Guide to Kissing' and (un)popularity . . . or interviewing . . . musicians like Carrie Brownstein and Morrissey, the writers, with their distinct voices and points-of-view, connect with their subjects." (School Library Journal)

Walters, Eric

 When elephants fight; written by Eric Walters and Adrian Bradbury. Orca Book Publishers 2008 89p il $19.95
Grades: 7 8 9 10   **305.23**
 1. Children and war
 ISBN 978-1-55143-900-6; 1-55143-900-X
"The authors detail the lives of children growing up in . . . [war torn nations]. They provide rich, detailed histories of each nation, and explain the current conflicts which have led to the destruction of families and normal childhood. . . . This would be an excellent supplemental text for a high school geography or world civilization program." Libr Media Connect

 ★ **Yell-oh** girls! emerging voices explore culture, identity, and growing up Asian American. {edited by} Vickie Nam. Quill 2001 xxxv, 297p il pa $13
 Grades: 11 12 Adult   **305.23**
 1. Girls 2. Teenagers 3. Asian Americans
 ISBN 0-06-095944-4
        LC 2001-18164

This is an "anthology of essays by young Asian American women. The contributors, from China, Hawaii, Laos, Vietnam, and even India, range in age from 13 to nearly 40. . . . Readers . . . who have felt the pain of being outsiders will be swept along by the authors' sincerity and their efforts to use writing to clarify who they are." Booklist

305.235   Young people twelve to twenty

Alifirenka, Caitlin

I will always write back; how one letter changed two lives. by Caitlin Alifirenka and Martin Ganda; with Liz Welch. Little, Brown & Co. 2015 400 p. (hardcover) $18

Grades: 6 7 8 9 10 11 12 Adult   **305.235**
1. Africans 2. Letter writing 3. Teenagers' writings 4. Friendship 5. Pen pals -- Zimbabwe 6. Pen pals -- United States 7. Teenagers -- Zimbabwe -- Social conditions 8. Teenagers -- United States -- Social conditions

ISBN 0316241318; 9780316241311
LC 2014030355

This memoir by Martin Ganda and Caitlin Alifirenka, with Liz Welch, "true story of an all-American girl and a boy from Zimbabwe and the letter that changed both of their lives forever. Everyone in Caitlin's class wrote to an unknown student somewhere in a distant place. Martin was lucky to even receive a pen-pal letter. There were only ten letters, and fifty kids in his class. But he was the top student, so he got the first one. That letter was the beginning of a correspondence that spanned six years and changed two lives." (Publisher's note)

"A feel-good, message-driven book that may appeal to adults more than teens." Kirkus

Ellis, Deborah

Kids of Kabul; living bravely through a never-ending war. Deborah Ellis. Groundwood Books 2012 143 p. $15.95

Grades: 6 7 8 9 10 11 12   **305.235**
1. Taliban 2. Interviews 3. Children -- Afghanistan

ISBN 1554981816; 9781554981816

This book is a collection of interviews with Afghani children who "mostly don't remember the Taliban's fall more than a decade ago, but they can't help but be shaped by the damage the Taliban did to their country. . . . One girl is imprisoned for fleeing a forced child marriage, while another's mother is a member of Parliament; one boy's damaged by a landmine, and another's proud to be a Scout. . . . [I]ntroductions to each young person provide historical, legal and social context." (Kirkus Reviews)

305.242   People in early adulthood

Burge, Kimberly

The born frees; writing with the girls of Gugule-thu. Kimberly Burge. W.W. Norton & Co. Inc. 2015 384 p. (hardcover) $26.95

Grades: 11 12 Adult   **305.242**
1. Creative writing 2. Women -- South Africa 3. Youth -- South Africa 4. South Africa -- Social life and customs 5. Post-apartheid era -- South Africa 6. Young women -- South Africa -- Social conditions 7. Creative writing (Study and teaching) -- South Africa

ISBN 0393239160; 9780393239164
LC 2015010037

In this book, by Kimberly Burge, a "creative writing group unites and inspires girls of the first South African generation 'born free.' Born into post-apartheid South Africa, the young women of the townships around Cape Town still face daunting challenges. . . . Yet, as . . . Burge discovered when she set up a writing group in the township of Gugule-thu, the spirit of these girls outshines their circumstances." (Publisher's note)

"Incredible and inspiring, this account belongs in every library and on every bookshelf." LJ

Includes bibliographical references

305.3   People by gender or sex

Bornstein, Kate

My gender workbook; how to become a real man, a real woman, the real you, or something else entirely. Kate Bornstein; with illustrations by Diane DiMassa. Routledge 1998 292p il

Grades: 7 8 9 10 11 12   **305.3**
1. Gender role 2. Transgender people

ISBN 0-415-91672-0; 0-415-91673-9 (pbk)
LC 98-134184

Written by Kate Bornstein and illustrated by Diane Di-Masa, this book "brings theory down to Earth and provides a practical approach to living with or without a gender. Bornstein starts from the premise that there are not just two genders performed in today's world, but countless genders lumped under the two-gender framework. Using a . . . workbook format, Bornstein gently but firmly guides you to discover your own unique gender identity." (Publisher's note)

"Artist and trans activist Bornstein (Gender Outlaw: On Men, Women, and the Rest of Us) has updated her 1997 introduction to gender, sexuality, and making your way in a world that has a lot of opinions about both. Goofy..., practical..., this updated workbook is full of clipart, tweets, and interactive exercises and quizzes...Bornstein dismantles some of the social mores we take the most for granted, and we are all the better for it." (Library Journal)

My new gender workbook; a step-by-step guide to achieving world peace through gender anarchy and sex positivity. Kate Bornstein. Routledge 2013 xiii, 293 p.p ill. (paperback) $39.95

Grades: 7 8 9 10 11 12   **305.3**
1. Sex 2. Gender role 3. Sex education 4. Sex -- Psychological aspects 5. Gender identity 6. Sex (Psychology)

ISBN 0415538653; 9780203109038; 9780415538640; 9780415538657
LC 2012033355

"Since its first publication in 1997, My Gender Workbook has been challenging, encouraging, questioning, and helping those trying to figure out how to become a 'real man,' a 'real woman,' or 'something else entirely.' In this exciting new edition of her classic text, Bornstein re-examines gender in light of issues like race, class, sexuality, and language. With new quizzes, new puzzles, new exercises, and plenty of Kate's playful and provocative style, My New Gender Workbook promises to help a new generation create their own unique place on the gender spectrum." (Publisher's note)

"It makes a sometimes-intimidating set of theories accessible and friendly for any reader, not just those already working on their gender. Bornstein dismantles some of the social mores we take the most for granted, and we are all the better for it. " LJ

305.38 Specific groups of men

McCall, Nathan

Makes me wanna holler; a young black man in America. Random House 1994 404p hardcover o.p. pa $14.95

Grades: 11 12 Adult **305.38**
    1. Journalists 2. Essayists 3. Memoirists 4. African Americans -- Biography
    ISBN 0-679-74070-8 pa

                         LC 93-30654
The author relates the "story of his rise from poverty to success as a journalist at the Washington Post. He uses graphic language, blunt descriptions, honest expression, introspection, and careful observation to describe his early years in Portsmouth, Virginia, as a young black male, the recipient of a 12-year prison sentence for armed robbery, whose life was dangerously out of control. Insensitivity, alienation, racial hatred, drugs (especially crack), guns, rape, robbery, the black American as an endangered species—McCall covers it all in a depressing yet spellbinding documentary." Libr J

305.4 Women

Collins, Gail

America's women; four hundred years of dolls, drudges, helpmates, and heroines. Morrow 2003 556p il $27.95; pa $15.95

Grades: 11 12 Adult **305.4**
    1. Women -- United States -- History
    ISBN 0-06-018510-4; 0-06-122722-6 pa

                        LC 2003-51011
This is a history of American women from colonial times to the present

"Collins elegantly and eruditely celebrates the hard-won victories, overwhelming obstacles, and selfless contributions of a captivating array of influential women." Booklist
Includes bibliographical references

When everything changed; the amazing journey of American women from 1960 to the present. Little, Brown and Co. 2009 471p il $27.99

Grades: 11 12 Adult **305.4**
    1. Women -- United States -- History
    ISBN 978-0-316-05954-1; 0-316-05954-4

                        LC 2008-54933
"Collins can be deadly serious and great fun to read at the same time. A revelatory book for readers of both sexes, and sure to become required reading for any American women's-studies course." Kirkus
Includes bibliographical references

★ The **essential** feminist reader; edited and with an introduction by Estelle B. Freedman. Modern Library 2007 472p pa $17.95

Grades: 11 12 Adult **305.4**
    1. Feminism
    ISBN 0-8129-7460-3; 978-0-8129-7460-7
This collection of writings by feminist authors "features primary source material from around the globe, including short works of fiction and drama, political manifestos, and the work of less well-known writers." Publisher's note
Includes bibliographical references

Gourley, Catherine

★ **Flappers** and the new American woman; perceptions of women from 1918 through the 1920s. Twenty-First Century Books 2008 144p il (Images and issues of women in the twentieth century) lib bdg $38.60

Grades: 7 8 9 10 **305.4**
    1. Women -- United States -- History 2. United States -- History -- 1919-1933
    ISBN 978-0-8225-6060-9; 0-8225-6060-7

                        LC 2006-28983
This describes images of women in the United States from 1918 through the 1920s.

"The sparkling and engaging [text is] generously expanded by numerous, well-placed black-and-white photographs and period reproductions. . . . Great for research or browsing." SLJ
Includes bibliographical references

★ **Gibson** girls and suffragists; perceptions of women from the turn of the century through 1918. Twenty-First Century Books 2008 144p il (Images and issues of women in the twentieth century) lib bdg $38.60

Grades: 7 8 9 10 **305.4**
    1. Women -- United States -- History 2. United States -- History -- 1898-1919
    ISBN 978-0-8225-7150-6; 0-8225-7150-1

                        LC 2007-1689
This describes the images of women in United States at the beginning of the twentienth century.

"The sparkling and engaging [text is] generously expanded by numerous, well-placed black-and-white photographs and period reproductions. . . . Great for research or browsing." SLJ
Includes bibliographical references

★ **Rosie** and Mrs. America; perceptions of women in the 1930s and 1940s. Twenty-First Century

Books 2008 144p il (Images and issues of women in the twentieth century) lib bdg $38.60

Grades: 7 8 9 10   **305.4**

1. Women -- United States -- History 2. United States -- History -- 20th century

ISBN 978-0-8225-6804-9; 0-8225-6804-7

LC 2006-28984

This describes images of women in the United States in the 1930s and 1940's.

"The sparkling and engaging [text is] generously expanded by numerous, well-placed black-and-white photographs and period reproductions. . . . Great for research or browsing." SLJ

Includes bibliographical references

Grunwald, Lisa

Women's letters; America from the Revolutionary War to the present. edited by Lisa Grunwald & Stephen J. Adler. Dial Press 2005 824p il hardcover o.p. pa $18; pa $18

Grades: 11 12 Adult   **305.4**

1. Women -- United States -- History -- Sources

ISBN 9780385335560; 0-385-33553-9; 0-385-33556-3 pa

LC 2005-41446

"Historical events of the last three centuries come alive through these women's singular correspondences—often their only form of public expression. In 1775, Rachel Revere tries to send financial aid to her husband, Paul, in a note that is confiscated by the British; First Lady Dolley Madison tells her sister about rescuing George Washington's portrait during the War of 1812; one week after JFK's assassination, Jacqueline Kennedy pens a heartfelt letter to Nikita Khrushchev; and on September 12, 2001, a schoolgirl writes a note of thanks to a New York City firefighter, asking him, "Were you afraid?" (Publisher's note)

"This collection of more than 400 entries begins with a letter written by Abigail Grant, accusing her husband of cowardice in battle, and ends with an e-mail by Wall Street Journal correspondent Farnaz Fassihi on the stark state of affairs in war-torn Iraq. In between, a wide variety of compelling subjects is covered. . . . The letters are accompanied by information about the topics included, biographical details about the author and the recipient, and other interesting facts." SLJ

Includes bibliographical references

Hemming, Heidi

Women making America; [by] Heidi Hemming, Julie Hemming Savage. Clotho Press 2009 378p il pa $28.95

Grades: 6 7 8 9 10   **305.4**

1. Women -- United States -- History 2. Women -- United States -- Biography

ISBN 978-0-9821271-0-0; 0-9821271-0-3

LC 2008-908741

"This hefty volume surveys the role of women in American history from 1770 to the present, focusing primarily on health issues, paid work, home, education, beauty, amusements, and the arts. Each chapter includes a brief summary of historical events and then examines the common threads. . . . The book's innovative and direct approach is sure to capture the attention of young women. Classroom teachers can utilize the plethora of facts to liven social studies and history lessons, and the format is appealing enough to attract browsers." SLJ

Includes bibliographical references

Hoogensen, Gunhild

Women in power; world leaders since 1960. [by] Gunhild Hoogensen and Bruce O. Solheim; foreword by Kim Campbell. Praeger Publishers 2006 179p $44.95

Grades: 11 12 Adult   **305.4**

1. Women in politics 2. Women -- Political activity

ISBN 978-0-275-98190-7; 0-275-98190-8

LC 2006-15398

This book "profiles 22 world leaders who have held the top positions of political power since 1960. Each chapter is devoted to a region of the world. In addition to providing an overview of the political careers of the women who emerged as leaders in these regions, the authors examine the political systems of each region in terms of the involvement of women in politics." Publisher's note

Includes bibliographical references

Lawler, Jennifer

Encyclopedia of women in the Middle Ages. McFarland & Co. 2001 279p $45

Grades: 9 10 11 12   **305.4**

1. Reference books 2. Middle Ages -- Encyclopedias 3. Women -- History -- Encyclopedias

ISBN 0-7864-1119-8

LC 2001-126809

"This encyclopedia contains several hundred entries on the culture, history and circumstances of women in the Middle Ages, from the years 500 to 1500 C.E. . . . There are entries on queens, empresses, and other women in positions of leadership as well as entries on topics such as work, marriage and family, households, employment, religion, and various other aspects of women's lives in the Middle Ages. Genealogies of queens and empresses accompany the text." Publisher's note

Includes bibliographical references

Mills, J. Elizabeth

Expectations for women; confronting stereotypes. Rosen Pub. 2010 112p il (A young woman's guide to contemporary issues) lib bdg $31.95

Grades: 7 8 9 10   **305.4**

1. Women 2. Body image 3. Self-perception

ISBN 978-1-4358-3543-6; 1-4358-3543-3

LC 2009-14429

"Facts are shared in a conversational tone, creating the sense of a chat with a big sister. . . . [Though] designed for personal reading and browsing, the data provided are accurate and also lend themselves to use in reports. This . . . will be of great interest." SLJ

Includes glossary and bibliographical references

Peavy, Linda Sellers

Pioneer women; the lives of women on the frontier. [by] Linda Peavy & Ursula Smith. Oklahoma paperbacks ed; University of Oklahoma Press 1998 144p il pa $21.95

Grades: 9 10 11 12 Adult   305.4

1. Women -- West (U.S.) 2. Frontier and pioneer life -- West (U.S.)

ISBN 0-8061-3054-7; 978-0-8061-3054-5

LC 97-40684

First published 1996 by Smithmark Pubs.

An illustrated exploration of women's lives on the Western frontier. Marriages between Anglo men and Indian and Hispanic women are examined as are the lives of women who found employment outside the homestead as teachers, physicians and journalists.

"YAs seeking primary source material for women's studies and on the westward movement will find this exceptional collection of journals, letters, oral histories, and rarely seen photographs an outstanding resource." Booklist

Includes bibliographical references

★ The **Quotable** woman, revised edition; the first 5,000 years. compiled and edited by Elaine Bernstein Partnow. Facts On File 2010 1038p (Facts on File library of language and literature) $95

Grades: 11 12 Adult   305.4

1. Quotations 2. Reference books 3. Women -- Quotations

ISBN 978-0-8160-7725-0

LC 2009-39139

First published 1992 as a combined edition of The quotable woman, from Eve to 1799 (1986) and The quotable woman, 1800-1981 (1983) with title: The New Quotable woman

"Entries are arranged chronologically then alphabetically by the names of the women quoted. Indexing is by name, career and occupation, ethnicity and nationality, and subject. . . . The quotations section makes up the first 832 pages of the book, and the bulk of the quotations are from the 20th century. The quotations are interesting and thoughtfully chosen; the women quoted are delightfully varied." Libr J

Rodriguez, Deborah

Kabul Beauty School; an American woman goes behind the veil. Random House 2007 275p $24.95; pa $14.95

Grades: 11 12 Adult   305.4

1. Beauty shops 2. Women -- Afghanistan 3. Kabul Beauty School (Afghanistan)

ISBN 978-1-4000-6559-2; 1-4000-6559-3; 978-0-8129-7673-1 pa; 0-8129-7673-8 pa

LC 2006-50384

"Rodriguez's experiences will delight readers as she recounts such tales as two friends acting as 'parents' and negotiating a dowry for her marriage to an Afghan man or her students puzzling over a donation of a carton of thongs. Most of all, they will share her admiration for Afghan women's survival and triumph in chaotic times." SLJ

Rosen, Ruth

The **world** split open; how the modern women's movement changed America. Rev. and updated; Penguin Books 2006 xlii, 482p il pa $19

Grades: 11 12 Adult   305.4

1. Feminism 2. Women's movement

ISBN 978-0-14-009719-1

First published 2000

"Rosen details the rebirth of feminism, from the liberalism of NOW through women's liberation, which grew out of the civil rights movement. Her focus is on the 'hidden injuries of sex' and how what had been construed as 'personal' problems—abortion, compulsory heterosexuality, rape and sexual violence, prostitution and pornography—became political issues." Publ Wkly

Includes bibliographical references

Schnall, Marianne

What will it take to make a woman president? conversations about women, leadership, and power. by Marianne Schnall. Seal Press 2013 384 p. $17

Grades: 9 10 11 12 Adult   305.4

1. Women politicians 2. Gender and politics 3. Presidential candidates -- United States 4. Women -- United States -- Interviews 5. Politicians -- United States -- Attitudes 6. Women political activists -- United States 7. Women presidential candidates -- United States

ISBN 158005496X; 9781580054966

LC 2013031218

Amelia Bloomer Project (2014)

This book, by Marianne Schnall, "features interviews with politicians, public officials, thought leaders, writers, artists, and activists in an attempt to discover the obstacles that have held women back and what needs to change in order to elect a woman into the White House. With insights and personal anecdotes . . . , this book addresses timely, provocative issues involving women, politics, and power." (Publisher's note)

"Through far-ranging conversations, Schnall gained insight into factors contributing to the country's failure to elect a woman to its highest office and sought advice as to how we can not only better prepare for the next presidential election but create a world in which today's young women feel empowered to break out of stereotypical roles. The good news is that there is universal agreement among those profiled that the country will, indeed, elect a woman president. The more disconcerting message is that there is still much work to do in order to achieve true gender parity." (Booklist)

★ **Voices** of resistance; Muslim women on war, faith, & sexuality. edited by Sarah Husain. Seal Press 2006 284p il map pa $16.95

Grades: 9 10 11 12   305.4

1. Muslim women

ISBN 978-1-58005-181-1; 1-58005-181-2

LC 2006-5459

This "collection of fiction, poetry, interviews, essays, letters, and artwork celebrates diversity across race, nation, sexuality, and gender. Most contributors live in the U.S., and the focus is on post-9/11 America, connecting multiple immigrant histories and memories of 'home' with the personal and political in contemporary daily life. . . . Sure to spark discussion in college classrooms and among feminist and peace activist groups." Booklist

Includes bibliographical references

Waisman, Charlotte S.

★ **Her** story; a timeline of the women who changed America. [by] Charlotte S. Waisman & Jill S. Tietjen. HarperCollins 2008 259p il $29.95

Grades: 9 10 11 12   **305.4**

1. Women -- United States -- History 2. United States -- History -- Chronology

ISBN 978-0-06-124651-7; 0-06-124651-4

LC 2007-29942

"This time line illuminates the ways in which hundreds of women changed America through their often-unrecognized contributions in science, education, arts, politics, and social activism, from the 1500s to the present." Booklist

Includes bibliographical references

Waking up American; coming of age biculturally. [edited by] Angela Jane Fountas. Seal Press 2005 232p pa $15.95

Grades: 11 12 Adult   **305.4**

1. Children of immigrants 2. Women -- United States

ISBN 1-58005-136-7; 978-1-58005-136-1

LC 2005-11765

"'Where are you from?' In one of the best of the recent anthologies by new immigrants, young women writers answer that question with immediacy and wit, displaying honesty about the pain, anger, and prejudice at home and outside." Booklist

Wolf, Naomi

The **beauty** myth; how images of beauty are used against women. Perennial 2002 348p pa $14.95

Grades: 11 12 Adult   **305.4**

1. Women 2. Gender role 3. Personal appearance 4. Sex role

ISBN 0-06-051218-0

LC 2002-72516

First published 1991 by Morrow

The author "presents a provocative and persuasive account of the pervasiveness of the beauty ideal in all facets of Western culture." Libr J

Includes bibliographical references

Women's lives in medieval Europe; a sourcebook. edited by Emilie Amt. 2nd ed.; Routledge 2009 277p $125; pa $39.95

Grades: 11 12 Adult   **305.4**

1. Women -- Europe 2. Europe -- History -- 476-1492

ISBN 978-0-415-46684-4; 978-0-415-46683-7 pa

LC 2009024316

First published 1993

This book "presents the everyday lives and experiences of women in the Middle Ages. . . . [It includes] sections on marriage and sexuality, and on peasant women and townswomen, as well as a . . . section on women and the law. . . . The book focuses not just on the Christian majority, but also present material about women in minority groups in Europe, such as Jews, Muslims, and those considered to be heretics." Publisher's note

★ **Women's** rights; people and perspectives. Crista DeLuzio, editor. ABC-CLIO 2010 xxxix, 296p il (Perspectives in American social history) $85

Grades: 9 10 11 12   **305.4**

1. Feminism 2. Women's rights

ISBN 978-1-59884-114-5

LC 2009-31359

"This enlightening source is much more than a roll call of persons and events that influenced women's rights and the suffrage movement. . . . This title will be extremely useful for research, and individual sections are interesting to peruse on their own. " SLJ

Includes bibliographical references

305.42   Social role and status of women

Feminist writings from ancient times to the modern world; a global sourcebook and history. Tiffany K. Wayne, editor. Greenwood 2011 2 v. (xlvi, 718 p.)p

Grades: 10 11 12   **305.42**

1. Anthologies 2. Feminist criticism 3. Feminism -- History 4. Feminist literature -- History 5. Feminism and literature -- History

ISBN 9780313345807; 9780313345814; 9780313345821; 9780313345838; 9780313345845; 9780313345852

LC 2011009468

"This two-volume anthology features feminist writings that focus on women's resistance to male privilege and power in cultures and religions around the world and in all time periods. The 230 entries include poems, letters, essays, speeches, court decisions, and other documents that address feminist thought. . . . This . . . set . . . includes well-known feminist writers such as Sappho, Mary Wollstonecraft, Margaret Fuller, Sojourner Truth, and Hillary Rodham Clinton as well as lesser-known feminists such as Enheduanna, of Sumer; Yeshe Tsogyal, of Tibet; and Nawal El Saadawi, of Egypt." (Booklist)

Includes bibliographical references and index

The **unfinished** revolution; voices from the global fight for women's rights. edited by Minky Worden. Seven Stories Press 2012 xviii, 361 p.p col. ill. (paperback) $25.95

Grades: 10 11 12 Adult   **305.42**

1. Human rights 2. Women's rights

ISBN 1609803876; 9781609803872

LC 2011052738

This book edited by Minky Worden is a collection of "essays assessing the progress of worldwide rights for women and girls since the UN's human rights conferences in the 1990s. The ongoing global struggle consists of three distinct spheres: economic issues (human trafficking, property rights); violence against women and their health rights (including genital mutilation); and harmful traditions (religious clothing restraints, so-called honor crimes)." (Booklist)

Includes bibliographical references and index

Zeilinger, Julie

A **little** f'd up; why feminism is not a dirty word. Julie Zeilinger. Seal Press 2012 ix, 249 p.p ill. $16

Grades: 9 10 11 12 **305.42**

1. Feminism 2. Body image 3. Feminism -- United States 4. Young women -- United States -- Attitudes

ISBN 1580053718; 9781580053716

LC 2011047093

Author Julie Zeilinger has "written a primer on feminism for teenagers and young women. Now a student at Barnard College, she draws on her own high-school experiences to connect to readers who may be put off by both the language and the ideas of feminism. She devotes the book's first third to the history of feminism. . . . Focusing on global issues, the Internet, and surviving high school, she describes feminism as both inclusive and empowering." (Library Journal)

Includes bibliographical references

305.5 People by social and economic levels

Ehrenreich, Barbara

★ **Nickel** and dimed; on (not) getting by in America. Metropolitan Bks. 2001 221p hardcover o.p. pa $15

Grades: 11 12 Adult **305.5**

1. Poverty 2. Minimum wage 3. Labor -- United States

ISBN 0-8050-6388-9; 0-8050-8838-5 pa

LC 00-52514

"No real answers to the problem but a compelling sketch of its reality and pervasiveness." Libr J

Issitt, Micah L.

Hippies; a guide to an American subculture. Greenwood Press/ABC-CLIO 2009 xxi, 164p il (Guides to subcultures and countercultures) $35

Grades: 11 12 Adult **305.5**

1. Hippies 2. Counter culture

ISBN 978-0-313-36572-0

LC 2009-29453

This book "explores the psyche and history of the American counterculture's influence on everything from music and fashion to war, peace, and the mainstream establishment. From hippie leaders and icons such as Timothy Leary to how 1960s America was transformed by the movement, HIPPIES is a powerful pick for any American history collection from high school to college levels." Midwest Book Rev

Includes bibliographical references

Painter, Nell Irvin

★ **Sojourner** Truth; a life, a symbol. Norton 1996 370p il hardcover o.p. pa $15.95

Grades: 11 12 Adult **305.5**

1. Feminism 2. Abolitionists 3. Memoirists 4. African American women -- Biography

ISBN 0-393-02739-2; 0-393-31708-0 pa

LC 95-47595

"Painter persuasively offers us the real woman behind the myth." Publ Wkly

Includes bibliographical references

Slave narratives. Library of Am. 2000 1,034 $40

Grades: 11 12 Adult **305.5**

1. Slaves 2. Authors 3. Novelists 4. Dramatists 5. Historians 6. Abolitionists 7. Domestics 8. Memoirists 9. Revolutionaries 10. Slavery -- United States 11. African Americans -- Biography

ISBN 1-88301-176-0

LC 99-40360

"Appearing in this collection are memoirs penned by well-known activists Nat Turner, Frederick Douglass, William Wells Brown, Henry Bibb, and Sojourner Truth. In addition, several powerful, evocative works by less celebrated writers are also featured. . . . Together these 10 narratives paint a vivid portrait of the cruelties of the institution of slavery. . . . A significant contribution to the literature of the African American experience." Booklist

Includes bibliographical references

305.8 Ethnic and national groups

★ The **African** American almanac; Christopher A. Brooks, editor; foreword by Benjamin Jealous. 11th ed; Gale Cengage Learning 2011 1601p il map $297

Grades: 8 9 10 11 12 Adult **305.8**

1. Reference books 2. African Americans

ISBN 978-1-4144-4547-2

First edition under the editorship of Harry A. Ploski published 1967 by Bellwether with title: The Negro almanac. Periodically revised. Editors vary

"Reference covering the cultural and political history of Black Americans. Includes generous amount of statistical information and biographies of Black Americans, both historical and contemporary." N Y Public Libr. Book of How & Where to Look It Up

Asante, Molefi K.

Erasing racism; the survival of the American nation. [by] Molefi Kete Asante. Rev. and expanded 2nd ed.; Prometheus Books 2009 370p il pa $19

Grades: 11 12 Adult **305.8**

1. Racism 2. United States -- Race relations 3. African Americans -- Civil rights 4. African Americans -- Social conditions

ISBN 978-1-591-02765-2; 1-591-02765-9

LC 2009020492

First published 2003

In this "analysis of the history of racism in America, Asante divides the nation into two camps: a white majority who perceives America as a land of promise, and a black minority that is relegated to exist in a wilderness on the margins of society. . . . The key to bridging the racial divide, he argues, lies in getting all Americans to understand and confront the history of slavery. . . . Anyone who has struggled to understand race relations in America or to engage others in open debate about it will glean something valuable from this book." Publ Wkly

Includes bibliographical references

The **Asian** Americans; Rodney P. Carlisle, general editor. Facts on File 2011 244p il map (Multicultural America) $55

Grades: 9 10 11 12   **305.8**
1. Asian Americans -- History
ISBN 978-0-8160-7814-1

This book "focuses on the social history, customs, and traditions of Asian Americans across U.S. history." Publisher's note

Includes glossary and bibliographical references

★ **Autobiography** of a people; three centuries of African American history told by those who lived it. [compiled by] Herb Boyd. Doubleday 2000 549p hardcover o.p. pa $15

Grades: 11 12 Adult   **305.8**
1. African Americans -- Biography 2. African Americans -- History -- Sources
ISBN 0-385-49278-2; 0-385-49279-0 pa

LC 99-16576

This volume contains excerpts from slave narratives, diaries, poems, letters, autobiographies, memoirs and speeches.

"Boyd includes the writers one would expect, such as Phyllis Wheatley, Frederick Douglass, W. E. B. Dubois, Reverend King, Malcolm X, and Colin Powell. But his collection may be most valuable to twenty-first century readers for the less familiar voices he gathers: slaves, freedmen and women, and, later, intellectuals, workers, and activists, whose experiences are captured in a protest or letter or memoir." Booklist

Includes bibliographical references

Bayoumi, Moustafa
How does it feel to be a problem? being young and Arab in America. Penguin Press 2008 290p pa $15; $24.95

Grades: 11 12 Adult   **305.8**
1. Arab American youth 2. Young men -- Psychology 3. Young men -- United States 4. Race awareness -- United States 5. United States -- Race relations 6. Arab Americans -- Ethnic identity 7. Arab Americans -- Social conditions 8. Brooklyn (New York, N.Y.) -- Ethnic relations
ISBN 978-0-14-311541-0 pa; 978-1-59420-176-9

LC 2007-49272

This book is based on interviews with seven young Arab Americans who live in Brooklyn. It "evaluates their daily encounters with such factors as prejudice, the Christian faith, and their relationships with friends and family members in the Middle East." (Publisher's note)

The author "wondered how younger generations of Arab Americans were faring in a post-9/11 U.S. against the backdrop of fear and suspicion. By focusing on the lives of seven young people living in Brooklyn, Bayoumi offers a revealing portrait of life for people who are often scrutinized but seldom heard from." Booklist

Includes bibliographical references

Coates, Ta-Nehisi, 1975-
★ **Between** the World and Me; Ta-Nehisi Coates. Random House Inc. 2015 176 p. illustrations (hardback) $24.00

Grades: 11 12 Adult   **305.8**
1. United States -- Race relations 2. African Americans -- Social conditions
ISBN 0812993543; 9780812993547

LC 2015008120

Pulitzer Prize Finalist: General Nonfiction (2016)
Kirkus Prize: Nonfiction (2015)
National Book Award: Nonfiction (2015)
Alex Award (2016)
National Book Critics Circle Award Finalist: Criticism (2015)
NAACP Image Award: Outstanding Literary Work- Biography/Autobiography (2016)

This book, by Ta-Nehisi Coates, argues "Americans have built an empire on the idea of 'race,' a falsehood that damages us all but falls most heavily on the bodies of black women and men--bodies exploited through slavery and segregation, and, today, threatened, locked up, and murdered out of all proportion. What is it like to inhabit a black body and find a way to live within it? And how can we all honestly reckon with this fraught history and free ourselves from its burden?" (Publisher's note)

"In this brief book, which takes the form of a letter to the author's teenage son, Coates . . . comes to grips with what it means to be black in America today. . . . There is awesome beauty in the power of his prose and vital truth on every page." Booklist

Curtis, Edward E., 1970-
Muslims in America; a short history. Oxford University Press 2009 144p il (Religion in American life) pa $12.95

Grades: 9 10 11 12 Adult   **305.8**
1. Muslims 2. Ethnic relations 3. Islam -- History 4. Muslims -- United States 5. Islam -- United States -- History 6. Muslims -- United States -- History 7. United States -- Religious life and customs
ISBN 978-0-19-536756-0

LC 2008-47566

The author "has authored a fine and succinct history that spans centuries. . . . Although geared toward non-Muslims, American Muslims would also learn a great deal from reading about their own history. . . . [Readers] will undoubtedly be intrigued by Curtis's compelling little read." Publ Wkly

Includes bibliographical references

Danalis, John
Riding the black cockatoo. Allen & Unwin 2009 262p pa $10.99

Grades: 9 10 11 12   **305.8**
1. Aboriginal Australians -- Antiquities
ISBN 978-174175-377-6

"While taking a course in Indigenous Writing, 40-year-old Danalis realized that the Aboriginal skull that sat on his family's mantle for years was morally wrong. . . . [This] is his account of first figuring out how and where to return it, and then the bureaucracy involved, the government's horrifying lack of respect for these people, and the appreciation and ceremony on the part of the Native people when it was returned. This memoir strikes the perfect balance between being informative and giving extraordinary insight into Aboriginal culture." SLJ

Du Bois, W. E. B.

The **souls** of Black folk; edited with an introduction and notes by Brent Hayes Edwards. Oxford University Press 2007 xxxvi, 223p il (Oxford world's classics) pa $12.95

Grades: 11 12 Adult   **305.8**

1. African Americans

ISBN 978-0-19-280678-9; 0-19-280678-5

LC 2006-35193

First published 1903 by McClurg

"A collection of fifteen essays and sketches by W.E.B. Du Bois. In it he describes the lives of African American farmers, sketches the role of music in their churches, details the history of the Freedman's Bureau, discusses the career of Booker T. Washington, and advocates a commitment to higher education for the most talented African American youth." Benet's Reader's Ency of Am Lit

Includes bibliographical references

Encyclopedia of African American history; Leslie M. Alexander and Walter C. Rucker, editors. ABC-CLIO 2010 3v il map (American ethnic experience) set $295

Grades: 9 10 11 12 Adult   **305.8**

1. Reference books 2. African Americans -- History -- Encyclopedias 3. African Americans -- Biography -- Encyclopedias

ISBN 978-1-85109-769-2; 978-1-85109-774-6 ebook

LC 2009-51262

"Each volume in this set begins with a list of entries. The first volume contains entries about Atlantic African, American, and European backgrounds, as well as a section on culture, identity, and community from slavery to the present. The second volume contains entries on political activity and resistance to oppression from the American Revolution to the Civil War. The third volume includes political activity, migration and urbanization from reconstruction to civil rights, and modern African Americans. . . . This is a valuable reference set." Libr Media Connect

Includes bibliographical references

Epstein, Lawrence J.

At the edge of a dream; the story of Jewish immigrants on New York's Lower East Side. Jossey-Bass 2007 299p il $40

Grades: 11 12 Adult   **305.8**

1. Jews -- New York (N.Y.) 2. United States -- Immigration and emigration

ISBN 978-0-7879-8622-3

LC 2007-4000

The author "explores why the immigrants left Eastern Europe, how they came here, and what they found when they arrived. He describes their journey in steerage, their life in tenements, and their search for jobs. Also under discussion are Yiddish theater, journalism, and literature, as well as such famous personalities as Jacob Adler, George Burns, Fanny Brice, Irving Berlin, George Gershwin, Sholom

Aleichem, Eddie Cantor, and Jack Benny. . . . Words and pictures combine to make this book a foremost chronicle of Jewish immigration." Booklist

Includes bibliographical references

The **European** Americans; Rodney P. Carlisle, general editor. Facts on File 2011 243p il map (Multicultural America) $55

Grades: 9 10 11 12   **305.8**

1. European Americans -- History

ISBN 978-0-8160-7816-5

"The European Americans examines the history of this ethnic group in America, as well as the foods they ate, how they dressed, entertainment, work, education, popular pastimes, political activity, and their contributions and conflicts in American society." Publisher's note

Includes glossary and bibliographical references

Franklin, John Hope

★ **From** slavery to freedom; a history of African Americans. [by] John Hope Franklin, Evelyn Higginbotham. 9th ed.; McGraw-Hill 2010 xxv, 710p il map $100.63

Grades: 11 12 Adult   **305.8**

1. Slavery -- United States 2. African Americans -- History

ISBN 978-0-07-296378-6; 0-07-296378-6

LC 2009-42935

First published 1947

A survey of African-Americans history from slavery to the present.

Includes bibliographical references

★ **Freedom** on my mind; the Columbia documentary history of the African American experience. Manning Marable, general editor; Nishani Frazier and John McMillian, assistant editors. Columbia University Press 2003 734p $80

Grades: 11 12 Adult   **305.8**

1. African Americans -- History -- Sources

ISBN 0-231-10890-7

LC 2003-51605

This "anthology features the works of noteworthy figures of African American history and culture . . . and provides a tapestry of personal correspondence, excerpts from slave narratives and autobiographies, leaflets, speeches, oral histories and interviews, political manifestos, song lyrics, and important statements of black institutions and organizations. . . . A necessary text of readings for both introductory and advanced African American studies courses." Choice

Includes bibliographical references

Gay, Kathlyn

Bigotry and intolerance; the ultimate teen guide. Kathlyn Gay. The Scarecrow Press, Inc. 2013 174 p. (It happened to me) (cloth: alk. paper) $50

Grades: 9 10 11 12   **305.8**

1. Toleration 2. Discrimination

ISBN 0810883600; 9780810883604

LC 2012043200

In this book, author Kathlyn Gay "looks at the various reasons why people of all age levels and backgrounds feel the need to disparage others. This book also offers help to teens who are the object of fear and hatred by showing them how to combat such behavior. . . . Aimed at young adults who are interested in fighting bigotry and intolerance, this book will help teens who suffer from the small-mindedness of others." (Publisher's note)

"This book examines bigotry throughout history: intolerance based on religion, race, sexual identification, and other personal traits; bullying in schools, online, and on the job; the language, symbols, music, and speech of bigotry; censorship; hate groups; and more. The final chapter supports the idea that concerted efforts of various groups and programs may help to lessen intolerance. The balanced text is informative, interesting, and straightforward." (School Library Journal)

Includes bibliographical references and index

Gonzalez, Juan

★ **Harvest** of empire; a history of Latinos in America. Rev. ed.; Penguin Books 2011 xxiv, 392p map pa $18

Grades: 11 12 Adult   **305.8**
1. Latinos (U.S.) 2. Hispanic Americans
ISBN 978-0-14-311928-9

                LC 2011006880

First published 2000

The author notes that with rising immigration "Latinos will constitute the largest minority in the nation by 2010. Gonzalez explores why Spanish and British colonization experiences were so different, particularly the divergence in attitudes on slavery and race. . . . This is an important book for understanding a major American ethnic group." Booklist

Includes bibliographical references

Griffin, John Howard

★ **Black** like me; the definitive Griffin estate edition, corrected from original manuscripts. foreword by Studs Terkel; with historic photographs by Don Rutledge; and an afterword by Robert Bonazzi. 2nd Wings Press ed., with index; Wings Press 2006 243p il $29.95

Grades: 11 12 Adult   **305.8**
1. Prejudices 2. African Americans -- Southern States
ISBN 978-0-930324-73-5

First published 1961 by Houghton Mifflin

The author, "who is white, a Catholic, and a Texan, conceived and carried out the unusual notion of blackening his skin with a newly developed pigment drug and traveling through the Deep South as a Negro. This book, part of which appeared in the Negro magazine Sepia, is a journal account of that experience." New Yorker

Includes bibliographical references

IndiVisible; African-Native American lives in the Americas. general editor, Gabrielle Tayac. Smithsonian Institution's National Museum of the American Indian in association with the National Mu 2009 256p il map pa $19.95

Grades: 11 12 Adult   **305.8**
1. Racially mixed people 2. Native Americans -- History 3. African Americans -- History 4. United States -- Ethnic relations
ISBN 978-1-58834-271-3

                LC 2009-34290

"This book complements the IndiVisible exhibition at the National Museum of the American Indian (NMAI). . . . [Tayac] brings together 27 scholars who share what being an African-Native means to them. The book is organized thematically, emphasizing racial policy, community identity issues, peaceful and physical resistance, and cultural lifeways. . . . The volume's photographic images and narrative approach speak well to the collaboration necessary for addressing identity politics—a complicated and often contentious subject." Choice

Includes bibliographical references

It's not all black and white; multiracial youth speak out. St. Stephen's Community House. Annick Press 2012 109 p. $12.95

Grades: 8 9 10 11 12   **305.8**
1. Prejudices 2. Minority youth 3. Identity (Psychology) 4. Racially mixed people
ISBN 1554513804; 9781554513802

In this collection of "poems, interviews, and short essays, a group of young people describe being biracial, multiracial, or of mixed race. . . . Themes include navigating mixed-race relationships, dealing with prejudice and the assumptions people make based on appearances, and working through identity confusion to arrive at a strong and positive sense of self." (Publisher's note)

Iyer, Deepa

We too sing America; South Asian, Arab, Muslim, and Sikh immigrants shape our multiracial future. Deepa Iyer. The New Press 2015 256 p. tables (hardback) $25.95

Grades: 11 12 Adult   **305.8**
1. Racism 2. Xenophobia 3. Hate crimes 4. Islamophobia -- United States 5. United States -- Race relations 6. United States -- Race relations -- 21st century 7. Racism -- United States -- History -- 21st century 8. Xenophobia -- United States -- History -- 21st century 9. Hate crimes -- United States -- History -- 21st century 10. Islamophobia -- United States -- History -- 21st century 11. Immigrants -- United States -- Social conditions -- 21st century
ISBN 9781620970140

                LC 2015020036

In this book, "activist Deepa Iyer catalogs recent racial flashpoints, from the 2012 massacre at the Sikh gurdwara in Oak Creek, Wisconsin, to the violent opposition to the Islamic Center of Murfreesboro, Tennessee, and to the Park 51 Community Center in Lower Manhattan. Iyer asks whether hate crimes should be considered domestic terrorism and explores the role of the state in perpetuating racism through detentions, national registration programs, police profiling, and constant surveillance." (Publisher's note)

"A welcome addition to the growing literature of race, ethnicity, and religion from the perspectives of immigrant groups within the United States. Both the general public and policymakers will benefit." LJ

Includes bibliographical references and index

Letters from Black America; edited by Pamela Newkirk. Farrar, Straus, and Giroux 2009 372p il $30

Grades: 9 10 11 12 Adult   **305.8**

1. African Americans -- Social conditions 2. American letters -- African American authors

ISBN 978-0-374-10109-1; 0-374-10109-4

LC 2008-41265

"This anthology features the writings of individuals who range from highly celebrated to barely literate and presents stories that are of vital historical importance and touchingly personal. Newkirk divides the letters by topic—covering family, courtship and romance, politics and social justice, education and scholarship, war, art and culture, and the African diaspora—and offers concise introductions to each. . . . While this unique collection of letters represents a frank depiction of the black experience, the great achievement is that these writings often go far beyond race and class to simply tell the story of the human experience in America." Libr J

Includes bibliographical references

Litwack, Leon F.

The **Harvard** guide to African-American history; Evelyn Brooks Higginbotham, editor-in-chief; Leon F. Litwack and Darlene Clark Hine, general editors; Randall K. Burkett, associate editor; foreword by Henry Louis Gates, Jr. Harvard Univ. Press 2001 xxxvi, 923p (Harvard University Press reference library) $125

Grades: 11 12 Adult   **305.8**

1. African Americans -- History

ISBN 0-674-00276-8

LC 00-53861

"The first section includes 12 essays on historical research aids divided by topics such as films, newspapers, Internet resources, primary sources on microform, government documents, manuscript collections, and oral history archives. The second section contains comprehensive bibliographies . . . further subdivided into specific themes such as race relations, religion, color and class, politics and voting, urban conditions, and science and technology. The third section provides sources related to special subject matters: autobiographies of African Americans, studies identified by geographic region, and studies of African American women." Libr J

Miller, Calvin Craig

Backlash; race riots in the Jim Crow Era. Calvin Craig Miller. Morgan Reynolds Pub. 2012 128 p.

Grades: 8 9 10 11 12   **305.8**

1. Racism -- History 2. Riots -- United States 3. African Americans -- History 4. Cities and towns -- United States 5. United States -- Race relations -- History 6. United States -- Race relations 7. African Americans -- Crimes against 8. Riots -- United States -- History -- 20th century 9. United States -- Race relations -- History -- 20th century 10. African Americans -- Crimes against -- History -- 20th century

ISBN 1599351838; 9781599351834

LC 2011005673

This book details the history of "violence against African Americans in the Jim Crow era. . . . In cities, without the protection of secrecy, violence manifested itself in white mob attacks against black communities. This . . . [book] recognizes seven of the worst attacks that occurred in cities across the United States. Starting with the 1898 riot in Wilmington, North Carolina, in which white supremacists overturned an elected government . . . and killed 30 blacks, the . . . text goes on to cover similar events in Atlanta, Springfield, East St. Louis, Chicago, Tulsa, and Detroit. In each case, [Calvin Craig] Miller notes numerous similarities, including rage among working-class whites over competition with blacks for jobs and affordable housing, and rumors fueled by racist media." (Booklist)

Includes bibliographical references (p. 123-124) and index

The **Native** Americans; Rodney P. Carlisle, general editor. Facts on File 2011 242p il map (Multicultural America) $55

Grades: 9 10 11 12   **305.8**

1. Native Americans -- History

ISBN 978-0-8160-7817-2

This book "explores the history and customs of [Native Americans,] . . . covering everything from the foods they ate and how they dressed to popular pastimes, political activity, and more." Publisher's note

Includes glossary and bibliographical references

Rose, Tricia

The **hip** hop wars; what we talk about when we talk about hip hop. BasicCivitas 2008 308p pa $15.95

Grades: 11 12 Adult   **305.8**

1. Hip-hop 2. Rap music 3. African Americans -- Social conditions

ISBN 978-0-465-00897-1; 0-465-00897-6

LC 2008-31637

"Rose's convincing arguments and challenges of assumptions . . . make this an important title. . . . This title definitely deserves readers." Libr J

Includes bibliographical references

Sanna, Ellyn

We shall all be free; survivors of racism. Mason Crest Publishers 2009 128p il (Survivors: ordinary people, extraordinary circumstances) lib bdg $24.95

Grades: 7 8 9 10   **305.8**

1. Racism 2. Minorities 3. Prejudices

ISBN 978-1-4222-0458-0; 1-4222-0458-8

LC 2008-50326

"Sanna covers racism of all kinds, including genocide in parts of Africa; the deplorable conditions of Native Americans; anti-Semitism; racism against the Roma, better known as Gypsies, and against African Americans; and the conditions faced by some immigrants. . . . [This title exposes] the underbelly of society, explaining terms that might be unfamiliar and providing multiple examples of the issues." SLJ

Includes bibliographical references

Scarpaci, Vincenza

The **journey** of the Italians in America; foreword by Gary R. Mormino. Pelican Pub. Co. 2008 319p il $40

Grades: 9 10 11 12 Adult   **305.8**

1. Italian Americans 2. Immigrants -- United States 3. United States -- Immigration and emigration

ISBN 978-1-58980-245-2; 1-58980-245-4

LC 2008-18199

"Primarily a photographic record accompanied by extensive captions and short chapter introductions, this fascinating historical account . . . is divided into nine chapters, from embarkation and arrival to assimilation and ethnic resurgence. The book does not dodge contentious issues, like organized crime and the lionization of Columbus. Its many rare illustrations, including period photos, sheet music, advertisements, and document facsimiles, tell individual stories of survival, persistence, ingenuity, and community with more immediacy than any essay." Libr J

Should America pay? slavery and the raging debate over reparations. {edited by} Raymond A. Winbush. Amistad 2003 396p hardcover o.p. pa $13.95

Grades: 11 12 Adult   **305.8**

1. African Americans 2. Slavery -- United States

ISBN 0-06-008310-7; 0-06-008311-5 pa

LC 2002-27927

The author addresses the issue "of paying reparations to black Americans for slavery. . . . He explores numerous voices within the reparations movement and commentary on the various stages and aspects of the movement. He also examines the significance of grassroots organizations in the development of the reparations movement, as well as legal perspectives and dissenting voices. This is a complete and balanced look at a controversial topic." Booklist

Includes bibliographical references

Wright, Simeon

Simeon's story; an eyewitness account of the kidnapping of Emmett Till. [by] Simeon Wright; with Herb Boyd. Lawrence Hill Books 2010 144p il map $19.95

Grades: 6 7 8 9 10   **305.8**

1. Racism 2. Children 3. Lynching 4. Trials (Homicide) 5. Murder victims 6. Mississippi -- Race relations 7. African Americans -- Mississippi

ISBN 978-1-55652-783-8; 1-55652-783-7

LC 2009-33631

"Simeon Wright was 12 years old when his cousin Emmett 'Bobo' Till came from Chicago to visit relatives in Mississippi. . . . One hot August night in 1955, Till whistled at a white female store clerk, setting off a chain of events that left an indelible mark not only on our nation's history, but also on the cousin who witnessed Till's gaffe and eventual kidnapping. Wright's story is chilling, and his honest account will hook readers from the beginning." SLJ

305.8924 Jews

Goldstein, Phyllis

A **convenient** hatred; the history of antisemitism. Phyllis Goldstein; foreword by Sir Harold Evans. Facing History & Ourselves 2012 405 p., [9] p. of platesp ill., maps $17.95

Grades: 11 12 Adult   **305.8924**

1. Prejudices 2. Antisemitism 3. Jews -- History 4. Antisemitism -- History 5. Jews -- Persecutions -- History

ISBN 0981954383; 9780981954387; 9780983787013

LC 2011935882

This book by Phyllis Goldstein presents an overview of anti-Semitism throughout Western history. "It raises important questions about the consequences of our assumptions and beliefs and the ways we, as individuals and as members of a society, make distinctions between "us" and "them," right and wrong, good and evil. These questions are both universal and particular." (Publisher's note)

Includes bibliographical references (p. [363]-374) and index

305.896 Africans and people of African descent

Du Bois, W. E. B.

★ The **Oxford** W. E. B. Du Bois reader; edited by Eric J. Sundquist. Oxford Univ. Press 1996 680p pa $34.95

Grades: 11 12 Adult   **305.896**

1. African Americans 2. United States -- Race relations

ISBN 0-19-509178-7

LC 95-21307

This reader covers Du Bois's "writing career, from the 1890s through the early 1960s. The volume selects key essays and longer works that portray the range of Du Bois's thought on such subjects as African American culture, the politics and sociology of American race relations, art and music, black leadership, gender and women's rights, Pan-Africanism and anti-colonialism, and Communism in the U.S. and abroad." Publisher's note

Includes bibliographical references

Feelings, Tom

The **middle** passage; white ships/black cargo. introduction by John Henrik Clarke. Dial Bks. 1995 un il map $75

Grades: 7 8 9 10   **305.896**

1. Blacks in art 2. Slavery -- Pictorial works

ISBN 0-8037-1804-7

LC 95-13866

"The Middle Passage is the name given to one of the most tragic ordeals in history: the cruel and terrifying journey of enslaved Africans across the Atlantic Ocean. In this seminal work, master artist Tom Feelings tells the complete story of this horrific diaspora in sixty-four extraordinary narrative paintings. Achingly real, they draw us into the lives of the millions of African men, women, and children who were savagely torn from their beautiful homelands, crowded into disease-ridden "death ships," and transported under nightmarish conditions to the so-called New World." (Publisher's note)

"Feelings's art speaks to the soul in this magnificent visual record of the Black Diaspora in the Americas. Clarke provides a concise narrative of the slave trade, and then readers pause at a double-spread image of a man, woman, bird, sun, and land before the pages become horrific. Guns, yokes, chains, whips,knives one can see anger, grief, sadness, pain, and almost hear the screams coming from the captives' open mouths. The crowded holes, ankle chains, branding, rats, and sharks swarming around the ship as bodies are thrown overboard all build, image byimage, to the reality of man's inhumanity to man. . . . A powerfully rendered reality that all teens deserve the opportunity to experience." SLJ

Includes bibliographical references

305.897 American native peoples--social aspects

Urban Tribes; Native Americans in the City. Edited by Lisa Charleyboy and Mary Beth Leatherdale. Firefly Books Ltd 2015 136 p. illustrations, color, b/w $21.95
Grades: 7 8 9 10 11 12   **305.897**
1. Native Americans
ISBN 1554517516; 9781554517510

This book, edited by Lisa Charleyboy and Mary Beth Leatherdale, "profiles young urban Natives from across North America, exploring how they connect with Native culture and values in their contemporary lives. Their stories are as diverse as they are. From a young Dene woman pursuing a MBA at Stanford to a Pima photographer in Phoenix to a Mohawk actress in New York, these urban Natives share their unique perspectives to bridge the divide between their past and their future." (Publisher's note)

"A refreshingly authentic, edgy, and captivating work that will appeal to young people." SLJ

companion to dreaming in Indian

305.9 People by occupation and miscellaneous social statuses; people with disabilities and illnesses, gifted people

Bergquist, James M.
Daily life in immigrant America, 1820-1870. Greenwood Press 2008 306p il (Greenwood Press 'Daily life through history' series) $49.95
Grades: 9 10 11 12   **305.9**
1. Immigrants -- United States 2. United States -- History -- 19th century 3. United States -- Immigration and emigration
ISBN 978-0-313-33698-0; 0-313-33698-9
LC 2007-35360

The author "has written the best history ever of . . . [this] subject. . . . The perfect history for those who want to learn more about the peopling of the US." Publ Wkly

Includes glossary and bibliographical references

Martinez, Ruben
The **new** Americans; photographs by Joseph Rodríguez. New Press 2004 251p il $25
Grades: 11 12 Adult   **305.9**
1. United States -- Immigration and emigration
ISBN 1-565-84792-X
LC 2003-70621

"Masterfully evoking such diverse settings as a Palestinian wedding in Chicago, a raucous ball game in Guatemala City and a torpid migrant trailer camp in California, Martínez's writing is clear-eyed and incisive—and sometimes heartbreaking and hilarious." Publ Wkly

Includes bibliographical references

Moorehead, Caroline
Human cargo; a journey among refugees. H. Holt 2005 330p maps $26; pa $16
Grades: 11 12 Adult   **305.9**
1. Refugees
ISBN 0-8050-7443-0; 0-312-42561-9 pa
LC 2004-54239

The author "tours a number of refugee milieus, visiting, among others, Liberian refugees in Cairo, Mexican migrants waiting to cross into the United States, Mideastern refugees detained in Australian internment camps and Palestinian refugees still nursing hopes of returning to a homeland they have never seen. . . . Moorehead draws sympathetic portraits of individual refugees, replete with horror stories of the travails they fled and their precarious but hopeful efforts to build new lives, but also pulls back to examine what she says are the sometimes counterproductive policies of aid organizations and the indifference and callousness of Western governments." Publ Wkly

Includes bibliographical references

306 Culture and institutions

★ **American** values: opposing viewpoints; David M. Haugen, book editor. Greenhaven Press 2009 227p il (Opposing viewpoints series) lib bdg $39.70; pa $27.50
Grades: 9 10 11 12   **306**
1. Social values 2. United States -- Moral conditions
ISBN 978-0-7377-4190-2 lib bdg; 0-7377-4190-2 lib bdg; 978-0-7377-4191-9 pa; 0-7377-4191-0 pa
LC 2008-31771

Articles in this anthology discuss what social values America considers important, whether or not they are threatened, the nature of patriotism, and whether American values can be shared with other nations.

Includes bibliographical references

Bales, Kevin
Slavery today; [by] Kevin Bales and Becky Cornell. Groundwood Books 2008 141p il (Groundwork guides) $18.95; pa $10
Grades: 7 8 9 10   **306**
1. Slavery
ISBN 978-0-88899-772-2; 0-88899-772-8; 978-0-88899-773-9 pa; 0-88899-773-6 pa

"Easy to read and extremely engaging, the work traces the existence and occurrence of slavery in modern factories, jungles, and farms around the world, and discusses prostitution and strategies for ending slavery in the global market. . . . Students will find this book of great use for research papers, but it is also highly readable for personal enrichment. The language used is not complicated, the prose is understandable, and the personal narratives are passionate, even when describing awful, inhumane acts." Libr Media Connect

Includes bibliographical references

★ **Growing** up in slavery; stories of young slaves as told by themselves. edited by Yuval Taylor; illustrations by Kathleen Judge. Lawrence Hill Books 2005 xxv, 230p il $22.95; pa $9.95

Grades: 9 10 11 12   **306**

1. Slavery -- United States

ISBN 1-55652-548-6; 1-55652-635-0 pa

"Ten African Americans—among them Frederick Douglass and Harriet Jacobs, as well as less well-known individuals—tell what it was like to be a child and teenager under slavery. . . . Invaluable for students in search of primary-source material, and many selections will make riveting read-alouds." Booklist

Includes bibliographical references

Hill, Jeff

★ **Life** events and rites of passage; the customs and symbols of major life-cycle milestones, including cultural, secular, and religious traditions observed in the United States. by Jeff Hill and Peggy Daniels; foreword by Clifton D. Bryant. Omnigraphics 2008 498p il lib bdg $71

Grades: 8 9 10 11 12   **306**

1. Rites and ceremonies 2. United States -- Social life and customs

ISBN 978-0-7808-0735-8

LC 2007-35420

"This book provides a good starting point for those needing basic information, especially since it approaches topics from a wide variety of cultural viewpoints." Libr J

Includes bibliographical references

Mark, Joan T.

★ **Margaret** Mead; coming of age in America. [by] Joan Mark. Oxford Univ. Press 1998 110p il (Oxford portraits in science) $28

Grades: 7 8 9 10   **306**

1. Anthropologists 2. Curators 3. Writers on science

ISBN 0-19-511679-8

LC 98-18604

This is a biography of the American anthropologist who wrote Coming of Age in Samoa. Bibliography. Index. "Grades six to ten." (Libr J)

An "account of the life and works of the influential, pioneering anthropologist. . . . Mark does a fine job of abstracting Mead's research and published works and showing why they were both critically acclaimed and criticized. The reader-friendly prose is peppered with fascinating anecdotes and photos. Mead herself is presented as a complex, intriguing figure, with fascinating, often contradictory, public and private lives." Booklist

Includes bibliographical references

Popular culture; Noah Berlatsky, book editor. Greenhaven Press 2011 220p il map (Global viewpoints) $37.30; pa $26.50

Grades: 9 10 11 12   **306**

1. Popular culture

ISBN 978-0-7377-5118-5; 978-0-7377-5119-2 pa

LC 2010019294

This "book hops all around the world, exploring how various laws affect pop culture such as music, manga, anime, and intellectual property rights. Some of the essays are quite sophisticated in legal content. It is a wide-ranging collection of topics that sound eclectic ('Jamaican Dancehall Performers Who Espouse Homophobia Should Be Prevented from Performing in Canada'), but that all come around to the same concept of free speech versus illegal content." SLJ

Includes bibliographical references

306.362   Slavery

Conkling, Winifred

Passenger on the Pearl; the true story of Emily Edmonson's flight from slavery. Winifred Conkling. First edition Algonquin Young Readers 2015 176 p. illustrations, maps $17.95

Grades: 7 8 9 10   **306.362**

1. Fugitive slaves 2. Pearl (Schooner) 3. Underground Railroad -- Washington Region 4. Fugitive slaves -- Washington Region -- History -- 19th century 5. Antislavery movements -- United States -- History -- 19th century

ISBN 1616201967; 9781616201968

LC 2014029246

This book presents a "historical narrative concerning several people involved in an attempted slave escape in 1848. The Pearl was to ferry 13-year-old Emily Edmonson and scores of other runaway slaves from Washington DC down the Potomac River and up the Chesapeake Bay. However, the ship was captured before reaching free soil. [Winifred] Conkling narrates the tumultuous stories of Edmonson, her family, and the others involved." (School Library Journal)

"By examining the intersecting experiences of enslaved people, abolitionists, free people of color, slave owners, and slave traders, this book provides an effective antidote to the oversimplified picture of slavery in America painted by some outdated textbooks." Booklist

Includes bibliographical references

Postma, Johannes

The **Atlantic** slave trade. Greenwood Press 2003 xxii, 177p map (Greenwood guides to historic events, 1500-1900) $45

Grades: 11 12 Adult   **306.362**

1. Slave trade

ISBN 0-313-31862-X

LC 2002-35338

The author "covers the entire Atlantic slave trade era, from the 1400s to the final abolition of chattel slavery in the New World in 1888. The focus is on Africa and the entire New World. While he describes the many horrors of the Middle Passage, he also examines how the slave trade contributed to the development of the modern international economy. The last chapters discuss the efforts to abolish the slave trade and its legacy." SLJ

Includes bibliographical references

306.4   Specific aspects of culture

★ **Are** athletes good role models? Kathy L. Hahn, book editor. Greenhaven Press 2010 122p (At issue. Sports) lib bdg $31.80; pa $22.50

Grades: 9 10 11 12   **306.4**

1. Athletes 2. Conduct of life
ISBN 978-0-7377-4646-4 lib bdg; 0-7377-4646-7 lib bdg; 978-0-7377-4647-1 pa; 0-7377-4647-5 pa
LC 2009-37394

The articles in this anthology weigh the merits and demerits of using athletes as role models.

Includes bibliographical references

Body image; Heidi Williams, book editor. Greenhaven Press 2009 112p il (Issues that concern you) lib bdg $33.70

Grades: 9 10 11 12   **306.4**

1. Body image
ISBN 978-0-7377-4182-7; 0-7377-4182-1
LC 2008-26756

This book about body image has an "accessible text and a clear layout. . . . Colorful charts and graphs, color photos with informative captions, and a list of sources to contact add to . . . [its] research value." SLJ

Includes bibliographical references

Celebrity culture: opposing viewpoints; Roman Espejo, book editor. Greenhaven Press 2011 191p il (Opposing viewpoints series) $41.70; pa $28.90

Grades: 9 10 11 12   **306.4**

1. Fame 2. Celebrities 3. Popular culture
ISBN 978-0-7377-5213-7; 978-0-7377-5214-4 pa
LC 2010032979

Articles in this anthology discuss whether celebrity culture is a problem, how it affects young people, whether celebrity activism benefits society, and what the future holds for celebrity culture.

Includes bibliographical references

★ The **culture** of beauty: opposing viewpoints; Roman Espejo, book editor. Greenhaven Press 2009 220p il (Opposing viewpoints series) lib bdg $38.50; pa $26.75

Grades: 8 9 10 11 12   **306.4**

1. Aesthetics 2. Personal appearance
ISBN 978-0-7377-4508-5 lib bdg; 0-7377-4508-8 lib bdg; 978-0-7377-4509-2 pa; 0-7377-4509-6 pa
LC 2009-33675

Examines both sides of the issues surrounding the obsession with image, from beauty standards to societal impact and from individual aspirations of beauty to effects of the beauty and fashion industries.

Includes bibliographical references

Fadiman, Anne

★ The **spirit** catches you and you fall down; a Hmong child, her American doctors, and the collision of two cultures. Anne Fadiman. Farrar, Straus & Giroux 1997 xi, 339p $25; (pbk.) $15

Grades: 11 12 Adult   **306.4**

1. Epilepsy 2. Medical care 3. Culture conflict 4. Hmong (Asian people) 5. Epilepsy in children 6. Hmong Americans -- Medicine 7. Intercultural communication 8. Hmong American children -- Medical care -- California 9. Transcultural medical care -- California -- Case studies
ISBN 0374267812; 9780374533403
LC 97005175

Los Angeles Times Book Prizes: Current Interest (1997), National Book Critics Circle Award: General Nonfiction (1997)

This book presents an "anthropological exploration of the Hmong population in Merced County, California. Following the case of Lia (a Hmong child with a progressive and unpredictable form of epilepsy), Fadiman maps out the controversies raised by the collision between Western medicine and holistic healing traditions of Hmong immigrants. Unable to enter the Laotian forest to find herbs for Lia that will 'fix her spirit,' her family becomes resigned to the Merced County emergency system, which has little understanding of Hmong animist traditions. [Anne] Fadiman reveals the rigidity and weaknesses of these two ethnographically separated cultures." (Library Journal)

Includes bibliographical references (p. [311]-324) and index.

Leonard, Annie

The **story** of stuff; how our obsession with stuff is trashing the planet, our communities, and our health--and a vision for change. [by] Annie Leonard with Ariane Conrad. Free Press 2010 xxxiv, 317p il $26

Grades: 11 12 Adult   **306.4**

1. Material culture 2. Consumption (Economics)
ISBN 978-1-4391-2566-3
LC 2009-42207

"Leonard explains that our consumer goods undergo extraction, production, distribution, consumption, and disposal processes that are trashing the planet, diminishing our resources, exploiting workers, and contributing to high levels of disease and death. She advocates an international cooperative effort to develop domestic and international policies and laws that will reverse our planet's ecological decline and leave a sustainable world for future generations." LJ

306.7   Sexual relations

Age of consent; Olivia Ferguson and Hayley Mitchell Haugen, book editors. Greenhaven Press 2010 93p (At issue. Teen issues) $31.80; pa $22.50

Grades: 9 10 11 12   **306.7**

1. Youth -- Sexual behavior   2. Youth -- Law and legislation

ISBN 978-0-7377-4669-3; 0-7377-4669-6; 978-0-7377-4670-9 pa; 0-7377-4670-X pa

       LC 2009-40551

"These 13 articles, ranging in length from four to seven pages, tackle the murky moral issue of legislating the age of first consensual sexual experiences. The authors address establishing uniform age-of-consent laws, the dilemma of teaching students about safe sex and then prosecuting them for sexual activity, what to do about sexting, applying a life-long sex-offender label to a teen, and parental notification of a minor seeking an abortion; and examine sources of pressure for reform. . . . These well-written entries provide solid report information, and the book should be considered for purchase where the curriculum requires material on early sexual circumstances in relation to the law." SLJ

Includes bibliographical references

Feinstein, Stephen

   Sexuality and teens; what you should know about sex, abstinence, birth control, pregnancy, and stds. Enslow Publishers 2010 104p il (Issues in focus today) lib bdg $31.93

Grades: 7 8 9 10   **306.7**

1. Youth -- Sexual behavior

ISBN 978-0-7660-3312-2; 0-7660-3312-0

       LC 2009-1373

"This text provides a well-balanced look at sexual attitudes and behaviors as they relate to today's youth. . . . The book could be useful for basic report and debate information or as a jumping-off point for class discussions." SLJ

Includes glossary and bibliographical references

Forssberg, Manne

   ★ **Sex** for guys; translated by Maria Lundin. Groundwood Books/House of Anansi 2007 142p il (Groundwork guides) $15.95; pa $9.95

Grades: 7 8 9 10 11 12   **306.7**

1. Sex education   2. Men -- Sexual behavior

ISBN 978-0-88899-770-8; 978-0-88899-771-5 pa

This "will prove invaluable to guys bombarded with less sensitive and comprehensive media messages. . . . This is a witty, sane treatment of the things that drive guys crazy—a must read for teens with questions." Bull Cent Child Books

   Includes bibliographical references

Howard-Barr, Elissa

   The **truth** about sexual behavior and unplanned pregnancy; Robert N. Golden, general editor, Fred Peterson, general editor; Elissa Howard-Barr and Stacey Barrineau, principal authors. 2nd ed.; Facts On File 2009 224p (Truth about series) $35

Grades: 9 10 11 12   **306.7**

1. Sexual hygiene   2. Teenage pregnancy   3. Sexual behavior

ISBN 978-0-8160-7634-5; 0-8160-7634-0

       LC 2009-8403

First published 2005 under the editorship of Mark J. Kittleson

Provides "information about everything from contraception to the media's portrayal of sex. . . . [This book offers] advice to teenagers and encourages discussion with parents and peers." Publisher's note

Includes glossary and bibliographical references

Teen sex; Olivia Ferguson, book editor. Greenhaven Press 2010 105p (At issue. Teen issues) $31.80; pa $22.50

Grades: 9 10 11 12   **306.7**

1. Sex education   2. Sexual abstinence   3. Youth -- Sexual behavior

ISBN 978-0-7377-5095-9; 978-0-7377-5096-6 pa

       LC 2010022997

The articles in this anthology discuss such topics as abstinence-only education, sex education, how teens view oral sex, and abortion among teens.

Includes bibliographical references

The **V-word;** true stories about first-time sex. [edited by] Amber J. Keyser. Beyond Words 2016 208 p. (hardcover: alk. paper) $19.99

Grades: 9 10 11 12   **306.7**

1. Sex   2. Women -- Sexual behavior   3. Virginity   4. First sexual experiences

ISBN 9781582705217; 9781582705224

       LC 2015019131

This book, edited by Amber J. Keyser, offers "an honest and poignant collection of essays by women about losing their virginity in their teens. . . . Deciding to have sex for the first time is a choice that's often fraught with anxiety and joy. . . . Some of their experiences happened too soon, some at just the right time, but all paint a broad picture of what first-time sex is really like." (Publisher's note)

"Occasionally, the tone is overly sentimental, and teens allergic to sincerity might bristle, but, overall, this is an excellent resource for teens interested in sex that gives them not only meaningful and important tools for health, such as concrete advice about contraceptives and consent, but a supportive, sex-positive voice in a culture that's still fairly uncomfortable addressing sexuality, in teen girls in particular." Booklist

   Includes bibliographical references and index

306.76   Sexual orientation, transgenderism, intersexuality

Andrews, Arin

   Some assembly required; the not-so-secret life of a transgender teen. Arin Andrews. Simon & Schuster Books for Young Readers 2014 256 p. (hardback) $17.99

Grades: 9 10 11 12   **306.76**

1. Autobiographies   2. Transgender people   3. Transgenderism -- United States   4. Transgender youth

-- United States -- Biography
ISBN 1481416758; 9781481416757; 9781481416764
LC 2014010948

In this memoir, "Seventeen-year-old Arin Andrews shares all the hilarious, painful, and poignant details of undergoing gender reassignment as a high school student. . . . Arin details the journey that led him to make the life-transforming decision to undergo gender reassignment as a high school junior. . . . Arin reveals the challenges he faced as a girl, the . . . anger he felt after getting kicked out of his private school, and . . . changes . . . once his transition began." (Publisher's note)

"This is an invaluable title that puts empathetic human faces on a condition that otherwise might be presented as coldly clinical." Booklist

Bausum, Ann

★ **Stonewall**; breaking out in the fight for gay rights. Ann Bausum. Viking Books for Young Readers 2015 128 p. illustrations (hardback) $16.99
Grades: 8 9 10 11 12 **306.76**
1. Gay rights 2. Civil rights 3. Stonewall Riots, New York, N.Y., 1969 4. Gay men -- United States -- History -- 20th century 5. Lesbians -- United States -- History -- 20th century 6. Greenwich Village (New York, N.Y.) -- History -- 20th century 7. Gay liberation movement -- United States -- History -- 20th century
ISBN 0670016799; 9780670016792
LC 2014039812

Author Ann Bausum presents this "exploration of the Stonewall Riots and the national Gay Rights movement that followed. In 1969 being gay in the United States was a criminal offense. It meant living a closeted life or surviving on the fringes of society. The Stonewall Inn, a Mafia-run, filthy, overpriced bar in New York City's Greenwich Village, was one of them." (Publisher's note)

"Bausum begins her history of the gay rights movement with a careful, detailed exposition of the June 1969 Stonewall riots, laying out the events leading up to the clash between the Greenwich Village gay community and the police and putting those events in the context of time and place. She dedicates the first half of the book to the riots themselves, drawing on reports, interviews, and other first-person accounts to put together a candid linear narrative that takes into consideration the perspectives of both sides of the conflict. . . . Bausum writes with the precision of a journalist; there is never any doubt as to what she wonders, what she conjectures, and what she knows." Horn Book

Includes filmography and bibliographical references (pages 111-115) and index

Dawson, James

★ This Book Is Gay; by James Dawson (Author), David Levithan (Introduction) Sourcebooks Inc 2015 272 p. illustrations (pbk.) $9.99
Grades: 9 10 11 12 **306.76**
1. LGBT people 2. LGBT literature
ISBN 1492617822; 1492617830; 9781492617822; 9781492617839
LC 2015002230

This book, by James Dawson, "is for everyone, regardless of gender or sexual preference. . . . Inside you'll find the answers to all the questions you ever wanted to ask: from sex to politics, hooking up to stereotypes, coming out and more. This . . . exploration of sexuality and what it's like to grow up LGBT also includes real stories from people across the gender and sexual spectrums." (Publisher's note)

"An insightful option for those with questions about what it's like to be LGBTQ." SLJ

The **Full** spectrum; a new generation of writing about gay, lesbian, bisexual, transgender, questioning, and other identities. edited by David Levithan & Billy Merrell. Knopf 2006 272p il hardcover o.p. pa $9.95
Grades: 8 9 10 11 12 **306.76**
1. Gay men 2. Lesbians 3. Gender role 4. Homosexuality 5. Sex role
ISBN 0-375-93290-9; 0-375-83290-4 pa
LC 2005-23435

"The 40 contributions to this invaluable collection about personal identity have two things in common: all are nonfiction and all are by writers under the age of 23. Beyond that, diversity is the order of the day, and the result is a vivid demonstration of how extraordinarily broad the spectrum of sexual identity is among today's gay, lesbian, bisexual, transgender, and questioning youth. . . . Insightful, extraordinarily well written, and emotionally mature, the selections offer compelling, dramatic evidence that what is important is not what we are but who we are." Booklist

The **gender** quest workbook; a guide for teens and young adults exploring gender identity. Rylan Jay Testa, PhD, Deborah Coolhart, PhD, Jayme Peta, MA, MS; foreword by Ryan K. Sallans, M.A.; afterword by Arlene Istar Lev, LCSW-R, CASAC. New Harbinger Publications, Inc. 2015 168 p. illustrations (pbk.: alk. paper) $16.95
Grades: 7 8 9 10 11 12 Professional **306.76**
1. Gender role 2. Transgender teenagers 3. Sex differences (Psychology) 4. Transgenderism 5. Gender identity 6. Sex differences (Psychology)
ISBN 9781626252974
LC 2015032696

This guidebook "incorporates skills, exercises, and activities from evidence-based therapies—such as cognitive behavioral therapy (CBT)—to help you address the broad range of struggles you may encounter related to gender identity, such as anxiety, isolation, fear, and even depression." (Publisher's note)

"From inconspicuous activities such as people watching to more task-oriented ideas for encouraging young people to broach their concerns to family members, this volume serves as a valuable resource. While this isn't the best acquisition for libraries (it is truly a workbook), librarians would do well to be informed of its availability." LJ

Hill, Katie Rain

Rethinking normal; a memoir in transition. by Katie Rain Hill. First edition Simon & Schuster 2014 272 p. illustrations (hardback) $17.99
Grades: 9 10 11 12 **306.76**
1. Autobiographies 2. Transgender people 3.

Transgender people -- Identity 4. Transgender youth
-- United States -- Biography
ISBN 1481418238; 9781481418232; 9781481418249
LC 2014013051

This memoir by Katie Rain Hill tells how she "never
felt comfortable in her own skin. . . . Suffocating under her
peers' bullying and the mounting pressure to be 'normal,'
Katie tried to take her life at the age of eight years old.
After several other failed attempts, she finally understood
that 'Katie'--the girl trapped within her--was determined to
live." (Publisher's note)

"[A] warm, conversational and sometimes-irreverent
memoir . . . [Rethinking Normal] [w]ill both educate cisgen-
der readers and strike sparks of recognition in those questioning their own gender identities." Kirkus

Huegel, Kelly

★ GLBTQ; the survival guide for gay, lesbian,
bisexual, transgender, and questioning teens. rev &
updated 2nd ed.; Free Spirit Pub. 2011 229p il
Grades: 7 8 9 10 11 12   **306.76**
1. LGBT youth 2. Lesbians 3. Bisexual people 4.
Transgender people 5. Gay youth
ISBN 1-57542-363-0; 978-1-57542-363-0
LC 2010-48196
First published 2003

Describes the challenges faced by gay, lesbian, bisexual,
and transgendered teens, offers practical advice, real-life
experiences, and accessible resources and support groups.

"The information . . . [this] provides for GLBTQ teens
makes it a valuable addition to any high school or public
library collection." Voice Youth Advcocates

Includes bibliographical references

It gets better; coming out, overcoming bullying, and
creating a life worth living. [edited by] Dan Savage [and] Terry Miller. Penguin 2012 352p pbk
$16.00
Grades: 6 7 8 9 10 11 12   **306.76**
1. Bullies 2. Happiness 3. Gay teenagers 4. Bullying
5. Coming out (Sexual orientation)
ISBN 9780452297616

"It Gets Better is a collection of original essays and
expanded testimonials written to teens from celebrities, political leaders, and everyday people, because while many
LGBT teens can't see a positive future for themselves, we
can." (Publisher's note)

"I wish I could have told you things get better." The
words that became a call to action were born in the comments
section on a blog post written by Savage about 15-year-old
Billy Lucas. Savage, an author (The Kid, 1999), gay activist,
and sex-advice columnist, together with his partner, Miller,
launched the It Gets Better project on YouTube as a reaction
to Lucas' and two other suicides precipitated by gay bullying
during the summer of 2010. . . . It Gets Better—the book—
expands on a selection of those videos, capturing stories
from people of every background, including a startling collection of famous writers, entertainers, and politicians. Particularly noteworthy are essays from President Obama and
David Sedaris and a bilingual entry from a Mexican student
now living in Canada. This a resource every library should
have on hand." Booklist

Kuklin, Susan

★ Beyond magenta; transgender teens speak
out. Susan Kuklin. Candlewick Press 2014 192 p.
ill. (some col.) $22.99
Grades: 9 10 11 12   **306.76**
1. Teenagers 2. Transgender people
ISBN 0763656119; 9780763656119
LC 2013943071

Stonewall Honor Book: Children's & Young Adult Literature (2015)

For this book, author Susan Kuklin "met and interviewed
six transgender or gender-neutral young adults . . . to represent them thoughtfully and respectfully before, during, and
after their personal acknowledgment of gender preference.
Portraits, family photographs, and candid images grace the
pages, augmenting the emotional and physical journey each
youth has taken." (Publisher's note)

"The level of detail about their lives, and the diversity of their identities--including gender, sexuality, ethnicity, religion, and geography--provide a powerful antidote
to the isolation and stigma that some transgender youth
experience." SLJ

Includes bibliographical references

The letter Q; queer writers' notes to their younger
selves. edited by Sarah Moon; with contributing
editor James Lecesne. Arthur A. Levine Books
2012 281 p.
Grades: 9 10 11 12   **306.76**
1. Letters 2. Gay youth 3. Adolescence 4. Self-
acceptance 5. Gays -- Identity 6. Coming out (Sexual
orientation)
ISBN 0545399327; 9780545399326; 9780545399333
LC 2011041181

In this anthology edited by Sarah Moon, "sixty-three
award-winning authors such as Michael Cunningham, Amy
Bloom, Jacqueline Woodson, Gregory Maguire, David
Levithan, and Armistead Maupin . . . [reflect on] their pasts,
telling their younger selves what they would have liked to
know then about their lives as Lesbian, Gay, Bisexual, or
Transgendered people." The authors give their past selves
"reasons to hold on for the better future ahead." (Publisher's note)

Marcus, Eric

What If? Answers to Questions About What It
Means to Be Gay and Lesbian. Eric Marcus. 2nd
edition Simon Pulse 2013 192 p. (hbk.) $18.99;
pbk $12.99
Grades: 8 9 10 11 12   **307.76**
1. Gays 2. Lesbians 3. LGBT youth
ISBN 1442482982; 9781442482982; 1442482974;
9781442482975
LC 2012945636

Previously published as What If Someone I Know
Is Gay?

"No question goes unanswered in this important book
about being gay. All the basics--and not-so-basics--are covered in more than one hundred questions asked by real teens.
Whether you're curious about your own sexual orientation
or looking to understand and support someone close to you,
this book contains an abundance of answers. Primarily tar-

geted at young adults, this indispensible guide also includes a chapter especially for parents as well as an appendix packed with additional resources." (Publisher's note)

Includes bibliographical references and index

Schwartz, John

Oddly normal; one family's struggle to help their teenage son come to terms with his sexuality. John Schwartz. 1st ed. Gotham Books 2012 xiv, 290 p.p ill. (hardcover) $26

Grades: 9 10 11 12 Adult **306.76**
1. Gay teenagers 2. Parents of gays 3. Families 4. Parent and teenager
ISBN 1592407285; 9781592407286
LC 2012014369

Includes bibliographical references (p. 279-290).

This book by John Schwartz is a "memoir by the father of a gay teen. . . . After mustering the courage to come out to his classmates, [Shwartz's] thirteen-year-old son, Joe, was in the hospital following a failed suicide attempt. . . . 'Oddly Normal' is Schwartz's . . . attempt to address his family's own struggles within a culture that is changing fast, but not fast enough to help gay kids like Joe." (Publisher's note)

Seba, Jaime A.

Homosexuality around the world; safe havens, cultural challenges. by Jaime A. Seba. Mason Crest Publishers 2011 64 p. ill. (chiefly col.) (hardcover) $22.95; (paperback) $9.95

Grades: 6 7 8 9 10 **306.76**
1. Gay rights 2. Homosexuality 3. Depression, Mental 4. Gays
ISBN 1422217531; 1422218724; 9781422217535; 9781422218723
LC 2010017917

This book looks at global views on homosexuality. Readers can "explore different countries and learn about their cultural attitudes toward lesbian, gay, bisexual, and transgender people, as gay men and women from around the globe share their personal stories and experiences. Find out how American policies compare with our North American neighbors, Canada and Mexico, [and] discover how gay equal rights are beginning to emerge in places such as India and South Africa." (Publisher's note)

Includes bibliographical references (p. 60-61) and index.

Speaking Out; Queer Youth in Focus. Rachelle Lee Smith. Independent Pub Group 2014 128 p. 7 plates; color photographs (paperback) $14.95

Grades: Adult **306.76**
1. LGBT youth 2. Documentary photography
ISBN 1629630411; 9781629630410

This book by Rachelle Lee Smith, is "a photographic essay that explores a wide spectrum of experiences told from the perspective of a diverse group of young people, ages 14-24, identifying as queer (lesbian, gay, bisexual, transgender, or questioning). . . . [It] presents portraits without judgment or stereotype by eliminating environmental influence with a stark white backdrop." (Publisher's note)

"A salutary addition to the growing body of LGBTQ literature." Booklist

Trans bodies, trans selves; a resource for the transgender community. edited by Laura Erickson-Schroth. Oxford University Press, USA 2014 672 p. illustrations (paperback) $41.95

Grades: Adult **306.76**
1. Transgender people 2. Transgenderism 3. Gender identity
ISBN 9780199325351
LC 2014007921

This book, edited by Laura Erickson-Schroth, is "a comprehensive, reader-friendly guide for transgender people, with each chapter written by transgender or genderqueer authors. . . . Each chapter takes the reader through an important transgender issue, such as race, religion, employment, medical and surgical transition, mental health topics, relationships, sexuality, parenthood, arts and culture, and many more." (Publisher's note)

"A glossary and biographical information for each contributor round out this much-needed and well-done workbook, suitable for all types of libraries." Booklist

Wright, Kai

Drifting toward love; black, brown, gay, and coming of age on the streets of New York. Beacon Press 2008 224p $24.95

Grades: 11 12 Adult **306.76**
1. African American gay men 2. Hispanic American gay men 3. New York (N.Y.)
ISBN 978-0-8070-7968-3; 0-8070-7968-5
LC 2007-15759

"Drifting Toward Love tells the stories of Manny, Julius, Carlos, and their friends, young gay men of color desperately searching for life's basic necessities: homes that provide more than shelter and security against more than violence or disease. As these teenagers navigate the rocky waters of adolescence, they wade through pains and passions that are typical of any young person coming of age. But they do so with few resources-material or emotional-in a world where the cards are stacked against their success." (Publisher's note)

"Three young men of color and their friends are profiled in an intricate, dense, and revealing book. Manny, Julius, and Carlos reside in New York and its boroughs, places where they are segregated not just by their race but also by their sexual orientation. In language that is both literary and urban, Wright profiles the three boys, their upbringings, and how they came to understand and accept their sexuality. In the course of these discoveries, the boys often engaged in unsafe sex practices both online and in the real world. Each struggles to understand who he is, often helped along the way by gay and lesbian peers. . . . Readers with a special interest in sociology or gender and sexuality studies will find this book informative, but the casual nonfiction reader may feel that the New York history and explanation of the formation of neighborhoods and communities detracts from Manny's, Julius's, and Carlos's stories. This one can be recommended to those interested in Jonathan Kozol's writings about New York's poor." VOYA

306.768   Transgenderism and intersexuality

Golio, Laurel

  We Are the Youth; Laurel Golio and Diana Scholl; edited by Stephani Gilmore and Cameron Russell. Space-Made 2014 96 p.

Grades: 9 10 11 12   **306.768**
  1. Teenagers 2. LGBT youth
  ISBN 1631732234; 9781631732232

  This book by Laurel Golio and Diana Scholl, edited by Stephani Gilmore and Cameron Russell, "is based on the online photojournalism project that shares the stories of lesbian, gay, bisexual, transgender and queer youth in the United States. Through portraits by photographer Laurel Golio, and 'as told to' personal essays by writer Diana Scholl, this book captures the incredible strength and diversity of LGBTQ youth." (Publisher's note)

Nutt, Amy Ellis

  Becoming Nicole; the transformation of an American family. Amy Ellis Nutt. Random House Inc 2015 304 p.

Grades: 11 12 Adult   **306.768**
  1. Family 2. Transgender people 3. Transgender teenagers 4. Families -- United States 5. Transgenderism -- United States 6. Transgender youth -- United States 7. Transgender people -- United States
  ISBN 9780812995411
               LC 2015031162
  Stonewall Honor Book in Non-Fiction (2016)

  "The inspiring true story of a transgender girl, her identical twin brother, and an ordinary American family's extraordinary journey to understand, nurture, and celebrate the right to be different—from the Pulitzer Prize–winning science reporter forThe Washington Post." (Publisher's note)

  "This poignant account of a transgender girl's transition offers a heartfelt snapshot of a family whose only objective is to protect their daughter. Tackling the subject from a biological, social, and psychological viewpoint, Pulitzer-winning reporter Nutt (Shadows Bright as Glass) weaves complex elements of what being transgender means into a compelling narrative about a young woman who has identified as female since early childhood. . . . Writing in a very journalistic tone, Nutt succeeds in placing Nicole's individual story within the more general narrative of transgender rights in the United States and humanizes the issues currently at play." PW

  Includes bibliographical references

306.8   Marriage and family

Barnes, Amber

  ★ The **truth** about family life; Robert N. Golden, general editor; Fred L. Peterson, general editor; Mark J. Kittleson, William Kane and Richelle Rennegarbe, advisers to the first edition; Amber Barnes and Julia Watkins, principal authors. 2nd ed.; Facts On File 2011 240p (Truth about series) $35

Grades: 9 10 11 12   **306.8**
  1. Family -- United States
  ISBN 978-0-8160-7641-3; 0-8160-7641-3
               LC 2010-49240
  First published 2005 under the authorship of Renée Despres

  This book provides "information on family types, their history and role in society, and how to cope with the basic issues that confront families of all kinds." Publisher's note
  Includes bibliographical references

Fakhrid-Deen, Tina

  ★ **Let's** get this straight; the ultimate handbook for youth with LGBTQ parents. [by] Tina Fakhrid-Deen with COLAGE. Seal Press 2010 203p il $15.95

Grades: 7 8 9 10   **306.8**
  1. Children of gay parents 2. Parent-child relationship
  ISBN 978-1-58005-333-4; 1-58005-333-5
               LC 2010-1775

  "This book is written for youth with a parent(s) that is lesbian, gay, bisexual, transgender, or questioning. Its purpose is informational, as well as introspective and affirming. . . . There are seven chapters focusing on a range of topics, from family dynamics, school, and social issues to religion and activism. . . . Quizzes add to the interactive feel. Youth and adults who were interviewed by the author share their experiences in their own words in a section called 'Our Voices.' These quotations, as well as original poetry, add to the feeling of community." Voice Youth Advocates
  Includes glossary and bibliographical references

Haskins-Bookser, Laura

  Dreams to reality; help for young moms: education, career, and life choices. illustrated by Jami Moffett. Morning Glory Press 2006 174p il $21.95; pa $14.95

Grades: 7 8 9 10   **306.8**
  1. Teenage mothers 2. Single parent family
  ISBN 978-1-932538-37-3; 978-1-932538-36-6 pa
               LC 2005-58090

  "The book reads easily, making it palatable for busy teen mothers struggling to get through the basics of education, but it covers a lot of important ground and it is highly recommended for school and public libraries." Voice Youth Advocates
  Includes bibliographical references

Shantz-Hilkes, Chloe

  My Girlfriend's Pregnant! A Teen's Guide to Becoming a Dad. Chloe Shantz-Hilkes. Firefly Books Ltd 2015 128 p. (hardcover) $19.95

Grades: 7 8 9 10 11 12   **306.8**
  1. Teenage fathers 2. Teenage pregnancy 3. Pregnancy -- Psychological aspects 4. Parenthood -- Psychological aspects 5. Teenage fathers -- Life skills guides
  ISBN 9781554517428; 9781554517435; 1554517435

  This book, by Chloe Shantz-Hilkes, seeks to help "teens faced with an unplanned pregnancy. . . . Teenage fathers also face a future filled with fear, doubt, and guilt. . . . With an extensive list of further readings and resources to help with issues ranging from child support to bonding with your child, this book illustrates to young dads that they are not alone and that there are positive ways of dealing with the difficult choices that lie ahead." (Publisher's note)

"Intended to provide teen fathers-to-be some support and guidance, this book sheds light on a variety of topics: pregnancy, childbirth, and parenting; the different options ahead (keeping the baby, adoption, abortion), how to deal with the relationship with the mother, and how to manage stress. Interspersed throughout are firsthand accounts from men who became fathers in their teens or early twenties. The style is matter-of-fact, and the author is reassuring ("There's simply no right or wrong answer when it comes to staying in a young relationship affected by pregnancy."). . . . This work could be a valuable resource for the targeted audience." SLJ

Winchester, Elizabeth

Sisters and brothers; the ultimate guide to understanding your siblings and yourself. [by] Elizabeth Siris Winchester. Franklin Watts 2008 112p il (Scholastic choices) lib bdg $27; pa $8.95

Grades: 6 7 8 9 10 **306.8**

1. Family 2. Siblings

ISBN 978-0-531-13870-0 lib bdg; 0-531-13870-4 lib bdg; 978-0-531-20528-0 pa; 0-531-20528-2 pa

LC 2007-51871

Real-life stories from teenagers about interacting with siblings, whether blood, adopted, foster, or step.

"Colorful and compact, with [an] attractive cover [and] . . . excellent black-and-white photographs of a diverse array of teens." SLJ

Includes glossary and bibliographical references

Worth, Richard

★ **Frequently** asked questions about teen fatherhood. Rosen Pub. 2010 64p il (FAQ: teen life) lib bdg $29.25

Grades: 7 8 9 10 **306.8**

1. Teenage fathers

ISBN 978-1-4358-5325-6; 1-4358-5325-3

LC 2008-51938

"While conversational, [this volume is] surprisingly helpful—even emotive. . . . [This book greets] its intended audience with encouragement and aplomb. Dealing with feelings of disbelief and blame quickly segue into preparing for a birth, staying in school, and considering part-time jobs. Adoption and abortion are given only brief mentions." Booklist

Includes glossary and bibliographical references

306.87 Intrafamily relationships

Apelqvist, Eva

LGBTQ families; the ultimate teen guide. Eva Apelqvist. Scarecrow Press, Inc. 2013 208 p. (It happened to me) (cloth: alk. paper) $50

Grades: 7 8 9 10 11 12 **306.87**

1. LGBT people 2. Families 3. Children of gay parents 4. Gays -- Family relationships 5. Sexual minorities

-- Family relationships

ISBN 0810885360; 9780810885363

LC 2013015488

This book by Eva Apelqvist is part of the It Happened to Me series. This entry "begins with an overview of each letter of the iconic acronym and progresses into a more thorough look at LGBTQ adolescents, LGBTQ parents, and how trans individuals may affect family dynamics. Other chapters investigate same-sex marriage, other issues (e.g., rights of sperm donors), LGBTQ rights around the world, bullying, . . . and the ongoing debate between the LGBTQ community and various religious, political, and business groups." (Booklist)

Includes bibliographical references and index

306.874 Parent-child relationship

Glatzer, Jenna

The **pregnancy** project; a memoir. Gaby Rodriguez with Jenna Glatzer. Simon & Schuster Books For Young Readers 2012 p. cm. (hardcover) $17.99

Grades: 9 10 11 12 **306.874**

1. Teenage pregnancy 2. Stereotype (Social psychology) 3. Stereotypes (Social psychology) 4. Teenage pregnancy -- United States

ISBN 9781442446229; 9781442446243

LC 2011038862

This memoir, by Gaby Rodriguez with Jenna Glatzer, tells of her experiences faking pregnancy in high school to experience and confront the social stereotypes and hardships it would bring. "[H]ow would she be treated if she 'lived down' to others' expectations? Would everyone ignore the years she put into being a good student and see her as just another pregnant teen statistic with no future? . . . What she learned changed her life forever." (Publisher's note)

Parks, Peggy J., 1951-

Teenage sex and pregnancy; Peggy J. Parks. ReferencePoint Press 2012 96 p. (hardback) $27.95

Grades: 9 10 11 12 **306.874**

1. Sex education 2. Teenage pregnancy 3. Teenagers -- Sexual behavior 4. Sex instruction for children

ISBN 1601521685; 9781601521682

LC 2011012468

This book about teenage sex and pregnancy, by Peggy J. Parks, "confronts . . . urgent, controversial issues; provides detailed information about both abstinence and contraception; and debates what should be taught in sex education, including the role of religious values. . . . [Readers] will find important facts as well as opposing viewpoints on issues such as the role of faith and religious counseling, the need for sex ed for nonheterosexual teens, and much more." (Publisher's note)

Includes bibliographical references and index

South Vista Education Center (Richfield, Minn.)

★ **Daycare** and diplomas; essays by teen mothers who stayed in school. by the students at South Vista Educational Center. Fairview Press 2000 89p il pa $9.95

Grades: 9 10 11 12   **306.874**
1. Teenage mothers   2. South Vista Education Center (Richfield, Minn.)
ISBN 1-57749-098-3

LC 00-37620

In this work 36 teen mothers share their experiences and views on pregnancy, parenting and staying in school

Wahls, Zach

My two moms; lessons of love, strength, and what makes a family. by Zach Wahls; with Bruce Littlefield. Gotham Books 2012 xix, 233 p.p ill. (hardcover) $26; (paperback) $16

Grades: 7 8 9 10 11 12   **306.874**
1. Same-sex marriage   2. Children of gay parents 3. Gay rights -- United States 4. Lesbian mothers -- United States 5. Same-sex marriage -- United States 6. Children of gay parents -- United States
ISBN 1592407137; 1592407633; 9781592407132; 9781592407637

LC 2011053087

In this book, "[Zach] Wahls writes about growing up as the son of gay parents in the heartland. In January 2011, the author, then a student at the University of Iowa, testified before the Iowa House Judiciary Committee as they considered a state constitutional amendment to ban same-sex marriage. . . . The speech was aimed at dismantling the myth that kids are damaged by having gay parents . . . Here the author expands on his speech, discussing the values that his parents helped to instill in him." (Kirkus)

306.9   Institutions pertaining to death

Noyes, Deborah

Encyclopedia of the end; mysterious death in fact, fancy, folklore, and more. Houghton Mifflin Co. 2008 143p il $25

Grades: 7 8 9 10 11 12   **306.9**
1. Death   2. Reference books   3. Funeral rites and ceremonies
ISBN 978-0-618-82362-8; 0-618-82362-X

LC 2008-1872

"This stylish A-to-Z encounter with all things related to death and dying shows Noyes . . . at her liveliest. . . . The author offers a broad illumination of spiritual, historical and biological aspects of death. Photos, paintings and engravings in homage to 'the end' make the book dynamic visually, too." Publ Wkly

307.2   Movement of people to, from, within communities

Harris, Laurie Lanzen

The **great** migration north, 1910-1970; by Laurie Lanzen Harris. Omnigraphics, Inc. 2012 xvi, 241 p.p

Grades: 7 8 9 10 11 12   **307.2**
1. Internal migration   2. African Americans -- History 3. United States -- History -- 20th century 4. African

Americans -- Migrations -- History -- 20th century   5. Rural-urban migration -- United States -- History -- 20th century
ISBN 0780811860; 9780780811867

LC 2011033540

This historical survey by Laurie Lanzen Harris "explains the social and economic factors that drove the African-American exodus out of the rural South to the industrial cities of the North during the first half of the twentieth century. The book also details the transformative impact of this migration on U.S. industry, culture, and race relations, as well as the daily experiences of the men, women, and children who built new lives for themselves in New York, Chicago, Philadelphia, Detroit, and other cities of the North. Finally, it explains how this multi-generational flight from oppression to opportunity changed the internal dynamics of African-American families and communities across America." (Publisher's note)

Includes bibliographical references and index.

307.7   Specific kinds of communities

Lorinc, John

Cities. Groundwood Books/House of Anansi Press 2008 144p (Groundwork guides) $18.95; pa $10

Grades: 7 8 9 10 11 12   **307.7**
1. Urbanization   2. Cities and towns
ISBN 978-0-88899-820-0; 0-88899-820-1; 978-0-88899-819-4 pa; 0-88899-819-8 pa

"This packed, highly readable [title] . . . does an excellent job of tracing urban history worldwide, raising the big social, political, and economic issues of poverty, migration, conservation, public health, crime, transportation, and much more, always rooted in specific examples of the problems and riches of city life." Booklist

Includes bibliographical references

317   General statistics of North America

★ **Proquest** Statistical Abstract of the United States 2013; ProQuest LLC. 1st ed. Rowman & Littlefield Pub Inc 2012 xvi, 1025 p.p (hardcover) $179

Grades: 8 9 10 11 12 Adult   **317**
1. Almanacs   2. United States -- Census
ISBN 159888591X; 9781598885910

This almanac, published by ProQuest, offers statistical summaries of Census data and socio-demographic information of the United States as of 2013. This annually compiled work "is the best-known statistical reference publication in the country. . . . As a carefully selected collection of statistics on the social, political, and economic conditions of the United States, it is a snapshot of America and its people." (Publisher's note)

320 Political science (Politics and government)

Anderson, Jodi Lynn

Americapedia; taking the dumb out of freedom. [by] Jodi Anderson, Daniel Ehrenhaft, Andisheh Nouraee. Walker Books for Young Readers 2011 240p il $24.99; pa $16.99

Grades: 7 8 9 10   **320**

1. Citizenship 2. World politics 3. United States -- Politics and government

ISBN 978-0-8027-9792-6; 0-8027-9792-X; 978-0-8027-9793-3 pa; 0-8027-9792-X pa

        LC 2010-38028

"This examination of the state of the union uses edgy humor to discuss pertinent matters in the worlds of politics, international relations, religion, and culture. Bullet points, footnotes, sidebars, and tongue-in-cheek graphics . . . lighten heady topics like nuclear proliferation and the Israel-Palestine conflict. Despite the irreverent tone . . . discussions of such topics as the stem cell debate, global warming, and gerrymandering remind readers of the seriousness behind the issues." Publ Wkly

Includes bibliographical references

★ **Governance**; Power, Politics, and Participation. Edited by Brian Duignan. Rosen Pub Group 2012 160 p. $176.25

Grades: 10 11 12   **320**

1. Political science 2. Comparative government

ISBN 1615308083; 9781615308088

This reference series looks at governance. "While seeking to maintain an ordered society, governing bodies at every level—local, regional, or national—must balance majority interests with socially and economically viable solutions. This . . . series examines many forms of government around the world and through the ages. Included are discussions of the structures, laws, and interests with which they must contend." (Publisher's note)

★ The **United** States government internet directory; edited by Shana Hertz Hattis. Bernan Press 2016 600 p. pa $72

Grades: 11 12 Adult   **320**

1. Reference books 2. Web sites -- Directories 3. Internet resources -- Directories 4. Government information -- Directories

ISBN; 9781598888331

        LC 2010237279

Annual. First published 2004 with title: The United States government Internet manual. Published in 2009 with title: E-government and web directory

This directory "contains more than 2,000 Web site records, organized into 20 subject-themed chapters; provides descriptions and URLs for each site; . . . includes information about the sponsoring agency; notes the useful or unique aspects of the site; lists some of the major government publications hosted on the site; evaluates the most important and frequently sought sites; provides a roster of congressional members with members' Web sites includes a one-page 'Quick Guide' to the major federal agencies and the leading online library, data source, and finding aid sites; [and] high-lights the Freedom of Information Act Web pages to access U.S. federal executive agency records." Publisher's note

Washington Information Directory 2014-2015. Congressional Quarterly, Inc. 2014 983 p. il. Hardcover $195

Grades: 11 12 Adult   **320**

1. Reference books 2. Washington (D.C.) -- Directories

ISBN 9781483347929

Annual. First published 1975/76

"This substantial and user-friendly guide . . . [is] a vital resource for navigating Washington's intricate bureaucratic web." Libr J

320.01 Philosophy and theory

The **politics** book; Big ideas simply explained. edited by Rebecca Warren and Kate Johnsen; illustrated by James Graham. 1st American ed. DK Pub. 2013 352 p. ill. (some col.) (Big ideas simply explained) (hardcover) $25.00

Grades: 8 9 10 11 12 Adult   **320.01**

1. Political philosophy

ISBN 1465402144; 9781465402141

        LC 2012533724

This book, part of the Big Ideas Simply Explained series, looks at political philosophy. "More than 100 political philosophers, among them Confucius, Plato, Machiavelli, Mary Wollstonecraft, Karl Marx, Ito Hirobumi, Emiliano Zapata, Jomo Kenyatta, and Mao Zedong, are covered in seven chronological sections ranging from 'Ancient Political Thought' to 'Postwar Politics.'" (Library Journal)

320.1 The state

Machiavelli, Niccolo

★ The **prince**. Knopf 1992 xxxi, 190p (Everyman's library) $16

Grades: 11 12 Adult   **320.1**

1. Political ethics 2. Political science

ISBN 0-679-41044-9

        LC 91-53225

Written in 1513

"A handbook of advice on the acquisition, use, and maintenance of political power, dedicated to Lorenzo de Medici." Haydn. Thesaurus of Book Dig

Social contract; essays by Locke, Hume, and Rousseau. with an introduction by Sir Ernest Barker. Oxford Univ. Press 1980 xliv, 307p pa $22.95

Grades: 11 12 Adult   **320.1**

1. State, The 2. Political science

ISBN 0-19-500309-8

First published 1947 in the United Kingdom; 1948 in the United States

This book contains three major essays dealing with the social contract theory of government, first published 1690, 1748 and 1762 respectively. The introduction by Sir Ernest

Barker discusses the history and transformations of the theory before focusing on the ideas of the three authors

320.4   Structure and functions of government

Han, Lori Cox
   Handbook   to American democracy;   Lori Cox Han and Tomislav Han. Facts On File 2011 224 p.
   Grades: 8 9 10 11 12 Adult   **320.4**
      1. United States -- History 2. Democracy -- United States -- History 3. United States -- Politics and government 4. United States -- Politics and government -- Handbooks, manuals, etc
   ISBN 0816078548; 9780816078547
                                        LC 2011005185
   The authors "address the foundations of American democracy and the three branches of American government. The books introduce offices, history, and issues in eight chapters each (e.g., 'The Founding Fathers and the American Revolution,' 'How Congress Is Organized,' and 'Vice Presidents, Presidential Advisers, and America's First Ladies'). The material is complemented by black-and-white photos and sidebars on legal cases, laws and legislation, statistics, maps, biographies of major figures such as Henry VIII, and other primary materials, and chapters close with a summary. . . . [The volumes] each include an individual glossary, index, selected bibliography, and table of contents." (Libr J)
   Includes bibliographical references and index

320.5   Political ideologies

Paine, Thomas
   Collected writings. Library of Am. 1995 906p $35
   Grades: 11 12 Adult   **320.5**
      1. Political science
   ISBN 1-883011-03-5
                                          LC 94-25756
   Includes bibliographical references

320.54   Nationalism, regionalism, internationalism

The **Malcolm** X encyclopedia; edited by Robert L. Jenkins, co-edited by Mfanya Donald Tryman. Greenwood Press 2002 643p il $74.95
   Grades: 11 12 Adult   **320.54**
      1. Reference books 2. Black Muslim leaders 3. Civil rights activists 4. Black Muslims -- Encyclopedias
   ISBN 0-313-29264-7
                                          LC 2001-23318
   "The major section of the volume consists of 500 essays that create a cross-disciplinary, textured description of the man, his life, his times, and events. . . . Topics include African nationalism, Civil rights movement, Police brutality, Socialism, and White liberals, among others. Also included are a detailed chronology as well as several thematic essays that provide a framework for the entries that follow. . . . All

encyclopedia entries have a short bibliography, but there is an extensive bibliography of books, articles, newspapers, electronic resources, and oral interviews included as a separate section in the volume. . . . The encyclopedia would add a first-stop resource for library users seeking information on this important figure of contemporary American history." Booklist
   Includes bibliographical references

321   Systems of governments and states

Davidson, Tish
   ★   **Theocracy**; Tish Davidson. Mason Crest 2013 64 p. col. ill. (Major forms of world government) (library) $22.95; (ebook) $28.95
   Grades: 6 7 8 9 10   **321**
      1. Theocracy 2. Political science
   ISBN 1422221431; 9781422221433; 9781422294604
                                          LC 2012027863
   This book, by Tish Davidson, as part of the publisher's "Major Forms of World Government" series, "examines theocratic governments, from ancient Egypt to present-day Iran. It explores how different theocracies arose, how their leaders maintained authority, and what it was like for ordinary people living under religious rule." (Publisher's note)
   Includes bibliographical references and index.

Stefoff, Rebecca
   Monarchy.   Marshall Cavendish Benchmark 2007 143p il (Political systems of the world) lib bdg $27.95
   Grades: 7 8 9 10 11 12   **321**
      1. Monarchy
   ISBN 978-0-7614-2630-1
                                          LC 2006-26384
   "Discusses monarchies as a political system, and details the history of monarchies throughout the world." Publisher's note
   Includes bibliographical references

321.8   Democratic government

Laxer, James
   Democracy. Groundwood Books 2009 143p (Groundwork guides) $18.95; pa $10
   Grades: 8 9 10 11 12   **321.8**
      1. Democracy
   ISBN 978-0-88899-912-2; 0-88899-912-7; 978-0-88899-913-9 pa; 0-88899-913-5 pa
   This title "stands out for its accessible introduction to historical and contemporary democracy across the globe. Laxer skillfully supports his arguments with examples and avoids pat definitions." Booklist
   Includes bibliographical references

322.342 Relation of the state to organized groups and their members

Judson, Karen

Religion and government; should they mix? Marshall Cavendish Benchmark 2009 127p il (Controversy!) $25.95

Grades: 7 8 9 10 **322.342**
1. Church and state -- United States
ISBN 978-0-7614-4235-6; 0-7614-4235-9

LC 2008-44483

"For readers fascinated with the ways in which religion and government work, or try not to work, together in America, this introduction will provide much food for thought. . . . Each chapter examines a different sphere of influence, from politics to education and social welfare, including influential court cases that form the backbone of current policy." SLJ

Includes bibliographical references

322.4 Political action groups

Bartoletti, Susan Campbell

★ **They** called themselves the K.K.K. the birth of an American terrorist group. Houghton Mifflin 2010 172p il map $19

Grades: 7 8 9 10 **322.4**
1. Racism 2. Ku Klux Klan 3. White supremacy movements 4. Reconstruction (1865-1876) 5. United States -- Race relations
ISBN 0-618-44033-X; 978-0-618-44033-7

LC 2009-45247

This is a history of the Ku Klux Klan. Bibliography. Index. "Middle school, high school." (Horn Book)

"In this comprehensive, accessible account, . . . [the author] draws from documentary histories, slave narratives, newspapers, congressional testimony, and other sources to chronicle the origins and proliferation of the Ku Klux Klan against the charged backdrop of Reconstruction politics and legislation. . . . The author lives up to her introductory promise to avoid censoring racist language and images, and includes some horrifying descriptions of lynchings and murders perpetuated during KKK raids. . . . Her account of attending a Klan meeting while researching the book is chilling to the core." Publ Wkly

Includes bibliographical references

The **Britannica** guide to political and social movements that changed the modern world; edited by Heather M. Campbell. Britannica Educational Pub. in association with Rosen Educational Services 2010 389p il (Turning points in history) lib bdg $45

Grades: 9 10 11 12 **322.4**
1. Social movements
ISBN 978-1-61530-016-7

LC 2009-37443

"This book traces an array of important political and social movements from their inception to their apex, with . . . side discussions of notable proponents." Publisher's note

Includes glossary

Chalmers, David Mark

Hooded Americanism: the history of the Ku Klux Klan; 3rd ed; Duke Univ. Press 1987 477p il hardcover o.p. pa $24.95

Grades: 11 12 Adult **322.4**
1. Ku Klux Klan
ISBN 0-8223-0772-3 pa

LC 86-29133

First published 1965 by Doubleday; this is a reissue of the 1981 edition published by Watts

This book recounts the history of the Klan. It describes the sociological and psychological forces behind the Klan, and sets forth its dogmas

"The book is written in a breezy, journalistic style. . . . Especially instructive and sobering is Chalmers' account of the role of the Klan in politics." J Am Hist

Includes bibliographical references

Esposito, John L.

Unholy war; terror in the name of Islam. Oxford Univ. Press 2002 196p hardcover o.p. pa $15.95

Grades: 11 12 Adult **322.4**
1. Islam and politics 2. Terrorism -- Religious aspects 3. United States -- Foreign opinion
ISBN 0-19-515435-5; 0-19-516886-0 pa

LC 2001-58009

"Engaging, evenhanded, and highly readable . . . this is essential reading for every concerned citizen and all those who wish to gain a deeper understanding of contemporary Islam and its internal struggles." Libr J

Includes bibliographical references

Gandhi, Mahatma

★ **Gandhi** on non-violence; selected texts from Mohandas K. Gandhi's Non-violence in peace and war. edited with an introduction by Thomas Merton; preface by Mark Kurlansky. New Directions 2007 101p pa $13.95

Grades: 11 12 Adult **322.4**
1. Passive resistance 2. India -- Politics and government
ISBN 978-0-8112-1686-9

LC 2007-32262

First published 1965

In an introductory essay Merton "considers Gandhi's ideas, not in relation to their Indian context, but in terms of their applicability to all men's lives. Brief quotations from Gandhi's writings make up most of the book." Asia: a Guide to Paperbacks

Includes bibliographical references

Hamilton, Neil A.

Rebels and renegades; a chronology of social and political dissent in the United States. Routledge 2002 361p il $100; pa. $48.95

Grades: 11 12 Adult **322.4**
1. Radicalism 2. Right and left (Political science)
ISBN 0-415-93639-X; 9780415869386

LC 2002-8916

The author "examines the historical role that radicals and reactionaries have played in shaping American society and culture. Arranged in nine chapters, the book features a chronological format that begins in 1620 with the Pilgrims and ends with the September 11, 2001 terrorist attacks. Each chapter opens with an overview of the time period, and individual entries consist of one- or two-page descriptions of radicals, their activities, and their impact." Libr J

Includes bibliographical references

Voices of protest; documents of courage and dissent. edited by Frank Lowenstein, Sheryl Lechner, and Erik Bruun. Distributed by Workman Pub. Co. 2007 560p il $24.95

Grades: 10 11 12   **322.4**
1. Dissent 2. History -- Sources
ISBN 978-1-57912-585-1

LC 2007-60380

"The bold cover of this book shouts out some of the famous dissenters quoted within: Martin Luther King, Jr.; Margaret Sanger; Pablo Picasso; Mohandas Gandhi; and even Ronald Reagan. . . . It is precisely the inclusion of such unexpected voices, manifested in song lyrics, speeches, essays, sermons, or images from around the globe and throughout time, that makes this comprehensive collection so fresh and groundbreaking." SLJ

Includes bibliographical references

323   Civil and political rights

Berry, Mary Frances
My face is black is true; Callie House and the struggle for ex-slave reparations. Knopf 2006 314p il $26.95; pa $14.95

Grades: 11 12 Adult   **323**
1. Needleworkers 2. Laundry workers 3. Social activists 4. African Americans -- Reparations 5. African American women -- Biography
ISBN 1-4000-4003-5 Knopf; 0-307-27705-4 pa, Vintage; 978-0-307-27705-3 pa, Vintage

LC 2004-51330

The author "unearths the intriguing story of Callie House (1861-1928), a Tennessee washerwoman and seamstress become activist, and the organization she led, the National Ex-Slave Mutual Relief, Bounty and Pension Association. . . . Students and scholars of African-American history, as well as those engaged in the current reparations debates, will be deeply informed by the rise and fall of the Ex-Slave Association." Publ Wkly

Includes bibliographical references

Brinkley, Douglas
★ **Rosa** Parks. Viking 2000 246p (Penguin lives series) hardcover o.p. pa $13

Grades: 11 12 Adult   **323**
1. Civil rights activists 2. African Americans -- Civil rights 3. African American women -- Biography
ISBN 0-670-89160-6; 0-14-303600-9 pa

LC 00-35916

"Rosa Parks' story takes readers from rural Alabama to the Montgomery Industrial School for Girls, marriage to barber Raymond Parks, quiet activism in the '30s and '40s, a first experience of integration at the Highlander Folk School, arrest in 1955 and the bus boycott, a move to Detroit, and

more than 20 years on the staff of Rep. John Conyers (D-Mich.)." Booklist

Includes bibliographical references

Civil liberties;   Lauri S. Friedman, book editor. Greenhaven Press 2010 144p il map (Introducing issues with opposing viewpoints) lib bdg $34.70

Grades: 7 8 9 10 11 12   **323**
1. Terrorism 2. Civil rights 3. National security
ISBN 978-0-7377-4732-4; 0-7377-4732-3

LC 2009-51887

This book "of pro/con essays . . . [is] intended to stimulate discussion of critical social issues and to open readers' minds to divergent opinions. Civil Liberties includes discussions of the Patriot Act, the rights of Muslims and Arab Americans, and racial profiling. . . . Active-reading questions preface the essays, which are followed by directions for evaluating the arguments presented. Color photos and other graphics throughout enliven the reading experience." SLJ

Includes bibliographical references

Osborne, Linda Barrett
★ **Women** of the civil rights movement. Library of Congress 2006 61p il (Women who dare) $12.95

Grades: 9 10 11 12   **323**
1. Women political activists 2. Civil rights demonstrations 3. African Americans -- Civil rights
ISBN 0-7649-3548-8; 978-0-7649-3548-0

LC 2005-49546

This history of the civil rights movement discusses the ways in which women participated in it, including Rosa Parks, Ella Baker and Daisy Bates.

Includes bibliographical references

Thompson, Cooper
White men challenging racism; 35 personal stories. {by} Cooper Thompson, Emmett Schaefer, and Harry Brod; with a foreword by James W. Loewen. Duke Univ. Press 2003 xxxvi, 353p $64.95; pa $21.95

Grades: 9 10 11 12   **323**
1. Racism 2. Civil rights 3. Political activists
ISBN 0-8223-3084-9; 0-8223-3096-2 pa

LC 2002-14628

This book contains interviews with "35 white men with a range of ages and backgrounds and from across the U.S. . . . who have spent their lives combating racism and social injustice via community organizing, teaching, civil rights advocacy, and a variety of other efforts . . . Among the subjects are Herbert Aptheker, radical historian; Stetson Kennedy, a Klan infiltrator in the 1940s; Richard Lapchick, advocate for racial and gender justice in sports. The contributors explore issues from immigrant rights to interracial relations to gay activism. Readers interested in different perspectives on social justice will enjoy this collection." Booklist

Includes bibliographical references (p. {351}-353)

323.1 Civil and political rights of nondominant groups

Aretha, David

★ **Freedom** Summer. Morgan Reynolds Pub. 2007 128p (The civil rights movement) lib bdg $27.95

Grades: 7 8 9 10 11 12 **323.1**

1. Mississippi Freedom Project 2. Mississippi -- Race relations 3. African Americans -- Civil rights

ISBN 978-1-59935-059-2; 1-59935-059-9

LC 2007-23815

This "discusses the collaborative strategies black and white Americans . . . devised to dismantle the restrictive, often violent measures used in the South to prevent most African Americans from voting. . . . [This title is] visually appealing with generous white space around the [text]. Throughout, mostly black-and-white historical photos . . . enhance the [narrative]. Also adding impact are numerous dramatic accounts by participants in the struggle." SLJ

Includes bibliographical references

★ **Montgomery** bus boycott. Morgan Reynolds Pub. 2009 128p il (The civil rights movement) $28.95

Grades: 7 8 9 10 **323.1**

1. African Americans -- Civil rights 2. Montgomery (Ala.) -- Race relations

ISBN 978-1-59935-020-2; 1-59935-020-3

LC 2008-18679

"The wrenching consequences of Rosa Parks's decision that sparked the Civil Rights Movement are depicted in this well-written book. Descriptions of civil rights activism dating back to 1865 . . . provide historical context and a sense of the fervor surrounding discrimination and segregation. The facts of the boycott are documented with supportive news articles, relevant quotations, moving individual stories, and significant court cases. . . . [Photographs] depict significant figures and document incidents such as meetings and car-pooling to avoid buses." SLJ

Includes bibliographical references

Bausum, Ann

★ **Marching** to the mountaintop; how poverty, labor fights, and civil rights set the stage for Martin Luther King, Jr.'s final hours. by Ann Bausum. National Geographic 2012 104 p.

Grades: 7 8 9 10 **323.1**

1. Memphis (Tenn.) -- History 2. African Americans -- Civil rights 3. Strikes -- United States -- History 4. African Americans -- Economic conditions 5. Sanitation Workers Strike, Memphis, Tenn., 1968 6. Memphis (Tenn.) -- Race relations -- History -- 20th century 7. Labor movement -- Tennessee -- Memphis -- History -- 20th century

ISBN 1426309392; 1426309406; 9781426309397; 9781426309403

LC 2011024661

"In early 1968 the grisly on-the-job deaths of two African-American sanitation workers in Memphis, Tennessee, prompted an extended strike by that city's segregated force of trash collectors. Workers sought union protection, higher wages, improved safety, and the integration of their work force. Their work stoppage became a part of the larger civil rights movement and drew an impressive array of national movement leaders to Memphis, including, on more than one occasion, Dr. Martin Luther King, Jr. . . . Marching to the Mountaintop explores how the media, politics, the Civil Rights Movement, and labor protests all converged to set the scene for one of King's greatest speeches and for his tragic death." (Publisher's note)

Includes bibliographical references (p. 100-102) and index

Boerst, William J.

★ **Marching** in Birmingham. Morgan Reynolds Pub. 2008 112p il map (The civil rights movement) $27.95

Grades: 7 8 9 10 11 12 **323.1**

1. Clergy 2. Nonfiction writers 3. Civil rights activists 4. Nobel laureates for peace 5. African Americans -- Civil rights 6. Birmingham (Ala.) -- Race relations

ISBN 978-1-59935-055-4; 1-59935-055-6

LC 2007-26640

This "focuses on Alabama and the organized efforts by both black and white Americans to end local-government-sanctioned segregation and inequality. [This title is] visually appealing with generous white space around the [text]. Throughout, mostly black-and-white historical photos . . . enhance the [narrative]. Also adding impact are numerous dramatic accounts by participants in the struggle." SLJ

Includes bibliographical references

Bowers, Rick

The **spies** of Mississippi; the true story of the spy network that tried to destroy the Civil Rights Movement. National Geographic 2010 120p il $16.95; lib bdg $26.90

Grades: 7 8 9 10 **323.1**

1. Mississippi -- Race relations 2. African Americans -- Civil rights 3. Mississippi State Sovereignty Commission

ISBN 978-1-4263-0595-5; 1-4263-0595-8; 978-1-4263-0596-2 lib bdg; 1-4263-0596-6 lib bdg

LC 2009-18944

"Bowers draws upon archival material, supplemented with his own extensive research, to document the activities of the Mississippi State Sovereignty Commission, a Civil Rights-era state agency that disseminated segregationist propaganda and used Soviet-style methods to spy upon, harass, and harm those who challenged white supremacy. . . . This book's unique perspective will help students understand the previously unknown history of the despicable actions of Mississippi leaders who opposed civil rights and the silent citizens who supported their activities." SLJ

Includes bibliographical references

Brimner, Larry Dane

★ **Black** & white; the confrontation of Reverend Fred L. Shuttlesworth and Eugene Bull O'Connor. Calkins Creek 2011 109p il

Grades: 7 8 9 10 11 12 **323.1**

1. Clergy 2. Police officials 3. Civil rights activists 4. Organization officials 5. African Americans -- Civil

rights 6. Birmingham (Ala.) -- Race relations
ISBN 1-59078-766-8; 978-1-59078-766-3

"Reverend Fred L. Shuttlesworth led the civil rights struggle for equality in Birmingham, Alabama. . . . Eugene 'Bull' Connor, backed by the Ku Klux Klan, became a symbol of racist hatred and violence against Shuttlesworth. With a spacious design that includes archival pictures and primary-source documents on almost every page, this accessible photo-essay recounts the events in three sections, which focus first on the preacher, then on the commisioner, and finally, on their confrontation. . . . Never simplistic in his depictions, Brimner shows the viewpoints from all sides. . . . A penetrating look at elemental national history." Booklist
Includes bibliographical references

Des Chenes, Betz

American civil rights: primary sources; [compiled by] Phillis Engelbert; edited by Betz Des Chenes. U.X.L 1999 xl, 200p il $58

Grades: 8 9 10 11 12   323.1
1. Civil rights
ISBN 0-7876-3170-1

LC 99-27167

Presents fifteen documents, including speeches, autobiographical texts, and proclamations, related to the civil rights movement and arranged by category under economic rights, desegregation, and human rights

"The uniqueness of this set lies in the range of people covered. Students will find it an excellent resource for reports and interesting reading." Booklist
Includes bibliographical references

Euchner, Charles

Nobody turn me around; a people's history of the 1963 march on Washington. Beacon Press 2010 226p $26.95

Grades: 11 12 Adult   323.1
1. Civil rights demonstrations 2. Washington (D.C.) 3. African Americans -- Civil rights
ISBN 978-0-8070-0059-5

LC 2009-46943

Draws on the oral histories of more than one hundred participants to provide a behind-the-scenes look at the historic 1963 March on Washington that culminated in Martin Luther King Jr.'s "I Have a Dream" speech.

"A sweeping, comprehensive look at a pivotal march in American history." Booklist
Includes bibliographical references

★ The **Eyes** on the prize civil rights reader; documents, speeches, and firsthand accounts from the black freedom struggle, 1954-1990. general editors, Clayborne Carson {et al.} Penguin Bks. 1991 764p pa $18

Grades: 11 12 Adult   323.1
1. United States -- Race relations 2. African Americans -- Civil rights
ISBN 0-14-015403-5

LC 91-9507

First published 1987 with title: Eyes on the prize: America's civil rights years, a reader and guide

"An anthology of primary material important in the historiography of this country's civil rights movement. . . . Not simply for reference use, this compilation makes provocative cover-to-cover reading and is extremely worthy of consideration by every library." Booklist
Includes bibliographical references

Hampton, Henry

Voices of freedom; an oral history of the civil rights movement from the 1950s through the 1980s. {by} Henry Hampton and Steve Fayer with Sarah Flynn. Bantam Bks. 1990 692p hardcover o.p. pa $24

Grades: 11 12 Adult   323.1
1. United States -- Race relations 2. African Americans -- Civil rights
ISBN 0-553-05734-0; 0-553-35232-6 pa

LC 89-18297

This companion to the PBS series "'Eyes on the Prize,' composed of interviews done originally for the TV program, is a riveting document of the civil rights movement of the 1960s and 1970s. The text is arranged in a chronological sequence that reconstructs major events from the murder of Emmett Till in Mississippi in 1955 and the Little Rock integration crisis to the affirmative action cases of the 1970s." Booklist
Includes bibliographical references

Jones, William P.

★ The **March** on Washington; jobs, freedom, and the forgotten history of civil rights. William P. Jones. 1st ed. W.W. Norton & Co. Inc. 2013 320 p. (hardcover) $26.95

Grades: 10 11 12 Adult   323.1
1. Civil rights demonstrations 2. African Americans -- Civil rights 3. March on Washington for Jobs and Freedom (1963: Washington, D.C.) 4. African Americans -- Civil rights -- History -- 20th century 5. Civil rights movements -- United States -- History -- 20th century 6. Civil rights demonstrations -- Washington (D.C.) -- History -- 20th century
ISBN 0393082857; 9780393082852

LC 2013006173

This book by William P. Jones presents "an account of the American civil rights movement leading up to the infamous 1963 March on Washington, which 'aimed not just to end racial segregation and discrimination in the South but also to ensure that Americans of all races had access to quality education, affordable housing, and jobs that paid a living wage.' . . . Much of the book focuses on A. Philip Randolph, an African-American trade unionist." (Kirkus Reviews)

"This excellent revisionist account places the march, on its 50th anniversary, in its historical context, while revealing the economic roots of the modern civil rights movement. General readers and scholars will appreciate this fine, accessible narrative." (Library Journal)
Includes bibliographical references and index.

King, Martin Luther

★ A **testament** of hope; the essential writings of Martin Luther King, Jr. edited by James Melvin

Washington. Harper & Row 1986 xxvi, 676p hardcover o.p. pa $23.95

Grades: 11 12 Adult **323.1**

1. United States -- Race relations 2. African Americans -- Civil rights

ISBN 0-06-250931-4; 0-06-064691-8 pa

LC 85-45370

"King's most important writings are gathered together in one source. The arrangement is topical: philosophy, sermons and public addresses, essays, interviews and excerpts of his books. The material within each of these categories is arranged chronologically. Included are Dr. King's writings on nonviolence, integration and politics." SLJ

Includes bibliographical references

Where do we go from here; chaos or community? [by] Martin Luther King, Jr.; [foreword by Coretta Scott King; introduction by Vincent Harding] Beacon Press 2010 xxiv, 223p (King legacy series) $24.95; pa $14

Grades: 11 12 Adult **323.1**

1. Racism 2. United States -- Race relations 3. African Americans -- Civil rights

ISBN 978-0-8070-0076-2; 978-0-8070-0067-0 pa

LC 2009035950

First published 1967 by Harper & Row

The author reaffirms his belief in the power of nonviolence to achieve full citizenship for black people in America and defines his attitude toward the Black Power movement and the white backlash.

Includes bibliographical references

★ **Why** we can't wait; [by] Martin Luther King, Jr. Harper & Row 1964 178p il hardcover o.p. pa $6.95

Grades: 11 12 Adult **323.1**

1. African Americans -- Civil rights 2. Birmingham (Ala.) -- Race relations

ISBN 0-06-012395-8; 0-451-52753-4 pa

The author first reviews the background of the 1963 civil rights demands. He then describes the strategy of the Birmingham campaign and outlines future action

Levinson, Cynthia Y.

We've got a job; the 1963 Birmingham Children's March. written by Cynthia Levinson. Peachtree Publishers 2012 176 p.

Grades: 6 7 8 9 **323.1**

1. Political activists 2. African American youth 3. African Americans -- Civil rights 4. Birmingham (Ala.) -- Race relations 5. Civil rights demonstrations -- Alabama 6. African American youth -- Alabama -- Birmingham -- History -- 20th century

ISBN 9781561456277

LC 2011031738

YALSA Award for Excellence in Nonfiction for Young Adults Finalist (2013)

In this book, "[c]overing the history of the Birmingham Children's March from inception to full impact, [author Cynthia Y.] Levinson traces the stories of four young people between the ages of 9 and 15 in 1963. Audrey Hendricks,

Washington Booker III, Arnetta Streeter, and James Stewart came from very different segments of the city's black community, but all risked their lives and spent time in jail to fight for their freedom." (School Library Journal)

Litwack, Leon F.

How free is free? The long death of Jim Crow. Harvard University Press 2009 187p (Nathan I. Huggins lectures) $18.95

Grades: 11 12 Adult **323.1**

1. African Americans -- Segregation 2. African Americans -- Civil rights 3. Southern States -- Race relations 4. African Americans -- Southern States

ISBN 978-0-674-03152-4

LC 2008-36468

"An interesting analysis of the dynamics of race and class and how they continue to affect progress." Booklist

Includes bibliographical references

Mayer, Robert H.

★ **When** the children marched; the Birmingham civil rights movement. Enslow Publishers 2008 176p il map (Prime) $34.60

Grades: 7 8 9 10 **323.1**

1. African American children 2. African Americans -- Civil rights 3. Birmingham (Ala.) -- Race relations

ISBN 978-0-7660-2930-9; 0-7660-2930-1

LC 2007-25590

"Children played a significant role in Birmingham's crucial civil rights struggle, and this stirring history of the movement, with many photos, news reports, and quotes from all sides, emphasizes the connections between the young people's power and that of the big leaders. . . . From the cover picture of police escorting African American children to jail, the numerous photos of youth in nonviolent confrontation—marching, attacked by dogs and fire hoses, crammed in prisons—will draw readers with their gripping drama." Booklist

Includes glossary and bibliographical references

Mitchell, Don

The **Freedom** Summer Murders; Don Mitchell. Scholastic 2014 256 p. $18.99

Grades: 7 8 9 10 **323.1**

1. Homicide 2. African Americans -- Civil rights 3. Mississippi Freedom Project 4. Civil rights workers -- Mississippi -- Biography 5. Mississippi -- Race relations -- History -- 20th century 6. Murder -- Mississippi -- Neshoba County -- History -- 20th century

ISBN 0545477255; 9780545477253

This young adult book by Don Mitchell tells how "In June of 1964, three idealistic young men . . . were lynched by the Ku Klux Klan in Mississippi. They were trying to register African Americans to vote as part of the Freedom Summer effort to bring democracy to the South. Their disappearance and murder caused a national uproar and was one of the most significant incidents of the Civil Rights Movement, and contributed to the passage of the Civil Rights Act of 1964." (Publisher's note)

"The murders of three young civil rights workers--James Chaney, Andrew Goodman, and Michael Schwerner--are the focus of Mitchell's absorbing book. He conducted interviews with friends and family members of the men, and provides a fascinating biographical sketch of each, along with a thorough account of the police investigation. This compelling book will grab you from its opening paragraphs and won't let go. Bib., ind." Horn Book

Nguyen, Tram

We are all suspects now; untold stories from immigrant communities after 9/11. Beacon Press 2005 187p pa $14

Grades: 11 12 Adult   **323.1**

1. Immigrants 2. September 11 terrorist attacks, 2001
3. War on terrorism 4. United States -- Ethnic relations
ISBN 0-8070-0461-8

LC 2005-11579

"Mesmerizing personal accounts of poor treatment by the US government, as well as everyday trials and tribulations that immigrants face in the aftermath of September 11th, make this book impossible to put down." Univ Press Books for Public and Second Sch Libr, 2006

Includes bibliographical references

Partridge, Elizabeth

★ **Marching** for freedom; walk together, children, and don't you grow weary. Viking 2009 72p il $19.99

Grades: 6 7 8 9 10 11 12   **323.1**

1. Selma (Ala.) -- Race relations 2. African Americans -- Civil rights 3. Civil rights movements 4. African American children
ISBN 978-0-670-01189-6; 0-670-01189-4

LC 2009-9696

Boston Globe-Horn Book Award: Nonfiction (2010)

An examination of the march from Selma to Montgomery in 1965 led by Dr. Martin Luther King, Jr., this book focuses on the children who faced terrifying violence in order to walk alongside him in their fight for freedom and the right to vote.

This is a "stirring photo-essay. . . . The vivid text is filled with quotes collected from Partridge's personal interviews with adults who remember their youthful experiences. . . . Filled with large black-and-white photos, every spread brings readers up close to the dramatic, often violent action." Booklist

Includes bibliographical references

★ **Reporting** civil rights. Library of Am. 2003 2v ea $40

Grades: 11 12 Adult   **323.1**

1. Journalism 2. United States -- Race relations 3. African Americans -- Civil rights
ISBN 1-931082-28-6 v1; 1-931082-29-4 v2

LC 2002-27459

"From A. Philip Randolph's defiant call in 1941 for African Americans to march on Washington to Alice Walker in 1973, Reporting Civil Rights presents firsthand accounts of the revolutionary events that overthrew segregation in the United States. This two-volume anthology brings together for the first time nearly 200 newspaper and magazine reports and book excerpts, and features 151 writers, including James Baldwin, Robert Penn Warren, David Halberstam, Lillian Smith, Gordon Parks, Murray Kempton, Ted Poston, Claude

Sitton, and Anne Moody. A newly researched chronology of the movement, a 32-page insert of rare journalist photographs, and original biographical profiles are included in each volume." (Publisher's note)

"An important anthology for readers interested in the history of the civil rights movement." Booklist

Sugarman, Tracy

We had sneakers, they had guns; the kids who fought for civil rights in Mississippi. Syracuse University Press 2009 332p il $34.95

Grades: 11 12 Adult   **323.1**

1. Mississippi -- Race relations 2. African Americans -- Civil rights
ISBN 978-0-8156-0938-4; 0-8156-0938-8

LC 2009-4618

The author, "a participant in Freedom Summer in Mississippi in 1964-65, where the Student Nonviolent Coordinating Committee (SNCC) worked for voter registration efforts and community organizing, writes an introspective memoir complete with many of his original illustrations composed that summer. . . . This book is a testament to the courageous civil rights workers whose perseverance and courage will inspire all readers." Libr J

Turck, Mary

Freedom song; young voices and the struggle for civil rights. [by] Mary C. Turck. Chicago Review Press 2009 146p il pa $18.95

Grades: 7 8 9 10   **323.1**

1. African American music 2. Chicago Children's Choir 3. Freedom Singers (Musical group) 4. African Americans -- Civil rights
ISBN 978-1-55652-773-9; 1-55652-773-X

LC 2008-29673

"The book is divided into chapters that represent the history of the Civil Rights Movement. 'Sunday of Song,' 'Singing in the Churches,' and 'South Africa,' for example, contain information about the factual events while including how the evolution of the music captured the mood and sentiment of the time. The importance of music in the lives of African Americans is described in depth. . . . The accompanying CD allows students to internalize the words and their emotional impact as they listen. Overall, this informative and well-written book is an excellent addition to any collection." SLJ

Includes bibliographical references

323.11 Ethnic and national groups

Freedman, Russell, 1929-

★ **Because** they marched; the people's campaign for voting rights that changed America. Russell Freedman. Holiday House 2014 83 p. (hardcover) $20

Grades: 6 7 8 9 10   **323.11**

1. Selma (Ala.) 2. African Americans -- Civil rights 3. Civil rights demonstrations -- Alabama 4. Selma (Ala.) -- Race relations 5. Civil rights movements -- Alabama -- Selma -- History -- 20th century 6. African

Americans -- Suffrage -- Alabama -- Selma -- History -- 20th century
ISBN 0823429210; 9780823429219

LC 2013038991

This book, by Russell Freedman, celebrates "the 50th anniversary of the 1965 march for voting rights from Selma to Montgomery, Alabama. . . . [The author] has written a riveting account of this pivotal event in the history of civil rights. . . . In the early 1960s, tensions in the segregated South intensified. Tired of reprisals for attempting to register to vote, Selma's black community began to protest." (Publisher's note)

"With characteristically clear prose sprinkled liberally with primary source quotes and carefully selected photographs, Freedman documents the historic 1965 Selma-to-Montgomery march that sparked the passing of the Voting Rights Act, "the crowning achievement of the civil rights movement." Freedman's opening chapter is particularly effective because it focuses on the teachers' march to the courthouse to register as a major trigger for the movement." Includes bibliographical references and index

Lowery, Lynda Blackmon

Turning 15 on the road to freedom; my story of the 1965 Selma to Montgomery March. by Lynda Blackmon Lowery; as told to Elspeth Leacock and Susan Buckley. Dial Books, an imprint of Penguin Group (USA) LLC 2015 128 p. (hardcover) $19.99
Grades: 7 8 9 10 11 12 **323.11**
1. African Americans -- Civil rights 2. Selma (Ala.) -- Race relations 3. Civil rights movements -- Alabama -- Selma -- History -- 20th century 4. African Americans -- Suffrage -- Alabama -- Selma -- History -- 20th century
ISBN 0803741235; 9780803741232

LC 2013047316

Robert F. Sibert Honor Book (2016)

This book, by Lynda Blackmon Lowery, is "a memoir of the Civil Rights Movement from one of its youngest heroes. As the youngest marcher in the 1965 voting rights march from Selma to Montgomery, Alabama, Lynda Blackmon Lowery proved that young adults can be heroes. Jailed eleven times before her fifteenth birthday, Lowery fought alongside Martin Luther King, Jr. for the rights of African-Americans." (Publisher's note)

"The illustrations are a mix of photographs and cartoonish drawings, which bring a graphic novel-like feel to this memoir. A concluding chapter explains the fight for voting rights and contains short biographies of those who died for the cause. This is an honest, powerful historical work, straight from the source." SLJ

323.3 Civil and political rights of other social groups

★ **Do** children have rights? Christine Watkins, book editor. Greenhaven Press 2010 129p (At issue. Civil liberties) $31.80; pa $22.50
Grades: 9 10 11 12 **323.3**
1. Youth -- Civil rights
ISBN 978-0-7377-4876-5; 978-0-7377-4877-2 pa

LC 2010021987

The articles in this anthology discuss different aspects of children's rights including child labor, sex education, and drug testing in schools.
Includes bibliographical references

323.44 Freedom of action (Liberty)

Freedom of expression; Alicia Cafferty Lerner and Adrienne Wilmoth Lerner, book editors. Greenhaven Press 2009 205p il map (Global viewpoints) $37.30; pa $25.70
Grades: 9 10 11 12 **323.44**
1. Censorship 2. Mass media 3. Freedom of speech 4. Freedom of the press
ISBN 978-0-7377-4154-4; 978-0-7377-4155-1 pa

LC 2009-8221

The articles in this anthology "focus on the censorship issues that face artists, journalists, and everyday citizens around the globe. Most of the writing concerns how countries restrict freedoms. Yet some of the most interesting essays center on how these very restrictions can be beneficial in other ways." Booklist
Includes bibliographical references

Fromm, Erich

★ **Escape** from freedom. 1941 305p hardcover o.p. pa $14
Grades: 9 10 11 12 **323.44**
1. Freedom 2. Totalitarianism 3. Social psychology
ISBN 0-8050-3149-9

"A searching inquiry into the meaning of freedom for modern man. . . . The author stresses the role of psychological factors in the social process, interpreting the historical development of freedom in terms of man's awareness of himself as a significant separate being." Libr J
Includes bibliographical references

January, Brendan

Information Insecurity; privacy under siege. Brendan January. Twenty-First Century Books 2016 96 p. (lib. bdg.: alk. paper) $34.65
Grades: 7 8 9 10 **323.44**
1. Privacy 2. Right of privacy 3. Internet -- Security measures
ISBN 9781467725170

LC 2014018682

This young adult nonfiction book, by Brendan January, explores how "the Internet gives us information, communication options, shopping opportunities, entertainment, and much more--all at the touch of a fingertip and much of it for free. But in exchange for these benefits, we may be losing a basic right: the right to privacy." (Publisher's note)

"With an engaging, direct tone and plenty of further reading suggestions, this informative title will provide valuable, accessible insight into an up-to-the-minute topic." Booklist
Includes bibliographical references and index

Senker, Cath

Privacy and surveillance; Cath Senker. Rosen Central 2012 48 p. (Ethical debates)

Grades: 7 8 9 10   323.44
1. Right of privacy 2. Electronic surveillance 3.
Privacy, Right of -- Case studies 4. Electronic
surveillance -- Case studies
ISBN 1448870119; 9781448860227; 9781448870110;
9781448870127

LC 2011028565
This book by Cath Senker, part of the Ethical Debates
series, "[d]iscusses the controversies regarding privacy and
surveillance, including the ethical aspects of electronic surveillance of citizens by the government, security of identity over the Internet, and students under surveillance at
schools." (WorldCat)
Includes bibliographical references and index

323.6   Citizenship and related topics

Ellis, Richard
★ To the flag; the unlikely history of the Pledge
of Allegiance. [by] Richard J. Ellis. University Press
of Kansas 2005 297p il hardcover o.p. pa $15.95
Grades: 11 12 Adult   323.6
1. Pledge of Allegiance
ISBN 0-7006-1372-2; 0-7006-1521-0 pa

LC 2004-23110
The author provides an "account not only of the pledge's
19th century beginnings, but also of its recent use as a political tool. A must read for political junkies of any age!" Univ
Press Books for Public and Second Sch Libr, 2006

324   The political process

★ Student's guide to elections; advisory editor,
Bruce J. Schulman. CQ Press 2008 394p il map
(Student's guide to the U.S. government series)
$85
Grades: 9 10 11 12   324
1. Reference books 2. Elections -- United States
ISBN 978-0-87289-552-2

LC 2008-13032
In this first volume of a projected four-volume series,
"Schulman takes a three-part approach to the topic of United
States' elections. He opens with three essays on the Electoral College, the role of political parties, and American
democracy. His second part covers more than one hundred
election-related topics in alphabetical order, including the
presidential elections from 1789 to the 2008 campaign. The
third part comprises a collection of primary source documents related to topics covered in the book. . . . This book
provides a thorough introduction to the political process."
Voice Youth Advocates
Includes bibliographical references

Thomas, Evan
A long time coming; the inspiring, combative
2008 campaign and the historic election of Barack
Obama. with exclusive, behind-the-scenes reporting
by the staff of Newsweek. PublicAffairs 2009 220p
il $22.95

Grades: 11 12 Adult   324
1. Lawyers 2. Presidents 3. Senators 4. State
legislators 5. Nobel laureates for peace 6. Presidents
-- United States -- Election -- 2008
ISBN 978-1-58648-607-5

LC 2008-51492
This book on the 2008 election is "compiled from the
reporting of the political writers of Newsweek. . . . [This is]
a perceptive, smoothly written and generally fair-minded account of both presidential campaigns." N Y Times Book Rev

324.2   Political parties

McNeese, Tim
The progressive movement; advocating social
change. Chelsea House 2007 144p il (Reform
movements in American history) $30
Grades: 8 9 10 11 12   324.2
1. Social change 2. Progressivism (United States
politics) 3. United States -- Politics and government
-- 1865-1898
ISBN 978-0-7910-9501-0; 0-7910-9501-0

LC 2007-14920
This chronological history of the progressive movement
discusses the events, legislation, and people associated with
the movements and includes a chronology and timeline.
Includes bibliographical references

Norton, Augustus R.
Hezbollah; a short history. [by] Augustus Richard Norton. Princeton University Press 2014 187p
il map (Princeton studies in Muslim politics) pa
$15.95
Grades: 11 12 Adult   324.2
1. Hezbollah (Lebanon) 2. Lebanon -- Politics and
government
ISBN 9780691160818
Norton "provides an objective account of the genesis and
development of Hezbollah, explaining its central role in contemporary Lebanon. . . . The author demonstrates why Hezbollah has solidified its role as a principal player in Lebanese
politics and enhanced its regional prestige." Choice
Includes bibliographical references

324.5   Nominating candidates

Congressional Quarterly, Inc.
National party conventions, 1831-2008. CQ
Press 2010 375p il pa $65
Grades: 11 12 Adult   324.5
1. Political parties 2. Political conventions
ISBN 978-1-60426-540-8

LC 2009040264
First published 1995 with title: National party conven-
tions, 1831-1992
This volume offers information about Republican and
Democratic Party national conventions including sites, del-
egates, chief officers and keynote speakers, party organi-

zation and rules, credential fights, platform fights, ballots, and candidates.

Includes bibliographical references

324.6 Election systems and procedures; suffrage

Aretha, David

Selma and the Voting Rights Act. Morgan Reynolds Pub. 2007 128p il (The civil rights movement) lib bdg $27.95

Grades: 7 8 9 10 11 12   **324.6**

1. Voting Rights Act of 1965 2. African Americans -- Suffrage 3. Selma (Ala.) -- Race relations 4. African Americans -- Civil rights

ISBN 978-1-59935-056-1; 1-59935-056-4

LC 2007-24655

The author discusses "mid-1960s Alabama and the black struggle to exercise the constitutional right to vote. Even those who know the story of the famous protest marches will be interested in the details here. . . . There are quotes from and photos of the famous as well as the unknown, as well as excerpts from speeches and news photos." Booklist

Includes bibliographical references

Benenson, Bob

Elections A to Z; Dave Tarr, Bob Benenson. 4th ed. SAGE Publications 2012 xxxvii, 793 p.p ill. (cloth) $125

Grades: 11 12 Adult   **324.6**

1. Suffrage 2. Elections 3. United States -- Politics and government 4. Elections -- United States -- Encyclopedias

ISBN 0872897699; 9780872897694

LC 2012008921

This book is a "resource on the history and process of U.S. national elections" that has been updated to include articles on the Tea Party political movement and "the Supreme Court's 2010 Citizens United decision. The approximately 225 alphabetically arranged articles cover topics from 'Absentee Voting' and 'Electoral Behavior' to 'Beauty Contest' and 'Scandals'; they also offer separate entries on black, women's, and youth suffrage." (School Library Journal)

Includes bibliographical references (p. 731-733) and index

Clift, Eleanor

Selecting a president; Eleanor Clift and Matthew Spieler. 1st ed. Thomas Dunne Books 2012 196 p. (hardback) $19.99

Grades: 9 10 11 12   **324.6**

1. Presidents -- United States -- Election 2. Political campaigns -- United States 3. United States -- Politics and government 4. Presidents -- United States -- Nomination

ISBN 1250004497; 9781250004499; 9781466802230

LC 2012008975

This book "explains the machinery of our presidential electoral system. . . . [T]he authors . . . cover the elements of a presidential contest from the early caucuses and primaries through the conventions, general election campaign, Elec-

tion Day and inauguration. . . . In addition to the glossary of elementary political terms, the appendix contains . . . and the complete text of four consequential pieces of campaign rhetoric." (Kirkus)

Congressional Quarterly, Inc.

★ **Presidential** elections 1789-2008. CQ Press 2010 295p il map pa $65

Grades: 11 12 Adult   **324.6**

1. Presidents -- United States -- Election

ISBN 978-1-60426-541-5

LC 2009-40267

First published 1995 with title: Presidential elections, 1789–1992

This book offers information about the electoral college, electoral votes and popular votes in each presidential election, voter turnout, primary returns, and Democratic and Republican Party conventions.

Includes bibliographical references

Frost-Knappman, Elizabeth

Women's suffrage in America; an eyewitness history. [by] Elizabeth Frost-Knappman and Kathryn Cullen-DuPont. Updated ed; Facts on File 2005 512p (Eyewitness history) $75

Grades: 9 10 11 12   **324.6**

1. Women -- Suffrage 2. Women -- United States -- History

ISBN 0-8160-5693-5

LC 2004-43339

First published 1992

This is "a lively and important sourcebook for students of American political and cultural history." SLJ [review of 1992 edition]

Includes bibliographical references

Hillstrom, Laurie

The **Voting** Rights Act of 1965; [by] Laurie Collier Hillstrom. Omnigraphics, Inc. 2009 244p il (Defining moments) $44

Grades: 11 12 Adult   **324.6**

1. Voting Rights Act of 1965 2. African Americans -- Suffrage 3. United States -- Politics and government -- 1961-1974

ISBN 978-0-7808-1048-8; 0-7808-1048-1

LC 2008-38392

"Explains the events that led to the Voting Rights Act of 1965. Details both the racial discrimination and violence that pervaded the South and the civil rights protests that changed American voting rights. Features include a narrative overview, biographies, primary source documents, chronology, glossary, bibliography, and index." Publisher's note

Includes glossary and bibliographical references

Marzilli, Alan

Election reform; 2nd ed.; Chelsea House 2010 119p il map (Point-counterpoint) lib bdg $35

Grades: 7 8 9 10   **324.6**

1. Politics 2. Elections -- United States 3. Campaign

funds -- United States
ISBN 978-1-60413-691-3; 1-60413-691-X
　　　　　　　　　　　　　　LC 2009-51401
First published 2004
This book "examines ongoing debates over voting rights and election laws and asks how the United States might reach the ideal of 'one person, one vote.'" Publisher's note
Includes bibliographical references

The **presidential** election process: opposing viewpoints; Tom Lansford, book editor. Greenhaven Press 2008 216p (Opposing viewpoints series) lib bdg $36.20; pa $24.95
Grades: 9 10 11 12　　　　　　　　　　**324.6**
1. Politics 2. Presidents -- United States -- Election 3. Presidents -- United States -- Nomination
ISBN 978-0-7377-3892-6 lib bdg; 0-7377-3892-8 lib bdg; 978-0-7377-3893-3 pa; 0-7377-3893-6 pa
　　　　　　　　　　　　　　LC 2007-35066
"This collection of essays addresses the American election process. Four chapters feature pro/con articles on the roles of primaries and conventions in the nomination process, campaign financing, media coverage, and the electoral college. Each chapter has four to six selections offering a wide range of opinions on these themes. . . . An excellent resource for students, teachers, and parents." SLJ
Includes bibliographical references

Ruth, Janice E.
　★ **Women** of the suffrage movement; by Janice E. Ruth & Evelyn Sinclair. Library of Congress 2006 64p il (Women who dare) $12.95
Grades: 9 10 11 12　　　　　　　　　　**324.6**
1. Suffragists 2. Women -- Suffrage
ISBN 0-7649-3547-X; 978-0-7649-3547-3
　　　　　　　　　　　　　　LC 2005-40190
This history of the women's suffrage movement includes brief profiles of several key women of that movement, including Elizabeth Smith Miller, Lucy Stone, and Adella Hunt Logan.
Includes bibliographical references

Should the voting age be lowered? Ronnie D. Lankford, book editor. Greenhaven Press 2008 114p (At issue. American politics) lib bdg $29.95; pa $21.20
Grades: 7 8 9 10 11 12　　　　　　　　　**324.6**
1. Voting age
ISBN 978-0-7377-3936-7 lib bdg; 0-7377-3936-3 lib bdg; 978-0-7377-3937-4 pa; 0-7377-3937-1 pa
　　　　　　　　　　　　　　LC 2007-35370
This is an anthology of essays discussing different perspectives on lowering the voting age.
Includes bibliographical references

Votes of Confidence; A Young Person's Guide to American Elections. by Jeff Fleischer. Turtleback Books 2016 240 p. $13.99
Grades: 6 7 8 9 10 11 12　　　　　　　**324.6**
1. Elections -- United States
ISBN 0606379827; 1936976900; 9780606379823; 9781936976904
In this book, author Jeff Fleischer "attempts to make Civics 101 a little more interesting. He breaks down many terms and aspects of the election process to bring some clarity to what seems to be a long, convoluted method of choosing our nation's leaders. The author provides many historical examples to illustrate his discussions of how and why elections work the way they do." (School Library Journal)

Voting rights: opposing viewpoints; Tom Lansford, book editor. Greenhaven Press 2008 225p il (Opposing viewpoints series) lib bdg $25.95; pa $37.40
Grades: 7 8 9 10 11 12　　　　　　　　**324.6**
1. Suffrage
ISBN 978-0-7377-4014-1 lib bdg; 978-0-7377-4015-8 pa
　　　　　　　　　　　　　　LC 2008-12800
This title "discusses current issues in the U.S. [related to voting] . . . and also looks at politics in many other countries: women's right to vote in the Arab world and parts of Latin America, the rulings of South Africa's post-apartheid Constitutional Court, and more. . . . For each article, a clear introduction discusses the issues raised, and the book includes an extensive bibliography of books, periodicals, and organizations to contact." Booklist
Includes bibliographical references

324.7　Conduct of election campaigns

Issenberg, Sasha
　The **victory** lab; the secret science of winning campaigns. Sasha Issenberg. 1st ed. Crown 2012 357 p. (hardcover) $26
Grades: 10 11 12　　　　　　　　　　　**324.7**
1. Elections 2. Political science 3. Political campaigns -- United States 4. Internet in political campaigns -- United States 5. Political campaigns -- United States -- Psychological aspects 6. Political campaigns -- Technological innovations -- United States
ISBN 030795479X; 9780307954794
　　　　　　　　　　　　　　LC 2012023774
This book looks "at the way political consultants and professional vote-getters manipulate people into casting their votes for certain candidates. Although the field has seen some serious innovations over the years--computer models, highly detailed research tools, the use of cutting-edge behavioral psychology to predict how voters will mark their ballots, and more--it's not a new endeavor." The history of the field is considered. (Booklist)
　Includes bibliographical references (p. [329]-344) and index.

Political campaigns: opposing viewpoints; Louise I. Gerdes, book editor. Greenhaven Press 2010 245p il (Opposing viewpoints series) lib bdg $38.50; pa $26.75

Grades: 8 9 10 11 12 **324.7**

1. Politics 2. Campaign funds -- United States 3. United States -- Politics and government

ISBN 978-0-7377-4540-5 lib bdg; 978-0-7377-4541-2 pa

LC 2009-36044

This collection of article excerpts "presents factors that may promote and hinder fair campaigns, including the perennial issue of redistricting and recent technological developments, such as Internet donations." Booklist

Includes bibliographical references

325 International migration and colonization

Bausum, Ann

★ **Denied,** detained, deported; stories from the dark side of American immigration. National Geographic 2009 111p il $21.95; lib bdg $32.90

Grades: 6 7 8 9 10 11 12 **325**

1. Essayists 2. Anarchists 3. Memoirists 4. Writers on politics 5. Family planning advocates 6. Immigrants -- United States 7. United States -- Immigration and emigration

ISBN 978-1-4263-0332-6; 1-4263-0332-7; 978-1-4263-0333-3 lib bdg; 1-4263-0333-5 lib bdg

"This volume deals frankly with the more troubling aspects of United States immigration policy. The author chose the stories of three immigrants. . . . Twelve-year-old German-Jew Herb Karliner was denied entry to the United States at the border when he attempted to escape Nazi Germany. Sixteen-year-old Japanese-American Mary Matsuda was detained with the rest of her family during World War II. Labor-activist Emma Goldman was deported for her 'un-American' views. . . . The themes of the three stories are unified by the introduction and conclusion, which deal with Chinese immigration during the late 19th century and the history of immigration across the southern border of the United States, respectively. Photographs throughout will help students relate to the narrative. . . . This is an interesting and readable book." SLJ

Includes bibliographical references

Immigration; Debra A. Miller, book editor. Greenhaven Press/Gale Cengage Learning 2010 191p (Current controversies) $39.70; pa $27.50

Grades: 9 10 11 12 **325**

1. United States -- Immigration and emigration

ISBN 978-0-7377-4709-6; 0-7377-4709-9; 978-0-7377-4710-2 pa; 0-7377-4710-2 pa

LC 2009044185

"Explores the extent to which both legal and illegal immigration are a problem in the United States, including the impact of immigration on the economy, natural resources, and security. Examines the current treatment of illegal immigrants, and potential changes to the U.S. response to ille-

gal immigration. Also looks at how U.S. immigration policy could be reformed to mitigate the problem." Publisher's note

Includes bibliographical references

Smith, Bonnie

Imperialism; a history in documents. Oxford Univ. Press 2000 175p il map (Pages from history) $32.95

Grades: 9 10 11 12 **325**

1. Imperialism 2. World history

ISBN 0-19-510801-9

LC 00-28552

The author "examines the 'high tide' of colonial imperialism, an era characterized by the expansion of European empires in Africa and Asia for financial gain and national power. She opens with background about the racial and economic rationales for imperialism, and then provides chapters about the rapid growth of empires, the role of technology and profits in imperialism, and its impact on the environment." SLJ

Includes bibliographical references and index

U.S. immigration and migration. Primary sources; [compiled by] James L. Outman; Lawrence W. Baker, editor. UXL 2004 xxxi, 232p il (U.S. immigration and migration reference library) $65

Grades: 9 10 11 12 **325**

1. United States -- Immigration and emigration

ISBN 0-7876-7669-1

LC 2004-3553

"The 17 excerpts begin with Lord Baltimore's 1649 Declaration of Religious Tolerance and end with Pat Buchanan's views on immigration policies. The letters, articles, government documents, Supreme Court rulings, and the reflections of authors such as Willa Cather and Mark Twain offer a wide variety of viewpoints." SLJ

Includes bibliographical references

Urrea, Luis Alberto

★ The **devil's** highway; a true story. Luis Alberto Urrea. Little, Brown 2004 xii, 239p (pbk.) $13.99

Grades: 11 12 Adult **325**

1. Unauthorized immigrants 2. Mexico -- Immigration and emigration 3. United States -- Immigration and emigration 4. Illegal aliens -- Crimes against -- Mexican-American Border Region

ISBN 9780316746717; 9780316010801

LC 2003058930

This book "tracks the paths" of "26 Mexican men" who in 2001 "scrambled across the border into an area of the Arizona desert known as the Devil's highway. Only 12 made it safely across. . . . Their enemies were many: the U.S. Border Patrol ('La Migra'); gung-ho gringo vigilantes bent on taking the law into their own hands; the Mexican Federales; rattlesnakes; severe hypothermia and the remorseless sun. . . . But while many point to the group's smugglers . . . as the prime villains of the tragedy, [Luis Alberto] Urrea unloads on . . . 'the politics of stupidity that rules both sides of the border.' Mexican and U.S. border policy is backward, Urrea finds, and it does little to stem the flow of immigrants. Since the policy results in Mexicans making the crossing in increasingly forbidding areas, it contributes to the conditions that kill those who attempt it." (Publishers Weekly)

326 Slavery and emancipation

Bailey, Anne C.

★ **African** voices of the Atlantic slave trade; beyond the silence and the shame. Beacon Press 2005 289p il map $26; pa $16

Grades: 11 12 Adult   **326**

1. Slave trade

ISBN 0-8070-5512-3; 0-8070-5513-1 pa

LC 2004-15082

The author "focuses on the slave trade from the African perspective. As there are few written African records, in contrast to those found in Europe and the Americas, on this topic, she centers her study on the oral tradition, what she refers to as 'African human libraries.' She primarily focuses on a region in Ghana around one particular oral remembrance told from various perspectives. . . . A fascinating perspective on slavery from the African continent." Booklist

Includes bibliographical references

Douglass, Frederick, 1818-1895

★ **Frederick** Douglass: selected speeches and writings; edited by Philip S. Foner; abridged and adapted by Yuval Taylor. Hill Bks. 1999 789p hardcover o.p. pa $32.95

Grades: 11 12 Adult   **326**

1. Speeches, addresses, etc., American 2. African Americans -- Civil rights -- History -- 19th century 3. Slaves -- United States -- Social conditions -- 19th century 4. Antislavery movements -- United States -- History -- 19th century

ISBN 1-55652-352-1 pa

LC 99-23180

Based on Foner's five-volume The life and writings of Frederick Douglass (1950-1975), this volume "covers Douglass' speeches and writings over a 54-year period. The breadth and depth of his focus and concerns reflected in more than 2,000 speeches, editorials, articles, and letters provide a wellspring of knowledge about the man and his intellect." Booklist

Includes bibliographical references

Fradin, Judith Bloom

5,000 miles to freedom; Ellen and William Craft's flight from slavery. [by] Judith Bloom Fradin and Dennis Brindell Fradin. National Geographic 2006 96p il $19.95; lib bdg $29.90

Grades: 5 6 7 8 9 10   **326**

1. Slaves 2. Memoirists 3. Slavery -- United States

ISBN 0-7922-7885-2; 0-7922-7886-0 lib bdg

"In 1848, light-skinned Ellen Craft, dressed in the clothing of a rich, white man, assumed the identity of Mr. William Johnson and, escorted by his black slave, William, traveled by railroad and boat to reach the North. With the passage of a more stringent Fugitive Slave Law in 1850, the couple . . . decided to travel to England. . . . In 1869, they returned to the United States, opening a school and operating a farm in Georgia. . . . This lively, well-written volume presents the events in their lives in an exciting, page-turner style that's sure to hold readers attention. Black-and-white photographs, illustrations, and reproductions enhance the text." SLJ

Includes bibliographical references

Gann, Marjorie

★ **Five** thousand years of slavery; [by] Marjorie Gann and Janet Willen. Tundra Books 2011 168p il map $27.95

Grades: 7 8 9 10   **326**

1. Slavery 2. Slavery -- History

ISBN 978-0-88776-914-6; 0-88776-914-4

"This well-researched global survey introduces readers to slavery practices, customs, suffering, uprisings, and revolts as well as antislavery efforts from ancient Greece and Rome to today's world. . . . Informative documentary photos and factually rich sidebars enhance the text. . . . [This is a] groundbreaking title." SLJ

Includes bibliographical references

Grant, Reg

★ **Slavery**; real people and their stories of enslavement. DK Pub. 2009 191p il $24.99

Grades: 7 8 9 10   **326**

1. Slavery

ISBN 978-0-7566-5169-5; 0-7566-5169-7

"This encyclopedic guide to the subject of slavery highlights its history from Mesopotamia through the Atlantic slave trade and into the present day. . . . Photographs, time lines, quotations from historical figures and paintings create a diverse panorama of information. . . . As thorough as it is socially pertinent." Publ Wkly

Grayson, Robert

The **Amistad**. ABDO Pub. 2011 112p il (Essential events) lib bdg $23.95

Grades: 7 8 9 10 11 12   **326**

1. Slave trade 2. Amistad (Schooner)

ISBN 978-1-61714-761-6; 1-61714-761-3

LC 2010044662

This "is dramatic history, focusing on the 1839-40 trial of the kidnapped Africans who rebelled on the slave ship from Cuba and were captured and tried in the U.S. on charges of piracy. Were the Africans property? . . . The spacious . . . design is inviting, with many color illustrations and screens, and the extensive back matter includes a detailed time line, glossary, bibliography and source notes." Booklist

Includes glossary and bibliographical references

Horton, James Oliver

★ **Slavery** and the making of America; [by] James Oliver Horton [and] Lois E. Horton. Oxford University Press 2004 254p il maps $35; pa $18.95

Grades: 11 12 Adult   **326**

1. Slavery -- United States 2. African Americans -- History

ISBN 0-19-517903-X; 0-19-530451-9 pa

LC 2004-13617

"The oft-told tale is made fresh through up-to-date slavery scholarship, the extensive use of slave narratives and archival photos and, especially, a focus on individual experience." Publ Wkly

Jewett, Clayton E.
Slavery in the South; a state-by-state history. [by] Clayton E. Jewett and John O. Allen; foreword by Jon L. Wakelyn. Greenwood Press 2004 xxxiii, 305p il $59.95
Grades: 11 12 Adult   **326**
1. Slavery -- United States
ISBN 0-313-32019-5
LC 2003-60004
"Although the book is organized by state, the information is valuable for students who are studying the institution of slavery as a whole." Libr Media Connect
Includes bibliographical references

Lester, Julius
To be a slave; paintings by Tom Feelings. 30th anniversary ed; Dial Bks. 1998 160p il hardcover o.p. pa $6.99
Grades: 6 7 8 9   **326**
1. Slavery -- United States
ISBN 0-8037-2347-4; 0-14-131001-4 pa
LC 98-5213
A reissue of the title first published 1968
"Through the words of the slave, interwoven with strongly sympathetic commentary, the reader learns what it is to be another man's property; how the slave feels about himself; and how he feels about others. Every aspect of slavery, regardless of how grim, has been painfully and unrelentingly described." Read Ladders for Hum Relat. 6th edition
Includes bibliographical references

Slavery in America; Orville Vernon Burton, editor. Gale 2008 2v il (Gale library of daily life) set $211
Grades: 9 10 11 12   **326**
1. Reference books 2. Slavery -- United States
ISBN 978-1-4144-3013-3; 1-4144-3013-2
LC 2007-38576
This is a "survey of slavery in the United States between 1619 and the Civil War. . . . Chapters are organized into sections covering subjects such as the Middle Passage and Africa; work; family and community; culture and leisure; health; religion; the business of slavery; resistance and rebellion; and historical reactions for and against the institution. . . . This thought-provoking and thorough reference work will appeal to both general and scholarly audiences. American history students will find it useful for reports and background information." SLJ
Includes bibliographical references

★ **Slavery** today; Ronald D. Lankford, Jr., book editor. Greenhaven Press 2010 137p (At issue. Social issues) $31.80; pa $22.50
Grades: 9 10 11 12   **326**
1. Slavery 2. Slave trade
ISBN 978-0-7377-4440-8; 0-7377-4440-5; 978-0-7377-4441-5 pa; 0-7377-4441-3 pa
LC 2009020987

The articles in this anthology discuss modern-day slavery and possible ways to end it.
Includes bibliographical references

Worth, Richard
Slave life on the plantation; prisons beneath the sun. Enslow Publishers 2004 128p il (Slavery in American history) lib bdg $26.60
Grades: 7 8 9 10   **326**
1. Plantation life 2. Slavery -- United States
ISBN 0-7660-2152-1
LC 2003-24291
"Worth frames his account within the sweep of history, but his focus is on daily life—the work, the hardship (especially the breakup of family life), punishment, and resistance—and he discusses the relationship between owners and slaves, the importance of cotton, and African American culture. [This title includes] several stirring page-long slave narratives as well as black-and-white drawings and photos. The documentation is exemplary." Booklist
Includes glossary and bibliographical references

326.8   Emancipation

Gann, Marjorie
Speak a word for freedom; women against slavery. Janet Willen, Marjorie Gann. Tundra Books of Northern New York 2015 216 p. illustrations, portraits (hardcover) $21.99
Grades: 7 8 9 10   **326.8**
1. Abolitionists 2. Women political activists
ISBN 9781770496514; 9781770496538
LC 2014939465
This book, by Janet Willen and Marjorie Gann, profiles women anti-slavery activism. "From the early days of the antislavery movement, when political action by women was frowned upon, British and American women were tireless and uncompromising campaigners. . . . And the commitment of today's women . . . descends directly from that of the early female activists. . . . [This volume] tells the story of fourteen of these women." (Publisher's note)
"With the exceptions of Harriet Tubman and Harriet Beecher Stowe, most of the women featured will be new to most readers. The powerful message, that the fight to end slavery is ongoing and depends on a wide variety of actions and individuals, will both educate teens on this important issue and inspire them to take active roles in civic life." Booklist

327   International relations

The **American** empire; [edited by] John C. Davenport. Chelsea House 2007 152p il (The world in focus) $35
Grades: 7 8 9 10   **327**
1. Imperialism 2. War on terrorism 3. United States -- Foreign relations
ISBN 978-0-7910-9195-1; 0-7910-9195-3
LC 2007-3656

"The first set of essays searches the past for the origins of American imperialism and the roots of American preeminence. The second section looks at how the United States applies—or sometimes misapplies—its unparalleled power and influence overseas, as well as the domestic implications of such actions. Each of the essays in the final section considers a future in which the United States acknowledges its imperial status and asserts itself accordingly, examining the beneficial and deleterious effects of a self-consciously active empire." Publisher's note

Includes bibliographical references

Global perspectives on the United States; a nation by nation survey. David Levinson and Karen Christensen, editors. Berkshire Pub. Group 2007 2v il map set $275

Grades: 11 12 Adult   327

1. United States -- Foreign opinion 2. United States -- Foreign relations

ISBN 978-1-9337820-6-5; 1-9337820-6-4

LC 2006-39331

"Not recommended reading for thin-skinned patriots; however, a great resource for academic, public, and high-school libraries." Booklist

Includes bibliographical references

Laxer, James

Empire. Groundwood Books 2006 144p il map (Groundwork Guides) $15.95

Grades: 8 9 10 11 12   327

1. Imperialism 2. United States -- Foreign relations

ISBN 978-0-88899-706-7; 0-88899-706-X

LC 2006-497080

This book "compares the American Empire to those of the past, finding much can be learned from the fates of the British, Roman, Chinese, Incan, and Aztec empires." Publisher's note

Includes bibliographical references

Margulies, Phillip

America's role in the world; foreword by James M. Goldgeier. Facts On File 2009 358p (Global issues) $45

Grades: 9 10 11 12   327

1. United States -- Foreign opinion 2. United States -- Foreign relations

ISBN 978-0-8160-7611-6; 0-8160-7611-1

LC 2008-32102

"This volume begins with a detailed history of American foreign policy and the debate over what direction it should take. Margulies examines America's role in the world from the perspectives of Europe, Latin America, the Islamic world, Asia, and the former Soviet Union. . . . Readers will also find a chapter on how to research America's role in the world, facts and figures, key players, organizations and agencies, chronology, glossary and and an annotated bibliography. The scholarship exhibited should be a model for all . . . books written for high school students." Libr Media Connect

Includes glossary and bibliographical references

327.12   Espionage and subversion

Espionage and intelligence; Debra A. Miller, book editor. Greenhaven Press 2007 234p (Current controversies) lib bdg $38.50; pa $26.75

Grades: 9 10 11 12   327.12

1. American espionage 2. Intelligence service -- United States

ISBN 978-0-7377-3719-6 lib bdg; 0-7377-3719-0 lib bdg; 978-0-7377-3720-2 pa; 0-7377-3720-4 pa

LC 2007-931891

Topics in this anthology include the use of torture to gather information, civil rights issues regarding intelligence gathering, and U.S. intelligence with regards to the 9/11 terrorist attacks and Iraq's possession of weapons of mass destruction.

Includes bibliographical references

Weiner, Tim

★ **Legacy** of ashes; the history of the CIA. Tim Weiner. Doubleday 2007 702p ill. (pbk.) $17.95; o.p.; o.p.

Grades: 11 12 Adult   327.12

1. United States -- History -- 1945- 2. Intelligence service -- United States 3. United States. Central Intelligence Agency 4. United States -- Central Intelligence Agency 5. United States. Central Intelligence Agency -- History

ISBN 9780307389008; 9780385514453; 038551445X

LC 2007004077

Los Angeles Times Book Prizes: History (2007); National Book Awards: Nonfiction (2007)

This book is a "chronicle of the [U.S.] Central Intelligence Agency . . . [and] C.I.A. incompetence. . . . The author has . . . studied the archival record, teased out newly declassified primary documents and done numerous interviews to glean as much as can be publicly known about the agency's history. Some of the most damning criticism of the C.I.A.'s past performance in this book comes . . . from ex-officials and long-secret authorized accounts by C.I.A. historians. . . . [Author Tim] Weiner argues that a bad C.I.A. track record has encouraged many of . . . [the U.S.'s] gravest contemporary problems: Iran, Iraq, Afghanistan, terrorism." (New York Times)

This book "takes the CIA from its creation after World War II, through its battles in the cold war and the war on terror, to its . . . [circumstances] after 9/11." Publisher's note

Includes bibliographical references and index

328   The legislative process

Barone, Michael

★ The **almanac** of American politics 2012; Michael Barone, Chuck McCutcheon. University of Chicago Press 2011 xviii, 1838 p.p (hardcover) $110; (paperback) $85.00

Grades: 11 12 Adult   328

1. Almanacs 2. United States -- Politics and government

-- 2001-
ISBN 0226038076; 0226038084; 9780226038070;
9780226038087

LC 2011929193

This book, by Michael Barone and Chuck McCutcheon, is a 2012 edition almanac on U.S. politics. It "includes profiles of every member of Congress and every governor. It offers in-depth and completely up-to-date narrative profiles of all 50 states and 435 House districts, covering everything from economics to history to, of course, politics." (Publisher's note)

Congressional Quarterly, Inc.

Congress and the Nation; a review of government and politics in the postwar years. Congressional Quarterly 1965
Grades: 11 12 Adult   **328**
1. Legislation 2. United States -- Congress 3. United States -- Politics and government -- 20th century
"Overview and detailed coverage of presidential, legislative, and political events in every major subject area." N Y Public Libr Book of How & Where to Look It Up

★ **CQ's** politics in America, 2010; the 111th Congress. by Congressional Quarterly staff; Chuck McCutcheon and Christina L. Lyons, editors. Congressional Quarterly, Inc. 2009 xxvi, 1214p il $125; pa $89
Grades: 11 12 Adult   **328**
1. Reference books 2. United States -- Congress 3. Elections -- United States
ISBN 978-1-60426-602-3; 978-1-60426-603-0 pa
Biennial. First published 1981
Provides an analysis of every lawmaker in the 111th Congress, including biographical data, contact information, election results, and committee assignments.
"An outstanding, highly detailed guide to contemporary politics." Libr J

Dewhirst, Robert E.

Encyclopedia of the United States Congress; [by] Robert E. Dewhirst; John David Rausch, Jr., associate editor. Facts on File 2006 578p il (Facts on File library of American history) $95
Grades: 11 12 Adult   **328**
1. Reference books 2. United States -- Congress
ISBN 0-8160-5058-9

LC 2005-28124

This encyclopedia covers "the people, events, and terms involved in the legislative branch of government. It also provides explanations of the relationships between the legislative and other branches of government, court cases, elections, political opponents, congressional leaders, scandals, controversial issues, and the inner workings of Congress." Publisher's note
Includes bibliographical references

Freedman, Eric

African Americans in Congress; a documentary history. [by] Eric Freedman, Stephen A. Jones. CQ Press 2008 574p il $115

Grades: 9 10 11 12   **328**
1. Reference books 2. Statesmen -- United States 3. United States -- Congress -- History 4. African Americans -- History -- Sources
ISBN 978-0-87289-385-6; 0-87289-385-5

LC 2007-40318

"For students of history, American studies, politics, and journalism, this volume is mandatory." SLJ
Includes bibliographical references

Lewis, John

Walking with the wind; a memoir of the movement. [by] John Lewis with Michael D'Orso. Harcourt 1999 526p il pa $16
Grades: 11 12 Adult   **328**
1. Members of Congress 2. Civil rights activists 3. African Americans -- Biography 4. African Americans -- Civil rights 5. United States -- Congress -- House 6. Student Nonviolent Coordinating Committee
ISBN 0-15-600708-8

LC 99-28356

First published 1998 by Simon & Schuster
"The strength of Lewis's powerful new book is not only the witness he bears but also the simplicity of his voice." Newsweek

★ **Official** Congressional directory, 2009-2010; 111th Congress convened January 6, 2009. Joint Committee on Printing, United States Congress. U.S. Government Printing Office 2009 xxiv, 1207p map $55; pa $45
Grades: 11 12 Adult   **328**
1. Reference books 2. United States -- Congress -- Directories
ISBN 978-0-16-083728-9; 978-0-16-083727-2 pa
Biennial
"Covers biographical information, committee assignments of members of Congress, and officers of Congress." N Y Public Libr Book of How & Where to Look It Up

Remini, Robert Vincent

The **House**: the history of the House of Representatives; [by] Robert V. Remini. HarperCollins Publishers 2006 614p il hardcover o.p. pa $19.95
Grades: 11 12 Adult   **328**
1. United States -- Congress -- House -- History
ISBN 978-0-06-088434-5; 0-06-088434-7; 978-0-06-134111-3 pa; 0-06-134111-8 pa

LC 2006-615801

"Published under the aegis of the House itself, Remini's work is nonpartisan, civic-minded, and deserving of every library's consideration." Booklist
Includes bibliographical references

Robert C. Byrd Center for Legislative Studies

Congress investigates; a critical and documentary history. edited by Roger A. Bruns, David L. Hostetter, Raymond W. Smock; Robert C. Byrd Center for Legislative Studies. Rev. ed; Facts on File 2011 2v il (Facts on File library of American history) set $195

Grades: 9 10 11 12 Adult   **328**
1. Reference books 2. Governmental investigations -- United States
ISBN 978-0-8160-7679-6; 978-1-4381-3545-8 ebook
LC 2010020268
First published 1975
The editors "have gathered here information on congressional investigations from the Colonial period to the 21st century. The entries, written by U.S. historians and archivists, each offer an overview, chronology, documents, excerpts from congressional committee reports and testimony, and a bibliography; many also include black-and-white illustrations, photographs, or political cartoons. They cover well-known events such as the Teapot Dome scandal, the burning of Washington in 1814, the Hurricane Katrina inquiry of 2005–06, and several lesser-known happenings—General St. Clair's defeat of 1792–93 and the Pujo Committee on the 'Money Trust,' for example. . . . This well-researched and richly detailed resource provides an excellent overview of major congressional investigations and will be a quality addition to a high school, public, or undergraduate academic library." Libr J
Includes bibliographical references

Stathis, Stephen W.
★ **Landmark** debates in Congress; from the Declaration of independence to the war in Iraq. CQ Press 2009 514p il map $145
Grades: 11 12 Adult   **328**
1. Reference books 2. American speeches 3. Parliamentary practice 4. United States -- Congress -- History 5. United States -- Politics and government -- Sources
ISBN 978-0-87289-976-6; 0-87289-976-4
LC 2008-41380
"Presenting excerpts of speeches delivered in the House of Representatives and the Senate, this volume seeks to give readers 'a window into how Congress, seemingly constituting a cross-section of society, has wrestled with some of the most thorny questions facing American democracy.' Such monumental issues as war, slavery, impeachment of the President, amendments to the Constitution, and other bones of contention illuminate the legislative process. . . . A depiction of real people struggling to solve real problems, this book helps to humanize 'the marble men'—and women—of our national legislative body." Libr J
Includes bibliographical references

★ **Student's** guide to Congress; advisory editor, Bruce J. Schulman. CQ Press 2009 379p il map (Student's guide to the U.S. government series) $75
Grades: 9 10 11 12   **328**
1. Reference books 2. United States -- Congress
ISBN 978-0-87289-554-6; 0-87289-554-8
LC 2008-28980
"Part 1 consists of essays that help students explain who gets elected, understand how Congress operates, and appreciate how Congress and the president must work together. Part 2 consists of 142 A-Z entries, from Abscam to Zone whips. . . . Part 3, Primary Source Library, includes portions of the Constitution, Henry Clay's explanation of his support

of the War of 1812, Joseph McCarthy's 1950 telegram to Harry Truman alleging that the State Department harbors a nest of communists and communist sympathizers, and the War Powers Resolution of 1973. . . . [This] volume provides a lot of information and thought-provoking material that will serve high-school students in addition to any older researchers interested in this topic." Booklist
Includes bibliographical references

330   Economics

Bussing-Burks, Marie
Money for minors; a student's guide to economics. Greenwood Press 2008 200p il $55
Grades: 9 10 11 12   **330**
1. Money 2. Economics
ISBN 978-0-313-34757-3
LC 2008-4496
"A wonderful reference for all monetary matters. . . . It's a great resource for beginners." SLJ
Includes bibliographical references

★ **Economic** literacy; a complete guide. Marshall Cavendish 2009 224p il $99.90
Grades: 9 10 11 12   **330**
1. Economics
ISBN 978-0-7614-7910-9; 0-7614-7910-4
LC 2009-9462
This book is "comprised of approximately 50 A-to-Z articles ranging in length from two to four pages. Economic Literacy provides clearly outlined historical perspectives on international trade, socialism, and tariffs, balanced with newsworthy items. . . . Articles on globalization, service economy, and sustainable development look toward future developments and include links to organizations, reports, inflation calculators, and more." SLJ
Includes glossary and bibliographical references

Outman, James L.
Industrial Revolution: biographies; [by] James L. Outman, Elisabeth M. Outman. U.X.L 2003 218p il (Industrial revolution reference library) $55
Grades: 8 9 10 11 12   **330**
1. Industrial revolution
ISBN 0-7876-6514-2
LC 2002-155421
"The 25 essays in [this volume] provide biographical information with an emphasis on each person's contribution or impact on the Industrial Revolution. . . . More than 50 black-and-white photographs complement the text. . . . This is an excellent adjunct to American and world history units and classes on economics and labor movements." Booklist
Includes bibliographical references

★ The **Statesman's** Yearbook 2014; The Politics, Cultures and Economies of the World. edited by Barry Turner. 150th ed. Palgrave Macmillan 2013 1608 p. (hardcover) $325

Grades: 8 9 10 11 12 Adult   **330**

1. Almanacs 2. Geopolitics

ISBN 0230377696; 9780230377691

This reference book "presents a political, economic and social account of every country of the world together with facts and analysis. The 2014 edition includes revised and updated biographical profiles of all current leaders," "revised economic overviews for every country," and a "chronology of key political events from April 2010 to March 2011." (Publisher's note)

330.01 Philosophy and theory

Furgang, Kathy

Understanding economic indicators; predicting future trends in the economy. Kathy Furgang. Rosen Pub. 2012 80 p. (library binding) $33.25

Grades: 9 10 11 12   **330.01**

1. Economic indicators 2. Gross national product

ISBN 1448855713; 9781448855711

     LC 2011017461

This book by Kathy Furgang, part of the Real World Economics series, "introduces readers to the . . . realm of economic indicators -- leading, lagging, and coincident indicators. Readers will be initiated into the mysteries of economic analysis and forecasting and learn exactly how economists 'read the signs' and come up with solid data that provides reliable and accurate information about the upward or downward direction in which the economy is headed." (Publisher's note)

Includes bibliographical references and index.

330.1 Systems, schools, theories

Heilbroner, Robert L.

The **worldly** philosophers; the lives, times, and ideas of the great economic thinkers. Rev. 7th ed.; Simon & Schuster 1999 365p pa $16

Grades: 11 12 Adult   **330.1**

1. Authors 2. Utopias 3. Economics 4. Capitalism 5. Economists 6. Depressions 7. Imperialism 8. Journalists 9. Social critics 10. Nonfiction writers 11. Patrons of the arts 12. Writers on politics 13. Political and social philosophers

ISBN 0-684-86214-X

     LC 99-14050

First published 1953

The author traces the story of economics and the great economists from Adam Smith, Malthus, Ricardo, the Utopians, Marx, Veblen and Keynes to those working with the problems of our contemporary world

Includes bibliographical references

330.9 Economic situation and conditions

Allport, Alan

The **British** industrial revolution. Chelsea House 2011 126p il (Milestones in modern world history) lib bdg $35

Grades: 7 8 9 10   **330.9**

1. Industrial revolution 2. Great Britain -- History -- 19th century 3. Great Britain -- Economic conditions -- 19th century

ISBN 978-1-60413-498-8; 1-60413-498-4

     LC 2010030579

"Allport introduces his subject with the intriguing premise of a time traveler from Roman Britain looking upon the world of 1750 and then 1850, and noting the extreme changes made in that single century compared to 1700 years before it. Chapters cover Britain before the Industrial Revolution, changes in agriculture and textiles, the rise of cities, and the reform movement that sprang up in response to the degrading conditions created in the newly industrialized world." SLJ

Includes bibliographical references

Benson, Sonia

Development of the industrial U.S.: Almanac; [by] Sonia G. Benson; Jennifer York Stock, project editor. UXL 2006 lv, 216p il (Development of the industrial U.S reference library) $63

Grades: 9 10 11 12   **330.9**

1. Reference books 2. Industrial revolution 3. Industries -- United States

ISBN 1-4144-0175-2

     LC 2005-15915

This book "consists of 14 chapters, each thoroughly examining one aspect of industrialization, such as railroads or early factories. User-friendly features (research and activity ideas, ample glossaries and word boxes, references to Web sites and print resources) further enhance this product's usefulness." Booklist

Includes bibliographical references

★ **Development** of the industrial U.S.: Primary sources; [by] Sonia G. Benson; Jennifer York Stock, project editor. UXL 2006 lii, 205p il (Development of the industrial U.S reference library) $63

Grades: 9 10 11 12   **330.9**

1. Industrial revolution 2. Industries -- United States

ISBN 1-4144-0179-5

     LC 2005-16349

This book "provides excerpts and explications of seminal sources, including legislative acts, accounts of daily life from regular citizens, political cartoons and more." Publisher's note

Includes bibliographical references

Encyclopedia of the age of the industrial revolution, 1700-1920; edited by Christine Rider. Greenwood Press 2007 2v il set $225

Grades: 11 12 Adult   **330.9**

1. Reference books 2. Industrial revolution --

Encyclopedias
ISBN 978-0-313-33503-7; 0-313-33501-X

LC 2007-1830

"The 150 signed essays in this set cover people, events, and inventions of the Industrial Revolution, and discuss how the movement affected not only business and trade, but also society, politics, and even ecology in many countries. The entries provide important facts, yet are often thoughtful and philosophical. . . . Many other volumes expound on inventions and inventors, but this one stands out for its treatment of Japan, Russia, and other countries, as well as its coverage of the sociological, ecological, and aesthetic implications of this period." SLJ

Includes bibliographical references

★ **Industrial** revolution; people and perspectives. Jennifer L. Goloboy, editor. ABC-CLIO 2008 224p il (Perspectives in American social history) $85

Grades: 11 12 Adult   330.9
1. Reference books 2. Industrialization 3. Industrial revolution 4. United States -- Social conditions
ISBN 978-1-59884-065-0; 1-59884-065-7

LC 2008-2366

"This clearly written and carefully researched volume documents . . . [the] early steps toward industrialization from roughly 1800 to 1860, calling attention to groups [such as] women, ethnic and cultural minorities, [and] laborers. . . . This work provides a useful timeline from 1748 to 1860, an abundance of photographs, an assortment of primary documents . . . a bibliography at the end of each chapter and a topical bibliography at the end of the study, and an adequate index. While certainly useful to scholars, this is a work for a general audience that would be a worthwhile addition to high school and university libraries." Am Ref Books Annu, 2009

Includes bibliographical references

Industrialization and empire, 1783 to 1914; edited by Louise Spilsbury. Brown Bear Books 2010 112p il map (Curriculum connections. Atlas of world history) lib bdg $39.95

Grades: 9 10 11 12   330.9
1. Imperialism 2. Modern history 3. Industrialization 4. Industrial revolution 5. World history -- 19th century
ISBN 978-1-933834-69-6

LC 2009-27837

This book "is divided into thematic and regional maps which are followed by short but very comprehensive articles. . . . [It includes] curriculum context sidebars, important terms students should know, and how the topic ties into other areas." Libr Media Connect

Includes bibliographical references

Lewis, Michael
The **big** short; inside the doomsday machine. W.W. Norton 2010 266p

Grades: 11 12 Adult   330.9
1. Financial crises 2. Global Financial Crisis, 2008-2009 3. Financial crises -- United States 4. United States -- Economic conditions 5. United States --

Economic conditions -- 2001-2009
ISBN 0-393-07223-1; 0-393-33882-7 pa; 978-0-393-07223-5; 978-0-393-33882-9 pa

LC 201004804

This is a study of the financial crisis that began in 2008. Michael Lewis, the author of Liar's Poker (1989) contends that "the roots of the meltdown of 2008 can be found in the 1980s, . . . when complex financial products like mortgage derivatives were developed." (N Y Times (Late N Y Ed))

"'The Big Short' manages to give us the truest picture yet of what went wrong on Wall Street—and why. At times, it reads like a morality play, at other times like a modern-day farce. But as with any good play, its value lies in the way it reveals character and motive and explores the cultural context in which the plot unfolds." Washington Post

Outman, James L.
Industrial Revolution: almanac; [by] James L. Outman, Elisabeth M. Outman. U.X.L 2003 242p il (Industrial revolution reference library) $55

Grades: 8 9 10 11 12   330.9
1. Reference books 2. Industrial revolution
ISBN 0-7876-6513-4

LC 2002-155422

"This is an excellent adjunct to American and world history units and classes on economics and labor movements." Booklist

Includes bibliographical references

330.973 Economic conditions--United States

Bair, Sheila, 1954-
The **Bullies** of Wall Street; this is how greedy adults messed up our economy. Sheila Bair. Simon & Schuster Books for Young Readers 2015 272 p. illustrations (hardcover) $17.99

Grades: 8 9 10 11 12   330.973
1. Working class 2. Financial crises 3. Global Financial Crisis, 2008-2009 4. United States -- Economic conditions 5. United States -- Economic conditions -- 2001-2009
ISBN 1481400851; 9781481400855; 9781481400862

LC 2014005948

In this book, author Sheila Bair "explains how the Great Recession impacted families on a personal level using language that everyone can understand. . . . [S]he describes the many ways in which a broken system led families into financial trouble, and also explains the decisions being made at the time by the most powerful people in the country-- from CEOs of multinational banks, to heads of government regulatory committees-- that led to the recession." (Publisher's note)

"The case studies themselves are interesting and clear, but the explanatory, bolded inserts are difficult to follow. Bair's personal story is interesting, but it contains information beyond the scope of youth understanding. A list of government agencies and their acronyms would be helpful throughout the book. Best used as supplemental reading for advanced finance classes." Booklist

Bullie$ of Wall St
Bullies of Wall Street

331 Economics of labor, finance, land, energy

Murray, R. Emmett

The **lexicon** of labor; more than 500 key terms, biographical sketches, and historical insights concerning labor in America. Rev. and updated ed.; New Press 2010 235p pa $16.95

Grades: 11 12 Adult **331**

1. Reference books 2. Labor -- United States -- Dictionaries

ISBN 978-1-59558-226-3

LC 2010-8276

First published 1998

This is an "encyclopedia of 500 entries for terms, concepts, people, legislation, places, and events in U.S. labor history." Booklist

Includes bibliographical references

331.1 Labor force and market

Affirmative action; a documentary history. edited by Jo Ann Ooiman Robinson. Greenwood Press 2001 400p (Primary documents in American history and contemporary issues) $49.95

Grades: 11 12 Adult **331.1**

1. Civil rights 2. Discrimination 3. Affirmative action programs

ISBN 0-313-30169-7

LC 00-49508

"Presents 400 documents, beginning in 1864 . . . and ending in mid-2000. In between are extracts from speeches, proceedings, legislation, court cases, articles, and more. Each document is accompanied by a brief explanation that puts it in context." Booklist

Includes bibliographical references

331.2 Conditions of employment

Paquette, Penny Hutchins

Apprenticeship; the ultimate teen guide. Scarecrow Press 2005 373p il (It happened to me) $42

Grades: 9 10 11 12 **331.2**

1. Apprentices 2. Vocational education 3. Occupational training

ISBN 0-8108-4945-3

LC 2005-8301

"An excellent starting point for teens." SLJ

Includes bibliographical references

331.3 Labor force by personal attributes

★ **Child** labor and sweatshops; Christine Watkins, book editor. Gale Cengage Learning 2011 124p (At issue. Social issues) $33.70; pa $23.85

Grades: 9 10 11 12 **331.3**

1. Child labor

ISBN 978-0-7377-4874-1; 978-0-7377-4875-8 pa

LC 2010012649

First published 1999

Articles in this anthology cover different aspects of child labor, such as whether legislation preventing child labor works.

Includes bibliographical references

331.4 Women workers

Povich, Lynn

The **good** girls revolt; how the women of Newsweek sued their bosses and changed the workplace. Lynn Povich. PublicAffairs 2012 xx, 249 p.p (hardcover) $25.99

Grades: Adult **331.4**

1. Sexism 2. Women journalists 3. Sex discrimination in employment 4. Sex discrimination -- Law and legislation 5. Newsweek 6. Women journalists -- United States 7. Sex discrimination in employment -- United States 8. Sex role in the work environment -- United States

ISBN 161039173X; 9781610391733; 9781610391740

LC 2012006936

Amelia Bloomer Project (2014)

This book by Lynn Povich explains how, in 1970, "forty-six 'Newsweek' women charged the magazine with discrimination in hiring and promotion. It was the first female class action lawsuit--the first by women journalists--and it inspired other women in the media to quickly follow suit. . . . 'The Good Girls Revolt' also explores why changes in the law didn't solve everything. Through the lives of young female journalists at Newsweek today, Lynn Povich shows what has--and hasn't--changed in the workplace." (Publisher's note)

Includes bibliographical references and index.

331.7 Labor by industry and occupation

150 great tech prep careers; 2nd ed.; Ferguson 2009 561p $85; pa $29.95

Grades: 9 10 11 12 **331.7**

1. Occupations 2. Technical education 3. Vocational education

ISBN 978-0-8160-7733-5; 0-8160-7733-9; 978-0-8160-7734-2 pa; 0-8160-7734-7 pa

LC 2008-34824

First published 1998 with title: From high school to work

This book describes "jobs in a number of fields that are attainable without a four-year degree—requiring only on-the-job training, an apprenticeship, a certificate, or an associate's degree." Publisher's note

Includes bibliographical references

Christen, Carol

What color is your parachute? for teens; discovering yourself, defining your future. [by] Carol Christen and Richard N. Bolles with Jean M. Blomquist. 2nd ed., rev.; Ten Speed Press 2010 178p il pa $15.99

Grades: 9 10 11 12   **331.7**
     1. Job hunting 2. Vocational guidance 3. Applications for positions
     ISBN 978-1-58008-141-2

                 LC 2010-483344

First published 2006 with Bolles' name appearing first

The authors "begin by prompting readers to consider their interests, the kinds of people they enjoy and their ideal work environment, and round out the text with quizzes, writing exercises and teen testimonials designed to get teens thinking. Then they offer concrete ideas on how to gain experience (internships, Web sites, etc.) and prepare for interviews." Publ Wkly [review of 2006 ed.]

Includes bibliographical references

Exploring tech careers; 4th ed.; Ferguson Pub. Co. 2006 2v il set $125

Grades: 9 10 11 12   **331.7**
     1. Occupations 2. Technology -- Vocational guidance
     ISBN 0-8160-6447-4; 978-0-8160-6447-2

                 LC 2005-19101

First published 1995 under the editorship of Halli R. Cosgrove

This "two-volume set covers more than 110 technician careers and features interviews with professionals already at work in the field." Publisher's note

Includes bibliographical references

Farrell, Courtney

Green jobs. ABDO Pub. 2011 112p il (Inside the industry) lib bdg $34.22

Grades: 8 9 10 11 12   **331.7**
     1. Occupations 2. Vocational guidance 3. Environmental protection
     ISBN 978-1-61714-801-9; 1-61714-801-6

                 LC 2010039122

"This book contains an interesting overview of jobs that fall beneath the 'green' umbrella. Farrell writes in clear prose about the wide range of career opportunities that students with environmental interests can pursue. She focuses on four fields: green architect, organic farmer, professional conservationist, and alternative-energy expert." SLJ

Includes glossary and bibliographical references

Ferguson Publishing

The **top** 100; the fastest growing careers for the 21st century. 5th ed.; Ferguson 2011 388p $75; pa $19.95

Grades: 9 10 11 12 Adult   **331.7**
     1. Occupations 2. Vocational guidance
     ISBN 978-0-8160-8367-1; 0-8160-8367-3; 978-0-8160-8359-6 pa; 0-8160-8359-2 pa; 978-1-4381-3767-4 ebook; 1-4381-3767-2 ebook

                 LC 2011004455

First published 1998

This book provides information "on jobs projected to experience the fastest growth, the greatest opportunity, and the best earnings through 2018, according to statistics from the U.S. Department of Labor. . . . Each job article describes the job duties; required education, training, and skills; expected earnings; and . . . more." Publisher's note

Gregory, Michael G.

The **career** chronicles; an insider's guide to what jobs are really like: the good, the bad, and the ugly from over 750 professionals. New World Library 2008 262p pa $15.95

Grades: 11 12 Adult   **331.7**
     1. Occupations 2. Professions 3. Vocational guidance
     ISBN 978-1-57731-573-5; 1-57731-573-1

                 LC 2008-4088

"This book belongs in every high school library and guidance office." SLJ

J.G. Ferguson Publishing Company

★ **Encyclopedia** of careers and vocational guidance; 15th ed.; Ferguson 2010 5v il set $249.95

Grades: 8 9 10 11 12 Adult   **331.7**
     1. Reference books 2. Occupations -- Encyclopedias 3. Vocational guidance -- Encyclopedias
     ISBN 978-0-8160-8313-8; 0-8160-8313-4

                 LC 2010-17724

First published 1967

"These five volumes contain more than 700 . . . [articles] on careers in nearly 100 industries. Each three to five-page entry provides a concise and engaging profile of fields like accounting, animal care, computers, the environment, publishing, sales, and the visual arts. Included in each job entry are an overview, a history, a description, requirements, employers, advancement, earnings, work environment, outlook, and more." Libr J [review of 2008 edition]

Includes bibliographical references

Porterfield, Deborah

Construction and trades. Ferguson 2007 126p il (Top careers in two years) $32.95

Grades: 9 10 11 12   **331.7**
     1. Building 2. Occupations 3. Vocational guidance 4. Industrial arts education
     ISBN 978-0-8160-6897-5; 0-8160-6897-6

                 LC 2007-14326

This book "explores the various career options in . . . [the construction and trade] field that students have with an associate's degree, comparable certification, or work/life experience." Publisher's note

Seupel, Celia W.

Business, finance, and government administration. Ferguson 2008 109p il (Top careers in two years) $32.95

Grades: 9 10 11 12   **331.7**

1. Occupations 2. Business education 3. Vocational guidance

ISBN 978-0-8160-6899-9; 0-8160-6899-2

LC 2007-19640

This book provides "information on careers in the business, finance, and government administration industries for students with two-year degrees." Publisher's note

Includes bibliographical references

United States. Dept. of Labor

O*NET; dictionary of occupational titles. 4th ed.; JIST Works 2007 672p $49.95; pa $39.95

Grades: 11 12 Adult   **331.7**

1. Reference books 2. Occupations -- Dictionaries

ISBN 978-1-59357-415-4; 1-59357-415-0; 978-1-59357-416-1 pa; 1-59357-416-9 pa

LC 2007-652

First published 1998 to replace Dictionary of occupational titles published by the government Printing Office. Frequently revised

This book "puts the official job descriptions and other important information from the U.S. Department of Labor's . . . Occupational Information Network (O*NET) database into [print form]. . . . Descriptions and data included for nearly 950 jobs, covering almost 100 percent of the workforce." Publisher's note

Wyckoff, Claire

Communications and the arts. Ferguson 2007 132p il (Top careers in two years) $32.95

Grades: 9 10 11 12   **331.7**

1. Arts 2. Mass media 3. Occupations 4. Vocational guidance

ISBN 978-0-8160-6898-2; 0-8160-6898-4

LC 2007-14328

This book examines "job opportunities in . . . [the field of arts and communications] for students with an associate's degree, comparable certification, or work/life experience." Publisher's note

Includes bibliographical references

331.702   Choice of vocation

Careers; the graphic guide to finding the perfect job for you. consultant and principal author, Sarah Pawlewski. DK Publishing 2015 320 p. color illustrations (softcover) $19.99

Grades: 6 7 8 9 10 11 12   **331.702**

1. Vocational guidance 2. Occupations 3. Professions

ISBN 1465429735; 9781465429735

LC 2015303113

"Covering more than 400 jobs, [this book on careers] is organized . . . [to] guide teen and tween readers. Check at-a-glance summary panels for chosen careers to learn about salary, working hours, training, and career paths. Cross-ref-

erenced job matrix tables offer another way to learn about all the options. Tweens and teens with no idea of what kind of job to look for can start with their favorite school subjects or hobbies and find relevant careers from there." (Publisher's note)

"A typical library's collection of career books can quickly become dated or out of touch. Enter this manual. With simple graphics, bright colors, and a vast compendium of information, this guide will engage teens who are wondering, "What now?" . . . This strong addition will be fun for browsers as well as for those selecting college majors and making job decisions." SLJ

McKenna, Amy

Nontraditional careers for women and men; more than 30 great jobs for women and men with apprenticeships through phds. by Andrew Morkes and Amy McKenna. College & Career Press 2012 280 p. $19.95

Grades: 11 12 Adult   **331.702**

1. Occupations 2. Professions 3. Vocational guidance 4. Men -- Employment -- United States 5. Vocational guidance -- United States 6. Women -- Employment -- United States

ISBN 0974525197; 9780974525198

LC 2011046915

This book about nontraditional employment with an emphasis on gender "is chock-full of career articles encompassing a wide variety of fields. Each career article includes salary information, skills needed, minimum education level, employment outlook, information about the career, certification and licensing information, tips for getting a job in this career, and industry resources." (Voice of Youth Advocates)

331.8   Labor unions, labor-management bargaining and disputes

Bridegam, Martha A.

Unions and labor laws; by Martha Bridegam. Chelsea House 2009 126p il map (Point-counterpoint) lib bdg $32.95

Grades: 7 8 9 10   **331.8**

1. Labor unions -- United States

ISBN 978-1-60413-511-4; 1-60413-511-5

LC 2009-15013

"The work of unions in previous generations helped to create benefits . . . such as weekends off, the 40-hour workweek, and medical benefits. . . . The power of unions, however, has also been responsible for the creation of often corrupt and bullying labor leaders and crippling strikes. 'Unions and Labor Laws' examines these complex issues from a variety of viewpoints." Publisher's note

Includes glossary and bibliographical references

Hillstrom, Kevin

Workers unite! the American labor movement. Omnigraphics 2011 236p il (Defining moments) $55

Grades: 8 9 10 11 12　　　**331.8**
1. Labor movement 2. Industrial relations
ISBN 978-0-7808-1130-0

LC 2010-26548

"Though basic and brief, this title is highly recommended for middle school and high school students researching the history of the labor movement. It's both a good place to begin research and a useful reference when reading other works." Libr J

Includes bibliographical references

McNeese, Tim

★ The **labor** movement; unionizing America. Chelsea House 2007 168p il (Reform movements in American history) lib bdg $30

Grades: 8 9 10 11 12　　　**331.8**
1. Labor unions 2. Working class 3. Labor movement 4. Industrial relations
ISBN 978-0-7910-9503-4; 0-7910-9503-7

LC 2007-14917

This history of the labor movement discusses the events, legislation, and people associated with the movement and includes a chronology and timeline.

Includes bibliographical references

Skurzynski, Gloria

Sweat and blood; a history of U.S. labor unions. Twenty-First Century Books 2008 112p il (People's history) lib bdg $31.93

Grades: 7 8 9 10　　　**331.8**
1. Labor unions 2. Working class
ISBN 978-0-8225-7594-8; 0-8225-7594-9

LC 2007-50270

This "begins with the roots of unionization in colonial America, cruises through the frenzy of industrialization in the twentieth century, and ends in the present day. . . . The period prints and photographs are well chosen to highlight and comment on the text. Classes studying any part of the industrial or social history of this country will be well served by this valuable resource." Booklist

Includes bibliographical references

332　Financial economics

Bostick, Nan

Managing Money. Saddleback Educational Pub. 2012 120 p. ill.

Grades: 8 9 10 11 12　　　**332**
1. Life skills 2. Banks and banking 3. Household budgets 4. Teenagers -- Personal finance 5. Economics -- Handbooks, manuals, etc. 6. Adult education 7. Finance, Personal 8. Life skills--Handbooks, manuals, etc.
ISBN 1616516593; 9781616516598

This book is a part of the "Life Skills Handbooks" series. "With the text split into four main topics—controlling your spending, banking basics, buying now and paying later, and improving your budgeting skills—young adults get a comprehensive look at the world of personal finance. . . . When it comes to sticking to a budget, teens are encouraged to keep

their needs and wants in sharp focus. There's even a chapter devoted to unexpected purchases and variable spending. . . . There are also helpful hints for paying those expenses without credit cards. Credit-card debt, loans, and spending more than one earns are issues that are addressed . . . . Basic advice, such as how to write out a check and read a bank statement, is included." (Booklist) Index.

"This entry in Saddleback's Life Skills Handbooks series is a keeper... Young adults get a comprehensive look at the world of personal finance in digestible doses." Booklist

332.024　Personal finance

Bellenir, Karen

★ **Debt** information for teens; tips for a successful financial life, including facts about the economy & personal finances, money management, interest rates, loans, credit cards... edited by Karen Bellenir. 2nd ed. Omnigraphics 2012 xi, 364 p.p ill.

Grades: 9 10 11 12　　　**332.024**
1. Debt 2. Money 3. Consumer credit 4. High school students 5. Teenagers -- Personal finance 6. Teenagers -- Finance, Personal
ISBN 0780812158; 9780780812154

LC 2011034700

This book "offer[s] students facing college and/or independence . . . financial advice and background information. The articles in 'Debt' are culled mainly from government documents published or themselves updated over the past four years (through mid-2011). They provide coverage ranging from general and statistical overviews of U.S. coinage and monetary policy to more personally relevant procedures and best practices related to budgeting, checking and savings accounts, identity theft, borrowing, credit cards, and resolving various debt-related problems. Paying for a car and for college are discussed in individual chapters." (School Libr J)

Includes bibliographical references and index

★ **Cash** and credit information for teens; tips for a successful financial life including facts about earning money, paying taxes, budgeting, banking, shopping, using credit, and avoiding financial pitfalls. edited by Karen Bellenir. 2nd ed.; Omnigraphics 2009 424p (Teen finance series) $69

Grades: 9 10 11 12　　　**332.024**
1. Personal finance
ISBN 978-0-7808-1065-5; 0-7808-1065-1

LC 2009012105

First published 2005

"Provides information for teens about earning and managing money, spending and using credit wisely, and avoiding fraud. Includes index, resource information, and a list of online money management tools." Publisher's note

Includes bibliographical references

★ **Debt:** opposing viewpoints; Christina Fisanick, book editor. Greenhaven Press 2010 200p il

(Opposing viewpoints series) lib bdg $38.50; pa $26.75

Grades: 8 9 10 11 12   **332.024**
1. Debt 2. Consumer credit
ISBN 978-0-7377-4202-2 lib bdg; 978-0-7377-4203-9 pa

LC 2009-27494

Examines both sides of the issues surrounding consumer debt, from attitudes towards debt and responsible debt management to national debt and resolving debt problems.
Includes bibliographical references

Gray, Farrah

Reallionaire; nine steps to becoming rich from the inside out. [by] Farrah Gray, with Fran Harris. Health Communications 2004 282p il pa $12.95

Grades: 11 12 Adult   **332.024**
1. Personal finance
ISBN 0-7573-0224-6

LC 2004-62555

The author "grew up in the projects in Chicago and formed his first business organization at age 7, inspired by his mother's will and determination. By age 15, he had developed his own food company for kids, Farr-Out Foods, which he sold for $1.5 million. . . . Although the book is punctuated with what he calls 'Real Points' for success and exercises for things like building a great team and seizing opportunities, the real inspiration is his personal story, which speaks strongly of the importance of mentoring to young people and sends the message that you should never underestimate anyone, especially yourself." Booklist

Lawless, Robert E.

The **student's** guide to financial literacy. Greenwood 2010 220p il $85

Grades: 9 10 11 12   **332.024**
1. Personal finance
ISBN 978-0-313-37718-1

LC 2009-50449

"This title covers everything young adults just starting out in the world should be thinking about with respect to their future financial decisions. . . . Beginning with savings, then investments, Lawless breaks the material down into small, digestible sections. . . . The chapters on Tax Considerations and Insurance are must-reads. Excellent charts and graphs support the text, and Guess What? and Beware! boxes offer fascinating related facts and cautions against such things as risky mortgage loans." SLJ
Includes bibliographical references

McGuire, Kara

The **teen** money manual; a guide to cash, credit, spending, saving, work, wealth, and more. by Kara McGuire. Capstone Young Readers 2015 208 p. **332.024**
1. Teenagers -- Personal finance 2. Life skills -- Handbooks, manuals, etc.
ISBN 9781623701352

LC 2014003725

Written by Kara McGuire, "This book offers today's teens the . . . tips on how to make money, how to spend it, how to invest and save it, and how to protect it. Learn how to land that first job, figure out your paycheck, and negotiate a raise. Discover how to stretch your money to cover all of your needs and (at least some of!) your wants. Learn to be a savvy saver to vastly improve your life." (Publisher's note)
Includes bibliographical references and index

Mooney, Carla

Smart savings and financial planning; by Carla Mooney. 1st ed. Rosen Pub. 2013 64 p. col. ill. (library) $31.95; (paperback) $12.95

Grades: 10 11 12   **332.024**
1. Personal finance 2. Saving and investment 3. Savings accounts
ISBN 1448882516; 9781448882519; 9781448882588; 9781448882595

LC 2012024917

This book is part of the Get Smart With Your Money series and looks at saving and financial planning. The series provides "teens with real-world tips on making the most of their financial opportunities." This entry "outlines methods for setting financial goals, budgeting, and adhering to a savings plan, as well as various types of savings accounts and financial investment plans." (Booklist)
Includes bibliographical references (p. 60) and index.

★ **Personal** finance; a guide to money and business. Marshall Cavendish 2009 186p il $99.90

Grades: 9 10 11 12   **332.024**
1. Personal finance
ISBN 978-0-7614-7909-3; 0-7614-7909-0

LC 2009-9461

This book is "comprised of approximately 50 A-to-Z articles ranging in length from two to four pages. . . . Personal Finance focuses on what readers will encounter in their daily lives, such as debit cards, credit history, job search, pricing, consumer protection, and interest rates. An entry on bundling goods and services looks at its pros and cons and includes a diagram of a computer connection and repair service. The numerous graphs, flow charts, maps, political cartoons, and tables help make sense of complicated concepts." SLJ
Includes glossary and bibliographical references

Peterson, Judy Monroe

Digital smarts; how to stay within a budget when shopping, living, and doing business online. by Judy Monroe Peterson. Rosen Pub. 2013 64 p. col. ill. (library) $31.95; (paperback) $12.95

Grades: 10 11 12   **332.024**
1. Internet shopping 2. Electronic commerce 3. Internet and teenagers 4. Teleshopping 5. Internet banking 6. Finance, Personal -- Computer network resources
ISBN 1448882567; 9781448882564; 9781448882625

LC 2012022099

This book by Judy Monroe Peterson is part of the Get Smart With Your Money series and focuses on staying within a budget while doing business and shopping online. The series provides "teens with real-world tips on making the most of their financial opportunities." This entry "describes various ways to use your money via online shopping sites, how to do online banking, and how to protect your money digitally." (Booklist)
Includes bibliographical references and index.

★ **Savings** and investment information for teens; tips for a successful financial life. edited by Karen Bellenir. 2nd ed.; Omnigraphics 2009 422p (Teen finance series) $69

Grades: 9 10 11 12   **332.024**
1. Personal finance 2. Saving and investment
ISBN 978-0-7808-1064-8

LC 2009-3482
First published 2005

"Provides information for teens about strategies for saving money, investment options, and economic factors that affect personal wealth. Includes index, resource information and recommendations for further reading." Publisher's note
Includes bibliographical references

332.6   Investment

Connolly, Sean
The **stock** market. Amicus 2010 46p il (World economy explained) lib bdg $34.25

Grades: 7 8 9 10   **332.6**
1. Stocks 2. Stock exchanges 3. Financial crises
ISBN 978-1-60753-082-4; 1-60753-082-4

LC 2009-29073
"Complex concepts like lending, earning, and charging interest are presented simply and with clear examples. Lively photos and 'Personal Account' asides bring home the ramifications for individuals of big-bank collapses." SLJ
Includes glossary

332.64   Exchange of securities and commodities; speculation

Blumenthal, Karen
★ **Six** days in October; the stock market crash of 1929. Atheneum Bks. for Young Readers 2002 156p il $17.95

Grades: 7 8 9 10   **332.64**
1. Great Depression, 1929-1939 2. New York Stock Exchange, Inc. 3. United States -- Economic conditions -- 1919-1933
ISBN 0-689-84276-7

LC 2001-46360
A comprehensive review of the events, personalities, and mistakes behind the Stock Market Crash of 1929, featuring photographs, newspaper articles, and cartoons of the day

"This fast-paced, gripping . . . account of the market crash of October 1929 puts a human face on the crisis." Publ Wkly
Includes bibliographical references

333.7   Natural resources and energy

Cunningham, Kevin
Soil. Morgan Reynolds Pub. 2010 111p il (Diminishing resources) $28.95

Grades: 8 9 10 11 12   **333.7**
1. Soils 2. Soil conservation
ISBN 978-1-59935-114-8; 1-59935-114-5

LC 2009-10487
"The first chapter of Soil discusses how depletion of this resource began as far back as the Neolithic age, and the book continues through time, closing with today's efforts to conserve soil in places such as Iceland. In addition to being great research resources, [this title is] interesting enough for pleasure reading. [It contains] beautiful, full-page photographs, as well as a helpful time line." SLJ
Includes bibliographical references

Encyclopedia of global resources; editor, Craig W. Allin. Salem Press 2010 4v il map set $395

Grades: 11 12 Adult   **333.7**
1. Reference books 2. Natural resources -- Encyclopedias
ISBN 978-1-58765-644-6; 1-58765-644-2

LC 2010-1984
First published 1998 with title: Natural resources
"This four-volume set provides a wide variety of perspectives about Earth's natural resources and explains the interrelationships among resource exploitation, environmentalism, geology, and biology. Allin . . . presents 576 articles on resources such as oil and tar sands, nations from Argentina to Zimbabwe, government laws and conventions, and historical events. . . . [This encyclopedia] offers real value and sheds important light on where we derive our mineral and biological resources, how they are processed, what they are used for, and how they fit into the global economy." Libr J
Includes bibliographical references

Magoc, Chris J.
Environmental issues in American history; a reference guide with primary documents. Greenwood Press 2006 xxxv, 328p il map (Major issues in American history) $85

Grades: 11 12 Adult   **333.7**
1. Human ecology 2. Nature conservation 3. Environmental protection 4. Environmental policy -- United States
ISBN 0-313-32208-2

LC 2005-34852
In this "study, primary documents support different sides of various questions, such as the use of water as an energy source, deforestation, gold mining in California, and the emergence of wildlife conservation." Publisher's note
Includes bibliographical references

Park, Chris
A **dictionary** of environment and conservation; by Chris Park. 2nd ed. Oxford University Press 2013 484 p. (Oxford paperback reference) (paperback) $21.95

Grades: 11 12 Adult   **333.7**
1. Environment 2. Conservation of natural resources 3. Environmental sciences -- Dictionaries 4. Conservation of natural resources -- Dictionaries
ISBN 0199641668; 9780199641666

LC 2008006450

This book by Michael Allaby and Chris Park "provides over 9,000 alphabetically arranged entries on scientific and social aspects of the environment, including concise and authoritative information on key thinkers, treaties, movements, organizations, concepts, and theories. For the second edition, Allaby has added over 700 new entries, including 'aerial plankton,' 'cyclone collector,' 'oasis,' and 'supertramp.'" (Publisher's note)

"The second edition of this user-friendly title is updated with 800 new entries, expanding the work to more than 500 pages...Students will appreciate having access to this information in one convenient source. This affordable title is recommended for public and academic libraries." (Booklist)

Rockliff, Mara
★ **Get** real. Running Press 2010 112p il pa $10.95
Grades: 6 7 8 9 10   **333.7**
1. Consumer education 2. Consumption (Economics)
ISBN 978-0-7624-3745-0; 0-7624-3745-6
This book "points out plenty of practical ways for kids to impact their world by making different choices about what food to eat, what clothes to wear, how often to replace a cell phone, and more. . . . Nicely designed, the book has colorful graphic elements on many pages, including photographs and eye-catching digital images incorporating photos. . . . A clearly written guide for reader who want to translate social and environmental awareness into action." Booklist
Includes filmography and bibliographical references

Tabak, John
Wind and water. Facts On File 2009 208p il map (Energy and the environment) $40
Grades: 9 10 11 12 Adult   **333.7**
1. Renewable energy resources
ISBN 978-0-8160-7087-9; 0-8160-7087-3
LC 2008-28247
This book "has value both for the explanations it offers and the questions it raises." SLJ
Includes glossary and bibliographical references

Wilkins, Thurman
John Muir; apostle of nature. University of Okla. Press 1995 xxvii, 302p il maps (Oklahoma western biographies) hardcover o.p. pa $21.95
Grades: 11 12 Adult   **333.7**
1. Authors 2. Naturalists 3. Writers on nature
ISBN 0-8061-2797-X pa
LC 95-11426
"Wilkins follows Muir from his Scottish boyhood, clouded by a harsh, fundamentalist father, to an adolescence of arduous farmwork in Wisconsin to a lifelong career of exploration and study of wildernesses, particularly those of the western U.S., and vividly relates some of Muir's more perilous adventures on cliffside and snowfield. . . . An affectionate, uncluttered tale of an American folk hero." Booklist
Includes bibliographical references

333.72   Conservation and protection

★ **Encyclopedia** of American environmental history; edited by Kathleen A. Brosnan. Facts On File 2010 4v il map (Facts on File library of American history) set $350
Grades: 11 12 Adult   **333.72**
1. Reference books 2. Environmental protection -- Encyclopedias 3. Environmental policy -- United States -- Encyclopedias
ISBN 978-0-8160-6793-0; 978-1-4381-3267-9 ebook
LC 2010-21963
"Approximately 775 entries written by more than 350 expert contributors bring together the natural, social, and political events; people; geography; and ideas that are important in understanding American environmental history. Documents, maps, charts, historic photographs, an extensive bibliography, and an extremely detailed index add depth and value to this work." Booklist
Includes bibliographical references

The **environment**; William Dudley, book editor. Greenhaven Press 2006 224p (History of issues) lib bdg $34.95
Grades: 9 10 11 12   **333.72**
1. Environmental movement 2. Environmental protection
ISBN 0-7377-2865-5; 978-0-7377-2865-1
LC 2005-46391
This book "leaves the reader with a balanced presentation of both sides." Voice Youth Advocates
Includes bibliographical references

Kostigen, Thomas M.
The **green** book; the everyday guide to saving the planet one simple step at a time. Elizabeth Rogers and Thomas M. Kostigen; with a foreword by Cameron Diaz and William McDonough. Three Rivers Press 2007 xix, 201p $13.95
Grades: 10 11 12 Adult   **333.72**
1. Environmental movement 2. Environmental protection 3. Environmentalism 4. Environmental protection -- Citizen participation
ISBN 9780307381354; 0307381358
LC 2007013222
It was the authors' intent to "address the fact that Americans endanger the balance of the ecosystem by the amount of waste we produce, the amount of water we use, and the amount of energy we consume." In order to influence readers' behavior, they present "observations and suggestions for living green" from "celebrities including Robert Redford, Ellen DeGeneres, Jennifer Aniston, Faith Hill, and Dale Earnhardt Jr." (Booklist) Topics include "ATM receipts . . . [t]urn[ing] off the tap while you brush your teeth . . . [and] voice-mail service for your home phone." (Publisher's notes)
Includes bibliographical references (p. [147]-197) and index.

McDaniel, Carl N.
Wisdom for a livable planet; the visionary work of Terri Swearingen, Dave Foreman, Wes Jackson,

Helena Norberg-Hodge, Werner Fornos, Herman Daly, Stephen Schneider, and David Orr. Trinity University Press 2005 277p hardcover o.p. pa $17.95

Grades: 11 12 Adult　　　**333.72**

1. Environmental sciences
ISBN 1-595-34008-4; 1-595-34009-2 pa

LC 2004-19081

The author personalizes "critical environmental issues via profiles of eight 'visionaries' agitating for a more livable planet. . . . His subjects are prominent in the areas of hazardous waste incineration, biodiversity, sustainable agriculture, appropriate technology, population control, rational economic planning, climate concerns and environmental education. . . . The stories of these eight ecological warriors are profoundly appealing in that they show the diverse ways that people can commit to a common cause." Publ Wkly

Includes bibliographical references

Melville, Greg

Greasy rider; two dudes, one fry-oil-powered car, and a cross-country search for a greener future. Algonquin Books of Chapel Hill 2008 257p pa $15.95

Grades: 11 12 Adult　　　**333.72**

1. Environmental movement 2. Alternative fuel vehicles 3. Voyages and travels -- Anecdotes
ISBN 978-1-56512-595-7; 1-56512-595-9

LC 2008-25991

"From its punny title, to its unique premise (a man decides to drive from coast to coast in a car powered by used french-fry oil), to its serious message (you, too, can be more environmentally conscious), to its easygoing writing style, this is just a splendid book. . . . It's an exciting and occasionally nail-biting adventure, but the author keeps the book from being a simple road trip by delving fairly deeply into the whole ecological, pro-environmental, self-sufficiency theme, taking the reader along on visits to such interesting places as Google headquarters, a wind farm, a renewable energy lab, and a green home. Melville . . . is a lively stylist, and the book is both entertaining and educational." Booklist

Includes bibliographical references

Mongillo, John F.

Teen guides to environmental science; [by] John Mongillo; with assistance from Peter Mongillo. Greenwood Press 2004 5v il map set $249.95

Grades: 9 10 11 12　　　**333.72**

1. Human ecology 2. Environmental sciences 3. Human influence on nature
ISBN 0-313-32183-3

LC 2004-44869

"This set would be useful for large public and school libraries with a curriculum that includes environmental studies." SLJ

Includes bibliographical references

Nagle, Jeanne

★ **Living** green; [by] Jeanne Nagle. Rosen Pub. 2009 64p il (In the news) lib bdg $21.95

Grades: 7 8 9 10　　　**333.72**

1. Environmental protection
ISBN 978-1-43585037-8; 1-435-85037-8

"Accessible and up-to-date. . . . Living Green presents theories of climate change and short biographies of green pioneers before examining the role of government and NGOs in environmental protection, as well as basic, earth-friendly lifestyle changes that individuals can make. Throughout, Nagle addresses the controversies that surround issues, encouraging readers to take a wide, nuanced view." Booklist

Power Scott, Jennifer

Green careers; you can make money and save the planet. Lobster Press 2010 240p il pa $16.95

Grades: 8 9 10 11 12　　　**333.72**

1. Vocational guidance 2. Environmental protection
ISBN 978-1-897550-18-2; 1-897550-18-9

"Written in a breezy, conversational style, this book recounts the stories of 30 young people who are working in environmental jobs. . . . They are eco-entrepreneurs, urban activists, green architects, organic gardeners, animal caretakers, artists, and fashion designers. . . . These inspirational stories are sure to spark interest and creative thinking." SLJ

Sonneborn, Liz

The **environmental** movement; protecting our natural resources. Chelsea House Publishers 2008 128p il (Reform movements in American history) $30

Grades: 8 9 10 11 12　　　**333.72**

1. Environmental movement
ISBN 978-0-7910-9537-9; 0-7910-9537-1

LC 2007-14914

This book "introduces readers to . . . [the environmental] movement, which arose in the United States in the late 1800s in response to the nation's dwindling forests and the pollution caused by a greater number of factories. . . . [This] book also details how environmentalism has become a global effort, led by organizations such as Greenpeace and the World Wildlife Fund." Publisher's note

Includes bibliographical references

333.75　Forest lands

Balliett, James Fargo

Forests; environmental issues, global perspectives. M.E. Sharpe 2010 152p il map (Environmental issues, global perspectives) $55

Grades: 9 10 11 12　　　**333.75**

1. Forests and forestry
ISBN 978-0-7656-8227-7

LC 2010-12120

"Case studies in Forests explore illegal logging in the Amazon rain forest, examine the effect of increased hunting in the Congo forest, and discuss encroachment on old-growth tropical forests on the Southern Pacific island of Borneo, among other issues relevant to the world's forests." Publisher's note

Includes glossary and bibliographical references

Dietrich, William

The **final** forest; big trees, forks, and the Pacific Northwest. 2010 ed. / with a new preface and afterword.; University of Washington Press 2010 336p map pa $19.95

Grades: 11 12 Adult   **333.75**

1. Forest conservation 2. Forests and forestry 3. Lumber and lumbering 4. Pacific Northwest

ISBN 978-0-295-99062-0

LC 2010031802

First published 1992 by Simon & Schuster

"Before Forks, a small town on Washington's Olympic Peninsula, became famous as the location for Stephenie Meyer's Twilight book series, it was the self-proclaimed 'Logging Capital of the World' and ground zero in a regional conflict over the fate of old-growth forests. . . . [This book] recounts how forest policy and practices have changed since the early 1990s and also tells us what has happened in Forks and where the actors who were so important to the timber wars are now." Publisher's note

Stenstrup, Allen

Forests. Morgan Reynolds Pub. 2009 112p il (Diminishing resources) lib bdg $28.95

Grades: 8 9 10 11 12   **333.75**

1. Forest conservation 2. Forests and forestry

ISBN 978-1-59935-116-2; 1-59935-116-1

LC 2009-31025

"This highly readable [book] provides a unique viewpoint on the utilization of natural resources, as scientific and environmental concerns are discussed from a historical perspective. . . . [It contains] beautiful, full-page photographs, as well as a helpful time line." SLJ

Includes bibliographical references

333.79 Energy

Allen, John

Thinking critically; renewable energy by John Allen. ReferencePoint Press, Inc. 2013 80 p. illustrations, color maps (hardback) $28.95

Grades: 9 10 11 12   **333.79**

1. Renewable energy resources

ISBN 1601526288; 9781601526281

LC 2013033656

This book, part of the Thinking Critically series, by John Allen, "examines the future of renewable energy. Topics include: Are Renewable Energy Sources Needed? How Practical Is Renewable Energy? Is Renewable Energy Too Expensive? Should the Government Help Develop Renewable Energy?" (Publisher's note)

"Renewable Energy asks whether developing and promoting alternative energy sources is necessary, practical, or affordable, and considers the role of government support. For teachers wishing to use a debate approach to consideration of current political and social issues, the entire series offers useful information and presents an excellent model." Booklist

Includes bibliographical references and index

Renewable energy

★ **Energy** alternatives: opposing viewpoints; David Haugen, Susan Musser, and Vickey Kalambakal, book editors. Greenhaven Press 2010 218p il (Opposing viewpoints series) $39.70; pa $27.50

Grades: 9 10 11 12   **333.79**

1. Energy resources 2. Renewable energy resources

ISBN 978-0-7377-4962-5; 978-0-7377-4963-2 pa

LC 2009-52253

Articles in this anthology address such topics as whether alternative energy sources are necessary, different types of alternative energy, and the government's role in advocating the use of alternative sources.

Includes bibliographical references

Heinrichs, Ann

★ **Sustaining** Earth's energy resources. Marshall Cavendish Benchmark 2010 128p il (Environment at risk) lib bdg $39.93

Grades: 6 7 8 9 10   **333.79**

1. Energy development 2. Renewable energy resources

ISBN 978-0-7614-4007-9; 0-7614-4007-0

LC 2008-42010

This book provides "information on Earth's sources of renewable and nonrenewable energy, how they are used, their benefits and disadvantages, their interrelationships with the natural world, and the future of Earth's sources of energy." Publisher's note

Includes bibliographical references

Kallen, Stuart A.

Renewable energy research. ReferencePoint Press 2010 96p il (Inside science) lib bdg $26.95

Grades: 7 8 9 10   **333.79**

1. Renewable energy resources

ISBN 978-1-60152-129-3; 1-60152-129-4

LC 2010-18102

This "offers the necessary information for stellar reports. Politics, debates, and ethical concerns are briefly and fairly mentioned, but the . . . [book concentrates] on consistent, documented, and well-balanced scientific coverage. The human stories sprinkled throughout will help kids identify with both scientists and patients." SLJ

Includes bibliographical references

Marcovitz, Hal

Can renewable energy replace fossil fuels? ReferencePoint Press 2010 95p il (In controversy) lib bdg $26.95

Grades: 10 11 12   **333.79**

1. Fuel 2. Renewable energy resources

ISBN 978-1-60152-113-2

LC 2009-50482

This book "looks at the costs, limitations, and liabilities of using fossil fuels as well as the practicality of various alternatives." Booklist

Includes bibliographical references

McPherson, Stephanie Sammartino

Arctic thaw; climate change and the global race for energy resources. Stephanie Sammartino McPherson. Twenty-First Century Books 2015 64

p. color illustrations, color map (library binding: alkaline paper) $34.60

Grades: 6 7 8 9 10　　　　　333.79

1. Global warming 2. International relations 3. Arctic regions -- Exploration 4. Climate change -- Arctic regions 5. Power resources -- Arctic regions 6. Natural resources -- Arctic regions 7. Economic development -- Arctic regions

ISBN 1467720437; 9781467720434

LC 2013025164

In this book on climate change, author Stephanie Sammartino McPherson "describe[s] the changes in polar ice cover that are encouraging exploration and allowing access to previously inaccessible energy resources. Subsequent chapters describe new, shorter ocean passages, the jockeying for territory as nearby nations lay claim and others look for ways to get involved, and the likely difficulties of development." (Kirkus Reviews)

"Succinct and clearly written, the text offers up-to-date information, illustrated with clear color photos and useful maps. An articulate introduction to the Arctic in a time of profound, striking changes." Booklist

Includes bibliographical references (pages 59-60) and index

Moan, Jaina L.

Energy use worldwide; a reference handbook. [by] Jaina L. Moan and Zachary A. Smith. ABC-CLIO 2007 337p il (Contemporary world issues) $55

Grades: 9 10 11 12　　　　　333.79

1. Energy resources 2. Energy consumption

ISBN 978-1-85109-890-3

LC 2007-7414

The authors "delineate energy consumption's influential political figures and principal challenges while clarifying prospective conservation solutions. The book is rich with illustrative tables and offers a glossary of essential terms." Libr J

Includes glossary and bibliographical references

Yount, Lisa

Energy supply. Facts on File 2005 296p il (Library in a book) $45

Grades: 11 12 Adult　　　　　333.79

1. Energy resources 2. Energy consumption

ISBN 0-8160-5577-7

LC 2004-21607

"This title summarizes . . . the many aspects of important energy issues, furnishing a concise overview of major points needed for doing research on this topic." Choice

Includes bibliographical references

333.792　Primary forms of energy

Ferguson, Charles D.

Nuclear energy; what everyone needs to know. Charles D. Ferguson. Oxford University Press 2011 xvii, 222 p.p (What everyone needs to know) (hardback) $74

Grades: 11 12 Adult　　　　　333.792

1. Nuclear energy 2. Nuclear power plants

ISBN 0199759456; 9780199759453; 9780199759460

LC 2010044449

In this book, "Charles D. Ferguson provides an authoritative account of the key facts about nuclear energy. What is the origin of nuclear energy? What countries use commercial nuclear power, and how much electricity do they obtain from it? How can future nuclear power plants be made safer? What can countries do to protect their nuclear facilities from military attacks? How hazardous is radioactive waste? Is nuclear energy a renewable energy source?" (Publisher's note)

"This compelling assembly of historical and scientific information deftly steps through the essential discoveries, definitions, and theory that led to the development of nuclear reactors and nuclear bombs. . . . [F]ollowing chapters . . . cover safety, climate change, nuclear proliferation concerns, security, and the politically charged options for disposal of radioactive waste." Choice

Includes bibliographical references and index

333.8　Subsurface resources

★ **Foreign** oil dependence; Susan C. Hunnicutt, book editor. Greenhaven Press 2008 106p (At issue. International politics) $31.80; pa $22.50

Grades: 9 10 11 12　　　　　333.8

1. Energy policy 2. Petroleum industry

ISBN 978-0-7377-4060-8; 978-0-7377-4061-5 pa

LC 2007-50858

The articles in this anthology cover topics such as government regulation of the energy industry, energy independence, Iraqi oil, and coal and ethanol as possible alternatives to oil.

Includes bibliographical references

Gardner, Timothy

Oil. Morgan Reynolds Pub. 2009 111p il (Diminishing resources) lib bdg $28.95

Grades: 8 9 10 11 12　　　　　333.8

1. Petroleum 2. Energy conservation 3. Greenhouse effect

ISBN 978-1-59935-117-9; 1-59935-117-X

LC 2009-10245

This book about oil "will draw activists, but even readers who do not think they care that much will find the facts devastating. Quotes from authoritative sources . . . about both the historic overview and the contemporary crisis accompany full-color double-page photos that show what is happening now. . . . [The book] discusses in detail the role of the Middle East, the effects of America's addiction to cars, and always, the current focus on global warming." Booklist

Includes bibliographical references

Laxer, James

Oil. Groundwood Books/House of Anansi Press 2008 144p il (Groundwork guides) $15.95; pa $11

Grades: 9 10 11 12 Adult **333.8**
1. Petroleum industry
ISBN 978-0-88899-815-6; 0-88899-815-5; 978-0-88899-816-3 pa; 0-88899-816-3 pa
LC 2008-411360
Provides an overview of the petroleum industry, its history, and its key players; examines the relationship between oil, finance, and politics; and explores the future of oil as supplies diminish and global warming threatens.

"This is an excellent choice for high school readers. . . . [The author] makes a complex subject clear with the aid of time lines of oil history, highlighted points of interest, and a solid list of sources for further reading." Libr J
Includes bibliographical references

Tabak, John
Coal and oil. Facts On File 2009 208p il (Energy and the environment) $40
Grades: 9 10 11 12 **333.8**
1. Coal 2. Petroleum as fuel
ISBN 978-0-8160-7083-1; 0-8160-7083-0
LC 2008-24343
"This terrifically informative volume . . . is a perfect resource for someone struggling to wrap their brain around some of the most complex energy issues of our time." Booklist
Includes glossary and bibliographical references

Natural gas and hydrogen. Facts On File 2009 203p il map (Energy and the environment) $40
Grades: 9 10 11 12 Adult **333.8**
1. Natural gas 2. Hydrogen as fuel
ISBN 978-0-8160-7084-8; 0-8160-7084-9
LC 2008-26072
An "overview of the complex relationship the world has with two significant sources of gaseous fuel. The book discusses the business of natural gas production and the energy futures markets that have evolved as vehicles for speculation and risk management. It also focuses on the possible advantages of adopting hydrogen as a viable source of energy, as well as on the inevitable obstacles that hamper large-scale fuel switching." Publisher's note
Includes glossary and bibliographical references

333.9   Other natural resources

Space exploration; Daniel A. Leone, book editor. Greenhaven Press 2005 95p (At issue) lib bdg $28.70; pa $19.95
Grades: 9 10 11 12 **333.9**
1. Outer space -- Exploration 2. Astronautics -- United States
ISBN 0-7377-2747-0 lib bdg; 0-7377-2748-9 pa
LC 2004-58028
The essays in this anthology explore NASA's space initiative involving manned missions to Mars and beyond, in addition to such issues as "weapons in space, privatizing space ventures, and protecting Earth from asteroids." Publisher's note
Includes bibliographical references

333.91   Water and lands adjoining bodies of water

Balliett, James Fargo
Oceans; environmental issues, global perspectives. M.E. Sharpe 2010 156p il map (Environmental issues, global perspectives) $55
Grades: 9 10 11 12 **333.91**
1. Ocean
ISBN 978-0-7656-8229-1
LC 2010-19428
"The case studies in Oceans include a discussion of the most remote locations along the Mid-Atlantic Ridge, where new ocean floor is being formed underwater; the Maldive Islands, where rising sea levels may force residents to abandon their communities; and the North Sea, where fishing stocks have been dangerously depleted as a result of multiple nations' unrelenting removal of certain species." Publisher's note
Includes glossary and bibliographical references

Wetlands; environmental issues, global perspectives. M.E. Sharpe 2010 155p il map (Environmental issues, global perspectives) $55
Grades: 9 10 11 12 **333.91**
1. Wetlands
ISBN 978-0-7656-8226-0
LC 2010-12119
This book "provides case studies that illuminate our changing perceptions of one of the world's richest and biologically productive biomes, including the Florida Everglades, the Aral Sea in Central Asia, and Lake Poyong in China. It also highlights efforts that have been undertaken to protect many of these areas." Publisher's note
Includes glossary and bibliographical references

Fishman, Charles
The **big** thirst; Charles Fishman. Free Press 2011 388p. ebook $12.99; $26.99
Grades: 10 11 12 Adult **333.91**
1. Water supply 2. Infrastructure (Economics) 3. Water resources development
ISBN 978-1-4391-2493-2 ebook; 978-1-4391-0207-7
LC 2010033989
This book presents an "assessment of the current politics, economics, and culture of water." It was the author's intent to demonstrate "that the water we have now is all the water we will ever have and that our 'golden age' of 'abundant, safe, and cheap' water may soon end, thanks to deteriorating infrastructure, . . . rising urban populations, and climate change. Both 'water complacency' and 'water poverty' are rampant. . . . Among his many case studies are Las Vegas' water extravaganzas and India's lack of 24/7 water even in its booming cities, which keeps millions of girls out of school to collect and carry each day's water supply. . . . Fishman praises tap water, observes that water consciousness is 'infectious,' and declares that 'most water problems are, in fact, solvable'." (Booklist)
This is a "lively and invaluable assessment of the current politics, economics, and culture of water. Lyrical in his descriptions of the beauty and wonder of water, Fishman is rigorous when explaining that the water we have now is

all the water we will ever have and that our 'golden age' of 'abundant, safe, and cheap' water may soon end, thanks to deteriorating infrastructure (7 billion gallons leak out of our water systems every day), rising urban populations, and climate change." Booklist

Includes bibliographical references and index.

Kallen, Stuart A.

Running dry; the global water crisis. by Stuart A. Kallen. Twenty-First Century Books 2015 64 p. illustrations (chiefly color) (lib. bdg.: alk. paper) $33.32

Grades: 4 5 6 7 8   **333.91**

1. Water supply 2. Water conservation 3. Water consumption 4. Water -- Pollution
ISBN 146772646X; 9781467726467; 9781467763080
LC 2014003223

This book, by Stuart A. Kallen "provides information on the growing water crisis. Looking at the subject globally, the discussion includes matters such as the dwindling supply of fresh water, its pollution by agriculture and industry, the dramatic effects of climate change, and the increasing competition for water. . . . Sidebars and full-page features spotlight pertinent topics such as the desalination of sea water." (Booklist)

"This title provides a clear and concise look at the importance of fresh water in sustaining life on earth . . . the book will appeal to those with little or no background on the subject. An excellent source for student research." SLJ

Includes bibliographical references and index

Kaye, Cathryn Berger

★ **Going** blue; a teen guide to saving our oceans & waterways. by Cathryn Berger Kaye; with Philippe Cousteau and Earth Echo International. Free Spirit Pub. 2010 151p il map pa $14.95

Grades: 6 7 8 9 10   **333.91**

1. Marine ecology 2. Marine pollution 3. Environmental protection
ISBN 978-1-57542-348-7; 1-57542-348-0
LC 2010-16589

Teaches young people about the Earth's water crisis and provides practical suggestions on how readers can identify water-related needs in the community and transform their ideas into action.

"This valuable how-to manual is suitable for an individual student, a family, a youth group, or a school wishing to protect our precious resource of water. This upbeat treasure will challenge anyone interested in environmental activism, whether water related or not. It is a must for any library serving youth." Voice Youth Advocates

Includes bibliographical references

Knapp, Bevil

America's wetland; Louisiana's vanishing coast. photographs by Bevil Knapp; text by Mike Dunne. Louisiana State University Press 2005 129p il $39.95

Grades: 11 12 Adult   **333.91**

1. Coasts 2. Wetlands
ISBN 0-8071-3115-6; 978-0-8071-3115-2
LC 2005-9329

"In an eerie prophesy of the flooding to come in New Orleans, this book discusses the job of wetlands in keeping storm surges and waves out of the low-lying areas. Superb color photographs detail fishing, the oil industry, and marine life in the wetlands areas of Louisiana." Univ Press Books for Public and Second Sch Libr, 2006

Leahy, Stephen

Your Water Footprint; The Shocking Facts About How Much Water We Use to Make Everyday Products. Stephen Leahy. Firefly Books Ltd 2014 144 p. col. illustrations, col. maps $35

Grades: 9 10 11 12   **333.91**

1. Drinking water 2. Natural resources 3. Water conservation
ISBN 1770854991; 9781770854994

This book by Stephen Leahy "reveals the true cost of our lifestyle. A 'water footprint' is the amount of fresh water used to produce the goods and services we consume, including growing, harvesting, packaging, and shipping. The 125 footprint facts in this book show the true cost of our lifestyle and what it is doing to Earth, including draining it dry." (Publisher's note)

"As irresistible as it is alarming, Leahy's water footprint primer is a catalyst for conservation of our most precious endangered resource." Booklist

Petersen, Christine

Renewing Earth's waters. Marshall Cavendish Benchmark 2010 112p il (Environment at risk) lib bdg $39.93

Grades: 6 7 8 9 10   **333.91**

1. Water pollution 2. Water conservation
ISBN 978-0-7614-4004-8; 0-7614-4004-6
LC 2008-20905

This book provides "information on the interrelationships of the natural world, environmental problems both natural and man-made, the relative risks associated with these problems, and solutions for resolving and/or preventing them." Publisher's note

Includes bibliographical references

333.95 Biological resources

Corwin, Jeff

100 heartbeats; the race to save earth's most endangered species. Rodale 2009 303p il $24.99

Grades: 11 12 Adult   **333.95**

1. Endangered species 2. Wildlife conservation
ISBN 978-1-60529-847-4; 1-60529-847-6
LC 2009-23449

The author looks at several "critically endangered [species] and examines what is being done to save them, beginning with a chapter that discusses the broad causes of extinction—global warming and the loss of habitat—and then examines specific threats to endangered species while looking at animals most at risk from these threats. . . . Corwin's conversational, upbeat style makes readers care about the species in peril." Booklist

Includes bibliographical references

★ **Endangered** oceans: opposing viewpoints; Louise I. Gerdes, book editor. Greenhaven Press 2009 234p il (Opposing viewpoints series) lib bdg $38.50; pa $26.75

Grades: 8 9 10 11 12   **333.95**

1. Marine ecology 2. Marine pollution 3. Environmental policy

ISBN 978-0-7377-4210-7 lib bdg; 978-0-7377-4211-4 pa

LC 2008-36462

Articles in this anthology cover such topics as overfishing and loss of coral reefs, government policies to protect ocean life, sustainable fishing, and the effects of human activities on marine mammals.

Includes bibliographical references

Hoekstra, Jonathan M.

The **atlas** of global conservation; changes, challenges and opportunities to make a difference. [by] Jonathan Hoekstra ... [et al.]; edited by Jennifer L. Molnar. University of California Press 2010 234p il map $49.95

Grades: 9 10 11 12 Adult   **333.95**

1. Atlases 2. Globalization 3. Reference books 4. Environmental protection 5. Conservation of natural resources

ISBN 978-0-520-26256-0

LC 2009-23617

"Focusing primarily on biomes and ecosystems, this valuable atlas promotes a deeper understanding of the challenges involved in preserving and maintaining these habitats and resources. Basically an analysis of the current state of the globe, the book highlights conservation challenges through chapters on habitats, species distributions, deforestation, global warming, coastal development, and pollution. . . . The book is unique and well done." Voice Youth Advocates

Includes bibliographical references

Kurlansky, Mark, 1948-

The **world** without fish; how could we let this happen? illustrations by Frank Stockton. Workman Pub. 2011 183p il $16.95

Grades: 5 6 7 8 9 10   **333.95**

1. Water pollution 2. Commercial fishing

ISBN 978-0-7611-5607-9; 0-7611-5607-0

LC 2011-15516

It was the author's intent to communicate that "our 'enduring misconception' about nature's bounty may lead to the extinction of many of the fish we eat (such as cod, salmon, swordfish, and tuna) and the subsequent collapse of marine ecosystems . . . . To avoid the dystopia he fears, Kurlansky stresses the importance of supporting sustainable fishing and hopes to enlist his readers to act to help 'change the way we do things!'" (Science)

"Brief sections in graphic-novel format follow a young girl, Ailat, and her father over a couple of decades as the condition of the ocean grows increasingly dire, eventually an orange, slimy mess mostly occupied by jellyfish and leatherback turtles. At the end, Ailat's young daughter doesn't even know what the word fish means. This is juxtaposed against nonfiction chapters with topics including types of fishing equipment and the damage each causes, a history of the destruction of the cod and its consequences, the international politics of the fishing industry and the effects of pollution and global warming. . . . Depressing and scary yet grimly entertaining." Kirkus

Lebbin, Daniel J.

The **American** Bird Conservancy guide to bird conservation; [by] Daniel J. Lebbin, Michael J. Parr, and George H. Fenwick; with a foreword by Jonathan Franzen. University of Chicago Press 2010 446p il map $45; ebook $27

Grades: 11 12 Adult   **333.95**

1. Wildlife conservation 2. Birds -- United States

ISBN 978-0-226-64727-2; 0-226-64727-7; 978-0-226-6472-6 ebook

LC 2010007646

The authors survey "the comprehensive status of bird conservation in the Americas, primarily focusing on North America. . . . 'WatchList Birds' provides accounts for 212 US birds—priority species for conservation—with a color plate, map, and text sections on distribution, threats, conservation, and action. 'Habitats' gives an overview of 12 major North American habitats (tundra, wetlands, grasslands, etc.) and includes several prime site descriptions within each, accompanied by the same features as the 'WatchList' accounts. The third major section, 'Threats,' includes sections such as 'Habitat Loss,' 'Pollution and Toxics,' and 'Climate Change,' and describes problems, solutions, and actions. . . . A beautiful production visually, the book is inviting as well as an unprecedented, rewarding conservation reference source." Choice

Includes glossary and bibliographical references

Orenstein, Ronald

Ivory, horn and blood; behind the elephant and rhinoceros poaching crisis. Ronald Orenstein. Firefly Books 2013 216 p. color illustrations $29.95

Grades: 9 10 11 12 Adult   **333.95**

1. Ivory 2. Poaching 3. Elephants 4. Rhinoceros 5. Ivory industry -- Corrupt practices 6. Rhinoceroses -- Effect of poaching on 7. African elephant -- Effect of poaching on 8. Asiatic elephant -- Effect of poaching on 9. Rhinoceros horn industry -- Corrupt practices

ISBN 1770852271; 9781770852273

LC 2013427986

This book, by Ronald Orenstein, describes how "today a new ivory crisis has arisen, fuelled by internal wars in Africa and a growing market in the Far East. . . . Bands of militia have crossed from one side of Africa to the other, slaughtering elephants with automatic weapons. A market surge in Vietnam and elsewhere has led to a growing criminal onslaught against the world's rhinoceroses. The situation, for both elephants and rhinos, is dire." (Publisher's note)

"Orenstein brings his considerable expertise to bear on this complex catastrophe, presenting all sides of some of the most polarizing issues." LJ

Includes bibliographical references (pages [194]-211)

and index

Riley, Laura

Nature's strongholds; the world's great wildlife reserves. [by] Laura and William Riley. Princeton University Press 2005 672p il maps $49.50

Grades: 9 10 11 12   **333.95**
1. Wildlife refuges 2. National parks and reserves
ISBN 0-691-12219-9

LC 2004-97392

"The authors present summaries of the major reserves on each continent, discuss the backgrounds of those reserves and the flora and fauna found there, and give . . . guidelines for visiting the sites." Sci Books Films

Includes bibliographical references

335.4   Marxian systems

Pipes, Richard

★ **Communism**: a history. Modern Lib. 2001 175p hardcover o.p. pa $10.95

Grades: 11 12 Adult   **335.4**
1. Communism
ISBN 0-679-64050-9; 0-8129-6864-6 pa

LC 2001-275458

"This is a short history on the essentials of communism—as an ideal, as a program outlined by Marx, and as a state established by Lenin to implement the program." Booklist

Includes bibliographical references

337   International economics

Steger, Manfred

Globalization: a very short introduction; [by] Manfred B. Steger. Oxford University Press 2009 147p il map (Very short introductions) pa $11.95

Grades: 11 12 Adult   **337**
1. Globalization
ISBN 978-0-19-955226-9

LC 2009-294674

First published 2003

This book covers "the major causes and consequences of globalization as well as the hotly contested question of whether globalization is, ultimately, a good or a bad thing. . . . The book also examines political movements both for and against globalization, from WTO protests to the recent rise in global jihadism; considers such concepts as 'Americanization' and 'McDonaldization'; and explores the role of the media and communication technologies in the process of cultural globalization." Publisher's note

Includes bibliographical references

338.1   Specific kinds of industries

Gay, Kathlyn

★ **Food**; the new gold. Kathlyn Gay. Twenty-First Century Books 2013 96 p. (lib. bdg.: alk. paper) $31.93

Grades: 9 10 11 12   **338.1**
1. Food relief 2. Climate change 3. Genetic engineering 4. Food supply 5. Food security
ISBN 0761346074; 9780761346074

LC 2011045486

In author Kathlyn Gay's book, she "explores the complicated interaction between food, business, politics, and the environment. She examines the international food aid system . . . [and] the genetic engineering of seeds, plants, and animals. These systems and practices promise to get more food to the people who need it--but the promises don't always pan out. Worse, many modern agricultural practices are harmful to the environment, to workers who produce the food, and even to consumers who eat it." (Publisher's note)

Includes bibliographical references and index.

Green, Jen

Food and farming; Jen Green. 1st ed. Heinemann Library 2012 64 p. (The impact of environmentalism) (hardcover) $35

Grades: 6 7 8 9 10   **338.1**
1. Environmental movement 2. Agriculture -- Environmental aspects 3. Food supply 4. Environmentalism
ISBN 1432965174; 9781432965174; 9781432965235

LC 2012001033

This book by Jen Green is part of the Impact on Environmentalism series. In "discussing the impact of the environmental movement on food and farming, Green also explores controversies surrounding modern agriculture and its distribution practices. A brief history of farming . . . leads to a discussion of more recent trends, including high-yield varieties of crops, monoculture, genetically modified foods, pesticides, water management, factory farming, organic farming, [and] fair trade." (Booklist)

Peacock, Kathy Wilson

★ **Food** security; Kathy Wilson Peacock; foreword by Mary K. Hendrickson. Facts On File 2011 344 p. (acid-free paper) $45.00

Grades: 11 12 Adult   **338.1**
1. Scarcity 2. Nutrition 3. Food supply 4. Food security 5. Food -- Safety measures
ISBN 0816082030; 9780816082032

LC 2011018414

This reference book "examines problems related to the amount, accessibility, and nutritional quality of the human food supply. Set up by a foreword by rural sociologist Mary Hendrickson, this topically arranged volume features three sections: a substantial introduction to global food security, with comprehensive case studies from representative countries (Bangladesh, China, the Democratic Republic of Congo, Haiti, the U.S., and Yemen); primary source documents; and research tools. The introduction defines food security and elucidates related topics such as global food supplies, causes and effects of food shortfalls, the potential effects of climate change and the global water crisis on food production, international history of food insecurity, and counterstrategies." (Booklist)

Includes bibliographical references and index.

Pollan, Michael

★ The **omnivore's** dilemma; the secrets behind what you eat. adapted by Richie Chevat. Young readers ed.; Dial Books 2009 298p il $17.99

Grades: 5 6 7 8 9 10 **338.1**

1. Food supply 2. Food chains (Ecology)
ISBN 0803734158; 9780803734159

LC 2009-9283

Adapted from: The omnivore's dilemma: a natural history of four meals, published 2006 by Penguin Press

This volume is adapted from Pollan's 2006 work for adults, The Omnivore's Dilemma: A Natural History of Four Meals. It presents information about food production in the United States and "encourages kids to consider the personal and global health implications of their food choices." (Publisher's note) Bibliography. Index. "Grades seven to ten." (Bull Cent Child Books)

"Adopting the role of food detective, the author 'peers behind the curtain' of the modern food industry and finds that the industrial approach to the food chain imperils our health and planet. The four sections of the volume describe differing types of meals: industrial; industrial organic; local sustainable; and hunted, gathered and found. Clear organization and lively writing rooted in fascinating examples make this accessible and interesting." Kirkus

Includes bibliographical references

338.2 Extraction of minerals

Black, Brian C.

Crude reality; petroleum in world history. Brian C. Black. Rowman & Littlefield Publishers 2012 277 p. ill. (cloth: alk. paper) $35.00; (ebook) $34.99

Grades: 11 12 **338.2**

1. Natural resources 2. Petroleum as fuel 3. Petroleum -- United States 4. Petroleum products -- History 5. Petroleum -- Economic aspects -- History 6. Petroleum industry and trade -- Social aspects -- History
ISBN 0742556549; 9780742556546; 9781442216112

LC 2011051805

Author Brian C. Black's book offers an "introduction to the history of oil tells the story of how petroleum shaped human life since it was first discovered leaking inconspicuously from the soil . . . [He] connects the subsequent exploitation of petroleum to patterns in world history while tracing the intricate links between energy and people after 1850 . . . Today, we see the disastrous results of environmental degradation, political instability, and world economic disparity in the waning years of a petroleum-powered civilization." (Publisher's note)

Includes bibliographical references and index.

338.4 Secondary industries and services

Pampel, Fred C.

Tobacco industry and smoking; Rev. ed; Facts On File 2009 314p map (Library in a book) $45

Grades: 11 12 Adult **338.4**

1. Smoking 2. Tobacco industry
ISBN 978-0-8160-7793-9; 0-8160-7793-2

LC 2009-396

First published 2004

This title about the tobacco industry "highlights emerging and accelerating trends in the worldwide battle over tobacco use, with . . . legal and historical overviews, reference resources, statistics, and a research guide." Publisher's note

Includes glossary and bibliographical references

338.5 General production economics

Galbraith, John Kenneth

★ The **great** crash, 1929; with a new introduction by the author; foreword by James K. Galbraith. Houghton Mifflin Co. 2009 206p pa $14.95

Grades: 11 12 Adult **338.5**

1. Great Depression, 1929-1939 2. United States -- Economic conditions -- 1919-1933
ISBN 978-0-547-24816-5

First published 1955

Beginning with the bull market of Coolidge and Hoover and continuing through the stock market crash, the author analyzes its causes and speculates about the chances of another crash.

Includes bibliographical references

Should the federal government bail out private industry? David Haugen, book editor. Greenhaven Press 2010 114p (At issue. Economy) $30.85; pa $21.85

Grades: 7 8 9 10 **338.5**

1. Banks and banking 2. Government lending 3. Economic policy -- United States 4. Industrial policy -- United States
ISBN 978-0-7377-4656-3; 0-7377-4656-4; 978-0-7377-4657-0 pa; 0-7377-4657-2 pa

LC 2009-37781

This "work effectively introduces the Trouble Asset Relief Program, the collapse of the subprime mortgage industry, and the highly charged issue of governmental economic regulation. The now-familiar style of the work couples diametrically opposed opinions drawn from diverse sources such as the New York Times, U.S. News & World Report, and SocialistAlternative.org with a focus on issues spanning executive bonuses, the auto industry, student loans, and numerous bailout shortcomings." SLJ

Includes bibliographical references

338.7 Business enterprises

Casnocha, Ben

My start-up life; what a (very) young CEO learned on his journey through Silicon Valley. Ben Casnocha; foreword by Marc Benioff. Jossey-Bass 2007 xiv, 189 p.p (cloth) $24.95

Grades: 11 12 Adult **338.7**

1. Entrepreneurship 2. New business enterprises 3.

Comcate (Firm) 4. Entrepreneurship -- United States 5. Computer software industry -- United States 6. Internet software industry -- United States 7. New business enterprises -- United States -- Management
ISBN 0787996130; 9780787996130

LC 2007007866

This book is written by "Ben Casnocha [who] discovered he was an entrepreneur at age 12 and hasn't slowed down since. In this . . . instructive book, Ben dissects the entrepreneurship 'gene,' explaining that everyone has inherited it if they have an idea to make the world a better place. In Casnocha's case, he found a better way for city governments to communicate with constituents on the Web. Six years later, Comcate has dozens of municipal clients, a growing staff, and a record of excellence. This book is the story of his start-up, but also a conversation with his mentors, clients and fellow entrepreneurs about how to make a business idea work and how to have the time of your life trying." (Publisher's note)

Includes bibliographical references (p. 185-188).

Frydenborg, Kay

Chocolate; sweet science and dark secrets of the world's favorite treat. Kay Frydenborg. Houghton Mifflin Harcourt 2015 272 p. 16 plates; color illustrations $18.99

Grades: 9 10 11 12   338.7

1. Cocoa 2. Science 3. Chocolate 4. Chocolate -- History 5. Cocoa trade
ISBN 9780544175662; 0544175662

LC 2014015885

In author Kay Frydenborg's book on the history of chocolate "cutting-edge genetic science whisked in with a strong social conscience, history, and culture yield one thought-provoking look into one of the world's most popular foods." (Publisher's note)

"Covering controversy over labor laws, the chemical makeup of chocolate, and recent attempts to map the cacao genome, Frydenborg offers a wealth of information that will likely encourage students to think critically about the ecological and human cost of their favorite candies and maybe even prompt them to choose sustainable alternatives. This is a great choice for school projects or chocolate fans curious about their beloved treat." Booklist

Includes bibliographical references

338.91 International development and growth

Prentzas, G. S.

The **Marshall** Plan; G. S. Prentzas. Chelsea House 2009 122 p. (Milestones in world history) (hardcover) $35

Grades: 7 8 9 10 11 12   338.91

1. American foreign aid 2. Reconstruction (1939-1951) 3. Europe -- Economic conditions 4. World War, 1939-1945 -- Economic aspects 5. Marshall Plan 6. Europe -- Economic conditions -- 1945- 7. Economic assistance, American -- Europe -- History -- 20th century
ISBN 1604134607; 9781604134605

LC 2010026904

This book on the Marshall Plan is part of the "Milestones in Modern World History" series of books that "give . . . explanations for major world events that continue to have an impact on today's world." Author G. S. Prentzas "discusses the U.S. financial aid plan to help Europe after WWII and to fight communisim at the same time" and includes "photographs, time lines, and maps." (Booklist) "This new title delves into the plan that transformed a war-ravaged Europe into a continent of vibrant economies." (Publisher's note)

Includes bibliographical references and index

339.2 Distribution of income and wealth

Gilbert, Geoffrey

Rich and poor in America; a reference handbook. ABC-CLIO 2008 275p il (Contemporary world issues) $55

Grades: 9 10 11 12   339.2

1. Wealth 2. Poverty 3. Economic policy -- United States
ISBN 978-1-59884-056-8; 1-59884-056-8

LC 2008-9350

"This work provides . . . [an] overview and analysis of the increasing gap between the Americans at the top and bottom of the economic scale." Publisher's note

Includes bibliographical references

339.3 Product and income accounts

Brezina, Corona

Understanding the gross domestic product and the gross national product; Corona Brezina. Rosen Pub. 2012 80 p. (library binding) $33.25

Grades: 9 10 11 12   339.3

1. Gross domestic product 2. Gross national product 3. National income 4. Economic indicators
ISBN 1448855691; 9781448855698

LC 2011014677

This book by Cornona Brezina explains the economic importance of the "Gross Domestic Product (GDP) . . . [and] the Gross National Product (GNP). . . . Together the GDP and GNP are perhaps the most important of all economic indicators, and for this reason it is essential that students understand what they are, how they are calculated, and what real-world economic realities they reflect and predict. Understanding the GDP and GNP is crucial to understanding the current economy." (Publisher's note)

Includes bibliographical references and index.

339.4 Factors affecting income and wealth

Should the U.S. reduce its consumption? David Haugen and Susan Musser, book editors. Greenhaven Press 2011 113p (At issue. Social issues) $33.70; pa $23.85

Grades: 9 10 11 12 **339.4**

1. Consumers 2. Consumption (Economics)

ISBN 978-0-7377-4894-9; 978-0-7377-4895-6 pa

LC 2010020771

Articles in this anthology cover issues such as U.S. oil consumption, food consumption, and sustainability.

Includes bibliographical references

340 Law

★ **Black's** law dictionary; Bryan A. Garner, editor in chief. 9th ed.; West 2009 xxxi, 1920p $80

Grades: 11 12 Adult **340**

1. Reference books 2. Law -- Dictionaries

ISBN 978-0-314-19949-2

LC 2009-459279

First published 1891 with title: A dictionary of law, under the authorship of Henry Campbell Black. Periodically revised to bring terms up to date

This law dictionary contains more than 45,000 terms, including archaic terms and references to statutes and cases.

Includes bibliographical references

Feinman, Jay M.

★ **Law** 101; 3rd ed.; Oxford University Press 2010 363p $27.95

Grades: 11 12 Adult **340**

1. Law -- United States

ISBN 978-0-19-539513-6

LC 2010-487303

First published 2000

This book "covers the main subjects taught in the first year of law school. Readers are introduced to every aspect of the legal system, from constitutional law and the litigation process to tort law, contract law, property law, and criminal law." Publisher's note

340.023 Law as a profession, occupation, hobby

Prentzas, G. S.

Careers as a paralegal and legal assistant; G. S. Prentzas. Rosen Publishing Group, Inc. 2014 80 p. color illustrations (Essential careers) (library binding) $34.25

Grades: 9 10 11 12 **340.023**

1. Lawyers 2. Legal aid 3. Legal assistants -- Vocational guidance -- United States

ISBN 1477717900; 9781477717905

LC 2013012399

This book, by G.S. Prentzas, "begins with a brief introduction to the U.S. legal system before delineating such paralegal tasks as investigations, legal research, and client relations. The book provide information on the skills, education, and training needed." (Booklist)

"Whether used by students with no professional direction or students with some interest in business who are in need of more specifics, these titles in the Essential Careers series offer clear and realistic choices." Booklist

Includes bibliographical references (p. 74-76) and index

341.23 United Nations

Alger, Chadwick F.

The **United** Nations system; a reference handbook. ABC-CLIO 2005 375p (Contemporary world issues) $50

Grades: 9 10 11 12 **341.23**

1. United Nations

ISBN 1-85109-805-4

LC 2005-25406

"This book is divided into chapters that cover background and history, problems, controversies and solutions, ambivalent participation of the Untied [sic] States in the UN system, chronologically the emergence and development of the UN system, facts and data, alternative futures of the UN system, directors of organizations, associations and agencies, biographical sketches of present heads of the UN system, selective print and nonprint resources of the United Nations, and an index and information about the author. . . . This book should be in all libraries that need up-to-date information on globalization, the United Nations, and the interrelationship between countries." Am Ref Books Annu, 2006

Includes bibliographical references

Fasulo, Linda M.

An **insider's** guide to the UN; [by] Linda Fasulo. 2nd ed; Yale University Press 2009 262p il pa $17

Grades: 11 12 Adult **341.23**

1. United Nations

ISBN 978-0-300-14197-9; 0-300-14197-1

LC 2008-52231

First published 2003

This "guide to the United Nations surveys the world body's programs and activities, and covers key issues including human rights, climate change, counterterrorism, nuclear proliferation, peacekeeping, and UN reform. It also offers guidelines for setting up a Model UN." Publisher's note

Includes bibliographical references

Gorman, Robert F.

Great debates at the United Nations; an encyclopedia of fifty key issues 1945-2000. Greenwood Press 2001 xli, 451p il $65

Grades: 11 12 Adult **341.23**

1. United Nations

ISBN 0-313-31386-5

LC 00-57652

The introduction "provides some historical background on the United Nations and the nature of its debates since its inception. Next come discussions of specific issues . . . that have appeared on its agenda. Each entry contains four sections: the significance of the issue; its historical, social, and economic background; the history of the UN discussions . . . and the outcome of the debate. . . . Each discussion ends with a list of suggested readings." SLJ

Includes bibliographical references

Moore, John Allphin

★ **Encyclopedia** of the United Nations; [by] John Allphin Moore, Jr., Jerry Pubantz. 2nd ed.; Facts On File 2008 2v il (Facts on File library of world history) set $125

Grades: 11 12 Adult **341.23**
1. United Nations 2. Reference books 3. International relations -- Encyclopedias
ISBN 978-0-8160-6913-2
LC 2007-29559
First published 2002

This set features entries on "the United Nations's institutions, procedures, policies, specialized agencies, historic personalities, initiatives, and involvement in world affairs. . . . The appendixes contain important UN documents, such as the Charter of the United Nations, the Universal Declaration of Human Rights, the Statute of the International Court of Justice, and the recent Security Council Resolution." Publisher's note

Includes bibliographical references

341.6 Law of war

Kenney, Karen Latchana

Korematsu v. the United States; World War II Japanese-American internment camps. by Karen Latchana Kenney; content consultant Richard D. Friedman. ABDO Pub. Co. 2013 160 p. ill. (some col.) (library) $35.64

Grades: 8 9 10 11 12 **341.6**
1. Korematsu v. United States (Supreme Court case) 2. Japanese Americans -- Evacuation and relocation, 1942-1945 3. United States -- Trials, litigation, etc.
ISBN 1617834734; 9781617834738
LC 2012001277

This book by Karen Latchana Kenney is part of the Landmark Supreme Court Cases series and focuses on the case of Korematsu v. the United States. It "looks at the historical impact of World War II and the internment of Japanese American citizens out of fear and hysteria following the bombing of Pearl Harbor." (School Library Journal)

Includes bibliographical references (p. 146-154) and index.

342 Branches of law; laws, regulations, cases; law of specific jurisdictions, areas, socioeconomic regions

Abrams, Floyd

Friend of the court; on the front lines with the First Amendment. by Floyd Abrams. Yale University Press 2013 488 p. (hardbound: alk. paper) $32.50

Grades: 10 11 12 Adult **342**
1. Freedom of speech 2. Lawyers -- United States 3. United States. Constitution. 1st-10th amendments 4. Lawyers -- United States -- Biography 5. Freedom of expression -- United States 6. United States.

Constitution. 1st Amendment
ISBN 0300190875; 9780300190878
LC 2012047962

"In this . . . collection of speeches, letters, testimony, and public debate, [author Floyd] Abrams explores the landscape of free-speech issues in the U.S. during the past 50 years. He argues that free speech is not an ideological concept, noting its use by liberals to defend organized labor and civil rights and antiwar protestors and by conservatives to defend antiabortion protestors and corporate support for political candidates." (Booklist)

"... highly accessible, page-turning collection that demonstrates that ultimately the most important client passionately defended across the years by Abrams is the expressive freedom clause of the First Amendment. Indeed, an important theme of this volume is that this provision has continuously needed defending from attacks by liberals and conservatives alike. The readers for whom this volume will be useful and informative will be as diverse as the myriad audiences for whom the original materials were intended." (Choice Reviews)

Includes bibliographical references and index

Amar, Akhil Reed

America's constitution; a biography. Random House 2005 657p il $29.95; pa $16.95

Grades: 11 12 Adult **342**
1. Constitutional history -- United States
ISBN 1-400-06262-4; 0-8129-7272-4 pa
LC 2004-61464

"Only rarely do you find a book that embodies scholarship at its most solid and invigorating; this is such a book." Publ Wkly

Includes bibliographical references

★ **Amendment** XV; race and the right to vote. Jeff Hay, book editor. Greenhaven Press 2009 154p il map (Constitutional amendments: beyond the Bill of Rights) $34.70

Grades: 7 8 9 10 11 12 **342**
1. African Americans -- Suffrage 2. United States -- Constitution -- 15th Amendment
ISBN 978-0-7377-4327-2; 0-7377-4327-1
LC 2009-4704

This book "examines the Fifteenth Amendment, which allowed all American citizens the right to vote, regardless of race. . . . . The sources reproduced . . . illuminate the controversy and philosophical debate that surround the amendments." Voice Youth Advocates

Includes bibliographical references

★ The **annotated** U.S. Constitution and Declaration of Independence; edited by Jack N. Rakove. Belknap Press 2009 354p il $24.95

Grades: 11 12 Adult **342**
1. United States -- Constitution 2. Constitutional law -- United States 3. Constitutional history -- United States 4. United States -- Declaration of Independence 5. United States -- Constitution -- 1st-10th amendments
ISBN 0-674-03606-9; 978-0-674-03606-2
LC 2009-22907

This is an explication of the Declaration of Independence, the Bill of Rights, and the Constitution. Bibliography.

The author "presents both the Declaration and the Constitution with carefully laid out annotation that's accessible to general readers as well as high school and college students. His extended introduction provides a readable and instructive analysis of how the writing of the Constitution progressed, especially on matters concerning representation, executive power, and creation of the amendments. His annotations often rely upon contemporary usage and meaning from the time of the Declaration of Independence and Constitution . . . and he compares such usage to other documents of the time." Libr J

Includes bibliographical references

Bowen, Catherine Drinker

★ **Miracle** at Philadelphia; the story of the Constitutional Convention, May to September, 1787. foreword by Warren E. Burger. Little, Brown 1986 346p hardcover o.p. pa $16.95

Grades: 11 12 Adult **342**
1. Constitutional history -- United States 2. United States -- Constitutional Convention (1787)
ISBN 0-316-10398-5 pa
LC 86-205421

A reissue of the title first published 1966

"Writing from sources—delegates' letters and diaries; contemporary reports; James Madison's faithful minutes—Catherine Drinker Bowen draws [a] . . . picture of the men, issues and background of the Constitutional Convention held at Philadelphia in the hot summer of 1787." Publ Wkly

Includes bibliographical references

★ **Civil** liberties and the Constitution; cases and commentaries. Lucius J. Barker ... [et al.] 9th ed.; Longman 2011 845p $112.60

Grades: 9 10 11 12 **342**
1. Civil rights 2. United States -- Supreme Court 3. Constitutional law -- United States
ISBN 978-0-13-092268-7; 0-13-092268-4
LC 2010027105

First published 1970

"This casebook explores civil liberty problems through a study of leading judicial decisions." Publisher's note

Includes bibliographical references

Civil liberties and war; Jamuna Carroll, book editor. Greenhaven Press 2006 173p il (Issues on trial) lib bdg $34.95

Grades: 9 10 11 12 **342**
1. Civil rights 2. War -- Public opinion 3. Military policy -- United States
ISBN 0-7377-2503-6; 978-0-7377-2503-2
LC 2005-52761

"This volume examines four significant Supreme Court cases: Charles T. Schenck v. United States (1919), involving suppressing speech that poses a clear and present danger; Toyosaburo Korematsu v. United States (1944), which deals with the evacuation of Japanese Americans; New York Times Co. v. United States (1971), which revolves around the publication of the Pentagon Papers and the issue of prior restraint; and Yaser Esam Hamdi et al. v. Donald H. Rums-

feld et al. (2004), which entails due-process rights and enemy combatants. . . . An important, timely addition for most collections." SLJ

Includes bibliographical references

The **Civil** Rights Act of 1964. Greenhaven Press 2004 128p il (At issue in history) lib bdg $29.95; pa $21.20

Grades: 9 10 11 12 **342**
1. Civil rights 2. Civil Rights Act of 1964
ISBN 0-7377-2304-1 lib bdg; 0-7377-2305-X pa
LC 2003-47288

"This book reviews the history of the landmark legislation, the debate that surrounded it, and its legacy through essays and articles written at the time and more recent pieces that examine the progress made and outlook for the future. . . . A useful collection of primary and secondary sources for reports." SLJ

Includes bibliographical references

Davis, Thomas J.

Plessy v. Ferguson; Thomas J. Davis. Greenwood 2012 xx, 238 p.p (Landmarks of the American mosaic) (hardcover) $58

Grades: 10 11 12 Adult **342**
1. Segregation 2. United States -- Race relations -- History 3. Segregation -- Law and legislation -- United States -- History 4. Segregation in transportation -- Law and legislation -- Louisiana -- History
ISBN 0313391874; 9780313391873
LC 2012011735

This book, by Thomas J. Davis, discusses the U.S. Supreme Court case Plessy v. Ferguson as part of the "Landmarks of the American Mosaic" series. "Contrary to popular misconceptions, Plessy v. Ferguson was not a simple case of black vs. white separation, but rather a challenging and complex protest for U.S. law to fully accept mixed ancestry and multiculturalism." (Publisher's note)

Includes bibliographical references (p. 219-222) and index.

★ **Encyclopedia** of the First Amendment; edited by John R. Vile, David L. Hudson Jr., David Schultz. CQ Press 2009 2v il set $275

Grades: 11 12 Adult **342**
1. Reference books 2. United States -- Constitution -- 1st-10th amendments -- Encyclopedias
ISBN 978-0-87289-311-5; 0-87289-311-1
LC 2008-36077

This "is an excellent resource for anyone who wants to learn more about broadcast regulation, the establishment of religion clause, students' rights, or a myriad of other topics involving the First Amendment and its political, cultural, and legal significance." Booklist

Includes bibliographical references

Feinberg, Barbara Silberdick

The **Articles** of Confederation; the first constitution of the United States. 21st Cent. Bks. (Brookfield) 2002 110p il maps lib bdg $24.90

Grades: 7 8 9 10   **342**
1. Constitutional history -- United States 2. United States -- Articles of Confederation 3. United States -- Politics and government -- 1775-1783, Revolution
ISBN 0-7613-2114-4

LC 2001-27441

"Feinberg introduces the history and text of 'The Articles of Confederation and Perpetual Union,' the constitution that guided the U.S. government from 1776 to 1787. . . . Attractively laid out, this solid choice includes many black-and-white illustrations, including portrait paintings, engravings, and maps." Booklist

Includes bibliographical references

Freedom of speech; edited by William Dudley. Greenhaven Press 2005 128p (Bill of Rights) lib bdg $32.45
Grades: 9 10 11 12   **342**
1. Censorship 2. Freedom of speech
ISBN 0-7377-1929-X

LC 2004-54149

"This interesting anthology examines the historical origins of the free speech clause of the First Amendment, the evolving interpretations of the First Amendment by the Supreme Court, and the changing public attitudes toward free speech. Included are discussions of such issues as wartime dissent, censorship, hate speech, and flag burning." Publisher's note

Includes bibliographical references

Freedom of the press; Rob Edelman, book editor. Greenhaven Press 2007 181p (Issues on trial) lib bdg $34.95
Grades: 9 10 11 12   **342**
1. Freedom of the press
ISBN 0-7377-3449-3; 978-0-7377-3449-2

LC 2006-41173

"This anthology offers . . . [an] examination of four landmark court cases involving freedom of the press, each of which was heard by the U.S. Supreme Court." Publisher's note

Includes bibliographical references

Haugen, David
Rights of the disabled; [by] David M. Haugen, with Susan Musser and Andrea DeMott. Facts on File 2008 296p (Library in a book) $45
Grades: 9 10 11 12 Adult   **342**
1. People with disabilities -- Civil rights 2. People with disabilities-- Legal status, laws, etc.
ISBN 978-0-8160-7128-9

LC 2007-34803

This book is an "overview of the history of this topic and opinions surrounding it, ranging from the formation of the League of the Physically Handicapped in 1935 to current efforts to enhance and modify the ADA." Publisher's note

Includes glossary and bibliographical references

Haynes, Charles C.
First freedoms; a documentary history of the First Amendment Rights in America. [by] Charles

C. Haynes, Sam Chaltain, Susan M. Glisson. Oxford University Press 2005 255p il $40
Grades: 8 9 10 11 12   **342**
1. Freedom of speech 2. Freedom of religion 3. Freedom of the press 4. Constitutional history -- United States 5. United States -- Constitution -- 1st-10th amendments
ISBN 978-0-19-515750-5; 0-19-515750-8

LC 2005-31880

This is "an excellent resource for all libraries, as well as enjoyable reading for history buffs." SLJ

Hennessey, Jonathan
★ The **United** States Constitution; a graphic adaptation. written by Jonathan Hennessey; art by Aaron McConnell. Hill and Wang 2008 149p il $35; pa $16.95
Grades: 9 10 11 12 Adult   **342**
1. Graphic novels 2. United States -- Constitution -- Graphic novels 3. Constitutional history -- United States -- Graphic novels
ISBN 978-0-8090-9487-5; 0-8090-9487-8; 978-0-8090-9470-7 pa; 0-8090-9470-3 pa

LC 2008-17927

The author and illustrator go "through the entire U. S. Constitution, article by article, amendment by amendment, explaining their meaning and implications—in comics format. Avoiding the didactic, the book succeeds in being both consistently entertaining and illuminating." Publ Wkly

Includes bibliographical references

Hinds, Maurene J.
You have the right to know your rights; what teens should know. Enslow Pubs. 2005 104p il (Issues in focus today) $31.93
Grades: 9 10 11 12   **342**
1. Youth -- Civil rights
ISBN 0-7660-2358-3

The author "outlines for readers the ways in which the rights of young people have changed over time in the United States, and she brings them up-to-date on the topic of young people's rights today. Hinds covers such issues as privacy and self-expression and explains what teens can do if their rights are violated." Publisher's note

Includes bibliographical references

Latimer, Christopher P.
Civil liberties and the state; a documentary and reference guide. [by] Christopher Peter Latimer. Greenwood 2011 367p il (Documentary and reference guides) $95
Grades: 9 10 11 12   **342**
1. Civil rights 2. United States -- History -- Sources
ISBN 978-0-313-37934-5; 978-0-313-37935-2 ebook

LC 2010041535

"Latimer provides 81 historical documents illustrating the history of due process, equal protection, the right to privacy, and the rights guaranteed by the First Amendment. The chronological presentation opens with the Magna Carta and closes with portions of the 2008 Democratic and Republican parties' respective 'Party Platform Concerning Civil Liberties.' . . . Especially useful to students in Advanced Placement government courses." SLJ

Includes bibliographical references

Lewis, Anthony

Freedom for the thought that we hate; a biography of the First Amendment. Basic Books 2007 221p (Basic ideas) $25

Grades: 11 12 Adult 342

1. Freedom of speech 2. Freedom of the press
ISBN 978-0-465-03917-3; 0-465-03917-0

LC 2007-40249

The author "does a remarkable job of presenting the history and scope of freedom of thought. He writes simply without oversimplifying. . . . Mr. Lewis has produced a concise and wise book. His conclusions are well worth pondering." Economist

Includes bibliographical references

Marzilli, Alan

★ **Fetal** rights. Chelsea House Publishers 2006 150p il map (Point-counterpoint) $32.95

Grades: 9 10 11 12 342

1. Fetus
ISBN 0-7910-8643-7

LC 2005-6533

"This book examines whether the law should recognize an unborn child—or fetus—as a person. Other relevant topics include whether or not women should be prosecuted for using drugs during pregnancy and whether or not a pregnant woman should be forced to undergo medical procedures for the benefit of a fetus." Publisher's note

Includes bibliographical references

Merino, Noel

What rights should illegal immigrants have? Noël Merino, book editor. Greenhaven Press 2010 106p (At issue. Civil liberties) $31.80; pa $22.50

Grades: 9 10 11 12 342

1. Civil rights 2. Unauthorized immigrants 3. Illegal aliens 4. United States -- Immigration and emigration
ISBN 978-0-7377-4902-1; 0-7377-4902-4; 978-0-7377-4903-8 pa; 0-7377-4903-2 pa

LC 2010-4546

This anthology of essays covers topics related to illegal immigration, such as whether immigration raids are justified and whether existing immigration law violates illegal immigrants' rights.

Includes bibliographical references

Native American rights; Uma Kukathas, book editor. Greenhaven Press 2008 199p (Issues on trial) lib bdg $37.40

Grades: 9 10 11 12 342

1. Native Americans -- Civil rights
ISBN 978-0-7377-4076-9

LC 2008-10057

"This book discusses and analyzes various Supreme Court rulings, both historical and contemporary, their impact on American society, and the controversies before and after the court's rulings by various experts in the related fields. .

. . This would be a great resource for schools wanting more materials on contemporary Native American issues for use in classes such as American History, English, and Current Events." Libr Media Connect

★ The **Oxford** guide to United States Supreme Court decisions; edited by Kermit L. Hall, James W. Ely, Jr. 2nd ed.; Oxford University Press 2009 499p $35

Grades: 11 12 Adult 342

1. Reference books 2. United States -- Supreme Court 3. Constitutional law -- United States
ISBN 978-0-19-537939-6

LC 2008-23763

First published 1999

The editors "assemble the scholarship of 161 field specialists, who summarize the Supreme Court's 440 most significant cases. Scholar-signed, multiparagraph entries are alphabetized by case name, include argued and decided dates, and detail vote divisions. The book closes with a glossary, an appendix containing the complete Constitution, a chronology of justices since 1789, and a list of presidential appointments. An outstanding single-volume reference." Libr J

Includes bibliographical references

Pendergast, Tom

Constitutional amendments: from freedom of speech to flag burning; [by] Tom Pendergast, Sara Pendergast, and John Sousanis; Elizabeth Shaw Grunow, editor. U.X.L 2001 3v set $165

Grades: 7 8 9 10 342

1. Civil rights 2. Constitutional law -- United States 3. United States -- Constitution -- 1st-10th amendments
ISBN 0-7876-4865-5

LC 00-67236

"Presentation is very clear. . . . This is definitely a set that belongs in school and public libraries." Booklist

Includes glossary and bibliographical references

Racial discrimination; Mitchell Young, book editor. Greenhaven Press 2006 183p il (Issues on trial) lib bdg $34.95

Grades 8 9 10 11 12 342

1. Hate crimes 2. Segregation 3. Race discrimination 4. Affirmative action programs
ISBN 0-7377-2787-X; 978-0-7377-2787-6

LC 2005-55092

This anthology examines four major court cases involving racial discrimination: Plessy v. Ferguson (1896), Brown v. Board of Education (1954), Wisconsin v. Mitchell (1993), and Grutter v. Bollinger (2003).

Includes bibliographical references

Savage, David G.

★ The **Supreme** Court and individual rights; 5th ed.; CQ Press 2009 570p il map pa $52

Grades: 9 10 11 12 342

1. Civil rights 2. United States -- Supreme Court 3. Constitutional law -- United States
ISBN 978-0-87289-424-2

LC 2009-19747

First published 1980 under the authorship of Elder Witt

The author "explores the personal impact of Supreme Court decisions made through 2008. He divides his content into six thematic chapters that explore our guaranteed rights, like Freedom of Speech, along with restricted facets, such as flag burning. With each topic, historic cases involving individuals' rights are carefully explained. Half-page sidebars further clarify complex issues, such as the Court's history regarding cases involving slavery's legality and state sedition laws." Libr J

Includes bibliographical references

Schultz, David A.

Encyclopedia of the United States Constitution; [by] David Schultz. Facts On File 2009 2v il (Facts on File library of American history) set $150

Grades: 9 10 11 12 Adult 342
1. Reference books 2. Constitutional law -- United States -- Encyclopedias
ISBN 978-0-8160-6763-3; 0-8160-6763-5
LC 2008-23349

"This reference source can help high-school students, the general public, and other interested parties comprehend the fundamental concepts, evolutionary character, and historic people and events that have shaped the [Constitution.] . . . The alphabetically arranged entries cover terms, events, people, landmark cases, and issues that help explain the Constitution's history. The appendix provides the Declaration of Independence, the Articles of Confederation, the Constitution, and the Bill of Rights as well as 'Other Amendments to the Constitution,' a 'U.S. Constitution Time Line,' and instructions on locating court cases." Booklist

Includes bibliographical references

Stearman, Kaye

Freedom of information; Kaye Stearman. Rosen Central Pub. 2012 48 p. (pbk.) $11.75

Grades: 7 8 9 10 342
1. Secrecy 2. Political ethics 3. United States -- Politics and government 4. Freedom of information -- United States
ISBN 1448860199; 1448870089; 1448870100; 9781448860197; 9781448870080; 9781448870103
LC 2011034070

Author Kaye Stearman presents "explanations of how freedom of information laws work and how they have been framed in different countries. . . . Most countries' laws contain limits on disclosure, and there are many debates about where the lines should be drawn. . . . Chapters explore the debate about how these laws should be applied so that they work well for both government officials and the public." (Publisher's note)

Includes bibliographical references and index.

Supreme Court Historical Society

Supreme Court decisions and women's rights; milestones to equality. edited by Clare Cushman; foreword by Ruth Bader Ginsburg; sponsored by the Supreme Court Historical Society. 2nd ed.; CQ Press 2010 310p il $67; pa $57

Grades: 9 10 11 12 342
1. Women's rights 2. Reference books 3. Sex discrimination 4. United States -- Supreme Court
ISBN 978-1-60871-406-3; 978-1-60871-407-0 pa
LC 2010-26076

First published 2001

"A great resource for reports and a handy reference tool for students and teachers alike." SLJ

Includes bibliographical references

Tischauser, Leslie V.

★ **Jim** Crow laws; Leslie V. Tischauser. Greenwood 2012 xxiii, 215 p.p

Grades: 9 10 11 12 342
1. Race relations 2. African Americans -- Civil rights 3. Race discrimination -- Law and legislation -- United States -- 20th century 4. African Americans -- Social conditions -- To 1964 5. African Americans -- Legal status, laws, etc. -- History 6. Race discrimination -- Law and legislation -- United States -- History
ISBN 0313386080; 9780313386084; 9780313386091
LC 2012007814

This book by Leslie V. Tischauser "presents the history of the discriminatory laws that segregated people by race in the American South from the end of the Civil War through passage of the 1965 Civil Rights Act. . . .[T]his book provides a detailed analysis of the creation, defense, justification, and fight against the Jim Crow system." (Publisher's note)

Includes bibliographical references (p. 193-204) and index.

Treaties with American Indians; an encyclopedia of rights, conflicts, and sovereignty. Donald L. Fixico, editor. ABC-CLIO 2008 3v il set $285

Grades: 9 10 11 12 Adult 342
1. Reference books 2. Native Americans -- Treaties -- Encyclopedias
ISBN 978-1-57607-880-8
LC 2007-27797

"This set is the most comprehensive source of information on Canadian-Indian treaties and U.S.-Indian treaties." Booklist

Includes bibliographical references

Van Zee, Amy

Dred Scott v. Sandford; slavery and freedom before the American civil war. by Amy Van Zee; content consultant, Earl Maltz. ABDO Pub. Co. 2013 160 p. ill. (some col.) (Landmark Supreme Court cases) (hbk.: alk. paper) $35.64

Grades: 8 9 10 11 12 342
1. Slavery -- United States 2. United States. Supreme Court 3. Slavery -- Law and legislation -- United States -- History -- 19th century
ISBN 1617834726; 9781617834721
LC 2012001276

This book is part of the Landmark Supreme Court Cases Series. This title focuses on Dred Scott v. Sandford and explains how "the origins of slavery in the United States in regard to societal acceptance and black inferiority, deeply ingrained throughout the growth and development of the country, played a major role in every aspect of the developing nation with the continuing struggle between both sides of the issue." (School Library Journal)

Includes bibliographical references (p. 146-153) and index

Vile, John R.
The **Constitutional** Convention of 1787; a comprehensive encyclopedia of America's founding. ABC-CLIO 2005 2v il set $185
Grades: 11 12 Adult   342
1. Reference books 2. Constitutional law -- United States -- Encyclopedias 3. Constitutional history -- United States -- Encyclopedias
ISBN 1-85109-669-8
LC 2005-24214
This "resource covers the people, events, committees, ideology, and documents related to the drafting of the Constitution." SLJ
Includes bibliographical references

Essential Supreme Court decisions; summaries of leading cases in U.S. constitutional law. 15th ed.; Rowman & Littlefield Publishers 2010 xxxvi, 535p $59.95; pa $24.95
Grades: 9 10 11 12   342
1. Reference books 2. United States -- Supreme Court 3. Constitutional law -- United States
ISBN 978-1-4422-0384-6; 978-1-4422-0385-3 pa
LC 2010-8375
First published 1954 with title: Summaries of leading cases on the Constitution
This volume presents summaries of major cases concerning constitutional law that have been decided by the Supreme Court since its establishment. It is written for students and laypersons.
This is "the most comprehensive single collection of the Court's decisions. . . . It is indispensable for the study of the work of the Supreme Court." Choice
Includes glossary

Weiner, Mark Stuart
Black trials; citizenship from the beginnings of slavery to the end of caste. [by] Mark S. Weiner. Alfred A. Knopf 2004 421p $26.95; pa $16.95
Grades: 11 12 Adult   342
1. Trials 2. African Americans -- Civil rights
ISBN 0-375-40981-5; 0-375-70884-7 pa
LC 2004-40860
The author "examines how court proceedings involving black people—and whites trying to assist them—have served as windows onto race relations and the power of whites over blacks in the U.S. from its earliest days. . . . This book is the best of its kind—a serious, deeply felt reflection on the weight of history on contemporary affairs." Publ Wkly
Includes bibliographical references

344 Labor, social service, education, cultural law

★ **Amendments** XVIII and XXI; prohibition and repeal. Sylvia Engdahl, book editor. Greenhaven Press 2009 218p il map (Constitutional amendments: beyond the Bill of Rights) $34.70
Grades: 7 8 9 10 11 12   344
1. Prohibition 2. United States -- Constitution -- 18th Amendment 3. United States -- Constitution -- 21st Amendment
ISBN 978-0-7377-4328-9; 0-7377-4328-X
LC 2008-51451
This book "examines the eighteenth and twenty-first amendments. This volume's historical essays examine both sides of the issue; both for and against Prohibition. . . . Other essays examine the impact of these amendments on the Constitution, and the controversies that still surround intoxicating substances in America." Voice Youth Advocates
Includes bibliographical references

American Bar Association
The **American** Bar Association guide to workplace law; [principle author, Barbara Fick] 2nd ed; Random House Reference 2006 301p pa $16.95
Grades: 11 12 Adult   344
1. Labor -- Law and legislation
ISBN 0-375-72140-1; 978-0-375-72140-3
LC 2006-45186
First published 1997
This guide covers laws affecting hiring, sexual harassment, leave time, health insurance, ending an employment relationship, retirement, unions, government employment and workplace rights.
Includes bibliographical references

Barbour, Scott
Should marijuana be legalized? ReferencePoint Press 2010 96p il map (In controversy) lib bdg $26.95
Grades: 9 10 11 12   344
1. Marijuana 2. Drugs -- Law and legislation
ISBN 978-1-60152-106-4; 1-60152-106-5
LC 2009-40002
This book "discusses medical, judicial, economic, and social concerns that come to light in the debate over legalizing marijuana." Booklist
Includes bibliographical references

The **environment;** Andrea C. Nakaya, book editor. Greenhaven Press 2006 163 p. ill. (library) $42.15
Grades: 9 10 11 12   344
1. Environmental policy -- United States
ISBN 0737727977; 9780737727975
LC 2005052713
"This anthology examines four court cases that offer insight into some of America's most important environmental conflicts. . . . There is a wealth of information in this title,

which serves as a meaningful reference tool and a prelude to the study of law as a force for major social change." SLJ

Includes bibliographical references (p. 154-158) and index.

Hillstrom, Laurie
Roe v. Wade; [by] Laurie Collier Hillstrom. Omnigraphics 2008 249p il (Defining moments) $49
Grades: 9 10 11 12 Adult   **344**
    1. Abortion -- Law and legislation
ISBN 978-0-7808-1026-6

           LC 2008-3524

"Explores the history of abortion in America, describing the Roe v. Wade case, explaining the decision and its implications, and examining the continuing debate over abortion rights and its impact on American society and politics. Features include a narrative overview, biographical profiles, primary source documents, detailed chronology, glossary, annotated sources for further study, bibliography, and index." Publisher's note

Includes glossary and bibliographical references

Hull, N. E. H.
Roe v. Wade; the abortion rights controversy in American history. [by] N.E.H. Hull and Peter Charles Hoffer. 2nd ed., rev. & expanded.; University Press of Kansas 2010 370p (Landmark law cases & American society) $39.95; pa $19.95
Grades: 11 12 Adult   **344**
    1. Roe v. Wade 2. District attorneys 3. Pro-choice activists 4. Abortion -- Law and legislation
ISBN 978-0-7006-1753-1; 0-7006-1753-1; 978-0-7006-1754-8 pa; 0-7006-1754-X pa

           LC 2010-21294

First published 2001

Thsi book "highlights the abortion issue's historical background; highlights Roe v. Wade's core issues, essential personalities, and key precedents; tracks the case's path through the courts; clarifies the jurisprudence behind the court's ruling in Roe; and gauges its impact on American society and subsequent challenges to it in Webster v. Reproductive Services (1989) and Casey v. Planned Parenthood (1992). . . . [It includes] chapters covering abortion politics and legal battles in the post-9/11 era." Publisher's note

Includes bibliographical references

Is gun ownership a right? Lea Sakora, book editor. Greenhaven Press 2010 107p (At issue. Civil liberties) $31.80; pa $22.50
Grades: 9 10 11 12   **344**
    1. Gun control 2. United States -- Constitution -- 1st-10th amendments
ISBN 978-0-7377-4428-6; 0-7377-4428-6; 978-0-7377-4429-3 pa; 0-7377-4429-4 pa

           LC 2009-26389

Articles in this anthology discuss the Second Amendment and issues related to gun ownership and gun regulation.

Includes bibliographical references

Mountjoy, Shane
Engel v. Vitale; school prayer and the establishment clause. Chelsea House 2007 128p il (Great Supreme Court decisions) lib bdg $30
Grades: 7 8 9 10   **344**
    1. Church and state 2. Religion in the public schools
ISBN 0-7910-9241-0; 978-0-7910-9241-5

           LC 2006-7328

This describes the 1962 Supreme Court case which ruled that official prayers in public schools were unconstitutional.

"Excellent period photos, magazine covers, and portraits of historical figures are closely cued to the [text]. . . . Handsomely packaged, accessible." SLJ

Includes glossary and bibliographical references

Perl, Lila
Cruzan v. Missouri; the right to die? Marshall Cavendish Benchmark 2007 143p il (Supreme Court milestones) $27.95
Grades: 7 8 9 10   **344**
    1. Metalworkers 2. Accident victims 3. Right to die -- Law and legislation
ISBN 978-0-7614-2581-6; 0-7614-258-0

           LC 2006-25740

"Perl discusses Nancy Cruzan's parents quest for her right to die following an auto accident and her resulting vegetative state. Highlights include the discussion of religious arguments, physician-assisted suicide, and the cases of Karen Ann Quinlan and Terry Schiavo. . . . Additional information is presented in sidebars. Occasional black-and-white photos add interest." SLJ

Includes bibliographical references

Reproductive rights; William Dudley, book editor. Greenhaven Press 2006 178p il (Issues on trial) lib bdg $34.95
Grades: 9 10 11 12   **344**
    1. Abortion -- Law and legislation 2. Birth control -- Law and legislation
ISBN 0-7377-2511-7; 978-0-7377-2511-7

           LC 2005-54268

"This book examines various issues related to the topic via a series of writings about famous Supreme Court cases, ranging from Buck v. Bell in 1927 and Griswold v. Connecticut in 1965 to Roe v. Wade in 1973 and A.Z. v. B.Z. in 2000. The essays include court decisions and dissenting opinions as well as contemporary journalism pieces and retrospective commentary. . . . Students of modern science, biology, genetics, and the law will find this volume informative and interesting." SLJ

Includes bibliographical references

Students' rights; Laura K. Egendorf, book editor. Greenhaven Press 2006 189p il (Issues on trial) lib bdg $34.95
Grades: 9 10 11 12   **344**
    1. Youth -- Civil rights 2. Students -- Civil rights 3. Students -- Law and legislation
ISBN 0-7377-2509-5; 978-0-7377-2509-4

           LC 2005-52690

"In this anthology judges and commentators explore four key students' rights cases." Publisher's note

Includes bibliographical references

345 Criminal law

Aretha, David

The **trial** of the Scottsboro boys. Morgan Reynolds Pub. 2007 128p il (The civil rights movement) lib bdg $27.95

Grades: 7 8 9 10 11 12   **345**

1. Trials 2. Scottsboro case 3. African Americans -- Civil rights

ISBN 978-1-59935-058-5; 1-59935-058-0

LC 2007-23818

This describes the case of nine young black men between the ages of 13 and 20 who were accused of rape in the 1930s in Alabama by two white women and were sentenced to death.

"Aretha writes clearly, with objectivity and compassion." SLJ

Includes bibliographical references

Capital punishment; Paul G. Connors, book editor. Greenhaven Press 2007 220p (Current controversies) $39.70; pa $27.50

Grades: 9 10 11 12   **345**

1. Capital punishment -- United States

ISBN 978-0-7377-3711-0; 0-7377-3711-5; 978-0-7377-3712-7 pa; 0-7377-3712-3 pa

LC 2007-25898

An anthology of essays discussing the ethical issues surrounding capital punishment, including whether or not it deters crime.

Includes bibliographical references

Cates, David

The **Scottsboro** boys; by David Cates. ABDO Pub. Co. 2012 112 p. ill. $34.22

Grades: 6 7 8 9   **345**

1. Scottsboro case 2. Civil rights -- United States -- History 3. Trials (Rape) -- Alabama -- Scottsboro 4. Scottsboro Trial, Scottsboro, Ala., 1931 5. African Americans -- Civil rights -- History

ISBN 161783310X; 9781617833106

LC 2011036128

This book "tells the story of the nine African American teenagers accused of raping two white women on a train in Scottsboro, Alabama in 1931, covering the arrests and . . . legal proceedings." The book "explores the history of America at the time of the trials, the accounts of the nine men on trial regarding their train ride from Tennessee to Alabama, their sentences, and the effects of this event on society." (Publisher's notes)

"These titles are excellent introductions to these important topics, particularly for developing an analytical framework for debate." SLJ

Includes bibliographical references (p. 104-109) and index

Cawthon, Elisabeth A.

★ **Famous** trials in history; Elisabeth A. Cawthon. Facts On File 2011 463 p.

Grades: 9 10 11 12   **345**

1. Law -- History 2. Courts -- History 3. Trials -- History 4. Trials

ISBN 9780816081677

LC 2010047037

In this book, Elisabeth A. Cawthon ""collects 100 significant legal trials" that date from the time of Socrates to today. . . . Ranging in length from two to several pages, the . . . entries provide a discussion of the key issues of the trial under examination, a history of the case, argument summaries, and the verdict. Also featured are the significance of the case and a . . . further-reading list. There is also a selected bibliography and chronological and topical lists of the trials (although the years are not part of the list)." (Libr J)

Includes bibliographical references and index

Crimes and trials of the century; edited by Steven Chermak and Frankie Y. Bailey. Greenwood Press 2007 2v il set $199.95

Grades: 9 10 11 12 Adult   **345**

1. Trials 2. Administration of criminal justice

ISBN 978-0-313-34109-0

LC 2007-30704

"From the Black Sox scandal of 1919 to the investigations of Abu Ghraib through 2006, this set looks closely at 35 particularly newsworthy American crimes. . . . Clear writing, strong organization, and involving subject matter make this a strong resource." SLJ

Includes bibliographical references

The **death** penalty; Samuel Brenner, book editor. Greenhaven Press 2006 190p il map (Issues on trial) lib bdg $34.95

Grades: 9 10 11 12   **345**

1. Capital punishment -- United States

ISBN 0-7377-2507-9; 978-0-7377-2507-0

LC 2005-58851

This book examines four major court cases involving capital punishment.

Includes bibliographical references

Freedom from cruel and unusual punishment; Kristin O'Donnell Tubb, book editor. Greenhaven Press 2005 144p (Bill of Rights) lib bdg $32.45

Grades: 9 10 11 12   **345**

1. Punishment 2. Capital punishment

ISBN 0-7377-1925-7

LC 2004-54223

"This anthology discusses the Eighth Amendment, including a history dating back to biblical times, its inseparable ties to the death penalty, and recent rulings and debates." Publisher's note

Includes bibliographical references

Individual rights and the police; Mark R. Nesbitt, book editor. Greenhaven Press 2006 188p (Issues on trial) lib bdg $34.95

Grades: 9 10 11 12   345

1. Civil rights 2. Criminal procedure
ISBN 0-7377-2505-2; 978-0-7377-2505-6

LC 2005-54542

This anthology examines four court cases involving the rights of the accused: Mapp v. Ohio (1961), Miranda v. Arizona (1966), Katz v. United States (1967), and Terry v. Ohio (1968).

Includes bibliographical references

Jacobs, Thomas A.

They broke the law, you be the judge; true cases of teen crime. edited by Al Desetta. Free Spirit Pub. 2003 213p il pa $15.95

Grades: 7 8 9 10   345

1. Juvenile courts 2. Administration of criminal justice
ISBN 1-57542-134-8

LC 2003-4814

"An excellent introduction to how juvenile justice works, this will be a great resource for classroom and group discussions." Booklist

Includes bibliographical references

Kelly-Gangi, Carol

Miranda v. Arizona and the rights of the accused; debating Supreme Court decisions. [by] Carol Kelly-Gangi. Enslow Publishers 2006 128p il (Debating Supreme Court decisions) lib bdg $26.60

Grades: 7 8 9 10   345

1. Criminals 2. Right to counsel
ISBN 0-7660-2477-6

LC 2006011737

This discusses the Supreme Court case involving a suspect's rights while being questioned by police.

Includes bibliographical references

Krygier, Leora

★ **Juvenile** court; a judge's guide for young adults and their parents. Scarecrow Press 2009 181p il $29.95

Grades: 9 10 11 12 Adult   345

1. Juvenile courts 2. Juvenile delinquency
ISBN 978-0-8108-6127-5; 0-8108-6127-5

LC 2008-32075

"This book is Krygier's attempt to inform and prepare young people who are facing a court hearing. From minor traffic violations and truancy charges to fighting and drug and alcohol-related offenses, Krygier unpacks some of the most common terms, procedures, facts, and myths of the juvenile court system so that young people—and their parents—might more efficiently navigate the process. . . . Her approach is serious and straightforward, but remains highly readable as a guide or a reference manual." Voice Youth Advocates

Includes bibliographical references

Larson, Edward J.

The **Scopes** trial; a photographic history. introduction by Edward Caudill; photo captions by Edward Larson; afterword by Jesse Fox Mayshark. University of Tenn. Press 1999 88p il hardcover o.p. pa $18.95

Grades: 11 12 Adult   345

1. Geologists 2. Science teachers 3. Evolution -- Study and teaching
ISBN 1-57233-080-5; 1-57233-081-3 pa

LC 99-50735

"Sandwiching a clutch of generously annotated documentary photos, Caudill's introduction explains what led to the trial. . . . Mayshark's afterword presents the trial's larger historical and political context and its long-lived effects on Tennessee, textbook publishing, and plain speech about hot topics. The slim, handsome book is an ideal primer on its notorious subject." Booklist

Includes bibliographical references

Lewis, Anthony

Gideon's trumpet. Random House 1964 262p hardcover o.p. pa $12.95

Grades: 11 12 Adult   345

1. Law -- United States 2. United States -- Supreme Court
ISBN 0-679-72312-9 pa

An account of the case of a Florida man convicted of burglary which brought about a historic decision of the Supreme Court decreeing that in all states a defendant is entitled to counsel.

Includes bibliographical references

Marzilli, Alan

The **Internet** and crime. Chelsea House 2010 120p il (Point-counterpoint) lib bdg $32.95

Grades: 7 8 9 10   345

1. Computer crimes 2. Consumer protection 3. Internet -- Law and legislation
ISBN 978-1-60413-506-0; 1-60413-506-9

LC 2009-22139

This book covers "crimes directly related to the Internet, such as stealing personal information or engaging in fraudulent schemes." Publisher's note

Includes bibliographical references

The **right** to a trial by jury; edited by Robert Winters. Greenhaven Press 2005 142p (Bill of Rights) $32.45

Grades: 9 10 11 12   345

1. Jury
ISBN 0-7377-1937-0

LC 2004-52282

This book "examines medieval origins and the colonial implementation of English-style trial processes and includes Supreme Court decisions. It then presents the modern arguments for and against the jury system, with a time line of significant decisions." Voice Youth Advocates

and framing, licensing, and electronic reserves are covered separately, bolstered by court-case examples, notes, and bibliographies. . . . An indispensable reference for all types of libraries." SLJ

Includes bibliographical references

Russell, Carrie

Complete copyright for K-12 librarians and educators; Carrie Russell. American Library Association 2012 xi, 173 p.p ill. (chiefly col.) (alk. paper) $50
Grades: Professional   **346.04**
1. Copyright 2. Fair use (Copyright) 3. Segregation -- Law and legislation 4. Fair use (Copyright) -- United States 5. Librarians -- Legal status, laws, etc. -- United States 6. School libraries -- Law and legislation -- United States
ISBN 0838910831; 9780838910832
           LC 2012016674
This book by Carrie Russell "is designed as a resource for educators, offering guidance for providing material to students while carefully observing copyright law. The book offers detailed advice on distinctive issues of intellectual property in the school setting; explores scenarios often encountered by educators . . . and precisely defines 'fair use,' by showing readers exactly what's possible within the law." (Education Digest)

Includes bibliographical references and index

Wherry, Timothy Lee

Intellectual property; everything the digital-age librarian needs to know. American Library Association 2008 141p il $50
Grades: Adult Professional   **346.04**
1. Patents 2. Copyright 3. Trademarks
ISBN 978-0-8389-0948-5; 0-8389-0948-5
           LC 2007-13893
The author "explains the difference between patents, copyrights, and trademarks and when one would want to obtain any one or a combination of the three. He goes on to instruct readers on how technology has simplified the process of both searching and acquiring these three types of intellectual property protection. . . . This informative and necessary volume is a must have for any professional reference collection." Voice Youth Advocates

347   Procedure and courts

Courts, law, and justice; general editor, William J. Chambliss. Sage Reference 2011 317p (Key issues in crime and punishment) $80
Grades: 10 11 12   **347**
1. Crime 2. Law enforcement 3. Administration of criminal justice
ISBN 978-1-4129-7857-6; 1-4129-7857-2
           LC 2011292310
This book covers topics such as "drug and gun control laws as well as the ins and outs of the criminal justice system as encountered by arrested suspects, during the trial process, and during the sentencing phase. This volume looks closely at Miranda rights and the impact of polygraphs and DNA testing; legal and procedural issues during prosecution, including exclusionary rules and double jeopardy; and sentencing and punishment for crimes, including for offenses such as DUI and sex offenses. The role of the victim during the prosecutorial process is also examined." Publisher's note

Includes bibliographical references

Finkelman, Paul

★ **Landmark** decisions of the United States Supreme Court; [by] Paul Finkelman, Melvin I. Urofsky. 2nd ed.; CQ Press 2008 791p il $250
Grades: 11 12 Adult   **347**
1. United States -- Supreme Court 2. Constitutional law -- United States
ISBN 978-0-87289-409-9
           LC 2007-42588
First published 2003
This "provides the historical context and constitutional perspective of more than 1,000 of the most important Supreme Court cases." Publisher's note

Includes bibliographical references

Leiter, Richard A.

Landmark Supreme Court cases; the most influential decisions of the Supreme Court of the United States. [by] Gary Hartman, Roy M. Mersky, [and] Cindy Tate Slavinski. Facts on File 2004 594p (Facts on File library of American history) $70; pa $21.95
Grades: 11 12 Adult   **347**
1. Law -- United States 2. United States -- Supreme Court
ISBN 0-8160-2452-9; 0-8160-6923-9 pa
           LC 2003-57776
This is "an excellent source for beginning researchers. . . . The discussion of the case's significance and its implications will be useful for students." SLJ

Includes bibliographical references

Marshall, Thurgood

Thurgood Marshall; his speeches, writings, arguments, opinions, and reminiscences. edited by Mark Tushnet; foreword by Randall Kennedy. Hill Bks. 2001 xxvi, 548p (Library of Black America) $40; pa $24.95
Grades: 11 12 Adult   **347**
1. Lawyers 2. Solicitors general 3. Civil rights activists 4. Supreme Court justices 5. African Americans -- Biography 6. United States -- Supreme Court 7. African Americans -- Civil rights
ISBN 1-55652-385-8; 1-55652-386-6 pa
           LC 2001-16793
"In a career ranging from his trial and appellate work for the NAACP to his tenure as an associate justice of the Court, Marshall wrought revolutionary changes in U.S. law and politics, and this collection of his legal briefs, writings, speeches, and judicial opinions, plus a never-before-published oral interview, gives us a superior analysis of the advocate, the democrat, the dissenter, and the unflagging fighter for equality." Libr J

Includes bibliographical references

Mauro, Tony

Illustrated great decisions of the Supreme Court; 2nd ed.; CQ Press 2006 415p il $81

Grades: 9 10 11 12 Adult   **347**

1. United States -- Supreme Court 2. Constitutional law -- United States

ISBN 1-56802-964-0; 978-1-56802-964-1

LC 2005-30474

First published 2000

For each of the nearly 100 cases summarized the author provides background facts, highlights of the decision and assesses the impact on American society. Illustrated with photos, portraits, political cartoons, and drawings. Includes a bibliography and a case and subject index.

Includes bibliographical references

The **Oxford** companion to the Supreme Court of the United States; editor in chief, Kermit L. Hall; editors, James W. Ely, Jr., Joel B. Grossman. 2nd ed.; Oxford University Press 2005 xxv, 1239p il $65

Grades: 11 12 Adult   **347**

1. Reference books 2. United States -- Supreme Court

ISBN 0-19-517661-8

LC 2004-29463

First published 1992

This encyclopedia includes over 1200 articles "on all aspects of the court's history, justices, operations, and cases. Over 300 experts contributed the entries, which vary in length; some have bibliographic references. The organization . . . [includes] alphabetical entries, portraits of the justices, cross-references, and indexes by both case name and topic." Choice

Patrick, John J.

The **Supreme** Court of the United States; a student companion. 3rd ed.; Oxford University Press 2006 415p il (Oxford student companions to American government) $60

Grades: 9 10 11 12   **347**

1. United States -- Supreme Court

ISBN 978-0-19-530925-6; 0-19-530925-1

LC 2006-8473

First published 1994 with title: The young Oxford companion to the Supreme Court of the United States

"Entries presented alphabetically include biographies of justices, decisions of the court, core concepts, ideas and issues, legal terms and phrases, and procedures, practices, and personnel. . . . The inclusion of so many illustrations makes this a welcome and necessary addition to every high school library." Libr Media Connect

Includes bibliographical references

Savage, David G.

★ **Guide** to the U.S. Supreme Court; 5th ed.; CQ Press 2010 2v il map set $410

Grades: 9 10 11 12 Adult   **347**

1. Reference books 2. United States -- Supreme Court

ISBN 978-0-87289-423-5; 0-87289-423-1

LC 2010-17634

First published 1979 with title: Congressional Quarterly's guide to the U.S. Supreme Court

This set "is not only timely but highly informative and readable. . . . Savage's understanding and experience with the Court have resulted in an insightful, authoritative source to rival all others." Choice

Includes bibliographical references

Schultz, David A.

The **encyclopedia** of the Supreme Court; [by] David Schultz. Facts on File 2005 562p il (Facts on File library of American history) $85

Grades: 11 12 Adult   **347**

1. Reference books 2. United States -- Supreme Court

ISBN 0-8160-5086-4

LC 2004-13174

"The ease with which one can search this volume, as well as the style of writing and depth of explanation make this a truly valuable resource." Libr Media Connect

Includes bibliographical references

Williams, Juan

Thurgood Marshall; American revolutionary. Times Bks. 1998 459p il hardcover o.p. pa $16

Grades: 11 12 Adult   **347**

1. Lawyers 2. Solicitors general 3. Civil rights activists 4. Supreme Court justices 5. African Americans -- Biography 6. United States -- Supreme Court 7. African Americans -- Civil rights

ISBN 0-8129-3299-4 pa

LC 98-9735

"Williams presents Marshall as a revolutionary 'of grand vision,' but this well-rounded portrait of the man also addresses his vanities and warts, from his ascension to his deflation and subsequent redemption. This is a must read for all Americans concerned with the struggle for civil and individual rights." Booklist

Includes bibliographical references

347.73   Civil procedure and courts of the United States

Coyle, Marcia

The **Roberts** court; the struggle for the constitution. Marcia Coyle. Simon & Schuster 2013 352 p. (hardcover) $28

Grades: Adult   **347.73**

1. Roberts, John G., 1955- 2. United States. Constitution 3. United States. Supreme Court 4. United States. Supreme Court -- History -- 21st century 5. Political questions and judicial power -- United States -- History -- 21st century

ISBN 1451627513; 9781451627510; 9781451627527; 9781451627534

LC 2012051637

In this book, author Marcia Coycle "reveals the fault lines in the conservative-dominated [U.S. Supreme] Court led by Chief Justice John Roberts Jr." It "captures four landmark decisions--concerning health care, money in elections, guns at home, and race in schools. Her analysis shows how dedicated conservative lawyers and groups are strategizing to find cases and crafting them to bring up the judicial road to the Supreme Court with an eye on a receptive conservative majority." (Publisher's note)

Includes bibliographical references and index

Cushman, Clare

Courtwatchers; eyewitness accounts in Supreme Court history. Clare Cushman. Rowman & Littlefield Publishers 2011 xiv, 312 p.p ill. (hardback: alk. paper) $39.95; (ebook) $35.00

Grades: 10 11 12   347.73
1. Courts -- United States 2. United States -- History 3. Administration of criminal justice -- United States 4. Judges -- United States -- History 5. United States. Supreme Court -- History 6. Clerks of court -- United States -- History 7. Judicial process -- United States -- History
ISBN 9781442212459; 9781442212473
LC 2011019794

Author Clare Cushman offers "a behind-the-scenes look at the [Supreme Court and] people, practices, and traditions that have shaped an American institution for more than 200 years. Each chapter covers one general thematic topic and weaves a narrative from memoirs, letters, diaries, and newspaper accounts by the Justices, their spouses and children, court reporters, clerks, oral advocates, court staff, journalists, and other eyewitnesses." (Publisher's note)

Includes bibliographical references (p. 263-300) and index.

Jost, Kenneth

★ The **Supreme** Court A to Z; Kenneth Jost. 5th ed. CQ Press 2012 xvii, 668 p.p ill. (hardcover: alk. paper) $125.00

Grades: 8 9 10 11 12 Adult   347.73
1. United States. Supreme Court -- Biography 2. United States. Supreme Court -- Encyclopedias
ISBN 1608717445; 9781608717446
LC 2012000642

This book by Kenneth Jost "offers . . . information about the Supreme Court, including its history, traditions, organization, dynamics, and personalities. The entries in The Supreme Court A to Z are arranged alphabetically and are . . . cross-referenced to related information. This volume also has a detailed index, reference materials on Supreme Court nominations, a seat chart of the justices, the U.S. Constitution, online sources of decisions, and a bibliography." (Publisher's note)

Includes bibliographical references (p. 617-630) and index.

Sotomayor, Sonia, 1954-

★ **My** beloved world; Sonia Sotomayor. Knopf 2013 ix, 315 p., [16] p. of platesp ill. (hardback) $27.95

Grades: 10 11 12 Adult   347.73
1. Hispanic American women 2. Hispanic American women -- Biography 3. Judges -- United States -- Biography 4. Hispanic American judges -- Biography 5. United States. Supreme Court -- Officials and employees -- Biography
ISBN 0307594882; 9780307594884
LC 2012031797

Author Sonia Sotomayor presents an autobiography as "the first Hispanic and third woman appointed to the United States Supreme Court . . . She determined to become a lawyer, . . . from valedictorian of her high school class to the highest honors at Princeton, Yale Law School, the New York County District Attorney's office, private practice, and appointment to the Federal District Court before the age of forty." (Publisher's note)

"Graceful, authoritative memoir from the country's first Hispanic Supreme Court justice. . . . The author vividly narrates her scholarly adventures at Princeton, where she advocated for Latino faculty, and Yale Law School, where she dealt with smaller cases in preparation for the complexities of work in the district attorney's office. In 1992, she received an appointment to the U.S. District Court for the Southern District of New York. The author's text forms a cultural patchwork of memories and reflections as she mines the nuances of her parents' tumultuous relationship, fondly recalls family visits in Puerto Rico and offers insight on a judicial career that's just beginning when the memoir ends. . . . Mature, life-affirmative musings from a venerable life shaped by tenacity and pride." Kirkus

The **Supreme** Court justices; illustrated biographies, 1789-2012. edited by Clare Cushman, the Supreme Court Historical Society; foreword by Chief Justice John G. Roberts, Jr. 3rd ed. CQ Press, an imprint of SAGE Publications 2013 xx, 562 p.p ill., ports. (hardcover) $135

Grades: 8 9 10 11 12 Adult   347.73
1. Judges -- Biography 2. Judges -- United States -- Biography 3. United States. Supreme Court -- History 4. United States. Supreme Court -- Officials and employees -- Biography
ISBN 1608718328; 9781608718320
LC 2012031502

This book, edited by Clare Cushman, is "a single-volume reference profiling every Supreme Court justice from John Jay through Elena Kagan. An original essay on each justice paints a . . . picture of his or her individuality as shaped by family, education, pre-Court career, and the times in which he or she lived. Each biographical essay also presents the major issues on which the justice presided. Essays are arranged in the order of the justices' appointments." (Publisher's note)

"Written by leading constitutional scholars, the well-researched essays are arranged in chronological order of the justices' appointment to the Court. The volume includes a revised bibliography organized by individual justices, and a thorough index. . . . Recommended." Choice

Includes bibliographical references (pages 516-538) and index.

349   Law of specific jurisdictions, areas, socioeconomic regions, regional intergovernmental organizations

Gale encyclopedia of American law; 3rd ed.; Gale/Cengage Learning 2011 14v il map set $1604

Grades: 9 10 11 12 Adult   349
1. Reference books 2. Law -- United States --

Encyclopedias
ISBN 978-1-4144-3684-5; 1-4144-3684-X; 978-1-
4144-4302-7 ebook; 1-4144-4302-1 ebook
LC 2010-45527
First published 1983-1985 with title: The Guide to
American law. Previous edition published with title: West's
encyclopedia of American law

Explains legal terms and concepts in everyday language,
covering a wide variety of persons, entities, and events that
have shaped the U.S. legal system and influenced public perceptions of it.

Includes bibliographical references

352.13   Administration of subordinate jurisdictions

The **book** of the states; [compiled by] the Council
of State Governments. 2010 ed; Council of State
Governments 2010 627p il map $125

Grades: 11 12 Adult   **352.13**
1. State governments
ISBN 978-0-87292-7667
Biennial, 1935-2001, Annual from 2002. Began
publication 1935

"In addition to general articles on various aspects of
state government, this source provides many statistical and
directory data, the principal state officials, and such information as the nickname, motto, flower, bird, song, and tree of
each state." Ref Sources for Small & Medium-sized Libr.
6th edition

352.23   Chief executives

Encyclopedia of the U.S. presidency; a historical
reference. edited by Nancy Beck Young. Facts
On File 2013 6 v., 2500 p.p ill., maps (hardcover) $550

Grades: 11 12 Adult   **352.23**
1. Presidents -- United States -- Encyclopedias
ISBN 0816067449; 9780816067442
LC 2010020746
This six-volume set looks at the American presidency.
The "opening volume includes 19 thematic essays dealing
with various topics surrounding the history of the presidency
including 'Origins of the Presidency,' 'Presidency and the
Politics of Race,' and 'The Presidency and Popular Culture.'
The ensuing volumes follow a chronological arrangement
of individually signed entries covering from Washington to
Obama." (Library Journal)

Includes bibliographical references and index

Fellow citizens; the Penguin book of U.S. presidential inaugural addresses. edited with an introduction and commentaries by Robert V. Remini and
Terry Golway. Penguin Books 2008 476p $16

Grades: 10 11 12 Adult   **352.23**
1. American speeches 2. Presidents -- United States

-- Inaugural addresses
ISBN 978-0-14-311453-6; 0-14-311453-0
LC 2008-19970
"Two distinguished historians round up every presidential inaugural address and preface it with commentary on the
rhetoric and historical context of the discourse. . . . Reflecting the major events of American history, as well as a rhetorical evolution from prolixity to brevity, this . . . is a great
resource." Booklist

Includes bibliographical references

★ **Guide** to the presidency and the executive branch;
Michael Nelson, editor. 5th ed. CQ Press 2013
2 v. (xix, 2141 p.)p ill. (cloth: alk. paper) $425

Grades: 11 12 Adult   **352.23**
1. Political science 2. Presidents -- United States
ISBN 9781608719068
LC 2012023291
This two-volume guide is a source "for researchers
seeking an understanding of those who have occupied the
White House and on the institution of the U.S. presidency."
Its chapters "explain the structure, powers, and operations
of the office and the president's relationship with Congress
and the Supreme Court." In this fifth edition, there is "coverage of the George W. Bush presidency, the 2008 election,
and the first 3 years of the presidency of Barack Obama."
(Publisher's note)

Includes bibliographical references and index

My fellow citizens; the inaugural addresses of the
presidents of the United States, 1789-2009. with
an introduction by Arthur M. Schlesinger, Jr. and
commentary by Fred L. Israel. Facts On File
2010 428p (Facts on File library of American
history) $45

Grades: 9 10 11 12 Adult   **352.23**
1. Presidents -- United States -- Inaugural addresses
ISBN 978-0-8160-8253-7; 0-8160-8253-7
LC 2009-32184
First published 2007
"Features the original text of all 56 inaugural speeches,
each with an explanatory essay." Publisher's note

Raphael, Ray

Mr. president; how and why the founders created
a chief executive. by Ray Raphael. Alfred A. Knopf
2012 324 p.

Grades: 11 12 Adult   **352.23**
1. Executive power -- United States 2. Founding Fathers
of the United States 3. Presidents -- United States --
Biography 4. Constitutional conventions -- United
States 5. United States -- Politics and government --
1783-1809 6. Presidents -- United States -- History --
18th century
ISBN 9780307595270
LC 2011033471
This book presents a "biography of the Constitutional
Convention and the herculean task faced by the representatives. The author paints a picture of heroes--Edmund Randolph, George Mason, James Wilson and James Madison,
among others--noting that the founders developed a government presupposing that George Washington would be the

first chief executive. . . . In order to show how their views evolved as they toiled, Raphael explores the founders' writings in chronological order." (Kirkus Reviews)

Includes bibliographical references (p. [289]-309) and index

Student's guide to the presidency; advisory editor, Bruce J. Schulman. CQ Press 2009 398p il (Student's guide to the U.S. government series) $85

Grades: 9 10 11 12   **352.23**
1. Reference books 2. Presidents -- United States 3. Executive power -- United States
ISBN 978-0-87289-555-3

LC 2008-50731

"The strength of . . . [this book] is not the entries on each president but rather the information regarding the election process and the executive branch. . . . [This is] a welcome addition to high-school media centers and public libraries." Booklist

Includes bibliographical references

Witcover, Jules

America's vice presidents; from irrelevance to power. Jules Witcover. Smithsonian Institution Press 2014 592 p. illustrations $34.95

Grades: 11 12 Adult   **352.23**
1. Vice-presidents -- United States 2. United States -- Politics and government 3. Vice-Presidents -- United States -- History 4. Vice-Presidents -- United States -- Biography
ISBN 1588344711; 9781588344717

LC 2014004242

This book by Jules Witcover is an "examination of the vice presidency throughout American history. Witcover chronicles each of the 47 vice presidents, including their personal biographies and their achievements--or lack thereof--during their vice presidential tenures." (Publisher's note)

"The essays included here are well-rounded, concise perspectives of the vice president's time in office, and in many cases, his pursuits after leaving that position. Adults and motivated high school students could pick and choose from among the entries or read straight through for an inside view of an oft-overlooked position." Library Jorunal

Includes bibliographical references

352.4   Financial administration and budgets

Kramer, Mattea

★ A **people's** guide to the federal budget; National Priorities Project; written by Mattea Kramer ... [et al.]; foreword by Barbara Ehrenreich; afterword by Josh Silver. Interlink Books 2012 219 p. (pbk.) $15.00

Grades: 10 11 12 Adult   **352.4**
1. Budget -- United States 2. United States. Congress 3. United States -- Appropriations and expenditures 4. Fiscal policy -- United States 5. Budget deficits -- United States 6. Government spending policy -- United

States
ISBN 1566568870; 9781566568876

LC 2012007930

This book focuses on U.S. fiscal policy, government spending, and the federal budget. It "addresses such issues as discretionary and mandatory spending; how the federal government creates a budget; where the money comes from and goes; and the federal debt. . . . Other important priorities include construction of roads and highways, law enforcement, and veterans' assistance." (Booklist)

Includes bibliographical references.

355   Military science

Axelrod, Alan

The **encyclopedia** of the American armed forces. Facts on File 2005 2v il (Facts on File library of American history) set $175

Grades: 11 12 Adult   **355**
1. Reference books 2. United States -- Armed forces -- Encyclopedias
ISBN 0-8160-4700-6

LC 2004-20549

"The four sections each document a major branch of the United States military: Army, Navy, Marine Corps, and Air Force. Each branch has an initial list of entries, a list of branch-specific abbreviations and acronyms, and a short bibliography." Choice

Includes bibliographical references

Barker, Geoff P.

War; [by] Geoff Barker. Smart Apple Media 2010 46p il (Voices) lib bdg $34.25

Grades: 7 8 9 10 11 12   **355**
1. War
ISBN 978-1-59920-2785; 1-59920-278-6

LC 2009-5418

This discusses "today's headline conflicts in Iraq, Afghanistan, and Gaza, as well as a look back at World War I, the bombing of Hiroshima and Nagasaki, and the fighting in Kosovo, Eritrea, and Cambodia. Ongoing issues include the role of child soldiers, WMDs, and the number of civilian deaths. The . . . blend of current political debate with witnesses' close-up experiences told through photos, narratives, and quotes will draw browsers, and many will go on to find out more." Booklist

Includes glossary and bibliographical references

The **encyclopedia** of Middle East wars; the United States in the Persian Gulf, Afghanistan, and Iraq conflicts. Spencer C. Tucker, editor; Priscilla Mary Roberts, editor, documents volume; foreword by Anthony C. Zinni. ABC-CLIO 2010 1887p 5v il map set $495

Grades: 11 12 Adult   **355**
1. Reference books 2. Iraq War, 2003- -- Encyclopedias 3. Afghan War, 2001- -- Encyclopedias 4. Persian Gulf War, 1991 -- Encyclopedias 5. Middle East -- Military

history -- Encyclopedias
ISBN 978-1-85109-947-4; 978-1-85109-948-1 ebook
LC 2010-33812
"An essential resource for anyone seeking detailed information and in-depth reading on U.S. actions and involvement in the Middle East region during the last 15 years." Libr J
Includes bibliographical references

Gale Group
Gale encyclopedia of U.S. history: war. Gale 2008 2v il map set $220
Grades: 9 10 11 12   355
1. Reference books 2. United States -- Military history -- Encyclopedias
ISBN 978-1-4144-3114-7; 1-4144-3114-7
LC 2007-33628
This set "examines the country's military history, beginning with the conflicts with Native Americans in the 1600s and ending with today's war in Iraq. Each chapter provides a brief overview of one major conflict, its causes, biographies of major figures, key battles, impact on the home front and nonmilitary events at home, the war in an international context, and its aftermath." SLJ
Includes bibliographical references

A **global** chronology of conflict; from the ancient world to the modern Middle East. Spencer C. Tucker, editor. ABC-CLIO 2010 6v il map set $395
Grades: 9 10 11 12 Adult   355
1. Reference books 2. Historical chronology 3. Military history -- Chronology
ISBN 978-1-85109-667-1; 1-85109-667-1
LC 2009-32434
This set "presents a concise, chronologically organized history of the major military actions and related events from the earliest recorded conflicts to the present day. The work examines the political and diplomatic forces driving world conflicts, revolutions, forced changes of governments, international treaties, and acts of aggression and terrorism. . . . This should be considered an essential resource for students, researchers, history aficionados, and general readers." Libr J
Includes bibliographical references

Grant, R. G.
Commanders; history's greatest military leaders. DK Pub. 2010 360p il map $40
Grades: 9 10 11 12 Adult   355
1. Generals 2. Leadership 3. Military history
ISBN 978-0-7566-6736-8; 0-7566-6736-4
LC 2010-282653
"Thirty-five hundred years of military leadership are covered in this attractive, concise presentation. The text opens with a detailed table of contents covering five major eras, divided by empires, conflicts, and/or type of warrior or soldier. Each era is introduced and followed by individual entries: Ramesses II is the first entry in the volume and Osama Bin Laden is the last. Biographical profiles begin with the subject's name in a tinted bar followed by his or her title, birth and death dates, key conflicts, and key battles." SLJ

Sunzi bing fa
★ The **illustrated** art of war; [by] Sun Tzu; the definitive English translation by Samuel B. Griffith. Oxford University Press 2005 272p il map $29.95
Grades: 11 12 Adult   355
1. Military art and science
ISBN 0-19-518999-X; 978-0-19-518999-5
LC 2005-10651
An illustrated version of The art of war, a military treatise written in China during the 6th century BC discussing different military tactics and strategies.
Includes bibliographical references

Sutherland, Jonathan
African Americans at war; an encyclopedia. [by] Jonathan D. Sutherland. ABC-CLIO 2004 2v set $185
Grades: 11 12 Adult   355
1. Reference books 2. African American soldiers 3. United States -- Armed forces -- Encyclopedias 4. African Americans -- Biography -- Encyclopedias
ISBN 1-57607-746-2
LC 2003-21501
"There are more than 250 [alphabetically arranged] entries conveying biographical, thematic, and conceptual information. Well-known leaders (Colin Powell), groups (Buffalo Soldiers), specific units [and battles] . . . have their own entries. . . . This is a superb resource for any . . . library looking to enrich its history, military or African American studies collections." Booklist

★ **Voices** of war; stories of service from the home front and the front lines. edited by Tom Wiener. National Geographic Society 2004 336p il $30; pa $6.95
Grades: 11 12 Adult   355
1. Veterans 2. United States -- Military history 3. United States -- Armed forces -- Military life
ISBN 0-7922-7838-0; 0-7922-4204-1 pa
LC 2004-49986
This book showcases "the oral histories collected by the Veteran's History Project, the Library of Congress's nationwide effort to collect and preserve the stories not only of war veterans, but also of those who served in support of the frontline troops. . . . The personal accounts cover the major conflicts of the 20th century, from World War I to the Persian Gulf War, and include letters, diaries, and journals. The chapters are nicely arranged to show the commonalities of military experience, e.g., basic training, daily life, combat, the home front, and returning home." Libr J

★ **War:** from ancient Egypt to Iraq; editorial consultant, Saul David. DK 2009 512p il $50
Grades: 9 10 11 12 Adult   355
1. Reference books 2. War -- Encyclopedias 3. Military history -- Encyclopedias
ISBN 978-0-7566-5572-3
LC 2010-278612
"From the Punic wars to the Crusades to the wars of the league of Cognac and modern conflicts like those in the former Yugoslavia, War is an outstanding catalog of conflict.

Each of the seven chapters . . . opens with a time line and is peppered with sidebars of military superlatives such as youngest commanders, famous female warriors, and even landmark war movies. . . . An essential reference title for all libraries." Libr J

355.009 Military science--History, geographic treatment, biography

Keegan, John

Fields of battle; the wars for North America. Knopf 1996 348p il maps hardcover o.p. pa $15
Grades: 11 12 Adult   **355.009**
  1. North America -- Military history
  ISBN 0-679-42413-X; 0-679-74664-1 pa
               LC 96-154385
First published 1995 in the United Kingdom with title: Warpaths: travels of a military historian in North America
The author "demonstrates how North America's geography has influenced its history: how its mountain chains and river systems have determined where people fought, and fought repeatedly. For example, the defenses that Cornwallis built at Yorktown to deter American forces were improved and reused by the Confederates almost a century later. Keegan's tour of the continent skips the Mexican War, and his book is atypically discursive. For Americans, the charm is the familiarity of its sites—Brooklyn, Pittsburgh, Laramie, and other home towns." New Yorker

355.2 Military resources

Military draft: opposing viewpoints; Viqi Wagner, book editor. Greenhaven Press 2007 238p (Opposing viewpoints series) lib bdg $36.20; pa $24.95
Grades: 9 10 11 12   **355.2**
  1. Draft 2. Voluntary military service
  ISBN 978-0-7377-3824-7 lib bdg; 978-0-7377-3825-4 pa
             LC 2007-38960
In this collection of essays, "the draft isn't the only issue brought up; related topics, such as gays in the military and the use of military contractors, are also covered." Booklist
Includes bibliographical references

355.3 Organization and personnel of military forces

Gays in the military: opposing viewpoints; Noah Berlatsky, book editor. Greenhaven Press 2011 199p (Opposing viewpoints series) $24.99; pa $16.99
Grades: 10 11 12   **355.3**
  1. Gays and lesbians in the military
  ISBN 978-0-7377-5221-2; 0-7377-5221-1; 978-0-7377-5222-9 pa; 0-7377-5222-X pa
             LC 2010039237

This volume explores the topic of gays in the military by presenting varied expert opinions that examine many of the different aspects that surround this issue.
"Although compiled before the repeal, this book provides much useful information. As the military readies to transition to open service, readers will see if any of the dire predictions made by opponents will come to pass." SLJ
Includes bibliographical references

355.4 Military operations

Merino, Noel

  ★ **U.S.** military deployment; Noel Merino, book editor. Greenhaven Press 2010 133p il map (At issue) $33.70; pa $23.85
Grades: 9 10 11 12   **355.4**
  1. Intervention (International law) 2. Military policy -- United States 3. United States -- Foreign relations -- Public opinion
  ISBN 978-0-7377-5373-8; 0-7377-5373-0; 978-0-7377-5411-7 pa; 0-7377-5411-7 pa; 978-0-7377-5530-5 ebook; 0-7377-5530-X ebook
             LC 2010029232
This book "examines the often vexing issue of U.S. military deployment abroad. Should the U.S. continue to maintain a military presence in 46 countries and territories around the globe, especially Iraq and Afghanistan? A variety of answers are offered in 14 previously published essays by a variety of experts whose views represent all sides and political takes on the issue. . . . All offer thought-provoking, sophisticated, and timely analyses that will be valuable for students of current events." Booklist
Includes bibliographical references

Tucker, Spencer C.

Battles that changed history; an encyclopedia of world conflict. ABC-CLIO 2010 655p il map $95
Grades: 9 10 11 12 Adult   **355.4**
  1. Reference books 2. Battles -- Encyclopedias 3. Military history -- Encyclopedias
  ISBN 978-1-59884-429-0; 978-1-59884-430-6 ebook
             LC 2010-32810
Tucker "has compiled over 200 battles that had a significant impact on history. About half of the battles are drawn from the 19th through 21st centuries. The earliest account is of the Battle of Megiddo that took place in May 1479 B.C.E., and the last entry is the Iraq war's battle for Baghdad, which took place from March 19 to May 1, 2003. Each entry includes the date, opponents (with the winner denoted by an asterisk), commanders, number of troops, and importance of the battle. . . . This clear and concise overview of the major battles from a number of wars and would be a great addition to the collection of any library." Libr J
Includes bibliographical references

355.5 Military training

Fisher, David

Basic; surviving boot camp and basic training. Colonel Jack Jacobs (Ret.) and David Fisher. Thomas

Dunne Books 2012 ix, 308 p (hardcover) $25.99; (paperback) $14.99

Grades: 9 10 11 12   **355.5**

1. Military camps 2. Military training camps 3. United States -- Military history 4. United States -- Armed Forces -- Military life -- Handbooks, manuals, etc 5. Basic training (Military education) -- United States -- Handbooks, manuals, etc

ISBN 0312622775; 9780312622770; 9781466802445; 9781250033727

LC 2012009382

In this book, authors Jack Jacobs and David Fisher discuss boot camp and basic training in the U.S. Military. The book provides a "history of how America has trained its military, told through the indelible memories of those who remember the experiences as if they happened yesterday. . . . If you've done it, you will recognize the Drill Instructors, the marching chants, the movie segments, the proper way to make a hospital corner, the jokes, the camaraderie and the shared feeling of triumph." (Publisher's note)

355.8   Military equipment and supplies (Materiel)

Diehl, Sarah J.

Nuclear weapons and nonproliferation; a reference handbook. [by] Sarah J. Diehl, James Clay Moltz. 2nd ed.; ABC-CLIO 2008 335p (Contemporary world issues) $55

Grades: 9 10 11 12   **355.8**

1. Arms race 2. Nuclear weapons
ISBN 978-1-59884-071-1

LC 2007-17651

First published 2002

The author provide a "subject history, a record of past U.S. involvement, an overview of ethical debates, a chronological survey of events, relevant biographical sketches, and lucid definitions of nuclear technologies. Two concluding chapters provide an exhaustive list of international, federal, and nongovernmental nonproliferation organizations. An essential one-stop resource on a timely subject." Libr J

Includes bibliographical references

Preston, Diana

★ **Before** the fallout; from Marie Curie to Hiroshima. Walker 2005 438p il $27

Grades: 11 12 Adult   **355.8**

1. Atomic bomb
ISBN 0-8027-1445-5

LC 2004-61953

"Avidly researched and gracefully constructed, Preston's revelatory history is rich in telling moments, powerful personalities, intense confrontations, and indelible images of the devastation delivered by nuclear weapons, our Damoclean sword." Booklist

Includes bibliographical references

Vander Hook, Sue

The **Manhattan** Project. ABDO Pub. 2011 112p il map (Essential events) lib bdg $23.95

Grades: 7 8 9 10 11 12   **355.8**

1. Atomic bomb 2. Manhattan Project
ISBN 978-1-61714-767-8; 1-61714-767-2

LC 2010041429

This describes the project that developed the first atomic bomb, and discusses the political, social, and technical issues pertaining to it.

Includes glossary and bibliographical references

356   Specific kinds of military forces and warfare

Fredriksen, John C.

Fighting elites; a history of U.S. special forces. John C. Fredriksen. ABC-CLIO 2012 ix, 392 p.p

Grades: 10 11 12   **356**

1. War -- History 2. Guerrilla warfare 3. Military art and science -- History 4. United States -- Armed forces -- History 5. Guerrilla warfare -- United States -- History 6. Irregular warfare -- United States -- History 7. United States Armed Forces -- Commando troops -- History 8. Special forces (Military science) -- United States -- History

ISBN 1598848100; 1598848119; 9781598848106; 9781598848113

LC 2011036624

This book "brings America's long history of small, well-trained special-forces units into . . . focus. Whether discussing the paramilitary forces of colonial New England or the U.S. Navy's "SEAL Team Six," [John C.] Fredriksen argues that the American proclivity toward individualism and the changing nature of warfare have pushed these units from "tactical novelties" to "standing strategic necessities." . . . All chapters include a . . . number of sidebars on such notable individuals as Daniel Morgan, Richard Marcinko, and David Petraeus and conclude with a . . . bibliography." (Booklist)

Includes bibliographical references (p. 375-379) and index

History of U.S. special forces

Haney, Eric L.

★ **Inside** Delta Force; the story of America's elite counterterrorist unit. Delacorte Press 2006 246p il hardcover o.p. pa $17

Grades: 8 9 10 11 12   **356**

1. United States -- Army -- Delta Force
ISBN 0-385-73251-1; 0-385-33936-4 pa

LC 2004-30945

"In this adaptation of an adult book, Retired Command Sergeant Major Haney relates a . . . story of the 1977 founding of the ultrasecret counterterrorist unit of the U.S. Army known as Delta Force. . . . Better stock up on copies; you won't want to ration this one." Booklist

358   Air and other specialized forces and warfare; engineering and related services

★ **Biological** and chemical weapons; Stefan Kiesbye, book editor. Greenhaven Press 2010 98p (At issue. International politics) $31.80; pa $22.50

Grades: 9 10 11 12 **358**

1. Chemical warfare 2. Biological warfare

ISBN 978-0-7377-4870-3; 978-0-7377-4871-0 pa

LC 2010-3357

Contributors to this anthology debating the potential threat of biological and chemical warfare include Andy Oppenheimer, Thomas Frank, and Stephen Maurer.

Includes bibliographical references

Marcovitz, Hal

Biological & chemical warfare. ABDO Pub. Co. 2010 112p il (Essential issues) lib bdg $22.95

Grades: 7 8 9 10 **358**

1. Chemical warfare 2. Biological warfare

ISBN 978-1-60453-951-6; 1-60453-951-8

LC 2009-29947

The text is "well-written, providing examples that put a human face to each problem. Quotes and facts are clearly attributed, and their sources are noted in the extensive back matter. . . . Sidebars provide further information, or, more compellingly, offer stories about those touched by the topic. . . . [This] will be of great assistance to students writing reports." SLJ

Includes glossary and bibliographical references

358.4   Air forces and warfare

Van Creveld, Martin L.

The **age** of airpower; Martin van Creveld. PublicAffairs 2011 498p il pa $18.99

Grades: 10 11 12 Adult **358.4**

1. Air power

ISBN 978-1-58648-981-6; 1-58648-981-X; 9781610391085; 161039108X

LC 2010-42365

"A brilliantly formulated, exhaustively researched, and engagingly written critique of America's once vaunted military service, this is sure to arouse much controversy among interested parties." LJ

Wildsmith, Snow

Joining the United States Air Force; a handbook. Snow Wildsmith. McFarland & Co. 2012 x, 229 p.p (Joining the military) (pbk.: alk. paper) $25

Grades: 10 11 12 Adult **358.4**

1. Employment 2. United States -- Armed forces 3. Military personnel -- United States 4. United States. Air Force -- Vocational guidance

ISBN 0786447583; 9780786447589

LC 2012010677

Author Snow Wildsmith presents a book on the U.S. Air Force. "This book is for the teenager or young adult who is interested in enlisting in the United States Air Force. It will walk him or her through the enlistment and recruit training process: making the decision to join the military, talking to recruiters, getting qualified, preparing for and learning what to expect at basic recruit training." (Publisher's note)

Includes bibliographical references and index

359.9   Specialized combat forces; engineering and related services

Bartlett, Merrill L.

Leathernecks: an illustrated history of the U.S. Marine Corps; [by] Merrill L. Bartlett and Jack Sweetman. Naval Institute Press 2008 xx, 479p il map $60

Grades: 10 11 12 Adult **359.9**

1. United States -- Marine Corps -- History

ISBN 978-1-59114-020-7; 1-59114-020-X

LC 2008-15582

First published 2001 with title: The U.S. Marine Corps: an illustrated history

A history of the U.S. Marines from the Revolutionary War to the War on Terror, with a brief look at the marines of antiquity.

Includes bibliographical references

361   Social problems and services

★ **Global** social issues; an encyclopedia. Christopher G. Bates and James Ciment, editors. M.E. Sharpe 2013 3 v., xvi, 1051, I-70 p.p ill. (alk. paper) $349

Grades: 9 10 11 12 **361**

1. Encyclopedias and dictionaries 2. Social problems -- Encyclopedias

ISBN 0765682923; 9780765682925

LC 2012021425

This three-volume reference book "presents discussion of problems that affect societies around the world along with efforts being made to address the problems. . . . The 136 entries are alphabetically arranged, signed essays balancing historical and contemporary aspects and including references (print and internet resources) and cross references." (Reference & Research Book News)

Includes bibliographical references and index

361.2   Social action

Drake, Jane

Yes you can! your guide to becoming an activist. [by] Jane Drake & Ann Love. Tundra Books 2010 136p pa $12.95

Grades: 7 8 9 10 **361.2**

1. Social action

ISBN 978-0-88776-942-9; 0-88776-942-X pa

"Young people who want to effect change are guided by a sequence of nine steps and inspirational examples of grassroots activism. . . . Each step, or chapter, includes a story, strategies, skills, and a time line of milestones and setbacks.

. . . The style is conversational and the tone offers realistic encouragement to teens looking to solve problems. . . . This title will primarily serve as a how-to, although the time lines, an accessible index, and factual information about anti-smoking campaigns, recycling, and children's rights make it a useful historical perspective of activism." SLJ

Halpin, Mikki

It's your world--if you don't like it, change it; activism for teenagers. Simon Pulse 2004 305p pa $8.99

Grades: 7 8 9 10　　　　　　　　　　**361.2**
　　1. Social action
　　ISBN 0-689-87448-0

"Animal rights, racism, war protest, AIDS, school violence and bullying, women's rights, and promoting tolerance are among the topics covered here. Halpin provides basic information about each one and then makes myriad suggestions for action at home, in the community, the 'five-minute activist,' etc. The ideas are easy to implement. . . .This is an important book that will empower any young adult who would like to make a difference." SLJ

　　Includes bibliographical references

361.6　Governmental action

Banerjee, Dillon

★ The **insider's** guide to the Peace Corps; what to know before you go. 2nd ed.; Ten Speed Press 2009 182p map pa $14.95

Grades: 11 12 Adult　　　　　　　　　**361.6**
　　1. Peace Corps (U.S.)
　　ISBN 978-1-58008-970-8; 1-58008-970-4

　　　　　　　　　　　　　　　LC 2008-43720

First published 2000 with title: So you want to join the Peace Corps

"A guide that tells potential Peace Corps volunteers what to expect, through first-hand advice from recent volunteers." Publisher's note

　　Includes bibliographical references

Streissguth, Thomas

Welfare and welfare reform; [by] Tom Streissguth. Facts on File 2009 282p (Library in a book) $45

Grades: 11 12 Adult　　　　　　　　　**361.6**
　　1. Public welfare
　　ISBN 978-0-8160-7114-2; 0-8160-7114-4

This book provides "information that readers need to understand and research welfare issues. . . . Resources include capsule biographies, summaries of key cases such as Standard Machine Company v. Davis, a research guide, an annotated bibliography, historic documents such as the Personal Responsibility and Work Opportunity Reconciliation Act of 1996, and an overview of the welfare debate in U.S. history beginning with the first public almshouses in the North American British colonies." Publisher's note

　　Includes glossary and bibliographical references

361.9　Social problems and services--History, geographic treatment, biography

Slavicek, Louise Chipley, 1956-

Jane Addams. Chelsea House 2011 126 p. ill (some col.) (Women of achievement) lib bdg $35

Grades: 6 7 8 9　　　　　　　　　　**361.9**
　　1. Authors 2. Philanthropists 3. Hull House (Chicago, Ill.) 4. Essayists 5. Pacifists 6. Social welfare leaders 7. Nobel laureates for peace 8. Chicago (Ill.) -- Social conditions
　　ISBN 978-1-60413-907-5; 1-60413-907-2

　　　　　　　　　　　　　　　LC 2011000038

This book "traces [Jane] Addams' life and considerable accomplishments in social welfare, labor reform, and women's suffrage . . . [and] portrays Addams' difficult path to good education and her determination to use her life well." It is "supplemented with sidebars and illustrations . . . [and] includes a chronology, notes for the many quotes, a source bibliography, and lists of recommended books and websites." (Booklist) Details on her role in "found[ing] the pioneering settlement house, Hull House, where she and a dedicated staff of volunteers, most of them college-educated women like herself, lived and worked among some of Chicago's most destitute residents" are also presented. (Publisher's note)

　　Includes bibliographical references and index.

362.1　People with illnesses and disabilities

Banish, Roslyn

★ **Focus** on living; portraits of Americans with HIV and AIDS. photographs and interviews by Roslyn Banish; introduction by Paul A. Volberding. University of Massachusetts Press 2003 xxiv, 263p il $50; pa $24.95

Grades: 9 10 11 12　　　　　　　　　**362.1**
　　1. AIDS (Disease)
　　ISBN 1-558-49394-8; 1-558-49395-6 pa

　　　　　　　　　　　　　　　LC 2002-14512

The author "has been interviewing and photographing Americans who are living with HIV or AIDS; this book collects 40 of her portraits along with transcriptions of her subjects' first-person testimony . . . Banish's unadorned portraits, often shot at her subjects' homes, are subtle and dignified, and the narratives have a lucid strength, even in despair . . . The disease crosses all lines of race, class, gender and sexual orientation, and Banish takes care to include people from all walks of life, fostering an expanded sense of community and further breaking the silence and statistics that surround people living with HIV and AIDS." Publ Wkly

Dreyer, ZoAnn

Living with cancer; ZoAnn Dreyer. Facts On File 2008 202p $34.95

Grades: 8 9 10 11 12　　　　　　　　**362.1**
　　1. Cancer
　　ISBN 978-0-8160-6484-7

　　　　　　　　　　　　　　　LC 2007-10675

"Although written for teens with these conditions, these titles will have more general appeal... Material in both titles is presented in a straightforward manner. "SLJ

Includes bibliographical references (p. 192-194) and index.

Eating disorders; Lorraine Savage, editor. Thomson / Gale 2008 144p il (Perspectives on diseases and disorders) lib bdg $34.95

Grades: 7 8 9 10   **362.1**
1. Eating disorders
ISBN 978-0-7377-3872-8; 0-7377-3872-3
     LC 2007-37455

This book "explores the debilitating illness of anorexia, bulimia and binge eating." Publisher's note
Includes glossary and bibliographical references

Farrell, Courtney
Mental disorders. ABDO Pub. Co. 2010 112p il (Essential issues) lib bdg $22.95

Grades: 7 8 9 10   **362.1**
1. Mental illness
ISBN 978-1-60453-956-1; 1-60453-956-9
     LC 2009-29942

The text is "well-written, providing examples that put a human face to each problem. Quotes and facts are clearly attributed, and their sources are noted in the extensive back matter. . . . Sidebars provide further information, or, more compellingly, offer stories about those touched by the topic. . . . [This] will be of great assistance to students writing reports." SLJ

Includes glossary and bibliographical references

Fast food; Lauri S. Friedman, book editor. Greenhaven Press 2010 122p il map (Introducing issues with opposing viewpoints) $34.70

Grades: 7 8 9 10 11 12   **362.1**
1. Obesity 2. Restaurants 3. Convenience foods
ISBN 978-0-7377-4733-1; 0-7377-4733-1
     LC 2009-51963

This is a collection of essays arguing various viewpoints about fast foods and their effects on health, and whether or not fast food restaurants should be banned, taxed, or regulated.

This "contains some fascinating arguments, including the central question of whether or not fast food makes people fat and sick. Active-reading questions preface the essays, which are followed by directions for evaluating the arguments presented. Color photos and other graphics throughout enliven the reading experience." SLJ

Includes bibliographical references

Gelletly, LeeAnne
AIDS and health issues; LeeAnne Gelletly. Mason Crest 2014 126 p. col. ill., col. maps $24.95

Grades: 9 10 11 12 Adult   **362.1**
1. Africa 2. Health 3. Public health 4. AIDS (Disease)
ISBN 9781422229354
     LC 2013013013

This book, by LeeAnne Gelletly, "explores the current health crisis in Africa, explaining the scope of the problems that the continent faces. It also describes efforts by humani-

tarian organizations and by African governments to train health-care professionals." (Publisher's note)

Kaufman, Miriam
★ **Easy** for you to say; Q & As for teens living with chronic illness or disability. Miriam Kaufman, M.D. Third edition Firefly Books 2012 320 p. 22 cm pa. $19.95

Grades: 9 10 11 12 Professional   **362.1**
1. Chronic diseases 2. Children with disabilities 3. Students with disabilities
ISBN 9781770850996
     LC 2012540055

This work, by Miriam Kaufman, is "aimed exclusively at teens who are disabled or who have a chronic illness. . . . [It] is filled with very personal, even courageous questions from teens with varied medical conditions—from spina bifida to cystic fibrosis, to kidney disease. There are a few fairly general chapters—on family dynamics, friendship, and recreation. But the best sections concern medical issues and sexuality." (Booklist)

Naden, Corinne J.
Patients' rights; [by] Corinne Naden. Marshall Cavendish Benchmark 2008 144p il (Open for debate) lib bdg $27.95

Grades: 7 8 9 10   **362.1**
1. Medical care
ISBN 978-0-7614-2576-2; 0-7614-2576-4
     LC 2006-21786

This book maintains a "balanced tone while providing an abundance of examples and factual information. Many captioned color photos enhance the text." SLJ

Includes bibliographical references

Shilts, Randy
★ **And** the band played on; politics, people, and the AIDS epidemic. 20th anniversary ed.; St Martin's Griffin 2007 630p pa $17.95

Grades: 11 12 Adult   **362.1**
1. AIDS (Disease)
ISBN 978-0-312-37463-1
First published 1987

The author traces the history of the AIDS epidemic in the United States.

"Shilts successfully weaves comprehensive investigative reporting and commercial page-turner pacing, political intrigue and personal tragedy into a landmark work." Publ Wkly

Includes bibliographical references

Waller, John C.
Health and wellness in 19th-century America; John C. Waller. Greenwood, an imprint of ABC-CLIO, LLC 2014 xiv, 287 p.p illustrations (Health and wellness in daily life) (hardback) $58

Grades: 9 10 11 12   **362.1**
1. Public health -- United States 2. Medical care -- United States -- History -- 19th century 3. Medicine -- United States -- History -- 19th century 4. Public health

-- United States -- History -- 19th century
ISBN 0313380449; 9780313380440

LC 2014010742

This book by John C. Waller "covers a period of dramatic change in the United States by examining our changing understanding of the nature of the disease burden, the increasing size of the nation, and our conceptions of sickness and health. With topics ranging from the unsanitary tenements of New York's Five Points, the field hospitals of the Civil War, and to the laboratories of Johns Hopkins Medical School, . . . Waller reveals a complex picture." (Publisher's note)

"As with others in the series, this title does a thorough job of covering broad health topics in a particular time period. High-school and college students requiring reference material on the history of health and wellness for different eras will be well served by this set." Booklist

Includes bibliographical references (pages 259-277) and index

White, Ryan

Ryan White: my own story; by Ryan White and Ann Marie Cunningham. Dial Bks. 1991 277p il hardcover o.p. pa $7.99

Grades: 11 12 Adult   **362.1**
1. Students 2. AIDS activists 3. AIDS (Disease) -- Personal narratives
ISBN 0-8037-0977-3; 0-451-17322-8 pa

LC 90-21038

Ryan White describes how he got AIDS, engaged in a legal battle to return to school, and became a celebrity and spokesman for issues concerning the deadly disease

The book contains "surprising snatches of humor and insight that lend dimension to the vulnerable young man whose positive outlook shines through so clearly. Not saccharine, not angry, not bitter, this unusual book, delivered without an ounce of self-pity, seems as honest as it is inspiring. It will touch both adults and teens." Booklist

Winick, Judd

Pedro & me; friendship, loss, & what I learned. Henry Holt and Co. 2009 187p il pa $16.99

Grades: 7 8 9 10 11 12   **362.1**
1. Graphic novels 2. Television personalities 3. Biographical graphic novels 4. AIDS patients 5. AIDS activists 6. Friendship -- Graphic novels 7. AIDS (Disease) -- Graphic novels 8. Real world (Television program) -- Graphic novels
ISBN 978-0-8050-8964-6
First published 2000

2001 Robert F. Sibert Honor Book for informational books for youth

In this "volume—part graphic novel, part memoir—professional cartoonist Winick pays tribute to his Real World housemate and friend Pedro Zamora, an AIDS activist who died of the disease in 1994." Publ Wkly

362.196   Specific conditions

Rawl, Paige

Positive; surviving my bullies, finding hope, and living to change the world: a memoir. by Paige Rawl with Ali Benjamin. HarperCollins 2014 288 p. **362.196**
1. Bullies 2. AIDS (Disease) 3. Autobiographies 4. Bullying -- Psychological aspects 5. HIV-positive children -- Biography 6. AIDS (Disease) in adolescence -- Social aspects 7. AIDS (Disease) in adolescence -- Patients -- Biography
ISBN 9780062342515

LC 2014005857

This memoir, co-written with Ali Benjamin, tells how author "Paige Rawl has been HIV positive since birth, but growing up, she never felt like her illness defined her. On an unremarkable day in middle school, she disclosed to a friend her HIV-positive status--and within hours the bullying began. From that moment forward, every day was like walking through a minefield. Paige was never sure when or from where the next text, taunt, or hateful message would come." (Publisher's note)

Stratton, Stephen E.

★ The **encyclopedia** of HIV and AIDS; Stephen E. Stratton, Evelyn J. Fisher; foreword by Edward A. Morales. 3rd ed. Facts On File 2012 414 p. (hardcover) $75

Grades: 11 12 Adult   **362.196**
1. AIDS (Disease) 2. HIV infections 3. Reference books 4. AIDS (Disease) -- Dictionaries
ISBN 0816077231; 9780816077236

LC 2011017597

First published 1998 with title: The AIDS dictionary

This book is the third edition of an encyclopedia of HIV and AIDS. "Coverage includes definitions of AIDS and HIV; information on medications used to treat the conditions--including side effects, dosage, and drug interactions; and related medical conditions. Further research is supported by the inclusion of a bibliography for each essay. The appendixes include frequently used abbreviations, lists of online resources, and U.S. and global HIV and AIDS statistics." (Library Journal)

This volume includes "entries covering the basic biological, medical, financial, legal, political, and social issues and terms associated with HIV and AIDS. Entries explain symptoms and treatments, opportunistic infections, prevention strategies, and much more. Appendixes include HIV/AIDS associations, education centers, clinical trials, hotlines, publications, and additional material." Publisher's note

Includes bibliographical references and index.

Therrien, Patricia

An **enemy** within; overcoming cancer and other life-threatening diseases. by Patty Therrien. Mason Crest Publishers 2009 128 p. col. ill. (library) $24.95

Grades: 7 8 9 10   **362.196**
1. Terminally ill 2. Cancer patients 3. Cancer in children -- Patients -- Biography
ISBN 1422204502; 9781422204504

LC 2008033776

This book offers a collection of "stories of courageous young people and how their lives have changed due to such a diagnosis [which] are told from their own viewpoint." The volume "includes full-color photographs, table of contents, for further reading and for more information sections, bibliography, index, and author and consultant profiles." (Publisher's note)

Includes bibliographical references (p. 125) and index.

362.2 People with mental illness and disabilities

Chastain, Zachary

★ **Cocaine**; the rush to destruction. Zachary Chastain. Mason Crest 2013 128 p. ill., map, photos
Grades: 9 10 11 12   **362.2**
1. Cocaine 2. Substance abuse 3. Drug abuse -- Juvenile nonfiction
ISBN 9781422224298

LC 2011032565

This book, by Zachary Chastain, "tells the story of cocaine, its history and role in medicine, religion, and even soda production . . . [and includes facts] about the biology behind the highs—and lows—of the drug's effects. . . . [It also] provides information on kicking the cocaine habit." (Publisher's note)

★ **Mental** Illness; Roman Espejo, Book Editor. Greenhaven Press 2012 215 p. pa $30.95
Grades: 9 10 11 12   **362.2**
1. Mental illness
ISBN 9780737757354

LC 2011011655

This book, edited by Roman Espejo, focuses on the topic of mental illness. Questions raised include: "Is Mental Illness a Serious Problem?; How Should Society Address Mental Illness?; What Mental Health Issues Do Youths Face Today?; What Treatments for Mental Illness Are Effective?" (Publisher's note)

362.28 Suicide

Galas, Judith C.

The **power** to prevent suicide; a guide for teens helping teens. [by] Richard E. Nelson, Judith C. Galas; foreword by Bev Cobain; edited by Pamela Espeland. Updated ed; Free Spirit 2006 115p pa $13.95
Grades: 7 8 9 10 11 12   **362.28**
1. Suicide
ISBN 1-57542-206-9; 978-1-57542-206-0
First published 1994

"The authors' premise is that, as trusted and caring friends, YAs have a special role in the prevention of suicide among their peers, and discuss what to do if they observe the danger signals. . . . This book provides clear, practical information and advice." SLJ

Marcovitz, Hal

Suicide. ABDO Pub. Co. 2010 112p il (Essential issues) lib bdg $22.95
Grades: 7 8 9 10   **362.28**
1. Suicide
ISBN 978-1-60453-958-5; 1-60453-958-5

LC 2009-30354

This is "well-written, providing examples that put a human face to each problem. Quotes and facts are clearly attributed, and their sources are noted in the extensive back matter. . . . Sidebars provide further information, or, more compellingly, offer stories about those touched by the topic. . . . [This] will be of great assistance to students writing reports." SLJ

Includes glossary and bibliographical references

Suicide; Paul Connors, book editor. Thomson/ Gale 2007 236p (Current controversies) lib bdg $36.20; pa $24.95
Grades: 9 10 11 12   **362.28**
1. Suicide 2. Euthanasia
ISBN 978-0-7377-2488-2 lib bdg; 978-0-7377-2489-9 pa

LC 2007-1989

First published 2000 under the editorship of Leslie A. Miller and Paul A. Rose

"This title compiles essays and articles that highlight the economic, ethical, political, racial, and religious dimensions of suicide. . . . Debaters and researchers will appreciate this title's diverse collection of primary sources, as well as the entries' concise introductions and the appended bibliography and directory of organizations." Booklist

Includes bibliographical references

★ **Suicide** information for teens; health tips about suicide causes and prevention: including facts about depression, risk factors, getting help, survivor support, and more. edited by Kim Wohlenhaus. 2nd ed.; Omnigraphics, Inc. 2010 380p (Teen health series) $69
Grades: 9 10 11 12   **362.28**
1. Suicide
ISBN 978-0-7808-1088-4

LC 2010015720

First published 2005 under the editorship of Joyce Brennfleck Shannon

"Provides basic consumer health information for teens about suicide risk factors, warning signs, intervention and treatment, and prevention strategies. Includes index, directory of crisis hotlines and support groups, and resource information." Publisher's note

Includes bibliographical references

Suicide: opposing viewpoints; Jacqueline Langwith, book editor. Greenhaven Press 2008 268p (Opposing viewpoints series) lib bdg $38.50; pa $26.75
Grades: 8 9 10 11 12   **362.28**
1. Suicide 2. Euthanasia
ISBN 978-0-7377-4012-7 lib bdg; 0737740124 lib bdg; 978-0-7377-4013-4 pa; 0-7377-4013-2 pa

LC 2008-1007

The articles in this anthology cover topics such as suicide among teens and other types of people, what causes suicide, assisted suicide, and how suicide can be prevented.

Includes bibliographical references

Teen suicide; Emily Schusterbauer, book editor. Greenhaven Press 2009 116p (At issue. Teen issues) $31.80; pa $22.50

Grades: 9 10 11 12   **362.28**

1. Suicide 2. Adolescent psychology 3. Depression (Psychology)

ISBN 978-0-7377-4418-7; 0-7377-4418-9; 978-0-7377-4419-4 pa; 0-7377-4419-7 pa

LC 2008-55845

A collection of articles discussing the problem of teen suicide and what parents, friends, teachers and society can do to prevent the tragedy.

Includes bibliographical references

362.29   Substance abuse

Adamec, Christine A.

Amphetamines and methamphetamine; [by] Christine Adamec; consulting editor, David J. Triggle. Chelsea House 2011 106p il (Understanding drugs) $34.95

Grades: 9 10 11 12   **362.29**

1. Drug abuse 2. Amphetamines 3. Methamphetamine

ISBN 978-1-60413-530-5; 978-1-4381-3820-6 ebook

This book provides "information on the nature and chemistry of . . . [amphetamines and methamphetamine], their effects, abuse, addiction, and addiction treatment." Publisher's note

Includes glossary and bibliographical references

★ **Addiction:** opposing viewpoints; Christina Fisanick, book editor. Greenhaven Press 2009 228p il (Opposing viewpoints series) lib bdg $39.70; pa $27.50

Grades: 8 9 10 11 12   **362.29**

1. Alcoholism 2. Drug abuse

ISBN 978-0-7377-4352-4 lib bdg; 0-7377-4352-2 lib bdg; 978-0-7377-4351-7 pa; 0-7377-4351-4 pa

LC 2008-53997

Articles in this anthology discuss the nature of addiction, including how addictions can be prevented and treated.

Includes bibliographical references

Bjornlund, Lydia

Marijuana; by Lydia Bjornlund. ReferencePoint Press 2012 136 p. (Compact research series) (hardcover) $27.95

Grades: 7 8 9 10 11 12   **362.29**

1. Marijuana 2. Drug education 3. Medical botany 4. Drugs -- Physiological effect 5. Drugs -- Law and legislation -- United States 6. Marijuana -- United States

ISBN 160152160X; 9781601521606

LC 2011007743

This book on marijuana is a part of the Compact Research: Drugs series and "focus[es] on three types of information: "objective single-author narratives, opinion-based primary source quotations, and facts and statistics." What this translates to on the page is an overview of the topic and an in-depth chapter-by chapter discussion of the points raised in the overview." Lydia Bjornlund "looks at questions such as whether marijuana is a dangerous drug, whether it should be legalized, and the most pressing dilemma: Should the drug be readily available for medical use?" (Booklist)

Includes bibliographical references and index.

Bjornlund, Lydia D.

How dangerous are performance-enhancing drugs? [by] Lydia Bjornlund. ReferencePoint Press 2011 96p il (In controversy) lib bdg $26.95

Grades: 10 11 12   **362.29**

1. Steroids 2. Drug abuse 3. Athletes -- Drug use

ISBN 978-1-60152-126-2; 1-60152-126-X

LC 2010-17131

This book "considers the effects of drug use on the integrity of sports as well as on athletes' achievements and health." Booklist

Includes bibliographical references

Teen smoking. Reference Point Press 2010 104p il (Compact research. Current issues) $25.95

Grades: 8 9 10 11 12   **362.29**

1. Smoking

ISBN 978-1-60152-098-2; 1-60152-098-0

LC 2009-28008

This addresses the following questions: How serious a problem is teen smoking?; Who is to blame for teen smoking?; How should teen smoking be regulated?; How can we prevent teen smoking?

"The straightforward presentation of serious subject matter, graphics, and easy access to facts . . . [make this book] excellent . . . for reports and debates." SLJ

Chastain, Zachary

★ **Tobacco**; through the smoke screen. Zachary Chastain. Mason Crest 2013 128 p. ill. (Chiefly col.) $24.95

Grades: 9 10 11 12   **362.29**

1. Smoking 2. Tobacco habit

ISBN 9781422224427

LC 2011032594

This book by Zachary Chastain, part of the Illicit and Misused Drugs series, "Presents the story of tobacco, its history, its role in culture, and its dangers. Also explains the power of tobacco over smokers and chewers, how cigarette makers help increase its hold and make it more difficult to live without it, and offers suggestions on how to kick the tobacco habit and reverse its ill effects." (Publisher's note)

Club drugs; Roman Espejo, book editor. Greenhaven Press 2009 101p (At issue. Drugs) $31.80; pa $22.50

Grades: 9 10 11 12   **362.29**

1. Ecstasy (Drug) 2. Designer drugs. 3. Gamma-hydroxybutyrate.

ISBN 978-0-7377-4290-9; 0-7377-4290-9; 978-0-7377-4289-3 pa; 0-7377-4289-5 pa

LC 2008039334

The articles in this anthology discuss the positives and negatives of drugs such as GHB and ecstacy.

Includes bibliographical references

Currie-McGhee, L. K.

Drug addiction; [by] Leanne Currie-McGhee. ReferencePoint Press 2010 96p il (Compact research. Diseases and disorders) lib bdg $26.95

Grades: 8 9 10 11 12   **362.29**

1. Drug abuse

ISBN 978-1-60152-109-5; 1-60152-109-X

LC 2009-45174

Through "overviews, primary sources, and full color illustrations this title examines [such topics as] What Is Drug Addiction? What Causes Drug Addiction? What Are the Dangers of Drug Addiction? and Can Drug Addiction Be Overcome?" Publisher's note

Includes bibliographical references

Drug abuse sourcebook; basic consumer health information about the abuse of cocaine, club drugs, hallucinogens, heroin, inhalants, marijuana, and other illicit substances, prescription medications, and over-the-counter medi. edited by Joyce Brennfleck Shannon. 3rd ed; Omnigraphics 2010 645p il (Health reference series) $95

Grades: 11 12 Adult   **362.29**

1. Drug abuse 2. Reference books

ISBN 978-0-7808-1079-2

LC 2010-748

First published 2000 under the editorship of Karen Bellenir

"Well organized and readily accessible to lay readers, this is recommended." Libr J

Includes bibliographical references

Encyclopedia of drugs, alcohol & addictive behavior; [edited by] Pamela Korsmeyer and Henry R. Kranzler. 3rd ed.; Macmillan Reference USA 2009 4v il set $620

Grades: 11 12 Adult   **362.29**

1. Reference books 2. Drug abuse -- Encyclopedias

ISBN 978-0-02-866064-6; 0-02-866064-1

LC 2008-12719

First published 1995 with title: Encyclopedia of drugs and alcohol

This encyclopedia addresses "social, medical, legal, and political issues related to substance use and addictive behavior." Publisher's note

Includes bibliographical references

Etingoff, Kim

★ **Abusing** over-the-counter drugs; illicit uses for everyday drugs. by Kim Etingoff. Mason Crest Publishers 2012 120 p.

Grades: 9 10 11 12   **362.29**

1. Drug abuse 2. Drugs, Nonprescription

ISBN 9781422224243; 9781422224250; 9781422224434; 9781422224441

LC 2011032590

This book details how "the abuse and misuse of over-the-counter medications are on the rise." It "presents the facts about this alarming trend. You'll learn what drugs are most misused, the effects of misused over-the-counter medications, and what the government is doing to stem the prob-

lem. You will also find suggestions on how to get help to stop abusing over-the-counter medications." (Publisher's note)

Includes bibliographical references (p. 122-124, 127) and index

★ **Methamphetamine**; unsafe speed. by Kim Etingoff. Mason Crest Publishers 2012 128 p.

Grades: 9 10 11 12   **362.29**

1. Methamphetamine abuse

ISBN 9781422224366; 9781422224557

LC 2011032570

This book examines how "methamphetamine has become one of the most abused and dangerous drugs in the world." It looks at "how methamphetamine was developed, how its use has spread, and how it is used for limited medical purposes. You'll also learn about methamphetamine abuse. Who becomes an abuser? What are the symptoms of meth abuse? How can addiction be overcome? What are the legal consequences of meth abuse?" (Publisher's note)

Includes bibliographical references and index

Flynn, Nora

★ **Inhalants** and solvents; sniffing disaster. Noa Flynn. Mason Crest 2012 128 p. ill. (some col.) $24.95

Grades: 9 10 11 12   **362.29**

1. Drugs 2. Solvent abuse

ISBN 9781422224342

LC 2011032587

This book, by Noa Flynn, offers case studies of young people "who have sniffed, bagged, or ingested inhalants. . . . Readers will also learn how inhalants and solvents act on the brain and body, producing the feelings sought by their users. The author also takes readers down the path of long and short-term effects of inhalant and solvent abuse, including the potential for death with just one use." (Publisher's note)

Hecht, Alan

Cocaine and crack; consulting editor David J. Triggle. Chelsea House 2011 109p il (Understanding drugs) $34.95

Grades: 9 10 11 12   **362.29**

1. Cocaine 2. Crack (Drug)

ISBN 978-1-60413-536-7; 1-60413-536-0; 978-1-4381-3704-9 ebook; 1-4381-3704-4 ebook

LC 2010-46555

This book "discusses the nature of cocaine and crack addiction, how it affects one's health, and how it can be treated." Publisher's note

Includes glossary and bibliographical references

Klosterman, Lorrie

The **facts** about drug dependence to treatment. Marshall Cavendish Benchmark 2008 126p il (Drugs) lib bdg $31.94

Grades: 7 8 9 10 11 12   **362.29**

1. Drug abuse

ISBN 978-0-7614-2676-9

LC 2007-8780

This discusses the beginnings of drug dependence, its costs, first steps to recovery, rehabilitation, and lifetime freedom from drugs.

This is "well-organized, attractively illustrated, current, and highly informative." Sci Books Films

Includes glossary and bibliographical references

Kuhar, Michael J.

Drugs of abuse; consultants, Michael J. Kuhar, Howard Liddle. Marshall Cavendish Corporation 2011 320p il $59.95

Grades: 9 10 11 12   **362.29**
   1. Drug abuse
   ISBN 978-0-7614-7944-4

                 LC 2011004717

"This A-to-Z reference includes . . . discussions of alcohol, prescription drugs such as pain relievers and antidepressants, common but readily abused products acting as hazardous inhalants, plant-based substances that can be poisonous when abused, illegal drugs, and the human body's natural chemicals that play decisive roles in promoting substance abuse." Publisher's note

Marijuana; Noah Berlatsky, book editor. Greenhaven Press 2012 219 p. ill. (Opposing viewpoints series) $44.95

Grades: 9 10 11 12   **362.29**
   1. Marijuana
   ISBN 0737757337; 9780737757330

                 LC 2011042809

This book, edited by Noah Berlatsky, "examines the many controversies plaguing marijuana: whether it harms the body, has potential for addiction, and impairs driving abilities; whether current marijuana legislation is fair and effective; whether the drug should be legalized and under what circumstances; and how its use should be discouraged." (Publisher's note)

This book "examines the many controversies plaguing marijuana: whether it harms the body, has potential for addiction, and impairs driving abilities; whether current marijuana legislation is fair and effective; whether the drug should be legalized and under what circumstances; and how its use should be discouraged." Publisher's note

Includes bibliographical references and index

May, Suellen

Steroids and other performance-enhancing drugs; consulting editor, David J. Triggle. Chelsea House 2011 113p il (Understanding drugs) $34.95

Grades: 9 10 11 12   **362.29**
   1. Steroids 2. Athletes -- Drug use
   ISBN 978-1-60413-552-7; 1-60413-552-2; 978-1-4381-3791-9 ebook; 1-4381-37915 ebook

                 LC 2011-1012

This book "explains what steroids are, their medical benefits when used properly, and the damage they do when abused." Publisher's note

Includes glossary and bibliographical references

Merino, Noel

Gateway drugs: opposing viewpoints; Noël Merino, book editor. Greenhaven Press 2008 198p il (Opposing viewpoints series) lib bdg $37.40; pa $25.95

Grades: 9 10 11 12   **362.29**
   1. Drug abuse
   ISBN 978-0-7377-4002-8 lib bdg; 0-7377-4002-7 lib bdg; 978-0-7377-4003-5 pa; 0-7377-4003-5 pa

                 LC 2008-8134

"This title presents different opinions on the gateway theory of drug use in a fair and unbiased manner. . . . Each article is introduced with a paragraph that provides an overview and the qualifications of the author followed by a list of questions for students to consider while reading that specific piece." SLJ

Includes bibliographical references

Smoking; Noël Merino, book editor. Greenhaven Press 2010 143p il (Introducing issues with opposing viewpoints) $35.75

Grades: 8 9 10 11 12   **362.29**
   1. Smoking 2. Tobacco habit
   ISBN 978-0-7377-5101-7; 0-7377-5101-0

                 LC 2010-26766

Replaces the edition published 2006 under the editorship of Laurie S. Friedman

"The articles in this anthology expose multiple sides of . . . [the smoking] debate." Publisher's note

Includes bibliographical references

Mooney, Carla

★ **Thinking** critically; Performance-enhancing drugs. by Carla Mooney. ReferencePoint Press, Inc. 2014 80 p. (Thinking critically series) $28.95

Grades: 9 10 11 12   **362.29**
   1. Steroids 2. Drug abuse 3. Sports -- Corrupt practices 4. Doping in sports
   ISBN 1601525842; 9781601525840

                 LC 2013002802

"—Encouraging analysis through engaging, well-researched examinations of hot topics, these books are exceptional in both writing and design. . . . The design is spare, with understated graphics; bright, compelling photos; and text boxes that pull out interesting quotes. Easy-to-read graphs and charts add another layer of visual information. Powerful anecdotes make the issues more relevant." SLJ

Includes bibliographical references (pages 74-75) and index.

Performance-enhancing drugs

Nelson, Sheila

Hallucinogens; unreal visions. Sheila Nelson. Mason Crest 2013 128 p. ill. (mostly col.), photograph (Illicit and misused drugs) (library) $24.95

Grades: 9 10 11 12   **362.29**
   1. Drug abuse 2. Hallucinogens
   ISBN 9781422224328

                 LC 2011032567

This book, by Sheila Nelson, "looks at hallucinogenic drugs, including their history, how they affect the body, their dangers, and their legal status." (Publisher's note)

This book details the history and dangers of hallucinogenic drugs.

Includes bibliographical references (p. 117-124) and index

Newton, David E.

Substance abuse; a reference handbook. ABC-CLIO 2010 298p (Contemporary world issues) $55

Grades: 9 10 11 12 Adult   362.29

1. Drug abuse 2. Reference books

ISBN 978-1-59884-509-9; 978-1-59884-510-5 ebook

LC 2010-7451

"A comprehensive look at the physical, historical, cultural, and legal aspects of drug use including information regarding drug regulations in foreign countries and the drug culture in the United States. . . . [This is] a valuable resource for those researching or debating drug, alcohol, and tobacco-related topics." SLJ

Includes glossary and bibliographical references

Olive, M. Foster

Ecstasy; consulting editor, David J. Triggle. Chelsea House Publishers 2010 109p il (Understanding drugs) lib bdg $34.95

Grades: 8 9 10 11 12   362.29

1. Ecstasy (Drug)

ISBN 978-1-60413-538-1; 1-60413-538-7

LC 2010-5458

This book "book delves into the effects of using Ecstasy, from the initial pleasure to the dangerous aftereffects." Publisher's note

Includes glossary and bibliographical references

Parks, Peggy J., 1951-

Bath salts and other synthetic drugs; by Peggy J. Parks. ReferencePoint Press, Inc. 2014 96 p. (Compact research series) (hardback) $28.95

Grades: 8 9 10 11 12   362.29

1. Drugs 2. Designer drugs 3. Drugs of abuse 4. Synthetic drugs

ISBN 1601525168; 9781601525161

LC 2013015820

This book, by Peggy J. Parks, "describes the rise in use of these newer and perhaps lesser known but potentially deadly drugs, as well as problems associated with elusive marketing and hard-to-track Internet sales. Additional back matter comprises lists of key people, advocacy groups, and related organizations." (Booklist)

"Backed by current facts, statistics, and first-person experiences, every chapter includes further documentation with concluding "Primary Source Quotes," from former addicts and law enforcement to health care workers and government officials. In this visual, by-the-numbers era, the series responds with end-of-chapter charts and graphs that display drug-related information." (Booklist)

Includes bibliographical references and index

Methamphetamine; by Peggy J. Parks. ReferencePoint Press, Inc. 2013 96 p. (Compact research series) (hardback) $28.95

Grades: 8 9 10 11 12   362.29

1. Drug abuse 2. Methamphetamine

ISBN 1601525206; 9781601525208

LC 2013009272

This book, by Peggy J. Parks, "looks at the serious dangers of meth production and abuse and the difficulties in treating meth addiction and passing laws to regulate the drug. Backed by current facts, statistics, and first-person experiences, every chapter includes further documentation with concluding 'Primary Source Quotes,' from former addicts and law enforcement to health care workers and government officials." (Booklist)

"In this visual, by-the-numbers era, the series responds with end-of-chapter charts and graphs that display drug-related information. Additional back matter comprises lists of key people, advocacy groups, and related organizations; a bibliography; and a chronology. This series is the next go-to resource for drug-abuse research." (Booklist)

Includes bibliographical references and index

★ **Performance** enhancing drugs; Louise Gerdes, book editor. Greenhaven Press 2008 105p (At issue. Drugs) lib bdg $29.95; pa $21.20

Grades: 9 10 11 12   362.29

1. Steroids 2. Athletes -- Drug use

ISBN 978-0-7377-3693-9 lib bdg; 0-7377-3693-3 lib bdg; 978-0-7377-3694-6 pa; 0-7377-3694-1 pa

LC 2007-32384

This book "is made up of articles written by people of a variety of backgrounds and viewpoints. Each entry gives a brief background of the author helping the reader understand the writer's viewpoint. Policy and controversy surrounding performance enhancing drugs is discussed from all perspectives. Entries give clear and up-to-date information about the health risk, regulation, and banning of performance enhancing drugs, and the effectiveness of drug testing." Libr Media Connect

Includes bibliographical references

Sanna, E. J.

★ **Heroin** and other opioids; poppies' perilous children. E.J. Sanna. Mason Crest Publishers 2012 128 p. ill. (chiefly col.), col. map (Illicit and misused drugs) $24.95

Grades: 9 10 11 12   362.29

1. Heroin 2. Narcotics 3. Heroin abuse

ISBN 1422224333; 9781422224335

LC 2011032568

This book, by E.J. Sanna, "takes readers on a trip through the history of opium production and use, and its role in political history. . . . [This book also provides information on] the opioids' effects on the body and brain, their long and short-term side effects, and their dangers." (Publisher's note)

Includes bibliographical references and index

★ **Marijuana**; mind-altering weed. by E.J. Sanna. Mason Crest 2013 128 p. ill. (chiefly col.), col. map (Illicit and misused drugs) $24.95

Grades: 9 10 11 12   362.29

1. Marijuana 2. Drug abuse

ISBN 142222435X; 9781422224359

LC 2011032569

This book, by E.J. Sanna, "describes the history of marijuana use, the dangers of its use, and the legal consequences. [Also included are] the controversies surrounding the drug-
-including the issues of decriminalization and the use of medical marijuana. Treatment options for marijuana dependency are also discussed." (Publisher's note)

"This book describes the history of marijuana use, the dangers of its use, and the legal consequences. [Also included are] the controversies surrounding the drug--including the issues of decriminalization and the use of medical marijuana. Treatment options for marijuana dependency are also discussed." Publisher's note

Includes bibliographical references (p. 121-124) and index

★ **Substance** abuse, addiction, and treatment. Marshall Cavendish Reference 2012 352p il $85.64; ebook $85.64

Grades: 9 10 11 12   362.29
1. Drug abuse
ISBN 978-0-7614-7943-7; 978-0-7614-9972-5 ebook
LC 2011009226

"Health care professionals summarize the medical basics and therapeutic strategies associated with efforts to promote healthy behaviors and prevent damage to individuals, families, and society. Subjects range from abstinence, detoxification, and mental disorders to risk factors, gateway drugs, liver diseases, and halfway houses." Publisher's note
Includes bibliographical references

Teen drug abuse: opposing viewpoints; David E. Nelson, book editor. Greenhaven Press 2010 235p il (Opposing viewpoints series) $39.70; pa $27.50

Grades: 8 9 10 11 12   362.29
1. Drug abuse 2. Youth -- Alcohol use 3. Teenagers -- Drug use
ISBN 978-0-7377-4992-2; 978-0-7377-4993-9 pa
LC 2010-18884

A collection of articles and speeches, book excerpts and quotations on various aspects of teen drug abuse.
Includes bibliographical references

Tobacco and Smoking; Roman Espejo, book editor. Greenhaven Press 2015 242 p. illustrations (Opposing viewpoints) (hardcover) $48.80; (pbk.) $33.80

Grades: 8 9 10 11 12   362.29
1. Smoking 2. Tobacco industry 3. Smoking -- United States
ISBN 0737772956; 0737772948; 9780737772944; 9780737772951
LC 2014026089

This high school book, edited by Roman Espejo, part of the publisher's "Opposing Viewpoints" series, "explores the questions of whether or not smoking is a serious problem, how tobacco use can be reduced, how smoking alternatives should be regulated, and how the media affects the choice to smoke or not to smoke." (Publisher's note)
Includes bibliographical references and index

Tobacco information for teens; health tips about the hazards of using cigarettes, smokeless tobacco, and other nicotine products: including facts about nicotine addiction, nicotine delivery systems, secondhand smoke, health consequ. edited by Karen Bellenir. 2nd ed.; Omnigraphics 2010 440p il (Teen health series) $69

Grades: 7 8 9 10 11 12   362.29
1. Smoking 2. Tobacco habit
ISBN 978-0-7808-1153-9; 0-7808-1153-4
LC 2010023716

First published 2007
"Provides basic consumer health information for teens on tobacco use, addiction, and related diseases, along with tips for quitting smoking. Includes index and resource information." Publisher's note
Includes bibliographical references

Walker, Ida

Addiction in America; society, psychology, and heredity. Mason Crest Publishers 2008 128p il (Illicit and misused drugs) $24.95

Grades: 7 8 9 10   362.29
1. Alcoholism 2. Drug abuse 3. Teenagers -- Drug use 4. Teenagers -- Alcohol use
ISBN 978-1-4222-0151-0
LC 2006-100092

This book "takes a look at what leads people to a life of addiction—the social, psychological, and hereditary factors that might make an individual susceptible to addiction." Publisher's note
Includes glossary and bibliographical references

★ **Addiction** treatment; escaping the trap. Mason Crest Publishers 2008 128p il (Illicit and misused drugs) $24.95

Grades: 7 8 9 10   362.29
1. Alcoholics -- Rehabilitation 2. Drug addicts -- Rehabilitation
ISBN 978-1-4222-0152-7
LC 2007-6739

This book aims to teach "some definitions important in the study of addiction treatment. Readers will also learn about the history of addiction treatment, including the work and continuing influence of the Washingtonians, the Emmanuel Movement, the Oxford Movement, and of course, Alcoholics Anonymous. Treatment philosophies are also presented." Publisher's note
Includes glossary and bibliographical references

Natural and everyday drugs; a false sense of security. Mason Crest Publishers 2008 128p il (Illicit and misused drugs) $24.95

Grades: 7 8 9 10   362.29
1. Caffeine 2. Drug abuse 3. Nonprescription drugs
ISBN 978-1-4222-0160-2
LC 2007-10780

This book details the negative health effects of caffeine and other legal drugs.
Includes glossary and bibliographical references

★ **Painkillers**; prescription dependency. Mason Crest Publishers 2008 128p il (Illicit and misused drugs) $24.95

Grades: 7 8 9 10   **362.29**
1. Narcotics 2. Analgesics 3. Drug abuse
ISBN 978-1-4222-0161-9; 1-4222-0161-9
LC 2006-23091

This book provides "information about painkillers and how they are abused. Special attention is given to OxyContin, which has expanded addiction to new groups of people. Treatment methods are also covered." Publisher's note
Includes glossary and bibliographical references

Recreational Ritalin; the not-so-smart drug. Mason Crest Publishers 2008 128p il (Illicit and misused drugs) $24.95

Grades: 7 8 9 10   **362.29**
1. Ritalin 2. Attention deficit disorder 3. Teenagers -- Drug use
ISBN 978-1-4222-0162-6
LC 2006-23975

This book offers an overview of ADHD and the drugs most often prescribed to treat it, and how those drugs are being abused.
Includes glossary and bibliographical references

★ **Sedatives** and hypnotics; deadly downers. Mason Crest Publishers 2008 128p il (Illicit and misused drugs) $24.95

Grades: 7 8 9 10   **362.29**
1. Drug abuse 2. Tranquilizing drugs
ISBN 978-1-4222-0163-3
LC 2006-29392

This book "reveals the long history of sedatives and hypnotics. . . . [It includes information on] how these drugs work and their effects—good and bad. Preventative measures are discussed, as well as treatment options for abuse and addiction." Publisher's note
Includes glossary and bibliographical references

362.292   Alcohol

Alcohol; Lauri S. Friedman, book editor. Greenhaven Press 2010 136p il (Introducing issues with opposing viewpoints) lib bdg $35.75

Grades: 9 10 11 12   **362.292**
1. Alcoholism 2. Drunk driving 3. Teenagers -- Alcohol use
ISBN 978-0-7377-4730-0; 0-7377-4730-7
LC 2009-50773

"Explores issues surrounding the use of alcohol and whether or not it constitutes a threat to society. Discusses the impact of underage drinking, and the effectiveness of banning alcohol advertising or lowering the drinking age. Looks at the problem of drunk driving and potential solutions like stricter laws, sobriety checkpoints, and ignition interlock devices." Publisher's note
Includes bibliographical references

R., John
The **12** steps unplugged; a young person's guide to Alcoholics Anonymous. John R. Hazelden 2011 121 p. pa $13.95

Grades: 9 10 11 12   **362.292**
1. Alcoholism 2. Teenagers -- Alcohol use 3. Twelve-step programs
ISBN 1616491108; 9781616491109

"In this simple and often funny guide, [the author] interprets the philosophies and stories of the Big Book in straightforward language that speaks to regular people. John will help you connect with the basic messages of getting honest with yourself, accepting the help of others, and finding a relevant spiritual support.

Through The 12 Steps Unplugged, you'll discover just how universal the AA program really is." (Publisher's note)

"Alcoholics Anonymous, more familiarly called The Big Book, was published in 1939. . . . The Big Book describes the basic AA 12-step program, including the personal story of Bill W., credited with founding AA. In this clearly written manual, John R. devotes an interpretive chapter that corresponds to each of the 11 chapters in The Big Book. . . . In addition to those in recovery, this guide will also be useful to their family, friends, counselors and teachers." Publ Wkly
Includes bibliographical references

Walker, Ida
Alcohol addiction; not worth the buzz. Mason Crest Publishers 2008 128p il (Illicit and misused drugs) $24.95

Grades: 7 8 9 10   **362.292**
1. Alcoholism 2. Alcoholics -- Rehabilitation
ISBN 978-1-4222-0153-4
LC 2006-25415

This book "provides readers with . . . information about alcohol addiction (alcoholism) and other drinking problems. Readers will learn about the history of alcohol use and early attempts to curb drinking, how alcohol affects the brain, and the effects it has on the body in the long and short term. The author also provides information on how individuals with alcohol problems can get help." Publisher's note
Includes glossary and bibliographical references

Youngerman, Barry
★ The **truth** about alcohol; Robert N. Golden, general editor; Fred L. Peterson, general editor; Barry Youngerman, principal author; Heath Dingwell, contributing author; Richelle Rennegarbe, adviser. 2nd ed.; Facts on File 2010 230p (Truth about series) $35

Grades: 8 9 10 11 12   **362.292**
1. Alcoholism 2. Teenagers -- Alcohol use
ISBN 978-0-8160-7639-0; 0-8160-7639-1
LC 2009-53476

First published 2004
This discusses such topics as binge drinking, underage drinking, the prevalence of drinking on college campuses, drunken driving, dealing with alcohol abuse in the family, alcohol advertising and counter-advertising, and seeking help for an alcohol problem.
Includes glossary and bibliographical references

362.4   People with physical disabilities

Encyclopedia of American disability history; edited by Susan Burch; foreword by Paul K. Longmore. Facts On File 2009 3v il (Facts on File library of American history) set $295

Grades: 9 10 11 12 Adult   **362.4**
1. Reference books 2. Peope with disabilities -- History 3. Peope with disabilities -- United States 4. People with disabilities -- Encyclopedias
ISBN 978-0-8160-7030-5; 0-8160-7030-X; 978-1-4381-2672-2 ebook; 1-4381-2672-7 ebook
LC 2008-30537

"The over 750 entries, contributed by over 350 authors nationwide, cover activists, disabled persons, authors, and inventors. Also covered are topics relating to disability in general, such as disorders, organizations, governmental institutes, acts and legal cases, publications, movements, sites of importance, events, major historical experiences, stereotypes, popular culture, autobiographical essays, and literature." Libr J

Includes bibliographical references

Laney, Dawn

People with disabilities; Dawn Laney, book editor. Greenhaven Press 2008 207p (The history of issues) lib bdg $37.40

Grades: 8 9 10 11   **362.4**
1. People with disabilities
ISBN 978-0-7377-3972-5
LC 2008-20216

"Four general sections, each of which contains six primary-source essays, address rights, treatments, and care; the ADA, institutions, and capital punishment; education, funding, and inclusion; and technology, surgical procedures, and genetic testing. . . . An excellent resource." SLJ

Includes bibliographical references

McHugh, Mary

★ **Special** siblings; growing up with someone with a disability. rev ed; Paul H. Brookes 2003 xxvii, 241p il pa $21.95

Grades: 9 10 11 12   **362.4**
1. Siblings 2. People with disabilities
ISBN 1-557-66607-5
LC 2002-28179

First published 1999 by Hyperion

"A look at what it is like to be a sibling of someone with a physical, mental, or emotional disability. McHugh's brother has both cerebral palsy and mental retardation, a fact that has shaped every aspect of her life. In the course of writing this book, she spoke to siblings ranging in age from 6 to 76 years of age who expressed feelings that ran the gamut from compassion to resentment. She writes with painful honesty and includes information about research studies, interviews with experts, and the experiences and stories of many siblings." SLJ

Includes bibliographical references

362.5   Poor people

Gifford, Clive

Poverty. Smart Apple Media 2010 46p il (Voices) lib bdg $34.25

Grades: 7 8 9 10 11 12   **362.5**
1. Poverty
ISBN 978-1-59920-277-8; 1-59920-277-8
LC 2008-50431

This book "focuses on poor countries and also the poor in rich countries, addressing poverty's causes, the role of welfare and foreign aid, and always, the hardships individuals in need face day to day. . . . [The] blend of current political debate with witnesses' close-up experiences told through photos, narratives, and quotes will draw browsers, and many will go on to find out more." Booklist

Includes glossary and bibliographical references

How can the poor be helped? Jennifer Dorman, book editor. Greenhaven Press 2011 107p (At issue. Social issues) $31.80; pa $22.50

Grades: 9 10 11 12   **362.5**
1. Poor 2. Poverty 3. Public welfare
ISBN 978-0-7377-5155-0; 978-0-7377-5156-7 pa
LC 2010050614

Articles in this anthology discuss possible ways to help the poor, including welfare reform, education, and marriage.

Includes bibliographical references

Lusted, Marcia Amidon

Poverty. ABDO Pub. Co. 2010 112p il map (Essential issues) lib bdg $22.95

Grades: 7 8 9 10   **362.5**
1. Poverty
ISBN 978-1-60453-957-8; 1-60453-957-7
LC 2009-30333

The text is "well-written, providing examples that put a human face to each problem. Quotes and facts are clearly attributed, and their sources are noted in the extensive back matter. . . . Sidebars provide further information, or, more compellingly, offer stories about those touched by the topic. . . . [This] will be of great assistance to students writing reports." SLJ

Includes glossary and bibliographical references

Merino, Noel

★ **Poverty** and homelessness; Noël Merino, book editor. Greenhaven Press 2009 210p (Current controversies) lib bdg $39.70; pa $27.50

Grades: 9 10 11 12   **362.5**
1. Poverty 2. Homeless persons
ISBN 978-0-7377-4458-3 lib bdg; 0-7377-4458-8 lib bdg; 978-0-7377-4459-0 pa; 0-7377-4459-6 pa
LC 2009-12041

Articles in this anthology discuss causes and possible solutions to poverty and homelessness.

Includes bibliographical references

★ Poverty; David M. Haugen and Matthew J. Box, book editors. Greenhaven Press 2006 108p il (Social issues firsthand) lib bdg $28.70
Grades: 8 9 10 11 12 **362.5**
1. Poverty 2. Poor -- United States
ISBN 0-7377-2899-X
LC 2005-45120
These "16 accounts from poverty's gritty trenches evaporate easy assumptions about the poor, and reveal the obstacles faced by stricken individuals and families hampered by catch-22 social policies, entrenched racial inequities, and logistics such as cleaning up for an interview." Booklist
Includes bibliographical references

Welfare; Margaret Haerens, book editor. Greenhaven Press 2012 223 p. ill. $42.95
Grades: 10 11 12 **362.5**
1. Public welfare -- United States
ISBN 0737754303; 9780737754308; 9780737754315
LC 2011021326
This book, part of the "Opposing Viewpoints" series, "presents essays with opposing viewpoints on problems associated with welfare and the welfare system. . . . The selections -- by experts, policy makers, and concerned citizens -- include complete articles and speeches, long book excerpts, and occasional cartoons and boxed quotations." (Publisher's note)
"...The scope of the material is outstanding... This would be a useful resource in any public or school library media collection.—" VOYA
Includes bibliographical references (p. 211-213) and index

362.7 Young people

Feuereisen, Patti
Invisible girls; the truth about sexual abuse. with Caroline Pincus. New and rev. ed.; Seal Press 2009 334p pa $16.95
Grades: 9 10 11 12 **362.7**
1. Child sexual abuse
ISBN 978-1-58005-301-3
LC 2010-483060
First published 2005
"This book sets personal narratives within a generalized discussion of sexual abuse of girls and young women. Feuereisen addresses myths about female sexuality and abuse, considers contributing family dynamics, and offers advice on preventing, reporting, and recovering from abuse. Individual chapters are given to father-daughter incest, other incest, abuse by teachers and clergy, and different types of rape. The writing is clear and frank, including sufficient details without becoming salacious." SLJ [review of 2005 edition]
Includes bibliographical references

Gordon, Sherri Mabry
★ **Beyond** bruises; the truth about teens and abuse. Enslow 2009 128p il (Issues in focus today) lib bdg $31.93

Grades: 7 8 9 10 **362.7**
1. Date rape 2. Invective 3. Child abuse 4. Domestic violence
ISBN 978-0-7660-3064-0; 0-7660-3064-4
LC 2008-12273
"Discusses the various types of abuse teenagers face, including both domestic and dating abuse, the impact abuse has on teens, and several ways to help teens who suffer from some form of abuse." Publisher's note
Includes glossary and bibliographical references

Lanchon, Anne
★ **All** about adoption; how to deal with the questions of your past. illustrated by Monike Czarnecki; edited by Tucker Shaw. Abrams/Amulet 2006 104p il (Sunscreen) pa $9.95
Grades: 7 8 9 10 **362.7**
1. Adoption
ISBN 0-8109-9227-2
"This guide covers an adopted child's traditional worries and concerns, such as establishing identity and living with overprotective parents. It also addresses such squirm-worthy issues as the fear of abandonment, racist comments, and discussing birth parents with adoptive parents. . . . Originally published in France, this handsomely designed self-help title . . . provides practical advice and reassurance for adopted teens and their families." Booklist
Includes bibliographical references

Langwith, Jacqueline
Adoption; Jacqueline Langwith, book editor. Greenhaven Press 2014 130 p (Introducing issues with opposing viewpoints) $38.45
Grades: 7 8 9 10 **362.7**
1. Adoption
ISBN 9780737769180
LC 2013033191
This book about adoption is part of the "Opposing Viewpoints series, which explores important issues, placing expert opinions from a wide range of sources in a unique pro/con format. . . . [It] features useful charts, graphs and cartoons, engaging fact boxes that provide at-a-glance information and questions that focus on vocabulary and reading comprehension." (Publisher's note)
This book "features useful charts, graphs and cartoons, engaging fact boxes that provide at-a-glance information and questions that focus on vocabulary and reading comprehension." Publisher's note
Includes bibliographical references and index

Slade, Suzanne
★ **Adopted:** the ultimate teen guide; [by] Suzanne Buckingham Slade; illustrations by Christopher Papile, Mary Sandage, and Odelia Witt; photographs by Chris Washburn. Scarecrow Press 2007 246p il (It happened to me) $45
Grades: 9 10 11 12 **362.7**
1. Adoption
ISBN 978-0-8108-5774-2; 0-8108-5774-X
LC 2007-13648

This "guide features interviews with adoptees, essays by adoptive and birth parents, as well as information on famous adoptees, statistics, and other facts about adoption. Slade offers comprehensive coverage on topics such as transracial, international, and open adoptions, and the pros and cons of seeking information about their birth parents." SLJ

Includes bibliographical references

William Gladden Foundation

Growing up in the care of strangers; the experiences, insights and recommendations of eleven former foster kids. compiled and edited by Waln K. Brown and John R. Seita. William Gladden Foundation Press 2009 175p pa $27.95

Grades: 10 11 12 Adult   **362.7**
1. Foster children 2. Adopted children 3. Foster home care
ISBN 978-0-9824510-0-7; 0-9824510-0-8
LC 2009-927375

Most of "the authors of the stories in this book . . . suffered dangerous and dysfunctional childhoods requiring removal from their families and placement in out-of-home care. They have chosen to reflect on their childhood experiences through the lens of adult professionals, so that their unique knowledge might reach receptive minds looking to improve services to today's youth." Publisher's note

Includes bibliographical references

362.76   Abused and neglected young people

Abuse And Violence Information For Teens; health tips about the causes & consequences of abusive & violent behavior. by Sandra Augustyn Lawton. Omnigraphics, Inc. 2008 411 p. $69

Grades: 8 9 10 11 12   **362.76**
1. Child abuse 2. Domestic violence 3. Domestic relations 4. Interpersonal relations
ISBN 0780810082; 9780780810082

This book, by Sandra Augustyn Lawton, is part of the Omnigraphics' Teen Health Series. It provides "excerpted interpretation of subjects like 'Hurting Yourself' and 'Is Your Relationship a Healthy One?' Each chapter includes an 'It's a Fact' box for each chapter referencing some government or other authoritative document, thereby introducing readers to different kinds of information and documentation." (Public Library Quarterly)

362.82   Families

Domestic violence: opposing viewpoints; Mike Wilson, book editor. Greenhaven Press 2008 217p (Opposing viewpoints series) lib bdg $39.70; pa $27.50

Grades: 8 9 10 11 12   **362.82**
1. Domestic violence
ISBN 978-0-7377-4206-0 lib bdg; 0-7377-4206-2 lib bdg; 978-0-7377-4207-7 pa; 0-7377-4207-0 pa
LC 2008-28517

Articles in this anthology discuss domestic violence, including its causes and possible remedies.

Includes bibliographical references

Zehr, Howard

What will happen to me? by Howard Zehr and Lorraine Stutzman Amstutz; portraits by Howard Zehr. Good Books 2010 94p il pa $14.95

Grades: 7 8 9 10   **362.82**
1. Children of prisoners
ISBN 978-1-56148-689-2
LC 2010-12419

This discusses issues facing "children of incarcerated parents. . . . In part one, the statements from the children interviewed are accompanied by full-color photo portraits. What comes through is that they all love their parents unequivocally, but here it is tangible and poignant both in their words and faces. . . . Part two offers advice for caregivers and includes 10 questions often asked by children whose parents are in jail." SLJ

Includes bibliographical references

362.83   Women

★ **Violence** against women; Kate Burns, book editor. Greenhaven Press 2008 221p (Current controversies) lib bdg $38.50; pa $26.75

Grades: 9 10 11 12   **362.83**
1. Violence 2. Abused women
ISBN 978-0-7377-3729-5 lib bdg; 0-7377-3729-8 lib bdg; 978-0-7377-3730-1 pa; 0-7377-3730-1 pa
LC 2007-29806

Topics covered in this anthology include rape, domestic violence, the influence of pornography, and violence against women worldwide.

Includes bibliographical references

362.88   Victims of war

Bickerstaff, Linda

Violence against women; public health and human rights. Rosen Pub. 2010 112p il (A young woman's guide to contemporary issues) lib bdg $31.95

Grades: 7 8 9 10   **362.88**
1. Violence 2. Abused women
ISBN 978-1-4358-3539-9; 1-4358-3539-5
LC 2009-12062

"Facts are shared in a conversational tone, creating the sense of a chat with a big sister. . . . [Though] designed for personal reading and browsing, the data provided are accurate and also lend themselves to use in reports." SLJ

Includes glossary and bibliographical references

Simons, Rae

Gender danger; survivors of rape, human trafficking, and honor killings. by Rae Simons with Joyce Zoldak. Mason Crest Publishers 2009 128p il (Survivors: ordinary people, extraordinary circumstances) lib bdg $24.95

Grades: 7 8 9 10 **362.88**
1. Rape 2. Violence 3. Sex crimes 4. Abused women 5. Women -- Social conditions
ISBN 978-1-4222-0451-1; 1-4222-0451-0
LC 2008-50322

The author discusses "the issues faced by women in this and other cultures. The book looks at rape as a weapon of war, honor killings, female circumcision, and the complex and often dangerous world of transgender individuals." SLJ

Includes bibliographical references

Surviving sexual violence; a guide to recovery and empowerment. edited by Thema Bryant-Davis. Rowman & Littlefield Publishers 2011 ix, 372 p.p (cloth: alk. paper) $49.95; (electronic) $49.95

Grades: Adult Professional **362.88**
1. Rape 2. Sex crimes 3. Sexual harassment 4. Sexual abuse victims -- Psychology 5. Sexual abuse victims -- Rehabilitation
ISBN 144220639X; 9781442206397; 9781442206410
LC 2011013937

Author Thema Bryant-Davis's "book outlines and describes the impact of particular types of sexual violation . . . [including] childhood sexual abuse, sexual assault during adulthood, marital rape, sexual harassment, sex trafficking, or sexual violence within the military. . . . [Readers] are introduced to various pathways to surviving sexual violence and moving forward. . . . Survivors can make use of the particular approaches, which include mind-body practices, counseling, group therapies, self-defense training, and others." (Publisher's note)

Includes bibliographical references and index.

362.883 Rape

Klein, Rebecca T.
Rape and sexual assault; healing and recovery. Rebecca T. Klein. Rosen Publishing 2013 80 p. colored illustrations (Helpline: teen issues and answers) (library binding) $33.25

Grades: 7 8 9 10 11 12 **362.883**
1. Rape 2. Rape victims
ISBN 9781448894499; 1448894492
LC 2012041016

"[A strong choice] for teens needing help with difficult situations." SLJ

Includes bibliographical references (pages 75-76) and index.

The **truth** about rape; Robert N. Golden, general editor, Fred Peterson, general editor; Kathryn Hilgenkamp, Judith Harper, Elizabeth Boskey con-

tributing author[s] 2nd ed.; Facts On File 2010 191p il (Truth about series) $35

Grades: 9 10 11 12 **362.883**
1. Rape
ISBN 978-0-8160-7642-0; 0-8160-7642-1
LC 2009-18452

First published 2005 under the editorship of Mark J. Kittleson

"The introduction includes a section on how to use the book as well as a brief discussion of 'Society and the Victims of Rape.' The entries, which are generally a few pages in length, are clear and concise. They answer basic questions that students will have through definitions, statistics, an examination of common myths associated with the subject, and a Q & A." SLJ

Includes glossary

Wilkins, Jessica
Date rape. Crabtree Pub. 2011 48p il (Straight talk about . . .) $29.27; pa $9.95

Grades: 7 8 9 10 **362.883**
1. Date rape
ISBN 978-0-7787-2128-4; 0-7787-2128-0; 978-0-7787-2135-2 pa; 0-7787-2135-3 pa
LC 2010-16397

This book about date rape "also spends a good deal of its pages covering dating violence, both verbal and physical, which girls don't always understand to be problematic. . . . The information . . . is strong and far reaching." Booklist

363.1 Public safety programs

Cell phones and driving; Stefan Kiesbye, book editor. Greenhaven Press 2011 95p (At issue. Social issues) $33.70; pa $23.95

Grades: 9 10 11 12 **363.1**
1. Traffic accidents 2. Automobile drivers 3. Cellular telephones
ISBN 978-0-7377-5145-1; 978-0-7377-5146-8 pa
LC 2010024370

Articles in this anthology take different perspectives on the subject of driving with cellular phones.

Includes bibliographical references

Chernobyl; David Erik Nelson, book editor. Greenhaven Press 2010 220p il map (Perspectives on modern world history) $38.50

Grades: 8 9 10 11 12 **363.1**
1. Chernobyl Nuclear Accident, Chernobyl, Ukraine, 1986
ISBN 978-0-7377-4555-9; 0-7377-4555-X
LC 2009-27203

"This volume contains a wealth of relevant information representing many viewpoints of the current discussions surrounding the 1986 disaster at the Chernobyl nuclear power plant in Ukraine, which led to an official death toll of 56 people. Each article, skillfully drawn from multinational secondary sources, provides researchers with an admirable base for reports." SLJ

Includes glossary and bibliographical references

Drunk driving; Stefan Kiesbye, book editor. Greenhaven Press 2011 105p (At issue. Social issues) $31.80; pa $22.50
Grades: 9 10 11 12   363.1
1. Drunk driving
ISBN 978-0-7377-5841-2; 978-0-7377-5842-9 pa
LC 2011-8689
Articles in this anthology present different opinions on drunk driving and possible ways to prevent it.
Includes bibliographical references

Espejo, Roman
★ **Fast** food; Roman Espejo, book editor. Greenhaven Press 2009 96p (At issue. Health) $31.80; pa $22.50
Grades: 9 10 11 12   363.1
1. Restaurants 2. Food industry 3. Convenience foods
ISBN 978-0-7377-4300-5; 0-7377-4300-X; 978-0-7377-4299-2 pa; 0-7377-4299-2 pa
LC 2008-52832
Articles in this book discuss the controversies surrounding fast food, including its possible links to obesity and other health problems.
Includes bibliographical references

Food safety; Judeen Bartos, book editor. Greenhaven Press 2011 99p (At issue. Health) lib bdg $31.80; pa $22.50
Grades: 9 10 11 12   363.1
1. Food contamination 2. Food adulteration and inspection
ISBN 978-0-7377-5149-9 lib bdg; 978-0-7377-5150-5 pa
LC 2010-43628
Among the topics discussed in these 10 reprinted articles are government regulations on food, genetically engineered crops, and imported foods.
Includes bibliographical references

★ **Genetically** modified food; Diane Andrews Henningfeld, book editor. Greenhaven Press 2009 114p (At issue. Environment) lib bdg $31.80; pa $22.50
Grades: 9 10 11 12   363.1
1. Genetically modified foods
ISBN 978-0-7377-4098-1 lib bdg; 0-7377-4098-1 lib bdg; 978-0-7377-4099-8 pa; 0-7377-4099-X pa
LC 2008-29477
Presents a series of essays with varying viewpoints on the subject of genetically modified food. Includes a list of organizations to contact.
Includes bibliographical references

Lusted, Marcia Amidon
The **Chernobyl** Disaster. ABDO Pub. 2011 112p il (Essential events) lib bdg $23.95
Grades: 7 8 9 10 11 12   363.1
1. Nuclear power plants 2. Chernobyl Nuclear Accident, Chernobyl, Ukraine, 1986
ISBN 978-1-6171-4763-0; 1-6171-4763-X
LC 2010045019

This describes "the technology and engineering detail of how a nuclear power plant generates electricity and why it is dangerous, as well as the politics of why the disaster happened. . . . The spacious . . . design is inviting, with many color illustrations and screens, and the extensive back matter includes a detailed time line, glossary, bibliography and source notes." Booklist
Includes glossary and bibliographical references

The **Three** Mile Island nuclear disaster; by Marcia Amidon Lusted. ABDO Pub. Company 2012 112 p. il (Essential events)
Grades: 6 7 8   363.1
1. Nuclear energy 2. Nuclear power plants 3. Nuclear power plants -- Accidents 4. Three Mile Island Nuclear Power Plant (Pa.)
ISBN 1617833118; 9781617833113
LC 2011036182
This children's educational book by Marcia Amidon Lusted "examines an important historic event — the Three Mile Island nuclear disaster near Middletown, Pennsylvania. . . . [It] explores the history of nuclear power in the United States, how a nuclear plant works, details of the emergency at Metropolitan Edison Company's nuclear power plant, handling of the disaster by the Nuclear Regulatory Commission, President Jimmy Carter's visit to Three Mile Island, the investigation into the disaster, and the effects of this event on society. Features include a table of contents, glossary, selected bibliography, Web links, source notes, and an index, plus a timeline and essential facts." (Publisher's note)
Includes glossary and bibliographical references.

Parks, Peggy J., 1951-
Drunk driving. ReferencePoint Press 2009 96p il (Compact research. Current issues) lib bdg $25.95
Grades: 7 8 9 10   363.1
1. Drunk driving
ISBN 978-1-60152-072-2; 1-60152-072-7
LC 2008-48499
This "title has an overview of [drunk driving] as well as topic-specific chapters such as 'Who Drives Drunk?' and 'How Should Drunk Drivers Be Punished?' It offers differing ideas on questions that have more than one answer. The colorful graphs and charts contain current information." SLJ
Includes bibliographical references

Petersen, Christine
★ **Protecting** earth's food supply. Marshall Cavendish Benchmark 2010 112p il (Environment at risk) lib bdg $39.93
Grades: 6 7 8 9 10   363.1
1. Diseases 2. Food poisoning 3. Food contamination 4. Food adulteration and inspection
ISBN 978-0-7614-4008-6; 0-7614-4008-9
LC 2008-35949
This book provides "information on Earth's food supply and its protection, the interrelationships of the natural world, environmental problems both natural and man-made, the relative risks associated with these problems, and solutions for resolving and/or preventing them." Publisher's note
Includes bibliographical references

Smith, Terry L.

Nutrition and food safety. Chelsea House 2010 180p il map (Healthy eating: a guide to nutrition) $35

Grades: 9 10 11 12   363.1

1. Nutrition 2. Food adulteration and inspection
ISBN 978-1-60413-776-7

LC 2010-21324

This book "explores the many risks to our food and water supplies, including bacterial contamination, agricultural pesticides, food additives, allergens, and industrial chemicals." Publisher's note

Includes glossary and bibliographical references

363.17 Hazardous materials

Kops, Deborah

The Great Molasses Flood; Boston, 1919. Deborah Kops. Charlesbridge 2012 102 p.

Grades: 6 7 8 9   363.17

1. Molasses 2. Industrial accidents 3. Boston (Mass.) -- History 4. Floods -- Massachusetts -- Boston -- History -- 20th century 5. Industrial accidents -- Massachusetts -- Boston -- History -- 20th century 6. Alcohol industry -- Accidents -- Massachusetts -- Boston -- History -- 20th century 7. Molasses industry -- Accidents -- Massachusetts -- Boston -- History -- 20th century
ISBN 1580893481; 9781580893480; 9781580893497

LC 2011000655

This historical survey by Deborah Kops follows the events of "January 15, 1919 . . . an unseasonable warm day in Boston, Massachusetts, and a day that would go down in history. One minute it was business as usual on the waterfront and the next - KABOOM! A large tank holding molasses exploded, sending shards of metal hundreds of feet away, collapsing buildings, and coating the harborfront community with a thick layer of sticky-sweet sludge." (Publisher's note)

"The combination of the sepia-toned photographs, the use of brown to highlight the chapter headings, and the choice of cream-colored paper gives this book a rich, elegant quality while staying consistent with the subject matter." Booklist

363.2 Police services

Bell, Suzanne

Fakes and forgeries. Facts On File 2008 108p il (Essentials of forensic science) $35

Grades: 7 8 9 10 11 12   363.2

1. Fraud 2. Forgery
ISBN 978-0-8160-5514-2; 0-8160-5514-9

LC 2008-4502

This is a "fascinating introduction to how scientists identify fraudulent copies, from signatures to oil paintings. . . . Bell moves from examples of the crime that date back to ancient Mesopotamian civilizations all the way through to today's high-tech counterfeiting cases." Booklist

Includes glossary and bibliographical references

Helvarg, David

Rescue warriors; the U.S. Coast Guard, America's forgotten heroes. Thomas Dunne Books 2009 xxiii, 356p il $25.95

Grades: 9 10 11 12 Adult   363.2

1. Lifesaving 2. Rescue work 3. United States -- Coast Guard
ISBN 978-0-312-36372-7; 0-312-36372-9

LC 2008-44633

"An informative history starting with the Coast Guard's beginnings in the 18th century, written in straightforward prose. The emphasis is on the fifth armed service's record during the 20th and 21st centuries, especially its unparalleled effectiveness and heroism during Hurricane Katrina. . . . This is an excellent title for students interested in the Coast Guard, especially as a possible career choice." SLJ

Includes bibliographical references

Newton, Michael

★ The encyclopedia of crime scene investigation; foreword by John L. French. Facts On File 2008 334p il (Facts on File crime library) $75; pa $21.95

Grades: 9 10 11 12 Adult   363.2

1. Reference books 2. Criminal investigation -- Encyclopedias
ISBN 978-0-8160-6814-2; 0-8160-6814-3; 978-0-8160-6815-9 pa; 0-8160-6815-1 pa

LC 2007-4406

This encyclopedia includes "300 alphabetically arranged articles that describe and discuss crime-solving procedures and technologies. The entries provide a broad treatment of historical and scientific breakthroughs that have attempted to keep pace with criminal ingenuity, such as fingerprinting techniques, ballistics, biometrics, and DNA analysis. . . . Newton's conversational tone and writing style are accessible to high school students, who may use the volume for research or to browse the case studies." SLJ

Includes glossary and bibliographical references

Orr, Tamra

Racial profiling. ABDO Pub. Co. 2010 112p il (Essential viewpoints) lib bdg $32.79

Grades: 7 8 9 10   363.2

1. Racial profiling in law enforcement 2. Racial profiling
ISBN 978-1-60453-535-8; 1-60453-535-0

LC 2008-34915

"This timely book covers racial profiling as practiced in the United States since the terrorist attacks of 9/11, when it has come to center on young men of Middle Eastern extraction. . . . Orr presents arguments for and against the practice in focused, clearly written essays that will help students become informed. . . . There are plenty of color photographs. This book will enhance most collections." SLJ

Includes bibliographical references

Owen, David

Hidden evidence; the story of forensic science and how it helped to solve 50 of the world's toughest

crimes. Rev. 2nd ed.; Firefly Books, Ltd. 2009 288p
il pa $24.95

Grades: 11 12 Adult   **363.2**
1. Forensic sciences 2. Criminal investigation
ISBN 978-1-55407-540-9; 1-55407-540-8
     LC 2010285527
First published 2000

Owen "looks at how forensic science has developed and
how techniques have evolved from methods of investigation used in ancient China to computerized DNA analysis.
. . . This is fascinating reading for a range of readers from
forensic scientists to professional and amateur sleuths, but
the graphic illustrations are not for the squeamish." Booklist

Police and law enforcement; general editor, William
     J. Chambliss. Sage Reference 2011 320p (Key
     issues in crime and punishment) $80
Grades: 10 11 12   **363.2**
1. Police 2. Law enforcement
ISBN 978-1-4129-7859-0; 1-4129-7859-9
     LC 2011292307

Examines many aspects of policing in society, including their common duties, legal regulations on those duties, problematic policing practices, and alternatives to
traditional policing.

"An excellent purchase for students interested in serious
research." SLJ

Includes bibliographical references

Police brutality; Sheila Fitzgerald, book editor.
     Greenhaven Press/Thomson Gale 2007 184 p.
     (lib.: alk. paper) $44.95
Grades: 8 9 10 11 12   **363.2**
1. Police brutality
ISBN 0737733586; 0737733594; 9780737733587;
9780737733594
     LC 2006022915

This book, edited by Sheila Fitzgerald, "presents a
collection of essays that cover varying opinions on police
brutality." Chapters include "Is Misconduct in Law Enforcement a Serious Problem?," "Racism Is a Factor in Police
Violence," and "Does the War on Terror Invite Law-En-
forcement Abuses?" (Publisher's note)

Includes bibliographical references (p. 173-176)
and index

Racial profiling; Kathy L. Hahn, book editor. Green-
     haven Press 2010 90p (At issue. Social issues)
     $31.80; pa $22.50
Grades: 9 10 11 12   **363.2**
1. Racial profiling in law enforcement 2. Racial
profiling
ISBN 978-0-7377-5093-5; 978-0-7377-5094-2 pa
     LC 2010-15895

This is an anthology of essays by writers offering different opinions on the issue of racial profiling.

Includes bibliographical references

Sapse, Danielle S.
     Legal aspects of forensics. Chelsea House 2007
114p il (Inside forensic science) $32.95

Grades: 9 10 11 12   **363.2**
1. Forensic sciences 2. Criminal investigation 3.
Administration of criminal justice
ISBN 978-0-7910-8925-5; 0-7910-8925-8
     LC 2006-12412

This book "is intended for students who would like to
become knowledgeable in the basic aspects of law, as a
preparation for the understanding of the scientific methods
currently used in the elucidation of crimes. Focusing on the
aspects of law that make use of forensic science methods,
it does not require a previous background in either law or
science, but does provide this background as far as law is
concerned." Publisher's note

Includes glossary and bibliographical references

Stefoff, Rebecca
     Crime labs. Marshall Cavendish Benchmark
2010 95p il (Forensic science investigated) $23.95
Grades: 6 7 8 9 10   **363.2**
1. Forensic sciences 2. Graphologists 3. Criminologists
ISBN 978-0-7614-4140-3; 0-7614-4140-9
     LC 2010-10536

The "titles in the Forensic Science Investigated series
stand out not only for their thorough overviews of how
forensic science is practiced today but also for their fascinating historical perspectives. . . . Crime labs introduces
nineteenth-century Frenchman Edmond Locard, creator of
the world's first forensic lab." Booklist

Includes bibliographical references

Wagner, E. J.
     The **science** of Sherlock Holmes; from Basker-
ville Hall to the Valley of Fear, the real forensics behind the great detective's greatest cases. Wiley 2006
244p il $24.95; pa $16.95
Grades: 11 12 Adult   **363.2**
1. Forensic sciences 2. Criminal investigation 3.
Holmes, Sherlock (Fictitious character)
ISBN 0-471-64879-5; 978-0-471-64879-6; 0-470-
12823-2 pa; 978-0-470-12823-7 pa
     LC 2005-22236

The author discusses forensic science in Arthur Conan
Doyle's stories of the 'consulting detective' Sherlock
Holmes. She compares Holmes's investigative techniques to
those used in actual cases such as the killing of Lizzie Borden's parents in 1892, the 1902 murder of Joseph Browne Elwell, and the disappearance of Dr. George Parkman in 1849.

This book "will intrigue readers with incredible stories
and amazing tales from the early days of forensic science."
Christ Sci Monit

Includes bibliographical references

Walker, Pamela
     Forensic science experiments; [by] Pamela
Walker, Elaine Wood. Facts on File 2009 150p il
(Facts on File science experiments) $35
Grades: 7 8 9 10   **363.2**
1. Forensic sciences 2. Science -- Experiments
ISBN 978-0-8160-7804-2; 0-8160-7804-1
     LC 2008-39900

This "contains 20 experiments that allow students to
actively engage in scientific inquiry. Projects are presented

in a uniform format, with an introduction to the topic, time requirements (35 minutes to 2 weeks), a materials list, numbered procedures, and several analysis questions. . . . The experiments themselves are timely and fascinating. . . . In [this book], a banana autopsy, blood-spatter inquiry, and 'Glitter as Trace Evidence' will hook CSI fans. Despite detailed instructions, close teacher supervision is a must." SLJ

Includes glossary and bibliographical references

Warner, Judith Ann

U.S. border security; a reference handbook. [by] Judith A. Warner. ABC-CLIO 2010 381p il (Contemporary world issues) $55

Grades: 9 10 11 12   **363.2**
1. United States -- Boundaries 2. United States -- Border Patrol
ISBN 978-1-59884-407-8

LC 2010-9662

"The eight chapters in this . . . work address history, contemporary issues, and the international context of security, and provide a chronology of events, biographies of major figures, selected documents and data, a directory of involved organizations and agencies, and a list of sources. . . . Its comprehensive coverage includes security concerns at land, sea, and air borders, such as unauthorized entry and smuggling of individuals (including human trafficking); drug trafficking and narcoterrorism; and property offensives such as theft, terrorism, and the smuggling of weapons of mass destruction. This useful compendium fills a gap on the reference shelf." Choice

Includes glossary and bibliographical references

Wright, John D.

Fire and explosives. Sharpe Focus 2008 96p (Forensic evidence) $39.95

Grades: 7 8 9 10 11 12   **363.2**
1. Fires 2. Explosives 3. Forensic sciences 4. Criminal investigation
ISBN 978-0-7656-8117-1

LC 2007-6750

This book focuses on how forensic science plays a role in investigating explosions and fires.

Includes glossary and bibliographical references

Hair and fibers. Sharpe Focus 2008 96p il (Forensic evidence) $39.95

Grades: 7 8 9 10 11 12   **363.2**
1. Hair 2. Fibers 3. Forensic sciences 4. Criminal investigation
ISBN 978-0-7656-8116-4

LC 2007-6752

"This volume, about the most familiar examples of trace evidence (hair and fibers), provides readers with well-detailed descriptions of how such fibers are handled at the scene, analyzed in the lab, and used in the courtroom, as well as how the science itself has evolved. . . . Make a place for this on the shelf; interest will be high." Booklist

Includes glossary and bibliographical references

363.25   Detection of crime (Criminal investigation)

Aronson, Marc

★ **Master** of deceit; J. Edgar Hoover and America in the age of lies. Marc Aronson. Candlewick Press 2012 230 p. $25.99

Grades: 9 10 11 12   **363.25**
1. United States -- History -- 20th century 2. United States -- Politics and government 3. United States. Federal Bureau of Investigation 4. United States -- Officials and employees -- Biography 5. Government executives -- United States -- Biography
ISBN 9780763650254

LC 2011046078

This book, by Marc Aronson, offers a "biography of J. Edgar Hoover. . . . In this . . . exploration of one of the most powerful Americans of the twentieth century, . . . [the author] unmasks the man behind the Bureau--his tangled family history and personal relationships; his own need for secrecy, deceit, and control; and the broad trends in American society that shaped his world." (Publisher's note)

Includes bibliographical references (p. 217-219) and index

Weiner, Tim

Enemies; the history of the FBI at war. Tim Weiner. 1st ed. Random House 2011 537 p. (alk. paper) $30

Grades: 11 12 Adult   **363.25**
1. National security -- United States 2. Intelligence service -- United States 3. United States -- History -- 20th century 4. Espionage -- United States -- History -- 20th century 5. United States. Federal Bureau of Investigation -- History -- 20th century
ISBN 9780679643890; 9781400067480

LC 2011005353

This book "delivers a . . . history of what has been, in effect, America's secret police.The history of the FBI is easily divided into two periods: the J. Edgar Hoover period and after. In 1924, before he was 30, Hoover took over a tiny, tawdry Bureau and built it into a fearsome empire he ruled as a personal fiefdom until his death in 1972. . . . Weiner focuses on the FBI's activities investigating and attempting to prevent subversion and terrorism." (Kirkus Reviews)

Includes bibliographical references and index

363.3   Other aspects of public safety

Cunningham, Kevin

Wildfires. Morgan Reynolds Pub. 2009 112p il (Extreme threats) lib bdg $28.95

Grades: 7 8 9 10   **363.3**
1. Wildfires
ISBN 978-1-59935-120-9; 1-59935-120-X

LC 2009-25709

This book about wildfires has "black-and-white and color photographs on almost every page. . . . Frequent sidebars, covering as much as a spread, discuss peripheral and often unusual information. The conclusion . . . explains what

scientists are doing, or what they anticipate doing, to ameliorate the threat." SLJ
Includes glossary and bibliographical references

Media violence: opposing viewpoints; David Haugen and Susan Musser, book editors. Greenhaven
Press 2009 232p il (Opposing viewpoints series)
lib bdg $37.40; pa $25.95
Grades: 8 9 10 11 12   363.3
1. Violence 2. Mass media
ISBN 978-0-7377-4218-3 lib bdg; 978-0-7377-4219-
0 pa
                                         LC 2008-30355
This anthology "begins with articles that probe the scope
and severity of the phenomenon and then moves on to sections about how violence in the media should be regulated, the
effects of violence in the news, and cyberbullying." Booklist
Includes bibliographical references

363.31 Censorship

Caso, Frank
 ★ **Censorship**; foreword by Richard B. Collins.
Facts On File 2008 342p (Global issues) $45
Grades: 9 10 11 12   363.31
1. Censorship
ISBN 978-0-8160-7123-4; 0-8160-7123-3
                                         LC 2007-47075
The author "lays out censorship's lengthy history and
follows with a thoughtful account of its various religious,
political, and social motives." Libr J
Includes bibliographical references

 ★ **Censorship**; Julia Bauder, book editor. Greenhaven Press 2007 275p (Current controversies)
lib bdg $34.95; pa $23.70
Grades: 9 10 11 12   363.31
1. Censorship
ISBN 978-0-7377-3277-1 lib bdg; 0-7377-3277-6 lib
bdg; 978-0-7377-3278-8 pa; 0-7377-3278-4 pa
                                         LC 2006-38688
Includes bibliographical references

 ★ **Censorship**: opposing viewpoints; Scott Barbour, book editor. Greenhaven Press 2010 217p il
(Opposing viewpoints series) $39.70; pa $27.50
Grades: 9 10 11 12   363.31
1. Censorship 2. Freedom of speech
ISBN 978-0-7377-4761-4; 978-0-7377-4762-1 pa
                                         LC 2009-40557
Articles in this anthology discuss issues relating to censorship including whether there should be limits to free
speech, censorship of the Internet, and censorship in other
nations including China.
Includes bibliographical references

Should music lyrics be censored for violence and
exploitation? Roman Espejo, book editor. Green-

haven Press 2008 137p (At issue. Mass media)
lib bdg $29.95; pa $21.20
Grades: 9 10 11 12   363.31
1. Rap music -- Censorship 2. Rap music -- History
and criticism
ISBN 978-0-7377-4064-6 lib bdg; 978-0-7377-4065-
3 pa
                                         LC 2007-50857
This book "explores the isses surrounding the censorship
of violent and misogynistic rap and hip-hop lyrics. Contributors address freedom of speech, the impact of song content
on young people's behavior, violence and sexism in our culture, and the rights and responsibilities of both recording artists and record companies." SLJ
Includes bibliographical references

363.32 Social conflict

Encyclopedia of terrorism; Peter Chalk, editor.
ABC-CLIO 2013 xviii, 871 p.p ill. (hardcopy)
$205; (ebook) $205.00
Grades: 11 12 Adult   363.32
1. Terrorism -- Encyclopedias
ISBN 0313308950; 9780313308956; 9780313385353
                                         LC 2012016710
This book, edited by Peter Chalk, "provides comprehensive coverage of the events, individuals, groups, incidents,
and trends in terrorism in the modern era. [It] . . . presents .
. . information on developments since the watershed events
of September 11, 2001, providing readers with an invaluable reference tool for understanding major developments
that have occurred in domestic and international terrorism."
(Publisher's note)
Includes bibliographical references and index

Evans, Kimberly Masters
 National security; [by] Kim Masters Evans.
Gale Cengage 2009 158p il map (Information Plus
reference series) pa $55
Grades: 9 10 11 12   363.32
1. National security -- United States
ISBN 978-1-4144-3380-6
This book discusses the war on terror and its effect on
civil liberties.
Includes bibliographic references

Friedman, Lauri S.
 Terrorist attacks. ReferencePoint Press 2008
128p il map (Compact research. Current issues) lib
bdg $24.95
Grades: 7 8 9 10 11 12   363.32
1. Terrorism
ISBN 978-1-60152-022-7; 1-60152-022-0
                                         LC 2007-9907
This "introduces theories as to why people carry out terrorist attacks, how they are executed, and how the attacks
might be prevented. . . . [The] volume includes people and
groups associated with the issue, a chronology of events,
related organizations, and suggestions for further research.
Chapters open and end with an array of quotes that argue

for or against a particular argument or aspect of the issue, complete with full citation." SLJ

Includes glossary and bibliographical references

Gupta, Dipak K.

Who are the terrorists? Chelsea House 2006 116p il map (The roots of terrorism) lib bdg $35
Grades: 7 8 9 10   **363.32**
1. Islam 2. Terrorism
ISBN 0-7910-8306-3

LC 2005021627

This "volume discusses the world history as well as the groups and individuals behind today's headlines. . . . Gupta emphasizes that equating Islam with the barbaric acts of a few terrorists is like making the burning crosses of the Ku Klux Klan the essence of Christianity. He also points out the role of the American invasion of Iraq and the images from Abu Ghraib. . . . This is sure to spark vehement group discussion." Booklist

Includes bibliographical references

Harris, Shane

The **watchers**; the rise of America's surveillance state. Penguin Press 2010 418p il $27.95; pa $17
Grades: 11 12 Adult   **363.32**
1. Terrorism 2. National security -- United States 3. Intelligence service -- United States
ISBN 978-1-59420-245-2; 978-0-14-311890-9 pa

LC 2009-37205

The author examines the development of domestic surveillance programs in the United States intended to prevent terrorist attacks.

"A sharply written, wise analysis of the complex mashup of electronic sleuthing, law, policy and culture." Kirkus

Includes bibliographical references

Netzley, Patricia D.

The **Greenhaven** encyclopedia of terrorism; by Patricia D. Netzley; Moataz A. Fattah, consulting editor. Greenhaven Press 2007 365p il (Greenhaven encyclopedia of) $77.45
Grades: 9 10 11 12   **363.32**
1. Reference books 2. Terrorism -- Encyclopedias
ISBN 978-0-7377-3235-1; 0-7377-3235-0

LC 2007-8156

An alphabetical presentation of definitions and descriptions of terms and events associated with terrorism.

Includes bibliographical references

★ **Terrorism;** David M. Haugen and Matthew J. Box, book editors. Greenhaven Press 2006 110p il (Social issues firsthand) lib bdg $28.70
Grades: 9 10 11 12   **363.32**
1. Terrorism
ISBN 0-7377-2501-X

LC 2005-40218

This book designed to discuss the personal aspects of controversial issues "includes articles written by Osama bin Laden, Timothy McVeigh, Hizbullah, and a member of Aum Shinrikyo. All of these are in a chapter titled, 'What Motivates a Terrorist?' Later chapters include reports by survi-

vors and family members of Sept. 11, 2001, the Oklahoma City bombing, Palestine, and other terrorist tragedies." Libr Media Connect

Includes bibliographical references

Terrorism: opposing viewpoints; Mike Wilson, book editor. Greenhaven Press 2008 209p il (Opposing viewpoints series) lib bdg $38.50; pa $26.75
Grades: 8 9 10 11 12   **363.32**
1. Terrorism
ISBN 978-0-7377-4234-3 lib bdg; 0-7377-4234-8 lib bdg; 978-0-7377-4235-0 pa; 0-7377-4235-6 pa

LC 2008-29140

The articles in this anthology cover such topics as whether terrorism is a serious threat, different types of terrorism, terrorism's causes, and ways to combat terrorism.

Includes bibliographical references

What motivates suicide bombers? Roman Espejo, book editor. Greenhaven Press 2009 118p (At issue. National security) $31.80; pa $22.50
Grades: 9 10 11 12   **363.32**
1. Terrorism 2. Suicide bombers
ISBN 978-0-7377-4448-4; 0-7377-4448-0; 978-0-7377-4449-1 pa; 0-7377-4449-9 pa

LC 2009028941

Essays in this anthology discuss the religious, social, and political motivations behind suicide bombings.

Includes bibliographical references

363.33   Control of firearms

Atkin, S. Beth

★ **Gunstories**; life-changing experiences with guns. interviews and photographs by S. Beth Atkin. HarperCollins Publishers 2006 245p il $16.99; lib bdg $17.89
Grades: 7 8 9 10 11 12   **363.33**
1. Guns 2. Firearms
ISBN 0-06-052659-9; 0-06-052660-2 lib bdg

LC 2005-2076

"This book should be useful for students involved in the debate about guns in our culture as well as for those with a general interest in the subject." SLJ

Doeden, Matt

Gun control; preventing violence or crushing constitutional rights? Twenty-First Century Books 2011 127p il map (USA Today's debate: voices and perspectives) lib bdg $35.93; ebook $26.95
Grades: 9 10 11 12   **363.33**
1. Guns 2. Gun control 3. Firearms
ISBN 978-0-7613-6433-7 lib bdg; 978-0-7613-8074-0 ebook

LC 2010051919

"This book examines the history of U.S. gun ownership as well as current federal, state, and local laws. It provides the opinions and perspectives of government leaders, historians, activists, and ordinary Americans on both sides of the issue." Publisher's note

Includes glossary and bibliographical references

Nakaya, Andrea C.

Thinking critically; Gun Control & Violence. by Andrea C. Nakaya. ReferencePoint Press, Inc. 2014 80 p. illustrations (Thinking critically) (hardback) $28.95

Grades: 7 8 9 10 11 12   **363.33**
1. Violence 2. Gun control 3. Gun control -- United States 4. Violent crimes -- United States
ISBN 1601526067; 9781601526069

LC 2013012392

This book about gun control and violence, written by Andrea C. Nakaya, is part of the Thinking Critically series, which "encourage[s] teens to view important social issues from different perspectives. . . . [It] considers whether Americans have a constitutional right to own guns and if stronger gun control measures might prevent mass shootings." (Booklist)

"Diagrams and sidebars (Social includes one stock photo) support these well-organized models for classroom discourse. First chapters introduce the debates surrounding cell phones, social networking, and gun control; subsequent chapters present pro and con responses to four key questions. Despite lots of graphic elements, the text-heavy pages may be off-putting. Two pages of facts and a list of related organizations are appended." Horn Book

Includes bibliographical references and index

363.34 Disasters

Are natural disasters increasing? Stefan Kiesbye, book editor. Greenhaven Press 2010 135p (At issue. Disasters) $31.80; pa $22.50

Grades: 7 8 9 10   **363.34**
1. Natural disasters
ISBN 978-0-7377-4665-5; 978-0-7377-4666-2 pa

LC 2009-42506

"This book includes a good selection of viewpoints on weather-related natural disasters, their frequency, and whether or not they are primarily caused by global warming or poor human planning. . . . The concepts are clearly laid out by well-respected professionals in the field, and the arguments are all supported with data." SLJ

Includes bibliographical references

Brown, Don, 1949-

★ **Drowned** City; Hurricane Katrina and New Orleans. by Don Brown. Houghton Mifflin Harcourt 2015 96 p. chiefly color illustrations $18.99; $18.99

Grades: 7 8 9 10   **363.34**
1. Hurricane Katrina, 2005 2. New Orleans (La.) -- History
ISBN 054415777X; 9780544157774

LC 2015458266

Eisner Nominee: Best Publication for Teens (2016)
Robert F. Sibert Honor Book (2016)

In this work of graphic nonfiction by Don Brown, "when the calamitous category five Katrina's gusty winds hurl into the city of New Orleans, most people have evacuated the city. The rest of the scared, stubborn, and simply stranded must face the dangers of what is to come--broken levees quickly swelling the city with water. Many families seek safety on their roofs or via floatation devices as a way to row to safety. However, some are not as fortunate." (Children's Literature)

"Brown's narrative is clear and precise, relying exclusively on data and statistics interspersed with quotes from residents, rescue crews, journalists, and news reports. Alone, the text might lack impact, but combined with the haunting imagery, it hits readers like a punch in the gut." Booklist

Includes bibliographical references

Campbell, Ballard C.

Disasters, accidents, and crises in American history; a reference guide to the nation's most catastrophic events. Facts On File 2008 461p il map (Facts on File library of American history) $95

Grades: 11 12 Adult   **363.34**
1. Accidents 2. Disasters 3. Reference books
ISBN 978-0-8160-6603-2; 0-8160-6603-5

LC 2007-27688

"Chronicling approximately 200 of the nation's worst catastrophes, chosen for their 'immense impact on American civilization,' this useful volume ranges chronologically from Columbus's first voyage through Hurricane Katrina. . . . The articles are informative and clear." SLJ

Includes bibliographical references

Hurricane Katrina; Diane Andrews Henningfeld, book editor. Greenhaven Press 2010 146p (At issue. Disasters) $31.80; pa $22.50

Grades: 9 10 11 12   **363.34**
1. Rescue work 2. Disaster relief 3. Hurricane Katrina, 2005
ISBN 978-0-7377-4882-6; 978-0-7377-4883-3 pa

LC 2010-3359

"This title looks at myriad topics related to the catastrophe and its aftermath. It follows the series format of offering reprinted articles that present positive and negative views. Researchers will be interested in some of the discussions, such as the effects of global warming on future storms, the need to restore wetlands, and the response of FEMA (Federal Emergency Management Agency) to help victims." SLJ

Includes bibliographical references

Katrina: state of emergency; introduction by Ivor van Heerden. Andrews McMeel Pub. 2005 176p il pa $19.95

Grades: 11 12 Adult   **363.34**
1. Disaster relief 2. Hurricane Katrina, 2005
ISBN 0-7407-5844-6; 978-0-7407-5844-7

LC 2005-935404

This book "provides a chronological account of the hurricane through a selection of CNN transcripts and photos documenting all facets of the disaster starting from past studies predicting such a tragedy to the path of the hurricane to the consequences surrounding the flooding and delayed rescue efforts." Publisher's note

Robson, David

Disaster response. ReferencePoint Press 2009 96p il map (Compact research. Current issues) lib bdg $25.95

Grades: 7 8 9 10 **363.34**

1. Disaster relief

ISBN 978-1-60152-081-4; 1-60152-081-6

LC 2009-2283

"Robson covers disasters ranging from manmade to weather-related and bioterrorism. . . . Hurricane Katrina is discussed in the overview and leads into chapters that question the ability of the United States to handle natural disasters and how it can be improved. . . . Colorful graphs and up-to-date statistics are included. [This title] would be [a] great [addition] for students needing print materials to help with research projects, and for those who require some kind of first-person account included in their research." SLJ

Includes bibliographical references

363.4 Controversies related to public morals and customs

Hill, Jeff

★ **Prohibition**. Omnigraphics 2004 xxv, 201p il (Defining moments) $38

Grades: 7 8 9 10 **363.4**

1. Prohibition

ISBN 0-7808-0768-5

LC 2004-22643

This book provides an "historical analysis of the Prohibition era (1920-33), including the politics of the Eighteenth Amendment; the Mob wars; the roles played by important public figures, from mobster Al Capone to Prohibition activist Carry Nation to President Warren Harding; and much more. . . . With a detailed glossary, a chronology, and an annotated bibliography, this is an important curriculum resource on the social and political history of an era." Booklist

Includes glossary and bibliographical references

Nathan, Debbie

Pornography. Groundwood Books 2007 144p (Groundwork guides) $15.95

Grades: 10 11 12 **363.4**

1. Pornography

ISBN 0-88899-766-3; 978-0-88899-766-1

This "title examines the controversial, multifaceted topic of pornography and its entry into modern culture, including the instantaneous and unrestricted availability of sexually explicit material on the Internet. . . . [This is] a provocative starting point for further research in media studies, censorship, and human sexuality." Booklist

Includes bibliographical references

★ **Online** pornography: opposing viewpoints; Emma Carlson Berne, book editor. Greenhaven Press 2007 229p il (Opposing viewpoints series) lib bdg $36.20; pa $24.95

Grades: 9 10 11 12 **363.4**

1. Censorship 2. Pornography 3. Internet and children

4. Internet -- Law and legislation

ISBN 978-0-7377-3657-1 lib bdg; 0-7377-3657-7 lib bdg; 978-0-7377-3658-8 pa; 0-7377-3658-5 pa

LC 2007-10677

"The articles here are organized to address the questions: 'Is online pornography harmful to society?,' 'Is online pornography a form of free speech?,' 'Should children be protected from online pornography?,' and 'Should limits be placed on online pornography?' Some of the arguments include whether or not pornography is a growing moral problem, whether or not it is addictive, [and] whether or not online laws should be the same as other pornography laws. . . . This is an excellent addition for middle and high school libraries." SLJ

Includes bibliographical references

363.45 Drug traffic

Drug trafficking; Julia Bauder, book editor. Thomson/Gale 2008 258p (Current controversies) lib bdg $37.40; pa $25.95

Grades: 7 8 9 10 11 12 **363.45**

1. Drug traffic

ISBN 978-0-7377-3281-8 lib bdg; 0-7377-3281-4 lib bdg; 978-0-7377-3282-5 pa; 0-7377-3282-2 pa

LC 2007-937459

An anthology of essays discussing topics such as whether or not drug trafficking can be stopped, if efforts to curb drug trafficking are harming the United States, and the effects of the War on Drugs on Latin America.

Includes bibliographical references

Merino, Noel

Drug legalization; Noël Merino, book editor. Greenhaven Press 2010 204p (Current controversies) $39.70; pa $27.50

Grades: 8 9 10 11 12 **363.45**

1. Drugs -- Law and legislation

ISBN 978-0-7377-5097-3; 978-0-7377-5098-0 pa

LC 2010-19299

"Contributors explore the political, social, and medical dilemma of liberalization and legalization of recreational drugs such as marijuana. Domestic and international prohibition, the war on drugs, and mandatory sentencing are all examined." Publisher's note

Includes bibliographical references

Parks, Peggy J., 1951-

Drug legalization. ReferencePoint Press 2009 112p il (Compact research. Current issues) lib bdg $25.95

Grades: 9 10 11 12 **363.45**

1. Drug abuse 2. Drugs -- Law and legislation

ISBN 978-1-60152-012-8; 1-60152-012-3

LC 2007-16582

"This book looks at marijuana [legalization], but also includes information regarding the legalization of a variety of other controlled substances. . . . Chapters begin by posing questions such as, 'Would legalizing drugs decrease crime?' or 'Would legalizing drugs increase drug addiction?' The book provides different opinions, documented facts, and primary-source quotes to guide readers in forming and articulating their own responses. . . . Useful for persuasive writing and speaking assignments." SLJ

Includes bibliographical references

Sherman, Jill

    Drug trafficking. ABDO Pub. Co. 2010 112p il (Essential issues) lib bdg $22.95

Grades: 7 8 9 10   **363.45**

    1. Drug abuse 2. Drug traffic

ISBN 978-1-60453-953-0; 1-60453-953-4

                LC 2009-29935

This is "well-written, providing examples that put a human face to each problem. Quotes and facts are clearly attributed, and their sources are noted in the extensive back matter. . . . [This] will be of great assistance to students writing reports." SLJ

Includes glossary and bibliographical references

The **war** on drugs; [edited by] David L. Hudson Jr. Chelsea House 2011 104p il (Point-counterpoint) lib bdg $35

Grades: 7 8 9 10   **363.45**

    1. Drug abuse 2. Drugs -- Law and legislation

ISBN 978-1-60413-758-3

                LC 2010-52649

Articles in this anthology present different views on the war on drugs.

Includes bibliographical references

363.46   Abortion

Abortion wars; a half century of struggle, 1950-2000. edited by Rickie Solinger. University of Calif. Press 1998 413p hardcover o.p. pa $21.95

Grades: 11 12 Adult   **363.46**

    1. Abortion

ISBN 0-520-20952-4 pa

                LC 97-12261

"A collection of 18 essays written by abortion providers, journalists, reproductive-rights activists, legal strategists, and philosophers. In the introduction the editor makes it clear that the book is 'unabashedly a pro-rights book.' . . . The time line alone is so valuable that it's practically worth the price of the book." SLJ

★ **Abortion:** opposing viewpoints; David Haugen, Susan Musser, and Kacy Lovelace, book editors. Greenhaven Press 2010 206p (Opposing viewpoints series) lib bdg $39.70; pa $27.50

Grades: 8 9 10 11 12   **363.46**

    1. Abortion

ISBN 978-0-7377-4747-8 lib bdg; 0-7377-4747-1 lib bdg; 978-0-7377-4748-5 pa; 0-7377-4748-X pa

                LC 2009-41649

Provides opposing viewpoints on the topic of abortion.

Includes bibliographical references

McBride, Dorothy E.

    Abortion in the United States; a reference handbook. ABC-CLIO 2008 303p (Contemporary world issues) $55

Grades: 9 10 11 12   **363.46**

    1. Abortion 2. Pro-life movement 3. Pro-choice movement

ISBN 978-1-59884-098-8; 1-59884-098-3

                LC 2007-25876

"This unbiased reference handbook clearly documents the historical background concerning abortion in the 19th century and beyond." Libr Media Connect

Includes bibliographical references

Rose, Melody

★ **Abortion**; a documentary and reference guide. Greenwood Press 2008 258p il $85

Grades: 11 12 Adult   **363.46**

    1. Abortion

ISBN 978-0-313-34032-1; 0-313-34032-3

                LC 2007-37489

This "reference work explores the evolution of America's abortion debate in a . . . selection of over 40 primary documents by doctors, feminists, religious leaders, politicians, extremists, and judges from the 19th century to the present day." Publisher's note

Includes bibliographical references

363.6   Public utilities and related services

Balliett, James Fargo

    Freshwater; environmental issues, global perspectives. M.E. Sharpe 2010 155p il map (Environmental issues, global perspectives) $55

Grades: 9 10 11 12   **363.6**

    1. Water supply 2. Freshwater ecology

ISBN 978-0-7656-8230-7

                LC 2010-12122

This book "tracks the complex history of the steady growth of humankind's water consumption. . . . The case studies in Freshwater look at the efforts to protect and transport water within systems such as New York City; examine how growth has affected freshwater quality in the Lake Baikal region of eastern Russia; and study the success story of the privatized freshwater system in Santiago, Chile, among other relevant issues." Publisher's note

Includes glossary and bibliographical references

Farabee, Charles R.

    National park ranger; an American icon. {by} Charles R. "Butch" Farabee Jr. Roberts Rinehart Publishers 2003 180p il pa $18.95

Grades: 11 12 Adult   **363.6**

    1. United States -- National Park Service 2. National parks and reserves -- United States

ISBN 1-570-98392-5

                LC 2003-1022

"In this study of the vocation of park ranger since Maryland's park caretakers in 1696 to the present day, former ranger Farabee not only explores a ranger's role but also touches on the establishment of the National Park Service, the introduction of women rangers, and early resource management. Readers will enjoy the abundance of archival photographs, ranger profiles, and numerous other features." Libr J

Includes bibliographical references

Workman, James G.

Water. Morgan Reynolds Pub. 2009 111p il (Diminishing resources) lib bdg $28.95

Grades: 8 9 10 11 12 **363.6**

1. Water supply 2. Water conservation

ISBN 978-1-59935-115-5; 1-59935-115-3

LC 2009-28708

This discussion of world water supply and conservation "will draw activists, but even readers who do not think they care that much will find the facts devastating. Quotes from authoritative sources—environmentalists, scientists, and survivors—about both the historic overview and the contemporary crisis accompany full-color double-page photos that show what is happening now. . . . The discussion ranges from the pros and cons of dams to the price of bottled water." Booklist

Includes bibliographical references

363.7 Environmental problems

Anderson, Michael, 1972-

Global Warming; edited by Michael Anderson. First Edition Britannica Educational Publishing in association with Rosen Educational Services 2012 79 p color illustrations (The Environment: Ours to Save) (library binding) $31.70

Grades: 9 10 11 12 **363.7**

1. Global warming

ISBN 9781615305063

LC 2010049962

This book, edited by Michael Anderson, focuses on global warming. "Scientist have observed and noted that over the past 100 years the temperature of our planet has been rising. . . . A growing number of scientists arc asserting that the rising surface temperature on Earth--a phenomenon known as global warming--is a global warning sign we need to heed. . . . Readers will learn about the greenhouse effect and how it is connected to global warming." (Publisher's note)

"Michael Anderson presents Global Warming as a crises waiting to happen with dire consequences for humanity. The seriousness of the problem is backed up with charts and statistics, complete with color photographs and interesting graphs and diagrams." VOYA

Includes bibliographical references (page 76) and index

Berners-Lee, Mike

★ **How** bad are bananas? the carbon footprint of everything. Greystone Books 2011 232p il pa $16.95

Grades: 11 12 Adult **363.7**

1. Carbon 2. Greenhouse effect

ISBN 978-1-55365-831-3 pa; 978-1-55365-832-0 ebook

First published 2010 in the United Kingdom

Discusses the carbon footprint—the carbon emissions used to manufacture and transport—of everyday items, including paper bags and imported produce, and provides information to help build carbon considerations into everyday purchases.

"A book like this risks being preachy or overly serious, but Berners-Lee approaches his topics with humor and curiosity. He rarely advocates radical change. Rather, he gives readers information." Christ Sci Monit

Includes bibliographical references

Black, Brian

Global warming; [by] Brian C. Black and Gary J. Weisel. Greenwood 2010 188p (Historical guides to controversial issues in America) $55

Grades: 9 10 11 12 **363.7**

1. Greenhouse effect 2. Environmental policy -- United States

ISBN 978-0-313-34522-7; 978-0-313-34523-4 ebook

LC 2010-7137

"Black and Weisel discuss climate processes, Earth's geology, past climates and how scientists determine if the Earth is warming, modern industry and its impact on the environment, national and international responses to global warming, the Kyoto Protocol, and more. . . . Each of the six chapters begins with an overview and contains many quotes and references." SLJ

Includes bibliographical references

Braasch, Gary

Earth under fire; how global warming is changing the world. Updated ed; University of California Press 2009 xxx, 267p il pa $24.95

Grades: 11 12 Adult **363.7**

1. Greenhouse effect 2. Climate -- Environmental aspects

ISBN 978-0-520-26025-2

First published 2007

"What sets Earth Under Fire apart from other books on the same topic are the inspiring photographs. These images are an effective tool that helps the reader understand what the implications of climate change are—for people, for other organisms, and for entire ecosystems." Sci Books Films

Includes bibliographical references

Carson, Rachel, 1907-1964

★ **Silent** spring; introduction by Linda Lear; afterword by Edward O. Wilson. 40th anniversary ed; Houghton Mifflin 2002 378p il

Grades: 11 12 Adult **363.7**

1. Pesticides and wildlife 2. Pesticides -- Environmental aspects

ISBN 0-618-24906-0 pa; 0-618-25305-X

First published 1962

In The silent spring, Carson "contended that the indiscriminate use of weed killers and insecticides constituted a hazard to wildlife and to human beings. Her provocative work inspired many subsequent environmental studies." Reader's Ency. 4th edition

Casper, Julie Kerr

Fossil fuels and pollution; the future of air quality. Facts on File 2010 268p il map (Global warming) $40

Grades: 9 10 11 12   **363.7**

1. Pollution 2. Environmental protection
ISBN 978-0-8160-7265-1; 0-8160-7265-5

LC 2009-12612

"In this valuable resource, detailed maps, charts, graphs, and sidebars offer useful data on subjects ranging from coal use and production to agriculture and from biofuels to green technology. The author includes an interesting history of technology and the concurrent rise of carbon-based fuels, documentation on current legislation, an outline of the future of emissions, and a discussion of recent public awareness of the effect of global dimming and its potential to mask the warming of the Earth." SLJ

Includes glossary and bibliographical references

Greenhouse gases; worldwide impacts. Facts on File 2010 270p il map (Global warming) $40

Grades: 9 10 11 12   **363.7**

1. Greenhouse effect
ISBN 978-0-8160-7264-4; 0-8160-7264-7

LC 2009-4727

This book explores the "role these gases play and their global impact on populations and ecosystems worldwide. The goal of this book is to provide readers with an understanding of the various sources of these gases, their interaction with the atmosphere, their effect on natural systems, and why controlling them is critical to the Earth's future climate. Other issues discussed . . . include the role of the ozone and a newly discovered concept called 'global dimming' and how it relates to global warming." Publisher's note

Includes glossary and bibliographical references

Cassio, Jim

Green careers; choosing work for a sustainable future. Jim Cassio & Alice Rush. New Society Publishers 2009 xvi, 351 p ill., ports. (pbk.) $19.95

Grades: 9 10 11 12   **363.7**

1. Environmental sciences -- Vocational guidance
ISBN 9780865716438

LC 2009483327

This career guidance book, by Jim Cassio and Alice Rush, "covers green jobs representing almost every area of career interest. The authors' extensive experience in workforce development will help you explore tomorrow's green career options by answering such questions as: What green careers are available? What salary can I expect? What education do I need? What is the demand for this profession? How do I change to a green career?" (Publisher's note)

"[C]overage is broad and not limited to occupations requiring high levels of math or science proficiency. . . . Sixty-five profiles of people working in green careers are included, and they provide an insider's view on how to get started in a particular field, as well as areas of future growth. Job seekers and career counselors will find the extensive listing of additional resources very helpful." Choice

Includes bibliographical references.

Climate change; Arthur Gillard, book editor. Greenhaven Press 2011 116p il map (Issues that concern you) $35.75

Grades: 9 10 11 12   **363.7**

1. Human influence on nature 2. Greenhouse effect 3. Climate -- Environmental aspects
ISBN 978-0-7377-5205-2

LC 2010-36735

Several articles discuss the issues surrounding climate change.

Includes bibliographical references

Conserving the environment; Debra A. Miller, book editor. Greenhaven Press 2010 211p (Current controversies) $39.70; pa $27.50

Grades: 8 9 10 11 12   **363.7**

1. Environmental movement 2. Environmental protection 3. Greenhouse effect
ISBN 978-0-7377-4661-7; 0-7377-4661-0; 978-0-7377-4662-4 pa; 0-7377-4662-9 pa

LC 2009-37782

"Explores the gravity of the global environmental problem with respect to climate, air pollution, overpopulation, water supply, and the health of the oceans. Examines the threat of global warming and the long-term impacts of biodiversity loss and extinction. Discusses potential steps to protect the environment, such as reducing emissions and supporting renewable energy sources, and the role of governments and markets in shaping a sustainable global economy." Publisher's note

Includes bibliographical references

Encyclopedia of environmental issues; editor, Craig W. Allin. Rev. ed.; Salem Press 2011 4v il map set $495

Grades: 9 10 11 12 Adult   **363.7**

1. Reference books 2. Pollution -- Encyclopedias 3. Environmental sciences -- Encyclopedias
ISBN 978-1-58765-735-1; 978-1-58765-740-5 ebook

LC 2011004176

First published 2000

"This set would be useful to general readers and students alike and would be a worthwhile resource for high-school, public, and undergraduate libraries." Booklist

Includes bibliographical references

The **environment:** opposing viewpoints; Louise I. Gerdes, book editor. Greenhaven Press 2009 224p il (Opposing viewpoints series) $39.70; pa $27.50

Grades: 8 9 10 11 12   **363.7**

1. Environmental sciences
ISBN 978-0-7377-4362-3; 978-0-7377-4361-6 pa

LC 2008-55846

This collection of essays offers varying viewpoints on environmental pollution and protection.

Includes bibliographical references

Evans, Kate

Weird weather; everything you didn't want to know about climate change but probably should

find out. [with an introduction by George Monbiot] Groundwood Books 2007 95p il $15.95; pa $9.95
Grades: 8 9 10 11 12   363.7
1. Graphic novels 2. Weather -- Graphic novels 3. Greenhouse effect -- Graphic novels 4. Climate -- Environmental aspects -- Graphic novels
ISBN 978-0-88899-838-5; 978-0-88899-841-5 pa
First published 2006 in the United Kingdom with title: Funny weather

This book, in graphic novel format, presents "the history of global warming, likely outcomes of current pollution patterns, and what can be done if we hope to survive as a species. Cleverly, the narrative unfolds through the voices of three main characters: an outraged young idealist, a scientist fascinated by the challenges of the situation, and a greedy consumer who is only interested in himself. Accessible and entertaining, this book will be adored by science teachers... . Important reading for secondary students and adults." SLJ

Includes bibliographical references

Farrell, Courtney

The **Gulf** of Mexico oil spill. ABDO Pub. 2011 112p il (Essential events) lib bdg $23.95
Grades: 7 8 9 10 11 12   363.7
1. Gulf of Mexico oil spill, 2010
ISBN 978-1-61714-765-4; 1-61714-765-6
LC 2010044976

This describes the political, social, and technical issues concerning the 2010 oil spill in the Gulf of Mexico.

Includes glossary and bibliographical references

Fleischman, Paul

★ **Eyes** wide open; what's behind the environmental headlines. Paul Fleischman. Candlewick Press 2014 208 p. illustrations hbk $17.99; pbk $9.99
Grades: 8 9 10 11 12   363.7
1. Environmental sciences 2. Environmental degradation 3. Environmental quality 4. Environmental protection
ISBN 0763671029; 0763675458; 9780763671020; 9780763675455
LC 2013953458

This book by Paul Fleischman describes how "we're living in an Ah-Ha moment. Take 250 years of human ingenuity. Add abundant fossil fuels. The result: a population and lifestyle never before seen. The downsides weren't visible for centuries, but now they are. Suddenly everything needs rethinking--suburbs, cars, fast food, cheap prices. It's a changed world. This book explains it." (Publisher's note)

"With simple, matter-of-fact language, an attractive layout and an abundance of references, this compact guide to addressing climate change is a must-read for millennials and for all who seek solutions to global warming. . . . Readers are offered advice on how to analyze and interpret what they hear in person and discover through the media." Kirkus

Includes bibliographical references, filmography and index

Friedman, Thomas L.

★ **Hot,** flat, and crowded; why we need a green revolution--and how it can renew America. Farrar, Straus & Giroux 2008 438p il $27.95

Grades: 11 12 Adult   363.7
1. Energy resources 2. Environmental movement 3. Climate -- Environmental aspects 4. Environmental policy -- United States
ISBN 978-0-374-16685-4; 0-374-16685-4
LC 2008-930589

"Friedman's big, passionate, and solidly specific ecological primer, social manifesto, and realistic plan for a green revolution aimed at restoring America's greatness and securing a sustainable future should serve as a playbook for innovators and civic leaders." Booklist

★ **Garbage** and recycling: opposing viewpoints; Mitchell Young, book editor. Greenhaven Press 2007 256p il map (Opposing viewpoints series) lib bdg $36.20; pa $24.95
Grades: 9 10 11 12   363.7
1. Recycling 2. Refuse and refuse disposal
ISBN 978-0-7377-3651-9 lib bdg; 0-7377-3651-8 lib bdg; 978-0-7377-3652-6 pa; 0-7377-3652-6 pa
LC 2007-4374

An anthology of essays with opposing arguments on the topic of recycling and garbage disposal.

Includes bibliographical references

Gates, Alexander E.

Encyclopedia of pollution; [by] Alexander E. Gates and Robert P. Blauvelt. Facts on File 2011 2v il map (Facts on File science library) set $170
Grades: 9 10 11 12 Adult   363.7
1. Pollution 2. Reference books 3. Pollution -- Encyclopedias
ISBN 978-0-8160-7002-2
LC 2009048190

"Broad topics encompass all aspects of pollutants, including properties, production, uses, environmental release and fate, regulations, and adverse health effects in response to exposure. Summary entries on general subjects, such as water pollution, provide topical overviews. Case studies of pollution events supply instructive background information." Booklist

Includes bibliographical references

Gelletly, LeeAnne

Ecological issues. Mason Crest Publishers 2007 112p il map (Africa: progress & problems) $24.95
Grades: 9 10 11 12   363.7
1. Environmental degradation 2. Environmental policy -- Africa
ISBN 978-1-59084-956-9; 1-59084-956-6
LC 2005-16306

"This book discusses the ecological issues facing Africa today, including deforestation and desertification, threats to the continent's biodiversity, pollution, and shortages of safe drinking water. It also explains steps some African leaders are taking to address and resolve these serious problems." Publisher's note

Includes bibliographical references

George, Rose

The **big** necessity; the unmentionable world of human waste and why it matters. Metropolitan Books 2008 288p il $26

Grades: 11 12 Adult   **363.7**

1. Sanitation 2. Sewage disposal

ISBN 978-0-8050-8271-5; 0-8050-8271-9

LC 2008-29999

The author "breaks the embarrassed silence over the economic, political, social and environmental problems of human waste disposal. . . . From the depths of the world's oldest surviving urban sewers in to Japan's robo-toilet revolution, George leads an intrepid, erudite and entertaining journey through the public consequences of this most private behavior." Publ Wkly

Includes bibliographical references

★ **Global** warming: opposing viewpoints; David Haugen, Susan Musser, and Kacy Lovelace, book editors. Greenhaven Press 2010 249p il map (Opposing viewpoints series) $39.70; pa $27.50

Grades: 8 9 10 11 12   **363.7**

1. Greenhouse effect

ISBN 978-0-7377-4631-0; 0-7377-4631-9; 978-0-7377-4632-7 pa; 0-7377-4632-7 pa

LC 2009-38723

"Explores whether global warming is a real phenomenon or a myth, addressing possible causes like carbon dioxide, deforestation, melting permafrost, and livestock agriculture. Examines the effects of global warming on the polar ice caps, polar bears and human health, and discusses some proposed strategies to mitigate the impact." Publisher's note

Includes bibliographical references

Gore, Al

★ An **inconvenient** truth; the planetary emergency of global warming and what we can do about it. Rodale 2006 325p il map pa $23.95

Grades: 11 12 Adult   **363.7**

1. Human ecology 2. Environmental protection 3. Greenhouse effect 4. Environmental policy -- United States

ISBN 978-1-59486-567-1; 1-59486-567-1

LC 2006-926537

"Gore has put together a coherent account of a complex topic that Americans desperately need to understand. . . . By telling the story of climate change with striking clarity . . . Al Gore may have done for global warming what [Rachel Carson's] Silent Spring [1962] did for pesticides." N Y Rev Books

Our choice; how we can solve the climate crisis. [text adapted by Richie Chevat] Young readers ed.; Puffin Books 2009 207p il map $24.99; pa $16.99

Grades: 6 7 8 9 10   **363.7**

1. Human ecology 2. Environmental policy 3. Environmental protection 4. Greenhouse effect

ISBN 978-0-670-01248-0; 0-670-01248-3; 978-0-14-240981-7 pa; 0-14-240981-2 pa

LC 2010-455157

"This colorful, well-designed volume presents the climate crisis in an easy-to-understand format. Covering many aspects of this complex problem, it addresses the effects of pollution on the environment, the search for alternative energy sources, and offers suggestions for conserving power and reducing the impact of human habitation on the planet. . . . Although the urgency of the current global situation is stressed, the chapters are also laced with hope. Suggestions for change offer positive steps that anyone can take to reduce his carbon footprint, and extend a call to unite globally to save the planet for future generations." Voice Youth Advocates

Kallen, Stuart A.

Toxic waste. Referencepoint Press 2011 96p il map (Compact research. Energy and the environment) lib bdg $26.95

Grades: 9 10 11 12   **363.7**

1. Hazardous wastes

ISBN 978-1-60152-124-8; 1-60152-124-3

LC 2009-52242

This "book discusses the seriousness of toxic and electronic waste, the effectiveness of cleanup efforts, and future challenges. . . . Primary-source quotations; short narrative texts, followed by relevant quotations; a section with a bulleted list of one-sentence facts; pertinent illustrations; and annotated lists of key people, organizations, and advocacy groups are included." SLJ

Includes bibliographical references

Kolbert, Elizabeth

★ **Field** notes from a catastrophe; man, nature, and climate change. Bloomsbury Pub. 2006 210p il map hardcover o.p. pa $14.95

Grades: 11 12 Adult   **363.7**

1. Climate 2. Greenhouse effect

ISBN 1-59691-125-5; 978-1-59691-125-3; 1-59691-130-1 pa; 978-1-59691-130-7 pa

LC 2005-30972

"On the burgeoning shelf of cautionary but occasionally alarmist books warning about the consequences of dramatic climate change, Kolbert's calmly persuasive reporting stands out for its sobering clarity." Publ Wkly

Includes bibliographical references

Lynas, Mark

High tide; the truth about our climate crisis. Picador 2004 xxxiii, 345p il map pa $14

Grades: 11 12 Adult   **363.7**

1. Greenhouse effect

ISBN 0-312-30365-3

LC 2004-44661

"In a series of . . . travel narratives, Lynas shows the human side of global warming, taking readers to Britain, North and South America, China, and the South Pacific. He introduces them to folks whose houses and roads are falling crazily through melting permafrost, who are going hungry because fishing lakes have disappeared, and who are becoming refugees because their grasslands have turned to desert. . . . The author clearly explains why these are not isolated incidents, but interrelated parts of a worldwide set of phenomena that soon will affect us all." SLJ

Includes bibliographical references

Macgillivray, Alex

Understanding Rachel Carson's Silent Spring. Rosen Pub. 2011 128p il (Words that changed the world) lib bdg $31.95

Grades: 7 8 9 10 **363.7**

1. Authors 2. Insect pests 3. Conservationists 4. Pesticides and wildlife 5. College teachers 6. Marine biologists 7. Writers on nature 8. Writers on science 9. Pesticides -- Environmental aspects

ISBN 978-1-4488-1670-5; 1-4488-1670-X

LC 2010-9260

"This focused title examines Rachel Carson's Silent Spring, zeroing in on the content and enduring impact of the watershed 1962 work. . . . The text begins with a brief introduction to Carson and her times before moving into an analysis of the text and its indictment of pesticide use, . . . the immediate postpublication response, and its hugely influential legacy today. . . . A useful supplement to environmental-science units, this will easily support student research." Booklist

Includes glossary and bibliographical references

McClelland, Carol L.

Green careers for dummies; [by] Carol McClelland. John Wiley 2010 340p pa $19.99

Grades: 9 10 11 12 Adult **363.7**

1. Environmental sciences -- Vocational guidance

ISBN 978-0-470-52960-7

LC 2009-941922

The author "has delivered an excellent volume for anyone interested in a career in the green economy. Whether just starting out or looking for a midlife change, readers will find extremely useful McClelland's descriptions of the development of the green economy, her details on different types of careers available, and her technical advice on using the latest methods for finding green jobs, writing résumés, and doing well in the interview process. She also provides plenty of ideas for further information. . . . An essential resource for anyone looking to take advantage of career opportunities in the green economy, at the right price and easy to use." Libr J

McKibben, Bill

★ **Fight** global warming now; the handbook for taking action in your community. [by] Bill McKibben and the Step It Up Team, Phil Aroneanu . . . [et al.] Henry Holt 2007 202p il $13

Grades: 11 12 Adult **363.7**

1. Social action 2. Environmental movement 3. Greenhouse effect

ISBN 978-0-8050-8704-8; 0-8050-8704-4

LC 2007-25492

The authors tell the "Step It Up creation story and offer a lively, convincing how-to for revitalizing social-change movements. A set of commonsensical and shrewd organizing principles and a realistic list of priorities are supported by detailed advice and examples, and all are wreathed with clearly stated information about global warming." Booklist

Includes bibliographical references

Miller, Debra A.

★ **Garbage** and recycling. Lucent Books 2009 112p il map (Hot topics) $32.45

Grades: 7 8 9 10 **363.7**

1. Recycling 2. Refuse and refuse disposal

ISBN 978-1-4205-0147-6; 1-4205-0147-X

LC 2009-18371

This is a "standout survey of what happens to what we throw away and how those decisions affect the globe. . . . This overview offers a balance of viewpoints in its clear comparison of traditional methods of waste management with more sustainable technologies, such as recycling and new landfill techniques. . . . [Sidebars] make for compelling reading, while numerous color photos, charts, and maps will further attract readers' attention." Booklist

Includes bibliographical references

Mooney, Chris

Storm world; hurricanes, politics, and the battle over global warming. Harcourt 2007 392p il map $26

Grades: 11 12 Adult **363.7**

1. Hurricanes 2. Greenhouse effect

ISBN 978-0-15-101287-9; 0-15-101287-3

LC 2007-09742

"This is certainly one of the most thought-provoking and accessible accounts of climate change to appear since Katrina." Booklist

Includes bibliographical references

Parks, Peggy J., 1951-

Coal power. ReferencePoint Press 2010 96p il (Compact research. Energy and the environment) $26.95

Grades: 8 9 10 11 12 **363.7**

1. Coal 2. Energy resources

ISBN 978-1-60152-107-1; 1-60152-107-3

LC 2009-40878

"—The first book discusses the seriousness of toxic and electronic waste, the effectiveness of cleanup efforts, and future challenges. The second title examines the global demand for coal power, environmental impacts of burning and mining it, and the future of the industry. In a concise, objective manner, the books investigate historical, economic, political, and environmental issues." SLJ

Includes bibliographical references

Petersen, Christine

★ **Controlling** Earth's pollutants. Marshall Cavendish Benchmark 2010 112p il (Environment at risk) lib bdg $39.93

Grades: 6 7 8 9 10 **363.7**

1. Pollution

ISBN 978-0-7614-4005-5; 0-7614-4005-4

LC 2008-30816

This book provides "information on pollution, the interrelationships of the natural world, environmental problems both natural and man-made, the relative risks associated with these problems, and solutions for resolving and/or preventing them." Publisher's note

Includes bibliographical references

Pielke, Roger A.

The **climate** fix; what scientists and politicians won't tell you about global warming. [by] Roger Pielke, Jr. Basic Books 2010 276p il $26

Grades: 11 12 Adult　　　　　　　363.7

1. Greenhouse effect 2. Climate -- Environmental aspects

ISBN 978-0-465-02052-2

　　　　　　　　　　　　LC 2010-21776

"An excellent primer for getting past the politically charged debate clouding the issues. Recommended for readers confused by the deluge of conflicting climate information and willing to revisit the quandary and make their own assessments." Libr J

Includes bibliographical references

★ **Pollution:** opposing viewpoints; Louise I. Gerdes, book editor. Greenhaven Press 2011 262p il (Opposing viewpoints series) lib bdg $39.70; pa $26.50

Grades: 8 9 10 11 12　　　　　　363.7

1. Pollution

ISBN 978-0-7377-5231-1 lib bdg; 0-7377-5231-9 lib bdg; 978-0-7377-5232-8 pa; 978-0-7377-5232-7 pa

　　　　　　　　　　　　LC 2010-51681

"The authors in this . . . anthology debate several controversial questions, including whether various forms of pollution continue to be a serious problem, whether pollution poses a public health threat, and what policies and programs will best reduce pollution." Publisher's note

Includes bibliographical references

Walker, Gabrielle

★ The **hot** topic; what we can do about global warming. [by] Gabrielle Walker and Sir David King. Harcourt 2008 276p il map pa $14

Grades: 11 12 Adult　　　　　　　363.7

1. Greenhouse effect

ISBN 978-0-15-603318-3

　　　　　　　　　　　　LC 2007-45080

"This is the best overview of global warming that this reviewer has read. . . . What is most valuable about this book is that the text clearly explains to lay readers a very complex and highly controversial topic." Libr J

Includes bibliographical references

363.738　Pollutants

Newman, Patricia

Plastic, ahoy! investigating the great Pacific garbage patch. Patricia Newman; photographs by Annie Crawley. Millbrook Press 2014 48 p. (lib. bdg.: alk. paper) $30.60

Grades: 5 6 7 8 9 10　　　　　　363.738

1. Plastics 2. Marine pollution 3. Refuse and refuse disposal 4. Waste disposal in the ocean 5. Marine pollution -- Pacific Ocean

ISBN 1467712833; 9781467712835

　　　　　　　　　　　　LC 2013017773

This book, by Patricia Newman, focuses on "what happens when [plastic] ends up where it doesn't belong--like in the Pacific Ocean? How does it affect ocean life? Is it dangerous? And exactly how much is out there? A team of researchers went on a scientific expedition to find out. They explored the Great Pacific Garbage Patch, where millions of pieces of plastic have collected. The plastic has drifted there from rivers, beaches, and ocean traffic all over the world." (Publisher's note)

"Here readers travel to the Pacific Garbage Patch with three graduate-student scientists as they try to determine the effect of plastics on the sea. There's solid explanation of their hypotheses and research, and emphasis on the researchers' experiences lends a personal feel. Questions of how plastic may harm the oceans, its inhabitants, and even humans encourage further inquiry." Horn Book

Streissguth, Tom

The **role** of industry; Tom Streissguth; Michael E. Mann consulting editor. Greenhaven Press 2011 158 p. (Confronting global warming) (hardcover) $37.10

Grades: 9 10 11 12　　　　　　　363.738

1. Climate change 2. Global warming 3. Industrial revolution 4. Renewable energy resources 5. Clean energy industries

ISBN 9780737751765

　　　　　　　　　　　　LC 2011005924

This book, a volume of the Confronting Global Warming series, explores the role and impact of industry on the environment. It covers areas related to global warming including the effects of industry emissions on the climate as well as various international commitments to curb them, such as the Montreal Protocol to curb ozone depletion and the 1997 Kyoto Protocol to the United Nations Framework Convention on Climate Change (UNFCCC). Also discussed are green industries active in promoting alternative energy.

Includes bibliographical references (p. 138-144) and index

363.8　Food supply

Food; Jan Grover, book editor. Greenhaven Press 2008 220p (Current controversies) lib bdg $37.40; pa $25.95

Grades: 7 8 9 10 11 12　　　　　　363.8

1. Diet 2. Nutrition

ISBN 978-0-7377-3793-6 lib bdg; 0-7377-3793-X lib bdg; 978-0-7377-3794-3 pa; 0-7377-3794-8 pa

　　　　　　　　　　　　LC 2007-39167

An anthology of essays offering different viewpoints on topics including nutrition, the safety of the food supply, childhood obesity's link to fast food and snack foods, and organic foods.

Includes bibliographical references

363.9　Population problems

Birth control: opposing viewpoints; Beth Rosenthal, book editor. Greenhaven Press 2009 221p (Opposing viewpoints series) lib bdg $37.40; pa $25.95

Grades: 7 8 9 10 11 12   **363.9**
1. Birth control
ISBN 978-0-7377-4194-0 lib bdg; 978-0-7377-4195-7 pa

LC 2008-26069

An anthology of essays featuring opposing views on the topic of birth control. "The chapters in Birth Control . . . move from broad inquiries ('How does birth control affect society?') to specific topics: should the government fund sex education?" Booklist

Includes bibliographical references

Wittenstein, Vicki Oransky

Reproductive rights; who decides? Vicki Oransky Wittenstein. Twenty-First-Century Books 2014 160 p. color illustrations $38.65

Grades: 8 9 10 11 12   **363.9**
1. Reproduction 2. Birth control 3. Birth control -- History 4. Family planning -- History 5. Reproductive rights -- History
ISBN 9781467741873; 1467741876

LC 2014040830

This book, by Vicki Oransky Wittenstein, examines how "as society changes--and as new reproductive technologies expand the possibilities for controlling and initiating pregnancy--Americans will continue to debate reproductive rights for all. Throughout history, men and women have always found ways to control reproduction. Others turned to methods that are still used in the twenty-first century, such as abstinence, condoms, and abortions." (Publisher's note)

"Well written and impeccably researched, this volume will appeal to budding activists and feminists and to those concerned about human rights." SLJ

Includes bibliographical references and index

364 Criminology

Crime and criminal behavior; general editor, William J. Chambliss. SAGE 2011 323p (Key issues in crime and punishment) $80

Grades: 10 11 12   **364**
1. Crime
ISBN 978-1-4129-7855-2; 1-4129-7855-6

LC 2011292306

Covers topics such as the age of consent, euthanasia and assisted suicide, gambling, guns, internet pornography, marijuana and other drug laws, religious convictions, and terrorism and extremism.

Includes bibliographical references

★ **Crime** and criminals: opposing viewpoints; Christina Fisanick, book editor. Greenhaven Press 2009 253p il (Opposing viewpoints series) lib bdg $39.70; pa $27.50

Grades: 9 10 11 12   **364**
1. Crime 2. Criminals 3. Administration of criminal

justice
ISBN 978-0-7377-4360-9 lib bdg; 978-0-7377-4359-3 pa

LC 2009-21918

Articles in this anthology cover issues regarding crime and punishment in America, including prisoners' rights, what can be done to deter crime, and rehabilitation of prisoners.

Includes bibliographical references

Ekirch, A. Roger

Birthright; the true story that inspired Kidnapped. W.W. Norton & Co. 2010 xxiii, 258p il map $24.95

Grades: 11 12 Adult   **364**
1. Kidnapping 2. Trials (Kidnapping)
ISBN 978-0-393-06615-9; 0-393-06615-0

LC 2009-33194

"Ekirch provides the necessary context for understanding the characters and events in the tale, including changing courtship and child-rearing practices, the deference that tied poverty-stricken Catholic tenants to landlords and, most important, the kidnapping trade that authorities had difficulty eliminating. An engrossing familial and legal tale told with dash and clarity." Kirkus

Includes bibliographical references

Juvenile crime and justice; general editor, William J. Chambliss. SAGE 2011 336p (Key issues in crime and punishment) $80

Grades: 10 11 12   **364**
1. Crime 2. Corrections 3. Law enforcement 4. Juvenile delinquency 5. Administration of criminal justice
ISBN 978-1-4129-7858-3; 1-4129-7858-0

LC 2011292309

Presents arguments both in favor of and opposed to various treatments, programs, and punishments, examining issues such as youth curfews, juveniles in adult courts, legal representation for juveniles, juvenile boot camps, group homes, and out-of-home placement.

"An excellent purchase for students interested in serious research." SLJ

Includes bibliographical references

Simpson, Colton

Inside the Crips; life inside L.A.'s most notorious gang. [by] Colton Simpson with Ann Pearlman. St. Martin's Press 2005 xxiii, 323p $24.95; pa $14.95

Grades: 11 12 Adult   **364**
1. Crips (Gang) 2. Gang members
ISBN 0-312-32929-6; 0-312-30930-X pa

LC 2005-42704

The author "provides an insider's perspective on day-to-day life in the Crips, the gang's history (including quite a bit about its rival, the Bloods), and the plight of growing up in the 'hood while wanting a better life. . . . This unvarnished portrayal of gang life is enlightening and even inspiring about a subject badly in need of illumination." Booklist

Wolcott, David B.

Crime and punishment in America; [by] David B. Wolcott and Tom Head. Facts on File 2010 417p il map (American experience) $85; pa $21.95

Grades: 11 12 Adult   **364**

1. Punishment 2. Reference books 3. Administration of criminal justice 4. Crime -- United States

ISBN 978-0-8160-6247-8; 978-0-8160-7897-4 pa

LC 2008-13372

This is a "fascinating glimpse into the history and development of the American criminal justice system and the social contexts that contributed to its evolution from 1500 to now. . . . The chronologically arranged chapters include narrative text describing the crimes and punishments of the period followed by a two to three-page chronicle of events and selections from relevant primary documents." Libr J

Includes glossary and bibliographical references

364.089   Racism--Criminology

African Americans and criminal justice; an encyclopedia. edited by Delores D. Jones-Brown, Beverly D. Frazier, and Marvie Brooks. Greenwood 2014 631 p. illustrations, portraits (pbk.: alk. paper) $100

Grades: Adult   **364.089**

1. African Americans 2. Administration of criminal justice -- United States 3. African American criminals 4. United States -- Race relations 5. Discrimination in capital punishment -- United States 6. Discrimination in criminal justice administration -- United States 7. Criminal justice, Administration of -- Moral and ethical aspects -- United States

ISBN 0313357161; 9780313357169

LC 2013042831

This book edited by Delores D. Jones-Brown, Beverly D. Frazier, and Marvie Brooks "comprises descriptive essays documenting the ways in which people of African descent have been victimized by oppressive laws enacted by local, state, and federal authorities in the United States. The entries also describe how Blacks became disproportionately represented in national crime statistics, largely through their efforts to resist legalized oppression in early American history." (Publisher's note)

"The text provides coverage of law and criminal justice practices from the precolonial period up to the present and a candid, inclusive assessment of how black Americans have come to be strongly identified with criminality. Summing Up: Recommended. Lower-division undergraduates and above; general readers." Choice

364.1   Criminal offenses

Bugliosi, Vincent

Helter skelter; the true story of the Manson murders. {by} Vincent Bugliosi with Curt Gentry. 25th anniversary ed; Norton 1994 528p il $25; pa $13.95

Grades: 11 12 Adult   **364.1**

1. Homicide 2. Prisoners 3. Murderers

ISBN 0-393-08700-X; 0-393-32223-8 pa

LC 94-20957

A reissue of the title published 1974

"This book by the prosecutor at the Tate-LaBianca murder trial tells the inside story of the Manson Family murders, the investigations, and the trial." Libr J

Capote, Truman

In cold blood; a true account of a multiple murder and its consequences. Random House 2002 343p $22; pa $13

Grades: 11 12 Adult   **364.1**

1. Homicide 2. Murderers

ISBN 0-375-50790-6; 0-679-74558-0 pa

LC 2002-282920

A reissue of the title first published 1966

"Truman Capote called his account of the 1959 murder of a Kansas farm family a nonfiction novel. Using information he collected through interviews with townspeople and the killers, Capote created a vivid portrait of the criminals and graphically described the crime, the criminals' escape to Mexico, capture, trial, appeals, and hanging." HarperCollins Reader's Ency of Am Lit. 2nd edition

Dolnick, Edward

The rescue artist; a true story of art, thieves, and the hunt for a missing masterpiece. HarperCollins Publishers 2005 270p il $25.95; pa $14.95

Grades: 11 12 Adult   **364.1**

1. Artists 2. Painters 3. Art thefts

ISBN 0-06-053117-7; 978-0-06-053117-1; 0-06-053118-5 pa; 978-0-06053118-8 pa

LC 2004-62060

This is an "account of the 1994 theft of one of the world's most famous paintings, The Scream. . . . This is a tightly woven, fast-paced story." SLJ

Includes bibliographical references

★ Gangs: opposing viewpoints; Adela Soliz, book editor. Greenhaven Press 2009 213p il (Opposing viewpoints series) $39.70; pa $27.50

Grades: 8 9 10 11 12   **364.1**

1. Gangs

ISBN 978-0-7377-4366-1; 0-7377-4366-2; 978-0-7377-4365-4 pa; 0-7377-4365-4 pa

LC 2009-10705

A compendium of viewpoints—both pro and con—on several issues relating to the prevalence of gangs in American society.

Includes bibliographical references

Geary, Rick

The Lindbergh child; America's hero and the crime of the century. written and illustrated by Rick Geary. NBM/ComicsLit 2008 un il map (Treasury of XXth century murder) pa $15.95

Grades: 8 9 10 11 12 Adult   **364.1**

1. Generals 2. Air pilots 3. Graphic novels 4. Mystery graphic novels 5. Memoirists 6. Air force officers 7.

Homicide -- Graphic novels 8. Kidnapping -- Graphic novels

ISBN 978-1-56163-529-0

Charles Lindbergh was an American hero following his solo crossing of the Atlantic in an airplane. He married into a wealthy family, he and his wife had a baby, they were building their dream home. Then, one night, the baby was abducted from the house. Geary's account retraces all the highly publicized events, ransom notes (false and otherwise), as well as the string of colorful characters who all claimed they could help but instead snookered the Lindberghs. While Bruno Hauptmann was arrested, tried, convicted, and executed, there remain many questions about what really happened. Geary brings them up for readers to consider.

"A good example of the origins of modern forensics, crime-scene investigation, and celebrity hysteria, this work is an excellent choice for most collections." SLJ

Hanel, Rachael

Identity theft. Marshall Cavendish Benchmark 2011 143p il (Controversy!) lib bdg $25.95

Grades: 8 9 10 11 12 **364.1**

1. Identity theft

ISBN 978-0-7614-4901-0; 0-7614-4901-9

"Hanel explores types of identity theft, common scams, and prevention, which is a contentious point. Many argue that governmental proposals to secure data are invading people's privacy and civil liberties. . . . With rapid changes in technology and legislation, [this book is] recommended for all libraries seeking quality and current materials on [this topic]." SLJ

Hate crimes; Jennifer Bussey, book editor. Greenhaven Press 2007 237p (The history of issues) lib bdg $37.40

Grades: 9 10 11 12 **364.1**

1. Hate crimes

ISBN 978-0-7377-2869-9; 0-7377-2869-8

LC 2007-40010

An anthology of essays presenting the history of hate crimes. Topics discussed include hate groups and hate crime legislation.

Includes bibliographical references

Jacobs, Thomas A.

★ **Teen** cyberbullying investigated; where do your rights end and consequences begin? Free Spirit Pub. 2010 195p il pa $15.99

Grades: 7 8 9 10 11 12 **364.1**

1. Bullies 2. Computer crimes

ISBN 978-1-57542-339-5; 1-57542-339-1

LC 2009-43293

This title deals with the "topic of online teen harassment, by both teens and by adults. The author, a former judge, focuses on recent landmark court cases, many of them still pending, and in an informal, interactive style, each chapter discusses one case in detail, bringing together the rights of the victim as well as those of the perpetrator." Booklist

Includes glossary and bibliographical references

Marcovitz, Hal

Gangs. ABDO Pub. Co. 2010 112p il (Essential issues) lib bdg $22.95

Grades: 7 8 9 10 **364.1**

1. Gangs

ISBN 978-1-60453-954-7; 1-60453-954-2

LC 2009-29862

The text is "well-written, providing examples that put a human face to each problem. . . . [This] will be of great assistance to students writing reports." SLJ

Includes glossary and bibliographical references

Sexual violence: opposing viewpoints; Louise I. Gerdes, book editor. Greenhaven Press 2008 193p il map (Opposing viewpoints series) lib bdg $38.50; pa $26.75

Grades: 9 10 11 12 **364.1**

1. Rape 2. Violence 3. Sex crimes

ISBN 978-0-7377-4010-3 lib bdg; 978-0-7377-4011-0 pa

LC 2008-8133

First published 1997

The articles in this anthology address such topics as rape, sexual predators, pornography, and possible ways to reduce sexual violence.

Includes bibliographical references

Swift, Richard

★ **Gangs**; Richard Swift. Groundwood 2011 144 p. (Groundwork guides)

Grades: 7 8 9 10 11 12 **364.1**

1. Gangs 2. Ethnic groups 3. Urban sociology 4. Crime -- History

ISBN 088899978X pa; 0888999798; 9780888999788 pa; 9780888999795

In this book, "[a] short history, definition, and insight into the romantic idea of gangs as opposed to the actual reality of gang life, provide an overview of the book's focus. The role of poverty, family and home environment, communities and schools is explained. An explanation of the hierarchy that governs their world, code of conduct, gang locations throughout the world, differences in ethnic gangs, and an explanation for institutionalized groups . . . [is provided]. Supplementary information, such as gray pages and sidebars within chapters, provide additional material. A page of unique gang vocabulary and a timeline, complete chapter notes, further reading, viewing, and web lists, and a detailed index complete this . . . book." (Library Media Connection)

"This riveting volume, which is both comprehensive and concise, explores a complex and potentially controversial issue. Swift frames the issue against the gross social inequities that create gangs and discusses the factors that contribute to their existence, such as racism, poverty, drug use and trafficking, lack of jobs, crumbling global economies, etc. . . . Despite its conveniently compact size, the book is packed with information. . . . This interesting and accessible volume is an essential purchase." SLJ

Szumski, Bonnie

Thinking critically; by Bonnie Szumski and Jill Karson. ReferencePoint Press, Inc. 2014 80 p. illustrations, maps (Thinking critically series) (hardback) $28.95

Grades: 9 10 11 12   364.1
1. Noncitizens -- United States 2. United States -- Immigration and emigration 3. Unauthorized immigrants

ISBN 1601526261; 9781601526267

LC 2013035556

This juvenile reference book, by Bonnie Szumski and Jill Karson, "through a narrative-driven pro/con format . . . examines issues related to social networking. Topics include: How Does Illegal Immigration Affect the Economy? How Does Illegal Immigration Impact America's Safety and Security? Should Illegal Immigrants Be Offered a Path to Citizenship? [And] how Should Illegal Immigration Laws Be Enforced?" (Publisher's note)

"Illegal Immigration looks at the phenomenon's effect on this country's economy, safety, and security; the appropriate government response; and the need for a path to citizenship. For teachers wishing to use a debate approach to consideration of current political and social issues, the entire series offers useful information and presents an excellent model." Booklist

Includes bibliographical references and index
Illegal immigration

Trost, Cathy

President Kennedy has been shot; by the Newseum with Cathy Trost and Susan Bennett. Sourcebooks 2003 300p il $29.95; pa $19.95

Grades: 11 12 Adult   364.1
1. Presidents 2. Senators 3. Members of Congress
ISBN 1-4022-0158-3; 1-4022-0317-9 pa

LC 2003-15512

This is a "multimedia reliving of Kennedy's assassination, beginning with Air Force One landing at Love Field and ending with the president's internment at Arlington National Cemetery. The commentaries from some of the nation's foremost journalists, including Mike Wallace, Dan Rather, and Walter Cronkite, have a clarity, drama, and intensity that only newsmen of their stature can provide. . . . The book-CD combination is so well done that many readers will feel as if they have experienced that fateful day." SLJ

Includes bibliographical references

364.15 Offenses against the person

Bascomb, Neal

★ The **Nazi** hunters; How a Team of Spies and Survivors Captured the World's Most Notorious Nazi. Neal Bascomb. Arthur A. Levine Books, an imprint of Scholastic Inc. 2013 256 p. (hardcover: alk. paper) $16.99

Grades: 6 7 8 9 10   364.15
1. War crimes 2. War criminals 3. Nazi hunters 4. Nazis -- Biography 5. Secret service -- Israel 6. Holocaust, Jewish (1939-1945) 7. World War, 1939-

1945 -- Atrocities
ISBN 0545430992; 9780545430999; 9780545431002; 9780545562393

LC 2012041757

YALSA Award for Excellence in Nonfiction for Young Adults (2014)

In this book, by Neal Bascomb, "Adolf Eichmann was among the Gestapo war criminals who managed to escape from Europe and establish new lives in Argentina. The search for him involved an international group of Nazi hunters who left no stone unturned to determine where and how he had fled, find him and bring him to justice." (Kirkus Reviews)

"This is a splendid example of fascinating storytelling blended with significant historical events." Booklist

Broyles, Janell

Frequently asked questions about hate crimes; Barbara Dunkell, Janell Broyles. Rosen Pub. 2012 64 p. col. ill. (FAQ: teen life) (library) $31.95

Grades: 7 8 9 10 11 12   364.15
1. Hate crimes 2. Discrimination
ISBN 1448855624; 9781448855629

LC 2011015910

This book, which looks at hate crimes, is part of the FAQ: Teen Life series, which "focuses on a wide variety of timely, high-interest issues for adolescents. . . . Each title provides excellent contextual information about the topic, dispels common myths, and answers key questions concerning each issue. The authors also provide lists of vital questions to ask teachers, guidance counselors, and other specialists." (Voice of Youth Advocates)

Includes bibliographical references and index

Coe, Alexis

Alice and Freda Forever; A Murder in Memphis. by Alexis Coe. Houghton Mifflin Harcourt 2014 208 p. illustrations, map $16.99

Grades: 9 10 11 12 Adult   364.15
1. Lesbians 2. Trials (Homicide) 3. Memphis (Tenn.) -- History 4. Mentally ill -- Institutional care
ISBN 1936976609; 9781936976607

This book, by Alexis Coe, focuses on a murder that took place in Tennessee in 1892. "[19]-year-old Alice Mitchell had planned to pass as a man in order to marry her [17]-year-old fiancée Freda Ward, but when their love letters were discovered, they were forbidden from ever speaking again. Freda adjusted to this fate with an ease that stunned a heartbroken Alice. Her desperation grew with each unanswered letter. . . .On January 25, Alice publicly slashed her ex-fiancée's throat." (Publisher's note)

"The year was 1892, and 19-year-old Alice Mitchell was in love with Freda Ward, 17. She determined that if she couldn't marry Freda, nobody else would, either. The two women devised a plan to marry, with Alice posing as a man. However, their scheme was uncovered, and their families forbade the relationship. Freda moved on with her life and discovered other loves. Alice was unable to accept life without Freda and decided to kill her former lover when she visited Memphis...Additionally, the book provides a foundation for discussion of sociocultural themes, such as how LGBT relationships have historically been viewed by society, gender and femininity, and even journalism." SLJ

Larson, Erik

The **devil** in the white city; murder, magic, and madness at the fair that changed America. Erik Larson. Crown 2003 xi, 447p ill., maps $25.95

Grades: 11 12 Adult **364.15**
1. Homicide 2. Murderers 3. World's Columbian Exposition (1893: Chicago, Ill.)
ISBN 0609608444; 9780609608449

LC 20020154046
International Horror Guild Awards: Best Nonfiction (2003); Edgar Allan Poe Awards: Best Fact Crime (2004)

This nonfiction "tale of Chicago Worlds' Fair of 1893 focuses primarily on two men: Daniel H. Burnham, the architect who was the driving force behind the fair, and Henry H. Holmes, a sadistic serial killer working under the cover of the busy fair. . . Burnham and his partner, John Root, the leading architects in Chicago, were tapped for the job, and they in turn called on Frederick Law Olmstead, Louis Sullivan, and Richard M. Hunt to help them build the world's greatest fair. . . . Unbeknownst to any of them, Holmes, a charismatic, handsome doctor, had arrived in the city and built a complex with apartments, a drugstore, and a vault, which he used to trap his victims until they suffocated." (Booklist)

This is an account of how "H.H. Holmes (born Herman Webster Mudget) dispatched somewhere between 27 and 200 people, mostly single young women, in the churning new metropolis of Chicago; many of the murders occurred during (and exploited) the city's finest moment, the World's Fair of 1893. Larson's breathtaking new history is a novelistic yet wholly factual account of the fair and the mass murderer who lurked within it." Publ Wkly

Includes bibliographical references (p. [423]-429) and index.

Sebold, Alice

Lucky; Alice Sebold. Scribner 1999 254p (hbk.) $25

Grades: 11 12 Adult **364.15**
1. Rape victims 2. Autobiographies 3. Victims of crimes 4. Rape victims -- United States -- Case studies 5. Trials (Rape) -- United States -- Case studies
ISBN 9780684857824; 0684857820

LC 99019697
This "memoir . . . [by] Alice Sebold reveals how her life was utterly transformed when, as an eighteen-year-old college freshman, she was brutally raped and beaten in a park near campus. What propels this chronicle of her recovery is Sebold's indomitable spirit - as she struggles for understanding; as her dazed family and friends sometimes bungle their efforts to provide comfort and support; and as, ultimately, she triumphs, managing through grit and coincidence to help secure her attacker's arrest and conviction." (Publisher's note)

364.152 Homicide

Alphin, Elaine Marie

An **unspeakable** crime; the prosecution and persecution of Leo Frank. Carolrhoda Books 2010 152p il lib bdg $22.95

Grades: 9 10 11 12 **364.152**
1. Children 2. Lynching 3. Trials (Homicide) 4. Atlanta (Ga.) 5. Murder victims 6. Factory managers
ISBN 978-0-8225-8944-0; 0-8225-8944-3

LC 2008-42300
"This detailed, fully documented account tells of the trial and lynching of a Jewish factory superintendent, falsely accused of the 1913 rape and murder of teenager Mary Phagan in Atlanta. Alphin digs into the roots of anti-Semitism that grew from post-Reconstruction hardship and shows that Leo Frank was viewed, and despised, by many in his community as a 'privileged Yankee Jew.' . . . The details are made even more horrific when accompanied by the numerous black-and-white photos, including court scenes and a picture postcard of the lynching." Booklist

Includes glossary and bibliographical references

Aretha, David

The **murder** of Emmett Till. Morgan Reynolds Pub. 2007 160p il (The civil rights movement) lib bdg $27.95

Grades: 7 8 9 10 11 12 **364.152**
1. Children 2. Lynching 3. Murder victims 4. Mississippi -- Race relations 5. African Americans -- Civil rights
ISBN 978-1-59935-057-8; 1-59935-057-2

LC 2007-26250
"The heinous murder of Emmett Till galvanized the civil rights movement and raised the nation's awareness of the extreme racism in the South. . . . This title . . . details the events surrounding Till's murder, the trial and acquittal of his killers, and the nation's racial climate before and after this milestone in civil rights history." Booklist

Includes bibliographical references

Crowe, Chris

Getting away with murder: the true story of the Emmett Till case. Phyllis Fogelman Bks. 2003 128p il map $18.99

Grades: 7 8 9 10 **364.152**
1. Racism 2. Children 3. Lynching 4. Trials (Homicide) 5. Murder victims 6. Mississippi -- Race relations
ISBN 0-8037-2804-2

LC 2002-5736
This is the story of "the black 14-year-old from Chicago who was brutally murdered while visiting relatives in the Mississippi Delta in 1954. . . . The gruesome, racially motivated crime and the court's failure to convict the white murderers was a powerful national catalyst for the civil rights movement. . . . Crowe's powerful, terrifying account does justice to its subject in bold, direct telling, supported by numerous archival photos and quotes from those who remember." Booklist

Includes bibliographical references

Cullen, Dave

★ **Columbine**. Twelve 2009 417p $26.99
Grades: 10 11 12 Adult **364.152**
1. School shootings 2. Columbine High School

(Littleton, Colo.)
ISBN 978-0-446-54693-5; 0-446-54693-3
LC 2008-31441

This is an account of the shootings at Columbine High School in 1999.

This book "is an excellent work of media criticism, showing how legends become truths through continual citation; a sensitive guide to the patterns of public grief . . . and, at the end of the day, a fine example of old-fashioned journalism." N Y Times Book Rev

Includes bibliographical references

Faryon, Cynthia J.

Guilty of being weird; the story of Guy Paul Morin. Cynthia J. Faryon. James Lorimer & Co. 2013 144 p. (Lorimer Real Justice) (hardcover) $18.95
Grades: 7 8 9 10 11 12   **364.152**
1. False accusation
ISBN 1459400933; 9781459400931

This book, by Cynthia J. Faryon, is part of the "Lorimer Real Justice" series. "At twenty-four, Guy Paul Morin was considered a bit strange. . . . So when the nine-year-old girl next door went missing, the police were convinced that Morin was responsible. . . . This book tells his story, showing how the justice system not only failed to help an innocent young man, but conspired to convict him." (Publisher's note)

"Structured like a data log, each chapter covers a specific date. . . . Teens interested in CSI can turn a critical eye to badly executed procedures and biased criminal investigation. . . . However, the choppy organization by date and the differences between the Canadian and American legal system will limit the book's appeal." SLJ

Geary, Rick

The **saga** of the bloody Benders; the infamous homicidal family of Labette County, Kansas. NBM/ComicsLit 2007 un il $15.95
Grades: 9 10 11 12 Adult   **364.152**
1. Graphic novels 2. Mystery graphic novels 3. Homicide -- Graphic novels
ISBN 978-1-56163-498-9

In Kansas, around the year 1870, the Bender family ran the Bender Inn and grocery store in Labette County, Kansas. Soon after they open their inn to travelers, people start to disappear, usually people with a fair amount of money with them. When the authorities investigate, the family disappears, and the people of Labette County make grisly discoveries in the Bender Inn's cellar. Geary includes just enough gory details for readers to comprehend the Benders' crimes. Earlier volumes in this series focused on famous nineteenth century murders and criminals, but the crimes of this more obscure family are just as dastardly for true crime aficionados.

The **terrible** Axe-Man of New Orleans; music and lyrics by Rick Geary. NBM Publishing/ComicsLit 2010 un il map (Treasury of XXth century murder) $15.99
Grades: 9 10 11 12 Adult   **364.152**
1. Graphic novels 2. Mystery graphic novels 3. Homicide -- Graphic novels 4. New Orleans (La.) --

History -- Graphic novels
ISBN 978-1-56163-581-8
LC 2010-926782

Geary tells the story of the Terrible Axe-Man, who murdered grocers in New Orleans right after World War I. In each case, the murderer removed a piece of the door to the house, borrowed an axe found at the property, then aimed straight for the head of his victim. From May 23, 1918 to October 27, 1919, the Axe-Man killed six people and badly wounded six more, then disappeared. Geary lays out the known facts, then shows some of the speculation. The black and white art helps to mitigate the violence and gore, so the book is suitable for teens who enjoy true-life mysteries.

"Geary's exacting, historically accurate approach makes this . . . a natural for true-crime fans as well as comics lovers." Booklist

Includes bibliographical references

Houser, Aimee

Tragedy in Tucson; the Arizona shooting rampage. by Aimee Houser. ABDO Pub. Co. 2012 112 p. col. ill., col. map (hc) $34.22
Grades: 6 7 8 9 10   **364.152**
1. Gun control 2. Schizophrenia 3. Murder -- Arizona -- Tucson 4. Mental health laws -- United States 5. Firearms and crime -- Arizona -- Tucson
ISBN 1617833126; 9781617833120
LC 2011038452

This book "examines . . . the shooting of Representative Gabrielle Giffords and 18 others in Tucson, Arizona." It "explores the man behind the shooting, Jared Loughner, and his history of mental illness, the disease schizophrenia, Giffords's rise in politics, [and] the political climate in America, including the hot button issue of health-care reform, Giffords's fight for her life, and the effects of this event on society. Also discussed are the gun laws in America." (Publisher's note)

"...These titles are excellent introductions to these important topics, particularly for developing an analytical framework for debate." SLJ

Includes bibliographical references (p. 104-109, 112) and index

364.16 Offenses against property

Hynson, Colin

Cyber crime; by Colin Hynson. Smart Apple Media 2012 44 p. col. ill. (Inside crime) (library) $35.65
Grades: 7 8 9 10   **364.16**
1. Computer crimes 2. Computer crimes -- Prevention
ISBN 1599203960; 9781599203966
LC 2010043232

This book, part of the Crime and Detection Series, focuses on cyber crime. "These titles examine the diversity of crimes committed around the world. Each . . . illustrated, oversized volume has a photograph or reproduction on every spread, many times taking up a full page." Andrew Grant-Adamson "looks at hackers, viruses, and computer crimes that have come to light in the age of the Internet." (School Library Journal)

Includes bibliographical references (p. 43) and index

Juettner, Bonnie

Blackmail and bribery; by Bonnie Juettner. Lucent Books 2009 104 p. col. ill. (Crime scene investigations) (hardcover) $35.45

Grades: 7 8 9 10 **364.16**
1. Bribery 2. Forensic sciences 3. Extortion 4. White collar crimes
ISBN 1420500686; 9781420500684
LC 2008025864

This book, part of the Crime Scene Investigations series, focuses on blackmail and bribery. This series "unveils the tools and techniques used by today's (and yesterday's) professionals. . . . Each title focuses on a particular type of crime, and includes features like crime stats, facts versus fiction sections, full-color photos and more." (Publisher's note)

Includes bibliographical references (p. 92-95) and index.

364.2 Causes of crime and delinquency

Gun violence: opposing viewpoints; Louise I. Gerdes, book editor. Greenhaven Press 2010 257p il map (Opposing viewpoints series) $39.70; pa $27.50

Grades: 8 9 10 11 12 **364.2**
1. Guns 2. Violence 3. Gun control 4. Firearms
ISBN 978-0-7377-4966-3; 978-0-7377-4967-0 pa
LC 2010-26764

Articles in this anthology cover the issues surrounding gun violence, including gun control.

Includes bibliographical references

364.3 Offenders

Stemple, Heidi E. Y.

Bad girls; sirens, Jezebels, murderesses, thieves, and other female villains. Jane Yolen and Heidi E. Y. Stemple; illustrated by Rebecca Guay. Charlesbridge 2012 176 p. (reinforced for library use) $18.95

Grades: 6 7 8 9 10 11 12 **364.3**
1. Women criminals 2. Criminals -- Biography 3. Femmes fatales -- Biography
ISBN 1580891853; 9781580891851
LC 2012000783

This book, by Jane Yolen and Heidi E. Stemple, illustrated by Rebecca Guay, examines the history of "twenty-six . . . notorious women. Each bad girl has a rotten reputation, but there are two sides to every tale. Decide whether Tituba was really a conspiring witch or just a humble housemaid. Analyze the evidence stacked for and against Lizzie Borden. And what made the brazen Cleopatra so dishonorable . . . or honorable?" (Publisher's note)

Includes bibliographical references and index

364.36 Juvenile delinquents

Merino, Noel

Juvenile crime; Noel Merino, book editor. Greenhaven Press 2010 146p il map (Introducing issues with opposing viewpoints) lib bdg $35.75

Grades: 7 8 9 10 **364.36**
1. Juvenile delinquency
ISBN 978-0-7377-4735-5; 0-7377-4735-8
LC 2009-48144

"Examines the causes of juvenile crime and school violence, including gang activity, single parenthood, bullying, and mental illness. Explores the treatment of juvenile offenders in the criminal justice system and the relative importance of rehabilitation and punishment in sentencing. Discusses what can and should be done to prevent crime and violence by children." Publisher's note

Includes bibliographical references

Mooney, Carla

★ **Teen** violence; by Carla Mooney. ReferencePoint Press 2013 96 p. (hardcover) $27.95

Grades: 9 10 11 12 **364.36**
1. Bullies 2. Violence 3. Teenagers
ISBN 160152496X; 9781601524966
LC 2012033700

This book by Carla Mooney is part of the Teenage Problems series and focuses on teen violence. It "looks at the reasons for the phenomenon, considers such issues as media influence, and speculates on how violence can be stopped. Bullying and violence around dating are also discussed." Charts and graphs are included. (Booklist)

Includes bibliographical references and index.

364.6 Penology

Corrections; general editor, William J. Chambliss. SAGE 2011 327p (Key issues in crime and punishment) $80

Grades: 10 11 12 **364.6**
1. Crime 2. Corrections 3. Administration of criminal justice
ISBN 978-1-4129-7856-9; 1-4129-7856-4
LC 2011292308

Covers the correctional system and offers arguments for and against the practice of the laws and policies that comprise corrections, from parole and probation to imprisonment, to the application of the death penalty.

Includes bibliographical references

Marcovitz, Hal

Exposing torture; centuries of cruelty. by Hal Marcovitz. Twenty-First Century Books 2015 112 p. illustrations (some color) (lib. bdg.: alk. paper) $34.65

Grades: 9 10 11 12 **364.6**
1. Torture -- History 2. Crimes against humanity
ISBN 1467750492; 9781467750493; 9781467763066
LC 2014003211

This book, by Hal Marcovitz, "tackles . . . complex questions, delving into the history of torture around the world, from the . . . methods of torture in ancient societies to the humiliating forms of psychological and sexual torture of the twenty-first century. . . . Readers will examine the ethical and moral dilemmas of torture, while learning more about the international efforts to ensure the humanitarian treatment of individuals in a variety of circumstances." (Publisher's note)

"Though none of the issues presented is explored in any great depth, this overview provides readers with a useful starting place for further exploration." Kirkus

Includes bibliographical references and index

Schenwar, Maya

Locked down, locked out; why prison doesn't work and how we can do better. Maya Schenwar. Berrett-Koehler Publishers 2014 240 p. (paperback) $18.95

Grades: Adult **364.6**

1. Reformatories 2. Prisons -- United States 3. Administration of criminal justice -- United States 4. Corrections -- United States 5. Imprisonment -- United States 6. Justice, Administration of -- United States 7. Criminals -- Rehabilitation -- United States 8. Alternatives to imprisonment -- United States

ISBN 9781626562691; 1626562695

LC 2014021463

This book, by Maya Schenwar, "shows how the institution that locks up 2.3 million Americans and decimates poor communities of color is shredding the ties that, if nurtured, could foster real collective safety. But looking toward a future beyond imprisonment, Schenwar profiles community-based initiatives that successfully deal with problems--both individual harm and larger social wrongs--through connection rather than isolation." (Publisher's note)

"This book should be read by students and professionals in criminal justice. Since it has an easy-to-read style, it should also be of interest to the general reader who simply wishes to know what it's like to be behind bars." LJ

364.66   Capital punishment

The **death** penalty; Lauri S. Friedman, book editor. Greenhaven Press 2011 143p il map (Introducing issues with opposing viewpoints) $35.75

Grades: 7 8 9 10 **364.66**

1. Capital punishment -- United States

ISBN 978-0-7377-4938-0

LC 2010-30748

"This collection of articles helps students hone in on the main arguments that are used to support and to condemn the death penalty." Publisher's note

Includes bibliographical references

The **Death** penalty; Jean Alicia Elster, book editor. Greenhaven Press 2005 237p (History of issues) lib bdg $34.95; pa $23.70

Grades: 9 10 11 12 **364.66**

1. Capital punishment -- United States

ISBN 0-7377-1911-7 lib bdg; 0-7377-1912-5 pa

LC 2004-43661

"This volume explores the history of capital punishment in America from the 17th century to the present while covering such . . . topics as cruel and unusual punishment, deterrence, race and gender discrimination, the morality of state-sanctioned killing, and protecting the innocent defendant." Publisher's note

Includes bibliographical references

The **death** penalty: opposing viewpoints; Diane Andrews Henningfeld, book editor; Bonnie Szumski, publisher; Helen Cothran, managing editor. Greenhaven Press 2006 223p il (Opposing viewpoints series) hardcover o.p. pa $23.70

Grades: 8 9 10 11 12 **364.66**

1. Capital punishment

ISBN 0-7377-2929-5; 0-7377-2930-9 pa

LC 2005-52743

"Powerful people and organizations contribute essays to the death-penalty debate. Supreme Court Justice Antonin Scala argues that the death penalty is just, and his former colleague, Sandra Day O'Connor, debates whether juveniles should be exempt from it. This nonbiased, comprehensive look at one of today's most difficult issues will be helpful for students writing persuasive essays and for debate groups." SLJ

Includes bibliographical references

★ The **ethics** of capital punishment; Christine Watkins, book editor. Greenhaven Press 2011 127p (At issue. Social issues) lib bdg $31.80; pa $22.50

Grades: 9 10 11 12 **364.66**

1. Capital punishment

ISBN 978-0-7377-5171-0 lib bdg; 978-0-7377-5172-7 pa

LC 2010-36737

A compendium of opinion on the moral and ethical issues surrounding capital punishment, including whether it deters murder and whether it's too expensive to retain.

Includes bibliographical references

Henderson, Harry

★ **Capital** punishment; 3rd ed; Facts on File 2006 316p il (Library in a book) $45

Grades: 11 12 Adult **364.66**

1. Capital punishment

ISBN 0-8160-5708-7

LC 2005-13671

First published 1991 under the authorship of Stephen A. Flanders

A look at both sides of this controversial issue from social, political, ethical, and religious perspectives. Includes a glossary, bibliographies, and Internet sources.

Includes bibliographical references

Kuklin, Susan

★ **No** choirboy; murder, violence, and teenagers on death row. Henry Holt and Co. 2008 212p il $17.95

Grades: 8 9 10 11 12   **364.66**

1. Capital punishment 2. Juvenile delinquency
ISBN 978-0-8050-7950-0; 0-8050-7950-5

LC 2007-46940

"The book opens with candid interviews that introduce three inmates, all of them teenagers when they committed their crimes. . . . This eye-opening account will likely open minds. . . . The book concludes with solid back matter—notes, glossary, bibliography, and index." Horn Book

Includes glossary and bibliographical references

364.973 Crime--United States

Kanefield, Teri, 1960-

Guilty; crime, punishment, and the changing face of criminal justice. by Teri Kanefield. Houghton Mifflin Harcourt 2014 144 p. illustrations $16.99

Grades: 5 6 7 8 9 10   **364.973**

1. Law -- United States 2. Administration of criminal justice 3. Guilt (Law) -- United States 4. Judicial process -- United States 5. Criminal justice, Administration of -- United States
ISBN 0544148967; 9780544148963

LC 2013042010

This book, by Teri Kanefield, "takes a look at the evolution of the American justice system. . . . [She] scrutinizes the judicial system by examining current and past crimes. The book opens by defining the word 'criminalize' (as 'an act that the law makes punishable') and goes on to argue that the American judicial system is flawed. . . . [She] offers both famous cases, such as Plessy v. Ferguson and more obscure ones." (School Library Journal)

"A series of case studies, the book's first section, about deciding what behavior to criminalize, is most successful; the second and third--on punishment and due process--are also provocative. Kanefield allows readers to understand how notions of right and wrong change over time and across cultures, helping them begin to understand the complexities of crime and punishment. Reading list. Bib., glos., ind." Horn Book

Includes bibliographical references (pages 123-130) and index

365 Penal and related institutions

★ **America's** prisons: opposing viewpoints; Noah Berlatsky, book editor. Greenhaven Press 2010 224p il map (Opposing viewpoints series) $39.70; pa $27.50

Grades: 8 9 10 11 12   **365**

1. Prisons -- United States
ISBN 978-0-7377-4956-4; 0-7377-4956-3; 978-0-7377-4957-1 pa; 0-7377-4957-1 pa

LC 2009-50927

"This collection of opposing viewpoints provides students an opportunity to weigh the merits of arguments that support or oppose the operation of America's prisons." Publisher's note

Includes bibliographical references

Edge, Laura Bufano

Locked up; a history of the U.S. prison system. by Laura B. Edge. Twenty-First Century Books 2009 112p il (People's history) lib bdg $31.93

Grades: 6 7 8 9 10   **365**

1. Prisons -- United States
ISBN 978-0-8225-8750-7; 0-8225-8750-5

LC 2008-26883

"Using primary resources, photographs, and solid research, Edge has written a well-organized and engaging history of our prison system. . . . This book can serve as an excellent resource for reports." SLJ

Includes bibliographical references

Ferro, Jeffrey

★ **Prisons**; Rev. ed; Facts On File, Inc. 2011 312p (Library in a book) $45

Grades: 11 12 Adult   **365**

1. Prisons -- United States
ISBN 978-0-8160-8236-0; 978-1-4381-3398-0 ebook

LC 2010-49855

First published 2006

This book "examines the state of U.S. prisons and related issues. It focuses on the development of prisons in the United States and how the competing goals of punishment and rehabilitation have shaped the evolution of criminal correction. An overview presents statistics on U.S. prisons and explores the issues behind those statistics, including racial disparity among prisoners and the causes of recidivism. The financial costs of running prisons and the mixed record of private prisons are examined, and laws and legislation relating to issues of incarceration are reviewed." Publisher's note

Includes bibliographical references

Fisher, Robin Gaby

The **boys** of the dark; a story of betrayal and redemption in the deep south. with Michael O'McCarthy and Robert W. Straley. St. Martin's Press 2010 247p $24.99

Grades: 11 12 Adult   **365**

1. Reformatories 2. Adult child abuse victims
ISBN 978-0-312-59539-5

LC 2009-45734

"A journalist collaborates with two former juvenile detention-center inmates to expose a scandal. With the assistance of O'McCarthy and Straley, who served time more than 50 years ago, [Fisher] . . . investigates the Florida School for Boys. For decades, misbehaving boys, many of them preteens, were committed by judges or extralegal authorities as punishment for offenses serious and frivolous alike. . . . During the '50s and '60s, when O'McCarthy and Straley were youthful residents, beatings with leather whips might have led to numerous deaths, and certainly led to physical and emotional scars. . . . A worthy exploration of a regrettably long-lasting true-crime nightmare." Kirkus

Hubner, John

Last chance in Texas; the redemption of criminal youth. Random House 2005 xxv, 277p $25.95

Grades: 11 12 Adult **365**
1. Juvenile delinquency 2. Giddings State School (Tex.)
ISBN 0-375-50809-0

LC 2005-42892

"Readers of this eye-opening account will find themselves reflecting on their own attitudes about juvenile justice as it's administered today." Booklist

Prisons; Sylvia Engdahl, book editor. Greenhaven Press 2010 230p (Current controversies) $39.70; pa $27.50

Grades: 9 10 11 12 **365**
1. Prisons -- United States
ISBN 978-0-7377-4460-6; 0-7377-4460-X; 978-0-7377-4461-3 pa; 0-7377-4461-8 pa

LC 2009024277

Articles in this anthology present differing opinions on the state of prisons in the United States.

Includes bibliographical references

368.4   Government-sponsored insurance

DeWitt, Larry

Social security; a documentary history. [by] Larry W. DeWitt, Daniel Béland, and Edward D. Berkowitz. CQPress 2008 557p il $115

Grades: 10 11 12 Adult **368.4**
1. Social security
ISBN 978-0-87289-502-7; 0-87289-502-5

LC 2007-30363

"Anyone who has an interest in the development of the Social Security program will find this to be an interesting and valuable resource." Am Ref Books Annu, 2008

Includes glossary and bibliographical references

370.117   Multicultural and bilingual education

★ **Bilingual** education; Janel D. Ginn, book editor. Greenhaven Press 2008 111p (At issue. Education) lib bdg $29.95; pa $21.20

Grades: 10 11 12 **370.117**
1. Bilingual education
ISBN 978-0-7377-3912-1 lib bdg; 0-7377-3912-6 lib bdg; 978-0-7377-3913-8 pa; 0-7377-3913-4 pa

LC 2007-938125

"This volume presents 12 signed essays from passionate proponents of and opponents to bilingual education. . . . This volume is well suited for debate topics and provides a list of organizations to contact for more information about the controversy." SLJ

Includes bibliographical references

370.71   Education

Growing schools; librarians as professional developers. Debbie Abilock, Kristin Fontichiaro, and Violet H. Harada, editors. Libraries Unlimited 2012 390 p. (pbk.) $45

Grades: Professional **370.71**
1. Teachers -- Training 2. Educational technology 3. School libraries -- Information technology 4. Libraries and teachers -- United States -- Case studies 5. Teachers -- Training of -- United States -- Case studies 6. Educational technology -- Study and teaching -- Case studies 7. Information technology -- Study and teaching -- Case studies 8. Technological literacy -- Study and teaching -- Case studies 9. Teachers -- In-service training -- United States -- Case studies 10. School librarian participation in curriculum planning -- Case studies 11. Academic libraries -- Relations with faculty and curriculum -- Case studies
ISBN 1610690419; 9781610690416

LC 2012016191

In this book, "editors [Debbie] Abilock, [Kristin] Fontichiaro, and [Violet H.] Harada examine ways school librarians can act as professional developers within their pedagogical communities. Thirty-two articles in sixteen thematic chapters offer real-world examples of how teacher librarians have leveraged their skills and expertise to provide learning experiences for other teachers, community members, and students." (Voice of Youth Advocates)

"This book promotes the role of the school librarian as a leader in school, district, and online professional development in 16 essays written by school librarians, school district personnel, and professors...A rich smorgasbord of ideas, this book would be invaluable for an individual librarian looking to become a professional development leader, and for district librarians to use in planning and implementing meaningful district-wide professional development." (Library Media Connection)

Includes bibliographical references and index

McKeown, Rosalyn

Into the classroom; a practical guide for starting student teaching. Rosalyn McKeown. University of Tennessee Press 2011 xv, 165 p.p (pbk.) $14.95

Grades: Adult Professional **370.71**
1. Teaching 2. Student teaching 3. Student teaching -- United States
ISBN 1572338164; 9781572338166

LC 2011011282

This book offers suggestions to those "just starting out in a secondary school classroom. . . . After exploring the pitfalls of inexperience and providing . . . guidance on maintaining order in the classroom, [Rosalyn] McKeown focuses on teaching skills. She advises readers on writing objectives and lesson plans, creating interesting ways to start and end class, introducing variety into the classroom, lecturing, asking meaningful questions, and using visual aids." (Amazon.com)

Includes bibliographical references and index.

370.9 Education--History, geographic treatment, biography

Friedman, Ian C.

Education reform; Rev. ed.; Facts on File 2011 264p il (Library in a book) $45

Grades: 9 10 11 12 Adult   **370.9**
1. Reference books 2. Education -- United States 3. Education -- Aims and objectives
ISBN 978-0-8160-8238-4

                LC 2010-43133

First published 2004

"Coverage includes: current developments regarding teacher incentives, curriculum standards, standardized tests, and homeschooling; the goals and requirements of 'Race to the Top,' a $5 billion education grant program rolled out as part of the Obama administration's Recovery and Reinvestment Act of 2009; . . . [a] survey of the events and major debates surrounding education reform in the United States, from earliest influences through the present; . . . [and] statistics on charter school enrollment and operations." Publisher's note

Includes bibliographical references

371 Schools and their activities; special education

★ **Education:** opposing viewpoints; David Haugen and Susan Musser, book editors. Greenhaven Press 2009 290p il (Opposing viewpoints series) lib bdg $39.70; pa $27.50

Grades: 9 10 11 12   **371**
1. School choice 2. Public schools 3. Multicultural education 4. Religion in the public schools
ISBN 978-0-7377-4208-4 lib bdg; 0-7377-4208-9 lib bdg; 978-0-7377-4209-1 pa; 0-7377-4209-7 pa

                LC 2008-31458

Articles in this anthology discuss the state of education in the United States, including standardized testing, alternatives to public education, the role of religion in public education, and ways to improve schools.

Includes bibliographical references

371.1 Schools and their activities

Kozol, Jonathan

Letters to a young teacher. Crown Publishers 2007 288p hardcover o.p. pa $14

Grades: 11 12 Adult Professional   **371.1**
1. Teaching
ISBN 978-0-307-39371-5; 0-307-39371-2; 978-0-307-39372-2 pa; 0-307-39372-0 pa

                LC 2007-2689

"The book will delight and encourage first-year (or for that matter, 40th-year) teachers who need Kozol's reminders of the ways that their beautiful profession can bring joy and beauty, mystery and mischievous delight into the hearts of little people in their years of greatest curiosity." Publ Wkly

Includes bibliographical references

371.2 School administration; administration of student academic activities

Mueller, Jonathan

★ **Assessing** critical skills; [by] Jon Mueller. Linworth Pub. 2008 132p pa $44.95

Grades: Adult Professional   **371.2**
1. Educational tests and measurements
ISBN 978-1-58683-282-7; 1-58683-282-4

                LC 2008-19609

"According to Mueller, educators need training to instruct students on skills such as problem-solving, information literacy, reasoning, collaboration, and critical thinking. In this thoroughly researched, organized, and concise book, Mueller stresses the need to incorporate authentic assessment throughout the curriculum in order to effectively teach and measure these skills. The author provides numerous detailed tasks and rubrics making it easy for the classroom teacher and media specialist to create authentic assessments." Libr Media Connect

Includes bibliographical references

Odden, Allan R.

Improving student learning when budgets are tight; Allan R. Odden. Corwin 2012 xxi, 184 p.p

Grades: Adult Professional   **371.2**
1. Schools -- Finance 2. Academic achievement 3. Schools -- Administration 4. School budgets -- United States 5. School improvement programs -- United States
ISBN 1452217084; 9781452217086

                LC 2011045908

This book by Allan R. Odden "offers a comprehensive framework to enhance student achievement in good times and in bad. . . . Odden outlines a school improvement action plan focused sharply on student learning and then shows how to target resources to implement each strategy in that plan. . . . Educators will find a wide range of real-life examples of schools and districts that have implemented these strategies and significantly improved student learning." (Publisher's note)

Includes bibliographical references and index

371.3 Methods of instruction and study

Harada, Violet H.

Collaborating for project-based learning in grades 9-12; [by] Violet H. Harada, Carolyn H. Kirio, Sandra H. Yamamoto. Linworth Pub. 2008 xxii, 226p il pa $44.95

Grades: Adult Professional   **371.3**
1. Project method in teaching 2. Instructional materials centers
ISBN 978-1-58683-291-9; 1-58683-291-3

                LC 2007-42180

"This resource offers school media specialists insight into learning opportunities available through project-based learning (PBL). . . . The text opens with a clear, detailed, and accessible definition of PBL, puts PBL in context with school reform and the issue of school dropout rates, moves toward explaining and illustrating the school media specialist's responsibilities in maintaining standards of information literacy throughout the PBL process, and reviews the necessary steps in planning actual projects. . . . The balance of theory and practical guidance make the book a sure fit for most high school-based professional collections." Voice Youth Advocates

Includes bibliographical references

Landy, Robert J.

Theatre for change; education, social action and therapy. Robert J. Landy and David Montgomery. Palgrave Macmillan 2012 xxviii, 309 p.p (pbk.) $29

Grades: Adult Professional   **371.3**

1. Drama in education 2. Drama -- Therapeutic use
ISBN 0230243665; 9780230243651; 9780230243668

LC 2012023003

This book by Robert Landy and David T. Montgomery "explores how Educational Theatre, Applied Theatre and Drama Therapy facilitate change within schools, community centres, prisons, and theatres." The book "provid[es] an international overview of the latest work and thinking in Drama and Education, and feature[es] interviews with a worldwide variety of leading practitioners and theorists." (Publisher's note)

Includes bibliographical references (p. 259-304) and index

November, Alan C.

Empowering students with technology; 2nd ed.; Corwin Press 2010 115p il pa $25.95

Grades: Adult Professional   **371.3**

1. Internet in education 2. Computer-assisted instruction
ISBN 978-1-4129-7425-7; 1-4129-7425-9

LC 2009-43649

First   published   2001   by   Skylight Professional Development

"Discusses the relationship of technology to today's learning environment and the potential for technology to encourage students to learn collaboratively. This . . . edition emphasizes current topics such as information literacy, global connectivity, and the educational applications of utilities such as digital cameras and cell phones. The book's usefulness is as a reasource for teachers and librarians to consult in creating, planning, and assisting with school projects in all subjects." Libr Media Connect

Includes bibliographical references

Richardson, Will

Blogs, wikis, podcasts, and other powerful Web tools for classrooms; 3rd ed.; Corwin 2010 171p il pa $31.95

Grades: Adult Professional   **371.3**

1. Weblogs 2. Podcasting 3. Internet in education 4. Online social networks 5. Wikis (Computer science) 6. Teaching -- Aids and devices
ISBN 978-1-4129-7747-0; 1-4129-7747-9

LC 2009-51376

First published 2006

"The book is well-written and comprehensive. The author's engaging writing style will instill confidence in readers that they will be able to easily integrate the same technologies with the same results in their classrooms. Readers will not want to stop reading this eye-opening and inspirational book. It is jam-packed with proven ideas, and individuals, especially educators, will want to try out these technologies." Libr Media Connect

Includes bibliographical references

Vascellaro, Salvatore

Out of the classroom and into the world; learning from field trips, educating from experience, and unlocking the potential of our students and teachers. Salvatore Vascellaro. Perseus Distribution Services 2011 xviii, 250 p.p ill. (paperback) $19.95

Grades: Adult Professional   **371.3**

1. Teaching 2. Education -- United States 3. Active learning -- United States 4. School field trips -- United States 5. School improvement programs -- United States
ISBN 1595586822; 9781595586827

LC 2011016423

In this book, author Salvatore Vascellaro "visits a rich variety of classrooms transformed by innovative field trip curricula--showing how students' hearts and minds are opened as they discover how a suspension bridge works, see what connects them to the people and places of their neighborhood, and come to understand the ecosystem of a river by following it to its source. Vascellaro also shows that what teachers can offer children is fueled by their own engagement with the world." (Publisher's note)

Includes bibliographical references (p. 221-237) and index.

371.33   Teaching aids, equipment, materials

Baule, Steven M.

Social networking for schools; by Steven M. Baule and Julie E. Lewis. Linworth 2012 220 p. (hardcopy: alk. paper) $45

Grades: Professional   **371.33**

1. Schools 2. Social media 3. Educational technology 4. Students -- Social networks 5. Educational technology -- Social aspects 6. Education -- Effect of technological innovations on
ISBN 1586835378; 9781586835378; 9781586835385

LC 2012014933

This book by Steven M. Baule and Julie E. Lewis "take[s] a comprehensive look at the topic of social media use in schools. Starting with the numerous justifications for integrating social media into schools, it provides real-world examples of how to seamlessly integrate social media within your classroom or library, examines the methodologies for crafting the necessary policies and procedures to ensure that staff members." (Publisher's note)

"This detailed book will help schools incorporate social media tools into communication, curriculum, and professional development...This is an excellent resource that provides a blueprint for utilizing social media to facilitate teaching and learning." (Library Media Connection)

Includes bibliographical references and index

371.4 Student guidance and counseling

Morgan, Genevieve

Undecided; navigating life and learning after high school. Genevieve Morgan. Zest Books 2014 256 p. $14.99

Grades: 9 10 11 12 Adult   **371.4**

1. College choice 2. Vocational guidance 3. Life skills -- Handbooks, manuals, etc.

ISBN 1936976323; 9781936976324

LC 2013951198

"This comprehensive handbook outlines the different options available to teens after high school and provides suggestions on how to follow each path. . . . It covers everything from SAT preparation and personal statements to trade school pros and cons and advice on how to prepare for life in the military. Full of checklists, anecdotes, brainstorming activities, and journal exercises, 'Undecided' leaves no stone unturned and no option unconsidered." (Publisher's note)

"A helpful guide full of good, sensible advice to teens feeling overwhelmed by the prospect of major life transitions." Kirkus

Includes bibliographical references and index

Zasloff, Beth

Hold fast to dreams; a college guidance counselor, his students, and the vision of a life beyond poverty. Beth Zasloff and Joshua Steckel. The New Press 2014 320 p. (hardcover: alk. paper) $25.95

Grades: Adult   **371.4**

1. Students 2. College choice 3. Academic achievement 4. Educational counseling 5. College choice -- United States 6. Academic achievement -- United States 7. Minority students -- Counseling of -- United States

ISBN 159558904X; 9781595589040; 9781595589286

LC 2013043224

This book, by Beth Zasloff and Joshua Steckel, "follows the lives of ten . . . students as they navigate the vast and obstacle-ridden landscape of college in America. . . . At a time when the idea of 'college for all' is alternately embraced and challenged, this . . . book uncovers . . . the many ways the American education system fails in its promise as a ladder to opportunity." (Publisher's note)

"This is more than a heart-wrenching look at the particular struggles of 10 inner-city students. It is a profound examination of the obstacles faced by low-income students to get into and through college and the kinds of reforms needed to make higher education and the upward mobility it promises more accessible." Booklist

Includes bibliographical references

371.5 School discipline and related activities

★ **Bully;** an action plan for teachers and parents to combat the bullying crisis. edited by Lee Hirsch and Cynthia Lowen; with Dina Santorelli. Perseus Books Group 2012 viii, 295 p.p ill. $15.99

Grades: Adult Professional   **371.5**

1. Bullies 2. Bullying 3. Bullying -- Prevention 4. Cyberbullying -- Prevention 5. Bullying in schools --

Prevention

ISBN 1602861846; 1602861854; 9781602861848; 9781602861855

LC 2012289039

"This companion book to the documentary film Bully was edited by filmmaker [Lee]Hirsch and writer/producer [Cynthia] Lowen, with contributing chapters by a number of celebrities, authors, experts, government officials, and educators. Part homage to the film, part resource, the book interweaves the stories of children who have been bullied with practical information and advice for parents and other readers." (Publishers Weekly)

Includes bibliographical references (p. 281-289) and index

371.7 Student welfare

Hunnicutt, Susan

School shootings; Susan Hunnicutt, book editor. Greenhaven Press 2006 102p (At issue. Crime) lib bdg $28.70; pa $19.95

Grades: 9 10 11 12   **371.7**

1. School violence

ISBN 0-7377-2416-1 lib bdg; 978-0-7377-2416-5 lib bdg; 0-7377-2417-X pa; 978-0-7377-2417-2 pa

LC 2005-54525

"This anthology explores various explanations for rampage school shootings, and examines ways communities have responded." Publisher's note

Includes bibliographical references

Lily, Henrietta M.

School violence and conflict resolution; Marilyn E. Smith, Matthew Monteverde, Henrietta M. Lily. Rosen Pub. 2013 48 p.

Grades: 9 10 11 12   **371.7**

1. School violence 2. Conflict management 3. Conflict management -- United States 4. School violence -- United States -- Prevention

ISBN 9781448868919

LC 2012003027

"These newest additions to the Teen Mental Health series tackle topics that are at once timely and timeless in adolescents' lives. Filled with statistics on the recent history of violence in schools, School Violence and Conflict Resolution explains potential warning signs of violent offenders and how schools are combating violence, particularly through peer mediation. All of these easy-to-read books emphasize seeking support from friends, family, and counselors and even suggest "10 Great Questions to Ask a Guidance Counselor." Other features include "Myths and Facts" (such as the myth that only females worry about their bodies and self-image), a glossary, and a list of related organizations. These titles are good beginning resources for both health reports and personal research." (Booklist)

Includes bibliographical references and index

Schier, Helga

The **causes** of school violence; by Helga Schier. ABDO Publishing 2008 112 p. ill. (chiefly col.) (library) $34.22

Grades: 7 8 9 10   **371.7**
1. School violence 2. School violence -- United States
ISBN 160453060X; 9781604530605
                      LC 2007031920
This book is part of the Essential Viewpoints series and looks at the causes of school violence. The series "examines critical debates occurring today, including the legislation that has shaped the issue as well as the numerous sides of each argument. Color photos, detailed maps, and informative sidebars accompany" the text. (Publisher's note)
Includes bibliographical references (p. 102-103) and index.

★ **School** violence; Lucinda Almond, book editor. Greenhaven Press 2008 232p (Current controversies) lib bdg $37.40; pa $25.95
Grades: 7 8 9 10 11 12   **371.7**
1. School violence
ISBN 978-0-7377-3795-0 lib bdg; 0-7377-3795-6 lib bdg; 978-0-7377-3796-7 pa; 0-7377-3796-4 pa
                      LC 2007-29879
An anthology of essays presenting differing viewpoints on topics such as school bullying, the factors that contribute to school violence, gun control laws, and alternative juvenile interventions.
Includes bibliographical references

371.82   Specific groups of students; schools for specific groups of students

Cahill, Sean
LGBT youth in America's schools; Jason Cianciotto and Sean Cahill. The University of Michigan Press 2012 236 p. (pbk.: alk. paper) $30
Grades: Adult Professional   **371.82**
1. Bullies 2. Gay youth 3. Discrimination 4. Schools -- Administration 5. Gay students -- United States 6. Sexual minorities -- Education 7. Lesbian students -- United States 8. Bisexual students -- United States 9. Homosexuality and education -- United States 10. Transgender youth -- Education -- United States
ISBN 0472031406; 9780472028320; 9780472031405; 9780472118229
                      LC 2011045478
In this book, "[Jason] Cianciotto and [Sean] Cahill use statistics and real-life anecdotes to show the pervasiveness of gender- and sexual orientation-based harassment in American schools, and argue for institutional reform and policy changes. . . . [R]esearch shows that . . . more young people are coming out . . . while still technically a minor, and thus subject to the rules of their educational institutions, and increasingly the abuse of their peers, teachers, and school administrators." (Publishers Weekly)
Includes bibliographical references and index.

Mortenson, Greg
Stones into schools; promoting peace with books, not bombs, in Afghanistan and Pakistan. Viking 2009 420p il map $26.95
Grades: 11 12 Adult   **371.82**
1. Humanitarian intervention 2. Schools -- Pakistan 3. Schools -- Afghanistan
ISBN 978-0-670-02115-4
                      LC 2009-30812
In this follow-up to Three cups of tea (2009), the author "continues the story of how the Central Asia Institute (CAI) built schools in northern Afghanistan. Descriptions of the harsh geography and more than one near-death experience impress readers as new faces join Mortenson's loyal 'Dirty Dozen' as they carefully plot a course of school-building through the Badakshan province and Wakhan corridor. . . . To blandly call this book inspiring would be dismissive of all the hard work that has gone into the mission in Afghanistan as well as the efforts to fund it. Mortenson writes of nothing less than saving the future, and his adventure is light years beyond most attempts." Booklist

Perez, William
We are Americans; undocumented students pursuing the American dream. foreword by Daniel Solorzano. Stylus 2009 xxxiv, 161p $70; pa $22.50
Grades: 9 10 11 12 Adult   **371.82**
1. Unauthorized immigrants 2. Discrimination in education 3. Illegal aliens 4. United States -- Immigration and emigration
ISBN 978-1-57922-375-5; 978-1-57922-376-2 pa
                      LC 2009-26206
The author "plumbs the stories of students living with the constant threat of deportation for an answer to the question, 'What does it mean to be an American?' Raised in this country by parents who gained access illegally, the 16 high school, college and postgraduate students profiled here (standing in for 65,000 nationwide) have each embraced our language, culture and collective dream, but are denied pathways to success. . . . No matter what one's position is on legalizing immigrants, this collection of inspiring, heartbreaking stories puts a number of unforgettable faces to the issue, making it impossible to defend any one side in easy terms or generalities." Publ Wkly
Includes bibliographical references

371.9   Special education

Cohen, Leah Hager
Train go sorry; inside a deaf world. Vintage Bks. 1995 296p pa $14.95
Grades: 11 12 Adult   **371.9**
1. Deaf -- Means of communication 2. Lexington School for the Deaf (New York, N.Y.)
ISBN 0-679-76165-9
                      LC 94-23501
First published 1994 by Houghton Mifflin
"Well organized and beautifully written." Booklist

Conroy, Pat
The **water** is wide. Dial Press Trade Paperbacks 2006 294p pa $14
Grades: 11 12 Adult   **371.9**
1. Children with social disabilities 2. African Americans

-- Education 3. Public schools -- South Carolina
ISBN 978-0-553-38157-3; 0-553-38157-1

LC 2005-285152

First published 1972 by Houghton Mifflin

"A young white teacher goes to an island off the coast of South Carolina to teach a group of functionally illiterate black children. Yamacraw Island is backward and primitive, a world for the most part left untouched by the 20th Century. . . . By ignoring the textbooks and concentrating on meaningful situations and dialogue . . . he begins to make headway. He also, unfortunately arouses the ire of the powers that be and, after fierce struggle, is fired." Libr J

Kozol, Jonathan

Savage inequalities; children in America's schools. HarperPerennial 1992 261p pa $14.95
Grades: 11 12 Adult   **371.9**
1. Public schools 2. Segregation in education 3. Children with social disabilities
ISBN 0-06-097499-0; 978-0-06-097499-2

First published 1991 by Crown

"Jonathan Kozol has written an impassioned book, laced with anger and indignation, about how our public education system scorns so many of our children. 'Savage Inequalities' is also an important book, and warrants widespread attention" N Y Times Book Rev

Includes bibliographical references

Paquette, Penny Hutchins

★ **Learning** disabilities; the ultimate teen guide. [by] Penny Hutchins Paquette, Cheryl Gerson Tuttle. Scarecrow Press 2003 301p il (It happened to me) lib bdg $32.50; pa $17.95
Grades: 7 8 9 10   **371.9**
1. Learning disabilities
ISBN 0-8108-4261-0 lib bdg; 0-8108-5643-3 pa

LC 2002-17588

"Far more detailed than similiar books from other publishers." Voice Youth Advocates
Includes bibliographical references

Parks, Peggy J., 1951-

Learning disabilities. ReferencePoint Press 2009 96p il (Compact research. Diseases and disorders) lib bdg $25.95
Grades: 7 8 9 10   **371.9**
1. Learning disabilities
ISBN 978-1-60152-077-7; 1-60152-077-8

LC 2009-13445

"Parks explains what learning disabilities are and discusses the causes and overcoming them. The book's strength is that it explains how learning disabilities differ from other types of disorders. . . . Teens will find the overall organization of [this] succinct and easy-to-read [book] useful and attractive." SLJ
Includes bibliographical references

Salzman, Mark

True notebooks. Alfred A. Knopf 2003 330p hardcover o.p. pa $13.95

Grades: 11 12 Adult   **371.9**
1. Creative writing 2. Juvenile delinquency
ISBN 0-375-41308-1; 0-375-72761-2 pa

LC 2002-43435

"While teaching writing to 17-year-olds detained in Los Angeles Central Juvenile Hall, Salzman found himself surprised by the boys' talent. The teens' heartwarming, funny voices are included in his irresistible, provocative memoir." Booklist

372   Specific levels of education

Lukenbill, W. Bernard

Health information in a changing world; practical approaches for teachers, schools, and school librarians. [by] W. Bernard Lukenbill and Barbara Froling Immroth. Libraries Unlimited 2010 244p il $45
Grades: Adult Professional   **372**
1. Health education 2. Youth -- Health and hygiene 3. Health -- Information services
ISBN 978-1-59884-398-9; 1-59884-398-2

LC 2010-7505

"This is quite an impressive book and a real treasure for any professional involved with health education, whether for the classroom, public health, or personal counseling." Voice Youth Advocates
Includes bibliographical references

Mary Elizabeth (Mary Elizabeth Miller)

Painless spelling; Mary Elizabeth. 3rd edition Barrons Educational Series, Inc. 2011 284 p. ill. pbk $9.99
Grades: 7 8 9 10   **372**
1. Spelling 2. English language -- Spelling
ISBN 0764147137; 9780764147135

LC 2010941464

First published 1998

Provides guidelines for spelling American English words; explains visual and sound patterns, letter combinations, syllables, compound words, and hyphenation; and includes practical exercises.

372.4   Reading

Bernadowski, Carianne

Research-based reading strategies in the library for adolescent learners; [by] Carianne Bernadowski and Patricia Liotta Kolencik. Libraries Unlimited 2010 108p il pa $40
Grades: Adult Professional   **372.4**
1. Reading 2. School libraries
ISBN 978-1-58683-347-3; 1-58683-347-2

LC 2009-21198

"This book explains six proven strategies—question/answer, think-alouds, reciprocal teaching, anticipation guides, questioning the author, and SQR3 (survey, question, read, recite, and review)—for reading comprehension and three strategies (Semantic Feature Analysis, word maps/journals,

and Frayer Models/word sorts) for vocabulary building. . .
. Although the strategies are standard approaches, weaving
in librarian roles makes this book useful for librarians who
serve teens." Booklist

Includes bibliographical references

Teaching literacy skills to adolescents using
Coretta Scott King Award winners. Libraries Unlimited 2009 136p il pa $35

Grades: Adult Professional   372.4
1. Coretta Scott King Award 2. African Americans in
literature 3. Teenagers -- Books and reading
ISBN 978-1-58683-337-4; 1-58683-337-5

LC 2009-15279

"The book includes award-winning book selections and
Coretta Scott King Honor Books. It is a showcase for African-American authors' works, and helps educators working
with adolescent students and their reading needs. . . . Each
chapter covers one title and contains an annotation, grade
level discussion starters, writing prompts, pre-reading activities, literary strategies for reading, post-reading activities, additional information about the author, and additional
resources. This book would be a great professional resource,
and a must have for those educators that teach adolescents."
Libr Media Connect

Includes bibliographical references

Grover, Sharon
Listening to learn; audiobooks supporting literacy. by Sharon Grover and Lizette D. Hannegan.
American Library Association 2011 xi, 188 p.p (alk.
paper) $45

Grades: Adult Professional   372.4
1. Literacy 2. Audiobooks 3. Educational technology
4. Reading -- United States 5. Children -- Books and
reading 6. Libraries -- Special collections -- Audiobooks
7. Literacy -- Study and teaching -- United States 8.
School librarian participation in curriculum planning
ISBN 0838911072; 9780838911075

LC 2011041814

Authors Sharon Grover and Lizette D. Hannegan "make
the case that audiobooks not only present excellent opportunities to engage the attention of young people but also
advance literacy. 'Listening to Learn' connects audiobooks
with K-12 curricula and demonstrates how the format can
support national learning standards and literacy skills."
(Publisher's note)

"This informative resource establishes the literacy benefits of audiobooks as an alternate reading delivery method...
Discussions of audiobook formats and recommended sources for building an audiobook collection are also included.
The authors provide a collaborative resource that would
benefit a classroom, library, or home setting." (Library
Media Connection)

Includes bibliographical references (p. 175-178)
and index

372.5   The arts

Art and social justice education; culture as commons. edited by Therese Quinn, John Ploof, and

Lisa Hochtritt. Routledge 2012 xxiii, 201 p.p
ill. (some col.)

Grades: Adult Professional   372.5
1. Culture 2. Educators 3. Education -- Curricula
4. Arts -- Study and teaching 5. Art in education --
Social aspects 6. Social justice -- Study and teaching 7.
Teaching -- Social aspects -- United States 8. Education
-- Social aspects -- United States
ISBN 0415879078; 9780203852477; 9780415879064;
9780415879071

LC 2011027006

Editor Therese Quinn "offers inspiration and tools for
educators to craft critical, meaningful, and transformative
arts education curriculum and arts integration projects. The
images, descriptive texts, essays, and resources are grounded within a clear social justice framework and linked to ideas
about culture . . . Proposing that art can contribute in a wide
range of ways to the work of envisioning and making a more
just world, this imaginative . . . sourcebook of contemporary
artists' works and education resources advances the field of
arts education." (Amazon)

Includes bibliographical references and index

372.6   Language arts (Communication skills)

Chatton, Barbara
Using poetry across the curriculum; learning to
love language. 2nd ed; Libraries Unlimited 2010
241p pa $40

Grades: Adult Professional   372.6
1. Poetry -- Study and teaching
ISBN 978-1-59158-697-5; 1-59158-697-6

LC 2009-36711

First published 1993

"With the emphasis in most schools on improving literacy, fluency, and reading and writing test scores, this book
is extremely valuable. Sections are divided into various curricula areas. Each section begins with the national standards
for that discipline, then a few paragraphs explain how the
poetry in the extensive listing can be used. . . . Because all
teachers must incorporate writing into their teaching, having
relevant poetry for their curriculum and ideas on how to use
it, will make this book popular." Libr Media Connect

Includes bibliographical references

372.62   Written and spoken expression

★ **Breakfast** on Mars and 37 Other delectable Essays; Edited by Rebecca Stern and Brad Wolfe.
Roaring Brook Press 2013 xii, 211p.p ill. (hardcover) $16.99

Grades: 6 7 8 9 10 11 12   372.62
1. American essays 2. Authorship -- Handbooks,
manuals, etc. 3. Essay -- Authorship 4. English language
-- Composition and exercises -- Study and teaching
(Elementary) 5. English language -- Composition and
exercises -- Study and teaching (Middle school)
ISBN 1596437375; 9781596437371

LC 2012040918

This book, edited by Rebecca Stern and Brad Wolfe, is a collection of essays meant for middle- and high-school students. "Thirty-eight short essays . . . come from Sloane Crosley, Sarah Prineas, Ned Vizzini, Scott Westerfeld, Rita Williams-Garcia, and more. Assigned a genre . . . and topic . . . , the contributors [wrote essays meant to] inspire and entertain." (Publishers Weekly)

"This handy volume fills a gap. Thirty-eight essays for young readers by contemporary writers demonstrate that "essays can be just as enjoyable to read as fiction"...An important collection that ought to become a staple in writing classes." Kirkus

373.1 Organization and activities in secondary education

Braun, Linda W.

★ **Teens,** technology, and literacy; or, Why bad grammar isn't always bad. Libraries Unlimited 2007 105p il pa $30

Grades: Adult Professional **373.1**
1. Literacy 2. Information technology 3. Bibliographic instruction 4. Computer-assisted instruction 5. Teenagers -- Books and reading
ISBN 1-59158-368-3; 978-1-59158-368-4
LC 2006-31714

"Braun shows teachers, administrators, and librarians how to incorporate today's technologies into the development of literacy skills. The author backs up the grammar used in IMs and text messaging by explaining how these technologies promote better literacy in the classroom. . . . This book is a must for most collections." SLJ
Includes bibliographical references

Fireside, Bryna J.

Choices for the high school graduate; a survival guide for the information age. 5th ed.; Infobase Pub. 2009 261p il $34.95; pa $16.95

Grades: 9 10 11 12 **373.1**
1. Vocational guidance
ISBN 978-0-8160-7617-8; 0-8160-7617-0; 978-0-8160-7618-5 pa; 0-8160-7618-9 pa
LC 2008-47835

First published 1997
"Presents students with a wide range of options available to them during and after high school—from early college admissions and entering a trade to joining the military and volunteering abroad." Publisher's note
Includes bibliographical references

Katz, Eric D.

High school's not forever; [by] Jane Bluestein and Eric Katz. HCI Teens 2005 302p il pa $12.95

Grades: 7 8 9 10 11 12 **373.1**
1. High school students
ISBN 0-7573-0256-4
LC 2005-50232

"Culled from the responses of some 2000 high and post-high school students, this title gives voice to young people who have lived through the experience and who offer both affirming and cautionary tales as they attempted to navigate the uncertain seas of friendship, depression, academic achievement, drugs, and sexuality. . . . There is no question that this book will enhance most YA collections." SLJ
Includes bibliographical references

Nichols, Beverly

★ **Improving** student achievement; 50 research-based strategies. Linworth Pub. 2008 110p il pa $44.95

Grades: Adult Professional **373.1**
1. Academic achievement 2. Instructional materials centers 3. Schools -- Administration
ISBN 978-1-58683-293-3; 1-58683-293-X
LC 2008-6918

"The text considers 50 data-driven interventions that represent a variety of affective and cognitive strategies. Each 'Research Tip' addresses a specific strategy, and is placed in broad categories such as literacy, curriculum alignment, and assessment. . . . Media specialists need to take leadership roles in building school improvement initiatives, and this resource will help them." Libr Media Connect
Includes bibliographical references

Streisel, Jim

★ **High** school journalism; a practical guide. McFarland & Co. 2007 224p il $35

Grades: 9 10 11 12 **373.1**
1. College and school journalism
ISBN 978-0-7864-3060-4; 0-7864-3060-5
LC 2007-7509

"The book offers chapters on information gathering, writing, alternative coverage, packaging, and . . . information about Web-based journalism and legal rights. Each section is broken into chapters about researching, interviewing, editing, visual design, and hooking nonreaders. Teachers and students will all find something to use in this book." Libr Media Connect

373.12 High school administration

Stewart, Gail B.

★ **Teenage** dropouts; by Gail B. Stewart. ReferencePoint Press 2013 96 p. (hardcover) $27.95

Grades: 9 10 11 12 **373.12**
1. Dropouts 2. Teenagers 3. Educational sociology
ISBN 1601525060; 9781601525062
LC 2012036648

This book by Gail B. Stewart is part of the Teenage Problems series and focuses on teenage dropouts. "Today, teens without high-school diplomas will earn much less throughout their lives than those who've obtained them. The book goes on to explain why teens drop out (pregnancy often plays a role for both young women and young men). It considers the question of how dropout rates can be reduced and what can be done to help those already out of school." (Booklist)
Includes bibliographical references and index.

373.18 Students--Secondary education

Muchnick, Justin Ross

Teens' guide to college & career planning; your high school roadmap for college and career success. Justin Ross Muchnick. 12 edition Peterson's 2016 242 p. illustrations $14.95

 Grades: 8 9 10 11 12   **373.18**
 1. Vocational guidance 2. College applications 3. Colleges and universities
 ISBN 9780768939903; 0768939909

 "Whether [teens are] planning to head to a two-year or four-year college, a technical school, an apprenticeship, the military, or directly into the workforce-or even if they are still undecided-Teens' Guide is where they'll find information on the various options available and which ones may best suit their skills, needs, and desires." (Publisher's note)

 Includes bibliographical references (pages 239-242)

375   Curricula

Nichols, Beverly

 Managing curriculum and assessment; a practitioner's guide. [by] Beverly Nichols . . . [et al.] Linworth Publishing 2006 170p pa $49.95

Grades: Adult Professional   **375**
 1. Evaluation 2. Education -- Curricula
 ISBN 1-58683-216-6

            LC 2006003202

 "This is a guide by practitioners who give advice on how to respond to the laws and requirements of No Child Left Behind. It is an invaluable resource that provides new insights. . . . There are three sections to the guide with an accompanying CD that contains everything in the book and more. . . . This guide is loaded with examples and is a must have for your professional library." Libr Media Connect

 Includes bibliographical references

378   Higher education (Tertiary education)

Asher, Donald

 Cool colleges for the hyper-intelligent, self-directed, late blooming, and just plain different; 2nd ed.; Ten Speed Press 2007 287p il pa $21.95

Grades: 9 10 11 12   **378**
 1. College choice 2. Reference books 3. Colleges and universities -- United States -- Directories
 ISBN 978-1-58008-839-8; 1-58008-839-2

            LC 2007-922323

First published 2000

Profiles more than 40 innovative and unusual schools of higher learning.

Barron's profiles of American colleges 2013; Barron's Educational Series, Inc. Barron's Educa-

tional Series 2012 xiii, 1644 p.p (paperback) $28.99

 Grades: 11 12 Adult   **378**
 1. College choice 2. Colleges and universities -- United States
 ISBN 0764147846; 9780764147845

 This book offers rankings of U.S. colleges and universities. "It gives college-bound students online information and guidance to help them match their academic plans and aptitudes with the admission requirements and academic programs of every accredited four-year college in the country." (Publisher's note)

Book of Majors 2014. Henry Holt & Co 2013 1368 p. (paperback) $27.99

 Grades: 10 11 12 Adult   **378**
 1. College majors 2. College students
 ISBN 1457300222; 9781457300226

 This book is a guide to college majors. "In-depth descriptions of 200 of the most popular majors are followed by complete listings of every major offered at more than 3,800 colleges, including four-year and two-year colleges and technical schools. The 2014 edition covers every college major identified by the U.S. Department of Education—over 1,200 majors are listed in all." (Publisher's note)

★ **College** Board Guide To Getting Financial Aid, 2014. Henry Holt & Co 2013 1000 p. (paperback) $22.99

 Grades: 11 12 Adult   **378**
 1. Student aid 2. College costs 3. Education -- Finance
 ISBN 1457300192; 9781457300196

 This book looks at financial aid for college students. The "FAFSA [Free Application for Federal Student Aid] form is explained with step-by-step instructions, and the College Board's CSS/Financial Aid PROFILE form is explained by the people who administer it. The guide includes information and advice from experts on how to apply for aid, plus easy-to-compare college profiles giving the 'financial aid picture' for more than 3,000 four-year and two-year colleges and technical schools." (Publisher's note)

Kravets, Marybeth

 ★ The **K** & W guide to colleges for students with learning disabilities or attention deficit hyperactivity disorder; [by] Marybeth Kravets and Imy F. Wax. 10th ed.; Random House 2010 831p pa $29.99

Grades: 9 10 11 12 Adult   **378**
 1. Reference books 2. Learning disabilities 3. Colleges and universities -- United States -- Directories
 ISBN 978-0-375-42961-3

 Biennial. First published 1991 with title: The K & W guide to colleges for the learning disabled

 This guide "includes profiles of over 300 schools, advice from specialists in the field of learning disabilities, and strategies to help students find the best match for their needs." Publisher's note

Logue, Robert

 ★ **Fiske** guide to colleges, 2012; [by] Edward B. Fiske with Robert Logue and the Fiske guide to colleges staff. 28th ed.; Sourcebooks 2011 xxxv, 812p pa $23.99

Grades: 11 12 Adult **378**

1. College choice 2. Reference books 3. Colleges and universities -- United States -- Directories
ISBN 978-1-4022-0962-8

Annual. First published 1982 with title: The New York Times selective guide to colleges

This guide to over 310 of the best colleges and universities nationwide includes information on admissions, costs, financial aid, housing, social life, and academic strengths and weaknesses.

Morkes, Andrew

★ **College** exploration on the internet; a student and counselor's guide to more than 1,000 websites and resources. by Andrew Morkes and Amy McKenna. 2nd ed.; College & Career Press 2009 xxxviii, 296p il pa $19.95

Grades: 9 10 11 12 Adult **378**

1. College choice 2. Reference books 3. Web sites -- Directories
ISBN 978-0-9745251-4-3

LC 2008-28982

First published 2004

"The book is organized into two main sections: college resource Web sites and college/career association Web resources. . . . The sites themselves are organized alphabetically by title and offer a concise summary, the best features, and important information about the site, including whether the site is fee based. . . . This book is an essential addition to college and career collections in school and public libraries." Voice Youth Advocates

Includes bibliographical references

★ **Peterson's** four-year colleges 2012; 42nd ed.; Peterson's 2011 1987p il pa $32.95

Grades: 11 12 Adult **378**

1. Reference books 2. Colleges and universities -- United States -- Directories
ISBN 978-0-7689-3279-9

Annual. First published 1966 as part of Peterson's annual guide to undergraduate study. Formerly titled Peterson's guide to four-year colleges

This reference compiles profiles of over 2,500 accredited institutions in the United States with four year undergraduate degree programs.

★ **Peterson's** two-year colleges 2012; 42nd ed; Peterson's Publishing 2011 498p il pa $29.95

Grades: 11 12 Adult **378**

1. Reference books 2. Colleges and universities -- United States -- Directories
ISBN 978-0-7689-3278-2

Annual. First published 1966 as part of Peterson's annual guide to undergradute study. Formerly titled Peterson's guide to two-year colleges

This reference compiles profiles of over 1,500 accredited institutions in the United States with two year associate degree programs.

They teach that in college; [managing editor, Andrew Morkes] 2nd ed.; College & Career Press 2008 344p il pa $22.95

Grades: 9 10 11 12 **378**

1. Reference books 2. Colleges and universities -- Curricula 3. Colleges and universities -- United States -- Directories
ISBN 978-0-9745251-7-4

First published 2006

"With 'ripped from the headlines' immediacy for students who are not interested in run-of-the-mill professions, this invaluable resource profiles careers that fill a job market deamnd and pay well; are offered as majors by no more than 25 percent of the nation's colleges; and are fun." Voice Youth Advocates

378.1 Organization and activities in higher education

Albom, Mitch, 1958-

Tuesdays with Morrie; an old man, a young man, and life's greatest lesson. Mitch Albom. Doubleday 1997 192 p. pa $13.99; $20.00

Grades: 11 12 Adult **378.1**

1. Amyotrophic lateral sclerosis 2. Sociologists 3. College teachers 4. Brandeis University -- Faculty -- Biography 5. Death -- Psychological aspects -- Case studies 6. Teacher-student relationships -- United States -- Case studies 7. Amyotrophic lateral sclerosis -- Patients -- United States -- Biography
ISBN 076790592X pa; 0385484518

LC 96052535

This book discusses the author's relationship with his former teacher and mentor, "sociologist Morrie Schwartz. Here [Mitch] Albom recounts how . . . as the old man was dying, he renewed his warm relationship with his revered mentor. This is the . . . record of the teacher's battle with muscle-wasting amyotrophic lateral sclerosis, or Lou Gehrig's disease. The dying man, largely because of his life-affirming attitude toward his death-dealing illness, became a sort of thanatopic guru, and was the subject of three Ted Koppel interviews on Nightline. That was how the author first learned of Morrie's condition. Albom . . . calls his weekly visits to his teacher his last class, and the present book a term paper. The subject: The Meaning of Life . . . . Albom does not present a full transcript of the regular Tuesday talks. Rather, he expands a little on the professor's aphorisms." (Kirkus)

Bain, Ken

What the best college students do; Ken Bain. The Belknap Press of Harvard University Press 2012 289 p. (alk. paper) $24.95

Grades: 11 12 Adult **378.1**

1. College students 2. Academic achievement 3. College students -- United States 4. Academic achievement -- United States
ISBN 0674066642; 9780674066649

LC 2012015548

In this book, author Ken Bain "identifies the key attitudes that distinguished the best college students from their peers. These individuals started out with the belief that intelligence and ability are expandable, not fixed. This led them to make connections across disciplines, to develop a 'metacognitive' understanding of their own ways of thinking, and to find ways to negotiate ill-structured problems rather than simply looking for right answers." (Publisher's note)

"A soundly encouraging guide for college students to think deeply and for as long as it takes." Kirkus

Includes bibliographical references and index

Bardin, Matt

Zen in the art of the SAT; how to think, focus, and achieve your highest score. [by] Matt Bardin and Susan Fine. Houghton Mifflin 2005 220p il pa $7.99

Grades: 9 10 11 12   378.1
1. Scholastic Assessment Test 2. Colleges and universities -- Entrance requirements
ISBN 0-618-57488-3

LC 2005-4326

"Each chapter explores how students can use principles of Zen Buddhism to move beyond anxiety, build their confidence, and focus on solving the SAT's inscrutable, koan-like questions. . . . It's the advice about mindfulness and transforming nervous energy and negative thoughts, which readers can apply to every life experience, that really distinguishes this title." Booklist

Includes bibliographical references

Berent, Polly

Getting ready for college. Random House 2003 209p il pa $12.95

Grades: 9 10 11 12   378.1
1. College students 2. Colleges and universities -- United States
ISBN 0-8129-6896-4

LC 2003-41375

This "will be useful to any young person getting ready to enter the college milieu. It's a quick, easy read, enriched by quotes from teens." Booklist

Berger, Larry

Up your score; the underground guide to the SAT. by Larry Berger ... [et al.]; illustrations by Chris Kalb. 2011-2012 ed.; Workman Pub. 2010 328p il pa $12.95

Grades: 9 10 11 12   378.1
1. Scholastic Assessment Test
ISBN 978-0-7611-5873-8

First published 1987 by New Chapter Press with title: Up your S.A.T. score. Frequently revised

Presents a study guide intended to improve the readers score on the SAT test, and includes vocabulary words, concentration and memory activities, and sample test questions.

Blackballed; the black and white politics of race on America's campuses. Lawrence Ross. St. Mar-

tin's Press 2016 288 p. 8 plates; illustrations (hardback) $25.99

Grades: 11 12 Adult   378.1
1. United States -- Race relations 2. Colleges and universities -- United States 3. Racism in higher education -- United States 4. College campuses -- Social aspects -- United States 5. Discrimination in higher education. -- United States 6. African American college students -- Social conditions 7. African Americans -- Education (Higher) -- United States
ISBN 125007911X; 9781250079114

LC 2015026361

This book, by Lawrence Ross, argues "America's colleges have fostered a racist environment that makes them a hostile space for African American students. Blackballed exposes the white fraternity and sorority system, with traditions of racist parties, songs, and assaults on black students; and the universities themselves, who name campus buildings after racist men and women. It also takes a deep dive into anti-affirmative action policies." (Publisher's note)

"Highly recommended for high school junior and seniors, college students, and educators." LJ

Burtnett, Frank

★ **Bound**-for-college guidebook; a step-by-step guide to finding and applying to colleges. Rowman & Littlefield Education 2009 156p $24.95

Grades: 9 10 11 12 Adult   378.1
1. College choice 2. College applications 3. Colleges and universities -- Entrance requirements
ISBN 978-1-57886-992-3; 1-57886-992-7

LC 2008-39425

In this guide to preparing for college, the author "focuses mainly on the admission process, offering checklists, outlines, and user-friendly qualitative exercises to help students get organized, meet deadlines, and determine which colleges fit their individual objectives. . . . This essential guide is highly recommended for all college-bound students and their parents." Libr J

Includes bibliographical references

Castleman, Benjamin L.

Summer melt; supporting low-income students through the transition to college. Benjamin L. Castleman, Lindsay C. Page. Harvard Education Press 2014 208 p. illustrations (library) $56.95

Grades: Professional   378.1
1. College applications 2. High school students
ISBN 9781612507415; 9781612507422

LC 2014940440

In this book, authors Benjamin L. Castleman and Lindsay C. Page explain that "summer can be a time of significant attrition among college-intending seniors—especially those from low-income families. . . . [They explore] the complex factors that contribute to this trend—the absence of school support, confusion over paperwork, lack of parental guidance, and the teenage tendency to procrastinate." (Publisher's note)

"Well researched and accessible, with notes, references, and appendixes (including a sample communication plan), this is a ready resource for education majors, high school counselors, college registrars, and first-year resource specialists." LJ

Cohen, Harlan

The **naked** roommate; and 107 other issues you might run into in college. 3rd ed.; Rev. and updated; Sourcebooks 2009 465p pa \$14.99

Grades: 9 10 11 12   **378.1**

1. College students

ISBN 978-1-4022-1901-6

First published 2004

This is "a hilarious and truthful book that gives high school students a look at college life. . . . The advice is sound; the tone is light." SLJ

Includes bibliographical references

Cohen, Katherine

The **truth** about getting in; a top college advisor tells you everything you need to know. Hyperion 2002 252p \$21.95; pa \$14.95

Grades: 9 10 11 12   **378.1**

1. College applications 2. Colleges and universities -- Entrance requirements

ISBN 0-7868-8747-8; 0-7868-8849-0 pa

LC 2003-266705

"Chapters cover a wide variety of topics—from gathering information about colleges and preparing for admissions tests to writing an effective essay and securing financial aid. . . . Cohen's approach is pleasant and positive." Booklist

Conley, David T.

★ **College** knowledge; what it really takes for students to succeed and what we can do to get them ready. Jossey-Bass 2005 xxii, 350p il (Jossey-Bass education series) hardcover o.p. pa \$19.95

Grades: 11 12 Adult   **378.1**

1. College students 2. Academic achievement

ISBN 0-7879-7397-1; 0-7879-9675-0 pa

LC 2004-30569

The author "recounts the preparation or lack thereof during the high school years of three college-bound students and makes it clear that there is a difference between college-eligible and college-ready. He lays out chapter by chapter what is wrong and how it can be remedied. . . . This valuable book belongs in every high school library." SLJ

Includes bibliographical references

Crossman, Anne

★ **Getting** the best out of college; insider advice for success from a professor, a dean, and a recent grad. Peter Feaver, Sue Wasiolek, Anne Crossman. Rev. and updated, 2nd ed. Ten Speed Press 2012 xiv, 289 p.p (pbk.) \$14.99

Grades: 9 10 11 12 Adult   **378.1**

1. Counseling 2. College students 3. Colleges and universities -- United States 4. College student orientation -- United States

ISBN 160774144X; 9781607741442

LC 2011051246

This book, by authors Peter Feaver, Sue Wasiolek, and Anne Crossman, "reveals insider advice that makes the hefty price tag worth it: how to impress professors, live with a roommate, pick the best courses (and do well in them), design a meaningful transcript, earn remarkable internships, prepare for a successful career after graduation, and much more." (Publisher's note)

DaSilva-Gordon, Maria

Your first year of college; from classroom to dorm room. Rosen Pub. 2010 80p il (Thinking about college) lib bdg \$30.60; pa \$14.15

Grades: 9 10 11 12   **378.1**

1. College students

ISBN 978-1-4358-3600-6 lib bdg; 1-4358-3600-6 lib bdg; 978-1-4358-8506-6 pa; 1-4358-8506-6 pa

LC 2009-15473

"This book provides an introduction to college life, highlighting what makes it different from the high school experience. . . . Chapters include tips on designing one's academic program, studying and staying organized, navigating social and extracurricular opportunities, staying physically and mentally healthy, and managing money." Publisher's note

Includes bibliographical references

Ehrenhaft, George

Barron's ACT; [by] George Ehrenhaft ... [et al.] 16th ed.; Barrons 2010 688p il pa \$18.99

Grades: 11 12 Adult   **378.1**

1. ACT assessment 2. Colleges and universities -- Entrance requirements

ISBN 978-0-7641-4482-0

First published 1972 with title: Barron's how to prepare for the American College Testing Program (ACT). Continues How to prepare for the ACT, American College Testing Assessment Program, Barron's How to prepare for the ACT assessment, and Barron's ACT assessment. Frequently revised. Editors vary

A guide to achieving higher scores on the ACT which includes subject reviews and practice exams with answers.

★ **Writing** a successful college application essay; 4th ed.; Barron's 2008 170p pa \$13.99

Grades: 9 10 11 12   **378.1**

1. College applications 2. Colleges and universities -- Entrance requirements

ISBN 978-0-7641-3637-5; 0-7641-3637-2

LC 2007-43441

First published 1987 with title: Write your way into college

The author gives "advice on deciding what to write, composing an essay, and the rewriting process. . . . The practical advice and concrete examples, especially in the section on editing and rewriting, will prove useful to any student facing the dreaded task of writing application essays." Voice Youth Advocates

★ **Fiske** guide to getting into the right college; [by] Edward B. Fiske & Bruce G. Hammond. 4th ed.; Sourcebooks 2010 352p pa \$16.99

Grades: 11 12 Adult   **378.1**

1. College choice 2. Colleges and universities -- Finance 3. Colleges and universities -- Entrance requirements

ISBN 978-1-4022-4309-7

First published 1997 by Times Bks.

This guide includes advice and information on constructing applications, writing essays, interviews, the application process, using the Internet when applying for college, and finanical aid.

Gardner, John N.

Step by step to college and career success; 4th ed; Bedford/St. Martin's 2010 xx, 179p il pa $35

Grades: 11 12 Adult   **378.1**
   1. Success 2. College students
   ISBN 978-0-312-68306-1
   First published 2006

This book "offers students . . . information and . . . strategies that they can apply toward their success . . . [Topics covered include] money management, emotional intelligence, technology, and diversity." Publisher's note

Gonsher, Debra

★ The **community** college guide; the essential reference from application to graduation. [by] Debra Gonsher and Joshua Halberstam. BenBella Books 2009 279p il pa $14.95

Grades: 9 10 11 12   **378.1**
   1. Junior colleges
   ISBN 978-1-933771-73-1

"Navigating the road of community college is not the most intuitive process, but this book serves as a map to making it through, from the application process to securing employment. The authors clearly outline the book in the table of contents, taking the reader from start to finish. Key areas addressed are handling difficult professors, taking ESL and remediation courses, the pitfalls of procrastination, and test-taking tips. . . . There is something for everyone in this essential purchase whether fresh out of high school, a student from abroad, or an adult returning to college. It will be both a handy reference tool and a treasure for circulation." Voice Youth Advocates

Includes bibliographical references

Gould, Jon B.

★ **How** to succeed in college (while really trying) a professor's inside advice. Jon B. Gould. The University of Chicago Press 2012 xi, 168 p.p (paperback: alkaline paper) $14.00

Grades: 9 10 11 12   **378.1**
   1. Study skills 2. College students 3. Academic achievement 4. Educational counseling -- Handbooks, manuals, etc 5. Counseling in higher education -- Handbooks, manuals, etc
   ISBN 0226304655; 0226304663; 9780226304656; 9780226304663
                  LC 2011037291

This book by Jon B. Gould "provides . . . help to [college] students, offering practical tips and specific study strategies that will equip them to excel in their new environment. . . . [S]tudents will learn how to identify the best instructors, how to choose classes and settle on a major, how to develop effective strategies for reading and note taking, and how to write good papers and successfully complete exams." (Publisher's note)

Includes bibliographical references and index.

Green, Sharon

★ **Barron's** SAT; [by] Sharon Weiner Green, Ira K. Wolf. 25th ed.; Barron's Educational Series 2010 920p il pa $18.99

Grades: 9 10 11 12 Adult   **378.1**
   1. Scholastic Assessment Test 2. Colleges and universities -- Entrance requirements
   ISBN 978-0-7641-4436-3
   Annual. Continues Barron's how to prepare for the SAT

"This manual explains all of the important tactics and strategies for taking the SAT and provides a . . . review of all test topics. It also presents a diagnostic test and five full-length SAT practice tests with all questions answered and explained." Publisher's note

Includes bibliographical references

Grossberg, Blythe N.

Applying to college for students with ADD or LD; a guide to keep you (and your parents) sane, satisfied, and organized through the admission process. by Blythe Grossberg. American Psychological Association 2011 143p il pa $14.95

Grades: 9 10 11 12   **378.1**
   1. College applications 2. Learning disabilities 3. Attention deficit disorder
   ISBN 978-1-4338-0892-0; 1-4338-0892-7
                  LC 2010-23130

"Beginning with an encouraging introduction, Grossberg then lays out the path to moving through the application process, which she expands upon in subsequent chapters. An early emphasis on figuring out strengths and weaknesses leads to a section on organization: what to do in your junior year, senior year, and the summer before college. Each time-frame is broken down into specific tasks, such as taking standardized tests and writing college essays, which are also explained in detail. . . . There's such good advice in this including wiping your social networking pages clean that teens without ADD or learning disabilities will find this eminently useful, too." Booklist

Gruber, Gary R.

Gruber's complete SAT guide 2011; 14th ed; Sourcebooks 2010 xxx, 1048p il pa $19.99

Grades: 9 10 11 12   **378.1**
   1. Scholastic Assessment Test 2. Colleges and universities -- Entrance requirements
   ISBN 978-1-4022-3777-5
   Annual. First published 1985 by Critical Thinking Book Co. with title: Gruber's complete preparation for the SAT

The author explains the principles behind the test, reviews necessary skills and develops test-taking strategies. Sample tests with answers are provided.

Hernandez, Michele A.

Acing the college application; how to maximize your chances for admission to the college of your choice. Updated; Ballantine Books 2007 262p pa $14.95

Grades: 9 10 11 12 **378.1**
1. College applications
ISBN 0-345-49892-5; 978-0-345-49892-2
LC 2007-281254
First published 2002

This guide to applying for college includes "step-by-step instructions on how to maximize a student's chance of getting into top colleges and universities across the country. . . . The author has successfully broken down what would normally be very dry material, making it sound as though she is discussing it face-to-face." Voice Youth Advocates

Jacobs, Lynn F.
★ The **secrets** of college success; [by] Lynn F. Jacobs and Jeremy S. Hyman. Jossey-Bass 2010 198p (Professors' guide) pa $15.95
Grades: 9 10 11 12 **378.1**
1. Conduct of life 2. Time management 3. College students
ISBN 978-0-470-87466-0

"While covering the basics found in other 'how to be successful in college'-type books (study skills, time management, test-taking tips), this one also has sections on other issues that students will likely face: how to get into a closed class, studying abroad, working with a professor, and getting one's money's worth. . . . [This] would be a great tool to incorporate into an adviser/advisee program for students on a college track. Learning to implement some of the tips will make them more successful in college, and they will likely reap benefits during their high school tenure as well." SLJ
Includes bibliographical references

Jager-Hyman, Joie
B + grades, A+ college application; how to present your strongest self, write a stand-out admissions essay, and get into the perfect school for you. by Joie Jager-Hyman, EdD. Random House Inc 2013 ix, 246 p.p (paperback) $14.99
Grades: 10 11 12 Adult **378.1**
1. Student aid 2. College applications 3. Exposition (Rhetoric) 4. Universities and colleges -- United States -- Admission
ISBN 1607743418; 9781607743415
LC 2013004970

In this book, college admissions consultant Joie Jager-Hyman "guides students (and their parents) through the college-admissions process, offering a wealth of insider advice. . . . Jager-Hyman covers the usual steps: developing a list of target, reach, and safety schools; writing essays; prepping for the college interview; taking the SATs; and demystifying financial aid." (Publishers Weekly)

The **Latino** student's guide to college success; Leonard A. Valverde, editor. Greenwood 2012 xiv, 270 p.p (alk. paper) $58
Grades: 9 10 11 12 Adult Professional **378.1**
1. Hispanic Americans -- Education (Higher) -- Handbooks, manuals, etc. 2. Universities and colleges -- United States -- Directories 3. Hispanic Americans

-- Education (Higher) -- Handbooks, manuals, etc
ISBN 031339797X; 0313397988; 9780313397974; 9780313397981
LC 2012010827

This book, edited by Leonard A. Valverde, provides "advice directed specifically to Latinos contemplating, preparing for, or already in the university or community college setting. This volume contains the 8 Steps to College Success, numerous vignettes of notable Latinos in many fields who give their personal story of how they succeeded in college and their advice for today's students, and a directory of top Latino universities and community colleges." (Publisher's note)

Mamlet, Robin
College admission; from application to acceptance, step by step. [by] Robin Mamlet, Christine VanDeVelde. Three Rivers Press 2011 405p il pa $19.99
Grades: 9 10 11 12 **378.1**
1. College choice 2. College applications 3. Colleges and universities -- United States
ISBN 978-0-307-59032-9
LC 2011-7978

"Starting off with an overview of the application process, replete with statistics, the authors draw upon their combined 23 years experience in college admissions to demystify an often overwhelming procedure. Their broad yet intricately detailed guide is intended for both parents and students alike and touches on everything from testing to interviews to financial aid." Kirkus
Includes bibliographical references

Marcus, David L.
Acceptance; a legendary guidance counselor helps seven kids find the right colleges--and find themselves. Penguin Press 2009 244p $25.95; pa $16
Grades: 11 12 Adult **378.1**
1. College choice 2. Educational counseling 3. Guidance counselors
ISBN 978-1-59420-214-8; 1-59420-214-1; 978-0-14-311764-3 pa; 0-14-311764-5 pa
LC 2009-8328

The author "chronicles the efforts of acclaimed guidance counselor Gweyth (pronounced to rhyme with Faith) 'Smitty' Smith and seven students to find the best colleges for them. . . . Marcus's poignant book will have readers wishing that they too had had Smitty as a guidance counselor and rooting for the students profiled." Libr J
Includes bibliographical references

Metcalf, Linda
How to say it to get into the college of your choice; application, essay, and interview strategies to get you the big envelope. Prentice Hall Press 2007 229p pa $15.95
Grades: 9 10 11 12 **378.1**
1. College applications
ISBN 978-0-7352-0420-1
LC 2007-3058

"This excellent, comprehensive, college application management guide addresses what to do as well as what to say when choosing and being chosen for post-high school education. . . . Using information from public as well as private schools and anticipating the needs of the homeschooler, she meticulously works through the tests, deadlines, common and specific applications, finances, recommendations, personal essay, parental communication, and appropriate interview attire." Voice Youth Advocates

★ **Navigating** your freshman year; how to make the leap to college life and land on your feet. [Natavi Guides, Inc.] Prentice Hall Press 2005 155p il (Students helping students) pa $12.95

Grades: 9 10 11 12   **378.1**
1. College students
ISBN 0-7352-0392-X
LC 2004-56976

This student-authored guide covers topics such as what to bring with you to college, how to deal with roommates, social activites and dating, and study tips

"There's lots of good advice in the pages of this guide. . . . Leaving home, doing laundry, forming good study habits, finding friends, and seeking help are all dealt with efficiently." Booklist

Includes bibliographical references

Nist, Sherrie L.

College rules! how to study, survive, and succeed in college. [by] Sherrie Nist-Olenjnik and Jodi Patrick Holschuh. 3rd ed; Ten Speed Press 2011 342p il pa $14.99

Grades: 9 10 11 12   **378.1**
1. Study skills 2. College students
ISBN 978-1-60774-001-8
First published 2002

This college survival primer by two college professors shares advice and strategies on topics ranging from stress management and test preparation to staying motivated and balancing academics with a social life

Pierce, Valerie

Countdown to college; 21 to-do lists for high school. [by] Valerie Pierce with Cheryl Rilly. 2nd ed.; Front Porch Press 2009 167p il pa $11.95

Grades: 9 10 11 12   **378.1**
1. College applications 2. Colleges and universities -- Entrance requirements
ISBN 978-0-9656086-8-8
First published 2003

The authors offer "academic and financial advice, such as connecting with couselors and teachers, planning an academic schedule, checking admission requirements at certified institutions, and launching a scholarship search. . . . The junior and senior year chapters include sources for getting through testing, campus visits, essays, Advanced Placement choices, application deadlines, 'senioritis,' and hidden costs as well as packing and planning for the big move." Voice Youth Advocates

Pine, Phil

Peterson's master the SAT 2011; Margaret Moran, editor. 11th ed.; Peterson's 2010 820p il pa $29.95

Grades: 9 10 11 12   **378.1**
1. Scholastic Assessment Test 2. Colleges and universities -- Entrance requirements
ISBN 978-0-7689-2881-5

Annual. First published with title Master the new SAT

This book provides "test-taking strategies and helps students prepare for the SAT with . . . reviews and 9 full-length practice tests to help sharpen math, writing, and critical reading skills." Publisher's note

Roberts, Andrew Lawrence

The **thinking** student's guide to college; 75 tips for getting a better education. [by] Andrew Roberts. University of Chicago Press 2010 174p (Chicago guides to academic life) $42; pa $14

Grades: 10 11 12 Adult   **378.1**
1. College choice 2. Conduct of life 3. Higher education 4. Colleges and universities -- United States
ISBN 978-0-226-72114-9; 978-0-226-72115-6 pa
LC 2009-49905

This "easy-to-read, informative book for students and parents on the college-selection process contains common-sense tips as well as helpful information that most would probably not initially consider when selecting a college. . . . This book is highly recommended for students and parents as a first step, before beginning to consider things like which schools to apply to and potential majors. It will give a larger picture of options to explore when making such an important decision and will help save money, sleep, and calm." Libr J

Includes bibliographical references

Robinson, Adam

Cracking the SAT; [by] Adam Robinson, John Katzman, and the staff of the Princeton Review. 2011 ed.; Random House 2010 716p il pa $21.99

Grades: 9 10 11 12   **378.1**
1. Scholastic Assessment Test 2. Colleges and universities -- Entrance requirements
ISBN 978-0-375-42982-8

Annual. First published 2005 with title Cracking the new SAT to partially replace Cracking the SAT & PSAT by Adam Robinson and John Katzman

This guide offers practical advice on how to prepare for the SAT college entrance exam. Practice tests are provided with detailed explanations for each answer. Free access to extra tests, lessons, and drills online is also included.

Rooney, John J.

Preparing for college; practical advice for students and their families. [by] John J. Rooney, John F. Reardon; foreword by Katherine Haley Will. Ferguson 2009 196p $34.95; pa $16.95

Grades: 9 10 11 12   **378.1**
1. College students 2. Colleges and universities --

United States
ISBN 978-0-8160-7377-1; 0-8160-7377-5; 978-0-8160-7378-8 pa; 0-8160-7378-3 pa
LC 2008-9025
"No other book on the market today gathers so much information into such a concise and user-friendly format." Voice Youth Advocates
Includes bibliographical references

Rosen, Louis
★ **College** is not for everyone; [by] Louis Rosen. ScarecrowEducation 2005 87p il pa $20.95
Grades: 9 10 11 12 **378.1**
1. Higher education 2. Vocational guidance
ISBN 1-578-86245-0
LC 2004-29878
The author argues "that schools from secondary through community college are not doing enough to prepare students who are not university bound. . . . This book will find the most use in the counselors' offices of schools where there are the largest number of students moving straight into the work force after high school." Voice Youth Advocates
Includes bibliographical references

Rubenstein, Jeff
Cracking the PSAT, NMSQT; [by] Jeff Rubenstein and Adam Robinson. 2011 ed.; Random House, Inc. 2010 386p il pa $14.99
Grades: 9 10 11 12 **378.1**
1. Scholastic Assessment Test 2. Colleges and universities -- Entrance requirements
ISBN 978-0-375-42981-1
Annual. First published 2005 to partially replace Cracking the SAT & PSAT by Adam Robinson and John Katzman
This guide on how to prepare for the PSAT exam includes practice tests, a listing of important vocabulary words, and the strategies and techniques needed to glean the correct answers to test questions.

Crash course for the SAT; the last-minute guide to scoring high. 4th ed; Random House 2011 230p il pa $9.99
Grades: 9 10 11 12 **378.1**
1. Scholastic Assessment Test 2. Colleges and universities -- Entrance requirements
ISBN 978-0-375-42831-9
First published 1999
This book provides strategies and practice questions for students who have little time left to study for the SAT.

Schoem, David
College knowledge for the Jewish student; 101 tips. University of Michigan 2010 232p pa $20.95
Grades: 10 11 12 Adult **378.1**
1. Life skills 2. College students 3. Jews -- Social life and customs
ISBN 978-0-472-03430-7
LC 2010-21415
This book "includes tips on the academic aspects of college life, like communicating with faculty, learning what is where on campus, where to go for help with coursework, how to manage one's time for a balanced experience, etc. In addition, it offers advice on dealing with family, finances, health, and safety, as well as the many social and emotional aspects of this . . . rite of passage." Publisher's note

Silivanch, Annalise
★ **Making** the right college choice; technical, 2-year, 4-year. Rosen Pub. Group 2010 80p il (Thinking about college) lib bdg $30.60; pa $14.15; ebook $30.60
Grades: 9 10 11 12 **378.1**
1. College choice
ISBN 978-1-4358-3598-6 lib bdg; 978-1-4358-8508-0 pa; 978-1-4488-0070-4 ebook
LC 2009-21848
"The major question asked by Silivanch is whether to attend college or not. The author concludes . . . that attending a two or four-year college is a must. She makes the case for college as a rite of passage for high school graduates, arguing that they deny themselves monetary gain and economic status when they do not choose to further their education, a position backed up by salary statistics. The book walks readers briefly through the college application process, and in a departure from the other books, outlines the economy's impact on college selection." SLJ
Includes bibliographical references

Steinberg, Jacques
The **gatekeepers**; inside the admissions process of a premier college. Viking 2002 xxiii, 292p hardcover o.p. pa $15
Grades: 11 12 Adult **378.1**
1. College applications 2. Wesleyan University (Middletown, Conn.)
ISBN 0-670-03135-6; 0-14-200308-5 pa
LC 2002-16884
"This insightful and readable book should be purchased by all academic and large public libraries." Libr J
Includes bibliographical references

Yaverbaum, Eric
Life's little college admissions insights; top tips from the country's most acclaimed guidance counselors. [by] Eric and Cole Yaverbaum. Morgan James Pub. 2010 125p il pa $14.95
Grades: 9 10 11 12 **378.1**
1. College choice 2. College applications
ISBN 978-1-60037-728-0
For this book, "experts from around the country were interviewed and have given many . . . opinions on what's important from their own first hand experience advising hundreds of thousands of students in their careers." Publisher's note

378.198 College students

Bondy, Halley
77 things you absolutely have to do before you finish college; Halley Bondy. Zest Books 2014 191 p. $14.99

Grades: 9 10 11 12   **378.198**
1. College students 2. Life skills -- Handbooks, manuals, etc. 3. College students -- Conduct of life
ISBN 1936976005; 9781936976003

LC 2013951194

This book by Halley Bondy, illustrated by James Lloyd, describes how "College is about way more than just frats and finals. . . The 77 entries included here cover everything from negotiating the terms of an apartment rental to attending a school-sponsored lecture event to hosting a movie marathon--and supplemental sidebars provide bonus tips for doing everything cheaply and well." (Publisher's note)

"This book offers college students a wide variety of experiences intended to maximize personal growth and fun during the college years...Readers will likely get the sense that they are receiving sound advice from a big sister who has been there, one who encourages a balance of fun, healthy risks with responsibility and an eye on the future. This would make a good gift for high school graduates." VOYA

378.3   Student aid and related topics

American Library Association
How to pay for college; a library how-to handbook. [by] editors of the American Library Association. American Library Association 2011 170p il $20; pa $14.95

Grades: 11 12 Adult   **378.3**
1. Student aid 2. Scholarships 3. College costs 4. Education -- Finance
ISBN 978-0-8389-1077-1; 978-1-61608-155-3 pa

LC 2010-47768

Readers "can use this guide to: fill out forms for financial aid, loans, and scholarships; find ways to plan and save for the high cost of college tuition; [and] narrow their search to those schools that are the best fit. . . . [This] guide emphasizes the help that the local library can offer in this process, using its reference materials, the Internet, and the advice of experienced researchers." Publisher's note

Includes bibliographical references

Bellenir, Karen
★ **College** financing information for teens; tips for a successful financial life. edited by Karen Bellenir. Omnigraphics, Inc. 2008 438p (Teen finance series)

Grades: 9 10 11 12   **378.3**
1. Student aid 2. College costs 3. Personal finance
ISBN 978-0-7808-0988-8

LC 2007043689

"This guide deserves a spot in every school, public, and community college library. Filled with information on helping students make choices about higher education, including college selection and applications, it will also help them make sense of the myriad ways to pay for it." SLJ

Includes bibliographical references

Bissonnette, Zach
Debt-free U; how I paid for an oustanding college education without loans, scholarships, or mooching off my parents. Portfolio 2010 290p pa $16

Grades: 10 11 12 Adult   **378.3**
1. College costs 2. Higher education 3. Personal finance
ISBN 978-1-59184-298-9

LC 2010-18510

Challenges popular beliefs that college finances must impose financial hardships for parents and students, posing strategies for attending non-private schools, avoiding student loans, and maximizing available resources.

"This is a timely guide to a decision that has important financial ramifications." Booklist

Includes bibliographical references

College Entrance Examination Board
2011 scholarship handbook; [by] College Board. 14th ed; College Board 2010 616p pa $28.99

Grades: 9 10 11 12   **378.3**
1. Reference books 2. Scholarships -- Directories
ISBN 978-0-87447-906-5

Annual. First published 1997. Alternate title: College Board scholarship handbook 2011

Information on more than 2,100 undergraduate scholarships, internships, and loan programs. Entries are indexed by category, among them gender, minority status, field of study, and career interest. Includes a planning worksheet to help students organize applications.

★ **College** financing information for teens; tips for a successful financial life including facts about planning, saving, & paying for postsecondary education, with information about college savings plans, grants, loans... edited by Elizabeth Magill. Omnigraphics 2011 387 p.

Grades: 9 10 11 12   **378.3**
1. Student aid 2. Scholarships 3. College costs 4. Teenagers -- Personal finance 5. Student aid -- United States 6. College costs -- United States 7. Finance, Personal -- United States
ISBN 078081214X; 9780780812147

LC 2011034082

This guide is "[f]illed with information on helping students make choices about higher education, including college selection and applications, [and] it will also help them make sense of the myriad ways to pay for it. Chapters on scholarships, loans, grants, and financial aid for specialized interests, including the military, survey what is out there. . . . Sidebars like "It's a Fact!" and "Quick Tip" remind students that study-abroad opportunities are for everyone, not just language majors, and that the Coast Guard does not offer ROTC programs. The last two chapters are directories of resources and state higher-education agencies. A[n] . . . index . . . includes many Web site addresses and phone numbers of various agencies and scholarship providers." (School Library Journal)

Includes bibliographical references and index

High school senior's guide to merit and other no-need funding, 2008-2010; [by] Gail Ann Schlachter, R. David Weber. Reference Service Press 2008 410p $29.95

Grades: 11 12 Adult   378.3

1. Reference books 2. Student aid -- Directories 3. Scholarships -- Directories

ISBN 978-1-58841-165-5

Biennial. First published 1996

Lists and describes more than 1000 merit scholarships and other no-need funding programs available to high school seniors and recent graduates.

Hollander, Barbara

★ **Paying** for college; practical, creative strategies. [by] Barbara Gottfried Hollander. Rosen Pub. 2010 80p il (Thinking about college) lib bdg $30.60; pa $14.15; ebook $30.60

Grades: 9 10 11 12   378.3

1. Student aid 2. College costs

ISBN 978-1-4358-3599-3 lib bdg; 1-4358-3599-9 lib bdg; 978-1-4358-8504-2 pa; 1-4358-8504-X pa; 978-1-4488-0071-1 ebook

LC 2009-18681

This book "discusses in clear detail the various governmental loans, grants, and scholarships that are available to students." SLJ

Includes bibliographical references

McCormick, Lisa

Financial aid smarts; getting money for school. by Lisa McCormick. 1st ed. Rosen Pub. 2013 64 p. col. ill. (library) $31.95; (paperback) $12.95

Grades: 10 11 12   378.3

1. Student aid 2. Scholarships 3. Student loan funds 4. Student aid -- United States 5. College costs -- United States -- Planning

ISBN 1448882524; 9781448882526; 9781448882663; 9781448882670

LC 2012024847

This book by Lisa McCormick is part of the Get Smart With Your Money series and focuses on student financial aid. The series provides "teens with real-world tips on making the most of their financial opportunities." This entry "imparts financial-aid basics (including how to fill out the necessary Free Application for Federal Student Aid), different opportunities to receive money (e.g. grants, loans, and scholarships), and ways to protect these investments." (Booklist)

Includes bibliographical references (p. 60-61) and index.

★ **Peterson's** how to get money for college; financing your future beyond federal aid. 28th ed.; Peterson's 2010 863p pa $33.95

Grades: 11 12 Adult   378.3

1. Scholarships 2. College costs 3. Student loan funds

ISBN 978-0-7689-2886-0

Annual. First published 1983. Variant titles: Paying less for college; College money handbook

A resource for anyone looking to supplement his or her federal financial-aid package with funds from colleges and universities, this directory features information on need-based and non-need gifts, loans, and more.

Schlachter, Gail A.

College student's guide to merit and other no-need funding, 2008-2010; [by] Gail Ann Schlachter, R. David Weber. Reference Service Press 2008 490p $32.50

Grades: 11 12 Adult   378.3

1. Reference books 2. Student aid -- Directories 3. Scholarships -- Directories

ISBN 978-1-58841-166-2

First published 1998. Frequently revised

Compiles over thirteen hundred scholarships and college funding programs that are based on merit rather than financial need.

★ **Directory** of financial aids for women 2009-2011; [by] Gail Ann Schlachter, R. David Weber. Reference Service Press 2009 552p $45

Grades: 11 12 Adult   378.3

1. Reference books 2. Scholarships -- Directories 3. Women -- Education -- Directories

ISBN 978-1-58841-194-5

Biennial. First published 1978

Describes "scholarships, fellowships, loans, grants, awards, and internships designed primarily or exclusively for women. . . . Lists state sources of educational benefits and offers an annotated bibliography of directories that list general financial aid programs. Program title, sponsoring organization, geographic, subject, and filing date indexes." Ref Sources for Small & Medium-sized Libr. 5th edition

★ **Financial** aid for the disabled and their families, 2010-2012; [by] Gail Ann Schlachter, R. David Weber. Reference Service Press 2010 480p $40

Grades: 11 12 Adult   378.3

1. Scholarships 2. People with physical disabilities

ISBN 978-1-58841-204-1

Biennial. First published 1988

"Provides information on a wide range of funding needs in such areas as education, career development, research, and travel. Includes multiple indexes; cross-referenced." N Y Public Libr Book of How & Where to Look It Up

379.2 Specific policy issues in public education

Aretha, David

With all deliberate speed; court-ordered busing and American schools. David Aretha. Morgan Reynolds Pub. 2012 128 p. ill. (some col.) (The civil rights movement) (lib. bdg.) $28.95

Grades: 7 8 9 10   379.2

1. School integration 2. Busing (School integration) 3. Boston (Mass.) -- Race relations

ISBN 1599351811; 1599352176; 9781599351810; 9781599352176

LC 2011019530

This book, part of the "Civil Rights Movement" series, "details the slow, painful, unpopular, and often ineffective process of integrating public schools by busing students outside their neighborhoods in the decades following the 1954 landmark Brown v. Board of Education decision. In addition to a detailed account of experiences in Boston, [David] Aretha includes specific information on busing in numerous large and small metropolitan areas around the country." (Booklist)

"The latest books from the Civil Rights Movement series offer well-researched and clearly-written discussions of events and issues that helped define their times." Booklist

Includes bibliographical references (p. 122-124) and index

381   Commerce (Trade)

Eltis, David
★ **Atlas** of the transatlantic slave trade; [by] David Eltis and David Richardson; foreword by David Brion Davis; afterword by David W. Blight. Yale University Press 2010 xxvi, 307p il map (The Lewis Walpole series in eighteenth-century culture and history) $50

Grades: 11 12 Adult   381
1. Atlases 2. Reference books 3. Slave trade -- Maps
ISBN 978-0-300-12460-6

"For nearly 20 years, the Trans-Atlantic Slave Trade Database project has been diligently tabulating all the slave ship crossings of the Atlantic Ocean, from 1500 to 1900. . . . With 189 informative and handsome maps, Eltis and Richardson relay and interpret the information contained in this rich database, mixing in beautiful historical illustrations and key passages from relevant texts. An accessible narrative, meanwhile, expands on the information in the maps. . . . This marvelous book will change how people think of the slave trade." Foreign Affairs

382   International commerce (Foreign trade)

Goldstein, Natalie
Globalization and free trade; Natalie Goldstein; foreword by Joanna G. Moss. 2nd ed. Facts On File 2012 428 p. (ebook) $54.00; (hardcover) $45.00; (paperback) $18.95; (hardcover) $45.00

Grades: 9 10 11 12 Adult   382
1. Free trade 2. Globalization 3. International economic relations 4. Free trade -- Case studies 5. Globalization -- Economic aspects -- Case studies 6. International economic integration -- Case studies
ISBN 9781438109008; 9780816068081; 9780816077397; 0816083657; 9780816083657
LC 2011004940

This encyclopedia, by Natalie Goldstein, examines international economic issues and "provides an overview of the history of globalization and how it has evolved into its present state." It gives "opinions by proponents and detractors of the issue, and case studies of the United States, East Asia, China, Cochabamba, and Iceland are presented to provide real-world context." (Publisher's note)

Includes bibliographical references and index.

384   Communications

Gertner, Jon
The **idea** factory; Bell Labs and the great age of American innovation. Jon Gertner. Penguin Press 2012 422 p. ill. $29.95

Grades: 11 12 Adult   384
1. Bell Telephone Laboratories 2. Telecommunication -- History 3. Technological innovations -- History 4. Inventors -- United States -- History -- 20th century 5. Bell Telephone Laboratories -- History -- 20th century 6. Creative ability -- United States -- History -- 20th century 7. Telecommunication -- United States -- History -- 20th century 8. Technological innovations -- United States -- History -- 20th century
ISBN 1594203288; 9781594203282
LC 2011040207

This book "traces the history of Bell Labs through more than five decades of brilliant thinking and innovation. From the transistor to lasers to satellites and cellular technology, Bell Labs and its scientists invented machines and techniques that . . . ultimately presaged all of modern communications. . . . Bell Labs became a haven for creative and technical minds due to a unique culture of encouraged interdisciplinary research." (Kirkus Reviews)

"The book is a celebration of basic exploratory research. . . . [T]he writing and the longitudinal biographical portraits are engaging." LJ

Includes bibliographical references (p. [409]-412) and index

Henderson, Harry
Communications and broadcasting; from wired words to wireless Web. rev ed.; Facts on File 2006 201p il (Milestones in discovery and invention) $35

Grades: 7 8 9 10 11 12   384
1. Telecommunication
ISBN 0-8160-5748-6; 978-0-8160-5748-1
LC 2006-5577

First published 1997
This is a "look at the development and interconnection of [the following] scientific ideas: electromagnetism, leading to the telegraph and telephone; Maxwell's wave theory, leading to radio and television; and communications and information theory, from Claude Shannon to the World Wide Web and beyond. In addition, there are . . . portraits of the inventors themselves." Publisher's note

Includes glossary and bibliographical references

Lapsley, Phil
Exploding the Phone; The Untold Story of the Teenagers and Outlaws Who Hacked Ma Bell. by Phil Lapsley; forward by Steve Wozniak. Grove Press 2013 xvi, 431 p.p (hardcover) $26

Grades: 11 12 Adult   384
1. Bell System 2. Telecommunication -- History
ISBN 080212061X; 9780802120618

In this book, Phil Lapsley "uses more than 100 interviews and 400 Freedom of Information Act requests to present the virtually unknown battle between phone companies and overcurious young tech whizzes determined to explore Ma Bell's networks." He "pieces together a . . . re-creation of 1967, a highly significant period in telecommunications history." (Library Journal)

385 Railroad transportation

Drabelle, Dennis

The **great** American railroad war; how Ambrose Bierce and Frank Norris took on the notorious Central Pacific Railroad. Dennis Drabelle. St. Martin's Press 2012 306 p. $26.99

Grades: 10 11 12 Adult   385

1. Whistle blowing 2. Central Pacific Railroad Company -- History 3. Norris, Frank, 1870-1902 -- Criticism and interpretation 4. Bierce, Ambrose, 1842-1914? -- Criticism and interpretation 5. Railroads -- California -- History -- 19th century 6. Political corruption -- Press coverage -- California

ISBN 0312667590; 9780312667597; 9781250015051

LC 2012010247

Author Dennis Drabelle "examines the role of literature in battling the Central Pacific Railroad monopoly. He recounts the financing of the transcontinental railroad with U.S. government bonds and how the railroad's owners such as Leland Stanford and Collis Huntington enriched themselves in various quasi-legal ways. Though the railroad worked to make itself untouchable by buying influence, Drabelle chronicles how writers Ambrose Bierce and Frank Norris challenged that position." (Library Journal)

Includes bibliographical references

Gimpel, Diane

The **transcontinental** railroad. ABDO Pub. Co. 2011 112p il (Essential events) lib bdg $23.95

Grades: 7 8 9 10 11 12   385

1. Railroads -- History 2. West (U.S.) -- History

ISBN 978-1-61714-768-5; 1-61714-768-0

LC 2010044830

Describes how and why the Transcontinental Railroad was built and tells how it affected the westward expansion of settlers.

Includes glossary and bibliographical references

388.3 Vehicular transportation

Bjornlund, Lydia

What is the future of alternative energy cars? by Lydia Bjornlund. ReferencePoint Press, Inc. 2014 80 p. color illustrations (Future of renewable energy series) (hardback) $28.95

Grades: 6 7 8 9   388.3

1. Alternative fuel vehicles 2. Automobiles -- Fuel consumption 3. Automobiles -- Technological innovations

ISBN 1601526105; 9781601526106

LC 2013036244

This book on alternative energy cars, by Lydia Bjornlund, is "organized around a narrative-driven, pro-con [design]. . . . [It] examine[s] . . . cost, environmental impact, practicality when measured against fossil fuels, and the role of government in renewable energy's future. Important ideas are supported throughout each book by current and relevant facts, quotes, full-color statistical illustrations, and anecdotes." (Publisher's note)

"Well written and understandable, the authors use a wide variety of source material to present each side fairly and completely. The question/answer format of the chapters breaks the topics into simplified arguments that can easily be absorbed." VOYA

Includes bibliographical references and index

390 Customs, etiquette, folklore

★ The **Greenwood** encyclopedia of daily life; a tour through history from ancient times to the present. Joyce E. Salisbury, general editor. Greenwood Press 2004 6v il map set $599.95

Grades: 11 12 Adult   390

1. Reference books 2. Civilization -- Encyclopedias 3. Manners and customs -- Encyclopedias

ISBN 0-313-32541-3

LC 2003-54724

This "work provides an overview of the material, domestic, recreational, religious, political, intellectual, and economic aspects of daily life in a selection of cultures from six broad historical periods. . . . Each of the six volumes gives a survey of the historical period in each culture covered, which is representative rather than exhaustive, then covers aspects of daily life from broad topics to narrower." Libr J

Includes bibliographical references

391 Customs

Albee, Sarah

Why'd They Wear That? Fashion As the Mirror of History. by Sarah Albee; foreword by Tim Gunn. Natl Geographic Soc Childrens books 2015 192 p. $19.99

Grades: 5 6 7 8 9   391

1. Fashion -- History 2. Clothing and dress -- History

ISBN 1426319193; 9781426319198

In this book, by Sarah Albee, "kids will learn about outrageous, politically-perilous, funky, disgusting, regrettable, and life-threatening creations people have worn throughout the course of human history, all the way up to the present day. From spats and togas to hoop skirts and hair shirts, why people wore what they did is an illuminating way to look at the social, economic, political, and moral climates throughout history." (Publisher's note)

"As the subtitle says, this hefty, extensively illustrated book uses fashion to discuss the ways and whys people dress and how it reflects what's happening in their civilization. . . . The many photographs are well chosen and reproduced, and Albee writes in a conversational style that, though occasionally repetitive, is instantly appealing to readers. Tim Gunn writes the foreword, and a timeline and bibliography conclude." Booklist

Ashenburg, Katherine

The **dirt** on clean; an unsanitized history. [by] Katherine Ashenburg. North Point Press 2007 358p il pa $15; $24

Grades: 11 12 Adult 391

1. Hygiene 2. Personal grooming 3. Hygiene -- History 4. Bathing customs -- History
ISBN 0-374-53137-4 pa; 0-86547-690-X; 978-0-374-53137-9 pa; 978-0-86547-690-5

LC 2007-32334

This is a study "of attitudes to hygiene through time." (Publisher's note) Index.

"Brimming with lively anecdotes, this well-researched, smartly paced and endearing history of Western cleanliness holds a welcome mirror up to our intimate selves, revealing deep-seated desires and fears spanning 2000-plus years." Publ Wkly

Includes bibliographical references

Bailey, Diane

Tattoo art around the world. Rosen Pub. 2011 64p il (Tattooing) lib bdg $30.60; pa $12.95

Grades: 7 8 9 10 391

1. Tattooing
ISBN 978-1-4488-4618-4 lib bdg; 1-4488-4618-8 lib bdg; 978-1-4488-4622-1 pa; 1-4488-4622-6 pa

LC 2010048428

This book "discusses how different cultures have used tattoos. . . . The design and the reading level are accessible without talking down to the audience, so this is a good choice for enticing reluctant readers with an interest in body art." Booklist

Includes bibliographical references

Brasser, Ted J.

Native American clothing; an illustrated history. [by] Theodore Brasser. Firefly Books 2009 368p il map $65

Grades: 9 10 11 12 Adult 391

1. Clothing and dress 2. Native American costume 3. Native Americans -- Antiquities
ISBN 978-1-55407-433-4; 1-55407-433-9

LC 2009-482555

A collection of photographs from museums, collectors and private dealers that documents five centuries of Native American artistry.

"Featuring an amazing breadth of clothing design, motif, and technique, Brasser's volume makes an excellent cross-collection resource for anyone interested in indigenous art or Native American history." Publ Wkly

Includes bibliographical references

Cosgrave, Bronwyn

★ The **complete** history of costume and fashion; from ancient Egypt to the present day. Checkmark Bks. 2001 256p il $37.95

Grades: 11 12 Adult 391

1. Costume -- History
ISBN 0-8160-4574-7

LC 00-64401

"This book explores the development of fashion from its simple and practical beginnings to the growth of the multi-billion dollar global industry that it is today. . . . Trends in clothing style, fabric, accessories, and footwear {are examined}." Publisher's note

Includes bibliographical references

Cumming, Valerie

★ The **dictionary** of fashion history; [by] Valerie Cumming, C.W. Cunnington and P.E. Cunnington. Berg 2010 286p il $99.95; pa $29.95

Grades: 11 12 Adult 391

1. Reference books 2. Fashion -- Encyclopedias 3. Clothing and dress -- History -- Encyclopedias
ISBN 978-1-84788-534-0; 978-1-84788-533-3 pa

"Concise yet detailed, academic, and fabulous, . . . [this book] is truly a dictionary—a compendium of fashion and fashion-related terms, defined in alphabetical order—and it covers 900 C.E. to the present day. . . . [This] is an essential purchase (and great value!) for any library serving patrons with an interest in fashion, clothing, art, history, theater, anthropology, or nearly any area of the social sciences." Libr J

Includes glossary and bibliographical references

DeJean, Joan E.

The **essence** of style; how the French invented high fashion, fine food, chic cafes, style, sophistication, and glamour. Free Press 2005 303p il $25; pa $15

Grades: 11 12 Adult 391

1. Kings 2. Fashion -- History 3. France -- Social life and customs
ISBN 0-7432-6413-4; 0-7432-6414-2 pa

LC 2005-40019

"An unusual and delightfully educational perspective on snob appeal." Booklist

Includes bibliographical references

DeMello, Margo

Encyclopedia of body adornment. Greenwood Press 2007 xx, 326p il $79.95

Grades: 9 10 11 12 Adult 391

1. Tattooing 2. Body piercing 3. Reference books 4. Body marking 5. Tattooing -- Encyclopedias 6. Scarification (Body marking) 7. Body, Human -- Social aspects 8. Body piercing -- Encyclopedias 9. Manners and customs -- Encyclopedias
ISBN 978-0-313-33695-9

LC 2007-16304

"Over 200 entries address the major adornments and modifications, their historical and cross-cultural locations, and the major cultural groups and places in which body modification has been central to social and cultural practices." Publisher's note

Includes bibliographical references

Flaherty, Somer

The **Book** of styling; an insider's guide to creating your own look. Somer Flaherty. Zest Books 2012 160 p. $16.99

Grades: 9 10 11 12 **391**
1. Fashion 2. Fashion design 3. Women's clothing
ISBN 0982732244; 9780982732243

LC 2012934246

This book, by Somer Flaherty, "explains the what's, why's, and how's of styling; . . . whether you're looking to update your wardrobe or curate your closet. . . . Somer Flaherty helps readers figure out what their look is (or ought to be), and how to tailor that look to their own particular body type. Also, . . . Flaherty helps readers understand the skills that are necessary to style others, and to even turn styling into a real career." (Publisher's note)

Gerber, Larry
Getting inked; what to expect when you get a tattoo. Rosen Pub. 2011 64p il (Tattooing) lib bdg $30.60; pa $12.95
Grades: 7 8 9 10 **391**
1. Tattooing
ISBN 978-1-4488-4616-0 lib bdg; 978-1-4488-4621-4 pa

LC 2010045970

This book "details how to find a competent tattoo artist, what the inking process is like, and how to care for the tattoo afterward. . . . Illustrations . . . are of high quality. . . . The design and the reading level are accessible without talking down to the audience, so this is a good choice for enticing reluctant readers with an interest in body art." Booklist
Includes bibliographical references

Graydon, Shari
★ **In** your face; the culture of beauty and you. Annick 2004 176p il hardcover o.p. pa $14.95
Grades: 7 8 9 10 **391**
1. Body image 2. Personal appearance
ISBN 1-55037-857-0; 1-55037-856-2 pa

The author "looks at fashion across time and cultures, and analyzes the underlying messages in today's focus . . . on thinness, long nails, and high heels. Along the way, she warns both young men and women of the very real dangers of eating disorders, plastic surgery, liposuction, and other body-image 'solutions.' . . . Graydon will make readers laugh as well as think about the issues." Booklist
Includes bibliographical references

The **Greenwood** encyclopedia of clothing through American history 1900 to the present; Amy T. Peterson, general editor [v. 1], Ann T. Kellogg, general editor [v. 2] Greenwood Press 2008 2v il set $199.95
Grades: 9 10 11 12 Adult **391**
1. Reference books 2. Clothing and dress -- History -- Encyclopedias
ISBN 978-0-313-35855-5; 0-313-35855-9

LC 2008-24624

This encyclopedia "surveys the impact of American social, cultural, and economic life on mainstream clothing and the fashion industry. . . . The encyclopedia's placement of fashion within its social and historical context will be interesting to many readers, including theater students and others doing costume research." Booklist
Includes glossary and bibliographical references

The **Greenwood** encyclopedia of clothing through world history; edited by Jill Condra. Greenwood Press 2007 3v il set $349.95
Grades: 11 12 Adult **391**
1. Reference books 2. Clothing and dress -- History -- Encyclopedias
ISBN 978-0-313-33662-1

LC 2007-30705

"Volume one (prehistory to 1500 C.E.) includes cultures such as ancient Greece and Persia; volume two (1501-1800) chronicles dress in places such as Europe, North America, India, and Japan; volume three (1801-present) has an international scope and is arranged chronologically. Each chapter targets a specific period and opens with an accurate and selectively detailed time line and an introduction to the era and the milestones in clothing and textiles, laying an appropriate foundation for the discussion that follows. . . . An outstanding purchase with an ambitious scope." SLJ
Includes bibliographical references

Kelly, Clinton
Dress your best; the complete guide to finding the style that's right for your body. [by] Clinton Kelly and Stacy London. Three Rivers Press 2005 255p il pa $18.95
Grades: 11 12 Adult **391**
1. Fashion 2. Clothing and dress
ISBN 0-307-23671-4

LC 2005-13681

This fashion guide describes specific male and female body types, and the kinds of outfits that match well with them. "Each type's section opens with a photo of an average-looking model sporting a basic swimsuit, along with comments from the model and the authors. . . . Ladies and gentlemen, start your shopping engines—and don't leave home without this book!" Publ Wkly

Nagle, Jeanne
Why people get tattoos and other body art. Rosen 2011 64p il (Tattooing) lib bdg $30.60; pa $12.95
Grades: 7 8 9 10 **391**
1. Tattooing
ISBN 978-1-4488-4617-7 lib bdg; 978-1-4488-4620-7 pa

LC 2011000276

This book "explains the appeal of tattoos for a wide variety of people as a way of expressing themselves aesthetically, religiously, or for other reasons. Illustrations . . . are of high quality. . . . The design and the reading level are accessible without talking down to the audience, so this is a good choice for enticing reluctant readers with an interest in body art." Booklist
Includes bibliographical references

Nunn, Joan
Fashion in costume, 1200-2000; 2nd ed; New Amsterdam Bks. 2000 280p pa $18.95
Grades: 11 12 Adult **391**
1. Costume -- History
ISBN 1-56663-279-X

LC 99-47516

First published 1984 by Schocken Bks. with title: Fashion in costume, 1200-1980

This history of American and European costume covers men's, women's, and children's dress, accessories and jewelry, fabrics, and color. Discusses how historical, social, economic, and artistic events influence fashion

Includes bibliographical references

Paterek, Josephine

Encyclopedia of American Indian costume. Norton 1996 516p il pa $24.95

Grades: 11 12 Adult   **391**

1. Reference books 2. Native American costume -- Encyclopedias

ISBN 0-393-31382-4

First published 1994 by ABC-CLIO

Paterek describes "the clothing used for everyday, war, rites, and ceremonies for men, women, and children in hundreds of tribes in diverse climates stretching over centuries. Well-organized text and 400 drawings and authentic photos plus the cultural essays prefacing the 10 regional groupings and each tribe put the costumes in historical, social, and geographic context. Appendixes cover terminology and the materials used in clothing. The excellent bibliographies in this classic work both document and encourage further reading." Am Libr

Includes bibliographical references

Spalding, Frank

Erasing the ink; getting rid of your tattoo. Rosen Pub. 2011 64p il (Tattooing) lib bdg $30.60; pa $12.95

Grades: 7 8 9 10   **391**

1. Skin 2. Tattooing

ISBN 978-1-4488-4615-3 lib bdg; 978-1-4488-4619-1 pa

LC 2010045920

This book "focuses . . . on the negatives of getting a tattoo and the difficulties of removing them. . . . Illustrations . . . are of high quality. . . . The design and the reading level are accessible without talking down to the audience, so this is a good choice for enticing reluctant readers with an interest in body art." Booklist

Includes bibliographical references

What people wore when; a complete illustrated history of costume from ancient times to the nineteenth century for every level of society. consultant editor Melissa Leventon. St. Martin's Griffin 2008 352p il pa $29.95

Grades: 11 12 Adult   **391**

1. Clothing and dress -- History

ISBN 978-0-312-38321-3; 0-312-38321-5

LC 2008-12938

"This attractive book will appeal to teens looking for quick answers for a last-minute assignment, and it will also be of interest to budding fashionistas and social historians. Leventon has combined current research on costume and dress through the ages with the detailed beauty of the work of two 19th-century illustrators, Auguste Racinet and Friedrich Hottenroth, to provide a historical and thematic examination of fashion and dress that is both comprehensive and readable." SLJ

Includes glossary and bibliographical references

391.6   Personal appearance

Hardy, Ed

Wear your dreams; my life in tattoos. Ed Hardy with Joel Selvin. Thomas Dunne Books 2013 304 p. (hardback) $26.99

Grades: 11 12 Adult   **391.6**

1. Tattooing 2. Tattoo artists -- Biography 3. Artists -- United States -- Biography 4. Tattoo artists -- United States -- Biography

ISBN 1250008824; 9781250008824

LC 2013003988

Author and tattoo artist Ed Hardy presents a memoir "from his beginnings in 1960s California, to leading the tattoo renaissance and building his name into a hugely lucrative international brand. Hardy recounts his genesis as a tattoo artist and leader in the movement to recognize tattooing as a valid and rich art form, through to the ultimate transformation of his career into a multi-billion dollar branding empire." (Publisher's note)

"Hardy's memoir/cautionary tale about art, commerce, skin and ink, written with the assistance of San Francisco Chronicle music writer Selvin...While the culture of tattoo art is clearly bold and sometimes risky, Hardy admits he would have become an academic if he hadn't plied his trade in this different medium. A coda about Audigier admits Hardy's inner conflict about the deal as he tells a friend, "This guy is at ground zero of everything that is wrong with contemporary culture," before ultimately taking the deal. "I just wanted to get paid and to be left alone," he says. Be careful what you wish for. The lesson in this surprisingly heartfelt memoir by an iconic American tattoo artist is that the man is not always the brand." (Kirkus)

Von D, Kat

The **tattoo** chronicles; by Kat Von D with Sandra Bark; photography by Kat Von D. Collins Design 2010 235 p. ill. (chiefly col.) $29.99

Grades: 11 12 Adult   **391.6**

1. Diaries 2. Television personalities 3. Reality television programs 4. Tattooing -- Pictorial works 5. Tattoo artists -- United States -- Diaries 6. Tattooing -- United States -- Pictorial works

ISBN 9780061953361

LC 2010926554

This book is "an illustrated diary that offers a . . . look at a . . . year in the personal and professional life of Kat Von D, the . . . tattooer and star of [the television program] 'LA Ink.' When Kat does a tattoo, she writes an entry about it in her journal, reflecting not only on the significance of the tattoo for the person who is receiving it but also on how the experience of creating this tattoo affects her personally. In these diary entries . . . Kat lays it on the line about how doing these tattoos influences her life and art. . . . [Included are] Kat's images, from sketches of her tattoos to the finished works, and . . . shots of her . . . personal collections—all photographed by Kat herself." (Publisher's note)

392 Customs of life cycle and domestic life

Alvarez, Julia, 1950-

Once upon a quinceanera; coming of age in the USA. Viking Adult 2007 278p hardcover o.p. pa $15

Grades: 11 12 Adult **392**

1. Quinceañera (Social custom) 2. Hispanic American women -- Biography 3. Hispanic Americans -- Social life and customs

ISBN 0-452-28830-4 pa; 0-670-03873-3; 978-0-452-28830-0 pa; 978-0-670-03873-2

LC 2006-37561

This is a study of the Latina coming-of-age ritual, celebrated when a young woman turns fifteen. The author of How the Garcia Girls Lost Their Accents (1991), In the Time of the Butterflies (1994), and Something to Declare (1998) "spent a year talking to women from Cuba, Mexico, the Dominican Republic, Puerto Rico and other countries." (Women's Rev Books)

This is an "enlightening look at an important event in the lives of Latinas in America." Booklist

Includes bibliographical references

Fifteen candles; 15 tales of taffeta, hairspray, drunk uncles, and other Quinceanera stories: an anthology. edited by Adriana Lopez. Rayo/HarperCollins 2007 332p il pa $14.95

Grades: 11 12 Adult **392**

1. Quinceañera (Social custom) 2. Hispanic Americans -- Social life and customs

ISBN 978-0-06-124192-5; 0-06-124192-X

LC 2007-14489

"This collection offers a memorable blend of the sweetness and pain that mark life's milestones." SLJ

394.1 Eating, drinking; using drugs

Albala, Ken

Food in early modern Europe. Greenwood Press 2003 360p il (Food through history) $49.95

Grades: 9 10 11 12 **394.1**

1. Eating customs 2. Food -- History 3. Europe -- Social life and customs

ISBN 0-313-31962-6

LC 2002-28431

"This very scholarly book provides interesting information for both the researcher and browser alike." Libr Media Connect

Includes bibliographical references

Amason, Jessica

This is why you're fat; where dreams become heart attacks. Jessica Amason & Richard Blakeley. HarperStudio 2009 133p. chiefly col. ill. (pbk.) $9.99

Grades: 10 11 12 **394.1**

1. Wit and humor 2. Eating customs 3. American cooking 4. Food -- Caloric content 5. Popular culture -- United States 6. Cooking, American 7. Food habits

-- North America

ISBN 0061936634; 9780061936630

LC 2009032820

This book is based on the food website called This Is Why You're Fat which features high caloric food combinations. "[T]here came a day when fancy vegetable towers came crashing down and $50 mushrooms were no longer acceptable. [Authors Jessica] Amason and [Richard] Blak[e]ley wanted see the old stand-bys, the carnival foods of their childhoods, the sticky mess of a deep-fried candy bar, the indulgence of a greasy burger with all the fixins. It was the birth of the nasty food web-trend. . . . The website This is Why You're Fat is an ode to this trend - whether seen as a commentary on North American dietary habits or a celebration of the deliciously bad - Amason and Blak[el]ey are devoted to the world's newfound obsession with over-the-top food." (Publisher's note)

Includes index.

Schlosser, Eric

Chew on this; everything you don't want to know about fast food. by Eric Schlosser and Charles Wilson. Houghton Mifflin Co. 2006 304p il $16; pa $9.99

Grades: 6 7 8 9 10 **394.1**

1. Eating habits 2. Food industry 3. Convenience foods

ISBN 0-618-71031-0; 0-618-59394-2 pa

LC 2005-27527

"An adaptation of Schlosser's Fast Food Nation (Houghton, 2001), Chew on This covers the history of the fast-food industry and delves into the agribusiness and animal husbandry methods that support it. . . . Equally disturbing is his revelation of the way that the fast-food giants have studied childhood behavior and geared their commercials and free toy inclusions to hook the youngest consumers. The text is written in a lively, layout-the-facts manner. Occasional photographs add bits of visual interest." SLJ

★ **Fast** food nation; the dark side of the all-American meal. Houghton Mifflin 2001 356p il $25

Grades: 11 12 Adult **394.1**

1. Restaurants 2. Food industry 3. Convenience foods

ISBN 0-395-97789-4

LC 00-53886

"Schlosser documents the effects of fast food on America's economy, its youth culture, and allied industries. . . . Starting with a young woman who makes minimum wage working at a Colorado fast-food restaurant, Schlosser relates the oft-told story of Ray Kroc's founding of McDonald's. The author also tells about the development of the franchise method of business ownership and the health and nutrition implications of fast-food consumption." Booklist

Includes bibliographical references

Tobacco in history and culture; an encyclopedia. Jordan Goodman, editor in chief. Thomson Gale

2005 2v il (Scribner turning points library) set $275

Grades: 11 12 Adult   **394.1**
1. Reference books 2. Tobacco -- Encyclopedias
ISBN 0-684-31405-3

LC 2004-7109

"This makes an excellent starting point for readers looking for quick entrance to the vast body of knowledge of the history and diversity of tobacco uses, tobacco health, addiction, social control issues, advertising, production, and distribution, among other topics." Choice
Includes bibliographical references

394.26   Holidays

Christianson, Stephen G.

The **international** book of days; edited by Lynn M. Messina; contributors, Jennifer Peloso, Norris Smith, Laura Ware. H.W. Wilson 2004 xxxi, 889p il map $140

Grades: 11 12 Adult   **394.26**
1. Holidays 2. Festivals
ISBN 0-8242-0975-3

LC 2004-42285

This "book presents an international tour of holidays and major historical events. Organized by day of the year, the book covers some 1500 key events in world history." Libr J

Encyclopedia of holidays and celebrations; a country-by-country guide. Matthew Dennis, editor. Facts on File 2006 3v il map (Facts on File library of world history) set $275

Grades: 11 12 Adult   **394.26**
1. Holidays 2. Festivals
ISBN 0-8160-6235-8; 978-0-8160-6235-5

LC 2005-27700

This is "a three-volume guide that explores holidays and festivals in 206 countries. Volumes I and II are organized alphabetically by country, and volume III contains overviews of major internationally observed holidays and religions. . . . This welcome addition to multicultural studies is attractively laid out, easy to use, great for browsing as well as fact finding, and is highly recommended for high school, public, and college libraries." Ref & User Services Quarterly
Includes bibliographical references

Forbes, Bruce David

Christmas; a candid history. University of California Press 2007 179p il $19.95; pa $12.95

Grades: 9 10 11 12 Adult   **394.26**
1. Christmas
ISBN 978-0-520-25104-5; 978-0-520-25802-0 pa

LC 2007-00366

The author "presents a brief social history of Christmas from pre-Christian winter celebrations to the commercialization of the holiday in American popular culture. The growth of the holiday to include Christmas cards, music and movies are included in this easy to read overview." Univ Press Books for Public and Second Sch Libr, 2008
Includes bibliographical references

Gulevich, Tanya

Encyclopedia of Christmas and New Year's celebrations; illustrated by Mary Ann Stavros-Lanning. Omnigraphics 2003 xx, 977p il $68

Grades: 11 12 Adult   **394.26**
1. New Year 2. Christmas
ISBN 0-7808-0625-5

LC 2003-40580

First published 2000 with title: Encyclopedia of Christmas

The author "covers a variety of secular and sacred aspects of Christmas and New Year's celebrations. . . . This encyclopedic work is useful for those schools where folklore is covered, or for those interested in origins of the holidays." Libr Media Connect
Includes bibliographical references

Hillstrom, Laurie

The **Thanksgiving** book; [by] Laurie C. Hillstrom. Omnigraphics 2008 328p il $65

Grades: 9 10 11 12 Adult   **394.26**
1. Thanksgiving Day
ISBN 978-0-7808-0403-6

LC 2007-25708

"This book is definitely a wonderful tribute to the holiday of Thanksgiving." Am Ref Books Annu, 2008
Includes bibliographical references

★ **Holiday** symbols and customs; 4th ed.; Omnigraphics 2009 1321p $94

Grades: 11 12 Adult   **394.26**
1. Holidays 2. Festivals
ISBN 978-0-7808-0990-1

LC 2008-28403

First published 1998 with title: Holiday symbols
"Describes the origins of 323 holidays around the world. Explains where, when, and how each event is celebrated, with detailed information on the symbols and customs associated with the holiday. Includes contact information and web sites for related organizations." Publisher's note
Includes bibliographical references

★ **Holidays,** festivals, and celebrations of the world dictionary; detailing more than 3,000 observances from all 50 states and more than 100 nations: a compendious reference guide to popular, ethnic, religious, national, and ancient holidays. . . edited by Cherie D. Abbey. 4th ed.; Omnigraphics 2010 1323p $144

Grades: 8 9 10 11 12 Adult   **394.26**
1. Reference books 2. Holidays -- Dictionaries 3. Festivals -- Dictionaries
ISBN 978-0-7808-0994-9

LC 2009-41138

First edition published 1994 compiled by Sue Ellen Thompson and Barbara W. Carlson

"A comprehensive dictionary that describes more than 3,000 holidays and festivals celebrated around the world. Features both secular and religious events from many different cultures, countries, and ethnic groups. Includes contact information for events; multiple appendices with background information on world holidays; extensive bibliography; multiple indexes." Publisher's note

Roy, Christian

Traditional festivals; a multicultural encyclopedia. ABC-CLIO 2005 2v il set $185
Grades: 9 10 11 12   **394.26**
1. Festivals
ISBN 1-57607-089-1

LC 2005-10444

"The work attempts to cover festivals from all major religions. Moreover, the text also takes into account festival and feast days from ancient or extinct societies. . . . Articles trace the historical development of festivals as well as geographical variations of these holy and feast days in a comparative framework. . . . This will be a very helpful resource for researchers in the field of comparative religion and culture." Choice

Includes bibliographical references

395   Etiquette (Manners)

Baldrige, Letitia

Letitia Baldrige's new manners for new times; a complete guide to etiquette. illustrations by Denise Cavalieri Fike. Scribner 2003 xxvi, 709p il $35
Grades: 11 12 Adult   **395**
1. Etiquette
ISBN 0-7432-1062-X

LC 2003-65666

First published 1990 with title: Letitia Baldrige's complete guide to the new manners for the 90's

"Combining correctness, consideration, and common sense in equal measure, Baldrige advises readers on proper ways to approach intricate situations. She addresses same-sex unions, pregnant brides, blended and extended families, and sexual harassment with aplomb." Libr J

Isaacs, Florence

What do you say when-- talking to people with confidence on any social or business occasion. Clarkson Potter Publishers 2009 151p $18
Grades: 9 10 11 12 Adult   **395**
1. Etiquette 2. Conversation
ISBN 978-0-307-40528-9

LC 2008-40535

"This small book lays out a strategy for successful networking and socializing through a series of simple tips related to a wide array of common business and social situations. The author offers up hundreds of conversation starters designed to elicit thoughtful responses from acquaintances, colleagues, and even complete strangers. . . . Written in a simple and engaging style, this practical guide is filled with real-world scenarios depicting job interviews, family gatherings, dating, and funerals." SLJ

Martin, Judith

Miss Manners' guide to excruciatingly correct behavior; illustrated by Gloria Kamen. freshly updated; Norton 2005 858p il $35

Grades: 11 12 Adult   **395**
1. Etiquette
ISBN 0-393-05874-3

LC 2005-00264

First published 1982 by Atheneum Pubs.

"Miss Manners is always as entertaining as she is civilized." Booklist

Post, Peggy

★ **Emily** Post's Etiquette; 17th ed.; HarperCollins Publishers 2004 876p $39.95
Grades: 7 8 9 10 11 12 Adult   **395**
1. Etiquette
ISBN 0-06-620957-9

LC 2004-40508

First published 1922 under the authorship of Emily Post. Periodically revised and updated. Title varies. 11th-15th editions revised by Elizabeth Post; 16th-17th editions revised by Peggy Post

"The classic reference for which fork to use has been expanded to include such modern situations as dating, living together, second marriages, and co-ed business traveling." N Y Public Libr Book of How & Where to Look It Up

Senning, Cindy Post

Emily Post prom and party etiquette. Collins 2010 134p il $15.99
Grades: 7 8 9 10 11 12   **395**
1. Parties 2. Etiquette
ISBN 978-0-06-111713-8; 0-06-111713-7

LC 2009-2795

"Covering parties and special occasions like prom, homecoming, quinceañera, and graduation, the authors have developed a modern set of rules for navigating today's more relaxed social customs with finesse and confidence. Myriad issues are tackled, from how to rent a tuxedo and who pays for what on prom night to table settings and crafting the perfect thank-you note, with important points highlighted. The comprehensive guide gives proper respect to religious occasions and thoughtfully explains how to determine from an invitation whether bringing a date is acceptable or not. Witty line drawings complement the text." SLJ

398   Folklore

De Vos, Gail

Tales, rumors, and gossip; exploring contemporary folk literature in grades 7-12. Libraries Unlimited 1996 xx, 405p $39
Grades: Adult Professional   **398**
1. Folklore
ISBN 1-56308-190-3

LC 95-19553

"Aimed at the professional, the book is divided into three sections: an introduction to contemporary legends, the role of these legends in the world around us, and a discussion of individual legends. If you are looking for legends on cults, demonology or Satanism, you'll find them here. . . . Librarians and teachers will use this as a resource for contemporary literature classes." Book Rep

Includes bibliographical references

Guiley, Rosemary Ellen

The **encyclopedia** of vampires & werewolves;
foreword by Jeanne Keyes Youngson. 2nd ed; Facts
On File 2011 430p il $85; pa $24.95

Grades: 9 10 11 12 Adult   **398**
1. Reference books 2. Monsters -- Encyclopedias
3. Vampires -- Encyclopedias 4. Werewolves --
Encyclopedias
ISBN 978-0-8160-8179-0; 0-8160-8179-4; 978-0-
8160-8180-6 pa; 0-8160-8180-8 pa; 978-1-4381-
3632-5 ebook; 1-4381-3632-3 ebook

LC 2010034839

First published 2004 with title: The encyclopedia of
vampires, werewolves, and other monsters

"Entries describe supposed true historical accounts, how
vampires and werewolves come into existence, beliefs about
vampires and werewolves, and real-life creatures and cases
that may have inspired their legends. . . . Fictional vampires
from a range of media are discussed, along with the people
who helped create them." Publisher's note

Includes bibliographical references

Hurston, Zora Neale

★ **Folklore,** memoirs, and other writings. Library of Am. 1995 1001p il $35

Grades: 11 12 Adult   **398**
ISBN 0-940450-84-4

LC 94-21384

Companion volume to Novels and stories (1995)

"This is the first time the unexpurgated version of Hurston's 1942 autobiography, Dust Tracks on the Road, is being published; sections deemed too provocative (dealing
with politics, race, and sex) have been restored. Mules and
Men (1935) is a collection of African American folklore she
gleaned on travels in the South, while Tell My Horse (1938)
tenders her personal findings on African-based religion in
Jamaica and Haiti. Additionally, 22 magazine and book articles with anthropological themes . . . that have never been
gathered into book form are corralled here." Booklist

Robson, David

Encounters with vampires. ReferencePoint
Press 2010 80p il (Vampire library) lib bdg $26.95

Grades: 7 8 9 10   **398**
1. Vampires
ISBN 978-1-6015-2133-0; 1-6015-2133-2

LC 2010-10100

The author "lays out both folklore and real-world reports
of bloodsucking beings. Expanding beyond familiar Transylvanian tales and stories of vampires in strictly human form,
the author's survey is global, from the Malaysian langsuyar,
believed to be responsible for many newborn deaths, to the
red-eyed, monstrous Latin American chupacabra, notorious
for preying on livestock. . . . Young vampire-fiction fans will
find much to ponder here, while the accounts of contemporary murders with purported vampire links may emerge as
the most chilling and grisly." Booklist

Includes bibliographical references

World folklore for storytellers; tales of wonder, wisdom, fools, and heroes. Josepha Sherman, editor.
Sharpe Reference 2010 368p il $95

Grades: 11 12 Adult   **398**
1. Folklore 2. Storytelling
ISBN 978-0-7656-8174-4

LC 2009-10525

This is "a wonderfully wide-ranging collection of nearly
200 ethnically diverse folktales. Particularly vital is that the
stories are organized thematically rather than geographically, allowing for broader symbolic and anthropological comparisons. Each narrative runs several pages, includes a brief
explanatory introduction, and consistently concludes with
at least two bibliographic references. Pockets of multipage
color plates offer images from native folktale anthologies
and other relevant artistic renderings." Libr J

Includes bibliographical references

398.2   Folk literature

★ **American** folklore; an encyclopedia. edited
by Jan Harold Brunvand. Garland 1996 794p
il (Garland reference library of the humanities)
hardcover o.p. pa $44.95

Grades: 11 12 Adult   **398.2**
1. Reference books 2. Folklore -- United States --
Encyclopedias
ISBN 0-8153-3350-1 pa

LC 95-53734

This volume contains "more than 500 articles covering
American and Canadian folklore from holidays, festivals,
and rituals to crafts, music, dance, and occupations. Well-
chosen black-and-white photographs illustrate many aspects
of our rich folklife tradition. Twenty-three ethnic groups
receive lengthy articles describing their traditional and contemporary folklore—with the exception of Native Americans." Am Libr

Includes bibliographical references

Asian-Pacific folktales and legends; edited by Jeannette L. Faurot. Simon & Schuster 1995 252p
pa $12

Grades: 11 12 Adult   **398.2**
1. Folklore -- Asia
ISBN 0-684-81197-9

LC 95-31549

"The 65 myths and folktales in this volume are gathered
from the rich heritage of legends in eight East and Southeast
Asian countries, with the largest number of stories coming
from China (17). The editor herself translates or retells 14 of
the Chinese stories for this collection, while the others are
reprinted from existing anthologies. . . . The collection gives
a quick, multinational overview of some favorite Asian legends." Libr J

Brunvand, Jan Harold

★ **Be** afraid, be very afraid; the book of scary
urban legends. [collected by] Jan Harold Brunvand.
Norton 2004 256p pa $13.95

Grades: 9 10 11 12 **398.2**
1. Legends 2. Folklore
ISBN 0-393-32613-6

LC 2004-11798

In this collection of urban legends, the author "has compiled the scariest, grisliest ones—some that are unfamiliar but many that have been heard at sleepovers and depicted in horror movies over the past several years. . . . This is a good addition where such titles are popular." SLJ

Includes bibliographical references

Bulfinch, Thomas
Bulfinch's mythology; foreword by Alberto Manguel. Modern Library pbk. ed.; Modern Library 2004 862p pa $17.95
Grades: 11 12 Adult **398.2**
1. Chivalry 2. Emperors 3. Mythology 4. Mabinogion 5. Folklore -- Europe
ISBN 0-375-75147-5

LC 2005-271850

First combined edition published 1913 by Crowell. Originally published in three separate volumes 1855, 1858 and 1862 respectively

"The classic work on mythology, Bulfinch's gives brief summations of Greek, Roman, Norse, Arthurian, and other miscellaneous myths and includes notes on the 'Iliad,' the 'Odyssey,' and the 'Aeneid.'" N Y Public Libr Book of How & Where to Look It Up

Includes bibliographical references

De Vos, Gail
What happens next? contemporary urban legends and popular culture. Gail de Vos. xxvii, 242 p.p
Grades: 11 12 **398.2**
1. Legends 2. Urban folklore 3. Literature and folklore 4. Mass media and folklore
ISBN 9781598846331; 9781598846348

LC 2012014930

"This fascinating book uncovers the history behind urban legends and explains how the contemporary iterations of familiar fictional tales provide a window into the modern concerns--and digital advancements--of our society. " (Publisher)

Includes bibliographical references and indexes

★ **Favorite** folktales from around the world; edited by Jane Yolen. Pantheon Bks. 1986 498p hardcover o.p. pa $18
Grades: 11 12 Adult **398.2**
1. Folklore 2. Fairy tales
ISBN 0-394-75188-4 pa

LC 86-42644

"Selections include tales from the American Indians, the brothers Grimm, Italo Calvino's Italian folk-tales, as well as stories from Iceland, Afghanistan, Scotland, and many other countries. Yolen provides each section with a relevant introduction, often including historical and literary factors, thus alerting readers as to what to look for." SLJ

Holt, David
Spiders in the hairdo; modern urban legends. collected and retold by David Holt & Bill Mooney. August House 1999 111p il pa $7.95
Grades: 11 12 Adult **398.2**
1. Folklore -- United States
ISBN 0-87483-525-9

LC 99-11973

This "collection of urban myths assembles 50 brief stories from modern oral tradition. Commonly attributed to FOAFs (friends of a friend), they are intriguing and often frightening tales passed along in casual conversation. These tales are the substance of modern folklore, an evolving treasury of evanescent narratives." Libr J

Includes bibliographical references

Latin American folktales; stories from Hispanic and Indian traditions. edited and with an introduction by John Bierhorst. Pantheon Bks. 2002 386p (Pantheon fairy tale & folklore library) hardcover o.p. pa $17
Grades: 11 12 Adult **398.2**
1. Folklore -- Latin America
ISBN 0-375-42066-5; 0-375-71439-1 pa

LC 2001-34056

Bierhorst "has collected and translated more than 100 folktales from the Spanish oral tradition as practiced in the Americas, from New Mexico to Nicaragua to Chile. . . . {His} introduction provides the context not only for the evolution and telling . . . of the folktales but also for their recording, primarily by early-twentieth-century folklorists and anthropologists. He then sets his readers loose in a vivid world of tricksters, witches, amorous young men, sneaky wives {and} animals with magical powers. . . . A glossary and registry of motifs adds to this volume's value and enjoyment." Booklist

Includes bibliographical references (p. 373-383)

Lester, Julius
Black folktales; illustrated by Tom Feelings; with an introduction by the author. 1st Evergreen ed; Grove Press 1992 110p il pa $12
Grades: 9 10 11 12 **398.2**
1. Blacks -- Folklore 2. Folklore -- Africa
ISBN 0-8021-3242-1

LC 91-7619

First published 1969 by Baron, R.W.

"Lester gives 12 African and Afro-American folk tales such twentieth-century touches as the Lord's reading of the 'TV Guide' and the mention of Rap Brown and Aretha Franklin but his sprightly versions retain the spirit and shape of the original story. . . . These stories of creation, love, folk heroes, and everyday people have a direct simplicity and laconic humor that is both effective and appealing." Booklist

Malory, Thomas
Le morte Darthur, or, The hoole book of Kyng Arthur and of his noble knyghtes of the Rounde Table; authoritative text, sources and backgrounds, criticism. [by] Sir Thomas Malory; edited by Stephen

H.A. Shepherd. Norton 2004 lii, 954p (A Norton critical edition) pa $16.95

Grades: 11 12 Adult	**398.2**
1. Kings
ISBN 0-393-97464-2

LC 2002-26534

Originally published 1485

"The work is a skillful selection and blending of materials taken from the mass of Arthurian legends. The central story consists of two main elements: the reign of King Arthur ending in catastrophe and the dissolution of the Round Table; and the quest of the Holy Grail." Oxford Companion to Engl Lit

Includes bibliographical references

Pickering, David
★ A **dictionary** of folklore. Facts on File 1999 324p $44

Grades: 11 12 Adult	**398.2**
1. Reference books 2. Folklore -- Dictionaries 3. Mythology -- Dictionaries
ISBN 0-8160-4550-0

The author provides entries "on such subjects as herbal remedies, the supersititions connected with various gemstones, the folklore associated with selected trees, plants, birds, and animals. He also covers the ritual tradition of holidays and festivals and the origins of proverbs and sayings. In addition, the dictionary mentions characters and heroes from selkies to Joe Magarac, fantasy beings such as sprites and pixies, and some urban myths." Libr J

Pyle, Howard
The **story** of King Arthur and his knights; written and illustrated by Howard Pyle. Scribner 1984 312p il $22.95

Grades: 1 2 8 9 10 11	**398.2**
1. Arthurian romances 2. Kings
ISBN 0-684-14814-5

LC 84-50167

A reissue of the title first published 1903

This is an account of the times "when Arthur, son of Uther-Pendragon, was Overlord of Britain and Merlin was a powerful enchanter, when the sword Excalibur was forged and won, when the Round Table came into being." Publisher's note

The **story** of Sir Launcelot and his companions. Dover Publications 1991 340p il pa $13.95

Grades: 8 9 10 11 12	**398.2**
1. Arthurian romances 2. Lancelot (Legendary character)
ISBN 0-486-26701-6

LC 90-22326

A reissue of the title first published 1907 by Scribner

This third book of the series follows "Sir Launcelot's adventures as he rescues Queen Guinevere from the clutches of Sir Mellegrans, does battle with the Worm of Corbin, wanders as a madman in the forest and is finally returned to health by the Lady Elaine." Best Sellers

The **story** of the champions of the Round Table; written and illustrated by Howard Pyle. Dover Publications 1968 328p il pa $11.95

Grades: 8 9 10 11 12	**398.2**
1. Arthurian romances
ISBN 0-486-21883-X

A reissue of the title first published 1905 by Scribner

"Pyle's second volume of Arthurian legends will be of interest to motivated students of literature and history, as well as useful in professional collections for comparisons and source work. In spite of the archaic language . . . the narrative depth and graphic force . . . will draw in readers." Booklist

The **story** of the Grail and the passing of Arthur. Dover Publications 1992 258p il pa $12.95

Grades: 8 9 10 11 12	**398.2**
1. Arthurian romances 2. Kings 3. Grail -- Fiction
ISBN 0-486-27361-X

LC 92-29058

A reissue of the title first published 1910 by Scribner

This fourth volume of the series follows the adventures of Sir Geraint, Galahad's quest for the holy Grail, the battle between Launcelot and Gawaine, and the slaying of Mordred

Tingle, Tim
Walking the Choctaw road. Cinco Puntos Press 2003 142p il $24.95; pa $10.95

Grades: 7 8 9 10	**398.2**
1. Choctaw Indians -- Folklore 2. Folklore -- Southern States
ISBN 0-938317-74-1; 0-938317-73-3 pa

LC 2003-1069

A collection of stories of the Choctaw people, including traditional lore arising from beliefs and myths, historical tales passed down through generations, and personal stories of contemporary life

"Sophisticated narrative devices and some subtle character nuances give these stories a literary cast, but the author's evocative language, expert pacing, and absorbing subject matter will rivet readers and listeners both." Booklist

Yivo Institute for Jewish Research
Yiddish folktales; edited by Beatrice Silverman Weinreich; translated by Leonard Wolf. Pantheon Bks. 1988 xxxii, 413p il (Pantheon fairy tale & folklore library) hardcover o.p. pa $18

Grades: 11 12 Adult	**398.2**
1. Jews -- Folklore
ISBN 0-8052-1090-3 pa

LC 88-42594

A "collection of Yiddish folktales divided into various categories, including allegories, children's tales, humor, legends, and the supernatural. The more than 200 selections from the world of Eastern European Jewry are drawn from the archives of the YIVO Institute of Jewish Research. . . . {This work} brings the Yiddish culture of long ago vividly to life." Booklist

Zitkala-Sa

American Indian stories, legends, and other writings; edited with an introduction and notes by Cathy N. Davidson and Ada Norris. Penguin Bks. 2003 xlvi, 268p il pa $13

Grades: 9 10 11 12 **398.2**
1. Native Americans -- Folklore 2. Native Americans -- Social conditions
ISBN 0-14-243709-3

LC 2002-32268

This is a collection of stories and nonfiction writings by the Sioux writer and activist. "Her work, surprisingly, seems undated. . . . This first comprehensive collection . . . reveals Zitkala-Sa as a crusading, spiritually aware woman." Booklist

Includes bibliographical references

398.21   Tales and lore on a specific topic

Hearne, Betsy Gould

Beauties and beasts; by Betsy Hearne; illustrated by Joanne Caroselli. Oryx Press 1993 179p il (Oryx multicultural folktale series) pa $33.95

Grades: 8 9 10 11 12 Adult **398.21**
1. Folklore 2. Mythology 3. Fairy tales
ISBN 0-89774-729-1

LC 93-16

"Professionals will be very grateful for this sensitively written, thoughtful, and accessible interpretive collection." J Youth Serv Libr

Includes bibliographical references

398.24   Tales and lore of plants and animals

Nigg, Joe

Wonder beasts; tales and lore of the phoenix, the griffin, the unicorn, and the dragon. Libraries Unlimited 1995 160p il $27.50

Grades: 7 8 9 10 **398.24**
1. Dragons 2. Unicorns 3. Animals -- Folklore
ISBN 1-56308-242-X

LC 94-46797

The author "has compiled material ranging from Herodotus, Ovid, Pliny the Elder, to Chinese and Native American folk tales, and fantasies by Edith Nesbit. Each entry is carefully documented and a reference list at the end provides dozens of full citations for those who'd like to delve deeper. Wonder Beasts will be useful to students who are researching myth and folklore, and to librarians and scholars who are looking for a comprehensive source list on the topic." Voice Youth Advocates

399   Customs of war and diplomacy

Wagner, Eduard

Medieval costume, armour, and weapons; selected and illustrated by Eduard Wagner; text by Zoro-

slava Drobná & Jan Durdik; with a new introduction by Vladimir Dolinek. Dover Publications 2000 72p il pa $39.95

Grades: 9 10 11 12 **399**
1. Armor 2. Weapons 3. Medieval civilization 4. Clothing and dress -- History
ISBN 0-486-41240-7

LC 00-38419

Original Czech edition, 1956

"Over 400 royalty-free illustrations trace the evolution of clothing styles, armor, and weapons during the medieval period in Central Europe—from simple tunics and robes of peasants to the battle equipment and armor of warriors and the fur-lined cloaks and brocaded garments of the aristocracy." Publisher's note

Includes bibliographical references

400   LANGUAGE

400   Language

Crystal, David

The **Cambridge** encyclopedia of language; 3rd ed; Cambridge University Press 2010 516p il map $99; pa $45

Grades: 11 12 Adult **400**
1. Reference books 2. Language and languages -- Encyclopedias
ISBN 978-0-521-51698-3; 978-0-521-73650-3 pa

LC 2010-502889

First published 1987

"A valuable and concise . . . handbook for linguistic beginners, linguistic researchers looking for a quick overview and, most of all, the general reader interested in language." Linguist List

Includes bibliographical references

Dalby, Andrew

★ **Dictionary** of languages; the definitive reference to more than 400 languages. Columbia Univ. Press 1999 734p il maps $73.50; pa $22.95

Grades: 11 12 Adult **400**
1. Reference books 2. Language and languages -- Dictionaries
ISBN 0-231-11568-7; 0-231-11569-5 pa

LC 98-87178

This dictionary includes alphabetical entries that "cover all languages with official status as well as those with a written literature and 175 minor languages with significant historical and/or anthropological interest. A preface explains the author's pronunciation scheme. . . . The entries themselves are from two to four pages long. Each one discusses a specific language. . . . With coverage of languages from Abkhaz to Zulu, explanations of Egyptian hieroglyphics and Sumerian script, and a discussion of Chinese dialects and characters, [this] . . . is a welcome addition to public and academic library collections." Booklist

410 Linguistics

Crystal, David

★ **Language** and the internet; 2nd ed.; Cambridge University Press 2006 304p $29.99

Grades: 11 12 Adult **410**

1. Internet 2. Language and languages

ISBN 978-0-521-86859-4; 0-521-86859-9

LC 2006-12916

First published 2001

"Covering a range of Internet genres, including e-mail, chat, and the Web, this is . . . [an] account of how the Internet is radically changing the way we use language." Publisher's note

Includes bibliographical references

411 Writing systems of standard forms of languages

Humez, Alexander

On the dot; the speck that changed the world. [by] Alexander Humez, Nicholas Humez. Oxford University Press 2008 256p $24.95

Grades: 9 10 11 12 Adult **411**

1. Dot (Symbol) 2. Dot (Symbol) -- History

ISBN 978-0-19-532499-0

LC 2008-3320

"Ideal for etymologists and trivia buffs, this book covers an array of information and innovations on the relevance of this 'speck.'" Publ Wkly

Includes bibliographical references

412 Etymology of standard forms of languages

Hayakawa, S. I.

Language in thought and action; {by} S.I. Hayakawa and Alan R. Hayakawa. 5th ed; Harcourt Brace Jovanovich 1990 287p il $49.95; pa $16

Grades: 11 12 Adult **412**

1. Semantics 2. English language 3. Thought and thinking

ISBN 0-15-550120-8; 0-15-648240-1 pa

LC 89-84371

First published 1939 with title: Language in action

The author analyzes the nature of language, discusses the processes of thinking and writing, and gives advice on thinking and writing clearly

Includes bibliographical references

418 Standard usage (Prescriptive linguistics)

Ostenson, Jonathan W.

Integrating young adult literature through the common core standards; Rachel L. Wadham and Jonathan W. Ostenson. Libraries Unlimited, an imprint of ABC-CLIO, LLC 2013 x, 260 p.p (paperback) $45

Grades: Adult Professional **418**

1. Reading 2. Young adult literature 3. Reading (Secondary) 4. Reading comprehension 5. Teenagers -- Books and reading -- United States 6. Language arts (Secondary) -- Standards -- United States 7. Young adult literature -- Study and teaching (Secondary)

ISBN 1610691180; 9781610691185

LC 2012036269

This text "examines the various components to be considered when determining the complexity of YA texts. The book is divided into two sections with the first part dealing with the various elements that make texts complex and the second section providing specific instructional suggestions for integrating the CCSS [common core standards] with YAL [young adult literature]." (New England Reading Association Journal)

Includes bibliographical references and indexes

419 Sign languages

Costello, Elaine

★ **Random** House Webster's American Sign Language dictionary: unabridged. Random House Reference 2008 xxxii, 1200p $55

Grades: 8 9 10 11 12 Adult **419**

1. Reference books 2. Sign language -- Dictionaries

ISBN 978-0-375-42616-2; 0-375-42616-7

First published 1994 with title: Random House American Sign Language dictionary

This dictionary includes "over 5,600 signs for the novice and experienced user alike. It includes complete descriptions of each sign, plus full-torso illustrations. There is also a subject index for easy reference as well as alternate signs for the same meaning." Publisher's note

Gallaudet University

★ The **Gallaudet** dictionary of American Sign Language; Clayton Valli, editor in chief; illustrated by Peggy Swartzel Lott, Daniel Renner, and Rob Hills. Gallaudet University Press 2005 xli, 558p il $49.95

Grades: 8 9 10 11 12 Adult **419**

1. Reference books 2. Sign language -- Dictionaries

ISBN 1-56368-282-6; 978-1-56368-282-7

LC 2005-51129

"This is a very valuable language resource for parents, students, and teachers learning ASL as a first language and as a second language." Choice

Includes bibliographical references

Grayson, Gabriel

★ **Talking** with your hands, listening with your eyes; a complete photographic guide to American Sign Language. Square One Pubs. 2002 373p il pa $26.95

Grades: 11 12 Adult **419**

1. Sign language

ISBN 0-7570-0007-X

LC 2002-1125

"An outstanding, user-friendly resource for those interested in learning ASL." SLJ

420 Specific languages

Crystal, David

★ The **Cambridge** encyclopedia of the English language; 2nd ed; Cambridge Univ. Press 2003 499p il hardcover o.p. pa $35
Grades: 11 12 Adult **420**
1. English language
ISBN 0-521-82348-X; 0-521-53033-4 pa
LC 2003-272259
First published 1995
This "volume is divided into six broad topics that cover the English language's history, vocabulary, grammar, writing and speech systems, usage, and acquisition. Within these major topics, the book is divided into logical subtopics and finally into the basic unit of the text—the two-page spread. . . . The clear and spirited text is stunning, enhanced with over 500 illustrations, making this a particularly rich reference work and a browser's dream." Libr J {review of 1995 edition}

McCrum, Robert

The **story** of English; [by] Robert McCrum, Willam Cran [and] Robert MacNeil. 3rd rev ed; Penguin Bks. 2003 xxi, 468p pa $16
Grades: 11 12 Adult **420**
1. English language -- History
ISBN 0-14-200231-3
LC 2002-29818
First published 1986 by Viking
A "companion to the PBS television series of the same name. . . . The text covers the history of our language from its roots in Latin through its transplanting to other shores and its infusions from other cultures and languages. . . . Good for browsing, this book is a must for word and history buffs." SLJ [review of 1986 edition]
Includes bibliographical references

421 Writing system, phonology, phonetics of standard English

Truss, Lynne

Eats, shoots & leaves; the zero tolerance approach to punctuation. Gotham Books 2004 xxvii, 209p $19.95; pa $12
Grades: 8 9 10 11 12 Adult **421**
1. Punctuation
ISBN 1-59240-087-6; 1-59240-203-8 pa
LC 2004-40646
First published 2003 in the United Kingdom
The author "dissects common errors that grammar mavens have long deplored (often, as she readily points out, in isolation) and makes . . . arguments for increased attention to punctuation correctness. . . . Truss serves up delightful, unabashedly strict and sometimes snobby little book, with cheery Britishisms ('Lawks-a-mussy!') dotting pages

that express a more international righteous indignation." Publ Wkly
Includes bibliographical references

422 Etymology of standard English

Adonis to Zorro; Oxford dictionary of reference and allusion. edited by Andrew Delahunty and Sheila Dignen. 3rd ed.; Oxford University Press 2010 406p $34.95
Grades: 11 12 Adult **422**
1. Allusions 2. Reference books
ISBN 978-0-19-956745-4; 0-19-956745-X
LC 2010-549367
First published 2001 with title: The Oxford dictionary of allusions
"This guide to allusions and common references is a moderately priced volume well worth adding to a public, school, community college, or college shelf. Neat and user-friendly, the 1,900 entries, their provenance, definitions, models, and starred cross-references identify a range of familiar terms, from 'Terminator' to 'hobbit,' and from 'My Lai' to the 'sword of Damocles' and 'thirty pieces of silver.' The text makes clever use of fonts, dingbats, and point count to identify authors, sources, and dates." Choice

★ **From** bonbon to cha-cha; Oxford dictionary of foreign words and phrases. edited by Andrew Delahunty. 2nd ed; Oxford University Press 2008 411p $24.95; pa $18.99
Grades: 11 12 Adult **422**
1. Reference books 2. English language -- Foreign words and phrases -- Dictionaries
ISBN 978-0-19-954369-4; 0-19-954369-0; 978-0-19-954368-7 pa; 0-19-954368-2 pa
LC 2008-482026
First published 1997 with title: The Oxford dictionary of foreign words and phrases. Paperback has title: Oxford dictionary of foreign words and phrases
This reference "offers coverage of more than 6,000 foreign words and phrases that are in regular use in English today." Publisher's note

Gorrell, Gena K.

Say what? the weird and mysterious journey of the English language. Tundra Books 2009 146p il pa $10.95
Grades: 7 8 9 10 11 12 **422**
1. English language -- Etymology
ISBN 978-0-88776-878-1; 0-88776-878-4
"Gorrell takes readers on a quick and amusing historical tour of the English language, looking at how it has been influenced by Latin, Old English, French, and German. . . . This clever and funny book also integrates explanations for tricky grammar and spelling problems as part of the historical explanation for our changing language. Readers are not only given examples of malapropisms but also a list of several words that are often confused. . . . Supplementary materials including a time line and a large number of illustrations

will make this book a valuable addition to both public and school libraries." Voice Youth Advocates

Hendrickson, Robert

★ The **Facts** on File encyclopedia of word and phrase origins; 4th ed., [Updated and expanded ed.]; Facts On File 2008 948p (Facts on File library of language and literature) $95; pa $27.95

Grades: 11 12 Adult   **422**

1. Reference books 2. English language -- Terms and phrases 3. English language -- Etymology -- Dictionaries

ISBN 978-0-8160-6966-8; 978-0-8160-6967-5 pa

LC 2007-48223

First published 1987

"Because the entries have both scholarly value and the capacity to entertain, the book is ideal for both linguists and lay readers." Libr J

Hitchings, Henry

The **secret** life of words; how English became English. Farrar, Straus and Giroux 2008 440p $27

Grades: 8 9 10 11 12 Adult   **422**

1. English language -- Etymology

ISBN 978-0-374-25410-0; 0-374-25410-9

LC 2008-26055

"Hitchings here provides a colorful, thematic history of the English language. Treating borrowings and coinages as psychological windows to history, the author takes the reader on a tour of the lexicon from Anglo-Saxon to the present day and shows how new words answer linguistic needs. . . . Hitchings treats the reader to some 3,000 word histories. . . . With 90-plus pages of notes, sources, and useful indexes, this is a fine choice for libraries and a 'smorgasbord' for language aficionados." Choice

Includes bibliographical references

More word histories and mysteries; from aardvark to zombie. from the editors of the American Heritage dictionaries. Houghton Mifflin 2006 288p il pa $12.95

Grades: 8 9 10 11 12 Adult   **422**

1. Reference books 2. English language -- Etymology

ISBN 978-0-618-71681-4; 0-618-71681-5

LC 2006020835

This "emphasizes the huge number of source languages from which English draws its vast vocabulary—from Sanskrit to French and beyond. The introductory pages give the reader a brief overview of the methods and aims of etymology and a potted history of the origins of English. . . . The editors then present an alphabetical listing of words and their etymology. Each of the 300-plus entries is about half a page to a page long and briefly outlines the origins of the word, its use, and the evolution of its meaning. . . . The book's informative yet informal writing style would appeal to the amateur enthusiast, and accessibility is further enhanced by a useful glossary of linguistic terms." Libr J

★ The **Oxford** dictionary of English etymology; edited by C. T. Onions; with the assistance of G.

W. S. Friedrichsen and R. W. Burchfield. Oxford Univ. Press 1966 1024p $65

Grades: 11 12 Adult   **422**

1. Reference books 2. English language -- Etymology -- Dictionaries

ISBN 0-19-861112-9

"Authoritative work tracing the history of common English words back to their Indo-European roots. The most complete and reliable etymological dictionary ever published, it serves as a complement to the OED." Ref Sources for Small & Medium-sized Libr. 6th edition

Word histories and mysteries; from abracadabra to Zeus. from the editors of the American Heritage dictionaries. Houghton Mifflin Co. 2004 xvi, 348p il pa $12.95

Grades: 8 9 10 11 12 Adult   **422**

1. Reference books 2. English language -- Etymology

ISBN 978-0-618-45450-1; 0-618-45450-0

LC 2004014798

"The 400 alphabetically arranged entries here illustrate the diversity from which the English language draws its vocabulary, particularly from the prehistoric base that linguists call Proto-Indo-European. As a result, the editors aim to demonstrate links between the ancient base and modern English. . . . An overall quality resource." Libr J

423   Dictionaries of standard English

The **American** Heritage abbreviations dictionary; 3rd ed., [updated]; Houghton Mifflin 2007 294p $6.95

Grades: 9 10 11 12 Adult   **423**

1. Reference books 2. Acronyms -- Dictionaries 3. Abbreviations -- Dictionaries

ISBN 978-0-618-85747-0

Presents commonly used acronyms and abbreviations along with their meanings.

★ The **American** Heritage dictionary of the English language; 5th ed.; Houghton Mifflin Harcourt 2011 xxvii, 2084p il map

Grades: Adult   **423**

1. Reference books 2. Encyclopedias and dictionaries 3. English language -- Usage -- Dictionaries 4. English language -- Dictionaries

ISBN 9780547041018

LC 2011004777

First published 1969

This book, "the fifth edition of "The American Heritage Dictionary of the English Language" (AHD)" includes 10,000 new words, with "color photos in the margin to illustrate the definitions. Countries all have a small map with their location and major cities. . . . [U]sage notes . . . . have been updated . . . AHD also includes example sentences, and many of these have been lengthened with the addition of quotations from writers . . . Synonyms for words have been added . . . The purchase of this print edition contains a passkey for a free app version, and there is a free online version at www.ahdictionary.com." (Booklist)

The **American** Heritage student grammar dictionary; by the editors of the American Heritage Dictionaries. Houghton Mifflin Harcourt 2011 154p il
Grades: 9 10 11 12 Adult   **423**
1. Reference books 2. English language -- Grammar 3. English language -- Dictionaries
ISBN 978-0-547-47265-2
LC 2010051670
"Although barely more than 150 pages long, this title provides a mother lode of grammatical information. The American Heritage editors introduce each grammatical term with an example sentence, followed by a definition or explanation of the term. The appropriate placement of the term in a sentence is noted with samples showing various locations—before a verb, after a noun, etc. Additional notes about the term, e.g., 'attributive adjective,' 'double genitive,' or 'indirect discourse,' are included in a 'Useful Tip' section; there are See also sections for the majority of terms along with many illustrative cartoons." Libr J

Ammer, Christine
The **Facts** on File dictionary of cliches; 3rd ed.; Facts On File 2011 556p (Facts on File library of language and literature) $60; pa $19.95
Grades: 9 10 11 12 Adult   **423**
1. Reference books 2. English language -- Usage 3. English language -- Terms and phrases
ISBN 978-0-8160-8353-4; 978-0-8160-8354-1 pa; 978-1-4381-3705-6 ebook
LC 2010049234
First published 1992 with title: Have a nice day--no problem!: a dictionary of clichés
This book "explains the meanings and origins of more than 4,000 clichés and common expressions. Each entry includes the meaning of the cliché or expression, its origin and early uses, its historical development, and its present-day usage." Publisher's note
Includes bibliographical references

★ **Concise** Oxford American thesaurus. Oxford University Press 2006 996p $19.95
Grades: 11 12 Adult   **423**
1. Reference books 2. English language -- Synonyms and antonyms
ISBN 0-19-530485-3; 978-0-19-530485-5
LC 2005-35868
First published 1997 in the United Kingdom with title: The concise Oxford thesaurus; Original American edition published 1999 with title: The Oxford American thesaurus of current English
This "thesaurus contains over 15,000 entries with more than 350,000 synonyms and is . . . arranged with the typical synonyms listed first. . . . This simple arrangement makes this thesaurus particularly user-friendly." Libr J

★ **Concise** Oxford English dictionary; edited by Catherine Soanes, Angus Stevenson. 11th ed.,

rev; Oxford University Press 2008 xx, 1681p $35
Grades: 11 12 Adult   **423**
1. Reference books 2. English language -- Dictionaries
ISBN 978-0-19-954841-5
LC 2008-30091
First published 1911 under the editorship of H. W. Fowler and F. G. Fowler with title: The Concise dictionary of current English
This work contains over 240,000 entries, including derivatives, compounds and abbreviations. It includes explanatory notes on pronunciation, grammatical inflection and etymology.
Includes bibliographical references

Davidson, Mark
★ **Right,** wrong, and risky; a dictionary of today's American English usage. Norton 2006 570p $29.95
Grades: 11 12 Adult   **423**
1. Americanisms 2. Reference books 3. English language -- Usage 4. English language -- Dictionaries
ISBN 0-393-06119-1
LC 2005-17628
The author "offers a dictionary that 'views the real world of today's American English, identifying usage questions that are debatable, citing conflicting answers, and offering risk-free solutions for each conflict.' . . . Browsers will enjoy the colorful, interesting backstories on the origins of terms such as ground zero, on the sudden warming to the phrase girl talk, and on the widely misunderstood use of the word Neanderthal." Booklist
Includes bibliographical references

Garner, Bryan A.
★ **Garner's** modern American usage; 3rd ed; Oxford University Press 2009 lx, 942p $45
Grades: 11 12 Adult   **423**
1. Reference books 2. Americanisms -- Dictionaries 3. English language -- Usage -- Dictionaries
ISBN 978-0-19-538275-4
LC 2009-9539
First published 1998 with title: A dictionary of modern American usage
"One would be tempted to say that this is clearly one of the best works on the topic, but doing so would be using one of Garner's weasel words (intensives such as clearly that 'actually have the effect of weakening a statement'). Suffice it to say that it is highly recommended for most libraries." Booklist
Includes bibliographical references (p. 925-938)

Historical thesaurus of the Oxford English dictionary; with additional material from A Thesaurus of Old English. [edited by] Christian Kay [et al.] Oxford University Press 2009 3952p 2v set $395
Grades: 9 10 11 12 Adult   **423**
1. Reference books 2. English language -- Synonyms

and antonyms
ISBN 978-0-19-920899-9

LC 2009-935029

"The knowledge compiled in this 40-year project is stunning, and promises to revolutionize the study of the language by making wholly new kinds of questions possible." Choice

Includes bibliographical references

Houghton Mifflin Co.
The **American** Heritage dictionary of phrasal verbs. Houghton Mifflin Co. 2005 466p $19.95

Grades: 11 12 Adult   **423**
1. Reference books 2. English language -- Terms and phrases
ISBN 0-618-59260-1; 978-0-618-59260-9

LC 2005-12835

"This unique resource belongs on the shelves of most libraries as a complement to standard English-language dictionaries. It will be useful to native English speakers as well as to ESL students." Booklist

Little, Brown & Co. Inc.
★ **Bartlett's** Roget's thesaurus. Little, Brown 1996 xxxii, 1415p $21.95; pa $16.95

Grades: 8 9 10 11 12 Adult   **423**
1. Americanisms 2. Reference books 3. English language -- Synonyms and antonyms
ISBN 0-316-10138-9; 0-316-73587-6 pa

LC 96-18343

This thesaurus "reflects the current state of American English, including terminology from the worlds of composers and television, with such sub-categories as 'Living Things,' 'The Arts,' 'Feelings.' But what really makes the book a joy to use is the tremendously useful lists—everything from phobias to styles and periods of furniture." Am Libr

The **Merriam**-Webster dictionary of synonyms and antonyms. Merriam-Webster 1992 443p pa $4.99

Grades: 8 9 10 11 12 Adult   **423**
1. Reference books 2. English language -- Synonyms and antonyms
ISBN 0-87779-906-7

LC 93-119503

First published 1942 with title: Webster's dictionary of synonyms

"This synonym dictionary is an outstanding work. . . . Synonyms and similar words, alphabetically arranged, are carefully defined, discriminated, and illustrated with thousands of quotations. The entries also include antonyms and analogous words." Nichols. Guide to Ref Books for Sch Media Cent. 4th edition

Merriam-Webster Inc.
Merriam-Webster's collegiate dictionary; Eleventh ed; Merriam-Webster 2003 1623p il $23.95

Grades: 11 12 Adult   **423**
1. Reference books 2. English language -- Dictionaries
ISBN 0-87779-808-7

LC 2003-3674

First published 1898

This edition includes over 165,000 entries, 10,000 new words and meanings, 38,000 etymologies, a handbook of style, an essay on the English language, a special section on signs and symbols, and a free one-year subscription to the Collegiate Web site.

Merriam-Webster's collegiate thesaurus; 2nd ed.; Merriam-Webster 2010 16a, 1162p $21.95

Grades: 11 12 Adult   **423**
1. Reference books 2. English language -- Synonyms and antonyms
ISBN 978-0-8777-9269-7; 0-8777-9269-0

LC 2009-42161

First published 1976 with title: Webster's collegiate thesaurus

"Employs a conventional dictionary arrangement, and gives synonyms, related terms, idiomatic equivalents, antonyms, and contrasted words as applicable. Cross-references in small capitals." Guide to Ref Books. 11th edition

★ **Merriam**-Webster's visual dictionary. Merriam-Webster, Inc. 2012 1112 p. (hbk.) $39.95

Grades: 6 7 8 9 10 11 12 Adult   **423**
1. English language -- Dictionaries
ISBN 0877791511; 9780877791515

This visual dictionary, edited by Jean-Claude Corbeil, has "more than 8,000 highly detailed, full-color illustrations, organized by subject in specialized fields from all aspects of life, . . . [and] nearly 25,000 . . . technical and everyday terms with clear, concise definitions. . . . Themes include a wide variety of fields: astronomy, the earth, human beings, the animal kingdom, plants and gardening, . . . food, arts and architecture, . . . sports and games" and more. (Publisher's note)

★ **Metaphors** dictionary; [edited by] Elyse Sommer, with Dorrie Weiss. Visible Ink Press 2001 xlvi, 612p $24.95

Grades: 11 12 Adult   **423**
1. English language -- Terms and phrases
ISBN 1-57859-137-6

First published 1995 by Gale Res.

"Any library serving patrons involved in creative writing, composition, public speaking, or literary criticism should add this volume." Am Ref Books Annu, 1996 [entry for 1995 edition]

Mitchell, Kevin M.
Hip-hop rhyming dictionary; for rappers, DJs and MCs. Firebrand Music; Distributed by Alfred Pub. 2003 183p pa $10.95

Grades: 9 10 11 12 Adult   **423**
1. Reference books 2. Hip-hop -- Dictionaries 3. English language -- Rhyme 4. Rap music -- Dictionaries
ISBN 0-7390-3333-6

LC 2003-107925

This rhyming dictionary includes "writing tips to inspire creative lyrics as well as a brief history of rap and the artists who sent hip-hop to the top of the charts." Publisher's note

★ **New** Oxford American dictionary; 3rd ed.; Oxford University Press 2010 xxvi, 2018p il map $60

Grades: 11 12 Adult **423**

1. Reference books 2. Americanisms -- Dictionaries 3. English language -- Dictionaries

ISBN 978-0-19-539288-3

LC 2010-20033

First published 1980 with title: The Oxford American dictionary. Editors vary

"This dictionary arranges definitions by most current usage and provides additional guidance in usage notes. Although U.S. English is the focus here, regionalisms from other English-speaking areas are also included. More than 1000 illustrations (e.g., photos, drawings, diagrams) clarify definitions. . . . A labor of love and an unparalleled gift to writers and readers worldwide, the New Oxford American Dictionary should be on the reference shelves of every library." Libr J

★ **Oxford** American writer's thesaurus; compiled by Christine A. Lindberg. 2nd ed.; Oxford University Press 2008 xxvi, 1052p $40

Grades: 9 10 11 12 Adult **423**

1. Reference books 2. English language -- Synonyms and antonyms

ISBN 978-0-19-534284-0; 0-19-534284-4

LC 2008-31259

First published 2004

"This expansive reference . . . is a functional treasure." Libr J

Princeton Language Institute

★ **Roget's** 21st century thesaurus in dictionary form; the essential reference for home, school, or office. edited by the Princeton Language Institute; Barbara Ann Kipfer, head lexicographer. 3rd ed; Bantam Dell 2005 962p $15; pa $5.99

Grades: 8 9 10 11 12 Adult **423**

1. Reference books 2. English language -- Synonyms and antonyms

ISBN 0-385-33895-3; 0-440-24269-X pa

First published 1992

This thesaurus, cross referencing each word with the same concept, provides 500,000 synonyms and antonyms in a dictionary format and includes recently coined and common slang terms and commonly used foreign terms.

★ **Random** House Webster's unabridged dictionary; 2nd ed.; Random House 2005 xxvi, 2230p il map $59.95

Grades: 8 9 10 11 12 Adult **423**

1. Reference books 2. English language -- Dictionaries

ISBN 0-375-42599-3

First published 1966 with title: The Random House dictionary of the English language

This dictionary contains over 315,000 entries. A new-words section and an essay on the growth of English are included. 2,400 spot maps and illustrations complement the text

Roget's II; the new thesaurus. by the editors of The American Heritage Dictionaries. 3rd ed.; Houghton Mifflin 2003 1200p $21

Grades: 8 9 10 11 12 Adult **423**

1. Reference books 2. English language -- Synonyms and antonyms

ISBN 0-618-25414-5

First published 1980

The work uses a dictionary format, with words and numbered definitions on the left column of a page, and corresponding numbered synonyms, near-synonyms, antonyms and near-antonyms on the right column.

Sheehan, Michael

★ **Word** parts dictionary; standard and reverse listings of prefixes, suffixes, roots, and combining forms. [by] Michael J. Sheehan. 2nd ed.; McFarland & Co. 2008 286p lib bdg $55

Grades: 11 12 Adult **423**

1. Reference books 2. English language -- Dictionaries

ISBN 978-0-7864-3564-7; 0-7864-3564-X

LC 2008-41

First published 2000

"The purpose of this dictionary is to provide convenient word parts to those who may be interested in inventing or deciphering words bearing an established and embedded meaning." Publisher's note

★ **Shorter** Oxford English dictionary on historical principles; [editor-in-chief, Lesley Brown] 6th ed.; Oxford University Press 2007 2v il map set $175

Grades: 11 12 Adult **423**

1. Reference books 2. English language -- Dictionaries

ISBN 978-0-19-923324-3; 0-19-923324-1

LC 2007-37226

First published 1933

This dictionary "has more than half a million definitions drawn from the Oxford English Corpus database of more than 1.5 billion words. . . . It includes 'all words in current English from 1700 to the present day, plus the vocabulary of Shakespeare, the Authorized Version of the Bible and other major works from before 1700.'" Booklist

Includes bibliographical references

Webster's New World College Dictionary; 5th edition. Webster's New World 2016 1703 p. $25.95

Grades: 9 10 11 12 Adult **423**

1. English language -- Dictionaries

ISBN 0544598229; 9780544598225

" A clear and accessible defining style, compelling feature notes, full-page tables and charts, hundreds of drawings that complement the definitions, and authoritative guidance on usage and style points make this the perfect dictionary for use at school, at the office, or at home. This edition has been updated for 2016 with dozens of new words and senses and hundreds of revisions." (Publisher's note)

Young, Sue

★ The **new** comprehensive American rhyming dictionary. Morrow 1991 622p hardcover o.p. pa $14.95

Grades: 8 9 10 11 12 Adult   **423**
1. Americanisms 2. Reference books 3. English language -- Rhyme
ISBN 0-380-71392-6 pa

LC 90-19165

This book contains over 65,000 words and phrases categorized by sound, rather than spelling. It includes many colloquialisms and slang expressions.

427 Historical and geographic variations, modern nongeographic variations of English

Dickson, Paul

★ **Slang!** the topical dictionary of Americanisms. Walker & Co. 2006 418p $24.95

Grades: 11 12 Adult   **427**
1. Reference books 2. Americanisms -- Dictionaries 3. English language -- Slang -- Dictionaries
ISBN 0-8027-1531-1; 978-0-8027-1531-9
First published 1990 by Pocket Bks.

"Informative, reliable, entertaining, and modern, this topical slang dictionary complements the more staid slang lexicons and more scholarly general dictionaries." Booklist

Includes bibliographical references

Green, Jonathon

Green's dictionary of slang. Chambers 2011 3v

Grades: 11 12 Adult   **427**
1. Reference books 2. English language -- Slang -- Dictionaries
ISBN 0-550-10440-2; 978-0-550-10440-3

Entries in this three-volume set "cover slang from the past five centuries right up to the present day, from all the different English-speaking countries and regions." (Publisher's note)

"This 6000-page compilation of some 110,000 choice unconventional English specimens is a verbivore's delight. Geographically wide-ranging, this work seeks out and samples vulgar English wherever it is spoken, e.g., South Africa, Australia, New Zealand, and parts of the Caribbean, though British and American slang are most prominent. . . . Each entry follows a standard format and includes a headword; word class (noun, adjective, etc.); variant spellings; word history/derivation; usage notes; meaning, broken down by sense; and citations, which comprise the bulk of the entry, listing date, title of literary work, and author." Libr J

Spears, Richard A.

McGraw-Hill's American idioms dictionary; 4th ed.; McGraw-Hill 2007 xxiii, 743p il pa $16.95

Grades: 9 10 11 12   **427**
1. Americanisms 2. Reference books 3. English language -- Idioms 4. English language -- Terms and phrases
ISBN 978-0-07-147893-9; 0-07-147893-0

LC 2006-46933

First published 1987 with title: NTC's American idioms dictionary

This dictionary contains more than 14,000 idiomatic phrases in American parlance. Meaning, usage and appropriate contexts are given for each idiomatic phrase.

Includes bibliographical references

★ **McGraw**-Hill's dictionary of American slang and colloquial expressions; 4th ed.; McGraw-Hill 2006 xxix, 546p pa $19.95

Grades: 11 12 Adult   **427**
1. Americanisms 2. Reference books 3. English language -- Slang -- Dictionaries
ISBN 0-07-146107-8; 978-0-07-146107-8

LC 2005-52220

First published 1989 with title: NTC's dictionary of American slang and colloquial expressions

This book offers "definitions of more than 12,000 slang and informal expressions from various sources, ranging from golden oldies such as . . . golden oldie, to recent coinages like shizzle (gangsta), jonx (Wall Street), and ping (the Internet). Each entry is followed by examples illustrating how an expression is used in everyday conversation and, where necessary, International Phonetic Alphabet pronunciations are given, as well as cautionary notes for crude, inflammatory, or taboo expressions." Publisher's note

Includes bibliographical references

428 Standard English usage (Prescriptive linguistics)

Adolescent literacy in the academic disciplines; general principles and practical strategies. edited by Tamara L. Jetton, Cynthia Shanahan. The Guilford Press 2012 xiv, 274 p.p ill. (paper) $30

Grades: Adult Professional   **428**
1. Reading 2. Literacy 3. Teaching 4. Secondary education 5. Language arts (Secondary) 6. Language arts -- Correlation with content subjects
ISBN 1462502806; 9781462502806; 9781462502837

LC 2011035689

This book, edited by Tamara L. Jetton and Cynthia Shanahan, "addresses the particular challenges of literacy learning in each of the major academic disciplines. Chapters focus on how to help students successfully engage with texts and ideas in English/literature, science, math, history, and arts classrooms. The book shows that . . . students also need to learn processing strategies that are quite specific to each subject and its typical tasks or problems." (Publisher's note)

Includes bibliographical references and index

Collis, Harry

101 American English proverbs; [enrich your English Conversation with colorful everyday sayings] illustrated by Mario Risso. McGraw-Hill 2009 105p il (101 proverbs) pa $12.95

Grades: 9 10 11 12   **428**
1. Proverbs 2. English language -- Conversation and

phrase books
ISBN 978-0-07-161588-4; 0-07-161588-1

LC 2008-935417

This book for English as a second language students presents common American English proverbs and explains how to use them.

A **dictionary** of modern English usage; H.W. Fowler; with an introduction and notes by David Crystal. Oxford University Press 2010 784 p.

Grades: 11 12 Adult **428**

1. English language -- Usage 2. English language -- Idioms 3. English language -- Etymology
ISBN 019958589X; 9780199585892

LC 2011389197

First published 1926

"Much loved for his firm opinions, passion, and dry humor, Fowler has stood the test of time and is still considered by many to be the best arbiter of good practice. Now Oxford is bringing back the original long-out-of-print first edition of this beloved work, enhanced with a new introduction by one of today's leading experts on the language, David Crystal. Drawing on a wealth of entertaining examples, Crystal offers an insightful reassessment Fowler's reputation and his place in the history of linguistic thought. Most important, Crystal examines nearly 300 of Fowler's entries in detail, offering a modern perspective on them, and showing how English has changed since the 1920s." (Publisher's note)

Farwell, Sybil M.

Supporting reading in grades 6-12; a guide. by Sybil M. Farwell and Nancy L. Teger. Libraries Unlimited 2012 xiii, 358 p.p

Grades: Professional **428**

1. Motivation (Psychology) 2. Children -- Books and reading 3. Reading (Secondary) 4. Motivation in education 5. School librarian participation in curriculum planning
ISBN 9781598848038; 9781598848045

LC 2012010826

This book, by Sybil M. Farwell and Nancy L. Teger, "addresses head-on the disturbing trend of declining leisure reading among students and demonstrates how school librarians can contribute to the development of lifelong reading habits as well as improve students' motivation and test scores. The book provides a comprehensive framework for achieving this: the READS curriculum, which stands for Read as a personal activity." (Publisher's note)

Includes bibliographical references and index

Fogarty, Mignon

Grammar girl presents the ultimate writing guide for students; with illustrations by Erwin Haya. Henry Holt and Co. 2010 294p il $19.99; pa $12.99

Grades: 6 7 8 9 10 **428**

1. Rhetoric 2. Report writing 3. English language -- Grammar
ISBN 978-0-8050-8943-1; 0-8050-8943-8; 978-0-8050-8944-8 pa; 0-8050-8944-6 pa

LC 2010011699

"This text is evenly divided into five sections: parts of speech, sentence structure, punctuation, usage, and a final

segment on how readers can improve their writing. Fogarty's style mimics her podcasts with pithy but helpful rules and advice laced with examples. Pop quizzes and cartoon illustrations are also included. Libraries should purchase this book for reference use if nothing else, but budding writers will find it invaluable." SLJ

Includes bibliographical references

Grammar Girl's 101 words every high school graduate needs to know. St. Martin's Griffin 2011 120p il (Quick and dirty tips) pa $5.99

Grades: 9 10 11 12 **428**

1. Vocabulary 2. English language -- Terms and phrases
ISBN 978-0-312-57345-4

LC 2011011240

This book features "simple, one-page explanations and sentences that cover a range of nouns, verbs, and other parts of speech to clarify use and meaning. . . . Graduate includes fun and functional choices such as 'bohemian,' 'kibosh,' 'rhetoric,' and 'ubiquitous.'" SLJ

Fuhrken, Charles

What every middle school teacher needs to know about reading tests (from someone who has written them) Charles Fuhrken. Stenhouse Publishers 2012 vii, 237 p.p ill. (pbk.: alk. paper) $24

Grades: Professional **428**

1. Achievement tests 2. Examinations -- Study guides 3. Educational tests and measurements 4. Reading (Middle school) -- Ability testing
ISBN 1571108858; 1571109455; 9781571108852; 9781571109453

LC 2011037287

This book's author, "Charles Furhrken, has spent years working with several major testing companies and contributing to the reading assessments of various testing programs." He "offers . . . strategies to help students perform well on test day." Particular focus is given to "information about reading tests, including . . . preparation materials, samples of the most frequently assessed reading standards, and . . . core-reading activities." (Publisher's note)

Includes bibliographical references and index.

Grammar the easy way

Barron's E-Z grammar; 2nd ed.; Barron's Educational Series 2009 208p pa $12.99

Grades: 9 10 11 12 Adult **428**

1. English language -- Grammar
ISBN 978-0-7641-4261-1; 0-7641-4261-5

LC 2008-42424

First published 2002 with title: Grammar the easy way

Reviews basic grammar, including parts of speech, sentence structure, and subject-verb agreement; provides a manual of usage, instruction on writing paragraphs and research papers, and how to develop one's own style; and includes exercises and a test.

Hellweg, Paul

★ The **American** Heritage student thesaurus; Paul Hellweg, Joyce LeBaron, Susannah LeBaron. Houghton Mifflin Harcourt 2012 vi, 378 p.p $18.95

Grades: 5 6 7 8 9 10   **428**
1. Vocabulary 2. English language -- Synonyms and antonyms
ISBN 0547659164; 9780547659169
LC 2012462955

This newly updated student thesaurus "includes advice to teen writers about choosing the best word for their purpose, how synonyms are presented in the text, and the use of other words like antonyms. . . . Pages are large, with the entry word in a blue sans-serif type, while the synonyms appear in a smaller black boldface type. An even smaller type is used for each explanatory sentence, followed by antonyms (marked with a blue arrow) where appropriate." (Children's Literature)

Langer de Ramirez, Lori
Empower English language learners with tools from the Web. Corwin 2010 163p il $70.95; pa $38.95

Grades: Adult Professional   **428**
1. Computer-assisted instruction 2. English language -- Study and teaching
ISBN 978-1-4129-7242-0; 1-4129-7242-6; 978-1-4129-7243-7 pa; 1-4129-7243-4 pa
LC 2009-36786

"With a hands-on approach, the rationale for the use of Web 2.0 tools is clearly explained and defended. K-12 project ideas for blogging, wikis, podcasts, video, visual media, social networking, social bookmarking, and virtual worlds in the context of the ELL classroom are explicitly explained. Each concept includes what, why, how, when, who, steps for doing it yourself, where to locate further information, suggested readings, and useful websites. . . . This resource fills a gap in any school striving to meet the instructional and social needs of English Language Learners." Libr Media Connect
Includes bibliographical references

Merriam-Webster Inc.
★ **Merriam**-Webster's dictionary of English usage. Merriam-Webster 1994 978p $24.95

Grades: 9 10 11 12   **428**
1. Reference books 2. English language -- Usage
ISBN 0-87779-132-5
LC 93-19289

First published 1989 with title: Webster's dictionary of English usage

This guide looks at English usage from both historical and contemporary perspectives. Over 20,000 quotations illustrate the discussion of usage issues. Provides explanations of how accomplished writers have dealt with usage problems. Grammar, spelling and punctuation points are also covered
Includes bibliographical references

O'Conner, Patricia T.
Woe is I; the grammarphobe's guide to better English in plain English. Riverhead Bks. 2003 240p $19.95; pa $14

Grades: 11 12 Adult   **428**
1. English language -- Usage 2. English language --

Grammar
ISBN 1-57322-252-6; 1-59448-006-0 pa
LC 2003-41416

First published 1996

This guide to good English offers advice on punctuation, usage, style and grammar as well as e-mail.

"The author doesn't take herself or the subject matter too seriously, offering a delightful romp through the intricacies of our language. . . . She knows her subject, can convey her message with wit and ease, and does it all in a compact, easy-to-read format. In short, this is an entertaining and useful grammar reference." Libr J
Includes bibliographical references

Peters, Pam
★ The **Cambridge** guide to English usage. Cambridge University Press 2004 608p il $35

Grades: 11 12 Adult   **428**
1. Reference books 2. English language -- Usage
ISBN 0-521-62181-X
LC 2004-301888

"Considering the abundance of peculiarities and challenges in English usage, Cambridge will strengthen even a library well stocked with other guides. It is a serious book for those serious about language." Booklist

433   Dictionaries of standard German

★ **Random** House Webster's German-English, English-German dictionary; Rev. ed; Random House Reference 2006 547p $12.95

Grades: 11 12 Adult   **433**
1. Reference books 2. German language -- Dictionaries
ISBN 0-375-72194-0; 978-0-375-72194-6

First published 1997 with title: Random House German-English English-German dictionary

In addition to more than 60,000 entries this dictionary also includes notes on pronunciation, lists of abbreviations, tables of irregular verbs and lists of geographical names.

440   French and related Romance languages

Cracking the SAT French Subject Test. Princeton Review/Random House

Grades: 9 10 11 12   **440**
1. Scholastic Assessment Test 2. French language -- Study and teaching 3. Colleges and universities -- Entrance requirements
Annual. First published 2005

This guide provides test-taking strategies and sample tests on the subject of French.

443   Dictionaries of standard French

Correard, Marie-Helene
★ The **Oxford**-Hachette French dictionary; French-English, English-French. edited by Marie-Hélène Corréard, Valerie Grundy. 4th ed.; Oxford

University Press/Hachette Livre 2007 xxxviii, 1945p
$55

Grades: 11 12 Adult   **443**
1. Reference books 2. French language -- Dictionaries
ISBN 978-0-19-861422-7; 0-19-861422-5

LC 2007-14213

First published 1994

This work provides coverage of French and English
vocabulary in general as well as scientific and technical areas with over 350,000 words and phrases and over 530,000
translations. Supplementary material includes information
on French society and culture, including famous places,
people and much practical information for those planning
to reside in France.

460   Spanish, Portuguese, Galician

Cracking the SAT Spanish Subject Test. Princeton
Review
Grades: 9 10 11 12   **460**
1. Scholastic Assessment Test 2. Spanish language
-- Study and teaching 3. Colleges and universities --
Entrance requirements
Annual, first published 2005
This guide provides test-taking strategies and sample
tests on the subject of Spanish.

463   Dictionaries of standard Spanish

★ The **concise** Oxford Spanish dictionary; Spanish-
English, English-Spanish / chief editors, Carol
Styles Carvajal, Jane Horwood. dirección edito-
rial, Carol Styles Carvajal, Jane Horwood. 4th
ed.; Oxford University Press 2009 xxii, 1479p
$29.95
Grades: 6 7 8 9 10 11 12 Adult   **463**
1. Reference books 2. Spanish language -- Dictionaries
ISBN 978-0-19-956094-3

LC 2009-464493

First published 1996

"Focusing on student users, the Concise Oxford Spanish
Dictionary contains more than 1450 pages, and two appendixes. Included are the familiar verb tables for both regular
and irregular forms. Other useful tools include endpapers
that offer Spanish/English proprietary names along with examples of personal and business correspondence (letters and
emails)." SLJ

Houghton Mifflin Co.
★ The **American** Heritage Spanish dictionary;
Spanish/English, ingles/espanol. 2nd ed; Houghton
Mifflin 2001 xxx, 1103p $26
Grades: 11 12 Adult   **463**
1. Reference books 2. Spanish language -- Dictionaries
ISBN 0-618-12770-4

LC 2001-24524

"With an emphasis on American English and Latin
American Spanish, . . . this bilingual dictionary includes new
technological, scientific, and business terms. Speakers of all

the Americas will appreciate the different meanings of more
than 120,000 words, presented in an easy-to-understand design. Notes on grammar usage are a plus." Booklist

Larousse concise dictionary: Spanish-English, English-Spanish; [project management/dirección,
Sharon J. Hunter] Larousse 2006 various paging
$22.95; pa $12.95
Grades: 9 10 11 12   **463**
1. Reference books 2. Spanish language -- Dictionaries
ISBN 2-03-542138-1; 978-2-03-542138-8; 2-03-
542137-3 pa; 978-2-03-542137-1 pa
First published 1999

"With more than 90,000 references and 120,000 translations, including English compounds, English phonetics, and
a supplement on life and culture in Spain, Latin America,
the United Kingdom, and the U.S., this concise bilingual
dictionary provides essential, everyday vocabulary for language learners." Booklist [review of 1999 edition]

★ **Multicultural** Spanish dictionary; how everyday Spanish differs from country to country. Schreiber Pub. 2006 281p pa $24.95
Grades: 9 10 11 12   **463**
1. Reference books 2. Spanish language -- Dictionaries
ISBN 978-0-884003-17-5; 0-884003-17-5

LC 2006-13957

First published 1999 under the editorship of
Agustín Martínez

"Divided into three parts (English-Spanish, Spanish-
English and subject areas) this guide includes the most commonly used words throughout Latin America and Spain in
the most common areas of everyday life. As stated in the
introduction, it 'is not meant to replace the standard Spanish-English dictionary'; rather, it is a useful basic guide to
a variety of common Spanish terms." Booklist [review of
1999 edition]

473   Dictionaries of classical Latin

Simpson, D. P.
Cassell's Latin dictionary; Latin-English, Eng-
lish-Latin. by D. P. Simpson. Macmillan 1977 883p
thumb-indexed $24.95
Grades: 8 9 10 11 12 Adult   **473**
1. Reference books 2. Latin language -- Dictionaries
ISBN 0-02-522580-4

LC 77-7670

First published 1854. This edition first published 1959.
Previous United States editions published by Funk & Wagnalls with title: Cassell's New Latin dictionary

"Cassell's incorporates current English idiom and Latin
spelling into the traditional presentation of classical Latin.
The 30,000 entries include generic terms, geographical and
proper nouns. Etymological notes and illustrative quotations
are provided within entries." Wynar. Guide to Ref Books for
Sch Media Cent. 3d edition

492.4   Hebrew

Zilkha, Avraham

Modern English-Hebrew dictionary. Yale Univ. Press 2002 457p (Yale language series) $55; pa $30

Grades: 11 12 Adult   **492.4**
    1. Reference books 2. Hebrew language -- Dictionaries
    ISBN 0-300-09004-8; 0-300-09005-6 pa

                         LC 2001-26830

This dictionary includes 30,000 entries, with listings for translating words with multiple meanings, newly coined and slang words, common idioms, vocalization of Hebrew words, acronyms, and gender identification and plural forms of irregular nouns

493   Non-Semitic Afro-Asiatic languages

McDonald, Angela

Write your own Egyptian hieroglyphs. University of California Press 2007 80p il pa $15.95

Grades: 7 8 9 10 11 12 Adult   **493**
    1. Hieroglyphics 2. Egyptian language
    ISBN 978-0-520-25235-6

                         LC 2006-51405

This book "covers the history of ancient Egyptian civilization and the context of this fascinating, early form of writing. Readers learn to create hieroglyphs for names, places, phrases and even insults! Kids from upper elementary through high school and adults will enjoy this fun book." Univ Press Books for Public and Second Sch Libr, 2008

Includes bibliographical references

495.6   Japanese

Kardy, Glenn

Manga University Presents . . . Kana de Manga Special Edition: Japanese Sound FX! writer, Glenn Kardy; artist, Chihiro Hattori. Japanime Co. Ltd./ Manga University 2007 110p il pa $9.99

Grades: 6 7 8 9 10 11 12 Adult   **495.6**
    1. Manga 2. Graphic novels 3. Japanese language
    ISBN 978-4-921205-12-6

What does a cat's meow sound like in Japanese? How about the grumble of an empty stomach, the wail of a police car's siren or the crash of an ocean wave? Japanese manga artists rely heavily upon onomatopoeia—sound-effect words—and this entry in the Kana de Manga / Kanji de Manga language-learning series includes illustrated examples of those sounds in action. It features more than 100 Japanese onomatopoeia and their English equivalents in categories such as "Humans," "Animals," "Machines" and "Nature." The text is written in both English and Japanese hiragana.

Lammers, Wayne P.

Japanese the manga way; an illustrated guide to grammar & structure. Stone Bridge Press 2005 xxviii, 282p il pa $24.95

Grades: 9 10 11 12   **495.6**
    1. Japanese language
    ISBN 1-880656-90-6

                         LC 2005-296444

The author "intends to teach absolute beginners how to use manga to learn to speak and read conversational Japanese. . . . For someone who has the patience, drive, and desire to learn the language, the book will be an immense help." SLJ

Includes bibliographical references

500   SCIENCE

500   Natural sciences and mathematics

Beyer, Rick

The **greatest** science stories never told; 100 tales of invention and discovery to astonish, bewilder & stupefy. Harper 2009 214p il $19.99

Grades: 9 10 11 12 Adult   **500**
    1. Science 2. Inventions
    ISBN 978-0-06-162696-8

                         LC 2009-32741

This book features miscellaneous stories about inventions and discoveries in science.

Includes bibliographical references

Bryson, Bill, 1951-

★ A **short** history of nearly everything. Broadway Bks. 2003 544p $27.50; pa $15.95

Grades: 9 10 11 12 Adult   **500**
    1. Science 2. Science -- Popular works
    ISBN 0-7679-0817-1; 0-7679-0818-X pa

                         LC 2003-46006

In presenting this history of science, Bryson's "interest is not simply to discover what we know but to find out how we know it. How do we know what is in the center of the earth, thousands of miles beneath the surface? How can we know the extent and the composition of the universe, or what a black hole is? How can we know where the continents were 600 million years ago?" Publisher's note

Includes bibliographical references

De Heer, Margreet

Science, a discovery in comics; Margreet de Heer. NBM Publishing 2013 192 p. (A discovery in comics) (hardcover) $19.99

Grades: 9 10 11 12 Adult   **500**
    1. Science
    ISBN 1561637505; 9781561637508

                         LC 2013939851

"This history of scientific discovery, [by Margreet de Heer] is presented as a series of conversations about understanding the laws that govern the universe. . . . Beginning with the ideals of scientific observation and inquiry, the book moves to detailed chronologies of the evolutions of biology, physics, geology, etc. Much of the information is organized in time-line form, which is used to depict the gradual accumulation and transformation of concepts." (School Library Journal)

"Although the information on any one topic is very basic, a great many topics are treated, thanks to the economy of de Heer's visual presentation, and they are all handled very well, thanks to the energy of her drawing style and the vividness of Kohl's coloring." Booklist

Etzkowitz, Henry

★ **Athena** unbound; the advancement of women in science and technology. {by} Henry Etzkowitz, Carol Kemelgor, Brian Uzzi, with Michael Neushatz {et al.} Cambridge Univ. Press 2000 282p $55; pa $21

Grades: 11 12 Adult   **500**
  1. Women scientists
  ISBN 0-521-56380-1; 0-521-78738-6 pa
              LC 00-20997

This is an "inquiry into why there are so few women scientists. . . . The authors balance their extremely detailed analysis with a humanistic perspective as they compare and contrast the status of women scientists in different countries, characterize both exclusionary and supportive forms of networking, and, ultimately, offer some surprising and hopeful conclusions." Booklist

Includes bibliographical references

Feynman, Richard Phillips

The **meaning** of it all; thoughts of a citizen scientist. Basic Books 2005 133p pa $13.95

Grades: 11 12 Adult   **500**
  1. Science 2. Religion
  ISBN 0-465-02394-0
  First published 1998 by Addison-Wesley

"Originally delivered as a three-part lecture series at the University of Washington in 1963, this collection touches on such far-ranging topics as the existence or nonexistence of God; the Constitution; and UFOs. . . . These memorable lectures confirm that Feynman's gift of insight extended from the subatomic world to the cosmic, and to the very human as well." Publ Wkly

Grant, John

Corrupted science. Facts, Figures & Fun 2007 336p il $12.95

Grades: 11 12 Adult   **500**
  1. Fraud in science
  ISBN 978-1-904332-73-2

Contains brief discussions of examples throughout history of science being corrupted for political, ideological, or fraudulent purposes, including Lysenkoism, science under the Nazis, the Piltdown Man hoax, and recent attempts to discredit global warming.

The **handy** science answer book; compiled by the Carnegie Library of Pittsburgh; [edited by] Naomi E. Balaban and James E. Bobick. 4th ed.; Visible Ink Press 2011 679p il pa $21.95

Grades: 11 12 Adult   **500**
  1. Science 2. Technology
  ISBN 978-1-57859-321-7
              LC 2011-429

First published 1994

"The text is divided into various subject areas including physics and chemistry, space, earth, climate and weather, minerals and other materials, energy, technology, and environment, gathering answers to reference questions. . . . A comprehensive index . . . makes the material accessible and easy to find. Pages are full of fascinating tidbits, complemented by illustrations, photos, charts, graphs, and maps." Voice Youth Advocates

Includes bibliographical references

Henderson, Mark

100 most important science ideas; key concepts in genetics, physics and mathematics. [by] Mark Henderson, Joanne Baker, Tony Crilly. Firefly Books 2009 431p il $19.95

Grades: 11 12 Adult   **500**
  1. Physics 2. Genetics 3. Mathematics
  ISBN 978-1-55407-527-0

This book aims to encourage the reader to explore "the 100 most important, groundbreaking ideas that have emerged from the scientific disciplines of genetics, physics, and mathematics. Divided into three sections, each written by one of the authors . . . this work presents complex scientific topics in a simple, understandable way. . . . Text boxes, entertaining quotations, frequent diagrams, and everyday examples hold the reader's attention and make this work engaging to anyone interested in the world of science." Libr J

History of modern science and mathematics; Brian S. Baigrie, editor. Scribner 2002 4v il set $605

Grades: 11 12 Adult   **500**
  1. Science -- History 2. Mathematics -- History
  ISBN 0-684-80636-3
              LC 2002-4042

This "set attempts to synthesize the history of scientific developments in anthropology, astronomy, biology, chemistry, mathematics, physics, psychology, and the earth sciences. . . . This work ranges from the 17th century to the present without trying to include the most recent developments." Libr J

Includes bibliographical references

Levy, Joel

A **bee** in a cathedral and 99 other scientific analogies. Firefly Books 2011 224p il $29.95

Grades: 9 10 11 12 Adult   **500**
  1. Science
  ISBN 978-1-55407-959-9; 1-55407-959-4
              LC 2011292445

Uses analogies to explain scientific truths and principles.

This book "would serve as an excellent resource for teachers looking to help students make that final connection or as a way to introduce 'big idea' thinking into a discussion. Outside of the classroom, an afternoon with this book will be time well spent for any level of science enthusiast." Sci Books Films

Oxford dictionary of scientific quotations; edited by W.F. Bynum and Roy Porter; assistant editors, Sharon Messenger, Caroline Overy. Oxford University Press 2005 712p $60; pa $18.95

Grades: 11 12 Adult　　　　　　　　**500**
1. Science 2. Quotations
ISBN 0-19-858409-1; 0-19-861443-8 pa
　　　　　　　　　　　　　　LC 2005-277260

"This hefty volume is a great reference but it is also a great read—open it up to any page and expand the mind with a sampling of scientific ideas and philosophy." Choice

Sagan, Carl
　Broca's brain; reflections on the romance of science. Random House 1979 347p hardcover o.p. pa $7.99

Grades: 11 12 Adult　　　　　　　　**500**
1. God 2. Science 3. Religion 4. Astronomy 5. Machinery 6. Philosophy 7. Physicians 8. Physicists 9. Psychologists 10. Writers on science 11. Nobel laureates for physics
ISBN 0-345-33689-5 pa
　　　　　　　　　　　　　　LC 78-21810

The author "is a lucid, logical writer with a gift for explaining science to the layman and infecting the reader with his own boundless enthusiasm and curiosity." Natl Rev
　Includes bibliographical references

The **science** book; everything you need to know about the world and how it works. authors, Matthias Delbrück ... et al. National Geographic 2008 431 p. (hbk.) $35

Grades: 9 10 11 12 Adult　　　　　　**500**
1. Reference books 2. Science -- Encyclopedias 3. Science -- Popular works 4. Science
ISBN 1426203373; 9781426203374; 9781426203695; 9781426203701
　　　　　　　　　　　　　　LC 2009280291

"A delight for the casual reader, yet so complete and wide-ranging that science buffs and students will welcome it,The Science Book encapsulates centuries of scientific thought in one richly illustrated volume. Natural phenomena, revolutionary inventions, and the most up-to-date investigations are explained in detailed text, and 2,000 vivid illustrations - including 3-D graphics and pictograms - make the information even more accessible and amazing to discover." (Publisher's Note)

"Over 2,000 images, including 3-D graphics, pictograms, and gatefold spreads cover major areas of science, including chemistry, biology, earth studies, cosmology, mathematics, physics, and technology. . . . This educational and entertaining book is an essential teaching guide that will appeal to a wide readership." Choice
　Science book

500.2　Physical sciences

Gothard, Lisa Quinn
　Encyclopedia of physical science; [by] Joe Rosen and Lisa Quinn Gothard. Facts on File 2009 2v il (Facts on File science library) set $170

Grades: 11 12 Adult　　　　　　　　**500.2**
1. Reference books 2. Physical sciences -- Encyclopedias
ISBN 978-0-8160-7011-4; 0-8160-7011-3
　　　　　　　　　　　　　　LC 2008-36444

"The layout, color illustrations, and numerous tables make this an accessible reference on an important topic." Libr J
　Includes bibliographical references

500.5　Space sciences

Krauss, Lawrence Maxwell
　The **physics** of Star Trek; with a foreword by Stephen Hawking. [Rev. and updated ed.]; Basic Books 2007 251p il pa $15

Grades: 11 12 Adult　　　　　　　　**500.5**
1. Space sciences 2. Star trek (Television program)
ISBN 978-0-465-00204-7; 0-465-00204-8
　　　　　　　　　　　　　　LC 2007-18981
　First published 1995

This book examines various aspects of the television series Star Trek from the perspective of a scientist.
　"This is interesting and entertaining and can lead to endless discussions on the science used in all the Star Trek series." Sci Books Films
　Includes bibliographical references

Launius, Roger D.
　Smithsonian atlas of space exploration; [by] Roger D. Launius & Andrew K. Johnston. Collins 2009 230p il map $34.99

Grades: 9 10 11 12 Adult　　　　　　**500.5**
1. Outer space -- Exploration -- Pictorial works
ISBN 978-0-06-156526-7
　　　　　　　　　　　　　　LC 2009-649

This book "relates the story of space exploration in text, photographs, illustrations, and maps from the earliest times to the present. Written at a level geared to the general reader, this topically arranged work is divided into seven parts. . . . Each part contains a number of two or four-page subsections covering topics ranging from the earliest observatories of the ancient world to the possibilities for space flight in the future. . . . Distinguished by outstanding color illustrations and photographs, the very reasonably priced atlas should appeal to a broad audience." Booklist
　Includes bibliographical references

Parks, Peggy J., 1951-
　Space research. ReferencePoint Press 2010 96p il (Inside science) $26.95

Grades: 8 9 10 11 12　　　　　　　**500.5**
1. Astronautics 2. Space sciences 3. Outer space --

Exploration
ISBN 978-1-60152-111-8; 1-60152-111-1

LC 2009-48159

"Parks piles on the research, digging deep into interstellar study, programs that reach into space, and what it all means to the common person, never shying away from detail and onerous proper nouns. . . . The color layout features plenty of photos, boxes, and charts, while Parks delivers a surprisingly spry text." Booklist

Includes bibliographical references

Zimmerman, Robert

★ The **chronological** encyclopedia of discoveries in space. Oryx Press 2000 410p il maps $95

Grades: 11 12 Adult **500.5**

1. Astronautics 2. Outer space -- Exploration
ISBN 1-57356-196-7

"Over 1,000 entries record the date of launch, name of the spacecraft(s), summary of the mission, names of the crew members, experiments, problems, and discoveries in a clear and concise fashion. Seemingly every single space mission is included, encompassing spaceflight with and without human crews, military and civilian ventures, public and commercial ventures, planetary probes, and communications satellites. . . . An excellent, cross-referencing system within the text, as well as extensive subject indices by satellite, mission, and nation or consortia, helps the reader follow particular interests in detail. . . . There is no comparable source to this volume for its comprehensiveness and conciseness." Sci Books Films

Includes bibliographical references

501   Philosophy and theory

This **will** change everything; ideas that will shape the future. edited by John Brockman; [introduction by Daniel C. Dennett] HarperCollins 2010 xxiii, 390p pa $14.99

Grades: 11 12 Adult **501**

1. Science 2. Forecasting
ISBN 978-0-06-189967-6

"With contributions from Ian McEwan, Steven Pinker, Lee Smolin, Craig Venter, Richard Dawkins and 130 others of their ilk, the book is like an intellectual lucky dip." New Sci

502   Miscellany

Echaore-Yoon, Susan

Career opportunities in science; [by] Susan Echaore-McDavid. 2nd ed; Ferguson 2008 332p $49.50; pa $18.95

Grades; 9 10 11 12 **502**

1. Science -- Vocational guidance
ISBN 978-0-8160-7132-6; 0-8160-7132-2; 978-0-8160-7133-3 pa; 0-8160-7133-0 pa

LC 2007-40659

First published 2003

This book "will be highly useful to a diverse population of readers. . . . This excellent book is easy to read and the information it presents is clear and concise." Sci Books Films

Includes glossary and bibliographical references

Lamothe, Matt

The **where,** the why, and the how; 75 artists illustrate wondrous mysteries of science. Matt Lamothe; Julia Rothman; Jenny Volvovski. Chronicle Books 2012 160 p. ill. (chiefly col.) (hardcover) $24.95

Grades: 9 10 11 12 Adult **502**

1. Physics 2. Life sciences 3. Earth sciences
ISBN 1452108226; 9781452108223

LC 2012289775

In this book by Matt Lamothe, Julia Rothman, and Jenny Volvovski, "some of the biggest (and smallest) mysteries of the natural world are explained in essays by real working scientists, which are then illustrated by artists given free rein to be as literal or as imaginative as they like. The result is a celebration of the wonder that inspires every new discovery." (Publisher's note)

Sullivan, Megan

All in a day's work; careers using science. by Megan Sullivan for The Science Teacher. 2nd ed; NSTA Press 2008 140p il pa $15.95

Grades: 9 10 11 12 **502**

1. Science -- Vocational guidance
ISBN 978-1-93353-145-8; 1-93353-145-2

LC 2008-24672

First published 2007

This is a compilation of "interviews from the Science Teacher journal. From astronaut to video-game level designer, each entry poses questions that go beyond basic education requirements and job responsibilities. . . . An excellent choice for career collections, Sullivan's book not only encourages students to take as much math and science as possible in high school, but also emphasizes the commitment to lifelong learning critical for most 21st-century jobs." SLJ

Includes bibliographical references

503   Dictionaries, encyclopedias, concordances

Clugston, M. J.

Penguin Dictionary of Science; ed. M.J. Clugston; author team, N.J. Lord... [et al.] 4th edition Penguin 2014 768 p. (Penguin reference) pa. $18

Grades: 9 10 11 12 Adult **503**

1. Science -- Dictionaries 2. Science -- Popular works
ISBN 0141979038; 9780141979038

"A dictionary that covers all the important topics in this key subject area including chemistry, physics, molecular biology, biochemistry, human anatomy, mathematics, astronomy and computing. It is suitable for anyone who needs to understand scientific terms, whether student, researcher or enthusiastic layperson." (Publisher's Note)

Encyclopedia of science, technology, and ethics; edited by Carl Mitcham. Macmillan Reference USA 2005 4v il map set $450

Grades: 11 12 Adult **503**

1. Reference books 2. Technology -- Encyclopedias 3. Science -- Ethical aspects -- Encyclopedias

ISBN 0-02-865831-0

LC 2005-6968

This "multivolume work on ethics provides a superb introduction to the issues presented." Booklist

Includes bibliographical references

McGraw-Hill Publishing Company

★ **McGraw**-Hill concise encyclopedia of science & technology; 6th ed.; McGraw-Hill 2009 2v il map set $295

Grades: 11 12 Adult **503**

1. Reference books 2. Science -- Encyclopedias 3. Technology -- Encyclopedias

ISBN 978-0-07-161366-8

LC 2008-50987

First published 1984

This encyclopedia features over 7100 articles on branches of technology and science ranging from acoustics to zoology.

Includes bibliographical references

★ The **new** book of popular science. Scholastic Library Pub. 2008 6v il set $399

Grades: 7 8 9 10 11 12 **503**

1. Reference books 2. Science -- Encyclopedias 3. Technology -- Encyclopedias

ISBN 978-0-7172-1226-2

LC 2007-41858

First published 1924 with title: The book of popular science. Frequently revised

The information in this set is classified under such broad categories as astronomy and space science, computers and mathematics, earth sciences, energy, environmental sciences, physical sciences, general biology, plant life, animal life, mammals, human sciences and technology.

Includes bibliographical references

Science; the definitive visual guide. editor in chief: Adam Hart-Davis. DK Pub. 2009 512p il $50

Grades: 9 10 11 12 Adult **503**

1. Reference books 2. Science -- Encyclopedias

ISBN 978-0-7566-5570-9

LC 2010-281802

This is "a beautiful pictorial history of science, ranging from the prehistoric harnessing of fire to the current race to minimize anthropogenic climate change. Each topic presented within the 512 pages of the text is succinctly described in a chronological sequence, together with a multitude of engaging color visuals. This combination makes the overall presentation as accessible and inviting as that of a coffee-table book, while still maintaining the necessary breadth and depth of detail to make the volume useful as an introductory reference." Sci Books Films

Swedin, Eric Gottfrid

Science in the contemporary world; an encyclopedia. [by] Eric G. Swedin. ABC-CLIO 2005 xxv, 382p il (ABC-CLIO's history of science series) $85

Grades: 9 10 11 12 **503**

1. Reference books 2. Science -- Encyclopedias

ISBN 1-85109-524-1

LC 2004-26950

This book "covers developments in the scientific disciplines from the end of World War II to the present day. . . . It makes a make good introductory text to the history of science in the late twentieth and early twenty-first centuries." Booklist

Includes bibliographical references

★ **Van** Nostrand's scientific encyclopedia; 10th ed.; Wiley 2008 3v il map set $450

Grades: 11 12 Adult **503**

1. Reference books 2. Science -- Encyclopedias

ISBN 978-0-471-74338-5

LC 2007-46658

First published 1938

This encyclopedia contains articles contains over 10,000 entries on topics such as biology, chemistry, earth science, mathematics and engineering, anatomy and physiology, physics, botany, and space science.

Includes bibliographical references

507.8 Use of apparatus and equipment in study and teaching

Downie, N. A.

Vacuum bazookas, electric rainbow jelly, and 27 other Saturday science projects; {by} Neil Downie. Princeton Univ. Press 2001 253p hardcover o.p. pa $18.95

Grades: 9 10 11 12 **507.8**

1. Science projects 2. Science -- Experiments

ISBN 0-691-00985-6; 0-691-00986-4 pa

LC 2001-36258

"This book is an excellent source of fun, light-hearted projects for young adults." Sci Books Films

Includes bibliographical references and index

Dutton, Judy

Science fair season; twelve kids, a robot named Scorch-- and what it takes to win. Hyperion 2011 271p $24.99

Grades: 11 12 Adult **507.8**

1. Science projects 2. Science -- Exhibitions 3. International Science and Engineering Fair

ISBN 978-1-4013-2379-0

"Following 12 teens to the Super Bowl of science fairs— the Intel International Science & Engineering Fair (Intel ISEF) brings together 1,500 kids from over 50 countries, and offers up to $4 million in prizes and scholarships—[the author] shows that science can be exciting, creative, even glamorous. . . . [This] is an incredibly fun read, and a reminder that scientists can be heroes, too." Maclean's

Includes bibliographical references

Johnson, George

The **ten** most beautiful experiments. Alfred A. Knopf 2008 192p il $22.95

Grades: 11 12 Adult   **507.8**

1. Science -- Experiments

ISBN 978-1-4000-4101-5; 1-4000-4101-5

LC 2007-27839

"Writing up Luigi Galvani's study of frog's legs, James Joule's of heat, Albert Michelson's of light's speed, and Robert Millikan's of the electron's charge, Johnson exerts classic appeal to science readers: presenting the lone genius making a great discovery. Good to go in any library." Booklist

Includes bibliographical references

Vecchione, Glen

Blue ribbon science fair projects. Sterling Pub. Co. 2005 224p il $19.95

Grades: 9 10 11 12   **507.8**

1. Science projects 2. Science -- Experiments

ISBN 978-1-4027-1073-5; 1-4027-1073-9

LC 2005-13557

"After an introduction to the process of creating science-fair projects and a summary of tips from an experienced science-fair judge, Vecchione . . . [presents] project ideas within the following subject areas: animals, the human body, magnetism, botany, equipment, chemistry, astronomy, physics, and math. . . . Students planning science-fair projects will find this a solid resource." Booklist

Vickers, Tanya M.

Teen science fair sourcebook; winning school science fairs and national competitions. Enslow Publishers 2009 160p il lib bdg $34.60

Grades: 7 8 9 10   **507.8**

1. Science projects 2. Science -- Exhibitions 3. Science -- Experiments

ISBN 978-0-7660-2711-4; 0-7660-2711-2

LC 2008-30779

"The book is clearly written, and its page design, which includes the occasional photo, is colorful. . . . A useful resource for highly motivated students." Booklist

Includes glossary and bibliographical references

Walker, Pamela

Environmental science experiments; [by] Pamela Walker, Elaine Wood. Facts on File 2010 153p il (Facts on File science experiments) $35

Grades: 7 8 9 10   **507.8**

1. Environmental science 2. Science -- Experiments

ISBN 978-0-8160-7805-9; 0-8160-7805-X

LC 2008-53715

This "contains 20 experiments that allow students to actively engage in scientific inquiry. Projects are presented in a uniform format, with an introduction to the topic, time requirements (35 minutes to 2 weeks), a materials list, numbered procedures, and several analysis questions. . . . Line drawings, colorful images, and data tables enhance instructions. . . . The experiments themselves are timely and fascinating. [The book] includes high-interest investigations into

what people throw away, the safety of reusing water bottles, and a 'bottled versus tap water' taste test." SLJ

Includes glossary and bibliographical references

508   Natural history

Carroll, Sean B.

Remarkable creatures; epic adventures in the search for the origins of species. Houghton Mifflin Harcourt 2009 331p il map $26; pa $14.95

Grades: 11 12 Adult   **508**

1. Evolution 2. Naturalists

ISBN 978-0-15-101485-9; 0-15-101485-X; 978-0-547-24778-6 pa; 0-547-24778-8 pa

LC 2008-25438

"A stirring introduction to the wonder of evolutionary biology." Kirkus

Includes bibliographical references

Daubert, Stephen

The **shark** and the jellyfish; more stories in natural history. Vanderbilt University Press 2009 213p il $24.95

Grades: 11 12 Adult   **508**

1. Natural history

ISBN 978-0-8265-1629-9; 0-8265-1629-7

LC 2008-29024

"This intriguing book is composed of eight short stories on various subjects in natural history, grouped into five sections: 'Field & Stream,' 'Air,' 'Sea and Shore,' 'Forest,' and 'Earth and Stars.' Each story weaves a narrative about the interconnections between life and the environment, built around findings that have been published in the scientific literature. . . . The book provides an engaging and interesting discourse on natural history that is backed by real science on the subject being covered." Sci Books Films

Includes bibliographical references

Threads from the web of life; stories in natural history. with illustrations by Chris Daubert. Vanderbilt University Press 2006 162p il $24.95

Grades: 11 12 Adult   **508**

1. Natural history

ISBN 0-8265-1509-6; 978-0-8265-1509-4

LC 2005-23117

The author "illustrates 16 ecological processes with lively narratives in which he envisions how it might feel to be at the center of the action: for example, traveling with a green sea turtle from its feeding grounds in Brazil to its nesting beaches 2,000 kilometers away on Ascension Island in the eastern Atlantic; riding whirling air currents with migrating American white pelicans; or fleeing from a predator swordfish with a school of neon flying squid. . . . His natural history tales are instructive and entertaining, and each is followed by an annotation explaining the science behind it." Publ Wkly

Includes bibliographical references

Fothergill, Alastair

★ **Planet** Earth; as you've never seen it before. [by] Alastair Fothergill [et al.]; foreword by David Attenborough. University of California Press 2007 309p il map $39.95

Grades: 11 12 Adult   **508**

1. Habitat (Ecology) 2. Earth
ISBN 978-0-520-25054-3; 0-520-25054-0

LC 2006-50073

In this collection of over 400 photographs of natural landscapes and wildlife, the author "takes readers on a kaleidoscopic tour of the flora, fauna and natural history of the Earth's poles, forests, plains, deserts, mountains and oceans." Publ Wkly

Gould, Stephen Jay

The **richness** of life; the essential Stephen Jay Gould. edited by Paul McGarr and Steven Rose; with an introduction by Steven Rose and a foreword by Oliver Sacks. Norton 2007 654p il $35

Grades: 11 12 Adult   **508**

1. Evolution 2. Natural history
ISBN 978-0-393-06498-8; 0-393-06498-0

LC 2006-29208

Frist published 2006 in the United Kingdom
"For collections that have room for only one volume of his writing, this is the essential one." SLJ
Includes bibliographical references

Hamilton, Neil A.

Scientific exploration and expeditions; from the age of discovery to the twenty-first century. [by] Neil Hamilton. M.E. Sharpe 2011 2v il map set $165

Grades: 7 8 9 10 11 12   **508**

1. Reference books 2. Scientific expeditions
ISBN 978-0-7656-8076-1; 0-7656-8076-9

LC 2010-12118

"Hamilton's 115 entries in this set describe the courses and discoveries of significant scientific expeditions from the early 15th century to mid 2009. . . . The presentations are systematic, carefully detailed, not exclusively Eurocentric, and when appropriate, skeptical. The currency of information and focus on science will make this work particularly useful." SLJ
Includes bibliographical references

Leopold, Aldo, 1886-1948

A **Sand** County almanac; Aldo Leopold. iltrated ed; Oxford University Press 2001 190p. col. ill. £36.99: CIP entry (Nov)

Grades: 10 11 12   **508**

1. Nature writing 2. American essays 3. Nature conservation
ISBN 0-19-514617-4; 9780195146172

LC 2001034038

National Outdoor Book Awards: Outdoor Classics (2000)

This book "combines . . . nature writing . . . with an . . . ethical regard for America's relationship to the land. Written with an . . . understanding of the ways of nature, the book includes a section on the monthly changes of the Wiscon-

sin countryside; another part that gathers informal pieces written by Leopold over a forty-year period as he traveled through the woodlands of Wisconsin, Iowa, Arizona, Sonora, Oregon, Manitoba, and elsewhere; and a final section in which Leopold addresses the philosophical issues involved in wildlife conservation." (Publisher's note)

Natural history; the ultimate visual guide to everything on Earth. [senior project editor, Kathryn Hennessy] DK 2010 648p il map $50

Grades: 10 11 12 Adult   **508**

1. Natural history 2. Reference books
ISBN 978-0-7566-6752-8; 0-7566-6752-6

LC 2010-283659

"This is an international encyclopedia of life-forms— e.g., fossils, fungi, plants, animals, mammals—that includes vital facts and two to three sentences about each as well as more than 5000 color illustrations in all. Each grouping is introduced by an essay that puts it in biological and evolutionary perspective." Libr J

Savage, Candace

★ **Prairie**: a natural history; principle photography by James R. Page; illustrations by Joan A. Williams. 2nd ed; Greystone Books 2011 305p il map pa $29.95

Grades: 9 10 11 12   **508**

1. Prairies
ISBN 978-1-55365-588-6

First published 2004

This "guide to the biology and ecology of the prairies, the Great Plains grasslands of North America . . . [includes information on] declining bird species, enhanced protection of bison, the effect of industrialization on the prairies, and the effect of the increase in coyote numbers on red foxes and swift foxes." Publisher's note

Schaller, George B.

A **naturalist** and other beasts; tales from a life in the field. with photographs by the author. Sierra Club Books 2007 272p il $24.95

Grades: 11 12 Adult   **508**

1. Wildlife
ISBN 978-1-57805-129-8; 1-57805-129-0

LC 2006-51153

"Schaller presents exciting animal lore that will inspire readers to learn more about these precious creatures." Booklist
Includes bibliographical references

Webster, Raymond B.

★ **African** American firsts in science and technology; foreword by Wesley L. Harris. Gale Group 1999 462p $80

Grades: 11 12 Adult   **508**

1. Scientists 2. African American inventors
ISBN 0-7876-3876-5

LC 99-27346

Presents capsule accounts of notable first achievements by African Americans, arranged in the categories "Agriculture and Everyday Life," "Dentistry and Nursing," "Life

Science," "Math and Engineering," "Medicine," "Physical Science," and "Transportation."
Includes bibliographical references

509 History, geographic treatment, biography

Alic, Margaret
  Hypatia's heritage; a history of women in science from antiquity through the nineteenth century. Beacon Press 1986 230p il pl $20; pa $9.95 **509**
    ISBN 0-8070-6730-X; 0-8070-6731-8 pa
    LC 86-47510
  Includes bibliographical references and index

American Council of Learned Societies
  Concise dictionary of scientific biography; 2nd ed; Scribner 2000 1097p il $135
  Grades: 9 10 11 12 **509**
    1. Reference books 2. Scientists -- Dictionaries
    ISBN 0-684-80631-2
    LC 00-61231
    First published 1981
  "This book would be useful as a quick introduction and as a starting point for further study." Am Ref Books Annu, 2001
    Includes index

Balchin, Jon
  Science; 100 scientists who changed the world. Jon Balchin. Enchanted Lion 2003 208p il $18.95
  Grades: 9 10 11 12 **509**
    1. Science -- History
    ISBN 1-592-70017-9
    LC 2003-47009
  "Each two-page entry offers a chronology, biographical material, scientific contributions, and a portrait of the individual. While the information is brief, it is more interesting reading than similar entries in an encyclopedia, and includes a discussion of the scientific theory or the discovery's impact on society." SLJ

The **Biographical** dictionary of women in science; pioneering lives from ancient times to the mid-20th century. Marilyn Ogilvie and Joy Harvey, editors. Routledge 2000 2v set $250
  Grades: 11 12 Adult **509**
    1. Reference books 2. Women scientists -- Dictionaries
    ISBN 0-415-92038-8
    LC 99-17668
  "This title includes approximately 2,500 women scientists. . . . Science is defined broadly to include related fields like anthroplogy and sociology. . . . Entries begin with a brief biographical description, with birth and death dates, educational background, and area of professional work. The essays, typically 250 to 750 words long, give only brief early life history before focusing on the subjects' principal scientific contributions. . . . Ogilvie and Harvey's work is a must-have reference tool." Am Ref Books Annu, 2001
    Includes bibliographical references and indexes

Bynum, William F.
  A **little** history of science; William Bynum. Yale University Press 2012 vi, 263 p.p ill. (hardcover) $25
  Grades: 10 11 12 Adult **509**
    1. DNA 2. Gravity 3. Planets 4. Science -- History 5. Science and civilization
    ISBN 0300136595; 9780300136593
    LC 2012026738
  Author W. F. Bynum's book presents "the history of science. It takes readers to the stars through the telescope, as the sun replaces the earth at the center of our universe. It delves beneath the surface of the planet, charts the evolution of chemistry's periodic table, introduces the physics that explain electricity, gravity, and the structure of atoms. It recounts the scientific quest that revealed the DNA molecule and opened unimagined new vistas for exploration." (Publisher's note)
  Noting biographical details of the scientists mentioned . . . Bynum connects their characters to whatever scientific mystery piqued their curiosity. In the process, he often approaches a topic by extrapolating from a common experience, as from bird-watching to dinosaurs. A super-accessible introduction to science." Booklist
    Includes bibliographical references and index

Crease, Robert P.
  The **great** equations; breakthroughs in science from Pythagoras to Heisenberg. W.W. Norton & Co. 2009 315p il $25.95
  Grades: 11 12 Adult **509**
    1. Equations 2. Science -- History 3. Science -- Philosophy
    ISBN 978-0-393-06204-5; 0-393-06204-X
    LC 2008-42494
  The author "explores 10 rather beautiful equations. He begins with the beguiling simplicity of the equation that bears Pythagoras' name . . . and moves on to Newton's second law of motion and law of universal gravitation, the second law of thermodynamics, Maxwell's celebrated equations, discoveries by Einstein and Schrödinger and, finally, Heisenberg's famous uncertainty principle. . . . Any reader who aspires to be scientifically literate will find this a good starting place." Publ Wkly
    Includes bibliographical references

  ★ The **prism** and the pendulum; the ten most beautiful experiments in science. Random House 2003 xxii, 244p il hardcover o.p. pa $14.95
  Grades: 11 12 Adult **509**
    1. Science -- History 2. Science -- Experiments
    ISBN 1-400-06131-8; 0-8129-7062-4 pa
    LC 2003-54765
  Each scientific experiment discussed here "is followed by an 'interlude,' or commentary, on how the experiment qualifies as most beautiful and how art and science both give meaning to the term 'beauty.'" Sci Books Films

Currie, Stephen

African American inventors; Stephen Currie. Lucent Books 2010 104 p. ill. (some col.) (hardcover) $36.10

Grades: 6 7 8 9 10 **509**

1. Inventions 2. African American inventors 3. Inventions -- United States -- History 4. African American inventors -- Biography

ISBN 1420501216; 9781420501216

LC 2009038456

This book is part of the Lucent Library of Black History and focuses on African-American Inventors and Inventions. "Each volume in the Lucent Library of Black History examines an event or time period of particular significance in African American history. . . . Each chapter contains sidebars that highlight relevant personalities and events. Numerous photos and illustrations" are included. (Publisher's note)

"Particular attention is given to historical, social, and political contexts and challenges faced by the inventors (e.g., institutionalized racism; difficulties with the patent system). The text is dense but informative." Horn Book

Includes bibliographical references (p. 93-98) and index.

Goddard, Jolyon

Concise history of science & invention; an illustrated time line. edited by Jolyon Goddard. National Geographic 2010 352p il map $40

Grades: 9 10 11 12 Adult **509**

1. Reference books 2. Science -- History 3. Inventions -- History 4. Science -- History -- Chronology 5. Inventions -- History -- Chronology

ISBN 978-1-4262-0544-6; 1-4262-0544-9

LC 2009-18460

This book presents "a panoramic perspective on humankind's restless quest for the laws, theories, and tools by which we can grasp and master our universe. . . . All human scientific endeavors and achievement are divided into four general fields of inquiry and arrayed into four basic geocultural regions . . . highlighted by 350 photographs, maps, illustrations, and diagrams that add graphic emphasis to key information." (Publisher's note)

This volume examines "our species' key scientific and innovative achievements, . . . presenting ten distinct eras from the first glimmers of intelligence to the cutting-edge technologies of the modern world." Publisher's note

Includes glossary and bibliographical references

Gribbin, John R.

★ The scientists; a history of science told through the lives of its greatest inventors. [by] John Gribbin. Random House 2003 xxii, 646p il hardcover o.p. pa $16.95

Grades: 11 12 Adult **509**

1. Scientists 2. Science -- History

ISBN 1-4000-6013-3; 0-8129-6788-7 pa

LC 2003-46607

First published 2002 in the United Kingdom with title: Science: a history, 1543-2001

"Replete with scientific clarity, Gribbin's work is the epitome of what a general-interest history of science should be." Booklist

Includes bibliographical references

Hakim, Joy

★ The story of science: Aristotle leads the way. Smithsonian Books 2004 282p (Story of science) $24.95

Grades: 8 9 10 11 12 **509**

1. Ancient civilization 2. Science -- History

ISBN 1-58834-160-7

"Hakim has interwoven creation myths, history, physics, and mathematics to present a seamless, multifaceted view of the foundation of modern science. . . . The entire volume is beautifully organized." SLJ

Includes bibliographical references

★ The story of science: Einstein adds a new dimension. Smithsonian Books 2007 468p il (Story of science) $27.95

Grades: 8 9 10 11 12 **509**

1. Cosmology 2. Quantum theory 3. Science -- History

ISBN 978-1-58834-162-4; 1-58834-162-3

LC 2007-14096

Hakim delivers a "brisk, intellectually challenging account of the development of quantum theory and modern cosmology. . . . She introduces a teeming cast of deep thinkers who . . . delivered a series of brilliant experiments and insights. . . . Supplemented by a digestible resource list and a generous assortment of illustrations." Booklist

Includes bibliographical references

★ The story of science: Newton at the center. Smithsonian Books 2005 463p (Story of science) $24.95

Grades: 8 9 10 11 12 **509**

1. Physics 2. Astronomy 3. Science -- History

ISBN 1-58834-161-5

LC 2004-58465

This "is an account of the history of astronomy and physics from c.1500 to 1900."

"Teachers will find anecdotal information to enliven their lessons; browsers will be fascinated by the sidebars and captioned illustrations that enhance the text or show related information." SLJ

Includes bibliographical references

Hellman, Hal

Great feuds in science; ten of the liveliest disputes ever. Wiley 1998 240p $24.95

Grades: 11 12 Adult **509**

1. Scientists 2. Science -- History

ISBN 0-471-16980-3

LC 97-39824

"Ranging from Galileo vs. Pope Urban VIII to Derek Freeman vs. Margaret Mead, this compilation of great scientific feuds covers an interesting variety of personalities as well as subject matter. . . . Hellman aims to show the human side of scientists, including all their petty frailties." Libr J

Includes bibliographical references

Horvitz, Leslie Alan

★ Eureka!: scientific breakthroughs that changed the world. Wiley 2002 246p il $24.95

Grades: 11 12 Adult **509**
1. Clergy 2. Chemists 3. Inventors 4. Physicists 5. Naturalists 6. Mathematicians 7. Biochemists 8. Geophysicists 9. Meteorologists 10. Travel writers 11. Microbiologists 12. College teachers 13. Science -- History 14. Writers on science 15. Writers on medicine 16. Mathematics teachers 17. Molecular biologists 18. Broadcasting engineers 19. Nobel laureates for physics 20. Nobel laureates for physiology or medicine
ISBN 0-471-40276-1
LC 2001-46890
This examines twelve scientific discoveries and their discoverers, including Joseph Priestley and oxygen, Friedrich Kekulé and the structure of carbon compounds, Dmitri Mendeleev and the periodic table, Isaac Newton and gravity, Einstein and the theory of relativity, Philo Farnsworth and television, Alexander Fleming and penicillin, Charles Townes and the laser, Alfred Wegener and continental drift, Darwin and the origin of species, Watson and Crick and the double helix, and Benoit Mandelbrot and fractal geometry.
Includes bibliographical references

Langone, John
Theories for everything; an illustrated history of science from the invention of numbers to string theory. [by John Langone, Bruce Stutz, and Andrea Gianopoulos] National Geographic 2006 407p il $40
Grades: 11 12 Adult **509**
1. Science -- History
ISBN 0-7922-3912-1; 978-0-7922-3912-3
LC 2006-21419
"With its profusion of illustrations, this is an inviting orientation to the fascinations of science." Booklist
Includes bibliographical references

Lawson, Russell M.
★ **Science** in the ancient world; an encyclopedia. ABC-CLIO 2004 xxv, 291p il (ABC-CLIO's history of science series) $85
Grades: 11 12 Adult **509**
1. Reference books 2. Science -- History -- Encyclopedias
ISBN 1-85109-534-9
LC 2004-17715
This book "describes scientific concepts in ancient societies, including the Egyptian, Babylonian, Greek, and Roman worlds until the fall of the Roman Empire. Most of the entries are about people, concepts, and locales of the Greco-Roman world. Arrangement is alphabetical, supported by good cross-references and indexing." Booklist
Includes bibliographical references

Life sciences in the twentieth century; biographical portraits. Everett Mendelsohn, editor; Brian S. Baigrie, consulting editor. Scribner 2001 207p il (Scribner science reference series) $80
Grades: 11 12 Adult **509**
1. Life sciences 2. Reference books 3. Scientists --

Dictionaries
ISBN 0-684-80647-9
LC 00-63789
A collection of about 90 biographical profiles of 20th century scientists in such fields as "anthropology, paleontology, bacteriology, immunology, organic chemistry, crystallography {and} biochemistry." Publisher's note
Includes bibliographical references (p. 195-196)

Lightman, Alan P.
★ The **discoveries**; great breakthroughs in 20th century science. [by] Alan Lightman. Pantheon Books 2005 553p il $32.50; pa $16.95
Grades: 11 12 Adult **509**
1. Science -- History
ISBN 0-375-42168-8; 0-375-71345-X pa
LC 2005-40854
This book "chronicles 25 landmark findings in astronomy, physics, chemistry, and biology in the 20th century. Beginning with Max Planck's quantum theory and ending with Paul Berg's recombinant DNA, these breakthroughs are academically and playfully explored via the nature of the unknown, the circumstances and influences of discovery, and, most originally, the actual words of the scientists." Libr J
Includes bibliographical references

Moser, Diane
The **birth** of science: ancient times to 1699; [by] Ray Spangenburg and Diane Kit Moser. Facts on File 2004 256p (History of science) $35
Grades: 7 8 9 10 **509**
1. Science -- History
ISBN 0-8160-4851-7
LC 2003-19470
First published 1993 with title: The history of science from the ancient Greeks to the scientific revolution
Discusses major scientists as well as scientific knowledge and discoveries from ancient times through the seventeenth century
"Very well written and thoroughly understandable, the book succeeds hugely in its objective to introduce the development of science in an interesting fashion to the intended audience without patronizing or oversimplifying." Sci Books Films [review of 1993 edition]
Includes glossary and bibliographical references

Nardo, Don
The **scientific** revolution; by Don Nardo. Lucent Books 2011 104 p. ill. (World history series) (library) $34.95
Grades: 6 7 8 9 **509**
1. Science -- History 2. Discoveries in science -- Europe
ISBN 1420506137; 9781420506136
LC 2011006556
This book by Don Nardo is part of the World History series and looks at the Scientific Revolution. The series entries offer an "overview of an important historical event or period. The series is designed both to acquaint readers with the basics of history and to make them aware that their lives and their own historical era are an intimate part of the ongoing human saga." (Publisher's note)
Includes bibliographical references (p. 96-98) and index.

Noyce, Pendred E.

Remarkable Minds; Seventeen More Pioneering Women in Science and Medicine. Penny Noyce. Tumblehome Learning, Inc 2015 192 p. illustrations $18.95

Grades: 6 7 8 9 10   **509**
1. Women scientists 2. Women in medicine
ISBN 0990782905; 9780990782902

LC 2015907841

This book, by Penny Noyce, "introduces the lives, sayings, and dreams of 16 women over four centuries and chronicles their contributions to mathematics, physics, chemistry, astronomy, and medicine. Some of the notable women portrayed in the book include French mathematician Marie-Sophie Germain . . . Scottish chemist Elizabeth Fulhame, . . . and Rita Levi-Montalcini, who . . . received the 1986 Nobel Prize in Physiology or Medicine for [the] discovery of nerve growth factor." (Publisher's note)

"This scholarly look at 17 remarkable, intelligent women devoted to research in science and medicine will round out science or biography collections." SLJ

The **Oxford** companion to the history of modern science; editor in chief, J.L. Heilbron; editors, James Bartholomew {et al.} Oxford Univ. Press 2003 xxviii, 941p il $110

Grades: 11 12 Adult   **509**
1. Science -- History
ISBN 0-19-511229-6

LC 2002-153783

This reference on the history of science from the Renaissance through the 20th century includes some 600 articles covering "a broad spectrum of topics in all scientific disciplines (e.g., biotechnology, geology) as well as disciplines that influenced science, such as religion and politics. Also included are the biographies of 100 leading figures (e.g., Isaac Newton, Marie Curie) and coverage of scientific instruments (e.g., microscopes, Geiger counters). Organized alphabetically, the well-written articles include plenty of cross references. Over 100 black-and-white illustrations appear within their appropriate articles, but the eight pages of color illustrations in the middle of the volume are not associated with any article." Libr J

Includes bibliographical references

The **Renaissance** and the scientific revolution; biographical portraits. Brian S. Baigrie, editor. Scribner 2001 210p il (Scribner science reference series) $80

Grades: 11 12 Adult   **509**
1. Reference books 2. Scientists -- Dictionaries
ISBN 0-684-80646-0

LC 00-63565

A collection of about 90 biographical profiles of scientists from 1500 to 1800.

Includes bibliographical references

The **Scientific** revolution; Mitchell Young, book editor. Greenhaven Press 2006 240p il (Turning points in world history) lib bdg $34.95

Grades: 9 10 11 12   **509**
1. Science -- History
ISBN 0-7377-2987-2

LC 2005-40268

"This volume offers many essays and articles discussing various aspects of a single subject—the scientific revolution. Each themed chapter includes about a half-dozen entries, introduced by the editor and written mainly by academics. . . . Though the book will be challenging for some students, others will find it a well-organized, informative resource." Booklist

Includes bibliographical references

Windelspecht, Michael

Groundbreaking scientific experiments, inventions, and discoveries of the 19th century; illustrated by Sandra Windelspecht. Greenwood Press 2003 xxvii, 270p il (Groundbreaking scientific experiments, inventions, and discoveries through the ages) $65

Grades: 9 10 11 12   **509**
1. Science -- History 2. Technology -- History
ISBN 0-313-31969-3

LC 2002-75305

This volume presents material "alphabetically by topic with information about the specific experiments, inventions, and discoveries of both women and men. . . . Each entry provides a brief historical discussion that allows the reader to understand the climate of the time of discovery and builds a foundation for understanding the methodology by which the scientists and inventors approached their discoveries, experiments, and inventions and for realizing the implications of these on man's future." Lib Media Connect

Includes bibliographical references

510   Mathematics

Acheson, D. J.

1089 and all that; a journey into mathematics. [by] David Acheson. Oxford Univ. Press 2002 178p il hardcover o.p. pa $17.95

Grades: 11 12 Adult   **510**
1. Mathematics
ISBN 0-19-851623-1; 0-19-959002-8 pa

LC 2002-71547

"Not a page passes without at least one intriguing insight. . . . Anyone who is baffled by mathematics should buy it." New Sci

Adam, John A.

A **mathematical** nature walk. Princeton University Press 2009 248p il $27.95

Grades: 10 11 12 Adult   **510**
1. Mathematics 2. Mathematical analysis
ISBN 978-0-691-12895-5; 0-691-12895-2

LC 2008-44828

"The general reader will find here a remarkably lucid explanation of how mathematicians create a formulaic model

that mimics the key features of some natural phenomenon. . . . Ordinary math becomes adventure." Booklist
Includes bibliographical references

Banks, Robert B.
Slicing pizzas, racing turtles, and further adventures in applied mathematics. Princeton Univ. Press 1999 286p il hardcover o.p. pa $26.95
Grades: 9 10 11 12 **510**
1. Mathematical recreations
ISBN 0-691-05947-0; 0-691-10284-8 pa
LC 98-53513
"Banks's style is entertaining but never condescending. Some of the math is pretty tough; it helps if you did well in trigonometry as well as introductory calculus and analytic geometry." Christ Sci Monit
Includes bibliographical references

Barrow, John D.
100 essential things you didn't know you didn't know; math explains your world. by John D. Barrow. W W Norton & Co Inc 2009 284 p. il $16.95
Grades: Adult **510**
1. Mathematics
ISBN 0393338673; 9780393070071; 9780393338676
LC 200855910
First published 2008 in the United Kingdom
In this book, author John D. Barrow "takes the most baffling of everyday phenomena and—with simple math, lucid explanations, and illustrations—explains why they work the way they do. His witty, crystal-clear answers shed light on the dark and shadowy corners of the physical world we all think we understand so well." (Publisher's note)
"Barrow (Mathletics), a Cambridge University professor of mathematical sciences and the director of the Millennium Mathematics Project, delves into the many ways mathematics informs art, and more broadly, our daily lives. Barrow is well versed in mathematics and is fascinated by the topics, but he does not consistently provide accessible explanations. That said, even when he misses, Barrow successfully conveys the idea that mathematics provides a key to understanding both ordinary and extraordinary phenomena." Pub Wkly.
Includes bibliographical references

Blastland, Michael
★ The **numbers** game; the commonsense guide to understanding numbers in the news, in politics, and in life. [by] Michael Blastland and Andrew Dilnot. Gotham Books 2009 210p il $22
Grades: 10 11 12 Adult **510**
1. Statistics 2. Mathematics 3. Number concept
ISBN 978-1-59240-423-0; 1-59240-423-5
LC 2008-30130
First published 2007 in the United Kingdom with title: The tiger that isn't
The authors "embark on a monumental task of interpreting numerical data and showing how its misinterpretation often leads to misinformation. . . . The authors take a close look at statistics that are accepted at face value—many stemming from scientific or medical discoveries." Publ Wkly
Includes bibliographical references

Boyer, Carl B.
★ A **history** of mathematics; [by] Carl B. Boyer and Uta Merzbach. 3rd ed.; Wiley 2010 xx, 668p il (pbk.) $39.95
Grades: 11 12 Adult **510**
1. Mathematics 2. Mathematics -- History
ISBN 9780470525487
LC 2010-3424
First published 1969
This book explores the "history of humankind's relationship with numbers, shapes, and patterns. This revised edition features up-to-date coverage of topics such as Fermat's Last Theorem and the Poincaré Conjecture, in addition to recent advances in areas such as finite group theory and computer-aided proofs." (Publisher's note)
"This good general history of mathematics is understandable to the student as well as authoritative for the mathematician." Malinowsky. Best Sci & Technol Ref Books for Young People
Includes bibliographical references

Bradley, Michael J.
The **birth** of mathematics; ancient times to 1300. Facts on File 2006 148p il (Pioneers in mathematics) $29.95
Grades: 7 8 9 10 **510**
1. Mathematicians 2. Mathematics -- History
ISBN 0-8160-5423-1
LC 2005-30563
The author "explores in exact detail the mathematical advances and other discoveries of 10 early mathematicians, from Thales of Miletus to Leonardo Fibonnaci. Illustrated with many mathematical figures and equations." Booklist
Includes glossary and bibliographical references

Darling, David J.
The **universal** book of mathematics; from Abracadabra to Zeno's paradoxes. [by] David Darling. Wiley 2004 383p il $40
Grades: 11 12 Adult **510**
1. Reference books 2. Mathematics -- Encyclopedias
ISBN 0-471-27047-4
LC 2003-24670
"The book's entries include numerous mathematical terms, brief biographies of mathematicians from ancient times to the present, and famous mathematical problems (both solved and unsolved), as well as problems and puzzles of a more recreational nature. It is a spirit of whimsy, the fanciful, and the outrageous that makes this book much more than a dry encyclopedia of mathematical terms, however. Darling's writing style and choice of entries make this an easy book to pick up and page through." Choice
Includes bibliographical references

Elwes, Richard
Mathematics 1001; absolutely everything that matters in mathematics in 1001 bite-sized explanations. Firefly Books 2010 415p il $24.95
Grades: 9 10 11 12 Adult **510**
1. Mathematics
ISBN 978-1-55407-719-9

"Concise essays about a variety of mathematical fields—numbers, algebra, geometry, logic—are arranged here by broad topics along with more specific subjects. The accessible text is written without troublesome jargon and terminology. . . . One can rarely call a mathematics book fun, but that's exactly what Elwes's book is." Libr J

★ The **Facts** on File dictionary of mathematics; edited by John Daintith, Richard Rennie. 4th ed; Facts on File 2005 262p il (Facts on File science library) $45; pa $17.95

Grades: 9 10 11 12   510

1. Reference books 2. Mathematics -- Dictionaries
ISBN 0-8160-5651-X; 0-8160-5652-8 pa
LC 2005-48762

First published 1980
Among the topics covered are: fractals, sets, chaos theory, computer graphics and hypertext.
Includes bibliographical references

Glazer, Evan

Real-life math; everyday use of mathematical concepts. [by] Evan M. Glazer and John W. McConnell. Greenwood Press 2002 165p il $49.95

Grades: 11 12 Adult   510

1. Mathematics
ISBN 0-313-31998-7
LC 2001-58635

The authors "have written this book as a reply to students' complaints that they'll never use the mathematical concepts they're being taught. They look at dozens of mathematical concepts and . . . show how these math ideas relate to the world in which students live. . . . The book is thorough and accurate." Libr Media Connect
Includes bibliographical references

Henderson, Harry

Mathematics: powerful patterns in nature and society. Facts on File 2007 170p il (Milestones in discovery and invention) $35

Grades: 7 8 9 10 11 12   510

1. Mathematics
ISBN 0-8160-5750-8; 978-0-8160-5750-4
LC 2006-24680

"Some mathematicians have discovered relatively simple yet exceedingly powerful patterns that yield insight into aspects of natural and human behavior. . . . [This book] presents 10 essays that profile the minds behind such patterns, many of which have surfaced in recent popular culture." Publisher's note
Includes glossary and bibliographical references

Lehmann, Ingmar

Mathematical curiosities; a treasure trove of unexpected entertainments. Alfred S. Posamentier, Ingmar Lehmann. Prometheus Books 2014 382 p. illustrations (pbk.) $19.95

Grades: 10 11 12 Adult   510

1. Mathematics -- Miscellanea 2. Mathematics -- Study

and teaching
ISBN 1616149310; 9781616149314
LC 2014006790

This book, by Alfred S. Posamentier and Ingmar Lehmann, offers an "innovative and appealing way for the layperson to develop math skills--while actually enjoying it. . . . This book will show you that the subject you learned to hate in high school can be as entertaining as a witty remark, as engrossing as the mystery novel you can't put down. . . . When you realize that doing math can be enjoyable, you open a door into a world of unexpected insights while learning an important skill." (Publisher's note)

"Posamentier (Mercy College) and Lehmann (formerly, Humboldt Univ., Germany), authors of many mathematics and mathematics education books, present a collection of mathematics tidbits, hoping to entertain readers. . . . This title is more readable than most recreational mathematics books. Physical production is superb. The book will be useful for libraries that serve mathematics recreation enthusiasts." Choice
Includes bibliographical references (pages 345-352) and index

Pask, Colin

Math for the frightened; facing scary symbols and everything else that freaks you out about mathematics. Prometheus Books 2011 380p il pa $19

Grades: 9 10 11 12   510

1. Mathematics 2. Mathematical notation
ISBN 978-1-61614-421-0
LC 2010048457

Pask's "examples and solutions are straight forward and uncomplicated. The 'anxious' math student and teacher will find his simplicity and humor very encouraging and easy to apply." Sci Books Films
Includes bibliographical references

Pickover, Clifford A.

The **math** book; from Pythagoras to the 57th dimension, 250 milestones in the history of mathematics. Clifford A. Pickover. Sterling 2009 527 p. il pbk $19.95; $29.95

Grades: 8 9 10 11 12 Adult   510

1. Mathematics -- History
ISBN 1402788290; 9781402788291; 9781402757969
LC 200843214

In this book, "beginning millions of years ago with ancient 'ant odometers' and moving through time to our modern-day quest for new dimensions, prolific polymath Clifford Pickover covers 250 milestones in mathematical history. Among the numerous concepts readers will encounter as they dip into this inviting anthology: cicada-generated prime numbers, magic squares, and the butterfly effect." (Publisher's note)

"Pickover's love of mathematics shines through the text and images, and it is likely that the reader will catch at least some of his enthusiasm." Choice
Includes bibliographical references

Rudman, Peter Strom

The **Babylonian** theorem; the mathematical journey to Pythagoras and Euclid. [by] Peter S. Rudman. Prometheus Books 2010 248p il $26

Grades: 11 12 Adult 510

1. Philosophers 2. Mathematicians 3. Writers on science 4. Mathematics -- History

ISBN 978-1-59102-773-7; 1-59102-773-X

LC 2009-39196

Sequel to How mathematics happened (2007)

"Topics covered include Pythagorean triplets, . . . similar triangles, square-root calculations, and calculations of the volume of a pyramid. . . . This is a well-researched volume on what forms of mathematics existed when similar ideas developed again and again in different cultures. The book's numerous mathematical equations would delight any math student." Sci Books Films

Includes bibliographical references

★ **How** mathematics happened; the first 50,000 years. [by] Peter S. Rudman. Prometheus Books 2007 314p il $26

Grades: 11 12 Adult 510

1. Mathematics -- History

ISBN 1-59102-477-3; 978-1-59102-477-4

LC 2006-20255

The author presents a "history of how numbers evolved beyond the finger and stone-counting of hunter-gatherer societies. It all started with the Babylonians, who fit very old body-part measurements into a powerful new arithmetic of squares and square roots. Rudman also probes the physiological logic that equipped the Mayans with base-20 numbers for mapping the heavens, and he scrutinizes the brilliance of Egyptian mathematicians who calculated complex volumes without calculus. Readers can deepen their understanding of ancient feats by working out the numerous 'Fun Questions' Rudman has embedded in his text to provide practical experience with key concepts." Booklist

Includes bibliographical references

Followed by The Babylonian theorem (2010)

Seife, Charles

Proofiness; the dark arts of mathematical deception. Viking 2010 295p il map $25.95

Grades: 9 10 11 12 Adult 510

1. Mathematics

ISBN 978-0-670-02216-8

LC 2010-12127

The author "examines the many ways that people fudge with numbers, sometimes just to sell more moisturizer but also to ruin our economy, rig our elections, convict the innocent and undercount the needy. . . . [This book] reveals the truly corrosive effects on a society awash in numerical mendacity. This is more than a math book; it's an eye-opening civics lesson." N Y Times Book Rev

Includes bibliographical references

Stewart, Ian

★ **Letters** to a young mathematician. Basic Books 2006 210p il (Art of mentoring) $22.95; pa $15

Grades: 11 12 Adult 510

1. Mathematics

ISBN 0-465-08231-9; 978-0-465-08231-5; 0-465-08232-7 pa; 978-0-465-08232-2 pa

LC 2005-30384

This book "takes the form of letters from a fictitious mathematician to his niece. The letters span a period of 20 years, from the time the niece is thinking about studying mathematics in high school through the early years of her academic career. The format works wonderfully well to introduce readers to the basics of the discipline of mathematics while providing a sense of what mathematicians actually do." Publ Wkly

The **magical** maze; seeing the world through mathematical eyes. Wiley 1998 268p il $24.95; pa $16.95

Grades: 11 12 Adult 510

1. Mathematics 2. Mathematical recreations

ISBN 0-471-19297-X; 0-471-35065-6 pa

LC 98-13185

Stewart presents various mathematical puzzles and problems through the metaphorical structure of a maze.

Chapters "contain good discussions of such topics as modular arithmetic, Marilyn vos Savant's Monty-Hall problem, depth-first and other search strategies, static and dynamic symmetry, Turing machines, optimization, fractals, and chaos. This is an excellent mix of topics and the material is very much up-to-date." Choice

★ **Professor** Stewart's hoard of mathematical treasures. Basic Books 2010 339p il pa $16.95

Grades: 9 10 11 12 Adult 510

1. Mathematics 2. Mathematical recreations

ISBN 978-0-465-01775-1; 0-465-01775-4

LC 2010-280702

Sequel to Professor Stewart's cabinet of mathematical curiosities (2009)

First published 2009 in the United Kingdom

This book features "puzzles, jokes, word problems, puns, and history and lore about math. . . . One never knows what's next: a proof that two plus two indeed equals four jostles with a spoof of proof itself. . . . The equal sign makes for a go-to topic for amusing vignettes, while stories about math underlying modern technology underscore the serious side of a subject with which Stewart makes such good sport. A great distraction for math mavens at any knowledge level." Booklist

Strogatz, Steven

★ The **joy** of X; a guided tour of math, from one to infinity. Steven Strogatz. Houghton Mifflin Harcourt 2012 336 p. (hardback) $27.00

Grades: 9 10 11 12 Adult 510

1. Mathematics

ISBN 0547517653; 9780547517650

LC 2012017320

In this book on mathematics, author Steven Strogatz "begins with arithmetic, by way of Sesame Street, then explores algebra, geometry, and, finally, the wonders of calculus. . . . From addition and subtraction, with a glimpse into negative numbers and 'the black art of borrowing,' it's a quick step into the hardcore detective work of algebra's search for the unknown x, with algorithms like the quadratic equation." (Publishers Weekly)

Tabak, John

★ **Mathematics** and the laws of nature; developing the language of science. Rev. ed.; Facts on File 2011 xx, 244p il (History of mathematics) $45
Grades: 9 10 11 12   510
  1. Science -- History 2. Mathematics -- History
  ISBN 978-0-8160-7943-8

LC 2010021599
First published 2004
This book "describes the evolution of the idea that nature can be described in the language of mathematics. . . . Chapters explore the earliest attempts to apply deductive methods to the study of the natural world . . . [and go] on to examine the development of classical conservation laws, including the conservation of momentum, the conservation of mass, and the conservation of energy." Publisher's note
  Includes bibliographical references

Tanton, James S.

★ **Encyclopedia** of mathematics; [by] James Tanton. Facts on File 2005 568p il (Facts on File science library) $75
Grades: 11 12 Adult   510
  1. Reference books 2. Mathematics -- Encyclopedias
  ISBN 0-8160-5124-0

LC 2004-16785
This encyclopedia "offers more than 800 entries from abacus and compound interest to Bertrand Russell and vector along with essays on the history and evolution of equations and algebra, calculus, functions, geometry, probability and statistics, and trigonometry." SLJ
  Includes bibliographical references

Tattersall, Graham

Geekspeak; how life + mathematics. Collins 2008 239p il pa $19.95
Grades: 10 11 12 Adult   510
  1. Mathematics
  ISBN 978-0-061-62924-2; 0-061-62924-3

LC 2008-16134
First published 2007 in the United Kingdom
Tattersall has rescued math from the prison of the classroom and put it to use explaining some of the oft-pondered questions of the world.
  "Leavened with armchair fun, such as estimating the weight of the moon or how many flies can power a car, Tattersall's amble might revive the fashion for pocket protectors and horn-rimmed spectacles." Booklist

511   General principles of mathematics

Kaplan, Robert

The **nothing** that is; a natural history of zero. illustrations by Ellen Kaplan. Oxford Univ. Press 2000 225p $40; pa $11.95

Grades: 11 12 Adult   511
  1. Zero (The number)
  ISBN 0-19-512842-7; 0-19-514237-3 pa

LC 99-29000
"Kaplan presents cultural, philosophical, historical, and mathematical developments that either encouraged or discouraged the recognition of the role of zero in counting and computation." Sci Books Films

Seife, Charles

Zero; the biography of a dangerous idea. Viking 2000 248p il hardcover o.p. pa $15
Grades: 11 12 Adult   511
  1. Zero (The number)
  ISBN 0-670-88457-X; 0-14-029647-6 pa

LC 99-36693
"The zero emerges as a daunting intellectual riddle in this . . . chronicle of a once controversial concept as Seife deftly traces the gradual acceptance of the zero and its role as catalyst for the evolution of everything from business to physics to moral thought." Booklist
  Includes bibliographical references

511.3   Mathematical logic (Symbolic logic)

Edwards, A. W. F.

Cogwheels of the mind; the story of Venn diagrams. foreword by Ian Stewart. Johns Hopkins University Press 2004 110p il $25
Grades: 11 12 Adult   511.3
  1. Philosophers 2. Symbolic logic
  ISBN 0-8018-7434-3

LC 2003-10633
"This title will appeal to readers studying mathematics and logic, to those who would like to know how scientific and mathematical research is carried out, and to those who are involved in graphic design and the study of the history of art as it relates to math." SLJ

512   Algebra

Gonick, Larry

The **cartoon** guide to algebra; by Larry Gonick. HarperCollins 2015 233 p. illustrations $18.99
Grades: 6 7 8 9 10   512
  1. Algebra
  ISBN 0062202693; 9780062202697

LC 2015458390
This book, by Larry Gonick, "offers a complete and up-to-date illustrated course to help students understand [algebra]. Using engaging graphics and lively humor, Gonick covers all of the algebra essentials, including linear equations, polynomials, quadratic equations, and graphing techniques. He also offers a concise overview of algebra's history and its many practical applications in modern life." (Publisher's note)
  "A valuable choice for visual learners or students in need of additional instruction." SLJ

McKellar, Danica

Hot X; algebra exposed. Hudson Street Press 2010 417p il $26.95

Grades: 9 10 11 12 **512**

1. Algebra

ISBN 978-1-59463-070-5

LC 2010-18163

"Facing down a 432-page book devoted to algebra could give even math whizzes pause, but McKellar makes it work, taking the textbook-meets-Seventeen approach by mixing the explanations and equations with boy talk, quizzes, and testimonials from successful women. While a tutor might use this title as a teaching aid, teen girls will want to explore it on their own. Navigation is easy; students are encouraged to hop from chapter to chapter as their homework demands. . . . While McKellar keeps her focus on how to solve math problems, her approach is both readable and even entertaining." Booklist

Miller, Robert

Bob Miller's algebra for the clueless; algebra. 2nd ed.; McGraw-Hill 2007 276p il (Bob Miller's clueless series) pa $12.95

Grades: 9 10 11 12 **512**

1. Algebra

ISBN 0-07-147366-1; 978-0-07-148846-4

LC 2006-8455

First published 1999

This guide to algebra explains such concepts as natural numbers, integers, equations, factoring, radicals and exponents and includes anxiety reducing features and tips for solving difficult problems.

Tabak, John

Algebra; sets, symbols, and the language of thought. Rev. ed.; Facts On File 2011 236p il (History of mathematics) $45

Grades: 9 10 11 12 **512**

1. Algebra

ISBN 978-0-8160-7944-5

LC 2010021597

First published 2004

This book "describes the history of both strands of algebraic thought. This . . . resource describes some of the earliest progress in algebra as well as some of the mathematicians in Mesopotamia, Egypt, China, and Greece who contributed to this early period. It goes on to explore the many breakthroughs in algebraic techniques as well as how letters were used to represent numbers." Publisher's note

Includes bibliographical references

Wingard-Nelson, Rebecca

★ Algebra I and algebra II. Enslow Publishers 2004 64p il (Math success) $22.60

Grades: 9 10 11 12 **512**

1. Algebra

ISBN 0-7660-2566-7

LC 2003-27620

"The book follows a concise algebraic format and is clearly and simply presented." Sci Books Films

Includes bibliographical references

513 Arithmetic

Bellos, Alex

Here's looking at Euclid; a surprising excursion through the astonishing world of math. Free Press hardcover ed.; Free Press 2010 319p il $25; ebook $11.99

Grades: 10 11 12 Adult **513**

1. Number concept

ISBN 978-1-4165-8825-2; 978-1-4165-9634-9 ebook

LC 2009-36815

The author "offers a lively romp through many different fields of mathematics as he incorporates ancient discoveries and modern developments alike. Topics include geometry, number theory, the development of sudoku, numerous aspects of pi and its calculation, statistics, probability and its application to gambling, and many other historical tidbits." Libr J

Includes bibliographical references

Tabak, John

Numbers; computers, philosophers, and the search for meaning. Rev. ed.; Facts On File 2011 243p il (History of mathematics) $45

Grades: 9 10 11 12 **513**

1. Numbers 2. Counting

ISBN 978-0-8160-7940-7

LC 2010-15830

First published 2004

This book "deals with numbers from the point of view of computation, beginning with the earliest number concepts from ancient Mesopotamian, Chinese, and Mayan mathematicians. It describes the origin and diffusion of Arabic numerals, and it concludes with a discussion of the way that the number system is represented within computers. . . . [It also] describes some of the IEEE standards for floating point arithmetic." Publisher's note

Includes bibliographical references

515 Analysis

Berlinski, David

A tour of the calculus. Pantheon Bks. 1995 331p il hardcover o.p. pa $14.95

Grades: 11 12 Adult **515**

1. Calculus

ISBN 0-679-74788-5 pa

LC 95-4042

"Berlinski tangibly grounds the abstract notions, so that attentive readers can ease into and grasp the several full-blown proofs he sets forth." Booklist

Kojima, Hiroyuki

★ The manga guide to calculus; [by] Hiroyuki Kojima, Shin Togami, and Becom Co., Ltd. No Starch Press 2009 238p il pa $19.95

Grades: 9 10 11 12 **515**

1. Manga 2. Graphic novels 3. Calculus -- Graphic

novels
ISBN 978-1-59327-194-7; 1-59327-194-8

LC 2008-50189

"Noriko is just getting started as a junior reporter for the Asagake Times. She wants to cover the hard-hitting issues, like world affairs and politics, but does she have the smarts for it? Thankfully, her overbearing and math-minded boss, Mr. Seki, is here to teach her how to analyze her stories with a mathematical eye. . . . [He teaches her] that calculus is a useful way to understand the patterns in physics, economics, and the world around us, with help from real-world examples like probability, supply and demand curves, the economics of pollution, and the density of Shochu (a Japanese liquor)." Publisher's note

Maor, Eli

★ The **Facts** on File calculus handbook. Facts on File 2003 164p il $35; pa $17.95

Grades: 9 10 11 12   **515**

1. Calculus

ISBN 0-8160-4581-X; 0-8160-6229-3 pa

LC 2003-49027

This resource is "a supplement to calculus or trigonometry course work. The Handbook's primary content is the glossary. Here, the author has compiled terms and expressions commonly used in calculus with . . . definitions and examples. . . . The other sections include a historical overview of the development of calculus, a selection of brief biographies of mathematicians, a timeline of calculus, a collection of charts and tables, and a list of recommended readings and Websites. . . . The conciseness of the definitions and examples, in addition to the historical data, make it a good 'study guide' or review resource for those high school students preparing for AP exams or similar college placement exams. For a quick look up of a definition that will be understandable to the non-math individual, this would be a practical ready-reference resource." Am Ref Books Annu, 2004

Includes bibliographical references

516 Geometry

Gorini, Catherine A.

★ The **Facts** on File geometry handbook; Rev ed; Facts on File 2009 342p il (Facts on File science library) $40

Grades: 11 12 Adult   **516**

1. Geometry

ISBN 978-0-8160-7389-4

LC 2009-5775

First published 2003

This includes a glossary of over 3,000 entries with labeled diagrams, biographies of over 300 scientists and mathematicians from ancient times to the present, a chronology of geometry history, charts, tables, recommended reading and websites.

Includes glossary and bibliographical references

Grigorieva, Ellina

Methods of solving complex geometry problems; Ellina Grigorieva. Birkhäuser 2013 xvi, 234 p.p (hardcover) $49.99

Grades: 10 11 12 Adult   **516**

1. Geometry 2. Mathematics -- Problems, exercises, etc. 3. Geometry -- Problems, exercises, etc

ISBN 3319007041; 9783319007045

LC 2013943010

This book, by Ellina Grigorieva, "is a unique collection of challenging geometry problems and detailed solutions that will build students' confidence in mathematics. By proposing several methods to approach each problem and emphasizing geometry's connections with different fields of mathematics, . . . [it] serves as a bridge to more advanced problem solving." (Publisher's note)

"his is a useful resource for geometry students, in particular Olympiad participants, to help them learn how to tackle hard problems." Choice

Includes bibliographical references and index

Lehmann, Ingmar

The **secrets** of triangles; a mathematical journey. by Alfred S. Posamentier and Ingmar Lehmann. Prometheus Books 2012 387 p. ill. (hardcover) $26

Grades: 11 12 Adult   **516**

1. Geometry 2. Triangle 3. Trigonometry

ISBN 1616145870; 9781616145873

LC 2012013635

This book offers "mathematical insights, intriguing relationships, and surprising results focused on the triangle." Topics include "noteworthy points, special lines, and concentric circles as related to triangles. Ultimately the book is a . . . compendium of results that" may surprise the reader with their simultaneous simplicity and complexity. (Choice)

Includes bibliographical references (p. 367-368) and index.

Mlodinow, Leonard

Euclid's window; the story of geometry from parallel lines to hyperspace. Free Press 2001 306p il hardcover o.p. pa $15

Grades: 11 12 Adult   **516**

1. Authors 2. Geometry 3. Physicists 4. Astronomers 5. Philosophers 6. Mathematicians 7. College teachers 8. Writers on science 9. Nobel laureates for physics

ISBN 0-684-86524-6 pa

LC 00-54351

"This engaging history does an excellent job of explaining the importance of the study of geometry without making the reader learn any geometry." Libr J

Includes bibliographical references

Tabak, John

Beyond geometry; a new mathematics of space and form. Facts on File 2011 xx, 217p il (History of mathematics) $45

Grades: 9 10 11 12   **516**

1. Geometry 2. Topology 3. Set theory

ISBN 978-0-8160-7945-2

LC 2010023887

This book "describes how set-theoretic topology developed and why it now occupies a central place in mathematics. Describing axiomatic method as well as providing a definition of what a geometric property is, this . . . resource examines how early analysts incorporated geometric thinking into their development of the calculus. It also looks at the various mathematicians who struggled to develop a new conceptual framework for mathematics and examines one of the sub-disciplines of set-theoretic topology called dimension theory." Publisher's note

Includes glossary and bibliographical references

★ **Geometry**; the language of space and form. Rev. ed.; Facts on File 2011 248p il (History of mathematics) $45

Grades: 9 10 11 12   **516**
  1. Geometry
  ISBN 978-0-8160-7942-1
                                          LC 2010018627
  First published 2004

This book "describes geometry in antiquity. Beginning with a brief description of some of the geometry that preceded the geometry of the Greeks, it takes up the story of geometry during the European Renaissance as well as the significant mathematical progress in other areas of the world. It also discusses the analytic geometry of René Descartes and Pierre Fermat, the alternative coordinate systems invented by Isaac Newton, and the solid geometry of Leonhard Euler." Publisher's note

Includes glossary and bibliographical references

516.2 Euclidean geometry

Livio, Mario
  The **golden** ratio; the story of phi, the world's most astonishing number. Broadway Bks. 2002 294p hardcover o.p. pa $14.95

Grades: 11 12 Adult   **516.2**
  1. Geometry
  ISBN 0-7679-0815-5; 0-7679-0816-3 pa
                                          LC 2002-23084

The author examines the history and myths of phi, the "golden ratio" of 1.6180339887 that has been related to phenomena as diverse as the arrangements of petals on roses and the breeding patterns of rabbits.

"Overall, an enjoyable work, amply supported by index, extensive references, and ten appendixes presenting mathematical elaborations of text material." Choice

Includes bibliographical references

Maor, Eli
  The **Pythagorean** theorem; a 4,000-year history. Princeton University Press 2007 259p il map $24.95

Grades: 9 10 11 12 Adult   **516.2**
  1. Mathematics -- History
  ISBN 978-0-691-12526-8; 0-691-12526-0
                                          LC 2006-50969

"This [is an] interesting and well-written book. . . . I recommend the book highly to students, teachers, and the intelligent general reader interested in a very old, beautiful, and useful result." Sci Books Films

Includes bibliographical references

516.22 Plane geometry

Blatner, David
  ★ The **joy** of pi. Walker & Co. 1997 129p il hardcover o.p. pa $12

Grades: 11 12 Adult   **516.22**
  1. Pi
  ISBN 0-8027-1332-7; 0-8027-7562-4 pa
                                          LC 97-23705

The author discusses the history of the number π, as well as the process of "calculating the ratio of a circle's circumference to its diameter, which has advanced from measuring lengths of string and the 'brute force' of measuring polygons to feeding supercomputers sophisticated algorithms. Sidebars . . . abound, containing a factoid, joke, or doggerel inspired by π." Booklist

Includes bibliographical references

519.2 Probabilities

Mazur, Joseph
  Fluke; the math and myth of coincidences. Joseph Mazur. Basic Books 2016 288 p. illustrations (hardcover) $26.99

Grades: 11 12 Adult   **519.2**
  1. Chance 2. Mathematics -- Popular works 3. Coincidence 4. Simultaneity (Physics) 5. Coincidence theory (Mathematics)
  ISBN 9780465060955
                                          LC 2015043288

In this book, "mathematician Joseph Mazur takes a second look at the seemingly improbable, sharing with us an entertaining guide to the most surprising mathematical concepts in our lives. He takes us on a tour of the mathematical concepts of probability, such as the law of large numbers and the birthday paradox, and combines these concepts with lively anecdotes of flukes from around the world." (Publisher's note)

"Like John Allen Paulos, in Innumeracy (1988), mathematician Mazur takes what could be difficult, abstruse subjects—probability and statistics—and makes them entertaining. The author's focus is coincidence, in particular our perception of coincidence. He astounds us with some eye-opening facts (it's actually quite likely that a squirrel might get hit by lightning while crossing a street, even though it sure doesn't seem all that likely), shows us that seemingly astounding things are actually not that astounding (the same person winning a lottery four times isn't all that improbable), and explains how it's our own lack of familiarity with mathematics and the nature of probability that makes things seem wildly unlikely (a certain event might seem rare and unique to us, but in terms of probability, it can be entirely expected). . . . An ideal book, then, for the lay reader who is curious about the nature of coincidence." Booklist

Includes bibliographical references and index

Rosenthal, Jeffrey
  Struck by lightning; the curious world of probabilities. [by] Jeffrey S. Rosenthal. HarperCollins Canada 2005 263p il pa $19.95

Grades: 11 12 Adult   **519.2**
1. Chance 2. Probabilities
ISBN 0-309-09734-7; 978-0-309-09734-5
LC 2005-37021

Rosenthal discusses ways in which probability theory affects such areas of everyday life as crime, travel, gambling, politics, and disease.

"The lighthearted presentation ensures that readers will not feel burdened by all the knowledge they are gaining and the concluding summary—disguised as a final exam—is sure to deliver an A to everyone, which is what Rosenthal deserves for this clever book." Publ Wkly

Tabak, John

★ **Probability** and statistics; the science of uncertainty. Rev. ed.; Facts on File 2011 252p il (History of mathematics) $45
Grades: 9 10 11 12   **519.2**
1. Statistics 2. Probabilities
ISBN 978-0-8160-7941-4
LC 2010026448

First published 2004

This book "deals with the history of probability, describing the modern concept of randomness and examining 'pre-probabilistic' ideas of what most people today would characterize as randomness. . . . [It] documents some historically important early uses of probability to illustrate some very important probabilistic questions." Publisher's note

Includes bibliographical references

519.5   Statistical mathematics

Adam, John A.

Guesstimation; solving the world's problems on the back of a cocktail napkin. [by] Lawrence Weinstein and John A. Adam. Princeton University Press 2008 301p il pa $19.95
Grades: 11 12 Adult   **519.5**
1. Problem solving 2. Approximate computation
ISBN 0-691-12949-5; 978-0-691-12949-5
LC 2007-33928

The authors "briefly review good 'guesstimation' techniques involving numbers (i.e., scientific notation, accuracy, unit conversion) and explain why the use of the geometric mean is preferred over the arithmetic mean. The authors then meander through a wide variety of fascinating problems, roughly arranged in 'world-type' categories: animals, people, transportation, energy, work, Earth's chemical elements, environment, atmosphere, and space. Some of the problems are easy, some are hard—and most will grab the reader's interest." Choice

Includes bibliographical references

Cohen, I. Bernard

The **triumph** of numbers; how counting shaped modern life. W. W. Norton 2005 209p il $24.95; pa $14.95

Grades: 11 12 Adult   **519.5**
1. Statistics
ISBN 0-393-05769-0; 978-0-393-05769-0; 0-393-32870-8 pa; 978-0-393-32870-7 pa
LC 2004-27322

"This book presents a persuasive narrative on how numbers have maintained a prominent role not only in science and government throughout time, but in the daily operations of life." Sci Books Films

Includes bibliographical references

Paulos, John Allen

★ **Once** upon a number; the hidden mathematical logic of stories. Basic Bks. 1998 214p hardcover o.p. pa $13
Grades: 11 12 Adult   **519.5**
1. Statistics 2. Symbolic logic
ISBN 0-465-05159-6 pa
LC 98-39252

"Paulos fills this book with so many intriguing nuggets of mathematically sound information about the stories we tell that it deserves rereading, which, because Paulos' voice is so enjoyable, seems no daunting task." Booklist

Includes bibliographical references

Wheelan, Charles

Naked statistics; stripping the dread from the data. Charles Wheelan. W W Norton & Co Inc 2013 304 p. (hardcover) $26.95
Grades: 11 12 Adult   **519.5**
1. Statistics
ISBN 0393071952; 9780393071955
LC 2012034411

Wheelan "has provided an intuitive presentation of statistical concepts without getting bogged down by extensive data lists or computation. The author begins by generally introducing each idea with an idealized situation to illustrate that statistical setting and its impact on effective interpretation, and then moves on to current real-world settings to legitimize his discussion. He also clearly discusses subtleties that can be encountered, showing how data users must be careful to avoid oversimplifying the implications of a given result. The presentation is nonthreatening, yet readers will find it a suitably thoughtful consideration of statistical ideas." Choice

Includes bibliographical references and index

520   Astronomy and allied sciences

Angelo, Joseph A.

★ **Encyclopedia** of space and astronomy; [by] Joseph A. Angelo, Jr. Facts on File 2006 740p il (Facts on File science library) $75
Grades: 11 12 Adult   **520**
1. Reference books 2. Astronomy -- Encyclopedias 3. Space sciences -- Encyclopedias
ISBN 0-8160-5330-8
LC 2004-30800

This encyclopedia presents "the main concepts, terms, facilities, and people in astronomy. . . . Coverage includes terms such as astrophysics, planetary science, and cosmology, as well as both American and international astronomy and space technology." Publisher's note

Includes bibliographical references

★ The **Facts** on File space and astronomy handbook; [by] Joseph A. Angelo, Jr. Rev. ed.; Facts on File 2009 342p il map (Facts on File science library) $40

Grades: 11 12 Adult   **520**

1. Astronomy 2. Space sciences 3. Reference books
ISBN 978-0-8160-7388-7

LC 2008-51761

First published 2002

This handbook is divided into four sections: a glossary of nearly 1,300 entries related to science and astronomy, biographies of over 400 scientists, a chronology, and a set of charts and tables.

Includes bibliographical references

Aveni, Anthony F.

★ **Stairways** to the stars; skywatching in three great ancient cultures. [by] Anthony Aveni. Wiley 1997 230p il hardcover o.p. pa $15.95

Grades: 11 12 Adult   **520**

1. Incas 2. Mayas 3. Ancient civilization 4. Astronomy -- History 5. Stonehenge (England)
ISBN 0-471-15942-5; 0-471-32976-2 pa

LC 96-36517

"An insightful and interesting blend of ancient anthropology and ancient astronomy." Choice

Includes bibliographical references

Bartusiak, Marcia

The **day** we found the universe. Pantheon Books 2009 337p il $27.95

Grades: 9 10 11 12 Adult   **520**

1. Astronomy -- History
ISBN 978-0-375-42429-8; 0-375-42429-6

LC 2008-34377

"This is a superb book that interweaves the fascinating story of a major scientific quest with a cast of characters, situations, painstaking observations, and imaginative thinking that reminds us all of the human side of scientific endeavors and the ways in which the universe itself continuously surprises us." Sci Books Films

Includes bibliographical references

Couper, Heather

The **history** of astronomy; [by] Heather Couper & Nigel Henbest; foreword by Arthur C. Clarke. Firefly Books 2007 285p il $59.95; pa $29.95

Grades: 11 12 Adult   **520**

1. Astronomy -- History
ISBN 978-1-55407-325-2; 1-55407-325-1; 978-1-55407-537-9 pa; 1-55407-537-8 pa

LC 2008-272095

This "history is pieced together through astronomer interviews and visits to historically important astronomy sites around the world. . . . This is a copiously illustrated, straightforwardly written volume that will appeal to readers

with and without an astronomy background. In addition to covering astronomy through the ages, the authors do an admirable job explaining current astronomical discoveries and personalities." Choice

Darling, David J.

The **universal** book of astronomy from the Andromeda Galaxy to the zone of avoidance; [by] David Darling. Wiley 2003 570p il $40

Grades: 11 12 Adult   **520**

1. Reference books 2. Astronomy -- Dictionaries
ISBN 0-471-26569-1

LC 2003-13941

"Designed for nonspecialists, Darling's volume fills a niche in astronomy ready reference. . . . The volume is . . . highly readable and provides bonuses in 22 star charts outlining all 88 constellations in both north and south celestial hemispheres, instructional aids throughout the text, and charts that accompany entries for many stars, galaxies, and clusters and show size, position, etc." Choice

Includes bibliographical references

Dickinson, Terence

★ The **universe** and beyond; foreword by Edward G. Gibson. 5th ed., Revised and expanded; Firefly Books 2010 204p il $45; pa $29.95

Grades: 9 10 11 12   **520**

1. Astronomy
ISBN 978-1-55407-640-6; 978-1-55407-748-9 pa

First published 1986

Illustrated with over 130 color illustrations and photographs, this describes the universe, comets, planets, black holes, galaxies, dark matter, quasars, and other topics.

Includes bibliographical references

Dyson, Marianne J.

Space and astronomy; decade by decade. Facts on File 2007 284p il map (Twentieth-century science) $49.50

Grades: 9 10 11 12   **520**

1. Space flight 2. Astronomy -- History
ISBN 978-0-8160-5536-4; 0-8160-5536-X

LC 2006-12547

"This chronology includes astronomical discoveries (the dwarf planet then called Pluto, pulsars), innovations in rocketry, exploration of space by crewed and uncrewed missions, the search for extraterrestrial life, and even some space-related fiction. . . . Chapters cover one decade each and include a two-page 'Scientist of the Decade' section that focuses on the career of one significant person and a time line of important events. . . . [This book] is extremely well detailed, the writing remains readable from start to finish, and an excellent index provides near-encyclopedic access. A fine history." SLJ

Includes bibliographical references

★ The **Facts** on File dictionary of astronomy; edited by John Daintith, William Gould. 5th ed.; Facts on File 2006 550p il (Facts on File science library) $59.50

Grades: 7 8 9 10 11 12   **520**

1. Reference books 2. Astronomy -- Dictionaries
ISBN 0-8160-5998-5; 978-0-8160-5998-0

LC 2006-40860

First published 1979 under the editorship of Valerie Illingworth

This dictionary includes "more than 3,700 entries . . . that reflect all aspects of astronomy, together with associated terms in spectroscopy, photometry, and particle physics." Publisher's note

Includes bibliographical references

Gater, Will

The **practical** astronomer; [by] Will Gater and Anton Vamplew; consultant Jacqueline Mitton. DK Pub. 2010 256p il map pa $19.95

Grades: 7 8 9 10 11 12   **520**

1. Astronomy 2. Astronomy -- Observers' manuals
ISBN 978-0-7566-6210-3; 0-7566-6210-9

LC 2010-281460

"This beautifully illustrated volume is a valuable and accurate guide to observing and understanding the wide variety and essential characteristics of fascinating astronomical objects that are visible from Earth. . . . [It enables] the reader to learn about coordinate systems; solar system motions; the nature of light; and how to use the eye, binoculars, telescopes, cameras, and astronomical atlases and catalogues to explore the heavens directly and efficiently." Sci Books Films

Gilliland, Ben

Rocket science for the rest of us; cutting-edge concepts made simple. written by Ben Gilliand; consultant, Jack Challoner. Dk Pub 2015 192 p. color illustrations (paperback) $15.99

Grades: 10 11 12   **520**

1. Science -- Popular works 2. Astrophysics
ISBN 9781465433657; 1465433651

LC 2015297118

In this book, by Ben Gilliand, readers will "get a grip on even the most mysterious and complex sciences with . . . [this] guide to dark matter, exo-planets, Planck time, earth sciences, and more. . . . [The author] breaks it all down so science and physics are easy to understand." (Publisher's note)

"This book is certain to appeal to students studying science as well as armchair enthusiasts and would be a solid choice for libraries looking to supplement their science collections." SLJ

Hetherington, Edith W.

★ **Astronomy** and culture; [by] Edith W. Hetherington and Norriss S. Hetherington. Greenwood Press/ABC-CLIO 2009 231p il (Greenwood guides to the universe) $65

Grades: 9 10 11 12   **520**

1. Astronomy 2. Science and civilization
ISBN 978-0-313-34536-4; 0-313-34536-8; 978-0-313-34537-1 ebook; 0-313-34537-6 ebook

LC 2009-7368

This "is a book of exceptional breadth. . . . [The authors] cover topics ranging from how ancient cultures in Mesopotamia, Greece, and the New World created mythology and calendars to make sense of the sky, to connections between astronomy and religion, to the history of the idea of extraterrestrial life. Besides combining diverse perspectives from the history of science, the history of astronomy, and archaeoastronomy, the book represents a unique attempt to present astronomy integrated with culture, broadly defined." Choice

Includes bibliographical references

Kanipe, Jeff

The **cosmic** connection; how astronomical events impact life on Earth. Prometheus Books 2009 296p il $27.95

Grades: 11 12 Adult   **520**

1. Astronomy
ISBN 978-1-59102-667-9; 1-59102-667-9

LC 2008-31877

"This extremely well written book would be an engaging read for any person with even the slightest interest in astronomy." Sci Books Films

Includes bibliographical references

Kidger, Mark R.

Astronomical enigmas; life on Mars, the Star of Bethlehem, and other Milky Way mysteries. Johns Hopkins University Press 2005 297p il map $29.95

Grades: 9 10 11 12   **520**

1. Astronomy
ISBN 0-8018-8026-2

LC 2004-8937

"This is a beautifully written book packed with narrative answers to major astronomical topics of current interest." Sci Books Films

Includes bibliographical references

Mitton, Jacqueline

★ **Cambridge** illustrated dictionary of astronomy. Cambridge University Press 2007 397p il map $35

Grades: 11 12 Adult   **520**

1. Reference books 2. Astronomy -- Dictionaries
ISBN 978-0-521-82364-7; 0-521-82364-1

LC 2008-295878

First published 1993 in the United Kingdom with title: The Penguin dictionary of astronomy

"With this dictionary Mitton . . . offers a welcome addition to the reference collection." Choice

★ **Night**Watch: a practical guide to viewing the universe; foreword by Timothy Ferris; illustrations by Adolf Schaller, Victor Costanzo, Roberta Cooke, Glenn LeDrew; principal photography by Terence Dickinson. 4th ed.; Firefly Books 2006 192p il $35

Grades: 8 9 10 11 12   **520**

1. Astronomy
ISBN 978-1-55407-147-0; 1-55407-147-X

LC 2006-491527

First published 1983

This "handbook for amateur astronomers combines a text both meaty and hard to put down with a great array of charts, boxes, tables, and dazzling full-color photos of the sky." SLJ [review of 1998 edition]

Includes bibliographical references

★ **Oxford** dictionary of astronomy; edited by Ian Ridpath. 2nd ed.; Oxford University Press 2007 561p il (Oxford paperback reference) pa $18.95

Grades: 11 12 Adult   **520**

1. Reference books 2. Astronomy -- Dictionaries

ISBN 978-0-19-921493-8

LC 2007-40707

First published 1997

This dictionary presents "4200 paragraph-sized definitions, along with illuminating technical graphs and charts. Included is an exhaustive, A-to-Z compilation of eminent figures and significant, if sometimes obscure, scientific phenomena, mission names, and project monikers." Libr J

Petersen, Carolyn Collins

Visions of the cosmos; {by} Carolyn Collins Petersen, John C. Brandt. Cambridge University Press 2003 218p il $40

Grades: 9 10 11 12   **520**

1. Astronomy

ISBN 0-521-81898-2

LC 2003-43043

"Almost every page holds stunningly detailed visual images. Full-page color digital photos such as the birth of a star or the Pillars of Creation captivate readers while the descriptive text explains how these visions were recorded and what they may mean. This book takes the scientific who, what, where, when, and why and puts them in terms a neophyte astronomer can comprehend." Libr Media Connect

Includes bibliographical references

Plait, Philip C.

★ **Death** from the skies! these are the ways the world will end . . . [by] Philip Plait. Viking 2008 326p il $25.95

Grades: 11 12 Adult   **520**

1. End of the world

ISBN 978-0-670-01997-7; 0-670-01997-6

LC 2008-22943

"The book is extremely informative: Plait explains not only what can destroy the planet but also how it would happen. It's a crash course in astronomy as well as a cautionary tale about the (possibly brief) future of our world." Booklist

Rhee, George

Cosmic dawn; the search for the first stars and galaxies. George Rhee. Springer 2013 xi, 279 p.p ill. (chiefly col.) $39.99

Grades: 10 11 12 Adult   **520**

1. Astronomy 2. Cosmology 3. Cosmology -- Popular works

ISBN 146147812X; 9781461478126

LC 2013940914

This book, by George Rhee, "takes the reader on an exploration of the structure and evolution of our universe. The basis for our knowledge is the Big Bang theory of the expanding universe. This book then tells the story of our search for the first stars and galaxies using current and planned telescopes." (Publisher's note)

" Rhee (Univ. of Nevada) begins the book with a discussion of humankind's historical attempts to find our place and time in the universe. While exploring the evidence that the universe began with an unimaginably huge explosion, the author also gives a pretty good primer on astronomy. The relatively recent discovery of dark matter and dark energy and what they imply for the present structure and future evolution of the universe is also very well described. . . . Part of the "Astronomers' Universe" series, this is one of the most readable books on cosmology around. Anyone with an interest in science will enjoy it." Choice

Includes bibliographical references (p. 275-276) and index

Schaaf, Fred

The **50** best sights in astronomy and how to see them; observing eclipses, bright comets, meteor showers, and other celestial wonders. John Wiley 2007 280p il pa $19.95

Grades: 11 12 Adult   **520**

1. Astronomy

ISBN 978-0-471-69657-5; 0-471-69657-9

LC 2006-36221

The author "begins with some basic information and terminology (altazimuth system, for example, or right ascension) and then plunges right in with the most easily accessible astronomical sight, the starry sky above our heads. For each sight, he not only explains what it is and the best conditions under which to observe it, he also tells us about its historical, mythological, or scientific importance and explores how these far-off wonders can have a very real effect on our humble home world. This could so easily have been a dry-as-dust tome, but Schaaf's enthusiasm overflows every page." Booklist

Includes bibliographical references

Sobel, Dava

A **more** perfect heaven; how Copernicus revolutionized the cosmos. Walker Pub. 2011 273p il map $25

Grades: 11 12 Adult   **520**

1. Astronomy 2. Astronomers 3. Solar system

ISBN 978-0-8027-1793-1

LC 2011024772

"Dava Sobel excels in telling the story of Nicholas Copernicus and his almost-shelved masterpiece, On the Revolutions. Along the way, she brings the social and political milieu of the times into sharp relief providing context for the sheer audacity of his insights into planetary motion and his reticence in pursuing their dissemination." Sci Books Films

Includes bibliographical references

Trefil, James

Space atlas; mapping the universe and beyond. James Trefil; foreword by Buzz Aldrin. National Geographic 2012 335 p, col. ill. (hardback) $50

Grades: 9 10 11 12 Adult   **520**

1. Galaxies 2. Astronomy 3. Solar system 4. Stars

-- Atlases 5. Galaxies -- Atlases 6. Solar system --
Atlases 7. Astronomy -- Charts, diagrams, etc
ISBN 1426209711; 9781426209710; 9781426210914
LC 2012020000

Author James Trefil presents a "guide to the planets,
stars and outer reaches of the universe." The book "explains
the nature of planets, stars, galaxies and exotic objects such
as black holes alongside photos and art . . . In addition to
the latest imagery coming from space telescopes and diagrams explaining key astronomical concepts, this atlas also
includes more than 90 pages of detailed maps." (Publisher's note)

Includes bibliographical references

★ **Universe**; general editor, Martin Rees. DK 2008
512p il pa $27.95
Grades: 11 12 Adult   **520**
1. Cosmology
ISBN 978-0-7566-3670-8; 0-7566-3670-1
LC 2008-299650
First published 2005
This is "a visually stunning reference that makes brows-
ing irresistible. Every page of this oversized volume is full
color, with an eye-pleasing balance of text and graphics."
Libr J

Watson, Fred
Star-Craving Mad; Tales from a Travelling Astronomer. Fred Watson. Allen & Unwin 2013 334
p. (paperback) $19.95
Grades: 10 11 12 Adult   **520**
1. Astronomers 2. Astronomy -- Popular works
ISBN 9781742373768; 1742373763
In this book, by Fred Watson, "everything the amateur
astronomer needs to know about the history of the universe,
from the transit of Venus to the Higgs boson, from ancient
Peruvian observatories to the world's largest particle accelerator. . . . [It explains how] astronomy . . . provide[s]
a broader framework than most sciences for deliberations
about issues big and small." (Publisher's note)
"Watson, Australia's most popular astronomer, offers a
lighthearted excursion into the history of mankind's understanding of the universe. The subtitle refers to the astronomy
tours he leads, which also inform the book's structure, and
the book is a combination of travelogue—incorporating time
spent aboard an astronomy cruise—and popular science, as
it explores several continents, eras, and scientists of historic
note. . . . " PW

Walker, Pamela
Space and astronomy experiments; [by] Pamela
Walker, Elaine Wood. Facts on File 2010 xx, 152p
il (Facts on File science experiments) $35
Grades: 7 8 9 10 11 12   **520**
1. Astronomy 2. Space sciences 3. Science --
Experiments
ISBN 978-0-8160-7809-7; 0-8160-7809-2
LC 2009-32825
This book "presents experiments designed to foster
understanding of space science and astronomy. Geared
to middle and high-school students and their teachers, the
20 experiments convey basic astronomy principles, draw

from historic experiments, or explore new technologies. . . .
Schools and libraries where students and teachers are looking for science experiments on space and astronomy will
find this volume a useful addition to the collection." Booklist
Includes glossary and bibliographical references

Yount, Lisa
Edward Pickering and his women "computers"
analyzing the stars. Lisa Yount. Chelsea House 2011
130 p. (Trailblazers in science and technology) (li-
brary) $35
Grades: 7 8 9 10 11 12   **520**
1. Women astronomers 2. Pickering, Edward C.
(Edward Charles), 1846-1919 3. Physicists -- United
States -- Biography 4. Astronomers -- United States --
Biography
ISBN 1604136642; 9781604136647
LC 2011002792
This book, by Lisa Yount, is part of the "Trailblazers in
Science and Technology" series. "In the 42 years that Edward Pickering directed the Harvard College Observatory,
he and his team of women 'computers' made strides in pro-
moting the new field of astrophotography. . . . The advances
these women made under Pickering's direction broadened
the window of professional opportunity for women as well
as our greater understanding of the universe." (Publisher's note)
Includes bibliographical references and index

**522 Techniques, procedures, apparatus,
equipment, materials**

Angelo, Joseph A.
Spacecraft for astronomy; [by] Joseph A. Angelo, Jr. Facts on File, Inc. 2006 288p il (Frontiers
in space) $39.50
Grades: 9 10 11 12   **522**
1. Space probes 2. Astronomical instruments 3.
Astronomical observatories
ISBN 0-8160-5774-5; 978-0-8160-5774-0
LC 2006-4875
This "volume describes the historic events, scientific
principles, and technical breakthroughs that allow complex
orbiting astronomical observatories to increase our understanding of the universe, its origin, and its destiny." Publisher's note
Includes glossary and bibliographical references

Harrington, Philip S.
Star ware; the amateur astronomer's guide to
choosing, buying, and using telescopes and accesso-
ries. 4th ed.; Wiley 2007 417p il pa $21.95
Grades: 11 12 Adult   **522**
1. Telescopes
ISBN 978-0-471-75063-5; 0-471-75063-8
LC 2006-25134
First published 1994
This guidebook on choosing and caring for telescopes
and related equipment also features advice on practical is-

sues such as keeping dew off a corrector plate, warding off mosquitoes, and staying warm outside.

Includes bibliographical references

Kerrod, Robin

★ **Hubble**; the mirror on the universe. [by] Robin Kerrod & Carole Stott. 3rd ed. updated, rev. and expanded.; Firefly Books 2011 224p il pa $29.95

Grades: 11 12 Adult 522

1. Hubble Space Telescope 2. Outer space -- Exploration

ISBN 978-1-55407-972-8; 1-55407-972-1

LC 2011292195

First published 2003

"Kerrod provides an excellent overview of Hubble's accomplishments (along with a history of the evolution of the telescope), thoughtfully organizing the spellbinding images from space, and clearly and avidly explaining exactly which phenomena they depict." Booklist

523 Specific celestial bodies and phenomena

★ **Firefly** atlas of the universe; foreword by Arnold Wolfendale. 3rd ed.; Firefly Books 2005 288p il $49.95

Grades: 11 12 Adult 523

1. Astronomy

ISBN 1-55407-071-6

LC 2006-275758

First published 1970 by Rand McNally; this edition first published 2003 in Canada. Variant title: Philip's atlas of the universe

This work begins with a "general historical overview, followed by individual sections on the solar system, the sun, the stars, the structure of the universe and our galaxy's place in it, and over 20 useful star maps, all incorporating the newest scientific data." Libr J [review of 2003 edition]

523.1 The universe, galaxies, quasars

Aguilar, David A.

Space encyclopedia; a tour of our solar system and beyond. written & illustrated by David A. Aguilar; contributing writers Christine Pulliam & Patricia Daniels. National Geographic 2013 191 p. color illustrations (National Geographic kids) (reinforced library binding) $24.95

Grades: 7 8 9 10 11 12 523.1

1. Planets 2. Astronomy 3. Cosmology 4. Outer space 5. Solar system

ISBN 1426309481; 1426315600; 1426316291; 9781426309489; 9781426315602; 9781426316296

LC 2013444119

This book on outer space by David A. Aguilar is "broken up into five sections. . . . Aguilar moves from the origins of the universe, to the planets and bodies of our Solar System, and then to the impressive phenomena from all corners of the universe. Everything from black holes to dark matter and theories about multiple universes is touched upon." (Children's Literature)

"This attractive compendium of information about space is encyclopedic in the sense that its scope is broad. The facts are presented in two- to eight-page highly illustrated articles within five thematic sections. . . . The articles are clearly written and informative, but the visuals steal the show." Booklist

Includes bibliographical references (page 191) and index

Bell, Jim, 1965-

The **space** book; from the beginning to the end of time, 250 milestones in the history of space & astronomy. Jim Bell. Sterling 2013 528 p. color illustrations; maps (hardcover) $29.95

Grades: 10 11 12 Adult 523.1

1. Universe 2. Cosmology 3. Physics -- History 4. Cosmology -- History

ISBN 9781402780714; 1402780710

LC 2013372035

This book by Jim Bell "presents 250 of the most ground-breaking astronomical events, from the formation of galaxies to the recent discovery of water ice on Mars. . . . Open the book to any page to discover some new wonder or mystery about the Universe around us." (Publisher's note)

"This is a fine coffee-table book, suitable for either deep study or a few moments' perusal. Recommended for readers with a casual interest in the history of astronomy and the universe, or for sparking such an interest in others." LJ

Includes bibliographical references (p. 518-525) and index

Chaisson, Eric

Epic of evolution; seven ages of the cosmos. illustrated by Lola Judith Chaisson. Columbia University Press 2005 478p il $34.50; pa $22.95

Grades: 11 12 Adult 523.1

1. Cosmology 2. Life -- Origin

ISBN 0-231-13560-2; 978-0-231-13560-3; 0-231-13561-0 pa; 978-0-231-13561-0 pa

LC 2005-45452

The author "has crafted a wonderful vehicle for exploring our universe." Sci Books Films

Includes bibliographical references

Cox, Brian, 1968-

Wonders of the universe; [by] Brian Cox and Andrew Cohen. Harper Design 2011 256p il $29.99; ebook $14.99

Grades: 11 12 Adult 523.1

1. Cosmology

ISBN 978-0-06-211054-1; 978-0-06-211561-4 ebook

The author "uses the evidence found in the natural world on Earth to . . . explain the truth of the cosmos. . . . [He shows] how the vast and unfathomable phenomena of deep space can be explained, and even experienced, by re-examining the familiar here on Earth." Publisher's note

Dunbar, James Lu

The **Universe** Verse; James Lu Dunbar. James & Kenneth Pub 2014 112 p. color illustrations $24.95

Grades: 5 6 7 8 9 10 523.1

1. Science -- Popular works 2. Universe -- Comic

books strips, etc. 3. Science 4. Cosmology 5. Human beings 6. Life -- Origin 7. Comic books, strips, etc.
ISBN 1888047259; 9781888047257

This comic book, by James Lu Dunbar, "is a scientifically-accurate rhyming comic book about the origins of the universe, life on Earth and the human race. It introduces and illuminates the most fundamental features of our existence in a way that is engaging and accessible to a wide audience. . . . This book contains most major scientific milestones known to humanity." (Publisher's note)

"The images slowly transition from black and white in the first section to unobtrusive color in last section....Young students will revel in the artwork, while older kids could use the text as an introduction to advanced high school science." SLJ

Gates, Evalyn

Einstein's telescope; the hunt for dark matter and dark energy in the universe. W.W. Norton 2009 305p il $25.95; pa $16.95

Grades: 11 12 Adult **523.1**

1. Dark energy (Astronomy) 2. Dark matter (Astronomy)
ISBN 978-0-393-06238-0; 978-0-393-33801-0 pa
LC 2008-44455

"Gates writes with a freshness and clarity that make complex ideas such as relativity, lensing, black holes, and the cosmic web understandable." Libr J
Includes bibliographical references

Hawking, Stephen, 1942-

Black holes and baby universes and other essays; [by] Stephen Hawking. Bantam Bks. 1993 182p hardcover o.p. pa $18

Grades: 11 12 Adult **523.1**

1. Cosmology 2. Science -- Philosophy
ISBN 0-553-37411-7 pa
LC 93-8269

A collection of essays and speeches ranging from autobiographical sketches to theoretical discussions of black holes, relativity and quantum mechanics.

The author "sprinkles his explanations with a wry sense of humor and a keen awareness that the sciences today delve not only into the far reaches of the cosmos, but into the inner philosophical world as well." N Y Times Book Rev

A brief history of time; {by} Stephen Hawking. Updated and expanded tenth anniversary ed; Bantam Bks. 1998 212p il $27.95; pa $16.95

Grades: 11 12 Adult **523.1**

1. Cosmology
ISBN 0-553-10953-7; 0-553-38016-8 pa
LC 98-21874
First published 1988

The author describes concepts about space and time, black holes, the origin and nature of the universe, the uncertainty principle, and the unification of physics. This edition includes a new introduction and a new chapter about wormholes and time travel

★ A briefer history of time; [by] Stephen Hawking and Leonard Mlodinow. Bantam Dell 2005 162p il $25

Grades: 11 12 Adult **523.1**

1. Cosmology
ISBN 0-553-80436-7
LC 2005-42949
First published 1988 with title: A brief history of time

The authors describe concepts about space and time, black holes, the origin and nature of the universe, the uncertainty principle, and the unification of physics. It also discusses string theory, dark matter, and dark energy.

"Hawking and Mlodinow provide one of the most lucid discussions of this complex topic ever written for a general audience. Readers will come away with an excellent understanding of the apparent contradictions and conundrums at the forefront of contemporary physics." Publ Wkly
Includes bibliographical references

Kaku, Michio

Parallel worlds; a journey through creation, higher dimensions, and the future of the cosmos. Doubleday 2005 428p il hardcover o.p. pa $15.95

Grades: 11 12 Adult **523.1**

1. Cosmology 2. String theory 3. Big bang theory
ISBN 0-385-50986-3; 1-4000-3372-1 pa
LC 2004-56039

"This is a riveting popular treatment of the string revolution in physics written by a pioneering theorist in the field. Kaku expounds comprehensibly on why astrophysicists love strings and branes and the way they resolve various vexatious cosmological paradoxes." Booklist

Miller, Ron

Recentering the universe; the radical theories of Copernicus, Kepler, and Galileo. by Ron Miller. Lerner Publishing Group 2013 88 p. (lib. bdg.: alk. paper) $31.93

Grades: 7 8 9 10 11 12 **523.1**

1. Astronomy 2. Religion and science 3. Astronomy -- History 4. Astronomy -- Religious aspects -- Christianity -- History
ISBN 0761358854; 9780761358855
LC 2012047665

In this book, author Ron Miller examines "scientists [who] risked their reputations—even their lives—to challenge the very heart of Catholic dogma and scientific tradition. In the 1500s and 1600s, men like Nicolaus Copernicus, Johanned Kepler, Galileo Galilei, and Isaac Newton began to ask questions. What if Earth actually orbited the sun, instead of the other way around? What if the universe was much bigger than anyone imagined?" (Publisher's note)
Includes bibliographical references (p. 83) and index

Panek, Richard

The 4 percent universe; dark matter, dark energy, and the race to discover the rest of reality. Houghton Mifflin Harcourt 2011 297 p. $26.00

Grades: 11 12 Adult **523.1**

1. Physics 2. Cosmology 3. Astrophysics 4. Dark

energy (Astronomy) 5. Dark matter (Astronomy)
ISBN 0618982442; 9780618982448

LC 2010-25838

This is an account of the scientific inquiry into the substance of the unseen dark matter and energy that makes up 96% of the universe. Index.

"This is a story about not just science, but also scientists, with enough dueling personalities, epic failures, inspirational triumphs, and out-and-out rivalries to carry a Hollywood blockbuster—should Hollywood ever turn its attention to the world of cosmology." Ad Astra

Includes bibliographical references

523.2   Planetary systems

Baker, David

The **50** most extreme places in our solar system; [by] David Baker and Todd Ratcliff. Belknap Press 2010 290p il $27.95

Grades: 9 10 11 12 Adult   **523.2**

1. Solar system 2. Extreme environments
ISBN 0-674-04998-5; 978-0-674-04998-7

LC 2010-06126

"Descriptions of physical phenomena are given around themes such as 'Surface and Interior' and 'Extreme Climates.'" (Sci Books Films) Glossary. Bibliography. Index.

The authors "discuss phenomena like the potential for diamond rain on Uranus and Neptune and the hardiness of extremophile life forms. As planetary scientists, they write clearly about the most extreme physical aspects of solar system bodies such as planets, moons, and comets, but deftly mix in more familiar comparisons from planet Earth as well." Choice

Includes bibliographical references

Benson, Michael

Beyond; a solar system voyage. Abrams Books for Young Readers 2009 121p il $19.95

Grades: 5 6 7 8 9 10   **523.2**

1. Astronomy 2. Solar system
ISBN 0-8109-8322-2; 978-0-8109-8322-9

LC 2008-22297

This book presents the solar system from the perspective of the space probes sent there. Glossary. Index. "Ages nine to twelve." (Sci Books Films)

"The book's focus is the exploration of the solar system by space probes, with many full-page photos. . . . The author skillfully blends lively narrative with the photos to contribute to the excitement of the explorations. . . . It is an inexpensive but valuable addition for any library." Voice Youth Advocates

Includes glossary and bibliographical references

Daniels, Patricia

The **new** solar system; ice worlds, moons, and planets redefined. foreword by Robert Burnham. National Geographic Society 2009 223p il map $35

Grades: 11 12 Adult   **523.2**

1. Solar system
ISBN 978-1-4262-0462-3; 1-4262-046-20

LC 2009-10117

This is "a sumptuously illustrated book describing the history, composition, and exploration of the solar system. Aimed at a general audience, the text is highly readable and contains numerous side notes providing fascinating anecdotes and facts about the planets, the sun, and astronomers." Choice

Includes bibliographical references

★ **Encyclopedia** of the solar system; editors, Lucy-Ann McFadden, Paul R. Weissman and Torrence V. Johnson. 2nd ed.; Academic 2007 xx, 966p il map $99.95

Grades: 9 10 11 12   **523.2**

1. Reference books 2. Astronomy -- Encyclopedias 3. Solar system -- Encyclopedias
ISBN 978-0-12-088589-3; 0-12-088589-1

LC 2006-937972

First published 1999

This encyclopedia covers "the origin and evolution of the solar system, historical discoveries, and details about planetary bodies and how they interact." Publisher's note

Includes bibliographical references

Jayawardhana, Ray

Strange new worlds; the search for alien planets and life beyond our solar system. Princeton University Press 2011 255p il $24.95

Grades: 11 12 Adult   **523.2**

1. Solar system 2. Extrasolar planets 3. Life on other planets 4. Astronomy -- History
ISBN 978-0-691-14254-8; 0-691-14254-8

LC 2010940350

An astronomer discusses the search for extrasolar planets and extraterrestrial life. Bibliography. Index.

"Everything you need to know about alien planet discovery is insightfully described in this engaging book, which will appeal to astronomers, general science buffs, and armchair UFOlogists." Libr J

Includes glossary and bibliographical references

Lemonick, Michael D.

Mirror Earth; the search for our planet's twin. Michael D. Lemonick. Walker 2012 294 p. (hardback) $26

Grades: 10 11 12 Adult   **523.2**

1. Earth 2. Extrasolar planets 3. Planetology
ISBN 080277900X; 9780802779007

LC 2012009787

AAAS Subaru SB & F Young Adult Science Book Finalist (2013)

This book by Michael Lemonick "offers readers . . . [a] view into the work of 'exoplaneteers': astronomers dedicated to searching out not just planets orbiting distant worlds, but 'Mirror Earths,' Earth-like planets that might harbor life. . . . Lemonick introduces planet-hunting pioneers like mild-mannered Bill Borucki, indefatigable Geoff Marcy . . . and nurse-turned-astrophysicist Debra Fischer, revealing personalities as well as research frustrations and successes." (Publishers Weekly)

"A solid overview of the cutting edge of astronomy and of the new breed of astronomers who are exploring it." Kirkus

Includes bibliographical references and index

Rivkin, Andrew S.

★ **Asteroids,** comets, and dwarf planets. Greenwood Press 2009 206p il (Greenwood guides to the universe) $65

Grades: 9 10 11 12   **523.2**

1. Comets 2. Asteroids 3. Solar system

ISBN 978-0-313-34432-9; 0-313-34432-9; 978-0-313-34433-6 ebook; 0-313-34433-7 ebook

LC 2009-16114

"Covering the solar system's non-moon smaller bodies, from comets plunging out of the distant Oort Cloud to NEO (Near Earth Objects) asteroids and hypothetical 'Vulcan Objects' spinning around the Sun inside Mercury's orbit, Rivkin devotes chapters to orbits, compositions, origins, and relevant space probe missions." SLJ

Includes glossary and bibliographical references

The **solar** system; editors, David G. Fisher, Richard R. Erickson. Salem Press 2009 3v il set $364

Grades: 9 10 11 12 Adult   **523.2**

1. Reference books 2. Solar system

ISBN 978-1-58765-530-2

LC 2009-13008

First published 1998 under the editorship of Roger Smith

"These 180 articles offer comprehensive views of the solar system's bodies, dynamics, and phenomena, as well as a thorough account of how they are studied via astronomical observation and space exploration..... The cross-references, lengthy subject index, continuous pagination throughout the volumes, and a thematic table of contents, in addition to one by volume, make access particularly easy." SLJ

Includes bibliographical references

523.4   Planets, asteroids, trans-Neptunian objects of solar system

Boyle, Alan

The **case** for Pluto; how a little planet made a big difference. Wiley 2010 258p il $22.95; ebook $14.99

Grades: 11 12 Adult   **523.4**

1. Solar system 2. Pluto (Planet)

ISBN 978-0-470-50544-1; 0-470-50544-3; 978-0-470-54188-3 ebook

LC 2009-15961

This volume examines the history of the discovery of planets. Boyle "chronicles the decision by the International Astronomical Union in 2006 to redefine the definition of a planet.... [Boyle argues] that Pluto has unjustly been cast out of the 'Planet Family' and recast as a 'dwarf planet.'" Sci Books Films

Includes bibliographical references

Brown, Mike

How I killed Pluto and why it had it coming; Mike Brown. Spiegel & Grau 2010 xiii, 267p 1 ill. (pbk.) $15.00; (alk. paper) o.p.; (alk. paper) o.p.; (ebook) $12.99

Grades: 11 12 Adult   **523.4**

1. Planets 2. Astronomers 3. Solar system 4. Pluto (Dwarf planet) 5. Discoveries in science

ISBN 9780385531108; 0385531087; 9780385531085; 9780385531092

LC 2010015074

This book relates the story of astronomer Mike Brown's research that led to the demotion of Pluto as a planet. "The solar system most of us grew up with included nine planets, with Mercury closest to the sun and Pluto at the outer edge. Then, in 2005, astronomer Mike Brown made the discovery of a lifetime: a tenth planet, Eris, slightly bigger than Pluto. But instead of adding one more planet to our solar system, Brown's find ignited a firestorm of controversy that culminated in the demotion of Pluto from real planet to the newly coined category of 'dwarf' planet. Suddenly Brown was receiving hate mail from schoolchildren and being bombarded by TV reporters—all because of the discovery he had spent years searching for and a lifetime dreaming about." (Publisher's note)

Chaikin, Andrew

A **passion** for Mars; intrepid explorers of the Red Planet. foreword by James Cameron. Abrams 2008 279p il $35

Grades: 11 12 Adult   **523.4**

1. Mars (Planet) -- Exploration

ISBN 978-0-8109-7274-2; 0-8109-7274-3

LC 2007-49007

The author "describes the quest to understand and travel to Mars through the eyes of the dreamers and scientists who make planetary exploration possible. . . . I cannot recommend this book highly enough. You will come away from reading it not only knowing more about the exploration of Mars, but also with a better understanding of the word 'passion.'" Sci Books Films

Chaple, Glenn F.

★ **Outer** planets. Greenwood Press 2009 199p il (Greenwood guides to the universe) $65

Grades: 9 10 11 12   **523.4**

1. Saturn (Planet) 2. Uranus (Planet) 3. Jupiter (Planet) 4. Neptune (Planet)

ISBN 978-0-313-36570-6; 0-313-36570-9

LC 2009-19682

"This book focuses on Jupiter, Saturn, Neptune, and Uranus in great detail, comparing the planets and delving into technical information on each planet. . . . The author's writing style takes a very complex, scientific subject and breaks it down into chapters that are understandable and interesting for the amateur enthusiast, with detailed information for the researcher looking for a credible source." Libr Media Connect

Includes glossary and bibliographical references

Grier, Jennifer A.

★ **Inner** planets; [by] Jennifer A. Grier and Andrew S. Rivkin. Greenwood Press 2010 212p il map (Greenwood guides to the universe) $65

Grades: 9 10 11 12　　　　　**523.4**
　1. Earth 2. Mars (Planet) 3. Venus (Planet) 4. Mercury (Planet)
　ISBN 978-0-313-34430-5; 0-313-34430-2

　　　　　　　　　　　　　　LC 2009-42491

"This volume eschews the conventional listing of the numerical data associated with astrophysical texts. Instead, the focus is on explaining processes of planetary formation and change. . . . [The authors] break these processes down into 13 thematic chapters, devoting each to a major concept like plate tectonics, magnetospheres, or atmospheres. Made up largely of engaging text arranged logically with subheadings, chapters are occasionally punctuated by monochromatic illustrations or informational sidebars. . . . A suitable subject primer for high schoolers and lay readers." Libr J
　Includes bibliographical references

Hartmann, William K.

A **traveler's** guide to Mars; the mysterious landscapes of the red planet. Workman Pub. 2003 468p map pa $18.95

Grades: 11 12 Adult　　　　　**523.4**
　1. Mars (Planet)
　ISBN 0-7611-2606-6

　　　　　　　　　　　　　　LC 2003-41149

"Following an opening chapter discussing what humans have believed and have come to verify about the red planet, the author discusses the three major eras of its 4.5 billion year history. He describes various regions, offering a geological tour of the craters, volcanoes, and the face of Mars. . . . Interspersed throughout are boxed inserts highlighting weather, hazards, financial considerations, geology, etc. Also appearing periodically are sections called 'My Martian Chronicles' in which the astronomer describes his own work and experiences in his quest to learn more about this unusual planet. His writing style will make teens want to keep reading. . . . If you can have only one title about Mars, this is the one to buy." SLJ
　Includes bibliographical references

Jones, Barrie William

Pluto; sentinel of the outer solar system. [by] Barrie W. Jones. Cambridge University Press 2010 231p il $35.99

Grades: 11 12 Adult　　　　　**523.4**
　1. Solar system 2. Pluto (Planet)
　ISBN 978-0-521-19436-5; 0-521-19436-9

　　　　　　　　　　　　　　LC 2010-15480

This is "a detailed, matter-of-fact, and thoroughly accessible look at Pluto's origins, its history, and what it can tell us about our solar system—especially its outer reaches. . . . The author writes in a clear, matter-of-fact style, including sidebars on related subjects from Kepler's laws of planetary motion to calculating a planet's surface temperature using nothing more complex than high school algebra." Publ Wkly
　Includes glossary and bibliographical references

Jones, Thomas D.

Planetology; unlocking the secrets of the solar system. [by] Tom Jones and Ellen Stofan. National Geographic 2008 217p il $35

Grades: 7 8 9 10 11 12　　　　　**523.4**
　1. Planets 2. Astrogeology
　ISBN 978-1-4262-0121-9; 1-4262-0121-4

　　　　　　　　　　　　　　LC 2008-10726

"This beautifully produced book provides an introduction to comparative planetology for a general audience. The large-format volume focuses on comparing and contrasting different processes that shape and form the primary planets in the solar system. . . . The writing is crisp and clear, and the choice of imagery and examples is very strong." Choice
　Includes bibliographical references

Karam, P. Andrew

Planetary motion; by P. Andrew Karam and Ben P. Stein. Chelsea House 2009 117p il (Science foundations) lib bdg $35

Grades: 9 10 11 12　　　　　**523.4**
　1. Planets 2. Galaxies
　ISBN 978-1-60413-017-1; 1-60413-017-2

　　　　　　　　　　　　　　LC 2009-2040

Learn how scientists have found new planets outside the solar system, and continue their search for planets like Earth.
　The title offers "a wealth of material, including useful further-reading lists. Great for curricular supplementation, report writers, and science buffs." SLJ
　Includes glossary and bibliographical references

Nardo, Don

Asteroids and comets. Morgan Reynolds Pub. 2009 112p il (Extreme threats) lib bdg $28.95

Grades: 7 8 9 10　　　　　**523.4**
　1. Comets 2. Asteroids
　ISBN 978-1-59935-121-6; 1-59935-121-8

　　　　　　　　　　　　　　LC 2009-26295

This book covers "evidence of impacts, types of impactors, giant impacts and mass extinctions, recent impacts and near misses, the current and future danger of near-earth-objects (NEOs), and scientific research on how to address the threat. . . . Features high-gloss pages in mottled green, full-color pictures, and informative sidebars. . . . [It is] well written, nicely designed, and interesting." Voice Youth Advocates
　Includes glossary and bibliographical references

Tyson, Neil deGrasse

The **Pluto** files; the rise and fall of America's favorite planet. W.W. Norton 2009 194p il $23.95; pa $15.95

Grades: 8 9 10 11 12 Adult　　　　　**523.4**
　1. Pluto (Dwarf planet)
　ISBN 978-0-393-06520-6; 0-393-06520-0; 978-0-393-33732-7 pa; 0-393-33732-4 pa

　　　　　　　　　　　　　　LC 2008-40436

The author, who is the director of the Hayden Planetarium and the Rose Center for Earth and Space at the American Museum of Natural History in New York City, discusses the "history of Pluto and the debate over its planethood. .

. [Tyson cites Pluto's] entrenchment in America's cultural and patriotic view of the cosmos to explain its considerable popularity and the reasons why so many people campaigned for the preservation of its status." (Publisher's note)

The author "uses an engaging mix of facts, photographs, cartoons, illustrations, songs, e-mails, and humor to explain what's up (and down) with Pluto." Christ Sci Monit

Includes bibliographical references

Weintraub, David A.

Is Pluto a planet? a historical journey through the solar system. Princeton University Press 2007 254p il $27.95

Grades: 11 12 Adult   **523.4**
1. Planets 2. Solar system 3. Pluto (Dwarf Planet)
ISBN 0-691-12348-9; 978-0-691-12348-6
LC 2006-929630

Weintraub "provides a very interesting and thought-provoking history concerning the whole idea of planets, and I recommend the book highly to anyone interested in the solar system." Sci Books Films

Includes bibliographical references

523.43   Mars

Miller, Ron

Curiosity's mission on Mars; exploring the red planet. by Ron Miller. TFCB, Twenty-First Century Books 2014 64 p. color illustrations (lib. bdg.: alk. paper) $33.26

Grades: 7 8 9 10 11 12   **523.43**
1. Mars (Planet) -- Exploration
ISBN 1467710873; 9781467710879
LC 2013009290

"This clearly written book provides a solid, basic introduction to the Curiosity rover, which NASA launched into space on November 26, 2011. It landed on Mars in August 2012, began drilling into rocks, and has found many key ingredients necessary for life...Sidebars provide additional information on related topics, such as the naming of Curiosity by Kansas sixth-grader Clara Ma, the likelihood of ice beneath the surface of Mars, and the layers of the planet's atmosphere. Rather small color photos and diagrams illustrate this succinct introduction." (Booklist)

Includes bibliographical references (pages 55-56) and index

523.5   Meteors, solar wind, zodiacal light

Norton, O. Richard

Field guide to meteors and meteorites; [by] O. Richard Norton, Lawrence A. Chitwood. Springer 2008 287p il (Patrick Moore's practical astronomy series) pa $39.95

Grades: 9 10 11 12 Adult   **523.5**
1. Meteors 2. Astrogeology
ISBN 978-1-84800-156-5 pa; 1-84800-156-8 pa; 978-1-84800-157-2 ebook; 1-84800-157-6 ebook
LC 2008-921357

This guide "goes beyond the well-illustrated guide to help meteorite hunters identify their prize (with detailed color or photos), and includes the astronomical context needed to understand meteorites and their Earth-bound predecessors, meteoroids. The authors cover astronomical origins, beginning with micrometeoroids, or space dust particles, through meteoroids' believed 'parent,' the asteroid. . . . The Guide offers useful advice on tools (e.g., metal detectors, magnets) to help identify objects and a beginner's guide to laboratory equipment, including microscopes and home chemical tests, to help amateur meteoriticists identify key characteristics for meteorite verification." Choice

Includes glossary

Smith, Caroline

Meteorites; [by] Caroline Smith, Sara Russell and Gretchen Benedix. Firefly Books 2009 112p il map $24.95

Grades: 9 10 11 12 Adult   **523.5**
1. Meteorites
ISBN 978-1-55407-515-7

This is an "introduction to meteorites and their scientific importance. . . . The authors describe what extraterrestrial rocks look like and the regions in which they are apt to be found and then delve into their significance to scientists such as themselves. . . . Including photos of recent space missions dedicated to meteoritic research, this is a capable title for libraries needing an introductory book on meteorites." Booklist

Includes bibliographical references

523.6   Comets

Burnham, Robert

★ **Great** comets; foreword by David H. Levy. Cambridge Univ. Press 2000 228p pa $22

Grades: 11 12 Adult   **523.6**
1. Comets
ISBN 0-521-64600-6
LC 98-50546

The author focuses on the comets Hyakutake in 1996 and Hale-Bopp in 1997, placing them in the context of their predecessors, including Halley's comet, profiles spaceprobes to the comets, and assesses the risks to humanity from comets

"The copious illustrations are . . . supported by a good deal of text. . . . The science is accurate and presented in a nontechnical way. . . . Overall, this is a very fine book." Sci Books Films

Includes bibliographical references

Levy, David H.

★ **David** H. Levy's guide to observing and discovering comets. Cambridge University Press 2003 177p il $70; pa $22.99

Grades: 11 12 Adult   **523.6**
1. Comets
ISBN 0-521-82656-X; 0-521-52051-7 pa
LC 2002-31547

The author "describes the observing techniques that have been developed over the years—from visual observations and searching, to photography, through to electronic charge-coupled devices (CCDs). He combines the history of comet hunting with the latest techniques, showing how our understanding of comets has evolved over time." Publisher's note

Includes bibliographical references

523.7 Sun

Alexander, David

★ The **sun**. Greenwood Press/ABC-CLIO 2009 228p il (Greenwood guides to the universe) $65
Grades: 9 10 11 12   523.7
1. Astronomy 2. Astrophysics 3. Sun
ISBN 978-0-313-34077-2; 0-313-34077-3
LC 2009-6640

This "is a guide to the sun and near-solar environment. The book is very wide-ranging in its scope, giving up-to-date information not only on the processes that power the sun, but also on the physical processes within its atmospheric layers (including the corona, photosphere, and chromosphere), as well as space weather and its effects on Earth and spacecraft. . . . The depth and breadth of this title is such that it will satisfy even the most serious amateur astronomers and science enthusiasts, while at the same time providing less serious readers enough practical information about the effects of solar phenomena on everyday life." Choice

Includes glossary and bibliographical references

Clark, Stuart

The **sun** kings; the unexpected tragedy of Richard Carrington and the tale of how modern astronomy began. Princeton Univ. Press 2007 211p il $24.95
Grades: 11 12 Adult   523.7
1. Astronomers 2. Photographers 3. Sun 4. Writers on science 5. Astronomy -- History
ISBN 978-0-691-12660-9; 0-691-12660-7
LC 2006-940123

"Clark's parade of historical characters dramatize the narrative nicely, and Clark conveys the significance of their scientific observations with plenty of context and thorough references, making this a fascinating work for both casual stargazers and serious astronomy buffs." Publ Wkly

Includes bibliographical references

Harrington, Philip S.

★ **Eclipse!** the what, where, when, why, and how guide to watching solar and lunar eclipses. Wiley 1997 280p il maps pa $16.95
Grades: 9 10 11 12   523.7
1. Lunar eclipses 2. Solar eclipses
ISBN 0-471-12795-7
LC 96-29777

This describes solar and lunar eclipses and offers advice on observing and photographing them

"This well-organized book . . . does a fine job of detailing the mechanics of solar and lunar eclipses. . . . Numerous black-and-white photographs and many line drawings and tables in the text are followed by seven helpful appendices and a good index." Sci Books Films

Includes bibliographical references

Lang, Kenneth R.

★ The **Cambridge** encyclopedia of the sun. Cambridge Univ. Press 2001 256p il $86
Grades: 11 12 Adult   523.7
1. Sun
ISBN 0-521-78093-4
LC 00-49365

"Each of the nine chapters addresses a different theme. These themes include physical properties, the magnetic solar atmosphere, solar winds and explosions, solar observations, and the Sun-Earth connection. The volume is well illustrated with figures and photographs in both color and black and white. A 35-page glossary provides definitions of terms and acronyms as well as information on telescopes, satellites, and instruments. A short annotated bibliography and an unannotated directory of Web sites are appended." Booklist

Includes bibliographical references

523.8 Stars

Jackson, Ellen B.

The **mysterious** universe; supernovae, dark energy, and black holes. text by Ellen Jackson; photographs and illustrations by Nic Bishop. Houghton Mifflin 2008 60p il $18
Grades: 5 6 7 8 9   523.8
1. Supernovas 2. Black holes (Astronomy)
ISBN 978-0-618-56325-8; 0-618-56325-3
LC 2007-41165

"Splitting its attention evenly between the scientist and his field, this handsomely designed volume displays the joys of being fascinated by one's work in a way that will encourage students to seek similar professional satisfaction for themselves." Booklist

Jones, Lauren V.

★ **Stars** and galaxies. Greenwood Press 2010 207p il (Greenwood guides to the universe) pa $65
Grades: 9 10 11 12   523.8
1. Stars 2. Galaxies
ISBN 978-0-313-34075-8; 0-313-34075-7
LC 2009-34909

"Moving from descriptions of star formation to an explanation of galaxy evolutions, ten highly engaging and accessible chapters make humorous references to pop culture and pose pertinent questions to foster reader interest and understanding. . . . Highly complex and specialized information in later chapters is presented clearly and with great attention to logical detail, along with explanatory sidebars and illustrations." Libr J

Includes bibliographical references

Kaler, James B.

The **hundred** greatest stars. Copernicus 2002 xxvii, 213p il $32.50
Grades: 11 12 Adult   523.8
1. Stars
ISBN 0-387-95436-8
LC 2002-19774

The author "picks a representative of the major star types, such as the red giant, and rounds out his group with a smattering of classical naked-eye stars. . . . Geared for popularity, the book's design presents one image of the star under discussion, either a field view of its position in a constellation or an exuberant HST closeup, faced by Kaler's one-page story about the star's characteristics and inferred history. For the astronomy buff, an alluring gallery of stars mysterious or simply odd awaits, from magnetars to pulsars to distended monsters on the verge of going supernova." Booklist

Includes bibliographical references

Ridpath, Ian

The **monthly** sky guide; Ian Ridpath; illustrated by Wil Tirion. 9th ed. Cambridge University Press 2012 71 p. col. ill. (paperback) $17.99

Grades: 8 9 10 11 12 Adult   **523.8**
1. Astronomy 2. Stars -- Atlases 3. Stars -- Identification 4. Stars -- Observers' manuals
ISBN 1107683157; 9781107683150

                                          LC 2012033599
This book, the ninth edition of Ian Ridpath and Wil Tirion's guide to the night sky, "is updated with planet positions and forthcoming eclipses to the end of the year 2017. It contains twelve chapters describing the main sights visible in each month of the year, providing" information for anyone "wanting to identify prominent stars, constellations, star clusters, nebulae and galaxies; to watch out for meteor showers . . .; or to follow the movements of the four brightest planets." (Publisher's note)

Includes bibliographical references and index.

Scagell, Robin

Stargazing with binoculars; [by] Robin Scagell, David Frydman. 2nd ed., updated and rev.; Firefly Books 2011 208p il pa $19.95

Grades: 9 10 11 12 Adult   **523.8**
1. Stars 2. Astronomy 3. Binoculars
ISBN 978-1-55407-821-9; 1-55407-821-0

                                          LC 2011-288021
First published 2008
This is a "guide to using binoculars to view the night sky for newcomers to astronomy. The book includes reviews of the wide range of binoculars on the market and provides advice on features to consider before making a purchase. The authors guide the beginner through the first steps of using binoculars to observe the night sky, describe what will be visible and show how to find specific objects." Publisher's note

Scharf, Caleb

Gravity's engines; how bubble-blowing black holes rule galaxies, stars, and life in the cosmos. Caleb Scharf. Scientific American/ Farrar, Straus and Giroux 2012 ix, 252 p.p (hardback) $26

Grades: 11 12 Adult   **523.8**
1. Gravity 2. Cosmology 3. Black holes (Astronomy)
ISBN 0374114129; 9780374114121

                                          LC 2011047089
Author Caleb Scharf presents a "journey through the endlessly colorful place we call our galaxy and reminds us that the Milky Way sits in a special place in the cosmic

zoo--a 'sweet spot' of properties. Is it coincidental that we find ourselves here at this place and time? Could there be a deeper connection between the nature of black holes and their role in the universe and the phenomenon of life?" (Publisher's note)

Includes bibliographical references and index.

Tyson, Neil deGrasse

Death by black hole; and other cosmic quandaries. Norton 2007 384p $24.95; pa $15.95

Grades: 11 12 Adult   **523.8**
1. Cosmology 2. Space biology 3. Religion and science 4. Black holes (Astronomy) 5. Solar system
ISBN 978-0-393-06224-3; 0-393-06224-4; 978-0-393-33016-8 pa; 0-393-33016-8 pa

                                          LC 2006-22058
"A wonderfully informed viewpoint on the slowly expanding boundaries of human knowledge." Boston Globe

Includes bibliographical references

526   Mathematical geography

Danson, Edwin

Weighing the world; the quest to measure the Earth. Oxford University Press 2005 289p il $29.95

Grades: 11 12 Adult   **526**
1. Surveying 2. Earth 3. Science -- History
ISBN 978-0-19-518169-2; 0-19-518169-7

                                          LC 2004-66284
The author "enlivens data about geodetic surveying, transforming them into greatly interesting dramas of science." Booklist

Includes bibliographical references

★ The **Map** book; edited by Peter Barber. Levenger Press 2006 360p il map $45

Grades: 11 12 Adult   **526**
1. Maps
ISBN 0-8027-1474-9
"More than 165 maps are chronologically arranged in this . . . volume, each with a descriptive and interpretative text by one of 68 international scholars. . . . This handsome collection of antique and modern cartography, brilliantly reproduced in full color, is highly recommended for all libraries, particularly those with cartographical or related collections." Libr J

Includes bibliographical references

Nicastro, Nicholas

Circumference; Eratosthenes and the ancient quest to measure the globe. St. Martin's Press 2008 223p il map $23.95

Grades: 9 10 11 12 Adult   **526**
1. Astronomers 2. Measurement 3. Weights and measures 4. Geographers 5. Writers on science
ISBN 978-0-312-37247-7; 0-312-37247-7

                                          LC 2008-25773
"Nicastro delivers the deeply human story of a multitalented genius whose tenure as the head of Alexandria's famed library occasioned remarkable achievements in literature,

history, linguistics, and philosophy despite the political turmoil that periodically rocked the Ptolemaic world." Booklist

Includes bibliographical references

Raymo, Chet

Walking zero; discovering cosmic space and time along the Prime Meridian. Walker & Co. 2006 194p il maps $22.95

Grades: 11 12 Adult **526**

1. Longitude 2. Great Britain -- Description and travel
ISBN 0-8027-1494-3; 978-0-8027-1494-7

LC 2006-282372

This is the author's "expression of his personal exploration of space, time, and scientific history, inspired partly by his walking the footpaths of southeast England in close proximity to the 0 degrees longitude line. . . . This work is a thought-provoking, highly enlightening discussion of some of the most fascinating concepts in physics, astronomy, and geology, among other subjects." Sci Books Films

Includes bibliographical references

Sobel, Dava

★ **Longitude**; the true story of a lone genius who solved the greatest scientific problem of his time. with a new foreword by Neil Armstrong. Hardcover anniversary ed., [10th anniversary ed., 2005 anniversary ed.]; Walker & Co. 2005 184p il $19

Grades: 11 12 Adult **526**

1. Longitude 2. Mechanical engineers 3. Clock and watch makers
ISBN 0-8027-1462-5; 978-0-8027-1462-6
First published 1995

"In 1714, Britain's Parliament offered the modern equivalent of $12 to anybody who could develop a means of determining longitude at sea. While the likes of Isaac Newton and Edmund Halley sought to calculate longitude by celestial measurement, John Harrison, an uneducated clockmaker, solved the problem with his invention of the chronometer. Science writer Sobel tells this story in a way that enables readers 'to see the globe anew.'" Libr J

Includes bibliographical references

528 Ephemerides

★ The **Astronomical Almanac** for the Year 2015. U.S. Govt. Printing Office 2014 620 pp $46.00

Grades: 9 10 11 12 Adult **528**

1. Almanacs 2. Astronomy 3. Nautical almanacs
ISBN 9780707741499

"Official publication prepared jointly with Her Majesty's Nautical Almanac Office of the United Kingdom Hydrographic Office and the United States Naval Observatory's Nautical Almanac Office. Designed in consultation with other astronomers of many countries, it provides current, accurate astronomical data for use in the making and reduction of observations and for general purposes." (Publisher's Note)

529 Chronology

Aveni, Anthony F.

Empires of time; calendars, clocks, and cultures. [by] Anthony Aveni. rev ed; University Press of Colo. 2002 332p il pa $22.95

Grades: 11 12 Adult **529**

1. Time
ISBN 0-87081-672-1

LC 2002-7120

First published 1989 by Basic Bks.

The author "traces the modern calendar's roots back to Greek pastoral poetry and prehistoric African bone markings, then compares Western, Chinese, Maya, Inca and tribal time systems. He also fathoms our division of time into days, weeks, months, seasons and years for clues to our psychology and worldview." Publ Wkly

Includes bibliographical references

Gleick, James

Faster; the acceleration of just about everything. Pantheon Bks. 1999 324p il hardcover o.p. pa $14

Grades: 11 12 Adult **529**

1. Time
ISBN 0-679-77548-X pa

LC 99-21640

The author's "shrewd dissection of the 'psychology of hurriedness' leads to many provocative observations." Booklist

Richards, E. G.

★ **Mapping** time; the calendar and its history. Oxford Univ. Press 1999 xxi, 438p il hardcover o.p. pa $43.50

Grades: 11 12 Adult **529**

1. Time 2. Calendars
ISBN 0-19-286205-7 pa

LC 98-24957

"An overview of astronomy, time, clocks, writing, arithmetic, and other theoretical issues lays the groundwork for a description of calendar systems from prehistory to the present. Illustrations, charts, and diagrams, including algorithms for the conversion of calendar systems, are also provided." Libr J

Includes bibliographical references

530 Physics

Balibar, Sebastien

The **atom** and the apple; twelve tales from contemporary physics. translated by Nathanael Stein. Princeton University Press 2008 190p il $24.95

Grades: 10 11 12 Adult **530**

1. Physics
ISBN 978-0-691-13108-5

LC 2008-18027

This "is a delightful ramble through many areas of science as well as through the experiences, opinions, passions and frustrations of a leading research physicist. . . . It is a

very refreshing read that will do much to bring an understanding of scientific culture to the reader." Times Higher Ed
Includes bibliographical references

Bloomfield, Louis

How everything works; making physics out of the ordinary. [by] Louis A. Bloomfield. Wiley 2007 720p il $40

Grades: 9 10 11 12   530
1. Physics
ISBN 978-0-471-74817-5; 0-471-74817-X
LC 2006-296744
"All but the most hard-core technophile should finy many . . . moments of enlightenment in this delightfully informative book." Am Sci

Christianson, Gale E.

★ Isaac Newton and the scientific revolution. Oxford Univ. Press 1996 155p il (Oxford portraits in science) lib bdg $28

Grades: 7 8 9 10   530
1. Physicists 2. Scientists 3. Mathematicians 4. Writers on science
ISBN 0-19-509224-4
LC 96-13179
Explores the life and scientific contributions of the famed English mathematician and natural philosopher
This book "reads easily and with a pleasant and comfortable flow. Structured around pivotal moments in Newton's life, the book is an excellent reference for biographical data on the great English scientist; in addition, it affords a fine historical perspective of the scientific revolution." Sci Books Films
Includes bibliographical references

Cropper, William H.

★ Great physicists; the life and times of leading physicists from Galileo to Hawking. Oxford Univ. Press 2001 500p il hardcover o.p. pa $21.95

Grades: 11 12 Adult   530
1. Authors 2. Chemists 3. Physicists 4. Astronomers 5. Mathematicians 6. People with disabilities 7. College teachers 8. Writers on science 9. Nobel laureates for physics 10. Nobel laureates for chemistry
ISBN 0-19-513748-5; 0-19-517324-4 pa
LC 2001-21611
The author "incorporates nothing beyond the ken of high-school calculus students. . . . His reworking of the abundant extant biographical material enhances the appeal of his book for reflective science students." Booklist
Includes bibliographical references

Darling, David J.

Gravity's arc; the story of gravity, from Aristotle to Einstein and beyond. [by] David Darling. J. Wiley 2006 278p $24.95

Grades: 11 12 Adult   530
1. Gravity
ISBN 0-471-71989-7; 978-0-471-71989-2
LC 2005-30772

This is a "historical review of the human understanding of gravity from the ancient Greeks to the 21st century. Included are examinations of Greek philosophers and their debates, medieval and Arabic developments, Galileo, Tycho, Kepler, Newton, Eotvos, [and] Einstein. . . . The writing style is clear and reader friendly. . . . Read this book to learn about gravity and experience a model scientific exposition for the scientist and general reader alike." Sci Books Films
Includes bibliographical references

Einstein, Albert

The ultimate quotable Einstein; collected and edited by Alice Calaprice; with a foreword by Freeman Dyson. Princeton University Press 2011 xxviii, 578p il $24.95; ebook $24.95

Grades: 11 12 Adult   530
1. Quotations
ISBN 978-0-691-13817-6; 0-691-13817-6; 978-1-4008-3596-6 ebook
LC 2010002855
This collection of Einstein's quotes includes "sections titled 'On and to Children' and 'On Race and Prejudice,' and a brief selection of Einstein's wry verses. The comments are few on the matters of physics and mathematics, concentrating more on personal, social, political, philosophical, and educational subjects." Choice
Includes bibliographical references

★ The Facts on File dictionary of physics; edited by John Daintith, Richard Rennie. 4th ed; Facts on File 2005 278p il (Facts on File science library) $45; pa $17.95

Grades: 9 10 11 12   530
1. Reference books 2. Physics -- Dictionaries
ISBN 0-8160-5653-6; 0-8160-5654-4 pa
LC 2005-40096
First published 1981
This dictionary contains over 2,500 entries. Among topics covered are: particle physics, cosmology, low-temperature physics, quantum theory, nanotechnology, and superconductivity. Tables list symbols for physical quantities and conversion factors.
Includes bibliographical references

Feynman, Richard Phillips

Six easy pieces; essentials of physics explained by its most brilliant teacher. [by] Richard P. Feynman; originally prepared for publication by Robert B. Leighton and Matthew Sands; introduction by Paul Davies. Basic Books 2005 xxix, 144p il pa $13.95

Grades: 11 12 Adult   530
1. Atoms 2. Physics 3. Gravitation 4. Quantum theory 5. Energy conservation
ISBN 978-0-465-02392-9
First published 1995 by Helix Bks.
This book reprints six chapters from Feynman's Lectures on Physics. "In these six chapters, Feynman introduces the general reader to the following: atoms, basic physics, the relationship of physics to other topics, energy, gravitation, and quantum force." Publisher's note

Hideo Nitta

The **manga** guide to physics; [by] Hideo Nitta, Keita Takatsu; Trend-pro Co., Ltd. No Starch Press 2009 232p il pa $19.95

Grades: 7 8 9 10 **530**

1. Manga 2. Graphic novels 3. Physics -- Graphic novels

ISBN 1-59327-196-4; 978-1-59327-196-1

LC 2009-12720

First published 2006 in Japan

"Megumi is a great tennis player but not so great at physics. Fortunately, Ryota, the stereotypical geek with a crush on Megumi, offers to help her with physics concepts. Using things Megumi already understands, like tennis and rollerblading, Ryota covers the basics of physics, including action and reaction, force and motion, momentum, and energy. Each concept is presented in graphic format and followed by several pages of text summary, with diagrams as needed. This book is unlikely to stand alone as an introduction to physics, but it could be very useful as a review of concepts or as a supplement to a high-school physics course." Voice Youth Advocates

Jargodzki, Christopher

Mad about physics; braintwisters, paradoxes, and curiosities. {by} Christopher Jargodzki and Franklin Potter. Wiley 2000 304p il pa $16.95

Grades: 11 12 Adult **530**

1. Physics

ISBN 0-471-56961-5

LC 00-39914

The authors present 397 questions and answers in physics and astronomy such as why the full moon is nine times brighter than the half moon, why backspin is important in basketball, and why race car drivers accelerate when going around a curve

"This entertaining book is sure to appeal to anyone with an interest in what makes the world work the way it does. . . . The authors' explanations of even the most complicated phenomena are always clear and precise." Booklist

Kakalios, James

The **Physics** of Superheroes; James Kakalios. Spectacular 2nd ed. Gotham Books 2009 424 p. $18

Grades: 11 12 Adult **530**

1. Comic books, strips, etc. 2. Physics -- Study and teaching 3. Heroes and heroines

ISBN 1592405088; 9781592405084

LC 2009028814

"With The Physics of Superheroes, named one of the best science books of 2005 by Discover, he introduced his colorful approach to an even wider audience. Now Kakalios presents a totally updated, expanded edition that features even more superheroes and findings from the cutting edge of science. With three new chapters and completely revised throughout with a splashy, redesigned package, the book that explains why Spider-Man's webbing failed his girlfriend, the probable cause of Krypton's explosion, and the Newtonian physics at work in Gotham City is electrifying from cover to cover." (Publisher's Note)

"By combining his love for physics with his love of comic books, . . . Kakalios has written a book for the general reader [that covers] all of the basic points in a first-level college physics course and is difficult to put down. . . . That all of this is accomplished with enough humor to make you laugh aloud is an added bonus." Pub Wkly

Includes bibliographical references and index

Kaku, Michio

Physics of the impossible; a scientific exploration into the world of phasers, force fields, teleportation, and time travel. Doubleday 2008 xxi, 329p $26.95

Grades: 11 12 Adult **530**

1. Physics

ISBN 978-0-385-52069-0; 0-385-52069-7

LC 2007-30290

"There is a surprising amount of heavyweight, cutting-edge science woven into the fabric of the book. String theory, dark energy, metamaterials and quantum theory are just a few topics—Physics of the Impossible is, in fact, an easy-to-read physics primer in disguise." New Sci

Includes bibliographical references

Krauss, Lawrence Maxwell

★ **Fear** of physics; a guide for the perplexed. [by] Lawrence M. Krauss. Rev ed; Basic Books 2007 257p il pa $29.95

Grades: 11 12 Adult **530**

1. Physics

ISBN 978-0-465-00218-4; 0-465-00218-8

LC 2007-04700

First published 1993

This overview describes what physics is and the work of physicists.

"The writing style genuinely keeps the reader interested. . . . This book is a great resource if you want insight into what physics really is and what physicists do." Sci Books Films

Includes bibliographical references

Matter; edited by Andrea R. Field. 1st ed. Britannica Educational Pub. in association with Rosen Educational Services 2013 77 p. ill. (some col.) (Introduction to physics) (library) $31.70

Grades: 7 8 9 10 **530**

1. Matter 2. Physics

ISBN 1615308393; 9781615308392

LC 2011052216

This book by Andrea R. Field is part of the Introduction to Physics series and focuses on Matter. The entry "covers the basic properties and states of matter; its relationship to energy, including Einstein's theory of special relativity; and physicists' quandaries with dark matter and antimatter." (Booklist)

Includes bibliographical references (p. 73) and index.

Muller, Richard A., 1944-

The **instant** physicist; [an illustrated guide] [by] Richard A. Muller; illustrations by Joey Manfre. W.W. Norton 2010 138p il $16.95

Grades: 9 10 11 12 Adult   **530**
1. Physics
ISBN 978-0-393-07826-8

LC 2010-25739

"On left-hand pages, there are brief examinations of interesting or little-known [physics] facts; on right-hand pages, there are Joey Manfre's humorous illustrations based on those facts. . . . Readers will learn a lot from the book: you can outrun a tsunami; plutonium is 1,000 times less toxic than Botox; antimatter isn't science fiction; organically grown foods have more carcinogens than foods sprayed with artificial pesticides. . . . Very entertaining and very informative—a winning combination." Booklist

Ohanian, Hans C.

Einstein's mistakes; the human failings of genius. W.W. Norton & Company 2008 394p il $24.95
Grades: 11 12 Adult   **530**
1. Physics 2. Physicists 3. Nobel laureates for physics
ISBN 978-0-393-06293-9; 0-393-06293-7

LC 2008-13155

This "clearly written, fascinating, and exciting book is a gem." Sci Books Films

Includes bibliographical references

Potter, Franklin

Mad about modern physics; braintwisters, paradoxes and curiosities. [by] Franklin Potter and Christopher Jargodzki. J. Wiley 2004 296p il pa $16.95
Grades: 9 10 11 12   **530**
1. Physics
ISBN 0-471-44855-9

LC 2004-14941

A collection of physics trivia, with diagrams and illustrations.

Includes bibliographical references

Rosen, Joe

★ **Encyclopedia** of physics. Facts on File 2004 386p il (Facts on File science library) $75
Grades: 11 12 Adult   **530**
1. Reference books 2. Physics -- Encyclopedias
ISBN 0-8160-4974-2

LC 2003-14963

The entries "cover physical concepts, prominent physicists (modern and historical), and physics laboratories, societies, and organizations. The alphabetically arranged entries are supplemented with 11 topical essays that aim to shed some light on physics in a philosophical or practical way. These essays cover such topics as beauty, the nature of the relationship between physics and philosophy, and the desire among some physicists to find the unifying laws governing all physical concepts. . . . The entries are well written, accurate, and include equations where appropriate." Booklist

Includes bibliographical references

The **science** of physics; edited by Andrea Field. Britannica Educational Pub. 2012 80 p. (Introduction to physics) (library binding) $31.70
Grades: 7 8 9 10   **530**
1. Physics
ISBN 1615306765; 9781615306763

LC 2011026548

This book, edited by Andrea R. Field, is part of the Introduction to Physics series. It "surveys some of the major branches of physics, the laws, and theories significant to each. Also chronicled are some of the historical milestones in the field by such great minds as Galileo and Isaac Newton." (Publisher's note)

Includes bibliographical references and index

530.01   Philosophy and theory

Cole, K. C.

The **hole** in the universe; how scientists peered over the edge of emptiness and found everything. Harcourt 2001 274p il hardcover o.p. pa $14
Grades: 11 12 Adult   **530.01**
1. Physics
ISBN 0-15-601317-7 pa

LC 00-44947

Cole discusses the history of nothing, "combining the history of zero (a mathematical nothing) with that of the vacuum (a physical nothing). . . . Until Einstein showed that light needed no tangible medium through which to travel, theorists filled the vacuum with 'ether'—the 'enfant terrible' of substances, as Einstein put it. It was subsequently banished." Atl Mon

Includes bibliographical references

530.092   Physicists

Baxter, Roberta

Ernest Rutherford and the birth of the atomic age; by Roberta Baxter. Morgan Reynolds Pub. 2011 ill. (Profiles in science) (library) $28.95
Grades: 7 8 9 10 11 12   **530.092**
1. Nuclear physics 2. Nuclear physics -- History 3. Physicists -- New Zealand -- Biography
ISBN 1599351714; 9781599351711; 9781599352756

LC 2010049096

This children's nonfiction book, by Roberta Baxter, is part of the "Profiles in Science" series, profiling the nuclear physicist Ernest Rutherford. Topics include a profile of his life as a child growing up in New Zealand, his work researching physics in Canada, his Nobel Prize, and the legacy of his work after his death.

"This is a well-rounded portrait of the 20th century's greatest experimental scientists. Baxter not only explains Rutherford's major accomplishments . . . in lucid but not oversimplified terms, but she also paints a vivid picture of an ambitious but not egotistical man with a big personality and close family ties. Enlightening diagrams and plenty of photographs . . . add solid visual elements. . ." SLJ

Includes bibliographical references and index

530.1 Theories and mathematical physics

Bodanis, David

E; a biography of the world's most famous equation. Walker & Company 2005 337p il $25

Grades: 11 12 Adult **530.1**

1. Physicists 2. Space and time 3. Force and energy 4. Nobel laureates for physics

ISBN 0-8027-1463-3

First published 2000

The author relates the story of "Einstein's formulation of the equation in 1905 and its association ever after with relativity and nuclear energy. Parallel with the science, Bodanis populates his tale with dramatic lives." Booklist [review of 2000 edition]

Ford, Kenneth W.

101 quantum questions; what you need to know about the world you can't see. [by] Kenneth W. Ford. Harvard University Press 2011 291p il

Grades: 11 12 Adult **530.1**

1. Quantum theory

ISBN 9780674050990

LC 2010-34791

"Ford explains the essential concepts of quantum reality, our small-fast world, full of uncertainty and probability, where all matter can exist in more than one state simultaneously. Ford brings interesting and entertaining anecdotal and historical material into his answers, organizing and shaping his book around 15 subjects. By using humor and straight talk to answer questions that often bedevil the nonscientist who attempts to grasp this knotty subject, Ford has created an entertaining read and an excellent companion piece to more detailed popular treatments of modern physics." Publ Wkly

Includes bibliographical references

Guillen, Michael

Five equations that changed the world; the power and poetry of mathematics. Hyperion 1995 277p hardcover o.p. pa $14.95

Grades: 11 12 Adult **530.1**

1. Physics 2. Chemists 3. Physicists 4. Mathematics 5. Mathematicians 6. College teachers 7. Writers on science 8. Nobel laureates for physics

ISBN 0-7868-6103-7; 0-7868-8187-9 pa

LC 95-15199

"A seamless blend of dramatic biography and mathematical documentary that links the personal with the scientific." Publ Wkly

Hawking, Stephen, 1942-

The grand design; [by] Stephen Hawking and Leonard Mlodinow. Bantam Books 2010 198p il $28; ebook $28

Grades: 11 12 Adult **530.1**

1. Universe 2. Cosmology 3. String theory 4. Quantum theory 5. Life -- Origin 6. Science -- Philosophy

ISBN 978-0-553-80537-6; 0-553-80537-1; 978-0-553-90707-0 ebook; 0-553-90707-7 ebook

"The three central questions of philosophy and science: Why is there something rather than nothing? Why do we exist? Why this particular set of laws and not some other? . . . Along with Caltech physicist Mlodinow . . . Hawking deftly mixes cutting-edge physics to answer those key questions. . . . This is an amazingly concise, clear, and intriguing overview of where we stand when it comes to divining the secrets of the universe." Publ Wkly

Includes bibliographical references

The **nature** of space and time; [by] Stephen Hawking and Roger Penrose. [New ed.]; Princeton University Press 2010 145p il (Isaac Newton Institute series of lectures) pa $14.95; ebook $14.95

Grades: 11 12 Adult **530.1**

1. Astrophysics 2. Quantum theory 3. Space and time

ISBN 978-0-691-14570-9 pa; 978-1-4008-3474-7 ebook

First published 1996

This volume "takes the form of a debate between Hawking and Penrose at Cambridge in 1994. At the center of the discussion is a pair of powerful theories: the quantum theory of fields and the general theory of relativity. The issue is how—if at all—one can merge the two into a quantum theory of gravity. . . . A substantial background in theoretical physics is needed for full comprehension." Libr J

Includes bibliographical references

The **universe** in a nutshell; [by] Stephen Hawking. Bantam Bks. 2001 216p il $35

Grades: 11 12 Adult **530.1**

1. Quantum theory

ISBN 0-553-80202-X

LC 2001-35757

Hawking "explains the basic laws of physics that govern the universe, beginning with a brief history of the concept of relativity, and then he is off and running to explore time, space, the future, and the possibility of time travel, among other fundamental rules of the universe's road. Admirers of Hawking's previous book will continue to appreciate his ability not only to air fresh, provocative ideas but also to say what he means clearly and without watering down his material or condescending to his audience—he even injects humor into his narrative. The profuse, beautifully rendered illustrations contribute greatly to the reader's understanding of his points." Booklist

Kakalios, James

The **amazing** story of quantum mechanics; a math-free exploration of the science that made our world. Gotham Books 2010 318p il $26

Grades: 9 10 11 12 Adult **530.1**

1. Quantum theory

ISBN 978-1-59240-479-7; 1-59240-479-0

LC 2010-29568

"Though the book does not quite live up to the subtitle's promise of a 'math-free' text, readers need no more than basic algebra to accompany comic-book heroes into well-illustrated explanations of quantum packets of light energy, of the wave functions of particles, and even of the angular spin inherent in both energy and matter. These basic principles illuminate the solid-state physics of semiconductors, the atomic magnetism of MRIs, and the nanotechnology of high-capacity storage batteries. And all of this conceptual heavy lifting comes with entertaining episodes from DC Comics and H. G. Wells' fiction. Physics has never been more fun!" Booklist

Includes bibliographical references

Orzel, Chad

How to teach physics to your dog. Scribner 2009 241p il $24

Grades: 11 12 Adult   **530.1**
  1. Physics 2. Quantum theory
  ISBN 978-1-4165-7228-2; 1-4165-7228-7
                                                LC 2009-21073

"Particle physicist Orzel has a smart and energetic German shepherd-mix, Emmy, who's interested in what he does for a living that keeps her in treats and kibble. So she asks him about it, and he tells her, with plenty of chaseable bunnies and squirrels illustratively standing-in for photons, electrons, and other particles. . . . It's hard to imagine a better way for the mathematically and scientifically challenged, in particular, to grasp basic quantum physics." Booklist

Includes bibliographical references

Rigden, John S.

★ **Einstein** 1905; the standard of greatness. Harvard University Press 2005 173p il $21.95; pa $14.95

Grades: 11 12 Adult   **530.1**
  1. Physicists 2. Quantum theory 3. Nobel laureates for physics
  ISBN 0-674-01544-4; 0-674-02104-5 pa
                                                LC 2004-54049

"The book is a delight to read, with a lot of interesting, useful information." Choice

Includes bibliographical references

Toomey, David M.

The **new** time travelers; a journey to the frontiers of physics. [by] David Toomey. W. W. Norton 2007 391p il $28

Grades: 11 12 Adult   **530.1**
  1. Space and time
  ISBN 978-0-393-06013-3; 0-393-06013-6
                                                LC 2007-11307

This book on the physics of time travel "illustrates dimension-bending concepts with space-time diagrams, M. C. Escher drawings, and the plot of H.G. Wells' Time Machine. Toomey gets a grip on bending the fourth dimension by historically chronicling physicists who have theorized about time travel . . . . If you dream of getting outside your personal light cone, Toomey shows how it might be imagined." Booklist

Includes bibliographical references

530.11   Relativity theory

Gott, J. Richard

Time travel in Einstein's universe; the physical possibilities of travel through time. {by} J. Richard

Gott, III. Houghton Mifflin 2001 291p il hardcover o.p. pa $14

Grades: 11 12 Adult   **530.11**
  1. Space and time 2. Fourth dimension
  ISBN 0-395-95563-7; 0-618-25735-7 pa
                                                LC 00-54243

"Gott tackles the complexities of attempting to turn the fantasy of time travel into a theoretical possibility in a lively and lucid discussion." Booklist

Includes bibliographical references

Orzel, Chad

How to teach relativity to your dog; Chad Orzel. Basic Books 2012 327 p.

Grades: 11 12 Adult   **530.11**
  1. Dogs -- Training 2. Physics -- Humor 3. Relativity (Physics) 4. Physics -- Study and teaching 5. Relativity (Physics) -- Humor
  ISBN 9780465023318; 9780465029372
                                                LC 2011044067

The author "follows his "How to Teach Physics to Your Dog" with a . . . walk through Einstein's theory of relativity, using the same conceit of lecturing to his preternaturally intelligent and curious dog, Emma. [Chad] Orzel . . . tackles this elusive subject in chapters with titles like "Time Slows When You're Chasing Bunnies", and "The Unified Theory of Critters."" (Publishers Wkly) "Emmy is the stand-in for the every-man . . . who has never quite managed to grasp the idea of spacetime, or why moving clocks tick slower than stationary ones. . . . Relativity has a rich history, and while Einstein . . . gets the credit, it took . . . many mathematicians and physicists to make the theory possible. Orzel gives a number of them their due, especially Albert Michelson and Edward Morley." (Science News)

Includes bibliographical references and index

530.4   States of matter

Angelo, Joseph A.

Gaseous matter. Facts on File 2011 238p il (States of matter) $45

Grades: 9 10 11 12   **530.4**
  1. Gases 2. Matter
  ISBN 978-0-8160-7607-9; 978-1-4381-3648-6 ebook
                                                LC 2010034289

Includes bibliographical references

This book "focuses on the many important discoveries that led to the scientific interpretation of matter in the gaseous state. This new, full-color resource describes the basic characteristics and properties of several important gases, including air, hydrogen, helium, oxygen, and nitrogen. The nature and scope of the science of fluids is discussed in great detail, highlighting the most important scientific principles upon which the field is based." (Publisher's note)

530.8 Measurement

★ The **Economist** desk companion; how to measure, convert, calculate, and define practically anything. Wiley 1998 272p il map $27.95

Grades: 11 12 Adult 530.8

1. Weights and measures

ISBN 0-471-24953-X

LC 98-17615

First published 1992 by Holt & Co.

"This reference manual provides essential information on measurements, formulas, and calculations on a wide variety of scientific, industrial, economic, and applied technological topics. The introductory section describes the three major world measurement systems, followed by sections containing conversion tables, local units of measurements around the world, and abbreviations and country codes. Subjects include agriculture, finance, health, and transport, among many other topics. . . . This ready-reference volume serves as a superb compilation of material scattered in numerous sources." Libr J

Robinson, Andrew

The **story** of measurement. Thames & Hudson 2007 224p il map $34.95

Grades: 11 12 Adult 530.8

1. Measurement

ISBN 978-0-500-51367-5; 0-500-51367-8

LC 2007-921450

"Robinson has the knack to explain any number of complex concepts lucidly and with simplicity, without being condescending. . . . He has produced a highly readable book." Times Lit Suppl

Includes bibliographical references

531 Classical mechanics

Energy; edited by Andrea R. Field. Britannica Educational Pub. in association with Rosen Educational Services 2012 79 p. ill. (some col.) (Introduction to physics)

Grades: 7 8 9 10 531

1. Force and energy -- Study and teaching (Middle school)

ISBN 9781615306732

LC 2011021493

"This series fills a gap in the high school library by truly being an introduction to physics, electronics, and energy. It introduces readers to the major figures who discovered the laws of physics, and gives definitions of terms while providing common examples of such things as electrostatic induction, applications of magnetism, or conductivity and resistance in a circuit." (Library Media Connection)

"With attractive, lively graphics, [this] will make a good supplement in libraries needing lots of science-experiment background information." Booklist

Includes bibliographical references (p. 72-75) and index

Gurstelle, William

Backyard ballistics; build potato cannons, paper match rockets, Cincinnati fire kites, tennis ball mortars, and more dynamite devices. William Gurstelle. 2nd ed Chicago Review Press 2012 210 p. ill. $16.95

Grades: 11 12 Adult 531

1. Science -- Experiments

ISBN 1613740646; 9781613740644

LC 2001017321

This book, by William Gurstelle, is a "DIY handbook [that] now features new and expanded projects, enabling ordinary folks to construct 16 awesome ballistic devices in their garage or basement workshops using inexpensive household or hardware store materials and this step-by-step guide. Clear instructions, diagrams, and photographs show how to build projects ranging from the simple match-powered rocket to the more complex tabletop catapult and the offbeat Cincinnati fire kite." (Publisher's note)

"Interspersed between projects are sections on history and scientific principles, adding depth to the mayhem. Cautions for safety are strongly stated and frequently. These are definitely not for unsupervised youth. The projects range from utterly simplistic to complicated construction, accompanied by clear instructions." LJ

Manning, Phillip

Gravity. Chelsea House 2010 139p il (Science foundations) lib bdg $35

Grades: 7 8 9 10 531

1. Gravity 2. Gravitation

ISBN 978-1-60413-296-0; 1-60413-296-5

LC 2010-15793

This book "explains how two of the greatest scientific minds in history—Isaac Newton and Albert Einstein—finally unraveled most of the mystery surrounding this peculiar force, and how scientists today are continuing to search for answers to the remaining questions." Publisher's note

Includes glossary and bibliographical references

533 Pneumatics (Gas mechanics)

Gardner, Robert

Air; green science projects for a sustainable planet. Enslow Publishers 2011 128p il (Team Green science projects) lib bdg $31.93

Grades: 6 7 8 9 10 533

1. Air 2. Air pollution 3. Science projects 4. Science -- Experiments

ISBN 978-0-7660-3646-8; 0-7660-3646-4

LC 2010-1120

This book offers science experiments that explain the properties of air, how to conserve energy while heating and cooling air, and how to reduce air pollution.

"Gardner provides plenty of information, well-designed experiments, and demonstrations, and then shares brief science-fair ideas. . . . Experiments and demonstrations are presented with clear step-by-step instructions and occasional illustrations and represent a wide range of complexity." SLJ

Includes glossary and bibliographical references

534   Specific forms of energy

The **Britannica** guide to sound and light; edited by Erik Gregersen. Britannica Educational Pub. 2011 347p il (Physics explained) lib bdg $64.65; ebook $64.65

Grades: 7 8 9 10   **534**
1. Light 2. Sound 3. Physics
ISBN 978-1-61530-300-7 lib bdg; 1-61530-300-6 lib bdg; 978-1-61530-374-8 ebook

LC 2010013444

This "volume explores the science behind acoustics and optics and the broad application they have to everything from listening to music and watching television to ultrasonic and laser technologies that are crucial to the medical field." Publisher's note

Includes glossary and bibliographical references

Sound; edited by Sherman Hollar. Britannica Educational Pub. in association with Rosen Educational Services 2013 79 p. ill. (Introduction to physics) (library) $31.70

Grades: 7 8 9 10   **534**
1. Sound
ISBN 1615308415; 9781615308415

LC 2012010563

This book on sound, edited by Sherman Hollar, is part of the "Introduction to Physics" series. It "describes how sound is produced, carried, and processed and features a chapter on acoustical engineers' applications in the life sciences, earth sciences, architecture, and the arts." (Booklist) "Also covered are functions and diseases of the human ear." (Publisher's note)

Includes bibliographical references and index.

535.6   Color

Finlay, Victoria

Color: a natural history of the palette. Ballantine Bks. 2002 448p il maps hardcover o.p. pa $14.95

Grades: 11 12 Adult   **535.6**
1. Color
ISBN 0-345-44430-2; 0-8129-7142-6 pa

This "book is a blend of travelogue and historical exploration about the myriad ways color takes on meaning for us, whether as a matter of aesthetics, economics, war or culture. . . . Thanks to Finlay's impeccable reportorial skills and a remarkable degree of engagement, this is an utterly unique and fascinating read." Publ Wkly

Includes bibliographical references

536   Heat

Heat; edited by Andrea R. Field. Britannica Educational Pub. 2013 76 p. ill. (some col.) (library) $31.70

Grades: 7 8 9 10   **536**
1. Heat 2. Physics
ISBN 1615308385; 9781615308385

LC 2011053232

This book looks at heat, or "the energy that is transferred from one object to another because of a difference in temperature," as well as "the related concepts of temperature, thermal energy, and thermodynamics and introduces readers to some of the great minds that furthered our understanding of this . . . area of physics." (Publisher's note)

Includes bibliographical references (p. 73) and index.

Shachtman, Tom

★ **Absolute** zero and the conquest of cold. Houghton Mifflin 1999 261p hardcover o.p. pa $14

Grades: 11 12 Adult   **536**
1. Thermodynamics 2. Low temperatures -- Research
ISBN 0-395-93888-0; 0-618-08239-5 pa

LC 99-33305

The author "analyzes the social impact of the chill factor, explains the science of cold and tells the curious tales behind inventions like the thermometer, the fridge and the thermos flask." N Y Times Book Rev

Includes bibliographical references

537   Electricity and electronics

Bodanis, David

★ **Electric** universe; the shocking true story of electricity. Crown Publishers 2004 308p hardcover o.p. pa $31

Grades: 11 12 Adult   **537**
1. Electricity
ISBN 1-4000-4550-9; 0-307-33598-4 pa

LC 2004-11275

"As a storyteller, author David Bodanis is wonderful. . . This book is directed at a general audience, but it should be required reading for all scientific professionals." Sci Books Films

Includes bibliographical references

Electricity; edited by Michael Anderson. Britannica Educational Pub. in association with Rosen Educational Services 2012 79 p. ill. (some col.) (Introduction to physics)

Grades: 7 8 9 10   **537**
1. Electricity 2. Electricity
ISBN 161530665X; 9781615306657

LC 2011017090

"...Features clear diagrams and is a narrow enough topic to be well covered, with chapters on circuits, magnetic fields, and generators." Booklist

Includes bibliographical references (p. 76) and index

Gibilisco, Stan

Electricity experiments you can do at home; Stan Gibilisco. McGraw-Hill 2010 xi, 339 p.p ill pbk $26

Grades: 10 11 12 Adult   537

1. Science -- Experiments 2. Electric apparatus and appliances

ISBN 9780071621649

LC 2010001953

This book, by Stan Gibilisco, "is a hands-on guide that helps you master the principles of electrical currents and magnetism. Each of the book's three sections--direct current, alternating current, and magnetism--begins with step-by-step instructions for setting up your lab for the experiments that follow. Using inexpensive, easy-to-find parts, the experiments progress from basic to more complex and will spark ideas and encourage inventiveness." (Publisher's note)

"Each of the book's three sections--direct current, alternating current, and magnetism--begins with step-by-step instructions for setting up [a] lab for the experiments that follow. Using inexpensive, easy-to-find parts, the experiments progress from basic to more complex and will spark ideas and encourage inventiveness." Publisher's note

Includes bibliographical references and index

538   Magnetism

Verschuur, Gerrit L.

★ **Hidden** attraction; the history and mystery of magnetism. Oxford Univ. Press 1993 256p il hardcover o.p. pa $14.95

Grades: 11 12 Adult   538

1. Magnetism

ISBN 0-19-506488-7; 0-19-510655-5 pa

LC 92-37690

The author "uses the history of magnetism to illustrate the development of scientific theory and method, from natural phenomena rooted in superstition to the accurate simulations of modern science. An informative study, with details about such scientists as Michael Faraday and James Maxwell and their pioneering work." Booklist

Includes bibliographical references

539.2   Radiation (Radiant energy)

Karam, P. Andrew

Radioactivity; [by] P. Andrew Karam and Ben P. Stein. Chelsea House 2009 124p il (Science foundations) lib bdg $35

Grades: 7 8 9 10 11 12   539.2

1. Radiation 2. Radioactivity

ISBN 978-1-60413-016-4; 1-60413-016-4

LC 2008-38067

This book "explains the science behind radiation, from the radiation in the body to the radiation in the environment; how radiation can create energy and cause destruction; and how it saves lives every day." Publisher's note

Includes glossary and bibliographical references

539.7   Atomic and nuclear physics

The **Britannica** guide to the atom; edited by Erik Gregersen. Britannica Educational Pub. 2011 320p il (Physics explained) lib bdg $64.65; ebook $64.65

Grades: 7 8 9 10   539.7

1. Atoms

ISBN 978-1-61530-319-9 lib bdg; 1-61530-319-7 lib bdg; 978-1-61530-384-7 ebook

LC 2010023231

Discusses the structure of the atom and reveals the ways the parts facilitate both radioactivity and nuclear reactions.

Includes glossary and bibliographical references

Campbell, Margaret Christine

★ **Discovering** atoms; Margaret Christine Campbell, Natalie Goldstein. 1st ed. Rosen Pub. 2012 112 p. ill. (The scientist's guide to physics) (library) $34.60

Grades: 5 6 7 8 9   539.7

1. Atoms 2. Atomic theory -- History 3. Atomic structure 4. Matter -- Constitution

ISBN 1448847001; 9781448847006

LC 2010048416

This book by Margaret Christine Campbell is part of the "Scientist's Guide to Physics" series. It "presents the . . . story of the atom's discovery, which is full of bizarre theories, false starts, dead ends, and . . . intellectual insight." (Publisher's note) "Campbell includes a . . . chronological foundation upon which the discovery of elements and the creation of the periodic table build up to the discovery of the atom, atomic rays, particles, models . . . and subatomic particles." (VOYA)

Includes bibliographical references and index.

Conkling, Winifred

Radioactive! how Irene Curie and Lise Meitner revolutionized science and changed the world. Winifred Conkling. Algonquin Young Readers 2016 240 p. illustrated $17.95

Grades: 7 8 9 10   539.7

1. Physicists 2. Radioactivity 3. Nuclear fission 4. Women scientists -- France -- Biography 5. Women scientists -- Germany -- Biography

ISBN 9781616204150; 161620415X

LC 2015017256

This book, by Winifred Conkling, "presents the story of [Irène Curie and Lise Meitner,] two women breaking ground in a male-dominated field, scientists still largely unknown despite their crucial contributions to cutting-edge research, in a nonfiction narrative that reads with the suspense of a thriller. Photographs and sidebars illuminate and clarify the science in the book." (Publisher's note)

"Readers interested in a more succinct and compelling look at Meitner's work on fission than what's presented here will find it in Steve Sheinkin's Bomb (2012). Flat writing and too many pages of dense text unrelieved by photographs or other visuals mar a volume that might have been suspenseful. An important if sometimes-awkward study of two scientists who helped to change the world." Kirkus

Includes bibliographical references and index

Henderson, Harry

The **Curie** family; exploring radioactivity. Harry Henderson. Chelsea House 2012 117 p. (Trailblazers in science and technology) $35

Grades: 7 8 9 10 11 12   **539.7**

1. Radioactivity 2. Curie, Maric, 1867-1934 3. Curie, Pierre, 1859-1906

ISBN 1604136758; 9781604136753

LC 2011011800

This book, by Harry Henderson, is part of the "Trailblazers in Science and Technology" series. "Marie and Pierre Curie, their daughter Irène Joliot-Curie, and her husband Frédéric Joliot-Curie were one of science's most remarkable and influential families. Their painstaking research into the mysteries of radioactivity allowed scientists to reach a new understanding about the structure of atoms and opened a new field of medical treatment." (Publisher's note)

Includes bibliographical references and index

Manning, Phillip

Atoms, molecules, and compounds. Chelsea House 2008 137p il (Essential chemistry) $35

Grades: 7 8 9 10   **539.7**

1. Atoms 2. Matter 3. Molecules 4. Chemical reactions

ISBN 978-0-7910-9534-8; 0-7910-9534-7

LC 2007-11403

"In relatively few pages, and with lots of colorful, clear illustrations, Manning takes us from Thompson's plum-pudding model of the atom to Rutherford's model to the quantum model, and through the discovery of atomic particles and the teasing out of atomic forces, in a very clear, compelling path. . . . The clear linkages he makes between the different types of chemical bonds and the nature of various materials will remain with the reader." Sci Books Films

Includes glossary and bibliographical references

540 Chemistry and allied sciences

Chemical compounds; Neil Schlager, Jayne Weisblatt, and David E. Newton, editors; Charles B. Montney, project editor. UXL 2006 3v il set $181

Grades: 7 8 9 10   **540**

1. Chemicals

ISBN 1-4144-0150-7; 978-1-4144-0150-8

LC 2005-23636

"This set discusses 180 molecules, both organic and inorganic, that have played an important role in human affairs. Each molecule is depicted by a structural formula and . . . [a] color image of a ball-and-stick model. . . . These pictorial representations are accompanied by a listing of physical properties, a description of how the compound is made, a discussion of common uses and hazards, and often a brief review of the compound's history. . . . The result—a unique way to introduce high school students to chemistry." Choice

Includes bibliographical references

Chemistry: foundations and applications. Macmillan Ref. USA 2004 4v il set $395

Grades: 9 10 11 12   **540**

1. Reference books 2. Chemistry -- Encyclopedias

ISBN 0-02-865721-7; 9780028659138

LC 2003-21038

The alphabetically arranged signed articles "range from concise definitions to multiple-page overviews. Broad areas covered include analytical chemistry applications, biochemistry, elements, energy, environmental chemistry, medicine, organic chemistry, physical chemistry, reactions, states of matter, and structure. . . . In addition to explaining scientific principles, this set relates chemistry to everyday life. . . . An 18-page glossary and 67-page subject index are included in each volume. Glossary definitions also appear in the margins next to the text. . . . Bibliographic references and related Internet resources are listed at the end of many articles." Booklist

Cobb, Cathy

The **joy** of chemistry; the amazing science of familiar things. [by] Cathy Cobb & Monty L. Fetterolf. Prometheus Books 2005 393p il hardcover o.p. pa $19

Grades: 11 12 Adult   **540**

1. Chemistry

ISBN 1-591-02231-2; 1-591-02771-3 pa

LC 2004-20144

The authors cover "the material of a general chemistry course along with organic, inorganic and analytical chemistry and biochemistry; there's even a chapter on forensic chemistry. . . . They explain everything from flatulence (the chemical composition of intestinal gas) to pizza cheese (why mozzarella rather than, say, parmesan?)." Publ Wkly

Includes bibliographical references

★ **Cracking** the SAT Chemistry subject test. Princeton Review/Random House illustrations

Grades: 9 10 11 12   **540**

1. Scholastic Assessment Test 2. Chemistry -- Study and teaching 3. Colleges and universities -- Entrance requirements

Annual; first published 2005

This guide provides test-taking strategies and sample tests on the subject of chemistry.

A **dictionary** of chemistry; edited by Richard Rennie and Jonathan Law. 7th edition Oxford University Press 2016 577 p. illustrations pbk $19.95

Grades: 9 10 11 12 Adult   **540**

1. Chemistry -- Dictionaries

ISBN 0198722826; 9780198722823

'Fully revised and updated, the seventh edition of this popular dictionary is the ideal reference resource for students of chemistry, either at school or at university. With over 5000 entries--over 175 new to this edition--it covers all aspects of chemistry, from physical chemistry to biochemistry. The seventh edition boasts broader coverage in areas such as nuclear magnetic resonance, polymer chemistry, nanotechnology and graphene, and absolute configuration." (Publisher's note)

The **Facts** on File chemistry handbook; the Diagram Group. Facts On File 2006 272 p. ill. (hardcover) $40; (ebook) $42.00
Grades: 8 9 10 11 12 **540**
1. Chemistry -- Dictionaries 2. Chemistry -- Handbooks, manuals, etc
ISBN 0816058784; 9780816058785 out of print; 9781438109558 pdf
LC 2005055496
This fact book for middle-grade readers, part of the Facts on File Handbook series, looks at chemistry. Each series entry "contains, in separate sections, a dictionary of around 1500 entries; 250-400 thumbnail biographies; a multipage chronology; and an array of field-specific charts, tables, and diagrams." (School Library Journal)
Includes bibliographical references (p. 262-264) and index

★ The **Facts** on File dictionary of chemistry; edited by John Daintith. 4th ed; Checkmark Books 2005 310p il (Facts on File science library) $45; pa $17.95
Grades: 9 10 11 12 **540**
1. Reference books 2. Chemistry -- Dictionaries
ISBN 0-8160-5649-8; 0-8160-5650-1 pa
LC 2005-43785
First published 1981
This reference work includes more than 3,000 cross-referenced entries that identify terms, reactions, techniques and applications in chemistry.
Includes bibliographical references

Greenberg, Arthur
★ **From** alchemy to chemistry in picture and story. Wiley-Interscience 2007 xxiii, 637p il $69.95
Grades: 11 12 Adult **540**
1. Chemistry -- History
ISBN 978-0-471-75154-0; 0-471-75154-5
LC 2006-33564
According to the author, this "is a combination of his two previous books, A Chemical History Tour and The Art of Chemistry, with some additions and revisions . . . One could open the book at almost any page to learn something about the remarkable history of the chemical sciences." Sci Books Films
Includes bibliographical references

★ **Lange's** handbook of chemistry; James G. Speight. 17th edition McGraw-Hill 2016 $199
Grades: 11 12 Adult **540**
1. Chemistry 2. Chemistry -- Tables
ISBN 9781259586095; 125958609X
First published 1934. Periodically revised
"Lange's Handbook of Chemistry, 17th Edition, is divided into six sections--general information and conversion tables, spectroscopy, inorganic chemistry, organic chemistry, petroleum and petroleum products, biomass and biofuels, and environmental science. Existing tables have been thoroughly overhauled and new tables have been added that cover the properties of coal, minerals, natural gas, oil shale, and petroleum." (Publisher's note)

Le Couteur, Penny
Napoleon's buttons; how 17 molecules changed history. [by] Penny Le Couteur, Jay Burreson. Jeremy P. Tarcher/Penguin Books 2003 375p il hardcover o.p. pa $14.95
Grades: 11 12 Adult **540**
1. Chemistry
ISBN 1-58542-220-7; 1-58542-331-9 pa
LC 2002-032247
"Napoleon's Buttons is a fascinating attempt at recognizing the role of chemistry in the wider world. With its many structural diagrams, the book can resemble a course in organic chemistry, but the chemist-authors are good guides. . . . The best chapter is the one on dyes." Quill & Quire
Includes bibliographical references

Rittner, Don
★ **Encyclopedia** of chemistry; [by] Don Rittner and Ronald A. Bailey. Facts on File 2005 342p il (Facts on File science library) $75
Grades: 11 12 Adult **540**
1. Reference books 2. Chemistry -- Encyclopedias
ISBN 0-8160-4894-0
LC 2004-11242
This encyclopedia "offers more than 2000 articles on topics from ABO blood groups to zwitterionic compound." SLJ
Includes bibliographical references

540.7 Education, research, related topics

Walker, Pamela
Chemistry experiments; [by] Pamela Walker, Elaine Wood. Facts on File 2011 xx, 177p il map (Facts on File science experiments) $40
Grades: 7 8 9 10 11 12 **540.7**
1. Chemistry 2. Science -- Experiments
ISBN 978-0-8160-8172-1
LC 2010-33149
A collection of twenty science projects. "Topics covered include ozone depletion, wood alcohol, heat energy, purifying water, and carbonation in beverages." Publisher's note
Includes glossary and bibliographical references

541 Chemistry

Atkins, Peter William, 1940-
Reactions; the private life of atoms. by Peter Atkins. Oxford University Press 2011 191 p.
Grades: 11 12 Adult **541**
1. Chemical reactions
ISBN 9780199695126; 0199695121
LC 2011275047
The author "provides detailed descriptions of the reactions that occur in everyday life, using language that, while elevated, will be accessible for the armchair scientist. Each chapter focuses on a particular type of reaction, including: precipitation, neutralization, combustion, reduction, oxidation separately and in combination, catalysis, and more." Publ Wkly

Cobb, Cathy

Magick, mayhem, and mavericks; the spirited history of physical chemistry. Prometheus Books 2002 420p il $29

Grades: 11 12 Adult   **541**

1. Physical chemistry -- History

ISBN 1-573-92976-X

LC 2002-70511

"The history moves from ancient astronomy, mathematics and natural philosophy through early modern developments in mathematics, physics, alchemy, medicinal remedies and chemistry, using the assumption that physical chemists could achieve their aims only after the foundations of mathematics, physics and chemistry were well laid. . . . Cobb's style is lively and swashbuckling." American Scientist

Includes bibliographical references

Manning, Phillip

Chemical bonds. Chelsea House 2009 134p il (Essential chemistry) lib bdg $35

Grades: 7 8 9 10   **541**

1. Chemistry

ISBN 978-0-7910-9740-3; 0-7910-9740-4

LC 2008-1981

Examines the nature of the chemical bonds, answering questions about how they form, how they are broken, and how they help define life as we know it

Includes glossary and bibliographical references

546   Inorganic chemistry

Gray, Theodore

★ The **elements**; a visual exploration of every known atom in the universe. photographs by Theodore Gray and Nick Mann. Black Dog & Leventhal Publishers 2009 240p il $29.95

Grades: 11 12 Adult   **546**

1. Periodic law 2. Chemical elements -- Pictorial works

ISBN 1579128149; 9781579128142

LC 2009-34931

This is a collection of "photographic representations of the 118 elements in the periodic table. . . . [The book also contains] facts, figures, and stories of the elements as well as data on the properties of each, including atomic weight, density, melting and boiling point, valence, electronegativity, and the year and location in which it was discovered." (Publisher's note) Index.

"This gorgeously photographed guide to the elements can be used as a visual reference, but its brief entries are packed with intriguing tidbits that also make it a fascinating read." Libr J

Includes bibliographical references

Green, Dan

The **elements**; Dan Green. Scholastic 2012 105 p. col. ill. (pbk.) $15.99

Grades: 7 8 9 10 11 12   **546**

1. Chemical elements

ISBN 054533019X; 9780545330190

LC 2011278730

This book on the elements, part of the "Discover More" series, is "arranged in single-topic spreads grouped in five chapters based on sections of the Periodic Table." It "highlights either selected single elements or related groups. The layout includes color photos, digital diagrams and images, fact boxes, explanatory captions, and other text in a variety of sizes and weights. . . . A downloadable ebook supplement . . . extends the overall topic." (School Library Journal)

"...This broad introduction is current enough to include mention of Element #117 (probably observed in 2010) and chock-full of basic information cranked up with a generous admixture of "gosh-wow" facts about our universe's building blocks.—" SLJ

Halka, Monica

Alkali & alkaline earth metals; [by] Monica Halka, Brian Nordstrom. Facts on File 2010 xxxv, 172p il (Periodic table of the elements) $40

Grades: 9 10 11 12   **546**

1. Periodic law 2. Chemical elements

ISBN 978-0-8160-7369-6

LC 2009-35152

This book "presents the current scientific understanding of the physics, chemistry, geology, and biology of these two families of elements, including how they are synthesized in the universe, when and how they were discovered, and where they are found on Earth. With information pertaining to the discovery and naming of these elements as well as new developments and dilemmas, this . . . book examines how humans use alkalis and alkaline earths and their benefits and challenges to society, health, and the environment." Publisher's note

Includes glossary and bibliographical references

Halogens and noble gases; [by] Monica Halka, Brian Nordstrom. Facts on File 2010 xxxiii, 157p il (Periodic table of the elements) $40

Grades: 9 10 11 12   **546**

1. Gases 2. Periodic law 3. Chemical elements

ISBN 978-0-8160-7368-9

LC 2009-31088

"Beginning with an overview of chemistry and physics, this volume is arranged into two sections: halogens and noble gases. Each one begins with an introduction to its family and is followed by chapters devoted to a single element or pairs of elements. The chapters focused on elements feature a chart highlighting key information: symbol, atomic number, melting and boiling point, etc. . . . The writing and explanations are clear and would be appropriate for generalists as well as chemistry students." SLJ

Includes glossary and bibliographical references

Lanthanides and actinides; [by] Monica Halka and Brian Nordstrom. Facts on File 2011 xxxiv, 190p il (Periodic table of the elements) $40

Grades: 9 10 11 12   **546**

1. Periodic law 2. Chemical elements

ISBN 978-0-8160-7372-6

LC 2010-6296

This book "explains how they were discovered, as well as the practical applications that these elements have in today's scientific, technological, medical, and military communities. Actinium, thorium, protactinium, uranium, and the transuranium elements are just some of the elements covered." Publisher's note

Includes glossary and bibliographical references

Metals and metalloids; [by] Monica Halka and Brian Nordstrom. Facts on File 2011 xxxiii, 158p il (Periodic table of the elements) $40

Grades: 9 10 11 12 **546**

1. Metals 2. Periodic law 3. Chemical elements

ISBN 978-0-8160-7370-2

LC 2009049369

This book "presents the current scientific understanding of the physics, chemistry, geology, and biology of these two families of elements, including the post-transition metals and metalloids." Publisher's note

Includes glossary and bibliographical references

Nonmetals; [by] Monica Halka and Brian Nordstrom. Facts on File 2010 xxxiv, 187p il (Periodic table of the elements) $40

Grades: 9 10 11 12 **546**

1. Periodic law 2. Chemical elements

ISBN 978-0-8160-7367-2

LC 2009-18453

This book discusses "developments in the research of nonmetals, including where they came from, how they fit into our current technological society, and where they may lead us. . . . Nonmetals explored in this volume include hydrogen, carbon, nitrogen, phosphorus, oxygen, sulfur, and selenium." Publisher's note

Includes glossary and bibliographical references

Transition metals; [by] Monica Halka and Brian Nordstrom. Facts on File 2011 xxxiv, 190p il (Periodic table of the elements) $40

Grades: 9 10 11 12 **546**

1. Metals 2. Periodic law 3. Chemical elements

ISBN 978-0-8160-7371-9

LC 2009054139

This book discusses "the chemical and physical properties of transition metals and how they are useful in everyday life. Some of the transition metals covered include scandium, yttrium, titanium, manganese, cobalt, and zinc." Publisher's note

Includes glossary and bibliographical references

Kean, Sam

★ The **disappearing** spoon; and other true tales of madness, love, and the history of the world from the periodic table of the elements. Little, Brown and Co. 2010 391p $24.99

Grades: 11 12 Adult **546**

1. Chemical elements

ISBN 978-0-316-05164-4; 0-316-05164-0

LC 2009-40754

"Kean's traipse among the elements leads him through a warren of subjects, as he examines how these basic building blocks have factored prominently in astronomy, biology, literature, history, politics, and even cryptozoology. With the anecdotal flourishes of Oliver Sacks and the populist acces-

sibility of Malcolm Gladwell, but without the latter's occasional facileness, he makes even the most abstract concepts graspable for armchair scientists. His keen sense of humor is a particular pleasure." Entertainment Wkly

Includes bibliographical references

Krebs, Robert E.

★ The **history** and use of our earth's chemical elements; a reference guide. illustrations by Rae Déjur. 2nd ed; Greenwood Press 2006 422p il $75

Grades: 11 12 Adult **546**

1. Chemical elements

ISBN 0-313-33438-2; 978-0-313-33438-2

LC 2006-12032

First published 1998

"The elements are examined within their groups, enabling students to make connections between elements of similar structure. In addition, the discovery and history of each element—from those known from ancient times to those created in the modern laboratory—is explained." Publisher's note

Includes bibliographical references

Lew, Kristi

Acids and bases. Chelsea House 2008 124p il (Essential chemistry) $35

Grades: 7 8 9 10 **546**

1. Acids 2. Bases (Chemistry)

ISBN 978-0-7910-9783-0; 0-7910-9783-8

LC 2008-24015

"Annotated, colorful photographs and illustrations appear on most spreads, and boxed areas and sidebars highlight specific subjects and areas. The explanations are clear and detailed." SLJ

Includes glossary and bibliographical references

Stwertka, Albert

★ A **guide** to the elements; 2nd ed; Oxford Univ. Press 2002 246p il $37.50; pa $18.95

Grades: 9 10 11 12 **546**

1. Chemical elements

ISBN 0-19-515026-0; 0-19-515027-9 pa

LC 2002-282309

First published 1996

Presents the basic concepts of chemistry and explains complex theories before offering a separate article on each of the building blocks that make up the universe

Includes bibliographical references

West, Krista

Carbon chemistry. Chelsea House 2008 117p il (Essential chemistry) lib bdg $35

Grades: 7 8 9 10 **546**

1. Carbon

ISBN 978-0-7910-9708-3; 0-7910-9708-0

LC 2007-51318

Explains how carbon is integrated into all facets of life as we know it and discusses the unique properties of this essential element.

"Annotated, colorful photographs and illustrations appear on most spreads, and boxed areas and sidebars highlight specific subjects and areas. The explanations are clear and detailed." SLJ

Includes glossary and bibliographical references

546.8   Periodic law and periodic table

Scerri, Eric R.

The **periodic** table; a very short introduction. Eric R. Scerri. Oxford University Press 2011 147 p. (pbk.) $11.95

Grades: Adult   **546.8**
1. Periodic law 2. Periodic table 3. Chemical elements 4. Periodic law -- Tables
ISBN 0199582491; 9780199582495

                      LC 2012359233

This book by Eric Scerri is about the periodic table of elements. "Scerri looks at the trends in properties of elements that led to the construction of the periodic table, and how the deeper meaning of its structure gradually became apparent with the development of atomic theory and quantum mechanics, so that physics arguably came to colonize an entirely different science, chemistry." (Publisher's note)

Includes bibliographical references (p. 139) and index

547   Organic chemistry

Organic chemistry and biochemistry; edited by Graham Bateman. Brown Bear Books 2010 64p il (Facts at your fingertips: introducing chemistry) lib bdg $35.65

Grades: 7 8 9 10   **547**
1. Biochemistry 2. Organic chemistry
ISBN 978-1-936333-14-1

                    LC 2010-16456

"The editorial team has assembled a dozen sections covering the basics of their topic, from the natural starting point of defining organic chemistry, through discussions of bonding, carbon chains and rings, and alcohols and other organic compound groups, to examinations of polymers, carbohydrates, lipids, proteins, and, finally, the biosynthesis of amino acids, nucleic acids, and genes. . . . The book would be a valuable reference in a high school or, possibly, middle school classroom and will be a good addition to secondary school libraries." Sci Books Films

549   Mineralogy

Chaline, Eric

Fifty minerals that changed the course of history; Eric Chaline. Firefly Books 2012 223 p. ill. (chiefly col.), ports. $29.95

Grades: 11 12 Adult   **549**
1. Minerals 2. Mines and mineral resources
ISBN 1554079845; 9781554079841

This book by Eric Chaline is a "guide to the minerals that have had the greatest impact on human civilization. These are the materials used from the Stone Age to the First and Second Industrial Revolutions to the Nuclear Age and

include metals, ores, alloys, salts, rocks, sodium, mercury, steel and uranium. The book also includes minerals used as currency, as jewelry and as lay and religious ornamentation when combined with gem minerals like diamonds, amber, coral, and jade." (Publisher's note)

Includes bibliographical references and index.

Pellant, Chris

Rocks and minerals; Helen Pellant, editorial consultant; photography by Harry Taylor. 2nd American ed; Dorling Kindersley 2002 256p il (Smithsonian handbooks) pa $20

Grades: 11 12 Adult   **549**
1. Rocks 2. Minerals
ISBN 0-7894-9106-0; 978-0-7894-9106-0

First published 1992 as part of the Eyewitness handbooks series

This field guide to identification of rocks and minerals includes techniques for collection and classification, and facts about physical and chemical composition and formation.

Pough, Frederick H.

★ A **field** guide to rocks and minerals; photographs by Jeff Scovil. 5th ed; Houghton Mifflin 1996 396p il hardcover o.p. pa $20

Grades: 8 9 10 11 12   **549**
1. Rocks 2. Minerals
ISBN 0-395-72778-2; 0-395-91096-X pa

                    LC 94-49005

First published 1953

This illustrated guide utilizes traditional identification methods and includes discussions of crystallography, mineralogy and home laboratory techniques.

Includes bibliographical references

550   Earth sciences

Calhoun, Yael

Earth science fair projects; revised and expanded using the scientific method. Enslow Publishers 2010 160p il lib bdg $34.60

Grades: 7 8 9 10   **550**
1. Earth sciences 2. Science projects 3. Science -- Experiments
ISBN 978-0-7660-3425-9 lib bdg; 0-7660-3425-9 lib bdg

"Each volume begins with an overview of the scientific method and safety, then presents a collection of activities encouraging readers to explore central concepts in the featured fields. The activities include step-by-step instructions and helpful color diagrams, interspersed with extended coverage of scientific ideas. The "Results" sections ask questions rather than giving away the answers. Reading list, websites." (Horn Book)

★ **Earth;** the definitive visual guide. editors-in-chief, James F. Luhr and Jeffrey E. Post. Revised and updated ed. DK Publishing 2013 528 p. ill. (chiefly col.) (hbk.) $50

Grades: 8 9 10 11 12 Adult **550**
1. Earth 2. Earth (Planet) 3. Earth (Planet) -- Pictorial works
ISBN 1465414371; 9781465414373

LC 2013444093

First published 2003

This book, edited by James F. Luhr, presents "insight into the forces and processes that formed our environment and which continue to influence its evolution. With thousands of . . . photographs and unique visual catalogues of the features and phenomena that take place on Earth -- such as rocks, minerals, and mountains to tropical rain forests and the different types of clouds -- [it] contains the most up-to-date ideas on how our world works." (Publisher's note)

"Specially commissioned new 3-D digital artwork provides a striking, informative guide to the features of our planet, explains the scientific processes that govern our world, and looks at the complex relationship between humans and the natural environment." Publisher's note

Gardner, Robert

Earth's cycles; green science projects about the water cycle, photosynthesis, and more. Enslow Publishers 2011 112p il (Team Green science projects) lib bdg $31.93

Grades: 6 7 8 9 10 **550**
1. Earth sciences 2. Science projects 3. Science -- Experiments
ISBN 978-0-7660-3644-4; 0-7660-3644-8

LC 2010-25816

"Gardner takes familiar experiments geared toward motivated science learners and gives them an eco-twist. Some are straightforward demonstrations of basic science while others explore aspects of alternative and sustainable science and technologies. Sections of background information further expand the green science coverage. Photographs and diagrams help illustrate the necessary equipment and setups"

Includes glossary and bibliographical references

Kusky, Timothy

Encyclopedia of Earth and space science; [by] Timothy Kusky; Katherine Cullen, managing editor. Facts on File 2010 2v il map (Facts on File science library) set $170

Grades: 9 10 11 12 Adult **550**
1. Earth sciences 2. Space sciences 3. Reference books 4. Earth sciences -- Encyclopedias 5. Space sciences -- Encyclopedias
ISBN 978-0-8160-7005-3

LC 2009-15655

"Topics are organized alphabetically and categorized by National Science Education Standards for Content, grades 9 through 12. Categories include Science as Inquiry, Energy in the Earth System, Geochemical Cycles, Origin and Evolution of the Earth System, Origin and Evolution of the Universe, Science and Technology, Science in Personal and Social Perspectives, History and Nature of Science, and Subdisciplines. Entries encompass beaches and shorelines, climate change, Copernicus, global warming, tsunamis, and volcanos. . . . This is an informative resource that displays the Earth's wonder. It will appeal to an audience of high school and college Earth science and astronomy classes." Libr J

Includes glossary and bibliographical references

Rybolt, Thomas R.

Environmental science fair projects; revised and expanded using the scientific method. [by] Thomas R. Rybolt and Robert C. Mebane. Enslow Publishers 2010 160p il lib bdg $34.60

Grades: 7 8 9 10 **550**
1. Earth sciences 2. Science projects 3. Environmental sciences 4. Science -- Experiments
ISBN 978-0-7660-3426-6 lib bdg; 0-7660-3426-7 lib bdg

"Each book focusing on earth science will be helpful to middle school students and contains a section about the scientific method as well as experiments that are outlined to cover the experimental question, hypothesis, materials, procedures, results and conclusions." (Publisher's Note)

551 Geology, hydrology, meteorology

Allaby, Michael

★ **Encyclopedia** of weather and climate; [illustrations by Richard Garratt] Rev ed; Facts on File 2007 2v il (Facts on File science library) set $165

Grades: 11 12 Adult **551**
1. Reference books 2. Meteorology -- Encyclopedias
ISBN 0-8160-6350-8; 978-0-8160-6350-5

LC 2006-18295

First published 2002

"The main body of the encyclopedia consists of . . . entries describing processes such as cloud formation, atmospheric phenomena such as rainbows, and some of the techniques and instruments used to study the atmosphere, as well as the units of measurement that scientists use. The . . . coverage also includes the classification systems that are used for climate types, winds, and clouds. Ten appendixes contain . . . supplementary material—such as biographical notes on scientists and lists of the most severe tropical cyclones and tropical storms, weather disasters, and milestones in atmospheric research." Publisher's note

Includes bibliographical references

Cobb, Allan B.

Earth chemistry. Chelsea House 2008 130p il map (Essential chemistry) $35

Grades: 7 8 9 10 **551**
1. Chemistry 2. Environmental sciences
ISBN 978-0-7910-9677-2; 0-7910-9677-7

LC 2007-51317

"Annotated, colorful photographs and illustrations appear on most spreads, and boxed areas and sidebars highlight specific subjects and areas. The explanations are clear and detailed." SLJ

Includes glossary and bibliographical references

Lambert, David

★ The **field** guide to geology; [by] David Lambert and the Diagram Group. New ed.; Checkmark Books 2006 304p il map $39.95; pa $16.95

Grades: 11 12 Adult   **551**

1. Geology

ISBN 0-8160-6509-8; 978-0-8160-6509-7; 0-8160-6510-1 pa; 978-0-8160-6510-3 pa

LC 2006-48533

First published 1988

This is an "overview of the processes that forged the planet and the technologies that have revolutionized the way that scientists investigate Earth's systems." Publisher's note

Includes bibliographical references

★ **Plate** tectonics, volcanoes, and earthquakes; edited by John P. Rafferty. Britannica Educational Pub. in association with Rosen Educational Services 2010 312p il map (Dynamic Earth) lib bdg $45

Grades: 6 7 8 9 10   **551**

1. Volcanoes 2. Earthquakes 3. Plate tectonics

ISBN 978-1-61530-106-5; 1-61530-106-2

LC 2009042303

"The 2010 earthquake in Haiti, threats to aviation from clouds of volcanic ash and aerosols, and recent changes in the Antarctic make . . . [this] a very updated resource. The process of plate tectonics and prior explanations of the dynamic nature of the earth is followed by explanations of volcanism and seismology. Charts and text describe significant volcanoes and earthquakes that have impacted humans throughout history. . . . [Recommended] for younger youth as well as high school youth since they are highly readable, with details concerning activities of interest to all ages." Voice Youth Advocates

Includes bibliographical references

551.1   Gross structure and properties of the earth

Tomecek, Steve

★ **Plate** tectonics. Chelsea House 2009 102p il (Science foundations) lib bdg $35

Grades: 9 10 11 12   **551.1**

1. Plate tectonics

ISBN 978-1-60413-014-0; 1-60413-014-8

LC 2008-6054

Examines the evolution of plate tectonic theory from its beginnings as a wild idea of drifting continents to its acceptance as the main concept that drives geology today.

This title offers "a wealth of material, including useful further-reading lists. Great for curricular supplementation, report writers, and science buffs." SLJ

Includes glossary and bibliographical references

551.2   Volcanoes, earthquakes, thermal waters and gases

Gates, Alexander E.

★ **Encyclopedia** of earthquakes and volcanoes; [by] Alexander E. Gates, PH.D and David Ritchie. 3rd ed.; Facts on File 2007 346p il map (Facts on File science library) pa $21.95; $75

Grades: 11 12 Adult   **551.2**

1. Reference books 2. Volcanoes -- Encyclopedias 3. Earthquakes -- Encyclopedias

ISBN 9780816071203; 0-8160-6302-8

LC 2005-46619

First published 1994

"The book's entries cover information on key environmental issues, economic dilemmas, ethical concerns, advances in research and technology, organizations, and individuals who have left their mark on the fields of volcanology and seismology." Publisher's note

Includes bibliographical references

Kusky, Timothy M.

★ **Earthquakes**; plate tectonics and earthquake hazards. [by] Timothy Kusky. Facts on File 2008 169p il map (Hazardous earth) $39.50

Grades: 9 10 11 12   **551.2**

1. Earthquakes 2. Plate tectonics

ISBN 978-0-8160-6462-5; 0-8160-6462-8

LC 2007-20832

"Presenting the main ideas of plate tectonics, this . . . reference provides readers with an understanding of how, why, and where most earthquakes occur. Coverage includes what happens during an earthquake, using many examples of hazards such as landslides, passage of seismic-earthquake waves through the ground, and other phenomena that people have encountered during real earthquakes." Publisher's note

Includes glossary and bibliographical references

Nardo, Don

Volcanoes. Morgan Reynolds Pub. 2009 112p il map (Extreme threats) lib bdg $28.95

Grades: 7 8 9 10   **551.2**

1. Volcanoes

ISBN 978-1-59935-118-6; 1-59935-118-8

LC 2009-25705

This book "begins with a vivid account of the 79 CE eruption of Vesuvius, the cataclysm that buried Pompeii and Herculaneum. Later chapters explore the development of volcanology, formation and location of volcanoes, volcanic avalanches, supervolcanoes and mass extinctions, and the bleak future of humanity with regard to volcanoes. Throughout, Nardo references specific volcanoes and eruptions and brings the disasters to life by including primary source quotes from witnesses and scientists." Voice Youth Advocates

Includes glossary and bibliographical references

Rooney, Anne

Volcanoes. New Forest Press 2010 64p il map lib bdg $34.25

Grades: 7 8 9 10 **551.2**
1. Volcanoes
ISBN 978-1-84898-319-9; 1-84898-319-0
"Both books present basic information about these natural disasters, including explanations of plate tectonics, the categories and causes of each, and historical examples of prominent events. Stock color photographs and diagrams help to illustrate the concepts. Additional information about current scientific research projects and the scientists leading them can be found in the numerous sidebars." (Horn Book)

551.3 Surface and exogenous processes and their agents

Fredston, Jill A.
★ **Snowstruck**; in the grip of avalanches. [by] Jill Fredston. Harcourt 2005 342p il $24; pa $14
Grades: 11 12 Adult **551.3**
1. Avalanches 2. Survival skills
ISBN 978-0-15-101249-7; 0-15-101249-0; 978-0-15-603254-4 pa; 0-15-603254-6 pa
LC 2005-20454
"As avalanche experts, . . . [the author and her husband] are often called upon to forecast, trigger, and teach about avalanches as well as rescue survivors—or, sadly, more often to recover remains. Fredston's decades of experience distilled into this instructive and personal narrative will leave readers with a newfound appreciation for the force, the fury, and the cold sorrow of avalanches." Libr J

Glaciers, sea ice, and ice formation; edited by John P. Rafferty. Britannica Educational Pub. in association with Rosen Educational Services 2010 253p il map (Dynamic Earth) lib bdg $45
Grades: 6 7 8 9 10 **551.3**
1. Ice 2. Glaciers
ISBN 978-1-61530-119-5; 1-61530-119-4
LC 2010000226
This book "examines the dynamic processes of [glaciers, sea ice, and ice formation]. . . . [It] provides the reader with an understanding of basic processes, historical background, and current phenomena. . . . [Recommended] for younger youth as well as high school youth." Voice Youth Advocates
Includes bibliographical references

Pollack, H. N.
A **world** without ice; [by] Henry Pollack. Avery 2009 287p il map $26; pa $16
Grades: 11 12 Adult **551.3**
1. Ice 2. Glaciers 3. Greenhouse effect
ISBN 978-1-58333-357-0; 978-1-58333-407-2 pa
LC 2009-30326
"Seldom has a scientist written so well and so clearly for the lay reader. Pollack's explanations of how researchers can tell that the climate is warming faster than normal are free of the usual scientific jargon and understandable. All readers concerned about global warming and students writing papers on the topic will want this excellent and important volume." Libr J
Includes bibliographical references

551.4 Geomorphology and hydrosphere

Aleshire, Peter
Mountains; foreword by Geoffrey H. Nash. Chelsea House Publishers 2008 144p il map (The extreme Earth) $35
Grades: 8 9 10 11 12 **551.4**
1. Mountains
ISBN 978-0-8160-5918-8; 0-8160-5918-7
LC 2007-20692
This describes how mountains were formed, how they have changed over the span of geologic time, and their contributions to the environment, and goes on to describe specific mountains and mountain ranges including Mount Everest, the Appalachians, the Alps, the Mid-Atlantic Ridge of North America, the Sierra Nevadas, the Andes, Mauna Kea in Hawaii, Mount Saint Helens, Mount Kilimanjaro, and Humphreys Peak, in the southwestern United States.
Includes bibliographical references

Balliett, James Fargo
Mountains; environmental issues, global perspectives. M.E. Sharpe 2010 155p il map (Environmental issues, global perspectives) $55
Grades: 9 10 11 12 **551.4**
1. Mountains
ISBN 978-0-7656-8228-4
LC 2010-12121
"The case studies in Mountains consider how global warming in East Africa is harming Mount Kenya's regional population, examine the fragile ecology of New Zealand's Southern Alps, and discuss the impact of mountain use over time in New Hampshire's White Mountains, among other critical issues." Publisher's note
Includes glossary and bibliographical references

Berlatsky, Noah
Water and ice; Michael E. Mann, consulting editor. Greenhaven Press 2011 120p il map lib bdg $37.10
Grades: 7 8 9 10 11 **551.4**
1. Ice 2. Glaciers 3. Greenhouse effect
ISBN 978-0-7377-4861-1; 0-7377-4861-3
LC 2010011348
"After useful introductions to climate change science and background information on related atmospheric and oceanic sciences, the volumes examine the rise of average global and ocean temperatures. Evidence for and against causal relationships between these increases and extreme weather events such as hurricanes, droughts, and heat waves are then thoughtfully discussed. Some color photographs and diagrams are included." (Horn Book)

Collier, Michael
Over the coasts. Mikaya Press 2009 120p il map (An aerial view of geology) $34.95
Grades: 9 10 11 12 **551.4**
1. Coasts 2. Aerial photography 3. Geology -- North America
ISBN 1-931414-42-4; 978-1-931414-42-5
LC 2009-75245

This volume of aerial photography examines "coastal processes: how waves interact with promontories, dunes, sand spits, barrier islands and human constructions." Publ Wkly

Includes glossary and bibliographical references

Hanson, Erik A.

Canyons; [by] Erik Hanson; foreword by Geoffrey H. Nash. Chelsea House 2007 206p il map (The extreme Earth) $35

Grades: 8 9 10 11 12   **551.4**
1. Canyons 2. Plate tectonics
ISBN 0-8160-6435-0; 978-0-8160-6435-9
LC 2006-15810

Profiles canyons around the world including the Grand Canyon, the Columbia River Gorge, Fish River Canyon, and Monterey Canyon; and describes how and when they were formed, how the landscape has changed over time, and the contribution of each to the environment.

"The story in this book may generate a longing within the reader to visit vistas and hike into canyons for an intimate view of earth history." Sci Books Films

Includes glossary and bibliographical references

Hanson, Jeanne K.

Caves; foreword by Geoffrey H. Nash. Chelsea House 2007 142p il map (The extreme Earth) $35

Grades: 8 9 10 11 12   **551.4**
1. Caves
ISBN 978-0-8160-5917-1; 0-8160-5917-9
LC 2006-11718

The describes types of caves and how they are formed, their exploration, and some specific caves including Mammoth Cave of Kentucky; the caves of Yucatan, Mexico; Lascaux Cave of southwestern France; Lubang Nasib Bagus and the Sarawak Chamber of Borneo, Malaysia; Kazumura Cave of Hawaii; Waitomo Cave of New Zealand; and Wind Cave of South Dakota.

Includes bibliographical references

551.41   Geomorphology

Streever, Bill

Heat; adventures in the world's fiery places. Bill Streever. Little, Brown, and Co. 2013 368 p. (hardback) $26.99

Grades: 11 12 Adult   **551.41**
1. Fire 2. Heat 3. Arid regions -- Description and travel
ISBN 0316105333; 9780316105330
LC 2012020861

In this book, Bill Streever "explores any place hot or anything that creates heat, like Death Valley, forest fires, coal, oil, nuclear bombs, cooking, and volcanoes. . . . In this . . . companion to 'Cold,' Streever is able to mix the pop science, personal experiences, and historic asides into a . . . commentary on a subject that few people think about." (Publishers Weekly)

551.45   Plane and coastal regions

Fagan, Brian

The **attacking** ocean; the past, present, and future of rising sea levels. Brian Fagan. 1st U.S. ed. Bloomsbury Press 2013 320 p. ill., maps $28; $18

Grades: 10 11 12 Adult   **551.45**
1. Ocean 2. Sea level 3. Ocean -- History 4. Sea level -- History
ISBN 1608196925; 9781608196920; 9781608196944
LC 2012043454

This book by Brian Fagan describes how "The past fifteen thousand years . . . have witnessed dramatic sea level changes, which began with rapid global warming at the end of the Ice Age, when sea levels were more than 700 feet below modern levels. . . . These rapid changes had little effect on those humans who experienced them, partly because there were so few people on earth, and also because they were able to adjust readily to new coastlines." (Publisher's note)

"In three absorbing, well-crafted sections, the author recounts some notable past storm surges and tsunamis, and predicts likely damages from future ocean-borne disasters. More than just another nervous admonition about climate change, Fagan's account relies on hard data to warn cities and governments worldwide to act now and forestall otherwise inevitable catastrophic flooding." Booklist

Includes bibliographical references and index

551.46   Oceanography and submarine geology

Aleshire, Peter

Ocean ridges and trenches; foreword by Geoffrey H. Nash. Chelsea House 2007 148p il map (The extreme Earth) $35

Grades: 8 9 10 11 12   **551.46**
1. Ocean bottom 2. Marine ecology
ISBN 978-0-8160-5919-5; 0-8160-5919-5
LC 2006-32058

Provides information about the formation of ocean ridges and trenches. Includes ten examples of ridges and trenches from around the world.

Includes bibliographical references

Casey, Susan

The **wave**; in pursuit of the rogues, freaks and giants of the ocean. Doubleday 2010 326p il map $27.95

Grades: 11 12 Adult   **551.46**
1. Surfing 2. Ocean waves
ISBN 978-0-7679-2884-7; 0-7679-2884-9
LC 2010-10193

Casey "estimates that freak waves might have a hand in sinking about two dozen large ships every year. She embarked on a five-year odyssey to meet the people who know these monsters best—from salvagers working a graveyard of ships off the South African coast to a convention of wave scientists, from researchers and mariners who have battled these beasts to surfers who roam the world in search of the ultimate thrill. Reading the 'The Wave' is almost like riding one, paddling in the expositional surf of vivid imagery and colorful description, thrown at you in ever-escalating surges." Cleveland Plain Dealer

Includes bibliographical references

Day, Trevor

Oceans; illustrations by Richard Garratt. rev ed; Facts on File 2008 318p il map (Ecosystem) $70

Grades: 8 9 10 11 12 Adult   551.46

1. Ocean 2. Oceanography

ISBN 0-8160-5932-2; 978-0-8160-5932-4

LC 2006-100769

First published 1999

This volume describes the oceans of the world with regard to their geography, geology, history, chemistry, biology, ecology, exploration, relationship to the atmosphere, economic resources, and management.

Includes glossary and bibliographical references

Friedman, Lauri S.

Oceans; Lauri S. Friedman, book editor. Greenhaven Press 2011 $36.82

Grades: 7 8 9 10   551.46

1. Ocean 2. Marine pollution

ISBN 978-0-7377-5200-7; 0-7377-5200-9

LC 2011005910

"These volumes present previously published articles and essays from journals, magazines, and websites to provide opposing viewpoints about alternative energy sources and environmental threats to Earth's oceans. Though the many photographs, sidebars, and charts make the books visually approachable, the lack of contextual information about primary sources makes for texts that are more inflammatory than useful." (Horn Book)

Hohn, Donovan

★ Moby-Duck; The True Story of 28,800 Bath Toys Lost at Sea. Donovan Hohn. Viking 2011 402p. map (pbk) $16

Grades: 10 11 12 Adult   551.46

1. Journalism 2. Oceanography

ISBN 0-670-02219-5; 978-0-670-02219-9; 9780143120506

LC 2010-33608

"When the writer Donovan Hohn heard of the mysterious loss of thousands of bath toys at sea, he figured he would interview a few oceanographers, talk to a few beachcombers, and read up on Arctic science and geography... Hohn's accidental odyssey pulls him into the secretive arena of shipping conglomerates, the daring work of Arctic researchers, the lunatic risks of maverick sailors, and the shadowy world of Chinese toy factories.' (Publisher's note)

"Like Bill Bryson on hard science, or John McPhee with attitude, journalist Hohn travels from beaches to factories to the northern seas in pursuit of a treasure that mystifies as much as it provokes. His quest is to determine what happened to a load of 28,800 Chinese manufactured plastic animals in a container that fell off a ship en route to Seattle in 1992... The resulting book is a thoroughly engaging environmental/travel title that crosses partisan divides with its solid research and apolitical nature. Rubber ducks as harmless, ubiquitous symbols of childhood? Not anymore, not by a long shot. This dazzles from start to finish." (Booklist)

Hutchinson, S.

★ Oceans: a visual guide; [by] Stephen Hutchinson [and] Lawrence E. Hawkins. Firefly Books 2005 303p il map $29.95

Grades: 11 12 Adult   551.46

1. Oceanography 2. Marine biology

ISBN 1-55407-069-4

"Beginning with the birth of the oceans, the 'cradle of life,' the authors explain tides, salinity, currents, waves, and the diverse and complex ecosystems of the polar, equatorial, and temperate oceans with diagrams, photographs, and concise and clear commentary." Booklist

Kusky, Timothy M.

Tsunamis; giant waves from the sea. [by] Timothy Kusky. Facts on File 2008 134p il (The hazardous Earth) $39.50

Grades: 8 9 10 11 12   551.46

1. Tsunamis

ISBN 978-0-8160-6464-9; 0-8160-6464-4

LC 2007-23477

"This detailed study of the causes and physics of massive waves covers not only the oceanic sort but also similar phenomena, 'seiches,' that occur in closed bodies of water. . . . After analyzing tsunamis' various forms and behaviors, Kusky delivers harrowing accounts of over a dozen disasters, from those centuries past to the devastating Indian Ocean tsunami in 2004. He then closes with a discussion of early-warning systems. Occasional photos capture the devastation of which these waves are capable." Booklist

Includes bibliographical references

Nichols, C. Reid

★ Encyclopedia of marine science; [by] C. Reid Nichols and Robert G. Williams. Facts on File 2009 626p il map (Facts on File science library) $85

Grades: 11 12 Adult   551.46

1. Reference books 2. Marine sciences -- Encyclopedias

ISBN 978-0-8160-5022-2; 0-8160-5022-8

LC 2007-45166

"The expert contributors have packed these pages with top-notch information that will be invaluable to students and reference librarians." SLJ

Includes bibliographical references

Prager, Ellen J.

Chasing science at sea; racing hurricanes, stalking sharks, and living undersea with ocean experts. [by] Ellen Prager. University of Chicago Press 2008 162p il $22.50; pa $13

Grades: 11 12 Adult   551.46

1. Oceanography

ISBN 978-0-226-67870-2; 0-226-67870-9; 978-0-226-67874-0 pa; 0-226-67874-1 pa

LC 2007-49486

"Written in a welcoming, conversational tone, the book not only entertains but delivers some important lessons that will prove useful to any student considering a career in field research." Choice

Includes bibliographical references

Roberts, Callum

The **ocean** of life; the fate of man and the sea. Callum Roberts. Viking 2012 405 p. paperback $17; hardcover o.p.

Grades: 11 12 Adult　　**551.46**

1. Ocean 2. Ocean mining 3. Human ecology 4. Climate change 5. Marine ecology 6. Ocean -- History 7. Ocean and civilization

ISBN 9780143123484; 9780670023547; 067002354X

LC 2012000252

This book by Callum Roberts addresses how the ocean "has been used as a dumping ground while being indiscriminately overharvested." It also looks at "noise pollution, invasive species, plastic pollution, and the effects of climate change on reefs and sea levels as well as ocean acidification. . . . Roberts . . . provides . . . arguments against some of the technological 'fixes' some scientists have proposed." (Choice: Current Reviews for Academic Libraries)

Includes bibliographical references and index.

Ulanski, Stan L.

The **Gulf** Stream; tiny plankton, giant bluefin, and the amazing story of the powerful river in the Atlantic. [by] Stan Ulanski. University of North Carolina Press 2008 212p il map $28; pa $22

Grades: 11 12 Adult　　**551.46**

1. Gulf Stream

ISBN 978-0-8078-3217-2; 0-8078-3217-0; 978-0-8078-8709-7 pa; 0-8078-8709-9 pa

LC 2008-4746

This "book provides the layperson a synopsis of the physical origin, general biology, and rich exploration history of the Gulf Stream. Ulanski . . . offers a concise, engaging blend of science and history for anyone interested in learning about the general flow dynamics, the intricate food webs, and the human use and exploitation of this vital western-boundary current of the North Atlantic Ocean." Choice

Includes bibliographical references

551.48 Hydrology

Burnham, Laurie

Rivers; foreword by Geoffrey H. Nash. Chelsea House 2007 176p il map (The extreme Earth) $35

Grades: 8 9 10 11 12　　**551.48**

1. Rivers

ISBN 0-8160-5916-0; 978-0-8160-5916-4

LC 2006-31302

This is a "portrait of 10 of the most unusual rivers that examines what was on-site before the river, how it was formed, how and why it has changed over time, and its contributions to the environment." Publisher's note

Includes glossary and bibliographical references

Collier, Michael

Over the rivers. Mikaya 2008 128p il (An aerial view of geology) $34.95

Grades: 9 10 11 12　　**551.48**

1. Rivers 2. Aerial photography 3. Geology -- North

America

ISBN 1-931414-21-1; 978-1-931414-21-0

LC 2008-60051

"This book contains stunning photographs illustrating the geological dynamics of many rivers in the continental United States, such as the Colorado, Mississippi, and Green rivers. This would be a great text for an Earth science classroom to enhance the study of weathering, erosion, and deposition in the development of landscapes sculpted by running water." National Science Teachers Association

Includes bibliographical references

Gardner, Robert

Water; green science projects for a sustainable planet. Enslow Publishers 2011 128p il (Team Green science projects) lib bdg $31.93

Grades: 6 7 8 9 10　　**551.48**

1. Water 2. Science projects 3. Science -- Experiments

ISBN 978-0-7660-3645-1; 0-7660-3645-6

LC 2009-37902

This book offers science experiments that explain the properties of water, the water cycle, and how you can conserve water.

"Gardner takes familiar experiments geared toward motivated science learners and gives them an eco-twist. Some are straightforward demonstrations of basic science while others explore aspects of alternative and sustainable science and technologies. Sections of background information further expand the green science coverage. Photographs and diagrams help illustrate the necessary equipment and set-ups.' (Horn Book)

Includes glossary and bibliographical references

Hanson, Jeanne K.

Lakes; foreword, Geoffrey H. Nash. Facts on File 2007 146p il map (The extreme Earth) $35

Grades: 8 9 10 11 12　　**551.48**

1. Lakes

ISBN 978-0-8160-5914-0; 0-8160-5914-4

LC 2005-34327

This describes how lakes are formed, the current environmental health of the lakes and their future prognosis, and some specific bodies of water including the Caspian Sea in the Middle East, the Aral Sea in Western Asia, Lake Superior in North America, Lake Baikal in Central Asia, and Lake Titicaca in South America.

Includes bibliographical references

551.5 Meteorology

Allaby, Michael

A **chronology** of weather; illustrations by Richard Garratt. Rev. ed.; Facts on File 2004 196p il (Dangerous weather) $35

Grades: 9 10 11 12　　**551.5**

1. Reference books 2. Weather -- Chronology 3. Natural disasters -- Chronology

ISBN 0-8160-4792-8; 978-0-8160-4792-5

LC 2003-4000

First published 1998

The author answers "questions students and non-specialists have about weather and provides a general overview of the . . . information that shapes the way weather is understood and studied. Features include discussion of how the climates of the world have changed over the centuries; a 5,000-year chronology of dangerous weather, from ca. 3200 BCE to the present; and a chronology of discoveries listing important developments in the understanding of weather." Publisher's note

Includes glossary and bibliographical references

Buckley, Bruce

Weather: a visual guide; [by] Bruce Buckley, Edward J. Hopkins [and] Richard Whitaker. Firefly Books 2004 303p il maps $29.95; pa $27.95

Grades: 11 12 Adult   **551.5**

1. Weather 2. Meteorology

ISBN 1-55297-957-1; 978-1-55297-957-0; 1-55407-430-4 pa; 978-1-55407-430-3 pa

LC 2004-303909

This is "a comprehensive academic resource with information and glorious color photographs on virtually every aspect of weather." SLJ

Desonie, Dana

Atmosphere; air pollution and its effects. Chelsea House 2007 194p il map (Our fragile planet) $35

Grades: 9 10 11 12   **551.5**

1. Weather 2. Atmosphere 3. Meteorology

ISBN 978-0-8160-6213-3; 0-8160-6213-7

LC 2007-8241

"From the basics defining what is atmosphere and its role in supporting and protecting all life to the more complex issues that have become front page news such as the hole in the ozone layer, air pollution, skin cancer, global warming, and . . . Hurricane Katrina, this book helps the reader delve into the background information that is necessary in understanding why things work the way they do." Libr Media Connect

Includes glossary and bibliographical references

Gunn, Angus M.

A **student** guide to climate and weather. Greenwood Press 2010 5v il map set $255

Grades: 9 10 11 12   **551.5**

1. Climate 2. Meteorology 3. Reference books

ISBN 978-0-313-35568-4; 978-0-313-35569-1 ebook

LC 2009-42256

"These volumes discuss the scientific processes that pertain to weather and climate, and the specific ways that weather and climate impact human life." Booklist

Includes glossary and bibliographical references

Streissguth, Thomas

Extreme weather; [by] Tom Streissguth; Michael E. Mann, consulting editor. Greenhaven Press/Gale, Cengage Learning 2011 116p il map (Confronting global warming) lib bdg $37.10

Grades: 7 8 9 10 11 12   **551.5**

1. Weather 2. Climate -- Environmental aspects

ISBN 978-0-7377-4859-8; 0-7377-4859-1

LC 2010-24973

"Presented in a scholarly design that will appeal to older readers. . . . The illustrations and pictures support the text, and the graphics and sidebars are well placed." Libr Media Connect

Includes glossary and bibliographical references

Walker, Gabrielle

An **ocean** of air; why the wind blows and other mysteries of the atmosphere. Harcourt 2007 272p il map $25

Grades: 11 12 Adult   **551.5**

1. Atmosphere

ISBN 978-0-15-101124-7; 0-15-101124-9

LC 2006-32359

The author "brings a new perspective to centuries-old stories of wonder and discovery and sheds light on the personalities of the 19th and 20th centuries who have also contributed to the world's body of knowledge. Witty and full of fascinating information, this is a captivating book." Libr J

Includes bibliographical references

Williams, Jack

★ The **AMS** weather book; the ultimate guide to America's weather. University of Chicago Press 2009 316p il map $35

Grades: 9 10 11 12 Adult   **551.5**

1. Climate 2. Weather 3. Meteorology

ISBN 0-226-89898-9; 978-0-226-89898-8

LC 2008-35916

This book "provides a clearly written, profusely illustrated narrative guide to weather that affects the US. . . . Topics in this 12-chapter volume range from how rainbows are formed and what makes the wind blow, to climate change and how weather satellites work. In addition, Williams highlights profiles of meteorologists and other scientists influential in weather prediction and research, including many women and minorities. This work, with its attractive, easy-to-understand graphics, offers a useful, engaging basic introduction to a wide variety of weather-related topics." Choice

Includes glossary

551.51 Composition, regions, dynamics of atmosphere

Amato, Joseph Anthony

★ **Dust**; a history of the small and the invisible. {by} Joseph A. Amato. University of Calif. Press 2000 288p il hardcover o.p. pa $15.95

Grades: 11 12 Adult   **551.51**

1. Dust 2. Science -- Philosophy

ISBN 0-520-21875-2; 0-520-23195-3 pa

LC 99-27115

The author "writes only incidentally about dust; rather, he reviews how humanity's view of the unseen world changed throughout the ages as the ability to see it, through magnification, increased. . . . Amato touches on such diverse topics as the role of light in art, germ theory and medical advances, particle physics, and the effect of artificially made dusts on the environment. He concludes with a philosophical view of the future of humanity as medical and scientific advances takes it into uncharted waters." Choice

Includes bibliographical references

Bowen, Mark

★ **Thin** ice; unlocking the secrets of climate in the world's highest mountains. Henry Holt 2005 463p il $30; pa $17

Grades: 11 12 Adult   **551.51**
1. Upper atmosphere 2. Climate -- Research
ISBN 0-8050-6443-5; 0-8050-8135-6 pa
LC 2005-40426

"This book will appeal to mountaineering and climatology buffs, but should be read by everyone concerned about the future of our planet." Publ Wkly

Holmes, Hannah

The **secret** life of dust; from the cosmos to the kitchen counter, the big consequences of little things. Wiley 2001 240p hardcover o.p. pa $14.95

Grades: 11 12 Adult   **551.51**
1. Dust 2. Science -- Philosophy
ISBN 0-471-37743-0; 0-471-42635-0 pa
LC 2001-22368

"Holmes explores how dust has been crucial in the birth of planets, how it affects the earth's environment and weather, and how humans create it as well. Out to communicate straight facts and science, she considers technical points in language that is clear and comprehensible even for those lacking a science background. In addition to the bibliography, Holmes provides a listing of web sites for each chapter so that readers may easily obtain current information and graphics." Libr J

Includes bibliographical references

551.55   Atmospheric disturbances and formations

Emanuel, Kerry A.

★ **Divine** wind; the history and science of hurricanes. [by] Kerry Emanuel. Oxford Univ. Press 2005 285p il $45

Grades: 11 12 Adult   **551.55**
1. Hurricanes
ISBN 0-19-514941-6
LC 2004-13078

This is a study of hurricanes.

"A gripping popular treatment of peril, that will have great resonance in light of recent disasters." Booklist

Includes bibliographical references

Levine, Mark

F5; devastation, survival, and the most violent tornado outbreak of the twentieth century. Miramax Books 2007 307p il map $25.95

Grades: Adult   **551.55**
1. Tornadoes
ISBN 978-1-4013-5220-2; 1-4013-5220-0

The author "turns the laconic detail, thorough compression and rhythmic nuance of his best verse to sensational use, producing a work of reportage so artfully structured that it looks pretty good next to 'In Cold Blood.'" N Y Times Book Rev

Includes bibliographical references

Longshore, David

Encyclopedia of hurricanes, typhoons, and cyclones; New ed; Facts on File 2008 468p il map (Facts on File science library) $75

Grades: 8 9 10 11 12 Adult   **551.55**
1. Reference books 2. Cyclones -- Encyclopedias 3. Typhoons -- Encyclopedias 4. Hurricanes -- Encyclopedias
ISBN 978-0-8160-6295-9; 0-8160-6295-1
LC 2007-32336

First published 1998

This encyclopedia describes named hurricanes, typhoons and cyclones, explains meteorological terms and instruments, and includes biographical data, a chronology, and a list of hurricane safety procedures.

"This is an excellent basic reference work that belongs in all school, public, and academic libraries." Sci Books Films

Includes bibliographical references

Storms, violent winds, and earth's atmosphere; edited by John P. Rafferty. Britannica Educational Pub. in association with Rosen Educational Services 2010 249p il (Dynamic Earth) lib bdg $45

Grades: 6 7 8 9 10   **551.55**
1. Winds 2. Storms 3. Atmosphere
ISBN 978-1-61530-114-0
LC 2009049109

"This book examines the science that gives us a greater understanding of the patterns that produce hurricanes, tornadoes, cyclones, and a host of related conditions." Publisher's note

Includes bibliographical references

551.6   Climatology and weather

Climate change; in context. Brenda Wilmoth Lerner & K. Lee Lerner, editors. Gale, Cengage Learning 2008 2v il map set $257

Grades: 9 10 11 12   **551.6**
1. Reference books 2. Climate -- Environmental aspects -- Encyclopedias
ISBN 978-1-4144-3614-2
LC 2007-51762

"An excellent resource for research papers and opposing-viewpoint debates that will motivate students to consider carefully all aspects of environmental changes while challenging them to discover solutions." Libr J

Includes bibliographical references

Dow, Kirstin, 1963-

The **atlas** of climate change; mapping the world's greatest challenge. Kirstin Dow and Thomas E. Downing. 3rd edition University of California Press 2011 128 p. col. ill., col. maps pbk $24.95

Grades: 11 12 Adult   **551.6**
1. Atlases 2. Climate 3. Reference books
ISBN 9780520268234

LC 2011922284
First published 2006
"This atlas examines the causes of climate change and considers its possible impact on subsistence, water resources, ecosystems, biodiversity, health, coastal megacities, and cultural treasures. It reviews historical contributions to greenhouse gas levels, progress in meeting international commitments, and local efforts to meet the challenge of climate change." Publisher's note
Includes bibliographical references

Fagan, Brian M.

The **long** summer: how climate changed civilization. Basic Books 2003 284p il hardcover o.p. pa $16

Grades: 11 12 Adult   **551.6**
1. Climate 2. Civilization -- History
ISBN 0-465-02281-2; 0-465-02282-0 pa

LC 2003-13917
"This book is highly recommended for general audiences considering the implications and the challenges posed by human-induced global climate change." Sci Books Films
Includes bibliographical references

Flannery, Tim F.

We are the weather makers; the history of climate change. [by] Tim Flannery; adapted by Sally M. Walker. Candlewick Press 2009 303p il map $17.99

Grades: 7 8 9 10   **551.6**
1. Greenhouse effect 2. Climate -- Environmental aspects
ISBN 978-0-7636-3656-2; 0-7636-3656-8

LC 2008-939840
An adaptation of The weather makers, published 2005 for adults by Atlantic Monthly Press
"Arguing that climate change and global warming affect us all and that we can be part of the solution, this comprehensive look at the issue includes a clear explanation of the mechanism of the carbon cycle, the role of greenhouse gases on Earth, historical instances of climate change and their causes, descriptions of effects on a variety of habitats, future scenarios and suggestions—both personal and global—about what might be done. . . . A copy belongs in every middle and high-school library." Kirkus
Includes bibliographical references

Fleming, James Rodger

Fixing the sky; the checkered history of weather and climate control. [by] James Rodger Fleming. Columbia University Press 2010 325p il (Columbia studies in international and global history) $27.95

Grades: 9 10 11 12 Adult   **551.6**
1. Global warming 2. Weather control 3. Human influence on nature 4. Climatic changes
ISBN 978-0-231-14412-4

LC 2010-15482
This book "should be read by all who want a better understanding of global climate change and the debate over geoengineering our environment." Sci Books Films
Includes bibliographical references

Fry, Juliane L.

★ The **encyclopedia** of weather and climate change; a complete visual guide. [authors, Juliane L. Fry ... [et al.] University of California Press 2010 512 p. col. ill., col. maps

Grades: 9 10 11 12 Adult   **551.6**
1. Reference books 2. Weather -- Encyclopedias 3. Climatology -- Encyclopedias 4. Meteorology -- Encyclopedias 5. Climatic changes -- Encyclopedias
ISBN 0520261011; 9780520261013

LC 2009943908
"Major sections fall under the following headings: Engine, Action, Extremes, Watching, Climate, and Change. Chapters within the sections begin with a broad overview of a particular topic, then move on to greater detail. The regional climate guide, focusing on 43 specific locations around the world, is particularly noteworthy. . . . The profuse illustrations carry the information; this title could be just the thing for visual learners." Libr J
Includes index.

Gardner, Robert

Weather science fair projects; revised and expanded using the scientific method. Enslow Publishers 2010 160p il lib bdg $34.60

Grades: 7 8 9 10   **551.6**
1. Weather 2. Science projects 3. Science -- Experiments
ISBN 978-0-7660-3424-2 lib bdg; 0-7660-3424-0 lib bdg
"Each volume begins with an overview of the scientific method and safety, then presents a collection of activities encouraging readers to explore central concepts in the featured fields. The activities include step-by-step instructions and helpful color diagrams, interspersed with extended coverage of scientific ideas. The "Results" sections ask questions rather than giving away the answers." (Horn Book)

Kusky, Timothy M.

Climate change; shifting glaciers, deserts, and climate belts. [by] Timothy Kusky. Facts on File 2009 156p il map (The hazardous Earth) $39.50

Grades: 8 9 10 11 12   **551.6**
1. Greenhouse effect 2. Climate -- Environmental aspects
ISBN 978-0-8160-6466-3; 0-8160-6466-0

LC 2008-5134
"This is a terrific collection of all of the pertinent science about how climate works, how human activity is affecting climate, and how the earth is responding. Not only is climate science well explained, but there are also detailed examples

of how various cultures and regions are being affected by changes in climate." Sci Books Films

Includes glossary and bibliographical references

Nardo, Don

Climate change. Morgan Reynolds Pub. 2009 112p il (Extreme threats) lib bdg $28.95

Grades: 7 8 9 10 **551.6**

1. Greenhouse effect 2. Climate -- Environmental aspects

ISBN 978-1-59935-119-3; 1-59935-119-6

LC 2009-25704

This book about climate change has "black-and-white and color photographs on almost every page. . . . Frequent sidebars, covering as much as a spread, discuss peripheral and often unusual information. The conclusion . . . explains what scientists are doing, or what they anticipate doing, to ameliorate the threat." SLJ

Includes glossary and bibliographical references

Philander, S. George

★ **Our** affair with El Nino; how we transformed an enchanting Peruvian current into a global climate hazard. Princeton University Press 2004 275p il maps hardcover o.p. pa $17.95

Grades: 11 12 Adult **551.6**

1. Climate 2. El Niño Current

ISBN 0-691-11335-1; 0-691-12622-4 pa

LC 2003-44235

"This is an exceptional book, enjoyable to read and educational at several levels. El Niño is the springboard for a book that thoroughly explains the phenomenon and even goes far beyond it." Sci Books Films

Includes bibliographical references

551.63 Weather forecasting and forecasts, reporting and reports

Cullen, Heidi

The **weather** of the future; heat waves, extreme storms, and other scenes from a climate-changed planet. HarperCollins 2010 329p il map $25.99; pa $15.99

Grades: 11 12 Adult **551.63**

1. Forecasting 2. Climate -- Environmental aspects

ISBN 978-0-06-172688-0; 0-06-172688-5; 978-0-06-172694-1 pa; 0-06-172694-X pa

"A lively and troubling but not entirely doomsday scenario of our warmer future, which will hopefully persuade readers to pay greater attention." Kirkus

Includes bibliographical references

552 Petrology

Bishop, A. C.

★ **Guide** to minerals, rocks & fossils. Firefly Books 2005 336p il pa $19.95

Grades: 9 10 11 12 **552**

1. Rocks 2. Fossils 3. Minerals

ISBN 1-55407-054-6

LC 2005-280972

First published 1974 in the United Kingdom with title: The Hamlyn guide to minerals, rocks, and fossils; 1999 edition published by Cambridge Univ. Press with title: Cambridge guide to minerals, rocks, and fossils

"Minerals, rocks, and fossils are described, illustrated, explained, and related to their natural environment in this splendid compact volume. . . . As a most useful field guide for explorers or as a straightforward, beautifully illustrated and written general reference, this book is unparalleled." Choice

Includes bibliographical references

Bonewitz, Ronald

Rock and gem; the definitive guide to rocks, minerals, gemstones, and fossils. Ronald Louis Bonewitz; consultants, Margaret Carruthers, Richard Efthim. DK Pub. 2008 360 p. pbk $24.95

Grades: 9 10 11 12 Adult **552**

1. Gems 2. Rocks 3. Fossils 4. Minerals 5. Precious stones

ISBN 0756633427; 9780756633424

LC 2008272981

"Published in association with the Smithsonian Institution, this lavishly illustrated reference provides a close-up look at the world's diverse rocks and gems, covering more than 450 different specimens, along with detailed descriptions, identification tips, classification information, and practical advice on gem and rock collecting." (Publisher's Note)

553.2 Carbonaceous materials

Freese, Barbara

Coal: a human history. Penguin Books 2004 304p il pa $15

Grades: 11 12 Adult **553.2**

1. Coal

ISBN 978-0-14-200098-4

First published 2003 by Perseus Bks.

This is "an engrossing account of the comparatively cheap, usually dirty fuel that supported the Industrial Revolution, inspired the building of canals and railroads to move it, and once made London and Pittsburgh famous for their air." N Y Times Book Rev

Includes bibliographical references

Marcovitz, Hal

What is the future of fossil fuels? by Hal Marcovitz. ReferencePoint Press, Inc. 2013 80 p. color illustrations, maps (Future of renewable energy series) (hardback) $28.95

Grades: 6 7 8 9 **553.2**

1. Fossil fuels

ISBN 1601526121; 9781601526120

LC 2013029017

This book, by Hal Marcovitz, "examines the future of fossil fuels. Topics include: Are Fossil Fuels Affordable? Can Fossil Fuels Be Compatible with the Environment? Can

Alternative Energy Take the Place of Fossil Fuels? Should the Government Continue to Support Fossil Fuels as an Energy?" (Publisher's note)

"Well written and understandable, the authors use a wide variety of source material to present each side fairly and completely. The question/answer format of the chapters breaks the topics into simplified arguments that can easily be absorbed. The author's style is rather dispassionate which elevates the quality of the works by allowing reader to come to their own conclusions." VOYA

Includes bibliographical references and index

Marrin, Albert, 1936-

Black gold; the story of oil in our lives. Albert Marrin. Alfred A. Knopf 2012 181 p. (hbk.) $19.99 Grades: 8 9 10 11   **553.2**
1. Petroleum as fuel 2. Petroleum industry 3. Petroleum -- United States 4. Petroleum -- United States -- History ISBN 0375866736; 0375966730; 9780375866739; 9780375966736

LC 2011013175

This book offers "perspectives on the role of fossil fuels in human history. . . . [Albert] Marrin opens with a petro-centric tale of wars. These range from an Egyptian conflict in the 4th century BCE to the War on Terror . . . and the U.S. invasion of Afghanistan. He also reviews the course of the Industrial Revolution . . . , then goes on to analyze the hazards of our oil dependence, recap major oil spills and consider both the benefits and dangers of alternative energy sources." (Kirkus)

Includes bibliographical references and index.

553.6   Other economic materials

Kurlansky, Mark

★ **Salt:** a world history. Penguin Books 2003 484p il map pa $16
Grades: 11 12 Adult   **553.6**
1. Salt
ISBN 0-14-200161-9

LC 2004-270006

First published 2002 by Walker & Co.

"Throughout his engaging, well-researched history, Kurlansky sprinkles witty asides and amusing anecdotes. A piquant blend of the historic, political, commercial, scientific and culinary, the book is sure to entertain as well as educate." Publ Wkly

Includes bibliographical references

553.7   Water

Fagan, Brian

Elixir; a history of water and humankind. Brian Fagan. 1st U.S. ed. Bloomsbury Press 2011 384 p. ill., maps $28
Grades: 11 12 Adult   **553.7**
1. Water supply 2. Human ecology 3. Drinking water 4. Water 5. Water -- History 6. Water and civilization

-- History 7. Water -- Social aspects -- History ISBN 160819003X (alk. paper); 9781608190034 (alk. paper)

LC 2010032082

Author Brian Fagan presents "anecdotes and historical episodes showing how pre-industrial people . . . properly appreciated water, from the San hunters of the Kalahari, who see the whole world as a sometimes grudging source of the substance, to John Wesley Powell's efforts to create political divisions in the American West not based on surveyors' straight lines but on natural watersheds." (Kirkus ReviewS)

"Supplying intriguing historical background, Fagan well informs those pondering freshwater's role in contemporary environmental problems." Booklist

Includes bibliographical references and index.

Kandel, Robert S.

Water from heaven; the story of water from the big bang to the rise of civilization, and beyond. [by] Robert Kandel. Columbia Univ. Press 2003 311p il maps $29.95; pa $24
Grades: 11 12 Adult   **553.7**
1. Water
ISBN 0-231-12244-6; 0-231-12245-4 pa

LC 2002-31229

Original French edition, 1998

The author "explains the earth's elaborate and essential-to-life water cycle . . . beginning cosmologically with the birth of the solar system and an analysis of various theories as to where the earth's water . . . originated." Booklist

Includes bibliographical references

Newton, David E.

Encyclopedia of water. Greenwood Press 2002 401p il $75
Grades: 11 12 Adult   **553.7**
1. Reference books 2. Water -- Encyclopedias
ISBN 1-57356-304-8

LC 2002-70031

"The 236 entries in this book comprise an A-Z overview of water's manifold roles in human society and the natural world throughout history." Publisher's note

Includes bibliographical references

553.8   Gems

Gemstones of the world; Walter Schumann; translated by Daniel Shea and Nicole Shea. 5th edition Sterling 2013 319 p. ill. (chiefly col.) hbk $24.95
Grades: 9 10 11 12   **553.8**
1. Precious stones
ISBN 1454909536; 9781454909538

"More than 1,500 full-color photos showcase each precious and semiprecious stone in its rough, natural, polished, and cut renditions. Each entry offers . . . information on the gemstone's formation, structure, physical properties, and characteristics, along with the best methods of working, cutting, and polishing it." Publisher's note

Oldershaw, Cally

★ **Firefly** guide to gems. Firefly Bks. 2004 224p il map $14.95

Grades: 11 12 Adult   **553.8**

1. Gems 2. Precious stones
ISBN 1-55297-814-1

This book "opens with extensive introductory material including history, various properties, and lore. Then, each gem is presented with text and charts of specific chemical properties. While most gems are discussed on a single page, some that are well known have longer articles." SLJ

Gems of the world. Firefly Books 2008 256p il hardcover o.p. pa $24.95

Grades: 11 12 Adult   **553.8**

1. Gems
ISBN 978-1-55407-367-2; 1-55407-367-7; 978-1-55407-539-3 pa; 1554075394 pa

                                    LC 2008-274904

Guide to the indentification and use of gemstones. Includes the geology, chemistry and properties of gemstones, what to look for when buying and how to care for them, plus information on the diamond industry.

Zoellner, Tom

The **heartless** stone; a journey through the world of diamonds, deceit, and desire. St. Martins Press 2006 293p map hardcover o.p. pa $16

Grades: 11 12 Adult   **553.8**

1. Diamonds
ISBN 0-312-33969-0; 978-0-312-33969-2; 0-312-33970-4 pa; 978-0-312-33970-8 pa

                                     LC 2005-33037

The author "probes how 'blood diamonds' are used to fund vicious civil wars in Africa; how De Beers, seeing new markets to exploit, linked diamonds to the ancient yuino ceremony in Japan and played on caste obsession in India; and how India is pushing Belgium and Israel out of the gem trade. . . . This is a superior piece of reportage." Publ Wkly

Includes bibliographical references

557   Earth sciences of North America

Collier, Michael

★ **Over** the mountains; an aerial view of geology. foreword by John S. Shelton. Mikaya Press 2007 un il map (An aerial view of geology) $29.95

Grades: 8 9 10 11 12   **557**

1. Mountains 2. Aerial photography 3. Geology -- North America
ISBN 1-931414-18-1; 978-1-931414-18-0

                                     LC 2006-47151

The author "expresses his passion for geology through awe-inspiring aerial photographs that reveal how mountains were formed and modified across the eons of time. . . . The four sections of this book explore what mountains are, why some are peaked and others rounded, and why they are often strung together in ranges. . . . Collier's love for the land is

contagious, and his flying field trips over the mountains are thrilling." Voice Youth Advocates

Includes bibliographical references

560   Paleontology

Ottaviani, Jim

★ **Bone** sharps, cowboys, and thunder lizards; a tale of Edwin Drinker Cope, Othniel Charles Marsh, and the gilded age of paleontology. by Jim Ottaviani & Big Time Attic. G.T. Labs 2005 165p il pa $22.95

Grades: 9 10 11 12 Adult   **560**

1. Zoologists 2. Graphic novels 3. Biographical graphic novels 4. Paleontologists 5. Fossils -- Graphic novels
ISBN 0-9660106-6-3; 978-0-9660106-6-4

                                     LC 2005-920326

"Ottaviani portrays the heyday of American dinosaur hunting with a ripsnorting Western feel. Rival scientist/dinosaur hunters Marsh and Cope play out their real-life drama in a mostly accurate historical telling. Copious notes at the back of the book point out where Ottaviani departs from the facts; science and history become fun in his hands." Voice Youth Advocates

Includes bibliographical references

Poinar, George O.

What bugged the dinosaurs? insects, disease, and death in the Cretaceous. [by] George Poinar, Jr. and Roberta Poinar; with photographs and drawings by the authors. Princeton University Press 2008 264p il map $29.95

Grades: 11 12 Adult   **560**

1. Fossils 2. Dinosaurs 3. Parasites 4. Insects as carriers of disease
ISBN 978-0-691-12431-5; 0-691-12431-0

                                     LC 2007-61024

The authors contend that in the Cretaceous period, insects "dominated life on the planet and played a significant role in the life and death of the dinosaurs. . . . [They argue that] insects infected with malaria, leishmania, and other pathogens, together with intestinal parasites, could have devastated dinosaur populations." Publisher's note

Includes bibliographical references

★ **Prehistoric** life; [authors, Douglas Palmer ... et al.; consultants, Simon Lamb ... et al.; senior editors, Angeles Gavira Guerrero, Peter Frances; project editors, Cressida Malins ... et al.; editors, Jamie Ambrose ... et al.] DK 2009 512p il map $40

Grades: 7 8 9 10 11 12 Adult   **560**

1. Fossils
ISBN 978-0-7566-5573-0

                                     LC 2010-278841

"Condensing millions of years of life on earth into a 512-page single-volume encyclopedia, this ambitious work presents earth's history from its formation through the Mesolithic period (Middle Stone Age). . . . Geared to adults, this work will find popularity with science enthusiasts and browsers alike." Booklist

Thompson, Ida

★ The **Audubon** Society field guide to North American fossils; with photographs by Townsend P. Dickinson; visual key by Carol Nehring. Knopf 1982 846p il maps flexible bdg $19.95

Grades: 11 12 Adult   **560**

1. Fossils

ISBN 0-394-52412-8

         LC 81-84772

"This softbound field guide to fossils is divided into a section of color photographs followed by a section of detailed descriptions. It covers 420 fossils of marine and freshwater invertebrates, insects, plants, and vertebrates that are likely to be found by the amateur." Malinowsky. Best Sci & Technol Ref Books for Young People

567 Fossil cold-blooded vertebrates

Holmes, Thom

The **first** vertebrates; oceans of the Paleozoic era. Chelsea House 2008 188p il (The prehistoric Earth) lib bdg $35

Grades: 7 8 9 10   **567**

1. Fossils 2. Vertebrates

ISBN 978-0-8160-5958-4; 0-8160-5958-6

        LC 2007-45329

Describes the first instances of vertebrate life in the oceans of the Paleozoic Era, tracing the development of early fish from jawless species to sharks and bony fish.

This "is a comprehensive, well-written, and easily readable text. . . . The chapters are well-organized." Sci Books Films

Includes glossary and bibliographical references

567.9 Reptiles

Barnes-Svarney, Patricia

The **handy** dinosaur answer book; [by] Patricia Barnes-Svarney and Thomas E. Svarney. 2nd ed.; Visible Ink Press 2010 274p il (Handy answer book series) pa $21.95

Grades: 9 10 11 12 Adult   **567.9**

1. Dinosaurs

ISBN 978-1-57859-218-0; 1-57859-218-6

        LC 2009-32573

First published 2000

"The student who simply cannot find enough information about dinosaurs will be delighted with this book that has an amazing wealth of information about dinosaurs. The place of the dinosaur in geologic time, theories about the origin and extinction of dinosaurs, anatomy and physiology, descriptions of various dinosaurs, and paleontological methods are all a part of this work. It is really a comprehensive study of dinosaurs, even if the format is asking simple questions." Voice Youth Advocates

Includes bibliographical references

Everhart, Michael J.

Sea monsters; prehistoric creatures of the deep. [by] Mike Everhart. National Geographic 2007 191p il map $30

Grades: 7 8 9 10   **567.9**

1. Fossils 2. Marine animals 3. Prehistoric animals

ISBN 978-1-4262-0085-4; 1-4262-0085-4

        LC 2007-18671

Featuring "computer-generated images and 3D film clips—with 3D glasses—field photography by National Geographic cameramen, and much more, the book interweaves dramatic scenes of the far, far distant past; up-to-the-minute scientific profiles of nearly two dozen sea monsters; and a group portrait of the eccentric Sternberg family, Kansas-bred pioneers of marine paleontology." Publisher's note

Holmes, Thom

Last of the dinosaurs; the Cretaceous period. Chelsea House 2009 232p il map (The prehistoric Earth) $35

Grades: 9 10 11 12   **567.9**

1. Fossils 2. Dinosaurs

ISBN 978-0-8160-5962-1; 0-8160-5962-4

        LC 2008-38331

This book "discusses how the changing ecological and geological conditions in the Early and Late Cretaceous periods created opportunities for the expansion of dinosaurs. It was also these very climatic and geologic shifts that contributed to the eventual extinction of large and small dinosaurs. . . . [Holmes] is thorough, clear, and informative in explaining theories relating to the mass extinction of dinosaurs and other creatures of the time. . . . Appealing in format and design, the text is supported with abundant color illustrations, charts, and graphs." Booklist

Includes glossary and bibliographical references

Holtz, Thomas R.

★ **Dinosaurs**; the most complete, up-to-date encyclopedia for dinosaur lovers of all ages. by Dr. Thomas R. Holtz, Jr.; illustrated by Luis V. Rey. Random House 2007 427p il $34.99; lib bdg $37.99

Grades: 7 8 9 10   **567.9**

1. Dinosaurs

ISBN 978-0-375-82419-7; 0-375-82419-7; 978-0-375-92419-4 lib bdg; 0-375-92419-1 lib bdg

        LC 2006-102491

This "covers everything from dinosaur eggs to taxonomy and cladistics to the history of paleontology, glued together with chapters on the dinosaurs themselves. . . . The illustrations range from small photos to larger sepia-toned drawings to even larger full-color paintings. . . . This eye-catching imagination grabber will be enjoyed (on different levels) by dinophiles of all ages." SLJ

Includes glossary

Naish, Darren

The **great** dinosaur discoveries. University of California Press 2009 192p il map $29.95

Grades: 7 8 9 10 11 12 **567.9**
1. Fossils 2. Dinosaurs
ISBN 978-0-520-25975-1; 0-520-25975-0
LC 2009-6140
"From the fragmentary remains of giant extinct animals found in the early 1800s to the dinosaur wars in the American West to the amazing near-complete skeletons found around the world today, Darren Naish tells how these discoveries have led not only to the recognition of new species and whole new groups, but also to new theories of evolutionary history." Publisher's note
Includes glossary and bibliographical references

Parker, Steve, 1952-
★ **Dinosaurus**; the complete guide to dinosaurs. Firefly Books 2004 448p il $49.95
Grades: 9 10 11 12 **567.9**
1. Dinosaurs
ISBN 1-55297-772-2
LC 2004-299417
This is "is a must-have source for libraries where dinosaur study is an annual research unit." Voice Youth Advocates
Includes bibliographical references

Paul, Gregory S.
★ The **Princeton** field guide to dinosaurs. Princeton University Press 2010 320p il map (Princeton field guides) $35
Grades: 9 10 11 12 Adult **567.9**
1. Dinosaurs
ISBN 978-0-691-13720-9; 0-691-13720-X
LC 2010-14916
"Though not a field guide to stuff in your backpack, this exciting addition to dinosaur reference is essential for high school through university libraries and is highly recommended for all students of dinosaurs." Libr J
Includes bibliographical references

Pim, Keiron
Dinosaurs the grand tour; everything worth knowing about dinosaurs from Aardonyx to Zuniceratops. Keiron Pim with field notes by Jack Horner; illustrated by Fabio Pastori. The Experiment 2014 352 p. illustrations (some color) (hardcover) $24.95
Grades: 10 11 12 Adult **567.9**
1. Fossils 2. Dinosaurs
ISBN 9781615192120; 1615192123
LC 2014018581
This book on dinosaurs, by Keiron Pim and Jack Horner provides "a chronological survey of the group by genus/species from their first appearances in the fossil record in the Triassic through the Jurassic and their final extinction at the end of the Cretaceous. They include information on the initial and later discoveries of parts or whole skeletons and information on many famous dinosaur collectors." (Choice: Current Reviews for Academic Libraries)
"This book provides detailed analyses of more than 300 different dinosaurs, grouped by the period (Triassic, Jurassic, or Cretaceous) in which they lived. Information is provided for each dinosaur on name pronunciation, the creature's diet and weight, where bones have been found, and when it lived. . . . This is a good, inexpensive choice for those who want the most up-to-date, comprehensive information on dinosaurs, and it is suitable for school and public libraries." Booklist
Includes bibliographical references and index

Sampson, Scott D.
Dinosaur odyssey; fossil threads in the web of life. University of California Press 2009 332p il map $29.95
Grades: 11 12 Adult **567.9**
1. Fossils 2. Dinosaurs
ISBN 978-0-520-24163-3; 0-520-24163-0
LC 2009-6150
"This book draws scientifically accurate pictures in a style that is accessible to researchers and general readers alike." Libr J
Includes bibliographical references

567.91 Specific dinosaurs and other archosaurs

Switek, Brian
My beloved Brontosaurus; on the road with old bones, new science, and our favorite dinosaurs. Brian Switek. Scientific American/Farrar, Straus and Giroux 2013 272 p. (hardback) $26
Grades: 9 10 11 12 **567.91**
1. Dinosaurs 2. Paleontology 3. Popular culture 4. Apatosaurus -- Miscellanea 5. Paleontology -- Miscellanea
ISBN 0374135061; 9780374135065
LC 2012034530
In this book, author Brian Switek "explores scientists' evolving perception of the wild, wonderful dinosaur world, emphasizing . . . the dynamic nature of their field despite its now inanimate subjects." He looks at "aspects of dinosaur anatomy, phytogeny, and behavior that paleontologists have wrestled with over the years. Switek intersperses his . . . scientific and historical discussions with personal anecdotes and cultural signposts." (Science)
"Today, most readers are aware that a catastrophic mass extinction 65 million years ago wiped out the dinosaurs. In another reassessment, paleontologists now believe that only "nonavian dinosaurs" vanished. One family had already evolved into birds. Readers will forgive Switek's detours into cuteness and bad jokes in exchange for a genuinely informative introduction to his favorite subject." (Kirkus)

569 Fossil mammals

Holmes, Thom
Primates and human ancestors; the Pliocene epoch. Chelsea House 2009 158p il (The prehistoric Earth) lib bdg $35
Grades: 7 8 9 10 **569**
1. Fossils 2. Primates 3. Evolution 4. Fossil hominids
ISBN 978-0-8160-5965-2; 0-8160-5965-9
LC 2008-38328
"The book traces the evolution of early hominids in three different sections. The first section provides an overview of

evolution, tracing the history of evolutionary thought and presenting the mechanism of evolution. . . . The second section focuses on primates. . . . The last section traces the evolution of the early hominids, pinpointing the transition from ape to hominin in a clear-cut fashion. The book concludes with a look at early human ancestors, including Australopithecus afarensis." Sci Books Films

Includes glossary and bibliographical references

Lister, Adrian

★ **Mammoths**; giants of the ice age. [by] Adrian Lister and Paul Bahn; foreword by Jean M. Auel. Rev ed; University of California Press 2007 192p il $29.95

Grades: 11 12 Adult   569
1. Mammoths
ISBN 978-0-520-25319-3; 0-520-25319-1
                                        LC 2007-26369
First published 1994 by Macmillan
This book integrates "research to piece together the story of mammoths, mastodons, and their relatives, icons of the Ice Age." Publisher's note

Includes glossary and bibliographical references

569.9   Humans and related genera

Aronson, Marc

★ The **skull** in the rock; how a scientist, a boy, and Google Earth opened a new window on human origins. by Marc Aronson and Lee Berger. National Geographic 2012 64 p. (hardcover: alk. paper) $18.95

Grades: 5 6 7 8 9 10   569.9
1. Human origins 2. Fossil hominids 3. Paleoanthropology 4. Excavations (Archeology) 5. Paleoanthropology 6. Human beings -- Origin 7. Fossil hominids -- South Africa -- Witwatersrand Region 8. Human evolution -- South Africa -- Witwatersrand Region 9. Excavations (Archaeology) -- South Africa -- Witwatersrand Region
ISBN 1426310102; 9781426310102; 9781426310539
                                        LC 2012012943
This book by Marc Aronson and Lee R. Berger tells the story of how "in 2008 [Berger]--with the help of his curious 9-year-old son--discovered two remarkably well preserved, two-million-year-old fossils . . . known as 'Australopithecus sediba'; a previously unknown species of ape-like creatures that may have been a direct ancestor of modern humans." (Publisher's note)

Includes bibliographical references and index.

Fagan, Brian

Cro-Magnon; how the Ice Age gave birth to the first modern humans. [by] Brian Fagan. Bloomsbury Press 2010 295p il map $28

Grades: 9 10 11 12 Adult   569.9
1. Ice Age 2. Evolution 3. Cro-Magnons 4. Neanderthals 5. Prehistoric peoples 6. Glacial epoch

7. Cro-Magnon man 8. Human evolution
ISBN 1-59691-582-X; 978-1-59691-582-4
                                        LC 2009-25242
Fagan examines "the Ice Age, describes subsequent climate change, and characterizes the lifeways of indigenous and diminishing Neanderthal populations and the evolution and expansion of early modern humans: the [Cro-Magnons]." (Sci Books Films) Index.

Fagan examines "the Ice Age, describes subsequent climate change, and characterizes the lifeways of indigenous and diminishing Neanderthal populations and the evolution and expansion of early modern humans. . . . Fagan's vivid imagination and eloquent writing style paint a fascinating picture of the struggle to adapt to a changing climate." Sci Books Films

Includes bibliographical references

Morse, Michael A.

Neanderthals rediscovered; how modern science is rewriting their history. Dimitra Papagianni, Michael A. Morse. Thames & Hudson 2013 208 p. ill (some color), maps, port. (hardcover) $29.95

Grades: 10 11 12 Adult   569.9
1. Neanderthals 2. Human remains (Archeology) 3. Fossil hominids
ISBN 0500051771; 9780500051771
                                        LC 2013930837
This book by Dimitra Papagianni and Michael A. Morse describes how "In recent years, the common perception of the Neanderthal has been transformed thanks to new discoveries and paradigm-shattering scientific innovations. . . . Meanwhile, advances in DNA technologies have forced a reassessment of the Neanderthals' place in our own past." (Publisher's note)

"Although focused on Neanderthals, the authors set their discussion accessibly within the deeper context of the scientific study of hominid evolution generally. . . . The authors describe the differing points of view among notable paleontologists, archaeologists, and anthropologists . . . about such matters as where Homo sapiens themselves evolved, Neanderthal burials, and Neanderthal-modern human interbreeding." LJ

Sarmiento, Esteban

The **last** human; a guide to twenty-two species of extinct humans. created by G.J. Sawyer and Viktor Deak; text by Esteban Sarmiento, G.J. Sawyer, Richard Milner; with contributions by Donald C. Johanson, Meave Leakey, and Ian Tattersall. Yale University Press 2006 256p il map $45

Grades: 11 12 Adult   569.9
1. Evolution 2. Human beings 3. Fossil hominids
ISBN 978-0-300-10047-1; 0-300-10047-7
"This is fascinating stuff, not least because it drives home just how much of our knowledge about the past is based on inference." New Sci

Includes bibliographical references

Walter, Chip

Last ape standing; the seven-million year story of how and why we survived. Chip Walter. Walker & Co. 2013 240 p. $17; $26

Grades: 11 12 Adult   **569.9**

1. Evolution 2. Human origins 3. Fossil hominids 4. Human evolution 5. Primates -- Evolution

ISBN 9781620405215; 080271756X; 9780802717566
LC 2012037484

In this book, Chip Walter considers human evolution. He "argues that neotony, 'the retention of juvenile features in the adult animal,' is most responsible for differences between humans and other hominids. . . . In the end, Walter posits that the next evolutionary step might be Cyber sapiens: immortal superhuman hybrids of humans and machines." (Publishers Weekly)

"An exceptionally well-written overview of man's evolutionary history as well as an accessible guide to the underappreciated field of paleoanthropology." Booklist

Includes bibliographical references and index

570   Biology

Cracking the SAT. Biology E/M subject test. Princeton Review/Random House illustrations

Grades: 9 10 11 12   **570**

1. Scholastic Assessment Test 2. Biology -- Study and teaching 3. Colleges and universities -- Entrance requirements

Annual. First published 2005. Continues Cracking the SAT II: biology subject test.

This guide provides test-taking strategies and sample tests for the subject of biology.

A **dictionary** of biology; editor, Robert S. Hine. 7th edition Oxford University Press 2015 662 p. illustrations pbk $19.95

Grades: 9 10 11 12 Adult   **570**

1. Biology -- Dictionaries

ISBN 9780198714378; 0198714378

"With more than 5,500 clear and concise entries, it provides comprehensive coverage of biology, biophysics, and biochemistry. Over 250 new entries include terms such as Broca's area, comparative genomic hybridization, mirror neuron, and Pandoravirus. Appendices include classifications of the animal and plant kingdoms, the geological time scale, major mass extinctions of species, model organisms and their genomes, Nobel prizewinners, and a new appendix on evolution." (Publisher's note)

Life sciences before the twentieth century; biographical portraits. Everett Mendelsohn, editor. Scribner 2002 211p il (Scribner science reference series) $80

Grades: 9 10 11 12   **570**

1. Life sciences 2. Reference books 3. Scientists -- Dictionaries

ISBN 0-684-80661-4

LC 2001-32045

A collection of about 90 biographical profiles of famous anatomists, biologists, bacteriologists, biochemists, and others involved in the life sciences from ancient times through the nineteenth century

Includes bibliographical references (p.   )

Stone, Carol Leth

The **basics** of biology; Carol Leth Stone. Greenwood Press 2004 280p il (Basics of the hard sciences) $75

Grades: 9 10 11 12   **570**

1. Biology

ISBN 0-313-31786-0

LC 2004-8510

This book "offers an overview of the discipline, including its history and key concepts and principles. Chapter coverage includes ecology, evolution, genetics, body systems, and the classes of living organisms. A handful of experiments accompanies each chapter. The final section is devoted to additional open-ended experiments for assignments or personal study. . . . This overview is well suited to novice students." SLJ

Includes bibliographical references

Wilson, Edward O., 1929-

★ **Letters** to a Young Scientist; by Edward O. Wilson. Liveright 2013 256 p. $21.95

Grades: 9 10 11 12 Adult   **570**

1. Science -- Vocational guidance 2. Observation (Scientific method) 3. Science 4. Biologists -- United States -- Correspondence 5. Naturalists -- United States -- Correspondence

ISBN 0871403773; 9780871403773

LC 2012051412

In this book, author Edward O. Wilson "draws on the experiences of a long career to offer encouraging advice to those considering a life in science. . . . After a prologue in which the author assures would-be scientists of their importance in our technoscientific world, he groups 20 letters into five sections. . . . In Part II, 'The Creative Process,' Wilson discusses the nature of science, the scientific method, how scientists think creatively and what it takes to succeed." (Kirkus Reviews)

"In five thematic sections, he presents 20 "letters" (five- to ten-plus pages each) examining the scientist's role in the 21st century, the foundations and credos that remain in place, and the manner in which the field has changed...Although the title and small format may suggest the book as a gift for graduates, it ought to be on the shelves of all high school and public libraries, as well as some undergraduate collections." (Library Journal)

570.1   Philosophy and theory

Bulletproof feathers; how science uses nature's secrets to design cutting-edge technology. edited by

Robert Allen. University of Chicago Press 2010 192p il $35

Grades: 11 12 Adult 570.1

1. Robots 2. Bionics

ISBN 978-0-226-01470-8

LC 2009037097

This book "is a fascinating introduction to the field of biomimetics, or bionics. Biomimetics refers to efforts to understand the design and complexity of natural, biological systems and the application of this knowledge to achieve useful new technologies. . . . This book, beautifully illustrated with many real-world examples and explanatory diagrams, will be a joy to read for any fan of science and technology." Choice

Includes bibliographical references

Lewis, Mark J.

Classification of living organisms. Rosen Pub. 2011 80p il (Understanding genetics) lib bdg $30.60

Grades: 9 10 11 12 570.1

1. Biology -- Classification

ISBN 978-1-4358-9535-5

Describes the classification system scientists use to identify and name all living organisms, and explains how animals are categorized based on certain characteristics.

570.7 Education, research, related topics

Calhoun, Yael

Plant and animal science fair projects; revised and expanded using the scientific method. Enslow Publishers 2010 160p il lib bdg $34.60

Grades: 7 8 9 10 570.7

1. Natural history 2. Science projects 3. Science -- Experiments

ISBN 978-0-7660-3421-1 lib bdg; 0-7660-3421-6 lib bdg

LC 2009-14805

"Each volume begins with an overview of the scientific method and safety, then presents a collection of activities encouraging readers to explore central concepts in the featured fields. The activities include step-by-step instructions and helpful color diagrams, interspersed with extended coverage of scientific ideas. The "Results" sections ask questions rather than giving away the answers." (Horn Book)

570.9 History, geographic treatment, biography

★ **Notable** women in the life sciences; a biographical dictionary. edited by Benjamin F. Shearer and Barbara S. Shearer. Greenwood Press 1996 440p il $52.50

Grades: 11 12 Adult 570.9

1. Reference books 2. Women scientists -- Dictionaries

ISBN 0-313-29302-3

LC 95-25603

"Biographical entries of 97 women who have made significant contributions to the life sciences from antiquity to the present. Essays vary in length from two pages to seven

and include a biographical essay, notes, bibliography, and a photograph if available." SLJ

Yount, Lisa

Craig Venter; dissecting the genome. by Lisa Yount. Chelsea House 2011 xix, 134 p.p col. ill. (Trailblazers in science and technology) (library) $35

Grades: 7 8 9 10 11 12 570.9

1. Human genome 2. Biologists -- United States -- Biography

ISBN 1604136626; 9781604136623

LC 2010050561

This book by Lisa Yount, part of the Trailblazers in Science and Technology series, looks at scientist Craig Venter. It "details the life and accomplishments of this trailblazing scientist, describing his early days in California and military service in Vietnam, his . . . work to map the human genome, and his other numerous scientific achievements." (Publisher's note)

Includes bibliographical references and index

571 Internal biological processes and structures

Roach, Mary, 1959-

★ **Packing** for Mars; the curious science of life in the void. W.W. Norton 2010 334p il

Grades: 9 10 11 12 Adult 571

1. Space biology

ISBN 0-393-06847-1; 978-0-393-06847-4

LC 2010-17113

This book examines space travel and life without gravity. (Publisher's note)

The author "explores the organic aspects of the space program, such as the dangerous bane of space motion sickness and the challenges of space hygiene. . . . She devotes one chapter to space food and another to zero-gravity elimination, which is a serious matter, even with a term like 'fecal popcorning.' An impish and adventurous writer with a gleefully inquisitive mind and a standup comic's timing, Roach celebrates human ingenuity (the odder the better), and calls for us to marshal our resources, unchain our imaginations, and start packing for Mars." Booklist

Includes bibliographical references

Toomey, David

Weird Life; The Search for Life That Is Very, Very Different from Our Own. David Toomey. 1st ed. W W Norton & Co Inc 2013 288 p. ill pbk $15.95; (hardcover) $25.95

Grades: 11 12 Adult 571

1. Life 2. Ecology 3. Organisms 4. Life (Biology) 5. Adaptation (Biology) 6. Extreme environments 7. Life on other planets 8. Curiosities and wonders

ISBN 9780393348262; 0393071588; 9780393071580

LC 2012042391

This book looks at living organisms. The "author begins by describing 'extremophiles,' which thrive in wildly harsh conditions: chemical hot springs, inside sea ice, . . . or at the ocean's bottom. Having dealt with creatures that, however weird, exist, he proceeds to even stranger life that may exist on Earth, the planets, elsewhere throughout the universe, and in the minds of writers and philosophers. Along the way, he addresses surprisingly difficult questions, such as how to define life." (Kirkus)

"Toomey manages to make this panoply of life forms at once strange and familiar, and in doing so will entrance his readers." LJ

Includes bibliographical references and index.

571.2 Plants and microorganisms

Chamovitz, Daniel

What a plant knows; a field guide to the senses. Daniel Chamovitz. 1st ed. Scientific American/Farrar, Straus and Giroux 2012 192 p. ill (alk. paper) $23

Grades: 9 10 11 12 Adult   **571.2**
1. Botany 2. Plants 3. Plant physiology
ISBN 0374288739; 9780374288730

LC 2011040179

This book discusses "the science behind how a plant senses and adapts to its environment. . . . Plants are confined to one spot. 'Because of this,' writes the author, 'plants have evolved complex sensory and regulatory systems that allow them to modulate their growth in response to ever-changing conditions.' Through extensive research and scientific models, [Daniel] Chamovitz explains . . . how plants have somewhat human-like sensory responses to stimuli." (Kirkus Reviews)

"In a lively and delightful discourse that aligns botany with human biology, [Chamovitz] articulates his findings about plants and the senses in accessible, often whimsical observations that make complex science not only comprehensible but fun to ponder." Booklist

Includes bibliographical references and index.

571.6 Cell biology

Panno, Joseph

★ The cell; nature's first life-form. Rev. ed; Facts on File 2010 286p il (The new biology) $40

Grades: 9 10 11 12   **571.6**
1. Cells
ISBN 978-0-8160-6849-4

LC 2009-40063

First published 2004

"The book traces the development of the cell from its first appearance in the 'primordial soup' of the oceans of ancient Earth 3 million years ago, through the emergence of simple bacteria, to the rise of multicellular organisms that eventually became today's plants and animals. The author provides . . . information about the structure and function of the cell, will special emphasis on cell division and cell-to-cell communication essential to the development of multicelled creatures." Publisher's note

Includes glossary and bibliographical references

Rainis, Kenneth G.

Cell and microbe science fair projects; revised and expanded using the scientific method. Enslow Publishers 2010 160p il lib bdg $34.60

Grades: 7 8 9 10   **571.6**
1. Cells 2. Biology 3. Microbiology 4. Science projects 5. Science -- Experiments
ISBN 978-0-7660-3420-4 lib bdg; 0-7660-3420-8 lib bdg

LC 2009019374

"Each book focusing on biology will be helpful to middle school students and contains a section about the scientific method as well as experiments that are outlined to cover the experimental question, hypothesis, materials, procedures, results and conclusions." (Publisher's Note)

Wolpert, L.

How we live and why we die; the secret lives of cells. [by] Lewis Wolpert. Norton 2009 240p $24.95

Grades: 11 12 Adult   **571.6**
1. Cells
ISBN 978-0-393-07221-1

LC 2009-9718

"Including discussion of stem cells and embryonic growth, Wolpert's work will absorb anyone fascinated by the universe inside the cell." Booklist

Includes bibliographical references

571.7 Biological control and secretions

Foster, Russell G.

Rhythms of life; the biological clocks that control the daily lives of every living thing. Yale University Press 2004 276p il $30; pa $18

Grades: 11 12 Adult   **571.7**
1. Biological rhythms
ISBN 0-300-10574-6; 978-0-300-10574-2; 0-300-10969-5 pa; 978-0-300-10969-6 pa

LC 2004-105609

The authors "survey the biological clocks that dictate circadian rhythms, the daily cycles that affect creatures from cockroaches to humans. . . . Biology buffs will marvel at the fascinating material." Publ Wkly

Includes bibliographical references

572 Biochemistry

Zimmer, Marc

Bioluminescence; Nature and Science at Work. by Marc Zimmer. Twenty-First Century Books 2016 72 p. color illustrations $34.65

Grades: 6 7 8 9 10   **572**
1. Bioluminescence 2. Green fluorescent protein
ISBN 1467757845; 9781467757843

LC 2014025675

This book, by Marc Zimmer, "takes readers into the world of bioluminescence, or the production and emission of light by living creatures. After providing a brief explanation of how 19th-century physiologist Raphaël Dubois discovered that bioluminescence is a product of the enzyme luciferase and the molecule luciferin, Zimmer presents many fascinating examples of animals making use of this ability." (School Library Journal)

"Featuring top-notch photos, this succinct presentation of a complex topic will make a stimulating addition to most science collections." SLJ

Includes bibliographical references and index

572.8 Biochemical genetics

Carroll, Sean B.

★ The **making** of the fittest; DNA and the ultimate forensic record of evolution. with illustrations by Jamie W. Carroll and Leanne M. Olds. W.W. Norton & Co. 2006 301p il map $25.95

Grades: 11 12 Adult   **572.8**
    1. DNA 2. Evolution
    ISBN 978-0-393-06163-5; 0-393-06163-9
                                        LC 2006-17197
The author presents "discoveries gathered from DNA evidence that confirm Charles Darwin's theory of evolution 'beyond any reasonable doubt.' . . . Readers will gain insight into the evolutionary process and expand their knowledge of how the 'fittest' species were made, from fish that live in subfreezing water to birds that communicate via ultraviolet colors." Libr J

Includes bibliographical references

Genome science; a practical and conceptual introduction to molecular genetic analysis in eukaryotes. David A. Micklos, Uwe Hilgert, Bruce Nash. Cold Spring Harbor Laboratory Press 2013 ix, 692 p.p illustrations (hard cover: alk. paper) $55

Grades: 10 11 12 Adult   **572.8**
    1. Genetics 2. Molecular biology 3. Genomics 4. Eukaryotic cells 5. Molecular genetics
    ISBN 0879698594; 9780879698591
                                        LC 2012007495
This textbook, by David A. Micklos, Uwe Hilgert, and Bruce Nash, "combines approachable narrative with extensively tested lab exercises that integrate key concepts of genome biology in humans, plants, and invertebrates. Each stand-alone lab merges bioinformatics methods with molecular technologies. The labs are organized into units, each with an introduction providing an historical and conceptual framework." (Publisher's note)

Includes bibliographical references and index

Rose, Hilary

Genes, cells, and brains; the Promethean promises of the new biology. Hilary and Steven Rose. Verso 2013 336 p.

Grades: 9 10 11 12 Adult   **572.8**
    1. Bioethics 2. Biotechnology 3. Genomics
    4. Bioethical Issues 5. Computational Biology
    6. Regenerative Medicine 7. Neurotechnology

(Bioengineering)
    ISBN 9781844678815; 9781844679171
                                        LC 2012029597
In this book, " feminist sociologist Hilary Rose and neuroscientist Steven Rose take on the bioscience industry and its claims. Examining the establishment of biobanks, the rivalries between public and private genesequencers, and the rise of stem cell research, they ask why the promised cornucopia of health benefits has failed to emerge and reveal the questionable enterprise that has grown out of bioethics." (Publisher's note)

"Although biotechnology has become a multibillion dollar business, the actual benefits to individuals have been surprisingly rare, according to the Roses (Alas Poor Darwin), she a sociologist and he a biologist in England... They offer both scientific and sociological explanations for the lack of results...Some will find this argument powerful, others strident, but many will find much to consider." (Publishers Weekly)

Includes bibliographical references and index

Segrè, Gino

Ordinary geniuses; Max Delbruck, George Gamow, and the origins of genomics and big bang cosmology. Gino Segrè. Viking 2011 xxi, 330 p.p $27.95

Grades: 11 12 Adult   **572.8**
    1. Physicists -- United States -- Biography 2. Molecular biologists -- United States -- Biography
    ISBN 9780670022762; 0670022764
                                        LC 2011009309
The author "explores the extraordinary lives and scientific accomplishments of two far-from-ordinary men, Max Delbrück and George Gamow. . . . An exuberant dual biography that integrates developments in quantum physics, cosmology and genetics since the 1920s with the lives of these two scientists." Kirkus

Includes bibliographical references (p. 309-318) and index

Takemura, Masaharu

★ The **manga** guide to molecular biology; [by] Masaharu Takemura, Sakura, Becom Co., Ltd. No Starch Press 2009 225p il pa $19.95

Grades: 9 10 11 12   **572.8**
    1. Manga 2. Graphic novels 3. Molecular biology -- Graphic novels
    ISBN 978-1-59327-202-9; 1-59327-202-2
                                        LC 2009-25876
"Rin and Ami have been skipping molecular biology class all semester, and Professor Moro has had enough—he's sentencing them to summer school on his private island. But they're in store for a special lesson. Using Dr. Moro's virtual reality machine to travel inside the human body, they'll get a closeup look at the . . . world of molecular biology. . . . [This guide follows them as they learn] all about DNA, RNA, proteins, amino acids, and more." Publisher's note

Watson, James D., 1928-

The **annotated** and illustrated double helix; James D. Watson; edited by Alexander Gann & Jan

Witkowski. Simon & Schuster 2012 345 p. (hardcover) $30

Grades: 11 12 Adult   **572.8**

1. DNA 2. Genetic Code 3. Molecular Biology
ISBN 1476715491; 9781476715490; 9781476715506; 9781476715513

LC 2012037483

This book, by James D. Watson, Alexander Gann and Jan Witkowski, was "published to mark the 50th anniversary of the Nobel Prize for Watson and Crick's discovery of the structure of DNA, an annotated and illustrated edition of . . . his 1968 memoir, 'The Double Helix,' the brash young scientist James Watson chronicled the drama of the race to identify the structure of DNA, a discovery that would usher in the era of modern molecular biology." (Publisher's note)

"Numerous appendices include a chapter about his Nobel Prize experiences, the first letters about the double helix, a previously unpublished chapter, and reviews of the original edition. Watson strikes a balance between science for the layman and science for the scientist, resulting in a memoir that will hold the interest of a broad, scientifically-minded audience." Pub Wkly

Includes bibliographical references and index

Yount, Lisa

Rosalind Franklin; photographing biomolecules. by Lisa Yount. Chelsea House 2011 xix, 125 p.p col. ill. (Trailblazers in science and technology) (library) $35.00

Grades: 7 8 9 10 11 12   **572.8**

1. Women scientists 2. DNA -- History 3. Molecular biologists -- Great Britain -- Biography
ISBN 160413660X; 9781604136609

LC 2010048229

This book by Lisa Yount is part of the Trailblazers in Science and Technology series and looks at Rosalind Franklin. "Tracing her life from her birth in Great Britain to her education at Cambridge, to her groundbreaking research [in X-ray crystallography], and to her tragic and untimely death," this book offers an "overview of the life and career of one of the most influential scientific figures of the 20th century." (Publisher's note)

Includes bibliographical references and index.

573   Specific physiological systems in animals, regional histology and physiology in animals

Morell, Virginia

Ancestral passions; the Leakey family and the quest for humankind's beginnings. Simon & Schuster 1995 638p il hardcover o.p. pa $28.95

Grades: 11 12 Adult   **573**

1. Human origins 2. Anthropologists 3. Archaeologists 4. Paleontologists 5. Government officials 6. Museum administrators
ISBN 0-684-82470-1 pa

LC 95-14306

"The Leakey family, now in its third generation of hunting hominid fossils in East Africa, is the subject of this exquisitely written biography about the search for the begin-

nings of humankind. . . . With access to volumes of personal and professional papers and extensive interviews with Mary, Richard, and Meave Leakey, as well as many others who played a role in the story of human origins, Virginia Morell has allowed the reader to gain unparalleled insight into the oftentimes complex lives of the world's 'first family of human evolution.'" Sci Books Films

Includes bibliographical references

576   General and external biological phenomena

Gardner, Robert

Genetics and evolution science fair projects; revised and expanded using the scientific method. Enslow Publishers 2010 160p il lib bdg $34.60

Grades: 7 8 9 10   **576**

1. Genetics 2. Evolution 3. Science projects 4. Science -- Experiments
ISBN 978-0-7660-3422-8 lib bdg; 0-7660-3422-4 lib bdg

LC 2009-14803

"Each volume begins with an overview of the scientific method and safety, then presents a collection of activities encouraging readers to explore central concepts in the featured fields. The activities include step-by-step instructions and helpful color diagrams, interspersed with extended coverage of scientific ideas. The "Results" sections ask questions rather than giving away the answers." (Horn Book)

Rainis, Kenneth G.

A guide to microlife; {by} Kenneth G. Rainis and Bruce J. Russell. Watts 1996 287p il lib bdg $40

Grades: 9 10 11 12   **576**

1. Microbiology 2. Microorganisms
ISBN 0-531-11266-7

LC 95-44973

Serves as a guide to be used for the identification of microorganisms and provides information about microlife forms and how they affect other life forms, including human

"A good resource for classrooms, this colorful volume is packed with information." SLJ

Includes bibliographical references

Schutten, Jan Paul

The mystery of life; how nothing became everything. Jan Paul Schutten; illustrated by Floor Rieder; translated by Laura Watkinson. Aladdin" "Beyond Word 2015 240 p. color illustrations (hardcover) $15.99

Grades: 7 8 9 10   **576**

1. Evolution 2. Life (Biology) 3. Life -- Origin 4. Discoveries in science 5. Evolution
ISBN 9781582705255

LC 2014039916

In this book, originally published in the Netherlands, author Jan Paul Schutten "looks into the miracle of life, whether the specimen in question is a microscopic bacterium or an invented sample human, 'Joe Schmo from Buffalo,' exploring the age of the planet, natural selection, and the development of life on Earth along the way." (Publishers Weekly)

"Though his discussion of hiccups is blurred by fuzzy logic, and virus es and extinction events rate barely a mention, his overall account of life's origins and tenure is as rich in detail as it is entertaining. Rieder likewise supplies a flood of line drawings that provide humorous visual commentary as well as additional information.A glib and occasionally spotty picture but eminently readable and generally on target." Kirkus

Includes bibliographical references and index

576.5   Genetics

Day, Trevor
  Genetics; investigating the function of genes and the science of heredity. Trevor Day. 1st ed. Rosen Central 2013 48 p. ill. (chiefly col.) (Scientific pathways) (library) $29.25
  Grades: 6 7 8 9   576.5
  1. Genetics 2. Scientists 3. Heredity
  ISBN 1448871999; 9781448871995
                                              LC 2011047887
  This book by Trevor Day is part of the Scientific Pathways series and looks at genetics. The series authors "look at science as a process of discovery and explain how each discipline developed in different cultures over time. Significant names and important terms are printed in bold . . . . Brief biographies of thinkers, inventors, and scientists are provided along with important experiments and the conclusions that were made in relation to them." (School Library Journal)
  Includes bibliographical references and index.

Endersby, Jim
  A **guinea** pig's history of biology. Harvard University Press 2007 499p il $27.95; pa $18.95
  Grades: 11 12 Adult   576.5
  1. Genetics 2. Heredity 3. Biology -- History
  ISBN 978-0-674-02713-8; 0-674-02713-2; 978-0-674-03227-9 pa; 0-674-03227-6 pa
                                              LC 2007-20824
  "This book would be of interest to anyone fascinated or intrigued by genetics or biological research, as well as any professional or lay student of history and science." Sci Books Films
  Includes bibliographical references

Hand, Carol
  Introduction to genetics. Rosen Pub. 2010 80p il (Understanding genetics) lib bdg $30.60
  Grades: 6 7 8 9 10 11 12   576.5
  1. Genetics 2. Heredity
  ISBN 978-1-4358-9531-7
                                              LC 2009-40364
  Provides an introduction to genetics, including information on the Punnett Square, inheritance patterns and alleles, mitosis, and gene mapping.
  "The moderately technical language in the other titles discusses significant discoveries, current directions in research and—superficially—ethical and other issues. Illustrations include helpful charts, microphotos, portraits of scientists, and color photos; extensive back matter provides plenty of support for further research." SLJ

Mooney, Carla
  Genetics; Breaking the Code of Your DNA. by Carla Mooney; illustrated by Samuel Carbaugh. Nomad Press 2014 128 p. illustrations (Inquire and Investigate) $21.95
  Grades: 6 7 8 9 10 11   576.5
  1. Genetics 2. DNA 3. Genes
  ISBN 161930208X; 9781619302082
  This book on genetics, by Carla Mooney, illustrated by Samuel Carbaugh, "presents the main concepts of the science, including what a chromosome does, how DNA is structured, and how genetic inheritance works. Students learn about new discoveries in the field of genetics and how those discoveries have helped to cure or even prevent certain diseases, as well as examine controversial issues in genetics such as genetically modified foods and stem cell research." (Publisher's note)
  "Although the book can be used independently, it will be better appreciated with some background knowledge. A solid resource that shows life science and biology students the practicalities and marvels of genetics." Booklist

New thinking about genetics; edited by Kara Rogers. Britannica Educational Pub. in association with Rosen Educational Services 2010 274p il (21st century science) lib bdg $45
  Grades: 9 10 11 12   576.5
  1. Genetics
  ISBN 978-1-61530-104-1
                                              LC 2009-44215
  This book introduces "the science of genetics as well as detailing the controversies and implications for future studies." Publisher's note
  Includes bibliographical references

Schultz, Mark
  ★ The **stuff** of life; a graphic guide to genetics and DNA. written by Mark Schultz; art by Zander Cannon and Kevin Cannon. Hill and Wang 2009 150p il $30; pa $14.95
  Grades: 9 10 11 12 Adult   576.5
  1. Graphic novels 2. Genetics -- Graphic novels
  ISBN 978-0-8090-8946-8; 978-0-8090-8947-5 pa
  Eisner and Harvey Award winning writer Schultz uses the device of an alien writing a report to describe genetics and DNA in five chapters, from molecular structure of Earth organisms to sexual reproduction to genetic inheritance to genetic counseling and the genome Project and beyond. The black and white cartoons add some humor to the sound information, and the book includes a list of suggested reading ranging from magazines and books to websites, along with a glossary of terms.
  Includes bibliographical references

Yount, Lisa
  Modern genetics; engineering life. rev ed.; Facts on File 2006 204p il map (Milestones in discovery and invention) $35

Grades: 7 8 9 10 11 12 **576.5**
1. Genetics 2. Genetic engineering
ISBN 0-8160-5744-3; 978-0-8160-5744-3

LC 2005-18152

First published 1997 with title: Genetics and genetic engineering

This book "profiles 14 men and women who were among the leaders in making important genetic discoveries in research and new technologies. Profiles include James Watson, Francis Crick, Herbert Boyer, Stanley N. Cohen, Michael Bishop, and Harold Varmus." Publisher's note

Includes glossary and bibliographical references

576.8 Evolution

Angelo, Joseph A.
Life in the universe. Facts on File 2007 338p il (Frontiers in space) $39.50
Grades: 9 10 11 12 **576.8**
1. Space biology 2. Life on other planets 3. Outer space -- Exploration
ISBN 0-8160-5776-1; 978-0-8160-5776-4

LC 2006-34860

"This volume prepares readers for some of the revelations that space technology may yield this century by discussing the historic events, scientific principles, and technical developments that allow sophisticated robot exploring machines to visit faraway worlds in the solar system as they hunt for signs of life—existent or extinct." Publisher's note

Includes glossary and bibliographical references

Bennett, Jeffrey O.
Beyond UFOs; the search for extraterrestrial life and its astonishing implications for our future. [by] Jeffrey Bennett. Princeton University Press 2008 211p il $26.95
Grades: 11 12 Adult **576.8**
1. Space biology 2. Life on other planets 3. Life -- Origin
ISBN 978-0-691-13549-6; 0-691-13549-5

LC 2007-37872

"The writing style is like that of a fireside chat with an expert in the field: an easy read, but thought provoking." Sci Books Films

Darwin, Charles
★ The **Darwin** reader; edited by Mark Ridley. 2nd ed; Norton 1996 315p il pa $21.30
Grades: 11 12 Adult **576.8**
1. Evolution 2. Natural selection
ISBN 0-393-96967-3

LC 95-50297

First published in the United Kingdom with title: The essential Darwin; first Norton edition published 1987

This collection presents excerpts from Darwin's most important works including Origin of the species, The descent of man and Coral reef. Illustrations are taken from the original editions

Includes bibliographical references

★ **On** the origin of species; David Quammen, general editor. Illustrated ed.; Sterling Pub. 2008 544p il $35
Grades: 10 11 12 Adult **576.8**
1. Heredity 2. Evolution 3. Human origins 4. Natural selection
ISBN 978-1-4027-5639-9

LC 2008-6902

Illustrated edition of the book first published 1859 with title: The origin of species by means of natural selection

"As a milestone not only in the history of science but also in cultural history, On the Origin of Species belongs in every library, high school and above. . . . [Quammen] offers a gloriously illustrated and richly annotated volume, which testifies to the book's enduring legacy. Throughout the text, relevant sidebars from other of Darwin's writings, including his Autobiography, field notes from the HMS Beagle, and his myriad letters, are presented for their insight. Illustrations include historical images, such as sketches, woodcuts, and portraits of people and places, but also included are contemporary photographs of the flora and fauna that Darwin described." Libr J

Includes bibliographical references

Davies, P. C. W.
The **eerie** silence; renewing our search for alien intelligence. [by] Paul Davies. Houghton Mifflin Harcourt 2010 241p il $27
Grades: 11 12 Adult **576.8**
1. Life on other planets 2. Extraterrestrial beings 3. Unidentified flying objects
ISBN 978-0-547-13324-9; 0-547-13324-3

LC 2010-3088

"After 50 years of scanning the skies for signs of extraterrestrial intelligence, astronomers have only silence to report — an eerie silence, Davies argues. Part history of the search, part road map for its future and (large) part mind-stretching exercise, the book provides Davies' perspective on profound questions that have implications far beyond alien hunting." Sci News

Includes bibliographical references

Evolution; Don Nardo, book editor. Greenhaven Press 2005 240p il (History of issues) lib bdg $34.95; pa $23.70
Grades: 9 10 11 12 **576.8**
1. Evolution
ISBN 0-7377-2098-0 lib bdg; 0-7377-2099-9 pa

LC 2004-47481

"In this volume, scientists, religious leaders, and others square off in pairs of pro and con essays. Topics include: the nineteenth-century controversy over evolution, modern advances in evolutionary theory, and the debate over teaching evolution in schools." Publisher's note

Includes bibliographical references

Hodge, Russ
Evolution; the history of life on earth. [by] Russ Hodge; foreword by Nadia Rosenthal. Facts On File 2009 252p il (Genetics & evolution) $39.50

Grades: 9 10 11 12 **576.8**
1. Evolution
ISBN 978-0-8160-6679-7; 0-8160-6679-5
LC 2008-29741

This book describes the "impact evolution has had on society and on modern medicine—including the birth of genetic science in the early 1900s and the discovery that genes were made of DNA in the 1950s." Publisher's note

Includes glossary and bibliographical references

Holmes, Thom
Evolution. Chelsea House 2010 109p il lib bdg $35
Grades: 7 8 9 10 **576.8**
1. Evolution
ISBN 978-1-60413-338-7; 1-60413-338-4
LC 2010015738

"A solid, competent history of the evolution of ideas and the theory of evolution itself. . . . Certainly not for browsing or easy light reading, but definitely of use to teachers or serious researchers." (School Library Journal)

Johnson, Sylvia A.
★ **Shaking** the foundation; Charles Darwin and the theory of evolution. by Sylvia A. Johnson. Twenty-First Century Books 2013 88 p. (library) $33.27
Grades: 6 7 8 9 **576.8**
1. Evolution
ISBN 0761354867; 9780761354864
LC 2012018075

This book offers an "overview of how [Charles] Darwin's theories of natural selection and evolution shook the foundations of religious beliefs and long-held scientific views. . . .[Sylvia A.] Johnson devotes the first half of her book to discussing the intellectual, philosophical and societal changes brought by the Enlightenment and Industrial Revolution that would make people receptive to Darwin's ideas. . . . The second half chronicles how Darwin formulated his theories." (Kirkus Reviews)

"In this thoughtful history of both Darwin and his theories of evolution, Johnson explains how the scientist lived and worked, religious and scientific challenges to his theories, and American legal challenges to evolution that continue in contemporary times. Numerous historical photographs and scientific illustrations, many from scientists of his time, greatly enhance the text." (Horn Book)

Includes bibliographical references and index

Kaufman, Marc
First contact; scientific breakthroughs in the hunt for life beyond Earth. Simon & Schuster 2011 213p il $26; ebook $12.99
Grades: 11 12 Adult **576.8**
1. Life on other planets
ISBN 978-1-4391-0900-7; 978-1-4391-3030-8 ebook
LC 2010-44630

Kaufman "takes us from beneath the surface of our planet, where scientists hunt for and study 'extremophile' microbes that alter our views of what is necessary for life to exist, to observatories and labs searching deep space for extraterrestrial signals or exoplanets, planets outside the solar system. Not only does the book suggest the breadth of the

effort, it reveals how each aspect reveals ideas and science never before suspected. . . . [The author] does what excellent science reporters do—he translates at times difficult concepts into language those of us who barely passed 'Bonehead Chemistry' can understand." Seattle Post-Intelligencer

Includes bibliographical references

Keller, Michael
★ **Charles** Darwin's On the Origin of Species; a graphic adaptation. [by] Michael Keller; art by Nicolle Rager Fuller. Rodale 2009 192p il $19.99; pa $14.99
Grades: 9 10 11 12 Adult **576.8**
1. Naturalists 2. Graphic novels 3. Travel writers 4. Writers on science 5. Heredity -- Graphic novels 6. Evolution -- Graphic novels 7. Human origins -- Graphic novels 8. Natural selection -- Graphic novels
ISBN 978-1-60529-697-5; 1-60529-697-X; 978-1-60529-948-8 pa; 1-60529-948-0 pa
LC 2009-11387

"The graphic novel follows Origin's original chapters, combining snippets of Darwin's text with quotes from letters, illustrative examples from his time and from the present, and occasional invented dialog. Fuller's images of people seem clumsy, but her full-color plants, animals, charts, maps, and scientific accoutrements are attractive and effective. . . . [This] version well conveys both the science and the wonder of Origin." Libr J

Kolbert, Elizabeth
★ **The sixth** extinction; an unnatural history. Elizabeth Kolbert. First edition. Henry Holt and Co 2014 336 p. illustrations, map (hardback) $28
Grades: 9 10 11 12 Adult **576.8**
1. Extinction (Biology) 2. Environmental degradation 3. Human influence on nature 4. Mass extinctions 5. Environmental disasters
ISBN 0805092994; 9780805092998
LC 2013028683

Pulitzer Prize: General Nonfiction (2015)
Carnegie Medal Shortlist: Nonfiction (2015)
Los Angeles Times Book Prize: Science and Technology

"In 'The Sixth Extinction,' [author] Elizabeth Kolbert draws on the work of scores of researchers in half a dozen disciplines, accompanying many of them into the field: geologists who study deep ocean cores, botanists who follow the tree line as it climbs up the Andes, marine biologists who dive off the Great Barrier Reef. She introduces us to a dozen species, some already gone, others facing extinction." (Publisher's note)

"Kolbert . . . weaves a relatable element into the at-times heavily scientific discussion, bringing the sites of past and present extinctions vividly to life with fascinating information that will linger with readers long after they close the book. A highly significant eye-opener rich in facts and enjoyment." Kirkus

Includes bibliographical references and index

Lew, Kristi
Evolution; the adaptation and survival of species. Rosen Pub. 2010 80p il (Understanding genetics) lib bdg $30.60

Grades: 9 10 11 12   **576.8**
1. Evolution
ISBN 978-1-4358-9534-8

LC 2009-46684

Discusses early theories of evolution, the work of Darwin, fossil and other evidence, and the effects of evolution on humans and the future.

Milner, Richard

Darwin's universe; evolution from A to Z. with a foreword by Ian Tattersall and a preface by Stephen Jay Gould. University of California Press 2009 487p il $39.95

Grades: 11 12 Adult   **576.8**
1. Naturalists 2. Reference books 3. Travel writers 4. Writers on science 5. Evolution -- Encyclopedias
ISBN 978-0-520-24376-7

LC 2008-35575

This encyclopedia "presents unusual details about Darwin's life and his famous theory. Entries range from the evolution of social behavior to the Creationist Museum, where dinosaurs are the contemporaries of humans. The style of writing is appropriate for a high-school or college audience, and the book is nicely illustrated and well laid out." Booklist

Includes bibliographical references

Switek, Brian

Written in stone; evolution, the fossil record and our place in nature. Brian Switek. 1st ed. Bellevue Literary Press 2010 320p il pa $17.95

Grades: 9 10 11 12 Adult   **576.8**
1. Fossils 2. Evolution 3. Fossil hominids 4. Human evolution
ISBN 1-934137-29-4 pa; 978-1-934137-29-1 pa

This is a "history of evolutionary discovery." (Publisher's note) Index

Young, Christian C.

Evolution and creationism; a documentary and reference guide. [by] Christian C. Young and Mark A. Largent. Greenwood Press 2007 298p il $85

Grades: 11 12 Adult   **576.8**
1. Evolution 2. Creationism
ISBN 978-0-313-33953-0; 0-313-33953-8

LC 2007-10682

"This reference work provides over 40 of the most important documents to help readers understand the [evolution versus creationism] debate in the eyes of the people of the time. Each document is from a major participant in the debates from the predecessors of Darwin to the judges of the influential court cases of the present day." Publisher's note

Includes bibliographical references

577 Ecology

Agosta, William C.

Thieves, deceivers, and killers; tales of chemistry in nature. {by} William Agosta. Princeton Univ. Press 2001 241p $26.95; pa $16.95

Grades: 11 12 Adult   **577**
1. Ecology 2. Animal communication
ISBN 0-691-00488-9; 0-691-09273-7 pa

LC 00-32627

The author "discusses chemical substances used for protection or communications in plants and animals and how these substances have found use as bactericides, repellents, and medicinals. This small book contains many detailed and fascinating descriptions of interspecies interactions and how nature uses chemical substances for communications, defense, and offense in the world of microbes, insects, and mammals." Choice

Includes bibliographical references (p.)

Roston, Eric

The **carbon** age; how life's core element has become civilization's greatest threat. Distributed to the trade by Macmillan 2008 309p il $25.99

Grades: 11 12 Adult   **577**
1. Carbon 2. Atmosphere
ISBN 978-0-8027-1557-9; 0-8027-1557-5

LC 2008-2754

"The first half traces carbon's history from the beginning of the universe, the Big Bang, and the nucleosynthesis (the formation of the elements) through the life cycle of stars, and then covers the development of life and dynamics of the 'natural' carbon cycle of Earth. The second section spans the last 150 years and delves into the impact of humans on the climate in creating what Roston calls the 'industrial carbon cycle.' Without using a great deal of scientific jargon, Roston leads us patiently and clearly through this complex issue." Libr J

Includes bibliographical references

Shaw, Daniel

Eco-tracking; on the trail of habitat change. with photographs by Melanie Keithley, Jon Livingston MacLake, and the author. University of New Mexico Press 2010 85p il (Worlds of wonder) $19.95

Grades: 6 7 8 9 10   **577**
1. Ecology 2. Environmental protection
ISBN 978-0-8263-4531-8; 0-8263-4531-X

LC 2010010319

"The authors tackle environmental issues with depth and rigor, attuned to both current events and the concerns of today's teens. Global Warming and Powering look at the science and human impact of climate change and alternative energies, while Eco-tracking encourages citizen-science investigation for young environmentalists. The excellent texts are enhanced by color photographs and diagrams that further explain scientific ideas. " (Horn Book)

Includes glossary

Stolzenberg, William

Where the wild things were; life, death, and ecological wreckage in a land of vanishing predators. Bloomsbury 2008 291p $24.99; $24.99

Grades: 11 12 Adult   **577**
1. Ecology 2. Predatory animals 3. Endangered species
ISBN 9781596912991; 978-1-59691-299-1; 1-59691-299-5

LC 2008-2392

A look at how the disappearance of the world's great predators has upset the delicate balance of the environment, and what their disappearance portends for the future.

This "is one of those rare books that provide not just an enriching story, but a new, clarifying lens through which to understand the world around us." Christ Sci Monit

Includes bibliographical references

577.2   Specific factors affecting ecology

Casper, Julie Kerr

Changing ecosystems; effects of global warming. Facts on File 2010 254p il map (Global warming) $40

Grades: 9 10 11 12   577.2
1. Ecology 2. Greenhouse effect
ISBN 978-0-8160-7263-7; 0-8160-7263-9
LC 2009-1411

In this book on global warming, the author examines "boreal and tropical forests, grasslands, deserts, mountains, and Arctic and marine environments. Within each section, specific problems such as drought, fire, and the extermination of species are considered, as is the resulting economic impact. The concluding chapter addresses the possibility of adaptation by animal species and vegetation and the need for decisions by qualified policy makers working in conjunction with knowledgeable scientists." SLJ

Includes glossary and bibliographical references

Montaigne, Fen

Fraser's penguins; a journey to the future in Antarctica. Henry Holt and Co. 2010 288p il map $26

Grades: 11 12 Adult   577.2
1. Penguins 2. Human influence on nature 3. Ecologists
4. Climate -- Environmental aspects 5. Antarctica --
Description and travel
ISBN 978-0-8050-7942-5; 0-8050-7942-4
LC 2010-07151

The author "spent five months tracking penguins through the breeding season on the northwestern Antarctica peninsula with the scientist Bill Fraser, and his book is a bittersweet account of the stark beauty of the continent and the climate change that threatens its delicate ecosystem. . . . Montaigne poetically portrays the daunting Antarctic landscape and gives readers an intimate perspective on its rugged, audacious, and charming penguin and human inhabitants." Publ Wkly

Includes bibliographical references

577.3   Ecology of specific environments

Allaby, Michael

Temperate forests; illustrations by Richard Garratt. rev ed; Facts on File 2008 336p il map (Ecosystem) $70

Grades: 7 8 9 10   577.3
1. Forest ecology 2. Forests and forestry
ISBN 0-8160-5930-6; 978-0-8160-5930-0
LC 2006-28859

First published 1999

"Those who are curious about or who are studying the environment and ecosystems . . . will find this book both fascinating and enlightening." Sci Books Films

Includes glossary and bibliographical references

Forsyth, Adrian

Nature of the rainforest; Costa Rica and beyond. photographs by Michael Fogden and Patricia Fogden; foreword by E.O. Wilson. Comstock Pub. Associates 2008 183p il pa $29.95

Grades: 11 12 Adult   577.3
1. Rain forest ecology
ISBN 978-0-8014-7475-0; 0-8014-7475-2
LC 2008-19291

First published 1990 by Camden House (Camden East) with title: Portraits of the rainforest

"There are 17 sections, plus a foreword by E. O. Wilson and a preface. Each section explores either a specific theme or a particular tropical place in Costa Rica (Guanacaste, Monteverde, Osa) or 'beyond' (Amazônia). The themes expore such topics as diversity, nutrient cycles in the tropics, and chemical defenses. . . . Although the book is so clearly and cleverly written that a layperson will easily enjoy it . . . an experienced tropical ecologist can read it and gain new insights. . . . This is an excellent book; come for the pictures and stay for the text!" Sci Books Films

Includes bibliographical references

Moore, Peter D.

Tropical forests; illustrations by Richard Garratt. Facts On File 2008 xx, 246p il map (Ecosystem) $70

Grades: 7 8 9 10   577.3
1. Rain forest ecology 2. Forests and forestry
ISBN 0-8160-5934-9; 978-0-8160-5934-8
LC 2006-37441

This book "explores the great biodiversity of [tropical] forests, from microbes to mammals, as well as the adaptations of organisms to their environment and to the other species surrounding them. The interactions between organisms and their physical surroundings are examined, as are the processes linking the two into an integrated ecosystem." Publisher's note

Includes glossary and bibliographical references

Preston, Richard

The wild trees; a story of passion and daring. Random House 2007 294p il map $25.95; pa $16

Grades: 11 12 Adult   577.3
1. Redwood 2. Botanists 3. College teachers
ISBN 978-1-4000-6489-2; 1-4000-6489-9; 978-0-8129-7559-8 pa; 0-8129-7559-6 pa
LC 2006-48646

The author tells the story of Steve Sillett, Marie Antoine and other naturalists and researchers who climb and explore giant redwoods in northern California

"There is something so elementally boyish in searching out the biggest and tallest, poring over maps and measurements, dubbing these trees with names lifted from J.R.R. Tolkein's Middle Earth. . . . Preston knows how to fold the science into the seams of his narrative, and his dry humor

crops up, pleasurably, at the edges of his observations."
Cleveland Plain Dealer

577.34   Rain forest ecology

Lowman, Margaret

Life in the treetops; adventures of a woman in
field biology. [by] Margaret D. Lowman. Yale Univ.
Press 1999 219p il maps hardcover o.p. pa $13.95
Grades: 11 12 Adult   **577.34**

  1. Botanists 2. Women scientists
  ISBN 0-300-07818-8; 978-0-300-07818-3; 0-300-
  08464-1 pa; 978-0-300-08464-1 pa

                  LC 98-48691

Lowman "gives a funny, unassuming and deeply idiosyncratic chronicle of her trials and triumphs as a field biologist of tree canopies and other ecosystems in Australia,
New England, Belize, Panama and elsewhere." N Y Times
Book Rev

  Includes bibliographical references

  Followed by It's a jungle up there! (2006)

577.4   Grassland ecology

Hoare, Ben

Temperate grasslands; Ben Hoare. Raintree
2011 64 p. col. ill., col. maps (Biomes atlases) (library) $34.00
Grades: 6 7 8 9   **577.4**

  1. Prairies 2. Grasslands 3. Prairie animals 4. Prairie
  ecology 5. Grassland ecology
  ISBN 143294181X; 9781432941819

              LC 2010013034

This book, by Ben Hoare, is part of the publisher's
"Biomes Atlases" nonfiction series. "Untouched temperate
grasslands can be hard to find, since the fertile soil is often
converted to farmland." This book presents a profile of the
wild flora and fauna which does exist in these areas. (Publisher's note)

"Each volume opens with a colorful world map featuring the eleven biomes of the world; individual books then
diverge into a specific biome. Five topics are covered in each
book: climate, plants, animals, people, and future of the biome. Each of these main sections is separated by a two-page
layout featuring a specific example of the region...While the
majority of the information is available online, students will
enjoy learning with these books much more than an electronic search." (Library Media Connection)

  Includes bibliographical references (p. 63) and index.

577.5   Ecology of miscellaneous environments

Allaby, Michael

  ★ **Deserts**; illustrations by Richard Garratt. rev
ed; Facts on File 2008 320p il map (Ecosystem)
$70

Grades: 7 8 9 10   **577.5**

  1. Deserts 2. Desert ecology
  ISBN 0-8160-5929-2; 978-0-8160-5929-4

              LC 2007-00477

First published 2001

"This book is a good mix of text, excellent maps, photographs, and scientific information." Sci Books Films

  Includes glossary and bibliographical references

Fothergill, Alastair

Frozen planet; a world beyond imagination.
Alastair Fothergill and Vanessa Berlowitz; foreword
by David Attenborough. BBC Books 2011 312 p
col. ill., maps $39.95
Grades: 9 10 11 12 Adult   **577.5**

  1. Polar regions
  ISBN 9781554079919

              LC 2012360040

This book "opens with an introduction by David Attenborough. This is followed by a section which contrasts the
conditions in the two Polar regions and the different kinds
of wildlife. The main portion of the book consists of four
chapters which follow the change of seasons and how wildlife copes with these changes. This is followed by a section
which recounts the experiences of the people who spent four
years in the Polar regions making the photographs and films
used in the book." (SB&F: Your Guide to Science Resources
for All Ages)

"This companion piece to the Frozen Planet documentary includes dozens of stunning photographs, a seasonal
exploration of the frozen climes, and a section detailing the
production of the show and the book. Fans of the series or
nature documentaries in general will find this tome enthralling as an educational text and as a stunning collection of
images." Pub Wkly

Gritzner, Charles F.

Deserts. Chelsea House 2006 127p il map (Geography of extreme environments) lib bdg $24.95
Grades: 9 10 11 12   **577.5**

  1. Deserts
  ISBN 0-7910-9234-8; 978-0-7910-9234-7

              LC 2006-25584

This book on deserts discusses desert weather and climate, geography, the ecosystem, the native cultures that live
there, and future prospects for the people that live there.

  Includes bibliographical references

Swan, Robert

Antarctica 2041; my quest to save the earth's
last wilderness. [by] Robert Swan with Gil Reavill.
Broadway Books 2009 290p il map $24.99
Grades: 11 12 Adult   **577.5**

  1. Environmental protection 2. Antarctica -- Description
  and travel
  ISBN 978-0-7679-3175-5

              LC 2009-10963

The author, "the first person to walk to both the North
and South Poles, combines adventure and environmentalism
in this thoughtful consideration of Antarctica. His lifelong
admiration for Robert Scott inspired him to follow in the
explorer's footsteps. . . . This is a man with a mission, and

his story is the sort to make you get up and do something— maybe even try to save the world." Booklist

Includes bibliographical references

577.7 Marine ecology

Carson, Rachel

The **edge** of the sea; with illustrations by Bob Hines. Houghton Mifflin 1955 276p il hardcover o.p. pa $14

Grades: 7 8 9 10 11 12 Adult   577.7
1. Seashore 2. Marine biology
ISBN 0-395-92496-0 pa

"The seashores of the world may be divided into three basic types: the rugged shores of rock, the sand beaches, and the coral reefs and all their associated features. Each has its typical community of plants and animals. The Atlantic coast of the United States [provides] clear examples of each of these types. I have chosen it as the setting for my pictures of shore life." Preface

Ellis, Richard

★ The **empty** ocean; plundering the world's marine life. written and illustrated by Richard Ellis. Island Press 2003 367p il hardcover o.p. pa $25; pa $37.50

Grades: 11 12 Adult   577.7
1. Marine ecology 2. Endangered species
ISBN 1-55963-974-1; 1-55963-637-8 pa;
9781559636377

"Rather than writing the 'Silent Spring' of the oceans, [Ellis] has produced a book that is likely to provide the inspiration and source materials for such a badly needed work . . . It is also a splendid example of history illuminating ecology, with well-chosen facts that enable us to picture a largely invisible catastrophe." N Y Times Book Rev

Includes bibliographical references

O'Neill, Michael Patrick

Wild waters photo journal. Batfish Books 2010 106p il $29.95

Grades: 6 7 8 9 10   577.7
1. Marine animals 2. Marine ecology
ISBN 978-0-9728653-6-4; 0-9728653-6-5

"This personal collection of stunning, full-color photographs highlights unique underwater habitats and the life found in select natural communities around the world. Full spreads provide either an overview of an ecosystem, e.g., Komodo National Park or Bali in Indonesia, or a signature animal, e.g., the great white shark at Guadalupe Island, Mexico, or a dwarf caiman in Brazil. . . . The photographs are compelling by themselves and beautiful to browse. This book informs readers and gives them a deeper understanding of the ever-present threats to the ecological diversity and beauty of the planet." SLJ

Walker, Pamela

★ The **coral** reef; [by] Pam Walker and Elaine Wood. Facts on File 2005 140p (Life in the sea) $35

Grades: 6 7 8 9 10   577.7
1. Coral reefs and islands
ISBN 0-8160-5703-6

"An opening chapter gives detailed coverage of how reefs are formed. Later chapters examine the reefs' inhabitants, from essential microbes to the larger, showier fish, reptiles, and other animals. The final chapter . . . mentions environmental hazards and conservation efforts. . . . The range and depth of information . . . make this a fine addition for science collections." Booklist

Zell, Len

The **great** barrier reef; a journey through the world's greatest natural wonder. Len Zell. Murdoch Books 2014 250 p. $49.95

Grades: 10 11 12 Adult   577.7
1. Coral reef ecology 2. Great Barrier Reef (Australia)
ISBN 1743361793; 9781743361795

This book about the Great Barrier Reef leads readers to "discover how [it] was formed, learn about life on the Reef, and meet the plants and animals that inhabit it. It also looks at the environmental challenges facing this incredibly delicate ecosystem, and what the future may hold. llustrated in . . . full-color photography throughout." Publisher's note

577.8 Synecology and population biology

Crump, Martha L.

Sexy orchids make lousy lovers & other unusual relationships; with illustrations by Alan Crump. The University of Chicago Press 2009 214p il $25

Grades: 11 12 Adult   577.8
1. Animal behavior
ISBN 978-0-226-12185-7; 0-226-12185-2
                                      LC 2009-11857

"Crump maintains a cheeky sense of humor as she dispels all sorts of myths about the animal kingdom and reveals a wealth of biological information. . . . With Alan Crump's drawings on every page, Marty Crump's discussions on animal and human connections are more friendly chat than lecture; as pleasant a sojourn into so many different worlds as any reader could want." Booklist

Includes bibliographical references

578.4 Adaptation

Barrington, Rupert

Life; extraordinary animals, extreme behaviour. [by] Martha Holmes and Mike Gunton; [with] Rupert Barrington ... [et al.] University of California Press 2010 311p il map

Grades: 11 12 Adult   578.4
1. Animal behavior 2. Adaptation (Biology)
ISBN 0-520-26537-8; 978-0-520-26537-0
                                      LC 2009-31158

First published 2009 in the United Kingdom

"In 2009, to commemorate the 200th anniversary of Charles Darwin's birth, the BBC premiered the ten-episode television documentary Life to great acclaim. . . . Written by the documentary's producers, this impressive companion volume showcases species of fish, amphibians, reptiles, insects, birds, mammals, and plants that have developed unique or unusual strategies for solving 'the eternal problems of life': finding food, escaping predators, attracting mates, and raising young. . . . Even the most casual reader will be awed by the beauty, complexity, and ingenuity of nature as celebrated here."

"In 2009, to commemorate the 200th anniversary of Charles Darwin's birth, the BBC premiered the ten-episode television documentary Life to great acclaim. . . . Written by the documentary's producers, this impressive companion volume showcases species of fish, amphibians, reptiles, insects, birds, mammals, and plants that have developed unique or unusual strategies for solving 'the eternal problems of life': finding food, escaping predators, attracting mates, and raising young. . . . Even the most casual reader will be awed by the beauty, complexity, and ingenuity of nature as celebrated here." Libr J

Bonner, John Tyler

Why size matters; from bacteria to blue whales. Princeton University Press 2006 161p il $16.95

Grades: 11 12 Adult   **578.4**

1. Size

ISBN 978-0-691-12850-4; 0-691-12850-2

LC 2006-04945

The author's "tone is warm and engaging, his illustrative examples are simple to grasp, while his prose is precise, clear and highly readable." Times Lit Suppl

Includes bibliographical references

Gross, Michael

Life on the edge; amazing creatures thriving in extreme environments. Plenum Trade 1998 200p il hardcover o.p. pa $15

Grades: 11 12 Adult   **578.4**

1. Stress (Physiology) 2. Adaptation (Biology) 3. Life -- Origin

ISBN 0-7382-0445-5 pa

LC 98-4622

"The book constitutes an accessible introduction to an exciting outpost on the scientific frontier." Booklist

Includes glossary and bibliographical references

578.6 Miscellaneous nontaxonomic kinds of organisms

Fleisher, Paul

Parasites; latching on to a free lunch. Twenty-First Century Books 2006 112p il (Discovery!) lib bdg $29.27

Grades: 7 8 9 10   **578.6**

1. Parasites

ISBN 978-0-8225-3415-0; 0-8225-3415-0

LC 2005-10521

This is "well organized and quite up to date. The photos . . . are plentiful, colorful, and excellent. . . . Clear, concise, and interesting." Voice Youth Advocates

Includes bibliographical references

Foster, Steven

★ A **field** guide to venomous animals and poisonous plants; North America, North of Mexico. [by] Steven Foster and Roger A. Caras. Houghton Mifflin 1994 244p il hardcover o.p. pa $21

Grades: 11 12 Adult   **578.6**

1. Poisonous plants 2. Poisonous animals

ISBN 0-395-93608-X pa

LC 94-1641

This guide includes "90 animals from the mildly irritating to the deadly venomous: stinging and biting insects, scorpions and spiders, mammals, and reptiles, with an emphasis on snakes. More than 250 plants are described: wildflowers, weeds and exotic aliens, shrubs, trees, ferns, and mushrooms. The list includes plants that often cause allergies or dermatitis, such as Poison Ivy, as well as those that are toxic to eat." Publisher's note

Includes glossary and bibliographical references

Hamilton, Garry

Super species; the creatures that will dominate the planet. Firefly Books 2010 271p il $35

Grades: 9 10 11 12 Adult   **578.6**

1. Nonindigenous pests 2. Biological invasions

ISBN 978-1-55407-630-7; 1-55407-630-7

LC 2011286604

"Well researched and written, with an abundance of excellent photos, this work provides an outstanding, balanced look at this group of species." Choice

Includes bibliographical references

578.68 Rare and endangered species

★ **Endangered** species: opposing viewpoints; Viqi Wagner, book editor. Greenhaven Press 2008 230p map (Opposing viewpoints series) lib bdg $38.50; pa $26.75

Grades: 8 9 10 11 12   **578.68**

1. Endangered species 2. Nature conservation

ISBN 978-0-7377-2931-3 lib bdg; 978-0-7377-2932-0 pa

LC 2007-38314

This collection of articles offers varying viewpoints on extinction, preservation, property rights, and international cooperation.

Includes bibliographical references

McLeish, Todd

Basking with humpbacks; tracking threatened marine life in New England waters. University Press of New England 2009 214p il $26.95

Grades: 11 12 Adult   **578.68**

1. Marine animals 2. Endangered species

ISBN 978-1-58465-676-0; 1-58465-676-X

LC 2009-15170

"This book profiles the biology of over a dozen (mostly) threatened or endangered marine organisms found in New England. Not a scientist himself, the author goes out in the field with marine scientists who are studying these animals, and through hands-on experiences and extensive conversations with the researchers gives the reader an understanding of the basic biology of these animals and the human-caused threats they face. . . . The book will be of interest to students, naturalists, and environmentalists, and will be an enjoyable read for professionals as well." Sci Books Films

Includes bibliographical references

578.7 Organisms characteristic of specific kinds of environments

Burt, William

Marshes; the disappearing Edens. Yale University Press 2007 179p il $35

Grades: 11 12 Adult   **578.7**
  1. Marshes
  ISBN 978-0-300-12229-9; 0-300-12229-2
                 LC 2006-26961

This book combines photographs of marsh life with information about wetland habitat in North America.

"This well-structured, readable book will be valuable for students, teachers, researchers, and sundry readers interested in a unique kind of wetland. Reading this book is an excellent way to understand marshes as wild places." Choice

Includes bibliographical references

Cramer, Deborah

Smithsonian ocean; our water, our world. Smithsonian Books 2008 295p il map $39.95

Grades: 11 12 Adult   **578.7**
  1. Marine biology 2. Marine ecology
  ISBN 978-0-06-134383-4; 0-06-134383-8
                 LC 2008-15633

"With its hundreds of beautiful photographs, the volume is visually enchanting. It is also a vividly, accurately, and clearly written survey of the state of our understanding . . . of the history and current condition of the ocean." Sci Books Films

Includes bibliographical references

Crist, Darlene Trew

World ocean census; a global survey of marine life. [by] Darlene Trew Crist, Gail Scowcroft, James M. Harding, Jr. Firefly Books 2009 256p il map $40

Grades: 10 11 12 Adult   **578.7**
  1. Marine animals 2. Marine biology 3. Science -- Methodology 4. Census of Marine Life (Project)
  ISBN 978-1-55407-434-1; 1-55407-434-7

The authors "have produced a highly readable text with stunning photos that should fully engage the public imagination." Publ Wkly

Includes bibliographical references

★ **Guide** to wetlands; Patrick Dugan, general editor. Firefly Books 2005 304p il maps pa $19.95
  Grades: 9 10 11 12   **578.7**
  1. Wetlands
  ISBN 1-55407-111-9
               LC 2006-276145

"This book would be a great resource for addressing the ecological role, diversity, and human use of wetlands." Sci Books Films

Kirby, Richard R.

Ocean drifters; a secret world beneath the waves. Firefly Books 2011 192p il $29.95

Grades: 5 6 7 8 9 10 11 12 Adult   **578.7**
  1. Marine plankton
  ISBN 978-1-55407-982-7; 1-55407-982-9
               LC 2011284690

"Kirby (Marine Inst. Research Fellow, Plymouth Univ., UK), who has published widely in scientific journals, combines in this book his area of expertise-plankton-with magnificent color photography of each species. He details the importance of the ocean's plankton layer to the health of the globe and its effects on sea and human life in the photos' descriptions...Recommended for readers interested in the smaller denizens of the natural world, the ocean, or microphotography." (Library Journal)

Marent, Thomas

★ **Rainforest;** [by] Thomas Marent with Ben Morgan. DK Pub. 2006 360p il map hardcover o.p. pa $24.95

Grades: 11 12 Adult   **578.7**
  1. Rain forests -- Pictorial works
  ISBN 0-7566-1940-8; 978-0-7566-1940-4; 0-7566-6599-X pa; 978-0-7566-6599-9 pa
               LC 2006-6774

This "book is the product of Swiss photographer Marent's passion for exploring rainforests on five continents and over 16 years. His spectacularly beautiful photographs show much about the nature of rainforests and their curious inhabitants, and the accompanying text explains what you are seeing and what it can tell you about these ecosystems. . . . An accompanying CD provides rainforest sounds from various locations. This book . . . is not only beautiful but an excellent source of information. It also shows the amazing diversity of species that makes rainforests unique and valuable." Libr J

Moore, Peter D.

★ **Wetlands;** illustrations by Richard Garratt. rev ed.; Facts on File 2008 270p il map (Ecosystem) $70

Grades: 7 8 9 10   **578.7**
  1. Wetlands
  ISBN 0-8160-5931-4; 978-0-8160-5931-7
               LC 2006-37399
  First published 2000

This book "examines the diversity of wetlands in the past, present, and future, how they work, and how they can be conserved." Publisher's note

Includes glossary and bibliographical references

Oldfield, Sara

Rainforest; photography by Bruce Coleman Collection; foreword by Mark Rose. MIT Press 2003 160p il map $29.95

Grades: 11 12 Adult   **578.7**
1. Rain forests
ISBN 0-262-15106-5
                                      LC 2002-29559
The author "presents a wonderful overview of both tropical and temperate rainforests. . . . An excellent primer on
this imperiled ecosystem." Booklist

Rice, Stanley A.
   Encyclopedia of biodiversity; author, Stanley A
Rice. Facts On File 2012 598 p. $95
Grades: 9 10 11 12 Adult   **578.7**
1. Biology -- Encyclopedias 2. Evolution --
Encyclopedias 3. Biodiversity -- Encyclopedias
ISBN 0816077266; 9780816077267
                                      LC 2010050557
This biology and evolutionary science encyclopedia,
by Stanley A. Rice, provides "information about groups of
organisms (from bacteria to mammals) and about ecological concepts and processes (such as biogeography and ecological succession). . . . Tables at the end of each entry .
. . allow . . . readers to see how environmental conditions
and biodiversity have changed through evolutionary time."
(Publisher's note)
   "The text is suitable for high school students but advanced enough for adult readers, too. Although there are
many encyclopedias on ecology, resources, and science,
this one presents important biodiversity topics in one volume, providing a handy overview for term papers and class
presentations." LJ
   Includes bibliographical references and index

Weis, Judith S.
   Salt marshes; a natural and unnatural history.
[by] Judith S. Weis and Carol A. Butler. Rutgers University Press 2009 254p il $49.95; pa $23.95
Grades: 11 12 Adult   **578.7**
1. Salt marshes
ISBN 978-0-8135-4548-6; 978-0-8135-4570-7 pa
                                      LC 2008-43710
This is "an outstanding study of North American salt
marshes, their natural histories, contributions to human
wellbeing, and what their destruction means from human
life and property. . . . This account should make an informative treat for any armchair conservationist." Publ Wkly
   Includes bibliographical references

Wolfe, David W.
   Tales from the underground; a natural history of
subterranean life. Perseus Bks. 2001 221p il hardcover o.p. pa $18
Grades: 11 12 Adult   **578.7**
1. Soil microbiology
ISBN 0-7382-0679-2 pa
The author discusses the ecology of life in the soil and
the earth's rocky crust, including Darwin's experiments with
earthworms, Lewis and Clark's first encounter with prairie
dogs, the use of genetic tools, and the possible role of primitive underground microbes in evolution.

Wolfe "explains in a straightforward, readable style that
there is probably as much biodiversity and even as much
biomass below ground as above." New Sci
   Includes bibliographical references

579   Natural history of microorganisms, fungi, algae

Ben-Barak, Idan
   The invisible kingdom; from the tips of our fingers to the tops of our trash, inside the curious world
of microbes. Basic Books 2009 204p $24
Grades: 10 11 12 Adult   **579**
1. Microbiology
ISBN 978-0-465-01887-1; 0-465-01887-4
                                      LC 2009-19655
The author "gives an enthusiastic tour of single-celled
life. . . . He touches on myriad microbes in a range of environments, from the abyss of the sea to the inside of humans, explaining how they defend themselves, eat, move,
and reproduce." Booklist
   Includes bibliographical references

Ingraham, John L.
   March of the microbes; sighting the unseen.
John L. Ingraham. Harvard University Press 2012
326 p. il $16.95
Grades: 11 12 Adult   **579**
1. Microbiology
ISBN 0674064097; 9780674064096
                                      LC 2009037712
Designed as a field guide, this work examines bacteria,
fungi and other microscopic life forms. Index.
   "In this engaging treatment, [Ingraham] shows readers
the invisible world through observations about its macro-
scopic manifestations in a range of environments, from the
kitchen to the abyss of the sea. . . . Ingraham's clarity, plus
touches of humor, augments the appeal of this fine contribution to popularizing science." Booklist
   Includes bibliographical references and index.

579.2   Viruses and subviral organisms

Panno, Joseph
   ★ **Viruses**; the origin and evolution of deadly
pathogens. Facts on File 2011 232p il (The new
biology) $40
Grades: 9 10 11 12   **579.2**
1. Viruses
ISBN 978-0-8160-6855-5; 978-1-4381-3626-4 ebook
                                      LC 2010023664
This book "describes the structure, function, and evolution of viruses with an emphasis on their dual role as infectious microorganisms and important members of Earth's
biosphere. Coverage includes the origin of viruses, viral
structure and behavior, viral taxonomy, and the history of
virology." Publisher's note
   Includes bibliographical references

579.6 Mushrooms

Laessoe, Thomas
Mushrooms; editorial consultant, Gary Lincoff; photography by Neil Fletcher. 2nd American ed.; DK Pub. 2002 304p il (Smithsonian handbooks) $20
Grades: 9 10 11 12   **579.6**
1. Mushrooms
ISBN 0-7894-8986-4
First published 1998 as part of the Eyewitness handbooks series
This is a "guide to more than 500 species of mushroom and other macrofungi found in northern temperate zones worldwide.... For each species, there are one to four sharp, detailed color photos with clues about their identity. There is also a small color painting of habitat suitable for the growth of the species.... This book should prove invaluable at any level, from casual nature observer to professional mycologist." Sci Books Films [review of 1998 edition]

Lincoff, Gary
★ The **Audubon** Society field guide to North American mushrooms; [by] Gary H. Lincoff; visual key by Carol Nehring. Knopf 1981 926p il $19.95
Grades: 7 8 9 10 11 12 Adult   **579.6**
1. Mushrooms
ISBN 0-394-51992-2
LC 81-80827
This guide to 703 species of common mushrooms provides 762 color photographs and descriptions as keys to identifying these plants.
"The author is an expert on mushroom toxins and instills responsible cautions. The photos are uncommonly beautiful." SLJ

McKnight, Kent H.
★ A **field** guide to mushrooms, North America; [by] Kent H. McKnight and Vera B. McKnight; illustrations by Vera B. McKnight. Houghton Mifflin 1987 429p il hardcover o.p. pa $21
Grades: 11 12 Adult   **579.6**
1. Mushrooms
ISBN 0-395-91090-0 pa
LC 86-27799
"More than 500 species [of mushrooms] are described and depicted.... Edibility of each species is noted and signified by marginal pictograms both in the text and on the color-plates.... Appended: a genial chapter of recipes by Anne Dow, glossary, selected references, and index." Booklist

579.8 Algae

Iselin, Josie
An **ocean** garden; the secret life of seaweed. Josie Iselin. Abrams 2014 143 p. color illustrations $17.95
Grades: 10 11 12 Adult   **579.8**
1. Seaweed 2. Marine biology 3. Kelps 4. Marine

algae
ISBN 9781419711701; 1419711709
LC 2013945600
In this book, author "Josie Iselin returns to the seashore to reveal the unexpected beauty of seaweed. Produced on a flatbed scanner, Iselin's vibrant portraits of ocean flora reveal the exquisite color and extraordinary forms of more than 200 specimens gathered from tidal pools along the California and Maine coasts. Her engaging text, which accompanies the images, blends personal observation and philosophical musings with scientific fact." (Publisher's note)

580 Natural history of plants and animals

Huxley, Anthony Julian
Green inheritance; the WWF book of plants. [by] Anthony Huxley; foreword by Sir David Attenborough. Rev.; University of California Press 2005 192p il map pa $29.95
Grades: 9 10 11 12   **580**
1. Plant conservation
ISBN 0-520-24359-5
LC 2005-52876
First published 1985
This book "draws attention to the problems facing the planet at large as well as the ways each individual can conserve natural resources. Overall, the educational and wide-ranging text promotes an appreciation for the wondrous properties of plant life, from basic sustenance and curative powers to the ecology of insects and flowers." Booklist
Includes bibliographical references

Magill's encyclopedia of science; plant life. editor, Bryan D. Ness. Salem Press 2002 4v il map set $457
Grades: 11 12 Adult   **580**
1. Reference books 2. Botany -- Encyclopedias
ISBN 1-58765-084-3
LC 2002-13319
This encyclopedia provides "information for any study related to plants, archaea, bacteria, algae, or fungi, from molecular-level processes to planet-wide economic or environmental issues. The 379 signed articles, about half of which are published with revisions and updated bibliographies from several of the publisher's earlier reference books, are arranged into a single alphabet." SLJ
Includes bibliographical references

Stuppy, Wolfgang
The **bizarre** and incredible world of plants; [by] Wolfgang Stuppy, Rob Kesseler, Madeline Harley; edited by Alexandra Papadakis. Firefly Books 2009 135p il $29.95
Grades: 11 12 Adult   **580**
1. Plants -- Pictorial works
ISBN 978-1-55407-533-1; 1-55407-533-5
LC 2009-675174
This is a "gorgeous and mind-blowing volume about the marvelous yet secret lives of plants. The astonishing pictures are matched by scientifically exacting explanations of

how plants, which produce oxygen and feed either directly or indirectly all life on Earth, have evolved sophisticated survival strategies, including symbiotic relationships with pollinators." Booklist

Includes bibliographical references

580.75   Museum activities and services

Silvey, Anita

The **plant** hunters; true stories of their daring adventures to the far corners of the Earth. Anita Silvey. Farrar Straus Giroux 2012 88 p. col. ill. $19.99

Grades: 6 7 8 9 10   **580.75**

1. Botanists 2. Collectors and collecting 3. Plants -- Collection and preservation 4. Plant collecting -- History

ISBN 0374309086; 9780374309084

LC 2011005161

This book "introduces European and North American plant hunters, primarily from the nineteenth and twentieth centuries. Driven by curiosity, commerce, and 'botonomania,' they sought to collect valuable plant specimens around the world. Likening Baron Alexander von Humboldt to Indiana Jones and calling the plant hunters' experiences 'amazing escapades,' [Anita] Silvey . . . recount[s] horrific experiences reported by various plant hunters." (Booklist)

"The slim, engaging narrative paints vivid portraits of these botanic adventurers. It is smoothly written, smartly paced and filled with exciting tales of risk taking and derring-do." Kirkus

581.4   Adaptation

Castaldo, Nancy

The **Story** of Seeds; From Mendel's Garden to Your Plate, and How There's More of Less to Eat Around the World. Nancy Castaldo. Houghton Mifflin Harcourt 2016 144 p. color illustrations (hardcover) $17.99

Grades: 6 7 8 9   **581.4**

1. Seeds 2. Agriculture

ISBN 9780544320239; 0544320239

This book, by Nancy Castaldo, "speaks to the current ways we think about our food, the more thoughtful and philosophical questions about regulating which crops farmers are allowed to grow, and what consumers are able to eat. Readers will discover just how important seeds are to the functioning of our global economy--and how much power we as a world-wide community have to keep seeds around, because once a seed disappears, it's gone forever." (Publisher's note)

This stellar interdisciplinary resource may need handselling to get readers beyond its plain packaging, but be prepared to satisfy readers' thirst for more information about, for instance, protecting Russia's international seed vaults during WWII, finding Glass Gem corn, and fighting biopiracy. A terrific, engrossing resource." Booklist

581.6   Miscellaneous nontaxonomic kinds of plants

Foster, Steven

Peterson field guide to medicinal plants and herbs of eastern and central North America; Steven Foster and James A. Duke; photographs by Steven Foster. Houghton Mifflin Harcourt 2014 456 p. col. ill. (Peterson field guides) $21

Grades: Adult   **581.6**

1. Medical botany 2. Plants -- Identification

ISBN 0547943989; 9780547943985

In this book, authors "Steven Foster and James A. Duke have used recent advances in the study of medicinal plants and their combined experience of over 100 years to completely update the 'Peterson Field Guide to Medicinal Plants.' The clear and concise text identifies the key traits, habitats, uses, and warnings for more than 530 of the most significant medicinal plants in the eastern and central United States and Canada including both native and alien species." (Publisher's note)

"A hefty handbook to haul over marsh and meadow, but invaluable to searchers and researchers alike.—" LJ

Includes bibliographical references (p. 422-425) and indexes

Laws, Bill

Fifty plants that changed the course of history; written by Bill Laws. Firefly Books 2010 223p il $29.95

Grades: 11 12 Adult   **581.6**

1. Economic botany 2. Plants

ISBN 978-1-55407-798-4; 1-55407-798-2

LC 2011-414731

This is a "guide to the plants that have had the greatest impact on human civilization. Entries feature a description of the plant, its botanical name, its native range and its primary functions edible, medicinal, commercial or practical." Publisher's note

Includes bibliographical references

581.7   Plant ecology, plants characteristic of specific environments

Bodden, Valerie

Critical plant life. Creative Education 2010 48p il (Earth issues) $23.95

Grades: 7 8 9 10   **581.7**

1. Plant ecology

ISBN 978-1-58341-984-7; 1-58341-984-5

"The scientific information is up to date, well written for a lay audience, and presented in a highly engaging and visually appealing format." Sci Books Films

Includes glossary and bibliographical references

Rice, Stanley A.

Green planet; how plants keep the Earth alive. [by] Stanley A. Rice. Rutgers University Press 2009 298p il map $27.95

Grades: 9 10 11 12 Adult **581.7**
1. Plant ecology
ISBN 0-8135-4453-X; 978-0-8135-4453-3
LC 2008-13964

"This work is notable for its breadth of coverage of not only how plants directly affect humans (e.g., agriculture and oxygen production), but also of how plants affect the functioning of the ecosystems that humans need for a range of goods and services (e.g., climate, soil renewal, habitat creation). . . . The 37 illustrations and 18 tables help clarify key points and simplify difficult concepts." Choice

Includes bibliographical references

582.13 Plants noted for their flowers

Burger, William C.
Flowers: how they changed the world. Prometheus Books 2006 337p il $23
Grades: 11 12 Adult **582.13**
1. Flowers
ISBN 1-59102-407-2; 978-1-59102-407-1
LC 2006-2739

This is "an engaging and beautifully written look at how flowering plants, over more than 100 million years, have 'transformed terrestrial ecosystems, supported the origin of primates, and helped us humans become the masters of our planet.'" Publ Wkly

Includes bibliographical references

Spellenberg, Richard
Familiar flowers of North America: eastern region; Ann H. Whitman, editor. Knopf 1986 192p il pa $9
Grades: 11 12 Adult **582.13**
1. Wild flowers
ISBN 0-394-74843-3
LC 86-045587

This guide to 80 eastern wildflowers is arranged by color and shape of the flower and includes color photos, drawings, and descriptions of the plants habitat and range, folklore and history

Familiar flowers of North America: western region; Ann H. Whitman, editor. Knopf 1986 192p il pa $4.95
Grades: 11 12 Adult **582.13**
1. Wild flowers
ISBN 0-394-74844-1
LC 86-045586

Eighty "color plates, arranged by the color and shape of the flower, fill the main section of this truly pocket-size field guide. Each entry also includes a line drawing, a description of the plant's habitat and range, and a paragraph explaining its place among other flowers and its folklore or history. . . . Appendices include a brief glossary and an alphabetic and a family index." BAYA Book Rev

★ **National** Audubon Society field guide to North American wildflowers, western region; 2nd ed rev; Knopf 2001 862p il map $19.95

Grades: 7 8 9 10 11 12 Adult **582.13**
1. Wild flowers
ISBN 0-375-40233-0
LC 2001-269242
First published 1979

"More than 940 . . . full-color images show the wildflowers of western North America close-up and in their natural habitats. . . . Images are grouped by flower color and shape and keyed to . . . descriptions that reflect current taxonomy." Publisher's note

Thieret, John W.
★ **National** Audubon Society field guide to North American wildflowers: eastern region; revising author, John W. Thieret; original authors, William A. Niering and Nancy C. Olmstead. Knopf 2001 879p il map (National Audubon Society field guide series) $19.95
Grades: 7 8 9 10 11 12 Adult **582.13**
1. Wild flowers
ISBN 0-375-40232-2
LC 2001-269241
First published 1979 under the authorship of William A. Niering and Nancy C. Olmstead

"Covers the area east of the Rockies and east of the Big Bend area of Texas to the Atlantic. Color photographs together with family and species descriptions make this a most useful field guide." Sci News {review of 1979 edition}

582.16 Trees

National Audubon Society
Familiar trees of North America: eastern region; Ann H. Whitman, editor; Jerry F. Franklin, John Farrand, Jr., consultants. Knopf 1986 192p il pa $9
Grades: 11 12 Adult **582.16**
1. Trees -- North America
ISBN 0-394-74851-4
LC 86-045585

This pocket field guide covers eighty trees commonly found in the eastern United States. Includes color photos and descriptions of characteristics, habitat, range, history, and uses

Familiar trees of North America: western region; Ann H. Whitman, editor; Jerry F. Franklin, John Farrand, Jr., consultants. Knopf 1986 192p il pa $9
Grades: 11 12 Adult **582.16**
1. Trees -- North America
ISBN 0-394-74852-2
LC 86-045584

This pocket field guide covers eighty trees commonly found in the western United States. "Each color plate is accompanied by a black silhouette of the tree and a small photo of its bark as well as a written description of its characteristics, its habitat and range, and its history and uses. . . . Introductory essays and illustrations provide a key to tree identification. Appendices include descriptions of tree families and an index to common and botanical names." BAYA Book Rev

Plotnik, Arthur

★ The **urban** tree book; an uncommon field guide for city and town. {by} Arthur Plotnik; in consultation with the Morton Arboretum; illustrated by Mary H. Phelan. Three Rivers Press (NY) 2000 432p il pa $18.95

Grades: 11 12 Adult   **582.16**
1. Trees -- United States
ISBN 0-8129-3103-3

LC 99-42452

An inquiry into the characteristics and survival strategies of nearly 200 species of trees

The author "expresses his sense of wonder about urban trees found all over the U.S. with warmth and wit as he recounts their history and lore and medicinal and spiritual legacies. . . . Plotnik also celebrates landmark trees, assesses the new urban forestry movement, and provides a wealth of useful resources." Booklist

Includes bibliographical references

Sibley, David

★ The **Sibley** guide to trees; written and illustrated by David Allen Sibley. Alfred A. Knopf 2009 xxxviii, 426p il map $39.95

Grades: 11 12 Adult   **582.16**
1. Trees -- North America
ISBN 978-0-375-41519-7

LC 2009-927625

This "is an outstanding book that should be available in all public libraries, schools, colleges, universities, and homes. The text is comprehensive and the illustrations are pertinent, accurate, and clear." Sci Books Films

587   Vascular seedless plants

Parker, Steve, 1952-

Ferns, mosses & other spore-producing plants. Compass Point Books 2010 48p il lib bdg $29.32

Grades: 6 7 8 9   **587**
1. Ferns 2. Mosses
ISBN 978-0-7565-4220-7 lib bdg; 0-7565-4220-0 lib bdg

LC 2009-12060

"This series gives an overview of a few of the main classifications of living things. Packed with text, photos, micrographs, and insets, these titles will compel readers to look closely. The main text meanders through the loaded pages providing background information, while visuals with italicized captions provide examples and detail. Scientific terms are often defined in the text and used again in later pages. Each spread focuses on a single aspect of the life-form and either moves through the life cycle or presents variations of the classification. Final spreads examine beneficial and harmful varieties. The books close with an overview of scientific classification with a specific example. With its compelling facts and visuals, this is a quality choice." (School Library Journal)

590   Animals

Campbell, Jeff

Daisy to the Rescue; True Stories of Daring Dogs, Paramedic Parrots, and Other Animal Heroes. by Jeff Campbell, illustrated by Ramsey Beyer. Houghton Mifflin Harcourt 2014 336 p. illustrations $17.99

Grades: 6 7 8 9 10   **590**
1. Human-animal relationship 2. Animal behavior 3. Cognition in animals 4. Animal heroes -- Anecdotes
ISBN 1936976625; 9781936976621

This book, by Jeff Campbell, illustrated by Ramsey Beyer, "celebrates over fifty . . . heroic animals with stunning illustrated portraits and detailed accounts of their exploits. The book asks important questions about why these animals act the way they do . . . often putting themselves in harm's way in the process." (Publisher's note)

"Inherent animal abilities are discussed alongside the accounts, as are animal traits and scientific theories in layman's terms. Individual stories of animal derring-do, illustrated with pencil portraits, make for quick, compelling reads that prompt the reader to wonder what really goes on in an animal's head and heart." Booklist

Conniff, Richard

Swimming with piranhas at feeding time; my life doing dumb stuff with animals. Norton 2009 299p $25.95; pa $15.95

Grades: 11 12 Adult   **590**
1. Dangerous animals
ISBN 978-0-393-06893-1; 978-0-393-30457-2 pa

LC 2008-51234

The author "offers a delightful collection of pieces about his encounters with spiders, crabs, leopards and other fauna. With warmth and simplicity, the author spins a beguiling web as he recalls his travels to rainforests, deserts, inner-city neighborhoods and other locales in search of interesting creatures and the often-quirky scientists who study them. . . . Bright entertainment from a great explainer of the lives of animals." Kirkus

Includes bibliographical references

A **dictionary** of zoology; edited by Michael Allaby. 3rd ed.; Oxford University Press 2009 689p il (Oxford paperback reference) pa $19.76

Grades: 9 10 11 12 Adult   **590**
1. Reference books 2. Zoology -- Dictionaries
ISBN 978-0-19-923341-0; 0-19-923341-1

LC 2009-419052

First published 1999 with title: Concise Oxford dictionary of zoology

"Illustrated with many line drawings, the book defines terms from animal behavior, evolution, earth history, zoogeography, genetics, and physiology, provides full taxonomic coverage of arthropods and other invertebrates, fish, reptiles, amphibians, birds, and mammals, and introduces . . . material on behavioral ecology and conservation biology." Publisher's note

Dinerstein, Eric

★ **Tigerland** and other unintended destinations. Island Press 2005 279p $25.95; pa $16.95

Grades: 9 10 11 12   **590**

1. Ecology 2. Nature conservation
ISBN 1-55963-578-9; 1-59726-152-1 pa

           LC 2005-13822

The author's "compelling tour of wild places and his vivid portraits of intrepid wildlife defenders offer convincing arguments for providing the treasures of nature with the same reverence and protection we accord cherished works of art." Booklist

★ The **encyclopedia** of animals; a complete visual guide. [text, Jenni Bruce . . . et al.] University of California Press 2004 608p il map $39.95

Grades: 7 8 9 10 11 12   **590**

1. Reference books 2. Animals -- Encyclopedias
ISBN 0-520-24406-0

           LC 2004-303646

"This lavishly illustrated chronicle of Earth's biodiversity is a visual delight." Booklist

Magill's encyclopedia of science: animal life; editor, Carl W. Hoagstrom. Salem Press 2002 4v il set $435

Grades: 11 12 Adult   **590**

1. Reference books 2. Zoology -- Encyclopedias
ISBN 1-58765-019-3

           LC 2001-49799

This "is a major revision and update of the six-volume Magill's Survey of Science: Life Science, published in 1991. . . . There are 385 signed main entries, ranging in length from 1000 to 3000 words each. . . . The entries cover a wide variety of topics related to animal life and include articles on subjects such as biodiversity and defense mechanisms as well as those on specific species or individual animals. Each entry begins with ready-reference information and a list of principal terms with definitions." Libr J

Includes bibliographical references

Piper, Ross, Dr.

Animal Earth; The Amazing Diversity of Living Forms. Ross Piper. Thames & Hudson 2013 320 p. color illustrations (hbk.) $45

Grades: 9 10 11 12 Adult   **590**

1. Animals 2. Zoology 3. Animal diversity
ISBN 0500516960; 9780500516966

This book, by zoologist Ross Piper, "showcases legions of oft-overlooked species. . . . Most of Piper's subjects are of the marine or microscopic varieties: parasitic nematodes, micro-colonies of barnacles and feather stars, water bears, and spindly sea spiders are just some of the creepy-crawlies awaiting readers. . . . But the book's main draw is its striking images." (Publishers Weekly)

"[A] fascinating look at the animal kingdom, with a decided emphasis on the obscure, the unusual, and the mysterious. . . . The book includes over 500 high-quality full-color photographs, with each accompanied by a brief comment or notable detail about the pictured animal." Choice

Includes bibliographical references (page 317) and index.

Smith, Lewis

Why the cheetah cheats; and other mysteries of the natural world. Firefly Books 2009 240p il $29.95

Grades: 11 12 Adult   **590**

1. Animals 2. Zoology 3. Natural history
ISBN 978-1-55407-534-8

"In 100 brief and lively dispatches accompanied by striking photographs, science journalist Smith captures telling moments on the nature research beat. . . . Whether the subject is dire (bats, trees, and corals are dying due to global warming) or fascinating (why female cheetahs are intrepidly promiscuous), Smith writes with equanimity, making for an intriguing, instructive, and up-to-date book of discoveries." Booklist

590.73   Collections and exhibits of living mammals

Anthony, Lawrence, 1950-2012

Babylon's ark; the incredible wartime rescue of the Baghdad Zoo. [by] Lawrence Anthony with Graham Spence. Thomas Dunne Books 2007 248p il hardcover o.p. pa $14.95

Grades: 11 12 Adult   **590.73**

1. Zoos 2. Iraq War, 2003-2011 3. Wildlife conservation 4. Iraq War, 2003- 5. Baghdad Zoo (Iraq)
ISBN 0-312-35832-6; 0-312-38215-4 pa; 978-0-312-35832-7; 978-0-312-38215-5 pa

           LC 2006-50573

"This remarkable story recounts the recent wartime rescue of the once-world-renowned Baghdad Zoo through the experiences of a South African conservationist and heroic Iraqi zookeepers." Booklist

French, Thomas

Zoo story; life in the garden of captives. Hyperion 2010 288p $24.99

Grades: 11 12 Adult   **590.73**

1. Zoos 2. Lowry Park Zoo
ISBN 978-1-4013-2346-2

The author "chronicles the rise of Lowry Park from one of the worst zoos in the country to one of the best. . . . This behind-the-scenes look will both entertain and enlighten animal lovers. It is a story that needs to be told, and French does it superbly." Libr J

Includes bibliographical references

Robinson, Phillip T.

★ **Life** at the zoo: behind the scenes with the animal doctors. Columbia University Press 2004 293p il $27.95; pa $17.95

Grades: 11 12 Adult   **590.73**

1. Zoos
ISBN 0-231-13248-4; 0-231-13249-2 pa

           LC 2004-43893

"It would be difficult to cover even one aspect, such as animal health, that might affect the overall management of a zoo, but Dr. Philip Robinson manages to provide an excellent coverage of just about everything that might be involved in the operation of a zoo." Sci Books Films

Includes bibliographical references

591   Specific topics in natural history of animals

Wildlife of the world; contributors Jamie Ambrose [and nine others] DK Publishing 2015 480 p. illustrations, color maps $50

Grades: K 1 2 3 4 5 6 7 8 9 10 11 12 Adult   **591**
1. Animals 2. Animals -- Pictorial works
ISBN 1465438041; 9781465438041

LC 2015458474

This book, by DK Publishing, foreword by Don E. Wilson and produced in association with the Smithsonian Institution,"takes you on a journey through some of the most scenic and rich animal habitats--from the Amazon rain forests to the Himalayas, the Sahara to the South Pole--meeting the most important animals in each ecosystem along the way.... An additional eighty-page illustrated reference section on the animal kingdom explains the animal groups and profiles additional species." (Publisher's note)

"A chart at the beginning of each section indicates the number of species in each order, class, or phylum. The table of contents has a small editing error in pagination for the end material, but this is an important, gorgeous, accessible introduction to hundreds of species and their habitats throughout the world at a very small price, and it belongs in all public and school libraries." Booklist

Smithsonian

591.3   Genetics, evolution, age characteristics

Arthur, Wallace

Creatures of accident; the rise of the animal kingdom. Hill & Wang 2006 255p hardcover o.p. pa $22

Grades: 11 12 Adult   **591.3**
1. Evolution 2. Natural selection
ISBN 0-8090-4321-1; 978-0-8090-4321-7; 0-8090-3701-7 pa; 978-0-8090-3701-8 pa

LC 2005-33540

The author "advances the argument that the process [of the evolution of life] tends toward greater complexity over time.... Arthur sketches out the main structural attributes of complexity in animals, from the cell to organs to embryology to body forms, and when they appeared.... Championing naturalistic clarity, Arthur's precision about the processes of evolution will benefit serious students of the topic." Booklist

Includes bibliographical references

Nielsen, Claus

Animal evolution; interrelationships of the living phyla. Claus Nielsen. Oxford University Press 2012 x, 402 p.p (hbk) $69.99

Grades: 9 10 11 12 Adult   **591.3**
1. Evolution 2. Developmental biology 3. Unicellular

organisms 4. Phylogeny
ISBN 0199606021; 019960603X; 9780199606023; 9780199606030

LC 2011941928

In this book, Claus Nielsen "examines the unity of the animal kingdom by tracing the evolution of all the 31 living phyla from their unicellar ancestor. The second edition incorporates new morphological data and new topic areas from the past decade, including histological/ultrastructural and embriological data, numerical cladistic analyses, DNA sequencing and developmental biology." (Booknews)

Includes bibliographical references and index.

591.47   Protective and locomotor adaptations, color

McDougall, Len

Tracking and reading sign; a guide to mastering the original forensic science. Skyhorse Pub. 2010 183p il pa $18.95

Grades: 11 12 Adult   **591.47**
1. Animal tracks 2. Animal behavior 3. Tracking and trailing
ISBN 978-1-61608-006-8; 1-61608-006-X

LC 2009-50543

This book "offers an introduction on the principles of tracking and reading sign by looking at tracks, prints, gaits, scats, scents, and animal behaviors. It provides the reader with tracking and stalking techniques such as cold hunting, camouflage, and using the stump method." Publisher's note

591.5   Behavior

American Museum of Natural History

Animal life; Charlotte Uhlenbroek, [editor in chief] DK Pub. 2008 512p il map $50

Grades: 9 10 11 12 Adult   **591.5**
1. Animal behavior 2. Animals -- Pictorial works
ISBN 978-0-7566-3986-0; 0-7566-3986-7

LC 2008-300010

This book "provides an excellent overview of the animal world written at a level accessible to students and the general public. Introductory sections cover basics of animal life such as evolution, animal history, classification, and anatomy. Animal behavior receives the most extensive treatment, encompassing living space, hunting and feeding, defense mechanisms, sex and reproduction, birth and development, society, communication, and intelligence." Booklist

Balcombe, Jonathan

Second nature; the inner lives of animals. foreword by J.M. Coetzee. Palgrave Macmillan 2010 242p il $27.00; $27.00

Grades: 10 11 12 Adult   **591.5**
1. Animal behavior 2. Animal intelligence 3. Animal psychology 4. Social behavior in animals
ISBN 0230613624; 9780230613621

LC 2009-30770

The author of Pleasurable Kingdom (2006) argues that animals are "sentient beings capable of feelings and pain and emotions." (Publisher's note) Index.

The author "draws on the latest research, observational studies and personal anecdotes to reveal the full gamut of animal experience—from emotions, to problem solving, to moral judgment. Balcombe challenges the widely held idea that nature is red in tooth and claw, highlighting animal traits we have disregarded until now: their nuanced understanding of social dynamics, their consideration for others, and their strong tendency to avoid violent conflict." Publisher's note

Includes bibliographical references

Boysen, Sarah Till

The **smartest** animals on the planet; with a contribution from Deborah Custance. Firefly Books 2009 192p il map $35

Grades: 9 10 11 12 Adult   591.5
 1. Animal behavior 2. Animal intelligence
 ISBN 978-1-5540-7456-3; 1-5540-7456-8

"Succinctly written and sumptuously illustrated with photographs and diagrams, this appealing book is sure to fascinate the general reader and inspire the science student considering a career in animal behavior or cognition." Libr J

Crump, Martha L.

Headless males make great lovers; & other unusual natural histories. [by] Marty Crump; with illustrations by Alan Crump. University of Chicago Press 2005 199p il $25; pa $14

Grades: 11 12 Adult   591.5
 1. Animal behavior
 ISBN 0-226-12199-2; 0-226-12202-6 pa

LC 2005-7592

"Illustrated throughout with line drawings, and bolstered with a chapter-by-chapter list of references, this marvelous introduction to the whys and wherefores of animal behavior will find an audience in all libraries." Booklist

Includes bibliographical references

Encyclopedia of animal behavior; edited by Marc Bekoff; foreword by Jane Goodall. Greenwood Press 2004 3v il set $349.95

Grades: 11 12 Adult   591.5
 1. Animal behavior
 ISBN 0-313-32745-9

LC 2004-56073

This encyclopedia describes "what makes animals tick using techniques that range from molecular approaches to analysis of species. The 300 entries, some stretching to 7000 words, discuss topics as diverse as concept learning in pigeons and stress in dolphins." Libr J

Includes bibliographical references

Grandin, Temple

★ **Animals** in translation; using the mysteries of autism to decode animal behavior. [by] Temple Grandin and Catherine Johnson. Scribner 2010 356p $28; ebook $18.99

Grades: 11 12 Adult   591.5
 1. Autism 2. Animal behavior
 ISBN 978-1-4391-8710-4; 978-1-4391-3084-1 ebook
 First published 2005

"This fascinating book will teach readers to see as animals see, to be a little more visual and a little less verbal, and, as a unique analysis of animal behavior, it belongs in all libraries." Booklist

Includes bibliographical references

McCarthy, Susan

Becoming a tiger; how baby animals learn to live in the wild. HarperCollins 2004 418p hardcover o.p. pa $13.95

Grades: 11 12 Adult   591.5
 1. Animal intelligence
 ISBN 0-06-620924-2; 0-06-093484-0 pa

LC 2003-67553

The author examines "the ways that animals figure out how to function in their worlds. . . . One of the basic things a baby animal must learn is how to get from one place to another in a manner appropriate to its species. Other basics involve learning to recognize your own species, to communicate, to find food, and not to become some other species' food. McCarthy discusses species as various as horses, bonobos, zebra finches, and fruit-fly maggots to illustrate the learning process." Booklist

Includes bibliographical references

Morell, Virginia

Animal wise; the thoughts and emotions of our fellow creatures. Virginia Morell. Random House Inc 2013 304 p. $26

Grades: 9 10 11 12 Adult   591.5
 1. Animal behavior 2. Thought and thinking 3. Cognition in animals 4. Human-animal communication
 ISBN 0307461440; 9780307461445

LC 2012031503

This book, by Virginia Morell, "explores the frontiers of research on animal cognition and emotion. . . . [The book] takes us . . . into the inner world of animals, from ants to elephants to wolves, and from sharp-shooting archerfish to pods of dolphins that rumble like rival street gangs. . . . She probes the moral and ethical dilemmas of recognizing that even 'lesser animals' have cognitive abilities such as memory, feelings, personality, and self-awareness." (Publisher's note)

591.56 Behavior relating to life cycle

Kostyal, K. M.

Great migrations; official companion to the National Geographic channel global television event. [by] K. M. Kostyal; afterword by series producer David Hamlin. National Geographic 2010 303p il $35

Grades: 9 10 11 12 Adult   591.56
 1. Animals -- Migration
 ISBN 978-1-4262-0644-3

LC 2010-20998

This book, "the official companion to the National Geographic Channel television film Great Migrations, follows the sequence of the film. The book is divided into sections, each of which emphasizes a feature that makes migration essential to the survival of a variety of animal species. Throughout, the author continuously emphasizes the instincts and internal and external forces that drive animals to make risky, yet deliberate, journeys of hundreds to thousands of miles annually. . . . Over one hundred excellent color pictures illustrate various aspects of migration and daily life for dozens of animal species." Sci Books Films

Includes bibliographical references

591.59　Communication

Friend, Tim

★ **Animal** talk; breaking the codes of animal language. Free Press 2004 274p il $25; pa $15

Grades: 11 12 Adult　　　　　　　　**591.59**

1. Animal communication

ISBN 0-7432-0157-4; 0-7432-0158-2 pa

LC 2003-63107

"The author describes the methods of, and reasons behind, animal communication and demonstrates that human and animal communication are not so widely disparate as once believed. Friend also gives background details on the basics of communication theory, genetics, evolution, and the progression of scientific thought regarding animal communication. . . . His humorous and engaging prose style makes this a captivating read." Libr J

Includes bibliographical references

591.6　Miscellaneous nontaxonomic kinds of animals

Hammond, Paula

The **atlas** of the world's most dangerous animals; mapping nature's born killers. Marshall Cavendish 2010 224p il map lib bdg $99.93

Grades: 7 8 9 10 11 12　　　　　　**591.6**

1. Dangerous animals

ISBN 978-0-7614-7870-6 lib bdg; 0-7614-7870-1 lib bdg

LC 2008-44960

First published 2004 in the United Kingdom

Explores each of the world's continents, featuring deadly species of animals.

"Each of these beautifully illustrated books features an appealing layout; logical organization; and plenty of full-color drawings, maps, and photographs. The volumes are organized by continent, with an additional chapter covering animals in the world's oceans...These volumes are ideal for reports, but animal lovers will enjoy perusing them as well." (School Library Journal)

591.68　Rare and endangered animals

Girling, Richard

The **Hunt** for the Golden Mole; All Creatures Great & Small and Why They Matter. Richard Girling. Counterpoint Press 2014 312 p. illustrations $26

Grades: 9 10 11 12 Adult　　　　　　**591.68**

1. Hunting 2. Rare animals 3. Moles (Animals) 4. Golden moles -- Somalia 5. Extinct animals -- Somalia 6. Biodiversity -- South Africa 7. Nature conservation -- South Africa 8. Hunting -- Moral and ethical aspects

ISBN 1619024500; 9781619024502

LC 2014022506

This book, "taking as its narrative engine the hunt for an animal that is legendarily rare, Richard Girling writes [a] . . . history of humankind's interest in hunting and collecting-what prompts us to do this? What good might come of our need to catalog all the living things of the natural world?" (Publisher's note)

"Though Girling presents a sobering assessment of the state of the world's fauna, he does so with the dramatic flair of a novelist and eye for detail of a travel journalist. The result is a page-turning, thought-provoking treatise on a desperate environmental crisis." Booklist

Includes bibliographical references and index

Goodall, Jane, 1934-

Hope for animals and their world; how endangered species are being rescued from the brink. [by] Jane Goodall, with Thane Maynard and Gail Hudson. Grand Central Pub. 2009 392p il $27.99; pa $15.99

Grades: 11 12 Adult　　　　　　　　**591.68**

1. Endangered species 2. Nature conservation 3. Wildlife conservation 4. Wildlife rescue 5. Wildlife reintroduction

ISBN 978-0-446-58177-6; 0-446-58177-1; 978-0-446-58178-3 pa; 0-446-58178-X pa

LC 2009-11215

"An upbeat compendium that will energize both hands-on and armchair conservationists." Kirkus

Includes bibliographical references

Hammond, Paula

★ The **atlas** of endangered animals; wildlife under threat around the world. Marshall Cavendish 2010 224p il map lib bdg $99.93

Grades: 7 8 9 10 11 12　　　　　　**591.68**

1. Atlases 2. Reference books 3. Endangered species

ISBN 978-0-7614-7872-0; 0-7614-7872-8

LC 2008-44956

First published 2006 in the United Kingdom

This "beautifully illustrated . . . . [book] features an appealing layout; logical organization; and plenty of full-color drawings, maps, and photographs. . . . Ideal for reports, but animal lovers will enjoy perusing them as well." SLJ

591.7 Animal ecology, animals characteristic of specific environments

Naskrecki, Piotr

The **smaller** majority; the hidden world of the animals that dominate the tropics. Belknap Press of Harvard University Press 2005 278p il $35

Grades: 11 12 Adult   **591.7**

1. Invertebrates 2. Tropics 3. Animals -- Pictorial works

ISBN 0-674-01915-6; 978-0-674-01915-7

LC 2005-46060

"Naskrecki's exuberant, expert knowledge of this microscopic world has been distilled down to the most arresting details. Crisp, enjoyable prose, clearly explains complex biological processes." Publ Wkly

Includes bibliographical references

591.75 Urban animals

Bears in the backyard; big animals, sprawling suburbs, and the new urban jungle. Edward R. Ricciuti. The Countryman Press 2014 248 p. (hardcover: alk. paper) $23.95

Grades: 10 11 12 Adult   **591.75**

1. Habitat (Ecology) 2. Human-animal relationship 3. Urban pests -- United States 4. Urban animals -- United States 5. Human-animal relationships -- United States

ISBN 1581572174; 9781581572179

LC 2014008488

In this book, scientist Edward R. Ricciuti "explores the increasing intersection between humans and wild animals. . . . As cities and suburbs sprawl, and conservation efforts enable wildlife populations to recover, large wild animals are encroaching on human turf. These creatures might be thrilling to see, but they can bite, scratch, and even kill, and attacks on humans will only increase as we come face to face in the man-made landscape." (Publisher's note)

591.9 Animals by specific continents, countries, localities

Bambaradeniya, Channa N. B.

The **illustrated** atlas of wildlife; [by] Channa Bambaradeniya [et al.] University of California Press 2009 288p il map $39.95

Grades: 9 10 11 12 Adult   **591.9**

1. Atlases 2. Biogeography 3. Reference books

ISBN 978-0-520-25785-6; 0-520-25785-5

LC 2008-40625

"This gorgeous book, featuring detailed, customized maps and more than 800 photographs . . . and original artworks, presents a spectacular visual survey of wild animals across the globe and describes in detail their habitats, physical characteristics, diet, and behavior. . . . [It also includes] conservation and preservation data, information about human impact upon the world's complex ecosystems, and chronicles of the evolution and adaptation of animals over the ages." Education Digest

Includes glossary and bibliographical references

592 Specific taxonomic groups of animals

Attenborough, David

Life in the undergrowth. Princeton University Press 2006 288p il $29.95

Grades: 11 12 Adult   **592**

1. Invertebrates

ISBN 0-691-12703-4

LC 2005-934727

"This wonderful exploration of invertebrates exceeds the requirements for a great nature book through the strength of its photographs and the quality of its prose." Publ Wkly

Stewart, Amy

The **earth** moved; on the remarkable achievements of earthworms. Algonquin Bks. 2004 223p $23.95; pa $12.95

Grades: 11 12 Adult   **592**

1. Worms 2. Earthworms

ISBN 1-56512-337-9; 1-56512-468-5 pa

LC 2003-52379

Stewart discusses earthworms. "This peaceful, delicate creature, Stewart writes, has posed a large task for scientists, who have taken more than 100 years to piece together a portrait of the earthworm's dark life. But the subterrestrials still have more to teach us, even as creatures like the giant Oregon earthworm are being pushed to the brink of extinction." (Christ Sci Monit)

The author explores "the impact worms have on humans and on our planet. . . . {She} educates on the vital roles these creatures play in growing crops, how they can neutralize the effects of nuclear waste on soil, and their ability to regenerate new body parts. . . . A book that's as enlightening as it is entertaining." SLJ

Includes bibliographical references

594 Mollusks and molluscoids

Rehder, Harald Alfred

The **Audubon** Society field guide to North American seashells; {by} Harald A. Rehder; with photographs by James H. Carmichael, Jr.; visual key by Carol Nehring and Mary Beth Brewer. Knopf 1981 894p il flexible bdg $19.95

Grades: 7 8 9 10 11 12 Adult   **594**

1. Shells 2. Mollusks

ISBN 0-394-51913-2

LC 80-84239

"[T]his guide explores more than 705 seashells, living mollusks, abalone, periwinkles, conchs, limpets, oysters, clams, mussels, and cockles found on the Atlantic, Pacific, and Gulf coasts of North America and the West Indies. The photographs are arranged by shape and color, making identification quick and easy." Publisher's note

Williams, Wendy

Kraken; the curious, exciting, and slightly disturbing science of squid. Abrams Image 2011 223p il $21.95

Grades: 11 12 Adult   594
  1. Squids
  ISBN 978-0-8109-8465-3

LC 2010032489

This book "traces sightings of the giant squid throughout the centuries. . . . Discussion of the anatomy, physiology, reproduction, evolution, and taxonomy of Architeuthis is provided, along with accounts of the author's visits to various scientific laboratories and descriptions of research studies being conducted on the animal. . . . This serves as a good introduction to the subject for general readers and an inspiration to young people interested in marine biology." Libr J

Includes filmography and bibliographical references

595 Arthropods

Fortey, Richard

Horseshoe crabs and velvet worms; the story of the animals and plants that time has left behind. by Richard Fortey. Alfred A. Knopf 2012 320 p. ill. (some col.) $28.95

Grades: 10 11 12 Adult   595
  1. Botany 2. Zoology 3. Paleontology 4. Worms 5. Plant conservation 6. Arthropoda -- Conservation 7. Invertebrates -- Conservation 8. Limulus polyphemus -- Conservation
  ISBN 9780307263612

LC 2011039941

This book by Richard Fortey introduces "the reader to organisms that seemingly have undergone little change since their ancient origins. . . . Evolution has never stopped, and Fortey discusses changes that occur at the molecular level in response to predation pressure and other changing environmental conditions. He starts his journey by witnessing the spectacular spawning of horseshoe crabs, the closest living relatives of his specialty, the trilobites." (Choice: Current Reviews for Academic Libraries)

"Informative, engrossing and delightful." Kirkus

595.4 Chelicerates

★ **Common** spiders of North America; Richard A. Bradley; illustrations by Steve Buchanon; sponsored by the American Arachnological Society. University of California Press 2013 x, 271 p.p leaves of plates: ill. (some (cloth: alk. paper) $85

Grades: 10 11 12 Adult   595.4
  1. Spiders 2. North America 3. Spiders -- North America -- Identification
  ISBN 0520274881; 9780520274884

LC 2012018390

This book, by Richard A. Bradley and illustrated by Steve Buchanan, is a "comprehensive guide to all 68 spider families in North America [and] . . . illustrates 469 of the most commonly encountered species. Group keys enable identification by web type and other observable details, and species descriptions include identification tips, typical habitat, geographic distribution, and behavioral notes." (Publisher's note)

"This book will interest anyone intrigued by spiders, regardless of the extent of his/her training or experience. The first section of the volume is a very good introduction to the natural history and scientific study of spiders. Bradley (Ohio State) considers aspects of spider anatomy, habitat, growth/development, courtship/mating, silk production, senses, and general behavior as well as hunting behavior. . . . A useful resource for a wide audience." Choice

Includes bibliographical references (p. 257-259) and index

Dalton, Stephen

★ **Spiders**; the ultimate predators. Firefly Books 2008 208p il lib bdg $34.95

Grades: 9 10 11 12 Adult   595.4
  1. Spiders
  ISBN 978-1-55407-346-7; 1-55407-346-4

This guide provides "information on the . . . array of techniques spiders use for catching their prey: trapping in webs, lassoing, jumping, stealing, chasing, ambushing, spitting, fishing, masquerading as other animals and even attracting prey by mimicking the prey's pheromones. . . . Chapters provide information on habitat, hunting techniques, anatomy, general characteristics and location in the world." Publisher's note

Includes bibliographical references

Kelly, Lynne

Spiders; learning to love them. Jacana Books 2009 264p il pa $19.95

Grades: 9 10 11 12 Adult   595.4
  1. Phobias 2. Spiders
  ISBN 978-1-74175-179-6; 1-74175-179-9

"Confirmed arachnophobe (she had nightmares of giant spiders attacking her) Kelly trained herself to love spiders, and in a few months of observing and photographing the spiders around her Melbourne home became a confirmed arachnophile. She first discusses arachnophobia in general and traces the theories as to its roots as a genuine phobia. Her method for overcoming her fear was to first locate spiders around her house and name them. . . . In the course of describing her spiders and their ways, Kelly also imparts what she learned from reading and from scientists, weaving an amazing amount of spider biology into her narrative. . . . This book is a triumph." Booklist

Includes bibliographical references

595.7 Insects

Brock, James P.

★ **Kaufman** field guide to butterflies of North America; [by] Jim P. Brock and Kenn Kaufman; with the collaboration of Rick and Nora Bowers and Lynn Hassler. Houghton Mifflin 2006 391p il map pa $19.95

Grades: 11 12 Adult 595.7

1. Butterflies

ISBN 0-618-76826-2; 978-0-618-76826-4

LC 2006-287515

First published 2003 with title: Butterflies of North America

"Each species is listed by common name and scientific name and receives a several-sentence description, including flight time and larval food plants. All except very local or accidental species also are shown on range maps. The illustrations are opposite the written description, with most species pictured in multiple images. . . . The illustrations are created by digital enhancement of photographs. . . . An essential purchase for all libraries." Booklist [review of 2003 edition]

Capinera, John L.

★ **Field** guide to grasshoppers, crickets, and katydids of the United States; [by] John L. Capinera, Ralph D. Scott, and Thomas J. Walker. Cornell University Press 2004 249p il maps hardcover o.p. pa $29.95

Grades: 11 12 Adult 595.7

1. Crickets 2. Grasshoppers

ISBN 0-8014-4260-5; 0-8014-8948-2 pa

LC 2004-10727

"The highlight is certainly the 50 pages of Scott's color illustrations. . . . For those who want to know what's plaguing them when locusts descend, this is the book." Publ Wkly

Includes bibliographical references

Dourlot, Sonia

Insect museum; describing 114 species of insects and other arthropods, including their natural history and environment. Firefly Books 2009 255p il $39.95

Grades: 9 10 11 12 Adult 595.7

1. Insects 2. Spiders

ISBN 978-1-55407-483-9

"Dourlot's galley of arthropods is a visually arresting introduction to insects and spiders. . . . [Each entry features] a full-page color image of the critter, magnified several times life-size to enhance its monsterlike appearance, and depicted as if set on mounting paper. The image is faced by a page of descriptive data, the etymologies of scientific and common names, and a sidebar of a fun fact or folk story associated with the insect, so the layout gives the effect of looking like the lab book of an enthusiastic collector. . . . Durable both physically and in content, Dourlot's striking tome promises active library usage." Booklist

Includes bibliographical references

Eisner, Thomas

Secret weapons; defenses of insects, spiders, scorpions, and other many-legged creatures. [by] Thomas Eisner, Maria Eisner, Melody V.S. Siegler. Belknap Press of Harvard University Press 2005 372p il $29.95; pa $18.95

Grades: 11 12 Adult 595.7

1. Insects 2. Spiders 3. Animal defenses

ISBN 0-674-01882-6; 0-674-02403-6 pa

LC 2005-41042

"This very readable and well-illustrated book will appeal to all those interested in disciplines like biology, entomology, and ecology." Choice

Includes bibliographical references

Ellis, Hattie

Sweetness & light; the mysterious history of the honeybee. Harmony Books 2004 243p il hardcover o.p. pa $13.95

Grades: 11 12 Adult 595.7

1. Bees 2. Beekeeping

ISBN 1-4000-5405-2; 1-4000-5406-0 pa

LC 2004-4116

"What a delightful volume on the honeybee this is: Not only is the reader treated to a wealth of information on the biology, ecology, and economic importance of that insect, but the interrelationship of the honeybee and humanity throughout history is very nicely presented." Sci Books Films

Includes bibliographical references

Evans, Arthur V.

National Wildlife Federation field guide to insects and spiders & related species of North America; written by Arthur Evans; foreword by Craig Tufts. Sterling Pub. 2007 496p il map pa $19.95

Grades: 7 8 9 10 11 12 Adult 595.7

1. Insects 2. Spiders

ISBN 978-1-4027-4153-1; 1-4027-4153-7

LC 2006-19491

"This guide presents a glimpse of the incredible array of colors, shapes, and forms found within the phylum Arthropoda. . . . Over 380 pages of color photographs follow, most showing two or three different species. . . . This is a very good guide that will find a wide audience." Choice

Holldobler, Bert

The **leafcutter** ants; civilization by instinct. [by] Bert Hölldobler and Edward O. Wilson. Norton 2010 160p il pa $19.95

Grades: 9 10 11 12 Adult 595.7

1. Ants

ISBN 978-0-393-33868-3

LC 2010-16202

The authors "introduce the general reader to earth's most evolved animal society. With the colony's queen as its reproductive organ; the various ages and types of workers as the brain, heart, and other organs; and the communication among the ants similar to the communication of nerves and ganglia, a leafcutter ant colony can be truly considered as a superorganism." Booklist

Includes bibliographical references

Marshall, Stephen A.

★ **Insects**: their natural history and diversity; with a photographic guide to insects of eastern North America. Firefly Books 2006 718p il $95

Grades: 11 12 Adult 595.7

1. Insects

ISBN 978-1-55297-900-6; 1-55297-900-8

LC 2006-389462

This "offers more than 4000 excellent color photographs and concise, accurate information about every major insect family worldwide. . . . This book is simply bigger, prettier, and more comprehensive than any previous publication on insects and will be useful to amateur and professional alike." Libr J

Includes bibliographical references

Milne, Lorus Johnson

The **Audubon** Society field guide to North American insects and spiders; [by] Lorus and Margery Milne; visual key by Susan Rayfield. Knopf 1980 989p il $19.95

Grades: 7 8 9 10 11 12 Adult   595.7
  1. Insects 2. Spiders
  ISBN 0-394-50763-0

                                        LC 80-7620

The authors "have based their field guide on 702 excellent color photographs (75 of which are of spiders and other arachnids). In addition to some general information, the text (two thirds of the book) is made up of brief comments on each kind of arthropod pictured." Choice

Includes glossary

Moffett, Mark W.

Adventures among ants; a global safari with a cast of trillions. University of California Press 2010 280p il $29.95

Grades: 11 12 Adult   595.7
  1. Ants 2. Ants -- Ecology 3. Ants -- Behavior
  ISBN 978-0-520-26199-0; 0-520-26199-2

                                       LC 2009-40610

"This superb book by a first-class writer with an unsurpassed feel for ants begins at the ground level as we come face to face with the creatures, move into their minds, and begin to understand what makes them tick. Moffett organizes his text around six ant lifestyles, each represented by an insect that dominates its habitat: Indian Marauder ants, African army ants, African Weaver ants, Amazon slavemaking ants, Neotropical leaf cutter ants, and the Argentine ant, a global invader. . . . This marvelous volume illustrated with the author's closeup photographs will delight biologists, naturalists, and general readers with a natural history bent." Libr J

Includes bibliographical references

Pyle, Robert Michael

The **Audubon** Society field guide to North American butterflies; visual key by Carol Nehring and Jane Opper. Knopf 1981 916p il $19.95

Grades: 7 8 9 10 11 12 Adult   595.7
  1. Butterflies
  ISBN 0-394-51914-0

                                        LC 80-84240

This guide "introduces more than 600 species of North American butterfly, including those native to the Hawaiian Islands. A section of brilliant color plates (more than 1,000 of them) featuring butterflies in their natural habitats, follows a general introduction and notes on text organization and use." Booklist

Savage, Candace

Bees; nature's little wonders. Greystone Books 2008 136p il $26; pa $16.95

Grades: 11 12 Adult   595.7
  1. Bees
  ISBN 978-1-55365-321-9; 978-1-55365-531-2 pa

"This book is a wonderful read for someone who wants to learn about bees but does not have a scientific background. The writing style is casual and pleasant. Historic poems and artwork pertaining to bees are scattered throughout the book." Sci Books Films

Includes bibliographical references

Turley, Windle

The **amazing** monarch; the secret wintering grounds of an endangered butterfly. photos & text by Windle Turley. Turley Gallery 2010 116 p. il $39.95

Grades: 9 10 11 12 Adult   595.7
  1. Nature photography 2. Monarch butterflies 3. Monarch butterfly
  ISBN 0989220109; 9780989220101

                                       LC 201041274

This book features "photographs of monarch butterflies at their overwintering grounds in Mexico. . . . The photographs are accompanied by short quotations, myths, poems, and stories about butterflies." (Sci Books Films)

In this book, "author and photographer Windle Turley chronicles the life cycle of the monarch butterfly." Publisher's note

Includes bibliographical references and index.

Waldbauer, Gilbert

A **walk** around the pond; insects in and over the water. Harvard University Press 2006 286p il hardcover o.p. pa $16.95

Grades: 11 12 Adult   595.7
  1. Insects 2. Freshwater animals
  ISBN 0-674-02211-4; 0-674-02765-5 pa

                                       LC 2005-44737

"Readers will be inspired to take a closer look at their favorite pond or stream." Booklist

Includes bibliographical references

What good are bugs? insects in the web of life. Harvard University Press 2003 384p il hardcover o.p. pa $17.50

Grades: 11 12 Adult   595.7
  1. Insects
  ISBN 0-674-01027-2; 0-674-01632-7 pa

                                       LC 2002-27335

This "is an excellent work about the beneficial insects, that vast majority of insect species of which we are generally unaware. . . . The author is an excellent writer and provides many interesting examples." Choice

Includes bibliographical references

Zuk, Marlene

Sex on six legs; lessons on life, love, and language from the insect world. [by] Marlene Zuk. Houghton Mifflin Harcourt 2011 262p $25

Grades: 11 12 Adult   **595.7**
  1. Insects 2. Sexual behavior in animals
  ISBN 978-0-15-101373-9

           LC 2010025829
"Despite the title, . . . the book gives clear accounts of a wide range of research beyond sex: insect personalities, wasp facial recognition, fruit flies artificially bred for intelligence, slave-making ants, hitchhiking blister beetles and much more." Sci News

Includes bibliographical references

597 Cold-blooded vertebrates

Benchley, Peter
  Shark trouble; true stories about sharks and the sea. Random House 2002 186p il hardcover o.p. pa $12.95
Grades: 11 12 Adult   **597**
  1. Sharks 2. Marine animals
  ISBN 0-375-50824-4; 0-8129-6633-3 pa

           LC 2002-283533
"Handy with statistics and quick to crack a joke with himself as the target, Benchley offers riveting accounts of his and his family's up close and personal encounters with sharks, a gigantic manta ray, a friendly killer whale, barracuda, and sundry other wild creatures." Booklist

Compagno, Leonard J. V.
  Sharks of the world; [by] Leonard Compagno, Marc Dando, Sarah Fowler. Princeton University Press 2005 368p il map (Princeton field guides) hardcover o.p. pa $29.95
Grades: 11 12 Adult   **597**
  1. Sharks
  ISBN 0-691-12071-4; 0-691-12072-2 pa

           LC 2004-111901
First published in the United Kingdom with title: Field guide to the sharks of the world

The authors cover "over 450 species, including many as-yet-unnamed species and some that are only known from a single specimen. Each is illustrated with both a line drawing and a beautifully rendered color painting; in most cases a ventral view of the head and illustrations of the teeth are included. . . . Packed with information, this is an invaluable guide for anyone interested in this fascinating group." Choice

Includes bibliographical references

Eilperin, Juliet
  Demon fish; travels through the hidden world of sharks. Pantheon Books 2011 xxi, 295p il $26.95
Grades: 11 12 Adult   **597**
  1. Sharks
  ISBN 978-0-375-42512-7

           LC 2010-30264
Eilperin "describes her travels throughout Asia, South Africa, and the United States in search of shark information and folklore. . . . The author provides a well-written overview of current and past attitudes toward sharks and

discusses shark species, physiology, genetics, reproduction, evolution, navigation, and attacks on swimmers." Libr J

Includes bibliographical references

Gilbert, Carter Rowell
  ★ **National** Audubon Society field guide to fishes, North America; [by] Carter R. Gilbert, James D. Williams. rev ed, 2nd ed, fully rev; Alfred A. Knopf 2002 607p il maps pa $19.95
Grades: 7 8 9 10 11 12 Adult   **597**
  1. Fishes -- North America
  ISBN 0-375-41224-7

           LC 2002-20773
First published 1983 with title: The Audubon Society field guide to North American fishes, whales, and dolphins

This guide covers over 600 freshwater and saltwater species in detail, with notes on 771 more species.

Page, Lawrence M.
  ★ **Peterson** field guide to freshwater fishes of North America north of Mexico; [by] Lawrence M. Page, Brooks M. Burr; illustrations by Eugene C. Beckham III . . . [et al.]; maps by Griffin E. Sheehy. 2nd ed.; Houghton Mifflin Harcourt 2011 663p il map pa $21
Grades: 7 8 9 10 11 12 Adult   **597**
  1. Fishes -- North America
  ISBN 978-0-547-24206-4; 0-547-24206-9

           LC 2010-49219
First published 1991 with title: A field guide to freshwater fishes: North America north of Mexico

This guide to identifying different species of freshwater fish in North America includes "maps and information showing where to locate each species of fish—whether that species can be found in miles-long stretches of river or small pools that cover only dozens of square feet." Publisher's note

Includes glossary and bibliographical references

Parker, Steve, 1952-
  The **encyclopedia** of sharks; New ed., completely rev. and updated; Firefly Books 2008 224p il map pa $24.95
Grades: 9 10 11 12   **597**
  1. Reference books 2. Sharks -- Encyclopedias
  ISBN 978-1-55407-409-9

           LC 2008279142
First published 1999

This encyclopedia contains "information on: evolution and design of the shark; classifications and orders; understanding the shark; the life of the shark—how it feeds, breeds and migrates; shark 'supersense'—how it survives in the aquatic environment; [and] the need for protection and conservation." Publisher's note

Pepperell, Julian G.
  Fishes of the open ocean; a natural history & illustrated guide. illustrated by Guy Harvey. University of Chicago Press 2010 266p il map $35

Grades: 11 12 Adult   **597**
1. Fishes
ISBN 978-0-226-65539-0; 0-226-65539-3
LC 2009032290

This book "details the biology and brief ecology of various open-ocean fishes. The first half of the book details the importance of pelagic fish in the oceans, the food web of oceanic life, and the relationship between form (fish shape) and function, along with a historical perspective of interactions between fish and humans. The second half of the book illustrates the distribution range, migratory patterns and behavior, reproductive patterns, and trophic information of various fishes. . . . the book is not exhaustive in detail, it provides a very useful overall description of various fishes and their life in the oceans." Choice

Includes bibliographical references

597.8   Amphibians

Beltz, Ellin

Frogs: inside their remarkable world. Firefly Books 2005 175p il $34.95
Grades: 5 6 7 8 9 10   **597.8**
1. Frogs 2. Toads
ISBN 1-55297-869-9
LC 2006-365517

The author gives a "picture of the history of the frog, its anatomical makeup, its place in the natural world and the threats that are seriously reducing its numbers around the world." Publisher's note

Includes bibliographical references

Elliott, Lang

★ The **frogs** and toads of North America; a comprehensive guide to their identification, behavior, and calls. [by] Lang Elliott, Carl Gerhardt, and Carlos Davidson. Houghton Mifflin 2009 343p il map pa $19.95
Grades: 9 10 11 12 Adult   **597.8**
1. Frogs 2. Toads
ISBN 978-0-618-66399-6; 0-618-66399-1
LC 2008-26090

"The title says it all for this beautiful field guide to all 101 species of frogs and toads found in the U.S. and Canada. Elliott has produced a masterpiece of photographs and particulars of all our native and introduced toads and frogs. Each species is covered in a minimum two-page spread, with common and Latin names, a range map, and a short discussion of appearance, range and habitat, behavior, and voice. . . . The major strength of this book, and one that almost demands its purchase, is the accompanying CD featuring recordings of the calls of every species (with the exception of the two that never vocalize)." Booklist

Includes bibliographical references

Solway, Andrew

Poison frogs and other amphibians; by Andrew Solway. Heinemann Library 2006 48 p. col. ill. (Adapted for success) (library) $32.00; (paperback) $8.99

Grades: 5 6 7 8 9   **597.8**
1. Frogs 2. Animal defenses 3. Amphibians 4. Dendrobatidae
ISBN 140348225X; 9781403482259; 9781403482327
out of print
LC 2006014294

This book by Andrew Solway is part of the Adapted for Success series and looks at poison frogs. "Poison Frogs are among the most poisonous animals in the world, but how have they, and other amphibians, adapted to become so successful? The series explores how some of our favorite animals are uniquely adapted to their environment. Each book . . . covers habitat, defenses, camouflage, and the way animals find food." (Publisher's note)

Includes bibliographical references and index.

597.9   Reptiles

Attenborough, David

Life in cold blood. Princeton University Press 2008 288p il $29.95
Grades: 11 12 Adult   **597.9**
1. Reptiles 2. Amphibians
ISBN 978-0-691-13718-6; 0-691-13718-8
LC 2007-938089

"The writing is crisp and lively, the examples are up to date, and the photography is beautiful. . . . This is a very interesting book, which provides many examples of organisms some of us often overlook." Am Biology Teacher

Conant, Roger

A **field** guide to reptiles & amphibians; eastern and central North America. [by] Roger Conant and Joseph T. Collins; illustrated by Isabelle Hunt Conant and Tom R. Johnson. 3rd ed, expanded; Houghton Mifflin 1998 616p il map (Peterson field guide series) pbk $21
Grades: 7 8 9 10 11 12 Adult   **597.9**
1. Reptiles 2. Amphibians
ISBN 9780395904527
LC 98-13622

First published 1958 with title: A field guide to reptiles and amphibians of the United States and Canada east of the 100th meridian

This guide describes 595 species and subspecies, featuring color photos, black and white drawings, and color distribution maps of reptiles and amphibians of the region. Also includes information on transporting live reptiles and amphibians

Includes glossary and bibliographical references

★ **Peterson** first guide to reptiles and amphibians; [by] Roger Conant, Robert C. Stebbins, Joseph T. Collins. Houghton Mifflin 1999 128p il pa $5.95
Grades: 9 10 11 12   **597.9**
1. Reptiles 2. Amphibians
ISBN 0-395-97195-0
First published 1992

This is a guide to identification of reptile and amphibian species.

This book is "easy to use. The information is accurate and easy to understand. . . . Useful for browsing as well as for identification in the field." Voice Youth Advocates

Ernst, Carl H.
Venomous reptiles of the United States, Canada, and northern Mexico; Carl H. Ernst and Evelyn M. Ernst. Johns Hopkins University Press 2011 424 p. ill. (some col.), maps (v. 2: alk. paper) $75
Grades: 11 12 Adult   **597.9**
1. Reptiles 2. Poisonous animals 3. Animals -- North America 4. Heloderma -- North America 5. Poisonous snakes -- North America
ISBN 0801898757; 0801898765; 9780801898754; 9780801898761
     LC 2010036966
This book presents a reference guide to the venomous reptiles of North America. "The first volume contains species accounts of the venomous lizards and elapid and viperid snakes found north of Mexico's twenty-fifth parallel. Volume 2 of this definitive work covers the twenty-one species of the genus Crotalus found in the United States, Canada, and . . . northern Mexico." (Publisher's note)
"A current, vital addition to herpetology collections." LJ
Includes bibliographical references and index

Orenstein, Ronald
Turtles, tortoises and terrapins; a natural history. Ronald Orenstein. Firefly Books 2012 448 p. ill. (chiefly col.) $59.95
Grades: 9 10 11 12   **597.9**
1. Turtles
ISBN 1770851194; 9781770851191
     LC 2012517857
This book on turtles "is laid out evolutionarily, meaning that [Ronald Orenstein] starts from their evolutionary beginnings, progresses through to the present and maintains that attention to categorization and geography as he proceeds through the groups of turtles and into their morphology and life cycles. Orenstein discusses the biology, social habits, predator prey relationships, reproductive habits, human uses and conservation, (or lack thereof)." (SB&F: Your Guide to Science Resources for All Ages)
"Notable for outstanding color photographs and highly accessible and engaging content." Booklist
Includes bibliographical references and index.

Stebbins, Robert C.
A **field** guide to Western reptiles and amphibians; text and illustrations by Robert C. Stebbins. 3rd ed newly rev; Houghton Mifflin 2003 533p il map (Peterson field guide series) pa $22
Grades: 7 8 9 10 11 12 Adult   **597.9**
1. Reptiles 2. Amphibians
ISBN 0-395-98272-3
     LC 2002-27561
First published 1966
This "covers all the species of reptiles and amphibians found in western North America. More than 650 full-color paintings and photographs show key details for making accurate identifications. . . . Color range maps give species'

distributions. . . . [Includes] information on conservation efforts and survival status." Publisher's note
Includes bibliographical references

597.92   Turtles

Safina, Carl
Voyage of the turtle; in pursuit of the Earth's last dinosaur. Holt 2006 383p il map $27.50; pa $17
Grades: 11 12 Adult   **597.92**
1. Turtles
ISBN 978-0-8050-7891-6; 0-8050-7891-6; 978-0-8050-8318-7 pa; 0-8050-8318-9 pa
     LC 2005-55023
"This is a well-written natural history/conservation narrative. General readers will enjoy the book and hopefully will become excited to learn more about critical environmental issues." Sci Books Films
Includes bibliographical references

Spotila, James R.
★ **Sea** turtles; a complete guide to their biology, behavior, and conservation. Johns Hopkins University Press 2004 227p il $24.95
Grades: 11 12 Adult   **597.92**
1. Sea turtles
ISBN 0-8018-8007-6
     LC 2004-8935
"The author is eloquent in his appeal for the conservation of sea turtles. The best single book on the subject." Booklist
Includes bibliographical references

597.96   Snakes

Ernst, Carl H.
★ **Snakes** of the United States and Canada; [by] Carl H. Ernst, Evelyn M. Ernst. Smithsonian Books 2003 668p il map $70
Grades: 11 12 Adult   **597.96**
1. Snakes
ISBN 1-58834-019-8
     LC 2002-26924
"This current and comprehensive volume contains all the information currently available on the 131 species of snakes living in North America." Libr J
Includes bibliographical references

Mattison, Christopher
The **new** encyclopedia of snakes. Princeton University Press 2007 272p il map $35
Grades: 9 10 11 12 Adult   **597.96**
1. Reference books 2. Snakes -- Encyclopedias
ISBN 0-691-13295-X; 978-0-691-13295-2
     LC 2007-922951
First published 1995 by Facts on File with title: The encyclopedia of snakes
This encyclopedia "covers all aspects of snake biology and habitat. This is not a field guide aimed at snake identification. . . . But the work contains a wealth of information

about our scaled friends, including patterns of distribution and matters relating to evolution and morphology, feeding, reproduction, and defensive strategies. . . . This captivating work will appeal to students and snake lovers everywhere." Libr J

Includes bibliographical references

O'Shea, Mark

★ **Venomous** snakes of the world. Princeton University Press 2005 160p il map $29.95

Grades: 11 12 Adult   **597.96**
1. Snakes 2. Poisonous animals
ISBN 0-691-12436-1

        LC 2005-920576

"Fascinating photographs and descriptions will make this title a favorite." Univ Press Books for Public and Second Sch Libr, 2006

Includes bibliographical references

598 Birds

Alderfer, Jonathan

★ **National** Geographic birding essentials; all the tools, techniques, and tips you need to begin and become a better birder. [by] Jonathan Alderfer and Jon L. Dunn. National Geographic 2007 224p il pa $15.95

Grades: 11 12 Adult   **598**
1. Bird watching
ISBN 978-1-4262-0135-6; 1-4262-0135-4

        LC 2007-30960

This "book offers data on how to begin and how to improve your bird-watching skills. Chapters deal with the pleasures of birding, getting started, where and when birds are found, how common or rare they are at different seasons, parts of a bird, how to identify them, and variations in birds. . . . With a helpful glossary, this is an essential volume for all bird-watchers." Booklist

Includes bibliographical references

★ The **atlas** of bird migration; tracing the great journeys of the world's birds. general editor Jonathan Elphick; foreword by Thomas E. Lovejoy. Firefly Books 2007 176p il map hardcover o.p. pa $24.95

Grades: 11 12 Adult   **598**
1. Birds -- Migration
ISBN 978-1-55407-248-4; 1-55407-248-4; 978-1-55407-971-1 pa; 1-55407-971-3 pa
First published 1995 by Random House

"The first section is a primer on bird migration and habitat usage patterns, consisting of short, illustrated essays on topics like the evolution of migration, the mechanics of flight, birds' navigational methods and how human development affects migration patterns. Succeeding sections examine different families of migrating birds according to geographical distribution, and each has carefully designed maps that show birds' seasonal ranges and migratory routes. The use of color to describe, clarify, distinguish and compare migration patterns is exceptional, and clear explanations of

complicated topics (e.g., how birds fly) make it an excellent text for middle and high school students as well as adults." Publ Wkly

Backhouse, Frances

Owls of North America. Firefly Books 2008 215p il map $34.95

Grades: 11 12 Adult   **598**
1. Owls
ISBN 978-1-55407-342-9; 1-55407-342-1

This book "takes an intimate look at the 22 species of typical owls and 1 species of barn owl found in North America. Eight preliminary chapters examine general owl anatomy, hunting and feeding behavior, communication, mating and care of young, and daily behaviors and migration. Profiles of the 23 species follow, covering all owls found in Canada, the U.S., and Mexico north of the Tropic of Cancer. Each species range is depicted on a map, with specifics of appearance, voice, time of daily activity, distribution, habitat, feeding, breeding, migration, and conservation discussed. Heavily illustrated with beautiful, clear photographs." Booklist

Includes bibliographical references

Berger, Cynthia

Owls; illustrations by Amelia Hansen. Stackpole Books 2005 131p il (Wild guide) pa $19.95

Grades: 11 12 Adult   **598**
1. Owls
ISBN 0-8117-3213-4

        LC 2005-2317

Berger "has produced a wonderfully complete yet compact introduction to owls." Booklist

Includes bibliographical references

Bull, John L.

★ The **National** Audubon Society field guide to North American birds, Eastern region; [by] John Bull and John Farrand, Jr.; revised by John Farrand, Jr.; visual key by Amanda Wilson and Lori Hogan. rev ed; Knopf 1994 797p il maps pa $19.95

Grades: 7 8 9 10 11 12 Adult   **598**
1. Birds -- North America
ISBN 0-679-42852-6

        LC 94-7768

This pictorial guide to 508 eastern species arranges birds by color and shape to simplify identification. It also includes information on bird-watching and conservation status

Chandler, Richard J.

Shorebirds of North America, Europe, and Asia; a photographic guide. [by] Richard Chandler. Princeton University Press 2009 448p il map pa $35

Grades: 11 12 Adult   **598**
1. Birds
ISBN 978-0-691-14281-4; 0-691-14281-5

        LC 2009-921111

"Opening with a comprehensive primer on shorebird geography, speciation, appearance and behavior, Chandler goes on to describe feed techniques in fascinating detail, with illustrations showing how birds disturb small prey on mud flats and marsh grasses. Each species is accompanied by a seasonal distribution map, and a thorough bibliography and index backs up clearly written text." Publ Wkly

Includes bibliographical references

Choiniere, Joseph

What's that bird? getting to know the birds around you, coast-to-coast. [by] Joseph Choiniere & Claire Mowbray Goldin; photography by Tom Vezo; ill. by James Robins. Storey Pub. 2005 117p il map $24.95; pa $14.95

Grades: 9 10 11 12   **598**

1. Birds 2. Bird watching

ISBN 1-58017-555-4; 1-58017-554-6 pa

LC 2004-17307

This book features "facts about bird nesting sites, habitat, song, diet, lifestyle, and migration patterns." Publisher's note

Includes bibliographical references

Chu, Miyoko

Songbird journeys; four seasons in the lives of migratory birds. Walker & Co. 2006 312p il map $23

Grades: 11 12 Adult   **598**

1. Birds -- Migration

ISBN 0-8027-1468-4; 978-0-8027-1468-8

LC 2006-278075

The author describes the "seasonal migrations of American songbirds. . . . In addition to descriptions of the birds' migrations, habits, and life histories for each season, there are details on hotspots for observing the birds, including web sites, addresses, when to go, and special activities. . . . An excellent overview of a compelling subject; highly recommended." Libr J

Includes bibliographical references

Couzens, Dominic

Extreme birds; the world's most extraordinary and bizarre birds. Firefly Books 2008 287p il $45

Grades: 11 12 Adult   **598**

1. Birds

ISBN 978-1-55407-423-5; 1-55407-423-1

"Each of 150 species of bizarre birds from around the world is portrayed in a short essay and a showcase color photograph. These superlative birds are organized in four categories: extreme form (e.g., heaviest flier, smallest species, biggest eyes); extreme ability (e.g., fastest swimmer, highest migration, sharpest hearing); extreme behavior (e.g., largest roost, oddest incubation); and extreme family life (e.g., strangest courtship, sibling rivalry, bigamy). The text is interesting, accurate, and up to date with recent discoveries." Am Ref Books Annu, 2009

Ehrlich, Paul R.

The birder's handbook; a field guide to the natural history of North American birds: including all species that regularly breed north of Mexico. [by] Paul R. Ehrlich, David S. Dobkin, Daryl Wheye. Simon & Schuster 1988 xxx, 785p il hardcover o.p. pa $21.95

Grades: 11 12 Adult   **598**

1. Birds -- North America

ISBN 0-671-65989-8 pa

LC 87-32404

This volume contains "basic information on each of the 646 species of birds in North America, enriched by 250 short essays on all aspects of avian behavior and biology. This book is a companion volume to any illustrated field guide." Am Libr

Includes bibliographical references

Erickson, Laura

The bird watching answer book; everything you need to know to enjoy birds in your backyard and beyond. Storey Pub. 2009 388p il pa $14.95

Grades: 9 10 11 12 Adult   **598**

1. Bird watching

ISBN 978-1-60342-452-3

LC 2009-23708

"Dividing the book into three parts—'For the Birds: Feeding, Watching and Protecting Our Feathered Friends'; 'Bird Brains: Avian Behavior and Intelligence'; and 'All about Birds, Inside and Out'—Erikson organizes a vast amount of bird biology and behavior into manageable snippets. Using a familiar question-and-answer format, the author covers such broad topics as feeding birds and bird migration." Booklist

Includes bibliographical references

Hanson, Thor

★ Feathers; the evolution of a natural miracle. Basic Books 2011 336p il

Grades: 11 12 Adult   **598**

1. Birds 2. Feathers

ISBN 0-465-02013-5; 978-0-465-02013-3

LC 2011003272

Hanson "presents the natural history of feathers, applying the findings of paleontologists, ornithologists, biologists, engineers and art historians to answer questions about the origin of feathers, their evolution and their uses throughout the ages." (Publisher's note) Index.

"Divided into sections that cover such categories as evolution, insulation, flight and adornment, 'Feathers' stretches from the ancient mists of the late Jurassic to the laboratories of today's Smithsonian Museum, where 'snarge'—science slang for what's produced when a bird meets a plane—is analyzed for data. In between, you learn that a falcon thrown out of an airplane can dive at a speed of 242 miles per hour, that the word pen is itself derived from the Latin word for feather and that the most valuable cargo on the Titanic wasn't gold or jewels but more than 40 cases of plumes intended for women's hats, a fashion craze that nearly caused the extinction of several species and led to the formation of the Audubon Society, as well as America's first National Wildlife Refuge, Florida's Pelican Island. Mr. Hanson may be a scientist but he writes like a man who believes in the value of story. . . . [He] offers more than a fanciful, associative style. He is a very good explainer of serious biology." Wall Street J

Includes bibliographical references

Jones, Mark

Albatross; their world, their ways. [by] Tui De Roy, Mark Jones, Julian Fitter. Firefly Books 2008 240p il map $49.95

Grades: 11 12 Adult   **598**

1. Albatrosses

ISBN 978-1-55407-415-0

LC 2008-274293

"In this magnificent book about a magnificent bird—the revered, now endangered albatross—wildlife photographer De Roy and contributing scientists cover all aspects of albatross beauty, biology, and conservation." Booklist

Includes bibliographical references

Kaufman, Kenn

Kaufman field guide to birds of North America; with the collaboration of Rick and Nora Bowers and Lynn Hassler Kaufman. Houghton Mifflin 2005 392p il map pa $18.95

Grades: 11 12 Adult   **598**

1. Birds -- North America

ISBN 0-618-57423-9; 978-0-618-57423-0

First published 2000 with title: Birds of North America

For this identification guide "Kaufman selected over 2000 digitally edited photographs, enhanced to improve contrast, color, and the like. The excellent result will appeal to beginning birders perhaps intimidated by illustrations. . . . Kaufman's text is simple and uncluttered, a plus for novices." Libr J

Lynch, Wayne

Penguins of the world; text and photographs by Wayne Lynch. 2nd ed.; Firefly Books 2007 175p il map $34.95; pa $24.95

Grades: 11 12 Adult   **598**

1. Penguins

ISBN 978-1-55407-334-4; 1-55407-334-0; 978-1-55407-274-3 pa; 1-55407-274-3 pa

LC 2007-299218

First published 1997

This is a "look at Lynch's discoveries about these flightless seabirds in the field and in scientific journals, during day-to-day as well as birth-to-death observations, and from the smallest to the largest type. While Lynch presents detailed descriptions of everything from mating rituals to eating habits, the best parts of his book are the photographs. Lynch's gorgeous and gorgeously printed images . . . display such a refined visual sensibility that even without accompanying text, the images would still achieve Lynch's goal of presenting the scientific and aesthetic appeal of this unique family of birds." Publ Wkly

Includes bibliographical references

McCarthy, Michael

Say goodbye to the cuckoo; migratory birds and the impending ecological catastrophe. Ivan R. Dee 2010 274p $26.95

Grades: 9 10 11 12 Adult   **598**

1. Endangered species 2. Birds -- Migration

ISBN 978-1-56663-856-2; 1-56663-856-9

In luminous prose, British writer McCarthy addresses the cultural significance of migratory songbirds, from nightingales to turtle doves to the European cuckoo, on the heart and soul. . . . Then, finally, he relates the devastating facts about global warming, which causes avian 'mistiming,' and other causes of the current migratory species crash. A stunning and profound book." Booklist

National Audubon Society

Bird; the definitive visual guide. Audubon; [senior editor, Peter Frances; contributors, BirdLife International, David Burnie] DK Pub. 2007 512p il map $50

Grades: 9 10 11 12 Adult   **598**

1. Birds

ISBN 978-0-7566-3153-6; 0-7566-3153-X

LC 2007-282186

"From flyleaf to fore edge, the visuals are astounding. . . . An enclosed CD with bird calls and songs adds yet another dimension to a glorious work." Libr J

Peterson, Roger Tory, 1908-1996

Peterson field guide to birds of Eastern and Central North America; [by] Roger Tory Peterson, with contributions from Michael DiGiorgio [et al.] 6th ed; Houghton Mifflin Harcourt 2010 445p il map (Peterson field guide series) $19.95

Grades: 5 6 7 8 9 10 11 12 Adult   **598**

1. Birds -- North America

ISBN 978-0-547-15246-2; 0-547-15246-9

LC 2009-37681

First published 1934 with title: A field guide to the birds

This guide to birds found east of the Rocky Mountains contains colored illustrations painted by the author, with a description of each species on the facing page. Views of young birds and seasonal variations in plumage are included.

Peterson, Roger Tory, 1908-1996

★ **Peterson** field guide to birds of North America; with contributions from Michael DiGiorgio . . . [et al.] Houghton Mifflin Co. 2008 527p il map (Peterson field guide series) $26

Grades: 5 6 7 8 9 10 11 12 Adult   **598**

1. Birds -- North America

ISBN 0-618-96614-5; 978-0-618-96614-1

LC 2007-39803

First published 1934 with title: A field guide to the birds. Previously published in two separate parts as A field guide to western birds (1990) and A field guide to the birds of eastern and central North America (2002)

This guide to birds found in North America contains colored illustrations painted by the author, with a description of each species on the facing page. Views of young birds and seasonal variations in plumage are included. The book also includes a URL to video podcasts.

"This field guide is of high quality and should be in millions of birders' and other nature lovers' backpacks." Sci Books Films

Peterson field guide to birds of Western North America; with contributions from Michael DiGior-

gio [et al.] 4th ed; Houghton Mifflin Harcourt 2010 493p il map (Peterson field guide series) pa $19.95
Grades: 5 6 7 8 9 10 11 12 Adult   **598**
1. Birds -- North America
ISBN 978-0-547-15270-7; 0-547-15270-1
    LC 2009-39158
First published 1941 with title: A field guide to western birds

This guide illustrates over 600 species of birds on 176 color plates. In addition, over 588 range maps are included.

The **Princeton** encyclopedia of birds; edited by Christopher Perrins. Princeton University Press 2009 656p il map pa $35
Grades: 9 10 11 12 Adult   **598**
1. Reference books 2. Birds -- Encyclopedias
ISBN 978-0-691-14070-4; 0-691-14070-7
First published 1985 by Facts on File with title: The encyclopedia of birds. Previous edition published 2003 by Firefly Bks. with title: Firefly encyclopedia of birds

The editor "combines the work of 150 contributors and more than 1000 great color photographs, maps, and other illustrations to produce a stunning book that informs both amateurs and experts. Coverage includes form and function, distribution, diet, breeding biology, and conservation and environment." Libr J

Includes bibliographical references

Sibley, David
★ The **Sibley** field guide to birds of Eastern North America; written and illustrated by David Allen Sibley. Knopf 2003 431p il pa $19.95
Grades: 11 12 Adult   **598**
1. Birds -- North America
ISBN 0-679-45120-X
    LC 2002-114931
"All the qualities to be expected in a field guide are here. . . . Image reproduction is crisp, colors are distinct, shading shows well, and despite the very small size, range map colors are clear. . . . Sibley has accomplished the difficult task of condensing . . . [The Sibley guide to birds] to practical field size." Libr J

★ The **Sibley** field guide to birds of Western North America; written and illustrated by David Allen Sibley. Knopf 2003 473p il pa $19.95
Grades: 11 12 Adult   **598**
1. Birds -- North America
ISBN 0-679-45121-8
    LC 2002-114930
"All the qualities to be expected in a field guide are here. . . . Image reproduction is crisp, colors are distinct, shading shows well, and despite the very small size, range map colors are clear. . . . Sibley has accomplished the difficult task of condensing . . . [The Sibley guide to birds] to practical field size." Libr J

★ The **Sibley** guide to bird life & behavior; illustrated by David Allen Sibley; edited by Chris Elphick, John B. Dunning, Jr., David Allen Sibley. Knopf 2001 588p il maps hardcover o.p. pa $39.95

Grades: 11 12 Adult   **598**
1. Birds -- North America
ISBN 0-679-45123-4; 1-4000-4386-7 pa
    LC 2001-33903
This companion volume to The Sibley guide to birds provides "information about birds' lives and behavior. . . . Part 1 ('The World of Birds') discusses basic avian biology, including form, distribution, population, and conservation, in about 100 pages. Part 2 ('Bird Families of North America'), to which over 40 ornithologists contributed, uses a standard format to describe taxonomy, foraging, breeding, range, nests, eggs, longevity, conservation, and more." Libr J

★ The **Sibley** guide to birds; written and illustrated by David Sibley. Knopf 2000 544p il maps pa $35
Grades: 11 12 Adult   **598**
1. Birds -- North America
ISBN 0-679-45122-6
    LC 00-41239
"This stunning volume stands out as a must have for even casual birders." SLJ

Sterry, Paul
Birds of Eastern North America; a photographic guide. [by] Paul Sterry & Brian E. Small. Princeton University Press 2009 336p il map $45; pa $18.95
Grades: 11 12 Adult   **598**
1. Birds -- North America
ISBN 978-0-691-13425-3; 978-0-691-13426-0 pa
    LC 2009-1494
The author "offer birders excellent state-of-the art digital photos and comprehensive, up-to-date data on North American birds. Species information includes common and scientific names, field marks, plumage variation, size, vocalization, range maps provided by Cornell Laboratory of Ornithology, and habitat. Conservation status and observation tips for each species are also included." Libr J

Includes bibliographical references

Birds of Western North America; a photographic guide. [by] Paul Sterry and Brian E. Small. Princeton University Press 2009 416p il map $45; pa $18.95
Grades: 11 12 Adult   **598**
1. Birds -- North America
ISBN 978-0-691-13427-7; 978-0-691-13428-4 pa
    LC 2009-1416
The authors "cover more than 500 species an variants—including birds that migrate down the Pacific and Rocky Mountain flyways and over the eastern Pacific Ocean, as well as Eastern birds known to visit—assembling photos, geographical data, species descriptions and field observations from the Cornell Laboratory of Ornithology. Experienced guidebook authors, Sterry and Small present their information in an organized, easy-to-use manner." Publ Wkly

Includes bibliographical references

Tennant, Alan
On the wing; to the edge of the earth with the peregrine falcon. Alfred A. Knopf 2004 304p il $26.95; pa $14.95

Grades: 11 12 Adult **598**
  1. Falcons
  ISBN 0-375-41551-3; 1-4000-3182-6 pa
                  LC 2003-69496

"An exhilarating and illuminating storyteller, Tennant offers exquisitely poetic descriptions of peregrine falcons—magnificently aerodynamic, keen-sighted, and fearless birds of prey—a galvanizing history of falconry, and a sobering accounting of the consequences of rampant chemical pollution and environmental destruction." Booklist

Udvardy, Miklos D. F.
  ★ **National** Audubon Society field guide to North American birds, Western region; revised by John Farrand, Jr.; visual key by Amanda Wilson and Lori Hogan. rev ed; Knopf 1994 822p il maps pa $19.95

Grades: 6 7 8 9 10 11 12 Adult **598**
  1. Birds -- North America
  ISBN 0-679-42851-8
                  LC 94-7415

In this guide, "virtually every bird found in North America is brought to life in a full-color photograph and with textual information on the bird's voice, nesting habits, habitat, range, and interesting behaviors. Accompanying range maps; overhead flight silhouettes; sections on bird-watching, accidental species, and endangered birds" are also included. (Publisher's note)

Unwin, Mike
  The **atlas** of birds; diversity, behavior, and conservation. Princeton University Press 2011 144p il map pa $22.95

Grades: 11 12 Adult **598**
  1. Birds 2. Atlases 3. Reference books
  ISBN 978-0-691-14949-3
                  LC 2011920367

This "is neither a textbook nor an encyclopedia but rather a compendium of interesting factoids and bird trivia, with each two-page layout addressing one aspect of bird biology. This is a book for general readers who enjoy studying birds." Choice

  Includes bibliographical references

Zickefoose, Julie
  Baby Birds; An Artist Looks into the Nest. Julie Zickefoose. Houghton Mifflin Harcourt 2016 352 p. color illustrations $28

Grades: 11 12 Adult **598**
  1. Birds 2. Nest building
  ISBN 0544206703; 9780544206700

In this book, by Julie Zickefoose, "more than 400 water-color paintings show the breathtakingly swift development of seventeen different species of wild birds. Sixteen of those species nest on Julie's wildlife sanctuary, so she knows the birds intimately, and writes about them with authority. Julie shares a lifetime of insight about bird breeding biology, growth, and cognition." (Publisher's note)

  "This is not a field guide; rather, it is for learning about baby birds and savoring watercolor paintings of them in more contemplative settings. It will appeal to lovers of nature art and bird-watching enthusiasts." Library Journal

  Includes bibliographical references (pages 326-327) and index

599 Mammals

Attenborough, David
  The **life** of mammals. Princeton University Press 2002 320p il $35

Grades: 11 12 Adult **599**
  1. Mammals
  ISBN 0-691-11324-6
                  LC 2002-106846

"Heavily illustrated with beautiful photographs and enlivened by Attenborough's friendly, informative writing style, this is a terrific introduction to the wonders of our hairy, milk-producing relatives." Booklist

Elbroch, Mark
  ★ **Mammal** tracks & sign; a guide to North American species. Stackpole Bks. 2003 779p il maps $44.95

Grades: 11 12 Adult **599**
  1. Mammals 2. Animal tracks
  ISBN 0-8117-2626-6
                  LC 2002-10549

The author "brings an ideal combination of practical experience and careful research to this work. . . . A definitive treatment, Elbroch's book will set the standard for years to come and is essential to anyone interested in tracking this continent's mammals." Libr J

  Includes bibliographical references

Forsyth, Adrian
  Mammals of North America. Firefly Bks. (Buffalo) 1999 352p il maps hardcover o.p. pa $29.95

Grades: 11 12 Adult **599**
  1. Mammals
  ISBN 1-55209-409-X; 1-55407-233-6 pa

"The author has limited his work to approximately 150 species that inhabit some of the same territory as humans. . . . Each chapter follows the same format: the common name of the species followed by the Latin name; a color photograph; a sidebar consisting of a map with the habitat shaded, a description, and vital statistics, including life span, diet, habitat, predators, and dental formula; and an article of a few paragraphs to several pages describing the mammal's life in the wild. . . . This resource can be used by students for reports because the text is clear and easy to comprehend." Booklist

Kays, Roland
  Mammals of North America; [by] Roland W. Kays and Don E. Wilson. 2nd ed.; Princeton University Press 2009 248p il map (Princeton field guides) $45; pa $19.95

Grades: 11 12 Adult **599**
  1. Mammals
  ISBN 978-0-691-14278-4; 978-0-691-14092-6 pa
                  LC 2009-1417

First published 2002

This "is a durable and portable field guide [to mammals] that should hold up to many years of use. Its range maps are clear, easy to interpret, and placed conveniently adjacent to accompanying text.... Kays and Wilson's inclusion of print, scat (carnivore and herbivore), and dive sequence illustrations may be particularly valuable to novices and occasional observers who are more likely to see signs of species than the species themselves." Sci Books Films

Includes bibliographical references

Mammals; editorial consultants, Juliet Clutton-Brock, Don E. Wilson. DK 2002 400p il map (Smithsonian handbooks) hardcover o.p. pa $20
Grades: 9 10 11 12   599
1. Mammals
ISBN 0-7513-3374-3; 0-7894-8404-8 pa
                                        LC 2001-47823
This book features over 500 profiles of mammals including descriptions, color photos, and facts about the animals.

Mammals of the Northern Hemisphere; edited by Tim Harris. Brown Bear Books 2011 64 p. col. ill., col. maps (Facts at Your Fingertips: endangered animals) (library binding) $35.65
Grades: 7 8 9   599
1. Mammals 2. Endangered species 3. Wildlife conservation 4. Rare mammals -- Northern Hemisphere
ISBN 1936333341; 9781936333349
                                        LC 2010053969
This book is part of the "Facts at Your Fingertips: Endangered Animals" series. "Each page has all benefits of a picture book with large, colorful photographs that accompany the encyclopedia-style text. Each new animal is accompanied by a 'data panel,' which summarizes . . . information such as location, size, habitat, population and diet. This series focuses on animals facing extinction all over the world. Factors contributing to the animal's endangered status as well as preservation techniques are also discussed." The book "talks about well-known animals like the Polar Bear and Giant Panda as well as lesser-known mammals such as the Ryukyu Flying Fox." (Children's Literature)

Includes bibliographical references (p. 63) and index.

Morris, Desmond

Monkey; Desmond Morris. University of Chicago Press 2013 224 p. (paperback) $19.95
Grades: 10 11 12 Adult   599
1. Monkeys 2. Human-animal relationship 3. Monkey -- history 4. Monkeys and civilization
ISBN 1780230966; 9781780230962
This book by Desmond Morris "unpacks human attitudes toward [monkeys]. Morris reveals that our fascination with monkeys extends through many cultures and eras--ancient Egyptians revered baboons, monkey deities featured prominently in ancient Chinese and Japanese religions, and sacred status was given to the langur monkey by some groups in India. He also describes how our relationship with monkeys has changed since [Charles] Darwin, and even become more troubled." (Publisher's note)

The **Princeton** encyclopedia of mammals; edited by David W. Macdonald. Princeton University Press 2009 936p il map pa $45
Grades: 9 10 11 12 Adult   599
1. Reference books 2. Mammals -- Encyclopedias
ISBN 978-0-691-14069-8; 0-691-14069-3
This encyclopedia features a "general introduction to mammals followed by . . . accounts of species and groups that . . . describe form, distribution, behavior, status, conservation, and more." Publisher's note

Includes bibliographical references

Whitaker, John O.

★ **National** Audubon Society field guide to North American mammals; rev ed; Knopf 1996 937p il maps pa $19.95
Grades: 6 7 8 9 10 11 12 Adult   599
1. Mammals
ISBN 0-679-44631-1
                                        LC 95-81456
First published 1980
This field guide describes 390 species of mammals of North America and includes keys for identification, range maps, information on tracks and anatomy, and 375 color photos

599.2   Marsupials and monotremes

Flannery, Tim F.

★ **Chasing** kangaroos; a continent, a scientist, and a search for the world's most extraordinary creature. Grove Press 2007 258p il map hardcover o.p. pa $14
Grades: 11 12 Adult   599.2
1. Kangaroos 2. Australia -- Description and travel
ISBN 978-0-8021-1852-3; 0-8021-1852-6; 978-0-8021-4371-6 pa; 0-8021-4371-7 pa
                                        LC 2006-52628
First published 2004 in Australia with title: Country
"In a time where pride in one's country is a rarity, Flannery has written a love letter to his. . . . Just as much as Chasing Kangaroos is about the evolution of a creature, it's also Flannery's acknowledgement of Australia's inherent uniqueness, a uniqueness he begs is not casually lost in the growing conformity of the global landscape." Paste

Moyal, Ann

Platypus; the extraordinary story of how a curious creature baffled the world. Smithsonian Institution Press 2001 226p il maps $21.95
Grades: 11 12 Adult   599.2
1. Platypus
ISBN 1-56098-977-7
                                        LC 2001-20892
The author offers an "account of this odd Australian mammal as she follows the story of its discovery, the scientific infighting over its place in taxonomy, and modern efforts to understand its biology and keep and breed it in captivity. The author captures the state of nineteenth-century scientific inquiry beautifully. Well illustrated with period engravings

of both the animal and the scientists who fought over it, as well as photographs of the living animal." Booklist

Includes bibliographical references (p.   )

599.4 Bats

Richardson, Phil

Bats. Firefly Books 2011 128p il pa $19.95

Grades: 9 10 11 12 Adult **599.4**

1. Bats

ISBN 978-1-55407-803-5

This book "describes these mammals' complex life cycles and explains how anyone can watch and study bats and help to conserve them." Publisher's note

Includes bibliographical references

599.5 Cetaceans and sea cows

Bortolotti, Dan

★ Wild blue; a natural history of the world's largest animal. Thomas Dunne Books 2008 315p il map $24.95

Grades: 11 12 Adult **599.5**

1. Whales

ISBN 978-0-312-38387-9; 0-312-38387-8

LC 2008-24933

The author "provides the most comprehensive title yet on blue whales for the general reader. Encapsulating everything from statistical analysis of geographic populations to the reports of whalers from centuries past, Wild Blue is an effective twenty-first-century fusion of marine biology and international politics." Booklist

Includes bibliographical references

Kelsey, Elin

★ Watching giants; the secret lives of whales. with photographs by Doc White; additional photographs by François Gohier. University of California Press 2009 201p il $24.95

Grades: 11 12 Adult **599.5**

1. Whales

ISBN 978-0-520-24976-9; 0-520-24976-3

LC 2008-7782

"An appealing, agitating foray into the world of whales that ignites both protective instincts and a hungry curiosity to know more." Kirkus

Includes bibliographical references

Nicklin, Flip

Among giants; a life with whales. Charles 'Flip' Nicklin. University of Chicago Press 2011 190 p. $40

Grades: 9 10 11 12 Adult **599.5**

1. Whales 2. Photography of animals

ISBN 0226580997; 9780226580999

LC 2010029430

This book "tells the story of [cetacean photographer Charles 'Flip'] Nicklin's life and career on the high seas, from his first ill-equipped shoots in the mid-1970s through his long association with the National Geographic Society to the present, when he is one of the founders of Whale Trust, a nonprofit conservation and research group." (Publisher's note)

"Nicklin has created an exciting tale combining the adventure (and drudgery) of field research and the discovery of what whales do and why." Booklist

Includes bibliographical references and index

Reep, Roger L.

The Florida manatee; biology and conservation. [by] Roger L. Reep and Robert K. Bonde. University Press of Florida 2006 189p il map $34.95

Grades: 11 12 Adult **599.5**

1. Manatees

ISBN 978-0-8130-2949-8; 0-8130-2949-X

LC 2005-58578

"The authors explore Sirenian history . . . and detail the manatee lifestyle. They explain, with expertise, the neuroanatomy, senses, perception, and behavior, revealing (in a comparative framework) how the aquatic environment demanded solutions very different from those found in terrestrial animals. No other source fulfills more admirably the goal of inspiring and recruiting young talent into the fold of Sirenian conservation around the world." Choice

Includes bibliographical references

599.66 Odd-toed ungulates

Hyde, Dayton O.

All the wild horses; preserving the spirit and beauty of the world's wild horses. photography by Rita Summers and Charles G. Summers, Jr. MBI Pub. Co. 2006 208p il pa $24.99

Grades: 9 10 11 12 Adult **599.66**

1. Horses

ISBN 978-0-7603-2590-2; 0-7603-2590-1; 978-0-7603-3648-9 pa; 0-7603-3648-2 pa

LC 2006-015586

"There is no better book for horse lovers or anyone interested in the horse as an icon of the American West." Booklist

599.67 Elephants

Anthony, Lawrence, 1950-2012

The elephant whisperer; my life with the herd in the African wild. [by] Lawrence Anthony with Graham Spence. Thomas Dunne Books/St. Martin's Press 2009 368p il $24.99

Grades: 11 12 Adult **599.67**

1. Elephants 2. Wildlife refuges

ISBN 978-0-312-56578-7

LC 2009-23815

This is the author's "robust portrait of Thula Thula, the game land he owns, in cooperation with a number of Zulu tribes, in Zululand—5,000 acres of raw landscape that is thought to have been part of the exclusive hunting grounds of the Zulu king. No longer, since Anthony now runs it as a conservationist lodge, but it continues to produce colorful tales of wild discovery. Most prominent are the many fascinating stories that surround his adoption of the elephants, an unruly bunch he endeavors to make at home on the reserve. With a combination of intuition and experience, the author intelligently discusses many aspects of elephant behavior." Kirkus

599.7 Carnivores

Ross, Mark

Predator; life and death in the African bush. [by] Mark C. Ross and David Reesor. Abrams 2007 207p il $35

Grades: 9 10 11 12   **599.7**

1. Predatory animals 2. Animals -- Africa

ISBN 978-0-8109-9301-3; 0-8109-9301-5

LC 2006-36127

"Ecological depth and plentiful insight make this an excellent addition to middle and high-school classrooms, while vivid photographs provide a fine virtual tour of the African bush and a great advert for conservation efforts." Publ Wkly

Includes bibliographical references

599.75 Cat family

Alderton, David

★ **Wild** cats of the world; photographs by Bruce Tanner. Facts on File 2002 192p il map $35

Grades: 7 8 9 10   **599.75**

1. Wild cats

ISBN 0-8160-5217-4

LC 2002-34736

First published 1993

This "volume explores the development and behavior of wild cats, with chapters covering form and function, evolution, and distribution. It also examines each species in detail, providing information on distinctive features such as sight, hearing, hunting techniques, and locomotion." Publisher's note

Includes bibliographical references

Caputo, Philip

Ghosts of Tsavo; stalking the mystery lions of East Africa. National Geographic Soc. 2002 275p il $27; pa $15

Grades: 11 12 Adult   **599.75**

1. Lions 2. Tsavo National Park (Kenya)

ISBN 0-7922-6362-6; 0-7922-4100-2 pa

LC 2002-22642

This is a study of the Tsavo lions of Kenya. Philip Caputo discusses "why they are bigger than their counterparts of the Serengeti plains, why the males do not normally grow manes, and why Tsavo lions are more prone than Serengeti lions to make humans a part of their diet. The observable differences between Tsavo lions and Serengeti lions have led some behavioral scientists whom Mr. Caputo interviews to believe that the Tsavo lions are actually a different species." N Y Times (Late N Y Ed)

599.77 Dog family

Grambo, Rebecca L.

Wolf: legend, enemy, icon; photographs by Daniel J. Cox. Firefly Books 2006 176p il $34.95

Grades: 11 12 Adult   **599.77**

1. Wolves

ISBN 1-55407-044-9

Shifting "between science and myth, with sociological, anthropological, and ethological stops along the way, Grambo explores all sides of the wolf, from both lupine and human perspectives. The many illustrations, which include Daniel Cox's images of wolves in the wild, reinforce the premise of the text." Booklist

Includes bibliographical references

McAllister, Ian

The **last** wild wolves; ghosts of the rain forest. with contributions by Chris Darimont; introduction by Paul C. Paquet. University of California Press 2007 191p il map $39.95

Grades: 11 12 Adult   **599.77**

1. Wolves

ISBN 978-0-520-25473-2; 0-520-25473-2

LC 2007-10887

"The text is particularly well written and engaging. . . . However, it is the dozens of unique photos sprinkled liberally throughout the book that provide the greatest appeal." Sci Books Films

Smith, Douglas W.

Decade of the wolf; returning the wild to Yellowstone. [by] Douglas W. Smith & Gary Ferguson. Lyons Press 2005 212p il maps $23.95; pa $16.95

Grades: 11 12 Adult   **599.77**

1. Wolves 2. Endangered species 3. Yellowstone National Park

ISBN 1-59228-700-X; 1-59228-886-3 pa

LC 2005-40767

"Well illustrated with black-and-white and color photographs, this intimate history of the return of the top predator to Yellowstone will find an eager audience." Booklist

Includes bibliographical references

Steinhart, Peter

The **company** of wolves. Knopf 1995 374p il maps hardcover o.p. pa $14.95

Grades: 11 12 Adult   **599.77**

1. Wolves

ISBN 0-679-41881-4; 0-679-74387-1 pa

LC 94-26913

This is "an examination of the relationship between humans and wolves in the wolves' last refuges in the Arctic and in places where the two species live together again as wolves move into new areas, either through their own natural movements or through attempts at reintroduction. Steinhart . . . speaks with wolf biologists, wildlife managers, trappers, ranchers, Native Americans, and others. Though it is clear where Steinhart's sympathies lie, the book is balanced between the wolves' advocates and their opponents." Libr J

Includes bibliographical references

Yuskavitch, Jim

In **wolf** country; the power and politics of reintroduction. Jim Yuskavitch. Globe Pequot 2015 224
p. $18.95

Grades: 10 11 12 Adult   **599.77**
1. Wolves 2. Rocky Mountains 3. Gray wolf --
Reintroduction -- Rocky Mountains Region 4. Gray
wolf -- Reintroduction -- Political aspects -- Rocky
Mountains Region
ISBN 0762797533; 9780762797530

LC 2014037561

This book, by Jim Yuskavitch, "tells the story of the first
groups of wolves that emigrated from reintroduced areas
in Idaho to re-colonize their former habitat in the Pacific
Northwest, how government officials prepared for their arrival, and the battles between the people who welcome them
and the people who don't, set against the backdrop of the
ongoing political controversy surrounding wolf populations
in the Northern Rockies." (Publisher's note)

Includes bibliographical references and index

599.78   Bears

Breiter, Matthias

Bears: [a year in the life] Firefly Books 2005
176p il $34.95

Grades: 11 12 Adult   **599.78**
1. Bears
ISBN 1-55407-077-5

LC 2006-295648

The author offers a "look at three species of bears by
following their lives through each month of the year. . . .
Breiter works a tremendous amount of natural history into
this calendar approach, and his photo illustrations are both
apt and beautiful." Booklist

Includes bibliographical references

Ellis, Richard

On thin ice; the changing world of the polar bear.
Alfred A. Knopf 2009 400p il $28.95

Grades: 11 12 Adult   **599.78**
1. Polar bear 2. Greenhouse effect
ISBN 978-0-307-27059-7; 0-307-27059-9

LC 2009-20017

This profile of the habitat and life cycle of the polar bear
covers the species' venerated position in Inuit culture, its
reproductive habits, and the environmental factors that are
compromising its ability to survive.

"The real strength of the book is its focus on the polar
bear as the poster child of global warming, of how tied the
bears are to the arctic ice and what will happen if the ice
melts, and of the national and international wrangling over
the politics of climate change and the listing of the bear as
an endangered species. The polar bear could not ask for a
better champion than Ellis in this highly recommended
work." Booklist

Includes bibliographical references

Rosing, Norbert

The **world** of the polar bear. Firefly Books 2006
203p il $45

Grades: 11 12 Adult   **599.78**
1. Polar bear
ISBN 978-1-55407-155-5; 1-55407-155-0

This book contains "a season-by-season account of the
life of the polar bear, including feeding, mating, rearing of
cubs and journeying from the ice; an intimate look at the
animals that share the polar bear's environment, including
seals, arctic foxes, walruses and muskoxen; a section on
such northern sky phenomena as sun dogs and the northern
lights; [and] many anecdotes and insights about the polar
bear." Publisher's note

Includes bibliographical references

599.784   Grizzly bear (Brown bear)

Busch, Robert

The **grizzly** almanac; [by] Robert H. Busch. Lyons Press 2000 229p il maps hardcover o.p. pa
$19.95

Grades: 11 12 Adult   **599.784**
1. Grizzly bear
ISBN 1-58574-143-4; 1-59228-320-9 pa

LC 00-58587

The author "traces the evolution of the 'big bear' from its
earliest days, describes its habitat and behavior, and recounts
grizzly folklore and tales of grizzly attacks. Maintaining that
the grizzly's reputation as a vicious killer is undeserved, he
makes recommendations for a more peaceful coexistence
with humans." Libr J

Includes bibliographical references

599.786   Polar bear

Mulvaney, Kieran

The **great** white bear; a natural and unnatural
history of the polar bear. Kieran Mulvaney. Houghton Mifflin Harcourt 2011 xiii, 251 p.p il $26

Grades: 11 12 Adult   **599.786**
1. Furbearing animals 2. Polar bear
ISBN 0547152426; 9780547152424

LC 2010017206

This book covers the polar bear's "natural history and its
historical and current encounters with humans." (Sci Books
Films) Annotated bibliography. Index.

"Mixing historical accounts, research data, and his own
observations, Mulvaney skillfully describes the harsh nomadic life of polar bears." Booklist

Includes bibliographical references (p. [221]-240)
and index

599.79   Marine carnivores

Miller, David

Seals & sea lions. Voyageur Press 1998 72p il
(World life library) pa $16.95

Grades: 9 10 11 12   **599.79**
1. Seals (Animals)
ISBN 0-89658-371-6

LC 97-44771
This describes the habits and habitats of seals and sea lions and threats to their existence
Includes bibliographical references (p. 72) and index

Williams, Terrie M.
The **odyssey** of KP2; an orphan seal, a marine biologist, and the fight to save a species from extinction. Terrie M. Williams. Penguin Press 2012 xvi, 283 p.p ill. (hardcover) $27.95
Grades: 9 10 11 12 Adult   **599.79**
1. Animal rescue 2. Seals (Animals) 3. Wildlife rehabilitation 4. Endangered species -- Hawaii 5. Wildlife conservation -- Hawaii 6. Wildlife rehabilitation -- Hawaii 7. Hawaiian monk seal -- Conservation
ISBN 1594203393; 9781594203398

LC 2011050415
AAAS/Subaru SB&F Prize for Excellence in Science Books: Young Adult Science Book (2013)
This book "chronicles . . . an orphaned Hawaiian monk seal's . . . rescue and first years of life. . . . [Terrie M.] Williams and her team of researchers began an intense study of the young male, and they collected important data on KP2's growth rates, feeding habits and sociability, with the 'survival of [the] entire species' resting on his shoulders." (Kirkus Reviews)

599.8 Primates

Among African apes; stories and photos from the field. edited by Martha M. Robbins and Christophe Boesch. University of California Press 2011 182p il map pa $29.95; ebook $29.95
Grades: 11 12 Adult   **599.8**
1. Apes
ISBN 978-0-520-26710-7 pa; 978-0-520-94883-9 ebook

LC 2010033131
This book on apes contains some violent content. "The authors want to raise awareness about the plight of African apes. To do so, they draw upon research careers that go back at least 30 years. Included in the text are day-to-day accounts of what it takes to organize and find a research site in Africa, what it's like to track a gorilla, what it's like to experience a chimp or bonobo community, and what happens to these communities as a result of their encounters with various human communities. . . . Rarely does a book so perfectly illustrate the scientific process. The interaction between researcher and subject comes alive in these pages." Sci Books Films
Includes bibliographical references

Goodall, Jane
★ **In** the shadow of man; photographs by Hugo van Lawick; [with a new preface; foreword by Richard Wrangham] Mariner Books 2009 xxx, 302p il map pa $15.95

Grades: 11 12 Adult   **599.8**
1. Chimpanzees
ISBN 978-0-547-33416-5

LC 2009044848
First published 1971
The author describes the chimpanzee group she studied during ten years of field observation in the Gombe Stream Chimpanzee Reserve in Tanzania.
Includes bibliographical references

★ **Through** a window; my thirty years with the chimpanzees of Gombe. [with a new preface and a new afterword] Houghton Mifflin Harcourt 2010 xx, 337p il map pa $15.95
Grades: 11 12 Adult   **599.8**
1. Chimpanzees
ISBN 978-0-547-33695-4; 0-547-33695-0

LC 2009045230
First published 1990
This continuation of In the shadow of man "tells two stories: first of how the chimps of Gombe in Tanzania have grown, changed and died, and second, how Goodall and her dedicated group of Tanzanian observers have survived the rigours of the past thirty years. It is beautifully written, and evokes both sympathy and understanding of these animals." Times Lit Suppl
Includes bibliographical references

Morris, Desmond
Planet ape; [by] Desmond Morris with Steve Parker. Firefly Books 2009 288p il $49.95
Grades: 9 10 11 12 Adult   **599.8**
1. Apes
ISBN 978-1-55407-566-9
Detail of the great apes, including: where they live, how they live and the challenges they face. Illustrations compare apes with human beings, including their anatomy, social life, physical and mental development, diet and communication.
"Published in a large format (approximately 10 by 11 inches) with hundreds of full-color glossy photographs and illustrations, this beautiful volume is a cross between a coffee-table book and a thorough compendium of ape behavior, anatomy, taxonomy, and lore. . . . The book reads well, is packed full of exciting information, and is just plain fun to browse for hours." Sci Books Films

Redmond, Ian
The **primate** family tree; the amazing diversity of our closest relatives. foreword by Jane Goodall. Firefly Books 2008 176p il map $35; pbk $24.95
Grades: 11 12 Adult   **599.8**
1. Primates
ISBN 978-1-55407-378-8; 1-55407-378-2; 9781554079643
"The book is structured according to the four main branches of the primate family tree and contains . . . information on the natural history, characteristics and behavior of . . . [some] 250 species, along with maps showing the ranges of the species." Publisher's note
Includes bibliographical references

Russon, Anne E.

Orangutans: wizards of the rainforest; rev ed.; Firefly Books 2004 240p il map pa $24.95

Grades: 8 9 10 11 12   **599.8**

1. Orangutan

ISBN 1-55297-998-9

LC 2005-357221

First published 1999 in the United Kingdom

A firsthand account of the lives of orangutans including a scientific history of orangutans, a description of orangutans and their natural habitat, their behavior patterns, rehabilitation operations, the politics of orangutan rescue work, and a look at orangutans released back into the forest.

Includes bibliographical references

★ **World** atlas of great apes and their conservation; edited by Julian Caldecott and Lera Miles; foreword by Kofi A. Annan. University of California Press, in association with UNEP-WCMC 2005 456p il map $45

Grades: 11 12 Adult   **599.8**

1. Apes 2. Atlases 3. Biogeography 4. Reference books 5. Wildlife conservation

ISBN 0-520-24633-0; 978-0-520-24633-1

LC 2006-272653

"Each great ape specie is given a separate chapter that contains information on behavior and ecology, communication and tool use, threats and conservation, and exceptionally detailed distribution maps. What sets this book apart is the section that details each country in which apes are found and exactly what conservation efforts are underway." Univ Press Books for Public and Second Sch Libr, 2006

Includes bibliographical references

599.88   Great apes and gibbons

Stanford, Craig B.

Planet without apes; Craig B. Stanford. Belknap Press of Harvard University Press 2012 262 p. ill. (hardcover) $25.95

Grades: 10 11 12 Adult   **599.88**

1. Apes 2. Endangered species 3. Extinct animals

ISBN 0674067045; 9780674067042

LC 2012023985

This book, by Craig B. Stanford, "warns that extinction of the great apes--chimpanzees, bonobos, gorillas, and orangutans--threatens to become a reality within just a few human generations. We are on the verge of losing the last links to our evolutionary past, and to all the biological knowledge about ourselves that would die along with them. The crisis we face is tantamount to standing aside while our last extended family members vanish from the planet." (Publisher's note)

"Stanford has brilliantly distilled scientific research, African and Asian economic issues, and ethical concerns surrounding the exploitation of these intelligent, highly social creatures into a powerful plea for primate protection." LJ

Includes bibliographical references and index

599.885   Chimpanzees

Halloran, Andrew R.

The **song** of the ape; Andrew R. Halloran. 1st ed. St. Martin's Press 2012 x, 276p.p

Grades: 11 12 Adult   **599.885**

1. Chimpanzees 2. Animal sounds 3. Animal communication 4. Zoo keepers 5. Primatologists

ISBN 9780312563110; 9781429933278

LC 2011041344

The premise for this book began when, "working as a zookeeper at a drive-through animal park in south Florida, [author and primatologist Andrew R.] Halloran witnessed the escape of a group of chimpanzees who capitalized on an unsecured boat to flee from their island habitat and an upstart group of rival chimps. To react so quickly and uniformly, the group, Halloran surmises, must have been communicating in a complex manner that allowed them to plan and orchestrate such an escape. To examine this idea further, Halloran . . . embarks on a . . . study of five of the chimps involved, delving into their histories, their calls, and the meaning of their calls. The result is an . . . account of communication development among these intelligent animals . . . showing how they communicate with each other on their own terms and how numerous factors cause dialects to emerge." (Publishers Weekly)

Includes bibliographical references and index

599.9   Humans

Deem, James M.

Faces from the past; forgotten people of North America. by James M. Deem. Houghton Mifflin Harcourt 2012 154 p. $18.99

Grades: 6 7 8 9 10   **599.9**

1. Skeleton 2. Human body 3. Physical anthropology 4. North America -- Population 5. Radiocarbon dating -- North America 6. Forensic anthropology -- North America 7. Human remains (Archaeology) -- North America 8. Facial reconstruction (Anthropology) -- North America

ISBN 0547370245; 9780547370248

LC 2012006819

This book by James M. Deem looks at "nine cases in which" facial "reconstructions help interpret a specific moment in American history. . . . This title brings to life such diverse figures as paleoamerican Spirit Cave Man; 'Pearl,' a slave from eighteenth-century upstate New York; a buffalo soldier whose corpse was reassembled and given an honorable burial; [and] nine persons among the 1,271 bodies found in pauper's graves in an almshouse cemetery." (Bulletin of the Center for Children's Books)

599.909   Physical anthropologists

Henderson, Harry, 1951-

The **Leakey** family; unearthing human ancestors. Harry Henderson. Chelsea House 2011 127

p. (Trailblazers in science and technology) (library) $35

Grades: 7 8 9 10 11 12 **599.909**
1. Olduvai Gorge (Tanzania) -- Antiquities 2. Fossil hominids -- Tanzania -- Olduvai Gorge 3. Excavations (Archaeology) -- Tanzania -- Olduvai Gorge 4. Paleoanthropolgists -- Tanzania -- Olduvai Gorge -- Biography 5. Physical anthropologists -- Tanzania -- Olduvai Gorge -- Biography
ISBN 160413674X; 9781604136746
LC 2011001972

This book, by Harry Henderson, profiles the Leakey family as part of the "Trailblazers in Science and Technology" series. "In the 20th century, the family name . . . became synonymous with paleoanthropology. . . . Louis S.B. Leakey explored East Africa and what is now Tanzania, finding skulls of human ancestors to fill in the evolutionary roadmap to modern man. Leakey worked alongside his wife, Mary, herself an experienced archaeologist and anthropologist." (Publisher's note)
Includes bibliographical references and index

599.93   Genetics, sex and age characteristics, evolution

★ **Encyclopedia** of human evolution and prehistory; editors, Eric Delson [et al.] 2nd ed; Garland 2000 xlv, 753p il (Garland reference library of the humanities) lib bdg $175
Grades: 9 10 11 12 **599.93**
1. Reference books 2. Human origins -- Encyclopedias
ISBN 0-815-31696-8
First published 1988 under the editorships of Ian Tattersall, Eric Delson, and John Van Couvering
"This is a very readable, thorough reference source covering every aspect of human evolution and prehistory. The scientific facts, theories, and philosophies pertaining to evolution are presented skillfully and understandably." Booklist

Gibbons, Ann
★ The **first** human; the race to discover our earliest ancestors. Doubleday 2006 306p il map hardcover o.p. pa $14.95
Grades: 11 12 Adult **599.93**
1. Evolution 2. Fossil hominids
ISBN 0-385-51226-0; 978-0-385-51226-8; 978-1-4000-7696-3 pa; 1-4000-7696-X pa
LC 2005-53780
This "is a near insider's account that still has the critical distance a nonpartisan can offer." Libr J
Includes bibliographical references

Hodge, Russ
Human genetics; race, population, and disease. foreword by Nadia Rosenthal. Facts on File 2010 228p il (Genetics & evolution) $39.50
Grades: 9 10 11 12 **599.93**
1. Genetics
ISBN 978-0-8160-6682-7; 0-8160-6682-5
LC 2009-10706

This book explores the "topic through a variety of perspectives. . . . Coverage also includes studies of human molecules that have been applied in some fascinating ways, for example to solve historical mysteries, and how modern doctors try to identify the factors that make the body healthy or sick. Finally, this . . . resource explores the rich variety of the human species—differences between individuals and groups, including questions like the genetic meaning of human races and how genes influence behavior and society." Publisher's note
Includes glossary and bibliographical references

Holmes, Thom
Early humans; the Pleistocene & Holocene epochs. Chelsea House 2009 151p il map (The prehistoric Earth) lib bdg $35
Grades: 7 8 9 10 **599.93**
1. Evolution 2. Human origins 3. Fossil hominids
ISBN 978-0-8160-5966-9; 0-8160-5966-7
LC 2008-38936
"The book consists of two sections. The first section describes the early hominins in Chapter 1 and the archaic species of Homo in Chapter 2. The second section reviews the origins and evolution of more modern Homo species in Chapters 3 and 4. The concluding chapter briefly discusses some contemporary topics, including the meaning of human races, the evolution of skin color, the human role in the evolution and extinction of other species, and the impact of the evolution of diseases. . . . [This] is an outstanding contribution to teaching junior high and high school students about evolution in general and human evolution in particular." Sci Books Films
Includes glossary and bibliographical references

Johanson, Donald C.
From Lucy to language; [by] Donald Johanson & Blake Edgar; principal photography, David L. Brill. Rev., updated, and expanded; Simon and Schuster 2006 288p il map $65
Grades: 11 12 Adult **599.93**
1. Human origins 2. Fossil hominids
ISBN 0-7432-8064-4; 978-0-7432-8064-8
LC 2007-270098
First published 1996
This is a "photographic showcase of the essential physical evidence of human origins. . . . Permitting a face-to-face encounter with human ancestors, this work furnishes essential information, [and] an incomparable visual experience." Booklist
Includes bibliographical references

Lucy: the beginnings of humankind; [by] Donald C. Johanson and Maitland A. Edey. Simon & Schuster 1981 409p il hardcover o.p. pa $16
Grades: 11 12 Adult **599.93**
1. Human origins 2. Fossil mammals
ISBN 0-671-72499-1 pa
LC 80-21759
In November 1974 at a place called Hadar in Ethiopia Donald Johanson "discovered the partial skeleton of an extremely primitive female, erect-walking primate or hominid. . . . The skeleton received the name 'Lucy.' Much later, Lucy

received the scientific name, Australopithecus afarensis, and it was determined she was some 3.5 million years old. . . . This book is Johanson's own story of the events leading up to and subsequent to Lucy's discovery." Best Sellers
Includes bibliographical references

Jolly, Alison
Lucy's legacy; sex and intelligence in human evolution. Harvard Univ. Press 1999 518p il hardcover o.p. pa $18.95
Grades: 11 12 Adult 599.93
1. Evolution 2. Intellect
ISBN 0-674-00069-2; 0-674-00540-6 pa
LC 99-32252
"Lucy is the name given to the fossil skeleton of an Australopithecine, a human ancestor, discovered in Ethiopia. The name may be a misnomer, since there's no way yet of telling whether Lucy was female. No matter. Primatologist Jolly's interest is not so much in Lucy as in the crucial role that females in general have played in human evolution. . . . In clear and clever prose, Jolly shows us how we got so smart, what sex had to do with it, and how our brains have become the central force in evolution." Booklist
Includes bibliographical references

Leakey, Richard E.
The origin of humankind; [by] Richard Leakey. Basic Bks. 1994 171p il maps (Science masters series) hardcover o.p. pa $14.95
Grades: 11 12 Adult 599.93
1. Human origins
ISBN 0-465-05313-0 pa
LC 94-3617
This "is a worthwhile addition to many kinds of libraries—public, general, science, biological, and psychological." Sci Books Films
Includes bibliographical references

Origins reconsidered; in search of what makes us human. [by] Richard Leakey and Roger Lewin. Doubleday 1992 375p il hardcover o.p. pa $16.95
Grades: 11 12 Adult 599.93
1. Human origins
ISBN 0-385-46792-3 pa
LC 92-6661
"Leakey and Lewin discuss how conceptions of human anatomical and behavioral development have been radically altered within the last 12 years by new discoveries and research in other fields. They review the developments and assert Leakey's own hypotheses based on these discoveries. . . . This is an engrossing book written for the layperson, fully explaining anthropological terms and theories when necessary. It's a solid introduction to current theory concerning human development." SLJ

Reilly, Philip
★ Is it in your genes? the influence of genes on common disorders and diseases that affect you and your family. [by] Philip R. Reilly. Cold Spring Harbor Laboratory Press 2004 288p hardcover o.p. pa $19.95

Grades: 9 10 11 12 599.93
1. Medical genetics
ISBN 0-87969-719-9; 0-87969-721-0 pa
LC 2004-2458
"Drawing on the many questions he has been asked (for example, 'My sister has multiple sclerosis. Am I at an increased risk?'), Reilly discusses over 90 common conditions, diseases, and disorders, arranged from conception to old age." Publisher's note
Includes bibliographical references

Stefoff, Rebecca
First humans. Marshall Cavendish Benchmark 2009 112p il map (Humans: an evolutionary history) lib bdg $37.07
Grades: 7 8 9 10 599.93
1. Human origins 2. Fossil hominids
ISBN 978-0-7614-4184-7; 0-7614-4184-0
LC 2008-34330
"Stefoff provides an enlightening and entertaining history of the evolution of Homo sapiens, their ancestors, and cousins, from primitive origins to today. The clear, insightful [text is] accented by intriguing sidebars and colorful photos, maps, and graphs." SLJ
Includes glossary and bibliographical references

Ice age Neanderthals. Marshall Cavendish Benchmark 2009 112p il map (Humans: an evolutionary history) lib bdg $37.07
Grades: 7 8 9 10 599.93
1. Neanderthals 2. Human origins 3. Fossil hominids
ISBN 978-0-7614-4186-1; 0-7614-4186-7
LC 2008-54830
"Stefoff provides an enlightening and entertaining history of the evolution of Homo sapiens, their ancestors, and cousins, from primitive origins to today. The clear, insightful [text is] accented by intriguing sidebars and colorful photos, maps, and graphs." SLJ
Includes glossary and bibliographical references

Modern humans. Marshall Cavendish Benchmark 2009 112p il map (Humans: an evolutionary history) lib bdg $37.07
Grades: 7 8 9 10 599.93
1. Genetics 2. Evolution 3. Human origins 4. Fossil hominids
ISBN 978-0-7614-4187-8; 0-7614-4187-5
LC 2009-12364
"Stefoff provides an enlightening and entertaining history of the evolution of Homo sapiens, their ancestors, and cousins, from primitive origins to today. The clear, insightful [text is] accented by intriguing sidebars and colorful photos, maps, and graphs." SLJ
Includes glossary and bibliographical references

Tattersall, Ian
Masters of the planet; Ian Tattersall. Palgrave Macmillan 2012 272p.

Grades: 11 12 Adult **599.93**
1. Biology 2. Evolution 3. Human origins
ISBN 9780230108752

LC 2011034415

'This book examines the evolution of humans. "When homo sapiens made their entrance 100,000 years ago they were confronted by a wide range of other early humans - homo erectus, who walked better and used fire; homo habilis who used tools; and of course the Neanderthals, who were brawny and strong. . . . [Author Ian Tattersall] explores how the physical traits and cognitive ability of homo sapiens distanced them from the rest of nature. Even more importantly, 'Masters of the Planet' looks at how our early ancestors acquired these superior abilities; it shows that their strange and unprecedented mental facility is not, as most of us were taught, simply a basic competence that was refined over unimaginable eons by natural selection. Instead, it is an emergent capacity that was acquired quite recently and changed the world definitively." (Publisher's note)

Includes bibliographical references and index.

Wade, Nicholas
Before the dawn; recovering the lost history of our ancestors. Penguin Press 2006 312p il map $24.95
Grades: 11 12 Adult **599.93**
1. Evolution 2. Social change
ISBN 1-59420-079-3; 978-1-59420-079-3

LC 2005-55293

"This is highly recommended for readers interested in how DNA analysis is rewriting the history of mankind." Publ Wkly

Includes bibliographical references

600 TECHNOLOGY

600 Technology (Applied sciences)

1001 inventions that changed the world; general editor, Jack Challoner; preface by Trevor Baylis. Barron's 2009 960 p. il $35
Grades: 9 10 11 12 Adult **600**
1. Inventions -- History 2. Technological innovations
ISBN 0764161369; 9780764161360

LC 2008927423

This book, edited by Jack Challoner, "tells the stories behind the inventions that have changed the world. . . . Inventors and pioneers of science and technology, including Eli Whitney, James Watt, Benjamin Franklin, Henry Bessemer, Thomas Edison, J.B. Dunlop, the Wright Brothers, Werner von Braun, Jonas Salk, J. Robert Oppenheimer, and many others are also discussed. Fascinating photos and illustrations complement authoritative summaries of each invention." (Publisher's note)

"This overview of creative thinking and innovation moves chronologically from one advancement to another. Photos, advertisements, and schematics . . . . enhance history with succinct captioning and color or black-and-white illustrations of the devices in use. Commentary and gloss-

es are succinct and inclusive without dumbing down the material." Booklist

One thousand and one inventions that changed the world

Harman, Jay
The **shark's** paintbrush; biomimicry and how nature is inspiring innovation. Jay Harman. White Cloud Press 2013 326 p. ill $26.95
Grades: 11 12 Adult **600**
1. Biomimicry 2. Sustainable development
ISBN 1935952846; 9781935952848

LC 2012015185

This book, by Jay Harman, describes how, "in a world of depleted natural resources, entrepreneurs and scientists are turning to nature to inspire future products that are more energy- and cost-efficient. Biomimicry, the science of employing nature to advance sustainable technology, is arguably one of the hottest new business concepts." Harman "shows business leaders and aspiring entrepreneurs how we can reconcile creating more powerful, lucrative technologies with maximizing sustainability." (Publisher's note)

"A useful update on recent developments in biomimicry and an intriguing case for innovative green technology that goes beyond sustainability." Kirkus

Woodford, Chris
★ **Cool** Stuff 2.0 and how it works; written by Chris Woodford and Jon Woodcock. DK Pub. 2007 256p il $24.99
Grades: 5 6 7 8 9 10 **600**
1. Inventions 2. Technology
ISBN 978-0-7566-3207-6; 0-7566-3207-2

LC 2007-299442

"More than 100 entries present a wide variety of topics with high child appeal, from robot cars to high-tech toilets. . . . Full but uncluttered layouts mix photos, text boxes, diagrams, and captions to highlight key elements. . . . Readers should have an easy time understanding the basics of what each item does, how it is used, and how it works. Along with up-to-date scientific information on high-interest topics, this title has very strong browsing appeal and great booktalk potential." SLJ

Cool stuff exploded. Dorling Kindersley 2008 256p il $24.99
Grades: 7 8 9 10 **600**
1. Inventions
ISBN 978-0-7566-4028-6; 0-7566-4028-8

"Photographs and computer-generated images provide an inside look at the mechanisms that make many transportation vehicles, home appliances, entertainment systems, and personal electronics function. Futuristic applications and environmental impacts of technology are also included." National Science Teachers Association

Includes glossary

604 Technical drawing, hazardous materials technology; groups of people

Sluby, Patricia Carter

★ The **inventive** spirit of African Americans; patented ingenuity. Praeger 2004 xxxviii, 313p il $39.95

Grades: 9 10 11 12 **604**

1. African American inventors
ISBN 0-275-96674-7

LC 2003-64767

This "portrait of many black inventors and scientists is derived from a comprehensive review of all the patents that have been issued to African Americans from the days of slavery to the present high-tech era. Sluby also includes a brief biography of many little-known male and female African Americans whose ingenuity contributed to American industry. . . . An important addition to the literature on contributions of African Americans to US history." Choice

Includes bibliographical references

609 History, geographic treatment, biography

The **Britannica** guide to inventions that changed the modern world; edited by Robert Curley. Britannica Educational Pub. in association with Rosen Educational Services 2010 386p il (Turning points in history) lib bdg $45

Grades: 9 10 11 12 **609**

1. Inventions -- History 2. Technology -- History
ISBN 978-1-61530-020-4; 1-61530-020-1

LC 2009-37539

Each chapter highlights an invention that was influential enough to alter the modern world.

Includes glossary and bibliographical references

Carlisle, Rodney P.

★ **Scientific** American inventions and discoveries; all the milestones in ingenuity--from the discovery of fire to the invention of the microwave oven. Wiley 2004 502p il $40

Grades: 9 10 11 12 **609**

1. Technological innovations 2. Inventions -- History
3. Technology -- History
ISBN 0-471-24410-4

LC 2003-23258

"This fact-filled compendium will delight students with a passion for science and technology, no matter what their age." Publ Wkly

Ferris, Julie

Ideas that changed the world; authors, Julie Ferris [et al.] DK Pub. 2010 256p il map $24.99

Grades: 6 7 8 9 10 **609**

1. Inventions -- History 2. Technology -- History
ISBN 978-0-7566-6531-9; 0-7566-6531-0

LC 2010282281

A guide to technological developments that changed the world describes each invention and explores its place in history and how it influenced civilization, discussing inventions from the wheel to computers.

"Brightly colored and packed with information, this reference volume delivers. . . . This book could be used in multiple subject areas. English classes might use it for general research or units on the decades, social studies for the major changes over time, and science due to the technological advancements." Libr Media Connect

Macdonald, Anne L.

★ **Feminine** ingenuity; women and invention in America. {by} Anne Macdonald. Ballantine Bks. 1992 xxiv, 514p il hardcover o.p. pa $25

Grades: 9 10 11 12 Adult **609**

1. Inventions 2. Women inventors
ISBN 0-345-38314-1 pa

LC 91-55502

This is a "study of American women's contribution to science, engineering, and technology as represented in the issuance of U.S. patents. From the first patent issued to a woman in 1809, Macdonald traces the uphill struggle women have faced in their efforts to obtain equal rights—in the area of patent awards as well as in the broader educational, economic, and social arenas." Libr J

Includes bibliographical references

★ The **Seventy** great inventions of the ancient world; edited by Brian M. Fagan. Thames & Hudson 2004 304p il $40

Grades: 9 10 11 12 Adult **609**

1. Inventions -- History 2. Technology -- History
ISBN 0-500-05130-5

LC 2004-100250

"Fagan organizes into six categories the 70 things his three dozen scholarly contributors present. The first category describes the basic natural materials—stone, clay, and wood—with which humanity began to alter the environment. Ensuing categories catalog their uses, such as in hunting, farming, or artwork. . . . Stuffed with hundreds of color photographs, Fagan's work is an estimable spruce-up option for any library." Booklist

Includes bibliographical references

Strapp, James

Science and technology. Sharpe Focus 2009 80p il (Inside ancient China) $31.45

Grades: 7 8 9 10 **609**

1. Science and civilization 2. Science -- China 3. Technology -- History
ISBN 978-0-7656-8169-0; 0-7656-8169-2

LC 2008-31168

"This colorful book surveys science and technology developed by the ancient Chinese. Strapp discusses early compasses and mapmaking, the building of canals, and the invention of . . . the wheelbarrow, water clocks, gunpowder, and the harness. The last chapter looks at Chinese medicine and feng shui. . . . The writing is clear and the format is inviting, with many sidebars and pictures. Illustrations include photos of artifacts and maps as well as period artwork and line-and-wash pictures." Booklist

Includes bibliographical references

Tobin, James

Great projects; the epic story of the building of America: from the taming of the Mississippi to the invention of the Internet. Free Press 2001 322p il maps hardcover o.p. pa $31.95

Grades: 11 12 Adult **609**

1. Engineering -- History
ISBN 0-7432-1064-6; 1-4516-1301-6 pa

LC 2001-33016

"The clearly written, nontechnical narratives are lively and comprehensive." Libr J

Includes bibliographical references

Van Dulken, Stephen

Inventing the 20th century; 100 inventions that shaped the world: from the airplane to the zipper. {by} Stephen Van Dulken; with an introduction by Andrew Phillips. New York Univ. Press 2000 246p il hardcover o.p. pa $17.95

Grades: 11 12 Adult **609**

1. Inventions
ISBN 0-8147-8808-4; 0-8147-8812-2 pa

LC 00-41141

This briefly describes inventions of the 20th century, arranged by decade, with text and diagrams from the patent applications

"A fascinating compendium for trivia seekers." Publ Wkly

Includes bibliographical references

Wearing, Judy

Edison's concrete piano; flying tanks, six-nippled sheep, walk-on-water shoes, and 12 other flops from great inventors. ECW Press 2009 270p il pa $14.95

Grades: 11 12 Adult **609**

1. Inventors 2. Inventions
ISBN 978-1-55022-863-2

LC 2009-675182

The author "details 16 inventions that never took off and lists the personality traits that typify the inventive mind. They include determination, rebelliousness, financial unrealism, and thinking in redemptive terms, such as the salvation of humanity. . . . She portrays lively personalities and eccentric projects in concrete prose." Booklist

Includes bibliographical references

609.2 Technology - biography

Helfand, Lewis

They Changed the World; Bell, Edison and Tesla. writer, Lewis Helfand; illustrator, Naresh Kumar. Random House Inc 2014 96 p. color illustrations $12.99

Grades: 7 8 9 10 **609.2**

1. Inventors -- Biography 2. Graphic novels 3. Inventors -- United States -- Biography -- Comic books, strips, etc.
ISBN 9380741871; 9789380741871

"Find out how Alexander Graham Bell, Thomas Edison and Nicola Tesla changed the world we live in forever! Three men, three great minds and three completely different approaches to science." (Publisher's note)

"Kumar shows not only the fundamental intelligence but also the hard work and productive attitudes these three geniuses brought to their work. Helfand's solid research is a great jumping-off point for student researchers, and the inclusion of a DIY project--building a rudimentary phone--adds to the appeal." Booklist

Vare, Ethlie Ann

★ Patently female; from AZT to TV dinners: stories of women inventors and their breakthrough ideas. [by] Ethlie Ann Vare, Greg Ptacek. Wiley 2002 220p il $27.95

Grades: 11 12 Adult **609.2**

1. Women inventors
ISBN 0-471-02334-5

LC 2001-26950

Sequel to: Mothers of invention (1988)

The authors "detail how women's ideas like the cotton gin, automatic sewing machine and even the Brooklyn Bridge have often been attributed to men and how history books and museums like the Smithsonian and the National Inventors Hall of Fame have ignored women's achievements." Publ Wkly

Includes bibliographical references

610 Medicine and health

Adler, Robert E.

Medical firsts; from Hippocrates to the human genome. Wiley 2004 232p il $24.95

Grades: 11 12 Adult **610**

1. Medicine -- History
ISBN 0-471-40175-7

LC 2003-14212

"Adler ably combines good storytelling, clear and cogent scientific explanations [and] a respect for science over superstition." Publ Wkly

Includes bibliographical references

Black's medical dictionary; 42nd ed.; A. & C. Black 2010 764p il $55

Grades: 9 10 11 12 **610**

1. Reference books 2. Medicine -- Dictionaries
ISBN 978-0-7136-8902-0

First published 1906. Frequently revised

"This dictionary, illustrated with line drawings and graphs, has longer entries than most. Many are several paragraphs long, with extensive information on diseases and parts of the body. The language is accessible to educated lay readers." Ref Sources for Small & Medium-sized Libr. 6th edition

Carroll, Aaron E.

Don 't cross your eyes-- they'll get stuck that way; Aaron E. Carroll and Rachel C. Vreeman. St. Martin's Griffin 2011 ix, 289 p (pbk.) $13.99

Grades: 11 12 Adult   **610**
1. Medicine -- Miscellanea
ISBN 9780312681876

LC 2011000021

This book, by Aaron E. Carroll and Rachel C. Vreeman, is a "myth-busting collection of quirky and curious facts about your body and health. . . . [Myths include]: Eggs give you high cholesterol, You should stretch before you exercise, Kids in day care catch more colds, Sit-ups or crunches will flatten your stomach, [and] A glass of warm milk will put you to sleep." (Publisher's note)

The authors explore "a wide range of myths and misconceptions about bodies and health." Publisher's note

Includes bibliographical references (p. 237-278) and index.

Davis, Sampson

The **pact**: three young men make a promise and fulfill a dream; by Samson Davis, George Jenkins, and Remeck Hunt; with Lisa Frazier Page. Riverhead Bks. 2002 248p hardcover o.p. pa $14

Grades: 11 12 Adult   **610**
1. Physicians 2. African Americans -- Biography
ISBN 1-57322-216-X; 1-57322-989-X pa

LC 2001-59647

"Three young black men in the medical professions (a dentist, an emergency-room physician, and an internist) recall an informal pact they made as youths that guided them out of their inner-city Newark neighborhoods and into successful careers. . . . In their own voices, these three young men tell a compelling story that will inspire other young people to form and value supportive, long-term friendships." Booklist

Dorland's illustrated medical dictionary; 32nd ed; Elsevier/Saunders 2011 xxvii, 2147p il $51.95

Grades: 11 12 Adult   **610**
1. Reference books 2. Medicine -- Dictionaries
ISBN 978-1-4160-6257-8

LC 2011-9789

First published 1900. Periodically revised

This standard reference includes terms used in medicine, surgery, dentistry, pharmacy, chemistry, nursing, veterinary science, biology, and medical biology. Pronunciation, derivation, and definitions are given.

"This is considered one of the most comprehensive medical dictionaries in print." N Y Public Libr Book of How & Where to Look It Up

Includes bibliographical references

Hellman, Hal

Great feuds in medicine; ten of the liveliest disputes ever. Wiley 2001 237p $24.95; pa $15.95

Grades: 11 12 Adult   **610**
1. Chemists 2. Biologists 3. Physicians 4. Scientists 5. Biochemists 6. Geochemists 7. Biophysicists 8. Physiologists 9. Psychoanalysts 10. Microbiologists 11. Writers on science 12. Medicine -- History 13. Writers on medicine 14. Public health officials 15. Nobel laureates for physiology or medicine
ISBN 0-471-34757-4; 0-471-20833-7 pa

LC 00-63349

This considers disputes involving such medical scientists as William Harvey, Galvani, Volta, Pasteur, Freud, Sabin, Salk, and Montagnier

"Hellman eschews comprehensiveness for pith and entertainment, neglecting no unusual 'twist,' 'strange coincidence,' 'cloud of suspicion' or 'lucky break' to heighten the drama of these medical milestones." Publ Wkly

Includes bibliographical references

Kelly, Kate

Early civilizations; prehistoric times to 500 C.E. Facts on File 2010 174p il map (The history of medicine) $40

Grades: 6 7 8 9 10   **610**
1. Ancient civilization 2. Medicine -- History
ISBN 978-0-8160-7205-7; 0-8160-7205-1

LC 2008-43441

"This eye-opening and information-rich [volume] . . . shows that ancient human beings were quite knowledgeable about health and well-being. This book discusses medical advances from prehistoric times through the Roman Empire. . . . Coverage is global. . . . Readers will gain a deepened appreciation of and insights into modern medicine by examining this book. Because of its inclusion of new research, it is recommended as a first purchase for most libraries." SLJ

Includes bibliographical references

Medicine becomes a science; 1840-1999. Facts on File 2010 168p il map (The history of medicine) $40

Grades: 9 10 11 12   **610**
1. Science -- History 2. Medicine -- History
ISBN 978-0-8160-7209-5; 0-8160-7209-4

LC 2009-11598

This book "covers the time period when medicine moved from guesswork to being a real, measurable science. Because of the sheer amount of material to discuss, the author details the history episodically by profiling specific people and their contributions, certain advances and how they were made, who contributed to them, etc. The text is highly engaging and readable. Students interested in a career in medicine or in history will enjoy this book." SLJ

Includes glossary and bibliographical references

Medicine today; 2000 to the present. Facts on File 2010 160p il map (The history of medicine) $40

Grades: 9 10 11 12   **610**
1. Medical ethics 2. Medicine -- History
ISBN 978-0-8160-7210-1; 0-8160-7210-8

LC 2009-16629

This book "describes some of the technology and discoveries that are currently being explored in the world of medicine, providing information on what some of these new developments might mean and the possibilities for tomorrow." Publisher's note

Includes glossary and bibliographical references

The **Middle** Ages; 500-1450. Facts on File 2010 158p il map (The history of medicine) $40

Grades: 9 10 11 12   **610**
1. Medicine -- History
ISBN 978-0-8160-7206-4; 0-8160-7206-X
LC 2008-48709
This book shows "what occurred during medieval times that affected future developments in medicine." Publisher's note
Includes glossary and bibliographical references

Old world and new; early medical care, 1700-1840. Facts On File 2010 150p il map (The history of medicine) $40
Grades: 9 10 11 12   **610**
1. Medicine -- History
ISBN 978-0-8160-7208-8; 0-8160-7208-6
LC 2009-5163
Discusses the concerns and advances in medicine that occurred during the Enlightenment, a time of significant progress in specific scientific fields.
Includes glosary and bibliographical references

The **scientific** revolution and medicine; 1450-1700. Facts on File 2010 158p il map (The history of medicine) $40
Grades: 9 10 11 12   **610**
1. Medicine -- History
ISBN 978-0-8160-7207-1; 0-8160-7207-8
LC 2008-55603
This book "examines the scientific revolution and how it has affected future developments in medicine." Publisher's note
Includes glossary and bibliographical references

★ The **Merck** manual of diagnosis and therapy; Robert S. Porter, editor-in-chief; Justin L. Kaplan, senior assistant editor. 19th ed.; Merck Sharp & Dohme Corp. 2011 xxxii, 3754p il $79.95
Grades: 11 12 Adult   **610**
1. Reference books 2. Medicine -- Handbooks, manuals, etc.
ISBN 978-0-911910-19-3
First published 1899
"A one-volume reference that attempts to cover all but the most obscure diseases. Sections are organized by type of disease or medical specialty." N Y Public Libr Book of How & Where to Look It Up

610.3 Medicine -- Dictionaries

Magill's medical guide; medical editors: Bryan C. Auday, Ph.D., Gordon College, Michael A. Buratovich, Ph.D., Spring Arbor University, Geraldine F. Marrocco, Ed.D., APRN, CNS, ANP-BC, Yale University School of Nursing, Paul Moglia, Ph.D., South Nassau Communities Hospital. Seventh edition Salem Press 2014 5 volumes ill
Grades: 11 12 Adult   **610.3**
1. Medicine -- Encyclopedias
ISBN 9781619252141; 1619252147

This medical reference book "covers diseases, disorders, treatments, procedures, specialties, anatomy, biology, and issues in an A-Z format, with sidebars addressing recent developments in medicine and concise information boxes for all diseases and disorders." (Publisher's note)
"Covers diseases, disorders, treatments, procedures, specialties, anatomy, biology, and issues in an A-Z format, with sidebars addressing recent developments in medicine and concise information boxes for all diseases and disorders." Publisher's note
Includes bibliographical references and index.

610.7 Education, research, nursing, services of allied health personnel

Kirkland, Kyle
Biological sciences; notable research and discoveries. Facts on File 2010 224p il (Frontiers of science) $39.50
Grades: 9 10 11 12   **610.7**
1. Biology 2. Medicine -- Research
ISBN 978-0-8160-7439-6; 0-8160-7439-9
LC 2009-15651
"This book covers diverse topics such as brain imaging, the human genome, proteins, biodiversity, viruses, and regeneration. Each section traces the history of developments in the field, current research and technology, and where such research is concentrated, and concludes with a recap that often includes new information." Libr Media Connect
Includes bibliographical references

610.73 Nursing and services of allied health personnel

Careers in health care; Barbara Sheen. ReferencePoint Press, Inc. 2015 80 p. color illustrations (Exploring careers) (hardback) $28.95
Grades: 9 10 11 12   **610.73**
1. Professions 2. Medical care 3. Vocational guidance
ISBN 1601526482; 9781601526489
LC 2013041611
Author Barbara Sheen's book on health care is part of a series in which books " take a field or industry-fashion, for example-and break down several different jobs in that area. Each job has its own chapter that describes what the work entails, the education requirements, and an estimated salary range. Most importantly, though, the text includes quotes from and interviews with real people about their jobs, as well as useful details about opportunities for growth in that position." (School Library Journal)
"These three resources develop awareness of some career possibilities within the broad categories. They contain much of the same material for jobs as the Occupations Outlook Handbook produced by the U.S. Department of Labor, but they are much more readable for students. . . . The career profiles inform the reader about the training required, future outlook for career opportunities, and salaries, as well as some of the expected tasks for a specific career. The small size and large print may well encourage students who are not

willing to tackle a large resource containing multiple career fields." VOYA

Includes bibliographical references and index
Other titles in this series are:
Careers in Biotechnology (2014)
Careers in Engineering (2014)

610.9 Medicine--history

Great discoveries in medicine; edited by William & Helen Bynum. Thames & Hudson 2011 304p il
Grades: 10 11 12 Adult   **610.9**
1. Medicine -- History 2. Medical sciences -- History
ISBN 9780500251805; 0500251800

LC 2011922602

This book provides an "account of the evolution of medical knowledge and practice from ancient Egypt, India, and China to the latest technology. . . . Topics include humors & pneumas, Islamic medicine, pathological anatomy, neuron theory, bedlam & beyond, parasites & vectors, hormones, the genetic revolution, defibrillators, the endoscope, medical robots, typhus, tuberculosis, smallpox, HIV, and more." (Publisher's note) "The volume is divided into sections that address different areas of medicine and studies of the body from the ancient world to modern times: tools, contagious diseases, remedies, surgery, and various technological innovations." (Publishers Weekly)

This beautifully designed, quarto-sized volume features 382 illustrations from classical art to medieval engravings to early photographs to the latest examples of medical imaging and electronic microscopes. Egyptian, Chinese, Indian, Islamic, and Greek medical traditions are covered both in the text and in the images, which enriches the dominant narrative of Western medical progress. . . . A striking and informative history." LJ

Includes bibliographical references (p. 295-304) and index.

Rooney, Anne
The **history** of medicine; Anne Rooney. Rosen Pub. Group 2013 208 p. (The history of science) (library) $42.60
Grades: 7 8 9 10 11 12   **610.9**
1. Medicine -- History
ISBN 1448872286; 9781448872282

LC 2012009971

This book, by Anne Rooney, is part of "The History of Science" series. "Organized thematically, this . . . entry . . . delves into the history of disease, diagnosis, treatment and surgery. Because of its broad scope, the book is able to make comparisons across eras, transforming . . . history into something relevant to today's teens. . . . Insets offer medical milestones, biographical sketches, and primary resources." (Booklist)

"Organized thematically, this enlightening entry into the History of Science series delves into the history of disease, diagnosis, treatment, and surgery... Rooney has crafted a highly readable tome about a dense topic." Booklist

Includes bibliographical references (p. 205) and index

610.92 Biography

Eule, Brian
Match day; one day and one dramatic year in the lives of three new doctors. Brian Eule. St. Martin's Press 2009 261 p. $24.95
Grades: 9 10 11 12 Adult   **610.92**
1. Physicians 2. Women physicians 3. Medicine -- Study and teaching 4. Interns (Medicine) 5. Physicians, Women -- Personal Narratives 6. Internship and Residency -- Personal Narratives
ISBN 0312377843; 9780312377847

LC 2008042228

This book, by Brian Eule, is an "informative account of three young doctors beginning their hospital residencies. Some 15,000 fourth-year U.S. medical students, nearly half women, are assigned residencies each spring in a national ritual called 'Match Day.' . . . He brings us deep into the lives of these young people and celebrates the real-world rigor of residence training." (Kirkus Reviews)

"Highly informative account of three young doctors beginning their hospital residencies.Some 15,000 fourth-year U.S. medical students, nearly half women, are assigned residencies each spring in a national ritual called "Match Day."...He brings us deep into the lives of these young people and celebrates the real-world rigor of residence training, though he notes that "this model pushed everything else in a person's life to the wayside."Required reading for future doctors." (Kirkus)

Includes bibliographical references (p. [251]-261).

611 Human anatomy, cytology, histology

Abrahams, Peter H., 1947-
McMinn & Abrahams' clinical atlas of human anatomy; By Peter H. Abrahams, Jonathan D. Spratt, Marios Loukas, and Albert-Neels van Schoor. Mosby / Elsevier 2014 400 p ill pa $82.95
Grades: 11 12 Adult   **611**
1. Reference books 2. Human anatomy -- Atlases
ISBN 9780723436973; 0723436975

This reference book, by Peter H. Abrahams, Jonathan D. Spratt, Marios Loukas, and Albert-Neels van Schoor, "delivers the straightforward visual guidance you need to confidently perform all of the dissections required during your medical training...while acquiring the practical anatomical knowledge needed in your future clinical practice." (Publisher's note)

This atlas contains "a vast array of excellent dissection photographs with radiological correlation and color diagrams." Publisher's note

Balaban, Naomi E.
★ The **handy** anatomy answer book; [by] Naomi E. Balaban and James E. Bobick. Visible Ink Press 2008 362p il pa $21.95
Grades: 9 10 11 12 Adult   **611**
1. Physiology 2. Human anatomy
ISBN 978-1-57859-190-9

"This book can provide an excellent way to read and self-test for health and human biology classes. Adults wanting to know more about the subjects covered will also find a wealth of useful and accessible information." Voice Youth Advocates

★ **Gray's** anatomy; the anatomical basis of clinical practice. 40th ed.; Churchill Livingstone 2008 xxiv, 1551p il $209
Grades: 11 12 Adult   **611**
1. Human anatomy 2. Reference books
ISBN 978-0-443-06684-9
First published 1858. Periodically revised. Publisher varies
A comprehensive standard reference work with illustrations, descriptions and definitions.
"Holds its place as a major and authoritative text on systematic anatomy. Recommended." Annals of Internal Medicine
Includes bibliographical references

Hall, Linley Erin
DNA and RNA. Rosen Pub. 2010 80p il (Understanding genetics) lib bdg $30.60
Grades: 7 8 9 10 11 12   **611**
1. DNA 2. RNA
ISBN 978-1-4358-9532-4
LC 2009-46612
"Introduces DNA and RNA, discussing how heredity works, what can happen when the code goes wrong, replication, and new advances in science and technology." (Publisher's note)
"...with the liberal use of color illustrations, color sidebars, subsections labeled in bold color fonts, and patterns of chemical bonds as backgrounds, will appeal to less able and reluctant readers." Libr Media Connect

Heos, Bridget
The **human** genome. Rosen Pub. 2010 80p il (Understanding genetics) lib bdg $30.60
Grades: 9 10 11 12   **611**
1. Genomes 2. Genetics
ISBN 978-1-4358-9533-1
LC 2009-47915
Presents an introduction to genetics, discussing genes, chromosomes, probability, DNA, mutation, and the Human Genome Project.

Hodge, Russ
★ The **molecules** of life; DNA, RNA, and proteins. foreword by Nadia Rosenthal. Facts On File 2009 222p il (Genetics & evolution) $39.50
Grades: 9 10 11 12   **611**
1. Proteins 2. Biochemistry 3. Nucleic acids 4. Molecular biology
ISBN 978-0-8160-6680-3; 0-8160-6680-9
LC 2008-37094
"This highly readable book about molecular biology explains how organic molecules drive processes between and within the cells. . . . For those schools wanting to develop a strong science collection, this is a needed resource for it can

be used in introductory and advanced biology classes." Libr Media Connect
Includes glossary and bibliographical references

Leonardo
Leonardo on the human body; {by} Leonardo da Vinci. Dover Publs. 1983 506p il pa $26.95
Grades: 9 10 11 12   **611**
1. Human anatomy
ISBN 0-486-24483-0
LC 82-18285
First published 1952 by H. Schuman with title: Leonardo Da Vinci on the human body
This volume includes 215 black-and-white plates containing some 1200 illustrations. Each plate is accompanied by explanatory notes

Roach, Mary
Stiff; the curious lives of human cadavers. Norton 2003 303p il $23.95; pa $13.95
Grades: 11 12 Adult   **611**
1. Dead 2. Dissection 3. Human experimentation in medicine
ISBN 0-393-05093-9; 0-393-32482-6 pa
LC 2002-152908
"For those who are interested in the fields of medicine or forensics and are aware of some of the procedures, this book makes excellent reading." SLJ
Includes bibliographical references

Shubin, Neil
★ **Your** inner fish; a journey into the 3.5-billion-year history of the human body. Pantheon Books 2008 229p il map $24
Grades: 11 12 Adult   **611**
1. Evolution 2. Human anatomy
ISBN 978-0-375-42447-2; 0-375-42447-4
LC 2007-24699
This is a "look at how the human body evolved into its present state. . . . Shubin excels at explaining the science, making each discovery an adventure, whether it's a Pennsylvania roadcut or a stony outcrop beset by polar bears and howling Arctic winds." Publ Wkly
Includes bibliographical references

612 Human physiology

Anatomy and physiology; an illustrated guide. Marshall Cavendish 2010 192p il (Marshall Cavendish reference) $99.80
Grades: 9 10 11 12   **612**
1. Anatomy 2. Physiology
ISBN 978-0-7614-7881-2; 0-7614-7881-7
LC 2009-2177
"This text begins with a study of the animal cell, its structure and function, and continues with detailed explanations of the major life functions such as reproduction, digestion, respiration/circulation, and locomotion. Each chapter provides a detailed overview of the system structures and how they function along with specific information on varia-

tions across species. . . . [This is] a well organized, sequential reference tool for individuals who need information on the animal cell, organ systems, or reproduction." Libr Media Connect

Includes bibliographical references

Carroll, Aaron E.

Don't swallow your gum! myths, half-truths, and outright lies about your body and health. [by] Aaron E. Carroll and Rachel C. Vreeman. St. Martin's Griffin 2009 221p pa $13.95

Grades: 11 12 Adult   **612**
1. Medical misconceptions
ISBN 978-0-312-53387-8; 0-312-53387-X
    LC 2009-7363

"Divided into six sections, each comprising approximately 10 'myths' in two pages each, the book covers issues about disease, sex and pregnancy, babies and children, what we eat, and 'controversial' topics. . . . It is easy to imagine teens browsing through and sharing fun tidbits with one another. In fact, with its offhand tone, liberal use of expressions like 'sucks' and 'BS,' the occasional gratuitous gross-out story, short chapters, and compact paperback format, the book reads as if it were written with teen appeal in mind. At the same time, the authors demonstrate clear research and documentation, including more than 40 pages of references." SLJ

Includes bibliographical references

★ The **complete** human body; the definitive visual guide. Alice Roberts [editor-in-chief] DK Publishing 2010 512p il $50

Grades: 8 9 10 11 12 Adult   **612**
1. Diseases 2. Human body
ISBN 978-0-7566-6733-7; 0-7566-6733-X
    LC 2010-282438

This incorporates "hundreds of stunning images and clearly written text. . . . The extraordinary detail of these pictures will give students an excellent understanding of the body's structure and organization." SLJ

Encyclopedia of human body systems; Julie McDowell, editor. Greenwood 2011 2v il set $125

Grades: 11 12 Adult   **612**
1. Reference books 2. Physiology -- Encyclopedias
ISBN 978-0-313-39175-0; 978-0-313-39176-7 ebook
    LC 2010-21682

"This two-volume set offers readers a concise description of the structure and function of 11 body systems. Sections explain each system's anatomy, cellular chemistry, and organization, together with its relationship to the other body systems. Good writing makes it easy for readers to understand the various systems, and ample tables and line drawings supplement the text." Choice

Includes glossary and bibliographical references

Hill, Z. B.

Exercise for physical & mental health; Z.B. Hill. Mason Crest 2015 64 p. color illustrations (An integrated life of fitness) (hardcover) $23.95

Grades: 11 12   **612**
1. Exercise 2. Mental health 3. Exercise -- Health aspects 4. Exercise -- Physiological aspects 5. Exercise -- Psychological aspects
ISBN 1422231569; 1422231615; 9781422231562; 9781422231616; 9781422231999
    LC 2014011345

This book by Z.B. Hill "introduces readers to various styles of exercise and their benefits, providing historical and scientific background as well as practical exercise routines. Explanations of how physical activity strengthens muscle groups and mental functioning will provide subtle motivation, and 'Text Dependent Questions' will assist with closer reading and research activity." (School Library Journal)

"The physiological information is detailed enough for a college course in exercise science. Each book touches on safety and common injuries. Despite a few missteps, this excellent series demonstrates how a physical education class can be interdisciplinary and academically rigorous." SLJ

Includes bibliographical references (page 59) and index
Exercise for physical and mental health

Holmes, Hannah

The **well**-dressed ape; a natural history of myself. Random House 2008 351p $25

Grades: 11 12 Adult   **612**
1. Human beings 2. Physical anthropology 3. Comparative physiology
ISBN 978-1-4000-6541-7
    LC 2008-16582

Explores how the human animal—the eponymous well-dressed ape—fits into the natural world, even as we humans change that world in both constructive and destructive ways.

"A pellucid spin through the contours of the human brain and the folds of the human body." Kirkus

Includes bibliographical references

Human body from A to Z. Marshall Cavendish Reference 2011 480p $79.95

Grades: 6 7 8 9   **612**
1. Human anatomy
ISBN 978-0-7614-7946-8
    LC 2011006783

Presents 168 entries that focus on all the elements that make up the human body, describing major body systems, physical features, and health issues.

"The writing is informal and readable, and... appropriate for upper-elementary through high-school readers." Booklist

Includes bibliographical references

Laberge, Monique

Biochemistry. Chelsea House 2008 112p il (Essential chemistry) lib bdg $35

Grades: 7 8 9 10 11 12   **612**
1. Biochemistry
ISBN 978-0-7910-9693-2; 0-7910-9693-9
    LC 2007-51316

This title discusses various aspects of biochemistry, including the Human Genome Project.

"The writing style is wholly accessible to a reader with only the most basic background in the life sciences and chemistry. . . . This book amiably introduces the field of biochemistry and could easily inspire further reading in a young reader interested in science." Sci Books Films

Includes glossary and bibliographical references

Macaulay, David

★ The **way** we work; getting to know the amazing human body. [by] David Macaulay, with Richard Walker. Houghton Mifflin 2008 336p il $35

Grades: 6 7 8 9 10   **612**

1. Human body

ISBN 978-0-618-23378-6; 0-618-23378-4

LC 2008-25109

Boston Globe-Horn Book Award honor book: Nonfiction (2009)

"The opening chapter introduces basic concepts of biology and chemistry at the cellular level while subsequent chapters take us through the various systems of the body. . . . [Humor] occasionally leavens the information, which, though often complex and technical, is clearly and succintly presented in double-page spreads, accompanied by an illuminating array of illustrations." Horn Book

Mai, Larry L.

★ The **Cambridge** Dictionary of human biology and evolution; [by] Larry L. Mai, Marcus Young Owl, M. Patricia Kersting. Cambridge University Press 2005 648p il pa $60

Grades: 9 10 11 12 Adult   **612**

1. Reference books 2. Biology -- Dictionaries 3. Evolution -- Dictionaries

ISBN 0-521-66486-1; 978-0-521-66486-8

LC 2004-43553

"This is one of those dictionaries that will keep even casual browsers intrigued." Choice

McMillan, Beverly

★ **Human** body; a visual guide. Firefly Books 2006 304p il $29.95

Grades: 9 10 11 12 Adult   **612**

1. Physiology 2. Human anatomy

ISBN 978-1-55407-188-3; 1-55407-188-7

This book provides "scientific information on the human body, using microphotography, advanced medical imaging and annotated illustrations. The book reveals all the intricacy and beauty of the human body and shows the structure and functions of all the systems that make up a human being." Publisher's note

Includes bibliographical references

Redd, Nancy Amanda

Body drama; real girls, real bodies, real issues, real answers. Gotham 2008 271p ebook $16.99

Grades: 6 7 8 9 10   **612**

1. Puberty 2. Human body 3. Physiology 4. Girls -- Health and hygiene

ISBN 9781101555002

Information for teenage girls about various issues pertaining to their changing physiology

"The author covers a myriad of physical as well as mental health issues, including cutting and depression. . . . It is likely to be a read-and-pass-along book not only for

the helpful advice and accurate information but also for the gross-out pictures of head lice, warts, and keloid scars." Voice Youth Advocates

Includes bibliographical references

612.2   Respiratory system

Petechuk, David

★ The **respiratory** system. Greenwood Press 2004 202p il (Human body systems) $65

Grades: 9 10 11 12 Adult   **612.2**

1. Respiratory system

ISBN 0-313-32434-4

LC 2004-40445

This book "discusses the functions of each organ and how they work together to allow us to breathe. Respiration is discussed both externally (breathing) and internally at the cellular level. The cardiovascular, nervous, and muscular systems are discussed in relation to the respiratory system." Publisher's note

Includes bibliographical references

612.3   Digestive system

Allman, Toney

Nutrition and disease prevention. Chelsea House 2010 191p il map (Healthy eating: a guide to nutrition) lib bdg $35

Grades: 7 8 9 10 11 12   **612.3**

1. Nutrition 2. Preventive medicine

ISBN 978-1-60413-777-4; 1-60413-777-0

LC 2009-41337

This "volume uses boldface type to introduce important and unknown words to the reader and explains them in an easy to understand manner so the reader can grasp the concept being discussed. . . . [For] classes needing information about the importance of good nutrition . . . [this] would be valuable." Libr Media Connect

Includes glossary and bibliographical references

Hill, Z. B.

Eating right & additional supplements for fitness; by Z.B. Hill. Mason Crest 2015 64 p. color illustrations (An integrated life of fitness) (hardback) $23.95

Grades: 9 10 11 12   **612.3**

1. Nutrition 2. Physical fitness 3. Dietary supplements

ISBN 1422231569; 1422231593; 9781422231562; 9781422231593

LC 2014014788

This book, by Z.B. Hill, "[d]iscusses the importance of making healthy food choices; provides information about the various food groups, organic foods, and nutritional supplements; and offers guidance in developing a food and fitness plan in order maintain a strong and healthy body." (Publisher's note)

"Despite a few missteps, this excellent series demonstrates how a physical education class can be interdisciplinary and academically rigorous." SLJ

Includes bibliographical references (page 58) and index

Eating right and additional supplements for fitness

Roach, Mary, 1959-

★ **Gulp**; adventures on the alimentary canal. Mary Roach. W W Norton 2013 336 p.

Grades: 10 11 12 Adult   **612.3**

1. Alimentary canal -- Popular works 2. Digestive organs -- Popular works 3. Gastrointestinal system -- Popular works

ISBN 9780393081572

LC 2012050391

In this book, science writer Mary Roach explores "the alimentary canal. Roach asks the questions that some readers may have always wondered: Does saliva have curative properties? Do pets taste food differently than their owners do? Could Jonah have survived three days in a whale's stomach? . . . As she investigates these questions, Roach encounters many an eccentric scientist who has worked tirelessly to unlock the mysteries of saliva, gastrointestinal gases, and mastication." (Library Journal)

"Roach's approach is grounded in science, but the virtuosic author rarely resists a pun, and it's clear she revels in giving readers a thrill... Adventurous kids and doctors alike will appreciate this fascinating and sometimes ghastly tour of the gastrointestinal system." Pub Wkly

Includes bibliographical references

Smolin, Lori A.

Basic nutrition; [by] Lori A. Smolin and Mary B. Grosvenor. 2nd ed.; Chelsea House 2010 224p il map (Healthy eating: a guide to nutrition) lib bdg $35

Grades: 9 10 11 12   **612.3**

1. Nutrition

ISBN 978-1-60413-801-6

LC 2010-5696

First published 2005

This book provides "information regarding the six classes of nutrients, how each is broken down and used by the body, and how much of each nutrient an individual needs." Publisher's note

Includes glossary and bibliographical references

612.4   Hematopoietic, lymphatic, glandular, urinary systems

McDowell, Julie

★ The **lymphatic** system; [by] Julie McDowell and Michael Windelspecht. Greenwood Press 2004 172p il (Human body systems) $65

Grades: 9 10 11 12 Adult   **612.4**

1. Lymphatic system

ISBN 0-313-32494-8

LC 2004-44218

In this book "the lymph system, including lymph nodes and lymphatic circulation are explored and lymphatic func-

tions of the spleen, appendix, and tonsils are discussed. The history of the research on the lymphatic system is presented and the future of research in this field is considered." Publisher's note

Includes bibliographical references

Watson, Stephanie

★ The **endocrine** system; [by] Stephanie Watson, and Kelli Miller. Greenwood Press 2004 210p il (Human body systems) $65

Grades: 9 10 11 12 Adult   **612.4**

1. Endocrine glands

ISBN 0-313-32699-1

LC 2004-40447

This book "discusses the anatomy and function of each organ in the endocrine system. . . . Discussions on insulin, metabolism and menopause are included. . . . The history of the research on the endocrine system is presented and the future of research in this field is considered. Current controversies and dilemmas of scientists performing this research are explored." Publisher's note

Includes bibliographical references

612.6   Reproduction, development, maturation

Brynie, Faith Hickman

101 questions about reproduction; or how 1 + 1. Twenty-First Century Books 2006 176p il (101 questions) lib bdg $27.90

Grades: 7 8 9   **612.6**

1. Pregnancy 2. Childbirth 3. Sex education

ISBN 0-7613-2311-2

LC 2003-16350

Uses a question-and-answer format to present information about physical, medical, and social issues surrounding human reproduction, including birth control, pregnancy, and childbirth.

"This is a splendid companion to Brynie's 101 Questions about Sex and Sexuality (21st Century Bks, 2003); together the books present informative, complementary coverage for browsers and researchers." SLJ

Includes bibliographical references

Nilsson, Lennart

A **child** is born; [photography], Lennart Nilsson; text, Lars Hamberger; translated from the Swedish by Linda Schenck. 4th ed, completely rev and updated; Delacorte Press 2003 239p il $35; pa $21

Grades: 11 12 Adult   **612.6**

1. Pregnancy 2. Childbirth 3. Embryology

ISBN 0-385-33754-X; 0-385-33755-8 pa

LC 2003-43854

Original Swedish edition, 1965; first United States edition, 1966

An illustrated look at male and female reproductive anatomy and physiology, the processes of ovulation and fertilization, fetal development, and labor and delivery.

Panno, Joseph

★ **Aging**; modern theories and therapies. Rev. ed.; Facts on File 2010 246p il (The new biology) $40

Grades: 9 10 11 12   **612.6**

1. Aging 2. Longevity

ISBN 978-0-8160-6846-3

LC 2009-47717

First published 2005

This book "describes the field of gerontology and the many theories that scientists have developed over the years to explain the age-related changes that occur in nearly all animals. . . . [Coverage includes] insight on the ways in which humans age, how the aging process has changed over the past thousand years, theoretical aspects of rejuvenation, and . . . studies and effective treatments for Alzheimer's, cardiovascular disease, and osteoporosis." Publisher's note

Includes glossary and bibliographical references

612.7   Musculoskeletal system, integument

Adams, Amy

★ The **muscular** system. Greenwood Press 2004 209p il (Human body systems) $65

Grades: 9 10 11 12 Adult   **612.7**

1. Muscles

ISBN 0-313-32403-4

LC 2004-47595

This book "discusses the parts of the muscular system and how they work together to help us move from place to place and to maintain many internal processes, such as a heart beat. Muscle contraction, development, and response during exercise are covered. . . . Muscular system diseases and disorders, symptoms and treatments are [also] explored." Publisher's note

Includes bibliographical references

Brynie, Faith Hickman

101 questions about muscles to stretch your mind and flex your brain; by Faith Hickman Brynie. Twenty-First Century Books 2008 176p il (101 questions) lib bdg $30.60

Grades: 8 9 10 11 12   **612.7**

1. Muscles

ISBN 978-0-8225-6380-8; 0-8225-6380-0

LC 2006-37041

This answers such questions as "What do tendons do? What causes muscle cramps? . . . [This book] makes human physiology accessible, with questions everyone has always wondered about and up-to-date, detailed answers that discuss the complex science in chatty but never condescending style. Like the text, the clear diagrams and photographs deal with everything from basic information . . . to the more advanced." Booklist

Includes glossary and bibliographical references

Kelly, Evelyn B.

★ The **skeletal** system; [by] Evelyn Kelly. Greenwood Press 2004 231p il (Human body systems) $65

Grades: 9 10 11 12 Adult   **612.7**

1. Bones 2. Skeleton

ISBN 0-313-32521-9

LC 2003-67643

In this book, "both the axial bones of the skeleton and the appendicular bones of the limbs are explored. Joints, ligaments, tendons and cartilage are discussed in relation to the bones of the skeletal system. . . . Skeletal system disorders, symptoms and treatments are [also] explored, including sprains, fractures, arthritis, lyme disease, and carpal tunnel syndrome." Publisher's note

Includes bibliographical references

612.8   Nervous system

Aamodt, Sandra

★ **Welcome** to your brain; why you lose your car keys but never forget how to drive and other puzzles of everyday life. [by] Sandra Aamodt and Sam Wang. Bloomsbury USA 2008 220p il $24.95

Grades: 11 12 Adult   **612.8**

1. Brain

ISBN 978-1-59691-283-0; 1-59691-283-9

LC 2007-26739

This is a "'user's guide' to our brains. . . . The text is divided into six main parts, covering the brain's basic structure and function, the senses, the brain's development, emotions, rational processes, and altered states. . . . Rather than didactically lecturing, the authors very effectively engage the reader in a comfortable, interesting, and informative dialog." Sci Books Films

Evans-Martin, Fay

The **nervous** system; [by] F. Fay Evans-Martin. Chelsea House 2009 222p il (The human body: how it works) lib bdg $35

Grades: 7 8 9 10   **612.8**

1. Nervous system

ISBN 978-1-60413-374-5; 1-60413-374-0

LC 2009-22141

Examines the parts, organization, and development of the nervous system, including information on diseases and injuries of the nervous system.

Includes glossary and bibliographical references

Rapport, Richard

Nerve endings; the discovery of the synapse. Norton 2005 240p il hardcover o.p. pa $18.95

Grades: 11 12 Adult   **612.8**

1. Biologists 2. Physicians 3. Nervous system 4. Writers on medicine 5. Public health officials 6. Nobel laureates for physiology or medicine

ISBN 0-393-06019-5; 0-393-33752-9 pa

LC 2005-942

"Teens studying biology and medicine will find that the book provides an accessible introduction to understanding the structure and function of the nervous system." SLJ

Includes bibliographical references

Turkington, Carol

The **encyclopedia** of the brain and brain disorders; [by] Carol Turkington and Joseph R. Harris. 3rd ed; Facts On File 2009 434p (Facts on File library of health and living) $75

Grades: 11 12 Adult   **612.8**
1. Reference books 2. Brain -- Encyclopedias
ISBN 978-0-8160-6395-6; 0-8160-6395-8
                                  LC 2007-33543

First published 1996 with title: The brain encyclopedia

With a large focus on memory this edition discusses the functions and elements of the brain, how it works, how it breaks down, and various diseases and disorders that affect it.

Includes bibliographical references

612.82   Central nervous system

Carter, Rita

The **human** brain book; Rita Carter, Susan Aldridge, Martyn Page, Steve Parker; consultants Chris Frith, Utal Frith Melanie Shulman. DK Publishing 2014 264 p color illustrations hc $40

Grades: 11 12 Adult   **612.82**
1. Brain 2. Human anatomy 3. Brain -- Physiology
ISBN 9781465416025; 1465416021
                                  LC 2013444872

Written by Rita Carter, this second edition uses "the latest findings from neuroscience with new brain imaging techniques, as well as developments on infant brains, telepathy, and brain modification, this new edition of DK's 'The Human Brain Book' covers brain anatomy, function, and disorders. . . . With its . . . 22-page atlas, illustrated with MRI scans, and an interactive DVD, 'The Human Brain Book' is a . . . resource for . . . human biology, anatomy, and neuroscience." (Publisher's note)

"Using computer-generated three-dimensional images, graphics, and clear explanatory text presented in brief sections, the follow-up to The Human Body Book (2007) examines each aspect of the brain's structure and functions... This is a valuable resource for any high-school, college, and public library collection. Libraries should be aware that it comes with a DVD." Booklist

613   Personal health and safety

Boston Women's Health Book Collective

★ **Our** bodies, ourselves; [by the] Boston Women's Health Book Collective. 40th anniversary ed.; Touchstone 2011 928p il pa $26; ebook $12.99

Grades: 11 12 Adult   **613**
1. Women -- Psychology 2. Women -- Health and hygiene
ISBN 978-1-4391-9066-1 pa; 1-4391-9066-6 pa; 978-1-4391-9665-6 ebook; 1-4391-9665-6 ebook
                                  LC 2011022749

First published 1971

This encyclopedia of women's health covers such topics as body image, food, alcohol and drugs, holistic healing, psychotherapy, occupational health, violence, relationships and sexuality, sexual health and controlling fertility, childbearing, aging and politics of women and health.

This is "the bible for women's health; an outstanding resource that belongs in all health collections." Libr J

Complementary and alternative medicine information for teens; health tips about diverse medical and wellness systems. edited by Lisa Bakewell. 2nd ed. Omnigraphics, Inc. 2013 xiii, 389 p.p (hardcover) $69

Grades: 7 8 9 10 11 12   **613**
1. Alternative medicine 2. Teenagers -- Health and hygiene 3. Alternative medicine -- Popular works 4. Teenagers -- Health and hygiene -- Popular works
ISBN 0780813111; 9780780813113
                                  LC 2012047548

This book offers information about alternative medicine for teenagers. The "volume is divided into 60 chapters, each focusing on a specific natural medicine or therapy that can be used in combination with or in place of conventional drugs to enhance health . . . . The nine parts address major categories, such as whole-medicine systems, manipulative and body-based practices, dietary and herbal remedies, and energy medicines, as well as sensory and emotional-based therapies." (School Library Journal)

Includes bibliographical references and index.

De la Bedoyere, Camilla

★ **Personal** hygiene and sexual health. Amicus 2010 46p il (Healthy lifestyles) lib bdg $32.80

Grades: 7 8 9 10   **613**
1. Puberty 2. Teenagers -- Health and hygiene
ISBN 978-1-60753-087-9; 1-60753-087-2
                                  LC 2009-47571

This book is "well-written and satisfyingly informative. . . . [The] magazine-like format includes numerous sidebars, color photos, and charts." SLJ

Includes glossary

Dicker, Katie

Diet and nutrition. Amicus 2011 45p il (Healthy lifestyles) lib bdg $32.80

Grades: 7 8 9 10   **613**
1. Diet 2. Nutrition 3. Physical fitness 4. Teenagers -- Health and hygiene
ISBN 978-1-60753-085-5; 1-60753-085-6
                                  LC 2009-44219

This book is "well-written and satisfyingly informative." SLJ

Includes glossary

Goldstein, Mark A.

Boys into men; staying healthy through the teen years. by Mark A. Goldstein and Myrna Chandler Goldstein. Greenwood Press 2000 197p il $45

Grades: 9 10 11 12   **613**
1. Boys -- Health and hygiene 2. Teenagers -- Health and hygiene
ISBN 0-313-30966-3
                                  LC 00-21045

"Dividing adolescence into three time frames—twelve to fourteen, fifteen to eighteen, and nineteen to twenty-one years old—the Goldsteins present information on various areas of physical and emotional growth and development." Voice Youth Advocates

Includes bibliographical references

Libal, Autumn

Can I change the way I look? a teen's guide to the health implications of cosmetic surgery, makeovers, and beyond. Mason Crest Publishers 2005 128p il (Science of health) $24.95

Grades: 7 8 9 10 **613**
1. Personal grooming 2. Teenagers -- Health and hygiene
ISBN 1-59084-843-8

LC 2004-1883

"Framing her discussion within an examination of the media influence on our culture's definition of beauty, Libal does an excellent job of discussing the risks and benefits of cosmetics, piercing and tattooing, diet, exercise, and cosmetic surgery. . . . The author also considers, in some detail, the dangers of anorexia nervosa, bulimia, and steroid use." SLJ

Includes bibliographical references

★ Mayo Clinic family health book; Scott Litin, editor-in-chief. 4th ed., completely rev. and updated; Time Inc. Home Entertainment 2009 1423p il $49.95

Grades: 11 12 Adult **613**
1. Medicine 2. Reference books
ISBN 978-1-60320-077-6; 1-60320-077-0

LC 2010-287052

First published 1990 by Morrow

This book covers over 1,000 illnesses and includes information on immunizations, breast health, genetics, sleep disorders, complementary and alternative medicine, pain management, and end-of-life issues.

McCoy, Kathleen

★ The teenage body book; [by] Kathy McCoy and Charles Wibbelsman; illustrations by Bob Stover and Kelly Grady. Rev and updated; Hatherleigh 2008 300p il pa $17.95

Grades: 7 8 9 10 11 12 **613**
1. Adolescence 2. Sex education 3. Teenagers -- Health and hygiene
ISBN 978-1-57826-277-9

LC 2009-368424

First published 1979 by Pocket Bks. with authors' names in reverse order

A handbook for teenagers discussing nutrition, health, fitness, emotions, and sexuality, including such topics as body image, drugs, STDs, fad diets and hazards and benefits of the Internet.

"This highly informative book . . . is at the same time easily readable, nonpreachy, and comprehensive. . . . This book should be not only in the library of every middle and high school, but also in the hands of every student and in health education classes." Sci Books Films

Natterson, Cara

The care & keeping of you 2; the body book for older girls. Dr. Cara Natterson; illustrated by Josee Masse. American Girl 2013 96 p. (paperback) $12.99

Grades: 5 6 7 8 **613**
1. Puberty 2. Life skills -- Handbooks, manuals, etc. 3. Teenage girls -- Health and hygiene
ISBN 1609580427; 9781609580421

LC 2012045813

This book, by Cara Natterson, illustrated by Josee Masse, is a body image and physiology guide written for girls going through puberty. "This . . . advice book will guide you through the next steps of growing up. . . . This book covers new questions about periods, your growing body, peer pressure, personal care, and more." (Publisher's note)

"The friendly illustrations support the overall tone and style. . . . Its neutral, matter-of-fact approach will help show readers . . . that all the changes they may be feeling are perfectly normal." SLJ

Reber, Deborah

Chill; stress-reducing techniques for a more balanced, peaceful you. Simon Pulse 2008 196p il pa $9.99

Grades: 8 9 10 11 12 **613**
1. Stress (Psychology) 2. Girls -- Health and hygiene
ISBN 978-1-4169-5526-9 pa; 1-4169-5526-7 pa

"This book has just the right combination of smart wit, know-it-all bravado, and advice from a pseudo big sister. The pages speed by, moving from topic to topic: time management, support systems, self-help therapy, exercise, nutrition, and more. Advice is free-flowing, complete with examples, exercises, and quizzes. . . . This helpful resource will appeal to a wide variety of young women." SLJ

Yancey, Antronette K.

Instant recess; building a fit nation 10 minutes at a time. [by] Toni Yancey. University of California Press 2010 263p il $55; pa $22.95

Grades: 11 12 Adult **613**
1. Exercise 2. Physical fitness
ISBN 978-0-520-26375-8; 978-0-520-26376-5 pa

LC 2010024933

"Yancey makes a compelling case for establishing ten-minute recesses—that is, aerobic breaks—in schools, churches, baseball stadiums, and offices around the country. Her goal: for people to think that prolonged sitting is as socially unacceptable as drinking and driving or smoking. . . . To liven up her text, the author shares poems she has written and fun photos, even as she stays focused on her call for an affordable, easy way to prevent chronic diseases and promote health." Booklist

Includes bibliographical references

613.2 Dietetics

Burke, Louise

The complete guide to food for sports performance; a guide to peak nutrition for your sport.

[by] Louise Burke, Greg Cox. 3rd ed., Updated and expanded; Allen & Unwin 2010 xxii, 522p il pa $24.95

Grades: 11 12 Adult   613.2
1. Physical fitness 2. Athletes -- Nutrition
ISBN 978-1-7411-4390-4; 1-7411-4390-X
LC 2010-537626
First published 1992

"This book presents nutrition as an integrated part of an athlete's total performance-enhancing package. General nutrition and exercise physiology information are converted into a plan for day-to-day practice for training and competition preparation. It outlines important differences in nutritional needs for different sports, including the timing of food and liquid intake, and the best foods to achieve maximum energy output." Publisher's note

Can diets be harmful? edited by Christine Watkins. Greenhaven Press 2012 101 p. (At issue) (library) $34.45; (paperback) $25.45

Grades: 8 9 10 11 12   613.2
1. Diet 2. Eating habits 3. Diet in disease 4. Reducing diets -- Heath aspects 5. Reducing diets -- Health aspects
ISBN 0737755563; 0737755571 pa; 9780737755565 lib bdg; 9780737755572
LC 2011020813

This book, edited by Christine Watkins, is part of the At Issue series and looks at diets. The series "provides a wide range of opinions on individual social issues. Each volume focuses on a specific issue and offers a variety of perspectives—eyewitness accounts, governmental views, scientific analysis, newspaper and magazine accounts, and many more—to illuminate the issue." (Publisher's note)
Includes bibliographical references (p. 93-97) and index.

Favor, Lesli J.
Weighing in; nutrition and weight management. Marshall Cavendish Benchmark 2007 128p il (Food and fitness) lib bdg $28

Grades: 7 8 9 10   613.2
1. Nutrition 2. Weight loss
ISBN 0761443673; 9780761443674
LC 2006-101930

This "offers an in-depth look at issues related to body weight. Chapters . . . discuss determining one's ideal weight; health risks associated with weight, from diabetes to anorexia; nutrition and wellness; teen dietary requirements and meal planning; and weight-loss strategies, with possible dangers highlighted. . . . Teens will find this a useful, often thought-provoking resource for personal or class research." Booklist
Includes bibliographical references

Gay, Kathlyn
★ The scoop on what to eat; what you should know about diet and nutrition. Enslow Publishers 2009 112p il (Issues in focus today) lib bdg $31.93
Grades: 7 8 9 10   613.2
1. Nutrition
ISBN 978-0-7660-3066-4; 0-7660-3066-0
LC 2008-40382

"Bolstered with well-integrated quotes and relevant statistics, [this book offers] an excellent starting point for students seeking [a] broad, thoroughly researched [introduction] to [diet and nutrition]. . . . Illuminating case studies, enhanced with multiple viewpoints, personalize the facts and place them in boarder context." Booklist
Includes glossary and bibliographical references

James, Delores C. S.
★ Nutrition and well-being A to Z; Delores C.S. James, editor in chief. Macmillan Reference USA 2004 2v il set $175
Grades: 9 10 11 12 Adult   613.2
1. Reference books 2. Nutrition -- Encyclopedias
ISBN 0-02-865707-1
LC 2004-6088

This is "a no-nonsense, comprehensive encyclopedia that will be of use to students researching health and food-science topics." SLJ
Includes bibliographical references

Kessler, David A.
Your food is fooling you; how your brain is hijacked by sugar, fat, and salt. David A. Kessler; adapted by Richie Chevat. Roaring Brook Press 2013 183 p. (paperback) $9.99
Grades: 9 10 11 12   613.2
1. Diet 2. Nutrition 3. Obesity -- Prevention 4. Health behavior -- United States 5. Nutrition -- Psychological aspects 6. Obesity -- Prevention -- United States
ISBN 1596438312; 9781596438316; 9781596438484
LC 2012032020

In this book, David A. Kessler "argues forcefully that our brain chemistry is being hijacked by the food we eat: that by consuming stimulating combinations of sugar, fat, and salt, we're conditioning our bodies to crave more sugar, fat, and salt--and consigning ourselves to a vicious cycle of overeating." This edition is adapted to a "format that's accessible, positive, and affirming for teenagers." (Publisher's note)

Rau, Dana Meachen
Going organic; a healthy guide to making the switch. by Dana Meachen Rau. Compass Point Books 2012 64 p. col. ill. (paperback) $8.95; (hardcover) $33.99
Grades: 6 7 8 9   613.2
1. Diet 2. Nutrition 3. Natural foods 4. Organic farming 5. Health
ISBN 0756545234; 0756545285; 9780756545239; 9780756545284
LC 2011040704

"[Rau] outlines the perils of factory farms and industrial food lots, both on an environmental and personal scale; distinguishes the often interrelated terms organic, sustainable, and local; offers a rundown of potentially misleading marketing terms; and even tosses in a few recipes, charts, and other helpful sidebars. Readers who find their interest piqued by this informative and concise treatment..." Booklist
Includes bibliographical references (p. 62) and index.

Rau, Dana Meachen, 1971-

Going vegetarian; a healthy guide to making the switch. by Dana Meachen Rau. Compass Point Books 2012 64 p. (hardcover) $33.99

Grades: 5 6 7 8 9   **613.2**

1. Nutrition 2. Vegetarianism 3. Vegetarian cooking
ISBN 0756545226; 9780756545222; 9780756545307
      LC 2011040836

Author Dana Meachen Rau presents a guide to becoming a vegetarian. "Learn about the benefits and challenges of a diet that does not include red meat, poultry, or fish. Helpful tips, delicious vegetarian recipes, and how tos will make the switch so much easier." The book also offers various organic, meatless, and vegan recipes and meal ideas. (Publisher"s note)

"Whether looking to go organic, ovo-lacto vegetarian, or vegan, kids will find the information necessary to make the switch in these titles...Organic focuses on the USDA's National Organic Program (NOP) regulations, making no mention of other certification programs. It does, however, warn kids about trusting organic labels implicitly and recommends that they go straight to the source when possible by researching and even visiting companies. Serve these up to budding health foodies.." (School Library Journal)

Includes bibliographical references (p. 62) and index

Smolin, Lori A.

Nutrition and weight management; [by] Lori A. Smolin and Mary B. Grosvenor. 2nd ed.; Chelsea House 2010 184p il map (Healthy eating: a guide to nutrition) lib bdg $35

Grades: 7 8 9 10 11 12   **613.2**

1. Nutrition 2. Weight loss
ISBN 978-1-60413-803-0; 1-60413-803-3
      LC 2009-41335

First published 2005

This "volume uses boldface type to introduce important and unknown words to the reader and explains them in an easy to understand manner so the reader can grasp the concept being discussed. . . . [For] classes needing information about the importance of good nutrition . . . [this] would be valuable." Libr Media Connect

Includes glossary and bibliographical references

613.208 Young people

★ **Diabetes** information for teens; health tips about managing diabetes and preventing related complications, including facts about insulin, glucose control, healthy eating, physical activity, and learning to live with diabetes. edited by Karen Bellenir. Omnigraphics 2012 397 p. ill. (hardcover: alk. paper) $69.00

Grades: 7 8 9 10 11 12   **613.208**

1. Diabetes 2. Teenagers -- Health and hygiene
ISBN 0780812182; 9780780812185
      LC 2011038652

This book for teenagers on the topic of diabetes, edited by Karen Bellenir, "examines the alarming trends in diabetes prevalence, and it provides information about positive steps that can be taken. The book provides facts about the different types of diabetes, its medical management, and the roles of nutrition and physical activity in averting its consequences. Suggestions are included for handling problematic situations, such as caring for diabetes at school." (Publisher's note)

Includes bibliographical references and index

★ **Diet** information for teens; health tips about nutrition fundamentals and eating plans including facts about vitamins, minerals, food additives, and weight-related concerns. edited by Zachary Klimecki and Karen Bellenir. 3rd ed. Omnigraphics, Inc. 2012 xiii, 427 p.p ill. (Teen health series) (hardcover: alk. paper) $69

Grades: 8 9 10 11 12   **613.208**

1. Diet 2. Health 3. Teenagers -- Health and hygiene 4. Teenagers -- Nutrition
ISBN 0780811569; 9780780811560
      LC 2011031595

This book is a "compendium of diet and nutrition" for teenagers comprising "articles on all facets of nutrition, drawn mainly from FDA documents.... Chapters of specialized appeal include 'Special Dietary Guidelines for Teenage Mothers' and 'Assessing School Lunches,' as well as coverage of teen snacking." (School Library Journal)

Includes bibliographical references and index

613.262 Vegetarian diet

Traugh, Susan M.

Vegetarianism. Lucent Books 2011 96p il lib bdg $30.85

Grades: 6 7 8 9   **613.262**

1. Vegetarianism
ISBN 978-1-4205-0272-5; 1-4205-0272-7
      LC 2010014015

"The attractively designed title in the Nutrition & Health series will help middle-grade and high-school students make good decisions about the food they eat. Unlike some nutrition books, the tone remains mostly positive, informing readers about the negative effects of poor choices such as obesity and disease while also encouraging them to take control of their own decisions by reading nutrition labels. Although it uses the nutrition pyramid, recently put aside for the newer 'plate' model, the information remains very current, and each book highlights recent scientific studies." Booklist

613.6 Personal safety and special topics of health

Doeden, Matt

Safety smarts; how to manage threats, protect yourself, get help, and more. Matt Doeden. Twenty-First Century Books 2013 64 p. col. ill. (USA today teen wise guides: lifestyle choices) (library) $31.93

Grades: 8 9 10 11 12   **613.6**

1. Safety education 2. Teenagers -- Crimes against --

Prevention
ISBN 0761370226; 9780761370222

LC 2011044268

This book, by Matt Doeden, offers advice for teen safety as part of the "USA Today Teen Wise Guides: Lifestyle Choices" series. "In a perfect world, everyone would be safe all the time: in the car, at home, at school, and online. Well, . . . cars sometimes crash, burglars break into houses, kids get bullied at school, and cyberstalkers and sexual predators prowl the Internet. But that's no reason to hide in your room and worry. You can stay safe if you use some safety smarts." (Publisher's note)

Includes bibliographical references (p. 61-63) and index.

Gervasi, Lori Hartman

Fight like a girl-- and win; defense decisions for women. St. Martin's Griffin 2007 285p pa $14.99

Grades: 11 12 Adult　　　　　　　　　**613.6**

1. Safety education 2. Self-defense for women
ISBN 978-0-312-35772-6; 0-312-35772-9

LC 2007-17216

"Although the author has a black belt in karate, she maintains that 90 percent of self-defense is awareness and common sense. She helps readers set up absolute rules and boundaries, sharpen their observation skills, and trust in their intuition. Physical fitness is stressed, and resources are provided for further training." Libr J

Includes bibliographical references

Piven, Joshua

The **worst**-case scenario survival handbook; by Joshua Piven and David Borgenicht. Chronicle Bks. 1999 176p il pa $14.95

Grades: 9 10 11 12　　　　　　　　　**613.6**

1. Safety education 2. Wilderness survival 3. Survival after airplane accidents, shipwrecks, etc.
ISBN 0-8118-2555-8

LC 2001-268229

This offers advice on safety and survival in emergencies from such dangers as quicksand, erupting volcanoes, terrorist attacks, sharks, plane crashes, and bombs.

Stilwell, Alexander

★ The **encyclopedia** of survival techniques. Lyons Press 2007 192p il map pa $19.95

Grades: 11 12 Adult　　　　　　　　　**613.6**

1. Survival skills 2. Wilderness survival
ISBN 978-1-59921-314-9

First published 2000

This guide covers preparation, basic skills, equipment, various terrains, natural disasters, and first aid.

Stroud, Les

Will to live; dispatches from the edge of survival. [by] Les Stroud with Michael Vlessides. Harper 2011 228p il pa $17.99

Grades: 11 12 Adult　　　　　　　　　**613.6**

1. Survival skills 2. Survival after airplane accidents, shipwrecks, etc.
ISBN 978-0-06-202657-6

First published 2010 in Canada

Analyzes survival stories, recounting the events that occurred, and evaluating the decisions made utilizing four critical survival elements, in a text that includes practical tips.

The author "offers intelligent tips—if you're traveling somewhere remote, tell people where you're going, take a well-stocked survival kit, and keep a cool head if you get lost—and he does an excellent job of putting readers into the situations he's discussing, making us feel the cold or the panic or the sheer desperation." Booklist

Includes bibliographical references

Survival wisdom & know-how; everything you need to know to subsist in the wilderness. from the editors of Stackpole Books; compiled by Amy Rost. Black Dog & Leventhal Publishers 2007 480p il pa $19.95

Grades: 9 10 11 12 Adult　　　　　　　**613.6**

1. Survival skills 2. Wilderness survival
ISBN 978-1-57912-753-4

LC 2007-25379

This oversized guide covers "every aspect of outdoor adventure and survival . . . Topics include Building Outdoor Shelter, Tracking Animals, Winter Camping, Tying Knots, Orienteering, Reading the Weather, Identifying Edible Plants and Berries, Surviving in the Desert, Bird Watching, Fishing and Ice Fishing, Hunting and Trapping, Canoeing, Kayaking, and White Water Rafting, First Aid, Wild Animals, Cookery, and . . . more." Publisher's note

Includes bibliographical references

Wiseman, John

SAS survival handbook; for any climate, in any situation. [by] John 'Lofty' Wiseman. Rev. ed.; Collins 2009 576p il pa $19.99

Grades: 11 12 Adult　　　　　　　　　**613.6**

1. Survival skills 2. Wilderness survival 3. Survival after airplane accidents, shipwrecks, etc.
ISBN 978-0-06-173319-2; 0-06-173319-9

LC 2009-502549

First published 1986 in the United Kingdom

This book "is the Special Air Service's complete course in being prepared for any type of emergency. John Wiseman presents real strategies for surviving in any type of situation, from accidents and escape procedures, including chemical and nuclear to successfully adapting to various climates (polar, tropical, desert), to identifying edible plants and creating fire." Publisher's note

613.66　　Self-defense

Soo-Warr, Lavinia

Self-defense for women; Lavinia Soo-Warr. Rosen Pub 2010 256 p. (A young woman's guide to health and well-being) (library binding) $42.60

Grades: 9 10 11 12 Adult　　　　　　　**613.66**

1. Martial arts 2. Self-defense for women
ISBN 143585358X; 9781435853584

LC 2009010436

This book "provides a solid introduction to basic self defense techniques and methods. . . . The content is readable and clear, with indexes to guide readers to key concepts." VOYA

613.7 Physical fitness

Bellenir, Elizabeth

Fitness Information for Teens; Health Tips About Exercise & Active Lifestyles. edited by Elizabeth Bellenir. 3rd ed. Omnigraphics 2012 xiii, 387 p.p ill. (Teen health series) (hardcover: alk. paper) $69.00

Grades: 7 8 9 10 11 12 **613.7**

1. Physical fitness 2. Teenagers -- Health and hygiene 3. Physical fitness for youth

ISBN 9780780812673; 0780812670

LC 2012024737

This book is "earmarked to provide the tools and information needed for teens to engage in a healthier lifestyle before entering adulthood. . . . Seven main sections cover information on the human body, personal fitness plans, exercise fundamentals, team activities, sports safety, obstacles to finding fitness, and resources." (Booklist)

"In this thorough, easy-to-follow single volume, seven main sections cover information on the human body, personal fitness plans, exercise fundamentals, team activities, sports safety, obstacles to finding fitness, and resources... Highly recommended." Booklist

Includes bibliographical references and index

Brignell, Roger

The **pilates** handbook. Rosen Pub. 2009 256p il (A young woman's guide to health and well-being) lib bdg $39.95

Grades: 9 10 11 12 **613.7**

1. Pilates method 2. Women -- Health and hygiene

ISBN 978-1-4358-5361-4

LC 2009-10317

This guide "looks at the origins and development of Pilates, and how it can enhance mental as well as physical well-being. The exercise section begins with some basic warmup movements, then works through a series of beginner, intermediate, and advanced exercises. It also demonstrates exercises using a Swiss ball and other equipment." Publisher's note

Includes bibliographical references

Dicker, Katie

Exercise. Amicus 2010 46p il (Healthy lifestyles) lib bdg $32.80

Grades: 7 8 9 10 **613.7**

1. Exercise 2. Physical fitness

ISBN 978-1-60753-086-2; 1-60753-086-4

LC 2009-47566

This book is "well-written and satisfyingly informative. . . . [The] magazine-like format includes numerous sidebars, color photos, and charts." SLJ

Includes glossary

Epstein, David

The **sports** gene; inside the science of extraordinary athletic performance. David Epstein. Current 2013 352 p. $26.95

Grades: 11 12 Adult **613.7**

1. Athletes 2. Genetics 3. Human genetics 4. Sports -- Physiological aspects

ISBN 1591845114; 9781591845119

LC 2013013443

In this book, David Epstein investigates the connection between genetics and athletic ability. "Drawing on interviews with athletes and scientists, he points out that 'a nation succeeds in a sport not only by having many people who practice prodigiously at sport-specific skills, but also by getting the best all-around athletes into the right sports in the first place.'" (Publishers Weekly)

"[T]his book is essential reading for sports fans interested in the science of sports, and for readers (not scholars) interested in the science of human differences." LJ

Includes bibliographical references and index

Fahey, Thomas D.

Basic weight training for men and women; 6th ed.; McGraw-Hill 2007 248p il pa $30.63

Grades: 11 12 Adult **613.7**

1. Weight lifting

ISBN 0-07-304688-4; 978-0-07-304688-4

LC 2005-53132

First published 1989 by Mayfield Pub. Co. with title: Basic weight training

This is a "guide to developing a personalized weight-training program with both free weights and machines. Weight training concepts and specific exercises are grouped by body region, and many photographs, illustrations, diagrams, and figures demonstrate proper technique and form." Publisher's note

Includes bibliographical references

Finney, Sumukhi

The **yoga** handbook. Rosen Pub. 2010 256p il (A young woman's guide to health and well-being) lib bdg $39.95

Grades: 9 10 11 12 **613.7**

1. Yoga 2. Women -- Health and hygiene

ISBN 978-1-4358-5359-1

LC 2009-10509

This guide "offers insight into both the physical and spiritual traditions associated with yoga. Clearly organized, the chapters discuss types of yoga; breathing, diet, and meditation suggestions; and, of course, the poses, which are described step by step, illustrated with small color photos, and bolstered with variations on the basic forms. Finney's experience shows in her enthusiastic tone and in the quotes she culls from ancient texts and contemporary teachers alike." Booklist

Includes bibliographical references

Frederick, Shane

Strength training for teen athletes; exercises to take your game to the next level. by Karen Latchana

Kenney. Capstone Press 2012 48 p. col. ill. (paperback) $7.95; (library binding) $31.32

Grades: 6 7 8 9   **613.7**

1. Athletes 2. Exercise 3. Weight lifting 4. Teenagers -- Health and hygiene 5. Muscle strength 6. Teenage athletes -- Training of

ISBN 1429676809; 9781429680028; 1429680024; 9781429676809

LC 2011033561

Author Karen Latchana Kenney provides a guide for teenage athletes on how to improve their performance with strength training. "With . . . strength building exercises and tips, you'll notice a big improvement in your game. Build the power behind your baseball or softball swing, soccer kick, or swimming stroke." (Publisher's note)

Includes bibliographical references and index.

Hesson, James L.

Weight training for life; 9th ed.; Wadsworth/Cengage Learning 2010 178p il $59.95

Grades: 11 12 Adult   **613.7**

1. Weight lifting

ISBN 978-0-495-55909-2; 0-495-55909-1

LC 2010291364

First published 1985 by Morton

"The text contains hundreds of full-color photos demonstrating exercises and proper techniques. It also contains forms for writing goals, planning a personal weight-training program, and recording circumference, strength, and muscle endurance measurements." Publisher's note

Includes bibliographical references

Hill, Z.B.

Cross-training; Z.B. Hill. Mason Crest 2015 64 p. color illustrations (hardback) $23.95

Grades: 9 10 11 12 Adult   **613.7**

1. Exercise 2. Physical education 3. Physical fitness 4. Physical education and training

ISBN 1422231585; 9781422231562; 9781422231586

LC 2014014787

This book by Z.B. Hill, part of the Integrated Life of Fitness series, "resents information about cross-training, looking at how athletes and regular people use it to improve athletic performance and health, and how to go about it in a safe and effective manner." (Publisher's note)

"Despite a few missteps, this excellent series demonstrates how a physical education class can be interdisciplinary and academically rigorous." SLJ

Includes bibliographical refeences and index

Endurance & cardio training; Z.B. Hill. Mason Crest 2015 64 p. color illustrations (Hardback) $23.95

Grades: 9 10 11 12   **613.7**

1. Exercise 2. Physical fitness 3. Cardiovascular system

ISBN 1422231607; 9781422231609

LC 2014011343

This book by author Z.B. Hill, part of the Integrated Life of Fitness series, "explains how cardio training strengthens the heart and lungs, improves mental health, and builds endurance; offers information on equipment and safety; and provides guidance for setting up an exercise plan." (Publisher's note)

"The physiological information is detailed enough for a college course in exercise science. Each book touches on safety and common injuries. Despite a few missteps, this excellent series demonstrates how a physical education class can be interdisciplinary and academically rigorous." SLJ

Endurance and cardio training

Hines, Emmett W.

Fitness swimming; [by] Emmett Hines. 2nd ed.; Human Kinetics 2008 224p il pa $18.95

Grades: 9 10 11 12 Adult   **613.7**

1. Swimming 2. Physical fitness

ISBN 978-0-7360-7457-5; 0-7360-7457-0

LC 2008-13353

First published 1999

The author "has created 60 . . . workouts and 16 sample programs, each arranged into suggested training zones to correspond to your fitness level and performance goals. . . . The text covers stretching, warm-up and cool-down methods, heart rate zone targets, expanded instruction for stroke efficacy, progressive drills, conditioning tips, and fitness assessments." Publisher's note

Includes bibliographical references

James, Sara

Flexibility & agility; Sara James. Mason Crest 2015 64 p. color illustrations (Hardback) $23.95

Grades: 9 10 11 12   **613.7**

1. Physical fitness 2. Stretching exercises

ISBN 1422231623; 9781422231623

LC 2014014791

This book by Sara James, part of the Integrated Life of Fitness series, "presents information on what flexibility and agility are and why they are important, as well as exercises for improving both and advice for making a plan for improving them." (Publisher's note)

Yoga & Pilates; Sara James. Mason Crest, an imprint of National Highlights 2015 64 p. color illustrations (An integrated life of fitness) (hardback) $23.95

Grades: 9 10 11 12   **613.7**

1. Hatha yoga 2. Pilates method

ISBN 1422231666; 9781422231661

LC 2014014800

This book, by Sara James, "introduces readers to [yoga and pilates] . . . and their benefits, providing historical and scientific background as well as practical exercise routines. . . . Explanations of how physical activity strengthens muscle groups and mental functioning will provide subtle motivation. . . . The physiological information is detailed enough for a college course in exercise science. Each book touches on safety and common injuries." (School Library Journal)

"Despite a few missteps, this excellent series demonstrates how a physical education class can be interdisciplinary and academically rigorous." SLJ

Part of a series

Pagano, Joan

★ **Strength** training for women; tone up, burn calories, stay strong. Dorling Kindersley 2005 160p il pa $15

Grades: 9 10 11 12 Adult **613.7**

1. Weight lifting 2. Physical fitness 3. Women -- Health and hygiene

ISBN 0-7566-0595-4; 978-0-7566-0595-7

LC 2005-295208

The author "begins with a three-part fitness test and questionnaire to assess whether the reader should consult a doctor before beginning her program. For true beginners, she provides an anatomy chart that depicts the major muscle groups and the exercises that are best suited to them. She dispels fitness myths like 'lifting weights will bulk you up' and 'you can spot reduce,' and talks about the risk factors, exercise guidelines and restrictions of osteoporosis. . . . This book may be one of the best substitutes for pricey gym memberships and personal trainers." Publ Wkly

Pawlett, Raymond

The **tai** chi handbook; [by] Ray Pawlet. Rosen Pub. 2009 246p il (A young woman's guide to health and well-being) lib bdg $39.95

Grades: 9 10 11 12 **613.7**

1. Tai chi 2. Women -- Health and hygiene

ISBN 978-1-4358-5360-7

LC 2009-10316

"The Tai Chi Handbook teaches readers . . . about the art, including its history, styles, applications, and moves." Publisher's note

Includes bibliographical references

Scott, Celicia

Sports & fitness; Celicia Scott. Mason Crest 2015 64 p. color illustrations (Hardback) $23.95

Grades: 9 10 11 12 **613.7**

1. Health 2. Sports 3. Recreation

ISBN 1422231631; 9781422231630

LC 2014011347

This book by Cecilia Scott "presents information on how playing sports helps people lose weight and stay fit and healthy, and looks at the different kinds of sports, how people train for them, and how to stay safe when playing them." (Publisher's note)

"The physiological information is detailed enough for a college course in exercise science. Each book touches on safety and common injuries. Despite a few missteps, this excellent series demonstrates how a physical education class can be interdisciplinary and academically rigorous." SLJ

Sports and fitness

Weight lifting & strength building; Celicia Scott. Mason Crest 2015 64 p. color illustrations (hardback) $23.95

Grades: 9 10 11 12 **613.7**

1. Exercise 2. Weight lifting 3. Bodybuilding

ISBN 1422231658; 9781422231562; 9781422231654

LC 2014011348

This book by Celicia Scott "presents information about weightlifting and strength training, covering how to get

started in it, the weights and equipment needed, how to lift weights safely, how to eat appropriately, and how to plan a lifting program." (Publisher's note)

"The physiological information is detailed enough for a college course in exercise science. Each book touches on safety and common injuries. Despite a few missteps, this excellent series demonstrates how a physical education class can be interdisciplinary and academically rigorous." SLJ

Includes bibliographical references and index

Smolin, Lori A.

★ **Nutrition** for sports and exercise; [by] Lori A. Smolin and Mary B. Grosvenor. 2nd ed.; Chelsea House 2010 192p il (Healthy eating: a guide to nutrition) lib bdg $35

Grades: 9 10 11 12 **613.7**

1. Exercise 2. Nutrition 3. Athletes -- Nutrition

ISBN 978-1-60413-804-7

LC 2010-5692

First published 2005

"The book explores the dangers that athletes may face when they neglect their nutritional needs and provides valuable information about how athletes can best achieve optimal nutrition." Publisher's note

Includes glossary and bibliographical references

613.8 Substance abuse (Drug abuse)

★ **Drug** information for teens; health tips about the physical and mental effects of substance abuse. edited by Elizabeth Magill. 3rd ed. Omnigraphics 2011 xiv, 490 p.p ill. (hardcover) $69

Grades: 7 8 9 10 11 12 **613.8**

1. Teenagers -- Drug use 2. Teenagers -- Health and hygiene 3. Drug abuse 4. Drugs -- Physiological effect 5. Teenagers -- Drug use -- United States 6. Alcoholism -- United States -- Prevention 7. Drug abuse -- United States -- Prevention 8. Teenagers -- Alcohol use -- United States 9. Teenagers -- Health and hygiene -- United States

ISBN 0780811542; 9780780811546

LC 2010048932

This book "provides updated facts about drug use, abuse, and addiction. It describes the physical and psychological effects of alcohol, marijuana, prescription drugs, inhalants, club drugs, stimulants, and many other commonly abused drugs and chemicals. It includes information about drug-related health concerns. . . . A section on substance abuse treatment describes care options and provides resources for addiction recovery." (Publisher's note)

613.81 Alcohol

★ **Alcohol** information for teens; health tips about alcohol use, abuse & dependence including facts about alcohol's effects on mental and physical health, the consequences of underage drinking & understanding alcoholic family members. edited by Karen Bellenir. 3rd ed. Omnigraphics, Inc.

2013 371 p. ill (Teen health series) (hardcover) $69

Grades: 7 8 9 10 11 12　　　　**613.81**

1. Alcoholism 2. Teenagers -- Alcohol use 3. Drinking of alcoholic beverages

ISBN 0780813138; 9780780813137

LC 2013000216

This book "provides updated information about the use and misuse of alcohol. It describes ways alcohol can affect mental and physical health. It discusses the special vulnerabilities of the teen brain and the changes in brain functioning that lead to dependency. A section on treatment and recovery discusses achieving and maintaining sobriety, and a section on alcohol abuse in the family addresses the special concerns of teens who live with an alcoholic relative." (Publisher's note)

Includes bibliographical references and index

613.9　Birth control, reproductive technology, sex hygiene, sexual techniques

Bell, Ruth

★ **Changing** bodies, changing lives; a book for teens on sex and relationships. [by] Ruth Bell and other co-authors of Our bodies, ourselves and Ourselves and our children, together with members of the Teen Book Project. expanded 3rd ed; Times Bks. 1998 411p il pa $24.95

Grades: 7 8 9 10 11 12　　　　**613.9**

1. Sex education

ISBN 0-8129-2990-X

LC 97-29249

First published 1980

This is a "book on sex, physical and emotional health, and personal relationships. . . . Readers . . . will find emotional support as well as specific answers to most of their questions in this nonjudgmental resource." Booklist

Bringle, Jennifer

Reproductive rights; making the right choices. Rosen Pub. 2010 112p il (A young woman's guide to contemporary issues) lib bdg $31.95

Grades: 7 8 9 10　　　　**613.9**

1. Pregnancy 2. Birth control 3. Teenage mothers

ISBN 978-1-4358-3542-9; 1-4358-3542-5

LC 2009-13721

"Facts are shared in a conversational tone, creating the sense of a chat with a big sister. . . . [Though] designed for personal reading and browsing, the data provided are accurate and also lend themselves to use in reports." SLJ

Includes glossary and bibliographical references

Fonda, Jane, 1937-

Being a teen; everything teen girls and boys should know about relationships, sex, love, health, identity & more. by Jane Fonda. Random House Trade Paperbacks 2014 288 p.

Grades: 9 10 11 12　　　　**613.9**

1. Teenage pregnancy 2. Teenagers -- Sexual behavior

3. Sex instruction for teenagers 4. Teenagers -- Health and hygiene

ISBN 9780812978612

LC 2013016042

"The book's strength is its factual information on puberty, with simple line drawings accompanying clearly explained information." Publ Wkly

Includes bibliographical references and index

Murray, Craig

Sexpectations; Sex Stuff Straight Up. Allen & Unwin 2012 111 p. $19.95

Grades: 7 8 9 10 11 12　　　　**613.9**

1. Sex education 2. Sexual hygiene 3. Teenagers -- Sexual behavior

ISBN 1741751438; 9781741751437

Includes bibliographical references.

This book, by Craig Murray and Leissa Pitts, offers a "teenage-friendly sex education and sexual health guide book, for both boys and girls, in one . . . volume. Designed to help teens make healthy, positive choices, . . . It takes teens through knowing themselves and their bodies, keeping safe, protecting themselves, thinking through pregnancy, knowing about relationships, and tapping into their personal power to make positive choices." (Publisher's note)

Pardes, Bronwen

Doing it right; making smart, safe, and satisfying choices about sex. by Bronwen Pardes. Simon Pulse 2013 146 p. il $17.99

Grades: 7 8 9 10 11 12　　　　**613.9**

1. Sex education

ISBN 1442483709; 9781442483705

LC 2006-928450

This book, by Bronwen Pardes, presents sex education for teenagers. "Chapters, which often use a question-and-answer format based on teens' actual queries, delve into sexual anatomy, questions to consider before sex, contraception, safe-sex practices, homosexuality, masturbation, and sexual violence. Throughout, Pardes avoids a heterosexual bias, and her discussion of sexual activity is explicit and inclusive." (Publisher's note)

The author "tackles the tough questions about sexual orientation, size, abuse, orgasm, pregnancy, STDs, and masturbation among others." Voice Youth Advocates

Includes bibliographical references

★ **Sexual** health information for teens; edited by Sandra Augustyn Lawton. 2nd ed.; Omnigraphics 2008 430p il (Teen health series) $69

Grades: 7 8 9 10 11 12　　　　**613.9**

1. Sex education 2. Teenagers -- Health and hygiene

ISBN 978-0-7808-1010-5; 0-7808-1010-4

LC 2007052454

First published 2003

"This offering represents the most up-to-date information available on an array of topics. . . . The range of coverage . . . is thorough and extensive. Each chapter includes a bibliographic citation, and the three back sections containing additional resources, further reading, and the index are all first-rate. The few illustrations and diagrams range in quality from good to excellent." SLJ

Includes bibliographical references

★ **Teenage** sexuality: opposing viewpoints; Ken R. Wells, book editor. Greenhaven Press 2006 224p il (Opposing viewpoints series) lib bdg $34.95; pa $23.70

Grades: 9 10 11 12 **613.9**

1. Sex education 2. Youth -- Sexual behavior
ISBN 0-7377-3362-4 lib bdg; 0-7377-3363-2 pa

LC 2005-52664

Issues covered include teenagers' attitudes about sex, teen pregnancy, sex education, and teenage homosexuality.

Includes bibliographical references

614 Forensic medicine; incidence of injuries, wounds, disease; public preventive medicine

Adelman, Howard C.

Forensic medicine. Chelsea House 2007 104p il map (Inside forensic science) $32.95

Grades: 9 10 11 12 **614**

1. Forensic sciences 2. Medical jurisprudence
ISBN 978-0-7910-8926-2; 0-7910-8926-6

LC 2006-20617

This book "is intended as an introduction to the topic [of forensic medicine], which is also known as forensic pathology. Many of the medical terms used in this specialty are defined, and basic physiologic processes are explained." Publisher's note

Includes glossary and bibliographical references

Bass, William M.

★ **Death's** acre; inside the legendary forensic lab the Body Farm where the dead do tell tales. [by] Bill Bass and Jon Jefferson; foreword by Patricia Cornwell. Putnam 2003 304p il $24.95; pa $15

Grades: 9 10 11 12 Adult **614**

1. Forensic anthropology
ISBN 0-399-15134-6; 0-425-19832-4 pa

LC 2003-46908

"The author explains the process of decomposition and how bones give clues to identify: approximate age, sex, height, and race, all of which are needed to bring the forensic scientist one step closer to putting a name to a corpse. He describes some of the cases he has been involved with and laughs at himself when he shares stories of mistakes and assumptions. Young adults will gain insight into the forensic process and appreciate Bass's dedication to the truth and his work." SLJ

Blum, Deborah

The **poisoner's** handbook; murder and the birth of forensic medicine in Jazz Age New York. Penguin Press 2010 319p pa $16; $25.95

Grades: 11 12 Adult **614**

1. Toxicology 2. Forensic sciences 3. Poisons and poisoning 4. Poisoning 5. Forensic toxicology 6. Forensic sciences -- History 7. Crime -- New York

(N.Y.) -- History -- 20th century
ISBN 0-14-311882-X pa; 1-59420-243-5; 978-0-14-311882-4 pa; 978-1-59420-243-8

LC 2009-26461

This "history of the development of forensics in New York City . . . spans the years from 1915 to 1936." (N Y Times Book Rev) Index.

"Blum effectively balances the fast-moving detective story with a clear view of the scientific advances that her protagonists brought to the field. Caviar for true-crime fans and science buffs alike." Kirkus

Includes bibliographical references

Kobilinsky, Lawrence F.

Forensic DNA analysis; [by] Lawrence Kobilinsky, Louis Levine, Henrietta Margolis-Nunno. Chelsea House 2007 114p il (Inside forensic science) $32.95

Grades: 9 10 11 12 **614**

1. DNA 2. Forensic sciences
ISBN 978-0-7910-8923-1; 0-7910-8923-1

LC 2006-25586

"DNA can be used for many applications, from figuring out whether someone is the father of a baby to determining whether a particular person was present at a crime scene. Forensic DNA Analysis takes readers through the analysis process and explains the possible results." Publisher's note

Includes glossary and bibliographical references

Mitchell, T. J.

Working stiff; two years, 262 bodies, and the making of a medical examiner. Judy Melinek, MD and T.J. Mitchell. First Scribner hardcover ed Scribner 2014 272 p. (hardback) $25

Grades: 10 11 12 Adult **614**

1. Forensic sciences 2. Medical jurisprudence 3. Forensic pathologists -- New York (State) -- New York -- Biography 4. Medical examiners (Law) -- New York (State) -- New York -- Biography
ISBN 1476727252; 9781476727257; 9781476727264

LC 2014017610

This book, by Judy Melinek and T. J. Mitchell, offers a "memoir of a young forensic pathologist's 'rookie season' as a NYC medical examiner, and the cases--hair-raising and heartbreaking and impossibly complex--that shaped her as both a physician and a mother. . . . [It] offers a firsthand account of daily life in one of America's most arduous professions, and the unexpected challenges of shuttling between the domains of the living and the dead." (Publisher's note)

"Though some sections call for a strong stomach, armchair detectives and would-be forensic pathologists will find Melinek's well-written account to be inspiring and engaging." Pub Wkly

Stripp, Richard A.

The **forensic** aspects of poisons. Chelsea House 2007 127p il (Inside forensic science) lib bdg $32.95

Grades: 9 10 11 12 **614**

1. Forensic sciences
ISBN 978-0-7910-9197-5

LC 2006-22825

This book "introduces students to the basic principles of forensic toxicology and the role of poisons in forensic science. Emphasis is placed on the common drugs and poisons that are encountered by a practicing forensic toxicologist and the approach to determining their medicolegal role in establishing the cause of death and disease. Topics explored include homicide by chemical means, the role of drugs and chemicals in other types of accidental and intentional deaths, and how the interpretation of such cases is utilized in the criminal court setting." Publisher's note

Includes glossary and bibliographical references

Wecht, Cyril H.

Tales from the morgue; forensic answers to nine famous cases including the Scott Peterson & Chandra Levy cases. [by] Cyril Wecht and Mark Curriden with Angela Powell. Prometheus Books 2005 314p il $26

Grades: 11 12 Adult   **614**
1. Forensic sciences 2. Criminal investigation
ISBN 1-59102-353-X
LC 2005-17805

Pathologist Wecht "sorts out the evidence, or lack thereof, in the scandalous circumstances of Scott Peterson and Chandra Levy, explains why he thinks the JFK assassination was a conspiracy and agrees with the original Marilyn Monroe autopsy that found no signs of foul play. . . . What makes Wecht's arguments so persuasive is that he lets scientific facts—or at least his expert interpretation of them—do the talking." Publ Wkly

Includes bibliographical references

Zedeck, Beth E.

Forensic pharmacology; [by] Beth E. Zedeck and Morris S. Zedeck; series editor, Lawrence Kobilinsky. Chelsea House Publishers 2006 138p il (Inside forensic science) $30

Grades: 9 10 11 12   **614**
1. Pharmacology 2. Forensic sciences
ISBN 0-7910-8920-7; 978-0-7910-8920-0
LC 2006-20624

"This book describes one aspect of forensic science: forensic pharmacology and toxicology of drugs and abuse. The reader is introduced to the daily work of the scientists, the principles of pharmacology and toxicology, the technical anaylsis of drugs, and the characteristics of eight major categories of drugs of abuse." Publisher's note

Includes glossary and bibliographical references

Zugibe, Frederick T.

Dissecting death; secrets of a medical examiner. [by] Frederick Zugibe and David L. Carroll. Broadway Books 2005 240p il $24.95; pa $14

Grades: 11 12 Adult   **614**
1. Forensic sciences 2. Medical jurisprudence 3. Criminal investigation
ISBN 0-7679-1879-7; 0-7679-1880-0 pa
LC 2004-62889

The authors' "straightforward style makes for clear and fascinating reading, and the cases chosen are intriguing." Booklist

614.4 Incidence of and public measures to prevent disease

Do infectious diseases pose a threat? Diane Andrews Henningfeld, book editor. Greenhaven Press 2009 144p (At issue. Health) $31.80; pa $22.50

Grades: 9 10 11 12   **614.4**
1. Epidemics 2. Public health 3. Communicable diseases
ISBN 978-0-7377-4294-7; 0-7377-4294-1; 978-0-7377-4293-0 pa; 0-7377-4293-3 pa
LC 2008049414

Discusses the return of epidemics in modern times, possible causes, and how they are tracked and controlled, and debates whether current preventative measures are effective.

Includes bibliographical references

★ **Encyclopedia** of plague and pestilence; from ancient times to the present. George Childs Kohn, editor. 3rd ed; Facts On File 2008 529p il map (Facts on File library of world history) $85

Grades: 11 12 Adult   **614.4**
1. Reference books 2. Epidemics -- Encyclopedias
ISBN 978-0-8160-6935-4; 0-8160-6935-2
LC 2006-41296

First published 1995

This encyclopedia provides "descriptions of more than 700 epidemics, listed alphabetically by location of the outbreak. Each . . . entry includes when and where a particular epidemic began, how and why it happened, whom it affected, how it spread and ran its course, and its outcome and significance." Publisher's note

Includes bibliographical references

Epidemics: opposing viewpoints; David Haugen and Susan Musser, book editors. Greenhaven Press 2011 273p (Opposing viewpoints series) lib bdg $39.70; pa $26.50

Grades: 8 9 10 11 12   **614.4**
1. Epidemics 2. Vaccination 3. Communicable diseases
ISBN 978-0-7377-5219-9; 0-7377-5219-X; 978-0-7377-5220-5 pa; 0-7377-5220-3 pa
LC 2010052249

Articles in this anthology present opposing viewpoints on the subject of epidemics.

Includes bibliographical references

Farrell, Jeanette

★ **Invisible** enemies; stories of infectious diseases. 2nd ed; Farrar, Straus & Giroux 2005 272p il $18

Grades: 7 8 9 10   **614.4**
1. Communicable diseases
ISBN 9780374336073; 0-374-33607-5
LC 2004-57668

First published 1998

The author "focuses on seven dreaded human diseases: smallpox, leprosy, plague, tuberculosis, malaria, cholera, and AIDS. Each chapter provides a description of the physical and psychological effects of the disease on its victims, early theories about its causes, and efforts made to avoid or cure it. Then the methods of research that revealed its cause and developed the means to control its spread are explained in fascinating detail. . . . If every science book for nonspecialists were written with such flair and attention to detail, science would soon become every student's favorite subject." SLJ

Includes glossary and bibliographical references

Grady, Denise
Deadly invaders; virus outbreaks around the world, from Marburg fever to avian flu. Kingfisher 2006 128p il map $16.95
Grades: 7 8 9 10 **614.4**
1. Viruses 2. Marburg virus 3. Communicable diseases
ISBN 978-0-7534-5995-9; 0-7534-5995-7
LC 2006004441
The "writing is informative and compelling. . . . The layout is appealing and includes good-quality, full-color, relevant photographs on almost every spread. . . . A fast-paced, timely, and important book." SLJ

Includes bibliographical references

McKenna, Maryn
Beating back the devil; on the front lines with the disease detectives of the Epidemic Intelligence Service. Free Press 2004 303p hardcover o.p. pa $21.95
Grades: 11 12 Adult **614.4**
1. Centers for Disease Control and Prevention (U.S.) -- Epidemic Intelligence Service Program
ISBN 0-7432-5132-6; 1-4391-2310-1 pa
LC 2004-53214
"This book should serve as an effective antidote for anyone suffering from the misconception that epidemiologists must lead boring lives." Sci Books Films

Includes bibliographical references

614.5 Incidence of and public measures to prevent specific diseases and kinds of diseases

Barbour, Scott
Is the world prepared for a deadly influenza pandemic? ReferencePoint Press 2010 96p il (In controversy) lib bdg $26.95
Grades: 9 10 11 12 **614.5**
1. Influenza
ISBN 978-1-60152-127-9; 1-60152-127-8
LC 2010-5859
In this book "the lessons of past pandemics are brought to bear on current realities, from lapses in internal cooperation to differing views on mandatory vaccination." Booklist

Includes bibliographical references

Byrne, Joseph Patrick
★ The **black** death; [by] Joseph P. Byrne. Greenwood Press 2004 xxx, 231p il map (Greenwood guides to historic events of the medieval world) $45

Grades: 9 10 11 12 **614.5**
1. Plague
ISBN 0-313-32492-1
LC 2004-43640
This book "describes the bubonic plague that destroyed large European populations in the 14th century. . . . [The author] has compiled an outstanding reference discussing many theories about the possible causes, transmission, societal implications, economic consequences, and impact on modern medicine." SLJ

Includes bibliographical references

Crosby, Molly Caldwell
The **American** plague; the untold story of yellow fever, the epidemic that shaped our history. Berkley Books 2006 308p il $24.95
Grades: 11 12 Adult **614.5**
1. Yellow fever 2. Yellow fever -- History
ISBN 0-425-21202-5; 978-0-425-21202-8
LC 2006050497
This is an "account of the 1878 yellow fever epidemic." (N Y Times Book Rev) Index.
The author "offers a forceful narrative of a disease's ravages and the quest to find its cause and cure." Publ Wkly

Includes bibliographical references

Cunningham, Kevin
The **bubonic** plague. ABDO Pub. Co. 2011 112p il map (Essential events) lib bdg $23.95
Grades: 7 8 9 10 11 12 **614.5**
1. Plague 2. Epidemics
ISBN 978-1-61714-762-3; 1-61714-762-1
LC 2010043852
A history of the plague which caused one of the most catastrophic losses of life in history.
"The spacious . . . . design is inviting, with many color illustrations and screens, and the extensive back matter includes a detailed time line, glossary, bibliography and source notes." Booklist

Includes glossary and bibliographical references

Flu. Morgan Reynolds Pub. 2009 176p il (Diseases in history) lib bdg $28.95
Grades: 8 9 10 11 12 **614.5**
1. Influenza
ISBN 978-1-59935-105-6; 1-59935-105-6
LC 2008-51620
"This informative title reveals the continued concerns surrounding this killer disease and the possibility of a future pandemic. The text, though somewhat scientific, will help students to better understand the history of the virus, how it has mutated and jumped from animals to humans, and new concerns regarding more dangerous forms. . . . Color and black-and-white archival photos, as well as reproduction of a three-dimensional rendering of the flu virus, enhance the text." SLJ

Includes glossary and bibliographical references

Malaria. Morgan Reynolds Pub. 2009 144p il (Diseases in history) lib bdg $28.95

Grades: 8 9 10 11 12   **614.5**
1. Malaria
ISBN 978-1-59935-103-2; 1-59935-103-X
LC 2008-51619
"Provides fascinating information about an ongoing scourge.... Here readers have an accessible, well presented account of the continuing struggle against a deadly disease." Voice Youth Advocates
Includes glossary and bibliographical references

Plague. Morgan Reynolds Pub. 2009 144p il (Diseases in history) lib bdg $28.95
Grades: 8 9 10 11 12   **614.5**
1. Plague
ISBN 978-1-59935-102-5; 1-59935-102-1
LC 2008-51618
"Chapters based upon plagues include one on Justinian's Plague, the Black Death, The Dreadful Pestilence, the Great Plague of London, and the current H1N1 swine flu pandemic. This detailed overview . . . will appeal to more advanced students. The research is thorough and the writing is insightful, thought provoking, and accessible." Voice Youth Advocates
Includes glossary and bibliographical references

Currie, Stephen
★ The **black** death; by Stephen Currie. ReferencePoint Press, Inc. 2013 94 p. (Understanding world history series) (hardcover) $27.95
Grades: 7 8 9 10   **614.5**
1. Plague -- History 2. Black Death -- History
ISBN 1601524803; 9781601524805
LC 2012021114
This book on the Black Death by Stephen Currie is part of the "Understanding World History" series. "Readers learn the surprising benefits of depopulation and how technology, medicine, and even religion changed as a result of this tragic epidemic. . . . While it briefly covers the beginnings of the plague in Asia and the many people killed there, the bulk of the book is about the impact of the disease on Europe." (School Library Journal)
Includes bibliographical references and index.

Goldsmith, Connie
The **ebola** epidemic; the fight, the future. Connie Goldsmith. Twenty-First Century Books 2016 112 p. illustrations, color maps (lb: alk. paper) $35.99
Grades: 9 10 11 12   **614.5**
1. Epidemics 2. Ebola virus
ISBN 9781467792448
LC 2015025963
This book, by Connie Goldsmith, explores how "Ebola has riveted and terrified the world since its reemergence from the jungle, killing more than eleven thousand people in West Africa since December 2013. . . . Readers will hear from Ebola survivors, learn what experts say about this devastating disease, and draw their own conclusions about whether another epidemic can be prevented." (Publisher's note)
"A solid, valuable look at a still-mysterious illness and a tumultuous time in recent history." Booklist
Includes bibliographical references and index

Influenza: the next pandemic? Twenty-First Century Books 2007 112p il (Twenty-first century medical library) lib bdg $27.93
Grades: 6 7 8 9 10   **614.5**
1. Influenza
ISBN 978-0-7613-9457-0; 0-7613-9457-5
LC 2005-23588
The author "traces the history of the flu, giving attention to past outbreaks and epidemics. She also describes flu viruses of today, explains treatments, and details health officials' concerns about bird flu. . . . Good for reports, and a worthy source to update collections." SLJ
Includes bibliographical references

Jarrow, Gail
★ **Bubonic** panic; when plague invaded America. Gail Jarrow. Calkins Creek 2016 200 p. illustrations (some color) (hardcover) $18.95
Grades: 5 6 7 8 9   **614.5**
1. Plague 2. Public health -- United States
ISBN 9781620917381; 9781629795621
LC 2015953543
This book, by Gail Jarrow, "tells the true story of America's first plague epidemic—the public health doctors who desperately fought to end it, the political leaders who tried to keep it hidden, and the brave scientists who uncovered the plague's secrets. Jarrow brings the history of a medical mystery to life in vivid and exciting detail for young readers. This title includes photographs and drawings, a glossary, a timeline, further resources, an author's note, and source notes." (Publisher's note)
"In her third book in this trilogy (Red Madness; Fatal Fever), Jarrow focuses on the nineteenth century, when the bubonic plague reared its ugly head in places like Hong Kong, Honolulu, and San Francisco. The thorough, fascinating treatment is complemented by a handsome design that includes numerous primary source artifacts. An exemplary contribution to the history of science and medicine." Horn Book

Fatal fever; tracking down Typhoid Mary. Gail Jarrow. Calkins Creek 2015 192 p. illustrations (some color) $16.95
Grades: 6 7 8 9 10   **614.5**
1. Typhoid fever
ISBN 1620915979; 9781620915974
LC 2014948476
This children's book by Gail Jarrow "tells the true story of [Typhoid Mary,] the woman who unwittingly spread deadly bacteria, the epidemiologist who discovered her trail of infection, and the health department that decided her fate. This gripping story follows this tragic disease as it shatters lives from the early twentieth century to today." (Publisher's note)
"In the second book by Jarrow about a deadly disease -- Red Madness was the first -- she takes on typhoid. At the turn of the twentieth century, typhoid was still very much a mystery...Jarrow has written a suspenseful medical mystery for inquisitive readers. Timeline, glossary, author's note, source notes, bibliography, and index are included among the extensive back matter." Horn Book

Johnson, Steven

The **ghost** map; the story of London's most terrifying epidemic--and how it changed science, cities, and the modern world. Riverhead 2006 299p il map $26.95

Grades: 11 12 Adult **614.5**

1. Cholera 2. Physicians 3. Writers on medicine

ISBN 1-59448-925-4; 978-1-59448-925-9

LC 2006-23114

"From Snow's discovery of patient zero to Johnson's compelling argument for and celebration of cities, this makes for an illuminating and satisfying read." Publ Wkly

Includes bibliographical references

Jurmain, Suzanne

The **secret** of the yellow death; a true story of medical sleuthing. Houghton Mifflin Books for Children 2009 104p il $19

Grades: 6 7 8 9 10 **614.5**

1. Epidemics 2. Physicians 3. Yellow fever 4. Army officers 5. Cuba -- History 6. Microbiologists 7. Writers on medicine 8. Medicine -- Research

ISBN 978-0-618-96581-6; 0-618-96581-5

LC 2009-22499

"This medical mystery is extremely interesting, easy to read, and well illustrated with period photos." SLJ

Includes glossary and bibliographical references

Nardo, Don

The **Black** Death. Lucent Books 2011 96p il lib bdg $33.45

Grades: 6 7 8 9 **614.5**

1. Plague 2. Medieval civilization

ISBN 978-1-4205-0348-7; 1-4205-0348-0

LC 2010043804

"Students are given a clear explanation of the disease and how it may have spread and some coverage of its social, economic, and cultural repercussions. The essays each speak to a specific issue. An appendix that includes 16 primary documents, a concise chronology, lists for further reading divided by content, and an index complete this valuable research tool." SLJ

Oshinsky, David M.

Polio; an American story. Oxford University Press 2005 342p il $30; pa $16.95

Grades: 11 12 Adult **614.5**

1. Poliomyelitis vaccine

ISBN 0-19-515294-8; 0-19-530714-3 pa

LC 2004-25249

This book "is a rich and illuminating analysis that convincingly grounds the ways and means of modern American research in the response to polio." N Y Times Book Rev

Includes bibliographical references

Pierce, John R.

Yellow jack; how yellow fever ravaged America and Walter Reed discovered its deadly secrets. [by] John R. Pierce, Jim Writer. J. Wiley 2005 278p il $24.95

Grades: 11 12 Adult **614.5**

1. Physicians 2. Yellow fever 3. Army officers 4. Microbiologists 5. Writers on medicine

ISBN 0-471-47261-1

LC 2004-13845

"This chronicle of the rise and eventual fall of yellow fever traces a substantial medical history." Booklist

Includes bibliographical references

Preston, Richard

The **hot** zone. Random House 1994 300p hardcover o.p. pa $14

Grades: 11 12 Adult **614.5**

1. Ebola virus 2. Animal experimentation

ISBN 0-385-49522-6 pa

LC 94-13415

This book by Richard Preston "tells the true story of how a deadly virus from the central African rain forest suddenly appears in a Washington, D.C., animal test lab. In a matter of days, 90% of the primates exposed to the virus are dead, and secret government forces are mobilized to stop the spread of this exotic 'hot' virus." (SB&F: Your Guide to Science Resources For All Ages)

"Ebola, a lethal virus that slumbers in an unknown host somewhere in the rain forest, sneaked into the United States in 1989 in a shipment of primates that ended up in a monkey house in Reston, Virginia. This virus jumps between species easily, and takes only weeks to kill its victim, with gory hemorrhaging from various orifices. Preston tells the suspenseful tale of its detection, and gives vivid life to the members of the SWAT team that, for eighteen bio-hazardous days, combatted the strain now known as Ebola Reston." New Yorker

Sehgal, Alfica

Leprosy; foreword by David Heymann. Chelsea House 2006 88p il (Deadly diseases and epidemics) $31.95

Grades: 9 10 11 12 **614.5**

1. Leprosy

ISBN 0-7910-8502-3

LC 2005-10391

Includes glossary and bibliographical references

Examines the biology, epidemiology, history, and treatment of leprosy.

Smith, Tara C.

Ebola and Marburg viruses; 2nd ed.; Chelsea House Publishers 2011 104p il (Deadly diseases and epidemics) lib bdg $34.95

Grades: 8 9 10 11 12 **614.5**

1. Ebola virus 2. Marburg virus

ISBN 978-1-60413-252-6; 1-60413-252-3

LC 2010032999

First published 2005

This describes the outbreaks of Marburg and Ebola viruses, their characteristics and ecology, detection and treatment, developing a vaccine, and other hemorrhagic fevers.

Includes glossary and bibliographical references

Spurlock, Morgan

★ **Don't** eat this book; fast food and the super-sizing of America. G. P. Putnam's Sons 2005 308p hardcover o.p. pa $14

Grades: 9 10 11 12 Adult   **614.5**
1. Restaurants 2. Food industry 3. Convenience foods
ISBN 0-399-15260-1; 0-425-21023-5 pa
LC 2005-43196

The author "describes America's obesity epidemic, its relation to the fast food industry, the industry's cozy relations to U.S. government agencies and how the problem is spreading worldwide. . . . His book is a powerful tool in his rip-roaring campaign to turn around America's love-hate relationship with fast food." Publ Wkly

Includes bibliographical references

Zahler, Diane

★ The **Black** Death. Twenty-First Century Books 2009 160p il map (Pivotal moments in history) lib bdg $38.60

Grades: 7 8 9 10   **614.5**
1. Plague 2. Middle Ages
ISBN 978-0-8225-9076-7; 0-8225-9076-X
LC 2008-26878

This book discusses the pivotal moment in history when one out of three people died and changed the course of world history, the Black Death.

"This is a well-written and well-researched volume. Full-color illustrations, a note explaining the value of primary sources, a who's who, and careful source notes make this book a valuable addition to history collections." SLJ

Includes glossary and bibliographical references

615   Pharmacology and therapeutics

Allman, Toney

Vaccine research. ReferencePoint Press 2010 96p il (Inside science) lib bdg $26.95

Grades: 7 8 9 10   **615**
1. Vaccination 2. Medicine -- Research
ISBN 978-1-60152-131-6; 1-60152-131-6
LC 2010-20635

This book "offers the necessary information for stellar reports. Politics, debates, and ethical concerns are briefly and fairly mentioned, but the . . . [book concentrates] on consistent, documented, and well-balanced scientific coverage. The human stories sprinkled throughout will help kids identify with both scientists and patients." SLJ

Includes bibliographical references

Bjornlund, Lydia

Oxycodone; by Lydia Bjornlund. ReferencePoint Press 2012 96 p. (Compact research series)

Grades: 7 8 9 10 11 12   **615**
1. Narcotics 2. Analgesics 3. Drug abuse 4. Drug education 5. Drugs -- Law and legislation -- United States
ISBN 1601521618; 9781601521613
LC 2011020202

This book on oxycodone is a part of the Compact Research: Drugs series and "focus[es] on three types of information: "objective single-author narratives, opinion-based primary source quotations, and facts and statistics." What this translates to on the page is an overview of the topic and an in-depth chapter-by chapter discussion of the points raised in the overview." Lydia Bjornlund "discuss[es] . . . the health dangers of the drug and its legitimacy in medical use, government regulation of the drug, and how oxycodone abuse can be prevented." (Booklist)

Includes bibliographical references and index

Foster, Steven

National Geographic desk reference to nature's medicine; [by] Steven Foster and Rebecca L. Johnson. National Geographic Society 2006 416p il map $40

Grades: 11 12 Adult   **615**
1. Materia medica 2. Medical botany 3. Reference books
ISBN 978-0-7922-3666-5; 0-7922-3666-1

The authors "offer an engaging, authoritative, and succinct work on traditional and current medicinal uses for a variety of plants, guidelines for cultivation and preparation, recent research, and cautions. Using a two-page format for each plant, the volume is arranged alphabetically. Sidebars feature colored botanical drawings, color photographs, habitat maps, and interesting information that enlivens the understanding of human experience with the plants." Choice

Includes bibliographical references

Goldsmith, Connie

Superbugs strike back; when antibiotics fail. Twenty-First Century Books 2007 112p il (Discovery!) lib bdg $29.27

Grades: 7 8 9 10   **615**
1. Bacteria 2. Antibiotics 3. Drug resistance
ISBN 978-0-8225-6607-6; 0-8225-6607-9
LC 2006-10726

"The emergence of 'superbugs'—antibiotic resistant bacteria—and the threat they pose to public health are examined in this detailed introduction. . . . Full-color tables, sidebars, diagrams, and good-quality photos and micrographs are interspersed throughout. The text is meticulous without being tedious." SLJ

Includes glossary and bibliographical references

Hager, Thomas

The **demon** under the microscope; from battle-field hospitals to Nazi labs, one doctor's heroic search for the world's first miracle drug. Harmony Books 2006 340p $24.95

Grades: 11 12 Adult   **615**
1. Sulfonamides 2. Microbiologists 3. Writers on science 4. Nobel laureates for physiology or medicine
ISBN 1-4000-8213-7; 978-1-4000-8213-1
LC 2006-4510

The author "narrates the story of the race [by doctors such as Gerhard Domagk] to find the 'magic bullet' to eliminate diseases such as pneumonia, childbed fever, and gonorrhea. . . . Hager connects early innovations in medicine to the fortuitous and intuitive leaps that allowed early 20th-century researchers to create sulfa, the first antibiotic. . . . One is left with a sense of gratitude for the relative safety of modern medical practices." Libr J

Includes bibliographical references

Kidd, J. S.

★ **Potent** natural medicines; Mother Nature's pharmacy. [by] J.S. Kidd and Renee A. Kidd. rev ed.; Chelsea House 2006 212p il (Science and society) lib bdg $35

Grades: 7 8 9 10   **615**

1. Pharmacology 2. Medical botany

ISBN 9781438122946; 0-8160-5607-2

LC 2005041741

This introduces "plants' medicinal properties, pioneers who hunted for sources of and applications for botanical treatments, and the ways phytochemical nutrients prevent disease. . . . [Also included] are chapters about recent research, including investigation into animal sources for medicine; the impact of field research on native peoples; and the federal regulation of herb and plant supplements. . . . This [is] a good choice to support research and debate projects." Booklist

Includes bibliographical references

Klosterman, Lorrie

The **facts** about drugs and the body. Marshall Cavendish Benchmark 2006 143p il (Drugs) lib bdg $42.79

Grades: 7 8 9 10 11 12   **615**

1. Drugs

ISBN 978-0-7614-2675-2; 0-7614-2675-2

LC 2007-2260

This discusses the effects of various drugs on the nervous, cardiovascular, respiratory, digestive, and reproductive systems of the body.

"Klosterman has done an excellent job of demonstrating how drugs affect the body functions. The illustrations and captions enhance the information to make it more understandable." SLJ

Includes glossary and bibliographical references

Lax, Eric

★ The **mold** in Dr. Florey's coat; the story of the penicillin miracle. Henry Holt and Co. 2004 307p il hardcover o.p. pa $15

Grades: 9 10 11 12 Adult   **615**

1. Penicillin

ISBN 0-8050-6790-6; 0-8050-7778-2 pa

LC 2003-56685

"In this fluent, entertaining report on the history of the arguably most significant medical discovery of the twentieth century, Lax delves into the lives of the colorful scientists who played significant roles in developing the antibiotic." Booklist

Includes bibliographical references

Rooney, Anne

Dealing with drugs. Amicus 2010 46p il (Healthy lifestyles) lib bdg $32.80

Grades: 7 8 9 10   **615**

1. Drugs

ISBN 978-1-60753-084-8; 1-60753-084-8

This book is "well-written and satisfyingly informative. . . . [The] magazine-like format includes numerous sidebars, color photos, and charts." SLJ

Includes glossary

Winner, Cherie

Circulating life; blood transfusion from ancient superstition to modern medicine. Twenty-First Century Books 2007 112p il (Discovery!) $30.60

Grades: 6 7 8 9 10   **615**

1. Blood -- Transfusion

ISBN 978-0-8225-6606-9; 0-8225-6606-0

LC 2006-29921

This is a study of how bloodletting was replaced by blood transfusion as a medical therapy. Index. "Grades seven to twelve." (Sci Books Films)

This "compendium is both a history of the art of transfusions and a scientific discourse on the chemistry of blood. From early 'bleeding treatments' to the discovery of the circulatory system; from the earliest attempts at transfusions to Charles Drew's heroic work with plasma in World War II, Winner's clear text takes readers on an epic trip." SLJ

Includes bibliographical references

615.1   Drugs (Materia medica)

Goldsmith, Connie

Dietary supplements; Harmless, Helpful, or Hurtful? by Connie Goldsmith. Twenty-First Century Books 2016 96 p. color illustrations (lib. bdg.: alk. paper) $34.65

Grades: 6 7 8 9   **615.1**

1. Dietary supplements

ISBN 9781467738484

LC 2014024851

This book, by Connie Goldsmith, "explores the value vs. the potential danger of [dietary supplements]. . . . Goldsmith devotes considerable detail to such hot-button topics as: vitamin and mineral supplements; herbal products, both those proven moderately effective and those that are dangerous; and weight-loss and sports supplements, legal and banned." (Kirkus Reviews)

"Excellent, detailed endmatter rounds out a balanced exploration of a timely topic. Equally apt for research projects and as a single go-to source of information." Kirkus

Includes bibliographical references and index

615.5   Therapeutics

The **Gale** encyclopedia of alternative medicine; edited by Laurie J. Fundukian, editor. 3rd ed.; Gale, Cengage Learning 2009 4v il set $540

Grades: 11 12 Adult   **615.5**

1. Reference books 2. Alternative medicine --

Encyclopedias
ISBN 978-1-4144-4872-5

LC 2008-16097

First published 2001
This encyclopedia "identifies 150 types of alternative medicine being practiced today, including reflexology, acupressure, acupuncture, chelation therapy, kinesiology, yoga, chiropractic, Feldenkrais, polarity therapy, detoxification, naturopathy, Chinese medicine, biofeedback, Ayurveda and osteopathy." Publisher's note

Includes bibliographical references

615.7   Pharmacokinetics

Newton, David E.

Marijuana; a reference handbook. David E. Newton. ABC-CLIO 2013 330 p. (Contemporary world issues) (alk. paper) $58

Grades: 9 10 11 12 Adult   **615.7**
1. Marijuana 2. Drug legalization 3. Cannabis 4. Government Regulation 5. Cannabinoids -- Therapeutic use 6. Marijuana Smoking -- Legislation & jurisprudence
ISBN 1610691490; 9781610691499; 9781610691505
LC 2012036276

This book, part of the Contemporary World Issues series, "examines the production, consumption, and regulation of the Cannabis plant; the plant's commercial, recreational, medicinal, and religious applications; and the various attempts to regulate the production and consumption of marijuana in the United States and other parts of the world. Additionally, it provides . . . the arguments for and against its legalization or decriminalization." (Publisher's note)

Includes bibliographical references and index

Parks, Peggy J., 1951-

Diet drugs; by Peggy J. Parks. Referencepoint Press 2013 96 p. (Compact research) (hardback) $28.95

Grades: 8 9 10 11 12   **615.7**
1. Drugs 2. Weight loss 3. Appetite depressants -- Miscellanea 4. Weight loss preparations industry -- Miscellanea 5. Weight loss preparations -- Side effects -- Miscellanea
ISBN 1601525184; 9781601525185
LC 2013021407

This book, by author Peggy J. Parks, "gives a history of early weight-loss drugs in the U.S. and their increasing popularity with the rise of obesity. It also relates the controversial effectiveness of diet drugs and the problem of diet-drug fraud. Additional back matter comprises lists of key people, advocacy groups, and related organizations." (Publisher's note)

"Backed by current facts, statistics, and first-person experiences, every chapter includes further documentation with concluding "Primary Source Quotes," from former addicts and law enforcement to health care workers and government officials. In this visual, by-the-numbers era, the series responds with end-of-chapter charts and graphs that display drug-related information." (Booklist)

Includes bibliographical references and index

Szumski, Bonnie

Thinking critically; Medical marijuana. by Bonnie Szumski and Jill Karson. ReferencePoint Press, Inc. 2013 80 p. color illustrations & maps (hardback) $28.95

Grades: 7 8 9 10 11 12   **615.7**
1. Marijuana 2. Marijuana -- United States 3. Marijuana -- Therapeutic use 4. Marijuana -- Law and legislation -- United States
ISBN 1601525826; 9781601525826
LC 2012047796

This book, by Bonnie Szumski and Jill Karson, is a "well-researched examination" of medical marijuana. "The first page of each chapter, 'The Debate at a Glance,' offers bullet points that summarize common arguments pro and con. The design is spare, with understated graphics; bright, compelling photos; and text boxes that pull out interesting quotes. Easy-to-read graphs and charts add another layer of visual information." (School Library Journal)

"Diagrams and sidebars (and one photo per volume) support these well-organized models for classroom discourse. First chapters provide an overview of the debates surrounding medical marijuana and stem cell research; subsequent chapters present pro and con responses to four key questions. Despite lots of graphic elements, the text-heavy pages may be off-putting. Two pages of facts and lists of related organizations are appended. Reading list, websites." Horn Book

Includes bibliographical references and index

615.8   Specific therapies and kinds of therapies

Marcovitz, Hal

Gene therapy research. ReferencePoint Press 2010 96p il (Inside science) lib bdg $26.95

Grades: 7 8 9 10 11 12   **615.8**
1. Gene therapy 2. Medicine -- Research
ISBN 978-1-60152-108-8; 1-60152-108-1
LC 2009-41686

"Opening with an account of successful gene therapy for a rare eye disease, this introduction to the research goes on to speculate about future applications for other inherited diseases. Beginning with basic definitions of such terms as gene, human genome, and DNA, the well-organized narrative explains the impact of viruses, drugs, cloning, and stem cells on gene therapy and describes recent research." Booklist

Panno, Joseph

★ **Gene** therapy; treatments and cures for genetic diseases. Rev. ed; Facts On File 2010 236p il (The new biology) $40

Grades: 9 10 11 12   **615.8**
1. Gene therapy
ISBN 978-0-8160-6850-0
LC 2009-45854

First published 2004
Thsi book "discusses the science behind gene therapy, as well as the ethical and legal issues associated with this therapy." Publisher's note

Includes glossary and bibliographical references

615.9 Toxicology

Grossman, Elizabeth

Chasing molecules; poisonous products, human health, and the promise of green chemistry. Island Press/Shearwater Books 2009 249p $26.95

Grades: 11 12 Adult   615.9

1. Toxicology 2. Commercial products 3. Environmental chemistry

ISBN 978-1-59726-370-2; 1-59726-370-2

LC 2009-28279

The author "tracks the migration of synthetic, petroleum-based molecules emitted by pesticides, cosmetics, food containers, and vinyl. . . . She accompanies scientists to China, the Great Lakes, and the Arctic, where these persistent and pernicious chemicals (82,000 and counting) are found in alarming quantities. . . . Green chemistry aims to replace hazardous synthetic chemicals with chemicals that are 'benign by design.' Grossman's clarion exposé should give this lifesaving initiative a big boost." Booklist

Includes bibliographical references

Landau, Elaine

Food poisoning and foodborne diseases. Twenty-First Century Books 2010 128p il (USA Today health reports: diseases and disorders) lib bdg $34.60

Grades: 7 8 9 10 11 12   615.9

1. Food poisoning 2. Communicable diseases

ISBN 978-0-8225-7290-9; 0-8225-7290-7

LC 2009-20325

This book "will drawn an audience with its everyday examples of food risks as well as instructions about how to buy, prepare, cook, and store food. . . . Also included are warnings about how to keep hands and kitchen surfaces clean and what to watch out for in cafeteria and fast-food outlets. . . . [The] accessible design extends the impressive educational data." Booklist

Includes bibliographical references

Satin, Morton

★ **Food** alert! the ultimate sourcebook for food safety. 2nd ed; Facts On File 2008 350p il $39.95; pa $14.95

Grades: 9 10 11 12 Adult   615.9

1. Diseases 2. Food contamination 3. Consumer protection

ISBN 978-0-8160-6968-2; 0-8160-6968-9; 978-0-8160-6969-9 pa; 0-8160-6969-7 pa

LC 2008-11038

First published 1999

The author "divides the text into four major segments: the complex history of food poisoning; major food sources and their characteristic pathogens; dangers extant at the consumer product and home-preservation levels; and pathogens' assorted forms. Three appendixes offer charts detailing various fungal, bacterial, and parasitic types; food preservation guidance; and informational web sites. [This is] accessibly written and extremely well-organized." Libr J

Includes bibliographical references

616 Diseases

Bakalar, Nick

★ **Where** the germs are; a scientific safari. {by} Nicholas Bakalar. Wiley 2003 262p il $24.95

Grades: 9 10 11 12 Adult   616

1. Bacteria 2. Microbiology 3. Germ theory of disease

ISBN 0-471-15589-6

LC 2003-271569

The author's "excellent chapter on childhood diseases and vaccines should be required reading for parents, and teenagers should be plunked down in a chair with the chapter on sexually transmitted diseases. . . . His writing is witty, and he gives all the details of germs and illnesses without medical school jargon." Publ Wkly

Includes glossary and bibliographical references

Diseases, disorders, and injuries. Marshall Cavendish Reference 2010 320p il $85.64

Grades: 9 10 11 12   616

1. Reference books 2. Diseases -- Encyclopedias 3. Medicine -- Encyclopedias 4. Wounds and injuries -- Encyclopedias

ISBN 978-0-7614-7935-2

LC 2010010057

This is "a simplified and much shorter version of Marshall Cavendish's 18-volume Encyclopedia of Health (2010). . . . More than 200 subjects are arranged A–Z. Articles for diseases and conditions include a description, with causes, symptoms, diagnosis, treatment, and prevention. Articles for parts of the body cover their function and location. Q&A sidebars (written as if by young people) are included in every article." Booklist

The **Gale** encyclopedia of genetic disorders; Laurie J. Fundukain, editor. 3rd ed.; Gale 2010 2v il set $445

Grades: 9 10 11 12   616

1. Reference books 2. Medical genetics -- Encyclopedias

ISBN 978-1-4144-7602-5; 1-4144-7602-7

LC 2010-2222

First published 2001 under the editorship of Stacey L. Blachford

This encyclopedia provides "information on genetic disorders, including conditions, tests, procedures, treatments and therapies. . . . [The disorders covered include] Down Syndrome, Trisomy, Hemophilia and Tourette Syndrome, and rarely seen diseases such as Meckel Syndrome, Neuraminidase Deficiency and Phenylketonuria." Publisher's note

Includes bibliographical references

★ **Human** diseases and conditions; Miranda Herbert Ferrara, project editor. 2nd ed.; Charles Scribner's Sons/Gale Cengage Learning 2010 4v il set $340

Grades: 9 10 11 12 Adult   616

1. Reference books 2. Medicine -- Encyclopedias

ISBN 978-0-684-31238-5; 0-684-31238-7

LC 2009-6533

First published 2000

"The entries include a brief definition and the phonetic spelling of the term and cover what the disease or condition is and its prevalence, etiology, symptoms, and prevention and treatment. Some entries begin with a brief story about someone who has the disease, and each ends with a list of relevant resources of articles, books, web sites, or health organizations, as well as cross-references. The illustrations are in color, as are term definitions in the margins. . . . The entries are accessible to patrons from a high school reading level and above, and the colorful display adds appeal." Libr J

Includes glossary and bibliographical references

Marcovitz, Hal

Stem cell research. ReferencePoint Press 2011 96p il (Inside science) lib bdg $26.95

Grades: 7 8 9 10   616

1. Stem cell research

ISBN 978-1-60152-130-9; 1-60152-130-8

LC 2010-4128

Discusses the science behind stem cell research and the ways in which stem cells can be used in treatment of disease.

This book "offers the necessary information for stellar reports. Politics, debates, and ethical concerns are briefly and fairly mentioned, but the . . . [book concentrates] on consistent, documented, and well-balanced scientific coverage. The human stories sprinkled throughout will help kids identify with both scientists and patients." SLJ

Includes bibliographical references

Panno, Joseph

Stem cell research; medical applications and ethical controversies. Rev. ed.; Facts On File 2010 262p il (The new biology) $40; pa $18.95

Grades: 9 10 11 12   616

1. Stem cell research

ISBN 978-0-8160-6851-7; 978-0-8160-8330-5 pa

LC 2009-30506

First published 2005

This book "discusses the different types of stem cells, how they are studied in the laboratory, and the diseases that may be treated with these cells. . . . [It includes] chapters that discuss the origin and evolution of ordinary cells, as well as a . . . discussion of human and animal stem cells, therapeutic cloning, and a new form of stem cell that is produced by reprogramming ordinary skin cells." Publisher's note

Includes glossary and bibliographical references

Shnayerson, Michael

The killers within; the deadly rise of drug-resistant bacteria. {by} Michael Shnayerson, Mark Plotkin. Little, Brown 2002 328p hardcover o.p. pa $14.95

Grades: 11 12 Adult   616

1. Bacteria 2. Antibiotics

ISBN 0-316-71331-7; 0-316-73566-3 pa

LC 2002-24177

The authors provide a "look at the overuse of antibiotics, the methods bacteria use to develop resistance, the role of antibiotics as animal growth promoters, and the outlook for antibiotics. . . . Shnayerson and Plotkin have managed to demonstrate their concern over the future of antibiotics

while keeping the scientific background manageable for lay readers." Libr J

Includes bibliographical references

Simon, Lizzie

Detour; my bipolar road trip in 4-D. Pocket Books 2001 211p hardcover o.p. pa $13

Grades: 11 12 Adult   616

1. Authors 2. Mentally ill 3. Mental illness 4. Memoirists

ISBN 0-7434-4659-3; 0-7434-4660-7 pa

LC 2001-60261

"In fall 1999, twentysomething Simon, who had suffered one full-blown manic episode in her late teens and who controlled her symptoms with lithium, decided to put aside her career as a theatrical producer to seek out other highly successful young manic-depressives. Instead, she encounters a differing array of bipolars, from a multimillionaire who can't control his drug and alcohol use to people who have been institutionalized. . . . This book will resonate with younger readers." Libr J

Skloot, Rebecca

The immortal life of Henrietta Lacks; by Rebecca Skloot. 1st paperback ed. Crown Publishers 2010 369 p ill. (some col.) (hardcover) $26.00; (paperback) $16.00

Grades: 6 7 8 9   616

1. Cancer 2. Homemakers 3. Medical ethics 4. Human experimentation in medicine 5. African American women -- Biography

ISBN 1400052173; 9781400052172; 9781400052189

LC 200931785

Here, Rebecca Skloot tells the story of Henrietta Lacks, an African American Virginia tobacco farmer who died of cervical cancer in 1951. Unbeknownst to Mrs. Lacks and her family, scientists harvested her cells to create a human cell line known as HeLa, from the first two letters of her first and last names, "that has been kept alive indefinitely, enabling discoveries in such areas as cancer research, in vitro fertilization and gene mapping." (Publisher's note)

Includes bibliographical references and index.

Van Tilburg, Christopher

Mountain rescue doctor; wilderness medicine in the extremes of nature. St. Martin's Press 2007 293p il hardcover o.p. pa $14.95

Grades: 11 12 Adult   616

1. Rescue work 2. Mountaineering

ISBN 978-0-312-35887-7; 0-312-35887-3; 978-0-312-35888-4 pa; 0-312-35888-1 pa

LC 2007-28304

The author "is a member of the Hood River Crag Rats, the oldest search-and-rescue (S&R) team in the United States. Both adults and teens will relish his vivid recountings of efforts to rescue sports enthusiasts who got lost or injured in the mountains." Libr J

Wynbrandt, James

★ The encyclopedia of genetic disorders and birth defects; [by] James Wynbrandt and Mark D.

Ludman. 3rd ed; Facts On File 2007 682p (Facts on File library of health and living) $75

Grades: 9 10 11 12 Adult   **616**

1. Reference books 2. Birth defects -- Encyclopedias

ISBN 978-0-8160-6396-3

LC 2006-100640

First published 1991

This "is an excellent resource for public and consumer-health libraries with limited budgets. It is a good starting point for research, too." Booklist

Includes bibliographical references

616.02   Special topics of diseases

American Medical Association

★ **American** Medical Association family medical guide; 4th ed., completely rev. and updated; John Wiley & Sons 2004 1184p il $45

Grades: 9 10 11 12 Adult   **616.02**

1. Medicine 2. Health self-care

ISBN 0-471-26911-5

LC 2004-5764

First published 1982

"This is a well-organized volume, considering the amount of information it covers." Publ Wkly

American Red Cross

★ The **American** Red Cross first aid and safety handbook; [prepared by] American Red Cross and Kathleen A. Handal; foreword by Elizabeth Dole. Little, Brown 1992 321p il hardcover o.p. pa $18.95

Grades: 9 10 11 12 Adult   **616.02**

1. First aid

ISBN 0-316-73645-7; 0-316-73646-5 pa

LC 91-24847

This first aid guidebook is based on course materials used by the Red Cross and covers how to handle such emergencies as allergic reactions, bleeding, choking, and heart attacks.

Anthes, Emily

★ **Frankenstein's** cat; cuddling up to biotech's brave new beasts. Emily Anthes. 1st ed. Scientific American / Farrar, Straus and Giroux 2013 256 p. (hardcover) $26

Grades: 9 10 11 12 Adult   **616.02**

1. Biotechnology 2. Transgenic animals

ISBN 0374158592; 9780374158590

LC 2012029045

This book, by Emily Anthes, "takes us from petri dish to pet store as she explores how biotechnology is shaping the future of our furry and feathered friends. . . . [Visiting] a 'frozen zoo' where scientists are storing DNA from the planet's most exotic creatures, she discovers how we can use cloning to protect endangered species, craft prosthetics to save injured animals, and employ genetic engineering to supply farms with disease-resistant livestock." (Publisher's note)

"[A] quick, often surprising review of current advances, giving accessible treatment to a weighty subject and employing clear descriptions of complex science." Booklist

Includes bibliographical references and index.

★ The **Merck** manual home health handbook; Robert S. Porter, editor-in-chief; Justin L. Kaplan, senior assistant editor; Barbara P. Homeier, assistant editor; editorial board, Richard K. Albert ... [et al.] [3rd ed.]; Merck Research Laboratories 2009 xlii, 2306p il $39.95

Grades: 11 12 Adult   **616.02**

1. Medicine -- Handbooks, manuals, etc.

ISBN 978-0-9119-1030-8

LC 2009-923536

First published 1997 with title: The Merck manual of medical information, Home ed

"An editorial board of 207 medical experts contributes to this comprehensive overview of medical practice today, with a special focus on geriatric medicine (including a chapter devoted to enhancing the quality of end-of-life care for patient, caregiver, friends and family). . . . Charts and illustrations aid the book's accessibility, making it Merck's most authoritative and easy-to-read home medical guide yet." Publ Wkly

Norton, Trevor

Smoking ears and screaming teeth; a celebration of scientific eccentricity and self-experimentation. Pegasus Books 2011 404p il $24.95

Grades: 11 12 Adult   **616.02**

1. Eccentrics and eccentricities 2. Human experimentation in medicine 3. Medicine -- Research

ISBN 978-1-60598-254-0

"Meet the dedicated (some might say demented) scientists who risked lives (sometimes their own) to advance scientific knowledge in the days before medical ethics and institutional review boards. Norton . . . introduces us to doctors who infected themselves or others with deadly diseases and parasites, inhaled noxious gases, irradiated themselves, and experimented on themselves in other painful and sometimes gruesome ways. The reader will also meet scientists who ascended to the stratosphere, plumbed the ocean's depths, and swam with sharks." Libr J

Includes bibliographical references

616.042   Genetic diseases (Hereditary diseases)

Gallagher, Kathleen

One in a Billion; The Story of Nic Volker and the Dawn of Genomic Medicine. Mark Johnson and Kathleen Gallagher. Simon & Schuster 2016 256 p. (hardcover) $26

Grades: 10 11 12 Adult   **616.042**

1. Medical genetics 2. Genomics 3. Medical genetics -- case studies

ISBN 9781451661330; 9781451661323; 1451661320

This book, by Mark Johnson and Kathleen Gallagher, "chronicle the story of Nic Volker, the Wisconsin boy at the center of a daring breakthrough in medicine—a complete gene sequencing to discover the cure for an otherwise undiagnosable illness. At just two years old, Nic experienced a searing pain that signaled the awakening of a new and deadly disease, one that would hurl Nic and his family up against the limits of modern medicine." (Publisher's note)

"In 2003, an international consortium of scientists finished sequencing the human genome, a process that took more than seven years and cost more than $600 million (by 2015, the cost had dropped to less than $1,000 and took only a few hours). . . . This is a moving, skillfully written book that's well positioned to introduce a broad audience to the profound clinical relevance of whole-genome and exome sequencing." PW

616.07　Pathology

Murray, Elizabeth A.
Death; corpses, cadavers, and other grave matters. Twenty-First Century Books 2010 112p il (Discovery!) lib bdg $31.93
Grades: 7 8 9 10　　　　　　　　　　**616.07**
1. Death 2. Forensic sciences
ISBN 978-0-7613-3851-2; 0-7613-3851-9
LC 2009-17436

The author "has written a book that deals with the scientific aspect of life and death. Her experience as a teacher of anatomy and physiology comes through as she explains the living body, what happens when systems shut down, and how postmortem remains can give evidence to solve crimes and the mysteries of diseases. . . . First-person accounts of terminally ill patients and those working in the fields of pathology, hospice, and anatomy clarify subjects presented in the chapters. Color photographs are included throughout, some of which are potentially disturbing. The glossary and bibliography are extensive and helpful. This book provides information for those who are curious about a subject that is not easy to discuss." SLJ

Includes glossary and bibliographical references

Segen, J. C.
★ The **patient's** guide to medical tests; everything you need to know about the tests your doctor orders. [by] Joseph C. Segen and Josie Wade. 2nd ed; Facts on File 2002 418p (Facts on File library of health and living) $44
Grades: 9 10 11 12 Adult　　　　　　**616.07**
1. Diagnosis
ISBN 0-8160-4651-4
LC 2002-18824

First published 1997 with Joseph Stauffer as joint author
This "guide presents information on more than 1,000 commonly prescribed tests and procedures. Each entry includes a description of the test, patient preparation required, a description of the procedure itself, the reference range, what abnormal values may signify, and the approximate cost of each test." Publisher's note

616.1　Specific diseases

Mertz, Leslie A.
★ The **circulatory** system; [by] Leslie Mertz. Greenwood Press 2004 xx, 217p il (Human body systems) $65
Grades: 11 12 Adult　　　　　　　　　**616.1**
1. Cardiovascular system
ISBN 0-313-32401-8
LC 2004-42449

In addition to the parts and functions of the circulatory system, "blood pressure, blood type and fetal circulation are covered. The history of research on the circulatory system is presented and the future of research in this field is considered. Current controversies and dilemmas, such as stem cell research, are explored." Publisher's note

Includes bibliographical references

616.2　Diseases of respiratory system

Apel, Melanie Ann
Cystic fibrosis; the ultimate teen guide. Scarecrow Press 2006 259p il (It happened to me) $42
Grades: 9 10 11 12　　　　　　　　　　**616.2**
1. Cystic fibrosis
ISBN 0-8108-4821-X
LC 2005-22073

"The first four chapters focus on the definition, source, diagnosis, and grueling treatments of cystic fibrosis before moving on to discuss patient and family reactions to the information and challenges. . . . Gripping personal accounts will pull in readers, teenage and adult, who are not familiar with the disease." Voice Youth Advocates

Includes bibliographical references

Asthma information for teens; health tips about managing asthma and related concerns including facts about asthma causes, triggers and symptoms, diagnosis, and treatment. edited by Kim Wohlenhaus. 2nd ed.; Omnigraphics 2010 427p il (Teen health series) $69
Grades: 7 8 9 10 11 12　　　　　　　**616.2**
1. Asthma
ISBN 978-0-7808-1086-0; 0-7808-1086-4
LC 2009048694

First published 2005 under the editorship of Karen Bellenir

"Provides basic consumer health information for teens about asthma causes and treatments, controlling triggers, and coping with asthma at home and school. Includes index, resource information and recommendations for further reading." Publisher's note

Includes bibliographical references

Berger, William E.
Living with asthma. Facts on File 2007 183p (Teen's guides) lib bdg $34.95

Grades: 7 8 9 10 11 **616.2**
1. Asthma
ISBN 978-0-8160-6483-0 lib bdg; 0-8160-6483-0 lib bdg; 0-8160-7560-3 pa; 9781438121055
LC 2007003664
Examines asthma and provides teens with the information they need to understand it.
"There is a great directory of referral and online resources in the appendix. Although there are no illustrations, the text is appealing, well-organized, and accessible for the teen reader." Voice Youth Advocates
Includes glossary

Giddings, Sharon
Cystic fibrosis. Chelsea House 2009 128p il (Genes & disease) lib bdg $35
Grades: 7 8 9 10 **616.2**
1. Cystic fibrosis
ISBN 978-0-7910-9694-9; 0-7910-9694-7
LC 2008-44771
"Cystic fibrosis is one of the most widespread fatal genetic diseases in the United States. . . . [This book] discusses this genetic disease, its history, current treatments, and how scientists are searching for a cure." Publisher's note
Includes glossary and bibliographical references

Goldsmith, Connie
Influenza. Twenty-First Century Books 2010 128p il (USA Today health reports: diseases and disorders) lib bdg $34.60
Grades: 7 8 9 10 11 12 **616.2**
1. Influenza
ISBN 9780761363767; 978-0-7613-5881-7; 0-7613-5881-1
LC 2010-01030
"This book provides information about flu, how it spreads, and how it is prevented and treated." (Introduction) Glossary. Bibliography. Index. "Grades seven to twelve." (Sci Books Films)
This book "talks about the science behind the highly contagious disease, how it has spread to millions, and how to prevent and treat it. . . . [The] accessible design extends the impressive educational data." Booklist
Includes bibliographical references

Kelly, Evelyn B.
Investigating influenza and bird flu; real facts for real lives. [by] Evelyn B. Kelly and Claire Wilson. Enslow Publishers 2010 160p il (Investigating diseases) lib bdg $34.60
Grades: 6 7 8 9 10 **616.2**
1. Influenza 2. Avian influenza
ISBN 978-0-7660-3341-2; 0-7660-3341-4
LC 2009-14802
"Provides information about influenza and bird flu, including treatment, diagnosis, history, medical advances, and true stories about people with the diseases." Publisher's note
Includes glossary and bibliographical references

★ **Lung** disorders sourcebook; edited by Dawn D. Matthews. Omnigraphics 2002 678p il (Health reference series) $78
Grades: 11 12 Adult **616.2**
1. Lungs -- Diseases
ISBN 0-7808-0339-6
LC 2002-16976
"This title is a great addition for public and school libraries because it provides concise health information on the lungs. Readers can start with this reference source and get satisfactory answers before proceeding to other medical reference tools for more in-depth information." Am Ref Books Annu, 2003

Parks, Peggy J., 1951-
Influenza. ReferencePoint Press 2011 96p il map (Compact research: diseases and disorders) lib bdg $26.95
Grades: 7 8 9 10 11 12 **616.2**
1. Influenza 2. Swine influenza
ISBN 978-1-60152-118-7; 1-60152-118-9
LC 2010-26063
This book about influenza "begins with a general overview followed by a focus on statistics, causes, symptoms, treatments, and prevention. [The book] discusses the virus that causes the disease; presents information on prevention through proper hygiene as well as vaccination, especially during epidemics; and warns against public apathy. . . . The readable page design features pull quotes and subtitles, with occasional photos throughout." Booklist
Includes bibliographical references

616.3 Diseases of digestive system

Chow, Cheryl
The **encyclopedia** of hepatitis and other liver diseases; [by] James H. Chow, Cheryl Chow. Facts on File 2005 372p (Facts on File library of health and living) $75
Grades: 11 12 Adult **616.3**
1. Reference books 2. Liver -- Diseases -- Encyclopedias
ISBN 0-8160-5710-9; 978-0-8160-5710-8
LC 2005-18489
"With more than 150 entries, coverage ranges from symptoms, treatments, and research to tests, social issues, and much more. Appendixes list . . . relevant organizations, transplantation and Internet resources, and support groups for those with liver-related issues." Publisher's note
Includes bibliographical references

Fredericks, Carrie
Obesity. Reference Point Press 2008 104p il map (Compact research. Current issues) lib bdg $24.95
Grades: 8 9 10 11 12 **616.3**
1. Obesity
ISBN 978-1-60152-040-1; 1-60152-040-9
LC 2007-42183

Examines the topic of obesity in a format with objective overviews, primary source quotes, illustrated facts, and statistics.

"Both general readers and serious researchers will find something useful in this volume. It facilitates research for less-motivated students and supplies excellent information for better researchers." SLJ

Includes bibliographical references

Goldsmith, Connie

Hepatitis. Twenty-First Century Books 2010 128p il (USA Today health reports: diseases and disorders) lib bdg $34.60

Grades: 7 8 9 10 11 12　　　　　　　　　**616.3**
1. Liver -- Diseases
ISBN 978-0-8225-6787-5; 0-8225-6787-3
　　　　　　　　　　　　　　　LC 2009-20720

This "reveals that an estimated five million Americans have viral Hepatitis A, B, and C, making it a major public health problem. . . . The detailed information is combined with photos and diagrams portraying transmission, vaccines, and effective treatment. . . . [The] accessible design extends the impressive educational data." Booklist

Includes bibliographical references

Minocha, Anil

★ The **encyclopedia** of the digestive system and digestive disorders; [by] Anil Minocha, Christine Adamec. 2nd ed; Facts on File 2010 xxvii, 353p il (Facts on File library of health and living) $75

Grades: 11 12 Adult　　　　　　　　　　**616.3**
1. Reference books 2. Digestive organs -- Encyclopedias
3. Gastrointestinal system -- Encyclopedias
ISBN 978-0-8160-7661-1; 0-8160-7661-8
　　　　　　　　　　　　　　　LC 2010-28790

First published 2004

"Entries explain the organs of the digestive system and how they work, the digestive process, disorders and infectious diseases of the digestive system, and how to maintain good digestive health." Publisher's note

Includes bibliographical references

Obesity; Tom and Gena Metcalf, editors. Thomson / Gale 2008 136p il (Perspectives on diseases and disorders) lib bdg $34.95

Grades: 7 8 9 10　　　　　　　　　　　**616.3**
1. Obesity
ISBN 978-0-7377-3873-5; 0-7377-3873-1
　　　　　　　　　　　　　　　LC 2007-37470

"This book explains what obesity is, provides insight into its causes, and takes a serious look at why it's becoming such an epidemic. Accounts by people who have firsthand experience dealing with being overweight add value to the book." SLJ

Includes glossary and bibliographical references

★ **Obesity:** opposing viewpoints; Scott Barbour, book editor. Greenhaven Press 2011 194p (Opposing viewpoints series) $39.70; pa $27.50

Grades: 9 10 11 12　　　　　　　　　　**616.3**
1. Obesity
ISBN 978-0-7377-4978-6; 978-0-7377-4979-3 pa
　　　　　　　　　　　　　　　LC 2010004515

Articles in this anthology discuss the causes of obesity and ways it can be reduced.

Includes bibliographical references

Palmer, Melissa

Dr. Melissa Palmer's guide to hepatitis & liver disease. Avery 2004 470p il pa $16.95

Grades: 11 12 Adult　　　　　　　　　　**616.3**
1. Liver -- Diseases
ISBN 1-58333-188-3
　　　　　　　　　　　　　　　LC 2003-63905

First published 1999

The author "discusses all facets of liver disease, from symptoms and tests to treatment options and lifestyle changes." Publisher's note

616.4　Diseases of endocrine, hematopoietic, lymphatic, glandular systems; diseases of male breast

Ambrose, Marylou

Investigating diabetes; real facts for real lives. Enslow Publishers 2010 160p il (Investigating diseases) lib bdg $34.60

Grades: 6 7 8 9 10　　　　　　　　　　**616.4**
1. Diabetes
ISBN 978-0-7660-3338-2; 0-7660-3338-4
　　　　　　　　　　　　　　　LC 2008-30778

"The book is a comprehensive primer that can well serve patients with newly diagnosed diabetes and their families with its detailed account of diabetes, the causes of the disease, and its potential consequences." Sci Books Films

Includes glossary and bibliographical references

American Diabetes Association

★ **American** Diabetes Association complete guide to diabetes; 5th ed.; American Diabetes Association 2011 499p il pa $22.95

Grades: 11 12 Adult　　　　　　　　　　**616.4**
1. Diabetes
ISBN 978-1-58040-330-6
　　　　　　　　　　　　　　　LC 2010-41272

First published 1996

This book describes types of insulin and the best ways to use them, insulin pumps and injection-free insulin techniques in research, new oral diabetes medications and therapies, the use of carbohydrate counting techniques as a meal planning tool as well as information on diabetes in the workplace, school, and day care.

Includes bibliographical references

Brill, Marlene Targ, 1945-

Diabetes. Twenty-First Century Books 2011
128p il (USA Today health reports: diseases and disorders) lib bdg $34.60

Grades: 7 8 9 10 11 12   **616.4**
1. Diabetes
ISBN 978-0-7613-6085-8; 0-7613-6085-9
LC 2010049454

This volume explores the history of diabetes, and explains the various treatments that are available today.

"This is an important endeavor from the author [that]
will be very helpful for patients and others who are looking
for basic information about diabetes. The author has done
a good job of helping readers understand how their bodies
function and the underlying mechahism of diabetes." Sci
Books Films

Includes glossary and bibliographical references

Hood, Korey K.

★ Type 1 teens; a guide to managing your life
with diabetes. illustrated by Bryan Ische. American
Psychological Association 2010 150p il pa $14.95

Grades: 9 10 11 12   **616.4**
1. Diabetes 2. Teenagers -- Health and hygiene
ISBN 978-1-4338-0788-6; 1-4338-0788-2
LC 2010-11063

A guide for teens on managing Type 1 diabetes offers
strategies and tips on making diabetes a high priority, fighting diabetes burnout, getting help from others, and coping
with school and relationships.

"With conversational prose, contemporary reference,
and scenarios that will resonate with teens, . . . Hood offers
an accessible, supportive resource for youth diagnosed with
type-1 diabetes." Booklist

Parker, Katrina

Living with diabetes. Facts On File 2007 170p
(Teen's guides) $34.95

Grades: 9 10 11 12   **616.4**
1. Diabetes
ISBN 978-0-8160-6346-8; 0-8160-6346-X
LC 2007-27679

"All issues relevant to diabetic teens are covered, from
the natures of Type 1 and Type 2 diabetes and the choices
available to regulate blood sugar, to the importance of diet
and exercise and the emotional challenges involved. . . . The
information is presented clearly and matter-of-factly and its
slightly 'scared-straight' approach lets teens know up front
what they are facing and how to deal with it." SLJ

Includes glossary and bibliographical references

Yuwiler, Janice

Diabetes. ReferencePoint Press 2009 96p il
(Compact research. Diseases and disorders) lib bdg
$25.95

Grades: 7 8 9 10   **616.4**
1. Diabetes
ISBN 978-1-60152-076-0; 1-60152-076-X
LC 2009-6173

"Yuwiler discusses type 1 diabetes and its management,
type 2 diabetes and its prevention, metabolic syndrome, and

medical advances. . . . Subtopics are delineated by brightly
colored burgundy headings; blocks of orange-colored sidebars with bright-red print and relevant color photos and illustrations appear throughout. Each chapter ends with several pages of primary-source quotes and facts and illustrations
that offer greater clarity to the text." SLJ

Includes bibliographical references

616.5   Diseases of integument

Juettner, Bonnie

Acne. Lucent Books 2010 104p il (Diseases and
disorders series) lib bdg $33.45

Grades: 7 8 9 10   **616.5**
1. Acne
ISBN 978-1-4205-0215-2; 1-4205-0215-8
LC 2009-33484

First published 2004

"Well-organized chapters present clear information on
the causes of acne, types of self-treatment, medical and 'alternative' paths to a cure, the future of treatment, and the
psychological ramifications for an affected person. . . . This
title will be useful for reports and is a solid addition to health
and/or disease collections." SLJ

Includes bibliographical references

Skin health information for teens; health tips about
dermatological disorders and activities that affect
the skin, hair, and nails. edited by Lisa Esposito.
3rd ed. Omnigraphics, Inc. 2013 424 p. (hardcover) $69.00

Grades: 7 8 9 10   **616.5**
1. Skin -- Care 2. Skin -- Diseases 3. Teenagers --
Health and hygiene 4. Beauty, Personal 5. Skin -- Care
and hygiene
ISBN 0780813170; 9780780813175
LC 2013009908

This book "provides updated information about the
skin, hair, and nails. It explains how the skin and its related
structures grow and how to keep them healthy. Common ail-
ments, including acne, eczema, impetigo, psoriasis, vitiligo,
and warts are explained, and a section on skin cancer provides information about cancer risks, prevention strategies,
warning signs, and treatments. The care of skin injuries,
including cuts, scrapes, burns, bites, and stings, is also discussed." (Publisher's note)

Includes bibliographical references and index.

Turkington, Carol

★ The encyclopedia of skin and skin disorders;
[by] Carol Turkington, Jeffrey S. Dover; medical illustrations, Birck Cox. 3rd ed; Facts on File 2007
459p (Facts on File library of health and living) $75;
pa $17.95

Grades: 11 12 Adult   **616.5**
1. Reference books 2. Skin -- Encyclopedias
ISBN 0-8160-6403-2; 978-0-8160-6403-8; 0-8160-
6404-0 pa; 978-0-8160-6404-5 pa
LC 2005-57402

First published 1996 with title: Skin deep

"More than 1,100 entries cover everything from the sun, skin, and acne to skin cancer, cosmetics, and skin lotions." Publisher's note

Includes bibliographical references

616.6   Diseases of urogenital system

The **kidneys** and the renal system; edited by Kara Rogers. Britannica Educational Pub. in association with Rosen Educational Services 2012 xvii, 174 p.p col. ill.

Grades: 7 8 9 10 11 12   **616.6**
1. Kidneys 2. Human anatomy 3. Urinary organs 4. Kidneys -- Diseases
ISBN 161530679X; 9781615306794

LC 2011026615

This biology reference work, edited by Kara Rogers, describes the Human waste system. "Responsible for managing the body's waste and regulating the balance of water and electrolytes, the kidneys and renal system, in a sense, make up the body's plumbing network. . . . This volume examines the various components of the renal, or urinary, system, and the consequences of dysfunction and disease." (Publisher's note)

Includes bibliographical references and index

Watson, Stephanie

★ The **urinary** system. Greenwood Press 2004 207p il (Human body systems) $65

Grades: 11 12 Adult   **616.6**
1. Urinary organs
ISBN 0-313-32402-6

LC 2003-67648

The author "discusses the role and function of each part of the urinary system. . . . Watson also explores how the urinary system maintains chemical balance and hydration in the body. The history of research related to the urinary system is presented and the future of research in this field is considered." Publisher's note

Includes bibliographical references

616.7   Diseases of musculoskeletal system

Sayler, Mary Harwell

★ The **encyclopedia** of the muscle and skeletal systems and disorders; foreword by Lori Siegel. Facts on File 2005 xx, 389p (Facts on File library of health and living) $75

Grades: 11 12 Adult   **616.7**
1. Reference books 2. Musculoskeletal system -- Encyclopedias
ISBN 0-8160-5447-9

LC 2003-26606

The author "writes each entry with wit and skill— amazing among health science encyclopedias. It will be useful to health care consumers and students for years to come." Choice

Includes bibliographical references

616.8   Diseases of nervous system and mental disorders

Bloom, Ona

Encephalitis; [by] Ona Bloom and Jennifer Morgan; foreword by David Heymann. Chelsea House 2006 125p il (Deadly diseases and epidemics) $31.95

Grades: 9 10 11 12   **616.8**
1. Encephalitis
ISBN 0-7910-8503-1

LC 2005-5518

Includes glossary and bibliographical references

Dougherty, Terri

Epilepsy. Lucent Books 2010 104p il (Diseases and disorders series) lib bdg $33.45

Grades: 7 8 9 10 11 12   **616.8**
1. Epilepsy
ISBN 978-1-4205-0218-3; 1-4205-0218-2

LC 2009-33344

This "offers a thorough explanation of [epilepsy], giving a basic definition; a discussion of the causes, symptoms, and treatments; a description of living with the disease; and ideas of future treatment and diagnoses. The color photographs and sidebars help to make the information in the dense text more easily understood, and personal stories provide insight into how individuals deal with their disease. . . . Different types of seizures and the varied triggers are explained." Voice Youth Advocates

Includes bibliographical references

Esherick, Joan

★ The **journey** toward recovery; youth with brain injury. Mason Crest Publishers 2004 127p il (Youth with special needs) hardcover o.p. pa $14.95

Grades: 7 8 9 10   **616.8**
1. Brain damaged children
ISBN 1-59084-734-2; 1-4222-0425-1 pa

LC 2003-18640

Through the story of Jerome, a teenager who suffers a traumatic brain injury from a bike accident, this book discusses different "forms of brain injury; how these injuries affect people's lives; and how schools, doctors, and lawmakers are helping youth with this form of special need." Publisher's note

Includes glossary and bibliographical references

Freedman, Jeri

Tay-Sachs disease. Chelsea House 2009 128p il (Genes & disease) lib bdg $35

Grades: 7 8 9 10   **616.8**
1. Tay-Sachs disease
ISBN 978-0-7910-9634-5; 0-7910-9634-3

LC 2008-44770

This book "discusses the nature of the disease, why it affects certain groups of people more often than others, how genetic screening can help detect carriers of the Tay-Sachs gene, and what options genetic testing and counseling provide for having children." Publisher's note

Includes glossary and bibliographical references

Goldstein, Natalie

Parkinson's disease. Chelsea House 2008 128p il (Genes & disease) lib bdg $35

Grades: 7 8 9 10 **616.8**

1. Parkinson's disease

ISBN 978-0-7910-9584-3; 0-7910-9584-3

LC 2008-10494

This book opens "with accounts of people who have [Parkinson's] disease . . . followed by information on history, symptoms, variations, diagnosis, treatments, and research. . . . Chapters devoted to current genetic research and therapies can become dense as they introduce complex topics but photos, diagrams and charts help to clarify the details. . . . [Controversial issues] are introduced fairly." SLJ

Includes glossary and bibliographical references

Sacks, Oliver W.

Uncle Tungsten; memories of a chemical boyhood. [by] Oliver Sacks. Knopf 2001 337p il hardcover o.p. pa $14

Grades: 11 12 Adult **616.8**

1. Physicians 2. Neurologists 3. Writers on science 4. Writers on medicine

ISBN 0-375-40448-1; 0-375-70404-3 pa

LC 2001-33738

"Sacks' first scientific love was chemistry, and he presents an avid history of the field within a memoir that pays tribute to his uncle, who welcomed Sacks into his lab, thus encouraging his passion for chemistry and learning." Booklist

Shmaefsky, Brian

Meningitis; [by] Brian R. Shmaefsky; consulting editor, Hilary Babcock; foreword by David L. Heymann. 2nd ed.; Chelsea House 2010 120p il (Deadly diseases and epidemics) $34.95

Grades: 7 8 9 10 **616.8**

1. Meningitis

ISBN 978-1-60413-241-0; 1-60413-241-8

LC 2010-8044

First published 2005

This book contains "information on the causes, spread, treatment, and prevention of the disease, as well as . . . [information on] recent meningitis outbreaks, which are a persistent problem in schools and on college campuses." Publisher's note

Includes glossary and bibliographical references

616.85 Miscellaneous diseases of nervous system and mental disorders

Ambrose, Marylou

Investigating eating disorders (anorexia, bulimia, and binge eating) real facts for real lives. [by] Marylou Ambrose and Veronica Deisler. Enslow Publishers 2011 160p il (Investigating diseases) lib bdg $34.60

Grades: 6 7 8 9 10 **616.85**

1. Eating disorders

ISBN 978-0-7660-3339-9; 0-7660-3339-2

LC 2009-6492

"This book is a well-organized, clear, succinct, and attractive presentation on anorexia, bulimia, and binge eating. In it, the authors have gathered helpful definitions, early religious history, international viewpoints, statistics, family issues, medical and psychological assessments, treatments, medications, and legislation to present information on the future outlook of, and research into, these eating disorders." Sci Books Films

Includes glossary and bibliographical references

Baish, Vanessa

Self-image and eating disorders; by Rita Smith ... [et al.] 1st ed. Rosen Pub. 2013 48 p. col. ill. (Teen mental health) (library) $29.25

Grades: 6 7 8 9 **616.85**

1. Body image 2. Eating disorders

ISBN 1448868947; 9781448868940

LC 2012003030

This book on self-image and eating disorders by Rita Smith is part of the "Teen Mental Health" series. It "addresses self-esteem and negative body image. Eating disorders include anorexia nervosa, bulimia nervosa, binge eating, orthorexia nervosa, and compulsive exercise, along with related health and emotional problems. The books discuss techniques for coping and encourage teens to seek out available resources such as professional help, support groups, or school programs." (School Library Journal)

Includes bibliographical references (p. 43-46) and index.

Cobain, Bev

★ **When** nothing matters anymore; a survival guide for depressed teens. edited by Elizabeth Verdick. rev and updated ed.; Free Spirit Pub. 2007 146p il pa $14.95

Grades: 7 8 9 10 **616.85**

1. Depression (Psychology)

ISBN 978-1-57542-235-0; 1-57542-235-2

LC 2006-36325

First published 1998

This book written for teens defines depression, describes the symptoms, and explains that depression is treatable

"This practical, reassuring book should be made available to all teens." Voice Youth Advocates

Includes bibliographical references

Denkmire, Heather

★ The **truth** about anxiety and depression; Heather Denkmire, principal author; John Perritano, contributing author; Robert N. Golden, general editor, Fred L. Peterson, general editor. 2nd ed.; Facts on File 2010 199p il (Truth about series) $35

Grades: 7 8 9 10 **616.85**

1. Anxiety 2. Depression (Psychology)

ISBN 978-0-8160-7643-7; 0-8160-7643-X

LC 2010005461

First published 2004 with title: The truth about fear and depression

Presents information on anxiety and depression, including the genetics of mood and anxiety disorders, gender and depression, types of treatments available, related disorders, and more.

Includes glossary and bibliographical references

★ **Eating** disorders information for teens; health tips about anorexia, bulimia, binge eating, and body image disorders, including information about risk factors, prevention, diagnosis, treatment, health consequences, and other related issues. edited by Elizabeth Bellenir. 3rd ed. Omnigraphics, Inc. 2013 xiii, 380 p.p ill. (hardcover) $69

Grades: 7 8 9 10 11 12   **616.85**
  1. Eating disorders 2. Teenagers -- Health and hygiene
  ISBN 0780812697; 9780780812697

                              LC 2012036612
This book "provides information about a wide range of eating and body image disorders. The volume is broken into six parts covering general information about eating disorders; specific disorders such as anorexia nervosa, bulimia nervosa, and others; the heath consequences of eating disorders; prevention, diagnosis, and treatment; healthy eating and exercise; and additional reading, research studies, and organizations." (Voice of Youth Advocates)
  Includes bibliographical references and index.

Evans-Martin, Fay
  Down syndrome; [by] F. Fay Evans-Martin. Chelsea House 2008 128p il (Genes & disease) lib bdg $35

Grades: 7 8 9 10   **616.85**
  1. Down syndrome
  ISBN 978-0-7910-9644-4; 0-7910-9644-0
                              LC 2008-44773
"Down syndrome is a developmental disorder caused by the presence of an extra copy of chromosome 21. . . . [This book] explains this genetic disease, its history and characteristics, and what scientists are doing to study it." Publisher's note
  Includes glossary and bibliographical references

Farrar, Amy
  ADHD. Twenty-First Century Books 2010 112p il (USA Today health reports: diseases and disorders) lib bdg $34.60

Grades: 7 8 9 10 11 12   **616.85**
  1. Attention deficit disorder
  ISBN 978-0-7613-5455-0; 0-7613-5455-7
                              LC 2010-870
This book describes attention deficit-hyperactivity disorder, its causes and treatments.
This is "liberally sprinkled with relevant articles and 'snapshots' (graphs showing statistical breakdowns of the topic at hand) from the newspaper, providing a competent introduction to primary-source material." SLJ
  Includes glossary and bibliographical references

Greene, Jessica R.
  Eating disorders; the ultimate teen guide. Jessica R. Greene. Rowman & Littlefield Pub Inc 2014

316 p. illustrations (It happened to me) (cloth: alk. paper) $45

Grades: 9 10 11 12   **616.85**
  1. Teenagers -- Conduct of life 2. Eating disorders in adolescence 3. Teenagers -- Life skill guides 4. Eating disorders in adolescence -- Popular works
  ISBN 0810887738; 9780810887732; 9780810887749
                              LC 2014005390
This book on eating disorders, by Jessica R. Greene, "examines the complex factors that contribute to pathological dieting and binging and purging behaviors in teenagers, as well as current thoughts on how to overcome them. The author reviews how types of eating disorders are classified per the latest edition of the Diagnostic and Statistical Manual of the American Psychiatric Association (DSM-5), points out the similarity to behavioral addictions, and showcases opinions from experts." (Publisher's note)

"There are many texts that deal with eating disorders, but this is one of the more comprehensive ones . . . [r]eaders will appreciate the many personal accounts from those who have dealt with eating disorders, as well as opinions from experts in the field. Contact information for these individuals is included, too, such as Twitter handles, email addresses, and websites, further enhancing students' ability to delve deeper in the subject." SLJ
  Includes bibliographical references and index

Hallowell, Edward M.
  ★ **Positively** ADD; real success stories to inspire your dreams. [by] Catherine A. Corman and Edward M. Hallowell. Walker 2006 172p il $16.95; lib bdg $17.85

Grades: 8 9 10 11 12   **616.85**
  1. Attention deficit disorder
  ISBN 978-0-8027-8988-4; 0-8027-8988-9; 978-0-8027-8071-3 lib bdg; 0-8027-8071-7 lib bdg
                              LC 2005037184
This "profiles 17 adults who began dealing with attention deficit disorder in childhood. Along with political strategist [James] Carville, subjects include a Pulitzer Prize-winning photographer, a major league pitcher, and a young Rhodes scholar. . . . [This is] an encouraging, helpful book for teens with ADD as well as for their parents, teachers, and friends." Booklist
  Includes bibliographical references

Hidalgo-Robert, Alberto, 1992-
  Fat no more; a teenager's victory over obesity. by Alberto Hidalgo-Robert. Pinata Books 2012 184 p.

Grades: 7 8 9 10 11 12   **616.85**
  1. Obesity 2. Lifestyles 3. Teenagers -- Health and hygiene 4. Weight loss -- Personal narratives
  ISBN 1558857451; 9781558857452
                              LC 2012003177
"A timely account of a teen's success in losing weight and improving his health. Hidalgo-Robert describes in a conversational style how he became so heavy. Nicknamed 'El Gorditio' by his family, he traces his weight issues beginning with his early childhood in El Salvador and continuing into his teen years in the United States. Hidalgo-Robert explains how relationships and environmental factors contrib-

uted to his emotional state and obesity. . . . With a change in attitude, the help of the program's staff, new 'tools,' and a more supportive family environment, the teen shed pounds and changed his lifestyle." (School Library Journal)

Honos-Webb, Lara

The **ADHD** workbook for teens; activities to help you gain motivation and confidence. Lara Honos-Webb. Instant Help Books 2010 vi, 132 p.p (pbk.: alk. paper) $15.95
Grades: 7 8 9 10 11 12   **616.85**
1. Adolescent psychology 2. Attention deficit disorder 3. Attention-deficit disorder in adolescence -- Popular works
ISBN 1572248653; 9781572248656
LC 2010040282
According to this workbook by Lara Honos-Webb, "Symptoms of attention deficit/hyperactivity disorder, or ADHD, can strike at any time-during class, when you're listening to a friend's story, while doing homework, and did we mention during class? You might find it difficult to pay attention and sit still when your impulses are constantly tempting you to do the opposite." (Publisher's note)

This book helps ADHD-affected teens "learn simple skills [they] can use to confidently handle school, make and keep friends, and organize and finish every project [they] start." Publisher's note

Kramer, Gerri Freid

★ The **truth** about eating disorders; Robert N. Golden, Fred L. Peterson general editors; Gerri Freid Kramer, principal author. 2nd ed.; Facts on File 2009 208p (Truth about series) $35
Grades: 7 8 9 10   **616.85**
1. Eating disorders
ISBN 978-0-8160-7633-8; 0-8160-7633-2
LC 2008-44036
First published 2004
This discusses anorexia, bulimia, fad diets, and laxative abuse, the causes of eating disorders, how to recognize the disorders, the portrayal of eating disorders in the media, and obesity and weight control

This title does "an excellent job of providing accurate information for teens. For reports or for self-help, [it belongs] in any library serving young adults." SLJ [review of 2004 edition]
Includes glossary and bibliographical references

Mackay, Jenny

Phobias. Gale Cengage Learning 2009 103p il (Diseases and disorders series) $33.45
Grades: 9 10 11 12   **616.85**
1. Phobias
ISBN 978-1-4205-0103-2; 1-4205-0103-8
LC 2008033762
Explains what phobias are, how they are caused, how people live with them, and offers the latest information about treatment.
Includes bibliographical references

Meloy, C. G.

Life & Spectrum; A Revealing Look at High Functioning Autism and Asperger's Syndrome. written by C.G. Meloy; illustrated by Z. Pullen. Createspace Independent Pub 2013 136 p. $15
Grades: 9 10 11 12   **616.85**
1. Autism 2. Asperger's syndrome
ISBN 1482704226; 9781482704228
"In this . . . resource for those who live or work with individuals on the autism spectrum, [C. G.] Meloy reflects on growing up and living with such a condition. . . . As an adult, with his family's support, he has been successful in . . . living independently. Realizing his limitations, particularly in multitasking and stress management, he knows the kind of work situation that fits, and because he has learned to live frugally, he knows when hs needs to quit a job and regroup." (Booklist)

Mooney, Carla

Mood disorders. ReferencePoint Press 2010 96p il (Compact research: diseases and disorders) lib bdg $26.95
Grades: 8 9 10 11 12   **616.85**
1. Depression (Psychology) 2. Manic-depressive illness
ISBN 978-1-60152-119-4; 1-60152-119-7
LC 2010-5868
This book about mood disorders "begins with a general overview followed by focus on statistics, causes, symptoms, treatments, and prevention. . . . [The book] discusses the two main categories [of mood disorders]: unipolar (if untreated the number-one risk for suicide) and bipolar (which swings between depression and mania.) . . . The readable page design features pull quotes and subtitles, with occasional photos throughout." Booklist
Includes bibliographical references

What is anxiety disorder? by Carla Mooney. ReferencePoint Press, Inc. 2016 80 p. (hardback) $28.95
Grades: 8 9 10 11 12   **616.85**
1. Anxiety -- Treatment 2. Anxiety 3. Anxiety disorders 4. Anxiety disorders -- Treatment
ISBN 1601529201; 9781601529206
LC 2015016548
This juvenile book, by Carla Mooney, part of the publisher's "Understanding mental disorders" series, presents an overview of clinical anxiety. "Experts estimate that as many as 40 million American adults experience anxiety disorder in a given year, making it the most common mental illness in the United States. . . . [The volume] examines what this disorder is, what causes it, what it is like to live with it, and how or whether it can be treated or cured." (Publisher's note)

"This explores what it is like to live with the illness as well as its causes and treatments, and the well-organized, jargon-free information allows readers not already familiar with the topic to easily understand. Graphs, color photos, and side boxes containing supplemental facts break up the text, but this volume, unlike many of its contemporaries, is ultimately more invested in providing substantive information than in creating an engaging reading experience. A list of chapter notes, organizations, and sources round up the reference credentials of the book, which will be of value to student researchers." Booklist

Includes bibliographical references and index

Nathan, Debbie

Sybil exposed; the extraordinary story behind the famous multiple personality case. Free Press 2011 xxi, 297p il $26; ebook $12.99

Grades: 11 12 Adult   616.85

1. Artists 2. Painters 3. Mentally ill 4. Multiple personality

ISBN 978-1-4391-6827-1; 978-1-4391-6829-5 ebook

LC 2011009164

The author "claims that the subject of the 1973 international bestseller, Sybil by Flora Schreiber, and the blockbuster film that followed, was a deliberate fabrication that not only fooled a mass popular audience but shaped the practice of psychiatry, opening the door to mass hysteria and misdiagnosis. . . . A nuanced, not-entirely-unsympathetic account of the women who perpetrated a sensational literary fraud." Kirkus

Includes bibliographical references

Parks, Peggy J., 1951-

Down syndrome. ReferencePoint Press 2009 104p il (Compact research. Diseases and disorders) $25.95

Grades: 7 8 9 10 11 12   616.85

1. Down syndrome

ISBN 978-1-60152-065-4; 1-60152-065-4

LC 2008-36644

"This up-to-date, excellent overview of Down syndrome addresses controversies and ethical issues associated with this genetic disorder. Parks also reports on current and potential scientific advances that may prevent it in the future and offer a better quality of life and opportunities for those born with it." SLJ

Includes bibliographical references

Obsessive-compulsive disorder. ReferencePoint Press 2010 96p il (Compact research: diseases and disorders) lib bdg $26.95

Grades: 8 9 10 11 12   616.85

1. Obsessive-compulsive disorder

ISBN 978-1-60152-120-0; 1-60152-120-0

LC 2010-5872

This book about obsessive-compulsive disorder is written "with objectivity and depth. . . . [It] begins with a general overview followed by a focus on statistics, treatments, and prevention. . . . [The book] shows that the irrational fears of OCD affect males and females across race and class. . . . The readable page design features pull quotes and subtitles, with occasional photos throughout." Booklist

Includes bibliographical references

Online addiction; by Peggy J. Parks. ReferencePoint Press, Inc. 2013 96 p. (hardcover) $27.95

Grades: 7 8 9 10 11 12   616.85

1. Internet 2. Internet gambling 3. Addiction

ISBN 1601522703; 9781601522702

LC 2012014191

In this book about online addiction, Peggy J. Parks "addresses four basic questions: Is online addiction real? Can people get addicted to social networking? How serious of a problem is compulsive online gaming and gambling? Can people recover from online addiction? . . . Parks addresses each of her four questions in separate sections of her book." (Booklist)

Includes bibliographical references and index.

Self-injury disorder. ReferencePoint Press 2011 96p il (Compact research: diseases and disorders) lib bdg $26.95

Grades: 8 9 10 11 12   616.85

1. Self-mutilation

ISBN 978-1-60152-112-5; 1-60152-112-X

LC 2009-50483

This book about self-injury disorder "begins with a general overview followed by a focus on statistics, causes, symptoms, treatments, and prevention. . . . [The book] states that the main cause of self-inflicted injury is to gain relief from unbearable emotional pain, and it also covers methods of treatment and prevention. The readable page design features pull quotes and subtitles, with occasional photos throughout." Booklist

Includes bibliographical references

Price, Janet

★ **Take** control of Asperger's syndrome; the official strategy guide for teens with Asperger's syndrome and nonverbal learning disorder. [by] Janet Price and Jennifer Engel Fisher. Prufrock Press 2010 168p pa $16.95

Grades: 6 7 8 9 10   616.85

1. Asperger's syndrome

ISBN 978-1-59363-405-6; 1-59363-405-6

LC 2009-50852

"Directly addressing teens diagnosed with Asperger's Syndrome or Nonverbal Learning Disorder, two educational consultants experienced in special-needs issues lay out feasible strategies for success in school and in social interactions." Booklist

Includes bibliographical references

Rompella, Natalie

Obsessive-compulsive disorder; the ultimate teen guide. Scarecrow Press 2009 177p il (It happened to me) lib bdg $40

Grades: 7 8 9 10   616.85

1. Obsessive-compulsive disorder

ISBN 978-0-8108-5778-0; 0-8108-5778-2

LC 2008-46242

Guide that helps teenagers understand obsessive-compulsive disorder, and explains different treatment options.

Includes bibliographical references

Sonenklar, Carol

Anorexia and bulimia. Twenty-First Century Books 2010 128p il (USA Today health reports: diseases and disorders) lib bdg $34.60

Grades: 7 8 9 10 11 12 **616.85**
1. Bulimia 2. Anorexia nervosa
ISBN 978-0-8225-6786-8; 0-8225-6786-5
This describes the symptoms and treatment of anorexia and bulimia.

This book "stands out for the substantial amount of information conveyed in a lively writing style. . . . Graphs, sidebars, diagrams, and other illustrations [are] used judiciously." Booklist

Turkington, Carol
★ The **encyclopedia** of autism spectrum disorders; [by] Carol Turkington, Ruth Anan. Facts on File 2007 324p $75
Grades: 11 12 Adult **616.85**
1. Reference books 2. Autism -- Encyclopedias
ISBN 0-8160-6002-9; 978-0-8160-6002-3
LC 2005-27227
"More than 300 entries address the different types of autism, causes and treatments, institutions, associations, leading scientists, research, social impact, and much more." Publisher's note
Includes bibliographical references

Zucker, Bonnie
Take control of OCD; the ultimate guide for kids with OCD. Prufrock Press 2010 179p il pa $16.95
Grades: 6 7 8 9 10 **616.85**
1. Obsessive-compulsive disorder
ISBN 978-1-59363-429-2; 1-59363-429-3
LC 2010-34863
The author "addresses affected young readers directly and offers a structured set of self-help strategies for coping with diagnosed obsessive-compulsive behavior. Suggesting that the chapters be read in order for best results, she opens with a nontechnical explanation of the disorder's genetic and neurological roots, then goes on to discuss creating written behavioral 'ladders,' using relaxation techniques effectively, building self-awareness, handling uncertainty, and managing stress." Booklist
Includes bibliographical references

616.89 Mental disorders

Carlson, Dale
Out of order; young adult manual of mental illness and recovery: mental illnesses, personality disorders, learning problems, intellectual disabilities, treatment and recovery. Dale Carlson, coauthor Dr. Michael Bower; pictures by Carol Nicklaus. Bick Publishing House 2013 256 p. (alk. paper: alk. paper) $14.95
Grades: 9 10 11 12 **616.89**
1. Adolescent psychiatry 2. Adolescent psychology 3. Mental health services 4. Adolescent psychiatry 5. Adolescent psychopathology 6. Youth -- Mental health services
ISBN 1884158374; 9781884158377
LC 2013003328

This book, by Dale Carlson and Dr. Michael Bower, "is a manual for teens and young adults to help them understand mental illness and recovery. It covers such topics as mental illnesses, suicidal thoughts, personality disorders, learning problems, intellectual disabilities, treatment, and recovery. This book will help answer questions like: What is mental illness? What are the symptoms? Do you need help? How do you find the right kind of help?" (Publisher's note)

"This sweeping synopsis of mental conditions is presented in four sections, each of which includes the perspective of someone who's "been there." Chapters provide descriptions of various symptoms, treatments, and causes along with prescriptions for coping and recovery. "Self-Test Questions," a "Mental Disorders Dictionary," and, finally, correlative resources, including websites, hotlines, and addresses for various organizations, are included...This accessible book offers a narrative enriched with first-person vignettes personalizing topics relating to mental disorders." SLJ
Includes bibliographical references and index

Hicks, James Whitney
★ **Fifty** signs of mental illness; a guide to understanding mental health. Yale University Press 2005 389p (Yale University Press health & wellness) hardcover o.p. pa $17
Grades: 11 12 Adult **616.89**
1. Mental illness 2. Abnormal psychology
ISBN 0-300-10657-2; 0-300-11694-2 pa
LC 2004-21535
"Organizing the text alphabetically by symptom, psychiatrist Hicks (director, clinical services, Kirby Forensic Psychiatric Ctr.) opens each chapter with a good story or character study, wasting no words and packing in much more than one might expect without getting heavy." LJ

Meisel, Abigail
Investigating depression and bipolar disorder; real facts for real lives. Enslow Publishers 2010 160p il (Investigating diseases) lib bdg $34.60
Grades: 6 7 8 9 10 **616.89**
1. Depression (Psychology) 2. Manic-depressive illness
ISBN 978-0-7660-3340-5; 0-7660-3340-6
LC 2008-50060
"Meisel discusses the history, science, diagnosis, and treatment of depression and bipolar disorder. In addition, she shows how these illnesses affect not just the patients, but their families, peers, and friends. She explains the science behind the two conditions, their possible causes, and the varying nature of the illnesses themselves. . . . This is an excellent book for persons from high school age to adults to read and become familiar with these important illnesses." Sci Books Films
Includes glossary and bibliographical references

Noll, Richard
★ The **encyclopedia** of schizophrenia and other psychotic disorders; foreword by Leonard George. 3rd ed.; Facts on File 2007 xx, 409p (Facts on File library of health and living) $75

Grades: 11 12 Adult   **616.89**
1. Reference books 2. Schizophrenia -- Encyclopedias
ISBN 0-8160-6405-9; 978-0-8160-6405-2

LC 2005-56749

First published 1992

"Biologically related schizophrenic disorders, genetics, antipsychotic drug treatments, and pathophysiology are a few of the topics explored in the more than 600 entries. . . . The language is clear, making this volume equally suitable for use by patients, scholars, and general readers. A solid addition for health collections." Booklist

Includes bibliographical references

616.9   Other diseases

Allman, Toney
  Infectious disease research; by Toney Allman. ReferencePoint Press 2012 96 p. (Inside science series) (hardback) $27.95
Grades: 6 7 8 9 10 11 12   **616.9**
1. Communicable diseases -- Encyclopedias 2. Communicable diseases
ISBN 1601521774; 9781601521774

LC 2011007745

This book, by Toney Allman, presents a research guide to infectious disease research. "Infectious diseases are responsible for untold global suffering and the loss of millions of human lives each year. This knowledge drives the research toward a fuller understanding of infectious microbial agents and the development of new treatment and prevention methods for infectious diseases." (Publisher's note)

Includes bibliographical references and index

Ashby, Bonnie
  ★ The **encyclopedia** of infectious diseases; [by] Carol Turkington, Bonnie Lee Ashby. 3rd ed; Facts On File 2007 412p (Facts on File library of health and living) $75
Grades: 11 12 Adult   **616.9**
1. Reference books 2. Communicable diseases -- Encyclopedias
ISBN 0-8160-6397-4; 978-0-8160-6397-0

LC 2006-13795

First published 1998

"The alphabetically arranged volume covers diseases, treatment options, and relevant organizations. . . . Information is provided for each disease and includes its cause, symptoms, treatment, and prevention. Major diseases that have had an impact on the world's population (tuberculosis, AIDS) are covered . . . and include a history. This feature makes the volume useful to researchers and students." Booklist [review of 2003 edition]

Includes bibliographical references

Coleman, William H.
  Cholera; [by] William Coleman; consulting editor, Hilary Babcock; foreword by David Heymann. Chelsea House 2009 142p il (Deadly diseases and epidemics) lib bdg $29.95

Grades: 9 10 11 12   **616.9**
1. Cholera
ISBN 978-1-60413-232-8; 1-60413-232-9

LC 2008-28627

First published 2004

"This book describes the history of this infectious disease and discusses characteristics that enable this microorganism to cause serious health problems. The book also discusses the basic bacteriology, immunology, treatment, and epidemiology of the disease. Research that seeks both to cure and to understand the cholera bacillus is also highlighted." Publisher's note

Includes glossary and bibliographical references

Decker, Janet M.
  Mononucleosis; [by] Janet Decker and Alan Hecht; consulting editor: Hilary Babcock; foreword by David Heymann. 2nd ed.; Chelsea House 2009 128p il (Deadly diseases and epidemics) lib bdg $34.95
Grades: 9 10 11 12   **616.9**
1. Mononucleosis 2. Epstein-Barr virus
ISBN 978-1-60413-234-2; 1-60413-234-5

LC 2008-28628

First published 2004

"Mononucleosis is caused by the Epstein Barr virus. This book explores the microbiology of the virus as well as treatment and prevention options." Publisher's note

Includes glossary and bibliographical references

Edlow, Jonathan A.
  Bull's-eye: unraveling the medical mystery of Lyme disease. Yale University Press 2003 285p il hardcover o.p. pa $17
Grades: 11 12 Adult   **616.9**
1. Lyme disease
ISBN 0-300-09867-7; 0-300-10370-0 pa

LC 2002-154119

"This well-documented book is . . . as important for the light it sheds on the nature of scientific inquiry within the contemporary social and political context as it is for its information about Lyme disease." Booklist

Includes bibliographical references

Emmeluth, Donald
  Botulism; consulting editor, Hilary Babcock; foreword by David L. Heymann. 2nd ed.; Chelsea House 2010 144p il map (Deadly diseases and epidemics) $34.95
Grades: 7 8 9 10   **616.9**
1. Botulism
ISBN 978-1-60413-235-9; 1-60413-235-3

LC 2010-8111

First published 2005

This book contains "information on this disease, exploring its history, causes, statistics, and . . . diagnostic and treatment breakthroughs. It also includes accounts of numerous recent outbreaks." Publisher's note

Includes glossary and bibliographical references

Freeman-Cook, Lisa

Staphylococcus aureus infections; [by] Lisa and Kevin Freeman-Cook. Chelsea House 2006 182p il (Deadly diseases and epidemics) $31.95

Grades: 9 10 11 12 **616.9**

1. Bacterial infections

ISBN 0-7910-8508-2

LC 2005-4958

Includes bibliographical references

Goldsmith, Connie

Battling malaria; on the front lines against a global killer. Twenty-First Century Books 2010 128p il map (Twenty-first century medical library) lib bdg $37.27

Grades: 8 9 10 11 12 **616.9**

1. Malaria

ISBN 978-0-8225-8580-0; 0-8225-8580-4

LC 2009-20324

"From the trained scientist who simply wants a review of this global disease to the high school student who is just beginning to understand the life-cycle complexities of a single-celled parasitic organism, readers will appreciate this very nice overview of the challenges that malaria poses for mankind." Sci Books Films

Includes bibliographical references

Guilfoile, Patrick

Antibiotic-resistant bacteria; [by] Patrick G. Guilfoile; founding editor, I. Edward Alcamo; foreword by David Heymann. Chelsea House Publishers 2006 128p il (Deadly diseases and epidemics) $31.95

Grades: 9 10 11 12 **616.9**

1. Drugs 2. Microorganisms

ISBN 0-7910-9188-0; 978-0-7910-9188-3

LC 2006-17589

This book "describes pathogens that have become particularly adept at evading a wide range of antibiotics, and highlights how scientists continue to strive to develop new treatments and countermeasures to fight this onslaught." Publisher's note

Includes glossary and bibliographical references

Tetanus; consulting editor, Hilary Babcock; foreword by David Heymann. Chelsea House 2008 100p il map (Deadly diseases and epidemics) $31.95

Grades: 9 10 11 12 **616.9**

1. Tetanus

ISBN 978-0-7910-9711-3; 0-7910-9711-0

LC 2007-37928

This book "describes the characteristics of the disease, which includes powerful muscle contractions and a form of paralysis called lockjaw, and details its prevention and treatment. The historical background of the disease and the future trends of treatment and prevention are also covered." (Publisher's note)

Includes glossary and bibliographical references

Kelly, Evelyn B.

Investigating tuberculosis and superbugs; real facts for real lives. [by] Evelyn B. Kelly, Ian Wilker, and Marylou Ambrose. Enslow Publishers 2010 160p il (Investigating diseases) lib bdg $34.60

Grades: 7 8 9 10 **616.9**

1. Tuberculosis 2. Drug resistance

ISBN 978-0-7660-3343-6; 0-7660-3343-0

LC 2009-37811

This "methodically presents medical and statistical information about major kinds of tuberculosis, malaria, AIDS/HIV, and other persistent bacterial, viral, and parasitic pandemics worldwide that are becoming ominously resistant to once-effective treatments. . . . [This is] massively documented with endnotes; supplemented by sidebar insertions, accounts of specific cases, and small color photos; and rounded off with digestible lists of relevant further sources." Booklist

Includes bibliographical references

Levy, Janey

The **world** of microbes; bacteria, viruses, and other microorganisms. Rosen Pub. 2010 80p il (Understanding genetics) lib bdg $30.60

Grades: 9 10 11 12 **616.9**

1. Bacteria 2. Microorganisms

ISBN 978-1-4358-9536-2

LC 2009-48520

Explains the impact of bacteria, viruses, and other microorganisms on human genetics.

Murphy, Jim

Invincible microbe; tuberculosis and the never-ending search for a cure. Jim Murphy, Alison Blank. Clarion Books 2012 149 p. (hardback) $18.99

Grades: 5 6 7 8 9 **616.9**

1. Tuberculosis 2. Lungs -- Diseases 3. Communicable diseases -- Treatment

ISBN 0618535748; 9780618535743

LC 2011025951

This book looks at tuberculosis. It "starts with archeologists finding evidence of tuberculosis in a 500,000 year old skull and continues through to the present day. Various 'cures' such as the medieval 'king's touch' . . . , bloodletting of the 19th century, twentieth century sanatoriums and modern day drug cocktails are all discussed." Also "covered is the socioeconomic side of the disease, with a discussion of how treatment often varied depending on the race and economic status of the patient." (Children's Literature)

Includes bibliographical references

Preston, Richard

★ The **demon** in the freezer; a true story. Random House 2002 240p hardcover o.p. pa $7.99

Grades: 11 12 Adult **616.9**

1. Smallpox 2. Biological warfare

ISBN 0-375-50856-2; 0-345-46663-2 pa

The author explains "the chemical properties of the smallpox virus; how a single infected person . . . can set off an epidemic; and what this horrendous disease can be like. . . . We learn how the disease was eliminated by an international vaccination campaign in the 1970's; why there are reasons to believe that the Soviet Union grew staggering quantities of the virus, allegedly in part to arm intercontinental missiles; and how the virus might now be used by others as a 'strategic weapon.'" N Y Times Book Rev

Sheen, Barbara

MRSA. Lucent Books 2010 104p il (Diseases and disorders series) $33.45

Grades: 7 8 9 10   **616.9**

1. Methicillin-Resistant Staphylococcus aureus
ISBN 978-1-4205-0144-5; 1-4205-0144-5

LC 2009-32644

This "offers a thorough explanation of [MRSA] giving a basic definition; a discussion of the causes, symptoms, and treatments; a description of living with the disease; and ideas of future treatment and diagnoses. Each volume lists source notes and organizations to contact. A glossary, index, and ideas for further reading are also included. The color photographs and sidebars help to make the information in the dense text more easily understood, and personal stories provide insight into how individuals deal with their disease." Voice Youth Advocates

Includes glossary and bibliographical references

Shmaefsky, Brian

Toxic shock syndrome; [by] Brian R. Shmaefsky; consulting editor, Hilary Babcock; foreword by David L. Heymann. 2nd ed.; Chelsea House 2010 127p il (Deadly diseases and epidemics) $34.95

Grades: 8 9 10 11 12   **616.9**

1. Toxic shock syndrome
ISBN 978-1-60413-243-4; 1-60413-243-4

LC 2010029222

First published 2003

This describes types of toxic shock syndrome, its causes, diagnosis and treatment.

Includes glossary and bibliographical references

616.95   Sexually transmitted diseases, zoonoses

Ambrose, Marylou

Investigating STDs (sexually transmitted diseases) real facts for real lives. [by] Marylou Ambrose and Veronica Deisler. Enslow Publishers 2010 160p il (Investigating diseases) lib bdg $34.60

Grades: 7 8 9 10   **616.95**

1. Sexually transmitted diseases
ISBN 978-0-7660-3342-9; 0-7660-3342-2

LC 2008-50061

The authors offer "facts about sexually transmitted diseases. Real-life examples of how teens deal with these issues are mixed with data from scientific studies, tips on how to live with and treat STDs, and the history of STDs." Publisher's note

Includes glossary and bibliographical references

Collins, Nicholas

Frequently asked questions about STDs; by Nicholas Collins and Samuel G. Woods. Rosen Pub. 2012 64 p. col. ill. (library) $31.95

Grades: 7 8 9 10   **616.95**

1. Teenagers -- Sexual behavior 2. Sexually transmitted diseases
ISBN 1448846307; 9781448846306

LC 2011000303

This book by Nicholas Collins looks at STDs. "Sexually transmitted diseases are clinically explained, including how they affect the body, how to recognize symptoms of infection, and how teens can protect themselves and their partner against, not only STDs, but HIV and AIDS as well." (Voice of Youth Advocates)

Includes bibliographical references (p. 83) and index.

Dougherty, Terri

Sexually transmitted diseases. Lucent Books 2010 96p il (Diseases and disorders series) $32.45

Grades: 7 8 9 10   **616.95**

1. Sexually transmitted diseases
ISBN 978-1-4205-0220-6

LC 2009-39583

"This book discusses the most common afflictions, diseases that are usually found in combinations, medical advances, and how the outlook for STDs is complicated by new trends such as drug-resistant strains. Information is also supplied about causes, prevention, diagnosis, and treatment. . . . A number of the photos show some of the horrific physical manifestations in individuals, including infants. . . . [This book] should be considered for first purchase." SLJ

Includes bibliographical references

616.97   Diseases of immune system

Cunningham, Kevin

HIV /AIDS. Morgan Reynolds Pub. 2009 144p il (Diseases in history) lib bdg $28.95

Grades: 8 9 10 11 12   **616.97**

1. AIDS (Disease)
ISBN 978-1-59935-104-9; 1-59935-104-8

LC 2008-51616

"Explores the origin of the two types of HIV viruses and the reasons why poverty, promiscuity, and the common use of world blood supplies enable its horrible and devastatingly rapid spread. . . . This detailed overview . . . will appeal to more advanced students. The research is thorough and the writing is insightful, thought provoking, and accessible." Voice Youth Advocates

Includes glossary and bibliographical references

Ehrlich, Paul

Living with allergies; [by] Paul M. Ehrlich, with Elizabeth Shimer Bowers. Facts On File 2009 168p (Teen's guides) $34.95; pa $14.95

Grades: 7 8 9 10 11 12   **616.97**

1. Allergy
ISBN 9781438129976; 978-0-8160-7327-6; 0-8160-7327-9; 0-8160-7742-8 pa

LC 2008-34352

This "book addresses allergy triggers, preventing allergic reactions, what to expect from treatment, paying for care, and how to help yourself, friends, or family members who may have allergies." Publisher's note

Includes glossary and bibliographical references

Hillstrom, Kevin

Food allergies; by Kevin Hillstrom. Lucent Books 2012 96 p. col. ill. (Nutrition and health) (hardcover) $30.95

Grades: 7 8 9 10 11 12   **616.97**

1. Food allergy

ISBN 1420507206; 9781420507201

LC 2012002945

This book on food allergies by Kevin Hillstrom is part of the "Nutrition and Health" book series. It "discusses the rising numbers of allergic young people, the physiology of the symptoms (with a clear diagram of an anaphylactic reaction), the search for a cure, and the social stigma." (Booklist) "Doctors, researchers, and people living with food allergies are quoted throughout the text." (Publisher's note)

Includes bibliographical references (p. 81-84) and index.

James, Otto

AIDS. Smart Apple Media 2010 46p il (Voices) lib bdg $34.95

Grades: 7 8 9 10 11 12   **616.97**

1. AIDS (Disease)

ISBN 978-1-59920-282-2; 1-59920-282-4

LC 2009-5417

"AIDS looks at causes, prevention, treatment, and the chances of a cure and also discusses abstinence, safe sex, the cost of AIDS drugs, and much more. . . . [The] blend of current political debate with witnesses' close-up experiences told through photos, narratives, and quotes will draw browsers, and many will go on to find out more." Booklist

Includes glossary and bibliographical references

Quicksand; HIV/AIDS in our world. by Anonymous. Candlewick Press 2009 103p $15.99

Grades: 6 7 8 9 10   **616.97**

1. AIDS (Disease)

ISBN 978-0-7636-1589-5; 0-7636-1589-7

LC 2009-7761

"The anonymous author explains her motivation for writing this book by telling readers that ten years ago, when HIV/AIDS was still considered a taboo subject, her brother-in-law was diagnosed with the disease. She writes in a truthful, open manner, addressing common questions about HIV/AIDS and providing easy-to-understand and honest advice. . . . The author's personal insight is what makes this book an important addition. Topics address everything from the history of HIV/AIDS to how to protect oneself from the disease. She also provides suggestions on how to cope with hearing that a family or friend has HIV/AIDS. . . . The author's focus on how the disease affects all people, whether they have contracted HIV/AIDS or not, makes this book a must-have for all teen collections." Voice Youth Advocates

Includes glossary and bibliographical references

Yount, Lisa

Luc Montagnier; identifying the AIDS virus. by Lisa Yount. Chelsea House 2011 xix, 123 p.p col. ill. (library) $35

Grades: 7 8 9 10 11 12   **616.97**

1. AIDS (Disease) 2. HIV (Viruses)

ISBN 1604136618; 9781604136616

LC 2010047006

This book by Lisa Yount is part of the Trailblazers in Science and Technology series and looks at Luc Montagnier. It "recounts the life and career of the Nobel Prize-winning French virologist whose contributions to the understanding of the nature of viruses led to a significant advance in cancer research and in discovering the HIV virus that causes AIDS." (Publisher's note)

Includes bibliographical references and index.

616.99   Tumors and miscellaneous communicable diseases

Casil, Amy Sterling

Pancreatic cancer; current and emerging trends in detection and treatment. Rosen Pub. 2009 64p il (Cancer and modern science) lib bdg $29.25

Grades: 7 8 9 10 11 12   **616.99**

1. Pancreas -- Cancer

ISBN 9781435856998; 978-1-4358-5008-8; 1-4358-5008-4

LC 2008-25132

This book describes pancreatic cancer and its treatment.

"Clearly aimed at teens who have cancer or know someone who does, . . . [this title combines] lots of technical detail about anatomy, physiology, and pathology with a personal, interactive style. . . . With a highly readable design, including crisp color photos and anatomical diagrams, the [book] will also serve the needs of student researchers. Also features excellent, extensive back matter." Booklist

Includes glossary and bibliographical references

Fies, Brian

Mom's cancer. Abrams ComicArts 2008 115p il $14.95

Grades: 9 10 11 12 Adult   **616.99**

1. Graphic novels 2. Biographical graphic novels 3. Cancer -- Graphic novels

ISBN 978-0-8109-7107-3

First published 2006

When writer/cartoonist Fies learned his mother had cancer and that it had already spread from her lungs, he used webcomics to depict what was happening to his mother and the rest of the family as Mom fought the cancer. All the pain, the heartache, the little battles won, the effects on Fies' relationships with his sisters, the ultimate hope are all on the page. In the end, Mom beat the cancer. In an afterword, Fies tells the reader that some of the medications just wore down his mother's body, and she died shortly before the book was published.

Freedman, Jeri

Brain cancer; current and emerging trends in detection and treatment. Rosen Pub. 2009 63p il (Cancer and modern science) lib bdg $29.25

Grades: 7 8 9 10 11 12   616.99
1. Brain -- Cancer
ISBN 9781435857025; 978-1-4358-5011-8; 1-4358-5011-4

LC 2008-22086

This book combines "lots of technical detail about anatomy, physiology, and pathology with a personal, interactive style. . . . Brain Cancer includes a section on Coping with School and Community that speaks directly to students with the disease and encourages them to stay active and involved. It also looks in detail at different types of brain cancer, detection and diagnosis, and present and future treatments." Booklist

Includes glossary and bibliographical references

Goldsmith, Connie

Skin cancer. Twenty-First Century Books 2010 128p il (USA Today health reports: diseases and disorders) lib bdg $34.60

Grades: 7 8 9 10 11 12   616.99
1. Cancer 2. Skin -- Diseases
ISBN 978-0-7613-5469-7; 0-7613-5469-7

LC 2010-10003

This describes causes, prevention, and treatments of skin cancer.

This is "liberally sprinkled with relevant articles and 'snapshots' (graphs showing statistical breakdowns of the topic at hand) from the newspaper, providing a competent introduction to primary-source material." SLJ

Includes glossary and bibliographical references

Panno, Joseph

★ **Cancer**; the role of genes, lifestyle, and environment. Facts On File 2010 246p il (The new biology) $40

Grades: 9 10 11 12   616.99
1. Cancer
ISBN 978-0-8160-6848-7

LC 2009-50783

First published 2004

This book "explores the many facets of cancer research, from basic genetic and cellular mechanisms to the danger of carcinogens and the influence of lifestyle. . . . Chapters focus on the unique characteristics of normal cells, cancer cells, cancer genes, and cancer progression, as well as the recent shift in the scientific community regarding the root cause of cancer." Publisher's note

Includes bibliographical references

Silver, Marc

My parent has cancer and it really sucks; Marc Silver, Maya Silver. Sourcebooks Fire 2013 272 p. $14.99

Grades: 6 7 8 9 10 11 12   616.99
1. Cancer -- Psychological aspects 2. Children of cancer patients
ISBN 9781402273070; 140227307X

LC 2012039095

This handbook "aims to guide teens through the experience of having an ill parent. . . . Short chapters include 'Let's Talk: How to Keep Your Family Communication Lines Wide Open,' 'How Things Will Change During Cancer,' 'Dealing

with Stress,' 'The Power (and the Limits) of Optimism and Faith,' 'Seeking Support,' 'Facing a Dire Prognosis,' and 'Losing a Parent to Cancer.'" (School Library Journal)

"Drawing on their experiences, the Silvers offer advice for finding solace in people who have been there and who have found ways to cope... It's admirable that the authors don't sugarcoat the realities of cancer and will speak with an honesty that teens will identify with and find comfort in." Booklist

Thornton, Denise

Living with cancer; the ultimate teen guide. Scarecrow Press 2011 il $40

Grades: 7 8 9 10   616.99
1. Cancer
ISBN 978-0-8108-7277-6

LC 2010044140

"Written primarily for teens surviving cancer, this guide is chock-full of advice, tips, and firsthand accounts. The views of teens with a sibling or a parent battling the disease are also presented. Honest and heart-wrenching, this title doesn't shy away from the brutal realities of the disease. . . . This is a valuable resource, reminding those affected that they are not alone." SLJ

617   Surgery, regional medicine, dentistry, ophthalmology, otology, audiology

Black, Keith

Brain surgeon; a doctor's inspiring encounters with mortality and miracles. [by] Keith Black, with Arnold Mann. Wellness Central 2009 226p $24.99

Grades: Adult   617
ISBN 9780446581097; 0446581097

LC 2008-46708

"Black, chair of the department of neurosurgery at Cedars-Sinai Medical Center, reflects on his extraordinary life and career. As an African-American growing up in Alabama and Ohio, Black benefited from the emphasis his scholarly parents put on learning: 'I was brought up to believe there was nothing that I could not do,' and he published his first scientific paper at age 17 and went on to pioneer blood-brain barrier research to enable chemotherapy drugs to reach brain tumors directly. Introducing the reader to his colleagues and patients, Black tours the interior of the brain with detailed accounts of delicate surgical procedures." Pub Wkly

617.1   Injuries and wounds

★ **Everyday** sports injuries. DK 2010 272p il pa $21.95

Grades: 9 10 11 12   617.1
1. Sports medicine 2. Wounds and injuries
ISBN 978-0-7566-5737-6

"Featuring more than 150 step-by step exercise routines for recovery after injury, improving strength and performance, and reducing risk of injury, . . . [this is a] guide to recognizing, treating, and preventing injury, with the goal of getting back in action as soon as possible." Publisher's note

Fainaru, Steve

League of Denial; The NFL, Concussions and the Battle for Truth. Mark Fainaru-Wada and Steve Fainaru. Random House Inc 2013 416 p. illustrations (chiefly color) $27

Grades: 11 12 Adult   **617.1**

1. Brain -- Concussion 2. National Football League 3. Sports medicine -- United States 4. Football injuries -- United States

ISBN 0770437540; 9780770437541

LC 2012276088

"Both ESPN investigative reporters, the authors reveal how the NFL, over a period of nearly two decades, sought to cover up and deny mounting evidence of the connection between football and brain damage. This narrative moves between the NFL trenches, America's research labs and the boardrooms where the NFL went to war against science; it examines how the league used its power and resources to attack independent scientists and elevate its own flawed research." Publisher's note

"The narrative is fast-paced and almost cinematic in the way it describes the culture of the gridiron, and in the picture it provides of the NFL research labs where scientists drew their conclusions, and the NFL boardrooms where football executives decided to go to war." Pub Wkly

★ **Sports** injuries information for teens; health tips about acute, traumatic, and chronic injuries in adolescent athletes. edited by Zachary Klimecki and Elizabeth Bellenir. 3rd ed. Omnigraphics, Inc. 2012 xiii, 401 p.p (hardcover) $69

Grades: 7 8 9 10 11 12   **617.1**

1. Athletes -- Wounds and injuries 2. Teenagers -- Health and hygiene 3. Sports injuries 4. Wounds and injuries 5. Teenagers -- Wounds and injuries -- Prevention

ISBN 0780812654; 9780780812659

LC 2012018884

This book offers teens a "guide to being a healthy athlete. It includes guidelines for participating safely in sports and avoiding injury. It also discusses how to deal with injuries when they occur. It explains diagnostic and treatment procedures and discusses issues related to rehabilitation, including suggestions for making decisions about returning to play. The book concludes with directories of resources for more information about sports-related injuries and fitness." (Publisher's note)

Includes bibliographical references and index.

617.4   Surgery by systems and regions

Goldsmith, Connie

Traumatic brain injury; from concussion to coma. Connie Goldsmith. Twenty-First Century Books 2014 88 p. illustrations (lib. bdg.: alk. paper) $34.60

Grades: 6 7 8 9 10 11   **617.4**

1. Nervous system 2. Brain -- Wounds and injuries

ISBN 1467713481; 9781467713481

LC 2013001346

This juvenile nonfiction book, by Connie Goldsmith, explores traumatic brain injury, including "the different types of TBIs, what causes them, and how they are diagnosed and treated. . . . [It also profiles] National Hockey League player Derek Boogaard and U.S. Representative Gabby Giffords, both of whom sustained TBIs, with dramatically different outcomes. . . . [Finally, it previews] medical technologies that help victims recover and promise hope for the future." (Publisher's note)

"Photographs, charts, and statistics are included, which expand the information. Appended are source notes, a glossary, a bibliography, and a list of websites and resources. The currency of this topic and its potential impact on teens make this a smart choice for school and public libraries." - Booklist

Includes bibliographical references and index

McClafferty, Carla Killough

Fourth down and inches; concussions and football's make-or-break moment. by Carla Killough McClafferty. Carolrhoda Books 2013 96 p. (lib. bdg.: alk. paper) $20.95

Grades: 6 7 8 9 10 11 12   **617.4**

1. Football injuries 2. Brain -- Concussion 3. Head -- Wounds and injuries 4. Football players -- Health and hygiene

ISBN 1467710679; 9781467710671

LC 2013004192

This book by Carla Killough McClafferty presents a "warning about the dangers of playing football, especially at the youth level. . . . The author . . . presents story after poignant story of high school and professional players who suffered brain damage or worse. Among their profiles are details of research studies, photos of MRI images and damaged brain tissue, and explanations of chronic traumatic encephalopathy (CTE) and second-impact syndrome." (Publishers Weekly)

Includes bibliographical references and index

Yount, Lisa

Alfred Blalock, Helen Taussig, and Vivien Thomas; mending children's hearts. by Lisa Yount. Chelsea House 2012 xviii, 127 p.p col. ill. (Trailblazers in science and technology) (library) $35

Grades: 7 8 9 10 11 12   **617.4**

1. Heart -- Surgery 2. Surgeons 3. Pediatric cardiology -- History 4. Heart surgeons -- United States -- Biography

ISBN 1604136588; 9781604136586

LC 2010035656

This book, part of the Trailblazers in Science and Technology series, focuses on medical professionals Alfred Blalock, Helen Taussig, and Vivien Thomas. The book "recounts the lives and careers of three medical pioneers—a white male surgeon (Blalock), a white female cardiologist (Taussig), and an African-American male laboratory technician (Thomas)—who combined their skills in 1944 to create a groundbreaking operation" for pediatric cardiology. (Publisher's note)

"Sidebars and captioned color and archival photographs round out the dense, though clearly written, texts." SLJ

Includes bibliographical references and index.

617.5   Regional medicine

Ear, nose, and throat; edited by Kara Rogers. Britannica Educational Pub. in association with Rosen Educational Services 2012 xvii, 186 p.p col. ill.
Grades: 7 8 9 10 11 12   **617.5**
1. Ear 2. Nose 3. Throat 4. Otolaryngology -- Popular works
ISBN 1615306579; 9781615306572

                         LC 2011013432
Editor Kara Rogers presents a book on otolaryngology. "The interconnectedness of the ear, nose, and throat is evident when you consider how the smell . . . can affect your perception of their taste, or how a runny nose and scratchy throat can lead to an ear infection. In addition to enabling sensory perception, the ear, nose, and throat perform a number of vital functions in the human body. This incisive volume examines the structure of each in turn and in concert with the other, also exploring the diseases and disorders that sometimes afflict them." (Publisher's note)
     Includes bibliographical references (p. 170-171) and index

617.9   Operative surgery and special fields of surgery

Cheney, Annie
    ★ **Body** brokers; inside America's underground trade in human remains. Broadway Books 2006 205p $23.95; pa $14
Grades: 11 12 Adult   **617.9**
    1. Procurement of organs, tissues, etc.
    ISBN 0-7679-1733-2; 978-0-7679-1733-9; 0-7679-1734-0 pa; 978-0-7679-1734-6 pa
                         LC 2005-54278
This book "speeds along like a circular saw through a thigh joint. It's a zippy, entertaining read, and more formal, scholarly works on the topic are not." N Y Times Book Rev
Includes bibliographical references

Cosmetic surgery: opposing viewpoints; Roman Espejo, book editor. Greenhaven Press 2011 180p il (Opposing viewpoints series) $39.70; pa $26.50
Grades: 10 11 12   **617.9**
1. Plastic surgery
ISBN 978-0-7377-4958-8; 0-7377-4958-X; 978-0-7377-4959-5 pa; 0-7377-4959-8 pa
                         LC 2010039234
This book "discusses liposuction, rhinoplasty, and breast augmentation, as well as nonsurgical procedures like Botox injections. With money seemingly the only obstacle to achieving the perfect you, this book helps students go beyond the media hype and weigh the complicated social, psychological, and medical issues behind cosmetic surgery." SLJ
Includes bibliographical references

Foran, Racquel
    ★ **Organ** transplants; Racquel Foran. Abdo Pub. Co. 2013 112 p. illustrations (chiefly color) $34.22

Grades: 6 7 8 9 10   **617.9**
    1. Medical technology 2. Transplantation of organs, tissues, etc.
ISBN 1617839043; 9781617839047
                         LC 2013932976
Written by Racquel Foran and part of the Medical Marvels series, "This title follows the development of organ transplants, including early attempts at transplantation, groundbreaking discoveries and the doctors who made them, and where the science is heading in the future. . . . Sidebars, full-color photos, a glossary, and well-placed graphs, charts, and maps, enhance this . . . title." (Publisher's note)
    "The book is handsomely designed, with interesting full-bleed photographs often facing a page of text. Sidebars, highlighted in yellow, pertain to the topic and never feel intrusive. Source notes and a bibliography . . . add to the title's usefulness for researchers." Booklist
    Includes bibliographical references and index

618   Gynecology, obstetrics, pediatrics, geriatrics

Hollen, Kathryn H.
    ★ The **reproductive** system. Greenwood Press 2004 xx, 193p il (Human body systems) $65
Grades: 11 12 Adult   **618**
1. Reproductive system
ISBN 0-313-32449-2
                         LC 2004-43638
This book "discusses the reproductive organs, hormones, conception through childbirth and development after birth including puberty. The history of research on the reproductive system is presented and the future of research in this field is considered. Current controversies and dilemmas are also explored." Publisher's note
    Includes bibliographical references

Krohmer, Randolph W.
    The **reproductive** system; [by] Randolph Krohmer. Chelsea House 2009 116p il (The human body: how it works) lib bdg $35
Grades: 7 8 9 10   **618**
1. Reproductive system
ISBN 978-1-60413-373-8; 1-60413-373-2
                         LC 2009-22140
Examines the workings of the male and female reproductive systems and the complex process of human reproduction.
    Includes glossary and bibliographical references

Zach, Kim K.
    ★ **Reproductive** technology. Lucent Books 2005 112p il (Great medical discoveries) $27.45
Grades: 9 10 11 12   **618**
1. Reproductive technology
ISBN 1-59018-344-4
                         LC 2003-15403
"For students studying ethics or science, this book will provide concise, clear information for reports. . . . Teens will find understandable, complete explanations for their assignments or clarification if there are fertility issues within their families" SLJ
    Includes bibliographical references

618.1 Gynecology and obstetrics

Waters, Sophie

 Seeing the gynecologist. Rosen Pub. Group 2007 47p il (Girls' health) $19.95

Grades: 7 8 9 10 11 12   **618.1**

 1. Girls -- Health and hygiene 2. Women -- Health and hygiene

 ISBN 978-1-4042-1948-9; 1-4042-1948-X

         LC 2007-1633

 "Introductory chapters include a brief introduction to the physiology of women's reproduction and menstruation, but the majority of the book covers the specifics of a gynecological visit, from choosing a doctor and insurance concerns to what happens during a pelvic exam. . . . The accessible text is informative and supportive." Booklist

 Includes bibliographical references

Weiss, Marisa C.

 Taking care of your 'girls' a breast health guide for girls, teens, and in-betweens. [by] Marisa C. Weiss and Isabel Friedman. Three Rivers Press 2008 237p il pa $15.95

Grades: 9 10 11 12   **618.1**

 1. Breast 2. Girls -- Health and hygiene

 ISBN 978-0-307-40696-5

         LC 2008-17457

 The authors "have surveyed 3,000 mothers and their daughters to produce this chatty but informative book on breast health for girls and adolescents. The text covers everything from getting the first bra to risk factors for breast cancer . . . and is peppered with questions posed by girls of all ages, ranging from when to start regular breast exams to why breasts sometimes feel painful or tender. . . . This empowering book will be an excellent impetus for honest conversations about breast health and development." Publ Wkly

 Includes bibliographical references

618.2 Obstetrics

Brewer, Sarah

 The **pregnant** body book; [by] Sarah Brewer [et al.] DK Pub. 2011 256 p. il $40

Grades: 9 10 11 12 Adult   **618.2**

 1. Physiology 2. Reproductive system 3. Pregnancy 4. Pregnant women

 ISBN 0756675596; 9780756675592

         LC 2011283116

 This book is accompanied by a DVD-ROM entitled Pregnant Body. The "book looks at the nature of human pregnancy, including how it's changed through evolution, and explores the anatomy and physiology of both the reproductive systems." (Publisher's note) Index.

 "This book, a revisiting of the universal human experiences of sex, pregnancy, and birth, stands out for its comprehensive pictorial representations and down-to-earth explanations." Pub Wkly

★ **Pregnancy** information for teens; health tips about teen pregnancy and teen parenting. edited

by Elizabeth Magill. 2nd ed. Omnigraphics 2012 xiii, 396 p.p ill. (hardcover) $69.00

Grades: 7 8 9 10   **618.2**

 1. Teenage pregnancy 2. Teenagers -- Health and hygiene 3. Teenage parents

 ISBN 0780812204; 9780780812208

         LC 2011042323

 This book uses "articles reprinted with permission from sources such as the March of Dimes and The National Campaign to Prevent Teen Pregnancy." This "second edition gives updated information on unplanned pregnancies. While part one features aspects of the phenomenon as a social issue, the rest of the book provides health tips and options for teens who are pregnant." (School Library Journal)

 Includes bibliographical references and index.

618.92 Pediatrics

★ **Allergy** information for teens; health tips about allergic reactions to food, pollen, mold, and other substances, including facts about diagnosing, treating, and preventing allergic responses and complications. edited by Karen Bellenir. 2nd ed. Omnigraphics, Inc. 2013 xiii, 388 p.p ill. (hardcover) $69

Grades: 8 9 10 11 12   **618.92**

 1. Allergy -- Encyclopedias 2. Teenagers -- Health and hygiene 3. Allergy 4. Food allergy 5. Insect allergy 6. Allergy in children

 ISBN 0780812883; 9780780812888

         LC 2012038514

 This book is a "51-chapter resource for reliable information about the many kinds of allergic reactions, triggers, symptoms, tests, treatments, and management strategies. Each chapter presents topics in short sections, using a handy question-and-answer format interwoven with many diagrams and sidebars. The volume concludes with lists of 19 additional titles, 10 cookbooks, and 24 articles, many with 2005 publication dates." (School Library Journal)

 Includes bibliographical references and index.

Attention deficit hyperactivity disorder; Heidi Williams, book editor. Greenhaven Press 2011 133p il map (Issues that concern you) $35.75

Grades: 9 10 11 12   **618.92**

 1. Attention deficit disorder

 ISBN 978-0-7377-4950-2; 0-7377-4950-4

         LC 2010-13958

 "Following a brief introduction, this volume contains 14 short articles on ADHD, current treatments, and controversies. . . . A useful resource for students with ADHD and their parents and teachers is appended." SLJ

 Includes bibliographical references

Chesner, Jonathan

 ADHD in HD; brains gone wild. by Jonathan Chesner. Free Spirit Pub. 2012 145 p. ill. (some col.) (pbk.) $14.99

Grades: 6 7 8 9   **618.92**

 1. Attention deficit disorder 2. Teenagers -- Conduct of

life 3. Abnormal psychology 4. Anxiety in adolescence 5. Teenagers -- Family relationships 6. Attention-deficit disorder in adolescence

ISBN 1575423863; 9781575423869; 9781575426716

LC 2011047036

This book, by actor Jonathan Chesner, "is a kinetic collection of frank personal stories of failure and success, hilarious anecdotes, wild ideas, and point-blank advice that will resonate with teens and young adults. . . . The book addresses the four main characteristics of ADHD: hyperactivity, impulsivity, inattention, and indecisiveness. It provides positive advice about school, family life, social life, dating, careers, medicine, and how to be like Mr. T." (Publisher's note)

"With much practical advice (for example, taking "baby steps" when trying to establish eating habits), this packs in plenty of valuable content—and is pretty enjoyable, too." Booklist

Currie-McGhee, Leanne K.

Childhood obesity; by Leanne K. Currie-McGhee. Lucent Books 2012 104 p. ill. (some col.) (Nutrition and health) (hardcover) $30.95

Grades: 7 8 9 10 11 12   **618.92**
1. Obesity in children

ISBN 1420507230; 9781420507232

LC 2012002939

This book by Leanne K. Currie-McGhee, part of the "Nutrition & Health" series, "explores global issue of childhood obesity. Causes of and proposed solutions to this public health issue are explored, and the findings of current studies are detailed. The text features comments from scientists and researchers, but also includes first-hand accounts from children and teens who have struggled with obesity." (Publisher's note)

Includes bibliographical references (p. 90-93) and index.

Nakaya, Andrea C.

ADHD. ReferencePoint Press 2009 108p il map (Compact research. Diseases and disorders) $25.95

Grades: 7 8 9 10 11 12   **618.92**
1. Attention deficit disorder

ISBN 978-1-60152-062-3; 1-60152-062-X

"ADHD thoroughly examines the disorder and incorporates numerous first-person accounts, including some from adults who find that the condition helps them excel in the workplace." Booklist

Includes bibliographical references

Rouba, Kelly

Juvenile arthritis; the ultimate teen guide. Scarecrow Press 2009 289p il (It happened to me) lib bdg $49

Grades: 7 8 9 10   **618.92**
1. Arthritis

ISBN 978-0-8108-6055-1; 0-8108-6055-4

LC 2008-42317

"Rouba gives advice on living with the disease, including treatment options, diet and exercise tips, and managing mental and physical health." Voice Youth Advocates

Includes bibliographical references

Sundquist, Josh, 1984-

We should hang out sometime; embarrassingly, a true story. Josh Sundquist. Little, Brown & Co. 2015 336 p. illustrations (hardcover) $18

Grades: Adult   **618.92**
1. Rejection (Psychology) 2. Dating (Social customs) 3. Motivational speakers -- United States -- Biography 4. Skiers with disabilities -- United States -- Biography 5. Ewing's sarcoma -- Patients -- United States -- Biography

ISBN 031625102X; 9780316251020

LC 2013041678

In this book, author Josh Sundquist explains he "only ever had one girlfriend. For twenty-three hours. In eighth grade. Why was Josh still single? To find out, he tracked down the girls he had tried to date and asked them straight up: What went wrong. The results of Josh's semiscientific, wholly hilarious investigation are captured here. . . . [T]his story is about looking for love--or at least a girlfriend--in all the wrong places." (Publisher's note)

Yamazaki, James N.

★ **Children** of the atomic bomb; an American physician's memoir of Nagasaki, Hiroshima, and the Marshall Islands. {by} James N. Yamazaki with Louis B. Fleming. Duke Univ. Press 1995 182p il maps (Asia-Pacific) $21.95

Grades: 11 12 Adult   **618.92**
1. Physicians 2. Japanese Americans 3. Atomic bomb victims 4. Pediatricians 5. Nagasaki (Japan) -- Bombardment, 1945 6. Hiroshima (Japan) -- Bombardment, 1945

ISBN 0-8223-1658-7

LC 95-6683

The author "describes the incredible destruction of lives and buildings, cooperation from Japanese officials and health care personnel (doctors, nurses, midwives), firsthand reports from survivors, and the medical studies of pregnancies and short- and long-term effects on children. . . . This autobiography is unique in the history of this genre." Choice

Includes bibliographical references

620   Engineering and allied operations

Berlow, Lawrence H.

★ The **reference** guide to famous engineering landmarks of the world; bridges, tunnels, dams, roads, and other structures. Oryx Press 1997 250p il $73.95

Grades: 11 12 Adult   **620**
1. Engineering -- History

ISBN 0-89774-966-9

LC 97-36051

"The main section is an alphabetically arranged, double-column compendium of facts and histories of 600 structures. The format of each entry begins with the structure's location and date of construction. Size is often given, including metric, and the basic facts of the construction are provided. . . . A biography section provides background on 52 significant engineers or designers. A chronology section begins with the oldest surviving dam in the world (in Egypt) and continues to 2010, when a monster skyscraper, Millennium Tower, will be completed in Tokyo." Booklist

Petroski, Henry, 1942-

To forgive design; understanding failure. Henry Petroski. Belknap Press of Harvard University Press 2012 xii, 410 p.p ill.

Grades: 11 12 Adult **620**
1. Design 2. Engineering 3. Structural failures 4. System failures (Engineering)
ISBN 0674065840; 9780674065840

LC 2011044194

This book, by Henry Petroski, "looks not only at how people contribute to the failure of engineering designs but also at how analyzing those failures can improve subsequent models. He considers many different types of failures, from several infamous bridge collapses to carefully designed intentional failures, which are engineered specifically to prevent greater failures." (Library Journal)

"Even the layman will find Petroski's study to be accessible, informative, and interesting." Pub Wkly

Includes bibliographical references and index.

Szumski, Bonnie

Careers in engineering; Bonnie Szumski. ReferencePoint Press, Inc. 2015 80 p. color illustrations (Exploring careers) (hardback) $28.95

Grades: 9 10 11 12 **620**
1. Engineers 2. Engineering 3. Vocational guidance
ISBN 1601526768; 9781601526762

LC 2013048093

Author Bonnie Szumski's book on engineering is part of a series in which books " take a field or industry-fashion, for example-and break down several different jobs in that area. Each job has its own chapter that describes what the work entails, the education requirements, and an estimated salary range. Most importantly, though, the text includes quotes from and interviews with real people about their jobs, as well as useful details about opportunities for growth in that position." (School Library Journal)

"These three resources develop awareness of some career possibilities within the broad categories. They contain much of the same material for jobs as the Occupations Outlook Handbook produced by the U.S. Department of Labor, but they are much more readable for students. . . . The career profiles inform the reader about the training required, future outlook for career opportunities, and salaries, as well as some of the expected tasks for a specific career. The small size and large print may well encourage students who are not willing to tackle a large resource containing multiple career fields." VOYA

Includes bibliographical references and index
Other titles in this series are:
Careers in Biotechnology (2014)
Careers in Health Care (2014)

620.1 Engineering mechanics and materials

Freinkel, Susan

Plastic; a toxic love story. Houghton Mifflin Harcourt 2011 324p $27

Grades: 11 12 Adult **620.1**
1. Plastics
ISBN 978-0-547-15240-0

LC 2010-43019

"At first a godsend, [plastic] reduced dependence on shrinking natural resources, such as the shell of the hawksbill turtle (combs) or elephants' ivory (billiard balls and piano keys.) Ultimately it democratized materialism, making everything available to everybody, cheaply. Now, the partner we've found in plastic 'can rightly inspire both our deepest admiration and our strongest disgust.' To describe its history, wonders and dangers, journalist Freinkel reviews eight products: the comb, the chair, the Frisbee, the IV bag, the disposable lighter, the grocery bag, the soda bottle and the credit card. You will not look casually at any of them again." Cleveland Plain Dealer

Includes bibliographical references

621 Applied physics

Alley, Richard B., 1957-

Earth; the operators' manual. W.W. Norton 2011 479p il $27.95

Grades: 11 12 Adult **621**
1. Energy development 2. Renewable energy resources 3. Greenhouse effect
ISBN 978-0-393-08109-1

LC 2010-54016

The author "presents a primer on combatting global warming. The book begins with a history of how fuel—from trees, whale oil, and petroleum—has been instrumental to civilization and how we tend to exhaust our sources. He goes on to explain how scientists study climate change and why the evidence is convincing, and ends with a call to action and an overview of possible solutions. . . . This optimistic book ought to convince even the most obstinate climate-change denier." Publ Wkly

Includes bibliographical references

621.3 Electrical, magnetic, optical, communications, computer engineering; electronics, lighting

Swanson, Jennifer

Amazing feats of electrical engineering; Jennifer Swanson. Essential Library 2015 112 p. $35.64 **621.3**
1. Electrical engineering 2. Electricity
ISBN 1624034284; 9781624034282

LC 2014932576

This book by Jennifer Swanson "examines amazing feats of electrical engineering. Engaging text explores the global positioning system, solar power plants, and self-driving cars. It also examines the engineers who made these projects a reality and traces the history of the discipline. Relevant sidebars, stunning photos, and a glossary aid readers' understanding of the topic. A hands-on project and career-planning chart give readers a sense of what it takes to become an engineer." (Publisher's note)

Includes bibliographical references (pages 104-109) and index

Yount, Lisa

Nikola Tesla; harnessing electricity. by Lisa Yount. Chelsea House 2012 xviii, 128 p.p col. ill. (Trailblazers in science and technology) (library) $35

Grades: 7 8 9 10 11 12　　　　　　621.3

1. Electricity 2. Tesla, Nikola, 1856-1943 3. Inventors -- United States -- Biography 4. Electrical engineers -- United States -- Biography

ISBN 1604136707; 9781604136708

LC 2010052627

This book by Lisa Yount is part of the Trailblazers in Science and Technology series and looks at Nikola Tesla. He "saw his fortunes reverse as many times." He "drew the attention of businessman George Westinghouse with his alternating current (AC), a method of delivering electricity more efficiently and over greater distances than Edison's direct current (DC). With Westinghouse's support, Tesla's method soon became dominant in the industry." (Publisher's note)

Includes bibliographical references and index.

621.38　Electronics, communications engineering

Gregory, Josh

From butterfly wings to display technology; by Josh Gregory. Cherry Lake Publishing 2014 32 p. color illustrations (Innovations from Nature) (lib. bdg.) $28.50

Grades: 6 7 8 9 10　　　　　　621.38

1. Biomimicry 2. Inventions 3. Butterflies 4. Biomimicry 5. Inventions 6. Flat panel displays

ISBN 1624317545; 9781624317545; 9781624317606

LC 2013030377

This book, by Josh Gregory, part of the Innovations from Nature series, "explores how researchers take ideas from plants and animals and turn them into projects with practical applications. . . . [It] explains the concept of structural color, such as the iridescent colors formed by the ridged scales on a butterfly's wings. This concept has led to the development of IMOD display screens for electronic devices." (Booklist)

"These creative books use a pleasantly unusual angle to show how aspects of nature can inspire scientists and engineers. For instance, some scientists, inspired by the way a gecko's feet allow it to stick to surfaces, are attempting to create an adhesive tape using the structure of the lizard's foot. High-resolution photographs and a dark black and purple layout give the books a slick, stylish look, while the narrative is both fascinating and informative. Intriguing additions to science collections." SLJ

Includes bibliographical references and index

Other titles in the series include:

From African Plants to Vaccine Preservation (2014)
From Bats to Radar (2013)

From Birds to Aircraft (2013)
From Cats' Eyes to Reflectors (2013)
From Gecko Feet to Adhesive Tape (2014)
From Kingfishers to Bullet Trains (2013)
From Locusts to Automobile Anti-Collision Systems (2013)
From Sharks to Swimsuits (2013)
From Termite Den to Office Building (2014)
From Thistle Burrs to Velcro (2013)
From Woodpeckers to Helmets (2013)

621.381　Electronics

Electronics; edited by Sherman Hollar. Britannica Educational Pub. in association with Rosen Educational Services 2012 80 p. (Introduction to physics) (library binding) $31.70

Grades: 7 8 9 10 11 12　　　　　　621.381

1. Electronics

ISBN 9781615306640; 1615306641

LC 2011017100

This book, edited by Sherman Hollar, is part of the Introduction to Physics series. It "examines various components, such as electron tubes and semiconductors, that have been essential to electronics over the years, as well as the history of the field in general and its applications in everyday life." (Publisher's note)

Includes bibliographical references and index

Platt, Charles

Encyclopedia of electronic components; Charles Platt. Maker Media 2013 296 p color illustrations pbk $24.99

Grades: 11 12 Adult　　　　　　621.381

1. Electric apparatus and appliances

ISBN 9781449333898

LC 2013434096

"This first book of a three-volume set includes key information on electronics parts . . . . complete with photographs, schematics, and diagrams." Publisher's note

Includes index.

Schultz, Mitchel E.

★ **Grob's** basic electronics; 11th ed.; McGraw-Hill 2011 xxvi, 1206p il $155.31

Grades: 11 12 Adult　　　　　　621.381

1. Electricity 2. Electronics

ISBN 978-0-07-351085-9; 0-07-351085-8

LC 2010-8273

First published 1959 under the authorship of Bernard Grob. Periodically revised

An introductory text on the fundamentals of electricity and electronics for technicians in radio, television, and industrial electronics.

Includes glossary

621.384 Radio and radar

Sequeira, Michele
Cell phone science; what happens when you call and why. [by] Michele Sequeira, Michael Westphal. University of New Mexico Press 2010 174p il (Barbara Guth worlds of wonder science series for young readers) $24.95

Grades: 6 7 8 9 **621.384**
1. Cellular telephones 2. Wireless communication systems
ISBN 978-0-8263-4968-2; 0-8263-4968-4
LC 2010028600

"The book sets out to help readers understand the complex science behind . . . [cell phones]. . . . The book features clear explanations, easy-to-read text, and colorful photographs and illustrations on almost every page. Boxed areas and information in the margins supplement the text. Students interested in learning the story of the science behind their cell phone will be well rewarded with this title." SLJ

Includes glossary and bibliographical references

621.388 Television

Grabowski, John
Television. Lucent Books 2011 112p il (Technology 360) $33.45

Grades: 7 8 9 10 **621.388**
1. Television
ISBN 978-1-4205-0169-8; 1-4205-0169-0
LC 2010033525

This book offers "clean design with clear explanations of sometimes-complicated scientific subjects. . . . This brings the information [about television] up to date with flat screens and 3-D. . . . A strong [title] for report writers and students with a serious interest in technology and its inventions." Booklist

Includes bibliographical references

621.46 Electric and related motors

Gabrielson, Curt
Kinetic contraptions; build a hovercraft, airboat, and more with a hobby motor. Chicago Review Press 2010 176p il pa $16.95

Grades: 7 8 9 10 **621.46**
1. Airplanes -- Models 2. Motorboats -- Models 3. Automobiles -- Models
ISBN 978-1-55652-957-3; 1-55652-957-0
LC 2009-25695

The author "describes projects intended to foster in students a passion for electrical experimentation as they construct more than 20 motor-powered devices. With sections dedicated to creating machines that run on land, water, and air, as well as spinning machines (such as a snow globe) and bizarre machines (such as a bubble maker), the book has projects designed to appeal to everyone." Education Digest

621.48 Nuclear engineering

Mahaffey, James A.
Fusion; James A. Mahaffey. Facts on File 2012 x, 142 p.p (ebook) $45.00; (hardcover) $45.00

Grades: 7 8 9 10 11 12 **621.48**
1. Sun 2. Nuclear fusion 3. Big bang theory 4. Nuclear reactors 5. Fusion -- Popular works
ISBN 9781438138435; 0816076537; 9780816076536
LC 2011012505

This book, by author James A. Mahaffey, "deliver[s] complex information including background on the theories, applications, devices, and future of fusion. [Topics include] . . . hydrogen fusion in the Sun . . . the big bang nucleosynthesis . . . [and] the International Tokamak Experimental Reactor and the Demonstration Power Plant." (School Library Journal)

Includes bibliographical references and index.

622 Mining and related operations

Reece, Erik
★ Lost mountain; a year in the vanishing wilderness: radical strip mining, and the devastation of Appalachia. foreword by Wendell Berry; photographs by John J. Cox. Riverhead Books 2006 250p il $24.95; pa $14

Grades: 11 12 Adult **622**
1. Coal mines and mining 2. Human influence on nature 3. Appalachian region
ISBN 1-59448-908-4; 1-59448-236-5 pa
LC 2005-52921

The author explores the effects of strip mining on the landscape of Eastern Kentucky.

Reece "has written an impassioned account of a business rife with industrial greed, devious corporate ownership and unenforced environmental laws. It's also a heartrending account of the rural residents whose lives are being ruined by strip-mining's relentless, almost unfettered, encroachment." Publ Wkly

Includes bibliographical references

623.4 Ordnance

Reinhardt, Hank
The book of swords. Baen Pub. Enterprises 2009 235p il $35; pa $20

Grades: 11 12 Adult **623.4**
1. Swords -- History 2. Weapons -- History
ISBN 978-1-439-13281-4; 978-1-439-13282-1 pa
LC 2009-18226

"Drawing on information from grave excavations, illustrations of battle scenes, and many classical and medieval literary sources, this book discusses how contemporaries showed swords were used." Publisher's note

Includes bibliographical references

Sheinkin, Steve

★ **Bomb**; the race to build and steal the world's most dangerous weapon. Steve Sheinkin. Roaring Brook Press 2012 266 p. ill. (hc) $19.99

Grades: 5 6 7 8 9 10 11 12 Adult   **623.4**

1. Nuclear warfare 2. Nuclear weapons 3. World War, 1914-1918 -- Chemical warfare 4. Atomic bomb -- History 5. Operation Freshman, 1942 6. Atomic bomb -- Germany -- History 7. World War, 1939-1945 -- Secret service -- Soviet Union 8. World War, 1939-1945 -- Secret service -- Great Britain 9. World War, 1939-1945 -- Commando operations -- Norway -- Vemork

ISBN 1596434872; 9781596434875

LC 2011044096

John Newbery Honor Book (2013)

Robert F. Sibert Informational Book Medal (2013)

YALSA Award for Excellence in Nonfiction for Young Adults (2013)

Author Steve Sheinkin's "story unfolds in three parts, covering American attempts to build the [atomic] bomb, how the Soviets tried to steal American designs and how the Americans tried to keep the Germans from building a bomb. It was the eve of World War II, and the fate of the world was at stake . . . all along the way spies in the United States were feeding sensitive information to the KGB." (Kirkus Reviews)

Includes bibliographical references (p. [243]-259) and index

623.88   Seamanship

Budworth, Geoffrey

A **handbook** of knots and knot tying; over 200 techniques with step-by-step photographs. Geoffrey Budworth. Southwater 2011 256 p. col. ill. $18.99

Grades: 11 12 Adult   **623.88**

1. Knots and splices

ISBN 9781780191164; 1780191162

This book, by Geoffrey Budworth, shows "how to tie over 200 essential knots, including bends, hitches, bindings, loops, mats, plaits, rings and slings, [and has] a key to usage from angling and fishing, boating and sailing, caving and climbing, general purpose and outdoor pursuits, all shown in 1200 clear step-by-step photographs." (Publisher's note)

Includes bibliographical references and index

624   Civil engineering

Carmichael, L.E.

Amazing Feats of Civil Engineering; by L.E. Carmichael. Essential Library 2015 112 p. $35.64

624

1. Civil engineering 2. Structural engineering

ISBN 1624034276; 9781624034275

LC 2014932575

This book by L.E. Carmichael "examines amazing feats of civil engineering. Engaging text explores massive bridges, the world's tallest skyscraper, and the Panama Canal. It also examines the engineers who made these projects a real-

ity and traces the history of the discipline. Relevant sidebars, stunning photos, and a glossary aid readers' understanding of the topic. A hands-on project and career-planning chart give readers a sense of what it takes to become an engineer." (Publisher's note)

Includes bibliographical references (pages 104-109) and index

Macaulay, David

Underground. Houghton Mifflin 1976 109p il hardcover o.p. pa $9.95

Grades: 5 6 7 8 9   **624**

1. Subways 2. Building 3. Sewerage 4. Electric lines 5. Public utilities 6. Civil engineering

ISBN 0-395-24739-X; 0-395-34065-9 pa

"Introduced by a visual index—a bird's eye view of a busy, hypothetical intersection with colored indicators marking the specific locations analyzed in subsequent pages—detailed illustrations are combined with a clear, precise narrative to make the subject comprehenssible and fascinating." Horn Book

Includes glossary

625.2   Railroad rolling stock

McDonnell, Greg

Locomotives; the modern diesel & electric reference. Boston Mills Press 2008 240p il $49.95; pa $29.95

Grades: 11 12 Adult   **625.2**

1. Locomotives

ISBN 978-1-55046-493-1; 978-1-55407-896-7 pa

LC 2009417490

First published 2002 by Kalmbach Publishing with title: Field guide to modern diesel locomotives

This book "covers all mainline models built for North American railroads from the mid-1970s to today, from EMD Dash 2s and GE Dash 7s to the latest 70 Series and Evolution Series models, as well as Green Goats, Gensets and mainline passenger electric-powered locomotives." Publisher's note

628   Sanitary engineering

Hand, Carol

Amazing feats of environmental engineering; Carol Hand. Essential Library 2015 112 p. $35.64

628

1. Sanitary engineering 2. Environmental science

ISBN 1624034292; 9781624034299

LC 2014932584

This book by author Carol Hand "examines amazing feats of environmental engineering. Engaging text explores projects that supply water to impoverished areas, structures in the Netherlands that hold back the Atlantic Ocean, and the cleanup of contaminated areas. It also examines the engineers who made these projects a reality and traces the history of the discipline. Relevant sidebars, stunning pho-

tos, and a glossary aid readers' understanding of the topic."
(Publisher's note)

Includes bibliographical references and index

628.4 Waste technology, public toilets, street cleaning

Gardner, Robert

Recycle; green science projects for a sustainable planet. Enslow Publishers 2011 128p il (Team Green science projects) lib bdg $31.93

Grades: 6 7 8 9 10   **628.4**

1. Recycling 2. Science projects 3. Science -- Experiments

ISBN 978-0-7660-3648-2; 0-7660-3648-0

      LC 2009-37903

This describes science projects about recycling, including experiments and information about plastics, solid waste and decomposition, composting, aluminum, and paper.

"Gardner provides plenty of information, well-designed experiments, and demonstrations, and then shares brief science-fair ideas. . . . Experiments and demonstrations are presented with clear step-by-step instructions and occasional illustrations and represent a wide range of complexity." SLJ

Includes glossary and bibliographical references

Humes, Edward

Garbology; our dirty love affair with trash. Edward Humes. Avery 2012 277 p.

Grades: Adult   **628.4**

1. Pollution 2. Consumption (Economics) 3. United States -- Social life and customs 4. Refuse and refuse disposal -- United States 5. Salvage (Waste, etc.) -- China 6. Environmental engineering -- United States

ISBN 1583334343; 9781583334348

      LC 2012001701

In this book, "Edward Humes . . . [makes the case] that the United States—the world's largest generator of trash—will soon confront a new crisis of garbage. . . . Humes spotlights a turning point in the history of American garbage: the postwar rise of consumer culture, birthed by a new generation of advertisers who saw their mission in life as persuading Americans to throw away perfectly good things in order to buy bigger, better replacements. . . . Humes argues that an economy whose health depends on how much disposable stuff people buy is driving us toward a precipice. Making and trashing all those things will generate economic activity and jobs, to be sure, but the waste-driven model of mass consumption also eats up tremendous amounts of increasingly scarce resources." (Bookforum)

Includes bibliographical references and index

Maczulak, Anne E.

Waste treatment; reducing global waste. [by] Anne Maczulak. Facts on File 2010 198p il (Green technology) $40

Grades: 9 10 11 12   **628.4**

1. Recycling 2. Waste minimization 3. Refuse and

refuse disposal

ISBN 978-0-8160-7204-0; 0-8160-7204-3

      LC 2008-45054

"Divided into eight chapters, this volume explains the various means to treat and eliminate waste. Emphasizing that waste management is a global issue, chapters explore incineration, vitrification, solidification and stabilization, compaction, and wastewater treatment. Each chapter begins with a concise overview introducing the main points and ends with a conclusion summarizing those items. . . . A useful resource and reference book for advanced science students." SLJ

Includes glossary and bibliographical references

628.5 Pollution control technology and industrial sanitation engineering

Maczulak, Anne E.

Cleaning up the environment; hazardous waste technology. [by] Anne Maczulak. Facts on File 2010 226p il (Green technology) $40

Grades: 9 10 11 12   **628.5**

1. Hazardous waste sites 2. Environmental protection

ISBN 978-0-8160-7198-2; 0-8160-7198-5

      LC 2008-42367

"This comprehensive and somewhat technical discussion of the various methods used for the cleanup of environmental waste will be a valuable addition to science units. . . . . . This is a vitally important subject not often discussed in environmental literature and is a welcome addition for use in classroom studies and for those considering a career in the field." SLJ

Includes glossary and bibliographical references

New thinking about pollution; edited by Robert Curley. Britannica Educational Pub. in association with Rosen Educational Services 2010 269p il map (21st century science) lib bdg $45

Grades: 9 10 11 12   **628.5**

1. Pollution

ISBN 978-1-61530-135-5

      LC 2010-9095

This "volume explores the root causes of pollution, as well as the local and global responses and constantly emerging technologies that allow governments and ordinary citizens to cope with an increasingly toxic environment and landscape." Publisher's note

Includes bibliographical references

628.9 Other branches of sanitary and municipal engineering

★ **Fire** fighters; stories of survival from the front lines of firefighting. edited by Clint Willis. Thunder's Mouth Press 2002 351p il pa $17.95

Grades: 11 12 Adult   **628.9**

1. Fire fighting

ISBN 1-56025-402-5

      LC 2002-18147

This is a collection of 21 accounts of fighting fires in urban, rural, and forest environments, previously published in books and magazines between 1963 and 2001, by such authors as Edward Abbey, Norman Maclean, Stephen Pyne, and Studs Terkel

"Mere display guarantees this collection's circulation." Booklist

Includes bibliographical references

629   Other branches of engineering

Van Pelt, Michel

Rocketing into the future; the history and technology of rocket planes. Michel Van Pelt. Springer 2012 384 p. (softcover: alk. paper) $44.95

Grades: 11 12 Adult   **629**
1. Rocket planes
ISBN 1461431999; 9781461431992

LC 2012932254

In this book, Michel Van Pelt "describes the technology, history, and future of rocket planes . . . . He recounts the history of rocket airplanes, from the early pioneers who attached simple rockets onto their wooden glider airplanes to the modern world of high-tech research vehicles. The author visits museums where rare examples of early rocket planes are kept and modern laboratories where future spaceplanes are being developed." (Publisher's note)

"There are good descriptions of German, Russian, and British rocket planes, and in-depth coverage of American rocket planes. . . . The book is well written, well organized, and well illustrated." Choice

629.1   Aerospace engineering

Branson, Richard

Reach for the skies; ballooning, birdmen, and blasting into space. Current 2011 343p il $26.95

Grades: 11 12 Adult   **629.1**
1. Aeronautics -- History
ISBN 978-1-61723-003-5

LC 2010-52340

"The Virgin Atlantic Airlines founder and billionaire adventurer celebrates the exploits of airborne daredevils—his own prominently among them—in this lively history of aviation pioneers. Branson ranges from the Montgolfier brothers' 1783 invention of the hot-air balloon to today's nascent space tourism industry . . . . highlighting men and women who risked their money and lives to advance aerial technology or just put on a good show. It's a colorful assemblage of engineers, test pilots, barnstormers, and fighter aces. . . . Branson's enthusiasm for avant-garde flight and his firsthand understanding of its rigors make this a rousing—sometimes even elevating—read." Publ Wkly

Includes bibliographical references

Hickam, Homer H.

★ **Rocket** boys; a memoir. [by] Homer H. Hickam, Jr. Delacorte Press 1998 368p $25.95; pa $14

Grades: 7 8 9 10 11 12 Adult   **629.1**
1. Authors 2. Novelists 3. Aerospace engineers 4. Memoirists 5. West Virginia 6. Authors, American 7. Writers on science
ISBN 0-385-33320-X; 0-385-33321-8 pa

LC 98-19304

"Even if Hickam stretched the strict truth to metamorphose his memories into Stand By Me-like material for Hollywood . . . the embellishing only converts what is a good story into an absorbing, rapidly readable one that is unsentimental but artful about adolescence, high school, and family life." Booklist

Smibert, Angie

Amazing Feats of Aerospace Engineering; Angie Smibert. Essential Library 2015 112 p. illustrations (chiefly color) $35.64

Grades: 7 8 9 10   **629.1**
1. Aeronautics 2. Aerospace engineering
ISBN 162403425X; 9781624034251

LC 2014932565

This book by Angi Smibert "examines amazing feats of aerospace engineering. Engaging text explores the Saturn V moon rocket, the International Space Station, and the world's largest passenger jet. It also examines the engineers who made these projects a reality and traces the history of the discipline. Relevant sidebars, stunning photos, and a glossary aid readers' understanding of the topic. A hands-on project and career-planning chart give readers a sense of what it takes to become an engineer." (Publisher's note)

"These substantial books begin with a brief introduction and history, then validate the "Amazing Feats" label with remarkable projects including the International Space Station, a thought-controlled bionic leg, the Canadian Confederation Bridge, and the driverless car; challenges and problem-solving are emphasized. Illustrations include both color photos and diagrams. Career advice, facts, and a hands-on project are appended." Horn Book

Includes bibliographical references (pages 104-109) and index

Other titles in the series are:
Amazing Feats of Biological Engineering (2014)
Amazing Feats of Civil Engineering (2014)
Amazing Feats of Electrical Engineering (2014)
Amazing Feats of Environmental Engineering (2014)
Amazing Feats of Mechanical Engineering (2014)
Aerospace Engineering

629.13   Aeronautics

Abrams, Michael

★ **Birdmen,** batmen, and skyflyers; wingsuits and the pioneers who flew in them, fell in them and perfected them. Harmony Books 2006 304p il $23.95; pa $13.95

Grades: 11 12 Adult   **629.13**
1. Aeronautics -- History
ISBN 1-4000-5491-5; 978-1-4000-5491-6; 1-4000-5492-3 pa; 1-978-1-4000-5492-3 pa; 1-978-1-4000-5492 pa

LC 2005-32409

"From ancient myths through China 'sometime in the sixth century A.D.' to present-day skydivers, Abrams chronicles the men and their various models of wings that have taken to the air in hope of flying like a bird. The tales of flight range from the silly and mysterious to the inspiring and unbelievable." Publ Wkly

Includes bibliographical references

Dick, Ron

The **early** years; [by] Ron Dick and Dan Patterson. Firefly Books 2003 240p il (Aviation century) $39.95

Grades: 11 12 Adult 629.13

1. Aeronautics -- History

ISBN 978-1-55046-407-8; 1-55046-407-8

"Dick's text carries the reader from the antics of the wing walkers and aerobatic pilots of the day to the sheer persistence of such distance flyers as Charles Lindbergh and the crew of the Southern Cross. The vying aircraft in these contests are captured in all of their antiquated beauty." Libr J

Includes bibliographical references

The **golden** age; [by] Ron Dick and Dan Patterson. Boston Mills Press 2004 287p il (Aviation century) $39.95

Grades: 11 12 Adult 629.13

1. Aeronautics -- History

ISBN 1-55046-409-4; 978-1-55046-409-2

LC 2005-298220

This book "chronicles the history of aviation from 1919 to 1939. . . . Any readers interested in the history of flying will treasure this profusely illustrated book." Booklist

Includes bibliographical references

War & peace in the air; [by] Ron Dick and Dan Patterson. Boston Mills Press 2006 352p il (Aviation century) $49.95

Grades: 11 12 Adult 629.13

1. Aeronautics -- History

ISBN 978-1-55046-430-6; 1-55046-430-2

This book "explores the influence of aviation in the major wars and minor conflicts since World War II. The authors also examine the dangers of flight, including airborne disasters, accident investigations and threats from terrorism, and speculate on the myriad ways in which aviation will change in the near and far future." Publisher's note

Includes bibliographical references

Wings of change. Boston Mills 2005 288p il (Aviation century) $39.95

Grades: 11 12 Adult 629.13

1. Aeronautics -- History

ISBN 978-1-55046-428-3; 1-55046-428-0

"This book takes an eclectic look at several strands of aviation history. Chapter 1 focuses on commercial airlines since 1945, but includes material on the business aviation sector as well as bush flying and the use of aircraft in fighting wildfires. The second chapter considers personal and private flying, but begins coverage in the 1930s and proceeds to the present, and includes the sport of soaring. Chapter 3 treats lighter-than-air subjects, from 18th-century hot-air balloons through current balloon meets, and incorporates a discussion of the dirigible era of the 1920s-30s. In chapter 4, autogiros and helicopters are analyzed through the 20th century, with coverage of both civil and military developments. Chapter 5 looks at high-speed research, primarily as a series of biographical sketches." Choice

Includes bibliographical references

Haynsworth, Leslie

★ **Amelia** Earhart's daughters; the wild and glorious story of American women aviators from World War II to the dawn of the space age. {by} Leslie Haynsworth and David Toomey. Morrow 1998 322p il hardcover o.p. pa $14

Grades: 11 12 Adult 629.13

1. Air pilots 2. Women air pilots 3. Women astronauts 4. Cosmetics industry executives

ISBN 0-380-72984-9 pa

LC 98-8727

This "study of American women aviators concentrates almost exclusively on the WASPs of World War II and the would-be female astronauts of the early 1960s." Booklist

Includes bibliographical references

Marshall, David

★ **Wild** about flying! dreamers, doers, and daredevils. [by] David Marshall & Bruce Harris. Firefly Books 2003 232p il $35

Grades: 9 10 11 12 629.13

1. Aeronautics -- History

ISBN 1-55297-849-4

LC 2004-297806

This is a "history of aviation told through brief biographies of the most central people in the saga of flight. . . . With its unique focus and accurate, understandable technical data, this volume is a great addition to YA collections." SLJ

Smithsonian atlas of world aviation; charting the history of flight from the first balloons to today's most advanced aircraft. [compiled by] Dana Bell. HarperCollins 2008 230p il map $39.95

Grades: 9 10 11 12 Adult 629.13

1. Reference books 2. Historical atlases 3. Aeronautics -- History

ISBN 978-0-06-125144-3; 0-06-125144-5

LC 2007-47574

"Bell's writing . . . adds immeasurably to the value of this atlas: it is articulate, clear, informative, and, above all, accurate." SLJ

Includes bibliographical references

Tobin, James

To conquer the air; the Wright Brothers and the great race for flight. Free Press 2003 433p il hardcover o.p. pa $16

Grades: 11 12 Adult 629.13

1. Inventors 2. Aeronautics -- History 3. Aircraft industry executives

ISBN 0-684-85688-3; 0-7432-5536-4 pa

LC 2002-44778

"This book represents the most forceful argument to date for the brothers' monumental legacy to the history of flight.

. . . This lucidly written and exhaustively researched study is recommended for all aviation collections and all libraries." Libr J

Includes bibliographical references

629.130   Biography of flight

Brown, Jeremy K.

Amelia Earhart; by Jeremy K. Brown. Chelsea House 2011 132p ill. (hardcover: acid-free paper) $35.00

Grades: 6 7 8 9   **629.130**
  1. Biography 2. Women air pilots 3. Air pilots --
  United States -- Biography
  ISBN 9781604139105

                                                       LC 2011000037

This book chronicles the life of female aviator Amelia Earhart. "From her . . . beginnings in a small Kansas town to her . . . solo flight across the Atlantic, Earhart defied expectations and rose to become the most famous female pilot of all time. Despite the restrictions placed on women of her era, she broke through barriers and refused to allow society to label her. As a result, she made history through her daring flights all over the world. In 1937, she disappeared without a trace while on a solo flight around the world." (Kids' Catalog Web)

Includes bibliographical references (p. 124-125) and index

629.133   Aircraft types

Aircraft; the definitive visual history. by DK Publishing. DK Publishing 2013 320 p. ill. $40

Grades: 9 10 11 12 Adult   **629.133**
  1. Airplanes 2. Airplanes -- History
  ISBN 9781465402127; 1465402128

                                                       LC 2012277485

"From the first prototypes of flying machines to today's supersonic jets, the history and roles of aircraft are explored in this . . . illustrated guide. . . . Planes are divided equally between military and commercial aircraft, and iconic aircraft of each era, such as the Supermarine Spitfire and Concorde, are showcased in . . . photographed spreads with 'virtual tours' that reveal the anatomy of these legendary planes." (Publisher's note)

"[T]he history and roles of aircraft are explored in this . . . illustrated guide. . . . Planes are divided equally between military and commercial aircraft, and iconic aircraft of each era, such as the Supermarine Spitfire and Concorde, are showcased in . . . photographed spreads with 'virtual tours' that reveal the anatomy of these legendary planes." Publisher's note

Chiles, James R.

The **god** machine; from boomerangs to black hawks, the story of the helicopter. Bantam Dell 2007 354p il hardcover o.p. pa $16

Grades: 11 12 Adult   **629.133**
  1. Helicopters
  ISBN 978-0-553-80447-8; 978-0-553-38352-2 pa

                                                       LC 2007-28575

This "is an engaging blend of pop science and pop culture." Publ Wkly

Includes bibliographical references

629.2   Motor land vehicles, cycles

Sobey, Ed

A **field** guide to automotive technology. Chicago Review Press 2008 207p il pa $14.95

Grades: 11 12 Adult   **629.2**
  1. Mechanics 2. Automobiles
  ISBN 978-1-55652-812-5

                                                       LC 2008046620

The author "helps readers identify items on, inside, and under the car, as well as under the hood, and explains what they do and why. He also painlessly reviews a few principles of science and mechanics here and there. The 130 entries range from basic to complex, from bumper and windshield to differential and constant velocity joint boot. . . . Most of the material concerns passenger vehicles, but there are also sections on off-road vehicles, motorcycles, buses, and human-powered conveyances." SLJ

629.22   Types of vehicles

Kettlewell, Caroline

★ **Electric** dreams; one unlikely team of kids and the race to build the car of their dreams. Carroll & Graf 2004 290p hardcover o.p. pa $14.95

Grades: 9 10 11 12   **629.22**
  1. Electric automobiles
  ISBN 0-7867-1271-6; 0-7867-1485-9 pa

"The word 'inspirational' is applied to too many books, but it comfortably fits this one, with its genuinely likable cast of unlikely achievers. This is essential reading for any serious environmentalist, as it makes the case that EVs might play even in the conservative South." Publ Wkly

Mackay, Jenny

Electric cars. Lucent Books 2011 104p il (Technology 360) $33.45

Grades: 7 8 9 10   **629.22**
  1. Electric automobiles
  ISBN 978-1-4205-0612-9; 1-4205-0612-9

                                                       LC 2011016597

This book describes the technology of electric cars.

Includes bibliographical references

629.28   Tests, driving, maintenance, repair

Downs, Todd

★ The **bicycling** guide to complete bicycle maintenance & repair; for road & mountain bikes.

Expanded and rev. 6th ed.; Rodale 2010 395p il pa $23.99

Grades: 11 12 Adult   **629.28**

1. Bicycles -- Maintenance and repair

ISBN 978-1-60529-487-2; 1-60529-487-X

LC 2010-26471

First published 1986 with title: Bicycling magazine's Complete guide to bicycle maintenance and repair

This illustrated guide includes step-by-step instructions for major and minor repairs and maintenance for many types of bicycles.

Ramsey, Dan

Teach yourself visually car care & maintenance; by Dan Ramsey and Judy Ramsey. Visual / Wiley 2009 210p il (Visual read less, learn more) pa $24.95

Grades: 11 12 Adult   **629.28**

1. Automobiles -- Maintenance and repair

ISBN 978-0-470-37727-7

LC 2009-920042

This book covers "how to change oil and other fluids; rotate tires; replace fuel pumps, air filters, and batteries; and . . . more." Publisher's note

Includes glossary

Stalder, Erika

In the driver's seat; a girl's guide to her first car. Zest Books 2009 127p il pa $14.95

Grades: 9 10 11 12   **629.28**

1. Automobiles -- Maintenance and repair

ISBN 978-0-9800732-4-9

LC 2009-933013

"This nifty hot-pink-and-black guide to buying, understanding, maintaining, and styling a first car will be a real help to new drivers, and it is the size and shape of an owner's manual, so it will store nicely in the glove compartment. The tips range from the very basic (how to release the hood latch and prop it open) to diagrams and descriptions of brake rotors and calipers, as well as directions for checking and replacing air filters. Charts of symptoms indicating possible problems and what to do about them are useful." Booklist

629.4 Astronautics

Angelo, Joseph A.

Space technology. Greenwood Press 2003 394p il (Sourcebooks in modern technology) $65

Grades: 9 10 11 12   **629.4**

1. Astronautics 2. Space sciences 3. Outer space -- Exploration

ISBN 1-57356-335-8

LC 2002-75310

"This book is a good source of general information, easily read and understood by most high school students, and will provide plenty of good information for reports and papers." Lib Media Connect

Includes bibliographical references

Carlisle, Rodney P.

Exploring space; rev ed.; Chelsea House 2010 120p il (Discovery and exploration) lib bdg $35

Grades: 7 8 9 10   **629.4**

1. Astronautics 2. Outer space -- Exploration

ISBN 978-1-60413-188-8; 1-60413-188-8

LC 2009-25585

First published 2005 by Facts on File

This describes the history of space exploration, from early astronomers to first steps into space by Germans, Soviets, and Americans, space flight to the Moon, space stations, space shuttles, unmanned space exploration, the Hubble space telescope, radio telescopes, and possible future explorations

Includes glossary and bibliographical references

Evans, Kimberly Masters

Space exploration; triumphs and tragedies. [by] Kim Masters Evans. 2010 ed; Gale, Cengage Learning 2011 184p il map (Information Plus reference series) pa $55

Grades: 9 10 11 12   **629.4**

1. Outer space -- Exploration

ISBN 978-1-4144-4122-1

This book is a brief history of space exploration, with chapters on NASA, the space shuttle program, and the international space station.

Hardesty, Von

Epic rivalry; the inside story of the Soviet and American space race. [by] Von Hardesty and Gene Eisman; foreword by Sergei Khrushchev. National Geographic Society 2007 275p il map $28; pa $16.95

Grades: 11 12 Adult   **629.4**

1. Cold war 2. Outer space -- Exploration 3. Astronautics -- Soviet Union 4. Astronautics -- United States

ISBN 978-1-4262-0119-6; 978-1-4262-0321-3 pa

LC 2007-17393

"This is a true saga, full of daring, danger, death, ego conflicts, and triumphs. . . . All readers should love this fabulous and profusely illustrated combined story." Sci Books Films

Includes bibliographical references

Tyson, Neil deGrasse, 1958-

★ **Space** chronicles; facing the ultimate frontier. Neil deGrasse Tyson; edited by Avis Lang. W.W. Norton 2012 364 p. ill. $26.95

Grades: 11 12 Adult   **629.4**

1. Space flight -- Forecasting 2. Astronautics -- United States 3. Astronautics and state -- United States 4. United States. National Aeronautics and Space Administration

ISBN 0393082105; 9780393082104

LC 2011032481

In this book, Neil DeGrasse Tyson "delivers . . . [an] argument for space exploration even in the face of a disastrous economy. In this collection of articles and talks, the author investigates what space travel means to us as a species and, more specifically, what NASA means to America. . . . 'When science does advance, when discovery does unfold . . . ,' he writes, 'they happen as an auxiliary benefit and not as a primary goal of NASA's geopolitical mission statement.'" (Kirkus Reviews)

"Tyson is an articulate popularizer of astrophysics. . . . His writing style, while necessarily a bit technical, is as engaging as his screen presence." LJ

Young, Karen Romano

Space junk; the dangers of polluting earth's orbit. Karen Romano Young. Twenty-First Century Books 2016 64 p. color illustrations (lb: alk. paper) $33.32
  Grades: 7 8 9 10   **629.4**
  1. Space debris 2. Artificial satellites
  ISBN 1467756008; 9781467756006
                                          LC 2015013396
In this book, by Karen Romano Young, readers can " learn about the dangers of space junk collisions, how scientists track them, and how space agencies are working to develop new technologies to clean up the space junk. Along the way, [readers] hear from the scientists who are working to ensure that outer space remains a safe place to travel and explore." (Publisher's note)

"Clearly written and concise, the book lays out the problem without sensationalizing it, while including human-interest details, such as your odds of being stuck by falling space junk (at 'one in several trillion,' decidedly low). Small, well-captioned color photos, helpful diagrams, and interesting sidebars enhance the text. A natural for booktalking to STEM-minded kids, this slender volume belongs in many libraries." Booklist

Includes bibliographical references and index

629.45   Manned space flight

Ackmann, Martha

★ The **Mercury** 13: the untold story of thirteen American women and the dream of space flight. Random House 2003 239p il hardcover o.p. pa $13.95
Grades: 11 12 Adult   **629.45**
  1. Women astronauts 2. Project Mercury
  ISBN 0-375-50744-2; 0-375-75893-3 pa
                                          LC 2002-37118
"Mercury 13 is both an outstanding work of research and an exceptionally readable and well-told story. Readers will gain new perspectives on space, medicine, women, and American culture, and will appreciate the magnitude of what was lost when the women were grounded." SLJ

Includes bibliographical references

Angelo, Joseph A.

Human spaceflight. Facts on File 2007 370p il (Frontiers in space) $39.50
Grades: 11 12 Adult   **629.45**
  1. Astronautics 2. Space flight 3. Space colonies 4. Outer space -- Exploration
  ISBN 0-8160-5775-3; 978-0-8160-5775-7
                                          LC 2006-29488
This book "follows the evolution of space technology from the dawn of the space age to the present day. Chap-

ters include 'The Dream of Human Spaceflight,' 'Living in Space,' 'Space Walks and the Gemini Project,' 'Moonwalks and the Apollo Project,' and 'Space Shuttle.'" Booklist

Includes glossary and bibliographical references

Doeden, Matt

Human travel to the moon and Mars; waste of money or next frontier? Twenty-First Century Books 2011 112p il (USA Today's debate: voices and perspectives) lib bdg $35.93; ebook $26.95
Grades: 9 10 11 12   **629.45**
  1. Outer space -- Exploration 2. Astronautics -- United States
  ISBN 978-0-7613-6436-8 lib bdg; 978-0-7613-8077-1 ebook
                                          LC 2010035644
"This book looks at the costs of crewed missions to Mars and the Moon, as well as the potential payoff; the dangers of space exploration, both physical and psychological; and the potential for human settlement on Mars." Publisher's note

Includes glossary and bibliographical references

French, Francis

★ In the shadow of the moon; a challenging journey to Tranquility, 1965-1969. [by] Francis French and Colin Burgess; with a foreword by Walter Cunningham. University of Nebraska Press 2007 425p il (Outward odyssey) $29.95
Grades: 11 12 Adult   **629.45**
  1. Apollo project 2. Space flight to the moon 3. Astronautics -- Soviet Union 4. Astronautics -- United States
  ISBN 978-0-8032-1128-5; 0-8032-1128-7
                                          LC 2006-103047
"This book will have an important place in the recorded history of space exploration." Sci Books Films

Includes bibliographical references

Jones, Chris

Out of orbit; the true story of how three astronauts found themselves hundreds of miles above the earth with no way home. Chris Jones. Broadway Books 2008 288p ill. (pbk.) $15
Grades: 10 11 12   **629.45**
  1. Astronauts 2. Space flight 3. Space vehicle accidents 4. Risk management 5. International Space Station 6. Columbia (Spacecraft) -- Accidents 7. Manned space flight -- Risk assessment
  ISBN 9780767919913
                                          LC 2007034216
This book takes place after "February 1, 2003, [when] the nation was stunned to watch the shuttle 'Columbia' disintegrate into a blue-green sky. Despite . . . numerous . . . reports, . . . the public remained largely unaware that three men, U.S. astronauts Donald Pettit and Kenneth Bowersox, and Russian flight engineer Nikolai Budarin, remained orbiting Earth. With the launch program suspended indefinitely, these astronauts, who were already near the end of a fourteen-week mission, had suddenly lost their ride home. 'Out of Orbit' is the . . . behind-the-scenes chronicle of the efforts of beleagured Mission Controls in Houston and Moscow,

who worked frantically against the clock to bring their men safely back to Earth." (Publisher's note)

Includes bibliographical references.

Kevles, Bettyann

Almost heaven; the story of women in space. [by] Bettyann Holtzmann Kevles. MIT Press 2006 280p il pa $16.95

Grades: 11 12 Adult **629.45**

1. Women astronauts

ISBN 978-0-262-61213-5; 0-262-61213-5

LC 2006-41945

First published 2003 by Basic Books

This is a "history of the U.S. space program, with special emphasis on, and stories about, the women who have had the courage to venture into space. Each one is special, the book reveals; yet they all share a spirit of adventure and a willingness to put up with hardship in order to fulfill their dream." Sci Books Films

Includes bibliographical references

Pyle, Rod

★ Destination moon; the Apollo missions in the astronauts' own words. HarperCollins Publishers 2005 192p il $24.95; pa $14.95

Grades: 11 12 Adult **629.45**

1. Space flight to the moon 2. Project Apollo

ISBN 0-06-087349-3; 0-06-087350-7 pa

LC 2005-51350

This "survey of the Apollo moon program includes a brief summary of each flight and attempted flight of the great effort, from the fatal fire on Pad 34 in 1967 to the landing of a scientist on the moon in Apollo 17 in 1972. . . . Space collections of all sizes should welcome Pyle's book, and smaller ones will find it invaluable." Booklist

Stone, Tanya Lee

★ Almost astronauts; 13 women who dared to dream. Candlewick Press 2008 133p il $24.99; pa $17.99

Grades: 5 6 7 8 9 10 **629.45**

1. Women astronauts 2. Sex discrimination 3. Project Mercury -- History

ISBN 0-7636-3611-8; 0-7636-4502-8 pa; 978-0-7636-3611-1; 978-0-7636-4502-1 pa

LC 2008-17487

Boston Globe-Horn Book Award honor book: Nonfiction (2009)

This book "explores the little known experiences of 13 brave, inspiring women who dreamed of becoming astronauts in the very early days of NASA's training program and submitted themselves to many of the tests undertaken by their male counterparts, the Mercury 7." Tanya Lee Stone "brings together a variety of primary and secondary sources, including her interviews with some of the women involved, to provide a unique view of the challenges faced by the female pilots of the day." (School Library Journal)

"In 1960, thirteen American women passed the physical exams required to become astronauts as surely as any of the men already involved in NASA's early space flight endeavors, but they were disqualified solely because of their gender. This book is their story. . . . Any girl with an interest in space flight or the history of women's rights will enjoy this account and applaud these courageous pioneers." Voice Youth Advocates

Includes bibliographical references

Wolfe, Tom

The right stuff. Picador 2008 352p pa $16

Grades: 11 12 Adult **629.45**

1. Astronauts 2. Astronautics -- United States

ISBN 0-312-42756-5; 978-0-312-42756-6

First published 1979 by Farrar, Straus & Giroux

This volume chronicles "the handful of adrenaline-junkie military test pilots who became the Mercury astronauts. Their story is juxtaposed against that of Chuck Yeager, the ace of aces pilot who broke the sound barrier but couldn't apply to the space program because he lacked a college degree. . . . A terrific read from beginning to end." Libr J

629.47 Astronautical engineering

Reynolds, David West

Kennedy Space Center; gateway to space. Firefly Books 2006 248p il $40

Grades: 11 12 Adult **629.47**

1. John F. Kennedy Space Center 2. Astronautics -- United States

ISBN 1-55407-039-2; 978-1-55407-039-8

Containing an "overview of the space program from the view of the facilities that launched the missions and the people who made it happen, Reynolds's work is full of elegant descriptions and compelling details that highlight the vast technology and the indomitable human spirit." Voice Youth Advocates

Includes bibliographical references

629.8 Automatic control engineering

Henderson, Harry

Modern robotics; building versatile machines. Chelsea House 2006 xx, 188p il (Milestones in discovery and invention) $35

Grades: 7 8 9 10 11 12 **629.8**

1. Robots

ISBN 0-8160-5745-1

LC 2005-31805

This book presents "biographies of the men and women who were and are the leaders in bringing about this change through research and new technologies." Publisher's note

Includes glossary and bibliographical references

Wallach, Wendell

Moral machines; teaching robots right from wrong. [by] Wendell Wallach and Colin Allen. Oxford University Press 2009 275p il $17.95; $29.95

Grades: 11 12 Adult **629.8**

1. Robots 2. Computers -- Social aspects. 3. Computers

-- Moral and ethical aspects.
ISBN 0199737975; 9780199737970; 978-0-19-537404-9; 0-19-537404-5

LC 2008-11800

This book examines "how one builds moral machines, or how one embeds (human) ethical principles in the decision making of machines that scientists build to do things instead of humans. . . . Written with an abundance of examples and lessons learned, scenarios of incidents that may happen, and elaborate discussions on existing artificial agents on the cutting edge of research/practice, Moral Machines goes beyond what is known as computer ethics into what will soon be called the discipline of machine morality." Choice

630 Agriculture and related technologies

Rothman, Julia
Farm anatomy; the curious parts & pieces of country life. Julia Rothman. Storey Pub. 2011 223 p. col. ill., col. maps
Grades: 7 8 9 10 11 12 **630**
1. Barns 2. Farms 3. Farm life 4. Farm produce 5. Domestic animals 6. Farm life -- Miscellanea 7. Farm life -- Pictorial works
ISBN 1603429816; 9781603429818

LC 2012360929

This book explains the "difference between a weanling and a yearling, or a farrow and a barrow . . . [in this] guide to the curious parts and pieces of rural living. Dissecting everything from tractors and pigs to fences, hay bales, crop rotation patterns, and farm tools, [Julia] Rothman gives a . . . tour of the quirky details of country life. From the shapes of squash varieties to the parts of a goat; from how a barn is constructed to what makes up a beehive, every corner of the barnyard is uncovered and celebrated." (Publisher's note)
Includes bibliographical references (p. 220-222).

631.4 Soil science

Gardner, Robert
Soil; green science projects for a sustainable planet. Enslow Publishers 2011 128p il (Team Green science projects) lib bdg $31.93
Grades: 6 7 8 9 10 **631.4**
1. Soils 2. Science projects 3. Science -- Experiments
ISBN 978-0-7660-3647-5; 0-7660-3647-2
This book offers science experiments that explain the properties of soil, erosion, and methods to conserve soil.
"Gardner provides plenty of information, well-designed experiments, and demonstrations, and then shares brief science-fair ideas. . . . Experiments and demonstrations are presented with clear step-by-step instructions and occasional illustrations and represent a wide range of complexity." SLJ
Includes glossary and bibliographical references

631.5 Cultivation and harvesting

Roberts, Jack L.
Organic agriculture; protecting our food supply or chasing imaginary risks? Twenty-First Century Books 2011 128p il (USA Today's debate: voices and perspectives) lib bdg $35.93; ebook $26.95
Grades: 9 10 11 12 **631.5**
1. Natural foods 2. Organic farming
ISBN 978-0-7613-6434-4 lib bdg; 978-0-7613-8075-7 ebook

LC 2011000188

"This book examines the history of the organic movement. It provides a variety of studies, reporting, and opinions from scientists, farmers, activists, agribusiness leaders, journalists, consumer groups, and ordinary Americans." Publisher's note
Includes glossary and bibliographical references

632 Plant injuries, diseases, pests

Stewart, Amy
Wicked bugs; the louse that conquered Napoleon's army & other diabolical insects. etchings and drawings by Briony Morrow-Cribbs. Algonquin Books of Chapel Hill 2011 271p il $18.95
Grades: 11 12 Adult **632**
1. Mites 2. Ticks 3. Spiders 4. Insect pests
ISBN 978-1-56512-960-3

LC 2011-3629

"Ranging from verdant South American jungles to Manhattan's cold concrete canyons, Stewart amusingly but analytically profiles the baddest bugs around in quick but attention-grabbing snapshots of little creatures that pack a lot of punch. Bed bugs and bookworms, rat fleas and filth flies all come under Stewart's curious gaze as she exposes their evil habits and lethal charms. No alarmist setting out to stoke preexisting phobias, Stewart shares her natural fascination with the insect world to help readers recognize both the threats and the wonders that could be lurking in corner crevices or come wafting in on the next gentle breeze." Booklist
Includes bibliographical references

Waldbauer, Gilbert
Insights from insects; what bad bugs can teach us. Prometheus Books 2005 311p il $18
Grades: 11 12 Adult **632**
1. Insect pests
ISBN 1-59102-277-0

LC 2004-26928

The author "profiles a rogue's gallery of unhealthful, unprofitable and unsavory creatures from the mosquito and house fly to an array of agricultural scourges. From their ingenious strategies for wreaking havoc and evading retribution from predators, toxic plant chemicals, insecticides and eradication programs, he gleans lessons about the Darwinian struggle for survival and the complex, easily upset balance of ecosystems. Waldbauer's lucid, engaging style, informed by accessible discussions of his and other scientists' research, maintains a lab-coated tone of interested objectivity." Publ Wkly

Includes bibliographical references

634.9 Forestry

Brown, Daniel

Under a flaming sky; the great Hinckley firestorm of 1894. [by] Daniel James Brown. Lyons Press 2006 256p il map $22.95

Grades: 11 12 Adult   634.9

1. Forest fires 2. Minnesota

ISBN 1-59228-863-4; 978-1-59228-863-2

"On September 1, 1894, a firestorm consumed timber-boomtown Hinckley, Minnesota, and three nearby hamlets. Brown, grandson of an 11-year-old survivor, makes riveting, affecting, white-knuckle reading of that horrifying, internationally reported day's lethal passage." Booklist

Includes bibliographical references

MacLean, Norman

Young men & fire. University of Chicago Press 1992 301p pl maps $19.95

Grades: 11 12 Adult   634.9

1. Forest fires 2. Fire fighters 3. Large print books 4. United States -- Forest Service

ISBN 0226500616; 9780226500614

LC 92-11890

"On Aug. 5, 1949, 16 Forest Service smoke jumpers landed at a fire in remote Mann Gulch, Mont. Within an hour, 13 were dead or irrevocably burned, caught in a 'blowup'--a rare explosion of wind and flame. . . . [A]n engrossing account of human fallibility and natural violence." Pub Wkly

Raven, Catherine

Forestry. Chelsea House Publishers 2006 126p il (Green world) $37.50

Grades: 7 8 9 10   634.9

1. Forest ecology 2. Forests and forestry

ISBN 0-7910-8752-2; 978-0-7910-8752-7

LC 2005-21244

This book "explores the science of forestry, from the types of trees and shrubs grown for commercial and medicinal use, to the impact of trees on the environment and human society. . . . [This] is an excellent book in its content, instructional value, technical quality, and photography." Sci Books Films

Includes bibliographical references

635 Garden crops (Horticulture)

Ellis, Barbara W.

Burpee complete gardener; a comprehensive, up-to-date, fully illustrated reference for gardeners at all levels. [by] Maureen Heffernan [et al.]; edited by Barbara W. Ellis. Macmillan 1995 422p il $29.95

Grades: 11 12 Adult   635

1. Gardening

ISBN 0-02-860378-8

LC 95-13141

This volume presents "information on 420 annuals, biennials, perennials, bulbs, roses, vegetables, herbs, ground covers, and vines. There's a description of each plant, along with growing instructions and its uses. Other chapters cover designing, starting, planting, and caring for a garden; tools and equipment; and pests and diseases." Booklist

Includes bibliographical references

Learn to garden; [contributors, Guy Barter ... [et al.]] 1st American ed.; DK Pub. 2008 352p il pa $22.95

Grades: 11 12 Adult   635

1. Gardening

ISBN 978-0-7566-3443-8; 0-7566-3443-1

LC 2008-297619

This book covers how to "plant perennials, annuals and bulbs; prune trees and shrubs; make a new lawn or a gravel garden; select and grow roses, grasses, and ferns; grow vegetables and herbs in containers; [and] keep pests and diseases under control." Publisher's note

Smith, Jeremy N.

Growing a garden city; how farmers, first graders, counselors, troubled teens, foodies, a homeless shelter chef, single mothers, and more are transforming themselves and their neighborhoods through the intersection of local. [by] Jeremy N. Smith; foreword by Bill McKibben; photographs by Chad Harder and Sepp Jannotta. Skyhorse Pub. 2010 225p il $24.95

Grades: 11 12 Adult   635

1. Community gardens

ISBN 978-1-61608-108-9

LC 2010-12369

"Bright, vibrant, and buoyantly accessible, this effervescent celebration of the local food movement thrums with regional, national, and international implications." Booklist

Smith, Miranda

Your backyard herb garden; a gardener's guide to growing over 50 herbs plus how to use them in cooking, crafts, companion planting, and more. Rodale Press 1997 160p map hardcover o.p. pa $16.95

Grades: 9 10 11 12   635

1. Herbs 2. Herb gardening

ISBN 0-87596-767-1; 0-87596-994-1 pa

LC 96-23153

This guide offers information about planning and preparing an herb garden, growing and caring for herbs, using them for cooking, health, and beauty, and includes an illustrated directory of more than 70 herbs

Includes bibliographical references

635.9 Flowers and ornamental plants

★ The American Horticultural Society A-Z encyclopedia of garden plants; Christopher Brickell,

H. Marc Cathey, editors-in-chief. Rev. US ed.;
DK Pub. 2004 1099p il map $80

Grades: 11 12 Adult   **635.9**

1. Reference books   2. Ornamental plants --
Encyclopedias

ISBN 0-7566-0616-0

LC 2004-559196

First published 1997

"Equal parts gem and tool, this book is like a diamond.
Clear, concise, and thoroughly useful, it fits the needs of all
gardeners." Am Ref Books Annu, 2005

Dirr, Michael A.

Dirr's encyclopedia of trees and shrubs; Michael
A. Dirr. Timber Press 2011 951 p. col. ill. $79.95

Grades: 11 12 Adult   **635.9**

1. Trees   2. Shrubs   3. Ornamental plants   4.
Ornamental trees -- Encyclopedias   5. Ornamental
shrubs -- Encyclopedias

ISBN 0881929018; 9780881929010

LC 2011007951

This reference book, by Michael A. Dirr, focuses on
trees and shrubs. "From majestic evergreens to delicate
vines and flowering shrubs, Dirr features thousands of plants
and all the essential details for identification, planting, and
care, plus full-color photographs showing a tree's habit in
winter, distinctive bark patterns, fall color, and more." (Publisher's note)

"With beautiful, artistic photographs and succinct text,
this volume is nearly as attractive as one of the gorgeous
blossoming shrubs discussed within. . . . The chatty descriptions incorporate information often limited to tables—disease resistance, size, shape, and zone hardiness as well as
some history and taxonomy. These descriptions are accompanied by high-quality photographs." Booklist

Includes bibliographical references and index

636   Animal husbandry

Halligan, Karen

★ **Doc** Halligan's What every pet owner should
know; prescriptions for happy, healthy cats and dogs.
illustrations by Liz Wells. HarperCollins Publishers
2007 324p il $24.95; pa $15.95

Grades: 9 10 11 12 Adult   **636**

1. Cats   2. Dogs   3. Pets -- Health and hygiene

ISBN 978-0-06-089859-5; 0-06-089859-3; 978-0-06-
089860-1 pa; 0-06-089860-7 pa

LC 2007-60869

"Emphasizing canine (and feline) wellness, . . . [the au-
thor] gives clear advice about preventing illness and injuries
through sensible nutrition, regular grooming, dental care,
and partnering with your veterinarian." Libr J

Wells, Jeff

All my patients have tales; favorite stories from
a vet's practice. St. Martin's Press 2009 226p il
$24.95; pa $13.99

Grades: 11 12 Adult   **636**

1. Veterinary medicine

ISBN 978-0-312-53739-5; 0-312-53739-5; 978-0-312-
60639-8 pa; 0-312-60639-7 pa

LC 2008-35868

"Newly minted veterinarian Wells is on one of his first
calls—a cow trying to deliver a dead calf—when after two
hours of unceasing labor, he decides to try another approach,
and one of the on-looking farmers says, 'That's what you
should have done to begin with!' So begins the education
of a young vet, the on-the-job training that no amount of
schooling can provide. . . . A move to Colorado didn't immediately improve his finances but did improve his buffalo-
wrangling skills and his ability to remove porcupine quills
from overzealous dogs and donkeys. Another winning veterinary memoir deserving of space next to the immortal James
Herriot and his heirs." Booklist

636.08   Specific topics in animal husbandry

Farthing, Pen

One dog at a time; saving the strays of Afghanistan. Thomas Dunne Books 2010 308p il $24.99

Grades: 11 12 Adult   **636.08**

1. Dogs   2. Afghan War, 2001- -- Personal narratives

ISBN 978-0-312-60774-6; 0-312-60774-1

LC 2010-20605

"Farthing, a British Royal Marine, describes his struggles to save stray dogs languishing and dying in the streets
of wartorn Afghanistan. . . . Farthing's remarkable story will
inspire, shock, and move readers, introducing them, perhaps
for the first time, to war's most voiceless and unintentional
victims." Publ Wkly

Includes bibliographical references

Winegar, Karin

Saved; rescued animals and the lives they transform. text by Karin Winegar; photographs by Judy
Olausen; foreword by Jane Goodall; preface by Temple Grandin. Da Capo Lifelong 2008 xxiii, 212p il
$25.95; pa $18

Grades: 11 12 Adult   **636.08**

1. Pets   2. Animal welfare

ISBN 978-0-7382-1276-0; 0-7382-1276-8; 978-0-306-
81842-4 pa; 0-306-81842-6 pa

LC 2008-20616

"This book is about people trying to heal the damage
done to animals and how animals heal suffering human beings." Publisher's note

Includes bibliographical references

636.089   Veterinary medicine

Kahn, Cynthia M.

The **Merck** /Merial manual for pet health; Cynthia M. Kahn, editor. Home ed.; Merck & Co. 2007
xxvii, 1345p il $29.95; pa $22.95

Grades: 11 12 Adult   **636.089**

1. Pets -- Health and hygiene   2. Veterinary medicine

-- Handbooks, manuals, etc.
ISBN 978-0-911910-22-3; 0-911910-22-0; 978-0-911910-99-5 pa; 0-911910-99-9 pa

LC 2007-933381

Covers basic care and diseases of dogs, cats, horses, and exotic pets.

"An in-depth, thoroughly indexed reference featuring high-quality information." Libr J

Nakaya, Shannon Fujimoto

★ **Kindred** spirit, kindred care; making health decisions on behalf of our animal companions. New World Library 2005 155p pa $13.95

Grades: 9 10 11 12 **636.089**
1. Pets -- Health and hygiene
ISBN 1-57731-507-3

LC 2005-880

"Devoting entire chapters to choosing a veterinarian, understanding diagnostic and treatment options, managing care, and coping with death and its aftermath, and providing sidebars filled with pertinent questions to ask at various stages of treatment management, Nakaya arms conscientious caregivers with the information they will need to make the best choices for their animal companions. A necessary and noble guide to easing those stressful situations every animal lover must face." Booklist

Includes bibliographical references

636.1 Horses

Faurie, Bernadette

The **horse** riding & care handbook. Lyons Press 2000 160p il hardcover o.p. pa $19.95

Grades: 11 12 Adult **636.1**
1. Horses 2. Horsemanship
ISBN 1-58574-058-6; 1-58574-517-0 pa

"Each section contains pictures or diagrams to clarify the explanations, from horse evolution and history with humans to markings, colors, and breeds. Topics such as tack, how to mount, a first riding lesson, and techniques of western riding are all simply described with wonderful graphics." Libr J

Price, Steven D.

The **horseman's** illustrated dictionary. Lyons Press 2000 214p il hardcover o.p. pa $16.95

Grades: 11 12 Adult **636.1**
1. Horses 2. Horsemanship
ISBN 1-58574-146-9; 1-59228-098-6 pa

LC 00-62147

This dictionary includes definitions and derivations of words about horses and horsemanship

636.4 Swine

Montgomery, Sy

The **good** good pig; the extraordinary life of Christopher Hogwood. Ballantine Books 2006 228p il $21.95; pa $13.95

Grades: 11 12 Adult **636.4**
1. Pigs
ISBN 0-345-48137-2; 978-0-345-48137-5; 0-345-49609-4 pa; 978-0-345-49609-6 pa

LC 2005-57094

This is a "description of the 14-year life of a 750-pound pet pig who was named after the conductor [Christopher Hogwood]. Anyone who has ever loved a pet can enjoy reading about the relationship between Montgomery and her Christopher." Sci Books Films

Whyman, Matt

Oink; my life with mini-pigs. Simon & Schuster 2011 314p il $24; ebook $10.99

Grades: 11 12 Adult **636.4**
1. Pets 2. Pigs
ISBN 1-4516-1828-X; 1-4516-1830-1 ebook; 978-1-4516-1828-0; 978-1-4516-1830-3 ebook

LC 2011007817

"Made up of enough material about the nature of families and happiness to make it more than just a pig tale, . . . [this book] should make readers laugh." Libr J

Includes bibliographical references

636.7 Dogs

American Kennel Club

★ The **complete** dog book; American Kennel Club. 20th ed.; Ballantine Books 2006 xxi, 858p il $35

Grades: 7 8 9 10 11 12 Adult **636.7**
1. Dogs
ISBN 0-345-47626-3; 978-0-345-47626-5

LC 2005-48263

First published 1935. Periodically revised

"The official guide to 124 AKC registered breeds and their history, appearance, selection, training, care and feeding, and first aid. Some color plates." N Y Public Libr. Ref Books for Child Collect. 2d edition

Arden, Andrea

★ **Dog**-friendly dog training; illustrations by Tracy Dockray. 2nd ed.; Wiley Pub. 2007 232p il $18.99

Grades: 9 10 11 12 Adult **636.7**
1. Dogs -- Training
ISBN 978-0-470-11514-5; 0-470-11514-9

LC 2007-7079

First published 2000 by Howell Book House

"This straightforward, color-illustrated book by a charter member of the APDT [Association of Pet Dog Trainers] focuses on a dog-friendly, positive approach [to training]. The essential title for libraries with tight budgets." Libr J

Burch, Mary R.

★ **Citizen** canine; ten essential skills every well-mannered dog should know. Kennel Club Books 2010 256p il pa $14.95

Grades: 9 10 11 12 Adult   **636.7**
1. Dogs -- Training
ISBN 978-1-593786-44-1

LC 2009-28847

"Often a component of therapy dog assessment, the Canine Good Citizen (CGC) test has become a popular way to document a dog's manners. . . . [The author] outlines the ten test items and demonstrates how to teach your dog these skills. . . . This well-indexed guide is essential reading for dog owners, whether the goal is obedience training, therapy dog work, or simply polite pets." Libr J

Coile, D. Caroline
The **dog** breed bible. Barron's Educational Series 2007 192p il $16.99
Grades: 9 10 11 12 Adult   **636.7**
1. Dogs
ISBN 978-0-7641-6000-4; 0-7641-6000-1

LC 2006-36904

"More than 160 American Kennel Club–recognized breeds in the areas of sporting, hound, working, terrier, toy, nonsporting, herding, and 'miscellaneous'—those not yet placed in an AKC group—are beautifully described here in a condensed version of Barron's Encyclopedia of Dog Breeds. . . . Full-page entries contain the breed name; brief descriptions of history, temperament, upkeep, and health concerns; a captioned color photo of the full body and close up of snout area; and highlighted data on the origin, function, coat, color, and height and weight of the breed. . . . This small, spiral-bound book is perfect for circulating or reference collections in school and public libraries." Booklist

Coppinger, Raymond
Dogs; a new understanding of canine origin, behavior, and evolution. [by] Raymond Coppinger and Lorna Coppinger. University of Chicago Press 2002 352p il pa $18
Grades: 11 12 Adult   **636.7**
1. Dogs
ISBN 0-226-11563-1

LC 2002-20404

First published 2001 by Scribner
"This important book belongs in all libraries." Booklist
Includes bibliographical references

Fogle, Bruce
★ **Dog**: the definitive guide for dog owners. Firefly Books 2010 384p il $39.95; pa $29.95
Grades: 11 12 Adult   **636.7**
1. Dogs
ISBN 978-1-55407-779-3; 978-1-55407-700-7 pa

This is a "one-volume compendium on everything canine. He begins with an explanation of the dog's evolution, genetics, and classification. Then he delves into the human-dog relationship, giving . . . information and advice about selecting and training a new puppy, surviving its adolescence, enjoying its adulthood, coping with its declining years, and, finally, coming to grips with its demise. . . . [This is] an easy-to-read, attractive, indispensable guide for the novice and veteran dog owner alike." Libr J
Includes bibliographical references

Foster, Stephen
Fetching Dylan; a true tale of canine domestication in leaps and bounds. Perigee 2009 273p il pa $13.95
Grades: 9 10 11 12 Adult   **636.7**
1. Dogs 2. Pets
ISBN 978-0-399-53511-6; 0-399-53511-X
Sequel to: Walking Ollie (2008)
First published 2008 in the United Kingdom with title: Along came Dylan

"In Walking Ollie . . . Foster introduced us to . . . Ollie, a saluki/greyhound cross with numerous emotional issues. Ollie, who had been afraid of everything, including the author, was beginning to act fed up, bored, and full of ennui, so the author decided that what he needed was a playmate. Enter Dylan, the saluki pup. . . . Full of wry, deadpan humor, the story of Ollie and little brother Dylan, along with their human and canine mates, will leave readers begging for more." Booklist

Walking Ollie, or, Winning the love of a difficult dog. Perigee Books 2008 177p il pa $12
Grades: 9 10 11 12 Adult   **636.7**
1. Dogs 2. Pets
ISBN 978-0-3995-3429-4

LC 2008-275298

First published 2006 in the United Kingdom
The author "chronicles the many trials and misadventures of first-time dog ownership as he and his girlfriend consider various breeds, traipse through the woods with an eccentric vizsla breeder, scour animal shelters—and finally meet their match in Ollie, a fearful, stubborn saluki-greyhound mix. . . . Ollie makes for an entertaining and completely unpredictable subject, and this book will delight animal lovers with its warmth and wit." Publ Wkly

Franklin, Jon
The **wolf** in the parlor; the eternal connection between humans and dogs. Henry Holt 2009 283p $25
Grades: 9 10 11 12 Adult   **636.7**
1. Dogs
ISBN 978-0-8050-9077-2; 0-8050-9077-0

LC 2009-2227

Building on evolutionary science, archaeology, behavioral science, and the firsthand experience of watching his own dog evolve from puppy to family member, Franklin posits that man and dog are more than just inseparable; they are part and parcel of the same creature.
"Among a plethora of books on breeding, disciplining, loving and lamenting the loss of man's best friend, this thoughtful discourse is a best of breed." Publ Wkly

Geeson, Eileen
Ultimate dog grooming; additional material by Barbara Vetter & Lia Whitmore. Firefly Books 2004 288p il $29.95; pa $27.95
Grades: 11 12 Adult   **636.7**
1. Dogs
ISBN 1-55297-873-7; 1-55407-328-6 pa
The author "offers a three-part introduction to grooming for both owners and professionals. In Part 1, she briefly addresses what an owner needs to know about grooming as

well as how to choose the right groomer. Part 2 is geared toward those who want to become professional groomers. . . . The bulk of the book offers well-done profiles of 170 dog breeds—arranged by coat type—that include worthwhile tips and hints. Supplementing the text are more than 500 color illustrations, ranging from detailed drawings to photographs." Libr J

Kihn, Martin

Bad dog; a love story. Pantheon Books 2011 213p

Grades: 11 12 Adult **636.7**
1. Dogs
ISBN 978-0-307-37915-3; 978-0-307-37987-0 ebook
LC 2010035355

"Meet Hola, a gorgeous purebred Bernese mountain dog so badly managed by her human that walks were 'a haphazard dance of death' and greetings 'full-body slam[s] . . . just this side of actionable.' Now meet the human: Kihn, a Yale grad with an M.B.A., a deep neurotic streak, and a serious drinking problem. When his wife leaves, Kihn realizes he must get his life under control, and that includes Hola. Soon man and dog are enrolled in various training programs so that Hola can earn her Canine Good Citizen certificate from the American Kennel Club. . . . This sharply written, darkly funny memoir-cum-dog story-cum-recovery tale is a quick, absorbing read that will serve a wide audience well." Libr J

Lufkin, Elise

To the rescue; found dogs with a mission. photographs by Diana Walker; foreword by Bonnie Hunt. Skyhorse Pub. 2009 150p il $19.95

Grades: 9 10 11 12 Adult **636.7**
1. Dogs 2. Animals and people with disabilities
ISBN 978-1-60239-772-9
LC 2009-12164

"This feel-good book should please animal and dog-lovers, especially those who live with a working dog." Publ Wkly

Includes bibliographical references

The **original** dog bible; the definitive source for all things dog. edited by Kristin Mehus-Roe. 2nd ed.; Bowtie Press 2009 831p il pa $29.95

Grades: 11 12 Adult **636.7**
1. Dogs
ISBN 978-1-933958-82-8
LC 2008-44402

First published 2005

This book "opens with an astute and wonderfully illustrated survey of dogs' considerable role in history and popular culture, using both period and artifact photographs. Because it is more a guide to responsible dog ownership than a breed standards guide, the book is subsequently divided into eight segments and 34 chapters, which offer indispensable guidance on pet-relevant emergencies, travel, exercise, training, health regimens, and end-of-life concerns. An informative, extremely enjoyable read, regardless of pet ownership." Libr J

Includes bibliographical references

Rogers, Tammie

4-H guide to dog training and dog tricks. Voyageur Press 2009 176p il pa $18.99

Grades: 5 6 7 8 9 10 **636.7**
1. Dogs -- Training
ISBN 978-0-7603-3629-8; 0-7603-3629-6
LC 2009-17040

"This is not simply a how-to-train book; it is also a guide to cultivating a respectful relationship with your dog. The excellent information is comprehensive, and it is presented in a clear and detailed style. The author covers different training methods, discussing the tools needed from food to collar selection. Using this manual, dog owners can move through the basics (sit, down, etc.) to obedience competition and fun tricks and activities." SLJ

Includes bibliographical references

636.72　Specific breeds and groups of dogs

Sexton, Linda Gray, 1953-

Bespotted; my family's love affair with thirty-eight Dalmatians. Linda Gray Sexton. Counterpoint Press 2014 288 p. illustrations $26

Grades: 9 10 11 12 **636.72**
1. Dalmatian dog 2. Human-animal relationship 3. Human-animal relationships
ISBN 1619023458; 9781619023451
LC 2014014414

This book, by Linda Gray Sexton, is "[t]he story of the Dalmatians that filled a woman's life. . . . Despite a stint of dogless years at the beginning of her marriage, for most of her life, Sexton has been surrounded by at least one Dalmatian. She highlights each dog in her life as she recounts how she learned to show them, to breed them and to love them unconditionally, despite the dogs that fought each other, chased cars or had the wrong markings for a champion." (Kirkus Reviews)

"The inside look at the rarefied environment of dog shows is a fascinating subplot; and the decisions that must be made as well as the mechanics of breeding for show dogs will be eye-opening for many dog lovers. Sexton's paean to dalmatians, the dogs she feels have genuinely saved her life, will resonate." Booklist

636.8　Cats

Bessant, Claire

★ **Cat** manual; the complete step-by-step guide to understanding and caring for your cat. Haynes 2009 143p il $32.95

Grades: 11 12 Adult **636.8**
1. Cats
ISBN 978-1-84425-675-4; 1-84425-675-8
LC 2009-923208

At head of title: Haynes

This manual to owning and caring for cats discusses cat personalities, training, and health issues.

Bradshaw, John, 1950-

Cat sense; how the new feline science can make you a better friend to your pet. John Bradshaw. Basic Books 2013 336 p. (hardcover) $27.99

Grades: 9 10 11 12 Adult   **636.8**

1. Cats 2. Pets 3. Animal intelligence 4. Cat owners 5. Cats -- Behavior 6. Cats -- Psychology 7. Human-animal relationships

ISBN 0465031013; 9780465031016

     LC 2013020749

In this book, author John Bradshaw takes readers "further into the mind of the domestic cat . . . using cutting-edge scientific research to dispel the myths and explain the true nature of our feline friends. Tracing the cat's evolution from lone predator to domesticated companion, Bradshaw shows that although cats and humans have been living together for at least eight thousand years, cats remain independent, predatory, and wary of contact with their own kind." (Publisher's note)

"Bradshaw teases out a better understanding of what our cats want (and need) from their owners. . . . This fascinating book will be a bible for cat owners." Booklist

Includes bibliographical references and index

Herriot, James

James Herriot's cat stories; with illustrations by Lesley Holmes. St. Martin's Press 1994 161p $17.95

Grades: 11 12 Adult   **636.8**

1. Cats

ISBN 0-312-11342-0

     LC 94-20131

A "collection of favorite cat tales from Herriot's veterinary practice. Retired after over 50 years in practice, Herriot continues to entertain young and old alike with his storytelling ability. His current collection includes 'Alfred, the Sweet-Shop Cat,' 'Boris and Mrs. Bond's Cat Establishment,' 'Moses Found Among the Rushes,' and others." Libr J

Page, Jake

Do cats hear with their feet? where cats come from, what we know about them, and what they think about us. illustrations by Jake Page; photographs by Susanne Page; preface by Michael W. Fox. Smithsonian Books 2008 204p il $24.95

Grades: 11 12 Adult   **636.8**

1. Cats 2. Wild cats

ISBN 978-0-06-145648-0; 0-06-145648-9

     LC 2008-6776

The author "traces cats from the time they first adapted their feline form about 20 million years ago. He gives readers a cat's-eye view of why cats hunt even when they are full, why territory is so important, and why no self-respecting cat would eat vegetables. . . . There is solid science content that will help readers recognize we should let cats be cats and what a darn good job they have done of domesticating us." Libr J

Includes bibliographical references

636.9   Other mammals

McKimmey, Vickie

Ferrets. T.F.H. Publications 2007 111p il (Animal Planet pet care library) $11.95

Grades: 9 10 11 12 Adult   **636.9**

1. Ferrets

ISBN 978-0-7938-3787-8

     LC 2007-14332

This book on ferret care features advice "from animal experts on a variety of topics, including feeding, housing, grooming, training, health care, and fun activities." Publisher's note

Includes bibliographical references

Russell, Geoff

Mini encyclopedia of rabbit breeds & care; a color directory of the most popular breeds and their care. Firefly Books 2009 208p il pa $19.95

Grades: 9 10 11 12 Adult   **636.9**

1. Rabbits

ISBN 978-1-55407-474-7; 1-55407-474-6

     LC 2010-483165

This "mini encyclopedia features more than 40 of the most popular breeds and varieties of rabbit. . . . [Each breed profile features information on:] character; appearance; typical weight; temperament; suitability as a pet; country of origin; [and] special features of coat types and colors." Publisher's note

Includes bibliographical references

Westoll, Andrew

The chimps of Fauna Sanctuary; a true story of resilience and recovery. Houghton Mifflin Harcourt 2011 268p il $25

Grades: 11 12 Adult   **636.9**

1. Chimpanzees 2. Wildlife refuges 3. Animal rescue 4. Fauna Foundation 5. Chimpanzees -- Behavior 6. Animal experimentation -- Moral and ethical aspects

ISBN 978-0-547-32780-8; 0-547-32780-3

     LC 2010049783

"This is both an inspiring and a disturbing book. It is inspiring because of the devotion of caregivers to welfare of the chimps; it is disturbing because of the callous treatment to which chimps in research are subjected." Sci Books Films

Includes bibliographical references

638   Insect culture

Benjamin, Alison

A world without bees; [by] Alison Benjamin, Brian McCallum. Pegasus Books 2009 298p il $26

Grades: 11 12 Adult   **638**

1. Bees 2. Beekeeping

ISBN 978-1-60598-065-2

"In 2007, newspapers began carrying reports of a strange and widespread disease affecting the hives of honeybees. The bees were dying in droves. The potentially catastrophic situation was dubbed colony collapse disorder (CCD), and it touched beekeepers and farmers throughout the world. .

.. The authors launch an intelligent, open-minded investigation into possible agents of collapse—first noting that such collapses have been periodic in the bee industry—including parasites, pesticides, global warming, genetically modified transgenic pollens and stress from long shipping times." Kirkus

Includes bibliographical references

Buchmann, Stephen

Honey bees; letters from the hive. Delacorte Press 2010 212p il $16.99; lib bdg $19.99

Grades: 7 8 9 10   **638**

1. Bees 2. Honey

ISBN 978-0-385-73770-8; 0-385-73770-X; 978-0-385-90683-8 lib bdg; 0-385-90683-8 lib bdg

LC 2010-6093

Based on the adult book, Letters from the hive: an intimate history of bees, honey, and humankind published by Delacorte Press in 2005

"This sweeping survey engagingly discusses bee biology and behavior and examines humanity's relationship with bees, from prehistoric times to the present, through their significant roles in art, religion, literature and medicine. Buchmann, a beekeeper and entomologist, also offers a great deal of information about honey..... The text is illustrated with black-and-white photographs and documented with source notes." Kirkus

Burns, Loree Griffin

The **hive** detectives; chronicle of a honey bee catastrophe. by Loree Griffin Burns with photographs by Ellen Harasimowicz. HMH Books for Young Readers 2010 80 p. il (Scientists in the field) $18.99

Grades: 5 6 7 8 9 10   **638**

1. Bees 2. Beekeeping 3. Insects -- Behavior 4. Honeybee 5. Bee culture

ISBN 0547152310; 9780547152318

LC 2009045249

In this book, author Loree Griffin Burns "profiles bee wranglers and bee scientists who have been working to understand colony collapse disorder, or CCD. In this dramatic and enlightening story, readers explore the lives of the fuzzy, buzzy insects and learn what might happen to us if they were gone." (Publisher's note)

"Not long after beekeepers encountered a devastating new problem in their hives in 2006, a team of bee scientists began working to discover the causes of colony collapse disorder (CCD), now attributed to a combination of factors possibly including pesticides, nutrition, mites and viruses... . Mock notebook pages break up the narrative with biographies of the individual scientists, information about who and what can be found inside the hive and the features of bee bodies. An appendix adds varied fascinating facts about bees—again using the format of an illustrated research journal. Harasimowicz's clear, beautifully reproduced photographs support and extend the text." Kirkus

Includes bibliographical references (p. 65) and index

Readicker-Henderson, Ed

A **short** history of the honey bee; humans, flowers, and bees in the eternal chase for honey. images by Ilona; text by E. Readicker-Henderson. Timber Press 2009 163p il $19.95

Grades: 9 10 11 12 Adult   **638**

1. Bees 2. Honey 3. Beekeeping

ISBN 978-0-88192-942-3; 0-88192-942-5

LC 2008-50286

"The author's passion for the subject shines through." Booklist

Includes bibliographical references

639.2   Commercial fishing, whaling, sealing

Dolin, Eric Jay

Leviathan; the history of whaling in America. W.W. Norton & Company 2007 479p il $27.95

Grades: 11 12 Adult   **639.2**

1. Whaling -- History

ISBN 978-0-393-06057-7; 0-393-06057-8

LC 2007-06113

Hand, Carol

Dead zones; why earth's waters are losing oxygen. by Carol Hand. Twenty-First Century Books 2016 80 p. color illustrations (lb: alk. paper) $35.99

Grades: 7 8 9 10   **639.2**

1. Anoxic zones 2. Marine pollution 3. Fish kills

ISBN 9781467775731

LC 2014041304

This juvenile book, by Carol Hand, explores how "currently the world has more than 400 identified dead zones. ... The good news is that people can eliminate dead zones by changing agricultural practices and reducing pollution. Using real-world examples, this book looks at the impact of pollution on global water resources, and discusses the interconnectedness of ecosystems and organisms." (Publisher's note)

"A significant overview for serious eco-activists or any students interested in our planet's oceans and waterways." SLJ

Kurlansky, Mark

The **last** fish tale; the fate of the Atlantic and survival in Gloucester, America's oldest fishing port and most original town. Riverhead Books 2009 xxix, 269p il map pa $16

Grades: 11 12 Adult   **639.2**

1. Commercial fishing 2. Gloucester (Mass.)

ISBN 978-1-59448-374-5

First published 2008 by Ballantine Books

The author "provides a delightful, intimate history and contemporary portrait of the quintessential northeastern coastal fishing town: Gloucester, Mass., on Cape Anne. Illustrated with his own beautifully executed drawings, Kurlansky's book vividly depicts the contemporary tension between the traditional fishing trade and modern commerce, which in Gloucester means beach-going tourists." Publ Wkly

Includes bibliographical references

639.3　Culture of cold-blooded vertebrates

Alderton, David

Firefly encyclopedia of the vivarium. Firefly Books 2007 224p il $39.95

Grades: 9 10 11 12 Adult　　　　639.3

1. Insects 2. Reptiles 3. Amphibians 4. Terrariums 5. Invertebrates

ISBN 978-1-55407-300-9; 1-55407-300-6

"With its vibrant photographs and easy reading level, this text is suggested for school and public libraries that are in need of a basic guide." Booklist

Includes bibliographical references

Bartlett, Richard D.

Lizard care from A to Z; [by] R.D. Bartlett & Patricia Bartlett. 2nd ed.; Barron's Educational Series 2008 186p il pa $12.99

Grades: 11 12 Adult　　　　639.3

1. Lizards

ISBN 978-0-7641-3890-4; 0-7641-3890-1

LC 2008-8533

First published 1997

"The authors describe differing dietary needs for herbivorous, insectivorous and omnivorous lizards. They also give advice on indoor and outdoor caging, and show you how to create terraria to suit different kinds of lizard: cool desert, warm desert, semi-aquatic, cool woodland, tropical woodland, and escarpment." Publisher's note

Includes glossary and bibliographical references

De Vosjoli, Philippe

The **art** of keeping snakes; from the experts at Advanced Vivarium Systems. Advanced Vivarium Systems 2004 232p il (Herpetocultural library) pa $16.95

Grades: 9 10 11 12 Adult　　　　639.3

1. Snakes

ISBN 978-1-882770-63-2; 1-882770-63-3

LC 2005-271302

This book covers "how to setup and maintain a vivaria . . . [as well as] which snakes are the best display snakes and how to handle, feed, and care for them." Publisher's note

Includes bibliographical references

639.34　Fish culture in aquariums

Alderton, David

★ **Encyclopedia** of aquarium & pond fish. Dorling Kindersley 2005 400p il hardcover o.p. pa $24.95

Grades: 11 12 Adult　　　　639.34

1. Reference books 2. Fishes -- Encyclopedias

ISBN 0-7566-0941-0; 0-7566-3678-7 pa

The author "has created the definitive work on the subject, with photos to match." Libr J

Boruchowitz, David E.

Mini aquariums. T.F.H. Publications 2008 256p il $34.95

Grades: 9 10 11 12 Adult　　　　639.34

1. Fishes 2. Aquariums

ISBN 978-0-7938-0573-0

LC 2007-30146

"The book discusses the important elements concerning setup, equipment, and the wide range of specimens including fish, vegetation, coral, invertebrates, and amphibians. The author dispels myths and misconceptions about goldfish and other types of misunderstood species. Although this volume focuses on small aquariums, it lends itself to responsible and creative larger aquarium systems and will educate and inspire those who enjoy them." Libr J

Includes bibliographical references

Jennings, Greg

The **new** encyclopedia of the saltwater aquarium. Firefly Books 2007 304p il $49.95

Grades: 11 12 Adult　　　　639.34

1. Reference books 2. Marine aquariums 3. Fishes -- Encyclopedias

ISBN 978-1-55407-182-1; 1-55407-182-8

LC 2007-296089

First published 2003 under the authorship of Nick Dakin with title: Complete encyclopedia of the saltwater aquarium

"Over 150 species of reef fish, invertebrates and algae are described: their distribution in the wild, size, behavior, diet, aquarium requirements and compatibility. A large, full color photograph appears for each featured species, with personal recommendations on the fish considered best for the beginner." Publisher's note

Includes bibliographical references

Maitre-Allain, Thierry

★ **Aquariums**; the complete guide to freshwater and saltwater aquariums. [by] Thierry Maitre-Allain and Christian Piednoir; [English translation by Matthew Clarke] Firefly Books 2006 281p il $39.95

Grades: 11 12 Adult　　　　639.34

1. Aquariums 2. Marine aquariums

ISBN 1-55407-085-6

The authors "walk the novice through all aspects of setting up and maintaining an underwater habitat. . . . Beautiful photos clearly illustrate this good all-in-one handbook that will fill the needs of beginning aquarists." Booklist

Includes bibliographical references

639.9　Conservation of biological resources

DeNapoli, Dyan

The **great** penguin rescue; 40,000 penguins, a devastating oil spill, and the inspiring story of the world's largest animal rescue. Free Press 2010 307p il map $26

Grades: 10 11 12 Adult　　　　639.9

1. Penguins 2. Oil spills

ISBN 978-1-4391-4817-4; 1-4391-4817-1

LC 2010-17156

This "firsthand account of the rescue of the oiled penguins (all of whom fought against their rescuers), repeated washing of each bird, force-feeding, and guano cleanup

plunges the reader into the maelstrom of animal rescue and rehabilitation on such a large scale." Booklist
Includes bibliographical references

640   Home and family management

★ The **experts'** guide to 100 things everyone should know how to do; created by Samantha Ettus. Clarkson Potter Publishers 2004 326p $19.95
Grades: 9 10 11 12   640
1. Life skills 2. Home economics
ISBN 1-4000-5256-4; 978-1-4000-5256-1
LC 2004-2546
"These experts and 94 more show you how to read a newspaper (New York Times publisher [Arthur] Sulzberger), tell a joke (comedian [Howie] Mandel), save money (financial guru [Suze] Orman), and, well, pretty much anything else you can think of. . . . The authors call the book 'Cliff Notes to life,' and that about sums it up. It's more fun than Cliff Notes, though." Booklist

Fagerstrom, Derek
Show me how; 500 things you should know, instructions for life from the everyday to the exotic. [by] Derek Fagerstrom, Lauren Smith & the Show Me team. Collins Design 2008 un il pa $24.99
Grades: 9 10 11 12   640
1. Life skills
ISBN 978-0-06-166257-7
"In a series of 500 nearly wordless, . . . step-by-step procedurals, readers learn how to do hundreds of . . . tasks, including: Perform CPR, dance the tango, pack a suitcase, win a bar bet, play the blues, make authentic sushi rolls, fight a shark . . . and 493 more essentials of modern life." Publisher's note

Nakone, Lanna
★ **Organizing** for your brain type; finding your own solution to managing time, paper, and stuff. St. Martin's Griffin 2005 xlvii, 222p pa $13.95
Grades: 11 12 Adult   640
1. Home economics 2. Time management
ISBN 0-312-33977-1
LC 2004-60159
"A quiz at the beginning assigns readers to the maintaining, harmonizing, innovating, or prioritizing style. Nakone then describes the strengths and weaknesses of each type and matches a prescription for how that type can best manage time. . . . This book should do well in most libraries." Libr J
Includes bibliographical references

641   Food and drink

Allen, Stewart Lee
In the devil's garden; a sinful history of forbidden food. Ballantine Bks. 2002 315p hardcover o.p. pa $13.95

Grades: 11 12 Adult   641
1. Food 2. Menus 3. Cooking 4. Eating customs
ISBN 0-345-44015-3; 0-345-44016-1 pa
LC 2001-43882
"The historical and cultural links between food, sex and religion make for fascinating reading." Publ Wkly
Includes bibliographical references

Davidson, Alan, 1924-2003
The **Oxford** companion to food; Alan Davidson; edited by Tom Jaine; illustrations by Soun Vannithone. 3rd ed Oxford University Press 2014 xxx, 921p illustrations $65
Grades: 11 12 Adult   641
1. Food 2. Reference books
ISBN 9780199677337
LC 2013957569
First published 1999
"There is new coverage of attitudes to food consumption, production and perception, such as food and genetics, food and sociology, and obesity. New entries include terms such as convenience foods, drugs and food, Ethiopia, leftovers, medicine and food, pasta, and many more. There are also new entries on important personalities who are of special significance within the world of food." Publisher's note
Includes bibliographical references and index

Rolland, Jacques L.
The **food** encyclopedia; over 8,000 ingredients, tools, techniques and people. [by] Jacques L. Rolland and Carol Sherman with other contributors. Robert Rose 2006 701p il $49.95
Grades: 11 12 Adult   641
1. Reference books 2. Food -- Encyclopedias 3. Cooking -- Encyclopedias
ISBN 978-0-7788-0150-4; 0-7788-0150-0
This encyclopedia "has 8,000 entries, with cross-reference on foods, wines, beverages, cooking methods and techniques, and biographies of prominent people." Publisher's note
Includes bibliographical references

641.3   Food

Aaron, Shara
Chocolate; a healthy passion. [by] Shara Aaron and Monica Bearden. Prometheus Books 2008 213p il $19.98
Grades: 11 12 Adult   641.3
1. Chocolate
ISBN 978-1-59102-653-2; 1-59102-653-9
LC 2008-26159
"Divided into six chapters, the book covers all facets of the confection. The authors begin by explaining what chocolate is and its origins before moving on to the history of chocolate and how it is grown and harvested. Of particular note are the last two chapters on chocolate and health and the various myths about the food. The authors do an excellent job of explaining the health benefits of chocolate, which is rich in antioxidants and flavonols. They also provide recipes

at the end of each chapter, including those for facials, lip balm, and soap." Libr J

Includes bibliographical references

Foer, Jonathan Safran

Eating animals. Little, Brown and Company 2009 341p $25.99; pa $14.99

Grades: 11 12 Adult   641.3

1. Vegetarianism

ISBN 978-0-316-06990-8; 978-0-316-06988-5 pa

LC 2009-34434

The novelist presents a critique of the food industry and explores arguments in favor of humane agriculture and vegetarianism.

"A blend of solid—and discomforting—reportage with fierce advocacy that will make committed carnivores squeal." Kirkus

Includes bibliographical references

Goldstein, Myrna Chandler

Controversies in food and nutrition; {by} Myrna Chandler Goldstein and Mark A. Goldstein. Greenwood Press 2002 260p il (Contemporary controversies) $45

Grades: 11 12 Adult   641.3

1. Food 2. Nutrition

ISBN 0-313-31787-9

LC 2002-69605

This book explains varying opinions and underlying issues that surround such topics as popular diets, vegetarianism, food irradiation, organic and imported food, vitamin supplementation, food allergies, and genetic modifications

"For anyone confused about the barrage of messages we get every day about nutrition, this is an excellent book. . . . Thoroughly enjoyable to read, the book is designed as a high school or college reference text, but it would also interest the general public." Choice

Includes bibliographical references

Kaufman, Cathy K.

★ Cooking in ancient civilizations. Greenwood Press 2006 liv, 224p il map (Greenwood Press 'Daily life through history' series) $45

Grades: 11 12 Adult   641.3

1. Cooking 2. Ancient civilization 3. Food -- History

ISBN 0-313-33204-5; 978-0-313-33204-3

LC 2006-15692

This cookbook focuses "on the main ancient peoples studied today—the Romans, Mesopotamians, Egyptians, and Greeks. . . . Each group is covered in a chapter that begins with a narrative overview of the environment and resources, cuisine and social class, and a note on sources." Publisher's note

Includes bibliographical references

Menzel, Peter

Hungry planet; what the world eats. photographed by Peter Menzel; written by Faith D'Aluisio. Ten Speed Press 2005 287p il map $40; pa $24.95

Grades: 11 12 Adult   641.3

1. Food -- Pictorial works

ISBN 978-1-58008-681-3; 978-1-58008-869-5 pa

LC 2005-13455

"This is a beautiful, quietly provocative volume." Publ Wkly

Includes bibliographical references

Organic food and farming; Lauri S. Friedman, book editor. Greenhaven Press 2009 138p il (Introducing issues with opposing viewpoints) $34.70

Grades: 6 7 8 9 10   641.3

1. Natural foods 2. Organic farming

ISBN 978-0-7377-4483-5; 0-7377-4483-9

LC 2009-36912

"This title first examines the difference between organic and conventional food in terms of human health. The articles have been successfully edited for brevity and clarity. Whether organic farming can improve the world is discussed in the second . . . section of the book. . . . The bulk of the final section discusses the future of organic food and looks at the debate within the organic community on the direction of sustainable agriculture and the label organic. . . . With its colorful graphs and photographs nicely breaking up the text, this . . . book will provide a starting point for assignments." SLJ

Includes bibliographical references

Ornelas, Kriemhild Conee

★ The Cambridge world history of food; editors, Kenneth F. Kiple, Kriemhild Coneè Ornelas. Cambridge Univ. Press 2000 2v set $190

Grades: 11 12 Adult   641.3

1. Diseases 2. Nutrition 3. Edible plants 4. Food -- History

ISBN 0-521-40216-6

LC 00-57181

"The two volumes are arranged in eight parts covering the diet of early man, staple foods, dietary liquids, nutrients and food-related disorders, food and drink around the world, nutrition and health, current food-related issues and concluding with a dictionary of plant foods. . . . The Cambridge World History of Food is a thorough study of a topic that is eternally popular. It should become a standard source in reference collections." Booklist

Includes bibliographical references

★ The Oxford encyclopedia of food and drink in America; Andrew F. Smith, editor in chief. Oxford University Press 2004 2v il set $250

Grades: 11 12 Adult   641.3

1. Beverages 2. Reference books 3. Food 4. Cookery, American 5. Food -- Encyclopedias

ISBN 0-19-515437-1; 978-0-19-515437-5

LC 2003-24873

In some 800 articles, this work "covers the significant events, inventions, and social movements in American history that have affected the way Americans view, prepare, and consume food and drink. In an A-Z format, this two-volume set details the regions, people, ingredients, foods, drinks, publications, advertising, companies, historical periods, and political and economic aspects pertinent to American cuisine."

This reference covers "the regions, people, ingredients, foods, drinks, publications, advertising, companies, historical periods, and political and economic aspects pertinent to American cuisine." Publisher's note

Rosenblum, Mort

    Chocolate: a bittersweet saga of dark and light. North Point Press 2005 290p il $24; pa $14

Grades: 11 12 Adult   **641.3**

   1. Chocolate

   ISBN 0-86547-635-7; 0-86547-730-2 pa

                       LC 2004-54734

The author "unveils chocolate's history and its various incarnations, including in his fresh and insightful discussions the origins of mole; the differences between, say, Hershey's kisses and Valrhona's products; the invention of Nutella; and the small boutique chocolate artisans found nearly everywhere. . . . A compelling and tasty read." Booklist

Tannahill, Reay

    Food in history; new, fully rev and updated ed; Crown 1989 424p il hardcover o.p. pa $16

Grades: 9 10 11 12   **641.3**

   1. Dining 2. Food -- History

   ISBN 0-517-88404-6

                       LC 89-671

First published 1973 by Stein & Day; this edition first published 1988 in the United Kingdom

   "A world history of food from prehistoric times . . . this book also traces the way in which food has influenced the entire course of human development." Publisher's note

   Includes bibliographical references

641.5   Cooking

American Institute for Cancer Research

    The **new** American plate cookbook; recipes for a healthy weight and a healthy life. American Institute for Cancer Research. University of California Press 2005 306p il $24.95

Grades: 11 12 Adult   **641.5**

   1. Cooking

   ISBN 0-520-24234-3

                       LC 2004-17993

The recipes in this book are "built around vegetables and whole grains, with an emphasis on brown rice, wheat pasta, and other healthful foods, rather than protein. . . . Recipes are appealing and easy to make and cover every course of a meal. Well-known dishes are reworked, e.g., New England Clam Chowder, to help with the transition to healthier eating." Libr J

Anderson, Pam

    How to cook without a book; recipes and techniques every cook should know by heart. Broadway Bks. 2000 290p $25

Grades: 11 12 Adult   **641.5**

   1. Cooking

   ISBN 0-7679-0279-3

                       LC 99-43776

   "Former executive editor of Cook's magazine and author of The Perfect Recipe, Anderson wants to teach Americans a new way to cook without relying on recipes. It's somewhat surprising, then, to discover that this book is full of recipes. However, readers may cotton to Anderson's method: each chapter consists of a simple technique, basic recipe, variations, key points and a little mnemonic device used to recall the technique. The techniques are, for the most part, terrific time-savers." Pub Wkly

Better homes and gardens

   ★   **Better** homes and gardens new cook book; 15th ed.; J. Wiley 2010 660p il $29.95

Grades: 11 12 Adult   **641.5**

   1. Cooking

   ISBN 978-0-470-55686-3

                       LC 2010-25417

First published 1930 with title: My Better Homes and Gardens cook book. Periodically revised

   "A standard cookbook . . . with staple recipes and types of cooking." N Y Public Libr. Book of How & Where to Look It Up

   ★   **Betty** Crocker cookbook; everything you need to know to cook today. 10th ed.; Wiley 2005 575p il $29.95; pa $17.95

Grades: 11 12 Adult   **641.5**

   1. Cooking

   ISBN 0-7645-6877-9; 978-0-7645-6877-0; 0-7645-8374-3 pa; 978-0-7645-8374-2 pa

                       LC 2006-281166

First published with this title 1969 by Golden Press. Periodically revised. Publisher varies. Variant title: Betty Crocker's new cookbook

   "This book gives easily readable and understandable recipes. Also has a glossary of cooking terms in back, as well as nutritional guidelines and 'special helps.'" N Y Public Libr. Book of How & Where to Look It Up

Carle, Megan

    Teens cook; how to make what you want to eat. [by] Megan and Jill Carle with Judi Carle. Ten Speed Press 2004 146p il pa $19.95

Grades: 7 8 9 10   **641.5**

   1. Cooking

   ISBN 1-58008-584-9

This cookbook features "recipes for a variety of dishes including chocolate chip scones, potato skins, broccoli cheese soup, steak fajitas, baked macaroni and cheese, and toffee bars. Because Megan is a vegetarian, there are several vegetarian recipes or vegetarian substitutes. . . . Attractive, engaging, and told from a teen perspective, this cookbook will make an excellent addition to any nonfiction collection." Voice Youth Advocates

Cunningham, Marion

   ★   The **Fannie** Farmer cookbook; illustrated by Lauren Jarrett. 13th ed; Knopf 1996 874p il $30

Grades: 11 12 Adult   **641.5**

   1. Cooking

   ISBN 0-679-45081-5

                       LC 97-162330

First published 1896 under the authorship of Fannie Merritt Farmer. Periodically revised

This standard cookbook focuses on the selection, preparation, and serving of a wide variety of foods

Gold, Rozanne

★ **Eat** fresh food; awesome recipes for teen chefs. by Rozanne Gold and her all-star team; photographs by Phil Mansfield. Bloomsbury Children's Books 2009 160p il $21.99; pa $17.99

Grades: 6 7 8 9 10   **641.5**

1. Cooking

ISBN 1-59990-282-6; 1-59990-445-4 pa; 978-1-59990-282-1; 978-1-59990-445-0 pa

LC 2008-42443

"This joyful recipe book features fresh, healthful ingredients and encourages ambitious young chefs to collaborate on such mature dishes as Grape-and-Pignoli Breakfast Cake, Crunchy Wasabi-Lime Salmon with red cabbage and sugar snaps and orange-ginger sweet potato puree. . . . A prime pick for adventurous eaters and a potential catalyst for those in a junk food rut." Publ Wkly

Grant, Mark

Roman cookery; ancient recipes for modern kitchens. Rev. ed; Serif 2008 187p il pa $18

Grades: 9 10 11 12 Adult   **641.5**

1. Roman cooking

ISBN 978-1-89795-960-2

First published 1999

The author's "theme is everyday Roman food: bread and olive oil form the basic of the simple cuisine that he tells us even emperors ate when not attending extravagant banquets. . . . [He] brings together recipes from the whole span of Roman cookery: . . . sources range from about 400 B.C. to A.D. 500, and from Egypt to northern France." Classical Rev

Includes bibliographical references

The **green** teen cookbook; [edited by] Laurane Marchive, Pam McElroy. Zest Books 2014 144 p. $14.99

Grades: 6 7 8 9 10   **641.5**

1. Cookbooks 2. Vegetarian cooking 3. Nutrition 4. Low-budget cooking

ISBN 1936976587; 9781936976584

LC 2013951195

Edited by Laurane Marchive and Pam McElroy, this book "cuts through the chaos and shows teens how to shop smarter, cook more consciously, and eat a healthier diet. . . . In addition to the 70+ . . . recipes . . . , the book also includes illuminating essays about freeganism, flexitarians, vegetarianism, and more; tips about how to shop on a budget and get the most out of what you already have in your pantry; a seasonal key that ensures the freshness of the recipes (and a minimal carbon footprint). (Publisher's note)

"Originally published in the U.K., Marchive and McElroy's cookbook gives teenage home cooks ideas for every meal of the day, including snacks and desserts, with an eye toward healthy, seasonal options (brief essays explore organic and fair-trade food, vegetarianism, and other topics)... Color photos, clear instructions, and quotes from the teens providing the recipes should help bolster the confidence of young cooks." PW

Ishihara, Yoko

The **manga** cookbook; presented by the Manga University Culinary Institute; illustrations by Chihiro Hattori; [with recipes by Yoko Ishihara] Japanime Co. Ltd. 2007 158p il pa $14.95

Grades: 4 5 6 7 8 9 10 11 12   **641.5**

1. Manga 2. Graphic novels 3. Japanese cooking -- Graphic novels

ISBN 978-4-921205-07-2

Food appears frequently in manga and in anime, but just what are the characters eating? This book is an illustrated step-by-step guide to preparing some Japanese dishes, from onigiri (rice balls) to yakitori (skewered grilled chicken), oshinko (pickled vegetables), udon (Japanese noodles), to traditional sweets and desserts. Definitions of terms and ingredients used, basic cooking guidelines, and instructions on how to properly use chopsticks are all included. The recipes are authentic but have been simplified somewhat so older children and teens with some basic kitchen skills can prepare the foods. Adult supervision is recommended for younger children and for children who aren't very experienced with using knives, measuring spoons, and cooking on the stove.

Lee, Jennifer 8.

The **fortune** cookie chronicles; adventures in the world of Chinese food. Twelve 2008 307p hardcover o.p. pa $13

Grades: 11 12 Adult   **641.5**

1. Restaurants 2. Eating customs 3. Chinese cooking

ISBN 978-0-446-58007-6; 0-446-58007-4; 978-0-446-69897-9 pa; 0-446-69897-0 pa

LC 2007-33432

"When a large number of Powerball winners in a 2005 drawing revealed that mass-printed paper fortunes were to blame, the author . . . . went in search of the backstory. She tracked the winners down to Chinese restaurants all over America, and the paper slips the fortunes are written on back to a Brooklyn company. This travellike narrative serves as the spine of her cultural history—not a book on Chinese cuisine, but the Chinese food of takeout-and-delivery—and permits her to frequently but safely wander off into various tangents related to the cookie. . . . Like the numbers on those lottery fortunes, the book's a winner." Publ Wkly

Includes bibliographical references

Locricchio, Matthew

Teen cuisine; illustrated by Janet Hamlin; photographs by James Peterson. Marshall Cavendish Children 2010 207p il $22.95

Grades: 6 7 8 9 10   **641.5**

1. Cooking

ISBN 978-0-7614-5715-2; 0-7614-5715-1

LC 2009-46847

"This contemporary collection of recipes will appeal to teen cooks and would make a great gift or an excellent addition to a library's cookbook collection." Voice Youth Advocates

Mackenzie, Jennifer

The **complete** trail food cookbook; [by] Jennifer MacKenzie, Jay Nutt & Don Mercer. R. Rose 2010 256p il pa $21.95

Grades: 11 12 Adult   641.5
1. Outdoor cooking
ISBN 978-0-778-80236-5

A collection of recipes that can be prepared before or during nature hikes or camping. Contains instructions on how to dehydrate food.

Manning, Ivy

The **adaptable** feast; satisfying meals for the vegetarians, vegans, and omnivores at your table. photography by Gregor Torrence. Sasquatch Books 2009 xxii, 249p il pa $23.95

Grades: 11 12 Adult   641.5
1. Cooking 2. Vegetarian cooking
ISBN 978-1-57061-583-2; 1-57061-583-7
LC 2009-18963

"Each basic recipe has a stopping point in its process where a quantity of the dish is set aside to feed the vegetarians before any meat products go in. In some cases, the meat-free portion is then enriched with the addition of beans or tofu. For the vegan, Manning indicates which ingredients may simply be left out altogether. She turns to meat substitutes, such as seitan, as advice on ensuring that vegans get sufficient complete proteins for sound nutrition." Booklist

Includes bibliographical references

New American Heart Association cookbook

★ The **new** American Heart Association cookbook; 8th ed.; Clarkson Potter 2010 xxi, 696p il $35

Grades: 11 12 Adult   641.5
1. Cooking 2. Low-cholesterol diet 3. Heart diseases -- Diet therapy
ISBN 978-0-307-40757-3
LC 2009-44692

First published 1973 with title: American Heart Association cookbook

"Each recipe comes with a breakdown of calories, protein content, carbohydrates, cholesterol, fats (broken down by saturated, polyunsaturated and monounsaturated) and sodium content, along with a table of dietary exchange. . . . This book remains a basic in many heart-conscious kitchens." Publ Wkly

Robertson, Robin

Vegan planet; 400 irresistible recipes with fantastic flavors from home and around the world. Harvard Common Press 2003 576p hardcover o.p. pa $21.95

Grades: 11 12 Adult   641.5
1. Vegetarian cooking
ISBN 1-55832-210-8; 1-55832-211-6 pa
LC 2002-7435

The author "offers dozens of imaginative vegan recipes inspired by a wide range of cuisines, from Five-Spiced Portobello Satays and Lebanese Fattoush (bread salad) to Cajun-Style Collards and Moroccan Fava Bean Stew." Libr J

Rombauer, Irma von Starkloff

★ **Joy** of cooking; [by] Irma S. Rombauer, Marion Rombauer Becker, Ethan Becker; illustrated by John Norton. 75th anniversary ed.; Scribner 2006 1132p il $30

Grades: 11 12 Adult   641.5
1. Cooking
ISBN 978-0-7432-4626-2; 0-7432-4626-8
LC 2006-51231

First published 1931

This is the "backbone for any library's cookery reference collection, its nearly 4,000 recipes defining essential American home cooking." Booklist

Segan, Francine

Shakespeare's kitchen; Renaissance recipes for the contemporary cook. photographs by Tim Turner. Random House 2003 270p il $35

Grades: 9 10 11 12   641.5
1. British cooking 2. Italian cooking
ISBN 0-375-50917-8
LC 2002-36839

"Updating dozens of classic Elizabethan recipes, Segan leads a culinary foray into Shakespeare's time. Each recipe is supplemented with a historical note that places the dish in context. . . . Its playful tone, fascinating side-notes, and apt citations from the Bard's plays make this book as fun to read as it is to cook from." Publ Wkly

Includes bibliographical references

Smith, Merril D.

History of American cooking; Merril D. Smith. ABC-CLIO 2013 xxxiv, 188 p.p (hardcopy: alk. paper) $37

Grades: 9 10 11 12 Adult   641.5
1. Cookbooks 2. American cooking -- History
ISBN 0313387117; 9780313387111
LC 2012035382

This book is a history of American cooking. "Following a historical introduction covering five centuries, independent scholar [Merril D.] Smith . . . discusses chronology, cooking methods, techniques, popular ingredients, and recipes in ten chapters, each devoted to a particular type of cooking, e.g., braising, broiling, and grilling. A concluding chapter looks at emerging technology and what it means for future cooking and eating." (Library Journal)

"This book will appeal to readers who eschew history as "his story," as it illuminates what has typically occupied a large part of female daily life. Plus, the "melting pot" that is America is examined in terms of its multicultural influences on what we create and consume...A concluding chapter looks at emerging technology and what it means for future cooking and eating. VERDICT A well-researched addition to school and academic libraries supporting humanities curricula." (Library Journal)

Includes bibliographical references and index

Splendid table (Radio program)

The **Splendid** table's how to eat supper; recipes, stories, and opinions from public radio's award-winning food show. [by] Lynne Rossetto Kasper and

Sally Swift. Clarkson Potter/Publishers 2008 338p il $35

Grades: Adult   641.5
1. Dining 2. Cooking
ISBN 978-0-307-34671-1

LC 2007-24749

"The recipes gathered here, ranging from Thai Cantaloupe Salad with Chile to Filipino-Style Chicken Adobo, were inspired by a variety of cuisines. Many of them include variations, and sidebars titled 'Cook to Cook' provide . . . information on all sorts of topics. There are also . . . digressions on various culinary matters and recommendations for favorite cookbooks." Libr J

Warren, Rachel Meltzer

The **smart** girl's guide to going vegetarian; how to look great, feel fabulous, and be a better you. Rachel Meltzer Warren, MS, RDN. Sourcebooks Fire 2014 240 p. (alk. paper) $12.99

Grades: 7 8 9 10 11 12   641.5
1. Veganism 2. Eating habits 3. Vegetarianism 4. Vegetarian cooking 5. Teenagers -- Nutrition
ISBN 1402284918; 9781402284915

LC 2013023334

In this book, author Rachel Meltzer Warren "encourages readers who are considering changing their diet to begin by participating in Meatless Mondays. Chapters include information on nutrients that are crucial to a healthy diet and what foods they can be found in for all types of diets (vegan, lacto-ovo, pescetarian). The book also includes types of restaurants with vegetarian-friendly options and an explanation of how to use the choosemyplate.gov resource to practice planning a healthy meal." (Publisher's note)

"A vegetarian herself since age 12, Warren knows the questions that teen girls ask and the arguments their parents raise when kids want to experience vegetarianism or veganism. Here, she offers sound advice for girls who are considering being or have chosen to go vegetarian or vegan and for those who waver about where they stand on the topic...The catchy, accessible text is broken up by generous topic headings and questions. Overall, a sound guide for any teenager, really, and her or his parents." (Booklist)

Includes bibliographical references and index

Webb, Lois Sinaiko

Holidays of the world cookbook for students; [by] Lois Sinaiko Webb and Lindsay Grace Roten. updated and rev.; Greenwood 2011 442p il map $95; pa $32.95

Grades: 5 6 7 8 9 10   641.5
1. Cooking 2. Holidays
ISBN 978-0-313-38393-9; 0-313-38393-6; 978-0-313-39790-5 pa; 0-313-39790-2 pa; 978-0-313-38394-6 ebook

LC 2011-8458

First published 1995 by Oryx Press

"The recipes appear with each country entry, and the countries are arranged in alphabetical order within each region: Africa, Asia and the South Pacific, the Caribbean, Europe, Latin America, the Middle East, and North America." Publisher's note

★ The **multicultural** cookbook for students; [by] Lois Sinaiko Webb and Lindsay Grace Roten. Updated & rev.; Greenwood Press 2009 354p map $85

Grades: 7 8 9 10   641.5
1. Cooking
ISBN 978-0-313-37558-3; 0-313-37558-5

LC 2009-26718

First published 1993 under the authorship of Carole Lisa Albyn

"This highly informative cookbook includes not only recipes, but also information on the country, its food staples, and ethnic and cultural divisions. Recipes are divided into seven sections according to geography: Africa, Asia and South Pacific, The Caribbean, Europe, Latin America, The Middle East, and North America. . . . Recipes are then divided by country with a description of the country concentrating on culinary information. A minimum of two recipes per country are also annotated with information about the ingredients or why the dish was important to the area. . . . This book is a great resource for cultural research even if the actual recipes will not be prepared. There is a comprehensive index by recipe name, country, and ingredients." Libr Media Connect

Includes glossary and bibliographical references

Weinstein, Jay

The **ethical** gourmet. Broadway 2006 353p il pa $18.95

Grades: 11 12 Adult   641.5
1. Cooking -- Natural foods
ISBN 0-7679-1834-7; 978-0-7679-1834-3

LC 2005-53630

"This book may be an eye-opener and mouth-closer for many teens accustomed to fast food." SLJ

Includes bibliographical references

641.509   Cooking -- History, geographic treatment, biography

Abrams, Dennis

Julia Child, chef; by Dennis Abrams. Chelsea House 2011 134 p. ill. (some col.)

Grades: 6 7 8 9   641.509
1. Cooks -- United States -- Biography
ISBN 9781604139129

LC 2011000039

'This book offers a biography of chef "Julia Child . . . [who] started a cooking revolution when she burst onto television screens in the 1960s. Before long, Americans inspired by her example began cooking French food at home in droves and truly appreciating the pleasure that preparing good food can provide. Yet Child did not grow up knowing how to cook or even with an interest in fine cuisine. Her story is one of an American woman's quest to find herself, to find her passion, and then to find a way to share that passion with the world. It is the story of how Julia McWilliams of Pasadena, California, transformed herself into Julia Child, 'The French Chef.'" (Publisher's note)

Includes bibliographical references and index

Samuelsson, Marcus

Make it messy; my perfectly imperfect life. Marcus Samuelsson with Veronica Chambers. Delacorte Press 2014 224 p. 8 plates; illustrations (trade hardcover) $16.99

Grades: 8 9 10 11 **641.509**

1. Cooks 2. Ambition 3. Motivation (Psychology) 4. Cooks -- Sweden -- Biography 5. African American cooks -- Biography 6. Cooks -- United States -- Biography

ISBN 9780375991448; 9780385744003; 0385744005

LC 2014017788

In this autobiography, author and chef Marcus Samuelsson "tells his extraordinary story and encourages young people to embrace their mistakes and follow their dreams. Based on his highly praised adult memoir, Yes, Chef, this young adult edition includes an 8-page black-and-white family photo insert." (Publisher's note)

"Samuelsson asserts, and his story evinces, that three things have stood him in good stead: he is humble, he works hard, and he loves food. This smoothly written account, co-authored with Chambers, brings the drama of the kitchen to vivid and memorable life. Bon appétit!" Booklist

641.59 Cooking characteristic of specific geographic environments, ethnic cooking

Locricchio, Matthew

The **cooking** of Brazil; Matthew Locricchio; with photos by Jack McConnell. 2nd ed. Marshall Cavendish Benchmark 2012 96 p. ill. (library) $35.64; (ebook) $35.64

Grades: 7 8 9 10 11 12 **641.59**

1. Cookbooks 2. Brazilian cooking

ISBN 1608705498; 9781608705498; 9781608707379

LC 2011004948

This book, by Matthew Locricchio, "invites . . . readers to the kitchen to experience the satisfaction of preparing authentic [Brazilian] recipes." The book "opens with a . . . look at the . . . country and their culinary traditions and contributions to international cuisine. This cultural introduction is followed with an overview of kitchen safety, food handling, and common sense nutrition, then on to a wide variety of recipes that range from soups and salads to main entrees and desserts." (Publisher's note)

Includes bibliographical references and index.

McFeely, Mary Drake

Can she bake a cherry pie? American women and the kitchen in the twentieth century. University of Mass. Press 2000 194p hardcover o.p. pa $16.95

Grades: 9 10 11 12 **641.59**

1. Cooking 2. Women -- United States

ISBN 1-55849-250-X; 1-55849-333-6 pa

LC 00-23452

"This book shows how cooking developed and evolved during the twentieth century. From Fannie Farmer to Julia Child, new challenges arose to replace the old. Women found themselves still tied to the kitchen, but for different reasons and with the need to acquire new skills." Publisher's note

Includes bibliographical references

Zanger, Mark H.

The **American** history cookbook. Greenwood Press 2003 xxiii, 459p il (Cookbooks for students) pa $29.95

Grades: 11 12 Adult **641.59**

1. Cooking 2. American cooking---History

ISBN 1-57356-376-5

LC 2002-69608

"This book uses historical commentary and recipes to trace the history of American cooking from the first European contact with Native Americans to the 1970s. Each of 50 chronologically arranged topical chapters contain 500-1,000 words of general commentary followed by descriptions and . . . step-by-step instructions for 3-4 recipes. The recipes are drawn from a wide variety of historical cookbooks and other historical sources." Publisher's note

Includes bibliographical references

641.8 Cooking specific kinds of dishes and preparing beverages

Blakeslee, Robert L.

Your time to bake; a first cookbook for the novice baker. by Robert L. Blakeslee. Square One Publishers 2012 384 p. (hardback) $29.95

Grades: 9 10 11 12 **641.8**

1. Baking 2. Desserts 3. Cookbooks 4. Cake decorating

ISBN 9780757003554

LC 2011014622

In this cookbook, "[Robert L.] Blakeslee includes 'step by step photo instructions, with a finished shot of each recipe.' . . . He provides recipes for every simple sweet treat imaginable. . . . Explaining that baking is 'more about chemistry,' Blakeslee . . . discusses 'important baking variables and how to control them,' with helpful tips: measuring ingredients exactly and making sure ingredients such as eggs and butter are the correct temperature. Also . . . [included] are sections on essential items needed for baking--such as different flours, sugars, spices and cheeses--important equipment, and baking terms from A to Z. . . . [T]here are more than 150 recipes . . . and a final chapter on decorating cookies, tarts, and cupcakes and making fondant." (Publishers Weekly)

Carle, Megan

Teens cook dessert; [by] Megan and Jill Carle, with Judi Carle. Ten Speed Press 2006 158p pa $19.95

Grades: 6 7 8 9 10 **641.8**

1. Cooking 2. Desserts

ISBN 978-1-58008-752-0; 1-58008-752-3

LC 2005-24343

The authors "start out with the all-around favorites, like classic chocolate chip cookies. There are holiday recipes for Halloween dirt pie, complete with cookie tombstones and gummy worms that seem to crawl out of the chocolate 'earth.' The final chapter has fancy foods like vanilla souffît with chocolate sauce or fresh raspberry napoleons. . . . Not only do the recipes sound delicious, they look delicious in glossy color pictures. . . . The instructions are easy to understand." Voice Youth Advocates

Tack, Karen

Hello, cupcake! [by] Karen Tack and Alan Richardson; text and photographs by Alan Richardson; recipes and food styling by Karen Tack. Houghton Mifflin 2008 230p il pa $15.95

Grades: 9 10 11 12 Adult   **641.8**
   1. Cake decorating 2. Cupcakes
   ISBN 978-0-618-82925-5
                   LC 2007-40029

The authors cover "the decorating of cupcakes for almost every conceivable occasion. They choose from a vast array of cupcake accessories, including designables (jelly beans), cuttables (licorice), and rollables (Tootsie Rolls), to name just a few. They also incorporate different techniques for building and dipping as well as 18 cake and frosting recipes. The eye-popping results include Oreo-laden pandas, raspberry-preserve-topped truffles, spaghetti and meatballs, an elegant wedding cake, and Christmas ornaments one could almost hang from a tree. An imaginative, well-illustrated book containing recipes that are so clearly explained and easy to make that kids can also enjoy the fun." Booklist

643   Housing and household equipment

Reader's Digest Association, Inc.

★ **Complete** do-it-yourself manual; with the editors of Family handyman. rev and updated; Reader's Digest 2005 528p il $35

Grades: 11 12 Adult   **643**
   1. Houses -- Maintenance and repair
   ISBN 0-7621-0579-8
                   LC 2004-50945

First published 1973 with title: Reader's Digest complete do-it-yourself manual

This manual for homeowners covers topics such as power tools, plumbing, landscaping, and storage projects with photos, diagrams and illustrations

"Intriguing sidebars on wood refinishers (the fastest drying versus the safest), the financial benefits of renting specialty tools for a large drywall project and other subjects round out this must-have guide." Publ Wkly

644.6   Plumbing

DiPiazza, Francesca Davis

Remaking the john; the invention and reinvention of the toilet. Francesca Davis DiPiazza. Twenty-First Century Books 2015 64 p. color illustrations (lib. bdg.: alk. paper) $34.60

Grades: 6 7 8 9   **644.6**
   1. Toilets 2. Sewage disposal 3. Toilets -- History
   ISBN 1467726451; 9781467726450
                   LC 2013040138

Readers of this book by Francesca Davis Dipiazza will "explore the many ways people across the globe and through the ages have invented--and reinvented--the toilet. You will learn about everything from ancient Roman sewers to the world's first flush toilets. You'll also find out about the twenty-first-century Reinvent the Toilet Challenge--an engineering contest designed to spur creation of an ecologically friendly, water-saving, inexpensive, and sanitary toilet." (Publisher's note)

"This honest, fact-filled little book should attract readers and researchers (who may even begin celebrating World Toilet Day every November 19)." SLJ

Includes bibliographical references (pages 58-59) and index

646   Sewing, clothing, management of personal and family life

Jones, Caroline

1001 little fashion miracles. Carlton Books 2008 224p il pa $12.95

Grades: 11 12 Adult   **646**
   1. Fashion 2. Women's clothing 3. Clothing and dress
   ISBN 978-1-84442-838-0

Offering advice on styles, accessorizing and shopping, this book provides ideas for looking best in different circumstances.

646.2   Sewing and related operations

Creative Publishing International, Inc.

The **complete** photo guide to sewing; 1200 full-color how-to photos. [created by the editors of Creative Publishing International] Rev. + expanded ed.; Creative Pub. International 2009 352p il pa $24.99

Grades: 9 10 11 12 Adult   **646.2**
   1. Sewing
   ISBN 978-1-58923-434-5; 1-58923-434-0
                   LC 2008-31264

First published 1999

"Sections include choosing the right tools and notions, using conventional machines and sergers, fashion sewing, tailoring, and home décor projects. Included are step-by-step instructions for basic projects like pillows, tablecloths, and window treatments." Publisher's note

Smith, Alison

Sew step by step. Dorling Kindersley 2011 224p il pa $15.95

Grades: 9 10 11 12 Adult   **646.2**
   1. Sewing 2. Dressmaking
   ISBN 978-0-7566-7164-8

First published 2009 in the United Kingdom with title: The sewing book

This book covers over 200 sewing techniques using contemporary styles and materials.

646.4 Clothing and accessories construction

Holkeboer, Katherine Strand

Patterns for theatrical costumes; garments, trims, and accessories from ancient Egypt to 1915. [by] Katherine Strand Holkeboer. Drama Book Publishers 1992 342p il pa $35

Grades: 9 10 11 12   **646.4**
  1. Sewing 2. Costume
  ISBN 0-89676-125-8

                LC 92-34985

First published 1984 by Prentice-Hall

Each design "includes black-and-white drawings of the completed garment, pattern pieces for enlarging embellishments to be copied, and, when necessary, illustrations of how to wear the particular costume. A few special costumes—clergy, animals, oriental—are featured as are notes on constructing important accessories." Booklist

Includes bibliographical references

Rannels, Melissa

Sew subversive; down and dirty DIY for the fabulous fashionista. [by] Melissa Rannels, Melissa Alvarado, Hope Meng; illustrated by Hope Meng & 3+Co.; photographs by Matthew Carden. The Taunton Press 2006 186p il pa $14.95

Grades: 11 12 Adult   **646.4**
  1. Sewing 2. Women's clothing
  ISBN 978-1-56158-809-1; 1-56158-809-1

                LC 2006-1502

The authors "give beginning sewers all the basics, plus 22 tempting projects. Their mission—'subverting' fashion—is all about 'embellishing and customizing clothes—refashioning them to make them uniquely your own.' . . . They start with a solid chapter on hand sewing (mending rips, hemming skirts), then tell you everything you've ever wanted to know about sewing machines but were afraid to ask. T-shirts are torn apart to make mini skirts, shoulder bags and tube tops. . . . With its casual approach and offbeat creations, this is definitely not your mother's sewing book." Publ Wkly

Includes bibliographical references

646.7 Management of personal and family life

Bergamotto, Lori

Skin; the bare facts. Zest Books 2009 97p il pa $18.95

Grades: 6 7 8 9 10   **646.7**
  1. Skin -- Care 2. Teenagers -- Health and hygiene
  ISBN 978-0-9800732-5-6; 0-9800732-5-1

Presents an overview on skin types, methods for treating common problems, and tips for skin care and makeup application.

"There's something for every girl here, whether she's just had her first breakout or needs a refresher on which sunscreen to use and when to reapply." SLJ

Brown, Bobbi

Bobbi Brown teenage beauty; everything you need to look pretty, natural, sexy & awesome. [by]

Bobbi Brown & Annemarie Iverson. Cliff St. Bks. 2000 200p il $25; pa $18.95

Grades: 9 10 11 12   **646.7**
  1. Personal grooming 2. Skin -- Care
  ISBN 0-06-019636-X; 0-06-095724-7 pa

                LC 00-711795

"Brown and Iverson give teens basic beauty tips and a large boost to their self-esteem. . . . The authors stress the importance of diet and exercise." SLJ

Earle, Liz

Skin care secrets; how to have naturally healthy beautiful skin. special photography by Patrick Drummond and Kate Whitaker; illustrations by Kathy Wyatt. Firefly Books 2010 192p il pa $24.95

Grades: 9 10 11 12 Adult   **646.7**
  1. Skin -- Care
  ISBN 978-1-55407-608-6

                LC 2010-459161

A guide to naturally beautiful skin at any age.

Fonseca, Christine

The **girl** guide; finding your place in a mixed-up world. by Christine Fonseca. Prufrock Press 2013 228 p. $14.95

Grades: 6 7 8 9   **646.7**
  1. Girls 2. Teenagers
  ISBN 1618210270; 9781618210272

This book, by Christine Fonseca, is designed "for girls in grades 6-8 as they enter the tumultuous world of adolescence. Worksheets and quizzes, as well as stories from older girls and women, [cover] everything a teenage girl needs to know on the journey toward her own identity. Proven strategies for dealing with stress management, confronting relational aggression, being safe online, navigating the changing mother-daughter relationship, and more make this [a] guide for any girl to get through the teen years." (Publisher's note)

"—Sporting a sassy, appealing cover, The Girl Guide elbows its way into the already-crowded market of self-help and self-esteem-building books...There's a bit of genius at play here as the author gives the gift of time to her readers-time for reflection and for de-stressing through the act of creating. Teens should not rush through this book. No quick fixes are offered, just reasonable suggestions for maintaining true north through the turbulent teen years.—" (School Library Journal)

Fornay, Alfred

★ **Born** beautiful; the African American teenager's complete beauty guide. John Wiley & Sons 2002 166p il pa $14.95

Grades: 8 9 10 11 12   **646.7**
  1. Personal grooming 2. Personal appearance 3. Teenagers -- Health and hygiene 4. African American women -- Health and hygiene
  ISBN 0-471-40275-3

                LC 2002-18131

This book on beauty and grooming for African American teenage girls includes information on makeup, hairstyles, nail and skin care, diet, and clothing.

Morgenstern, Julie

★ **Organizing** from the inside out for teens; the foolproof system for organizing your room, your time, and your life. [by] Julie Morgenstern and Jessi Morgenstern-Colón; illustrations by Janet Pedersen. Holt & Co. 2002 238p il pa $15

Grades: 7 8 9 10   **646.7**

     1. Life skills 2. Time management
     ISBN 0-8050-6470-2

                      LC 2002-68552

The authors "offer practical advice to teenagers who want to get organized. After considering what might be holding them back and the three steps to success (analyze, strategize, attack), the discussion shifts to the two major areas of concern: managing space and managing time. . . . Useful advice in an accessible paperback format." Booklist

The **New** York Times practical guide to practically everything; the essential companion for everyday life. edited by Amy D. Bernstein and Peter W. Bernstein. St. Martin's Press 2006 834p il map $29.95

Grades: 11 12 Adult   **646.7**

     1. Life skills
     ISBN 0-312-35388-X; 978-0-312-35388-9

                      LC 2006-45081

This "guide covers a wide range of topics—from 'Getting and Staying Trim' to 'The Braille System'—broken up into broad subject categories such as 'Health,' 'Food & Drink,' 'Money,' 'Careers,' 'House & Garden,' 'Sports & Games,' 'Arts & Entertainment' and 'Everyday Science.' . . . This is a browse-worthy collection of general knowledge that should come in handy next time you're traveling to the Galapagos, building an igloo, or in any of more than 800 other 'everyday' situations." Publ Wkly

Parrish, J. R.

You don't have to learn the hard way; making It in the real world: a guide for graduates. BenBella Books 2009 283p il $19.95

Grades: 11 12 Adult   **646.7**

     1. Success 2. Life skills
     ISBN 978-1933771-74-8

This book offers advice for teens and college graduates on topics "including: nailing that first big job interview; avoiding dangerous relationship mistakes; mastering the art of managing your finances; circumventing the typical pitfalls of adjusting to the adult world; making friends and forging career alliances; [and] choosing the right mentors." Publisher's note

Shipp, Josh

The **teen's** guide to world domination; advice on life, liberty, and the pursuit of awesomeness. St. Martin's Griffin 2010 285p il pa $14.99

Grades: 8 9 10 11   **646.7**

     1. Life skills 2. Conduct of life 3. Interpersonal relations
     ISBN 978-0-312-64154-2; 0-312-64154-0

                      LC 2010-22069

The author "provides a funny, compassionate, and straight-talking blueprint for teens to achieve fulfillment personally, socially, and professionally. . . . Shipp's fresh and honest approach should make sense to teens seeking guidance and avoids feeling preachy or heavy-handed." Publ Wkly

Shoket, Ann

Seventeen ultimate guide to beauty; the best hair, skin, nails & makeup ideas for you. Ann Shoket & the editors of Seventeen Magazine. Running Press 2012 191 p.

Grades: 7 8 9 10   **646.7**

     1. Hair 2. Cosmetics 3. Personal appearance 4. Beauty, Personal 5. Skin -- Care and hygiene
     ISBN 0762445246; 9780762445240

                      LC 2012935723

This book, by Ann Shoket and the editors of "Seventeen" magazine, "is a girl's handbook to celebrating her natural beauty. It's packed with clear, customized service that helps make the most of her skin tone, her face shape, her hair texture, and her style! Each chapter is filled with detailed how-tos, amazing inspiration, and awesome advice from 'Seventeen's' editors." (Publisher's note)

"illed with great fashion photography featuring the Beauty Smarties, this guide highlights real girls' personal styles... The detailed photographs and step-by-step instructions will have readers practicing braids, up-dos, and smoky eye makeup for hours. A fine addition to the 646.7 shelves." (School Library Journal)

Spencer, Kit

★ **Pro** makeup; salon secrets of the professionals. Firefly Books 2009 255p il $29.95

Grades: 8 9 10 11 12 Adult   **646.7**

     1. Cosmetics
     ISBN 978-1-55407-477-8

                      LC 2009-279649

This book "provides an organized, attractive overview of makeup application techniques from everyday to costume. The text is enhanced throughout by useful highlights offering tips from professionals on everything from achieving the perfect eyebrow arch to taking the attention away from a wide nose. Bridal and costume party makeup are covered as well. . . . There is a section on developing looks, dealing with skin conditions, choosing equipment, and even applying makeup to men and children." Voice Youth Advocates

Toselli, Leigh

★ **Pro** nail care; salon secrets of the professionals. Firefly Books 2009 254p il $29.95

Grades: 8 9 10 11 12 Adult   **646.7**

     1. Manicuring 2. Personal grooming
     ISBN 978-1-55407-478-5

                      LC 2009-288700

This book "goes well beyond the typical manicure or pedicure. An intriguing history of nail care is provided (who knew they had manicures in ancient Babylon?), as well as a history of nail polish fashion. The anatomy of the hand and foot are examined in detail. Nail diseases and problems are explained with suggested remedies. There are sections on massage, overlay systems, the chemistry of nail products, and a gallery of nail 'looks.' Most interesting is the section on nail art. The looks are explained with step-by-step instructions accompanied by clear photographs." Voice Youth Advocates

Willdorf, Nina

City chic; the modern girl's guide to living large on less. [New ed.]; Sourcebooks 2009 271p il pa $14.99

Grades: 9 10 11 12 Adult   **646.7**
    1. Life skills 2. Young women 3. Personal finance
    ISBN 978-1-4022-1785-2; 1-4022-1785-4
                  LC 2008-38831
    First published 2003
This is a "guide to living well on a dime. Although aimed at women in their twenties and thirties, women in other age brackets will also appreciate the author's hints for saving money in many realms of their lives, including home furnishings, makeup, entertainment, and laundry. Moneysaving ideas range from exercising at home to storing food properly." Libr J
    Includes bibliographical references

Yellin, Susan

  ★ Life after high school; a guide for students with disabilities and their families. [by] Susan Yellin and Christina Cacioppo Bertsch. Jessica Kingsley Publishers 2010 269p pa $19.95

Grades: Adult   **646.7**
    1. Vocational guidance 2. Students with disabilities 3. People with disabilities -- Employment
    ISBN 978-1-84905-828-5
                  LC 2010-4298
The authors "provide students with disabilities and their parents an outstanding and highly readable guide to preparing for and transitioning to life after high school. They start by examining the legal landscape and cover defining a disability and creating a paper trail to document the disability and previous accommodations. They move on to college-entrance exams, how to select a college, and the admissions process, and then discuss the transition to full-time work. There is also a chapter devoted to dealing with medical issues without mom." Libr J
    Includes bibliographical references

647.9   Specific kinds of public households and institutions

Chalmers, Irena

Food jobs; 150 great jobs for culinary students, career changers and food lovers. Beaufort Books 2008 xxiii, 326p il pa $19.95

Grades: 11 12 Adult   **647.9**
    1. Food service 2. Vocational guidance
    ISBN 978-0-8253-0592-4; 0-8253-0592-6
                  LC 2008-26124
"The book's strength lies in exposing readers to new possibilities and in further illuminating some of the more familiar or traditional jobs and fields. . . . [It] is meant to be both entertaining and helpful as a resource, ideally project-

ing readers along the paths of their personal and professional aspirations. In short—this book is useful." Gastronomica
    Includes bibliographical references

647.95   Eating and drinking places

Food. Ferguson's 2011 122 p. (Discovering careers series) (hardcover: alk. paper) $30

Grades: 7 8 9 10   **647.95**
    1. Food service -- Vocational guidance 2. Food industry and trade -- Vocational guidance
    ISBN 0816080577; 9780816080571
                  LC 2011022916
"Each volume breaks down broad career umbrellas into 20 specific subsets and examines them from the vantage point of "Education and Training," "Outlook," "Earnings," and so on. A clean design, sidebars, and the occasional on-the-job action photo add to the appeal. Food moves from the ground (farmers and fishers) to the plate (personal chefs)... both younger and older kids will find tempting—perhaps before unheard-of—career options to get them thinking about down the road." (Booklist)
    Includes bibliographical references and index

649   Child rearing; home care of people with disabilities and illnesses

Lindsay, Jeanne Warren

  ★ Teen dads; rights, responsibilities, and joys. Rev. [3rd] ed.; Morning Glory Press 2008 224p il pa $12.95

Grades: 9 10 11 12   **649**
    1. Parenting 2. Child rearing 3. Teenage fathers
    ISBN 978-1-932538-86-1
    First published 1993
"This upbeat presentation instructs young men on how to be supportive of their partner and the new baby, assist with the baby's labor and delivery, care for and nurture the child through infancy and the toddler years, and better understand their changing relationship with the mother. Short chapters cover, in chronological order, all the issues young parents must face, from the pregnancy test to learning how to properly love, feed, and discipline a curious, growing child." Voice Youth Advocates
    Includes bibliographical references

649.1   Child rearing

Bondy, Halley

Don't sit on the baby; the ultimate guide to sane, skilled, and safe babysitting. Halley Bondy. Zest Books 2012 127 p. (pbk.) $12.99

Grades: 7 8 9 10 11 12   **649.1**
    1. Child care 2. Babysitting 3. Infants -- Care
    ISBN 0982732236; 9780982732236
                  LC 2011942757
This book is a "how to guide [that] covers everything . . . that a teen might need to know to become a babysitter.

The first section covers topics such as . . . what to expect from kids ages newborn to ten. Section two covers essential skills such as feeding, dressing, playing, bathing, bedtime, and keeping kids healthy. The final section includes tips on how to get a job, how to interview, how much to charge, and even how to quit a job." (Children's Literature)

Includes web resources and index.

650   Management and auxiliary services

★ The **business** book; senior editor, Sam Atkinson. Dk Pub 2014 352 p. illustrations (chiefly color) (Big Ideas Simply Explained) $25

Grades: Adult   **650**

1. Business 2. Encyclopedias and dictionaries

ISBN 1465415858; 9781465415851

               LC 2013478653

A "comprehensive coverage of business, addressing such topics as money management, leadership and human resources, starting and growing a business, marketing, production, and operations. Discussed is not only what has worked for successful businesses but also what has not worked, and why being the first with an idea is not always the best." VOYA

Trueit, Trudi Strain

Animal trainer; Trudi Strain Trueit. Cavendish Square 2014 64 p. color illustrations $34.21

Grades: 6 7 8 9 10   **650**

1. Animal trainers 2. Animal training -- Vocational guidance

ISBN 1627124616; 9780761480754; 9780761480822; 9781627124614

               LC 2012027729

This book, by Trudi Strain Trueit, focuses on "professionals engaged in a wide range of careers with animals and . . . [describes] their daily work to bring to life numerous options for animal trainers and wildlife conservationists. After a general introduction to animal training, . . . [the author] includes focus chapters for those working with dogs, horses, and marine mammals." (School Library Journal)

"The books include color pictures and a section with more resources. There is enough information in each book to give students an idea of the working conditions and job requirements for each career." Lib Med Con

Includes bibliographical references and index

Wildlife Conservationist; Trudy Strain Trueit. Cavendish Square 2014 64 p. color illustrations (Careers with Animals) $34.21

Grades: 6 7 8 9 10   **650**

1. Vocational guidance 2. Wildlife conservation 3. Wildlife conservation -- Vocational guidance 4. Environmental protection -- Vocational guidance

ISBN 1627124675; 9781627124676

This children's book by Trudi Strain Trueit, part of the Careers with Animals series, discusses career options in the field of wildlife conservation. It aims to help readers to "Explore the job duties, career specialties, educational requirements, and job outlook in this growing field." (Publisher's note)

"While offering encouragement to animal lovers, Trueit does not minimize hard work and long hours involved, sometimes in adverse conditions. A list of relevant websites provides additional resources to expand the information supplied in these readable and realistic career overviews." SLJ

650.1   Personal success in business

Roza, Greg

Great networking skills. Rosen Pub. 2008 64p il (Work readiness) lib bdg $29.25

Grades: 9 10 11 12   **650.1**

1. Vocational guidance 2. Interpersonal relations

ISBN 978-1-4042-1420-0

               LC 2007-34841

The author "explains what networking is and what it isn't. Topics include working with friends, family, and academic contacts; staying organized; writing; preparing résumés; making connections; and selling youself." SLJ

Includes glossary and bibliographical references

Sommers, Michael A.

Great interpersonal skills. Rosen Pub. 2008 64p il (Work readiness) lib bdg $29.25

Grades: 9 10 11 12   **650.1**

1. Social skills 2. Interpersonal relations

ISBN 978-1-4042-1423-1; 1-4042-1423-2

               LC 2007-23663

This book "discusses groundwork such as developing conversational skills, creating a good first impression, teamwork, assertiveness, and conflict resolution." SLJ

Includes glossary and bibliographical references

650.14   Success in obtaining jobs and promotions

Berger, Lauren

All work, no pay; finding an internship, building your resume, making connections, and gaining job experience. Lauren Berger. Ten Speed Press 2012 xii, 194 p.p $12.99

Grades: 11 12 Adult   **650.14**

1. Job hunting 2. Internship programs 3. Employees -- Training 4. Vocational guidance

ISBN 1607741687; 9781607741688

               LC 2011034540

This book is a "guide [that] reveals insider secrets to scoring the perfect internship, building invaluable connections, boosting transferable skills, and ultimately moving toward your dream career." Topics include "internship opportunities," writing "effective resumes and cover letters," and "network[ing] like a pro." (Publisher's note)

Includes bibliographical references and index.

Enelow, Wendy S.

Best resumes for people without a four-year degree. Impact Publications 2004 185p pa $19.95

Grades: 9 10 11 12 **650.14**
1. Résumés (Employment)
ISBN 1-57023-204-0

LC 2003-100522

This collection of professionally-written résumés "includes four . . . résumé-writing exercises as well as contact information for the professional résumé writers who contributed to this book." Publisher's note

Includes bibliographical references

Henneberg, Susan

Internship smarts; by Susan Henneberg. 1st ed. Rosen Pub. 2013 64 p. col. ill. (library) $31.95; (paperback) $12.95

Grades: 10 11 12 **650.14**
1. Internship programs 2. Teenagers -- Employment
ISBN 1448882559; 9781448882557; 9781448882687; 9781448882694

LC 2012022064

This book by Susan Henneberg, part of the Get Smart With Your Money series, looks at internships. It "focuses on the purposes of intern experiences, how to land an internship, tactics for making a good first impression, and reflecting on the experience as a means of determining future interests and career paths." (Booklist)

Includes bibliographical references (p. 60-62) and index.

Hinds, Maurene J.

★ The **Ferguson** guide to resumes and job hunting skills; a step-by-step guide to preparing for your job search. Ferguson 2005 248p il $45; pa $16.95

Grades: 9 10 11 12 **650.14**
1. Job hunting 2. Résumés (Employment)
ISBN 0-8160-5792-3; 0-8160-5796-6 pa

LC 2004-24445

"Included are an annotated roundup of assessment tests, from Myers-Briggs to the Strong Interest Inventory; a litany of common job-hunters' mistakes (for instance, not looking an interviewer directly in the eyes); and, of course, a variety of resumes and cover letters." Booklist

Reeves, Ellen Gordon

Can I wear my nose ring to the interview? the crash course: finding, landing, and keeping your first real job. Workman Pub. 2009 227p pa $13.95

Grades: 10 11 12 Adult **650.14**
1. Job hunting 2. Interviewing 3. Résumés (Employment)
ISBN 978-0-7611-4145-7; 0-7611-4145-6

LC 2009-279010

This book discusses how to search for a job; create a résumé, cover letter, and list of references; and prepare for job interviews.

Salvador, Evelyn U.

Step-by-step cover letters; build a cover letter in 10 easy steps using personal branding. Evelyn U. Salvador. JIST Works 2011 xiii, 226 p.p (bound-in cd-rom: alk. paper) $19.95

Grades: 11 12 Adult **650.14**
1. Job hunting 2. Cover letters
ISBN 159357780X; 9781593577803

LC 2010027700

This book, by Evelyn U. Salvador, offers guidance on writing and editing cover letters for job resumes. "Professional resume writer . . . Evelyn Salvador leads you through the steps of writing a compelling first paragraph, showing the value you bring, developing and communicating your brand in your letter, summarizing your key accomplishments, editing your letter, and compelling the employer to pick up the phone and call you for an interview." (Publisher's note)

Step-by-step resumes; build an outstanding resume in 10 easy steps! Evelyn U. Salvador. JIST Works 2011 xvi, 295 p.p (pbk.: alk. paper): $19.95

Grades: 11 12 Adult **650.14**
1. Job hunting 2. Résumés (Employment)
ISBN 1593577788 $19.95; 9781593577780 $19.95

LC 2010025503

This book, by Evelyn U. Salvador, offers guidance for writing resumes. Through the steps provided in this volume, "readers can pull together an effective resume with ease. [This book] also includes an exhaustive collection of thousands of powerful resume keywords. . . . New for this edition is a section on integrating your resume into your social networking strategy, as well as new personal branding worksheets and expanded tips on e-mailing resumes." (Publisher's note)

Troutman, Kathryn K.

Creating your high school resume; a step-by-step guide to preparing an effective resume for jobs, college, and training programs. [by] Kathryn Kraemer Troutman. 3rd ed; JIST Works 2009 150p il pa $16.95

Grades: 9 10 11 12 **650.14**
1. Résumés (Employment)
ISBN 978-1-59357-662-2
First published 1998

This book "explains why high school students need to work on a resume and keep updating it. In addition to job searching, students will be able to use a resume when applying for college, asking people for recommendations, and applying for scholarships. There are examples from teenagers that demonstrate how to present oneself in the best possible light." Libr Media Connect

Withers, Jennie

Hey, get a job! a teen guide for getting and keeping a job. Jennie Withers 2009 89p il pa $14.99

Grades: 8 9 10 11 12 **650.14**
1. Occupations 2. Vocational guidance
ISBN 978-0-9842354-0-7

This guide "covers all the basics and more for teens about to enter the working world with a style and approach that tells it like it is. . . . Seven chapters cover everything from finding employment opportunities, filling out applications, brainstorming relevant strengths and experience for resumes to interview prep and completing standard employment forms." Voice Youth Advocates

651.7 Communication

Geffner, Andrea B.

★ **How** to write better business letters; 4th ed.; Barron's 2007 173p il pa $14.99

Grades: 9 10 11 12   **651.7**

1. Business letters

ISBN 0-7641-3539-2; 978-0-7641-3539-2

LC 2006-42953

First published 1982

"This book instructs on how to write effective examples of every kind of business letter. It presents about 75 model letters in categories that include credit applications, letters of inquiry, orders of goods and services, formal business announcements, letters of recommendation, and sales promotional letters of the type used by direct marketers. This book also features examples of different letter formatting styles." Publisher's note

Thomason-Carroll, Kristi L.

★ **Young** adult's guide to business communications. Business Books 2004 117p il $14.95

Grades: 9 10 11 12   **651.7**

1. Interviewing 2. Business communication 3. Résumés (Employment)

ISBN 0-9723714-4-3

LC 2002-115501

This "guide covers writing a résumé, filling out job applications, interviewing skills, and work etiquette (e.g., the proper form for memos, e-mails, and reports, and interactions with others). Throughout the lively text, the author stresses the importance of making a good impression through careful preparation and presentation." SLJ

Includes bibliographical references

652 Processes of written communication

Butler, William S.

Secret messages; concealment, codes, and other types of ingenious communication. {by} William S. Butler and L. Douglas Keeney. Simon & Schuster 2001 192p il $23

Grades: 11 12 Adult   **652**

1. Ciphers 2. Cryptography

ISBN 0-684-86998-5

LC 00-46368

"Through a series of short stories and anecdotes, this book gives . . . {a} quick tour of codes used by common folk as well as spies. . . . Much of the book is devoted to codes used to convey messages in everyday life. Those used by hospitals, police officers, restaurant staff, and bridge players are addressed. . . . An engaging book that may entice readers to pursue a more in-depth exploration of the topic." SLJ

Includes bibliographical references

658.002 General management--Miscellany

Harmon, Daniel E.

Careers as a marketing and public relations specialist; Daniel E. Harmon. Rosen Publishing Group, Inc. 2014 80 p. color illustrations (Essential careers) (library binding) $34.25

Grades: 9 10 11 12   **658.002**

1. Marketing 2. Public relations 3. Marketing -- Vocational guidance 4. Public relations -- Vocational guidance

ISBN 1477717935; 9781477717936

LC 2013016223

This book, by author Daniel E. Harmon, "explains the relationship and differences between these two fields as it describes marketing and PR relations managers and related jobs (art directors, technical writers, etc.). [The series] provide information on the skills, education, and training needed." (Booklist)

"Whether used by students with no professional direction or students with some interest in business who are in need of more specifics, these titles in the Essential Careers series offer clear and realistic choices." Booklist

Includes bibliographical references (pages 71-76) and index

658.1 Organization and financial management

Bielagus, Peter G.

Quick cash for teens; be your own boss and make big bucks. Sterling Pub. 2009 249p pa $12.95

Grades: 7 8 9 10 11 12   **658.1**

1. Small business 2. Entrepreneurship 3. Money-making projects for children

ISBN 978-1-4027-6038-9; 1-4027-6038-8

LC 2008-42793

"Young entrepreneurs wanting to own and operate their own businesses will find this practical, introductory guide an excellent source of advice. . . . Bielagus' conversational style and the frequent insertion of anecdotes from successful teen entrepreneurs make the text accessible." Booklist

658.3 Personnel management (Human resource management)

Freedman, Jeri

Careers in human resources; Jeri Freedman. Rosen Publishing Group, Inc. 2014 80 p. illustrations (some color) (library binding) $34.25

Grades: 9 10 11 12   **658.3**

1. Vocational guidance 2. Personnel management

ISBN 1477717919; 9781477717912

LC 2013012402

In this book on human resources, by Jeri Freedman, "[t]eens investigate the vital roles of staffing a company, training employees, learning HR policies and benefits, employee relations, and the types of jobs that are available in HR. Headhunting and recruitment firms and payroll processing firms are considered, as well as education requirements for the HR profession." (Publisher's note)

"Whether used by students with no professional direction or students with some interest in business who are in need of more specifics, these titles in the Essential Careers series offer clear and realistic choices." Booklist

Includes bibliographical references and index

658.4 Executive management

Encyclopedia of leadership; editors, George R. Goethals, Georgia J. Sorenson, James MacGregor Burns. Sage Publications 2004 4v il map set $595

Grades: 11 12 Adult   **658.4**

1. Reference books 2. Leadership -- Encyclopedias
ISBN 0-7619-2597-X

      LC 2004-1252

"What is leadership? What is a great leader? What is a great follower? What are the types of leadership? And how does someone become a leader? This set was designed with the needs of several user communities in mind, including students, scholars, and professionals who want to explore such questions." Booklist

Includes bibliographical references

658.8 Management of marketing

Underhill, Paco

Why we buy; the science of shopping. Updated and rev.; Simon & Schuster Pbks. 2009 306p pa $16; ebook $12.99

Grades: 11 12 Adult   **658.8**

1. Shopping 2. Consumers 3. Marketing
ISBN 978-1-4165-9524-3 pa; 1-4165-9524-4 pa; 978-1-4165-6174-3 ebook; 1-4165-6174-9 ebook

      LC 2010-483248

First published 1999

"Each chapter delves into a particular aspect of a store environment and its interface with customers: the importance of signage and why less is more, how men shop, . . . and clues about waiting time. Throughout, insights are peppered with one or several examples." Booklist [review of 1999 edition]

Weinick, Suzanne

Increasing your tweets, likes, and ratings; marketing your digital business. Suzanne Weinick. 1st ed. Rosen Pub. 2013 64 p. col. ill. (Digital entrepreneurship in the age of apps, the web, and mobile devices) (library) $31.95; (paperback) $12.95

Grades: 8 9 10 11 12   **658.8**

1. Marketing 2. Social media 3. Internet marketing 4. Electronic commerce -- Marketing
ISBN 1448869285; 9781448869282; 9781448869763; 9781448869770

      LC 2012006836

This "entry in the . . . Digital Entrepreneurship in the Age of Apps, the Web, and Mobile Devices series . . . focuses

on marketing minutiae, including giving your app a savvy name, choosing a useful Twitter image, monitoring your Facebook page, vlogging, and knowing your SEO [search engine optimization] from your PPC [pay per click] and CPM [cost per impression]." (Booklist)

Includes bibliographical references (p. 57-62) and index

658.85 Personal selling

Mozer, Mindy

Careers as a commissioned sales representative; Mindy Mozer. Rosen Publishing Group, Inc. 2014 80 p. color illustrations (Essential careers) (library binding) $34.25

Grades: 9 10 11 12   **658.85**

1. Retail trade 2. Sales personnel
ISBN 1477717943; 9781477717943

      LC 2013013521

This book, by author Mindy Mozer, "devotes separate chapters to various types of sales, including advertising, retail, and real estate, and discusses related duties, products or services, and work environments. It also covers what it means to work on commission and how to calculate one." (Booklist)

"Whether used by students with no professional direction or students with some interest in business who are in need of more specifics, these titles in the Essential Careers series offer clear and realistic choices." Booklist

Includes bibliographical references and index

659.1 Advertising

★ **Advertising:** opposing viewpoints; Roman Espejo, book editor. Greenhaven Press 2010 207p il (Opposing viewpoints series) $39.70; pa $27.50

Grades: 9 10 11 12   **659.1**

1. Advertising
ISBN 978-0-7377-4751-5; 0-7377-4751-X; 978-0-7377-4752-2 pa; 0-7377-4752-8 pa

      LC 2009050761

Articles in this anthology discuss whether advertising is harmful, if it exploits children, and political advertising.

Includes bibliographical references

★ **How** does advertising impact teen behavior? David M. Haugen, book editor. Greenhaven Press 2008 88p (At issue. Teen issues) lib bdg $29.95; pa $21.20

Grades: 9 10 11 12   **659.1**

1. Mass media 2. Advertising 3. Teenagers -- Attitudes
ISBN 978-0-7377-3922-0 lib bdg; 0-7377-3922-3 lib bdg; 978-0-7377-3923-7 pa; 0-7377-3923-1 pa

      LC 2007-48660

This "is a well-rounded assortment of essays that covers the most salient discussion points in the debate about what impact advertising has on teen behavior. Authors address the role it plays in childhood obesity, smoking, and brand loyalty." SLJ

Includes bibliographical references

660.6 Biotechnology

Careers in biotechnology; Bonnie Szumski. ReferencePoint Press, Inc. 2015 80 p. (hardback) $28.95

Grades: 9 10 11 12   660.6

1. Professions 2. Biotechnology 3. Vocational guidance

ISBN 1601527020; 9781601527028

LC 2014015009

Author Bonnie Szumski's book on biotechnology is part of a series in which books " take a field or industry-fashion, for example-and break down several different jobs in that area. Each job has its own chapter that describes what the work entails, the education requirements, and an estimated salary range. Most importantly, though, the text includes quotes from and interviews with real people about their jobs, as well as useful details about opportunities for growth in that position." (School Library Journal)

"These three resources develop awareness of some career possibilities within the broad categories. They contain much of the same material for jobs as the Occupations Outlook Handbook produced by the U.S. Department of Labor, but they are much more readable for students. . . . The career profiles inform the reader about the training required, future outlook for career opportunities, and salaries, as well as some of the expected tasks for a specific career. The small size and large print may well encourage students who are not willing to tackle a large resource containing multiple career fields." VOYA

Includes bibliographical references and index

Other titles in this series are:

Careers in Engineering (2014)

Careers in Health Care (2014)

George, Linda

Biotech research; by Charles and Linda George. ReferencePoint Press 2012 96 p. (Inside science) (hardback) $27.95

Grades: 6 7 8 9 10 11 12   660.6

1. Discoveries in science 2. Biotechnology

ISBN 1601521766; 9781601521767

LC 2011007744

This book, by Charles George and Linda George, presents an overview of bio-technological research in the 21st century. "Biotech research has expanded exponentially since the mapping of the Human Genome. This knowledge drives the research toward finding genetic causes and cures for thousands of human conditions and diseases, and toward enhancing agricultural products, improving industrial processes, and toward environmental reclamation and conservation." (Publisher's note)

Includes bibliographical references and index

Hartman, Eve

What are the issues with genetic technology? by Eve Hartman and Wendy Meshbesher. Raintree 2012 48 p. (Sci-hi: science issues) (pb) $8.99

Grades: 6 7 8 9 10   660.6

1. Genetic engineering 2. Genetics

ISBN 1410944719; 9781410944641; 9781410944719

LC 2011015013

This book, written by authors Eve Hartman and Wendy Meshbesher, "explains what genetic technology is, what can be done with it, what will be possible in the future, and what the ethical concerns are regarding this evolving technology." (Publisher's note)

"Tackling intriguing and sometimes controversial topics, these hi/lo titles provide a thorough, yet approachable exploration of their subjects...Readers are encouraged to think critically and actively engage in the scientific and ethical debates. Suitable for reports or simply to satisfy readers' curiosity." (School Library Journal)

Includes bibliographical references and index

Hodge, Russ

Genetic engineering; manipulating the mechanisms of life. foreword by Nadia Rosenthal. Facts on File 2009 219p il map (Genetics & evolution) $39.50

Grades: 9 10 11 12   660.6

1. Genetic engineering

ISBN 978-0-8160-6681-0; 0-8160-6681-7

LC 2008-33700

This book "traces the history of genetic science up to the present day and proposes some thoughts about how it is likely to affect the future. This . . . resource describes some of the developments in the first few years of the 21st century and how society is coping with some of the ethical challenges that accompany them." Publisher's note

Includes glossary and bibliographical references

Panno, Joseph

Animal cloning; the science of nuclear transfer. Rev ed; Facts on File 2010 228p il (The new biology) $40

Grades: 9 10 11 12   660.6

1. Cloning

ISBN 978-0-8160-6847-0

LC 2009-49945

First published 2005

"Beginning chapters discuss cloning within the context of a natural process that many animals use as a survival strategy, followed by the historical development of the nuclear transfer procedure, the cloning of Dolly the sheep, the medical applications of cloning technology, and . . . more." Publisher's note

Includes glossary and bibliographical references

662 Technolgy of explosives, fuels, related products

Tabak, John

Biofuels. Facts on File 2009 204p il (Energy and the environment) $40

Grades: 9 10 11 12   662

1. Biomass energy

ISBN 978-0-8160-7082-4; 0-8160-7082-2

LC 2008-24349

This book "has value both for the explanations it offers and the questions it raises." SLJ

Includes glossary and bibliographical references

664 Food technology

Aronson, Marc

★ **Sugar** changed the world; a story of magic, spice, slavery, freedom, and science. by Marc Aronson and Marina Budhos. Clarion Books 2010 166p il map

Grades: 7 8 9 10 11 12   664

1. Slavery 2. World history 3. Sugar -- History
ISBN 0618574921; 9780618574926

LC 2009033579

The book discusses the history of sweet substances. "Sugar was the substance that drove the bloody slave trade and caused the loss of countless lives but it also planted the seeds of revolution that led to freedom in the American colonies, Haiti, and France." (Publisher's note) Chronology. Bibliography. Index. "Grades seven to twelve." (Bull Cent Child Books)

"From 1600 to the 1800s, sugar drove the economies of Europe, the Americas, Asia and Africa and did more 'to reshape the world than any ruler, empire, or war had ever done.' Millions of people were taken from Africa and enslaved to work the sugar plantations throughout the Caribbean, worked to death to supply the demand for sugar in Europe. . . . Maps, photographs and archival illustrations, all with captions that are informative in their own right, richly complement the text, and superb documentation and an essay addressed to teachers round out the fascinating volume." Kirkus

Includes bibliographical references

Hayhurst, Chris

Everything you need to know about food additives. Rosen Pub. Group 2002 64p il (Need to know library) lib bdg $27.95

Grades: 9 10 11 12   664

1. Food additives
ISBN 0-8239-3548-5

LC 2001-1980

This book "introduces common additives and explains reasons for their use, including consumers' finicky preferences; discusses health risks associated with many additives; and offers exciting alternatives to processed foods, such as produce from community-supported agriculture programs." Booklist

Includes bibliographical references

Winter, Ruth

★ A **consumer's** dictionary of food additives; 7th ed.; Three Rivers Press 2009 595p pa $17.95; ebook $17.95

Grades: 11 12 Adult   664

1. Reference books 2. Food additives -- Dictionaries
ISBN 978-0-307-40892-1 pa; 978-0-307-45259-7 ebook

LC 2008-40601

First published 1972. Periodically revised

This guide provides "facts about the safety and side effects of more than 12,000 ingredients—such as preservatives, food-tainting pesticides, and animal drugs—that end up in food as a result of processing and curing." Publisher's note

Includes bibliographical references

667 Cleaning, color, coating, related technologies

Garfield, Simon

Mauve; how one man invented a color that changed the world. Norton 2001 222p il hardcover o.p. pa $13.95

Grades: 11 12 Adult   667

1. Chemists 2. Dyes and dyeing 3. Mauve 4. Dye industry -- Great Britain 5. Chemists -- England -- Biography
ISBN 0-393-32313-7 pa

LC 00-69533

This volume discusses how a British student, William Henry Perkin, while trying to synthesize quinine from coal tar, developed mauve, "the first mass-produced artificial dye. . . . By the turn of the 20th century, because of Perkin's novel idea, dye makers had 2,000 synthesized colors at their disposal." (N Y Times Book Rev) Index.

"The text is understandable by the average layman and is enjoyable reading for the scientist and non-scientist alike." Sci Books Films

Includes bibliographical references

668 Technology of other organic products

Mara, Wil

From gecko feet to adhesive tape; by Wil Mara. Cherry Lake Publishing 2014 32 p. illustrations (chiefly color) (Innovations from Nature.) (lib. bdg.) $28.50

Grades: 6 7 8 9 10   668

1. Geckos 2. Adhesives 3. Biomimicry 4. Inventions
ISBN 1624317529; 9781624317521; 9781624317583

LC 2013030375

This book, by Wil Mara, part of the Innovations from Nature series, "explores how researchers take ideas from plants and animals and turn them into projects with practical applications. . . . [It] discusses the gecko's remarkable climbing ability. Studies of the setae (tiny hairs), the motion, and the tendons of geckos' feet are leading to the development of new adhesives." (Publisher's note)

"These creative books use a pleasantly unusual angle to show how aspects of nature can inspire scientists and engineers . . . High-resolution photographs and a dark black and purple layout give the books a slick, stylish look, while the narrative is both fascinating and informative. Intriguing additions to science collections." SLJ

Includes bibliographical references and index

674   Lumber processing, wood products, cork

Edlin, Herbert L.
  What wood is that? A manual of wood identification. Viking 1969 160p il $32.95

Grades: 9 10 11 12 Adult   **674**
1. Wood
ISBN 0-670-75907-4

                          LC 69-15933

The book discusses timber cutting and sawing, wood identification, including keys for naming timbers, and descriptions of each of the forty trees listed as examples

"The text is of British origin, and does consider some woods little used in our country; it also omits others very much used here. The language is universal, however, and both text and illustrations constitute a notable addition to the woodworker's library." Libr J

★ The **Encyclopedia** of wood; a tree-by-tree guide to the world's most versatile resource. general editor, Aidan Walker. Facts on File 2005 192p il map $35

Grades: 11 12 Adult   **674**
1. Reference books 2. Wood -- Encyclopedias
ISBN 0-8160-6181-5

                        LC 2004-60849

First published 1989

"A nice addition to libraries with strong interior design or DIY collections." Libr J

Includes bibliographical references

679   Other products of specific kinds of materials

Walker, John Frederick
  Ivory's ghosts; the white gold of history and the fate of elephants. John Frederick Walker. Atlantic Monthly Press 2009 312p ill., map pa $15

Grades: 9 10 11 12 Adult   **679**
ISBN 9780802144522; 9780871139955; 0871139952

"Nominally protected by an international prohibition of commerce in their tusks, elephants continue to be poached and, occasionally, legally killed. Walker's review of the arguments by proponents (mainly African countries) and opponents (mainly Western conservationists) of permitting some level of trade in ivory caps his history of the material's allures and applications throughout human history." (Booklist)

Includes bibliographical references (p. [259]-290) and index.

682   Small forge work (Blacksmithing)

Weitzman, David
★ **Skywalkers**; Mohawk ironworkers build the city. Roaring Brook Press/Flash Point 2010 124p il $19.99

Grades: 8 9 10 11 12 Adult   **682**
1. Bridges 2. Building 3. Skyscrapers 4. Mohawk

Indians 5. Steel construction
ISBN 1-59643-162-8; 978-1-59643-162-1

Weitzman relates the history of Mohawks from Kahnawàke, Québec, known for their ability to navigate heights, who worked on the construction of bridges and tall buildings in Canada and New York City. "Intermediate, middle school." (Horn Book)

"Stunning photographs complement Weitzman's comprehensive research and clear text in this memorable tribute to Mohawk ironworkers. . . . Weitzman wisely intersperses passages of construction history and technical technique with numerous personal stories. . . . Plentiful black and white archival photographs . . . are chilling or breathtaking. Throughout, Weitzman's admiration and respect for the Mohawk people shine through." Voice Youth Advocates

Includes glossary and bibliographical references

683.4   Small firearms

Blumenthal, Karen
★ **Tommy**; the gun that changed America. by Karen Blumenthal. Roaring Brook Press 2015 240 p. (hardcover) $19.99

Grades: 7 8 9 10   **683.4**
1. Guns -- United States -- History 2. Thompson submachine gun -- History
ISBN 9781626720848

                        LC 2014040642

This book, by Karen Blumenthal, describes how "the Tommy gun became the weapon of choice for a generation of bootleggers and bank-robbing outlaws, and became a deadly American icon. Following a bloody decade--and eighty years before the mass shootings of our own time--Congress moved to take this weapon off the streets, igniting a national debate about gun control." (Publisher's note)

"This biography of a gun traces the Thompson submachine gun (a.k.a. the Tommy) from its 1918 invention--by former Army officer John Thompson as a potential military weapon--to its use by crooks and bootleggers terrorizing people throughout the next two decades. With thorough research and impeccable documentation, Blumenthal also examines the history of American gun laws, showing the complexity of gun culture. Bib., ind." Horn Book

Includes bibliographical references and index

684   Furnishings and home workshops

Bird, Lonnie
  Taunton's complete illustrated guide to woodworking; [by] Lonnie Bird . . . [et al.]. Taunton Press 2005 311p il $29.95

Grades: 11 12 Adult   **684**
1. Woodwork
ISBN 1-56158-769-9

                        LC 2004-28678

This "guide covers a wide array of woodworking topics. . . . The arrangement is consistent and well thought out, with illustrated referencing at the beginning of each chapter." Libr J

Woodwork; a step-by-step photographic guide to successful woodworking. [writers, Alan Bridgewater . . . [et al]; illustrator, Simon Rodway] DK Pub. 2010 400p il $40

Grades: 10 11 12 Adult **684**
1. Woodwork
ISBN 978-0-7566-4306-5

LC 2010-279214

Thsi book "offers instruction in basic woodworking techniques and pairs profiles of common and exotic woods with great photos. The 25 projects, including furnishings and household products, start from simple and build to complex. While the projects are not particularly distinctive, the supporting materials make this a key purchase for any woodworking collection. Highly recommended." Libr J

688.7   Recreational equipment

Sobey, Ed
The **way** toys work; the science behind the magic 8 ball, etch a sketch, boomerang, and more. [by] Ed Sobey and Woody Sobey. Chicago Review Press 2008 178p il pa $14.95

Grades: 11 12 Adult **688.7**
1. Toys
ISBN 978-1-55652-745-6

LC 2008-1303

"This is really quite a nifty book, perfect for collectors, for anyone daring enough to build homemade versions of these classic toys, and even for casual browsers." Booklist
Includes bibliographical references

Stone, Tanya Lee
The **good,** the bad, and the Barbie; a doll's history and her impact on us. Viking 2010 130p il $19.99

Grades: 6 7 8 9 10 **688.7**
1. Barbie dolls 2. Mattel Inc. 3. Toy industry executives
ISBN 978-0-670-01187-2; 0-670-01187-8

LC 2010-7507

"Stone tantalizes with her brief and intriguing survey of Barbie. She begins with the history of Mattel, started by self-made businesswoman Ruth Handler in the 1940s, and moves onto materialism, body image, portrayals of ethnicity, nudity, taboo and art." Kirkus
Includes bibliographical references

690   Construction of buildings

Macaulay, David
Unbuilding. Houghton Mifflin 1980 78p il $18; pa $9.95

Grades: 4 5 6 7 8 9 **690**
1. Building 2. Skyscrapers 3. Empire State Building (New York, N.Y.)
ISBN 0-395-29457-6; 0-395-45425-5 pa

LC 80-15491

This fictional account of the dismantling and removal of the Empire State Building describes the structure of a skyscraper and explains how such an edifice would be demolished

"Save for the fact that one particularly stunning double-page spread is marred by tight binding, the book is a joy: accurate, informative, handsome, and eminently readable." Bull Cent Child Books

Woolf, Alex
Buildings; by Alex Woolf. Heinemann Library 2013 56 p. ill. (chiefly col.) (library) $33.50; (paperback) $9.49

Grades: 6 7 8 9 **690**
1. Building 2. Architecture
ISBN 1432970291; 9781432970291; 9781432970345

LC 2012013465

This book by Alex Woolf examines the life cycle of a building, covering "the stages from its design, construction, and opening to its use, maintenance, and demolition and disposal at the end of its useful life. This book explains what happens during these stages, such as planning, the sourcing of materials, the construction process, the decisions made by designers and engineers, and refurbishing and recycling." (Publisher's note)

"Books in the Design and Engineering for STEM series offer an up-to-date introduction to an industry in a time of change..Buildings emphasizes the impact of architecture, construction, and demolition on the environment and shows how that impact can be minimized at different stages. Appearing on nearly every page, illustrations include many color photos and the occasional graph, digital drawing, or map. This attractive, informative series tackles meaningful topics and doesn't talk down to readers." (Booklist)

Includes bibliographical references (page 55) and index.

700   ARTS

700   The arts

Delacampagne, Ariane
Here be dragons; a fantastic bestiary. {by} Ariane Delacampagne and Christian Delacampagne. Princeton University Press 2003 199p il $45

Grades: 9 10 11 12 **700**
1. Animals in art 2. Mythical animals
ISBN 0-691-11689-X

LC 2003-51741

After an "assessment of animals in art as dream imagery and religious symbols, the Delacampagnes' five subsequent chapters consider, respectively, the evolution of the bestiary of nonexistent creatures, portrayals of unicorns and partially human beasts, images of four-footed flying things and dragons, the issue of influence versus coincidence in accounting for the similarity of fantastic animals in disparate cultures, and fantastic animals in contemporary art . . . The pictures of everything from the two-horned unicorn . . . on the walls of the Lascaux caves to a yeti from the pages of Tintin au Tibet (1960) are invariably gorgeous." Booklist
Includes bibliographical references

★ **Encyclopedia** of the Harlem Renaissance; Cary D. Wintz, Paul Finkelman, editors. Routledge 2004 2v il map set $325

Grades: 11 12 Adult   **700**
1. Reference books 2. African American arts 3. Harlem Renaissance -- Encyclopedias
ISBN 1-57958-389-X

LC 2004-16353

This encyclopedia features "essays on the life and works of major writers, artists, and musicians of the period as well as broader articles on the impact of contemporary political, social, economic, and legal issues on the movement. . . . This thorough and well-organized reference work should appeal to a wide range of users from high school to graduate school students and is recommended for all libraries." Libr J

Includes bibliographical references

Encyclopedia of the romantic era, 1760-1850; Christopher John Murray, general editor. Fitzroy Dearborn 2003 2v il set $325

Grades: 11 12 Adult   **700**
1. Romanticism
ISBN 1-57958-361-X

LC 2003-42406

"This two-volume cultural encyclopedia contains 770 entries on the arts and sciences of the Romantic Era, including, but not limited to, the Romantic movement. The strengths of this encyclopedia are many, including its geographical coverage (Britain, continental Europe, and the Americas); entries on individuals; discussions of specific works of literature, art, and music; and thematic entries that focus on a broad-range of subjects (e.g. the Dandy, Orientalism, and the Sublime)." Libr Media Connect

Includes bibliographical references

Fallon, Michael

How to analyze the works of Andy Warhol. ABDO Pub. Co. 2011 112p il (Essential critiques) $34.22

Grades: 9 10 11 12   **700**
1. Artists 2. Art criticism 3. Art appreciation 4. Motion picture directors
ISBN 978-1-61613-534-8

LC 2010-15882

This book looks at the works of Andy Warhol "through the lenses of prevalent schools of criticism. The first chapters introduce the concept of critical theory, its purpose, and how to develop and support a thesis statement. In subsequent chapters, an overview of each work is followed by a critique using a particular theory. . . . Critical theories are applied to 32 Campbell's Soup Cans, Turquoise Marilyn, 16 Jackies, Brillo Boxes, and Mickey Mouse." SLJ

Includes bibliographical references

Makosz, Rory

★ **Latino** arts and their influence on the United States; songs, dreams, and dances. Mason Crest Publishers 2005 112p il (Hispanic heritage) $22.95

Grades: 7 8 9 10   **700**
1. Latin American art 2. Arts -- United States
ISBN 1-59084-938-8

LC 2004022968

This "book begins with a general discussion of the ways in which cultures express themselves through their arts. It goes on to discuss the arts of Latin American cultures and their growing prominence in the United States, with emphasis on dance and music. Writing, painting, theater arts, and holidays are also included. . . . [This is] an excellent resource both for students researching Latino arts for reports and for general readers." SLJ

Includes bibligraphical references

The **muses** go to school; inspiring stories about the importance of arts in education. edited by Herbert Kohl and Tom Oppenheim. New Press 2012 xxvii, 200 p.p

Grades: Adult Professional   **700**
1. Celebrities 2. Arts -- Study and teaching 3. Education -- Aims and objectives
ISBN 1595585397; 9781595585394

LC 2011042803

In this book, edited by Herbert Kohl and Tom Oppenheim, "autobiographical pieces with well-known artists and performers are paired with . . . essays by . . . educators to produce a . . . case for positioning the arts at the center of primary and secondary school curriculums. Spanning a range of genres from acting and music to literary and visual arts, these . . . voices make surprising connections between the arts and the development of intellect, imagination, spirit, emotional intelligence, self-esteem, and self-discipline of young people." (Publisher's note)

Smith, Anna Deavere

Letters to a young artist; straight-up advice on making a life in the arts--for actors, performers, writers, and artists of every kind. Anchor Books 2006 227p il pa $13

Grades: 11 12 Adult   **700**
1. Artists 2. Conduct of life 3. Creation (Literary, artistic, etc.)
ISBN 1-4000-3238-5; 978-1-4000-3238-9

LC 2005-48318

The author "casts her reflections on the creative process, the artist's life and the acting profession as a series of brief letters addressed to a fictitious teenager. . . . With a pithiness that wards away the preachy, Smith succeeds in conveying the pain, the joy and the effort that characterize a life on the stage and in the world." Publ Wkly

Includes bibliographical references

700.9 History, geographic treatment, biography of the arts

Fitzgerald, Kenneth

Volume; writings on graphic design, music, art, and culture. written by Kenneth FitzGerald; liner notes by Rudy VanderLans. Princeton Architectural Press 2010 254 p. (alk. paper) $24.95

Grades: 10 11 12 Adult **700.9**
1. Graphic design 2. American essays 3. Cultural critique 4. Arts, Modern -- 20th century 5. Arts, Modern -- 21st century 6. Graphic arts -- United States -- History -- 20th century 7. Graphic arts -- United States -- History -- 21st century
ISBN 1568989644; 9781568989648

LC 2009045011

This book is a "collection of both new and classic writings by . . . educator Kenneth FitzGerald that survey the discipline of graphic design in context with the parallel creative fields of contemporary music and art. The topics of the writings are diverse: the roles of class in design, design education, Lester Bangs and 'Creem' magazine, pornography, album cover art, independent record labels, anonymity and imaginary creative identities, and design as cultural chaosmaker." (Publisher's note)

702.8 Auxiliary techniques and procedures; apparatus, equipment, materials

Colston, Valerie
Aspire: 200 projects to strengthen your art skills. Barron's 2008 128p il pa $21.99
Grades: 10 11 12 Adult **702.8**
1. Art -- Technique
ISBN 978-0-7641-3811-9

LC 2006-940776

"Written with art students in mind, . . . [this book] includes a section on putting together a portfolio and examples of art-school applicants' sketchbooks and portfolios. The text takes a do-it-yourself approach to learning a full complement of basic and intermediate techniques. Colston gathers examples and prescribes an assortment of observation exercises and projects that explore such concepts as shadow, distortion, mood, and collage. . . . Colston does a good job of providing an overview of the fundamentals and introducing a wide range of techniques." SLJ

The **Grove** encyclopedia of materials and techniques in art; edited by Gerald W.R. Ward. Oxford University Press 2008 828p il lib bdg $150
Grades: 11 12 Adult **702.8**
1. Reference books 2. Art -- Technique -- Encyclopedias 3. Artists' materials -- Encyclopedias
ISBN 978-0-19-531391-8; 0-19-531391-7

LC 2008-2486

Ward "has revised and updated approximately 1440 entries and full-length articles . . . from the venerable 34-volume Grove Dictionary of Art and added some new entries on topics of 'emerging importance' to produce a comprehensive one-volume resource on all aspects of materials and techniques of the fine arts and crafts, from acrylic painting, alabaster, and aquatint to upholstery, varnish, wood-engraving, and zinc. . . . An essential work for artists, historians, and art students and for the libraries that serve them." Libr J
Includes bibliographical references

Kallen, Stuart A.
★ The **artist's** tools. Lucent Books 2007 104p il (Eye on art) $33.45

Grades: 9 10 11 12 Adult **702.8**
1. Artists' materials
ISBN 1-59018-957-4

LC 2006-17409

"This book describes the origins and characteristics of tools, from charcoal to computers. The focus is on introducing mediums and giving background information rather than on project ideas. An informative overview of paints, ceramics, and technology." SLJ
Includes bibliographical references

Smith, Ray
★ The **artist's** handbook; [equipment, materials, procedures, techniques] 3rd. ed.; DK Pub. 2009 384p il pa $21.95
Grades: 11 12 Adult **702.8**
1. Artists' materials 2. Art -- Technique
ISBN 978-0-7566-5722-2; 0-7566-5722-9

LC 2010-502586

First published 1987 by Knopf
An illustrated handbook offers step-by-step projects, reproductions of works by master artists, and instruction in creative techniques, covering everything from drawing and painting to printmaking and digital media.

704 Special topics in fine and decorative arts

Bolden, Tonya
★ **Wake** up our souls; a celebration of Black American artists. Published in association with Smithsonian American Art Museum. Harry N. Abrams 2004 128p il $24.95
Grades: 6 7 8 9 10 **704**
1. African American art
ISBN 0-8109-4527-4

Presents a history of African American visual arts and artists from the days of slavery to the present
"Bolden's writing is rich and lyrical. She smoothly incorporates the historical context, explaining pivotal events and relevant artistic movements clearly and succinctly." SLJ

704.03 Ethnic and national groups

★ **Dreaming** in Indian; Contemporary Native American Voices. edited by Lisa Charleyboy and Mary Leatherdale. Firefly Books Ltd 2014 128 p. color illustrations $19.95
Grades: PreK 7 8 9 10 11 12 **704.03**
1. Native Americans 2. Indian artists -- United States -- Biography
ISBN 1554516870; 9781554516872

LC 2014045769

This book, edited by Lisa Charleyboy and Mary Leatherdale, is an "anthology from some of the most groundbreaking Native artists working in North America today. . . . Emerging and established Native artists, including acclaimed author Joseph Boyden, renowned visual artist Bunky Echo Hawk, and stand-up comedian Ryan McMahon, contribute thoughtful and heartfelt pieces on their experiences growing up Indigenous." (Publisher's note)

"Original and accessible, both an exuberant work of art and a uniquely valuable resource." Kirkus

Companion title:

Urban Tribes (2015)

704.9 Iconography

Patel, Sanjay

The **little** book of Hindu deities; from the Goddess of Wealth to the Sacred Cow. Plume 2006 141p il pa $14

Grades: 9 10 11 12   **704.9**

1. Hinduism 2. Gods and goddesses

ISBN 0-452-28775-8; 978-0-452-28775-4

LC 2006-12110

The author describes "the exploits of various deities while drawing us in—literally—with his joyous and unexpected full-color illustrations. . . . Both funny and informative, this is a fresh and breezy introduction to the Hindu gods." Publ Wkly

706 Organizations and management of fine and decorative arts

Bostic, Mary Burzlaff

Artist's & graphic designer's market 2014; by Mary Burzlaff Bostic. North Light Books 2013 671 p. ill. $34.99

Grades: 11 12 Adult   **706**

1. Graphic arts 2. Art -- Marketing 3. Art -- Vocational guidance

ISBN 9781440329432

This book presents a "reference guide for any artist who wants to establish or expand a career in fine art, illustration or graphic design." It includes "contact information for more than 1,700 art market resources, including galleries, magazines, book publishers, greeting card companies, ad agencies, syndicates, art fairs and more" as well as "information on grants, residencies, organizations, publications and websites that offer support and direction for visual artists." (Publisher's note)

708 Galleries, museums, private collections of fine and decorative arts

An **eye** for art; focusing on great artists and their work. National Gallery of Art with Chicago Review Press, Incorporated 2013 180 p. (pbk.) $19.95

Grades: 4 5 6 7 8 9 10 11 12   **708**

1. Art 2. Art appreciation 3. National Gallery of Art (U.S.)

ISBN 1613748973; 9781613748978

LC 2013009403

This book is an "introduction to the works collected in the National Gallery of Art. More than 50 great artists are highlighted, from the 13th to the 21st centuries. The artists and their works and techniques are . . . arranged stylistically in categories that include 'Studying Nature,' 'Observing Everyday Life,' 'Exploring Places,' and 'Telling Stories.'" (School Library Journal)

National Gallery of Art (U.S.)

National Gallery of Art; [foreword by Earl A. Powell III] 2nd ed.; Thames and Hudson 2006 332p il (World of art) pa $18.95

Grades: 11 12 Adult   **708**

1. National Gallery of Art (U.S.)

ISBN 0-500-20390-3; 978-0-500-20390-3

LC 2005-904459

First published 2004 by National Gallery of Art; Based on John Walker's National Gallery of Art, published 1984

"The collection of the National Gallery of Art in Washington includes works by the greatest masters of Western art from the twelfth century to the present. . . . [In this] look at the National Gallery's masterpieces . . . the works are illustrated in full color, and the curators have written the texts." Publisher's note

709 History, geographic treatment, biography

The **Art** Book; Phaidon Press. Phaidon Press 2012 592 p. (hardcover) $59.95

Grades: 10 11 12 Adult   **709**

1. Art 2. Artists

ISBN 0714864676; 9780714864679

This book by Phaidon Press is an "A - Z guide to artists from medieval times to the present day . . . including paintings, photographs, sculptures, video, installations and performance art. Each artist is represented on a full page with a definitive work and explanatory . . . information." The book features "examples of all periods, schools, visions and techniques." (Publisher's note)

★ **Atlas** of world art; edited by John Onians. Oxford University Press 2004 352p il maps $150

Grades: 11 12 Adult   **709**

1. Art -- History -- Maps

ISBN 0-19-521583-4

LC 2003-55029

"Groundbreaking and handsomely produced, this is a welcome addition to any reference collection." Libr J

Includes bibliographical references

Bearden, Romare

★ **A history** of African-American artists; from 1792 to the present. {by} Romare Bearden & Harry Henderson. Pantheon Bks. 1992 541p il $75

Grades: 11 12 Adult   **709**

1. American art 2. Harlem Renaissance 3. African American artists

ISBN 0-394-57016-2

LC 89-42782

"Richly illustrated and written with resounding empathy and pride, this is a major contribution to the literature on African American history and to the annals of American art." Booklist

Farrington, Lisa E.

★ **Creating** their own image; the history of African-American women artists. Oxford University Press 2005 354p il $55

Grades: 11 12 Adult **709**
1. Women artists 2. African American women 3. African American artists
ISBN 0-19-516721-X

LC 2003-66171

"A richly detailed yet fluent work of trailblazing research, fresh interpretations, and cogent argument, Farrington's treatise discusses vital aesthetic as well as social and cultural issues and creates a vibrant context for such seminal artists as Augusta Savage, Faith Ringgold, Barbara Chase-Riboud, Kara Walker, and many more." Booklist

Gardner, Helen

★ **Gardner's** art through the ages; a global history. [revised by] Fred S. Kleiner. Enhanced 13th ed.; Wadsworth, Cengage Learning 2010 1088p il map $165.99

Grades: 11 12 Adult **709**
1. Art -- History
ISBN 978-0-495-79986-3; 0-495-79986-6

LC 2009-932089

First published 1926 by Harcourt Brace & Co.

This book surveys world art from prehistoric times to the present day. Painting, sculpture, architecture and some decorative arts are considered. Although the focus is on European art, there are also chapters on ancient Near Eastern, Asian, pre-Columbian, American Indian, African and Oceanic art.

Includes bibliographical references

Gombrich, E. H.

★ The **story** of art; 16th ed rev and expanded; Phaidon Press 1995 688p il $49.95; pa $29.95

Grades: 11 12 Adult **709**
1. Art -- History
ISBN 0-7148-3355-X; 0-7148-3247-2 pa

LC 96-140698

First published 1950

This survey of art examines artistic achievements in historical context to consider how prevailing social, political, and economic factors may have influenced the succession and popularity of certain artistic styles.

Includes bibliographical references

Hartt, Frederick

★ **Art**: a history of painting, sculpture, architecture. Prentice Hall 2003 2v il map pa $122.80

Grades: 9 10 11 12 **709**
1. Art -- History
ISBN 978-0-13-184155-0; 0-13-184155-6

A reprint of the volumes first published 1976 by Abrams. Periodically revised

An illustrated chronological history of art from prehistory to the contemporary period. Timelines link the political

history, religions, literature, science and technology, with the painting, sculpture and architecture of each era.

Hirst, Michael

★ **Michelangelo** and his drawings. Yale Univ. Press 1988 132p il hardcover o.p. pa $25

Grades: 11 12 Adult **709**
1. Artists 2. Painters 3. Sculptors 4. Architects
ISBN 0-300-04796-7 pa

LC 88-50431

"An informative, insightful, and eminently readable book. . . . This is an important contribution to Michelangelo scholarship." Choice

Janson, H. W.

★ **Janson's** history of art; the western tradition. Penelope J.E. Davies ... [et. al] 8th ed.; Prentice Hall 2011 xxxi, 1152p il map $170.40

Grades: 11 12 Adult **709**
1. Art -- History
ISBN 978-0-205-68517-2; 0-205-68517-X

LC 2009-22617

First published 1962 by Abrams with title: History of art

A history of art from prehistoric cave paintings to video art. While the focus is primarily on Western art, brief discussions of Oriental, Near Eastern, Islamic, African and Latin American arts are included.

Includes bibliographical references

Kampen O'Riley, Michael

★ **Art** beyond the West; the arts of Africa, West and Central Asia, India and Southeast Asia, China, Japan and Korea, the Pacific, Africa, and the Americas. 2nd ed.; Pearson Prentice Hall 2006 368p il map pa $121

Grades: 11 12 Adult **709**
1. Art
ISBN 0-13-175152-2

LC 2006-43185

First published 2001 in the United Kingdom by Abrams

The author "has attempted to encapsulate the entirety of non-Western art in one volume. . . . [Chapters] range over Africa, India, Southeast Asia, China, Japan and Korea, the Americas, and the Pacific and consider such issues as post and intercolonialism and postmodernism." Libr J

Includes bibliographical references

Khalili, Nasser D.

★ **Islamic** art and culture; a visual history. Overlook Press 2006 186p il $60

Grades: 11 12 Adult **709**
1. Islamic art 2. Islamic civilization
ISBN 1-58567-839-2; 978-1-58567-839-6

This "visual history of Islamic art introduces readers to the diverse peoples, cultures, and styles making up Islam today. Spanning 12 centuries and covering everything from miniature painting to architecture, it shows, e.g., various Qur'ans, coins, armor, and scientific instruments. . . . This is an excellent introduction to the subject that combines aptly chosen and beautifully reproduced photographs with a concise and informative text." Libr J

Includes bibliographical references

Khanduri, Kamini

Japanese art & culture. Raintree 2004 56p il map (World art & culture) lib bdg $33.50

Grades: 6 7 8 9 10   709

1. Japanese arts 2. Japan -- Civilization
ISBN 978-0-7398-6609-2; 0-7398-6609-5

LC 2003-1957

This offers a history of the arts of Japan including painting, woodblock prints, sculpture, metalwork, pottery, lacquerware, architecture, gardens, calligraphy, and theater, and explains their places in Japanese culture.

Includes glossary and bibliographical references

King, Ross

Art: over 2,500 works from cave to contemporary; foreword by Ross King. DK Pub. 2008 612p il $50

Grades: 11 12 Adult   709

1. Reference books 2. Art appreciation 3. Art -- History
ISBN 978-0-7566-3972-3; 0-7566-3972-7

LC 2008-301471

Within each time period, provides examples of significant works in painting, sculpture, drawing and other media. Highlights themes that were important at various times such as nudes, landscape, still life, and love. Includes brief biographies of some artists and a "closer look" in depth for the most significant works.

"Easy to read and use, . . . both newcomers to art and art connoisseurs will enjoy this picturesque work." Libr J

Includes glossary

Lewis, Elizabeth

Mexican art & culture. Raintree 2004 56p il map (World art & culture) lib bdg $33.50

Grades: 6 7 8 9 10   709

1. Mexican art 2. Mexico -- Civilization
ISBN 978-0-7398-6610-8; 0-7398-6610-9

LC 2003-1958

This offers a history of the arts of Mexico including architecture, carvings and sculpture, pottery and ceramics, masks, lacquering, textiles and clothing, jewelry, painting, music and musical instruments, fiestas and festivals, death and burial customs, and toys, and explains their roles in Mexican culture.

The text is "straightforward and concise, but it's the excellent selection of high-quality color photos that really stand out." Booklist

Includes glossary and bibliographical references

Little, Stephen

★ . . . isms: understanding art. Universe 2004 159p il pa $16.95

Grades: 11 12 Adult   709

1. Art -- History
ISBN 0-7893-1209-3

LC 2004-94996

The author "identifies four types of isms: trends specific to the visual arts (perspectivism), broad cultural trends (romanticism), artist-defined movements (cubism),

and retrospectively named movements (mannerism). He then moves forward chronologically, deftly defining more than 50 isms, naming key artists, and showcasing splendid examples." Booklist

Mason, Antony

A **history** of Western art; from prehistory to the 20th century. edited by John T. Spike. Abrams Books for Young Readers 2007 128p il $22.50

Grades: 7 8 9 10   709

1. Art -- History
ISBN 978-0-8109-9421-8; 0-8109-9421-6

LC 2007-10291

This is a survey of "Western art's 50,000-year history. . . . With a few exceptions, each spread focuses on a different time period or movement, spotlighting representative work, from prehistoric cave paintings and ancient artifacts to contemporary new media. . . . A short narrative paragraph accompanies beautifully reproduced color images, extensive captions, and text boxes. . . . This overview gives students a strong visual introduction to Western art." Booklist

National Museum of the American Indian (U.S.)

★ **Creation's** journey; Native American identity and belief. edited by Tom Hill and Richard W. Hill, Sr. Smithsonian Institution Press 1994 255p il $45

Grades: 11 12 Adult   709

1. Native American art 2. National Museum of the American Indian (U.S.)
ISBN 1-56098-453-8

LC 94-4757

This "volume links stories, anecdotes, descriptions of rituals, and spiritual beliefs to specific art objects, including an Osage cradleboard and a Winnebago bandolier bag. In each essay, the connection between spirituality and the making of art is articulated; each pattern, image, and symbol is shown to be an expression of dreams, visions, and beliefs." Booklist

Includes bibliographical references

Scott, John F.

★ **Latin** American art; ancient to modern. University Press of Fla. 1999 xxiv, 240p il $49.95; pa $29.95

Grades: 11 12 Adult   709

1. Latin American art
ISBN 0-8130-1645-2; 0-8130-1826-9 pa

LC 98-46535

A study "of Latin American art from pre-Columbian times to the present, encompassing media ranging from sculpture, pottery, and painting to architecture. Scott . . . addresses the major styles and artists that define each period." Libr J

Includes bibliographical references

Strickland, Carol

The **annotated** Mona Lisa; a crash course in art history from prehistoric to post-modern. [by] Carol Strickland and John Boswell. 2nd ed.; Andrews McMeel Pub. 2007 206p il pa $22.99

Grades: 11 12 Adult **709**
1. Art -- History
ISBN 978-0-7407-6872-9; 0-7407-6872-7
LC 2009-293905
First published 1992
Presents the history of art from prehistoric times to the present day, describes major artists and movements, and details the influence of art on society through the ages.

Tregear, Mary
★ **Chinese** art; rev ed; Thames & Hudson 1997 216p il maps (World of art) pa $14.95
Grades: 11 12 Adult **709**
1. Chinese art
ISBN 0-500-20299-0
First published 1980 by Oxford Univ. Press
An introduction to major decorative, ceremonial, figurative and narrative aspects of Chinese art. Coverage ranges from works of Neolithic groups and the bronzes of the Shang dynasty to Buddhist sculpture, ceramics, garden design and architecture. Emphasis is also placed on the interaction of poetry, painting and calligraphy.
Includes bibliographical references

709.02 6th-15th centuries, 500-1499

Snyder, James
★ **Art** of the Middle Ages; [by] James Snyder, Henry Luttikhuizen, Dorothy Verkerk. 2nd ed.; Prentice Hall 2006 530p il map hardcover o.p. pa $134.40
Grades: 11 12 Adult **709.02**
1. Medieval art 2. Christian art 3. Medieval architecture
ISBN 0-13-193825-8; 0-13-192970-4 pa
LC 2004-60135
First published 1989 with title Medieval art
"Church architecture and decoration receive the bulk of Snyder's attention, with manuscript illumination and sumptuary and secular arts presented rather briefly. The volume is well illustrated, though chiefly in black-and-white photographs." Libr J [review of 1989 edition]
Includes bibliographical references

709.04 20th century, 1900-1999

Arnason, H. Harvard
★ **History** of modern art; painting, sculpture, architecture, photography. [by] H.H. Arnason, Elizabeth C. Mansfield. 6th ed.; Pearson Prentice Hall 2009 830p il $130.67; pa $122.67
Grades: 11 12 Adult **709.04**
1. Modern art
ISBN 0-205-67367-8; 978-0-205-67367-4; 0-13-606206-7 pa; 978-0-13-606206-6 pa
LC 2009-15436
First published 1969
This covers artists and movements in art from the 19th century to the present, discussing such schools as cubism, surrealism, and abstract impressionism. Video, installation and performance art, sculpture, architecture, and photography are also surveyed.
"An ideal primer on modern art." Libr J
Includes glossary and bibliographical references

Hodge, Susie
How to survive modern art. Tate 2009 127p il pa $19.95
Grades: 6 7 8 9 10 **709.04**
1. Modern art
ISBN 978-1-85437-749-4; 1-85437-749-3
LC 2009-928894
The author "offers a lucid and understandable guide for anyone puzzled or horrified by art that does not exemplify photographic realism. . . . For anyone who has ever struggled with the idea of urinals, soup cans, or monochrome canvasses as art, this book is a thoroughly delightful necessity." Voice Youth Advocates

711 Area planning (Civic art)

Macaulay, David
★ **City**: a story of Roman planning and construction. Houghton Mifflin 1974 112p il $18; pa $10.99
Grades: 4 5 6 7 8 9 10 **711**
1. Civil engineering 2. Roman architecture 3. City planning -- Rome
ISBN 0-395-19492-X; 0-395-34922-2 pa
LC 74-4280
"By following the inception, construction, and development of an imaginary Roman city, the account traces the evolution of Verbonia from the selection of its site under religious auspices in 26 B.C. to its completion in 100 A.D." Horn Book
Includes glossary

720 Architecture

Burden, Ernest E., 1934-
Illustrated dictionary of architecture; Ernest Burden. 3rd ed. McGraw-Hill 2012 564 p. col. ill. (pbk.) $60
Grades: 11 12 Adult **720**
1. Reference books 2. Architecture -- Dictionaries
ISBN 9780071772938; 0071772936
LC 2011534273
"This revised and expanded edition of a standard lexicon . . . contains twice the number of new entries as the last edition, along with some definitions that are completely rewritten. A modest redesign makes for some improvement in the layout. Published in full color for the first time, this dictionary also features 1,000 more images than the second edition and twice as many as the first. . . . This is an economically designed but surprisingly comprehensive dictionary. It encompasses famous buildings, styles, and architects' biographies, along with materials and individual architectural elements." Choice

★ **Dictionary** of architecture & construction; edited by Cyril M. Harris. 4th ed.; McGraw-Hill 2005 1089p il $74.95

Grades: 11 12 Adult   **720**

1. Reference books 2. Building -- Dictionaries 3. Architecture -- Dictionaries

ISBN 0-07-145237-0

LC 2005-42340

First published 1975

"The handy one-volume format, the reasonable cost, the clarity and accuracy of entries, the legible type and drawings, and the inclusive approach to current developments in the design, building, and scholarly professions related to architecture make this publication a crucial tool." Choice

Macaulay, David

★ **Building** big. Houghton Mifflin 2000 192p il $30; pa $12.95

Grades: 5 6 7 8 9 10   **720**

1. Dams 2. Bridges 3. Tunnels 4. Engineering 5. Skyscrapers 6. Architecture

ISBN 0-395-96331-1; 0-618-46527-8 pa

LC 00-28116

"Macaulay combines his detailed yet vaguely whimsical illustrations with simple, straightforward prose that breaks down complex architectural and engineering accomplishments into easily digestible tidbits that don't insult the intelligence of the reader of any age." N Y Times Book Rev

Includes glossary

Watkin, David, 1925-2008

A **history** of Western architecture; David Watkin. Watson-Guptill Publications 2005 720 p. (paperback) $40.00

Grades: Adult   **720**

1. Architecture -- History 2. Classicism in architecture

ISBN 0823022773; 1856697908; 9781856697903

LC 2005921992

This book by David Watkin "traces the history of western architecture from the earliest times in Mesopotamia and Egypt to the eclectic styles of the twenty-first century. The author emphasizes the ongoing vitality of the Classical language of architecture, underlining the continuity between, say, the work of Ictinus in fifth-century BC Athens and that of McKim, Mead and White in twentieth-century New York." (Publisher's note)

Includes bibliographical references (p. 704-708) and index

720.23   Architecture -- Careers

Waldrep, Lee W.

Becoming an architect; a guide to careers in design. Lee W. Waldrep, PhD. Third edition John Wiley & Sons, Inc. 2014 352 p. (pbk.) $44.95

Grades: 11 12 Adult   **720.23**

1. Architecture -- Vocational guidance

ISBN 9781118612132

LC 2013042097

This book, by Lee W. Waldrep, "highlights the risks and rewards on the path to a career as an architect. You'll find new insight and tons of helpful resources, as well as a complete outline of the trajectory of an architect's early career, from higher education through internship and licensure." (Publisher's note)

"[T]his guide provides a complete overview of the profession, including educational requirements, design specialties, registration requirements, and the paths of a career in architecture." Publisher's note

Includes bibliographical references and index

720.3   Architecture -- Dictionaries, encyclopedias, concordances

Ching, Francis D. K.

A **visual** dictionary of architecture; Francis D. K. Ching. 2nd ed. Wiley 2012 viii, 328 p.p ill paperback $55

Grades: 11 12 Adult   **720.3**

1. Reference books 2. Architecture -- Dictionaries

ISBN 9780470648858

LC 2011028227

This book, by Francis D. K. Ching, "is organized thematically around the basic aspects of architecture, art history, design, and the mechanics of construction, including foundations, roofing, lighting, heating, cooling, plumbing, and accessibility. With its detailed drawings, this dictionary will definitely appeal to visual learners." (Choice)

720.9   History, geographic treatment, biography

Clements, Gillian

A **picture** history of great buildings. Frances Lincoln Children's 2007 61p il map $19.95

Grades: 7 8 9 10   **720.9**

1. Buildings 2. Architecture -- History

ISBN 978-1-84507-488-3; 1-84507-488-2

An illustrated history of over 9,000 years of great buildings around the world from the tombs of ancient Egypt to the modern skyscrapers of today.

This is "an excellent resource, jam-packed with information for anyone interested in a basic study of architecture throughout the ages." Libr Media Connect

Includes glossary

Glancey, Jonathan

★ The **story** of architecture. Dorling Kindersley 2000 240p il hardcover o.p. pa $25

Grades: 11 12 Adult   **720.9**

1. Architecture -- History

ISBN 0-7894-5965-5; 0-7894-9334-9 pa

LC 00-30434

"Devoting nearly half the text to the modern period, Glancey condenses history's panorama into a series of colorful vignettes, each described as having some contemporary relevance. Driven by a contagious enthusiasm, the narrative is enlivened by chatty, sometimes offbeat commentary." Libr J

The **Seventy** wonders of the modern world; 1500 years of extraordinary feats of engineering and construction. edited by Neil Parkyn. Thames & Hudson 2002 304p il $40

Grades: 11 12 Adult **720.9**

1. Architecture 2. Curiosities and wonders

ISBN 0-500-51047-4

LC 2002-100549

Published in the United Kingdom with title: The seventy architectural wonders of our world

"Most of the featured 'wonders' date from the second half of the 20th century. The selections are divided into seven categories: churches, palaces, public buildings, towers and skyscrapers, bridges and railways, canals and dams, and statues. Each entry includes basic information on history, structural and engineering details, innovations, aesthetics, and a sidebar 'fact-file.'" Libr J

Includes bibliographical references

Watkin, David

A **history** of Western architecture; 4th ed; Laurence King 2005 720p il pa $40

Grades: 9 10 11 12 Adult **720.9**

1. Architecture -- History

ISBN 978-1-85669-459-9

First published 1986 by Watson-Guptill Publications

This study focuses on the development of architecture in Europe and the United States and includes chapters on Mesopotamian and Egyptian architecture.

"The book is persuasively written, its illustrations are numerous and well chosen, and readers are often introduced to buildings known only to specialists." Choice

Includes bibliographical references

722 Architectural schools and styles

The **Grove** encyclopedia of classical art and architecture; edited by Gordon Campbell. Oxford University Press 2007 2v il map set $250

Grades: 11 12 Adult **722**

1. Reference books 2. Greek art -- Encyclopedias 3. Roman art -- Encyclopedias 4. Greek architecture -- Encyclopedias 5. Roman architecture -- Encyclopedias

ISBN 978-0-19-530082-6; 0-19-530082-3

LC 2007-487

"One cannot speak too highly of this publication; it should grace the library of every scholar and library interested in the subject. It is a fundamental resource—from the most basic entry to the most in-depth reading and research." Choice

Includes bibliographical references

726 Buildings for religious and related purposes

King, Ross

Brunelleschi's dome; how a Renaissance genius reinvented architecture. Penguin Books 2001 194p il pa $14

Grades: 11 12 Adult **726**

1. Artists 2. Sculptors 3. Architects 4. Church buildings 5. Santa Maria del Fiore (Cathedral: Florence, Italy)

ISBN 0-14-200015-9

LC 2001-280068

First published 2000 by Walker & Co.

"King illuminates the mysterious sources of inspiration and the secretive methods of architectural genius Filippo Brunelleschi in a fascinating chronicle of the building of his masterwork, the dome of Santa Maria del Fiore in Florence. A remarkable saga of how one incandescent mind performed the one matchless feat that would forever transform architecture from a mechanical craft into a creative art." Booklist

Includes bibliographical references

Macaulay, David

★ **Mosque**. Houghton Mifflin 2003 96p il $18

Grades: 4 5 6 7 8 9 10 **726**

1. Mosques -- Design and construction

ISBN 0-618-24034-9

LC 2003-177

"Once again Macaulay uses clear words and exemplary drawings to explore a majestic structure's design and construction. . . . In his respectful, straightforward explanation of the mosque's design, Macaulay offers an unusual, inspiring perspective into Islamic society." Booklist

Includes glossary

★ **Pyramid**. Houghton Mifflin 1975 80p il $20; pa $9.95

Grades: 4 5 6 7 8 9 10 **726**

1. Pyramids 2. Egypt -- Civilization

ISBN 0-395-21407-6; 0-395-32121-2 pa

LC 75-9964

The construction of a pyramid in 25th century B.C. Egypt is described. "Information about selection of the site, drawing of the plans, calculating compass directions, clearing and leveling the ground, and quarrying and hauling the tremendous blocks of granite and limestone is conveyed as much by pictures as by text." Horn Book

Includes glossary

729 Design and decoration of structures and accessories

Macaulay, David

★ **Built** to last. Houghton Mifflin Harcourt 2010 272p il $24.99

Grades: 4 5 6 7 8 9 10 **729**

1. Castles 2. Cathedrals 3. Architecture 4. Mosques -- Design and construction

ISBN 978-0-547-34240-5; 0-547-34240-3

"Significantly updating the Caldecott Honor-winning Castle (1977) and Cathedral (1973) with new text and full-color illustrations, this hefty volume combines them with a very lightly revised Mosque (2003) for a three-in-one architectural spree. No mere colorization of the black-and-white originals of the first two books, . . . the all-new, often breathtaking images have been drawn by hand and then digitally colored to harmonize, beautifully with the look of Mosque. .

.. Take a moment to mourn the originals, then celebrate this entirely worthy revision." Kirkus

731.4 Techniques and procedures

Hessenberg, Karin

★ **Sculpting** basics; everything you need to know to create fantastic three-dimensional artwork. Barron's 2005 128p il $23.99

Grades: 10 11 12 Adult 731.4

1. Sculpture -- Technique
ISBN 978-0-7641-5843-8; 0-7641-5843-0

The author "presents a fine overview for beginning sculptors. . . . [The book] touches on a wide range of sculptural forms and styles, including the traditional figure, symbolic compositions, and abstract reliefs. . . .For such a slight book, [it] bundles a surprising amount of information." Libr J

Includes bibliographical references

732 Schools and styles of sculpture

Priwer, Shana

Ancient monuments; [by] Cynthia Phillips and Shana Priwer. Sharpe Focus 2009 112p il (Frameworks) lib bdg $39.95

Grades: 7 8 9 10 732

1. Ancient architecture 2. Megalithic monuments
ISBN 978-0-7656-8123-2; 0-7656-8123-4

LC 2007-40697

This book "presents monuments from ancient civilizations. As well as discussing Egyptian pyramids, Greek temples, Roman buildings, and megalithic monuments in Britain, the book includes interesting chapters on architecture in Mesoamerica, the early Middle East, and ancient China and Japan." Booklist

Includes glossary and bibliographical references

736 Other plastic arts

Engel, Peter

★ **10**-fold origami; fabulous paperfolds you can make in just 10 steps! Tuttle 2009 96p il $19.95

Grades: 8 9 10 11 12 Adult 736

1. Origami
ISBN 978-4-8053-1069-4

LC 2009-920075

This craft book features 26 origami models, all of which can be completed with ten major folds. All models are rated in difficulty from Easy to Advanced.

The author's "art subjects range from the wonderfully whimsical to the eminently practical. . . . Who could resist a plateful of sunny-side up eggs and bacon or the stolidly silent black-and-white penguin? Or not be tempted to use a brightly patterned picture frame or decorative party pinwheels?" Booklist

Hayakawa, Hiroshi

Kirigami menagerie; 38 paper animals to copy, cut & fold. Sterling Pub. 2009 128p il pa $17.95

Grades: 8 9 10 11 12 Adult 736

1. Paper crafts 2. Animals in art
ISBN 978-1-60059-318-5

LC 2008-50622

The author shows how to cut and fold paper shapes to make 38 different types of animals, including sheep, pandas, and dragons.

737.4 Coins

Cuhaj, George S.

★ **2012** standard catalog of world coins, 1901-2000; George S. Cuhaj, editor; special contributors: Mahdi Bseiso, Ivan Rakitin, Joeseph Zaffern. 39th ed; Krause Pub. 2011 2345p il map pa $65

Grades: 11 12 Adult 737.4

1. Coins
ISBN 978-1-4402-1572-8

Annual. First published 1972

This illustrated volume covers coins from throughout the world minted 1901-2000. Prices are provided for each coin in up to four grades of preservation. Includes commemorative issues.

Yeoman, R. S.

★ A **guide** book of United States coins; [by] R.S. Yeoman; editor, Kenneth Bressett; research editor, Q. David Bowers; valuations editor, Jeff Garrett. 64th ed; Whitman Pub. 2010 429p il (Official red book series) $16.95

Grades: 11 12 Adult 737.4

1. Coins 2. Reference books
ISBN 978-0-7948-3148-6

Annual. First published 1946 by Whitman

This guide "known as the 'Red Book' is an outstanding reference on U.S. coins designed for use in identifying and grading coins. All issues from 1616 to the present are covered. The guide provides historical data, statistics, values, and detailed photographs for each coin. Additional sections deal with specialties such as Civil War and Hard Times tokens, misstruck coins, and uncirculated and proof sets." Nichols. Guide to Ref Books for Sch Media Cent. 4th edition

738.1 Techniques, procedures, apparatus, equipment, materials

Muller, Kristin

The **potter's** studio handbook; a start-to-finish guide to hand-built and wheel-thrown ceramics. Quarry Books 2007 192p il (Back yard series) pa $24.99

Grades: 9 10 11 12 Adult 738.1

1. Pottery
ISBN 978-1-59253-373-2; 1-59253-373-6

LC 2007-16693

The author "guides beginners through advanced students in equipping a ceramic studio, handling the design, preparing the clay, constructing slab projects, throwing on a wheel, glazing, and firing. The 16 clay projects featured here include teapots, vases, and dinner plates. Readers can draw inspiration from the creative painting and underglazing examples, as well as the unusual firing techniques for color and texture." Libr J

Nelson, Glenn C.
★ **Ceramics**: a potter's handbook; [by] Glenn C. Nelson, Richard Burkett. 6th ed; Wadsworth/Thomson Learning 2002 439p il pa $90.95
Grades: 11 12 Adult **738.1**
1. Pottery 2. Ceramics
ISBN 0-03-028937-8
LC 2001-96329
First published 1960. Periodically revised
This manual for beginner to advanced potters presents forming and decorating techniques, body and glaze recipes, and sources for raw materials and equipment.
Includes bibliographical references

739.27 Jewelry

Michaels, Chris Franchetti
★ **More** teach yourself visually jewelry making; techniques to take your projects to the next level. Chris Franchetti Michaels, Marie Morris, Laura M. Reckford. Wiley Pub., Inc. 2012 320 p. (pbk: alk. paper) $24.99
Grades: 9 10 11 12 Adult **739.27**
1. Jewelry 2. Handicraft
ISBN 9781118083345
LC 2012930551
This book, by Chris Franchetti Michaels, presents a guide to jewelry-making. "Beginning with a concise overview of jewelry making tools and essential techniques, the book gives you technique-specific chapters covering: basic metal work, . . . sculpting with metal clay, . . . designing with chain, using adhesives, and working with art glaze. . . . Plus, a . . . chapter devoted to example projects . . . for making 12 unique pieces to add to your jewelry collection." (Publisher's note)

740 Graphic arts

Kidd, Chip
Go; a Kidd's guide to graphic design. Chip Kidd. Workman Publishing Company, Inc. 2013 160 p. (alk. paper) $17.95
Grades: 5 6 7 8 9 10 11 12 **740**
1. Graphic design 2. Children and design 3. Graphic arts -- Technique
ISBN 076117219X; 9780761172192
LC 2013032394
YALSA Award for Excellence in Nonfiction for Young Adults: Finalist (2014)

This book is an introduction to graphic design for children. It introduces "the aspiring designer to the thought processes behind typography and visual organization. Among the topics are color, juxtaposition, typography, design history, and the use of design to convey concepts such as irony and metaphor." (Library Journal)
Includes bibliographical references and index

741 Drawing and drawings

Bogaert, Harmen Meyndertsz van den
★ **Journey** into Mohawk Country; as written by H.M. van den Bogaert, with artwork by George O'Connor and color by Hilary Sycamore. First Second 2006 144p il pa $17.95
Grades: 8 9 10 11 12 **741**
1. Graphic novels 2. United States -- History -- 1600-1775, Colonial period -- Graphic novels 3. New York (State) -- History -- 1600-1775, Colonial period -- Graphic novels
ISBN 1-59643-106-7
In 1634, young Dutch trader Harmen Meyndertsz van den Bogaert, several companions, and some native guides traveled deep into what is now New York State, trading tools and weapons and trying to establish new tribal friendships to bolster Dutch trade. van den Bogaert kept a journal throughout his journeys. O'Connor has kept the original text and conducted extensive research in order to make his illustrations as authentic as possible.

Eisner, Will
Eisner /Miller: a one-on-one interview; conducted by Charles Brownstein. Dark Horse Books 2005 347p il pa $19.95
Grades: 9 10 11 12 **741**
1. Artists 2. Authors 3. Cartoonists 4. Illustrators 5. Comic books, strips, etc. 6. Screenwriters 7. Comic book writers 8. Publishing executives 9. Motion picture directors
ISBN 1-56971-755-9
"In 2002, cartoonist Frank Miller visited with Will Eisner for a free-ranging discussion across several days. Brownstein provided shape to their encounters, giving the two artists a medium in which they could use words to explore the history of American graphic-novel expression, the business concerns of comics publishing, the relationship between art forms such as comics and film, and the meanings of success to each individual. . . . Students will find it valuable both for curriculum support and casual reading." SLJ
Includes bibliographical references

Say, Allen
The **Inker's** Shadow; by Allen Say. Scholastic Press 2015 80 p. illustrations (some color) $19.99
Grades: 5 6 7 8 **741**
1. Schools 2. Japanese 3. Bildungsromans 4. Father-son relationship
ISBN 0545437768; 9780545437769
In this book, by Allen Say, "life as teen in Southern California was a cold existence. His father, one of the leading

hamburger salesmen in Japan, ran a booming burger business, much like McDonald's, and sent Allen to an American military academy, so that his son could learn English and 'become a success in life.' As the school's first and only Japanese student, he experienced immediate racism among his fellow cadets and his teachers." (Publisher's note)

"A deceptively simple story, given depth by technically excellent illustrations that require a sophisticated level of visual and cultural literacy to successfully interpret." SLJ

741.2   Techniques, procedures, apparatus, equipment, materials

Baggetta, Marla

Pastel step by step. Distributed by Black Rabbit Books 2011 64p il (Artist's library series) lib bdg $34.25

Grades: 9 10 11 12   **741.2**
    1. Pastel drawing 2. Drawing -- Technique
    ISBN 978-1-936309-25-2
                                                LC 2010005937
First published 2004

"The book begins with basic information on composition, color theory, value, and special techniques, such as scumbling, glazing, and cross-hatching. Then . . . . Marla Baggetta teaches [the reader] how to paint still lifes and more in hard and soft pastel." Publisher's note

Edwards, Betty

Drawing on the Right Side of the Brain; A Course in Enhancing Creativity & Artistic Confidence. Betty Edwards. 4th ed. Tarcher/Penguin 2012 xxxiii, 284 p.p ill. (hbk.) $32.95; (pbk.) $19.95; (deluxe) $29.95; (hbk.) $32.95; (pbk.) $19.95; (deluxe) $29.95

Grades: 9 10 11 12 Adult   **741.2**
    1. Laterality 2. Drawing -- Technique 3. Visual perception 4. Cerebral dominance
    ISBN 1585429198; 1585429201; 158542921X;
9781585429196; 9781585429202; 9781585429219
                                                LC 2012001232

"This new edition of the hugely popular and influential drawing manual first published over 30 years ago incorporates new findings from neuroscience, like the discovery of brain plasticity, together with the tried-and-true exercises included in past editions." LJ

Includes bibliographical references (p. 270-274) and index

Franks, Gene

Pencil drawing. Distributed by Black Rabbit Books 2011 64p il (Artist's library series) lib bdg $34.25

Grades: 9 10 11 12   **741.2**
    1. Pencil drawing 2. Drawing -- Technique
    ISBN 978-1-936309-24-5; 1-936309-24-6
                                                LC 2010009448
First published 1988

This book "includes comprehensive instructions for drawing a variety of subjects in pencil. . . . Gene Franks

explains how to develop . . . drawings from start to finish, teaching specific fundamental techniques for shading, contrast, texture, detail, and more." Publisher's note

Goldman, Ken

Charcoal drawing. Distributed by Black Rabbit Books 2011 64p il (Artist's library series) lib bdg $34.25

Grades: 9 10 11 12   **741.2**
    1. Charcoal drawing 2. Drawing -- Technique
    ISBN 978-1-936309-26-9; 1-936309-26-2
                                                LC 2010005935

This book offers tips and techniques for drawing with charcoal.

Kutch, Kristy Ann

Drawing and painting with colored pencil; basic techniques for mastering traditional and watersoluble colored pencils. Watson-Guptill Publications 2005 144p il pa $24.95

Grades: 9 10 11 12   **741.2**
    1. Watercolor painting -- Technique 2. Colored pencil drawing -- Technique
    ISBN 0-8230-1568-8; 978-0-8230-1568-9
                                                LC 2005-10466

"This excellent book will inspire artists and wannabe artists alike." Voice Youth Advocates

Includes bibliographical references

Micklewright, Keith

Drawing: mastering the language of visual expression. Harry N. Abrams 2005 168p il (Abrams studio) pa $29.95

Grades: 11 12 Adult   **741.2**
    1. Drawing -- Technique
    ISBN 0-8109-9238-8
                                                LC 2005-5862

"Using examples of master artists such as Ingres and Michelangelo as well as more contemporary work of Cezanne, Hockney, and others, different aspects of drawing are examined. Each chapter ends with 'Ideas to Explore,' in which the reader is given suggestions for practice. . . . This book is valuable for those learning the theory behind the elements of drawing and for those looking for practical instruction." Voice Youth Advocates

Includes bibliographical references

Scott, Damion

★ **How** to draw hip-hop; [by] Damion Scott and Kris Ex. Watson-Guptill 2006 144p il pa $19.95

Grades: 7 8 9 10   **741.2**
    1. Drawing 2. Hip-hop
    ISBN 0-8230-1446-0
                                                LC 2005-29156

"This book combines the bold and energetic lines of graffiti art with the bright colors of cel-shaded video games and an obvious Japanese manga influence. . . . [It discusses] genre-specific concepts like wild style lettering [and] hip-hop clothing. . . . There is no other book of this kind on the market, making it a necessary and relevant purchase." SLJ

Webb, David

Drawing handbook; materials, techniques, theory. David and Charles 2008 320p il pa $24.99
Grades: 9 10 11 12 Adult   **741.2**
1. Artists' materials 2. Drawing -- Technique
ISBN 978-0-7153-2653-4

"The author encourages readers to keep a daily sketchbook and clearly demonstrates essential aspects of drawing, including paper, pencils, color, shading, and more. The book's English origin is reflected in the writing style. Readers willing to practice stand to benefit greatly." SLJ

741.5 Cartoons, graphic novels, caricatures, comics

Abadzis, Nick

★ **Laika.** First Second Books 2007 205p il
Grades: 5 6 7 8 9 10 11 12 Adult   **741.5**
1. Graphic novels 2. Space flight -- Graphic novels 3. Soviet Union -- History -- 1953-1991 -- Graphic novels
ISBN 1-59643-101-6; 978-1-59643-101-0
LC 2006-51907

Laika was the abandoned puppy destined to become Earth's first space traveler. This is her journey. Along with Laika, there is Korolev, once a political prisoner and now a driven engineer at the top of the Soviet space program, and Yelena, the lab technician responsible for Laika's health and life. The book depicts the dedication and struggles of the scientists and technicians who worked in the Soviet space program, based on research Abadzis did before writing this book. The book includes a bibliography of books and websites.

"Abadzis's tear-inducing and solidly researched graphic novel treatment of Laika's surpassingly tragic story is a standout." Publ Wkly

Abel, Jessica

Drawing words & writing pictures; making comics: from manga, graphic novels, and beyond. [by] Jessica Abel & Matt Madden. First Second Books 2008 xxi, 282 p.p il $34.99
Grades: 9 10 11 12 Adult   **741.5**
1. Drawing -- Technique 2. Cartooning -- Technique 3. Graphic novels -- Authorship 5. Comic books, strips, etc. -- Authorship
ISBN 1596431318; 9781596431317
LC 2007044125

Authors Jessica Abel and Matt Madden present "a course on comic creation -- for college classes or for independent study -- that centers on storytelling and concludes with making a finished comic. With chapters on lettering, story structure, and panel layout, the fifteen lessons offered -- each complete with homework, extra credit activities and supplementary reading suggestions -- provide a solid introduction for people interested in making their own comics." (Publisher's note)

This "book offers step-by-step entry into a complicated series of skills in a nonscary and approachable way." Libr J

Includes bibliographical references (p. 261-265) and index

La Perdida; Jessica Abel. Pantheon 2006 272p ill. hbk 34.95
Grades: 11 12 Adult   **741.5**
ISBN 9781594973673; 0-375-42365-6

"Carla, an American estranged from her Mexican father, heads to Mexico City to 'find herself.' She crashes with a former fling, Harry, who has been drinking his way through the capital in the great tradition of his heroes, William S. Burroughs and Jack Kerouac. Harry is good-humored about Carla's reappearance on his doorstep--until he realizes that Carla, who spends her days soaking in the city, exploring Frida Kahlo's house, and learning Spanish, has no intention of leaving." (Publisher's note)

Life sucks; [text by] Jessica Abel, Gabe Soria; [art by] Warren Pleece; coloring by Hilary Sycamore. First Second Books 2008 186p il $19.95
Grades: 10 11 12 Adult   **741.5**
1. Graphic novels 2. Horror graphic novels 3. Romance graphic novels 4. Humorous graphic novels 5. Vampires -- Graphic novels
ISBN 978-1-59643-107-2; 1-59643-107-5

Anyone who thinks the vampire life is all romantic and ethereal better have another think. Dave can tell them, it sucks. He's the night manager for a convenience store, and he's a vampire, "made" by his boss (master), Radu. He's not the only one; in their neighborhood, most of the shops are owned by vampires who make their night managers vampires. Dave can't make himself drink from humans, so he drinks bottled blood. His roommate is human but tolerant. Then Dave sees the perfect girl, Rosa, one of the goth vampire groupies who hangs out in the neighborhood. However, surfer/slacker Wes, whom Dave replaced as the night manager, also has his eye on Rosa, and Wes isn't above killing to get his way. The book includes some violence (including the tearing off of one girl's head), and some harsh language.

"Warren Pleece's art marvelously captures the humor of the mundane that lends the book's crew of late-night wage-slave vamps believability and energy. A really fun read!" Booklist

Mastering comics; drawing words & writing pictures continued. by Jessica Abel and Matt Madden. 1st ed. First Second 2012 xvii, 318 p.p chiefly ill. (some col.) (hardcover) $34.99
Grades: 9 10 11 12 Adult   **741.5**
1. Drawing 2. Cartoonists 3. Cartooning -- Technique 4. Comic books, strips, etc. -- Technique
ISBN 1596436174; 9781596436176
LC 2011037023

Jessica Abel's book "Mastering Comics," written with her husband Matt Madden, is a "course of study for the budding cartoonist. Covering advanced topics such as story composition, coloring, and file formatting, [the book] is a vital companion to the introductory content of the first volume" entitled "Drawing Words & Writing Pictures." (Publisher's note)

Above the Dreamless Dead; World War I in Poetry and Comics. edited by Chris Duffy. First Second 2014 144 p. illustrations $24.99

Grades: 9 10 11 12 Adult　　　**741.5**

1. Comic books, strips, etc. 2. World War, 1914-1918 -- Poetry 3. World War, 1914-1918 -- Comic books, strips, etc.

ISBN 1626720657; 9781626720657

In this book edited by Chris Duffy, "various artists adapt the works of some of the most famous WWI poets, including Wilfred Owen, Siegfried Sassoon, and Isaac Rosenberg. The . . . cartoonists, including Hunt Emerson, Sarah Glidden, and Stuart Immomen, use different approaches to illuminate poems known for its bitter irony and brutal honesty." (Publishers Weekly)

"The work of 'Trench Poets' from WWI is brought vividly to life by accomplished cartoonists. This stunningly effective presentation does much to inform readers of the emotional and physical horrors of war. The volume's small format renders some of the detail difficult to decipher, but anything larger might be overwhelming. There's very mature content, especially in lyrics of soldiers' songs. Reading list." Horn Book

Includes bibliographical references and index

Aguirre-Sacasa, Roberto

Afterlife with Archie; Escape from Riverdale. story by Roberto Aguirre-Sacasa; artwork by Francesco Francavilla; lettering by Jack Morelli. Archie Comic Publications 2014 160 p. chiefly color illustrations (Afterlife with Archie) $17.99

Grades: 10 11 12 Adult　　　**741.5**

1. Dogs -- Fiction 2. Witches -- Fiction 3. Zombies -- Fiction 4. Comic books, strips, etc.

ISBN 1619889080; 9781619889088

LC 2014430277

In this book, by Roberto Aguirre-Sacasa, "[w]hen Jughead's beloved pet Hot Dog is killed in a hit and run, Jughead turns to the only person he knows who can help bring back his furry best friend—Sabrina the Teenage Witch. Using dark, forbidden magic, Sabrina is successful and Hot Dog returns to the land of the living. But he's not the same... and soon, the darkness he brings back with him from beyond the grave begins to spread." (Publisher's note)

"Not parody but serious drama, this graphic novel casts off the typical Archie comic lightheartedness and goes deep into the gut. . . .. Paired with Francavilla's dead-on illustrations, the excellent writing from Aguirre-Sacasa . . . brings constant surprises while confronting the dilemma of remaining humane through crisis." LJ

Alanguilan, Gerry

Elmer; written & illustrated by Gerry Alanguilan. SLG 2010 un il pa $12.95

Grades: 11 12 Adult　　　**741.5**

1. Graphic novels 2. Fantasy graphic novels 3. Racism -- Graphic novels 4. Chickens -- Graphic novels

ISBN 978-1-59362-204-6

Jake Gallo, an intelligent chicken, returns to the farm where his father, Elmer, one of the first sentient chickens, is dying, where he reads Elmer's diary and talks to the man who protected his parents before chickens were declared human.

"This unusual and affecting story is bound to evoke what-if discussions. Strongly recommended for teens and up in classrooms as well as libraries. Violence, strong language, and occasional sexual references and nudity." Libr J

Alberto Urrea, Luis

Mr. Mendoza's paintbrush; artwork by Christopher Cardinale; color masking and compositing, Anthony Cardinale; design, Anne M. Giangiulio. Cinco Puntos Press 2010 un il pa $17.95

Grades: 7 8 9 10 11 12 Adult　　　**741.5**

1. Graphic novels 2. Humorous graphic novels 3. Mexico -- Graphic novels 4. Artists -- Graphic novels

ISBN 978-1-933693-23-1

LC 2008-11636

Rosario is a small town in the Sinaloa region of Mexico, nestled into a wet, green, mango-sweet subtropical landscape. There, Mr. Mendoza wields his paintbrush to write graffiti with a purpose. When Mr. Mendoza catches the young narrator and his best friend Jaime spying on the girls who are swimming, he strips them, writes graffiti all over their bodies, and chases the naked boys down the street through town. He also appoints himself as the town's conscience and angers the authorities with his graffiti on the town's whorehouse, bridge, and other places. Then, one day, he takes his paint and paintbrush to the center square and paints steps into the sky and walks up until he disappears. Women and girls are shown in their underwear, and the naked boys are shown only from the back. The talk of sex, the way the boys sneak peeks at the girls and one of the town's women, make this book suitable for teens even though the format resembles a picture book.

"Not only does the art perfectly capture the mood of the piece—from the blocky woodcuts to the muted earth tones—but it also reinforces the lucid dreamlike quality of its magical realism, serving as an enticing invitation to further explore the genre." Horn Book Guide

Allen, Brooke A.

A **home** for Mr. Easter. NBM Publishing, Inc. 2010 197p il pa $13.99

Grades: 8 9 10 11 12 Adult　　　**741.5**

1. Graphic novels 2. Humorous graphic novels 3. Rabbits -- Graphic novels

ISBN 978-1-56163-580-1; 1-56163-580-4

High school student Tesana is large, not too bright, strong, and has always gotten into trouble. A lonely misfit, she tries to fit in better by joining a pep rally planning committee. Once she finds the white rabbits that will be used in the pep rally, she discovers one that is very different: it lays colorful eggs that grant wishes. Tesana believes this is the real Easter Bunny, and she calls him Mr. Easter—and he talks to her. When the football team tries to take Mr. Easter away, Tesana takes them all down and then runs away. Soon they're pursued by cops, an unscrupulous and greedy pet shop owner, laboratory scientists, animal rights protesters, television news crews, a magician/con man, and her mom. Allen was a student at the Savannah School of Art and Design when she wrote this book.

"This is for mature readers who understand the humor, and would be a welcome addition for your multicultural section—female, robust, ethnic." Libr Media Connect

Allison, John

Bad machinery; 1 the case of the team spirit. John Allison; [edited by] James Lucas Jones. Oni Press 2013 112 p. chiefly color illustrations $19.99

Grades: 7 8 9 10 11 12 Adult   **741.5**

1. Mystery graphic novels 2. School stories -- Graphic novels

ISBN 1620100843; 9781620100844

LC 2012953355

"Shauna. Charlotte. Mildred. Three schoolgirl sleuths. Jack. Linton. Sonny. Three schoolboy investigators. Tackleford. One mid-sized city with a history of countless mysteries. Is there enough room at Griswalds Grammar School for two groups of kid detectives? There better be, because once these kids have set their sights on solving a mystery there's nothing that can derail them. Nothing, except maybe gossip, classwork, new football player cards, torment from siblings, or any number of childhood distractions." (Publisher's note)

"Allison is a triple threat: he plots deftly, draws confidently, and writes dead-on adolescent dialogue. Set in a grammar school in a British working-class community, this first book in his Bad Machinery series--originally published as a webcomic--has three earnest boys vying against three sharp-tongued girls to solve mysteries." Pub Wkly

Other Bad Machinery volumes are:

The case of the good boy (2014)

The case of the simple soul (2014)

The case of the lonely one (2015)

The case of the fire inside (2016)

Amberlyn, J. C.

Drawing manga; animals, chibis, and other adorable creatures. Watson-Guptill 2009 160p il $21.99

Grades: 9 10 11 12 Adult   **741.5**

1. Manga -- Drawing 2. Cartooning -- Technique

ISBN 978-0-8230-9533-9

LC 2009-21667

The author "explores traditional pen-and-ink techniques and describes how to create images with computer software. The first part of the volume is devoted to the basic elements of drawing characters, including the anatomical proportions necessary for realistic creatures and ways to manipulate proportions to devise a variety of images. How to convey expression and movement are among other topics discussed. The second section highlights various creatures important to Japanese culture and legend. . . . This is a solid addition to manga-instruction collections." SLJ

An **Anthology** of graphic fiction, cartoons, and true stories; edited by Ivan Brunetti. Yale University Press 2006 400p il $28

Grades: 11 12 Adult   **741.5**

1. American wit and humor 2. Comic books, strips, etc.

ISBN 978-0-300-11170-5; 0-300-11170-3

LC 2006-14095

Brunetti presents "an overview of the art-comics movement, complete with a handful of the classic newspaper strips that informed today's creators. He finds room for such established veterans as R. Crumb, Lynda Barry, Gilbert and Jaime Hernandez, Daniel Clowes, Gary Panter, and Chester Brown as well as many less-familiar creators. . . . Brunetti admits that his selection criteria are highly personal, but as a cartoonist himself, whose work combines a socially transgressive spirit and impressive formal capability, his idiosyncratic approach is based in professional expertise. If his choices are sometimes arguable, his iconoclasm makes the book livelier and less predictable than such anthologies are wont to be." Booklist

Arakawa, Hiromu

★ **Fullmetal** alchemist; by Hiromu Arakawa. Viz 2005 192 p. chiefly ill. $9.99

Grades: 8 9 10 11 12   **741.5**

1. Manga 2. Shonen manga 3. Alchemy -- Fiction 4. Brothers -- Fiction

ISBN 1591169208; 9781591169208

"Alchemy: the mystical power to alter the natural world. . . . When two brothers, Edward and Alphonse Elric, dabbled in this power to grant their dearest wish, one of them lost an arm and a leg...and the other became nothing but a soul locked into a body of living steel. Now Edward is an agent of the government, a slave of the military-alchemical complex, using his unique powers to obey orders." (Publisher's note)

Volume 1 of 27

Also available in VIZBIG omnibus editions

Ashihara, Hinako

Sand chronicles vol. 1; story & art by Hinako Ashihara; [translation, Kinami Watabe; English adaptation, John Werry] Viz Media/Shojo Beat 2008 un il pa $8.99

Grades: 9 10 11 12   **741.5**

1. Manga 2. Shojo manga 3. Graphic novels

ISBN 978-1-4215-1477-2

After her parents divorce, twelve-year-old Ann Uekusa and her mother move from Tokyo to rural Shimane, to stay with Ann's grandparents. Ann finds it difficult to adjust to a small town where everybody knows everybody, and she especially has a hard time with local boy Daigo, whom she finds to be obnoxious. But when Ann's mother deliberately gets lost in the mountains around New Year's Day and dies of exposure, Ann needs the comfort of the people in Shimane, and she finally bonds with her grandmother. The publisher rates this series for older teens, citing "mature themes."

Volume 1 of a 10-volume series

Azuma, Kiyohiko

★ **Azumanga** Daioh omnibus; translation, Stephen Paul. Yen Press 2009 675p il pa $24.99

Grades: 8 9 10 11 12   **741.5**

1. Manga 2. Graphic novels 3. Humorous graphic novels 4. School stories -- Graphic novels 5. High school students -- Graphic novels

ISBN 978-0-316-07738-5

First published 2001 in Japan

An omnibus edition of a humorous four-volume manga series featuring a Japanese suburban high school class with a ditzy teacher. The adult teachers go drinking occasionally, and there's one male teacher who ogles the girls in their P.E. uniforms.

B., David

Epileptic. Pantheon Books 2005 361p il $25; pa $18.95

Grades: 11 12 Adult   **741.5**
1. Graphic novels 2. Autobiographical graphic novels 3. Epilepsy -- Graphic novels
ISBN 0-375-42318-4; 0-375-71468-5 pa; 9780375423185

LC 2004-53419

Original French edition, 2002

The author's "artwork is magnificent—gorgeously bold, impressionistic representations of the world not as it is but as he's taught himself to perceive it. . . . B.'s illustrations constantly underscore his writing's wrenching psychological depth; readers can literally see how the chaos of his childhood shaped his vision and mind." Publ Wkly

Backderf, Derf

Trashed; a graphic novel. by Derf Backderf. Abrams ComicArts 2015 256 p. chiefly illustrations (hardcover) $24.95

Grades: 10 11 12 Adult   **741.5**
1. Refuse and refuse disposal -- Fiction 2. Sanitation workers -- Fiction
ISBN 9781419714535; 9781419714542

LC 2015011115

This graphic novel, by Derf Backderf, "is an ode to the crap job of all crap jobs--garbage collector. . . . [It] follows the raucous escapades of three 20-something friends as they clean the streets of pile after pile of stinking garbage, while battling annoying small-town bureaucrats, bizarre townfolk, sweltering summer heat, and frigid winter storms." (Publisher's note)

"The blocky grotesquerie of Backderf's art is well-suited to the material, and the episodic, slackerish narrative is spiked here and there by brief lessons on the history of the garbage truck, the ecology of the landfill, and an answer to the question of whether rich or poor neighborhoods generate the most trash (hint: it's not the poor). A downbeat but entertaining ode to the odiferous realities of getting by." Pub Wkly

Includes bibliographical references

Bailey, Neal

Female force; Neal Bailey, writer; Ryan Howe & Joshua LaBello, penciliers. Bluewater 2009 un il pa $15.99

Grades: 7 8 9 10   **741.5**
1. Mayors 2. Lawyers 3. Governors 4. Graphic novels 5. Senators 6. Nonfiction writers 7. Secretaries of state 8. Spouses of presidents 9. Children of presidents 10. Hospital administrators 11. Presidential candidates 12. Women in politics -- Graphic novels
ISBN 978-1-42763858-8

This graphic novel includes stories on Hillary Clinton, Sarah Palin, Michelle Obama, and Caroline Kennedy.

"Although the art here is cartoony, and the women can appear middle-aged even in sections about their girlhoods, Bailey's analyses are respectful, insightful, and prowoman." Booklist

Includes bibliographical references

Baker, Kyle

★ **How** to draw stupid and other essentials of cartooning. Watson-Guptill 2008 110p il pa $16.95

Grades: 8 9 10 11 12 Adult   **741.5**
1. Cartooning -- Technique 2. Graphic novels -- Drawing
ISBN 978-0-8230-0143-9

LC 2008-922161

"Baker, an award-winning cartoonist and graphic-novel illustrator, gives aspiring cartoonists irreverent advice about how to succeed in their chosen field. He offers instruction in basic drawing techniques such as choosing the right tools and discusses the importance of learning to draw shapes, exaggerating, and using references. But the author's most inspiring advice focuses on how to succeed as a cartoonist." SLJ

Balak (Animator)

Last man; 1 The stranger. Bastien Vivés, Michaël Sanlaville, Balak; English translation by Alexis Siegel. First Second 2015 207 p. chiefly illustrations (paperback) $9.99

Grades: 9 10 11 12   **741.5**
1. Magic -- Fiction 2. Martial arts -- Comic books, strips, etc
ISBN 1626720460; 9781626720466

LC 2014045696

In this book, "Adrian has been preparing for the annual Games for years, and he's crushed when his assigned partner manages to get sick right before the event. Richard Aldana arrives late at the Games, and he's . . . clearly from another world. . . . Aldana is also seeking a partner in order to compete, and thus magically trained boy Adrian and brutish man Aldana team up and eventually become friends." (Bulletin of the Center for Children's Books)

"Recommend to graphic novel fans looking for something new—they will not be disappointed." SLJ

Other titles in this series are:
2, The royal cup
3, The chase
4, The show

Barry, Lynda

Picture this; the near-sighted monkey book. with guest watercolorist Kevin Kawula. Drawn and Quarterly 2010 224 p. chiefly col. ill. $29.95

Grades: 9 10 11 12 Adult   **741.5**
1. Graphic novels 2. Humorous graphic novels 3. Animals -- Graphic novels 4. Animals/Graphic novels 5. American wit and humor, Pictorial
ISBN 1897299648; 9781897299647

LC 2010399443

In author Lynda Barry's book, she "asks 'Why do we stop drawing?' and 'Why do we start?' It features the return of" the character "Marlys, and introduces a new one, the Nearsighted Monkey." The book is a "graphic-memoir-how-to" and a "take home extension of Barry's traveling" writing workshop which focuses on literature illustration. (Publisher's note)

★ **What** it is. Drawn & Quarterly 2008 209p il $24.95

Grades: 7 8 9 10 11 12 Adult   **741.5**
1. Authorship -- Graphic novels 2. Creative writing

-- Graphic novels
ISBN 978-1-897299-35-7; 1-897299-35-4

LC c2007-9047319

Independent cartoonist Lynda Barry presents an unconventional book that encourages its readers to write by using her colorful art and asking questions such as "How are monsters different? And how are they the same?" "Can/Do images exist without thinking?" "What is the difference between lying and pretending?" Each question appears with illustrated writing prompts and Barry's own ruminations on the topics. It's a workbook of sorts, but it also exists as a book to be read for itself.

"Every so often a book comes along that surpasses expectations, taking readers on an inspirational voyage that they don't want to leave. This is one such book." SLJ

Beagle, Peter S.

The **last** unicorn; original story by Peter S. Beagle; adaptation by Peter B. Gillis; art by Renae De Liz. IDW 2011 167p il rpt $16.00; $24.99
Grades: 6 7 8 9 10   **741.5**
1. Graphic novels 2. Unicorns -- Fiction
ISBN 9780451450524 rpt; 978-1-60010-851-8;
1-60010-851-2

Presents a graphic novel adaptation of the famous novel, in which a unicorn, alone in an enchanted wood, discovers she might be the last of her kind and sets out on a journey to find others like her.

"A beloved story is now a graphic novel in this excellent adaptation. . . . Much of the original novel's lyrical language has been included, and readers will be eager to find out if the unicorn will give up her quest for love, or if any of Schmendrick's spells will ever turn out right. . . . The illustrations are graceful and detailed, and inked in warm, glowing colors. This is a worthy successor to the classic novel and film." SLJ

Beaton, Kate

Hark! A vagrant. Drawn and Quarterly 2011 168p il
Grades: Adult   **741.5**
1. Comic books, strips, etc.
ISBN 1770460608; 9781770460607

LC 2011505458

The book offers a collection of comic strips by author Kate Beaton, "a series of short gag cartoons, primarily about history and literature, with a particularly Canadian bent. . . . Comics about long-suffering heroines like Jane Eyre, Laura Secord, and 'Every Lady Scientist in History Who Ever Did Anything Until Now' highlight the absurdities of gender disparity. . . . A number of these comics are driven simply by absurdity itself: a kingdom whose royal mascot is a fat pony; a sexy Batman; and teens who solve crimes in a real-life fashion: by hiding behind the school, smoking weed, and lying about it later." (Quill & Quire)
Includes index.

Beatty, Scott

Batgirl/Robin; Year One. Scott Beatty and Chuck Dixon; art by Marcos Martin and Javier Pulido. DC Comics 2013 un color illustrations $24.99

Grades: 9 10 11 12 Adult   **741.5**
1. Superhero graphic novels
ISBN 9781401240332; 140124033X

"Here it is: Robin's baptism by fire as dons the costume of Robin, the Boy Wonder for the first time and patrols the night by Batman's side. In his earliest adventures, Robin learns very quickly that what he thought would be fun is actually a matter of life and death. And in the action-packed origin of the original Batgirl, explore Barbara Gordon's transformation from average citizen into costumed superheroine." (Publisher's note)

The **DC** Comics encyclopedia; the definitive guide to the characters of the DC universe. text by Scott Beatty . . . [et al.]; updated text by Dan Wallace. Updated and expanded; DK Pub. 2008 399p il $40
Grades: 9 10 11 12 Adult   **741.5**
1. Reference books 2. DC Comics Group 3. Comic books, strips, etc. -- Encyclopedias
ISBN 978-0-7566-4119-1; 0-7566-4119-5

LC 2008-300609

First published 2004

The authors "meticulously profile 1000 DC heroes and villains created since DC's 1935 founding. The entries are organized alphabetically, by character name, while introductory insets consistently detail first appearance, hero/villain status, physical statistics, and special powers. A genuinely essential DC character reference." Libr J

Beyer, Ramsey

Little fish; a memoir from a different kind of year. Ramsey Beyer. Zest Books 2013 272 p. chiefly illustrations $15.99
Grades: 9 10 11 12   **741.5**
1. Youth 2. College students 3. City and town life
ISBN 1936976188; 9781936976140; 9781936976188

LC 2013932098

This graphic memoir, by Ramsey Beyer, is a "coming-of-age story illustrates the transformation of an 18-year-old girl from a small-town teenager into an independent city-dwelling college student." This book "shows the challenges of being a young person facing the world on her own for the very first time and the unease--as well as excitement--that comes along with that challenge." (Publisher's note)

"Wary college-bound students will find comfort in this sincere and endearing look at freshman year." Booklist

Black, Holly

The **Good** Neighbors; book one: Kin. Graphix 2008 117p (The Good Neighbors) $16.99
Grades: 7 8 9 10 11 12   **741.5**
1. Graphic novels 2. Fantasy graphic novels 3. Fairies -- Graphic novels
ISBN 978-0-439-85562-4; 0-439-85562-4

LC 2007-49008

Sixteen-year-old Rue has grown up in a world much like ours, except that the human world and the world of faerie have co-existed, as good neighbors, for a long time. When Rue's mother disappears and her professor father becomes the main suspect in the murder of a young woman, Rue's life turns strange. As she digs for information to figure out what is happening in her life, Rue discovers that her mother is a faerie and has returned to that realm because of a broken promise.

"This sophisticated tale is well served by Naifeh's stylish, angular illustrations." SLJ

Other titles in this series are:

Kith (2009)

Kind (2010)

Bowers, Rick

Superman vs. the Ku Klux Klan; the true story of how the iconic superhero battled the men of hate. by Rick Bowers. National Geographic 2012 160 p.

Grades: 7 8 9 10 11 12   **741.5**

1. Ku Klux Klan 2. Comic books, strips, etc. -- History and criticism 3. United States -- Social life and customs -- History 4. Ku Klux Klan (1915-)

ISBN 1426309155; 1426309163; 9781426309151; 9781426309168

LC 2011024660

This book by Richard Bowers relates how "In 1946 . . . the powers behind the Superman franchise decided to use the superhero (in his radio incarnation) to take on a growing concern: the reemergence of the Ku Klux Klan . . . . [Rick] Bowers begins with the story of Superman's creators, two Jewish kids who grew up in Cleveland. In alternating sections, he also follows the evolution of the Klan, from its beginnings after the Civil War to its renaissance . . . . in the 1920s and beyond. A dual biography of both the hero and the hate group, this book also chronicles the early years of comics . . . and discusses how both Superman and the Klan came with values they wanted to impress upon young people." (Booklist)

Includes bibliographical references and index.

Brosgol, Vera

★ **Anya's** ghost. First Second 2011 221p il $19.99; pa $15.99

Grades: 6 7 8 9 10   **741.5**

1. Graphic novels 2. Ghosts -- Graphic novels 3. School stories -- Graphic novels

ISBN 978-1-59643-713-5; 1-59643-713-8; 978-1-59643-552-0 pa; 1-59643-552-6 pa

LC 2010036251

"A deliciously creepy page-turning gem from first-time writer and illustrator Brosgol. . . . A moodily atmospheric spectrum of grays washes over the clean, tidy panels, setting a distinct stage before the first words appear. . . . In addition to the supernatural elements, Brosgol interweaves some savvy insights about the illusion of perfection and outward appearance. . . . A book sure to haunt its reader long after the last page is turned—exquisitely eerie." Kirkus

Buhle, Paul

A **people's** history of American empire: a graphic adaptation. Henry Holt and Company/Metropolitan Books 2008 275p $30; pa $17

Grades: 10 11 12 Adult   **741.5**

1. Historians 2. Graphic novels 3. United States -- History 4. College teachers 5. Social activists 6. Nonfiction writers 7. United States -- History -- Graphic novels 8. United States -- Foreign relations -- Graphic novels 9. United States -- Territorial expansion --

Graphic novels

ISBN 978-0-8050-7779-7; 978-0-8050-8744-4 pa

LC 2007-31150

First published in 1980, A People's History of the United States triggered a revolution in the way history is told, chronicling events as they were lived, from the bottom up. Now Howard Zinn, historian Paul Buhle, and cartoonist Mike Konopacki have collaborated to retell a chapter of A People's History: the centuries-long story of America's actions in the world. Narrated by Zinn, this version opens with the events of 9/11 and then jumps back to explore the cycles of U.S. expansionism from Wounded Knee to Iraq, stopping along the way at World War I, Central America, Vietnam, and the Iranian revolution. The book also follows the story of Zinn, the son of poor Jewish immigrants, from his childhood in the Brooklyn slums to his role as one of America's leading historians. The Civil Rights Movement is also included. The book includes images of violence, both in photographs and drawn art.

Byrne, John

Cartooning; the best one-stop guide to drawing cartoons, caricatures, comic strips, and manga. [by] John M. Byrne. Collins 2008 191p il hardcover o.p. pa $16.95

Grades: 9 10 11 12 Adult   **741.5**

1. Cartooning -- Technique

ISBN 978-0-06-147794-2 o.p.

LC 2008-7587

The author "touches on all aspects of cartooning—history, drawing exercises, types of tools and materials, basic drawing skills, lettering, paneling, storytelling, humor, using computers, marketing, and much more. Various styles are included, with special chapters devoted to caricatures and manga. . . . A solid title with useful information for both beginners and more advanced artists." SLJ

Includes bibliographical references

Card, Orson Scott

Laddertop. Tor 2011 un il pa $10.99

Grades: 6 7 8 9 10   **741.5**

1. Graphic novels 2. Science fiction graphic novels

ISBN 978-0-7653-2460-3; 0-7653-2460-1

"Preteens Robbi and Azure are best friends, though the girls couldn't be more opposite: Robbi is a sensitive dreamer, while Azure is a driven go-getter with a short temper. Azure's biggest dream is to be picked for Laddertop. This is a program of the Givers, aliens who claim to help conserve Earth's resources by building power-providing space stations 36,000 feet above the Earth; these are reached by giant ladders. . . . The main characters in this volume are largely female, strong and intelligent, a wonderful departure from male-dominated extraterrestrial offerings. Ibardolaza's muscular art blends manga and Western aesthetics." Kirkus

Carroll, Emily

★ **Through** the woods; Emily Carroll. 1st ed Margaret K. McElderry Books 2014 208 p. chiefly color illustrations (trade paper) $14.99; (hardcover) $21.99

Grades: 8 9 10 11 12 Adult   **741.5**

1. Horror fiction 2. Comic books, strips, etc. 3. Short

stories 4. Graphic novels
ISBN 9781442465961; 9781442465954

LC 2013030969

Ignatz Award: Outstanding Artist (2015)

Eisner Award: Best Graphic Album--Reprint (2015)

In this book, Emily Carroll "crafts five unsettling tales in graphic-novel format inspired by common folkloric themes--from wolves in the woods to peculiar visitors to dark possessions. In 'Our Neighbor's House,' three sisters who find themselves alone in a cabin are taken, one by one, in the middle of the night by a smiling stranger. . . . 'The Nesting Place' focus on malevolent spirit possession." (Horn Book Magazine)

"All the tales in Carroll's debut graphic novel are fairly standard ghost stories, but it is her eerie illustrations--popping with bold color on black, glossy pages--that masterfully build terrifying tension and a keep-the-lights-on atmosphere." Booklist

Castellucci, Cecil

Janes in love; by Cecil Castellucci and Jim Rugg; with lettering by Rob Clark Jr. and gray tones by Jasen Lex. DC Comics/Minx 2008 176p il (Plain Janes) pa $9.99

Grades: 7 8 9 10 11 12   **741.5**

1. Graphic novels 2. Romance graphic novels 3. Art -- Graphic novels 4. Friendship -- Graphic novels 5. School stories -- Graphic novels 6. High school students -- Graphic novels

ISBN 978-1-4012-1387-9 pa; 1-4012-1387-1 pa

"Castellucci deftly deals with a number of serious issues, including anxiety and depression, mortality, body image, gay relationships, and community activism. Fortunately, they never weigh down the narrative: this is a sweet, quirky story with some uplifting (though never pedantic) messages. Rugg's clean, crisp illustrations are the perfect accompaniment." SLJ

The **Plain** Janes; [illustrated by] Jim Rugg. DC Comics/Minx 2007 un il pa $9.99

Grades: 7 8 9 10 11 12   **741.5**

1. Graphic novels 2. Art -- Graphic novels 3. Friendship -- Graphic novels 4. School stories -- Graphic novels 5. High school students -- Graphic novels

ISBN 978-1-4012-1115-8

After a bomb attack in Metro City, Jane's parents move to suburban Kent Waters, where Jane feels lost. Then she meets three other Janes at the "reject" table in the high school lunch room, and she convinces them to help her form their own secret club: P.L.A.I.N.—People Loving Art in Neighborhoods. However, their "art attacks" cause the authorities to think that P.L.A.I.N. is a terrorist group.

"The art, inspired by Dan Clowes' work, is absolutely engaging. Packaged like manga this is a fresh, exciting use of the graphic-novel format." Booklist

Another title about the Janes is:

Janes in love (2008)

Cherrywell, Steph

Pepper Penwell and the land creature of Monster Lake; [written and drawn by Steph Cherrywell]. SLG Publishing 2011 un il pa $14.95

Grades: 7 8 9 10 11 12 Adult   **741.5**

1. Graphic novels 2. Horror graphic novels 3. Mystery graphic novels 4. Humorous graphic novels 5. Monsters -- Graphic novels

ISBN 978-1-59362-205-3

British teenager Pepper Penwell prefers solving mysteries over school work and wants to be a detective like her father. When the latest school boots her out, Pepper takes on the case of a missing drum majorette named Lucy. Accompanied by her brother Alex, who inexplicably (it was some kind of accident) has the body of a bird, Pepper travels to Monster Lake, a town trying to establish itself as a tourist attraction based on its local monster, which is a land creature. In the town, Pepper meets strange people, any of whom could be guilty of kidnapping the wealthy and annoying Lucy. However, after Pepper does find Lucy, there's still the matter of the land monster, which is all too real. British slang (arse, bum) provides the mildly harsh language.

Chiarello, Mark

The **DC** Comics guide to coloring and lettering comics; [by] Mark Chiarello and Todd Klein; introduction by Jim Steranko. Watson-Guptill Publications 2004 144p il pa $19.95

Grades: 9 10 11 12   **741.5**

1. Drawing 2. Cartoons and caricatures 3. Comic books, strips, etc.

ISBN 0-8230-1030-9

LC 2004-9753

"This is a great resource for YAs seriously interested in graphic storytelling; it will also find an appreciative audience among adults." Booklist

Chmakova, Svetlana

Nightschool: the weirn books, volume one; [by] Svetlana Chmakova; toning artist, Dee DuPuy; lettering, JuYoun Lee. Yen Press 2009 190p il pa $12.99

Grades: 7 8 9 10 11 12   **741.5**

1. Graphic novels 2. Mystery graphic novels 3. Supernatural graphic novels 4. Witches -- Graphic novels

ISBN 978-0-7595-2859-8

PS 13W is a regular public high school during the day, but after dark it is the Nightschool attended by werewolves, vampires, and weirns (a particular breed of witch). Sarah has just started her job as the new Night Keeper when she disappears from the school; when her younger sister Alex, a young weirn who's been homeschooled, discovers that Sarah's existence has been wiped out from everyone's memory but hers, she sets out to investigate. Dark forces have caused Sarah's disappearance, and they seem to be watching Alex, too. Meanwhile, Daemon, the teacher of the hunters, must try to figure out what young seer Marina has seen in her visions of a broken seal and what this has to do with his students who were severely injured while they were out on a class trip to the cemetery. This urban fantasy was first published in Yen Press's manga magazine, Yen Plus.

"Manga fans and teens looking for vampire stories will devour this one and will want to find out more about these characters." SLJ

Volume 1 of 4

Chwast, Seymour

★ The **odyssey**; [Homer]; adapted by Seymour Chwast. 1st U.S. ed. Bloomsbury 2012 128 p. ill. (All-action classics) (hardcover) $20.00

Grades: Adult   **741.5**
1. Epic literature 2. Adventure graphic novels 3. Odysseus (Greek mythology) 4. Graphic novels
ISBN 9781608194865

LC 2012010047

In this graphic retelling of Homer's "The Odyssey," "Odysseus faces storm and shipwreck, a terrifying man-eating Cyclops, the alluring but deadly Sirens, and the fury of the sea-god Poseidon as he makes his ten-year journey home from the Trojan War. While Odysseus struggles to make it home, his wife, Penelope, fights a different kind of battle as her palace is invaded by forceful, greedy men who tell her that Odysseus is dead and she must choose a new husband." (Publisher's note)

This graphic novel adaptation of Homer's classic epic is "a crackling adventure that also penetrates the recessess of the human heart. . . . Caldwell's art has the force and vibrant life of a Samurai Jack cartoon." Booklist

Cliff, Tony

★ **Delilah** Dirk and the Turkish Lieutenant; by Tony Cliff. First Second 2013 176 p. ill. (paperback) $15.99

Grades: 9 10 11 12   **741.5**
1. Adventure fiction 2. Historical fiction 3. Istanbul (Turkey) -- Fiction 4. Women adventurers -- Fiction
ISBN 1596438134; 9781596438132

LC 2013947230

In this book, "Delilah Dirk has abandoned conventional court life and become a globe-trotting soldier of fortune. She is captured and held prisoner in 1800s Constantinople. Eventually she escapes, taking along the astonished Turkish Lieutenant Erdemogul Selim, whose quiet life centers around a proper cup of tea. This unlikely pair embarks on a wild journey that includes flying a ship, outwitting the Evil Pirate Captain Zakul, and escaping burning buildings." (School Library Journal)

"Plenty of fight scenes will attract male readers, in addition to females looking for strong heroines. All in all, this is a carefree romp across the Ottoman Empire with an upbeat tone that is refreshing." Lib Med Con

Crilley, Mark

Brody's ghost: book 1; story and art by Mark Crilley. Dark Horse Books 2010 88p il pa $6.99

Grades: 8 9 10 11 12 Adult   **741.5**
1. Graphic novels 2. Fantasy graphic novels 3. Mystery graphic novels 4. Adventure graphic novels 5. Ghosts -- Graphic novels
ISBN 978-1-59582-521-6

In what looks like a near-future city, Brody is down and out, eking out a living by playing guitar on the streets and working part-time as a stock clerk. Then, one day, while playing his guitar, he sees the ghost of a young woman; he thinks he's seeing things, but she won't let him alone until he talks with her. Talia, the ghost, needs to do a great deed before she can get into heaven, and she has decided to solve the mystery of a serial killer called the Penny Murderer, but she needs Brody, who is a ghostseer, to help her. First, though, he needs training to bring out his ghostseer powers, because he doesn't think he has any. Enter Kagemura, the ghost of a samurai, who decides, half-unwillingly, to train Brody. This book is much grittier than Crilley's earlier works, which were more suitable for younger readers; it is aimed more at teen and adult readers and includes some fighting violence but no graphically violent content.

"The setting—an unidentified future city partially in ruins—is a masterpiece of drawing, and Brody and the other characters are equally well crafted. . . . The story is more than a match for the art: humor, action, and mystery butt up against the reality of Brody's sad life, giving him the opportunity to change who he is." Booklist

Book 1 of 6

Miki Falls, Book One: Spring. HarperCollins/HarperTeen 2007 176p il pa $7.99

Grades: 7 8 9 10 11 12   **741.5**
1. Graphic novels 2. Friendship -- Graphic novels 3. School stories -- Graphic novels 4. High school students -- Graphic novels
ISBN 978-0-06-084616-9

"Crilley uses mystery to drive the narrative and creates characters that the reader will care about. The black-and-white, manga-style art is beautiful." Voice Youth Advocates

Other titles in this series are:
Miki Falls, Book Two: Summer
Miki Falls, Book Three: Autumn
Miki Falls, Book Four: Winter

Dawson, Mike

Troop 142; Mike Dawson. Secret Acres 2011 1 v. (unpaged) chiefly ill. (trade pbk.) $20

Grades: 9 10 11 12   **741.5**
1. Camping -- Graphic novels 2. Comic books, strips, etc. 3. Scouts and scouting -- Graphic novels 4. Boy Scouts -- Comic books, strips, etc
ISBN 9780979960994

LC 2011924536

This graphic novel, originally published online where it won the 2010 Ignatz Award for Outstanding Online Comic, "follows a group of campers and counselors at a week-long scout retreat in the woods of New Jersey. It is a story as much about adults as it is adolescents, the blurred line between childhood and manhood, and the consequences of authoritative posturing. Dispensing with idyllic notions, [author Mike] Dawson describes . . . truths about boys and men, the hypocrisy of institutional morality and the resilience of Spam and the human spirit." (Publisher's note)

Delisle, Guy

★ **Pyongyang**: a journey in North Korea; translated by Helge Dascher. Drawn & Quarterly 2005 176p il map hardcover o.p. pa $14.95

Grades: 11 12 Adult   **741.5**
1. Graphic novels 2. Korea (North) -- Graphic novels
ISBN 1-896597-89-0; 1-897299-21-4 pa

"Pyongyang will appeal to multiple audiences: current events buffs, Persepolis fans and those who just love a good yarn." Publ Wkly

Denson, Abby

★ **Tough** Love: High School Confidential. Manic D Press 2006 144p il $12.95

Grades: 8 9 10 11 12 Adult 741.5

1. Graphic novels 2. Romance graphic novels 3. Homosexuality -- Graphic novels
ISBN 978-1-933149-08-0

Dorkin, Evan

★ **Beasts** of Burden: animal rites; written by Evan Dorkin; art by Jill Thompson; lettering by Jason Arthur and Jill Thompson. Dark Horse Comics 2010 184p il $19.99

Grades: 8 9 10 11 12 Adult 741.5

1. Graphic novels 2. Mystery graphic novels 3. Supernatural graphic novels 4. Cats -- Graphic novels 5. Dogs -- Graphic novels
ISBN 978-1-59582-513-1

2010 Eisner Award for Best Publication for Teens; 2010 Eisner Award to Jill Thompson for Best Painter/Multimedia Artist for Beasts of Burden and Magic Trixie; 2005 Eisner Award for Best Short Story for 'Unfamiliar;' 2004 Eisner Award to Jill Thompson for Best Painter/Multimedia Artist (interior art) for 'Stray.'

Burden Hill is just a nice, quiet suburban town full of houses with yards and white picket fences, demonic frogs, zombie roadkill, ghosts, etc. The humans who live in Burden Hill seem to be totally oblivious to the dangers, but the dogs, and one cat, work together to keep their town safe. Jack the beagle, Pugsley (go figure), Ace the husky, Rex the Doberman, Whitey the terrier, and Orphan the cat deal with a haunted dog house, witches, undead dogs, a werewolf, and other monsters. The book includes some mild bad language ("crap" usually from Pugs) and a fair amount of violence. This book includes the four-issue miniseries plus all of the short stories that originally appeared in The Dark Horse Book of Hauntings, The Dark Horse Book of Witchcraft, The Dark Horse Book of the Dead, and The Dark Horse Book of Monsters. Sarah Dyer co-wrote "A Dog and His Boy" with Evan Dorkin.

"Gorgeous artwork and a smart, witty script elevate this tale of household pets who unite to fight occult menaces in idyllic Burden Hill." Publ Wkly

Drooker, Eric

Blood song; a silent ballad. introduction by Joe Sacco. 2nd ed.; Dark Horse 2009 un il pa $19.95

Grades: 11 12 Adult 741.5

1. Graphic novels 2. Stories without words
ISBN 978-1-59582-389-2

First published 2002 by Harcourt

"Driven by war from their rural home in Southeast Asia, a young woman and her dog ride the ocean currents to a city in the West. A deeply moving graphic novel, masterfully done." SLJ

Dunning, John Harris

Salem Brownstone; all along the watchtowers. [by] John Harris Dunning and Nikhil Singh. Candlewick Press 2010 un il lib bdg $18.99

Grades: 9 10 11 12 741.5

1. Graphic novels 2. Fantasy graphic novels 3. Supernatural graphic novels 4. Circus -- Graphic novels 5. Magicians -- Graphic novels
ISBN 978-0-7636-4735-3; 0-7636-4735-7

LC 2009-47413

Upon his father's death, Salem inherits a mansion as well as an unfinished battle with creatures from another world, which requires him to seek the help of his guardian familiar and the colorful performers of Dr. Kinoshita's Circus of Unearthly Delights.

"Salem's world is a haunting one, made only more so by the mysterious and enthralling images that accompany the storyline. The gothic elements, combined with the carnivalesque nature of Dr. Kinoshita's Circus and his performers, mesmerize readers and keep them grounded in the story long after it has ended." Voice Youth Advocates

Eisner, Will

★ **Comics** and sequential art; principles and practices from the legendary cartoonist. W.W. Norton 2008 175p il (The Will Eisner library) pa $22.95

Grades: 9 10 11 12 Adult 741.5

1. Drawing -- Technique 2. Graphic novels -- Authorship 3. Comic books, strips, etc. -- Authorship
ISBN 978-0-393-33126-4; 0-393-33126-1

LC 2008-20042

First published 1985 by Poorhouse Press

This book offers the author's ideas, theories, and advice about graphic storytelling and the uses to which the comic book art form can be applied.

Fairfield, Lesley

★ **Tyranny**. Tundra Books 2009 114p il pa $10.95

Grades: 8 9 10 11 12 741.5

1. Graphic novels 2. Eating disorders -- Graphic novels
ISBN 0-88776-903-9; 978-0-88776-903-0

This graphic novel portrays teenager Anna's struggle with anorexia, "personified as her tormentor, Tyranny." (Publisher's note) "Age eleven and up." (Quill Quire)

"This is one of the most moving and important graphic novels to come along in years. Many stories have been written about teens who try to change what they see in the mirror through anorexia and bulimia, but this one features a girl who is driven by her own personal demon. That demon is called Tyranny, and it is represented by an angry and chaotic swirl of lines that form the shape of a person. . . . Fairfield treats this important subject with intelligence and empathy. . . . The simple yet powerful black-and-white drawings do wonders in bringing the book's message to its readers." SLJ

Fleming, Ann Marie

The **Magical** Life of Long Tack Sam; An Illustrated Memoir. Ann Marie Fleming. Riverhead Books 2007 170 p. ill. (some col.) $20

Grades: 11 12 Adult 741.5

1. Magicians 2. Graphic novels 3. Biographical graphic novels 4. Magicians -- Graphic novels
ISBN 1594482640; 9781594482649

LC 2007060352

This graphic memoir, by Ann Marie Fleming, was "inspired by the award-winning documentary-and the life and mystery of China's greatest magician. Who was Long Tack Sam? He was born in 1885. He ran away from Shangdung Province to join the circus. He was an acrobat. A magician. A comic. An impresario. A restaurateur. A theater owner. A world traveler. An East-West ambassador. A mentor to Orson Welles. He was considered the greatest act in the history of vaudeville." (Publisher's note)

"Born in a Chinese village, Fleming's great-grandfather was a world-class magician who called places on four continents home during his 70 years. Fleming brilliantly illuminates how dramatically international politics affected his life." Booklist

Includes bibliographical references (p. 168-169)

Flight v2; [editor/art director, Kazu Kibuishi] Villard 2007 432p il pa $24.95

Grades: 10 11 12 Adult   **741.5**
1. Graphic novels 2. Fantasy graphic novels 3. Short stories -- Graphic novels
ISBN 978-0-345-49637-9

In this themed story collection, "more than 30 accomplished young artists take off on the theme, sometimes loosely construed, of flight. . . . At more than 400 pages, there is something in this elegantly produced collection for everyone, including readers who usually snub comics." Booklist

Flight v3; [editor/art director, Kazu Kibuishi]. Ballantine Books 2006 351p il pa $24.95

Grades: 9 10 11 12 Adult   **741.5**
1. Graphic novels 2. Fantasy graphic novels 3. Short stories -- Graphic novels
ISBN 978-0-345-49039-1; 0-345-49039-8
                LC 2006-45883

Sequel to Flight v2 (2005)

This third volume of Flight includes 26 short stories by mostly young writers, many of whom have webcomics. Some, such as Michael Gagne and Becky Cloonan, have published a number of books. The stories range from whimsical interludes to ironic fables to mini-epics of derring-do; ironically, most of the stories have only a tangential connection to the theme of flight.

Flight: Volume Four. Random House/Villard 2007 344p il $24.95

Grades: 9 10 11 12 Adult   **741.5**
1. Graphic novels 2. Fantasy graphic novels 3. Short stories -- Graphic novels
ISBN 978-0-345-49040-7

This fourth volume of the graphic novel anthology series includes 25 stories by creators ranging from veterans such as Michel Gagne and Graham Annable to newer creators such as Clio Chiang and Neil Babra. Most of the artists have webcomics; a number of them work in animation (Gagne most recently worked on the motion picture Ratatouille); some have worked on major graphic novel projects - Lark Pien colored Gene Yang's American Born Chiense, and Raina Telgemeier works on the graphic novel adaptations of The Baby-Sitters Club. While there is little harsh language and no nudity, some of the stories have more mature themes.

Gaiman, Neil, 1960-

★ The **graveyard** book graphic novel Volume 1; based on the novel by Neil Gaiman; adapted by P. Craig Russell; illustrated by Kevin Nowlan, P. Craig Russell, Tony Harris, Scott Hampton, Galen Showman, Jill Thompson, Stephen B. Scott; colorist, Lovern Kindzierski; letterer, Rick Parker. HarperCollins 2014 188 p. color illustrations $19.99

Grades: 5 6 7 8 9 10   **741.5**
1. Graphic novels 2. Orphans -- Fiction 3. Cemeteries -- Fiction
ISBN 9780062194817; 006219481X
                LC 2013953799

This graphic novel is an adaptation of the "Newbery Medal-winning novel, [where] Bod is an unusual boy . . . , the only living resident of a graveyard. Raised from infancy by the ghosts, werewolves, and other cemetery denizens, Bod has learned the antiquated customs of his guardians' time as well as their ghostly teachings." (Publisher's note)

"Russell brings his decades of comics know-how to this lovely, lyrical adaptation of [Gaiman's] well-loved, Newbery Medal--winning book. Not content to rely exclusively on his own distinctive talents, Russell has enlisted some of the industry's greatest contemporary illustrators as contributors, who fill the panels with appropriately gothic tones. In order to give ample room to the novel's twists and turns, the adaptation has been divided into two parts." Booklist

★ The **graveyard** book graphic novel Volume 2; based on the novel by Neil Gaiman; adapted by P. Craig Russell; illustrated by David LaFuente, Scott Hampton, P. Craig Russell, Kevin Nowlan, Galen Showman; colorist, Lovern Kindzierski; letterer, Rick Parker. HarperCollins 2014 188 p. color illustrations (hardcover) $19.99

Grades: 5 6 7 8 9 10   **741.5**
1. Dead -- Fiction 2. Orphans -- Fiction 3. Cemeteries -- Fiction 4. Supernatural graphic novels 5. Graphic novels 6. Supernatural -- Fiction
ISBN 0062194836; 9780062194831
                LC 2013497350

"Russell concludes the two-part adaptation of Gaiman's Newbery Medal winner, encompassing the final three chapters of the novel. Bod, raised by the ghostly denizens of a graveyard, is a young adult now, yearning for knowledge of the world of the living. After a showdown with a pair of school bullies . . . Bod finally confronts the ancient order who murdered his family and overcomes them with his supernatural know-how and his innate courage and cleverness." (Booklist)

"Russell and his team of illustrators continue to do this amazing story justice with images that lead readers down a path into Bod's dark and magical graveyard world. Gaiman has the ability to weave beauty and intrigue into a story that has a strong potential to frighten." VOYA

Geary, Rick

The **lives** of Sacco and Vanzetti; Rick Geary. NBM Comics Lit 2011 80 p. chiefly ill. $15.99

Grades: 9 10 11 12 Adult   **741.5**
1. Sacco-Vanzetti case 2. Anarchism and anarchists --

Graphic novels 3. United States -- History -- 1919-1933 -- Graphic novels 4. Sacco-Vanzetti Trial, Dedham, Mass., 1921 -- Comic books, strips, etc. 5. Trials (Murder) -- Massachusetts -- Dedham -- Comic books, strips, etc.

ISBN 1561636053; 9781561636051

LC 2011927818

"Geary lays out what is known and not known about the case, in which two Italian anarchist immigrants were put to death after being found guilty of robbery and murder. The . . . narrative not only details the events of the crime, manhunt, and trial but also includes information about the lives of Sacco and Vanzetti and their families." (Publishers Weekly)

Includes bibliographical references.

Giffen, Keith

Blue Beetle: Shellshocked; writers, Keith Giffen & John Rogers; Cully Hamner . . . [et al], pencillers; Phil Balsman, Pat Brosseau, letterers; David Self, Guy Major, colorists; Cully Hamner, Phil Moy, Duncan Rouleau, Jack Purcell, inkers. DC Comics 2006 144p il pa $12.99

Grades: 8 9 10 11 12 Adult   **741.5**

1. Graphic novels 2. Adventure graphic novels 3. Superhero graphic novels 4. Blue Beetle (Fictional character)

ISBN 978-1-4012-0965-0

Ted Kord, the Blue Beetle, is dead; but the Blue Beetle scarab has chosen a new guardian, El Paso teenager Jaime Reyes. Supernatural powers can be a blessing or a curse, and when it comes to the powers of the Scarab, you don't get one without the other. The new hero will now have to deal with increasingly strange and dangerous days ahead, as he learns to handle his new skills while intergalactic trouble comes looking for him.

Gillen, Kieron

Young avengers; style > substance. Kieron Gillen, writer; Jamie McKelvie, Mike Norton, artist; Matthew Wilson, color artist; VC's Clayton Cowles, letterer. Marvel Enterprises 2013 128 p. ill pbk $15.99

Grades: 10 11 12 Adult   **741.5**

1. Teenagers -- Fiction 2. Superhero graphic novels

ISBN 9780785167082; 0785167080

Author Kieron Gillen and illustrator Jamie McKelvie tell the story of "Wiccan, Hulkling and Kate 'Hawkeye' Bishop with Kid Loki, Marvel Boy and Ms. America. . . . As a figure from Loki's past emerges, Wiccan makes a horrible mistake that comes back to bite everyone on their communal posteriors. Fight scenes! Fake IDs! And plentiful feels! (aka 'meaningful emotional character beats' . . .)" (Publisher's note)

"The story . . . flies by, thanks to clever banter and lightning pacing. . . . McKelvie turns in clean, polished pages with eye-popping character work and shows some real and very welcome imagination with action sequences." Booklist

Young Avengers; Volume 2 alternative cultures. Kieron Gillen, illustrated by Kate Brown and Jamie McKelvie. Marvel Enterprises 2014 112 p. chiefly col. ill. (Young Avengers) $15.99

Grades: 9 10 11 12 Adult   **741.5**

1. Fantasy fiction 2. Comic books, strips, etc. 3. Superhero comic books, strips, etc. 4. Heroes 5. Graphic novels 6. Young adult fiction 7. Science fiction comic books, strips, etc.

ISBN 0785167099; 9780785167099

"Existential horror turns cosmic horror as something emerges from the shadows of the past . . . and it seems that the Young Avengers have one more thing to worry about. The team races desperately across the multi-verse in pursuit of their missing friend, but their road trip goes crazy as it reaches its destination." (Publisher's note)

"As with the previous one, this slim volume is a quick read with snappy dialogue and fast, cleanly depicted action that pops with cinematic digital coloring effects." Booklist

Gipi

Notes for a war story; translated by Spectrum. First Second Books 2007 126p il pa $16.95

Grades: 10 11 12 Adult   **741.5**

1. Graphic novels 2. War -- Graphic novels 3. Crime -- Graphic novels

ISBN 978-1-59643-261-1

LC 2006-49716

Original Italian edition, 2004

Giuliano, a loner among outsiders, is one of three young drifters caught up in the whirlwind of a war in the Balkans. The three boys are like passing shadows; they live in abandoned houses, dodge the occasional bomb, and steal car parts for money. Meeting Felix—a powerful, fast-talking mercenary—changes everything for them. Felix is an expert manipulator; he speaks to their ambition and to their desires for power, wealth, and purpose. They're instantly hooked, especially the trio's unofficial leader, Stefano, and they soon escalate from petty crime to working on behalf of a mafia-style militia, bullying and extorting money in Felix's name. But as Giuliano comes to realize, they don't know what they're fighting for—if they're even fighting for anything. There's some naturally occurring violence and harsh language.

Goldstein, Nancy

Jackie Ormes; the first African American woman cartoonist. University of Michigan Press 2008 225p il $35

Grades: 10 11 12 Adult   **741.5**

1. Cartoonists 2. African American women -- Biography

ISBN 978-0-472-11624-9; 0-472-11624-X

LC 2007-35395

This book covers the life and career of Jackie Ormes, who was the first African American woman cartoonist. She wrote and drew comic strips that ran in Black newspapers such as the Pittsburgh Courier and the Chicago Defender. She was part of the Black elite in Chicago and knew other luminaries such as singer Eartha Kitt and musician/composer/conductor Duke Ellington. She was also investigated by the FBI because of her Leftist political ideas and activities. While she did such things as create Torchy paper dolls, based on her beautiful and sexy cartoon character, and cute Patty-Jo dolls, Ormes also used her comic strips to put forth her political views. This book reproduces some of her cartoons and comic strips, in both black and white and in color.

Includes bibliographical references

Gonick, Larry

The **cartoon** history of the modern world; Part 1: from Columbus to the U.S. Constitution. Collins 2007 259p il pa $17.95

Grades: 9 10 11 12 Adult   **741.5**

1. Graphic novels 2. Modern history -- Graphic novels
ISBN 978-0-06-076004-5; 0-06-076004-4

LC 2006-49146

The book begins with a "15-page distillation of pre-Columbian America; and while Europe and North America receive most of the attention, Gonick does include at least some highlights from other parts of the world. Covering such topics as the Protestant Reformation, the British defeat of the Spanish Armada, the Copernican model of the universe, and the American Revolution, he writes and draws with considerable wit and authority, and is obviously well versed in his subject." SLJ

Followed by:

The Cartoon History of the Modern World Part 2: From the Bastille to Baghdad (2009)

Graphic Classics volume eight: Mark Twain; edited by Tom Pomplun. 2nd ed.; Eureka Productions 2007 144p il pa $11.95

Grades: 9 10 11 12 Adult   **741.5**

1. Authors 2. Humorists 3. Novelists 4. Graphic novels 5. Humorous graphic novels 6. Adventure graphic novels 7. Essayists 8. Satirists 9. Memoirists 10. Travel writers 11. Short story writers 12. Short stories -- Graphic novels
ISBN 978-0-9787919-2-6

First published 2004

This book includes an adaptation of "Tom Sawyer Abroad" by Tom Pomplun and George Sellas, "The Mysterious Stranger" by Rick Geary, "A Dog's Tale" by Lance Tooks, "The Celebrated Jumping Frog of Calaveras County" by Kevin Atkinson, and "The Carnival of Crime in Connecticut" by Antonella Caputo and Nick Miller. Also in this volume are "Is He Living or Is He Dead?," "A Curious Pleasure Excursion," and eight women artists interpret Mark Twain's "Advice to Little Girls."

"With a terrific lineup of artists and unbeatable material, Pomplun has assembled a collection of Mark Twain's work that should delight graphic novel fans and anyone seeking to boost their general cultural knowledge." Publ Wkly [review of 2004 edition]

Graphic Classics volume eleven: O. Henry; edited by Tom Pomplun. Eureka Productions 2005 144p il pa $11.95

Grades: 7 8 9 10 11 12 Adult   **741.5**

1. Authors 2. Graphic novels 3. Short story writers 4. Short stories -- Graphic novels
ISBN 978-0-9746648-2-0

This volume of Graphics Classics adapts some of the short stories by O. Henry, the master of the surprise ending. Stories include 'The Ransom of Red Chief,' illustrated by Johnny Ryan, 'The Gift of the Magi,' illustrated by Lisa We-

ber, 'The Caballero's Way' (the original story of the Cisco Kid), illustrated by Mark A. Nelson, and more.

Grayson, Devin

Uglies; Shay's story. created by Scott Westerfeld; written by Scott Westerfeld and Devin Grayson; illustrations by Steven Cummings. Del Rey 2012 160 p. chiefly ill. (prebind) $22.10; (paperback) $10.99

Grades: 7 8 9 10   **741.5**

1. Dystopian graphic novels 2. Conformity -- Graphic novels 3. Plastic surgery -- Graphic novels 4. Graphic Novels 5. Science fiction 6. Friendship -- Fiction 7. Beauty, Personal -- Fiction
ISBN 9780606264754; 0345527224; 9780345527226

LC 2012374898

This young adult graphic novel retells the story of author Scott Westerfeld's dystopia "Uglies" from "the point of view of recurring frenemy Shay." It is "set in a . . . future time when discord is suppressed through ruthlessly enforced conformity and obligatory plastic surgery at age 16. . . . Shay yearns for freedom. An encounter with the flawed and alluring David, a covert envoy from the Smoke, a secret community of nonconformists, may offer Shay the escape she craves." (Publishers Weekly)

Followed by:

Uglies: Cutters (2012);

Greenberg, Isabel

The **encyclopedia** of early earth; a novel. Isabel Greenberg. Little, Brown and Co. 2013 176 p. $23

Grades: 10 11 12 Adult   **741.5**

1. Fables 2. Earth -- Fiction 3. Travel -- Fiction
ISBN 0316225819; 9780316225816

LC 2013939419

Author Isabel Greenberg presents a "series of illustrated and linked tales [which] chronicles the explorations of a young man as he paddles from his home in the North Pole to the South Pole. There, he meets his true love, but their romance is ill-fated. Early Earth's unusual and finicky polarity means the lovers can never touch." (Publisher's note)

"Greenberg deeply immerses readers in the themes and lessons of world mythology, but she remarkably never merely apes classic myths—the way each of Early Earth's cultures tweaks the same ideas and characters for their own myths is a veritable lesson in comparative theology." Booklist

Gulledge, Laura Lee

Page by Paige. Amulet Books 2011 un il $18.95; pa $9.95

Grades: 7 8 9 10 11 12   **741.5**

1. Graphic novels 2. Humorous graphic novels 3. Artists -- Graphic novels 4. Friendship -- Graphic novels 5. Young adult literature -- Works 6. New York (N.Y.) -- Graphic novels
ISBN 0-8109-9721-5; 0-8109-9722-3 pa; 978-0-8109-9721-9; 978-0-8109-9722-6 pa

Teenage Paige Turner (blame her writer parents) moves to New York City from Virginia, and she finds the big city rather overwhelming. She decides to buy a sketchbook and sort out her thoughts and feelings in drawings. Soon she does make some friends, and she explores more of the city, but as she begins to feel happier, she clashes with her parents. All of this goes into her sketchbook journal, which she starts to show to her new friends—Jules, Longo, and Gabe. The book is organized by Paige's "rules," which she uses to try to change herself, such as "Rule #2: Draw what you know. If you feel it or see it . . . DRAW IT!"

"Gulledge's b&w illustrations are simple but well-suited to their subject matter; the work as a whole is a good-natured, optimistic portrait of a young woman evolving toward adulthood." Publ Wkly

Will & whit; Laura Lee Gulledge. Abrams Book 2013 192 p. ill. (paperback) $12.95
Grades: 7 8 9 10   **741.5**
  1. Grief -- Graphic novels 2. Fear of the dark -- Graphic novels
ISBN 1419705466; 9781419705465
                                          LC 2012955192
In this graphic novel, by Laura Lee Gulledge, "Wilhelmina 'Will' Huxstep is a creative soul struggling to come to terms with a family tragedy. She crafts whimsical lamps, in part to deal with her fear of the dark. . . . She longs for unplugged adventures with her fellow creative friends, Autumn, Noel, and Reese. Little does she know that she will get her wish in the form of an arts carnival and a blackout . . . which forces Will to face her fear of darkness." (Publisher's note)

Hambly, Barbara
  Anne Steelyard: the garden of emptiness, act I; an honorary man. Penny Farthing Press 2008 un il pa $14.95
Grades: 9 10 11 12 Adult   **741.5**
  1. Graphic novels 2. Adventure graphic novels 3. Archeology -- Graphic novels 4. Middle East -- Graphic novels
ISBN 978-0-9719012-9-2
In 1908, the Middle East is a region in turmoil; while Germany and Great Britain posture at each other in a prelude to the First World War, men called the Young Turks challenge the Turkish Sultans for control of the Ottoman Empire. Archeologists excavate relics and treasures from the desert sands, their work beginning to demystify human history and managing to bring wealth and fame (or infamy) to those archeologists. Anne Steelyard is a British archeologist who wants to make that one huge discovery which will make her reputation, free her from her father and force the male-dominated field to recognize her as an equal. However, even as she tries to set up an expedition, the politics of the place and time provide obstacles from the Turkish government, from the British, and from society itself. The book includes some violence.
  Other titles in this series are:
  The gate of dreams and starlight (2009)
  A thousand waters (2011)

Hamilton, Tim
  ★ **Ray** Bradbury's Fahrenheit 451; the authorized adaptation. introduction by Ray Bradbury. Hill and Wang 2009 148p il $30; pa $16.95
Grades: 10 11 12 Adult   **741.5**
  1. Authors 2. Novelists 3. Graphic novels 4. Science fiction graphic novels 5. Screenwriters 6. Children's authors 7. Short story writers 8. Science fiction writers
ISBN 978-0-8090-5100-7; 978-0-8090-5101-4 pa
                                          LC 2009-4804
"It's no wonder Hamilton's comic novelization is authorized by Bradbury himself: this evocative button-pusher will almost certainly entice readers to seek out the original. . . . When Montag, the fireman whose job it is to 'fix' forbidden libraries by reducing them to cinder, becomes enticed by the printed word, his treason unleashes no less than subterfuge, paranoia, thuggery, and even robotic killer dogs. Hamilton renders much of the story in triptych panels and moody, two-tone palettes that blot characters' features into Munch-like skulls." Booklist

Hart, Christopher
  Figure it out! human proportions; draw the head and figure right every time. Christopher Hart. Sixth & Spring Books 2014 143 p. illustrations pbk $19.95
Grades: 9 10 11 12 Adult   **741.5**
  1. Figure drawing 2. Drawing -- Technique
ISBN 1936096730; 9781936096732
                                          LC 2013034431
"Most artists whose work features the human head and figure don't have the time or opportunity to draw directly from models, so it's essential that they acquire the skills and tools to draw them accurately without using direct reference. Now, thanks to Chris Hart's foolproof method, even beginners can quick-check the proportions of their head and figure drawings, identify errors, and swiftly fix mistakes." (Publisher's note)

The **master** guide to drawing anime; how to draw original characters from simple templates. Christopher Hart. Sixth&Spring Books 2015 144 p. color illustrations pbk $19.95
Grades: 7 8 9 10 11 12   **741.5**
  1. Manga -- Drawing 2. Cartooning -- Technique
ISBN 9781936096862; 1936096862
                                          LC 2014030200
Nothing brings anime artists more satisfaction than creating original characters to use in a comic strip or graphic novel. . . . Christopher Hart helps them reach this goal by providing insight into the six most popular anime types: schoolgirls, schoolboys, preteens, vengeful bad guys, humorous personalities, and fantasy figures. He supplies templates for each; an extensive array of 'menus' of head and body types, outfits, and accessories; and detailed, accessible, step-by-step demonstrations and drawing exercises." (Publisher's note)

Hartzell, Andy
  Fox bunny funny. Top Shelf Productions 2007 102p il pa $10
Grades: 9 10 11 12 Adult   **741.5**
  1. Graphic novels 2. Fantasy graphic novels 3. Animals -- Graphic novels 4. Stories without words -- Graphic novels
ISBN 978-1-891830-97-6
The rules are simple: you're either a fox or a bunny. Foxes oppress and devour, bunnies suffer and die. Everyone knows their place. Everyone's satisfied. So what happens

461

when a secret desire puts you at odds with your society? Starting from a simple premise—and without using a single word—this book leads the reader on a zigzag chase in and out of rabbit holes, and through increasingly strange landscapes where funny animals have serious identity problems. The tale swerves from slapstick to horror and back again before landing at the inevitable climax, in which all the old rules are shattered. Some moments of violence and dismemberment might be disturbing for some readers.

"Deftly presented in crisp black-and-white, block-print-like panels, this is a must for libraries supporting LGBT collections." Booklist

Harvey, Robert C.

★ The **art** of the comic book; an aesthetic history. University Press of Miss. 1996 288p il (Studies in popular culture) hardcover o.p. pa $22

Grades: 11 12 Adult   **741.5**

1. Comic books, strips, etc. 2. Popular culture -- United States

ISBN 0-87805-758-7

                         LC 95-377

Harvey "attempts to situate the comic book in terms of its evolution from the comic strip to the world of publishing as a whole. . . . {He describes the} change brought upon comics by the institution of the Comics Code in 1954, which put horror and detective stories out of business and ushered in the primacy of superheroes. He also {examines} . . . the art itself, focusing on the development of the vocabulary of panel, layout, story, and style, and the relationship between writer and artist during various stages of comic book history. In addition, he . . . {discusses Will Eisner}, Gil Kane, Frank Miller, and Robert Crumb." Libr J

Includes bibliographical references

Heinberg, Allan

Young Avengers Vol. 1: Sidekicks; writer, Allan Heinberg; pencils, Jim Cheung; inks, John Dell, Mark Morales & Drew Geraci; colors, Justin Ponsor; letters, Virtual Calligraphy's Cory Petit. Marvel Entertainment 2006 un il $14.99

Grades: 9 10 11 12 Adult   **741.5**

1. Graphic novels 2. Superhero graphic novels

ISBN 978-0-7851-2018-6

"In the wake of Avengers Disassembled, a mysterious new group of teen super heroes appears. But who are they? Where did they come from? And what right do they have to call themselves the Young Avengers?" (Publisher's note)

Helfer, Andrew

★ **Malcolm** X; a graphic biography. written by Andrew Helfer; art by Randy DuBurke. Hill and Wang 2006 102p il $15.95

Grades: 10 11 12 Adult   **741.5**

1. Graphic novels 2. Biographical graphic novels 3. Black Muslim leaders 4. Civil rights activists 5. Black Muslims -- Graphic novels 6. African Americans -- Biography -- Graphic novels

ISBN 978-0-8090-9504-9; 0-8090-9504-1

                       LC 2006-13743

The authors "tell the story of Malcolm X's short life—his meeting with Dr. Martin Luther King Jr., the two leaders describing the opposite ideological ends of the fight for civil rights; and his eventual assassination by other members of the Nation of Islam (NOI)—in narration and detailed b&white drawings, sharp as photographs in a newspaper. . . . Helfer and DuBurke have created an evocative and studied look at not only Malcolm X but the racial conflict that defined and shaped him." Publ Wkly

Ronald Reagan; a graphic biography. written by Andrew Helfer; art by Steve Buccellato and Joe Staton. Hill and Wang 2007 102p il $16.95

Grades: 9 10 11 12 Adult   **741.5**

1. Actors 2. Governors 3. Presidents 4. Graphic novels 5. Biographical graphic novels 6. Presidents -- United States -- Graphic novels

ISBN 978-0-8090-9507-0

                       LC 2006-16437

This graphic novel biography covers the life of Ronald Reagan, who began as an actor and ended his career as the fortieth president of the U.S. The book discusses Reagan's work as a union president (Screen Actor's Guild), a General Motors pitchman on television, Governor of California, and his terms as President. It also covers some of the scandals that occurred during his gubernatorial and presidential terms, including the Iran/Contra arms-for-hostages deal, and the assassination attempt by John Hinkley.

Includes bibliographical references

Henson, Jim, 1936-1990

Jim Henson's tale of sand; written by Jim Henson and Jerry Juhl; as realized by Ramón K. Pérez; colors by Ian Herring with Ramón K. Pérez; lettering and font design by Deron Bennett based on the handwriting of Jim Henson; edited by Stephen Christy. Archaia Entertainment 2012 152 p.

Grades: 10 11 12 Adult   **741.5**

1. Fantasy graphic novels 2. Adventure graphic novels 3. Deserts -- Graphic novels 4. Southwestern States -- Graphic novels

ISBN 1936393093; 9781936393091

This graphic novel "follows its hapless protagonist as he is cast out into the desert by the cheerful Sheriff Tate. . . . The scruffy hero is a pawn in a game whose rules are concealed from him, pursued across a surrealistic southwest U.S. by an implacable hunter and hindered by the eccentric, bizarre inhabitants of the great desolation. The prize waiting for him at the end of the chase, should he survive to reach the end, is one he will never guess at." (Publishers Weekly)

Heuvel, Eric

A **family** secret; [English translation, Lorraine T. Miller] Farrar, Straus and Giroux 2009 62p il pa $9.99; $18.99

Grades: 7 8 9 10 11 12   **741.5**

1. Graphic novels 2. Jews -- Graphic novels 3. Grandmothers -- Graphic novels 4. Holocaust, 1933-

1945 -- Graphic novels
ISBN 0-374-32271-6; 978-0-374-42265-3 pa; 0-374-42265-6 pa; 978-0-374-32271-7

LC 2009-13943

Original Dutch edition, 2003

While searching his Dutch grandmother's attic for yard sale items, Jeroen finds a scrapbook which leads Gran to tell of her experiences as a girl living in Amsterdam during the Holocaust, when her father was a Nazi sympathizer and Esther, her Jewish best friend, disappeared

This is a "moving graphic novel. . . . The art is in ink and watercolor, with very clear, highly detailed panels. . . . [A] gripping story." Booklist

Hickman, Troy

Common Grounds: Baker's dozen. Image Comics/Top Cow Productions 2004 144p il pa $14.99
Grades: 9 10 11 12 Adult   741.5
1. Graphic novels 2. Superhero graphic novels
ISBN 978-1-58240-841-5

Superheroes and supervillains need a place where they can relax, unwind, and not worry about the next battle. Common Grounds is just such a place—a chain of coffee shops with bakery counters, totally neutral ground. Here, hero and villain can relax and take a break in the restroom ("Head Games"), a teenage superhero who doubts herself and an older superpowered religious Jew can encourage each other ("Sanctuary"), a group of overweight heroes can meet ("Fat Chance"), or formerly evil monsters can get custom takeout and shoot the breeze ("Where Monsters Dine"). The book includes a baker's dozen (thirteen) stories.

Hicks, Faith Erin

The **Nameless** City; Faith Erin Hicks; color by Jordie Bellaire. First Second 2016 240 p. chiefly color illustrations (trade pbk.) $14.99
Grades: 5 6 7 8 9 10   741.5
1. Friendship -- Fiction 2. Fantasy graphic novels 3. Survival skills -- Fiction 4. Cities and towns -- Fiction 5. Survival -- Fiction
ISBN 1626721564; 9781626721562; 9781626721579
LC 2015020651

"Every nation that invades the City gives it a new name. . . . The natives don't let themselves get caught up in the unending wars. To them, their home is the Nameless City. . . . Kaidu is . . . a Dao born and bred--a member of the latest occupying nation. Rat is a native of the Nameless City. At first, she hates Kai for everything he stands for, but his love of his new home may be the one thing that can bring these two unlikely friends together." (Publisher's note)

"With comprehensive world building, well-rounded characters, and entertaining action, this expertly executed story will find a home with a wide variety of readers, all of whom will be eagerly awaiting the next installment." Booklist

Zombies calling. SLG Publishing 2007 104p il pa $9.95
Grades: 8 9 10 11 12 Adult   741.5
1. Graphic novels 2. Horror graphic novels 3. Humorous graphic novels 4. Zombies -- Graphic novels
ISBN 978-1-59362-079-0

Anglophile/zombie movie fan/college student Joss is going crazy in the middle of exams week, but when her college campus is overrun with actual zombies, she knows what to do. With her roommate Sonnet and their buddy Robyn, Joss uses the Rules gleaned from years of watching zombie movies to fight the undead hordes. When the first rule is that the ordinary person suddenly becomes a total ass-kicking cool fighter able to beat off zombies with no fighting lessons, yeah, it's cool. Except the zombies just keep coming and coming. . . . The book has some harsh language and lots of black and white zombie fighting action without gore.

Hill, Joe

Locke & key: welcome to Lovecraft; written by Joe Hill; art by Gabriel Rodriguez. IDW Publishing 2008 158p il $24.99; pa $19.99
Grades: 10 11 12 Adult   741.5
1. Graphic novels 2. Horror graphic novels 3. Mystery graphic novels
ISBN 978-1-60010-237-0; 978-1-60010-384-1 pa

After Rendell Locke is murdered by a former student, Sam Lesser, who then tried to find and kill the rest of the family, Nina Locke takes her children, Tyler, Kinsey, and Bode to Lovecraft, Massachusetts, to live with Rendell's brother Duncan in Keyhouse. Tyler needs to deal with the guilt he feels because of a conversation with Sam Lesser, in which he said Sam should kill his dad. Kinsey had taken Bode and hidden him from Sam, keeping them both safe, but she feels as though she'll never be safe again. Bode finds a door at Keyhouse, and when he goes through it, he dies and his ghost wanders around. There's definitely something weird at Keyhouse, and something is living at the bottom of the well in the well house—something that uses both Bode and Sam Lesser—and wants revenge. The book includes bloody violence. Joe Hill is the son of Stephen King.

"This first of . . . several volumes delivers on all counts, boasting a solid story bolstered by exceptional work from Chilean artist Rodriguez . . . that resembles a fusion of Rick Geary and Cully Hamner with just a dash of Frank Quitely." Publ Wkly

Other titles in this series are:
Vol 2: Head Games (2009)
Vol 3: Crown of Shadows (2010)
Vol 4: Keys to the Kingdom (2011)
Vol 5: Clockworks (2012)
Vol 6: Alpha & Omega (2014)

Hinds, Gareth

★ **Beowulf**; adapted and illustrated by Gareth Hinds. Candlewick Press 2007 un il $21.99; pa $9.99
Grades: 8 9 10 11 12 Adult   741.5
1. Graphic novels 2. Adventure graphic novels 3. Beowulf -- Graphic novels 4. Monsters -- Graphic novels
ISBN 978-0-7636-3022-5; 0-7636-3022-5; 978-0-7636-3023-2 pa; 0-7636-3023-3 pa

LC 2006-49023

Graphic novel adaptation of the Old English epic poem, Beowulf

"For fantasy fans both young and old, this makes an ideal introduction to a story without which the entire fantasy genre would look very different; many scenes may be too intense for very young readers." Publ Wkly

★ **King** Lear; a play by William Shakespeare; adapted and illustrated by Gareth Hinds. Candlewick Press 2009 123p il $22.99; pa $11.99
Grades: 7 8 9 10 11 12   **741.5**
1. Poets 2. Authors 3. Dramatists 4. Graphic novels
ISBN 978-0-7636-4343-0; 0-7636-4343-2; 978-0-7636-4344-7 pa; 0-7636-4344-0 pa
A reissue of the title first published 2007 by Thecomic.com

"Employing a range of artistic styles that convey dramatic mood, the artist begins the play almost as a fairy tale, featuring bright, softly washed drawings. Once Cordelia is cast out and things sour, the images become darker and more compact. As the king descends into madness, the art becomes downright menacing, with Lear appearing as a jagged, ghostly figure drawn with white pencil on a dark background." (Kirkus)

The **merchant** of Venice; a play. by William Shakespeare; adapted and illustrated by Gareth Hinds. Candlewick Press 2008 68p il $21.99; pa $11.99
Grades: 8 9 10 11 12 Adult   **741.5**
1. Poets 2. Authors 3. Dramatists 4. Graphic novels
ISBN 978-0-7636-3024-9; 978-0-7636-3025-6 pa
LC 2007-938349
Hinds uses a sketchy art style and blue and gray tones to illustrate his graphic adaptation of Shakespeare's controversial play. He sets the play in modern Venice and uses more modern language, including prose, at the beginning of the play and then gradually returns to Shakespeare's original language for the courtroom scenes. The play tells the story of a debt owed to a Jewish merchant of Venice, of a strong-willed young woman who is determined to choose her own husband, and of the quest to save a young man from the fate of having a pound of flesh cut from him.

"Fans of the play will find this an intriguing adaptation." Publ Wkly

★ The **Odyssey**; a graphic novel. by Gareth Hinds. Candlewick Press 2010 248 p. col. ill. $24.99
Grades: 7 8 9 10 11 12 Adult   **741.5**
1. Poets 2. Authors 3. Graphic novels 4. Odyssey 5. Greek mythology -- Graphic novels
ISBN 0763642665; 0763642681; 9780763642662; 9780763642686
LC 2010007512
"Retells, in graphic novel format, Homer's epic tale of Odysseus, the ancient Greek hero who encounters witches and other obstacles on his journey home after fighting in the Trojan War." (Publisher's note)

This is "the most lavish retelling of Homer yet. . . . Hinds lets the epic story take its time, with a slow build and pages that aren't afraid to alternate packed dialogue with titanic action. The sumptuous art, produced with grain, texture, and hue, evokes a time long past while detailing every line and drop of sweat on Odysseus' face and conveying the sheer grandeur of seeing a god rise out of the ocean." Booklist

Hosoda, Mamoru, 1967-
Wolf children Ame & Yuki; original story: Mamoru Hosoda; art: Yu; character design: Yoshiyuki Sadamoto; translation: Jocelyne Allen; lettering: Tania Biswas, Lys Blakeslee. Yen Press 2014 538 p. chiefly color illustrations $26
Grades: 10 11 12 Adult   **741.5**
1. Manga 2. Widows -- Fiction 3. Werewolves -- Fiction
ISBN 031640165X; 9780316401654
"When Hana falls in love with a young interloper she encounters in her college class, the last thing she expects to learn is that he is part wolf. Instead of rejecting her lover upon learning his secret, she accepts him with open arms. . . . But after what seems like a mere moment of bliss to Hana, the father of her children is tragically taken from her." (Publisher's note)

"This emotion-laden work focuses on family and community issues. . . . The soft color palette of these watercolors complements the tender emotion of the plot." Lib Med Con

Igarashi, Daisuke
Children of the sea, vol. 1. Viz Media/Viz Signature 2009 320p il pa $14.99
Grades: 7 8 9 10 11 12   **741.5**
1. Manga 2. Graphic novels 3. Fantasy graphic novels 4. Mystery graphic novels 5. Adventure graphic novels 6. Ocean -- Graphic novels
ISBN 978-1-4215-2914-1; 1-4215-2914-9
"Igarashi's storytelling is quiet, thoughtful, and thought provoking, but it is his drawings that make this manga so amazing. Extremely detailed settings turn panels into mini-masterpieces." Booklist
Volume 1 of a 5 volume series

Inoue, Takehiko
★ **Real,** volume 1; story & art by Takehiko Inoue. Viz Media 2008 222p il pa $12.99
Grades: 10 11 12 Adult   **741.5**
1. Manga 2. Graphic novels 3. Sports -- Graphic novels 4. Basketball -- Graphic novels 5. Wheelchair basketball -- Graphic novels
ISBN 978-1-4215-1989-0
Original Japanese edition, 2001
Nomiya was the controlling rider on a motorcycle when he got into an accident that paralyzed the young woman riding with him; now he has dropped out of high school in his senior year and feels guilty. Togawa is stuck in a wheelchair but still plays basketball, which was the only thing Nomiya was good at in school. Togawa has quit the wheelchair basketball team, but he still plays. Nomiya starts playing while in a wheelchair, and they soon start a bit of a scam against regular players. They each have their own goals, but can they work together and find a better life for themselves? The book includes some harsh language, partial nudity, and Nomiya commits a bodily act against his school when he leaves.

"A compelling story of tragedy and struggle, Real is sure to appeal to teens—especially to male readers." SLJ
Volume 1 of an ongoing series

★ **Slam** dunk, volume 1; Sakuragi. story and art by Takehiko Inoue; English adaptation Kelly Sue DeConnick. Viz Media/Shonen Jump 2008 197p il pa $7.99

Grades: 8 9 10 11 12   **741.5**

1. Manga 2. Shonen manga 3. Graphic novels 4. Basketball -- Graphic novels

ISBN 978-1-4215-0679-1

Original Japanese edition, 1991

Hanamichi Sakuragi is a first year student at Shohoku Prefecture High School; he's got a reputation as a bruising fighter and has suffered 50 rejections from girls who were scared of his fighting. He's looked down on sports all his life, but on this first day of high school, he meets Haruko Akagi; she's not scared of him, and she loves basketball. He falls for her completely, enough to try to play basketball. But, he has competition—Kaeda Rukawa is another first year student; he's a star basketball player, and Haruko has a huge crush on him. Then Sakuragi gets on the bad side of the basketball team captain, who happens to be Haruko's older brother. Sakuragi does everything he can to convince Takenori Akagi to let him join the team. However, he has a long way to go before he can build the fundamental skills to play basketball effectively; will he stick it out? There's some fighting, one male student's buttocks get exposed accidentally, but there's no bad language.

Volume 1 of a 31 volume series

Inzana, Ryan

Ichiro; written & illustrated by Ryan Inzana. Houghton Mifflin/Houghton Mifflin Harcourt 2012 288 p. ill. (chiefly col.)

Grades: 7 8 9 10   **741.5**

1. Fantasy graphic novels 2. Supernatural graphic novels 3. Japan -- History -- Graphic novels 4. Folklore -- Japan -- Graphic novels 5. Japanese Americans -- Graphic novels 6. Graphic novels 7. Japan -- Fiction 8. Monsters -- Fiction 9. Grandfathers -- Fiction 10. Supernatural -- Fiction 11. Gods and goddesses -- Fiction

ISBN 0547252692; 9780547252698

LC 2011277558

This graphic novel depicts the story of Ichiro, "a young American teen, son of a Japanese immigrant and an American soldier killed in combat, [who] goes to Japan with his mother for an extended visit and begins to grapple with sophisticated cultural complexities. . . . After his mother and Japanese grandfather tell him stories of Japanese history and folklore, Ichiro has a fantastical adventure involving the Japanese myth of the shape-shifting tanuki spirit." (Kirkus Reviews)

Isabella, Tony

1,000 comic books you must read. Krause Publications 2009 271p il $29.99

Grades: 9 10 11 12 Adult   **741.5**

1. Best books 2. Comic books, strips, etc. -- Bibliography

ISBN 978-0-89689-921-6; 0-89689-921-7

Isabella "has the great fortune of not having to decide the thousand finest but rather the thousand that he finds compelling. This lends his hardcover a kaleidoscopic approach to deconstructing the evolution of the American comic rather than focusing on the creme de la creme alone. With its chapters predominantly broken up by decade ('The Fighting Forties,' 'The Fearful Fifties,' etc.), 1000 Comic Books provides short summaries (under 75 words) for each title as well as clear cover scans and creator/ publishing information. A plethora of obscure information is sprinkled through the book. . . . There is no discrimination of subject matter, and even the most ardent comic book reader is bound to learn something new." Cincinnati City Beat

Isayama, Hajime

Attack on Titan 1; Hajime Isayama. Kodansha 2012 186 p. chiefly ill. (Attack on Titan) (paperback) $10.99

Grades: 8 9 10 11 12   **741.5**

1. Shonen manga 2. Horror graphic novels 3. Giants -- Graphic novels 4. Horror comic books, strips, etc. 5. Good and evil -- Comic books, strips, etc.

ISBN 1612620248; 9781612620244

"Humanity has been devastated by the bizarre, giant humanoids known as the Titans. Little is known about . . . why they are bent on consuming mankind. . . . People believe their 100-meter-high walls will protect them from the Titans, but the sudden appearance of an immense Titan is about to change everything." (Publisher's note)

"Along with the setting and intricate, twisting plot, Attack on Titan derives its appeal from its willingness to bend the conventions of shounen manga. Here, friendship and burning spirit do not conquer all, and your favorite character stands a good chance of getting eaten without the opportunity to give a cool speech first." LJ

Volume 1 of an ongoing series

Ishida, Sui

Tokyo Ghoul 1; by Sui Ishida; translation, Joe Yamazaki. Viz 2015 224 p. chiefly ill. $12.99

Grades: 10 11 12 Adult   **741.5**

1. Manga 2. Seinen 3. Horror fiction 4. College students -- Fiction

ISBN 1421580365; 9781421580364

"Ghouls live among us, the same as normal people in every way—except their craving for human flesh. Ken Kaneki is an ordinary college student until a violent encounter turns him into the first half-human half-ghoul hybrid. Trapped between two worlds, he must survive Ghoul turf wars, learn more about Ghoul society and master his new powers." (Publisher's note)

Volume 1 of an ongoing series

Iwaoka, Hisae

★ **Saturn** apartments, volume 1; [translation, Matt Thorn]. Viz signature ed.; Viz Signature 2010 184p il pa $12.99

Grades: 7 8 9 10   **741.5**

1. Manga 2. Graphic novels 3. Science fiction graphic novels

ISBN 978-1-4215-3364-3; 1-4215-3364-2

Far in the future, humankind has left Earth to live in a gigantic ringlike structure that circles the planet. In this structure, humans have developed a class structure based on where one lives: the higher the floor on which you live, the greater your status. Mitsu has just graduated from junior high and is now expected to work as a window washer, just like his father before him. The thing is, his father disappeared while washing windows and is presumed dead. Window washing means one must get into a space suit and go out of the structure into outer space, 35 kilometers above the Earth's surface; space winds and other hazards make the work dangerous and expensive. Even as he wonders still, five years after his father's disappearance, what happened to him, Mitsu finds his job gives him a unique perspective on the lives of those who live in the Saturn Apartments. This is science fiction from the viewpoint of the mundane service work rather than heroics of space action.

"This story of a young teen struggling to live alone will appeal to YAs, and the introspective nature of the narrative will have plenty of crossover appeal for adult readers as well." Booklist

Volume 1 of 7

Jacobson, Sidney

★ The **9** /11 report; a graphic adaptation. by Sid Jacobson and Ernie Colón; [with a foreword by Thomas H. Kean and Lee H. Hamilton] Hill and Wang 2006 133p il $30; pa $16.95

Grades: 9 10 11 12 Adult **741.5**

1. Graphic novels 2. September 11 terrorist attacks, 2001 -- Graphic novels

ISBN 0-8090-5738-7; 978-0-8090-5738-2; 0-8090-5739-5 pa; 978-0-8090-5739-9 pa

"The book aims to make . . . [The 9/11 Commission Report] more accessible to all readers and draw in young adults. . . . This graphic adaptation is an important and necessary part of any collection." Libr J

Jones, Gerard

★ **Men** of tomorrow; geeks, gangsters and the birth of the comic book. Basic Books 2004 320p il $26; pa $15

Grades: 11 12 Adult **741.5**

1. Cartoonists 2. Comic books, strips, etc.

ISBN 0-465-03656-2; 0-465-03657-0 pa

LC 2004-9031

This book tells "the surprising story of the young Jewish misfits, hustlers and nerds who invented the superhero and the comic book industry. . . . Springing unheralded out of working-class Jewish immigrant neighborhoods in the depths of the Depression, these young men transformed an odd mix of geekdom, science fiction, and outsider yearnings into blue-eyed chisel-nosed crime-fighters and adventurers who quickly captured the mainstream imagination. . . . He chronicles how the comics sparked a frightened counterattack that nearly destroyed the industry in the 1950's and how later they surged back at an underground level, to inspire a new generation to transmute those long-ago fantasies into art, literature, blockbuster movies and graphic novels." Publisher's note

Kallen, Stuart A.

Manga. Lucent Books 2011 112p il (Eye on art) lib bdg $33.45

Grades: 9 10 11 12 **741.5**

1. Manga 2. Comic books, strips, etc.

ISBN 978-1-4205-0535-1; 1-4205-0535-1

LC 2011002418

This book "digs into the deep roots of Japanese comics. Kallen touches on centuries-old artwork that can be seen as rudimentary comics, describes how the loosening of cultural borders at the end of the nineteenth and beginning of the twentieth centuries helped bring American comic strips into Japan, and then moves into the widespread embrace of the medium from the 1940s on. . . . Those serious about getting a complete picture of the history of manga and brushing up on some of the bigger titles will find much to relish." Booklist

Includes bibliographical references

Kashyap, Keshni

Tina's mouth; Keshni Kashyap; illustrated by Mari Araki. Houghton Mifflin Harcourt 2011 242 p. ill. $18.95

Grades: 9 10 11 12 **741.5**

1. Graphic novels 2. Girls -- Graphic novels 3. Teenagers -- Graphic novels 4. Schools -- Fiction 5. High schools -- Fiction 6. Individuality -- Fiction 7. California, Southern -- Fiction 8. East Indian Americans -- Fiction

ISBN 9780618945191; 0618945199

LC 2011030439

"Tina, an Indian-American living in San Francisco, writes an illustrated diary to Jean-Paul Sartre as part of a semesterlong existentialism class. . . . Tina's best friend ditches her for a boy and Tina has a crush on someone but has trouble making it work. All the while, Tina observes her older siblings' love anxiety, her sister's move back home after a broken heart, and her brother's disastrous exploration of Indian dating sites.." (Publishers Weekly)

Katin, Miriam

We are on our own; a memoir. Drawn & Quarterly 2006 122p il $19.95

Grades: 9 10 11 12 Adult **741.5**

1. Artists 2. Animators 3. Cartoonists 4. Illustrators 5. Autobiographical graphic novels 6. Holocaust, 1933-1945 -- Graphic novels 7. World War, 1939-1945 -- Graphic novels

ISBN 1-896597-20-3

LC 2005-9063602

In this WWII memoir, the author recounts "how she and her mother faked their deaths and fled Budapest after the Nazis occupied the city. With forged papers obtained from a black marketer, they escaped to the countryside in the guise of a servant girl and her illegitimate child. Katin relates their harrowing lives there and her mother's desperate search for her missing husband after the war. . . . This impressive book belongs in all serious graphic novel collections and is also a natural for Jewish studies." Booklist

Kim, Derek Kirk

Same difference; Derek Kirk Kim. First Second 2011 90p. chiefly ill.

Grades: 9 10 11 12 Adult **741.5**

1. Short stories 2. Graphic novels 3. Love -- Fiction

4. Youth -- Fiction 5. Family -- Fiction
ISBN 9781596436572; 1596436573

LC 2010052663

This collection of short stories is concerned with young people, and gives particular focus to romantic and familial relationships. "The title story focuses on 20-somethings Nancy and Simon, who are racked with guilt. Why? Simon has turned down a date with a friend because she is blind, and Nancy has read love letters meant for someone else-and answered them, giving the jilted ex-boyfriend false hope. Through a series of credible coincidences, both eventually make amends. . . . [The] collection also includes stories about high school track, weed wacking, familial relationships, celebrity interviews, and autobiographical tales." (School Libr J)

Kim, Susan

Brain camp; by Susan Kim and Laurence Klavan; illustrated by Faith Erin Hicks. First Second 2010 151p il pa $16.99

Grades: 7 8 9 10   741.5

1. Graphic novels 2. Horror graphic novels 3. Mystery graphic novels 4. Science fiction graphic novels 5. Camps -- Graphic novels
ISBN 978-1-59643-366-3; 1-59643-366-3

Jenna and Lucas are both under-achieving young teens who suddenly receive invitations to join the Fielding Camp for the summer. Pressed by their respective parents to attend, Jenna and Lucas both notice some strange things at the camp, and neither feels like eating the nasty slop served at every meal. The other campers are either intellectually challenged bullies, misfits, or supersmart zombies. At first Dwayne, a self-described spaz, befriends them, but when his cabin "wins" ice cream treats at dinner, Lucas sees the camp counselors sneaking in that night to "inoculate" all his cabin mates. Lucas and Jenna work against time to escape the camp and develop an antidote. Jenna is shown in one panel sitting on a commode when her period comes, and one short sequence shows Lucas having a wet dream and then washing out his stained undies; both situations are nonverbal and drawn with restraint, but school librarians will need to decide whether these two scenes meet their own schools' standards.

The authors present a "well-rounded adventure here, as the far-out (and kind of gross) climax mixes with genuine insight into dealing with parents, fitting into a new crowd, and handling the pressures of performance. Hicks' line work is cool enough to assuage older readers who might be suspicious of the summer-camp setting." Booklist

Kishimoto, Masashi

Naruto. vol. 1, The tests of the Ninja; story and art by Masashi Kishimoto; [English adaptation by Jo Duffy] Viz 2003 186p il pa $7.95

Grades: 7 8 9 10 11 12   741.5

1. Manga 2. Shonen manga 3. Graphic novels 4. Martial arts -- Graphic novels
ISBN 1-56931-900-6; 978-1-56931-900-0

First published 1999 in Japan

"Teen orphan Naruto wants to become the greatest ninja of all, despite the fact that most people in his village have despised him from birth because a terrible demon has been imprisoned in his body. . . . Teens love this series." Voice Youth Advocates

Volume 1 of 72

Knisley, Lucy

Relish; My Life in the Kitchen. by Lucy Knisley. First Second 2013 192 p. (paperback) $17.99

Grades: 9 10 11 12 Adult   741.5

1. Food 2. Cooking
ISBN 1596436239; 9781596436237

Alex Award (2014)

This book is a memoir from food-lover Lucy Knisley. "Having grown up surrounded by delicious food, thanks to her gourmand father and earthy superchef mother, Knisley looks back on her childhood and adolescence through her roving palette and voracious appetite for new tastes and experiences. With each memory Knisley shares, she shows that life, like a good meal, should be savored and that all food--even junk food--is more than 'just fuel.'" (Publishers Weekly)

"Knisley tempers any navel-gazing impulses with humor, humility, and honesty. . . . Just about everything in this rambling memoir is handled with good cheer." Booklist

Kubo, Tite

Bleach, Vol. 1; [story and art by Tite Kubo; English adaptation, Lance Caselman; translation, Joe Yamazaki] Viz Shonen Jump 2004 190p il pa $7.95

Grades: 9 10 11 12   741.5

1. Manga 2. Shonen manga 3. Graphic novels 4. Adventure graphic novels 5. Supernatural graphic novels
ISBN 1-59116-441-9

Teenage Ichigo Kurasaki has always been able to see ghosts, but that never really affected his life, until the night a Hollow, an evil spirit that preys on humans, attacks him. Soul Reaper Rukia Kuchiki tries to help Ichigo save himself and his family, but somehow he manages to absorb all her powers. Now he's a Soul Reaper, and he must work to protect the innocent from the Hollows. This is the first volume of an ongoing manga series that is full of fighting action and irreverent humor.

Volume 1 of 74

Kuper, Peter

The jungle; [based on the story by] Upton Sinclair; adapted by Peter Kuper. Papercutz 2010 un il (Classics Illustrated) pa $9.99

Grades: 9 10 11 12 Adult   741.5

1. Authors 2. Novelists 3. Graphic novels 4. Biographers 5. Socialist leaders 6. Immigrants -- Graphic novels 7. Meat industry -- Graphic novels 8. Chicago (Ill.) -- Graphic novels
ISBN 978-1-59707-192-5

First published 1991 by First Publishing

"Jurgis and his family have immigrated to America from Lithuania, settled in Chicago, and found jobs in the meatpacking plant. The family seems to be living the American dream: having their own home, and a means of support, even if the work is hard and disgusting. Peter Kuper's dark, colored, cartoon-style illustrations, framed in black, bring to life Sinclair's original work and highlight the atrocities perpetuated upon the Rudkus family." Libr Media Connect

Lagos, Alexander

The **sons** of liberty; created and written by Alexander Lagos and Joseph Lagos; art by Steve Walker; color by Oren Kramek; letters by Chris Dickey. Random House 2010 un il $18.99; lib bdg $21.99; pa $12.99

Grades: 6 7 8 9 10 11 12   **741.5**

1. Graphic novels 2. Adventure graphic novels 3. Superhero graphic novels 4. African Americans -- Graphic novels 5. United States -- History -- 1600-1775, Colonial period -- Graphic novels

ISBN 978-0-375-85670-9; 0-375-85670-6; 978-0-375-95667-6 lib bdg; 0-375-95667-6 lib bdg; 978-0-375-85667-9 pa; 0-375-85667-9 pa

In the mid-eighteenth century American colonies, Graham and Brody work as slaves on a tobacco plantation not far from Philadelphia. When they run away after injuring the plantation owner's son for threatening another slave, they seek Benjamin Lay, an eccentric abolitionist who might give them shelter. Instead, William Franklin, son of Benjamin Franklin, finds them and conducts unknown experiments on them.

"History offers few villains as vile as slaveholders, but this graphic novel is far from being a simple revenge thriller. The use of historical figures and well-researched (but embellished) history, and a willingness to flesh out characters and set up situations to pay off in future installments, makes for an uncommonly complex, literate, and satisfying adventure." Booklist

The **sons** of liberty 2; death and taxes. created and written by Alexander Lagos and Joseph Lagos; art by Steve Walker; color by Oren Kramek; letters by Chris Dickey. Random House Children's Books 2011 un il $18.99; pa $12.99

Grades: 6 7 8 9 10 11 12   **741.5**

1. Scientists 2. Graphic novels 3. Adventure graphic novels 4. Superhero graphic novels 5. African Americans -- Graphic novels 6. United States -- History -- 1600-1775, Colonial period -- Graphic novels

ISBN 978-0-375-85671-6; 978-0-375-85668-6 pa

"Graham and Brody, escaped slaves gifted with superpowers, remain at the center of this continuing pre–Revolutionary War saga of political intrigue and reimagined history. As Benjamin Franklin seeks to stop the stamp tax from falling on the colonies and enemies attack his good name, Graham attempts to arrange an escape back to Africa along with his love, the slave girl Isabel. . . . The embellishments, literate dialogue, and several historical truths—effectively counterpointed with glossy contemporary art—keep things fun and suspenseful." Booklist

Larson, Hope

Mercury. Atheneum Books for Young Readers 2010 234p il $19.99; pa $9.99

Grades: 8 9 10 11 12   **741.5**

1. Graphic novels 2. Supernatural graphic novels 3.

Nova Scotia -- Graphic novels

ISBN 978-1-4169-3585-8; 1-4169-3585-1; 978-1-4169-3588-9 pa; 1-4169-3588-6 pa

            LC 2009-903638

This book, "relates two coming-of-age stories in tandem, showing how the past interweaves with the present. In the present, Tara and her mother have lost their old farmhouse in a fire, and Tara's mother is struggling to support them from far away while Tara lives with relatives. . . . In 1859, Josey, Tara's ancestor, falls in love with a gold dowser who has convinced her father to open a mine. Her mother, who has supernatural sight, is sure that the dowser means no good." (School Library Journal)

"The storytelling, both in words and pictures, brilliantly offers details from Canadian history and modern life. The dialogue varies from funny to poignant. An excellent graphic novel." SLJ

Lat

★ **Kampung** boy. First Second 2006 141p il pa $16.95

Grades: 7 8 9 10 11 12 Adult   **741.5**

1. Graphic novels 2. Muslims -- Graphic novels 3. Malaysia -- Graphic novels 4. Family life -- Graphic novels

ISBN 1-59643-121-0

            LC 2005-34135

First published 1979 in Malaysia with title: Lat, the kampung boy

"Malaysian cartoonist Lat uses the graphic novel format to share the story of his childhood in a small village, or kampung. From his birth and adventures as a toddler to the enlargement of his world as he attends classes in the village, makes friends, and, finally, departs for a prestigious city boarding school, this autobiography is warm, authentic, and wholly engaging." Booklist

★ **Town** boy. First Second Books 2007 191p il pa $16.95

Grades: 7 8 9 10 11 12 Adult   **741.5**

1. Graphic novels 2. Humorous graphic novels 3. Malaysia -- Graphic novels 4. Bildungsromans -- Graphic novels

ISBN 978-1-59643-331-1; 1-59643-331-0

            LC 2006-102857

In this sequel to Kampung Boy, it's the late 1960s and Mat is now a teenager attending a boarding school in the town of Ipoh, far from his kampung. He discovers bustling streets, hip music, heady literature, budding romance, and through it all his growing passion for art.

Lee, Stan, 1922-

Stan Lee's How to draw comics; from the legendary co-creator of Spider-Man, the Incredible Hulk, Fantastic Four, X-Men, and Iron Man. Watson-Guptill Publication 2010 224p il pa $24.99

Grades: 9 10 11 12 Adult   **741.5**

1. Graphic novels 2. X-Men (Fictional characters) 3. Fantastic Four (Fictional characters) 4. Drawing -- Technique 5. Comic books, strips, etc. -- Authorship

ISBN 978-0-8230-0083-8

            LC 2010-5781

The author "includes chapters on creating comics with computer programs and online resources and how to get work in the 21st century. The book begins with a brief history of comics, then focuses on action-adventure style, romance, humor, horror, and Japanese manga. This is the one book anyone interested in drawing comics should own." Libr J

Includes bibliographical references

Lee, Tony

Excalibur; the legend of King Arthur, a graphic novel. written by Tony Lee; illustrated, colored, and lettered by Sam Hart. Candlewick Press 2011 un il
Grades: 7 8 9 10   **741.5**
1. Graphic novels 2. Fantasy graphic novels 3. Kings 4. Middle Ages -- Graphic novels 5. Young adult literature -- Works 6. Kings and rulers -- Graphic novels 7. Knights and knighthood -- Graphic novels 8. Merlin (Legendary character) -- Graphic novels 9. Great Britain -- History -- 0-1066 -- Graphic novels
ISBN 0-7636-4643-1 pa; 0-7636-4644-X; 978-0-7636-4643-1 pa; 978-0-7636-4644-8
LC 2010-39163

Retells, in graphic novel form, the tale of Arthur Pendragon who, raised in obscurity, draws a legendary sword from a stone and begins the life he was born to lead, guided by the elusive wizard Merlin.

The author is "a master of graphic-novel adaptations. Teaming up with illustrator and colorist Hart, . . . Lee negotiates the terrain of medieval legend with finesse, rendering it easily accessible for a new generation of readers." Kirkus

★ **Outlaw**: the legend of Robin Hood; a graphic novel. written by Tony Lee; illustrated by Sam Hart; colored by Artur Fujita. Candlewick Press 2009 un il $21.99; pa $11.99
Grades: 7 8 9 10 11 12   **741.5**
1. Graphic novels 2. Adventure graphic novels 3. Robin Hood (Fictional character) 4. Great Britain -- History -- 1154-1399, Plantagenets -- Graphic novels
ISBN 978-0-7636-4399-7; 0-7636-4399-8; 978-0-7636-4400-0 pa; 0-7636-4400-5 pa
LC 2008-943331

In this retelling of the Robin Hood legend, it's the year 1192, and Robin of Loxley has returned home from the Crusades after receiving news of his father's death. The Sheriff of Nottingham and Sir Guy of Gisburn govern Nottingham at the pleasure of Prince John. When Gisburn treacherously stabs Robin in a murder attempt, Robin escapes to Sherwood Forest, where the outlaws befriend him. With the help of such men as Little John and Friar Tuck, he organizes the outlaws and they start hurting Prince John where it matters—in his moneybags.

"Lee's excellent rendition of the famed selfless hero goes hand-in-hand with Hart's expressive illustrations, featuring lots of closeups and dramatic lighting and a beautiful jewel-toned palette. Teens will get caught up in this exciting page-turner." SLJ

Lemire, Jeff

Essex County, Vol. 1: Tales from the Farm. Top Shelf Productions 2007 un il $9.95

Grades: 10 11 12 Adult   **741.5**
1. Graphic novels 2. Orphans -- Graphic novels 3. Farm life -- Graphic novels 4. Friendship -- Graphic novels
ISBN 978-1-891830-88-4

Orphaned ten-year-old Lester lives with his bachelor uncle Ken on a southwestern Ontario farm. He constantly wears a mask and cape, imagining that he's protecting the place from invading space aliens. Uncle Ken doesn't know how to deal with Lester, and their relationship becomes strained. Only one grown-up, Jimmy, who runs the gas station and convenience store, can connect with Lester on his level.

"Lemire enriches this rather familiar scenario with telling, particularizing detail, ensuring that this time the old heartwarming routine is unforgettably special." Booklist
Volume 1 of 3

Trillium; Jeff Lemire, writer & artist; Jeff Lemire, Jose Villarrubia, colorists; Carlos M. Mangual, letterer. DC Comics/Vertigo 2014 192 p. color illustrations (paperback) $16.99
Grades: 11 12 Adult   **741.5**
1. Love stories 2. Time travel -- Graphic novels 3. Science fiction graphic novels
ISBN 1401249000; 9781401249007
LC 2014011939

Eisner Nominee: Best Limited Series (2014)

This graphic novel, by Jeff Lemire, with color by Jose Villarrubia and lettering by Carlos M. Mangual, "spins the tale of two star-crossed loved through space in time. . . . [In] the year 3797, . . . botanist Nika Temsmith is researching a strange species on a remote science station near the outermost rim of colonized space. . . . [In] 1921, . . . English explorer William Pike leads an expedition into the dense jungles of Peru in search of the fabled 'Lost Temple of the Incas.'" (Publisher's note)

"Lemire's art excels, combining his trademark sketchiness with gorgeous watercolors. But it's the layouts that take the book to new heights of creativity. Lemire tells two stories at once by turning the panels upside down, disorienting the reader as much as his heroes." Pub Wkly

Love, Jeremy

★ **Bayou,** volume one; created by Jeremy Love; colors by Patrick Morgan. Zuda Comics/DC Comics 2009 un il pa $14.99
Grades: 9 10 11 12 Adult   **741.5**
1. Graphic novels 2. Fantasy graphic novels 3. Monsters -- Graphic novels 4. African Americans -- Graphic novels
ISBN 978-1-4012-2382-3

2009 Glyph Comics Awards: Story of the Year, Best Writer, Best Artist, Best Female Character (Lee), Best Comic Strip

In a little southern town called Charon in 1933, Lee Wagstaff lives the kind of precarious life that African Americans under Jim Crow laws had to live. She's friends with white Lily Westmoreland, but that friendship doesn't protect her when Lily's mother accuses Lee of theft. Then Lily disappears, victim of a swamp monster, and the town's white men haul her father off to jail, most likely to face a lynching.

Lee has to find Lily to save her father, but when she goes to the swamp where Lily disappeared, she falls into a strange land of monsters. There she meets Bayou, a blues-singing swamp monster who helps her, and Lee faces the evil in the strange land to find and save her friend. This book collects the first four chapters of the webcomic by Love, which was one of the first webcomics from Zuda, run by DC Comics. The book includes disturbing images of hanged people, and a white man hits Lee so hard she flies through the air and lands on her back with her face torn up. The "n" word is represented by "n*****" while other harsh language is plainly written. The book contains enough violence to bother squeamish and sensitive readers.

"Extremely beautiful, scary and wonderful, this . . . comic takes readers to a pair of almost familiar, frequently threatening worlds." Publ Wkly

Volume 1 of 2

Lovecraft, H. P. (Howard Phillips), 1890-1937

Graphic Classics volume four: H. P. Lovecraft; edited by Tom Pomplun. 2nd ed.; Eureka Productions 2007 144p il pa $11.95

Grades: 7 8 9 10 11 12 Adult   **741.5**

1. Authors 2. Graphic novels 3. Horror graphic novels 4. Essayists 5. Fantasy writers 6. Mystery writers 7. Short story writers 8. Short stories -- Graphic novels

ISBN 978-0-9746648-9-7

First published 2002

Here are comic book adaptations of stories by Lovecraft, master of the macabre and creator of the Cthulhu Mythos. It includes adaptations of "The Shadow Over Innsmouth," illustrated by Simon Gane and "Dreams in the Witch House," by Pedro Lopez. Plus: "Sweet Ermengarde," a rare comedy by Lovecraft. Returning from the previous edition are "Reanimator," "The Shadow Out of Time," "The Terrible Old Man" and "The Cats of Ulthar." Illustrations of headless corpses and monstrous beings might disturb more tender sensibilities.

Lutes, Jason

★ **Houdini**: the handcuff king. Hyperion Books for Children/Jump at the Sun 2007 90p il (Center for Cartoon Studies presents) $16.99; pa $9.99

Grades: 4 5 6 7 8 9 10   **741.5**

1. Magicians 2. Graphic novels 3. Biographical graphic novels 4. Nonfiction writers 5. Magicians -- Graphic novels

ISBN 978-0-7868-3902-5; 978-0-7868-3903-2 pa

On May 1, 1908, magician Harry Houdini performed one of his famous handcuff escapes, this time in handcuffs and leg irons, while jumping off the Cambridge Bridge in Massachusetts into the frigid Boston River. This graphic novel takes the reader through Houdini's day, from 5:00 a.m. as he makes his preparations, makes a practice jump, coaches his wife Bess on how she's to help him, and then makes the jump.

This is a "fascinating graphic novel. . . . The format will instantly draw a lot of attention from readers and then hold on to it. Lutes and Bertozzi use grayscale comic panels to share their story about the life of Harry Houdini in a unique way. . . . The book resembles a hybrid between fiction and nonfiction, and the ingenious choice of format will appeal to a broad age range of readers." Voice Youth Advocates

Mairowitz, David Zane

Kafka; [by] David Zane Mairowitz and Robert Crumb; edited by Richard Appignanesi. Fantagraphics Books 2007 176p il pa $14.95

Grades: 10 11 12 Adult   **741.5**

1. Poets 2. Authors 3. Novelists 4. Graphic novels 5. Biographical graphic novels 6. Short story writers

ISBN 978-1-56097-806-0

This book combines a biography of Kafka with illustrated plot descriptions of many of his works, including The Metamorphosis. Crumb renders the stories in comic book form, while the biographical information is presented mostly in text.

Mashima, Hiro

Fairy tail vol. 1; translated and adapted by William Flanagan; lettered by North Market Street Graphics. Del Rey Manga 2008 202p il pa $10.95

Grades: 8 9 10 11 12   **741.5**

1. Manga 2. Graphic novels 3. Fantasy graphic novels 4. Humorous graphic novels

ISBN 978-0-345-50133-2

Cute girl wizard Lucy wants to join the Fairy Tail, a club for the most powerful wizards (and the most troublesome — they tend to do stuff such as blow up harbors while fighting the bad guys). However, her ambitions land her in the clutches of a gang of unsavory pirates led by a devious magician, who plan to sell her into slavery. Her only hope is Natsu, a strange boy she has met on her travels. Natsu is not the typical hero: he gets motion sickness, eats like a pig, and his best friend is a talking cat. He is a member of the Fairy Tail, however. The book includes some mild fan service (usually cleavage shots), consumption of alcohol, and lots of magical fighting.

Volume 1 of an ongoing series

McCloud, Scott

Making comics; storytelling secrets of comics, manga, and graphic novels. HarperCollins 2006 264p il pa $22.95

Grades: 11 12 Adult   **741.5**

1. Graphic novels -- Drawing 2. Comic books, strips, etc. -- Authorship

ISBN 0-06-078094-0; 978-0-06-078094-4

The author "explores practical matters, including comics devices such as panels, word balloons, and sound effects; facial expressions and body language; the creation of convincing and evocative settings; and the different tools artists can use for the job, from pencils to computers. He also delves into the framing of images in panels, the flow of panels on a page, and the relationships between words and pictures in comics. . . . This is thoughtful, fascinating, stimulating, potentially controversial, and inspiring." Libr J

Includes bibliographical references

Reinventing comics; how imagination and technology are revolutionizing an art form. Paradox Press 2000 237p il pa $22.95

Grades: 11 12 Adult   **741.5**
1. Cartoons and caricatures 2. Comic books, strips, etc.
ISBN 0-06-095350-0

                                    LC 00-710457

The author maps out "'12 revolutions', which, he believes, need to take place for comics to survive and finally be recognized as a legitimate art form. The topics progress from the oldest of comic-related arguments (seeking respect) to the use of computer technology to renew and expand its audience. These brilliantly presented discussions concern comics as literature, comics as art, creators' rights, industry innovation, and public perception, among other topics." Libr J

★ **Understanding** comics; the invisible art. HarperPerennial 1994 215p il pa $22.95
Grades: 9 10 11 12 Adult   **741.5**
1. Comic books, strips, etc.
ISBN 0-06-097625-X; 9780060976255
First published 1993 by Kitchen Sink Press

McCloud "conducts a genial, well-researched and funny tour of virtually every historical and perceptual aspect of comics, which he calls 'sequential art,' that is, art that consists of sequences of words and pictures. Beginning in the 11th century with the Bayeux tapestry, he examines pre-Columbian picture languages and the printing press, presenting a quick survey of the historical development of early sequential pictures into the specialized visual language of comics. . . . He dissects the vocabulary of the medium, cheerfully analyzing the psychological power of comics and their central role in our ultra-visual culture." (Publishers Weekly)

The author "traces the 3,000-year history (from Egyptian paintings on) of telling stories through pictures; describes the language of comics—its 'grammar' and 'vocabulary'; explains the use of different types of images ranging from ironic to realistic; depicts how artists convey movement and the passage of time and use various symbols as shorthand; and [seeks to demonstrate] the expressive emotional qualities of different drawing styles." Booklist [review of 1993 edition]

Includes bibliographical references

McCreery, Conor

Kill Shakespeare, vol. 1; a sea of troubles. created and written by Conor McCreery and Anthony Del Col; art by Andy Belanger; colors by Ian Herring; lettering by Chris Mowry, Robbie Robbins, and Neil Uyetake. IDW Publishing 2010 un il pa $19.99
Grades: 10 11 12 Adult   **741.5**
1. Poets 2. Authors 3. Dramatists 4. Graphic novels
5. Fantasy graphic novels 6. Adventure graphic novels
ISBN 978-1-60010-781-8

A shipwrecked Hamlet finds himself in England with Richard III, who wants his help to find and kill the wizard, Will Shakespeare, so that Richard can rule with impunity. Haunted by his father's ghost, who tells Hamlet that killing Shakespeare will let him live again, Hamlet agrees to help the English king. Then he discovers that the Lady Juliet Capulet leads an army of rebellion, aided by Othello and Falstaff. They fight against the corrupt Richard, who consults the witch Hecate (who has her own agenda). Falstaff says that Hamlet is the prophesied Shadow King, who will aid the rebellion, while Richard and his allies only want to use Hamlet to destroy Shakespeare, but all agree that only Hamlet can lead them to the wizard. The book includes bloody action and sexual situations, making this more suited to older teens.

"McCreery and Del Col spin an engrossing action-adventure tale of satisfying complexity, full of mystery, deceit, and gory violence, starring a hero who once again must marshal his determination and decide his path." Libr J

Other titles in this series are:
Volume two: the blast of war (2011)
Volume three: the tide of blood (2013)

Mechner, Jordan

Solomon's thieves; artwork by LeUyen Pham & Alex Puvilland. First Second 2010 139p il pa $12.99
Grades: 6 7 8 9 10   **741.5**
1. Graphic novels 2. Middle Ages -- Graphic novels
3. Knights and knighthood -- Graphic novels 4. France
-- History -- 0-1328 -- Graphic novels
ISBN 978-1-59643-391-5; 1-59643-391-4

                                    LC 2010-282641

Life as a Templar Knight returning from the Crusades is dull— bread, beans, and lots and lots of walking. But after Martin stumbles upon his lost love (now married—to someone else), things begin to get more interesting very quickly. There's a vast conspiracy afoot to destroy the Templar Order and steal their treasure. Soon, Martin finds himself one of the only Templars out of prison—and out for revenge!

"Pham and Puvilland . . . are again in top form, balancing grainy, hatched textures and clean spaces to lend a weighty historical feel as a vibrant sense of kineticism brings the action sequences to life." Booklist

Includes bibliographical references

Medley, Linda

★ **Castle** waiting; the definitive edition Fantagraphics 2006 456p il $29.95
Grades: 5 6 7 8 9 10 11 12   **741.5**
1. Graphic novels 2. Fantasy graphic novels 3. Fairy tales -- Graphic novels
ISBN 1-56097-747-7

All of Medley's previously self-published comics are collected here in one volume for the first time. The titular castle was the home of Sleeping Beauty, whose story is retold from the viewpoint of the flibbertigibbet ladies in waiting. After the flighty princess awakens with the kiss of a handsome but not too bright prince, the castle becomes a sanctuary for various misfits. Readers will find references to many fairy tales, folk tales, and nursery rhymes in Medley's book, and her clean, clear black-and-white art reflects the works of classic illustrators such as Arthur Rackham.

MOONSHOT; The Indigenous Comics Collection. edited by Hope Nicholson. Alternate History Comics Inc 2015 176 p. chiefly illustrations $17.99
Grades: 6 7 8 9 10 11 12 Adult   **741.5**
1. Graphic novels 2. American literature -- Native American authors
ISBN 0987715259; 9780987715258

This comic anthology, edited by Hope Nicholson, "from traditional stories to exciting new visions of the future, . . . presents some of the finest comic book and graphic novel work in North America. The traditional stories presented in the book are with the permission from the elders in their respective communities, making this a truly genuine, never-before-seen publication." (Publisher's note)

"This collection of folklore from a powerhouse team of Native authors, including Buffy Sainte-Marie and Richard Van Camp, will wow readers with traditional and futuristic tales based on tribal-specific cultural teachings. . . . The full-page illustrations in some selections and the bright colors in others add depth and understanding to the narratives. The artwork is as diverse as the stories collected." SLJ

Moore, Alan, 1953-
  Watchmen; Alan Moore, writer; Dave Gibbons, illustrator/letterer; John Higgins, colorist. DC Comics 2005 il
  Grades: 11 12 Adult   741.5
    1. Graphic novels 2. Superhero graphic novels 3. Comic books, strips, etc.
    ISBN 1-4012-0713-8; 978-0-930289-23-2 pa
  Originally published in single magazine form as Watchmen 1-12; trade paperback edition still available
  Hugo Award: Other Forms (1988)
  Eisner Award: Best Graphic Album (1988)
  Eisner Award: Best Finite Series (1988)
  "It all begins with the paranoid delusions of a half-insane hero called Rorschach. But is Rorschach really insane or has he infact uncovered a plot to murder super-heroes and, even worse, millions of innocent civilians? On the run from the law, Rorschach reunites with his former teammates in a desperate attempt to save the world and their lives, but what they uncover will shock them to their very core and change the face of the planet!" (Publisher's note)
  "Nearly 20 years after the original publication, 'Watchmen' shows an eerie prescience: the symmetry between current events and the conclusion of its story, concerning a villain who believes he can stave off real war by distracting the populace with a trumped-up one, and an act of mass murder perpetrated in the heart of New York City, is almost too fearful to bear." N Y Times Book Rev

Morrison, Grant
  All-Star Superman, Volume One; written by Grant Morrison; pencilled by Frank Quitely. DC Comics 2007 160p il hardcover o.p. pa $12.99
  Grades: 8 9 10 11 12 Adult   741.5
    1. Graphic novels 2. Superhero graphic novels 3. Superman (Fictional character)
    ISBN 978-1-4012-0914-8; 978-1-4012-1102-8 pa
  Eisner Award: Best New Series (2006)
  Writer Morrison and artist Quitely present several episodes in the life of the iconic superhero, Superman. When he saves a group of scientists from burning up in the sun, what no one realizes is that uber-villain Lex Luthor set up everything in order to kill Superman, who absorbed so much solar radiation that it is now slowly killing him. Once Superman learns that he is dying, he sets out to give Lois Lane a birthday she will never forget, by giving her his powers for one day. Then, when Jimmy Olsen takes charge of the science think tank P.R.O.J.E.C.T. for one day, they discover black kryptonite, which makes Superman turn evil. And, in his guise as Clark Kent, he interviews Lex Luthor in prison, but super-villain Parasite is taken from his shielded cell and begins to absorb Superman's powers, causing chaos.
  Volume 1 of 2

Murata, Yusuke
  ★ **One**-punch man; Volume 1 story by One; art by Yusuke Murata. Viz 2015 189 p. chiefly illustrations $9.99
  Grades: 8 9 10 11 12 Adult   741.5
    1. Manga 2. Superheroes 3. Graphic novels
    ISBN 1421585642; 9781421585642
  Eisner Nominee: Best U.S. Edition of International Material--Asia (2015)
  "Nothing about Saitama passes the eyeball test when it comes to superheroes, from his lifeless expression to his bald head to his unimpressive physique. However, this average-looking guy has a not-so-average problem--he just can't seem to find an opponent strong enough to take on! Every time a promising villain appears, he beats the snot out of 'em with one punch!" (Publisher's note)
  "The story is fast-paced, humorous, and entertaining in a way that looks and feels like an action movie." SLJ
  Volume 1 of an ongoing series

Myers, Walter Dean, 1937-2014
  Monster; a graphic novel. by Walter Dean Myers; adapted for graphic novel by Guy A. Sims; illustrated by Dawud Anyabwile. HarperTeen, an imprint of HarperCollinsPublishers 2015 160 p. illustrations (hardcover) $17.99
  Grades: 8 9 10 11 12   741.5
    1. Teenagers -- Graphic novels 2. Trials (Homicide) -- Fiction 3. Bildungsromans -- Graphic novels 4. Graphic novels 5. Prisons -- Fiction 6. Self-perception -- Fiction 7. Trials (Murder) -- Fiction 8. African Americans -- Fiction
    ISBN 0062275003; 9780062274991; 9780062275004
                                          LC 2013043138
  This graphic novel by Guy Sims, illustrated by Dawud Anyabwile, and adapted from the novel by Walter Dean Myers, is a "coming-of-age story about Steve Harmon, a teenager awaiting trial for a murder and robbery. As Steve acclimates to juvenile detention and goes to trial, he envisions the ordeal as a movie." (Publisher's note)
  "Using panels like a filmstrip, Sims and Anyabwile achieve several remarkably cinematic effects: alternating grids and splash pages captures the tension between close-up and long shots; the use of jittery lettering and uneven word balloons injects deeper anxiety into the sound design; having a jury view the events recounted in testimony as a movie audience creates incisive visual metaphors." Booklist

Nakahara, Aya
  Love*Com Vol. 1; story and art by Aya Nakahara; [translation & English adaptation, Pookie Rolf] Viz Media/Shojo Beat 2007 un il pa $8.99
  Grades: 8 9 10 11 12   741.5
    1. Manga 2. Shojo manga 3. Graphic novels 4.

Romance graphic novels 5. Humorous graphic novels
ISBN 978-1-4215-1343-0

First published 2001 in Japan

Risa Koizumi is the tallest girl in class, and the last thing she wants is the humiliation of standing next to Atsushi Otoni, the shortest guy. Fate and the whole school have other ideas, and the two find themselves cast as the unwilling stars of a bizarre romantic comedy duo. Rather than bow to the inevitable, Risa and Atsushi join forces to pursue their true objects of affection. But in the quest for love, will their budding friendship become something more complex?

Volume 1 of 17

Neri, Greg

★ **Yummy**; the last days of a Southside Shorty. by G. Neri; illustrated by Randy DuBurke. Lee & Low Books 2010 94p il pa $16.95

Grades: 8 9 10 11 12   741.5

1. Children 2. Graphic novels 3. Biographical graphic novels 4. Gang members 5. Murder victims 6. Gangs -- Graphic novels 7. Violence -- Graphic novels 8. Chicago (Ill.) -- Graphic novels 9. African Americans -- Graphic novels

ISBN 978-1-58430-267-4 pa; 1-58430-267-4 pa

LC 2006-17771

Coretta Scott King Author Award honor book, 2011

"Neri's straightforward, unadorned prose is the perfect complement to DuBurke's stark black-and-white inks; great slabs of shadow and masterfully rendered faces breathe real, tragic life into the players." Publ Wkly

North, Ryan

The **unbeatable** Squirrel Girl; Volume 1 Squirrel power! Ryan North; illustrated by Erica Henderson. Marvel Enterprises 2015 136 p. chiefly color illustrations $15.99

Grades: 7 8 9 10 11 12 Adult   741.5

1. Squirrels -- Fiction 2. Superheroes -- Fiction 3. Female superhero graphic novels 4. Squirrel Girl (Fictional character)

ISBN 0785197028; 9780785197027

Eisner Nominee: Best New Series (2016)

"Supervillains and criminals meet their match with Tony Stark's friend Squirrel Girl, aka Doreen Green, a college freshman with the appearance, speed, and agility of a squirrel. Fitting in proves to be challenging, as normal girls do not talk to or have a squirrel sidekick, nor do they have super strength. Then there is Squirrel Girl's roommate, who has a tough exterior and is obsessed with knitting and her cat. Luckily, Squirrel Girl has a knack for winning people over. When Galactus threatens Earth, the heroine must rely on more than strength to defeat the Devourer of Worlds. She may have extraordinary strength, an army of squirrels at her disposal, a collection of Deadpool villain trading cards, and nut-inspired catchphrases, but it is her ability to form connections with people that proves to be her most powerful asset.:" (School Library Journal)

Volume 1 of an ongoing series

Novgorodoff, Danica

Slow storm. First Second 2008 172p il pa $17.95

Grades: 9 10 11 12   741.5

1. Graphic novels 2. Immigrants -- Graphic novels
ISBN 978-1-5964-3250-5; 1-5964-3250-0

LC 2007-46202

"Novgorodoff writes a very literate and rich graphic novel. The illustrations are masterfully done and often wordlessly tell the story as well as convey the mood." Voice Youth Advocates

O'Malley, Bryan Lee

★ **Scott** Pilgrim's Precious Little Life, Vol. 1. Oni Press 2004 un il $11.95

Grades: 10 11 12 Adult   741.5

1. Graphic novels 2. Romance graphic novels 3. Humorous graphic novels 4. Martial arts -- Graphic novels

ISBN 1-932664-08-4

Other titles in this series are:

Scott Pilgrim vs. the World (2005)
Scott Pilgrim & the Infinite Sadness (2006)
Scott Pilgrim Gets It Together (2007)
Scott Pilgrim vs. the Universe (2009)
Scott Pilgrim's Finest Hour (2010)

Seconds; Bryan Lee O'Malley. Ballantine Books 2014 336 p. chiefly color illustrations $25

Grades: 10 11 12 Adult   741.5

1. Graphic novels 2. Restaurants -- Fiction
ISBN 0345529375; 9780345529374

LC 2013456979

In this graphic novel by Bryan Lee O'Malley, "Katie's got it pretty good. She's a talented young chef, she runs a successful restaurant, and she has big plans to open an even better one. Then, all at once, progress on the new location bogs down, her charming ex-boyfriend pops up, her fling with another chef goes sour, and her best waitress gets badly hurt. And just like that, Katie's life goes from pretty good to not so much." (Publisher's note)

"O'Malley's engaging narrative voice hasn't diminished----even the self-absorbed Katie is likeable enough to root for, although it's obvious that she's making things worse for herself. O'Malley's sweet, nimble art, now in color, has acquired more confidence: the plot unfolds cinematically, and his character designs are more appealing than ever." Pub Wkly

O'Neil, Dennis

The **DC** comics guide to writing comics; introduction by Stan Lee. Watson-Guptill 2001 128p il $19.95

Grades: 11 12 Adult   741.5

1. Comic books, strips, etc. -- Authorship
ISBN 0-8230-1027-9

LC 2001-26101

"O'Neil addresses the universals of writing in a way that makes the book useful to all aspiring scripters, regardless of their knowledge of comics." Booklist

O, Se-Yong

Buja's diary. NBM 2005 280p il pa $19.95

Grades: 11 12 Adult **741.5**

1. Graphic novels 2. Korea (South) -- Graphic novels
ISBN 1-56163-448-4; 978-1-56163-448-4

LC 2005-50519

The thirteen "stories by this Korean 'manwha' (comic book) author relate poignant tales of distressed humanity struggling with family, history, and culture. . . . Although O's eye is not unsympathetic, the world he depicts is unforgiving, sometimes graphically so. . . . Originally published in 1995, this book is a thoughtful examination of the human condition in the Korea of the recent past as well as universally." Voice Youth Advocates

Obata, Yuki

★ **We** were there, vol. 1; story & art by Yuki Obata. Viz Media/Shojo Beat 2008 un il pa $8.99
Grades: 10 11 12 **741.5**

1. Manga 2. Shojo manga 3. Graphic novels 4. Romance graphic novels
ISBN 978-1-4215-2018-6

Original Japanese edition, 2002

Fifteen-year-old Nanami Takahashi has just started high school, with high hopes for making friends and doing well, but things don't go as smoothly as she had hoped. She struggles with math, then she gets sort of railroaded into being the class president. She also falls for Motoharu Yano, an irresponsible boy who somehow is the most popular person in the class. His carefree attitude covers his grief for the death of his girlfriend, an older girl whose younger sister is their classmate, Yuri Yamamoto. Nanami struggles with classwork, with the responsibilities of being class president, and with her conflicting feelings about Motoharu. Some of the black and white art looks airbrushed; these pages occur at the beginning of each chapter. Viz has rated this series for older teens due to sexual themes, but they don't occur in this first volume.

Volume 1 of 18

Oima, Yoshitoki

A **silent** voice; Volume 1 Yoshitoki Oima; translation, lettering, Steven LeCroy. Kodansha 2015 186 p. chiefly illustrations (pbk.) $10.99

Grades: 7 8 9 10 **741.5**

1. Bullies -- Graphic novels 2. Deaf children -- Graphic novels 3. School stories -- Graphic novels
ISBN 163236056X; 9781632360564

Eisner Nominee: Best U.S. Edition of International Material--Asia (2016)

"Shoya is a bully. When Shoko, a girl who can't hear, enters his elementary school class, she becomes their favorite target. . . . But the children's cruelty goes too far. Shoko is forced to leave the school, and Shoya ends up shouldering all the blame. Six years later, the two meet again. Can Shoya make up for his past mistakes, or is it too late?" (Publisher's note)

Volume 1 of 7

Okabayashi, Kensuke

Manga for dummies. Wiley Publishing, Inc. 2007 416p il (--For dummies) pa $19.99

Grades: 9 10 11 12 Adult **741.5**

1. Manga 2. Graphic novels -- Drawing
ISBN 978-0-470-08025-2

LC 2006-939589

This guide, written and illustrated by Okabayashi, who teaches art at the Educational Alliance Art School in New York City and who has interned with manga creators in Japan, shows aspiring manga artists how to create characters, how to draw weapons, cars, animals, and more, how to create plotlines and storyboards, how to convey motion and emotion, and more.

Ottaviani, Jim

Levitation: physics and psychology in the service of deception; [by] Jim Ottaviani and Janine Johnston; lettering by Tom Orzechowski. G. T. Labs 2007 71p il pa $12.95

Grades: 6 7 8 9 10 11 12 Adult **741.5**

1. Graphic novels 2. Magic tricks -- Graphic novels
ISBN 978-0-9788037-0-4

This book tells the story of how John Neville Maskelyne developed the stage magic trick of levitation, of the American Harry Kellar, who acquired the trick through devious means, of the old school engineer Guy Jarrett, who perfected the magicians' tricks, and of stage performer Howard Thurston, who inherited the levitation trick from Kellar and ruined it. Or did he? The book includes notes and reprints of old posters and other information on the magicians.

Includes bibliographical references

Primates; The Fearless Science of Jane Goodall, Dian Fossey, and Biruté Galdikas. Jim Ottaviani; illustrated by Maris Wicks. First edition First Second 2013 133 p. chiefly color illustrations (hardcover) $19.99

Grades: 5 6 7 8 9 10 Adult **741.5**

1. Primates
ISBN 1596438657; 9781596438651

LC 2013427678

This book presents an "account of the three greatest primatologists of the last century: Jane Goodall, Dian Fossey, and Biruté Galdikas. These three ground-breaking researchers were all students of the great Louis Leakey, and each made profound contributions to primatology--and to our own understanding of ourselves." (Publisher's note)

"More story than study, the book provides an accessible introduction to Goodall's, Fossey's and Galdikas' lives and work." Kirkus

Includes bibliographical references, page 138

Pope, Paul

Battling Boy; Paul Pope; colors by Hilary Sycamore. First Second 2013 208 p. chiefly ill. (paperback) $15.99; (hardcover) $24.99

Grades: 7 8 9 10 11 12 **741.5**

1. Fantasy graphic novels 2. Superhero graphic novels
ISBN 1596438053; 9781596431454; 9781596438057

LC 2013030815

Eisner Award: Best Publication for Teens (2014)

In this book, "the hero Haggard West helps battle the evil forces of Sadisto and his hooded ghouls. However, in a shocking turn of events, evil triumphs over good, and the metropolis is left without protection. In a world far, far away, a 13-year-old son of a god has been chosen to help Earth fight the onslaught of monsters as a rite of passage. Sent with only a few possessions, including an array of magical T-shirts, Battling Boy helps the city—but he finds he cannot do it alone." (Kirkus Reviews)

"This is a sophisticated tale for younger readers, but Pope manages to both grant full-scale wish fulfillment and acknowledge the limitations of young boys with equal aplomb. His art, meanwhile, looks like nothing else in comics, with ropy, sinewy figures, dynamic action, and gritty urban design all captured in panels that have the rough, subversive tone of classic punk album covers." Booklist

Powell, Nate

Swallow me whole. Top Shelf Productions 2008 un il pa $20.95

Grades: 10 11 12 Adult   **741.5**

1. Graphic novels 2. Mental illness -- Graphic novels
ISBN 978-1-60309-033-9

Stepsiblings Ruth and Perry share their secrets with each other; Ruth hears insects talking to her, and Perry has to deal with a tiny wizard who forces him to draw all the time. In high school, Ruth is diagnosed as an obsessive compulsive with schizophrenic tendencies, while Perry manages to hide his wizard. Ruth sees cicadas and other insects always surrounding her, to the point that she thinks she's completely covered with them and she can fly. Her Memaw (grandmother) warns her that what she sees can swallow her whole. This book includes considerable use of foul language, especially the f-bomb, and the story takes a very thoughtful, mature reader to comprehend what is happening.

Prince, Liz

Tomboy; A Graphic Memoir. by Liz Prince. Zest Books 2014 256 p. illustrations $15.99

Grades: 7 8 9 10 11 12 Adult   **741.5**

1. Gender role 2. Sex differences (Psychology) 3. Stereotype (Social psychology) 4. Sex role 5. Graphic novels 6. Gender identity 7. Cartoonists -- Caricatures and cartoons 8. Cartoonists -- United States -- Biography
ISBN 1936976552; 9781936976553

LC 2014034070

This memoir, by Liz Prince, "is a graphic novel about refusing gender boundaries, yet unwittingly embracing gender stereotypes at the same time, and realizing later in life that you can be just as much of a girl in jeans and a T-shirt as you can in a pink tutu." (Publisher's note)

"Prince's honest voice and self-deprecating humor help make young Liz a sympathetic and relatable character. The simply rendered black-and-white panel drawings have an unpretentious quality, in keeping with the narrative tone." Horn Book

Raven, Nicky

Bram Stoker's Dracula; adapted by Nicky Raven; illustrated by Anne Yvonne Gilbert. Candlewick Press 2010 96p il $19.99

Grades: 7 8 9 10   **741.5**

1. Graphic novels 2. Horror graphic novels 3. Vampires

-- Graphic novels
ISBN 978-0-7636-4793-3; 0-7636-4793-4

LC 2009-22116

A modern, illustrated retelling of the Bram Stoker classic, in which young Jonathan Harker first meets and then must destroy the vampire, Count Dracula, in order to save those closest to him.

Raven "successfully abridges a vaunted classic. . . . Raven does a great job fleshing out characters that even in Stoker's original felt bloodless. . . . Gilbert's gothic drawings, the crosshatches of which often conceal layers of spooky elements, are a perfect fit for the somber tone." Booklist

Reed, M. K.

Americus; written by MK Reed; art by Jonathan Hill. First Second 2011 215p il pa $14.99

Grades: 8 9 10 11 12   **741.5**

1. Graphic novels 2. Libraries -- Fiction 3. Censorship -- Fiction 4. Books and reading -- Fiction 5. Christian fundamentalism -- Fiction
ISBN 978-1-59643-601-5; 1-59643-601-8

LC 2010051586

"Neil Barton finds the transition from middle school to high school to be challenging. He finds solace reading and listening to music, and working at the library. A censorship challenge by a fundamentalist Christian group forces him to courageously stand up before the public library board." (Library Media Connection)

"The clever mix of fantasy and realistic fiction, thoughtful pacing, authentic dialogue, and expressive art perfectly captures the angst of a nerdy teen who is at first ostracized but then finds his niche as he finds his voice." Booklist

Richardson, Mike

47 Ronin; writer, Mike Richardson; artist, Stan Sakai. Dark Horse 2014 151 p. chiefly color illustrations $19.99

Grades: 11 12 Adult   **741.5**

1. Comic books, strips, etc. 2. Samurai -- Graphic novels
ISBN 1595829547; 9781595829542

Written by Mike Richardson and illustrated by Stan Sakai, "this collection of the acclaimed [comic book] miniseries recounts this sweeping saga of honor and violence in all its grandeur. Opening with the tragic incident that sealed the fate of Lord Asano, 47 Ronin follows a dedicated group of Asano's vassals on their years-long path of vengeance!" (Publisher's note)

"Richardson, founder of Dark Horse Comics, and Sakai, creator of the long-running and award-laden Usagi Yojimbo samurai series, combine talents to produce this terrific graphic interpretation of one of Japan's most important sagas. . . . The level of talent, the research, and the attention to both narrative and artistic detail shine through in this volume." LJ

Roman, Dave

Agnes Quill; an anthology of mystery. all transcripts written by Dave Roman; illustrated by Jason Ho, Raina Telgemeier, Jeff Zornow and Dave Roman. SLG Publishing 2006 130p il pa $10.95

Grades: 7 8 9 10 11 12   **741.5**

1. Graphic novels 2. Horror graphic novels 3. Mystery

graphic novels
ISBN 978-1-59362-052-3

Orphaned teen Agnes Quill lives in the city of Legerdemain and carries on a family tradition; she can see and communicate with ghosts, and she works as a detective to help them. Her cases range from recovering the mummified head of a ghost's old body in order to save the valuable necklace hidden there, to helping a little girl ghost find her doll, to helping a man find his legs, and more. Roman works with artists including Raina Telgemeier, and their styles range from childlike cartoons to gloomy, atmospheric art full of shadows.

"The variety of drawing styles and Agnes' story of being a teenage detective who can see the dead among the living combine in an interesting read that will likely keep readers' attention." Voice Youth Advocates

Rucka, Greg

Batwoman; elegy. Greg Rucka, writer; J.H. Williams III, artist; Dave Stewart, colorist; Todd Klein, letters. Deluxe ed. DC Comics 2010 1 v. chiefly col. ill. $24.99

Grades: 11 12 Adult   741.5
1. Graphic novels 2. Superheroes -- Fiction 3. Mentally ill -- Fiction 4. Batwoman (Fictitious character) -- Comic books, strips, etc.
ISBN 9781401226923; 1401226922

LC 2010283560

"Batwoman battles a madwoman known only as Alice, inspired by Alice in Wonderland, who sees her life as a fairy tale and everyone around her as expendable! Batwoman must stop Alice from unleashing a toxic death cloud over all of Gotham City--but Alice has more up her sleeve than just poison, and Batwoman's life will never ever be the same." (Publisher's note)

"[A] nuanced, literary, and culturally charged story, but the real knockout element is Williams' art nouveau inspired compositions." Booklist

Sakai, Stan

Usagi Yojimbo, book one; The Ronin. Stan Sakai. Fantagraphics Books 1999 144p il pa $15.95
Grades: 7 8 9 10 11 12   741.5
1. Graphic novels 2. Adventure graphic novels 3. Japan -- Graphic novels 4. Rabbits -- Graphic novels 5. Samurai -- Graphic novels 6. Usagi Yojimbo (Fictional character)
ISBN 0-930193-35-0; 978-0-930193-35-5

LC 93-239124

First published 1987
This series contains the adventures of Miyamoto Usagi, a ronin samurai rabbit in 17th-century Japan.
Volume 1 of an ongoing series

Usagi Yojimbo: Yokai; created, written, and illustrated by Stan Sakai. Dark Horse Books 2009 62p il pa $14.95
Grades: 6 7 8 9 10 11 12 Adult   741.5
1. Graphic novels 2. Adventure graphic novels 3. Japan -- Graphic novels 4. Samurai -- Graphic novels 5. Monsters -- Graphic novels 6. Usagi Yojimbo

(Fictional character)
ISBN 978-1-59582-362-5

LC 2009-20024

As he walks through a spooky forest at night, samurai rabbit Usagi Yojimbo encounters a woman who begs him to find her daughter, who was kidnapped and dragged into the forest. That night, the yokai—monsters, demons, and spirits from Japanese folklore—are amassing for a once-a-century attempt to take over the living world. Armed only with his swords and his wit, Usagi can't hope to win against so many supernatural beings, but luckily Sasuke the Demon Queller has come, knowing about the yokais' plan, and together they fight the gathered monsters. The fighting is not graphic or bloody, and the monsters and demons aren't too scary looking for most younger readers.

"Sakai's art deftly demonstrates that comics can be simultaneously cartoony and scary. . . . Usagi Yojimbo is a genuine pleasure for readers of all ages." Publ Wkly

Satrapi, Marjane, 1969-

★ The **complete** Persepolis. Pantheon Books 2007 341p il pa $24.95
Grades: 11 12 Adult   741.5
1. Artists 2. Authors 3. Novelists 4. Cartoonists 5. Graphic novels 6. Autobiographical graphic novels 7. Memoirists 8. Iran -- Graphic novels
ISBN 978-0-375-71483-2

LC 2007-60106

Originally published in two separate volumes 2003-2004
Ignatz Award: Outstanding Graphic Novel (2005)

"Persepolis is the story of Satrapi's unforgettable childhood and coming of age within a large and loving family in Tehran during the Islamic Revolution; of the contradictions between private life and public life in a country plagued by political upheaval; of her high school years in Vienna facing the trials of adolescence far from her family; of her homecoming--both sweet and terrible; and, finally, of her self-imposed exile from her beloved homeland. It is the chronicle of a girlhood and adolescence at once outrageous and familiar, a young life entwined with the history of her country yet filled with the universal trials and joys of growing up." (Publisher's note)

Schweizer, Chris

Crogan's march. Oni Press 2009 212p il $14.95
Grades: 8 9 10 11 12 Adult   741.5
1. Graphic novels 2. Adventure graphic novels 3. Imperialism -- Graphic novels 4. North Africa -- World history -- 20th century -- Graphic novels
ISBN 978-1-934964-24-8
Sequel to: Crogan's vengeance (2008)

When brothers Eric and Cory squabble at the dinner table, their father tells them the story of Peter Crogan, one of their ancestors, who fought in the French Foreign Legion in 1912. Crogan's five-year term of service is one month from completion when he's asked to stay and become an officer. His unit is stationed in North Africa, where the French hold territory and depend on the French Foreign Legion to police the territory, putting down the rebellious attacks of the Tuaregs. He finds himself torn between the heroic Captain Poitelet (who tends to be the sole survivor of various battles) and the grizzled sergeant who actually cares about the people the Legion polices. When Crogan's unit escorts a caravan that endures an attack by Tuaregs, the captain's reckless actions endanger everyone, and Crogan must find help. Schweizer's story includes the kind of violence military actions cause, but very little in the way of bad language. Some may wince at the heavily French-accented English of some of the characters ("zee Daughters of France send zem out to all of zee units," etc.). This action-packed historical fiction graphic novel will appeal to teens, but adults who remember such novels as Beau Geste by Percival Christopher Wren (and the movies, of course) will also enjoy reading Schweizer's tale.

★ **Crogan's** vengeance; book design by Keith Wood; edited by James Lucas Jones with Jill Beaton. Oni Press 2008 185p il pa $14.95

Grades: 8 9 10 11 12 Adult   741.5
1. Graphic novels 2. Adventure graphic novels 3. Pirates -- Graphic novels
ISBN 978-1-934964-06-4

Catfoot Crogan serves as an honest and honorable sailor on a ship commanded by an unjust captain when the ship is taken over by pirates. In order to save their lives, the sailors all take the oath to become pirates, but Crogan immediately runs afoul of D'Or, a brutal man who enjoys torturing others. Catfoot is a pirate, but he's determined to remain as honest and honorable as he can be, which continually puts him in danger. This swashbuckling tale shows a less romantic story than Rafael Sabatini's Captain Blood, with more violence, but it is more action-oriented than merely violent.

"Filled with mutiny, ferocious storms, shark-infested waters, commandeering of ships, and—of course—swashbuckling sword fights, this book has high teen appeal." SLJ

★ **Secret** identities; the Asian American superhero anthology. [edited by] Jeff Yang . . . [et al.]; New Press 2009 194p il pa $21.95

Grades: 9 10 11 12 Adult   741.5
1. Graphic novels 2. Superhero graphic novels 3. Asian Americans -- Graphic novels
ISBN 978-1-59558-398-7

LC 2009-1536
Yang, Shen, Chow, and coeditor Jerry Ma have put together a collection of twenty-six stories by Asian American creators about Asian American superheroes. The book is divided into sections: War and Remembrance, Many Masks, When Worlds Collide, Girl Power, Ordinary Heroes, and From Headline to Hero. The Preface, the Prologue, all section introductions, and the Epilogue, are all done in comic book format. Creators include Gene Luen Yang, Greg Pak, Dustin Nguyen, Kazu Kibuishi, Cliff Chiang, Christine Norrie, and many more. Some stories deal with the Nisei soldiers of the 100th Battalion/442nd Regimental Combat Team during World War II, others confront the idea that the Asian character can only be the sidekick, still others explore the stereotypical attitudes of some Americans toward Asian Americans. The book includes some violence and some harsh language.

Sfar, Joann

The **professor's** daughter; [story by] Joann Sfar & [illustrated by] Emmanuel Guibert; translated by Alexis Siegel. First Second Books 2007 63p il pa $16.95

Grades: 7 8 9 10 11 12 Adult   741.5
1. Graphic novels 2. Romance graphic novels 3. Humorous graphic novels 4. Mummies -- Graphic novels
ISBN 978-1-59643-130-0; 1-59643-130-X

LC 2006-22177
In Victorian London, Lillian, the daughter of a famed archeologist, has fallen in love with the mummy of Imhotep IV; he thinks that Lillian bears a strong resemblance to this long-dead wife. Their love faces many obstacles, from Lillian's father, the police, a pirate who is actually Imhotep III (yes, the father and another mummy), even Queen Victoria herself. Dainty Victorian manners mix with broad farce and black comedy in a beautifully illustrated book with muted colors and sepia tones.

The **rabbi's** cat. Pantheon Books 2005 142p il $21.95; pa $16.95

Grades: 11 12 Adult   741.5
1. Graphic novels 2. Jews -- Graphic novels 3. Rabbis -- Graphic novels 4. North Africa -- Graphic novels 5. France -- History -- 1914-1940 -- Graphic novels
ISBN 0-375-42281-1; 0-375-71464-2 pa

LC 2004-61406
"A slinky gray cat lives with a rabbi and his beautiful young daughter. One day, the feline eats their parrot, only to find that he has gained the bird's ability to talk. Witty and highly intelligent, the cat immediately decides that he wants to learn more about Judaism, from the Kabbalah to the Torah. . . . There is plenty for teens to like—humor, romance, and theological questioning combined with a folkloric quality to bring to life a multifaceted work." SLJ

Shakespeare, William, 1564-1616

The **most** excellent and lamentable tragedy of Romeo & Juliet; a play by William Shakespeare. by William Shakespeare, adapted and illustrated by Gareth Hinds. Candlewick Press 2013 128 p. (hardcover) $21.99; (pbk.) $12.99

Grades: 7 8 9 10   741.5
1. Graphic novels
ISBN 0763659487; 0763668079; 9780763659486; 9780763668075

LC 2012950561
This book by Gareth Hinds presents a graphic novel adaptation of William Shakespeare's play "Romeo and Juliet." "The most notable change between this story and Shakespeare's original is the creative license that Hinds takes with ethnicity--he makes the characters of African, Indian, and Caucasian descent in order to promote the universality of the story. The Shakespearean language is abridged but not adapted into contemporary English." (School Library Journal)

"Cleaving to Shakespeare's words and dramatic arc, Hinds (The Merchant of Venice) creates another splendid graphic novel, tracing each scene in taut, coherent dialogue. The characters, in period dress modified by a few more contemporary touches, are poignantly specific yet universal. Hinds delivers the play's essence and beauty, its glorious language, furious conflict, yearning love, and wrenching tragedy." (Horn Book)

Shanower, Eric

Age of Bronze; Betrayal part 2. by Eric Shanower. Image Comics 2013 176 p. chiefly illustrations
Grades: 10 11 12 Adult   **741.5**
1. Graphic novels 2. Greece -- Fiction 3. Trojan War -- Fiction
ISBN 1607067579; 9781607067573

In this graphic novel, written and illustrated by Eric Shanower, "the Trojan plain fills with death as Achaean forces clash in blood with the Trojan army. In the city of Troy, Pandarus pulls the strings to put Troilus in Cressida's bed. But when Cressida is ripped away to the enemy camp, how far will Troilus fight? (Publisher's note)

"Shanower's graphic-novel retelling of the Trojan War is one of the great artistic visions of the comics medium. Where both mythology and heroic-adventure comics typically lean toward vast spectacle and archetypal characters, Shanower is uncompromising in his sharp, humanizing focus. Betrayal, Part 2, the second part of the third part of Shanower's projected seven-part series, begins with Achilles and his Myrmidons invading the beach of Troy and ends with Troilus' breakdown during a bloody skirmish with a squad of Achaeans. . . . Seldom has a work shined so brightly on every page." Booklist

Age of Bronze vol. 1: A Thousand Ships. Image Comics 2001 223p il (Age of bronze) hardcover o.p. pa $19.95
Grades: 10 11 12   **741.5**
1. Graphic novels 2. Trojan War -- Graphic novels 3. Greek mythology -- Graphic novels
ISBN 1-58240-212-4; 1-58240-200-0 pa

Shanower includes frank sex scenes and doesn't shy away from the brutal violence of war.

"This series retells the story of the Trojan War, going back to the young Trojan prince Paris and the petty rivalry of several goddesses that set the events into motion. Shanower conducted extensive reasearch of the world of that time—its technology, architecture, clothing, armor, and weapons. His books are more 'real' than any Hollywood movie depiction." Voice Youth Advocates

Includes bibliographical references
Other books in the Age of Bronze series include:
Betrayal (2008)
Sacrifice (2004)

Age of bronze volume 3A: Betrayal part one. Image Comics 2007 176p il $17.99
Grades: 10 11 12 Adult   **741.5**
1. Graphic novels 2. Adventure graphic novels 3. Greek mythology -- Graphic novels 4. Troy (Extinct city) -- Graphic novels
ISBN 978-1-58240-755-5
Sequel to Sacrifice (2004)

The graphic novel retelling of the story of the Trojan War continues, as High King Agamemnon's army passes the island of Tenedos on its journey to conquer Troy. When a snake bites Philoktetes on the foot, his cries of pain bother the army so much that Odysseus must find a solution. Then, the Achaeans send an embassy to Troy in hopes of preventing a war. This book includes some nudity and sexual situations as well as some violence. Shanower includes a lengthy bibliography of historical sources.

Age of Bronze: Sacrifice. Image Comics 2004 223p il map (Age of bronze) hardcover o.p. pa $19.95
Grades: 10 11 12 Adult   **741.5**
1. Graphic novels 2. Trojan War -- Graphic novels 3. Greek mythology -- Graphic novels
ISBN 1-58240-360-0; 1-58240-399-6 pa

This is the second book in the author's projected seven-volume graphic novel about the Trojan War. The first volume, A thousand ships, was published in 2001

"Sacrifice begins by recapitulating the story thus far. Paris sails back to Troy, just as self-regarding and shortsighted as when he left. Thrilled with his own prize (Helen), he has no understanding of the political complications. Priam does, but he is swayed by the machinations of Helen and by Hecuba's generosity. Not only are the major characters (Achilles, Klytemnestra, Odysseus) complex, but even a minor player like Telephus is carefully developed." SLJ

Includes bibliographical references
Followed by Betrayal (2008)

Shelley, Mary Wollstonecraft, 1797-1851

★ **Frankenstein**; the graphic novel. [by] Mary Shelley; script adaptation Jason Cobley; American English adaptation: Joe Sutliff Sanders; linework: Declan Shalvey; coloring: Jason Cardy & Kat Nicholson; lettering: Terry Wiley. Classical Comics 2008 141p il pa $16.95
Grades: 6 7 8 9 10 11 12 Adult   **741.5**
1. Authors 2. Novelists 3. Graphic novels 4. Horror graphic novels 5. Frankenstein (Fictional character)
ISBN 978-1-906332-49-5

Young scientist Victor Frankenstein becomes obsessed with the idea that technology can create life, and works to prove his theories. However, his success doesn't bring him glory, but a living nightmare for himself and everyone around him. This graphic adaptation brings the entire book to the reader, using Shelley's original text for the dialog and narrative. Back matter includes a brief biography of Shelley, her family tree, a description of how she came to write the novel, and information on some of the various adaptations of the story to the stage and to film.

"More than a straightforward retelling, this edition invites readers to explore important social issues such as alienation, the consequences and ethics of scientific studies, as well as the nature of creation and destruction." SLJ

Shiga, Jason

Empire State; a love story (or not) colors by John Pham. Abrams ConnieArts 2011 un il $17.95
Grades: 9 10 11 12 Adult   **741.5**
1. Graphic novels 2. Romance graphic novels 3. New York (N.Y.) -- Graphic novels
ISBN 978-0-8109-9747-9

LC 2010934622

"This dialogue-driven comic stars nerdy young Oakland librarian Jimmy, whose blatant inexperience with this whole being-grown-up thing isn't limited to just matters of the heart. . . . When his one friend moves back to New York, he goes on a surprise cross-country trek to see if just maybe he can inspire a Sleepless in Seattle moment with her. The mildly disastrous results might have been soul-crushing if they weren't handled with Shiga's terrifically wry wit and Jimmy's cheery ability to roll with the punches, even when they land a bit harder than expected." Booklist

Siddell, Thomas

Gunnerkrigg Court: orientation; [by] Tom Siddell. Archaia Studios Press 2009 296p il $26.95
Grades: 6 7 8 9 10 11 12 **741.5**
1. Graphic novels 2. Fantasy graphic novels
ISBN 978-1-932386-34-9; 1-932386-34-3

"Antimony Carver is a precocious and preternaturally self-possessed young girl starting her first year of school at gloomy Gunnerkrigg Court, a very British boarding school that has robots running around along side body-snatching demons, forest gods, and the odd mythical creature. The opening volume in the series follows Antimony through her orientation year: the people she meets, the strange things that happen, and the things she causes to happen as she and her new friend, Kat, unravel the mysteries of the Court and deal with the everyday adventures of growing up." (Publisher's note)

"The first 14 chapters of Siddell's popular webcomic are collected here in an alluring hardcover. The premise, best described as science-fantasy, involves a young girl named Antimony plopped into a strange boarding-school/industrial-complex which . . . she knows nothing about. Discrete chapters . . . all feature varying levels of jaw-dropping peculiarity, devilish bursts of humor, and sublime creativity that lurk at the ends of the school's corridors. The darkly hued artwork is deceptively simplistic and displays a flair for the crucial details of setting and atmosphere." Booklist

Other titles in this series are:
Vol. 2: Research (2009)
Vol. 3: Reason (2011)
Vol. 4: Materia (2013)
Vol. 5: Refine (2015)

Slate, Barbara

You can do a graphic novel. Alpha Books 2010 187p il pa $19.95
Grades: 7 8 9 10 **741.5**
1. Graphic novels -- Authorship
ISBN 978-1-59257-955-6; 1-59257-955-8
LC 2009-930703

"This is a practical book for those who aspire to create their own graphic novels. Slate . . . is fair handed with the advice she gives to writers as well as artists. . . . The instructions and illustrations are easy to follow, and the format is colorful and eye-catching." SLJ

Small, David, 1945-

★ **Stitches**; a memoir. W.W. Norton 2009 329p il $23.95
Grades: 10 11 12 Adult **741.5**
1. Artists 2. Authors 3. Illustrators 4. Graphic novels 5. Comic books, strips, etc. 6. Autobiographical graphic novels 7. Art teachers 8. Children's authors 9. Cancer

-- Graphic novels 10. Family life -- Graphic novels
ISBN 978-0-393-06857-3; 0-393-06857-9
LC 2009-22526

David Small grew up in a dysfunctional family, with a radiologist father who was distant, an angry mother who expressed her anger in eloquent silences, and an older brother who played drums a lot to express his frustrations. When he was eleven, he had a lump, a growth, on the side of his neck. Nothing was done until he was fourteen. He thought he was going in for a minor surgery to remove the cyst from his neck; instead, there were two surgeries, and when he woke up, he had no voice—a vocal cord was removed. He later learned he had cancer, something his parents refused to discuss. After he finds his mother in bed with another woman and his father confesses that he exposed him to x-rays when he was very young, Small leaves home at age sixteen, with little except his dreams that his art could be his life. In one early scene, Small shows the indignities wrought upon his body by his father, including an enema. In another scene, young Small and his older brother look at their father's medical books and see a woman's breast and a man's penis; towards the end of the book, Small draws his grandmother stripping all her clothes off and dancing wildly after setting her house on fire. Other than these few images, Small's depictions of his horrible childhood and teen years are quiet and low-key.

"Emotionally raw, artistically compelling and psychologically devastating graphic memoir of childhood trauma." Kirkus

Smith, Brian

The **stuff** of legend; Omnibus two by Mike Raicht and Brian Smith; illustrated by Charles Paul Wilson III. Th3rd World Studios 2014 270 p. chiefly col. ill. (The Stuff of Legend) $34.99
Grades: 8 9 10 11 12 Adult **741.5**
1. Graphic novels 2. Toys -- Fiction 3. Toys 4. Kidnapping 5. Horror comic books, strips, etc.
ISBN 0989574490; 9780989574495

The second omnibus edition "finds our toys at a crossroads. Unable to find their boy, our loyal toys' bonds have been tested and broken. Now scattered across The Dark, the toys must decide whether to continue their search or admit defeat and return home." (Publisher's note)

The **Stuff** of Legend; Omnibus one by Mike Raicht and Brian Smith; illustrated by Charles Paul Wilson III. Th3rd World Studios 2014 284 p. chiefly col. ill. (The Stuff of Legend) $29.99
Grades: 8 9 10 11 12 Adult **741.5**
1. Graphic novels 2. Toys -- Fiction 3. Toys 4. Rescues 5. Kidnapping
ISBN 9780983216193; 0989574482; 9780989574488

"This hardcover collection brings together the first two volumes. . . . As Allied forces fight the enemy on Europe's war-torn beaches, another battle begins in a child's bedroom in Brooklyn when the nightmarish Boogeyman snatches a boy and takes him to the realm of the Dark. The child's playthings, led by the toy soldier known as the Colonel, band together to stage a daring rescue. On their perilous mission they will confront the boy's bitter and forgotten toys, as well as betrayal in their own ranks." (Publisher's note)

"Wilson renders the harrowing closet netherworld with full-fleshed detailing and sepia tones that nail both the 1940s time frame and the classicism of children's stories. But don't mistake this for a kids' comic—the violence is often explicit, and the Boogeyman creepy enough to slither his way right back onto grownups' most-terrifying lists." Booklist

Stassen, Jean-Philippe

Deogratias; a tale of Rwanda. [by] Stassen; translated by Alex Siegel. Roaring Brook 2006 79p il pa $17.95

Grades: 11 12 Adult　　　741.5

1. Graphic novels 2. Rwanda -- Graphic novels 3. Genocide -- Graphic novels

ISBN 1-59643-103-2; 978-1-59643-103-4

LC 2005-17576

In this "fictionalized account of the Rwandan genocide, readers meet Deogratias, a teenaged Hutu. His friends Benina and Apollinaria are Tutsi—a race that is being ethnically cleansed by Hutu extremists. As the conflict escalates, Deogratias witnesses murders and is forced to become involved in brutal acts of violence. He suffers a mental breakdown. The story is told through a series of flashbacks while he skates the line between rational and insane. Stassen spares his readers none of the brutality and visceral cruelties of this atrocity. Scenes of rape, harsh language, and some sexual content solidly designate this book for a mature audience. . . . A masterful work with vibrant, confident art, this book will stay with and haunt its readers." SLJ

Stevenson, Noelle

Lumberjanes; Volume 1 Beware the kitten holy. by Noelle Stevenson, Grace Ellis, Brooke Allen, and Shannon Watters. Boom! Studios 2015 128 p. ill. (chiefly col.) (Lumberjanes) pbk $14.99

Grades: 6 7 8 9 10 11 12 Adult　　　741.5

1. Camps -- Fiction 2. Adventure fiction 3. Summer -- Fiction 4. Monsters -- Fiction 5. Female friendship -- Graphic novels

ISBN 1608866874; 9781608866878

Eisner Award: Best New Series (2015)

Harvey Award: Best New Series (2015)

Eisner Award: Best Publication for Teens (2015)

Harvey Award: Best Original Graphic Publication For Young Readers (2015)

"[This] graphic novel begins mid-adventure as five campers are out after hours investigating a strange event that they all witnessed: a woman turning into a giant bear. This is just the first of many odd occurrences that Jo, April, Molly, Mal, and Ripley encounter at the summer camp for 'Hardcore Lady Types.' The Lumberjanes, as the scouts are called, band together to solve puzzles, defeat three-eyed creatures, and escape the ire of their watchful counselor Jen." (School Library Journal)

"Humorously riffing on everything from scout badges to the X-Men to feminist heroes . . ., it's a sharp, smart, and most of all fun celebration of sisterhood." Pub Wkly

Volume 1 of an ongoing series

★ **Nimona**; by Noelle Stevenson. HarperCollins Childrens Books 2015 272 p. $17.99

Grades: 7 8 9 10 11 12　　　741.5

1. Fantasy graphic novels 2. Magic -- Graphic novels 3. Good and evil -- Fiction 4. Heroes and heroines -- Graphic novels 5. Shapeshifting -- Comic books, strips, etc.

ISBN 0062278231; 9780062278234

Eisner Nominee: Best Digital/Web Comic (2015)

National Book Award Finalist: Young People's Literature (2015)

Eisner Nominee: Best Graphic Album--Reprint (2016)

In this graphic novel, by Noelle Stevenson, "Nimona is an impulsive young shapeshifter with a knack for villainy. Lord Ballister Blackheart is a villain with a vendetta. As sidekick and supervillain, Nimona and Lord Blackheart are about to wreak some serious havoc. Their mission: prove to the kingdom that Sir Ambrosius Goldenloin and his buddies at the Institution of Law Enforcement and Heroics aren't the heroes everyone thinks they are." (Publisher's note)

"This celebrated webcomic, a mash-up of medieval culture with modern science and technology, is now available in print. . . . Action scenes dominate as Nimona shifts with Hulk-like ferocity from frightful creatures such as a fire-breathing dragon to a docile cat or a timid child. Dialogue is fresh and witty with an abundance of clever lines." SLJ

Sturm, James

James Sturm's America; God, gold, and golems. Drawn & Quarterly 2007 192p il $24.95

Grades: 10 11 12 Adult　　　741.5

1. Graphic novels 2. Baseball -- Graphic novels 3. Revivals -- Graphic novels 4. Gold mines and mining -- Graphic novels 5. United States -- History -- Graphic novels

ISBN 978-1-897299-05-0

This book compiles three of Sturm's stories that are set in quieter periods of American history, during relatively peaceful non-war and pre-Depression times. "The Revival," set around 1801, portrays frontier life and early religious revival movements as a couple makes their way from Ohio westward and stop off at a camp where people push themselves into religious frenzies. "Hundreds of Feet Below Daylight" examines the people who continue gold mining after the euphoria has died down and life becomes tough. Some readers may be shocked by the brutality exhibited by some of the miners who so desperately hunt for money. "The Golem's Mighty Swing" features a Jewish professional baseball team traveling the country just trying to get by in the 1920s. Facing racial and religious taunts and sometimes violence, they try a gimmick—disguising their African American player as a golem—in order to generate ticket sales.

"Social issues, including racial prejudice and intolerance, poverty, and family dynamics, are broached via both plot and character. . . . This [is] an easy crossover graphic novel for readers who enjoy American history made into well-told stories." Booklist

★ **Satchel** Paige; striking out Jim Crow. by James Sturm & Rich Tommaso; with an introduction by Gerald Early. Jump at the Sun 2007 89p il $16.99; pa $9.99

Grades: 6 7 8 9 10 11 12　　　741.5

1. Graphic novels 2. Baseball players 3. Baseball

-- Graphic novels
ISBN 0-7868-3900-7; 0-7868-3901-5 pa

LC 2007-61362

This graphic novel is "about fictional Emmet Wilson, a black farmer whose moment of glory as a player in the Negro Leagues came when he scored a run off the great pitcher, Satchel Paige. . . . This visually powerful, suspenseful, even profound story makes an excellent choice for readers interested in baseball or in the history of race relations." Booklist

Suburbia, Liz

Sacred Heart; Liz Suburbia. Fantagraphics 2015 312 p. chiefly ill. $24.99

Grades: 11 12 Adult   **741.5**

1. Mystery fiction 2. Teenagers -- Graphic novels
ISBN 1606998412; 9781606998410

LC 2015942121

Alex Award (2016)

In this graphic novel, by Liz Suburbia, "the children of . . . Alexandria are just trying to live like normal teens until their parents' promised return from a mysterious, four-year religious pilgrimage, and Ben Schiller is no exception. She's just trying to take care of her sister . . . and get through her teen years. But her relationship with her best friend is changing, her younger sister is hiding a dark secret, and a terrible tragedy is coming for them all." (Publisher's note)

Takahashi, Rumiko

One-pound gospel, vol. 1; 2nd ed.; Viz Media 2008 242p il pa $9.99

Grades: 10 11 12 Adult   **741.5**

1. Manga 2. Shonen manga 3. Graphic novels 4. Humorous graphic novels 5. Boxing -- Graphic novels
ISBN 978-1-4215-2030-8

Kosaku Hatanaka is a talented boxer, but he suffers from an insatiable appetite that makes it extremely difficult to make weight for his boxing matches (he's a featherweight who should weigh 126 pounds). He drives his poor coach crazy and tends to lose matches because he has to starve himself to lose weight, which saps his strength. Then he meets Sister Angela, a novice nun who tries to help him; she's so cute, Kosaku has a crush on her. Between his coach at Mukaida's Gym and Sister Angela's prayers, Kosaku starts to win his bouts—but usually with such bizarre circumstances and incredible luck that his opponents hate him. The boxing action is pretty well done and fairly graphic; this volume doesn't include much at all in the way of strong language, but Viz has put a warning about strong language and realistic violence on the title page. This series was originally published starting in 1989 and is now released in Viz's now standard unflipped tankobon size book.

Volume 1 of 4

Takechi, Naoko

★ **Sailor** Moon; Volume 1 Naoko Takeuchi; translator/adapter, William Flanagan. Kodansha Comics 2011 240 p. chiefly ill. (some col.) (pbk.) $10.99

Grades: 5 6 7 8 9 10   **741.5**

1. Shojo manga 2. Good and evil -- Fiction 3. Teenage girls -- Fiction 4. Women heroes -- Comic books, strips,

etc 5. Teenage girls -- Japan -- Comic books, strips, etc
ISBN 1935429744; 9781935429746

LC 2012374271

"Usagi Tsukino is a normal girl until she meets up with Luna, a talking cat, who tells her that she is Sailor Moon. As Sailor Moon, Usagi must fight evils and enforce justice, in the name of the Moon and the mysterious Moon Princess. She meets other girls destined to be Sailor Senshi (Sailor Scouts), and together, they fight the forces of evil!" (Publisher's note)

Volume 1 of 12

Talbot, Bryan

The **tale** of one bad rat; 2nd ed.; Dark Horse 2010 un il $19.99

Grades: 9 10 11 12 Adult   **741.5**

1. Graphic novels 2. Runaway teenagers -- Graphic novels 3. Child sexual abuse -- Graphic novels
ISBN 978-1-59582-493-6

First published 1995

This book's "heroine is teenager Helen Potter, who has run away from an abusive father and whose path to recovery takes her from a squat in London to refuge at an inn in the British countryside. Along the way, she meets characters and situations that Talbot derives from the work of Helen's namesake, Beatrix Potter, whose life he symbolically links to Helen's. Talbot's vivid, realistic full-color illustration brilliantly evokes the story's settings, yet even more effective are his compassionate characterizations." Booklist

Tamaki, Jillian

SuperMutant Magic Academy; Jillian Tamaki. Drawn & Quarterly 2015 274 p. chiefly illustrations (pbk.) $22.95

Grades: 10 11 12 Adult   **741.5**

1. School stories 2. Teenagers -- Fiction 3. Fantasy graphic novels 4. Comic books, strips, etc. -- Canada 5. Teenagers -- Comic books, strips, etc 6. Private schools -- Comic books, strips, etc
ISBN 1770461981; 9781770461987

LC 2015376543

Eisner Nominee: Best Publication for Teens (2016)

In this graphic novel, author Jillian Tamaki "paints a teenaged world filled with just as much ennui and uncertainty, but also with a sharp dose of humor and irreverence. . . . The SuperMutant Magic Academy is a prep school for mutants and witches, but their paranormal abilities take a backseat to everyday teen concerns. Science experiments go awry, bake sales are upstaged, and the new kid at school is a cat who will determine the course of human destiny." (Publisher's note)

"There are flickering moments of transcendent wisdom and kindness, but the overall tone is one of insouciant, salty resignation to the mundane realities of existence. Simultaneously heartbreaking and hilarious." Booklist

Tamaki, Mariko

Skim; words by Mariko Tamaki; drawings by Jillian Tamaki. Groundwood Books 2008 144p il PB 12.95; HC $18.95

Grades: 7 8 9 10 11 12   **741.5**

1. Graphic novels 2. Humorous graphic novels 3.

Friendship -- Graphic novels 4. School stories -- Graphic novels

ISBN 088899964X; 0-88899-753-1; 9780888999641; 978-0-88899-753-1

Ignatz Award: Outstanding Graphic Novel (2008)

Skim is Kimberly Keiko Cameron, a not-slim half-Japanese would-be Wiccan goth who attends a private school. When classmate Katie Matthews' ex-boyfriend commits suicide, concerned guidance counselors descend upon the school because so many of the student body goes into mourning overdrive. The popular clique starts a new club, Girls Celebrate Life, and make Katie their project, especially after she falls off her roof and breaks both arms. Kim and her best friend Lisa observe all this, but counselors target Kim for her goth tendencies and are convinced she'll become suicidal any moment. All she is, is in love with her English teacher, Ms. Archer, who seems to reciprocate and then leaves the school. As Lisa starts to get sucked into the GLC, Kim and Katie tentatively begin a new friendship. There is only one rather chaste kiss between Kim and Ms. Archer. Artist Jillian Tamaki draws Kim to look like a classical Heian period Japanese woman.

★ **This** One Summer; Mariko Tamaki, [art by] Jillian Tamaki. First Second 2014 320 p. chiefly ill. pbk 17.99; hbk $21.99; pbk 17.99; hbk 21.99

Grades: 7 8 9 10 11 12 Adult   **741.5**

1. Graphic novels 2. Vacations -- Fiction 3. Friendship -- Fiction

ISBN 159643774X; 9781626720947; 9781596437746; 1626720940

Harvey Nominee: Best Artist (2015)

Eisner Award: Best Graphic Album--New (2015)

Harvey Nominee: Best Graphic Album of Original Work (2015)

Caldecott Honor Book (2015)

Ignatz Award: Outstanding Graphic Novel (2014)

Harvey Nominee: Best Original Graphic Publication For Young Readers (2015)

Printz Honor Book (2015)

"Every summer, Rose goes with her mom and dad to a lake house in Awago Beach. . . . Rosie's friend Windy is always there, too, like the little sister she never had. But this summer is different. . . . It's a summer of secrets, and sorrow, and growing up, and it's a good thing Rose and Windy have each other." (Publisher's note)

"This captivating graphic novel presents a fully realized picture of a particular time in a young girl's life, an in-between summer filled with yearning and a sense of ephemerality." SLJ

Tan, Shaun

★ The **arrival**. Arthur A. Levine Books 2007 un il $19.99

Grades: 6 7 8 9 10   **741.5**

1. Graphic novels 2. Stories without words 3. Immigrants -- Graphic novels

ISBN 0-439-89529-4; 9780439895293

LC 2006-21706

Boston Globe-Horn Book Award special citation (2008)

In this wordless graphic novel, a man leaves his homeland and sets off for a new country, where he must build a new life for himself and his family.

"Young readers will be fascinated by the strange new world the artist creates. . . . They will linger over the details in the beautiful sepia pictures and will likely pick up the book to pore over it again and again." SLJ

TenNapel, Doug

Bad Island; created, written, and drawn by Doug TenNapel. Graphix 2011 218p il $24.99

Grades: 6 7 8 9 10   **741.5**

1. Adventure graphic novels 2. Family life -- Graphic novels 3. Extraterrestrial beings -- Graphic novels 4. Father-son relationship -- Graphic novels 5. Survival after airplane accidents, shipwrecks, etc. -- Graphic novels

ISBN 0545314798; 0545314801 pa; 9780545314794; 9780545314800 pa

LC 2011276008

"Dad has decided to take Reese, who is too cool for family outings, and his sister, Janine, on a fishing trip. The vacation takes an unexpected turn when their boat capsizes during a storm and they find themselves marooned on a strange island. To their horror, the family slowly realizes that the island is the submerged body of a giant creature, escaped from another world. The story alternates between the shipwreck survivors and the faraway world that created this "island." Both stories feature conflict between an adolescent son and his father. . . . Ultimately, both rebellious adolescents grow up and find their place as young men." (School Libr J)

"Though father, mother, teenage son, and tween daughter face the various dangers like a gang of Indiana Joneses, their family stresses are believable. . . . A clever, old-fashioned adventure with some modern twists and a lighthearted tone." Booklist

Tezuka, Osamu

★ **Black** Jack, volume 1. Vertical, Inc. 2008 287p il pa $16.95

Grades: 9 10 11 12 Adult   **741.5**

1. Manga 2. Graphic novels 3. Surgeons -- Graphic novels 4. Medical practice -- Graphic novels

ISBN 978-1-934287-27-9

Black Jack is the only known name for a mysterious, scarred surgeon from Japan who can perform surgical miracles but is considered to be a creepy mercenary. He will perform highly risky surgeries for an exorbitant price, and he's unlicensed. However, most people don't realize that he actually does a lot for more altruistic reasons as well. In this first volume that reprints the original stories by pioneer mangaka (manga creator) Tezuka, stories include one in which Black Jack operates on a crime boss's son using the body of an unjustly convicted man; and one where he removes a teratoid cystoma from a unidentified wealthy and famous woman, but he refuses to kill the cystoma, which contains the body parts of the woman's unborn twin. While there are some surgical scenes that might not be for the squeamish, the stories offer little in the way of graphic violence or bad language while providing action and some thought about ethics and morals.

"With genre-spanning stories—horror, sci-fi, romance—and Tezuka's signature blend of drama, bathos and extreme broad comedy jammed together on every page, Black Jack is a wild but extravagantly entertaining ride." Publ Wkly

Volume 1 of 17

Thompson, Craig

★ **Blankets**; an illustrated novel. Top Shelf 2003 582p il pa $29.95

Grades: 10 11 12 Adult **741.5**

1. Graphic novels 2. Autobiographical graphic novels 3. Artists 4. Cartoonists 5. Illustrators 6. Family life -- Graphic novels

ISBN 1-891830-43-0; 9781891830433

LC 2004-297892

This "memoir recreates the confusion, emotional pain and isolation of the author's rigidly fundamentalist Christian upbringing, along with the trepidation of growing into maturity. Skinny, naive and spiritually vulnerable, Thompson and his younger brother manage to survive their parents' overbearing discipline (the brothers are sometimes forced to sleep in 'the cubbyhole,' a forbidding and claustrophobic storage chamber) through flights of childhood fancy and a mutual love of drawing . . . Thompson manages to explore adolescent social yearnings, the power of young love and the complexities of sexual attraction with a rare combination of sincerity, pictorial lyricism and taste. His exceptional b&w drawings balance representational precision with a bold and wonderfully expressive line for pages of ingenious, inventively composed and poignant imagery." Publ Wkly

Toboso, Yana

Black butler, vol. 1; by Yana Toboso [translation: Tomo Kimura; lettering: Tania Biswas]. Yen Press 2010 184p il pa $10.99

Grades: 10 11 12 Adult **741.5**

1. Manga 2. Graphic novels 3. Fantasy graphic novels 4. Mystery graphic novels 5. Household employees -- Graphic novels

ISBN 978-0-316-08084-2

In an alternate England, the young Earl Phantomhive, Ciel, lives just outside London; he's only twelve years old, but he runs a massive toy manufacturing company, aided by his butler Sebastian. In this world, magic coexists with science and technology, cars from the early twentieth century drive the roads and Ciel tests video games. Sebastian commands the other workers: Finnian the Gardener (who tends to kill plants), Mey-Rin the klutzy housemaid, and Baldroy the chef, who always has a cigarette dangling from the corner of his mouth. The dapper butler always finds a way to save the day, whether it's transforming a destroyed courtyard into a Japanese rock garden, teaching his young charge to dance the waltz, or saving him from gangsters. He is too good to be true; he is, as he says, "a devil of a butler." The book includes some graphic violence and occasional, mildly bad language ("bastard," "damned").

Volume 1 of an ongoing series

Tollison, Hal

Cartooning. Distributed by Black Rabbit Books 2011 64p il (Artist's library series) lib bdg $34.25

Grades: 9 10 11 12 **741.5**

1. Cartooning -- Technique

ISBN 978-1-936309-29-0

LC 2010009450

First published 1989

Focuses on how to master the materials, practical exercises, and easy techniques for drawing your own cartoons.

Tran, G. B. (Gia-Bao), 1976

Vietnamerica; a family's journey. written and illustrated by GB Tran. Villard Books 2010 279 p. chiefly col. ill. $30

Grades: 11 12 Adult **741.5**

1. Artists 2. Illustrators 3. Graphic novels 4. Vietnamese Americans -- Biography 5. Cartoonists 6. Vietnamese refugees -- Graphic novels 7. Vietnamese Americans -- Graphic novels 8. Vietnam War, 1961-1975 -- Graphic novels

ISBN 0345508726; 9780345508720

LC 2011283144

"GB Tran is a young Vietnamese American artist who grew up distant from (and largely indifferent to) his family's history. Born and raised in South Carolina as a son of immigrants, he knew that his parents had fled Vietnam during the fall of Saigon. But even as they struggled to adapt to life in America, they preferred to forget the past--and to focus on their children's future. It was only in his late twenties that GB began to learn their extraordinary story. When his last surviving grandparents die within months of each other, GB visits Vietnam for the first time and begins to learn the tragic history of his family, and of the homeland they left behind." (Publisher's note)

"The comic utilizes a dizzying barrage of effects to depict the characters' confusing experience: different lettering styles, realistic action set against full-page government posters, sound effects swirling from panel to panel, action-packed panoramas breaking apart as South Vietnam collapses." Pub Wkly

Unita, Yumi

Bunny drop vol. 1; [translation, Kaori Inoue; lettering, Alexis Eckerman]. Yen Press 2010 196p il pa $12.99

Grades: 8 9 10 11 12 Adult **741.5**

1. Manga 2. Josei manga 3. Graphic novels 4. Unmarried fathers -- Graphic novels

ISBN 978-0-7595-3122-2

First published 2006 in Japan

Thirty-year-old bachelor Daikichi is a salaryman, a junior executive, living on his own in Tokyo. When he goes home for his grandfather's funeral, he discovers that his grandfather had a younger lover who left him with a little girl, Rin (which makes her his aunt). The lover is nowhere to be found, and none of Daikichi's relatives will have anything to do with Rin, who won't talk to anyone but sticks close to Daikichi, who closely resembles his grandfather. When no one will step forward to take care of the six-year-old, Daikichi impulsively decides he will. Once he brings Rin home, the reality of his new situation finally dawns on him; Daikichi is now a single father and has to provide care for Rin. There's one scene with Rin and Daikichi together in their furo bath (a very typical Japanese family scene), and a few panels with Rin and Daikichi in their underwear. In one chapter, Daikichi has to deal with Rin's night time bedwetting, and Rin is shown changing her clothes.

"This sweet-natured manga shows the joys, frustrations, and quirks of family life; and while it is aimed at teens, it would also be more than welcome in the hands of adult readers." Booklist

Volume 1 of 9

Urasawa, Naoki

★ **Pluto**; by Naoki Urasawa & Osamu Tezuka; co-authored with Takashi Nagasaki; translation, Jared Cook & Frederick L. Schodt. Viz Media 2009 200 p. il $12.99

Grades: 9 10 11 12 Adult   **741.5**

1. Manga 2. Robots -- Fiction 3. Mystery graphic novels 4. Graphic novels 5. Robots -- Graphic novels 6. Astro Boy (Fictional character)

ISBN 1421519186; 9781421519180

Original Japanese edition, 2004

"In a distant future where sentient humanoid robots pass for human, someone or some thing is out to destroy the seven great robots of the world. Europol's top detective Gesicht is assigned to investigate these mysterious robot serial murders--the only catch is that he himself is one of the seven targets." (Publisher's note)

"In a tribute to Osamu Tezuka's (the 'God of Manga') classic Astro Boy, Urasawa takes one of Tezuka's story arcs and reimagines it as a noir detective story. Along the way, he brings in themes of racism, war, and what it means to be human." Booklist

Volume 1 of 8

Vaughan, Brian K.

Runaways, Vol. 1: Pride & Joy. Marvel Entertainment 2004 un il $7.99

Grades: 7 8 9 10 11 12   **741.5**

1. Graphic novels 2. Superhero graphic novels 3. Science fiction graphic novels 4. Runaways (Fictional characters)

ISBN 0-7851-1379-7

All young people believe their parents are evil ... but what if they really are? Meet Alex, Karolina, Gert, Chase, Molly and Nico - whose lives are about to take an unexpected turn. When these six young friends discover their parents are all secretly super-powered villains, the shocked teens find strength in one another. Together, they run away from home and straight into the adventure of their lives - vowing to turn the tables on their evil legacy. This is the first volume of an ongoing series.

Other Runaways volumes are:

2: Teenage Wasteland
3: The Good Die Young
4: True Believers
5: Escape to New York
6: Parental Guidance
7: Live Fast
8: Dead End Kids
9: Dead Wrong
10: Rock Zombies
11: Homeschooling

Watsuki, Nobuhiro

Rurouni Kenshin; Meiji swordsman romantic story [Vol. 1] story and art by Nobuhiro Watsuki; [English adaptation, Gerard Jones; translation, Kenichiro Yagi; touch-up art & lettering, Steve Dutro]. Vizbig ed; Viz 2008 576p il pa $17.99

Grades: 10 11 12   **741.5**

1. Manga 2. Graphic novels 3. Japan -- History --

1868-1945 -- Graphic novels
ISBN 978-1-4215-2073-5

This twenty-eight volume series was completed in late 2006

"The story of a young wandering samurai—who bears a reverse blade sword and strives not to kill after seeing and committing much bloodshed in the battles to bring the Emperor back to power in 1868—becomes much more than mere historical saga. Kenshin's relationships with new and old friends and enemies makes compelling storytelling." Voice Youth Advocates

Weiner, Stephen

101 outstanding graphic novels; Stephen Weiner; [edited by] Daniel J. Fingeroth. 3rd edition NBM Pub. 2015 80 p. (hardcover) $15.99

Grades: Adult Professional   **741.5**

1. Graphic novels

ISBN 1561639443; 9781561639441

    LC 2014958652

Previously called 101 Best Graphic Novels

"The popular primer on the best graphic novels, initially called The 101 Best Graphic Novels, is back in its third updated edition. Expert librarian Stephen Weiner--with the crowdsourcing help of professionals in the field, from artists to critics to leading comic store owners--has sifted through the bewildering thousands of graphic novels now available to come up with an outstanding, not-to-be-missed 101." (Publisher's note)

Weing, Drew

Set to sea. Fantagraphics 2010 un il $16.99

Grades: 8 9 10 11 12   **741.5**

1. Graphic novels 2. Poets -- Graphic novels 3. Sea stories -- Graphic novels 4. Seafaring life -- Graphic novels

ISBN 978-1-60699-368-2; 1-60699-368-2

The author "has produced a beautiful gem here, with minimal dialogue, one jolting battle scene, and each small page owned by a single panel filled with art whose figures have a comfortable roundness dredged up from the cartoon landscapes of our childhood unconscious, even as the intensely crosshatched shadings suggest the darkness that sometimes traces the edges of our lives. . . . [This book] is playful, atmospheric, dark, wistful, and wise." Booklist

Weinstein, Lauren

Girl stories; by Lauren R. Weinstein. Henry Holt 2006 237p il pa $16.95

Grades: 7 8 9 10 11 12 Adult   **741.5**

1. Graphic novels 2. Humorous graphic novels 3. Girls -- Graphic novels 4. Friendship -- Graphic novels

ISBN 978-0-8050-7863-3; 0-8050-7863-0

    LC 2005-46205

"Smart, creative Lauren sheds her geeky rep in high school in Weinstein's collection of comic strips, which have to intimacy of a teen's diary. The color-washed sketches have an edgy quality." Booklist

White, Tracy

How I made it to eighteen; a mostly true story. Roaring Brook 2010 151p il $16.99

Grades: 8 9 10 11 12 **741.5**
1. Graphic novels 2. Autobiographical graphic novels
3. Mental illness -- Graphic novels
ISBN 978-1-59643-454-7; 1-59643-454-6

"White's story of a 17-year-old girl's ordeals with depression, addiction, and body image issues is all the more powerful because of its basis in truth. The story follows Stacy Black, whose nervous breakdown leads to her decision to check into the Golden Meadows Hospital for mental health. . . . White's very simple hand-drawn, b&w artistic style enhances the personal touch of the work, creating the effect of an illustrated diary. While text-heavy, the narration is clear-eyed and affecting." Publ Wkly

Wilson, G. Willow

Cairo; written by G. Willow Wilson; art by M.K. Perker; lettered by Travis Lanham. DC Comics/Vertigo 2007 160p il $24.99
Grades: 9 10 11 12 Adult **741.5**
1. Graphic novels 2. Fantasy graphic novels 3. Adventure graphic novels
ISBN 978-1-4012-1140-0

A stolen hookah, a spiritual underworld, and a genie on the run change the lives of five strangers in Cairo. A drug runner, a down-on-his-luck journalist, an American expatriate, a troubled young student, and a female Israeli soldier end up all working together to help the jinn that Lebanese American Shaheed calls Shams to recover a special box from the evil magic-wielding drug lord Nar. The book includes some violence.

"Scripting and art complement each other well in an adventure with lots of appeal for readers willing to try a literary graphic novel and for those simply looking for the next good one." Booklist

Ms. Marvel; Volume 3 Crushed. G. Willow Wilson; illustrated by Takeshi Miyazawa and Elmo Bondoc. Marvel Enterprises 2015 112 p. chiefly color illustrations $15.99
Grades: 9 10 11 12 Adult **741.5**
1. Female superhero graphic novels 2. Valentine's Day -- Graphic novels 3. Superhero comic books, strips, etc. 4. Teenage girls -- Comic books, strips, etc. 5. Pakistani Americans -- Comic books, strips, etc.
ISBN 0785192271; 9780785192275

"Love is in the air in Jersey City as Valentine's Day arrives! Kamala Khan may not be allowed to go to the school dance...but Ms. Marvel is! Well sort of - by crashing it attempting to capture Asgard's most annoying trickster! Yup, it's a special Valentine's Day story featuring Marvel's favorite charlatan, Loki!" (Publisher's note)

"As always, Wilson's rollicking superhero action is sprinkled with both hilarity and meaningful cultural commentary, and Kamala herself is as appealing as ever." Booklist

★ **Ms.** Marvel 1; No Normal. writer, G. Willow Wilson; artist, Adrian Alphona. Marvel Enterprises 2014 120 p. chiefly color illustrations $15.99
Grades: 9 10 11 12 Adult **741.5**
1. Muslim women -- Fiction 2. Female superhero comic books, strips, etc.
ISBN 078519021X; 9780785190219

Hugo Award: Best Graphic Story (2015)

In this comic, written by G. Willow Wilson and illustrated by Adrian Alphona, "Kamala Khan is an ordinary girl from Jersey City--until she is suddenly empowered with extraordinary gifts. But who truly is the all-new Ms. Marvel? Teenager? Muslim? Inhuman? Find out as . . . Kamala discovers the dangers of her newfound powers [and] she unlocks a secret behind them as well." (Publisher's note)

"Wilson's story touches on many issues bubbling up around comics today--diversity, gender, culture, sexuality--though never with a heavy hand. The story is the focus here, and together with Alphona's playful and stylish artwork, Wilson offers a superhero comic full to bursting with heart and charm." Booklist

Volume 1 of an ongoing series

Ms. Marvel 2; Generation Why. by G. Willow Wilson; illustrated by Jacob Wyatt and Adrian Alphona. Marvel Enterprises 2015 136 p. chiefly color illustrations $15.99
Grades: 9 10 11 12 Adult **741.5**
1. Female superhero comic books, strips, etc. 2. Women superheroes 3. Muslim women -- Fiction 4. Teenage girls -- Fiction 5. Pakistani Americans -- Fiction
ISBN 0785190228; 9780785190226

"Who is the Inventor, and what does he want with the all-new Ms. Marvel and all her friends? Maybe Wolverine can help! Kamala may be fan-girling out when her favorite (okay maybe Top Five) super hero shows up, but that won't stop her from protecting her hometown." (Publisher's note)

"Alphona's distinctive panels make great use of exaggerated angles and distorted figures, and his line work, more intricate than most comic-book artists', packs each page with captivating, tongue-in-cheek detail." Booklist

Yakin, Boaz

Marathon; by Boaz Yakin; [illustrations by Joe Infurnari] First Second 2012 186 p. $16.99
Grades: 8 9 10 11 12 **741.5**
1. Adventure graphic novels 2. Greece -- History -- Graphic novels 3. Marathon, Battle of, 490 B.C. -- Graphic novels 4. Graphic novels 5. Greece -- History -- Persian Wars, 500-449 B.C. -- Fiction 6. Greece -- History -- Persian Wars, 500-449 B.C. -- Juvenile fiction
ISBN 9781596436800; 1596436808

LC 2011030472

This book is a graphical "account of the battle of Marathon" in which "Hippias, former king of Athens, is on his way back with a huge army of Persians to reclaim the throne and crush Athenian democracy. . . . Eucles, Athens' best runner, is charged to race the 153 miles to Sparta in hopes of finding an ally, . . . [returning] with the dismaying news that the Spartans will not be coming in time. He joins the savage fight and then runs 26 more miles over rugged mountains to Athens . . . warning of an impending surprise attack by sea." (Kirkus Reviews)

Yang, Gene Luen, 1973-

★ **American** born Chinese; by Gene Luen Yang; color by Lark Pien. First Second 2006 233p il pa $16.95

Grades: 7 8 9 10 11 12   **741.5**
1. Graphic novels 2. Chinese Americans -- Graphic novels
ISBN 1-59643-152-0; 978-1-59643-152-2
LC 2005-58105
Eisner Award: Best Graphic Album--New (2007)
National Book Award Finalist: Young People's Literature (2006)
Printz Award (2007)
"Jin Wang is the only Asian American boy in his new school; Danny is a young man deeply embarrassed by his visiting Chinese cousin, portrayed deliberately by the author as an ethnic cliché; and the Monkey King, a figure from Chinese lore, is desperate to be treated like a god. This . . . story relates how three characters overcome hurdles to find satisfaction within themselves." (Library Journal)

"True to its origin as a Web comic, this story's clear, concise lines and expert coloring are deceptively simple yet expressive. Even when Yang slips in an occasional Chinese ideogram or myth, the sentiments he's depicting need no translation. Yang accomplishes the remarkable feat of practicing what he preaches with this book: accept who you are and you'll already have reached out to others." Publ Wkly

Animal crackers; by Gene Luen Yang. Slave Labor Graphics 2010 un il pa $14.95
Grades: 7 8 9 10   **741.5**
1. Graphic novels 2. Humorous graphic novels 3. Science fiction graphic novels 4. Dreams -- Graphic novels 5. Bullies -- Graphic novels 6. Chinese Americans -- Graphic novels
ISBN 978-1-59362-183-4; 1-59362-183-3
"In the first story, a kinda-bully befriends a nerd whose hatred of his awful father has anthropomorphized into huge, murderous animal crackers. In . . . [Loyola Chin], a girl falls for a dream-spirit named Saint Danger, who plans to save humanity from an alien invasion by deciding who is unfit enough for survival. The two stories share a few tangential relationships, cast of characters, and a secret society of microbots who store data up people's nostrils. The power of Yang's work comes from his ability to juggle a lot of ideas while working on several different levels all at once." Booklist

★ **Boxers**; Gene Luen Yang; color by Lark Pien. First Second 2013 328 p. (pbk.) $18.99
Grades: 7 8 9 10 11 12 Adult   **741.5**
1. Historical fiction 2. China -- History -- Boxer Rebellion, 1899-1901 -- Graphic novels
ISBN 1596433590; 9781596433595
LC 2013947229
National Book Award for Young People's Literature: Finalist (2013)
Boston Globe-Horn Book Honor: Fiction (2014)
"Life in Little Bao's peaceful rural village is disrupted when . . . a priest and his phalanx of soldiers . . . arrive." They start "smashing the village god, appropriating property, and administering vicious beatings for no reason. Little Bao and his older brothers train in kung fu and swordplay." . . . Little Bao "becomes the leader of a peasant army, eventually marching to Beijing." (School Library Journal)

"China's Boxer Rebellion is the unlikely backdrop for this graphic treatment of young villagers on the opposite sides of history. Bao wants to drive out the white devils that poison his country with opium and Christianity. Four-Girl is an unwanted daughter who finds purpose in the missionary life. Their stories collide in a moment of grace that could only be penned by the Printz Award-winning author of 'American Born Chinese.'" LJ

★ The **eternal** smile; three stories. Gene Luen Yang and Derek Kirk Kim. First Second 2009 170p il pa $16.95
Grades: 9 10 11 12   **741.5**
1. Graphic novels 2. Fantasy graphic novels 3. Short stories -- Graphic novels
ISBN 978-1-59643-156-0; 1-59643-156-3
"Three tales evince very different realities and viewpoints. . . . Duncan, the hero of the first, is desperately seeking the approval of the Princess, though something in his kingdom doesn't seem quite right. In the next, an anthropomorphized, avaricious amphibian named Gran'pa Greenbax seeks to be the richest frog in the land, only to discover that his domain isn't quite what he thought it was. In the last, a painfully shy office worker distorts her own perception—and judgment—to create a reality more pleasing. . . . Begging for multiple readings, this exceptionally clever examination of fantasy and perception is one to be pored over and ruminated upon." Kirkus

Level up; Gene Luen Yang; [illustrated by Thien Pham]. First Second Books 2011 160p il $15.99
Grades: 10 11 12 Adult   **741.5**
1. Graphic novels 2. Angels -- Graphic novels 3. Bildungsromans -- Graphic novels 4. College students -- Graphic novels 5. Chinese Americans -- Graphic novels
ISBN 978-1-59643-235-2
LC 2010-36257
"Pham's watercolor artwork, mostly in muted pallet, is a perfect match for Yang's story. This gentle tale of loss and redemption, family responsibility, and dreams might not be to all teens' tastes (especially by the end), but the mix of fantasy and realism will please the right crowd." Voice Youth Advocates

Prime baby; [by] Gene Luen Yang, colors by Derek Kirk Kim. First Second Books 2010 56p il pa $6.99
Grades: 6 7 8 9 10 11 12   **741.5**
1. Graphic novels 2. Humorous graphic novels 3. Science fiction graphic novels 4. Siblings -- Graphic novels 5. Extraterrestrial beings -- Graphic novels
ISBN 978-1-59643-612-1
Thaddeus K. Fong always preferred to be the center of his family's attention, so the birth of his little sister Maddie has really bothered him. When she's eighteen months old, he notices something about the sounds she makes; her "gaga's" come out in prime numbers. Then his math teacher says that if aliens were ever to try to make contact with humans, it would be through prime numbers. Oh no, Maddie is an intergalactic conduit for invading aliens! Except no one believes Thaddeus. Until Maddie starts burping up strange things that turn out to be little ships for sluglike aliens. They're peaceful missionary types, but that doesn't stop Thaddeus from

making them seem hostile. When their parents finally believe Thaddeus, Maddie gets locked up in a research facility. Thaddeus should be ecstatic, his dumb little sister has been put away. So why is he feeling sad? This story was originally serialized in the New York Times magazine and has been printed to preserve the original comic strip format.

"Sf readers who value humor and humanity (not just slam-bang action), Christians, newcomers to graphic novels, and fans of Yang's simultaneously childlike and sophisticated ability to create and maintain tension should all be satisfied by his new book." Booklist

★ **Saints**; by Gene Luen Yang; color by Lark Pien. First Second 2013 170 p. (pbk.) $15.99
Grades: 7 8 9 10 11 12 Adult   741.5
1. Historical fiction 2. China -- History -- Boxer Rebellion, 1899-1901 -- Graphic novels
ISBN 1596436891; 9781596436893
LC 2013947228
Boston Globe-Horn Book Honor: Fiction (2014)
National Book Award for Young People's Literature: Finalist (2013)

This graphic novel, by Gene Luen Yang and Lark Pien, "follows a lonely girl . . . . Unwanted by her family, Four-Girl isn't even given a proper name until she converts to Catholicism and is baptized by the very same priest who bullics Little Bao's village. Four-Girl, now known as Vibiana, leaves home and finds fulfillment in service to the Church, while Little Bao roams the countryside committing acts of increasing violence as his army grows." (School Library Journal)

"Yang presents a 'diptych' of graphic novels set during China's Boxer Rebellion. Boxers follows Little Bao, who learns to harness the power of ancient gods to fight the spread of Christianity; Saints centers on Four-Girl, who sits squarely on the other side of the rebellion. Yang's characteristic infusions of magical realism, bursts of humor, and distinctively drawn characters make for a compelling read." (Horn Book)

The **Shadow** Hero; story by Gene Luen Yang; art by Sonny Liew; lettering by Janice Chiang. First Second 2014 176 p. chiefly color illustrations $17.99
Grades: 6 7 8 9 10   741.5
1. Superheroes -- Fiction 2. Comic books, strips, etc. 3. Chinese Americans -- Fiction
ISBN 1596436972; 9781596436978

This book, by Gene Luen Yang, is about "Green Turtle, a 1940s comic book hero. . . . The Green Turtle is cast as an unlikely 19-year-old young man, Hank, the son of Chinese immigrants who own a grocery store in 1940s America. When his mother is rescued by a superhero, the loving but overbearing woman decides that it's Hank's fate to become a hero himself, and she does everything in her power to push her son in that direction." (School Library Journal)

"Yang and Liew have crafted an origin story for the Green Turtle, a little-known . . . World War II-era comic superhero created by cartoonist Chu Hing in 1944. Much about the series remains a mystery, as Yang shares in an author's note, but according to rumors Hing wanted his star to be Chinese, and, not surprisingly for the era, his publishers balked at the idea. Now seventy years later, Yang and Liew vindi-cate the cartoonist by imagining the Green Turtle as 'perhaps . . . the first Asian American superhero.'" Horn Book

Yolen, Jane
Foiled; written by Jane Yolen; artwork by Mike Cavallaro. First Second 2010 160p il pa $15.99
Grades: 7 8 9 10   741.5
1. Graphic novels 2. Fantasy graphic novels 3. Fencing -- Graphic novels
ISBN 978-1-59643-279-6; 1-59643-279-9

"Besting competitors twice her age in tournaments, and keeping a strict routine of fencing practice, homework, and role-playing games, Aliera is a loner and likes it that way— until she becomes lab partners with the cutest boy in school. . . . Turns out her new ruby-handled foil is the key to his interest in her, and to the yet-unseen magical dimension she must keep in balance. . . . [Yolen] has created a strong, conflicted, and relatable girl hero. . . . Cavallaro's artwork suits Aliera's monochrome existence, but burst into life when she finally sees (in color!) the faerie beasties cheering her on." Booklist

Yoshizaki, Seimu
Kingyo used books, vol. 1; story & art by Seimu Yoshizaki; translation, Adrienne Weber, Mini Eda; editor, Eric Scarleman. Viz Media/Viz Signature 2010 191p il pa $12.99
Grades: 9 10 11 12 Adult   741.5
1. Manga 2. Graphic novels 3. Books and reading -- Graphic novels
ISBN 978-1-4215-3362-9

This manga collects several stories based in or connected to Kingyo Used Books, a used manga store in Tokyo. An art student finds inspiration in a manga series based on the life of the famous artist Hokusai; a silly gag manga helps an archer regain his focus in time for a match; a young Japanese man raised in the U.S. uses an old detective manga series from the 1950s to model his life; the manga store owner's son tries to get away from manga by living in Europe, where he discovers that comics are everywhere; a busy housewife rekindles the passion in her life when she rediscovers a shojo manga featuring a dreamy male protagonist. While there is no violence or bad language, all the main characters are adults.
Volume 1 of 4

Yumi, Kiiro
Library wars, vol. 1: love & war; story and art by Kiiro Yumi; original concept by Hiro Arikawa; [English translation & adaptation, Kinami Watabe] Shojo beat ed.; Viz Media/Shojo Beat 2010 166p il pa $9.99
Grades: 9 10 11 12 Adult   741.5
1. Manga 2. Shojo manga 3. Graphic novels 4. Censorship -- Graphic novels 5. Librarians -- Graphic novels
ISBN 978-1-4215-3488-6
First published 2008 in Japan

In Japan of the near future, the federal government passes the Media Betterment Act, and the Media Betterment Committee goes on book hunts to destroy any "unsuitable" book. The libraries strike back with the Library Defense

Force, a paramilitary organization dedicated to protecting the freedom to read. Iku Kasahara started to work for libraries and wants more than anything to join the Library Defense Force; she's physically very capable, but drill instructor Sergeant Dojo doesn't seem to like her very much and pushes her very hard. Iku must improve her library skills as well as her physical skills if she's to work effectively as a soldier librarian.

This book "delivers an appealing, determined female lead in the midst of an intriguing war on censorship being waged in bookstores and libraries." SLJ

Volume 1 of 14

741.6 Graphic design, illustration, commercial art

Bancroft, Tom

Creating characters with personality; introduction by Glen Keane. Watson-Guptill 2006 160p il pa $19.95

Grades: 9 10 11 12   **741.6**
    1. Graphic arts 2. Cartoons and caricatures
    ISBN 0-8230-2349-4; 978-0-8230-2349-3
                                                LC 2005-28462
This book "shows artists how to create a distinctive character, then place that character in context within a script, establish hierarchy, and maximize the impact of pose and expression." Publisher's note

741.672 Fashion drawing

Nothdruft, Dennis

How to draw vintage fashion; Celia Joicey, Dennis Nothdruft. Thames & Hudson 2014 96 p. illustrations (some color) (paper) $19.95

Grades: 9 10 11 12   **741.672**
    1. Drawing 2. Fashion 3. Fashion design 4. Vintage clothing
    ISBN 0500650373; 9780500650370
                                                LC 2014932778
This book, by Celia Joicey and Dennis Nothdruft, "encourages people to draw inspiration from fashion looks of the past to create their own unique designs. . . . The first section of the book focuses on interviews with designers, models, stylists, and fashion bloggers about iconic photographs and garments that have helped to shape their work. The next section features a hands-on guide to drawing a range of vintage fashion including 1960s and 1970s looks." (Publisher's note)

"In this guide, Joicey and Nothdruft, the head and curator, respectively, of London's Fashion and Textile Museum, offer younger audiences a fresh look at vintage fashion through drawing it. . . . This fun survey of 20th-century fashion is surprisingly informative, particularly for tweens and teenagers, whether or not they choose to follow the drawing lessons." LJ

742 Perspective in drawing

DuBosque, Doug

Draw 3-D; a step-by-step guide to perspective drawing. Peel Productions 1999 63p il pa $8.99

Grades: 6 7 8 9 10   **742**
    1. Drawing 2. Perspective
    ISBN 0-939217-14-7
                                                LC 98-42174
"Using easy-to-follow, step-by-step sketches, DuBosque introduces readers to the techniques of three-dimensional drawing. Beginning with such elementary concepts as depth, he progresses logically through shading, reflections, and multiple vanishing points. The supportive tone encourages novices to keep trying and not become discouraged." SLJ

Powell, William F.

Perspective; an essential guide featuring basic principles, advanced techniques, and practical applications. Distributed by Black Rabbit Books 2011 64p il (Artist's library series) lib bdg $34.25

Grades: 9 10 11 12   **742**
    1. Perspective 2. Drawing -- Technique
    ISBN 978-1-936309-28-3; 1-936309-28-9
                                                LC 2010009449
First published 1989

This book covers what readers "need to know to make objects in . . . drawings and paintings look three dimensional. [Readers will] practice the methods of measuring and dividing areas proportionately; then learn how we perceive depth and distance, and how to render it correctly on paper or canvas. . . . [This book also covers] the basics and beyond, covering concepts like foreshortening; cast shadows; reflections; and even one, two, and three-point perspective." Publisher's note

743 Drawing and drawings by subject

Butkus, Mike

How to draw zombies; discover the secrets to drawing, painting, and illustrating the undead. by Mike Butkus and Merrie Destefano. Walter Foster 2011 128p il map $48.95

Grades: 8 9 10 11 12   **743**
    1. Zombies 2. Monsters in art 3. Drawing -- Technique
    ISBN 978-1-936309-63-4; 1-936309-63-7
                                                LC 2010052983
"For young artists fascinated by the living dead, this sophisticated drawing book gives step-by-step instructions for creating a variety of unexpected characters. . . . Most of the drawings are done in pencil, but acrylic paints are also occasionally featured. An added bonus is the instructions for giving a final digital touch to the drawings on the computer. . . . Extra bits of zombie lore are added. Fans of the truly terrifying will appreciate the fact that the featured pictures attain a high level of creepiness. . . . Those looking for a zombie drawing book with added bite will find hours of fun with this one." Booklist

Eggleton, Bob

Dragons' domain; the ultimate dragon painting workshop. foreword by John A. Davis. Impact 2010 127p il pa $22.99

Grades: 7 8 9 10 **743**

1. Drawing 2. Dragons in art

ISBN 978-1-60061-457-6; 1-60061-457-4

"Here is a book for those dragon lovers who are bored with beginner drawing books. Eggleton starts with a thorough discussion of materials and some basic drawing and painting techniques. Then he spends an entire page on each of several key dragon body parts, such as feet, wings, frills, and tails. After some insightful discussion of finding inspiration and references from nature and fantasy pop culture, the artist demonstrates how to create a handful of different types of dragons. . . . The book is full of Eggleton's own work in progressive stages of completion, photographed in color and attractively placed on backgrounds with fantasy-themed borders." SLJ

Graves, Douglas R.

★ **Drawing** portraits. Watson-Guptill 1974 159p il hardcover o.p. pa $16.95

Grades: 9 10 11 12 **743**

1. Drawing 2. Artistic anatomy

ISBN 0-8230-1431-2

The author discusses "the art and craft of portraiture from beginning to end—seeing and drawing the anatomy of the head and hands, posing and lighting the sitter, conveying the weight, texture, and drape of the sitter's clothing, composing the portrait (individual as well as group), and dealing with such auxiliary problems as the relationship between the artist and his sitter." Introduction

Includes bibliographical references

743.4 Drawing human figures

Hart, Christopher

★ **Human** anatomy made amazingly easy. Watson-Guptill 2000 114p il pa $19.95

Grades: 11 12 Adult **743.4**

1. Figure drawing 2. Artistic anatomy

ISBN 0-8230-2497-0

LC 00-43514

In this work for the beginning artist "Hart simplifies the process in an accessible manual that concentrates on line and forgoes the complexity of color." Libr J

745.5 Handicrafts

Dobson, Jolie

The **duct** tape book; 25 Projects to Make With Duct Tape. Firefly Books Ltd 2012 144 p. (paperback) $14.95

Grades: 7 8 9 10 11 12 **745.5**

1. Duct tape 2. Handicraft

ISBN 1770850988; 9781770850989

This book by Jolie Dobson on crafting with duct tape "contains 25 . . . projects" with "instructions and color pho-

tographs." The projects include a "bike pannier . . . vest . . . purse . . . piggy bank . . . wallet . . . bow ties . . . picture frames . . . knapsack . . . skirt and chaps . . . [and] tissue box." (Publisher's note)

745.54 Papers

Perdana, Julius

Build your own paper robots; 100s of mecha model designs on CD to print out and assemble. [by] Julius Perdana and Josh Buczynski; with Axel Bernal . . . [et al.] St. Martin's Griffin 2009 96p il $18.95

Grades: 8 9 10 11 12 Adult **745.54**

1. Paper crafts 2. Robots -- Models

ISBN 978-0-312-57370-6

LC 2009-517888

"Cleverly designed miniature robots, some resembling figures from Star Wars, are ready be cut out and glued together following the exploded diagrams. Color templates can be printed from the enclosed CD or color-copied from the book. Figures include high-tech humanoids, dogs, and war machines." Libr J

Reeder, Dan

Papier-mache monsters; turn trinkets and trash into magnificent monstrosities. photographs by Julie, Jeff and Dan Reeder. Gibbs Smith 2009 144p il pa $16.99

Grades: 9 10 11 12 Adult **745.54**

1. Paper crafts 2. Monsters in art

ISBN 978-1-4236-0555-3; 1-4236-0555-1

LC 2009-3827

"For lovers of the truly grotesque, Reeder . . . provides detailed photo instructions for large figures constructed of clothes hangers, newspaper, and glue. Cloth skin, teeth, and slathered-on paint finish them off. The toothy dragons are particularly effective." Libr J

Sowell, Sharyn

★ **Paper** cutting techniques for scrapbooks & cards. Sterling Pub. 2005 128p il hardcover o.p. pa $12.95

Grades: 11 12 Adult **745.54**

1. Scrapbooks 2. Paper crafts 3. Greeting cards

ISBN 1-4027-1921-3; 1-4027-5387-X pa

LC 2005-15043

"Both experienced and novice paper users will learn something from this beautifully illustrated book, which is pretty enough to be an art book in and of itself." Booklist

745.58 Beads, found and other objects

BeadStyle magazine

Discover beading; compiled by Lesley Weiss. Kalmbach Books 2006 96p il pa $19.95

Grades: 9 10 11 12 Adult **745.58**
1. Beads 2. Jewelry 3. Beadwork
ISBN 0-8711-6239-3

LC 2007-273183

"This visually pleasing beading book for crafters is a smart purchase. . . . This book will appeal to crafting teens and adults and would be a nice addition to any size public library." Voice Youth Advocates

745.592 Toys, models, miniatures, related objects

Hrachovec, Anna
Super-scary mochimochi; 20+ cute & creepy creatures to knit. Anna Hrachovec; photography by Brandi Simons. Potter Craft 2012 144 p. (pbk.: alk. paper) $19.99
Grades: 9 10 11 12 **745.592**
1. Knitting 2. Soft toy making 3. Needlework -- Patterns 4. Amigurumi -- Patterns
ISBN 0307965767; 9780307965769

LC 2011046773

This book, by Anna Hrachovec, offers patterns for knitting stuffed Amigurumi monsters. "What creatures lurk in the darkest shadows of Mochimochi Land? Only the most adorable assortment of knitted monsters, such as tiny vampire brats, a teenage werewolf, and a miniature gang of killer bees. . . . After all, nothing is scarier than a clever knitter armed with yarn, needles, and a wild imagination." (Publisher's note)

745.594 Decorative objects

Fox, Danielle
Simply modern jewelry; designs from the editor of Stringing magazine. Interweave Press 2008 120p il pa $21.95
Grades: 9 10 11 12 Adult **745.594**
1. Jewelry 2. Beadwork
ISBN 978-1-59668-048-7

LC 2007-27338

"The first two dozen pages provide a crash course in identifying the different components of jewelry and the terms that apply to them as well as the tools and techniques used in the projects shown. . . . Each project starts with a chart of materials, tools, and techniques necessary to complete the piece, the finished size, and a simplicity scale. . . . The projects are chic and satisfying, and range from a simple tied-leather-thong necklace to complicated chandelier earrings. For the most part they could be made in a day and worn that evening. A great resource." SLJ

745.6 Calligraphy, heraldic design, illumination

Marsh, Don
Calligraphy. North Light Bks. 1996 128p (First steps series) $18.99

Grades: 11 12 Adult **745.6**
1. Calligraphy
ISBN 0-89134-666-X

LC 96-4014

This guide to calligraphy is aimed at the beginner and includes various projects such as greeting cards and invitations
"Excellent for secondary school age and above." Libr J
Includes bibliographical references

745.7 Decorative coloring

Fisher, Diana
The **art** of rock painting. Distributed by Black Rabbit Books 2011 64p il (Artist's library series) lib bdg $34.25
Grades: 9 10 11 12 **745.7**
1. Rocks 2. Acrylic painting
ISBN 978-1-936309-31-3; 1-936309-31-9

LC 2010005936

First published 2003
This book offers tips and techniques for painting rocks.

746 Textile arts

Searle, Teresa
Felt jewelry; 25 pieces to make using a variety of simple felting techniques. St. Martin's Griffin 2008 128p il pa $21.95
Grades: 11 12 Adult **746**
1. Fabrics 2. Jewelry 3. Handicraft
ISBN 978-0-312-38356-5; 0-312-38356-8

LC 2008-40066

"The book is filled with detailed, eye-catching color photographs that will aid beginners and inspire the more accomplished felters." SLJ

746.43 Knitting, crocheting, tatting

Eckman, Edie
The **crochet** answer book; solutions to every problem you'll ever face, answers to every question you'll ever ask. Edie Eckman. 2nd edition Storey Publishing 2015 408 p. illustrations $14.95
Grades: 11 12 Adult **746.43**
1. Crocheting
ISBN 1612124062; 9781612124063

LC 2014033696

In this book, by Edie Eckman, "you'll find helpful answers to . . . crochet questions, including . . . questions on broomstick lace, linked stitches, crochet cables, and much more. You'll also find illustrations for left-handed crocheters; up-to-the-minute information on new internet resources; and an expanded section on unusual techniques like Tunisian crochet." (Publisher's note)
Eckman "presents a definitively revised guide that reflects the latest trends. In her inimitable question-and-answer style, she features the most recently unearthed techniques (do remember: what's old is new again in this and

other needlework books), like Tunisian crochet and Bruges and Clones laces. There are brief illustrations, now, for both left- and right-handed stitchers. And new yarns and new tools (or adaptive ones) are explored with helpful tips and caveats." Booklist

Haden, Christen

Creepy cute crochet; zombies, ninjas, robots, and more! Quirk Books 2008 96p il $14.95

Grades: 7 8 9 10 11 12 Adult **746.43**

1. Toys 2. Crocheting

ISBN 978-1-5947-4232-3; 1-5947-4232-4

"Japanese-inspired amigurumi (literal translation: 'knitted stuffed toy') is one of the latest crafting crazes, and Haden's first book puts a unique spin on amigurumi by focusing on the creepy side of crocheted creatures. . . . There are . . . . crocheted ninjas, a Grim Reaper, Day of the Dead figures, and vampires, all lovingly rendered. Although some beginner information is provided, a basic knowledge of crochet stitches and techniques is assumed." Libr J

Keen, Sarah

Knitted wild animals; 15 adorable, easy-to-knit toys. Watson-Guptill 2010 127p il pa $19.99

Grades: 9 10 11 12 Adult **746.43**

1. Toys 2. Knitting

ISBN 978-0-82303-318-8

First published 2009 in the United Kingdom

"Knitted toys are popular, and Keen's creative designs for wild animals will please children and adults alike. The patterns are easy to follow and range from simple to complex, and the finished products are adorable." Libr J

Obaachan, Annie

Amigurumi animals; 15 patterns and dozens of techniques for creating cute crochet creatures. St. Martin's Griffin 2008 128p il pa $21.95

Grades: 9 10 11 12 Adult **746.43**

1. Toys 2. Knitting 3. Crocheting

ISBN 978-0-312-37820-2; 0-312-37820-3

LC 2008-299792

Introduces amigurumi, the Japanese art of crocheting or knitting small stuffed animals, and provides tips on how to design one using patterns and step-by-step instructions for fifteen projects.

"This book would be useful not only for beginners, but also for those who could use technique refreshers or who need to be inspired by the great variety of photographs of completed projects." SLJ

Okey, Shannon

★ **Knitgrrl**; learn to knit with 15 fun and funky projects. photography by Shannon Fagan, Christine Okey, and Tamas Jakab; illustrations by Kathleen Jacques. Watson-Guptill 2005 96p il pa $9.95

Grades: 7 8 9 10 **746.43**

1. Knitting

ISBN 0-8230-2618-3

This offers instructions for basic knitting techniques and for such projects as scarves, hats, leg warmers, mittens, and bags.

"A lively, teen-friendly book with all the basics, plenty of additional information, and appealing color photos and illustrations." SLJ

Radcliffe, Margaret

The **knitting** answer book; solutions to every problem you'll ever face; answers to every question you'll ever ask. by Margaret Radcliffe. 2nd edition Storey Publishing 2015 439 p. illustrations pbk $14.95

Grades: 9 10 11 12 Adult **746.43**

1. Knitting 2. Knitting -- Miscellanea

ISBN 9781612124056; 9781612124049; 1612124046

LC 2014033661

"Margaret Radcliffe's classic Q&A guide is better than ever! This thoroughly revised and updated new edition gives expert answers to scores of new questions that knitters have asked since the first edition was published. You'll find more than a dozen new cast ons and bind offs; new techniques for beading and knitting backwards; tips for making smooth stripes when knitting in the round and for measuring gauge on tricky fabrics, such as ribbing and lace; fresh information on interpreting patterns and adjusting patterns to fit; and much more." (Publisher's note)

Includes bibliographical references (pages 415-428) and index

Taylor, Kathleen

Knit one, felt too; discover the magic of knitted felt with 25 easy patterns. Storey Books 2003 176p il pa $18.95

Grades: 11 12 Adult **746.43**

1. Knitting

ISBN 1-58017-497-3

LC 2003-50558

"If you knit a loose, oversize garment and then shrink it on purpose, you have turned a wool object into felt . . . Taylor offers 25 projects, first showing how to knit the item, then how to get the desired look. The projects are quite inventive, from toddler slippers shaped like bunnies to wine bags decorated with grapes. Taylor's enthusiasm combined with the straightforward and eye-catching color photos will entice knitters." Booklist

746.46 Patchwork and quilting

Beyer, Jinny

Quiltmaking by hand; simple stitches, exquisite quilts. Breckling Press 2003 262p il pa $29.95

Grades: 11 12 Adult **746.46**

1. Quilting

ISBN 0-9721218-2-X

LC 2003-15827

In this guide to the "traditional methods of quilt assembly—all by hand, the author begins with threading the needle and progresses to perfecting hand quilting stitches." Libr J

Includes bibliographical references

746.9   Other textile products

Faerm, Steven

Fashion: design course. Barron's 2010 144p il pa $23.99

Grades: 11 12 Adult   **746.9**
1. Fashion design
ISBN 978-0-7641-4423-3

LC 2009-940543

The author "takes readers through a thorough exploration of the fashion industry, from history to inspiration to the design process to landing a job. There are also 14 practical assignments to help budding designers learn more about the industry. Teens exploring careers in fashion will enjoy the practical advice from industry insiders, and fashion-mad readers of all ages will appreciate the information about how fashion design works." Libr J

Iverson, Annemarie

In fashion; from runway to retail, everything you need to know to break into the fashion industry. Clarkson Potter 2010 324p il pa $16.99

Grades: 9 10 11 12   **746.9**
1. Clothing industry 2. Fashion -- Vocational guidance
ISBN 978-0-307-46383-8; 0-307-46383-4

LC 2009-48121

The author "has written a comprehensive guide for budding fashionistas desiring a career in the competitive fashion world. . . . Chapters like 'Fashionista Boot Camp' and 'Fashionista Survival Guide' provide straight talk and professional direction about educational choices, portfolios, résumés, what to wear, internships, character, ethics, and more. . . . This smart, savvy fashion career guide is packed with practical knowledge and expert guidance from an industry insider." Libr J

Stalder, Erika

Fashion 101; a crash course in clothing. illustrations by Ariel Krietzman. Zest Books 2008 128p il pa $17.95

Grades: 9 10 11 12   **746.9**
1. Fashion 2. Clothing and dress
ISBN 978-0-9790173-4-6; 0-9790173-4-3

LC 2007-939159

This book is "divided into apparel categories, from underwear to overcoats, the chapters introduce archetypal styles (e.g., sailor pants and skinny jeans) with clear line drawings, background history about each style ('Who Made It'), the cultural icons who popularized it ('Who Made It Hot'), and tips for making outfits ('How to Rock It'). . . . Any teen interested in clothing will devour this compendium of quick historical facts and practical advice." Booklist

The **teen vogue** handbook; an insider's guide to careers in fashion. Razorbill 2009 276p il pa $24.95

Grades: 7 8 9 10 11 12   **746.9**
1. Clothing industry 2. Fashion -- Vocational guidance
ISBN 978-1-59514-261-0; 1-59514-261-4

LC 2009-10626

"Any teen interested in a career in fashion should read this handbook. It is filled with advice from top designers, photographers, models, stylists, makeup artists, writers, and their interns and assistants. They share how they got started and give tips to those interested in a fashion career. This book looks and reads like a magazine on glossy pages filled with photographs and sidebars, but the interviews give pertinent information on every aspect of work in fashion." Voice Youth Advocates

Includes bibliographical references

Vendittelli, Marie

The **Fashion** Book; written by Marie Vendittelli; illustrated by Sophie Griotto; translated by Annie Barton; edited by Jen Wainwright; concept and design by Laëtitia Robaeys; cover design by Barbara Ward. Trafalgar Square Books 2013 128 p. $15.99

Grades: 6 7 8 9 10   **746.9**
1. Fashion design 2. Fashion designers
ISBN 1780551134; 9781780551135

This book is a guide to becoming a confident fashion designer. Marie Vendittelli and Sophie Griotto offer "numerous ideas and tips for drawing, working with color and fabric, designing with the seasons in mind, and accessorizing. . . . There are brief profiles of famed designers, including Coco Chanel, Yves St. Laurent, and Alexander McQueen." (Publishers Weekly)

746.92   Costume

Angus, Emily

The **fashion** encyclopedia; a visual resource for terms, techniques, and styles. Emily Angus, Macushla Baudis, Philippa Woodcock. Barron's 2015 352 p. ill. (chiefly col.) $29.99

Grades: 9 10 11 12 Adult   **746.92**
1. Clothing and dress 2. Fashion -- Encyclopedias
ISBN 9780764167676; 0764167677

"As complete as any 352-page reference could hope to be, The Fashion Encyclopedia admirably covers fabrics, fashion movements, techniques, terms, styles, and more, with full-color photos on nearly every page. Divided into four major sections ('Fashion Terminology'; 'Styles and Components of Dress';'Design, Tailoring, and Stitching'; and 'Textiles and Embellishments'), with subsections for each, the book follows a logical path of exploration for the fashion novice, with plenty of interest for those more steeped in couture." (Booklist)

Black, Alexandra

The **fashion** book; author, Alexandra Black. DK Publishing 2014 160 p. ill. (chiefly col.)

Grades: 6 7 8 9 10 11 12   **746.92**
1. Fashion 2. Fashion -- History
ISBN 1465422846; 9781465422842

"From corsets and camis to tailoring and textiles, 'The Fashion Book' is a sassy style guide for teenage girls who want to discover the stories behind their favorite looks, find their own style, and learn what makes the fashion world tick. Packed with gorgeous images, this illustrated book for young adults takes a unique look at fashion. It reveals how modern-day looks, from catwalk to high-street fashions, draw on the styles of the past from the Middle Ages to the Renaissance and from the rebel attire of the 50s to the sport-inspired looks of the 80s." (Publisher's note)

751 Techniques, procedures, apparatus, equipment, materials, forms

Ganz, Nicholas

★ **Graffiti** world; street art from five continents. edited by Tristan Manco. Updated ed.; Abrams 2009 391p il $35

Grades: 11 12 Adult **751**
1. Graffiti 2. Street art 3. Mural painting and decoration
ISBN 978-0-8109-8049-5

LC 2009-922509

First published 2004

Ganz's survey of graffiti art includes "upward of 2,000 full-color photographs. . . . An ephemeral, often despised, yet irrefutably powerful mode of expression, graffiti has always been political, and although many of the street artists Ganz succinctly profiles have moved away from illegal spray painting, they have not compromised the inherent subversiveness of their work. . . . Ganz's global array captures the power and synergy of this vibrant alternative art world in which artists form crews and collectiveness to ensure that their art is seen." Booklist [review of 2004 edition]

Includes bibliographical references

Sanmiguel, David

Complete guide to materials and techniques for drawing and painting; [text, David Sanmiguel; translation, Michael Brunelle and Beatriz Cortabarria] English language ed.; Barrons Educational Series 2008 239p il $26.99

Grades: 9 10 11 12 Adult **751**
1. Artists' materials 2. Drawing -- Technique 3. Painting -- Technique
ISBN 978-0-7641-6111-7; 0-7641-6111-3

LC 2007-931258

Original Spanish edition, 2007

"From applicators like pencils and spatulas to auxiliary materials such as fillers and cleaners . . . [this book] covers a variety of artistic media including paint, paper, canvas, and cardboard. . . . The second half of the book describes drawing and painting techniques. . . . Basic enough for a beginning art student and complete enough to hold the interest of practicing artists, this book is a good choice for any collection." Voice Youth Advocates

751.4 Techniques and procedures

All about techniques in acrylics; an indispensable manual for artists. {author, Parramón's Editorial Team} Barron's 2004 143p il (All about techniques) $26.95

Grades: 11 12 Adult **751.4**
1. Acrylic painting -- Technique
ISBN 0-7641-5710-8

LC 2003-68843

Originally published in Spain

"The book is a delight for anyone interested in acrylics." Voice Youth Advocates

751.42 Use of water-soluble mediums

Craig, Diana

The **new** encyclopedia of watercolor techniques; [by] Diana Craig & Hazel Harrison. Running Press 2010 144p il pa $19.95

Grades: 9 10 11 12 **751.42**
1. Watercolor painting -- Technique
ISBN 978-0-7624-4050-4; 0-7624-4050-3

LC 2009943398

First published 1990 with title: The encyclopedia of watercolor techniques

The authors offer lessons on how to use water-based media.

Crawshaw, Alwyn

Watercolour for the absolute beginner; [by] Alwyn Crawshaw, Sharon Finmark & Trevor Waugh. Collins 2006 224p il pa $16.95

Grades: 9 10 11 12 Adult **751.42**
1. Watercolor painting -- Technique
ISBN 978-0-00-723606-0; 0-00-723606-9

LC 2008-360702

Chapter one first published 2000 with title: You can paint watercolour. Chapter two first published 2002 with title: You can paint people in watercolour. Chapter three first published 2002 with title: You can paint animals in watercolour. All three chapters first published in one volume 2004

"This is a compilation of three books by three fine British artists. . . . Condensed into a single volume, the three make a good, inexpensive manual for beginners. There are basic techniques for brushstrokes, color mixing, and design, and instruction on tone, texture, pattern, and movement." Libr J

Hammond, Lee

Paint realistic animals in acrylic with Lee Hammond. North Light Books 2007 127p il pa $24.99

Grades: 9 10 11 12 **751.42**
1. Animals in art 2. Acrylic painting -- Technique
ISBN 1-58180-912-3; 978-1-58180-912-1

LC 2006-36386

"An appealing array of wild and domesticated animals are presented as acrylic painting projects. The basics are covered as well as the usefulness of grids for accuracy. Sidebars list exactly which colors are to be used, and the author gives special attention to tricky elements such as noses and paws." SLJ

Swenson, Brenda

Steps to success in watercolor. Distributed by Black Rabbit Books 2011 64p il (Artist's library series) $34.25

Grades: 9 10 11 12   **751.42**
1. Watercolor painting -- Technique
ISBN 978-1-936309-27-6

LC 2010005939

First published 2007

"In this book, watercolor artist Brenda Swenson explores practical ways to plan your painting to avoid common mistakes. . . . [It covers] art theory and techniques, including composition, perspective, [and] color mixing." Publisher's note

Wang, Lucy

The **art** of Chinese brush painting. Distributed by Black Rabbit Books 2011 64p il (Artist's library series) lib bdg $34.25

Grades: 9 10 11 12   **751.42**
1. Ink painting
ISBN 978-1-9363093-0-6; 1-9363093-0-0

LC 2010005938

First published 2004

"Lucy Wang covers the fundamentals of this medium, such as handling the brush and creating elegant strokes, as well as information on the history of the art form. Then she guides [the reader] step by step through a series of painting lessons, from flowers and animals to a landscape and a traditional figure." Publisher's note

751.45   Oil painting

Willenbrink, Mark

Oil painting for the absolute beginner; a clear & easy guide to successful oil painting. by Mark and Mary Willenbrink. North Light Books 2010 127p il pa $24.99

Grades: 10 11 12 Adult   **751.45**
1. Painting -- Technique
ISBN 978-1-60061-784-3

LC 2010-5056

"Unlike less successful art books for beginners, this one starts simply and takes the rank amateur to a satisfying level of accomplishment. . . . The accompanying DVD offers useful demonstrations of two complete paintings." Libr J

751.7   Specific forms

Felisbret, Eric

Graffiti New York; Eric Felisbret DEAL CIA; contributions by Luke Felisbret SPAR ONE; foreword by James Prigoff. Abrams 2009 339 p. ill. (chiefly col.)

Grades: 9 10 11 12 Adult   **751.7**
1. Street art 2. Artists -- United States 3. Mural painting and decoration 4. Graffiti -- New York (N.Y.) -- History 5. Graffiti -- New York (State) -- New York 6. Street art -- New York (State) -- New York 7. Mural painting and decoration, American -- New York (State) -- New York
ISBN 0810951460; 9780810951464

LC 2009011736

This book explores the history and influence of New York City as a "mecca of graffiti culture. . . . This is the city where it all began, yet few know the back story. 'Graffiti New York' fills that gap, detailing the concepts, aesthetics, ideals, and social structures that have served as a cultural blueprint for graffiti movements across the world. The book features approximately 1,000 images, complemented by texts by the authors and relevant players in the movement, as well as descriptive graphics and sidebars. [The book describes] . . . the birth of simple signature tags to today's vibrant murals, and covering the ups and downs of the movement, the culture's value system, its social framework, the various forms of graffiti, and significant artists and crews." (Publisher's Note)

Ganz, Nicholas

Graffiti women; street art from five continents. foreword by Swoon; introduction by Nancy Macdonald. Abrams 2006 223p il $29.95

Grades: 9 10 11 12 Adult   **751.7**
1. Street art 2. Women artists 3. Mural painting and decoration
ISBN 0-8109-5747-7; 978-0-8109-5747-3

LC 2006-15287

"More than 1,000 images from prominent female graffiti and street artists show women challenging stereotypes and succeeding in the male-dominated field of tagging." Booklist
Includes bibliographical references

753   Iconography

★ **How** to read a painting; lessons from the old masters. [edited by] Patrick de Rynck. H.N. Abrams 2004 383p il $35

Grades: 11 12 Adult   **753**
1. Art appreciation 2. Symbolism in art
ISBN 0-8109-5576-8

LC 2004-9511

The editor "presents 150 paintings and frescoes that have attained the status of masterpieces. Each work is displayed on a full-color two-page spread that includes detailed closeups and a meticulous decoding of the painting's subject, symbols, and intent. This is a truly felicitous approach, and the selections are supreme." Booklist
Includes bibliographical references

759   History, geographic treatment, biography

Hartt, Frederick

★ **Michelangelo** Buonarroti. H.N. Abrams 2004 126p il (Masters of art) pa $19.95

Grades: 11 12 Adult **759**
1. Artists 2. Painters 3. Sculptors 4. Architects
ISBN 0-8109-9144-6

LC 2003-22522

Concise edition of the author's Michelangelo, originally published 1964

The forty colorplates in this book include broad views and close details of Michelangelo's frescoes in the Sistine Chapel and of his other paintings.

Includes bibliographical references

Lucie-Smith, Edward

Toulouse-Lautrec; rev and enl ed; Phaidon Press 1983 31p il hardcover o.p. pa $9.95
Grades: 9 10 11 12 **759**
1. Artists 2. Painters 3. Lithographers
ISBN 1-7148-2761-4
First published 1977

"The introductory overview of the artist's life is followed by 48 chronologically arranged color plates and concise, paragraph-length analyses of individual works. . . . An intelligently written and well-illustrated survey." Choice

Marani, Pietro C.

★ **Leonardo** da Vinci--the complete paintings; appendices edited by Pietro C. Marani and Edoardo Villata. Abrams 2000 384p il $85
Grades: 11 12 Adult **759**
1. Artists 2. Painters 3. Scientists 4. Writers on science
ISBN 0-8109-3581-3

LC 00-27556

Original Italian edition, 1999

This guide covers Leonardo's 31 paintings "intensively, recording possible precedents for design and technique in the work of other artists, calling attention to significant details, offering preparatory drawings and cartoons for comparison with the finished, which is not to say completed, works, and presenting X rays to elucidate the gestation of the Mona Lisa and other paintings Leonardo spent years striving to perfect. Such scrupulous attention to Leonardo's total creative process boosts the number of illustrations, mostly colorplates, to 295." Booklist

Includes bibliographical references

Morris, Catherine

The **essential** Claude Monet. Harry N. Abrams 1999 112p il (Essential series) $12.95
Grades: 9 10 11 12 **759**
1. Artists 2. Painters
ISBN 0-8109-5802-3; 978-0-8109-5802-9

This book examines the work of Impressionist painter Claude Monet.

Wasserman, Jack

Leonardo da Vinci; Concise, pbk. ed.; Harry N. Abrams 2003 126p il (Masters of art) pa $21.95
Grades: 11 12 Adult **759**
1. Artists 2. Painters 3. Scientists 4. Writers on science
ISBN 978-0-8109-9130-9; 0-8109-9130-6

LC 2003013703

First published 1984

This is a collection of 40 colorplates of Leonardo da Vinci's works, including Last Supper and Mona Lisa.

759.03 Art history 1400-1599

D'Elia, Una Roman

Painting in the Renaissance; [by] Una D'Elia. Crabtree Pub. Co. 2009 32p il pa $8.95; lib bdg $26.60
Grades: 6 7 8 9 **759.03**
1. Art -- 15th and 16th centuries
ISBN 978-0-7787-4612-6; 978-0-7787-4592-1

LC 2008-52600

"–Ideal introductions to concepts, people, and events of the Renaissance... succinct and thorough." SLJ

759.05 Art history 1800-1899

Bingham, Jane

Impressionism. Heinemann Library 2008 48p il (Art on the wall) lib bdg $32.86
Grades: 5 6 7 8 9 10 **759.05**
1. French painting 2. Impressionism (Art)
ISBN 978-1-4329-1371-7; 1-4329-1371-9

LC 2008020468

This title succeeds "in presenting a bird's-eye view of [Impressionism] without oversimplification. Information on individual artists is included in the broader context of the movement. Visually exciting, with plenty of color, [the layout is] hip and should appeal to the target audience." SLJ

Includes glossary and bibliographical references

Post-Impressionism. Heinemann Library 2009 48p il (Art on the wall) lib bdg $32.86
Grades: 5 6 7 8 9 10 **759.05**
1. French painting 2. Postimpressionism (Art)
ISBN 978-1-4329-1369-4; 1-4329-1369-7

LC 2008020464

This book "discusses how Post-Impresssionism developed, examines the distinctive styles of individual Post-Impressionist artists, and looks at how the Post-Impressionists used colour, shape, and composition." Publisher's note

Includes glossary and bibliographical references

759.13 Art -- United States

Fallon, Michael

How to analyze the works of Georgia O'Keeffe. ABDO Pub. Co. 2011 112p il (Essential critiques) $34.22
Grades: 9 10 11 12 **759.13**
1. Artists 2. Painters 3. Art criticism 4. Art appreciation
ISBN 978-1-61613-535-5

LC 2010-15883

This book looks at the works of Georgia O'Keeffe "through the lenses of prevalent schools of criticism. The first chapters introduce the concept of critical theory, its purpose, and how to develop and support a thesis statement. In subsequent chapters, an overview of each work is followed by a critique using a particular theory. . . . Georgia O'Keeffe's Evening Star No. V, The Black Iris, Red Hills with White Shell, and Pelvis Series Red with Yellow are addressed." SLJ

Includes bibliographical references

759.9 Other geographic areas

Schaffner, Ingrid

★ The **essential** Vincent van Gogh. Harry N. Abrams 1998 112p il (Essential series) $12.95

Grades: 9 10 11 12   **759.9**

1. Artists 2. Painters

ISBN 0-8109-5813-9; 978-0-8109-5813-5

LC 98-71931

This book examines the art of disturbed Dutch painter Vincent Van Gogh.

Sweet, Christopher

The **essential** Johannes Vermeer. Harry N. Abrams 1999 112p il (Essential series) $12.95

Grades: 9 10 11 12   **759.9**

1. Artists 2. Painters

ISBN 0-8109-5801-5; 978-0-8109-5801-2

This book examines the art of great Dutch painter Jan Vermeer.

769.5 Forms of prints

Friedberg, Arthur

Paper money of the United States; a complete illustrated guide with valuations: the standard reference work on paper money. by Arthur L. and Ira S. Friedberg; based on the original work by Robert Friedberg. Coin and Currency Institute 2010 304p il $49.50

Grades: 9 10 11 12   **769.5**

1. Paper money 2. Reference books

ISBN 978-0-87184-519-1

First published 1953. Periodically revised

A guide to paper money of the United States from 1861 to the present. Contains descriptions, valuations, and illustrations of notes, fractional currency, and certificates.

770 Photography, computer art, cinematography, videography

Goldberg, Vicki

The **power** of photography; how photographs changed our lives. Abbeville Press 1991 279p hardcover o.p. pa $35

Grades: 11 12 Adult   **770**

1. Photography

ISBN 1-55859-467-1

LC 91-3116

This study of photography "traces the medium from its beginnings with the French daguerreotype of the 1840s to the powerful social tool and all-pervasive 'eye' {the author considers} it has become." SLJ

Includes bibliographical references

Kallen, Stuart A.

Photography. Lucent Books 2007 112p il (Eye on art) $32.45

Grades: 7 8 9 10 11 12   **770**

1. Photography -- History

ISBN 978-1-59018-986-3

LC 2007015978

"This volume surveys the history of photography, from the ancient camera obscura to the digital camera. . . . This title offers a clear overview of an art form that many teens both practice and appreciate." Booklist

Includes bibliographical references

Matter, Jordan

Dancers among us; a celebration of joy in the everyday. Jordan Matter. Workman Publishing 2012 229 p. color illustrations (alk. paper) $17.95

Grades: 9 10 11 12 Adult   **770**

1. Dance in art 2. Dance -- Pictorial works 3. Dancers -- Portraits 4. Portrait photography

ISBN 0761171703; 9780761171706

LC 2012033655

This book by Jordan Matter presents photographs of "dancers leaping, laughing, reclining, and soaring in some of the most unconventional spots: in offices, crossing a busy street, high up in a leafy tree limb, and even in the shower!" The "images [are] around themes like work, play, love, exploration, and dreaming." Also included are "Matter's personal anecdotes about life, learning, and family". (Dance Magazine)

Partridge, Elizabeth

★ **Restless** spirit: the life and work of Dorothea Lange. Viking 1998 122p il hardcover o.p. pa $12.99

Grades: 6 7 8 9   **770**

1. Photographers 2. Women photographers

ISBN 0-670-87888-X; 0-14-230024-1 pa

LC 98-9807

A biography of Dorothea Lange, whose photographs of migrant workers, Japanese American internees, and rural poverty helped bring about important social reforms

"Generously placed throughout this accessibly written biography are the photographic images that make Lange a pre-eminent artist of the century. The book is elegantly designed and the photographic reproductions are excellent." Bull Cent Child Books

Includes bibliographical references

770.9 History, geographical treatment, biography

Sandler, Martin W.
Photography: an illustrated history. Oxford Univ. Press 2002 156p il (Oxford illustrated histories) $29.95
Grades: 11 12 Adult   **770.9**
1. Photography -- History
ISBN 0-19-512608-4

LC 2001-36602
Presents the history of photography from the daguerreotypes of the mid-1800s to its acceptance as an art form and more
"Most exciting are the images . . . . which range from famous examples of photojournalism . . . . to fine art. . . . {A} well-done, clearly written overview." Booklist
Includes bibliographical references

770.92 Biography

Willis, Deborah
Reflections in Black; a history of Black photographers, 1840-1999. Norton 2000 348p il $50; pa $35
Grades: 11 12 Adult   **770.92**
1. African Americans in art 2. African American photographers 3. Photography -- History
ISBN 0-393-04880-2; 0-393-32280-7 pa

LC 99-55185
Companion volume to A Smithsonian traveling exhibition
"Willis sketches important figures and traces both developments in photographic techniques and the practice of photography by African Americans. . . . A beautiful and informative album." Booklist
Includes bibliographical references and index

778.9 Photography of specific subjects

Caputo, Robert
★ **National** Geographic photography field guide; people & portraits: secrets to making great pictures. National Geographic Soc. 2001 159p il $21.95
Grades: 11 12 Adult   **778.9**
1. Photography
ISBN 0-7922-6499-1

LC 2001-44918
This guide explains "the best angles, lighting, and lenses to capture candid photos and portraits of family, friends, and everyone else. How to evoke a subject's true character on film {and} how to compose a formal family portrait." Publisher's note
Includes bibliographical references

779 Photographic images

Latana
Barely exposed. ORO Editions 2009 133p il $40
Grades: 7 8 9 10   **779**
1. Portrait photography
ISBN 978-0-9820607-0-4; 0-9820607-0-X
"The work is a compilation of black-and-white photographs depicting sixty young adults from all over the world in—literally and figuratively—a barely exposed state. On the opposite side of the page is a quote intended to express how the subject sees him or herself in the context of life, and/or where and how they might ultimately fit into this world. These passages are usually expressed in the teen's own words, which often prove to be not only insightful but are also sometimes in sharp contrast to the outward appearance of the subject. . . . This book is highly recommended for libraries of all types; if a picture is worth a thousand words, then this one is surely worth a million." Voice Youth Advocates

National Geographic Society (U.S.)
In focus; National Geographic greatest portraits. National Geographic Society 2004 504p il $30
Grades: 11 12 Adult   **779**
1. Portrait photography
ISBN 0-7922-7363-X

LC 2004-44953
"Comprising 280 portraits by 150 of National Geographic's celebrated photographers . . . the book spans over 100 years and covers the entire globe. Organized chronologically as well as thematically and enriched with essays on the development of photographic styles through decades, it is a tasteful celebration of the medium but even more so of human diversity." Libr J

Through the lens; National Geographic greatest photographs. National Geographic Soc. 2003 504p il $30
Grades: 11 12 Adult   **779**
1. Documentary photography
ISBN 0-7922-6164-X

LC 2003-52757
This is a "collection of 250 photos, mostly in color and drawn from the National Geographic Society's archive. . . . The society's signature blend of dramatic, rigorously composed natural shots and 'family of nations'-style culture peeps are backed by broad captions and text. . . . The six sections ('Europe'; 'Asia'; 'Africa & the Middle East'; 'The Americas'; 'Oceans and Isles'; 'The Universe') include the first color underwater photographs, as well as collaborative work with NASA, and prominently credit the 84 photographers whose work is featured." Publ Wkly

★ **Photos** that changed the world; the 20th century. edited by Peter Stepan; with contributions by

Claus Biegerd [et al.] Prestel-Verlag 2000 183p il pa $19.95

Grades: 11 12 Adult   779
1. Photojournalism
ISBN 3-7913-2395-4; 3-7913-3628-2 pa

Stepan provides "105 images that had the lasting visual power to capture a moment that could be the image of an era held in the instant of a shutter's click for distribution to a generation. . . . The photos are well reproduced and gain from the explanations of time, place, and context included in the excellent short essays that accompany each." Libr J

780   Music

The **complete** classical music guide; general editor, John Burrows with Charles Wiffen and contributions from Robert Ainsley ... [et al.] DK Pub. 2012 352 p. ill. (hc) $25

Grades: 10 11 12 Adult   780
1. Music 2. Musical instruments 3. Music appreciation
ISBN 0756692563; 9780756692568

                                    LC 2012562384

This "illustrated guide is arranged by period—'early' (ie 1000-1600), baroque, classical, romantic (with additional chapters on romantic opera and national schools) and modern. Each period is introduced by an overview, and the book opens with a general guide to classical music—its elements, instruments and performance." (Classical Music)

Forney, Kristine
   ★ The **enjoyment** of music; an introduction to perceptive listening. Kristine Forney, Joseph Machlis. W. W. Norton 2011 xxxiii, 595 p.p ill. (chiefly col.), col. maps (hardcover) $116.45

Grades: 11 12 Adult   780
1. Music appreciation 2. Music -- Social aspects 3. Music -- History and criticism
ISBN 0393935205; 9780393935202

                                    LC 2010026215

This book by Kristine Forney and Joseph Machlis "reflects how today's students learn, listen to, and live with music. . . . It emphasizes context to show how music fits in the everyday lives of people throughout history, and connects culture, performance, and technology to the lives of students today. The new edition features . . . cultural and historical context, and in-text features that encourage and develop critical thinking skills." (Publisher's note)

Includes bibliographical references and index

   ★ The **Harvard** concise dictionary of music and musicians; edited by Don Michael Randel. Belknap Press 1999 757p il hardcover o.p. pa $18.95

Grades: 11 12 Adult   780
1. Reference books 2. Music -- Dictionaries 3. Music -- Bio-bibliography
ISBN 0-674-00084-6; 0-674-00978-9 pa

                                    LC 99-40644

"Entries are arranged alphabetically and encompass terms, musical forms and styles, individual works,

and instruments, as well as composers, performers, and theorists." Booklist

Marsalis, Wynton
   Marsalis on music. Norton 1995 171p il music $29.95

Grades: 9 10 11 12 Adult   780
1. Music
ISBN 0-393-03881-5

                                    LC 95-4470

"An outstanding companion to a PBS series. . . . A superb resource for students and for other readers." Booklist

Includes glossary

   ★ The **Oxford** companion to music; edited by Alison Latham. Oxford Univ. Press 2002 1434p il $65

Grades: 11 12 Adult   780
1. Reference books 2. Music -- Dictionaries 3. Musicians -- Dictionaries
ISBN 0-19-866212-2

                                    LC 2002-537302

"Among the 8000 entries are articles on composers, theorists, and some performers; instruments, forms, and terms; subjects like electronic music, individual countries, and politics and music; and some pieces (and even some famous arias). Each entry is presented in a dictionary format, with a select index of names appended and sometimes with bibliographic references. . . . The bias is still English, but the book provides cross references to American terms and includes plenty of American composers and musical subjects. A solid reference with a grand pedigree, usefully improved for home and general library use, this is highly recommended for all public libraries." Libr J

Includes bibliographical references

780.89   Ethnic and national groups

Floyd, Samuel A.
   The **power** of black music; interpreting its history from Africa to the United States. {by} Samuel A. Floyd, Jr. Oxford Univ. Press 1995 316p il hardcover o.p. pa $18.95

Grades: 11 12 Adult   780.89
1. African American music
ISBN 978-0-19-510975-7

                                    LC 94-21

The range of genres the author discusses includes "slaves' ring shouts, turn-of-the-century cotillion dances, jazz, R & B, etc. . . . Complementing the discourse are plenty of musical examples. Academics, critics, scholars, and fans alike stand to gain much from carefully reading this impressive work." Booklist

Includes   discography,   filmography,   and bibliographical references

Southern, Eileen
   ★ The **music** of black Americans; a history. 3rd ed; Norton 1997 xxii, 678p il music hardcover o.p. pa $53.65

Grades: 11 12 Adult **780.89**
1. African American musicians 2. African American
music -- History and criticism
ISBN 978-0-393-03843-9; 0-393-03843-2; 978-0-393-
97141-5 pa; 0-393-97141-4 pa

LC 96-28811
First published 1971
A chronological survey of African American music in
the United States tracing black music from its origin in Af-
rica through colonial America and up to the present
Includes discography and bibliographical references

780.9 History, geographic treatment, biography

Perlis, Vivian
Composer's voices from Ives to Ellington; an
oral history of American music. [by] Vivian Perlis
and Libby Van Cleve. Yale University Press 2005
477p il $50
Grades: 11 12 Adult **780.9**
1. Jazz musicians 2. Composers -- United States
ISBN 0-300-10673-4; 9780300106732

LC 2005-361
"This volume offers the reader a unique perspective on
the composers who created ragtime, 'new' music, and early
jazz. A very enjoyable read supplemented by 2 compact
discs that contain excerpts of interviews." Univ Press Books
for Public and Second Sch Libr, 2006
Includes bibliographical references

Terkel, Studs, 1912-2008
And they all sang; adventures of an eclectic disc
jockey. New Press 2005 xxii, 301p $25.95; pa
$16.95
Grades: 11 12 Adult **780.9**
1. Musicians
ISBN 978-1-59558-003-0; 1-59558-003-4; 978-1-
59558-118-1 pa; 1-59558-118-9 pa

LC 2005-43866
In this "collection of 40 interviews, . . . Terkel recalls
his venerable radio program, The Wax Museum, which
premiered shortly after the end of WWII in 1945, profiling
composers, entertainers and impresarios of nearly every type
of music. . . . Insightful and daring, Terkel always asks the
right questions, whether culturally or musically." Publ Wkly

780.92 Biography

★ **Baker's** biographical dictionary of musicians;
Nicolas Slonimsky, editor emeritus; Laura Kuhn,
Baker's series advisory editor. Centennial ed;
Schirmer Bks. 2001 6v set $800
Grades: 11 12 Adult **780.92**
1. Reference books 2. Music -- Bio-bibliography 3.
Musicians -- Dictionaries
ISBN 0-02-865525-7

LC 00-46375
First published 1900 in one volume under the authorship
of Theodore Baker

"This monumental work collocates information from
classical, popular, and jazz music on a scale greater than any
other source. Essential for all libraries." Choice
Includes bibliographical references and discographies

Earls, Irene
Young musicians in world history. Greenwood
Press 2002 139p il $44.95
Grades: 8 9 10 11 12 **780.92**
1. Musicians
ISBN 0-313-31442-X

LC 2001-40559
Profiles thirteen musicians who achieved high honors
and fame before the age of twenty-five, representing many
different time periods and musical styles
"A useful introduction to some of the musical giants of
the last four centuries." SLJ
Includes glossary and bibliographical references

Roberts, Russell, 1953-
Scott Joplin; by Russell Roberts. Mitchell Lane
Publishers 2012 47 p. ill. (chiefly col.) (library)
$29.95
Grades: 6 7 8 9 **780.92**
1. Jazz music 2. Composers -- United States --
Biography
ISBN 1612282733; 9781612282732

LC 2012008633
This book by Russ Roberts is part of the American Jazz
series and looks at musician Scott Joplin. Within each entry,
"information about the subjects' childhoods and preparation
for their musical careers is included, as are the positive and
negative aspects of their adult lives. Their contributions to
the world of jazz are . . . explored." (School Library Journal)
Includes bibliographical references (pages 44-45), chronology (pages 40-41) and index.

781.6 Traditions of music

Swafford, Jan
★ The **Vintage** guide to classical music. Vin-
tage Bks. 1992 xxi, 597p il pa $17
Grades: 11 12 Adult **781.6**
1. Music appreciation 2. Music -- History and criticism
ISBN 0-679-72805-8

LC 91-50217
This guide contains "chronologically arranged essays
on nearly 100 composers, from Guillaume de Machaut (ca.
1300-1377) to Aaron Copland (1900-1990), that combine biography with detailed analyses of the major works while assessing their role in the social, cultural, and political climate
of their times." Publisher's note
Includes glossary and bibliographical references

781.64   Western popular music

Chang, Jeff

★ **Can't** stop, won't stop; a history of the hip-hop generation. introduction by D.J. Kool Herc. St. Martin's Press 2005 546p il hardcover o.p. pa $16
Grades: 11 12 Adult   **781.64**
    1. Rap music
    ISBN 0-312-30143-X; 0-312-42579-1 pa
                                         LC 2004-56656
"A fascinating, far-reaching must for pop-music and pop-culture collections." Booklist
    Includes bibliographical references, discography, and filmography

Morales, Ed

★ The **Latin** beat; the rhythms and roots of Latin music from bossa nova to salsa and beyond. Da Capo Press 2003 xxviii, 372p pa $18.95
Grades: 9 10 11 12   **781.64**
    1. Music -- Latin America
    ISBN 0-306-81018-2
                                         LC 2003-16423
"Displaying an incredible depth of historical and musical knowledge and insight, this book will be a joy to read both for those already steeped in the Latin musical tradition as well as for those recently introduced to the music of, for instance, Tito Puente." Publ Wkly
    Includes bibliographical references

781.643   Blues

King, B. B.

Blues all around me; the autobiography of B.B. King. [by] B.B. King with David Ritz. Avon Bks. 1996 336p il pa $15.99
Grades: 11 12 Adult   **781.643**
    1. Singers 2. Guitarists 3. Blues music 4. Blues musicians 5. African American musicians
    ISBN 0-380-97318-9; 0-06-206103-8 pa
                                         LC 96-27773
King recounts his humble beginnings and his career as a prominent blues guitarist.
"This is one of the best recent pop-music bios. King speaks straight from the soul, it seems, just like he plays the guitar." Booklist

781.644   Soul

Mendelson, Aaron A

★ **American** R & B; Gospel grooves, funky drummers, and soul power. Aaron Mendelson. Twenty-First Century Books 2013 64 p. (lib. bdg.: alk. paper) $30.60
Grades: 7 8 9 10 11 12   **781.644**
    1. Blues music 2. American songs 3. African American music 4. Soul music -- History and criticism 5. Rhythm and blues music -- History and criticism
    ISBN 0761345019; 9780761345015
                                         LC 2011045636
Author Aaron Mendelson's book focuses on R&B music. "Rhythm and blues music evolved from all sorts of sounds: swinging jazz, gritty blues, and African American spiritual songs. The music's smooth mix of styles made it unique, and its passionate performers made it a sensation. Ever since Ray Charles hit the charts in the 1950s, R & B fans have held it down on dance floors. And R & B singers have belted out messages of love and calls for social change." (Publisher's note)
    Includes bibliographical references and index.

Pinkney, Andrea Davis

★ **Rhythm** ride; a road trip through the Motown sound. Andrea Davis Pinkney. Roaring Brook Press 2015 176 p. illustrations (hardback) $22.99
Grades: 5 6 7 8 9   **781.644**
    1. Rhythm and blues music -- Sound recordings 2. Motown Record Corporation
    ISBN 9781596439733; 1596439734
                                         LC 2014045894
NAACP Image Award Nominee: Outstanding Literary Work- Youth/Teens (2016)
"Berry Gordy began Motown in 1959. . . . He converted the garage of a residential house into a studio and recruited teenagers . . . Smokey Robinson, Mary Wells, Marvin Gaye, Stevie Wonder, and Diana Ross to sing for his new label. Meanwhile, the country was on the brink of a cultural revolution, and one of the most powerful agents of change in the following decade would be this group of young black performers from urban Detroit." (Publisher's note)
"An ebullient, wonderfully told introduction to music that had an indelible influence on a generation and its times." Kirkus

781.65   Jazz

Gioia, Ted

The **history** of jazz; 2nd ed.; Oxford University Press 2011 444p il pa $19.95
Grades: 11 12 Adult   **781.65**
    1. Jazz music -- History and criticism
    ISBN 978-0-19-539970-7; 0-19-539970-6
                                         LC 2010-23182
First published 1997
The author "relates the story of African American music from its roots in Africa to the international respect it enjoys today. . . . This well-researched, extensively annotated volume covers the major trends and personalities that have shaped jazz. The excellent bibliography and list of recommended listening make this a valuable purchase for libraries building a jazz collection." Libr J
    Includes discography and bibliographical references

Marsalis, Wynton

Jazz A-B-Z; [by] Wynton Marsalis and Paul Rogers; with biographical sketches by Phil Schaap. Candlewick Press 2005 un il $24.99

Grades: 5 6 7 8 9 10   **781.65**
1. Jazz music 2. Jazz musicians
ISBN 978-0-7636-3434-6

LC 2005-48448

This is an illustrated alphabetically arranged introduction to jazz musicians.

This is a "witty, stunningly designed alphabet catalog. . . . The biographical sketches and notes on poetic forms by Phil Schaap are concise and genuinely informative. . . . Rogers's pastiche full-page portraits, his use of expressive typography and the smaller vignettes he sprinkles throughout are bound to heighten any reader's appreciation of both the musicians and the music. . . . [Marsalis offers] clever . . . poems, wordplays, odes and limericks." N Y Times Book Rev

Moving to higher ground; how jazz can change your life. [by] Wynton Marsalis with Geoffrey C. Ward. Random House 2008 181p il
Grades: 10 11 12 Adult   **781.65**
1. Jazz music -- History and criticism
ISBN 1400060788; 9781400060788

LC 2008-16560

The author "explains in lay readers' terms how jazz works as a diverse musical genre and, more important, how an understanding and appreciation of jazz can enrich one's life. . . . This work is highly recommended." Libr J

Szwed, John F.
★ **Jazz** 101; a complete guide to learning and loving jazz. {by} John Szwed. Hyperion 2000 354p pa $14.95
Grades: 11 12 Adult   **781.65**
1. Jazz music
ISBN 0-7868-8496-7

LC 00-35055

Szwed "proceeds chronologically through jazz history, managing to explore the different trends in jazz that often overlapped and the key players who often reinvented themselves over decades. There even are accounts of the famous nightclubs where jazz history was made. Strong, descriptive reviews of key albums are included as sidebars to give the reader good places to start listening. Very worthwhile." Booklist
Includes bibliographical references

Ward, Geoffrey C.
★ **Jazz**; a history of America's music. based on a documentary film by Ken Burns written by Geoffrey C. Ward; with a preface by Ken Burns. Knopf 2000 489p il $65; pa $29.95
Grades: 11 12 Adult   **781.65**
1. Jazz music
ISBN 0-679-44551-X; 0-679-76539-5 pa

LC 00-22604

"The illustrations are copious, including about 500 pieces and running from cover to cover; the text, picture captions, and sidebars reflect the research that went into the six-year project. A very competent and lovingly rendered history." Booklist
Includes bibliographical references

781.66   Rock (Rock 'n' roll)

Beaujon, Andrew
Body piercing saved my life; inside the phenomenon of Christian rock. Da Capo Press 2006 291p il $16.95
Grades: 11 12 Adult   **781.66**
1. Christian rock music
ISBN 0-306-81457-9; 978-0-306-81457-0

LC 2006-6254

The author "chronicles the Christian rock subculture, beginning with the 'Jesus People' of the early 1970s to its substantial popularity today. . . . This important, well-written study of the Christian rock phenomenon brings the personalities to life." Libr J
Includes bibliographical references

Hopper, Jessica
The **girl's** guide to rocking; how to start a band, book gigs, and get rolling to rock stardom. Workman Pub. 2009 229p il pa $13.95
Grades: 9 10 11 12   **781.66**
1. Rock musicians 2. Women -- Vocational guidance 3. Music industry -- Vocational guidance
ISBN 978-0-7611-5141-8

LC 2008-52803

"This guide is a necessary handbook for any aspiring Alicia Keys or Joan Jett." Booklist

Marcus, Sara
Girls to the front; the true story of the Riot grrrl revolution. HarperPerennial 2010 367p il pa $14.99
Grades: 11 12 Adult   **781.66**
1. Feminism 2. Riot grrrl movement
ISBN 978-0-06-180636-0; 0-06-180636-6

This book is "a brash, gutsy chronicle of the empowering music and feminist movement of the early 1990s." Publ Wkly

Nichols, Travis
Punk rock etiquette; the ultimate how-to guide for punk, underground, DIY, and indie bands. Roaring Brook Press 2008 128p il pa $10.95
Grades: 7 8 9 10 11 12   **781.66**
1. Punk rock music 2. Music industry -- Vocational guidance
ISBN 978-1-59643-415-8; 1-59643-415-5

LC 2008-11706

"Lively, knowledgeable, witty, and wise, this title offers a sound foundation in the social economics of indie rock. . . . From how to put together a band that functions rather than fights, to designing and creating appealing merchandise and running a successful tour, this heavily illustrated guide covers every aspect of how to be a bona fide DIY rock star for the twenty-first century." Voice Youth Advocates

Roberts, Jeremy
The **Beatles**; music revolutionaries. Twenty-First Century Books 2011 112p il (USA Today lifeline biographies) lib bdg $33.26

Grades: 6 7 8 9 10　　　　781.66
1. Rock musicians 2. Beatles
ISBN 978-0-7613-6421-4; 0-7613-6421-8
LC 2010031041

This "takes readers on an accessible tour of the band's rollicking run from Liverpool's underground scene to its nearly decade-long perch atop the charts. Written in a straightforward, reportorial style, . . . the book offers a fine dissection of the Beatle phenomenon. . . . As easy on the eyes as it is fun to read." Booklist

Includes discography, filmography, and bibliographical references

Rock and roll is here to stay; an anthology. edited by William McKeen; introduction by Peter Guralnick. Norton 2000 672p il $35
Grades: 11 12 Adult　　　　781.66
1. Rock music
ISBN 0-393-04700-8
LC 99-31759

McKeen "presents 94 excerpts from novels, rock criticism, lyrics, interviews, speeches, personal recollections, and other sources to weave together the history of rock'n'roll." Libr J

★ The **Rolling** Stone illustrated history of rock & roll; the definitive history of the most important artists and their music. edited by Anthony DeCurtis and James Henke with Holly George-Warren; original editor: Jim Miller. new ed; Random House 1992 710p il pa $36.95
Grades: 7 8 9 10　　　　781.66
1. Rock music
ISBN 0-679-73728-6
LC 92-6339

First published 1976
This history of four decades of rock music includes essays and photographs covering individual artists, groups, trends and styles

Talevski, Nick
The **unofficial** encyclopedia of the Rock and Roll Hall of Fame. Greenwood Press 1998 402p il $60
Grades: 11 12 Adult　　　　781.66
1. Rock music 2. Rock musicians 3. Rock & Roll Hall of Fame and Museum
ISBN 0-313-30032-1
LC 97-41928

"This book covers the first 150 inductees into the Rock and Roll Hall of Fame. . . . Individuals and groups who have been inducted into the Rock and Roll Hall of Fame are listed alphabetically, with the entries providing both personal and professional information. Each description includes not only dry factual annotations about the individual's achievements, records, etc., but also interesting personal information, anecdotes, comments, and insights. At the end of each entry is a bibliography for further reading." Voice Youth Advocates

Includes bibliographical references (p. {363}-366) and index

782.1　Vocal forms

Bordman, Gerald
American musical theatre; a chronicle. Gerald Bordman, Richard Norton. Oxford University Press 2011 xiv, 1017 p.p $160
Grades: 11 12 Adult　　　　782.1
1. Musicals 2. Theater -- United States -- History 3. Musicals -- United States -- History and criticism
ISBN 0199729700; 9780199729708
LC 2010033708

This book by Gerald Bordman and Richard Norton "covers more than 250 years of musical theatre in the United States, from a 1735 South Carolina production of Flora, or Hob in the Well to The Addams Family in 2010. Authors Gerald Bordman and Richard Norton . . . blend history, critical analysis, and . . . description to illustrate the transformation of American musical theatre through such incarnations as the ballad opera, revue, Golden Age musical, [and] rock musical." (Publisher's note)

782.25　Small-scale vocal forms

We'll understand it better by and by; pioneering African American gospel composers. edited by Bernice Johnson Reagon. Smithsonian Institution Press 1992 384p il music hardcover o.p. pa $27.95
Grades: 11 12 Adult　　　　782.25
1. Clergy 2. Singers 3. Pianists 4. Teachers 5. Composers 6. Gospel music 7. Conductors (Music) 8. African American musicians 9. Songwriters 10. Hymn writers 11. Gospel musicians 12. Music publishers 13. Choral conductors
ISBN 1-56098-167-9
LC 91-37954

"Reagon and her contributors explore every aspect of gospel's history, spiritual significance, and influence on secular music, but the primary focus is on individuals. The lives and achievements of six pioneering gospel music composers are examined in detail. . . . A splendidly comprehensive and invaluable history." Booklist

Includes discography and bibliographical references

782.42　Songs

The **anthology** of rap; edited by Adam Bradley, Andrew DuBois; foreword by Henry Louis Gates, Jr.; afterword by Chuck D and Common. Yale University Press 2010 867p il
Grades: 11 12 Adult　　　　782.42
1. Rap (Music) 2. Rap music -- History and criticism 3. Rap (Music) -- History and criticism
ISBN 0300141904; 9780300141900
LC 2010-23316

This "anthology brings together more than three hundred lyrics written over thirty years." (Publisher's note) Index.

"For fans, this is an obvious treasure. For skeptical listeners and readers, this mega-anthology strips away rap's performance elements and allows the language itself to pulse, break, spin, and strut in poems of audacity, outrage, insight, sweetness, and nastiness. Here is meter and rhyme, distillation, metaphor, misdirection, leaps of imagination, appropriation, improvisation, and a 'vivid vocabulary' that can be explicit, offensive, funny, dumb, and transcendent." Booklist

Includes bibliographical references

Bynoe, Yvonne

★ **Encyclopedia** of rap and hip-hop culture. Greenwood Press 2006 449p il $69.95

Grades: 11 12 Adult   **782.42**

1. Reference books 2. Hip-hop -- Encyclopedias 3. Rap music -- Encyclopedias
ISBN 0-313-33058-1

LC 2005-19215

This encyclopedia describes "the separate elements embraced by rap and hip-hop: the verbal (MCing), and the musical (DJing), break dancing, and aerosol painting. The alphabetical entries cover all these elements and include most of the well-known rap artists and groups, along with some less-familiar names. The articles also acknowledge some of rap's detractors. . . . This title will be of interest to browsers and report writers." SLJ

Includes bibliographical references

Furia, Philip

The **poets** of Tin Pan Alley; a history of America's great lyricists. Oxford Univ. Press 1990 322p hardcover o.p. pa $14.95

Grades: 11 12 Adult   **782.42**

1. Lyricists 2. Popular music 3. American songs
ISBN 0-19-507473-4

LC 90-35937

This work examines "lyrics from stage and movie musicals and the work of ten lyricists: Irving Berlin, Lorenz Hart, Ira Gershwin, Cole Porter, Oscar Hammerstein, Howard Dietz, Yip Harburg, Dorothy Fields, Leo Robin, and Johnny Mercer. . . . Although primarily a record of one aspect of show business, the book is a good history of American popular culture." Choice

Includes bibliographical references

Guerinot, Jim

Legends, icons & rebels; music that changed the world. by Robbie Robertson, Jim Guerinot, Sebastian Robertson, and Jared Levine. Tundra Books 2013 128 p. (hardcover) $29

Grades: 6 7 8 9 10 11 12   **782.42**

1. Musicians 2. Music -- History and criticism
ISBN 1770495711; 9781770495715; 9781770495739
LC 2013931040

Authors Robbie Robertson, Jim Guerinot, Jared Levine, and Sebastian Robertson discuss "twenty-seven musical legends. Short profiles chronicle personal stories and achievements of extraordinarily talented artists whose innovations changed the landscape of music for generations to come. Carefully compiled like any great playlist, the line-up features . . . Ray Charles to Johnny Cash, Chuck Berry to Bob Dylan." (Publisher's note)

"In this oversize, weighty volume, music-industry-veteran authors offer collected anecdotal sketches, including per-

sonal memories, of twenty-seven music "risk-takers" such as Aretha Franklin, the Beatles, and Bob Dylan. Their meteoric careers, many touched by tragedy, are justly celebrated. A timeline of these artists' first recordings (1925-1968) ends the book; includes two CDs of sparkling audio quality with one iconic song by each." (Horn Book)

Hatfield, Greg

Songwriter's market; Greg Hatfield, editor. 34th annual ed; Writer's Digest 362p il

Grades: 11 12 Adult   **782.42**

1. Popular music -- Writing and publishing
ISBN

Annual. First published 1978

The main section of this guide consists of listings of music publishers, record companies, producers, managers, booking agents, and firms interested in original music. Also included are articles which present an overview of the songwriting field, and listings of resources such as organizations, workshops, and contests.

★ **National** anthems of the world; edited by Michael Jamieson Bristow. 11th ed.; Weidenfeld & Nicolson 2006 629p $90

Grades: 5 6 7 8 9 10 11 12 Adult   **782.42**

1. National songs
ISBN 0-304-36826-1

First published 1943 in the United Kingdom with title: National anthems of the United Nations and France

This volume contains national anthems of about 198 nations, including melody and accompaniment. Words are presented in the native language with transliteration provided where necessary. English translations follow. Brief historical notes on the adoption of each anthem are included

"An essential reference resource for all libraries." Libr J

782.421   Rock (Rock 'n' roll) songs

The **Beatles** anthology. Chronicle Bks. 2000 367p il $60; pa $35

Grades: 11 12 Adult   **782.421**

1. Beatles
ISBN 0-8118-2684-8; 0-8118-3636-3 pa

LC 00-23685

The story of the Beatles as "told through quotes from John, Paul, George, and Ringo, as well as the group's closest aides: George Martin, Neil Aspinall, and Derek Taylor. . . . The density of the text is daunting, but the book's browsability makes it as appealing to casual readers as it is indispensable to Beatlemaniacs." Libr J

Includes bibliographical references

Carlin, Peter Ames

Bruce; Peter Ames Carlin. Simon & Schuster 2012 xi, 494 p.p ill.

Grades: 10 11 12 Adult   **782.421**

1. Rock musicians -- Biography 2. Rock musicians

-- United States -- Biography
ISBN 9781439191828; 9781439191835; 9781439191842

LC 2012020890

This book describes how, "For more than four decades, Bruce Springsteen has reflected the heart and soul of America with a career that includes twenty Grammy Awards, more than 120 million albums sold, two Golden Globes, and an Academy Award. [Author] Peter Ames Carlin . . . encompasses the breadth of Springsteen's astonishing career and explores the inner workings of a man who managed to redefine generations of music." (Publisher's note)

"A painstakingly traced chronicle of the remarkable career of powerhouse proletarian rocker Bruce Springsteen... The author presents his subject as a supremely gifted musician and truly heroic figure, albeit one with a lot on his troubled mind... An epic look at the man and his music." Kirkus

Includes bibliographical references and index.

Dunn, Jancee

Cyndi Lauper; a memoir. Cyndi Lauper with Jancee Dunn. Atria Books 2012 338 p. 16 unnumbered pages of plates $26
Grades: 10 11 12 Adult   **782.421**
1. Women rock musicians 2. Singers -- United States -- Biography
ISBN 143914785X; 9781439147856

LC 2013560375

Author Cyndi Lauper "left her home in Ozone Park, Queens, at age 17 to escape a sexually abusive stepfather and the limitations on life—especially for women—imposed by a hardscrabble working-class neighborhood and male-dominated family culture. . . . Her life changed in 1983, however, with the release of She's So Unusual, which . . . made Lauper an instant star. . . . Inevitably, her superstar aura faded, but her eclectic musical output did not." (Kirkus)

Feinstein, Michael, 1956-

The **Gershwins** and me; a personal history in twelve songs. by Michael Feinstein with Ian Jackman. Simon & Schuster 2012 351 p. illustrations (some color) (hc: alk. paper) $45
Grades: 10 11 12 Adult   **782.421**
1. Popular music -- Writing and publishing -- United States
ISBN 1451645309; 9781451645309; 9781451645316; 9781451645323; 9781451645330

LC 2012006833

Here, author Michael Feinstein "begins with a swift account of how he met Ira Gershwin, the lyricist of the celebrated duo, and how he subsequently went to work for him for six years. . . . Although he tells the Gershwins' stories, childhood to grave, he also . . . discusses the Gershwins' love lives, the significant performers of their work (from Fred Astaire to Ethel Merman), their successes and flops, their experiences in Hollywood and the devastation of George's shocking death at 38 (brain tumor)." (Kirkus)

Includes bibliographical references and index

784.19   Instruments

Baines, Anthony

The **Oxford** companion to musical instruments; written and edited by Anthony Baines. Oxford University Press 1992 404p il $85
Grades: 8 9 10 11 12 Adult   **784.19**
1. Reference books 2. Musical instruments -- Dictionaries
ISBN 0-19-311334-1

LC 92-8635

Based on The New Oxford companion to music (1983)

This volume presents alphabetically arranged entries for musical instruments. "The individual entries cover specific instruments and families thereof (e.g., Wind Instruments) as well as their representation in different countries (e.g., Africa) and time periods (e.g., Baroque). . . . Playing techniques, a brief history, and a list of the major repertory are [discussed]." Booklist

784.192   Techniques and procedures for instruments themselves

Pagliaro, Michael

The **musical** instrument desk reference; a guide to how band and orchestral instruments work. Michael J. Pagliaro. Scarecrow Press 2012 189 p. (cloth: alk. paper) $65
Grades: Adult Professional   **784.192**
1. Musical instruments 2. Wind instruments -- Construction 3. Bowed stringed instruments -- Construction
ISBN 0810882701; 9780810882706; 9780810882713

LC 2012007244

This book "begins with an 'easy-reference quick start' section on woodwinds, followed by more in-depth chapters on the flute, clarinet, saxophone, oboe, and the bassoon. For the brass instruments, there are fingering charts, an expanded in-depth study chapter, and a chapter on functioning. Nonfretted string instruments . . . are also given a chapter on producing sound and an expanded in-depth study chapter. The final chapter consists of an overview of percussion instruments." (Booklist)

784.2   Full orchestra (Symphony orchestra)

Steinberg, Michael

★ The **symphony**; a listener's guide. Oxford Univ. Press 1995 678p music $42.50; pa $25
Grades: 11 12 Adult   **784.2**
1. Symphony 2. Composers 3. Music appreciation
ISBN 0-19-506177-2; 0-19-512665-3 pa

LC 95-5568

"Steinberg describes 36 composers and, movement by movement, 118 symphonies, including all the standard repertory . . . as well as a few by less well known composers such as Gorecki, Harbison, Martinu, and Sessions. The writing varies from formal and factual to chatty, with candid asides and stories relevant to the composer, the composition, or an important performance." Libr J

Includes bibliographical references

784.8 Wind band

Bailey, Wayne

The **complete** marching band resource manual; techniques and materials for teaching, drill design, and music arranging. Wayne Bailey, Cormac Cannon, and Brandt Payne. 3rd edition University of Pennsylvania Press 2015 x, 306 p.p illustrations, music pbk $47.50

Grades: 9 10 11 12 **784.8**

1. Music 2. Marching bands -- Instruction and study

ISBN 0812223292; 9780812223293

LC 2014026612

First published 1994

"Supplemented with musical arrangements, warm-up exercises, and over a hundred drill charts, this manual presents both the fundamentals and the advanced techniques that are essential for successful marching band leadership. The materials in this volume cover every stage of musical direction and instruction, from selecting music and choreographing movements to improving student memorization and endurance to the creation of striking visual configurations through uniform and auxiliary units." (Publisher's note)

787.87 Guitars

Bacon, Tony

The **ultimate** guitar book; {by} Tony Bacon & Paul Day. Knopf 1991 192p il pa $27.50

Grades: 11 12 Adult **787.87**

1. Guitars

ISBN 0-375-70090-0

LC 91-52714

This is a "chronological history of the guitar, beginning with an example from 1552 and continuing through current times. Covering acoustic, electrical, and bass guitars, including all the big-name manufacturers such as Fender, Gibson, Martin, and Stratocaster, this informative and beautifully illustrated work will have wide appeal." SLJ

Chapman, Richard

The **new** complete guitarist; rev American ed; DK 2003 208p il pa $20

Grades: 11 12 Adult **787.87**

1. Guitars

ISBN 0-7894-9701-8

LC 2004-271630

First published 1993 with title: The complete guitarist

This work ranges "from fundamentals such as tuning, scales, chords, picking, and strumming, to advanced techniques of various styles such as rock, blues, and jazz. . . . [It also] includes discussions on such topics as sound and amplification, choosing a guitar, studio and home recording, plus care and maintenance of the instrument. An appealing

book in the style of the 'Eyewitness' series." SLJ [review of 1993 edition]

Includes bibliographical references

Chappell, Jon

Guitar All-in-one for Dummies; by Jon Chappell. 2nd edition Wiley 2014 628 p. pa. $34.99

Grades: Adult **787.87**

1. Guitars 2. Guitars -- Study and teaching

ISBN 978-0-470-48133-2

This book, by Jon Chappell, is a "complete compendium of guitar instruction, written in clear, concise For Dummies style. It covers everything from positioning and basic chords to guitar theory and playing styles, and even includes maintenance advice to keep your instrument sounding great. It's an amazing resource for newbies and veterans alike, and offers you the opportunity to stretch beyond your usual genre." (Publisher's Note)

Denyer, Ralph

★ The **guitar** handbook; [rev ed]; Knopf 1992 256p il pa $25

Grades: 11 12 Adult **787.87**

1. Guitars

ISBN 0-679-74275-1

LC 92-53164

First published 1982

Contains a learning program covering the range of guitar techniques from simple chords to improvised lead solos, profiles of famous and influential guitarists, an illustrated chord dictionary, chapters on guitar customizing and recording techniques, and sections on a variety of acoustic and electric guitars, amplification, special effects and stage sound systems.

Hodge, David

The **complete** idiot's guide to playing bass guitar. Alpha Books 2006 xxii, 308p il pa $22.95

Grades: 9 10 11 12 Adult **787.87**

1. Guitars

ISBN 978-1-59257-311-0; 1-59257-311-8

"This book provides a . . . foundation in reading music, purchasing the right equipment, and care and maintenance of the bass guitar. [It includes] a CD of original music." Publisher's note

Includes bibliographical references

788.7 Saxophones

Rice, Earle

★ **Charlie** Parker; by Earle Rice Jr. Mitchell Lane Publishers 2012 47 p. ill. (library) $29.95

Grades: 6 7 8 9 **788.7**

1. Jazz musicians -- Biography 2. African American musicians -- Biography

ISBN 1612282660; 9781612282664

LC 2012008628

This biography of musician Charlie Parker, part of the American Jazz series, presents an "account of Parker's drug-abuse-shortened life and stellar career--along with a . . . technical, specific analysis of his musical education and innovations." It includes "period photos of 'Bird' and his bandmates, plus a time line, a discography, and . . . sets of print and web resources for children and adults alike." (Booklist)

Includes discography (p. [41]), bibliographical references (p. 44), and index.

788.9   Brass instruments (Lip-reed instruments)

Boone, Mary

★ **Dizzy** Gillespie; by Mary Boone. Mitchell Lane Publishers 2013 47 p. ill. (some col.) (library) $29.95

Grades: 6 7 8 9   **788.9**

1. Jazz musicians -- Biography 2. Gillespie, Dizzy, 1917-1993 3. Bop (Music) -- History and criticism
ISBN 9781612282725

               LC 2012008630

This book by Mary Boone, part of the "American Jazz" series, presents a "biography of Jazz great Dizzy Gillespie written for intermediate through middle school age readers. . . . Gillespie owed much of his success to an elementary school teacher who worked to harness his energy and anger by recruiting him for the school band. . . . In the 1940s, the trumpet virtuoso and respected improviser teamed up with musician Charlie Parker to lay the foundations for bebop." (Publisher's note)

Orr, Tamra

★ **Miles** Davis; by Tamra Orr. Mitchell Lane Publishers 2012 47 p. ill. (library) $29.95

Grades: 6 7 8 9   **788.9**

1. Picture books for children 2. Jazz musicians -- United States
ISBN 1612282652; 9781612282657

               LC 2012008632

This book by Tamra Orr is part of the American Jazz series and looks at Miles Davis. "Known to jazz lovers around the world as the Prince of Darkness, Miles Davis lived a roller-coaster life of highs and lows. . . . You can follow his lows of grappling with the power of drug and alcohol addiction and racial prejudice to his highs of achieving world fame and appreciation, plus becoming a husband, father, and grandfather." (Publisher's note)

Includes discography (pages 41-42), bibliographical references (pages 44-45), and index.

790.1   General kinds of recreational activities

Ferrer, J. J.

The **art** of stone skipping and other fun old-time games; stoopball, jacks, string games, coin flipping, line baseball, jump rope, and more. by J.J. Ferrer; illustrated by Todd Dakins. Charlesbridge Pub., Inc. 2012 192 p. (paperback) $14.95

Grades: K 1 2 3 4 5 6 7 8 9 10 11 12 Adult   **790.1**

1. Games
ISBN 1936140748; 9781936140749

               LC 2012015052

This book, by J. J. Ferrer, offers a "collection of timeless games that guarantees kids a good time- by themselves, with a group of friends, or with family. Includes ball games . . . , card games . . . , sack races, and old favorites such as Duck, Duck, Goose and Red Rover. There is also a chapter for car games. Simple instructions explain the rules, how many people can play, the object of the game, and what you need." (Publisher's note)

Includes bibliographical references and index.

Rowell, Victoria

Tag, toss & run; 40 classic lawn games. Paul Tukey & Victoria Rowell. Storey Pub. 2012 207 p. (pbk.: alk. paper) $14.95

Grades: Adult Professional   **790.1**

1. Games 2. Outdoor recreation
ISBN 1603425608; 9781603425605

               LC 2011049410

This book on "family lawn games" presents a "guide to 40 time-tested favorites -- from classics like capture the flag, croquet, badminton, and bocce to the lesser-known Cherokee marbles, cornhole, and Kubb. The authors offer a quick overview of the basic structure of each game, as well as strategies for playing and tips for creating fun variations." (Publisher's note)

Includes bibliographical references and index.

791.4   Motion pictures, radio, television

Patmore, Chris

Movie Making Course: Expanded and Updated for the Digital Generation; For the Digital Generation. Chris Patmore. 2nd Edition Barron's 2012 176 p. color illustrations $23.99

Grades: 9 10 11 12   **791.4**

1. Motion pictures 2. Vocational education 3. Motion pictures -- Production and direction
ISBN 9781438001128

"If you're a budding filmmaker, you'll find the information you need for making short digital films on a tight budget. . . . Gain a practical working knowledge of pre-production and post-production as they relate to low-budget filmmaking. Get experience working in different genres, from ten-minute documentaries to pop videos and action sequences. Learn from a professional how to get your finished film seen. Gain valuable experience as you complete the book's self-teaching assignments, then put together a showreel, and get started on a rewarding career." (Publisher's Note)

791.43   Motion pictures

Dixon, Wheeler W., 1950-

A **Short** History of Film; Wheeler Winston Dixon & Gwendolyn Audrey Foster. 2nd edition Rutgers University Press 2013 449 p. illustrations (some color) pa. $29.95

Grades: Adult   **791.43**

1. Motion picture industry 2. Motion picture industry -- History 3. Motion pictures -- History. 4. Motion

picture industry -- History.
ISBN 9780813560557

LC 2012533144

This book, by Wheeler Winston Dixon and Gwendolyn Audrey Foster, "provides a concise and accurate overview of the history of world cinema, detailing the major movements, directors, studios, and genres from 1896 through 2012. Accompanied by more than 250 rare color and black-and-white stills - including many from recent films - the new edition . . . [conveys] a sense of cinema's sweep in the twentieth and early twenty-first centuries." (Publisher's note)

"This excellent introduction stands out in a crowded field with its lively, accessible writing, broad coverage, and particular focus on traditionally marginalized figures in film history...The most striking aspect of the book is the coverage of women, African Americans, and Third World filmmakers, which strongly complements its solid coverage of American and European film. Illustrations abound, and even the best-versed cineaste will find new films to track down after reading the breezy, enthusiastic analysis in this book. Highly recommended for all collections, this text would also make an excellent textbook for introductory film-studies courses.—" (Library Journal)

Landis, Deborah Nadoolman

Dressed; a century of Hollywood costume design. Deborah Nadoolman Landis. Collins Design 2007 xxv, 566 p.p ill. (some col.) (hbk.) $75.00
Grades: 11 12 Adult **791.43**
1. Costume 2. Fashion 3. Motion picture industry 4. Fashion in motion pictures
ISBN 9780060816506

LC 2007030375

This book explores "one hundred years of Hollywood's most tantalizing costumes and the characters they helped bring to life. Drawing on years of . . . research, [author Deborah Nadoolman] Landis has uncovered both a . . . trove of costume sketches and photographs—many of them previously unpublished—and a[n] . . . array of first-person anecdotes that inform and enhance the images. Along the way she also provides a . . . behind-the-scenes look at the evolution of the costume designer's art, from its emergence as a key element of cinematic collaboration to its limitless future in the era of CGI." (Publisher's note)

Includes bibliographical references and index.

Lanier, Troy

Filmmaking for teens; pulling off your shorts. [by] Troy Lanier & Clay Nichols. Michael Wiese Productions 2010 197p il pa $20.95
Grades: 9 10 11 12 **791.43**
1. Cinematography 2. Video recording 3. Motion pictures -- Production and direction
ISBN 978-1-932907-68-1

LC 2009-29891

First published 2005

A guide to filmmaking for teens that covers picking a subject, writing a script, production, schedules, expenses, directing, equipment, lighting, sound, editing, and distribution. It also provides tips on techniques.

Richmond, Simon

The **rough** guide to anime. Rough Guides 2009 292p il pa $18.99
Grades: 9 10 11 12 Adult **791.43**
1. Anime 2. Animated films
ISBN 978-18-58282-053

"The author covers a set of canonical films; popular anime television series; creator and director mini-bios; technical terms described accessibly and with reference to the 50 canonical titles; and includes many two-tone stills from adventure, romance, children's interest, suspense, and historical anime productions. . . . Teens who love anime will find this guide validates their interests, and library staff can turn to it as a reliable way to learn the vocabulary, icons, and plots of a good variety of examples of the popular art." SLJ
Includes bibliographical references

792 Stage presentations

Aliki

★ **William** Shakespeare & the Globe; written & illustrated by Aliki. HarperCollins Pubs. 1999 48p il hardcover o.p. pa $6.99
Grades: 4 5 6 7 8 9 **792**
1. Poets 2. Authors 3. Dramatists 4. Globe Theatre (London, England) 5. Shakespeare's Globe (London, England)
ISBN 0-06-027820-X; 0-06-443722-1 pa

LC 98-7903

"A logically organized and engaging text, plenty of detailed illustrations with informative captions, and a clean design provide a fine introduction to both bard and theater." Horn Book Guide

The **Cambridge** guide to American theatre; edited by Don B. Wilmeth; assistant to the editor, Leonard Jacobs. 2nd hardcover ed.; Cambridge University Press 2007 757p il $150
Grades: 11 12 Adult **792**
1. Reference books 2. Theater -- United States -- Dictionaries
ISBN 978-0-521-83538-1; 0-521-83538-0

LC 2008-270062

First published 1993

This guide covers different "aspects of the American theatre from its earliest history to the present. Entries include people, venues and companies scattered through the USA, plays and musicals, and theatrical phenomena." Publisher's note

Includes bibliographical references

Caruso, Sandra

★ The **young** actor's book of improvisation; dramatic situations from Shakespeare to Spielberg: ages 12-16. [by] Sandra Caruso with Susan Kosoff. Heinemann (Portsmouth) 1998 xx, 259p $22.95
Grades: 9 10 11 12 **792**
1. Acting
ISBN 0-325-00049-2

LC 97-46817

A sourcebook of techniques designed to develop improvisional skills in young actors

Scenes "are divided thematically—confrontation, fantasy, solo moment, relationships, etc.—and according to the number and gender of the actors. Each brief entry includes the source, characters, place, and time period if relevant, an explanation of the situation, and comments, including tips, notes, and supplemental information to 'enhance the actors' understanding of story and character.'" Booklist

Includes bibliographical references

Corson, Richard

★ **Stage** makeup; [by] Richard Corson, Beverly Gore Norcross, James Glavan. 10th ed.; Ally & Bacon/Pearson 2009 xx, 407p il $141.40

Grades: 11 12 Adult   792

1. Theatrical makeup
ISBN 978-0-205-64454-4

LC 2008-53845

First published 1942 by Appleton. Periodically revised

The authors discuss the art and technique of theatrical makeup, covering such topics as facial anatomy, various methods for applying greasepaint and other makeup, and the use of beards, wigs, and prosthetic pieces.

Lamedman, Debbie

The **ultimate** audition book for teens; 111 one-minute monologues. Smith & Kraus (Young actor series)

Grades: 7 8 9 10 11 12   792

1. Acting 2. Monologues

A series of collections of 111 original monologues, all about one minute long, to be used by male and female teenage actors in auditions.

"Some suggestive sexual situations described here will not be acceptable in some classrooms. Drama teachers may, however, welcome some of this material for beginning acting students." Book Rep [review of volume one]

Levy, Gavin

112 acting games; a comprehensive workbook of theatre games for developing acting skills. Meriwether Pub. 2005 237p il pa $17.95

Grades: 9 10 11 12   792

1. Games 2. Acting
ISBN 1-56608-106-8; 978-1-56608-106-1

LC 2005-1784

"The games in this workbook for acting students are divided into twenty different categories, including Relaxtion, Memorization, and Improvisation. The author explains the instructions for each game in a clear manner, including tips on student placement, the appropriate number of participants, and modifications for varying ages. . . . This book is a definite asset to any drama teacher." Voice Youth Advocates

Includes bibliographical references

Marasco, Ron

Notes to an actor. Ivan R. Dee 2007 214p $24.95

Grades: 11 12 Adult   792

1. Acting
ISBN 978-1-56663-757-2; 1-56663-757-0

LC 2007-11653

This is "a compendium of suggestions, inspirations, warnings, and musings about the art of acting. Marasco speaks to actors who already possess at least a basic knowledge of their craft, seeking to heighten their abilities, clarify their artistic choices, eliminate blocks, and make their work more exciting and enriching. . . . This book is truly unique among acting resources. Useful both to those seeking to further their development as actors and to those for whom acting has long been a profession, this is an insightful, invaluable, and definitive work." Choice

Includes bibliographical references

Millennium monologs; 95 contemporary characterizations for young actors. edited by Gerald Lee Ratliff. Meriwether 2002 261p pa $15.95

Grades: 8 9 10 11 12   792

1. Acting 2. Monologues 3. American drama -- Collections
ISBN 1-56608-082-7

LC 2002-13009

An anthology of monologues by contemporary writers, divided into four categories: "Hope and Longing," "Spirit and Soul," "Fun and Fantasy," and "Doubt and Despair." Includes audition techniques

"This fine collection of American monologues is notable for its diversity as well as for the high quality of the material." Booklist

Rogers, Barb

★ **Costumes,** accessories, props, and stage illusions made easy. Meriwether Pub. 2005 205p il pa $19.95

Grades: 8 9 10 11 12   792

1. Costume 2. Theater -- Production and direction
ISBN 978-1-56608-103-0; 1-56608-103-3

LC 2005-4359

This book details ways to make theater "costumes with simple tools such as scissors, glue guns, and paint. In addition, there are chapters on how to make hats, gloves, armor, and animal heads, as well as other props and accessories from rummage-sale finds and a little imagination. . . . This is a useful volume for schools and community theaters with little or no budgets for costumes and props." SLJ

Includes bibliographical references

Varley, Joy

★ **Places,** please! a manual for high-school theater directors. Smith & Kraus 2001 196p (Young actor series) pa $16.95

Grades: 9 10 11 12   792

1. Theater -- Production and direction
ISBN 1-57525-282-1

LC 01-20316

This guide offers guidance on choosing a script, casting, costuming, working with faculty, rehearsing, directing young actors, stage design and lighting

792.02 Miscellany

Rapkin, Mickey

Theater geek; the real life drama of a summer at Stagedoor Manor, the famous performing arts camp. Free Press 2010 220p il $15

Grades: 8 9 10 11 12 Adult   **792.02**

1. Camps 2. Acting 3. Actors

ISBN 1-4391-4576-8; 9781439145777

LC 2009-48797

This book, by Mickey Rapkin, focuses on "Stagedoor Manor, a theater camp in the Catskills where big-time Hollywood casting directors came to find the next generation of stars. . . . Rapkin . . . [follows] three determined teen actors through the rivalries, heartbreak, and triumphs of a summer at Stagedoor Manor." (Publisher's note)

"A 31-year-old senior editor for GQ, Rapkin indulges his inner theater geek by spending a session at Stagedoor Manor, a celebrated performing-arts summer camp for kids...He also writes of the changes that this age of American Idol and YouTube have visited on the Stagedoor culture. But overall this is an unabashed love letter to a facility that remains a microcosm of the New York theater scene. Definitely not for cynical readers, but theater geeks will, well, . . . geek out over it." Booklist

792.6 Musical plays

Bloom, Ken

Broadway musicals; the 101 greatest shows of all time. [by] Ken Bloom & Frank Vlastnik; new preface by Broadway's leading ladies; foreword by Jerry Orbach. Rev. and updated ed.; Black Dog & Leventhal 2010 344p il $40

Grades: 11 12 Adult   **792.6**

1. Musicals

ISBN 978-1-57912-849-4

First published 2004

This is a history of Broadway musicals from the past 100 years. Each entry features commentary, photos and brief features on performers and creators.

Kantor, Michael

★ Broadway: the American musical; [by] Michael Kantor; Laurence Maslon. Bulfinch Press 2004 480p il $60

Grades: 11 12 Adult   **792.6**

1. Musicals

ISBN 0-8212-2905-2

LC 2003-69715

This companion volume to a PBS documentary includes interviews and photographs of Broadway musicals from 1893 to 2004

"With its beguiling blend of entertainment and history, this splendid work is a must-have." Publ Wkly

Includes bibliographical references

792.7 Variety shows and theatrical dancing

Kohen, Yael

We killed; the rise of women in American comedy. Yael Kohen. Sarah Crichton Books 2012 xxviii, 308 p.p ill.

Grades: 10 11 12 Adult   **792.7**

1. Stand-up comedy -- United States 2. Women comedians -- United States -- Biography 3. Women comedians -- United States -- Interviews

ISBN 9780374287238

LC 2012018565

In this book, Yael Kohen "pieces together the revolution that happened to (and by) women in American comedy, gathering the country's most prominent comediennes and the . . . colleagues who revolved around them. She starts in the 1950s, when comic success meant ridiculing and de-sexualizing yourself; when Joan Rivers and Phyllis Diller emerged as America's favorite frustrated ladies. . . . Kohen brings us into the sixties and seventies, when the appearance of smart, edgy comedians (Elaine May, Lily Tomlin) and the women's movement brought a new wave of radicals." (Publisher's note)

Nevraumont, Edward J.

The ultimate improv book; a complete guide to comedy improvisation. {by} Edward J. Nevraumont and Nicholas P. Hanson, with additional material from Kurt Smeaton. Meriwether 2001 272p pa $16.95

Grades: 9 10 11 12   **792.7**

1. Acting 2. Comedy

ISBN 1-56608-075-4

LC 2001-51396

"Suggestions for assembling a capable, compatible team of players, setting up performances guidelines, and keeping the action flowing and on target for the audience preface set-ups for 60 games. The game-exercises . . . are specifically designed to assist players in using language, literature, song, and movement in their skits." Booklist

Includes bibliographical references

792.8 Ballet and modern dance

Balanchine, George, 1904-1983

101 stories of the great ballets; George Balanchine and Francis Mason. First edition Dolphin Books 1975 xiv, 541 p.p $18.95

Grades: 5 6 7 8 9 10 11 12 Adult   **792.8**

1. Ballet -- Stories, plots, etc.

ISBN 0385033982; 9780385033985

LC 73009140

This book, by George Balanchine and Francis Mason, "includes scene-by-scene retellings of the most popular classic and contemporary ballets, as performed by the world's leading dance companies. Certain to delight long-time fans as well as those just discovering the beauty and drama of ballet." (Publisher's note)

"Accessible books on ballet are few and far between . . . [but] George Balanchine and Francis Mason's 101 Stories of

the Great Ballets is considered the bible of ballet librettos."
Christian Science Monitor

Craine, Debra
  ★ The **Oxford** dictionary of dance; [by] Debra
Craine, Judith Mackrell. 2nd ed.; Oxford University
Press 2010 502p il (Oxford paperback reference)
pa $18.95
Grades: 11 12 Adult   **792.8**
    1. Reference books 2. Dance -- Dictionaries
    ISBN 978-0-19-956344-9; 0-19-956344-6
                                        LC 2010-930321
  Based on The concise Oxford dictionary of ballet by
Horst Kroegler. First published 2000
  "The work covers all aspects of the diverse dance world
from classical ballet to modern, from flamenco to hip-hop,
from tap to South Asian dance forms and includes . . . entries
on technical terms, steps, styles, works and countries, in addition to many biographies of dancers, choreographers, and
companies." Publisher's note
  Includes bibliographical references

Freedman, Russell
  ★ **Martha** Graham, a dancer's life. Clarion Bks.
1998 175p il $18
Grades: 7 8 9 10   **792.8**
    1. Dancers 2. Modern dance 3. Choreographers 4.
    Dance teachers
    ISBN 0-395-74655-8
                                          LC 97-15832
  A photo-biography of the American dancer, teacher, and
choreographer who was born in Pittsburgh in 1895 and who
became a leading figure in the world of modern dance
  "A showstopping biography that captures its dynamic
subject's personality, vision, and artistry." SLJ
  Includes bibliographical references

Minden, Eliza Gaynor
  The **ballet** companion; a dancer's guide to the
technique, traditions, and joys of ballet. Eliza Gaynor
Minden. Touchstone Books 2005 xv, 331 p.p illustrations (some color) $29.95
Grades: 6 7 8 9 10 11 12 Adult   **792.8**
    1. Ballet 2. Ballet dancers 3. Ballet dancing --
    Handbooks, manuals, etc
    ISBN 9780743264075; 074326407X
                                        LC 2005044102
  This book, by Eliza Gaynor Minden "is a fresh, comprehensive, and thoroughly up-to-date reference book for the
dancer. With 150 stunning photographs of ballet stars Maria
Riccetto and Benjamin Millepied demonstrating perfect execution of positions and steps, this elegant volume brims with
everything today's dance student needs" (Publisher's note)
  "[The Author's] explanation of the differences between
the six major ballet styles, along with the superb glossaries
of terms and dance history timeline, make this book a valuable resource for dance studios and a great primer for dancers in the early stages of training." Publishers Weekly
  Includes bibliographical references (p. [316]-317)
and index

Reynolds, Nancy
  No fixed points; dance in the twentieth century. [by] Nancy Reynolds and Malcolm McCormick.
Yale Univ. Press 2003 907p il $50
Grades: 11 12 Adult   **792.8**
    1. Dance 2. Ballet 3. Modern dance
    ISBN 0-300-09366-7
                                        LC 2003-10754
  "Although everyone will be using the book for reference, Reynolds and McCormick have produced a work that
is completely unlike a standard reference book; you don't
just look things up in it—you read it. Here is a coherent,
reasoned and entertaining chronicle of dance performance
in the West over the hundred years that are unquestionably
the fullest and most complicated in the long history of this
fragmented and elusive art." N Y Times
  Includes bibliographical references

Warren, Gretchen
  Classical ballet technique; {by} Gretchen Ward
Warren; photographs by Susan Cook. University of
S. Fla. Press 1989 395p il hardcover o.p. pa $39.95
Grades: 11 12 Adult   **792.8**
    1. Ballet
    ISBN 0-8130-0895-6; 0-8130-0945-6 pa
                                          LC 89-31141
  Text and numerous photographs explain the correct ex-
ecution of ballet steps
  "General material on basic concepts, body structure and
proportion, and ballet class proceed this extraordinary man-
ual and guide." Booklist
  Includes glossary and bibliographical references

792.802 Specific aspects of ballet and modern dance

Bernstein, Richard
  A **girl** named Faithful Plum; Richard Bernstein.
Alfred A. Knopf Books for Young Readers 2011
270p. ill. $15.99; lib bdg $18.99
Grades: 7 8 9 10 11 12   **792.802**
    1. Dancers 2. Arts -- China 3. Dance directors 4.
    China -- Biography
    ISBN 978-0-375-86960-0; 0-375-86960-3; 978-0-375-
    96960-7 lib bdg; 0-375-96960-8 lib bdg
                                        LC 2010048722
  This book tells the childhood story of dancer "Zhongmei
. . . [who] is a young Chinese girl from a rural family so poor
that though they raise chickens, she herself is allowed only
one boiled egg a year. At the age of 11, she hears the Beijing Dance Academy is holding open auditions for the first
time since the Cultural Revolution. Without any connections
to the Communist Party or even money for the train ride,
Zhongmei's parents at first refuse to let her audition. But
after Zhongmei stages a hunger strike, her parents borrow
money to send her on the grueling trip to Beijing. There,
Zhongmei endures an even more demanding seven-stage
audition and beats out over 20,000 girls to enter the school.
Soon she discovers that was the easy part." (N Y Times)

792.9 Stage productions

Grove, Elliot

★ **130** projects to get you into filmmaking. Barron's Educational Series 2009 128p il $21.99

Grades: 10 11 12 Adult   **792.9**

1. Cinematography 2. Motion pictures -- Production and direction

ISBN 978-0-7641-4296-3

                    LC 2009-928377

"This may be the most engaging and visually demonstrative introduction to filmmaking available in print. Actual filmic examples of diagrammed screenshots, storyboards, script breakdown sheets, business forms, equipment, lighting, makeup, and shot catalogs help to flesh out attractively the author's attainable 130 steps from idea to direction to postproduction to marketing and publicity." Libr J

Includes glossary

794.1 Chess

King, Daniel

★ **Chess**; from first moves to checkmate. New ed.; Kingfisher 2010 64p il pa $8.99

Grades: 5 6 7 8 9 10 11 12   **794.1**

1. Chess

ISBN 978-0-7534-1930-4

First published 2000

Introduces the rules and strategies of chess, as well as its history and some of the great players and matches.

Naroditsky, Daniel

Mastering positional chess; practical lessons of a junior world champion. [by] Daniel A. Naroditsky. New in Chess 2010 239p il pa $23.95

Grades: 7 8 9 10 11 12   **794.1**

1. Chess

ISBN 978-90-5691-310-6

"Every chapter focuses on a different aspect of playing the game. For example, one of the chapters simply deals with defense and how a player can make a comeback. The author uses many pictures to show positions of the pieces and different moves required to win. There is fabulous dialogue in the different scenarios cited. Each chapter also contains various chess exercises that the reader can try to solve. . . Although this book is very thorough, it is definitely for the more skilled chess player. Experienced chess players will find it a must read." Voice of Youth Advocates

794.8 Electronic games

Adams, Suellen S.

Crash course in gaming; Suellen S. Adams. Libraries Unlimited, an imprint of ABC-CLIO, LLC 2014 xi, 125 p.p (Libraries unlimited crash course series) (pbk.) $45

Grades: Adult Professional   **794.8**

1. Video games

ISBN 161069046X; 9781610690461

                    LC 2013031465

This book, by Suellen S. Adams, "discusses the pros and cons of gaming, the types of games and game systems, circulating collections, and game programs. It explains how a library's video game program can—and should—do much more than simply draw younger users to the library, providing examples of how everyone from parents to senior citizens can benefit from a patron-oriented computer gaming program." (Publisher's note)

Includes bibliographical references (pages 121-122) and index

Neiburger, Eli

★ **Gamers** . . . in the library?! the why, what, and how of videogame tournaments for all ages. American Library Association 2007 178p pa $42

Grades: Adult Professional   **794.8**

1. Video games 2. Computer games 3. Young adults' libraries

ISBN 978-0-8389-0944-7; 0-8389-0944-2

                    LC 2007-10512

"With the writing as vibrant as its topic, . . . [this book] is a must-have professional tool." Voice Youth Advocates

Includes bibliographical references

Parks, Peggy J., 1951-

Video games. ReferencePoint Press 2008 104p il map (Compact research. Current issues) $25.95

Grades: 8 9 10 11 12   **794.8**

1. Video games

ISBN 978-1-60152-053-1; 1-60152-053-0

                    LC 2007-49886

This "book opens with descriptions of the growing popularity of video games and the regulation and legislation of content and sales; ratings; connections with violent crime; and health effects, including addiction. An overview provides further background and context to these issues, and . . . chapters follow addressing related questions and providing other related material." SLJ

Includes bibliographical references

796 Athletic and outdoor sports and games

Blumenthal, Karen

Let me play; the story of Title IX, the law that changed the future of girls in America. Atheneum Books for Young Readers 2005 152p il $19.95

Grades: 6 7 8 9 10   **796**

1. Women athletes 2. Sex discrimination 3. Education Amendments of 1972 -- Title IX

ISBN 0-689-85957-0

                    LC 2004-1450

Title IX legislation assured "that 'no one could be closed out of any educational program or activity receiving federal money simply because of sex.' After explaining the genesis of the legislation, . . . Blumenthal discusses how evolving guidelines and interpretations brought girls' school athletic programs into its purview. Grades nine to twelve." (Bull Cent Child Books)

"The author looks at American women's evolving rights by focusing on the history and future of Title IX, which bans sex discrimination in U.S. education. . . . The images are . . . gripping, and relevant political cartoons and fact boxes add further interest. Few books cover the last few decades of American women's history with such clarity and detail." Booklist

Includes bibliographical references

Encyclopedia of sports in America; a history from foot races to extreme sports. edited by Murry R. Nelson. Greenwood Press 2009 2v il set $175
Grades: 7 8 9 10 11 12 Adult   796
1. Reference books 2. Sports -- Encyclopedias
ISBN 978-0-313-34790-0

LC 2008-34749

The editor "presents a work tracing the history of sports in America from the Colonial era through about 2007. . . . Horse racing, billiards, basketball, football, cycling, bowling, sports broadcasting, hockey, golf, baseball, and NASCAR count among the diverse topics. . . . Written for general readers, this set could easily fill a niche in middle school and high school libraries, as well as public libraries, particularly where research on sports history is a popular topic." Libr J

Includes bibliographical references

Gifford, Clive
Sports. Amicus 2010 46p il (Healthy lifestyles) lib bdg $32.80
Grades: 7 8 9 10   796
1. Sports 2. Physical fitness
ISBN 978-1-60753-088-6; 1-60753-088-0

LC 2009-47567

This book is "well-written and satisfyingly informative. . . . [The] magazine-like format includes numerous sidebars, color photos, and charts." SLJ

Includes glossary and bibliographical references

Li, WenFang
Extreme sports. Mason Crest Publishers 2010 96p il (Getting the edge: conditioning, injuries, and legal & illicit drugs) lib bdg $24.95
Grades: 7 8 9 10   796
1. Extreme sports
ISBN 978-1-4222-1729-0; 1-4222-1729-9

LC 2010-7229

This book "offers a general introduction to . . . [extreme sports], its rules, and its history before zeroing in on health and safety concerns. . . . Scanning a broad range of activities, from parachuting to rock climbing to snowboarding, . . . [it] provides useful information and advice on topics such as coping with fear and dealing with environmental injuries." Booklist

Includes bibliographical references

Morris, Jim
The **oldest** rookie; big-league dreams from a small-town guy. {by} Jim Morris with Joel Engel. Little, Brown 2001 276p $22.95; pa $13.95

Grades: 11 12 Adult   796
1. Teachers 2. Baseball players 3. Baseball -- Biography
ISBN 0-316-59156-4; 0-446-67837-6 pa

LC 00-64269

"Morris, a high-school baseball coach and former minor-league pitcher, makes a deal with the kids on his team: if they make the play-offs, he'll try for the majors one last time. They do, and he does. It's a fabulous baseball story, full of wonderful humor, but it isn't all about dreams coming true; it also shows how much dreams cost, to the dreamers and to their loved ones." Booklist

Musiker, Liz Hartman
The **smart** girl's guide to sports; a hip handbook for women who don't know a slam dunk from a grand slam. Hudson Street Press 2005 301p il hardcover o.p. pa $15
Grades: 9 10 11 12   796
1. Sports
ISBN 1-59463-011-9; 0-452-28950-5 pa

LC 2005-18858

This book "covers all the major professional sports: football, basketball, baseball, hockey, golf, soccer, boxing, and even car racing. Each chapter includes a 'Here's How It Works' section that explains the basics of the game; [and] profiles of each sport's timeless greats and 'contemporary cool' players." Publisher's note

Includes bibliographical references

Nike is a goddess; the history of women in sports. edited by Lissa Smith; introduction by Mariah Burton Nelson. Atlantic Monthly Press 1998 331p il hardcover o.p. pa $14
Grades: 11 12 Adult   796
1. Sports 2. Women athletes
ISBN 0-87113-761-5

LC 98-27049

"The quality of writing in the different sections varies but each writer is well connected with her field and all give a good background history as well as an assessment of current developments in the sport. Controversial issues are not ignored, and lesbianism is addressed." SLJ

Sokolove, Michael Y.
Warrior girls; protecting our daughters against the injury epidemic in women's sports. [by] Michael Sokolove. Simon & Schuster 2008 308p $25; pa $21.95
Grades: 9 10 11 12 Adult   796
1. Sports medicine 2. Sports for women 3. Wounds and injuries
ISBN 978-0-7432-9755-4; 0-7432-9755-4; 978-0-7432-9756-1 pa; 0-7432-9756-3 pa

LC 2008-12176

This is an "examination of the prevalence and sometimes life-altering effect of injuries in women's sports. . . . [The author] examines the differences in male and female anatomy, compares the competitiveness in men's and women's sports, and focuses on a handful of specific individuals to explore how an athlete's drive for perfection can lead to disaster. . .

. This well-researched, well-reasoned, and forcefully argued book makes an important contribution to the literature of sports." Booklist

Includes bibliographical references

★ Sports illustrated 2011 almanac; by the editors of Sports illustrated. Time Home Entertainment 2010 559p il pa $14.99

Grades: 7 8 9 10 11 12 Adult   **796**

1. Sports 2. Reference books

ISBN 978-1-60320-863-5

Annual. First published 1991 with title: Sports illustrated . . . sports almanac

"Provides team and individual records and highlights for all major sports. . . . A brief essay opens the section on each sport, followed by page upon page of records, both current and retrospective. Interspersed throughout . . . are black-and-white and color photographs and notable quotations by sports figures." Am Ref Books Annu, 1993

Wheeler, Dion

★ The **sports** scholarships insider's guide; getting money for college at any division. 2nd ed.; Sourcebooks 2009 377p il pa $16.99

Grades: 9 10 11 12   **796**

1. Athletes 2. Scholarships 3. College sports

ISBN 978-1-4022-1884-2

First published 2005

"Topics include the recruiting process, financial-aid opportunities, academic requirements, preparing credentials, school visits, and negotiating for financial assistance from NCAA division I, II, III and NAIA institutions. The second half of the book includes listings of sports for the various divisions, institution names, and Web addresses." SLJ

Includes glossary

Why a curveball curves; the incredible science of sports. edited by Frank Vizard; foreward by Robert Lipsyte. Hearst Books 2008 224p il (Popular mechanics) $19.95

Grades: 11 12 Adult   **796**

1. Sports 2. Science

ISBN 978-1-58816-475-9; 1-58816-475-6

LC 2007-29702

This collection of articles from Popular Mechanics explains the science behind different sports. In addition to baseball, the book "talks about basketball, soccer, hockey, golf, and several other sports, and it answers some very interesting questions, such as why Gretzky really was the greatest (an innate ability to translate physical cues into action) and how you, too, can bend it (a soccer ball, that is), like Beckham. A must-read for sports fans, physics buffs, and general audiences, too." Booklist

796.21   Roller skating

Werner, Doug

In-line skater's start-up; a beginner's guide to in-line skating and roller hockey. Tracks Pub. 1995 159p il (Start-up sports) pa $9.95

Grades: 9 10 11 12   **796.21**

1. In-line skating

ISBN 1-884654-04-5

LC 95-60153

This work discusses the various techniques and equipment required for both skating and hockey. This illustrated guide also provides safety tips

796.22   Skateboarding

Beal, Becky

Skateboarding; the ultimate guide. Becky Beal. ABC-CLIO, LLC 2013 xx, 150 p.p ill. (Greenwood guides to extreme sports) (hardcover) $37.00; (ebook) $37.00

Grades: 9 10 11 12 Adult   **796.22**

1. Skateboarding

ISBN 0313381127; 9780313381126; 9780313381133 pdf

LC 2012035631

This book, by Becky Beal, part of the "Greenwood Guides to Extreme Sports," profiles skateboarding. "In the last half century, skateboarding has evolved from a simple, idyllic child's pastime that originated in southern California to becoming a worldwide youth culture phenomenon. This now-mainstream action sport has spawned a multi-billion-dollar commercial market." (Publisher's note)

Includes bibliographical references (p. 125-135) and index.

796.3   Ball games

Chetwynd, Josh

The **secret** history of balls; Josh Chetwynd; Illustrations by Emily Stackhouse. Perigee Trade 2011 xiv, 221p ill.

Grades: 7 8 9 10 11 12 Adult   **796.3**

1. Ball games 2. Sporting goods 3. Sports -- History

ISBN 9780399536748

LC 2010054221

This book "mines the stories and lore of sports and recreation to offer insight into 60 balls - whether they're hollow, solid, full of air, or stuffed with twine or made of leather, metal, rubber, plastic, or polyurethane - that give us joy on playing fields and in every arena from backyards to stadiums around the globe." (Publishers' note)

796.323   Basketball

Blais, Madeleine

In these girls, hope is a muscle. Warner Bks. 1996 266p pa $13.95

Grades: 11 12 Adult   **796.323**

1. Basketball 2. Cathedral High School (Springfield, Mass.)

ISBN 0-446-67210-6; 978-0-446-67210-8

First published 1995 by Atlantic Monthly Press

"Alternately funny, exciting and moving, the book should be enjoyed not only by girls and women who have played sports but also those who wanted to but let themselves be discouraged." Publ Wkly

D'Orso, Michael

★ **Eagle** blue; a team, a tribe, and a high school basketball season in Arctic Alaska. Bloomsbury Pub. 2006 323p il map $23.95

Grades: 11 12 Adult **796.323**
1. Basketball 2. School sports 3. Fort Yukon (Alaska)
ISBN 978-1-58234-623-6; 1-58234-623-2
LC 2005-25430

The author "follows the Fort Yukon Eagles through their 2005 season to the state championship, shifting between a mesmerizing narrative and the thoughts of the players, their coach and their fans. What emerges is more than a sports story; it's a striking portrait of a community consisting of a traditional culture bombarded with modernity, where alcoholism, domestic violence and school dropout rates run wild." Publ Wkly

Doeden, Matt

The **Final** Four; the pursuit of college basketball glory. Matt Doeden. Millbrook Press 2016 64 p. illustrations (lb: alk. paper) $33.32

Grades: 4 5 6 7 8 **796.323**
1. College basketball 2. Sports tournaments 3. NCAA Basketball Tournament -- History
ISBN 1467787809; 9781467787802
LC 2015025429

This book, by Matt Doeden, examines how "the NCAA men's basketball tournament is one of the most popular sports events in the United States. By the time the tournament of 68 teams has been whittled down to the Final Four, excitement reaches a fever pitch. From the first intercollegiate basketball game played in 1895 all the way to the thrills and drama of the most recent Final Four, read about the shocking moments and stunning upsets that give March Madness its name." (Publisher's note)

"Though the book's appeal will be limited to serious basketball fans, the historical perspective and engaging presentation make it a solid choice." SLJ

Includes bibliographical references and index

Dohrmann, George

Play their hearts out; a coach, his star recruit, and the youth basketball machine. Ballantine Books 2010 422p il $26

Grades: 10 11 12 Adult **796.323**
1. Basketball 2. Basketball coaches 3. Basketball players
ISBN 978-0-345-50860-7; 0-345-50860-2
LC 2010-15470

The author "follows California phenom Demetrius Walker through the cycle of Amateur Athletic Union (AAU) summer league hoops, from playing for ambitious hustler and coach Joe Keller to the face of grassroots basketball, longtime coach Pat Barrett. In a constant search for the next Lebron, just as before for the next Michael Jordan, AAU coaches, with support and financing from shoe giants Nike and Adidas, woo youngsters to their summer league basketball teams with gear, shoes, and promises of a college scholarship. . . . [Dohrmann's] insights into the seamy side of youth basketball are investigative journalism at its best." Libr J

FreeDarko presents the macrophenomenal pro basketball almanac; styles, stats and stars in today's game. Bloomsbury USA 2008 219p il $23

Grades: 9 10 11 12 Adult **796.323**
1. Basketball 2. National Basketball Association
ISBN 978-1-59691-561-9; 1-59691-561-7

"This is a wonderful basketball book that blends a unique perspective, arresting presentation, and superior knowledge of its subject." Booklist

Grange, Michael

Basketball's greatest stars; Michael Grange. 3rd edition Firefly Books 2015 248 p. color illustrations pbk $24.95

Grades: 9 10 11 12 Adult **796.323**
1. National Basketball Association 2. Basketball players -- United States -- Biography
ISBN 1770855777; 9781770855779
LC 2015510411

"The spectacular success of the NBA is based on its stars, their performances and personalities, which excite fans game after game, championship after championship. Michael Grange has profiled the 50 greatest and most exciting of these players in 'Basketball's Greatest Stars.' They're all here: the score-at-will centers, the quick-dishing guards, the take-it-to-the-hoop power forwards, and the three-point shooters. The book also features a chapter on the future greats who are starting on NBA hardwood now." (Publisher's note)

Joravsky, Ben

Hoop dreams; a true story of hardship and triumph. introduction by Charles Barkley. Turner Pub. (Atlanta) 1995 301p il hardcover o.p. pa $13.50

Grades: 9 10 11 12 **796.323**
1. Basketball 2. Chicago (Ill.) -- Social conditions
ISBN 0-06-097689-6 pa
LC 94-46398

"Based on the documentary film of the same name, this book . . . looks at the dream of ghetto youths to play in the NBA." Publ Wkly

McCallum, Jack

★ **Dream** team; how Michael, Magic, Larry, Charles, and the greatest team of all time conquered the world and changed the game of basketball forever. Jack McCallum. Ballantine Books 2012 xxix, 352 p.p col. ill. (hardback) $28

Grades: 9 10 11 12 Adult **796.323**
1. Olympic games 2. Basketball -- History 3. Basketball players -- United States -- Biography 4. Basketball -- United States -- History 5. Basketball teams -- United States -- History
ISBN 0345520483; 0345520505; 9780345520487; 9780345520500
LC 2012006253

In this book "sports journalist Jack McCallum delivers the . . . story of . . . the 1992 U.S. Olympic Men's Basketball Team that captivated the world. . . . He offers a . . . look at the controversial selection process. . . . [a]nd he narrates . . . the legendary July 1992 intrasquad scrimmage that pitted the Dream Teamers against one another in what may have been the greatest pickup game--and the greatest exhibition of trash talk--in history." (Publisher's note)

"...[McCallum] effectively evokes the remarkable team while placing it within the larger historical context. Basketball and Olympics fans will welcome this nostalgic trip through the recent past." Kirkus

Rosen, Charles, 1941-
Crazy basketball; a life in and out of bounds. foreword by Phil Jackson. University of Nebraska Press 2011 301p $24.95
Grades: 11 12 Adult **796.323**
1. Authors 2. Sportswriters 3. Basketball coaches 4. Basketball -- Biography 5. Continental Basketball Association
ISBN 978-0-8032-1793-5
LC 2010-26921
The author "recalls his years as a coach in the Continental Basketball Association. . . . The shining star here isn't Rosen or any of the players, it's the game itself. The last half-dozen pages will bring a tear to the eye of anyone for whom the game was or is a passion." Booklist

Simmons, Bill
★ The **book** of basketball; the NBA according to the sports guy. Ballantine/ESPN Books 2009 715p il $30; pa $18
Grades: 11 12 Adult **796.323**
1. Basketball 2. National Basketball Association
ISBN 978-0-345-51176-8; 0-345-51176-X; 978-0-345-52010-4 pa; 0-345-52010-6 pa
LC 2009-36006
The author "summarizes the history of the league, discusses his personal fandom, includes a great 'what if?' chapter (what if Michael Jordan had been drafted second by Portland instead of third by Chicago?), analyzes Most Valuable Player choices through the years, and dissects the careers of the league's all-time best players. The true NBA fan will dive into this hefty volume and won't resurface for about a week, emerging from the man cave unshaven, smelling of beer and pizza, grinning, and armed with NBA history, insight, anecdotes, statistics, and a dozen new examples of Simmons' Unintentional Comedy Scale. This is just plain fun. Expect significant demand from hoops junkies." Booklist
Includes bibliographical references

796.325 Volleyball

Crisfield, Deborah
Winning volleyball for girls; [by] Deborah W. Crisfield, John Monteleone; foreword by Maria Nolan. 3rd ed.; Chelsea House 2009 189p il (Winning sports for girls) lib bdg $44.95; pa $11.96

Grades: 7 8 9 10 11 12 **796.325**
1. Volleyball
ISBN 978-0-8160-7720-5 lib bdg; 0-8160-7720-7 lib bdg; 978-0-8160-7721-2 pa; 0-8160-7721-5 pa
LC 2009-5733
First published 1995 by Facts on File
This includes a brief history of volleyball followed by descriptions of the rules, court and equipment, training, techniques such as the spike, the serve, the block, and the pass, offensive and defensive play, putting a team together, and game strategies.
Includes glossary and bibliographical references

Dearing, Joel
Volleyball fundamentals. Human Kinetics 2003 135p il (Sports fundamentals series) pa $14.95
Grades: 9 10 11 12 **796.325**
1. Volleyball
ISBN 0-7360-4508-2
LC 2002-15234

796.332 American football

Bissinger, H. G.
Friday night lights; a town, a team, and a dream. Da Capo Press 2000 367p il pa $15.95
Grades: 11 12 Adult **796.332**
1. Football 2. Permian High School (Odessa, Tex.)
ISBN 0-306-80990-7
LC 00-40510
First published 1990 by Addison-Wesley
"It is a tricky balancing act, but Mr. Bissinger carries it off: 'Friday Night Lights' offers a biting indictment of the sports craziness that grips not only Odessa but most of American society, while at the same time providing a moving evocation of its powerful allure." N Y Times Book Rev

Doeden, Matt
The **college** football championship; the fight for the top spot. Matt Doeden. Millbrook Press 2016 64 p. illustrations (some color) (lb: alk. paper) $33.32
Grades: 7 8 9 10 **796.332**
1. College sports 2. College football 3. College football coaches 4. Football -- United States -- History
ISBN 9781467718974
LC 2014041355
This book on college football, by Matt Doeden, "takes readers on a journey from the disorganized games of the early years to the most recent playoffs to determine the best college team in the nation. Along the way, discover some of the most incredible moments, games, blunders, and statistics in the history of college football championships." (Publisher's note)
"Highly recommended for sports enthusiasts." SLJ

McIntosh, J. S.
Football. Mason Crest Publishers 2010 96p (Getting the edge: conditioning, injuries, and legal & illicit drugs) lib bdg $24.95

Grades: 7 8 9 10   **796.332**
  1. Football
  ISBN 978-1-4222-1733-7; 1-4222-1733-7
                                    LC 2010-7230
This book covers basic safety training, equipment, preparation, and precautions related to football. It also covers
how to recover quickly from football-related injuries.
  Includes bibliographical references

796.334   Soccer (Association football)

Ayub, Awista
  However tall the mountain; a dream, eight girls,
and a journey home. Hyperion 2009 235p $23.99;
pa $14.99
Grades: 11 12 Adult   **796.334**
  1. Soccer 2. Women -- Afghanistan
  ISBN 978-1-4013-2249-6; 978-1-4013-1025-7 pa
                                    LC 2009-23225
"Ayub, an Afghan-born American, founded the Afghan
Youth Sports Exchange (AYSE) to draw Afghan girls into
soccer as a method of empowerment. She weaves together
the personal stories of the eight girls who pioneered the program, including their training trip to the United States and
their return to form teams and compete in Afghanistan. . .
. The courage of these eight girls will inspire readers of all
backgrounds." Libr J

Crisfield, Deborah
  ★ **Winning** soccer for girls; [by] Deborah W.
Crisfield; foreword by Bill Hawkey and Patrick Murphy. 3rd ed.; Chelsea House 2010 164p il (Winning sports for girls) lib bdg $39.50; pa $14.95
Grades: 7 8 9 10   **796.334**
  1. Soccer
  ISBN 978-0-8160-7714-4 lib bdg; 0-8160-7714-2 lib
bdg; 978-0-8160-7715-1 pa; 0-8160-7715-0 pa
                                    LC 2008-50595
  First published 1996 by Facts on File
This soccer guidebook contains "material on developing
agility, power, and strength and improving ball control and
handling. The history and rules of the game are also examined, and a glossary lists soccer terms." Publisher's note
  Includes glossary and bibliographical references

Longman, Jere
  ★ **The girls** of summer; the U.S. women's soccer team and how it changed the world. HarperCollins Pubs. 2000 318p il hardcover o.p. pa $14
Grades: 11 12 Adult   **796.334**
  1. Soccer 2. Women athletes
  ISBN 0-06-019657-2; 0-06-093468-9 pa
This "retelling of the 1999 Women's World Cup championship match between the U.S. and China weaves together
gender issues, the influence of Title IX, and biographies and
interviews with key players." Booklist
  Includes bibliographical references

McIntosh, J. S.
  Soccer. Mason Crest Publishers 2010 96p il
map (Getting the edge: conditioning, injuries, and
legal & illicit drugs) lib bdg $24.94
Grades: 7 8 9 10   **796.334**
  1. Soccer
  ISBN 978-1-4222-1739-9; 1-4222-1739-6
                                    LC 2010-15259
This book covers basic safety training, equipment, preparation, and precautions related to soccer. It also covers how
to recover quickly from soccer-related injuries.
  Includes bibliographical references

St. John, Warren
  Outcasts united; a refugee team, an American
town. Spiegel & Grau 2008 307p hardcover o.p.
pa $15
Grades: 11 12 Adult   **796.334**
  1. Soccer 2. Refugees 3. Soccer coaches 4.
Maintenance services executives
  ISBN 978-0-385-52203-8; 0-385-52203-7; 978-0-385-
52204-5 pa; 0-385-52204-5 pa
                                    LC 2008-40697
This is a "book about an unlikely soccer program in the
outlying Atlanta burb of Clarkston, Georgia. . . . Clarkston's
residents woke up one morning and found that the city's
housing projects had become havens of resettlement for
refugee families from war-ravaged locales including Libe-
ria, Afghanistan and Bosnia. Soccer is a pastime like sandlot
baseball or touch football to the often-traumatized boys on
the Fugees, a ramshackle intramural team of nine to 17-year-
olds that St. John follows, along with its Jordanian founder
Luma Hassan Mufleh, a Smith-educated woman whose
role as volunteer coach quickly expands to extended family member and social worker. St. John's aim is to draw a
portrait of small-town America in transition, and his eye for
detail is compelling from start to finish." Time Out N Y
  Includes bibliographical references

796.34   Racket games

Hinkson, Jim
  Lacrosse for dummies; by Jim Hinkson and Joe
Lombardi. 2nd ed.; John Wiley & Sons Canada, Ltd.
2010 xxvi, 330p il (--For dummies) pa $21.99
Grades: 9 10 11 12 Adult   **796.34**
  1. Lacrosse
  ISBN 978-0-470-73855-9; 0-470-73855-3
                                    LC 2010-282483
  First published 2003
"The book offers everything the beginning player needs
to know, from the necessary equipment to the basic rules
of the game, with explanations of the women's game and
the indoor game, too. It also offers . . . information for the
experienced player, including winning offensive and defensive strategies, along with skill-building exercises and drills.
Finally, there's information on how armchair lacrosse players can get their fix of the sport on television, online, on in
print." Publisher's note
  Includes bibliographical references

McAfee, Richard

Table tennis; steps to success. Human Kinetics 2009 xx, 203p il (Steps to success sports series) pa $18.95

Grades: 9 10 11 12 Adult **796.34**

1. Table tennis

ISBN 978-0-7360-7731-6; 0-7360-7731-6

LC 2009-4824

First published 1993 under the authorship of Larry Hodges

This book describes the skills and concepts used in table tennis.

Swissler, Becky

★ **Winning** lacrosse for girls; foreword by Katie Bergstrom. 2nd ed.; Chelsea House 2010 212p il (Winning sports for girls) lib bdg $44.95; pa $14.95

Grades: 7 8 9 10 **796.34**

1. Lacrosse

ISBN 978-0-8160-7712-0 lib bdg; 0-8160-7712-6 lib bdg; 978-0-8160-7713-7 pa; 0-8160-7713-4 pa

LC 2008-51346

First published 2004 by Facts on File

This lacrosse guidebook "teaches the game's basic skills, strategies, and drills and how to master them. Chapters cover the history of the game, the basics of stick handling, the rules of play, passing and receiving, offense and defense, key strategies, skills and tactics, conditioning, and . . . more." Publisher's note

Includes bibliographical references

Vanderhoof, Gabrielle

Lacrosse. Mason Crest Publishers 2010 96p il (Getting the edge: conditioning, injuries, and legal & illicit drugs) lib bdg $24.95

Grades: 7 8 9 10 **796.34**

1. Lacrosse

ISBN 978-1-4222-1737-5; 1-4222-1737-X

LC 2010-12754

This book covers basic safety training, equipment, preparation, and precautions related to lacrosse. It also covers how to recover quickly from lacrosse-related injuries.

Includes bibliographical references

796.342 Tennis (Lawn tennis)

Ashe, Arthur

Days of grace; a memoir. by Arthur Ashe and Arnold Rampersad. Knopf 1993 317p il hardcover o.p. pa $6.99

Grades: 11 12 Adult **796.342**

1. AIDS (Disease) 2. African American athletes 3. Tennis players 4. Nonfiction writers 5. Tennis -- Biography

ISBN 0-679-42396-6; 0-345-38681-7 pa

LC 92-54919

"This is a truly gripping book. It's gripping, it's moving, it's admirable; and what makes it so is Ashe's capacity for evaluating himself and the world with intelligence and honor." N Y Times Book Rev

796.352 Golf

Echikson, William

Shooting for Tiger; how golf's obsessed new generation is transforming a country club sport. PublicAffairs 2009 269p il $24.95

Grades: 11 12 Adult **796.352**

1. Golf

ISBN 978-1-58648-578-8; 1-58648-578-4

LC 2009-2003

"Who will be the next Tiger Woods? Echikson profiles the lives of many promising teenage golfers. The behind-the-scenes look at these young people, with their dedicated instructors, overzealous parents, and elite golf academies, provides a glimpse into the psyche of each of the players." SLJ

Includes bibliographical references

796.357 Baseball

Adair, Robert Kemp

The **physics** of baseball; 3rd ed, rev, updated, and expanded; Perennial 2002 169p il pa $12.95

Grades: 11 12 Adult **796.357**

1. Physics 2. Baseball 3. Force and energy

ISBN 0-06-008436-7

LC 2001-39886

A look at how some physical principles are applied to the game of baseball. Pitching, batting and the properties of bats are discussed

Includes bibliographical references

The **Baseball** anthology; 125 Years of stories, poems, articles, photographs, drawings, interviews, cartoons, and other memorabilia. general editor, Joseph Wallace; foreword by Sparky Anderson. Abrams 2004 296p il pa $19.95 **796.357**

1. Baseball

ISBN 0-8109-9179-9

LC 2005-284304

"Organized chronologically, the book combines a photo history of the game with a running narrative composed largely of excerpts from a wealth of well-known baseball writers. . . . The pictures are delightful, both for their excellent reproduction and for their content." Booklist

Baseball, the perfect game; an all-star anthology celebrating the game's greatest players, teams, and moments. Josh Leventhal, editor. Voyageur Press 2005 223p il $29.95

Grades: 11 12 Adult **796.357**

1. Baseball

ISBN 0-89658-668-5

LC 2004-23541

"Hardcore fans of 'America's Game' have a gem in this book. . . . The selections, all beautifully written, clearly are intended for older teens comfortable with documentary-style descriptions." Voice Youth Advocates

★ **Biographical** dictionary of American sports. Baseball; edited by David L. Porter. rev and expanded ed; Greenwood Press 2000 3v set $295
Grades: 11 12 Adult **796.357**
1. Baseball
ISBN 0-313-29884-X

LC 99-14840

First published 1987

This set "contains 1,450 signed entries. Individuals were chosen because of their 'impressive statistical records' or because they 'made a major impact on professional baseball' and include major league players; prominent minor league, Negro League, and Girls League players; and various executives, coaches, managers, and umpires. . . . Any library that wants to have a serious baseball reference section will need [this work]." Booklist

Includes bibliographical references

Cain, James T.

The **physics** of pitching; learn the mechanics, science, and psychology of pitching to success. [by] James T. Cain and Len Solesky; photography by Bruce Curtis. MVP: Quayside 2011 192p il $24.99
Grades: 11 12 Adult **796.357**
1. Force and energy 2. Human locomotion 3. Pitching (Baseball)
ISBN 978-0-7603-3850-6

LC 2010-45070

"A welcome title for any youth baseball coach or player, this pitching how-to guide illustrates each important step or movement in the successful delivery of the horsehide and instructs ably on injury avoidance, preparation (both physical and mental), and health and medicine, with an especially useful concluding chapter on 'Choosing Your Post High School Path.' Curtis's clear and focused color photos make plain the correct mechanics leading to optimum success." Libr J

Encyclopedia of women and baseball; edited by Leslie A. Heaphy and Mel Anthony May; foreword by Laura Wulf. McFarland & Co. 2006 438p il $49.95
Grades: 11 12 Adult **796.357**
1. Reference books 2. Baseball -- Encyclopedias 3. Women athletes -- Encyclopedias
ISBN 0-7864-2100-2; 978-0-7864-2100-8

LC 2006-8719

The editors "have produced a valuable resource on a seldom studied area of baseball." Choice

Includes bibliographical references

Fussman, Cal

After Jackie; pride, prejudice, and baseball's forgotten heroes: an oral history. ESPN Books 2007 243p il $24.95
Grades: 11 12 Adult **796.357**
1. Baseball players 2. African American athletes 3. Army officers 4. Baseball -- Biography
ISBN 1-93306-018-2; 978-1-93306-018-7

The author "traces Robinson's enormous legacy in sports, politics, and the civil rights movement through the men and women who came after him." Publisher's note

Garman, Judi

Softball skills & drills; [by] Judi Garman, Michelle Gromacki. 2nd ed.; Human Kinetics 2011 314p il pa $21.95
Grades: 9 10 11 12 **796.357**
1. Softball
ISBN 978-0-7360-9074-2; 0-7360-9074-6

LC 2010-48654

First published 2001

This book provides "coverage on strategies for every area of the game: hitting, fielding, pitching, catching, and baserunning. . . . [It includes] over 230 drills appropriate for players of all abilities." Publisher's note

Gola, Mark

★ **Winning** softball for girls; foreword by Gretchen Cammiso. 2nd ed.; Chelsea House 2009 220p il (Winning sports for girls) pa $14.95; lib bdg $44.95
Grades: 7 8 9 10 **796.357**
1. Softball
ISBN 0-8160-7716-9 lib bdg; 978-0-8160-7717-5 pa; 0-8160-7717-7 pa; 978-0-8160-7716-8 lib bdg

LC 2008-54453

First published 2002 by Facts on File

"Gola covers the history, rules of the game, and necessary equipment as well as tips for hitting, pitching, and base running. The fundamentals of defense and offense are covered, along with a number of drills in each area. In addition, the author details the various positions and gives advice on conditioning. . . . This title could prove useful in balancing baseball-laden collections." SLJ

Includes bibliographical references

Hogan, Lawrence D.

★ **Shades** of glory; the Negro Leagues and the story of African-American baseball. with a foreword by Jules Tygiel. National Geographic 2006 422p il $26
Grades: 11 12 Adult **796.357**
1. Baseball 2. Negro leagues 3. African American athletes
ISBN 0-7922-5306-X; 978-0-7922-5306-8

LC 2006-273216

"This is an important, informative, and entertaining contribution to sports history." Booklist

Kahn, Roger

Beyond the boys of summer; the very best of Roger Kahn. edited by Rob Miraldi. McGraw-Hill 2005 xxxvi, 364p hardcover o.p. pa $16.95
Grades: 11 12 Adult **796.357**
1. Baseball
ISBN 0-07-144727-X; 0-07-148119-2 pa

LC 2004-24851

"Kahn is a giant among sports journalists, and this is a fine sampling of his most memorable work." Booklist

Includes bibliographical references

Kelley, Brent P.

★ **Voices** from the Negro leagues; conversations with 52 baseball standouts of the period 1924-1960. McFarland & Co. 1998 334p il $45

Grades: 11 12 Adult   **796.357**

1. Baseball 2. African American athletes
ISBN 0-7864-2279-3

LC 97-37332

This "book is divided into two sections: the first comprises those who played prior to Jackie Robinson's breaking the color barrier; the second section features those who continued to play in the Negro leagues after Robinson's debut. . . . Kelley also provides biographies of each subject for context and whatever statistics are available. A wonderful book that should be exceedingly popular among fans with an interest in the game's history." Booklist

Includes bibliographical references

Posnanski, Joe

The **soul** of baseball; a road trip through Buck O'Neil's America. Morrow 2007 276p $24.95

Grades: 11 12 Adult   **796.357**

1. Baseball 2. Baseball players 3. Baseball coaches 4. Baseball managers 5. United States -- Description and travel
ISBN 978-0-06-085403-4; 0-06-085403-0

An account of how the author "spent a year on the road with the iconic Negro Leagues player and manager Buck O'Neil (1911-2006), recording the magnanimous 94-year-old's encounters with scores of fans and his vast repertoire of entertaining stories." Publ Wkly

Ripken, Cal

Play baseball the Ripken way; the complete illustrated guide to the fundamentals. [by] Cal Ripken, Jr. and Bill Ripken with Larry Burke. Random House 2004 236p il hardcover o.p. pa $15.95

Grades: 11 12 Adult   **796.357**

1. Baseball
ISBN 1-4000-6122-9; 0-8129-7050-0 pa

LC 2003-66725

"This book is the next best thing to a personal lesson with the man who broke Lou Gehrig's record of playing in 2,632 consecutive games; it's a comprehensive look at all aspects of how to play baseball that will benefit young players and adult weekend warriors." Publ Wkly

Vecsey, George

★ **Baseball**: a history of America's favorite game. Modern Library 2006 252p il (Modern Library chronicles) $21.95

Grades: 11 12 Adult   **796.357**

1. Baseball
ISBN 0-679-64338-9; 978-0-679-64338-8

LC 2006-45033

This history of baseball "unfolds much like a highlights tape, with a breezy background narrative of the game from

its pre-Civil War roots to its current drug scandals, structured around set pieces spotlighting the outsized deeds of luminaries like Babe Ruth, Jackie Robinson, Branch Rickey and George Steinbrenner. . . . Vivid, affectionate and clear-eyed, Vecsey's account makes for an engaging sports history." Publ Wkly

Includes bibliographical references

Wendel, Tim

Far from home; Latino baseball players in America. [by] Tim Wendel, José Luis Villegas. National Geographic Society 2008 159p il $28

Grades: 11 12 Adult   **796.357**

1. Baseball 2. Hispanic American athletes
ISBN 978-1-4262-0216-2; 1-4262-0216-4

LC 2007-61240

This "book offers revealing photographs of both the star and the lesser-known Latino players, accompanied by concise, insightful text. . . . The book mainly points to Cuban, Puerto Rican, Dominican, and Venezuelan stars. A useful time line is included." Libr J

The **new** face of baseball; the one-hundred year rise and triumph of Latinos in America's favorite sport. foreword by Bob Costas; color photographs by Victor Baldizon. Rayo 2003 266p il hardcover o.p. pa $13.95

Grades: 11 12 Adult   **796.357**

1. Baseball 2. Latinos (U.S.) 3. Hispanic Americans
ISBN 0-06-053631-4; 0-06-053632-2 pa

LC 2004-300834

"Fans will recognize names like Minoso, Clemente, Cepeda, or Sosa, but it is enlightening to see them presented as part of a single accomplished group . . . This is an excellent overview." Libr J

Includes bibliographical references

Wilson, Nick

★ **Voices** from the pastime; oral histories of surviving major leaguers, Negro leaguers, Cuban leaguers, and writers, 1920-1934. McFarland & Co. 2000 208p il pa $29.95

Grades: 11 12 Adult   **796.357**

1. Baseball
ISBN 0-7864-0824-3

LC 00-26695

The players and sportswriters not only recount their own careers, they talk of some of the greatest players in the history of the game, including Babe Ruth, Josh Gibson, Satchel Paige, Walter Johnson and Martin Dihigo

Includes bibliographical references

796.4   Weight lifting, track and field, gymnastics

Bobrick, Benson

A **passion** for victory: the story of the Olympics in ancient and early modern times; the story of the Olympics in ancient and early modern times. Benson

Bobrick. Alfred A. Knopf 2012 xvi, 143 p.p ill. (hardback) $19.99

Grades: 4 5 6 7　　　　　　　　　　　**796.4**

1. Olympic games 2. Sports tournaments

ISBN 9780375868696; 9780375968693

LC 2011016036

The book offers an "account of the Olympic Games and their place in history. . . . [Athletes] Milo of Croton, Jim Thorpe, Johnny Weissmuller and Jesse Owens are given their due here. The photo-essay format conveys their stories . . . as well as the glory, shenanigans and pettiness of the Olympics throughout history. Almost every full-page spread includes at least one photograph, and the text . . . addresses the cultural context of the games." (Kirkus Reviews)

Includes bibliographical references.

796.42　Track and field

Brant, John

14 minutes; a running legend's life and death and life. Alberto Salazar and John Brant. Rodale Books 2012 xiv, 258 p.p ill. (hardcover) $25.99; (paperback) $15.99

Grades: 9 10 11 12　　　　　　　　　**796.42**

1. Athletes 2. Biography 3. Marathon running 4. Runners (Sports) -- United States -- Biography

ISBN 1609613147; 9781609613143; 9781609619985

LC 2012002366

In this book long distance runner Alberto Salazar "reflects on an action-packed life that brought him fame for his successive marathon victories in New York City and Boston in the early 1980s, and made him a contender for the Olympics in 1984 and 1988. However, his successes came at a cost. In 2007 Salazar collapsed on the Nike campus and was counted dead for 14 minutes . . . claim[ing] a deeper religious awareness after the [near-death] experience." (Kirkus Reviews)

Burfoot, Amby

Runner's world complete book of running; everything you need to run for weight loss, fitness, and competition. edited by Amby Burfoot. Rev. & updated ed.; Rodale; Distributed by Macmillan 2009 312p il pa $21.99

Grades: 11 12 Adult　　　　　　　　**796.42**

1. Running

ISBN 978-1-60529-579-4 pa

LC 2009-33150

First published 1997

Topics covered include: nutrition, injury prevention and treatment, shoe selection, mental readiness, and marathon preparation.

Cantor, George

Usain Bolt; by George Cantor. Lucent Books 2011 96 p. col. ill. (People in the News) (hardcover) $33.95

Grades: 6 7 8 9　　　　　　　　　　**796.42**

1. Sprinters 2. Olympic athletes 3. Track and field

athletes -- Jamaica -- Biography

ISBN 1420503413; 9781420503418

LC 2011006980

This book offers a biography of Olympic sprinter Usain Bolt, a Jamaican athlete who set several world records, by author George Cantor. It is part of the "People in the News" series, which "profiles the lives and careers of some of today's most prominent newsmakers. Whether covering contributions and achievements or notorious deeds, books in this series examine why these well-known individuals garnered public attention." (Publisher's note)

Includes bibliographical references and index

Housewright, Ed

Winning track and field for girls; foreword by Jason-Lamont Jackson. 2nd ed.; Chelsea House 2009 194p il (Winning sports for girls) lib bdg $44.95; pa $11.96

Grades: 7 8 9 10 11 12　　　　　　　**796.42**

1. Track athletics

ISBN 978-0-8160-7718-2 lib bdg; 0-8160-7718-5 lib bdg; 978-0-8160-7719-9 pa; 0-8160-7719-3 pa

LC 2009-9019

First published 2004 by Facts on File

This includes a brief history of women's track, followed by topics including sprints, hurdles, middle and long distances, relays, jumping events, throwing events, the heptathlon, cross-country, and the triathlon, mental preparations and nutrition, stetches and weight lifting.

Includes bibliographical references

Scott, Dagny

Runner's world complete book of women's running; the best advice to get started, stay motivated, lose weight, run injury-free, be safe, and train for any distance. [by] Dagny Scott Barrios. Rev. and updated ed.; Distributed to the trade by Holtzbrinck Publishers 2007 324p il pa $16.95

Grades: 11 12 Adult　　　　　　　　**796.42**

1. Running

ISBN 978-1-59486-758-3; 1-59486-758-5

LC 2007-30645

First published 2000

Topics covered include racing, nutrition, running during pregnancy, weight loss, and proper clothing.

796.44　Gymnastics

James, Sara

Step aerobics & aerobic dance; Sara James. Mason Crest 2015 64 p. color illustrations (Hardback) $23.95

Grades: 9 10 11 12　　　　　　　　　**796.44**

1. Aerobics 2. Physical fitness

ISBN 142223164X; 9781422231647

LC 2014014801

This book by Sara James "presents information about what step aerobics and aerobic dance are, illustrates the benefits of these forms of exercise, and discusses the importance of appropriate workout attire and safety." (Publisher's note)

"The physiological information is detailed enough for a college course in exercise science. Each book touches on safety and common injuries. Despite a few missteps, this excellent series demonstrates how a physical education class can be interdisciplinary and academically rigorous." SLJ

McIntosh, J. S.

Gymnastics. Mason Crest Publishers 2010 96p il (Getting the edge: conditioning, injuries, and legal & illicit drugs) lib bdg $24.95

Grades: 7 8 9 10 **796.44**

1. Gymnastics

ISBN 978-1-4222-1734-4; 1-4222-1734-5

LC 2010-10053

This book "offers a general introduction to . . . [gymnastics], its rules, and its history before zeroing in on health and safety concerns. . . . [It] covers mental preparation as well as the dangers of using drugs such as diuretics and amphetamines." Booklist

Includes bibliographical references

796.48 Olympic games

Mallon, Bill

★ **Historical** dictionary of the Olympic movement; [by] Bill Mallon, Jeroen Heijmans. 4th ed; Scarecrow Press 2011 xcviii, 507p (Historical dictionaries of sports) $99; ebook $94.99

Grades: 9 10 11 12 **796.48**

1. Reference books 2. Olympic games -- Dictionaries

ISBN 978-0-8108-7249-3; 978-0-8108-7522-7 ebook

LC 2011002799

First published 1995

The authors "provide a 60-page opening segment with a brief synopsis of each of the modern Olympic Games, listing where each was held, other cities that competed for the honor, and the course of that particular Olympics. Making up the bulk of the book, the A-to-Z listing describes competitive events and their histories, biographies of selected athletes, organizational leaders, participating and host countries, and others who have contributed to the events. Biographical entries include birth and death information and a brief history of their involvement in the games or behind the scenes." Libr J

Includes bibliographical references

796.5 Outdoor life

Paulsen, Gary

Woodsong. Bradbury Press 1990 132p map hardcover o.p. pa $6.99

Grades: 7 8 9 10 **796.5**

1. Outdoor life 2. Sled dog racing 3. Minnesota

ISBN 0-02-770221-9; 1-4169-3939-3 pa

LC 89-70835

ALA YALSA Margaret A. Edwards Award (1997)

For the author and his family, life in northern Minnesota is a wild experience involving wolves, deer, and the sled dogs that make their way of life possible. Includes an account of Paulsen's first Iditarod, a dogsled race across Alaska

"The book is packed with vignettes that range among various shades of terror and lyrical beauty." Voice Youth Advocates

796.51 Walking

Hart, John

★ **Walking** softly in the wilderness; the Sierra Club guide to backpacking. 4th ed, complete rev and updated; Sierra Club Books 2005 508p il map (Sierra Club outdoor adventure guide) pa $16.95

Grades: 8 9 10 11 12 Adult **796.51**

1. Backpacking 2. Wilderness areas

ISBN 1-57805-123-1

LC 2004-56554

First published 1977

This guide for both the novice and experienced hiker reflects the environmental concerns of the Sierra Club. Among topics covered are: clothing and equipment; making and breaking camp; problem animals and plants; hiking and camping with kids. Listings of conservation and wilderness travel organizations, map and equipment sources, land management agencies, and Internet contacts are appended.

Includes bibliographical references

796.522 Mountains, hills, rocks

Climb: stories of survival from rock, snow, and ice; edited by Clint Willis. Thunder's Mouth Press 2000 259p il pa $16.95

Grades: 11 12 Adult **796.522**

1. Mountaineering

ISBN 1-56025-250-2

LC 99-26747

This anthology brings together "writings by some of the world's best climbers, such as American Jim Wickwire, Scotsman Hamish MacInnes, and literary icons Evelyn Waugh and H. G. Wells. This collection will surely appeal to die-hard veterans of the sport and newcomers intrigued by risk taking. . . . For all readers, lessons abound—although the writers may have survived their ordeals presented here, some did not survive others." Booklist

Coburn, Broughton

Everest: mountain without mercy; introduction by Tim Cahill, afterword by David Breashears. National Geographic Soc. 1997 256p il maps hardcover o.p. pa $24

Grades: 11 12 Adult **796.522**

1. Mountaineering 2. Mount Everest Expedition (1996)

ISBN 0-7922-7014-2; 0-7922-6984-5 pa

LC 97-10765

"Bringing an understated yet powerful Buddhist/Sherpa ethical perspective to the tragedy on Everest chronicled in Jon Krakauer's Into Thin Air, Coburn reports on the IMAX film crew who participated in the rescue effort when the May

1996 expeditions led by guides Rob Hall and Scott Fischer ended in death and crippling injury." Publ Wkly

Krakauer, Jon, 1954-
★ **Into** thin air; a personal account of the Mount Everest disaster. Villard Bks. 1997 xx, 293p il $25.95; pa $14.95
Grades: 11 12 Adult   796.522
    1. Mountaineering 2. Mount Everest Expedition (1996) 3. Mountaineering -- Personal narratives
    ISBN 0-679-45752-6; 0-385-49478-5 pa
                       LC 96-30031
This is an account of the author's May 1996 Mount Everest climbing expedition in which twelve fellow climbers died during a snow storm
  "This tense, harrowing story is as mesmerizing and hard to put down as any well-written adventure novel." SLJ
  Includes bibliographical references

Ralston, Aron
  Between a rock and a hard place. Atria Books 2004 354p il map hardcover o.p. pa $15
Grades: 11 12 Adult   796.522
    1. Mountaineering 2. Wilderness survival 3. Mountaineers
    ISBN 0-7434-9281-1; 0-7434-9282-X pa
                    LC 2004-303427
  "With precious little water or food, his right arm pinned for nearly five days by a boulder in a narrow canyon shaft in central-eastern Utah, Ralston amputated the arm with his pocketknife, then rappelled and hiked his way to his own rescue. What makes his account of his ordeal extraordinary, too, is the detail and precision Ralston, a former mechanical engineer, brings to the telling, from the almost minute-by-minute chronology of his ordeal to topographical descriptions of the ground he's covered in his life as an outdoor adventurer." Booklist
  Includes bibliographical references

Robinson, Victoria
  Rock climbing; the ultimate guide. Victoria Robinson. Greenwood 2013 165 p. (Greenwood guides to extreme sports) (hardcover) $37
Grades: 9 10 11 12 Adult   796.522
    1. Mountaineering 2. Rock climbing
    ISBN 0313378614; 9780313378614; 9780313378621
                    LC 2012031304
  This book, by Victoria Robinson, presents a guide to rock climbing as part of the "Greenwood Guides to Extreme Sports" series. The book "covers the history of rock climbing in the United States from its origins to the present day. . . . The chapters address topics such as the technicalities of the equipment and clothing, training methods, key places and events where the sport takes place, . . . and the evolution of the sport over the years." (Publisher's note)
  Includes bibliographical references and index.

Trailside (Television program)
  Rock climbing; a trailside guide. illustrations by Ron Hildebrand. Norton 2003 191p il (Trailside series guide) pa $18.95

Grades: 11 12 Adult   796.522
    1. Mountaineering
    ISBN 0-393-31653-X
                    LC 96-52821
  "Designed to be carried on the trail, this will ease beginners into the sport of rock climbing, with step-by-step illustrated tutorials, safety and first-aid tips, and more." Libr J
  Includes bibliographical references

796.525   Caves

Felix, Rebecca
  Exploring caves; by Rebecca Felix. Essential Library 2014 144 p. color illustrations (Story of exploration) $35.64
Grades: 5 6 7 8 9 10   796.525
    1. Caves 2. Exploration
    ISBN 1624032494; 9781624032493
                    LC 2013946594
  "This title offers a wonderful presentation about caves and exploration of them. The vivid photos provide a glimpse into various types of caves and aid in understanding the text, which offers plenty of information about the formation of caves, as well as the history of cave exploration. The author makes certain to impress upon the reader how far the study of these natural formations has come. The reader is also introduced to what caves can tell us about prehistoric civilizations." (VOYA)
  Includes bibliographical references and index

796.6   Cycling and related activities

Bicycling
  ★ **Bicycling** magazine's 1,000 all-time best tips; top riders share their secrets to maximize fun, safety, and performance. edited by Ben Hewitt. Fully rev and updated; Rodale 2005 168p il pa $10.95
Grades: 11 12 Adult   796.6
    1. Cycling
    ISBN 978-1-59486-051-5; 1-59486-051-3
                    LC 2005-638
  Replaces Bicycling magazine's 900 all-time best tips
  A collection of information on such topics as bicycle models, accessories, riding styles, and repair techniques

796.63   Mountain biking (All-terrain cycling)

Bicycling magazine's mountain biking skills; skills and techniques to master any terrain. Rodale 2005 122p pa $9.95
Grades: 9 10 11 12 Adult   796.63
    1. Mountain biking
    ISBN 978-1-59486-299-1; 1-59486-299-0
                    LC 2005-23045
  First published 1990
  This guide to mountain biking covers basic and intermediate skills and techniques including "ways to handle tough

terrain, steer clear of hazardous obstacles, and even crash properly to avoid injury." Publisher's note

Crowther, Nicky

★ The **ultimate** mountain bike book; the definitive illustrated guide to bikes, components, techniques, thrills and trails. maintenance section by Melanie Allwood. rev 3rd ed; Firefly Bks. 2002 191p il pa $24.95

Grades: 9 10 11 12 Adult   **796.63**

1. Mountain bikes

ISBN 1-55297-653-X

First published 1996 by Motorbooks International

"Some of the topics covered are as basic as how to choose a bike, required accessories, and nitty-gritty instructions on how to maintain and care for your equipment. Crowther also includes information about racing, downhill, cross-country, and stunt riding. Although certain topics are written with advanced and competitive riders in mind . . . the book is jam-packed with everything beginner and experienced bikers need to know." SLJ

796.72   Automobile racing

Leslie-Pelecky, Diandra L.

The **physics** of NASCAR; how to make steel + gas + rubber. Dutton 2008 286p il $25.95

Grades: 9 10 11 12   **796.72**

1. Automobile racing 2. Automobiles -- Design and construction 3. National Association for Stock Car Auto Racing

ISBN 978-0-525-95053-0; 0-525-95053-2

LC 2007-46081

"The author, a physicist and devoted NASCAR fan, explains in clear, simple terms what goes into making a NASCAR vehicle, from design to development to construction to test-driving. . . . She introduces us to some of the sport's key players and teaches us (painlessly) more about the physics of speed . . . Fans will flock to this book." Booklist

Includes bibliographical references

O'Malley, J. J.

★ **Daytona** 24 hours; the definitive history of America's great endurance race. foreword by Hurley Haywood; design by Tom Morgan; photos edited by Buzz McKim; results and index by János Wimpffen. David Bull Pub. 2009 452p il $99.95

Grades: 9 10 11 12   **796.72**

1. Automobile racing

ISBN 978-1-935007-00-5

LC 2008-941266

First published 2003

The author delivers a "chronicle of the race, year by year (1974 was the only year it wasn't run), and the clear, mostly full-color photos, one on nearly every page, show the crew, the cars, the drivers, the track, and the pulsing action." Booklist

Thunder and glory; the 25 most memorable races in NASCAR Winston Cup history. [from the editors

of NASCAR scene] Triumph Books 2004 160p il $34.95; pa $19.95

Grades: 9 10 11 12   **796.72**

1. Automobile racing 2. National Association for Stock Car Auto Racing

ISBN 1-57243-677-8; 1-57243-830-4 pa

LC 2006-297046

"The focus is on 25 of the editors' most memorable Winston Cup races, which are analyzed and recounted with utter reverence. . . . Even nonracing fans will find the drama compelling." Booklist

796.8   Combat sports

Kreidler, Mark

★ **Four** days to glory; wrestling with the soul of the American heartland. HarperCollins Publishers 2007 262p il hardcover o.p. pa $13.99

Grades: 11 12 Adult   **796.8**

1. Wrestling 2. School sports

ISBN 978-0-06-082318-4; 0-06-082318-6; 978-0-06-082319-1 pa; 0-06-082319-4 pa

LC 2007-272997

Jay Borschel and Dan LeClere aspire to be four-time high school wrestling champions in Iowa.

The author's "deftness in 'Four Days' is in turning a niche sport into one as accessible as baseball or basketball." N Y Times Book Rev

McIntosh, J. S.

Wrestling. Mason Crest Publishers 2010 96p il (Getting the edge: conditioning, injuries, and legal & illicit drugs) lib bdg $24.95

Grades: 7 8 9 10   **796.8**

1. Wrestling

ISBN 978-1-4222-1743-6; 1-4222-1743-4

LC 2010-17923

This book covers basic safety training, equipment, preparation, and precautions related to wrestling and how to recover quickly from wrestling-related injuries.

Includes bibliographical references

Pawlett, Raymond

★ The **karate** handbook; [by] Ray Pawlett. Rosen Pub. Group 2008 256p il (Martial arts) $39.95

Grades: 7 8 9 10 11 12   **796.8**

1. Karate

ISBN 978-1-4042-1394-4; 1-4042-1394-5

LC 2007-32795

This "offers a thorough introduction to karate that covers both the underlying philosophy and the physical practice. A thoughtful, sophisticated history opens the book and discusses karate's roots in Zen Buddhism, the styles of karate, and dojo etiquette. Later spreads feature lucid, step-by-step instructions." Booklist

Includes bibliographical references

Polly, Matthew

★ **American** Shaolin; flying kicks, Buddhist monks, and the legend of iron crotch: an odyssey in the new China. Gotham Books 2007 366p il $26; pa $15

Grades: 11 12 Adult   **796.8**
1. Martial arts 2. China -- Description and travel
ISBN 978-1-592-40262-5; 978-1-59240-337-0 pa
LC 2006-25384

"Scrawny, bullied since childhood, and sick of living with his 'Things Wrong with Matt' list, . . . [the author] recounts how he rode out pure instinct to leave college, travel to China, and best his inner demons through the art of kung fu fighting. What follows are fun and fascinating stories of his training with the famous monks at the world-renowned Shaolin temple, the birthplace of martial arts and Zen Buddhism." Libr J

796.83   Boxing

Stratton, W. K.

Floyd Patterson; the fighting life of boxing's invisible champion. W. K. Stratton. Houghton Mifflin Harcourt 2012 xiv, 269 p.p ill. (hardback) $25.00

Grades: 9 10 11 12 Adult   **796.83**
1. Boxers (Sports) 2. African Americans -- Civil rights 3. African American boxers -- Biography 4. Boxers (Sports) -- United States -- Biography
ISBN 0151014302; 9780151014309
LC 2012017319

This biography "examines one of the most complex fighters ever to wear the heavyweight crown," boxer Floyd Patterson. "Patterson started boxing [in high school] and . . . caught the eye of trainer Cus D'Amato . . . . By focusing on historical context, Stratton clarifies how Patterson could be trumpeted as a hero of the civil rights movement, then labeled an 'Uncle Tom' a few years later." (Publishers Weekly)

Includes bibliographical references and index.

796.91   Ice skating

Uschan, Michael V., 1948-

Apolo Anton Ohno; by Michael V. Uschan. Lucent Books 2011 104 p. (People in the News) (hbk.) $33.95

Grades: 7 8 9 10   **796.91**
1. Speed skating 2. Olympic athletes 3. Speed skaters -- United States 4. Speed skaters -- United States -- Biography
ISBN 142050603X; 9781420506037
LC 2011003418

This book offers a biography of Olympic speed skater Apolo Anton Ohno, an athlete who has won eight Olympic medals as of 2012, by author Michael V. Uschan. It is part of the "People in the News" series, which "profiles the lives and careers of some of today's most prominent newsmakers. Whether covering contributions and achievements or notorious deeds, books in this series examine why these well-known individuals garnered public attention." (Publisher's note)

Includes bibliographical references and index.

796.93   Skiing and snowboarding

Kleh, Cindy

Snowboarding skills; the back-to-basics essentials for all levels. [photographer, Jed Jacobson] Firefly Books 2007 128p il pa $16.95

Grades: 7 8 9 10 11 12 Adult   **796.93**
1. Snowboarding
ISBN 1-55297-626-2
LC 2003-467271

"Kleh's combination of dead-on practical advice, insider lingo, and near-religious enthusiasm makes this guide to snowboarding an invaluable resource for anyone wanting to try the sport or to advance his or her skills." Booklist

Trailside (Television program)

★ **Cross**-country skiing; a complete guide. illustrations by Ron Hildebrand. Norton 1995 192p il (Trailside series guide) flexible bdg $17.95

Grades: 11 12 Adult   **796.93**
1. Skiing
ISBN 0-393-31335-2
LC 95-5529

This illustrated guide to cross-country skiing covers equipment, techniques, backcountry skiing, clothing, safety, and fitness, and lists organizations, mail-order sources, and information sources

796.962   Ice hockey

Coffey, Wayne R.

The **boys** of winter; the untold story of a coach, a dream, and, the 1980 U.S. olympic hockey team. foreword by Jim Craig. Crown Publishers 2005 272p il hardcover o.p. pa $13.95

Grades: 9 10 11 12 Adult   **796.962**
1. Hockey 2. Olympic games
ISBN 1-4000-4765-X; 1-4000-4766-8 pa
LC 2004-14163

The author "offers a nuanced portrait of the 1980 Olympics 'miracle on ice' and the gold medal-winning U.S. hockey team." SLJ

Vanderhoof, Gabrielle

Hockey. Mason Crest Publishers 2010 96p il (Getting the edge: conditioning, injuries, and legal & illicit drugs) lib bdg $24.95

Grades: 7 8 9 10   **796.962**
1. Hockey
ISBN 978-1-422217-35-1; 1-42217-35-3
LC 2010-10054

This book "offers a general introduction to . . . [hockey], its rules, and its history before zeroing in on health and safety concerns. . . . [It] comments on typical injuries to hockey players and spells out NCAA and NHL penalties for using drugs such as steroids and human growth hormone." Booklist

Includes bibliographical references

796.98 Winter Olympic games

Wallechinsky, David

The **complete** book of the Winter Olympics; [by] David Wallechinsky and Jaime Loucky. 2010 ed.; Aurum 2009 322p il pa $24.95

Grades: 11 12 Adult **796.98**

1. Olympic games

ISBN 978-1-84513-491-4

First published 1984 by Overlook Press

"While the statistics will delight sports geeks, everyone can savor the readable prose accounts that draw out the athletes' character and high points." SLJ

797.1 Aquatic sports

American Canoe Association

Kayaking; editors, Pamela S. Dillon, Jeremy Oyen. Human Kinetics 2009 237p il (Outdoor adventures) pa $22.95

Grades: 9 10 11 12 Adult **797.1**

1. Canoes and canoeing

ISBN 978-0-7360-6716-4; 0-7360-6716-7

LC 2008-32111

"Part I of Kayaking explains the background knowledge, fitness fundamentals, equipment and gear selection, nutritional needs, and safety and survival skills for a successful adventure. Part II helps build basic techniques, strokes, and maneuvers. . . . [It includes] tips and instruction for the three most popular types of kayaking: sea, river, and whitewater. This book also includes the Quick-Start Your Kayak DVD to reinforce the paddling strokes and safety information found in the book. It features videos of kayaking maneuvers." Publisher's note

Includes bibliographical references

Sleight, Steve

New complete sailing manual; Rev ed., 1st American ed.; DK 2005 448p il map $35

Grades: 9 10 11 12 Adult **797.1**

1. Sailing

ISBN 0-7566-0944-5; 978-0-7566-0944-3

LC 2005-277514

First published 1999 with title: DK complete sailing manual

This sailing manual covers such topics as navigation, ropes and knots, boating safety, boat maintenance, and handling emergencies.

Stuhaug, Dennis O.

Kayaking made easy; a manual for beginners with tips for the experienced. 3rd ed.; Globe Pequot Press 2006 264p il (Made easy series) pa $17.95

Grades: 9 10 11 12 **797.1**

1. Canoes and canoeing

ISBN 0-7627-3859-6

LC 2006-43437

First published 1995

This guide offers "a step-by-step approach, first familiarizing you with the gear, then proceeding through the various strokes, and finally covering the complexities of long-distance navigation." Publisher's note

Trailside (Television program)

Canoeing; illustrations by Ron Hildebrand. Norton 1997 192p il (Trailside series guide) flexible bdg $18.95

Grades: 11 12 Adult **797.1**

1. Camping 2. Canoes and canoeing

ISBN 0-393-31489-8

LC 96-2151

This guide to canoeing covers equipment, safety, paddling techniques, camping, moving water and white water canoeing. Grant provides lists of organizations, schools, tour organizers and guides, information sources, mail-order sources of equipment, and canoe manufacturers.

798.4 Horse racing

Hillenbrand, Laura

★ **Seabiscuit**; an American legend. Random House 2001 399p il $25.95; pa $15.95

Grades: 11 12 Adult **798.4**

1. Horse racing 2. Seabiscuit (Race horse)

ISBN 0-375-50291-2; 0-449-00561-5 pa

LC 2001-267852

"This is a remarkable tale well told by a writer who deftly blends history and sport." Economist

Includes bibliographical references

Ours, Dorothy

Man o' War; a legend like lightning. St Martin's Press 2006 342p il $24.95

Grades: 11 12 Adult **798.4**

1. Horse racing 2. Man o' War (Race horse)

ISBN 0-312-34099-0; 978-0-312-34099-5

LC 2006-41631

This is an account of the thoroughbred racehorse Man o' War, also known as Big Red.

This book "is clearly a labor of love, and it certifies Big Red's claim to immortality." N Y Times Book Rev

Includes bibliographical references

798.8 Dog racing

Paulsen, Gary

Winterdance; the fine madness of running the Iditarod. Harcourt Brace & Co. 1994 256p il $26; pa $15

Grades: 6 7 8 9 10 **798.8**

1. Sled dog racing 2. Iditarod Trail Sled Dog Race, Alaska 3. Authors 4. Sledding 5. Sled dog racers

6. Children's authors 7. Short story writers 8. Young adult authors
ISBN 0-15-126227-6; 0-15-600145-4 pa
LC 93-42096

"The Alaskan Iditarod is an annual 1180-mile dogsled race from Anchorage to Nome that generally takes two to three weeks to complete. Paulsen . . . ran the race in 1983 and 1985 and was again in training when a heart condition forced him to retire. This book is primarily an account of Paulsen's first Iditarod." (Libr J)

"This book is primarily an account of Paulsen's first Iditarod and its frequent life-threatening disasters. . . . However, the book is more than a tabulation of tribulations; it is a meditation on the extraordinary attraction this race holds for some men and women." Libr J

799   Fishing, hunting, shooting

Paulsen, Gary
Father water, Mother woods; essays on fishing and hunting in the North Woods. with illustrations by Ruth Wright Paulsen. Delacorte Press 1994 159p il hardcover o.p. pa $4.99
Grades: 9 10 11 12   **799**
1. Fishing 2. Hunting
ISBN 0-440-21984-1
LC 94-2737

"This collection of autobiographical essays, identifies {Paulsen's} youthful experiences in the woods and rivers of northern Minnesota. . . . Throughout it all, descriptions of light and water, of fish and wildlife, kindle in the reader a measure of the author's own complex respect for nature." Publ Wkly

799.1   Fishing

Trailside (Television program)
★ **Fly** fishing; a Trailside guide. illustrations by Ron Hildebrand. Norton 1996 192p il (Trailside series guide) flexible bdg $19.95
Grades: 11 12 Adult   **799.1**
1. Fishing 2. Fly casting
ISBN 0-393-31476-6
LC 96-2141

This illustrated guide to fly fishing covers equipment, tying knots, types of flies, fly casting techniques for different types of fish, and lists organizations, schools, mail-order sources, and information sources.
Include bibliographical references

799.3   Shooting other than game

Engh, Douglas
Archery fundamentals. Human Kinetics 2005 125p il (Sports fundamentals series) pa $15.95

Grades: 9 10 11 12 Adult   **799.3**
1. Archery
ISBN 0-7360-5501-0; 978-0-7360-5501-7
LC 2004-11221

This book provides instruction in the basic skills of archery, including shooting techniques, improving aim, and how to keep score as well as information on care and repair of bows, arrows and other equipment.

800   LITERATURE, RHETORIC & CRITICISM

800   Literature (Belles-lettres) and rhetoric

Amend, Allison
Cracking the SAT. Literature subject test; [by] Allison Amend and Adam Robinson. 2011-2012 ed.; Random House 2011 242p (Princeton Review series) pa $19.99
Grades: 9 10 11 12   **800**
1. Scholastic Assessment Test 2. Literature -- Study and teaching 3. Colleges and universities -- Entrance requirements
ISBN 978-0-375-42811-1

Annual. First published 2005. Continues Cracking the SAT II: Writing and literature subject tests

This guide provides test-taking strategies and sample tests on the subject of literature.

Baker, Nancy L.
A **research** guide for undergraduate students; English and American literature. [by] Nancy L. Baker and Nancy Huling. 6th ed; Modern Language Association of America 2006 96p il pa $12
Grades: 11 12 Adult   **800**
1. Reference books 2. Literature -- Research 3. English literature -- Bibliography 4. American literature -- Bibliography
ISBN 978-0-8735-2924-2; 0-8735-2924-3
LC 2006-7360

First published 1982

This book "provides dozens of research samples from the library's online catalog to new databases. Includes a . . . chapter with bibliographic citation managers." Univ Press Books for Public and Second Sch Libr, 2007

Includes bibliographical references

803   Dictionaries, encyclopedias, concordances

Abrams, M. H.
★ A **glossary** of literary terms; with contributions by Geoffrey Galt Harpham. 8th ed.; Thomson, Wadsworth 2005 370p pa $34.95
Grades: 11 12 Adult   **803**
1. Reference books 2. Literature -- Dictionaries
ISBN 1-4130-0218-8; 978-1-4130-0218-8
LC 2004-111345

First published 1957

In a series of essays, the author discusses literary terms and definitions ranging from the traditional to the avant-garde. Subsidiary terms are included under major or generic terms.

Ayto, John

★ **Brewer's** dictionary of modern phrase & fable; by John Ayto & Ian Crofton. 2nd ed.; Chambers Harrap Pub. Ltd. 2010 853p $39.95

Grades: 9 10 11 12 Adult **803**

1. Allusions 2. Reference books 3. Literature -- Dictionaries

ISBN 978-0550-105-646

First published 2000 by Cassell

"Focusing on the 20th and 21st centuries, . . . [this book covers a] selection of buzzwords, catchphrases, slang, nicknames, fictional characters and . . . cultural phenomena from pop culture to politics, literature to technology." Publisher's note

Baldick, Chris

★ The **Oxford** dictionary of literary terms; 3rd ed; Oxford University Press 2008 361p (Oxford paperback reference) hardcover o.p. pa $16.95

Grades: 11 12 Adult **803**

1. Reference books 2. Literature -- Dictionaries 3. English language -- Terms and phrases

ISBN 978-0-19-923891-0; 0-19-923891-X; 978-0-19-920827-2 pa; 0-19-920827-1 pa

LC 2008-299352

First published 1990 with title: The concise Oxford dictionary of literary terms

This work defines more than 1,200 literary terms. Also provides coverage of traditional drama, rhetoric, literary history, and textual criticism. Includes pronunciation guides on over 200 terms.

Includes bibliographical references

★ **Benet's** reader's encyclopedia; edited by Bruce F. Murphy. 5th ed.; Collins 2008 1210p $60

Grades: 8 9 10 11 12 Adult **803**

1. Reference books 2. Literature -- Dictionaries

ISBN 978-0-06-089016-2

LC 2008-31430

First published 1948 under the editorship of William Rose Benet

This encyclopedia contains over 10,000 entries and covers world literature from early times to the present. Includes entries on authors, literary movements, principal characters, plot synopses, terms, awards, myths and legends, etc.

This is "an edifying staple for any literary library." Libr J

Harmon, William

★ A **handbook** to literature; Twelfth ed.; Longman 2011 655p il pa $53.33

Grades: 11 12 Adult **803**

1. Reference books 2. Literature -- Dictionaries

ISBN 978-0-205-02401-8; 0-205-02401-7

LC 2010-49056

First published 1936 by Doubleday under the authorship of William Flint Thrall and Addison Hibbard; later editions by William Harmon and C. Hugh Holman

This work provides "explanations of terms, concepts, schools, and movements in literature. Alphabetical arrangement with numerous cross-references as well as bibliographic references for some entries." Guide to Ref Books. 11th edition

Includes bibliographical references

Lewis, Catherine

★ **Thrice** told tales; Catherine Lewis. Atheneum Books for Young Readers 2013 144 p. (hardcover) $16.99

Grades: 7 8 9 10 **803**

1. Literary style 2. Authorship -- Handbooks, manuals, etc. 3. Literature -- Terminology

ISBN 1416957847; 9781416957843; 9781442460768

LC 2012010644

In this book, Catherine Lewis makes "use of the 'Three Blind Mice' nursery rhyme to illustrate nearly 100 elements of writing and literature—plot, dialogue, flashbacks, coincidence, and more. . . . Lewis expands on each term in brief 'Snip of the Tale' summaries and an extensive appendix." (Publishers Weekly)

"Three blind mice. See how they run—and how they take your writing to a new level. This clever review of literary terms will delight students and experts looking for a concise way to understand exposition and point-of-view or discern an epic from a bildungsroman." (Library Journal)

★ **Oxford** dictionary of phrase and fable; edited by Elizabeth Knowles. 2nd ed.; Oxford University Press 2005 805p $40; pa $18.95

Grades: 11 12 Adult **803**

1. Allusions 2. Reference books 3. Literature -- Dictionaries

ISBN 978-0-19-860981-0; 978-0-19-920246-1 pa

First published 2000

This work seeks to define words and phrases of British cultural history.

This "is a highly useful tool to help understand what phrases mean and where they come from and should definitely be added to all reference collections." Booklist

Quinn, Edward

★ A **dictionary** of literary and thematic terms; 2nd ed.; Facts on File 2006 474p (Facts on File library of language and literature) $55; pa $19.95

Grades: 11 12 Adult **803**

1. Reference books 2. Literature -- Dictionaries

ISBN 0-8160-6243-9; 978-0-8160-6243-0; 0-8160-6244-7 pa; 978-0-8160-6244-7 pa

LC 2005-29826

First published 1999

In addition to basic definitions of terms "this general literary dictionary . . . covers common themes in literature such as love, death, alienation, and time. Literary schools are treated with just enough depth to offer a basic understanding of the major tenets." Libr J [review of 1999 edition]

Includes bibliographical references

Rockwood, Camilla

★ **Brewer's** dictionary of phrase & fable; edited by Camilla Rockwood. 18th ed.; Brewer's 2009 xxv, 1460p il $49.95

Grades: 5 6 7 8 9 10 11 12 Adult   **803**

1. Allusions 2. Reference books 3. Mythology -- Dictionaries 4. Literature -- Dictionaries 5. English language -- Terms and phrases

ISBN 978-0-550-10411-3

LC 2009-379960

First published 1870 under the editorship of Ebenezer Cobham Brewer

"Over 15,000 brief entries give the meanings and origins of a broad range of terms, expressions, and names of real, fictitious and mythical characters from world history, science, the arts and literature." N Y Public Libr. Ref Books for Child Collect. 2d edition

808   Rhetoric and collections of literary texts from more than two literatures

826 Valencia (Organization)

The **autobiographer's** handbook; the 826 National guide to writing your memoir. edited by Jennifer Traig; introduction by Dave Eggers. Henry Holt and Co. 2008 242p pa $15

Grades: 9 10 11 12   **808**

1. Autobiography 2. Biography as a literary form

ISBN 978-0-8050-8713-0; 0-8050-8713-3

LC 2007-47355

"Put out by 826 Valencia, the San Francisco-based nonprofit Eggers started to provide creative writing instruction for middle and high school students, this book presents straightforward, practical ideas and advice from a double-handful of contemporary writers. . . . Their guidance, complemented by writing exercises and work plans, should prove useful, informative and motivating for writers at just about any level." Publ Wkly

Includes bibliographical references

American Psychological Association

Concise rules of APA style; 6th ed.; American Psychological Association 2009 280p il $28.95

Grades: 11 12 Adult   **808**

1. Reference books 2. Authorship -- Handbooks, manuals, etc.

ISBN 978-1-4338-0560-8; 1-4338-0560-X

LC 2009-11709

First published 2005

This book offers "writing and formatting standards for students, teachers, researchers, and clinicians in the social and behavioral sciences. . . . Readers will learn how to avoid the grammatical errors most commonly reported by journal editors; how to choose the appropriate format for statistics, figures, and tables; how to credit sources and avoid charges of plagiarism; and how to construct a reference list." Publisher's note

Includes bibliographical references

The **Chicago** manual of style; 16th ed; The University of Chicago Press 2010 1026p

Grades: 11 12 Adult   **808**

1. Writing 2. Authorship 3. English language -- Usage 4. Printing -- Style manuals 5. Publishers and publishing 6. Authorship -- Style manuals 7. Authorship -- Handbooks, manuals, etc. 8. Publishers and publishing -- Handbooks, manuals, etc.

ISBN 0226104206; 9780226104201

LC 2009053612

First published 1906 with title: A manual of style

This style manual includes journals and electronic publications, descriptive headings on all numbered paragraphs, and chapters on grammar, usage, and documentation, including guidance on citing electronic sources.

Includes glossary and bibliographical references

Dowhan, Adrienne

★ **Essays** that will get you into college; [by] Adrienne Dowhan, Chris Dowhan, and Dan Kaufman. 3rd ed.; Barron's 2009 178p pa $13.99

Grades: 9 10 11 12   **808**

1. Rhetoric 2. College applications

ISBN 978-0-7641-4210-9; 0-7641-4210-0

LC 2009-13487

First published 1998 under the authorship of Amy Burnham, Daniel Kaufman and Chris Dowhan

"The 50 model essays presented in this book were written by successful Ivy League college applicants. Each essay is followed by critical comments that reveal both strong and weak points in its author's style and content. Also presented is . . . essay-writing advice and instruction." Publisher's note

Dunn, Jessica

★ A **teen's** guide to getting published; publishing for profit, recognition, and academic success. [by] Jessica Dunn & Danielle Dunn. 2nd ed.; Prufrock Press 2006 249p pa $14.95

Grades: 7 8 9 10 11 12   **808**

1. Authorship 2. Publishers and publishing

ISBN 1-59363-182-0

LC 2006005109

First published 1997

"In addition to standard advice on publishers and agents, the authors give practical suggestions for finding a writing environment that is accessible to teens, such as school publication staffs and local newspaper internships. . . . Annotated appendixes list Web sites, books, journals, and contests. Also provided is information on mentors, writing camps, and courses catering to young authors, and a valuable list of mainstream publishers who have expressed openness to submissions from teens. This compact, sensible book discusses all kinds of writing." SLJ

Gaines, Ann

★ **Don't** steal copyrighted stuff! avoiding plagiarism and illegal internet downloading. [by] Ann Graham Gaines. Enslow Publishers 2008 192p il (Prime) $38.60

Grades: 7 8 9 10　　　　　**808**
1. Copyright 2. Plagiarism 3. Bibliographical citations
ISBN 978-0-7660-2861-6; 0-7660-2861-5

LC 2007-8370

"The first three chapters explain just what plagiarism is, the types of plagiarism, and what copyright and fair use are. Two chapters explain how to find sources, take notes properly, and construct a project or paper using proper citations in MLA format. . . . Every student should be required to read this. . . . Librarians and teachers who are looking for explanations of copyright and plagiarism and illustrative examples will find this book to be a good resource." Libr Media Connect

Includes bibliographical references

Johnson, Sarah Anne
The **art** of the author interview; and interviewing creative people. University Press of New England 2005 158p pa $19.95
Grades: 11 12 Adult　　　　　**808**
1. Interviewing 2. Reporters and reporting
ISBN 1-58465-397-3

LC 2004-23688

This book "shows readers how to initiate, research, conduct, and publish interviews with authors and other creative people." Publisher's note

Lasch, Christopher
Plain style; a guide to written English. edited and with an introduction by Stewart Weaver. University of Pa. Press 2002 121p hardcover o.p. pa $14.95
Grades: 11 12 Adult　　　　　**808**
1. Rhetoric 2. English language -- Grammar
ISBN 0-8122-3673-4; 0-8122-1814-0 pa

LC 2002-19163

"The guide is divided into six parts, covering the principles of literary construction; conventions governing punctuation, capitalization, typography, and footnotes; characteristics of bad writing; words often misued; words often mispronounced; and a table of proofreaders' marks." Booklist

Includes bibliographical references

Modern Language Association of America
★ **MLA** handbook for writers of research papers; 7th ed.; Modern Language Association of America 2009 xxi, 292p il pa $22
Grades: 9 10 11 12 Adult　　　　　**808**
1. Report writing
ISBN 978-1-60329-024-1

LC 2008-47484

First published 1977 with title: MLA handbook for writers of research papers, theses, and dissertations

This manual discusses research strategies, formatting, documenting sources, writing basics and utilizing electronic sources.

Includes bibliographical references

★ **MLA** style manual and guide to scholarly publishing; 3rd ed.; Modern Language Association of America 2008 xxiv, 336p $32.50
Grades: 11 12 Adult　　　　　**808**
1. Authorship -- Handbooks, manuals, etc.
ISBN 978-0-87352-297-7; 0-87352-297-4

LC 2008-2894

First published 1985 under authorship of Walter S. Achtert and Joseph Gibaldi

This book offers "guidance on writing scholarly texts, documenting research sources, submitting manuscripts to publishers, and dealing with legal issues surrounding publication." Publisher's note

Includes bibliographical references

Plotnik, Arthur
Spunk & bite; a writer's guide to punchier, more engaging language & style. Random House 2005 263p hardcover o.p. pa $12.95
Grades: 11 12 Adult　　　　　**808**
1. Rhetoric
ISBN 0-375-72115-0; 0-375-72227-0 pa

LC 2005-44934

The author "demonstrates how . . . unexpected humor, loquaciousness, and apt description can jolt a writer into engaged authorship. This primer is dotted with illustrative examples that range from Shakespeare and J.K. Rowling to Dave Barry and Maeve Binchy. . . . This is an entertaining and engaging choice for writers." Libr J

Prose, Francine
Reading like a writer; a guide for people who love books and for those who want to write them. HarperCollins Publishers 2006 273p
Grades: 11 12 Adult　　　　　**808**
1. Rhetoric 2. Creative writing 3. Books and reading 4. English language -- Rhetoric
ISBN 0-06-077704-4; 0-06-077705-2 pa; 978-0-06-077704-3; 978-0-06-077705-0 pa

LC 2005-58457

The author argues that "would-be writers should turn to the classics for inspiration." (N Y Times Book Rev)

This book "should be greatly appreciated in and out of the classroom. Like the great works of fiction, it's a wise and voluble companion." N Y Times Book Rev

Stop plagiarism; a guide to understanding and prevention. edited by Vibiana Bowman Cvetkovic, Katie Elson Anderson. Neal-Schuman Publishers 2010 220p il
Grades: Adult Professional　　　　　**808**
1. Plagiarism
ISBN 978-1-55570-716-3

LC 2010-24860

"The authors organize the book's ten chapters in three sections: 'Understanding the Problem,' which explains the meaning of plagiarism; 'Finding Remedies,' which suggests answers to the problem; and 'A Practitioner's Toolkit,' which provides sensible resources that will aid in changing the ways students address plagiarism. . . . The accompanying CD-ROM offers Web site connections, tutorials, and a video presentation that can be used in the classroom. Though intended primarily for professionals, the essays in this book are written in a conversational and practical style that makes them accessible to anyone confronting or wishing to know more about plagiarism." Choice

Includes bibliographical references

Strunk, William

★ The **elements** of style; with revisions, an introduction, and a chapter on writing by E.B. White. 4th ed; Allyn & Bacon 1999 105p $14.95; pa $7.95

Grades: 11 12 Adult   **808**

1. Rhetoric

ISBN 0-205-31342-6; 0-205-30902-X pa

LC 99-16419

First privately printed in 1918

This work provides guidelines for proper usage and composition. Misused expressions and commonly misspelled words are discussed. Includes examples.

This work is "prescriptive, conservative, and humorous; in sum, it is the best book available on how to write English prose." Nichols. Guide to Ref Books for Sch Media Cent. 4th edition

★ **Student's** guide to writing college papers; 4th ed; The University of Chicago Press 2010 281p il (Chicago guides to writing, editing, and publishing) $39; pa $15; ebook $15

Grades: 9 10 11 12 Adult   **808**

1. Dissertations 2. Report writing

ISBN 978-0-226-81630-2; 978-0-226-81631-9 pa; 978-0-226-81633-3 ebook

LC 2009-31583

First published 1963 with title: Student's guide for writing college papers

This guide covers selecting a topic, collecting material, planning and writing the paper, and preparing footnotes and bibliographies.

Includes bibliographical references

Walker, Janice R.

The **Columbia** guide to online style; [by] Janice R. Walker and Todd Taylor. 2nd ed.; Columbia University Press 2006 xxi, 288p il $45; pa $19.50

Grades: 11 12 Adult   **808**

1. Bibliographical citations 2. Authorship -- Data processing -- Handbooks, manuals, etc.

ISBN 0-231-13210-7; 978-0-231-13210-7; 0-231-13211-5 pa; 978-0-231-13211-4 pa

LC 2006-24383

First published 1998

This is a "resource for citing electronic and electronically accessed sources. It is also a . . . style guide for creating documents electronically for submission for print or electronic publication." Publisher's note

Includes bibliographical references

Where we are, what we see; the best young artists and writers in America: a Push anthology. edited

by David Levithan. PUSH/Scholastic 2005 220p il pa $7.99

Grades: 7 8 9 10   **808**

1. Teenagers' writings 2. American literature -- Collections

ISBN 0-439-73646-3

LC 2005-296492

The "young writers and artists in this anthology have been selected from the winners of the Scholastic Art & Writing Awards program. The offerings range from an intense recollection, 'What Cancer Meant,' to a whimsical dictionary of words that don't exist but should. . . . This collection is a real boon for budding writers and artists, who will feel the encouragement and see the possibility of publication." Booklist

Winkler, Anthony C.

Writing the research paper; a handbook. [by] Anthony C. Winkler, Jo Ray McCuen-Metherell. 2009 MLA updated ed., 7th ed; Heinle & Heinle 2009 356p il $59.95

Grades: 9 10 11 12   **808**

1. Research 2. Report writing

ISBN 978-0-495-79965-8

First published 1979 by Harcourt Brace Jovanovich

Among the topics addressed are: choosing a topic, finding background sources, punctuation, outlining and using the library.

Writing and publishing; the librarian's handbook. edited by Carol Smallwood. American Library Association 2010 189p (ALA guides for the busy librarian) pa $65

Grades: Adult Professional   **808**

1. Authorship 2. Library science

ISBN 978-0-8389-0996-6; 0-8389-0996-5

LC 2009-25047

"This important writer's guide is readable from cover to cover or by bits and pieces and is a helpful and handy read for every librarian." Libr Media Connect

Includes bibliographical references

808.02 Authorship techniques, plagiarism, editorial techniques

The **new** digital scholar; exploring and enriching the research and writing practices of NextGen students. edited by Randall McClure and James P. Purdy. American Society for Information Science and Technology by Information Today, Inc. 2013 xv, 400 p.p (ASIS&T Monograph Series) $59.50

Grades: Professional   **808.02**

1. Research -- Study and teaching 2. Authorship -- Study and teaching 3. Research 4. Generation Y 5. Report writing

ISBN 1573874752; 9781573874755

LC 2012046801

In this book, the authors "propose that writing teachers and librarians must meet students where they research, rethink what research is, and design assignments that capitalize on students' strengths." Evidence supporting this approach is "contributed by writing instructors, librarians, and technical professionals," who discuss topics including paraphrasing, digital resources, and college first-year writing programs. (Library Journal)

Includes bibliographical references and index

808.06   Rhetoric of specific kinds of writing

Turabian, Kate L.

★ A **manual** for writers of research papers, theses, and dissertations; Chicago Style for students and researchers. Kate L. Turabian; revised by Wayne C. Booth, Gregory G. Colomb, Joseph M. Williams, and the University of Chicago Press editorial staff. University of Chicago Press 2013 xv, 448 p.p illustrations (Chicago guides to writing, editing, and publishing) (cloth: alkaline paper) $42.50

Grades: 9 10 11 12 Adult   **808.06**
1. Dissertations 2. Report writing 3. Academic writing -- Handbooks, manuals, etc 4. Dissertations, Academic -- Handbooks, manuals, etc
ISBN 0226816370; 9780226816371; 9780226816388
LC 2012036981

This book, by Kate L. Turabian, "[begins] with an overview of the steps in the research and writing process . . . [and] provides an overview of citation practices with detailed information on the two main scholarly citation styles. . . . The final section treats all matters of editorial style, with advice on punctuation, capitalization, spelling, abbreviations, table formatting, and the use of quotations." (Publisher's note)

"This edition's new graphic design updates the look and feel of this resource and further develops rules and advice for the use and citation of online sources. In addition to featuring new templates for citing e-books, websites, blogs, social networks, discussion groups, online videos, and podcasts, the eighth edition offers new general advice to help students make good decisions about what information to include for online sources that may not have all the traditional elements useful in citing a print source." Choice

Includes bibliographical references (pages 409-433) and index

808.1   Rhetoric in specific literary forms

Deutsch, Babette

★ **Poetry** handbook: a dictionary of terms; 4th ed; HarperResource 2002 203p pa $14

Grades: 11 12 Adult   **808.1**
1. Reference books 2. Poetry -- Terminology 3. Poetics -- Dictionaries
ISBN 0-06-463548-1
First published 1957 by Funk & Wagnalls

"The craft of verse described in dictionary form. Terms and techniques are defined and illustrated." N Y Public Libr. Ref Books for Child Collect. 2d edition

Drury, John

★ The **poetry** dictionary; foreward by Dana Gioia. 2nd ed.; Writer's Digest Books 2006 374p pa $14.99

Grades: 11 12 Adult   **808.1**
1. Poetics 2. Reference books 3. Poetry -- Dictionaries
ISBN 1-58297-329-6; 978-1-58297-329-6
LC 2005-15113
First published 1995 by Story Press (Cincinnati)

"Spanning the centuries from ode to rap, The Poetry Dictionary contains 284 entries that define movements and schools of poetry, forms of verse, rhyme and stress patterns, and poetic devices. Entries range in length from a paragraph for canto to more than seven pages for sonnet." Booklist [review of 1995 edition]

Fooling with words; a celebration of poets and their craft. edited by Bill Moyers. Morrow 1999 230p hardcover o.p. pa $12

Grades: 11 12 Adult   **808.1**
1. Poets 2. Authors 3. Poetics 4. Novelists 5. Editors 6. Essayists 7. Feminists 8. Memoirists 9. Translators 10. Poets laureate 11. College teachers 12. Literary critics 13. Magazine editors 14. Short story writers 15. Science fiction writers
ISBN 0-688-17346-2; 0-688-17792-1 pa
LC 99-34965

"Moyers here interviews 11 American poets (e.g., Robert Pinsky, Mark Doty, Shirley Geok-lin Lim, and Paul Muldoon) whose voices echo the diversity of the United States—a wonderful jumble of genders, ethnic groups, and religions. This book is not a how-to; interviews (accompanied by the interviewee's poetry) focus on the poet as an individual, the creative process, and enjoying poetry and reveling in its sound." Libr J

Higginson, William J.

★ The **haiku** handbook; how to write, teach, and appreciate haiku. [by] William J. Higginson and Penny Harter; foreword by Jane Reichhold. 25th anniversary ed.; Kodansha International 2009 331p pa $18

Grades: 11 12 Adult   **808.1**
1. Haiku
ISBN 978-4-770-03113-6; 4-770-03113-0
LC 2009-36628
First published 1985 by McGraw-Hill

This book "presents haiku poets writing in English, Spanish, French, German, and five other languages on an equal footing with Japanese poets. Not only are the four great Japanese masters of the haiku represented (Bash□o, Buson, Issa, and Shiki) but also several major Western authors not commonly known to have written haiku. The book presents a . . . history of the Japanese haiku, including the dynamic changes throughout the twentieth century as the haiku has been adapted to suburban and industrial settings. Full chapters are offered on form, the seasons in haiku, and haiku craft, plus background on the Japanese poetic tradition, and the effect of translation on our understanding of haiku." Publisher's note

Includes bibliographical references

Hirsch, Edward

How to read a poem; and fall in love with poetry.
Harcourt Brace & Co. 1999 352p $23; pa $15

Grades: 11 12 Adult **808.1**

1. Poetics 2. Poetry -- History and criticism
ISBN 0-15-100419-6; 0-15-600566-2 pa

LC 98-50065

The author "has gathered an eclectic group of poems
from many times and places, with selections as varied as
postwar Polish poetry, works by Keats and Christopher
Smart, and lyrics from African American work songs. A prolific, award-winning poet in his own right, Hirsch suggests
helpful strategies for understanding and appreciating each
poem. The book is scholarly but very readable and incorporates interesting anecdotes from the lives of the poets."
Libr J

Includes bibliographical references

Jerome, Judson

The **poet's** handbook. Writer's Digest Bks. 1980
224p hardcover o.p. pa $15.99

Grades: 9 10 11 12 **808.1**

1. Poetics
ISBN 1-58297-136-6

LC 80-17270

"This is not the usual alphabetized handbook. It gives a
brief but scholarly background of the poet's place in early
times and later history and moves on to discuss in individual
chapters the craft of poetry: syllable-counting, meter, rhyme,
free verse, the rhythms of the English language, and so on.
It is more personal than one usually finds such a book to be,
and it presents almost everything a beginning poet, as well
as one who has mastered the craft, should know." Choice

Kooser, Ted

★ The **poetry** home repair manual; practical
advice for beginning poets. University of Nebraska
Press 2005 163p $19.95; pa $13.95

Grades: 11 12 Adult **808.1**

1. Poetics
ISBN 0-8032-2769-8; 0-8032-5978-6 pa

LC 2004-24700

"Among the many books offering advice on writing poetry, . . . [this book] stands out for its usefulness and, at the
same time, for its inspiring view of the purposes of poetry."
Midwest Quarterly

Includes bibliographical references

Myers, Jack Elliott

★ **Dictionary** of poetic terms; [by] Jack Myers,
Don Charles Wukasch. University of N. Tex. Press
2003 434p pa $22.95

Grades: 11 12 Adult **808.1**

1. Reference books 2. Poetics -- Dictionaries
ISBN 1-57441-166-7

LC 2003-11482

First published 1985 by Longman Press with title: Longman dictionary and handbook of poetry

"Particularly useful is the plethora of samples from the
works of such greats as James Joyce, Edna St. Vincent Millay, Ezra Pound, and Ogden Nash. Although some of the

vocabulary is lofty, the definitions, fascinating history, and
brief essays combine to form a useful handbook." Libr J

Includes bibliographical references

Oliver, Mary

A **poetry** handbook. Harcourt Brace & Co. 1994
130p pa $13

Grades: 11 12 Adult **808.1**

1. Poetics
ISBN 0-15-672400-6

LC 93-49676

A "handbook for young poets on the formal aspects and
structure of poetry. Oliver excels at explaining the sound and
sense of poetry—from scansion to imagery, diction to voice.
She stresses the importance of reading poetry, since, in order to write well, 'it is entirely necessary to read widely and
deeply.' Sage advice is given in an entire chapter dedicated
to revision, wherein Oliver urges poets to consider their first
draft 'an unfinished piece of work' that can be polished and
improved later. Written in a pleasant and lucid style, this
book is a wonderful resource." Libr J

Seeing the blue between; advice and inspiration
for young poets. compiled by Paul B. Janeczko.
Candlewick Press 2002 132p $18.99; pa $7.99

Grades: 7 8 9 10 **808.1**

1. Poetics 2. American poetry -- Collections
ISBN 0-7636-0881-5; 0-7636-2909-X pa

LC 2001-25882

"The letters are personal, friendly, and supportive. . . .
A valuable addition to public and school libraries, with the
potential for much classroom and personal use." SLJ

808.3 Rhetoric of fiction

Gratton, Tessa

The **anatomy** of curiosity; by Tessa Gratton,
Maggie Stiefvater, Brenna Yovanoff. Carolrhoda Lab
2015 296 p. (lb: alk. paper) $18.99

Grades: 8 9 10 11 **808.3**

1. Authorship 2. Creation (Literary, artistic, etc.) 3.
Fiction -- Authorship 4. Young adult fiction, American
5. American fiction -- 21st century 6. Young adult
fiction -- Authorship
ISBN 9781467723985

LC 2014046862

In this book, authors Tessa Gratton, Maggie Stiefvater,
and Brenna Yovanoff "have assembled a new trio of vignettes. . . . Each short work sheds light on one aspect of
writing: characterization, world-building, and the development of an idea." (School Library Journal)

"At its best, this is an accessible guidebook for creating
fiction that illustrates the complexity of the process while
offering practical tips for managing it." Kirkus

Includes bibliographical references and index

Henry, Laurie

★ The **fiction** dictionary. Story Press (Cincinnati) 1995 324p hardcover o.p. pa $20.99

Grades: 11 12 Adult **808.3**
1. Reference books 2. Fiction -- Technique 3. Fiction -- Dictionaries
ISBN 1-884910-05-X; 1-884910-54-8 pa

LC 95-4269

Henry provides "definitions of 345 terms relating to fiction, including genres, narrative devices, elements of fictional works, and critical theories. In addition to citing examples of works that illustrate a term, she frequently supplements her explanations with brief excerpts from novels and short stories." Booklist

Lukeman, Noah
The **plot** thickens; 8 ways to bring fiction to life. St. Martin's Press 2002 221p $19.95; pa $12.95
Grades: 11 12 Adult **808.3**
1. Fiction -- Technique
ISBN 0-312-28467-5; 0-312-30928-7 pa

LC 2001-58564

"Lukeman focuses on the mechanics of storytelling. He introduces budding writers to the techniques of characterization (ask yourself questions about the people you've created), the various ways of generating suspense (danger, a ticking clock), and the importance of conflict." Booklist

Piercy, Marge
So you want to write; how to master the craft of writing fiction and memoir. [by] Marge Piercy and Ira Wood. 2nd ed.; Leapfrog Press 2005 324p pa $16.95
Grades: 11 12 Adult **808.3**
1. Biography as a literary form 2. Fiction -- Technique
ISBN 0-9728984-5-X

First published 2001

This book "uses talks, exercises, anecdotes and examples proven in the classroom, to address: How to begin a piece by seducing your reader, How to create characters that embody the infinite contradictions of human behavior, How to master the elements of plotting fiction, How to create a strategy for telling the story of your life, How to learn to read critically, like a professional writer, How to write about painful personal material without coming off as a victim, [and] How to proceed if your work is continually rejected by publishers." Publisher's note

Includes bibliographical references

808.4 Rhetoric of essays

Orr, Tamra
★ **Extraordinary** essays. Franklin Watts 2005 128p il (F. W. Prep) $31; pa $9.95
Grades: 7 8 9 10 **808.4**
1. Essay 2. Authorship
ISBN 0-531-16761-5; 0-531-17576-6 pa

"This concise, appealingly designed writing guide offers practical advice to students on how to successfully complete essay assignments. Topics covered include choosing a topic, brainstorming, researching, crafting and defending a thesis statement, and revising." Booklist

Includes bibliographical references

808.5 Rhetoric of speech

Pinsky, Robert
★ The **sounds** of poetry; a brief guide. Farrar, Straus & Giroux 1998 129p hardcover o.p. pa $13
Grades: 11 12 Adult **808.5**
1. Poetry
ISBN 0-374-52617-6

LC 98-18873

"By bringing his passion for the sound of language—so evident in his own poems—to his expert interpretations of the work of others, Pinsky cracks open the glass case that seems to separate poetry from everyday language, allowing the song of each poem to ring bright and clear." Booklist

Includes bibliographical references

Ryan, Margaret
★ **Extraordinary** oral presentations. Franklin Watts 2005 128p il (F. W. Prep) $31; pa $9.95
Grades: 7 8 9 10 **808.5**
1. Public speaking
ISBN 0-531-16758-5; 0-531-17577-4 pa

This offers advice on preparing oral presentations
This book provides "good, practical ideas for students." SLJ

Includes bibliographical references

808.53 Debating

★ The **debatabase** book; a must-have guide for successful debate. [by] the editors of IDEA; introduction by Robert Trapp. International Debate Education Association 2011 227p il pa $27.95
Grades: 9 10 11 12 **808.53**
1. Debates and debating
ISBN 978-1-61770-015-6

LC 2010-52964

First published 2003

Presents background, arguments, and resources on approximately 150 debate topics in diverse areas. Includes the resolution, context, pro and con, sample motions, and web links and print resources.

Includes bibliographical references

Miller, Joe
Cross-X; a turbulent, triumphant season with an inner-city debate squad. Farrar, Straus & Giroux 2006 480p hardcover o.p. pa $17
Grades: 11 12 Adult **808.53**
1. Debates and debating
ISBN 978-0-374-13194-4; 0-374-13194-5; 978-0-312-42697-2 pa; 0-312-42697-6 pa

LC 2005-29829

"The reporting is both lively and engrossing, and even at nearly 500 pages, the book encourages most readers to learn more about these remarkable teens." Publ Wkly

Trapp, Robert
★ **Discovering** the world through debate; a practical guide to educational debate for debaters, coaches

and judges. [by] Robert Trapp . . . [et al.]; with the assistance of Judith K. Bowker. 3rd ed.; International-al Debate Education Association 2005 258p il pa $29.95

Grades: 9 10 11 12   **808.53**
   1. Debates and debating
   ISBN 1-932716-06-8

                                LC 2005-10911
   First published 2000 under the authorship of William Driscoll
   This book discusses how to prepare, structure, and carry out a debate. Includes chapters on judging and the appendix presents 50 debate exercises.

808.8   Collections of literary texts from more than two literatures

Flake, Sharon G.
   You don't even know me; stories and poems about boys. Hyperion/Jump at the Sun 2010 195p $16.99

Grades: 7 8 9 10   **808.8**
   1. Short stories 2. Boys -- Poetry 3. Boys -- Fiction 4. African Americans -- Poetry 5. African Americans -- Fiction
   ISBN 978-1-4231-0014-0; 1-4231-0014-X
   "This memorable collection of short stories and poems offers a glimpse into the urban lives of several African American boys. . . . Flake offers a vivid, unforgettable col-lection. . . . The voices ring true. . . . The stories and poetry are quite thought provoking." Voice Youth Advocates

★ **I** can't keep my own secrets; six-word memoirs by teens famous & obscure: from Smith maga-zine. edited by Rachel Fershleiser and Larry Smith. HarperTeen 2009 184p il pa $8.99

Grades: 7 8 9 10   **808.8**
   1. Autobiographies 2. Teenagers' writings
   ISBN 978-0-06-172684-2; 0-06-172684-2

                                  LC 2009-14584
   "The ruminations span from the haunting . . . to the fun-ny . . . to the inspirational. . . . A razor focus is put on issues that hit youths the hardest. . . . It has just the right proportion of humor and heartbreak." Booklist

Jocelyn, Marthe
   Scribbling women; true tales from astonishing lives. Tundra Books 2011 197p il $19.95

Grades: 6 7 8 9 10   **808.8**
   1. Literature -- Biography 2. Literature -- Women authors
   ISBN 978-0-88776-952-8; 0-88776-952-7
   Profiles women authors who have defied something that would have held others back, from societal convention to oppression, including Nellie Bly, Daisy Ashford, and Dang Thuy Tram.
   "Liberally using each writer's own words, Jocelyn's lyri-cal prose takes us deep into their lives, but mostly into their

spirits and courageous souls. Young readers can share the obstacles, joys, and/or sorrows each women faced," Kirkus
   Includes bibliographical references

Journalistas; 100 years of the best writing and re-porting by women journalists. edited by Eleanor Mills with Kira Cochrane. Carroll & Graf 2005 xx, 364p pa $14.95

Grades: 11 12 Adult   **808.8**
   1. Women journalists 2. Literature -- Collections
   ISBN 0-7867-1667-3
   This anthology contains work by such authors as "Mar-tha Gellhorn, Rebecca West, Susan Sontag and Mary Mc-Carthy. . . . The book is divided into subject areas." N Y Times Book Rev

Read all about it! great read-aloud stories, poems, and newspaper pieces for preteens and teens. ed-ited by Jim Trelease. Penguin Bks. 1993 489p il pa $13.95

Grades: 8 9 10 11 12   **808.8**
   1. Authors 2. Literature -- Collections
   ISBN 0-14-014655-5

                                  LC 93-21781
   This is a collection of 52 selections of fiction, poetry, and nonfiction from newspapers, magazines, and books by such authors as Cynthia Rylant, Jerry Spinelli, Howard Pyle, Rudyard Kipling, Robert W. Service, Maya Angelou, Moss Hart, Pete Hamill, and Leon Garfield. Includes biographical information about the authors

Webber, Carlie
   Gay, lesbian, bisexual, transgender, and question-ing teen literature; a guide to reading interests. [by] Carlisle K. Webber. Libraries Unlimited 2010 131p (Genreflecting advisory series) $45

Grades: Adult Professional   **808.8**
   1. Reference books 2. Homosexuality in literature 3. Libraries -- Special collections 4. Young adult literature -- Bibliography
   ISBN 978-1-59158-506-0

                                    LC 2010-2577
   "This slim volume will be a welcome guide for librar-ians who want to diversify their collections with current materials or who need readers? advisory assistance for their patrons. The titles are divided into six broad categories, and then subdivided into themes. . . . Each entry is annotated, with notations for awards, reading level, and sexual-identity appropriateness. The final chapter includes a discussion of collection development and the author's core list of fiction and nonfiction." SLJ
   Includes bibliographical references

808.81   Collections in specific forms

A **Book** of women poets from antiquity to now; edited by Aliki Barnstone & Willis Barnstone. rev ed; Schocken Bks. 1992 xxiv, 822p pa $22
Grades: 9 10 11 12   **808.81**
1. Poetry -- Women authors -- Collections
ISBN 0-8052-0997-2
LC 91-52701
First published 1980
An anthology of representative work by women poets of various literary traditions

City lights pocket poets anthology; edited by Lawrence Ferlinghetti. City Lights Bks. 1995 259p $18.95
Grades: 11 12 Adult   **808.81**
1. Poetry -- Collections
ISBN 0-87286-311-5
LC 95-31608
"Celebrating 40 years of publishing, this anthology contains selections from all 52 volumes of the 'Pocket Poets' series. Opening with Ferlinghetti's self-published 'Pictures of the Gone World,' the book {includes poems by} . . . Denise Levertov, Kenneth Patchen, Robert Duncan, . . . La Loca, Charles Upton, {and} Adam Cornford." (Libr J)
"Drawing from the 52 volumes published in the Pocket Poets series since 1956, this selection provides a handy sampler of many of the prominent avant-garde and leftist poets of the post-WW II era. . . . The series' extensive international scope is highlighted in poems culled from German, Russian, Italian, Dutch, Nicaraguan and Spanish poets." Publ Wkly

The **Columbia** Granger's dictionary of poetry quotations; edited by Edith P. Hazen. Columbia Univ. Press 1992 1132p $131
Grades: 11 12 Adult   **808.81**
1. Quotations 2. Reference books
ISBN 0-231-07546-4
LC 91-42240
This work contains the "most memorable lines written by the greatest poets of English. Quotations are organized alphabetically by poet, and coded so one can find full text in hundreds of current anthologies. With keyword and subject indexing." Univ Press Books for Public and Second Sch Libr

Crush: love poems. Word of Mouth Books/KA Productions 2007 72p pa $10
Grades: 8 9 10 11 12   **808.81**
1. Love poetry 2. Poetry -- Collections
ISBN 978-1-88801-840-0
"Alexander offers a cosmopolitan menu of tanka, haiku, long titles that lead into short first lines, verbal formulas that lead to sung discoveries, French phrases, prose poems, and poems written in Spanglish. The book is divided into three sections with various speakers, and a fourth section that includes poems by Sherman Alexie, Pablo Neruda, Nikki Giovanni, and the title poem, 'Crush' by Naomi Shihab Nye. . . . This well-crafted anthology will capture the interest of teens." SLJ

Faith & doubt; an anthology of poems. edited by Patrice Vecchione. Henry Holt and Co. 2006 138p $16.95
Grades: 9 10 11 12   **808.81**
1. Poetry -- Collections
ISBN 978-0-8050-8213-5; 0-8050-8213-1
LC 2006-18228
A collection of poems from around the world that explores the many facets of faith and doubt.
"This book will be read, considered, and discussed. Some who have been lost will find themselves; others will realize that there is direction even on the misguided path. Lucky are those who stumble upon this unassuming but powerful read." Voice Youth Advocates
Includes bibliographical references

Favorite Poem Project
★ **Americans'** favorite poems; the Favorite Poem Project anthology. edited by Robert Pinsky and Maggie Dietz. Norton 1999 327p $27.50
Grades: 11 12 Adult   **808.81**
1. Poetry -- Collections
ISBN 0-393-04820-9
LC 99-31979
"People across America, including many teens, share the poetry they love, and talk about what it means in their lives. Their choices—from John Keats to Lucille Clifton—defy stereotypes, and their comments are heartfelt." Booklist

★ **Fire** in the soul; 100 poems for human rights. edited by Dinyar Godrej. New Internationalist 2009 184p pa $16.95
Grades: 9 10 11 12 Adult   **808.81**
1. Poetry -- Collections 2. Human rights -- Poetry
ISBN 978-1-906523-16-9
"The selections come from a wide array of nations and voices. Some were written originally in English, others in Russian, Portuguese, Turkish, Tagalog, Hebrew, Tigrinya, and other languages. All are from the 20th century and are presented here in English. Every one of these poems comes from a place of great pain, of nearly unimaginable suffering, and all offer stubborn rays of hope. The themes range from the ravages of war and genocide to political and gender persecution, from famine to censorship, from child labor to neglect of the elderly." SLJ
Includes bibliographical references

Greenberg, Jan
★ **Side** by side; new poetry inspired by art from around our world. collected by Jan Greenberg. Abrams Books for Young Readers 2008 88p il $19.95
Grades: 8 9 10 11 12   **808.81**
1. Art -- Poetry 2. Poetry -- Collections
ISBN 978-0-8109-9471-3; 0-8109-9471-2
LC 2007-11973
This is an "anthology of accomplished poems inspired by artworks. . . . [Greenberg brings] together the work of poets and artists from around the globe. . . . The poems are grouped loosely into categories, defined in Greenberg's inspirational introduction. . . . Each spread features a poem in

its original language, the English translation, and an artwork, usually from the same country or culture as the poem. With a few exceptions, the reproductions of the art, which ranges from ancient to contemporary work, are sharp and clear, and the moving, often startling poems invite readers to savor the words and then look closely at each image." Booklist

I feel a little jumpy around you; a book of her poems & his poems collected in pairs. [by] Naomi Shihab Nye and Paul B. Janeczko. Simon & Schuster Bks. for Young Readers 1996 256p hardcover o.p. pa $10
Grades: 7 8 9 10   **808.81**
1. Poetry -- Collections
ISBN 0-689-81341-4
LC 95-44904

A collection of poems, by male and female authors, presented in pairings that offer insight into how men and women look at the world, both separately and together

"Though the gender counterpoint really plays little part in the juxtaposition, the pairings are piquant and provide a manageable way to start talking about a very large collection of poetry. An engaging marginal dialogue, taken from Nye's and Janeczko's collaborative fax correspondence, appears alongside the appendix and permits a revealing peek behind the scences. Highly readable notes from contributors are included, as is an index of poems and a gender-segregated index of poets." Bull Cent Child Books

I just hope it's lethal; poems of sadness, madness, and joy. collected by Liz Rosenberg and Deena November. Houghton Mifflin 2005 190p pa $7.99
Grades: 9 10 11 12   **808.81**
1. Poetry -- Collections
ISBN 0-618-56452-7
LC 2005-4257

"This interesting and rich collection of poetry will have special significance for teen readers." Voice Youth Advocates

Love poems. Knopf 1993 256p (Everyman's library pocket poets) $12.50
Grades: 11 12 Adult   **808.81**
1. Love poetry 2. Poetry -- Collections
ISBN 0-679-42906-9
LC 93-11427

Among the poets included are Robert Graves, W. B. Yeats, Pablo Neruda, Boris Pasternak, William Carlos Williams, Anna Akhmatova, Robert Browning and Christina Rossetti. An index of first lines is appended

Milosz, Czeslaw

A **Book** of luminious things; an international anthology of poetry. edited and with an introduction by Czeslaw Milosz. Harcourt Brace & Co. 1996 xx, 320p hardcover o.p. pa $15
Grades: 11 12 Adult   **808.81**
1. Poetry -- Collections
ISBN 0-15-600574-3
LC 95-38060

"Nobel laureate Milosz states in his introduction that the purpose of this personal and eclectic collection is to present poetry that is 'short, clear, readable, and . . . realistic, that is, loyal toward reality and attempting to describe it as concisely as possible.' . . . Most of the selections are from classical Chinese and 20th-century American and European (primarily Eastern European, Scandinavian, and French) poets." Libr J

Music of a distant drum; classical Arabic, Persian, Turkish, and Hebrew poems. translated and introduced by Bernard Lewis. Princeton Univ. Press 2001 222p il hardcover o.p. pa $17.95
Grades: 11 12 Adult   **808.81**
1. Arabic poetry -- Collections 2. Hebrew poetry -- Collections 3. Persian poetry -- Collections 4. Turkish poetry -- Collections
ISBN 0-691-15010-9 pa; 0-691-08928-0
LC 2001-19858

"Lewis, one of the foremost scholars of the Middle East, has devoted much of his career to the history of Islam; this volume collects his translations of poems—nearly all appearing in English for the first time—that span eleven centuries and four major Middle Eastern traditions. Many of the most striking works address, in spare, stirring lines, the twin demands of serving the self and serving God." New Yorker

Includes bibliographical references

The **Oxford** book of war poetry; chosen and edited by Jon Stallworthy. Oxford University Press 2008 xxxi, 358 p.p (paperback) $19.95
Grades: 8 9 10 11 12 Adult   **808.81**
1. War poetry 2. Poetry -- Collections 3. War poetry/Collections
ISBN 0199554536; 9780199554539
LC 8319303

This book is a collection of war poetry, arranged chronologically by conflict. The "250 poems in John Stallworthy's . . . anthology span centuries of human experience of war, from David's 'Lament for Saul and Jonathan,' and Homer's 'Iliad,' to the finest poems of the First and Second World Wars, and beyond." (Publisher's note)

Includes bibliographical references and indexes.

★ **Poems** to read; a new favorite poem project anthology. edited by Robert Pinsky and Maggie Dietz. Norton 2002 xxv, 352p $27.95
Grades: 11 12 Adult   **808.81**
1. Poetry -- Collections
ISBN 0-393-01074-0
LC 2002-321

"A graceful, sometimes jubilant, sometimes lyrical, sometimes brooding, but always welcoming and stirring collection." Booklist

Includes bibliographical references

The **Poetry** of our world; an international anthology of contemporary poetry. edited by Jeffrey Paine.

HarperCollins Pubs. 2000 xxviii, 511p hardcover o.p. pa $18.95

Grades: 11 12 Adult **808.81**

1. Poetry -- Collections

ISBN 0-06-055369-3; 0-06-095193-1 pa

LC 99-34921

In this global anthology "each section is preceded by a thoughtful introduction of several pages by the selector in that area. . . . A stunning and highly readable anthology." Libr J

★ **Poetry** speaks: who I am; poems of discovery, inspiration, independence, and everything else. Sourcebooks Jabberwocky 2010 136p $19.99

Grades: 5 6 7 8 9 10 **808.81**

1. Poetry -- Collections

ISBN 978-1-4022-1074-7; 1-4022-1074-4

This collection "aims at middle-grade readers with more than 100 strikingly diverse poems by writers including Poe, Frost, Nikki Giovanni, and Sandra Cisneros. The works are slotted together in mindful thematic order, beside occasional spot art. . . . Pairing a contemporary poem like Toi Derricotte's 'Fears of the Eighth Grade' alongside Keats's 'When I Have Fears That I May Cease to Be,' results in a refreshing lack of literary hierarchy that enables disparate works to build and reflect upon one another. An accompanying CD features recordings of 44 of the poems. . . . A sound and rewarding introduction to the joys of poetry." Publ Wkly

Revenge and forgiveness; an anthology of poems. edited by Patrice Vecchione. Henry Holt 2004 148p $16.95

Grades: 7 8 9 10 **808.81**

1. Poetry -- Collections

ISBN 0-8050-7376-0

LC 2003-56631

A collection of nearly sixty poems dealing with revenge and forgiveness, plus suggested readings about each contributing poet

"For students who are of a philosophical bent and for teachers of poetry, this book of poems about love, hate, and war will be a useful resource." Libr Media Connect

Includes bibliographical references

Risking everything; 110 poems of love and revelation. edited by Roger Housden. Harmony Bks. 2003 173p $20

Grades: 11 12 Adult **808.81**

1. Poetry -- Collections

ISBN 1-400-04799-4

LC 2002-14410

This is "an inspirational anthology sans inspirational chestnuts." Booklist

★ **This** same sky; a collection of poems from around the world. selected by Naomi Shihab Nye. Four

Winds Press 1992 212p il hardcover o.p. pa $9.99

Grades: 9 10 11 12 **808.81**

1. Poetry -- Collections

ISBN 0-02-768440-7; 0-689-80630-2 pa

LC 92-11617

A poetry anthology in which 129 poets from sixty-eight different countries celebrate the natural world and its human and animal inhabitants

"Notes on the contributors, a map, suggestions for further reading, an index to countries, and an index to poets are appended, adding additional luster to a book which should prove invaluable for intercultural education as well as for pure pleasure." Horn Book

War and the pity of war; edited by Neil Philip; illustrated by Michael McCurdy. Clarion Bks. 1998 96p il $20

Grades: 5 6 7 8 9 10 **808.81**

1. War poetry 2. Poetry -- Collections

ISBN 0-395-84982-9

LC 97-32897

"The selections, covering conflicts from ancient Persia to modern-day Bosnia, are by a wide variety of poets, from the well known (Tennyson, Whitman, Sandburg, Auden), to the obscure (Anakreon from ancient Greece and 11th-century Chinese poet Bunno). . . . The stark and simple scratchboard drawings are reminiscent of the Ernie Pyle illustrations from World War II and are as memorable as the best propaganda." SLJ

★ **World** poetry; an anthology of verse from antiquity to our time. Katharine Washburn and John S. Major, editors; Clifton Fadiman, general editor. Norton 1998 xxii, 1338p $45

Grades: 11 12 Adult **808.81**

1. Poetry -- Collections

ISBN 0-393-04130-1

LC 97-10879

The anthology's "stated aim—'to surprise and delight the common reader'—may seem rather quaint; yet it is a worthy one, and is, on the whole, impressively fulfilled." Times Lit Suppl

Includes bibliographical references

808.82 Collections of drama

100 great monologues from the neo-classical theatre; edited by Jocelyn A. Beard. Smith & Kraus 1994 157p (Monologue audition series) pa $9.95

Grades: 9 10 11 12 **808.82**

1. Acting 2. Monologues

ISBN 1-88039-960-1

LC 94-33114

"Among the neoclassical soliloquies chosen for inclusion are excerpts from the works of Congreve, Dryden, and Comielle. Molière is perhaps the most prominently featured of all the assembled playwrights. Dramatic plays such as Racine's Phedre are drawn upon to provide some very potent material, while more comic passages are contained in Sheridan's splendid The Rivals." Booklist

24 favorite one-act plays; edited by Bennett Cerf and Van H. Cartmell. Doubleday 1958 455p pa $14.95

    Grades: 11 12 Adult   **808.82**

    1. One act plays 2. Drama -- Collections

    ISBN 0-385-06617-1

A wide assortment of one-act plays includes comedies, tragedies, new and old, Irish, American, Russian, English, and Austrian. Includes the work of such playwrights as Eugene O'Neill, Noel Coward, George S. Kaufman, William Inge, and Dorothy Parker

"A good collection showing the variety of form and subject used by modern masters of the short play." Good Read

Actor's choice; monologues for teens. edited by Erin Detrick. Playscripts 2008 131p pa $14.95

    Grades: 6 7 8 9 10   **808.82**

    1. Acting 2. Monologues 3. Drama -- Collections

    ISBN 978-0-9709046-6-9; 0-9709046-6-5

                                 LC 2007-50166

"This volume of highly entertaining monologues is gleaned from one-act and full-length plays published by Playscripts, Inc. . . . This is an excellent volume to help students prepare for competitions as well as to use in drama, speech, or English classes." SLJ

★ **2010:** the best men's stage monologues and scenes; edited and foreword by Lawrence Harbison. Smith & Kraus 2010 176p (Monologue and scene study series) pa $14.95

    Grades: 11 12 Adult   **808.82**

    1. Acting 2. Monologues

    ISBN 978-1-57525-773-0

Annual. First published 1991 for the 1990 theater season under the editorship of Jocelyn Beard

This is a "selection of monologues and scenes from plays that were produced and/or published in the 2009-2010 theatrical season. Most are for younger performers (teens through thirties), but there are also some . . . pieces for men in their forties and fifties, and even a few for older performers. Some are comic (laughs), some are dramatic (generally, no laughs)." Publisher's note

★ **2010:** the best women's stage monologues and scenes; edited and with a foreword by Lawrence Harbison. Smith & Kraus Book 2010 193p (Monologue and scene study series) pa $14.95

    Grades: 11 12 Adult   **808.82**

    1. Acting 2. Monologues

    ISBN 978-1-57525-774-7

Annual. First published 1991 for the 1990 theater season under the editorship of Jocelyn Beard

This is a "selection of monologues and scenes from plays that were produced and/or published in the 2009-2010 theatrical season." Publisher's note

Allen, Laurie

    ★ **Comedy** scenes for student actors; short sketches for young performers. Meriwether Pub. 2009 197p pa $17.95

    Grades: 9 10 11 12   **808.82**

    1. Acting 2. Comedy 3. Drama -- Collections

    ISBN 978-1-56608-159-7; 1-56608-159-9

                                 LC 2008-41734

"This collection of 31 skits has a nice mix of female and male actors and works well in drama or speech classes. Each piece has a range of two to seven actors with options of up to a dozen, as well as suggested props and stage actions. The scenes are written with a superb sense of comic timing and portray authentic teen characters in high school settings." SLJ

★ The **Book** of monologues for aspiring actors; [edited by] Marsh Cassady. NTC Pub. Group 1995 212p il pa $23.96

    Grades: 7 8 9 10   **808.82**

    1. Acting 2. Monologues 3. Drama -- Collections

    ISBN 0-8442-5771-0

                                 LC 94-66239

"The selections range from the classical Greeks to Sam Shepard and Oscar Wilde; they give YA's the opportunity to develop characters of like ages in many different settings. Several questions to probe the actors' imaginations appear at the end of each monologue." SLJ

Cassady, Marsh

    The **book** of scenes for aspiring actors. NTC Pub. Group 1995 202p il pa $16.95

    Grades: 9 10 11 12   **808.82**

    1. Acting 2. Drama -- Collections

    ISBN 0-8442-5769-9

                                 LC 94-66240

"A collection of scripts for characters between the ages of 12-21. An introductory chapter analyzes the scene and the characters and gives information for both directors and actors on diagraming the set and blocking the action. . . . The selections come from Shakespeare, Jean Anouilh, and Maxwell Anderson and range in diversity from William Gillette's Secret Service to Brandon Thomas's Charley's Aunt and Arthur Laurents's West Side Story." Libr J

Great monologues for young actors; Craig Slaight, Jack Sharrar, editors. Smith & Kraus 1992 3v v1 pa $11.95; v2-v3 pa ea $14.95

    Grades: 8 9 10 11 12   **808.82**

    1. Acting 2. Monologues 3. Drama -- Collections

    ISBN 1-880399-03-2 v1; 0-57525-106-X v2; 1-57525-408-1 v3

These volumes provide an introduction and acting notes for monologues for men and women drawn from contemporary and classic works

★ **International** plays for young audiences; contemporary works from leading playwrights. edited by Roger Ellis. Meriwether 2000 419p pa $16.95

Grades: 9 10 11 12 **808.82**
1. Drama -- Collections
ISBN 1-56608-065-7

LC 00-55921

"The 12 short plays feature young characters in a variety of settings and situations. While some of the selections are straightforward in style (such as Gustavo Ott's Minor Leagues), others require a creative stretch in order to be able to read and produce them (such as Neil Duffield's racial fable Skin and Bones). . . . All, however, have characters that would be intriguing to young people and all deal with themes of cultural conflict and understanding." SLJ

Includes bibliographical references

Kehret, Peg
Tell it like it is; fifty monologs for talented teens. Meriwether Pub. 2007 117p pa $15.95

Grades: 9 10 11 12 **808.82**
1. Acting 2. Monologues
ISBN 978-1-56608-144-3; 1-56608-144-0

LC 2007-83

"The scenes range from funny to sweet to sad. Several entries concern animals, rites of passage, and historical events. Both contemporary and historical characters display a wide range of emotion, and there is enough flow and peak in all of the monologues for both beginners and advanced students. . . . This excellent book would make a smart purchase in preparation for forensics season." SLJ

More scenes and monologs from the best new plays; an anthology of new dramatic writing from professionally produced plays. edited by Roger Ellis. Meriwether Pub. 2007 233p pa $15.95

Grades: 9 10 11 12 **808.82**
1. Acting 2. Monologues
ISBN 978-1-56608-142-9; 1-56608-142-4

LC 2006-35093

Companion volume to Scenes & monologs from the best new plays (1992)

"The selections range from under a minute to approximately 10 minutes long, making them appropriate for competition or in the classroom. . . . Most of the characters range in age from middle teens to middle 20s. Students can choose from scenes for two women, scenes for two men, scenes for a man and woman, or monologs that don't specify gender. There is a good mix of comic, seriocomic, and serious pieces. . . . High school students and teachers will be pleased with the breadth and depth of the character selections and genres represented." SLJ

Includes bibliographical references

★ **Multicultural** scenes for young actors; Craig Slaight and Jack Sharrar, editors. Smith & Kraus 1995 237p (Young actor series) pa $11.95

Grades: 9 10 11 12 **808.82**
1. Acting 2. Drama -- Collections
ISBN 1-880399-48-2

LC 94-44187

This collection "is organized according to cast requirements, and each of the cuttings from over 40 plays is pre-

ceded by source notes and a brief plot summary. Information regarding performance rights is appended. Although a few of the plays have been included in standard compilations, the multicultural theme makes this collection unique." SLJ

The **Scenebook** for actors; great monologs & dialogs from contemporary & classical theatre. edited by Norman A. Bert. Meriwether 1990 246p pa $15.95

Grades: 9 10 11 12 **808.82**
1. Acting 2. Drama -- Collections
ISBN 0-916260-65-8

LC 90-52983

A collection of scenes, monologues and dialogues from scripts produced after 1975. Selections are for characters aged 18 to 30 and several are written for Afro-American and Hispanic actors

Includes bibliographical references

★ **Scenes** from classic plays, 468 B.C. to 1970 A.D. Jocelyn A. Beard, editor. Smith & Kraus 1993 310p pa $11.95

Grades: 9 10 11 12 **808.82**
1. Acting 2. Drama -- Collections
ISBN 1-880399-36-9

LC 93-33010

"Arranged chronologically, the selected scenes average three pages in length and involve two to three characters. A one-line description of the setting and of each character is given, as well as a one- to two-sentence synopsis of what is occurring at the opening of the scene. This book must be commended for such a well-balanced representation of time-honored classics." Booklist

Stevens, Chambers
Sensational scenes for teens; the scene studyguide for teen actors. Sandcastle Pub. 2001 104p il (Hollywood 101) $14.95

Grades: 9 10 11 12 **808.82**
1. Acting 2. Drama -- Collections
ISBN 1-883995-10-8

LC 99-76948

"Stevens presents more than 30 short comedy and drama scenes, all written for two actors with an even mix of boy-boy, girl-girl, and boy-girl casts. The contemporary urban and suburban settings coupled with culturally neutral names allow for racial and ethnic diversity." SLJ

Includes bibliographical references

★ The **Ultimate** audition book; 222 monologues, 2 minutes & under. edited by Jocelyn A. Beard. Smith & Kraus 1997 2v + v4 (Monologue audition series) ea pa $19.95

Grades: 11 12 Adult **808.82**
1. Acting 2. Monologues
ISBN 1-57525-066-7 v1; 1-57525-270-8 v2; 1-57525-420-4 v4

LC 97-10471

This collection draws "upon lesser-known works from significant writers and those of contemporary favorites and reflects a wide range of tone, age, time period, and voice. Divided among female, male, and unisex categories, all meet the obligatory two minutes or less time limit imposed by most directors and auditions." Libr J [review of volume 2]

Includes bibliographical references

808.85 Collections of speeches

Burns, William E.

Speeches in world history; [compiled by] Suzanne McIntire; with additional contribution by William E. Burns. Facts on File 2008 648p il (Facts on File library of world history) $85

Grades: 9 10 11 12 Adult   **808.85**
1. Speeches
ISBN 978-0-8160-7404-4; 0-8160-7404-6

LC 2008-5620

"From presidents to religious leaders to the common man, this reference of over 200 speeches provides students with a wide-ranging list of discourses that have had an impact on world history. . . . This outstanding resource will provide students with a well-rounded list of resources as well as tools for their own persuasive speech making." Libr Media Connect

Includes bibliographical references

★ **Lend** me your ears; great speeches in history. selected and introduced by William Safire. rev and expanded ed; Norton 1997 1055p $39.95

Grades: 8 9 10 11 12 Adult   **808.85**
1. Speeches
ISBN 0-393-05931-6

LC 96-43423

First published 1992
Pope Urban II, Bob Dole, Cicero, Jesus, Boris Yeltsin, Richard Nixon and Colin Powell are among the orators represented in this anthology of over 200 speeches grouped chronologically into thematic categories

★ The **Penguin** book of twentieth-century speeches; edited by Brian MacArthur. 2nd rev ed; Penguin Books 1999 xxix, 525p pa $15.95

Grades: 9 10 11 12   **808.85**
1. Speeches
ISBN 0-14-028500-8

LC 00-267955

First published 1992 in the United Kingdom
"Nelson Mandela, Winston Churchill, Emmeline Pankhurst, Martin Luther King, Jr., and Adolf Hitler are among the more than 140 famous speakers whose words are collected in this anthology that teens will use for reference and for browsing." Booklist [review of 1992 edition]

Words that ring through time; from Moses and Pericles to Obama: fifty-one of the most important speeches in history and how they changed our world. [compiled by] Terry Golway; foreword by Lewis Lapham. Overlook Press 2009 416p $30

Grades: 9 10 11 12 Adult   **808.85**
1. Speeches
ISBN 978-1-59020-231-9

LC 2010-275754

"Selected and introduced by historian Golway, the historically significant speeches in this anthology either crystallized a philosophy or addressed war, revolution, or national liberation. Prefacing them with the immediate contexts of their delivery, Golway permits the words to speak for themselves, without much analysis of their rhetorical arrangement. Readers are immediately immersed in scriptural excerpts from the Bible and the Koran and other declamations from the ancient world, such as Pericles' funeral oration. . . . Good browsing material for history collections." Booklist

Includes bibliographical references

808.88 Collections of miscellaneous writings

★ **Concise** Oxford dictionary of quotations; edited by Susan Ratcliffe. 5th ed.; Oxford University Press 2006 580p (Oxford paperback reference) pa $17.95

Grades: 11 12 Adult   **808.88**
1. Quotations 2. Reference books
ISBN 0-19-861417-9; 978-0-19-861417-3

LC 2006-48714

First published 1964
Collected here are quotations by over 2,000 authors from around the world ranging in time from the 8th century BC to the present. Arrangement is alphabetical by the names of authors with sections such as Anonymous, Ballads, The Bible, the Mass in Latin, etc. included in the alphabetical order. Foreign quotations are given in the original language followed by the English translation. Indexed by key words.

Heart full of grace; a thousand years of black wisdom. edited by Venice Johnson. Simon & Schuster 1995 un hardcover o.p. pa $19.95

Grades: 11 12 Adult   **808.88**
1. African Americans -- Quotations
ISBN 0-684-82542-2

LC 95-38106

"This is a diverse anthology of quotations, from the sayings of Martin Luther King and Langston Hughes to political speeches and African proverbs." Libr J

O'Brien, Geoffrey

Bartlett's familiar quotations; a collection of passages, phrases, and proverbs traced to their sources in ancient and modern literature. by John Bartlett; Geoffrey O'Brien, general editor. 18th ed. Little, Brown, and Co. 2012 lxi, 1438 p.p (hardcover) $50.00

Grades: 8 9 10 11 12 Adult   **808.88**
1. Quotations 2. Quotations, English
ISBN 0316017590; 9780316017596

LC 2012019870

This book, in its 18th edition, presents a collection of quotations "from the times of ancient Egyptians to the present day." (Publisher's note) It "includes 2500 new quotes and more than 800 newcomers, from Julia Child to David Foster Wallace. Quotes have been culled to bring in more foreigners and women and more material from fiction and poetry." (Library Journal)

Oxford dictionary of humorous quotations; edited by Ned Sherrin; with a foreword by Alistair Beaton. 4th ed; Oxford University Press 2008 536p hardcover o.p. pa $24.95

   Grades: 11 12 Adult   **808.88**

   1. Quotations 2. Wit and humor 3. Reference books
ISBN 978-0-19-923716-6; 0-19-923716-6; 978-0-19-957006-5 pa; 0-19-957006-X pa

                    LC 2008-486673

First published 1995 with title: The Oxford book of humorous quotations

This dictionary "features 5,000 quotations organized into more than 200 subject categories. Quips are arranged by broad themes. . . . Coverage spans the centuries, and you are as likely to find lines by Johnny Depp, Ricky Gervais, and Eddie Izzard are you are those by Noel Coward, William Shakespeare, and George Bernard Shaw. . . . An amusing addition to the reference collection." Booklist

Oxford dictionary of modern quotations; edited by Elizabeth Knowles. 3rd ed.; Oxford University Press 2007 479p $39.95; pa $18.95

   Grades: 9 10 11 12 Adult   **808.88**

   1. Quotations 2. Reference books
ISBN 978-0-19-920895-1; 0-19-920895-6; 978-0-19-954746-3 pa; 0-19-954746-7 pa

                    LC 2007-36871

First published 1991

"Containing more than 5,000 quotations from authors . . . [such] as Bertolt Brecht, George W. Bush, Homer Simpson, Carl Sagan, William Shatner, and Desmond Tutu, the dictionary is organized alphabetically by author, with . . . cross-referencing and keyword and thematic indexes." Publisher's note

Oxford dictionary of phrase, saying, and quotation; edited by Susan Ratcliffe. 3rd ed.; Oxford University Press 2006 xxi, 689p $39.95

   Grades: 9 10 11 12   **808.88**

   1. Proverbs 2. Quotations 3. Reference books 4. English language -- Terms and phrases
ISBN 978-0-19-280650-5; 0-19-280650-5

First published 1997

This book "brings together a profusion of proverbs, phrases, and quotations, arranged by subject or themes from Ability to Youth. The design and layout are clear and well organized. More than 12,000 bon mots from around the globe are included, and the origins and links of these treasured sayings in our language are traced through numerous cross-references." Booklist

★ **Oxford** dictionary of quotations; edited by Elizabeth Knowles. 7th ed.; Oxford University Press 2009 xxvi, 1155p $50

   Grades: 11 12 Adult   **808.88**

   1. Quotations 2. Reference books
ISBN 978-0-19-923717-3; 0-19-923717-4

                    LC 2009-464901

First published 1941

Collected here are around 20,000 quotations by nearly 3,500 authors from around the world ranging in time from the 8th century BC to the present. Arrangement is alphabetical by the names of authors with sections such as Advertising Slogans, Epitaphs, Film Lines, Prayers, etc. included in the alphabetical order. Indexed by key words.

Includes bibliographical references

809   History, description, critical appraisal of more than two literatures

★ **African** literature and its times; [edited by] Joyce Moss & Lorraine Valestuk. Gale Group 2000 xlv, 544p il (World literature and its times) lib bdg $145.25

   Grades: 11 12 Adult   **809**

   1. African literature -- History and criticism
ISBN 0-7876-3727-0

                    LC 00-24488

Contributors discuss "50 literary works in relation to their social and historical contexts. Each article begins with comments on the genre, setting, and the historical period in which the work takes place, along with information about the author. . . . The work of key writers such as Athol Fugard, Camara Laye, Doris Lessing and Wole Soyinka is discussed as is the writing of others who have more recently emerged on the scene." SLJ

Includes bibliographical references

Bloom, Harold

Dramatists and dramas. Chelsea House Publishers 2005 306p (Bloom's literary criticism 20th anniversary collection) $38.95

   Grades: 9 10 11 12   **809**

   1. Drama -- History and criticism
ISBN 0-7910-8226-1

                    LC 2005-3094

"Bloom's coverage ranges from the Ancient Greeks to modern day and includes writers like Aristophanes, Shakespeare, Moliere, Anton Chekhov, Tennessee Williams, and Arthur Miller." Publisher's note

The **epic**. Chelsea House Publishers 2005 265p (Bloom's literary criticism 20th anniversary collection) $38.95; pa $19.95

   Grades: 9 10 11 12   **809**

   1. Epic literature -- History and criticism
ISBN 0-7910-8229-6; 0-7910-8368-3 pa

                    LC 2005-5379

"In this volume, Bloom writes on the ancient works of Homer through more modern epics such as Hart Crane's 'The Bridge'." Publisher's note

Novelists and novels. Chelsea House Publishers 2005 588p (Bloom's literary criticism 20th anniversary collection) $38.95

Grades: 9 10 11 12   **809**
1. Fiction -- History and criticism
ISBN 0-7910-8227-X

LC 2005-3269

The author discusses "the world's great novelists including Miguel de Cervantes, Charles Dickens, Jane Austen, Franz Kafka, Ernest Hemingway, William Faulkner, and more." Publisher's note
Includes bibliographical references

Short story writers and short stories. Chelsea House Publishers 2005 188p (Bloom's literary criticism 20th anniversary collection) $38.95

Grades: 9 10 11 12   **809**
1. Short stories -- History and criticism
ISBN 0-7910-8228-8

LC 2005-6399

This book contains the author's "considerations on those writers who shaped the art of the short story; [including] Guy de Maupassant, Edgar Allan Poe, and Sherwood Anderson." Publisher's note

Burt, Daniel S.

The **literary** 100; a ranking of the most influential novelists, playwrights, and poets of all time. Rev ed; Facts on File 2009 541p (Facts on File library of world literature) $50; pa $19.95

Grades: 11 12 Adult   **809**
1. Authors 2. Literature -- History and criticism
ISBN 978-0-8160-6267-6; 978-0-8160-6268-3 pa

LC 2008-10066

First published 2001

Burt profiles not only familiar authors such as Tolstoy, Shakespeare, Dickens, and Jane Austen, but non-western writers such as Murasaki Shikibu, Du Fu, and Cao Xueqin.

"With definitive worth applied to Eastern and Western literary icons, the ranking equals a debate-spurring thesis, while engaging profiles are an essential literary primer." Libr J
Includes bibliographical references

Campbell, Patricia J.

Campbell's scoop; reflections on young adult literature. [by] Patty Campbell. Scarecrow Press 2010 245p (Scarecrow studies in young adult literature) $40

Grades: Adult Professional   **809**
1. Teenagers -- Books and reading 2. Young adult literature -- History and criticism
ISBN 978-0-8108-7293-6; 0-8108-7293-5

LC 2009-45563

"This resource represents the accumulated wisdom of a veteran librarian, author, speaker, critic, and pioneer of young adult services. Selected from several sources over many years, these essays and articles present a broad collection of critical writing. The articles are grouped into categories that include 'How We Got Here,' 'Trends and Tendencies,' 'Defining YA,' and 'Censorship Near and Far.' . . . Campbell's Scoop is a solidly useful professional title that weighs in on a diversity of topics. Unlike professional books that discuss and recommend specific YA titles, Campbell's Scoop is timeless. The information will not become dated and the breadth of the articles makes the collection relevant to a wide audience." Voice Youth Advocates
Includes bibliographical references

Civil disobedience; edited and with an introduction by Harold Bloom; volume editor, Blake Hobby. Bloom's Literary Criticism 2010 274p (Bloom's literary themes) $45

Grades: 10 11 12   **809**
1. Passive resistance 2. Resistance to government 3. Literature -- History and criticism
ISBN 978-1-60413-439-1; 1-60413-439-9

LC 2009-38087

The essays in this compilation explore "classical works of literature—novels, plays, short stories, letters, or speeches—with a common thematic thread. Sources analyzed in Civil Disobedience include excerpts from George Orwell's 1984, Herman Melville's 'Bartleby, the Scrivener,' Arthur Miller's The Crucible, and speeches by Malcolm X." SLJ
Includes bibliographical references

Contemporary literary criticism. Gale Res.

Grades: 11 12 Adult   **809**
1. Literature -- History and criticism

LC 76-38938

Irregular. Started publication in 1973

"This multivolume, onging series offers significant passages from contemporary criticism on authors who are now living or who have died since December 31, 1959. . . . Brief author sketches are followed by critical excerpts, presented in chronological order. The number of authors covered in each volume has varied over the years." Ref Sources for Small & Medium-sized Libr. 6th edition

Critical survey of drama; edited by Carl Rollyson. 2nd rev ed; Salem Press 2003 8v set $499

Grades: 11 12 Adult   **809**
1. Reference books 2. Drama -- Dictionaries 3. English drama -- Dictionaries 4. American drama -- Dictionaries
ISBN 1-58765-102-5

LC 2003-2190

This set contains "about 630 essays, of which 570 discuss individual dramatists and 60 cover overview topics. . . . Each essay on a dramatist provides . . . . material as birth and death dates, lists of the author's major dramatic works (with dates of first production and publication). Each essay opens with a brief survey of the author's publications in literary forms other than drama, a summary of the writer's professional achievements and awards, an extended biographical sketch that centers on the writer's development as a dramatist, and an extensive critical analysis of the writer's major dramatic works. Following this discussion is a list of major publications in fields other than drama and an annotated bibliography of critical works about the author." Publisher's note

Includes bibliographical references

★ **Encyclopedia** of world writers; Thierry Boucquey, general editor; Gary Johnson, advisor; Nina Chordas advisor; [written and developed by Book Builders LLC] Facts on File 2005 3v (Facts on File library of world literature) set $225

Grades: 9 10 11 12   **809**

1. Reference books 2. Authors -- Dictionaries

ISBN 0-8160-6143-2

     LC 2004-20551

Vol. 3 first published 2003 with title: Encyclopedia of world writers: 19th and 20th centuries

"This reference will stand out for its scope, particularly the accessible entries on the earliest literary activity." SLJ

Includes bibliographical references

Enslavement and emancipation; edited and with an introduction by Harold Bloom; volume editor, Blake Hobby. Bloom's Literary Criticism 2010 288p (Bloom's literary themes) $45

Grades: 10 11 12   **809**

1. Slavery in literature 2. Literature -- History and criticism

ISBN 978-1-60413-441-4

     LC 2009-38089

The essays in this compilation "explore classical works of literature—novels, plays, short stories, letters, or speeches—with a common thematic thread. . . . Excerpts in Enslavement and Emancipation discuss Toni Morrison's Beloved, the Declaration of Independence, various slave narratives, and some of Elie Wiesel's novels." SLJ

Includes glossary and bibliographical references

Griffiths, Trevor R.

The **Ivan** R. Dee guide to plays and playwrights. Ivan R. Dee 2003 424p il pa $28.95

Grades: 11 12 Adult   **809**

1. Reference books 2. Drama -- Dictionaries 3. Theater -- Dictionaries

ISBN 1-566-63566-7

     LC 2003-70127

First published 2003 in the United Kingdom with title: The theatre guide

This book "provides something that similar guides often omit: scribes, however obscure, who are being published and produced today. . . . Readers will find big names like George Abbott, Aeschylus, and Edward Albee as well as newcomers like Welsh dramatist Gary Owen and Briton Amanda Whittington." Libr J

Herz, Sarah K.

From Hinton to Hamlet; building bridges between young adult literature and the classics. [by] Sarah K. Herz and Donald R. Gallo. 2nd ed., rev. and expanded; Greenwood Press 2005 256p $39.95

Grades: Adult Professional   **809**

1. Youth -- Books and reading 2. Young adult literature

-- Study and teaching

ISBN 0-313-32452-2

     LC 2005-12728

First published 1996

"Aimed at teachers and librarians, the text offers personal experiences, testimonials, data, and theory for incorporating young adult literature into classrooms. . . . This resource is a must-have for all school libraries." Voice Youth Advocates

Includes bibliographical references

Highet, Gilbert

The **classical** tradition; Greek and Roman influences on Western literature. Oxford Univ. Press 1949 xxxviii, 764p hardcover o.p. pa $29.95

Grades: 11 12 Adult   **809**

1. Drama 2. Poets 3. Clergy 4. Judges 5. Satire 6. Authors 7. Romances 8. Humorists 9. Mythology 10. Novelists 11. Dramatists 12. Epic poetry 13. Renaissance 14. English literature 15. Italian literature 16. Classical literature 17. Comparative literature 18. Symbolism in literature 19. Essayists 20. Satirists 21. Pamphleteers 22. Short story writers 23. Writers on medicine 24. Writers on politics 25. Poetry -- History and criticism 26. Literature -- History and criticism 27. English literature -- Old English period 28. French literature -- History and criticism

ISBN 0-19-500206-7

"The twenty-four chapters fall into four main sections. The first takes in the Dark and Middle Ages—Anglo-Saxon poetry and prose, French epic and romance, Dante, Petrarch, Boccaccio, Chaucer. The second section comprises eight chapters on the Renaissance—drama, epic, pastoral and romance, lyric, the literature of translation, Rabelais, Montaigne. . . . [The] third section [is] 'The Baroque Age.' . . . After baroque, we come to our fourth and last section, the romantic, or . . . the revolutionary period 'and afterwards.'" Spectator

Includes bibliographical references

Kurian, George Thomas

★ **Timetables** of world literature. Facts on File 2003 457p $65

Grades: 11 12 Adult   **809**

1. Literature -- Chronology

ISBN 0-8160-4197-0

     LC 2002-3891

Chronicles world literature from the Classical Age through the twentieth century, discussing literary developments and the relationship between literature and the political and social climate of each historical period

"This comprehensive reference . . . helps academic researchers place major works of literature from 58 countries in historical and cultural context." Libr J

Includes bibliographical references

Literary movements for students; presenting analysis, context, and criticism on literary movements,

David Galens, project editor. Gale Group 2002
2v il set $185
Grades: 11 12 Adult　　　　　　　　**809**
1. Literature -- History and criticism
ISBN 0-7876-6517-7

LC 2002-10928

Entries provide "historical background information on
each movement as well as modern critical interpretation of
each movement's characteristic styles and themes. Approximately 25 movements are covered, including absurdism,
Greek drama, modernism, science fiction/fantasy, surrealism
and many others." Publisher's note
Includes bibliographical references

★ **Literature** and its times; profiles of 300 notable
literary works and the historical events that influenced them. Gale Res. 1997 5v set $741
Grades: 11 12 Adult　　　　　　　　**809**
1. Literature -- History and criticism
ISBN 0-7876-0606-5

LC 97-34339

"The editors chose the selections (fiction, poetry, short
stories, plays, biographies, and speeches) with the input of
public libraries and secondary-school teachers.... Each volume covers a time range subdivided by dates and a general
description . . . and begins with a brief overview of the historical events of the era, with a time-line providing a synopsis of each period." Libr J

Literature and its times: Supplement 1; profiles of
notable literary works and the historical events
that influenced them. Gale Group 2002 2v set
$190
Grades: 9 10 11 12　　　　　　　　**809**
1. Literature -- History and criticism
ISBN 0-7876-6550-9
These two volumes cover 100 additional titles

Literature of developing nations for students; Mi-
chael L. LaBlanc, Elizabeth Bellalouna, and Ira
Mark Milne, editors. Gale Group 2000 2v set
$160
Grades: 11 12 Adult　　　　　　　　**809**
1. Developing countries in literature 2. Fiction --
History and criticism
ISBN 0-7876-4928-7

LC 00-56023

"Each entry begins with an introduction of a few paragraphs to the author and specific novel and then . . . provides plot summary and analysis. Excerpts from essays and
articles about the novel are provided . . . and short summaries of major characters, an overview of important themes,
historical context, a critical overview, and a bibliography are
also included." Libr J
Includes bibliographical references

Magill's survey of world literature; edited by Steven
G. Kellman. Rev ed; Salem Press 2009 6v il
set $499
Grades: 11 12 Adult　　　　　　　　**809**
1. Reference books 2. Literature -- Bio-bibliography 3.

Literature -- History and criticism
ISBN 978-1-58765-431-2

LC 2008-46042

First published 1992 under the editorship of Frank
Northen Magill
"A solid choice for anyone in need of an inexpensive,
broad biocritical literary reference title on world literature."
Libr J
Includes glossary and bibliographical references

Patterson, Michael
★ The **Oxford** dictionary of plays. Oxford Uni-
versity Press 2005 xxxv, 523p $50
Grades: 11 12 Adult　　　　　　　　**809**
1. Reference books 2. Drama -- Dictionaries
ISBN 0-19-860417-3

LC 2004-23698

This is a "digest of 1000 works that span the history of
theater from Aristophanes to Michael Frayn's Democracy
(2003). The entries, which run between 200 and 400 words,
include the date and place of first performance, genre (descriptions of which are included in the preface), setting, cast
required, and a synopsis of the action with a one-paragraph
assessment of the play." Libr J
Includes bibliographical references

Ruud, Jay
Encyclopedia of medieval literature. Facts on
File 2005 734p (Facts on File library of world lit-
erature) $75
Grades: 11 12 Adult　　　　　　　　**809**
1. Reference books 2. Medieval literature --
Encyclopedias
ISBN 0-8160-5497-5

LC 2004-31066

"Each article focuses on key authors, characters, titles,
and aspects of works that exemplify the importance of the
Middle Ages. The selections are from Europe and Asia and
represent various cultural backgrounds. . . . Individuals interested in a source of basic information from which to begin
a study of the Middle Ages will find this volume to be especially useful." Am Ref Books Annu, 2006
Includes bibliographical references

Short stories for students. Gale Group
Grades: 9 10 11 12　　　　　　　　**809**
Started publication 1997
"Each volume contains entries for 20 stories arranged
alphabetically by title. . . . Each entry includes a brief biographical sketch of the writer; a plot summary; descriptions
of characters; a discussion of the major themes and style
(use of irony, symbolism, points of view, etc.); an introduction to the historical and cultural period during which the
story was written; a critical overview; and an essay written
for this resource along with excerpts from the work of other
critics." SLJ

★ **Short** story writers; edited by Charles E. May. Rev. ed.; Salem Press 2008 3v il (Magill's choice) set $217

Grades: 9 10 11 12 Adult   **809**

1. Short stories -- History and criticism
ISBN 978-1-58765-389-6

LC 2007-32789

First published 1997

This set "covers writers from Giovanni Boccaccio and Geoffrey Chaucer to Anton Chekhov and Sandra Cisneros. . . . Readers, whether in need of a brief critical overview or in search of what to read next, will find this set extremely useful. Each entry includes a brief biography, a list of principal works, a note on other literary forms the author explored, and a concise list of achievements as well as brief essays . . . on particular stories." SLJ

Includes bibliographical references

Women in literature; reading through the lens of gender. edited by Jerilyn Fisher and Ellen S. Silber; foreword by David Sadker. Greenwood Press 2003 xxxix, 358p $65

Grades: 9 10 11 12   **809**

1. Women in literature 2. Literature -- History and criticism
ISBN 0-313-31346-6

LC 2002-35212

This is a "collection of two- to three-page signed essays looking at 96 works of fiction (both canonical works and newer/less familiar titles) . . . . The literary works run the gamut from Homer and William Shakespeare to Alice Walker and Amy Tan. . . . Teachers looking for ways to shake up their traditional reading lists and students looking for a different approach to some classics will find this book of interest." SLJ

Includes bibliographical references

Yagoda, Ben

Memoir; a history. Riverhead Books 2009 291p $25.95

Grades: 11 12 Adult   **809**

1. Autobiography
ISBN 1-59448-886-X; 978-1-59448-886-3

LC 2009-30859

"Yagoda traces the memoir from its birth in early Christian writings and Roman generals' journals . . . [through the] year of 2007." (Publisher's note) Index.

"With its mixture of literary criticism, cultural history and just enough trivia, Yagoda's survey is sure to appeal to scholars and bibliophiles alike." Publ Wkly

Includes bibliographical references

809.1   Literature in specific forms other than miscellaneous writings

Arana, R. Victoria

The **Facts** on File companion to world poetry; 1900 to the present. Facts on File 2008 532p (Facts on File library of world literature) $85

Grades: 11 12 Adult   **809.1**

1. Reference books 2. Poetry -- History and criticism
ISBN 978-0-8160-6457-1

LC 2007-1831

"Arana classifies world poetry in broad terms, excluding only those poets from Britain, Ireland, and the US. This volume contains signed entries of moderate length that describe recognized and anthologized poets, significant individual poems, and related aesthetic movements (e.g., French rap, colonialism, hip-hop). . . . The volume's ease of use and inclusion of contemporary poets and movements make it a useful addition to most collections." Choice

Includes bibliographical references

Bloom, Harold

Poets and poems. Chelsea House Publishers 2005 487p (Bloom's literary criticism 20th anniversary collection) $38.95

Grades: 9 10 11 12   **809.1**

1. Poetry -- History and criticism
ISBN 0-7910-8225-3

LC 2005-8636

"In this volume, Bloom considers poets Emily Dickinson, Walt Whitman, Hart Crane, William Shakespeare, Samuel Taylor Coleridge, William Butler Yeats, and many others." Publisher's note

Johanson, Paula

World poetry, evidence of life. Enslow Publishers 2010 160p il (Poetry rocks!) lib bdg $34.60

Grades: 9 10 11 12   **809.1**

1. Poetry -- Authorship 2. Poetry -- History and criticism
ISBN 978-0-7660-3280-4; 0-7660-3280-9

LC 2009-44156

The author discusses "some of the poetry of famed world poets, including: Sin-leqi-unninni, Vyasa, Homer, Du Fu, Omar Khayyam, Rumi, Dante, Bash□o, Shevchenko, Tagore, Ahkmatova, Lorca, Neruda, Walcott, and Cohen." Publisher's note

Includes glossary and bibliographical references

809.3   Fiction--Criticism

Brave new words; the Oxford dictionary of science fiction. edited by Jeffrey Prucher; introduction by Gene Wolfe. Oxford University Press 2007 xxxi, 342p $29.95

Grades: 7 8 9 10 11 12 Adult   **809.3**

1. Reference books 2. Science fiction -- Dictionaries
ISBN 978-0-19-530567-8; 0-19-530567-1

LC 2006-37280

This is a "dictionary of the language of science fiction based on historical principles. . . . Entries include part of speech, etymology, definition with cross references to related terms, usage status (e.g., historical, jocular, derogatory, obsolete), variant forms, and . . . dated citations and quotations illustrating the usage of the word over time." Libr J

Includes bibliographical references

810   Literatures of specific languages and language families

911: the book of help; edited by Michael Cart; with Marianne Carus and Marc Aronson. Cricket Bks. 2002 178p $17.95; pa $9.95

Grades: 8 9 10 11 12   810

1. Terrorism 2. September 11 terrorist attacks, 2001 3. American literature -- Collections

ISBN 0-8126-2659-1; 0-8126-2676-1 pa

LC 2002-4707

A collection of essays, poems, and short fiction, created in response to the terrorist attacks of September 11, 2001. Contributors include Katherine Paterson, Joan Bauer, Walter Dean Myers, Nikki Giovanni, Arnold Adoff, and Russell Freedman

This "stands out for its rich prose, its unusual reporting, its search for context, its reminder of wonders." NY Times Book Rev

Acosta-Belen, Edna

The **Norton** anthology of Latino literature; Ilan Stavans, general editor; [editors], Edna Acosta-Belen [et al.] W.W. Norton & Co. 2010 2489p il map $59.95

Grades: 11 12 Adult   810

1. American literature -- Hispanic American authors -- Collections

ISBN 978-0-393-08007-0; 0-393-08007-2

LC 2010-15108

"With a great array of writers celebrated and too little known, and invaluable supporting materials, this grand and affecting treasury of culturally rich and aesthetically dynamic poems, fiction, drama, letters, diaries, and essays illuminates every aspect of Latino life." Booklist

Includes bibliographical references

Amend, Allison

Hispanic-American writers. Chelsea House 2010 128p il (Multicultural voices) $35

Grades: 7 8 9 10 11 12   810

1. Latino authors 2. Hispanic American authors 3. American literature -- Hispanic American authors -- History and criticism

ISBN 978-1-60413-312-7; 1-60413-312-0

LC 2009-46535

Profiles notable Hispanic Americans and their work in the field of literature, including Sandra Cisneros, Julia Alvarez, and Junot Diaz.

"This volume opens with a succinct yet thorough introduction to the historical and cultural context of eight authors. The overview explains the origins and uses of the terms Chicano, Hispanic, and Latino and sketches the histories of the nations where most Hispanic-Americans have their roots. Amend also identifies common themes in Hispanic-American literature such as language and family; however, she also notes each community's unique concerns. . . . Amend also suggests books by other Latino writers for further reading." SLJ

Includes bibliographical references

The **American** renaissance; edited and with an introduction by Harold Bloom. Chelsea House 2003 370p (Bloom's period studies) $37.95

Grades: 9 10 11 12   810

1. United States -- Intellectual life 2. American literature -- History and criticism

ISBN 0-7910-7676-8

LC 2003-19991

"Ralph Waldo Emerson's transcendental writings influenced Henry David Thoreau and Walt Whitman, whose works are considered cornerstones of the American literary movement. This volume examines the impact of the American Renaissance on the Western canon of literature." Publisher's note

Includes bibliographical references

American women writers, 1900-1945; a bio-bibliographical critical sourcebook. edited by Laurie Champion; Emanuel S. Nelson, advisory editor. Greenwood Press 2000 407p $95

Grades: 11 12 Adult   810

1. Reference books 2. American literature -- Women authors -- Bio-bibliography

ISBN 0-313-30943-4

LC 00-22336

"This reference book profiles 58 American women writers who published their significant works between 1900 and 1945. . . . The information is arranged in four sections: 'Biography,' 'Major Works and Themes,' 'Critical Reception,' and 'Bibliography.' . . . The biographical information is brief and includes the most basic details, while the overview of the major works and themes is quite substantive and will be very useful for research. 'Critical Reception,' considers reactions both at the time of publication and today. . . . This book will be a valuable tool for research because it balances coverage of the prominent and the lesser known." Booklist

Includes bibliographical references

Anesko, Michael

Romanticism and transcendentalism; 1800-1860. Jerry Phillips, general editor; Michael Anesko, adviser and contributor; Andrew Ladd, Karen Meyers, principal authors. 2nd ed.; Facts On File 2010 126p il (Backgrounds to American literature) $40

Grades: 9 10 11 12   810

1. Romanticism 2. Transcendentalism 3. American literature -- History and criticism

ISBN 978-1-60413-486-5

LC 2009-29630

First published 2005

This "guide to the romantic and transcendentalist era in American literature . . . [provides] information on the foundations of romantic thought, romanticism and the new nation, gothic romance and sentimentalism, transcendentalism, Nathaniel Hawthorne and Herman Melville, and romanticism and poetic voice." Publisher's note

Includes bibliographical references

Asian-American writers; edited and with an introduction by Harold Bloom. New ed; Chelsea House 2009 219p (Modern critical views) $45

Grades: 11 12 Adult **810**

1. American literature -- History and criticism 2. American literature -- Asian American authors

ISBN 978-1-60413-401-8

LC 2008-43031

First published 1999

This book offers "critical evaluations of this . . . body of American literature. Canonical writers such as Maxine Hong Kingston and Amy Tan are discussed in addition to the voices and traditions that have emerged from the United States' diverse South and East Asian communities." Publisher's note

Includes bibliographical references

Beat culture; lifestyles, icons, and impact. edited by William T. Lawlor. ABC-CLIO 2005 liv, 390p il $85

Grades: 9 10 11 12 **810**

1. Reference books 2. Beat generation -- Encyclopedias

ISBN 1-85109-400-8

LC 2005-2772

This "single-volume work is possibly the best overview of the topic for high school students." SLJ

Includes bibliographical references

The **Beat** generation; a Gale critical companion. Lynn M. Zott, project editor. Gale 2003 3v (Gale critical companion collection) set $350

Grades: 11 12 Adult **810**

1. Beat generation 2. American literature -- History and criticism

ISBN 0-7876-7569-5

LC 2002-155786

"Volume 1 gathers a variety of sources that place the movement in cultural context. . . . Volumes 2-3 supply entries for 28 Beat authors. . . . Author entries include a brief biography, notes on major works and critical reception, a list of principal works, a selection of primary sources and secondary criticism, and further readings. . . . The selections include contributions by major Beat Generation scholars and provide a well-balanced, representative view of the Beats." Choice

Includes bibliographical references

Censored books {I}-II; critical viewpoints. edited by Nicholas J. Karolides, Lee Burress, John M. Kean. Scarecrow Press 1993 2v v1 pa $39.50; v2 $45

Grades: 9 10 11 12 **810**

1. Censorship 2. American literature -- History and criticism

ISBN 0-8108-4038-3 v1; 0-8108-4147-9 v2

Authors, librarians, and teachers contribute essays in support of books that are frequently challenged. They examine each work as literature and assess its content relative to societal values

The **Chronology** of American literature; America's literary achievements from the colonial era to modern times. edited by Daniel S. Burt. Houghton Mifflin 2004 805p il $40

Grades: 11 12 Adult **810**

1. American literature -- Collections

ISBN 0-618-16821-4

LC 2003-51142

"This chronology includes more than 8,400 literary works by more than 5,000 writers. Sections for each year are grouped in five chapters by period, from 1582 to 1999. Within each year, entries are grouped by genre, such as diaries and other personal writings, fiction, essays, literary criticism and scholarship, nonfiction, poetry, and drama. Within each genre, authors are listed alphabetically, generally with birth and death dates and short descriptions of named works for the year. . . . The Chronology of American Literature is easy to browse and, for book lovers, difficult to put down." Booklist

Includes bibliographical references

Crossing into America; the new literature of immigration. edited by Louis Mendoza and S. Shankar. New Press (NY) 2003 xxvi, 365p hardcover o.p. pa $18.95

Grades: 11 12 Adult **810**

1. Immigrants 2. American literature -- Collections

ISBN 1-56584-720-2; 1-56584-895-0 pa

LC 2002-41055

"A beautiful piece by Cuban American Achy Obejas captures the intergenerational conflict without heroics, and there are electrifying selections from Sandra Cisneros, Jamaica Kincaid, and other famous writers as well as some exciting new voices." Booklist

Includes bibliographical references

Crossing the danger water; three hundred years of African-American writing. edited and with an introduction by Deirdre Mullane. Anchor Bks. (NY) 1993 xxii, 769p pa $20

Grades: 11 12 Adult **810**

1. American literature -- African American authors -- Collections

ISBN 0-385-42243-1

LC 93-17194

This anthology "includes fiction, autobiography, poetry, songs, and letters by such writers as Frederick Douglass, Sojourner Truth, W.E.B. Du Bois, Zora Neale Hurston, and Richard Wright. Many topics are covered, from slavery, education, the Civil War, Reconstruction, and political issues to spirituals, songs of the Civil Rights movement, and rap music." Libr J

Includes bibliographical references

Davis, Cynthia J.

★ **Women** writers in the United States; a timeline of literary, cultural, and social history. [by] Cynthia Davis and Kathryn West. Oxford Univ. Press 1996 488p $60

Grades: 11 12 Adult **810**

1. Women -- United States 2. American literature --

Chronology 3. American literature -- Women authors
ISBN 0-19-509053-5

LC 95-31815

In a timeline format, the authors "present information on the full spectrum of women's writing—including fiction, poetry, biography, political manifestos, essays, advice columns, and cookbooks, alongside a chronology of developments in social and cultural history that are especially pertinent to women's lives." Publisher's note

Encyclopedia of African-American writing; five centuries of contribution: trials & triumphs of writers, poets, publications and organizations. Shari Dorantes Hatch, editor. 2nd ed.; Grey House Pub. 2009 xxii, 863p il $165

Grades: 11 12 Adult **810**

1. Reference books 2. American literature -- African American authors -- Encyclopedias 3. American literature -- African American authors -- Bio-bibliography

ISBN 978-1-59237-291-1

First published 2000 by ABC-CLIO with title: African-American writers: a dictionary

"This voluminous and inclusive collection consists of 738 entries that cover authors and other topics related to African American writing, such as newspapers, magazines, journals, and publishers and figures such as educators, playwrights, journalists, academics, editors, and librarians from the past 500 years. . . . Although unsigned, the entries are highly accessible, very current, and chock-full of information for a range of audiences." Libr J

Includes bibliographical references

Encyclopedia of American Indian literature; [edited by] Jennifer McClinton-Temple, Alan Velie. Facts on File 2007 466p (Encyclopedia of American ethnic literature) $75

Grades: 11 12 Adult **810**

1. Reference books 2. Native American literature -- Encyclopedias 3. Native Americans in literature -- Encyclopedias

ISBN 0-8160-5656-0; 978-0-8160-5656-9

LC 2006-23762

"This book brings together solid information from scattered sources, facilitating research on an esoteric subject." Libr J

Includes bibliographical references

Facts on File, Inc.

★ **Encyclopedia** of American literature; 2nd ed; Facts on File 2008 4v il (Facts on File library of American literature) set $375

Grades: 11 12 Adult **810**

1. Reference books 2. American literature -- Encyclopedias

ISBN 978-0-8160-6476-2

LC 2007-25662

First published 2002

Entries in this encyclopedia cover works, writers, movements and other American literature-related topics

from colonial times to the present. Each volume includes a chronology.

Includes bibliographical references

Fernandez Olmos, Margarite

U.S. Latino literature; a critical guide for students and teachers. edited by Harold Augenbraum and Margarite Fernández Olmos under the auspices of the Mercantile Library of New York. Greenwood Press 2000 215p $49.95

Grades: 9 10 11 12 **810**

1. Hispanic Americans in literature 2. American literature -- Hispanic American authors -- History and criticism

ISBN 0-313-31137-4

LC 99-462065

Among the works discussed in these eighteen essays are Rudolfo A. Anaya's Bless me, Ultima, Richard Rodriguez's Hunger of memory, Sandra Cisneros' The house on Mango Street, and Julia Alvarez's How the Garcia girls lost their accents

"The critical essays begin with a brief biography of the author and then center on an analysis of the work's themes and forms. The essays also include ideas for teaching the work and suggestions for further reading. . . . An excellent addition to the professional shelf as well as literary criticism collections." Book Rep

Includes bibliographical references and index

GirlSpoken: from pen, brush & tongue; edited by Jessica Hein, Heather Holland and Carol Kauppi. Second Story Press 2007 202p il pa $18.95

Grades: 9 10 11 12 **810**

1. Teenagers' writings 2. Girls -- Poetry

ISBN 978-1-897187-30-2; 1-897187-30-0

"This collection of poetry, short prose, and art is the culmination of a Canadian research and action project designed to effect change by giving creative voice to teen girls. The book is divided into sections with four central themes: Voice, Beauty, Strength, and Becoming. . . . This collection is a welcome addition to the teen poetry genre and will appeal to teen girls who enjoy expressing themselves through creative writing and art." Voice Youth Advocates

Includes bibliographical references

★ **Growing** up ethnic in America; contemporary fiction about learning to be American. edited by Maria Mazziotti Gillan and Jennifer Gillan. Penguin Bks. 1999 374p pa $16.95

Grades: 9 10 11 12 **810**

1. Short stories

ISBN 0-14-028063-4

LC 99-25762

This anthology of 35 stories illustrates the various ways young people of distinct ethnic communities come to terms with their identities, negotiating the differences between their cultures and American society. Among the writers included are Amy Tan, Toni Morrison, Gary Soto, Sherman Alexie, Veronica Chambers, and E. L. Doctorow

"This kind of collection, with its literary quality and multiple perspectives, is the best answer to those who expect only messages with multiculturalism and who sneer 'P.C.' at the mention of diversity." Booklist

Growing up Latino; memoirs and stories. edited with an introduction by Harold Augenbraum and Ilan Stavans; foreword by Ilan Stavans. Houghton Mifflin 1993 xxix, 344p hardcover o.p. pa $15

Grades: 6 7 8 9 10   **810**

1. American literature -- Hispanic American authors -- Collections

ISBN 0-395-66124-2

LC 92-32624

A collection of short stories and excerpts from novels and memoirs written by twenty-five Latino authors. Among the contributors are Julia Alvarez, Oscar Hijuelos, Denise Chávez, Rolando Hinojosa, and Sandra Cisneros.

Includes bibliographical references

Guys write for Guys Read; edited by Jon Scieszka. Viking 2005 272p il $16.99; pa $11.99

Grades: 6 7 8 9 10   **810**

1. American literature -- Collections

ISBN 0-670-06007-0; 0-670-01144-4 pa

LC 2004-28984

This is a collection of short stories, essays, columns, cartoons, anecdotes, and artwork by such writers and illustrators as Brian Jacques, Jerry Spinelli, Chris Crutcher, Mo Willems, Chris Van Allsburg, Matt Groening, and Neil Gaiman, selected by voters at the Guys Read web site.

This is "a diverse and fast-paced anthology . . . that deserves a permanent place in any collection. . . . There's something undeniably grand about this collective celebration of the intellectual life of the common boy." SLJ

The **Harlem** Renaissance; edited and with an introduction by Harold Bloom. Chelsea House 2003 336p (Bloom's period studies) $37.95

Grades: 9 10 11 12   **810**

1. Harlem Renaissance 2. American literature -- African American authors -- History and criticism

ISBN 0-7910-7679-2

LC 2003-16873

"This volume examines the defining themes and style of African-American literature during . . . {the Harlem Renaissance} which laid the groundwork for contemporary African-American writers." Publisher's note

Includes bibliographical references

The **Harlem** Renaissance: a Gale critical companion; foreword by Trudier Harris-Lopez; Janet Witalec, project editor. Gale Res. 2003 3v il (Gale critical companion collection) set $325

Grades: 11 12 Adult   **810**

1. Harlem Renaissance 2. American literature -- African American authors -- History and criticism

ISBN 0-7876-6618-1

LC 2002-10076

"Volume 1 focuses on five topic areas, starting with an overview and background information, then moving on to chapters on social, economic, and political factors; publishing and periodicals; performing arts; and the visual arts. . . . Volumes 2 and 3 are devoted to writers. Eleven female and twenty-two male authors are discussed, among them Arna Bontemps, Marcus Garvey, Angelina Weld Grimké, James Weldon Johnson, and Dorothy West. . . . Most author entries include biographical profiles, lists of principal works, some primary source material, critical essays, and further reading lists. . . . The breadth and depth of Harlem Renaissance make it a valuable and unique reference source for academic, public, and high-school libraries." Booklist

Includes bibliographical references

Harlem speaks; a living history of the Harlem Renaissance. edited by Cary D. Wintz. Sourcebooks MediaFusion 2007 xxi, 502p il $29.95

Grades: 9 10 11 12   **810**

1. Harlem Renaissance 2. African Americans -- Intellectual life 3. American literature -- African American authors -- History and criticism

ISBN 978-1-4022-0436-4; 1-4022-0436-1

Includes audio CD

"The visual and auditory impact of this title, paired with an in-depth, accessible text, makes it a good choice for browsing or research." SLJ

Includes bibliographical references

Hart, James David

★ The **Oxford** companion to American literature; [by] James D. Hart; with revisions and additions by Phillip W. Leininger. 6th ed; Oxford Univ. Press 1995 779p $49.95

Grades: 11 12 Adult   **810**

1. Reference books 2. American literature -- Dictionaries

ISBN 0-19-506548-4

LC 94-45727

First published 1941

In addition to over 2000 entries for individual authors and more than 1,100 for important works this reference includes entries for literary movements, awards, magazines, printers, book collectors and newspapers. A chronological index of literary and social history is appended.

Hill, Laban Carrick

★ **Harlem** stomp! a cultural history of the Harlem Renaissance. Little, Brown 2004 151p il hardcover o.p. pa $12.99

Grades: 7 8 9 10   **810**

1. Harlem Renaissance 2. African American arts 3. African Americans -- Intellectual life

ISBN 0-316-81411-3; 0-316-03424-X pa

LC 2002-73067

"The vibrancy, energy, and color of the Harlem Renaissance come to life in this gem of a book packed with poetry, prose, song lyrics, art, and photography created by some of the period's most influential figures. . . . Informative and highly entertaining, it deserves to be shelved in any library." Voice Youth Advocates

Includes bibliographical references

Hillstrom, Kevin

The **Harlem** Renaissance. Omnigraphics 2008 228p il map (Defining moments) $49

Grades: 7 8 9 10　　　　　　　　　**810**

1. Harlem Renaissance 2. African American arts

ISBN 978-0-7808-1027-3; 0-7808-1027-9

LC 2007-51132

"This an insightful, highly accessible subject primer for general collections." Libr J

Includes glossary and bibliographical references

Hispanic-American writers; edited and with an introduction by Harold Bloom. New ed; Bloom's Literary Criticism 2008 187p (Modern critical views) $45

Grades: 9 10 11 12　　　　　　　　**810**

1. American literature -- Hispanic American authors -- History and criticism

ISBN 978-0-7910-9623-9

LC 2008-31221

First published 1998

This book "offers critical perspectives on the many Hispanic authors who have staked out a vibrant and burgeoning presence on the American literary scene." Publisher's note

Includes bibliographical references

Jewish American literature; a Norton anthology. [compiled and edited by] Jules Chametzky [et al.] Norton 2000 xxiv, 1221p il $39.95

Grades: 11 12 Adult　　　　　　　　**810**

1. American literature -- Collections 2. American literature -- Jewish authors

ISBN 0-393-04809-8

LC 00-55393

The editors have attempted "to encompass Jewish literature from 1654 to the present in this collection of poems, cartoons, sermons, diaries, letters, stories, speeches, plays, prayers, novel excerpts, and critical writings either translated from Hebrew or Yiddish or written in English. Major sections group the literature chronologically to help identify large movements. . . . This great anthology is essential for Jewish studies and American literature collections." Libr J

Includes bibliographical references

Johnson, Claudia D.

Labor and workplace issues in literature; [by] Claudia Durst Johnson. Greenwood Press 2006 183p (Exploring social issues through literature) $49.95

Grades: 9 10 11 12　　　　　　　　**810**

1. Work in literature 2. Fiction -- History and criticism

ISBN 0-313-33286-X

LC 2005-25974

"Each chapter examines the historical background and plot of the work, and discusses the labor and workplace issues raised by the author. It then overviews the history of these issues since the publication of the work and relates the literary text to modern concerns. The volume discusses such issues as low wages, long hours, workplace dangers, unemployment, sexual harassment, lack of job security or medical care, and the struggle of immigrants." Publisher's note

Includes bibliographical references

Magill's survey of American literature; edited by Steven G. Kellman. Rev. ed; Salem Press 2007 6v il set $499

Grades: 11 12 Adult　　　　　　　　**810**

1. Reference books 2. Literature -- Bio-bibliography 3. Literature -- History and criticism

ISBN 978-1-58765-285-1; 1-58765-285-4

LC 2006-16503

First published 1992 with two volume supplement published 1996 under the editorship of Frank Northen Magill

"Examining selected works of 339 U.S. and Canadian writers, from Anne Bradstreet and Benjamin Franklin to Edward Bloor and Octavia E. Butler, this clearly written resource provides sturdy support for assignments, and will also be popular with discussion groups and with general readers of literature." SLJ

Includes bibliographical references

Modern American women writers; edited by Elaine Showalter, Lea Baechler, and A. Walton Litz. Collier Bks. 1993 416p pa $15

Grades: 11 12 Adult　　　　　　　　**810**

1. Women authors 2. American literature -- History and criticism

ISBN 0-02-082025-9

LC 93-22193

First published 1991 by Scribner

"This work focuses on 41 representative American women who have published since 1870. Among those included are Anne Tyler, Alice Walker, and Emily Dickinson. The essays, ranging from 8 to 22 pages, emphasize the social and historical environment in which each wrote." Nichols. Guide to Ref Books for Sch Media Cent. 4th edition

Molin, Paulette Fairbanks

American Indian themes in young adult literature; [by] Paulette F. Molin. Scarecrow Press 2005 183p (Scarecrow studies in young adult literature) $40

Grades: Adult Professional　　　　　　**810**

1. Native Americans in literature 2. Young adult literature -- History and criticism

ISBN 0-8108-5081-8

LC 2004-26420

This "is a useful reference work, especially for the readers she targets—teachers, librarians, and even publishers and editors of young adult literature—and it provides the most complete bibliography of the genre in print." Amer Indian Culture and Research Journal

Includes bibliographical references

National Story Project (U.S.)

I thought my father was God and other true tales from the National Story Project; edited and introduced by Paul Auster; Nelly Reifler, assistant editor. Holt & Co. 2001 xxi, 383p il hardcover o.p. pa $15

Grades: 11 12 Adult　　　　　　　　**810**

1. American literature -- Collections

ISBN 0-8050-6714-0; 0-312-42100-1 pa

LC 00-54397

"These are stop-you-in-your-tracks stories about hair-raising coincidences, miracles, tragedies, redemption, and moments of pure hilarity." Booklist

Native American writers; edited and with an introduction by Harold Bloom. New ed; Bloom's Literary Criticism 2010 285p (Modern critical views) $45
Grades: 9 10 11 12 **810**
1. American literature -- Native American authors 2. Native American literature -- History and criticism
ISBN 978-1-60413-591-6; 978-1-4381-3439-0 ebook
LC 2010-6006
First published 1998
"This volume examines some of the finest Native American writers, including Joy Harjo, Louise Erdrich, James Welch, Sherman Alexie, N. Scott Momaday, Samsom Occom, Zitkala-□Sa, and Leslie Marmon Silko." Publisher's note
Includes bibliographical references

Nineteenth-century American women writers; a bio-bibliographical critical sourcebook. edited by Denise D. Knight; Emmanuel S. Nelson, advisory editor. Greenwood Press 1997 534p $110
Grades: 11 12 Adult **810**
1. Reference books 2. American literature -- Women authors -- Bio-bibliography
ISBN 0-313-29713-4
LC 96-35351
This volume "contains entries for 77 writers whose inclusion was determined by the fact that their best-known works were published during the nineteenth century. . . . Designed as a primary reference guide for researchers, the book includes fiction writers, poets, autobiographers, essayists, and abolitionists." Booklist

★ The **Norton** anthology of African American literature; Henry Louis Gates, Jr., general editor, Nellie Y. McKay, general editor. 2nd ed; Norton 2003 2800p 2 computer laser optical discs pa $70.30
Grades: 11 12 Adult **810**
1. American literature -- African American authors -- Collections
ISBN 0-393-97778-1
LC 2003-66176
First published 1996
"The anthology is divided into seven sections, each with a separate introduction giving the sociopolitical factors that impacted on the material included therein. Featured are 120 writers, 52 of whom are women, richly representing African American vernacular literature, poetry, drama, short stories, novels, slave narratives, and autobiographies." Libr J [review of 1996 edition]
Includes bibliographical references

Oh, Seiwoong
★ **Encyclopedia** of Asian-American literature. Facts On File 2007 384p (Facts on File library of American literature) $75
Grades: 11 12 Adult **810**
1. Reference books 2. American literature -- Asian

American authors -- Encyclopedias 3. American literature -- Asian American authors -- Bio-bibliography
ISBN 0-8160-6086-X; 978-0-8160-6086-3
LC 2006-26181
The author "traces American writers whose roots are in all parts of Asia, including China, Korea, Japan, Southeast Asia, the Philippines, the Indian subcontinent, and the Middle East. Coverage emphasizes works that are important in the high school and college literary canon, as well as the historically significant and the contemporary." Publisher's note
Includes bibliographical references

Otfinoski, Steven
Native American writers. Chelsea House 2010 126p il (Multicultural voices) $35
Grades: 8 9 10 11 12 **810**
1. American literature -- Native American authors 2. Native American literature -- History and criticism
ISBN 978-1-60413-314-1; 1-60413-314-7
LC 2009-41334
"This title introduces 10 major Native American poets and writers, such as N. Scott Momaday, Louise Erdrich, James Welch, and Sherman Alexie. An overview preceding the author entries explains the impact of white settlers on the culture of Native Americans, as well as the utilization of Native American storytelling and traditions in their literature and development of their writings. . . . The easily accessible information and fascinating details of the lives and writings of these authors make this a useful resource for both informative reading and research." SLJ
Includes bibliographical references

★ The **Oxford** book of women's writing in the United States; edited by Linda Wagner-Martin, Cathy N. Davidson. Oxford Univ. Press 1995 596p hardcover o.p. pa $27.50
Grades: 11 12 Adult **810**
1. American literature -- Women authors -- Collections
ISBN 0-19-513245-9 pa
LC 95-1499
This anthology provides "samples of the public and private work of 99 women of diverse racial and ethnic backgrounds who write in English and were born in or have lived in the United States over the past four centuries. They include short fiction (almost half of the book), poems, essays, plays, and speeches but have also gone beyond traditional genre categories to include performance pieces, erotica, diaries, letters, and recipes." Libr J

★ The **Oxford** encyclopedia of American literature; Jay Parini, editor-in-chief. Oxford University Press 2004 4v il set $495
Grades: 11 12 Adult **810**
1. Reference books 2. American literature -- Encyclopedias
ISBN 0-19-515653-6
LC 2002-156325
This set "provides a wealth of reliable information on standard bearers of American literature in an easy-on-the-eyes format for students and general readers." SLJ

★ The **Portable** sixties reader; edited by Ann Charters. Penguin Bks. 2003 xli, 628p il pa $16

Grades: 11 12 Adult   810

1. American literature -- Collections 2. United States -- History -- 1961-1974

ISBN 0-14-200194-5

LC 2002-32266

This reader includes "essays, poetry, and fiction under thematic subjects, such as civil rights; women's rights; the sexual revolution; environmental issues; the antiwar, free-speech, and black-arts movements; and the use of drugs in pursuit of enlightenment. . . . [Includes works by] James Baldwin, Thomas Merton, Susan Sontag, Gary Snyder, Allen Ginsburg, Rachel Carson, Kate Millett, Nikki Giovanni, and many more." Booklist

Includes bibliographical references

Ramirez, Luz Elena

★ **Encyclopedia** of Hispanic-American literature. Facts On File 2008 430p (Encyclopedia of American ethnic literature) $75

Grades: 11 12 Adult   810

1. Reference books 2. American literature -- Hispanic American authors -- Encyclopedias

ISBN 978-0-8160-6084-9; 0-8160-6084-3

LC 2007-34805

This encyclopedia provides "information on over 250 important works, writers, and related topics. . . . Organized in an A-Z format, entries include significant works, movements, and topics. . . . The appealing writing makes this a very readable and fascinating source." Libr Media Connect

Includes bibliographical references

Sidman, Joyce

The **world** according to dog; poems and teen voices. with photographs by Doug Mindell. Houghton Mifflin 2003 71p il hardcover o.p. pa $7.95

Grades: 8 9 10 11 12   810

1. Dogs 2. Teenagers' writings 3. American literature -- Collections

ISBN 0-618-17497-4; 0-618-28381-1 pa

LC 2002-476

A collection of poems about dogs is accompanied by essays by young people about the dogs in their lives

"The teen essays are heartfelt and honest. . . . Sidman's poetic form is succinct, evoking images, memories, and even smells. . . . Readers of all ages who appreciate their canine companions will thoroughly enjoy this slim book." Voice Youth Advocates

Student's encyclopedia of American literary characters; edited by Matthew J. Bruccoli, Judith S. Baughman. Facts On File 2008 4v (Facts on File library of American literature) set $340

Grades: 9 10 11 12   810

1. Reference books 2. American literature -- Encyclopedias 3. Characters and characteristics in literature -- Encyclopedias

ISBN 978-0-8160-6498-4; 0-8160-6498-9

LC 2008-1704

"Some 300 contributors to this set provide 1200-word summaries and analyses of about 900 characters from American novels, short stories, poems, plays, and musical theater." Libr J

Includes bibliographical references

Things I have to tell you; poems and writing by teenage girls. edited by Betsy Franco; photographs by Nina Nickles. Candlewick Press 2001 63p il hardcover o.p. pa $8.99

Grades: 7 8 9 10   810

1. Girls 2. Teenagers' writings 3. American literature -- Collections

ISBN 0-7636-0905-6; 0-7636-1035-6 pa

LC 99-46884

A collection of poems, stories, and essays written by girls twelve to eighteen years of age and revealing the secrets which enabled them to overcome the challenges they faced

War is-- soldiers, survivors, and storytellers talk about war. edited by Marc Aronson and Patty Campbell. Candlewick Press 2008 200p $17.99; pa $6.99

Grades: 8 9 10 11 12   810

1. War poetry 2. War stories 3. American literature -- Collections

ISBN 978-0-76363-625-8; 0-76363-625-8; 978-0-7636-4231-0 pa; 0-7636-4231-2 pa

LC 2007-52026

An anthology of fiction, speeches, poems, and essays about war

"With this collection, Aronson and Campbell have provided an uncommonly valuable source of hard information and perceptive insight." Booklist

Wilson, Charles E.

★ **Race** and racism in literature; [by] Charles E. Wilson, Jr. Greenwood Press 2005 154p (Exploring social issues through literature) $49.95

Grades: 9 10 11 12   810

1. Race in literature 2. American literature -- History and criticism

ISBN 0-313-32820-X; 978-0-313-32820-6

LC 2005-1494

"The novels discussed here were chosen to represent various racial and ethnic identities (e.g., black, Asian, Hispanic, Jewish, Italian, Native American). Each novel . . . is summarized, discussed in terms of its historical and social significance, and then discussed again as a work of literature. . . . [The author] is to be commended for drawing together a dozen novels that focus on race, and treating these works in a thoughtful and focused way." Am Ref Books Annu, 2006

Includes bibliographical references

You hear me? poems and writing by teenage boys. edited by Betsy Franco. Candlewick Press 2000 107p hardcover o.p. pa $6.99

Grades: 7 8 9 10   810

1. Boys 2. Teenagers' writings 3. American literature

-- Collections

ISBN 0-7636-1158-1; 0-7636-1159-X pa

LC 99-57129

"The voices range from painfully honest to playfully ironic, but all are controlled and powerful as they speak to subjects that teen readers will be familiar with." Voice Youth Advocates

811 American poetry

The **100** best African American poems; (*but I cheated) edited by Nikki Giovanni. Sourcebooks MediaFusion 2010 228p $22.99

Grades: 10 11 12 Adult **811**

1. African Americans -- Poetry 2. American poetry -- African American authors -- Collections

ISBN 978-1-4022-2111-8

Giovanni's "vivid and affecting selections add up to a complexly pleasurable anthology. The delight is in the musical, inventive, and vivid language; the astute insights and humor, passion and tenderness. But these are poems born of suffering and injustice, even as they reach for truth and wisdom. . . . Poets and other performers read 36 poems on the accompanying CD." Booklist

100 essential American poems; edited by Leslie M. Pockell. Thomas Dunne Books 2009 288p $24.95; pa $14.99

Grades: 9 10 11 12 Adult **811**

1. American poetry -- Collections

ISBN 978-0-312-36980-4; 0-312-36980-8; 978-0-312-62397-5 pa; 0-312-62397-6 pa

LC 2008-38641

In this collection, the editor "focuses on poems that have fueled the American identity. Covering 400 years, the poems range from classic, to familiar (and for nostalgics, poems most likely memorized and recited), to those that touch upon the seminal events in America's history. The collection aims to present an evolving American 'voice' while following the country's growth in human rights, feminism and diversity. . . . A work that serves as reference, comfort, and a reminder poetry's significance in the everyday experience of American life, this is a volume worthy of any shelf." Publ Wkly

180 more; extraordinary poems for every day. selected and with an introduction by Billy Collins. Random House 2005 xxiii, 373p pa $14.95

Grades: 11 12 Adult **811**

1. American poetry -- Collections

ISBN 0-8129-7296-1

LC 2005-42798

Sequel to: Poetry 180

This is a second collection of 180 poems for each day of the school year, designed to expose high school students to poetry.

★ **African**-American poets; volume 1: 1700s-1940s. edited and with an introduction by Har-

old Bloom. New ed; Chelsea House 2009 264p (Modern critical views) lib bdg $45

Grades: 9 10 11 12 **811**

1. African Americans in literature 2. American poetry -- African American authors -- History and criticism

ISBN 978-1-60413-400-1

LC 2008-54305

First published 2002

"This volume focuses on the principal African-American poets from colonial times to the Harlem Renaissance and the World War II era. . . . Poets covered in this volume include Phillis Wheatley, author of the first volume of verse published by an African American, and the seminal figures Gwendolyn Brooks, Countee Cullen, Paul Lawrence Dunbar, Langston Hughes, Claude McKay, and Jean Toomer." Publisher's note

Includes bibliographical references

Alexie, Sherman

Face. Hanging Loose Press 2009 159p $28; pa $15

Grades: 11 12 Adult **811**

1. Poetry -- By individual authors

ISBN 978-1-931236-71-3; 1-931236-71-2; 978-1-931236-70-6 pa; 1-931236-70-4 pa

LC 2008-46580

The author "has mastered both the metrical dance and fixed forms. A sequence of sonnets finds the Seven Deadly Sins in marriage, for instance; a villanelle begins with Mount Rushmore but eases into a consideration of America's Presidents, complemented by wry and smart footnotes. . . . There are a lot of serious undercurrents in his poetry, and they are always a pleasure to find." Libr J

Alvarez, Julia

The **woman** I kept to myself; poems. Algonquin Books of Chapel Hill 2004 155p hardcover o.p. pa $14.95

Grades: 11 12 Adult **811**

1. Poetry -- By individual authors

ISBN 1-56512-406-5; 1-61620-072-3 pa

LC 2003-70807

This "collection of 75 poems is divided into three sections, and each poem has three stanzas, exactly . . . The poet, who is from the Dominican Republic, writes about being raised with her sisters in New York. The subjects are personal—love, marriage, rejection, divorce, death, religion—but also universal." SLJ

★ **American** poetry, the twentieth century. Library of Am. 2000 2v ea $35

Grades: 11 12 Adult **811**

1. American poetry -- Collections

ISBN 1-88301-177-9 v1; 1-88301-178-7 v2

LC 99-43721

These volumes represent a "remarkable feat of assemblage, with excellent capsule biographies and explanatory notes at the end of each volume—the biographies, especially, are well worth reading." N Y Times Book Rev

Includes bibliographical references

★ **American** poetry: the nineteenth century; edited by John Hollander. Library of Am. 1993 2v ea $35

Grades: 11 12 Adult   **811**
1. American poetry -- Collections
ISBN 0-940450-60-7 v1; 0-940450-78-X v2

       LC 93-10702

An anthology of more than 1,000 poems by nearly 150 poets. Arrangement is chronological by poet's date of birth. Biographical sketches of the poets, a chronology of significant events from 1800 to 1900, and an essay on textual selection are included

Hollander has compiled "a selection of nineteenth-century American verse so wonderfully catholic that it not just augments but supersedes every other similar collection." Booklist

★ **American** poetry: the seventeenth and eighteenth centuries; edited by David Shields. Library of America 2007 xxiii, 952p $40

Grades: 11 12 Adult   **811**
1. American poetry -- Collections
ISBN 978-1-931082-90-7; 1-931082-90-1

       LC 2007-929763

"Besides hefty helpings of the few figures meagerly represented in general American-lit surveys—Anne Bradstreet, Edward Taylor, John Trumbull, Timothy Dwight, Philip Freneau, Phyllis Wheatley—here are poems short and . . . long by dozens of others, most of them obscure to even thoroughgoing, historically minded poetry lovers. . . . The subject matter isn't all religion and politics. Work, family, leisure, and exceptional events and lives (one man recounts escape from the limited slavery that was indenture) are all written up. And, in regular rhymes and meters, it's all quite readable. Early-American history buffs as much as, if not more than, poetry readers may consider the book a gold mine." Booklist
Includes bibliographical references

American religious poems; an anthology by Harold Bloom. Harold Bloom and Jesse Zuba, editors. Library of America 2006 685p $40

Grades: 11 12 Adult   **811**
1. Religious poetry 2. American poetry -- Collections
ISBN 1-931082-74-X

       LC 2006-41031

An anthology of "verse on Christian, Jewish, Islamic, Buddhist, Native American spiritual, Transcendentalist and even agnostic themes, from 17th-century European colonists (one poet is Roger Williams, who founded Rhode Island) to up-and-comers in contemporary verse. Pious readers will have no trouble finding high-quality poetry that confirms their beliefs—from the monk Thomas Merton, the Anglican T.S. Eliot, the Jewish liturgical poet Esther Schor and the Louisiana-based Christian poet Martha Serpas. Yet from the 19th century to the present, from the decidedly heterodox Emily Dickinson forwards, the anthology often highlights the ways in which American spirituality has challenged all doctrines about who God is and what God does. . . . More than half of the book is taken up by 20th-century poets, who offer varied takes on what religion has come to mean in America." Publ Wkly

★ **American** war poetry; an anthology. edited by Lorrie Goldensohn. Columbia University Press 2006 413p $27.95

Grades: 11 12 Adult   **811**
1. War poetry 2. American poetry -- Collections
ISBN 0-231-13310-3

       LC 2005-54762

"Arranged by war, the book begins with the Colonial period and proceeds through Whitman admiring Civil War soldiers crossing a river to end with Brian Turner, who published his first book in 2005, beckoning a bullet in contemporary Iraq. Many voices, by turns elegiac, outraged, rhetorical and ecstatic are represented." Publ Wkly

Includes bibliographical references

Angelou, Maya
★ The **complete** collected poems of Maya Angelou. Random House 1994 273p $24.95

Grades: 11 12 Adult   **811**
1. Poetry -- By individual authors
ISBN 0-679-42895-X

       LC 94-14501

This volume contains all of Angelou's published poems including her inaugural poem On the pulse of morning

Appelt, Kathi
Poems from homeroom; a writer's place to start. Holt & Co. 2002 114p hardcover o.p. pa $14.95

Grades: 7 8 9 10   **811**
1. Poetics 2. Poetry -- By individual authors
ISBN 0-8050-6978-X; 0-8050-7596-8 pa

       LC 2002-67886

A collection of poems about the experiences of young people and a section with information about how each poem was written to enable readers to create their own original poems

Appelt's "poems are at times sensual, dramatic, or violent, and always rhythmic. They are fascinating, smooth, and 'with it.'" SLJ

Includes bibliographical references

Atkins, Jeannine
★ **Borrowed** names; poems about Laura Ingalls Wilder, Madam C. J. Walker, Marie Curie, and their daughters. Henry Holt & Co. 2010 209p il $16.99

Grades: 6 7 8 9 10   **811**
1. Authors 2. Chemists 3. Novelists 4. Physicists 5. Entrepreneurs 6. Philanthropists 7. Cosmeticians 8. Western writers 9. College teachers 10. Children's authors 11. Nonfiction writers 12. Patrons of the arts 13. Young adult authors 14. Nobel laureates for physics 15. Cosmetics industry executives 16. Nobel laureates for chemistry 17. Poetry -- By individual authors 18. Mother-daughter relationship -- Poetry
ISBN 978-0-8050-8934-9; 0-8050-8934-9

       LC 2009-23446

"In 1867, three women who achieved great success were born: writer Laura Ingalls Wilder, entrepreneur Madam C. J. Walker, and scientist Marie Curie. All three had complicated relationships with their daughters, relationships that Atkins explores in this unusual volume of poetry. . . . In vivid scenes written with keen insight and subtle imagery, the poems offer a strong sense of each daughter's personality as well as the tensions and ties they shared with their notable mothers." Booklist

Auden, W. H.

Collected poems; edited by Edward Mendelson. Vintage Bks. 1991 xxvii, 926p pa $24

Grades: 11 12 Adult **811**

1. Poetry -- By individual authors

ISBN 0-679-73197-0

LC 91-158031

Originally published in hardcover in different form by Random House in 1976

A compilation of all the poems Auden wished to preserve, in his final revisions. Previous collected editions and later shorter poems are included. There is also an absurdist play written 1928: Paid on both sides

Beauty is a verb; edited by Jennifer Bartlett, Sheila Black, & Michael Northen. Cinco Puntos Press 2011 383p pa $19.95

Grades: 11 12 Adult **811**

1. People with disabilities 2. American poetry -- Collections

ISBN 978-1-935955-05-4

LC 2011022269

"This powerful anthology attempts to—and succeeds at—intimately showing (meaning, at various times and among many other aims, sharing the experience of, defining the self in terms of, refusing to define the self in terms of, trying to define, exploring the indefiniteness of) disability through the lenses of poetry. . . . Coming from across the aesthetic spectrum, these poets and poems demonstrate the deep truth of what Vassar Millar writes in a poem anthologized here: 'No man's sickness has a synonym.'" Publ Wkly

Bernier-Grand, Carmen T.

Diego; bigger than life. illustrated by David Diaz. Marshall Cavendish Children 2009 64p il $18.99

Grades: 8 9 10 11 12 **811**

1. Artists 2. Painters 3. Poetry -- By individual authors

ISBN 978-0-7614-5383-3; 0-7614-5383-0

LC 2007-13761

ALA ALSC Belpre Author Medal Honor Book (2010)

ALA ALSC Belpre Illustrator Medal Honor Book (2010)

This is a "well written and beautifully illustrated volume. . . . Almost all written in first-person from the artist's point of view, the poems convey information succinctly within a context of colorful narrative and clearly expressed emotion. . . . Apart from four reproductions of Rivera's paintings and one photo of the artist, the illustrations are mixed-media pictures by Diaz. Depicting Rivera and his world, these iconic images glow with warmth, light, and color." Booklist

Includes bibliographical references

★ **Frida**; viva la vida = long live life. by Carmen T. Bernier-Grand. Marshall Cavendish Children 2007 64 p. ill. $14.24

Grades: 8 9 10 11 12 **811**

1. Artists 2. Painters 3. Poetry -- By individual authors

4. Painters -- Mexico -- Biography

ISBN 9780761453369

LC 2006014479

In this book, "Frida Kahlo, a native of Mexico, is described . . . in biographical poems accompanied by her own artwork. Both text and images reveal the anguish and joy of her two marriages to muralist Diego Rivera, her life-long suffering from a crippling bus accident, and her thirst for life, even as she tasted death. . . . Back matter includes excerpts from Frida's diary and letters, a prose biography, a chronology of the artist's life, a glossary of Spanish words, sources, and notes." (Publisher's note)

"Bernier-Grand introduces a famous life with lyrical free-verse poems. Nearly every double-page spread pairs a well-reproduced painting by Frida Kahlo with an original poem that defines turning points in the artist's life. Bernier-Grand's words expertly extend the autobiographical imagery so evident in the art." Booklist

Includes bibliographical references (p. 61).

★ **Black** poets; [a new anthology] Bantam Books 1985 xxvi, 353p pa $7.99

Grades: 11 12 Adult **811**

1. American poetry -- African American authors -- Collections

ISBN 0-553-27563-1; 978-0-553-27563-6

This anthology covers African American poetry from slave songs to the works of Gwendolyn Brooks and Nikki Giovanni.

Block, Francesca Lia

How to (un)cage a girl. Joanna Cotler Books 2008 119p $15.99; lib bdg $16.89

Grades: 8 9 10 11 12 **811**

1. Love poetry 2. Girls -- Poetry 3. Poetry -- By individual authors

ISBN 978-0-06-135836-4; 0-06-135836-3; 978-0-06-135837-1 lib bdg; 0-06-135837-1 lib bdg

LC 2008-00629

A collection of love poems for girls.

"A stirring exploration of female suffering and empowerment, this will attract Block's adult readers, too." Booklist

Borus, Audrey

A **student's** guide to Emily Dickinson. Enslow Publishers 2005 152p il (Understanding literature) $27.93

Grades: 7 8 9 10 **811**

1. Poets 2. Authors

ISBN 0-7660-2285-4

LC 2004-18098

"A short discussion of Dickinson's life and times is followed by a chapter on how to read and analyze her poems, which would be particularly useful for students reading her work for the first time. Subsequent chapters focus on particular themes in the poems such as death and eternity, truth, faith and reality, the natural world, and the influence of the Civil War." SLJ

Includes bibliographical references

Brooks, Gwendolyn

In Montgomery, and other poems. Third World Press 2003 146p $22.95

Grades: 11 12 Adult   **811**

1. African Americans -- Poetry 2. Poetry -- By individual authors

ISBN 0-88378-232-4

      LC 2003-50749

This is a "posthumous collection consisting primarily of dramatic monologues in a stunning variety of voices, from those of urban children to Winnie Mandela's. Reading the title sequence resembles randomly tuning a radio dial to listen to the diverse voices of Montgomery, Alabama, a city of 'leaning and lostness, glazed paralysis.' . . . Especially moving are the children's monologues. . . . Brooks captures the fierce purity of these children's needs and desires. Her loving witness never sounded more clearly than in these late poems." Booklist

★ **Selected** poems. Harper & Row 1963 127p hardcover o.p. pa $12.95

Grades: 11 12 Adult   **811**

1. Poetry -- By individual authors

ISBN 0-06-088296-4

      LC 63-16503

"The subject of this poetry is the lives of African American residents of Northern urban ghettos, particularly women, and Brooks has been praised for her depiction of that experience in forms ranging from terza rima to blues meter." Benet's Reader's Ency of Am Lit

Buckwalter, Stephanie

Early American poetry, beauty in words. Enslow Publishers 2010 160p il (Poetry rocks!) lib bdg $34.60

Grades: 9 10 11 12   **811**

1. Poets, American 2. Poetry -- Authorship 3. American poetry -- History and criticism

ISBN 0-7660-3277-9; 978-0-7660-3277-4

      LC 2008-53658

"Discusses early American poetry from the early 17th century into the late 19th century, including short biographies of poets like Phillis Wheatley and Walt Whitman; also has examples of poems, poetic techniques, and explication." Publisher's note

Includes glossary and bibliographical references

Casale, Frank D.

Bloom's how to write about Walt Whitman; introduction by Harold Bloom. Chelsea House 2010 264p (Bloom's how to write about literature) $45

Grades: 9 10 11 12   **811**

1. Poets 2. Authors 3. Report writing 4. Essayists

ISBN 978-1-60413-310-3

      LC 2009-4596

This book offers paper topics and advice on writing an essay about the works of Walt Whitman.

Includes bibliographical references

★ The **Columbia** anthology of American poetry; edited by Jay Parini. Columbia Univ. Press 1995 757p $40.95

Grades: 11 12 Adult   **811**

1. American poetry -- Collections

ISBN 0-231-08122-7

      LC 94-32423

"Ranging from Anne Bradstreet to Louise Glück, editor Parini aims to represent 'the main schools of poetry that have co-existed in the United States . . . in proportion to their influence,' including more poetry by women and minorities 'than one generally finds' in older anthologies." Libr J

The **Columbia** book of Civil War poetry; Richard Marius, editor; Keith W. Frome, associate editor. Columbia Univ. Press 1994 xxxvi, 543p il $37.95

Grades: 11 12 Adult   **811**

1. American poetry -- Collections 2. United States -- History -- 1861-1865, Civil War -- Poetry

ISBN 0-231-10002-7

      LC 94-6481

"Bret Harte, Walt Whitman, and Robert Frost are but three of the many writers whose poems about the Civil War fill this noteworthy collection." Booklist

★ **Cool** salsa; bilingual poems on growing up Latino in the United States. edited by Lori M. Carlson; introduction by Oscar Hijuelos. Holt & Co. 1994 xx, 123p il hardcover o.p. pa $6.99

Grades: 5 6 7 8 9 10   **811**

1. Bilingual books -- English-Spanish 2. American poetry -- Hispanic American authors -- Collections

ISBN 0-8050-3135-9; 978-0-449-70436-3 pa; 0-449-70436-X pa

      LC 93-45798

"This collection presents poems by 29 Mexican-American, Cuban-American, Puerto Rican, and other Central and South American poets, including Sandra Cisneros, Luis J. Rodriguez, Pat Mora, Gary Soto, Ana Castillo, Oscar Hijuelos, Ed J. Vega, Judith Ortiz-Cofer, and other Latino writers both contemporary and historical. Brief biographical notes on the authors are provided. All the poems deal with experiences of teenagers." Book Rep

Crisler, Curtis L.

★ **Tough** boy sonatas; illustrations by Floyd Cooper. Wordsong 2007 86p il $19.95

Grades: 8 9 10 11 12   **811**

1. Indiana -- Poetry 2. African Americans -- Poetry 3. City and town life -- Poetry 4. Poetry -- By individual authors

ISBN 978-1-932425-77-2; 1-932425-77-2

      LC 2006-11836

"Crisler presents a collection of potent, hard-hitting poems about growing up in Gary, Indiana. Written mostly in voices of young African American males, the poems evoke the grit and ash of crumbling, burned-out streets as well as the realities of hardscrabble life. . . . Written with skillful manipulation of sound, rhythm, and form, the poems are filled with sophisticated imagery and graphic words . . . and

Cooper's illustrations extend . . . the poems' impact. Created in sooty black and gray, the powerful drawings are mostly portraits of anguished young men." Booklist

Cruz, Victor Hernandez

Paper dance; 55 Latino poets. edited by Victor Hernández Cruz, Leroy V. Quintana, and Virgil Suarez. Persea Bks. 1995 242p $14

Grades: 11 12 Adult   **811**
1. American poetry -- Hispanic American authors -- Collections
ISBN 0-89255-201-8

LC 94-15586

"This collection of poetry attests to the richness of culture in the Hispanic diaspora in the U.S., and includes well-known writers such as Julia Alvarez, Luis J. Rodriguez, and Lucha Corpi, to name a few. . . . The poets' themes are as varied as they are intriguing. Ranging in scope from contemplations on race and ethnicity to love and death, they demand that readers pay attention to vital threads in the fabric of the American literary tapestry." SLJ

Cummings, E. E.

★ **Complete** poems, 1904-1962; containing all the published poetry. edited by George J. Firmage. rev corr & expanded ed; Norton 1994 xxxii, 1102p $50

Grades: 9 10 11 12 Adult   **811**
1. Poetry -- By individual authors
ISBN 978-0-87140-152-6; 0-87140-152-5

LC 91-29158

Expanded version of Complete poems, 1913-1962 (1972)

"This volume has been prepared directly from the poet's original manuscripts, preserving the original typography and format. It includes all the previously published works, from Tulips (1922) to Etcetera (1983), as well as 36 uncollected poems that originally appeared in little magazines or anthologies." Libr J

Dickinson, Emily, 1830-1886

★ The **complete** poems of Emily Dickinson; edited by Thomas H. Johnson. Little, Brown 1960 770p $35; pa $19.95

Grades: 11 12 Adult   **811**
1. Poetry -- By individual authors
ISBN 0-316-18414-4; 0-316-18413-6 pa
A chronological arrangement of all known Dickinson poems and fragments

Final harvest; Emily Dickinson's poems. selection and introduction by Thomas H. Johnson. Little, Brown 1961 331p hardcover o.p. pa $14.99

Grades: 11 12 Adult   **811**
1. Poetry -- By individual authors
ISBN 0-316-18415-2
A selection of 575 poems from: The complete poems of Emily Dickinson. The editor's aim has been to allow the reader to realize the full scope and diversity of the poet's work

★ The **selected** poems of Emily Dickinson. Modern Lib. 1996 295p hardcover o.p. pa $9.95

Grades: 11 12 Adult   **811**
1. Poetry -- By individual authors
ISBN 0-679-60201-1; 0-679-78335-0 pa
This "edition presents the more than four hundred poems that were published between Dickinson's death and 1900. They express her concepts of life and death, of love and nature, and of what Henry James called 'the landscape of the soul.'" Publisher's note

Dove, Rita

American smooth; poems. W.W. Norton 2004 143p $22.95; pa $13.95

Grades: 11 12 Adult   **811**
1. Poetry -- By individual authors
ISBN 0-393-05987-1; 0-393-32744-2 pa

LC 2004-11793

"In these free-verse poems, Dove speaks from her own perspective—as well as from that of biblical characters, black soldiers from World War I, a ten-year-old girl from Harlem, several musicians, and a pair of dancers. The selections work by lists, line breaks where ideas collide, and a juxtaposition of voices. Then using razor-sharp metaphors, Dove goes for the jugular and usually finds it. Although the book's sense of audience seems inconsistent, with some poems suitable for A Child's Garden of Verses and others for The Kama Sutra, the poems are evocative." Libr J

Mother love; poems. Norton 1995 77p $17.95; pa $11

Grades: 11 12 Adult   **811**
1. Poetry -- By individual authors
ISBN 0-393-03808-4; 0-393-31444-8 pa

LC 95-5394

"Most poems included here are autobiographical. Dove writes of childhood bullies, rock songs crooned in the driveway, and, in the long poem, 'Persephone in Hell,' a stay in Paris over 20 years ago. Her language is simple and clear." Libr J

On the bus with Rosa Parks; poems. Norton 1999 95p hardcover o.p. pa $12.95

Grades: 11 12 Adult   **811**
1. Poetry -- By individual authors
ISBN 0-393-32026-X

LC 98-45057

Dove's "poems effortlessly suggest grand narratives and American myths, yet ground themselves tersely in localities, characters, practicalities and particulars. This seventh collection leads off with a Dove specialty, the historical sequence: her 'Cameos' lend broad, social relevance to an intermittently abandoned Depression-era wife and her family." Publ Wkly

★ **Selected** poems. Vintage Bks. 1993 xxvi, 210p pa $13

Grades: 11 12 Adult   **811**
1. Poetry -- By individual authors
ISBN 0-679-75080-0

LC 93-26112

"This volume places three previous collections under one cover. . . . The selection begins with The Yellow House on the Corner, Dove's first book, most notable for its poems derived from slave narratives. Museum, her second book, offers a potpourri of work that ranges over several continents and many millenia; Dove's tirelessly exact language illuminates the lives of saints, contemporary lifestyles, and Greek myths." Booklist

Eight American poets; an anthology: Theodore Roethke, Elizabeth Bishop, Robert Lowell, John Berryman, Anne Sexton, Sylvia Plath, Allen Ginsberg, James Merrill. edited by Joel Conarroe. Random House 1994 xxiv, 306p il hardcover o.p. pa $14.95

Grades: 11 12 Adult   **811**
1. American poetry -- Collections
ISBN 0-679-77643-5 pa

LC 94-10186
This anthology contains representative work by eight 20th century American confessional poets

Eliot, T. S.
★ **Collected** poems, 1909-1962. Harcourt Brace Jovanovich 1963 221p $23

Grades: 11 12 Adult   **811**
1. Poetry -- By individual authors
ISBN 0-15-118978-1
This volume contains the complete text of 'Collected poems, 1909-1935,' the 'Four quartets,' and several other poems accompanied by brief prefatory notes

★ The **complete** poems and plays, 1909-1950. Harcourt Brace & Co. 1952 392p $35

Grades: 11 12 Adult   **811**
1. Poetry -- By individual authors
ISBN 0-15-121185-X

★ The **waste** land, and other poems. Harcourt Brace Jovanovich 1955 88p pa $8

Grades: 9 10 11 12   **811**
1. Poetry -- By individual authors
ISBN 0-15-694877-X
In addition to Eliot's long poem of despair this volume contains a representative selection of his best known shorter works

Emerson, Ralph Waldo
★ **Collected** poems & translations. Library of Am. 1994 637p $35

Grades: 11 12 Adult   **811**
1. Poetry -- By individual authors
ISBN 0-940450-28-3

LC 93-40245
Contains Emerson's published poetry, plus selections of his unpublished poetry from journals and notebooks, and some of his translations of poetry from other languages, notably Dante's La vita nuova

★ **Encyclopedia** of American poetry, the twentieth century; edited by Eric L. Haralson. Fitzroy Dearborn Pubs. 2001 846p $125

Grades: 11 12 Adult   **811**
1. Reference books 2. Poets, American -- Dictionaries 3. American poetry -- Bio-bibliography
ISBN 1-57958-240-0
"The volume features more than 400 entries written by academic contributors on individual poets, landmark poems, and major topics. The poet entries are usually 1,000 to 2,000 words long and offer critical treatment of the poet's career and major achievements along with a capsule biography. . . . Approximately one-third of the poet entries include subentries for one or more landmark poems. The 'major topics' entries are longer (around 3,000 words) and include periods or movements (Black Arts movement, Dada), verse traditions (often ethnic, such as Asian American poetry), and styles and themes (Confessional poetry, War and antiwar poetry)." Booklist

Engle, Margarita
★ The **surrender** tree; poems of Cuba's struggle for freedom. Henry Holt and Co. 2008 169p $17.95

Grades: 7 8 9 10 11 12   **811**
1. Novels in verse 2. Cuba -- Fiction
ISBN 978-0-8050-8674-4; 0-8050-8674-9

LC 2007-27591
A Newbery Medal honor book, 2009
Pura Belpre Author Award, 2009
This "book is written in clear, short lines of stirring free verse. . . . [The author] draws on her own Cuban American roots . . . to describe those who fought in the nineteenth-century Cuban struggle for independence. At the center is Rosa, a traditional healer, who nurses runaway slaves and deserters in caves and other secret hideaways. . . . Many readers will be caught by the compelling narrative voices and want to pursue the historical accounts in Engle's bibliography." Booklist

Every shut eye ain't asleep; an anthology of poetry by African Americans since 1945. edited by Michael Harper and Anthony Walton. Little, Brown 1994 327p hardcover o.p. pa $19

Grades: 11 12 Adult   **811**
1. American poetry -- African American authors -- Collections
ISBN 0-316-34710-8 pa

LC 93-10788
"Using Robert Hayden and Gwendolyn Brooks's poetry as 'emblematic' successes, this anthology selects 35 African American poets (spanning three generations) who were born between 1913 and 1962 and came of age after 1945. Besides the well-known Imamu Baraka, Lucille Clifton, Rita Dove, and Etheridge Knight, the editors feature little-known or younger poets like Elizabeth Alexander, Gerald Barrax, Jayne Cortex, and Dolores Kendrick." Libr J

★ The **Facts** on File companion to American poetry; [New ed.]; Facts On File 2008 2v (Facts on File library of American literature) set $140
Grades: 11 12 Adult   **811**
1. American poetry -- History and criticism
ISBN 978-0-8160-6950-7
LC 2006-35417

Volume 2 first published 2004 with title: The Facts on File companion to 20th-century poetry

"Volume 1 includes members of the literary pantheon such as Ralph Waldo Emerson, Walt Whitman, and Emily Dickinson and represents literary schools ranging from Quaker poetry to poetry in translation. . . . [Volume 2] includes the pathos of Sylvia Plath's poetry, the Roman Catholic/Buddhist-influenced Beat works of Jack Kerouac, plus the imagist school, objectivist poetry, and the New York school." Libr J

Includes bibliographical references

Fagan, Deirdre
Critical companion to Robert Frost; a literary reference to his life and work. Facts on File 2007 454p il $75
Grades: 9 10 11 12 Adult   **811**
1. Poets 2. Authors
ISBN 0-8160-6182-3; 978-0-8160-6182-2
LC 2006-13269

"This encyclopedic guide offers critical entries on each of Frost's published poems, including such classics as 'The Road Not Taken,' 'Stopping By Woods on a Snowy Evening,' and 'The Death of the Hired Man.'" Publisher's note

Includes bibliographical references

Falling hard; 100 love poems by teenagers. edited by Betsy Franco. Candlewick Press 2008 144p $15.99
Grades: 9 10 11 12   **811**
1. Love poetry 2. Teenagers' writings 3. American poetry -- Collections
ISBN 978-0-7636-3437-7; 0-7636-3437-9
LC 2007-22401

This is a collection of love poems by young writers, ranging in age from twelve to eighteen.

"The quality here is head and shoulders above most young writers' collections, and in fact it's well above many adult anthologies as well. . . . This will inspire creativity, imitation, and perhaps, around Valentine's Day, a spot of appreciative plagiarism." Bull Cent Child Books

Ferlinghetti, Lawrence
How to paint sunlight; lyric poems & others (1997-2000) New Directions 2001 94p $19.95; pa $13.95
Grades: 11 12 Adult   **811**
1. Poetry -- By individual authors
ISBN 0-8112-1463-X; 0-8112-1463-X pa
LC 00-67860

"A late-career miscellany divided into four sections, this . . . collection draws some of life's great polarities—light and dark, tragedy and comedy, ecstasy and despair—into the

quotidian whorl of this beloved West Coast-transplant poet." Publ Wkly

★ **These** are my rivers; new & selected poems, 1955-1993. New Directions 1993 308p il hardcover o.p. pa $13.95
Grades: 11 12 Adult   **811**
1. Poetry -- By individual authors
ISBN 0-8112-1273-4
LC 93-10383

"Reading this hefty selection from 12 previous volumes, plus 50 pages of new poems, we realize how accurately the poet described himself in 1979: a man who 'thinks he's Dylan Thomas and Bob Dylan rolled together with Charlie Chaplin thrown in.' . . . His style is recognizable throughout—phlegmatic poems running several pages, often lacking stanza breaks, with short lines at the left margin or moving across the page as hand follows eye." Libr J

From both sides now; the poetry of the Vietnam War and its aftermath. edited by Phillip Mahony. Scribner 1998 314p hardcover o.p. pa $16
Grades: 11 12 Adult   **811**
1. American poetry -- Collections 2. Vietnam War, 1961-1975 -- Poetry
ISBN 0-684-84946-1; 0-684-84947-X pa
LC 98-16628

The editor "arranges poems by 135 poets in chronological order 'to simulate the progression of the Vietnam War.' Poems of the North and South Vietnamese, 'boat people,' and postwar Vietnamese American second-generation poets appear beside well-known names (e.g., Ehrhart, Komunyakaa, and Weihl)." Libr J

From totems to hip-hop; edited by Ishmael Reed. Thunder's Mouth Press 2003 xxx, 523p $34.95; pa $17.95
Grades: 11 12 Adult   **811**
1. American poetry -- Collections
ISBN 1-56025-500-5; 1-56025-458-0 pa
LC 2002-75691

This is "a dynamic and original anthology, an unprecedented amalgam of poets representing many facets of American culture and society." Booklist

Frost, Robert
★ **Collected** poems, prose, & plays. Library of Am. 1995 1036p $35
Grades: 11 12 Adult   **811**
1. Poetry -- By individual authors
ISBN 1-883011-06-X
LC 94-43693

This volume contains "all of the plays, a generous selection of prose, all collected poems, and 94 uncollected poems, as well as 17 poems that were previously unpublished." Libr J

★ The **poetry** of Robert Frost; edited by Edward Connery Lathem. Holt & Co. 1969 607p hardcover o.p. pa $18

Grades: 11 12 Adult **811**
1. Poetry -- By individual authors
ISBN 0-8050-0502-1; 0-8050-6986-0 pa

"A one-volume edition of Frost's eleven volumes of poetry and two short blank-verse plays. The collection ranges in time from A Boy's Will (1913) to In the Clearing (1962). . . . {There is} an appendix of bibliographical and textual notes for each of the poems." Nation

Gibran, Kahlil
★ The **Prophet**. Knopf 1923 107p il $15
Grades: 11 12 Adult **811**
1. Poetry -- By individual authors
ISBN 0-394-40428-9

A collection of poems by the mystical writer/artist, who was born in Lebanon and died in the United States, in which the prophet Almustafa deals with fundamental aspects of human life such as love, friendship, good and evil, self-knowledge, passion and reason, joy and sorrow, freedom, work, marriage and children, prayer and death

Ginsberg, Allen
Collected poems, 1947-1997. HarperCollins Publishers 2006 xx, 1189p il hardcover o.p. pa $25.99
Grades: 11 12 Adult **811**
1. Poetry -- By individual authors
ISBN 978-0-06-113974-1; 0-06-113974-2; 978-0-06-113975-8 pa; 0-06-113975-0 pa
LC 2006-41191

First published 1984 with title: Collected poems, 1947-1980

This books "reprints the complete text of 1984's Collected Poems 1947-1980, along with the collections that followed: White Shroud, Cosmopolitan Greetings, and Death and Fame, including the original book attributes of each collection. A poet of extremes at times too trusting of his instincts, Ginsberg could be playful, angry, strident, obscene, graceful, and hilarious in the space of a page, and by now his readers know they are likely to encounter as many embarrassing poems as enlightening ones. Still, this compendium provides the most complete edition of Ginsberg available." Libr J

Giovanni, Nikki
Blues; for all the changes: new poems. Morrow 1999 100p $15
Grades: 11 12 Adult **811**
1. Poetry -- By individual authors
ISBN 0-688-15698-3
LC 98-50996

"Giovanni never loses sight of the people in her work. In poems built with broken lines and paragraphs of prose, she spars with the ills that confront us, but every struggle has a human face." Libr J

Quilting the black-eyed pea; poems and not quite poems. William Morrow 2002 110p $16.95
Grades: 11 12 Adult **811**
1. Poetry -- By individual authors
ISBN 978-0-06-009952-7; 0-06-009952-6
LC 2002-66025

Giovanni "entwines the political and the personal and celebrates womanhood and black society and culture. Hers is an embracing, uplifting, and sustaining voice, one given to both anger and humor." Booklist

★ The **selected** poems of Nikki Giovanni (1968-1995) Morrow 1996 224p $22
Grades: 11 12 Adult **811**
1. Poetry -- By individual authors
ISBN 0-688-14047-5
LC 95-31646

"Writing as an African American and as a woman, Giovanni speaks with powerful music about politics, love, feminism, and family." Booklist

Good poems; selected and introduced by Garrison Keillor. Viking 2002 xxvi, 476p $25.95; pa $15
Grades: 11 12 Adult **811**
1. English poetry -- Collections 2. American poetry -- Collections
ISBN 0-670-03126-7; 0-14-200344-1 pa
LC 2002-16881

Keillor "has put together a collection of close to 300 poems he has read during . . . [the] PBS broadcast, The Writer's Almanac. . . . Poems are arranged by 19 general themes, such as 'Snow,' 'Failure,' and 'A Good Life.' Authors range from well-known oldies like Emily Dickinson and Robert Frost to unknowns like C.K. Williams. . . . An outstanding feature of this collection is that the selections are all so accessible—even folks who say they don't like poetry can find something here to enjoy." SLJ

Grandits, John
Blue lipstick; concrete poems. Clarion Books 2007 un il $15; pa $5.95
Grades: 5 6 7 8 9 10 **811**
1. Poetry -- By individual authors
ISBN 978-0-618-56860-4; 0-618-56860-3; 978-0-618-85132-4 pa; 0-618-85132-1 pa
LC 2006-23332

"This selection introduces readers to Jessie, who impulsively purchases blue lipstick, but later, regretfully decides to give it 'the kiss-off.' Jessie is big sister to Robert, who was featured in Grandits's Technically, It's Not My Fault (Clarion, 2004). As he did in that terrific collection, the author uses artful arrangements of text on the page, along with 54 different typefaces, to bring his images and ideas to life. . . . This irreverent, witty collection should resonate with a wide audience." SLJ

Harjo, Joy
The **woman** who fell from the sky; poems. Norton 1994 69p hardcover o.p. pa $12.95
Grades: 11 12 Adult **811**
1. Poetry -- By individual authors
ISBN 0-393-31362-X pa
LC 96-23014

"Harjo sets 25 prayer-like prose poems in a spooky land of myth . . . depicting an ongoing moral 'war' between forces of creation (northern lights, wolves) vs. destruction (alcoholism, Vietnam). Like contemporary Jobs, the people in these pieces search for an intelligible response to 'the wreck of culture,' their efforts symbolizing the impact of alienation on the psyche." Libr J

Harper's anthology of 20th century Native American poetry; edited by Duane Niatum. Harper & Row 1988 xxxii, 396p hardcover o.p. pa $24.95
Grades: 11 12 Adult   **811**
1. American poetry -- Native American authors
ISBN 0-06-250666-8 pa

LC 86-45023

This collection "contains the work of 36 native American poets, with hearty selections from each. Among the 36 are poets near the mainstream (Scott Momaday, James Welch, Louise Erdrich); those in academe (Gerald Vizenor, Linda Hogan, Jim Barnes); those writing in the tribal oral tradition (Barney Bush, Peter Blue Cloud, Wendy Rose); and those working in a modernist voice (Gladys Cardiff, Paula Gunn Allen). This book belongs in every collection that claims to represent the multiple voices of American literature today." Booklist
Includes bibliographical references

★ **Heart** to heart; new poems inspired by twentieth-century American art. edited by Jan Greenberg. Abrams 2001 80p il map $19.95
Grades: 5 6 7 8 9 10   **811**
1. American art 2. Art -- 20th century 3. American poetry -- Collections
ISBN 0-8109-4386-7

LC 99-462335

Michael L. Printz Award honor book, 2002
A compilation of poems by Americans writing about American art in the twentieth century, including such writers as Nancy Willard, Jane Yolen, and X. J. Kennedy.
"From a tight diamante and pantoum to lyrical free verse, the range of poetic styles will speak to a wide age group.... Concluding with biographical notes on each poet and artist, this rich resource is an obvious choice for teachers, and the exciting interplay between art and the written word will encourage many readers to return again and again to the book." Booklist

Hemphill, Stephanie
★ **Your** own, Sylvia; a verse portrait of Sylvia Plath. Alfred A. Knopf 2007 261p $15.99; lib bdg $18.99
Grades: 8 9 10 11 12   **811**
1. Poets 2. Authors 3. Novelists 4. Poetry -- By individual authors
ISBN 978-0-375-83799-9; 978-0-375-93799-6 lib bdg

LC 2006-07253

Michael L. Printz Award honor book, 2008
The author interprets the people, events, influences and art that made up the brief life of Sylvia Plath.
"Hemphill's verse, like Plath's, is completely compelling: every word, every line, worth reading." Horn Book
Includes bibliographical references

★ A **Historical** guide to Walt Whitman; edited by David S. Reynolds. Oxford Univ. Press 2000

280p il (Historical guides to American authors) $39.95; pa $19.95
Grades: 9 10 11 12   **811**
1. Poets 2. Authors 3. Essayists
ISBN 0-19-512081-7; 0-19-512082-5 pa

LC 99-12608

Following a brief biography contributors discuss Whitman's poetics, themes and influence. An illustrated chronology and a bibliographical essay are included.
Includes bibliographical references

Holbrook, Sara
More than friends; poems from him and her. [by] Sara Holbrook and Allan Wolf. Wordsong 2008 64p il $16.95
Grades: 6 7 8 9 10   **811**
1. Love poetry 2. Poetry -- By individual authors
ISBN 978-1-59078-587-4; 1-59078-587-8

LC 2007-50282

"In these parallel poems, a boy and a girl describe their progression from friendship to romance.... The simple language expresses strong feelings in a variety of poetic forms. ... Small black-and-white photos never get in the way of the words, which tell the edgy truth of romance in all its joy and confusion." Booklist

Hughes, Langston
Poems; selected and edited by David Roessel. Knopf 1999 252p $12.50
Grades: 11 12 Adult   **811**
1. African Americans -- Poetry 2. Poetry -- By individual authors
ISBN 0-375-40551-8

LC 98-55136

The editor presents a representative selection of poetry by the prominent African American writer

★ **I** am the darker brother; an anthology of modern poems by African Americans. edited and with an afterword by Arnold Adoff; drawings by Benny Andrews; introduction by Rudine Sims Bishop; foreword by Nikki Giovanni. rev ed; Simon & Schuster Bks. for Young Readers 1997 208p il hardcover o.p. pa $5.99
Grades: 6 7 8 9 10   **811**
1. American poetry -- African American authors -- Collections
ISBN 0-689-81241-8; 0-689-80869-0 pa

LC 97-144181

First published 1968
This anthology presents "the African-American experience through poetry that speaks for itself.... Because of the historical context of many of the poems, the book will be much in demand during Black History Month, but it should be used and treasured as part of the larger canon of literature to be enjoyed by all Americans at all times of the year. An indispensable addition to library collections." SLJ

Indivisible; poems for social justice. edited by Gail Bush & Randy Meyer; foreword by Common.

Norwood House Press 2013 94 p. (pbk.: alk. paper) $14.60

Grades: 7 8 9 10 11 12　　**811**

1. Poetry 2. Social justice 3. Social problems 4. Social justice -- Poetry 5. Social problems -- Poetry
ISBN 9781603574174

　　　　　　　　　　　　　　LC 2012021600

In this book of poetry, editors Gail Bush and Randy Meyer "have selected 54 previously published works by twentieth-century poets. The work represents a broad variety of races, cultures, and ethnicities and deals with such issues as bigotry and injustice, as well as with freedom, equality, and comity. Divided into five sections, the poems essentially chart a course from outside our culture to an inside where we can celebrate common dreams." (Booklist)

"From Langston Hughes and Amiri Baraka to Joy Harjo and Toi Derricotte, the poets discuss perspective, misguided pity, stereotyping, patriarchy, and thousands of other sticky issues. This carefully selected collection is not only poetically breathtaking, but will undoubtedly prove useful time and again as we seek to provide resources for educating empathetic global citizens.—" (School Library Journal)

Includes bibliographical references and index.

Jarrell, Randall

★ The **complete** poems. Farrar, Straus & Giroux 1969 507p hardcover o.p. pa $22

Grades: 11 12 Adult　　**811**

1. Poetry -- By individual authors
ISBN 0-374-51305-8 pa

Collected here are the entire contents of three published volumes Selected poems (1955), The woman at the Washington Zoo (1960), and The Lost World (1965) plus poems published from 1934 to 1964 but never collected and some never before published

Johnson, James Weldon

★ **Complete** poems; edited with an introduction by Sondra Kathryn Wilson. Penguin Bks. 2000 xxxiii, 202p pa $14

Grades: 11 12 Adult　　**811**

1. Poetry -- By individual authors
ISBN 0-14-118545-7

　　　　　　　　　　　　　　LC 00-39969

This volume contains Fifty years and other poems (1917), God's trombones (1927), Saint Peter relates an incident of the resurrection day (1935), and a number of previously unpublished poems. The editor's introduction considers Johnson's achievements and influence

Includes bibliographical references

Kerouac, Jack

★ **Pomes** all sizes; introduction by Allen Ginsberg. City Lights Bks. 1992 175p pa $13.95

Grades: 11 12 Adult　　**811**

1. Poetry -- By individual authors
ISBN 0-87286-269-0

　　　　　　　　　　　　　　LC 92-1204

"This book, which Kerouac prepared for publication before his death in 1969, collects poems written between 1954 and 1965. Most are playful—comments about friends, variations on the sounds of words. Yet a few extremely sensitive

longer pieces appear, including 'Caritas,' in which the poet runs after a barefoot beggar boy to give him money for shoes and then begins to doubt the boy's veracity. Other intriguing poems reflect the poet's religious concerns of the moment, running the gamut of Eastern and Western religions." Libr J

Kirk, Connie Ann

★ A **student's** guide to Robert Frost. Enslow Pubs. 2006 160p il (Understanding literature) $27.93

Grades: 7 8 9 10　　**811**

1. Poets 2. Authors
ISBN 0-7660-2434-2

　　　　　　　　　　　　　　LC 2005-13392

In this book, "the career of this literary giant is examined. . . . Poems are put into historical and biographical context, with special emphasis placed on curriculum-related works, including 'Stopping by Woods on a Snowy Evening,' 'The Road Not Taken,' 'The Gift Outright,' and 'Fire and Ice.'" Publisher's note

Leiter, Sharon

Critical companion to Emily Dickinson; a literary reference to her life and work. Facts on File 2006 448p il $75

Grades: 11 12 Adult　　**811**

1. Poets 2. Authors
ISBN 0-8160-5448-7; 978-0-8160-5448-0

　　　　　　　　　　　　　　LC 2005-28123

This book "opens with a foreword by poet and Dickinson scholar Gregory Orr and includes an introduction; an approximately 20-page biography of Dickinson; explications of 150 of her best-known poems (e.g., 'Because I Could Not Stop for Death'); an A-to-Z dictionary of relevant persons, places, and ideas illustrated with black-and-white photos; a chronology; bibliographies; and a comprehensive index." Libr J

Includes bibliographical references

★ **Letters** to America; contemporary American poetry on race. edited by Jim Daniels. Wayne State Univ. Press 1995 230p pa $21.95

Grades: 9 10 11 12　　**811**

1. American poetry -- Collections 2. United States -- Race relations -- Poetry
ISBN 0-8143-2542-4

　　　　　　　　　　　　　　LC 95-19996

This volume collects "the probings of several dozen American poets on their nation's nightmare. . . . If a large proportion of the poets selected are black, Indian, Chicano, or Asian, that is unsurprising, for they are the ones upon whom the subject thrusts itself most insistently." Booklist

Lewis, J. Patrick

Black cat bone; [by] J. Patrick Lewis; illustrations by Gary Kelley. Creative Editions 2006 48p il $19.95

Grades: 6 7 8 9 10　　**811**

1. Singers 2. Guitarists 3. Blues musicians 4. Songwriters 5. Blues music -- Poetry 6. Mississippi -- Poetry 7. Poetry -- By individual authors 8. African

American musicians -- Poetry
ISBN 978-1-56846-194-6

LC 2005-52298

"Robert Johnson, the celebrated blues musician, is said to have sold his soul to the devil for his skills on the guitar. . . . Lewis's verse echoes Johnson's music. . . . A single line of text parades ghostlike across the bottom of each page, explaining the aspect of the man's life that the poem sings of, and becoming a cumulative mini-bio in itself. A couple of Johnson's own lyrics appear with the sequence of Lewis's poems where they add to the narrative tension. Kelley's mixed-media illustrations in blues and browns add to the mood and enliven the layout." SLJ

Little, Michael R.
Bloom's how to write about Robert Frost; introduction by Harold Bloom. Chelsea House 2009 248p (Bloom's how to write about literature) $45
Grades: 9 10 11 12   **811**
1. Poets 2. Authors 3. Report writing
ISBN 978-1-60413-347-9

LC 2009-22860

This book offers paper topics and advice on writing an essay about the works of Robert Frost.
Includes bibliographical references

Llanas, Sheila Griffin
Contemporary American poetry, not the end, but the beginning. Enslow Publishers 2010 160p il (Poetry rocks!) lib bdg $34.60
Grades: 9 10 11 12   **811**
1. Poets, American 2. Poetry -- Authorship 3. American poetry -- History and criticism
ISBN 978-0-7660-3279-8; 0-7660-3279-5

LC 2009-23802

The author discusses "some of the poetry of leading contemporary American poets, including: Roethke, Bishop, Stafford, Lowell, Brooks, Wilbur, Ginsberg, Merwin, Rich, Plath, Collins, and Gluck." Publisher's note
Includes glossary and bibliographical references

Modern American poetry, echoes and shadows. Enslow Publishers 2009 160p il (Poetry rocks!) lib bdg $34.60
Grades: 9 10 11 12   **811**
1. Poets, American 2. Poetry -- Authorship 3. American poetry -- History and criticism
ISBN 978-0-7660-3275-0; 0-7660-3275-2

LC 2009-11529

"Explores modern American poetry, including biographies of twelve poets such as Robert Frost, Ezra Pound, and Langston Hughes; excerpts of poems, literary criticism, poetic technique, and explication." Publisher's note
Includes glossary and bibliographical references

Longfellow, Henry Wadsworth
★ **Poems** and other writings. Library of Am. 2000 854p $35

Grades: 11 12 Adult   **811**
1. Poetry -- By individual authors
ISBN 1-88301-185-X

LC 00-26678

This volume includes "Hiawatha, Evangeline, The Courtship of Miles Standish and 'The Midnight Ride of Paul Revere.' Here, too, are some surprisingly powerful lyric and meditative poems—well made, deeply felt, and not much like the schoolhouse favorites." Publ Wkly
Includes bibliographical references

Longsworth, Polly
The **world** of Emily Dickinson. Norton 1990 136p il maps hardcover o.p. pa $19.95
Grades: 11 12 Adult   **811**
1. Poets 2. Authors 3. Women poets 4. Poets, American
ISBN 0-393-31656-4 pa

LC 90-31672

Drawings, maps, and photographs illustrate the home, friends, landscape and influence of the nineteenth-century American poet.

Lowell, Robert
★ **Selected** poems; Expanded ed; Farrar, Straus and Giroux 2006 420p pa $18
Grades: 11 12 Adult   **811**
1. Poetry -- By individual authors
ISBN 0-374-53006-8; 978-0-374-53006-8

LC 2005-54313

A selection of over 200 poems tracing the development of one of the premier confessional poets of his generation.
Includes bibliographical references

MacLeish, Archibald
Collected poems, 1917-1982; with a prefatory note to the newly collected poems by Richard B. McAdoo. Houghton Mifflin 1985 524p hardcover o.p. pa $19
Grades: 11 12 Adult   **811**
1. Poetry -- By individual authors
ISBN 0-395-39569-0 pa

LC 85-14392

Collects all the known poetry of the author/public servant. As an expatriate in Paris his early work was heavily influenced by Pound and Eliot. After returning to the States his verse concerned itself more with America's political, social, and cultural heritage

Masters, Edgar Lee
★ **Spoon** River anthology; edited and with an introduction and annotations by John E. Hallwas. University of Ill. Press 1992 436p il map hardcover o.p. pa $19
Grades: 9 10 11 12   **811**
1. Poetry -- By individual authors
ISBN 0-252-01561-4; 0-252-06363-5 pa

LC 91-16968

First published 1915 by Macmillan
"The men and women of Spoon River narrate their own biographies from the cemetery where they lie buried. Re-

alistic and sometimes cynical, these free-verse monologues often contradict the pious and optimistic epitaphs written on the gravestones." Reader's Ency. 4th edition

Meltzer, Milton

Walt Whitman; a biography. 21st Cent. Bks. (Brookfield) 2002 160p il lib bdg $31.90

Grades: 7 8 9 10   **811**

1. Poets 2. Authors 3. Essayists 4. Poets, American
ISBN 0-7613-2272-8

LC 2001-27798

"The book honestly explores Whitman's character and actions, including his racial prejudice and his tendency to write anonymous (and effective) praises of his own writing. Ultimately, this has a definite edge and relevance that gives it more resonance than blander overviews of the poet. . . . Photographs of Whitman and his family, images of his work, and reproductions of period illustrations . . . liven up the formatting." Bull Cent Child Books

Includes bibliographical references

Merrell, Billy

Talking in the dark; a poetry memoir. PUSH 2003 136p pa $6.99

Grades: 9 10 11 12   **811**

1. Poetry -- By individual authors
ISBN 0-439-49036-7

Merrell has "packed away a lot of wisdom about life, death, self-acceptance, and the vararies of love and lust. Likewise, he has honed his writing craft, and his free-verse memoir is rich with metaphor, words carefully chosen to say enough but not to much." Booklist

Millay, Edna St. Vincent

★ **Collected** poems; edited by Norma Millay. Harper & Row 1956 xxi, 738p hardcover o.p. pa $22.95

Grades: 11 12 Adult   **811**

1. Poetry -- By individual authors
ISBN 0-06-090889-0 pa

The poems in this collection "are divided into two separate sections of lyrics and sonnets, arranged chronologically and printed in groups under the titles of the original volumes, ranging from 'Renascence' of 1917 to 'Mine the harvest,' published in 1954, four years after the poet's death." Booklist

Moore, Marianne

★ The **poems** of Marianne Moore; edited by Grace Schulman. Viking 2003 449p hardcover o.p. pa $18

Grades: 11 12 Adult   **811**

1. Poetry -- By individual authors
ISBN 0-14-303908-3 pa

LC 2003-50159

"The great modernist poet finally gets her due with this outstanding compliation." Libr J

Includes bibliographical references

Mora, Pat

Dizzy in your eyes; poems about love. Alfred A. Knopf 2010 165p il $15.99; lib bdg $18.99

Grades: 7 8 9 10   **811**

1. Love poetry 2. Poetry -- By individual authors
ISBN 978-0-375-84375-4; 0-375-84375-2; 978-0-375-94565-6 lib bdg; 0-375-94565-2 lib bdg

LC 2009-04300

"From family and school to dating and being dumped, the subjects in these 50 poems cover teens' experiences of love in many voices and situations. . . . Mora writes in free verse, as well as a variety of classic poetic forms—including haiku, clerihew, sonnet, cinquain, and blank verse—and for each form, there is an unobtrusive explanatory note on the facing page. The tight structures intensify the strong feelings in the poems, which teens will enjoy reading on their own or hearing aloud in the classroom." Booklist

My own true name; new and selected poems for young adults, 1984-1999. {by} Pat Mora with line drawings by Anthony Accardo. Piñata Bks. 2000 81p il $11.95

Grades: 9 10 11 12   **811**

1. Mexican Americans -- Poetry 2. Poetry -- By individual authors
ISBN 1-55885-292-1

LC 00-23969

"Interlaced with Mexican phrases and cultural symbols, these powerful selections, representing more than 15 years of work, address bicultural life and the meaning of family. Mora speaks very much from an adult perspective, but her poems are about universal experiences." Booklist

Murphy, Russell E.

Critical companion to T.S. Eliot; a literary reference to his life and work. [by] Russell Elliott Murphy. Facts on File 2007 614p il (Facts on File library of American literature) $75

Grades: 9 10 11 12 Adult   **811**

1. Poets 2. Authors 3. Dramatists 4. Editors 5. Essayists 6. Literary critics 7. Nobel laureates for literature
ISBN 978-0-8160-6183-9; 0-8160-6183-1

LC 2006-34076

"This is an excellent and exhaustive resource and a good buy for most libraries." Booklist

Includes bibliographical references

Myers, Walter Dean, 1937-2014

Harlem; a poem. pictures by Christopher Myers. Scholastic 1997 un il $16.95

Grades: 5 6 7 8 9 10   **811**

1. African Americans -- Poetry 2. Poetry -- By individual authors 3. Harlem (New York, N.Y.) -- Poetry
ISBN 0-590-54340-7

LC 96-8108

A Caldecott Medal honor book, 1998

A poem celebrating the people, sights, and sounds of Harlem

"Myers's paean to Harlem sings, dances, and swaggers across the pages, conveying the myriad sounds on the streets. . . . Christopher Myers's collages add an edge to his father's words, vividly bringing to life the sights and scenes of Lenox Avenue." Horn Book Guide

Here in Harlem; poems in many voices. written by Walter Dean Myers. Holiday House 2004 88p il $16.95

Grades: 7 8 9 10   811

1. African Americans -- Poetry 2. Poetry -- By individual authors 3. Harlem (New York, N.Y.) -- Poetry
ISBN 0-8234-1853-7

LC 2003-67605

"In each poem here, a resident of Harlem speaks in a distinctive voice, offering a story, a thought, a reflection, or a memory. The poetic forms are varied and well chosen. . . . Expressive period photos from Myers' collection accompany the text of this handsome book." Booklist

Nelson, Marilyn, 1946-

Carver, a life in poems. Front St. 2001 103p il $16.95

Grades: 7 8 9 10   811

1. Botanists 2. Poetry -- By individual authors
ISBN 1-88691-053-7

LC 00-63624

A Newbery Medal honor book, 2002

"A series of fifty-nine poems portrays George Washington Carver as a private, scholarly man of great personal faith and social purpose. Nelson fills in the trajectory of Carver's life with details of the cultural and political contexts that shaped him even as he shaped history. As individual works, each poem stands as a finely wrought whole of . . . high caliber." Horn Book Guide

Fortune's bones; the manumission requiem. Front Street 2004 32p il $16.95

Grades: 7 8 9 10   811

1. Slavery -- Poetry 2. African Americans -- Poetry 3. Poetry -- By individual authors
ISBN 1-932425-12-8

LC 2004-46917

"This requiem honors a slave who died in Connecticut in 1798. His owner, a doctor, dissected his body, boiling down his bones to preserve them for anatomy studies. The skeleton . . . hung in a local museum until 1970. . . . The museum . . . uncovered the skeleton's provenance, created a new exhibit, and led to the commissioning of these six poems. The selections . . . arc from grief to triumph. . . . The facts inform the verse and open up a full appreciation of its rich imagery and rhythmic, lyrical language." SLJ

Includes bibliographical references

★ The **freedom** business; including a narrative of the life & adventures of Venture, a native of Africa. Wordsong 2008 72p il $18.95

Grades: 8 9 10 11 12   811

1. Slavery -- Poetry 2. Connecticut -- Poetry 3. African Americans -- Poetry
ISBN 978-1-932425-57-4; 1-932425-57-8

LC 2008-04437

"Venture Smith, born Broteer Furro in Guinea, was captured and enslaved at the age of six and brought to America

in 1738. . . . His narrative, published in 1798, appears continuously on the left-hand page of each spread; Nelson's luminous poems appear on the right. Both are thrown into relief by Dancy's mixed-media artwork, which includes images of birds, ropes, chains and blood to heighten the visceral emotions of both texts. . . . Tragic, important, breathtaking." Kirkus

★ **How** I discovered poetry; by Marilyn Nelson and illustrated by Hadley Hooper. Dial Books 2014 112 p. (hardcover: alk. paper) $17.99

Grades: 7 8 9 10 11 12   811

1. American poets 2. Civil rights -- United States -- History 3. Authorship -- Poetry 4. Poetry -- Authorship
ISBN 0803733046; 9780803733046

LC 2013005289

Coretta Scott King Author Award Honor Book (2015)

In this memoir, author Marilyn Nelson "tells the story of her development as an artist and young woman through fifty eye-opening poems. Readers are given an intimate portrait of her growing self-awareness and artistic inspiration along with a larger view of the world around her: racial tensions, the Cold War era, and the first stirrings of the feminist movement." (Publisher's note)

"In this fictionalized memoir in verse, renowned poet Nelson lyrically recounts her passage from ages 4 to 14, from numerous military base homes; through friends, schools, and dogs; and from developmental stages of initiative through industry to identity..Hooper's line-and-shade illustrations, along with Nelson's family photos, set a quiet and respectful tone and offer readers the feeling of taking an unsolicited peek behind a heavy curtain. For fans of Nelson's impressive body of children's and adult poetry, including the brilliant A Wreath for Emmett Till (2005), this insight into her modulated memories gratifies that heartfelt belief that here writes a woman of great substance." (Booklist)

★ **My** Seneca Village; by Marilyn Nelson. Namelos 2015 98 p. $21.95

Grades: 6 7 8 9 10   811

1. Central Park (New York, N.Y.) 2. American poetry -- African American authors
ISBN 1608981967; 9781608981960

LC 2016007993

Los Angeles Times Book Prize: Young Adult Literature (2015)

In this poetry collection, author Marilyn Nelson "recreates the long lost community of Seneca Village. A multi-racial, multi-ethnic neighborhood in the center of Manhattan, it thrived in the middle years of the 19th century. . . . Then work crews arrived to build Central Park, and Seneca Village disappeared. Illustrated in the poet's own words -- with brief prose descriptions of what she sees inside her poems -- this collection takes readers back in time." (Publisher's note)

"Nelson chooses prose narrative to connect these 40-some lyric fictional portraits that include schoolchildren, a mariner, a bootblack, a hairdresser, a musician, bar owners, lovers, and a fortuneteller, among others, along with poignant snapshots of famous historical figures Frederick Douglass and Maria Stewart, the first African-American woman to lecture on politics and religion." Kirkus

★ A **wreath** for Emmett Till; illustrated by Philippe Lardy. Houghton Mifflin 2005 un il $17
Grades: 8 9 10 11 12 **811**
1. Children 2. Murder victims 3. Lynching -- Poetry 4. Mississippi -- Poetry 5. African Americans -- Poetry 6. Poetry -- By individual authors
ISBN 0-618-39752-3
LC 2004-9205
Michael L. Printz Award honor book, 2006
This is a "poetry collection about Till's brutal, racially motivated murder. The poems form a heroic crown of sonnets—a sequence in which the last line of one poem becomes the first line of the next. . . . The rigid form distills the words' overwhelming emotion into potent, heart-stopping lines that speak from changing perspectives. . . . When matched with Lardy's gripping, spare, symbolic paintings of tree trunks, blood-red roots, and wreaths of thorns, these poems are a powerful achievement that teens and adults will want to discuss together." Booklist

Nye, Naomi Shihab
★ **19** varieties of gazelle; poems of the Middle East. Greenwillow Bks. 2002 142p $16.95; pa $6.99
Grades: 7 8 9 10 **811**
1. Middle East -- Poetry 2. Poetry -- By individual authors
ISBN 0-06-009765-5; 0-06-050404-8 pa
LC 2002-771
In this "volume, Nye collects her poems about growing up as an Arab American (her ancestry is Palestinian), including previously published poems and newly written pieces. This rich and varied volume offers insights into the experience of childhood in two very different worlds. . . . This volume will fill a need for classroom use, for young people seeking a more personal understanding of the Middle East, and for readers seeking a connection with their own Middle Eastern background." Bull Cent Child Books

Honeybee; poems & short prose. Greenwillow Books 2008 164p $16.99; lib bdg $17.89
Grades: 8 9 10 11 12 **811**
1. Poetry -- By individual authors
ISBN 978-0-06-085390-7; 0-06-085390-5; 978-0-06-085391-4 lib bdg; 0-06-085391-3 lib bdg
LC 2007-36742
This poetry "anthology is a rallying cry, a call for us to rediscover such beelike traits as interconnectedness, strong community, and honest communication. . . . Teens at the very start of their questioning years will recognize their own angst in Nye's sense of irony, their idealistic optimism in her simple wonder." SLJ

You & yours: poems. BOA Editions 2005 87p (American poets continuum series) hardcover o.p. pa $15.50
Grades: 11 12 Adult **811**
1. Poetry -- By individual authors
ISBN 1-929918-68-2; 1-929918-69-0 pa
LC 2005-11360
"Tender yet forceful, funny and commonsensical, reflective and empathic, Nye writes radiant poems of nature and piercing poems of war, always touching base with homey details and radiant portraits of family and neighbors." Booklist

Oliver, Charles M.
Critical companion to Walt Whitman; a literary reference to his life and work. Facts on File 2005 408p il (Facts on File library of American literature) $65
Grades: 11 12 Adult **811**
1. Poets 2. Authors 3. Essayists
ISBN 0-8160-5768-0
LC 2005-4172
The author "begins this work with a biographical essay that includes several illustrations. A large portion of this book addresses Whitman's works, with entries for the individual poems and for the complete volumes. Each entry describes when and where the book was published and includes a brief account of the poem and its context. The third section of the volume covers people, places, publications, and topics related to Whitman's life and work." Choice
Includes bibliographical references

Oliver, Mary
New and selected poems. Beacon Press 2005 2v v1 $28.50; v1 pa $16; v2 $24.95; v2 pa $16
Grades: 11 12 Adult **811**
1. Poetry -- By individual authors
ISBN 0-8070-6878-0 v1; 0-8070-6877-2 v1 pa; 0-8070-6886-1 v2; 0-8070-6887-X v2 pa
Vol. 1 first published 1992; redesigned ed. to accompany the publication of vol. 2
Volume one contains poems written from 1965 to 1992. Volume two contains poems written from 1994 to 2005.

★ The **Oxford** anthology of African-American poetry; edited by Arnold Rampersad; associate editor, Hilary Herbold. Oxford University Press 2006 432p $32.50
Grades: 11 12 Adult **811**
1. American poetry -- African American authors -- Collections
ISBN 0-19-512563-0; 978-0-19-512563-4
LC 2005-15242
"Predicated on the fact that there is a vast body of poetry written by gifted black poets, this . . . anthology tells the story of African American culture and explicates its crucial role within the larger literary tradition. . . . There is much to admire about the artistry of the poems, and even more to discover about the African American experience." Booklist

★ The **Oxford** book of American poetry; chosen and edited by David Lehman; associate editor, John Brehm. Oxford University Press 2006 lvii, 1132p $35
Grades: 8 9 10 11 12 Adult **811**
1. American poetry -- Collections
ISBN 0-19-516251-X; 978-0-19-516251-6
LC 2005-36590
First published 1950 with title: The Oxford book of American verse

"The book is not only a sound historical survey, but also gives the reader a powerful taste of poetry's impact upon the wider world." Economist

Includes bibliographical references

★ The **Penguin** anthology of twentieth-century American poetry; edited with an introduction by Rita Dove. Penguin Books 2011 lii, 599 p.p

Grades: 9 10 11 12 Adult **811**

1. American poetry -- Collections 2. American poetry -- 20th century

ISBN 9780143106432

LC 2011036342

The book provides an anthology of 20th century U.S. poetry. "Selecting from the canon of American poetry throughout the twentieth century, [Rita] Dove has created an anthology that represents the full spectrum of aesthetic sensibilities. . . . Featuring poems both classic and contemporary, this collection reflects both a dynamic and cohesive portrait of modern American poetry and outlines its trajectory over the past century." (Publisher's note)

Phillips, Wendy

Fishtailing. Coteau Books for Teens 2010 196p pa $14.95

Grades: 8 9 10 11 12 **811**

1. School stories 2. Novels in verse 3. Violence -- Fiction 4. Authorship -- Fiction

ISBN 978-1-55050-411-8; 1-55050-411-8

Through a series of poems written for English class, interspersed with teacher comments and letters to and from parents, high school students Natalie, Tricia, Kyle, and Miguel describe their lives.

"The poetry is touching, painful, and jarring as Phillips presents their stories through their hesitations, hopes, pains, and fears. The plot constantly twists and turns, keeping the reader guessing what will happen next." Voice Youth Advocates

Plath, Sylvia

★ The **collected** poems; edited by Ted Hughes. Harper & Row 1981 351p hardcover o.p. pa $17.95

Grades: 11 12 Adult **811**

1. Poetry -- By individual authors

ISBN 0-06-155889-3 pa

"Although her best poems deal with suffering and death, others are exhilarating and affectionate, and her tone is frequently witty as well as disturbing." Concise Oxford Companion to Engl Lit

Please excuse this poem; 100 new poets for the next generation. Brett Fletcher Lauer and Lynn Melnick, editors. Viking 2015 304 p. (hardcover) $16.99

Grades: 9 10 11 12 **811**

1. American poets 2. American poetry 3. Poetry -- Collections 4. American poetry -- 21st century

ISBN 0670014796; 9780670014798

LC 2014007144

This poetry collection, edited by Brett Fletcher Lauer and Lynn Melnick, "features one hundred acclaimed younger poets from truly diverse backgrounds and points of view,

whose work has appeared everywhere from The New Yorker to Twitter, tackling a . . . range of subjects in a . . . range of poetic forms. Dealing with the aftermath of war; unpacking the meaning of 'the rape joke'; sharing the tender moments at the start of a love affair: these poems tell the world as they see it." (Publisher's note)

"This generous collection of their previously published work offers ample evidence that poetry is in good hands to ensure its viability for readers of the next generation." Booklist

Includes bibliographical references

Poe, Edgar Allan

★ **Complete** poems; edited by Thomas Ollive Mabbott. University of Ill. Press 2000 xxx, 627p il pa $25

Grades: 11 12 Adult **811**

1. Poetry -- By individual authors

ISBN 0-252-06921-8

LC 00-38639

This book contains 101 poems and their variants. In addition to classic poems such as The raven, The bells, and Annabel Lee, this volume contains previously uncollected poems, fragments, verses published in reviews, and poems attributed to Poe

Includes bibliographical references

Poems and poetics; Richard Wilbur, editor. Library of Am. 2003 xxv, 179p (American poets project) $20

Grades: 11 12 Adult **811**

1. Poetry -- By individual authors

ISBN 1-931082-51-0

LC 2003-46637

"Wilbur wants Poe to be appreciated as a transcendental cosmic theorist and 'the most difficult of the symbolist writers of his century,' and he appends selections from Poe's writings about poetics to help understanding of his cosmology and discusses some of Poe's most intense stories to exemplify his symbolism. The poems, presented chronologically, show again what a young prodigy Poe was, formulating his poetic thought while still in his teens, and what a sonorous Romantic musician he became." Booklist

Includes bibliographical references

Poetry 180; a turning back to poetry. selected and with an introduction by Billy Collins. Random House Trade Paperbacks 2003 xxiv, 323p pa $13.95

Grades: 11 12 Adult **811**

1. American poetry -- Collections

ISBN 0-8129-6887-5

LC 2002-36949

The editor "has collected 180 accessible modern poems: one for each day of the school year and together signifying a 180° turning back to poetry. These are poems, he says, you can 'get' the first time around, and he hopes that high schools will expose students to a poem a day via public address system or assemblies. A fine gathering of contemporary poets." Libr J

Includes bibliographical references

The **Poetry** anthology, 1912-2002; ninety years of America's most distinguished verse magazine. edited by Joseph Parisi & Stephen Young; with an introduction by Joseph Parisi. Ivan R. Dee 2002 lv, 509p $29.95; pa $16.95

Grades: 11 12 Adult   **811**
1. American poetry -- Collections
ISBN 1-56663-468-7; 1-56663-604-3 pa

LC 2002-31178

A collection of 600 poems previously published in Poetry magazine, written by such poets as W.H. Auden, Elizabeth Bishop, Sylvia Plath, James Merrill, and Susan Hahn

This is a "comprehensive and thrilling anthology, a veritable history of twentieth-century poetry in English." Booklist

★ **Poetry** speaks expanded; hear poets from Tennyson to Plath read their own work. Elise Paschen & Rebekah Presson Mosby, editors; Charles Osgood, narrator. [2nd ed.]; Sourcebooks 2007 384p il $49.95

Grades: 11 12 Adult   **811**
1. English poetry -- Collections 2. American poetry -- Collections
ISBN 978-1-4022-1062-4; 1-4022-1062-0

LC 2007-37080

First published 2001 with title: Poetry speaks

"Reluctant poetry readers may find themselves drawn to the printed page by the spoken work, and poetry fans are likely to find much to love here." Publ Wkly

The **poets** laureate anthology; edited and with introductions by Elizabeth Hun Schmidt; foreword by Billy Collins. W.W. Norton & Co. 2010 liii, 762p $39.95

Grades: 11 12 Adult   **811**
1. American poetry -- Collections
ISBN 978-0-393-06181-9

LC 2010-21692

Poems by each of the forty-three poets who have been named our nation's Poet Laureate since the post (originally called Consultant in Poetry to the Library of Congress) was established in 1937.

"A hefty and worthy read that everyone will want to savor. Essential for all contemporary poetry collections." Libr J

A **Poke** in the I; [selected by] Paul Janeczko; illustrated by Chris Raschka. Candlewick Press 2001 35p il hardcover o.p. pa $7.99

Grades: 4 5 6 7 8 9 10   **811**
1. American poetry -- Collections
ISBN 0-7636-0661-8; 0-7636-2376-8 pa

LC 00-33675

"Thirty concrete poems of all shapes and sizes are carefully laid on large white spreads, extended by Raschka's quirky watercolor and paper-collage illustrations. . . . Beautiful and playful, this title should find use in storytimes, in the classroom, and just for pleasure anywhere." SLJ

Postmodern American poetry; a Norton anthology. edited by Paul Hoover. 2nd ed. W W Norton & Co Inc 2013 lvii, 982 p.p (paperback) $39.95

Grades: 11 12 Adult   **811**
1. Postmodernism 2. American poetry 3. American poetry -- 20th century 4. American poetry -- 21st century 5. Postmodernism (Literature) -- United States
ISBN 0393341860; 9780393341867

LC 2012039473

This book, edited by Paul Hoover, is a the second edition of an anthology of poems written after 1950, by such authors as "Robert Duncan, Denise Levertov, James Schuyler, Robert Creeley, Allen Ginsberg, Gary Snyder, Ted Berrigan, Clarence Major, Mei-Mei Berssenbrugge, and David Shapiro." (Booklist) It includes "important recent movements such as Newlipo, conceptual poetry, and Flarf." (Publisher's note)

Includes bibliographical references and index.

Pound, Ezra
★ **Selected** poems; new ed; New Directions 1957 184p pa $8.95

Grades: 11 12 Adult   **811**
1. Poetry -- By individual authors
ISBN 0-8112-0162-7
First published 1949

This "provides a good sampling of the Pound who wrote 'A Virginal,' the latter-day Renaissance poet, as well as the reincarnate Li Po and the other 'personae' that Ezra wore during the years he spent absorbing the styles (and not the political thinking) of other centuries." Saturday Rev

Priddy, Anna
Bloom's how to write about Emily Dickinson; introduction by Harold Bloom. Chelsea House 2008 262p (Bloom's how to write about literature) $45

Grades: 9 10 11 12   **811**
1. Poets 2. Authors 3. Report writing
ISBN 978-0-7910-9492-1

LC 2006-100573

This book offers "paper-topic suggestions, . . . strategies on how to write a strong essay, and an . . . introduction by Harold Bloom on writing about Dickinson. This . . . volume is designed to help students develop their analytical writing skills and critical comprehension of this important poet and her works." Publisher's note

Includes bibliographical references

Reef, Catherine
Walt Whitman. Clarion Bks. 1995 148p il hardcover o.p. pa $7.95

Grades: 7 8 9 10   **811**
1. Poets 2. Authors 3. Essayists 4. Poets, American
ISBN 0-395-68705-5; 0-618-24616-9 pa

LC 94-7405

"This is not a biography for pleasure reading, but it could be a source for those interested in historical events of 19th century America. It also would be a good resource for students doing a critique of Whitman's work for an American literature course." Book Rep

Includes bibliographical references

Reflections on a gift of watermelon pickle--and other modern verse; [compiled by] Stephen Dunning, Edward Lueders, Hugh Smith. Lothrop, Lee & Shepard Bks. 1967 139p il $19.99

Grades: 6 7 8 9 10 **811**

1. American poetry -- Collections

ISBN 0-688-41231-9

First published 1966 by Scott, Foresman in a text edition

"Although some of the [114] selections are by recognized modern writers, many are by minor or unknown poets, and few will be familiar to the reader. Nearly all are fresh in approach and contemporary in expression. . . . Striking photographs complementing or illuminating many of the poems enhance the attractiveness of the volume." Booklist

Reynolds, Jason

My name is Jason. Mine too; by Jason Reynolds and Jason Griffin. HarperTeen 2009 un il pa $12.99

Grades: 7 8 9 10 **811**

1. Artists -- Poetry 2. New York (N.Y.) -- Poetry 3. Poetry -- By individual authors

ISBN 978-0-06-154788-1; 0-06-154788-3

LC 2008-43824

"Two former college roommates, both named Jason, set off for New York City to seek their collective fortunes. . . . As money and food quickly become rare commodities, the cruel realities of life in the City are all-too evident for the struggling artists. . . . Touching and endearing yet gritty and hip, this story should be highly appealing to older teens and indeed, many adults." Voice Youth Advocates

Roethke, Theodore

★ The **collected** poems of Theodore Roethke. Doubleday 1966 279p hardcover o.p. pa $14.95

Grades: 11 12 Adult **811**

1. Poetry -- By individual authors

ISBN 0-385-08601-6 pa

Roethke's "refreshingly original rhythms are keenly articulated and often hypnotic. Although his work is uneven and he sometimes gives way to self-indulgence or to surprising naiveté, many of his best poems recreate disconcertingly intense psychic or mystical experience. He also had a flair for the seductively lyrical and the brashly irreverent. He ranks as one of the best poets of the first postmodern generation." Benet's Reader's Ency of Am Lit

Sandburg, Carl

The **complete** poems of Carl Sandburg; rev and expanded ed; Harcourt Brace Jovanovich 1970 xxxi, 797p $40

Grades: 11 12 Adult **811**

1. Poetry -- By individual authors

ISBN 0-15-100996-1

First published 1950

A collection of seven of the author's books: Chicago poems, 1916; Cornhuskers, 1918; Smoke and steel, 1920; Slabs of the sunburnt West, 1922; Good morning, America, 1925; The people, yes, 1936; Honey and salt, 1963

"Known for his free verse, written under the influence of Walt Whitman and celebrating industrial and agricul-

tural America, American geography and landscape, figures in American history, and the American common people, {Sandburg} frequently makes use of contemporary American slang and colloquialisms." Herzberg. Reader's Ency of Am Lit

★ **Selected** poems; edited by George Hendrick and Willene Hendrick. Harcourt Brace & Co. 1996 xxix, 285p pa $16

Grades: 11 12 Adult **811**

1. Poetry -- By individual authors

ISBN 0-15-600396-1

LC 95-50686

"With a preface that puts the poet and his work in perspective, this 'one-volume edition of Sandburg's best and most characteristic poetry' is ideal for student and poetry enthusiast alike." Booklist

Includes bibliographical references

Sendak, Maurice, 1928-2012

My brother's book; Maurice Sendak; [edited by] Michael di Capua. HarperCollins 2013 32 p. (hardcover bdg.) $18.95

Grades: 4 5 6 7 8 **811**

1. Poetry 2. Poetry -- Collections

ISBN 0062234897; 9780062234896

LC 2012942549

In this book, "with influences from Shakespeare and William Blake, [Maurice] Sendak pays homage to his late brother, Jack, whom he credited for his passion for writing and drawing. Pairing Sendak's . . . poetry with his . . . artwork, . . . Sendak's tribute to his brother is an expression of both grief and love. . . . Pulitzer Prize--winning literary critic and Shakespearean scholar Stephen Greenblatt contributes a[n] . . . introduction." (Publisher's note)

Sexton, Anne

★ The **complete** poems; with a foreword by Maxine Kumin. Houghton Mifflin 1981 xxiv, 622p hardcover o.p. pa $19

Grades: 11 12 Adult **811**

1. Poetry -- By individual authors

ISBN 0-395-95776-1 pa

LC 81-2482

"Even before her death in 1974, Sexton's work was the subject of critical controversy, often dismissed as mere confessionalism. But, as Maxine Kumin observes in an insightful introductory essay, Sexton 'delineated the problematic position of women—the neurotic reality of the time' and in so doing 'earned her place in the canon.'" Choice

Shimmy shimmy shimmy like my sister Kate; looking at the Harlem Renaissance through poems. [edited by] Nikki Giovanni. Holt & Co. 1995 186p $17.95

Grades: 8 9 10 11 12 **811**

1. Harlem Renaissance 2. American poetry -- African American authors -- Collections

ISBN 0-8050-3494-3

LC 95-38617

This anthology includes poems by such authors as Paul Laurence Dunbar, Langston Hughes, Countee Cullen, Gwendolyn Brooks, and Amiri Baraka. Commentary and a discussion of the development of African American arts known as the Harlem Renaissance is provided by editor Giovanni

Includes bibliographical references

Sidman, Joyce

★ **What** the Heart Knows; chants, charms, and blessings. written by Joyce Sidman and illustrated by Pamela Zagarenski. Houghton Mifflin Harcourt 2013 80 p. $16.99

Grades: 6 7 8 9 10 11 12   811

1. Children's poetry 2. Blessing and cursing 3. Children's poetry, American

ISBN 0544106164; 9780544106161

LC 2012047836

This book, by Joyce Sidman and illustrated by Pamela Zagarenski, "is a collection of poems to provide comfort, courage, and humor at difficult or daunting moments in life. It conjures forth laments, spells, invocations, chants, blessings, promises, songs, and charms. Here are pleas on how to repair a friendship, wishes to transform one's life or to slow down time, charms to face the shame of a disapproving crowd, invocations to ask for forgiveness, [and] to understand the mysteries of happiness." (Publisher's note)

"Sidman and Zagarenski present "Chants & Charms," "Spells & Invocations," "Laments & Remembrances," and "Praise Songs & Blessings" in a variety of poetic forms. Each poem speaks directly from Sidman's heart to the reader's, addressing subjects of deep importance: forgiveness, friendship, bravery, death, illness, moving. Zagarenski's illustrations beautifully extend the poems with her dreamy style and deft use of white space, symbolism, and images." (Horn Book)

Silverstein, Shel

★ **Where** the sidewalk ends; the poems & drawings of Shel Silverstein. 30th anniversary special ed; HarperCollins 2004 183p il $17.99; lib bdg $18.89

Grades: 3 4 5 6 7 8 9 10   811

1. Humorous poetry 2. Nonsense verses 3. Poetry -- By individual authors

ISBN 0-06-057234-5; 0-06-058653-2 lib bdg

LC 2004-269335

First published 1974

"There are skillful, sometimes grotesque line drawings with each of the 127 poems, which run in length from a few lines to a couple of pages. The poems are tender, funny, sentimental, philosophical, and ridiculous in turn, and they're for all ages." Sat Rev

Six American poets; an anthology. edited by Joel Connaroe. Random House 1991 xxxiv, 281p il hardcover o.p. pa $14.95

Grades: 11 12 Adult   811

1. American poetry -- Collections

ISBN 0-679-74525-4 pa

LC 91-15375

This anthology contains 247 representative poems by Walt Whitman, Emily Dickinson, Wallace Stevens, William Carlos Williams, Robert Frost and Langston Hughes

Songs from this Earth on turtle's back; contemporary American Indian poetry. edited by Joseph Bruchac. Greenfield Review Press 1983 294p il pa $14.95

Grades: 11 12 Adult   811

1. American poetry -- Native American authors

ISBN 0-912678-58-5

LC 82-82420

"The collection provides a balance to the volumes of compiled chants and translated (or mistranslated) songs already in most libraries. . . . Writing in English, they display a variety of styles and themes and draw from urban, rural, and reservation backgrounds, yet they share a reverence for the earth and the natural world and a keen understanding of the power of language to create and shape that world." Choice

Soto, Gary

★ **Partly** cloudy; poems of love and longing. Harcourt 2009 100p $16

Grades: 7 8 9 10   811

1. Love poetry 2. Poetry -- By individual authors

ISBN 978-0-15-206301-6; 0-15-206301-3

LC 2008-22267

Poet Gary Soto captures the voices of young people as they venture toward their first kiss, brood over bruised hearts, and feel the thrill of first love.

"Soto's new book of verse about adolescent love is remarkable. . . . The language of the poems is spare but evocative, with not one word wasted. . . . Teens will find these poems very engaging and will relate to how the emotion of love is expressed in everyday moments." Voice Youth Advocates

Spires, Elizabeth

★ **I** heard God talking to me; William Edmondson and his stone carvings. Farrar, Straus and Giroux 2009 56p il $17.95

Grades: 8 9 10 11 12 Adult   811

1. Artists 2. Sculptors 3. Religious poetry 4. Artists -- Poetry 5. Sculpture -- Poetry 6. African Americans -- Poetry 7. Poetry -- By individual authors

ISBN 978-0-374-33528-1; 0-374-33528-1

LC 2008-02343

"Moved by a religious vision at age 57, Nashville janitor William Edmondson began carving tombstones and whimsical figures out of stone in 1931 and went on to attract the attention of international collectors, eventually becoming the first African American artist to have a solo show at the Museum of Modern Art in New York. This handsome picture-book-sized poetry collection pairs full-page, black-and-white photos of Edmondson and his works with poems inspired by the images. . . . Supported by an appended prose biography, these playful, thought-provoking poems introduce a fascinating artist." Booklist

★ The **Spoken** word revolution; slam, hip-hop, & the poetry of a new generation. edited by Marc Eleveld; advised by Marc Smith; introduction by Billy Collins. Sourcebooks 2003 241p il $24.95; pa $19.95

Grades: 11 12 Adult **811**

1. American poetry -- Collections

ISBN 1-4022-0037-4; 1-4022-0246-6 pa

LC 2003-841

The editors "trace the evolution of spoken-word poetry from the Beats to rap, hip-hop, and performance art. The result is a dynamic and clarifying volume chock-full of fresh and informative commentary by the likes of Billy Collins, Marvin Bell, and Jerry Quickley and an exciting array of knock-out poems by Patricia Smith, Tara Betts, Jeff McDaniel, Roger Bonair-Agard . . . and many more. Eleveld and his contributors not only celebrate the verve, artistry, and significance of performance poetry but also anchor it firmly within the splendid, age-old, and life-sustaining universe of poetry. . . . An accompanying CD presents poets performing their work." Booklist

Stevens, Wallace

The **collected** poems of Wallace Stevens. Knopf 1954 534p $40; pa $16

Grades: 11 12 Adult **811**

1. Poetry -- By individual authors

ISBN 0-394-40330-4; 0-679-72669-1 pa

Steven's "poems range from descriptive and dramatic lyrics to meditative and discursive discourse, but all show a deep engagement in experience and in art. His musical verse, rich in tropic imagery but precise and intense in statement, is marked by concern with means of knowledge, with the contrast between reality and appearance, and the emphasis upon imagination as giving an aesthetic insight and order to life." Oxford Companion to Am Lit. 6th edition

Swenson, May

Nature; poems old and new. Houghton Mifflin 1994 xxiii, 240p hardcover o.p. pa $15

Grades: 11 12 Adult **811**

1. Poetry -- By individual authors

ISBN 0-618-06408-7 pa

LC 93-45642

This collection of Swenson's poetry "brings together poems from several earlier books, as well as poems published only in magazines, and introduces us to nine splendid poems published here for the first time. This collection . . . is brought together with special attention to poems describing the environment; poems of tides and the sea, of birds and gardens, of moods and seasons, of self and others. . . . This is a collection to be treasured; it belongs in all libraries with even a modest selection of poetry." Libr J

Sylvia Plath; edited by Harold Bloom. Chelsea House 2000 96p (Bloom's major poets) lib bdg $21.95

Grades: 9 10 11 12 **811**

1. Poets 2. Authors 3. Novelists

ISBN 0-7910-5935-9

LC 00-55590

Literary scholars analyze The colossus, The arrival of the bee box, Daddy, Ariel, and Lady Lazarus.

Includes bibliographical references

T.S. Eliot's The waste land; edited & with an introduction by Harold Bloom. Chelsea House 2007 117p (Bloom's guides) $30

Grades: 9 10 11 12 **811**

1. Poets 2. Authors 3. Dramatists 4. Editors 5. Essayists 6. Literary critics 7. Nobel laureates for literature 8. Poetry -- By individual authors

ISBN 978-0-7910-9361-0; 0-7910-9361-1

LC 2006-101020

This study guide on T.S. Eliot's poem includes a brief biographical sketch of Eliot, a list of characters, a summary and analysis, and selections from critical essays by different scholars about the work.

Includes bibliographical references

Tell the world; teen poems from WritersCorps. HarperTeen 2008 116p $16.99; pa $8.99

Grades: 7 8 9 10 11 12 **811**

1. Teenagers' writings 2. American poetry -- Collections

ISBN 978-0-06-134505-0; 0-06-134505-9; 978-0-06-134504-3 pa; 0-06-134504-0 pa

LC 2007-49577

"This worthy collection of brief poems offers an array of teen voices. . . . An essay by WritersCorps teacher Michelle Matz adds a vivid picture of her students and their lives. This fine collection should inspire creativity and resonate with teens who find their own hopes, fears, and dreams eloquently voiced in the works of these young poets." SLJ

★ **Time** you let me in; 25 poets under 25. selected by Naomi Shihab Nye. Greenwillow Books 2010 236p $16.99; lib bdg $17.89

Grades: 8 9 10 11 12 **811**

1. American poetry -- Collections

ISBN 978-0-06-189637-8; 0-06-189637-3; 978-0-06-189638-5 lib bdg; 0-06-189638-1 lib bdg

LC 2009-19387

"This lively collection by young contemporary writers is rooted in the strong, emotional particulars of family, friendship, childhood memories, school, dislocation, war, and more. . . . Teens will connect with the passionate, unmoderated feelings that are given clarity and shape in each poem." Booklist

Includes bibliographical references

★ **Twentieth**-century American poetry; edited by Dana Gioia, David Mason, Meg Schoerke. McGraw Hill 2004 xlvi, 1143p il pa $79.69

Grades: 11 12 Adult **811**

1. American poetry -- Collections

ISBN 0-07-240019-6

LC 2003-61449

"The text is divided into sections like 'Realism and Naturalism' and 'The Harlem Renaissance,' with each section prefaced by a penetrating overview and each poet introduced by a biographical essay. Included are poets as diverse as Sherman Alexie, Ezra Pound, and Lucille Clifton, along with Nuyorican poets, New Formalists, Beats, imagists, and surrealists. Make room for this affordable, remarkable volume." Libr J

Includes bibliographical references

Unsettling America; an anthology of contemporary multicultural poetry. edited by Maria Mazziotti Gillan and Jennifer Gillan. Penguin Bks. 1994 xxv, 406p hardcover o.p. pa $18
Grades: 11 12 Adult   811
1. American poetry -- Collections
ISBN 0-14-023778-X pa

LC 94-722

This "anthology provides exposure to poets, emerging and established—Louis Simpson, Rita Dove, Luis Rodriguez—who write directly from the immigrant, ethnic and/or religious experience. . . . This collection is a must for anyone seeking an inclusive, unwincing catalogue of the American experience." Publ Wkly

★ The **Vintage** book of African American poetry; edited and with an introduction by Michael S. Harper and Anthony Walton. Vintage Bks. 2000 xxxiii, 403p pa $14.95
Grades: 11 12 Adult   811
1. American poetry -- African American authors -- Collections
ISBN 0-375-70300-4

LC 99-39428

"Included in chronological order here are over two centuries of poets, from Jupitor Hammon (1720-1800) to Reginald Shepherd (b.1963). . . . The editors' eloquent, outspoken vision provides a springboard for further examination of what constitutes the mainstream of American poetry." Libr J
Includes bibliographical references

★ The **Vintage** book of contemporary American poetry; edited and with an introduction by J.D. McClatchy. 2nd ed., newly rev. and expanded ed.; Vintage Books 2003 xxxiv, 617p pa $17.95
Grades: 11 12 Adult   811
1. American poetry -- Collections
ISBN 1-400-03093-5

LC 2003-269652

First published 1990

"With selections from 65 poets writing over the last 40 years, and with brief notes on their lives and work, this anthology will introduce YAs to much of the best modern poetry." Booklist [review of 1990 edition]
Includes bibliographical references

Walcott, Derek
★ **Collected** poems, 1948-1984. Farrar, Straus & Giroux 1986 515p hardcover o.p. pa $20
Grades: 11 12 Adult   811
1. Poetry -- By individual authors
ISBN 0-374-52025-9 pa

LC 85-20688

"It is difficult to think of a poet in our century who—without ever betraying his native sources—has so organically assimilated the evolution of English literature from the Renaissance to the present, who has absorbed the Classical and Judeo-Christian past, and who has mined the history of Western painting as Walcott has. Throughout his entire body

of work he has managed to hold in balance his passionate moral concerns with the ideal of art." Poetry
Includes bibliographical references

Omeros. Farrar, Straus & Giroux 1990 325p hardcover o.p. pa $16
Grades: 11 12 Adult   811
1. Poetry -- By individual authors
ISBN 0-374-52350-9 pa

LC 90-33592

"No poet rivals Mr. Walcott in humor, emotional depth, lavish inventiveness in language or in the ability to express the thoughts of his characters and compel the reader to follow the swift mutations of ideas and images in their minds. This wonderful story moves in a spiral, replicating human thought." N Y Times Book Rev

Walker, Alice
Hard times require furious dancing; new poems. foreword and illustrations by Shiloh McCloud. New World Library 2010 165p il $18
Grades: 11 12 Adult   811
1. Poetry -- By individual authors
ISBN 978-1-57731-930-6

LC 2010-29972

In this poetry collection, the author "writes of loss and disappointment, and the strength that rises from meeting them unflinchingly. . . . These are powerful anthems of womanhood and age, although just as likely to be empowering to men and to the not-yet-old." Booklist

Her blue body everything we know; earthling poems, 1965-1990, complete. Harcourt Brace Jovanovich 1991 463p hardcover o.p. pa $15
Grades: 11 12 Adult   811
1. Poetry -- By individual authors
ISBN 0-15-602861-1 pa

LC 90-5160

"Here, in an inspiring compilation of her earlier poetry, Walker offers a historical perspective on the political and spiritual issues spanning three decades of injustice, perseverance, and hope. Revelatory introductions to each group of poems become essential threads in the tapestry that is Alice Walker, tightly weaving a special insight into the evolving consciousness of one of the most remarkable and provocative literary voices of our time." (Publisher's Note)

In this volume of Walker's "complete earlier work, joined to new, previously uncollected poems, we see a quarter century of impressive artistic development." Booklist

Warren, Robert Penn
The **collected** poems of Robert Penn Warren; edited by John Burt; with a foreword by Harold Bloom. Louisiana State Univ. Press 1998 xxvi, 830p $44.95
Grades: 11 12 Adult   811
1. Poetry -- By individual authors
ISBN 0-8071-2333-1

LC 98-26104

"This immense volume gathers 15 books of poetry—as well as uncollected verse from the beginning and end of his writing life—from a formidable American man of letters and our first poet laureate. . . . Scholars will especially cherish the careful, copious textual and explanatory notes provided by Warren's literary executor Burt . . . and fans of American poetry and literary history alike should welcome this opportunity to explore the prodigious oeuvre of one of the New Criticism's most forceful, convincing proponents." Publ Wkly

Whitman, Walt

★ **Complete** poetry and collected prose. Library of Am. 1982 1380p $35; pa $17.95
Grades: 11 12 Adult   **811**
    1. Poetry -- By individual authors
    ISBN 0-940450-02-X; 1-883011-35-3 pa

LC 81-20768
"Presented here is the great culminating edition of 1891-92, the last supervised by Whitman himself. Whitman's prose, no less extraordinary, includes reminiscences of 19th-century New York City and notes on the Civil War, especially his service in Washington hospitals and glimpses of President Lincoln." Publisher's Note

★ **Leaves** of grass; edited and with a new afterword by David S. Reynolds. 150th anniversary ed.; Oxford University Press 2005 167p $23
Grades: 11 12 Adult   **811**
    1. Poetry -- By individual authors
    ISBN 0-19-518342-8

LC 2004-26509
First published 1855
"The book, radical in form and content, takes its title from the themes of fertility, universality, and cyclical life. . . . As he revised and added to the original edition, Whitman arranged the poems in a significant autobiographical order." Reader's Ency. 4th edition

Williams, William Carlos

★ The **collected** poems of William Carlos Williams. New Directions 1986 2v v1 $40; v1 pa $23.95; v2 $38; v2 pa $22.95
Grades: 11 12 Adult   **811**
    1. Poetry -- By individual authors
    ISBN 0-8112-0999-7 v1; 0-8112-1187-8 v1 pa; 0-8112-1063-4 v2; 0-8112-1188-6 v2 pa
"Williams's poetry is firmly rooted in the commonplace detail of everyday American life. He conceived of the poem as an object: a record of direct experience that deals with the local and the particular. He abandoned conventional rhyme and meter in an effort to reduce the barrier between the reader and his consciousness of his immediate surroundings. . . . Williams's original approach to poetry, his insistence on the importance of the ordinary, and his successful attempts at making his verse as 'tactile' as the spoken word had a far-reaching effect on American poetry." Reader's Ency. 4th edition

Word of mouth; poems featured on NPR's All things considered. edited and introduced by Catherine

Bowman. Random House 2003 xx, 182p pa $12
Grades: 11 12 Adult   **811**
    1. American poetry -- Collections
    ISBN 0-375-71315-8

LC 2002-28077
This collection includes works by 33 poets, such as Lucille Clifton, Kevin Young, C.D. Wright, Naomi Shihab Nye, Lucia Perillo, and Marilyn Chin
"These inspired selections . . . make for a fresh and enjoyable poetry anthology." Booklist

WritersCorps

Paint me like I am; teen poems from WritersCorps. HarperTempest 2003 128p hardcover o.p. pa $6.99
Grades: 7 8 9 10   **811**
    1. Teenagers' writings 2. American poetry -- Collections
    ISBN 0-06-029288-1; 0-06-447264-7 pa

LC 2002-5942
"The teen voices in these poems, collected from the WritersCorps youth program, are LOUD—raging, defiant, giddy, lusty, and hopeful. Grouped into arbitrary categories, the poems explore identity, creative expressions, family, neighborhood, drugs, and relationships. . . . A foreword from Nikki Giovanni rounds out this moving collection, which also includes a few thoughtful writing exercises." Booklist

812 American drama in English

Abbotson, Susan C. W.

Critical companion to Arthur Miller; a literary reference to his life and work. Facts on File 2006 518p il (Facts on File library of American literature) $75
Grades: 9 10 11 12 Adult   **812**
    1. Authors 2. Dramatists 3. Screenwriters
    ISBN 0-8160-6194-7; 978-0-8160-6194-5

LC 2006-22902
This book "covers Miller's entire canon, including plays, screenplays, fiction, short stories, and poetry, as well as many of his important essays and critical pieces. Also included are . . . entries on literary, theatrical, and personal figures important to Miller; key terms and topics connected to his work; and various theatrical companies and places with which he has been associated." Publisher's note
Includes bibliographical references

★ **Student** companion to Arthur Miller. Greenwood Press 2000 169p (Student companions to classic writers) lib bdg $35
Grades: 9 10 11 12   **812**
    1. Authors 2. Dramatists 3. Screenwriters
    ISBN 0-313-30949-3

LC 99-89069
A biographical section is followed by "discussion of eight of Miller's major plays that incorporates the impact of other literature and historical events on his work and links themes, language, and characters to events and periods in the writer's life. Chapters on each play address the develop-

ment of setting and plot, characters, and point of view; provide a historical context; and touch on other relevant literary devices. A bibliography of Miller's play and other works, as well as extensive listings of critical studies, reviews, and criticisms complete the text." SLJ

Includes bibliographical references

Albee, Edward

★ **Who's** afraid of Virginia Woolf? Scribner Classics 2003 243p $24

Grades: 11 12 Adult **812**

ISBN 0-7432-5525-9

LC 2003-54206

A reissue of the title first published 1962 by Atheneum Pubs.

Characters: 2 men, 2 women. 3 acts. First produced at the Billy Rose Theatre, New York City, October 13, 1962

"The play is a virulent unveiling of the relationship between George, a history professor, and his wife, Martha, the college president's daughter. Another couple, Nick and Honey, get caught in the crossfire of George and Martha's verbal and emotional lacerations, and it becomes clear that each character is engaged in an isolated struggle through a personal hell." Reader's Ency. 4th edition

Arthur Miller; edited with an introduction by Harold Bloom. New ed.; Chelsea House 2007 238p (Modern critical views) $45

Grades: 11 12 Adult **812**

1. Authors 2. Dramatists 3. Screenwriters

ISBN 978-0-7910-9549-2; 0-7910-9549-5

LC 2006-102701

First published 1987

A collection of critical essays focusing on the works of the author of Death of a salesman and The crucible.

Includes bibliographical references

Arthur Miller's Death of a salesman; edited and with an introduction by Harold Bloom. New ed; Bloom's Literary Criticism 2011 127p (Bloom's guides) $30

Grades: 9 10 11 12 **812**

1. Authors 2. Dramatists 3. Screenwriters

ISBN 978-1-60413-875-7; 1-60413-875-0

LC 2010027238

First published 2004

This collection "of critical excerpts about this . . . play includes an annotated bibliography of Miller's works, an index, and an introduction by literary critic Harold Bloom." Publisher's note

Includes bibliographical references

Arthur Miller's The crucible; edited & with an introduction by Harold Bloom. New ed; Bloom's Literary Criticism 2010 109p (Bloom's guides) $30

Grades: 9 10 11 12 **812**

1. Authors 2. Dramatists 3. Screenwriters

ISBN 978-1-60413-815-3

LC 2010-1312

First published 2004

Examines different aspects of Miller's classic play, with a biographical sketch of the author and critical essays on this work.

Includes bibliographical references

August Wilson; edited and with an introduction by Harold Bloom. Chelsea House 2009 192p (Modern critical views) $45

Grades: 9 10 11 12 **812**

1. Authors 2. Dramatists 3. Essayists 4. Theatrical directors

ISBN 978-1-60413-393-6

LC 2008-40762

This collection of critical essays explores the works of the author of Fences and The Piano Lesson.

Includes bibliographical references

Banach, Jennifer

Bloom's how to write about Tennessee Williams; introduction by Harold Bloom. Chelsea House 2009 248p (Bloom's how to write about literature) $45

Grades: 9 10 11 12 **812**

1. Authors 2. Novelists 3. Dramatists 4. Report writing 5. Short story writers

ISBN 978-1-60413-346-2

LC 2009-6653

This book offers paper topics and advice on writing an essay about the works of Tennessee Williams.

Includes bibliographical references

★ **Black** theatre USA; plays by African Americans, 1847 to today. edited by James V. Hatch, Ted Shine. rev and expanded ed; Free Press 1996 916p pa in 2v hardcover o.p. v1 pa $39.95; v2 pa $26

Grades: 11 12 Adult **812**

1. American drama -- African American authors -- Collections

ISBN 0-684-82306-3; 1-45163650-4 v1 pa; 0-684-82307-1 v2 pa

LC 95-40329

First published 1974

Among the plays are: Star of Ethiopia, by W. E. B. Du Bois; A soldier's play, by C. Fuller; Sally's rape, by R. Mc-Cauley; Contribution, by T. Shine; Fires in the mirror, by A. D. Smith.

Includes bibliographical references

Cervantes Saavedra, Miguel de

Man of La Mancha; a musical play. lyrics by Joe Darion; music by Mitch Leigh. Random House 1966 82p il hardcover o.p. pa $9.95

Grades: 11 12 Adult **812**

ISBN 0-394-40621-4; 0-394-40619-2 pa

Winner of the New York Drama Critics Circle award 'Best Musical 1966'

Characters: 14 men, 5 women, extras. First produced at the ANTA Washington Square Theatre, New York City, November 22, 1965

Children's Theatre Company (Minneapolis,

Minn.)

Fierce & true; plays for teen audiences. Peter & Elissa Adams, editors; The Children's Theatre Company. University of Minnesota Press 2010 219p il pa $17.95

Grades: 7 8 9 10 11 12 **812**

1. Drama -- Collections

ISBN 978-0-8166-7311-7; 0-8166-7311-X

The Children's Theatre Company "located in Minneapolis, wanted to broaden its audience, so it commissioned four playwrights to create works with young people (ages 12-18) specifically in mind. The results are the full-length plays in this anthology. . . . 'Anon(ymous)' is a contemporary retelling of Homer's Odyssey, set in a dirty North American city, and 'Five Fingers of Funk' is a mature musical celebrating the roots of hip-hop while dealing with issues of poverty and drugs. In 'The Lost Boys of Sudan,' three Dinka refugees flee the horrors of war and begin a harrowing yet humorous journey that takes them to Fargo, ND. And 'Prom' is played out as a frenetic battle between students and chaperones. Each of these selections has a distinctive voice, honoring adolescents as both actor and audience capable of understanding and engaging in today's complex issues." SLJ

Dabrowski, Kristen

Twenty 10-minute plays for teens. Smith & Kraus 2004 129p (Young actor series) pa $14.95

Grades: 9 10 11 12 **812**

1. Acting 2. One act plays

ISBN 1-57525-405-0

"These brief plays deal with typical adolescent concerns, including dating, parties, sports, and school life, as well as some more controversial topics like being gay, drinking, and suicide. There are roles for up to 14 females and 11 males, but the number of characters can easily be reduced or increased. . . . The content and language make the plays teen-friendly but more appropriate for older high school students, who will recognize the lingo and situations and will enjoy performing them." SLJ

Death of a salesman, by Arthur Miller; editor, Brenda Murphy. Salem Press 2010 285p (Critical insights) lib bdg $85

Grades: 9 10 11 12 **812**

1. Authors 2. Dramatists 3. Screenwriters

ISBN 978-1-58765-610-1; 1-58765-610-8

LC 2009-26317

"Contains an editor's introduction to the author or work, a perspective from the editors of the . . . literary magazine The Paris Review, and a biography of the author. Following these ready-reference chapters is a section, 'Critical Contexts,' that presents four original essays by current scholars." Publisher's note

Includes bibliographical references

Dowling, Robert M.

Critical companion to Eugene O'Neill; a literary reference to his life and work. Facts On File 2009 2v il (Facts on File library of American literature) set $150

Grades: 11 12 Adult **812**

1. Authors 2. Dramatists 3. Nobel laureates for literature

ISBN 978-0-8160-6675-9; 0-8160-6675-2

LC 2008-24135

"These volumes are wonderfully organized and very easy to use. . . . Entries are of a length to provide a good background of O'Neill's works and life." Booklist

Includes bibliographical references

Dunkleberger, Amy

★ A **student's** guide to Arthur Miller. Enslow Publs. 2005 160p il (Understanding literature) lib bdg $27.93

Grades: 7 8 9 10 **812**

1. Authors 2. Dramatists 3. Screenwriters

ISBN 0-7660-2432-6

This discusses the life of Arthur Miller and his works All My Sons, Death of a Salesman, The Crucible, A View From the Bridge, After the Fall, Incident at Vichy, and The Price

"Engaging and informative. . . . The very accessible format and the solid information make [this book] useful to students, and the engaging style should interest casual readers." SLJ

Includes glossary and bibliographical references

Ellis, Roger

Audition monologs for student actors {I}-{II} selections from contemporary plays. edited by Roger Ellis. Meriwether 1999 2v pa ea $15.95

Grades: 9 10 11 12 **812**

1. Acting 2. Monologues

ISBN 1-56608-055-X v1; 1-56608-073-8 v2

LC 99-37962

"An introduction discusses choosing and performing the monologues, including specific sections on characterization and staging. The selections are evenly divided between those for males and females, and many are for minority actors. Each selection is prefaced by thoughtful character insights and performance suggestions. An excellent, up-to-the-minute resource for serious teen actors." Booklist {review of volume 1}

Fairbanks, Stephanie S.

Spotlight; solo scenes for student actors. Meriwether 1996 115p pa $14.95

Grades: 9 10 11 12 **812**

1. Acting 2. Monologues

ISBN 1-56608-020-7

LC 96-6169

"Fifty five monologues that feature typical teenage concerns. They run an average of 55 lines each; require minimal props and costumes; and have numbered lines for easy directing and practicing." SLJ

Garner, Joan

Stagings; short scripts for middle and high school students. written and illustrated by Joan Garner. Teacher Ideas Press 1995 233p il pa $27

Grades: 9 10 11 12   **812**
1. Acting 2. One act plays
ISBN 1-56308-343-4

LC 95-19013

"This book presents nine science fiction and fantasy one-act plays for young people to perform. . . . Each script begins with a thorough description of characters and costumes, followed by a scene design, set description and a props list. Other notes describe how a teacher could use the play in the classroom and specifically discuss the best staging possibilities for the script." Book Rep

Gibson, William

★ The **miracle** worker. Scribner 2008 112p pa $12.99

Grades: 11 12 Adult   **812**
1. Deaf 2. Blind 3. Authors 4. Memoirists 5. Humanitarians 6. Teachers of the deaf 7. Inspirational writers 8. Teachers of the blind 9. Social welfare leaders
ISBN 978-1-4165-9084-2; 1-4165-9084-6

LC 2008-275273

First published 1957

A text of the television play, intended for reading, of Anne Sullivan Macy's attempts to teach her pupil, Helen Keller, to communicate.

"The present text is meant for reading, and differs from the telecast version in that I have restored some passages that read better than they play and others omitted in performance for simple lack of time." Author's note

Goodrich, Frances

The **diary** of Anne Frank; by Frances Goodrich and Albert Hackett; newly adapted by Wendy Kesselman. Dramatists Play Service 2000 70p il pa $7.50

Grades: 9 10 11 12 Adult   **812**
1. World War, 1939-1945 -- Jews -- Drama 2. Netherlands -- History -- 1940-1945, German occupation -- Drama
ISBN 0-8222-1718-X

LC 2006-455205

First published 1956 by Random House

Awarded the Pulitzer Prize and the New York Drama Critics Circle Award for 1956

Characters: 5 men, 5 women. 2 acts. First produced at the Cort Theatre, New York City, October 5, 1955.

★ **Great** scenes from minority playwrights; seventy-four scenes of cultural diversity. edited by Marsh Cassady. Meriwether 1997 341p pa $16.95

Grades: 9 10 11 12   **812**
1. Acting 2. Minorities in literature 3. American drama -- Collections
ISBN 1-56608-029-0

LC 97-298

A collection of scenes from Hispanic as well as Native-American, African-American, Jewish-American, and Asian-American theater

"Cassady introduces the plays and precedes each scene with questions intended to clarify characters' motivations or the playwright's intentions. Most plays concern the tragic aspects of prejudice, but two playwrights have chosen a sa-

tirical approach. A useful collection for drama classes and theater groups." Booklist

Gurney, A. R.

Love letters and two other plays: The golden age and What I did last summer; with an introduction by the playwright. Penguin Bks. 1990 209p pa $14

Grades: 11 12 Adult   **812**
1. American drama -- 20th century
ISBN 978-0-452-26501-1; 0-452-16501-0

LC 90-34177

Love letters dramatizes the 30-year epistolary "exchange between an upper-class man and an upper-upper-class woman. . . . The Golden Age is an updated, romantic-comic variation upon Henry James' Aspern Papers in which a young academic locates an old woman who may possess a missing chapter of The Great Gatsby and schemes to get it from her. What I did Last Summer is about 14-year-old Charlie's bohemian season with Anna, the Pig Woman, who fosters his creativity as she once did his mother's." Booklist

Hansberry, Lorraine

★ A **raisin** in the sun. Modern Lib. 1995 xxvi, 135p $14.95; pa $6.50

Grades: 11 12 Adult   **812**
ISBN 0-679-60172-4; 0-679-75533-0 pa

LC 95-16074

First published 1959

Awarded the New York Drama Critics Circle Award for the 1958-1959 season

Characters: 8 men, 3 women. 6 scenes in 3 acts. First produced at the Ethel Barrymore Theatre, New York City, March 11, 1959

"Hansberry's drama focuses on the Youngers, a 1950s African-American working-class family in Chicago striving to realize their individual dreams of prosperity and education, and their collective dream of a better life. It was the first play by an African-American woman to be produced on Broadway." Reader's Ency. 4th edition

Heintzelman, Greta

Critical companion to Tennessee Williams; [by] Greta Heintzelman, Alycia Smith Howard. Facts on File 2005 436p il (Facts on File library of American literature) $65; pa $19.95

Grades: 11 12 Adult   **812**
1. Authors 2. Novelists 3. Dramatists 4. Short story writers
ISBN 0-8160-4888-6; 0-8160-6429-6 pa

LC 2004-7362

The authors "offer an excellent resource for those studying Williams's life and extensive body of work." Choice

Includes bibliographical references

Hermann, Spring

A **student's** guide to Tennessee Williams. Enslow Publishers 2007 160p il (Understanding literature) lib bdg $27.93

Grades: 7 8 9 10   **812**
1. Authors 2. Novelists 3. Dramatists 4. Short story

writers

ISBN 978-0-7660-2706-0; 0-7660-2706-6

LC 2006-36458

"The life and work of Williams are examined. . . . Each work is placed in historical and biographical context, with special emphasis placed on curriculum-related works The Glass Menagerie, A Streetcar Named Desire, and Cat On a Hot Tin Roof, in addition to many other lesser-known works." Publisher's note

Includes glossary and bibliographical references

Hughes, Langston

Five plays; edited with an introduction by Webster Smalley. Indiana Univ. Press 1963 258p hardcover o.p. pa $14.95

Grades: 11 12 Adult   812

ISBN 0-253-32230-8; 0-253-20121-7 pa

Contents: Mulatto; Soul gone home; Little Ham; Simply heavenly; Tambourines to glory

Inge, William

4 plays. Grove Press 1979 304p pa $16

Grades: 11 12 Adult   812

ISBN 0-8021-3209-X

LC 78-73032

First published 1958 by Random House

The author was awarded the Pulitzer Prize, 1953, for Picnic

Krell-Oishi, Mary

Perspectives; relevant scenes for teens. Meriwether 1997 241p pa $14.95

Grades: 9 10 11 12   812

1. Acting 2. Teenagers -- Drama

ISBN 1-56608-030-4

LC 97-5405

Consists of 23 original scenes in a variety of styles for high school and college acting students

The scripts "vary in length and tone but have an equal number of male and female parts. Several scenes deal with sensitive subjects (premarital sex, abortion, homosexuality), but they are thoughtfully presented, and the occasional use of strong language is never gratuitous." Booklist

Kushner, Tony

Angels in America; a gay fantasia on national themes. 1st combined pbk. ed.; Theatre Communications Group 2003 289p pa $15.95

Grades: 11 12 Adult   812

1. Lawyers 2. Government officials

ISBN 1-55936-231-6

LC 2003-17904

Part one awarded the Pulitzer Prize, 1993

Millennium approaches first presented at the Eureka Theatre Company, San Francisco, May 1991. Perestroika first presented at the Mark Taper Forum, Los Angeles, November 1992.

Loos, Pamela

A **reader's** guide to Lorraine Hansberry's A raisin in the sun. Enslow Publishers 2008 128p il (Multicultural literature) lib bdg $31.93

Grades: 7 8 9 10   812

1. Authors 2. Dramatists 3. African Americans in literature 4. Essayists 5. Newspaper editors 6. Nonfiction writers 7. American drama -- History and criticism

ISBN 978-0-7660-2830-2; 0-7660-2830-5

LC 2006-17900

"A Raisin in the Sun has become part of the literary canon and is required reading for many students. This guide is intended to help them better appreciate the social milieu out of which this play emerged . . . making this volume a fine resource." SLJ

Includes bibliographical references

Lorraine Hansberry's A raisin in the sun; edited & with an introduction by Harold Bloom. Chelsea House 2008 174p (Bloom's guides) $30

Grades: 9 10 11 12   812

1. Authors 2. Dramatists 3. Essayists 4. Newspaper editors 5. Nonfiction writers

ISBN 978-1-60413-202-1

LC 2008-33184

This study guide on Hansberry's classic play includes a brief biographical sketch, a list of characters, a summary and analysis, and selections from critical essays by different scholars about the work.

Includes bibliographical references

McCullers, Carson

★ The **member** of the wedding; a play. an introduction by Dorothy Allison. New Directions 2006 118p pa $11.95

Grades: 11 12 Adult   812

ISBN 0-8112-1655-1; 978-0-8112-1655-5

LC 2005-36493

First published 1951

Awarded the New York Drama Critics Circle Award for 1950

Characters: 6 men, 7 women. 3 acts with 3 scenes in the last act. First produced at the Empire Theatre, New York City, January 3, 1950

Based on the author's book of the same title, this is "a study of the loneliness of an overimaginative young Georgian girl." Saturday Rev

McNally, Terrence

★ **15** short plays. Smith & Kraus 1994 373p (Contemporary playwrights series) pa $16.95

Grades: 11 12 Adult   812

ISBN 1-880399-34-2

LC 94-10070

"By providing a sampling of McNally's plays from the late 1960s to the early 1990s, the entire span of his career, this volume allows a great deal of insight into the range and depth of his development as he courses his way through some of the social, political, and sexual forces that have shaped the American temperament. . . . This is a splendid collection and these plays cut to the emotional bone." Voice Youth Advocates

Medoff, Mark Howard

Children of a lesser god; by Mark Medoff. Dramatists Play Service 1998 87p pa $7.50

Grades: 11 12 Adult   812
    1. Deaf -- Drama
    ISBN 0-8222-0203-4

LC 81-132181

Characters: 3 men, 4 women. 2 acts. First produced at the Longacre Theatre, New York City, March 30, 1980

"The sensitive drama of the love and growth of James Leeds, a speech teacher at a state school for the deaf, and Sarah Norman, one of his students, may lack some impact in reading since the effect of Sarah's isolation and skilled signing is lost, but Medoff's story remains a powerful, valuable one." Booklist

Includes bibliographical references

Miller, Arthur

The **crucible**; a play in four acts. Viking 1953 145p hardcover o.p. pa $12

Grades: 11 12 Adult   812
    1. Witchcraft -- Drama 2. Salem (Mass.) -- Drama
    ISBN 0-14-048138-9 pa

Characters: 11 men, 10 women. First produced at the Martin Beck Theatre in New York City, January 22, 1953

★ **Death** of a salesman; certain private conversations in two acts and a requiem. with an introduction by Christopher Bigsby. Penguin 1998 xxvii, 113p (Penguin twentieth-century classics) pa $12

Grades: 11 12 Adult   812
    ISBN 0-14-118097-8

LC 97-37223

First published 1949

Winner of the New York Drama Critics Circle Award and the Pulitzer Prize, 1949

Characters: 8 men, 5 women. First produced at the Morosco Theatre, New York City, February 10, 1949.

"The tragedy of a typical Americana salesman who at the age of sixty-three is faced with what he cannot face: defeat and disillusionment. It is a bitter and moving experience of groping for values and for material success." Wis Libr Bull

Includes bibliographical references

★ The **portable** Arthur Miller; original introduction by Harold Clurman; revised edition edited with an introduction by Christopher Bigsby. Penguin Books 2003 xli, 575p (Penguin classics) pa $17

Grades: 11 12 Adult   812
    ISBN 0-14-243755-7

LC 2003-276344

First published 1955

This volume contains the complete texts of Death of a salesman, The crucible, After the fall, The American clock, The last Yankee, and Broken glass. An excerpt from a radio play thought lost for years and two very brief selections from the memoir Timebends are also included.

Includes bibliographical references

O'Neill, Eugene

The **iceman** cometh; a play. Vintage Bks. 1946 260p pa $12

Grades: 11 12 Adult   812
    ISBN 0-375-70917-7

Characters: 16 men, 3 women. First produced at the Martin Beck Theatre, New York City, October 9, 1946

Long day's journey into night; a play. with a foreword by Harold Bloom. 2nd ed; Yale Univ. Press 2002 179p $22.95; pa $12.95

Grades: 11 12 Adult   812
    ISBN 0-300-09410-8; 0-300-09305-5 pa

LC 2001-97735

First published 1956

Awarded the Pulitzer Prize, 1957

Characters: 3 men, 2 women. 4 acts, 5 scenes. First produced in Stockholm, Sweden, February, 1956

"Among the papers Eugene O'Neill left when he died in 1953 was the manuscript of an autobiography. Not an autobiography in the usual sense, however. For 'Long Day's Journey Into Night' is in the form of a play—a true O'Neill tragedy, set in 1912 in the summer home of a theatrical family that is isolated from the community by a kind of ingrown misery and a sense of doom." N Y Times Book Rev

Rose, Reginald

Twelve angry men; introduction by David Mamet. Penguin Books 2006 73p (Penguin classics) pa $11

Grades: 9 10 11 12 Adult   812
    ISBN 0-14-310440-3; 978-0-14-310440-7

LC 2006-46006

First published 1955 by Dramatic Pub.

Characters: 12 men. 3 acts. Original television broadcast on CBS program Studio One, September 20, 1954.

Shange, Ntozake

★ **For** colored girls who have considered suicide, when the rainbow is enuf; a choreopoem. 1st Scribner trade pbk. ed.; Scribner 2010 96p il $23; pa $12; ebook $15.99

Grades: 11 12 Adult   812
    1. African American women -- Drama
    ISBN 978-1-4516-2420-5; 1-4516-2420-4; 978-1-4391-8681-7 pa; 1-4391-8681-2 pa; 978-1-4516-2415-1 ebook

LC 2011381105

First published 1977 by Macmillan

Choreopoem performed by seven women exploring the joys and sorrows of being a black woman. Includes two new poems and a reading group guide.

Simon, Neil

★ **Brighton** Beach memoirs. Plume 1995 130p pa $12

Grades: 11 12 Adult   812
    ISBN 0-452-27528-8

LC 95-21788

First published 1984 by Random House

Awarded the New York Drama Critics Circle Award for best play, 1983

"Sex and baseball are the primary preoccupations of 15-year-old Eugene Jerome, narrator of a seriocomic slice of lower-middle-class Jewish family life in Depression-era New York City. The several adolescent characters in the extended family add to the teenage appeal of Simon's . . . play." Booklist

★ The **collected** plays of Neil Simon; with an introduction by Neil Simon. New Am. Lib. 1986 4v v1-2 pa ea $19.95

Grades: 9 10 11 12 **812**
ISBN 0-452-25870-7 v1; 0-452-26358-1 v2
LC 86-12639

Lost in Yonkers. Plume 1993 120p (Plume drama) pa $12

Grades: 11 12 Adult **812**
ISBN 0-452-26883-4
LC 92-29111

First published 1991 by Random House
Awarded the Pulitzer Prize, 1991

Characters: 4 men, 3 women. 2 acts. First presented at the Stevens Center for the Performing Arts, Winston-Salem, December 31, 1990.

This play, "set in 1940s New York, is a sad-funny portrait of a dysfunctional family, headed by a woman who provided for her children but never showed them love." Booklist

Soto, Gary

★ **Novio** boy; a play. Harcourt 2006 78p pa $5.95

Grades: 7 8 9 10 **812**
1. Mexican Americans -- Drama 2. Dating (Social customs) -- Drama
ISBN 978-0-15-205863-0; 0-15-205863-X
LC 2007-271308

First published 1997

Rudy anxiously prepares for and then goes out on a first date with an attractive girl who is older than he is.

Stuyvesant High School (New York, N.Y.)

With their eyes; September 11th: the view from a high school at ground zero. edited by Annie Thoms; created by Taresh Batra [et. al.]; photos by Ethan Moses. HarperTempest 2002 228p il hardcover o.p. pa $6.99

Grades: 7 8 9 10 **812**
1. Teenagers' writings 2. American drama -- Collections 3. Stuyvesant High School (New York, N.Y.) 4. September 11 terrorist attacks, 2001 -- Drama
ISBN 0-06-051806-5; 0-06-051718-2 pa
LC 2002-4552

"The speakers reveal their emotions with painful honesty. . . . The book is an obvious choice for reader's theater and for use across the curriculum; its deeply affecting contents will also make compelling personal-interest reading." Booklist

Surface, Mary Hall

Most valuable player and four other all-star plays for middle and high school audiences. Smith & Kraus 1999 176p il (Young actor series) pa $16.95

Grades: 9 10 11 12 **812**
1. Children's plays, American
ISBN 1-57525-178-7
LC 99-30018

"The title play is a compelling piece about Jackie Robinson's early days in the major leagues. The other selections deal with Mozart's childhood and issues such as high school drug dealing, racial conflict, learning disability, and the need for artistic expression. They all move along at a fast clip, the characters speak simply and directly, and the language is realistic and occasionally rough. In most cases, the staging is fairly simple." SLJ

Tennessee Williams; edited and with an introduction by Harold Bloom. Chelsea House 2002 138p (Bloom's biocritiques) lib bdg $25.95

Grades: 9 10 11 12 **812**
1. Authors 2. Novelists 3. Dramatists 4. Short story writers
ISBN 0-7910-6185-X
LC 2002-14665

Critics assess the works of the influential southern dramatist. The volume includes a biographical essay and a chronology of Williams' life

Includes bibliographical references

The **Tennessee** Williams encyclopedia; edited by Philip C. Kolin. Greenwood Press 2004 xxx, 350p $89.95

Grades: 11 12 Adult **812**
1. Authors 2. Novelists 3. Dramatists 4. Short story writers
ISBN 0-313-32101-9
LC 2003-59583

The contributors "provide approximately 160 entries on individuals, places, works, and concepts of special significance in Williams's life and career. Entries are alphabetical. . . . This reviewer cannot imagine a more engaging or more useful reference resource for students and scholars of Williams." Choice

Includes bibliographical references

Tennessee Williams's A streetcar named desire; edited and with an introduction by Harold Bloom. New ed.; Chelsea House 2009 180p (Modern critical interpretations) $45

Grades: 11 12 Adult **812**
1. Authors 2. Novelists 3. Dramatists 4. Short story writers
ISBN 978-1-60413-389-9
LC 2008-49231

First published 1988

A collection of critical essays on Williams's play "A Streetcar Named Desire" arranged in chronological order of publication.

Includes bibliographical references

Tennessee Williams's The glass menagerie; edited & with an introduction by Harold Bloom. Chelsea House Publishers 2007 113p (Bloom's guides) $30

Grades: 9 10 11 12   **812**

1. Authors 2. Novelists 3. Dramatists 4. Short story writers

ISBN 0-7910-9297-6; 978-0-7910-9297-2

LC 2006-25341

This study guide on Tennessee Williams' classic play includes a brief biographical sketch of Williams, a list of characters, a summary and analysis, and selections from critical essays by different scholars about the work.

Williams' play "is analyzed in depth, scene by scene. . . An outstanding addition to high school libraries." Voice Youth Advocates

Includes bibliographical references

Ullom, Shirley

Tough acts to follow; seventy-five monologs for teens. Meriwether 2000 155p pa $14.95

Grades: 9 10 11 12   **812**

1. Acting 2. Monologues

ISBN 1-56608-057-6

LC 00-24678

This collection of original short character sketches "is overflowing with one-of-a kind monologues of equal length for both guys and girls, each with a clever title that provides quick insight into the subject matter." Voice Youth Advocates

Under 30; plays for a new generation. edited by Eric Lane and Nina Shengold. Vintage 2004 639p pa $17

Grades: 9 10 11 12   **812**

1. One act plays 2. American drama -- Collections

ISBN 1-4000-7616-1

LC 2004043041

"This collection offers thespians plenty of characters to portray in situations that crackle with teen appeal." SLJ

Wasserstein, Wendy

The **Heidi** chronicles and other plays. Vintage Bks. 1991 249p pa $13.95

Grades: 11 12 Adult   **812**

ISBN 0-679-73499-6

LC 90-55681

First published 1990 by Harcourt Brace Jovanovich

This collection traces "three decades of changing styles, mores, life objectives, and intellectual challenges. Wasserstein examines her characters and their times with great good humor, complexity, depth of feeling, and a firm refusal to accept trite and easy images." Libr J

Wilder, Thornton

Our town; a play in three acts. foreword by Donald Margulies. HarperCollins Pubs. 2003 xx, 181p $19.95; pa $9.95

Grades: 11 12 Adult   **812**

ISBN 0-06-053525-3; 0-06-051263-6 pa

A reissue with a new foreword of the title first published 1938 by Coward-McCann

Large mixed cast. First produced at McCarter's Theatre, Princeton, N.J., January 22, 1938.

"Presented without scenery of any kind, utilizing a narrator and loose episodic form, adventurous and imaginative in style, this unique play . . . is one of the most distinguished in the modern repertoire. It deals with the simplest and most touching aspects of life in a small town." HarperCollins Reader's Ency of Am Lit

★ **Three** plays: Our town, The skin of our teeth, The matchmaker; with a preface. Harper & Row 1957 401p hardcover o.p. pa $15.95

Grades: 11 12 Adult   **812**

ISBN 0-06-051264-4 pa

A collection of three titles first copyrighted 1938, 1942, and 1955 respectively. An earlier version of: The matchmaker, was first copyrighted 1939 with title: The merchant of Yonkers

Wilder was awarded the Pulitzer Prize, 1938 for Our town, and 1943 for The skin of our teeth

Our town is a portrait of family life in small town America. The skin of our teeth is an allegorical fantasy about man's struggle to survive. The matchmaker is a romantic farce set in the 1880's

Williams, Tennessee

★ The **glass** menagerie; introduction by Robert Bray. New Directions 1999 xxii, 105p pa $7.95

Grades: 9 10 11 12   **812**

ISBN 0-8112-1404-4

LC 98-54624

First published 1945 by Random House; this reissue of New Directions 1949 edition contains Williams' essay The catastrophe of success and production notes. A new critical introduction has been added

Awarded the New York Drama Critics Circle Award for 1945

Characters: 2 men, 2 women. 2 parts. One set of scenery. First produced at the Civic Theatre, Chicago, December 26, 1944

"A poignant and painful family drama set in St. Louis, in which a frigid and frustrated mother's dreams of her glamorous past as a Southern belle conflict with the grimness of her reduced circumstances, as she persuades her rebellious son Tom to provide a 'gentleman caller' for her crippled daughter, Laura." Oxford Companion to Engl Lit. 6th edition

A **streetcar** named desire; with an introduction by Arthur Miller. New Directions 2004 192p pa $9.95

Grades: 11 12 Adult   **812**

ISBN 0-8112-1602-0

LC 2004-11654

First published 1947

Characters: 6 women, 7 men. 11 scenes. First produced at the Barrymore Theatre, New York City, December 3, 1947

"A study of sexual frustration, violence, and aberration, set in New Orleans, in which Blanche Dubois' fantasies of refinement and grandeur are brutally destroyed by her brother-in-law, Stanley Kowalski, whose animal nature fascinates and repels her." Oxford Companion to Engl Lit. 5th edition

Wilson, August

★ **Fences**; a play. introduction by Lloyd Richards. New Am. Lib. 1986 101p pa $12

Grades: 11 12 Adult   **812**

ISBN 978-0-452-26401-4

LC 86-5264

Awarded the Pulitzer Prize, 1987

Characters: 5 men, 1 woman, 1 girl. 2 acts, 9 scenes. First produced at the Yale Repertory Theatre, New Haven, Connecticut, April 30, 1985

Jitney. Overlook Press 2001 96p hardcover o.p. pa $14.95

Grades: 11 12 Adult   **812**

ISBN 978-158567-370-4; 1-58567-370-6

LC 2001-33962

Winner of the New York Drama Critics Circle Award, 2000

Characters: 8 men, 1 woman. 2 acts, 8 scenes. This is a revised version of a play written 1979

Joe Turner's come and gone; a play in two acts. New Am. Lib. 1988 94p pa $12

Grades: 11 12 Adult   **812**

ISBN 978-0-452-26009-2; 0-452-26009-4

LC 88-1660

Characters: 6 men, 5 women. 2 acts, 10 scenes. 1 setting. First produced at the Yale Repertory Theatre, New Haven, Connecticut, April 29, 1986

Ma Rainey's black bottom; a play in two acts. New Am. Lib. 1985 111p pa $12

Grades: 11 12 Adult   **812**

ISBN 978-0-452-26113-6; 0-452-26113-9

LC 84-27156

Characters: 8 men, 2 women. 2 acts. First produced at the Yale Repertory Theatre, New Haven, Connecticut, April 6, 1984

★ The **piano** lesson. New Am. Lib. 1990 108p hardcover o.p. pa $12

Grades: 11 12 Adult   **812**

ISBN 978-0-452-26534-9; 0-452-26534-7

LC 90-38734

Awarded the Pulitzer Prize and the New York Drama Critics Circle Award, 1990

Characters: 5 men, 3 women. 2 acts, 7 scenes. First presented at the Yale Repertory Theatre, New Haven, November 26, 1987

Zindel, Paul

★ The **effect** of gamma rays on man-in-the-moon marigolds; a drama in two acts. drawings by Dong Kingman. Harper & Row 1971 108p il hardcover o.p. pa $6.99

Grades: 11 12 Adult   **812**

ISBN 0-06-075738-8 pa

ALA YALSA Margaret A. Edwards Award (2002)

Characters: 5 women. First produced at the Mercer-O'Casey Theatre, New York City, April 7, 1970

"The play, in the naturalistic tradition, deals with a widow and her two daughters, the imagination of one of whom has been captured by the atom and the possibilities it offers of producing mutations." McGraw-Hill Ency of World Drama

813   American fiction in English

Alexie, Sherman

★ **Ten** little Indians; stories. Grove Press 2003 243p hardcover o.p. pa $13

Grades: 11 12 Adult   **813**

1. Short stories 2. Native Americans -- Fiction

ISBN 0-8021-1744-9; 0-8021-4117-X pa

LC 2003-44832

"These short stories feature Spokane Indians from many urban walks of life. Alexie's characters include a student, a lawyer, a basketball player, and a feminist mother; their stories might be angry, tragic, humorous, or ironic—but they are all believable, and irresistibly engaging." SLJ

Alice Walker; edited and with an introduction by Harold Bloom. New edition; Bloom's Literary Criticism; an imprint of Infobase Publishing 2007 223p (Modern critical views) $45

Grades: 11 12 Adult   **813**

1. Poets 2. Authors 3. Novelists 4. Editors 5. Essayists 6. College teachers 7. Short story writers

ISBN 978-0-7910-9611-6

First published 1989

A collection of critical essays discussing the work of The Color Purple author Alice Walker.

Includes bibliographical references

Alice Walker's The color purple; edited and with an introduction by Harold Bloom. New ed.; Bloom's Literary Criticism 2008 191p (Modern critical interpretations) $45

Grades: 9 10 11 12 Adult   **813**

1. Poets 2. Authors 3. Novelists 4. Editors 5. Essayists 6. College teachers 7. Short story writers

ISBN 978-0-7910-9614-7; 0-7910-9614-9

LC 2008-2775

First published 2000

A collection of ten essays providing international appraisal and interpretation of Walker's novel.

Includes bibliographical references

Am I blue? coming out from the silence. edited by Marion Dane Bauer. HarperCollins Pubs. 1994 273p hardcover o.p. pa $7.99

Grades: 9 10 11 12   **813**

1. Short stories 2. Homosexuality -- Fiction

ISBN 0-06-024253-1; 0-06-440587-7 pa

LC 93-29574

This "collection includes stories by Bruce Coville, Lois Lowry, Jane Yolen, Nancy Garden, and others. While all the pieces center on themes of coming to terms with homosexuality, they also are stories of love, coming of age, adventure, and self-discovery. A powerful commentary about our social and emotional responses to homosexuality and our human need for love and acceptance." Horn Book Guide

Amy Tan; critical essays. edited and with an introduction by Harold Bloom. New ed; Bloom's Literary Criticism 2008 205p (Modern critical views) $45

Grades: 9 10 11 12   **813**
1. Authors 2. Novelists 3. Essayists 4. Children's authors 5. Short story writers
ISBN 978-1-60413-179-6

LC 2008-28039

First published 2000
Analytical essays explore the work of the Chinese American author whose fiction has achieved both critical and popular success.
Includes bibliographical references

Amy Tan's The Joy Luck Club; edited and with an introduction by Harold Bloom. Chelsea House Publishers 2001 223p (Modern critical interpretations) $45

Grades: 9 10 11 12 Adult   **813**
1. Authors 2. Novelists 3. Essayists 4. Children's authors 5. Short story writers
ISBN 0-7910-6338-0

LC 2001-47496

A collection of critical essays on the novel about Chinese American women.
Includes bibliographical references

Becnel, Kim E.
Bloom's how to write about F. Scott Fitzgerald; [introduction by Harold Bloom] Chelsea House 2008 232p (Bloom's how to write about literature) $45

Grades: 9 10 11 12   **813**
1. Authors 2. Novelists 3. Report writing 4. Screenwriters 5. Short story writers
ISBN 978-0-7910-9482-2

LC 2006-101321

This book offers "paper-topic suggestions, . . . strategies on how to write a strong essay, and an . . . introduction by Harold Bloom on writing about Fitzgerald. This . . . volume is designed to help students develop their analytical writing skills and critical comprehension of this modern master and his major works." Publisher's note
Includes bibliographical references

Blasingame, James B.
★ **Gary** Paulsen. Greenwood Press 2007 164p (Teen reads: student companions to young adult literature) $45

Grades: 7 8 9 10 11 12   **813**
1. Authors 2. Sled dog racers 3. Children's authors 4. Short story writers 5. Young adult authors
ISBN 978-0-313-33532-7; 0-313-33532-X

LC 2007-21446

"This volume examines a sample of . . . books by Paulsen. A biographical chapter demonstrates how Paulsen's life experiences, notably the Iditarod, have influenced his writing. Each book is analyzed for plot, characterization, setting, and themes." Publisher's note
Includes bibliographical references

Bloom, Harold
Herman Melville's Moby-Dick; edited and with an introduction by Harold Bloom. Updated ed; Chelsea House 2007 246p (Modern critical interpretations) $45

Grades: 9 10 11 12 Adult   **813**
1. Authors 2. Novelists
ISBN 0-7910-9363-8; 978-0-7910-9363-4

LC 2006-31155

First published 1986
A collection of eight critical essays on Melville's novel "Moby Dick" arranged in chronological order of publication.
Includes bibliographical references

Brothers, Meagan
Weird Girl and What's His Name; Meagan Brothers. Three Rooms Press 2015 336 p. $16.95

Grades: 9 10 11 12   **813**
1. LGBT youth 2. Friendship -- Fiction 3. Teenagers -- Sexual behavior -- Fiction
ISBN 1941110274; 9781941110270

LC 2015935226

In this novel by Meagan Brothers "Rory and Lulu share an affinity for all things geek. When Lulu discovers that underage Rory had an explicit relationship with his divorced boss and hid it from Lulu because of her crush on him, she begins to question her own sexual orientation. After she is rebuffed by her favorite teacher, Lulu decides to hunt down the skeletons in her family's closet." (School Library Journal)
"Recommended for fans of realistic fiction with relationship drama and an LGBTQ focus." SLJ

Buckwalter, Stephanie
A **student's** guide to Jack London. Enslow Publishers 2007 160p il (Understanding literature) lib bdg $27.93

Grades: 7 8 9 10   **813**
1. Authors 2. Novelists 3. Short story writers
ISBN 978-0-7660-2707-7; 0-7660-2707-4

LC 2006-32815

"The career of this literary giant is examined. . . . Each of his works is placed in historical and biographical context, with special emphasis placed on curriculum-related works. These include The Call of the Wild, White Fang, and several other autobiographical works and short stories." Publisher's note
Includes glossary and bibliographical references

Burkhead, Cynthia
★ **Student** companion to John Steinbeck. Greenwood Press 2002 180p (Student companions to classic writers) lib bdg $35.95

Grades: 9 10 11 12   **813**
1. Authors 2. Novelists 3. Screenwriters 4. Nobel laureates for literature
ISBN 0-313-31457-8

LC 2002-17134

"Examines the life, career, and works of John Steinbeck. . . . Each criticism explores plot and character development, major themes, symbolism, and literary devices. An alternative critical theme is also included. . . . Because

Steinbeck is required reading in many high school curriculums, this would be a valuable resource for students." Libr Media Connect

Includes bibliographical references

Burton, Zisca

Bloom's how to write about Toni Morrison; [by] Zisca Isabel Burton; [introduction by Harold Bloom] Chelsea House 2008 212p (Bloom's how to write about literature) $45

Grades: 9 10 11 12   **813**
1. Authors 2. Novelists 3. Dramatists 4. Report writing 5. Essayists 6. College teachers 7. Literary critics 8. Nobel laureates for literature
ISBN 978-0-7910-9548-5

LC 2007-8096

This book offers "paper-topic suggestions, . . . strategies on how to write a strong essay, and an . . . introduction by Harold Bloom on writing about Morrison. This . . . volume is designed to help students develop their analytical writing skills and critical comprehension of this important author and her works." Publisher's note

Includes bibliographical references

Campbell, Patricia J.

Robert Cormier; daring to disturb the universe. Delacorte Press 2006 287p pa $41.95; lib bdg $17.99

Grades: 9 10 11 12   **813**
1. Authors 2. Novelists 3. Young adult authors
ISBN 0-385-73046-2 pa; 978-0-385-73046-4 pa; 0-385-90074-0 lib bdg; 978-0-385-90074-4 lib bdg

LC 2005-23595

"Campbell treats . . . [Cormier's] fans to rare glimpses of his process, and, with her wide perspective on YA literature, puts Cormier's work—including such landmark novels as The Chocolate War and I Am the Cheese—and its widereaching reverberations in a context for today's readers and writers." Publ Wkly

Includes bibliographical references

★ Carson McCullers; edited and with an introduction by Harold Bloom. New ed; Chelsea House 2009 192p (Modern critical views) $45

Grades: 9 10 11 12   **813**
1. Authors 2. Novelists 3. Dramatists 4. Short story writers
ISBN 978-1-60413-394-3

LC 2008-38918

First published 1986

Scholars evaluate the author of The ballad of the sad cafe, The heart is a lonely hunter, and The member of the wedding.

Includes bibliographical references

Cart, Michael

The **heart** has its reasons; young adult literature with gay/lesbian/queer content, 1969-2004. [by] Michael Cart [and] Christine A. Jenkins. Scarecrow Press 2006 207p (Scarecrow studies in young adult literature) $42

Grades: Adult Professional   **813**
1. Homosexuality in literature 2. Teenagers -- Books and reading 3. Young adult literature -- History and criticism
ISBN 0-8108-5071-0

LC 2005-31320

"Both a comprehensive overview and a lively, detailed discussion of individual landmark books, this highly readable title . . . discusses 35 years of YA books with gay, lesbian, bisexual, transgender, and queer/questioning (GLBTQ) content. . . . With fully annotated bibliographies, including a chronological list, this is a valuable YA and adult resource, sure to be in great demand for personal reference and group discussion." Booklist

Includes bibliographical references

A **Century** of great Western stories; edited by John Jakes. Forge 2000 525p hardcover o.p. pa $18.95

Grades: 11 12 Adult   **813**
1. Short stories 2. Western stories
ISBN 0-312-86986-X; 0-312-86985-1 pa

LC 99-462096

This anthology of 30 short stories includes pieces by such writers as Owen Wister, Zane Grey, Max Brand, Bill Pronzini, Elmer Kelton and Marcia Muller.

"Romance, murder, action, mystery and suspense are mixed with hefty doses of moral dilemma, guilt and redemption in these carefully plotted tales. . . . Many of the stories are appearing here for the first time since they were published in the pulps of the '30s, '40s and '50s, but their appeal is as fresh as ever." Publ Wkly

Includes bibliographical references

Chaim Potok's The chosen; edited & with an introduction by Harold Bloom. Chelsea House Publishers 2004 133p (Bloom's guides) $30

Grades: 9 10 11 12   **813**
1. Authors 2. Novelists 3. Historians 4. Nonfiction writers
ISBN 0-7910-8173-7; 978-0-7910-8173-0

LC 2004-13704

This study guide on Potok's novel about Jewish life in America includes a brief biographical sketch of Potok, a list of characters, a summary and analysis, and selections from critical essays by different scholars about the work.

Includes bibliographical references

★ The **Columbia** companion to the twentieth-century American short story; Blanche H. Gelfant, editor. Columbia Univ. Press 2000 660p $83.50; pa $24.50

Grades: 11 12 Adult   **813**
1. Reference books 2. American fiction -- Bio-bibliography 3. Short stories -- History and criticism 4. American fiction -- History and criticism
ISBN 0-231-11098-7; 0-231-11099-5 pa

LC 00-31610

"The first 100 pages are devoted to thematic essays that focus on the form of the short story, the development of the genre, several distinct subject types (e.g., short stories of the Holocaust or of the working class), and four different ethnic groups (African American, Asian American, Chicano Latino American, and Native American). . . . The remainder of the book is devoted to over 100 individual author essays that focus on reading for pleasure and understanding rather than critical interpretation. Entries discuss the development of each author and the content and meaning of his or her major short stories." Libr J

Includes bibliographical references

★ **Coming** of age in America; a multicultural anthology. edited by Mary Frosch; foreword by Gary Soto. New Press (NY) 1994 274p hardcover o.p. pa $14.95
Grades: 11 12 Adult   813
1. Short stories
ISBN 1-56584-146-8; 1-56584-147-6 pa
                                         LC 93-46921
This collection consists of sixteen short stories and excerpts from five novels, written by noted authors from a variety of ethnic backgrounds. Among the authors represented are Dorothy Allison, Cynthia Kadohata, Julia Alvarez, Frank Chin, Tobias Wolff, and Chaim Potok.

Cormac McCarthy; edited and with an introduction by Harold Bloom. New ed; Chelsea House 2009 216p (Modern critical views) $45
Grades: 10 11 12   813
1. Authors 2. Novelists
ISBN 978-1-60413-395-0
                                         LC 2008-40110
First published 2002
A selection of critical essays explore the works of the author of The road, All the pretty horses, and No country for old men.
Includes bibliographical references

Crane, Stephen, 1871-1900
★ **Prose** and poetry. Library of Am. 1984 1379p $40; pa $15.95
Grades: 11 12 Adult   813
1. Short stories
ISBN 0-940450-17-8; 1-883011-39-6 pa
                                         LC 83-19908
"This collection also includes both Crane's collections of epigrammatic free verses—'The Black Riders' and 'War is kind'—and selections from his uncollected poems." Publisher's note

Crayton, Lisa A.
★ **A student's** guide to Toni Morrison. Enslow Publs. 2006 160p il (Understanding literature) lib bdg $27.93
Grades: 7 8 9 10   813
1. Authors 2. Novelists 3. Dramatists 4. Essayists 5. College teachers 6. Literary critics 7. Nobel laureates for literature
ISBN 0-7660-2436-9
                                         LC 2005-19069
"Each work is placed in historical and biographical context, with special emphasis placed on curriculum-related material, including The Bluest Eye, Song of Solomon, and

Beloved, along with several other noteworthy works." Publisher's note

Includes glossary and bibliographical references

Crew, Hilary S.
Experiencing America's story through fiction; historical novels for grades 7-12. Hilary Crew. ALA Editions, An imprint of the American Library Association 2014 xii, 193 p.p (paper) $57
Grades: Professional   813
1. Library science 2. American fiction -- Bibliography 3. Historical fiction -- Bibliography 4. Historical fiction, American 5. Historical fiction, American -- Bibliography 6. Young adult fiction, American -- Bibliography 7. United States -- In literature -- Bibliography 8. Teenagers -- Books and reading -- United States 9. United States -- History -- Fiction -- Bibliography
ISBN 0838912257; 9780838912256
                                         LC 2014008471
This annotated bibliography by Hillary Susan Crew "highlights more than 150 titles of historical fiction published since 2000 appropriate for seventh to twelfth graders." (Publisher's note)
"Historical fiction is a popular and effective way to connect literature to curriculum. Although the new Common Core Curriculum emphasizes informational texts, fiction can introduce different viewpoints and provide unique opportunities for evaluation and critical thinking. This book seeks to help history teachers and school and public librarians discover new historical fiction (most of the titles included were published between 2000 and 2013) and find ways to effectively use these titles to support their curriculum...The selection of books embodies a multitude of perspectives and truly represents the diversity of the United States. This outstanding bibliography is perfect for teachers, librarians, or history fans searching for just the right book." Horn Book
Includes bibliographical references (pages 183-185) and index

Diorio, Mary Ann L.
★ **A student's** guide to Herman Melville. Enslow Publs. 2006 160p il (Understanding literature) lib bdg $27.93
Grades: 7 8 9 10   813
1. Authors 2. Novelists
ISBN 0-7660-2435-0
                                         LC 2005-10159
"Each work is placed in historical and biographical context, with special emphasis placed on curriculum-related works, including his masterpiece, Moby Dick, along with Billy Budd, several of his short stories, including 'Bartleby the Scrivener,' and several of his poetic works." Publisher's note
Includes glossary and bibliographical references

Don, Katherine
Real courage; the story of Harper Lee. by Katherine Don. Morgan Reynolds Pub. 2013 128 p. ill. (some col.) $28.95
Grades: 7 8 9 10   813
1. Women -- Biography 2. American authors --

Biography
ISBN 9781599353487; 9781599353494

LC 2012016871

This book examines author Nelle Harper Lee and "the publication and film adaptation of her novel 'To Kill a Mockingbird.'" The book looks at "the turbulent 1960's civil rights movement and how Lee's book, which spoke of racial injustice, struck a nerve with the public. Lee grew up in a small Mississippi town that experienced segregation, which she later used as the fictional setting for 'Mockingbird.' The biography describes Lee's rise to fame and the legacy she left." (Voice of Youth Advocates)

"Students and teachers looking for a solid, accessible biography will find this to be a fine choice as the writing is straightforward and engaging." SLJ
Includes bibliographical references and index

Edgar Allan Poe's The tell-tale heart and other stories; edited and with an introduction by Harold Bloom. New ed; Chelsea House 2009 212p (Modern critical interpretations) $45
Grades: 9 10 11 12 **813**
1. Poets 2. Authors 3. Essayists 4. Short story writers
ISBN 978-1-60413-388-2

LC 2008-54307

First published 1987 with title: The Tales of Poe
A collection of critical essays on Poe's tales of horror arranged in chronological order of publication.
Includes bibliographical references

Ernest Hemingway; edited and with an introduction by Harold Bloom. New ed.; Bloom's Literary Criticism 2011 205p (Modern critical views) $45
Grades: 9 10 11 12 **813**
1. Poets 2. Authors 3. Novelists 4. Short story writers
5. Nobel laureates for literature
ISBN 978-1-60413-364-6

LC 2010036211

First published 2005
Scholars evaluate Hemingway's novels and short stories.
Includes bibliographical references

Ernest Hemingway's A farewell to arms; edited & with an introduction by Harold Bloom. Chelsea House 2009 135p (Bloom's guides) $30
Grades: 9 10 11 12 **813**
1. Poets 2. Authors 3. Novelists 4. Short story writers
5. Nobel laureates for literature
ISBN 978-1-60413-572-5

LC 2009-19581

Hemingway's "work is examined in . . . critical excerpts, and features an annotated bibliography, a biography of Hemingway, an index, and an introductory essay from literature scholar Harold Bloom." Publisher's note
Includes bibliographical references

Ernest Hemingway's The old man and the sea; edited and with an introduction by Harold Bloom.

New ed; Bloom's Literary Criticism 2008 246p (Modern critical interpretations) $45
Grades: 9 10 11 12 Adult **813**
1. Poets 2. Authors 3. Novelists 4. Short story writers
5. Nobel laureates for literature
ISBN 978-1-60413-147-5

LC 2008-7061

First published 1999
A collection of critical essays discussing Hemingway's classic novel.
Includes bibliographical references

Ernest Hemingway's The sun also rises; edited and with an introduction by Harold Bloom. New ed.; Bloom's Literary Criticism 2010 197p (Modern critical interpretations) $45
Grades: 9 10 11 12 **813**
1. Poets 2. Authors 3. Novelists 4. Short story writers
5. Nobel laureates for literature
ISBN 978-1-60413-890-0

LC 2010-19961

First published 1987
A collection of nine critical essays on Hemingway's novel The Sun Also Rises arranged in chronological order of publication.
Includes bibliographical references

F. Scott Fitzgerald's The great Gatsby; edited and with an introduction by Harold Bloom. Chelsea House Publishers 2004 230p (Modern critical interpretations) $45
Grades: 9 10 11 12 Adult **813**
1. Authors 2. Novelists 3. Screenwriters 4. Short story writers
ISBN 0-7910-7577-X

LC 2003-6917

A collection of twelve essays on Fitzgerald's classic Jazz Age novel.
Includes bibliographical references

Facts on File, Inc.
★ The **Facts** on File companion to the American novel; edited by Abby H.P. Werlock; assistant editor, James P. Werlock. Facts on File 2005 3v (Facts on File library of American literature) set $195
Grades: 11 12 Adult **813**
1. Reference books 2. American fiction -- Encyclopedias
3. American fiction -- Bio-bibliography
ISBN 0-8160-4528-3; 978-0-8160-4528-0

LC 2005-12437

"This A-to-Z reference contains 450 biographical overviews of American and foreign-born authors living in the United States and 500 signed analytical essays on their novels. . . . Libraries will value this compact set for including classics as well as hard-to-find contemporary authors." SLJ
Includes bibliographical references

The **Facts** on File companion to the American short story; edited by Abby H.P. Werlock; assistant editor, James P. Werlock. 2nd ed; Facts On File 2009

2v (Facts on File library of American literature) set $150

Grades: 11 12 Adult   **813**

1. Reference books 2. Short stories -- History and criticism

ISBN 9780-8160-6895-1

LC 2009-4725

First published 2000

The alphabetically arranged entries cover authors, characters, and major short stories. Literary terms, themes, and motifs are covered. Winners of prizes and awards are noted.

Includes bibliographical references

Fargnoli, A. Nicholas

★ **Critical** companion to William Faulkner; a literary reference to his life and work. [by] A. Nicholas Fargnoli, Michael Golay, Robert W. Hamblin. Facts On File 2008 562p il (Facts on File library of American literature) $75 **813**

1. Authors 2. Novelists 3. Screenwriters 4. Short story writers 5. Nobel laureates for literature

ISBN 978-0-8160-6432-8

LC 2007-32361

First published 2001 with title: William Faulkner A to Z

"Coverage includes: Faulkner's major works, including novels, short stories, poetry, and nonfiction; descriptions of characters in Faulkner's fiction, such as Benjy and Quentin from The Sound and the Fury; details about Faulkner's family, friends, colleagues, and critics; real and fictional places important to Faulkner's life and literary development, from Yoknapatawpha County, Mississippi to Hollywood; interviews and speeches given by Faulkner; [and] ideas and events that influenced his life and works, including slavery, the Civil War, World War I, and civil rights." Publisher's note

Includes bibliographical references

Farrell, Susan Elizabeth

Critical companion to Kurt Vonnegut; a literary reference to his life and work. [by] Susan Farrell. Facts On File 2008 532p il (Facts on File library of American literature) $75

Grades: 11 12 Adult   **813**

1. Authors 2. Novelists 3. Journalists 4. Biographers 5. Short story writers 6. Science fiction writers

ISBN 978-0-8160-6598-1

LC 2007-37900

This "book covers all his works, including his novels, such as the unforgettable Slaughterhouse-Five; his short stories, such as 'Harrison Bergeron'; and his lectures and essays. . . . Entries on his life, related people, places, and topics are also included." Publisher's note

Includes bibliographical references

Critical companion to Tim O'Brien; a literary reference to his life and work. [by] Susan Farrell. Facts on File 2011 480p (Facts on File library of American literature) $75

Grades: 11 12 Adult   **813**

1. Authors 2. Novelists 3. Essayists 4. Memoirists 5.

Short story writers

ISBN 978-0-8160-7870-7; 978-1-4381-3661-5 ebook

LC 2010038664

This book features a "biography of O'Brien; entries on all O'Brien's works, including his war novels, Going After Cacciato, The Things They Carried, and In the Lake of the Woods; his memoir, If I Die in a Combat Zone, Box Me Up and Ship Me Home; and all his other published novels and short stories, including The Nuclear Age, July, July, and more; [and] entries on related people, places, and topics, such as Green Berets, Ernest Hemingway, metafiction, and Viet Cong." Publisher's note

Includes bibliographical references

Gantos, Jack

★ **Hole** in my life. Farrar, Straus & Giroux 2002 199p il $16; pa $8

Grades: 7 8 9 10   **813**

1. Authors 2. College teachers 3. Authors, American 4. Children's authors

ISBN 0-374-39988-3; 0-374-43089-6 pa

LC 2001-40957

Michael L. Printz Award honor book, 2003

The author relates how, as a young adult, he became a drug user and smuggler, was arrested, did time in prison, and eventually got out and went to college, all the while hoping to become a writer

"Gantos' spare narrative style and straightforward revelation of the truth have, together, a cumulative power that will capture not only a reader's attention but also empathy and imagination." Booklist

Gillespie, Carmen

Critical companion to Alice Walker; a literary reference to her life and work. Facts on File 2011 452p il (Facts on File library of American literature) $75

Grades: 11 12 Adult   **813**

1. Poets 2. Authors 3. Novelists 4. Editors 5. Essayists 6. College teachers 7. Short story writers

ISBN 978-0-8160-7530-0; 978-1-4381-3488-8 ebook

LC 2010-18639

"Gillespie does an excellent job of creating readable entries geared for high-school students and undergraduates. This book is highly recommended for high-school libraries, university libraries serving undergraduates, and large public libraries." Booklist

Includes bibliographical references

Critical companion to Toni Morrison; a literary reference to her life and work. Facts On File 2008 484p il (Facts on File library of American literature) $75

Grades: 9 10 11 12 Adult   **813**

1. Authors 2. Novelists 3. Dramatists 4. Essayists 5. College teachers 6. Literary critics 7. Nobel laureates for literature

ISBN 978-0-8160-6276-8

LC 2006-38231

This book "examines Morrison's life and writing, featuring critical analyses of her work and themes, as well as . .

. entries on related topics and relevant people, places, and influences." Publisher's note

Includes bibliographical references

The **girl** who was on fire; your favorite authors on Suzanne Collins' Hunger games trilogy. edited by Leah Wilson. BenBella Books 2011 211p pa $12.95

Grades: Adult Professional **813**

1. Authors 2. Novelists 3. Fantasy writers 4. Young adult authors

ISBN 978-1-935618-04-1; 1-935618-04-0

LC 2011007180

"Fans of the trilogy will undoubtedly enjoy exploring elements of the series through the eyes of the author's contemporaries, each with a different expertise. The selections address the deeper social and political issues as well as the development of multilayered characters through witty and sometimes raw essays that ask readers to look deeper. . . . Essays explore . . . subjects from within Katniss's world of Panem with humor, irreverence, and social understanding. This thought-provoking text will be especially useful for educators or librarians utilizing the multidiscplinary themes in this trilogy with their students." SLJ

Includes bibliographical references

Gloria Naylor: critical perspectives past and present; edited by Henry L. Gates, Jr., and K.A. Appiah. Amistad Press 1993 322p (Amistad literary series) hardcover o.p. pa $14.95

Grades: 11 12 Adult **813**

1. Authors 2. Novelists 3. Dramatists 4. Essayists 5. Television scriptwriters 6. Afro-American women in literature

ISBN 1-56743-030-9 pa

LC 92-45758

This volume collects critical responses to Mama Day, The women of Brewster Place, Linden Hills and Bailey's Cafe

Includes bibliographical references

★ The **great** Gatsby, by F. Scott Fitzgerald; editor, Morris Dickstein. Salem Press 2009 291p (Critical insights) lib bdg $85

Grades: 9 10 11 12 **813**

1. Authors 2. Novelists 3. Screenwriters 4. Short story writers

ISBN 978-1-58765-608-8; 1-58765-608-6

LC 2009-26346

Purchase of the volume "allows online access to the print content in its entirety. Students can search the easy-to-navigate database and print out and/or email the desired material, along with a prepared citation. Overall, a fresh take . . . and an excellent choice." SLJ

Includes bibliographical references

Haralson, Eric L.

Critical companion to Henry James; a literary reference to his life and work. [by] Eric Haralson and Kendall Johnson. Facts On File 2009 516p il (Facts on File library of American literature) $75

Grades: 11 12 Adult **813**

1. Authors 2. Novelists

ISBN 978-0-8160-6886-9

LC 2008-36451

This book "covers the life and works of Henry James as well as the related people, places, and topics that shaped his writing. Other features in this . . . title include a chronology of James's life, bibliographies of his works and of secondary sources, and black-and-white photographs and illustrations." Publisher's note

Includes bibliographical references

★ **Harper** Lee's To kill a mockingbird; edited & with an introduction by Harold Bloom. New ed.; Bloom's Literary Criticism 2010 107p (Bloom's guides) $30

Grades: 9 10 11 12 **813**

1. Authors 2. Novelists 3. Essayists 4. Short story writers

ISBN 978-1-60413-811-5

LC 2009-49160

First published 2003

Examines different aspects of Harper Lee's novel about race relations in 1930s Alabama, with a biographical sketch of the author and critical essays on this work.

Includes bibliographical references

Harriet Beecher Stowe's Uncle Tom's cabin; edited & with an introduction by Harold Bloom. Chelsea House 2008 102p (Bloom's guides) $30

Grades: 9 10 11 12 **813**

1. Authors 2. Novelists 3. Abolitionists 4. Children's authors 5. Nonfiction writers 6. Short story writers

ISBN 978-0-7910-9789-2

LC 2007-43292

This book "examines the structure and characters of the novel and provides critical analysis. Essays discuss the novel as an agent of social change, fairness in the novel, the novel as an abolitionist tract, and more. An annotated bibliography and a listing of other works by the author complement the text." Publisher's note

Includes bibliographical references

Hickam, Homer H.

The **Coalwood** way; by Homer H. Hickam, Jr. Delacorte Press 2000 318p hardcover o.p. pa $6.99

Grades: 7 8 9 10 11 12 Adult **813**

1. Authors 2. Novelists 3. Aerospace engineers 4. Memoirists 5. West Virginia 6. Authors, American 7. Writers on science

ISBN 0-440-23716-5

LC 00-35884

This sequel to Rocket boys "continues the author's life story with his senior year in high school, 1959, in the declining West Virginia mining town of Coalwood. The rocket club, featured in the last book, is pushed to the periphery, and the focus shifts to Hickam's teenage problems, which include his parents, girls, and a sadness whose cause he cannot divine." Booklist

Sky of stone; {by} Homer Hickam. Delacorte Press 2001 365p hardcover o.p. pa $7.99

Grades: 11 12 Adult **813**
1. Authors 2. Novelists 3. Aerospace engineers 4. Memoirists 5. Writers on science
ISBN 0-385-33522-9; 0-440-24092-1 pa

LC 2001-32475

"This coming-of-age tale celebrates the virtues of community and family without a hint of preachiness, and provides a rousing good story into the bargain." SLJ

★ A **Historical** guide to Ernest Hemingway; edited by Linda Wagner-Martin. Oxford Univ. Press 1999 248p il (Historical guides to American authors) $45; pa $16.95
Grades: 11 12 Adult **813**
1. Poets 2. Authors 3. Novelists 4. Short story writers 5. Nobel laureates for literature
ISBN 0-19-512151-1; 0-19-512152-X pa

LC 99-10910

Following a brief biography contributors discuss nature, machismo, gender, war and wilderness as themes in Hemingway's fiction. An illustrated chronology and a bibliographical essay are included

Includes bibliographical references

★ A **Historical** guide to Nathaniel Hawthorne; edited by Larry J. Reynolds. Oxford Univ. Press 2001 223p il (Historical guides to American authors) $34.95; pa $15.95
Grades: 9 10 11 12 **813**
1. Authors 2. Novelists 3. Short story writers
ISBN 0-19-512413-8; 0-19-512414-6 pa

LC 00-58917

This Historical Guide collects a number of original essays by Hawthorne scholars that place the author in historical context. Like other volumes in the series, A Historical Guide to Nathaniel Hawthorne includes an introduction, a brief biography, a bibliographical essay, and an illustrated chronology of the author's life and times. Combining cultural criticism with historical scholarship, this volume addresses a wide range of topics relevant to Hawthorne's work, including his relationship to slavery, children, mesmerism, and the visual arts. (Publisher's note)

Includes bibliographical references

Hogan, Walter
Humor in young adult literature; a time to laugh. Scarecrow Press 2005 223p (Scarecrow studies in young adult literature) $40
Grades: Adult Professional **813**
1. Teenagers -- Books and reading 2. Wit and humor -- History and criticism
ISBN 0-8108-5072-9

LC 2004-18903

"As a reader's advisory tool, this book is invaluable, paving the way for many laughter-filled hours to come." Voice Youth Advocates

Includes bibliographical references

Hough, Robert
Diego's Crossing; by Robert Hough. Firefly Books Ltd 2015 152 p. $21.95

Grades: 9 10 11 12 **813**
1. Mystery fiction 2. Mexico -- Fiction 3. Violence -- Fiction 4. Drug traffic -- Fiction
ISBN 1554517575; 9781554517572

In this book, by Robert Hough, "Seventeen-year-old Diego lives in a broken-down town in Mexico, not too far from the U.S. border. The area has been ravaged by drug wars, leaving a trail of dead bodies. To make matters worse, Diego's older brother is a drug dealer with a healthy ego. After his brother is injured during a night of partying, Diego is forced to take his brother's place in the next drug run in order to protect his family." (School Library Journal)

"This short page-turner will appeal to reluctant readers and those looking to read unique, high-stakes YA." SLJ

Hurston, Zora Neale
★ **Novels** and stories. Library of Am. 1995 1041p $35
Grades: 11 12 Adult **813**
1. Short stories 2. African Americans -- Fiction
ISBN 0-940450-83-6

LC 94-25757

Companion volume to Folklore, memoirs, and other writings

This collection contains Hurston's four novels: Jonah's gourd vine, Their eyes were watching God, Moses, man of the mountain, and Seraph on the Suwanee. Also included are nine short stories

"Libraries without a complete set of Hurston's fiction will find this volume a necessary and easy purchase to fill that unfortunate gap." Booklist

J.D. Salinger; edited with an introduction by Harold Bloom. New ed; Chelsea House 2008 254p (Modern critical views) $45
Grades: 9 10 11 12 Adult **813**
1. Authors 2. Novelists 3. Short story writers
ISBN 978-0-7910-9813-4

LC 2007-44662

First published 1987

This collection of nine essays provides a view of Salinger's critical reception. Among the contributors are David Galloway, Anthony Kaufman and Robert Coles.

Includes bibliographical references

J.D. Salinger's The catcher in the rye; edited and with an introduction by Harold Bloom. New ed; Bloom's Literary Criticism 2009 215p (Modern critical interpretations) $45
Grades: 9 10 11 12 **813**
1. Authors 2. Novelists 3. Short story writers
ISBN 978-1-60413-183-3

LC 2008-45784

First published 2000

This collection of critical essays analyzes J.D. Salinger's classic novel featuring Holden Caulfield.

Includes bibliographical references

J.R.R. Tolkien's The lord of the rings; edited and with an introduction by Harold Bloom. New ed;

Chelsea House 2008 208p (Modern critical interpretations) $45

Grades: 9 10 11 12 Adult **813**

1. Authors 2. Novelists 3. Linguists 4. Philologists 5. Fantasy writers 6. Children's authors

ISBN 978-1-60413-145-1

LC 2008-7062

First published 2000

"Nine critics and scholars give various interpretive evaluations of the classic fantasy trilogy. . . . Each author evaluates the Tolkien novels using different criteria, some discussing their appeal, some their literary merit. Each essay is well defined and laboriously researched, and each opinion is defended within its context. . . . The book is a useful tool for students needing to examine the themes and context of Tolkien's work." SLJ [review of 2000 edition]

Includes bibliographical references

Jack London; edited and with an introduction by Harold Bloom. New ed; Bloom's Literary Criticism 2011 158p (Modern critical views) $45

Grades: 9 10 11 12 **813**

1. Authors 2. Novelists 3. Short story writers

ISBN 978-1-60413-366-0

LC 2010-36210

A selection of critical essays explore the works of the author of White Fang.

Includes bibliographical references

Jamaica Kincaid; edited and with an introduction by Harold Bloom. Updated ed; Chelsea House 2008 228p (Modern critical views) $45

Grades: 9 10 11 12 **813**

1. Authors 2. Novelists 3. Essayists 4. Memoirists 5. Short story writers

ISBN 978-0-7910-9812-7

LC 2007-37660

First published 1998

A collection of critical essays discussing the works of the author of Annie John and A Small Place.

Includes bibliographical references

Jocelyn, Marthe

A **Big** Dose of Lucky; Marthe Jocelyn. Orca Book Publishers 2015 264 p. $14.95

Grades: 7 8 9 10 11 12 **813**

1. Orphans -- Fiction 2. Teenage girls -- Fiction 3. Racially mixed people -- Fiction

ISBN 1459806689; 9781459806689

LC 2015935534

In this novel, by Marthe Jocelyn, "Malou has just turned sixteen . . . and all she knows for sure is that she's of mixed race and that she was left at an orphanage as a newborn. When the orphanage burns to the ground, she finds out that she may have been born in a small town in Ontario. Parry Sound turns out to have quite a few young brown faces, but Malou can't believe they might be related to her. After she finds work . . . an Aboriginal boy . . . helps her find answers to her questions." (Publisher's note)

"Sharp writing keeps this dramatic coming-of-age story from taking a turn toward the saccharine or melodramatic, despite the casual and not-so-casual racism Malou endures outside the sheltered confines of the orphanage. Lovely and easily digestible historical fiction." Booklist

Secrets Part of "Secrets" series. Other titles in series:
Innocent (2015)
Shattered Glass (2015)
My Life Before Me (2015)
Stones on a Grave (2015)
Small Bones (2015)

John Knowles's A separate peace; edited and with an introduction by Harold Bloom. New ed; Bloom's Literary Criticism 2009 124p (Modern critical interpretations) $45

Grades: 11 12 Adult **813**

1. Authors 2. Novelists 3. Travel writers

ISBN 978-1-60413-185-7

LC 2008-49797

First published 1999

A collection of ten essays on Knowles' novel about two boys in prep school during World War II.

Includes bibliographical references

John Steinbeck; edited and with an introduction by Harold Bloom. New ed; Bloom's Literary Criticism 2008 176p (Modern critical views) $45

Grades: 9 10 11 12 Adult **813**

1. Authors 2. Novelists 3. Screenwriters 4. Nobel laureates for literature

ISBN 978-0-7910-9787-8; 0-7910-9787-0

LC 2007-38676

First published 1987

A selection of criticism, arranged in chronological order of publication, devoted to the fiction of John Steinbeck.

Includes bibliographical references (p. 167-9)

John Steinbeck's Of mice and men; edited & with an introduction by Harold Bloom. Chelsea House Publishers 2006 134p (Bloom's guides) $30

Grades: 9 10 11 12 **813**

1. Authors 2. Novelists 3. Screenwriters 4. Nobel laureates for literature

ISBN 0-7910-8581-3; 978-0-7910-8581-3

LC 2005-38038

This is a "literary guide to one of John Steinbeck's greatest American novels. . . . Key features include: An introduction by . . . Harold Bloom that considers each work and its significance; a brief biographical sketch that offers insight into John Steinbeck's life; 'The Story Behind the Story' details the circumstances surrounding the inception and development of the work; summaries with analysis review that explain key points of the work; selections from critical essays . . . [and] an annotated bibliography that directs readers to additional materials on the subject and explains the importance of each." Publisher's note

Includes bibliographical references

John Steinbeck's The grapes of wrath; edited & with an introduction by Harold Bloom. Chelsea House Publishers 2005 100p (Bloom's guides) $30

Grades: 9 10 11 12 **813**

1. Authors 2. Novelists 3. Screenwriters 4. Nobel

laureates for literature
ISBN 0-7910-8239-3; 978-0-7910-8239-3
LC 2004-27519
Examines different aspects of Steinbeck's classic Dust Bowl-era novel, with a biographical sketch of the author and critical essays on this work.
Includes bibliographical references

Jones, Sharon L.
Critical companion to Zora Neale Hurston; a literary reference to her life and work. Facts On File 2008 288p il (Facts on File library of American literature) $75
Grades: 11 12 Adult   **813**
1. Authors 2. Novelists 3. Dramatists 4. Memoirists 5. Folklorists 6. Short story writers
ISBN 978-0-8160-6885-2; 0-8160-6885-2
LC 2008-10052
This "covers all her writings, including Their Eyes Were Watching God; her landmark works of folklore and anthropology, such as Mules and Men; and shorter works." Publisher's note
Includes bibliographical references

Joseph Heller's Catch-22; edited and with an introduction by Harold Bloom. New ed; Bloom's Literary Criticism 2008 281p (Modern critical interpretations) $45
Grades: 9 10 11 12 Adult   **813**
1. Authors 2. Novelists 3. Short story writers
ISBN 978-0-7910-9617-8
LC 2007-42768
First published 2001
A collection of essays providing international appraisal and interpretation of Joseph Heller's novel.
Includes bibliographical references

The **Joy** Luck Club, by Amy Tan; editor, Robert C. Evans. Salem Press 2010 323p (Critical insights) lib bdg $85
Grades: 9 10 11 12   **813**
1. Authors 2. Novelists 3. Essayists 4. Children's authors 5. Short story writers
ISBN 978-1-58765-626-2; 1-58765-626-4
LC 2009-26304
This book introduces The Joy Luck Club's narrative in its "historical context, [provides] a short biography of the author, and offer 'The Paris Review Perspective' on the [work], followed by a series of articles by academics under the headings of 'Critical Contexts' or 'Critical Readings.'" SLJ
Includes bibliographical references

Ken Kesey's One flew over the cuckoo's nest; edited and with an introduction by Harold Bloom. New ed; Bloom's Literary Criticism 2008 202p (Modern critical interpretations) $45
Grades: 9 10 11 12 Adult   **813**
1. Authors 2. Novelists
ISBN 978-0-7910-9616-1
LC 2007-45157

First published 2002
A collection of thirteen essays providing international appraisal and interpretation of Kesey's classic novel.
Includes bibliographical references

Kerr, Christine
Bloom's how to write about Alice Walker; [introduction by Harold Bloom] Bloom's Literary Criticism 2009 296p (Bloom's how to write about literature) $45
Grades: 9 10 11 12   **813**
1. Poets 2. Authors 3. Novelists 4. Report writing 5. Editors 6. Essayists 7. College teachers 8. Short story writers
ISBN 978-0-7910-9745-8
LC 2008-5707
This book offers "suggestions for paper topics, . . . strategies on how to write a strong essay, and an . . . introduction by Harold Bloom on writing about Walker. This . . . volume is designed to help students develop their analytical writing skills and critical comprehension of the author and her major works." Publisher's note
Includes bibliographical references

Bloom's how to write about J.D. Salinger; introduction by Harold Bloom. Chelsea House 2008 280p (Bloom's how to write about literature) $45
Grades: 9 10 11 12   **813**
1. Authors 2. Novelists 3. Report writing 4. Short story writers
ISBN 978-0-7910-9483-9
LC 2006-100570
"For librarians who want to counter the daily student complaint 'I don't know where to start!' with concrete direction, Kerr's book might be the answer." SLJ
Includes bibliographical references

Kincaid, Jamaica
My brother. Farrar, Straus & Giroux 1997 197p hardcover o.p. pa $10
Grades: 11 12 Adult   **813**
1. Authors 2. Novelists 3. Women authors 4. Essayists 5. Memoirists 6. Short story writers
ISBN 0-374-21681-9; 0-374-52562-5 pa
LC 97-16190
"Honest, unapologetic, and pure, this is an eloquent and searching elegy for the dead and a prayer of thankfulness for the living." Booklist

King, Stephen, 1947-
On writing; a memoir of the craft. Scribner 2000 288p hardcover o.p. pa $14.95
Grades: 11 12 Adult   **813**
1. Authors 2. Novelists 3. Authorship 4. Authors, American 5. Short story writers 6. Science fiction writers
ISBN 0-684-85352-3; 0-671-02425-6 pa
LC 00-30105
The author recounts "his life from early childhood through the aftermath of the 1999 accident that nearly killed him. Along the way, King touts the writing philosophies of

William Strunk and Ernest Hemingway, advocates a healthy appetite for reading, expounds upon the subject of grammar, critiques a number of popular writers, and offers the reader a chance to try out his theories. . . . Recommended for anyone who wants to write and everyone who loves to read." Libr J

Kirk, Connie Ann

Critical companion to Flannery O'Connor. Facts on File 2008 415p il (Facts on File library of American literature) $75

Grades: 9 10 11 12 Adult **813**
1. Authors 2. Novelists 3. Short story writers
ISBN 978-0-8160-6417-5

LC 2007-6512

This book examines O'Connor's "life and works, and includes critical analyses of some of the themes in her writing, as well as entries on related topics and relevant people, places, and influences." Publisher's note

Includes bibliographical references

The **kite** runner; edited & with an introduction by Harold Bloom. Bloom's Literary Criticism 2009 91p (Bloom's guides) $30

Grades: 9 10 11 12 **813**
1. Authors 2. Novelists 3. Physicians
ISBN 978-1-60413-199-4

LC 2008-35050

This study guide on Hosseini's work includes a brief biographical sketch of the author, a list of characters, a summary with analysis, and selections from critical essays by different scholars about the work.

Includes bibliographical references

Kordich, Catherine J.

Bloom's how to write about John Steinbeck; [introduction by Harold Bloom] Bloom's Literary Criticism 2008 264p (Bloom's how to write about literature) $45

Grades: 9 10 11 12 **813**
1. Authors 2. Novelists 3. Report writing 4. Screenwriters 5. Nobel laureates for literature
ISBN 0-7910-9486-3; 978-0-7910-9486-0

LC 2006-100571

This book offers "paper-topic suggestions, . . . strategies on how to write a strong essay, and an . . . introduction by Harold Bloom on writing about Steinbeck. This . . . volume is designed to help students develop their analytical writing skills and critical comprehension of this legendary author and his works." Publisher's note

Includes bibliographical references

Kramer, Barbara

Toni Morrison; a biography of a nobel prize-winning writer. by Barbara Kramer. Enslow Publishers 2012 104 p. (library) $26.60

Grades: 7 8 9 10 **813**
1. Morrison, Toni 2. African American novelists -- Biography 3. Novelists, American -- 20th century -- Biography
ISBN 0766039897; 9780766039896

LC 2011024344

In this biography of African American author Toni Morrison, "Barbara Kramer explores the life and career of this talented writer. From her childhood in Loraine, Ohio, to her creative expressions of African-American culture, Morrison has always remembered her past. She has taught at several universities, as well as being the author of novels, short stories essays, and a play." (Publisher's note)

Includes bibliographical references (p. 88-99) and index.

Kurt Vonnegut; edited and with an introduction by Harold Bloom. New ed; Bloom's Literary Criticism 2008 198p (Modern critical views) $45

Grades: 11 12 Adult **813**
1. Authors 2. Novelists 3. Journalists 4. Biographers 5. Short story writers 6. Science fiction writers
ISBN 978-1-60413-167-3

LC 2008-37161

First published 2000

A collection of critical essays on the author of Slaughterhouse-Five.

Includes bibliographical references

Kurt Vonnegut's Slaughterhouse-five; edited and with an introduction by Harold Bloom. New ed; Bloom's Literary Criticism 2009 183p (Modern critical interpretations) $45

Grades: 9 10 11 12 **813**
1. Authors 2. Novelists 3. Journalists 4. Biographers 5. Short story writers 6. Science fiction writers
ISBN 978-1-60413-585-5

LC 2009-16269

First published 2000

This collection of critical essays on Vonnegut's novel includes "information about the author's life and other works, . . . notes on the contributing writers, and an introductory essay by . . . Harold Bloom." Publisher's note

Includes bibliographical references

Lewis, Sinclair

Main Street & Babbitt. Library of Am. 1992 898p $40

Grades: 11 12 Adult **813**
1. Minnesota -- Fiction
ISBN 0-940450-61-5

LC 91-58224

In addition to Main Street, this book also features Babbitt (1922), a satire on American middle-class conventions. Set in the Midwest, it focuses on the life of George Babbitt, a prosperous and self-satisfied real estate man.

Litwin, Laura Baskes

A **reader's** guide to Zora Neale Hurston's Their eyes were watching god. Enslow Publishers 2010 128p il (Multicultural literature) lib bdg $31.93

Grades: 8 9 10 11 12 **813**
1. Authors 2. Novelists 3. Dramatists 4. African Americans in literature 5. Memoirists 6. Folklorists 7. Short story writers
ISBN 978-0-7660-3164-7; 0-7660-3164-0

LC 2008-38524

An introduction to Zora Neale Hurston's novel Their eyes were watching God for high school students, which includes biographical background on the author, explanations of various literary devices and techniques, and literary criticism for the novice reader.

Includes glossary and bibliographical references

London, Jack

★ The **portable** Jack London; edited by Earle Labor. Penguin Bks. 1994 xxxvii, 563p pa $15.95

Grades: 11 12 Adult   **813**

ISBN 0-14-017969-0

LC 93-38740

This volume contains selected short stories, the complete text of The call of the wild, personal letters, and a sampling of journalistic pieces.

Includes bibliographical references

Lusted, Marcia Amidon

How to analyze the works of Stephen King. ABDO Pub. Co. 2011 112p il (Essential critiques) $34.22

Grades: 9 10 11 12   **813**

1. Authors 2. Novelists 3. Short story writers 4. Science fiction writers 5. Horror fiction -- History and criticism

ISBN 978-1-61613-536-2

LC 2010-15007

This book looks at the works of Stephen King "through the lenses of prevalent schools of criticism. The first chapters introduce the concept of critical theory, its purpose, and how to develop and support a thesis statement. In subsequent chapters, an overview of each work is followed by a critique using a particular theory. . . . Feminist criticism is applied to Carrie, archetypal theory to The Green Mile, historical criticism to The Stand, and structuralist criticism to the 'Dark Tower' series." SLJ

Includes bibliographical references

Magistrale, Tony

★ **Student** companion to Edgar Allan Poe. Greenwood Press 2001 139p (Student companions to classic writers) $35

Grades: 9 10 11 12   **813**

1. Poets 2. Authors 3. Essayists 4. Short story writers

ISBN 0-313-30992-2

LC 00-49071

An introduction to the life, times and major works. Includes contemporary interpretations of The raven and The purloined letter

Includes bibliographical references

Margaret Atwood's The handmaid's tale; edited and with an introduction by Harold Bloom. Chelsea House 2001 188p (Modern critical interpretations) $45

Grades: 9 10 11 12 Adult   **813**

1. Poets 2. Authors 3. Novelists 4. Essayists 5. Children's authors 6. Short story writers

ISBN 0-7910-5926-X

LC 00-65839

A collection of essays discussing Margaret Atwood's novel about a futuristic society where women have no rights.

Includes bibliographical references

★ **Mark** Twain's The adventures of Huckleberry Finn; edited and with an introduction by Harold Bloom. Updated ed; Chelsea House 2007 248p (Modern critical interpretations) $45

Grades: 9 10 11 12 Adult   **813**

1. Authors 2. Humorists 3. Novelists 4. Essayists 5. Satirists 6. Memoirists 7. Travel writers 8. Short story writers

ISBN 0-7910-9426-X; 978-0-7910-9426-6

LC 2006-36858

First published 1986

A collection of twelve critical essays on Mark Twain's classic novel.

Includes bibliographical references

McCafferty, Megan

Sloppy firsts; by Megan McCafferty. Crown Publishers 2001 280 p. $13.99

Grades: 9 10 11 12 Adult   **813**

1. Friendship -- Fiction 2. New Jersey -- Fiction 3. Family life -- Fiction 4. Teenage girls -- Fiction 5. High school students -- Fiction 6. Darling, Jessica (Fictitious characters)

ISBN 0609807900; 9780609807903

LC 2001028143

In this book, by Megan McCafferty, "[w]hen her best friend, Hope Weaver, moves away, . . . sixteen-year-old Jessica Darling is devastated. A fish out of water at school and a stranger at home, Jessica feels more lost than ever. . . . How is she supposed to deal with the . . . girls at school, her dad's obsession with her track meets, her mother salivating over big sister Bethany's lavish wedding, and her nonexistent love life?" (Publisher's note)

Part of a series

★ **My** true love gave to me; twelve holiday stories. edited and with a story by Stephanie Perkins. St. Martin's Griffin 2014 336 p. (hardback) $18.99

Grades: 9 10 11 12   **813**

1. Love stories 2. Holidays -- Fiction 3. Christmas -- Fiction 4. Love stories, American 5. Short stories, American 6. Young adult fiction, American

ISBN 1250059305; 9781250059307

LC 2014030943

This book presents "twelve tales of holiday romance by notable YA authors. . . . Rainbow Rowell's opening 'Midnights' provides snapshots of Noel and Mags' relationship on each New Year's Eve of their high school years. . . . David Levithan provides an alternative to the collection's otherwise predominant heteronormativity with his portrayal of two boys finding warmth and solace on Christmas Eve in their romance even as their family foundations are shaken." (Bulletin of the Center for Children's Books)

Myers, Walter Dean, 1937-2014

★ **Bad** boy; a memoir. HarperCollins Pubs. 2001 214p $15.95; pa $6.99

Grades: 7 8 9 10   **813**
1. Poets 2. Authors 3. Novelists 4. African American authors 5. Editors 6. Authors, American 7. Children's authors 8. Young adult authors
ISBN 0-06-029523-6; 0-06-447288-4 pa
     LC 00-52978
This "is a story full of funny anecdotes, lofty ideals, and tender moments." SLJ

Nadel, Ira Bruce
Critical companion to Philip Roth; a literary companion to his life and work. [by] Ira B. Nadel. Facts On File, Inc. 2011 356p il (Facts on File library of American literature) $75
Grades: 11 12 Adult   **813**
1. Authors 2. Novelists 3. Short story writers
ISBN 978-0-8160-7795-3; 978-1-4381-3555-7 ebook
     LC 2010022769
"Coverage includes: a . . . biography of Roth; entries on all of Roth's works; . . . entries on related people, places, and topics, such as anti-Semitism, Claire Bloom, Newark, satire, and . . . more; [and] appendixes, including a chronology, a bibliography of Roth's works, and a secondary-source bibliography." Publisher's note
Includes bibliographical references

Nathaniel Hawthorne; edited and with an introduction by Harold Bloom. Chelsea House 2003 148p (Bloom's biocritiques) $35
Grades: 9 10 11 12   **813**
1. Authors 2. Novelists 3. Short story writers
ISBN 0-7910-7383-1
     LC 2003-1603
This book on the life and work of Hawthorne contains a "biography, literary criticism, a list of works by and about the author, and more." Publisher's note
Includes bibliographical references

Nathaniel Hawthorne's The scarlet letter; edited & with an introduction by Harold Bloom. New ed.; Bloom's Literary Criticism 2010 103p (Bloom's guides) $30
Grades: 9 10 11 12   **813**
1. Authors 2. Novelists 3. Short story writers
ISBN 978-1-60413-874-0
     LC 2010-24814
First published 2004
Examines different aspects of Hawthorne's novel, with a biographical sketch of the author and critical essays on the work.
Includes bibliographical references

Newman, Gerald
★ A **student's** guide to John Steinbeck; [by] Gerald Newman, Eleanor Newman Layfield. Enslow Publs. 2004 176p il (Understanding literature) $27.93
Grades: 9 10 11 12   **813**
1. Authors 2. Novelists 3. Screenwriters 4. Nobel

laureates for literature
ISBN 0-7660-2259-5
     LC 2004-2304
"The authors discuss . . . [Steinbeck's] books in terms of characters, themes, plots, and symbolism. They devote separate chapters to Of Mice and Men, The Grapes of Wrath, and East of Eden but include other writings as well. . . . A good choice for reports and for a general understanding of this much-studied writer's works." SLJ
Includes glossary and bibliographical references

Nilsen, Alleen Pace
Joan Bauer. Greenwood Press 2007 160p il (Teen reads: student companions to young adult literature) $45
Grades: 9 10 11 12   **813**
1. Authors 2. Children's authors
ISBN 978-0-313-33550-1; 0-313-33550-8
     LC 2007-8191
This book on the works of Joan Bauer includes an "interview with Bauer that is broken into topical sections, a discussion of Bauer's writing style, an examination of Bauer's short stories, and a chapter devoted to each of her novels. . . . This book is a most appropriate and welcome addition for high school libraries as well as high school English teachers' classrooms." Voice Youth Advocates
Includes bibliographical references

★ The **Norton** book of American short stories. Norton 1988 779p $29.95
Grades: 11 12 Adult   **813**
1. Short stories
ISBN 0-393-02619-1
     LC 88-14181
"The 70 stories Prescott chose for inclusion in this comprehensive anthology show to great effect the sterling quality of American short stories, from the dawn-days of Poe and Hawthorne to the . . . minimalism of Raymond Carver. A collection full of treasures." Booklist

O'Connor, Flannery
★ **Collected** works. Library of Am. 1988 1281p $35
Grades: 11 12 Adult   **813**
1. Short stories
ISBN 0-940450-37-2
     LC 87-37829

Oliver, Charles M.
Critical companion to Ernest Hemingway; a literary reference to his life and work. Facts on File 2006 630p il (Facts on File library of American literature) $75
Grades: 9 10 11 12 Adult   **813**
1. Poets 2. Authors 3. Novelists 4. Short story writers 5. Nobel laureates for literature
ISBN 0-8160-6418-0; 978-0-8160-6418-2
     LC 2006-7970
First published 1999 with title: Ernest Hemingway A to Z

"This volume features entries on all of Hemingway's major and minor works, places and events related to his works, major figures in his life, and more. Appendixes include a complete list of Hemingway's works; a chronology; a genealogy; a . . . map for readers of Islands in the Stream; a list of film, stage, and radio adaptations; and a bibliography of secondary sources." Publisher's note

Includes filmography and bibliographical references

Paulsen, Gary

The **beet** fields; memories of a sixteenth summer. Delacorte Press 2000 x, 160 p.p hardcover o.p. pa $5.99

Grades: 11 12 Adult   **813**

1. Authors, American 2. Teenage boys -- United States -- Biography 3. Authors, American -- 20th century -- Biography

ISBN 0-385-32647-5; 0-440-41557-8 pa; 0385326475

LC 00023184

The author recalls his experiences as a migrant laborer and carnival worker after he ran away from home at age sixteen.

"Paulsen's coming-of-age memoir is nearly Steinbeckian in its unadorned but effective prose, and the events of the author's young life have a universality that will draw in readers heading for their own rites of passage." Bull Cent Child Books

Peer pressure in Robert Cormier's The chocolate war; Dedria Bryfonski, book editor. Greenhaven Press 2010 178p il (Social issues in literature) $37.30; pa $25.70

Grades: 9 10 11 12   **813**

1. Authors 2. Novelists 3. Peer pressure 4. Young adult authors

ISBN 978-0-7377-4620-4; 0-7377-4620-3; 978-0-7377-4621-1 pa; 0-7377-4621-1 pa

LC 2009-18275

The "reprinted articles [in this book] are broken into three groups: those that focus on the author; those that focus on how the headline issue is exercised within the book itself; and those that expand that issue into contemporary settings. One of the first pieces in Peer Pressure in Robert Cormier's The Chocolate War is by Cormier himself, explaining how he adores happy endings even as he finds himself unable to write them. After taking on the novel's famous plot twists, the book moves on to such topics as cyberbullying." Booklist

Includes bibliographical references

Perez, Rene S., II

Seeing off the Johns; by Rene S. Perez II. Cinco Puntos Press 2015 256 p. (hardback: alk. paper) $16.95

Grades: 9 10 11 12   **813**

1. Texas -- Fiction 2. Athletes -- Fiction 3. City and town life -- Fiction 4. High school students -- Fiction

ISBN 9781941026113; 9781941026120

LC 2014032016

In this book, by Rene S Perez II, "People in the small town of Greenton mark their lives from that day in late summer when crowds lined the streets to see off high school athletic stars John Robison and John Mijias. That was the day the Johns, . . . left for state college, and never made it there—or back. . . . For Concepcion 'Chon' Gonzales, the days that the Johns headed out and didn't return was the first day of his new life." (Publisher's note)

"An atmospheric, refreshing read that will resonate with readers from towns both small and large." Kirkus

Pingelton, Timothy J.

★ A **student's** guide to Ernest Hemingway. Enslow Publishers 2005 160p il map (Understanding literature) lib bdg $27.93

Grades: 7 8 9 10   **813**

1. Poets 2. Authors 3. Novelists 4. Short story writers 5. Nobel laureates for literature

ISBN 0-7660-2431-8

This discusses Hemingway's life and his novels In Our Time, The Sun Also Rises, A Farewell to Arms, and The Old Man and the Sea

"Engaging and informative. . . . The very accessible format and the solid information make [this book] useful to students, and the engaging style should interest casual readers." SLJ

Includes glossary and bibliographical references

Powell, Kelley

The **Merit** Birds; by Kelley Powell. Dundurn 2015 240 p. $14.99

Grades: 9 10 11 12   **813**

1. Laos -- Fiction 2. Culture conflict -- Fiction 3. Mother-son relationship -- Fiction

ISBN 1459729315; 9781459729315

In this book, by Kelley Powell, "Cam's mood is further worsened when he is torn away from his friends, school, and basket-ball team and must contend with the 'Dark Ages' quality of life in Laos, its slow pace, and his inability to communicate. Things don't really get better for Cam in Laos. Sure, he meets a girl and develops a friendship, but when tragedy strikes, Cam's situation becomes much worse than he could have imagined." (Quill & Quire)

"While the book may not have wide appeal, it is a thought-provoking story that will appeal to older teens willing to expand their worldview." SLJ

Ralph Ellison; edited and with an introduction by Harold Bloom. New ed; Bloom's Literary Criticism 2009 238p (Modern critical views) $45

Grades: 9 10 11 12   **813**

1. Authors 2. Novelists 3. Essayists 4. Literary critics 5. Short story writers

ISBN 978-1-60413-578-7

LC 2009-8055

First published 1986

This "study guide contains a selection of . . . contemporary criticism on this great American author, plus an introduction by literary scholar Harold Bloom, a . . . chronology of Ellison's life, a bibliography for further study, and . . . [an] index." Publisher's note

Includes bibliographical references

Ralph Ellison's Invisible man; edited and with an introduction by Harold Bloom. Chelsea House 2008 83p (Bloom's guides) $30
Grades: 9 10 11 12 **813**
1. Authors 2. Novelists 3. Essayists 4. Literary critics 5. Short story writers
ISBN 978-0-7910-9790-8
LC 2007-36553
Along with excerpts of criticism on Ralph Ellison's classic work, this book "includes a brief biography of the author, . . . character profiles, structural and thematic analysis, an annotated bibliography, and more." Publisher's note

Ray Bradbury; edited and with an introduction by Harold Bloom. New ed; Bloom's Literary Criticism 2010 237p (Modern critical views) $45
Grades: 9 10 11 12 **813**
1. Authors 2. Novelists 3. Screenwriters 4. Children's authors 5. Short story writers 6. Science fiction writers
ISBN 978-1-60413-805-4; 1-60413-805-X
LC 2009-30891
First published 2000
A selection of critical essays explore the works of the author of Fahrenheit 451 and The Martian Chronicles.
Includes bibliographical references

Ray Bradbury's Fahrenheit 451; edited and with an introduction by Harold Bloom. New ed; Chelsea House 2008 133p (Modern critical interpretations) $45
Grades: 9 10 11 12 Adult **813**
1. Authors 2. Novelists 3. Screenwriters 4. Children's authors 5. Short story writers 6. Science fiction writers
ISBN 978-1-60413-144-4
LC 2008-8776
First published 2001
A collection of nine critical essays on Ray Bradbury's dystopian novel.
Includes bibliographical references

Reed, Arthea J. S.
Norma Fox Mazer; a writer's world. Scarecrow Press 2000 140p (Scarecrow studies in young adult literature) $36
Grades: 7 8 9 10 **813**
1. Authors 2. Novelists 3. Children's authors 4. Young adult authors
ISBN 0-8108-3814-1
LC 00-38759
"Quoting heavily from the author herself and published reviews of her work, the author provides a chronology of major events in Mazer's life and then goes into deeper detail about her subject's childhood and adolescence and how her upbringing played a vital role in her novels and partnership with her husband, Harry Mazer. Several works are comprehensively analyzed." SLJ
Includes bibliographical references

Reef, Catherine
John Steinbeck. Clarion Bks. 1996 163p il $17.95; pa $8.95
Grades: 7 8 9 10 **813**
1. Authors 2. Novelists 3. Screenwriters 4. Authors, American 5. Nobel laureates for literature
ISBN 0-395-71278-5; 0-618-43244-2 pa
LC 95-11500
"The book traces Steinbeck's life from his childhood in California, to his burgeoning writing career and his passion for social justice, to his worldwide recognition. Reef does an excellent job of synthesizing Steinbeck's work, his private life, and his politics and philosophy." Bull Cent Child Books
Includes bibliographical references

Rehak, Melanie
Girl sleuth; Nancy Drew and the women who created her. Harcourt 2005 364p il $25; pa $14
Grades: 11 12 Adult **813**
1. Authors 2. Mystery writers 3. Children's authors 4. Young adult authors 5. Drew, Nancy (Fictitious character)
ISBN 0-15-101041-2; 0-15-603056-X pa
LC 2005-9129
"Packed with revealing anecdotes, Rehak's meticulously researched account of the publishing phenomenon that survived the Depression and WWII . . . will delight fans of the beloved gumshoe whose gumption guaranteed that every reprobate got his due." Booklist
Includes bibliographical references

Richard Wright; edited and with an introduction by Harold Bloom. New ed; Bloom's Literary Criticism 2009 215p (Modern critical views) $45
Grades: 11 12 Adult **813**
1. Authors 2. Novelists 3. Dramatists 4. Essayists 5. Nonfiction writers 6. Short story writers
ISBN 978-0-7910-9622-2
LC 2008-31807
First published 1987
A collection of critical essays on the African American author and his works, including Native Son.
Includes bibliographical references

Richard Wright's Native son; edited and with an introduction by Harold Bloom. Bloom's Literary Criticism 2008 213p (Modern critical interpretations) $45
Grades: 11 12 Adult **813**
1. Authors 2. Novelists 3. Dramatists 4. Essayists 5. Nonfiction writers 6. Short story writers
ISBN 978-0-7910-9625-3
First published 1988
A collection of critical essays on Wright's classic portrayal of the black experience, arranged chronologically in the order of their original publication.

Rollyson, Carl
Critical companion to Herman Melville; a literary reference to his life and work. [by] Carl Rollyson, Lisa Paddock, and April Gentry. Facts on File 2006 394p il (Facts on File library of world literature) $75

Grades: 9 10 11 12 Adult **813**
1. Authors 2. Novelists
ISBN 0-8160-6461-X; 978-0-8160-6461-8
LC 2005-36733
First published 2000 with title: Herman Melville A to Z
Entries in this "volume examine the characters and settings of Melville's novels and short stories, the critics and scholars who commented on his work, and his friends and associates, including such prominent literary figures as Oliver Wendell Holmes and Nathaniel Hawthorne." Publisher's note
Includes bibliographical references

Russell, Sharon A.
★ **Revisiting** Stephen King; a critical companion. Greenwood Press 2002 171p (Critical companions to popular contemporary writers) $34.95
Grades: 9 10 11 12 **813**
1. Authors 2. Novelists 3. Short story writers 4. Science fiction writers
ISBN 0-313-31788-7
LC 2001-58641
This volume discusses the plot review, character development, and theme of eight of King's books from Desperation (1996) through Dreamcatcher (2001)
"Easy to read and understand, this title would be a good choice for secondary researchers. It's also interesting enough for King fans to enjoy." Libr Media Connect
Includes bibliographical references

★ **Stephen** King: a critical companion. Greenwood Press 1996 171p (Critical companions to popular contemporary writers) $35
Grades: 9 10 11 12 **813**
1. Authors 2. Novelists 3. Short story writers 4. Science fiction writers
ISBN 0-313-29417-8
LC 95-50460
"Biographical information about King and background information on the horror genre in which he writes are contained in the first two chapters. The chapters that follow cover in detail the author's most important, most popular, and most recent works in chronological order, examining plot and character development and theme." Voice Youth Advocates
Includes bibliographical references

Sandra Cisneros's The house on Mango Street; edited and with an introduction by Harold Bloom. New ed; Bloom's Literary Criticism 2010 121p (Bloom's guides) $30
Grades: 9 10 11 12 **813**
1. Poets 2. Authors 3. Novelists 4. Essayists 5. Short story writers
ISBN 978-1-60413-812-2; 978-1-4381-3341-6 ebook
LC 2010-5023
First published 2003
A collection of essays exploring various aspects of Sandra Cisneros' novel The House on Mango Street, with biographical data and other information.

"Given its popularity as a coming of age novel widely used in high school language arts classes, this volume should be on the high school library shelf." Libr Media Connect
Includes bibliographical references

Schroeder, Heather Lee
A **reader's** guide to Marjane Satrapi's Persepolis. Enslow Publishers 2010 152p il map (Multicultural literature) lib bdg $34.60
Grades: 8 9 10 11 12 **813**
1. Artists 2. Authors 3. Novelists 4. Cartoonists 5. Memoirists
ISBN 978-0-7660-3166-1; 0-7660-3166-7
LC 2008-51820
An introduction to Marjane Satrapi's graphic novel Persepolis for high school students, which includes biographical background on the author, explanations of various literary devices and techniques, and literary criticism for the novice reader.
Includes glossary and bibliographical references

Schultz, Jeffrey D.
★ **Critical** companion to John Steinbeck; a literary reference to his life and work. [by] Jeffrey Schultz, Luchen Li. Facts on File 2005 406p il (Facts on File library of American literature) $65; pa $19.99
Grades: 11 12 Adult **813**
1. Authors 2. Novelists 3. Screenwriters 4. Nobel laureates for literature
ISBN 0-8160-4300-0; 0-8160-4301-9 pa
LC 2004-26100
"Useful, succinct, and reasonably priced, it packs an abundance of information into one compact resource." Libr J
Includes bibliographical references

Sorrentino, Paul
★ **Student** companion to Stephen Crane; [by] Paul M. Sorrentino. Greenwood Press 2006 171p (Student companions to classic writers) $39.95
Grades: 9 10 11 12 **813**
1. Authors 2. Novelists
ISBN 0-313-33104-9
LC 2005-26301
The author "includes facts about Crane's family, background on the Civil War, critical commentaries, as well as discussions about his writings, his literary heritage, and his revered place in American literature. . . . This volume includes a wealth of useful material that will help students better understand and interpret the writings of this great 19th-century author." SLJ
Includes bibliographical references

Stefoff, Rebecca
Jack London; an American original. Oxford Univ. Press 2002 127p il maps (Oxford portraits) lib bdg $28
Grades: 7 8 9 10 **813**
1. Authors 2. Novelists 3. Authors, American 4. Short story writers
ISBN 0-19-512223-2
LC 2001-53087

"This volume does an excellent job of illuminating London's extraordinary life and career. The narrative is exciting and accessible. . . . The text is supplemented by interesting and informative illustrations, and includes excerpts from primary-source material." SLJ

Includes bibliographical references

Stephen Crane's The red badge of courage; edited and with an introduction by Harold Bloom. New ed.; Bloom's Literary Criticism 2010 162p (Modern critical interpretations) $45

Grades: 9 10 11 12   **813**

1. Authors 2. Novelists

ISBN 978-1-60413-889-4

LC 2010-19263

First published 2004

A collection of ten essays discussing Crane's Civil War novel.

Includes bibliographical references

Stephen King; edited and with an introduction by Harold Bloom. Updated ed; Chelsea House 2006 228p (Modern critical views) $45

Grades: 9 10 11 12   **813**

1. Authors 2. Novelists 3. Short story writers 4. Science fiction writers

ISBN 0-7910-9317-4

LC 2006-25199

First published 1998

A collection of critical essays discussing the work of the prolific horror writer Stephen King.

Includes bibliographical references

Sterling, Laurie A.

Bloom's how to write about Herman Melville; [introduction by Harold Bloom] Bloom's Literary Criticism 2009 296p (Bloom's how to write about literature) $45

Grades: 9 10 11 12   **813**

1. Authors 2. Novelists 3. Report writing

ISBN 978-0-7910-9744-1

LC 2008-5708

This book offers "paper-topic suggestions, . . . strategies on how to write a strong essay, and an . . . introduction by Harold Bloom on writing about Hawthorne." Publisher's note

Includes bibliographical references

Bloom's how to write about Nathaniel Hawthorne; [introduction by Harold Bloom] Chelsea House 2008 344p (Bloom's how to write about literature) $45

Grades: 9 10 11 12   **813**

1. Authors 2. Novelists 3. Report writing 4. Short story writers

ISBN 978-0-7910-9481-5

LC 2006-101324

This book offers "paper-topic suggestions, . . . strategies on how to write a strong essay, and an . . . introduction by Harold Bloom on writing about Hawthorne. This . . . volume is designed to help students develop their analytical writ-

ing skills and critical comprehension of this important writer and his works." Publisher's note

Includes bibliographical references

Stowe, Harriet Beecher

★ The **Oxford** Harriet Beecher Stowe reader; edited with an introduction by Joan D. Hedrick. Oxford Univ. Press 1999 560p pa $34.95

Grades: 11 12 Adult   **813**

ISBN 0-19-509117-5

LC 97-32020

The editor provides an "introduction that assesses Stowe's vital impact on nineteenth-century American literature, politics, and culture. The readings are divided into three sections: Early Sketches, Antislavery Writings, and Domestic Culture and Politics. Early Sketches presents the finest writing of Stowe's literary apprenticeship. Antislavery Writings includes Uncle Tom's Cabin in its entirety. . . . Domestic Culture and Politics shows the scope of Stowe's thinking on the Victorian home, for which she was a major propagandist." Publisher's note

Includes bibliographical references

Sylvia Plath's The bell jar; edited & with an introduction by Harold Bloom. Bloom's Literary Criticism 2009 175p (Bloom's guides) $30

Grades: 9 10 11 12   **813**

1. Poets 2. Authors 3. Novelists

ISBN 978-1-60413-203-8

LC 2008-36547

This study guide to Plath's novel includes a brief biographical sketch of the author, a list of characters, a summary with analysis, and selections from critical essays by different scholars about the work.

Includes bibliographical references

The **tales** of Edgar Allan Poe; editor, Steven Frye. Salem Press 2010 293p il (Critical insights) lib bdg $85

Grades: 9 10 11 12   **813**

1. Poets 2. Authors 3. Essayists 4. Short story writers

ISBN 978-1-58765-616-3; 1-58765-616-7

LC 2009-26318

"Contains an editor's introduction to the author or work, a perspective from the editors of the . . . literary magazine The Paris Review, and a biography of the author. Following these ready-reference chapters is a section, 'Critical Contexts,' that presents four original essays by current scholars." Publisher's note

Includes bibliographical references

Tate, Mary Jo

★ **Critical** companion to F. Scott Fitzgerald; a literary reference to his life and work. foreword by Matthew J. Bruccoli. Facts on File 2006 464p il (Facts on File library of American literature) $75

Grades: 9 10 11 12 Adult   **813**

1. Authors 2. Novelists 3. Screenwriters 4. Short story writers

ISBN 0-8160-6433-4; 978-0-8160-6433-5

LC 2006-11393

First published 1998 with title: F. Scott Fitzgerald A to Z

This book "studies the legacy of this writer, highlighting significant themes and historical references of his various works." Publisher's note

Includes bibliographical references

Toni Morrison; edited and with an introduction by Harold Bloom. Chelsea House Publishers 2002 108p (Bloom's biocritiques) $35

Grades: 9 10 11 12 **813**

1. Authors 2. Novelists 3. Dramatists 4. Essayists 5. College teachers 6. Literary critics 7. Nobel laureates for literature

ISBN 0-7910-6180-9

LC 2002-7265

"Critical work in this volume covers topics such as the fictional world of Morrison, mixed genres and the logic of slavery in Beloved, and community and nature of Morrison's novels. Also included is . . . [a] biography of the writer, a complete bibliography of her work, and a list of critical work about the writer." Publisher's note

Includes bibliographical references

Toni Morrison's Beloved; edited and with an introduction by Harold Bloom. New ed; Bloom's Literary Criticism 2009 221p (Modern critical interpretations) $45

Grades: 9 10 11 12 **813**

1. Authors 2. Novelists 3. Dramatists 4. Essayists 5. College teachers 6. Literary critics 7. Nobel laureates for literature

ISBN 978-1-60413-184-0

LC 2009-9816

First published 1999

"Acclaimed as the greatest American novel of the last quarter century, Beloved confronts the legacy of slavery and its aftermath. . . . [The] full-length essays in this volume provide a . . . critical overview of this modern classic. This study guide also features a chronology of the author's life, a bibliography, an index, notes on the contributing writers, and an introduction by literature professor Harold Bloom." Publisher's note

Includes bibliographical references

Toni Morrison's The bluest eye; edited and with an introduction by Harold Bloom. Updated ed.; Bloom's Literary Criticism 2007 247p (Modern critical interpretations) $45

Grades: 9 10 11 12 **813**

1. Authors 2. Novelists 3. Dramatists 4. Essayists 5. College teachers 6. Literary critics 7. Nobel laureates for literature

ISBN 978-0-7910-9615-4

LC 2006-102701

First published 1999

A collection of fourteen essays discussing Morrison's debut novel, "the story of Pecola Breedlove, a young black girl who prays for her eyes to turn blue so that she will be as beautiful as all the blond, blue-eyed children in America." Publisher's note

Includes bibliographical references

Tyson, Edith S.

Orson Scott Card; writer of the terrible choice. Scarecrow Press 2003 xxv, 187p (Scarecrow studies in young adult literature) $40

Grades: 8 9 10 11 12 Adult Professional **813**

1. Authors 2. Novelists 3. Editors 4. Fantasy writers 5. Short story writers 6. Science fiction writers

ISBN 0-8108-4790-6

LC 2003-5730

"Tyson begins her book with a . . . preface gleaned from Card's own explanation of the purpose of his writing, followed by a light biographical skimming of his life and development as a writer. The best features of the book are Tyson's excellent analyses of Card's books. Each book is summarized . . . and then enriched with different perspectives on the meaning, or some relevant background information, or something that Card himself wrote about that particular book. The sequence and interrelatedness of his books are also well documented. This book is a must-have for both professional and circulating collections." Voice Youth Advocates

Includes bibliographical references

Upton Sinclair's The jungle; edited and with an introduction by Harold Bloom. Chelsea House Publishers 2002 176p (Modern critical interpretations) $45

Grades: 9 10 11 12 Adult **813**

1. Authors 2. Novelists 3. Biographers 4. Socialist leaders

ISBN 0-7910-6341-0

LC 2001-47152

A collection of nine essays discussing Sinclair's novel about an immigrant working in the meat processing industry.

Includes bibliographical references

Wharton, Edith

★ **Novellas** and other writings. Library of Am. 1990 1137p il $45

Grades: 11 12 Adult **813**

ISBN 0-940450-53-4

LC 89-62930

This volume contains the following novelettes: Madame de Troyes (1907); Ethan Frome (1911); Summer (1917); The mother's recompense (1925). Old New York (1924) is a collection of four novelettes: False dawn; The old maid; The spark; New Year's day. Also included is the autobiographical A backward glance (1934)

Includes bibliographical references

Willa Cather's My Antonia; edited and with an introduction by Harold Bloom. New ed; Bloom's Literary Criticism 2008 182p (Modern critical interpretations) $45

Grades: 11 12 Adult **813**

1. Authors 2. Novelists 3. Western writers 4. Short story writers

ISBN 978-0-7910-9626-0

LC 2008-7336

First published 1987

A collection of eleven essays on Willa Cather's novel about an immigrant woman on the Nebraska prairie.
Includes bibliographical references

William Faulkner; edited and with an introduction by Harold Bloom. New ed.; Bloom's Literary Criticism 2008 269p (Modern critical views) $45
Grades: 11 12 Adult **813**
1. Authors 2. Novelists 3. Screenwriters 4. Short story writers 5. Nobel laureates for literature
ISBN 978-0-7910-9786-1
LC 2007-33754
First published 1986
"This volume of . . . critical essays examines The Sound and the Fury, Light in August, As I Lay Dying, Absalom, Absalom!, and other key works by this preeminent writer of the twentieth century." Publisher's note
Includes bibliographical references

Winchell, Mike
Been There, Done That; Writing Stories from Life. edited by Mike Winchell. Penguin Group USA 2015 304 p. illustrations $17.99
Grades: 4 5 6 7 Professional **813**
1. Authorship 2. Creative writing 3. Creation (Literary, artistic, etc.)
ISBN 0448486725; 9780448486727
LC 2015026311
This anthology, edited by Mike Winchell, " looks at the process of taking real-life experiences and turning them into works of engaging fiction. The collection features award-winning and bestselling middle-grade authors who provide both original fictional short stories as well as the nonfiction accounts that inspired them. The contributing authors include Julia Alvarez, Karen Cushman, [and] Margarita Engle." (Publisher's note)
"Each story is prefaced with the author's account of what really happened, proving that the old adage 'Write what you know' can take a story in so many rich directions. This collection offers a little something for everyone and plenty of opportunities for classroom writing exercises." Booklist

Wright, Sarah Bird
Critical companion to Nathaniel Hawthorne; a literary reference to his life and work. Facts on File 2006 392p il (Facts on File library of American literature) $75
Grades: 11 12 Adult **813**
1. Authors 2. Novelists 3. Short story writers
ISBN 0-8160-5583-1; 978-0-8160-5583-8
LC 2005-34648
This book "offers critical entries on Hawthorne's novels, short stories, travel writing, criticism, and other works, as well as portraits of characters, including Hester Prynne and Roger Chillingworth. This . . . reference also provides entries on Hawthorne's family, friends—ranging from Herman Melville to President Franklin Pierce—publishers, and critics, as well as periodicals that published his work and important places and events in his life." Publisher's note
Includes bibliographical references

Zora Neale Hurston; edited and with an introduction by Harold Bloom. New ed; Chelsea House Publishers 2008 238p (Modern critical views) $45
Grades: 10 11 12 Adult **813**
1. Authors 2. Novelists 3. Dramatists 4. Memoirists 5. Folklorists 6. Short story writers
ISBN 978-0-7910-9610-9
LC 2007-49161
First published 1986
"Featuring supplemental material such as a chronology, a bibliography, and an index, [this book is a] critical look at Hurston's work and its influence on contemporary themes, such as race and gender in American society." Publisher's note
Includes bibliographical references

Zora Neale Hurston's Their eyes were watching God; edited & with an introduction by Harold Bloom. Chelsea House 2010 109p (Bloom's guides) $30
Grades: 9 10 11 12 **813**
1. Authors 2. Novelists 3. Dramatists 4. Memoirists 5. Folklorists 6. Short story writers
ISBN 978-1-60413-571-8
LC 2009-15016
"This study guide to the novel features short excerpts of critical essays, an annotated bibliography, an index, and an introductory essay by . . . Harold Bloom." Publisher's note
Includes bibliographical references

813.54   American fiction--1945-1999

Wolny, Philip
Isaac Asimov; Philip Wolny. Rosen Publishing 2015 112 p. illustrations (some color) (Great science writers) (library bound) $35.60
Grades: 10 11 12 **813.54**
1. Scientists 2. Science writers -- United States -- Biography 3. Authors, American -- 20th century -- Biography
ISBN 1477776893; 9781477776896
LC 2013049327
This book by Philip Wolny examines how "as he was earning a Ph.D. in chemistry, [Isaac] Asimov was continuing his literary writing, both nonfiction and science fiction. Back matter includes an extensive timeline, glossary, further reading, bibliography and index." (Publisher's note)
"Throughout his biography, Tyson's passion for space exploration is palpable. Dynamic, understated artwork does not distract from excellent writing here. Strong additions." SLJ
Includes bibliographical references and index

814   American essays in English

Angelou, Maya
Wouldn't take nothing for my journey now. Random House 1993 141p hardcover o.p. pa $6.99

Grades: 11 12 Adult **814**
ISBN 0-679-42743-0; 0-553-56907-4 pa
LC 93-5904

The author "shares her thoughts about humankind: how to respect others of different cultures, opinions, and values as taught by universal philosophies. . . . Angelou's prose is brisk, fluid, and entrancing. This work will provide a taste of wisdom to all who read it." Libr J

Baldwin, James
Collected essays. Library of Am. 1998 869p $35
Grades: 11 12 Adult **814**
ISBN 1-883011-52-3
LC 97-23496

The essays in this volume were selected by Toni Morrison. "Morrison has reprinted all of the material contained in Baldwin's previous collected essays, The Price of the Ticket (1985). She has added eleven pieces, the earliest of which dates from 1947—Baldwin's first published review, of a biography of Frederick Douglass, in the Nation—and the latest from 1984." Times Lit Suppl

The **beholder's** eye; a collection of America's finest personal journalism. edited and with an introduction by Walt Harrington. Grove Press 2005 xxii, 256p pa $14
Grades: 11 12 Adult **814**
ISBN 0-8021-4224-5
LC 2005-46242

"Each writer takes a unique approach to the subject, drawing the reader into the experience of pit-bull fighting or hunting with the Inuit. Among the collection: Harrington, who is married to a black woman, explores his evolving attitudes on race through the lens of his relationship with his in-laws, Pete Earley returns to his hometown in search of the meaning of a sister's death in their youth, Ron Rosenbaum explores his own outlook on life in a philosophical discourse with then-New York governor Mario Cuomo, Davis Miller is unabashedly starstruck in a comfortable and closeup look at Muhammad Ali at the home of Ali's mother, and Stephen S. Hall is personally probing in his exploration, via MRI, of his own brain and its functioning. These stories are amusing, insightful, and touching in a way that only something personal can be." Booklist

★ The **Best** American essays of the century; Joyce Carol Oates, editor; Robert Atwan, coeditor; with an introduction by Joyce Carol Oates. Houghton Mifflin 2000 596p hardcover o.p. pa $18
Grades: 11 12 Adult **814**
ISBN 0-618-04370-5; 0-618-15587-2 pa

"Oates has assembled a provocative collection of masterpieces reflecting both the fragmentation and surprising cohesiveness of various American identities." Publ Wkly
Includes bibliographical references

Bradbury, Ray
Bradbury speaks; too soon from the cave, too far from the stars. William Morrow 2005 243p hardcover o.p. pa $14.95

Grades: 11 12 Adult **814**
ISBN 0-06-058568-4; 0-06-058569-2 pa
LC 2005-41489

In this collection of essays, the author "weighs in on a medley of topics, including the allure of Paris, his enthusiasm for trains, the genesis of his most popular novels, and his reasons for remaining a diehard optimist. . . . By turns whimsical, insightful, and unabashedly metaphoric, his prose is immediately accessible as well as thought-provoking. Fans and nonfans alike should enjoy." Booklist

Du Bois, W. E. B.
★ **Writings**. Library of Am. 1986 1334p $40; pa $15.95
Grades: 11 12 Adult **814**
ISBN 0-940450-33-X; 1-883011-31-0 pa
LC 86-10565

Includes bibliographical references

Everything I needed to know about being a girl I learned from Judy Blume. Pocket Books 2007 275p hardcover o.p. pa $14
Grades: 11 12 Adult **814**
1. Authors 2. Novelists 3. Children's authors 4. Young adult authors
ISBN 978-1-4165-3104-3; 1-4165-3104-1; 978-1-4391-0265-7 pa; 1-4391-0265-1 pa

"This collection of 24 essays . . . pays tribute to the influence of Judy Blume and her work about coming-of-age as a girl in America. In each piece, the writer reveals what O'Connell calls her 'Judy Blume moment,' telling a heartfelt and revealing story that reflects the same social awkwardness and true-to-life experiences Blume conveys in her novels, from menstruation to childhood bullying to masturbation. . . . Readers who similarly found solace and support in Blume's work should relate easily to these writers through the Blumian characters and themes they evoke." Publ Wkly

A **Historical** guide to Ralph Waldo Emerson; edited by Joel Myerson. Oxford Univ. Press 2000 322p il (Historical guides to American authors) $45; pa $17.95
Grades: 11 12 Adult **814**
1. Poets 2. Authors 3. Philosophers 4. Essayists
ISBN 0-19-512093-0; 0-19-512094-9 pa
LC 99-13122

Contributors discuss the prominent transcendentalist's views on religion, slavery, women's rights, natural science and individualism. Includes a biographical essay and a chronology
Includes bibliographical references

In fact; the best of Creative nonfiction. edited by Lee Gutkind; introduction by Annie Dillard. Norton 2005 xxxvi, 440p pa $15.95
Grades: 9 10 11 12 **814**
ISBN 0-393-32665-9
LC 2004-16506

This anthology of 25 essays from the literary journal Creative Nonfiction "covers the creative nonfiction universe from the personal essay to nature writing, literary journalism, and science writing. . . . This stellar volume will stand as an exciting and defining creative nonfiction primer." Booklist

Kingsolver, Barbara

Small wonder; essays. illustrations by Paul Mirocha. HarperCollins Pubs. 2002 267p $23.95; pa $12.95

Grades: 11 12 Adult   814

ISBN 0-06-050407-2; 0-06-050408-0 pa

LC 2002-276255

"This set of 19 penetrating autobiographical musings on humankind and how we treat each other and the rest of nature coalesced in the stunned aftermath of September 11. . . . Food, motherhood, gardening, literature, television, homelessness, globalization, scientific illiteracy, selfishness, and forgiveness all come under sharp and revelatory scrutiny." Booklist

Kirk, Andrew

Understanding Thoreau's Civil disobedience. Rosen Pub. 2010 128p il (Words that changed the world) lib bdg $31.95

Grades: 7 8 9 10   814

1. Authors 2. Naturalists 3. Resistance to government 4. Essayists 5. Pacifists 6. Writers on nature 7. Nonfiction writers

ISBN 978-1-4488-1671-2; 1-4488-1671-8

LC 2010-10221

First published 2004 by Barrons with title: Civil disobedience

This considers Thoreau's Civil Disobedience, including its "'Context and Creator,' 'Immediate Impact,' 'Legacy,' and 'Aftermath.' . . . [Exploring] the historical context of transcendentalism and resistance to big government. . . . [The] author provides a balance of deep context, expressive writing, and pertinent information." SLJ

Includes glossary and bibliographical references

Walker, Alice

Anything we love can be saved; a writer's activism: essays, speeches, statements & letters. Random House 1997 xxv, 225p hardcover o.p. pa $15.95

Grades: 11 12 Adult   814

ISBN 0-345-40796-2 pa

LC 96-41159

Walker has assembled a "wide-ranging collection of personal essays, remarks, letters, speeches and statements, many previously published. . . . Constantly testing and stretching her readers' imaginations and boundaries, Walker expresses her warmth, her anger, her optimism in this provocative, lively collection." Publ Wkly

815 American speeches in English

★ **American** Heritage book of great American speeches for young people; edited by Suzanne McIntire. Wiley 2001 292p il pa $14.95

Grades: 7 8 9 10   815

1. American speeches

ISBN 0-471-38942-0

LC 00-43749

This is a "compendium of more than 100 speeches that span nearly 400 years of American history, from Powhatan (1609) to Senator Charles Robb (2000). Prominent orators include Patrick Henry, Thomas Jefferson, John Kennedy, Richard Nixon, Martin Luther King, Jr., and Malcolm X. . . . The speeches inform readers and provide examples of how the spoken word has affected Americans throughout our past." SLJ

American speeches. Library of America 2006 2v ea $35

Grades: 9 10 11 12 Adult   815

1. American speeches

ISBN 1-931082-97-9 v1; 1-931082-98-7 v2

LC 2006-40928

This is a collection of over 120 historical speeches delivered between 1761 and 1997.

Includes bibliographical references

★ **Historic** speeches of African Americans; introduced and selected by Warren J. Halliburton. Watts 1993 192p il (African-American experience) lib bdg $23

Grades: 7 8 9 10 11 12   815

1. American speeches 2. African Americans -- History

ISBN 0-531-11034-6

LC 92-39318

Presents speeches by various African American religious and political leaders from the days of slavery to the present, along with biographical information and historical background.

"Kids will dip into this for personal reading, and for curriculum research; they'll also find stirring pieces to read aloud and think about. The detailed sources at the end of the book make it easy to find out more about the individuals and their ideas." Booklist

★ **In** our own words; extraordinary speeches of the American century. edited by Robert G. Torricelli and Andrew Carroll. Kodansha Int. 1999 xxx, 450p $28

Grades: 11 12 Adult   815

1. American speeches

ISBN 1-56836-291-9

LC 99-29995

"Arranged by decade from the Progressive Era to the '90s Technological Revolution, this book includes eulogies, sermons, fireside chats, public tributes, commencement addresses, and more. . . . Entries are attributed to Jane Addams, Clarence Darrow, Al 'Scarface' Capone, General George S. Patton, Jack Kerouac, Vince Lombardi, Jane Fonda, Ronald Reagan, and others." SLJ

Includes bibliographical references

Representative American speeches. Wilson, H.W. (Reference shelf)

Grades: 11 12 Adult   815

1. American speeches

Annual. First published 1937-1938

A compilation containing a selection of speeches of the year made by eminent men and women on major trends and events. Each speech is prefaced by a note about the speaker and the occasion. The appendix in each volume contains biographical notes.

★ **U-X-L** Asian American voices; edited by Deborah Gillan Straub. 2nd ed; U.X.L 2004 xxv, 315p il $58

Grades: 7 8 9 10 11 12   **815**

1. Asian Americans 2. American speeches
ISBN 0-7876-7600-4

LC 2003-110048

First published 1997 with title: Asian American voices

This "reference presents full or excerpted speeches, sermons, orations, poems, testimony and other notable spoken words of Asian Americans. Each entry is accompanied by an introduction and boxes explaining terms and events to which the speech refers. The volume is illustrated with photographs and drawings." Publisher's note

816   American letters in English

★ **Letters** of the century; America, 1900-1999. edited by Lisa Grunwald and Stephen J. Adler. Dial Press (NY) 1999 741p il hardcover o.p. pa $18

Grades: 11 12 Adult   **816**

1. American letters 2. United States -- Civilization
ISBN 0-385-31590-2; 0-385-31593-7 pa

LC 99-16808

Among the letter writers gathered are "Carl Van Doren, Huey Long, Franklin D. Roosevelt, Lillian Hellman and a Vietnam soldier named Dusty. This is one of the most original literary tributes to the closing century." Publ Wkly

Includes bibliographical references

817   American humor and satire in English

Honey, hush! an anthology of African American women's humor. edited by Daryl Cumber Dance; foreword by Nikki Giovanni. Norton 1997 xxxix, 673p il hardcover o.p. pa $17.95

Grades: 11 12 Adult   **817**

1. African American women 2. American wit and humor
ISBN 0-393-31818-4 pa

LC 97-6772

The editor "has collected folktales, proverbs, slave narratives, and cartoons reflecting the humor of African American women. Among those included are authors Audre Lorde and Toni Morrison and comedian Whoopi Goldberg." Libr J

Includes bibliographical references

★ **Russell** Baker's book of American humor. Norton 1993 598p $30

Grades: 11 12 Adult   **817**

1. American wit and humor
ISBN 0-393-03592-1

LC 93-22733

"Two hundred years of American humor have gone into the making of this anthology. . . . In the lineup are many of the old pros—Mark Twain, Fred Allen, James Thurber—and

several relative newcomers—Fran Lebowitz, Nora Ephron, P.J. O'Rourke, and Dave Barry. The selections are nicely assorted in substance and are arranged by theme rather than chronology." Libr J

Includes bibliographical references

818   American miscellaneous writings in English

Alex Haley's The autobiography of Malcolm X; edited & with an introduction by Harold Bloom. Chelsea House 2008 173p (Bloom's guides) $30

Grades: 9 10 11 12   **818**

1. Authors 2. Novelists 3. Historians 4. Journalists 5. Biographers 6. Short story writers 7. Black Muslim leaders 8. Civil rights activists
ISBN 978-0-7910-9832-5

LC 2007-51313

This study guide on Malcolm X's autobiography includes a brief biographical sketch, a list of characters, a summary and analysis, and selections from critical essays by different scholars about the work.

Includes bibliographical references

Amper, Susan

Bloom's how to write about Edgar Allan Poe; [introduction by Harold Bloom] Chelsea House 2007 232p (Bloom's how to write about literature) $45

Grades: 9 10 11 12   **818**

1. Poets 2. Authors 3. Report writing 4. Essayists 5. Short story writers
ISBN 978-0-7910-9488-4

LC 2007-8120

This book offers "paper-topic suggestions, . . . strategies on how to write a strong essay, and an . . . introduction by Harold Bloom on writing about Poe. This volume is designed to help students develop their analytical writing skills and critical comprehension of this important author's turbulent life and unforgettable works." Publisher's note

Includes bibliographical references

The **Best** of the West; an anthology of classic writing from the American West. edited by Tony Hillerman. HarperCollins Pubs. 1991 528p hardcover o.p. pa $18

Grades: 11 12 Adult   **818**

1. West (U.S.) in literature
ISBN 0-06-092352-0 pa

LC 90-55930

This anthology's "nonfiction sources run from 500 B.C. to the late nineteenth century; fictional selections by Harte, Crane, Scarborough, Davis, Stegner, and Norris are included. . . . Hillerman's subject groupings (e.g., explorers, settlers, Navajos, Hispanics, cowboys, miners, women, travel, and the military) make sense, and his juxtapositions encourage a thoughtful response." Booklist

Capote, Truman

A **Christmas** memory, One Christmas, & The Thanksgiving visitor. Modern Lib. 1996 107p $13.95

Grades: 9 10 11 12 **818**
ISBN 0-679-60237-2

LC 96-26022

In addition to two autobiographical stories A Christmas memory (1966) and The Thanksgiving visitor (1968), this volume includes the memoir One Christmas (1983)

One Christmas describes the Christmas Capote spent with his father in New Orleans when he was six years old. A Christmas memory and The Thanksgiving visitor "center on the author's early years with a family of distant relatives in rural Alabama. Both pay loving tribute to an eccentric old-maid cousin, Miss Sook Faulk, who became his best friend." Publisher's note

Dillard, Annie

The **Annie** Dillard reader. HarperCollins Pubs. 1994 455p hardcover o.p. pa $15.95
Grades: 11 12 Adult **818**
ISBN 0-06-092660-0 pa

LC 94-19482

This reader includes Holy the firm; excerpts from Pilgrim at Tinker Creek, An American childhood, and Teaching a stone to talk; and a reworked version of the 1978 short story The living

"This selection of writings, chosen by Dillard herself, provides a perfect sampling of her incisive, versatile, and impeccable achievements." Booklist

Pilgrim at Tinker Creek. Harper & Row 1974 271p hardcover o.p. pa $14.95
Grades: 9 10 11 12 Adult **818**
1. Natural history -- Virginia
ISBN 0-06-123332-3 pa; 978-0-06-123332-6 pa

This work is "in an honored tradition of literature, not quite environmentalism and not the philosophy of science, it is rather the refraction of natural philosophy through the prismatic conscience of art. Highly recommended for the general reader—any general reader, anywhere—who wishes to deepen his awareness of his yard of world and to reflect upon it more profoundly." Choice

★ **Edgar** Allan Poe; edited and with an introduction by Harold Bloom. Chelsea House Publishers 2001 99p (Bloom's biocritiques) $35
Grades: 9 10 11 12 **818**
1. Poets 2. Authors 3. Essayists 4. Short story writers
ISBN 0-7910-6173-6

LC 2001-53901

"This title offers a . . . biography of Poe, critical essays of his works, and an introduction by Professor Bloom." Publisher's note
Includes bibliographical references

Eliot, T. S.

Eliot; poems and prose. Knopf 1998 221p (Everyman's library pocket poets) $12.50
Grades: 11 12 Adult **818**
ISBN 0-375-40185-7

A representative selection of work by the influential modernist poet and critic

Emerson, Ralph Waldo

★ The **portable** Emerson; [rev ed]; Penguin Bks. 1981 xxxix, 670p pa $16.95
Grades: 11 12 Adult **818**
1. Authors 2. Emperors 3. Religion 4. Agriculture 5. Naturalists 6. Conservatism 7. Philosophers 8. Learning and scholarship 9. British national characteristics 10. Essayists 11. Pacifists 12. Writers on nature 13. Nonfiction writers 14. Great Britain -- Civilization
ISBN 0-14-015094-3

LC 81-4047

First published 1946 by Viking

The editors have provided the following selections: essays, including History, Self-reliance, The over-soul, Circles and The poet; The complete texts of Nature and English traits; biographical essays on Plato, Napoleon, Henry David Thoreau, Thomas Carlyle, and others as well as twenty-two poems.
Includes bibliographical references

The **environment** in Henry David Thoreau's Walden; Gary Wiener, book editor. Greenhaven Press 2010 219p il (Social issues in literature) $38.45; pa $26.50
Grades: 9 10 11 12 **818**
1. Authors 2. Naturalists 3. Nature in literature 4. Environmental protection 5. Essayists 6. Pacifists 7. Writers on nature 8. Nonfiction writers
ISBN 978-0-7377-4654-9; 0-7377-4654-8; 978-0-7377-4655-6 pa; 0-7377-4655-6 pa

LC 2009-40566

This book "is organized in three sections, beginning with background information about the author and providing insight into how the author's experiences influenced his or her work. Another section presents articles that analyze the relationship between the work and the social issue, all from a variety of perspectives. A final chapter brings the highlighted social issue into contemporary times, discussing its status in society today. . . . [This book] highlights issues of concern and shows how the issues that compelled Thoreau to retreat to Walden Pond are just as important to students today." Voice Youth Advocates
Includes bibliographical references

Franklin, Benjamin

★ **Autobiography,** Poor Richard, and later writings; letters from London, 1757-1775, Paris, 1776-1785, Philadelphia, 1785-1790, Poor Richard's almanack, 1733-1758, The autobiography. Library of America 1997 816p $30
Grades: 11 12 Adult **818**
ISBN 1-883011-53-1

LC 97-21611

"This collection of Franklin's works begins with letters sent from London (1757-1775) describing the events and diplomacy preceding the Revolutionary War. The volume also contains political satires, bagatelles, pamphlets, and letters written in Paris (1776-1785), where he represented the revolutionary United States at the court of Louis XVI, as well as his speeches given in the Constitutional Convention and other works written in Philadelphia (1785-1790), including his last published article, a . . . satire against slavery. Also included are the . . . prefaces to Poor Richard's Almanack (1733-1758). . . . [The] Autobiography, Franklin's last word on his greatest literary creation—his own invented personality—is presented here in a new edition." Publisher's note

Includes bibliographical references

Hawthorne, Nathaniel

The **portable** Hawthorne; edited with an introduction by William C. Spengemann. Penguin Books 2005 439p (Penguin classics) pa $18

Grades: 11 12 Adult   **818**

ISBN 0-14-303928-8; 978-0-14-303928-0

LC 2004-65791

This collection "includes writings from each major stage in the career of Nathaniel Hawthorne: a number of his . . . early tales, all of The Scarlet Letter, excerpts from his three subsequently published romances—The House of Seven Gables, The Blithedale Romance, and The Marble Faun—as well as passages from his European journals and a sampling of his last, unfinished works." Publisher's note

Includes bibliographical references

Henry David Thoreau; edited and with an introduction by Harold Bloom. Updated ed; Chelsea House 2007 244p (Modern critical views) $45

Grades: 9 10 11 12 Adult   **818**

1. Authors 2. Naturalists 3. Essayists 4. Pacifists 5. Writers on nature 6. Nonfiction writers

ISBN 0-7910-9348-4; 978-0-7910-9348-1

LC 2006-34841

Ethel Seybold, John Hildebidle, and Robert Sattelmeyer are among the contributors who discuss Thoreau's language, narrative technique and philosophy.

Includes bibliographical references

★ A **Historical** guide to Edgar Allan Poe; edited by J. Gerald Kennedy. Oxford Univ. Press 2001 247p il (Historical guides to American authors) $39.95; pa $15.95

Grades: 11 12 Adult   **818**

1. Poets 2. Authors 3. Essayists 4. Short story writers

ISBN 0-19-512149-X; 0-19-512150-3 pa

LC 00-20192

Following an introduction this volume presents a "capsule biography situating Poe in his historical context. The subsequent essays in this book cover such topics as Poe and the American publishing industry, Poe's sensationalism, his relationships to gender constructions, and Poe and American privacy. The volume also includes a bibliographic essay, a chronology of Poe's life, a bibliography, illustrations, and an index." Publisher's note

Includes bibliographical references

★ A **Historical** guide to Henry David Thoreau; edited by William E. Cain. Oxford Univ. Press 2000 285p il maps (Historical guides to American authors) $95; pa $50

Grades: 9 10 11 12   **818**

1. Authors 2. Naturalists 3. Essayists 4. Pacifists 5.

Writers on nature 6. Nonfiction writers

ISBN 0-19-513862-7; 0-19-513863-5 pa

LC 99-55276

Scholars assess the essays, social criticism, and natural history writing of the influential Transcendentalist. Includes a biographical essay and chronology

Includes bibliographical references

Hughes, Langston

The **return** of Simple; edited by Akiba Sullivan Harper; introduction by Arnold Rampersad. Hill & Wang 1994 xxii, 218p hardcover o.p. pa $11

Grades: 11 12 Adult   **818**

ISBN 0-8090-1582-X pa

LC 93-45373

This collection brings together the "narrations of the fictional Jesse B. Semple, or 'Simple,' which first appeared in 1943 in [Hughes] column in the Chicago Defender and, later, in the New York Post. Here, edited by a teacher at Spelman College, is an enlightening collection of these social commentaries." Publ Wkly

★ **I** know why the caged bird sings, by Maya Angelou; editor, Mildred R. Mickle. Salem Press 2009 285p (Critical insights) lib bdg $85

Grades: 9 10 11 12   **818**

1. Poets 2. Actors 3. Singers 4. Dramatists 5. Essayists 6. Memoirists 7. Children's authors

ISBN 978-1-58765-624-8; 1-58765-624-8

LC 2009-26306

This book discusses the historical context of Maya Angelou's book and includes a biography of the author as well as critical essays on the work.

Includes bibliographical references

Ironside, Fabian

Bloom's how to write about Ralph Waldo Emerson; [introduction by Harold Bloom] Bloom's Literary Criticism 2009 280p (Bloom's how to write about literature) $45

Grades: 11 12 Adult   **818**

1. Poets 2. Authors 3. Philosophers 4. Report writing 5. Essayists

ISBN 978-0-7910-9833-2

LC 2008-5710

This book offers "paper-topic suggestions, . . . strategies on how to write a strong essay, and an . . . introduction by Harold Bloom on writing about Emerson." Publisher's note

Includes bibliographical references

James Baldwin; edited and with an introduction by Harold Bloom. Updated ed; Chelsea House 2007 226p (Modern critical views) $45

Grades: 11 12 Adult   **818**

1. Authors 2. Novelists 3. Dramatists 4. Essayists 5. Screenwriters 6. Short story writers 7. Young adult authors

ISBN 0-7910-9365-4; 978-0-7910-9365-8

LC 2006-31146

First published 1986

A collection of critical essays discussing the work of the essayist, novelist and playwright James Baldwin.
Includes bibliographical references

Jefferson, Thomas, 1743-1826

★ **Writings**. Library of Am. 1984 1600p $35
Grades: 11 12 Adult 818
ISBN 0-940450-16-X

LC 83-19917

This is "the largest and most skillfully edited single-volume Jefferson ever published." N Y Times Book Rev
Includes bibliographical references

Kelley, James B.

Bloom's how to write about Langston Hughes; introduction by Harold Bloom. Bloom's Literary Criticism 2009 200p (Bloom's how to write about literature) $45
Grades: 9 10 11 12 818
1. Poets 2. Authors 3. Novelists 4. Dramatists 5. Report writing 6. Short story writers 7. Young adult authors
ISBN 978-1-60413-329-5

LC 2009-19583

This book offers paper topics and advice on writing an essay about the works of Langston Hughes.
Includes bibliographical references

Kerouac, Jack

★ The **portable** Jack Kerouac; edited by Ann Charters. Viking 1995 xxv, 625p hardcover o.p. pa $17
Grades: 11 12 Adult 818
ISBN 0-14-310506-X pa

LC 94-20120

"Charters has chosen selections from each of Kerouac's 14 novels, which comprise a complex and evocative autobiographical series Kerouac called the Legend of Duluoz. . . . Charters has also included poetry from San Francisco Blues and Book of Haikus, as well as a group of essays that cover Kerouac's main passions and interests: writing, traveling, jazz, and Buddhism." Booklist
Includes bibliographical references

Langston Hughes; edited and with an introduction by Harold Bloom. New ed; Blooms Literary Criticism 2008 247p (Modern critical views) $45
Grades: 9 10 11 12 818
1. Poets 2. Authors 3. Novelists 4. Dramatists 5. Short story writers 6. Young adult authors
ISBN 978-0-7910-9612-3

LC 2007-43405

First published 1989
A collection of critical essays discussing the works of Harlem Renaissance author Langston Hughes.
Includes bibliographical references

Lines of velocity; [executive editor, Keren Taylor; associate editors, Cindy Collins . . . [et al.]]
WriteGirl 2007 236p pa $19.95
Grades: 9 10 11 12 818
1. Teenagers' writings
ISBN 978-0-9741251-5-2

WriteGirl is "a creative writing and mentoring organization for teen girls in the Los Angeles area. Unlike many such anthologies, this collection includes the work of experienced mentors who volunteered their time to the project, as well as the teen participants. . . . This appealing volume is broken into 10 sections: self, writing, Los Angeles, friendship, love, rants, family, place, origins, and writing experiments. The poetry and prose found in each one are sincere and personal, and one gets the feeling of having discovered a dog-eared, doodle-laden journal among the refuse of a high school parking lot. . . . This anthology is sure to be picked up by aspiring young writers as well as educators looking for inspired samples and interactive exercises." SLJ

Margaret Atwood; edited and with an introduction by Harold Bloom. Bloom's Literary Criticism 2009 204p (Modern critical views) $45
Grades: 11 12 Adult 818
1. Poets 2. Authors 3. Novelists 4. Essayists 5. Children's authors 6. Short story writers
ISBN 978-1-60413-181-9

LC 2008-28128

First published 2000
This "collection of critical essays examines . . . [The Handmaid's Tale and other works] including Oryx and Crake, Cat's Cradle, The Robber Bride, and more." Publisher's note
Includes bibliographical references

Mark Twain; edited and with an introduction by Harold Bloom. Chelsea House 2003 163p (Bloom's biocritiques) $35
Grades: 9 10 11 12 818
1. Authors 2. Humorists 3. Novelists 4. Essayists 5. Satirists 6. Memoirists 7. Travel writers 8. Short story writers
ISBN 0-7910-6372-0

LC 2002-152672

This book features a brief biography of the American humorist along with several critical essays discussing his work.
Includes bibliographical references

★ **Maya** Angelou; edited and with an introduction by Harold Bloom. New ed; Bloom's Literary Criticism 2009 178p (Modern critical views) $45
Grades: 9 10 11 12 818
1. Poets 2. Actors 3. Singers 4. Dramatists 5. Essayists 6. Memoirists 7. Children's authors
ISBN 978-1-60413-177-2

LC 2008-44406

First published 1998
Scholars explore social, political and religious themes in Angelou's prose and poetry.
Includes bibliographical references

Maya Angelou's I know why the caged bird sings; edited and with an introduction by Harold Bloom. [New ed.]; Bloom's Literary Criticism 2009 141p (Modern critical interpretations) $45

Grades: 11 12 Adult   **818**

1. Poets 2. Actors 3. Singers 4. Dramatists 5. Essayists 6. Memoirists 7. Children's authors

ISBN 978-1-60413-187-1

LC 2009-12580

First published 1998

Critical essays analyze Angelou's classic autobiography. Contributors include Carol E. Neubauer, Elizabeth Fox-Genovese, Lucinda Moore, and Ian Marshall.

Includes bibliographical references

Poe, Edgar Allan

★ The **collected** tales and poems of Edgar Allan Poe. Modern Lib. 1992 1026p $20

Grades: 11 12 Adult   **818**

ISBN 0-679-60007-8

LC 92-50231

A reissue of The complete tales and poems of Edgar Allan Poe published 1938

This volume contains short stories, poems, and a sampling of Poe's essays, criticism and journalistic writings

Rasmussen, R. Kent

Bloom's how to write about Mark Twain; introduction by Harold Bloom. Chelsea House 2007 324p (Bloom's how to write about literature) $45

Grades: 9 10 11 12   **818**

1. Authors 2. Humorists 3. Novelists 4. Report writing 5. Essayists 6. Satirists 7. Memoirists 8. Travel writers 9. Short story writers

ISBN 978-0-7910-9487-7

LC 2007-7248

This book offers "paper-topic suggestions, . . . outlined strategies on how to write a strong essay, and an . . . introduction by Harold Bloom on writing about Twain. This volume is designed to help students develop their analytical writing skills and critical comprehension of this important author and his works." Publisher's note

Includes bibliographical references

Critical companion to Mark Twain; a literary reference to his life and work. with critical commentary by John H. Davis and Alex Feerst. Rev ed; Facts on File 2007 2v il map (Facts on File library of American literature) set $125

Grades: 11 12 Adult   **818**

1. Authors 2. Humorists 3. Novelists 4. Essayists 5. Satirists 6. Memoirists 7. Travel writers 8. Short story writers

ISBN 0-8160-5398-7; 978-0-8160-5398-8

LC 2004-46910

First published 1995 in one volume with title: Mark Twain A to Z

This companion to the life and works of Mark Twain includes a biography, synopses and critical commentaries on each of his works, discussions about major characters and

places in his works, and entries on important people, places, and other aspects of his life.

Includes glossary, filmography and bibliographical references

Richard Wright's Black boy; edited and with an introduction by Harold Bloom. Chelsea House Publishers 2006 197p (Modern critical interpretations) $45

Grades: 11 12 Adult   **818**

1. Authors 2. Novelists 3. Dramatists 4. Essayists 5. Nonfiction writers 6. Short story writers

ISBN 0-7910-8585-6; 978-0-7910-8585-1

LC 2006-1772

This book "details the themes and history of this seminal American classic with . . . critical essays . . . [and a] chronology of Wright's life and times." Publisher's note

Includes bibliographical references

Social and psychological disorder in the works of Edgar Allan Poe; Claudia Durst Johnson, book editor. Greenhaven Press 2010 163p il (Social issues in literature) $38.45; pa $26.50

Grades: 9 10 11 12   **818**

1. Poets 2. Authors 3. Social problems in literature 4. Essayists 5. Short story writers

ISBN 978-0-7377-5016-4; 0-7377-5016-2; 978-0-7377-5017-1 pa; 0-7377-5017-0 pa

LC 2010-83

This book "is organized in three sections, beginning with background information about the author and providing insight into how the author's experiences influenced his or her work. Another section presents articles that analyze the relationship between the work and the social issue, all from a variety of perspectives. A final chapter brings the highlighted social issue into contemporary times, discussing its status in society today. The articles, all signed, and all from individual contributors, are brief and clearly written, with students in mind. . . . They delve into the aspects of madness, murder, and obsession that make Poe's tales so fascinating to students." Voice Youth Advocates

Includes bibliographical references

Sova, Dawn B.

★ **Critical** companion to Edgar Allan Poe; a literary reference to his life and work. Facts on File 2007 458p il (Facts on File library of American literature) $75

Grades: 11 12 Adult   **818**

1. Poets 2. Authors 3. Essayists 4. Short story writers

ISBN 0-8160-6408-3; 978-0-8160-6408-3

LC 2006-29466

First published 2001 with title: Edgar Allan Poe, A-Z

"Biographical, historical, and critical material on Poe's life and work is presented in alphabetical order in three sections. The entries on Poe's works each provide a synopsis, a publication history, and character descriptions, while major works such as 'The Cask of Amontillado' and 'The Purloined Letter' have . . . [a] commentary and . . . further-reading suggestions." SLJ

Includes bibliographical references

Stein, Gertrude

Selected writings; edited with an introduction and notes by Carl Van Vechten and with an essay on Gertrude Stein by F. W. Dupee. Modern Lib. 1962 706p hardcover o.p. pa $18

Grades: 11 12 Adult **818**
1. France -- History -- 1945-1958 2. France -- History -- 1940-1945, German occupation
ISBN 0-679-72464-8 pa

In addition to the autobiography of Alice B. Toklas and the libretto Four saints in three acts, this volume contains representative selections of Stein's poetry, prose, drama, and criticism.

Writings, 1932-1946. Library of Am. 1998 844p $40

Grades: 11 12 Adult **818**
ISBN 1-883011-41-8
LC 97-28916

In addition to theater pieces, fiction, and poetry "memoir, philosophical speculation, literary criticism and theory, all sorts of briefer forms that are hard to account for but easy to marvel at and even to delight in, pack these volumes, and constitute, as the editors surely intended us to discover, the most consistently achieved representation of new ways of responding to life and new possibilities of getting experience into words that American literature has to show." N Y Times Book Rev

Steinbeck, John

★ The **grapes** of wrath and other writings, 1936-1941. Library of Am. 1996 1067p $35

Grades: 9 10 11 12 **818**
ISBN 1-883011-15-9
LC 96-3725

This volume contains the short story collection The long valley (1938) and the novel The grapes of wrath. Also included is The log from the Sea of Cortez (1941) Steinbeck's narrative about marine research in the Gulf of California and The harvest gypsies, a series of newspaper articles on migrant labor that was published with title Their blood is strong (1938)

Stephen Crane; edited and with an introduction by Harold Bloom. Updated ed.; Chelsea House 2007 220p (Modern critical views) $45

Grades: 11 12 Adult **818**
1. Authors 2. Novelists
ISBN 978-0-7910-9429-7; 0-7910-9429-4
LC 2006-101024

First published 1987

A collection of critical essays discussing the work of the author and poet Stephen Crane.
Includes bibliographical references

Thoreau, Henry David

★ **Collected** essays and poems. Library of Am. 2001 703p $35

Grades: 11 12 Adult **818**
ISBN 1-883011-95-7
LC 00-46234

Among the 27 essays included are Civil disobedience, Walking, Martyrdom of John Brown, A Yankee in Canada, and Life without principle. Many of the poems were taken from Thoreau's journals and manuscripts
Includes bibliographical references

★ **Walden,** or, Life in the woods; with an introduction by Verlyn Klinkenborg. Knopf 1992 xxxi, 295p $19

Grades: 11 12 Adult **818**
ISBN 0-679-41896-2
LC 92-54444

First published 1854

"Philosophy of life and observations of nature drawn from the author's solitary sojourn of two years in a cabin on Walden Pond near Concord, Massachusetts." Pratt Alcove
Includes bibliographical references

Thurber, James

Writings and drawings. Library of Am. 1996 1004p il $40

Grades: 11 12 Adult **818**
1. American wit and humor
ISBN 978-1-883011-22-2; 1-883011-22-1
LC 96-5853

"These stories, parodies, reminiscences, cartoons, and drawings present Thurber's unique and masterful take on work, psychotherapy, fantasizing, domesticity, and the battle between the sexes." Booklist

Thursby, Jacqueline S.

Critical companion to Maya Angelou; a literary reference to her life and work. Facts On File 2011 430p il (Facts on File of American literature) $75

Grades: 11 12 Adult **818**
1. Poets 2. Actors 3. Singers 4. Dramatists 5. Essayists 6. Memoirists 7. Children's authors
ISBN 978-0-8160-8093-9; 978-1-4381-3610-3 ebook
LC 2010032716

Coverage includes a "biography of Angelou; entries on all of Angelou's major works, including all six of her book-length autobiographies, her major poems and poetry collections, her major essays and essay collections, her children's books, and more; entries on the autobiographical works contain subentries on the main figures in the work; entries on related people, places, and topics, such as Harlem, Michelle Obama, racism, San Francisco, and more; [and] appendixes, including chronologies, a bibliography of Angelou's works, and a secondary source bibliography." Publisher's note
Includes bibliographical references

Twain, Mark, 1835-1910

The **innocents** abroad {and} Roughing it. Library of Am. 1984 1027p il $35

Grades: 9 10 11 12 **818**
1. Voyages and travels
ISBN 0-940450-25-9
LC 84-11296

The innocents abroad (1869) is Twain's humorous account of his adventures in the Holy Land, Italy, and Paris.

Roughing it (1872) recounts a trip across the plains to California and then Hawaii in the early 1860s

★ **Life** on the Mississippi; with an introduction by James M. Cox. Penguin Books 1984 450p (Penguin Classics) pa $9.95
Grades: 9 10 11 12   **818**
   1. Mississippi River valley
   ISBN 0-14-039050-2
                                                LC 84-1194
A reissue of the title first published 1874
"Its historical sketches, its frequent passages of vivid description, and its humorous episodes combine to make [this] a masterpiece of the literature of the Middle West." Eng and Pope's What to Read

Roughing it; edited with an introduction by Hamlin Hill. Penguin 1981 590p il (The Penguin American library) pa $14
Grades: 11 12 Adult   **818**
   1. Hawaii -- Description and travel
   ISBN 0-14-039010-3
                                                LC 81-10593
First published 1872
A humorous account of a trip across the plains to California and then to Hawaii in the early 1860s.
Includes bibliographical references

Ward, Geoffrey C.
Mark Twain; by Geoffrey C. Ward and Dayton Duncan; based on a documentary film directed by Ken Burns; written by Dayton Duncan and Geoffrey C. Ward; with a preface by Ken Burns; picture research by Susanna Steisel and Pam Tubridy Baucom, and contributions by Russell Banks [et al.] Knopf 2001 269p il map $40
Grades: 11 12 Adult   **818**
   1. Authors 2. Humorists 3. Novelists 4. Essayists 5. Satirists 6. Memoirists 7. Travel writers 8. Authors, American 9. Short story writers
   ISBN 0-375-40561-5
                                                LC 2001-33820
"This fascinating biography of Twain contains a treasure trove of photographs and pictures." Booklist
Includes bibliographical references

Wayne, Tiffany K.
Critical companion to Ralph Waldo Emerson; a literary reference to his life and work. Facts On File 2010 444p il (Facts on File library of American literature) $75
Grades: 11 12 Adult   **818**
   1. Poets 2. Authors 3. Philosophers 4. Essayists
   ISBN 978-0-8160-7358-0; 978-1-4381-3048-4 ebook
                                                LC 2009-24809
"This reference book examines the life and works of a central thinker in American history. . . . It begins with Emerson's biography for context. Part 2 focuses on 140 significant (in the view of scholars) individual works, including 60 poems (most with one to three pages of synopses, critical commentary, and further reading). Part 3 covers related

people, places, and topics. . . . The final appendixes offer a chronology of Emerson's life and times, bibliographies of both his works and relevant secondary sources." Choice
Includes bibliographical references. 'Bibliography of Emerson's works': p. 406-407. (BLCM)

Wright, Richard
★ **Works**. Library of Am. 1991 2v ea $35
Grades: 11 12 Adult   **818**
   1. African Americans 2. African Americans -- Fiction
   ISBN 0-940450-66-6 v1; 0-940450-67-4 v2
                                                LC 91-60540
This set contains the complete novels Native son; The outsider (1953); and Lawd today! (1963); the story collection Uncle Tom's children; and the memoir Black boy

820   English and Old English (Anglo-Saxon) literatures

Ahmad, Dohra
Rotten English; a literary anthology. Dohra Ahmad. W.W. Norton & Co. 2007 535p. (pbk.) $15.95
Grades: 10 11 12   **820**
   1. English literature 2. Poetry -- Collections 3. Dialect literature, English 4. English-speaking countries -- Literary collections
   ISBN 9780393329605; 0393329607
                                                LC 2007005013
This book offers a "global anthology of fiction and poetry in vernacular English. . . . [The book] spans the globe to offer an overview of . . . non-standard English writing of the past two centuries, with a focus on the most recent decades. During the last twelve years, half of the Man Booker awards went to novels written in non-standard English. What would once have been derogatorily termed 'dialect literature' has come into its own in a language known variously as slang, creole, patois, [and] pidgin. . . . [It covers] vernacular literature from around the English-speaking world, from Robert Burns, Mark Twain, and Zora Neale Hurston to Papua New Guinea's John Kasaipwalova and Tobago's Marlene Nourbese Philip." (Publisher's note)
Includes bibliographical references (p. 519-527).

Backgrounds to English literature. Facts on File 2002 5v set $150
Grades: 11 12 Adult   **820**
   1. Great Britain -- Civilization 2. English literature -- History and criticism
   ISBN 0-8160-5125-9
                                                LC 2002-71284
"Will be useful for students studying the social, historical, and cultural influences on authors of the post-war period." SLJ
Includes bibliographical references

The **Cambridge** guide to literature in English; edited by Dominic Head. 3rd ed; Cambridge University Press 2006 xxiii, 1241p il $50
Grades: 11 12 Adult   **820**
   1. Reference books 2. English literature -- Dictionaries 3. American literature -- Dictionaries 4. English

literature -- Bio-bibliography
ISBN 978-0-521-83179-6; 0-521-83179-2

LC 2006-271458

First published 1988 under the editorship of Ian Ousby

"The scope of material covered . . . extends to the literature of the United Kingdom and well beyond: Africa, Asia, Australia, Canada, the Caribbean, India, New Zealand, and the U.S. are all well represented. . . . Literary terms are explained, literary movements are summarized, and literary magazines are sketched in unsigned entries ranging in length from a few lines to a few paragraphs or more. . . . With its broad coverage, clearly written and accessible text, and relatively modest price, this is a must purchase for most reference collections." Booklist

Encyclopedia of British writers, 1800 to the present; general editors, George Stade, Karen Karbiener. 2nd ed; Facts On File 2009 2v (Facts on File library of world literature) set $170

Grades: 9 10 11 12 Adult **820**

1. Reference books 2. Authors, English -- Dictionaries 3. English literature -- Bio-bibliography 4. English literature -- History and criticism
ISBN 978-0-8160-7385-6

LC 2008-22264

First published 2003 with title: Encyclopedia of British writers, 19th and 20th centuries

"This set treats more than 900 authors. Coverage encompasses a range of genres. . . . Volume 1 traverses the nineteenth century, and volume 2 presents writers from the twentieth century on. Within each volume, arrangement is alphabetical. In addition to author entries, the editors have provided short essays on important literary movements such as the Irish Literary Renaissance, Romanticism, and Theater of the Absurd. . . . The entries are engaging and provide enough content to give readers a basic understanding of the life and work of each writer. High-school, college, and public libraries will find this a very useful resource." Booklist

Includes bibliographical references

Encyclopedia of themes in literature. Facts On File 2011 3v (Facts on File library of world literature) set $195

Grades: 9 10 11 12 Adult **820**

1. Reference books 2. English literature -- Encyclopedias 3. American literature -- Encyclopedias
ISBN 978-0-8160-7161-6; 978-1-4381-3268-6 ebook

LC 2009-47605

"A useful volume for writing research papers and gaining insight into literary theme." Libr J

Includes bibliographical references

★ The **Norton** anthology of literature by women; the traditions in English. [compiled by] Sandra M. Gilbert, Susan Gubar. 3rd ed.; W.W. Norton & Co. 2007 2v map set $76.25

Grades: 11 12 Adult **820**

1. English literature -- Women authors -- Collections 2. American literature -- Women authors -- Collections
ISBN 978-0-393-93015-3; 0-393-93015-7

LC 2006101170

First published 1985

The editors provide representative selections of prose and poetry by women. Period introductions, biographical headnotes and bibliographies are provided.

Includes bibliographical references

The **Oxford** anthology of English literature; general editors: Frank Kermode and John Hollander. Oxford Univ. Press 1973 6v in 2 il maps v1 2v pa set $65.95; v2 2v pa set $65.95

Grades: 11 12 Adult **820**

1. English literature -- Collections
ISBN 0-19-501657-2 v1 2v pa; 0-19-501658-0 v2 2v pa

★ The **Oxford** companion to English literature; edited by Dinah Birch. 7th ed; Oxford University Press 2009 1164p $150

Grades: 11 12 Adult **820**

1. Reference books 2. English literature -- Dictionaries 3. American literature -- Dictionaries 4. English literature -- Bio-bibliography 5. American literature -- Bio-bibliography
ISBN 978-0-19-280687-1

LC 2009-455948

First published 1932 under the editorship of Sir Paul Harvey

"The subjects of the entries include literary works, authors, themes, archetypes, journals, and forms. . . . This companion is a highly authoritative resource, with clear, concise, and approachable entries on literary topics of high interest to students and scholars of English literature. An essential reference for most public, high school, and academic libraries." Libr J

Pool, Daniel

What Jane Austen ate and Charles Dickens knew; from fox hunting to whist: the facts of daily life in nineteenth-century England. Simon & Schuster 1993 416p il maps hardcover o.p. pa $14

Grades: 11 12 Adult **820**

1. Great Britain -- Social life and customs 2. English literature -- History and criticism
ISBN 0-671-88236-8 pa

LC 93-16240

"Modern American readers of 19th-century English novels are often brought up short by bizarre references and puzzling words that did not need explaining when the books were written. Now they do, and Daniel Pool does a charming job of clearing things up in a witty, informal survey of daily life in the Hanoverian-Victorian era." N Y Times Book Rev

Includes bibliographical references

Stewart, Bruce

★ The **Oxford** companion to Irish literature; edited by Robert Welch, assistant editor, Bruce Stewart. Oxford Univ. Press 1996 xxv, 614p maps $55

Grades: 11 12 Adult **820**

1. Reference books 2. Irish literature -- Dictionaries
ISBN 0-19-866158-4

LC 95-44943

Encompassing "Ireland's literary heritage from the bardic poets and Celtic sagas to twentieth-century authors like Brian Friel, Edna O'Brien, and Nuala Ni Dhomhnaill, the more than 2,000 unsigned entries cover writers, titles of major works, literary genres and motifs, folklore, mythology, periodicals, associations, and historical figures and events." Booklist

The **Victorian** novel; edited and with an introduction by Harold Bloom. Chelsea House 2004 412p (Bloom's period studies) $37.95

Grades: 9 10 11 12   **820**
1. English literature -- History and criticism
ISBN 0-7910-7678-4

This study of the Victorian novel examines the work of major influential authors including "Charles Dickens, The Brontës, Anthony Trollope, George Eliot, Mrs. Elizabeth Gaskell, William Makepeace Thackeray, and Thomas Hardy." Publisher's note

Includes bibliographical references and index

821   English poetry

★ **100** essential modern poems; selected and introduced by Joseph Parisi. Ivan R. Dee 2005 305p $24.95

Grades: 11 12 Adult   **821**
1. English poetry -- Collections 2. American poetry -- Collections
ISBN 1-56663-612-4

LC 2005-9897

"Preceded by wonderfully conversational and expertly appreciative biocritical essays about each poet, his choices are superb as he lingers over Yeats and Stevens and includes often-overlooked witty and satirical poets, among them Dorothy Parker, Ogden Nash, Kay Ryan, Frank O'Hara, and Billy Collins." Booklist

100 great poems of the twentieth century; [edited by] Mark Strand. Norton 2005 320p $24.95

Grades: 11 12 Adult   **821**
1. English poetry -- Collections 2. American poetry -- Collections
ISBN 0-393-05894-8

LC 2005-2150

The editor "has selected works by poets of Europe and North and South America, and because there are so many gifted American poets, he restricted himself to those born before 1927. The result is a marvelously graceful, shimmering cosmos of poems by the likes of Anna Akhmatova, A. R. Ammons, Amy Clampit, Robert Desnos, Robert Frost, Nazim Hikmet, Kenneth Koch, Edna St. Vincent Millay, Gabriela Mistral, Eugenio Montale, Octavio Paz, and Derek Walcott." Booklist

Auden, W. H.

Auden; poems. selected by Edward Mendelson. Knopf 1995 256p (Everyman's library pocket poets) $12.50

Grades: 11 12 Adult   **821**
1. Poetry -- By individual authors
ISBN 0-679-44367-3

A representative selection of lyrics that span the influential poet's career

★ The **Best** poems of the English language; from Chaucer through Robert Frost. selected and with commentary by Harold Bloom. HarperCollins Publishers 2004 xxviii, 972p $34.95; pa $19.95

Grades: 11 12 Adult   **821**
1. English poetry -- Collections 2. American poetry -- Collections
ISBN 0-06-054041-9; 0-06-054042-7 pa

LC 2003-51104

"Arranged chronologically by author, the poems are preceded by commentaries that extol their specific virtues and place them in historical context. Taken together, they provide an overview of Bloom's own theories of writing, such as his notion that the greatest poems manifest an 'inevitability' of phrasing . . . Bloom rarely bores, and at his best he achieves a cogency . . . worthy of the poets he so deeply admires." Libr J

Includes bibliographical references

Blake, William

The **complete** poetry and prose of William Blake; edited by David V. Erdman; with a new foreword and commentary by Harold Bloom. Newly rev. ed., 1st Calif. ed.; University of California Press 2008 xxvi, 990p il $70

Grades: Adult   **821**
1. Poetry -- By individual authors
ISBN 978-0-520-04473-9

First published 1965 with title: Poetry and prose of William Blake

In addition to all of Blake's poetry, this volume also includes miscellaneous prose, marginalia, and letters

"The crucial preliminary problem [in establishing Blake's text] is simply to make out what Blake wrote. . . . Erdman has used modern aids such as infrared photography and microphotography. . . but his real achievement has been to look at Blake's text more closely and intelligently than any previous editor." N Y Rev Books

★ The **essential** Blake; selected and with an introduction by Stanley Kunitz. Ecco Press 1987 92p (Essential poets) hardcover o.p. pa $9.95

Grades: 11 12 Adult   **821**
1. Poetry -- By individual authors
ISBN 0-88001-138-6; 0-06-088793-1 pa

LC 86-24087

The editor has selected the poems he feels provide the best introduction to Blake's craft.

★ **Poems**. Knopf 1994 283p (Everyman's library pocket poets) $12.50

Grades: 11 12 Adult   **821**
1. Poetry -- By individual authors
ISBN 0-679-43633-2

A collection of representative and epic poems by the visionary Romantic poet, painter and engraver

Bronte, Emily

Bronte: poems. Knopf 1996 255p (Everyman's library pocket poets) $12.50

Grades: 11 12 Adult   **821**

1. Poetry -- By individual authors

ISBN 0-679-44725-3

A representative selection of Brontë's poetical output including many of her mythical works

Browning, Elizabeth Barrett

★ **Sonnets** from the Portuguese; a celebration of love. St. Martin's Press 1986 [63] il $9.95

Grades: 11 12 Adult   **821**

1. Poetry -- By individual authors

ISBN 0-312-74501-X

LC 86-13755

A series of sonnets which "were written during a period of seven years and are considered by some scholars to have been inspired by her love for her husband poet Robert Browning." New Century Handb of Engl Lit

Browning, Robert

★ **Robert** Browning's poetry; authoritative texts, criticism. selected and edited by James F. Loucks and Andrew M. Stauffer. 2nd ed.; W. W. Norton & Co. 2007 689p (A Norton critical edition) pa $14.50

Grades: 11 12 Adult   **821**

1. Poetry -- By individual authors

ISBN 978-0-393-92600-2; 0-393-92600-1

LC 2006-47308

First published 1980

This collection of Browning's poetry, which includes Pauline, "reprints the texts of the seventeen-volume 'Fourth and complete edition' (Smith, Elder), of which all but the final volume were approved by Browning before his death. The poems are ordered chronologically according to their first appearance in book form." Publisher's note

Byron, George Gordon Byron

★ **Byron**; poems. [this selection by Peter Washington] Knopf 1994 288p (Everyman's library pocket poets) $12.50

Grades: 11 12 Adult   **821**

1. Poetry -- By individual authors

ISBN 0-679-43630-8

A selection of lyric and dramatic poetry by the English Romantic poet and satirist.

Chaucer, Geoffrey

★ The **Canterbury** tales; translated into modern English by Nevill Coghill. Penguin Books 2003 504p (Penguin Classics) pa $10

Grades: 11 12 Adult   **821**

1. Poetry -- By individual authors

ISBN 0-14-042438-5

LC 2003-265749

"A collection of twenty-four stories, all but two of which are in verse, written by Geoffrey Chaucer mainly between 1386 and his death in 1400. The stories are supposed to be related by members of a company of thirty-one pilgrims (including the poet himself) who are on their way to the shrine of St. Thomas at Canterbury. The prologue which tells of their assembly at the Tabard Inn in Southwark and their arrangement that each shall tell two stories on the way to Canterbury and two on the return journey, is a remarkable picture of English social life in the fourteenth century, inasmuch as every class is represented from the gentlefolks to the peasantry." Keller. Reader's Dig of Books

★ The **portable** Chaucer; selected, translated and edited by Theodore Morrison. rev ed; Viking 1975 611p hardcover o.p. pa $15.95

Grades: 11 12 Adult   **821**

1. Poetry -- By individual authors

ISBN 0-14-015081-1 pa

First published 1949

Contains Troilus and Cressida, The Canterbury tales, selections from The book of the duchess and The bird's parliament, and some short verse.

Includes bibliographical references

★ The **Columbia** anthology of British poetry; edited by Carl Woodring and James Shapiro. Columbia Univ. Press 1995 xxxi, 891p $41

Grades: 11 12 Adult   **821**

1. English poetry -- Collections

ISBN 0-231-10180-5

LC 94-46333

This anthology "contains major British poetry from Beowulf to the present day. Poets receive a short biographical introduction along with their poetry. . . . It includes more female poets than most comparable anthologies, and is conducive to browsing. Major poems such as Coleridge's 'Rime of the Ancient Mariner,' Britain's best-loved poems, and newly rediscovered poems are part of this collection." SLJ

Donne, John

The **complete** poetry and selected prose of John Donne; edited by Charles M. Coffin; introduction by Denis Donoghue; notes by W. T. Chmielewski. Modern Lib. 2001 xxxii, 697p pa $14.95

Grades: 11 12 Adult   **821**

1. Poetry -- By individual authors

ISBN 0-375-75734-1

LC 2001-30077

A reissue of the Modern Library edition published 1994

This volume contains Donne's love poetry, satires, epigrams, verse letters and holy sonnets. Also includes selected prose and a sampling of private letters.

Flesch, William

The **Facts** on File companion to British poetry, 19th century. Facts On File 2010 468p (Facts on File library of world literature) $85

Grades: 10 11 12 Adult   **821**

1. Reference books 2. English poetry -- History and criticism

ISBN 978-0-8160-5896-9

LC 2008-32028

"Over 335 entries explore a wide range of poets, poems, poetic movements, influential journals, and significant terms and concepts. Flesch ... explores both biographical and critical themes, often at surprising length. Entries focused on specific works are especially detailed and useful for students interested in placing poetry within the context of historical events." Choice

Includes glossary and bibliographical references

Gawain and the Grene Knight (Middle English poem)

★ **Sir** Gawain and the Green Knight; a new verse translation by W. S. Merwin. Knopf 2002 hardcover o.p. pa $14

Grades: 9 10 11 12   **821**

1. Arthurian romances 2. Poetry -- By individual authors

ISBN 0-375-41476-2; 0-375-70992-4 pa

LC 2002-20815

"Merwin's Sir Gawain replicates the propulsive alliteration and the rhymed-quatrain stanza endings of the original, and the translation appears face-to-face with the Middle English original. A major translation of a major English, and a major horror, classic." Booklist

Geoffrey Chaucer; edited & with an introduction by Harold Bloom. Updated ed; Bloom's Literary Criticism 2007 259p (Modern critical views) $45

Grades: 11 12 Adult   **821**

1. Poets 2. Authors 3. Poetry -- By individual authors
ISBN 978-0-7910-9438-9; 0-7910-9438-3

LC 2007-10198

First published 1985

A collection of critical essays discussing the work of Canterbury Tales author Geoffrey Chaucer.

Includes bibliographical references

Geoffrey Chaucer's The Canterbury tales; edited and with an introduction by Harold Bloom. New ed; Chelsea House 2008 286p (Modern critical interpretations) $45

Grades: 9 10 11 12 Adult   **821**

1. Poets 2. Authors 3. Poetry -- By individual authors
ISBN 978-0-7910-9618-5

LC 2007-49158

First published 1988 in three separate editions focusing on the Prologue, The knight's tale, and The pardoner's tale

A collection of eleven critical essays on Chaucer's well-known work, arranged in chronological order of their original publication.

Includes bibliographical references

Glancy, Ruth F.

Thematic guide to British poetry; [by] Ruth Glancy. Greenwood Press 2002 303p $64.95

Grades: 9 10 11 12   **821**

1. English poetry -- History and criticism
ISBN 0-313-31379-2

LC 2002-23252

This is a "well-organized, easy-to-navigate, authoritative volume." SLJ

Includes bibliographical references

Hardy, Thomas

Poems. Knopf 1995 254p (Everyman's library pocket poets) $10.95

Grades: 11 12 Adult   **821**

1. Poetry -- By individual authors
ISBN 0-679-44368-1

A representative selection of the English author's verse. An index of first lines is included

Heaney, Seamus

Electric light. Farrar, Straus & Giroux 2001 98p hardcover o.p. pa $13

Grades: 11 12 Adult   **821**

1. Poetry -- By individual authors
ISBN 0-374-14683-7; 0-374-52841-1 pa

LC 00-67278

Heaney's "book of poems is a compendium of poetic genres set in an array of forms and tuned to many kinds of experience, the work of a mature poet and world citizen, aware of his cultural authority as a public man and of the rights and responsibilities that go with it." N Y Times Book Rev

Opened ground; selected poems, 1966-1996. Farrar, Straus & Giroux 1998 443p hardcover o.p. pa $16

Grades: 11 12 Adult   **821**

1. Poetry -- By individual authors
ISBN 0-374-52678-8 pa

LC 98-4331

"The best of nobel laureate Heaney's poems, gathered from 12 previous collections, create a substantial volume that charts the course of one man's thoroughly examined personal life and reflects a volatile era in the life of his troubled country, Northern Ireland, though the particulars Heaney renders so vibrantly become archetypal and unbounded in their tragedy and bliss." Booklist

Houle, Michelle M.

Modern British poetry, the world is never the same. Enslow Publishers 2010 160p il (Poetry rocks!) lib bdg $34.60

Grades: 9 10 11 12   **821**

1. Poets, English 2. Poetry -- Authorship 3. English poetry -- History and criticism
ISBN 978-0-7660-3278-1; 0-7660-3278-7

LC 2009-15880

"This collection introduces readers to eleven British poets born between 1806 and 1914, including Elizabeth Barrett Browning, Lord Alfred Tennyson, W. B. Yeats, W. H. Auden, and Dylan Thomas. Includes biographical information, historical background, poetry analysis, and several poems by each writer." Publisher's note

Includes glossary and bibliographical references

Housman, A. E.

The **collected** poems of A. E. Housman. Holt & Co. 1965 254p pa $16

Grades: 11 12 Adult   **821**
1. Poetry -- By individual authors
ISBN 0-8050-0547-1

This anthology "constitutes the authorized canon of A. E. Housman's verse as established in 1939." Note on the text

Hughes, Ted, 1930-1998

Selected poems, 1957-1994. Farrar, Straus & Giroux 2002 333p hardcover o.p. pa $15

Grades: 11 12 Adult   **821**
1. Poetry -- By individual authors
ISBN 0-374-25875-9; 0-374-52864-0 pa

LC 2002-21603

"With poems that are characteristically alert to the processes of creation as well as self-destruction, this selection displays Hughes's mighty, even terrifying, talent." N Y Times Book Rev

Johanson, Paula

Early British poetry, words that burn. Enslow Publishers 2010 160p il (Poetry rocks!) lib bdg $34.60

Grades: 9 10 11 12   **821**
1. Poets, English 2. Poetry -- Authorship 3. English poetry -- History and criticism
ISBN 978-0-7660-3276-7; 0-7660-3276-0

LC 2008-53657

"This is a great resource for many poetry assignments and English teachers themselves. Students will appreciate the organization of the book including the bright colors, clear headings, portraits, and backgrounds of the poems." Libr Media Connect

Includes glossary and bibliographical references

Keats, John

The **major** works; edited with an introduction and notes by Elizabeth Cook. Oxford Univ. Press 2001 xxxvi, 667p pa $16.95

Grades: 9 10 11 12   **821**
1. Poetry -- By individual authors
ISBN 0-19-284063-0

LC 2001-272404

First published 1990

This volume contains all the poetry published during Keats' lifetime, including Endymion in its entirety, the Odes, Lamia, and both versions of Hyperion. A number of posthumously published poems are presented along with a selection of Keats' letters. Includes a bibliography, chronology, and a glossary of classical names

Includes bibliographical references (p. {642}-644) and indexes

★ **Poems**. Knopf 1994 253p (Everyman's library pocket poets) $12.50

Grades: 11 12 Adult   **821**
1. Poetry -- By individual authors
ISBN 0-679-43319-8

LC 94-2495

A representative collection by the influential English romantic.

Includes bibliographical references

Kipling, Rudyard, 1865-1936

★ **Complete** verse; definitive edition. Doubleday 1989 850p hardcover o.p. pa $20

Grades: 11 12 Adult   **821**
1. Poetry -- By individual authors
ISBN 0-385-26089-X pa

LC 88-7364

Replaces Rudyard Kipling's verse: definitive edition, published 1940

This edition includes all of Kipling's published poetry and, in addition, more than 20 poems which have not previously appeared in the inclusive edition of his verse

★ The **New** Oxford book of Irish verse; edited, with translations, by Thomas Kinsella. Oxford Univ. Press 2001 xxx, 423p pa $16.95

Grades: 11 12 Adult   **821**
1. Irish poetry -- Collections
ISBN 0-19-280192-9

LC 2001-278442

Replaces The Oxford Book of Irish verse, XVIIth century-XXth century, chosen by Donagh MacDonagh and Lennox Robinson (1958); this is a reissue of the 1986 edition

"This selection is divided into three parts. Book I opens with the earliest pre-Christian poetry in Old Irish and ends in the fourteenth century with the first Irish poetry in the English language. Book II covers the fourteenth to the eighteenth centuries and Book III the nineteenth and twentieth centuries." Publisher's note

★ The **New** Oxford book of Victorian verse. Oxford Univ. Press 1987 xxxiv, 654p hardcover o.p. pa $25.95

Grades: 11 12 Adult   **821**
1. English poetry -- Collections
ISBN 978-0-19-955631-1 pa

LC 86-23701

Replaces The Oxford book of Victorian verse, edited by Sir Arthur Quiller-Couch (1912)

An anthology of 19th century English poetry. Among the poets prominently featured are: Clough, Morris, Arnold, the Decadents, Emily Brontë, Clare, Barnes, and Christina Rossetti.

"While general collections should all add Ricks, those retaining [the Quiller-Couch edition] should dust him off and keep him available in order to represent fully Victorian verse and changing attitudes toward it." Libr J

★ The **Norton** anthology of modern and contemporary poetry; edited by Jahan Ramazani, Richard Ellmann, Robert O'Clair. 3rd ed; Norton 2003 2v pa set $75

Grades: 11 12 Adult   **821**
1. English poetry -- Collections 2. American poetry -- Collections
ISBN 0-393-32429-X

LC 2002-37990

First published 1973 with title: The Norton anthology of modern poetry

This volume includes "1596 poems by 195 poets. . . . The anthology includes the works of such masters as Walt Whitman, Ezra Pound, Dylan Thomas, Langston Hughes, Gertrude Stein, Lucille Clifton, Louise Erdrich, and Allen Ginsberg. . . . Extensive, and beautifully composed introductions provide insight, observations, and historical context for the selections. . . . This ambitious, highly successful work is a veritable tribute to the enduring power of literature and language." SLJ

Includes bibliographical references

The **Norton** book of light verse; edited by Russell Baker; with the assistance of Kathleen Leland Baker. Norton 1986 447p $29.95

Grades: 11 12 Adult **821**

1. Humorous poetry 2. English poetry -- Collections 3. American poetry -- Collections

ISBN 0-393-02366-4

LC 86-18172

Arranged by subject, this anthology presents some four hundred British and American light verse selections. The poems date from the sixteenth-century to the present

★ The **Oxford** book of English verse; edited by Christopher Ricks. Oxford Univ. Press 1999 xxxii, 690p $39.95

Grades: 11 12 Adult **821**

1. English poetry -- Collections

ISBN 0-19-214182-1

LC 99-20831

First published 1900 under the editorship of Sir Arthur Quiller-Couch with title: The Oxford book of English verse, 1250-1900. Present edition replaces The New Oxford book of English verse, 1250-1950, edited by Helen Gardner published 1972

This collection "starts with anonymous 13th-century lyric and ends with Seamus Heaney; in between are seven centuries' worth of poems in English from Britain and Ireland. . . Ricks brings in plenty of dialect verse, excerpts from long poems and verse plays, and a few translations into English. . . Long after reviewers stop debating how Ricks chose each item, readers will keep returning to these pages to find yet another good poem they've not before seen." Publ Wkly

Poets of World War I: Rupert Brooke & Siegfried Sassoon; edited and with an introduction by Harold Bloom. Chelsea House 2003 83p (Bloom's major poets) lib bdg $22.95

Grades: 9 10 11 12 **821**

1. Poets 2. Authors 3. Novelists

ISBN 0-7910-7388-2

LC 2003-6927

This volume includes biographies of the two poets and critical analysis of their poems.

Includes bibliographical references

Poets of World War I: Wilfred Owen & Isaac Rosenberg; Harold Bloom, editor. Chelsea House 2002 111p (Bloom's major poets) lib bdg $22.95

Grades: 9 10 11 12 **821**

1. Poets 2. Artists 3. Authors 4. Painters

ISBN 0-7910-5932-4

LC 2001-28515

"This volume contains a short biography of each poet and the analysis of eight poems (four from each poet) from thematic and structural foundations. These criticisms are supported by primary source material, such as letters, diaries, and notes." Book Rep

Rossetti, Christina Georgina

Poems. Knopf 1993 256p (Everyman's library pocket poets) $12.50

Grades: 11 12 Adult **821**

1. Poetry -- By individual authors

ISBN 0-679-42908-5

LC 93-14362

The poems in this collection are grouped under the following headings: Lyric poems, Dramatic and narrative poems, Rhymes and riddles, Sonnet sequences, Prayers and meditations. An index of first lines is included

Rossignol, Rosalyn

Critical companion to Chaucer; a literary reference to his life and work. Facts on File 2006 648p il $85

Grades: 11 12 Adult **821**

1. Poets 2. Authors

ISBN 0-8160-6193-9; 978-0-8160-6193-8

LC 2006-99

First published 1999 with title: Chaucer A to Z

This book on the works of Chaucer includes a biography of Chaucer, synopses and critical commentary on his works (including the Canterbury Tales), and lists of related people, places and topics.

Includes bibliographical references

Shakespeare, William, 1564-1616

★ **Poems**. Knopf 1994 252p (Everyman's library pocket poets) $12.50

Grades: 11 12 Adult **821**

1. Poetry -- By individual authors

ISBN 0-679-43320-1

LC 94-2494

A representative selection of Shakespeare's verse.

★ The **sonnets**; edited by Rex Gibson. Cambridge Univ. Press 1997 204p il pa $12.50

Grades: 9 10 11 12 **821**

1. Poetry -- By individual authors

ISBN 0-521-55947-2

LC 97-149257

"Each of Shakespeare's 154 sonnets is given at least one page, which includes the text of the sonnet, its theme and meaning, one possible interpretation, an explanation of difficult phrases and imagery, and a glossary of the unfamiliar words. The information is not thrust on the reader as the final and only 'correct' interpretation." Book Rep

T.S. Eliot; edited and with an introduction by Harold Bloom. New ed.; Bloom's Literary Criticism 2010 194p (Modern critical views) $45
Grades: 9 10 11 12 **821**
1. Poets 2. Authors 3. Dramatists 4. Editors 5. Essayists 6. Literary critics 7. Nobel laureates for literature
ISBN 978-1-60413-879-5
LC 2010-19960
First published 1985
A selection of critical essays explore the works of the author of The Waste Land.
Includes bibliographical references

Thomas, Dylan
★ The **poems** of Dylan Thomas; edited with an introduction and notes by Daniel Jones; with a preface by Dylan Thomas. rev ed; New Directions 2003 xxix, 320p il $34.95
Grades: 11 12 Adult **821**
1. Poetry -- By individual authors
ISBN 978-0-8112-1541-1; 0-8112-1541-5
LC 2002-155790
First published 1971
"To the 90 poems Thomas published in Collected Poems, 1934-1952 Jones has added 102 and placed the total, as far as he could determine, in the chronological order of their composition. Some of the poems were still in manuscript form when Thomas died; others had been published in periodicals and anthologies. In an appendix, Jones offers Thomas' early poems—including one written when the poet was 12." Libr J [review of 1971 edition]
Includes bibliographical references

Selected poems, 1934-1952; rev ed; New Directions 2003 214p pa $14.95
Grades: 11 12 Adult **821**
1. Poetry -- By individual authors
ISBN 0-8112-1542-3
LC 2002-155792
First published 1953 with title: The collected poems of Dylan Thomas
"The prologue in verse, written for this collected edition of my poems, is intended as an address to my readers, the strangers. This book contains most of the poems I have written, and all, up to the present year, that I wish to preserve. Some of them I have revised a little." Preface {of 1953 edition}

The **Top** 500 poems; edited by William Harmon. Columbia Univ. Press 1992 xxx, 1132p $36.95
Grades: 11 12 Adult **821**
1. English poetry -- Collections 2. American poetry -- Collections
ISBN 0-231-08028-X
LC 91-42239
"Harmon devises an interesting method (collecting the 500 most anthologized shorter English and American poems as indexed in the Columbia Granger's Index to Poetry, 8th and 9th eds.) to bring together poetry of the last 750 years that he calls the 'greatest successes'. . . . Each of the 500

poems, arranged in chronological order, has a biographical headnote and editorial comments by the editor." Libr J

Understanding poetry; {edited by} Cleanth Brooks, Robert Penn Warren. 4th ed; Holt, Rinehart & Winston 1976 xxii, 602p pa $55.50
Grades: 9 10 11 12 **821**
1. English poetry -- Collections 2. American poetry -- Collections 3. Poetry -- History and criticism
ISBN 0-03-076980-9
First published 1938
This volume explores the meaning and structure of poetry with discussions of the nuances of theme, dramatic structure and metrics. Approximately 350 English and American poems ranging from the 16th century to the present are included in this collection

Wordsworth, William
★ **Poems**. Knopf 1995 256p (Everyman's library pocket poets) $12.50
Grades: 11 12 Adult **821**
1. Poetry -- By individual authors
ISBN 0-679-44369-X
A selection of work representative of the prominent Romantic's poetic legacy

Yeats, W. B.
★ The **poems**; edited by Richard J. Finneran. 2nd ed; Scribner 1997 xxix, 752p il $40; pa $20
Grades: 11 12 Adult **821**
1. Poetry -- By individual authors
ISBN 0-684-83935-0; 0-684-80731-9 pa
LC 97-23065
First published 1983 by Macmillan
This edition of the Nobel Laureate's verse contains complete texts of all the poems Yeats is known to have written. Yeats' original rhetorical punctuation has been restored. The editor provides textual histories

822 English drama

100 great monologues from the Renaissance theatre; edited by Jocelyn A. Beard. Smith & Kraus 1994 186p pa $9.95
Grades: 9 10 11 12 **822**
1. Acting 2. Monologues
ISBN 1-880399-59-8
LC 94-19393
A collection of monologues for men and women selected to represent the range of English Renaissance stage roles

Armitage, Simon
The **odyssey**; a dramatic retelling of Homer's epic. W.W. Norton & Co. 2008 266p pa $14.95 **822**
ISBN 978-0-393-33081-6
LC 2008-1290
First published 2006 in Great Britain with title: Homer's Odyssey
"Armitage's play will entertain . . . anyone interested in the fresh ways that Homer's story can be told." Publ Wkly

Ben Jonson; edited and with an introduction by Harold Bloom. Chelsea House 2001 104p (Bloom's major dramatists) $21.95

Grades: 9 10 11 12　　**822**

1. Poets 2. Authors 3. Dramatists 4. Poets laureate

ISBN 0-7910-6359-3

LC 2001-53677

Includes a biographical essay, plot summaries, and critical interpretations of the plays and their characters.

Includes bibliographical references

Bolt, Robert

A **man** for all seasons; a play in two acts. Random House 1962 xxv, 163p il hardcover o.p. pa $9.50

Grades: 11 12 Adult　　**822**

1. Saints 2. Authors 3. Statesmen 4. Writers on law 5. Writers on religion 6. Great Britain -- History -- 1485-1603, Tudors -- Drama

ISBN 0-679-72822-8 pa

Characters: 11 men, 2 women. First produced in the United States at the ANTA Theatre, New York City, November 22, 1961

Fugard, Athol

Master Harold-- and the boys. Vintage Books 2009 60p pa $12.95

Grades: 11 12 Adult　　**822**

1. South Africa -- Race relations -- Drama

ISBN 978-0-307-47520-6; 0-307-47520-4

LC 2010-292381

First published 1982 by Random House

Characters: 3 men. 1 act. First produced at the Yale Repertory theatre, New Haven, Connecticut, 1982.

Pinter, Harold

The **birthday** party, and The room; two plays. Grove Press 1961 120p il pa $10

Grades: 9 10 11 12　　**822**

ISBN 0-8021-5114-0

The birthday party, first performed in 1958 and published in 1959, portrays the mental destruction of a young pianist living obscurely in an English seaside town. In The room, first produced in 1957, an elderly couple seems about to be evicted from their boarding house

Pomerance, Bernard

The **Elephant** Man; a play. Grove Press 1979 71p hardcover o.p. pa $11

Grades: 11 12 Adult　　**822**

1. People with disabilities 2. People with disabilities -- Drama

ISBN 0-8021-3041-0 pa

LC 79-7792

Characters: 5 men, 2 women. 21 scenes. First produced at the Hampstead Theatre, London, 1977

Shaffer, Peter

Peter Shaffer's Amadeus; with an introduction by the director Sir Peter Hall and a wholly new preface by the author. Perennial Bks. 2001 xxxiv, 124p pa $15

Grades: 11 12 Adult　　**822**

1. Composers

ISBN 0-06-093549-9

LC 2001-278382

First published 1980 in the United Kingdom

Characters: 9 men, 1 woman, extras. 2 acts. First produced at the National Theater of Great Britain, November 1979

Shaw, Bernard

Pygmalion . . . and My fair lady; [Pygmalion] by George Bernard Shaw; and My fair lady/based on Shaw's Pygmalion; adaptation and lyrics by Alan Jay Lerner; music by Frederick Loewe. 50th anniversary ed.; Signet Classic 2006 219p pa $5.95

Grades: 11 12 Adult　　**822**

ISBN 0-451-53009-8

My fair lady was awarded the New York Drama Critics Circle Award for 1956

This volume includes the complete texts of Shaw's Pygmalion and Lerner's musical adaptation My fair lady.

Sheridan, Richard Brinsley

The **rivals**; [by] Sheridan; edited with introduction and notes by C. J. L. Price. Oxford Univ. Press 1968 140p pa $19.95

Grades: 9 10 11 12　　**822**

ISBN 0-19-831908-8

In this satirical comedy, first presented in 1775, two gentlemen woo Lydia Languish, a young woman with highly romantic ideas concerning love whose fortune will be forfeited if she marries without the consent of her aunt. The aunt, Mrs. Malaprop, has become famous for her eccentric use of the English language

Stoppard, Tom

Rosencrantz and Guildenstern are dead. Grove Press 1967 126p hardcover o.p. pa $12

Grades: 11 12 Adult　　**822**

1. Poets 2. Authors 3. Dramatists

ISBN 0-8021-3275-8 pa

Characters: 13 men, 2 women, extras. First produced in this form April 11, 1967 in London

This play "took the theatre world on both sides of the Atlantic by storm. The originality of the idea which put Hamlet's two insignificant friends centerstage was matched by the brilliance of the dialogue between these bewildered nonentities." Reader's Ency. 4th edition

Thomas, Dylan

Under milk wood; a play for voices. New Directions 1954 107p music pa $8.95

Grades: 11 12 Adult　　**822**

ISBN 0-8112-0209-7

"A radio play for voices. Written in poetic, inventive prose, this play is full of humor, a joyful sense of the goodness of life and love, and a strong Welsh flavor. It is an impression of a spring day in the lives of the people of Llareggub, a Welsh village situated under Milk Wood. It has no plot, but a wealth of characters who dream aloud, converse with one another, and speak in choruses of alternating voices." Reader's Ency. 4th edition

Tom Stoppard; edited and with an introduction by Harold Bloom. Chelsea House 2003 152p (Bloom's major dramatists) lib bdg $22.95

Grades: 9 10 11 12   **822**
1. Authors 2. Dramatists
ISBN 0-7910-7032-8

LC 2002-152060

Includes a biographical essay, plot summaries, and critical interpretations of the plays and their characters.
Includes bibliographical references

Wilde, Oscar

The **importance** of being earnest and other plays; introduction by Terrence McNally; notes by Michael F. Davis. Modern Library 2003 257p pa $9.95

Grades: 11 12 Adult   **822**
ISBN 0-8129-6714-3

LC 2003-44566

The title play, written in 1895, is a drawing room comedy exposing quirks and foibles of Victorian society with plot revolving around amorous pursuits of two men who face social obstacles when they woo young ladies of quality. The book also features Lady Windermere's fan (1893), a four act comedy about a woman who has an affair when she suspects her husband of adultery, and An ideal husband (1895), a comedy about a blackmail scheme involving a lord's investment in the Suez Canal days before the British government's purchase of it, and his wife's reaction to her husband's past misdeeds.

822.3   Drama of Elizabethan period, 1558-1625

Andersen, Richard

Macbeth; introduction by Joseph Sobran. Marshall Cavendish Benchmark 2008 127p il (Shakespeare explained) lib bdg $29.95

Grades: 7 8 9 10 11 12   **822.3**
1. Poets 2. Authors 3. Dramatists
ISBN 978-0-7614-3029-2; 0-7614-3029-6

LC 2008-14408

"A literary analysis of the play Macbeth. Includes information on the history and culture of Elizabethan England." Publisher's note
Includes glossary and bibliographical references

Baker, William

The **facts** on file companion to Shakespeare; William Baker and Kenneth Womack. Facts On File 2011 5 v. (acid-free paper) $375.00 **822.3**
1. English drama -- History and criticism
ISBN 0816078203; 9780816078202

LC 2010054012

This book focuses on the author William Shakespeare. "Volume 1 is made up of background essays and more on Shakespeare's times and texts. Poems and sonnets are covered in volume 2, offering for each analysis and a bibliography. In volumes 3, 4, and 5, plays are covered in a 'complete

works' fashion designed for use as a textbook. . . . These are followed by an overview essay and excerpts from 'classic criticism.'"(Booklist)
Includes bibliographical references and index

Bloom, Harold

Shakespeare: the invention of the human. Riverhead Bks. 1998 xx, 745p hardcover o.p. pa $18

Grades: 11 12 Adult   **822.3**
1. Poets 2. Authors 3. Dramatists
ISBN 1-57322-751-X pa

LC 98-21325

"The passion and obsessiveness of Bloom's approach are its greatest recommendation." N Y Rev Books

Boyce, Charles

★ **Critical** companion to William Shakespeare; a literary reference to his life and work. Rev. ed; Facts on File 2005 2v il (Facts on File library of world literature) set $104.50

Grades: 11 12 Adult   **822.3**
1. Poets 2. Authors 3. Dramatists
ISBN 0-8160-5373-1

LC 2004-25769

First published 1990 with title: Shakespeare A to Z
"The first two-thirds [of this set] covers the plays. Arranged alphabetically by title, the 3000 entries generally consist of a scene-by-scene summary, a commentary, sources, theatrical history, and character sketches. The last one-third features entries for actors, composers, musicians, places that figured in the plays, and miscellaneous items." Libr J
Includes bibliographical references

Bryson, Bill

Shakespeare; the world as stage. Atlas Books/ HarperCollins 2007 199p (Eminent lives) $19.95

Grades: 9 10 11 12   **822.3**
1. Poets 2. Authors 3. Dramatists
ISBN 978-0-06-074022-1; 0-06-074022-1

LC 2007-21647

In this biography, the author marshals "the usual little facts that others might overlook—for example, that in Shakespeare's day perhaps 40% of women were pregnant when they got married—to paint a portrait of the world in which the Bard lived and prospered. . . . Bryson is a pleasant and funny guide to a subject at once overexposed and elusive—as Bryson puts it, he is a kind of literary equivalent of an electron—forever there and not there." Publ Wkly
Includes bibliographical references

Butler, Colin

★ The **practical** Shakespeare; the plays in practice and on the page. Ohio University Press 2005 205p $39.95; pa $19.95

Grades: 11 12 Adult   **822.3**
1. Poets 2. Authors 3. Dramatists
ISBN 0-8214-1621-9; 0-8214-1622-7 pa

LC 2004-30580

"Notes on staging, acting behaviors, scenes not shown, entrances, exits, characterizations, prologues, choruses, and staging are each featured in the text. References to specific scenes in the plays are used to illustrate and support the material. Any group preparing a production of one of the plays should find this a useful reference." Univ Press Books for Public and Second Sch Libr, 2006

Includes bibliographical references

Cahn, Victor L.
The **plays** of Shakespeare; a thematic guide. Greenwood Press 2001 361p $49.95

Grades: 9 10 11 12　　　　　　　　　　**822.3**
1. Poets 2. Authors 3. Dramatists
ISBN 0-313-30981-7
　　　　　　　　　　　　　　　　LC 00-22337

The author approaches Shakespeare "through an analysis of his major themes across several plays. The book contains 19 separate thematic essays devoted to such topics as Fate, Honor, Justice, Love, Money, and Power. Each analysis is abundantly supported with quotations from well-known and often-studied plays." Book Rep

Includes bibliographical references

Coye, Dale F.
Pronouncing Shakespeare's words; a guide from A to Zounds. [by] Dale Coye. Routledge 2002 342p pa $27.95

Grades: 11 12 Adult　　　　　　　　　**822.3**
1. Poets 2. Authors 3. Dramatists 4. Reference books
ISBN 0-415-94182-2
　　　　　　　　　　　　　　　　LC 2002-9622

First published 1998 by Greenwood Press

This work provides the correct pronunciation of over 300 words from Shakespeare's plays and poems. An "introduction precedes a phonetic pronunciation guide that includes definitions. Organized by play or poem, words are given in the order in which they appear in a linear reading. Lists at the beginning of each work contain pronunciation guides for place and proper names, the most common 'hard' words, and the most common reduced forms." Libr J

Includes bibliographical references

Fallon, Robert Thomas
★ A **theatergoer's** guide to Shakespeare. Dee, I.R. 2001 479p $29.95; pa $18.95

Grades: 11 12 Adult　　　　　　　　　**822.3**
1. Poets 2. Authors 3. Dramatists
ISBN 1-56663-342-7; 1-56663-508-X pa
　　　　　　　　　　　　　　　　LC 00-57018

Fallon "begins each summary with a brief scholarly introduction that places the particular play in the Shakespearean canon and in some cases provides helpful historical information. Thereafter Fallon maps out, with faultless accuracy, the twists and turns of every play from King Lear to The Two Noble Kinsmen." Booklist

Includes bibliographical references

Garber, Marjorie
Shakespeare after all. Pantheon Books 2004 989p hardcover o.p. pa $20

Grades: 11 12 Adult　　　　　　　　　**822.3**
1. Poets 2. Authors 3. Dramatists
ISBN 0-375-42190-4; 0-385-72214-1 pa
　　　　　　　　　　　　　　　　LC 2004-40063

The author "provides a handbook on Shakespeare's plays. After an introduction supplying standard overviews of the Renaissance theater and Shakespeare's life, she offers a critical essay on each play, complete with bibliographies and filmographies. The strength of this work is that Garber shows how the plays are interrelated by recurring language, characters, and themes, how each era has interpreted Shakespeare for itself, and how Shakespeare continues to shape today's culture." Libr J

Includes bibliographical references

Garfield, Leon
Shakespeare stories [I]-II; illustrated by Michael Foreman. Houghton Mifflin 1991 2v il hardcover o.p. v1 pa $19.95; v2 pa $17

Grades: 7 8 9 10 11 12　　　　　　　　**822.3**
1. Poets 2. Authors 3. Dramatists
ISBN 0-395-56397-6 v1; 0-395-86140-3 v1 pa; 0-395-70893-1 v2; 0-395-89109-4 v2 pa
Original volume first published 1985 by Schocken Bks.

In these volumes Garfield has rewritten twenty-one of Shakespeare's plays in narrative form, retaining much of the original language

Gleed, Paul
Bloom's how to write about William Shakespeare; [introduction by Harold Bloom] Chelsea House 2008 244p (Bloom's how to write about literature) $45

Grades: 9 10 11 12　　　　　　　　　　**822.3**
1. Poets 2. Authors 3. Dramatists 4. Report writing
ISBN 978-0-7910-9484-6
　　　　　　　　　　　　　　　　LC 2006-102770

This book offers "paper-topic suggestions, . . . strategies on how to write a strong essay, and an . . . introduction by Harold Bloom on writing about Shakespeare. This . . . volume is designed to help students develop their analytical writing skills and critical comprehension of the legendary Bard of Avon and his timeless works." Publisher's note

Includes bibliographical references

★ The **Greenwood** companion to Shakespeare; a comprehensive guide to students. edited by Joseph Rosenblum. Greenwood Press 2005 4v set $299.95

Grades: 11 12 Adult　　　　　　　　　**822.3**
1. Poets 2. Authors 3. Dramatists
ISBN 0-313-32779-3
　　　　　　　　　　　　　　　　LC 2004-28690

"Each of the set's four volumes relates to a specific genre—Overviews and the History Plays (Vol. 1), The Comedies (Vol. 2), The Tragedies (Vol. 3), and The Romances and Poetry (Vol. 4)—and is organized in 'Cliff Notes' fashion, devoting each entry to a single play, long poem, sonnet, or sonnet pair. . . . A great introduction to the Bard." Libr J

Includes bibliographical references

Hamlet; edited and with an introduction by Harold Bloom; volume editor, Brett Foster. Bloom's

Literary Criticism 2008 443p (Bloom's Shakespeare through the ages) $50

Grades: 9 10 11 12 **822.3**

1. Poets 2. Authors 3. Dramatists

ISBN 978-0-7910-9592-8; 0-7910-9592-4

LC 2007-50853

This "study guide to one of Shakespeare's greatest plays contains a selection of . . . criticism through the centuries on Hamlet. . . . [It also features] an introduction by Harold Bloom, . . . [a] summary, analysis of key passages, a comprehensive list of characters, a biography of Shakespeare, and more." Publisher's note

Includes bibliographical references

Hester, John

Performing Shakespeare. Crowood 2008 160p il pa $34.95

Grades: 9 10 11 12 Adult **822.3**

1. Poets 2. Acting 3. Authors 4. Dramatists

ISBN 978-1-84797-073-2

This is a "sensible introduction to the mechanics of Shakespearean performance. Voice, movement, verse, character study, interpretation, and ensemble bonding are each treated in distinctive chapters, with exercises. The presentation is excellent; color photographs of recent English productions are juxtaposed with shots of young student actors engaged in various rehearsals." Libr J

Julius Caesar; edited and with an introduction by Harold Bloom; volume editor, Pamela Loos. Bloom's Literary Criticism 2007 314p (Bloom's Shakespeare through the ages) $50

Grades: 9 10 11 12 **822.3**

1. Poets 2. Authors 3. Dramatists

ISBN 978-0-7910-9593-5; 0-7910-9593-2

LC 2007-26814

This "study guide to one of Shakespeare's greatest plays contains a selection of . . . criticism through the centuries on Julius Caesar." Publisher's note

Includes bibliographical references

King Lear; edited and with an introduction by Harold Bloom; volume editor, Neil Heims. Bloom's Literary Criticism 2008 356p (Bloom's Shakespeare through the ages) $50

Grades: 10 11 12 **822.3**

1. Poets 2. Authors 3. Dramatists

ISBN 978-0-7910-9574-4

LC 2007-29708

This "study guide to one of Shakespeare's most renowned works contains a selection of . . . criticism through the centuries on King Lear." Publisher's note

Includes bibliographical references

Krueger, Susan Heidi

The **tempest**; [by] Susan H. Krueger; introduction by Joseph Sobran. Marshall Cavendish Benchmark 2009 127p il (Shakespeare explained) lib bdg $29.93

Grades: 7 8 9 10 11 12 **822.3**

1. Poets 2. Authors 3. Dramatists

ISBN 978-0-7614-3423-8; 0-7614-3423-2

LC 2009-2587

This book offers an "engaging [introduction] to the Bard's work. . . . Krueger's lively, opinionated, and knowledgeable analysis of the complex play . . . will easily draw students into further discussion." Booklist

Includes glossary and bibliographical references

Macbeth; edited and with an introduction by Harold Bloom; volume editor, Janyce Marson. Bloom's Literary Criticism 2008 402p (Bloom's Shakespeare through the ages) $50

Grades: 9 10 11 12 **822.3**

1. Poets 2. Authors 3. Dramatists

ISBN 978-0-7910-9594-2

LC 2007-32378

This "study guide to one of Shakespeare's greatest tragedies contains a selection of . . . criticism through the centuries on Macbeth, including commentaries by such . . . critics as Elizabeth Montagu, Samuel Taylor Coleridge, Thomas DeQuincey, John Berryman, Cleanth Brooks, and many others." Publisher's note

Includes bibliographical references

Mussari, Mark

Othello; [by] Mark Mussari; introduction by Joseph Sobran. Marshall Cavendish Benchmark 2009 111p il (Shakespeare explained) lib bdg $29.95

Grades: 7 8 9 10 11 12 **822.3**

1. Poets 2. Authors 3. Dramatists

ISBN 978-0-7614-3422-1; 0-7614-3422-4

LC 2008-37506

"A literary analysis of the play Othello. Includes information on the history and culture of Elizabethan England." Publisher's note

Includes glossary and bibliographical references

The **sonnets.** Marshall Cavendish Benchmark 2010 127p il (Shakespeare explained) lib bdg $42.79

Grades: 9 10 11 12 **822.3**

1. Poets 2. Authors 3. Dramatists

ISBN 978-1-60870-018-9

LC 2009-41727

"A literary analysis of Shakespeare's sonnets. Includes information on the history and culture of Elizabethan England." Publisher's note

Includes glossary and bibliographical references

Naden, Corinne J.

Romeo and Juliet. Marshall Cavendish Benchmark 2008 127p il (Shakespeare explained) lib bdg $29.95

Grades: 7 8 9 10 11 12 **822.3**

1. Poets 2. Authors 3. Dramatists

ISBN 978-0-7614-3031-5; 0-7614-3031-8

LC 2008-14407

The "book opens with a discussion of Shakespeare's life, Elizabethan England, and the theatre. A glossary defines literary terms, and another translates Shakespeare's language into modern English. Overviews and analysis of individual scenes will help students follow the action. . . . Easily comprehended writing and an attractive layout make [this an] excellent choice for students." Libr Media Connect

Includes glossary and bibliographical references

Nostbakken, Faith

Understanding Macbeth; a student casebook to issues, sources, and historical documents. Greenwood Press 1997 235p (Greenwood Press literature in context series) $39.95

Grades: 9 10 11 12   822.3
1. Poets 2. Authors 3. Dramatists
ISBN 0-313-29630-8

LC 96-35013

This work "cites primary 17th-century documents showing the political events that may have influenced Shakespeare's decision to write a tragedy based on royal treason and the evils of witchcraft. The casebook also includes a dramatic analysis of Macbeth, showing the elements—character and theme—that shape the play and guiding the reader to a critical understanding of the work." Book Rep

Includes bibliographical references

Olsen, Kirstin

★ **All** things Shakespeare; an encyclopedia of Shakespeare's world. Greenwood Press 2002 2v il maps set $150

Grades: 11 12 Adult   822.3
1. Poets 2. Authors 3. Dramatists 4. Reference books
ISBN 0-313-31503-5

LC 2002-69732

This "encyclopedia describes Shakespeare's physical environment, including common objects, daily activities, and popular beliefs and attitudes. Information is grouped into general topic clusters such as 'Behavior,' 'Clothing and Dress,' 'Furniture,' 'Fire,' and 'War and Peace.' . . . Within the 200-plus entries, references are made to the play, act, and scene in which Shakespeare mentions the item or activity being discussed." Libr J

Othello; edited and with an introduction by Harold Bloom; volume editor, Neil Heims. Bloom's Literary Criticism 2008 325p (Bloom's Shakespeare through the ages) $50

Grades: 9 10 11 12   822.3
1. Poets 2. Authors 3. Dramatists
ISBN 978-0-7910-9575-1

LC 2007-26815

This "study guide to one of Shakespeare's greatest plays contains a selection of . . . criticism through the centuries on Othello." Publisher's note

Includes bibliographical references

★ The **Oxford** companion to Shakespeare; general editor, Michael Dobson; associate general editor,

Stanley Wells. Oxford Univ. Press 2001 xxix, 541p il maps hardcover o.p. pa $39.95

Grades: 11 12 Adult   822.3
1. Poets 2. Authors 3. Dramatists 4. Reference books
ISBN 0-19-280614-9 pa; 0-19-811735-3

LC 2001-277478

This volume "illuminates not only Shakespeare's life and works but also the many forms that interpretation of Shakespeare has taken in the centuries since his death." Booklist

Includes bibliographical references

Richert, Scott P.

King Lear. Marshall Cavendish Benchmark 2010 127p il (Shakespeare explained) lib bdg $42.79

Grades: 8 9 10 11 12   822.3
1. Poets 2. Authors 3. Dramatists
ISBN 978-1-60870-016-5

LC 2010-7060

"A literary analysis of the play 'King Lear.' Includes information on the history and culture of Elizabethan England." Publisher's note

Includes glossary and bibliographical references

Riley, Dick

The **bedside,** bathtub & armchair companion to Shakespeare; {by} Dick Riley & Pam McAllister. Continuum 2001 288p il hardcover o.p. pa $19.95

Grades: 11 12 Adult   822.3
1. Poets 2. Authors 3. Dramatists
ISBN 0-8264-1250-5 pa; 0-8264-1249-1

LC 2001-17332

"Provides synopses of plays, information about the period in which each play is set, possible plot sources, and notable features and productions of 36 of Shakespeare's plays (Pericles and The Two Noble Kinsmen are not included). Interspersed with chapters on each play are short discussions about topics such as Shakespeare's sonnets, authorship problems, women's roles in 15th- and 16th-century society, and Shakespeare's language." Libr J

Includes bibliographical references

Romeo and Juliet; edited and with an introduction by Harold Bloom; volume editor, Janyce Marson. Bloom's Literary Criticism 2008 339p (Bloom's Shakespeare through the ages) $50

Grades: 9 10 11 12   822.3
1. Poets 2. Authors 3. Dramatists
ISBN 978-0-7910-9596-6

LC 2007-50854

This study guide contains a selection of criticism through the centuries on the play, plus a summary, analysis of key passages, a list of characters, and a biography of Shakespeare.

Includes bibliographical references

Saccio, Peter

Shakespeare's English kings; history, chronicle, and drama. 2nd ed; Oxford Univ. Press 2000 284p il map hardcover o.p. pa $14.95

Grades: 9 10 11 12   822.3
1. Poets 2. Authors 3. Dramatists 4. Great Britain

-- History 5. Great Britain -- Kings and rulers
ISBN 0-19-512318-2; 0-19-512319-0 pa

LC 99-43297

First published 1977

This book explores the medieval histories and Tudor chronicles that served as source material for Shakespeare's ten history plays. In addition to explicating the plots, the author also discusses where Shakespeare deviated from his sources. Includes genealogical charts and an appendix of names and titles

Includes bibliographical references (p. 257-273) and index

Scheeder, Louis

★ **All** the words on stage; a complete pronunciation dictionary for the plays of William Shakespeare. {by} Louis Scheeder and Shane Ann Younts. Smith & Kraus 2002 292p (Career development series) pa $24.95

Grades: 11 12 Adult   **822.3**
1. Poets 2. Authors 3. Dramatists
ISBN 1-57525-214-7

LC 2001-20182

"This reference work is first a pronunciation dictionary, but also can aid in understanding the rhythm and variants of the iambic pentameter and the interweaving of word ahd rhythm produced by Shakespeare's blank verse. . . . Schools that read or perform Shakespeare in their curriculum will want to have this fine dictionary in the reference collection." Book Rep

Includes glossary and bibliographical references

Schupack, Sara

The **merchant** of Venice. Marshall Cavendish Benchmark 2009 127p il (Shakespeare explained) lib bdg $29.95

Grades: 7 8 9 10 11 12   **822.3**
1. Poets 2. Authors 3. Dramatists
ISBN 978-0-7614-3421-4; 0-7614-3421-6

LC 2009-3166

"A literary analysis of Shakespeare's play The Merchant of Venice. Includes information on the history and culture of Elizabethan England." Publisher's note

Includes glossary and bibliographical references

Shakespeare; editor, Joseph Rosenblum; managing editor, Christina J. Moose. Salem Press 1998 xx, 482p il (Magill's choice) $68

Grades: 11 12 Adult   **822.3**
1. Poets 2. Authors 3. Dramatists
ISBN 0-89356-966-6

LC 97-43460

This work "divides the plays into histories, comedies, tragedies, and romances. The plays are indexed alphabetically and a time line also is included. Shakespeare begins with background of the man, the dramatist, and the poet. Each play is examined, including a summary, critical analysis, and bibliography. The poetry section explains each poem, analyzes it, and offers theories on theme." Book Rep

Includes bibliographical references

The **Shakespeare** encyclopedia; the complete guide to the man and his works. Firefly Books 2009 304p il map $35

Grades: 9 10 11 12 Adult   **822.3**
1. Poets 2. Authors 3. Dramatists 4. Reference books
ISBN 978-1-55407-479-2

LC 2010-291927

"This text is a must-have for any school library; accessible for students, librarians, and teachers alike, it provides far more than a simple overview of the writer and his work. In fact, it provides detailed histories and summaries of his major works and poems, including lists of characters, depictions of family trees, and analyses of dominant imagery, motifs, themes, and related quotes. . . . The encyclopedia is both intellectually and aesthetically pleasing." Voice Youth Advocates

Includes glossary and bibliographical references

Shakespeare for students; critical interpretations of Shakespeare's plays and poetry. 2nd ed.; Thomson Gale 2007 3v il set $308

Grades: 9 10 11 12   **822.3**
1. Poets 2. Authors 3. Dramatists
ISBN 978-1-4144-1255-9; 1-4144-1255-X

LC 2007-8901

First published as three separate volumes 1992-2000

"Covering 28 works of Shakespeare, including his sonnets, . . . [this set] provides the following information: a brief overview of each work, a plot summary, characters, themes, stylistic and literary devices, the historical context, a critical overview, a collection of criticism by scholars, a list of sources, and an annotated list for further reading. . . . This three-volume set is of great value to a beginning Shakespeare scholar seeking an introduction to a specific work." Libr J

Includes bibliographical references

Shakespeare's histories; edited and with an introduction by Harold Bloom. Chelsea House 2000 117p (Bloom's major dramatists) $19.95

Grades: 9 10 11 12   **822.3**
1. Poets 2. Authors 3. Dramatists
ISBN 0-7910-5241-9

LC 99-36774

This "title contains criticism on Richard III, Henry IV, Parts 1 and 2, and Henry V. Discussion of the individual plays is prefaced by an introduction and a three-page biography of Shakespeare. The entry on each play gives a succinct plot summary, brief descriptions of major characters, and six to eight critical excerpts. A list of the bard's works, further reading, and indexes of themes and ideas complete this comprehensive volume." SLJ

Includes bibliographical references

Shakespeare, William, 1564-1616

The **Columbia** dictionary of quotations from Shakespeare; [selected by] Mary and Reginald Foakes. Columbia Univ. Press 1998 516p $63

Grades: 11 12 Adult   **822.3**
1. Poets 2. Authors 3. Dramatists 4. Quotations
ISBN 0-231-10434-0

LC 97-44894

"The book is organized by topics ('Age,' 'Duplicity,' 'Fish'), followed by passages of about five or six lines. After each selection, the citation, the character, and usually the context of the lines are given. If a reference is obscure, the explanation is more elaborate. Indexes provide access by play and poem, by character, and by keyword." SLJ

★ The **complete** works; general editors, Stanley Wells and Gary Taylor; editors, Stanley Wells . . . [et al.]; with introductions by Stanley Wells. 2nd ed.; Clarendon Press; Oxford University Press 2005 lxxv, 1344p il $40
Grades: 11 12 Adult   **822.3**
    ISBN 0-19-926717-0
                                          LC 2005-47272
First published 1986
This anthology "features a brief introduction to each work as well as [a] General Introduction. . . . [The volume includes] essay on language, a list of contemporary allusions to Shakespeare, an index of Shakespearean characters, a glossary, a consolidated bibliography, and an index of first lines of the Sonnets." Publisher's note

The **essential** Shakespeare; selected and with an introduction by Ted Hughes. Ecco Press 1991 230p (Essential poets) hardcover o.p. pa $8
Grades: 11 12 Adult   **822.3**
    ISBN 0-06-088795-8 pa
                                          LC 91-17522
Ted Hughes has selected a "combination of sonnets, songs, speeches, and poetry that best illustrate the incredible breadth of Shakespeare's genius. In his introduction, Hughes explores the origins of Shakespeare's language." Publisher's note

★ The **first** part of King Henry the Fourth; edited by Claire McEachern. Penguin Books 2000 xlii, 117p il (The Pelican Shakespeare) pa $5
Grades: 9 10 11 12   **822.3**
    ISBN 0-14-071456-1
                                          LC 00-269943
Drama concerning problems arising from the deposition and murder of Richard II, of which Henry of Bolingbroke has had a part. Now king and faced with rebellion in Scotland and Wales, Henry and his sons Prince Hal (the Prince of Wales) and Prince John defeat the Percys and wage war against the armies of Northumberland and the Archbishop of York
Includes bibliographical references

★ **King** Lear; edited by Stephen Orgel. New ed; Penguin Books 1999 142p il (The Pelican Shakespeare) pa $5
Grades: 9 10 11 12   **822.3**
    ISBN 0-14-071476-6
                                          LC 00-503596
The King of Britain divides his kingdom between his two scheming elder daughters and estranges himself from his favorite daughter when she speaks out against him

★ **Macbeth**; edited by Stephen Orgel. Penguin Books 2000 xlvi, 98p il (The Pelican Shakespeare) pa $5
Grades: 9 10 11 12   **822.3**
    ISBN 0-14-071478-2
                                          LC 00-266703
Tragedy concerning a general who murders his king after hearing the prophecies of three witches. Spurred on by his wife, Lady Macbeth, they instigate a series of murders, as well as a war, in his quest (and her ambitions) for the throne of Scotland, ultimately leading to their demise
Includes bibliographical references

★ The **merchant** of Venice; edited by A. R. Braunmuller. Penguin Books 2000 lii, 103p (The Pelican Shakespeare) pa $5
Grades: 9 10 11 12   **822.3**
    ISBN 0-14-071462-6
                                          LC 00-702935
In this dark comedy, a young man, Bassiano, squanders his fortune and, in order to woo the wealthy lady he loves, must borrow money from his friend, Antonio, a Venetian merchant. Antonio, whose own money is invested in merchant ships, must borrow the sum from Shylock, the Jewish moneylender, who later demands a pound of Antonio's flesh when the merchant falls into his debt

★ A **midsummer** night's dream; edited by Russ McDonald. Penguin Books 2000 liii, 88p (The Pelican Shakespeare) pa $5
Grades: 9 10 11 12   **822.3**
    ISBN 0-14-071455-3
                                          LC 00-33635
Comedy about the strange events that take place in a forest inhabited by fairies who magically transform the romantic fate of two young couples
Includes bibliographical references

★ **Much** ado about nothing; edited by Peter Holland. [New ed.]; Penguin Books 1999 xliv, 98p (The Pelican Shakespeare) pa $5
Grades: 9 10 11 12   **822.3**
    ISBN 0-14-071480-4
                                          LC 99-462498
Romantic comedy about two couples, Hero and Claudio, and Beatrice and Benedick, who, despite personal and familial obstacles, finally unite through the forces of local constables Dogberry and Verges
Includes bibliographical references

★ The **Norton** Shakespeare; Stephen Greenblatt, general editor; Walter Cohen, Jean E. Howard, Katharine Eisaman Maus [editors]; with an essay on the Shakespearean stage by Andrew Gurr. 2nd ed.; W.W. Norton 2008 3419p il $77.50
Grades: 11 12 Adult   **822.3**
    ISBN 978-0-393-92991-1
                                          LC 2007-46599
First published 1997
The editors' "mission is to make Shakespeare accessible to modern readers. With lengthy introductions providing

insight into Shakespeare's life and times as well as textual notes, marginal glosses, footnotes, and bibliographies, they more than achieve their aim . . . [Includes] an illustrated chronology of Shakespeare's life, and over 150 illustrations. The result is a work of immense scope, scholarship, and richness." Libr J [review of 1997 edition]

Includes bibliographical references

Othello; [by] William Shakespeare; advisory editors, David Bevington, Barbara Gaines, and Peter Holland. Sourcebooks MediaFusion 2005 402p il (Sourcebooks Shakespeare) pa $14.95

Grades: 9 10 11 12 **822.3**
ISBN 1-4022-0102-8

LC 2005-23285

This book features the full text of Othello with performance annotations and glossary. The audio CD included features a 1944 performance of the play by Paul Robeson.

Romeo and Juliet; [by] William Shakespeare; advisory editors, David Bevington, Barbara Gaines, and Peter Holland. Sourcebooks MediaFusion 2005 360p il (Sourcebooks Shakespeare) pa $14.95

Grades: 9 10 11 12 **822.3**
ISBN 1-4022-0101-X

LC 2005-23286

This book features the full text of the play Romeo and Juliet with performance annotations and a glossary. The audio CD included features recordings of both Ellen Terry and Kate Beckinsale in the roles of Juliet.

★ The **tempest**; edited by Peter Holland. [New ed.]; Penguin Books 1999 xliv, 84p (The Pelican Shakespeare) pa $5

Grades: 9 10 11 12 **822.3**
ISBN 0-14-071485-5

LC 99-462496

Prospero, the exiled Duke of Milan, living on an island with his daughter Miranda, raises a tempest that brings his shipwrecked enemies ashore. Now, faced with advancing age, he has the opportunity to punish and forgive his enemies as well as relinquish his magic powers

Includes bibliographical references

★ The **tragedy** of Julius Caesar; edited by William Montgomery; with an introduction by Douglas Trevor. Penguin Books 2000 xlvi, 114p (The Pelican Shakespeare) pa $5

Grades: 9 10 11 12 **822.3**
ISBN 0-14-071468-5

LC 2001-266965

Brutus, best friend of the Roman ruler Caesar, reluctantly joins a successful plot to murder Caesar and subsequently destroys himself

★ The **tragedy** of Othello, the Moor of Venice; edited by Russ McDonald. Penguin Books 2001 xxix, 145p il (The Pelican Shakespeare) pa $5

Grades: 9 10 11 12 **822.3**
ISBN 0-14-071463-4

LC 2001-33135

A general serving the Venetian state, Othello is duped by a jealous ensign into thinking that his wife, Desdemona, has been unfaithful. Succumbing to jealousy, he murders her and then, upon learning the truth, commits suicide

★ The **tragical** history of Hamlet prince of Denmark. Penguin Books 2001 lviii, 148p (The Pelican Shakespeare) pa $5

Grades: 9 10 11 12 **822.3**
ISBN 0-14-071454-5

LC 2001-31340

Story about the Prince of Denmark who, upon learning of the death of his father at the hands of his uncle, Claudius, seeks revenge.

Includes bibliographical references

Shewmaker, Eugene F.

★ **Shakespeare's** language; a glossary of unfamiliar words in his plays and poems. 2nd ed.; Facts On File 2008 xxvii, 628p (Facts on File library of world literature) $75; pa $21.95

Grades: 9 10 11 12 **822.3**
1. Poets 2. Authors 3. Dramatists
ISBN 978-0-8160-7125-8; 978-0-8160-7557-7 pa

LC 2007-16138

First published 1996

"This would be a useful addition to any literature reference section." Libr Media Connect

Includes bibliographical references

Sobran, Joseph

Hamlet. Marshall Cavendish Benchmark 2008 127p il (Shakespeare explained) lib bdg $29.95

Grades: 7 8 9 10 11 12 **822.3**
1. Poets 2. Authors 3. Dramatists
ISBN 978-0-7614-3027-8; 0-7614-3027-X

LC 2008-7090

"A literary analysis of the play Hamlet. Includes information on the history and culture of Elizabethan England." Publisher's note

Includes glossary and bibliographical references

Henry IV, part 1. Marshall Cavendish Benchmark 2009 111p il (Shakespeare explained) lib bdg $29.95

Grades: 7 8 9 10 11 12 **822.3**
1. Poets 2. Authors 3. Dramatists
ISBN 978-0-7614-3419-1; 0-7614-3419-4

LC 2008-37510

"A literary analysis of the play Henry IV, part 1. Includes information on the history and culture of Elizabethan England." Publisher's note

Includes glossary and bibliographical references

A **midsummer** night's dream; Joseph Sobran. Marshall Cavendish Benchmark 2008 111p. ill. (some col.) lib bdg $29.95

Grades: 7 8 9 10 11 12 **822.3**
1. Poets 2. Authors 3. Dramatists
ISBN 978-0-7614-3030-8; 0-7614-3030-X

LC 2008007079

"A literary analysis of the play A Midsummer Night's Dream. Includes information on the history and culture of Elizabethan England." Publisher's note

"[This book] provides practical information, skillfully presented, making the complexities of Shakespearean theater accessible to present-day students. [The] author's contagious enthusiasm and attractive presentation make [it] imminently useful for high school and public libraries.—" VOYA

Includes glossary and bibliographical references

The **sonnets;** edited and with an introduction by Harold Bloom; volume editor, Brett Foster. Bloom's Literary Criticism 2008 388p (Bloom's Shakespeare through the ages) $50

Grades: 10 11 12   **822.3**
1. Poets 2. Authors 3. Dramatists
ISBN 978-0-7910-9597-3

LC 2008-12830

This "study guide contains a selection of . . . criticism through the centuries of Shakespeare's sonnets." Publisher's note

Includes bibliographical references

Spurgeon, Caroline F. E.

Shakespeare's imagery and what it tells us; with charts and illustrations. Cambridge Univ. Press 1935 408p il hardcover o.p. pa $29.95

Grades: 9 10 11 12   **822.3**
1. Poets 2. Authors 3. Dramatists
ISBN 0-521-09258-2 pa

"A distinctive contribution to Shakespeare's criticism, bold and original in idea, scrupulous and exhaustive in method, and of all things, readable as a detective story." N Y Times Book Rev

The **tempest;** edited and with an introduction by Harold Bloom; volume editor, Neil Heims. Bloom's Literary Criticism 2008 276p (Bloom's Shakespeare through the ages) $50

Grades: 10 11 12   **822.3**
1. Poets 2. Authors 3. Dramatists
ISBN 978-0-7910-9577-5

LC 2007-29605

This "study guide to one of Shakespeare's greatest plays contains a selection of . . . criticism through the centuries on The Tempest." Publisher's note

Includes bibliographical references

William Shakespeare; edited and with an introduction by Harold Bloom. Chelsea House 2002 142p (Bloom's biocritiques) lib bdg $25.95

Grades: 9 10 11 12   **822.3**
1. Poets 2. Authors 3. Dramatists
ISBN 0-7910-6171-X

LC 2002-5480

Cleanth Brooks, Ralph Waldo Emerson, Yoojin Grace Kim, and Samuel Johnson provide critical readings of the Shakespearean canon. A biographical profile and a chronology are included

Includes bibliographical references

William Shakespeare's Hamlet; edited and with an introduction by Harold Bloom. New ed; Bloom's Literary Criticism 2009 211p (Modern critical interpretations) $45

Grades: 9 10 11 12   **822.3**
1. Poets 2. Authors 3. Dramatists
ISBN 978-1-60413-632-6

LC 2009-18234

First published 1986

This "study guide to one of Shakespeare's greatest plays contains a selection of . . . contemporary criticism of Hamlet." Publisher's note

Includes bibliographical references

William Shakespeare's Julius Caesar; edited and with an introduction by Harold Bloom. New ed; Chelsea House 2009 178p (Modern critical interpretations) $45

Grades: 9 10 11 12   **822.3**
1. Poets 2. Authors 3. Dramatists
ISBN 978-1-60413-639-5

LC 2009-22143

First published 1988

A collection of critical essays on the Shakespeare tragedy, arranged in chronological order of their original publication.

Includes bibliographical references

William Shakespeare's Macbeth; edited & with an introduction by Harold Bloom. New ed; Bloom's Literary Criticism 2010 119p (Bloom's guides) $30

Grades: 9 10 11 12   **822.3**
1. Poets 2. Authors 3. Dramatists
ISBN 978-1-60413-877-1

LC 2010-28809

First published 2004

This study guide on Shakespeare's classic work includes a brief biographical sketch of Shakespeare, a list of characters, a summary and analysis, and selections from critical essays by scholars about the work.

Includes bibliographical references

William Shakespeare's Romeo and Juliet; edited & with an introduction by Harold Bloom. New ed; Bloom's Literary Criticism 2010 121p (Bloom's guides) $45

Grades: 9 10 11 12   **822.3**
1. Poets 2. Authors 3. Dramatists
ISBN 978-1-60413-813-9

LC 2009-53107

First published 2005

This book "begins with a brief biography of Shakespeare, a discussion of the play's sources, and a list of characters. The body of the book consists of a fairly lengthy summary and analysis written by Bloom and . . . critical essays, reprinted from other scholarly sources, analyzing various aspects of the play. . . . Because this play is so frequently taught at the high school level, this guide would be a useful addition to most collections." SLJ

Includes bibliographical references

Woodford, Donna

Understanding King Lear; a student casebook to issues, sources, and historical documents. Greenwood Press 2004 183p il (Greenwood Press literature in context series) $45

Grades: 9 10 11 12 **822.3**

1. Poets 2. Authors 3. Dramatists

ISBN 0-313-31936-7

LC 2004-3576

"By using documents and literature from Shakespeare's own time as well as from the present, Woodford illuminates the text of King Lear. . . . Anyone interested in King Lear could learn much from this book." SLJ

Includes bibliographical references

823 English fiction

Alan Paton's Cry, the beloved country; edited and with an introduction by Harold Bloom. New ed; Bloom's Literacy Criticism 2010 185p (Modern critical interpretations) $45

Grades: 9 10 11 12 **823**

1. Authors 2. Novelists 3. Essayists 4. Biographers

ISBN 978-1-60413-583-1

LC 2010-1314

Examines different aspects of Paton's novel about race relations in South Africa via critical essays on this work.

Includes bibliographical references

Aldous Huxley; edited and with an introduction by Harold Bloom. New ed; Bloom's Literary Criticism 2010 246p (Modern critical views) $45

Grades: 9 10 11 12 **823**

1. Authors 2. Novelists 3. Essayists 4. Screenwriters

ISBN 978-1-60413-866-5; 978-1-4381-3437-6 ebook

LC 2010-6251

First published 2003

"This volume contains a collection of . . . contemporary criticism on Huxley, plus a bibliography, a chronology of the author's life, and an index." Publisher's note

Includes bibliographical references

Aldous Huxley's Brave new world; edited & with an introduction by Harold Bloom. New ed.; Bloom's Literary Criticism 2010 133p (Bloom's guides) $30

Grades: 9 10 11 12 **823**

1. Authors 2. Novelists 3. Essayists 4. Screenwriters

ISBN 978-1-60413-878-8

LC 2010-28994

First published 2003

This study guide on Aldous Huxley's dystopian novel includes a brief biographical sketch of Huxley, a list of characters, a summary and analysis, and selections from critical essays by different scholars about the work.

Includes bibliographical references

Anelli, Melissa

Harry, a history; the true story of a boy wizard, his fans, and life inside the Harry Potter phenomenon. Pocket Books 2008 356p il pa $16

Grades: 9 10 11 12 **823**

1. Authors 2. Novelists 3. Fantasy writers 4. Children's authors 5. Young adult authors 6. Harry Potter (Fictional character)

ISBN 978-1-4165-5495-0; 1-4165-5495-5

LC 2008-21530

"With infectious, at times frenetic, excitement, Anelli presents two narratives in this hip report on how a boy wizard became a rock star. . . . Fans will recognize themselves in these pages, and the curious might finally understand their friends." Publ Wkly

Includes bibliographical references

Baker, William

Critical companion to Jane Austen; a literary reference to her life and work. Facts on File 2008 644p il (Facts on File library of world literature) $75

Grades: 9 10 11 12 Adult **823**

1. Authors 2. Novelists

ISBN 978-0-8160-6416-8

LC 2006-102848

"Janeites (and others) will find . . . [this book] a useful and accessible one-stop resource." Booklist

Includes bibliographical references

Brackett, Virginia

Bloom's how to write about the Brontes; [introduction by Harold Bloom] Bloom's Literary Criticism 2009 281p (Bloom's how to write about literature) $45

Grades: 9 10 11 12 **823**

1. Poets 2. Authors 3. Novelists 4. Report writing

ISBN 978-0-7910-9794-6

LC 2008-5709

This book offers paper topics and advice on writing papers on the works of the Brontë sisters.

Includes bibliographical references

The **Brontes**; edited and with an introduction by Harold Bloom. New ed; Bloom's Literary Criticism 2009 219p (Modern critical views) $45

Grades: 9 10 11 12 **823**

1. Poets 2. Authors 3. Novelists

ISBN 978-0-7910-9620-8; 0-7910-9620-3

LC 2008-32550

First published 1987

This is a compilation of "analyses of the Brontë sisters—Charlotte, Emily, and Anne. Several works of the authors are examined, including the classics Jane Eyre and Wuthering Heights." Publisher's note

Includes bibliographical references (p. 205-8)

Charles Dickens; edited and with an introduction by Harold Bloom. Chelsea House Publishers 2003 154p (Bloom's biocritiques) $35
Grades: 9 10 11 12   **823**
1. Authors 2. Novelists
ISBN 0-7910-6365-8
LC 2002-7683
Includes bibliographical references

Charles Dickens's A tale of two cities; edited & with an introduction by Harold Bloom. Chelsea House 2006 131p (Bloom's guides) $30
Grades: 9 10 11 12   **823**
1. Authors 2. Novelists
ISBN 0-7910-9293-3; 978-0-7910-9293-4
LC 2006-31096
This study guide on Charles Dickens' historical novel includes a brief biographical sketch of Dickens, a list of characters, a summary and analysis, and selections from critical essays by different scholars about the work.
Includes bibliographical references

Charles Dicken[s]'s Great expectations; edited and with an introduction by Harold Bloom. Chelsea House Publishers 2000 310p (Modern critical interpretations) $45
Grades: 9 10 11 12 Adult   **823**
1. Authors 2. Novelists
ISBN 0-7910-5661-9
LC 99-51594
A collection of fourteen critical essays on Dickens' novel arranged in chronological order of publication.
Includes bibliographical references

Charlotte Bronte's Jane Eyre; edited and with an introduction by Harold Bloom. Chelsea House 2006 235p (Modern critical interpretations) $45
Grades: 9 10 11 12   **823**
1. Poets 2. Authors 3. Novelists
ISBN 0-7910-9304-2; 978-0-7910-9304-7
LC 2006-15135
First published 1987
A collection of nine critical essays on Charlotte Bronte's historical novel arranged in chronological order of publication.
Includes bibliographical references

Chinua Achebe's Things fall apart; edited and with an introduction by Harold Bloom. new ed; Chelsea House Publishers 2009 221p (Modern critical interpretations) $45
Grades: 9 10 11 12   **823**
1. Poets 2. Authors 3. Novelists 4. Essayists 5. Short story writers
ISBN 978-1-60413-581-7
LC 2009-20349
First published 2002
A collection of essays discussing Achebe's novel.
Includes bibliographical references

Davis, Paul B.
★ **Critical** companion to Charles Dickens; a literary reference to his life and work. Rev ed; Facts on File 2007 676p il (Facts on File library of world literature) $75
Grades: 9 10 11 12 Adult   **823**
1. Authors 2. Novelists
ISBN 0-8160-6407-5; 978-0-8160-6407-6
LC 2006-3026
First published 1998 with title: Charles Dickens A-Z
This "reference contains entries on this writer's works, including the characters in each work, . . . historical and thematic information, and critical discussion. It also includes entries on related people, places, themes, topics, and influences. Additional features include 116 illustrations, a chronology, a bibliography of primary and secondary sources, and much more." Publisher's note
Includes bibliographical references

Dracula, by Bram Stoker; editor, Jack Lynch. Salem Press 2009 339p (Critical insights) lib bdg $85
Grades: 9 10 11 12   **823**
1. Authors 2. Novelists 3. Short story writers
ISBN 978-1-58765-612-5; 1-58765-612-4
LC 2009-26314
This book introduces Dracula's narrative in its "historical context, provide a short biography of the author, and offer 'The Paris Review Perspective' on . . . [the book,] followed by a series of articles by academics under the headings of 'Critical Contexts' or 'Critical Readings.'" SLJ
Includes bibliographical references

Emily Bronte's Wuthering Heights; edited & with introduction by Harold Bloom. Chelsea House 2008 96p (Bloom's guides) $30
Grades: 9 10 11 12   **823**
1. Poets 2. Authors 3. Novelists
ISBN 978-0-7910-9831-8
LC 2007-48752
This study guide on the classic romance novel includes a brief biographical sketch of Emily Bronte, a list of characters, a summary and analysis, and selections from critical essays by different scholars about the work.
Includes bibliographical references

★ The **Facts** on File companion to the British novel. Facts on File 2005 2v (Facts on File library of world literature) set $140
Grades: 9 10 11 12 Adult   **823**
1. English fiction -- History and criticism
ISBN 0-8160-6377-X; 978-0-8160-6377-2
LC 2004-20914
"With more than one thousand entries, each with a selected bibliography and a set of very usable appendixes, this work accomplishes much in a compact set." Ref & User Services Quarterly
Includes bibliographical references

Fargnoli, A. Nicholas
Critical companion to James Joyce; a literary companion to his life and work. [by] A. Nicholas

Fargnoli, Michael Patrick Gillespie. Rev ed; Facts On File 2006 450p il (Facts on File library of world literature) $65; pa $19.95

Grades: 11 12 Adult   **823**

1. Poets 2. Authors 3. Novelists 4. Dramatists 5. Short story writers

ISBN 0-8160-6232-3; 978-0-8160-6232-4; 0-8160-6689-2 pa; 978-0-8160-6689-6 pa

LC 2005-15721

First published 1995 with title: James Joyce A to Z

The authors "divide this reference to the writer's life and work into four parts. Part 1 is a brief biography. Part 2 focuses on individual works (e.g., Dubliners), including its publication date, a brief history, a synopsis, early critical reception, contemporary perspectives, and one or two recommended titles for further reading. The entries in Part 3 cover people (including friends and relatives), places, and ideas related to Joyce. Part 4 contains an appendix, a bibliography of the writer's work, a bibliography of secondary sources, chronologies, family trees, and more. . . . [This is] a great primer for those needing a detailed introduction into Joyce's world." Libr J

Includes bibliographical references

Fonstad, Karen Wynn

The **atlas** of Middle-earth; rev ed; Houghton Mifflin 2001 210p il maps pa $24

Grades: 9 10 11 12   **823**

1. Authors 2. Novelists 3. Linguists 4. Philologists 5. Fantasy writers 6. Children's authors

ISBN 0-618-12699-6

First published 1981

A guide to the journeys, lands, peoples, and history of Tolkien's imaginary kingdom

Includes bibliographical references

George Orwell's 1984; edited and with an introduction by Harold Bloom. Updated ed.; Chelsea House 2007 205p (Modern critical interpretations) $45

Grades: 9 10 11 12 Adult   **823**

1. Authors 2. Novelists 3. Essayists

ISBN 0-7910-9300-X; 978-0-7910-9300-9

LC 2006-25343

First published 1987

A collection of essays providing international appraisal and interpretation of Orwell's apocalyptic novel.

Includes bibliographical references

George Orwell's Animal farm; edited and with an introduction by Harold Bloom. New ed; Chelsea House 2009 166p (Modern critical interpretations) $45

Grades: 9 10 11 12   **823**

1. Authors 2. Novelists 3. Essayists

ISBN 978-1-60413-582-4

LC 2009-18851

First published 1999

This collection "of critical essays examining Animal Farm provides 10 to 12 full-length critical essays for students of literature, plus a chronology of the author's life, a bibliography, an index, and notes on the contributing writers." Publisher's note

Includes bibliographical references

Great expectations, by Charles Dickens; editor, Eugene Goodheart. Salem Press 2009 312p (Critical insights) lib bdg $85

Grades: 9 10 11 12   **823**

1. Authors 2. Novelists

ISBN 978-1-58765-614-9; 1-58765-614-0

LC 2009-26312

"Contains an editor's introduction to the author or work, a perspective from the editors of the . . . literary magazine The Paris Review, and a biography of the author. Following these ready-reference chapters is a section, 'Critical Contexts,' that presents four original essays by current scholars." Publisher's note

Includes bibliographical references

Horror: another 100 best books; edited by Stephen Jones and Kim Newman; with a foreword by Peter Straub. Carroll & Graf Publishers 2005 456p pa $16.95

Grades: 11 12 Adult   **823**

1. Best books 2. Horror fiction -- History and criticism

ISBN 0-7867-1577-4

First published 1988

"Horror fans seeking what to read next will not only find out here; they'll also have their taste and appreciative capacity refined by the intelligent, passionate commentary of the 100 writers who selected these 100 books." Booklist

J.R.R. Tolkien; edited and with an introduction by Harold Bloom. New ed; Bloom's Literary Criticism 2008 180p (Modern critical views) $45

Grades: 9 10 11 12 Adult   **823**

1. Authors 2. Novelists 3. Linguists 4. Philologists 5. Fantasy writers 6. Children's authors

ISBN 978-1-60413-146-8

LC 2008-5711

First published 2000

A selection of criticism, arranged in chronological order of publication, devoted to the works of J.R.R. Tolkien.

Includes bibliographical references

James Joyce; edited and with an introduction by Harold Bloom. Chelsea House 2003 142p (Bloom's biocritiques) $35

Grades: 9 10 11 12   **823**

1. Poets 2. Authors 3. Novelists 4. Dramatists 5. Short story writers

ISBN 0-7910-7382-3

LC 2003-805

This book "includes . . . [a] biography, literary criticism, a list of works by and about the author, and more." Publisher's note

Includes bibliographical references

Jane Austen; edited and with an introduction by Harold Bloom. New ed; Chelsea House 2009 315p
(Modern critical views) $45

Grades: 11 12 Adult   **823**

1. Authors 2. Novelists

ISBN 978-1-60413-397-4

LC 2008-44616

First published 1986

A collection of critical essays on Austen and her works. Also includes a chronology of events in her life.

Includes bibliographical references

Jane Austen's Pride and prejudice; edited and with an introduction by Harold Bloom. Updated ed; Chelsea House 2007 246p (Modern critical interpretations) $45

Grades: 9 10 11 12 Adult   **823**

1. Authors 2. Novelists

ISBN 978-0-7910-9437-2; 0-7910-9437-5

LC 2006-101022

First published 1987

A collection of eleven critical essays on the classic Jane Austen novel.

Includes bibliographical references

Jonathan Swift's Gulliver's travels; edited and with an introduction by Harold Bloom. New ed; Bloom's Literary Criticism 2008 256p (Modern critical interpretations) $45

Grades: 9 10 11 12 Adult   **823**

1. Poets 2. Clergy 3. Authors 4. Satirists 5. Pamphleteers 6. Writers on politics

ISBN 978-0-7910-9628-4

LC 2008-29375

First published 1986

This collection of critical essays on Swift's satirical novel discusses "topics such as the philosophical background of the work, satire, and more." Publisher's note

Includes bibliographical references

Jones, Diana Wynne, 1934-2011

Reflections; on the magic of writing. by Diana Wynne Jones. Greenwillow Books 2012 368 p. (hardback) $24.99

Grades: 7 8 9 10 11 12   **823**

1. Fantasy fiction -- Authorship 2. Children's stories -- Authorship

ISBN 0062219898; 9780062219893

LC 2012018080

This book, by Diana Wynne Jones, was arranged "after being informed that she had terminal cancer in 2010." It "pull[s] together" a "group of essays, lectures, and articles . . . about writing fantasy for children. . . . The selected pieces are thematically arranged, beginning with . . . a contemplative piece about watching children at play that sets the stage for her subsequent arguments regarding the importance of imagination and creativity." (Bulletin of the Center for Children's Books)

Includes bibliographical references and index

Joseph Conrad; edited and with an introduction by Harold Bloom. New ed; Bloom's Literary Criticism 2010 215p (Modern critical views) $45

Grades: 9 10 11 12   **823**

1. Authors 2. Novelists 3. Short story writers

ISBN 978-1-60413-808-5

LC 2009-36969

First published 1986

This volume offers a "selection of contemporary critical commentary on the author of such classic works as Lord Jim, Nostromo, and Heart of Darkness. . . . [It] also contains an introduction penned by literary scholar Harold Bloom, a bibliography, a chronology of the author's life, and an index for reference." Publisher's note

Includes bibliographical references

Joseph Conrad's Heart of darkness; edited and with an introduction by Harold Bloom. New ed; Chelsea House 2008 163p (Modern critical interpretations) $45

Grades: 9 10 11 12   **823**

1. Authors 2. Novelists 3. Short story writers

ISBN 978-0-7910-9825-7

LC 2007-51300

First published 1987

A collection of nine essays providing international appraisal and interpretation of Conrad's colonial novel.

Includes bibliographical references

Joyce, James

★ **Dubliners**. Knopf 1991 lxvii, 287p $19

Grades: 11 12 Adult   **823**

1. Short stories 2. Ireland -- Fiction

ISBN 0-679-40574-7

LC 91-53001

First published 1914 in the United Kingdom; first United States edition published 1916 by Huebsch

"This collection of 15 stories provides an introduction to the style and motifs found in Joyce's writing. The stories stand alone as individual scenes of Dublin society and are intertwined by the use of autobiography and symbolism." Shapiro. Fic for Youth. 3d edition

Kipling, Rudyard, 1865-1936

Collected stories; selected and introduced by Robert Gottlieb. Knopf 1994 xxxvii, 911p $25

Grades: 11 12 Adult   **823**

1. Short stories

ISBN 0-679-43592-1

LC 94-5854

"There is an enormous range of subject matter, genre, styles, and tones in Kipling's prose work. . . . {He} is undoubtedly one of the great short-story writers in English and the subtlety of his early narrative technique has led some to claim him as a proto-Modernist." Oxford Companion to 20th Cent Lit in Engl

Includes bibliographical references

Kirk, Connie Ann

J.K. Rowling: a biography. Greenwood Press 2003 141p il (Greenwood biographies) $29.95

Grades: 9 10 11 12 **823**
1. Authors 2. Novelists 3. Women authors 4. Fantasy writers 5. Authors, English 6. Children's authors 7. Young adult authors
ISBN 0-313-32205-8
LC 2002-75330
"Although there is information about the author herself, the majority of the content is devoted to analyzing her writing. . . . The scholarly writing style and evaluative content make this volume useful to high school students studying Rowling and her work." SLJ
Includes bibliographical references

Kordich, Catherine J.
Bloom's how to write about Jane Austen; [introduction by Harold Bloom] Bloom's Literary Criticism 2008 230p (Bloom's how to write about literature) $45 **823**
1. Authors 2. Novelists 3. Report writing
ISBN 978-0-7910-9743-4
LC 2008-4865
This book offers paper topics and advice on writing essays about the works of Jane Austen.
Includes bibliographical references

Martin, Darragh
The **Keeper**; Darragh Martin. Little Island 2013 280 p. $15.99
Grades: 7 8 9 10 **823**
1. Fantasy fiction 2. Magic -- Fiction 3. Orphans -- Fiction 4. Kidnapping -- Fiction 5. Books and reading -- Fiction 6. Brothers and sisters -- Fiction
ISBN 1908195843; 9781908195845
LC 2014407173
In this book, by Darragh Martin, "Oisín is not sure he wants to be Keeper of the Book of Magic, but when his little sister Sorcha is kidnapped by the Morrígan, a raven-goddess with a heart as dark as her feathers, he has to learn how to use the Book for good. Soon Oisín has a long journey ahead of him with only Stephen, his annoying older brother, and Antimony, a headstrong orphan with her own quest, to help him." (Publisher's note)
"Fans of Percy Jackson and Harry Potter will enjoy this fast-paced high fantasy adventure that adds a refreshing twist to Celtic myths and legends." SLJ

Mary Shelley's Frankenstein; edited and with an introduction by Harold Bloom. Updated ed; Chelsea House 2006 256p (Modern critical interpretations) $45
Grades: 9 10 11 12 **823**
1. Authors 2. Novelists
ISBN 0-7910-9303-4; 978-0-7910-9303-0
LC 2006-20214
First published 1987
A collection of critical essays bringing various interpretations to the novel about a monster created by a scientist.
Includes bibliographical references

Mary Wollstonecraft Shelley; edited and with an introduction by Harold Bloom. New ed; Bloom's

Literary Criticism 2009 198p (Modern critical views) $34.95
Grades: 9 10 11 12 **823**
1. Authors 2. Novelists
ISBN 978-0-7910-9619-2
LC 2008-30259
First published 1985 with title: Mary Shelley
This collection of critical essays looks at Frankenstein and more of Shelley's works.
Includes bibliographical references

McParland, Robert
Bloom's how to write about Joseph Conrad; [by] Robert P. McParland; introduction by Harold Bloom. Bloom's Literary Criticism 2010 247p (Bloom's how to write about literature) $45
Grades: 9 10 11 12 **823**
1. Authors 2. Novelists 3. Report writing 4. Short story writers
ISBN 978-1-60413-714-9
LC 2010-17430
This book offers paper topics and advice on writing an essay about the works of Joseph Conrad.
Includes bibliographical references

Mellor, Anne Kostelanetz
★ **Mary** Shelley, her life, her fiction, her monsters. Methuen 1988 xx, 275p il hardcover o.p. pa $26.95
Grades: 11 12 Adult **823**
1. Authors 2. Novelists
ISBN 0-415-90147-2 pa
LC 87-31249
The author "blends biography and informed criticism here to give a feminist reevaluation of Mary Shelley and her fiction, especially Frankenstein. . . . Mellor's book is clearly written and forcefully argued." Choice
Includes bibliographical references

Nardo, Don
★ **Understanding** Frankenstein. Lucent Bks. 2003 128p il (Understanding great literature) lib bdg $27.45
Grades: 7 8 9 10 **823**
1. Authors 2. Novelists
ISBN 1-59018-147-6
LC 2002-12560
Discusses Mary Shelley's sources of ideas for the compelling plot, well-developed characters, and universal themes of "Frankenstein" which have led to its enduring popularity.
"The text is easy to understand. A solid introduction for middle school students." SLJ
Includes bibliographical references

Olsen, Kirstin
★ **All** things Austen; an encyclopedia of Austen's world. Greenwood Press 2005 2v il maps set $157.95

Grades: 11 12 Adult **823**
1. Authors 2. Novelists 3. Reference books
ISBN 0-313-33032-8
LC 2004-28664
"This well-written and meticulously researched work provides a convenient means for general readers, students, and scholars to gain a better understanding of the social, cultural, and political climate of Austen's time." Booklist

The **Oxford** book of English short stories; edited by A.S. Byatt. Oxford Univ. Press 1998 xxx, 439p hardcover o.p. pa $19.95
Grades: 11 12 Adult **823**
1. Short stories
ISBN 0-19-214238-0; 0-19-956160-5 pa
LC 97-44998
In this anthology Byatt "includes necessary masters—Rudyard Kipling, Saki, D. H. Lawrence, and V. S. Pritchett, to name a few. But . . . she draws into the fold the work of several extremely talented writers of which few readers on this side of the Atlantic will have heard. Falling into this category are such writers as Malachi Whitaker, H. E. Bates, Sylvia Townsend Warner, and Charlotte Mew." Booklist

Pasachoff, Naomi E.
A **student's** guide to the Bronte sisters; [by] Naomi Pasachoff. Enslow Publishers 2010 160p il (Understanding literature) lib bdg $27.93
Grades: 7 8 9 10 **823**
1. Poets 2. Authors 3. Novelists
ISBN 978-0-7660-3267-5; 0-7660-3267-1
LC 2008-15165
"An introduction to the work of Charlotte, Emily, and Anne Bronte for high school students, which includes relevant biographical background on the authors, explanations of various literary devices and techniques, and literary criticism for the novice reader." Publisher's note
Includes glossary and bibliographical references

Poplawski, Paul
★ A **Jane** Austen encyclopedia. Greenwood Press 1998 411p il $95
Grades: 11 12 Adult **823**
1. Authors 2. Novelists
ISBN 0-313-30017-8
LC 97-44880
This volume "examines the life, works, characters, and minutiae of Austeniana. The alphabetically arranged entries include extensive plot summaries that end with lists of major and minor characters, brief character descriptions, and short articles on the author's family and friends." SLJ
Includes bibliographical references

Reef, Catherine
★ The **Bronte** sisters; the brief lives of Charlotte, Emily and Anne. by Catherine Reef. Clarion Books 2012 240 p. ill. (hardcover) $18.99
Grades: 7 8 9 10 **823**
1. Bronte family 2. Women authors -- Biography 3.

Women authors, English -- Biography
ISBN 0547579667; 9780547579665
LC 2011043559
"This collective biography of the Brontë family fills in . . . detail of their personal and public lives: what they wrote, their family stories as a minister's unmarried daughters, how they published under men's names, and how their groundbreaking novels were received at a time when women were expected to 'stay home and be quiet.'" (Booklist)
"A solid and captivating look at these remarkable pioneers of modern fiction." Kirkus
Includes bibliographical references (p. 212-217) and index.

Shields, Carol
Jane Austen. Viking 2001 185p (Penguin lives series) hardcover o.p. pa $13
Grades: 11 12 Adult **823**
1. Authors 2. Novelists 3. Women authors 4. Authors, English
ISBN 0-670-89488-5; 0-14-303516-9 pa
LC 00-43807
"In chronicling her subject's life and personality, Shields emphasizes Austen's keen ability to listen, observe, and capture clearly the social mores of her time and explore human nature in her writing. Shields contends that historical references are behind many of the scenes and characters in Austen's novels, and as a way of more clearly personalizing Austen's experiences or feelings, she interjects commentary regarding writing and publishing that is presumably based on personal experience." Libr J

Smiley, Jane
★ **Charles** Dickens. Viking 2002 212p (Penguin lives series) $19.95
Grades: 11 12 Adult **823**
1. Authors 2. Novelists 3. Authors, English
ISBN 0-670-03077-5
LC 2001-45607
This "biography examines Dickens' life through his work, starting not with his birth but rather the beginnings of his literary career. After writing short essays for a monthly magazine, Dickens began the serialization of his first novel, The Pickwick Papers. Dickens quickly became both a bestselling novelist and a famous man, who had to contend with both the envy of other authors and, much later on, the very public dissolution of his marriage. . . . Smiley's superb and thoughtful analysis should appeal to anyone familiar with the great author's work." Booklist

★ **Thomas** Hardy; edited and with an introduction by Harold Bloom. Chelsea House 2003 160p (Bloom's major novelists) lib bdg $22.95
Grades: 9 10 11 12 **823**
1. Poets 2. Authors 3. Novelists 4. Short story writers
ISBN 0-7910-6348-8
LC 2002-151007
This title includes a biographical essay, plot summaries, and critical interpretations of the novels and their characters.
Includes bibliographical references

Wagner, Hank

Prince of stories; the many worlds of Neil Gaiman. [by] Hank Wagner, Christopher Golden, and Stephen R. Bissette. St. Martin's Press 2008 546p il $29.95

Grades: 11 12 Adult **823**

1. Authors 2. Novelists 3. Comic book writers 4. Short story writers 5. Science fiction writers

ISBN 978-0-312-38765-5; 0-312-38765-2

LC 2008-24762

The authors "have conducted extensive research and interviews in their effort to create a compendium of data about one of fantasy's finest writers. . . . Encyclopedic in scope, this book offers reprints of articles by Gaiman, back stories, interviews with illustrators and others who work with Gaiman, photos, illustrations, and sneak peeks at future works. . . . Well written, well organized, and fun to peruse, this book can be enjoyed as a cover-to-cover read or a random browse. Readers will learn a lot about Gaiman, storytelling and the writing process." Voice Youth Advocates

Includes bibliographical references

Watkin, Amy S.

Bloom's how to write about Charles Dickens; [introduction by Harold Bloom] Bloom's Literary Criticism 2009 247p (Bloom's how to write about literature) $45

Grades: 9 10 11 12 **823**

1. Authors 2. Novelists 3. Report writing

ISBN 978-0-7910-9850-9

LC 2008-5713

This book offers paper topics and advice on writing an essay about the works of Charles Dickens.

Includes bibliographical references

William Golding's Lord of the flies; edited and with an introduction by Harold Bloom. New ed; Chelsea House 2008 176p (Modern critical interpretations) $45

Grades: 9 10 11 12 Adult **823**

1. Authors 2. Novelists 3. Essayists 4. Travel writers 5. Short story writers 6. Nobel laureates for literature

ISBN 978-0-7910-9826-4

LC 2008-2451

First published 1999

These "critical essays on Lord of the Flies are supplemented by a chronology of the author's life, a bibliography, and notes about the essay contributors." Publisher's note

Includes bibliographical references

828 English miscellaneous writings

Blake, William

★ The **portable** Blake; selected and arranged with an introduction by Alfred Kazin. Viking 1946 713p il hardcover o.p. pa $15.95

Grades: 11 12 Adult **828**

ISBN 0-14-015026-9 pa

A "generous selection of verse, prose, letters, and essays. Blake is shown as an artist and poet against all institutions but ever seeking unity (though his was the mystic's quest) while hunting for realism and naturalism." Cincinnati Public Libr

Includes bibliographical references

Brunsdale, Mitzi

★ **Student** companion to George Orwell; [by] Mitzi M. Brunsdale. Greenwood Press 2000 173p (Student companions to classic writers) $35

Grades: 9 10 11 12 **828**

1. Authors 2. Novelists 3. Essayists

ISBN 0-313-30637-0

LC 99-49690

The author explores the works of the noted novelist and social critic. Particular emphasis is placed on Animal farm and Nineteen eighty-four.

Includes bibliographical references

Conrad, Joseph

★ The **portable** Conrad; edited with an introduction by Michael Gorra. Penguin Books 2007 xlvi, 702p (Penguin classics) pa $20

Grades: 11 12 Adult **828**

ISBN 978-0-14-310511-4; 0-14-310511-6

LC 2007-60130

First published 1947

Contains "The Secret Agent, Heart of Darkness, and The Nigger of the 'Narcissus,' as well as shorter tales like 'Amy Forster' and 'The Secret Sharer,' a selection of letters, and his observations on the sinking of the Titanic." Publisher's note

Includes bibliographical references

DeGategno, Paul J.

Critical companion to Jonathan Swift; a literary reference to his life and works. [by] Paul J. DeGategno, R. Jay Stubblefield. Facts on File 2006 474p il (Facts on File library of world literature) $75

Grades: 11 12 Adult **828**

1. Poets 2. Clergy 3. Authors 4. Satirists 5. Pamphleteers 6. Writers on politics

ISBN 0-8160-5093-7; 978-0-8160-5093-2

LC 2005-25470

This "work is divided into five parts. These parts consist of a ten-page biography of satirist Jonathan Swift (1667-1745); a 'Works A-Z' section that includes synopses and commentaries that generally run to several hundred words on virtually all of Swift's poems, essays, and books; a 'Related Entries' section with similar brief articles on persons, topics, and places relevant to Swift studies; appendixes that include a chronology of Swift's life; a . . . bibliography of primary and secondary works; and an index." Libr J

Includes bibliographical references

Hopkins, Gerard Manley

Poems and prose of Gerard Manley Hopkins; selected with an introduction and notes by W.H. Gardner. Penguin 1984 xxxvi, 260p (Penguin classics) pa $16

Grades: 11 12 Adult **828**

ISBN 0-14-042015-0

"On entering the Society of Jesus at the age of twenty-four, . . . [the author] burnt all his poetry and 'resolved to write no more, as not belonging to my profession, unless by the wishes of my superiors'. The poems, letters and journal entries selected for this edition were written in the following twenty years of his life, and published posthumously in 1918." Publisher's note

Includes bibliographical references

Huxley, Aldous

★ **Brave** new world: and, Brave new world revisited; foreword by Christopher Hitchens. HarperCollins 2004 xxi, 340p $23.95

Grades: 11 12 Adult　　　　　　　　**828**

ISBN 0-06-053526-1

LC 2004-40611

First published 1960; a combined edition of the two titles published 1932 and 1958 respectively

Brave new world is a satirical novel "set in the year 632 AF (After Ford), it is a grim picture of the world which Huxley thinks our scientific and social developments have already begun to create." Reader's Ency. 4th edition

Kipling, Rudyard, 1865-1936

The **portable** Kipling; edited and with an introduction by Irving Howe. Viking 1982 xlii, 687p hardcover o.p. pa $18

Grades: 9 10 11 12　　　　　　　　**828**

1. Authors 2. Humorists 3. Novelists 4. Essayists 5. Satirists 6. Memoirists 7. Travel writers 8. Short story writers

ISBN 0-14-015097-8 pa

LC 81-52466

This volume collects short stories and verse. Included are about 50 poems. "The twenty-eight stories included give about equal weight to 'Stories of India' and 'Soldiers' Tales' and analyses of the effects of world war on disappointed idealists and activists." Christ Sci Monit

Means, A. L.

★ A **student's** guide to George Orwell. Enslow Pubs. 2005 176p il (Understanding literature) lib bdg $27.93

Grades: 7 8 9 10　　　　　　　　**828**

1. Authors 2. Novelists 3. Essayists

ISBN 0-7660-2433-4

An introduction to the life and work of the author of 1984, Animal Farm and other works

Includes glossary and bibliographical references

Milton, John

★ The **portable** Milton; edited and with an introduction by Douglas Bush. Viking 1949 693p hardcover o.p. pa $15.95

Grades: 11 12 Adult　　　　　　　　**828**

ISBN 0-14-015044-7 pa

A selection of the early poems and sonnets; "Areopagitica" complete; lengthy selections from the other chief prose works; and the three major poems, "Paradise lost," "Paradise regained," and "Samson Agonistes," complete

Includes glossary and bibliographical references

The **New** Oxford book of literary anecdotes. Oxford University Press 2006 385p il hardcover o.p. pa $16.95

Grades: 11 12 Adult　　　　　　　　**828**

1. Authors, English -- Anecdotes 2. Authors, American -- Anecdotes 3. English literature -- Anecdotes

ISBN 0-19-280468-5; 978-0-19-280468-6; 0-19-954341-0 pa; 978-0-19-954341-0 pa

LC 2005-33698

First published 1975 under the editorship of James Sutherland with title: The Oxford book of literary anecdotes

The editor "has compiled more than 700 anecdotes about English-language writers, from Geoffrey Chaucer to J.K. Rowling. The brief, chronologically-arranged (by subject's birth date) entries offer a glimpse into the personalities and times of these authors." Libr J

Includes bibliographical references

Quinn, Edward

Critical companion to George Orwell; a literary reference to his life and work. Facts On File 2009 450p il (Facts on File library of world literature) $75

Grades: 11 12 Adult　　　　　　　　**828**

1. Authors 2. Novelists 3. Essayists

ISBN 978-0-8160-7091-6

LC 2008-26727

This volume provides a "review of Orwell's life and covers all his novels, nonfiction, and other writings. . . . It is a superb resource for those desiring an introduction to George Orwell, the man and the writer." Booklist

Includes bibliographical references

Shippey, T. A.

★ **J.R.R.** Tolkien; author of the century. Houghton Mifflin 2001 xxxv, 347p $26; pa $13

Grades: 11 12 Adult　　　　　　　　**828**

1. Authors 2. Novelists 3. Linguists 4. Philologists 5. Fantasy writers 6. Children's authors 7. Fantasy fiction -- History and criticism

ISBN 0-618-12764-X; 0-618-25759-4 pa

LC 2001-16973

First published 2000 in the United Kingdom

"Shippey examines Tolkien's published and many unfinished works (such as The Silmarillion), as well as the shorter poems and stories. He convincingly argues that Tolkien deserves to be ranked as a major literary figure." Libr J

Includes bibliographical references

Thomas, Dylan

★ A **child's** Christmas in Wales; illustrated by Chris Raschka. Candlewick Press 2004 un il $17.99

Grades: 2 3 4 5 6 7 8 9　　　　　　　　**828**

1. Christmas -- Wales

ISBN 0-7636-2161-7

LC 2003-65274

The Welsh poet Dylan Thomas recalls the celebration of Christmas with his family and the feelings it evoked in him as a child.

"Applied to torn paper, the ink and watercolors spread through the fibers, freely forming soft outlines and shadows. The result is an intriguing contemporary take on a story that is by now part of the rather staid canon of Christmas classics." N Y Times Book Rev

Wilde, Oscar

★ The **portable** Oscar Wilde; selected and edited by Richard Aldington and Stanley Weintraub. rev ed; Viking 1981 741p hardcover o.p. pa $15.95
Grades: 11 12 Adult   **828**
　ISBN 0-14-015093-5 pa
　　　　　　　　　　　　　　　　　　LC 80-39827
　First published 1946
This volume contains The critic as artist, The picture of Dorian Gray, Salomé, The importance of being Earnest, De profundis, and selected poems, reviews, letters and phrases from other works.

Woolf, Virginia

★ The **Virginia** Woolf reader; edited by Mitchell A. Leaska. Harcourt Brace Jovanovich 1984 371p hardcover o.p. pa $16
Grades: 11 12 Adult   **828**
　ISBN 0-15-693590-2 pa
　　　　　　　　　　　　　　　　　　LC 84-4478
Excerpts from Woolf's "novels form less than 20 percent of a reader whose selections of short stories, essays, letters, and diary entries are excellent. This collection will be useful to those already familiar with Woolf's novels and seeking an introductory selection of her other writings." Libr J

Yeats, W. B.

★ The **Yeats** reader; a portable compendium of poetry, drama, and prose. edited by Richard J. Finneran. Rev. ed.; Scribner Poetry 2002 xxii, 566p il $35; pa $18
Grades: 11 12 Adult   **828**
　ISBN 0-7432-3315-8; 0-7432-2798-0
　　　　　　　　　　　　　　　　　LC 2002-70670
　First published 1997
This book "presents more than one hundred and fifty of his best-known poems . . . plus eight plays, a sampling of his prose tales, and excerpts from his published autobiographical and critical writings. In addition, an appendix offers six early texts of poems that Yeats later revised. Also included are selections from the memoirs left unpublished at his death and complete introductions written for a projected collection that never came to fruition." Publisher's note
Includes bibliographical references

829　Old English (Anglo-Saxon) literature

Beowulf; edited and with an introduction by Harold Bloom. Updated ed; Chelsea House 2007 280p (Modern critical interpretations) $45
Grades: 11 12 Adult   **829**
1. Epic poetry 2. Beowulf 3. English literature -- Old English period
ISBN 0-7910-9301-8; 978-0-7910-9301-6
　　　　　　　　　　　　　　　　　LC 2006-31072
　First published 1988

A collection of critical essays on the Old English epic poem.
Includes bibliographical references

830　German literature and literatures of related languages

★ The **Cambridge** history of German literature; edited by Helen Watanabe-O'Kelly. Cambridge Univ. Press 1997 613p $90; pa $32
Grades: 11 12 Adult   **830**
1. German literature -- History and criticism
ISBN 0-521-43417-3; 0-521-78573-1 pa
　　　　　　　　　　　　　　　　　LC 95-52412
A "briskly written survey of German literature that grounds literary practice in the social and historical context of each period and yet does not shortchange the aesthetic qualities of the representative works discussed." Choice

Garland, Henry B.

★ The **Oxford** companion to German literature; by Henry and Mary Garland. 3rd ed; Oxford Univ. Press 1997 951p maps $95
Grades: 11 12 Adult   **830**
1. Reference books 2. German literature -- Dictionaries
3. German literature -- Bio-bibliography
ISBN 0-19-815896-3
　　　　　　　　　　　　　　　　　LC 96-53309
　First published 1976
Entries include biographies, synopses of important works, literary terms and movements, historical events and figures, and material relevant to the social and intellectual background of German literature from the earliest records to the present.

831　German poetry

Rilke, Rainer Maria

★ **Selected** poems of Rainer Maria Rilke; a translation from the German and commentary by Robert Bly. Harper & Row 1981 224p hardcover o.p. pa $15
Grades: 9 10 11 12   **831**
1. Poetry -- By individual authors
ISBN 0-06-090727-4 pa
　　　　　　　　　　　　　　　　　LC 78-2114
A bilingual edition of the German poet's verse selected from A Book for the Hours of Prayer, The Book of Pictures, New Poems, The Uncollected and Occasional Poems, and Sonnets to Orpheus. The translator also includes five introductory essays
"Bly's comments make us see Rilke's work in relation to events of the poet's life and to creative inner tensions within certain periods. They also afford an awareness of Rilke's specific inwardness, a sensibility and disposition of soul very different from that of any American poet." Libr J

832   German drama

Brecht, Bertolt

Galileo; English version by Charles Laughton; edited and with an introduction by Eric Bentley. Grove Weidenfeld 1991 155p pa $6.95

Grades: 9 10 11 12   **832**

1. Astronomers 2. Writers on science

ISBN 0-8021-3059-3

LC 91-22966

Written 1938-39, first performed 1943

"The play concerns Galileo Galilei's conflict with the church over the application of the Copernican system, which the church viewed as anathema. Brecht deliberately portrays Galileo as a self-serving and decidedly unheroic character, willing to compromise his principles in the face of pressure." Reader's Ency. 4th edition

833   German fiction

Erich Maria Remarque's All quiet on the western front; edited & with an introduction by Harold Bloom. Chelsea House 2008 128p (Bloom's guides) $30

Grades: 9 10 11 12   **833**

1. Authors 2. Novelists

ISBN 978-0-7910-9830-1

LC 2008-1209

This study guide on Remarque's World War I novel includes a brief biographical sketch, a list of characters, a summary and analysis, and selections from critical essays by different scholars about the work.

Includes bibliographical references

Franz Kafka; edited and with an introduction by Harold Bloom. New ed; Bloom's Literary Criticism 2010 235p (Modern critical views) $45

Grades: 9 10 11 12   **833**

1. Poets 2. Authors 3. Novelists 4. Short story writers

ISBN 978-1-60413-806-1

LC 2009-32385

First published 1986

A collection of critical essays on Kafka and his work arranged in chronological order of publication.

Includes bibliographical references

Franz Kafka's The metamorphosis; edited and with an introduction by Harold Bloom. New ed.; Bloom's Literary Criticism 2008 190p (Modern critical interpretations) $45

Grades: 11 12 Adult   **833**

1. Poets 2. Authors 3. Novelists 4. Short story writers

ISBN 978-0-7910-9827-1; 0-7910-9827-3

LC 2007-46277

First published 1988

James Rolleston, Allen Thiher, and Margit M. Sinka are among the contributors to this collection of critical assessments of Kafka's classic.

I Don't Live Here Anymore; Gabi Kreslehner; translated by Shelley Tanaka. Groundwood Books 2015 128 p. $16.95

Grades: 7 8 9 10 11 12   **833**

1. Moving 2. Bildungsromans 3. Children of divorced parents -- Fiction

ISBN 1554988039; 9781554988037

In this novel by Gabi Kreslehner, translated by Shelley Tanaka, "Charlotte's life is changed forever when her parents' marriage breaks up, and Charlotte has to leave her beloved house and her old life behind. Then two very different boys cross her path, and a new emotion creeps into her sadness and anger. As she watches her parents cope, . . . with changes in their own personal lives, and as she deals with a new baby brother, a potential stepfather and unexpected house moves, she realizes that love is a messy business." (Publisher's note)

"It's an immersive, believable portrait of how adolescents cope, or not, with divorce, drawn from an inside view. Powerful and deeply resonant" Kirkus

838   German miscellaneous writings

★ **Hermann** Hesse; edited and with an introduction by Harold Bloom. Chelsea House 2002 246p (Modern critical views) $37.95

Grades: 9 10 11 12   **838**

1. Poets 2. Authors 3. Novelists 4. Short story writers 5. Nobel laureates for literature

ISBN 0-7910-7398-X

LC 2002-152671

"Essays here include discussions of Hesse's personal life, writing style, themes, characters, philosophy, and influences. His novels Siddhartha, Narcissus and Goldmund, The Glass Bead Game, Steppenwolf, and Demian are analyzed as is some of his poetry. Similarities of Hesse's writings with those of André Gide, Marcel Proust, and James Joyce are discussed in several essays. Excerpts of his poems are included in both German and English." SLJ

Includes bibliographical references

839.3   Netherlandish literatures

Frank, Anne

★ **Anne** Frank's Tales from the secret annex; with translations by Ralph Manheim and Michel Mok. Doubleday 1984 136p hardcover o.p. pa $4.95

Grades: 11 12 Adult   **839.3**

ISBN 0-553-58638-6 pa

LC 82-45871

Original Dutch edition copyrighted 1949. First English translation published 1960 in the United Kingdom with title: Tales from the house behind

This volume presents all of Anne Frank's existing stories, sketches and drafts as well as her personal reminiscences and essays

"The themes and plots of her brief fables are not extraordinary. But their very ordinariness reminds readers that the writer who kept one of the world's most widely read diaries was an ordinary child." Horn Book

839.8 Danish and Norwegian literatures

Henrik Ibsen; edited and with an introduction by Harold Bloom. New ed; Bloom's Literary Criticism 2011 128p (Modern critical views) lib bdg $45

Grades: 11 12 Adult **839.8**
1. Poets 2. Authors 3. Dramatists
ISBN 978-1-60413-577-0

LC 2010-44810

First published 1999
A selection of critical essays explore the works of the author of A Doll's House.
Includes bibliographical references

Ibsen, Henrik
★ **Ibsen**: four major plays; translated by Rick Davis and Brian Johnston. Smith & Kraus 1995 286p (Great translations for actors) pa $19.95

Grades: 11 12 Adult **839.8**
ISBN 1-880399-67-9

LC 95-13632

"All four of these versions have been 'production-tested,' which shows in their graceful and believable dialogue and their sheer theatricality. Davis and Johnston have unlocked the power in Ibsen's works and made it clear why Ibsen was once the playwright for firebrands, Fabians, and other progressives throughout the world." Booklist

840 French literature and literatures of related Romance languages

★ The **New** Oxford companion to literature in French; edited by Peter France. Oxford Univ. Press 1995 li, 865p maps $80

Grades: 11 12 Adult **840**
1. Reference books 2. French literature -- Dictionaries 3. French literature -- Bio-bibliography
ISBN 0-19-866125-8

First published 1959 with title: The Oxford companion to French literature

"This work views literature from the perspective of its greater cultural context. Accordingly, topics discussed go beyond the poets, novelists, and dramatists of the traditional French canon, and include philosophy, science, art, history, linguistics, and cinema. Even strip cartoons and pamphlets are treated. . . . The more than 3,000 entries are written by approximately 130 international experts. In addition to brief entries, there are long articles on general topics, such as Québec, feminism, Occitan literature, and the history of the French language." Am Ref Books Annu, 1996

841 French poetry

Baudelaire, Charles
Poems. Knopf 1993 256p (Everyman's library pocket poets) $12.50

Grades: 11 12 Adult **841**
1. Poetry -- By individual authors
ISBN 0-679-42910-7

LC 93-14363

A representative selection of poetry by the French symbolist.

Chanson de Roland
★ The **song** of Roland; translated, with an introduction, by W.S. Merwin. Modern Library 2001 137p pa $11.95

Grades: 11 12 Adult **841**
1. Roland (Legendary character)
ISBN 0-375-75711-2

LC 00-48989

"This heroic poem celebrates the mighty feats of Roland, the great French hero in the time of Charlemagne. The medieval legend has replaced and transformed the actual facts of history to a great extent but the epic poem has continued in popularity." Bookman's Manual
Includes bibliographical references

Rimbaud, Arthur
Poems; [selected by Peter Washington] Knopf 1994 288p (Everyman's library pocket poets) $12.50

Grades: 11 12 Adult **841**
1. Poetry -- By individual authors
ISBN 978-0-679-43321-7; 0-679-43321-X

LC 94-2496

A collection of work by the French Symbolist known for his daring images and pioneering prose poems

842 French drama

Anouilh, Jean
Antigone; a play. translated by Jeremy Sams. French 2002 48p pa $6.50

Grades: 11 12 Adult **842**
ISBN 0-573-62819-X
Characters: 7 men, 3 women. 1 act.

Beckett, Samuel
Waiting for Godot; tragicomedy in 2 acts. Grove Press 1954 60p il hardcover o.p. pa $13

Grades: 11 12 Adult **842**
ISBN 0-8021-3034-8 pa
Originally written in French. The play was first produced in Paris during the winter of 1952
"There are strong biblical references throughout, but Beckett's powerful and symbolic portrayal of the human condition as one of ignorance, delusion, paralysis, and intermittent flashes of human sympathy, hope, and wit has been subjected to many varying interpretations. The theatrical vitality and versatility of the play have been demonstrated by

performances throughout the world." Oxford Companion to Engl Lit. 5th edition

Ionesco, Eugene

Four plays; translated by Donald M. Allen. Grove Press 1958 160p pa $13

Grades: 9 10 11 12   **842**

ISBN 0-8021-3079-8

Original French edition, 1954

The bald soprano is a comedy satirizing English middle class life, while Jack, concerns a sulky young man who disappoints his family by refusing to marry the girl of their choice. An avant-garde drama, The chairs focuses on an old couple who receives many imaginary guests. The murder of a young student by his elderly teacher ends a bizarre lesson in The lesson

Rhinoceros, and other plays; translated by Derek Prouse. Grove Press 1960 141p pa $10

Grades: 11 12 Adult   **842**

ISBN 0-8021-3098-4

Three satirical comedies by a leading dramatist of the "theater of the absurd." In Rhinoceros, one man resists the pressure to conform as everyone about him accepts their transformation into rhinoceroses and he finds himself socially isolated. In The future is in eggs, a couple must produce eggs destined to become intellectuals. The leader is a satire on the mass adulation of political figures in which the leader turns out to be a headless figure

Moliere

The **misanthrope** and other plays. Signet Classics 2005 524p pa $7.95

Grades: 11 12 Adult   **842**

ISBN 0-451-52987-1; 978-0-451-52987-9

LC 2006-276841

★ **Moliere.** Chelsea House 2003 122p (Bloom's major dramatists) lib bdg $22.95

Grades: 9 10 11 12   **842**

1. Actors 2. Authors 3. Dramatists

ISBN 0-7910-7034-4

LC 2002-155108

Includes a biographical essay, plot summaries, and critical interpretations of the plays and their characters.

Includes bibliographical references

Samuel Beckett's Waiting for Godot; edited and with an introduction by Harold Bloom. New ed; Chelsea House 2008 172p (Modern critical interpretations) $45

Grades: 11 12 Adult   **842**

1. Poets 2. Authors 3. Novelists 4. Dramatists 5. Short story writers 6. Nobel laureates for literature

ISBN 978-0-7910-9793-9

LC 2007-49864

First published 1987

Critical interpretations of Beckett's classic tragicomedy illustrating the apparent meaninglessness of life.

Includes bibliographical references

Sartre, Jean Paul

★ **No** exit, and three other plays. Vintage Bks. 1989 275p pa $12

Grades: 11 12 Adult   **842**

ISBN 0-679-72516-4

LC 89-40097

No exit is a modern morality play; The flies is a reworking of the Orestes-Electra story. The third play concerns a young Communist intellectual's attempt to maintain his integrity as party line changes and personal relationships alter perceptions of his murder of a party boss who had fallen out of favor, but whose memory is later rehabilitated. The last play concerns a prostitute's involvement in false charges of rape against a murdered black man and his companion in a town in the American South

843 French fiction

Albert Camus's The stranger; edited and with an introduction by Harold Bloom. New ed; Bloom's Literary Criticism 2011 166p (Modern critical interpretations) $45

Grades: 9 10 11 12   **843**

1. Authors 2. Novelists 3. Dramatists 4. Essayists 5. Nobel laureates for literature

ISBN 978-1-60413-580-0

LC 2011018174

First published 2001

A collection of essays discussing Camus' classic novel.

Includes bibliographical references

De Fombelle, Timothée, 1973-

A **prince** without a kingdom; a prince without a kingdom. Timothee de Fombelle. Candlewick Press 2015 464 p. (sequel to Vango) $17.99

Grades: 7 8 9 10 11 12   **843**

1. Adventure fiction 2. Europe -- Fiction 3. Orphans -- Fiction

ISBN 9780763679507; 076367950X

LC 2014957056

In this novel, by Timothee de Fombelle and translated by Sarah Ardizzone, "fleeing dark forces and unfounded accusations across Europe in the years between World Wars, . . . Vango has been in danger for as long as he can remember. He has spent his life . . . evading capture across Russia, Paris, New York, and Italy. Narrow escapes, near misses, and a dash of romantic intrigue will rivet [readers] to their seats as Vango continues to unravel the mysteries of his past." (Publisher's note)

"The story runs from 1936 through 1942, which means that it is touched by WWII and the German occupation of France, where meaningful portions of the story are set. But whatever the setting, the story is rich in mysteries, enlivened by surprises, and suffused with suspense. It is so beautifully wrought, it reminds us why we love to read, and there can be no higher praise." Booklist

844 French essays

Camus, Albert

★ The **myth** of Sisyphus, and other essays; translated from the French by Justin O'Brien. Knopf 1955 212p hardcover o.p. pa $12.95

Grades: 11 12 Adult **844**

ISBN 0-679-73373-6 pa

Personal reflections on the meaning of life and the philosophical questions surrounding suicide

848 French miscellaneous writings

Voltaire

★ The **portable** Voltaire; edited, and with an introduction by Ben Ray Redmen. Viking 1949 569p hardcover o.p. pa $17

Grades: 11 12 Adult **848**

ISBN 0-14-015041-2 pa

The selections from Voltaire's works include: Candide, part one; Three stories: Zadig, Micromegas, and Story of a good Brahmin; Letters, and selections from the Philosophical Dictionary and other works. The editor's introduction gives a biographical sketch of Voltaire.

850 Literatures of Italian, Dalmatian, Romanian, Rhaetian, Sardinian, Corsican languages

The **Cambridge** history of Italian literature; edited by Peter Brand and Lino Pertile. Cambridge Univ. Press 1996 xxi, 701p map hardcover o.p. pa $36.99

Grades: 11 12 Adult **850**

1. Italian literature -- History and criticism

ISBN 0-521-43492-0; 0-521-66622-8 pa

LC 95-50622

"Contemporary readers will no doubt be delighted to learn more about such topics as the evolution of opera, compositions by Italian women writers, and the development of feminism." Choice

Ruud, Jay

Critical companion to Dante; a literary reference to his life and work. Facts on File 2008 566p il (Facts on File library of world literature) $75

Grades: 11 12 Adult **850**

1. Poets 2. Authors

ISBN 978-0-8160-6521-9

LC 2007-33473

This title covers the works of Dante, including The Divine Comedy, La Vita Nuova, and his philosophical works.

"Ruud has written a useful introductory resource that students and lay readers alike can enjoy." Booklist

Includes bibliographical references

851 Italian poetry

Dante Alighieri

★ The **portable** Dante; translated, edited, and with an introduction and notes by Mark Musa. Penguin Bks. 1995 xliii, 654p pa $17

Grades: 11 12 Adult **851**

1. Poetry -- By individual authors

ISBN 0-14-243754-9

LC 94-15988

First published 1947

Contains complete verse translations of The Divine comedy and La vita nuova

This book "contains complete verse translations of Dante's two masterworks, The Divine Comedy and La Vita Nuova, as well as a bibliography, notes, and an introduction by . . . Mark Musa." Publisher's note

Includes bibliographical references

Dante Alighieri; edited and with an introduction by Harold Bloom. New ed.; Bloom's Literary Criticism 2010 234p (Modern critical views) $45

Grades: 9 10 11 12 **851**

1. Poets 2. Authors

ISBN 978-1-60413-880-1

LC 2010-21315

First published 2004

A selection of critical essays explore the works of the author of The Divine Comedy.

Includes bibliographical references

860 Literatures of Spanish, Portuguese, Galician languages

★ **Concise** encyclopedia of Latin American literature; editor, Verity Smith. Fitzroy Dearborn Pubs. 2000 xxi, 678p $75

Grades: 11 12 Adult **860**

1. Reference books 2. Latin American literature -- Encyclopedias 3. Latin American literature -- Bibliography

ISBN 1-57958-252-4

Based on the Encyclopedia of Latin American literature (1997)

Contains entries on 50 leading writers and 50 important works of Latin American and Caribbean literature. Also includes survey articles on the literature of individual countries and topical essays. Bibliographies of primary and secondary sources are listed

Includes bibliographical references

Cortes, Eladio

Dictionary of Mexican literature; edited by Eladio Cortés. Greenwood Press 1992 xliii, 768p $115

Grades: 11 12 Adult **860**

1. Reference books 2. Mexican literature -- Dictionaries

ISBN 0-313-26271-3

LC 91-10529

This volume contains "500 entries covering the most important writers, literary schools, and cultural movements in

Mexican literary history. The 41 contributors include American, Mexican, and Hispanic scholars with assistance from some of the authors themselves." Libr J

Includes bibliographical references

Miguel De Cervantes' Don Quixote; edited and with an introduction by Harold Bloom. New ed; Bloom's Literary Criticism 2010 185p (Modern critical interpretations) $45

Grades: 9 10 11 12　　　　　　　　　　**860**

1. Poets 2. Authors 3. Novelists 4. Dramatists
ISBN 978-1-60413-821-4

LC 2009-53338

First published 2001

A collection of eight critical essays on Cervantes' satirical novel arranged in chronological order of publication.

Includes bibliographical references

Moss, Joyce

Latin American literature and its times; [by] Joyce Moss, Lorraine Valestuk. Gale Group 1999 xxxix, 562p il (World literature and its times) $125

Grades: 11 12 Adult　　　　　　　　　　**860**

1. Latin American literature -- History and criticism
ISBN 0-7876-3726-2

LC 99-29292

"Highlights Latin American literature and Latino works 'produced in the United States.' Arrangement is alphabetical by title. Lengthy, informative essays discuss individual poems and fiction and nonfiction titles with a focus on the political, economical, social contexts in which the pieces were written.... Each essay concludes with a list 'For More Information.' Black-and-white photographs, movie stills, and reproductions are sprinkled throughout." SLJ

Includes bibliographical references

★ The **Tree** is older than you are; a bilingual gathering of poems & stories from Mexico with paintings by Mexican artists. selected by Naomi Shihab Nye. Simon & Schuster Bks. for Young Readers 1995 111p il hardcover o.p. pa $13.95

Grades: 7 8 9 10　　　　　　　　　　**860**

1. Mexican literature -- Collections 2. Bilingual books -- English-Spanish
ISBN 0-689-82097-8; 0-689-82087-9 pa

LC 95-1565

"This bilingual anthology of poems, stories, and paintings by Mexican writers and artists brims over with a sense of wonder and playful exuberance, its themes as varied and inventive as a child's imagination." Voice Youth Advocates

861　Spanish poetry

Borges, Jorge Luis

Selected poems; edited by Alexander Coleman. Viking 1999 477p hardcover o.p. pa $20

Grades: 11 12 Adult　　　　　　　　　　**861**

1. Poetry -- By individual authors
ISBN 0-14-058721-7 pa

LC 99-10318

"Poetry is the heart of Borges' metaphysical, mythical, and cosmopolitan oeuvre. . . . Editor Coleman commissioned a wealth of new translations for this unprecedented and invaluable collection, and the roster of translators includes such luminaries as Robert S. Fitzgerald, W.S. Merwin, Mark Strand, and John Updike." Booklist

Cid

★ The **poem** of the Cid; translated by Rita Hamilton and Janet Perry; with an introduction and notes by Ian Michael. Penguin 1984 242p map pa $14

Grades: 11 12 Adult　　　　　　　　　　**861**

1. Poetry -- By individual authors
ISBN 0-14-044446-7

"The poem is based on the exploits of Rodrigo or Ruy Diaz de Bivar (c.1043-1099), who was known as 'el Cid.' . . . Similar in form to the 'Chanson de Roland,' the poem is notable for its simplicity and directness and for its exact, picturesque detail. Despite the inclusion of much legendary material, the figure of the Cid who is depicted as the model Castilian warrior, is not idealized to an extravagant degree." Reader's Ency. 4th edition

Neruda, Pablo

The **poetry** of Pablo Neruda; edited and with an introduction by Ilan Stavans. Farrar, Straus and Giroux 2003 996p hardcover o.p. pa $20

Grades: 11 12 Adult　　　　　　　　　　**861**

1. Poetry -- By individual authors
ISBN 0-374-29995-1; 0-374-52960-4 pa

LC 2002-32548

"Stavans has assembled the most complete anthology of Neruda yet available in English, drawing evenhandedly from the various stages of the poet's long and complex career. Neruda was, it seems, at least half a dozen poets, many of them in competition with the others. Needless to say, there are wonders in these pages that will delight readers unfamiliar with the tumultuously varied planet known as Neruda." Nation

Includes bibliographical references

★ **Twenty** love poems and a song of despair; translated by W. S. Merwin; introduction by Cristina García; illustrations by Pablo Picasso. Penguin Books 2004 94p il pa $13

Grades: 9 10 11 12　　　　　　　　　　**861**

1. Poetry -- By individual authors
ISBN 0-14-243770-0

LC 2003-67611

Original Spanish edition 1924; this translation first published 1971 by Grossman Pubs.

This bilingual collection presents a series of poems that contains "sea and nature imagery that associates woman with the productive forces of Mother Earth." Choice

Includes bibliographical references

Paz, Octavio

Selected poems; edited by Eliot Weinberger; translated from the Spanish by G. Aroul [et al.] New Directions 1984 147p hardcover o.p. pa $11.95

Grades: 11 12 Adult **861**
1. Poetry -- By individual authors
ISBN 0-8112-0899-0 pa

LC 84-9856

"The 67 well-chosen selections show Paz in his several phases and guises—in lyrics and prose poems, in long, free-form pieces and short, impressionistic works—a range of styles representing the best modes of East and West as practiced South over the last half-century. Many of the translations are by his peers (Elizabeth Bishop, Mark Strand, W. C. Williams)." Booklist

863 Spanish fiction

Gabriel Garcia Marquez; edited and with an introduction by Harold Bloom. Chelsea House 2006 xx, 129p (Bloom's biocritiques) $35
Grades: 9 10 11 12 **863**
1. Authors 2. Novelists 3. Journalists 4. Short story writers 5. Nobel laureates for literature
ISBN 0-7910-8115-X

LC 2005-8632

This book features a brief biography of the South American author along with several critical essays discussing his work.
Includes bibliographical references

Miguel de Cervantes; edited and with an introduction by Harold Bloom. Chelsea House Publishers 2005 157p (Bloom's biocritiques) $35
Grades: 9 10 11 12 **863**
1. Poets 2. Authors 3. Novelists 4. Dramatists
ISBN 0-7910-8116-8

LC 2004-14609

This book features a brief biography of the author of Don Quixote along with several critical essays discussing his work.
Includes bibliographical references

870 Latin literature and literatures of related Italic languages

Atchity, Kenneth John
★ The **classical** Roman reader; new encounters with Ancient Rome. edited by Kenneth J. Atchity; associate editor, Rosemary McKenna. Oxford University Press 1998 xxxvi, 438p il pa $24.95
Grades: 11 12 Adult **870**
1. Latin literature -- Collections
ISBN 0-19-512740-4

LC 98-29785

First published 1996 by Holt & Co.
"Excerpts by well-known authors are here—Virgil, Horace, Ovid, Juvenal—but so too are nonartistic authors who exemplify Rome's characteristic emphasis on the practical over the abstract. . . . For those uninitiated to Rome's written legacy but eager to meet it, this varied set of readings makes a memorable match." Booklist
Includes bibliographical references

Hamilton, Edith
★ The **Roman** way. Norton 1932 281p hardcover o.p. pa $12.95
Grades: 11 12 Adult **870**
1. Poets 2. Statesmen 3. Historians 4. Philosophers 5. Orators 6. Rome -- Civilization 7. Latin literature -- History and criticism
ISBN 0-393-31078-7 pa
Companion volume to The Greek way
An interpretation of Roman life from the descriptions in the works of great writers from Plautus and Terence to Virgil and Juvenal.

★ The **Portable** Roman reader; edited, and with an introduction by Basil Davenport. Viking 1951 656p hardcover o.p. pa $18
Grades: 11 12 Adult **870**
1. Latin literature -- Collections
ISBN 0-14-015056-0 pa
This anthology includes selections from Plautus, Terence, Caesar, Virgil, Seneca, Juvenal as well as complete plays by Plautus and Terence and the anonymous poem Vigil of Venus

871 Latin poetry

★ The **Roman** poets; selected and edited by Peter Washington. Knopf 1997 253p il (Everyman's library pocket poets) $12.50
Grades: 11 12 Adult **871**
1. Latin poetry -- Collections
ISBN 0-375-40071-0

LC 98-124022

A representative selection of classical Latin verse.

873 Latin epic poetry and fiction

Ovid
Metamorphoses; [by] Ovid; translated and with notes by Charles Martin; introduction by Bernard Knox. W.W. Norton & Co 2004 xxvi, 597p $57; pa $17.95
Grades: 11 12 Adult **873**
ISBN 0-393-05810-7; 0-393-32642-X pa

LC 2003-14491

"A series of tales in Latin verse. . . . Dealing with mythological, legendary, and historical figures, they are written in hexameters, in fifteen books, beginning with the creation of the world and ending with the deification of Caesar and the reign of Augustus." Reader's Ency. 4th edition
Includes bibliographical references

★ **Tales** from Ovid; [translated by] Ted Hughes. Farrar, Straus & Giroux 1997 257p hardcover o.p. pa $14

Grades: 11 12 Adult   **873**
1. Poetry -- By individual authors
ISBN 0-374-52587-0 pa

LC 97-36061

Hughes retells 24 Greco-Roman myths from Ovid's
Latin epic Metamorphoses.

This is "an inspired act of translation that stands as vigorous poetry in its own right." N Y Times Book Rev
Includes bibliographical references

878   Latin miscellaneous writings

Caesar, Julius
★ The **Gallic** War; with an English translation
by H. J. Edwards. Harvard Univ. Press 1958 xxii,
616p il maps $21.50
Grades: 11 12 Adult   **878**
1. Rome -- History
ISBN 0-674-99080-3

Caesar's account of his campaign (58-50 B.C.) to bring
the province of Gaul (France) under his control.

880   Classical Greek literature and literatures of related Hellenic languages

Ancient Greek literature; K.J. Dover, editor [et al.]
2nd ed; Oxford Univ. Press 1997 187p maps
pa $21.95
Grades: 9 10 11 12   **880**
1. Poets 2. Authors 3. Historians 4. Ancient
philosophy 5. Greek literature -- History and criticism
ISBN 0-19-289294-0

LC 98-120951

First published 1980

A historical survey of Greek poetry, tragedy, comedy,
history, science, philosophy, and oratory from 700 BC to
550 AD. Passages from the works of principal authors are
provided in translation.

Includes bibliographical references

Hamilton, Edith
★ The **Greek** way. Norton 1943 347p hardcover o.p. pa $12.95
Grades: 11 12 Adult   **880**
1. Poets 2. Comedy 3. Authors 4. Tragedy 5.
Dramatists 6. Historians 7. Art -- Philosophy 8.
Greece -- Religion 9. Greece -- Civilization 10. Greek
literature -- History and criticism
ISBN 0-393-31077-9 pa
Companion volume to The Roman way
First published 1930. Variant title: The great age of
Greek literature

An account of writers and literary forms of the Periclean
Age including discussions of Pindar, Aristophanes, Aeschylus, tragedy, Greek religion and philosophy

★ The **Norton** book of classical literature; edited by
Bernard Knox. Norton 1993 866p $29.95
Grades: 11 12 Adult   **880**
1. Greek literature -- Collections
ISBN 0-393-03426-7

LC 92-10378

"A comprehensive volume of more than 300 pieces
of classical literature, primarily Greek but also some
Roman." Booklist

★ The **Oxford** companion to classical literature; edited by M.C. Howatson. 3rd ed.; Oxford University Press 2011 un map $65
Grades: 11 12 Adult   **880**
1. Reference books 2. Classical literature -- Dictionaries
ISBN 978-0-19-954854-5
First published 1937 under the editorship of Sir
Paul Harvey

This work "covers classical literature from the appearance of the Greeks, around 2200 B.C., to the close of the
Athenian philosophy schools in A.D. 529. It includes articles
on authors, major works, historical notables, mythological
figures, and topics of literary significance. Short summaries
of major works, chronologies, charts, and maps are special
features." Nichols. Guide to Ref Books for Sch Media Cent.
4th edition

★ The **Portable** Greek reader; edited, and with an
introduction by W. H. Auden. Viking 1948 726p
hardcover o.p. pa $18
Grades: 11 12 Adult   **880**
1. Greek literature -- Collections
ISBN 0-14-015039-0 pa

"Selections from representative Greek writers, from
Homer to Galen, aimed at providing the reader with an introduction to all facets of Greek culture, rather than to its
literature alone. Mr. Auden's preface deals chiefly with the
various Greek concepts of the hero, in comparison with our
own, and points up the immense differences between the two
civilizations." New Yorker

Thorburn, John E.
The **Facts** on File companion to classical drama.
Facts on File 2005 680p map (Facts on File library
of world literature) $71.50
Grades: 11 12 Adult   **880**
1. Reference books 2. Classical drama -- Encyclopedias
ISBN 0-8160-5202-6

LC 2004-16803

"It is difficult to think of any other resource quite this
thorough that combines all of Greek and Roman drama into
a convenient single-volume publication." Libr J
Includes bibliographical references

881   Classical Greek poetry

★ The **Oxford** book of classical verse in translation; edited by Adrian Poole and Jeremy Maule. Oxford University Press 1995 xlix, 606p $45
Grades: 11 12 Adult **881**
1. Classical poetry -- Collections
ISBN 0-19-214209-7
A "collection of classical verse from Homer to Boethius. Translations, modern and older, are brought together in a rich blending of Greek and Latin writings. Some of the greatest poets in the English language—Dryden, Pope, Tennyson, Poe, Byron, Yeats, Browning, Houseman, Wilde, Shelley, and Pound are among the translators. They emphasize the debt English poetry owes to the classics." SLJ

882   Classical Greek dramatic poetry and drama

Aristophanes
Lysistrata; translated, with notes and topical commentaries by Sarah Ruden. Hackett Pub. Co 2003 126p $24.95; pa $5.95
Grades: 11 12 Adult **882**
ISBN 0-87220-604-1; 0-87220-603-3 pa
LC 2002-38750
This is a translation of Aristophanes' comedy with notes and commentary. "The 'topical commentaries' are essays on 'Athenian Democracy', 'Ancient Greek Warfare', 'Athenian Women', and 'Greek Comedy'. . . . The volume is topped off with a selected bibliography and an index to the commentaries." Classical Rev

★ **Seven** famous Greek plays; edited, with introductions by Whitney J. Oates and Eugene O'Neill, Jr. Modern Lib. 1950 xxv, 446p hardcover o.p. pa $10
Grades: 9 10 11 12 **882**
1. Greek drama -- Collections
ISBN 0-394-70125-9 pa
Includes bibliographical references

Sophocles' Oedipus rex; edited & with an introduction by Harold Bloom. Bloom's Literary Criticism 2007 118p (Bloom's guides) $30
Grades: 9 10 11 12 **882**
1. Authors 2. Dramatists 3. Oedipus (Tale)
ISBN 978-0-7910-9360-3; 0-7910-9360-3
LC 2007-10028
This study guide on the classic play includes a brief biographical sketch of Sophocles, a list of characters, a summary and analysis, and selections from critical essays by different scholars about the work.
Includes bibliographical references

883   Classical Greek epic poetry and fiction

Hecht, Jamey
Bloom's how to write about Homer; introduction by Harold Bloom. Bloom's Literary Criticism 2010 236p (Bloom's how to write about literature) $45
Grades: 9 10 11 12 **883**
1. Poets 2. Authors 3. Report writing
ISBN 978-1-60413-716-3
LC 2010-15753
This book offers paper topics and advice on writing an essay about the works of Homer.
Includes bibliographical references

Homer
★ The **Iliad**; translated by Robert Fagles; introduction and notes by Bernard Knox. Viking 1990 683p $40; pa $15.95
Grades: 8 9 10 11 12 Adult **883**
1. Poetry -- By individual authors
ISBN 978-0-670-83510-2; 978-0-14-027536-0 pa
LC 89-70695
Homer's epic of the Trojan War.
"Fagles gives us a stark and terrible poem, an Iliad about, as its first word announces, rage. He conveys, far better than either Lattimore or Fitzgerald, the psychological experience of combat and war." Classical World

★ The **Odyssey**; translated by Robert Fagles; introduction and notes by Bernard Knox. Viking 1996 541p $35; pa $16
Grades: 8 9 10 11 12 Adult **883**
1. Poetry -- By individual authors
ISBN 978-0-670-82162-4; 978-0-14-026886-7 pa
LC 96-17280
This is a verse translation of Homer's epic poem
"Fagles' Odyssey is the one to put into the hands of younger, first-time readers, not least because of its paucity of notes, which, though sometimes frustrating, is a sign that translation has been used to do the work of explanation. Altogether, an outstanding piece of work." Booklist
Includes bibliographical references

Homer; edited and with an introduction by Harold Bloom. Updated ed; Chelsea House 2006 221p (Modern critical views) $45
Grades: 9 10 11 12 **883**
1. Poets 2. Authors
ISBN 0-7910-9313-1; 978-0-7910-9313-9
LC 2006-25325
First published 1986
This book "explores Homer's transformative effect on epic and bardic poetry, as well as his narrative technique and use of language and meter." Publisher's note
Includes bibliographical references

Homer's The Iliad; edited and with an introduction by Harold Bloom. Updated ed; Chelsea House

Publishers 2006 212p (Modern critical interpretations) $45

Grades: 9 10 11 12   **883**

1. Poets 2. Authors

ISBN 0-7910-9306-9; 978-0-7910-9306-1

LC 2006-31068

First published 1987

A collection of nine critical essays discussing the epic Greek poem.

Includes bibliographical references (p. 199-201)

Homer's The Odyssey; edited with an introduction by Harold Bloom. Updated ed.; Chelsea House 2007 263p (Modern critical interpretations) $45

Grades: 9 10 11 12 Adult   **883**

1. Poets 2. Authors

ISBN 0-7910-9425-1; 978-0-7910-9425-9

LC 2006-35201

First published 1988

A collection of eleven critical essays on Homer's epic poem, arranged chronologically in order of their original publication.

Includes bibliographical references

Odyssey

The **Odyssey**; translated by Robert Fitzgerald; with an introduction by Seamus Heaney. Knopf 1992 xxvii, 509p (Everyman's library) $21

Grades: 9 10 11 12 Adult   **883**

1. Poetry -- By individual authors

ISBN 978-0-679-41047-8; 0-679-41047-3

LC 92-52903

This translation first published 1961 by Anchor Press/Doubleday

"Fitzgerald's new Odyssey . . . deserves to be singled out for what it is—a masterpiece." Nation

Includes bibliographical references

Willcock, Malcolm M.

A **companion** to the Iliad; based on the translation by Richmond Lattimore. University of Chicago Press 1976 293p il maps hardcover o.p. pa $14

Grades: 9 10 11 12   **883**

1. Poets 2. Authors

ISBN 0-226-89855-5 pa

"The notes here are directed mostly toward the explanation of words, expressions, and allusions in the text; but they also include summaries of books and sections, and assistance toward the appreciation of Homer's broader composition, by drawing attention to the implications of the narrative and the very effective characterization of the major heroes." Preface

Includes bibliographical references

888   Classical Greek miscellaneous writings

Aristotle, 384-322 B.C.

The **basic** works of Aristotle; edited, and with an introduction by Richard McKeon. Random House 1941 xxxix, 1487p $49.95; pa $19.95

Grades: 11 12 Adult   **888**

ISBN 0-394-41610-4; 0-375-75799-6 pa

Contains entire texts of the following: Physica; De generatione et corruptione; De anima; Parva naturalia; Metaphysica; Ethica Nicomachea; Politica; De poetica

Includes bibliographical references

890   Literatures of other specific languages and language families

Foster, John L.

★ **Ancient** Egyptian literature; an anthology. translated by John L. Foster. University of Tex. Press 2001 272p hardcover o.p. pa $19.95

Grades: 11 12 Adult   **890**

1. Egyptian literature -- Collections

ISBN 0-292-72526-4; 0-292-72527-2 pa

LC 00-61607

An anthology of ancient Egyptian poetry, stories, hymns, prayers, and wisdom texts. Includes a discussion of translation, as well as brief information about authorship and date of each selection

Includes bibliographical references

The **Literature** of ancient Egypt; an anthology of stories, instructions, and poetry. edited and with an introduction by William Kelly Simpson; with translations by Robert K. Ritner . . . {et al.} 3rd. ed., rev. and expanded; Yale Univ. Press 2003 544p il pa $20

Grades: 9 10 11 12   **890**

1. Egyptian literature

ISBN 0-300-09920-7

First published 1973

This is a collection of ancient Egyptian literature, including writings from the late Demotic period

Includes bibliographical references

891   East Indo-European and Celtic literatures

The **essential** Rumi; translated by Coleman Barks, with John Moyne, A.A. Arberry, Reynold Nicholson. Harper 1995 302p $23.95; pa $14.95

Grades: 11 12 Adult   **891**

1. Poetry -- By individual authors

ISBN 978-0-06-250958-1; 0-06-250958-6; 978-0-06-250959-8 pa; 0-06-250959-4 pa

LC 94-44995

A collection of ecstatic verse by the 13th-century Sufi mystic

Narayan, R. K.

★ The **Ramayana**; a shortened modern prose version of the Indian epic (suggested by the Tamil version of Kamban) introduction by Pankaj Mishra. Penguin Books 2006 157p (Penguin classics) pa $13

Grades: 11 12 Adult   **891**
ISBN 0-14-303967-9

LC 2006-45201

First published 1972

A retelling of Prince Rama's courtship of the fourteen-year-old Sita, their exile, Sita's abduction, the search, and the great battle with her abductor Ravana, involving a pantheon of gods, heroes, and evil spirits.

891.7   Russian literature and related East Slavic literatures

Chekhov, Anton Pavlovich

★ The **plays** of Anton Chekhov; a new translation by Paul Schmidt. HarperCollins Pubs. 1997 387p hardcover o.p. pa $15.95
Grades: 11 12 Adult   **891.7**
ISBN 0-06-092875-1 pa

LC 96-42456

Handbook of Russian literature; edited by Victor Terras. Yale Univ. Press 1985 558p hardcover o.p. pa $42
Grades: 11 12 Adult   **891.7**
1. Reference books 2. Russian literature -- Dictionaries
ISBN 0-300-04868-8 pa

LC 84-11871

"A valuable resource for students, scholars, and general readers." Libr J

Includes bibliographical references

★ The Portable nineteenth-century Russian reader; edited by George Gibian. Penguin Bks. 1993 xxii, 641p pa $15.95
Grades: 11 12 Adult   **891.7**
1. Russian literature -- Collections
ISBN 0-14-015103-6

LC 92-39863

This collection includes Pushkin's poem 'The Bronze Horseman'; Gogol's 'The Overcoat'; Turgenev's 'First Love'; Chekhov's 'Uncle Vanya'; Tolstoy's 'The Death of Ivan Ilych'; and 'The Grand Inquisitor' episode from Dostoyevsky's 'The Brothers Karamazov'; plus poetry, plays, short stories, novel excerpts, and essays by such writers as Griboyedov, Pavlova, Herzen, Goncharov, Saltykov-Shchedrin, and Maksim Gorky

★ The **Portable** twentieth-century Russian reader; edited with an introduction and notes by Clarence Brown. Rev. and updated ed.; Penguin Books 1993 615p (Penguin classics) pa $18
Grades: 9 10 11 12   **891.7**
1. Russian literature -- Collections
ISBN 0-14-243757-3

LC 2003-283124

First published 1985

This collection "includes stories by Chekhov, Gorky, Bunin, Zamyatin, Babel, Nabokov, Solzhenitsyn, and Voinovich; excerpts from Andrei Bely's Petersburg, Mikhail Bulgakov's The Master and Margarita, Boris Pasternak's

Dr. Zhivago, and Sasha Solokov's A School for Fools; the complete text of Yuri Olesha's 1927 masterpiece Envy; and poetry by Alexander Blok, Anna Akhmatova, and Osip Mandelstam." Publisher's note

892   Afro-Asiatic literatures

Gilgamesh

★ **Gilgamesh**; a new English version [by] Stephen Mitchell. Free Press 2004 290p $25; pa $14
Grades: 11 12 Adult   **892**
ISBN 0-7432-6164-X; 0-7432-6169-0 pa

LC 2004-50072

"Relying on existing translations (and in places where there are gaps, on his own imagination), Mitchell seeks language that is as swift and strong as the story itself. . . . This wonderful new version of the story of Gilgamesh shows how the story came to achieve literary immortality—not because it is a rare ancient artifact, but because reading it can make people in the here and now feel more completely alive." Publ Wkly

Includes bibliographical references

892.7   Arabic and Maltese literatures

★ **Anthology** of modern Palestinian literature; edited and introduced by Salma Khadra Jayyusi. Columbia Univ. Press 1992 xxxiii, 744p hardcover o.p. pa $30.50
Grades: 11 12 Adult   **892.7**
1. Arabic literature -- Collections
ISBN 0-231-07508-1; 0-231-07509-X pa

LC 92-5189

"Presented here are translations of poems, stories, and excerpts from novels, as well as works by Palestinian poets who write in English. Also included are personal narratives by Palestinian writers depicting the varied aspects of Palestinian life from the turn of the century to the present. . . . Biographical sketches introduce the authors, and a chronology of modern Palestinian history provides background for some of the events and places referred to in the selections. The introduction by the editor provides a concise but comprehensive political history of Palestinian literature during the twentieth century." Publisher's note

Includes bibliographical references

★ **Night** and horses and the desert; an anthology of classical Arabic literature. edited by Robert Irwin. Anchor Books 2001 462p pa $16
Grades: 11 12 Adult   **892.7**
1. Arabic literature -- Collections 2. Arabic literature -- History and criticism
ISBN 0-385-72155-2

LC 2001-53721

First published 2000 by Overlook Press

"The chapter on the Qur'an is perhaps the most essential as it examines just how vital the dogma of Islam has been for the Arabic understanding of culture and art. . . . This persuasive work will surely fill in the gap in the study of Arabic literature in this country." Publ Wkly

Includes bibliographical references

895.1 Chinese literature

★ **Anthology** of modern Chinese poetry; edited and translated by Michelle Yeh. Yale Univ. Press 1993 245p hardcover o.p. pa $21

Grades: 11 12 Adult   **895.1**

1. Chinese poetry -- Collections
ISBN 0-300-05947-7 pa

LC 92-16322

"Arranged chronologically, this selection of twentieth-century poetry from China and Taiwan offers a few poems by each of 67 poets born between 1891 and 1963. Its scope is enormous, its range impressive. Editor Yeh's translations are accessible and fluid; her introduction and notes are helpful without being overbearingly scholarly." Booklist

Includes bibliographical references

Liu Siyu

★ A **thousand** peaks; poems from China. [by] Siyu Liu and Orel Protopopescu; illustrated by Siyu Liu. Pacific View Press 2002 52p il $19.95

Grades: 5 6 7 8 9 10   **895.1**

1. Chinese poetry 2. Bilingual books -- English-Chinese
ISBN 1-88189-624-2

LC 2001-34008

A collection of thirty-five poems spanning nineteen centuries, representing both famous and lesser-known poets, including both the Chinese text and a literal translation.

This "is an anthology of considerable fascination and broad utility. . . . The layout is neat, tidily fitting each poem's material on a single page and adding a line drawing featuring a relevant Chinese character. The wealth of material here provides a more stimulating entree to Chinese history than any dry textbook." Bull Cent Child Books

Includes bibliographical references

★ **One** hundred poems from the Chinese; {edited and translated} by Kenneth Rexroth. New Directions 1956 159p hardcover o.p. pa $11.95

Grades: 11 12 Adult   **895.1**

1. Chinese poetry -- Collections
ISBN 0-8112-0180-5 pa

"Nine poets, who lived centuries ago, speak with the poignancy of understatement of unchanging things; the brevity of life, the richness of friendship, the beauties of nature, the inevitability of old age and death." Booklist

Includes bibliographical references

The **Shorter** Columbia anthology of traditional Chinese literature; Victor H. Mair, editor. Columbia Univ. Press 2000 xxx, 741p map (Translations from the Asian classics) $65; pa $26

Grades: 11 12 Adult   **895.1**

1. Chinese literature -- Collections
ISBN 0-231-11998-4; 0-231-11999-2 pa

LC 00-35878

Abridged version of Columbia anthology of traditional Chinese literature, published 1994

This "abridged volume, which, like the original includes selections of Chinese literature from the beginnings to 1919 . . . retains the characteristics of the original in that it is arranged according to genre rather than chronology and interprets 'literature' very broadly to include not just literary fiction, poetry, and drama, but folk and popular literature, lyrics and arias, elegies and rhapsodies, biographies, autobiographies and memoirs, letters, criticism and theory, and travelogues and jokes. It also contains fresh translations by newer voices in the field." Publisher's note

Includes bibliographical references

895.6 Japanese literature

Anthology of Japanese literature from the earliest era to the mid-nineteenth century; edited by Donald Keene. Grove Press 1955 442p il pa $14.50

Grades: 9 10 11 12   **895.6**

1. Japanese literature -- Collections
ISBN 0-8021-5058-6

"Covers the period from 712 A.D., when 'Record of Ancient Matters,' the earliest surviving Japanese book, was completed to about 1850. . . . The selections here include self-contained episodes from plays and novels (among them the classic 'The Tale of Genji'), fairy tales, short stories, and personal reminiscences, and numerous . . . poems." New Yorker

The **Classic** Noh theatre of Japan; {edited and translated} by Ezra Pound and Ernest Fenollosa. New Directions 1959 163p pa $10.95

Grades: 9 10 11 12   **895.6**

1. N□o plays
ISBN 0-8112-0152-X

A collection of classical Japanese No verse dramas, dealing with various aspects of social life and incorporating folklore

From the country of eight islands; an anthology of Japanese poetry. edited and translated [from the Japanese] by Hiroaki Sato and Burton Watson; with an introduction by Thomas Rimer; associate editor: Robert Fagan. Columbia Univ. Press 1987 xliv, 652p pa $29.50

Grades: 11 12 Adult   **895.6**

1. Japanese poetry -- Collections
ISBN 0-231-06395-4

LC 86-7881

First published 1981 by University of Wash. Press

This anthology ranges "from the Kojiki (Record of Ancient Matters) . . . to a nineteenth-century transcript of a cycle of rice-planting songs, and from Kakinomoto no Hitimaro, [a] writer of elegies, who lived in the sixth century, to such recent poets as Tomioka Taeko. . . . Also included are Fujiwara no Teika's anthology of one hundred three 'tanka,' a no play, six sequences of 'renga' or linked verse, the 'frog

matches' in which Basho participated, and some longer modern poems rendered in full." Publisher's note [1981 edition]
Includes bibliographical references

★ **One** hundred poems from the Japanese; {edited and translated} by Kenneth Rexroth. New Directions 1956 143p hardcover o.p. pa $11.95
Grades: 11 12 Adult   895.6
1. Japanese poetry -- Collections
ISBN 0-8112-0181-3 pa

A bilingual collection of poems drawn chiefly from the traditional Man□oshu, Kokinsh□u, and Hyakunin Isshu collections and also containing examples of haiku and other later forms. The translator's introduction provides background information on the history and nature of Japanese poetry
Includes bibliographical references

896   African literatures

★ The **Penguin** book of modern African poetry; edited by Gerald Moore and Ulli Beier. 4th ed.; Penguin Books 2007 xxvi, 448p pa $17
Grades: 11 12 Adult   896
1. African poetry -- Collections
ISBN 978-0-14-042472-0; 0-14-042472-5
First published 1963 in the United Kingdom with title: Modern poetry from Africa
This anthology includes over 200 poems by 67 poets from 23 countries.
Includes bibliographical references

897   Literatures of North American native languages

Coltelli, Laura
★ **Winged** words: American Indian writers speak; [reported by] Laura Coltelli. University of Neb. Press 1990 211p il (American Indian lives) hardcover o.p. pa $9.95
Grades: 11 12 Adult   897
1. Poets 2. Artists 3. Authors 4. Singers 5. Novelists 6. Dramatists 7. Illustrators 8. Anthropologists 9. Editors 10. Essayists 11. Memoirists 12. Biographers 13. College teachers 14. Literary critics 15. Children's authors 16. Short story writers 17. Television scriptwriters 18. American literature -- Native American authors
ISBN 0-8032-6351-1 pa

LC 89-39323
A compilation of interviews with Louise Erdrich, N. Scott Momaday, James Welch and eight other Native American writers.
"Coltelli's questions probe the writers' sources of inspiration, methods of composition, and perceptions of their own and their works' relationship to tribal culture, among other broad areas. But it's the questions Coltelli has tailored to each individual that hit pay dirt and result in some illuminating moments." Booklist
Includes bibliographical references

Coming to light; contemporary translations of the native literatures of North America. edited and with an introduction by Brian Swann. Random House 1994 801p hardcover o.p. pa $22
Grades: 11 12 Adult   897
1. Native American literature 2. American literature -- Native American authors -- Collections
ISBN 0-679-74358-8 pa

LC 94-13457
"Swann has gathered intact texts from storytellers, singers, and orators. Arranged by region and tribe, each set of translations is prefaced by a lengthy introduction by the translator that sets the stories in context. The focus varies, depending on whether the translator is a linguist, anthropologist, or educator and whether he or she is a Native speaker, of which a fair number are. This wide-ranging collection goes far toward achieving Swann's goal of presenting a collection of reliable translations placed in their cultural and historical environments." Libr J
Includes bibliographical references

900   HISTORY

900   History, geography, and auxiliary disciplines

Freedman, Grace Roegner
Cracking the SAT. U.S. & world history subject tests; [by] Grace Roegner Freedman; revised by Dan Komarek, Casey Paragin, and Christine Parker. 2011-2012 ed.; Random House 2011 449p (Princeton Review series) pa $19.99
Grades: 9 10 11 12   900
1. Scholastic Assessment Test 2. History -- Study and teaching 3. Colleges and universities -- Entrance requirements
ISBN 978-0-375-42816-6
Annual. First published 2005. Continues Cracking the S A T II: U.S. and world history subject tests
This guide provides test-taking strategies and sample tests on the subjects of both American and world history.

901   Philosophy and theory of history

The **Britannica** guide to theories and ideas that changed the modern world; edited by Kathleen Kuiper. Britannica Educational Pub. in association with Rosen Educational Services 2010 383p il (Turning points in history) lib bdg $45
Grades: 9 10 11 12   901
1. Intellectual life 2. Modern philosophy 3. Modern civilization 4. Science -- History
ISBN 978-1-61530-029-7

LC 2009-48166

This book "covers the development of the sciences and arts with such topics as string theory, musical harmony, and contemporary democracy." Libr Media Connect

Includes glossary and bibliographical references

902 Miscellany of history

Grun, Bernard

The **timetables** of history; a historical linkage of people and events. 4th ed.; Simon & Schuster 2005 835p $25

Grades: 11 12 Adult   902

1. Historical chronology

ISBN 0-7432-7003-7; 978-0-7432-7003-8

LC 2005-49766

Original German edition, 1946; first published in the United States 1975

This chronology "includes material from 4500 BCE to 2004. . . . The information is listed by year in seven columns labeled 'History, Politics', 'Literature, Theater', 'Religion, Philosophy, Learning', 'Visual Arts', 'Music', 'Science, Technology, Growth', and 'Daily Life.' . . . This work is an excellent chronological tool, and should be found in all libraries." Choice

★ The **timetables** of American history; Laurence Urdang, editor; with an introduction by Henry Steele Commager and a new foreword by Arthur Schlesinger, Jr. Simon & Schuster 2001 534p il pa $24

Grades: 11 12 Adult   902

1. Historical chronology

ISBN 0-7432-0261-9

First published 1982

Presents information chronologically in tabular form. Each double-page spread has columns for history and politics, the arts, science and technology, and miscellaneous.

902.2 Illustrations, models, miniatures

National Geographic Society (U.S.)

★ **National** Geographic visual history of the world; [authors, Klaus Berndl . . . et al.]. National Geographic Society 2005 656p il $35

Grades: 11 12 Adult   902.2

1. World history

ISBN 0-7922-3695-5

LC 2005-541553

"Over 4,000 illustrations and photographs cover individuals and events from prehistory (the beginning to ca. 4000 BCE) to the contemporary world (1945 to the present). . . . This educational and entertaining volume of social, cultural, and military history will appeal to a wide readership." Choice

903 Dictionaries, encyclopedias, concordances of history

Berkshire encyclopedia of world history; William H. McNeill, Jerry H. Bentley [and] David Christian, editors. 2nd ed.; Berkshire Pub. Group 2010 6v il map set $875

Grades: 11 12 Adult   903

1. Reference books 2. World history -- Encyclopedias

ISBN 978-1-933782-65-2

LC 2010021635

First published 2004

"To cover 250,000 years of human history, knowledge from various disciplines is synthesized, summarized, and presented in an easy-to-read fashion. Emphasis is placed on social change and cultural contact over time and place." Booklist

Includes bibliographical references

Encyclopedia of world history; edited by Marsha E. Ackermann . . . [et al.] Facts on File 2008 7v il map (Facts on File library of world history) set $650

Grades: 9 10 11 12 Adult   903

1. Reference books 2. World history -- Encyclopedias

ISBN 978-0-8160-6386-4; 0-8160-6386-9

LC 2007-5158

"This set deserves a place on the shelves of every high school library." Voice Youth Advocates

Includes bibliographical references

Takacs, Sarolta A.

The **modern** world; Sarolta Takács, general editor. M.E. Sharpe 2008 5v il map set $399

Grades: 7 8 9 10 11 12   903

1. Reference books 2. World history -- Encyclopedias 3. Modern civilization -- Encyclopedias

ISBN 978-0-7656-8096-9

LC 2007-44253

"This engaging, well-written set masterfully chronicles world history from 500 C.E. to the present, with a particular emphasis on how changes throughout the years helped shape contemporary society." SLJ

Includes bibliographical references

904 Collected accounts of events

Beyer, Rick

The **greatest** stories never told; 100 tales from history to astonish, bewilder, & stupefy. HarperResource 2003 214p il $17.95

Grades: 7 8 9 10   904

1. History -- Miscellanea

ISBN 0-06-001401-6

LC 2004-296419

"Beginning with the year 46 B.C. and ending in 1990, Beyer presents a chronological account of one hundred unknown, partially known, and familar tales about an array of people and events that have shaped the world. . . . They range from the mundane to the fantastic. . . . Extensive research went into the production of this charming work. Primary documents in the form of letters, laws, illustrations, and photographs bring to life these unique and incredible anecdotes." Voice Youth Advocates

Includes bibliographical references

Davis, Lee Allyn

Natural disasters; [by] Lee Davis. New ed; Facts On File 2008 464p (Facts on File science library) $75

Grades: 9 10 11 12   **904**
1. Natural disasters
ISBN 978-0-8160-7000-8; 0-8160-7000-8
                                                        LC 2007-50846
First published 1992

A worldwide survey of natural disasters throughout history. Over 500 alphabetical entries, organized by disaster type, cover a range of events, including: earthquakes, floods, typhoons, snowstorms, hurricanes, and tornadoes.

Includes bibliographical references

Diacu, Florin

Megadisasters; the science of predicting the next catastrophe. Princeton University Press 2010 195p il $24.95

Grades: 9 10 11 12 Adult   **904**
1. Forecasting 2. Natural disasters
ISBN 978-0-691-13350-8
                                                        LC 2009-29193

The author "presents a civilian-friendly guide to methods, like numerical modeling, used to understand, quantify, and possibly predict disasters. Written simply but without being simplistic, Diacu's text is driven by enthusiasm for his field and its potential for solving some of humanity's big problems." Publ Wkly

Includes bibliographical references

909   World history

Africana: the encyclopedia of the African and African American experience; editors, Kwame Anthony Appiah, Henry Louis Gates, Jr. 2nd ed; Oxford University Press 2005 5v set $550

Grades: 11 12 Adult   **909**
1. Reference books 2. Africa -- Encyclopedias 3. Blacks -- Encyclopedias 4. African diaspora -- Encyclopedias 5. African Americans -- Encyclopedias
ISBN 978-0-19-517055-9; 0-19-517055-5
                                                        LC 2004-20222
First published 1999 by Basic Civitas Bks.

This encyclopedia covers "prominent individuals, events, trends, places, political movements, art forms, business and trade, religions, ethnic groups, organizations, and countries on both sides of the ocean. . . . There are articles on contemporary nations of sub-Saharan Africa, ethnic groups from various regions of Africa, African American Academy award winners, Caribbean musical styles, African religions in Brazil, and European colonial powers." Booklist [review of 1999 edition]

Includes bibliographical references

Badcott, Nicholas

★ **Pocket** timeline of Islamic civilizations. Interlink 2009 32p il $13.95

Grades: 7 8 9 10   **909**
1. Reference books 2. Islamic civilization -- Chronology
ISBN 978-1-56656-758-9; 1-56656-758-0

"Badcott takes readers on a colorful and captivating tour of Islamic civilizations from the 7th to the 20th century. He discusses the rise and fall of dynasties, along with their achievements and contributions in art, medicine, architecture, commerce, and science. . . . The writing style is easy to read. . . . Attractive color photographs of buildings, pottery, jewelry, art, and inventions help maintain readers' interest throughout." SLJ

Includes bibliographical references

Boorstin, Daniel J.

The **creators**. Random House 1992 811p il hardcover o.p. pa $18.95

Grades: 11 12 Adult   **909**
1. Arts 2. Civilization 3. Creation (Literary, artistic, etc.)
ISBN 0-394-54395-5; 0-679-74375-8 pa
                                                        LC 91-39948

In this volume "Boorstin undertakes an interpretive history of creativity in Western civilization. Packed with shrewd, entertaining profiles of Dante, Goethe, Benjamin Franklin and dozens of others, this stimulating synthesis sets the achievements of individual geniuses into a coherent narrative of humanity's advance from ignorance." Publ Wkly

Includes bibliographical references

The **discoverers**. Random House 1983 745p hardcover o.p. pa $18.95

Grades: 11 12 Adult   **909**
1. Exploration 2. Civilization 3. Science -- History
ISBN 0-394-40229-4; 0-394-72625-1 pa
                                                        LC 83-42766

The author "leads his reader through . . . anecdotal information of the discoveries of timekeeping, mapmaking, observations of nature, both large and small, and of insights into human social organizations, past and present, in this popularized, general history of 'mankind's need to know.'" Choice

Includes bibliographical references

The **seekers**; the story of man's continuing quest to understand his world. Random House 1998 298p hardcover o.p. pa $15.95

Grades: 11 12 Adult   **909**
1. Civilization -- History
ISBN 0-679-43445-3; 0-375-70475-2 pa
                                                        LC 98-15430

Concluding volume of author's trilogy begun with The discoverers and The creators

"This is an account, generally chronological, of how the Western world's heritage of ideas of meaning and purpose was shaped by the thinking of the great philosophers and religious leaders from ancient times to the present. Until the rise of scientific thinking in the 17th century, Boorstin observes, answers were sought from history and human events, but in modern times, ideologies and dogmas overcame that way of thinking." Libr J

Includes bibliographical references

Cahill, Thomas

The **gifts** of the Jews; how a tribe of desert nomads changed the way everyone thinks and feels. Talese 1998 291p (Hinges of history) $23.50; pa $14

Grades: 11 12 Adult   **909**

1. Jews -- History 2. Judaism -- History 3. Bible -- O.T. -- History of Biblical events

ISBN 0-385-48248-5; 0-385-48249-3 pa

LC 97-45139

In this colloquial look at the influence of the Hebrew Bible on civilization, the author gives "the Jews credit for revolutionizing the concepts of democracy, universal law, monotheism, linear time, personal vocation, destiny, self-improvement and the belief in the equality of all humans. He stumbles on the odd aside and occasionally is surprisingly insensitive. . . Still, his passion and breadth of knowledge are admirable." N Y Times Book Rev

Includes bibliographical references

Sailing the wine-dark sea; why the Greeks matter. Talese 2003 304p (Hinges of history) $27.50; pa $14.95

Grades: 11 12 Adult   **909**

1. Greece -- Civilization

ISBN 0-385-49553-6; 0-385-49554-4 pa

LC 2003-50725

This author "begins with a discussion of Homer's Iliad and Odyssey and how these two epic poems relate to the history of Greece. He then focuses on such themes as the Greek alphabet, literature, and political system, and its playwrights, philosophers, and artists. A final chapter examines the effects that Greco-Roman and Judeo-Christian traditions had on each other." Booklist

Includes bibliographical references

The **Cambridge** illustrated history of the Islamic world; edited by Francis Robinson. Cambridge Univ. Press 1996 xxiii, 328p map (Cambridge illustrated history) hardcover o.p. pa $36.99

Grades: 11 12 Adult   **909**

1. Islamic countries -- History

ISBN 0-521-43510-2; 0-521-66993-6 pa

LC 95-37562

"Facts about Islam's history and practice are presented, along with its economic, societal, and intellectual structures. Excellent graphics support the text. Maps are extensive and exact." SLJ

Includes bibliographical references

Cocker, Mark

Rivers of blood, rivers of gold; Europe's conquest of indigenous peoples. Grove Press 2000 416p il hardcover o.p. pa $16

Grades: 11 12 Adult   **909**

1. Colonies 2. Genocide 3. Imperialism

ISBN 0-8021-1666-3; 0-8021-3801-2 pa

LC 99-87927

The author "looks in detail at the Spanish conquest of Mexico, the British near-extermination of the Tasmanian Aborigines, the white settlers' dispossession of the Apaches, and the German subjugation of the Herero and Nama of South-West Africa. Cocker shows that European imperialism involved the deaths of millions and the complete extinction of numerous distinct peoples." Booklist

Includes bibliographical references

★ **Daily** life through world history in primary documents; Lawrence Morris, general editor. Greenwood Press 2009 3v il set $299.95

Grades: 9 10 11 12 Adult   **909**

1. Reference books 2. Civilization -- History -- Sources 3. Manners and customs -- History -- Sources

ISBN 978-0-313-33898-4

LC 2008-8925

"Each of the three volumes . . . begins with a chronology of the era covered as well as a clear, concise historical overview that provides readers with core knowledge of the cultures discussed. The more than 530 entries are grouped into seven categories: domestic, economic, intellectual, material, political, recreational, and religious life." Booklist

Includes bibliographical references

Encyclopedia of the developing world; Thomas M. Leonard, editor. Routledge 2005 3v set $625

Grades: 11 12 Adult   **909**

1. Reference books 2. Developing countries -- Encyclopedias

ISBN 1-57958-388-1

LC 2005-49976

The entries "detail developments from 1945 forward. In addition to basic statistical and geographical information, country-focused entries detail history, economy, and political situation. Thematic entries cover people (e.g., Jomo Kenyatta), historical topics (e.g., colonialism), economic and government models (e.g., communism), the environment (e.g., water) and organizations (e.g., WTO)." Libr J

Includes bibliographical references

★ **Encyclopedia** of the Palestinians; edited by Philip Mattar. Rev. ed; Facts on File 2005 684p il map (Facts on File library of world history) $90

Grades: 9 10 11 12   **909**

1. Reference books 2. Palestinian Arabs -- Encyclopedias

ISBN 0-8160-5764-8

LC 2004-57673

First published 2000

This book focuses on "Palestinian history, politics, and society from the late Ottoman period to the present. . . . [This is] the most objective reference compendium to treat Palestinian history as a subject in its own right." Choice

Includes bibliographical references

Evans, Colin

Great feuds in history; ten of the liveliest disputes ever. Wiley 2001 242p hardcover o.p. pa $15.95

Grades: 11 12 Adult **909**
1. History -- Miscellanea
ISBN 0-471-38038-5; 0-471-22588-6 pa
LC 00-43919
This discusses the following feuds: Elizabeth I vs. Mary, Parliament vs. Charles I, Burr vs. Hamilton, Hatfields vs. McCoys, Stalin vs. Trotsky, Amundsen vs. Scott, Duchess of Windsor vs. Queen Mother, Montgomery vs. Patton, Johnson vs. Kennedy, Hoover vs. King.

This places "emphasis on the global issues often at stake and how, for better or worse, the feuds changed history. Evans . . . captures all the drama and controversy in these streamlined accounts brimming with invigorated, well-paced prose." Publ Wkly

Includes bibliographical references

Events that changed the world through the sixteenth century; edited by Frank W. Thackeray and John E. Findling. Greenwood Press 2001 223p il (Greenwood Press 'Events that changed the world' series) $39.50
Grades: 9 10 11 12 **909**
1. World history -- 15th century 2. World history -- 16th century
ISBN 0-313-29079-2
LC 00-52132
This volume focuses "on the fifteenth and sixteenth centuries, with 10 events ranging from the Reconquista (circa 711-1492) to the defeat of the Spanish Armada in 1588." Booklist

Includes bibliographical references and index

Great events from history, The 17th century, 1601-1700; editor, Larissa Juliet Taylor. Salem Press 2005 2v il map set $160
Grades: 11 12 Adult **909**
1. Reference books 2. World history -- 17th century
ISBN 1-58765-225-0; 978-1-58765-225-7
LC 2005-17362
Companion volume to Great lives from history, The 17th century, 1601-1700

Some of the essays in this work were originally published in Chronology of European history, 15,000 B.C. to 1997 (1997) and Great events from history: North American series. Rev. ed. (1997)

This set "offers two to three-page essays that detail the major milestones of the century as well as social developments that were reflective of daily life during the period. The perspective here is international and spans a variety of categories, including religion and theology, cultural and intellectual history, expansion and land acquisition, and natural disasters. A list of key figures involved in each event is provided." SLJ

Includes bibliographical references

Great events from history, The Renaissance & early modern era, 1454-1600; editor, Christina J. Moose. Salem Press 2005 2v il map set $160
Grades: 11 12 Adult **909**
1. Renaissance 2. Reference books 3. World history

-- 15th century 4. World history -- 16th century
ISBN 1-58765-214-5; 978-1-58765-214-1
LC 2004-28878
Companion volume to Great lives from history, The Renaissance & early modern era, 1454-1600

Some of the essays were previously published in various works

This collection of essays covers events in the scientific, intellectual, literary, sociological, political and military disciplines that happened worldwide during the Renaissance.

Includes bibliographical references

A **Historical** atlas of the Jewish people; from the time of the patriarchs to the present. general editor, Eli Barnavi; English edition editor, Miriam Eliav-Feldon; cartography, Michel Opatowski; new edition revised by Denis Charbit. new ed; Schocken Bks. 2002 321p il maps $45
Grades: 11 12 Adult **909**
1. Jews -- History -- Maps
ISBN 0-8052-4226-0
LC 2003-279553
First published 1992 by Knopf

"Covering three millennia of Jewish history and culture through a combination of concise text, accurate and well-drawn maps, and a sumptuous array of photographs, diagrams, and reproductions of paintings, this atlas succeeds in covering all the main themes of the Jewish experience. The material is arranged chronologically and systematically. . . . The result is a reference that will profit both scholars and lay readers." Libr J [review of 1992 edition]

★ The **Islamic** world; past and present. John L. Esposito, editor in chief . . . {et al.} Oxford University Press 2004 3v il map set $325
Grades: 9 10 11 12 **909**
1. Reference books 2. Islam -- Encyclopedias
ISBN 0-19-516520-9
LC 2003-19665
This book "contains more than 300 entries, ranging in length from a few paragraphs to several pages; many black-and-white photos; color inserts; numerous sidebars, including definitions of unfamiliar terms; an extensive bibliography; and (in each volume) a chronology, glossary, and list of 'People and Places.' The material is accessible, browsable, and current; topics treated include religion and history ('Prayer,' 'Prophets,' 'Crusades'), culture and customs, and political and social issues ('Architecture,' 'Clothing,' 'Intifadah,' 'Taliban,' 'Sexuality')." SLJ

James, Lawrence
The **rise** and fall of the British Empire. St. Martin's Press 1995 704p il hardcover o.p. pa $21.95
Grades: 11 12 Adult **909**
1. Great Britain -- Colonies 2. Commonwealth countries -- History
ISBN 0-312-14039-8; 0-312-16985-X pa
LC 95-38774
First published 1994 in the United Kingdom
The author "surveys the major periods and events in Britain's rise and decline as a global power without attempting to be the definitive study of any one of those periods or events.

. . . James' focus rests primarily on individuals—those who built the British Empire, those who maintained it, and those who, when it came time, eased it out of existence." Booklist

McKitterick, Rosamond
Atlas of the medieval world. Oxford University Press 2004 304p il map $45
Grades: 11 12 Adult   909
1. Middle Ages 2. Reference books 3. Historical atlases
ISBN 0-19-522158-3

LC 2004-56816

This atlas explores "through maps and narrative the millennium from the end of the Roman Empire to the colonization of the Americas. . . . The work features more than 90 digitally produced color political and thematic maps as well as hundreds of sumptuous photographs of art and architecture." Libr J
Includes bibliographical references

★ Milestone documents in world history; exploring the primary sources that shaped the world. Brian Bonhomme, editor in chief; Cathleen Boivin, consulting editor. Schlager Group 2010 4v il (Milestone documents) set $395
Grades: 9 10 11 12 Adult   909
1. World history -- Sources
ISBN 978-0-9797758-6-4

This set "provides and analyzes 125 important primary-source documents and covers a broad range of world history—from the 2350 B.C.E. Reform Edict of Urukagina to 2000's Constitutive Act of the African Union—and targets all geographic regions. It includes influential documents such as Christopher Columbus's letter to Raphael Sanxis on the discovery of America, Martin Luther's 95 theses, Winston Churchill's 'The sinews of peace' speech, and the Northern Ireland peace agreement." Libr J
Includes glossary

Morgan, Michael Hamilton
Lost history; the enduring legacy of Muslim scientists, thinkers, and artists. [foreword by King Abdullah II of Jordan] National Geographic 2007 301p il map $26; pa $15.95
Grades: 11 12 Adult   909
1. Islamic civilization
ISBN 978-1-4262-0092-2; 1-4262-0092-7; 978-1-4262-0280-3 pa; 1-4262-0280-6 pa

LC 2007-7207

This "is an entertaining popular work that traces a vivid picture of the history of Arabo-Islamic scientific thought. Each chapter opens with a brief narrative passage in which present-day fictional characters of Eastern descent realize that something in their knowledge of themselves and of their history is missing. These vignettes are the starting point for Morgan's story of the Arabo-Islamic sciences and their legacy in modern Western societies." Chemical Heritage
Includes bibliographical references

National Geographic concise history of the world; an illustrated timeline. edited by Neil Kagan. Re-

vised edition National Geographic Society 2013 416 p. ill. (some col.), maps $40
Grades: 6 7 8 9 10 11 12 Adult   909
1. World history 2. Historical chronology
ISBN 1426211783; 9781426211782

LC 2015430064

"For readers of all ages, world history is easily accessible, depicted as never before—so that events occurring simultaneously around the world can be viewed at-a-glance together. . . . The book's innovative time line truly sets it apart, allowing readers to scan across a spread and explore a single area or compare contemporary societies across the globe." (Publisher's note)
Includes bibliographical references (pages 405-406) and index

The **Oxford** encyclopedia of the Islamic world; John L. Esposito, editor in chief. Oxford University Press 2009 3110p 6v il map set $750
Grades: 10 11 12 Adult   909
1. Reference books 2. Islam -- Encyclopedias 3. Islamic countries -- Encyclopedias
ISBN 978-0-19-530513-5; 0-19-530513-2

LC 2008-40486

"The encyclopedia's 1050 A-to-Z entries, written by an international community of 550 scholars, cover such topics as history, geography, law, religious belief, culture, politics, economics, and mysticism. . . . Written in clear, jargon-free language, this is a balanced, well-rounded, and evenhanded resource for both scholars and general readers interested in understanding Islam and its place in the world." Libr J
Includes bibliographical references

Pagden, Anthony
Peoples and empires; a short history of European migration, exploration, and conquest from Greece to the present. Modern library ed; Modern Lib. 2001 xxv, 206p hardcover o.p. pa $10.95
Grades: 11 12 Adult   909
1. Colonies 2. World history 3. Immigration and emigration
ISBN 0-679-64096-7; 0-8129-6761-5 pa

LC 00-66204

This "overview of European empire building and colonization commences with the diffusion of Greek civilization and traces the subsequent evolution of the ensuing Roman, Spanish, French, and British empires. More interesting than how those empires physically expanded is the insightful discussion on what motivated individual men and entire nations to migrate and conquer." Booklist
Includes bibliographical references

Popular controversies in world history; investigating history's intriguing questions. Steven L. Danver, editor. ABC-CLIO 2011 4v il map set $380
Grades: 9 10 11 12   909
1. Reference books 2. Curiosities and wonders 3. History -- Miscellanea
ISBN 978-1-59884-077-3; 1-59884-077-0; 978-1-59884-078-0 ebook; 1-59884-078-9 ebook

LC 2010036572

"Rather than a collection of stale facts and dates, these volumes present world history in a way that allows students to exercise their analytical-thinking skills, moving them beyond knowledge and comprehension and ultimately to the levels of synthesis and evaluation." Booklist

Includes bibliographical references

Smith, Tom

★ **Discovery** of the Americas, 1492-1800; rev ed.; Chelsea House 2010 134p il map (Discovery and exploration) lib bdg $35

Grades: 7 8 9 10 11   **909**
1. Explorers 2. America -- Exploration
ISBN 978-1-60413-195-6; 1-60413-195-0

LC 2009-22330

First published 2005

"The chapters are well-illustrated with color and black and white historic photos, illustrations and maps. Chapter layout is clearly organized with helpful subtitles; sidebars develop related themes in eye-catching colors." Libr Media Connect

Includes glossary and bibliographical references

Technology in world history; W. Bernard Carlson, editor. Oxford University Press 2005 7v il maps set $299

Grades: 7 8 9 10   **909**
1. Reference books 2. Technology and civilization
ISBN 0-19-521820-5; 978-0-19-521820-6

LC 2003-55300

"Seeking to explore how people have used technology to shape societies, Carlson and 10 other scholars examine the distinctive development and effects of technology in 18 cultures—defined either geographically (Pacific Peoples, Sub-Saharan Africa) or by historical period (Stone Age, The World Since 1970)." SLJ

Includes bibliographical references

The **Third** World: opposing viewpoints; David M. Haugen, book editor. Greenhaven Press 2006 230p il (Opposing viewpoints series) lib bdg $34.95; pa $23.70

Grades: 11 12   **909**
1. Developing countries
ISBN 0-7377-2965-1 lib bdg; 978-0-7377-2965-8 lib bdg; 0-7377-2966-X pa; 978-0-7377-2966-5 pa

LC 2005-54544

This book is a collection of essays on the problems facing Third World countries.

"This volume would be an excellent resource for more advanced students researching the subject or looking for debate topics." SLJ

Includes bibliographical references

Treuer, Anton

Everything you wanted to know about Indians but were afraid to ask; Anton Treuer. Borealis Books 2012 190 p. (pbk.: alk. paper) $15.95

Grades: 9 10 11 12 Adult   **909**
1. Native Americans 2. Indians -- History 3. Indians

in popular culture 4. Indians -- Social life and customs
ISBN 0873518616; 0873518624; 9780873518611; 9780873518628

LC 2011053026

In this book Anton Treuer "endeavors to address misconceptions held by non-natives about the American Indian experience in the United States. He accomplishes his task by posing and answering approximately 125 questions divided into ten categories: 'Terminology,' 'History,' 'Religion, Culture & Identity,' 'Powwow,' 'Tribal Languages,' 'Politics,' 'Economics,' 'Education,' 'Perspectives: Coming to Terms and Future Directions,' and 'Finding Ways to Make a Difference.'" (Library Journal)

Includes bibliographical references and index

909.07   General historical periods

Andrea, Alfred J.

★ **Encyclopedia** of the crusades. Greenwood Press 2003 xxiii, 356p il, maps $75

Grades: 11 12 Adult   **909.07**
1. Reference books 2. Crusades -- Encyclopedias 3. Europe -- Church history -- Encyclopedias
ISBN 0-313-31659-7

LC 2003-48544

This encyclopedia includes "more than 200 entries, each one between approximately 10 lines and four pages in length. . . . The introduction gives the entries some historical context and defines the term crusade for the reader. The entries are in alphabetical order and include cross-references in bold type to other entries in the book. Many entries also include suggested readings, both primary sources and historical studies. At the end of the work, the author has included a chronology of important dates and events, a 'Basic Crusade Library' of further readings in bibliographic essay style, and a general index. . . . This encyclopedia is recommended for high-school, undergraduate, and public libraries." Booklist

Includes bibliographical references

★ The **Crusades;** an encyclopedia. Alan V. Murray, editor. ABC-CLIO 2006 4v il map set $385

Grades: 11 12 Adult   **909.07**
1. Reference books 2. Crusades -- Encyclopedias
ISBN 1-57607-862-0; 978-1-57607-862-4

LC 2006-19410

This encyclopedia "surveys all aspects of the crusading movement from its origins in the 11th century to its decline in the 16th century." Publisher's note

Includes bibliographical references

Currie, Stephen

The **Medieval** crusades; by Stephen Currie. Lucent Books 2009 96 p. ill. (chiefly col.), col. map (library) $34.95

Grades: 6 7 8 9   **909.07**
1. Crusades 2. Middle Ages
ISBN 1420500627; 9781420500622

LC 2008046532

This book by Stephen Currie is part of the World History series and looks at the medieval crusades. It "begins with an explanation of early Christendom and Islam and the schisms that existed within each religion. . . . The focus of the book falls on the long-term effects of the Crusades, creating European awareness of other countries and cultures that led to increased commerce and trade, which in turn led to the Age of Exploration and the Renaissance." (Voice of Youth Advocates)

Includes bibliographical references and index.

Encyclopedia of society and culture in the medieval world; Pam J. Crabtree, editor in chief. Facts On File 2008 4v il map (Facts on File library of world history) set $360
Grades: 9 10 11 12 Adult　　　　**909.07**
1. Reference books　2. Medieval civilization -- Encyclopedias
ISBN 978-0-8160-6936-1;　0-8160-6936-0
　　　　　　　　　　　　　　LC 2007-36571
"This well-organized resource covers a wide range of topics relating to medieval society. . . . A useful and important set." SLJ

Includes bibliographical references

Great events from history, The Middle Ages, 477-1453; editor, Brian A. Pavlac; consulting editors, Byron Cannon, . . . [et al.] Salem Press 2005 2v il map set $160
Grades: 11 12 Adult　　　　**909.07**
1. Middle Ages　2. Reference books　3. Medieval civilization
ISBN 1-58765-167-X; 978-1-58765-167-0
　　　　　　　　　　　　　　LC 2004-16640
Companion volume to Great lives from history, The Middle Ages, 477-1453

Some essays were previously published in Great events from history (1972-1980), Chronology of European history: 15,000 B.C. to 1997 (1997), Great events from history: North American series, revised edition (1997), Great events from history: ancient and medieval series (1972), and Great events from history: modern European series (1973)

This set "offers 322 essays, beginning with Confucianism arrives in Japan (fifth or sixth century) and ending with Fall of Constantinople (May 29, 1453)." Booklist

Includes bibliographical references

Jones, J. Sydney
★ The **Crusades,** Primary sources; written by J. Sydney Jones; edited by Marcia Merryman Means and Neil Schlager. UXL 2005 xxvii, 179p il (The Crusades reference library) $63
Grades: 11 12 Adult　　　　**909.07**
1. Crusades
ISBN 0-7876-9178-X
　　　　　　　　　　　　　　LC 2004-18001
This book "consists of 24 full or excerpted documents, first-person accounts, treaties, and speeches; the complete Magna Carta; and a section from the epic poem The Song of Roland. . . . All excerpts from the primary sources are followed by text that illuminates the history of the document and poses discussion questions." Booklist

Includes bibliographical references

Knight, Judson
Middle ages: almanac; edited by Judy Galens. U.X.L 2001 lxv, 226p il map (Middle Ages reference library) $60
Grades: 8 9 10 11 12　　　　**909.07**
1. Middle Ages　2. World history　3. Reference books　4. Medieval civilization
ISBN 0-7876-4856-6
　　　　　　　　　　　　　　LC 00-59442
This reference's 19 chapters review world history from the fall of the Roman Empire in 500 A.D. to the beginning of the Renaissance in 1500 A.D.

"The volume's strength is its broad coverage; it includes material on India, Southeast Asia, China, Japan, the Americas, and Africa as well as Europe and the Middle East, making it unique among other books for this age group." SLJ

Includes bibliographical references

The **Middle** Ages, 600 to 1492; edited by Helen Dwyer. Brown Bear Books 2009 102p map (Curriculum connections. Atlas of world history) lib bdg $39.95
Grades: 9 10 11 12　　　　**909.07**
1. Middle Ages　2. Medieval civilization　3. Europe -- History -- 476-1492
ISBN 978-1-933834-67-2
　　　　　　　　　　　　　　LC 2009-27835
This book "is divided into thematic and regional maps which are followed by short but very comprehensive articles. . . . [It includes] curriculum context sidebars, important terms students should know, and how the topic ties into other areas." Libr Media Connect

Includes bibliographical references

★ **Middle** ages: primary sources; [compiled by] Judson Knight; Judy Galens, editor. U.X.L 2000 xxxiv, 161p il (Middle Ages reference library) $60
Grades: 8 9 10 11 12　　　　**909.07**
1. Middle Ages
ISBN 0-7876-4860-4
　　　　　　　　　　　　　　LC 00-59441
This volume contains "19 full or excerpted documents written during this period, including the work of celebrated writers such as St. Augustine, Marco Polo, and Dante as well as less familiar individuals such as Anna Comnena and Lo Kuan-chung. Each selection is placed in its historical context and followed by a section entitled 'What happened next'. . . . Unfamiliar words or terms are defined in sidebars. Each entry has a box profiling the author of the documents and at least two illustrations." Booklist

Includes bibliographical references

O'Neal, Michael
The **Crusades,** Almanac; written by Michael J. O'Neal; edited by Marcia Merryman Means and Neil Schlager. UXL 2005 xxv, 207p il (The Crusades reference library) $63

Grades: 11 12 Adult **909.07**
1. Crusades
ISBN 0-7876-9176-3
LC 2004-18003

This book "discusses such topics as the conquering of Jerusalem by the caliph Umar, pilgrimages to the Holy Land, the traditions of chivalry, and territorial expansion and colonization as motivations for the Crusades. Its explanation of the difference and divisions between Sunni and Shiite Islam alone is useful reading for a wider audience." Booklist
Includes bibliographical references

★ The **Oxford** illustrated history of the Crusades; edited by Jonathan Riley-Smith. Oxford Univ. Press 1995 436p il maps hardcover o.p. pa $26.50
Grades: 11 12 Adult **909.07**
1. Crusades
ISBN 0-19-820435-3; 0-19-285428-3 pa
LC 94-24229

Scholars explore the complex religious, economic, and military aspects of the Crusades.
Includes bibliographical references

909.08 Modern history, 1450/1500-

The **early** modern world, 1492 to 1783; [editor, Helen Dwyer] Brown Bear Books 2009 112p map (Curriculum connections. Atlas of world history) lib bdg $39.95
Grades: 9 10 11 12 **909.08**
1. Modern history 2. World history -- 16th century 3. World history -- 17th century 4. World history -- 18th century
ISBN 978-1-933834-68-9
LC 2009-27836

This book "is divided into thematic and regional maps which are followed by short but very comprehensive articles. . . . [It includes] curriculum context sidebars, important terms students should know, and how the topic ties into other areas." Libr Media Connect
Includes bibliographical references

The **Oxford** encyclopedia of the modern world; Peter N. Stearns, editor in chief. Oxford University Press 2008 8v il set $1,255
Grades: 9 10 11 12 Adult **909.08**
1. Reference books 2. Modern history -- Encyclopedias 3. Modern civilization -- Encyclopedias
ISBN 978-0-19-517632-2; 0-19-517632-4
LC 2007-39891

"This comprehensive and outstanding resource covers much more than Western civilization. It presents a balanced, inclusive perspective on historical, social, political, and economic issues that students will need in order to function in a global society. . . . Ideal for social studies classes that need well-written and researched information with a global perspective." SLJ
Includes bibliographical references

Tuchman, Barbara Wertheim
The **march** of folly; from Troy to Vietnam. [by] Barbara W. Tuchman. Knopf 1984 447p il hardcover o.p. pa $16.95
Grades: 11 12 Adult **909.08**
1. Popes 2. Trojan War 3. Reformation 4. Modern history 5. Vietnam War, 1961-1975 6. Great Britain -- Colonies -- America 7. United States -- History -- 1600-1775, Colonial period
ISBN 0-345-30823-9 pa
LC 83-22206

The author analyzes examples of governmental bumbling including the Trojan horse, the U.S. involvement in Vietnam, and the British loss of the American colonies.
Includes bibliographical references

909.7 Specific historical periods since 1700

Great events from history, The 18th century, 1701-1800; editor John Powell. Salem Press 2006 2v il map set $160
Grades: 11 12 Adult **909.7**
1. Reference books 2. World history -- 18th century
ISBN 978-1-58765-279-0; 1-58765-279-X
LC 2006-5406

Companion volume to Great lives from history, The 18th century, 1701-1800
Some essays previously published in Great events from history: North American series (1997) and Chronology of European history (1997)

"Topics include geopolitical events, social and intellectual issues, scientific developments, philosophy, and the arts. The global coverage emphasizes turning points that redirected and shaped history and helped create the modern world. Essays have an average length of 1600 words. Each one begins with a short summary of the topic and includes dates, locales, categories, key figures, text, significance, further reading, see-also references, and cross-referencing to other essays in this set and in the rest of the series. . . . An informative resource." SLJ
Includes bibliographical references

909.8 World history--1800-

Winkler, Allan M.
The **Cold** War; a history in documents. by Allan M. Winkler. 2nd ed. Oxford University Press 2011 ix, 160 p.p ill., maps (Pages from History) (paperback) $34.95; (hardcover) $42.95
Grades: 8 9 10 11 12 **909.8**
1. Cold War 2. United States -- Foreign relations -- Soviet Union 3. Cold War -- Sources 4. World politics -- 1945-1989 -- Sources 5. Russia -- Foreign relations -- United States -- Sources 6. United States -- Foreign relations -- Russia -- Sources
ISBN 0199765995; 9780199765980; 9780199765997
LC 2010049111

This book by Allan M. Winkler is part of the Pages from History series and "traces the evolution of the Cold War . . . .

By addressing the key issues of the Cold War via documents, the author provides a . . . look into a time that set the table for the modern era. Topics such as nuclear proliferation, McCarthyism, censorship, the Vietnam War and the Civil Rights Movement are all" addressed. (Children's Literature)

Includes bibliographical references and index.

909.81 World history--19th century, 1800-1899

Great events from history, The 19th century, 1801-1900; editor, John Powell. Salem Press 2006 4v il map set $360

Grades: 11 12 Adult   **909.81**
1. Reference books 2. World history -- 19th century
ISBN 978-1-58765-297-4; 1-58765-297-8

LC 2006-19789

Companion volume to Great lives from history, The 19th century, 1801-1900

Some of the essays in this work appeared in various other Salem Press sets

"These volumes cover the world's most important events and developments from 1801 through 1900. . . . Essays address important social and cultural developments in daily life: major literary movements, significant developments in art and music, trends in immigration, and progressive social legislation." Publisher's note

Includes bibliographical references

909.82 World history--20th century, 1900-1999

Cold War; a student encyclopedia. Spencer C. Tucker, volume editor; Priscilla Roberts, editor, documents volume; Paul G. Pierpaoli, Jr., associate editor; Timothy C. Dowling, Gordon E. Hogg, Priscilla Roberts, assistant editors; personal perspective foreword by John S.D. Eisenhower. ABC-CLIO 2007 5v il map set $495

Grades: 9 10 11 12   **909.82**
1. Reference books 2. Cold war -- Encyclopedias 3. World politics -- 1945- -- Encyclopedias
ISBN 978-1-85109-847-7

LC 2007-19820

Entries in this encyclopedia "focus on the years 1945 through 1995 and will help students understand the conflicts, the arms race, and the tense climate between the superpowers and their allies. . . . Volume five contains 171 primary-source documents, each preceded by an introduction to help readers grasp the situation surrounding the document's creation. Back matter includes the rank structure for selected Cold War militaries, brief country profiles, and essays on how to read primary sources, maps, charts, tables, and graphs. The comprehensiveness and clarity of this work make it a useful resource." SLJ

Includes bibliographical references

Encyclopedia of conflicts since World War II; edited by James Ciment. 2nd ed; M.E. Sharpe 2007 4v set $439

Grades: 11 12 Adult   **909.82**
1. Reference books 2. World politics -- 1945- -- Encyclopedias
ISBN 978-0-7656-8005-1; 0-7656-8005-X

LC 2006-14011

First published 1999

"The illustrations are strong and the maps helpful, and the thumbnail biographies and glossary are useful. A valuable resource for most school and public libraries." SLJ

Includes bibliographical references

Gaddis, John Lewis

The **Cold** War; a new history. Penguin Press 2005 333p il hardcover o.p. pa $16

Grades: 11 12 Adult   **909.82**
1. Cold war 2. World politics -- 1945-1991
ISBN 1-594-20062-9; 0-14-303827-3 pa

LC 2005-53406

"Energetically written and lucid, . . . [this book] makes an ideal introduction to the subject." N Y Times (Late N Y Ed)

Includes bibliographical references

Great events from history: The 20th century, 1901-1940; editor, Robert F. Gorman. Salem Press 2007 6v il map set $495

Grades: 11 12 Adult   **909.82**
1. Reference books 2. World history -- 20th century
ISBN 978-1-58765-324-7; 1-58765-324-9

LC 2007-1930

Some of the essays in this work originally appeared in various Salem Press publications

"This set provides access to clear, objective information, especially on topics in the sciences and mathematics." Libr J

Includes bibliographical references

Great events from history: The 20th century, 1941-1970; editor, Robert F. Gorman. Salem Press 2008 6v il map set $495

Grades: 11 12 Adult   **909.82**
1. Reference books 2. World history -- 20th century
ISBN 978-1-58765-331-5; 1-58765-331-1

LC 2007-37204

Some of the essays in this work originally appeared in various Salem Press publications

The articles in this set "cover everything from the bombing of Pearl Harbor to the celebration of the First Earth Day. Each article lists a locale, key figures, categories, and a summary of events; readers can search for additional information based on categories or key figures. The sixth volume contains a bibliography, personage, subject, category, and geographical indexes and a chronological list of entries. . . . An excellent cross-reference tool." Libr J

Includes bibliographical references

Great events from history: The 20th century, 1971-2000; editor, Robert F. Gorman. Salem Press 2008 6v il map set $495

Grades: 11 12 Adult   **909.82**

1. Reference books 2. World history -- 20th century

ISBN 978-1-58765-338-4; 1-58765-338-9

      LC 2007-51351

Some of the essays originally appeared in other Salem Press sets

This set "provides extended coverage of 1,083 major events between 1971 and 2000." Publisher's note

Includes bibliographical references

Hillstrom, Kevin

The **Cold** War; foreward by Christian Ostermann. Omnigraphics 2006 xx, 536p il (Primary sourcebook series) $65

Grades: 11 12 Adult   **909.82**

1. Cold war 2. World politics -- 1945-1991

ISBN 0-7808-0934-3; 978-0-7808-0934-5

      LC 2006-15330

"The wide-ranging scope of documents compiled in this volume will provide AP history and social studies classes with a wealth of information for research and analysis." Libr Media Connect

Includes glossary and bibliographical references

Kaufman, Michael T.

★ **1968**. Roaring Brook Press 2009 148p il $22.95

Grades: 7 8 9 10 11 12   **909.82**

1. World history -- 20th century

ISBN 978-1-59643-428-8; 1-59643-428-7

      LC 2008-15471

Kaufman "expertly draws young readers into the worldwide events of a single, watershed year: 1968. . . . Each chapter focuses on a different hot spot around the globe, beginning with the Tet Offensive and the Vietnam War and moving through uprisings in New York, Paris, Prague, Chicago, and Mexico City, as well as the assassinations of Martin Luther King Jr. and Robert F. Kennedy. . . . The images, drawn from the [New York] Times archives, are riveting and will easily draw young people into the fascinating, often horrifying events." Booklist

Knauer, Kelly

TIME History's Greatest Images; the World's 100 Most Influential Photographs. Time Home Entertainment 2012 154 p. $29.95

Grades: 10 11 12 Adult   **909.82**

1. World history 2. Photojournalism

ISBN 1603201971; 9781603201971

This book is a compilation of photographs that "TIME" magazine considers the "most significant and influential photos in history." Here are "scientific breakthroughs, political upheavals and social revolutions, from the first photographs of an embryo in a human womb to the indelible images of America's Civil Rights movement. Here are sailors kissing nurses, a single man defying a Chinese tank, firefighters raising the American flag over the ruins of the World Trade Center." (Publisher's note)

Palmowski, Jan

★ A **dictionary** of contemporary world history; from 1900 to the present day. 3rd ed.; Oxford University Press 2008 767p il map $50; pa $16.95

Grades: 9 10 11 12 Adult   **909.82**

1. Reference books 2. Modern history -- Dictionaries

ISBN 978-0-19-929567-8; 978-0-19-929566-1 pa

      LC 2008-273688

First published 1997 with title: A dictionary of twentieth-century world history

This dictionary's "2500-plus entries are clear and concise and cover everything from world leaders, both past and present, to . . . information on all the world's nations. . . . [This is a] simple and easy-to-use research tool." Libr J

Schwartz, Richard Alan

★ The **1990s**; [by] Richard A. Schwartz. Facts on File 2006 496p il (Eyewitness history) $75

Grades: 11 12 Adult   **909.82**

1. United States -- History -- 1989- 2. United States -- Politics and government -- 1989-

ISBN 0-8160-5696-X

      LC 2004-28884

This book "provides hundreds of firsthand accounts of the 1990s—including diary entries, letters, speeches, and newspaper accounts—that illustrate how historical events appeared to those who lived through them. Each chapter provides an introductory essay and a chronology of events." Publisher's note

Includes bibliographical references

Tuchman, Barbara Wertheim

The **proud** tower; a portrait of the world before the war, 1890-1914. [by] Barbara W. Tuchman. 1st Ballantine Books ed; Ballantine Books 1996 528p il pa $15.95

Grades: 11 12 Adult   **909.82**

1. Composers 2. Socialism 3. Anarchism and anarchists 4. Army officers 5. Europe -- Social conditions 6. World history -- 19th century 7. World history -- 20th century 8. United States -- Social conditions

ISBN 0-345-40501-3

      LC 96-96511

First published 1966 by Macmillan

The author describes prewar social conditions in the U.S., France, England and Germany.

Includes bibliographical references

World wars and globalization, 1914 to 2010; edited by Louise Spilsbury. Brown Bear Books 2010 112p map (Curriculum connections. Atlas of world history) lib bdg $39.95

Grades: 9 10 11 12   **909.82**

1. Globalization 2. Modern history 3. World history -- 20th century

ISBN 978-1-933834-70-2

      LC 2009-27838

This book "is divided into thematic and regional maps which are followed by short but very comprehensive articles. . . . [It includes] curriculum context sidebars, important terms students should know, and how the topic ties into other areas." Libr Media Connect

909.83   World history--21st century, 2000-2099

Snapshot; the visual almanac for our world today. commissioning editors, Jon Asbury, Peter Taylor; produced for Mitchell Beazley by CIRCA and Heritage Editorial. Mitchell Beazley; distributed by Octopus Books USA 2009 224p il $29.99

Grades: 9 10 11 12 Adult   **909.83**
1. Almanacs 2. Reference books 3. World history -- 21st century -- Pictorial works
ISBN 978-1-84533-523-6

"Broad thematic areas—environment, finance, culture—and specific topics within them—e.g., water, voting, music—are addressed on spreads covered with charts and graphs, archival photos, perceptive and concise comments tightly focused on important details, and Web resources. Intended to be bias free, the volume is highly successful and will appeal to nonfiction, fact-addicted browsers, teen researchers, and activists." SLJ

910   Geography and travel

Allaby, Michael

The **encyclopedia** of Earth; a complete visual guide. [authors, Michael Allaby ... [et al.]] University of California Press 2008 608p il map $39.95

Grades: 9 10 11 12 Adult   **910**
1. Reference books 2. Earth sciences -- Encyclopedias
ISBN 978-0-520-25471-8; 0-520-25471-6

LC 2008-6956

This "source includes six main sections. 'Birth' is an overview of Earth's history and evolution; 'Fire' covers its inner workings, structure, and landscape; 'Land' covers rocks, minerals, and habitats; 'Air' covers weather; 'Water' includes information on oceans, rivers, and lakes; and 'Humans' is about humankind's relationship with Earth, including management of its resources. . . . This is a stunning, reasonably priced resource, especially useful for those in need of illustrations or a visual representation of a phenomenon or concept." Choice

Elliott, Lynne

Exploration in the Renaissance; [by] Lynne Elliott. Crabtree 2009 32p il pa $8.95; lib bdg $26.60

Grades: 6 7 8 9   **910**
1. Renaissance 2. America -- Exploration 3. Discoveries in geography -- European
ISBN 978-0-7787-4613-3 pa; 978-0-7787-4593-8 lib bdg

LC 2008-52601

"Ideal introductions to concepts, people, and events of the Renaissance... succinct and thorough." SLJ

Wojtanik, Andrew, 1989-

The **National** Geographic Bee ultimate fact book; countries A to Z. Andrew Wojtanik. National Geographic 2012 384 p. maps (pbk.) $21.90; (reinforced library binding) $21.90

Grades: 5 6 7 8 9 10   **910**
1. Atlases 2. Nations 3. Geography 4. Geography -- Encyclopedias
ISBN 1426309473; 1426309635; 9781426309472; 9781426309632

LC 2011282873

This book "provides statistical information for the world's 195 countries at a glance. The book starts off with a world map and full-page continental maps. Individual entries for countries are listed alphabetically. . . . A glossary explains terms that may be unfamiliar to students . . . . Each country entry includes a map with longitude and latitude and basic facts: continent, size, population, and capital." (Voice of Youth Advocates)

Includes bibliographical references (p. 382)

910.2   Geography--Miscellany; world travel guides

100 great journeys; consultant editor, Keith Lye. Hammond World Atlas Corp 2008 191p il map $24.95

Grades: 8 9 10 11 12   **910.2**
1. Reference books 2. Voyages and travels
ISBN 978-0-8437-0994-0; 0-8437-0994-4

"The title covers road trips, historical journeys, explorations, voyages, sacred routes, military campaigns and trails, treks, 'natural splendors,' and literary jaunts, with each spread focusing on one. The colorful maps are prominent against the white pages but not always the main focus; quality color photos and reproductions, multiple shaded sidebars (including short lists of relevant titles), and pull quotes compete for attention. . . . It would be a shame to limit copies of this book to the reference shelves." SLJ

Hillstrom, Laurie Collier

Global positioning systems. Lucent Books 2011 96p il map (Technology 360) lib bdg $33.45

Grades: 7 8 9 10   **910.2**
1. Global Positioning System
ISBN 978-1-4205-0325-8; 1-4205-0325-1

LC 2010030623

This offers "clean design with clear explanations of sometimes-complicated scientific subjects. . . . Global Positioning Systems discusses how GPS was developed, from its origins in the military to everyday life uses, such as tracking pets. . . . . A strong [title] for report writers and students with a serious interest in technology and its inventions." Booklist

Includes bibliographical references

Unesco

World heritage sites; a complete guide to 911 UNESCO world heritage sites. Rev. and updated; Firefly Books 2011 856p il map pa $29.95

Grades: 9 10 11 12 Adult   **910.2**
1. Historic sites 2. Reference books 3. Historic buildings 4. Unesco -- World Heritage Committee
ISBN 978-1-55407-827-1; 1-55407-827-X
LC 2010-671075

First published 2009
Each site has an entry explaining its historical and cultural significance, with a description and location map.

"UNESCO's World Heritage mission is to encourage the identification, protection, and preservation of cultural and natural heritage around the world considered to be of outstanding value to humanity. This treasure trove of a book reinforces that mission and, through spectacular photographs, shows how remarkable and beautiful our planet truly is. An excellent (and affordable) addition to any library." Libr J

910.3 Geography--Dictionaries, encyclopedias, concordances, gazetteers

The **Columbia** gazetteer of the world; edited by Saul B. Cohen. 2nd ed.; Columbia University Press 2008 3v set $595
Grades: 11 12 Adult   **910.3**
1. Gazetteers 2. Reference books
ISBN 978-0-231-14554-1
LC 2008-9181

First published 1952 with title: The Columbia Lippincott gazetteer of the world
"The 170,000-plus entries cover political, physical, and special places, including monuments and historic sites. . . . Historically accurate, this title can be considered a reference standard." Libr J

★ **Merriam**-Webster's geographical dictionary; 3rd ed; Merriam-Webster 1997 1361p maps $32.95
Grades: 11 12 Adult   **910.3**
1. Reference books 2. Geography -- Dictionaries
ISBN 0-87779-546-0
LC 96-52365

First published 1949 with title: Webster's geographical dictionary
This guide contains data about countries, cities, and physical features. More than 48,000 entries and over 250 maps provide population, size, economic data and historical notes. Pronunciations are included and a table of foreign terms used in English is provided.

The **Oxford** companion to world exploration; David Buisseret, editor in chief. Oxford University Press 2007 2v il map set $250
Grades: 9 10 11 12 Adult   **910.3**
1. Exploration
ISBN 0-19-514922-X; 978-0-19-514922-7
LC 2006-27968

"The entries are presented in alphabetical order and cover not only individual explorers, but also some geographic regions, wars, commercial operations, and religious organizations. . . . This work will become the first stop for students and general readers who seek either basic information or a starting point for further reading." Sci Books Films
Includes bibliographical references

Worldmark encyclopedia of the nations; [Timothy L. Gall and M. Hobby, editors] 12th ed; Thomson Gale 2007 5v set il map $535.00
Grades: 11 12 Adult   **910.3**
1. United Nations 2. Reference books 3. History 4. Economics 5. Geography 6. Political science 7. Geography -- Encyclopedias 8. World history -- Encyclopedias 9. World politics -- Encyclopedias
ISBN 1414410891
First published 1960
"Factual and statistical information on the countries of the world, exhibited in uniform format under such rubrics as topography, population, public finance, language, and ethnic composition. Country articles appear in volumes 2 through 5, arranged geographically by continent. Volume 1 is devoted to the United Nations and its affiliated agencies. Illustrations, maps." Ref Sources for Small & Medium-sized Libr. 6th edition

910.4 Accounts of travel and facilities for travelers

Anderson, Harry S.
Exploring the polar regions; rev ed.; Chelsea House 2010 116p il map (Discovery and exploration) lib bdg $35
Grades: 7 8 9 10   **910.4**
1. Polar regions -- Exploration
ISBN 978-1-60413-190-1; 1-60413-190-X
LC 2009-22863

First published 2004 by Facts on File
Covers exploration and discovery of the Arctic and Antarctic regions.
"The chapters are well-illustrated with color and black and white historic photos, illustrations and maps. Chapter layout is clearly organized with helpful subtitles; sidebars develop related themes in eye-catching colors. . . . [This book] attractively and effectively surveys an important . . . area in world studies." Libr Media Connect
Includes glossary and bibliographical references

The **Britannica** guide to explorers and explorations that changed the modern world; edited by Kenneth Pletcher. Britannica Educational Pub., in association with Rosen Educational Services 2010 350p il (Turning points in history) lib bdg $45
Grades: 9 10 11 12   **910.4**
1. Explorers 2. Exploration
ISBN 978-1-61530-028-0
LC 2009-37672

Details discovery expeditions and explorers from throughout history, including exploration of North America, the polar regions, and Mount Everest, and describes archaeological finds including Machu Picchu, Pompeii, and Easter Island.
Includes glossary and bibliographical references

Butler, Daniel Allen
Unsinkable: the full story of the RMS Titanic. Stackpole Bks. 1998 292p il $19.95

Grades: 11 12 Adult   **910.4**
1. Shipwrecks 2. Titanic (Steamship)
ISBN 0-8117-1814-X

LC 98-9294

This is a history "of the disaster and aftermath, drawing on first-person accounts and solid secondary sources." Libr J
Includes bibliographical references

Delaney, Frank
Simple courage; a true story of peril on the sea. Random House 2006 300p il hardcover o.p. pa $14.95
Grades: 11 12 Adult   **910.4**
1. Shipwrecks 2. Ship captains 3. Flying Enterprise (Ship)
ISBN 1-4000-6524-0; 978-1-4000-6524-0; 0-8129-7595-2 pa; 978-0-8129-7595-6 pa

LC 2006-41766

This book tells the story "of Captain Kurt Carlsen and the Flying Enterprise. On Christmas Day 1951, the World War II Liberty ship Flying Enterprise began splitting apart in a North Atlantic gale, and her cargo of pig iron shifted. Captain Carlsen saw to the safe abandonment of passengers and crew, then remained aboard to help with salvage efforts. He remained aboard, accompanied only by a young radioman who leaped aboard from a rescue ship, until the Flying Enterprise was about to sink under him." Booklist
Includes bibliographical references

Fleming, Fergus
Off the map; tales of endurance and exploration. as told by Fergus Fleming. Atlantic Monthly Press 2005 518p il maps $24.95; pa $16
Grades: 11 12 Adult   **910.4**
1. Explorers 2. Exploration
ISBN 0-8711-3899-9; 0-8021-4272-9 pa

LC 2005-47849

First published 2004 in the United Kingdom
"Almost comprehensive enough to serve as a reference, this densely packed tome supplies a bewildering wealth of information about some of humanity's most compelling adventures." Publ Wkly
Includes bibliographical references

Gilkerson, William
A **thousand** years of pirates. Tundra Books 2009 96p il map $32.95
Grades: 6 7 8 9 10   **910.4**
1. Pirates
ISBN 978-0-88776-924-5; 0-88776-924-1
"Pirates are given scholarly scrutiny in this handsome and invigorating overview. Short but dense chapters introduce the major factions, characters, and incidents that connect the scattered history of seagoing bandits. . . . Gilkerson's grasp of the politics surrounding each nation's pirates . . . is most impressive." Booklist
Includes bibliographical references

Heyerdahl, Thor
Kon-Tiki; across the Pacific by raft. translated by F.H. Lyon. Washington Square Press 1984 240p map (Enriched classics series) pa $5.99
Grades: 11 12 Adult   **910.4**
1. Pacific Ocean 2. Ethnology -- Polynesia 3. Kon-Tiki Expedition (1947)
ISBN 0-671-72652-8

LC 84-42785

Original Norwegian edition, 1948
The "story of the six men who crossed the Pacific from Peru to the Polynesians on a primitive balsa-log raft such as Peruvian natives of the fifth century used, to prove that it was possible that the legendary race that came to Easter Island and the Polynesians could have come from Peru." Wis Libr Bull

Jacobson, Mark
12,000 miles in the nick of time; a semi-dysfunctional family circumnavigates the globe. with additional commentary by Rae Jacobson. Atlantic Monthly Press 2003 271p il maps hardcover o.p. pa $13
Grades: 11 12 Adult   **910.4**
1. Voyages around the world
ISBN 0-8021-4138-2 pa

LC 2003-41821

"The book is very funny—the trip doesn't go exactly as the parents plan—but it is also hugely educational, history presented as a grand adventure. The kids learned a lot, and so do we." Booklist
Includes bibliographical references

Junger, Sebastian
The **perfect** storm; a true story of men against the sea. Norton 1997 226p il map $23.95; pa $14.95
Grades: 11 12 Adult   **910.4**
1. Storms 2. Shipwrecks
ISBN 0-393-04016-X; 0-393-33701-4 pa

LC 96-42412

"With waves as high as a hundred feet and winds so strong that anemometers were torn from their moorings, the storm of the title struck unsuspecting mariners off the coast of Nova Scotia in October, 1991. Junger traces the last voyage of the Andrea Gail—a commercial swordfishing boat that was lost, with all six hands, in the storm—and his account is relentlessly suspenseful." New Yorker

Kinder, Gary
Ship of gold in the deep blue sea. Atlantic Monthly Press 1998 507p hardcover o.p. pa $16.95
Grades: 11 12 Adult   **910.4**
1. Shipwrecks 2. Central America (Steamship)
ISBN 978-0-8021-4425-6

LC 97-49812

"On September 12, 1857, the steamship Central America sank in a great storm off the coast of South Carolina and settled a mile and a half beneath the waves. Most of the 423 souls on board perished. Lost, too, was $2,189,000 (now worth $1 billion) in California gold. . . . In 1989, a group of investors and treasure salvagers equipped with the latest underwater equipment was able to bring back much of the cargo, including the largest treasure ever recorded. The discovery of this vessel and its riches led to protracted litigation between various claimants, and the case is still in the courts. Kinder has followed the story from its beginning." Libr J

Konstam, Angus

★ The **world** atlas of pirates; treasures and treachery on the seven seas, in maps, tall tales, and pictures. The Lyons Press 2010 247p il map $29.95

Grades: 10 11 12 Adult   910.4

1. Pirates

ISBN 978-1-59921-474-0

The author "explains how piracy grew and flourished from the early buccaneers to the rogues of popular legends, how it has been snuffed out, and how it has reared its head again with the machine-gun-toting pirates operating on today's high seas." Publisher's note

Lavery, Brian

The **conquest** of the ocean; the illustrated history of seafaring. Brian Lavery. Dk Pub 2013 400 p. $30

Grades: 8 9 10 11 12   910.4

1. Seafaring life 2. Maritime history

ISBN 146540841X; 9781465408419

This book offers a "survey of humanity's history on the seas." It "begins about 30,000 years ago with Polynesian seafarers' colonization of Pacific islands and continues through to address harrowing accounts of modern-day piracy. Ports of call between these distant coasts include the treasure voyages of Ming official Zheng He, the discovery of the New World, the invention of the Fresnel lens, the Battle of Midway, and many others." (Publishers Weekly)

Macleod, Alasdair

Explorers; great tales of adventure and endurance. Royal Geographical Society; [written by Alasdair Macleod] DK in association with the Smithsonian Institution 2010 360p il $40

Grades: 11 12 Adult   910.4

1. Explorers 2. Exploration

ISBN 978-0-7566-6737-5

"The book covers the history of exploration from the discovery of the ancient Egyptians in Nubia to the exploration of space by the Soviet Union and the United States in the 20th century. . . . [It] is a wonderful introduction to the various personalities who, over a period of several thousand years, devoted themselves, to studying the world and revealing its fascinatingly diverse landscapes, conditions, and cultures." Sci Books Films

Nardo, Don

Polar explorations; by Don Nardo. Lucent Books 2011 104 p. ill., col. maps, photographs (library) $34.95

Grades: 6 7 8 9   910.4

1. Polar regions -- Exploration 2. Exploration 3. Explorers -- Polar regions -- Biography

ISBN 142050360X; 9781420503609

LC 2010039667

This book by Don Nardo is part of the World History series and looks at polar explorations. The series "examines the eras, events, civilizations, and movements that have shaped human history, providing readers with insight into the past and its many legacies. Vivid writing, full-color photographs and extensive use of fully cited primary and secondary source quotations provide a sense of immediacy." (Publisher's note)

Includes bibliographical references and (p. 95-97) index.

National Geographic Society (U.S.)

Return to Titanic; a new look at the world's most famous lost ship. [by] Robert D. Ballard with Michael Sweeney. National Geographic Society 2004 192p il map $30

Grades: 11 12 Adult   910.4

1. Shipwrecks 2. Underwater exploration 3. Titanic (Steamship)

ISBN 0-7922-7288-9

LC 2004-55930

The author reviews Titanic's "history and the catastrophic events that led to her demise. He describes his dream of turning the ship into a museum on the ocean floor, easily explored from above by computer. . . . It's Ballard's passion and expertise that make this book tick." Publ Wkly

Includes bibliographical references

Netzley, Patricia D.

Encyclopedia of women's travel and exploration. Oryx Press 2000 259p il $88.95

Grades: 11 12 Adult   910.4

1. Reference books 2. Women -- Travel -- Encyclopedias 3. Voyages and travels -- Encyclopedias

ISBN 1-573-56238-6; 978-1-57356-238-6

LC 00-10720

"The 315 entries, arranged alphabetically, focus on a wide variety of women explorers, adventurers, and travelers throughout history and across continents. Most entries are biographical, but some examine related topics such as accommodations, solo travel, guide books, and mountaineering, occasionally offering perceptive insights into women's travel experiences and motivations." Choice

Includes bibliographical references

Paine, Lincoln P.

Ships of discovery and exploration. Houghton Mifflin 2000 188p il maps pa $17

Grades: 11 12 Adult   910.4

1. Ships 2. Exploration

ISBN 0-395-98415-7

LC 00-40802

A look at 125 vessels that have played significant roles in voyages of geographical exploration and scientific discovery. The physical characteristics, construction, and history of each ship is described. Chronologies cover underwater archaeology sites, maritime technology, exploration, and disasters at sea. Illustrated with drawings paintings, photographs, and maps

Includes bibliographical references (p.)

Philbrick, Nathaniel

In the heart of the sea; the tragedy of the whaleship Essex. Viking 2000 302p il pa $15; $24.95

Grades: 11 12 Adult   **910.4**

1. Shipwrecks 2. Essex (Whaleship) 3. Shipwrecks -- Pacific Ocean

ISBN 0141001828 pa; 0670891576

LC 99-53740

Philbrick examines the events on which Melville's novel Moby-Dick was based. In November 1820, "halfway around the world from its home port of Nantucket, Mass., while chasing whales in the South Seas, the 238-ton whaler Essex was rammed and sunk by an angry sperm whale. . . . After the whale struck, Captain George Pollard Jr. and his crew took to their whaleboats." (Time) Bibliography. Index.

"On November 20, 1820, the Nantucket whaleship Essex was rammed by a large sperm whale and sank in the Pacific, 'just about as far from land as it was possible to be anywhere on earth.' The episode inspired Melville, but this climactic moment proves less interesting than the story of the survivors' voyage in the ship's whaleboats, a months-long ordeal that included madness and cannibalism. Philbrick nicely links the experiences aboard ship with the values of Nantucket society." New Yorker

Read, Piers Paul

Alive; sixteen men, seventy-two days, and insurmountable odds--the classic adventure of survival in the Andes. Harper Perennial 2005 398p il pa $13.95

Grades: 11 12 Adult   **910.4**

1. Survival after airplane accidents, shipwrecks, etc. 2. Andes

ISBN 0-06-077866-0

First published 1974 by Lippincott

The author describes the extraordinary hardships endured by the survivors of a horrific plane crash in the Andes.

Scieszka, Casey

To Timbuktu; words, Casey Scieszka; art, Steven Weinberg. Roaring Brook Press 2011 478p il pa $19.99

Grades: 9 10 11 12   **910.4**

1. American travelers 2. Voyages around the world

ISBN 978-1-59643-527-8

LC 2010-27627

This "is a travelogue that will provide great inspiration for teenagers and young adults who are looking for adventure and self-discovery. After college graduation, Scieszka and her boyfriend set off on an almost two-year jaunt to various parts of Asia and Africa where they lived, worked, and learned far from their homes in the States. She journaled with words while Weinberg did so with sketched illustrations, and the result is an appealing and engaging tale of the ups and downs of their journey." SLJ

Vail, Martha

Exploring the Pacific; [by] Martha Vail; John S. Bowman and Maurice Isserman, general editors. rev

ed.; Chelsea House 2010 120p il map (Discovery and exploration) $35

Grades: 7 8 9 10   **910.4**

1. Explorers 2. Pacific Ocean

ISBN 978-1-60413-197-0; 1-60413-197-7

LC 2009-22106

First published 2005 by Facts on File

"The chapters are well-illustrated with color and black and white historic photos, illustrations, and maps. Chapter layout is clearly organized with helpful subtitles; sidebars develop related themes in catching colors." Libr Media Connect

Includes glossary and bibliographical references

White, Pamela

Exploration in the world of the Middle Ages, 500-1500; Pamela White, John S. Bowman, and Maurice Isserman, general editors. Rev. ed.; Chelsea House 2010 132p il map (Discovery and exploration) $35

Grades: 7 8 9 10   **910.4**

1. Explorers 2. Exploration 3. Middle Ages

ISBN 978-1-60413-193-2; 1-60413-193-4

LC 2009-30202

First published 2005 by Facts On File

This describes world exploration in the Middle Ages by pilgrims and missionaries, the Vikings, Muslim travelers, Europeans seeking Asia, Marco Polo, and Portuguese sailors, and describes Medieval legends of mythical monsters and lands

Includes glossary and bibliographical references

911   Historical geography

Atlas of classical history; edited by Richard J.A. Talbert. Routledge 1988 217p maps pa $37.95

Grades: 9 10 11 12   **911**

1. Reference books 2. Historical atlases

ISBN 0-415-03463-9

LC 89-162237

First published 1985 by Macmillan

"Covers Greek and Roman history from Troy and Knossos to the Roman Empire in 314 CE. The black-and-white maps, though small, are very clear. Many city maps. The text is brief, in many cases good mainly for identification, a skeletal history, or verification of a few key dates." Guide to Ref Books. 11th edition

★ **Atlas** of exploration; cartography by Philip's; foreword by John Hemming. Oxford University Press 2008 256p il map $50

Grades: 9 10 11 12 Adult   **911**

1. Reference books 2. Exploration -- Atlases

ISBN 978-0-19-534318-2

LC 2008-626565

First published 1998 with title: Oxford atlas of exploration

"This atlas describes many of the explorations and participants that changed history and enhanced man's knowledge and perception of the world. . . . The volume is a visual delight, festooned with more than 100 specially drawn maps and 300 b&w and color photographs, period paintings, and illustrations on the various explorations." Libr Media Connect

Goetzmann, William H.

The **atlas** of North American exploration; from the Norse voyages to the race to the Pole. [by] William H. Goetzmann, Glyndwr Williams; [cartographic director, Malcolm Swanston; maps created by Isabelle Lewis and Jacqueline Land] University of Okla. Press 1998 222p il map pa $29.95

Grades: 9 10 11 12   **911**
1. Explorers 2. Reference books 3. Historical atlases 4. America -- Exploration
ISBN 0-8061-3058-X
     LC 97-45731

First published 1992

"This survey atlas, emphasizing exploration from the late 1400s to the late 1800s, is firmly directed toward a general audience. It features excellent color maps and illustrations with two-page 'spreads,' each devoted to the analysis of a particular explorer and each with extracts from the explorer's journals (translated to English if necessary). The atlas takes Columbus and his predecessors as a starting point, and covers all of North America. . . . The writers have endeavored to maintain an objective tone, and in the bibliography give full citations for works mentioned in the text." Libr J

Includes bibliographical references

Hayes, Derek

Historical atlas of the United States; with original maps. University of California Press 2007 280p il map $45

Grades: 11 12 Adult   **911**
1. Atlases 2. Reference books 3. United States -- Historical geography -- Maps
ISBN 978-0-520-25036-9; 0-520-25036-2
     LC 2006-42405

"Hayes has produced an excellent visual history of the land that became the US. The work includes 535 maps gathered from a variety of international collections, coupled with more than 60 other illustrations to chronicle the expansion and development of the nation over the last 500 years." Choice

Includes bibliographical references

Magocsi, Paul R.

Historical atlas of Central Europe; [by] Paul Robert Magocsi. rev and expanded ed; University of Wash. Press 2002 274p maps (History of East Central Europe) hardcover o.p. pa $45

Grades: 11 12 Adult   **911**
1. Atlases 2. Reference books 3. Central Europe -- Historical geography -- Maps
ISBN 0-295-98146-6
     LC 2001-27907

First published 1993 with title: Historical atlas of East Central Europe

"The volume is arranged chronologically, with coverage beginning about A.D. 400 (roughly the time of the demise

of the Roman Empire) and continuing through the end of the 20th century. The maps and tables provide information on military affairs; population and population movements; economy; ethnolinguistic distributions; and religious, cultural, and educational institutions. All are extremely well done." SLJ

Nash, Gary B.

★ **Atlas** of American history; [by] Gary B. Nash and Carter Smith. Facts on File 2006 346p il map (Facts on File library of American history) $95

Grades: 9 10 11 12   **911**
1. Atlases 2. Reference books 3. United States -- Historical geography -- Maps
ISBN 0-8160-5952-7; 978-0-8160-5952-2
     LC 2006-15915

This book "uses more than 200 full-color maps to help bring into focus both the dramatic events and enduring developments that have shaped our national heritage." Publisher's note

Includes bibliographical references

The **new** cultural atlas of China; edited by Tim Cooke. Marshall Cavendish Corp. 2010 192p il map lib bdg $99.93

Grades: 7 8 9 10   **911**
1. Atlases 2. Reference books 3. China -- Maps
ISBN 978-0-7614-7875-1; 0-7614-7875-2
     LC 2009-8600

An account of the world's oldest living civilization, exploring Chinese culture and society from the earliest times to the glories of the imperial age.

Includes glossary and bibliographical references

912   Graphic representations of surface of earth and of extraterrestrial worlds

Aczel, Amir D.

The **riddle** of the compass; the invention that changed the world. Harcourt 2001 178p il maps hardcover o.p. pa $13

Grades: 11 12 Adult   **912**
1. Compass
ISBN 0-15-100506-0; 0-15-600753-3 pa
     LC 00-47153

This book tracks "down the roots of the compass and tells the story of navigation through the ages." Publisher's note

Includes bibliographical references

★ **Atlas** of the World; [prepared by National Geographic Maps for the Book Division] Random House Inc 2014 448 p. 1 atlas; color maps; color ils $195

Grades: 4 5 6 7 8 9 10 11 12 Adult   **912**
1. Atlases
ISBN 1426213549; 9781426213540
     LC 200445002

This book presents "illustrated maps and informational graphics [that] chart rapidly changing global themes such as population trends, urbanization, health and longevity, human migration, climate change, communications, and the world economy. The core of any atlas is the reference mapping section and the 10th Edition boasts the largest and most comprehensive collection of political maps ever published by National Geographic." (Publisher's note)

Firefly atlas of North America; United States, Canada & Mexico. Firefly Books 2006 272p il map $55

Grades: 11 12 Adult　　　　　　　　　**912**
1. Atlases 2. Reference books
ISBN 978-1-55407-207-1; 1-55407-207-7

This atlas is "divided into three sections covering the United States (including Puerto Rico and the U.S. Pacific Territories), Canada and Mexico. . . . Each country section opens with a map and a color-coded legend to the regional maps that follow. All 50 U.S. states (plus Washington, D.C.), the 13 Canadian provinces and territories (including Nunavut) and Mexico's 32 states are illustrated." Publisher's note

Hollingum, Ben
Maps and mapping the world; [Ben Hollingum, editor] Gareth Stevens Pub. 2010 48p il map lib bdg $31; pa $14.95

Grades: 6 7 8 9　　　　　　　　　　**912**
1. Maps
ISBN 978-1-4339-3498-8 lib bdg; 1-4339-3498-1 lib bdg; 978-1-4339-3501-5 pa; 1-4339-3501-5 pa
LC 2009-37275

"These fascinating books open with an identical whirlwind time line of cartographic history, beginning with a map of the world as 15th-century Europeans knew it and ending with the first photos of Earth taken from space...Related events and topics also spring up... The books' further-reading lists, which include print and Web materials, are particularly extensive. Wonderful resources." SLJ

Travel maps; [Ben Hollingum, editor] Gareth Stevens Pub. 2010 48p il map lib bdg $31; pa $14.95

Grades: 6 7 8 9　　　　　　　　　　**912**
1. Maps
ISBN 978-1-4339-3506-0 lib bdg; 1-4339-3506-6 lib bdg; 978-1-4339-3507-7 pa; 1-4339-3507-4 pa
LC 2009-37277

"These fascinating books open with an identical whirlwind time line of cartographic history...descriptions of cartographic challenges, old and new, result in a lot of valuable extras–. Wonderful resources." SLJ

National Geographic Society (U.S.)
National Geographic Atlas of China. National Geographic Society 2008 128p il map $26

Grades: 11 12 Adult　　　　　　　　　**912**
1. Atlases 2. Reference books 3. China -- Maps
ISBN 978-1-4262-0136-3
LC 2008-299395

This atlas of China "maps the entire country with sections covering all provinces—including towns, cities, and transportation networks." Publisher's note

National Geographic student world atlas; 4th edition Natl Geographic Soc Childrens books 2014 143 p. lib bdg $28.90; hbk $19.99; pbk $12.99

Grades: 6 7 8 9 10　　　　　　　　　**912**
ISBN 9781426317767; 9781426317774; 1426317751; 1426317778; 142631776X; 9781426317750
Previously titled Student Atlas of the World

"Topics covered include information about maps in general, the history of the earth, global climates, political systems, elevations, populations, cultures, economies, and more. Maps are easy to read with clear legends and symbols. A featured topic related to each continent is highlighted and explained in more depth. Interesting fun facts are added to each page." Lib Med Conn

★ **National** Geographic visual atlas of the world. National Geographic Society 2009 416p il map $100

Grades: 11 12 Adult　　　　　　　　　**912**
1. Atlases 2. Reference books
ISBN 978-1-4262-0332-9
LC 2008-627044

This atlas "has the usual atlas features but emphasizes the more than 850 UNESCO World Heritage Sites. . . . Double-page spreads of regional maps are framed with four to six color photographs of the heritage sites that are indicated on the map. . . . Beautiful color photography and clear topical material combined with detailed maps of areas not covered as well in other world atlases make the Visual Atlas a recommended purchase. This is a first choice for any library needing a new medium-priced atlas." Booklist
Includes bibliographical references

★ The **new** atlas of the Arab world. American University in Cairo Press 2010 144p il map $39.50

Grades: 11 12 Adult　　　　　　　　　**912**
1. Atlases 2. Reference books 3. Arab countries -- Maps
ISBN 978-977-416-419-4

This atlas contains maps of the Arab world "showing physical features, political boundaries, towns, and communication networks. In addition, each of the twenty-two countries is the subject of an illustrated essay, with notes and . . . statistics on the geography, population, history and politics, and economy of the country. The countries covered are: Algeria, Bahrain, Comoros, Djibouti, Egypt, Iraq, Jordan, Kuwait, Lebanon, Libya, Mauritania, Morocco, Oman, Palestine, Qatar, Saudi Arabia, Somalia, Sudan, Syria, Tunisia, United Arab Emirates, Yemen." Publisher's note

★ **Oxford** Atlas of the world; [cartography by Philip's] 19th ed. Oxford University Press 2012 448 p. il map (hardcover) $89.95

Grades: 7 8 9 10 11 12 Adult　　　　　　**912**
1. Atlases 2. Earth -- Maps 3. Physical geography 4. Reference books
ISBN 0199937826; 9780199937820
LC 20100594813

First published 1992. Frequently revised. Variant title: Atlas of the world

This world atlas offers "new census information, dozens of city maps . . . satellite images of Earth, and a geographical glossary." It " provides details on such topics as climate, the greenhouse effect, employment and industry, standards of living, agriculture, population and migration, and global conflicts." (Publisher's note)

"...[U]pdated annually, this large-format resource continues to earn pride of place on the atlas case's top shelf for its combination of currency and eye-widening graphics. The physical, political, and country and regional maps that make up the volume's core are works of art-brilliantly designed for easy comprehension, rendered in bright colors and sharp detail... Atlases are among the quickest reference sources to age, so for classroom or library collections in which students search in vain...this makes a first-rate replacement." SLJ

Oxford new concise world atlas; [cartography by Philip's; text, Keith Lye]. 3rd ed; Oxford University Press 2010 1 atlas (224 p.) col. ill., col. maps $39.95
Grades: 6 7 8 9 10 11 12 Adult 912
1. Atlases 2. Reference books
ISBN 0195393295; 9780195393293
LC 2009292676
Containing over 100 pages of the most up-to-date topographic and political maps, the New Concise World Atlas also features a unique overview of the planet's human and natural processes in photographs, accessible text, and thematic maps. (Publisher's note)

"This update of the 2006 edition contains 128 pages of full-color, computer-generated maps by Philip's, a division of Octopus Publishing, with detailed and dramatic terrain modeling... This condensed and abridged version of the premium Oxford Atlas of the World offers all libraries outstanding value in an up-to-date, medium-sized atlas for an amazingly low price.—" LJ
Includes index.

Panchyk, Richard
Charting the world; geography and maps from cave paintings to GPS with 21 activities. by Richard Panchyk. Chicago Review Press 2011 xi, 132 p.p ill., maps (some col.) (paperback) $18.95
Grades: 7 8 9 10 912
1. Maps 2. Cartography -- Maps
ISBN 1569763445; 9781569763445
LC 2011019317
Author "[Richard] Panchyk's book helps explain why maps are exciting, how they expand our world, and have done so for generations. . . . Maps document the lay of the land, the placement of cities, and the height of mountains, among many other things. Panchyk walks us through these mapmaking skills, offering activities along the way. . . .Panchyk also provides sidebars about such notable explorers as Amerigo Vespucci, for whom America was named." (Children's Literature)
Includes bibliographical references (p. 126-127) and index.

Rand McNally Goodes World Atlas; edited by Howard Veregin. Rand McNally 2009 400 p. $45
Grades: 4 5 6 7 8 9 10 11 12 Adult 912
1. Maps 2. Atlases
ISBN 0528877542; 9780528877544

This book, edited by Howard Veregin, "features over 250 pages of maps, from definitive physical and political maps to important thematic maps that illustrate the spatial aspects of many important topics. [It] includes 160 pages of new, digitally produced reference maps, as well as new thematic maps on global climate change, sea level rise, CO_2 emissions, polar ice fluctuations, deforestation, extreme weather events, infectious diseases, water resources, and energy production." (Publisher's note)

The **Times** comprehensive atlas of the world; by The Times UK. 14th edition Trafalgar Square 2014 544 p. illustrations, maps $200
Grades: 9 10 11 12 Adult 912
1. Atlases
ISBN 0007551401; 9780007551408
LC 2012358515
This book is a "prestigious and authoritative world atlas. . . . New features include a double page map of the Arctic Ocean, new maps of sub-ice features in the Arctic Ocean and the Antarctic, and physical maps of all the continents. Major updates include 5,000 place name changes; . . . a beautifully illustrated section on current issues from climate to economy; updated national parks and conserved areas; . . . and towns and populations in Brazil and Japan." (Publisher's note)

913 Geography of and travel in ancient world

Bowman, John Stewart
Exploration in the world of the ancients; by John S. Bowman; John S. Bowman and Maurice Isserman, general editors. Rev. ed.; Chelsea House 2010 109p il map (Discovery and exploration) $35
Grades: 7 8 9 10 913
1. Explorers 2. Exploration 3. Ancient geography
ISBN 978-1-60413-191-8; 1-60413-191-8
LC 2009-18849
First published 2005 by Facts On File
"This book examines some of the earliest accounts of Egyptian and Mesopotamian explorations, as well as covering the Romans, Greeks, Phoenicians, and other ancient peoples. It concludes at the beginning of the Middle Ages." Publisher's note
Includes glossary and bibliographical references

915 Geography of and travel in Asia

Belliveau, Denis
In the footsteps of Marco Polo; [by] Denis Belliveau and Francis O'Donnell. Rowman & Littlefield Publishers 2008 280p il map $29.95
Grades: 9 10 11 12 Adult 915
1. Travelers 2. Travel writers 3. Asia -- Description and travel
ISBN 978-0-7425-5683-6; 0-7425-5683-2
LC 2008-23411
"The stunning photographs in this elegant book should please even the most casual reader, while the authors' un-

pretentious observations will satisfy those who want to know more about a still alien world. A travel/adventure book rather than a study of Marco Polo the man or a history of his travels, this volume deserves many readers. Warmly recommended." Libr J

Includes bibliographical references

Polo, Marco

The **travels** of Marco Polo; edited and revised from William Marsden's translation, by Manuel Komroff; introduction by Jason Goodwin. Modern Library pbk. ed.; Modern Library 2001 322p map pa $13.95

Grades: 11 12 Adult   915

1. Voyages and travels 2. Asia -- Description and travel
ISBN 0-375-75818-6

LC 2001-45030

An autobiographical account of Marco Polo's thirteenth century travels in Asia.

916 Geography of and travel in Africa

Benanav, Michael

Men of salt; across the Sahara with the caravan of white gold. Lyons Press 2006 220p il map $23.95

Grades: 11 12 Adult   916

1. Salt 2. Sahara Desert -- Description and travel
ISBN 1-59228-772-7; 978-1-59228-772-7

LC 2005-23205

"Even if readers don't find the idea of spending 40 harrowing days with a caravan crossing some of the world's most unforgiving desert as enticing as Benanav does, that doesn't mean they won't quickly devour his thrilling account of that otherworldly journey." Publ Wkly

Includes bibliographical references

917 Geography of and travel in North America

The **Columbia** gazetteer of North America; edited by Saul B. Cohen. Columbia Univ. Press 2000 1157p il $156

Grades: 11 12 Adult   917

1. North America -- Gazetteers
ISBN 0-231-11990-9

LC 00-27512

"This work includes more than 50,000 entries covering every incorporated place and country in the United States, along with many unincorporated places and physical features throughout North America. Arranged alphabetically, each entry includes a pronunciation guide, location information, and longitude and latitude where appropriate. If the listing is a municipality, brief population figures are provided as well. . . . Color maps of the physical regions of North America, along with political maps of the region, are included as reference points." Am Ref Books Annu, 2001

Cox, Caroline

★ **Opening** up North America, 1497-1800; [by] Caroline Cox and Ken Albala. Rev. ed.; Chelsea House 2009 140p il map (Discovery and exploration) $35

Grades: 7 8 9 10   917

1. Explorers 2. America -- Exploration
ISBN 978-1-60413-196-3; 1-60413-196-9

LC 2009-27794

First published 2005 by Facts On File

"Integrates in a chronological narrative the voyages taken from Florida to Newfoundland, covering the first recorded contact of John Cabot in 1497 through Alexander Mackenzie's journey across the Rocky Mountains to the Pacific in 1793." Publisher's note

Includes glossary and bibliographical references

Duncan, Dayton

★ **Lewis** & Clark; the journey of the Corps of Discovery. based on a documentary film by Ken Burns, written by Dayton Duncan; with a preface by Ken Burns and conributions by Stephen E. Ambrose, Erica Funkhouser, William Least Heat-Moon. Knopf 1997 248p il maps $45

Grades: 11 12 Adult   917

1. Lewis and Clark Expedition (1804-1806) 2. West (U.S.) -- Exploration
ISBN 0-679-45450-0

LC 97-73823

This is a companion volume to PBS television film "Lewis and Clark: The journey of the Corps of Discovery," by Ken Burns.

An "attractive book with a well-written text and an excellent presentation of historic paintings, photographs, maps, and original quotations from various of Lewis and Clark's journals." Sci Books Films

Hayes, Derek

America discovered; a historical atlas of exploration. Douglas & McIntyre 2004 224p il maps hardcover o.p. pa $35

Grades: 9 10 11 12 Adult   917

1. Reference books 2. Historical atlases 3. America -- Exploration -- Maps 4. North America -- Historical geography -- Maps
ISBN 1-553-65049-2; 1-553-65450-1 pa

LC 2004-52704

The author "chronicles the discovery and exploration of North America. The narrative text of this handsome volume provides the historical context for 280 carefully selected maps from North American and European collections, faithfully reproduced in full color and ranging in date from the early 16th century to several computer-generated images from the late 20th century. . . . Hayes has chosen maps that fascinate the intellect as well as please the eye." Libr J

Includes bibliographical references

Isserman, Maurice

★ **Exploring** North America, 1800-1900; [by] Maurice Isserman; John S. Bowman and Maurice

Isserman, general editors. Rev. ed.; Chelsea House 2010 151p il map (Discovery and exploration) $35
Grades: 7 8 9 10   **917**
1. Explorers 2. West (U.S.) -- Exploration
ISBN 978-1-60413-194-9; 1-60413-194-2
LC 2009-27860
First published 2005 by Facts On File
"Traces the history of the exploration of western North America and the impact it had on the histories of both the United States and Canada." Publisher's note
Includes glossary and bibliographical references

Krakauer, Jon, 1954-
★ **Into** the wild; Jon Krakauer. Villard Bks. 1996 xi, 207 p.p maps hardcover o.p. (pbk.) $12.95; (hbk.) $26
Grades: 11 12 Adult   **917**
1. Alaska -- Description and travel 2. Alaska -- Biography 3. Alaska -- Description 4. Biography, Individual 5. West (U.S.) -- Biography
ISBN 0385486804; 067942850X; 9780679428503
LC 95020008
This book, by Jon Krakauer, is the "story of a young man on a quest for knowledge and experience. . . . Chris Mc-Candless loved the road, the unadorned life, the Tolstoyan call to asceticism. After graduating college, he took off on another of his long destinationless journeys, this time cutting all contact with his family and changing his name to Alex Supertramp. . . . Ultimately, in 1992, his terms got him into mortal trouble when he ran up against something--the Alaskan wild." (Kirkus Reviews)
"A wonderful page-turner written with humility, immediacy, and great style. Nothing came cheap and easy to McCandless, nor will it to readers of Krakauer's narrative." Kirkus

MacGregor, Greg
Lewis and Clark revisited; a photographer's trail. Iris Tillman Hill, editor. Center for Documentary Studies in association with the University of Washington Press 2003 199p il map hardcover o.p. pa $29.95
Grades: 9 10 11 12   **917**
1. Lewis and Clark Expedition (1804-1806) 2. West (U.S.) -- Description and travel
ISBN 0-295-98342-6; 0-295-98343-4 pa
LC 2003-53110
This is a photo "album of nearly 100 black-and-white images, which set forth places along . . . [Lewis and Clark's] 1804-06 route as they appear today. Although generally not a pretty sight, with dams, power plants, and grain elevators having supplanted waterfalls, campfires, and wildlife, there yet remain refuges of original scenery whose beauty so transported Lewis and which MacGregor ably arrests in an ethereal timelessness." Booklist

National Geographic Society (U.S.)
★ **National** Geographic guide to the national parks of the United States; [project manger, Caroline Hickey] 6th ed.; National Geographic 2009 480p il pa $26

Grades: 9 10 11 12 Adult   **917**
1. National parks and reserves -- United States
ISBN 978-1-4262-0393-0
First published 1989
This guide provides information on each of the fifty-eight national parks, including things to do, campgrounds and accommodations, and facilities for the disabled.
"You can't do better than this guide. . . . Highly detailed and beautiful, this one is a must for all collections." Libr J

World and its peoples: the Americas. Marshall Cavendish Reference 2008 11v il map set $499.95
Grades: 7 8 9 10 11 12   **917**
1. Reference books 2. Human geography -- Encyclopedias
ISBN 978-0-7614-7802-7; 0-7614-7802-7
LC 2008-62303
Each volume in this set "begins with a well-defined overview of its region, organized by color-coded pages into sections covering 'Geography and Climate' and 'History and Movement of Peoples.' The country entries that follow include a time line, flag, and map; key facts on population, government, and transportation; and a closer analysis that varies in length. . . . The Americas is an ideal reference to use for social studies and history, and it will even benefit students in music, language, art, literature, family consumer science, and health and economics classes." SLJ
Includes glossary and bibliographical references

917.304   Travel

National Geographic Guide to the State Parks of the United States; 4th edition National Geographic Society 2012 384 p. illustrations, maps $25
Grades: 9 10 11 12 Adult   **917.304**
1. Parks -- United States 2. United States -- Guidebooks
ISBN 1426208898; 9781426208898
"Of the state parks' 25,000 miles of trails and recreation, the authors have selected favorites for hiking and biking, horseback riding, and wildflower gazing as well as ample opportunities for the birdwatcher or rock climber, the wildlife observer or the amateur archaeologist. The guide features more than 200 gorgeous, color photographs that capture the spendor of the parks, insider tips from state parks staff that are invaluable planning tools, and 32 easy-to-use maps that highlight sites, trails and campgrounds, as well as information on recreational activities, camping, and lodging." (Publisher's note)

919   Geography of and travel in Australasia, Pacific Ocean islands, Atlantic Ocean islands, Arctic islands, Antarctica and on extraterrestrial worlds

Armstrong, Jennifer
★ **Shipwreck** at the bottom of the world; the extraordinary true story of Shackleton and the Endurance. Crown 1998 134p il maps pbk $12.95

Grades: 7 8 9 10 11 12   **919**
1. Explorers 2. Endurance (Ship) 3. Imperial Trans-Antarctic Expedition (1914-1917) 1914-1917:
ISBN 0-517-80014-4; 9780375810497

LC 97-52063

This book describes the events of the 1914 Shackleton Antarctic expedition when, after being trapped in a frozen sea for nine months, their ship, Endurance, was finally crushed, forcing Shackleton and his men to make a very long and perilous journey across ice and stormy seas to reach inhabited land. (Booklist)

A book that will capture the attention and imagination of any reader." SLJ

Gurney, Alan

The **race** to the white continent; voyages to the Antarctic. Norton 2000 320p il maps hardcover o.p. pa $15.95

Grades: 11 12 Adult   **919**
1. Antarctica -- Exploration
ISBN 0-393-05004-1; 0-393-32321-8 pa

LC 00-38673

This is an account "of the expeditions that paved the way for the race to the South Pole. All took place in the late 1830s and early 1840s. . . . One was French, another English, and the third was American. Their leaders were, respectively, Jules Sébastien César Dumont d'Urville, James Clark Ross and Charles Wilkes. They were all naval officers, sent out by their governments." Publ Wkly

Includes bibliographical references

Solomon, Susan

The **coldest** March. Yale Univ. Press 2001 xxii, 383p il maps hardcover o.p. pa $16.95

Grades: 11 12 Adult   **919**
1. Explorers 2. South Pole 3. Antarctica -- Exploration 4. British Antarctic ("Terra Nova") Expedition (1910-1913)
ISBN 0-300-08967-8; 0-300-09921-5 pa

LC 00-54996

"In November 1911, Capt. Robert Falcon Scott and his British team set out to be the first to reach the South Pole. Battling the brutal weather of Antarctica, they reached the pole in January 1912 only to discover that a Norwegian team had beat them there by nearly a month. On their return from the Pole, Scott and four of his companions died in harsh conditions. Ever since, history has not known whether to label them heroes or bunglers. Solomon . . . analyzes all the factors present during Scott's expedition in an attempt to explain that his failure was due not to incompetence but to a combination of unpredictable weather, erroneous choices and bad luck." Libr J

Includes bibliographical references

919.89   Antarctica--Geography

Bertozzi, Nick

Shackleton; Antarctic odyssey. Nick Bertozzi. First edition First Second 2014 128 p. illustrations, maps $16.99

Grades: 5 6 7 8 9 10   **919.89**
1. Antarctica -- Exploration 2. Graphic novels 3. Explorers -- Great Britain -- Biography 4. Antarctica -- Discovery and exploration -- British
ISBN 1596434511; 9781596434516

This book by Nick Bertozzi describes how "Ernest Shackleton was one of the last great Antarctic explorers, and he led one of the most ambitious Antarctic expeditions ever undertaken. This is his story, and the story of the dozens of men who threw in their lot with him--many of whom nearly died in the unimaginably harsh conditions of the journey." (Publisher's note)

"Bertozzi eschews all narrative explanation, relying solely on dialogue among the crew and the detailed black-and-white panels to tell the story. The snow- and ice-bound journey is the perfect match for Bertozzi's minimal style--vast stretches of white become gasp-worthy, desolate vistas." Booklist

92   Individual biography

Aaron, Hank, 1934-

★ Stanton, Tom. **Hank** Aaron and the home run that changed America. William Morrow 2004 249p il hardcover o.p. pa $13.95

Grades: 7 8 9 10   **92**
1. Baseball players 2. African American athletes 3. Baseball -- Biography 4. United States -- Race relations
ISBN 0-06-057976-5; 0-06-072290-8 pa

LC 2004-46092

"Stanton deftly balances the story of Aaron's professional career, his personal life, and the changes in baseball between the years of Jackie Robinson and today's megastars, such as Ken Griffey, Jr. and Barry Bonds. . . . This book is a must for young adult collections." Voice Youth Advocates

Includes bibliographical references

Abbott, Berenice, 1898-1991

Sullivan, George. **Berenice** Abbott, photographer; an independent vision. Clarion Books 2006 170p il $20

Grades: 7 8 9 10   **92**
1. Photographers 2. Women photographers
ISBN 978-0-618-44026-9; 0-618-44026-7

LC 2005-30736

A biography of Berenice Abbott, who was a pioneer in the field of professional photography and is particularly acclaimed for her photographs of the streets and buildings of New York City before they were replaced by skyscrapers during a building boom in the 1920s and early 1930s.

"Sullivan brings together an enormous amount of information about Abbott and presents it in a clear, thoughtful manner. . . . Large, clear reproductions of Abbott's photos appear throughout the book." Booklist

Includes bibliographical references

Abdul-Jabbar, Kareem, 1947-

Abdul-Jabbar, Kareem. **On** the shoulders of giants; my journey through the Harlem Renaissance. [by] Kareem Abdul-Jabbar with Raymond Obstfeld.

Simon & Schuster 2007 274p il hardcover o.p. pa $18.99

Grades: 11 12 Adult   **92**
1. Harlem Renaissance 2. Basketball players 3. Nonfiction writers 4. African Americans -- Biography
ISBN 1-4165-3488-1; 978-1-4165-3488-4; 1-4165-3489-X pa; 978-1-4165-3489-1 pa

LC 2006-51776

"By mixing personal anecdotes with traditional research and reporting, . . . [Abdul-Jabbar] acts as a knowledgeable, passionate tour guide through the artistic and social history of one America's most dynamic creative eras." N Y Times Book Rev

Includes bibliographical references

Abeel, Samantha, 1977-

Abeel, Samantha. **My** thirteenth winter; a memoir. Orchard Bks. 2003 203p $15.95; pa $15.95

Grades: 9 10 11 12   **92**
1. Learning disabilities
ISBN 0-439-33904-9; 0-439-33905-6 pa

LC 2003-40465

"This introspective book provides a valuable resource for teachers or counselors working with youth with learning disabilities." VOYA

Achebe, Chinua, 1930-2013

Achebe, Chinua, 1930-2013. The **education** of a British-protected child; essays. A.A. Knopf 2009 172p $24.95; pa $14.95

Grades: 11 12 Adult   **92**
1. Poets 2. Racism 3. Authors 4. Novelists 5. Authors, Nigerian 6. Nigeria 7. Essayists 8. Short story writers 9. Nigeria -- Colonization 10. African literature -- History and criticism
ISBN 978-0-3072-7255-3; 9780307473677

LC 2009017480

This is a collection of essays by the author of Things Fall Apart. In the title piece, Achebe discusses "growing up in colonial Nigeria and inhabiting its 'middle ground,' recalling both his happy memories of reading novels in secondary school and the harsher truths of colonial rule. . . . Politics and history figure in 'What Is Nigeria to Me?,' 'Africa's Tarnished Name,' and 'Politics of the Politicians of Language.' And Achebe's . . . family comes into view in 'My Dad and Me' and 'My Daughters.'" (Publisher's note)

"With African literature emerging as a world force, it's good to have Achebe back after more than 20 years, offering 17 sterling essays." (Library Journal)

Includes bibliographical references

Addams, Jane, 1860-1935

★ Fradin, Judith Bloom. **Jane** Addams; champion of democracy. by Judith Bloom Fradin and Dennis Brindell Fradin. Clarion Books 2006 216p il $21

Grades: 7 8 9 10   **92**
1. Authors 2. Philanthropists 3. Hull House (Chicago, Ill.) 4. Essayists 5. Pacifists 6. Social welfare leaders 7. Nobel laureates for peace 8. Chicago (Ill.) -- Social conditions
ISBN 0-618-50436-1

A biography of the social activist, pacifist, author, founder of Hull House in Chicago, and winner of the Nobel Peace Prize.

"A fascinating and rich life is related in strong, unfussy prose." Booklist

Includes bibliographical references

Knight, Louise W. **Jane** Addams; spirit in action. W. W. Norton 2010 334p il $28.95

Grades: 9 10 11 12 Adult   **92**
1. Authors 2. Philanthropists 3. Hull House (Chicago, Ill.) 4. Essayists 5. Pacifists 6. Social welfare leaders 7. Nobel laureates for peace 8. Chicago (Ill.) -- Social conditions
ISBN 978-0-393-07165-8

LC 2010-20648

"Knight, the author of Citizen (2006), provides the first full-length biography of Jane Addams in 35 years. She carefully traces Addams' philosophical progression as she Addams evolved from a passive reformer into an active collaborator, who tirelessly worked with, not for, others to usher in a new era of democracy and social justice." (Booklist)

Includes bibliographical references

Akeley, Carl Ethan, 1864-1926

Kirk, Jay. **Kingdom** under glass; a tale of obsession, adventure, and one man's quest to preserve the world's great animals. Henry Holt 2010 387p il $27.50

Grades: 11 12 Adult   **92**
1. Artists 2. Explorers 3. Inventors 4. Sculptors 5. Taxidermy 6. Naturalists 7. Taxidermists 8. Zoological specimens -- Collection and preservation
ISBN 978-0-8050-9282-0

LC 2009-50706

This is "a rollicking biography of Carl Akeley, an American taxidermist who preserved realistic-looking beasts complete with aura of 'will,' for 20th-century natural history museums. . . . The author spends most of the book following Akeley's African safaris, where he hunts big game and touring tycoons who might fund his projects. . . . [This] is a beguiling, novelistic portrait of a man and an era straining to hear the call of the wild." Publ Wkly

Includes bibliographical references

Al Jundi, Sami, 1962-

Al Jundi, Sami. The **hour** of sunlight; one Palestinian's journey from prisoner to peacemaker. by Sami al Jundi and Jen Marlowe. Nation Books 2010 344p il pa $16.99

Grades: 11 12 Adult   **92**
1. Prisoners 2. Palestinian Arabs 3. Israel-Arab conflicts 4. Pacifists
ISBN 978-1-56858-448-5

LC 2010-29340

The authors "trace al Jundi's evolution from Palestinian militant to peacemaker. As teenagers, al Jundi and two friends joined the PLO, but when a bomb exploded as they were building it, one boy was killed, and the other two badly injured—and on the receiving end of Israeli interrogations and torture. Sentenced to a decade in prison, al Jundi dedicates himself to an extensive education program maintained by the prisoners themselves, ultimately committing himself to nonviolence and to bridging the Israeli-Palestinian divide." Publ Wkly

Includes bibliographical references

Al-Maria, Sophia

Al-Maria, Sophia. The **Girl** Who Fell to Earth; A Memoir. HarperCollins 2012 288 p. (paperback) $14.99

Grades: 9 10 11 12 Adult   92

1. Arab Americans 2. Culture conflict
ISBN 006199975X; 9780061999758

In this memoir, "when Sophia Al-Maria's mother sends her away from rainy Washington State to stay with her husband's desert-dwelling Bedouin family in Qatar, she intends it to be a sort of teenage cultural boot camp. What her mother doesn't know is that there are some things about growing up that are universal. In Qatar, Sophia is faced with a new world she'd only imagined as a child. She sets out to find her freedom, even in the most unlikely of places." (Publisher's note)

Alexander, the Great, 356-323 B.C.

Arrian. **Alexander** the Great; selections from Arrian. {translated by} J. G. Lloyd. Cambridge Univ. Press 1981 104p il maps (Translations from Greek and Roman authors) pa $17.95

Grades: 9 10 11 12   92

1. Kings and rulers 2. Kings 3. Greece -- History
ISBN 0-521-28195-4

      LC 81-9453

Born over four hundred years after the death of Alexander the Great, Arrian served in the Roman army and devoted his life's work to the study of Alexander's empire, a section of which he governed under the auspices of Rome. Here are selections from his history which focus primarily on Alexander's military campaigns

"This book may seem to be a military account, but first and foremost it is the story of a man." Introduction

Includes bibliographical references

Romm, James. **Alexander** the Great: Selections from Arrian, Diodorus, Plutarch, and Quintus Curtius; edited, with introduction, by James Romm; translated by Pamela Mensch and James Romm. Hackett Pub Co Inc 2005 193 p. $14.00

Grades: 9 10 11 12 Adult   92

1. Generals -- Greece 2. Greece -- Biography 3. Greece -- History -- 0-323
ISBN 9780872207271

"Comprised of relevant selections from the writings of four ancient historians, this volume provides a complete narrative of the important events in the life of Alexander the Great. The Introduction sets these works in historical context, from the conclusion of the Peloponnesian War through Alexander's conquest of Asia, and provides an assessment of Alexander's historical importance, as well as a survey of the central controversies surrounding his personality, aims and intentions." (Publisher's Note)

Alhazen, 965-1039

Steffens, Bradley. **Ibn** al-Haytham; first scientist. Morgan Reynolds Pub. 2007 128p il (Profiles in science) lib bdg $27.95

Grades: 7 8 9 10   92

1. Physicists 2. Scientists 3. Mathematicians
ISBN 978-1-59935-024-0; 1-59935-024-6

      LC 2006-23970

The author "has organized what is known of his subject's life and work into a coherent narrative. . . . Like the history of mathematics, the history of science is incomplete without an acknowledgment of early scholars in the Middle East. This clearly written introduction to al-Haytham, his society, and his contributions does that." Booklist

Includes bibliographical references

Ali, Muhammad, 1942-2016

Ezra, Michael. **Muhammad** Ali; the making of an icon. Temple University Press 2009 233p (Sporting) $69.50; pa $24.95

Grades: 11 12 Adult   92

1. Boxers (Persons) 2. Boxing -- Biography
ISBN 9781592136612; 9781592136629

      LC 2008-34323

This is a biography of the heavyweight boxing champion. "This book increases our understanding of how difficult it is to know the real Ali, a simple man paradoxically imbued with great complexity." Libr J

Includes bibliographical references

Micklos, John. **Muhammad** Ali; I am the greatest. [by] John Micklos, Jr. Enslow Publishers 2010 160p il (American rebels) lib bdg $34.60

Grades: 6 7 8 9 10   92

1. African American athletes 2. Boxers (Persons) 3. Boxing -- Biography
ISBN 978-0-7660-3381-8; 0-7660-3381-3

      LC 2009-17593

"This biography of the three-time heavyweight world champion, Vietnam War protester, and Nobel Peace Prize nominee includes useful context-setting background; Micklos's play-by-play descriptions of Ali's bouts provide just enough detail for boxing fans." Horn Book Guide

Includes bibliographical references

Allende family

Allende, Isabel. **Paula**; translated from the Spanish by Margaret Sayers Peden. HarperPerennial 2008 330, 23p pa $14.99

Grades: 11 12 Adult   92

1. Authors 2. Novelists 3. Dramatists 4. Journalists 5. Authors, Chilean 6. Children's authors
ISBN 978-0-06-156490-1
First published 1995

Allende "interweaves the story of her own life with the slow dying of her 28-year-old daughter, Paula." Publ Wkly

Allende, Isabel

Allende, Isabel. **Paula**; translated from the Spanish by Margaret Sayers Peden. HarperPerennial 2008 330, 23p pa $14.99

Grades: 11 12 Adult **92**
1. Authors 2. Novelists 3. Dramatists 4. Journalists 5. Authors, Chilean 6. Children's authors
ISBN 978-0-06-156490-1
First published 1995
Allende "interweaves the story of her own life with the slow dying of her 28-year-old daughter, Paula." Publ Wkly

Axelrod-Contrada, Joan. **Isabel** Allende. Marshall Cavendish Benchmark 2010 159p il (Today's writers and their works) $42.79
Grades: 8 9 10 11 12 **92**
1. Authors 2. Novelists 3. Dramatists 4. Journalists 5. Women authors 6. Authors, Chilean 7. Children's authors
ISBN 978-0-7614-4116-8; 0-7614-4116-6
This biography of Isabel Allende places the author in the context of her times and discusses her work.
This book provides "excellent information for reports. . . [The text is] organized well, lending [itself] to be read in [its] entirety or used as needed for research, and [includes] full-color photos and illustrations." SLJ
Includes bibliographical references

Allred, Lance, 1981-
Allred, Lance. **Longshot**; the adventures of a deaf fundamentalist Mormon kid and his journey to the NBA. HarperOne 2009 250p $25.99
Grades: 11 12 Adult **92**
1. Deaf 2. Athletes 3. Deafness 4. Basketball players 5. Athletes with physical disabilities
ISBN 978-0-06-171858-8; 0-06-171858-0
LC 2009-517317
"Allred played basketball with the University of Utah, then Weber State, before eventually joining the Cleveland Cavaliers in 2008, and recounts in folksy, unpretentious prose his long, arduous dream fulfilled to make the NBA. . . Allred's voice is humorously self-deprecating and youthfully winning. Frank about his shortcomings . . . he delivers an accessible, competent narrative, with highly unusual details about his Mormon roots." Publ Wkly

Anderson, Laurie Halse, 1961-
★ Glenn, Wendy J. **Laurie** Halse Anderson; speaking in tongues. Scarecrow Press 2010 169p (Scarecrow studies in young adult literature) $40
Grades: 8 9 10 11 12 **92**
1. Authors 2. Novelists 3. Women authors 4. Authors, American 5. Young adult authors
ISBN 978-0-8108-7281-3
LC 2009-30545
"This book is a comprehensive look at the life, work, and thoughts of Laurie Halse Anderson. . . . Any teen with a research paper on Laurie Halse Anderson who is lucky enough to have access to this title will walk away with a high mark." Voice Youth Advocates
Includes bibliographical references

Anderson, Marian, 1897-1993
Keiler, Allan. **Marian** Anderson; a singer's journey. University of Illinois Press 2002 447p hardcover o.p. pa $21.95
Grades: 11 12 Adult **92**
1. African American singers 2. Opera singers 3. African American women -- Biography
ISBN 0-684-80711-4; 0-252-07067-4 pa
LC 99-43319
First published 2000 by Scribner
The author's "clear, succinct prose, initially lacking narrative coherence, gains strength and momentum as his subject matures from a young and struggling artist into one of the enduring voices of our century." Publ Wkly
Includes discography and bibliographical references

Angelou, Maya 1928-2014
★ Angelou, Maya. **I** know why the caged bird sings. Random House 2002 281p $21.95
Grades: 11 12 Adult **92**
1. Poets 2. Actors 3. Singers 4. Dramatists 5. Women authors 6. African American authors 7. Essayists 8. Memoirists 9. Children's authors
ISBN 0-375-50789-2
LC 2001-41914
First published 1969
The first volume in the author's autobiographical series covers her childhood and adolescence in rural Arkansas, St. Louis, and San Francisco.
"Angelou is a skillful writer; her language ranges from beautifully lyrical prose to earthy metaphor, and her descriptions have power and sensitivity." Libr J
Followed by Gather together in my name (1974); Singin' and swingin' and gettin' merry like Christmas (1976); The heart of a woman (1981); All God's children need traveling shoes (1986); A song flung up to heaven (2002)

★ Angelou, Maya, 1928-2014. **Letter** to my daughter. Random House 2008 166p $25
Grades: 9 10 11 12 Adult **92**
1. Poets 2. Actors 3. Singers 4. Dramatists 5. Women authors 6. African American authors 7. Essayists 8. Memoirists 9. Children's authors
ISBN 978-1-4000-6612-4
LC 2008-28843
"A slim volume packed with nourishing nuggets of wisdom." Kirkus

★ Gillespie, Marcia Ann. **Maya** Angelou; a glorious celebration. [by] Marcia Ann Gillespie, Rosa Johnson Butler and Richard A. Long; foreword by Oprah Winfrey. Doubleday 2008 191p il $30
Grades: 11 12 Adult **92**
1. Poets 2. Actors 3. Singers 4. Dramatists 5. Women authors 6. African American authors 7. Essayists 8. Memoirists 9. Children's authors
ISBN 978-0-385-51108-7
LC 2007-31301
This look at Maya Angelou's life as well as her myriad interests and accomplishments by the people who know her best (longtime friends Marcia Ann Gillespie and Richard

Long and niece Rosa Johnson Butler) features over 150 sepia portraits, family photographs, and letters. Includes a bibliography of her works.

"A loving tribute to one of the most renowned authors today, this work is highly recommended." Libr J

Anthony, Susan B., 1820-1906

Colman, Penny. **Elizabeth** Cady Stanton and Susan B. Anthony; a friendship that changed the world. Henry Holt and Company 2011 256p il $18.99

Grades: 7 8 9 10	**92**

1. Feminism 2. Suffragists 3. Women -- Suffrage
ISBN 978-0-8050-8293-7; 0-8050-8293-X

LC 2010-39762

"Elizabeth Cady Stanton, a married mother of four boys at the time they met, and Susan B. Anthony, an unmarried schoolteacher, formed a friendship that lasted until Elizabeth's death more than 50 years later. Their tireless work, including advocacy, speeches, organizing and writing, placed them at the center of tumultuous events in the middle of the 19th century. . . . This [is a] lively, very readable narrative. . . . This thoughtful portrayal to two complex women is . . . enhanced by comprehensive backmatter, making this an invaluable addition to the literature of suffrage." Kirkus

Includes bibliographical references

Archimedes, ca. 287-212 B.C.

Hasan, Heather. **Archimedes**: the father of mathematics. Rosen Pub. Group 2006 112p il (The library of Greek philosophers) lib bdg $33.25

Grades: 9 10 11 12	**92**

1. Mathematicians 2. Writers on science
ISBN 1-4042-0774-0

LC 2005-9992

"This biography charts the life of Archimedes while . . . explaining his mathematical postulates." Publisher's note

Includes bibliographical references

Armstrong, Karen

Armstrong, Karen. The **spiral** staircase; my climb out of darkness. Knopf 2004 xxii, 305p hardcover o.p. pa $14

Grades: 11 12 Adult	**92**

1. Nuns 2. Religious scholars
ISBN 0-375-41318-9; 0-385-72127-7 pa

LC 2003-47550

This "is the story of Armstrong's personal spiritual quest, which led her at age 17 to join a convent. However, she found that her own skeptical nature and the physical constraints of convent life crippled her intellectually and spiritually. . . . After seven years, Armstrong left the convent." SLJ

Armstrong, Louis, 1901-1971

★ Orr, Tamra. **Louis** Armstrong; by Tamra Orr. Mitchell Lane Publishers 2012 47 p. ill. (chiefly col.) (library) $29.95

Grades: 6 7 8 9	**92**

1. Jazz musicians -- United States -- Biography
ISBN 1612282644; 9781612282640

LC 2012008631

This book by Tamra Orr is part of the American Jazz series and looks at musician Louis Armstrong. Within each entry, "information about the subjects' childhoods and preparation for their musical careers is included, as are the positive and negative aspects of their adult lives. Their contributions to the world of jazz are . . . explored." (School Library Journal)

Includes bibliographical references (pages 44-45) and index.

Arnold, Benedict, 1741-1801

★ Murphy, Jim. The **real** Benedict Arnold. Clarion Books 2007 264p il map $20

Grades: 7 8 9 10	**92**

1. Spies 2. Generals 3. Army officers 4. United States -- History -- 1775-1783, Revolution
ISBN 978-0-395-77609-4; 0-395-77609-0

LC 2007-5700

"Using Arnold's surviving military journals and political documents, Murphy carefully contrasts popular myth with historical fact. . . . As far as possible, he meticulously traces Arnold's life, revealing a complex man who was actually as much admired as he was loathed." Booklist

Includes bibliographical references

★ Sheinkin, Steve. The **notorious** Benedict Arnold; a true story of adventure, heroism, & treachery. Steve Sheinkin. Roaring Brook Press 2010 337p. ill. $19.99

Grades: 7 8 9 10	**92**

1. Spies 2. Generals 3. American Loyalists 4. Army officers
ISBN 1-59643-486-4; 978-1-59643-486-8

LC 201034797

Boston Globe-Horn Book Awards: Nonfiction (2012)

YALSA Award for Excellence in Nonfiction for Young Adults (2012)

This is a biography of the Continental Army officer who won battles for the Americans during the Revolutionary War but felt ill-used and unappreciated by the Continental Congress. He obtained command of the fort at West Point, New York, and plotted to surrender it to the British. After the plot was exposed in September 1780, he was commissioned into the British Army. Bibliography. Index. "Middle school, high school." (Horn Book)

"Sheinkin sees Arnold as America's 'original action hero' and succeeds in writing a brilliant, fast-paced biography that reads like an adventure novel. . . . The author's obvious mastery of his material, lively prose and abundant use of eyewitness accounts make this one of the most exciting biographies young readers will find." Kirkus

Includes bibliographical references

Arthur, King

Ashe, Geoffrey. The **discovery** of King Arthur; New pbk. ed.; Sutton 2005 244p il map pa $14.95

Grades: 11 12 Adult	**92**

1. Great Britain -- Kings and rulers 2. Great Britain -- History -- 0-1066 3. Kings
ISBN 0-7509-4211-8; 978-0-7509-4211-9

LC 2008383248

First published 1985 by Anchor Press/Doubleday

The author explores archeological findings that support the theory that Arthur was a real leader in the 5th century. Arthurian themes in literature and art are also examined.

Includes bibliographical references

Asayesh, Gelareh

Asayesh, Gelareh. **Saffron** sky; a life between Iran and America. Beacon Press 1999 222p hardcover o.p. pa $15

Grades: 11 12 Adult   92
1. Journalists 2. Iranian Americans 3. Women journalists 4. Iran -- History -- 20th century 5. Memoirists
ISBN 0-8070-7210-9; 0-8070-7211-7 pa
LC 99-27889

The author "chronicles her life as a series of trips to and from Iran—as a child who spoke no English, on the eve of the 1992 Gulf War as a green card-holding adult, and as the parent of a young biracial American citizen—and in doing so, tells the story of both her family's and Iran's tumultuous recent history. This beautifully written narrative provides a rare, humanizing glimpse into the politics, culture, and geography of {Iran}." Libr J

Aseel, Maryam Qudrat, 1974-

★ Aseel, Maryam Qudrat. **Torn** between two cultures; an Afghan-American woman speaks out. {by} Maryam Qudrat. Capital Bks. 2003 191p $22.95; pa $14.95

Grades: 11 12 Adult   92
1. Muslim women 2. Afghan Americans 3. Afghanistan -- History 4. Memoirists 5. Afghanistan 6. Social activists 7. Muslims -- United States
ISBN 1-931868-36-0; 1-931868-70-0 pa
LC 2002-41108

"Aseel, a first-generation Afghan American woman, is an activist in the Muslim community in general and the Afghani community in particular. Woven around her commentary on current events is the fascinating story of her life, including a childhood that balanced both modernity and tradition. Throughout the . . . . engaging narrative, Aseel manages to clear up numerous misconceptions about her culture and religion." Booklist

Includes bibliographical references

Atanasoff, John V.

Smiley, Jane. The **man** who invented the computer; the biography of John Atanasoff, digital pioneer. Doubleday 2010 246p il $25.95

Grades: 11 12 Adult   92
1. Inventors 2. Physicists 3. Mathematicians 4. Computer scientists
ISBN 978-0-385-52713-2; 0-385-52713-6
LC 2010-18887

"Engrossing. Smiley takes science history and injects it with a touch of noir and an exciting clash of vanities." Kirkus

Includes bibliographical references

Audubon, John James, 1785-1851

Rhodes, Richard. **John** James Audubon; the making of an American. Knopf 2004 528p il $30; pa $16

Grades: 11 12 Adult   92
1. Artists 2. Painters 3. Naturalists 4. Ornithologists 5. Writers on science 6. Biography, Individual 7. Artists -- United States
ISBN 0-375-41412-6; 0-375-71393-X pa
LC 2003-69489

This is a biography of the American ornithologist and painter.

The author "chronicles Audubon's ineluctable sense of mission, phenomenal skills, and triumph over adversity. . . . Rhodes sets Audubon's engrossing tale within the context of the War of 1812, the Louisiana Purchase, the wars against Native Americans (whom Audubon profoundly admired), and the rapid decimation of the American wilderness. . . . Full of passion and discovery, hardship and transcendence, Audubon's story is at once intimate and mythic, and Rhodes' fresh, comprehensive biography will capture the imagination of readers everywhere." Booklist

Includes bibliographical references

Aung San Suu Kyi

O'Keefe, Sherry. **Champion** of freedom; Aung San Suu Kyi. Sherry O'Keefe. Morgan Reynolds Pub. 2011 160 p. ill. (some col.), col. maps $28.95

Grades: 7 8 9 10 11 12   92
1. Myanmar 2. Political activists 3. Democracy -- Burma 4. Burma -- Politics and government -- 1988- 5. Women Nobel Prize winners -- Burma -- Biography 6. Women political activists -- Burma -- Biography 7. Women political prisoners -- Burma -- Biography
ISBN 1599351684; 9781599351681; 9781599353142
LC 2011035740

Author Sherry O'Keefe tells the story of politician Aung San Suu Kyi. "Knowing that the military regime will not allow her to return if she leaves, the Nobel Peace Prize laureate has remained in Burma, enduring extreme isolation, the threat of death, and personal pain and sacrifice, including the chance to see her dying husband one last time. . . . [Suu Kyi] remains as determined as ever to see Burma emerge from its isolation and join the family of democratic nations in the world." (Publisher's note)

Includes bibliographical references and index.

Austen, Jane, 1775-1817

Haggerty, Andrew. **Jane** Austen; Pride and Prejudice and Emma. Marshall Cavendish Benchmark 2007 127p il (Writers and their works) $39.93

Grades: 9 10 11 12   92
1. Authors 2. Novelists 3. Authors, English
ISBN 978-0-7614-2589-2
LC 2006-39179

This book features a biography of Jane Austen, a description of the times in which she lived, and a critical discussion of her novels Pride and Prejudice and Emma.

Includes filmography and bibliographical references

★ Reef, Catherine. **Jane** Austen; a life revealed. Clarion Books 2011 192p il $18.99

Grades: 6 7 8 9 10   **92**

1. Authors 2. Novelists 3. Women authors 4. Novelists, English

ISBN 0-547-37021-0; 978-0-547-37021-7

LC 2011008146

In this biography of the English novelist, Reef "combines firsthand accounts of Austen written by relatives and friends, historical information about Britain in the late 1700s, the basic facts of Austen's life, . . . and Austen's own novels and surviving letters. . . . A family tree, notes, a selected bibliography, a list of Austen's work, and an index are appended. . . . Middle school, high school." (Horn Book)

Reef "combines firsthand accounts of Austen written by relatives and friends, historical information about Britain in the late 1700s, the basic facts of Austen's life that are readily known, and Austen's own novels and surviving letters, presented in a chronological format. . . . Reef's account also focuses on Austen's large family and many friends, highlighting the connections between Austen's novels and her life. . . . For devout Janeites it's fascinating to see all this information combined, and for others it's a worthwhile introduction to a masterful writer's life." Horn Book

Includes bibliographical references

Ayers, Nathaniel Anthony

★ Lopez, Steve. The **soloist**; a lost dream, an unlikely friendship, and the redemptive power of music. G. P. Putnam's Sons 2008 273p hardcover o.p. pa $15

Grades: 11 12 Adult   **92**

1. Violinists 2. Homeless persons 3. Homeless 4. Schizophrenics 5. Street entertainers

ISBN 978-0-399-15506-2; 0-399-15506-6; 978-0-425-23836-3 pa; 0-425-23836-9 pa

LC 2007-46314

The true story of Nathaniel Ayers, a musician who becomes schizophrenic and homeless, and his friendship with Steve Lopez, the Los Angeles columnist who discovers and writes about him in the newspaper.

"With self-effacing humor, fast-paced yet elegant prose and unsparing honesty, Lopez tells an inspiring story of heartbreak and hope." Publ Wkly

Baker, Josephine

Caravantes, Peggy. The **many** faces of Josephine Baker; dancer, singer, activist, spy. Peggy Caravantes. Chicago Review Press 2015 208 p. (Women of action) (hardback) $19.95

Grades: 9 10 11 12   **92**

1. Women spies 2. African American dancers 3. African American entertainers 4. World War, 1939-1945 -- Secret service -- France 5. Spies -- France -- Biography

ISBN 1613730349; 9781613730348

LC 2014026074

This book, by Peggy Caravantes, "follows [Josephine] Baker's life from her childhood in the depths of poverty to her comedic rise in vaudeville and fame in Europe. . . . [It] covers her outspoken participation in the U.S. Civil Rights Movement, espionage work for the French Resistance during World War II, and adoption of 12 children. . . . Also included are informative sidebars on relevant topics such as the 1917 East St. Louis riot, Pullman railway porters, the Charleston, and more." (Publisher's note)

"A fascinating, compelling story of a remarkably resilient woman who overcame poverty and racial prejudice to become an international celebrity." Kirkus

Includes bibliographical references and index

Balanchine, George, 1904-1983

Gottlieb, Robert Adams. **George** Balanchine: the ballet maker. HarperCollins\Atlas Books 2004 224p (Eminent lives) $19.95; pa. $13.99

Grades: 11 12 Adult   **92**

1. Ballet 2. Dancers 3. Choreographers

ISBN 0-06-075070-7; 9780060750718

LC 2004-48856

"This loving tribute captures Balanchine's legacy: his energy, confidence, lack of pretension and, most important, his joy in creation." Publ Wkly

Includes bibliographical references

Barakat, Ibtisam

★ Barakat, Ibtisam. **Tasting** the sky; a Palestinian childhood. Farrar, Straus & Giroux 2007 176p $16

Grades: 6 7 8 9 10   **92**

1. Poets 2. Authors 3. Palestinian Arabs 4. Israel-Arab conflicts 5. Memoirists 6. College teachers 7. Young adult authors

ISBN 0-374-35733-1; 978-0-374-35733-7

LC 2006-41265

"In 1981 the author, then in high school, boarded a bus bound for Ramallah. The bus was detained by Israeli soldiers at a checkpoint on the West Bank, and she was taken to a detention center before being released. The episode triggers sometimes heart-wrenching memories of herself as a young child, at the start of the 1967 Six Days' War, as Israeli soldiers conducted raids, their planes bombed her home, and she fled with her family across the border to Jordan. . . . What makes the memoir so compelling is the immediacy of the child's viewpoint, which depicts both conflict and daily life without exploitation or sentimentality." Booklist

Barrowcliffe, Mark

Barrowcliffe, Mark. The **elfish** gene; dungeons, dragons and growing up strange. Soho Press 2008 277p $25

Grades: 11 12 Adult   **92**

1. Authors 2. Comedians 3. Novelists 4. Journalists 5. Fantasy games 6. Dungeons & dragons (Game) 7. Memoirists 8. Authors, English

ISBN 978-1-56947-522-5; 1-56947-522-9

LC 2008-12471

First published 2007 in the United Kingdom

In this attempt to understand the true inner nerd of the adolescent male, Barrowcliffe relates how he and twenty million other boys grew up in the '70s and '80s absorbed in the world of fantasy roleplaying games like Dungeon & Dragons.

"Barrowcliffe, whose own schoolboy nickname was Spaz, wonderfully captures the insensitivity, insecurity and selfishness of the adolescent male. . . . [He] renders all the comedy and sorrow of early manhood, when boys flee the wretchedness of their real status for a taste of power in imaginary domains." Publ Wkly

Barton, Clara, 1821-1912

Oates, Stephen B. A **woman** of valor: Clara Barton and the Civil War. Free Press 1994 527p il map hardcover o.p. pa $16.95; pa $23.95

Grades: 11 12 Adult   92

1. Nurses 2. Red Cross officials 3. Social welfare leaders 4. United States -- History -- 1861-1865, Civil War

ISBN 0-02-923405-0; 0-02-874012-2 pa; 9780028740126

LC 93-38830

"This is a carefully written and researched work that brings to life both the Civil War and a period of Barton's life that was to affect her forever." Libr J

Includes bibliographical references

Basie, Count, 1904-1984

Basie, Count. **Good** morning blues: the autobiography of Count Basie; as told to Albert Murray. Da Capo Press 1995 399p il pa $17.95

Grades: 11 12 Adult   92

1. Pianists 2. Jazz musicians 3. African American musicians 4. Band leaders

ISBN 0-306-81107-3

LC 94-44697

"Basie pays tribute to his colleagues and managers (and to John Hammond for 'discovering' him), but does not hesitate to discuss their weaknesses and short-comings; his language is direct and earthy. Although some of the book reads more like a catalogue or itinerary than an autobiography, it will have strong appeal for jazz buffs and fans of the late bandleader." Publ Wkly

Bauman, Jeff

Witter, Bret. **Stronger**; Jeff Bauman, with Bret Witter. Grand Central Publishing 2014 244 p. illustrations (hardcover) $26

Grades: 11 12 Adult   92

1. Terrorism victims 2. Amputees -- Rehabilitation 3. Boston Marathon Bombing, Boston, Mass., 2013

ISBN 1455584371; 9781455584376

LC 2013050788

Jeff Bauman was next to the bomb when it exploded at the Boston Marathon on April 15, 2013. Pictures of him flooded the media as he became the iconic image of the tragedy: Bauman in a wheel chair, legs missing from the knees down. The following weeks of speculation and the eventual police shootout with the Tsarnaev brothers is well documented. Bauman and co-author Bret Witter are telling a different story, a personal story. . . . Bauman does not sugar coat the heroism of his situation. He's upfront about the difficulties of amputation, of his family adjusting to new realities, [and] of being a sudden media personality." (Publishers Weekly)

"Only a misanthrope would fail to be moved by Bauman's guileless narration of the horrors of rehabilitation or his frustration with learning to live with his new prosthetic legs. This is the simple story of one decent guy who fights hard to stay strong in the face of adversity." LJ

Beah, Ishmael

★ Beah, Ishmael, 1980- A **long** way gone; memoirs of a boy soldier. Farrar, Straus & Giroux 2007 229p map pa $12; $22

Grades: 11 12 Adult   92

1. Refugees 2. Soldiers 3. Children and war 4. Memoirists 5. Social activists 6. Sierra Leone -- History -- Civil War, 1991- 7. Sierra Leone -- History -- Civil War, 1991-2002

ISBN 0-374-53126-9 pa; 0-374-95191-8; 978-0-374-10523-5; 978-0-374-53126-3 pa

LC 2006-17101

The author writes about his experiences as a recruit in the Sierra Leone Army.

"In 1993, when the author was twelve, rebel forces attacked his home town, in Sierra Leone, and he was separated from his parents. For months, he straggled through the war-torn countryside, starving and terrified, until he was taken under the wing of a Shakespeare-spouting lieutenant in the government army. Soon, he was being fed amphetamines and trained to shoot an AK-47. . . . Beah's memoir documents his transformation from a child into a hardened, brutally efficient soldier who high-fived his fellow-recruits after they slaughtered their enemies—often boys their own age—and who 'felt no pity for anyone.'" New Yorker

Beck, Glenn

Novak, Amy. **Glenn** Beck; by Amy Novak. Lucent Books 2011 112 p. col. ill. (hbk.) $33.95; (hbk.) $33.95

Grades: 6 7 8 9   92

1. Radio broadcasting 2. Conservatism -- United States 3. Conservatives -- United States -- Biography 4. Radio personalities -- United States -- Biography 5. Television personalities -- United States -- Biography

ISBN 1420506056; 9781420506051

LC 2011005084

This book offers a biography of Conservative radio and television personality Glenn Beck by author Amy Novak. It is part of the "People in the News" series, which "profiles the lives and careers of some of today's most prominent newsmakers. Whether covering contributions and achievements or notorious deeds, books in this series examine why these well-known individuals garnered public attention." (Publisher's note)

Includes bibliographical references (p. 103-105) and index

Beethoven, Ludwig van, 1770-1827

★ Morris, Edmund, 1940- **Beethoven**: the universal composer. HarperCollins Publishers 2005 243p (Eminent lives) $21.95; pa $13.99

Grades: 11 12 Adult   92

1. Composers

ISBN 0-06-075974-7; 978-0-06-075974-2; 9780060759759

LC 2006-274925

This is a biography of the German composer.

The author "clearly admires his subject not only for the work but also for his constant fight against the odds, and he has written an ideal biography for the general reader." Publ Wkly

Includes bibliographical references

Bernstein, Leonard, 1918-1990

Bernstein, Burton. **Leonard** Bernstein; American original; how a modern renaissance man transformed music and the world during his New York Philharmonic years, 1943-1976. [by] Burton Bernstein and Barbara B. Haws. HarperCollins 2008 223p il $29.95

Grades: 11 12 Adult   92
1. Composers 2. Musicians 3. Conductors (Music) 4. New York Philharmonic 5. Composers -- United States
ISBN 978-0-06-153786-8; 0-06-153786-1

LC 2008-13702
"A flat-out wonderful book." Booklist

Bernstein, Paula

Schein, Elyse. **Identical** strangers; a memoir of twins separated and reunited. [by] Elyse Schein, Paula Bernstein. Random House 2007 270p il pa $16.00; $25.95

Grades: 11 12 Adult   92
1. Twins 2. Journalists 3. Adopted children 4. Memoirists 5. Motion picture directors
ISBN 9780812975659; 978-1-4000-6496-0; 1-4000-6496-1

LC 2007-14488
"Reunited at the age of 35, . . . [the authors, who are identical twins,] embarked on a journey to uncover the story of their separation. Research into their genealogical background revealed an ethically questionable study on identical twins performed by the doctors associated with the agency that facilitated their adoptions. In alternating voices, the women detail their emotional struggles as they navigated their developing relationship and the realities of the circumstances surrounding their birth and separation. . . . Teens will be pulled in by the mystery surrounding the study and the identity of the authors' birth mother." SLJ

Birkeland, Kristian, 1867-1917

Jago, Lucy. The **northern** lights. Knopf 2001 297p hardcover o.p. pa $14

Grades: 11 12 Adult   92
1. Auroras 2. Physicists 3. Scientists 4. College teachers
ISBN 0-375-40980-7; 0-375-70882-0 pa

LC 2001-29895
"Instead of a stiff, scholarly biography, British journalist Jago has written a poignantly human story filled with minute, extensively researched details." Libr J

Includes bibliographical references

Black Elk, 1863-1950

Black Elk. **Black** Elk speaks; being the life story of a holy man of the Oglala Sioux. [as told through] John G. Neihardt; foreword by Vine Deloria, Jr.; with illustrations by Standing Bear; essays by Alexis N.

Petri and Lori Utecht. University of Nebraska Press 2004 xxix, 270p il map pa $19.95; pa $14.95

Grades: 11 12 Adult   92
1. Shamans 2. Oglala Indians 3. Indian leaders 4. Native Americans -- Biography
ISBN 9780803283916; 0-8032-8385-7

LC 2004-12692
A reprint of the title first published 1932 by Morrow

The Indian whose life story this is, was born in 1863. He was a famous warrior and hunter in his youth, and became a practicing medicine man among his people. Of him Neihardt says, "As an indubitable seer, he seemed to represent the consciousness of the Plains Indian more fully than any other I had ever known."

This "is about as near as you can get to seeing life and death, war and religion, through an Indian's eyes." Outlook

Blume, Judy

Tracy, Kathleen. **Judy** Blume; a biography. Greenwood Press 2008 127p (Greenwood biographies) $35

Grades: 9 10 11 12   92
1. Authors 2. Novelists 3. Women authors 4. Authors, American 5. Children's authors 6. Young adult authors
ISBN 978-0-313-34272-1; 0-313-34272-5

LC 2007-37491
"The book was hard to put down, and will appeal to high school students and adults. It is an inspiration to those who want to be authors." Libr Media Connect

Includes bibliographical references

Bly, Nellie, 1864-1922

Bankston, John. **Nellie** Bly; journalist. John Bankston. Chelsea House 2011 155 p. ill. (hc) $35.00

Grades: 7 8 9 10   92
1. Women journalists 2. Journalists -- United States -- Biography
ISBN 1604139080; 9781604139082

LC 2011000040
This book offers a biography journalist Elizabeth Cochrane, better known as Nellie Bly. An angry letter she wrote in response to a newspaper article about the role of women "earned her a job and a new name: Nellie Bly. As her alter ego, she gave a voice to women who worked in factories and were being treated in asylums. And she would travel around the world faster than anyone ever had. By the time she was 25, Nellie Bly was the most famous reporter in the world." (Google Books)

Includes bibliographical references (p. 144-147) and index

Bohr, Niels

Spangenburg, Ray. **Niels** Bohr; atomic theorist. [by] Ray Spangenburg and Diane Kit Moser. Rev ed; Chelsea House 2008 141p bibl il (Makers of modern science) $35

Grades: 7 8 9 10 11 12   92
1. Scientists
ISBN 978-0-8160-6178-5; 0-8160-6178-5

LC 2008-1196

"Spangenburg and Moser delve into Bohr's background and present him as a loving, talkative, and inquisitive person who liked soccer. He was also concerned about the consequences of his work with nuclear weapons and was involved in many humanitarian efforts... New content includes informational sidebars and a discussion of string theory." SLJ

Includes bibliographical references

Bohr, Niels Henrik David, 1885-1962

★ Ottaviani, Jim. **Suspended** in language; Niels Bohr's life, discoveries, and the century he shaped. written by Jim Ottaviani; illustrated and lettered by Leland Purvis. 2nd ed; G.T. Labs 2009 318p il pa $24.95

Grades: 10 11 12 Adult 92

1. Physicists 2. Graphic novels 3. Biographical graphic novels 4. Nobel laureates for physics 5. Physicists -- Graphic novels 6. Quantum theory -- Graphic novels
ISBN 978-0-9788037-2-8

First published 2004

"Quantum physics gets an accessible yet substantive introduction through art that mixes fantasy and realism. Great for teens who like science." Booklist

Includes bibliographical references

Bolt, Usain, 1986-

Bolt, Usain, 1986- **9.58**; my story: being the world's fastest man. [by] Usain Bolt with Shaun Custis. HarperSport 2010 252p il

Grades: 11 12 Adult 92

1. Running 2. Olympic athletes 3. Runners (Athletes)
ISBN 978-0-00-737139-6

This book follows "the world's fastest man through his mercurial path from a small outlying region of Jamaica to being one of the world's best-known sports personalities. . . . [The author] is brutally frank in relating his development as an athlete, circumstances in Jamaica, training methods, love of nightlife and fast cars, and how he will triumph in London in 2012 and in 2016 Brazil. . . . [This is] is a rich and textured outline of a life of present accomplishment and of future promise lived in the fast lane. A delight for readers of all ages and backgrounds." Libr J

Bonhoeffer, Dietrich, 1906-1945

Martin, Michael J. **Champion** of freedom; Dietrich Bonhoeffer. by Michael Martin. Morgan Reynolds Pub. 2012 144 p. ill. (some col.) (hbk.) $28.95

Grades: 7 8 9 10 11 12 92

1. Clergy 2. Theologians
ISBN 1599351692; 9781599351698

LC 2010049095

This book looks at "Dietrich Bonhoeffer [who in 1943] was arrested and imprisoned by the Gestapo for crimes [against] the government. . . . [This] German Lutheran Pastor was integrally involved in the plot to assassinate Adolf Hitler. During his two years of imprisonment, Bonhoeffer manages extreme circumstances, including interrogation and isolation, but is able to protect both himself and his co-conspirators through careful rhetorical practices. How does a pastor and a loyal German justify his involvement in the plot? . . . How could a pastor who penned a book titled Ethics, ethically justify his actions? This book considers some of those questions and is for theologians, ethicists, and rhetoricians as it examines the intersection of faith, politics, and classic rhetorical theory. (Amazon.com)

Includes bibliographical references (p. 140) and index.

Bosch, Carl

Hager, Thomas. The **alchemy** of air; a Jewish genius, a doomed tycoon, and the scientific discovery that fed the world but fueled the rise of Hitler. Harmony Books 2008 316p $24.95; pa $15

Grades: 11 12 Adult 92

1. Chemists 2. Fertilizers 3. Nobel laureates for chemistry
ISBN 978-0-307-35178-4; 0-307-35178-5; 978-0-307-35179-1 pa; 0-307-35179-3 pa

LC 2008-3192

"A fast-paced account of the early-20th-century quest to develop synthetic fertilizer. . . . Science writing of the first order." Kirkus

Includes bibliographical references

Bowman-Kruhm, Mary

The **Leakeys**; a biography. Greenwood Press 2005 150p il (Greenwood biographies) $29.95

Grades: 9 10 11 12 92

1. Anthropologists 2. Archaeologists 3. Paleontologists 4. Government officials 5. Museum administrators
ISBN 0-313-32985-0; 978-0-313-32985-2

LC 2005-16821

"Accurate, accessible biographies that go beyond facts to create engaging profiles of exceptional personalities." SLJ

Includes glossary and bibliographical references

Boyle, Robert, 1627-1691

Baxter, Roberta. **Skeptical** chemist; the story of Robert Boyle. Morgan Reynolds Pub. 2006 128p il (Profiles in science) lib bdg $27.95

Grades: 7 8 9 10 92

1. Chemists 2. Physicists 3. Scientists 4. Nonfiction writers 5. Writers on science
ISBN 978-1-59935-025-7; 1-59935-025-4

LC 2006-23969

The author makes a "case for Boyle's significance as a key figure in the field of scientific experimentation as well as his contributions to modern chemistry and physics. Well organized and clearly written, her book offers a good view of changes in science and society at this pivotal time and presents a well-rounded view of Boyle, whose interests extended beyond scientific inquiry and discussion." Booklist

Includes bibliographical references

Bradbury, Ray, 1920-2012

Bankston, John. **Ray** Bradbury; foreword by Kyle Zimmer. Chelsea House 2011 140p il (Who wrote that?) lib bdg $35.00

Grades: 6 7 8 9 10 92

1. Authors 2. Novelists 3. Screenwriters 4. Authors, American 5. Children's authors 6. Short story writers 7. Science fiction writers
ISBN 1-60413-778-9; 978-1-60413-778-1

This discusses the life and work of author Ray Bradbury. Includes bibliographical references

Eller, Jonathan R. **Becoming** Ray Bradbury. University of Illinois Press 2011 324p il $34.95
Grades: 11 12 Adult   92
1. Authors 2. Novelists 3. Screenwriters 4. Authors, American 5. Children's authors 6. Short story writers 7. Science fiction writers
ISBN 978-0-252-03629-3
LC 2011008562
The author "provides a detailed account of the experiences that shaped Ray Bradbury's life and writing career from his childhood until he embarked on the screenplay for John Huston's Moby Dick in late 1953. . . . Eller's work is thorough and enlightening on the subject of one of science fiction's greatest minds. Highly recommended not just for Bradbury fans but for all students of science fiction." Libr J
Includes bibliographical references

Brady, Tom
Doeden, Matt. **Tom** Brady; unlikely champion. Twenty-First Century Books 2011 112p il (USA today lifeline biographies) lib bdg $33.26
Grades: 7 8 9 10   92
1. Football players 2. Football -- Biography
ISBN 978-0-7613-6423-8; 0-7613-6423-4
LC 2010031518
This is a biography of the quarterback for the New England Patriots.
Includes glossary and bibliographical references

Brown, Bradford B., 1929-2012
Brown, Bradford B. **While** you're here, Doc; farmyard adventures of a Maine veterinarian. Tilbury House 2006 174p il pa $15
Grades: 9 10 11 12   92
1. Veterinarians 2. Veterinary medicine 3. Memoirists
ISBN 978-0-8844-8279-6; 0-8844-8279-0
LC 2005-32418
This veterinary memoir features "tales of animal doctoring in a small coastal town in 1950s Maine. . . . Full of laconic farmers, hysterical owners, and more feisty animal patients than one can imagine, these stories of backwoods veterinary care are sure to be popular among James Herriot lovers." Booklist

Brown, Claude, 1937-2002
★ Brown, Claude. **Manchild** in the promised land. Touchstone 1999 415p pa $19.95; pa $14.95
Grades: 11 12 Adult   92
1. Authors 2. Journalists 3. Essayists 4. Memoirists 5. African Americans -- Biography 6. African Americans -- Harlem (New York, N.Y.)
ISBN 9781451626674; 0-684-86418-5
First published 1965 by Macmillan
This is "the autobiography of a young black man raised in Harlem. It is a realistic description of life in the ghetto. . . . The core of the book concerns the 'plague' of heroin addiction that swept through Harlem in the 1950s taking the lives of many of Brown's contemporaries." Publ Wkly

Brown, John, 1800-1859
Sterngass, Jon. **John** Brown. Chelsea House 2009 144p il (Leaders of the Civil War era) lib bdg $30
Grades: 7 8 9 10   92
1. Abolitionists
ISBN 978-1-60413-305-9; 1-60413-305-8
LC 2008-44622
This is a biography of the abolitionist, John Brown.
This is an "even-keeled and well-written account of the man's life and times. . . . Sterngrass displays a sharp awareness that what makes the man so controversial is also what makes him so fascinating. . . . [This book] should add depth to Civil War studies." Booklist
Includes glossary and bibliographical references

Bruchac, Joseph, 1942-
Bruchac, Joseph. **Bowman's** store; a journey to myself. 1st Lee & Low ed; Lee & Low Books 2001 315p il pa $9.95
Grades: 7 8 9 10   92
1. Poets 2. Authors 3. Abnaki Indians 4. Storytellers 5. College teachers 6. Magazine editors 7. Authors, American 8. Children's authors 9. Nonfiction writers 10. Native Americans -- Biography
ISBN 1-58430-027-2; 978-1-58430-027-4
LC 2001-16435
A reissue of the title first published 1997 by Dial Books
"Each episode is constructed with a true storyteller's attention to language and plot development. Students of modern Native American cultures will find plenty of food for thought." Booklist

Bullard, Eugene Jacques, 1894-1961
Greenly, Larry. **Eugene** Bullard; world's first Black fighter pilot. Larry W. Greenly. Junebug Books 2012 160 p. illustrations $19.95
Grades: 8 9 10 11 12   92
1. Fighter pilots -- France -- Biography 2. African American fighter pilots -- Biography 3. World War, 1914-1918 -- Aerial operations, French 4. World War, 1939-1945 -- Aerial operations, French 5. African American fighter pilots -- France -- Biography 6. Race discrimination -- United States -- History -- 20th century
ISBN 158838280X; 9781588382801
LC 2012036425
This book, by Larry Greenly, "tells the story of pioneering black aviator Eugene Bullard from his birth in 1895 to his combat experiences in both World War I and II and, finally, his return to America. . . . He ran away from home at twelve and eventually made his way to France, where he joined the French Foreign Legion and later the Lafayette Flying Corps, to become the world's first black fighter pilot." (Publisher's note)
"The incredible story of Eugene Bullard—an African American honored by the French, yet shunned by the Americans—is one too long neglected. . . . Though his heroic deeds brought recognition from the French, a white American doctor in Paris became a constant stumbling block for further progress in Eugene's life and career. . . . Using Bullard's memoirs and other sparse information about him, Greenly crafts a moving, novelistic biography that portrays Bullard's

courage throughout his life. Meanwhile, the black-and-white photos, of everything from a teenage Bullard boxing to wartime aircrafts, add plenty of historical flavor." Booklist

Includes bibliographical references

Bunche, Ralph J. (Ralph Johnson), 1904-1971

Urquhart, Brian E. **Ralph** Bunche; an American life. [by] Brian Urquhart. Norton 1993 496p il maps hardcover o.p. pa $15.95

Grades: 11 12 Adult 92

1. Diplomats 2. Political scientists 3. United Nations officials 4. Nobel laureates for peace 5. African Americans -- Biography 6. United States -- Race relations

ISBN 0-393-03527-1; 0-393-31859-1 pa

LC 92-46564

The author "describes Bunche's itinerant childhood, academic background, teaching and research, OSS service in World War II, significant contributions at the Dumbarton Oaks Conference of Allied leaders, and troubleshooting and mediation on behalf of the UN throughout the Middle East, Africa, and Asia. . . . Urquhart has made a fascinating narrative of the accomplishments of an American-born international diplomat." Booklist

Includes bibliographical references

Burcaw, Shane

Burcaw, Shane. **Laughing** at my nightmare; Shane Burcaw. Roaring Brook Press 2014 256 p. illustrations (hardback) $17.99

Grades: 10 11 12 Adult 92

1. Wit and humor 2. People with disabilities 3. Spinal muscular atrophy -- Patients

ISBN 162672007X; 9781626720077

LC 2014010634

YALSA Award for Excellence in Nonfiction for Young Adults: Finalist (2015)

Author Shane Burcaw "describes the challenges he faces as a twenty-one-year-old with spinal muscular atrophy. From awkward handshakes to having a girlfriend and everything in between, Shane handles his situation with humor. While he does talk about everyday issues that are relatable to teens, he also offers an eye-opening perspective on what it is like to have a life threatening disease." (Publisher's note)

"Burcaw demonstrates mastery in expressing accessible insights that are well padded in humor, as well as a realistic awareness of his situation, leavened by tongue-in-cheek hyperbole, none of which gives way to off-putting egoism or navel gazing." Booklist

Burr, Aaron, 1756-1836

★ St. George, Judith. The **duel**: the parallel lives of Alexander Hamilton and Aaron Burr. Viking 2009 97p il $16.99

Grades: 6 7 8 9 10 92

1. Statesmen 2. Vice-presidents 3. Secretaries of the treasury 4. Politicians -- United States

ISBN 978-0-670-01124-7; 0-670-01124-X

LC 2009-5660

"After a prologue following the steps of Alexander Hamilton and Aaron Burr on the morning of their famous duel, St. George backtracks to trace the 'parallel lives' mentioned

in the subtitle. . . . Well researched and organized, the book offers insights into the personalities, lives, and times of Burr and Hamilton." Booklist

Calcines, Eduardo F., 1955-

★ Calcines, Eduardo F. **Leaving** Glorytown; one boy's struggle under Castro. Farrar, Straus & Giroux 2009 221p il $17.95

Grades: 7 8 9 10 92

1. Businesspeople 2. Cuban refugees 3. Memoirists 4. Cuba -- History -- 1959-

ISBN 0-374-34394-2; 978-0-374-34394-1

LC 2008-7506

Eduardo F. Calcines was "three years old when Castro came to power in January 1959. After that, everything changed for his family and his country. When he was ten, his family applied for an exit visa to emigrate to America. . . . His father was sent to an agricultural cultural reform camp to do hard labor as punishment for daring to want to leave Cuba. During the years to come, as he grew up in Glorytown, a neighborhood in the city of Cienfuegos, Eduardo hoped . . . that their exit visa would be granted before he turned fifteen, the age at which he would be drafted into the army. In [this memoir, Calcines] . . . recounts his boyhood and chronicles the conditions that led him to wish above all else to leave behind his beloved extended family and his home." (Publisher's note) "Grades seven to ten." (Bull Cent Child Books)

"Calcines's spirited memoir captures the political tension, economic hardship, family stress, and personal anxiety of growing up during the early years of the Castro regime in Cuba. . . . The author shares startling, clear memories about his life in the Glorytown barrio of Cienfuegos. . . . Calcines writes about Cuba with immediacy, nostalgia, and passion. This personal account will acquaint readers with the oppressive and ironic effects of communism." SLJ

Carroll, Lewis, 1832-1898

Rubin, C. M. The **real** Alice in Wonderland; a role model for the ages. [by] C.M. Rubin with Gabriella Rose Rubin. AuthorHouse 2010 134p il $29.95

Grades: 7 8 9 10 92

1. Authors 2. Children 3. Novelists 4. Mathematicians 5. Characters and characteristics in literature 6. Children's authors 7. Writers on science

ISBN 978-1-4490-8131-7; 1-4490-8131-2

LC 2010-901865

"Readers will follow this title down the rabbit hole to discover the world of the real Alice who inspired Lewis Carroll's Alice in Wonderland. The book moves seamlessly through the life of Alice Pleasance Liddell. . . . This offering paints a full picture of Alice, not only as a child who has captivated literature but also as a woman who was truly ahead of her time. This is a purchase that will do well with a range of people and should be offered as a standard accompaniment to Alice in Wonderland. The illustrations and pictures will make it quite popular in a public library." Voice Youth Advocates

Includes bibliographical references

Carson, Kit, 1809-1868

Remley, David. **Kit** Carson; the life of an American border man. by David Remley. University of Oklahoma Press 2011 289p il map (Oklahoma western biographies) $24.95

Grades: 11 12 Adult   92

1. Scouts 2. Pioneers 3. Frontier and pioneer life -- West (U.S.)

ISBN 978-0-8061-4172-5

LC 2010-37350

The author "separates the myth from the man in this engrossing portrait of frontiersman Carson (1809–1868) . . . Contrasting dangerous days and rip-roaring action with poignant moments of Carson's family life, Remley challenges recent revisionist representations of Carson as a 'trigger-happy' outlaw and scoundrel. Instead, the nomadic Carson emerges as an aggressive, helpful, and caring man, who 'matured intellectually and ethically as he grew older.' Remley's Old West overview permeates this rich and rewarding work of scholarship." Publ Wkly

Includes bibliographical references

Carter, Robert, 1728-1804

Levy, Andrew. The **first** emancipator; the forgotten story of Robert Carter, the founding father who freed his slaves. Random House 2005 310p hardcover o.p. pa $15.95

Grades: 11 12 Adult   92

1. Plantation owners 2. Biography, Individual 3. Slavery -- United States

ISBN 0-375-50865-1; 0-375-76104-7 pa

LC 2004-54054

"In 1791, [Robert] Carter began a manumission process that would eventually free some 450 people on his northern Virginia plantations and beyond. . . . [Levy focuses] on Carter's psychic and religious struggles as he progressed haltingly toward the act of manumission." (N Y Times Book Rev) Index.

"This well-written and thoroughly engaging book will certainly appeal to readers interested in the history of 18th- and 19th-century Virginia, but also to those interested in the history of slavery and racism in America and in historical biography." Publ Wkly

Includes bibliographical references

Cary, Lorene

Cary, Lorene. **Black** ice. Knopf 1991 237p hardcover o.p. pa $10

Grades: 11 12 Adult   92

1. Authors 2. Novelists 3. Journalists 4. Memoirists 5. St. Paul's School (Concord, N.H.) 6. African American women -- Biography

ISBN 0-394-57465-6; 0-679-73745-6 pa

LC 90-52988

"In the early 1970's, an Eastern prep school recruiting minority students opened its doors to Cary, then a 15-year-old Philadelphia high school girl. These affecting recollections explore her experiences—interactions with teachers, an affair with another student, friendships, and problems with prejudice—as well as her struggle to determine her own black identity." Booklist

Castro, Fidel, 1926-

★ Coltman, Leycester. The **real** Fidel Castro; with a foreword by Julia E. Sweig. Yale Univ. Press 2003 335p il map $30; pa $20

Grades: 11 12 Adult   92

1. Presidents 2. Communist leaders 3. Cuba -- Politics and government

ISBN 0-300-10188-0; 0-300-10760-9 pa

LC 2003-12942

This biography "offers a fresh assessment of the revolutionary leader. . . . It chronicles the events of Castro's extraordinary life and explores the contradiction between the private character and the public reputation." Univ Press Books for Public and Second Sch Libr, 2004

Includes bibliographical references

Cather, Willa, 1873-1947

★ Meltzer, Milton. **Willa** Cather; a biography. Twenty-First Century Books 2008 160p il (Literary greats) $33.26

Grades: 7 8 9 10 11 12   92

1. Authors 2. Novelists 3. Women authors 4. Western writers 5. Authors, American 6. Short story writers

ISBN 978-0-8225-7604-4; 0-8225-7604-X

LC 2007-25629

A biography of the author of such novels as O Pioneers! and My Antonia.

"With signature clarity, Meltzer's . . . biography . . . sets his detailed discussion of Cather's life and work against the larger backdrop of her times. . . . The book's handsome, inviting design includes photos on almost every spread." Booklist

Includes bibliographical references

Catherine II, the Great, Empress of Russia, 1729-1796

★ Whitelaw, Nancy. **Catherine** the Great and the Enlightenment in Russia. Morgan Reynolds Pub. 2005 160p il map (European queens) lib bdg $24.95

Grades: 9 10 11 12   92

1. Empresses 2. Russia -- Kings and rulers

ISBN 1-931798-27-3; 978-1-931798-27-3

LC 2004-14711

The author "follows Catherine from her youth as a struggling German princess to Russia, where at 16 she wed the profoundly unimpressive Grand Duke Peter, whom she embraced as a means to the throne. . . . In language both straightforward and compelling, Whitelaw describes the formidable czarina's reign, her love affairs, her vast cultural influence, and the political treachery that surrounded her court." Booklist

Includes bibliographical references

Catlin, George, 1796-1872

★ Reich, Susanna. **Painting** the wild frontier: the art and adventures of George Catlin. Clarion Books 2008 160p il map $21

Grades: 7 8 9 10 11 12   92

1. Artists 2. Painters 3. West (U.S.) in art 4. Native

Americans in art 5. Artists -- United States
ISBN 978-0-618-71470-4; 0-618-71470-7
LC 2007-38847

This is a "biography of nineteenth-century painter George Catlin, famous for his portraits of Native American life. . . . A great introduction to Catlin's work as well as an excellent title to use in social studies, history, and art classes." Booklist

Includes bibliographical references

Chavez, Cesar, 1927-1993

Haugen, Brenda. **Cesar** Chavez; crusader for social change. by Brenda Haugen. Compass Point Books 2008 112p il map $35.32

Grades: 6 7 8 9   92
1. Labor leaders. 2. Mexican Americans -- Biography. 3. Mexican American migrant agricultural laborers. 4. Labor leaders -- United States -- Biography..
ISBN 978-0-7565-3321-2 (lib bdg); 0-7565-3321-X (lib bdg)
LC 2007003939

Profiles the Mexican American who helped create a union to protect the rights of migrant agricultural laborers. (Publisher's note)

"Provides solid basic information... attractively packaged with many photos, interesting sidebars, and reader-friendly text arrangement." VOYA

Stavans, Ilan, 1961- **Cesar** Chavez; a photographic essay. Cinco Puntos Press 2010 91p il pa $13.95

Grades: 7 8 9 10   92
1. Agricultural laborers 2. Migrant agricultural laborers 3. Labor leaders 4. Mexican Americans -- Biography
ISBN 1-933693-22-3; 978-1-933693-22-4
LC 2009044179

"Chavez secured better working conditions for thousands with his 1970 victory for the United Farm Workers Union by bargaining with the table-grape growers. This photo-biography covers the high points of his career, including ample and pointed quotes by him and touching on his global recognition and interactions with activist Fred Ross Jr., Dolores Huerta, Pope Paul VI, and Senator Robert F. Kennedy. The full-page black-and-white photos give a sense of the man at various ages, of the migrant workers' lives, and of being on the road demonstrating and striking. The book also includes a comprehensive time line. It is an excellent introduction to social activism from the 1950s through the 1980s." SLJ

Chinmoy, Sri

Tamm, Jayanti. **Cartwheels** in a sari; a memoir of growing up cult. Harmony Books 2009 288p $22.99

Grades: 11 12 Adult   92
1. Gurus 2. College teachers
ISBN 978-0-307-39392-0; 0-307-39392-5
LC 2008-36450

The author "recounts her youth as the chosen disciple of Sri Chinmoy, the wildly charismatic leader of a New York-based spiritual sect that counts celebrities and heads of nations among its millions of followers. . . . Witty, compassionate, and often heartbreaking, Tamm's story offers crucial insight into a cult's inner workings and methods of indoctrination. All readers, though, will recognize universal coming-of-age themes as Tamm discards unwanted childhood lessons and begins to shape an independent adult life." Booklist

Clemente, Roberto, 1934-1972

★ Maraniss, David. **Clemente**; the passion and grace of baseball's last hero. Simon & Schuster 2006 401p il maps hardcover o.p. pa $15

Grades: 11 12 Adult   92
1. Baseball players 2. Baseball -- Biography
ISBN 0-7432-1781-0; 978-0-7432-1781-1; 0-7432-9999-X; 978-0-7432-9999-2 pa
LC 2006-42235

The author "has produced a baseball-savvy book sensitive to the social context that made Clemente, a black Puerto Rican, a leading indicator of baseball's future." N Y Times Book Rev

Includes bibliographical references

Santiago, Wilfred. **21**; the story of Roberto Clemente: a graphic novel. Wilfred Santiago. Fantagraphics 2011 148p. chiefly ill. $22.99

Grades: 11 12 Adult   92
1. Graphic novels 2. Baseball players -- Graphic novels 3. Baseball -- Graphic novels
ISBN 978-1-56097-892-3

This book "is an all-ages graphic biography of baseball star Roberto Clemente: No other baseball player dominated the 1960s like him and no other Latin American player achieved his numbers. '21' chronicles his early days growing up in rural Puerto Rico, the highlights of his career (including the 1960s World Series), the prejudice he faced, his private life and his humanitarian mission." (trplteens.wordpress.com)

"Santiago opens his dazzlingly drawn comics biography of the pioneering Puerto Rican ballplayer on the final game of the 1972 season, with Clemente just one hit shy of joining the 3,000-hit club. Fans will know, of course, that 3,000 would also be his final tally, as he would die in a plane crash delivering relief supplics to the earthquake-rocked Nicaragua that winter. Santiago skitters around formative scenes from Clemente's childhood—striking a complex chord of family, homeland, and a driving passion for baseball—before tracing significant moments from his professional career: staring down racism with the same resolute demeanor with which he faced a high heater, snagging batting championships and fans' hearts many times over, and always looking for ways to honor his heritage." Booklist

Includes bibliographic references.

Cleopatra, Queen of Egypt, d. 30 B.C.

★ Nardo, Don. **Cleopatra**. Lucent Books 2005 112p il map (Lucent library of historical eras, Ancient Egypt) $28.70

Grades: 7 8 9 10   92
1. Queens 2. Egypt -- History
ISBN 1-59018-660-5; 978-1-59018-660-2
LC 2004-22071

This biography of the Egyptian queen "features quotations from ancient authors, along with Nardo's discussion of how many of these authors were biased, for or against one of the most powerful women in history. He includes her romantic liaisons with Julius Caesar and Marc Antony. . . . A final chapter looks at how Cleopatra has been rendered in literature." SLJ

Includes bibliographical references

★ Roller, Duane W. **Cleopatra**; a biography. Oxford University Press 2010 252p il map (Women in antiquity) $24.95

Grades: 11 12 Adult   **92**

1. Queens 2. Egypt -- History

ISBN 978-0-19-536553-5; 0-19-536553-4

           LC 2009-24061

"Basing this chronicle exclusively on primary sources culled from classical antiquity, the author painstakingly separates myth from reality, discounting . . . [Cleopatra's] undeserved reputation as a seductress and concentrating on her impressive—but often overlooked or minimized—political, military, and administrative achievements. This revisionist portrait of one of the most powerful women in the ancient world adds substance and heft to her exotic legacy." Booklist

Includes bibliographical references

Clinton, Hillary Rodham

Hillary Rodham **Clinton**; a woman living history. Karen Blumenthal. Feiwel & Friends 2016 448 p. illustrations (hardcover) $18.99

Grades: 7 8 9 10 11 12   **92**

1. Women politicians 2. Legislators -- United States -- Biography 3. United States. Congress. Senate -- Biography 4. Cabinet officers -- United States -- Biography

ISBN 1250060141; 9781250060143

           LC 2015026916

In this biography "author Karen Blumenthal gives . . . an intimate and unflinching look at the public and personal life of Hillary Rodham Clinton. Illustrated throughout with black-and-white photographs and political cartoons, this is a . . . biography about a woman who has fascinated--and divided--the public, who continues to push boundaries, and who isn't afraid to reach for one more goal." (Publisher's note)

"As astounding as Clinton's many accomplishments are, readers receive a balanced, wholly human portrait with all the flaws it entails. A richly detailed study that is as perceptive as it is engaging." Kirkus

Colvin, Claudette

★ Hoose, Phillip. **Claudette** Colvin; twice toward justice. by Phillip Hoose. Melanie Kroupa Books 2009 133p il $19.95

Grades: 6 7 8 9 10   **92**

1. Civil rights activists 2. African Americans -- Civil rights 3. African American women -- Biography

ISBN 978-0-374-31322-7; 0-374-31322-9

           LC 2008-05435

ALA ALSC Newbery Medal Honor Book (2010)

"Teenager Claudette Colvin's significant contribution to the struggle for equal accommodation is presented in this biography that smoothly weaves excerpts from Hoose's extensive interviews with Colvin and his own supplementary commentary. . . . [Readers learn] why her arrest for refusing to give up her bus seat to a white passenger never became the crucial incident to spark the Montgomery Bus Boycott. . . . Plenty of black-and-white photographs and well-deployed sidebars enhance the text." Bull Cent Child Books

Includes bibliographical references

Cooper, Ilene

★ **Jack**; the early years of John F. Kennedy. by Ilene Cooper. 1st ed. Penguin Group USA 2013 168 p. ill. (paperback) $12.99

Grades: 5 6 7 8 9 10 11 12   **92**

1. Catholics 2. Presidents 3. Presidents -- United States

ISBN 0147510317; 9780147510310

           LC 2002075912

This book by Ilene Cooper offers a "portrait of [John F.] Kennedy's "youth and the forces that shaped it. . . . Readers discover what it was like for Jack to grow up under the paradoxical influences of privilege and prejudice. His father's wealth . . . couldn't remove the perceived taint of the family's Irish Catholic heritage . . . . To compensate, Joseph and Rose Kennedy pushed their children to excel at everything they did," leading to rivalry between Jack and his brother Joe. (Horn Book Magazine)

"Intelligent design and numerous fabulous, well-placed, and well-captioned black-and-white photographs enrich Cooper's clear prose. . . . This sensitive, well-researched biography will enhance any collection." Voice Youth Advocates

Includes bibliographical references and index.

Cornwell, John, 1940-

Cornwell, John. **Seminary** boy. Doubleday 2006 321p il $24.95

Grades: 11 12 Adult   **92**

1. Authors 2. Journalists 3. Nonfiction writers

ISBN 978-0-385-54186-6; 0-385-51486-7

           LC 2005-56026

The author "tells the story of his life at an all-male school in the 1950s. Son of a struggling working-class family in London, John was sent to Cotton College to become a Catholic priest. Here, during his teen years, he experienced the best and worst of pre-Vatican II seminary life. Some of his teachers were pious and dedicated men; others were sexual predators. . . . Part spiritual odyssey, part boarding school story, Cornwell's well-crafted memoir is filled with vivid descriptions of people and places and a young boy's struggle to find himself." Libr J

Cosell, Howard, 1918-1995

Bloom, John. **There** you have it; the life, legacy, and legend of Howard Cosell. University of Massachusetts Press 2010 220p il $80; pa $24.95

Grades: 11 12 Adult   **92**

1. Lawyers 2. Television personalities 3. Television broadcasting of sports 4. Sportscasters

ISBN 978-1-55849-836-5; 1-55849-836-2; 978-1-55849-837-2 pa; 1-55849-837-0 pa

           LC 2010037284

"Many of the contradictions of his character and the finer intricacies of his legacy are teased out in this carefully observed portrait." Publ Wkly

Includes bibliographical references

Cousteau, Jacques Yves, 1910-1997

Matsen, Bradford. **Jacques** Cousteau; the sea king. [by] Brad Matsen. Pantheon Books 2009 296p il $27.95

Grades: 11 12 Adult 92

1. Authors 2. Oceanography 3. Divers 4. Naval officers 5. Oceanographers 6. Nonfiction writers

ISBN 978-0-375-42413-7; 0-375-42413-X

LC 2009-11640

This biography "places Cousteau's films, books, and fame into the context of the rest of his life—ambitions, childhood, family relationships, friendships, and disagreements. . . . Readers who dive, who are interested in ecology or the oceans, or who simply recognize the name Cousteau, will want to read this full, well-rounded portrait of one of the world's greatest explorers and conservationists. Highly recommended." Libr J

Includes bibliographical references

Craft, Jerry, 1937-

Craft, Jerry. **Our** white boy; [by] Jerry Craft, with Kathleen Sullivan; foreword by Larry Lester. Texas Tech University Press 2010 xxx, 241p il (Sport in the American West) $29.95

Grades: 11 12 Adult 92

1. Mayors 2. Negro leagues 3. Baseball players 4. Ranchers 5. Baseball -- Biography 6. Texas -- Race relations

ISBN 978-0-89672-674-1

LC 2009046591

"On one level, this is a simple baseball story about a team and its successes and failures. On another level, it is the story of how a young white man in rural Texas learned firsthand not only about how profoundly painful and limiting segregation was for both whites and blacks but also about how segregation could promote black pride and entrepreneurialism. This is a wonderful book in every respect." Choice

Includes bibliographical references

Curie, Marie, 1867-1934

Borzendowski, Janice. **Marie** Curie; mother of modern physics. Sterling Pub 2009 124p il map (Sterling biographies) $12.95; pa $5.95

Grades: 7 8 9 10 92

1. Chemists 2. Physicists 3. Women scientists 4. Nobel laureates for physics

ISBN 978-1-4027-6543-8; 1-4027-6543-6; 978-1-4027-5318-3 pa; 1-4027-5318-7 pa

LC 2008-30701

"This interesting, informative biography of the scientist and Nobel Prize winner explores both Curie's personal and professional life. It includes numerous archival and modern photos and reproductions. . . . The book is far more thorough and satisfying than most biographies of Curie for teens." SLJ

Includes bibliographical references

D'Amboise, Jacques

D'Amboise, Jacques. **I** was a dancer. Alfred A. Knopf 2011 439p il map $35

Grades: 10 11 12 Adult 92

1. Dancers 2. Ballet dancers 3. Choreographers 4. Dance teachers 5. New York City Ballet

ISBN 978-1-4000-4234-0; 1-4000-4234-8

LC 2010-45356

"In this spirited memoir, Jacques d'Amboise, one of America's most celebrated classical dancers, and former principal dancer with the New York City Ballet for more than three decades, tells the story of his life in dance, and of America's most renowned and admired dance companies. He writes of his mother dragging her son and daughter to ballet class. We see him, a neighborhood tough, on the streets, fighting with neighborhood gangs, and taking ten classes a week at the School of American Ballet; being taught by Balanchine and other great teachers. We meet Balanchine's succession of ballerina muses who inspired him to near-obsessive passion, dancers with whom d'Amboise partnered; of going to Hollywood and being offered a long-term contract at MGM; and of the moment when he realizes his dancing career is over and he begins a new life teaching children all over the world about the arts through the magic of dance."--From publisher description

Dahl, Roald

Sturrock, Donald. **Storyteller**; the authorized biography of Roald Dahl. Simon & Schuster 2010 655p il $30

Grades: 9 10 11 12 Adult 92

1. Authors 2. Authors, English 3. Children's authors 4. Short story writers

ISBN 978-1-4165-5082-2; 1-4165-5082-8

LC 2010-07175

"In this authorized biography of Dahl, Sturrock, the artistic director of the Roald Dahl Foundation, reveals a life marked by tragedy: the early deaths of Dahl's father and sister, his son's tragic accident, the death of a daughter at seven, and the debilitating stroke of his wife, Patricia Neal, at age 39...This carefully researched and unflinching portrait of an immensely complicated and talented writer will appeal to Dahl's fans and other serious readers of biography." (Library Journal)

Includes bibliographical references

Dalai Lama XIV, 1935-

★ Bstan-'dzin-rgya-mtsho, Dalai Lama XIV, 1935- **Freedom** in exile; the autobiography of the Dalai Lama. HarperCollins Pubs. 1990 288p il maps hardcover o.p. pa $15

Grades: 11 12 Adult 92

1. Buddhism 2. Tibet (China) 3. Buddhist leaders 4. Political leaders 5. Nobel laureates for peace

ISBN 0-06-098701-4

LC 89-46523

"The Dalai Lama's story is, in part, a chapter in the 2,500-year history of Buddhism as well as a testament to the 'mendacity and barbarity' of Communist China. He shares the details of his amazing life, a glimpse at some of the mysteries of Tibetan Buddhism, and his unshakable belief in the basic good of humanity." Booklist

★ Iyer, Pico. The **open** road; the global journey of the fourteenth Dalai Lama. Bloomsbury 2008 288p $24

Grades: 11 12 Adult   **92**
   1. Buddhist leaders 2. Political leaders 3. Nobel laureates for peace
ISBN 978-0-307-26760-3; 0-307-26760-1
                    LC 2007-43991

"The combination of Iyer's exacting observations, incisive analysis, and frank respect for the unknowable results in a uniquely internalized, even empathic portrait of one of the world's most embraced and least understood guiding lights." Booklist

Includes bibliographical references

Dang, Thuy Tram, 1943-1970

Dang, Thuy Tram. **Last** night I dreamed of peace; the diary of Dang Thuy Tram. translated by Andrew X. Pham; introduction by Frances FitzGerald; notes by Jane Barton Griffith, Robert Whitehurst, and Dang Kim Tram. Harmony Books 2007 225p il map $19.95

Grades: 11 12 Adult   **92**
   1. Physicians 2. Diarists 3. Vietnam War, 1961-1975 -- Medical care
ISBN 978-0-307-34737-4; 0-307-34737-0
                    LC 2007-8201

"The volume will generate much discussion. It is an excellent source for nonfiction booktalks, book groups, World History and English classes, and public libraries everywhere." SLJ

Danticat, Edwidge, 1969-

★ Danticat, Edwidge, 1969- **Brother,** I'm dying. Alfred A. Knopf 2007 272p hardcover o.p. pa $15

Grades: 11 12 Adult   **92**
   1. Authors 2. Novelists 3. Dramatists 4. Women authors 5. Editors 6. Essayists 7. Children's authors 8. Short story writers 9. Biography, Individual
ISBN 1-4000-3430-2 pa; 1-4000-4115-5; 978-1-4000-3430-7 pa; 978-1-4000-4115-2
                    LC 2007-06887

This family memoir by the author of The Dew Breaker (2004) centers on the experiences of "her father, Mira, and his older brother, Joseph." (Publisher's note)

The author "has written a fierce, haunting book about exile and loss and family love, and how that love can survive distance and separation, loss and abandonment and somehow endure, undented and robust." N Y Times (Late NY Ed)

Danton, Georges Jacques, 1759-1794

Lawday, David. The **giant** of the French Revolution; Danton, a life. Grove Press 2010 294p il map $27.50

Grades: 11 12 Adult   **92**
   1. Revolutionaries 2. France -- History -- 1789-1799, Revolution
ISBN 978-0-8021-1933-9

"This is the best biography of Danton to be written since Hilaire Belloc's over 100 years ago. Both the scholar and the general reader will find this biography an informative and lively read." Libr J

Includes bibliographical references

Darwin, Charles, 1809-1882

Eldredge, Niles. **Charles** Darwin and the mystery of mysteries; by Niles Eldredge and Susan Pearson. Rb Flash Point 2010 135p il map lib bdg $19.99

Grades: 7 8 9 10   **92**
   1. Naturalists 2. Travel writers 3. Writers on science 4. Beagle Expedition (1831-1836)
ISBN 978-1-59643-374-8; 1-59643-374-4

Follows Charles Darwin on his journey aboard the HMS Beagle and presents the thinking that led him to the theory of evolution and the writing of The origin of the species. Includes historical photographs and passages from Darwin's personal diary.

"Numerous quotations from Darwin's works and correspondence bring his voice to readers. . . . Eldredge and Pearson have done a fine job of summarizing both Darwin's life and work." SLJ

★ Heiligman, Deborah. **Charles** and Emma; the Darwins' leap of faith. Henry Holt and Company 2009 268p il $18.95

Grades: 7 8 9 10 11 12   **92**
   1. Naturalists 2. Travel writers 3. Writers on science 4. Spouses of prominent persons
ISBN 978-0-8050-8721-5; 0-8050-8721-4
                    LC 2008-26091

ALA YALSA Printz Award Honor Book (2010)

ALA Excellence in Nonfiction Award (2010)

"This rewarding biography of Charles Darwin investigates his marriage to his cousin Emma Wedgwood. . . . Embracing the paradoxes in her subjects' personalities, the author unfolds a sympathetic and illuminating account, bolstered by quotations from their personal writings as well as significant research into the historical context." Publ Wkly

Includes bibliographical references

Darwin, Emma Wedgwood, 1808-1896

★ Heiligman, Deborah. **Charles** and Emma; the Darwins' leap of faith. Henry Holt and Company 2009 268p il $18.95

Grades: 7 8 9 10 11 12   **92**
   1. Naturalists 2. Travel writers 3. Writers on science 4. Spouses of prominent persons
ISBN 978-0-8050-8721-5; 0-8050-8721-4
                    LC 2008-26091

ALA YALSA Printz Award Honor Book (2010)

ALA Excellence in Nonfiction Award (2010)

"This rewarding biography of Charles Darwin investigates his marriage to his cousin Emma Wedgwood. . . . Embracing the paradoxes in her subjects' personalities, the author unfolds a sympathetic and illuminating account, bolstered by quotations from their personal writings as well as significant research into the historical context." Publ Wkly

Includes bibliographical references

Davis, Jefferson, 1808-1889

Aretha, David. **Jefferson** Davis; [by] David A. Aretha. Chelsea House Publishers 2009 112p il (Leaders of the Civil War era) lib bdg $30

Grades: 7 8 9 10   **92**

1. Statesmen 2. Presidents 3. Senators 4. Political leaders 5. Secretaries of war 6. Confederate States of America 7. United States -- History -- 1861-1865, Civil War

ISBN 978-1-60413-297-7; 1-60413-297-3

LC 2008-44764

Biography of Jefferson Davis, the president of the confederacy during the Civil War.

Includes glossary and bibliographical references

Dawidoff, Nicholas

Dawidoff, Nicholas. The **crowd** sounds happy; a story of love, madness, and baseball. Pantheon Books 2008 271p $24.95

Grades: 11 12 Adult   **92**

1. Authors 2. Sportswriters 3. Nonfiction writers 4. Baseball -- Biography

ISBN 978-0-375-40028-5; 0-375-40028-1

LC 2007-30525

In this memoir, the author describes how his love of baseball helped him through rough periods of his youth, including his father descent into mental illness.

"Essential reading for anyone who wishes a balm for heartbreaks in youth, torn family life, love, and seventh-game losses." Libr J

Dinesen, Isak, 1885-1962

Leslie, Roger. **Isak** Dinesen; Gothic storyteller. M. Reynolds 2004 128p il (World writers) lib bdg $21.95

Grades: 11 12 Adult   **92**

1. Authors 2. Novelists 3. Women authors 4. Authors, Danish 5. Memoirists 6. Short story writers

ISBN 1-931798-17-6

LC 2003-22484

"Danish author Dinesen, born 1885, was a strong-willed spirit who sought independence and adventure. With her long battle with syphilis figuring prominently in this accounting, this traces the path the writer followed, which led her away from her bourgeois upbringing in Denmark to the unfettered life she enjoyed on her coffee farm at the foot of the Ngong Hills of Nairobi." Booklist

Includes bibliographical references

Dornstein, David Scott, 1963-1988

Dornstein, Ken. The **boy** who fell out of the sky; a true story. Random House 2006 304p il $23.95; pa $13.95

Grades: 11 12 Adult   **92**

1. Travelers 2. Pan Am Flight 103 Bombing Incident, 1988 3. Murder victims

ISBN 0-375-50359-5; 0-375-70769-7 pa

LC 2005-42683

"Dornstein's account of his relationship with his brother and of his own self-examination is a startlingly honest, completely absorbing look at loss and brotherly love." Booklist

Includes bibliographical references

Douglass, Frederick, 1817?-1895

★ Adler, David A. **Frederick** Douglass; a noble life. Holiday House 2010 138p il $18.95

Grades: 7 8 9 10   **92**

1. Slaves 2. Authors 3. Abolitionists 4. Memoirists 5. African Americans -- Biography

ISBN 978-0-8234-2056-8; 0-8234-2056-6

LC 2009-29970

A biography of Frederick Douglass, who was born into slavery in 1818 and raised on a Maryland plantation under brutal conditions and who grew up to become a famous orator, journalist, author, and adviser to U.S. presidents.

This is "a thoroughly researched, lucidly written biography. . . . Adler does an excellent job of exploring the atrocities and dehumanizing indignities . . . visited on those who lived in slavery." Booklist

Includes bibliographical references

Esty, Amos. **Unbound** and unbroken: the story of Frederick Douglass. Morgan Reynolds Pub. 2010 143p il map (Civil rights leaders) lib bdg $28.95

Grades: 7 8 9 10   **92**

1. Slaves 2. Authors 3. Abolitionists 4. Memoirists 5. African Americans -- Biography

ISBN 978-1-59935-136-0; 1-59935-136-6

LC 2009-54287

Traces the life and historical impact of the noted abolitionist, detailing his birth into slavery and harsh upbringing, his subsequent escape, and his emergence as a leader.

"Multiple biographies have been written about Douglass; however, few capture the depth of his intellect as an orator and writer. Through interwoven quotes from his autobiography, speeches, and pictures, this story also serves as prime research material. Douglass's ingenious case for the Constitution and fifth of July speech make the biography accessible from cover to cover." Voice Youth Advocates

Includes bibliographical references

Driskell, David C., 1931-

McGee, Julie L. **David** C. Driskell; artist and scholar. Pomegranate 2006 216p il $45

Grades: 11 12 Adult   **92**

1. Artists 2. Painters 3. African American artists 4. Printmakers 5. Art teachers 6. Art historians

ISBN 0-7649-3747-2; 978-0-7649-3747-7

LC 2006-43184

In this "inquiry into Driskell's life and work, . . . McGee analyzes with great empathy Driskell's philosophical struggles as he sought to both express his feelings about racial strife in America and stay true to his art. . . . With an abundance of incandescent reproductions of Driskell's searching and vital work, photographs documenting his life, and multifaceted and involving commentary, this unprecedented volume extends the reach of a great artist and tireless arts advocate." Booklist

Includes bibliographical references

Du Bois, W. E. B. (William Edward Burghardt), 1868-1963

Bolden, Tonya. **W.E.B.** Du Bois; a twentieth-century life. Viking Children's Books 2008 224p il (Up close) $16.99

Grades: 7 8 9 10   92

1. Authors 2. Novelists 3. Historians 4. Editors 5. Essayists 6. Sociologists 7. Nonfiction writers 8. Civil rights activists 9. African Americans -- Biography 10. African Americans -- Civil rights

ISBN 978-0-670-06302-4; 0-670-06302-9

LC 2007-52380

"The author covers her subject's life, which spanned 95 years, from Reconstruction to the modern Civil Rights Movement. . . . This balanced, lively account records his many contributions as a teacher, speaker, Civil Rights activist, sociologist, writer, and cofounder of several organizations, including the NAACP, as well as his failings." SLJ

Includes bibliographical references

Dylan, Bob, 1941-

Brown, Donald. **Bob** Dylan; American troubadour. Donald Brown. Rowman & Littlefield Publishers, Inc. 2014 308 p. (Tempo: a Rowman & Littlefield music series on rock, pop, and culture) (cloth: alk. paper) $40

Grades: 9 10 11 12 Adult   92

1. Musicians -- United States

ISBN 0810884208; 9780810884205; 9780810884212

LC 2013044394

This biography, by Daniel Brown, "follows [Bob] Dylan chronologically through his career, from young troubadour in Greenwich Village who unwittingly became the spokesman of a generation through his controversial electric transformation to the 'rural glory' of the Basement Tapes to his richly creative Blood on the Tracks period to his born-again phase to his current renaissance as a rock elder and cultural force." (Booklist)

"While it covers familiar territory, the book's strength is a thorough assessment of Dylan's career, album by album, song by song." LJ

Includes bibliographical references, discography, and index

Earhart, Amelia, 1898-1937

Winters, Kathleen C. **Amelia** Earhart; the turbulent life of an American icon. Palgrave Macmillan 2010 242p il map $25

Grades: 11 12 Adult   92

1. Air pilots 2. Missing persons 3. Women air pilots 4. Memoirists

ISBN 978-0-230-61669-1

LC 2010-20026

"With erudite analysis of everything from Earhart's flying to her marriage and longtime financial support of her parents and sister, Winters proves there is still much to learn about this American icon." Booklist

Includes bibliographical references

Ebrahim, Zak, 1983-

Ebrahim, Zak. The **Terrorist's** Son; A Story of Choice. by Zak Ebrahim with Jeff Giles. First TED Books hardcover edit Simon & Schuster 2014 96 p. $14.99

Grades: 11 12 Adult   92

1. Terrorism 2. Terrorism -- Psychological aspects

ISBN 1476784809; 9781476784809

Alex Award (2015)

This book, by Zak Ebrahim, is the story "of an American boy raised by his terrorist father—the man who planned the 1993 World Trade Center bombing. . . . Ebrahim dispels the myth that terrorism is a foregone conclusion for people trained to hate. Based on his own remarkable journey, he shows that hate is always a choice—but so is tolerance. Though Ebrahim was subjected to a violent, intolerant ideology throughout his childhood, he did not become radicalized." (Publisher's note)

Eckford, Elizabeth, 1942-

★ Margolick, David. **Elizabeth** and Hazel; two women of Little Rock. Yale University Press 2011 310p il $26

Grades: 11 12 Adult   92

1. School integration 2. Arkansas -- Race relations 3. Little Rock (Ark.) -- Race relations 4. Central High School (Little Rock, Ark.) 5. School integration -- Arkansas -- Little Rock -- History -- 20th century

ISBN 978-0-300-14193-1; 0-300-14193-9

LC 2011-14101

"When Elizabeth Eckford braved the gauntlet of white hecklers leading to the newly desegregated Central High School in Little Rock, Arkansas, in 1957, photographers captured her image and that of the angry young white woman behind her. Elizabeth, the stoic, and Hazel Bryan, the tormentor, were frozen as icons. Elizabeth was part of the Little Rock Nine, the black teens who became the targets of race hatred as well as national and international inspirations. . . . Margolick draws on interviews and press reports of the time to present a very nuanced analysis of how Elizabeth and Hazel were affected by the scene that made them famous. . . . A complex look at two women at the center of a historic moment." Booklist

Includes bibliographical references

Einstein, Albert, 1879-1955

McCormick Lisa Wade. **Albert** Einstein. Rosen Publishing 2015 112 p. illustrations (some color) (Great Science Writers) (library bound) $35.60

Grades: 10 11 12   92

1. Science 2. Physicists -- Biography

ISBN 1477776877; 9781477776872

LC 2013044291

This children's book on Albert Einstein by Lisa Wade McCormick is part of a series that shows "even famous science experts struggle in school, as readers learn in this series, which sheds light on the human face of geniuses. Some titles emphasize the science writers' literary background more than others." (School Library Journal)

Includes bibliographical references (pages 104-108) and index

Eisner, Will, 1917-2005

Schumacher, Michael. **Will** Eisner; a dreamer's life in comics. Bloomsbury 2010 359p il $28

Grades: 11 12 Adult 92

1. Authors 2. Cartoonists 3. Comic book writers 4. Publishing executives

ISBN 978-1-60819-013-3

LC 2010-11283

"Born in 1917, Will Eisner, now known as the father of the graphic novel, grew up in the Bronx poor but resourceful. . . . [The author] zeroes in on the essence of Eisner's success: his rare ability to unite art (he inherited his phenomenal gift for drawing from his immigrant artist father) with practicality (his mother's specialty). . . . Propelled by Eisner's geyserlike energy and output, Schumacher keenly chronicles Eisner's brilliant career within a lively history of American comics and creates an inspiring portrait of a perpetually diligent and innovative artist whose belief in comics as fine art fueled a new and fertile creative universe." Booklist

Includes bibliographical references

Emerson, Ralph Waldo, 1803-1882

Caravantes, Peggy. **Self**-reliance: the story of Ralph Waldo Emerson. Morgan Reynolds Pub. 2010 143p il map (World writers) lib bdg $28.95

Grades: 7 8 9 10 92

1. Poets 2. Authors 3. Philosophers 4. Essayists 5. Authors, American

ISBN 978-1-59935-124-7; 1-59935-124-2

LC 2010-8143

Presents the life and career of the eighteenth century New England essayist, poet, and lecturer who advocated a philosophy of self-reliance and individualism and was an important figure in the American Transcendental Movement.

This volume treats "young adult readers with respect and . . . [works] to ease them into scholarly research and writing in an engaging manner." Voice Youth Advocates

Includes bibliographical references

Engle, Margarita

★ Engle, Margarita. **Enchanted** air; a Cold War memoir. Margarita Engle. Atheneum Books for Young Readers 2015 208 p. illustrations (hardcover) $17.99

Grades: 6 7 8 9 10 92

1. Cuban Americans 2. Cuban Americans -- Biography 3. Women authors, American -- 20th century -- Biography

ISBN 9781481435222; 9781481435239

LC 2014017408

YALSA Award for Excellence in Nonfiction for Young Adults: Shortlist (2016)

Pura Belpre Author Award (2016)

This book is a memoir in poetry by Margarita Engle. "She narrates growing up in Los Angeles in the 1950s and early '60s torn by her love of two countries: the United States, where she was born and raised, and Cuba, where her mother was from and where she spent vacations visiting family. Woven into the fabric of her childhood is the anxiety of deteriorating relations between the two countries as the Cuban revolution takes place, affecting both her family and the two countries at large." (Kirkus Reviews)

"A deeply personal memoir-in-verse filled with Engle's trademark intricately woven lyricism. . . . Engle captures the heart of a quiet, young girl torn between two cultures." SLJ

Erlbaum, Janice, 1969-

Erlbaum, Janice. **Girlbomb**; a halfway homeless memoir. Villard 2006 252p $21.95; pa $13.95

Grades: 11 12 Adult 92

1. Authors 2. Comedians 3. Runaway teenagers 4. Columnists 5. Memoirists

ISBN 1-4000-6422-8; 978-1-4000-6422-9; 0-8129-7456-5 pa; 978-0-8129-7456-0 pa

LC 2005-48643

"At 14, Erlbaum . . . became fed up with her mother's latest abusive husband and left their Brooklyn apartment. This memoir chronicles Erlbaum's teenage years, rife with typical issues that were intensified and complicated by her ongoing search for a place to call home. . . . Erlbaum perfectly captures the gritty landscape of the shelters, streets, and social scene of 1980s Manhattan and the gritty thoughts and feelings of a teenager immersing herself in flaky friends, lewd boys, violence, and drugs." Libr J

Farmer, Paul, 1959-

★ Kidder, Tracy. **Mountains** beyond mountains; the quest of Dr. Paul Farmer, a man who would cure the world. by Tracy Kidder; adapted for young people by Michael French. Delacorte Press 2013 288 p. hardcover o.p. (hardcover trade) $16.99

Grades: 7 8 9 10 11 12 Adult 92

1. Physicians 2. Access to health care 3. Human rights 4. Right to health

ISBN 0385743181; 9780307980885; 9780375990991; 9780385743181

LC 2012024905

This book is a study of Paul Farmer, an American doctor who opened a healthcare center for the poor in Haiti. "By Farmer's decree, no patient can be turned away. But medical aid alone is not enough. He also emphasizes the need to eliminate problems that contribute to illness: dirty water, inadequate nutrition, poor sanitation, illiteracy. . . . Encouraged by the success of his clinic, Farmer wants to replicate it as 'a laboratory for the world.'" (Christian Science Monitor)

This is a "portrait of Paul Farmer (MacArthur 'genius' grant, 1993), a driven, dedicated, rigidly idealistic doctor who commutes between Harvard and Haiti, where he works . . . to relieve the suffering of some of the poorest people on earth." N Y Times Book Rev

Includes bibliographical references

Faulkner, William, 1897-1962

Weinstein, Philip. **Becoming** Faulkner; the art and life of William Faulkner. [by] Philip Weinstein. Oxford University Press 2009 250p il

Grades: 11 12 Adult 92

1. Authors 2. Novelists 3. Screenwriters 4. Novelists, American 5. Short story writers 6. Biography, Individual 7. Nobel laureates for literature 8. Southern States -- Civilization

ISBN 0-19-534153-8; 978-0-19-534153-9

LC 2009-13181

Weinstein contends that William "Faulkner's troubled interactions with time, place, and history, with antebellum practices and southern heritage, form a pattern that played out over the course of his entire life. At the same time, [he beleives], these incidents take on their fullest meanings in his fiction. It was in meditating on his failures, his own unreadiness, Weinstein argues, that Faulkner came up with his singular language, one that captured human consciousness under stress as never before." (Publisher's note) Index.

"In his prologue, Weinstein . . . explains his concept of a biography as a work that does more than recount the events of a person's life in chronological order. He seeks to convey something of the disturbing stresses of Faulkner's life as he might have experienced them at the time and to explore how those experiences shaped the great works he produced between 1929 and 1942. . . . This rich work will be well received by Faulknerian students and scholars. Highly recommended." Libr J

Includes bibliographical references

Feynman, Richard Phillips, 1918-1988

★ Henderson, Harry. **Richard** Feynman; quarks, bombs, and bongos. Chelsea House 2010 138p il (Makers of modern science) $35

Grades: 7 8 9 10   **92**

1. Authors 2. Physicists 3. Writers on science 4. Nobel laureates for physics

ISBN 978-0-8160-6176-1; 0-8160-6176-9

A biography of physicist Richard Feyman.

"The mark of a good biography is when it makes people you may never have heard of, in fields you might not be interested in, fascinating. [This book] does this with [a] well-chosen [subject], engaging writing, plenty of sidebars that take the text in new directions, and perhaps most importantly, the determination to present a fully-rounded person, not just a scientist." Booklist

Krauss, Lawrence Maxwell. **Quantum** man; Richard Feynman's life in science. [by] Lawrence M. Krauss. W.W. Norton 2011 350p il (Great discoveries) $24.95

Grades: 11 12 Adult   **92**

1. Authors 2. Physicists 3. Writers on science 4. Nobel laureates for physics

ISBN 978-0-393-06471-1; 0-393-06471-9

LC 2010-45512

"This book is highly recommended for readers who want to get to know one of the preeminent scientists of the 20th century." Publ Wkly

Includes bibliographical references

Ottaviani, Jim. **Feynman**; written by Jim Ottaviani; art by Leland Myrick; coloring by Hilary Sycamore. 1st ed. First Second 2011 262 p. chiefly ill. (some col.) (hardcover) $29.99; (paperback) $19.99; (prebind) $33.99

Grades: 9 10 11 12 Adult   **92**

1. Atomic bomb 2. Nobel Prizes 3. Musicians -- Biography 4. Biography, Individual 5. Physicists --

Graphic novels

ISBN 1596432594; 9781596432598; 9781596438279; 9781451722406

LC 2010036260

Author Jim Ottaviani presents a "graphic novel biography . . . [of] Nobel-winning quantum physicist, adventurer, musician, world-class raconteur, and one of the greatest minds of the twentieth century: Richard Feynman . . . [The book] tells the story of the great man's life from his childhood in Long Island to his work on the Manhattan Project and the Challenger disaster." (Publisher's note)

"This is a fascinating look at the life of an eccentric genius, a man who worked on the Manhattan Project, won a Nobel Prize, was the first great physicist to teach freshmen classes, and was the investigator into the cause of the Challenger explosion who discovered the problem was the 0-rings. This work was so entertaining it was difficult to put down." Voice Youth Advocates

Fillmore, Millard, 1800-1874

Finkelman, Paul. **Millard** Fillmore. Times Books 2011 171p (American presidents series) $23; ebook $10.99

Grades: 11 12 Adult   **92**

1. Presidents 2. Vice-presidents 3. Members of Congress 4. Presidents -- United States 5. United States -- Politics and government -- 1815-1861

ISBN 978-0-8050-8715-4; 978-1-4299-2301-9 ebook

LC 2010-47174

The author "describes Millard Fillmore's nearly forgotten presidency by rigidly contrasting him with Abraham Lincoln, another self-made man who wrestled with racial and regional tensions as president. . . . This book is an enlightening view into the often overlooked beginnings of the Civil War, which history buffs and students alike will find enjoyable." Publ Wkly

Includes bibliographical references

Flynn, Elizabeth Gurley

Vapnek, Lara. **Elizabeth** Gurley Flynn; modern American revolutionary. Lara Vapnek. Westview Press 2015 160 p. illustrations (paperback) $22

Grades: 11 12 Adult   **92**

1. Women's rights 2. Women political activists 3. Communists -- United States -- Biography 4. Women labor leaders -- United States -- Biography 5. Women revolutionaries -- United States -- Biography

ISBN 9780813348094; 0813348099

LC 2014027690

In this book by Lara Vapnek, "weaving together [Elizabeth Gurley] Flynn's personal and political life, this biography reveals previously unrecognized connections between feminism, socialism, free love, and free speech. Flynn's remarkable career casts new light on the long and varied history of radicalism in the United States." (Publisher's note)

"A brief encapsulation of the fury and disillusionment that characterized the career of this significant American activist." Kirkus

Includes bibliographical references and index

Ford, Henry, 1863-1947

Curcio, Vincent. **Henry** Ford; by Vincent Curcio. Oxford University Press 2013 304 p. (Llives and legacies series) (hardback) $24.95

Grades: 9 10 11 12 Adult 92

1. Automobile industry 2. United States -- Biography 3. Industrialists -- United States -- Biography 4. Automobile industry and trade -- United States -- History

ISBN 0195316924; 9780195316926

LC 2012043539

In this book author Vincent Curcio "tracks [Henry] Ford's life and accomplishments, beginning with his. . . childhood. Here Ford first revealed his fascination with machines and their practical application.Curcio indicates, Ford didn't 'invent' the modern automobile, but he . . . understood how to get man and machines to work in tandem. He was also a social visionary whose efforts to provide high wages helped foster the expansion of the middle class to include industrial workers." (Booklist)

"Curcio... provides here an in-depth review of the life of Henry Ford. Covering his life from Ford's humble, rural beginnings to his rise as one of the world's first billionaires, Curcio examines the many facets of the entrepreneur's often contradictory persona." (Library Journal)

Includes bibliographical references and index

Fortunate Eagle, Adam, 1929-

Eagle, Adam Fortunate. **Pipestone**; my life in an Indian boarding school. afterword by Laurence M. Hauptman. University of Oklahoma Press 2010 193p il

Grades: 9 10 11 12 92

1. Private schools 2. Indian leaders 3. Native Americans -- Biography

ISBN 0-8061-4114-X; 978-0-8061-4114-5

LC 2009-41302

"Adam Fortunate Eagle entered the Pipestone Indian Training School at the age of six. From that time until his graduation at age 16, he spent each school year and many summers under the care of the teachers and wardens at Pipestone. Growing up with other children, some sent by their families and others enrolled as orphans, Fortunate Eagle experienced the loneliness of separation, the camaraderie of school life, and the absence of his culture. . . . [His story] is filled with school pranks, tender memories, and a growing sense of the world at large between 1935 and 1945. . . . Fortunate Eagle's memories of his time in an Indian boarding school fill a vital need in the canon of available literature about the American Indian experience." SLJ

Includes bibliographical references

Fossey, Dian

★ De la Bedoyere, Camilla. **No** one loved gorillas more; Dian Fossey, letters from the mist. with photographs by Bob Campbell. National Geographic Society 2005 191p il $30

Grades: 11 12 Adult 92

1. Authors 2. Gorillas 3. Women scientists 4. Murder victims 5. Primatologists 6. Writers on science

ISBN 0-7922-9344-4

LC 2004-57944

This biography featuring an assemblage of Dian Fossey's letters to family and friends "reveals both the intense joy and immense suffering Fossey experienced during her 18-year sojourn among Rwanda's mountain gorillas." Booklist

Includes bibliographical references

France, Diane L.

Hopping, Lorraine Jean. **Bone** detective; the story of forensic anthropologist Diane France. Franklin Watts 2005 118p il (Women's adventures in science) lib bdg $31.50

Grades: 7 8 9 10 92

1. Anthropologists 2. Women scientists 3. Forensic anthropology 4. Forensic scientists Individual

ISBN 0-531-16776-3

LC 2005-0784

This book by Lorraine Jean Hopping is part of the Women's Adventures in Science series. It presents a biography of forensic anthropologist Diane France. "The book describes her marriages and divorce, a battle with cancer, experiences with sexism on the job, working at the World Trade Center site, and how one must learn to put personal feelings 'in a box' when working on forensic cases." (SB&F: Your Guide to Science Resources for All Ages)

This "introduces the life and work of a contemporary forensic anthropologist, from her rural childhood to her work identifying the victims of the 9/11 tragedies. . . . The extensive detail gives readers a vivid sense of the daily work of a 'bone detective,' and clear explanations of the science will intrigue and inspire readers." Booklist

Includes glossary and bibliographical references

Francis, John

Francis, John. **Planetwalker**; 22 years of walking, 17 years of silence. text and illustrations by John Francis. National Geographic 2008 288p il map $26

Grades: 11 12 Adult 92

1. Silence 2. Walking 3. Conservationists 4. Environmental movement 5. Social activists

ISBN 978-1-4262-0275-9; 1-4262-0275-X

First published 2005 by Elephant Mountain Press

This "is an inspiring story that will make . . . [readers] think and may help them to realize that global change is possible through individual action." SLJ

Frank family

Gies, Miep. **Anne** Frank remembered; the story of the woman who helped to hide the Frank family. [by] Miep Gies and Alison Leslie Gold. Simon & Schuster trade pbk. ed.; Simon and Schuster Paperbacks 2009 264p il pa $15

Grades: 11 12 Adult 92

1. Holocaust, 1933-1945 2. Amsterdam (Netherlands) 3. Netherlands -- History -- 1940-1945, German occupation

ISBN 978-1-4165-9885-5; 1-4165-9885-5

LC 2009294295

First published 1987

"A memoir by the courageous Dutch woman who helped hide the Frank family, this book augments the Anne Frank story. Perceptive characterizations, with insight into life in Amsterdam during the Nazi occupation." SLJ

Frank, Anne, 1929-1945

Barnouw, David. The **diary** of Anne Frank: the critical edition; rev Critical ed; Doubleday 2003 851p il $75

Grades: 11 12 Adult   **92**
1. Children 2. Diarists 3. Holocaust victims 4. Jews -- Netherlands 5. Holocaust, 1933-1945 6. World War, 1939-1945 -- Jews 7. Netherlands -- History -- 1940-1945, German occupation
ISBN 0-385-50847-6

LC 2003-269527
First published 1989
This volume brings together "the three known versions of Frank's diary—the original, a self-edited version . . . {and} another edited by her father. It also contains . . . handwriting and paper analyses, new documentation regarding the Frank family's arrest, and . . . information about the diary's troubled publication history." Libr J {review of 1989 edition}
Includes bibliographical references

★ Frank, Anne. The **diary** of a young girl: the definitive edition; edited by Otto H. Frank and Mirjam Pressler; translated by Susan Massotty. Bantam 1997 340p $29.95; pa $7.99

Grades: 5 6 7 8 9 10 11 12 Adult   **92**
1. Children 2. Diarists 3. Holocaust victims 4. Jews -- Netherlands 5. Holocaust, 1933-1945 6. World War, 1939-1945 -- Jews 7. Netherlands -- History -- 1940-1945, German occupation
ISBN 0-385-47378-8; 9780553577129

LC 94-41379
"This new translation of Frank's famous diary includes material about her emerging sexuality and her relationship with her mother that was originally excised by Frank's father, the only family member to survive the Holocaust." Libr J

Jacobson, Sidney. **Anne** Frank; the Anne Frank House authorized graphic biography. [by] Sid Jacobson and Ernie Colón. Hill and Wang 2010 152p il $30; pa $16.95

Grades: 9 10 11 12 Adult   **92**
1. Children 2. Graphic novels 3. Biographical graphic novels 4. Diarists 5. Holocaust victims 6. Jews -- Netherlands -- Graphic novels 7. Holocaust, 1933-1945 -- Graphic novels 8. World War, 1939-1945 -- Jews -- Graphic novels
ISBN 978-0-8090-2684-5; 978-0-8090-2685-2 pa

LC 2010-5776
"Panel arrangements effectively show simultaneous events happening in the life of the family and in the world, while brief 'snapshots' provide enough historical information to make motives, fears, and expectations sensible to anyone unfamiliar with the Holocaust's machinery. More than simply poignant, this biography elucidates the complex

emotional aspects of living a sequestered adolescence as a brilliant, budding writer." Booklist
Includes bibliographical references

Müller, Melissa, 1967- **Anne** Frank; the biography. by Melissa Muller; translated by Rita and Robert Kimber. 2nd U.S. ed. Metropolitan Books/ Henry Holt and Company 2013 480 p. hardcover o.p. (hardcover) $35

Grades: 7 8 9 10 11 12 Adult   **92**
1. Children 2. Amsterdam (Netherlands) -- Biography 3. Jewish children in the Holocaust -- Biography 4. Jews -- Netherlands -- Amsterdam -- Biography 5. Holocaust, Jewish (1939-1945) -- Netherlands -- Amsterdam -- Biography
ISBN 0805087311; 9780805087314

LC 2013000297
This biography of Anne Frank "was originally published in 1998, but this expanded edition takes into account diary entries that had previously been redacted by Anne's father [Otto], as well as recently discovered letters from Otto to relatives in the United States and unpublished documents provided to [Melissa] Müller during interviews with those who knew Anne and her family." (Publishers Weekly)
"Müller includes a family tree; a family history; and considerable insight into the character, personality, and quality of life of Anne's parents, relatives, and friends. Interviews with many of these surviving people give a clearer idea of the situation and Anne's reactions to it." SLJ

Franklin, Benjamin, 1706-1790

Dash, Joan. A **dangerous** engine; Benjamin Franklin, from scientist to diplomat. pictures by Dusan Petricic. Frances Foster Books 2006 246p il $17

Grades: 7 8 9 10   **92**
1. Authors 2. Diplomats 3. Inventors 4. Statesmen 5. Scientists 6. Writers on science 7. Members of Congress 8. Statesmen -- United States
ISBN 0-374-30669-9

LC 2004-63204
"Franklin's long, productive, and interesting life is vividly recounted in a lively manner. Familiar aspects are covered, from his days as a printer in Philadelphia to his diplomatic service and his role in the development of the fledgling United States democracy. What may be new to some readers is Franklin's dedication to, and life-long love of, science and invention. . . . Witty pen-and-ink illustrations appear throughout." SLJ

★ Franklin, Benjamin. **Not** your usual founding father; selected readings from Benjamin Franklin. edited by Edmund S. Morgan. Yale University Press 2006 303p il map hardcover o.p. pa $16

Grades: 11 12 Adult   **92**
1. Authors 2. Diplomats 3. Inventors 4. Statesmen 5. Scientists 6. Writers on science 7. Members of Congress 8. Statesmen -- United States
ISBN 0-300-11394-3; 978-0-300-11394-5; 0-300-12688-3 pa; 978-0-300-126884 pa

LC 2006-45706

The editor "explains that this anthology differs from the typical selections of writings by founders, which showcase themes of revolution, war, and political philosophy. Here Morgan pursues the man himself, particularly Franklin's fascination with the curiosities of human behavior. . . . Franklin's humane solicitude and observational acuity surface in varied places (on ship, in Parisian salons) and in varied formats (personal letters, published satires) in such a way that readers encounter directly Franklin's seeming simplicity, which actually masked a deep complexity and which continually makes him the most interesting founder." Booklist

Franklin, Rosalind, 1920-1958

★ Polcovar, Jane. **Rosalind** Franklin and the structure of life. Morgan Reynolds 2006 144p il lib bdg $26.95

Grades: 7 8 9 10   92

1. DNA 2. Chemists 3. Biologists 4. Women scientists 5. Geochemists

ISBN 978-1-59935-022-6; 1-59935-022-X

LC 2006-16864

A biography of the scientist whose unpublished research led to the discovery of the structure of DNA

"Polcovar writes a rattling good story on two fronts: a woman becoming a scientist in an age when that was still unusual and the complex dynamics of personalities in a field sometimes thought of as impersonal." Booklist

Includes bibliographical references

Fugard, Athol

Fugard, Athol. **Cousins**; a memoir. Theatre Communications Group 1997 152p $19.95

Grades: 11 12 Adult   92

1. Actors 2. Dramatists 3. Theatrical directors

ISBN 1-55936-132-8

LC 97-6241

In this "memoir, South Africa's best-known contemporary playwright pays homage to two men who strongly influenced him when he was an impressionable young artist—his cousins Johnnie and Garth. . . . In passing, Fugard also tells a little about his family and boyhood in Port Elizabeth and environs, and he reveals, in tantalizing, brief snatches, which moments in his plays are taken from his life." Booklist

Gadaryan, Heranus, 1905-2000

Cetin, Fethiye. **My** grandmother; a memoir. translated by Maureen Freely. Verso 2008 114p il $21.95

Grades: 11 12 Adult   92

1. Converts 2. Homemakers 3. Armenian massacres, 1915-1923 4. Kidnap victims 5. Armenians -- Turkey

ISBN 978-1-84467-169-4; 1-84467-169-0

LC 2008-396857

"Cetin recounts the 1915 Armenian genocide, when the Turks sent thousands of Armenian people to their deaths. . . . [Cretin's grandmother] Christian-born Heranus was rescued from death by a Muslim gendarme who brought her up as the Muslim girl Seher. . . . Cetin was an adult when she learned of these horrors and of her grandmother's original family. . . . [This] is a fascinating account of a story that needs to be heard." SLJ

Garrison, William Lloyd, 1805-1879

Esty, Amos. The **liberator**: the story of William Lloyd Garrison. Morgan Reynolds Pub. 2010 144p il (Civil rights leaders) lib bdg $28.95

Grades: 7 8 9 10   92

1. Abolitionists 2. Newspaper editors 3. Slavery -- United States

ISBN 978-1-59935-137-7; 1-59935-137-4

LC 2009-54290

This biography of abolitionist William Lloyd Garrison "will hook readers with discussions of the larger political issues as well as [Garrison's] personal struggles. . . . The design . . . is readable, with spacious type and many kinds of illustrations, including color and sepia photos, paintings, and reproductions of famous documents." Booklist

Includes bibliographical references

Genghis Khan, 1162-1227

★ Rice, Earle. **Empire** in the east: the story of Genghis Khan. Morgan Reynolds Pub. 2005 160p il $26.95

Grades: 9 10 11 12   92

1. Kings 2. Mongolia -- Kings and rulers

ISBN 1-931798-62-1

LC 2004-30743

"The biography offers background information about social customs of the times as well as details on the personal history of the man originally called Temujin. . . . A good introduction to the leader's life and brutal times." Booklist

Includes bibliographical references

Geronimo, Apache Chief, 1829-1909

Sullivan, George. **Geronimo**; Apache renegade. Sterling 2010 124p il map (Sterling biographies) lib bdg $12.95; pa $5.95

Grades: 7 8 9 10   92

1. Apache Indians 2. Indian chiefs 3. Native Americans -- Biography

ISBN 978-1-4027-6843-9 lib bdg; 1-4027-6843-5 lib bdg; 978-1-4027-6279-6 pa; 1-4027-6279-8 pa

LC 2009-24135

"Geronmino describes how the Apache leader was feared and hated as he led violent clashes with whites, pursuing bloody vengeance for the massacre of his family and all that his people had lost, an identity far from the romanticized image that glorified him. . . . [The] spacious design is highly scannable, with color background screens, photos, maps, and historic prints throughout." Booklist

Includes glossary and bibliographical references

Ghahramani, Zarah, 1981-

Ghahramani, Zarah. **My** life as a traitor; [by] Zarah Ghahramani , with Robert Hillman. Farrar, Straus and Giroux 2008 242p $23

Grades: 11 12 Adult   92

1. Political prisoners 2. Dissenters 3. Memoirists 4. Women -- Iran

ISBN 978-0-374-21730-3; 0-374-21730-0

LC 2007-17983

"Zarah Ghahramani wrote 'My Life as a Traitor' soon after fleeing Iran for Australia. Born in 1981, she never knew a prerevolutionary Iran. . . . In 2001, when she was 20, Ghah-ramani was tortured and imprisoned at Evin for her role in a protest at Tehran University." N Y Times Book Rev

Goldsworthy, Anna, 1974-

Goldsworthy, Anna. **Piano** lessons; a memoir. St. Martin's Press 2010 243p $24.99

Grades: 11 12 Adult   **92**
   1. Pianists 2. Classical musicians
   ISBN 978-0-312-64628-8

                                              LC 2010-40105
"Australian pianist Goldsworthy was nine years old when she began instruction with the renowned Russian pianist Eleonora Sivan, now relocated to Adelaide. Their pupil-master relationship grew and deepened over the next decade, rendered here in serene, clear, elegant prose, as Goldsworthy, the child of two doctors and musicians, blossomed into a stunning stage force and a vessel of Sivan's deeply intuitive music instruction." Publ Wkly

González, Rigoberto, 1970-

González, Rigoberto. **Butterfly** boy; memories of a Chicano mariposa. University of Wisconsin Press 2006 207p (Writing in Latinidad) $24.95

Grades: 11 12 Adult   **92**
   1. Poets 2. Authors 3. Gay men 4. Memoirists 5. Mexican Americans 6. Children's authors 7. Biography, Individual 8. Mexican Americans -- Biography
   ISBN 0-299-21900-3; 978-0-299-21900-0

                                               LC 2006-6990
González, the author of "So Often the Pitcher Goes to Water Until it Breaks, 1999 [and] Other Fugitives and Other Strangers, 2006, . . . has written an autobiographical coming-of-age story." (MultiCult Rev)
   "This moving memoir of a young Chicano boy's maturing into a self-accepting gay adult is a beautifully executed portrait of the experience of being gay, Chicano and poor in the United States." Publ Wkly

Goodall, Jane, 1934-

Jane Goodall; Carol Hand. Rosen Publishing 2015 112 p. illustrations (some color) (library bound) $35.60

Grades: 10 11 12   **92**
   1. Women scientists 2. Primatologists -- England -- Biography 3. Chimpanzees -- Tanzania -- Gombe Stream National Park
   ISBN 1477776850; 9781477776858

                                              LC 2013042195
This children's book by Carol Hand focuses on Jane Goodall. "Readers will be intrigued to learn, for example, that Jane Goodall kept pet guinea pigs as a child. Some titles emphasize the science writers' literary background more than others. For example, Goodall's book focuses heavily on her work as a scientist." (Publisher's note)
   "Throughout his biography, Tyson's passion for space exploration is palpable. Dynamic, understated artwork does not distract from excellent writing here. Strong additions." SLJ
   Includes bibliographical references (pages 106-108) and index

★ Greene, Meg. **Jane** Goodall; a biography. Greenwood Press 2005 146p il (Greenwood biographies) $29.95

Grades: 9 10 11 12   **92**
   1. Women scientists 2. Primatologists 3. Writers on nature 4. Nonfiction writers
   ISBN 0-313-33139-1; 978-0-313-33139-8

                                              LC 2005-16818
"Goodall's life is revealed from her earlier days growing up in England and the influence of her mother, to her experiences living and observing chimpanzees in Africa, and her undying efforts to promote conservation of wildlife." Publisher's note
   Includes bibliographical references

Goodman, Benny, 1909-1986

★ Mattern, Joanne. **Benny** Goodman; by Joanne Mattern. Mitchell Lane Publishers 2013 47 p. ill. (some col.) (library) $29.95

Grades: 6 7 8 9   **92**
   1. Jazz musicians 2. Clarinetists -- United States -- Biography 3. Jazz musicians -- United States -- Biography
   ISBN 1612282695; 9781612282695

                                              LC 2012008483
This book by Joanne Mattern is part of the American Jazz series and looks at musician Benny Goodman. Within each entry, "information about the subjects' childhoods and preparation for their musical careers is included, as are the positive and negative aspects of their adult lives. Their contributions to the world of jazz are . . . explored." (School Library Journal)
   Includes bibliographical references (p. 44-45) and index.

Gorokhova, Elena

Gorokhova, Elena. A **mountain** of crumbs; a memoir. Simon & Schuster 2010 308p il $26

Grades: 11 12 Adult   **92**
   1. Linguists 2. Memoirists 3. College teachers 4. Soviet Union -- History 5. Saint Petersburg (Russia)
   ISBN 978-1-4391-2567-0; 1-4391-2567-8

                                               LC 2009-474
In this memoir, Elena Gorokhova discusses growing up in Leningrad, her love of languages and her eventual move to the United States.
   "Gorokhova vividly evokes the bleak years of the latter half of the 20th century in Russia, when the Great Patriotic War was followed by the Cold War and food shortages were the norm. . . . Articulate, touching and hopeful." Kirkus

Grahl, Gary A.

★ Grahl, Gary A. **Skinny** boy; a young man's battle and triumph over anorexia. American Legacy Media 2007 243p pa $17.95

Grades: 9 10 11 12   **92**
   1. Anorexia nervosa 2. Student counselors
   ISBN 978-0-976154-74-7
"Challenging the assumption that anorexia is an exclusively female affliction, . . . [this memoir describes] how a young man overcame this often fatal disorder." Publisher's note

Grant, Ulysses S. (Ulysses Simpson), 1822-1885

Mosier, John. **Grant**; a biography. John Mosier. Palgrave Macmillan 2006 193 p. ill., maps $21.95

Grades: 9 10 11 12 Adult **92**

1. Strategy -- History -- 19th century 2. Command of troops -- History -- 19th century

ISBN 9781403971364; 1403971366

LC 2005056370

"[A]n engaging biography of Ulysses S. Grant as general . . . this book is completed with a time line, a foreword by series editor Gen. Wesley K. Clark, black-and-white photographs, and extensive chapter notes." LJ

Includes bibliographical references (p. [175]-186) and index

★ Rice, Earle. **Ulysses** S. Grant: defender of the Union; [by] Earle Rice, Jr. Morgan Reynolds 2005 176p il map lib bdg $24.95

Grades: 9 10 11 12 **92**

1. Generals 2. Presidents 3. Presidents -- United States

ISBN 1-931798-48-6

LC 2004-22345

The author "presents Ulysses S. Grant, touching upon his Ohio boyhood, education at West Point, service in the Mexican War, military leadership during the Civil War, and two terms as president. Rice portrays Grant in an even-handed manner, making good use of source materials for apt quotations." Booklist

Includes bibliographical references

Grealy, Lucy, 1963-2002

Patchett, Ann. **Truth** & beauty; a friendship. HarperCollins Publishers 2004 257p hardcover o.p. pa $13.95

Grades: 11 12 Adult **92**

1. Poets 2. Authors 3. Novelists 4. Women authors 5. Memoirists

ISBN 0-06-057214-0; 0-06-057215-9 pa

LC 2003-67586

"As young writers. Patchett and Lucy Grealy began an intense friendship that lasted until Grealy's tragic death. With intimacy, gracy, and humor, Patchett's memoir captures Lucy's exuberance and her roller-coaster struggles with disfigurement and depression." Booklist

Greene, Nathanael, 1742-1786

Carbone, Gerald M. **Nathanael** Greene; a biography of the American Revolution. Palgrave Macmillan 2008 268p il map $27.95

Grades: 11 12 Adult **92**

1. Generals 2. United States -- Continental Army 3. United States -- History -- 1775-1783, Revolution -- Campaigns

ISBN 978-0-230-60271-7; 0-230-60271-1

LC 2007-47595

This is a biography of the American Revolutionary War general.

"A lucid account of the Revolutionary War from the point of view of its most successful general." Kirkus

Includes bibliographical references

Gregory, Julie

Gregory, Julie. **Sickened**; the memoir of a Munchausen by proxy childhood. foreword by Marc D. Feldman. Bantam Books 2003 244p il hardcover o.p. pa $13

Grades: 9 10 11 12 **92**

1. Authors 2. Child abuse 3. Memoirists

ISBN 0-553-80307-7; 0-553-38197-0 pa

LC 2003-52405

"Gregory's childhood was marred by a particularly insidious form of child abuse. Her mother used a combination of malnutrition, overwork, and prescription drugs to keep the girl in a perpetual state of ill health. . . . She relays her story not as a victim but as a strong survivor. . . . As well as being a fascinating read, this book could give others in similar situations a lifeline back to health." SLJ

Greitens, Eric, 1974-

Greitens, Eric, 1974- The **Warrior's** Heart; Becoming a Man of Compassion and Courage. Eric Greitens, Navy SEAL. Houghton Mifflin Harcourt 2012 264 p. $16.99

Grades: 9 10 11 12 **92**

1. Courage 2. Compassion 3. Humanitarian assistance, American 4. United States. Navy. SEALs -- Biography 5. United States. Navy -- Officers -- Biography 6. United States -- Armed Forces -- Civic action 7. United States. Navy -- Officers -- Training of

ISBN 0547868529; 9780547868523

LC 2012454795

This book adapts Eric Greitens' memoir for teens, emphasizing compassion and courage. Compassion is exemplified by his voluntary service to those in great need, including tours of service aiding refugees in Croatia and Rwanda following the genocides in those countries. . . . Greitens's courage is demonstrated by extreme physical and mental toughness developed during amateur boxing, . . . Navy Seal training, and military service on battlefields in Iraq." (Voice of Youth Advocates)

Includes bibliographical references

Griner, Brittney

Griner, Brittney, 1990- **In** my skin; my life on and off the basketball court. Brittney Griner. It Books 2014 224 p. 8 plate pages; ills (color) (hardback) $25.99

Grades: 9 10 11 12 Adult **92**

1. Autobiographies 2. Basketball for women 3. Women athletes -- Biography 4. Basketball players -- United States -- Biography 5. Women basketball players -- United States -- Biography

ISBN 0062309331; 9780062309334; 9780062309358

LC 2013050667

In this autobiography co-written with Sue Hovey, "Brittney Griner, the dunking phenom and national sensation who is shattering stereotypes and breaking boundaries, now shares her coming-of-age story, revealing how she found her strength to overcome bullies and to embrace her authentic self. . . . In her . . . memoir, she reflects on painful episodes in her life and describes how she came to celebrate what makes her unique--inspiring lessons she now shares." (Publisher's note)

"WNBA star Griner's memoir explores her childhood, college basketball experience at Texas's Baylor University, and transition to playing professionally for the Phoenix Mercury...Best suited to general readers interested in basketball, bullying, LGBT issues, or female identity in sport. Readers may also enjoy Kate Fagan's "The Reappearing Act: Coming Out as Gay on a College Basketball Team Led by Born-Again Christians." LJ

Grinnell, George Bird, 1849-1938

Punke, Michael. **Last** stand; George Bird Grinnell, the battle to save the buffalo, and the birth of the new West. Smithsonian Books/Collins 2007 286p il map $25.95

Grades: 11 12 Adult   92
1. Bison 2. Authors 3. Explorers 4. Naturalists 5. Wildlife conservation 6. Magazine editors 7. Writers on nature 8. Children's authors 9. West (U.S.) -- History
ISBN 978-0-06-089782-6; 0-06-089782-1
       LC 2007-60392

The author "ties together the fascinating story of Grinnell and the threatened treasures he loved. The decline of the buffalo is a very human story, and the author leads readers through the hunting culture of the Indians and the even more ferocious killers from the East that superseded it." SLJ

Guevara, Ernesto, 1928-1967

Kallen, Stuart A. **Che** Guevara; by Stuart A. Kallen. Twenty-First Century Books 2013 88 p. (lib. bdg.: alk. paper) $33.27

Grades: 8 9 10 11 12   92
1. Cuba -- History -- 1958-1959, Revolution 2. Cuba -- History -- 1959-1990 3. Revolutionaries -- Cuba -- Biography 4. Latin America -- History -- 1948-1980 5. Guerrillas -- Latin America -- Biography
ISBN 0822590352; 9780822590354
       LC 2011045480

In author Stuart A. Kallen's book on Che Guevara, "the charismatic Argentinian revolutionary had been leading guerilla fighters in the jungles of Bolivia and was captured by the Bolivian army. Mario Terán, a sergeant in the Bolivian army, volunteered to execute the prisoner. He carried out the bloody assignment with nine point-blank shots to Guevara's body . . . In this chronicle of an assassination, find out what inspired the myth of Che Guevara and what brought him to this bloody crossroads of history." (Publisher's note)

Includes bibliographical references and index.

★ Miller, Calvin Craig. **Che** Guevara; in search of revolution. Morgan Reynolds Pub. 2006 192p il map (World leaders) lib bdg $27.95

Grades: 7 8 9 10   92
1. Guerrillas 2. Physicians 3. Revolutionaries 4. Cuba -- History -- 1959-
ISBN 978-1-931798-93-8; 1-931798-93-1
       LC 2006-5975

This biography of the guerilla leader is "woven into . . . [an] account of the global politics of his day, including his role in the Cuban revolution and the showdown with the

U.S. The design is appealing, with clear type, occasional photos, and maps, and teens will be drawn to the account of the young leader who made a difference in spite of an inglorious defeat." Booklist

Includes bibliographical references

Gunther, John, 1929-1947

Gunther, John. **Death** be not proud; a memoir. Harper & Row 1949 261p il hardcover o.p. pa $13.95

Grades: 7 8 9 10   92
1. Sick 2. Cancer 3. Brain -- Tumors
ISBN 0-06-123097-9

A memoir of John Gunther's seventeen-year-old son, who died after a series of operations for a brain tumor. Not only a tribute to a remarkable boy but an account of a brave fight against disease

Guthrie, Woody, 1912-1967

Kaufman, Will. **Woody** Guthrie, American radical. University of Illinois Press 2011 270p il (Music in American life)

Grades: 11 12 Adult   92
1. Singers 2. Folk musicians 3. Memoirists 4. Songwriters
ISBN 0-252-03602-6; 978-0-252-03602-6
       LC 2010040240

In this biography, Will "Kaufman shares many previously unpublished essays, letters, and lyrics to more accurately capture [folk musician Woody] Guthrie's complex personality and his far-left political agenda, which previously remained largely hidden by the Will Rogers-inspired camouflage Guthrie skillfully created. Kaufman undermines this camouflage and reveals a more sophisticated and progressive thinker than the 'rube' persona Guthrie frequently presented to the world." (Notes)

"Drawing on previously unseen letters, song lyrics, essays, and interviews with family and friends, Kaufman traces Guthrie's involvement in the workers' movement and his development of protest songs. He portrays Guthrie as a committed and flawed human immersed in political complexity and harrowing personal struggle." Libr J

Includes bibliographical references

Haber, Fritz, 1868-1934

Hager, Thomas. The **alchemy** of air; a Jewish genius, a doomed tycoon, and the scientific discovery that fed the world but fueled the rise of Hitler. Harmony Books 2008 316p $24.95; pa $15

Grades: 11 12 Adult   92
1. Chemists 2. Fertilizers 3. Nobel laureates for chemistry
ISBN 978-0-307-35178-4; 0-307-35178-5; 978-0-307-35179-1 pa; 0-307-35179-3 pa
       LC 2008-3192

"A fast-paced account of the early-20th-century quest to develop synthetic fertilizer. . . . Science writing of the first order." Kirkus

Includes bibliographical references

Hakakian, Roya

Hakakian, Roya. **Journey** from the land of no; a girlhood caught in revolutionary Iran. Crown Publishers 2004 245p map hardcover o.p. pa $13

Grades: 9 10 11 12   92

1. Poets 2. Authors 3. Television producers 4. Iran -- History -- 1979- 5. Motion picture directors

ISBN 1-4000-4611-4; 0-609-81030-8 pa

LC 2003-21662

"Political upheavals like the fall of the Shah of Iran and the rise of Islamic fundamentalism may be analyzed endlessly by scholars, but eyewitness accounts like Hakakian's help us understand what it was like to experience such a revolution firsthand. . . . Hakakian's story—so reminiscent of the experiences of Jews in Nazi Germany—is haunting." Publ Wkly

Hale, Nathan, 1755-1776

Phelps, M. William. **Nathan** Hale; the life and death of America's first spy. Thomas Dunne Books 2008 306p $25.95

Grades: 11 12 Adult   92

1. Spies 2. Revolutionaries 3. Soldiers -- United States 4. United States -- History -- 1775-1783, Revolution

ISBN 978-0-312-37641-3; 0-312-37641-3

LC 2008-21471

This is a biography of the American Revolutionary War hero.

"This is a well-done, balanced account of a short but interesting life." Booklist

Includes bibliographical references

Hall, Meredith

Hall, Meredith. **Without** a map; a memoir. Beacon Press 2007 221p $24.95

Grades: 11 12 Adult   92

1. Authors 2. Essayists 3. Memoirists 4. College teachers 5. Authors, American

ISBN 978-0-8070-7273-8; 0-8070-7273-7

LC 2006-27507

"The year: 1965. The place: a small, insular New Hampshire community where church and home life are dominant forces. When Hall becomes pregnant at 16, she is shunned by family members and friends she's known throughout her school years. After traveling to the Middle East and suffering the indignities of loneliness and poverty, which include selling her own blood, she returns to the United States and creates a new life out of her still-palpable grief. . . . The message of redemptive compassion makes this a worthwhile and moving read." Libr J

Hall, Shyima

Hall, Shyima. **Hidden** girl; the true story of a modern-day child slave. Shyima Hall with Lisa Wysocky. Simon & Schuster Books for Young Readers 2014 240 p. (hardcover) $17.99

Grades: 9 10 11 12   92

1. Autobiography 2. Slave narratives 3. Child abuse -- United States 4. Child slaves -- United States 5. Foster parents -- United States

ISBN 1442481684; 9781442481688

LC 2013011860

This book by Shyima Hall and Lisa Wysocky is a "memoir from a young woman who lost her childhood to slavery- -and built a new life grounded in determination and justice. Shyima Hall was born in Egypt on September 29, 1989, the seventh child of desperately poor parents. When she was eight, her parents sold her into slavery. . . . When she was ten, her captors moved to Orange County, California, and smuggled Shyima with them." (Publisher's note)

"Shyima Hall was eight years old when her parents sold her into slavery. Before this, she was living with them and her 10 siblings in poverty in a small town near Alexandria, Egypt. She worked tirelessly for her captors, receiving no medical care or schooling and developed a general mistrust of people...Teens will be interested in learning how Shyima adjusted to foster care and adoption, school, dating, working, and being a regular young adult. The book ends on an uplifting note as Shyima becomes a mother and continues working toward her goal of becoming a police officer or working for the ICE in order to save others forced into bondage. The specific details of her eye-opening account provide an excellent introduction to the terrible plight of thousands of slaves who are brought into the U.S. each year." (School Library Journal)

Hamilton, Alexander, 1757-1804

★ St. George, Judith. The **duel**: the parallel lives of Alexander Hamilton and Aaron Burr. Viking 2009 97p il $16.99

Grades: 6 7 8 9 10   92

1. Statesmen 2. Vice-presidents 3. Secretaries of the treasury 4. Politicians -- United States

ISBN 978-0-670-01124-7; 0-670-01124-X

LC 2009-5660

"After a prologue following the steps of Alexander Hamilton and Aaron Burr on the morning of their famous duel, St. George backtracks to trace the 'parallel lives' mentioned in the subtitle. . . . Well researched and organized, the book offers insights into the personalities, lives, and times of Burr and Hamilton." Booklist

Hammel, Heidi B.

Bortz, Fred. **Beyond** Jupiter; the story of planetary astronomer Heidi Hammel. [by] Fred Bortz. Franklin Watts 2005 110p il (Women's adventures in science) lib bdg $31.50

Grades: 7 8 9 10   92

1. Astronomers 2. Women astronomers 3. College teachers

ISBN 0-531-16775-5

LC 2005-0778

This book by Fred Bortz is part of the Women's Adventures in Science series. It profiles "Heidi Hammel . . . a planetary astronomer, a scientist who uses the world's most powerful telescopes to learn about planets. By making remarkable discoveries in the farthest reaches of our solar system, Heidi also helps us better understand the planet we call home. The giant planets Neptune and Uranus are Heidi's specialties." (Publisher's note)

The author "has captured some of the engaging qualities of Heidi Hammel's personality through extensive work with her and with the cooperation of her friends and family." Sci Books Films

Includes glossary and bibliographical references

Hansberry, Lorraine, 1930-1965

★ Hansberry, Lorraine. **To** be young, gifted, and Black; Lorraine Hansberry in her own words. adapted by Robert Nemiroff; with drawings and art by Lorraine Hansberry; introduction by James Baldwin; and a new preface by Jewell Handy Gresham Nemiroff. 1st Vintage Books ed; Vintage Books 1995 xxx, 261p il pa $8.95; pa $13.95

Grades: 11 12 Adult **92**

1. Authors 2. Dramatists 3. Essayists 4. Newspaper editors 5. Nonfiction writers 6. Dramatists, American 7. African American women -- Biography
ISBN 9780451531780; 0-679-76415-1

LC 96-119999

First published 1969 by Prentice-Hall
Work on this book and on the script for the play of the same title, which was presented at New York's Cherry Lane Theatre in 1969, "proceeded concurrently, each drawing upon the experiences and creative discoveries of the other, but ultimately diverging quite drastically." Postscript

Hargreaves, Alice Pleasance Liddell, 1852-1934

Rubin, C. M. The **real** Alice in Wonderland; a role model for the ages. [by] C.M. Rubin with Gabriella Rose Rubin. AuthorHouse 2010 134p il $29.95

Grades: 7 8 9 10 **92**

1. Authors 2. Children 3. Novelists 4. Mathematicians 5. Characters and characteristics in literature 6. Children's authors 7. Writers on science
ISBN 978-1-4490-8131-7; 1-4490-8131-2

LC 2010-901865

"Readers will follow this title down the rabbit hole to discover the world of the real Alice who inspired Lewis Carroll's Alice in Wonderland. The book moves seamlessly through the life of Alice Pleasance Liddell. . . . This offering paints a full picture of Alice, not only as a child who has captivated literature but also as a woman who was truly ahead of her time. This is a purchase that will do well with a range of people and should be offered as a standard accompaniment to Alice in Wonderland. The illustrations and pictures will make it quite popular in a public library." Voice Youth Advocates

Includes bibliographical references

Hari, Daoud

Hari, Daoud. The **translator**; a tribesman's memoir of Darfur. Random House 2008 204p hardcover o.p. pa $13

Grades: 7 8 9 10 11 12 Adult **92**

1. Refugees 2. Memoirists 3. Guides (Persons) 4. Sudan -- History -- Darfur conflict, 2003-
ISBN 978-1-4000-6744-2; 1-4000-6744-8; 978-0-8129-7917-6 pa; 0-8129-7917-6 pa

LC 2007-42308

In this memoir, the author recounts his life in Darfur, Sudan before and after the conflict in 2003.

"Those with the courage to join Hari's odyssey may find this a life-changing read." Publ Wkly

Harmon, Adam

Harmon, Adam. **Lonely** soldier; the memoir of an American in the Israeli Army. Ballantine Books 2006 256p il $25.95

Grades: 11 12 Adult **92**

1. Soldiers 2. Memoirists 3. Soldiers -- Israel
ISBN 0-89141-874-1; 978-0-89141-874-0

LC 2005-58656

This is an "account of a sincere New Englander's move to Israel in 1990, where he enlists as a paratrooper just before the beginning of the Gulf War. . . . An illuminating account of a much-covered conflict, this is a memoir for anyone who wants a look behind the daily headlines." Publ Wkly

Hartzler, Aaron

Hartzler, Aaron. **Rapture** practice; a memoir. by Aaron Hartzler. 1st ed. Little, Brown and Co. 2013 400 p. (hardcover) $17.99

Grades: 9 10 11 12 **92**

1. Christian life 2. High school students -- Religious life 3. Teenagers -- Religious life 4. Christian biography -- United States
ISBN 031609465X; 9780316094658

LC 2012028746

Lambda Literary Award Finalist (2014)
This memoir, by Aaron Hartzler, tells how the author "was taught that at any moment Jesus might come down in the twinkling of an eye, . . . but as he turns sixteen, Aaron finds himself more and more attached to his life on Earth, and curious about all the things his family forsakes for the Lord. He begins to realize he doesn't want the Rapture to happen, just yet. . . . Before long, Aaron makes the plunge from conflicted do-gooder to full-fledged teen rebel." (Publisher's note)

Hawking, Stephen

Kamberg, Mary-Lane. **Stephen** Hawking. Rosen Publishing 2015 112 p. (library bound) $35.60

Grades: 10 11 12 **92**

1. Physicists 2. Black holes (Astronomy) 3. Physicists -- Great Britain -- Biography
ISBN 1477776834; 9781477776834

LC 2013043306

This children's book by Mary-Lane Kamberg on physicist Stephen Hawking is part of a series "which sheds light on the human face of geniuses. Some titles emphasize the science writers' literary background more than others." (School Library Journal)

"Throughout his biography, Tyson's passion for space exploration is palpable. Dynamic, understated artwork does not distract from excellent writing here. Strong additions." SLJ

Includes bibliographical references (pages 105-107) and index

Hayslip, Le Ly

Hayslip, Le Ly. **When** heaven and earth changed places; a Vietnamese woman's journey from war to peace. [by] Le Ly Hayslip with Jay Wurts. Plume 1990 368p pa $16

Grades: 11 12 Adult   **92**

1. Authors 2. Refugees 3. Businesspeople 4. Memoirists 5. Humanitarians 6. Vietnam War, 1961-1975 -- Personal narratives

ISBN 0-452-27168-1

    LC 89-13711

First published 1989 by Doubleday

"The book is a searing and human account of Vietnam's destruction and self-destruction. Lucidly, sometimes even lyrically, Ms. Hayslip paints an intensely intimate portrait." N Y Times Book Rev

Hemingway, Ernest, 1899-1961

★ Reef, Catherine. **Ernest** Hemingway; a writer's life. Clarion Books 2009 183p il $20

Grades: 8 9 10 11 12   **92**

1. Poets 2. Authors 3. Novelists 4. Authors, American 5. Short story writers 6. Nobel laureates for literature

ISBN 978-0-618-98705-4; 0-618-98705-3

    LC 2008-32885

"Reef creates a memorable portrait of the writer and his times, and even readers too young for most of Hemingway's oeuvre will enjoy armchair traveling to the bullfights in Spain, fishing expeditions to the Dry Tortugas and the Marquesas Keys, big-game hunting on the Serengeti and covering the Spanish Civil War. Along the way, they will gain a sense of the writer and his times and will even pick up some writing tips." Kirkus

Includes bibliographical references

★ Strathern, Paul. **Hemingway** in 90 minutes. Ivan R. Dee 2005 117p (Great writers in 90 minutes) $16.95; pa $8.95

Grades: 9 10 11 12   **92**

1. Poets 2. Authors 3. Novelists 4. Authors, American 5. Short story writers 6. Nobel laureates for literature

ISBN 1-56663-659-0; 1-56663-658-2 pa

    LC 2005-7511

In this book, the author offers an "account of Hemingway's life and ideas, and explains their influence on literature and on man's struggle to understand his place in the world." Publisher's note

Includes bibliographical references

Herriot, James

Herriot, James. **All** creatures great and small; 20th anniversary ed; St. Martin's Press 1992 442p $21.95; pa $13.95

Grades: 11 12 Adult   **92**

1. Authors 2. Veterinarians 3. Veterinary medicine 4. Memoirists

ISBN 0-312-08498-6; 0-312-33085-5 pa

    LC 92-18975

First published 1972

The first volume of Herriot's autobiographical account of the practice of veterinary medicine in Yorkshire, England in the 1930s

Followed by All things bright and beautiful (1974), All things wise and wonderful (1977), and The Lord God made them all (1981)

Herschel, Caroline Lucretia, 1750-1848

Lemonick, Michael D. The **Georgian** star; how William and Caroline Herschel revolutionized our understanding of the cosmos. W.W. Norton 2009 199p il map (Great discoveries) $23.95; pa $14.95

Grades: 11 12 Adult   **92**

1. Astronomers

ISBN 978-0-393-06574-9; 0-393-06574-X; 978-0-393-33709-9 pa; 0-393-33709-X pa

    LC 2008-29820

A tribute to the scientific contributions of William Herschel and his pioneering sister, Caroline, describes their establishment of surveying techniques that are still in use, Caroline's cataloging of nebulae, and William's discovery of infrared radiation.

"A rewarding account of two scientists who not only made great discoveries but enjoyed world recognition during their long, eventful lives." Kirkus

Includes bibliographical references

Herschel, William Sir, 1738-1822

Lemonick, Michael D. The **Georgian** star; how William and Caroline Herschel revolutionized our understanding of the cosmos. W.W. Norton 2009 199p il map (Great discoveries) $23.95; pa $14.95

Grades: 11 12 Adult   **92**

1. Astronomers

ISBN 978-0-393-06574-9; 0-393-06574-X; 978-0-393-33709-9 pa; 0-393-33709-X pa

    LC 2008-29820

A tribute to the scientific contributions of William Herschel and his pioneering sister, Caroline, describes their establishment of surveying techniques that are still in use, Caroline's cataloging of nebulae, and William's discovery of infrared radiation.

"A rewarding account of two scientists who not only made great discoveries but enjoyed world recognition during their long, eventful lives." Kirkus

Includes bibliographical references

Hirsi Ali, Ayaan, 1969-

Hirsi Ali, Ayaan. **Infidel**. Free Press 2007 353p il $26; pa $15

Grades: 11 12 Adult   **92**

1. Refugees 2. Muslim women 3. Feminists 4. Memoirists 5. Members of Parliament

ISBN 0-7432-8968-4; 978-0-7432-8968-9; 0-7432-8969-2 pa; 978-0-7432-8969-6 pa

    LC 2006-49762

"A Somali by birth and a recently elected member of the Dutch Parliament, Ms. Hirsi Ali had waged a personal crusade to improve the lot of Muslim women. Her warnings about the dangers posed to the Netherlands by unassimilated Muslims made her Public Enemy No. 1 for Muslim extremists, a feminist counterpart to Salman Rushdie. The circuitous, violence-filled path that led Ms. Hirsi Ali from Somalia to the Netherlands is the subject of 'Infidel,' her brave, inspiring and beautifully written memoir." N Y Times (Late N Y Ed)

Hitler, Adolf, 1889-1945

★ Rice, Earle. **Adolf** Hitler and Nazi Germany. Morgan Reynolds 2005 176p il map lib bdg $28.95
Grades: 7 8 9 10   92
1. Dictators 2. Heads of state 3. National socialism 4. Nazi leaders 5. Germany -- Politics and government -- 1933-1945
ISBN 978-1-931798-78-5; 1-931798-78-8
LC 2005-17825
"Clear, concise writing coupled with impressive illustrations that include black-and-white and color photos of cityscapes and individuals make this book a useful resource." SLJ

Holiday, Billie, 1915-1959

★ Holiday, Billie. **Lady** sings the blues; [Billie Holiday with William Dufty] 50th anniversary ed.; Harlem Moon 2006 231p il pa $15.95
Grades: 11 12 Adult   92
1. Singers 2. Blues musicians 3. African American singers
ISBN 978-0-7679-2386-6; 0-7679-2386-3
LC 2007-271682
First published 1956 by Doubleday
"A hard, bitter and unsentimental book, written with brutal honesty and having much to say not only about Billie Holiday, the person, but about what it means to be poor and black in America." N Y Her Trib Books
Includes discography

Holman, James, 1786-1857

Roberts, Jason. A **sense** of the world; how a blind man became history's greatest traveler. HarperCollins Publishers 2006 382p il $26.95; pa $14.95
Grades: 11 12 Adult   92
1. Blind 2. Naval officers 3. Travel writers
ISBN 0-00-716106-9; 978-0-00-716106-5; 0-00-716126-3 pa; 978-0-00-716126-3 pa
LC 2005-58166
The author "narrates the life of a 19th-century British naval officer who was mysteriously blinded at 25, but nevertheless became the greatest traveler of his time. . . . Roberts does Holman justice, evoking with grace and wit the tale of this man once lionized as 'The Blind Traveler.'" Publ Wkly
Includes bibliographical references

Houze, David, 1965-

Houze, David. **Twilight** people; one man's journey to find his roots. University of California Press 2006 329p il $24.95
Grades: 11 12 Adult   92
1. Apartheid 2. Journalists 3. Memoirists 4. African Americans -- Civil rights
ISBN 0-520-24398-6; 978-0-520-24398-9
LC 2005-35322

This "graceful memoir is a sensitive look into racial history in Africa and America, as well as a riveting personal narrative." Publ Wkly
Includes bibliographical references

Hughes, Langston, 1902-1967

★ Leach, Laurie F. **Langston** Hughes; a biography. Greenwood Press 2004 xx, 176p (Greenwood biographies) $29.95
Grades: 9 10 11 12   92
1. Poets 2. Authors 3. Novelists 4. Dramatists 5. Poets, American 6. Short story writers 7. Young adult authors
ISBN 0-313-32497-2
LC 2003-60131
This book covers the poet's life "from his tumultuous relationship with his father, various patrons, and romantic associations to his desire for recognition as an accomplished African-American literary artist. . . . This book would be a welcome addition to a high school library with a collection of in-depth biographies on literary artists." Libr Media Connect
Includes bibliographical references

Hunter-Gault, Charlayne

★ Hunter-Gault, Charlayne, 1942- **To** the mountaintop! Charlayne Hunter-Gault. Roaring Brook Press 2012 v, 198 p.p ill
Grades: 6 7 8 9 10 11 12   92
1. Colleges and universities 2. Women political activists 3. African Americans -- Civil rights 4. Southern States -- Race relations
ISBN 9781596436053
LC 2011020894
This book is written by Charlayne "Hunter-Gault . . . [who along with her] classmate Hamilton Holmes . . . [was one of] the first African Americans to be admitted to the University of Georgia, Athens. . . . [It] recalls the turbulent years from 1959, when she was first approached to challenge the system by seeking admission, through two years of legal battles for her admission to be finalized, through the campus protests and challenges unleashed by her actual enrollment, to graduation and her full-time position in 1965 at the 'New Yorker.' Organized by year, Hunter-Gault's personal experiences are set within the context of the larger civil rights movement." (Bulletin of the Center for Children's Books)
Includes bibliographical references and index

Hurston, Zora Neale, 1891-1960

★ Hurston, Zora Neale. **Dust** tracks on a road; an autobiography. with a foreword by Maya Angelou. 1st Harper Perennial Modern Classic ed; Harper Perennial Modern Classics 2006 308p il pa $13.95
Grades: 11 12 Adult   92
1. Authors 2. Novelists 3. Dramatists 4. African American authors 5. Memoirists 6. Folklorists 7. Short story writers 8. African American women -- Biography
ISBN 0-06-085408-1; 978-0-06-085408-9
LC 2005-52616
First published 1942 by Lippincott

The author describes her wanderings in and out of schools and jobs as a young girl, finishing her course work at Barnard, and beginning her life's work.

Includes bibliographical references

Sapet, Kerrily. **Rhythm** and folklore; the story of Zora Neale Hurston. Morgan Reynolds Pub. 2008 160p il lib bdg $27.95

Grades: 7 8 9 10 11 12   92
1. Authors 2. Novelists 3. Dramatists 4. Women authors 5. African American authors 6. Memoirists 7. Folklorists 8. Short story writers
ISBN 978-1-59935-067-7; 1-59935-067-X

LC 2008-844

A biography of the African American author and folklorist "With lots of personal quotes, this lively biography stays true to Hurston's defiant, independent spirit. . . . Sapet give a strong sense of the times, including the Harlem Renaissance. . . . With lots of full-page photos, this biography will encourage teens to read and discuss Hurston's work." Booklist

Includes bibliographical references

IraqiGirl

IraqiGirl. **IraqiGirl**; diary of a teenage girl in Iraq. Haymarket 2009 205p pa $13

Grades: 6 7 8 9 10   92
1. Weblogs 2. Bloggers 3. Iraq War, 2003- -- Personal narratives
ISBN 978-1-931859-73-8; 1-931859-73-6

"In 2004 in Mosul (the third largest city in Iraq), a 15-year-old girl started a blog detailing her life in the midst of the Iraq War. Her journal encompasses the day-to-day trauma the American invasion has caused her city, her family and friends. . . . [The author's] authentically teenage voice, emotional struggles and concerns make her story all the more resonant." Publ Wkly

Irwin, Cait

Irwin, Cait. **Monochrome** days; a firsthand account of one teenager's experience with depression. [by] Cait Irwin with Dwight L. Evans and Linda Wasmer Andrews. Oxford University Press 2007 160p il $30; pa $9.95

Grades: 9 10 11 12   92
1. Students 2. Mentally ill 3. Depression (Psychology)
ISBN 978-0-19-531004-7; 978-0-19-531005-4 pa

LC 2006-23381

"The book combines the firsthand experiences of the author with medical information and recommendations for teens struggling with depression." Voice Youth Advocates

Includes bibliographical references

Jackson, Andrew, 1767-1845

Wilentz, Sean. **Andrew** Jackson. Times Books 2005 195p (American presidents series) $20

Grades: 11 12 Adult   92
1. Generals 2. Presidents 3. Presidents -- United States
ISBN 0-8050-6925-9

LC 2005-52857

The author "shows that our complicated seventh president was a central figure in the development of American democracy. . . . It is rare that historians manage both Wilentz's deep interpretation and lively narrative." Publ Wkly

Includes bibliographical references

Jackson, Michael, 1958-2009

O'Keefe, Sherry. **Spin**; the story of Michael Jackson. Morgan Reynolds 2010 144p il (Modern music masters) lib bdg $28.95

Grades: 7 8 9 10   92
1. Singers 2. Rock musicians 3. African American singers 4. Songwriters 5. Pop musicians
ISBN 978-1-59935-134-6

LC 2009-54191

Discusses the singer's rise to stardom, his changing personal appearance, legal battles, family life, and unexpected death at the age of fifty.

Includes bibliographical references

Sullivan, Randall. **Untouchable**; the strange life and tragic death of Michael Jackson. Randall Sullivan. Grove Press 2012 776 p. ill $35

Grades: 9 10 11 12 Adult   92
1. Musicians -- Biography 2. African American musicians 3. African American singers -- Biography 4. Singers -- United States -- Biography
ISBN 080211962X; 9780802119629

LC 2013565073

This biography by Randall Sullivan "portrays Michael Jackson's life and death in unprecedented depth. Beginning with his last departure from Neverland, Sullivan captures Jackson's final years shuttling around the world, and plans to recapture his wealth and reputation with a comeback album and planned series of fifty mega-concerts." (Publisher's note)

"Some of Jackson's most ardent fans have been up in arms about Sullivan's latest take on the pop icon, and this book doesn't ignore the superstar's blemishes. For everyone but the most devoted, this is the Michael Jackson book the public wanted to read when he was still alive. Surprisingly, it makes him a more sympathetic figure than readers might expect." (Library Journal)

Includes bibliographical references (p. [611]-776)
Strange life and tragic death of Michael Jackson

Jackson, Robert Houghwout, 1892-1954

Jarrow, Gail. **Robert** H. Jackson; New Deal lawyer, Supreme Court Justice, Nuremberg prosecutor. Calkins Creek 2008 128p il $18.95

Grades: 7 8 9 10   92
1. Judges 2. Lawyers 3. Nuremberg Trial of Major German War Criminals, 1945-1946 4. Attorneys general 5. Government officials 6. Supreme Court justices
ISBN 978-1-59078-511-9

LC 2007-18858

"Framed by Jackson's famous speech as chief American prosecutor at the 1945 international Nuremberg trial of Nazi war criminals, this detailed biography sets his law career within the history and politics of his time and raises essential issues of human rights." Booklist

Includes bibliographical references

Jackson, Stonewall, 1824-1863

Koestler-Grack, Rachel A. **Stonewall** Jackson; by Rachel Koestler-Grack. Chelsea House 2009 136p il (Leaders of the Civil War era) lib bdg $30
Grades: 7 8 9 10   92
   1. Generals
   ISBN 978-1-60413-299-1; 1-60413-299-X
                  LC 2008-44611
A biography of Confederate general Stonewall Jackson. Includes glossary and bibliographical references

James, Kelle

James, Kelle. **Smile** for the camera. Simon & Schuster 2010 392p $16.99
Grades: 10 11 12   92
   1. Fashion models 2. Memoirists 3. Models (Persons)
   ISBN 978-1-4424-0623-0
                  LC 2009-53000
"This completely absorbing memoir follows the author from age 16, when she escaped from an abusive home in the late 1970s to become a model in New York City. Although Kelle ultimately succeeds, her path from squalor to security takes her through more abusive relationships, homelessness and a sensational murder trial. . . . James pulls no punches in her descriptions of the sexual and physical abuse she suffered at the hands of predatory men in the city and in flashback memories of her violent father. . . . Stark in its honesty, the book propels readers forward with a sense of suspense worthy of a thriller." Kirkus

Jefferson, Thomas, 1743-1826

Bober, Natalie. **Thomas** Jefferson; draftsman of a nation. [by] Natalie S. Bober. University of Virginia Press 2007 360p il $22.95
Grades: 9 10 11 12   92
   1. Architects 2. Presidents 3. Vice-presidents 4. Essayists 5. Presidents -- United States
   ISBN 978-0-8139-2632-2
                  LC 2006-32722
First published 1988 by Atheneum Pubs. with title: Thomas Jefferson: man on a mountain
This is a biography of the author of the Declaration of Independence and third president of the United States, who was also an inventor, architect, farmer, and educator.
"Jefferson's story is one every YA needs to know, and this excellent, well-documented edition is a must-have." SLJ
Includes bibliographical references

Jennings, Kevin, 1963-

Jennings, Kevin. **Mama's** boy, preacher's son; a memoir. Beacon Press 2006 267p $24.95; pa $15
Grades: 11 12 Adult   92
   1. Gay men 2. Educators 3. Political activists 4. Gay rights activists 5. Organization officials
   ISBN 0-8070-7146-3; 978-0-8070-7146-5; 0-8070-7147-1 pa; 978-0-8070-7147-2 pa
                  LC 2006-1275
"Jennings writes of his journey with graciousness and candor." Voice Youth Advocates

Jeter, Derek, 1974-

Greenberg, Keith Elliot. **Derek** Jeter; spectacular shortstop. Twenty-First Century Books 2011 112p il (USA today lifeline biographies) lib bdg $33.26
Grades: 7 8 9 10   92
   1. Baseball players 2. Baseball -- Biography
   ISBN 978-0-7613-6422-1; 0-7613-6422-6
                  LC 2010032162
This is a biography of the New York Yankees' baseball player.
Includes glossary and bibliographical references

Jeter, Derek. The **life** you imagine; ten steps to ultimate achievement. Crown 2000 xxii, 279p il hardcover o.p. pa $12
Grades: 11 12 Adult   92
   1. Baseball players 2. Baseball -- Biography 3. New York Yankees (Baseball team)
   ISBN 0-609-60786-3; 0-609-80718-8 pa
                  LC 00-34533
In this autobiography, Jeter outlines the "ten practical steps, . . . {he} used to fulfill his dream of playing baseball in the major leagues. The ten principles, which reflect the author's journey as an athlete, are based on input from family members, whom he credits for his success." Libr J

Joan, of Arc, Saint, 1412-1431

Pernoud, Regine. **Joan** of Arc: her story; Régine Pernoud, Marie-Véronique Clin; translated and revised by Jeremy duQuesnay Adams; edited by Bonnie Wheeler. St. Martin's Griffin 1999 xxii, 304p il map hardcover o.p. pa $16.95
Grades: 11 12 Adult   92
   1. Saints 2. Christian saints 3. France -- History -- 1328-1589, House of Valois
   ISBN 0-312-21442-1; 0-312-22730-2 pa
                  LC 98-45059
Original French edition, 1986
This work "traces the appearance of Joan as a documented historical character rather than adhering to a standard chronological sequence. Informing the narrative is a novel interpretation of Joan as a political prisoner. Moving beyond the narrative, the American translator . . . has added a series of appendixes containing valuable contextual material. . . . These materials discuss key historical events, provide biographical information on Joan's contemporaries, and discuss Joan's afterlife in history, literature, folklore, art, and iconography." Libr J
Includes bibliographical references

Jobs, Steve, 1955-2011

Blumenthal, Karen. **Steve** Jobs; the man who thought different: a biography. by Karen Blumenthal. Feiwel and Friends 2012 310 p. ill., ports.
Grades: 7 8 9 10   92
   1. Apple Computer, Inc. 2. Inventors -- United States -- Biography 3. Businesspeople -- United States -- Biography 4. Computer industry -- United States --

History

ISBN 125001445X; 125001557X; 9781250014450; 9781250015570

LC 2012376637

YALSA Award for Excellence in Nonfiction for Young Adults Finalist (2013)

This book is a biography of technology executive Steve Jobs. "[Karen] Blumenthal weaves her portrait on the thematic frame used by Jobs himself in his autobiographical 2005 Stanford commencement address." She chronicles "his adoption as an infant through his 'phone phreaking' days to a spectacular rise and just as meteoric fall from corporate grace in the 1980s. Following a decade of diminished fortunes and largely self-inflicted complications in personal relationships, he returned to Apple." (Kirkus)

Includes bibliographical references (p. [278]-283) and index

Hartland, Jessie. **Steve** Jobs; insanely great. Jessie Hartland. Schwartz & Wade Books 2015 272 p. chiefly illustrations (alk. paper) $22.95

Grades: 9 10 11 12 Adult   **92**
1. Entrepreneurs 2. Computer programming 3. Graphic novels 4. Computer engineers -- United States -- Biography 5. Computer engineers -- United States -- Biography -- Comic books, strips, etc

ISBN 0307982955; 9780307982957; 9780307982964

LC 2014005768

Author Jessie Hartland presents this "biography in graphic format [as a] complement to more text-heavy books on Steve Jobs like Walter Isaacson's biography. Presenting the story of the ultimate American entrepreneur, who brought us Apple Computer, Pixar, Macs, iPods, iPhones and more, this unique and stylish book is sure to appeal to the legions of readers who live and breathe the techno-centric world Jobs created." (Publisher's note)

"Luddites and iFans alike should find this volume an illuminating introduction to Jobs's life and the recent history of consumer electronics." SLJ

Includes bibliographical references and index

Quinn, Jason. **Steve** Jobs; genius by design. by Jason Quinn; illustrated by Amit Tayal. Random House Inc 2012 104 p. ill. (chiefly col.) $12.99

Grades: 7 8 9 10 11 12 Adult   **92**
1. Computer industry 2. Biographical graphic novels
ISBN 9380028768; 9789380028767

This graphic novel, by Jason Quinn, illustrated by Amit Tayal, presents a biography of the 20th-century technology entrepreneur and Apple Inc. founder Steve Jobs. "Steve Jobs and his inventions changed the world we live in." The book ranges "from his birth and his adoption, through the advent of the computer age and on into the digital age. Forced out of the company he created, his indomitable vision allowed him to change the world of computers, movies, music and telecommunications." (Publisher's note)

"This cleverly designed volume provides a concise but well-balanced view of Steve Jobs the wunderkind, including his difficult personality and complex genius." Booklist

John Paul II, Pope, 1920-2005

★ Renehan, Edward J. **Pope** John Paul II; [by] Edward J. Renehan, Jr. Chelsea House 2007 109p il (Modern world leaders) lib bdg $30

Grades: 7 8 9 10 11 12   **92**
1. Popes
ISBN 978-0-7910-9227-9 lib bdg; 0-7910-9227-5 lib bdg

LC 2006-10612

This "biography follows the arch of the pontiff's life in the context of world politics." Publisher's note

Includes bibliographical references

Johnson, Andrew, 1808-1875

Gordon-Reed, Annette. **Andrew** Johnson. Times Books/Henry Holt and Company 2011 166p il (American presidents series) $23

Grades: 11 12 Adult   **92**
1. Governors 2. Presidents 3. Vice-presidents 4. Members of Congress 5. Presidents -- United States 6. United States -- Politics and government -- 1865-1898
ISBN 978-0-8050-6948-8

LC 2010-32595

"Andrew Johnson rose from humble beginnings in the South to serve as Lincoln's second vice president, thus becoming President just as the Civil War was ending. He showed none of his predecessor's political finesse and is often viewed as among the worst to hold the office. . . . [The author] argues that the nation went from the best President to the worst during this most crucial period of its history. This slim study does cover Johnson from birth to death (1808–75), but the focus is assuredly on his presidency." Libr J

Includes bibliographical references

Johnson, Lyndon B. (Lyndon Baines), 1908-1973

Peters, Charles. **Lyndon** B. Johnson. Times Books 2010 199p (American presidents series) $23

Grades: 11 12 Adult   **92**
1. Presidents 2. Vice-presidents 3. Senators 4. Members of Congress 5. Presidents -- United States 6. United States -- Politics and government -- 1945-
ISBN 978-0-8050-8239-5

LC 2009-45612

"Peters describes Johnson's Texas childhood, his years in Congress, his frustrating years as Kennedy's vice president, and the triumphs and failures of his presidency (1963-68). . . . This book is aimed at general readers who want a brief account of this controversial President. . . . Its intended audience will not be disappointed with this fast-moving story." Libr J

Includes bibliographical references

Johnson, Robert, 1911-1938

Wald, Elijah. **Escaping** the delta; Robert Johnson and the invention of the blues. Amistad 2004 342p $24.95; pa $14.95

Grades: 11 12 Adult   **92**
1. Singers 2. Guitarists 3. Blues music 4. Blues musicians 5. African American musicians 6.

Songwriters
ISBN 0-06-052423-5; 0-06-052427-8 pa
LC 2003-52287
The author "writes better than anyone else ever has about the blues. If you read only one book about blues—maybe ever—read this one." Booklist
Includes bibliographical references

Joplin, Janis, 1943-1970

★ Angel, Ann. **Janis** Joplin; rise up singing. introduction by Sam Andrew. Amulet Books 2010 120p il $19.95
Grades: 9 10 11 12   92
1. Singers 2. Rock musicians
ISBN 978-0-8109-8349-6
LC 2010-5558
"From interviews with her friends and letters that Joplin wrote home, Angel pieces together her subject's short life, contrasting her conservative upbringing in a small Texas town with the wild 1960s, vividly portrayed both in descriptions and in excellent-quality, full-color and black-and-white photos on almost every page." SLJ
Includes bibliographical references

Joseph, Nez Percé Chief, 1840-1904

Hopping, Lorraine Jean. **Chief** Joseph; the voice for peace. Sterling 2010 124p il map (Sterling biographies) lib bdg $12.95
Grades: 7 8 9 10   92
1. Indian chiefs 2. Nez Percé Indians 3. Native Americans -- Biography
ISBN 978-1-4027-6842-2; 1-4027-6842-7
LC 2009-24132
This biography is "packed with fast action and detailed analysis. . . . Hopping tells of Joseph's painful decision to leave his land to save Nez Percé lives, choosing peace because he knew they could not win against the U.S. . . . [The] spacious design is highly scannable, with color background screens, photos, maps, and historic prints throughout." Booklist
Includes glossary and bibliographical references

★ Moulton, Candy Vyvey. **Chief** Joseph; guardian of the people. [by] Candy Moulton. Forge Books 2005 239p map (American heroes series) $19.95; pa $12.95
Grades: 11 12 Adult   92
1. Indian chiefs 2. Nez Percé Indians 3. Native Americans -- Biography
ISBN 0-7653-1063-5; 0-7653-1064-3 pa
LC 2004-56318
The author "focuses on Chief Joseph of the Nez Perce tribe, who, after trying for years to accommodate encroaching white men on his tribal lands, gave up and attempted, in the fall of 1877, to lead his people to safety in Canada. . . . Moving and well documented, this is a superb addition to the American Heroes series." Booklist
Includes bibliographical references

Julian, Percy L., 1899-1975

Stille, Darlene R. **Percy** Lavon Julian; pioneering chemist. Compass Point Books 2009 112p il map (Signature lives) lib bdg $34.65
Grades: 6 7 8 9 10   92
1. Chemists 2. Pharmaceutical executives
ISBN 978-0-7565-4089-0; 0-7565-4089-5
LC 2008-38462
Details the life of chemist Percy Lavon Julian and his accomplishments
The "inviting page design features photos and boxed screens on each spread, and . . . includes a detailed bibliography, source notes, time line and glossary." Booklist
Includes glossary and bibliographical references

Kamara, Mariatu, 1987-

★ Kamara, Mariatu. The **bite** of the mango; [by] Mariatu Kamara with Susan McClelland. Annick Press 2008 216p
Grades: 9 10 11 12   92
1. Amputees 2. Refugees 3. Children and war 4. Memoirists
ISBN 1-55451-158-5 pa; 1-55451-159-3; 978-1-55451-158-7 pa; 978-1-55451-159-4
"As a child in a small rural village in Sierra Leone, Mariatu Kamara lived peacefully surrounded by family and friends. Rumors of rebel attacks were no more than a distant worry. But when 12-year-old Mariatu set out for a neighboring village, she never arrived. Heavily armed rebel soldiers, many no older than children themselves, attacked and tortured [her]. . . . As told to her by Mariatu, journalist Susan McClelland has written the . . . story of the brutal attack, its aftermath and Mariatu's eventual arrival in Toronto. . . . Now 22 years old, Mariatu Kamara has been named a UNICEF Special Representative for Children in Armed Conflict." (Publisher's note) "Age fourteen and up." (Quill Quire)

"Relaying her experiences as a child in Sierra Leone during the 1990s, Kamara chillingly evokes the devastating effects of war. Mariatu is 11 when her tiny village is decimated by rebel soldiers, many of them children like her. Forced to watch as peaceful villagers are tortured and murdered, Mariatu is finally allowed to go free—but only after boy soldiers cut off her hands. . . . This book will unsettle readers—and then inspire them with the evidence of Mariatu's courage." Publ Wkly

Kamkwamba, William, 1987-

★ Kamkwamba, William. The **boy** who harnessed the wind; William Kamkwamba and Bryan Mealer. William Morrow 2009 273 p. (hbk.) $25.99; pa $14.99
Grades: 11 12 Adult   92
1. Windmills -- Malawi 2. Malawi -- Rural conditions 3. Water-supply, Rural -- Malawi 4. Rural electrification -- Malawi 5. Electric power production -- Malawi 6. Mechanical engineers -- Malawi -- Biography
ISBN 0-06-173032-7; 0-06-173033-5 pa; 0061730327; 978-0-06-173032-0; 978-0-06-173033-7 pa; 9780061730320
LC 2010275963
Autobiography of a teenager in Malawi who builds a windmill and brings electricity to his village.

"This exquisite tale strips life down to its barest essentials, and once there finds reason for hopes and dreams, and is especially resonant for Americans given the economy and increasingly heated debates over health care and energy policy." Publ Wkly

Kantner, Seth, 1965-

Kantner, Seth. **Shopping** for porcupine; a life in arctic Alaska. Milkweed Editions 2008 240p il $28; pa $18

Grades: 11 12 Adult   **92**

1. Authors 2. Novelists 3. Photographers 4. Alaska 5. Trappers 6. Fishermen 7. Arctic regions 8. Authors, American 9. Young adult authors

ISBN 978-1-57131-301-0; 978-1-57131-311-9 pa

LC 2007-46477

"Crafted with the precision and verve acquired by living off the land, this is a powerful and important book of remembrance, protest, and warning." Booklist

Karr, Mary

Karr, Mary. The **Liars'** Club; a memoir. [with a new introduction by the author] 10th anniversary ed.; Penguin Books 2005 320p pa $15

Grades: 11 12 Adult   **92**

1. Poets 2. Authors 3. Essayists 4. Memoirists 5. College teachers

ISBN 0-14-303574-6; 978-0-14-303574-9

LC 2005-276148

First published 2005

"This barbed memoir of a close and calamitous family from a Texas oil town moves with the same quickness as its doubledad title. . . . The revelations continue to the final page, with a misleading carelessness as seductive as any world-class liar's." New Yorker

Kay, Jackie

★ Kay, Jackie. **Red** dust road; an autobiographical journey. Atlas Books 2010 288p $24

Grades: 11 12 Adult   **92**

1. Poets 2. Authors 3. Adoption 4. Novelists 5. Dramatists 6. Authors, Scottish 7. Children's authors 8. Short story writers

ISBN 978-1-935633-34-1

"Adopted by Communists, poet Kay was atheist, gay, and mixed raced in 1960s Scotland. Her efforts to track down her biological parents result in a complete revision of the family lore she had so carefully absorbed over the years. A fire-and-brimstone-spouting Nigerian preacher and a mousy Scottish Alzheimer's patient were not what she was looking for, but it was what Kay—and her adoptive family—found. . . . This is a book about what makes a family and what makes a story. The humor and understanding with which Kay talks about all of her parents is poetic in the largest sense of the word." Libr J

Keat, Nawuth, 1964-

Keat, Nawuth. **Alive** in the killing fields; surviving the Khmer Rouge genocide. by Nawuth Keat with Martha E. Kendall. National Geographic 2009 127p il map $15.95; lib bdg $23.90

Grades: 7 8 9 10 11   **92**

1. Authors 2. Cambodian refugees 3. Political refugees 4. Young adult authors

ISBN 978-1-4263-0515-3; 1-4263-0515-X; 978-1-4263-0516-0 lib bdg; 1-4263-0516-8 lib bdg

LC 2008-39805

"Told with stark simplicity, Nawuth's narrative is memorable yet accessible to young readers." Voice Youth Advocates

Includes bibliographical references

Keckley, Elizabeth, ca. 1818-1907

Fleischner, Jennifer. **Mrs.** Lincoln and Mrs. Keckley; the remarkable story of the friendship between a first lady and a former slave. Broadway Bks. 2003 372p il map hardcover o.p. pa $15.95; pa $16.99

Grades: 11 12 Adult   **92**

1. Memoirists 2. Dressmakers 3. Spouses of presidents 4. African American women -- Biography 5. Presidents' spouses -- United States

ISBN 0-7679-0258-0; 0-7679-0259-9 pa; 9780767902595

LC 2002-34493

"The book gives an in-depth look at a time, a friendship, and two very different women. The author's almost conversational writing style will keep readers engrossed." SLJ

Includes bibliographical references

Keegan, Kyle

Keegan, Kyle. **Chasing** the high; a firsthand account of one young person's experience with substance abuse. [by] Kyle Keegan, with Howard B. Moss. Oxford University Press 2008 170p (The Annenberg Foundation Trust at Sunnylands' adolescent mental health initiative) $30; pa $9.95

Grades: 9 10 11 12   **92**

1. Drug abuse 2. Divers 3. Narcotic addicts

ISBN 978-0-19-531471-7; 978-0-19-531472-4 pa

LC 2007-35423

"Keegan grew up in a loving, middle-class family in a small town in New York and wound up homeless and hopeless in California. He recounts his life from his teens through the present; now in his early 30s, he has been clean for two years. By detailing his own 'often-harrowing' experiences, the depths of his heroin addiction, and his steps to recovery, Keegan hopes to reach at-risk young people who have experimented with drugs or who are using. . . . This heartfelt, powerfully written book is an easy read and a first choice for all collections." SLJ

Includes bibliographical references

Keller, Helen, 1880-1968

Herrmann, Dorothy. **Helen** Keller; a life. University of Chicago Press 1999 394p il pa $22

Grades: 11 12 Adult   **92**

1. Deaf 2. Blind 3. Authors 4. Memoirists 5. Humanitarians 6. Inspirational writers 7. Social welfare leaders

ISBN 0-226-32763-9; 978-0-226-32763-1

LC 99-23242

First published 1998 by Knopf

The author "takes us beyond the image of Helen Keller portrayed in The Miracle Worker to unearth a passionate, politically radical woman whose inspiration and teacher, Annie Sullivan, is equally fiery and brilliant. Herrmann brings us into the every day lives of the famous pair, but the story is hardly mundane. . . . Herrmann gives us fascinating details via archives and unpublished memoirs to show how society's view of disabled people was greatly shaped by Keller and Sullivan." Libr J

Includes bibliographical references

Keller, Helen. Helen Keller: selected writings; edited by Kim E. Nielsen; consulting editor, Harvey J. Kaye. New York University Press 2005 317p il (History of disability series) $35

Grades: 11 12 Adult   92

1. Deaf 2. Blind 3. Authors 4. Memoirists 5. Humanitarians 6. Inspirational writers 7. Social welfare leaders

ISBN 0-8147-5829-0

LC 2004-28974

This is a collection "of Keller's personal letters, political writings, speeches, and excerpts of her published materials from 1887 to 1968." Univ Press Books for Public and Second Sch Libr, 2006

Includes bibliographical references

★ Keller, Helen. The **story** of my life; edited and with a preface by James Berger. The restored ed.; Modern Library 2003 xlvi, 343p il hardcover o.p. pa $9.95

Grades: 8 9 10 11 12 Adult   92

1. Deaf 2. Blind 3. Authors 4. Memoirists 5. Humanitarians 6. Inspirational writers 7. Social welfare leaders

ISBN 0-679-64287-0; 0-8129-6886-7 pa

LC 2002-40971

First published 1903

This biography of the inspirational Keller contains accounts of her home life and her relationship with her devoted teacher Anne Sullivan.

Includes bibliographical references

Kennedy, Edward Moore, 1932-2009

Boston globe. **Ted** Kennedy; scenes from an epic life. Simon & Schuster 2009 p. cm.

Grades: 11 12 Adult   92

1. Senators 2. Siblings of presidents 3. Presidential candidates 4. United States -- Congress -- Senate

ISBN 1439138060 (alk. paper)

LC 2008046870

Includes bibliographical references and index.

English, Bella. **Last** lion; the fall and rise of Ted Kennedy. Simon & Schuster 2009 464p il $28

Grades: Adult   92

1. Senators 2. Siblings of presidents 3. Presidential candidates 4. United States -- Congress -- Senate

ISBN 978-1-4391-3817-5; 1-4391-3817-6

LC 2008-50491

Sapet, Kerrily. **Ted** Kennedy. Morgan Reynolds Pub. 2009 144p il (Political profiles) lib bdg $28.95

Grades: 6 7 8 9 10   92

1. Senators 2. Siblings of presidents 3. Presidential candidates 4. Statesmen -- United States

ISBN 978-1-59935-089-9; 1-59935-089-0

LC 2008-34943

This offers "a detailed examination of the senator's life and career. . . . This is a meaty offering that is especially good at setting Kennedy's story against the events of his time. . . . Black-and-white and color photos are well chosen." Booklist

Includes bibliographical references

Kennedy, John F. (John Fitzgerald), 1917-1963

Burner, David. **John** F. Kennedy and a new generation; 3rd ed; Pearson Longman 2008 210p il (Library of American biography) pa $23.60

Grades: 11 12 Adult   92

1. Presidents 2. Senators 3. Members of Congress 4. Presidents -- United States 5. United States -- Politics and government -- 1961-1974

ISBN 978-0-205-60345-9; 0-205-60345-9

LC 2008-34627

First published 1988 by Little, Brown

"Burner discusses John F. Kennedy (1917-1963) as both an individual and a leader, allowing the reader to examine the changes that took place in the American political and social systems as reflected in the hopeful days of Kennedy's 'Camelot.'" Publisher's note

Includes bibliographical references

Dallek, Robert. **Let** every nation know; John F. Kennedy in his own words. [by] Robert Dallek and Terry Golway. Sourcebooks MediaFusion 2006 289p il $29.95; pa $19.95

Grades: 9 10 11 12 Adult   92

1. Presidents 2. Senators 3. Members of Congress 4. Presidents -- United States 5. United States -- Politics and government -- 1961-1974

ISBN 1-4022-0647-X; 978-1-4022-0647-4; 1-4022-0922-3 pa; 978-1-4022-0922-2 pa

LC 2005-37973

"The voice of John F. Kennedy is burned into the brains of people of a certain age. But younger citizens may not be familiar with his ideas and the distinctive way in which he expressed himself. There have been past recordings of JFK's presidential speeches, but this unique package pairs a CD of the speeches with a collection of essays on them by historians Golway and Dallek (the latter wrote his own JFK book, An Unfinished Life, 2003). The result is nothing short of terrific..." (Booklist)

Includes bibliographical references

Kennedy, Robert F., 1925-1968

Aronson, Marc. **Robert** F. Kennedy; a twentieth-century life. Viking 2007 204p il (Up close) $15.99

Grades: 8 9 10 11 12   92

1. Senators 2. Attorneys general 3. Siblings of presidents 4. Presidential candidates 5. Politicians --

United States
ISBN 978-0-670-06066-5; 0-670-06066-6

LC 2006-102150

Explores Robert F. Kennedy's life from his childhood to his adult years as Attorney General, New York state senator, and candidate for the presidency of the United States.

"Aronson draws on a wide variety of sources and is very honest in examining his subject as a complete human being, warts and all. . . . This text stands as an unbiased and illuminating resource." SLJ

Includes bibliographical references

Khomeini, Ruhollah

Moin, Baqer. **Khomeini**; life of the Ayatollah. I. B. Tauris 2009 352p pa $29.50

Grades: 11 12 Adult 92

1. Islamic leaders 2. Political leaders 3. Iran -- Politics and government
ISBN 978-1-84511-790-0

LC 2010293496

First published 1999 in the United Kingdom

The author "describes the harsh side of the cleric who forever changed the course of Iran's history. . . . The most interesting parts of the book deal with the human side of a man who was little known before his ascent to power and widely misunderstood both before and after." N Y Times Book Rev

Includes bibliographical references

Kim, Jong Il, 1942-2011

Wyborny, Sheila. **Kim** Jong Il; by Sheila Wyborny. Lucent Books 2009 104 p. ill. (some col.), map (People in the News) (library) $35.95

Grades: 6 7 8 9 92

ISBN 9781420500912; 1420500910

LC 2008049567

This book by Sheila Wyborny is part of the People in the News series and focuses on late North Korean leader Kim Jong Il. The series "profiles the lives and careers of some of today's most prominent newsmakers. Whether covering contributions and achievements or notorious deeds, books in this series examine why these well-known people garner public attention." (Publisher's note)

Includes bibliographical references (p. 90-91) and index.

King, Martin Luther, Jr., 1929-1968

★ Anderson, Ho Che. **King**; a comics biography. Special ed.; Fantagraphics 2010 312p il $34.99

Grades: 10 11 12 Adult 92

1. Clergy 2. Graphic novels 3. Biographical graphic novels 4. Nonfiction writers 5. Civil rights activists 6. Nobel laureates for peace 7. African Americans -- Biography -- Graphic novels 8. African Americans -- Civil rights -- Graphic novels
ISBN 978-1-60699-310-1

First published 2005

"Much of the book (packaged nicely with previously unprinted material, sketches, and a somewhat beside-the-point modern-day 'prelude' titled Black Dogs) tracks King from his college days in the 1950s to his death, jamming each page with noirishly drawn frames and tightly packed political debates. Though all the great moments of his civil rights battle are here (from the March on Washington to his

less-successful housing campaign in Chicago), Anderson doesn't resort to the cheap cinematic trick of success and fadeout. There is more disappointment here than celebration, suffused with the sorrowful sense of a long, long battle just barely begun. A crowning achievement, like the man it portrays." Publ Wkly

★ Aretha, David. **Martin** Luther King Jr. and the 1963 March on Washington; by David Aretha. Morgan Reynolds Pub. 2014 112 p. illustrations (some color) $28.95

Grades: 7 8 9 10 11 12 92

1. African Americans -- Civil rights 2. March on Washington for Jobs and Freedom (1963: Washington, D.C.) 3. Civil rights demonstrations -- Washington (D.C.) -- History -- 20th century
ISBN 1599353725; 9781599353722

LC 2012035355

In this book, author David "Aretha begins his look at the historic 1963 March on Washington with a review of Jim Crow in the American South and the early days of the modern Civil Rights Movement. . . . Aretha offers considerable detail about the march, including the peaceful, racially integrated crowd and the rousing speeches, which culminated with Dr. King's 'Dream' speech." (Publisher's note)

"Black-and-white archival photographs, boxed quotes, and excerpts from notable speeches enhance this series documenting pivotal laws and incidents of the civil rights movement. Each title builds up to the featured event, though Brown more successfully sets the stage with historical context and what follows. Both are well researched additions to library collections. Timeline, websites. Bib., ind." (Horn Book)

Includes bibliographical references

★ Flowers, Arthur. **I** see the promised land; a life of Martin Luther King Jr. [text by] Arthur Flowers, [illustrations by] Manu Chitrakar, [design by] Guglielmo Rossi. Groundwood Books/House of Anansi Press 2013 154 p. il $16.95

Grades: 8 9 10 11 12 Adult 92

1. Clergy 2. Graphic novels 3. Biographical graphic novels 4. Nonfiction writers 5. Civil rights activists 6. Nobel laureates for peace 7. African Americans -- Civil rights -- Graphic novels
ISBN 1554983282; 9781554983285

This book is an illustrated biography of civil rights activist Martin Luther King Jr. by African American novelist and performance poet Arthur Flowers. "He weaves the entire history of the enslavement of black Americans into King's story, refers to unspecified gods taking an interest in affairs, and comments on King's speeches." (School Library Journal)

"A myth-making take on King's life that has both emotional and intellectual impact, the Flowers/Chitrakar collaboration supplies fresh color and richness to the oft-told history of this game-changer. . . . Designed for adults but fine for teens and up; recommended for all libraries." Libr J

King, Melissa

King, Melissa. **She's** got next; a story of getting in, staying open, and taking a shot. Houghton Mifflin 2005 181p pa $13

Grades: 11 12 Adult   **92**

1. Sportswriters 2. Basketball -- Biography

ISBN 0-618-26456-6

LC 2004-62756

"King grew up in Arkansas shooting baskets in the driveway with her brother. At 27, she moved to Chicago and found herself yearning for the court in an effort to erase an inner emptiness. Her tender memoir chronicles her playing pickup basketball, meandering from playground to gym to YMCA...Transformed from casual player to coach, King evolves from a slightly removed participant to a passionate leader. Her growth is a surprising, satisfying ending to a story with wide appeal. " (Publishers Weekly)

King, Stephen, 1947-

Rogak, Lisa Angowski. **Haunted** heart; the life and times of Stephen King. [by] Lisa Rogak. Thomas Dunne Books 2009 310p il $25.95

Grades: 11 12 Adult   **92**

1. Authors 2. Novelists 3. Authors, American 4. Short story writers 5. Science fiction writers 6. Horror fiction -- Authorship

ISBN 978-0-312-37732-8; 0-312-37732-0

LC 2008-34209

The author "has produced an unauthorized biography of one of America's most popular novelists. Using King's novels and movies, as well as numerous articles and interviews, as well as other books and web sites about the author, Rogak covers all of the major events of King's life and career. . . . For King's many fans, this is a good introduction to the writer and his work." Libr J

Includes bibliographical references

★ Stefoff, Rebecca, 1951- **Stephen** King. Marshall Cavendish Benchmark 2010 175p il (Today's writers and their works) lib bdg $42.79

Grades: 8 9 10 11 12   **92**

1. Authors 2. Novelists 3. Authors, American 4. Short story writers 5. Science fiction writers

ISBN 0-7614-4122-0; 978-0-7614-4122-9

This biography of Stephen King places the author in the context of his times and discusses his work.

This book provides "excellent information for reports." SLJ

Includes bibliographical references

Kingston, Maxine Hong

The **woman** warrior; China men. Maxine Hong Kingston; with an introduction by Mary Gordon. Everyman's Library 2005 xxix, 541 p.p $25

Grades: 11 12 Adult   **92**

1. Chinese Americans -- History 2. California -- Biography 3. Chinese Americans -- California -- Biography 4. Authors, American -- 20th century -- Biography 5. Chinese Americans -- California -- Social

life and customs

ISBN 1400043840; 9781400043842

LC 2004061143

National Book Critics Circle Award for General Nonfiction (1976)

This volume, by Maxine Hong Kingston, reprints of her award winning books "The Woman Warrior" and "China Men." The first work "is Kingston's disturbing and fiercely beautiful account of growing up Chinese-American in California." The second is "Kingston's unforgettable imaginative journey into the hearts and minds of generations of Chinese men in America, from those who worked on the transcontinental railroad in the 1840s to those who fought in Vietnam." (Publisher's note)

Klein, Stephanie, 1975-

Klein, Stephanie. **Moose**; a memoir of fat camp. William Morrow 2008 310p $24.95

Grades: 11 12 Adult   **92**

1. Camps 2. Obesity 3. Weight loss 4. Photographers 5. Bloggers 6. Memoirists

ISBN 978-0-06-084329-8; 0-06-084329-2

LC 2008-2728

"Follows the coming-of-age years of the author, whose life profoundly changed in her twelfth year when she spent a summer at a weight-loss camp, a personal journey that shaped her subsequent philosophies about body image and self-acceptance." Publisher's note

Kohler, Dean Ellis

Kohler, Dean Ellis. **Rock** 'n' roll soldier; with Susan VanHecke. HarperTeen 2009 278p il $16.99

Grades: 9 10 11 12   **92**

1. Singers 2. Soldiers 3. Veterans 4. Guitarists 5. Rock musicians 6. Advertising executives 7. Public relations consultants 8. Vietnam War, 1961-1975 -- Personal narratives

ISBN 978-0-06-124255-7; 0-06-124255-1

LC 2008-47702

"Kohler's younger self is appealing, and his reconstructed dialogue sounds genuine. . . . Occasional four-letter words, references to sex, and descriptions of maimed and dead bodies make this quick read best suited for older high school students." Voice Youth Advocates

Kopelman, Jay

Kopelman, Jay. **From** Baghdad, with love; a Marine, the war, and a dog named Lava. [by] Jay Kopelman with Melinda Roth. Globe Pequot 2006 196p il $22.95

Grades: 11 12 Adult   **92**

1. Dogs 2. Memoirists 3. Marine corps officers 4. Iraq War, 2003- -- Personal narratives

ISBN 978-1-59228-980-6; 1-59228-980-0

LC 2006-22144

The author, an Iraq War veteran, describes his "efforts to safely transport Lava, the stray dog his Marine unit found in the wreckage of Fallujah, back to the U.S. . . . The story of Lava's journey out of Iraq is exciting, but it's to Kopelman and Roth's credit that it's not nearly as harrowing as the story of what the dog left behind." Publ Wkly

Includes bibliographical references

Kramer, Clara, 1927-

★ Kramer, Clara. **Clara's** war; one girl's story of survival. [by] Clara Kramer with Stephen Glantz. Ecco 2009 339p il $25.99

Grades: 11 12 Adult   **92**

1. Holocaust survivors 2. Memoirists 3. Jews -- Poland 4. Holocaust, 1933-1945 -- Personal narratives
ISBN 978-0-06-172860-0; 0-06-172860-8
First published 2008 in the United Kingdom
ALA RUSA Sophie Brody Award Honor Book (2010)

"Based on her wartime diary, which she kept while hiding in a basement in Poland, Kramer's book vividly recalls the tensions within her hidden community after the Nazis overtook the town of Zolkiew in 1942. Of particular interest are revelations about the family who hid the Kramers, particularly how an anti-Semitic Polish householder demonstrated great courage in shielding Jews in his basement." Libr J

Kraus, Caroline

Kraus, Caroline. **Borderlines**; a memoir. Broadway Bks. 2004 360p hardcover o.p. pa $12.95

Grades: 9 10 11 12   **92**

1. Authors 2. Editors 3. Memoirists 4. Short story writers
ISBN 0-7679-1403-1; 0-7679-1428-7 pa
LC 2003-69592

"Caroline, an intelligent but somewhat naive college graduate, finds herself in a severely dysfunctional and dangerous friendship with troubled and manipulative Jane. Her downward spiral and recovery make for a compelling and suspenseful read." SLJ

Kristofic, Jim, 1982-

Kristofic, Jim. **Navajos** wear Nikes; a reservation life. University of New Mexico Press 2011 211p il map $26.95

Grades: 11 12 Adult   **92**

1. Historians 2. Navajo Indians 3. Memoirists 4. Guides (Persons) 5. High school teachers 6. Native Americans -- Reservations
ISBN 978-0-8263-4946-0
LC 2010-37428

The author "shares his story of being transported at age seven from Pittsburgh to Ganado, Arizona, on the Navajo Indian Reservation by his mother, a nurse who had long nurtured her 'Indian Dream.' Jimmy is the only bilagaana, or white person, in his class, and he struggles with racial teasing from day one. By the third grade, he's learning to escape the daily taunting by helping his 'Navajo enemies' with their schoolwork." Booklist
Includes bibliographical references

LaNier, Carlotta Walls, 1942-

★ LaNier, Carlotta Walls. A **mighty** long way; my journey to justice at Little Rock Central High School. with Lisa Frazier Page. One World Ballantine Books 2009 284p il $26; pa $16

Grades: 11 12 Adult   **92**

1. School integration 2. Real estate brokers 3. Civil rights activists 4. Arkansas -- Race relations 5. African American women -- Biography 6. Central High School

(Little Rock, Ark.)
ISBN 978-0-345-51100-3; 978-0-345-51101-0 pa
LC 2009-28429

"At 14, Lanier was the youngest of the 'Little Rock Nine,' who integrated Little Rock Central High School in 1951; she went on to become the first African American young woman to receive a diploma from the school. Her memoir provides a firsthand account of a seismic shift in American history. . . . [This is] a worthy contribution to the history of civil rights in America." Publ Wkly
Includes bibliographical references

Lacks, Henrietta

Skloot, Rebecca, 1972- The **immortal** life of Henrietta Lacks. Crown Publishers 2010 369p il $26

Grades: 11 12 Adult   **92**

1. Cancer 2. Homemakers 3. Human experimentation in medicine 4. Cancer patients 5. African American women -- Biography
ISBN 978-1-4000-5217-2
LC 2009-31785

"A thorny and provocative book about cancer, racism, scientific ethics and crippling poverty, 'The Immortal Life of Henrietta Lacks' also floods over you like a narrative dam break, as if someone had managed to distill and purify the more addictive qualities of 'Erin Brockovich,' 'Midnight in the Garden of Good and Evil' and 'The Andromeda Strain.' More than 10 years in the making, it feels like the book Ms. Skloot was born to write." N Y Times Book Rev
Includes bibliographical references

Lang, Lang, 1982-

★ Lang, Lang. **Journey** of a thousand miles; my story. [by] Lang Lang with David Ritz. Spiegel & Grau 2008 239p il $24.95

Grades: 11 12 Adult   **92**

1. Pianists 2. Classical musicians
ISBN 978-0-385-52456-8
LC 2008-732

An autobiography of the Chinese classical piano prodigy.
"Lang tells the story of his childhood without self-pity or bitterness, making his success, and the book itself, all the more satisfying." N Y Times Book Rev

Lauren, Ralph

Mattern, Joanne. **Ralph** Lauren. Chelsea House 2011 101p il (Famous fashion designers) lib bdg $35

Grades: 6 7 8 9 10   **92**

1. Fashion designers
ISBN 978-1-60413-978-5; 1-60413-978-1
LC 2010036192

This is a biography of fashion designer Ralph Lauren.
Includes glossary and bibliographical references

Lawrence, Sarahlee

Lawrence, Sarahlee. **River** house; a memoir. Tin House Books 2010 272p pa $16.95

Grades: 11 12 Adult   **92**

1. Farmers 2. Rafting (Sports) 3. Adventure and

adventurers

ISBN 978-0-9825691-3-9

LC 2010-7702

"Handy with tools and rafts, a good neighbor, and a mighty fine horsewoman, Lawrence is also adept with language, writing with arresting lucidity and a driving need to understand her father, her legacy, the land, community, work, and herself. A true adventure story of rare dimension." Booklist

Le Guin, Ursula K., 1929-

Brown, Jeremy K. **Ursula** K. Le Guin; foreword by Kyle Zimmer. Chelsea House Publishers 2010 128p il (Who wrote that?) lib bdg $35

Grades: 6 7 8 9 10   92

1. Authors 2. Novelists 3. Women authors 4. Fantasy writers 5. College teachers 6. Authors, American 7. Children's authors 8. Short story writers 9. Science fiction writers

ISBN 978-1-60413-724-8; 1-60413-724-X

LC 2010006600

"Le Guin's work raises questions about identity and morality, and Brown explores her treatment of these themes in a way that readers, whether they're reading for pleasure or for reports, will appreciate. . . . This title does a fine job of conveying both the story of an author's long career and the vision that fuels it." SLJ

Includes bibliographical references

Lee, Bruce, 1940-1973

Lee, Bruce. **Bruce** Lee; artist of life. compiled and edited by John Little. Tuttle 1999 269p il $24.95; pa $16.95

Grades: 11 12 Adult   92

1. Actors 2. Martial arts 3. Martial artists

ISBN 0-8048-3131-9; 0-8048-3263-3 pa

LC 99-33401

"Lee's writings are inspired and inspirational, of interest to his fans and to the multitudes seeking the meaning of life." Booklist

Includes bibliographical references

★ Miller, Davis. The **Tao** of Bruce Lee; a martial arts memoir. Harmony Bks. 2000 193p hardcover o.p. pa $15

Grades: 11 12 Adult   92

1. Actors 2. Martial arts 3. Martial artists

ISBN 0-609-60477-5; 0-609-80538-X pa

LC 99-87697

Miller chronicles the life of film star and martial arts legend Bruce Lee and the impact Lee had on his life

This book "is equally a study of the nature and role of the hero in popular culture, a poignant and unusual coming-of-age story, and an informative biography." Booklist

Lee, Harper, 1926-2016

★ Madden, Kerry. **Harper** Lee; a twentieth-century life. Viking Children's Books 2009 223p il map (Up close) $16.99

Grades: 7 8 9 10   92

1. Authors 2. Novelists 3. Women authors 4. Essayists

5. Authors, American 6. Short story writers

ISBN 978-0-670-01095-0; 0-670-01095-2

LC 2008-53911

"A narrative both well paced and richly detailed . . . this biography will appeal to fans of the novel and to newcomers. . . . Extensive source notes and an excellent bibliography round out this superb biography." Kirkus

Includes bibliographical references

★ Shields, Charles J., 1951- **I** am Scout: the biography of Harper Lee. Henry Holt & Co. 2008 245p il $18.95

Grades: 7 8 9 10   92

1. Authors 2. Novelists 3. Women authors 4. Essayists

5. Authors, American 6. Short story writers

ISBN 0-8050-8334-0; 978-0-8050-8334-7

LC 2007-27572

This is a biography of the author of To Kill a Mockingbird (1960). It is an abridged version of Shields's adult biography Mockingbird (2006). Bibliography. Index. "Grades seven to ten." (Bull Cent Child Books)

Shields "offers a fascinating look at the unconventional Lee, which captures his elusive subject and her lifelong friend, Truman Capote. . . . Shields' formidable research . . . will impress any student who has ever written a term paper." Booklist

Includes bibliographical references

Lee, Robert E. (Robert Edward), 1807-1870

Robertson, James I. **Robert** E. Lee; Virginian soldier, American citizen. [by] James I. Robertson, Jr. Atheneum Books for Young Readers 2005 159p il maps $21.95

Grades: 7 8 9 10   92

1. Generals 2. College presidents 3. United States -- History -- 1861-1865, Civil War

ISBN 0-689-85731-4

LC 2003-22108

This portrait of the Confederate general "puts particular emphasis on his life during the Civil War years but provides plenty of information on his youth, his early military career, and his postwar years. . . . Useful for reports and interesting in its own right, this well-researched biography will be a solid addition to library collections." Booklist

Includes bibliographical references

Lemon, Alex

Lemon, Alex. **Happy**; a memoir. Scribner 2010 292p $25

Grades: 11 12 Adult   92

1. Poets 2. Authors 3. Poets, American 4. Brain -- Diseases

ISBN 978-1-4165-5023-5; 1-4165-5023-2

LC 2009-27293

The author, a poet, "was a carefree, hard partying, baseball-playing college student at Macalester College in Minnesota in 1997 when he suffered a stroke and later two brain bleeds. Readers are swept along on his rough ride during the next two years, through his nasty travails of frenetic drug and alcohol use, terribly misguided attempts to cope with his deteriorating and frightening condition. . . . Lemon offers a raw and honest narration of his college life, his relationships with girlfriends and family members, especially his loving and quirky mother. . . . [This] is a voltaic narrative that is alternately horrifying and touching." Publ Wkly

Lennon, John, 1940-1980

★ Partridge, Elizabeth. **John** Lennon; all I want is the truth. a photographic biography by Elizabeth Partridge. Viking 2005 232p il $24.99

Grades: 8 9 10 11 12   **92**

1. Singers 2. Rock musicians 3. Beatles 4. Songwriters
ISBN 0-670-05954-4

LC 2005-11850

Michael L. Printz Award honor book, 2006

"This handsome book will be eagerly received by both Beatles fans, who are legion, and their elders, who will enjoy reliving the glory days of the Fab Four and exploring the inner workings of a creative talent." SLJ

Includes bibliographical references

Lewin, W. H. G. (Walter H. G.)

Goldstein, Warren. **For** the love of physics; from the end of the rainbow to the edge of time--a journey through the wonders of physics. [by] Walter Lewin and Warren Goldstein. Free Press 2011 302p il $26; ebook $12.99

Grades: 11 12 Adult   **92**

1. Physicists 2. Physics -- Study and teaching 3. Colleges and universities -- Faculty
ISBN 978-1-4391-0827-7; 978-1-4391-2354-6 ebook

LC 2010-47737

"MIT's Lewin is deservedly popular for his memorable physics lectures . . . and this quick-paced autobiography-cum-physics intro fully captures his candor and lively teaching style. . . . [This text] glows with energy and should please a wide range of readers." Publ Wkly

Lewis, C. S. (Clive Staples), 1898-1963

Hamilton, Janet. **C.** S. Lewis; twentieth century pilgrim. Morgan Reynolds Pub. 2010 128p il (World writers) lib bdg $28.95

Grades: 7 8 9 10   **92**

1. Authors 2. Novelists 3. Theologians 4. Essayists 5. Satirists 6. Authors, English 7. Literary critics 8. Children's authors
ISBN 978-1-59935-112-4; 1-59935-112-9

LC 2009-7134

In this biography of the British author, "Lewis' childhood is well-documented, as is his love of literature as an escape from the real world. Hamilton clearly shows the importance religion played in Lewis's life. The impact that war, and the resulting loss of the imaginative worlds he could find in literature, and his struggle with religious belief are tied directly to his writing." Voice Youth Advocates

Includes bibliographical references

Lewis, John, 1940

★ Lewis, John. **March**; Book Two. by John Lewis and Andrew Aydin; illustrated by Nate Powell. Top Shelf Productions 2015 192 p. chiefly ill. (pbk) $19.95

Grades: 8 9 10 11 12 Adult   **92**

1. African Americans -- Civil rights -- Graphic novels 2. Civil rights movements 3. African American legislators 4. Legislators -- United States 5. African Americans -- Civil rights 6. African American civil rights workers 7. Civil rights workers -- United States 8. Autobiographical comic books, strips, etc.
ISBN 9781603094009; 1603094008

LC bl2015004150

Eisner Nominee: Best Reality-Based Work (2016)
Eisner Nominee: Best Publication for Teens (2016)

This graphic novel, by John Lewis and Andrew Aydin, illustrated by Nate Powell, "takes us behind the scenes of some of the most pivotal moments of the Civil Rights Movement. . . . After the success of the Nashville sit-in campaign, John Lewis is more committed than ever to changing the world through nonviolence -- but as he and his fellow Freedom Riders board a bus into the vicious heart of the deep south, they will be tested like never before." (Publisher's note)

"Heroism and steadiness of purpose continue to light up Lewis' frank, harrowing account of the civil rights movement's climactic days. . . . The contrast between the dignified marchers and the vicious, hate-filled actions and expressions of their tormentors will leave a deep impression on readers." Kirkus

★ Lewis, John R., **March**; Book One. John Lewis; [co-written by] Andrew Aydin; [art by] Nate Powell. Top Shelf Productions 2013 121 p. chiefly ill. (acid-free paper) $14.95

Grades: 8 9 10 11 12 Adult   **92**

1. African Americans -- Civil rights -- Graphic novels 2. Civil rights movements -- United States -- Comic books, strips, etc
ISBN 9781603093002

LC 2013218903

Coretta Scott King (Author) Honor Book (2014)

This graphic novel, by U.S. congressman John Lewis, "in collaboration with co-writer Andrew Aydin and New York Times best-selling artist Nate Powell . . . spans John Lewis' youth in rural Alabama, his life-changing meeting with Martin Luther King, Jr., the birth of the Nashville Student Movement, and their battle to tear down segregation through nonviolent lunch counter sit-ins, building to a . . . climax on the steps of City Hall." (Publisher's note)

"This is superb visual storytelling that establishes a convincing, definitive record of a key eyewitness to significant social change." SLJ

Leyson, Leon, 1929-2013

★ Leyson, Leon, 1929-2013. The **boy** on the wooden box; Leon Leyson; with Marilyn J Harran and Elisabeth B Leyson. Atheneum Books for Young Readers 2013 240 p. (hardcover) $16.99

Grades: 6 7 8 9   **92**

1. Holocaust survivors 2. World War, 1939-1945 -- Jews -- Rescue 3. Narewka (Poland) -- Biography 4. Jews -- Poland -- Narewka -- Biography 5. Płaszów (Concentration camp) 6. Concentration camp inmates -- Poland -- Płaszów -- Biography 7. Jewish children in the Holocaust -- Poland -- Kraków -- Biography 8.

Holocaust, Jewish (1939-1945) -- Poland -- Kraków -- Personal narratives
ISBN 1442497815; 9781442497818; 9781442497832
LC 2013017987

In this book, "Leon Leyson (born Leib Lezjon) was only ten years old when the Nazis invaded Poland and his family was forced to relocate to the Krakow ghetto. With incredible luck, perseverance, and grit, Leyson was able to survive the sadism of the Nazis, including that of the demonic Amon Goeth, commandant of Plaszow, the concentration camp outside Krakow. Ultimately, it was the generosity and cunning of one man, a man named Oskar Schindler, who saved Leon Leyson's life, and the lives of his mother, his father, and two of his four siblings, by adding their names to his list of workers in his factory—a list that became world renowned: Schindler's List." (Publisher's Note)

"This powerful memoir of one of the youngest boys on Schindler's list deserves to be shared...This memoir is a natural curriculum addition to WWII units for upper-elementary- and middle-school readers. Be sure to have additional materials on hand about Oskar Schindler, as readers will want to do more research into Leyson's story." (Booklist)

Li, Charles N., 1940-

Li, Charles N. The **bitter** sea; coming of age in a China before Mao. HarperCollins Publishers 2008 283p il hardcover o.p. pa $14.99

Grades: 11 12 Adult   **92**

1. Anthropologists 2. Linguists 3. College teachers 4. China -- History -- 1949-
ISBN 978-0-06-134664-4; 0-06-134664-0; 978-0-06-170954-8 pa; 0-06-170954-9 pa
LC 2007-25697

The author, "who had an extraordinary life growing up in pre-Communist China, shares his story of betrayal, loss, hope, and triumph in this lyrical account. . . . This brilliant memoir is as much about modern Chinese history as it is about familial relationships." Libr J

Li, Moying, 1954-

★ Moying Li. **Snow** falling in spring; coming of age in China during the cultural revolution. Farrar, Straus and Giroux 2008 176p $16

Grades: 7 8 9 10 11 12   **92**

1. Memoirists 2. Financial consultants
ISBN 978-0-374-39922-1; 0-374-39922-0
LC 2006-38356

"This memoir . . . offers a highly personal look at China's Cultural Revolution. The author is four years old when Mao initiates the Great Leap Forward in 1958. . . . Li effectively builds the climate of fear that accompanies the rise of the Red Guard, while accounts of her headmaster's suicide and the pulping of her father's book collection give a harrowing, closeup view of the persecution. Sketches about her grandparents root the narrative within a broader context of Chinese traditions as well as her own family's values." Publ Wkly

Lincoln, Abraham, 1809-1865

★ Fleming, Candace. The **Lincolns**; a scrapbook look at Abraham and Mary. Schwartz & Wade Books 2008 177p il map $24.99; lib bdg $28.99

Grades: 7 8 9 10 11 12   **92**

1. Lawyers 2. Presidents 3. State legislators 4. Members of Congress 5. Spouses of presidents 6. Presidents -- United States 7. Presidents' spouses -- United States 8. United States -- History -- 1861-1865, Civil War
ISBN 978-0-375-83618-3; 0-375-83618-7; 978-0-375-93618-0 lib bdg; 0-375-93618-1 lib bdg
LC 2007-44113

Boston Globe-Horn Book Award: Nonfiction (2009)

Fleming twines "accounts of two lives—Abraham and Mary Todd Lincoln—into one fascinating whole. On spreads that combine well-chosen visuals with blocks of headlined text, Fleming gives a full, birth-to-death view of the 'inextricably bound' Lincolns." Booklist

★ Freedman, Russell. **Lincoln**: a photobiography. Clarion Bks. 1987 149p il $18; pa $7.95

Grades: 5 6 7 8 9 10   **92**

1. Lawyers 2. Presidents 3. State legislators 4. Members of Congress 5. Presidents -- United States 6. United States -- History -- 1861-1865, Civil War
ISBN 0-89919-380-3; 0-395-51848-2 pa
LC 86-33379

Awarded the Newbery Medal, 1988

This is "a balanced work, elegantly designed and enhanced by dozens of period photographs and drawings, some familiar, some refreshingly unfamiliar." Publ Wkly

Includes bibliographical references

★ Lincoln, Abraham. **Abraham** Lincoln the writer; a treasury of his greatest speeches and letters. compiled and edited by Harold Holzer. Boyds Mills Press 2000 106p il lib bdg $15.95

Grades: 7 8 9 10   **92**

1. Lawyers 2. Presidents 3. State legislators 4. Members of Congress 5. Presidents -- United States 6. United States -- History -- 1861-1865, Civil War
ISBN 1-56397-772-9
LC 99-66551

"Lincoln's writings include personal letters, notes on the law, excerpts from speeches, debates, and inaugural addresses, letters to parents of fallen soldiers, and telegrams to his family. Reproductions of period photos, portraits, and documents illustrate the text effectively. . . . Highly interesting and a fine resource for students seeking quotations or for those wanting to meet Lincoln through his own words." Booklist

McGovern, George S. **Abraham** Lincoln; [by] George McGovern. Times Books/Henry Holt and Co. 2009 184p il (American presidents series) $22

Grades: 9 10 11 12 Adult   **92**

1. Lawyers 2. Presidents 3. State legislators 4. Members of Congress 5. Presidents -- United States
ISBN 978-0-8050-8345-3; 0-8050-8345-6
LC 2008-29869

In this biography of Abraham Lincoln, former U.S. senator McGovern "assesses Lincoln's greatness in terms of his ability to use his humble origins, empathy, keen sense of justice, uncommon skill in seeing the essence of an issue, faith in American democracy, gifts of language, and personal self-confidence—all to become a masterly lawyer, a party leader, commander in chief, and a heroic figure with both the vision and the practicality to realize his purposes. . . . This biography warrants reading to catch the sense of Lincoln's greatness, both for his own day and ours." Libr J

Includes bibliographical references

★ McPherson, James M. **Abraham** Lincoln. Oxford University Press 2009 79p $12.95
Grades: 11 12 Adult   **92**
1. Lawyers 2. Presidents 3. State legislators 4. Members of Congress 5. Presidents -- United States
ISBN 978-0-19-537452-0; 0-19-537452-5

LC 2008-35623

"McPherson, America's leading authority on Lincoln and his times, demonstrates his complete command of his subject in this concise but remarkably rich and perceptive biography. . . . This little book is bigger than its pages and should be in every library, schoolhouse, and home." Libr J

Includes bibliographical references

McPherson, James M., 1936- **Tried** by war; Abraham Lincoln as commander in chief. Penguin Press 2008 329p il map hardcover o.p. pa $17
Grades: 11 12 Adult   **92**
1. Lawyers 2. Presidents 3. State legislators 4. Members of Congress 5. Presidents -- United States 6. Executive power -- United States -- History 7. United States -- History -- 1861-1865, Civil War
ISBN 0-14-311614-2 pa; 1-594-20191-9; 978-0-14-311614-1 pa; 978-1-594-20191-2

LC 2008-25229

This is an account of the ways in which Lincoln "worked with, or against, his senior commanders to defeat the Confederacy and reshape the presidential role." (Publisher's note) Index.

This book "is a perfect primer, not just for Civil War buffs or fans of Abraham Lincoln, but for anyone who wishes to understand the evolution of the president's role as commander in chief." N Y Times Book Rev

Includes bibliographical references

Sandler, Martin W. **Lincoln** through the lens; how photography revealed and shaped an extraordinary life. Walker Pub. Co. 2008 97p il $19.99; lib bdg $20.89
Grades: 6 7 8 9 10   **92**
1. Lawyers 2. Presidents 3. State legislators 4. Members of Congress 5. Photography -- History 6. Presidents -- United States 7. United States -- History -- 1861-1865, Civil War -- Pictorial works
ISBN 978-0-8027-9666-0; 0-8027-9666-4; 978-0-8027-9667-7 lib bdg; 0-8027-9667-2 lib bdg

LC 2008-0219

"When Lincoln became president, photography was new and he joined the 'very first generation of human beings ever to be photographed.' . . . This extraordinary book is a tribute to the way contemporary and future generations came to view Lincoln. . . . Part biography, part history of of the Civil War, the book touches on many interesting topics. . . . Every step of the way there are fascinating photographs. . . . Although it's the pictures that provide the

'wow factor,' Sandler's perceptive words have their own elegance." Booklist

★ Van Sciver, Noah. The **Hypo**; The Melancholic Young Lincoln. Noah Van Sciver. Fantagraphics 2012 192 p. chiefly ill. $24.99
Grades: 11 12 Adult   **92**
1. Depression (Psychology) 2. Biographical graphic novels
ISBN 1606996193; 9781606996195

This graphic novel, by Noah Van Sciver, "is based on [Abraham] Lincoln's battle with depression. . . . [It] follows the twenty-something Abraham Lincoln as . . . a rising Whig in the state's legislature as he arrives in Springfield, IL to practice law. . . . But, as time passes and uncertainty creeps in, young Lincoln is forced to battle a dark cloud of depression brought on by a chain of defeats and failures culminating into a nervous breakdown that threatens his life and sanity." (Publisher's note)

"A thoroughly engaging graphic novel that seamlessly balances investigation and imagination." Pub Wkly

Lincoln, Mary Todd, 1818-1882

Fleischner, Jennifer. **Mrs.** Lincoln and Mrs. Keckley; the remarkable story of the friendship between a first lady and a former slave. Broadway Bks. 2003 372p il map hardcover o.p. pa $15.95; pa $16.99
Grades: 11 12 Adult   **92**
1. Memoirists 2. Dressmakers 3. Spouses of presidents 4. African American women -- Biography 5. Presidents' spouses -- United States
ISBN 0-7679-0258-0; 0-7679-0259-9 pa; 9780767902595

LC 2002-34493

"The book gives an in-depth look at a time, a friendship, and two very different women. The author's almost conversational writing style will keep readers engrossed." SLJ

Includes bibliographical references

Lloyd, Rachel

LLoyd, Rachel. **Girls** like us; fighting for a world where girls are not for sale, an activist finds her calling and heals herself. Harper 2011 277p $24.99
Grades: 11 12 Adult   **92**
1. Juvenile prostitution 2. Women political activists 3. Youth workers 4. Girls Educational and Mentoring Services (Organization)
ISBN 978-0-06-158205-9

LC 2010-32458

"In 1998 at age 23, Lloyd founded GEMS (Girls Educational and Mentoring Services), a New York City-based nonprofit organization to help commercially sexually exploited young women and girls. Her memoir recounts her journey from a 13-year-old school dropout in England trying to support her unstable mother through years as a commercially exploited worker in the German sex industry before finding stability and safety. Arriving in the United States, she set out to break the system that had abused her, ultimately altering laws and helping to protect victims from criminal prosecution. . . . This consciousness-shifting book shreds stereotypes and perceptions of prostitution." Libr J

London, Jack, 1876-1916

Adam, Philip. **Jack** London, photographer; [by] Jeanne Campbell Reesman, Sara S. Hodson, & Philip Adam. University of Georgia Press 2010 271p il $49.95

Grades: 11 12 Adult   **92**
1. Authors 2. Novelists 3. Photographers 4. Authors, American 5. Short story writers
ISBN 978-0-8203-2967-3

           LC 2010005973

"This book will be of great appeal to a broad range of audiences interested in history, American literature, and photography." Libr J
Includes bibliographical references

Low, Juliette Gordon, 1860-1927

★ Wadsworth, Ginger. **First** Girl Scout; Ginger Wadsworth. Clarion Books 2012 xiii, 210p ill. $17.99

Grades: 7 8 9 10 11 12   **92**
1. Biography 2. Girl Scouts 3. Philanthropists 4. Scout leaders 5. Girl Scouts of the United States of America
ISBN 978-0-547-24394-8; 0-547-24394-4

           LC 2011009642

This book offers a biography of the founder of the Girl Scouts organization. "Juliette (Daisy) Gordon Low [who] was a . . . woman with ideas that were ahead of her time. She witnessed important eras in U.S. history, from the Civil War and Reconstruction to westward expansion to post–World War I. And she made history by founding the first national organization to bring girls from all backgrounds into the out-of-doors. Daisy created controversy by encouraging them to prepare not only for traditional homemaking but also for roles as professional women—in the arts, sciences, and business—and for active citizenship outside the home. Her group also welcomed girls with disabilities at a time when they were usually excluded." (Publisher's note)

"Low's personality really comes to life through the details in the narrative. Wadsworth shows readers that this remarkable woman was a skilled leader and hostess in spite of having suffered severe hearing loss that made conversation difficult. . . . The attractive book design features chapter headings that look like Girl Scout badges, and most spreads include period photos or reproductions of primary-source documents." SLJ
Includes bibliographical references (p. 201-204) and index.

Lowman, Margaret

Lowman, Margaret. **It's** a jungle up there; more tales from the treetops. [by] Margaret D. Lowman, Edward Burgess & James Burgess; foreword by Sir Ghillean T. Prance. Yale University Press 2006 291p il $27.50

Grades: 11 12 Adult   **92**
1. Botanists 2. Women scientists
ISBN 978-0-300-10863-7; 0-300-10863-X

           LC 2005-54133

"The chapters of the book focus on field biology questions, the canopy access methods developed to answer the

questions, and conservation or education components of each expedition." Publisher's note
Includes bibliographical references

Lyons, Maritcha Rémond, 1848-1929

Bolden, Tonya. **Maritcha**; a nineteenth-century American girl. Abrams 2005 47p il $17.95

Grades: 4 5 6 7 8 9 10   **92**
1. Teachers 2. Civic leaders 3. New York (N.Y.) -- Race relations 4. African American women -- Biography 5. African Americans -- New York (N.Y.)
ISBN 0-8109-5045-6

           LC 2004-05849

"The high quality of writing and the excellent documentation make this a first choice for all collections." SLJ

Ma, Yo-Yo, 1955-

Worth, Richard. **Yo**-Yo Ma. Chelsea House 2006 119p bibl il por lib bdg $30

Grades: 7 8 9 10   **92**
1. Chinese Americans 2. Cellists 3. Violoncellists 4. Classical musicians
ISBN 978-0-7910-9270-5 lib bdg; 0-7910-9270-4 lib bdg

           LC 2006026335

"World-famous cellist Ma was born in Paris to a family originally from China. He was taught the cello at the age of four by his father, and early on it became obvious that he was a musical genius. The book has information about Ma's teachers, influences, and favorite composers." (School Library Journal)

This is "well-researched . . . attractive . . . solid." SLJ

Maathai, Wangari, 1940-2001

Maathai, Wangari. **Unbowed**; a memoir. [by] Wangari Muta Maathai. Knopf 2006 314p il hardcover o.p. pa $15

Grades: 11 12 Adult   **92**
1. Biologists 2. Conservationists 3. Environmentalists 4. Kenya 5. Nobel laureates for peace 6. Green Belt Movement (Kenya)
ISBN 0-307-26348-7; 978-0-307-26348-3; 0-307-27520-5 pa; 978-0-307-27520-2 pa

           LC 2006-44729

"Nobel Peace Prize winner Maathai tells the unforgettable story of her Kenya girlhood, struggles as a biologist and professor, and founding of the Green Belt Movement to restore Kenya's decimated forests and provide women with work." Booklist

MacArthur, Douglas, 1880-1964

★ Frank, Richard B. **MacArthur**; foreword by Wesley K. Clark. Palgrave Macmillan 2007 224p (Great generals series) hardcover o.p. pa $12.95

Grades: 9 10 11 12 Adult   **92**
1. Generals
ISBN 1-4039-7658-9; 978-1-4039-7658-1; 0-230-61397-7 pa; 978-0-230-61397-3 pa

This biography of the World War II general is an "assessment of both the man and the soldier, covering the failures and triumphs in an assured and dispassionate tone. . . . A good starting point for generalists." Libr J

Malcolm X, 1925-1965

★ Malcolm X. The **autobiography** of Malcolm X; with the assistance of Alex Haley; introduction by M. S. Handler; epilogue by Alex Haley; afterword by Ossie Davis. Ballantine Bks. 1992 500p $25; pa $15

Grades: 11 12 Adult   **92**

1. Black Muslims 2. Black Muslim leaders 3. Civil rights activists 4. African Americans -- Biography
ISBN 0-345-37975-6; 0-345-37671-4 pa

LC 92-52659

First published 1965 by Grove Press

Based on tape-recorded conversations with Alex Haley, this account of the life of the Black Muslim leader was completed shortly before his murder

Alex Haley "did his job with sensitivity and with devotion. . . . {The book} will have a permanent place in the literature of the Afro-American struggle." N Y Rev Books

Manning, Lauren

Manning, Lauren. **Unmeasured** strength. Henry Holt and Co. 2011 252p il $25; ebook $11.99

Grades: 11 12 Adult   **92**

1. Burns and scalds 2. September 11 terrorist attacks, 2001 3. Securities brokers
ISBN 978-0-8050-9463-3; 978-1-4299-9688-4 ebook

LC 2011024019

"A partner at Cantor Fitzgerald, Manning was burned over 80 percent of her body during the World Trade Center attacks on 9/11. Here she recalls ten long years of recovery while detailing the early experiences that taught her the will to survive." Libr J

Manzano, Juan Francisco, 1797-1854

★ Engle, Margarita. The **poet** slave of Cuba: a biography of Juan Francisco Manzano; art by Sean Qualls. Henry Holt 2006 183p il $16.95

Grades: 7 8 9 10   **92**

1. Poets 2. Slaves 3. Authors 4. Slavery -- Cuba
ISBN 0-8050-7706-5; 978-0-8050-7706-3

LC 2005-46200

Awarded the Pura Belpré Author Award, 2008

This is a "biography of a Cuban slave who escaped to become a celebrated poet." (Publisher's note) "Grades seven to twelve." (Bull Cent Child Books)

"This is a book that should be read by young and old, black and white, Anglo and Latino." SLJ

Manzano, Sonia

★ **Manzano**, Sonia. Becoming Maria; love and chaos in the South Bronx. Sonia Manzano. Scholastic Press 2015 272 p. illustrations (black & white) (hardback) $17.99 **92**

1. Hispanic American women 2. Hispanic American women -- Biography 3. Coming of age -- Bronx (New York, N.Y.) 4. Television writers -- United States -- Biography.
ISBN 9780545621847; 9780545621854; 9780545621861

LC 2015007490

In this memoir, "actress Manzano, best known as Maria from Sesame Street, provides a[n] . . . account of her tough Nuyorican upbringing in the South Bronx. Split into three parts, this touching memoir is a chronological series of vignettes in the author's life, starting with her earliest memories as a diaper-clad toddler witnessing her father's drunken outbursts and meeting a mysterious 'dark little girl,' who turns out to be her older half sister." (Kirkus Reviews)

"This beautifully rendered coming-of-age story calls to mind Betty Smith's classic A Tree Grows in Brooklyn. Though it's a bit slow moving at times and would have benefited from a time line to help ground readers, this is nevertheless an inspiring portrait of resiliency and a time capsule for a New York that now feels like a distant memory." Booklist

Mao Zedong, 1893-1976

Naden, Corinne J. **Mao** Zedong and the Chinese Revolution. Morgan Reynolds Pub. 2009 144p il map (World leaders) lib bdg $28.95

Grades: 7 8 9 10 11 12   **92**

1. Heads of state 2. Communist leaders 3. Political leaders 4. China -- History -- 1949-1976
ISBN 978-1-59935-100-1; 1-59935-100-5

LC 2008-27829

This "discusses Chariman Mao Zedong's rise to power and his crucial role in national and international history. . . . Naden's analysis of the significant role of young people will draw YA readers for reports and for personal interest. The readable design, with clear type and lots of historic color photos as well as screens and detailed maps, includes spacious back matter." Booklist

Includes bibliographical references

Marie Antoinette, Queen, consort of Louis XVI, King of France, 1755-1793

Lever, Evelyne. **Marie** Antoinette; the last queen of France. translated from the French by Catherine Temerson. Farrar, Straus & Giroux 2000 357p il hardcover o.p. pa $16.95

Grades: 11 12 Adult   **92**

1. Queens 2. France -- History -- 1589-1789, Bourbons
ISBN 0-312-28333-4 pa

LC 00-28763

The author examines "the opulent Versailles subculture and the queen whose royal excesses served as a major catalyst for the revolutionary upheaval of 1789. Through the skillful use of memoirs and other primary documents, Lever creates an empathic picture of Louis XVI's headstrong wife." Libr J

Includes bibliographical references

Marley, Bob

★ Miller, Calvin Craig. **Reggae** poet: the story of Bob Marley. Morgan Reynolds Pub. 2007 128p il $27.95

Grades: 7 8 9 10

1. Singers 2. Musicians 3. Reggae music 4. Reggae

musicians
ISBN 978-1-59935-071-4; 1-59935-071-8

LC 2007-27476

In this biography of the Jamaican musician "Miller does a fine job showing the effect the music and the politics had on each other. He also skillfully weaves in the complicated topic of the Rastaferian religion and the part ganja (marijuana) plays in it, and he doesn't hesitate when explaining Marley's complicated romantic life. The . . . photos are well chosen." Booklist

Includes bibliographical references

Talamon, Bruce. **Bob** Marley; spirit dancer. {by} Bruce W. Talamon; text by Roger Steffens; foreword by Timothy White. Norton 1994 128p il hardcover o.p. pa $13

Grades: 11 12 Adult   92

1. Singers 2. Black musicians 3. Reggae musicians
ISBN 0-393-32173-8 pa

LC 94-18321

This book consists mainly of Talamon's photographs of the Jamaican reggae musician, with brief text by Steffens

"Tasteful and well done, Talamon's photographic essay stands in stark contrast to some of the raw, slapdash products intended primarily to cash in on Marley's fame. . . . A moving portrait of a great musician." Booklist

Marshall, Thurgood, 1908-1993

★ Crowe, Chris. **Thurgood** Marshall; a twentieth-century life. Viking 2008 248p il (Up close) $16.99

Grades: 6 7 8 9 10   92

1. Judges 2. Lawyers 3. Solicitors general 4. Civil rights activists 5. Supreme Court justices 6. African Americans -- Biography 7. United States -- Supreme Court
ISBN 978-0-670-06228-7; 0-670-06228-6

LC 2007-042794

"This is a captivating portrait of a heroic champion of justice that also offers great insight into the most pivotal moments of the Civil Rights Movement." Kirkus

Marton, Endre, 1910-2005

Marton, Kati. **Enemies** of the people; my family's journey to America. Simon & Schuster 2009 272p il $26

Grades: 11 12 Adult   92

1. Authors 2. Journalists 3. Political prisoners 4. Hungary -- History 5. Nonfiction writers
ISBN 978-1-4165-8612-8; 1-4165-8612-1

LC 2009-14480

"An American journalist trolls the archives of the Hungarian secret police (AVO) to piece together her parents' imprisonment in and flight from Hungary in the mid-1950s. . . . The author's probing work effectively renders an enormously unsettled, painful time of shifting allegiances and political treachery. . . . A dark, compelling narrative of secrecy and betrayal." Kirkus

Includes bibliographical references

Marton, Ilona, 1912-2004

Marton, Kati. **Enemies** of the people; my family's journey to America. Simon & Schuster 2009 272p il $26

Grades: 11 12 Adult   92

1. Authors 2. Journalists 3. Political prisoners 4. Hungary -- History 5. Nonfiction writers
ISBN 978-1-4165-8612-8; 1-4165-8612-1

LC 2009-14480

"An American journalist trolls the archives of the Hungarian secret police (AVO) to piece together her parents' imprisonment in and flight from Hungary in the mid-1950s. . . . The author's probing work effectively renders an enormously unsettled, painful time of shifting allegiances and political treachery. . . . A dark, compelling narrative of secrecy and betrayal." Kirkus

Includes bibliographical references

Marton, Kati

Marton, Kati. **Enemies** of the people; my family's journey to America. Simon & Schuster 2009 272p il $26

Grades: 11 12 Adult   92

1. Authors 2. Journalists 3. Political prisoners 4. Hungary -- History 5. Nonfiction writers
ISBN 978-1-4165-8612-8; 1-4165-8612-1

LC 2009-14480

"An American journalist trolls the archives of the Hungarian secret police (AVO) to piece together her parents' imprisonment in and flight from Hungary in the mid-1950s. . . . The author's probing work effectively renders an enormously unsettled, painful time of shifting allegiances and political treachery. . . . A dark, compelling narrative of secrecy and betrayal." Kirkus

Includes bibliographical references

Martí, José, 1853-1895

★ Sterngass, Jon. **Jose** Marti. Chelsea House Publishers 2007 123p il (Great Hispanic heritage) lib bdg $30

Grades: 9 10 11 12   92

1. Poets 2. Authors 3. Novelists 4. Journalists 5. Essayists 6. Cuba -- History 7. Revolutionaries
ISBN 0-7910-8841-3; 978-0-7910-8841-8

LC 2006-19601

This book "follows the life of the dynamic Cuban poet, journalist, and patriot." Publisher's note

Includes bibliographical references

Marx, Karl, 1818-1883

Rossig, Wolfgang. **Karl** Marx. Morgan Reynolds 2009 112p il (Profiles in economics) lib bdg $28.95

Grades: 8 9 10   92

1. Philosophers 2. Writers on politics 3. Political and social philosophers
ISBN 978-1-59935-132-2; 1-59935-132-3

LC 2009-29563

"This book presents the life of Karl Marx and places his social and economic theories within the useful context of his youth in a prosperous German family. . . . [The author] provides a well-researched account of Marx's life and his work." Booklist

Includes bibliographical references

Maryam Jameelah, 1934-2012

Baker, Deborah. The **convert**; a tale of exile and extremism. Graywolf Press 2011 246p il $23

Grades: 11 12 Adult   **92**

1. Converts 2. Muslim women 3. Biography, Individual

ISBN 1-55597-582-8; 978-1-55597-582-1

This is a biography of the Islamic polemicist Maryam Jameelah. Jameelah was "born as Margaret Marcus in 1934 in New Rochelle, N.Y." (N Y Times Book Rev)

This "is a cogent, thought-provoking look at a radical life and its rippling consequences." Publ Wkly

Includes bibliographical references

Massery, Hazel Bryan, 1942-

★ Margolick, David. **Elizabeth** and Hazel; two women of Little Rock. Yale University Press 2011 310p il $26

Grades: 11 12 Adult   **92**

1. School integration 2. Arkansas -- Race relations 3. Little Rock (Ark.) -- Race relations 4. Central High School (Little Rock, Ark.) 5. School integration -- Arkansas -- Little Rock -- History -- 20th century

ISBN 978-0-300-14193-1; 0-300-14193-9

LC 2011-14101

"When Elizabeth Eckford braved the gauntlet of white hecklers leading to the newly desegregated Central High School in Little Rock, Arkansas, in 1957, photographers captured her image and that of the angry young white woman behind her. Elizabeth, the stoic, and Hazel Bryan, the tormentor, were frozen as icons. Elizabeth was part of the Little Rock Nine, the black teens who became the targets of race hatred as well as national and international inspirations. . . . Margolick draws on interviews and press reports of the time to present a very nuanced analysis of how Elizabeth and Hazel were affected by the scene that made them famous. . . . . A complex look at two women at the center of a historic moment." Booklist

Includes bibliographical references

Masters, Jarvis

Masters, Jarvis. **That** bird has my wings; the autobiography of an innocent man on death row. [by] Jarvis Jay Masters. HarperOne 2009 281p $24.99

Grades: 11 12 Adult   **92**

1. Prisoners 2. African Americans -- Biography

ISBN 978-0-06-173045-0; 0-06-173045-9

LC 2009-22124

"A heartbreaking memoir; the brutal conditions of Masters's boyhood will be difficult for some readers to take, but his ultimate message of hope and reconciliation is moving and inspiring." Libr J

McCarthy, Joseph, 1908-1957

★ Giblin, James Cross, 1933- The **rise** and fall of Senator Joe McCarthy; [by] James Cross Giblin. Clarion Books 2009 294p il $22.00

Grades: 8 9 10 11 12   **92**

1. Anticommunist movements 2. Senators 3. United States -- History -- 1953-1961

ISBN 0-618-61058-8; 978-0-618-61058-7

LC 2009015005

Giblin examines the life of Joseph Mccarthy, the junior senator from Wisconsin. The book "discusses the Cold War tensions that shaped his beliefs and the unconstitutional methods he used to further his ends." (Publisher's note) Bibliography. Index. "Grades eight to twelve." (Bull Cent Child Books)

"YAs will see the contemporary parallels in this biography of the anti-Communist crusader who rose to power over 50 years ago. . . . Giblin's title, formatted with an open, photo-filled design and written in easy, direct style, makes no superficial connections, and the afterword, 'Another McCarthy?' will prompt discussion about the accusations of terrorism in the aftermath of 9/11. Just as memorable is the scathing commentary from famous journalist Edward Murrow about the differences between dissent and disloyalty." Booklist

Includes bibliographical references

McCartney, Stella

Aldridge, Rebecca. **Stella** McCartney. Chelsea House 2011 112p il (Famous fashion designers) lib bdg $35

Grades: 6 7 8 9 10   **92**

1. Fashion designers

ISBN 978-1-60413-982-2; 1-60413-982-X

LC 2010033972

A biography of fashion designer Stella McCartney.

"Biography collections in need of a bit of sprucing up should find [this title] helpful." SLJ

Includes glossary and bibliographical references

McCourt, Frank

McCourt, Frank, 1930-2009. **Angela's** ashes; a memoir. Scribner 1996 364p il pa $14; $25

Grades: 11 12 Adult   **92**

1. Authors 2. Irish Americans 3. Memoirists 4. High school teachers 5. Biography, Individual

ISBN 0-684-84267-X pa; 0-684-87435-0

LC 96-5335

This is a memoir by a New York City high school teacher. "Born to Irish immigrants in Depression-era Brooklyn, McCourt's mother (Angela) and father . . . return to family in Ireland. . . . A baby sister dies in Brooklyn, and two more brothers die in Ireland. . . . {McCourt suffers from} afflictions brought on by the starvation and squalor in his family's . . . Limerick slum, including a bout of typhoid." (Commonweal)

"Frank McCourt, a teacher, grandfather and occasional actor, was born in New York City, but grew up in the Irish town of Limerick during the grim 1930's and 40's before he came back here as a teen-ager. His recollections of childhood are mournful and humorous, angry and forgiving." N Y Times Book Rev

McElwain, Jason

★ McElwain, Jason. The **game** of my life; a true story of challenge, triumph, and growing up autistic. [by] Jason "J-Mac" McElwain with Daniel Paisner. New American Library 2008 243p il hardcover o.p. pa $14

Grades: 11 12 Adult 92

1. Autism 2. Students 3. Basketball players 4. Basketball -- Biography

ISBN 978-0-451-22301-2; 0-451-22301-2; 978-0-451-22619-8 pa; 0-451-22619-4 pa

LC 2007-32261

This is the autobiography of Jason McElwain, a.k.a. "J-Mac," a severely autistic high school basketball player and manager of the Greece Athena Trojans high school basketball team.

"Teens and adults, especially those touched by the challenges of autism, will welcome this encouraging story." Voice Youth Advocates

McGough, Matthew

McGough, Matthew. **Bat** boy; my true life adventures coming of age with the New York Yankees. Doubleday 2005 273p il hardcover o.p. pa $12.95

Grades: 11 12 Adult 92

1. Lawyers 2. Bat boys 3. Memoirists 4. New York Yankees (Baseball team)

ISBN 0-385-51020-9; 0-307-27864-6 pa

LC 2004-61756

This "memoir is much more than an all-access pass to Yankee Stadium and baseball—it is an exquisitely written and observed book about growing up and the beauty of the game." SLJ

McMullan, James, 1934-

McMullan, James. **Leaving** China; an artist paints his World War II childhood. James McMullan. Algonquin Young Readers 2014 128 p. color illustrations (alk. paper) $19.95

Grades: 7 8 9 10 11 12 92

1. Artists 2. World War, 1939-1945 -- Art and the war 3. China -- History -- 1937-1945 -- Anecdotes 4. Illustrators -- United States -- Biography 5. Children of missionaries -- China -- Biography 6. World War, 1939-1945 -- Personal narratives, American

ISBN 1616202556; 9781616202552

LC 2013035241

"A memoir of celebrated artist McMullan's early years, from age 2 to 11. His was a hopscotch childhood, thanks to WWII. Born in 1934 in Tsingtao, China, he subsequently lived in Shanghai, Canada, India, then China and Canada again and, finally, in the U.S. . . . The book consists of 54 chronologically arranged full-page illustrations, each accompanied by a facing page of text. The exquisite full-color pictures are filled with air and space, reminiscent of the Chinese scrolls that fascinated McMullan as a child. These pictures and the evocative text are a happy exercise in harmony." Booklist

Includes bibliographical references and index

Mead, Margaret, 1901-1978

★ Hess, Aimee. **Margaret** Mead. Pomegranate 2007 63p il (Women who dare) $12.95

Grades: 9 10 11 12 92

1. Anthropologists 2. Curators 3. Writers on science

ISBN 978-0-7649-3875-7

LC 2006-50343

This biography "traces Mead's life, exploring her youth, her studies and her research, her pioneering fieldwork techniques, and the controversies that often swirled around her." Publisher's note

Includes bibliographical references

Mee, Benjamin

Mee, Benjamin. **We** bought a zoo. Weinstein 2008 261p il $24.95; pa $14.95

Grades: 11 12 Adult 92

1. Zoos 2. Journalists 3. Zoo directors 4. Dartmoor Zoological Park (Sparkwell, England)

ISBN 978-1-60286-048-3; 978-1-60286-095-7 pa

"Following the death of his father, Mee took on the challenge of helping his 76-year-old mother find a new home. This relatively simple task resulted in life-altering, unexpected outcomes, not the least of which was taking on the responsibility of owning and renovating a dilapidated zoo in rural England. . . . Readers will delight in his anecdotes, most notably about escapees Sovereign the jaguar and Parker the wolf, who attracted a fair share of media attention and antizoo feeling from the public. . . . This engaging adventure will appeal to animal lovers." Libr J

Melendez, Benjy

Voloj, Julian. **Ghetto** Brother; Warrior to Peacemaker. Julian Voloj; illustrated by Claudia Ahlering. NBM Publishing 2015 128 p. chiefly b&w ill. $12.99

Grades: 11 12 Adult 92

1. Peace movements 2. Gangs -- Graphic novels 3. Puerto Ricans -- New York (N.Y.)

ISBN 1561639486; 9781561639489

This graphic novel by Julian Voloj, illustrated by Claudia Ahlering, "tells the true story of Benjy Melendez, a Bronx legend, son of Puerto-Rican immigrants, who founded, at the end of the 1960s, the notorious Ghetto Brothers gang. From the seemingly bombed-out ravages of his neighborhood, wracked by drugs, poverty, and violence, he managed to extract an incredibly positive energy from this riot ridden era: his multiracial gang promoted peace rather than violence." (Publisher's note)

"Using Melendez as narrator-protagonist, Voloj places the seminal events of November and December 1971 in the contexts of post–WWII Puerto Rican immigration and difficult assimilation to New York, and of Melendez's personal development as he learned of and adopted his Jewish heritage. Ahlering bases her artwork partly on news and documentary photography, although she doesn't incorporate or copy photos but draws on them for detail, composition, and tonal variety." Booklist

Meltzer, Milton, 1915-2009

Meltzer, Milton. **Milton** Meltzer; writing matters. Franklin Watts 2004 160p il lib bdg $29

Grades: 7 8 9 10 92

1. Authors 2. Historians 3. Biographers 4. Authors,

American 5. Children's authors 6. Nonfiction writers
ISBN 0-531-12257-3

LC 2004-2947

"The author includes clear, interesting explanations about the American historical and economic events that influenced his life. While this book is a pleasure to read for general interest, it would also supplement units on American history." SLJ

Includes bibliographical references

Melville, Herman, 1819-1891

★ Reiff, Raychel Haugrud. **Herman** Melville; Moby Dick and other works. Marshall Cavendish Benchmark 2007 156p il (Writers and their works) $39.93

Grades: 9 10 11 12   **92**

1. Authors 2. Novelists 3. Authors, American
ISBN 978-0-7614-2592-2

LC 2006-32673

This book features a biography, a description of the times in which he lived, and critical discussions of several of his works, including Typee, Moby Dick, "Bartleby, The Scrivener," and Billy Budd.

Includes filmography and bibliographical references

Menchú, Rigoberta

Menchu, Rigoberta. **I,** Rigoberta Menchu; an Indian woman in Guatemala. edited and introduced by Elisabeth Burgos-Debray; translated by Ann Wright. 2nd English-language ed.; Verso 2009 294p map $95; pa $22.95

Grades: 9 10 11 12   **92**

1. Political activists 2. Memoirists 3. Indian leaders 4. Human rights activists 5. Nobel laureates for peace 6. Native Americans -- Biography 7. Native Americans -- Guatemala
ISBN 978-1-84467-445-9; 978-1-84467-418-3 pa

LC 2010292478

First published 1984

This is the story of a twenty-three year old Guatemalan Indian woman. "It was recorded in the course of a single week in Paris, during January 1982, by a Venezuelan friend and admirer, Elizabeth Burgos-Debray. She then edited it as Rigoberta's autobiography, excluding her original questions and inserting linking passages." Times Lit Suppl

Includes bibliographical references

Michelangelo Buonarroti, 1475-1564

Somervill, Barbara A. **Michelangelo**; sculptor and painter. Compass Point Books 2005 112p il map (Signature lives) $30.60; pa $9.95

Grades: 6 7 8 9 10   **92**

1. Artists 2. Painters 3. Sculptors 4. Architects 5. Artists, Italian
ISBN 0-7565-0814-2; 978-0-7565-0814-2; 0-7565-1060-0 pa; 978-0-7565-1060-2 pa

LC 2004-17116

This is a biography of the Renaissance painter and sculptor.

The author "presents a candid introduction to her famous Renaissance subject. Her text has a casual tone, and her di-

rect, sometimes colloquial language will capture some reluctant readers." Booklist

Includes bibliographical references

Middleton, Earl M., 1919-2007

Barnes, Joy W. **Knowing** who I am; a Black entrepreneur's struggle and success in the American South. [by] Earl M. Middleton, with Joy W. Barnes. University of South Carolina Press 2008 183p il map $29.95

Grades: 11 12 Adult   **92**

1. Air pilots 2. African American businesspeople 3. State legislators 4. Real estate brokers 5. Civil rights activists
ISBN 978-1-57003-715-3; 1-57003-715-9

LC 2007-43037

The author, "a successful real-estate broker who has been profiled in the Wall Street Journal, looks back on the extraordinary history of his family, three generations of African Americans struggling against racial limitations in a small southern town. . . . An inspirational autobiography by a man who understands the importance of strong racial and personal identity." Booklist

Includes bibliographical references

Milk, Harvey

Aretha, David. **No** compromise: the story of Harvey Milk. Morgan Reynolds 2010 128p il (Civil rights leaders) lib bdg $28.95

Grades: 7 8 9 10 11 12   **92**

1. Gay rights activists 2. Gay men -- Civil rights 3. Local government officials
ISBN 1-59935-129-3; 978-1-59935-129-2

LC 2009-25708

This is a biography of the gay-rights activist and San Francisco politician who was killed in 1973.

This is written "with simple and engaging prose. . . . Full-color and black-and-white photos are interspersed throughout, giving a sense of the time period." SLJ

Miller, Arthur, 1915-2005

★ Andersen, Richard. **Arthur** Miller. Marshall Cavendish Benchmark 2005 144p il (Writers and their works) lib bdg $25.95

Grades: 7 8 9 10   **92**

1. Authors 2. Dramatists 3. Screenwriters 4. Authors, American
ISBN 0-7614-1946-2

This "attractive, well-organized [book fills] a gap in literary criticism for intermediate readers. Heavily illustrated with color and black-and-white photographs, [it] will appeal to students who might be intimidated by longer or more scholarly titles." SLJ

Milton, John, 1608-1674

Forsyth, Neil. **John** Milton; a biography. Lion 2008 254p pa $14.95

Grades: 11 12 Adult   **92**

1. Blind 2. Poets 3. Authors 4. Poets, English 5.

Essayists
ISBN 978-0-7459-5310-6; 0-7459-5310-7
LC 2009-291343

In this biography of the seventeenth-century English poet, the author "blends into the biographical data Milton's literary achievements, so where he was in his development can be appreciated. In addition, Forsyth offers a good amount of social/political/religious information of 17th-century England, which allows an even fuller understanding of Milton's world. The audience for this work should be familiar with Milton's body of literature as well as some English history. . . . Forsyth's engrossing and informative book is essential for anyone following classic English literature." Libr J

Includes bibliographical references

Miró, Asha, 1967-

Miro, Asha. **Daughter** of the Ganges; a memoir. translated by Jamal Mahjoub. Atria Books 2006 274p il hardcover o.p. pa $19.95

Grades: 11 12 Adult   92
1. Adoptees 2. Television personalities 3. Memoirists 4. Music teachers
ISBN 0-7432-8672-3; 978-0-7432-8672-5; 0-7432-8673-1 pa; 978-0-7432-8673-2 pa
LC 2006-40791

"A unique memoir with wide appeal." SLJ

Moaveni, Azadeh, 1976-

Moaveni, Azadeh. **Lipstick** jihad; a memoir of growing up Iranian in America and American in Iran. Public Affairs 2005 249p $25; pa $13

Grades: 11 12 Adult   92
1. Authors 2. Journalists 3. Iran 4. Memoirists
ISBN 1-58648-193-2; 1-58648-378-1 pa
LC 2004-43184

"Moaveni, an Iranian-American who grew up in California, decided to embark on a journey in spring 2000 to rediscover her Iranian heritage. In this account, she . . . conveys the tensions she observed between the fundamentalist mullahs and younger Iranians, who are pushing for a more Westernized, modern Iran. . . . A charming and informative memoir." Libr J

Monaque, Mathilde

Monaque, Mathilde. **Trouble** in my head; a young girl's fight with depression. translated by Lorenza Garcia. Trafalgar Square 2009 167p pa $15.95

Grades: 7 8 9 10   92
1. Depression (Psychology)
ISBN 978-0-09-191723-4 pa; 0-09-191723-9 pa

Monet, Claude, 1840-1926

Kallen, Stuart A. **Claude** Monet. Lucent Books 2009 112p il (Eye on art) lib bdg $32.45

Grades: 7 8 9 10   92
1. Artists 2. Painters 3. Artists, French 4. Impressionism (Art)
ISBN 978-1-4205-0074-5; 1-4205-0074-0
LC 2008-20640

An introduction to the life and career of the artist Claude Monet, and how he painted his way into history.

"This biography paints a clear picture of the artist's life, work, and legacy. . . . The accompanying color reproductions of the artworks and black-and-white photographs of Monet contribute to the book's clean and attractive design. . . . This work stands out as a balanced description of the man's legacy and an enjoyable read." SLJ

Includes glossary and bibliographical references

Monroe, James, 1758-1831

Hart, Gary. **James** Monroe. Times Books 2005 170p il (American presidents series) $20

Grades: 11 12 Adult   92
1. Presidents 2. Secretaries of state 3. Presidents -- United States
ISBN 978-0-8050-6960-0; 0-8050-6960-7
LC 2005-41928

The author "studies James Monroe, the last of the Virginia dynasty, who, although president at an important time in U.S. history (1817-25), is often overlooked. Hart argues that in the years after the disastrous War of 1812, Monroe was 'the first "national security president."' . . . [This] is a satisfying and informative read." Libr J

Includes bibliographical references

Mooney, Jonathan

Mooney, Jonathan. The **short** bus; a journey beyond normal. H. Holt 2007 272p hardcover o.p. pa $14.99

Grades: 11 12 Adult   92
1. Students with disabilities 2. Memoirists 3. Social activists 4. Motivational speakers
ISBN 978-0-8050-7427-7; 0-8050-7427-9; 978-0-8050-8804-5 pa; 0-8050-8804-0 pa
LC 2006-52588

The author's "target audience is not policy makers but his fellow misfits, and his boundless empathy will surely console those who also face the worst that cruel schoolchildren and the educational bureaucracy have to offer." N Y Times Book Rev

Muller, Salomé, b. ca. 1809

Bailey, John. The **lost** German slave girl; the extraordinary true story of the slave Sally Miller and her fight for freedom. Atlantic Monthly Press 2004 268p hardcover o.p. pa $14

Grades: 11 12 Adult   92
1. Slaves 2. German Americans 3. Racially mixed people 4. Slavery -- United States
ISBN 0-87113-921-9; 0-8021-4229-X pa
LC 2004-50264

"A series of highly contentious trials was held in the mid-1800s to determine whether Sally Miller, a New Orleans woman, was born a multiracial slave or was in fact a German immigrant trapped in bondage from childhood. The stuff of television miniseries, this sensational and emotional cause celebre of its time is revived into a fresh drama from the vantage point of the present." Libr J

Includes bibliographical references

Murakami, Haruki, 1949-

Mussari, Mark. **Haruki** Murakami. Marshall Cavendish Benchmark 2010 127p il (Today's writers and their works) lib bdg $42.79

Grades: 8 9 10 11 12   92

1. Authors 2. Novelists 3. Authors, Japanese 4. Nonfiction writers 5. Short story writers

ISBN 978-0-7614-4124-3; 0-7614-4124-7

This biography of Haruki Murakami places the author in the context of his times and discusses his work.

Includes bibliographical references

Murrow, Edward R.

Edwards, Bob. **Edward** R. Murrow and the birth of broadcast journalism; {by} Robert A. Edwards. Wiley 2004 174p (Turning points) $19.95

Grades: 11 12 Adult   92

1. Journalists 2. Radio reporters 3. Government officials 4. Television reporters 5. Television news anchors

ISBN 0-471-47753-2

LC 2003-21223

"The author chronicles Murrow's innovations in radio and television broadcasting, including live radio reports of the war in progress in Europe in 1940; exposure of the despotism of Senator Joseph McCarthy on CBS in 1953; the powerful television documentary Harvest of Shame on the deplorable conditions of migrant workers in the U.S.; and the first in-depth television news program, See It Now. . . . Edwards brings to life the early days of radio and television and the innovations that Murrow sparked. . . . Readers interested in journalism will enjoy this slim book." Booklist

Includes bibliographical references

Nelson, Horatio Nelson, Viscount, 1758-1805

★ Czisnik, Marianne. **Horatio** Nelson; a controversial hero. Hodder Arnold 2005 192p il pa $35

Grades: 11 12 Adult   92

1. Admirals 2. Great Britain -- Royal Navy

ISBN 0-340-90021-0 pa; 978-0-340-90021-5 pa

LC 2006-298161

This work on the British admiral "is a collection of essays, offering reflections on aspects of his career, and on his contemporary and posthumous reputation." Engl Hist Rev

Includes bibliographical references

Nemat, Marina

★ Nemat, Marina. **Prisoner** of Tehran; a memoir. Free Press 2007 306p $26

Grades: 11 12 Adult   92

1. Political prisoners 2. Memoirists 3. Iran -- History -- 1979-

ISBN 1-4165-3742-2; 978-1-4165-3742-7

LC 2006-50191

Nemat was sixteen when she was arrested in Iran in early 1982 for political protests against the new fundamentalist regime. This is an account of her prison experiences.

The author's "story is not so much a political history lesson than it is a memoir of faith and love, a protest against violence that cannot be silenced. . . . Her persistence in standing for goodness is a lesson for us all." Christ Sci Monit

Newton, Isaac Sir, 1642-1727

Ackroyd, Peter. **Newton**. Nan A. Talese/Doubleday 2006 176p il (Ackroyd's brief lives) $21.95

Grades: 11 12 Adult   92

1. Physicists 2. Scientists 3. Mathematicians 4. Writers on science

ISBN 978-0-385-50799-8; 0-385-50799-2

LC 2006-45619

This is a biography of the physicist and mathematician.

"Readers will . . . marvel at how many logic-defying complexities fill the life of the genius famous for recognizing in the fall of an apple the force unifying the universe." Booklist

Includes bibliographical references

Boerst, William J. **Isaac** Newton; organizing the universe. Morgan Reynolds Pub. 2004 144p il (Renaissance scientists) lib bdg $23.95

Grades: 7 8 9 10   92

1. Physicists 2. Scientists 3. Mathematicians 4. Writers on science

ISBN 1-931798-01-X

LC 2003-14571

"Boerst describes Newton's life from his premature birth through an isolated adulthood dominated by study and experimentation to his death at the age of 84. The author deftly explores his subject's accomplishments in relation to the scientific community and notable historical events of the time and includes information concerning his religious views. . . . This well-written book makes an excellent choice for teens exploring scientists or just looking for a good biography." SLJ

Includes bibliographical references

Nez, Chester

Nez, Chester. **Code** talker; [by] Chester Nez, with Judith Schiess Avila. Berkley Caliber 2011 310p il map $26.95

Grades: 11 12 Adult   92

1. Veterans 2. Cryptography 3. Navajo Indians 4. United States -- Marine Corps 5. World War, 1939-1945 -- Native Americans 6. World War, 1939-1945 -- Personal narratives

ISBN 978-0-425-24423-4

LC 2011023701

"While the Japanese could figure out many World War II American codes and transmissions, they could not crack the Navajo Code Talkers. Nez was one of the original Code Talkers serving with the Marines. Here, with Avila, . . . he tells of a hard New Mexico childhood in the Great Depression; the discrimination against Native Americans; how the code was developed from a language with no written background; his dangerous wartime experiences on Guadalcanal, Bougainville, Guam, and Peleliu; and his postwar life. . . . Accessible and compelling, this is recommended for general readers as well as World War II history buffs." Libr J

Includes bibliographical references

Ngugi wa Thiongo, 1938-

Ngugi wa Thiongo. **Dreams** in a time of war; a childhood memoir. Pantheon Books 2010 256p il $24.95

Grades: 11 12 Adult   **92**

1. Authors 2. Novelists 3. Kikuyu (African people) 4. Kenya 5. Essayists 6. College teachers 7. Short story writers

ISBN 978-0-307-37883-5; 0-307-37883-7

LC 2009-34107

"When Ngugi is accepted into an elite high school in Kenya, worried about where to get a pair of shoes, his brother is a Mau Mau guerrilla in the mountains. The world-renowned Kenyan writer looks back at his growing up in the 1950s in this crisp, clearly told memoir, which evokes the rising African nationalism of the era in all its conflict and complexity." Booklist

Nuñez Cabeza de Vaca, Alvar, 16th cent.

Childress, Diana. **Barefoot** conquistador; Cabeza de Vaca and the struggle for Native American rights. Twenty-First Century Books 2008 160p il map lib bdg $30.60

Grades: 7 8 9 10   **92**

1. Explorers 2. Historians 3. Travel writers 4. Government officials 5. America -- Exploration 6. Colonial administrators

ISBN 978-0-8225-7517-7; 0-8225-7517-5

LC 2007-22059

"This clearly written biography introduces a 16th-century Spanish explorer who made two expeditions to North and South America and eventually became a champion for Native Americans. . . . Childress's well-researched, lively text will fascinate readers. . . . The pages are sprinkled with period illustrations and maps." SLJ

Includes bibliographical references

Nye, Naomi Shihab, 1952-

Nye, Naomi Shihab. **I'll** ask you three times, are you ok? tales of driving and being driven. Greenwillow Books 2007 242p $15.99; lib bdg $16.89

Grades: 7 8 9 10 11 12   **92**

1. Poets 2. Authors 3. Voyages and travels 4. Editors 5. Essayists 6. Children's authors

ISBN 978-0-06-085392-1; 978-0-06-085393-8 lib bdg

LC 2006-36548

The author "writes about sudden intimate connections with strangers, especially taxi drivers, who often yield glimpses of family and exile that can sometimes change us. . . . The prose is chatty, fast, and unpretentious, and teens will enjoy the driving stuff and the idea of her kissing in the backseat, and they'll feel her sense of control when she is behind the wheel herself." Booklist

Obama, Barack, 1961-

Abramson, Jill. **Obama**; the historic journey. Callaway 2009 237p il map $40

Grades: 10 11 12 Adult   **92**

1. Lawyers 2. Presidents 3. Racially mixed people 4. Senators 5. State legislators 6. Nobel laureates for peace 7. Presidents -- United States 8. African

Americans -- Biography 9. Presidents -- United States -- Election -- 2008

ISBN 978-1-59448-893-1; 1-59448-893-2

LC 2009-5050

This title "showcases both the Obama campaign and the Times's own staff expertise on the subject. The photographs, from both documentary and color reproduction perspectives, are the best you'll find. Contributions by Times writers and editors includes both new pieces and reprints from the paper, with new biographical text by Jill Abramson going back to Obama's beginnings." Libr J

Mundy, Liza. **Michelle**; a biography. Simon & Schuster 2008 217p il $25

Grades: 11 12 Adult   **92**

1. Lawyers 2. Presidents 3. Women lawyers 4. Senators 5. State legislators 6. Spouses of presidents 7. Hospital administrators 8. Nobel laureates for peace 9. African American women -- Biography 10. Presidents' spouses -- United States

ISBN 1-4165-9943-6; 978-1-4165-9943-2

LC 2008-33595

This is a "comprehensive look at Michelle Obama and her relationship with Barack Obama." Libr J

Includes bibliographical references

Obama, Barack. **Dreams** from my father; a story of race and inheritance. Crown Publishers 2007 442p $25.95

Grades: 7 8 9 10 11 12 Adult   **92**

1. Lawyers 2. Presidents 3. Racially mixed people 4. Senators 5. State legislators 6. Nobel laureates for peace 7. Presidents -- United States 8. African Americans -- Biography

ISBN 978-0-307-38341-9

LC 2007-271892

First published 1995 by Times Books

This is the autobiography of the Illinois senator who would later become the 44th president of the United States.

The author "offers an account of his life's journey that reflects brilliantly on the power of race consciousness in America. . . . Obama writes well; his account is sensitive, probing, and compelling." Choice [review of 1995 edition]

Obama, Michelle

Mundy, Liza. **Michelle**; a biography. Simon & Schuster 2008 217p il $25

Grades: 11 12 Adult   **92**

1. Lawyers 2. Presidents 3. Women lawyers 4. Senators 5. State legislators 6. Spouses of presidents 7. Hospital administrators 8. Nobel laureates for peace 9. African American women -- Biography 10. Presidents' spouses -- United States

ISBN 1-4165-9943-6; 978-1-4165-9943-2

LC 2008-33595

This is a "comprehensive look at Michelle Obama and her relationship with Barack Obama." Libr J

Includes bibliographical references

Ochoa, Ellen, 1958-

Hasday, Judy L. **Ellen** Ochoa. Chelsea House Publishers 2007 106p il (Great Hispanic heritage) lib bdg $30

Grades: 9 10 11 12   **92**

1. Astronauts 2. Women astronauts 3. NASA officials
ISBN 0-7910-8842-1; 978-0-7910-8842-5

LC 2006-19632

This book "follows the life of the first Hispanic female astronaut who traveled in space." Publisher's note

Includes bibliographical references

Orwell, George, 1903-1950

Boon, Kevin A. **George** Orwell; Animal farm and Nineteen eighty-four. by Kevin Alexander Boon. Marshall Cavendish Benchmark 2009 143p il (Writers and their works) lib bdg $42.79

Grades: 9 10 11 12   **92**

1. Authors 2. Novelists 3. Essayists 4. Authors, English
ISBN 978-0-7614-2960-9; 0-7614-2960-3

LC 2007-33743

"A biography of writer George Orwell that describes his era, his major works—the novels Animal Farm and Nineteen Eighty-Four—his life, and the legacy of his writing." Publisher's note

Includes filmography and bibliographical references

Osceola, Seminole chief, 1804-1838

Sanford, William R. **Seminole** chief Osceola; by William R. Sanford. Enslow Publishers 2013 48 p. (library) $21.26

Grades: 6 7 8 9   **92**

1. Native Americans -- United States 2. Seminole Indians -- Kings and rulers -- Biography
ISBN 0766041174; 9780766041172

LC 2011050996

This book is part of the Native American Chiefs and Warriors series and looks at Seminole Chief Osceola. "Osceola led his people, the Seminoles, in one of the longest struggles of the Indian Wars. In a game of hide and seek in the Florida wetlands, the Seminoles struck deadly blows to the U.S. Army. Osceoloa was never defeated, but was finally double-crossed and captured." (Publisher's note)

Includes bibliographical references and index.

Oufkir, Malika

Oufkir, Malika. **Freedom**: the story of my second life; translated by Linda Coverdale. Hyperion 2006 241p $23.95

Grades: 9 10 11 12   **92**

1. Political prisoners
ISBN 1-4013-5206-5; 978-1-4013-5206-6

The author, "whose first book, Stolen Lives, recounted her family's 20 years in Moroccan prisons, now continues her story up to the present, revealing what it was like to be thrust into the free world after years of confinement. . . . Ever charming and gracious, Oufkir is a delight to spend time with." Libr J

Owens, Jesse, 1913-1980

Schaap, Jeremy. **Triumph**; the untold story of Jesse Owens and Hitler's Olympics. Houghton Mifflin 2007 272p il $24; pa $14.95

Grades: 11 12 Adult   **92**

1. African American athletes 2. Olympic games, 1936 (Berlin, Ger.) 3. Olympic athletes 4. Runners (Athletes)
ISBN 978-0-618-68822-7; 0-618-68822-6; 978-0-618-91910-9 pa; 0-618-91910-4 pa

LC 2006-26926

"Schaap's chronicle of Jesse Owens's journey to and glorious triumph at the 1936 Berlin Olympics is snappy and dramatic, with an eye for the rousing climax." Publ Wkly

Includes bibliographical references

Padilla Peralta, Dan-el

Padilla Peralta, Dan-el. **Undocumented**; A Dominican Boy's Odyssey from a Homeless Shelter to the Ivy League. by Dan-el Padilla Peralta. Penguin Group USA 2015 320 p. illustrations $27.95

Grades: 11 12 Adult   **92**

1. Homeless persons 2. Dominican Americans 3. Unauthorized immigrants 4. United States -- Immigration and emigration
ISBN 159420652X; 9781594206528

Alex Award (2016)

This book, by Dan-el Padilla Peralta, is an "undocumented immigrant's journey from a New York City homeless shelter to the top of his Princeton class. . . . As a boy, he came here legally with his family. Together they left Santo Domingo behind, but life in New York City was harder than they imagined. Their visas lapsed. . . . Without papers, [they] faced tremendous obstacles." (Publisher's note)

Padilla Peralta "writes candidly about hard times including a period spent in a dangerous homeless shelter, breaking through the harsh immigrant clichés to a pure humanistic level that any reader can embrace." Pub Wkly

Paine, Thomas, 1737-1809

★ Collins, Paul. The **trouble** with Tom: the strange afterlife and times of Thomas Paine. Bloomsbury 2005 278p map hardcover o.p. pa $15

Grades: 11 12 Adult   **92**

1. Essayists 2. Pamphleteers 3. Writers on politics 4. Writers on religion 5. Political and social philosophers
ISBN 1-58234-502-3; 1-58234-613-5 pa

LC 2005-45240

The author "traces the bizarre story of Thomas Paine's remains through nearly two centuries of American and English history. . . . Part travelogue, part memoir and part historical mystery, this book reads like a wry, witty novel and offers a delicious twist at the end." Publ Wkly

Includes bibliographical references

Palden Gyatso

Palden Gyatso. The **autobiography** of a Tibetan monk; {by} Palden Gyatso, with Tsering Shakya; foreword by the Dalai Lama; translated from the Tibetan by Tsering Shakya. Grove Press 1997 232p il maps $24; pa $13

Grades: 9 10 11 12   **92**

1. Tibet (China)

ISBN 0-8021-1621-3; 0-8021-3574-9 pa

LC 97-39679

Published in the United Kingdom with title: Fire under the snow

This is a "wrenching memoir of extraordinary suffering, resistance and endurance." N Y Times Book Rev

Paolini, Christopher

Bankston, John. **Christopher** Paolini; foreword by Kyle Zimmer. Chelsea House Publishers 2010 132p il (Who wrote that?) lib bdg $35

Grades: 6 7 8 9 10   **92**

1. Authors 2. Novelists 3. Fantasy writers 4. Authors, American 5. Young adult authors

ISBN 978-1-60413-727-9; 1-60413-727-4

LC 2010001366

This discusses the life and work of author Christopher Paolini.

Includes bibliographical references

Patel, Eboo, 1975-

Patel, Eboo. **Acts** of faith; the story of an American Muslim, the struggle for the soul of a generation. Beacon Press 2010 195p pa $14

Grades: 11 12 Adult   **92**

1. Multiculturalism 2. Sociologists 3. Youth leaders 4. Religious leaders 5. Writers on religion 6. Organization officials 7. Muslims -- United States

ISBN 978-0-8070-0622-1; 0-8070-0622-X

LC 2010-537438

First published 2007

"Eboo Patel's story as an American Muslim is a powerful account of one hopeful man's struggle against biases in America and how young people can bring together a purpose of common humanity and advance peace in the world." Univ Press Books for Public and Second Sch Libr, 2008

Includes bibliographical references

Paterson, Katherine

Paterson, Katherine. **Stories** of my life; by Katherine Paterson. Dial Books for Young Readers 2014 320 p. illustrations (hardcover) $17.99

Grades: 9 10 11 12 Adult Professional   **92**

1. Autobiographies 2. Women authors -- Biography 3. Children's stories -- Authorship 4. Authors, American -- 20th century -- Biography

ISBN 0803740433; 9780803740433

LC 2013042628

Author Katherine "Paterson's tales reveal details about her life from her childhood with missionary parents, to living as a single woman in Japan, to raising four children in suburban Maryland with her minister husband. . . . Filled with personal photos and letters, this . . . history from a legendary writer lets fans in on the making of literary classics." (Publisher's note)

"Written in a conversational style, these 'kitchen sink stories' will perhaps be received best by professional adults and readers who grew up with her books; much of what she recounts is about the distant past, courtship, and motherhood. What absolutely shines through is Paterson's warm, self-effacing humor, and the extraordinary humility of a writer who has won two National Book Awards, two Newbery Medals, and the Hans Christian Andersen Medal." Pub Wkly

Patrick, Danica, 1982-

Sirvaitis, Karen. **Danica** Patrick; racing's trailblazer. Twenty-First Century Books 2010 112p il (USA Today: lifeline biographies) lib bdg $33.26

Grades: 7 8 9 10 11 12   **92**

1. Women athletes 2. Automobile racing 3. Automobile racing drivers

ISBN 978-0-7613-5222-8; 0-7613-5222-8

LC 2009-45846

This biography is "both informative and eye-catching. . . . Even young readers with little interest in car racing will be caught up in the story behind Danica Patrick. . . . This involving story does more than recount the high times. Teammates are killed, loyalties switch, and personal criticism is a fact of life in the limelight." Booklist

Patrick, Saint, 373?-463?

Bury, John Bagnell. **Ireland's** saint; the essential biography of St. Patrick. [by] J.B. Bury; edited with introduction and annotations by Jon M. Sweeney. Rev ed; Paraclete Press 2008 205p il map $21.95

Grades: 9 10 11 12 Adult   **92**

1. Saints 2. Christian saints 3. Missionaries

ISBN 978-1-55725-557-0; 1-55725-557-1

LC 2008-17071

First published 1905 with title: The life of St. Patrick and his place in history

Sweeney "takes Bury's original text and fashions a contemporary English rendering from it, . . . adding sidebars that highlight recent scholarship and provide new insights into Patrick's life and thought. . . . This edition will . . . appeal to a popular audience." Libr J

Includes bibliographical references

Patterson, Floyd

★ Levy, Alan Howard. **Floyd** Patterson; a boxer and a gentleman. [by] Alan H. Levy. McFarland & Co. 2008 289p il pa $35

Grades: 11 12 Adult   **92**

1. African American athletes 2. Boxers (Persons) 3. Boxing -- Biography

ISBN 978-0-7864-3950-8; 0-7864-3950-5

LC 2008-32250

This is a "biography of the man who was the youngest world heavyweight champion in boxing history as well as the first boxer to regain the championship after losing it. . . . This book is not only an excellent study of Patterson but a superior source on professional boxing from the mid-1950s through the mid-1970s." Libr J

Includes bibliographical references

Peery, Nelson, 1925-

Peery, Nelson. **Black** radical; the education of an American revolutionary. New Press 2007 242p $24.95

Grades: 11 12 Adult **92**
1. Revolutionaries 2. Social activists 3. Communism -- United States 4. African Americans -- Biography 5. African Americans -- Civil rights
ISBN 978-1-59558-145-7; 1-59558-145-6
LC 2007-9181
Sequel to Black fire (1995)
This is the memoir of an African-American World War II veteran who became a member of the Communist Party in 1946.
"Some readers may chafe at Peery's avowedly Marxist terminology, but the development of [his] revolutionary consciousness is absorbing." Publ Wkly

Pei, I. M., 1917-
★ Rubalcaba, Jill. **I.M.** Pei; architect of time, place, and purpose. Marshall Cavendish 2011 92p il map $23.99; ebook $23.99
Grades: 6 7 8 9 10 11 12 **92**
1. Architects 2. Chinese Americans
ISBN 978-0-7614-5973-6; 0-7614-5973-1; 978-0-7614-6081-7 ebook; 0-7614-6081-0 ebook
LC 2011001910
"An exquisite package, much like one of Pei's buildings." Kirkus
Includes bibliographical references

Peterson, Brenda
Peterson, Brenda. **I** want to be left behind; finding rapture here on Earth. Da Capo Press 2010 277p $25
Grades: 11 12 Adult **92**
1. Authors 2. Novelists 3. End of the world 4. Essayists 5. Nature -- Religious aspects
ISBN 978-0-306-81804-2
LC 2009-22803
This is a "memoir about growing up among Southern Baptists and not quite fitting in. Peterson's story is told through . . . a series of vignettes, tied together by two themes, faith and the environment. She looks back at her childhood, college, and then adulthood, stopping here and there, selecting scenes from her life that show why she finds God outdoors, and why the rapture-obsessed family and community of her youth quickly loses its appeal. . . . Readers interested in a story about leaving behind theologically conservative Christianity and other types of extremism will find Peterson's collection of anecdotes and remembered conversations engaging." Publ Wkly

Picasso, Pablo, 1881-1973
Kallen, Stuart A. **Pablo** Picasso. Lucent Books 2009 104p il (Eye on art) lib bdg $32.45
Grades: 7 8 9 10 **92**
1. Cubism 2. Artists 3. Painters 4. Artists, French
ISBN 978-1-4205-0045-5; 1-4205-0045-7
LC 2008-13338
"Kallen tackles the complicated man that was Pablo Picasso and gives readers a look at both his genius and his eccentricities. . . . Visually, this is supported by the many photos of Picasso's art that appear throughout. Excellent sidebars offer solid information on such topics as communism

or the influence of the Impressionists. This is just the kind of book that engages enough to become a gateway." Booklist
Includes bibliographical references

Pierce, Franklin, 1804-1869
Holt, Michael F. **Franklin** Pierce. Times Books/ Henry Holt and Co. 2010 154p (American presidents series) $23
Grades: 11 12 Adult **92**
1. Generals 2. Presidents 3. Senators 4. Members of Congress 5. Presidents -- United States 6. United States -- Politics and government -- 1815-1861
ISBN 978-0-8050-8719-2
LC 2009-36425
The author "creates a solid portrait of both man and President. Pierce, a New Englander known for his charm and good looks, traditionally ranks as one of our nation's worst leaders. Holt does not dispel or challenge any previous assessments but rather tries to explain the pre-Civil War President's actions." Libr J
Includes bibliographical references

Pirsig, Robert M., 1928-
Pirsig, Robert M. **Zen** and the art of motorcycle maintenance; an inquiry into values. Morrow 1974 412p $26; pa $13.95
Grades: 11 12 Adult **92**
1. Authors 2. Novelists 3. Essayists
ISBN 0-688-00230-7; 0-06-083987-2 pa
A collection of the author's philosophical musings inspired by a motorcycle trip with his son

Plath, Sylvia
Reiff, Raychel Haugrud. **Sylvia** Plath. Marshall Cavendish Benchmark 2008 144p il (Writers and their works) lib bdg $39.93
Grades: 9 10 11 12 **92**
1. Poets 2. Authors 3. Novelists 4. Poets, American
ISBN 978-0-7614-2962-3; 0-7614-2962-X
LC 2007-23799
"A biography of writer Sylvia Plath that describes her era, her major works—the novel The Bell Jar and her poetry—her life, and the legacy of her writing." Publisher's note
Includes filmography and bibliographical references

Pocahontas, d. 1617
Jones, Victoria Garrett. **Pocahontas**; a life in two worlds. Sterling 2010 124p il map (Sterling biographies) lib bdg $12.95; pa $9.95
Grades: 7 8 9 10 **92**
1. Princesses 2. Powhatan Indians 3. Indian leaders 4. Jamestown (Va.) -- History 5. Native Americans -- Biography
ISBN 978-1-4027-6844-6 lib bdg; 1-4027-6844-3 lib bdg; 978-1-4027-5158-5 pa; 1-4027-5158-3 pa
LC 2009-24136
A biography of the daughter of Chief Powhatan and her friendship with the colonists of the Jamestown settlement.
Includes glossary and bibliographical references

Woodward, Grace Steele. **Pocahontas**. University of Okla. Press 1969 227p il (Civilization of the American Indian series) hardcover o.p. pa $17.95
Grades: 9 10 11 12   **92**
1. Farmers 2. Princesses 3. Powhatan Indians 4. Colonists 5. Indian chiefs 6. Indian leaders 7. Travel writers 8. Jamestown (Va.) -- History 9. Spouses of prominent persons 10. Native Americans -- Biography 11. United States -- History -- 1600-1775, Colonial period
ISBN 0-8061-1642-0 pa
This is the "story of the appealing daughter of Chief Powhatan and her friendship with the colonists of the Jamestown settlement. . . . Her marriage and brief life in England are vividly re-created." Booklist
Includes bibliographical references

Poe, Edgar Allan, 1809-1849

Ackroyd, Peter. **Poe**; a life cut short. Nan A. Talese/Doubleday 2008 205p il (Ackroyd's brief lives) $21.95
Grades: 9 10 11 12 Adult   **92**
1. Poets 2. Authors 3. Essayists 4. Authors, American 5. Short story writers
ISBN 978-0-385-50800-1; 0-385-50800-X
LC 2008-18244
Explores Poe's literary accomplishments and legacy against the background of his erratic, dramatic, and sometimes sordid life, including his marriage to his thirteen-year-old cousin and his much-written-about problems with gambling and alcohol.
This "readable account should appeal to Poe devotees and newcomers alike." Publ Wkly
Includes bibliographical references

★ Meltzer, Milton. **Edgar** Allan Poe; a biography. Twenty-First Century Books 2003 144p $31.90
Grades: 7 8 9 10   **92**
1. Poets 2. Authors 3. Essayists 4. Authors, American 5. Short story writers
ISBN 0-7613-2910-2
LC 2002-155802
"More than most other biographers for young people, Meltzer places his subject within the framework of his society. Readers will come away not only with greater knowledge of Poe's life and accomplishments but also a clearer picture of American life in the first half of the nineteenth century." Booklist
Includes bibliographical references

Reiff, Raychel Haugrud. **Edgar** Allan Poe; tales and poems. Marshall Cavendish Benchmark 2008 157p il (Writers and their works) lib bdg $39.93
Grades: 9 10 11 12   **92**
1. Poets 2. Authors 3. Essayists 4. Authors, American 5. Short story writers
ISBN 978-0-7614-2963-0; 0-7614-2963-8
"A biography of writer Edgar Allan Poe that describes his era, his major works, and the legacy of his writing." Publisher's note
Includes filmography and bibliographical references

Powhatan, ca. 1550-1618

Woodward, Grace Steele. **Pocahontas**. University of Okla. Press 1969 227p il (Civilization of the American Indian series) hardcover o.p. pa $17.95
Grades: 9 10 11 12   **92**
1. Farmers 2. Princesses 3. Powhatan Indians 4. Colonists 5. Indian chiefs 6. Indian leaders 7. Travel writers 8. Jamestown (Va.) -- History 9. Spouses of prominent persons 10. Native Americans -- Biography 11. United States -- History -- 1600-1775, Colonial period
ISBN 0-8061-1642-0 pa
This is the "story of the appealing daughter of Chief Powhatan and her friendship with the colonists of the Jamestown settlement. . . . Her marriage and brief life in England are vividly re-created." Booklist
Includes bibliographical references

Prado, Edgar, 1967-

Prado, Edgar. **My** guy Barbaro; a jockey's journey through love, triumph, and heartbreak with America's favorite horse. Harper 2008 202p il $25.95
Grades: 11 12 Adult   **92**
1. Horse racing 2. Barbaro (Race horse) 3. Jockeys
ISBN 978-0-06-146418-8; 0-06-146418-X
The author relates the "story of Barbaro's rise and fall. One of the most successful jockeys in history, Prado sensed Barbaro's special qualities during a race in Maryland. After going undefeated in their first three races together, Prado and Barbaro shared an easy 2006 Kentucky Derby victory that positioned Barbaro to win the Triple Crown. Disaster struck at the Preakness, however, when Barbaro shattered a leg into more than two dozen pieces just out of the gate. . . [The author's] journey from a one-room house in Lima, Peru—which he shared with his parents and 10 brothers and sisters—to a place at the top of his profession is fascinating in its own right." Publ Wkly

Presley, Elvis, 1935-1977

★ Mason, Bobbie Ann. **Elvis** Presley. Viking 2002 178p (Penguin lives series) hardcover o.p. pa $13
Grades: 11 12 Adult   **92**
1. Actors 2. Singers 3. Rock musicians
ISBN 0-670-03174-7; 0-14-303889-3 pa
LC 2002-28873
The author "chronicles Elvis' sad story: humble origins, 1954 breakthrough, adoption by 'the Colonel' (manager Tom Parker), early TV appearances, army hitch, the death of his mother, marriage to Priscilla, Hollywood, 1968 'comeback', Las Vegas headliner, prescription drug abuse, meeting with Nixon, and death at 42 in 1977." Booklist
Includes discography, filmography and bibliographical references

Proulx, Annie

Proulx, Annie, 1935- **Bird** cloud; a memoir. Scribner 2011 234p il map $26; ebook $12.99
Grades: 11 12 Adult   **92**
1. Authors 2. Novelists 3. Journalists 4. Women authors 5. Editors 6. Nonfiction writers 7. Short story

writers 8. Biography, Individual 9. Natural history --
Wyoming 10. Wyoming -- Description and travel
ISBN 978-0-7432-8880-4; 978-1-4391-7171-4 ebook

"'Bird Cloud' is the name Annie Proulx gave to 640
acres of Wyoming wetlands and prairie and four-hundred-
foot cliffs plunging down to the North Platte River. On the
day she first visited, a cloud in the shape of a bird hung in the
evening sky. Proulx also saw pelicans, bald eagles, golden
eagles, great blue herons, ravens, scores of bluebirds, harri-
ers, kestrels, elk, deer and a dozen antelope. She fell in love
with the land, then owned by the Nature Conservancy, and
she knew what she wanted to build on it—a house in harmony with her work, her appetites and her character, a library
surrounded by bedrooms and a kitchen. . . . Bird Cloud is
the story of designing and constructing that house—with its
solar panels, Japanese soak tub, concrete floor and elk horn
handles on kitchen cabinets. It is also a . . . natural history
and archaeology of the region—inhabited for millennia by
Ute, Arapaho and Shoshone Indians—and a family history,
going back to nineteenth-century Mississippi riverboat captains and Canadian settlers." (Publisher's note)

"Proulx bought a 640-acre nature preserve by the North
Platte River in Wyoming and started building her dream
house, a project that took years and went hundreds of thousands of dollars over budget. In her bustling account, Proulx
salivates over the prospect of a Japanese soak tub, polished
concrete floor, solar panels, and luxe furnishings that often
turn into pricey engineering fiascoes. . . . [This] is a fine evocation of place that becomes a meditation on the importance
of a home, however harsh and evanescent." Publ Wkly

Includes bibliographical references

Pullman, Philip, 1946-

Speaker-Yuan, Margaret. **Philip** Pullman. Chel-
sea House 2006 118p il (Who wrote that?) lib bdg
$30
Grades: 6 7 8 9   **92**
1. Authors 2. Novelists 3. Fantasy writers 4. Authors,
English 5. Young adult authors
ISBN 0-7910-8658-5
LC 2005-8184

This "draws upon an impressive array of sources—particularly Pullman's own writings—to present the groundbreaking author's life and work. . . . What may thrill readers
most . . . are the insights into the writing process." Booklist
Includes bibliographical references

Pung, Alice, 1981-

Pung, Alice. **Unpolished** gem; my mother, my
grandmother, and me. Penguin Group 2009 282p pa
$15 **92**
1. Lawyers 2. Cambodian refugees 3. Children of
immigrants 4. Australia 5. Memoirists
ISBN 978-0-452-29000-6
LC 2008-30365
First published 2006 in Australia

The author "recounts the journey her family made over
the decades—from China, her grandparents' birthplace, to
Cambodia, where her parents are born, through Vietnam and
Thailand to Australia where, one month after their arrival,
Pung is born. . . . The non-European-immigrant-girl-grows-
up story is a familiar one to American readers. What's new

about Pung's book is the Australian setting. That twist of
focus reveals how more alike than different the experience
is." Publ Wkly

Pythagoras

★ Karamanides, Dimitra. **Pythagoras**: pioneer-
ing mathematician and musical theorist of Ancient
Greece. Rosen Pub. Group 2006 112p il map (The
library of Greek philosophers) lib bdg $33.25
Grades: 9 10 11 12   **92**
1. Philosophers 2. Mathematicians
ISBN 1-4042-00500-4
LC 2005-11968

This is a biography of Greek mathematician
and philosopher.
Includes bibliographical references

Quiñones-Hinojosa, Alfredo

Quiñones-Hinojosa, Alfredo. **Becoming** Dr. Q;
my journey from migrant farm worker to brain surgeon. with Mim Eichler Rivas. University of California Press 2011 317p il $27.50
Grades: 11 12 Adult   **92**
1. Surgeons 2. Migrant labor 3. Mexican Americans
4. Neurologists 5. Neurosurgeons
ISBN 978-0-520-27118-0; 0-520-27118-1
LC 2011011531

"When the callow Quiñones-Hinojosa, or Dr. Q, made
up his mind to pursue a better life and, especially, an education in the U.S., no border or barrier could have kept him
from his destiny: a fate that led eventually to his becoming
a Johns Hopkins University neurosurgeon, professor, and
brain-cancer research scientist. Indeed, the brash teenager
left all that was familiar in his native Mexico and, with less
than $70 in his pocket, climbed the fence. In fact, he scaled
it twice because he was caught the first time and sent back. .
. . Quiñones-Hinojosa's story is gripping, inspiring, and just
plain awesome." Booklist

Ragusa, Kym

Ragusa, Kym. The **skin** between us; a memoir
of race, beauty, and belonging. W.W. Norton 2006
238p $23.95
Grades: 11 12 Adult   **92**
1. Racially mixed people 2. Motion picture directors
ISBN 978-0-393-05890-1; 0-393-05890-5
LC 2005-33673

"The particulars of Ragusa's story reveal the universal anxiety about belonging and about finding a home in
America." Booklist

Ramirez, Manny, 1972-

Rhodes, Jean E. **Becoming** Manny; inside the
life of baseball's most enigmatic slugger. [by] Jean
Rhodes and Shawn Boburg. Scribner 2009 304p
il $25
Grades: 11 12 Adult   **92**
1. Baseball players 2. Baseball -- Biography
ISBN 978-1-4165-7706-5; 1-4165-7706-8
LC 2009-2348

Authorized biography of Manny Ramirez.

"The authors don't dwell on Ramirez's shortcomings, but neither do they ignore them. On balance, an interesting biography of a baseball lightning rod." Booklist

Randolph, Asa Philip, 1889-1979

Miller, Calvin Craig. **A.** Philip Randolph and the African American labor movement. Morgan Reynolds 2005 160p il (Portraits of Black Americans) $24.95

Grades: 8 9 10 11 12   **92**

1. Labor unions 2. Labor leaders 3. Civil rights activists 4. African Americans -- Biography 5. African Americans -- Civil rights
ISBN 1-931798-50-8

LC 2004-23706

A biography of the African American leader

"Miller lucidly traces Randolph's spectacular career while presenting a case study in the effective use of hardnosed rhetoric and nonviolent tactics to achieve breakthroughs in the fight against segregation. Profusely illustrated with photographs, sometimes in color, and capped by resource lists." Booklist

Includes bibliographical references

Rapp, Emily

Rapp, Emily. **Poster** child; a memoir. Bloomsbury 2007 229p $23.95; pa $14.95

Grades: 11 12 Adult   **92**

1. Authors 2. People with disabilities 3. Essayists 4. Memoirists 5. Short story writers
ISBN 978-1-59691-256-4; 1-59691-256-1; 978-1-59691-505-3 pa; 1-59691-505-6 pa

LC 2006-12555

"Rapp was an extraordinary child. Born with a congenital defect, she had her left ankle amputated at the age of four. Four years later, after dozens of surgeries, her entire leg below the knee was gone. . . . She became the March of Dimes poster child, an amputee skier, and eventually won a Fulbright Scholarship to Korea. But this is not the story of her achievements. Instead, the book chronicles her poignant journey to make peace with her flaws. . . . Young adults, often obsessed with defects both real and imagined, will identify with the author's need at first to be extraordinary, and then her final acceptance of the imperfect, but valued person she really is." SLJ

Rather, Dan

Diehl, Digby. **Rather** outspoken; my life in the news. Dan Rather with Digby Diehl. Grand Central Pub. 2012 vi, 309 p.p (regular edition) $27.99

Grades: Adult   **92**

1. CBS Inc. 2. Television broadcasting of news 3. Television journalists -- United States -- Biography
ISBN 1455502413; 9781455502417; 9781455513468

LC 2011052227

This book by Dan Rather presents an "investigation of how the news media has become dangerously intertwined with politics and corporate interests." It focuses on "the circumstances behind his firing from CBS News, where he had worked as a reporter since 1962. . . . In between, he provides . . . portraits of the presidents he has interviewed . . . and expresses concern for the future of independent media in an industry that is increasingly kowtowing to the almighty bottom line." (Kirkus Reviews)

Reagan, Ronald, 1911-2004

Schaller, Michael. **Ronald** Reagan. Oxford University Press 2011 105p $12.95

Grades: 11 12 Adult   **92**

1. Actors 2. Governors 3. Presidents 4. Presidents -- United States
ISBN 978-0-19-975174-7

LC 2010-15726

"A fine steppingstone to the vast literature on Reagan, pro and con, Schaller's summary belongs in virtually all U.S. libraries." Booklist

Includes bibliographical references

Reyes, Guillermo, 1962-

Reyes, Guillermo. **Madre** and I; a memoir of our immigrant lives. University of Wisconsin Press 2010 278p il (Writing in Latinidad) pa $18.95

Grades: 11 12 Adult   **92**

1. Authors 2. Dramatists 3. Hispanic American gay men 4. Drama teachers 5. Immigrants -- United States
ISBN 978-0-299-23624-3

LC 2009-41310

The author "had an atypical Latino immigrant experience that provides ample material for this entertaining and stirring memoir. He bares his soul . . . as he tells his story of growing up in Chile, fatherless but with his father's name, and of his journey to Los Angeles, all the while coping with sexuality and body issues. But more than his own coming-of-age, this is the story of his mother, Maria, and her struggles, at times unconventionally approached, to provide a better life for her son. Reyes's recountings of his mother's and her family's adventures are the glue that holds this story together while he writes of shaping his own identity and finding his voice as a writer." Libr J

Rhodes-Courter, Ashley Marie

Rhodes-Courter, Ashley Marie. **Three** little words; a memoir. Atheneum Books for Young Readers 2008 304p il $17.99; pa $9.99

Grades: 8 9 10 11 12 Adult   **92**

1. Foster children 2. Adopted children 3. Foster home care 4. Memoirists 5. Child benefactors
ISBN 978-1-4169-4806-3; 1-4169-4806-6; 978-1-4169-4807-0 pa; 1-4169-4807-4 pa

LC 2007-21629

"This memoir lends a powerful voice to thousands of 'boomerang kids' who repeatedly wind up back in foster care." SLJ

Rice, Condoleezza, 1954-

Rice, Condoleezza, 1954- **Condoleezza** Rice; a memoir of my extraordinary, ordinary family and me. Delacorte Press 2010 319p il $16.99; lib bdg $19.99; e-book $9.99

Grades: 7 8 9 10 11 12   **92**

1. Women politicians 2. College teachers 3. Government officials 4. Political scientists 5. Secretaries of state 6. Presidential advisers 7. College administrators 8.

African American women -- Biography
ISBN 978-0-385-73879-8; 0-385-73879-X; 978-0-385-90747-7 lib bdg; 0-385-90747-8 lib bdg; 978-0-375-89613-2 e-book

LC 2010-29878

"The former Secretary of State recounts her life, beginning with her family history and childhood in Birmingham, AL, during the 1950s and '60s. . . . A 16-page insert of black-and-white and color photos adds detail, and the glossary has more information on the many political leaders whom Rice refers to in the book. This valuable memoir about breaking glass ceilings may inspire readers to test their own potential." SLJ

Richardson, Kevin

Richardson, Kevin. **Part** of the pride; my life among the big cats of Africa. with Tony Park. St. Martin's Press 2009 243p il $25.99

Grades: 11 12 Adult   92

1. Lions 2. Wild cats 3. Zookeepers 4. Zoologists 5. Behavioral scientists
ISBN 978-0-312-55674-7; 0-312-55674-8

LC 2009-16258

"Lion keeper and animal behaviorist Richardson . . . chronicles his life and career while explaining his unique ability to gain the trust of predators like lions and hyenas. . . . An engrossing account of a young life in Africa, this adventurous tale also provides amazing insight into the minds of Africa's most beautiful and dangerous creatures." Publ Wkly

Rickey, Branch, 1881-1965

Breslin, Jimmy. **Branch** Rickey. Viking 2010 147p (Penguin lives series) $19.95

Grades: 11 12 Adult   92

1. Baseball managers 2. Baseball executives 3. Baseball -- Biography 4. Biography, Individual 5. Brooklyn Dodgers (Baseball team)
ISBN 0-670-02249-7; 978-0-670-02249-6

LC 2010-35008

This is a biography of Branch Rickey, the president and general manager of the Brooklyn Dodgers, who, in 1947, brought Jackie Robinson to the team.

"Breslin reveals much about the development of baseball, the Dodgers' last years in Brooklyn, and the struggle to overcome the national pastime's racism while tracing the life, deeds, and some (but not all) of Branch Rickey's warts. A breezy read, this 'Penguin Life' is nonetheless insightful, humorous, and biting at times as it traces how the man dubbed 'the Mahatma' by sportswriters emerged from obscurity as an Idaho lawyer to develop the baseball farm system, multiple MLB winners, Vero Beach spring training, the scientific teaching of skills, and the MLB expansion that brought New York the Mets." Libr J

Includes bibliographical references

Ride, Sally

Sherr, Lynn. **Sally** Ride; America's first woman in space. Lynn Sherr. Simon & Schuster 2014 400 p. illustrations (hardcover) $28

Grades: 11 12 Adult   92

1. Women astronauts 2. Women -- Biography 3.

Astronauts -- United States -- Biography
ISBN 1476725764; 9781476725765; 9781476725772

LC 2013039647

This book is "The definitive biography of Sally Ride, America's first woman in space, with exclusive insights from Ride's family and partner, by [journalist Lynn Sherr] who covered NASA during its transformation from a test-pilot boys' club to a more inclusive elite. . . . Sally Ride made history as the first American woman in space." (Publisher's note)

"This is an intimate and enormously appealing biography of a fascinating woman, a triumph of research and sensitivity that lives up to its subject." Booklist

Includes bibliographical references and index

Riis, Jacob A. (Jacob August), 1849-1914

Pascal, Janet B. **Jacob** Riis. Oxford University Press 2006 175p il $28

Grades: 9 10 11 12   92

1. Reformers 2. Journalists 3. Memoirists 4. Photojournalists 5. Social reformers
ISBN 978-0-19-514527-4; 0-19-514527-5

LC 2005-7757

"This biography traces Riis's life and evolution into a progressive social reformer. . . . [This is] an insightful work that is sure to hold readers' interest." SLJ

Includes bibliographical references

Ripken, Cal, Jr.

Ripken, Cal. The **only** way I know; [by] Cal Ripken, Jr., and Mike Bryan. Viking 1997 326p il hardcover o.p. pa $12.95

Grades: 11 12 Adult   92

1. Baseball players 2. Baseball -- Biography 3. Baltimore Orioles (Baseball team)
ISBN 0-670-87193-1; 0-14-026626-7 pa

LC 97-9159

"Cal Junior chronicles his moves through the minor leagues and into the majors in great detail, always pointing out what he learned at each step of the journey and who taught it to him. There are some great baseball anecdotes—especially involving fiery Oriole skipper Earl Weaver—and plenty of the behind-the-scenes detail." Booklist

Robinson, Jackie, 1919-1972

★ Robinson, Jackie. **I** never had it made; an autobiography. by Jackie Robinson as told to Alfred Duckett; foreword by Cornel West; introduction by Hank Aaron. Ecco Press 1995 xxii, 275p il hardcover o.p. pa $13.95

Grades: 11 12 Adult   92

1. Baseball players 2. African American athletes 3. Army officers 4. Baseball -- Biography
ISBN 0-06-055597-1

LC 94-45279

A reissue of the title first published 1972 by Putnam

"Included are introductions by Hank Aaron and Cornel West that provide fresh perspectives on the significance of the legendary star's breaking of major league baseball's color barrier. With each retelling, it is clear that Robinson's story has become less a baseball story than a major cultural milestone in the nation's history." Libr J

Robison, John Elder, 1957-

★ Robison, John Elder. **Look** me in the eye; my
life with Asperger's. Crown Publishers 2007 288p
$25.95

Grades: 11 12 Adult   **92**
1. Photographers 2. Asperger's syndrome 3. Mechanics
(Persons) 4. Restorers 5. Memoirists
ISBN 978-0-307-39598-6; 0-307-39598-7

LC 2007-13139

In this memoir, the author describes growing up with
Asperger's syndrome (which went undiagnosed until he
was 40 years old), dealing with an alcoholic father and a
mentally unstable mother, and developing an affinity for machines that would eventually lead him to a career restoring
classic cars.

"Robison's memoir is must reading for its unblinking (as
only an Aspergian can) glimpse into the life of a person who
had to wait decades for the medical community to catch up
with him." Booklist

Includes bibliographical references

Rodriguez, Richard, 1944-

Rodriguez, Richard. **Hunger** of memory; the
education of Richard Rodriguez: an autobiography.
Bantam trade pbk. ed.; Bantam Books 2004 212p
pa $15

Grades: 11 12 Adult   **92**
1. Poets 2. Authors 3. Television personalities 4.
Essayists 5. Memoirists 6. Mexican Americans --
Biography
ISBN 0-553-38251-9

LC 2004-269979

First published 1982 by Godine

An account "of the coming of age of a person of Mexican descent and culture in American society and the inevitable transition in the private life of his family. Rodriguez
focuses on his educational experiences, from his parochial
elementary school . . . to his university years and subsequent
experience as an educator." Libr J

Rolfe, John, 1585-1622

Woodward, Grace Steele. **Pocahontas**. University of Okla. Press 1969 227p il (Civilization of the
American Indian series) hardcover o.p. pa $17.95

Grades: 9 10 11 12   **92**
1. Farmers 2. Princesses 3. Powhatan Indians 4.
Colonists 5. Indian chiefs 6. Indian leaders 7. Travel
writers 8. Jamestown (Va.) -- History 9. Spouses of
prominent persons 10. Native Americans -- Biography
11. United States -- History -- 1600-1775, Colonial
period
ISBN 0-8061-1642-0 pa

This is the "story of the appealing daughter of Chief
Powhatan and her friendship with the colonists of the Jamestown settlement. . . . Her marriage and brief life in England
are vividly re-created." Booklist

Includes bibliographical references

Roosevelt family

★ Renehan, Edward J. The **lion's** pride: Theodore Roosevelt and his family in peace and war; [by]

Edward J. Renehan, Jr. Oxford Univ. Press 1998
289p il $55; pa $44.99

Grades: 11 12 Adult   **92**
1. Governors 2. Presidents 3. Vice-presidents 4.
Nobel laureates for peace 5. Presidents -- United States
ISBN 0-19-512719-6; 0-19-513424-9 pa

LC 98-23998

Although this work explores Roosevelt's influential role
as a former president, it primarily explores his relationship
with his four sons and daughter.

"Renehan's portraits of the children further enrich a superb, real-life family saga." Booklist

Includes bibliographical references

Roosevelt, Eleanor, 1884-1962

★ Keating, Anjelina Michelle. **Eleanor** Roosevelt. Library of Congress 2006 64p il (Women
who dare) $12.95

Grades: 9 10 11 12   **92**
1. Diplomats 2. Columnists 3. Humanitarians 4.
Social activists 5. Spouses of presidents 6. United
Nations officials 7. Presidents' spouses -- United States
ISBN 0-7649-3543-7; 978-0-7649-3543-5

LC 2005-49544

This autobiography "traces Eleanor's life story, exploring the childhood that left her lonely and insecure, and surveying the challenges and opportunities that spurred her
transformation into one of the twentieth century's most admired and respected public citizens." Publisher's note

Includes bibliographical references

**Roosevelt, Franklin D. (Franklin Delano), 1882-
1945**

Brinkley, Alan. **Franklin** Delano Roosevelt. Oxford University Press 2010 116p $12.95

Grades: 9 10 11 12 Adult   **92**
1. Governors 2. Presidents 3. People with disabilities
4. Philatelists 5. Presidents -- United States
ISBN 978-0-19-973202-9

LC 2009-27690

This "biography chronicles Franklin Delano Roosevelt's
rise from a childhood of privilege to a presidency that forever changed the face of international diplomacy, the American party system, and the government's role in global and
domestic policy." Publisher's note

Includes bibliographical references

Roosevelt, Theodore, 1858-1919

★ Cooper, Michael L. **Theodore** Roosevelt; a
twentieth-century life. Viking 2009 208p il (Up
close) $16.99

Grades: 7 8 9 10   **92**
1. Governors 2. Presidents 3. Vice-presidents 4.
Nobel laureates for peace 5. Presidents -- United States
ISBN 978-0-670-01134-6; 0-670-01134-7

LC 2010-279534

"This biography presents an evenhanded account of
the life and presidency of Theodore Roosevelt. . . . This
clearly written biography includes many anecdotes and
well-chosen quotes that help bring Roosevelt to life. . . .

Cooper offers a solid portrayal of this noteworthy American president." Booklist

Includes bibliographical references

DiSilvestro, Roger L. **Theodore** Roosevelt in the Badlands; a young politician's quest for recovery in the American West. Walker & Co. 2011 352p il map $27

Grades: 11 12 Adult   92

1. Governors 2. Presidents 3. Ranch life 4. Vice-presidents 5. Nobel laureates for peace 6. Presidents -- United States 7. Frontier and pioneer life -- North Dakota

ISBN 978-0-8027-1721-4

LC 2010-44297

"Focused on TR in his twenties, DiSilvestro's work elaborates on the future president's days devoted to hunting and ranching in the Dakota Territory. . . . With its sources fully researched and capably integrated, DiSilvestro's account definitively fills in this part of TR's story." Booklist

Includes bibliographical references

★ Renehan, Edward J. The **lion's** pride: Theodore Roosevelt and his family in peace and war; [by] Edward J. Renehan, Jr. Oxford Univ. Press 1998 289p il $55; pa $44.99

Grades: 11 12 Adult   92

1. Governors 2. Presidents 3. Vice-presidents 4. Nobel laureates for peace 5. Presidents -- United States

ISBN 0-19-512719-6; 0-19-513424-9 pa

LC 98-23998

Although this work explores Roosevelt's influential role as a former president, it primarily explores his relationship with his four sons and daughter.

"Renehan's portraits of the children further enrich a superb, real-life family saga." Booklist

Includes bibliographical references

Rosenberg, Ethel, 1915-1953

Philipson, Ilene J. **Ethel** Rosenberg; beyond the myths. by Ilene Philipson. Rutgers University Press 1993 390p pa $22

Grades: 11 12 Adult   92

1. Spies 2. Trials (Espionage)

ISBN 0-8135-1917-9; 978-0-8135-1917-3

LC 92-23750

First published 1988 by Watts

This is "a fine psycho-historical study of a complex figure." BAYA Book Rev

Includes bibliographical references

Runyon, Brent

★ Runyon, Brent. The **burn** journals. Alfred A. Knopf 2004 373p hardcover o.p. pa $13.95

Grades: 7 8 9 10   92

1. Authors 2. Suicide 3. Burns and scalds 4. Essayists 5. Memoirists

ISBN 0-375-82621-1; 1-4000-9642-1 pa

LC 2004-5643

"One February day in 1991, Runyon came home from eighth grade . . . and set himself on fire. . . . The dialogue

between Runyon and his nurses, parents, and especially his hapless psychotherapists is natural and believable, and his inner dialogue is flip, often funny, and sometimes raw. . . . The authentically adolescent voice of the journals will engage even those reluctant to read such a dark story." SLJ

Rusesabagina, Paul

Rusesabagina, Paul. An **ordinary** man; an autobiography. [by] Paul Rusesabagina with Tom Zoellner. Viking 2006 207p map pa $14; $23.95

Grades: 11 12 Adult   92

1. Rwanda 2. Humanitarians 3. Hotel employees 4. Biography, Individual 5. Rwanda -- History -- Civil War, 1994 -- Personal narratives

ISBN 0-14-303860-5 pa; 0-670-03752-4; 978-0-14-303860-3 pa; 978-0-670-03752-0

LC 2005-43488

Paul Rusesabagina, whose story inspired the film Hotel Rwanda, discusses "his life before, during, and after the genocide. In early April 1994, hotel manager Rusesabagina filled his rooms with 1,268 people and helped them survive by drinking swimming pool water and eating scavenged food." (Christ Today)

Paul Rusesabagina, whose story inspired the film Hotel Rwanda, discusses "his life before, during, and after the genocide. In early April 1994, hotel manager Rusesabagina filled his rooms with 1,268 people and helped them survive by drinking swimming pool water and eating scavenged food." Christ Today

Rustin, Bayard, 1910-1987

Miller, Calvin Craig. **No** easy answers; Bayard Rustin and the civil rights movement. Morgan Reynolds Pub. 2005 160p il lib bdg $24.95

Grades: 7 8 9 10   92

1. Civil rights activists 2. African Americans -- Biography 3. African Americans -- Civil rights

ISBN 1-931798-43-5

LC 2004-18518

"Miller combines the life story of a great social activist with the history of the struggle for civil rights in the U.S. The politics are exciting, with details of the radical campaigns in the 1940s and 1950s, Rustin's impassioned call for nonviolent protest, and his role in organizing both the Montgomery Bus Boycott and the 1963 March on Washington." Booklist

Includes bibliographical references

Ruth, Babe, 1895-1948

Hampton, Wilborn. **Babe** Ruth; a twentieth-century life. Viking 2009 203p il (Up close) $16.99

Grades: 6 7 8 9 10   92

1. Baseball players 2. Baseball -- Biography

ISBN 978-0-670-06305-5; 0-670-06305-3

LC 2008-21550

"Hampton announces early in this biography of Babe Ruth that his emphasis is on separating fact from legend, and he is not afraid to dig up some of the more tawdry aspects of the slugger's life. . . . The focus here is on Ruth's sad early life and his career as a pitcher with the Boston Red Sox. Throughout, an attempt is made to give some sense of the grace, power, and skill of Ruth on the field. . . . [This title,] illustrated with a nice selection of photos, has the advantage of telling the complete, unvarnished story in a snappy, concise style." Booklist

Includes bibliographical references

Rutherford, Ernest, 1871-1937

Reeves, Richard. A **force** of nature; the frontier genius of Ernest Rutherford. W. W. Norton & Co. 2008 207p il (Great discoveries) $23.95

Grades: 11 12 Adult   92

1. Physicists 2. Nobel laureates for chemistry
ISBN 978-0-393-05750-8; 0-393-05750-X

           LC 2007-33184

The author "re-introduces Ernest Rutherford, one of the founding geniuses of nuclear physics. . . . This biography does an outstanding job of capturing the excitement and almost breathless pace of physics research in the 20th century's first four decades." Publ Wkly

Includes bibliographical references

Sís, Peter, 1949-

★ Sis, Peter, 1949- The **wall**; growing up behind the Iron Curtain. Farrar, Straus and Giroux 2007 un il $18

Grades: 4 5 6 7 8 9 10   92

1. Artists 2. Authors 3. Cold war 4. Animators 5. Illustrators 6. Set designers 7. Children's authors 8. Prague (Czech Republic)
ISBN 978-0-374-34701-7; 0-374-34701-8

           LC 2006-49149

Boston Globe-Horn Book Award: Nonfiction (2008)

"The author pairs his remarkable artistry with journal entries, historical context and period photography to create a powerful account of his childhood in Cold War-era Prague." Publ Wkly

Sacagawea, b. 1786

Berne, Emma Carlson. **Sacagawea**; crossing the continent with Lewis & Clark. Sterling 2010 124p il map (Sterling biographies) lib bdg $12.95; pa $5.95

Grades: 7 8 9 10   92

1. Lewis and Clark Expedition (1804-1806) 2. Interpreters 3. Guides (Persons) 4. Shoshone Indians 5. West (U.S.) -- Exploration 6. Native Americans -- Biography
ISBN 978-1-4027-6845-3 lib bdg; 1-4027-6845-1 lib bdg; 978-1-4027-5738-9 pa; 1-4027-5738-7 pa

           LC 2009-24139

"Contrary to myth, Sacagawea explains that the Shoshone teen was not a princess, her relationship with Clark was platonic, and she was a peace symbol rather than a guide until they finally reached the Shoshone tribe. . . . [The] spacious design is highly scannable, with color background screens, photos, maps, and historic prints throughout." Booklist

Includes glossary and bibliographical references

Sagan, Carl

Gabrielle Borisovna. Rosen Publishing 2015 112 p. illustrations (some color) (library bound) $35.60

Grades: 10 11 12   92

1. Scientists 2. Astronomers -- United States --

Biography
ISBN 1477776818; 9781477776810

           LC 2013039272

This children's book on Carl Sagan by Gabrielle Borisovna is part of a series that shows "even famous science experts struggle in school, as readers learn in this series, which sheds light on the human face of geniuses. Some titles emphasize the science writers' literary background more than others." (School Library Journal)

"Throughout his biography, Tyson's passion for space exploration is palpable. Dynamic, understated artwork does not distract from excellent writing here. Strong additions." SLJ

Includes bibliographical references (pages 107-109) and index

Salbi, Zainab

Salbi, Zainab. **Between** two worlds; escape from tyranny: growing up in the shadow of Saddam. [by] Zainab Salbi and Laurie Becklund. Gotham Books 2005 295p $26; pa $14

Grades: 11 12 Adult   92

1. Presidents 2. Feminists 3. Women -- Iraq 4. Human rights activists 5. Organization officials
ISBN 1-59240-156-2; 978-1-59240-156-7; 1-59240-244-5 pa; 978-1-59240-244-1 pa

           LC 2006-276819

The author discusses her childhood in Iraq, how life was changed by the accession to power of Saddam Hussein, her arranged marriage in America to an abusive husband, and her founding of an organization called Women for Women International.

"Through a journey colored with loss and hope, readers encounter a story of self-awakening and of realizing the will to live and survive." Libr J

Salinger, J. D., 1919-2010

★ Reiff, Raychel Haugrud. **J.D.** Salinger; The Catcher in the Rye and other works. Marshall Cavendish Benchmark 2007 158p il (Writers and their works) $39.93

Grades: 9 10 11 12   92

1. Authors 2. Novelists 3. Authors, American 4. Short story writers
ISBN 978-0-7614-2594-6

           LC 2006-19236

This book contains a biography of J.D. Salinger, a description of the times in which he wrote his most famous works, and critical discussions of his works including The Catcher in the Rye.

Includes filmography and bibliographical references

Salk, Jonas, 1914-1995

★ Kluger, Jeffrey. **Splendid** solution: Jonas Salk and the conquest of polio. G.P. Putnam's Sons 2004 373p il hardcover o.p. pa $15

Grades: 11 12 Adult   92

1. Physicians 2. Poliomyelitis 3. Microbiologists 4. Writers on medicine
ISBN 0-399-15216-4; 0-425-20570-3 pa

           LC 2004-50527

"Can't-put-it-down medical-science history." Booklist
Includes bibliographical references

Sherrow, Victoria. **Jonas** Salk; beyond the microscope. 2nd rev ed; Chelsea House 2008 146p il (Makers of modern science) $35

Grades: 7 8 9 10 **92**
1. Physicians 2. Scientists 3. Poliomyelitis vaccine 4. Microbiologists 5. Writers on medicine
ISBN 978-0-8160-6180-8; 0-8160-6180-7

LC 2006-33429

First published 1993 by Facts on File
This biography of Jonas Salk "describes this respected immunologist's medical research and his lifelong efforts to promote scientific and human progress on a global scale." Publisher's note
Includes glossary and bibliographical references

Samancı, Özge

Dare to disappoint; growing up in Turkey. Özge Samancı. Farrar, Straus & Giroux 2015 190 p. illustrations (paperback) $16.99

Grades: 6 7 8 9 10 **92**
1. Turkey 2. Artists 3. Family life 4. Turkey -- History -- 1960- 5. Artists -- Turkey -- Biography 6. Turkey -- History -- 1960- -- Comic books, strips, etc 7. Artists -- Turkey -- Biography -- Comic books, strips, etc
ISBN 0374316988; 9780374316983

LC 2015000704

In this graphic memoir, author Ozge Samanci "recounts her story using inventive collages, weaving together images of the sea, politics, science, and friendship.Growing up on the Aegean Coast, Ozge loved the sea and imagined a life of adventure while her parents and society demanded predictability. Her dad expected Ozge, like her sister, to become an engineer. She tried to hear her own voice over his and the religious and militaristic tensions of Turkey and the conflicts between secularism and fundamentalism." (Publisher's Note)
"In the growing body of graphic novel memoirs, this one is a standout." SLJ

Santiago, Esmeralda

Santiago, Esmeralda. **Almost** a woman; 1st Vintage Books ed.; Vintage Books 1999 314p il pa $13.95

Grades: 11 12 Adult **92**
1. Authors 2. Novelists 3. Memoirists 4. Screenwriters 5. Puerto Ricans -- United States
ISBN 0-375-70521-X

LC 99-25592

Sequel to When I was Puerto Rican
First published 1998 by Perseus Bks.
"Santiago's descriptive prose and lively dialog draw the reader in; we are reminded of the pains and pleasures of adolescence and wonder what happens next in her life." Libr J
Followed by The Turkish lover

Santiago, Esmeralda. **When** I was Puerto Rican; [a memoir] Da Capo Press 2006 278p pa $13.95

Grades: 11 12 Adult **92**
1. Authors 2. Novelists 3. Memoirists 4. Screenwriters 5. Puerto Ricans -- United States
ISBN 0-306-81452-8; 978-0-306-81452-5
First published 1993 by Addison-Wesley
"At once heart-wrenching and remarkably inspirational, this lyrical account depicts rural life in Puerto Rico amid the hardships and tensions of everyday life and Santiago's awakening as a young woman, who, although startled by culture shock, valiantly confronted New York head-on. When in the epilogue Santiago refers to her studies at Harvard, it is both a stirring and poignant reminder of the capacities of the human spirit." Booklist
Other autobiographical titles by the author are:
Almost a woman (1998)
The Turkish lover (2004)

Sayrafiezadeh, Saïd

Sayrafiezadeh, Saïd. **When** skateboards will be free; a memoir of a political childhood. Dial Press 2009 287p $22; pa $15

Grades: 11 12 Adult **92**
1. Authors 2. Socialism 3. Dramatists 4. Memoirists 5. Biography, Individual 6. Socialist Workers' Party (U.S.)
ISBN 0-385-34068-0; 0-385-34069-9 pa; 978-0-385-34068-7; 978-0-385-34069-4 pa

LC 2008-51096

The author presents a memoir "of growing up with (and without) his parents, ardent members of the Socialist Workers' Party." (N Y Times (Late N Y Ed))
"An enormously talented writer, Sayrafiezadeh ably conveys a complex blend of affection and anger toward his deeply flawed parents in deftly controlled prose. An excellent memoir." Kirkus

Scdoris, Rachael

Scdoris, Rachael. **No** end in sight; my life as a blind Iditarod racer. [by] Rachael Scdoris and Rick Steber. St. Martin's Press 2006 278p il $22.95; pa $13.95

Grades: 8 9 10 11 12 **92**
1. Blind 2. Women athletes 3. Sled dog racing 4. Sled dog racers 5. Athletes with physical disabilities
ISBN 0-312-35273-5; 978-0-312-35273-8; 0-312-36437-7 pa; 978-0-312-36437-3 pa

LC 2005-20897

First published 2005 by Two Star
"Readers will feel every twist and turn in the course, and will eagerly follow the progress of this inspiring athlete." SLJ

Scheeres, Julia, 1967-

Scheeres, Julia. **Jesus** land; a memoir. Counterpoint 2005 356p $23; pa $14

Grades: 11 12 Adult **92**
1. Adoption 2. Siblings 3. Child abuse 4. Journalists 5. Christian life 6. Memoirists 7. United States -- Race relations
ISBN 1-58243-338-0; 1-58243-354-2 pa

LC 2005-14816

"Tinged with sadness yet pervaded by a sense of triumph, Scheeres's book is a crisply written and earnest examination of the meaning of family and Christian values." Publ Wkly

Schein, Elyse

Schein, Elyse. **Identical** strangers; a memoir of twins separated and reunited. [by] Elyse Schein, Paula Bernstein. Random House 2007 270p il pa $16.00; $25.95

Grades: 11 12 Adult 92

1. Twins 2. Journalists 3. Adopted children 4. Memoirists 5. Motion picture directors
ISBN 9780812975659; 978-1-4000-6496-0; 1-4000-6496-1

LC 2007-14488

"Reunited at the age of 35, . . . [the authors, who are identical twins,] embarked on a journey to uncover the story of their separation. Research into their genealogical background revealed an ethically questionable study on identical twins performed by the doctors associated with the agency that facilitated their adoptions. In alternating voices, the women detail their emotional struggles as they navigated their developing relationship and the realities of the circumstances surrounding their birth and separation. . . . Teens will be pulled in by the mystery surrounding the study and the identity of the authors' birth mother." SLJ

Schiaparelli, Elsa, 1890-1973

Hot pink; the life and fashions of Elsa Schiaparelli. Susan Goldman Rubin. Abrams Books For Young Readers 2015 56 p. illustrations (chiefly color) (hardcover) $21.95

Grades: 5 6 7 8 9 S C

1. Fashion design 2. Fashion -- France -- History -- 20th century
ISBN 9781419716423

LC 2014032527

This book, by Susan Goldman Rubin, explores how "shocking pink—hot pink, as it is called today—was the signature color of Elsa Schiaparelli (1890–1973) and perhaps her greatest contribution to the fashion world. Schiaparelli was one of the most innovative designers in the early 20th century. Many design elements that are taken for granted today she created and brought to the forefront of fashion." (Publisher's note)

"With accessible text, an inviting format, and a comprehensive list of multimedia resources in the back matter, this concise biography is well suited to classroom use, particularly for students who prefer to approach history through art." Booklist

Schindler, Oskar, 1908-1974

★ Leyson, Leon, 1929-2013. The **boy** on the wooden box; Leon Leyson; with Marilyn J Harran and Elisabeth B Leyson. Atheneum Books for Young Readers 2013 240 p. (hardcover) $16.99

Grades: 6 7 8 9 92

1. Holocaust survivors 2. World War, 1939-1945 -- Jews -- Rescue 3. Narewka (Poland) -- Biography 4. Jews -- Poland -- Narewka -- Biography 5. Płaszów (Concentration camp) 6. Concentration camp inmates

-- Poland -- Płaszów -- Biography 7. Jewish children in the Holocaust -- Poland -- Kraków -- Biography 8. Holocaust, Jewish (1939-1945) -- Poland -- Kraków -- Personal narratives
ISBN 1442497815; 9781442497818; 9781442497832

LC 2013017987

In this book, "Leon Leyson (born Leib Lezjon) was only ten years old when the Nazis invaded Poland and his family was forced to relocate to the Krakow ghetto. With incredible luck, perseverance, and grit, Leyson was able to survive the sadism of the Nazis, including that of the demonic Amon Goeth, commandant of Plaszow, the concentration camp outside Krakow. Ultimately, it was the generosity and cunning of one man, a man named Oskar Schindler, who saved Leon Leyson's life, and the lives of his mother, his father, and two of his four siblings, by adding their names to his list of workers in his factory—a list that became world renowned: Schindler's List." (Publisher's Note)

"This powerful memoir of one of the youngest boys on Schindler's list deserves to be shared...This memoir is a natural curriculum addition to WWII units for upper-elementary- and middle-school readers. Be sure to have additional materials on hand about Oskar Schindler, as readers will want to do more research into Leyson's story." (Booklist)

Schultz, Philip, 1945-

★ Schultz, Philip. **My** dyslexia. W. W. Norton & Co. 2011 120p $21.95

Grades: 11 12 Adult 92

1. Poets 2. Authors 3. Dyslexia 4. Poets, American 5. College teachers
ISBN 978-0-393-07964-7

LC 2011015859

The author "tackles his struggle with dyslexia—a condition he only learned he had when his son was diagnosed. Schultz paints a precise and compelling picture of how his brain works, how he sees himself, and how he thinks others have seen him throughout his life. . . . His affecting prose will inspire compassion and leave readers with an understanding not only of dyslexia, but of the lifelong challenges that someone with disabilities may face." Publ Wkly

Schutz, Samantha, 1978-

Schutz, Samantha. **I** don't want to be crazy; a memoir of anxiety disorder. PUSH Books 2006 280p $16.99

Grades: 8 9 10 11 12 92

1. Anxiety 2. Panic disorders 3. Editors 4. Memoirists
ISBN 0-439-80518-X

LC 2005028964

"In this moving memoir, Schutz details her struggle with anxiety disorder. . . . Written in verse, this memoir successfully conveys what it is like to suffer from panic attacks." Voice Youth Advocates

Scott, Wendell, 1921-1990

Donovan, Brian. **Hard** driving: the Wendell Scott story; the odyssey of NASCAR'S first Black driver. Steerfort Press 2008 311p il hardcover o.p. pa $16.99

Grades: 11 12 Adult 92

1. Automobile racing 2. African American athletes 3.

Automobile racing drivers
ISBN 978-1-58642-144-1; 978-1-58642-160-1 pa
LC 2008-24287

For this biography, the author "interviewed Scott extensively over the last 14 months of his life. He also interviewed more than 200 other individuals, including Scott's widow and children. The result is the gripping story of a fascinating, brave man who deserves serious recognition for his solitary accomplishment. . . . A must-read for NASCAR fans." Booklist
Includes bibliographical references

Sediqi, Kamela, 1977-
Lemmon, Gayle Tzemach. The **dressmaker** of Khair Khana; five sisters, one remarkable family, and the woman who risked everything to keep them safe. Harper 2011 256p
Grades: 11 12 Adult   92
1. Dressmaking 2. Businesswomen 3. Taliban 4. Afghanistan 5. Dressmakers
ISBN 978-0-06-173237-9
LC 2010-20774

This book "is a fascinating window on Afghan life under the Taliban and a celebration of women the world over who support their loved ones with tenacity, inventiveness and sheer guts." People

Seeger, Pete
Wilkinson, Alec. The **protest** singer; an intimate portrait of Pete Seeger. Alfred A. Knopf 2009 151p il $22.95; pa $14
Grades: 11 12 Adult   92
1. Singers 2. Folk musicians 3. Songwriters
ISBN 978-0-307-26995-9; 978-0-307-39098-1 pa
LC 2008-54387

The author "draws on interviews with Seeger and others to present a seamless chronicle of his life and music, vivifying his passion for humanity, love of the environment, and deep curiosity about music." Libr J

Seuss, Dr.
Pease, Donald E. **Theodor** Seuss Geisel. Oxford University Press 2010 178p il
Grades: 11 12 Adult   92
1. Artists 2. Authors 3. Humorists 4. Illustrators 5. Authors, American 6. Children's authors 7. Biography, Individual
ISBN 9780195323023
LC 2009036478

This is a biography of the American writer and cartoonist. This "biography offers a succinct, thoroughly researched, and engaging introduction to one of children's literature's most influential creators." Booklist
Includes bibliographical references

Shakur, Tupac
Dyson, Michael Eric. **Holler** if you hear me: searching for Tupac Shakur. Basic Bks. 2001 292p il hardcover o.p. pa $15
Grades: 11 12 Adult   92
1. Poets 2. Actors 3. Hip-hop 4. Rap music 5.

African American musicians 6. Rap musicians
ISBN 0-465-01755-X; 0-465-01728-2 pa
LC 2001-36564

"Dyson's discussion goes beyond slogans and poses to the actualities of 'thug life' and the consequences of Shakur's passions and allegiances. Piquant and analytical." Booklist
Includes bibliographical references

Golus, Carrie. **Tupac** Shakur; hip-hop idol. Twenty-First Century Books 2010 112p il (USA Today: lifeline biographies) lib bdg $33.26
Grades: 7 8 9 10 11 12   92
1. Poets 2. Actors 3. Rap music 4. African American musicians 5. Rap musicians
ISBN 978-0-7613-5473-4; 0-7613-5473-5
LC 2009-38127

"The story told in Tupac Shakur will be inspirational for some and a cautionary tale for others. Born into poverty, Shakur became one of hip-hop's biggest stars. But even as he climbed up the ladder of success, drugs and violence were always there to pull him back down." Booklist
Includes bibliographical references

White, Armond. **Rebel** for the hell of it; the life of Tupac Shakur. [new foreword by S.H. Fernando] New ed.; Thunder's Mouth Press 2002 xxii, 230p il pa $14.95
Grades: 11 12 Adult   92
1. Poets 2. Actors 3. Hip-hop 4. Rap music 5. African American musicians 6. Rap musicians
ISBN 1-56025-461-0
First published 1997

In this biography of the rap musician and actor, "White outlines his stint as a dancer with the Digital Underground, his breakthrough second album, his three subsequent multiplatinum efforts, and his various roles in such movies as Juice and Poetic Justice. He also details the rapper's trouble with the law, his incarceration at Riker's Island prison, and his untimely death. . . . This will appeal mostly to fans of standard rock biography." Libr J
Includes discography and filmography

Shen, Fan, 1955-
Shen, Fan. **Gang** of one; memoirs of a Red Guard. University of Nebraska Press 2004 279p (American lives) $24.95; pa $15.95
Grades: 9 10 11 12   92
1. Authors 2. Memoirists 3. College teachers 4. Communism -- China 5. China -- History -- 1949-1976 -- Personal narratives
ISBN 0-8032-4308-1; 0-8032-9336-4 pa
LC 2003-17901

"Teens will strongly identify with Shen's maneuverings around repressive regulations." Booklist

Shepard, Sadia
Shepard, Sadia. The **girl** from foreign; a search for shipwrecked ancestors, forgotten histories, and a sense of home. Penguin Press 2008 364p il map $25.95; pa $16

Grades: 11 12 Adult   **92**
1. Memoirists 2. Jews -- India 3. Motion picture directors
ISBN 978-1-59420-151-6; 978-0-14-311577-9 pa
LC 2008-3912
A young Muslim-Christian woman travels to an insular Jewish community in India to unlock her family's secret history.
"A readable account that gives a vivid taste of life in present-day India as well as a poignant glimpse of complicated family relations." Kirkus
Includes bibliographical references

Sheppard, Ella, 1851-1914
Lowinger, Kathy. **Give** Me Wings; How a Choir of Former Slaves Took on the World. Kathy Lowinger. Firefly Books Ltd 2015 144 p. illustrations, portraits (hardcover) $21.95
Grades: 6 7 8 9   **92**
1. Freedmen 2. Choirs (Music)
ISBN 1554517478; 9781554517473
This book, by Kathy Lowinger, tells the story of Ella Sheppard, a former slave who "became a founding member of a traveling choir, the Jubilee Singers, to help raise funds for the Fisk Free Colored School, later known as Fisk University. The Jubilee Singers traveled from Cincinnati to New York, following the path of the Underground Railroad. With every performance they endangered their lives . . . , but they also broke down barriers between blacks and whites." (Publisher's note)

Sherman, William T. (William Tecumseh), 1820-1891
Woodworth, Steven E. **Sherman**; [foreword by Wesley K. Clark] Palgrave Macmillan 2009 198p il map (Great generals series) $21.95
Grades: 9 10 11 12 Adult   **92**
1. Generals 2. Memoirists 3. Secretaries of war 4. United States -- History -- 1861-1865, Civil War
ISBN 0-230-61024-2; 978-0-230-61024-8
LC 2008-22060
This is a biography of the Civil War general.
"An excellent brief life of a major and controversial figure." Booklist
Includes bibliographical references

Shivack, Nadia
Shivack, Nadia. **Inside** out; portrait of an eating disorder. written and illustrated by Nadia Shivack. Atheneum Books for Young Readers 2007 un il $17.99
Grades: 7 8 9 10 11 12   **92**
1. Graphic novels 2. Memoirists 3. Bulimia -- Graphic novels
ISBN 0-689-85216-9; 978-0-689-85216-9
LC 2004016096

Shockley, William, 1910-1989
Shurkin, Joel N. **Broken** genius; the rise and fall of William Shockley, creator of the Electronic Age. Macmillan 2006 378p

Grades: 11 12 Adult   **92**
ISBN 9781403988157; 1-403-98815-3
LC 2006041039
This is a biography of William Shockley, "the Nobel Prize winner widely credited with inventing the transistor [who is] more frequently remembered for his pseudo-scientific, racist views on IQ. . . . Shurkin portrays Shockley as a consummately driven man in all of his endeavors, who was, ultimately, driven to self-destruction." LJ

Shostakovich, Dmitrii Dmitrievich, 1906-1975
★ Anderson, M. T., 1968- **Symphony** for the city of the dead; Dmitri Shostakovich and the siege of Leningrad. M. T. Anderson. Candlewick Press 2015 464 p. illustrations $25.99
Grades: 9 10 11 12   **92**
1. Composers, Russian 2. Saint Petersburg (Russia) 3. World War, 1939-1945 -- Campaigns -- Soviet Union
ISBN 0763668184; 9780763668181
LC 2015936915
YALSA Award for Excellence in Nonfiction for Young Adults: Shortlist (2016)
Boston Globe Horn Book Nonfiction Honor Book (2016)
This book, by M. T. Anderson, "delivers a brilliant and riveting account of the Siege of Leningrad and the role played by Russian composer Shostakovich and his Leningrad Symphony. In September 1941, Adolf Hitler's Wehrmacht surrounded Leningrad. . . . Trapped between the Nazi invading force and the Soviet government itself was composer Dmitri Shostakovich, who would write a symphony that roused, rallied, eulogized, and commemorated his fellow citizens." (Publisher's note)
"This ambitious and gripping work is narrative nonfiction at its best. Anderson expertly sets the scene of the tumultuous world into which Dmitri Shostakovich was born in 1906 and traces his development as an artist and a public figure. He also tells the story of the composer's beloved Leningrad, focusing on the creation and legacy of the symphony written in its honor at the height of World War II. . . . Through it all, Anderson weaves the thread of the composer's music and the role it played in this larger-than-life drama. VERDICT A must-have title with broad crossover appeal." SLJ

Siana, Jolene
Siana, Jolene. **Go** ask Ogre; letters from a death-rock cutter. Process 2005 188p il pa $18.95
Grades: 11 12 Adult   **92**
1. Artists 2. Self-mutilation 3. Memoirists
ISBN 0-9760822-1-7; 978-0-9760822-1-7
"When she was 17, Siana wrote a series of letters to punk rocker Ogre, the front man of the '80s band Skinny Puppy. The letters speak of depression and cutting, drug abuse and sex, music and poetry. At one concert, Ogre told her that he saved all her letters and one day would return them. True to his word, two boxes arrived at her door nine years later; inside were illustrated letters and journals filled with her most intimate thoughts and fears. . . . Almost every page of the book is filled with heartbreaking artwork and photos, which brilliantly link the journal entries and letters together, allowing readers to get a look inside the mind of a very creative but disturbed young woman." SLJ

Simon, Rachel, 1959-

Simon, Rachel. **Riding** the bus with my sister; a true life journey. Plume 2003 296p pa $15

Grades: 11 12 Adult   92

1. Authors 2. Novelists 3. People with mental disabilities 4. College teachers 5. Short story writers
ISBN 0-452-28455-4

First published 2002 by Houghton Mifflin

"Clear writing and repeated conversations allow readers to hear the voices of both sisters. There is much to mull over, to enjoy, and to savor in this book." SLJ

Sitting Bull, Dakota Chief, 1831-1890

Stanley, George Edward. **Sitting** Bull; great Sioux hero. Sterling 2010 124p il map (Sterling biographies) lib bdg $12.95

Grades: 7 8 9 10   92

1. Dakota Indians 2. Indian chiefs 3. Native Americans -- Biography
ISBN 978-1-4027-6846-0 lib bdg; 1-4027-6846-X lib bdg

LC 2009-24141

This is a biography of the Sioux Indian chief.
Includes glossary and bibliographical references

Smith, Alison, 1968-

Smith, Alison. **Name** all the animals; a memoir. Scribner 2004 319p hardcover o.p. pa $13

Grades: 9 10 11 12   92

1. Authors 2. Memoirists
ISBN 0-7432-5522-4; 0-7432-5523-2 pa

LC 2003-60432

"When Smith was 15, her beloved older brother died suddenly. In a poignant, ultimately hopeful memoir that reads like fiction, Smith describes her own and her parents' journeys through grief and the thrill of a first love that was taboo in her religious community." Booklist

Smith, John, 1580-1631

Woodward, Grace Steele. **Pocahontas**. University of Okla. Press 1969 227p il (Civilization of the American Indian series) hardcover o.p. pa $17.95

Grades: 9 10 11 12   92

1. Farmers 2. Princesses 3. Powhatan Indians 4. Colonists 5. Indian chiefs 6. Indian leaders 7. Travel writers 8. Jamestown (Va.) -- History 9. Spouses of prominent persons 10. Native Americans -- Biography 11. United States -- History -- 1600-1775, Colonial period
ISBN 0-8061-1642-0 pa

This is the "story of the appealing daughter of Chief Powhatan and her friendship with the colonists of the Jamestown settlement. . . . Her marriage and brief life in England are vividly re-created." Booklist
Includes bibliographical references

Smith, Joseph, 1805-1844

★ Remini, Robert Vincent. **Joseph** Smith. Viking 2002 190p (Penguin lives series) $19.95

Grades: 11 12 Adult   92

1. Mormons 2. Mormon leaders
ISBN 0-670-03083-X

LC 2001-56762

"A masterful evenhanded précis that will engross history and religion readers alike." Booklist
Includes bibliographical references

Snyder, Kurt

Snyder, Kurt. **Me,** myself, and them; a first-hand account of one young person's experience with schizophrenia. with Raquel E. Gur, and Linda Wasmer Andrews. Oxford University Press 2007 164p il $30; pa $9.95

Grades: 9 10 11 12 Adult   92

1. Schizophrenia 2. Memoirists 3. Schizophrenics 4. Computer personnel 5. State government employees
ISBN 978-0-19-531123-5; 0-19-531123-X; 978-0-19-531122-8 pa; 0-19-531122-1 pa

LC 2007-16619

"Each chapter begins with Snyder's recollection of his difficulties, starting when he was eighteen, followed by detailed but extremely readable medical information. Many gray-scale sidebars share voices of other schizophrenics as well as history. . . . [Gur and Andrews] review medications, side effects, hospitalization, insurance issues, legal issues, diagnoses, symptoms, treatments, and related problems (substance abuse, depression, anxiety, etc.). Besides compelling thoroughness and readability, Snyder's story provides honesty and not a magic wand." Voice Youth Advocates
Includes bibliographical references

Stalin, Joseph, 1879-1953

★ Cunningham, Kevin. **Joseph** Stalin and the Soviet Union. M. Reynolds 2006 208p il map (World leaders) lib bdg $27.95

Grades: 9 10 11 12   92

1. Dictators 2. Heads of state 3. Communist leaders 4. Political leaders 5. Soviet Union -- History
ISBN 978-1-93179-894-5; 1-93179-894-X

LC 2005-32540

"This biography reviews the life of Soviet leader Joseph Stalin and the changes within the country during his long tenure. Although not ignoring his youth and his personal life, the discussion centers on his political leadership and its far-reaching effects. . . . This attractive volume offers a solid biography of Stalin." Booklist
Includes bibliographical references

Stanton, Elizabeth Cady, 1815-1902

Colman, Penny. **Elizabeth** Cady Stanton and Susan B. Anthony; a friendship that changed the world. Henry Holt and Company 2011 256p il $18.99

Grades: 7 8 9 10   92

1. Feminism 2. Suffragists 3. Women -- Suffrage
ISBN 978-0-8050-8293-7; 0-8050-8293-X

LC 2010-39762

"Elizabeth Cady Stanton, a married mother of four boys at the time they met, and Susan B. Anthony, an unmarried schoolteacher, formed a friendship that lasted until Elizabeth's death more than 50 years later. Their tireless work, including advocacy, speeches, organizing and writing, placed them at the center of tumultuous events in the middle of the 19th century. . . . This [is a] lively, very readable narrative. . . . This thoughtful portrayal to two complex women is . . . enhanced by comprehensive backmatter, making this an invaluable addition to the literature of suffrage." Kirkus

Includes bibliographical references

★ Ginzberg, Lori D. **Elizabeth** Cady Stanton; an American life. Hill and Wang 2009 254p il $25
Grades: 11 12 Adult   92
1. Feminism 2. Suffragists 3. Women -- Suffrage 4. Biography, Individual 5. Women -- Suffrage -- History
ISBN 0-8090-9493-2; 978-0-8090-9493-6
LC 2008-54395

This is a biography of the women's rights activist and author of Eighty Years and More (1898). Bibliography. Index.

The author "makes a convincing case for Stanton as the founding philosopher of the American women's rights movement in a lively voice that enhances her eccentric subject. . . . Ginzberg has created a vibrant portrait of a key, often misrepresented figure in American history." Am Hist

Includes bibliographical references

Steiner, Matt

Warren, Andrea. **Escape** from Saigon; how a Vietnam War orphan became an American boy. Farrar, Straus and Giroux 2004 110p il map hardcover o.p. pa $9.95
Grades: 6 7 8 9 10   92
1. Refugees 2. Physicians 3. Interracial adoption 4. Vietnamese Americans 5. Racially mixed people 6. Vietnam War, 1961-1975
ISBN 978-0-374-32224-3; 0-374-32224-4; 978-0-374-40023-1 pa; 0-374-40023-7 pa
LC 2003-60672

Chronicles the experiences of Matt Steiner, an orphaned Amerasian boy, from his birth and early childhood in Saigon through his departure from Vietnam in the 1975 Operation Babylift and his subsequent life as the adopted son of an American family in Ohio.

"The child-at-war story and the facts about the Operation Babylift rescue are tense and exciting. Just as gripping is the boy's personal conflict." Booklist

Stone, Toni, 1921-1996

Ackmann, Martha. **Curveball**; the remarkable story of Toni Stone, the first woman to play professional baseball in the Negro League. Lawrence Hill Books 2010 274p il $24.95
Grades: 11 12 Adult   92
1. Negro leagues 2. Baseball players 3. African American athletes 4. Baseball -- Biography
ISBN 978-1-55652-796-8
LC 2010-7019

This "book vividly details the trials and triumphs of this sports pioneer, a lifelong 'tomboy' who went on to play with the Indianapolis Clowns and the Kansas City Monarchs. . . . Ackmann has done a commendable job of celebrating the accomplishments of this forgotten gem. It's a grand slam." Jet

Includes bibliographical references

Stowe, Harriet Beecher, 1811-1896

Sonneborn, Liz. **Harriet** Beecher Stowe. Chelsea House Publishers 2009 120p il (Leaders of the Civil War era) lib bdg $30
Grades: 7 8 9 10   92
1. Authors 2. Novelists 3. Abolitionists 4. Authors, American 5. Children's authors 6. Nonfiction writers 7. Short story writers
ISBN 978-1-60413-302-8; 1-60413-302-3
LC 2008-44608

Biography of abolitionist and author, Harriet Beecher Stowe.

Includes glossary and bibliographical references

Stringer, Caverly

Stringer, Caverly. **Sleepaway** school; stories from a boy's life. [by] Lee Stringer. A Seven Stories Press 1st ed; Seven Stories Press 2004 227p $21.95; pa $13.95
Grades: 11 12 Adult   92
1. Authors 2. Homeless 3. Memoirists 4. African Americans -- Biography
ISBN 1-58322-478-5; 1-58322-701-6 pa
LC 2004-3610

The author "deftly tells a believable, candid and vivid tale of a person scarred by his past." Publ Wkly

Sui, Anna

Darraj, Susan Muaddi. **Anna** Sui. Chelsea House Publishers 2009 120p il (Asian Americans of achievement) $30
Grades: 7 8 9 10   92
1. Fashion designers
ISBN 978-1-60413-570-1; 1-60413-570-0
LC 2009-14608

"Anna Sui is known for her youthful 'baby doll' designs and extravagant combinations inspired by the hippie and rock-'n'-roll fashions of the '60s and early '70s. Readers learn about the setbacks and hard work required to become successful. . . . The quality of research and in-depth coverage broadens [the book's] usefulness. . . . [This book is] inspiring." SLJ

Includes glossary and bibliographical references

Swift, Jonathan, 1667-1745

★ Aykroyd, Clarissa. **Savage** satire; the story of Jonathan Swift. Morgan Reynolds Pub. 2006 160p il (World writers) lib bdg $27.95
Grades: 7 8 9 10   92
1. Poets 2. Clergy 3. Authors 4. Authors, Irish 5. Satirists 6. Pamphleteers 7. Writers on politics
ISBN 1-59935-027-0; 978-1-59935-027-1
LC 2006-18142

A biography of the Anglo-Irish writer who enjoyed shocking his readers.

"High-school students will find this a useful, informative introduction to the man's life, politics, and writings." Booklist

Includes bibliographical references

Tamm, Jayanti, 1970-

Tamm, Jayanti. **Cartwheels** in a sari; a memoir of growing up cult. Harmony Books 2009 288p $22.99

Grades: 11 12 Adult 92

1. Gurus 2. College teachers
ISBN 978-0-307-39392-0; 0-307-39392-5

LC 2008-36450

The author "recounts her youth as the chosen disciple of Sri Chinmoy, the wildly charismatic leader of a New York-based spiritual sect that counts celebrities and heads of nations among its millions of followers. . . . Witty, compassionate, and often heartbreaking, Tamm's story offers crucial insight into a cult's inner workings and methods of indoctrination. All readers, though, will recognize universal coming-of-age themes as Tamm discards unwanted childhood lessons and begins to shape an independent adult life." Booklist

Tammet, Daniel, 1979-

★ Tammet, Daniel. **Born** on a blue day; inside the extraordinary mind of an autistic savant: a memoir. Free Press 2007 226p il $24; pa $14

Grades: 11 12 Adult 92

1. Autism 2. Asperger's syndrome 3. Savants (Savant syndrome) 4. Mental calculators
ISBN 1-4165-3507-1; 978-1-4165-3507-2; 1-4165-4901-3 pa; 978-1-4165-4901-7 pa

LC 2006-41331

First published 2006 in the United Kingdom

This "autobiography is as fascinating as Benjamin Franklin's and John Stuart Mill's, both of which are, like his, about the growth of a mind." Booklist

Tan, Amy

Mussari, Mark. **Amy** Tan. Marshall Cavendish Benchmark 2010 125p il (Today's writers and their works) lib bdg $42.79

Grades: 8 9 10 11 12 92

1. Authors 2. Novelists 3. Women authors 4. Essayists 5. Authors, American 6. Children's authors 7. Short story writers 8. Chinese Americans -- Biography
ISBN 978-0-7614-4127-4; 0-7614-4127-1

This biography of Amy Tan places the author in the context of her times and discusses her work.

Includes bibliographical references

O'Keefe, Sherry. **From** China to America; the story of Amy Tan. Morgan Reynolds Pub. 2011 112p il lib bdg $28.95

Grades: 7 8 9 10 92

1. Authors 2. Novelists 3. Women authors 4. Essayists 5. Authors, American 6. Children's authors 7. Short story writers 8. Chinese Americans -- Biography
ISBN 978-1-59935-138-4; 1-59935-138-2

LC 2010-7594

"Born in California, the daughter of Chinese immigrants, Tan grew up as an American on the outside and Chinese on the inside. . . . Growing up, Tan faced the loss of her brother and father and the morbid outlook of her mother. Their tumultuous relationship led her to write stories about mother-and-daughter conflict, which later became the basis for The

Joy Luck Club. This book gives readers a brief overview of the novelist's life and a greater understanding of the inspiration behind her novels." SLJ

Includes bibliographical references

Tarbell, Ida M. (Ida Minerva), 1857-1944

McCully, Emily Arnold, 1939- **Ida** M. Tarbell; the woman who challenged big business--and won! by Emily Arnold McCully. Clarion Books/Houghton Mifflin Harcourt 2014 288 p. illustrations (hardcover) $18.99

Grades: 7 8 9 10 92

1. Women journalists 2. Journalists -- Biography 3. Journalists 4. Women -- Biography 5. Journalists -- United States -- Biography
ISBN 0547290926; 9780547290928

LC 2012039650

YALSA Award for Excellence in Nonfiction for Young Adults: Finalist (2015)

"Born in 1857 and raised in oil country, Ida M. Tarbell was one of the first investigative journalists and probably the most influential in her time. Her series of articles on the Standard Oil Trust, a complicated business empire run by John D. Rockefeller, revealed to readers the underhanded, even illegal practices that had led to Rockefeller's success." (Publisher's note)

"McCully expertly brings to life the story of a unique and determined woman in this well-written and thoroughly researched biography, filled with numerous and pertinent photographs." SLJ

Includes bibliographical references and index

Taylor, Major, 1878-1932

Balf, Todd. **Major**; a Black athlete, a White era, and the fight to be the world's fastest human being. Crown Publishers 2008 306p il $24; pa $13.95

Grades: Adult 92

1. Bicycle racing 2. African American athletes 3. Cyclists
ISBN 978-0-307-23658-6; 0-307-23658-7; 978-0-307-23659-3 pa; 0-307-23659-5 pa

LC 2007-20747

The author "chronicles the life of the unlikeliest of stars in the early years of cycling: Marshall 'Major' Taylor. Taylor was an incomparable athlete, poet and celebrity, but he was also a black man living during a time when the scars of the Civil War and slavery were still fresh in the minds of Americans. Balf . . . does great work presenting the complex nature of Taylor's life, including his upbringing in poverty in Indianapolis, the years he was treated as a son by a rich white family, the fans who both worshipped and vilified him and his close relationships with his white trainer and promoter." Publ Wkly

Includes bibliographical references

Tecumseh, Shawnee Chief, 1768-1813

Zimmerman, Dwight Jon. **Tecumseh**; shooting star of the Shawnee. Sterling 2010 124p il map (Sterling biographies) lib bdg $12.95

Grades: 7 8 9 10 92

1. Shawnee Indians 2. Indian chiefs 3. Native

Americans -- Biography
ISBN 978-1-4027-6847-7; 1-4027-6847-8

LC 2009-24142

"Lots of detailed physical battles dominate Tecumseh, with a strong focus on the Shawnee's brutal displacement by white settlers and the Indians caught up in the tensions between the U.S. and Great Britain. . . . [The] spacious design is highly scannable, with color background screens, photos, maps, and historic prints throughout." Booklist

Includes glossary and bibliographical references

Telfair, Sebastian, 1985-

O'Connor, Ian. The **jump**; Sebastian Telfair and the high stakes business of high school ball. Rodale 2005 307p il $23.95; pa $13.95

Grades: 11 12 Adult   **92**
1. Basketball players 2. Basketball -- Biography
ISBN 1-59486-107-2; 1-59486-447-0 pa

LC 2004-26366

In this biography of the up-and-coming basketball player, the author "chronicles Telfair's senior year at Brooklyn's Lincoln High. . . . This will be the most discussed book of the NBA season." Booklist

Teresa, Mother, 1910-1997

Slavicek, Louise Chipley. **Mother** Teresa; caring for the world's poor. Chelsea House 2007 113p bibl il por lib bdg $30

Grades: 7 8 9 10   **92**
1. Nuns 2. Missionaries 3. Nobel laureates for peace
ISBN 0-7910-9433-2 lib bdg; 978-0-7910-9433-4 lib bdg

LC 2006028383

This "book is well organized and well written, and reads like a story. It is balanced in that it points out the critics of Mother Teresa's selection for the Nobel Peace Prize . . . . as well as her admirers." SLJ

Spink, Kathryn. **Mother** Teresa; a complete authorized biography. by Kathryn Spink. HarperOne 2011 336 p. ill. $15.99

Grades: 9 10 11 12 Adult   **92**
1. Nuns 2. Nobel Prizes 3. Missions -- India 4. Christian missionaries 5. Biography, Individual 6. Missionaries of Charity
ISBN 0062026143; 9780062026149

LC 2011001621

"Spink's biography benefits from her own 18-year involvement with the work of the Missionaries of Charity Order as well as from the intimate relationship she developed over the years with Mother Teresa. . . . A final chapter in the book provides glimpses of Mother Teresa's affection for Princess Diana, a brief description of Mother Teresa's funeral and a short account of the election of Sister Nirmal as her successor." (Publ Wkly)

Tesla, Nikola, 1856-1943

Burgan, Michael. **Nikola** Tesla; physicist, inventor, electrical engineer. Compass Point Books 2009 112p il map (Signature lives) lib bdg $34.65

Grades: 6 7 8 9 10   **92**
1. Inventors 2. Electrical engineers
ISBN 978-0-7565-4086-9; 0-7565-4086-0

LC 2008-35725

A biography of Nikola Tesla, physicist, inventor, and electrical engineer

The "inviting page design features photos and boxed screens on each spread, and . . . includes a detailed bibliography, source notes, time line and glossary." Booklist

Includes glossary and bibliographical references

Carlson, W. Bernard. **Tesla**; inventor of the electrical age. W. Bernard Carlson. Princeton University Press 2013 xiii, 500 p.p ill. (hardcover) $29.95

Grades: 11 12 Adult   **92**
1. Electricity -- History 2. Inventors -- United States -- Biography 3. Electrical engineers -- United States -- Biography
ISBN 0691057761; 9780691057767

LC 2012049608

This book, by W. Bernard Carlson, presents a biography of the inventor Nikola Tesla, "a major contributor to the electrical revolution . . . at the turn of the twentieth century. His inventions, patents, and theoretical work formed the basis of modern AC electricity, and contributed to the development of radio and television. . . . An astute self-promoter and gifted showman, he cultivated a public image of the eccentric genius." (Publisher's note)

"Carlson provides not only a more detailed explanation of Tesla's science but also a . . . focused psychological account of Tesla's inventive process." Booklist

Includes bibliographical references and index

Thomas, Aquinas, Saint, 1225?-1274

Strathern, Paul. **Thomas** Aquinas in 90 minutes. Ivan R. Dee 1998 90p (Philosophers in 90 Minutes) $14.95; pa $7.95

Grades: 9 10 11 12   **92**
1. Saints 2. Theologians 3. Philosophers
ISBN 1-56663-193-9; 1-56663-194-7 pa

LC 98-13264

The author offers an "account of Aquinas' life and ideas, and explains their influence on man's struggle to understand his existence in the world. The book also includes selections from Aquinas' writings; a brief list of suggested reading for those who wish to push further; and chronologies that place Aquinas within his own age and in the broader scheme of philosophy." Publisher's note

Includes bibliographical references

Thoreau, Henry David, 1817-1862

★ Sullivan, Robert. The **Thoreau** you don't know; what the prophet of environmentalism really meant. Collins 2009 354p $25.99

Grades: 11 12 Adult   **92**
1. Authors 2. Naturalists 3. Essayists 4. Pacifists 5. Authors, American 6. Writers on nature 7. Nonfiction writers
ISBN 978-0-06-171031-5; 0-06-171031-8

LC 2008-34495

The author "endeavors to free Henry David Thoreau from his calcified reputation as a cantankerous hermit and nature worshipper. Sounding like your favorite teacher who manages to make history fun and relevant, Sullivan vibrantly portrays the sage of Walden as a geeky, curious, compassionate fellow of high intelligence and deep feelings who loved company, music, and long walks." Booklist

Thorpe, Jim, 1888-1953

Crawford, Bill. **All** American; the rise and fall of Jim Thorpe. John Wiley & Sons, Inc 2004 284p il $24.95

Grades: 11 12 Adult   **92**
1. Athletes 2. Decathletes 3. Pentathletes 4. Olympic athletes 5. Native Americans -- Biography
ISBN 0-471-55732-3
             LC 2004-14376

This "terse, punchy biography of sports legend Thorpe (1888–1953) illuminates the current debate over the exploitation of unpaid college athletes by moneymaking, headline-grabbing educational institutions." Publ Wkly

Includes bibliographical references

Thrash, Maggie

★ Thrash, Maggie. **Honor** girl; a graphic memoir. Maggie Thrash. Candlewick Press 2015 272 p. color illustrations (hardcover) $19.99

Grades: 9 10 11 12   **92**
1. Camps 2. Lesbians 3. Teenage girls
ISBN 076367382X; 9780763673826
             LC 2014951805

LA Times Book Prize Finalist: Graphic Novel/Comics (2015)

This graphic memoir, by Maggie Thrash, relates how the author "has spent basically every summer of her fifteen-year-old life at the one-hundred-year-old Camp Bellflower for Girls, set deep in the heart of Appalachia. . . . A split-second of innocent physical contact pulls Maggie into a gut-twisting love for a . . . female counselor named Erin. But Camp Bellflower is an impossible place for a girl to fall in love with another girl." (Publisher's note)

"Thrash finds both heartwarming support from her friends and smarmy disapproval from adults in the southern camp, and although she doesn't deny her burgeoning feelings, her revelation doesn't result in easy confidence, either. Though the understated artwork might not appeal to all readers, this honest, raw, and touching graphic memoir will resonate with teens coming to terms with identities of all stripes." Booklist

Tillage, Leon, 1936-

Tillage, Leon. **Leon's** story; [by] Leon Walter Tillage; collage art by Susan L. Roth. Farrar, Straus & Giroux 1997 107p il hardcover o.p. pa $6.95

Grades: 4 5 6 7 8 9 10   **92**
1. African Americans -- Biography 2. North Carolina -- Race relations
ISBN 0-374-34379-9; 0-374-44330-0 pa
             LC 96-43544

The son of a North Carolina sharecropper recalls the hard times faced by his family and other African Americans in the first half of the twentieth century and the changes that the civil rights movement helped bring about

Traig, Jennifer

Traig, Jennifer. **Devil** in the details; scenes from an obsessive girlhood. Little, Brown 2004 246p il hardcover o.p. pa $14.99

Grades: 9 10 11 12   **92**
1. Authors 2. Obsessive-compulsive disorder 3. Memoirists
ISBN 0-316-15877-1; 0-316-01074-X pa
             LC 2004-1417

The author's "efforts to adhere, in a vacuum, to Jewish law, are particularly amusing. She also writes affectionately about her long-suffering family members, who are funny enough to stage their own sitcom. In the end, she succeeds in overcoming her illness, providing a provocative yet entertaining memoir in the process." Libr J

Transue, Emily R.

Transue, Emily R. **On** call; a doctor's days and nights in residency. St. Martin's Press 2004 242p hardcover o.p. pa $13.95

Grades: 9 10 11 12   **92**
1. Physicians 2. Internists 3. Memoirists 4. College teachers
ISBN 0-312-32483-9; 0-312-32484-7 pa
             LC 2004-46893

"During her three years as a resident in internal medicine at the University of Washington in Seattle, Transue wrote about her patients as a way to guard against burnout and share her experiences with friends and family. This [is a] moving collection of her stories. . . . Her descriptions of medical procedures can be graphic, but she presents an intriguing picture of a side of medicine many people never see." Publ Wkly

Trebing, Katie, 2002-

Whitehouse, Beth. The **match**; savior siblings and one family's battle to heal their daughter. Beacon Press 2010 255p $24.95; pa $16

Grades: 11 12 Adult   **92**
1. Sick 2. Fertilization in vitro 3. Procurement of organs, tissues, etc. 4. Bone marrow -- Transplantation
ISBN 978-0-8070-7286-8; 0-8070-7286-9; 978-0-8070-0121-9 pa; 0-8070-0121-X pa
             LC 2009035949

The author "tracks Stacy and Steve Trebing and their decision to create a baby boy selected as an embryo as a genetic match for a sister suffering from Diamond-Blackfan anemia, a rare and fatal disease." Publ Wkly

Truman, Harry S., 1884-1972

Dallek, Robert. **Harry** S. Truman; Robert Dallek. Times Books 2008 xviii, 183p.p $22

Grades: 11 12 Adult   **92**
1. Presidents 2. Vice-presidents 3. Senators 4.

Presidents -- United States
ISBN 978-0-8050-6938-9

LC 2008-10193

This book is "the best starting point for knowledge of Truman's life and for an astute assessment of his career." Publ Wkly

Donald, Aida D. **Citizen** soldier; a life of Harry S. Truman. Aida D. Donald. Basic Books 2012 xvi, 265 p.p (hardcover: alk. paper) $26.99
Grades: 9 10 11 12 Adult   92
1. Soldiers -- United States -- Biography 2. Presidents -- United States -- Biography 3. United States -- Politics and government -- 1945-1953
ISBN 046503120X; 9780465031207

LC 2012025583

This book by Aida D. Donald is a biography of former U.S. President Harry S. Truman. "When Franklin Roosevelt passed away in April 1945, Truman unexpectedly found himself at the helm of the American war effort--and in command of the atomic bomb, the most lethal weapon humanity had ever seen. Truman's decisive leadership during the remainder of World War II and the period that followed reshaped American politics, economics, and foreign relations." (Publisher's note)

Includes bibliographical references and index

Tubman, Harriet, 1820?-1913

Malaspina, Ann. **Harriet** Tubman. Chelsea House 2009 120p il (Leaders of the Civil War era) lib bdg $30
Grades: 7 8 9 10   92
1. Abolitionists 2. Underground railroad 3. African American women -- Biography
ISBN 978-1-60413-303-5; 1-60413-303-1

LC 2008-42412

Biography of Harriet Tubman, former slave and a "conductor" on the Underground Railroad.

Includes glossary and bibliographical references

Turing, Alan Mathison, 1912-1954

Corrigan, Jim. **Alan** Turing. Morgan Reynolds Pub. 2008 112p il (Profiles in mathematics) lib bdg $27.95
Grades: 7 8 9 10   92
1. Mathematicians
ISBN 978-1-59935-064-6; 1-59935-064-5

LC 2007-11704

"Corrigan's descriptions of English mathematician Turing as sporting 'ragged, wrinkled clothes' and few social graces will fit many readers' mental image of a numbers genius. But other aspects of this portrait push against stereotypes. . . . Throughout, candid mentions of Turing's homosexuality help readers contextualize the scandal he endured after running afoul of the era's discriminatory legislation. Equal sensitivity distinguishes Corringan's handling of Turing's death, officially (but not decisively) a suicide." Booklist

Includes bibliographical references

★ Henderson, Harry. **Alan** Turing; computing genius and wartime code breaker. Chelsea House 2011 133p il (Makers of modern science) $35
Grades: 7 8 9 10   92
1. Mathematicians
ISBN 978-0-8160-6175-4; 0-8160-6175-0

LC 2010-15798

A biography of code breaker and computer pioneer Alan Turing.

"The mark of a good biography is when it makes people you may never have heard of, in fields you might not be interested in, fascinating. [This book] does this with [a] well-chosen [subject], engaging writing, plenty of sidebars that take the text in new directions, and perhaps most importantly, the determination to present a fully-rounded person, not just a scientist." Booklist

Includes bibliographical references

The **Imitation** Game; Alan Turing Decoded. Jim Ottaviani; illustrated by Leland Purvis. Harry N Abrams Inc 2016 240 p. chiefly illustrations $24.95
Grades: 9 10 11 12 Adult   92
1. Biographical graphic novels 2. Mathematicians -- Biography 3. Turing, Alan Mathison, 1912-1954
ISBN 1419718932; 9781419718939

This book, by Jim Ottaviani and illustrated by Leland Purvis, "present[s] a historically accurate graphic novel biography of English mathematician and scientist Alan Turing. [It covers] Turing's life and groundbreaking research--as an unconventional genius who was arrested, tried, convicted, and punished for being openly gay, and whose innovative work still fuels the computing and communication systems that define our modern world." (Publisher's note)

Turner, Nat, 1800?-1831

Baker, Kyle. **Nat** Turner. Abrams 2008 207p il pa $14.95
Grades: 10 11 12 Adult   92
1. Slaves 2. Graphic novels 3. Biographical graphic novels 4. Revolutionaries 5. Slavery -- Graphic novels
ISBN 978-0-8109-9535-2; 0-8109-9535-2

LC 2008-6911

Originally published 2006 in four volumes

This book "follows the dark legacy of the Virginia slave rebellion and subsequent murders of at least 55 white slave owners and their families in 1831. . . . Turner is presented as a fiercely intelligent, angry, yet steadfast individual whose potential was dashed in an era of hate and inhumanity. Those characteristics are mirrored in the actions of the slaves' rebellion, in illustrations that are not for the faint of heart or the weak of stomach. The ideas brought forth here are sure to ignite debate and discussion." SLJ

Includes bibliographical references

Baker, Kyle. **Nat** Turner Vol. 2: revolution. Image Comics 2006 96p il pa $10
Grades: 10 11 12 Adult   92
1. Slaves 2. Graphic novels 3. Biographical graphic novels 4. Revolutionaries 5. Slavery -- Graphic novels
ISBN 978-1-58240-792-0
Sequel to Nat Turner Encore Edition Vol. 1 (2006)

Originally published as Nat Turner issues #3 and 4 by Kyle Baker Publishing

In this concluding volume, excerpts from The Confessions of Nat Turner alternate with wordless panels to depict the series of murders carried out by Turner and his followers as they tried to start a slave revolution based on Turner's vision. He is eventually captured and hanged. Baker doesn't editorialize with narration, instead he allows readers to draw their own conclusions about Turner and the society against which he rebelled. Some of the images will be disturbing because of the brutal acts they depict.

Twain, Mark, 1835-1910

Caravantes, Peggy. A **great** and sublime fool; the story of Mark Twain. Morgan Reynolds Pub. 2009 176p il map (World writers) lib bdg $28.95
Grades: 7 8 9 10   **92**
  1. Authors 2. Humorists 3. Novelists 4. Essayists 5. Satirists 6. Memoirists 7. Travel writers 8. Authors, American 9. Short story writers
ISBN 978-1-599-35088-2; 1-599-35088-2
                         LC 2008-34139
This "offers a workmanlike but readable account of one of America's first great writers. . . . A nice selection of photographs and artwork complement the narrative. . . . Detailed source notes and an in-depth time line round out this even and reliable . . . biography." Booklist
Includes bibliographical references

Sonneborn, Liz. **Mark** Twain; foreword by Kyle Zimmer. Chelsea House Publishers 2010 125p il (Who wrote that?) lib bdg $35
Grades: 6 7 8 9 10   **92**
  1. Authors 2. Humorists 3. Novelists 4. Essayists 5. Satirists 6. Memoirists 7. Travel writers 8. Authors, American 9. Short story writers
ISBN 978-1-60413-728-6; 1-60413-728-2
                         LC 2010006601
This biography of Mark Twain "begins with the writer's memorable visit to his Missouri hometown in 1902, then tracks back to his early days and his well-known transformation from Sam Clemens to Mark Twain. Sonneborn deals with her material well, hitting all the highlights and keeping the narrative moving along. Good use of details adds interest. . . . A solid purchase." SLJ
Includes bibliographical references

Typhoid Mary, 1869-1938

Bartoletti, Susan Campbell. **Terrible** typhoid Mary; the most harmless and yet most dangerous woman in America: a true story of the deadliest cook in America. by Susan Campbell Bartoletti. Houghton Mifflin Harcourt 2015 240 p. illustrations $17.99
Grades: 6 7 8 9 10   **92**
  1. Typhoid fever 2. Communicable diseases 3. Cooks -- New York (State) -- New York -- Biography
ISBN 0544313674; 9780544313675
                         LC 2014023057
This biography of Mary Mallon, by Susan Campbell Bartoletti, "looks beyond the tabloid scandal of Mary's controversial life. How she was treated by medical and legal officials reveals a lesser-known story of human and consti-

tutional rights, entangled with the science of pathology and enduring questions about who Mary Mallon really was. How did her name become synonymous with deadly disease? And who is really responsible for the lasting legacy of Typhoid Mary?" (Publisher's note)

"This well-researched biography of Mary Mallon, also known as Typhoid Mary, begins in 1906, when Mallon was hired as a cook for a wealthy family vacationing in Oyster Bay, Long Island. The outbreak of typhoid that swept through the household a few weeks later turned out to be a pivotal event that forever changed her life. . . . Middle grade biography lovers will gravitate toward this compelling title." SLJ
Includes bibliographical references

Tyson, Neil deGrasse

Neil deGrasse **Tyson**; Jennifer Culp. Rosen Publishing 2015 112 p. illustrations (some color) (library bound) $35.60
Grades: 10 11 12   **92**
  1. Astrophysics 2. African American scientists 3. Universe 4. Astronautics -- United States
ISBN 1477776915; 9781477776919
                         LC 2013043307
This book by author Jennifer Culp profiles astrophysicist Neil deGrasse Tyson. "Quotes from Neil deGrasse Tyson's writing are scattered throughout his biography, helping students connect to his voice. Readers will be swept away by his journey as an African American astrophysicist who first stargazed atop a Bronx apartment building and later walked dogs to earn money for a telescope. Throughout his biography, Tyson's passion for space exploration is palpable." (School Library Journal)
Includes bibliographical references (pages 104-107) and index

Umrigar, Thrity N.

Umrigar, Thrity N. **First** darling of the morning; selected memories of an Indian childhood. Harper Perennial 2008 294, 18p pa $14.95
Grades: 11 12 Adult   **92**
  1. Authors 2. Novelists 3. Journalists 4. Essayists 5. Bombay (India) 6. Literary critics 7. Authors, American
ISBN 978-0-06-145161-4; 0-06-145161-4
First published 2004 in India
In this memoir, the author "alternates between sweet and biting accounts of her middle-class Parsi upbringing in 1960s and 1970s Bombay. With a mixture of rawness and warmth, she recalls moments from her tumultuous childhood through her teenage years, and finally into her early 20s when she leaves India for the U.S. . . . Umrigar's memoir is colorful and moving." Publ Wkly

Underwood, Rosamond

Wickenden, Dorothy. **Nothing** daunted; the unexpected education of two society girls in the West. Scribner 2011 286p il $26; ebook $12.99
Grades: 11 12 Adult   **92**
  1. Teachers 2. Women teachers 3. Colorado 4.

Socialites 5. Biography, Individual
ISBN 978-1-4391-7658-0; 978-1-4391-7660-3 ebook
LC 2011-08949
"On July 24, 1916, the Syracuse Daily Journal printed the headline: 'Society Girls Go to Wilds of Colorado.' The two young women were Dorothy Woodruff and Rosamond Underwood, recent graduates of Smith College who, in order to defy their family's expectation of marriage, sought work in the small town of Hayden, Colo. Woodruff was the grandmother of . . . [the author], who herself becomes a central character in an informative and engaging narrative. Using letters from her grandmother, newspaper articles, and interviews with descendants, Wickenden retells how Woodruff and Underwood traveled to the newly settled state of Colorado to teach at a ramshackle grade school." Publ Wkly
Includes bibliographical references

Ung, Chou

Ung, Loung. **Lucky** child; a daughter of Cambodia reunites with the sister she left behind. HarperCollins Publishers 2005 268p il $24.95; pa $13.95
Grades: 11 12 Adult   92
1. Homemakers 2. Cambodian Americans 3. Memoirists 4. Social activists 5. Cambodia -- History -- 1975-
ISBN 0-06-073394-2; 0-06-073395-0 pa
LC 2004-54346
Sequel to First they killed my father
In this "memoir, Ung picks up where her first . . . left off, with the author escaping a devastated Cambodia in 1980 at age 10 and flying to her new home in Vermont. . . . She and her eldest brother, with whom she escaped, left behind their three other siblings. This book is alternately heart-wrenching and heartwarming, as it follows the parallel lives of Loung Ung and her closest sister, Chou, during the 15 years it took for them to reunite." Publ Wkly
Includes bibliographical references

Ung, Loung, 1970-

Ung, Loung. **Lucky** child; a daughter of Cambodia reunites with the sister she left behind. HarperCollins Publishers 2005 268p il $24.95; pa $13.95
Grades: 11 12 Adult   92
1. Homemakers 2. Cambodian Americans 3. Memoirists 4. Social activists 5. Cambodia -- History -- 1975-
ISBN 0-06-073394-2; 0-06-073395-0 pa
LC 2004-54346
Sequel to First they killed my father
In this "memoir, Ung picks up where her first . . . left off, with the author escaping a devastated Cambodia in 1980 at age 10 and flying to her new home in Vermont. . . . She and her eldest brother, with whom she escaped, left behind their three other siblings. This book is alternately heart-wrenching and heartwarming, as it follows the parallel lives of Loung Ung and her closest sister, Chou, during the 15 years it took for them to reunite." Publ Wkly
Includes bibliographical references

Unger, Zac

Unger, Zac. **Working** fire; the making of an accidental fireman. Penguin Press 2004 262p hardcover o.p. pa $15
Grades: 11 12 Adult   92
1. Firefighters 2. Fire fighters -- Biography
ISBN 1-59420-001-7; 0-14-303495-2 pa
LC 2003-50676
"A young rookie provides a look behind the firehouse doors, bringing close the danger, excitement, and challenge of fighting fire in a big city." Booklist

Valentino

Reis, Ronald A. **Valentino.** Chelsea House 2011 119p il (Famous fashion designers) lib bdg $35
Grades: 6 7 8 9 10   92
1. Fashion designers
ISBN 978-1-60413-983-9; 1-60413-983-8
LC 2010034101
This is a biography of fashion designer Valentino.
Includes glossary and bibliographical references

Van Buren, Martin, 1782-1862

Widmer, Edward L. **Martin** Van Buren; [by] Ted Widmer. Times Bks. 2005 189p (American presidents series) $20
Grades: 11 12 Adult   92
1. Presidents 2. Vice-presidents 3. Secretaries of state 4. Presidents -- United States
ISBN 0-8050-6922-4
LC 2004-53652
The author "keenly evokes the environment that enabled Van Buren to thrive. . . . Widmer also lends a certain dignity to Van Buren's post-presidential attempts to resolve the sectional crisis." N Y Times Book Rev
Includes bibliographical references

Vasishta, Madan, 1941-

Vasishta, Madan. **Deaf** in Delhi; a memoir. Gallaudet University Press 2006 220p il (Deaf lives) pa $29.95
Grades: 11 12 Adult   92
1. Deaf 2. Memoirists 3. Delhi (India) 4. Teachers of the deaf 5. College administrators 6. School superintendents
ISBN 1-56368-284-2; 978-1-56368-284-1
LC 2005-55214
"A bout with mumps and typhoid left 11-year-old Vasishta deaf. In an India where the word for deaf in at least three languages means someone less than human, there was not much hope for his future. . . . The author weaves stories, set in the India of the 1950s and early '60s, of the holy men to whom his family turned for a cure for him, of his arranged marriage, and of the class system. . . . This book is a must for collections accessed by deaf teens, and it will appeal to young adults interested in Indian culture, multicultural studies, or disabilities." SLJ
Includes bibliographical references

Versace, Gianni, 1946-1997

Davis, Daniel K. **Versace**. Chelsea House 2011 116p il (Famous fashion designers) lib bdg $35

Grades: 6 7 8 9 10   92

1. Fashion designers

ISBN 978-1-60413-980-8; 1-60413-980-3

LC 2010034103

This is a biography of fashion designer Gianni Versace. "Biography collections in need of a bit of sprucing up should find [this title] helpful." SLJ

Includes glossary and bibliographical references

Volpe, Lou

Sokolove, Michael. **Drama** high; the incredible true story of a brilliant teacher, a struggling town, and the magic of theater. by Michael Sokolove. Riverhead Hardcover 2013 352 p. ill (hardback) $27.95

Grades: 9 10 11 12 Adult   92

1. College and school drama 2. Performing arts -- Study and teaching 3. English teachers -- Pennsylvania -- Levittown -- Biography 4. High school teachers -- Pennsylvania -- Levittown -- Biography 5. Theater -- Producers and directors -- Pennsylvania -- Levittown -- Biography

ISBN 1594488223; 9781594488221

LC 2013019393

In this book, author Michael Sokolove "chronicles the [Harry S Truman High School] drama director [Lou Volpe's] last school years and follows a group of student actors as they work through riveting dramas both on and off the stage. This is a story of an economically depressed but proud town finding hope in a gifted teacher and the magic of theater." (Publisher's note)

"During the season Sokolove spends at Truman, Volpe and his kids put on the play Good Boys and True and the musical Spring Awakening—both of which address teen sexuality, angst, and reckless behavior. Volpe pushes his student actors hard, but for most of them, being in one of his productions is transformative. Many alums go on to pursue careers in theater or the arts. A powerful look at the way a dynamic and dedicated teacher can change lives." (Booklist)

Von Braun, Wernher, 1912-1977

★ Spangenburg, Ray. **Wernher** von Braun; rocket visionary. [by] Ray Spangenburg and Diane Kit Moser. Rev ed; Chelsea House 2008 164p il (Makers of modern science) $29.95

Grades: 9 10 11 12   92

1. Rocketry 2. Scientists 3. Aerospace engineers 4. NASA officials

ISBN 978-0-8160-6179-2; 0-8160-6179-3

LC 2007-52220

First published 1995

This book "examines the life and career of the famed rocket scientist who supervised the development of the powerful rockets used by Apollo astronauts to reach the moon." Publisher's note

Includes glossary and bibliographical references

Walls, Jeannette

★ Walls, Jeannette. The **glass** castle; a memoir. Scribner 2005 288p $25; pa $14

Grades: 11 12 Adult   92

1. Authors 2. Novelists 3. Memoirists 4. Gossip columnists

ISBN 0-7432-4753-1; 0-7432-4754-X pa

LC 2004-58907

"Shocking, sad, and occasionally bitter, this gracefully written account speaks candidly, yet with surprising affection, about parents and about the strength of family ties—for both good and ill." Booklist

Warhol, Andy, 1928?-1987

★ Greenberg, Jan. **Andy** Warhol; prince of pop. [by] Jan Greenberg & Sandra Jordan. Delacorte Press 2004 193p il hardcover o.p. pa $6.99

Grades: 7 8 9 10   92

1. Artists 2. Pop art 3. Artists -- United States 4. Motion picture directors

ISBN 0-385-73056-X; 0-385-73275-9 pa

LC 2003-24102

A biography of the 20th century American artist famous for his Pop art images of Campbell's soup cans and Marilyn Monroe.

"Greenberg and Jordan offer a riveting biography that humanizes their controversial subject without making judgments or sensationalizing." Booklist

Includes glossary and bibliographical references

Wasdin, Howard E.

★ Wasdin, Howard E. **I** am a SEAL Team Six warrior; memoirs of an American soldier. Howard E. Wasdin and Stephen Templin. 1st ed. St. Martin's Griffin 2012 vi, 182 p.p ill. (paperback) $7.99

Grades: 8 9 10 11 12   92

1. Snipers -- United States -- Biography 2. United States. Navy. SEALs -- Biography 3. United States. Navy -- Commando troops -- Biography

ISBN 1250016436; 9781250016430

LC 2012376658

This book offers an "[a]bridged, . . . young-readers version of an ex-SEAL sniper's account ('SEAL Team Six,' 2011) of his training and combat experiences in Operation Desert Storm and the first Battle of Mogadishu. . . . In later chapters he retraces his long, difficult physical and emotional recovery from serious wounds received during the 'Black Hawk Down' operation, his increasing focus on faith and family after divorce and remarriage and his second career as a chiropractor." (Kirkus Reviews)

Includes bibliographical references (p. [181]-182).

Washington, Booker T., 1856-1915

Smock, Raymond W. **Booker** T. Washington; black leadership in the age of Jim Crow. [by] Raymond W. Smock. Ivan R. Dee 2009 223p il (Library of African-American biography) $26

Grades: 11 12 Adult   92

1. Slaves 2. Authors 3. Educators 4. African American educators 5. Memoirists 6. Nonfiction writers 7. Tuskegee Institute 8. Civil rights activists 9. African

Americans -- Biography
ISBN 978-1-56663-725-1; 1-56663-725-2

LC 2009-3277

The author "examines Washington's legacy and how he came to be alternately lauded and lambasted for his practical approach to racism following Reconstruction: to build a school to prepare blacks to occupy the unchallenged place set aside for them in the Jim Crow South. . . . This is a nuanced portrait of an enigmatic man of enduring contribution to black leadership." Booklist

Includes bibliographical references

★ Washington, Booker T. **Up** from slavery; edited with an introduction and notes by William L. Andrews. Oxford University Press 2008 xxvii, 196p (Oxford world's classics) pa $9.95

Grades: 7 8 9 10 11 12 Adult　　　**92**

1. Slaves 2. Authors 3. Educators 4. African American educators 5. Memoirists 6. Nonfiction writers 7. Tuskegee Institute 8. Civil rights activists 9. African Americans -- Biography
ISBN 978-0-19-955239-9

LC 2008-279129

First published 1901

"The classic autobiography of the man who, though born in slavery, educated himself and went on to found Tuskegee Institute." N Y Public Libr

Includes bibliographical references

Washington, George, 1732-1799

★ Ellis, Joseph J. **His** Excellency; George Washington. Knopf 2004 320p il hardcover o.p. pa $15

Grades: 11 12 Adult　　　**92**

1. Generals 2. Presidents 3. Presidents -- United States
ISBN 1-4000-4031-0; 1-4000-3253-9 pa

LC 2004-46576

The author "offers a magisterial account of the life and times of George Washington, celebrating the heroic image of the president whom peers like Jefferson and Madison recognized as 'their unquestioned superior' while acknowledging his all-too-human qualities." Publ Wkly

Includes bibliographical references

Johnson, Paul. **George** Washington: the Founding Father. HarperCollins Publishers 2005 126p (Eminent lives) $19.95

Grades: 11 12 Adult　　　**92**

1. Generals 2. Presidents 3. Presidents -- United States
ISBN 0-06-075365-X

LC 2004-52907

This is a biography of the first president of the United States.

The author "submits a beautifully cogent, enthrallingly perceptive, and . . . startlingly fresh take on the ultimate American icon." Booklist

Includes bibliographical references

Washington, Martha, 1731-1802

Brady, Patricia. **Martha** Washington; an American life. Viking 2005 276p il $24.95; pa $15

Grades: 11 12 Adult　　　**92**

1. Spouses of presidents 2. Presidents' spouses -- United States
ISBN 0-670-03430-4; 0-14-303713-7 pa

LC 2004-61242

In this book, the original first lady "is depicted as a very human but true heroine who remained steadfast through personal adversity and the uncertainties of war and revolution." Libr J

Includes bibliographical references

Wells, H. G. (Herbert George), 1866-1946

Abrams, Dennis. **H.G.** Wells; foreword by Kyle Zimmer. Chelsea House 2011 128p il (Who wrote that?) lib bdg $35

Grades: 6 7 8 9 10　　　**92**

1. Authors 2. Novelists 3. Historians 4. Authors, English 5. Writers on science 6. Writers on politics 7. Science fiction writers
ISBN 978-1-60413-770-5; 1-60413-770-3

LC 2010030588

This discusses the life and work of author H. G. Wells.

Includes bibliographical references

Wells-Barnett, Ida B., 1862-1931

Hinman, Bonnie. **Eternal** vigilance: the story of Ida B. Wells-Barnett. Morgan Reynolds Pub. 2010 128p il (Civil rights leaders) $28.95

Grades: 7 8 9 10　　　**92**

1. Authors 2. Lynching 3. Journalists 4. Women journalists 5. African American educators 6. Essayists 7. Nonfiction writers 8. Newspaper executives 9. Civil rights activists 10. United States -- Race relations 11. African Americans -- Civil rights 12. African American women -- Biography 13. African Americans -- Social conditions
ISBN 978-1-59935-111-7; 1-59935-111-0

LC 2010-8144

"Hinman tells of Wells-Barnett's tireless efforts as an antilynching crusader and civil rights advocate. . . . Hinman paints an engaging portrait of the activist who was instrumental in the formation of the NAACP. Each stage of Wells-Barnett's life is placed in historical context, providing students with a better understanding of the world in which she lived. Well-chosen black-and-white photographs and other period materials are included throughout the text." SLJ

Includes bibliographical references

Welty, Eudora, 1909-2001

★ Welty, Eudora. **One** writer's beginnings. Harvard Univ. Press 1984 104p il (William E. Massey, Sr. lectures in the history of American civilization) hardcover o.p. pa $12

Grades: 11 12 Adult　　　**92**

1. Authors 2. Novelists 3. Authors, American 4. Short story writers
ISBN 0-674-63925-1; 0-674-63927-8 pa

LC 83-18638

A series of lectures in which the author reflects on her Southern heritage and her early artistic influences.

Wharton, Edith, 1862-1937

Wooldridge, Connie Nordhielm. The **brave** escape of Edith Wharton; a biography. Clarion Books 2010 184p il $20

Grades: 7 8 9 10 **92**

1. Authors 2. Novelists 3. Women authors 4. Authors, American 5. Nonfiction writers 6. Short story writers

ISBN 978-0-547-23630-8; 0-547-23630-1

LC 2009-33574

"In this thoroughly researched, humanizing biography, Wooldridge writes with lively specifics about both the author and her time. . . . Frequent, well-woven quotes from Wharton's family and friends contribute to a strong sense of an energetic, groundbreaking, and ferociously intelligent writer, but it's the many quotes in Wharton's own voice that leave the most indelible impact." Booklist

Wiesel, Elie, 1928-2016

★ Wiesel, Elie. **Night**; translated from the French by Marion Wiesel; [with a new preface by the author; foreword by Francoise Mauriac] Hill and Wang 2006 xxi, 120p $19.95; pa $9

Grades: 9 10 11 12 **92**

1. Authors 2. Novelists 3. Journalists 4. Holocaust survivors 5. Human rights activists 6. Nobel laureates for peace 7. Holocaust, 1933-1945 -- Personal narratives

ISBN 0-374-39997-2; 978-0-374-39997-9; 0-374-50001-0 pa; 978-0-374-50001-6 pa

LC 2005-936797

Original French edition, 1958

This is "the autobiographical account of an adolescent boy and his father in Auschwitz. Wiesel writes of their battle for survival, and of his battle with God for a way to understand the wanton cruelty he witnesses each day." Publisher's note

Wilder, Laura Ingalls, 1867-1957

Zochert, Donald. **Laura**: the life of Laura Ingalls Wilder. Avon 1977 241p pa $5.99

Grades: 11 12 Adult **92**

1. Authors 2. Novelists 3. Women authors 4. Frontier and pioneer life 5. Western writers 6. Authors, American 7. Children's authors 8. Young adult authors

ISBN 0-380-01636-2

First published 1976 by Regnery

This biography of the author of the "Little House" books describes her early life and offers insight into her works.

Williams, Roger, 1604?-1683

Gaustad, Edwin Scott. **Roger** Williams; [by] Edwin S. Gaustad. Oxford University Press 2005 150p il (Lives and legacies) $17.95

Grades: 11 12 Adult **92**

1. Clergy 2. Puritans 3. Colonial leaders 4. Writers on religion 5. United States -- History -- 1600-1775, Colonial period

ISBN 0-19-518369-X

LC 2004-25246

The author "provides not just an excellent introduction to the man but a deep analysis of his largely unacknowledged influence on our political and cultural life." Reason

Wilson, Jacqueline

Bankston, John. **Jacqueline** Wilson. Chelsea House 2011 128p il (Who wrote that?) lib bdg $35

Grades: 6 7 8 9 10 **92**

1. Authors 2. Novelists 3. Women authors 4. Authors, American 5. Young adult authors

ISBN 978-1-60413-773-6; 1-60413-773-8

LC 2010047679

"Wilson knew from an early age that writing was her calling. Growing up in a turbulent home and dropping out of school at 16 pushed her to start writing for Jackie, a magazine for teenage girls. This well-written biography includes a quick-paced, fact-filled synopsis of her life." SLJ

Includes bibliographical references

Wilson, Woodrow, 1856-1924

Lukes, Bonnie L. **Woodrow** Wilson and the Progressive Era. Morgan Reynolds 2005 192p il lib bdg $26.95

Grades: 7 8 9 10 **92**

1. Governors 2. Presidents 3. College presidents 4. Nobel laureates for peace 5. Presidents -- United States 6. United States -- Politics and government -- 1898-1919

ISBN 978-1-93179-879-2; 1-93179-879-6

LC 2005-15999

"This well-documented, chronological account begins with Wilson's birth in 1856, describes his varied careers, and continues through his death in 1924. . . . The author describes the intense political conflicts of the time, mostly concerning Americas involvement in World War I and then in the League of Nations. Lukes's approach is balanced. . . . Good-quality, full-color and black-and-white photos and reproductions appear throughout." SLJ

Includes bibliographical references

Wolff, Tobias, 1945-

Wolff, Tobias. **This** boy's life: a memoir. Atlantic Monthly Press 1989 288p hardcover o.p. pa $14

Grades: 11 12 Adult **92**

1. Authors 2. Novelists 3. Memoirists 4. College teachers 5. Authors, American 6. Nonfiction writers 7. Short story writers

ISBN 0-871-13248-6; 0-8021-3668-0 pa

LC 88-17600

The novelist and short story writer "offers an engrossing and candid look into his childhood and adolescence in his first book of nonfiction. In unaffected prose he recreates scenes from his life that sparkle with the immediacy of narrative fiction. The result is an intriguingly guileless book, distinct from the usual reflective commentary of autobiography." Libr J

Woodruff, Dorothy, 1887-1979

Wickenden, Dorothy. **Nothing** daunted; the unexpected education of two society girls in the West. Scribner 2011 286p il $26; ebook $12.99

Grades: 11 12 Adult **92**

1. Teachers 2. Women teachers 3. Colorado 4. Socialites 5. Biography, Individual

ISBN 978-1-4391-7658-0; 978-1-4391-7660-3 ebook

LC 2011-08949

"On July 24, 1916, the Syracuse Daily Journal printed the headline: 'Society Girls Go to Wilds of Colorado.' The two young women were Dorothy Woodruff and Rosamond Underwood, recent graduates of Smith College who, in order to defy their family's expectation of marriage, sought work in the small town of Hayden, Colo. Woodruff was the grandmother of . . . [the author], who herself becomes a central character in an informative and engaging narrative. Using letters from her grandmother, newspaper articles, and interviews with descendants, Wickenden retells how Woodruff and Underwood traveled to the newly settled state of Colorado to teach at a ramshackle grade school." Publ Wkly
Includes bibliographical references

Woolf, Virginia, 1882-1941

★ Brackett, Virginia. **Restless** genius; the story of Virginia Woolf. Morgan Reynolds Pub 2004 144p il (World writers) lib bdg $24.95
Grades: 9 10 11 12   92
1. Authors 2. Novelists 3. Women authors 4. Essayists 5. Authors, English 6. Short story writers
ISBN 1-931798-37-0
LC 2003-25043
This biography "begins with the people, events, and dynamics of Woolf's childhood, then quickly progresses to her adult life. Throughout, Brackett discusses in some detail the writer's relationships with her father, sister, husband, and, to a lesser extent, other relatives and members of the Bloomsbury group while focusing increasingly on her writings and her mental health." Booklist
Includes bibliographical references

Mills, Cliff. **Virginia** Woolf; introduction by Betty McCollum. Chelsea House Publishers 2004 130p il (Women in the arts) $22.95; pa $13.25
Grades: 9 10 11 12   92
1. Authors 2. Novelists 3. Women authors 4. Essayists 5. Authors, English 6. Short story writers
ISBN 0-7910-7459-5; 0-7910-7953-8 pa
LC 2003-9505
Discusses the life and work of the twentieth-century English author, Virginia Woolf.
Woolf's "history is presented in an interesting manner as are the controversies that swirled around her. There are many color illustrations and pictures including insets giving more insight." Libr Media Connect
Includes bibliographical references

Worden, Alfred M., 1932-

Worden, Al, 1932- **Falling** to Earth; an Apollo 15 astronaut's journey. [by] Al Worden with Francis French. Smithsonian Books 2011 300p il
Grades: 11 12 Adult   92
1. Astronauts 2. Apollo project 3. Space flight to the moon 4. Air force officers 5. Biography, Individual 6. Apollo 15 (Spacecraft)
ISBN 1-58834-309-X; 978-1-58834-309-3
LC 2011003440
"Worden is eloquent, witty, and brutally honest, still in awe of the company he kept and the history he belongs to. A solid addition to space-literature collections."

"Worden is eloquent, witty, and brutally honest, still in awe of the company he kept and the history he belongs to. A solid addition to space-literature collections." Booklist
Includes bibliographical references

Wright, Orville, 1871-1948

★ Freedman, Russell. The **Wright** brothers: how they invented the airplane; with original photographs by Wilbur and Orville Wright. Holiday House 1991 129p il hardcover o.p. pa $14.95
Grades: 5 6 7 8 9 10   92
1. Inventors 2. Aeronautics -- History 3. Aircraft industry executives
ISBN 0-8234-0875-2; 0-8234-1082-X pa
LC 90-48440
A Newbery Medal honor book, 1992
In this "combination of photography and text, Freedman reveals the frustrating, exciting, and ultimately successful journey of these two brothers from their bicycle shop in Dayton, Ohio, to their Kitty Hawk flights and beyond. . . . An essential purchase for younger YAs." Voice Youth Advocates
Includes bibliographical references

★ Wright, Orville. **How** we invented the airplane; an illustrated history. edited with an introduction and commentary by Fred C. Kelly; additional text by Alan Weissman. Dover Publs. 1988 87p il pa $9.95
Grades: 11 12 Adult   92
1. Inventors 2. Aeronautics -- History 3. Aircraft industry executives
ISBN 0-486-25662-6
LC 87-33037
First published 1953 by D. McKay
This "account by the two inventors . . . covers experiments, discovery of aeronautical principles, construction of planes and motors, first flights, and much more. Also included is a later account written by both brothers." Publisher's note
Includes bibliographical references

Wright, Richard, 1908-1960

Wright, Richard. **Black** boy; (American hunger): a record of childhood and youth. foreword by Edward P. Jones. 60th anniversary ed., 1st ed.; HarperCollinsPublishers 2005 419p $24.95; pa $14.95
Grades: 11 12 Adult   92
1. Authors 2. Novelists 3. Dramatists 4. African American authors 5. Essayists 6. Nonfiction writers 7. Short story writers 8. African Americans -- Social conditions
ISBN 0-06-083400-5; 978-0-06-083400-5; 0-06-113024-9 pa; 978-0-06-113024-3 pa
LC 2005-52698
First published 1945 by World Publishing Company
This autobiographical work concludes with Wright "newly arrived in Chicago in 1927 as a fugitive from the white South that never knew him. [It] relates his nomadic life in Tennessee, Arkansas, and Mississippi, abandoned by

his father and with his mother working at menial jobs or incapacitated by illness." Benet's Reader's Ency of Am Lit

Includes bibliographical references

Wright, Wilbur, 1867-1912

★ Freedman, Russell. The **Wright** brothers: how they invented the airplane; with original photographs by Wilbur and Orville Wright. Holiday House 1991 129p il hardcover o.p. pa $14.95

Grades: 5 6 7 8 9 10   **92**

1. Inventors 2. Aeronautics -- History 3. Aircraft industry executives

ISBN 0-8234-0875-2; 0-8234-1082-X pa

LC 90-48440

A Newbery Medal honor book, 1992

In this "combination of photography and text, Freedman reveals the frustrating, exciting, and ultimately successful journey of these two brothers from their bicycle shop in Dayton, Ohio, to their Kitty Hawk flights and beyond. . . . An essential purchase for younger YAs." Voice Youth Advocates

Includes bibliographical references

★ Wright, Orville. **How** we invented the airplane; an illustrated history. edited with an introduction and commentary by Fred C. Kelly; additional text by Alan Weissman. Dover Publs. 1988 87p il pa $9.95

Grades: 11 12 Adult   **92**

1. Inventors 2. Aeronautics -- History 3. Aircraft industry executives

ISBN 0-486-25662-6

LC 87-33037

First published 1953 by D. McKay

This "account by the two inventors . . . covers experiments, discovery of aeronautical principles, construction of planes and motors, first flights, and much more. Also included is a later account written by both brothers." Publisher's note

Includes bibliographical references

Yoshitsune, Minamoto

★ **Samurai** rising; the epic life of Minamoto Yoshitsune. Pamela S. Turner; with illustrations by Gareth Hinds. Charlesbridge 2015 256 p. illustrations, maps (reinforced for library use) $16.95

Grades: 7 8 9 10   **92**

1. Samurai 2. Japan -- History 3. Samurai -- Japan -- Biography

ISBN 9781580895842

LC 2014049179

This book, by Pamela S. Turner, illustrated by Gareth Hinds, is an "epic tale of warriors and bravery, rebellion and revenge. . . . When Yoshitsune was just a baby, his father went to war with a rival samurai family—and lost. His father was killed, his mother captured, and his brothers sent away. Yoshitsune was raised in his enemy's household. . . . But . . . when the time came for the Minamoto to rise up against their enemy once again, Yoshitsune was there." (Publisher's note)

"The back cover warns: 'Very few people in this story die of natural causes.' Turner delivers on the promise of that

hook, and it will leave lovers of military history clamoring for more of this type." Horn Book

Yousafzai, Malala, 1997-

Lamb, Christina. **I** am Malala; The Girl Who Stood Up for Education and Was Shot by the Taliban. Malala Yousafzai. Little, Brown and Co. 2013 viii, 327 p.p (hardcover) $26.00

Grades: 9 10 11 12 Adult   **92**

1. Terrorism 2. Women -- Pakistan 3. Girls -- Education

ISBN 0316322407; 9780316322409

LC 2013941811

Amelia Bloomer Project (2014)

This memoir, by Malala Yousafzai, "is the . . . tale of a family uprooted by global terrorism, of the fight for girls' education, of a father who, himself a school owner, championed and encouraged his daughter to write and attend school, and of . . . parents who have a . . . love for their daughter in a society that prizes sons." (Publisher's note)

"On October 9, 2012, the teenaged Yousafzai was very nearly assassinated by members of the Taliban who objected to her education and women's rights activism in Pakistan. Currently, she lives in England, under threat of execution by the Taliban if she returns home. Lamb, who has been reporting from Pakistan for 26 years and was named Foreign Correspondent of the Year five times, helps Yousafzai tell her hugely significant story." (Library Journal)

Zaharias, Babe Didrikson, 1911-1956

Cayleff, Susan E. **Babe**: the life and legend of Babe Didrikson Zaharias. University of Ill. Press 1995 327p il (Women in American history) $29.95; pa $15.95

Grades: 11 12 Adult   **92**

1. Women athletes 2. Golfers 3. Hurdlers 4. High jumpers 5. Javelin throwers 6. Olympic athletes

ISBN 0-252-01793-5; 0-252-06593-X pa

LC 94-35584

The author "presents a feminist analysis of the life, sports career, and legacy of Mildred Ella 'Babe' Didrikson Zaharias. . . . Cayleff examines Babe's amateur athletic career from high school through the 1932 Olympics, as well as her professional and amateur golf accomplishments. . . . Although it will undoubtedly be controversial, Babe is a very important book about a unique and significant figure in US sports." Choice

Includes bibliographical references

Louis Zamerpini

Hillenbrand, Laura, 1967- **Unbroken**; an Olympian's journey from airman to castaway to captive. Laura Hillenbrand. Delacorte Press 2014 320 p. illustrations, maps (hardcover: alk. paper) $19.99

Grades: 9 10 11 12   **92**

1. Olympic athletes 2. World War, 1939-1945 -- Prisoners and prisons 3. Prisoners of war -- Japan -- Biography 4. Olympic athletes -- United States -- Biography 5. Long-distance runners -- United States

-- Biography
ISBN 0385742517; 9780307975652; 9780375990625;
9780385742511

LC 2014014794

This young adult biography, by Laura Hillenbrand, looks at athlete Louis Zamerpini, whose "gutsy performances earned him a slot on the 1938 Olympic track team. With the outbreak of World War II, he joined the Air Corps, surviving a plane crash and forty-seven days adrift on a raft only to be captured and interred in various Japanese POW camps until war's end. He returned to California alive but emotionally scarred." (Horn Book Magazine)

"Heavily illustrated with black-and-white photographs, this is sure to attract a wide audience, not only of survival story fans but also of those looking for a story of one man's heroic triumph over all odds." Booklist

Includes bibliographical references and index

Zellner, Robert, 1939-

Zellner, Robert. The **wrong** side of Murder Creek; a White southerner in the freedom movement, [by] Bob Zellner, with Constance Curry; foreword by Julian Bond. NewSouth Books 2008 351p il $27.95
Grades: 11 12 Adult   **92**
1. Historians 2. Civil rights demonstrations 3. College teachers 4. Civil rights activists 5. Southern States -- Race relations 6. Student Nonviolent Coordinating Committee
ISBN 978-1-58838-222-1; 1-58838-222-2

LC 2008-25962

"Zellner's memoir focuses on his experiences as a civil rights activist from 1960 to 1967. He tells a story that is sometimes horrific, always interesting, and ultimately inspirational about a white Southerner's commitment to racial justice. . . . This powerful portrait of a courageous man is highly recommended." Libr J

Zenatti, Valérie, 1970-

Zenatti, Valerie. **When** I was a soldier; a memoir. translated by Adriana Hunter. Bloomsbury Children's Books 2005 235p $16.95
Grades: 7 8 9 10   **92**
1. Authors 2. Soldiers 3. Novelists 4. Women soldiers 5. Israel 6. Memoirists 7. Translators 8. Children's authors
ISBN 1-58234-978-9

A "fast, wry, present-tense memoir. . . . Readers on all sides of the war-peace continuum, here and there, will find much to talk about." Booklist

920   Biography, genealogy, insignia

Abdul-Jabbar, Kareem

Black profiles in courage; a legacy of African American achievement. [by] Kareem Abdul-Jabbar and Alan Steinberg; foreword by Henry Louis Gates, Jr. Morrow 1996 xxiv, 232p il hardcover o.p. pa $13
Grades: 11 12 Adult   **920**
1. Slaves 2. Authors 3. Children 4. Explorers 5.

Inventors 6. Abolitionists 7. Sheriffs 8. Colonists 9. Dissenters 10. Memoirists 11. Murder victims 12. Revolutionaries 13. Writers on science 14. Civil rights activists 15. African Americans -- Biography
ISBN 0-688-13097-6; 0-380-81341-6 pa

LC 96-26245

The authors have provided "interesting and nuanced accounts of heroic African Americans whose accomplishments changed U.S. history. . . . Although Abdul-Jabbar is highly critical of past and present racism in the U.S., he gives credit to the abolitionist movement and leaders such as William Lloyd Garrison for their efforts toward ending slavery." Publ Wkly

Includes bibliographical references

African American lives; edited by Henry Louis Gates, Jr. and Evelyn Brooks Higginbotham. Oxford University Press 2004 xxvi, 1025p $55
Grades: 11 12 Adult   **920**
1. African Americans -- Biography
ISBN 0-19-516024-X

LC 2003-23640

"This work opens multiple fresh vistas on proper African American history. . . . Essential for any serious African American collection." Libr J

Includes bibliographical references

Almanac of Famous People; A Comprehensive Reference Guide to More Than 40,000 Famous and Infamous Newsmakers from Biblical Times to the Present. edited by Kristin Mallegg. 10th ed. Gale / Cengage Learning 2011 2887 p. (hardcover) $280
Grades: 7 8 9 10 11 12 Adult   **920**
1. Celebrities -- Encyclopedias
ISBN 1414445482; 9781414445489

This reference book offers "biographical information on more than 30,000 famous individuals and groups." Entries provide the "subject's best-known name, complete name, nickname, [and] name of group," "dates and places of birth and death," and "nationality and occupation. Most entries include citations to sources that provide additional biographical information." (Publisher's note)

American Council of Learned Societies

Invisible giants; fifty Americans that shaped the nation but missed the history books. edited by Mark C. Carnes. Oxford Univ. Press 2002 316p il hardcover o.p. pa $19.95
Grades: 11 12 Adult   **920**
1. United States -- Biography
ISBN 0-19-515417-7; 0-19-516883-6 pa

LC 2001-58785

The publisher of American National Biography recruited "50 well-known contemporary authors to pick from it a once-significant, now-obscure person, and reprint the ANB article prefaced by the selector's one-page justification. . . . As varied as the individal subjects, some selectors, such as Jacques Barzun (on critic John Jay Chapman) or Arthur Schlesinger Jr. (on historian George Bancroft), concisely point to changing tastes. . . . Each of these ANB subjects left a mark perceptible in modern America, filling this volume with surprises for even the most widely read." Booklist

Includes bibliographical references (p. 289-310) and index

Baker, Rosalie F.

Ancient Egyptians; people of the pyramids. [by] Rosalie F. and Charles F. Baker. Oxford Univ. Press 2001 189p il maps (Oxford profiles) $50

Grades: 7 8 9 10   **920**

    1. Egypt -- Biography 2. Egypt -- Civilization
    ISBN 0-19-512221-6

        LC 2001-21209

"Divided into five periods from the Old Kingdom, about 2686 B.C., to the declining New Kingdom, about 245 B.C., this book profiles some 30 Egyptian leaders, devoting a three- to seven-page chapter to each one. . . . The entries are well written and researched. . . . A useful addition for report writers and subject enthusiasts." SLJ

Includes glossary and bibliographical references

Bascomb, Neal

The **perfect** mile; three athletes, one goal, and less than four minutes to achieve it. Houghton Mifflin Co 2004 322p il hardcover o.p. pa $14.95

Grades: Adult   **920**

    1. Running 2. Neurologists 3. Olympic athletes 4. Runners (Athletes)
    ISBN 0-618-39112-6; 0-618-56209-5 pa

        LC 2004-40535

This is the story of the attempts of three athletes—Wes Santee, John Landy and Roger Bannister—to run the four-minute mile.

"Neal Bascomb skillfully transforms [the runners'] efforts into a compelling human drama. His crisp, detailed narrative helps readers step into the milers' spikes." Christ Sci Monit

Includes bibliographical references

Benson, Sonia

Development of the industrial U.S.: Biographies; [by] Sonia G. Benson; Carol Brennan, contributing writer; Jennifer York Stock, project editor. UXL 2006 lvi, 252p il (Development of the industrial U.S reference library) $63

Grades: 9 10 11 12   **920**

    1. Industrial revolution 2. Industries -- United States
    ISBN 1-4144-0176-0

        LC 2005-16350

"Subjects range from social workers to society divas and from industrialists to labor organizers and political activists. Articles average about 10 pages and include portraits, illustrations, and sidebars." Booklist

Includes bibliographical references

Berry, Bertice

The **ties** that bind; a memoir of race, memory, and redemption. Broadway Books 2009 205p $26.95

Grades: 11 12 Adult   **920**

    1. Farmers 2. Abolitionists 3. Sharecroppers 4.

Slavery -- United States 5. African Americans -- Biography 6. United States -- Race relations
ISBN 978-0-7679-2414-6; 0-7679-2414-2

        LC 2008-25555

"Berry continues to demonstrate an uncanny aptitude for weaving African-American history into entertaining, empowering stories both fictional and personal." Kirkus

Black firsts; 4,000 ground-breaking and pioneering events. [edited by] Jessie Carney Smith. Visible Ink Press 2013 700 p. $33.95

Grades: 9 10 11 12 Adult   **920**

    1. Blacks -- History -- Encyclopedias 2. African Americans -- History -- Encyclopedias 3. Blacks -- History -- Miscellanea 4. African Americans -- History -- Miscellanea 5. World records -- United States -- Miscellanea
    ISBN 1480621153; 9781480621152; 9781578593699

        LC 2012034407

This book, edited by Jessie Carney Smith, "collects and celebrates the thousands of world-moving people and hard-to-find facts and accomplishments [by people of African descent] that have helped shape society and culture. It recognizes and honors both renowned and lesser-known barrier-breaking trailblazers in all fields--arts, entertainment, business, civil rights, education, government, invention, journalism, religion, science, sports, music, and more." (Publisher's note)

"Carney presents major accomplishments ranging from firsts in cartooning and jazz to sporting firsts for jockeys in the Kentucky Derby. Brief profiles are presented chronologically and cover major figures such as Michael Jackson and Jackie Robinson as well as lesser-known figures such as Moses Fleetwood Walker, the first black member of a varsity collegiate baseball club...This is an excellent resource for starting research on black history, but its sheer volume may be overwhelming to casual researchers. The lesser-known figures, however, make the title worth digging into." LJ

Includes bibliographical references and index

★ **Black** leaders of the nineteenth century; edited by Leon Litwack and August Meier. University of Ill. Press 1988 344p il (Blacks in the new world) hardcover o.p. pa $22

Grades: 9 10 11 12   **920**

    1. African Americans -- Biography
    ISBN 0-252-06213-2 pa

        LC 87-19439

"Including individual essays on the famous, such as Frederick Douglass and Harriet Tubman, as well as a general discussion of black Reconstructionist leaders at the grass roots, this scholarly collection provides in-depth information." Booklist

Includes bibliographical references

Bradley, Michael J.

The **age** of genius; 1300 to 1800. Facts On File 2006 162p il (Pioneers in mathematics) $29.95

Grades: 7 8 9 10   **920**

    1. Mathematicians 2. Mathematics -- History
    ISBN 0-8160-5424-X

        LC 2005-32354

This volume presents profiles of mathematicians such as "Viete, Napier, Fermat, Pascal, Newton, Leibniz, Euler, and Agnesi. . . . The last chapter profiles Benjamin Banneker, an African-American from the colonial period in America." Sci Books Films

Includes glossary and bibliographical references

The **foundations** of mathematics; 1800 to 1900. Facts On File 2006 162p il (Pioneers in mathematics) $29.95

Grades: 7 8 9 10   **920**

1. Mathematicians 2. Mathematics -- History
ISBN 0-8160-5425-8

LC 2005-33736

This volume presents information on mathematicians such as Augusta Ada Lovelace, Marie-Sophie Germain, Mary Fairfax Somerville, Evariste Galois, Georg Cantor, and Henri Poincare.

Includes glossary and bibliographical references

Mathematics frontiers; 1950 to the present. Facts on File 2006 148p il (Pioneers in mathematics) $29.95

Grades: 7 8 9 10   **920**

1. Mathematicians 2. Mathematics -- History
ISBN 0-8160-5427-4

LC 2005-36154

This volume presents profiles of mathematicians such as John Nash, Stephen Hawking, Julia Robinson, Ernest Wilkins, Jr., John Conway, Fan Chung, Andrew Wiles, and Sarah Flannery.

Includes glossary and bibliographical references

Modern mathematics; 1900 to 1950. Facts on File 2006 164p il (Pioneers in mathematics) $29.95

Grades: 7 8 9 10   **920**

1. Mathematicians 2. Mathematics -- History
ISBN 0-8160-5426-6

LC 2005-36152

This volume presents profiles of mathematicians such as Alan Turing, David Hilbert, Norbert Wiener, Grace Chisholm Young, Amalie Emmy Noether, and Grace Murray Hopper.

Includes glossary and bibliographical references

Bruns, Roger

Icons of Latino America; Latino contributions to American culture. foreword by Ilan Stavans. Greenwood Press 2008 2v il (Greenwood icons) set $175

Grades: 11 12 Adult   **920**

1. Hispanic Americans -- Biography
ISBN 978-0-313-34086-4; 0-313-34086-2

LC 2008-13646

"This set employs a broad definition of 'icon' and includes real personages, cartoon characters, and Mexican food among the entries. The engaging articles average 20 to 30 pages in length and contain substantive, documented information. Entries are detailed and interesting." SLJ

Includes bibliographical references

Butts, Edward

She dared; true stories of heroines, scoundrels, and renegades. [by] Ed Butts; illustrated by Heather Collins. Tundra Bks. 2005 121p il pa $8.95

Grades: 6 7 8 9 10   **920**

1. Women -- Biography 2. Canada -- Biography
ISBN 0-88776-718-4

This "details the lives of some of Canada's most famous and infamous women. The stories showcase explorers, spies, criminals, and pioneers in a variety of career fields. Organized chronologically from the 16th to the mid-20th century, this 12-chapter offering is historically sound and well researched." SLJ

Carey, Charles W.

★ **American** inventors, entrepreneurs & business visionaries; [by] Charles W. Carey, Jr. Rev. ed; Facts On File 2010 xxi, 455p il (Facts on File library of American history) $95

Grades: 11 12 Adult   **920**

1. Inventors 2. Businesspeople 3. Reference books 4. United States -- Biography
ISBN 978-0-8160-8146-2; 978-1-4381-3336-2 ebook

LC 2009-54269

First published 2002

"This biographical dictionary includes profiles of more than 300 individuals who have made significant and lasting contributions to American industry dating from the Colonial era to the present. Each entry addresses the subject chronologically through his or her life, focusing on major professional achievements as well as personal triumphs and tragedies. . . . The book paints a fascinating portrait of American ingenuity. A well-written biographical dictionary that will appeal to anyone interested in the history of American invention and entrepreneurialism." Libr J

Includes bibliographical references

Caroli, Betty Boyd

First ladies; from Martha Washington to Michelle Obama. Rev. and updated ed.; Oxford University Press 2010 xxii, 437p il pa $17.95

Grades: 11 12 Adult   **920**

1. Presidents' spouses -- United States
ISBN 978-0-19-539285-2; 0-19-539285-X

LC 2010-14673

First published 1987

In addition to profiling each woman who has served as First Lady the author examines the ways the role has evolved over the years.

Includes bibliographical references

D'Agnese, Joseph

Signing their rights away; the fame and misfortune of the men who signed the United States Constitution. by Denise Kiernan & Joseph D'Agnese. Quirk Books 2011 254p il $19.95

Grades: 8 9 10 11 12 Adult   **920**

1. Statesmen -- United States 2. Presidents -- United States 3. United States -- Constitution 4. United States -- History -- 1775-1783, Revolution -- Biography 5. United States -- Politics and government -- 1775-1783,

Revolution

ISBN 978-1-59474-520-1

Presents the lives, deaths, and scandals involving the thirty-nine signers of the United States Constitution, including Benjamin Franklin, Alexander Hamilton, and James McHenry.

"For readers of American history, this is both educational and entertaining." Booklist

Includes bibliographical references

Day, Sara

★ **Women** for change. Library of Congress 2007 64p il (Women who dare) $12.95

Grades: 9 10 11 12   920

1. Political activists 2. Women -- United States -- Biography

ISBN 978-0-7649-3876-4

LC 2006-50349

This book "connects the stories of two dozen women who defied expectations in many different ways, speaking out, holding high office, leading strikes, challenging entrenched dogma." Publisher's note

Includes bibliographical references

Denlinger, Elizabeth Campbell

★ **Before** Victoria; extraordinary women of the British Romantic era. by Elizabeth Campbell Denlinger; foreword by Lyndall Gordon. Columbia University Press 2005 188p il $41.50

Grades: 11 12 Adult   920

1. Women -- Great Britain 2. Great Britain -- History -- 19th century

ISBN 0-231-13630-7

LC 2004-59267

This book "offers portraits of a group of women who were scientists, artists, writers, poets, philanthropists and reformers during the Romantic Era and details how their accomplishments changed the social and economic landscape for women." Univ Press Books for Public and Second Sch Libr, 2006

Includes bibliographical references

Dunn, Brad

When they were 22; 100 famous people at the turning point in their lives. Andrews McMeel Pub. 2006 179p $12.95

Grades: 9 10 11 12   920

1. Celebrities

ISBN 978-0-7407-5810-2; 0-7407-5810-1

LC 2005-57170

This book "tells the stories of famous people and the fateful events and choices they faced at the all-important age of 22. . . . [The personalities profiled range from] writers, actors, and musicians to politicians, hip-hop moguls, criminals, and porn stars." Publisher's note

Includes bibliographical references

Ellsberg, Robert

Blessed among all women; women saints, prophets, and witnesses for our time. Crossroad Pub. 2005 316p $19.95; pa $16.95

Grades: 9 10 11 12   920

1. Christian saints 2. Religious biography 3. Women -- Biography

ISBN 0-8245-2251-6; 0-8245-2439-X pa

LC 2005-11363

Companion volume to All saints (1997)

The author presents short biographies of 136 women he considers holy. The "entries are grouped according to the virtues of the Beatitudes, an arrangement that reflects Ellsberg's definition of saints as 'people who made the Gospel concrete'. . . . Although Ellsberg is yet another man narrating tales of women saints, his accounts are far from one-dimensional. The women he depicts are fully human, which makes them useful spiritual guides." America

Includes bibliographical references

Evans, Harold

★ **They** made America; [by] Harold Evans, with Gail Buckland and David Lefer. Little, Brown 2004 496p $40; pa $18.95

Grades: 11 12 Adult   920

1. Inventors 2. Inventions

ISBN 0-316-27766-5; 0-316-01385-4 pa

LC 2003-65954

The author "profiles 70 of America's leading inventors, entrepreneurs and innovators, some better known than others. Along with such obvious choices as Henry Ford, Thomas Edison and the Wright brothers, Evans profiles Lewis Tappan (an abolitionist who dreamed up the idea of credit ratings), Gen. Georges Doriot (pioneer of venture capital) and Joan Ganz Cooney, of the Children's Television Workshop." Publ Wkly

Fleischer, Jeff

Rockin' the Boat; 50 Iconic Rebels and Revolutionaries-from Joan of Arc to Malcom X. Jeff Fleischer. Houghton Mifflin Harcourt 2015 224 p. $13.99

Grades: 9 10 11 12   920

1. Individuality 2. Revolutionaries

ISBN 1936976749; 9781936976744

In this book author Jeff Fleischer "tells the stories of 50 . . . legends throughout the world, from people fed up with the Roman Empire and the revolutionaries who helped create America. Whether they fail, succeed, or succeed only to become what they once fought against, people who can rally others to their cause and shake up the status quo tend to be inherently interesting." (Publisher's note)

"Readers expecting all the revolutionaries to be virtuous do-gooders will be in for a surprise. Whether they read cover to cover or dip in, they will find many treats to further explore." Booklist

Garrison, Mary

★ **Slaves** who dared; the stories of ten African-American heroes. White Mane Kids 2002 142p il $19.95

Grades: 9 10 11 12   920

1. Clergy 2. Nurses 3. Slaves 4. Authors 5. Educators 6. Abolitionists 7. Cowboys 8. Porters 9. Domestics 10. Memoirists 11. State legislators 12. Nonfiction writers 13. Members of Congress 14. Civil

rights activists 15. Slavery -- United States 16. African Americans -- History
ISBN 1-57249-272-4

LC 2002-22666

"Garrison does a great job of weaving into each narrative many actual quotes, illustrations . . . and the drama of how and where the stories were recorded." Booklist
Includes bibliographical references

Haley, Alex

★ **Roots**; the saga of an American family: the 30th anniversary edition. Vanguard Books 2007 899p pa $15.95
Grades: 11 12 Adult   **920**
1. African American families. 2. African Americans -- Biography.
ISBN 978-1-59315-449-3; 1-59315-449-6

LC 2007-8822

First published 1976 by Doubleday
This book details Haley's "search for the genealogical history of his family. He describes his trip to Gambia, the African homeland of his ancestors, and recounts the lives of his forebears." Benet's Reader's Ency of Am Lit

Hanes, Richard Clay

Crime and punishment in America: biographies; [by] Richard C. Hanes and Kelly Rudd; Sarah Hermsen, project editor. UXL 2005 191, lixp il (Crime and punishment in America reference library) $60
Grades: 9 10 11 12   **920**
1. Criminals 2. Administration of criminal justice
ISBN 0-7876-9167-4

LC 2004-17066

This book "includes entries on important figures, such as Jane Addams, Allan Pinkerton, Clarence Darrow, Senator Estes Kefauver and others." Publisher's note
Includes bibliographical references

Hannon, Sharon M.

★ **Women** explorers. Library of Congress 2007 64p il map (Women who dare) $12.95
Grades: 9 10 11 12   **920**
1. Explorers 2. Women -- Biography
ISBN 978-0-7649-3892-4

LC 2006-50706

This book profiles "extraordinary women from the past two centuries who have eagerly sought out high adventure in far-flung corners of the world." Publisher's note
Includes bibliographical references

Hardesty, Von

Black wings; courageous stories of African Americans in aviation and space history. HarperCollins Publishers 2007 180p il $21.95
Grades: 11 12 Adult   **920**
1. African American pilots 2. African American astronauts
ISBN 978-0-06-126138-1

LC 2007-21270

"This book companion to the Smithsonian National Air and Space Museum exhibit of the same name offers a look at the little-known and long-neglected history of black pioneers in aviation. . . . [Along with] the Tuskegee Airmen, Hardesty profiles barnstormers, including the Blackbirds; William J. Powell, founder of an aviation club; military flyers, including Benjamin O. Davis Jr.; and astronauts Guy Bluford, Ronald McNair, and Mae Jemison. This is an inspiring look at the adventurous individuals who pushed against the limits of racial discrimination to realize their passion for flying." Booklist
Includes bibliographical references

Harlem Renaissance lives from the African American national biography; general editors, Henry Louis Gates, Jr., Evelyn Brooks Higginbotham. Oxford University Press 2009 595p il $50
Grades: 11 12 Adult   **920**
1. Harlem Renaissance 2. African Americans -- Biography 3. African Americans -- Intellectual life
ISBN 0195387953; 9780195387957; 978-0-19-538795-7; 0-19-538795-3

LC 2008-51794

"This authoritative reference work will prove a useful acquisition for high school, public, and academic libraries, particularly for smaller institutions that lack the African American National Biography."
"This authoritative reference work will prove a useful acquisition for high school, public, and academic libraries, particularly for smaller institutions that lack the African American National Biography." Libr J
Includes bibliographical references

Harris, Cecil

Charging the net; a history of blacks in tennis from Althea Gibson and Arthur Ashe to the Williams sisters. [by] Cecil Harris and Larryette Kyle-DeBose with a foreword by James Blake and an afterword by Robert Ryland. Ivan R. Dee 2007 267p il $26.95
Grades: 11 12 Adult   **920**
1. Tennis 2. African American athletes
ISBN 978-1-56663-714-5; 1-56663-714-7

LC 2007-2747

"This book will appeal to teens interested in black athletes' contributions to sports, in tennis generally, or in sports facts. It is well documented and may be read for pleasure or for assignments. It also portrays new role models for succeeding in sports and in life, while struggling with discrimination." SLJ
Includes bibliographical references

Haskins, James

African American religious leaders; [by] Jim Haskins and Kathleen Benson. Wiley 2008 162p il (Black stars) lib bdg $24.95
Grades: 6 7 8 9 10 11 12 Adult   **920**
1. African Americans -- Religion 2. African Americans -- Biography
ISBN 978-0-471-73632-5; 0-471-73632-5

LC 2007-27347

"It's great to have all these figures between two covers, and even a sampling of the entries captures the importance of religion, and its leaders, in African American life." Booklist
Includes bibliographical references

Henderson, Harry

Larry Page and Sergey Brin; information at your fingertips. author, Harry Henderson. Chelsea House 2012 134 p. (Trailblazers in science and technology) (library) $35

Grades: 7 8 9 10 11 12 **920**
1. Google 2. Google (Firm) 3. Web search engines 4. Webmasters -- United States -- Biography 5. Computer programmers -- United States -- Biography
ISBN 1604136766; 9781604136760

LC 2011032584

This book, by Harry Henderson, is a biography of the founders of the Internet company Google Inc. as part of the "Trailblaizers in Science and Technology" series. "When . . . Larry Page and Sergey Brin collaborated on the search engine Google, they didn't realize that their invention would soon become so ingrained in Web culture that its name would be used as a verb." (Publisher's note)

Includes bibliographical references and index

In the Shadow of Liberty; the hidden history of slavery, four presidents, and five black lives. Henry Holt & Co. 2016 304 p. hardcover $17.99

Grades: 6 7 8 9 10 **920**
1. Slavery -- United States 2. Presidents -- United States 3. United States -- Race relations -- History 4. African Americans -- Biography.
ISBN 9781627793117

LC 2015035204

"Here are the stories of five enslaved people who witnessed the birth of America: Billy Lee, valet to George Washington; Ona Judge, who escaped from Martha Washington; Isaac Granger, servant of Thomas Jefferson; Paul Jennings, who witnessed the War of 1812 in James Madison's White House; and Alfred Jackson, "owned" by Andrew Jackson. These true stories explore our country's great, tragic contradiction--that a nation "conceived in liberty" was also born in shackles." (Publisher's note)

"This well-researched book offers a chronological history of slavery in America and features five enslaved people and the four U.S. presidents who owned them. . . . Always referring to enslaved people rather than slaves, Davis organizes a great deal of factual material, personal accounts, and quotes into a very readable history book. Ties to familiar historical figures give the information about the five lesser-known African Americans a greater sense of context. In turn, the book offers a particularly realistic and nuanced view of these presidents. The illustrations include black-and-white reproductions of paintings, prints, and photos of artifacts and historic sites. A valuable, broad perspective on slavery, paired with close-up views of individuals who benefited from it and those who endured it." Booklist

Kane, Joseph Nathan

★ **Facts** about the presidents; a compilation of biographical and historical information. Joseph Nathan Kane, Janet Podell [editors] 8th ed; Wilson, H.W. 2009 720p $150

Grades: 8 9 10 11 12 Adult **920**
1. Reference books 2. Presidents -- United States
ISBN 9780824210878

LC 2008056016

First published 1959

The main part of this work provides an individual chapter on each President, from Washington through Barack Obama, presenting such information as family, education, election, Vice President, main events and accomplishments of his administration, and First Lady. Part two contains tables and lists presenting comparative data on all the Presidents

Kennedy, John F.

★ **Profiles** in courage. HarperCollins Pubs. 2003 xxii, 245p $19.95; pa $13.95

Grades: 7 8 9 10 11 12 Adult **920**
1. Judges 2. Courage 3. Lawyers 4. Governors 5. Statesmen 6. Presidents 7. Senators 8. Army officers 9. Political leaders 10. State legislators 11. Members of Congress 12. Newspaper executives 13. Secretaries of state 14. Territorial governors 15. Supreme Court justices 16. Presidential candidates 17. Secretaries of the interior 18. Politicians -- United States
ISBN 0-06-053062-6; 0-06-085493-6 pa

LC 2003-40676

A reissue of the title first published 1956

This series of profiles of Americans who took courageous stands at crucial moments in public life includes John Quincy Adams, Daniel Webster, Thomas Hart Benton, Sam Houston, Edmund G. Ross, Lucius Q. C. Lamar, George Norris, Robert A. Taft and others.

Includes bibliographical references

Kennedy, Kerry

Speak truth to power; human rights defenders who are changing our world. photographs by Eddie Adams; edited by Nan Richardson. Crown 2000 256p il hardcover o.p. pa $34.95

Grades: 7 8 9 10 **920**
1. Human rights
ISBN 0-8129-3062-2; 1-88416-733-0 pa

LC 00-34557

This book "is composed of fifty three-page interviews with people who have made strides in the global fight to ensure basic human rights for everyone. . . . The Dalai Lama, Desmond Tutu, and Elie Wiesel are included, but most subjects are everyday people who have survived imprisonment, death threats, and torture to bring about change. . . . Their reports are sad but inspiring. . . . The haunting photographs and stories are gripping." Voice Youth Advocates

Killam, G. D.

Student encyclopedia of African literature; [by] Douglas Killam and Alicia L. Kerfoot. Greenwood Press 2008 xxiii, 339p $85

Grades: 8 9 10 11 12 **920**
1. Reference books 2. African literature -- Encyclopedias
ISBN 978-0-313-33580-8; 0-313-33580-X

LC 2007-35356

"This alphabetically arranged volume provides brief information about authors, individual works, and issues related to the literature of the African continent, and a few themed articles that cover the literature of its diaspora. The articles are concise, if academic, and the coverage reasonably comprehensive." SLJ

Includes bibliographical references

Malone, John Williams

It doesn't take a rocket scientist; great amateurs of science. {by} John Malone. Wiley 2002 232p $24.95

Grades: 11 12 Adult   **920**
1. Clergy 2. Authors 3. Chemists 4. Novelists 5. Architects 6. Physicists 7. Presidents 8. Scientists 9. Astronomers 10. Vice-presidents 11. Essayists 12. Geneticists 13. Photometrists 14. Microbiologists 15. Writers on science 16. Short story writers 17. Science fiction writers
ISBN 0-471-41431-X
LC 2003-269159

This examines the lives and work of ten amateur scientists, including Gregor Mendel, David H. Levy, Henrietta Swan Leavitt, Joseph Priestley, Michael Faraday, Grote Reber, Arthur C. Clarke, Thomas Jefferson, Susan Hendrickson, and Felix d'Herelle

Includes bibliographical references

Matuz, Roger

★ **Reconstruction** era: biographies; Lawrence W. Baker, project editor. UXL 2004 xxiv, 246p il (Reconstruction Era reference library) $60

Grades: 11 12 Adult   **920**
1. Reconstruction (1865-1876)
ISBN 0-7876-9218-2
LC 2004-17300

This "volume covers political and military leaders as well as activists, artists, writers, and more. Among them are Louisa May Alcott, Frederick Douglass, Ulysses S. Grant, and Zebulon Vance. Within each biographical entry are cross-references to other individuals covered in this volume." Booklist

Includes bibliographical references

Morgan, Edmund Sears

★ **American** heroes; profiles of men and women who shaped early America. [by] Edmund S. Morgan. W.W. Norton & Co. 2009 278p il $27.95

Grades: 11 12 Adult   **920**
1. Heroes and heroines 2. United States -- History -- 1783-1809 3. United States -- History -- 1775-1783, Revolution 4. United States -- History -- 1600-1775, Colonial period
ISBN 978-0-393-07010-1; 0-393-07010-7
LC 2009-714

"This book is a perfect gem. . . . Both specialists and general readers will find this book both authoritative and fun to read." Libr J

★ **My** folks don't want me to talk about slavery; twenty-one oral histories of former North Carolina slaves. edited by Belinda Hurmence. Blair 1984 103p hardcover o.p. pa $6.95

Grades: 9 10 11 12   **920**
1. Slavery -- United States 2. African Americans -- Biography
ISBN 0-89587-038-X; 0-89587-039-8 pa
LC 84-16891

The narratives presented here were part of a Federal Writers' project during which some 2,000 former slaves were interviewed during the 1930s

A "unique glimpse of slavery viewed from the less well-recorded side, the side of the subjugated." Sci Books Films

Includes bibliographical references

Not quite what I was planning; six-word memoirs by writers famous and obscure: from Smith magazine. edited by Rachel Fershleiser and Larry Smith. HarperPerennial 2008 225p il pa $12

Grades: 9 10 11 12 Adult   **920**
1. Autobiographies
ISBN 978-0-06-137405-0; 0-06-137405-9

"The editors of SMITH magazine invited readers to contribute brief life stories in the vein of Hemingway's bravura tale, 'For sale: baby shoes, never worn.' The hundreds selected for publication include offerings from children and adults, professional writers, bereaved parents, recovering broken hearts, and people with great pride in showing off their wit. . . . A good combination of inspired, inspiring, and entertaining, this title is eminently browsable and shareable." SLJ

Open the unusual door; true life stories of challenge, adventure, and success by black Americans. edited and with an introduction by Barbara Summers. Graphia 2005 206p pa $7.99

Grades: 7 8 9 10   **920**
1. African Americans -- Biography
ISBN 0-618-58531-1

"A wonderful cross section of excerpts from published autobiographies. The 16 stories tell of challenges met and opportunities recognized and realized. Colin Powell's recollection of his introduction to the military life at City College in New York City stands alongside Russell Simmons's retelling of the turning point in his life when, at 16 years of age, he shot at and missed a fellow drug dealer. . . . This little gem of a book should be a first purchase for public and school libraries." SLJ

Ottaviani, Jim

★ **Dignifying** science; stories about women scientists. written by Jim Ottaviani and illustrated by Donna Barr . . . [et al.] 3rd ed; G.T. Labs 2009 142p il pa $16.95

Grades: 6 7 8 9 10 11 12   **920**
1. Graphic novels 2. Biographical graphic novels 3. Women scientists -- Graphic novels
ISBN 978-0-9788037-3-5; 0-9788037-3-5
First published 1999

Ottaviani provides biographical sketches of women scientists such as Lise Meitner, Rosalind Franklin, Barbara McClintock, and Hedy Lamarr (yes, the actress was also an inventor); all the stories are illustrated by women comics artists, including Lea Hernandez, Linda Medley, Anne Timmons, and others.

Outman, James L.

★ **U.S.** immigration and migration. Biographies; James L. Outman, Roger Matuz, Rebecca Valentine;

Lawrence W. Baker, editor. UXL 2004 2v il (U.S. immigration and migration reference library) set $115

Grades: 9 10 11 12   **920**
1. United States -- Immigration and emigration
ISBN 0-7876-7733-7

LC 2004-3552

This set "profiles 50 men and women who either immigrated to this country or influenced the debate on the treatment of immigrants." SLJ

Includes bibliographical references

Pendergast, Tom

★ The **sixties** in America. Biographies; [by] Tom Pendergast and Sara Pendergast; Kathleen J. Edgar, project editor. UXL 2005 lvi, 204p il (U-X-L the sixties in America reference library) $63

Grades: 9 10 11 12   **920**
1. United States -- History -- 1961-1974
ISBN 0-7876-9247-6

LC 2004-16600

"Biographical entries cover counterculture icons (Bob Dylan, Abbie Hoffman), politicians and newsmakers (John F. Kennedy, Ralph Nader), mainstream celebrities (Vince Lombardi, Walter Cronkite), and individuals associated with specific events." Booklist

Includes bibliographical references

Profiles in courage for our time; edited and introduced by Caroline Kennedy. Hyperion 2002 354p $23.95; pa $14.95

Grades: 11 12 Adult   **920**
1. Judges 2. Courage 3. Lawyers 4. Governors 5. Presidents 6. Vice-presidents 7. Prisoners of war 8. Senators 9. State legislators 10. District attorneys 11. Members of Congress 12. Secretaries of labor 13. Civil rights activists 14. School superintendents 15. Presidential candidates 16. Politicians -- United States
ISBN 0-7868-6793-0; 0-7868-8678-1 pa

LC 2001-51894

"Unabashedly liberal and pro-government, this collection is a stirring look at people who rarely thought about what they could do for themselves, but always about what they could do for their country." Publ Wkly

Reef, Catherine

Frida & Diego; art, love, life. Catherine Reef. Houghton Mifflin Harcourt 2014 176 p. illustrations (some color) (hardcover) $18.99

Grades: 7 8 9 10   **920**
1. Artists -- Biography 2. Painters -- Mexico -- Biography 3. Artist couples -- Mexico -- Biography
ISBN 0547821840; 9780547821849

LC 2013021340

"Nontraditional, controversial, rebellious, and politically volatile, the Mexican artists Frida Kahlo and Diego Rivera are remembered for their provocative paintings as well as for their deep love for each other. Their marriage was one of the most tumultuous and infamous in history--filled with passion, pain, betrayal, revolution, and, above all, art that helped define the twentieth century." (Publisher's note)

"Reef points out each individual's artistic development and unique qualities as a painter. Archival photos and color reproductions of artworks further enhance the narrative. Writing a dual biography is challenging, but in this case, the portrayal of each person would seem incomplete without an understanding of the other." Booklist

Includes bibliographical references and index

Ross, Michael Elsohn

★ **Salvador** Dali and the surrealists; their lives and ideas: 21 activities. Chicago Review Press 2003 132p il pa $17.95

Grades: 9 10 11 12   **920**
1. Artists 2. Painters 3. Surrealism 4. Artists, Spanish
ISBN 1-556-52479-X

LC 2002-155628

Examines the lives and creative work of the surrealist artist Salvador Dali and other artists and friends who shared his new ways of exploring art. Features art activities that engage the subconscious thoughts and spontaneity of the reader

"This visually stunning work enhances the body of material on the artist and his contemporaries. Eminently readable, the crisply written text is detailed and thorough, including pronunciations of many place and personal names. Dali's life is presented familiarly, drawing in many details of life as an artist during that period in Europe and the relationships among the surrealists. . . . The attractive layout includes numerous excellent-quality reproductions of the work of Dali and many of the other artists mentioned in the text, and period photographs. . . . A valuable addition to any collection." SLJ

Includes bibliographical references

Rubin, Susan Goldman

Everybody paints! the lives and art of the Wyeth family. by Susan Goldman Rubin. Chronicle Books 2013 105 p. illustrations (chiefly color) (alk. paper) $16.99

Grades: 6 7 8 9 10   **920**
1. American painting 2. Artists -- United States -- Biography 3. Wyeth family
ISBN 0811869849; 9780811869843

LC 2013006595

Author Susan Goldman Rubin "shares the . . . story of the Wyeths--N.C., Andrew, and Jamie--three generations of painters and arguably the First Family of American Art. The . . . text traces the events that shaped their art and the ways their art influenced them in return, while the . . . design showcases . . . reproductions of the works that have made the Wyeth family legendary." (Publisher's note)

"This small-trim book celebrates the artistic Wyeth family, mostly the work of revered illustrator N. C. Wyeth; his son Andrew, popular modern realist best-known for Christina's World; and grandson Jamie, an acclaimed painter working today. Rubin's prose is fluid, and seamlessly worked-in quotes from her subjects add to the narrative's personal feel. The handsome, clean design showcases the excellent reproductions." Horn Book

Schiff, Karenna Gore

Lighting the way; nine women who changed modern America. Miramax Books/Hyperion 2006 528p il $25.95; pa $17.95

Grades: 11 12 Adult   **920**

1. Women -- United States -- Biography

ISBN 1-4013-5218-9; 1-4013-6015-7 pa

LC 2005-56247

"This is an inspirational collection of biographies of women of various social, ethnic, and racial backgrounds fighting for social justice." Booklist

Includes bibliographical references

See, Lisa

On Gold Mountain; the one-hundred-year odyssey of my Chinese-American family. 1st Vintage Books ed; Vintage Books 1996 xxi, 394p il, maps pa $15.95

Grades: 11 12 Adult   **920**

1. Chinese Americans

ISBN 0-679-76852-1

LC 96-11821

First published 1995 by St. Martin's Press

"Facing the nimble shell game her family plays with its history, Ms. See has done a gallant and fair-minded job of fashioning anecdote, fable and fact into an engaging account." N Y Times Book Rev

Includes bibliographical references

Sickels, Amy

★ **African**-American writers. Chelsea House 2010 141p il (Multicultural voices) $35

Grades: 9 10 11 12   **920**

1. African Americans in literature 2. African Americans -- Intellectual life 3. American literature -- African American authors

ISBN 978-1-60413-311-0

LC 2009-37856

"In this clearly written, informative overview, Sickels examines the lives and major works of writers over the last 40 years. Eight authors are showcased, including Toni Morrison, Maya Angelou, Alice Walker, and Walter Dean Myers. Each chapter opens with a black-and-white photo and a brief biography, with the remainder of it dealing with a critical analysis of one or more of the writer's best-known works. . . . This is an outstanding contribution and should be a first purchase for high-school libraries." SLJ

Includes bibliographical references

★ **Sifters:** Native American women's lives; edited by Theda Perdue. Oxford Univ. Press 2001 260p (Viewpoints on American culture) $55; pa $19.95

Grades: 11 12 Adult   **920**

1. Native American women

ISBN 0-19-513080-4; 0-19-513081-2 pa

LC 00-39950

"From Pocahontas, a Powhatan woman of the seventeenth century, to Ada Deer, the Menominee woman who headed the Bureau of Indian Affairs in the 1990s, the essays span four centuries. Each one recounts the experiences of

women from vastly different cultural traditions. . . . Contributors focus on the ways in which different women have fashioned lives that remain firmly rooted in their identity as Native women." Publisher's note

Includes bibliographical references

Spitz, Bob

Yeah! yeah! yeah! the Beatles, Beatlemania, and the music that changed the world. Little, Brown 2007 234p il $18.99

Grades: 7 8 9 10   **920**

1. Rock musicians 2. Beatles

ISBN 978-0-316-11555-1; 0-316-11555-X

LC 2006-39575

Based on the author's title for adults: The Beatles (2005)

This is "packed with all the fun and fabulousness that were the Beatles. The book begins at the church festival where John and Paul met as teens, and ends with Paul's formal declaration to leave the group. . . . [This is] comprehensive, sensitive to its subjects, and told with a flow that carries readers along. Many smartly chosen black-and-white photographs help re-create the times." Booklist

Stark, Steven D.

Meet the Beatles; a cultural history of the band that shook youth, gender, and the world. HarperEntertainment 2005 344p il $26.95; pa $14.95

Grades: 11 12 Adult   **920**

1. Rock musicians 2. Beatles

ISBN 0-06-000892-X; 0-06-000893-8 pa

LC 2004-59794

In this biography of the Beatles, the author focuses "as much on the cultural trends that produced the Beatles—and the trends they created—as on the Fab Four themselves. . . . Throughout, Stark is sharp and insightful, even when he wades into the psychoanalytic waters of the John/Yoko and Paul/Linda relationships." Publ Wkly

★ **Stolen** voices; young people's war diaries from World War I to Iraq. edited with commentaries by Zlata Filipovic and Melanie Challenger; foreword by Olara A. Otunnu. Penguin 2007 xxiii, 293p il pa $14

Grades: 11 12 Adult   **920**

1. Children and war

ISBN 978-0-14-303871-9; 0-14-303871-0

The editors have "compiled 14 diaries that were kept by children during wartime, from World War I to Iraq. Their poignant voices will break your heart." Libr J

Terkel, Studs, 1912-2008

Hope dies last; keeping the faith in difficult times. New Press 2003 xxix, 326p hardcover o.p. pa $16.95

Grades: 11 12 Adult   **920**

1. Hope 2. United States -- Social conditions

ISBN 1-56584-837-3; 1-56584-937-X pa

LC 2003-50989

"Terkel talks with objectors, dissenters, observers, protestors, and do-gooders to find out what makes these committed and generous souls tick. He speaks with Ohio congressman and Democratic presidential candidate Dennis Kucinich, a doctor who treats the homeless, teachers, labor activists, recent immigrants, Pete Seeger, and John Kenneth Galbraith. . . . As a collector of true stories and a guardian of free speech, Terkel ensures that grass-root alternatives to the 'official word' are heard from sea to shining sea." Booklist

Watad, Mahmoud

Teen voices from the Holy Land; who am I to you? [by] Mahmoud Watad and Leonard Grob. Prometheus Books 2007 221p il pa $19

Grades: 9 10 11 12   **920**

1. Youth -- Israel

ISBN 978-1-59102-535-1

LC 2007-1565

"Based on interviews of thirty-four Palestinian and Israeli teenagers, . . . [this book presents] first-person narratives of their day-to-day lives. These young people describe their ordinary lives, including their interests, facts about their families, friendships, and neighborhoods, as well as their spiritual concerns and dreams for the future." Publisher's note

Includes bibliographical references

What my father gave me; daughters speak. edited by Melanie Little. Annick Press 2010 129p $21.95; pa $12.95

Grades: 10 11 12   **920**

1. Women authors 2. Father-daughter relationship

ISBN 978-1-55451-255-3; 978-1-55451-254-6 pa

"In this collection of first-person essays, seven women discuss their adolescent relationships with their fathers and how they affected their adult lives. . . . These and the other essays are intensely personal and honest, and the writers do not shy away from discussing some very painful subjects. Teens will appreciate this honesty and openness, making this anthology a good choice for YA collections." SLJ

Windows into my world; Latino youth write their lives. edited by Sarah Cortez; with an introduction by Virgil Suárez. Piñata Books 2007 210p pa $14.95

Grades: 10 11 12   **920**

1. Hispanic Americans -- Biography

ISBN 978-1-55885-482-6; 1-55885-482-7

LC 2006-52470

Autobiographies of Latino youth who struggle with issues such as death, anorexia, divorce, sexuality, etc.

"For young adults of all backgrounds, this collection illuminates both the familiar coming-of-age experiences that transcend cultural differences and the moments that are unique to young Latinos in the States." SLJ

920.003   Dictionaries, encyclopedias, concordances of biography as a discipline

Aaseng, Nathan

★ **African**-American athletes; Rev. ed.; Facts On File 2010 280p il (A to Z of African Americans) $49.50

Grades: 11 12 Adult   **920.003**

1. Reference books 2. African American athletes -- Dictionaries

ISBN 978-0-8160-7869-1

LC 2010-10023

First published 2003

This book "highlights athletes who have competed at the highest levels in one or more sports. Each entry provides . . . [a] biographical profile, concentrating on the events in that person's life related to his or her accomplishments in sports, followed by . . . [a] further reading list on that individual." Publisher's note

Includes bibliographical references

African American biographies. Grolier 2006 10v il set $529

Grades: 6 7 8 9 10 11 12   **920.003**

1. Reference books 2. African Americans -- Biography -- Dictionaries

ISBN 978-0-7172-6090-4

LC 2005-50391

"Entries cover a gamut of achievers: leaders of abolition, slaves, politicians, civil-rights activists, lawyers, educators, physicians, scientists, religious figures, military personnel, journalists, business leaders, artists, astronauts, entertainers, and sports figures. . . . It is nearly impossible to find fault with this important and visually appealing set. From the high quality of the paper to the layout of the pages, the attention given to creating a superior source is evident. For the student researcher, the material is clear, concise, and user-friendly in presentation." Booklist

Includes bibliographical references

★ The **African** American national biography; editors in chief, Henry Louis Gates, Jr., Evelyn Brooks-Higginbotham. Oxford University Press 2008 8v il set $995

Grades: 11 12 Adult   **920.003**

1. Reference books 2. African Americans -- Biography -- Dictionaries

ISBN 978-0-19-516019-2

LC 2007-44671

"A supplement to the 24-volume American National Biography . . . [this biographical encyclopedia] records the contributions of more than 4,000 African Americans—slaves, architects, entertainers, dentists, political leaders, artists, poets, and activists. . . . [This] is a major . . . standard reference work that most libraries of any size will want to have." Booklist

Includes bibliographical references

American Indian biographies; edited by Carole Barrett, Harvey Markowitz, project editor, R. Kent Rasmussen. rev ed.; Salem Press 2005 623p il map (Magill's choice) $62

Grades: 8 9 10 11 12 Adult   **920.003**

1. Reference books 2. Native Americans -- Biography

ISBN 1-58765-233-1; 978-1-58765-233-2

LC 2004-28872

First published 1999; some essays originally appeared in Dictionary of world biography, Great lives from history:

the Renaissance & early modern era, 1454-1600 (2005), and American ethnic writers (2000)

"The book contains essays on religious, social, and political leaders; warriors; and reformers from the past as well as modern activists, writers, artists, entertainers, scientists, and athletes. . . . A great bargain and an asset in any library that supports an American history curriculum." Booklist

Includes bibliographical references

Bader, Philip

★ **African**-American writers; revised by Catherine Reef. Rev. ed; Facts On File 2010 340p il (A to Z of African Americans) $49.50

Grades: 9 10 11 12 Adult   920.003
1. Reference books 2. African American authors -- Dictionaries 3. American literature -- African American authors -- Bio-bibliography
ISBN 978-0-8160-8141-7

LC 2010-05463

First published 2004

This book "profiles popular and prominent African-American writers across many genres of literature. Each entry in this . . . resource provides a biographical profile, concentrating on the major literary works and accomplishments of each author as well as an outline of his or her contributions to American literature." Publisher's note

Includes bibliographical references

Barthelmas, Della Gray

The **signers** of the Declaration of Independence; a biographical and genealogical reference. with a foreword by Frank Borman. McFarland & Co. 1997 334p il hardcover o.p. pa $35

Grades: 11 12 Adult   920.003
1. Reference books 2. United States -- Declaration of Independence 3. United States -- History -- 1775-1783, Revolution -- Biography
ISBN 0-7864-0318-7; 0-7864-1704-8 pa

LC 97-11663

Entries begin "with a full-page portrait of the signer and a facsimile of his signature as it appears on the document. The biographies range from one to 10 pages, followed by family information on the person (wives and children), then by genealogies of his and his spouse's ancestors for as many generations as possible." Book Rep

★ **Biographical** encyclopedia of artists; Sir Lawrence Gowing, general editor. Facts on File 2005 4v il set $260

Grades: 11 12 Adult   920.003
1. Reference books 2. Artists -- Biography -- Encyclopedias
ISBN 0-8160-5803-2

LC 2005-40500

First published 1983 by Prentice-Hall as volume two of Encyclopedia of visual art

"The artists covered include Laurie Anderson, Frank Gehry, Anselm Kiefer, Jan Vermeer, and Andy Warhol. . . . A visual chronology of artists by country and era functions as an index to artists, and an alphabetical artist/subject index concludes the work." Libr J

Includes bibliographical references

Black women in America; Darlene Clark Hine, editor in chief. 2nd ed; Oxford University Press 2005 3v il set $325

Grades: 11 12 Adult   920.003
1. Reference books 2. African American women -- Dictionaries
ISBN 0-19-515677-3

LC 2005-1532

First published 1993 by Carlson Pub.

"The essays offer fascinating glimpses into black women's economic, social, and political contributions, even at the grassroots level, and explore issues such as spirituality, domestic servitude, and mixed-race identity in terms of how they have shaped history." SLJ

Includes bibliographical references

Blanchard, Mary Loving

★ **Poets** for young adults; their lives and works. [by] Mary Loving Blanchard and Cara Falcetti. Greenwood Press 2006 287p il $59.95

Grades: 9 10 11 12   920.003
1. Reference books 2. Poets, American -- Dictionaries 3. American poetry -- Bio-bibliography
ISBN 0-313-32884-6; 978-0-313-32884-8

LC 2006-29475

This book "examines the lives and works of seventy-five poets that are read and loved by teens. . . . [The poets covered range] from the modern songwriters such as Bob Dylan and Tupac Shakur, to the nineteen sixties icons Jack Kerouac and Sylvia Plath, to such traditional poets as Edgar Allan Poe and William Blake." Publisher's note

Includes bibliographical references

British writers; edited under the auspices of the British Council; Ian Scott-Kilvert, general editor. Scribner 1979 7v + supplement I-IV set $2379

Grades: 11 12 Adult   920.003
1. Reference books 2. Authors, English -- Dictionaries 3. English literature -- Bio-bibliography 4. English literature -- History and criticism
ISBN 0-684-80587-1

"This work presents articles by distinguished contributors on major British writers from the fourteenth century to the present. . . . The biographical sketch that opens each entry is followed by a survey of the author's principal works, a critical evaluation, and an updated bibliography." Ref Sources for Small & Medium-sized Libr. 6th edition

Butler, Alban

★ **Butler's** Lives of the saints. Christian Classics 1956 4v set $149.95; pa set $109.95

Grades: 11 12 Adult   920.003
1. Reference books 2. Christian saints -- Dictionaries
ISBN 0-87061-045-7; 0-87061-137-2 pa

A reprint of the four volume set published 1956 by Kenedy; New edition of a work first published 1756-1759. The calendar arrangement is retained, but the number of entries has almost doubled and many of the entries have been rewritten in whole or part

"The biographies of the saints and beati are arranged by their feast days with each of the four volumes containing three months. . . . Each volume has a table of contents arranged by the days of the month with a list of the feasts for each day." Booklist

Carey, Charles W.

★ **African** Americans in science; an encyclopedia of people and progress. [by] Charles W. Carey, Jr. ABC-CLIO 2008 2v il set $195

Grades: 9 10 11 12 Adult   **920.003**
1. Reference books 2. Scientists -- Encyclopedias 3. African Americans -- Biography -- Encyclopedias
ISBN 978-1-85109-998-6

LC 2008-24609

This resource takes "a detailed look at the accomplishments of African American scientists. . . . Part 1 addresses the accomplishments of individual scientists. Part 2 covers the issues that are of critical importance to the African American scientific community, including science education and careers for blacks and a whole range of topics related to health disparities (e.g., cancer, obesity, cardiovascular issues, and diabetes). Part 3 outlines in more general terms the contributions made by the scientists in Part 1. Part 4 focuses on scientific research and training." Libr J
Includes bibliographical references

African-American political leaders; [by] Charles W. Carey, Jr.; revised by Liz Sonneborn. Rev. ed.; Facts On File 2011 374p il (A to Z of African Americans) $49.50

Grades: 11 12 Adult   **920.003**
1. Reference books 2. Politicians -- Dictionaries 3. Political activists -- Dictionaries 4. African Americans -- Biography -- Dictionaries
ISBN 978-0-8160-8120-2; 978-1-4381-3487-1 ebook

LC 2010-42294

First published 2004

This book "covers more than 180 individuals, from a handful who were born in the 1820s to contemporary figures such as Corey Booker and Adrian M. Fenty. . . . A nine-page introduction, a bibliography, and lists of 'Entries by Office Held' and 'Entries by Year of Birth' enhance the volume's usefulness." Booklist
Includes bibliographical references

Duncan, Joyce

Shapers of the great debate on women's rights; a biographical dictionary. Greenwood Press 2008 232p (Shapers of the great American debates) $75

Grades: 9 10 11 12 Adult   **920.003**
1. Reference books 2. Women -- Biography -- Dictionaries 3. Women political activists -- Dictionaries
ISBN 978-0-313-33869-4; 0-313-33869-8

LC 2008-23050

"The three waves of feminism are explored through the lives of the women who made history in bringing women's issues to the forefront of American society. . . . Many notable women, such as Susan B. Anthony, Elizabeth Cady Stanton, Billie Jean King, Betty Friedan, Helen Gurley Brown, Jane Fonda, and Sandra Day O'Connor, are included in this history of the women's movement in America." Publisher's note
Includes bibliographical references

★ **Encyclopedia** of women's autobiography; edited by Victoria Boynton and Jo Malin; Emmanuel S. Nelson, advisory editor. Greenwood Press 2005 2v set $249.95

Grades: 11 12 Adult   **920.003**
1. Autobiography 2. Reference books 3. Women -- Biography -- Encyclopedias
ISBN 0-313-32737-8

LC 2005-8526

This set's "encyclopedic and culturally diverse nature should appeal to a wide audience and provide a valuable starting point for further research." Libr J
Includes bibliographical references

Friedman, Ian C.

★ **Latino** athletes. Facts on File 2007 278p il (A to Z of Latino Americans) $44

Grades: 11 12 Adult   **920.003**
1. Reference books 2. Athletes -- Dictionaries 3. Hispanic Americans -- Dictionaries
ISBN 978-0-8160-6384-0; 0-8160-6384-2

LC 2006-16901

"Gymnast Trent Dimas, mountain biker Juli Furtado, and speed skater Derek Parra are among the 176 athletes profiled in this volume. . . . Following the entries, athletes are listed by sport, year of birth, and ethnicity or country of origin." Booklist
Includes bibliographical references

Great athletes; edited by The Editors of Salem Press; special consultant Rafer Johnson. Salem Press 2010 13v il set $1,020

Grades: 7 8 9 10 11 12   **920.003**
1. Reference books 2. Athletes -- Dictionaries
ISBN 978-1-58765-473-2; 1-58765-473-3

LC 2009-21905

"This massive undertaking totals 1,470 entries covering athletes in baseball, basketball, boxing, football, golf, auto racing, soccer, tennis, and Olympic sports. Additionally, well-known athletes in other, less recognized sports—such as cycling, skateboarding, stunt riding, martial-arts and chess—are included. . . . Overall, this is a well-put-together and wide-ranging set." Booklist
Includes bibliographical references

Great lives from history

Great lives from history, The 18th century, 1701-1800; editor, John Powell; editor, first edition, Frank N. Magill. Salem Press 2006 2v il map set $160

Grades: 11 12 Adult   **920.003**
1. Reference books 2. Biography -- Dictionaries 3. World history -- 18th century
ISBN 978-1-58765-276-9; 1-58765-276-5

LC 2006-5336

Companion volume to Great events from history, The 18th century, 1701-1800

First published as part of the Great lives from history series, published 1987-1995 under the editorship of Frank N. Magill; previously published as half of volume 4 of Dictionary of world biography, published 1998-1999

"The alphabetically listed subjects encompass 36 areas of expertise and include John Newbery, Pontiac, Qianlong, Hannah More, Pius IV, Paul Revere, and Shah Wali Allah, among others. Each article is approximately three pages long and lists the subject's major accomplishments, important dates, and areas of achievement. . . . A well-written, useful set." SLJ

Includes bibliographical references

Great lives from history, The 17th century, 1601-1700; editor, Larissa Juliet Taylor. Salem Press 2005 2v il set $160

Grades: 11 12 Adult   **920.003**
1. Reference books 2. Biography -- Dictionaries 3. World history -- 17th century
ISBN 1-58765-222-6; 978-1-58765-222-6

LC 2005-17804

Companion volume to Great events from history, The 17th century, 1601-1700

First published as part of the Great lives from history series, published 1987-1995 under the editorship of Frank N. Magill; previously published as half of volume 4 of Dictionary of world biography, published 1998-1999

This "is a collection of biographical essays, ranging from three to five pages in length and documenting the lives of those individuals who helped to shape the history of the 17th century. The coverage is also global and includes both well-known and lesser-known figures." SLJ

Includes bibliographical references

Great lives from history, The 19th century, 1801-1900; editor, John Powell. Salem Press 2006 4v il map set $360

Grades: 11 12 Adult   **920.003**
1. Reference books 2. Biography -- Dictionaries 3. World history -- 19th century
ISBN 978-1-58765-292-9; 1-58765-292-7

LC 2006-20187

Companion volume to Great events from history, The 19th century, 1801-1900

First published as part of the Great lives from history series, published 1987-1995 under the editorship of Frank N. Magill; previously published as volumes 5 and 6 of Dictionary of world biography, published 1998-1999

"A total of 737 essays covering 757 major figures including 123 on women make up the set. . . . Major world leaders appear here, as well as the giants of religious faith who dominated the century: monarchs, presidents, popes, philosophers, writers, social reformers, educators, and military leaders who left their imprint on political as well as spiritual institutions." Publisher's note

Includes bibliographical references

Great lives from history, The ancient world, prehistory-476 C.E; editor, Christina A. Salowey. Salem Press 2004 2v il, maps set $160

Grades: 11 12 Adult   **920.003**
1. Ancient history 2. Reference books 3. Biography -- Dictionaries
ISBN 1-587-65152-1; 978-1-58765-164-9

LC 2004-705

Companion volume to Great events from history, The ancient world, prehistory-476 C.E

First published as part of the Great lives from history series, published 1987-1995 under the editorship of Frank N. Magill; previously published as volume 1 of Dictionary of world biography, published 1998-1999

This "set provides three-to-six-page biographies on major personages from the ancient world. Arranged alphabetically, each article gives basic information such as when and where the individual was born and also where and when he or she died, a description of his or her early life and life's work, the significance of the individual, an annotated bibliography, and related entries in both this set and in the . . . [Great events from history] set." Ref & User Services Quarterly

Includes bibliographical references

Great lives from history, the Middle Ages, 477-1453; editor, Shelley Wolbrink. Salem Press 2005 2v il map set $160

Grades: 11 12 Adult   **920.003**
1. Reference books 2. Middle ages -- Biography 3. Biography -- Dictionaries
ISBN 1-58765-164-5; 978-1-58765-164-9

LC 2004-16696

Companion volume to Great events from history, the Middle Ages, 477-1453

First published as part of the Great lives from history series, published 1987-1995 under the editorship of Frank N. Magill; previously published as volume 2 of Dictionary of world biography, published 1998-1999

These "volumes focus on the people throughout the world from after the Fall of Rome, in 476 C.E., to 1453. Coverage is worldwide. . . . Each entry begins with ready-reference information, followed by a summary of the person's life, a paragraph or two on 'Significance,' a list of further readings, and cross-references to entries both within the set and within the [Great events in history] companion set." Booklist

Includes bibliographical references

Great lives from history, the Renaissance & early modern era, 1454-1600; editor, Christina J. Moose. Salem Press 2005 2v il map set $160

Grades: 11 12 Adult   **920.003**
1. Renaissance 2. Reference books 3. Biography -- Dictionaries
ISBN 1-58765-211-0; 978-1-58765-211-0

LC 2004-28875

Companion volume to Great events from history, the Renaissance & early modern era, 1454-1600

First published as part of the Great lives from history series, published 1987-1995 under the editorship of Frank N. Magill; previously published as volume 3 of Dictionary of world biography, published 1998-1999

"This two-volume work offers biographies of 338 historical figures in entries that range from two to five pages in length. A publisher's note in volume 1 explains the set's format and use. All the biographies include name, nationality or ethnicity, historical role, dates, and area(s) of achievement; description of early life, work, and significance; an annotated bibliography; and cross-references." Choice

Includes bibliographical references

Great lives from history: the 20th century, 1901-2000; editor, Robert F. Gorman. Salem Press 2008 10v il set $795

Grades: 11 12 Adult **920.003**
1. Reference books 2. Biography -- Dictionaries 3. World history -- 20th century
ISBN 978-1-58765-345-2

LC 2008-17125

First published as part of the Great lives from history series, published 1987-1995 under the editorship of Frank N. Magill; previously published as volumes 7-9 of Dictionary of world biography, published 1998-1999

"This ten-volume set offers 1,330 . . . biographies of major personages in world history (many still living) from 1901-2000. . . . The personages covered are identified with one or more of the following regions: Africa, Asia, Australia, Caribbean, Europe, Latin America, Middle East, North America, South America, and Southeast Asia." Publisher's note

Includes bibliographical references

Grossman, Mark

World military leaders; a biographical dictionary. Facts on File 2007 414p il (Facts on File library of world history) $75

Grades: 9 10 11 12 Adult **920.003**
1. Reference books 2. Biography -- Dictionaries 3. Military history -- Dictionaries
ISBN 0-8160-4732-4; 978-0-8160-4732-1

LC 2005-8908

"Spanning the centuries from 3500 BCE to the present, this . . . A-to-Z dictionary presents the stories of the military leaders whose actions precipitated enormous change in the world around them." Publisher's note

Includes bibliographical references

Hamilton, Neil A.

★ **Presidents**; a biographical dictionary. Ian C. Friedman, reviser. 3rd ed; Facts on File 2010 496p il (Facts on File library of American history) $85; pa $19.95

Grades: 11 12 Adult **920.003**
1. Reference books 2. Presidents -- United States -- Dictionaries
ISBN 978-0-8160-7708-3; 978-0-8160-8247-6 pa

LC 2009-10191

First published 2001

This book "contains biographies and portraits of all presidents, a . . . chronology of the life of each president, and suggested further reading about each president." Publisher's note

Includes bibliographical references

Heaphy, Maura

Science fiction authors; a research guide. Libraries Unlimited 2009 xxx, 318p (Author research series) pa $40

Grades: Adult Professional **920.003**
1. Reference books 2. Authors -- Dictionaries 3.

Science fiction -- Bio-bibliography
ISBN 978-1-59158-515-2

LC 2008-25708

"This volume will be invaluable to reader's advisory librarians and as a 'what to read next' guide for fans of the genre." SLJ

Includes bibliographical references

Holy people of the world; a cross-cultural encyclopedia. Phyllis G. Jestice, editor. ABC-CLIO 2004 3v il set $285

Grades: 11 12 Adult **920.003**
1. Reference books 2. Religious biography -- Encyclopedias
ISBN 1-576-07355-6

LC 2004-22606

"This edition deserves to become well-worn by the time a second appears." Libr J

Includes bibliographical references

Jones, J. Sydney

The **Crusades,** Biographies; written by J. Sydney Jones; edited by Marcia Merryman Means and Neil Schlager. UXL 2005 xxii, 230p il (The Crusades reference library) $63

Grades: 11 12 Adult **920.003**
1. Crusades
ISBN 0-7876-9177-1

LC 2004-18000

This book "includes entries on 25 key figures. Both well-known figures, such as the Muslim leader Saladin and Eleanor of Aquitaine, and those who are maybe less familiar, such as Anna Comnena, the twelfth-century author and Byzantine princess, are covered. Each entry has a boxed quotation by its subject, and most include portraits. The entries are readable and well organized." Booklist

Includes bibliographical references

Kort, Carol

A to Z of American women writers; Rev ed; Facts on File 2007 398p il (Facts on File library of American history) $60

Grades: 11 12 Adult **920.003**
1. Reference books 2. American literature -- Women authors -- Dictionaries
ISBN 978-0-8160-6693-3

LC 2007-20534

First published 2000

This dictionary "profiles 186 . . . women, among them poets, essayists, journalists, editors, novelists, memoirists, and numerous other types of writers." Publisher's note

Includes bibliographical references

Levin, Carole

Extraordinary women of the Medieval and Renaissance world; a biographical dictionary. [by] Carole Levin [et al.] Greenwood Press 2000 327p il $65

Grades: 11 12 Adult **920.003**
1. Renaissance 2. Reference books 3. Middle ages

-- Biography 4. Women -- Biography -- Dictionaries
ISBN 0-313-30659-1

LC 99-55218

This volume presents seventy women who "lived between the tenth and seventeenth centuries. . . . The entries are arranged in alphabetical order, with a brief subheading noting country and occupation. As much information as is known about the person is summarized, including education, family, and achievements. Each article ends with a bibliography of additional sources of information. A number of the articles include portraits." Booklist
Includes bibliographical references

★ The **Lincoln** Library of Sports Champions; 9th edition Lincoln Library 2013 14 v. illustrations $523

Grades: 7 8 9 10 11 12   **920.003**
1. Sports 2. Athletes
ISBN 0912168005; 9780912168005
First published 1975
Presents brief, alphabetically arranged biographies of nearly 300 great sports personalities, past and present, from around the world. Features a table of contents arranged by sport and a supplementary reading list.

Mandel, David
Who's who in the Jewish Bible. Jewish Publication Society 2007 xx, 422p pa $30

Grades: 9 10 11 12 Adult   **920.003**
1. Reference books 2. Bible -- O.T. -- Biography -- Dictionaries
ISBN 978-0-8276-0863-4; 0-8276-0863-2

LC 2007-27288

"Using only the Bible as its basis, this encyclopedia catalogues 3,000 characters from A to Z. General readers and students interested in past Jewish life will find this work most useful as a quick reference for information and a starting point for research." Booklist
Includes bibliographical references

Martinez Wood, Jamie
★ **Latino** writers and journalists. Facts on File 2007 294p il (A to Z of Latino Americans) $44

Grades: 11 12 Adult   **920.003**
1. Reference books 2. Hispanic Americans -- Dictionaries 3. American literature -- Hispanic American authors -- Bio-bibliography
ISBN 0-8160-6422-9; 978-0-8160-6422-9

LC 2006-17394

This book "brings together 150 writers identified as Latino Americans. Approximately one-third of the profiles are accompanied by photographs." Booklist
Includes bibliographical references

Musicians & composers of the 20th century; editor Alfred W. Cramer. Salem Press 2009 5v il set $399

Grades: 9 10 11 12 Adult   **920.003**
1. Reference books 2. Music -- Bio-bibliography 3. Musicians -- Dictionaries
ISBN 978-1-58765-512-8

LC 2009-2980

"The work covers 614 composers, performers, and teachers, chosen for musical influence as well as fame. All major genres are covered, from classical to rap, along with many subgenres, such as rockabilly, atonal, and funk. . . . This work provides valuable, basic information on the topic as well as multiple, easy-access routes to it. Highly recommended." Libr J
Includes bibliographical references

New dictionary of scientific biography; Noretta Koertge, editor in chief. Scribner's 2008 8v il set $995

Grades: 11 12 Adult   **920.003**
1. Reference books 2. Scientists -- Dictionaries
ISBN 978-0-684-31320-7

LC 2007-31384

First published 1970-1980 in 16 volumes with title: Dictionary of scientific biography
This biographical dictionary "contains thousands of biographies of mathematicians and natural scientists from all countries and from all historical periods." Publisher's note
Includes bibliographical references

Newton, David E.
★ **Latinos** in science, math, and professions. Facts on File 2007 274p il (A to Z of Latino Americans) $44

Grades: 11 12 Adult   **920.003**
1. Reference books 2. Scientists -- Dictionaries 3. Mathematicians -- Dictionaries 4. Hispanic Americans -- Dictionaries
ISBN 978-0-8160-6385-7; 0-8160-6385-0

LC 2006-16769

Among the figures profiled in this biographical dictionary "are sociology expert Maxine Baca Zinn; Ellen Ochoa, the first Latina in space; and research entomologist Fernando E. Vega." Libr J
Includes bibliographical references

Oakes, Elizabeth H.
★ **Encyclopedia** of world scientists; Rev. ed.; Facts on File 2007 2v il (Facts on File science library) set $170

Grades: 9 10 11 12 Adult   **920.003**
1. Reference books 2. Scientists -- Encyclopedias
ISBN 978-0-8160-6158-7; 0-8160-6158-0

LC 2007-6076

First published 2001
This work contains "stories of nearly 1,000 scientists—almost half of whom are female—who have contributed significantly to their fields. All scientific disciplines are represented, as well as all periods of history as far back as 600 BCE." Publisher's note
Includes bibliographical references

Otfinoski, Steven
African Americans in the performing arts; Rev. ed.; Facts On File 2010 280p il (A to Z of African Americans) $49.50

Grades: 11 12 Adult   **920.003**
1. Reference books 2. African American actors --

Dictionaries 3. African American dancers -- Dictionaries 4. African American musicians -- Dictionaries 5. African Americans -- Biography -- Dictionaries
ISBN 978-0-8160-7838-7

LC 2009-12400

First published 2003

"Profiling actors, dancers, singers, musicians, composers, and choreographers (the latter two categories only when they are performers as well as creators), alphabetically arranged entries were selected based on 'personal preference, historical importance, variety, and level of achievement.' . . . Entries describe each subject's life and discuss how personal experience affected his or her art. . . . A sound and inexpensive addition for high-school and public libraries." Booklist

Includes bibliographical references

African Americans in the visual arts; Rev. ed.; Facts on File 2010 272p il (A to Z of African Americans) $49.50

Grades: 11 12 Adult   **920.003**

1. Reference books 2. African American artists -- Dictionaries 3. African Americans -- Biography -- Dictionaries
ISBN 978-0-8160-7840-0; 978-1-4381-3768-1 ebook

LC 2009-27202

First published 2003

"Each entry in this . . . volume provides a brief biographical sketch of the artist, addressing the major achievements, events, and contributions of the artist's career." Publisher's note

Includes bibliographical references

★ **Latinos** in the arts. Facts on File 2007 277p il (A to Z of Latino Americans) $44

Grades: 11 12 Adult   **920.003**

1. Reference books 2. Actors -- Dictionaries 3. Artists -- Dictionaries 4. Musicians -- Dictionaries 5. Hispanic Americans -- Dictionaries
ISBN 978-0-8160-6394-9; 0-8160-6394-X

LC 2006-16900

"This volume profiles more than 178 individuals in the performing and visual arts 'who were born in the United States or who settled here permanently,' among them Marc Anthony, Cameron Diaz, Carmen Miranda, Tito Punete, and Shakira. Each entry concludes with a list of 'Further Reading' . . . and, in many cases, 'Further Listening' and 'Further Viewing.'" Booklist

Includes bibliographical references

Radcliffe Institute for Advanced Study

Notable American women; a biographical dictionary completing the twentieth century. Susan Ware, editor; Stacy Braukman, assistant editor. Belknap Press 2004 xxx, 729p $45

Grades: 11 12 Adult   **920.003**

1. Reference books 2. Women -- United States -- Biography 3. United States -- Biography -- Dictionaries
ISBN 0-674-01488-X

LC 2004-48859

This volume includes "stars of the golden ages of radio, film, dance, and television; scientists and scholars; politicians and entrepreneurs; authors and aviators; civil rights activists and religious leaders; Native American craftspeople and world-renowned artists. Women from a broad spectrum of ethnic , class, political, religious, and sexual identities are all acknowledged." Publisher's note

Includes bibliographical references

Reef, Catherine

African Americans in the military; Rev ed; Facts On File 2010 284p bibl il (A to Z of African Americans) $49.50

Grades: 11 12 Adult   **920.003**

1. Reference books 2. African American soldiers -- Dictionaries
ISBN 978-0-8160-7839-4

LC 2009-31298

First published 2004

This book "covers African American contributions to military efforts from the American Revolution to the present. The more than 130 entries also include selected persons from the British and French armies as well as the Canadian armed forces, although the U.S. military is the main focus." Booklist

Includes bibliographical references

Rich, Mari

World authors, 2000-2005; editors, Jennifer Curry, David Ramm, Mari Rich, Albert Rolls. Wilson, H. W. 2007 800p il (Authors series) $170

Grades: 11 12 Adult   **920.003**

1. Reference books 2. Authors -- Dictionaries 3. Literature -- Bio-bibliography
ISBN 978-0-8242-1077-9

This book "covers some 300 novelists, poets, dramatists, essayists, scientists, biographers, and other authors whose books [were] published 2000 through 2005." Publisher's note

Schneider, Dorothy

★ **First** ladies; a biographical dictionary. [by] Dorothy Schneider, Carl J. Schneider. 3rd ed; Facts on File 2010 436p il (Facts on File library of American history) $85

Grades: 11 12 Adult   **920.003**

1. Reference books 2. Presidents' spouses -- United States -- Dictionaries
ISBN 978-0-8160-7724-3

LC 2009-9047

First published 2001

This book "covers all the women who have held this esteemed 'office' since the founding of the United States. . . . Arranged chronologically by term of presidency, each biographical entry includes a . . . biography emphasizing each first lady's life during the presidency, as well as a chronology, appendixes, and suggestions for further reading." Publisher's note

Includes bibliographical references

The **Scribner** encyclopedia of American lives; Kenneth T. Jackson, editor in chief; Karen Markoe,

general editor; Arnold Markoe, executive editor.
Scribner 1998 8v il set $768
Grades: 11 12 Adult   **920.003**
1. Reference books 2. United States -- Biography --
Dictionaries
ISBN 0-684-31292-1

LC 98-33793

"Scribner envisions SEAL as the continuation of the
Dictionary of American Biography (DAB). . . . Selection criteria are that the biographees made significant contributions
to American life and culture. . . . An appreciable number of
women and people of color are recognized. All biographies
are signed contributions by 332 scholars." Libr J [review of
first two volumes]

Snodgrass, Mary Ellen

Who's who in the Middle Ages; illustrations re-
search by Linda Campbell Franklin. McFarland &
Co. 2001 312p il $75
Grades: 11 12 Adult   **920.003**
1. Reference books 2. Medieval civilization --
Dictionaries 3. Middle ages -- Biography -- Dictionaries
ISBN 0-7864-0774-3

LC 00-56243

"Entries are alphabetical; the scope is from the fifth century to the fifteenth. Each entry, giving an array of names
and alternate names for the person, includes both personal
and historical details. References are included with each entry, and a bibliography accompanies the whole. Appendices
cover the colleges and universities that educated many of
the people, and the period's noteworthy events, major monasteries, abbeys and convents and their founders and dates,
individuals listed by occupation or contribution, and popes,
emperors and monarchs." Publisher's note
Includes bibliographical references

Sonneborn, Liz

★ **A to Z of American Indian women**; rev ed;
Facts on File 2007 320p il map (Facts on File li-
brary of American history) $60
Grades: 8 9 10 11 12   **920.003**
1. Reference books 2. Native American women --
Dictionaries
ISBN 978-0-8160-6694-0

LC 2007-8162

First published 1998 with title: A to Z of Native
American women
"This resource is of exceptionally high quality." SLJ
Includes bibliographical references

Student's encyclopedia of great American writers;
Patricia Gantt, general editor. Facts on File 2009
5v (Facts on File library of American literature)
set $425
Grades: 9 10 11 12 Adult   **920.003**
1. Reference books 2. Authors, American --
Encyclopedias 3. American literature -- Encyclopedias
ISBN 978-0-8160-6087-0

LC 2009-30783

"More than 180 writers currently studied are profiled in
this set. chronologically, the volumes begin with colonists

such as Anne Bradstreet and revolutionary writers such as
Thomas Paine and Thomas Jefferson. Subsequent volumes
feature both canonical figures identified with America's literary movements and lesser-known writers gaining public
and scholarly interest. . . . This title stands out for its recognition and inclusion of a large number of female writers and
writers of a variety of ethnicities." SLJ
Includes bibliographical references

Vice presidents; a biographical dictionary. edited by
L. Edward Purcell. 4th ed; Facts On File 2010
554p il (Facts on File library of American his-
tory) $85
Grades: 9 10 11 12   **920.003**
1. Reference books 2. Vice-Presidents -- United States
-- Dictionaries
ISBN 978-0-8160-7707-6

LC 2009-26068

First published 1998
This is a "compendium that details the lives and careers
of America's vice presidents. . . . [It] contains biographies
of each vice president . . . portraits of each vice president, a
. . . chronology of their lives, and suggested further reading
about each vice president." Publisher's note
Includes bibliographical references

Wayne, Tiffany K.

American women of science since 1900. ABC-
CLIO 2011 2v il set $180
Grades: 9 10 11 12   **920.003**
1. Reference books 2. Women scientists -- Dictionaries
ISBN 978-1-59884-158-9; 978-1-59884-159-6 ebook

LC 2010-26838

Combined and updated version of American women in
science (1994) and American women in science, 1950 to the
present (1998), both written by Martha J. Bailey
"Along with providing significant support for research
in women's studies and the history of science—particularly
since much of the information here is not easily found elsewhere—this resource is chock-full of role models for young
women contemplating science careers." SLJ
Includes bibliographical references

★ **Who** was who in America; with world notables.
Marquis Who's Who 1942 23v set $999.95
Grades: 11 12 Adult   **920.003**
1. Reference books 2. United States -- Biography --
Dictionaries
ISBN 978-0-8379-0282-1
"Includes sketches removed from 'Who's who in Amer-
ica' because of death of the biographee; date of death and,
often, interment location is added." Guide to Ref Books.
11th edition

World cultural leaders of the twentieth and twenty-
first centuries; [by] Jennifer Durham Bass. 2nd
ed.; Grey House Publishing 2007 2v il set $195
Grades: 11 12 Adult   **920.003**
1. Reference books 2. Arts -- Biography 3. Biography
-- Dictionaries
ISBN 978-1-59237-118-1; 1-59237-118-3

First published 2000 by ABC-CLIO with title: World cultural leaders of the twentieth century

"The presentation, straightforward and accessible writing style, and 225 images make this source easy, appealing, and likely to be used." Libr J

Includes bibliographical references

Writers of the American Renaissance; an A-to-Z guide. edited by Denise D. Knight. Greenwood Press 2003 458p $99.95

Grades: 9 10 11 12 **920.003**
1. Reference books 2. Literature -- Bio-bibliography 3. Authors, American -- Dictionaries
ISBN 0-313-32140-X

LC 2003-52846

This "book is intended as a primary reference guide to 74 authors who wrote during the 19th century. Arranged alphabetically by author last name, each entry in the book includes a biography of the author; a discussion of the author's major works and themes; an overview of the critical reception of the author's works; works cited; and a two-part bibliography that includes works by the author and studies about the author. . . . This volume provides a comprehensive reference tool for students doing author studies and will add greatly to any high school library collection." Libr Media Connect

Includes bibliographical references

Yount, Lisa
★ **A to Z of women in science and math**; rev ed; Facts on File 2007 368p il (Facts on File library of world history) $60

Grades: 8 9 10 11 12 **920.003**
1. Reference books 2. Women scientists -- Dictionaries 3. Women mathematicians -- Dictionaries
ISBN 978-0-8160-6695-7; 0-8160-6695-7

LC 2007-23966

First published 1999

"More than 195 alphabetically arranged articles detail the lives of women from antiquity through modern day, including well-known scientists and mathematicians and less well-documented individuals. . . . The usefulness of this resource lies not only in the balanced group of profiles that have been assembled, providing a valuable tool for teachers and curriculum developers, but also in the readable and engaging entries themselves." Booklist

Includes bibliographical references

929 Genealogy, names, insignia

Ball, Edward
The **genetic** strand; exploring a family history through DNA. Simon & Schuster 2007 265p il $25

Grades: 11 12 Adult **929**
1. Genetics 2. DNA fingerprinting 3. Slaveholders 4. Plantation owners
ISBN 0-7432-6658-7; 978-0-7432-6658-1

LC 2007-11513

"Using locks of hair collected as family keepsakes, [the author] . . . analyzed DNA samples to trace his family history. He learned that, probably like most people, his lineage is a diverse racial mixture." Libr J

929.4 Personal names

★ **Dictionary** of American family names; Patrick Hanks, editor. Oxford Univ. Press 2003 3v set $295

Grades: 11 12 Adult **929.4**
1. Personal names -- United States
ISBN 0-19-508137-4

LC 2003-3844

"This set will be useful for genealogists, historians, and others curious about their family roots." SLJ

Includes bibliographical references

Hanks, Patrick
A **dictionary** of first names; [by] Patrick Hanks, Kate Hardcastle, and Flavia Hodges. 2nd ed.; Oxford University Press 2006 xxvii, 434p (Oxford paperback reference) pa $16.99

Grades: 11 12 Adult **929.4**
1. Reference books 2. Personal names -- Dictionaries
ISBN 978-0-19-861060-1; 0-19-861060-2

LC 2006-49845

First published 1990

This book "covers over 6,000 names in common use in English, including newly created names and traditional names that have been newly discovered. . . . [Entries list] the age, origin, and meaning of the name, as well as how it has fared in terms of popularity, and notes famous bearers (both historical and fictional). . . . [The book] covers alternative spellings, short forms and pet forms, and masculine and feminine forms, as well as help with pronunciation." Publisher's note

Includes bibliographical references

929.9 Forms of insignia and identification

Leepson, Marc
Flag: an American biography. Thomas Dunne Books/St. Martin's Press 2005 334p il $24.95; pa $14.95

Grades: 11 12 Adult **929.9**
1. Flags -- United States
ISBN 978-0-312-32308-0; 0-312-32308-5; 978-0-312-32309-7 pa; 0-312-32309-3 pa

LC 2004-65920

"From reverence to kitsch, Americans' attitudes to their flag and its mythology have changed over the years, and Leepson does a creditable job of recounting those changes." Publ Wkly

Includes bibliographical references

Minahan, James
The **complete** guide to national symbols and emblems. Greenwood Press 2010 2v il set $180

Grades: 8 9 10 11 12 Adult **929.9**
1. Reference books 2. Signs and symbols 3. National

emblems -- Encyclopedias 4. National characteristics -- Encyclopedias

ISBN 978-0-313-34496-1; 978-0-313-34497-8 ebook

LC 2009-36963

"This set is an impressive compilation of material that should be quite useful for anyone looking for current information about flags, anthems, athletic teams, cuisines, and such. The 200-plus entries cover independent nations of the world and some dependent states and territories that seek greater visibility, such as Wallonia (an autonomous region within Belgium) and Puerto Rico. Volume 1 covers Asia and Oceania, Central and South America, and Europe. Volume 2 covers the Middle East and North Africa, North America and the Caribbean, and sub-Saharan Africa. National flags and coats of arms are shown in color." Booklist

Includes bibliographical references

Shearer, Benjamin F.

State names, seals, flags, and symbols; a historical guide. [by] Benjamin F. Shearer and Barbara S. Shearer. 3rd ed, rev and expanded; Greenwood Press 2001 495p il $73.95

Grades: 8 9 10 11 12 Adult   **929.9**

1. Reference books 2. Seals (Numismatics) 3. Flags -- United States 4. Geographic names -- United States

ISBN 0-313-31534-5

LC 2001-23525

First published 1987

"Chapters on mottoes, flowers, trees, birds, songs, holidays, and license plates are just a sampling of what is covered, and the format is such that the concisely written material can be found as expeditiously as possible. Even though the book is touted predominantly as a reference tool, the information provided makes fascinating and enlightening reading." Libr J [review of 1994 edition]

Includes bibliographical references

Znamierowski, Alfred, 1940-

The World Encyclopedia of Flags; The definitive guide to international, flags, banners, standards and ensigns, with over 1400 illustration. by Alfred Znamierowski. Lorenz Books 2013 256 p. $16.99

Grades: 5 6 7 8 9 10 11 12 Adult   **929.9**

1. Flags

ISBN 0754826295; 9780754826293

This book, by Alred Znamierowski, presents "a directory of flags and a fascinating history of their development and usage, featuring over 600 flags including military signs, royal standards, civic flags, ensigns and national flags, expertly illustrated throughout." (Publisher's note)

930   History of ancient world (to ca. 499)

The classical world, 500 BCE to AD 600 CE; [edited by Clare Collinson] Brown Bear Books 2009

112p il map (Curriculum connections. Atlas of world history) lib bdg $39.95

Grades: 9 10 11 12   **930**

1. Ancient civilization 2. Classical civilization

ISBN 978-1-933834-66-5

LC 2009-27834

This book "is divided into thematic and regional maps which are followed by short but very comprehensive articles. . . . [It includes] curriculum context sidebars, important terms students should know, and how the topic ties into other areas." Libr Media Connect

Includes bibliographical references

Encyclopedia of the ancient world; editor, Thomas J. Sienkewicz. Salem Press 2002 3v il maps set $341

Grades: 11 12 Adult   **930**

1. Reference books 2. Ancient civilization -- Encyclopedias

ISBN 0-89356-038-3

LC 2001-49896

This reference work encompasses "not only Greece and Rome but also 'the civilizations, cultures, traditions, monuments and artifacts, significant wars and battles, and important personages of the rest of the world: Europe (outside Greece and Rome), Africa, the Americas, Asia, and Oceania.' The time span is from prehistory to approximately 700 C.E." Booklist

Includes bibliographical references

The **first** civilizations to 500 BC; edited by Clare Collinson. Brown Bear Books 2010 112p map (Curriculum connections. Atlas of world history) lib bdg $39.95

Grades: 9 10 11 12   **930**

1. Ancient history 2. Ancient civilization

ISBN 978-1-933834-65-8

LC 2009-27833

This book "is divided into thematic and regional maps which are followed by short but very comprehensive articles. . . . [It includes] curriculum context sidebars, important terms students should know, and how the topic ties into other areas." Libr Media Connect

Great events from history, The ancient world, prehistory-476 C.E. editor, Mark W. Chavalas; consulting editors, Mark S. Aldenderfer . . . [et al.] Salem Press 2004 2v il map set $160

Grades: 11 12 Adult   **930**

1. Ancient history 2. Reference books

ISBN 1-58765-155-6; 978-1-58765-155-7

LC 2004-1360

Companion volume to Great lives from history, The ancient world, prehistory-476 C.E.

Some essays previously published in Great events from history (1972-1980), Chronology of European history, 15,000 B.C. to 1997 (1997), and Great events from history, North American series (1997)

"Articles are arranged chronologically, beginning around 25,000 B.C.E. with the San Peoples, who created the first discernible art in Africa, and ends on September 4, 476 C.E. with the fall of Rome, when the last Roman emperor,

Romulus Augustulus, was deposed. Articles cover the entire world, with special attention paid to non-European areas. . . . . All articles maintain the same structure and give the locale of the event, its category, a summary of the event, its significance, an annotated list of further readings, and cross references to related events." Ref & User Services Quarterly
Includes bibliographical references

Howitt, Carolyn
500 things to know about the ancient world. Barrons Educational Series, Inc. 2007 152p il pa $9.99
Grades: 7 8 9 10   **930**
1. Ancient civilization
ISBN 978-0-7641-3863-8; 0-7641-3863-4
                                          LC 2007-21750
This collection of facts about the ancient world includes "facts about marriage and divorce in ancient cultures, the different kinds of clothes the ancients wore and how they fastened them in a time before zippers and Velcro, the magical ways in which ancient Egyptians interpreted dreams, the plants that were used as medicines in ancient civilizations, and . . . more." Publisher's note
Includes bibliographical references

Obregon, Mauricio
Beyond the edge of the sea; sailing with Jason and the Argonauts, Ulysses, the Vikings, and other explorers of the Ancient World. Random House 2001 132p il maps hardcover o.p. pa $11.95
Grades: 11 12 Adult   **930**
1. Explorers 2. Ancient geography
ISBN 0-679-46326-7; 0-679-78344-X pa
                                           LC 00-27173
"Sweeping in scope . . . this book offers several surprisingly provocative and plausible conclusions. . . . The fascinating history of the sea, its mythic and historical figures, and the boats that changed the world are brought into a fresh and interesting perspective." Booklist
Includes bibliographical references

Starr, Chester G.
★ A **history** of the ancient world; 4th ed; Oxford Univ. Press 1991 742p il maps $49.95
Grades: 11 12 Adult   **930**
1. Ancient history
ISBN 0-19-506629-4
                                          LC 90-34970
First published 1965
Incorporating recent archaeological and anthropological discoveries, the author surveys the changing economic and social structures of societies, from prehistory to the fifth century A.D. Egyptian, Assyrian, Chinese and Greek are among the civilizations discussed
Includes bibliographical references

Takacs, Sarolta A.
The **ancient** world; general editor, Eric Cline; consulting editor, Sarolta Takács. Sharpe Reference 2007 5v il map set $399
Grades: 7 8 9 10   **930**
1. Reference books 2. Ancient civilization --

Encyclopedias
ISBN 978-0-7656-8082-2
                                          LC 2006-101384
This encyclopedia "presents a cultural and societal investigation of ancient Africa, Europe, the Americas, the Near East, Southwest Asia, and Asia and the Pacific. Lucid, fact-packed entries are arranged alphabetically and cover topics such as civilizations and peoples, culture, agriculture, key places, and war and military affairs." SLJ
Includes bibliographical references

930.1   Archaeology

Ceram, C. W.
Gods, graves, and scholars; the story of archaeology. translated from the German by E. B. Garside and Sophie Wilkins. 2nd rev and substantially enl ed; Knopf 1967 441p il maps hardcover o.p. pa $11.16
Grades: 11 12 Adult   **930.1**
1. Mayas 2. Aztecs 3. Archeology 4. Hieroglyphics 5. Babel, Tower of 6. Cuneiform inscriptions 7. Rosetta stone inscription 8. Kings 9. Crete (Greece) 10. Egypt -- Antiquities
ISBN 0-394-74319-9 pa
Original German edition, 1949; first English language edition, 1951
"The story of Champollion and the reading of the Rosetta Stone, the decipherment of the inscriptions on the monument of Darius the Great, Leonard Woolley's famous excavations at Ur, and John Lloyd Stephens' discovery of the ruins of a great Mayan city are . . . told in this book." Doors to More Mature Read
Includes bibliographical references

Hunt, Patrick
Ten discoveries that rewrote history. Plume 2007 226p pa $27.95
Grades: 11 12 Adult   **930.1**
1. Antiquities 2. Ancient civilization 3. Archeology -- History
ISBN 978-0-452-28877-5; 0-452-28877-0
                                          LC 2007-19808
The author "has produced a wonderful volume of of archaeological history. In doing so, he has provided a seldom seen look at some of the most important scientific developments in the field." Sci Books Films
Includes bibliographical references

McIntosh, Jane
Handbook to life in prehistoric Europe. Facts on File 2006 404p il map (Facts on File library of world history) $70
Grades: 11 12 Adult   **930.1**
1. Ancient history 2. Ancient civilization 3. Europe -- History -- To 476
ISBN 978-0-8160-5779-5; 0-8160-5779-6
                                          LC 2005-19775
This book "focuses primarily on the period from 7000 B.C.E., when agricultural communities first began appearing in southeastern Europe, to the first century C.E., when west-

ern Europe was progressively incorporated into the Roman imperium." Publisher's note

Includes bibliographical references

The **Oxford** Companion to Archaeology; Edited by Neil Asher Silberman. 2nd edition Oxford University Press 2012 3 vol. illustrations $595
Grades: 11 12 Adult   **930.1**
1. Archeology
ISBN 0199735786; 9780199735785

LC 2011051893

"Much has changed in the field [of archaeology] since 1996. Recent developments in methods and analytical techniques (e.g., laser-based mapping and survey systems, new applications of the scanning electron microscope) have revolutionized the ways excavations are performed. Cultural tourism, cultural resource management, heritage, and conservation have been redefined as areas within archaeology, and have been newly emphasized by scholars and administrators. Major site discoveries have expanded our understanding of prehistory and human developments through time. The second edition explores each of these advances in the field, adding approximately 150 entries." (Publisher's note)

Rubalcaba, Jill
Every bone tells a story; hominid discoveries, deductions, and debates. [by] Jill Rubalcaba and Peter Robertshaw. Charlesbridge 2010 185p il map lib bdg $18.95
Grades: 8 9 10 11 12   **930.1**
1. Archeology 2. Fossil hominids 3. Prehistoric peoples 4. Excavations (Archeology)
ISBN 978-1-58089-164-6; 1-58089-164-0

LC 2008-26961

"Archaeology and paleontology are the exciting focus in this accessible account of four hominins who lived long before recorded history. . . . The informal style never oversimplifies the engaging science and technology, and the authors raise as many questions as they answer in the detailed chapters." Booklist

931   China to 420

Hardy, Grant
The **establishment** of the Han empire and imperial China; [by] Grant Hardy and Anne Behnke Kinney. Greenwood Press 2005 xxx, 170p il (Greenwood guides to historic events of the ancient world) $45
Grades: 9 10 11 12   **931**
1. China -- History
ISBN 0-313-32588-X

LC 2004-22475

This "is a promising eastward expansion of this series on the ancient world." SLJ

Includes bibliographical references

Kleeman, Terry F.
The **ancient** Chinese world; [by] Terry Kleeman & Tracy Barrett. Oxford University Press 2005 174p il map (World in ancient times) $32.95
Grades: 7 8 9 10   **931**
1. China -- History
ISBN 0-19-517102-0

LC 2004-14408

"Readers seriously interested in history, in archaeology—or in China—will be well served by this engrossing book." SLJ

Includes bibliographical references

Shaughnessy, Edward L.
Exploring the life, myth, and art of ancient China. Rosen 2009 144p il map (Civilizations of the world) lib bdg $29.95
Grades: 7 8 9 10 11 12   **931**
1. Chinese mythology 2. Arts -- China 3. China -- Civilization
ISBN 978-1-4358-5617-2; 1-4358-5617-1

LC 2009-10290

This is an introduction to ancient Chinese civilization

"This beautifully illustrated and well-written [title] . . . is perfect for those assignments where students must look at the culture of a civilization. Artwork and pictures blend seamlessly with the information and the reader is taken on a journey of discovery. Myths are used as the story of how the people view themselves, blended with the discussion of the reality of life. Everyday life is tied to the belief systems and is explained in light of those beliefs. The pictures are beautifully done and there is almost as much information in the captions as there is in the text." Libr Media Connect

Includes glossary and bibliographical references

932   Egypt to 640

Brier, Bob
The **murder** of Tutankhamen; a true story. Berkley Books 2005 xx, 264p il pa $14
Grades: 11 12 Adult   **932**
1. Kings 2. Egypt -- History
ISBN 0-425-20690-4; 978-0-425-20690-4

LC 2005-41085

First published 1998 by Putnam

"Brier obviously knows his subject and is impassioned by it. Readers who enjoy history or true-crime stories will be intrigued by this work." SLJ

Includes bibliographical references

Bunson, Margaret R.
Encyclopedia of ancient Egypt; Margaret R. Bunson. 3rd edition Facts On File 2012 xxviii, 516 p.p ill., maps (alk. paper) $95
Grades: 9 10 11 12 Adult   **932**
1. Egypt -- History 2. Egypt -- Antiquities -- Encyclopedias 3. Egypt -- Civilization -- Encyclopedias 4. Egypt -- Antiquities -- Dictionaries 5. Egypt --

Civilization -- To 332 B.C. -- Dictionaries
ISBN 0816082162; 9780816082162

LC 2011026433

"Entries are detailed and concise; some have bibliographies, and many summarize why a subject is notable, with references to related entries. The volume explores every aspect of Egyptian culture, from warfare to burial rites. Interesting entries include the ones on Akhenaten, the heretical pharaoh who introduced monotheism; his famous wife Nefertiti; and son Tutankhamun. Alexander the Great's conquest of Egypt and its historical impact are covered extensively in a detailed entry. Deities are discussed for many of the historical periods, and the information concerning Hatshepsut, the female pharaoh, is detailed and enlightening. This volume features a list of illustrations and maps, brief introduction, historical/geographical overview, chronology, and glossary." (Choice)

"This is a useful one-stop, ready-reference resource for general readers interested in ancient Egyptian civilization." LJ

Includes bibliographical references and index

Casson, Lionel

Everyday life in ancient Egypt; rev and expanded ed; Johns Hopkins Univ. Press 2001 163p il hardcover o.p. pa $15.95

Grades: 9 10 11 12   **932**

1. Egypt -- Civilization
ISBN 0-8018-6600-6; 0-8018-6601-4 pa

LC 00-59091

First published 1975 by American Heritage Pub. with title: The Horizon book of daily life in ancient Egypt

The author describes the structure of ancient Egyptian society including social classes, family, the role of women, farm life, leisure, the professions and craftsmen, religion, and travel.

Includes bibliographical references

David, A. Rosalie

★ **Handbook** to life in ancient Egypt; [by] Rosalie David. rev ed; Facts on File 2003 417p il map (Facts on File library of world history) $50

Grades: 11 12 Adult   **932**

1. Egypt -- Civilization
ISBN 0-8160-5034-1

LC 2002-35229

First published 1998

This covers such topics as the geography of Ancient Egypt, society and government, religion, funerary beliefs and customs, architecture, trade and transport, the army and navy, economy and industry, and everyday life.

Includes bibliographical references

Fletcher, Joann

Exploring the life, myth, and art of ancient Egypt. Rosen Pub. 2009 144p il map (Civilizations of the world) $29.95

Grades: 7 8 9 10 11 12   **932**

1. Egypt -- Antiquities 2. Egypt -- Civilization
ISBN 978-1-4358-5616-5; 1-4358-5616-3

LC 2009-8792

"This attractively designed and handsomely illustrated book offers a rich and informative introduction to ancient Egyptian culture. Abundantly illustrated with beautifully rendered color representations of architecture, works of art, and other artifacts, the book offers insight into the beliefs and rituals, economy, and social organization of ancient Egyptian civilization." Booklist

Includes glossary and bibliographical references

George, Charles, 1949-

★ The **pyramids** of Giza; by Charles and Linda George. ReferencePoint Press 2012 80 p. (Ancient Egyptian wonders) (hardcover) $28.95

Grades: 8 9 10 11 12   **932**

1. Pyramids 2. Egypt -- Antiquities
ISBN 1601522584; 9781601522580

LC 2012000282

This book by Charles George is part of the Ancient Egyptian Wonders series and looks at the pyramids of Giza. "Three of the grandest of all the pyramids built by the pharaohs of Egypt still stand on the Giza Plateau. These monuments serve as reminders of their builders but also of the glory and grandeur that was ancient Egypt." (Publisher's note)

Includes bibliographical references and index.

Hawass, Zahi A.

Tutankhamun and the golden age of the pharaohs; [by] Zahi Hawass; photographs by Kenneth Garrett. National Geographic Books 2005 285p il map $35

Grades: 11 12 Adult   **932**

1. Kings 2. Egypt -- Antiquities
ISBN 0-7922-3873-7

LC 2005-41678

This companion to an exhibition displaying about 130 items found in the tombs of Tutankhamun and other kings from the same dynasty "describes the physical and symbolic attributes of each object and explains its purpose in the afterlife. . . . An arrestingly visual album destined for high demand." Booklist

Includes bibliographical references

Lace, William

★ **King** Tut's curse; by William W. Lace. ReferencePoint Press 2012 80 p. ill. (Ancient Egyptian wonders series.) (hardcover) $27.95

Grades: 8 9 10 11 12   **932**

1. Egypt -- Antiquities 2. Tutankhamen, King of Egypt -- Tombs 3. Valley of the Kings (Egypt) -- Antiquities 4. Excavations (Archaeology) -- Egypt -- Valley of the Kings
ISBN 1601522509; 9781601522504

LC 2011048987

This book by William W. Lace is part of the Ancient Egyptian Wonders series and looks at King Tut's curse. Topics include "its origin, how it spread, and the remaining mysteries and search for answers. The title opens with Lord Carnarvon's 1923 death . . . and continues on to discuss Tutankhamen's life, rule, and death (including recent DNA testing, which indicates he had malaria) as well as the endeavors of those involved in the tomb's discovery." (Booklist)

This "explores Egyptian history, mummy making, the discovery and opening of the tomb of Tutankhamen in 1922, and the events that happened after that. Much of the book is based on archaeologist Howard Carter's diaries and letters, and on period newspaper articles. The color photographs in [this attractive [book] are excellent, and the readable [text is] interesting." SLJ

★ **Mummification** and death rituals of ancient Egypt; by William W. Lace. ReferencePoint Press, Inc. 2013 80 p. (Ancient Egyptian wonders) (hardcover) $27.95

Grades: 8 9 10 11 12   932
1. Egypt -- Antiquities 2. Ancient civilization 3. Mummies -- Egypt 4. Egypt -- Civilization -- 332-30 B.C. 5. Funeral rites and ceremonies -- Egypt -- History
ISBN 1601522541; 9781601522542
LC 2012011481

This book is part of the Ancient Egyptian Wonders series and focuses on mummification and death rituals of ancient Egypt. "Each book contains a timeline, important facts highlighted in sidebars, and websites." Each book "includes quotes from experts and ancient texts." (Library Media Connection)

Includes bibliographical references and index.

Mertz, Barbara
★ **Temples,** tombs, & hieroglyphs; a popular history of ancient Egypt. 2nd ed., 1st William Morrow ed.; William Morrow 2007 xxvi, 324p il map $26.95

Grades: 9 10 11 12 Adult   932
1. Queens 2. Hieroglyphics 3. Egyptian language 4. Kings 5. Syria 6. Egypt -- Antiquities 7. Egypt -- Civilization 8. Thebes (Egypt: Extinct city)
ISBN 978-0-06-125276-1; 0-06-125276-X
LC 2007-29118

First published 1964 by Coward-McCann

This is an "introduction to the history of ancient Egypt and Egyptology. . . . Mertz gives special attention to such topics as the kingship (yes) of Queen Hatshepsut, the exploits of Thutmose III, and the Amarna Period with its intriguing players Akhenaten, Nefertiti, and Tutankhamen. Presenting both pros and cons of current theories, Mertz also explains in simple language archaeological techniques such as carbon 14 dating and historical chronology. . . . [This is] an excellent introduction for patrons interested in the land of the pharaohs." Libr J

Netzley, Patricia D.
The **Greenhaven** encyclopedia of ancient Egypt. Greenhaven Press 2003 336p (Greenhaven encyclopedia of) $74.95

Grades: 8 9 10 11 12   932
1. Reference books 2. Egypt -- Antiquities -- Encyclopedias
ISBN 0-7377-1150-7
LC 2002-6965

"Alphabetical entries range from prehistory to the time of Greco-Roman domination and are generally between a paragraph and a page in length. Coverage includes individual pharaohs, places, practices, trades, beliefs, artwork, and aspects of daily and family life with entries such as 'furniture,' 'children,' and 'entertaining guests.' Important individuals such as archaeologist Howard Carter are also included." SLJ

Includes bibliographical references

★ The **Oxford** encyclopedia of ancient Egypt; Donald B. Redford, editor in chief. Oxford Univ. Press 2001 3v set $450

Grades: 11 12 Adult   932
1. Reference books 2. Egypt -- Antiquities -- Encyclopedias 3. Egypt -- Civilization -- Encyclopedias
ISBN 0-19-510234-7
LC 99-54801

ALA RUSA Dartmouth Medal (2002)

This reference work covers "archaeology, biography, history, language, social history, and more. . . . [It features] essays from more than 250 contributors from various countries and scholarly pursuits, all with solid academic credentials. . . . One is not likely to encounter another work of this magnitude on a subject of such universal interest for some time." Booklist

Includes bibliographical references

Taylor, John H.
Unwrapping a mummy; the life, death and embalming of Horemkenesi. University of Tex. Press 1996 111p il (Egyptian bookshelf) pa $18.95

Grades: 9 10 11 12   932
1. Mummies 2. Egypt -- Civilization
ISBN 0-292-78141-5
LC 95-61446

An exploration of ancient Egyptian civilization based on the study of the mummy of Horemkenesi. Customs surrounding death and the process of mummification are discussed in detail

Includes bibliographical references

932.01   Egypt--Early history to 332 B.C.

Brier, Bob
Ancient Egypt; Everyday Life in the Land of the Nile. by Bob Brier and Hoyt Hobbs. Sterling Pub Co Inc 2013 320 p. illus. (some color), color map $17.95

Grades: 9 10 11 12   932.01
1. Ancient history 2. Egypt -- History 3. Ancient civilization 4. Egypt -- Antiquities 5. Egypt -- Civilization -- To 332 B.C. 6. Egypt -- Social life and customs -- To 332 B.C.
ISBN 1454909072; 9781454909071
LC 2013387375

This book, by Bob Brier and Hoyt Hobbs, provides "[a] vivid view of life in ancient Egypt. More than 5,000 years ago, the ancient Egyptians founded one of the world's oldest civilizations. . . . Through deep investigative research, the authors explore the social and material existence in ancient Egypt-from what people ate and drank to how they worked, lived, played, and prayed." (Publisher's note)

"Pharaonic Egypt and ancient Greece are probably the most studied ancient civilizations in our schools. General-reader interest in the two cultures broadens to include everyday life, making these two works a welcome addition to most libraries .... For the price and level of coverage, both works are well suited for school projects that require students to go beyond their standard textbooks, and also for general readers interested in ancient Greece or pharaonic Egypt." Booklist

Kallen, Stuart A.

★ **Pharaohs** of Egypt; by Stuart A Kallen. ReferencePoint Press, Inc. 2013 80 p. (Ancient Egyptian wonders series) (hardcover) $27.95

Grades: 8 9 10 11 12   932.01

1. Pharaohs -- Egypt 2. Egypt -- Civilization 3. Pharaohs -- History 4. Egypt -- Antiquities 5. Egypt -- Civilization -- To 332 B.C 6. Egypt -- Politics and government -- To 332 B.C

ISBN 1601522568; 9781601522566

LC 2012000360

This book is part of the Ancient Egyptian Wonders series and looks at the pharaohs of Egypt. The series provides an "overview of ancient Egyptian civilization. . . . Each book contains a timeline, important facts highlighted in sidebars, and websites." Photographs and artwork are included. (Library Media Connection)

Includes bibliographical references and index

Whiting, Jim

★ **Life** along the ancient Nile; by Jim Whiting. ReferencePoint Press, Inc. 2013 80 p. (Ancient Egyptian wonders series.) (hardcover) $27.95

Grades: 8 9 10 11 12   932.01

1. Egypt -- History 2. Ancient civilization 3. Nile River Valley -- Civilization 4. Egypt -- Civilization -- To 332 B.C

ISBN 1601522525; 9781601522528

LC 2012000358

This book is part of the Ancient Egyptian Wonders series and focuses on life along the ancient Nile. It offers "coverage of marriage, fashion, medicine, and social classes" as well as dental procedures and wild parties. "Each book contains a timeline, important facts highlighted in sidebars, and websites." (Library Media Connection)

Includes bibliographical references and index.

933   Palestine to 70

Burleigh, Nina

Unholy business; a true tale of faith, greed, and forgery in the holy land. Smithsonian Books 2008 271p $27.50

Grades: 11 12 Adult   933

1. Forgery 2. Engineers 3. Entrepreneurs 4. Antiquarians 5. Israel -- Antiquities

ISBN 978-0-06-145845-3

LC 2008-23425

"In 2002, the James Ossuary, an ancient limestone box for bones with an inscription on it that said 'James, son of Jo-

seph, brother of Jesus' was publicized as the first real physical evidence of Jesus Christ's existence. The plot thickened when the ossuary went on tour, creating lots of publicity, a book by advocate Hershel Shanks, and a Discovery Channel documentary. Then the ossuary's owner, Oded Golan, and his antique-dealer associates were charged with forgery. . . . Whether or not readers believe the ossuary is authentic, they will thoroughly enjoy this book." Libr J

935   Mesopotamia to 637 and Iranian Plateau to 637

Bertman, Stephen

Handbook to life in ancient Mesopotamia. Facts on File 2002 396p il map (Facts on File library of world history) $70

Grades: 11 12 Adult   935

1. Iraq -- Civilization

ISBN 0-8160-4346-9

LC 2002-3516

"The Handbook to Life in Ancient Mesopotamia describes the culture, history, and people of this land, as well as their struggle for survival and happiness, from about 3500 to 500 BCE." Publisher's note

Includes bibliographical references

936   Europe north and west of Italian Peninsula to ca. 499

Cunliffe, Barry

The **ancient** Celts. Penguin Books 1999 324p il map pa $21.95

Grades: 11 12 Adult   936

1. Celts

ISBN 0-14-025422-6

First published 1997 by Oxford Univ. Press

This is a "survey of the origins of the Celts and their expansion during the Iron Age through their largely successful subjection by the Romans. . . . [Cunliffe] has written a readable and informative book with many attractive illustrations." Libr J

Includes bibliographical references

936.1   British Isles to 410

Burl, Aubrey

The **stone** circles of Britain, Ireland and Brittany. Yale Univ. Press 2000 462p il $60; pa $30

Grades: 9 10 11 12   936.1

1. Ireland -- Antiquities 2. Great Britain -- Antiquities

ISBN 0-300-08347-5; 0-300-11406-0 pa

LC 99-87909

First published 1976 with title: The stone circles of the British Isles

This describes the prehistoric stone circles built some 6000 years ago, such as Stonehenge in England, Callanish in Scotland and the cromlechs in Brittany, how and why they were constructed, and how they have been excavated and studied.

"Burl's authoritative book is indispensable for anyone pursuing this tantalizing enigma." Publ Wkly

Includes bibliographical references

937   Italian Peninsula to 476 and adjacent territories to 476

Adkins, Lesley

★ **Handbook** to life in ancient Rome; [by] Lesley Adkins and Roy A. Adkins. Updated ed; Facts on File 2004 450p il, maps (Facts on File library of world history) $85

Grades: 9 10 11 12   **937**
     1. Rome -- Civilization   2. Rome -- Social life and customs
     ISBN 0-8160-5026-0
                           LC 2003-49255

First published 1994

This work covers politics, military affairs, literature, religion, architecture, geography, and social life in ancient Rome from the 8th century B.C. to the 5th century A.D. Illustrated with site-specific photographs and line drawings.

Includes bibliographical references

Aldrete, Gregory S.

Daily life in the Roman city; Rome, Pompeii and Ostia. Greenwood Press 2004 278p il map (The Greenwood Press Daily life through history series) $55

Grades: 11 12 Adult   **937**
     1. Rome -- Social life and customs
     ISBN 0-313-33174-X
                           LC 2004-20943

This "study of life in the ancient Roman city explains how the city functioned, who lived there, and what the inhabitants' lives were like. . . . Included are accounts of Rome's history, infrastructure, government, and inhabitants, as well as chapters on life and death, the dangers and pleasures of urban living, entertainment, religion, the emperors, and the economy." Publisher's note

Includes bibliographical references

Allan, Tony

Exploring the life, myth, and art of ancient Rome; Tony Allan. Rosen Pub. 2012 144 p. (lib. bdg.) $39.95

Grades: 7 8 9 10 11   **937**
     1. Roman art 2. Roman mythology 3. Rome -- History 4. Rome -- Civilization 5. Art, Roman
     ISBN 9781448848317
                           LC 2011009799

This book on Ancient Rome "offers an informative overview of . . . political and social history as well as its art, architecture, and mythology, all bolstered with plenty of . . . details and narratives. . . . [T]he illustrations include artworks, documents, and handsome maps as well as photos of significant sites and artifacts. . . . Besides showing how the great city rose to domination, 'Ancient Rome' looks at how

it changed and was changed by the civilizations it housed." (Booklist)

The book "put[s] the art . . . in context, explaining how a society's religious beliefs, legends, and cultural traditions manifest themselves through images and iconography. The . . . layout features full-color photographs of architecture, sculpture, and painting on every page, accompanied by informative captions." (School Libr J)

Includes bibliographical references (p. 138-139) and index

★ **Life,** myth, and art in Ancient Rome. J. Paul Getty Museum 2005 144p il pa $19.95

Grades: 11 12 Adult   **937**
     1. Roman art 2. Roman mythology 3. Rome -- Antiquities 4. Rome -- Civilization
     ISBN 0-89236-821-7
                           LC 2004-114326

This is an "illustrated guide to the cultural and political heritage of ancient Rome, including the enduring legacy of its art and architecture, the engineering innovations of its vast system of roads and aqueducts, the . . . myths of its gods and goddesses, and the power of its emperors and legions." Publisher's note

Includes bibliographical references

Baker, Rosalie F.

Ancient Romans; expanding the classical tradition. {by} Rosalie F. and Charles F. Baker III. Oxford Univ. Press 1998 267p il (Oxford profiles) $40

Grades: 9 10 11 12   **937**
     1. Rome -- History 2. Rome -- Biography
     ISBN 0-19-510884-1
                           LC 97-21531

"Challenging reading, the book will best serve college-bound students with a basic knowledge of ancient Roman culture and history." Booklist

Includes glossary and bibliographical references

Berry, Joanne

The **complete** Pompeii. Thames & Hudson 2007 256p il map $40

Grades: 11 12 Adult   **937**
     1. Pompeii (Extinct city)
     ISBN 978-0-500-05150-4; 0-500-05150-X
                           LC 2007-922095

This book "covers the origins and evolution of the city, the daily life of its residents, the geography of the region, and the eruption of Mt. Vesuvius, as well as a history of the excavation of the site. Easy to read and with full color pictures of the excavation, along with maps, time lines, diagrams, and vivid art reproductions, this book gives a broad and comprehensive introduction to the Pompeian world. . . . High school libraries should be advised that there is a section on eroticism that contains visually and verbally explicit sexual material." Libr J

Includes bibliographical references

Bunson, Matthew

Encyclopedia of ancient Rome; Matthew Bunson. 3rd ed. Facts On File 2012 xxxvii, 788 p.p ill., maps (acid-free paper) $95.00

Grades: 9 10 11 12 Adult **937**
1. Rome -- Antiquities 2. Rome -- Civilization 3. Rome -- History -- Encyclopedias 4. Rome -- History -- Empire, 30 B.C.-476 A.D. -- Encyclopedias
ISBN 0816082170; 9780816082179
LC 2011038366

This encyclopedia, by Matthew Bunson, "provides . . . coverage of the people, places, events, and ideas of ancient Rome. Each entry . . . reflect[s] recent advances in archaeology, historical and literary criticism, and social analysis. In addition, the scope . . . include[s] the entire history of ancient Rome, from the first founding of the city . . . to the final collapse of Roman power in the fifth century CE." (Publisher's note)

"A superb source of detailed, engaging information on the ever fascinating and often perplexing ancient Roman civilization, Bunson's work is a handy reference for classics students and enthusiasts alike." LJ

Includes bibliographical references (p. 757-760) and index

★ **Encyclopedia** of the Roman Empire; rev ed; Facts on File 2002 636p il maps $75
Grades: 11 12 Adult **937**
1. Reference books 2. Rome -- History -- Encyclopedias
ISBN 0-8160-4562-3
LC 2001-53253
First published 1994

This reference work provides information on the key places, people, events, and culture of Roman history, from the reign of Julius Caesar to the fall of the last Roman emperor in 476 A.D.

"An excellent ready-reference source." Booklist [review of 1994 edition]

Includes bibliographical references

The **Cambridge** illustrated history of the Roman world; edited by Greg Woolf. Cambridge University Press 2003 384p il map (Cambridge illustrated history) $45
Grades: 11 12 Adult **937**
1. Rome -- History
ISBN 0-521-82775-2
LC 2004-298480

This book explores such topics as "religion, Rome's relationship with Greece, warfare and Empire, and science and culture." Publisher's note

Includes bibliographical references

Ermatinger, James William
The **decline** and fall of the Roman Empire; [by] James W. Ermatinger. Greenwood Press 2004 xxxi, 187p il map (Greenwood guides to historic events of the ancient world) $45
Grades: 9 10 11 12 **937**
1. Rome -- History
ISBN 0-313-32692-4
LC 2004-14674

"An overview of the period is presented in the introduction, and is followed by chapters on late Roman culture, society, and economics in late antiquity; religious conflicts in Christian Rome; enemies of Rome; and why and when Rome fell. The narrative chapters conclude with a section placing Rome's fall in modern perspective." Publisher's note

Includes bibliographical references

Hinds, Kathryn, 1962-
Everyday life in the Roman Empire. Marshall Cavendish Benchmark 2010 320p il lib bdg $42.79
Grades: 7 8 9 10 **937**
1. Holy Roman Empire 2. Rome -- History
ISBN 978-0-7614-4484-8; 0-7614-4484-X
LC 2009-5913

A compilation of four titles in the Everyday Life in the Roman Empire series, published 2004: The city; The countryside; The Patricians; Religion

This book combines "clear, bold text with vivid reproductions of period paintings, frescoes, and sculptures, making for [a] stunning [presentation]." SLJ

Includes glossary and bibliographical references

Nardo, Don
Classical civilization; by Don Nardo. Morgan Reynolds Pub. 2011 128 p. col. ill., maps (World history) (library) $28.95
Grades: 6 7 8 9 **937**
1. Rome -- History 2. Rome -- Civilization
ISBN 1599351749; 9781599351742
LC 2011005672

This book by Don Nardo on ancient Rome is part of the World History series. "Nardo provides a framework of history, then discusses aspects of the culture with far-reaching effects, such as its government, laws, architecture, roads, and language. The section called 'The First Urban Civilization' reveals surprising similarities between ancient Roman cities and their modern counterparts." (Booklist)

Includes bibliographical references (p. 120-121) and index.

938 Greece to 323

Adkins, Lesley
★ **Handbook** to life in ancient Greece; [by] Lesley Adkins and Roy A. Adkins. Updated ed; Facts on File 2005 514p il map (Facts on File library of world history) $70
Grades: 11 12 Adult **938**
1. Greece -- Civilization
ISBN 0-8160-5659-5
LC 2004-47105

This book covers "all aspects of ancient Greek life— from the beginnings of the Minoan civilization in Crete to the final defeat by the Roman world in 30 BCE." Publisher's note

Includes bibliographical references

Ancient Greece; edited by Thomas J. Sienkewicz. Salem Press 2007 3v il map (Magill's choice) set $207

Grades: 11 12 Adult   **938**

1. Reference books 2. Greece -- History -- Encyclopedias
ISBN 1-58765-281-1; 978-1-58765-281-3

LC 2006-16525

Some of the essays in this work appeared in various other Salem Press sets

This is a "comprehensive examination of Greek civilization and its impact on Western history, 'from its earliest archaeological remains until the Battle of Actium in 31 B.C.E.' . . . [The essays included] cover art, daily life and customs, government, literature, medicine and science, war, the role of women, and mythology. Biographical entries profile statesmen, artists, writers, scientists, and philosophers, and relevant entries probe battles, philosophical movements, and types of literature." SLJ

Includes bibliographical references

Cartledge, Paul

Ancient Greece; a history in eleven cities. Oxford University Press 2009 261p il map $19.95

Grades: 10 11 12 Adult   **938**

1. Greece -- Civilization 2. Greece -- History -- 0-323
ISBN 978-0-19-923338-0

LC 2009-26999

"Aiming for a general audience, Cartledge achieves a fast-paced, highly engaging romp through ancient Greece. An excellent choice for anyone seeking an introduction to the topic; for all its readability, this book doesn't skimp on the research." Libr J

Includes bibliographical references

Classical Greek civilization, 800-323 B.C.E; edited by John T. Kirby. Gale Group 2001 xxxi, 395p il maps (World eras) $99

Grades: 11 12 Adult   **938**

1. Greece -- Civilization
ISBN 0-7876-1707-5

LC 00-47648

This book's "comprehensive coverage of the entire classical Greek period makes it a valuable addition for your library's ancient history collection." Book Rep

Includes glossary and bibliographical references

Garland, Robert, 1947-

Ancient Greece; everyday life in the birthplace of western civilization. Robert Garland. Sterling Pub Co Inc 2013 xvii, 365 p.p color illus., color maps $17.95

Grades: 9 10 11 12   **938**

1. Ancient history 2. Greece -- History 3. Ancient civilization 4. Greece -- Antiquities 5. Greece -- Social life and customs 6. Greece -- Civilization -- To 146 B.C
ISBN 1454909080; 9781454909088

LC 2013474163

This book, by Robert Garland, presents a "vibrant portrait of the daily lives of ordinary people--men and women, children and the elderly, slaves and foreigners, rich and poor. . . . Did Greeks share our notion of romantic love? How sta-

ble was the family? How did they relax? What did they eat? Why was it more desirable to be a slave than a day laborer? Were they really more cultivated than we are? . . . [I]ncludes images throughout, as well as maps." (Publisher's note)

"Pharaonic Egypt and ancient Greece are probably the most studied ancient civilizations in our schools. General-reader interest in the two cultures broadens to include everyday life, making these two works a welcome addition to most libraries . . . . For the price and level of coverage, both works are well suited for school projects that require students to go beyond their standard textbooks, and also for general readers interested in ancient Greece or pharaonic Egypt." Booklist

Includes bibliographical references (pages 342-357) and index

Marcovitz, Hal

★ **Ancient** Greece; by Hal Marcovitz. ReferencePoint Press 2012 96 p. (Understanding world history) (hardcover) $27.95

Grades: 7 8 9 10   **938**

1. Greece -- History 2. Greece -- Civilization 3. Greece -- Civilization -- To 146 B.C.
ISBN 9781601522849; 1601522843

LC 2011048991

This book on ancient Greece by Hal Marcovitz is part of "Understanding World History, a series that surveys the political, social, and cultural trends of major periods and events in world history."(Publisher's note) It "combines mythology, history, and politics and provides an enlightening perspective on the treatment of women in the cultures of Athens and Sparta." (Booklist)

Includes bibliographical references and index.

Nardo, Don

Classical civilization; by Don Nardo. Morgan Reynolds Pub. 2011 112 p. ill. (some col.), col. map (World history) (library) $28.95

Grades: 6 7 8 9   **938**

1. Greece -- History 2. Greece -- Civilization 3. Greece -- History -- To 146 B.C. 4. Greece -- Civilization -- To 146 B.C.
ISBN 1599351730; 9781599351735

LC 2011000235

This book by Don Nardo on ancient Greece is part of the World History series. It "encompasses not only political history but also influential developments in political thinking, philosophy, science, literature, architecture, sports, and the military. The section on the Olympics debunks the notion that early Olympic athletes were amateurs without financial backing." (Booklist)

Includes bibliographical references and index.

★ The **Oxford** classical dictionary; general editors, Simon Hornblower and Antony Spawforth; assistant editor, Esther Eidinow. 4th ed; Oxford University Press 2012 lv, 1592 p

Grades: 11 12 Adult   **938**

1. Classical dictionaries 2. Classical civilization -- Dictionaries
ISBN 0199545561; 9780199545568

LC 2012009579

First published 1949 under the editorship of M. Cary and others

This reference book "offers nearly 1600 pages of entries that detail important topics of the Classical world from agriculture to war, social history to science, biography to religion. . . .Two focus areas are new to this edition: anthropology and reception, an area of study that examines how a Classical idea or concept affected various societies during different periods of history, depending on the context of the people reading the narrative, viewing the art . . . etc." (Library Journal)

"A scholarly dictionary, with signed articles, covering biography, literature, mythology, philosophy, religion, science, geography, etc. Most of the articles are brief, but there are some longer survey articles, e.g. Rome, music, scholarship, etc." Guide to Ref Books. 11th edition

Includes bibliographical references

Sacks, David

Encyclopedia of the ancient Greek world; editorial consultant, Oswyn Murray; revised by Lisa R. Brody. Rev ed; Facts on File 2005 xx, 412p il map (Facts on File library of world history) $75

Grades: 11 12 Adult   **938**
1. Reference books 2. Greece -- History -- Encyclopedias
ISBN 0-8160-5722-2

LC 2004-56429

First published 1995

This encyclopedia covers "ancient Greece, from the dawning of Minoan civilization to the conquest of Rome—2000 years of a remarkable civilization that left an indelible imprint on human history. . . . This is a first-rate purchase for libraries on a topic of endless inquiry and fascination." SLJ

Includes bibliographical references

Skelton, Debra

Empire of Alexander the Great; [by] Debra Skelton & Pamela Dell. Rev. ed.; Chelsea House 2009 152p il (Great empires of the past) $35

Grades: 7 8 9 10   **938**
1. Kings 2. Greece -- History
ISBN 978-1-60413-162-8

LC 2009-5723

First published 2005

This book "looks at what made Alexander a brilliant military tactician and a charismatic leader. It also explores what the Eastern world learned through contact with Alexander, and what Alexander brought to the West from the Persian Empire." Publisher's note

Includes glossary and bibliographical references

Stafford, Emma, 1968-

Exploring the life, myth, and art of ancient Greece; Emma J. Stafford. Rosen Pub. 2012 144 p. (lib. bdg.) $42.60

Grades: 7 8 9 10 11   **938**
1. Greek art 2. Greek mythology 3. Greece -- Religion 4. Greece -- Civilization 5. Greece -- History -- 0-323 6. Greece -- Civilization -- To 146 B.C.
ISBN 9781448848300

LC 2011009898

This book on Ancient Greece "offers an informative overview of . . . political and social history as well as its art, architecture, and mythology, all bolstered with plenty of . . . details and narratives. . . . [T]he illustrations include artworks, documents, and handsome maps as well as photos of significant sites and artifacts. "Ancient Greece" traces the development of Greek society and its expression through mythology and the arts." (Booklist) The book "put[s] the art . . . in context, explaining how a society's religious beliefs, legends, and cultural traditions manifest themselves through images and iconography. The . . . layout features full-color photographs of architecture, sculpture, and painting on every page, accompanied by informative captions." (School Libr J)

Includes bibliographical references (p. 137) and index

Tritle, Lawrence A.

The **Peloponnesian** War; [by] Lawrence Tritle. Greenwood Press 2005 xxiv, 206p il map (Greenwood guides to historic events of the ancient world) $45

Grades: 9 10 11 12   **938**
1. Greece -- History -- 431-404 B.C., Peloponnesian War
ISBN 0-313-32499-9

LC 2004-47506

This book features "biographical sketches, and annotated primary documents. An overview of the war is presented, followed a presentation of Thucydides' account of the war's causes. A look at the intertwined . . . relation of democracy and empire is offered, as are chapters on how the war was represented in plays, statuary, and pottery." Publisher's note

Includes bibliographical references

Wood, Michael

★ **In** the footsteps of Alexander the Great; a journey from Greece to Asia. University of Calif. Press 1997 256p il maps hardcover o.p. pa $18.95

Grades: 11 12 Adult   **938**
1. Historic sites 2. Kings 3. Asia -- Description and travel
ISBN 0-520-21307-6; 0-520-23192-9 pa

LC 97-19188

This book is "illustrated with a mixture of Alexandrine art from a variety of cultures, landscapes that capture the wide range of geographies through which Alexander and his imperial armies passed, and portraits of cultures . . . in which the influence of that long-ago juggernaut is still visible." Booklist

Includes bibliographical references

939 Other parts of ancient world

★ **Civilizations** of the Ancient Near East; Jack M. Sasson, editor in chief; John Baines, Gary Beckman, Karen S. Rubinson, associate editors. Hen-

drickson Publishers 2000 4v in 2 il map set
$169.95

Grades: 11 12 Adult   **939**
1. Middle East -- Civilization
ISBN 1-56563-607-4

LC 00-63144

First published 1995 by Scribner

This "work concentrates on the Near East, broadly defined to include a region from Northeast Africa to India,
Pakistan, and Burma, with principal focus on the core areas
of Egypt, Syro-Palestine, Mesopotamia, and Anatolia. The
time span ranges from the third millennium B.C.E., when
writing was invented, to 330 B.C.E., when Alexander triumphed over the Persian Empire. The 189 contributors from
five continents and 16 countries include some of the world's
finest scholars." Libr J [review of 1995 edition]

Includes bibliographical references

Thomas, Carol G.

★ The **Trojan** War; [by] Carol G. Thomas and
Craig Conant. Greenwood Press 2005 209p il map
(Greenwood guides to historic events of the ancient
world) $45

Grades: 9 10 11 12   **939**
1. Trojan War
ISBN 0-313-32526-X

LC 2004-17660

"An overview of Troy and the world of the late Bronze
Age is presented in the first chapter, followed by sections
on: finding Troy and the Trojan War, Homer and the epic
tradition, the force of legend, and Troy in the 21st century."
Publisher's note

Includes bibliographical references

939.4   Middle East to 640

Dictionary of the ancient Near East; edited by Piotr
Bienkowski and Alan Millard. University of Pa.
Press 2000 342p il maps hardcover o.p. pa
$34.95

Grades: 11 12 Adult   **939.4**
1. Reference books 2. Middle East -- Antiquities --
Dictionaries
ISBN 0-8122-3557-6; 0-8122-2115-X pa

LC 00-21715

"The volume's easy-to-follow format, very readable
content and affordable price assure its use by general readers, students and scholars." Choice

Includes bibliographical references

940   History of Europe

Davies, Norman

Europe: a history. HarperCollins Publishers
1998 1365p il map pa $25.95

Grades: 9 10 11 12   **940**
1. Europe -- History
ISBN 0-06-097468-0

LC 97-32889

First published 1996 by Oxford Univ. Press

This book covers "the rise and fall of Rome, the sweeping invasions of Alaric and Atilla, the Norman Conquests,
the Papal struggles for power, the Renaissance and the Reformation, the French Revolution and the Napoleonic Wars,
Europe's rise to become the powerhouse of the world, and its
eclipse in our own century, following two devastating World
Wars." Publisher's note

Includes bibliographical references

Marshall Cavendish Corporation

World and its peoples: Europe. Marshall Cavendish Reference 2010 13v il map set $714.21

Grades: 8 9 10 11 12   **940**
1. Reference books 2. Human geography --
Encyclopedias 3. Europe -- History -- Encyclopedias
4. Europe -- Civilization -- Encyclopedias
ISBN 978-0-7614-7883-6

LC 2009-4321

"Each book details the geographical features and climate
of the entire region, along with an overview of the history
and movement of people in the area. This overview is followed by in-depth coverage of each country (dependencies
and the Russian Federation are included), focusing on particulars such as statistics, culture, government, economics,
symbols, and national history. . . . With copious resources
offered for further research and a meticulous index, this set
is an ideal resource for geography, history, and social-studies
assignments." SLJ

Includes bibliographical references

940.1   Europe--Early history to 1453

English, Edward D.

★ **Encyclopedia** of the medieval world. Facts
on File 2004 2v il map (Facts on File library of
world history) set $150

Grades: 11 12 Adult   **940.1**
1. Reference books 2. Middle Ages -- Encyclopedias
ISBN 0-8160-4690-5

LC 2003-27825

This encyclopedia "covers the time period from the late
antique world to about 1500 C.E and includes events, people, institutions, and culture in western and eastern Europe,
Scandinavia, North Africa, Byzantium, and the Near East.
The 2,000 entries discuss significant people, art, politics, literature, religion, economics, law, science, and warfare in an
A-Z format." Booklist

Includes bibliographical references

Gies, Frances

The **knight** in history. Harper & Row 1984
255p il maps hardcover o.p. pa $14.99

Grades: 11 12 Adult   **940.1**
1. Middle Ages 2. Knights and knighthood
ISBN 0-06-015399-3; 0-06-091413-0 pa

LC 84-47571

This book describes the rise and fall of the institution of knighthood and the influence of the medieval knight throughout history.

Includes bibliographical references

Life in a medieval village; [by] Frances and Joseph Gies. Harper & Row 1990 257p il maps hardcover o.p. pa $14.95

Grades: 11 12 Adult 940.1

1. Middle Ages 2. Medieval civilization
ISBN 0-06-016215-5; 0-06-092046-7 pa

LC 89-33759

"Elton, England, is the focal point of the authors' efforts to portray the everyday life and social structure of the High Middle Ages. After giving a brief summary of Elton's origins and development in the Roman and Anglo-Saxon periods, the book examines just how the residents lived and worked within the feudal structure at the beginning of the fourteenth century." Booklist

Includes bibliographical references

Gies, Joseph

Life in a medieval city; [by] Joseph and Frances Gies. HarperPerennial 1981 274p il map pa $13.95

Grades: 11 12 Adult 940.1

1. Middle Ages 2. Medieval civilization
ISBN 0-06-090880-7

First published 1969 by Crowell

"A portrait of a medieval city [Troyes], a flourishing settlement of a type not known in Europe before the Middle Ages." Cincinnati Public Libr

Includes bibliographical references

The **Greenwood** encyclopedia of global medieval life and culture; Joyce E. Salisbury, general editor. Greenwood Press 2009 3v il map set $349.95

Grades: 7 8 9 10 11 12 Adult 940.1

1. Reference books 2. Medieval civilization -- Encyclopedias
ISBN 978-0-313-33801-4; 0-313-33801-9

LC 2008-36709

"This set is a much-expanded version of the Greenwood Encyclopedia of Daily Life, Volume II (2004). . . . As its title suggests, the new set extends the coverage of medieval life around the globe. . . . The global nature of this encyclopedia sets it apart from other works on the medieval period. Because of its depth and breadth of coverage, it is recommended for high-school, college, and public libraries that need reference works on medieval history." Booklist

Includes bibliographical references

Hamm, Jean S.

★ **Term** paper resource guide to medieval history; [by] Jean Shepherd Hamm. Greenwood Press 2010 371p $65

Grades: 10 11 12 940.1

1. Report writing 2. Reference books 3. Middle Ages -- Bibliography 4. Medieval civilization -- Bibliography
ISBN 978-0-313-35967-5; 0-313-35967-9

LC 2009-36249

This book "provides coverage of an extensive time period (410-1485), condensed into 100 significant historical

events from the Middle Ages. Organized chronologically, the guide reliably represents cultures from Asia, Africa, and the Americas, but largely focuses on European history. Although not intended to be a comprehensive history, this volume will be an exceedingly useful tool for advanced high school students and beginning undergraduates charged with writing papers on the medieval period. For each entry, the author gives a broad overview of a historical event; recommends related term paper topics and alternative projects; and provides excellent suggestions for primary, secondary, Web, and multimedia sources." Choice

Includes bibliographical references

★ **History** of the ancient and medieval world; 2nd ed.; Marshall Cavendish Reference 2009 11v il map set $714.21

Grades: 7 8 9 10 11 12 940.1

1. Middle Ages 2. Ancient history 3. Reference books 4. Medieval civilization
ISBN 978-0-7614-7789-1

LC 2008-60052

First published 1996

This "will become the resource for students seeking information on this time period." SLJ

Includes bibliographical references

Horizon book of the Middle Ages

★ The **Middle** Ages; 1st Mariner Books ed.; Houghton Mifflin Co. 2001 350p il pa $17

Grades: 9 10 11 12 940.1

1. Commerce 2. Religion 3. Peasantry 4. Amusements 5. Middle Ages 6. Medieval art 7. Medieval civilization
ISBN 0-618-05703-X

LC 2001-271448

First published 1968 by American Heritage with title: The Horizon book of the Middle Ages

This volume covers the period from the conversion of Constantine in 312 A.D. through the conclusion of the Hundred Years War in 1461.

Knights; in history and in legend. chief consultant Constance Brittain Bouchard. Firefly Books 2009 304p il map $40

Grades: 11 12 Adult 940.1

1. Knights and knighthood 2. Military art and science -- History
ISBN 978-1-55407-480-8

The history of knights, from their everyday lives to their clothing, training, heraldry and orders, as well as their role in literature and film, and the decline of traditional knighthood.

"Aimed at history and art history lovers, this work would be excellent reading for medieval history enthusiasts and should be welcomed as a library reference resource." Libr J

Includes bibliographical references

Nardo, Don

Medieval Europe; by Don Nardo. 1st ed. Morgan Reynolds Pub. 2011 128 p. col. ill., maps (World history) (library) $28.95

Grades: 6 7 8 9 940.1

1. Middle Ages 2. Great Britain -- History -- 1066-

1485, Medieval period 3. Civilization, Medieval
ISBN 1599351722; 9781599351728

LC 2010054477

This book by Don Nardo, part of the World History series, focuses on Medieval Europe. Medieval Europe "was the bridge that led from the ancient world to the modern one." Topics include the Roman Catholic Church, the stone castles built by kings and nobles, the Crusades, and the Renaissance. (Publisher's note)

Includes bibliographical references　(p. 120-121) and index.

The **Oxford** dictionary of the Middle Ages; edited by Robert E. Bjork. Oxford University Press 2010 4v il map set $595

Grades: 11 12 Adult　　　　　　　**940.1**
1. Reference books 2. Middle Ages -- Dictionaries 3. Middle Ages -- Encyclopedias 4. Civilization, Medieval -- Dictionaries 5. Medieval civilization -- Encyclopedias
ISBN 9780198662624 set

LC 2010-923327

"The ODMA's 5,000 entries range in length from one or two sentences (Gargoyle, Drollery) to 10,000 or more words and are consistently well written. . . . The ODMA encompasses areas of Asia, Africa, and the Middle East as well as topics of current scholarship, such as gender studies and Islam. Entries include individuals (Attila, Hildegard of Bingen); technical terms (Hammer beam, squinch); and places (Sutton Hoo)." Booklist

Includes bibliographical references

★ The **Oxford** history of medieval Europe; edited by George Holmes. Oxford Univ. Press 2001 395p il maps pa $16.95

Grades: 11 12 Adult　　　　　　　**940.1**
1. Europe -- History -- 476-1492
ISBN 0-19-280133-3

LC 2002-281715

This is an abridged edition of The Oxford illustrated history of medieval Europe, published 1988

This compact edition covers such subjects as the chivalric code of knights, popular festivals, new art forms, the Black Death, the fall of Rome, and the emergence of the Reformation

Includes bibliographical references

Singman, Jeffrey L.

★ **Daily** life in medieval Europe. Greenwood Press 1999 268p il $57.95; pa $25

Grades: 9 10 11 12　　　　　　　**940.1**
1. Medieval civilization 2. Europe -- History -- 476-1492 3. Europe -- Social life and customs
ISBN 0-313-30273-1; 0-313-36076-6 pa

LC 98-46816

The author "focuses on details that help readers picture rural and urban medieval life among peasants, monks, and the aristocracy—medieval heating and lighting, bedchambers in cottages and castles, clothing, money and prices, even sanitation. Singman narrows his focus to the years 1100-1300, portraying life in Northern France, England, the Low Countries, and some of Germany." Voice Youth Advocates

Includes bibliographical references

940.2　Europe--1453-

Allport, Alan

The **Congress** of Vienna; by Alan Allport. Chelsea House 2009 126 p. (Milestones in modern world history)

Grades: 7 8 9 10 11 12　　　　　　　**940.2**
1. Vienna (Austria) 2. International arbitration 3. Napoleonic Wars, 1800-1815 -- Treaties 4. Europe -- Politics and government -- 1789-1900
ISBN 9781604134971

LC 2009022862

This book on the Congress of Vienna is part of "the Milestones in Modern World History series" of books that "give . . . explanations for major world events that continue to have an impact on today's world." Author Alan Allport describes how the "Congress of Vienna took place after the defeat of Napoleon, when the fragmented nations of Europe agreed on some ground rules to avoid another war." (Booklist) The book "discusses what the statesmen hoped to achieve in Vienna, analyzes the mixed fortunes of the "Congress System" they established, and looks at the congress's legacy of international mediation in our era through such institutions as the United States Security Council." (Publisher's note)

Includes bibliographical references　(p. 117-119) and index

Currie, Stephen

★ The **Renaissance**; by Stephen Currie. ReferencePoint Press, Inc. 2012 96 p. (hardcover) $27.95

Grades: 7 8 9 10　　　　　　　**940.2**
1. Renaissance
ISBN 1601521898; 9781601521897

LC 2011048993

This book by Stephen Currie is part of the "Understanding World History" series. It "opens with an . . . overview of the circumstances that came together to inspire a Renaissance." (School Library Journal) It profiles "artists and philosophers . . . along with scientists like [Isaac] Newton. Also discussed is the tension between religion and humanism." (Booklist)

Includes bibliographical references and index.

Davis, Robert C.

Renaissance people; lives that shaped the modern age. [by] Robert C. Davis [and] Beth Lindsmith. J. Paul Getty Museum 2011 336p il $39.95

Grades: 9 10 11 12　　　　　　　**940.2**
1. Renaissance 2. Reference books 3. Middle ages -- Biography 4. Europe -- History -- 476-1492 5. Europe -- History -- 1492-1789
ISBN 978-1-60606-078-0; 1-60606-078-3

LC 2011006141

"Well-organized and well-executed, this work guides readers through the years 1400–1600 in chapters covering seven overlapping periods ranging from 25 to 50 years in length each. Each section provides a brief summary of the time in question, followed by 10 to 15 short biographies of some of the intriguing and influential figures who lived then. This clever chronological device makes the book stand out in that it is not an alphabetically organized encyclopedia of the people of the age, but, rather, a guide to the Renaissance as it unfolds through personal actions. . . . A valuable starting point for further research and study." SLJ

Includes bibliographical references

The **eighteenth** century; Europe, 1688-1815. edited by T.C.W. Blanning. Oxford University Press 2000 301p il map (Short Oxford history of Europe) hardcover o.p. pa $43.95

Grades: 10 11 12 Adult **940.2**

1. Europe -- Civilization 2. Europe -- Social conditions 3. Europe -- Economic conditions 4. Europe -- History -- 18th century

ISBN 0-19-873181-7; 0-19-873120-5 pa

LC 00711763

"In this book, six experts analyse . . . . the major developments [that occured in eighteenth-century Europe] in politics, society, the economy, religion and culture, warfare and international relations, and in Europe's relations with the world overseas." Publisher's note

Includes bibliographical references

Elliott, Lynne

The **Renaissance** in Europe; [by] Lynne Elliott. Crabtree Pub. Co. 2009 32p il lib bdg $26.60; pa $8.95

Grades: 6 7 8 9 **940.2**

1. Renaissance 2. Europe -- Civilization

ISBN 978-0-7787-4591-4 lib bdg; 0-7787-4591-0 lib bdg; 978-0-7787-4611-9 pa; 0-7787-4611-9 pa

LC 2008-52410

"Ideal introductions to concepts, people, and events of the Renaissance... succinct and thorough. "SLJ

Encyclopedia of the Enlightenment; Alan Charles Kors, editor in chief. Oxford Univ. Press 2003 4v il set $685

Grades: 11 12 Adult **940.2**

1. Reference books 2. Philosophy -- Encyclopedias 3. Enlightenment -- Encyclopedias

ISBN 0-19-510430-7

LC 2002-3766

This reference includes over 700 articles about "philosophic and social changes engendered by the Enlightenment. It {covers} . . . not only France, England, Scotland, the Low Countries, Italy, English-speaking North America, the German states, and Hapsburg Austria but also Iberian, Ibero-American, Jewish, Russian, and Eastern European cultures." Publisher's note

Includes bibliographical references

Europe 1789 to 1914; encyclopedia of the age of industry and empire. Merriman and Jay Winter, editors in chief. Charles Scribner's Sons 2006 5v il map (Scribner library of modern Europe) set $595

Grades: 11 12 Adult **940.2**

1. Reference books 2. Europe -- Civilization -- Encyclopedias 3. Europe -- History -- 1789-1900 -- Encyclopedias 4. Europe -- History -- 1871-1918 --

Encyclopedias

ISBN 0-684-31359-6; 978-0-684-31359-7

LC 2006-7335

This encyclopedia covers "the time period between the onset of the French Revolution to the outbreak of World War I." Publisher's note

Includes bibliographical references

★ The **European** Renaissance and Reformation, 1350-1600; edited by Norman J. Wilson. Gale Group 2001 xxix, 522p il maps (World eras) $130.75

Grades: 11 12 Adult **940.2**

1. Reformation 2. Renaissance

ISBN 0-7876-1706-7

LC 00-52802

This resource "is comprised of 10 chapters. The first two, focusing on world events and geography, respectively, provide users a global perspective and context for the culture and time period in question. Remaining chapters treat other cultural elements. . . . Each chapter is subdivided into five types of material: chronological, overview, topical, biographical, and documentary. . . . This volume, in addition to its fine organization, structure, and arrangement, is equally impressive for its inclusive, well-written content." Booklist

Includes bibliographical references

Gies, Joseph

Life in a medieval castle; [by] Joseph and Frances Gies. Harper & Row 1979 272p il pa $14.95

Grades: 11 12 Adult **940.2**

1. Castles 2. Feudalism 3. Middle Ages 4. Knights and knighthood 5. Hunting -- Great Britain

ISBN 0-06-090674-X

LC 79-103901

First published 1974 by Crowell

Using Chepstow Castle on the Welsh border as a model, the authors provide "descriptions of the medieval world where the castle was household, feudal center, and military target, and by concentrating on Anglo-Norman examples illustrate what existence was like as the dark ages began to brighten." Booklist

Includes glossary and bibliographical references

Hinds, Kathryn, 1962-

Everyday life in the Renaissance. Marshall Cavendish Benchmark 2010 327p il lib bdg $42.79

Grades: 7 8 9 10 **940.2**

1. Renaissance 2. Europe -- Civilization

ISBN 978-0-7614-4483-1; 0-7614-4483-1

LC 2008-54829

A compilation of four titles in the Everyday Life in the Renaissance series, published 2004: The church; The city; The countryside; The court

This book combines "clear, bold text with vivid reproductions of period paintings, frescoes, and sculptures, making for [a] stunning [presentation]." SLJ

Includes glossary and bibliographical references

The **nineteenth** century; Europe, 1789-1914. edited by T.C.W. Blanning. Oxford University Press

2000 304p il map (Short Oxford history of Europe) hardcover o.p. pa $43.95

Grades: 10 11 12 Adult   **940.2**
1. Europe -- Civilization 2. Europe -- Social conditions 3. Europe -- Economic conditions 4. Europe -- History -- 1789-1900
ISBN 0-19-873136-1; 0-19-873135-3 pa
                                  LC 00703223

"In six chapters, experts tackle the big questions relating to the political, international, social, economic, cultural, and imperial history of [nineteenth-century Europe]." Publisher's note

Includes bibliographical references

★ The **Oxford** illustrated history of modern Europe; edited by T. C. W. Blanning. Oxford Univ. Press 1996 362p il maps hardcover o.p. pa $24.95

Grades: 11 12 Adult   **940.2**
1. Europe -- History -- 1789-1900 2. Europe -- History -- 20th century
ISBN 0-19-820374-8; 0-19-285426-7 pa
This volume covers "politics, economics, warfare, class structure, art, and culture from the time of the revolution through 1995. Central themes include the idea that revolution against established order was possible, successful, and, once underway, perhaps unstoppable." Libr J

Includes bibliographical references

★ The **Renaissance;** Raymond Obstfeld and Loretta Obstfeld, book editors. Greenhaven Press 2002 220p il (History firsthand) hardcover o.p. pa $21.20

Grades: 9 10 11 12   **940.2**
1. Renaissance
ISBN 0-7377-1080-2 lib bdg; 0-7377-1079-9 pa
                                  LC 2001-51296

This anthology gathers primary accounts from religious, artistic, scientific and secular leaders dealing with social and political topics of the day

Includes bibliographical references

Renaissance and Reformation; editor, James A. Patrick. Marshall Cavendish 2007 6v il set $671.36

Grades: 9 10 11 12 Adult   **940.2**
1. Reference books 2. Reformation -- Encyclopedias 3. Renaissance -- Encyclopedias
ISBN 978-0-7614-7650-4; 0-7614-7650-4
                                  LC 2006-42600

This encyclopedia provides a "background on the historical period that bridged the medieval and modern worlds, roughly 1300-1700, with emphasis on 1350-1650. . . . This is an extremely impressive publication, lavishly presented, informative, and remarkably enjoyable to read. . . . A must-have for all high-school collections and for public libraries patronized by young adults. Adults will find it appealing as well." Booklist

Includes bibliographical references

Sider, Sandra
Handbook to life in Renaissance Europe. Facts on File 2005 382p il map (Facts on File library of world history) $70

Grades: 11 12 Adult   **940.2**
1. Renaissance 2. Europe -- Civilization
ISBN 0-8160-5618-8
                                  LC 2004-20088

This book "furnishes a good, general introduction to the Renaissance, and does so succinctly and with some of the breadth usually found in longer works." Choice

Includes bibliographical references

Streissguth, Thomas
The **Napoleonic** wars; defeat of the Grand Army. Lucent Books 2003 112p il map (History's great defeats) $27.45

Grades: 9 10 11 12   **940.2**
1. Emperors 2. France -- History -- 1799-1815 3. France -- Armeé -- Grande Armeé
ISBN 1-590-18065-8
                                  LC 2002-151712

Provides a look at how Napoleon Bonaparte's egotism, unrealistic dreams, and tendency to underestimate enemies led to the downfall of his Grand Armée during the Napoleonic Wars.

Includes bibliographical references

★ The **Renaissance**; by Tom Streissguth; Konrad Eisenbichler, consulting editor. Greenhaven Press 2008 353p il map (Greenhaven encyclopedia of) $77.45

Grades: 9 10 11 12   **940.2**
1. Reference books 2. Renaissance -- Encyclopedias
ISBN 978-0-7377-3216-0
                                  LC 2007-938127

Alphabetically arranged essays provide information about the Renaissance, discussing artistic, social, philosophical, theological, political, and scientific topics, and featuring biographical sketches of significant individuals as well as photographs, illustrations, maps, cross-references, and time lines.

"Entries are well written and concise and provide an excellent introduction to each subject for high-school students. Advanced middle-school social-studies classes could also utilize this resource." Booklist

Wilson, Ellen Judy
★ **Encyclopedia** of the Enlightenment; Peter Hanns Reill, consulting editor; Ellen Judy Wilson, principal author. rev ed; Facts on File 2004 670p $75

Grades: 11 12 Adult   **940.2**
1. Reference books 2. Europe -- Intellectual life 3. Philosophy -- Encyclopedias 4. Enlightenment -- Encyclopedias
ISBN 0-8160-5335-9
                                  LC 2003-22973

First published 1996

This reference provides a "review of the important ideas, people, and events that shaped the world during the Enlightenment. [It] covers the major changes in science, education, philosophy, art and architecture, and politics which took place during the 17th and 18th centuries and led to the birth of the modern era. . . . The biographical entries cover such notables as Robespierre, Schiller, Fielding, Kant, and Voltaire. . . . Larger public, school, and academic libraries looking for a comprehensive overview of the subject for the student or interested reader will find this a valuable and accessible resource." Libr J

Includes bibliographical references

940.3   World War I, 1914-1918

Barber, Nicola

World War I; by Nicola Barber. Heinemann Library 2012 80 p. ill. (some col.), col. maps (Living through) (library) $36.50; (paperback) $10.99
Grades: 6 7 8 9   **940.3**
1. World War, 1914-1918
ISBN 1432960105; 9781432960018; 9781432960100
LC 2011015931

In this book on World War I, part of the "Living Through" series, "[Nicola] Barber explains the European political powder keg of the late 1800s and the turn of the last century before telling of the assassination of Archduke Franz Ferdinand." (VOYA) Other topics include " the role of women in the war, propaganda, and the misalignment of the Peace Treaty of Versailles." (Children's Literature)

Includes bibliographical references (p. 76-78) and index.

Bausum, Ann

Unraveling freedom; the battle for democracy on the home front during World War I. National Geographic 2010 88p il $19.95; lib bdg $28.90
Grades: 7 8 9 10   **940.3**
1. Civil rights 2. German Americans 3. World War, 1914-1918 -- United States 4. United States -- Politics and government -- 1898-1919
ISBN 978-1-4263-0702-7; 1-4263-0702-0; 978-1-4263-0703-4 lib bdg; 1-4263-0703-9 lib bdg
LC 2010-10631

"Bausum describes the events that would eventually lead the U.S. into the European conflict that ultimately led to World War I. She then turns her attention to describing the destruction of civil liberties by President Wilson, Congress, and those in control of political power during the country's campaign to 'make the world safe for democracy.' . . . Black-and-white archival photos and political cartoons are arranged in an artistic manner with informative captions. Appropriate quotations by various people of the time are displayed in elegant fonts. Make this unique and timely offering a definite first purchase." SLJ

Includes bibliographical references

Bosco, Peter I.

World War I; Rev. ed.; Chelsea House 2010 182p il map (America at war) $45
Grades: 9 10 11 12   **940.3**
1. World War, 1914-1918 -- United States
ISBN 978-0-8160-8188-2
LC 2009-28627

First published 1991

This book provides a "portrait of this great conflict, with an emphasis on the critical role played by the United States. . . . [It includes a chapter on] the military innovations in tactics and weaponry." Publisher's note

Burg, David F.

Almanac of World War I; [by] David F. Burg and L. Edward Purcell; introduction by William Manchester. University Press of Ky. 1998 320p il maps hardcover o.p. pa $22
Grades: 11 12 Adult   **940.3**
1. World War, 1914-1918
ISBN 0-8131-2072-1; 0-8131-9087-8 pa; 9780813190877
LC 98-26625

"The bulk of the text is arranged chronologically by year and date, listing almost daily occurrences from 1914 through 1918. . . . The work is international in scope, covering political and military happenings from around the world. . . . There is really nothing comparable to this volume." Booklist

Includes bibliographical references

Carlisle, Rodney P.

World War I. Facts on File 2006 454p il map (Eyewitness history) $75
Grades: 8 9 10 11 12   **940.3**
1. World War, 1914-1918 -- Personal narratives
ISBN 0-8160-6061-4; 978-0-8160-6061-0
LC 2005-27236

First published 1992 under the authorship of Joe H. Kirchberger with title: The First World War

This book "provides hundreds of firsthand accounts— from diary entries, letters, speeches, and newspaper accounts—that focus on different warfare issues and on the social and cultural impacts of the war on Europe and the United States. . . . This volume also includes critical documents related to this topic, as well as capsule biographies of key figures, narrative sections, eyewitness testimonies, 102 black-and-white photographs, maps and graphs, a bibliography, notes, a glossary, chronologies, appendixes, and an index." Publisher's note

Includes bibliographical references

Coetzee, Marilyn Shevin

★ World War I; a history in documents. [by] Marilyn Shevin-Coetzee and Frans Coetzee. 2nd ed; Oxford University Press 2011 182p il (Pages from history) $39.95; pa $24.95
Grades: 7 8 9 10   **940.3**
1. World War, 1914-1918 -- Sources
ISBN 978-0-19-973151-0; 978-0-19-973152-7 pa
LC 2009049519

First published 2002 with authors' names in reverse order

Offering an "account of the war as more than a purely military phenomenon, . . . [this book] also addresses its profound social, cultural, and economic implications. Authors Marilyn Shevin-Coetzee and Frans Coetzee use editorials, memoirs, newspaper articles, poems, and letters to recreate the many facets of the war." Publisher's note

Includes bibliographical references

Freedman, Russell

★ The **war** to end all wars; World War I. Clarion Books 2010 176p il map $22

Grades: 6 7 8 9 10   **940.3**
1. World War, 1914-1918
ISBN 978-0-547-02686-2; 0-547-02686-2

LC 2009-28971

"In his signature lucid style, Freedman offers a photo-essay that examines World War I, the first global war in which modern weapons inflicted mass slaughter and an estimated 20 million people were killed. Interwoven into the big picture of the war's causes and consequences are unforgettable vignettes of German and Allied soldiers, drawn from reports, letters, and diaries, and the personal details are heartbreaking." Booklist

Gilbert, Martin

The **First** World War; a complete history. Holt & Co. 1994 xxiv, 615p il maps hardcover o.p. pa $25

Grades: 11 12 Adult   **940.3**
1. World War, 1914-1918
ISBN 0-8050-1540-X; 0-8050-7617-4 pa

LC 94-27268

"What Mr. Gilbert seeks to do, and frequently succeeds in doing, is to humanize, indeed to personalize, World War I. His effort and accomplishment make this a rewarding and significant book." N Y Times Book Rev

Includes bibliographical references

Grant, R. G.

World War I; The Definitive Visual History: from Sarajevo to Versailles. R. G. Grant. Dk Pub. 2014 360 p. ill. (some color), color maps $40

Grades: Adult   **940.3**
1. Weapons -- History 2. World War, 1914-1918
ISBN 1465419381; 9781465419385

LC 2013387827

"Written by historian R. G. Grant, and created by DK's award-winning editorial and design team, World War I charts the . . . war. . . . Using illustrated timelines, detailed maps, and personal accounts, readers will see the oft-studied war in a new light. Key episodes are set clearly in the wider context of the conflict, in-depth profiles look at the key generals and political leaders, and full-color photo galleries showcase . . . weapons, inventions, and new technologies." (Publisher's note)

"This is a broad, moving, informative account of the war that's perfect for both the young, budding historian and the well-versed WWI reader." Pub Wkly

Heyman, Neil M.

World War I. Greenwood Press 1997 xxiii, 257p il maps (Greenwood Press guides to historic events of the twentieth century) $45

Grades: 11 12 Adult   **940.3**
1. World War, 1914-1918
ISBN 0-313-29880-7

LC 97-1686

This work is "divided into three sections. The first gives an overview of the causes, issues, and ultimately the conse-

quences of a world at war. . . . The second section of the book is a series of biographies of the major political and military participants in the war. . . . The third section of the book is devoted to primary documents from the period." Book Rep

Includes bibliographical references

Stokesbury, James L.

A **short** history of World War I. Morrow 1981 348p maps hardcover o.p. pa $14.95

Grades: 11 12 Adult   **940.3**
1. World War, 1914-1918
ISBN 0-688-00128-9; 0-688-00129-7 pa

LC 80-22206

This chronologically arranged history of World War I presents both the political and military perspectives.

Includes bibliographical references

Stone, Norman

★ **World** War One. Basic Books 2009 226p il map $25

Grades: 9 10 11 12 Adult   **940.3**
1. World War, 1914-1918
ISBN 978-0-465-01368-5; 0-465-01368-6
First published 2007 in the United Kingdom

The author presents a narrative history of the First World War.

"Stone is as unconventional as he is brilliant, and this provocative interpretation of the Great War combines impressive command of the literature with a telling eye for relevant facts and a sensitive ear for telling epigrams." Publ Wkly

Includes bibliographical references

Strachan, Hew

The **First** World War. Viking 2004 364p il maps hardcover o.p. pa $16

Grades: 11 12 Adult   **940.3**
1. World War, 1914-1918
ISBN 0-14-303518-5 pa; 0-670-03295-6

LC 2003-62191

This book examines "the causes, the major campaigns, and the consequences of the First World War." (Publisher's note) Index.

"Readers already familiar with the sequence of events in strict order will benefit most. But all readers will eventually be gripped, and even the most seasoned ones will praise the insights and the original choice of illustrations." Publ Wkly

Includes bibliographical references

★ The **Treaty** of Versailles; Jeff Hay, book editor. Greenhaven Press 2002 124p il (At issue in history) hardcover o.p. pa $18.70

Grades: 9 10 11 12   **940.3**
1. Treaty of Versailles (1919) 2. World War, 1914-1918 -- Peace
ISBN 0-7377-0827-1 lib bdg; 0-7377-0826-3 pa

LC 2001-40609

This collection of articles examines "the expectations of those who negotiated the treaty, the responses to the treaty by those who were close observers or participants in the ne-

gotiations, and more recent assessments of the treaty." Publisher's note
Includes bibliographical references

Tuchman, Barbara Wertheim
The **guns** of August; [by] Barbara W. Tuchman; [with a new foreword by Robert K. Massie] 1st Ballantine Books ed; Ballantine 1994 xxiv, 511p il, maps pa $14
Grades: 11 12 Adult   **940.3**
  1. World War, 1914-1918
  ISBN 0-345-38623-X
          LC 93-90461
First published 1962 by Macmillan
A history of the negotiations that preceded World War I and the course of the war's first month.
Includes bibliographical references

The **Zimmermann** telegram. Ballantine Books 1985 244p il pa $14
Grades: 11 12 Adult   **940.3**
  1. World War, 1914-1918 -- Causes
  ISBN 0-345-32425-0
          LC 84-91737
First published 1958 by Macmillan
The author discusses the German plan to induce Mexico to attack the U.S. during World War I.
Includes bibliographical references

★ The **United** States in the First World War; an encyclopedia. editor, Anne Cipriano Venzon; consulting editor, Paul L. Miles. Garland 1995 xx, 830p maps (Garland reference library of the humanities) $155; pa $45
Grades: 11 12 Adult   **940.3**
  1. Reference books   2. World War, 1914-1918 -- Encyclopedias
  ISBN 0-8240-7055-0; 0-8153-3353-6 pa
          LC 95-1782
"Biography, economics, civil rights, women's issues, foreign relations, battles, armaments, and conferences are among the topics included. Arrangement is alphabetical, and most articles are brief—between one column and a page. . . . Most articles include brief bibliographies. There are six maps, but no other illustrations." Libr J

Woodward, David R.
World War I almanac. Facts On File 2009 554p il map (Almanacs of American wars) $95
Grades: 9 10 11 12 Adult   **940.3**
  1. Almanacs 2. Reference books 3. World War, 1914-1918
  ISBN 978-0-8160-7134-0; 978-1-4381-1896-3 ebook
          LC 2008-41575
This book "would be a welcome addition to public, school, and academic libraries where a student needs to find basic information quickly." Booklist
Includes glossary and bibliographical references

World War I: a student encyclopedia; Spencer C. Tucker, editor; Priscilla Mary Roberts, editor,

documents volume. ABC-CLIO 2005 5v il map set $485
Grades: 9 10 11 12   **940.3**
  1. Reference books   2. World War, 1914-1918 -- Encyclopedias
  ISBN 1-85109-879-8
          LC 2005-25638
"More than 900 A-to-Z entries that range in length from one to 20 pages cover major campaigns, individual battles, countries, biographies, weapons, diplomatic efforts, and the social and cultural impacts of the war. . . . This well-written and accessible resource is highly recommended for school and public libraries." Libr J
Includes bibliographical references

940.4   Military history of World War I

Eisenhower, John S. D.
Yanks: the epic story of the American Army in World War I; {by} John S. D. Eisenhower with Joanne Thompson Eisenhower. Free Press 2001 353p il maps hardcover o.p. pa $16
Grades: 11 12 Adult   **940.4**
  1. United States -- Army 2. World War, 1914-1918 -- Campaigns
  ISBN 0-684-86304-9; 0-7432-2385-3 pa
          LC 2001-23124
"This is an important work that should help alter the historical picture of the American role in the conflict." Booklist
Includes bibliographical references

Farwell, Byron
★ **Over** there; the United States in the Great War, 1917-1918. Norton 1999 336p $27.95; pa $15.95
Grades: 11 12 Adult   **940.4**
  1. World War, 1914-1918 -- United States
  ISBN 0-393-04698-2; 0-393-32028-6 pa
          LC 98-35705
This history of American intervention in World War I focuses primarily on the military aspects of the war but also discusses its social and economic impact
"This title does provide good coverage on the intervention in Russia and the role of women in the war, notably the 'Hello Girls.' " Libr J
Includes bibliographical references

Mosier, John
The **myth** of the Great War; a new military history of World War I. HarperCollins Pubs. 2001 381p il hardcover o.p. pa $14.95
Grades: 11 12 Adult   **940.4**
  1. World War, 1914-1918 -- Campaigns
  ISBN 0-06-019676-9; 0-06-008433-2 pa
          LC 00-46103
"After dissecting the major campaigns on the western front, Mosier concludes that Germany's ultimate defeat was the direct result of the influx of American soldiers into France in 1917 and 1918. . . . This is revisionist history that convincingly smashes the myths that Allied governments,

leaders, and propagandists worked so hard to promulgate. Mosier's masterful account is a welcome addition." Booklist

Includes bibliographical references

940.5 Europe--1918-

Europe since 1914; encyclopedia of the age of war and reconstruction. John Merriman and Jay Winter, editors in chief. Charles Scribner's Sons/ Thomson Gale 2006 5v il map (Scribner library of modern Europe) set $595

Grades: 11 12 Adult **940.5**

1. Reference books 2. Europe -- Civilization -- Encyclopedias 3. Europe -- History -- 20th century -- Encyclopedias

ISBN 0-684-31365-0; 978-0-684-31365-8

LC 2006-14427

This encyclopedia "details European history from the Bolshevik Revolution to the European Union, linking it to the history of the rest of the world." Publisher's note

Includes bibliographical references

940.53 World War II, 1939-1945

Ackerman, Diane, 1948-

The **zookeeper's** wife. W.W. Norton 2007 368p il $24.95

Grades: 11 12 Adult **940.53**

1. Zoos 2. Jews -- Poland 3. Holocaust, 1933-1945 4. World War, 1939-1945 -- Jews -- Rescue

ISBN 978-0-393-06172-7; 0-393-06172-8

LC 2007-12635

This is an account of how the director of the Warsaw Zoo and his wife, Jan and Antonina Zabinski, respectively, saved 300 Jews during World War II.

"An exemplary work of scholarship and an 'ecstasy of imagining,' Ackerman's affecting telling of the heroic Zabinskis' dramatic story illuminates the profound connection between humankind and nature, and celebrates life's beauty, mystery, and tenacity." Booklist

Includes bibliographical references

Altman, Linda Jacobs

Hidden teens, hidden lives; primary sources from the Holocaust. Enslow Publishers 2010 128p il (True stories of teens in the Holocaust) lib bdg $31.93

Grades: 8 9 10 11 12 **940.53**

1. Holocaust survivors 2. Holocaust, 1933-1945 3. World War, 1939-1945 -- Children 4. World War, 1939-1945 -- Personal narratives

ISBN 978-0-7660-3271-2; 0-7660-3271-X

LC 2009-6504

"Altman does a great job of providing historical context and realistic commentary for the individual experiences. Photos of teens and news pictures . . . add further dimensions to the text." Booklist

Includes bibliographical references

★ **And** justice for all; an oral history of the Japanese American detention camps. [compiled by] John Tateishi; foreword by Roger Daniels. University of Washington Press 1999 xxvii, 262p il, map pa $19.95

Grades: 9 10 11 12 **940.53**

1. World War, 1939-1945 -- United States 2. Japanese Americans -- Evacuation and relocation, 1942-1945

ISBN 0-295-97785-X

LC 98-49105

First published 1984 by Random House

"Recollections from 30 Japanese Americans who were placed in government detention camps following Japan's attack on Pearl Harbor lend valuable insight into this tragic event in U.S. history." Booklist

Axelrod, Alan

Encyclopedia of World War II; consulting editor, Jack A. Kingston. Facts on File 2007 2v il (Facts on File library of world history) set $150

Grades: 11 12 Adult **940.53**

1. Reference books 2. World War, 1939-1945 -- Encyclopedias

ISBN 0-8160-6022-3; 978-0-8160-6022-1

LC 2006-26155

This encyclopedia "provides entries on the people, groups, events, equipment, and concepts on both sides that were integral to the war. . . . [This] is an outstanding resource that makes it appropriate for any library serving patrons with questions about World War II." Am Ref Books Annu, 2008

Includes bibliographical references

Beyond Rosie; a documentary History of Women and World War II. edited by Julia Brock, Jennifer W. Dickey, Richard J. W. Harker. University of Arkansas Press 2015 245 p. (pbk.: alk. paper) $22.95

Grades: 9 10 11 12 Adult **940.53**

1. World War, 1939-1945 -- Women 2. World War, 1939-1945 -- United States

ISBN 9781557286697; 9781557286703; 9781610755573

LC 2014949011

This book, edited by Julia Brock, Jennifer W. Dickey, Richard Harker, and Catherine Lewis, "offers readers an opportunity to see the numerous contributions [women] made to the fight against the Axis powers and how American women's roles changed during the war. The primary documents (newspapers, propaganda posters, cartoons, excerpts from oral histories and memoirs, speeches, photographs, and editorials) collected here represent cultural, political, economic, and social perspectives on the diverse roles women played during World War II." (Publisher's note)

"The editors indicate that their intent in assembling this collection was to interest high-school history students and readers of wartime history, as well as students in universities supporting research in women's studies, history, and social-science disciplines. Summing Up: Recommended. All academic audiences; general readers." Choice

Bitton-Jackson, Livia

I have lived a thousand years; growing up in the Holocaust. by Livia E. Bitton-Jackson. Simon & Schuster Bks. for Young Readers 1997 224p hardcover o.p. pa $5.99

Grades: 7 8 9 10   **940.53**
1. Jews -- Hungary 2. Holocaust, 1933-1945 -- Personal narratives
ISBN 0-689-81022-9; 0-689-82395-9 pa
         LC 96-19971

Based on the author's book for adults, Elli: coming of age in the Holocaust (1980)

"This is a memorable addition to the searing accounts of Holocaust survivors." Horn Book

Includes glossary

Byers, Ann

Saving children from the Holocaust; the Kindertransport. Enslow Publishers 2011 128p il (The Holocaust through primary sources) lib bdg $31.93

Grades: 7 8 9 10 11 12   **940.53**
1. Holocaust, 1933-1945 2. World War, 1939-1945 -- Jews -- Rescue
ISBN 978-0-7660-3323-8; 0-7660-3323-6
         LC 2010014215

Discusses the Kindertransport, including the people who organized the operation, how the transports worked, the children's lives who escaped on a transport, and how ten thousand children were saved from the Holocaust.

Includes glossary and bibliographical references

California Historical Society

★ **Only** what we could carry; the Japanese American internment experience. edited with introduction by Lawson Fusao Inada; preface by Patricia Wakida; afterword by William Hohri. Heyday Bks. 2000 xxiii, 439p il maps pa $18.95

Grades: 11 12 Adult   **940.53**
1. Japanese Americans -- Evacuation and relocation, 1942-1945
ISBN 1-89077-130-9
         LC 00-9182

This anthology includes "poetry, prose, biography, news accounts, formal government declarations, letters, and autobiography along with photographs, sketches, and cartoons. . . . Readers will come away from this book with a deep understanding of the times, the sense of betrayal, and the conflicting feelings among the three major groups of Japanese who went through the ordeal." SLJ

Includes bibliographical references

Competing voices from World War II in Europe; edited by Harold J. Goldberg. Greenwood 2010 xxxi, 319p map (Fighting words) $65

Grades: 10 11 12 Adult   **940.53**
1. Reference books 2. World War, 1939-1945 -- Sources 3. World War, 1939-1945 -- Personal narratives
ISBN 978-1-84645-033-4; 1-84645-033-0
         LC 2009-50073

This book "amplifies the voices best equipped to communicate the complicated viewpoints and raw emotion of World War II. These texts tell the story more vividly than any neatly linear, retrospectively composed narrative could." Libr J

Includes bibliographical references

Daniels, Roger

Prisoners without trial; Japanese Americans in World War II. Rev. ed.; Hill and Wang 2004 162p il (Critical issue series) pa $12

Grades: 11 12 Adult   **940.53**
1. World War, 1939-1945 -- United States 2. Japanese Americans -- Evacuation and relocation, 1942-1945
ISBN 0-8090-7896-1
         LC 2004-47328

First published 1993

An account of "the relocation of Japanese Americans during World War II, an injustice prompted not by military necessity but by political and racial motivations. The purpose of this volume is to tell the story in light of the redress legislation enacted in 1988." Libr J [review of 1993 edition]

Includes bibliographical references

Davenport, John

★ The **internment** of Japanese Americans during World War II; detention of American citizens. [by] John C. Davenport. Chelsea House Publishers 2010 122p il (Milestones in American history) lib bdg $35

Grades: 6 7 8 9 10   **940.53**
1. Japanese Americans -- Evacuation and relocation, 1942-1945
ISBN 978-1-60413-681-4; 1-60413-681-2
         LC 2009-29613

The "chapters outline the impact of the bombing [of Pearl Harbor], the history of Japanese immigrants and citizens in the United States, Executive Order 9066 (permitting evacuation and internment of Japanese citizens on the West coast), Japanese American participation in the armed forces, reparations, and the legacy left by the internment. . . . A sound reference and research work." SLJ

Includes bibliographical references

Deem, James M.

Auschwitz; voices from the death camp. Enslow Publishers 2011 128p il map (The Holocaust through primary sources) lib bdg $31.93

Grades: 7 8 9 10 11 12   **940.53**
1. Holocaust, 1933-1945 2. Jews -- Persecutions 3. Auschwitz (Poland: Concentration camp)
ISBN 978-0-7660-3322-1; 0-7660-3322-8
         LC 2010003064

Examines Auschwitz, a death camp during the Holocaust, including its construction and daily workings, true accounts from prisoners of the camp and Nazi perpetrators, and how more than 1 million people were murdered there.

Includes glossary and bibliographical references

Kristallnacht; the Nazi terror that began the Holocaust. Enslow Publishers 2011 128p il (The Holocaust through primary sources) lib bdg $31.93

Grades: 7 8 9 10 11 12   **940.53**
1. Kristallnacht, 1938 2. Jews -- Germany 3. Holocaust,
1933-1945 4. Jews -- Persecutions
ISBN 978-0-7660-3324-5; 0-7660-3324-4
                                    LC 2010015696
Discusses Kristallnacht, a four-day pogrom instigated by
the Nazis against Germany's Jews, including stories from
the victims, witnesses and perpetrators of the attack, and
how it marked the beginning of the Holocaust.
  "Personal testimony is a powerful way to tell history....
These accounts . . . are tightly edited, drawing on the memories of victims, perpetrators, and witnesses.... Each chapter
blends an individual's testimony with historical background
and commentary as well as photos of the witness and of the
brutal events." Booklist
  Includes glossary and bibliographical references

The **prisoners** of Breendonk; personal histories
from a World War II concentration camp. written by
James M. Deem. Houghton Mifflin Harcourt 2015
352 p. illustrations, maps $18.99
Grades: 8 9 10 11 12   **940.53**
1. Concentration camps 2. World War, 1939-1945
-- Prisoners and prisons, German 3. Breendonk
(Concentration camp) 4. World War, 1939-1945 --
Prisoners and prisons, German -- Biography
ISBN 9780544096646
                                    LC 2015010722
This book, by James M. Deem, looks at Breendonk, a
Nazi concentration camp which "held about 3,600 prisoners
between 1940 and 1945. Jews, communists, common criminals, and freedom fighters all found themselves subject to
incarceration. Life in Breendonk was no different than that
in any of the better-known camps.... This narrative is told
through the lives of various prisoners who lived (and died)
there." (School Library Journal)
  "The overall quality of this volume makes this title about
a little-known camp a strong choice." SLJ

Drez, Ronald J.
  Twenty-five yards of war; the extraordinary courage of ordinary men in World War II. Hyperion 2001
xxii, 296p il hardcover o.p. pa $16
Grades: 11 12 Adult   **940.53**
1. World War, 1939-1945 2. United States -- Armed
forces
ISBN 0-7868-6783-3; 0-7868-8668-4 pa
                                    LC 2001-39077
Based on interviews with World War II veterans, Drez
describes the experiences of ten soldiers in such battles as
Midway, Tarawa, and Iwo Jima.
  "To be sure, some of these veterans' stories have been
previously published . . . but Drez manages to present them
with freshness and adequate context." Booklist
  Includes bibliographical references

Edsel, Robert M.
  The **monuments** men; Allied heros, Nazi thieves,
and the greatest treasure hunt in history. Robert M.
Edsel with Bret Witter. Center Street 2009 p. cm.
Grades: Adult   **940.53**
1. Art thefts 2. World War, 1939-1945 3. Europe --

History
ISBN 9781599951492
                                    LC 2009012255
Includes bibliographical references.

**Fortunoff Video Archive for Holocaust Testimo-
nies**
  ★ **Witness**; voices from the Holocaust. edited by
Joshua M. Greene and Shiva Kumar in consultation
with Joanne Weiner Rudof; foreword by Lawrence
L. Langer; in association with the Fortunoff Video
Archive for Holocaust Testimonies, Yale University.
Free Press 2000 xxx, 270p il $26; pa $15
Grades: 11 12 Adult   **940.53**
1. Holocaust, 1933-1945 -- Personal narratives
ISBN 0-684-86525-4; 0-684-86526-2 pa
                                    LC 99-58401
In this companion to the PBS series the editors "have
woven together the testimonies of 27 individuals into an
unforgettable narrative of the Holocaust: starting with pre-
WWII Jewish life, they go on to describe the war's out-
break, ghettos, resistance and hiding, death camps, death
marches, liberation and life after the Holocaust." Publ Wkly
  Includes bibliographical references

Heinrichs, Ann
  The **Japanese** American internment; innocence,
guilt, and wartime justice. Marshall Cavendish
Benchmark 2010 112p il (Perspectives on) $39.93
Grades: 7 8 9 10   **940.53**
1. Japanese Americans -- Evacuation and relocation,
1942-1945
  ISBN 978-0-7614-4983-6; 0-7614-4983-3
  "A solid resource for school reports, this straightforward
account includes an overview of the events that led up to
the signing of Executive Order 9066, which authorized the
relocation of Japanese Americans; details about life in the
internment camps; and an examination of the long-term
ramifications for the Japanese-American community. Information is accompanied by photographs and illustrations in
color and black-and-white. A balanced view of the internment is presented." SLJ

Hoose, Phillip M., 1947-
  ★ The **boys** who challenged Hitler; Knud Pedersen and the Churchill Club. Phillip Hoose. First
edition Farrar, Straus, Giroux 2015 208 p. illustra-
tions (hardback) $19.99
Grades: 7 8 9 10 11 12   **940.53**
1. Resistance to government 2. World War, 1939-1945
-- Underground movements 3. Heroes -- Denmark --
Biography 4. Sabotage -- Denmark -- History -- 20th
century 5. Boys -- Political activity -- Denmark --
Biography 6. Denmark -- History -- German occupation,
1940-1945
ISBN 0374300224; 9780374300227
                                    LC 2014026101
Robert F. Sibert Honor Book (2016)
This book, by Phillip Hoose, describes how "at the out-
set of World War II, Denmark did not resist German occupa-
tion. Deeply ashamed of his nation's leaders, fifteen-year-

old Knud Pedersen resolved with his brother and a handful of schoolmates to take action against the Nazis if the adults would not. . . . The boys' exploits and eventual imprisonment helped spark a full-blown Danish resistance." (Publisher's note)

"Hoose brilliantly weaves Pedersen's own words into the larger narrative of Denmark's stormy social and political wartime climate, showing how the astonishing bravery of otherwise ordinary Danish teens started something extraordinary." Horn Book

Includes bibliographical references and index

Houston, Jeanne Wakatsuki

Farewell to Manzanar; a true story of Japanese American experience during and after the World War II internment. [by] Jeanne Wakatsuki Houston and James D. Houston. Houghton Mifflin 2002 188p $15

Grades: 7 8 9 10   **940.53**
1. Manzanar War Relocation Center 2. World War, 1939-1945 -- United States 3. Japanese Americans -- Evacuation and relocation, 1942-1945
ISBN 0-618-21620-0

                LC 2002-727748

A reissue with a new afterword of the title first published 1973

"A spare, powerful memoir." Rochman. Against borders

Isserman, Maurice

World War II; John S. Bowman, general editor. rev ed; Chelsea House 2010 256p il map (America at war) lib bdg $45

Grades: 8 9 10 11 12   **940.53**
1. United States -- History -- 1933-1945 2. World War, 1939-1945 -- United States
ISBN 978-0-8160-8185-1; 0-8160-8185-9

                LC 2009-52541

First published 1991

This book describes and interprets the role of the United States in World War II.

Includes glossary and bibliographical references

Kris, 1972-

A **bag** of marbles; based on the memoir by Joseph Joffo; adapted by Kris; illustrated by Vincent Bailly; translated by Edward Gauvin. Graphic Universe 2013 126 p. color illustrations (pbk) $9.95

Grades: 6 7 8 9 10   **940.53**
1. Holocaust, 1939-1945 2. Children and war -- Fiction 3. World War, 1939-1945 -- France 4. Graphic novels 5. Jews -- France -- Fiction 6. World War, 1939-1945 -- France -- Fiction 7. Holocaust, Jewish (1939-1945) -- France -- Fiction
ISBN 1467715166; 9781467707008; 9781467715164; 9781467716512

                LC 2013002284

"Ten years old at the start of the story, Joffo recalls his Jewish family planning their escape from Occupied France during World War II. Tension runs through the story as he and his brother set off on the long journey to the Free Zone, where they plan to meet up with their older brothers. Along

the way the boys must hide their Jewish identity, evade train security, and find a passeur, or guide, to take them past guard posts and fences to safe territory." (School Library Journal)

"This graphic-novel adaptation of Joffo's 1973 memoir of the same name succeeds in melding sensitive and accurate imagery with the original narrative flow of a young secular Jewish boy's experiences in occupied France." Booklist

Langley, Andrew

World War II; by Andrew Langley. Heinemann Library 2012 80 p. ill. (some col.), col. maps (Living through) (library) $36.50; (paperback) $10.99

Grades: 6 7 8 9   **940.53**
1. Picture books for children 2. World War, 1939-1945
ISBN 1432960024; 9781432960025; 9781432960117

                LC 2011016056

This book by Andrew Langley is part of the Living Through series and looks at World War II. It answers questions including "why was World War II so devastating, and how had the world become so divided into armed camps? How did the war affect people on both sides of the conflict, and why are its consequences still felt today?" (Publisher's note)

Includes bibliographical references (p. 76-78) and index.

Madison, James H.

★ **World** War II; a history in documents. Oxford University Press 2010 163p il map (Pages from history) pa $24.95

Grades: 8 9 10 11 12   **940.53**
1. World War, 1939-1945 -- Sources
ISBN 978-0-19-533812-6; 0-19-533812-X

                LC 2009-576

"Arranged in eight chapters of broad topics, the text is a collection of excerpts from primary sources. . . . A variety of sources has been used to convey the thoughts of people of many nationalities and walks of life. There are quotes from official documents and laws, personal letters, books, and music lyrics. . . . [It also] contains primary sources from China, Japan, Germany, and Russia, in addition to the U.S. It belongs in most secondary collections." SLJ

Includes bibliographical references

Mara, Wil

Kristallnacht; Nazi persecution of the Jews in Europe. Marshall Cavendish Benchmark 2009 112p il (Perspectives on) lib bdg $39.93

Grades: 7 8 9 10   **940.53**
1. Kristallnacht, 1938 2. Jews -- Germany 3. Holocaust, 1933-1945
ISBN 978-0-7614-4026-0; 0-7614-4026-7

                LC 2008-42971

"The text is supplemented with sidebars and photos and illustrations, and . . . has source notes, lists of resources for further information, a timeline, and a comprehensive bibliography. . . . [This will be] useful to researchers and report writers." Libr Media Connect

Includes bibliographical references

Mullenbach, Cheryl

★ **Double** victory; how African American women broke race and gender barriers to help win World War II. Cheryl Mullenbach. Chicago Review Press 2012 272 p. (Women of action) (hardcover) $19.95

Grades: 7 8 9 10 11 12   **940.53**

1. World War, 1939-1945 -- Women 2. African American women -- Biography 3. United States -- Race relations -- History 4. African Americans -- Employment 5. African Americans -- Civil rights 6. World War, 1939-1945 -- African Americans 7. World War, 1939-1945 -- Women -- United States 8. African American women -- History -- 20th century 9. United States -- Race relations -- History -- 20th century 10. African American women -- Employment -- History -- 20th century 11. African American women -- Civil rights -- History -- 20th century

ISBN 1569768080; 9781569768082

LC 2012021343

Amelia Bloomer Project (2014)

This book, by Cheryl Mullenbach, is part of the "Women of Action" series. "African American women . . . did extraordinary things to help their country during World War II. In these pages young readers meet a range of remarkable women: war workers, political activists, military women, volunteers, and entertainers. . . . But many others fought discrimination at home and abroad in order to contribute to the war effort." (Publisher's note)

Includes bibliographical references and index

Oppenheim, Joanne

★ **Dear** Miss Breed; true stories of the Japanese American incarceration during World War II and a librarian who made a difference. foreword by Elizabeth Kikuchi Yamada; afterword by Snowden Becker. Scholastic 2006 287p il $22.99

Grades: 7 8 9 10   **940.53**

1. Librarians 2. World War, 1939-1945 -- United States 3. Japanese Americans -- Evacuation and relocation, 1942-1945

ISBN 0-439-56992-3; 978-0-439-56992-7

LC 2004-59009

This "account focuses on Clara Breed, a children's librarian at the San Diego Public Library, and the Japanese-American children she served prior to World War II and whom she continued to serve after their families were sent to an Arizona internment camp. . . . Illustrated with numerous photographs . . . and incorporating copious letters and documents, the book is . . . compelling." Horn Book

Includes bibliographical references

Prins, Marcel

Hidden like Anne Frank; fourteen true stories of survival. Marcel Prins and Peter Henk Steenhuis; translated by Laura Watkinson. Arthur A. Levine Books, An Imprint of Scholastic Inc. 2014 256 p. illustrations, maps (hardback) $16.99

Grades: 7 8 9 10 11 12   **940.53**

1. Holocaust, 1939-1945 2. Hidden children (Holocaust) 3. Jewish children in the Holocaust 4. World War, 1939-1945 -- Children 5. Netherlands -- Biography 6. Hidden children (Holocaust) -- Netherlands -- Biography 7. World War, 1939-1945 -- Netherlands -- Personal narratives 8. Jewish children in the Holocaust -- Netherlands -- Biography 9. Holocaust, Jewish (1939-1945) -- Netherlands -- Personal narratives

ISBN 0545543622; 9780545543620; 9780545543637; 9780545543644

LC 2013040908

This book, by Marcel Prins and Peter Henk Steenhuis, presents "fourteen . . . true stories of children hidden away during World War II. . . . Some children were only three or four years old when they were hidden; some were teenagers. Some hid with neighbors or family, while many were with complete strangers. But all know the pain of losing their homes, their families, even their own names. They describe the secret network of brave people who kept them safe." (Publisher's note)

"This volume includes compelling first-person accounts of survival during the Holocaust and WWII in Holland, including coauthor Prins's mother's experience. Readers will encounter incredible acts of courage, both from the subjects themselves and the Resistance fighters and ordinary people willing to risk their lives. Family photos and archival images appear throughout; a glossary and pictures of the survivors today are appended." Horn Book

Rappaport, Doreen, 1939-

★ **Beyond** courage; the untold story of Jewish resistance during the Holocaust. by Doreen Rappaport. 1st ed. Candlewick Press 2012 228 p. ill., maps (hardcover) $22.99

Grades: 6 7 8 9 10 11 12   **940.53**

1. Biography 2. Jews -- History 3. Resistance to government 4. Holocaust, Jewish (1939-1945) 5. Righteous Gentiles in the Holocaust 6. World War, 1939-1945 -- Jews -- Rescue

ISBN 0763629766; 9780763629762

LC 2011048116

In this book, Doreen Rappaport offers "more than 20 stories of Jewish resistance to the Holocaust, some never before told. From all corners of Nazi-occupied Europe, these harrowing accounts . . . pay tribute to the brave thousands who defied their oppressors in ways large and small. In one, 12-year-old Mordechai Shlayan . . . blows up a hotel where German officers are dining. In another, 22-year-old Marianne Cohn is caught smuggling children into Switzerland." (Publishers Weekly)

Includes bibliographical references (p. 209-221) and index.

Regis, Margaret

When our mothers went to war; an illustrated history of women in World War II. NavPublishing 2008 175p il map pa $29.95

Grades: 11 12 Adult   **940.53**

1. World War, 1939-1945 -- Women

ISBN 978-1-879932-05-0; 1-879932-05-9

LC 2008-2833

"This important story tells of the myriad roles women played during the massive U.S. mobilization for World War II. Brilliantly illustrated with black-and-white photos, maps, and posters, and including a well-paced, articulate text based on careful research. . . . This marvelous history tells it all, including the entertainers who raised morale and the war correspondents who were as likely as male journalists to get as close to the fighting as permitted." SLJ

Includes bibliographical references

★ **Reporting** World War II. Library of Am. 1995 2v ea $35

Grades: 11 12 Adult   **940.53**
1. World War, 1939-1945 2. Reporters and reporting
ISBN 1-883011-04-3 v1; 1-883011-05-1 v2
     LC 94-45463

This "collection of some 200 entries by nearly 90 writers, drawn from newspapers, magazine articles, broadcast transcripts and book excerpts, recalls WW II campaigns and battles in all theaters but pays attention to the home front as well. It begins with an excerpt from William L. Shirer's Berlin Diary and ends with one from John Hersey's Hiroshima. . . . This is a treasure trove of war reporting, featuring writing of the highest order." Publ Wkly

Robinson, Greg
★ **By** order of the president; FDR and the internment of Japanese Americans. Harvard Univ. Press 2001 322p $27.95; pa $19.95

Grades: 11 12 Adult   **940.53**
1. Governors 2. Presidents 3. People with disabilities
4. Philatelists 5. World War, 1939-1945 -- United States
6. Japanese Americans -- Evacuation and relocation, 1942-1945
ISBN 0-674-00639-9; 0-674-01118-X pa
     LC 2001-24609

This is a "lucid, comprehensive and balanced examination." Publ Wkly

Includes bibliographical references

Samuel, Wolfgang W. E.
The **war** of our childhood; memories of World War II. {reported by} Wolfgang W.E. Samuel. University Press of Miss. 2002 356p il $30

Grades: 11 12 Adult   **940.53**
1. World War, 1939-1945 -- Children 2. World War, 1939-1945 -- Personal narratives
ISBN 1-57806-482-1
     LC 2002-6172

These "memories by 27 German survivors of World War II relate how as children—ages 3 to 12—they endured air raids, hunger, terror, invading armies, and deprivation. Samuel tells of their resilience under the most trying circumstances and the critical role their mothers played in their lives." Booklist

Sandler, Martin W.
Imprisoned; the betrayal of Japanese Americans during World War II. by Martin W. Sandler. Walker Books For Young Readers 2013 176 p. (hardcover) $22.99; (library) $23.89

Grades: 7 8 9 10   **940.53**
1. World War, 1939-1945 2. Japanese Americans -- Evacuation and relocation, 1942-1945 3. World War,

1939-1945 -- Japanese Americans
ISBN 0802722776; 0802722784; 9780802722775; 9780802722782
     LC 2012032295

YALSA Award for Excellence in Nonfiction for Young Adults: Finalist (2014)

This book offers a "survey of Executive Order 9066 and its aftermath. The order authorized the U.S. military to relocate over 100,000 Japanese-Americans--many were U.S. citizens--from their homes in Washington, Oregon and California to detention camps. . . . A few government officials did object to the order, questioning its constitutionality." (Kirkus Reviews)

"Sandler's earnest telling is complemented by well-chosen primary sources, not just the words . . . but also the black-and-white photographs that present striking images." Horn Book

Schneider, Carl J.
World War II; [by] Carl J. Schneider and Dorothy Schneider. Facts on File 2003 472p il map (Eyewitness history) $75; pa $21.95

Grades: 9 10 11 12   **940.53**
1. United States -- History -- 1933-1945 2. World War, 1939-1945 -- United States
ISBN 0-8160-4484-8; 0-8160-4485-6 pa
     LC 2002-15268

This volume includes letters, speeches and newspaper articles as well as excerpts from documents and from capsule biographies of key figures.

"This useful volume offers a good blend of historical fact and primary-source material." SLJ

Includes bibliographical references

Setterington, Ken
★ **Branded** by the Pink Triangle; by Ken Setterington. Orca Book Publishers 2013 196 p. $15.95

Grades: 9 10 11 12   **940.53**
1. LGBT people -- Nazi persecution 2. World War, 1939-1945 -- Atrocities
ISBN 1926920961; 9781926920962

Stonewall Honor Book: Children and Young Adult (2014)

Rainbow List (2014)

This book presents a "history of the persecution of gay men during the Holocaust. . . . [Ken] Setterington introduce readers to early-20th-century Berlin, a bastion of gay tolerance. . . . He goes on to chronicle the Nazis' crackdown on gay men, their deportation to concentration camps, the experiences of both Jewish and Gentile gay men, and the aftermath of the war." (Kirkus Reviews)

"Though homosexuality had been illegal in Germany since 1871, Berlin was widely regarded as the gay capital of Europe in the early twentieth century, when attitudes toward homosexuals were generally relaxed. All that changed with the rise of Nazism in the 1930s...He also includes an overview of the distressing condition of being gay in postwar Germany and, finally, brings the story up to date with a hopeful chapter titled, "It Gets Better." Setterington's is a significant contribution to LGBT history and one that deserves a wide readership. " (Booklist)

Shermer, Michael

Denying history; who says the Holocaust never happened and why do they say it? [by] Michael Shermer & Alex Grobman; foreword by Arthur Hertzberg. Updated and expanded ed; University of California Press 2009 334p il (S. Mark Taper Foundation imprint in Jewish studies) pa $19.95

Grades: 11 12 Adult   940.53

1. Holocaust, 1933-1945 -- Historiography

ISBN 978-0-520-26098-6

First published 2000

"Using the deniers' own words to tear down their arguments, Shermer and Grobman provide a clear method for determining the reality of past events and supply a powerful weapon for anyone who cares about learning from the credible historical record." Publ Wkly

Includes bibliographical references

Spiegelman, Art

★ **Maus**; a survivor's tale. Art Spiegelman. 25th anniversary ed. Pantheon Bks. 1996 295 p. 2v in 1 ill., maps (some col.) $35

Grades: 7 8 9 10 11 12 Adult   940.53

1. Graphic novels 2. Biographical graphic novels 3. Holocaust, 1933-1945 -- Graphic novels

ISBN 0-679-40641-7

LC 96-32796

A combined edition of Maus I: My father bleeds history (1986) and Maus II: And here my troubles began (1991)

Awards: 1992 Pulitzer Prize Special Award; Eisner Award for Best Graphic Album: Reprint for Maus II; Harvey Award for Best Graphic Album of Previously Published Work (for Maus II); 1993 Los Angeles Times Book Prize for Fiction (for Maus II)

"An undisputed classic and award-winning title (including a Pulitzer Prize in 1992) in which renowned cartoonist Spiegelman depicts his father's experiences as a World War II Nazi concentration camp survivor. The memoir is also a chronicle of Spiegelman's relationship with his father as we witness their visits and disagreements. The black-and-white drawings are straightforward, but with an interesting twist: all of the Jews are depicted as mice and the Nazis as cats." LJ

Spiegelman, Art, 1948-

★ **MetaMaus**. Pantheon Books 2011 299p il $35

Grades: 11 12 Adult   940.53

1. Authors 2. Cartoonists 3. Graphic novels 4. Autobiographical graphic novels 5. Nonfiction writers 6. Cartoonists -- Graphic novels 7. Holocaust survivors -- Graphic novels 8. Holocaust, 1933-1945 -- Graphic novels

ISBN 978-0-375-42394-9

LC 2010052045

The New York cartoonist traces the creative process that went into drawing his Pulitzer Prizewinning classic, revealing the sources of his inspiration and describing his parents' emotional struggles as Holocaust survivors after the end of World War II.

"Informative about everything you may or may not have thought to ask about Maus and the Spiegelmans, this exhaustive purgative has been well organized and packaged and succeeds in being grimly entertaining, indeed almost addictive." Libr J

Stargardt, Nicholas

Witnesses of war; children's lives under the Nazis. Distributed by Random House 2006 493p il map $30; pa $16.95

Grades: 11 12 Adult   940.53

1. World War, 1939-1945 -- Children

ISBN 1-4000-4088-4; 978-1-4000-4088-9; 1-4000-3379-9 pa; 978-1-4000-3379-9 pa

LC 2005-50409

First published 2005 in the United Kingdom

This is "a sharp and taut account of misery." Publ Wkly

Includes bibliographical references

Takaki, Ronald T.

★ **Double** victory; a multicultural history of America in World War II. [by] Ronald Takaki. Little, Brown 2000 282p il hardcover o.p. pa $19.99

Grades: 11 12 Adult   940.53

1. United States -- Race relations 2. World War, 1939-1945 -- United States

ISBN 0-316-83155-7; 0-316-83156-5 pa

LC 99-40374

"Takaki discusses the experiences of African Americans, Indians, Chicanos, Asian Americans from several nations, German and Italian Americans, and Jewish Americans. . . . Despite Jim Crow, internment camps, neglected slums, barrios, reservations, and rejection of Jewish refugees, the nation's not-quite-Americans fought bravely in World War II." Booklist

Includes bibliographical references

World War II; Don Nardo, book editor. Greenhaven Press 2005 203p il (Opposing viewpoints in world history) hardcover o.p. pa $23.70

Grades: 9 10 11 12   940.53

1. World War, 1939-1945

ISBN 0-7377-2587-7 lib bdg; 0-7377-2588-5 pa

LC 2004-52277

"Four chapters discuss the assessment of blame for the attack on Pearl Harbor, the justification for the internment of Japanese Americans, the necessity and morality of using the atomic bomb, and whether the war deserves its nostalgic 'good war' image." SLJ

Includes bibliographical references

★ **World** War II: a student encyclopedia; Spencer C. Tucker, editor; Priscilla Mary Roberts, editor, Documents volume; Jack Greene . . . [et al.], assistant editors. ABC-CLIO 2005 5v il map set $485

Grades: 9 10 11 12   940.53

1. Reference books 2. World War, 1939-1945 -- Encyclopedias

ISBN 1-85109-857-7; 978-1-85109-857-6

LC 2004-29951

This "encyclopedia covers the entire scope of the Second World War, from its earliest roots to its continuing impact on global politics and human society." Publisher's note

Includes bibliographical references

WWII: the people's story; Nigel Fountain, general editor. Reader's Digest 2003 315p il map $39.95

Grades: 9 10 11 12   **940.53**
1. World War, 1939-1945
ISBN 0-7621-0376-0

LC 2003-43172

"Through letters, speeches, diaries, and interviews, this title provides insight into the thoughts and feelings of presidents and prime ministers during this period as well as soldiers, journalists, and children. Between excerpted comments, the text fills in the background information. . . . Pages are peppered with black-and-white and color photographs and reproductions depicting numerous aspects of the war. . . . An accompanying CD will allow students to hear the firsthand accounts included in the book." SLJ

Includes bibliographical references

Yellin, Emily

★ **Our** mothers' war; American women at home and at the Front during World War II. Free Press 2004 447p il hardcover o.p. pa $14

Grades: 11 12 Adult   **940.53**
1. World War, 1939-1945 -- Women
ISBN 0-7432-4514-8; 0-7432-4516-4 pa

LC 2004-40496

"Yellin reveals all of the responsibilities held by women, including helping to manufacture aircraft, ships, and other munitions; and, in the process, outproducing all of America's allies and enemies, by far. Readers see war brides who worked hard to maintain the morale of their husbands while surviving long separation, fear, and shortages of virtually everything necessary to support a family. . . . [This book] is an important book because the role played by women in World War II has been regularly ignored." SLJ

Includes bibliographical references

940.54   Military history of World War II

Allport, Alan

The **Battle** of Britain; by Alan Allport. Chelsea House 2012 128 p. (Milestones in modern world history) (hardcover) $35

Grades: 7 8 9 10 11 12   **940.54**
1. Britain, Battle of, 1940 2. World War, 1939-1945 -- Aerial operations 3. World War, 1939-1945 -- Great Britain
ISBN 160413920X; 9781604139204

LC 2011023053

This book, part of the Milestones in Modern World History series, "describes the air campaign waged by the Luftwaffe (German air force) against England's Royal Air Force during WWII. It starts with a look at [Adolph] Hitler's rise to power and continues with such pivotal conflicts as the Blitz.

The author also notes how important the burgeoning radar technology of the time aided England's defense." (Booklist)

Includes bibliographical references and index

Atkinson, Rick

D-Day; the invasion of Normandy, 1944. Rick Atkinson with Kate Waters. Henry Holt & Co. 2014 224 p. (hardcover) $18.99

Grades: 6 7 8 9 10 11 12   **940.54**
1. World War, 1939-1945 2. Normandy (France), Attack on, 1944 3. World War, 1939-1945 -- Campaigns -- France -- Normandy
ISBN 1627791116; 9781627791113; 9781627791120

LC 2014005162

Written by Rick Atkinson, "Adapted for young readers from . . . 'The Guns at Last Light,' 'D-Day' captures the events and the spirit of that day--June 6, 1944--the day that led to the liberation of western Europe from Nazi Germany's control. They came by sea and by sky to reclaim freedom from the occupying Germans, turning the tide of World War II." (Publisher's note)

"With Kate Waters. Adapted from Atkinson's adult book The Guns at Last Light, this young readers' edition focuses, effectively and excitingly, on the invasion of Normandy but provides enough context for WWII both before and after June 6, 1944. Copious photographs and a vibrant design will invite war buffs in; appended lists of interesting facts add appeal. Reading list, timeline, websites. Bib., glos., ind." Horn Book

Includes bibliographical references and index

The **attack** on Pearl Harbor; David Haugen and Susan Musser, book editors. Greenhaven Press 2011 204p il map (Perspectives on modern world history) lib bdg $39.70

Grades: 8 9 10 11 12   **940.54**
1. Pearl Harbor (Oahu, Hawaii), Attack on, 1941
ISBN 978-0-7377-5004-1; 0-7377-5004-9

LC 2010033590

In "discussing the events of December 7, 1941. . . [this] well-organized [volume presents] a wealth of clearly written analyses from a rich variety of viewpoints. With the inclusion of historical background, firsthand experiences, and discussions of particular points of controversy, [it helps] to familiarize readers with the [attack on Pearl Harbor] and [serves] as [an exercise] in the development of analytical thinking skills." SLJ

Includes bibliographical references

Atwood, Kathryn

Women heroes of World War II; 26 stories of espionage, sabotage, resistance, and rescue. Chicago Review Press 2011 266p il map $19.95

Grades: 7 8 9 10   **940.54**
1. World War, 1939-1945 -- Women 2. World War, 1939-1945 -- Underground movements
ISBN 978-1-55652-961-0; 1-55652-961-9

LC 2010-41830

"The 26 women profiled in this collective biography served on the front lines and behind enemy lines in Europe as correspondents, couriers, propagandists, Resistance fighters, saboteurs and spies. . . . Atwood's admiration and enthusiasm for her subjects is apparent in these engaging profiles, and readers will likely be inspired to investigate these fascinating women further." Kirkus

Ballard, Robert D.

Graveyards of the Pacific; from Pearl Harbor to Bikini Atoll. {by} Robert D. Ballard with Michael Hamilton Morgan. National Geographic Soc. 2001 255p il maps $45

Grades: 11 12 Adult   **940.54**
1. Shipwrecks 2. World War, 1939-1945 -- Naval operations
ISBN 0-7922-6366-9

This "overview of the Pacific war begins with {an} . . . account of Ballard's search for an elusive midget sub sunk just prior to the attack on Pearl Harbor, and ends with the American nuclear tests on Bikini Island, where captured German and Japanese craft were scuttled." Publisher's note
Includes bibliographical references

Bradley, James

★ Flags of our fathers; [by] James Bradley with Ron Powers. Bantam Bks. 2000 376p $24.95; pa $14

Grades: 11 12 Adult   **940.54**
1. Iwo Jima, Battle of, 1945 2. Photojournalists 3. United States -- Marine Corps
ISBN 0-553-11133-7; 0-553-38415-5 pa
LC 00-25803

This is the "story of the most famous photograph to come out of World War II, the flag-raising on Mount Suribachi during the Battle of Iwo Jima in February 1945. Bradley is the son of one of the six men immortalized in that remarkable photo, and his gripping narrative, vivid descriptions, and heartfelt style make this a powerful story of courage, humility, and tragedy." Libr J
Includes bibliographical references

Burgan, Michael

★ Hiroshima; birth of the nuclear age. Marshall Cavendish Benchmark 2009 128p il (Perspectives on) lib bdg $27.95

Grades: 8 9 10 11 12   **940.54**
1. Atomic bomb 2. Hiroshima (Japan) -- Bombardment, 1945
ISBN 978-0-7614-4023-9; 0-7614-4023-2
LC 2008-29249

This provides information on the Manhattan Project, the bombing of Hiroshima, and its legacy.

"Utilizing an unbiased and chronological narrative, [the author delves] deeply into the [topic], providing an overall representation as well as a substantial degree of insight. . . . The potency of [this title] lies in the excellent arrangement of numerous well-chosen sidebars and photos, and fluent, concise prose." SLJ
Includes bibliographical references

Cornioley, Pearl Witherington

Code name Pauline; memoirs of a World War II special agent. Pearl Witherington Cornioley with Hervé Larroque; edited by Kathryn J. Atwood. Chi-

cago Review Press 2013 208 p. (Women of action) (hardback) $19.95

Grades: 8 9 10 11 12   **940.54**
1. World War, 1939-1945 -- Secret service 2. World War, 1939-1945 -- Underground movements -- France 3. World War, 1939-1945 -- Secret service -- Great Britain
ISBN 1613744870; 9781613744871
LC 2013008734

In this memoir, "one of the most celebrated female World War II resistance fighters shares . . . her experiences as a special agent for the British Special Operations Executive. French-born British citizen [Pearl Witherington] Cornioley tells her story through a series of reminiscences, including . . . her recruitment and training as a special agent, and parachuting into a remote, rural area of occupied France." (Kirkus Reviews)

"Cornioley's detailed account of her time as a British special agent in Nazi-occupied France is suited for readers already familiar with the basic events of World War II. She narrates with short sentences and a matter-of-fact tone that keeps readers at a distance from her story, but the material is well documented and thorough. Appropriate for students needing primary source material. " (Horn Book)
Includes bibliographical references and index

Dick, Ron

World War II; [by] Ron Dick and Dan Patterson. Firefly Bks. 2004 352p il (Aviation century) $49.95

Grades: 11 12 Adult   **940.54**
1. Aeronautics -- History 2. World War, 1939-1945 -- Aerial operations
ISBN 978-1-55046-426-9; 1-55046-426-4
LC 2005-278795

This "volume begins with the Battle of Britain and concludes with the Japanese surrender following the destruction of Hiroshima and Nagasaki. Patterson's . . . color photography combines with works of contemporary aviation artists to depict aircraft vividly from all major theaters of war." Libr J
Includes bibliographical references

Farrell, Mary Cronk

Pure grit; how American World War II nurses survived battle and prison camp in the Pacific. by Mary Cronk Farrell. Abrams Books for Young Readers 2014 160 p. illustrations, color maps (hardcover: alk. paper) $24.95

Grades: 7 8 9 10 11 12   **940.54**
1. Nurses 2. Military medicine 3. World War, 1939-1945 -- Medical care 4. World War, 1939-1945 -- Prisoners and prisons 5. Prisoners of war -- Philippines 6. Prisoners of war -- United States 7. Military nursing -- United States -- History 8. World War, 1939-1945 -- Campaigns -- Philippines 9. Nurses -- United States -- History -- 20th century 10. World War, 1939-1945 -- Medical care -- United States 11. World War, 1939-1945 -- Prisoners and prisons, Japanese
ISBN 1419710281; 9781419710285
LC 2013017134

This book, by Mary Cronk Farrell, focuses on American World War II Navy and Army nurses who were stationed in the Pacific. "Nurses, deeply engaged in caring for desperately wounded soldiers, were sent to Bataan. After living on near-starvation rations, the nurses on Bataan were evacuated to Corregidor. . . . A few were rescued from Corregidor before it too fell to enemy forces. . . . The remaining nurses were then imprisoned . . . and not released until late winter of 1945." (Kirkus Reviews)

"Using historical interviews and modern correspondence with the subjects' relatives, Farrell presents a fascinating account of the more than one hundred army and navy nurses who served in the South Pacific in WWII. Through every battle and retreat, and even in POW camps, these nurses cared for the injured under the most primitive of conditions. The book's utilitarian design features archival photographs." Horn Book

Includes bibliographical references and index

Frank, Richard B.

Downfall; the end of the Imperial Japanese Empire. Penguin 2001 484p il map pa $18

Grades: 11 12 Adult **940.54**

1. Japan -- History -- 1868-1945 2. World War, 1939-1945 -- Japan 3. World War, 1939-1945 -- Aerial operations

ISBN 0-14-100146-1

First published 1999 by Random House

"Weaving together the strands of military and diplomatic events, Frank contends that absent the bombings of Hiroshima and Nagasaki the war would have continued for at least several more months, at a cost in Japanese and Allied civilian and combatant lives far in excess of the admittedly awful toll that the atomic bombs exacted. A powerful work of history." Libr J

Includes bibliographical references

Fussell, Paul

The **boys'** crusade; the American infantry in Northwestern Europe, 1944-1945. Modern Lib. 2003 184p hardcover o.p. pa $12.95

Grades: 11 12 Adult **940.54**

1. World War, 1939-1945 -- Europe 2. World War, 1939-1945 -- Campaigns

ISBN 0-679-64088-6; 0-8129-7488-3 pa

LC 2003-44556

This memoir of World War II includes "a series of essays dealing with strategy, tactics, and leadership from the landings at Normandy to the fall of Berlin. . . . Fussell describes the typical GI as 18 to 20 years old, from all types of social and educational backgrounds, taken from minimal training and thrown into ground combat of the fiercest kind. . . . This work is aimed at correcting the sanitized works of 'sentimental' history the war has inspired. Highly recommended." Libr J

Includes bibliographical references

Goldstein, Donald M.

The **way** it was; Pearl Harbor, the original photographs. [by] Donald M. Goldstein, Katherine V. Dillon and J. Michael Wenger. Pergamon-Brassey's 1991 181p il maps hardcover o.p. pa $19.95

Grades: 11 12 Adult **940.54**

1. Pearl Harbor (Oahu, Hawaii), Attack on, 1941 --

Pictorial works

ISBN 0-08-040573-8; 1-57488-359-3 pa

LC 90-49572

This is a collection of photographs of the Japanese attack on Pearl Harbor in 1941.

"The 430 prints in this . . . collection were gathered from various Japanese and U.S. sources, and most have never been seen by the general public. The majority were taken during the height of the air raid itself, many from Japanese cockpits. . . . The overall effect is to give the reader an uncanny sense of being present at the battle." Libr J

★ The **good** war; an oral history of World War Two. [edited by] Studs Terkel. New Press 1997 589p pa $16.95

Grades: 11 12 Adult **940.54**

1. World War, 1939-1945 -- Personal narratives

ISBN 1-56584-343-6

LC 2003-389322

First published 1984 by Pantheon Bks.

In a series of interviews Terkel depicts how WWII affected the lives of average Americans.

Hastings, Max

Overlord: D-Day and the battle for Normandy. Simon & Schuster 1984 368p il maps hardcover o.p. pa $22.95

Grades: 11 12 Adult **940.54**

1. Operation Overlord 2. Normandy (France), Attack on, 1944

ISBN 0-671-46029-3; 0-671-55435-2 pa

LC 83-20439

"Hastings' reportage of the battle is not unworthy to stand with that of the best journalists and writers who witnessed it. . . . He has managed to recreate what it was like for almost everyone who was there." N Y Times Book Rev

Includes bibliographical references

Hersey, John

★ **Hiroshima**; a new edition with a final chapter written forty years after the explosion. Knopf 1985 196p il $26; pa $6.50

Grades: 11 12 Adult **940.54**

1. Atomic bomb 2. World War, 1939-1945 -- Japan 3. Hiroshima (Japan) -- Bombardment, 1945

ISBN 0-394-54844-2; 0-679-72103-7 pa

LC 85-40346

First published 1946

An account of the aftermath of the first atomic bomb as reflected in the lives of six survivors

Hillstrom, Laurie

The **attack** on Pearl Harbor; [by] Laurie Collier Hillstrom. Omnigraphics 2009 237p il (Defining moments) $49

Grades: 7 8 9 10 11 12 **940.54**

1. Reference books 2. Pearl Harbor (Oahu, Hawaii), Attack on, 1941

ISBN 978-0-7808-1069-3; 0-7808-1069-4

LC 2009-4236

"This book is divided into three well-organized sections. Part one provides a narrative overview detailing the events leading up to the attack, the attack itself, and the aftermath, including the U.S. victory in the Pacific as well as the occupation and reconstruction of Japan after World War II. Part two is composed of eight two to three-page biographies of the important figures such as Yamamoto, Roosevelt, and Doris Miller, the first African-American to receive the Navy Cross. A final section of primary documents from the Japanese attack plan to Truman's announcement of the end of the war provides insight into the war in the Pacific. . . . This work is a must-have for reports and assignments." SLJ

Includes glossary and bibliographical references

Holm, Tom

Code talkers and warriors; Native Americans and World War II. Chelsea House 2007 168p il map (Landmark events in Native American history) $35

Grades: 7 8 9 10   **940.54**

1. World War, 1939-1945 -- Native Americans
ISBN 978-0-7910-9340-5; 0-7910-9340-9

LC 2006102263

"In this title about Native Americans in World War II, Holm . . . expands considerably on his specific topic to highlight significant miliary roles played by Native Americans in conflicts dating back to the sixteenth century. . . . [This is] outstanding. . . . [A] valuable resource." Booklist

Includes bibliographical references

Kurson, Robert

Shadow divers; the true adventure of two Americans who risked everything to solve one of the last mysteries of World War II. Random House 2004 375p il $26.95; pa $14.95

Grades: 9 10 11 12   **940.54**

1. Shipwrecks 2. Underwater exploration 3. Excavations (Archeology) 4. U-869 (Submarine)
ISBN 0-375-50858-9; 0-375-76098-9 pa

LC 2003-60362

This book "features undersea thrills, a gripping mystery, incredible discoveries, true-blue friendship, life-or-death crises and history unfolding before the reader's eyes." N Y Times (Late N Y Ed)

Includes bibliographical references

Lord, Walter

★ **Day** of infamy; [60th anniversary ed]; Holt & Co. 2001 241p il hardcover o.p. pa $14

Grades: 9 10 11 12   **940.54**

1. Pearl Harbor (Oahu, Hawaii), Attack on, 1941
ISBN 0-8050-6809-0; 0-8050-6803-1 pa

LC 00-54247

A reissue of the title first published 1957

Based on over 500 eyewitness reports, this book provides a minute-by-minute account of the Japanese attack on Pearl Harbor.

Megellas, James

All the way to Berlin; a paratrooper at war in Europe. Presidio Press 2003 xxi, 309p il maps $25.95

Grades: 11 12 Adult   **940.54**

1. World War, 1939-1945 -- Europe 2. World War, 1939-1945 -- Campaigns 3. World War, 1939-1945 -- Personal narratives
ISBN 0-89141-784-2

LC 2002-192563

This is the author's account of "the September 1944 assault across the Waal River. . . . The attrition Megellas witnessed over months on the front line, at Anzio and in the Battle of the Bulge, shapes his narrative, but his observations about the craft of killing lend it a distinctive tone. . . . Strongly put and unsentimental, this memoir is a must for the World War II collection." Booklist

Meltzer, Milton

Never to forget: the Jews of the Holocaust. Harper & Row 1976 217p maps hardcover o.p. pa $9.99

Grades: 6 7 8 9   **940.54**

1. Holocaust, 1933-1945
ISBN 0-06-446118-1 pa

"The mass murder of six million Jews by the Nazis during World War II is the subject of this compelling history. Interweaving background information, chilling statistics, individual accounts and newspaper reports, it provides an excellent introduction to its subject." Interracial Books Child Bull

Includes bibliographical references

Moore, Kate

The **Battle** of Britain. Osprey 2010 200p il map $29.95

Grades: 7 8 9 10   **940.54**

1. Britain, Battle of, 1940 2. World War, 1939-1945 -- Great Britain
ISBN 978-1-84603-474-9; 1-84603-474-4

"In the summer and autumn of 1940, Britain faced an unparalleled challenge. Forced to beat a quick retreat from Dunkirk with the German Luftwaffe in hot pursuit, the British dug in for what was to be one of the most remarkable feats in the history of human endurance. In this spectacular oversize volume, Moore recounts with notable lucidity and depth the events and characters from both the British and German home fronts during this critical moment in world history and offers an excellent analysis of prewar preparations by both sides. The most outstanding feature of the work is without a doubt the stunning visuals. The book is packed with a fantastic range of archival photos, maps, and war posters." SLJ

Nelson, Pete

★ **Left** for dead; a young man's search for justice for the USS Indianapolis. [by] Peter Nelson; with a preface by Hunter Scott. Delacorte Press 2002 xx, 201p il hardcover o.p. pa $8.95

Grades: 7 8 9 10   **940.54**

1. Children 2. Students 3. Naval officers 4. Indianapolis (Cruiser) 5. World War, 1939-1945 -- Naval operations
ISBN 0-385-72959-6; 0-385-73091-8 pa

LC 2001-53774

Recalls the sinking of the U.S.S. Indianapolis at the end of World War II, the navy cover-up and unfair court martial of the ship's captain, and how a young boy helped the survivors set the record straight fifty-five years later.

"Written in simple chronological order, it tells a powerful story." Book Rep

Includes bibliographical references

The **Pacific** War; from Pearl Harbor to Hiroshima. editor, Daniel Marston. Pbk. ed.; Osprey Pub. 2010 272p il map pa $19.95

Grades: 11 12 Adult   940.54
1. World War, 1939-1945 -- Campaigns -- Pacific Ocean
ISBN 978-1-84908-382-9

LC 2010-292672
First published 2005 with title: The Pacific war companion

"These essays on the Pacific theater of WW II, written by a group of international scholars representing Australia, Great Britain, Japan, and the US, cover the wellknown events at Pearl Harbor, the Coral Sea, and Midway; MacArthur's push to the Philippines; Nimitz's island campaign in the central Pacific; Okinawa; and the dropping of the atomic bomb on Hiroshima and Nagasaki. . . . A chronology, detailed maps, and photographs greatly enhance this excellent volume on the Pacific phase of WW II." Choice

Includes bibliographical references

Takaki, Ronald T.

★ **Hiroshima**; why America dropped the atomic bomb. [by] Ronald Takaki. Little, Brown 1995 193p il $28; pa $14.95

Grades: 11 12 Adult   940.54
1. Atomic bomb 2. World War, 1939-1945 -- United States 3. Hiroshima (Japan) -- Bombardment, 1945
ISBN 0-316-83122-0; 0-316-83124-7 pa

LC 95-13546
This study of the bombings of Hiroshima and Nagasaki focuses on the psychological motivations of the American decision-makers, especially Harry Truman.

"Right or wrong, the study is a provocative addition to the unresolved debate over the dropping of the atomic bombs." Publ Wkly

Includes bibliographical references

Tomblin, Barbara

★ **G.I.** nightingales; the Army Nurse Corps in World War II. [by] Barbara Brooks Tomblin. University Press of Ky. 1996 254p il hardcover o.p. pa $22

Grades: 11 12 Adult   940.54
1. United States -- Army Nurse Corps
ISBN 0-8131-1951-0; 0-8131-9079-7 pa

LC 96-1018
This is "an account of the 80,000 army nurses who served during World War II. These nurses participated in every theater of the war; some died while on duty, and many were decorated for their bravery. Along with their deserving stories, the reader learns the history of women nurses in the military." Libr J

Includes bibliographical references

Wukovits, John F., 1944-

The **bombing** of Pearl Harbor; by John F. Wukovits. Lucent Books 2011 112 p. ill. (some col.), photographs (World history) (library) $34.95

Grades: 6 7 8 9   940.54
1. World War, 1939-1945 -- Causes 2. Pearl Harbor (Oahu, Hawaii), Attack on, 1941
ISBN 1420503308; 9781420503302

LC 2010035993
This book by John Wukovits is part of the World History series and looks at the bombing of Pearl Harbor. Each book in the series offers an "overview of an important historical event or period. The series is designed both to acquaint readers with the basics of history and to make them aware that their lives and their own historical era are an intimate part of the ongoing human saga." (Publisher's note)

Includes bibliographical references (p. 97-100) and index.

940.55   Europe--1945-1999

Living through the end of the Cold War; edited by Jeff Hay. Greenhaven Press 2005 141p il (Living through the Cold War) lib bdg $32.45

Grades: 9 10 11 12   940.55
1. Cold war 2. World politics -- 1945-1991
ISBN 0-7377-2132-4

LC 2004-42437
This book "captures the drama and historical significance of declining hostilities between the United States and Russia. The text offers speeches by Reagan, Gorbachev, Yelstin, and Havel, plus commentary on change in Russian lives and the collapse of the Iron Curtain." Libr Media Connect

Includes bibliographical references

941   British Isles

Burns, William E.

★ A **brief** history of Great Britain. Facts On File 2010 xxiv, 296p il map (Brief history) $49.50; pa $19.95

Grades: 9 10 11 12 Adult   941
1. Great Britain -- History
ISBN 978-0-8160-7728-1; 978-0-8160-8124-0 pa

LC 2009-8217
This book "narrates the history of Great Britain from the earliest times to the 21st century, covering the entire island—England, Wales, and Scotland—as well as associated archipelagos such as the Channel Islands, the Orkneys, and Ireland as they have influenced British history. The central story of this volume is the development of the British kingdom, including its rise and decline on the world stage." Publisher's note

Includes bibliographical references

★ The **Lives** of the kings & queens of England; edited by Antonia Fraser. rev and updated; Univer-

sity of Calif. Press 1998 384p il maps hardcover
o.p. pa $27.50

Grades: 9 10 11 12   **941**
1. Great Britain -- Kings and rulers
ISBN 0-520-21938-4; 0-520-22460-4 pa

LC 99-169506

First published 1975 in the United Kingdom; first United
States edition 1995

"A collection of biographical sketches that encompasses
the period from the establishment of monarchical power by
the early Norman kings through the reign of Elizabeth II. . .
. Accompanying the text are 175 contemporary illustrations
and drawings of the royal coats of arms." Publisher's note

The **Oxford** illustrated history of Britain; edited by
Kenneth O. Morgan. New ed., Updated ed. for
the 21st century.; Oxford University Press 2009
683p il map pa $34.95

Grades: 11 12 Adult   **941**
1. Great Britain -- History
ISBN 978-0-19-954475-2

LC 2009293870

First published 1984
This work, the product of ten British historians, is a
study of the last two thousand years of British history.
Includes bibliographical references

941.081   British Isles--Reign of Victoria, 1837- 1901

Mitchell, Sally
   ★ **Daily** life in Victorian England; 2nd edition;
Greenwood Press 2009 336p il (Greenwood Press
'Daily life through history' series) $49.95

Grades: 11 12 Adult   **941.081**
1. Great Britain -- Civilization 2. Great Britain --
History -- 19th century
ISBN 978-0-313-35034-4

LC 2008-31363

First published 1996
This volume offers a "glimpse into Victorian daily living, including women's roles; 'Victorian Morality'; leisure;
health and medicine; and life in all settings, from workhouses to country estates." Publisher's note
Includes glossary and bibliographical references

941.5   Ireland

State, Paul F.
   A **brief** history of Ireland. Facts On File 2009
xxiv, 408p il map (Brief history) $49.50; pa $19.95

Grades: 9 10 11 12 Adult   **941.5**
1. Ireland -- History
ISBN 978-0-8160-7516-4; 0-8160-7516-6; 978-0-
8160-7517-1 pa; 0-8160-7517-4 pa

LC 2008-29243

The author "opens this vibrant reference with an introduction to Ireland's landscape, people, economics, natural
resources, and current government. Following this essay-

style overview are 11 chronologically organized chapters.
Each is devoted to a significant historical watershed, tracing
events from Ireland's prehistory to its contemporary prosperity. Appendixes provide at-a-glance portraits of Northern
Ireland and the Irish Republic, including a list of presidents,
prime ministers, and a time line of notable dates." Libr J
   Includes bibliographical references

941.508   Ireland 1800-1899

Bartoletti, Susan Campbell
   ★ **Black** potatoes; the story of the great Irish
famine, 1845-1850. Houghton Mifflin 2001 184p il
hardcover o.p. pa $9.95

Grades: 7 8 9 10   **941.508**
1. Famines 2. Ireland -- History 3. Ireland -- History
-- Famine, 1845-1852
ISBN 0-618-00271-5; 0-618-54883-1 pa

LC 2001-24156

Bartoletti discusses "the potato blight, its . . . causes, and
the societal attitudes and political legacies that exacerbated
the famine. {Chronology. Annotated bibliography. Index.}
Grades five to ten." (Bull Cent Child Books)

"The bibliography (also narrative) provides some of the
most fascinating historical reading in the book. Overall, a
useful addition to collections, for both personal and research
uses." SLJ
   Includes bibliographical references

941.6   Northern Ireland; Donegal, Monaghan, Cavan counties of Republic of Ireland

Cottrell, Robert C.
   Northern Ireland and England; the troubles.
foreword by George J. Mitchell; introduction by
James I. Matray. Chelsea House 2005 139p il map
(Arbitrary borders) $31.50

Grades: 9 10 11 12   **941.6**
1. Northern Ireland
ISBN 0-7910-8020-X

LC 2004-14440

This book deals with the conflicts involved in the establishment of Northern Ireland and the Peace Line.
   Includes bibliographical references

942.01   England--Early history to 1066

Lacey, Robert
   The **year** 1000; what life was like at the turn of
the first millennium: an Englishman's world. {by}
Robert Lacey, Danny Danziger. Little, Brown 1999
230p hardcover o.p. pa $13.99

Grades: 11 12 Adult   **942.01**
1. Great Britain -- History -- 0-1066
ISBN 0-316-55840-0; 0-316-51157-9 pa

LC 98-31254

"This is a superb time capsule, and the authors distill a wealth of historical information into brightly entertaining reading." Publ Wkly

Includes bibliographical references

942.02 England--Norman period, 1066-1154

Howarth, David Armine

★ **1066**: the year of the conquest; [by] David Howarth; illustrations to chapter headings by Gareth Floyd. Viking 1978 207p il hardcover o.p. pa $14

Grades: 11 12 Adult   **942.02**

1. Hastings (East Sussex, England), Battle of, 1066 2. Great Britain -- History -- 1066-1154, Norman period

ISBN 0-670-69601-3; 0-14-005850-8 pa

LC 77-21694

First published 1977 in the United Kingdom

A history of the invasion of England by the Normans and William the Conqueror's victory at the Battle of Hastings.

Includes bibliographical references

942.03 England--Period of House of Plantagenet, 1154-1399

Forgeng, Jeffrey L.

★ **Daily** life in Chaucer's England; [by] Jeffrey L. Forgeng and Will McLean. 2nd ed; Greenwood Press 2009 302p il (Greenwood Press 'Daily life through history' series) $49.95

Grades: 11 12 Adult   **942.03**

1. Poets 2. Authors 3. Great Britain -- History -- 1154-1399, Plantagenets

ISBN 978-0-313-35951-4

LC 2008-37469

First published 1995

"This volume examines . . . [different] aspects of life in medieval England, . . . [including] basic fundamentals like nutrition, waste management, and table manners. Readers will explore, seasons, holidays and holy days, the prevalence and normalcy of death, the average workday, crafts and trade, decorating practices, and recreational activities like archery and falconry." Publisher's note

Includes glossary and bibliographical references

942.04 England--Period of Houses of Lancaster and York, 1399-1485

Weir, Alison

The **Wars** of the Roses. Ballantine Bks. 1995 462p il hardcover o.p. pa $15.95

Grades: 11 12 Adult   **942.04**

1. Great Britain -- History -- 1455-1485, War of the Roses

ISBN 0-345-39117-9; 0-345-40433-5 pa

"No history collection should do without this perfectly focused and beautifully unfolded account." Booklist

942.05 England--Period of House of Tudor, 1485-1603

Aronson, Marc

Sir Walter Ralegh and the quest for El Dorado. Clarion Bks. 2000 222p il map $20

Grades: 7 8 9 10   **942.05**

1. Poets 2. Authors 3. Explorers 4. Historians 5. Courtiers 6. Travel writers

ISBN 0-395-84827-X

LC 99-43096

"Incorporating critical examinations of period art and poetry as well as standard historical documentary evidence and pausing frequently to review and explicitly support its thesis, this title is at once lively, accessible, and challenging. Period illustrations, an index, and fastidiously annotated endnotes and bibliography are included." Bull Cent Child Books

Includes bibliographical references

Forgeng, Jeffrey L.

★ **Daily** life in Elizabethan England; 2nd ed.; Greenwood Press 2010 xx, 276p il (Greenwood Press 'Daily life through history' series) $49.95

Grades: 11 12 Adult   **942.05**

1. Great Britain -- History -- 1485-1603, Tudors

ISBN 978-0-313-36560-7

LC 2009-27600

First published 1995

This "book easily could be used as a supplemental text in an advanced history course or sections could be used by English teachers to give broader meaning to students studying Shakespeare's plays. The well-written material is divided by headings, sub-headings, graphs, pictures, and illustrations. Chapters include a history of Tudor England; society and the course of life; clothing, food and drink; and the Elizabethan world." Libr Media Connect

Includes glossary and bibliographical references

Kallen, Stuart A.

★ **Elizabethan** England; by Stuart A. Kallen. ReferencePoint Press 2013 96 p. (Understanding world history series) (hardcover) $27.95

Grades: 7 8 9 10   **942.05**

1. Great Britain -- History -- 1558-1603, Elizabeth 2. England -- Civilization -- 16th century 3. England -- Social conditions -- 16th century 4. Great Britain -- History -- Elizabeth, 1558-1603

ISBN 1601524846; 9781601524843

LC 2012026174

This book, part of the Understanding World History series, looks at Elizabethan England. It "relates Queen Elizabeth I's advance to power and considers the hardships of life in London, the rise of the arts during the Renaissance, and Elizabeth's role as 'pirate queen,' endorsing privateering, slave trading, and the defeat of the Spanish Armanda." (Booklist)

Includes bibliographical references and index

Starkey, David

★ **Six** wives: the queens of Henry VIII. HarperCollins Pubs. 2003 xxvii, 852p il hardcover o.p. pa $16.95

Grades: 11 12 Adult   **942.05**

1. Queens 2. Great Britain -- History -- 1485-1603, Tudors

ISBN 0-694-01043-X; 0-06-000550-5 pa

"Solidly researched and delightfully told, this is highly recommended." Libr J

Includes bibliographical references

942.06   England--House of Stuart and Commonwealth periods to present, 1603-

Trevelyan, George Macaulay

The **English** Revolution, 1688-1689; [by] G. M. Trevelyan. Oxford University Press 1965 136p pa $30

Grades: 11 12 Adult   **942.06**

1. Great Britain -- History -- 1688, Revolution

ISBN 978-0-19-500263-8; 0-19-500263-6

First published 1938 in the United Kingdom

This study covers not only the revolution itself but also the events of the reign of James II, which led up to it and the political changes which followed.

Includes bibliographical references

943   Germany and neighboring central European countries

Coy, Jason Philip

A **brief** history of Germany; [by] Jason P. Coy. Facts on File 2011 288p il map (Brief history) $49.50; pa $19.95

Grades: 9 10 11 12 Adult   **943**

1. Germany -- History

ISBN 978-0-8160-8142-4; 978-0-8160-8329-9 pa

             LC 2010-23139

This book provides an "account of the events, people, and special customs and traditions that have shaped Germany from ancient times to the present." Publisher's note

Includes bibliographical references

Fulbrook, Mary

A **concise** history of Germany; 2nd ed; Cambridge University Press 2004 277p il, maps (Cambridge concise histories) hardcover o.p. pa $22

Grades: 11 12 Adult   **943**

1. Princes 2. Statesmen 3. Heads of state 4. Prime ministers 5. National socialism 6. Nazi leaders 7. Germany -- History

ISBN 0-521-83320-5; 0-521-54071-2 pa

             LC 2004-271599

First published 1990 in the United Kingdom

This history of Germany "spans the early Middle Ages to the present day. . . . Mary Fulbrook explores the interrela-

tionships between social, political and cultural factors in the light of the latest scholarly controversies." Publ Wkly

Includes bibliographical references

Nardo, Don

Hitler in Paris; how a photograph shocked a world at war. by Don Nardo. Compass Point Books 2014 64 p. (library binding) $33.99

Grades: 6 7 8 9   **943**

1. World War, 1939-1945 -- France -- Paris 2. France -- History -- 1940-1945, German occupation 3. Photographs -- Political aspects

ISBN 0756547334; 9780756547332; 9780756547899

             LC 2013030415

This book, by Don Nardo, focuses on a photograph of dictator Adolf Hitler in Paris, France during World War II. "Only days before, on June 14, 1940, German soldiers had overrun the city, shocking the world. . . . He posed for a photo in front of the Eiffel Tower, the beloved symbol of France and the country's free, democratic people. The photo, taken by his personal photographer, Heinrich Hoffmann, would show the world that Nazi Germany had triumphed over its bitter enemy." (Publisher's note)

"Analyzing visual images and setting them in a larger historical and cultural context is an important skill. This volume uses Heinrich Hoffmann's 1940 photograph of Hitler in front of the Eiffel Tower to discuss the dictator's rise to power and Hoffmann's image-crafting of his subject. A spacious page design, which includes plenty of photos, enhances the presentation. Reading list, timeline. Bib., glos., ind." Horn Book

Includes bibliographical references (page 63) and index

Other titles in the series include:

Assassination and its Aftermath (2014)

The Blue Marble (2014)

Breaker Boys (2012)

Civil War Witness (2014)

Little Rock Girl 1957 (2012)

Man on the Moon (2011)

Migrant Mother (2011)

Raising the Flag (2011)

Summiting Everest (2014)

Tank Man (2014)

943.086   Germany--Period of Third Reich, 1933-1945

Ayer, Eleanor H.

Parallel journeys; [by] Eleanor H. Ayer with Helen Waterford and Alfons Heck. Atheneum Bks. for Young Readers 1995 244p il hardcover o.p. pa $5.99

Grades: 7 8 9 10   **943.086**

1. Hitler-Jugend 2. Jews -- Germany 3. Holocaust, 1933-1945 4. Germany -- History -- 1933-1945

ISBN 0-689-31830-8; 0-689-83236-2 pa

             LC 94-23277

"Alternating chapters contrast the wartime experiences of two young Germans—Waterford, who was interned in a Nazi concentration camp, and Heck, a member of the Hitler Youth. The volume is composed mainly of excerpts from their published autobiographies, connected by Ayer's overall account of the era. A powerful and painful picture emerges, vividly describing life before, during, and, most impressively, after the Holocaust." Horn Book Guide

Includes bibliographical references

Bartoletti, Susan Campbell

★ **Hitler** Youth; growing up in Hitler's shadow. Scholastic Nonfiction 2005 176p il map $19.95

Grades: 7 8 9 10   **943.086**
1. National socialism 2. Holocaust, 1933-1945 3. Germany -- History -- 1933-1945
ISBN 0-439-35379-3

LC 2004-51040

A Newbery Medal honor book, 2006

"Bartoletti draws on oral histories, diaries, letters, and her own extensive interviews with Holocaust survivors, Hitler Youth, resisters, and bystanders to tell the history from the viewpoints of people who were there. . . . The stirring photos tell more of the story. . . . The extensive back matter is a part of the gripping narrative." Booklist

Includes bibliographical references

Dumbach, Annette E.

Sophie Scholl and the white rose; [by] Annette Dumbach, Jud Newborn. New ed; Oneworld 2007 238p il pa $14.95

Grades: 11 12 Adult   **943.086**
1. Students 2. National socialism 3. Dissenters 4. Underground leaders 5. Weisse Rose (Resistance group)
ISBN 978-1-85168-536-3; 1-85168-536-7

First published 1986 with title: Shattering the German night

This book tells "the story of five German university students and their professor, who formed a Nazi-resistance group dubbed the White Rose." Libr J

Includes bibliographical references

944   France and Monaco

Haine, W. Scott

Culture and customs of France. Greenwood Press 2006 315p il map (Culture and customs of Europe) $49.95

Grades: 9 10 11 12   **944**
1. France -- Civilization
ISBN 0-313-32892-7; 978-0-313-32892-3

LC 2006-17935

Includes bibliographical references

944.04   France since 1789

Anderson, James Maxwell

Daily life during the French Revolution; [by] James M. Anderson. Greenwood Press 2007 268p il map (Greenwood Press 'Daily life through history' series) $49.95

Grades: 9 10 11 12   **944.04**
1. France -- History -- 1789-1799, Revolution
ISBN 0-313-33683-0; 978-0-313-33683-6

LC 2006-34084

"Chapters include the physical makeup of France; the social and political background of the revolution; the First Republic; religion, church and state; urban life; rural life; family life; the fringe society; clothes and fashion; food and drink; the role of women; military life; education; health and medicine; and writers, artists, musicians and entertainment." Publisher's note

Includes bibliographical references

Doyle, William

The **Oxford** history of the French Revolution; 2nd ed; Oxford University Press 2003 481p maps pa $19.95

Grades: 9 10 11 12   **944.04**
1. Europe -- History -- 1789-1900 2. France -- History -- 1789-1799, Revolution
ISBN 0-19-925298-X

LC 2002-29004

First published 1989

"Beginning with the accession of Louis XVI in 1774, . . . William Doyle traces the history of France through revolution, terror, and counterterror, to the triumph of Napoleon in 1802, along the way analyzing the impact of these events in France upon the rest of Europe." Publisher's note

Includes bibliographical references

944.05   Period of First Empire, 1804-1815

Johnson, Paul

★ **Napoleon**. Viking 2002 190p (Penguin lives series) hardcover o.p. pa $13

Grades: 11 12 Adult   **944.05**
1. Emperors 2. France -- Kings and rulers
ISBN 0-670-03078-3; 0-14-303745-5 pa

LC 2001-45605

Johnson "presents a concise appraisal of Napoleon's career and a precise understanding of his enigmatic character. The author views Napoleon, not as an 'idea man' whose ideology was the ladder by which he propelled himself to heights of power, but as an opportunist who took advantage of a series of events and situations he could manipulate into achieving supreme control." Booklist

Includes bibliographical references

945   Italy, San Marino, Vatican City, Malta

The **Oxford** history of Italy; edited by George Holmes. Oxford Univ. Press 1997 386p il maps hardcover o.p. pa $29.95

Grades: 11 12 Adult   **945**
1. Italy -- History
ISBN 0-19-820527-9; 0-19-285444-5 pa

LC 98-100006

Twelve scholars survey Italian social, political and cultural history from the time of the Roman Empire to the present.

"An excellent choice for readers wanting either a refresher course on Italian history or those who have no background whatsoever in the subject but have a desire to learn the basics." Booklist

946   Spain, Andorra, Gibraltar, Portugal

Fuentes, Carlos

The **buried** mirror; reflections on Spain and the New World. Houghton Mifflin 1992 399p il hardcover o.p. pa $29.95

Grades: 11 12 Adult   946
1. Spain -- Civilization 2. Latin America -- Civilization
ISBN 0-395-47978-9; 0-395-92499-5 pa
LC 91-34312
"Every page in this lapidary essay offers profound insight into the Spanish American psyche." Libr J
Includes bibliographical references

947   Russia and neighboring east European countries

Gottfried, Ted

The **road** to Communism; illustrated by Melanie Reim. 21st Cent. Bks. (Brookfield) 2002 144p il lib bdg $28.90

Grades: 8 9 10 11 12   947
1. Soviet Union -- History -- 1917-1921, Revolution
ISBN 0-7613-2557-3
LC 2001-52252
Chronicles the Czarist Russian Empire in the 1800s, the birth of Bolshevism, events leading to the Russian Revolution of 1917, and the development of new political structures in its aftermath

"Gottfried writes with clarity and distance even as he narrates the dramatic details of the political conflict and the emotion of the 'dream that failed.'" Booklist
Includes glossary and bibliographical references

Kort, Michael

★ A **brief** history of Russia. Facts On File 2007 xxiii, 310p il map (Brief history) $45; lib bdg $19.95

Grades: 9 10 11 12 Adult   947
1. Russia -- History
ISBN 978-0-8160-7112-8; 0-8160-7112-8; 978-0-8160-7113-5 lib bdg; 0-8160-7113-6 lib bdg
LC 2007-32723
"Detailing the social, economic, and political changes and crises that the people of Russia have had to endure, . . . [this book provides an] account of this vast country's history." Publisher's note
Includes bibliographical references

Riasanovsky, Nicholas V.

A **history** of Russia; 8th ed; Oxford University Press 2011 various paging il map pa $64.95

Grades: 11 12 Adult   947
1. Russia -- History 2. Soviet Union -- History
ISBN 978-0-19-534197-3
LC 2010-23174
First published 1963
This narrative history includes discussions of economics, social organization, religion, and culture.
Includes bibliographical references

947.08   Russia since 1855

Fleming, Candace

★ The **family** Romanov; murder, rebellion, and the fall of imperial Russia. Candace Fleming. Schwartz & Wade Books 2014 304 p. il, maps, genealogical table $18.99

Grades: 7 8 9 10 11 12   947.08
1. Russia -- History -- 1917-1921, Revolution 2. Russia -- History -- Nicholas II, 1894-1917 3. Soviet Union -- History -- Revolution, 1917-1921
ISBN 0375867821; 9780375867828; 9780375967825
LC 2013037904
Robert F. Sibert Honor Book (2015)
YALSA Award for Excellence in Nonfiction for Young Adults: Finalist (2015)
Boston Globe-Horn Book Award: Nonfiction (2015)
This book, by Candace Fleming, describes how "when Russia's last tsar, Nicholas II, inherited the throne in 1894, he was unprepared to do so. With their four daughters (including Anastasia) and only son, a hemophiliac, Nicholas and his reclusive wife, Alexandra, buried their heads in the sand, living a life of opulence as World War I raged outside their door and political unrest grew into the Russian Revolution." (Publisher's note)

"Fleming crafts an exciting narrative from this complicated history and its intriguing personalities. It is full of rich details about the Romanovs, insights into figures such as Vladimir Lenin and firsthand accounts from ordinary Russians affected by the tumultuous events. A variety of photographs adds a solid visual dimension." Kirkus
Includes bibliographical references and index

Massie, Robert K., 1929-

The **Romanovs**; the final chapter. Random House 1995 308p il hardcover o.p. pa $14.95

Grades: 11 12 Adult   947.08
1. Emperors 2. Empresses 3. Forensic anthropology 4. Impostors 5. Royal pretenders 6. Russia -- Kings and rulers
ISBN 0-394-58048-6; 0-345-40640-0 pa
LC 95-4718
This book "is divided into three major parts. The first segment—by far the most fascinating and original—focuses on the complex scientific process used in identifying the Romanovs' remains. . . . The second part concerns the various impostors who have claimed to be members of the Russian imperial family. . . . [The] third segment [is] a report on those

Romanov émigrés—close relatives of the Czar's—who survived the Bolsheviks' persecution." N Y Times Book Rev

Includes bibliographical references

947.084 Russia (Soviet Union)--1917-1991

Gay, Kathlyn

The **aftermath** of the Russian Revolution. Twenty-First Century Books 2009 160p il (Aftermath of history) lib bdg $38.60

Grades: 8 9 10 11 12   **947.084**

1. Soviet Union -- History

ISBN 978-0-8225-9092-7; 0-8225-9092-1

LC 2008-25276

This book "begins with an overview of the Czar's Russia and the political machinations that brought about revolution. The disputes between different revolutionary groups led to the eventual triumph of the Bolsheviks and the reigns of Lenin and Stalin. Stalin's brutality in particular receives a lot of attention. The final chapters cover the transition to a more open society, the fall of the Soviet Union, and the age of Putin." SLJ

Includes glossary and bibliographical references

Wade, Rex A.

★ The **Bolshevik** revolution and Russian Civil War. Greenwood Press 2001 xxiii, 220p il maps (Greenwood Press guides to historic events of the twentieth century) $45

Grades: 11 12 Adult   **947.084**

1. Soviet Union -- History -- 1917-1921, Revolution

ISBN 0-313-29974-9

LC 00-35322

"A narrative history of the political, economic, and social background; causes and events of the revolution and civil war. . . . This book is a product of solid scholarship and an excellent choice for libraries." SLJ

Includes glossary and bibliographical references

Weinberg, Robert

Revolutionary Russia; a history in documents. [by] Robert Weinberg, Laurie Bernstein. Oxford University Press 2010 239p il map (Pages from history) $39.95; pa $24.95

Grades: 9 10 11 12   **947.084**

1. Soviet Union -- History -- 1917-1921, Revolution -- Sources

ISBN 978-0-19-512225-1; 0-19-512225-9; 978-0-19-533794-5 pa; 0-19-533794-8 pa

LC 2009-38666

This "is a solid historical overview of the October Revolution and rick Bolshevik culture as well as the terror of the purges and the horrendous conditions of the gulags. The authors show how forced collectivization led to famine and the deaths of millions, as well as how the country's successful transformation from an oppressed agricultural society to a highly industrialized nation made it able to withstand a German invasion during the Second World War." Booklist

Includes bibliographical references

947.085 Russia (Soviet Union)--1953-1991

Langley, Andrew

The **collapse** of the Soviet Union; the end of an empire. Compass Point Books 2006 96p il map (Snapshots in history) lib bdg $31.93

Grades: 7 8 9 10   **947.085**

1. Soviet Union -- History

ISBN 978-0-7565-2009-0; 0-7565-2009-6

LC 2006003003

This "describes leaders, their plans, and their ultimate downfalls, from the removal of Tsar Nicholas II to the problems of present-day Russia. [This book is] great for research . . . brief but comprehensive." SLJ

Includes glossary and bibliographical references

Stokes, Gale

The **walls** came tumbling down; the collapse of communism in Eastern Europe. Oxford Univ. Press 1993 319p hardcover o.p. pa $31.95

Grades: 11 12 Adult   **947.085**

1. Communism 2. Eastern Europe -- Politics and government

ISBN 0-19-506644-8; 0-19-506645-6 pa

LC 92-44862

This book "can be recommended as a coherent, well-written history that defines its time frame well, provides sound coverage, makes prudent judgments, and wears its analysis lightly. . . . Stokes's overview traces the ebb and flow of personalities and events in a manner that is both accessible to lay readers and informative to scholars." Libr J

948 Scandinavia

Allan, Tony

Exploring the life, myth, and art of the Vikings; Tony Allan. Rosen Pub. 2012 144 p. (Civilizations of the world)

Grades: 7 8 9 10 11   **948**

1. Vikings 2. Viking art 3. Norse mythology 4. Viking civilization

ISBN 9781448848331

LC 2011008856

This book on the Vikings "offers an informative overview of . . . political and social history as well as its art, architecture, and mythology, all bolstered with plenty of . . . details and narratives. . . . [T]he illustrations include artworks, documents, and handsome maps as well as photos of significant sites and artifacts. . . . "Vikings" explores heritage that the Norse people shared and their history as traders, raiders, and settlers in other lands." (Booklist) The book "put[s] the art . . . in context, explaining how a society's religious beliefs, legends, and cultural traditions manifest themselves through images and iconography. The . . . layout features full-color photographs of architecture, sculpture, and painting on every page, accompanied by informative captions." (School Libr J)

Includes bibliographical references (p. 136-137) and index

Nardo, Don

The **Vikings**. Lucent Books 2010 112p il lib
bdg $33.45

Grades: 6 7 8 9   **948**
1. Vikings
ISBN 978-1-4205-0316-6; 1-4205-0316-2
                     LC 2010010500

This "shines as it provides a contemporaneous writing
as well as work by scholars that offer plenty of drama—and
lots of facts too. . . . [It also] provides a solid time line, plenty of photographs, sourced quotes, and a list of books and
websites for further investigation. Excellent for reports and
research." Booklist

★ The **Oxford** illustrated history of the Vikings; edited by Peter Sawyer. Oxford Univ. Press 1997
298p il maps hardcover o.p. pa $27.50

Grades: 11 12 Adult   **948**
1. Vikings
ISBN 0-19-820526-0; 0-19-285434-8 pa
                     LC 97-16649

This illustrated collection of articles includes discussion of the Vikings' impact on England, Iceland, Greenland,
Russia, and the Frankish and Danish Empires; Viking ships
and ship-building; Viking religion; and the ways in which
Vikings have been portrayed throughout history. Significant
archaeological finds are featured.

Includes bibliographical references

Wolf, Kirsten

Daily life of the Vikings. Greenwood Press 2004
187p il map (Greenwood Press 'Daily life through
history' series) $55

Grades: 11 12 Adult   **948**
1. Vikings
ISBN 0-313-32269-4
                     LC 2004-15184

"The work is organized into chapters covering all aspects
[of Viking] life: domestic, economic, intellectual, material,
political, recreational, and religious. It includes a historical
timeline of Viking history, complementary pictures, illustrations, and maps, and a bibliography." Publisher's note

949.6   Balkan Peninsula

Mazower, Mark

The **Balkans**: a short history. Modern Lib. 2000
xliii, 188p maps (Modern Library chronicles) hardcover o.p. pa $11.95

Grades: 11 12 Adult   **949.6**
1. Balkan Peninsula -- History
ISBN 0-679-64087-8; 0-8129-6621-X pa
                     LC 00-56244

This "is an excellent primer on the region's history, especially the growth of the nation-state in the 19th
century." Economist

Includes bibliographical references

949.7   Serbia, Croatia, Slovenia, Bosnia and Hercegovina, Montenegro, Macedonia

Judah, Tim

The **Serbs**; history, myth and the destruction of
Yugoslavia. 3rd ed.; Yale University Press 2009
414p il map pa $19

Grades: 11 12 Adult   **949.7**
1. Yugoslav War, 1991-1995 2. Serbia 3. Yugoslavia
-- History
ISBN 978-0-300-15826-7; 0-300-15826-2
                     LC 2009039429

First published 1997

Judah explores the role of the Serbs in the Yugoslav conflict. "The early part is devoted to a summary of Serbian
history since the Middle Ages, and the remaining two-thirds
to recent events." London Rev Books

Includes bibliographical references

949.702   Yugoslavia, 1918-1991

Sacco, Joe

Safe area Gorazde. Fantagraphics Bks. 2000
227p il $28.95; pa $19.95

Grades: 10 11 12 Adult   **949.702**
1. Graphic novels 2. Bosnia and Hercegovina -- Graphic
novels 3. Yugoslav War, 1991-1995 -- Graphic novels
ISBN 1-56097-392-7; 1-56097-470-2 pa

Sacco "spent five months in Bosnia in 1996, immersing himself in the human side of life during wartime, researching stories that are rarely found in conventional news
coverage. The book focuses on the Muslim-held enclave of
Gorazde, which was besieged by Bosnian Serbs during the
war. Sacco lived for a month in Gorazde, entering before
the Muslims trapped inside had access to the outside world,
electricity or running water." (Publisher's note)

The author "spent four months in Bosnia, focusing on
the Muslim enclave of Gorazde, where he interviewed survivors of the city's siege by the Serbs. . . . Most of the book
is devoted to townspeople's accounts of how they endured
shelling and starvation, and to portrayals of their efforts at
resuming their lives while grappling with the question of
how their neighbors could have turned on them so cruelly.
Sacco's precise, expressive drawings tell the victims' stories
more compellingly than the text does and in more sustained
fashion than broadcast journalism does. As keen as is his
eye, his ear for eliciting these devastating, heartfelt stories
gives the book its undeniable power." Booklist

Includes bibliographical references

950   History of Asia

Lane, George

★ **Genghis** Khan and Mongol rule. Greenwood
Press 2004 xlv, 224p il map (Greenwood guides to
historic events of the medieval world) $45

Grades: 9 10 11 12 **950**
1. Mongols 2. Kings
ISBN 0-313-32528-6

LC 2004-43639

"The book tells a grand story in the brief compass of seven chapters." Hist Teach

Includes bibliographical references

Wood, Frances

The **Silk** Road; two thousand years in the heart of Asia. University of Calif. Press 2002 270p il maps $29.95; pa $19.95

Grades: 9 10 11 12 **950**
1. Central Asia -- History
ISBN 0-520-23786-2; 0-520-24340-4 pa

LC 2003-273631

"This historical journey through the byways of the old Silk Road is a beautifully rendered tribute to the thousands of years in which these routes served as the center of trade." Publ Wkly

Includes bibliographical references

951 China and adjacent areas

Abrams, Dennis

The **Treaty** of Nanking. Chelsea House 2011 120p il map (Milestones in modern world history) lib bdg $35

Grades: 7 8 9 10 **951**
1. China -- History -- Opium War, 1840-1842 2. China -- Foreign relations -- Great Britain 3. Great Britain -- Foreign relations -- China
ISBN 978-1-60413-495-7; 1-60413-495-X

LC 2010026903

This book is "about the Opium Wars begun by Britain in an effort to get China to open its trade to the West. Abrams offers a nice summation of the effect on Chinese foreign policy of the wars and the 'humiliating' treaty that ended them. The book is a fascinating glimpse into what was a mostly closed society, as well as into the ruthlessness of trade relations." SLJ

Includes bibliographical references

★ **China:** opposing viewpoints; Noah Berlatsky, book editor. Greenhaven Press 2010 214p il (Opposing viewpoints series) $41.70; pa $28.90

Grades: 9 10 11 12 **951**
1. China
ISBN 978-0-7377-4765-2; 0-7377-4765-X; 978-0-7377-4766-9 pa; 0-7377-4766-8 pa

LC 2009045725

"Explores the status of human rights and democracy in China, as well as China's economy and its potential as a military threat. Issues discussed include the global recession, trade imbalances, intellectual property piracy, nuclear nonproliferation, Taiwan and North Korea. Also looks at how China is addressing environmental concerns in the region." Publisher's note

Includes bibliographical references

Ebrey, Patricia Buckley

The **Cambridge** illustrated history of China; 2nd ed; Cambridge University Press 2010 384p il map (Cambridge illustrated history) $90; pa $45

Grades: 11 12 Adult **951**
1. China -- History
ISBN 978-0-521-19620-8; 978-0-521-12433-1 pa

LC 2010-292643

First published 1996

"Ebrey traces the origins of Chinese culture from prehistoric times to the present. She follows its development from the rise of Confucianism, Buddhism, and the great imperial dynasties to the Mongol, Manchu, and Western intrusions and the modern communist state." Publisher's note

Includes bibliographical references

Pelleschi, Andrea

China. ABDO 2012 144p. il lib bdg $35.64

Grades: 6 7 8 9 **951**
1. China
ISBN 978-1-61783-107-2

LC 2011019959

" Chapters then cover all the expected details for reportwriters... Vivid photographs and useful maps in an eyepleasing design enliven the presentation." Horn Book

Slavicek, Louise Chipley

★ The **Great** Wall of China; foreword by George J. Mitchell; intro. by James I. Matray. Chelsea House 2004 118p il map (Arbitrary borders) $31.50

Grades: 9 10 11 12 **951**
1. Great Wall of China 2. China -- History
ISBN 0-7910-8019-6

LC 2004-10127

"Chronicles the construction and history of the great fortified wall that was built across sections of northern China at differing times, concluding with what the wall has presently come to symbolize." (Publisher's note)

Includes bibliographical references

Ting, Renee

Chinese history stories; edited by Renee Ting; translated from Chinese by Qian Jifang. Shens Books 2009 2v il ea $19.95

Grades: 6 7 8 9 **951**
1. China -- History
ISBN 978-1-885008-37-4 v1; 1-885008-37-6 v1; 978-1885008-38-1 v2; 1-885008-38-4 v2

LC 2009027288

"These first two entries in a planned series of 12 volumes offer gripping introductions to China's cultural narratives. From the initial two-page condensation of 3000 years of history to the suggestions to 'Learn More' after (often more useful to read before), the well-told stories and the attractively varied illustrations are riveting. . . . Multiple illustrators provide changing art styles and historical allusions, but all are detailed, lively, and colorful." SLJ

951.04　China--Period of Republic, 1912-1949

Gay, Kathlyn

The **aftermath** of the Chinese nationalist revolution. Twenty-First Century Books 2008 160p il (Aftermath of history) lib bdg $38.60

Grades: 7 8 9 10　　　　　　　　　　　951.04

1. China -- History -- 1912-1949
ISBN 978-0-8225-7601-3; 0-8225-7601-5

LC 2007-15082

This book "offers a lucid account of the civil turmoil that began in China with the successful revolution led by Dr. Sun Yat-sen in 1911, and culminated in the establishment of the People's Republic in 1949." Booklist

Includes bibliographical references

951.05　China--Period of People's Republic, 1949-

Gay, Kathlyn

Mao Zedong's China. Twenty-First Century Books 2008 160p il map (Dictatorships) lib bdg $38.60

Grades: 7 8 9 10　　　　　　　　　　　951.05

1. Heads of state 2. Communist leaders 3. Political leaders 4. China -- History -- 1949-1976
ISBN 978-0-8225-7285-5

LC 2007-5083

The author "places Mao in context with other rulers of China and paints an extraordinary picture of how this young peasant rose nearly to the level of a deity in the eyes of the Chinese people." Voice Youth Advocates

Jiang, Ji-li

Red scarf girl; a memoir of the Cultural Revolution. foreword by David Henry Hwang. HarperCollins Pubs. 1997 285p $16.99; pa $6.99

Grades: 6 7 8 9 10　　　　　　　　　　951.05

1. Communism -- China 2. China -- History -- 1949-1976 -- Personal narratives
ISBN 0-06-027585-5; 0-06-446208-0 pa

LC 97-5089

"This is an autobiographical account of growing up during Mao's Cultural Revolution in China in 1966. . . . Jiang describes in terrifying detail the ordeals of her family and those like them, including unauthorized search and seizure, persecution, arrest and torture, hunger, and public humiliation. . . . Her voice is that of an intelligent, confused adolescent, and her focus on the effects of the revolution on herself, her family, and her friends provides an emotional focal point for the book, and will allow even those with limited knowledge of Chinese history to access the text." Bull Cent Child Books

Schoppa, R. Keith

★ **Twentieth** century China; a history in documents. 2nd ed.; Oxford University Press 2011 214p il map (Pages from history) $39.95; pa $24.95

Grades: 9 10 11 12　　　　　　　　　　951.05

1. China -- History -- 20th century -- Sources
ISBN 978-0-19-973201-2; 978-0-19-973200-5 pa

LC 2010010474

First published 2004

Using primary sources "including official reports and public statements, articles, political posters, cartoons, poetry, songs, and advertisements, R. Keith Schoppa paints a picture of a society undergoing drastic changes, both social and political." Publisher's note

Includes bibliographical references

Slavicek, Louise Chipley

The **Chinese** Cultural Revolution. Chelsea House Publishers 2010 128p il (Milestones in modern world history) lib bdg $35

Grades: 8 9 10 11 12　　　　　　　　　951.05

1. China -- History -- 1949-1976
ISBN 978-1-60413-278-6; 1-60413-278-7

LC 2008-54885

"From the cover photo onward, young people are front and center in [this book,] . . . which focuses on the Red Guards who heard the anti-establishment call of their leader, Mao Zedong, in 1966. This political upheaval led to the deaths of up to four million Chinese over 10 years." Booklist

Includes bibliographical references

Uschan, Michael V., 1948-

China since World War II; by Michael V. Uschan. Lucent Books 2008 104 p. ill. (some col.), col. map (library) $34.95

Grades: 6 7 8 9　　　　　　　　　　　　951.05

1. China -- History -- 1949-
ISBN 142050097X; 9781420500974

LC 2008014727

This book by Michael V. Uschan looks at the history of China since World War II. "Mao [Zedong] naturally dominates, the focus of five chapters. . . . One of the remaining two chapters is devoted to Deng Xiaoping, and the other to the Chinese economy. . . . There is no mention of the environmental consequences of China's prosperity, the human costs of the disappearance of social security . . . or the widespread corruption reflected in such recent events as collapsing schools." (School Library Journal)

Includes bibliographical references and index.

951.9　Korea

Edwards, Paul M.

Korean War almanac. Facts on File 2006 592p il map (Almanacs of American wars) $85

Grades: 11 12 Adult　　　　　　　　　　951.9

1. Korean War, 1950-1953
ISBN 0-8160-6037-1

LC 2005-9374

First published 1990 under the authorship of Harry G. Summers

This book "contains a day-by-day chronology of the events and the people involved in this important war." Publisher's note

Includes bibliographical references

Hastings, Max

The **Korean** War. Simon & Schuster 1987 391p il maps hardcover o.p. pa $16

Grades: 11 12 Adult   **951.9**

1. Korean War, 1950-1953

ISBN 0-671-52823-8; 0-671-66834-X pa

             LC 87-16547

The author covers the political and military background of the Korean War, and also discusses how it served as a prelude to the American involvement in the Vietnam War, 15 years later.

This is a "readable, informative and sensible study." Booklist

Includes bibliographical references

Isserman, Maurice

★ **Korean** War; John S. Bowman, general editor. Rev. ed.; Chelsea House 2010 162p il map (America at war) $45

Grades: 9 10 11 12   **951.9**

1. Korean War, 1950-1953

ISBN 978-0-8160-8186-8

             LC 2009-36873

First published 1992

Examines the political climate and military situation that led to the Korean War and discusses the key people and events involved in the conflict itself.

Includes glossary and bibliographical references

The **Korean** War; Dennis Nishi, book editor. Greenhaven Press 2003 240p (Interpreting primary documents) hardcover o.p. pa $23.70

Grades: 7 8 9 10   **951.9**

1. Korean War, 1950-1953

ISBN 0-7377-1202-3 lib bdg; 0-7377-1201-5 pa

             LC 2002-40890

"This anthology contains documents by influential Washington policy makers as well as popular editorialists of the day." Publisher's note

Includes bibliographical references

Peterson, Mark

★ A **brief** history of Korea; [by] Mark Peterson with Phillip Margulies. Facts On File 2010 328p il map (Brief history) $49.50

Grades: 9 10 11 12 Adult   **951.9**

1. Korea -- History

ISBN 978-0-8160-5085-7

             LC 2009-18889

This book "covers the history of Korea from the origins of the Korean people in prehistoric times to the economic and political situation in North and South Korea today." Publisher's note

Includes bibliographical references

Reece, Richard

The **Korean** War. ABDO Pub. 2011 112p il map (Essential events) lib bdg $23.95

Grades: 7 8 9 10 11 12   **951.9**

1. Korean War, 1950-1953

ISBN 978-1-61714-766-1; 1-61714-766-4

             LC 2010044661

This describes the Korean War and discusses the political and social issues pertaining to it.

Includes glossary and bibliographical references

Stokesbury, James L.

A **short** history of the Korean War. Morrow 1988 276p maps hardcover o.p. pa $13.95

Grades: 11 12 Adult   **951.9**

1. Korean War, 1950-1953

ISBN 0-688-06377-2; 0-688-09513-5 pa

             LC 88-5229

"Stokesbury's combination of scholarship, clear writing, balanced judgments, and wit has reached a new high. It would be hard to imagine better personality portraits or better coverage of the prisoner-of-war issue." Booklist

Includes bibliographical references

951.93   North Korea (People's Democratic Republic of Korea)

Kummer, Patricia K.

North Korea; by Patricia K. Kummer. Children's Press 2008 144p il map (Enchantment of the world, second series) lib bdg $38

Grades: 5 6 7 8 9   **951.93**

1. Korea (North)

ISBN 978-0-531-18485-1 lib bdg; 0-531-18485-4 lib bdg

             LC 2007025693

In this introduction to North Korea "geography is the focus, but Kummer also discusses ancient and recent history, . . . the economy, religion, sports, education, and more. Without discounting the rich culture, the book doesn't shy away from more sensitive issues. . . . The open design will draw readers, with clear type on thick, high-quality paper; numerous maps and color photos and spacious back matter are also included." Booklist

Includes bibliographical references

952   Japan

Dunn, Charles James

Everyday life in traditional Japan. C.E. Tuttle Co. 1972 197p il map (TUT books) pa $16.95

Grades: 9 10 11 12   **952**

1. Japan -- Civilization 2. Japan -- Social life and customs

ISBN 4-8053-1005-7

             LC 72-186748

First published 1969 by Putnam

"A description of Japanese life during the stable . . . reign of the Tokugawa shoguns [1600-1850]." Cincinnati Public Libr

Includes bibliographical references

952.03   Japan--1868-1945

Buruma, Ian
Inventing Japan, 1853-1964. Modern Lib. 2003 194p hardcover o.p. pa $12.95
Grades: 11 12 Adult   **952.03**
   1. Japan -- History
   ISBN 0-679-64085-1; 0-8129-7286-4 pa
                LC 2002-26346
"Buruma traces the remarkable metamorphosis that transformed an isolated island shogunate into an expansive military empire and then into a pacified and prosperous democracy. . . . An excellent introductory study." Booklist

Includes bibliographical references

953.8   Saudi Arabia

Wynbrandt, James
A **brief** history of Saudi Arabia; foreword by Fawaz A. Gerges. 2nd ed; Facts On File 2010 364p il map (Brief history) $49.50; pa $19.95
Grades: 9 10 11 12 Adult   **953.8**
   1. Saudi Arabia -- History
   ISBN 978-0-8160-7876-9; 978-0-8160-8250-6 pa
                LC 2010-5466
   First published 2004
This history of Saudi Arabia covers "pre-Islamic Arabia; Bedouin society and culture; the birth and spread of Islam; the development of and philosophy behind Wahhabism; the origins of House Saud; Saudi Arabia's role in the Middle East; Saudi Arabia's relationship to the United States; the battle between conservative and progressive elements in the monarchy today; [and] the reign of King Abdullah." Publisher's note

Includes glossary and bibliographical references

954   India and neighboring south Asian countries

McLeod, John
★ The **history** of India. Greenwood Press 2002 xx, 223p (Greenwood histories of the modern nations) $39.95
Grades: 11 12 Adult   **954**
   1. Mogul Empire 2. India -- History -- 1526-1765
   ISBN 0-313-31459-4
                LC 2002-276829
The author presents "in broad outlines some of the major events and episodes that make up India's history. . . . This is a useful compilation of important facts relating to Indian history. Its strength lies primarily in the last six chapters in which brief narratives of the struggle for independence and post-independence India down to the close of the twentieth century are nicely presented. All in all, this is a book that all libraries should have." Recomm Ref Books for Small & Medium-sized Libr & Media Cent, 2003

Includes bibliographical references

Ram-Prasad, Chakravarthi
Exploring the life, myth, and art of India. Rosen 2009 144p il map (Civilizations of the world) lib bdg $29.95
Grades: 7 8 9 10 11 12   **954**
   1. Indic mythology 2. Indic art 3. India -- Civilization
   ISBN 978-1-4358-5615-8; 1-4358-5615-5
                LC 2009-9274
This describes the civilization, mythology and art of ancient India

"This beautifully illustrated and well-written [title] . . . is perfect for those assignments where students must look at the culture of a civilization. Artwork and pictures blend seamlessly with the information and the reader is taken on a journey of discovery. Myths are used as the story of how the people view themselves, blended with the discussion of the reality of life. Everyday life is tied to the belief systems and is explained in light of those beliefs. The pictures are beautifully done and there is almost as much information in the captions as there is in the text." Libr Media Connect

Includes glossary and bibliographical references

Walsh, Judith E.
A **brief** history of India; 2nd ed.; Facts On File, Inc. 2010 414p il map (Brief history) $49.50; pa $19.95
Grades: 9 10 11 12 Adult   **954**
   1. India -- History
   ISBN 978-0-8160-8143-1; 978-0-8160-8362-6 pa
                LC 2010-26316
   First published 2006
Includes bibliographical references

954.03   India--Period of British rule, 1785-1947

Darraj, Susan Muaddi
The **Indian** Independence Act of 1947; by Susan Muaddi Darraj. Chelsea House 2011 120 p. (Milestones in modern world history)
Grades: 7 8 9 10 11 12   **954.03**
   1. India -- History -- 1947- 2. Constitutional history -- India 3. India -- Politics and government 4. India -- History -- Autonomy and independence movements
   ISBN 9781604134964

                LC 2011004476
This book on the Indian Independence Act of 1947 is part of the "Milestones in Modern World History" series of books that "give . . . explanations for major world events that continue to have an impact on today's world." Author Susan Muaddi Darraj "sorts out the complicated and violent events before and after the act and the partitioning of India and Pakistan." (Booklist) In the book, one can "[r]ead how Indian independence continues to impact the world in terms of politics, religion, and culture." (Publisher's note)

Includes bibliographical references (p. 109-113)

and index

954.91   Pakistan

Wynbrandt, James

★ A **brief** history of Pakistan; foreword by Fawaz A. Gerges. Facts On File 2008 324p il map (Brief history) $49.50

Grades: 11 12 Adult   **954.91**
1. Pakistan -- History
ISBN 978-0-8160-6184-6; 0-8160-6184-X
LC 2008-8921

This book about the history of Pakistan includes "dramatic events, notable people, and special customs and traditions that have shaped this country." Publisher's note

Includes glossary and bibliographical references

955   Iran

Wagner, Heather Lehr

The **Iranian** Revolution. Chelsea House 2010 111p il (Milestones in modern world history) lib bdg $35

Grades: 7 8 9 10 11 12   **955**
1. Iran -- History -- 1941-1979
ISBN 978-1-60413-490-2; 1-60413-490-9
LC 2009-22336

"Chapters cover the origin of the Pahlavi dynasty, [Ayatollah] Khomeini's early life and how he came to symbolize opposition to the shah's regime, and the shah's aggressive campaigns of reform and Westernization. . . . A solid addition to the series." SLJ

Includes bibliographical references

955.05   Iran--1906-2005

Wright, Robin

The **last** great revolution; turmoil and transformation in Iran. Knopf 2000 xxiv, 339p il hardcover o.p. pa $14

Grades: 11 12 Adult   **955.05**
1. Iran -- Politics and government
ISBN 0-375-40639-5; 0-375-70630-5 pa
LC 99-27798

The author "talks to journalists, educators, politicians, entertainers, and others to present a picture of the cultural and political changes in Iran: the softening of cultural restrictions, the empowerment of women, and the modernization of industry and the economy." Booklist

Includes bibliographical references

956   Middle East (Near East)

Agoston, Gabor

Encyclopedia of the Ottoman Empire; [edited by] Gábor Ágoston and Bruce Masters. Facts On File 2009 xxxvi, 650p il map (Facts on File library of world history) $85

Grades: 11 12 Adult   **956**
1. Reference books 2. Turkey -- History -- Ottoman Empire, 1288-1918 -- Encyclopedias
ISBN 978-0-8160-6259-1; 0-8160-6259-5
LC 2008-20716

This encyclopedia provides an "overview of the history and civilization of the Ottomans, with more than 400 A-to-Z entries focusing on major events, personalities, institutions, and terms." Publisher's note

Includes bibliographical references

The **Middle** East; Debra A. Miller, book editor. Greenhaven Press 2008 224p (Current controversies) lib bdg $37.40; pa $25.95

Grades: 7 8 9 10 11 12   **956**
1. Iraq War, 2003-2011 2. Israel-Arab conflicts 3. Iraq War, 2003- 4. War on terrorism 5. Middle East -- Foreign relations -- United States 6. United States -- Foreign relations -- Middle East
ISBN 978-0-7377-3960-2 lib bdg; 978-0-7377-3961-9 pa
LC 2007-37428

An anthology of essays presenting differing opinions on topics such as why the Middle East an area of conflict, whether or not the United States should withdraw its troops from Iraq, if the Israel-Palestinian conflict can be resolved, and if the United States should be involved in the Middle East's problems.

Includes bibliographical references

The **Middle** East: opposing viewpoints; David M. Haugen, Susan Musser and Kacy Lovelace, book editors. Greenhaven Press 2009 261p il map (Opposing viewpoints series) lib bdg $38.50; pa $26.75

Grades: 8 9 10 11 12   **956**
1. Middle East -- Politics and government 2. Middle East -- Foreign relations -- United States 3. United States -- Foreign relations -- Middle East
ISBN 978-0-7377-4532-0 lib bdg; 0-7377-4532-0 lib bdg; 978-0-7377-4533-7 pa; 0-7377-4533-9 pa
LC 2008-55848

The articles in this anthology cover such topics as U.S. relations with Middle Eastern nations, the Israeli/Palestinian conflict, whether Iran is a threat to the United States, and counterterrorism efforts in Middle Eastern nations.

Includes bibliographical references

Pouwels, Randall L.

★ The **African** and Middle Eastern world, 600-1500. Oxford University Press 2006 175p il map (Medieval and early modern world) $32.95

Grades: 9 10 11 12   **956**
1. Islamic civilization 2. Africa -- History 3. Middle East -- History
ISBN 0-19-517673-1; 978-0-19-517673-5
LC 2004-21476

"The author places readers in the midst of the action, allowing them to witness what it might have been like to live as a young caravan guide in A.D. 600. Thereafter, chapters are enlivened by the lives and exploits of Muhammad and his various successors, an in-depth discussion of the appeal of Islam, and a review of the leadership of men such as Mansa Musa and Sundiata. . . . This accessible and attractive volume is a wonderful introduction to the medieval Islamic world." SLJ

Includes bibliographical references

956.04   Middle East--1945-1980

Woolf, Alex

The **Arab**-Israeli War since 1948; by Alex Woolf. 1st ed. Heinemann Library 2011 80 p. ill. (some col.), col. maps (library) $36.50; (paperback) $10.99

Grades: 6 7 8 9   **956.04**
1. Israel-Arab conflicts 2. Arab-Israeli conflict
ISBN 1432959956; 9781432959951; 9781432960049
                                           LC 2011015920
"In this volume of the illustrated 'Living Through' series, readers are given a . . . summary of the critical events that shaped what we now think of as the Arab-Israeli Wars. . . . Readers will encounter some of the individuals, causes, and ongoing contradictions that make this international issue so seemingly unsolvable." (Children's Literature)
Includes bibliographical references (p. 76-78) and index.

956.7   Iraq

American Security Project

Iraq uncensored; perspectives. edited by James M. Ludes [for the] American Security Project; foreword by John Kerry. Fulcrum 2009 xxiv, 162p il (Speaker's corner) $22.95

Grades: 10 11 12 Adult   **956.7**
1. Iraq War, 2003-2011 2. Military policy -- United States 3. National security -- United States
ISBN 978-1-55591-703-6; 1-55591-703-8
                                           LC 2009-11509
"Although this is not strictly a book for young adults, the length of the essays (most are under 10 pages) and the well-balanced viewpoints make it a good choice for teens looking to learn about the Iraq war beyond the headlines. Sections cover planning for the war, its conduct, the Department of Defense, and the use of national power. Contributors include senators, military leaders, academics, and foreign-policy experts." SLJ
Includes bibliographical references

Campbell, Donovan

Joker one; a Marine platoon's story of courage, sacrifice, and brotherhood. Random House 2009 313p map hardcover o.p. pa $16.00

Grades: 11 12 Adult   **956.7**
1. Memoirists 2. Marine corps officers 3. Beverage industry executives 4. Iraq War, 2003- -- Campaigns 5. United States -- Marine Corps 6. Iraq War, 2003- --

Personal narratives
ISBN 0812979567; 1400067731; 9780812979565 pa; 9781400067732
                                           LC 2008-23896
This is an account of the seven-month street, to street, house to house battle fought in Ramadi by Marine platoon "Joker One" and the platoon's commander, Lt. Campbell.
This is "a harrowing narrative of [the author's] time as an infantry officer in Ramadi from March to September of 2004. . . . Campbell is a gifted writer who describes his own marines with deep care and attention." Washington Post

Carlisle, Rodney P.

★ **Iraq** War; John S. Bowman, general editor. Rev. ed.; Chelsea House 2010 208p il map (America at war) $45

Grades: 9 10 11 12   **956.7**
1. Iraq War, 2003-2011 2. Iraq -- History 3. Iraq War, 2003-
ISBN 978-0-8160-8191-2
                                           LC 2009-34823
First published 2004
This history of the Iraq War "explores the history of the region as well as the recent events leading up to and culminating in this war." Publisher's note
Includes glossary and bibliographical references

Ellis, Deborah

Children of war; voices of Iraqi refugees. Groundwood Books 2009 128p il $15.95; pa $9.95

Grades: 7 8 9 10 11 12   **956.7**
1. Refugees 2. Children and war 3. Iraq War, 2003-2011 4. Iraq War, 2003-
ISBN 978-0-88899-907-8; 0-88899-907-0; 978-0-88899-908-5 pa; 0-88899-908-9 pa
Ellis "interviews child refugees from Iraq, now living in Jordan, and a few who have made it to Canada. . . . Accompanying each of the . . . interviews with young people is a brief introduction and a photo. . . . What is haunting are their graphic recent memories of what they witnessed. . . . An important, current title that will have lasting significance." Booklist
Includes glossary

Fattah, Hala Mundhir

★ A **brief** history of Iraq; [by] Hala Fattah with Frank Caso. Facts On File 2008 318p il map (Brief history) $49.50

Grades: 11 12 Adult   **956.7**
1. Iraq -- History
ISBN 978-0-8160-5767-2; 0-8160-5767-2
                                           LC 2008-8451
This book about the history of Iraq "focuses primarily on the societies, peoples, and cultures of Iraq, as well as the regional influences that helped shape the destiny of the ethnicities, religions, sects, and national groups in this country." Publisher's note
Includes glossary and bibliographical references

★ **Iraq:** opposing viewpoints; David M. Haugen, Susan Musser, and Kacy Lovelace, book editors.

Greenhaven Press 2009 186p il map (Opposing viewpoints series) lib bdg $38.50; pa $26.75

Grades: 8 9 10 11 12 **956.7**

1. Iraq War, 2003-2011 2. Iraq War, 2003-

ISBN 978-0-7377-4524-5 lib bdg; 978-0-7377-4525-2 pa

LC 2008-51446

The articles in this anthology cover such topics as whether or not Iraq is becoming stable after the overthrow of Saddam Hussein and how much the United States should be involved in the rebuilding of Iraq.

Includes bibliographical references

Munier, Gilles

Iraq; an illustrated history. Interlink Books 2003 230p il $18

Grades: 11 12 Adult **956.7**

1. Iraq -- History

ISBN 1-566-56513-8

LC 2003-13372

This work "betrays the French view of recent events on the Middle East. Its usefulness, however, lies in its offering an excellent introduction to Iraq's 4000-year history and culture. . . . Features like a glossary, sidebars with statistics, schematic maps, a list of relevant web sites, and the book's compact size make this a timely, useful choice for anyone interested in learning more about Iraq." SLJ

Includes bibliographical references

Skiba, Katherine M.

Sister in the Band of Brothers; embedded with the 101st Airborne in Iraq. University Press of Kansas 2005 257p il (Modern war studies) $29.95

Grades: 11 12 Adult **956.7**

1. Iraq War, 2003- -- Personal narratives 2. United States -- Army -- Airborne Division, 101st

ISBN 0-7006-1382-X

LC 2004-26475

The author "was the only woman embedded with the 101st Airborne when the United States invaded Iraq in 2003. She has written a fascinating memoir of her time within the training with other reporters, waiting to invade Iraq and spending the first few months of the war with soldiers in Iraq." Univ Press Books for Public and Second Sch Libr, 2006

Slavicek, Louise Chipley, 1956-

The **establishment** of the state of Israel; by Louise Chipley Slavicek. Chelsea House 2012 125 p. (hardcover) $35

Grades: 7 8 9 10 11 12 **956.7**

1. Zionism 2. Jews -- History 3. Israel -- History 4. Palestine -- History 5. Jewish-Arab relations

ISBN 9781604139174

LC 2011011609

This book on the establishment of Israel is part of "the Milestones in Modern World History series" of books that "give . . . explanations for major world events that continue to have an impact on today's world." Author Louise Chipley Slavicek "cover[s] both Jewish and Arab perspectives." (Booklist) The book explains how "the new Jewish state was founded . . . after Palestine's Roman conquerors exiled the Jews . . . and . . . after Jewish immigrants began returning to their ancient homeland as part of the Zionist movement. Within hours of Israel's establishment, armies of the five neighboring Arab countries had already begun assembling along the new nation's borders. . . . [The book] goes in depth to explain how this conflict has affected the history of the region and the Middle East peace process. (Publisher's note)

Includes bibliographical references and index.

Smithson, Ryan

Ghosts of war; my tour of duty. HarperTeen 2009 321p il $16.99; lib bdg $17.89

Grades: 8 9 10 11 12 **956.7**

1. Soldiers -- United States 2. Iraq War, 2003- -- Personal narratives

ISBN 978-0-06-166468-7; 0-06-166468-5; 978-0-06-166470-0 lib bdg; 0-06-166470-7 lib bdg

LC 2008-35420

"Ryan Smithson was a typical 16-year-old high-school student until 9/11. . . . Smithson enlisted in the Army Reserve the following year and, a year into the Iraq war, was deployed to an Army engineer unit as a heavy-equipment operator. His poignant, often harrowing account, especially vivid in sensory details, chronicles his experiences in basic training and in Iraq. . . . This memoir is a remarkable, deeply penetrating read that will compel teens to reflect on their own thoughts about duty, patriotism and sacrifice." Kirkus

Includes glossary and bibliographical references

The **war** in Iraq; Tom Lansford, book editor. Greenhaven Press 2009 241p il map (Global viewpoints) $37.30; pa $25.70

Grades: 9 10 11 12 **956.7**

1. Iraq War, 2003-2011 2. Iraq War, 2003-

ISBN 978-0-7377-4162-9; 0-7377-4162-7; 978-0-7377-4163-6 pa; 0-7377-4163-5 pa

LC 2008-53992

"This collection of 21 essays reprinted from a variety of magazines and newspapers aims to provide a broad, international overview of the complex issues surrounding the conflict. The four chapters cover the war as it relates to United States foreign relations, the Arab-Israeli conflict, international terrorism, and democracy. . . . This work will be a useful tool in current-events classes, and its evenhanded approach offers plenty of substance for classroom discussions." SLJ

Includes bibliographical references

★ **What** was asked of us; an oral history of the Iraq War by the soldiers who fought it. [compiled by] Trish Wood. Little, Brown and Co. 2006 309p il map pa $14.99

Grades: 11 12 Adult **956.7**

1. Iraq War, 2003- -- Personal narratives

ISBN 978-0-316-01670-4; 0-316-01670-5; 978-0-316-01671-1 pa; 0-316-01671-3 pa

LC 2006-930963

"Colloquial, coarse and compelling, these narratives flash with humor, horror, nihilism and poesy." Publ Wkly

Zeinert, Karen

The **brave** women of the Gulf Wars; Operation Desert Storm and Operation Iraqi Freedom. [by] Karen Zeinert & Mary Miller. 21st Century Bks. 2006 112p il $30.60

Grades: 7 8 9 10 **956.7**

1. Iraq War, 2003 2. Women in the armed forces 3. Persian Gulf War, 1991 -- Women

ISBN 0-7613-2705-3

"Zeinert and Miller reinforce the argument that women do, indeed, belong in the U.S. military by highlighting their contributions in Operations Desert Storm (Kuwait) and Iraqi Freedom. . . . The narrative paints a picture of consistent courage under fire and, one terse mention of the abuses at Abu Ghraib Prison aside, of professional conduct. The authors extend their purview with a chapter on women journalists in the campaigns, and while thoroughly villainizing Saddam Hussein, they also indicate that the official justifications for the war in Iraq turned out to be weak at best. A utilitarian but cogent assessment of the topic, well supported by notes and sources." Booklist

Includes bibliographical references

956.704 Iraq--1979-

Bingham, Jane

The **Gulf** wars with Iraq; by Jane Bingham. Heinemann Library 2012 80 p. ill., maps (library) $36.50; (paperback) $10.99

Grades: 6 7 8 9 **956.704**

1. Iraq War, 2003-2011 2. Persian Gulf War, 1991

ISBN 1432959972; 9781432959975; 9781432960063

LC 2011015922

This book by Jane Bingham is part of the Living Through series and looks at the U.S. Gulf Wars with Iraq. Here, "Bingham takes her readers back through the twists and turns of fact and fiction that are part and parcel of these connected conflicts." Topics include "the falsification of intelligence linked to Saddam Hussein's weapons program, the ruthless nature of the Iraqi dictator and his family, and the human cost of these two wars." (Children's Literature)

Includes bibliographical references (p. 77-78) and index.

Chandrasekaran, Rajiv

Imperial life in the emerald city; inside Iraq's green zone. Rajiv Chandrasekaran. Alfred A. Knopf 2006 x, 320p maps (alk. paper) $25.95

Grades: 11 12 Adult **956.704**

1. Iraq 2. Iraq War, 2003-2011 3. Political corruption 4. United States -- Politics and government 5. Iraq War, 2003- 6. Iraq -- Coalition Provisional Authority 7. United States -- Politics and government -- 2001- 8. United States -- Politics and government -- 2001-2009

ISBN 1400044871; 9781400044870

LC 2006041014

BBC Samuel Johnson Prize for Non-Fiction (2007)

This book discusses "the Green Zone in Baghdad, headquarters for the American occupation in Iraq, . . . [and provides a] portrait of the Green Zone and the Coalition Provisional Authority (which ran Iraq's government from April 2003 to June 2004) that becomes a metaphor for the [U.S.] administration's larger failings in Iraq. An insular, often blinkered approach to decision making; a reluctance to listen to experts; Pollyannaish expectations leading to inadequate allocations of resources and staff; a willful ignorance of Iraqi culture and history; and an obliviousness to realities on the ground: all are on unfortunate display in the Emerald City." (New York Times)

Includes bibliographical references (p. [303]-306) and index.

Maraniss, David

They marched into sunlight; war and peace in Vietnam and America, October 1967. Simon & Schuster 2003 592p il map hardcover o.p. pa $16

Grades: 11 12 Adult **956.704**

1. Vietnam War, 1961-1975

ISBN 0-7432-1780-2; 0-7432-6104-6 pa

LC 2003-52885

This is a "narrative by a reporter who juxtaposes a ghastly little battle in Vietnam with an antiwar and anti-Dow demonstration at the University of Wisconsin, Madison, on the same day; it captures moral ambiguity everywhere, without stereotyping or condescension." N Y Times Book Rev

Includes bibliographical references

Schwartz, Richard Alan

Encyclopedia of the Persian Gulf War. McFarland & Co. 1998 216p il maps hardcover o.p. pa $45

Grades: 11 12 Adult **956.704**

1. Reference books 2. Persian Gulf War, 1991 -- Encyclopedias

ISBN 0-7864-0451-5; 0-7864-4103-8 pa

LC 97-51886

"Beginning with a seven-page overview, this encyclopedia presents alphabetically arranged entries that describe the conflict, including key figures, places, battles, diplomacy, and more." SLJ

Includes bibliographical references

Swofford, Anthony

★ **Jarhead**: a Marine's chronicle of the Gulf War and other battles. Scribner 2003 260p hardcover o.p. pa $15

Grades: 11 12 Adult **956.704**

1. United States -- Marine Corps 2. Persian Gulf War, 1991 -- Personal narratives

ISBN 0-7432-3535-5; 0-7432-8721-5 pa

LC 2002-30866

This book offers "an unflinching portrayal of the loneliness and brutality of modern warfare and sophisticated analyses of—and visceral reactions to—its politics." Publ Wkly

956.91 Syria

Gelfand, Dale Evva

Syria; by Dale Evva Gelfand. ABDO Pub. Co. 2013 144 p. (library) $35.64

Grades: 8 9 10 11 12   **956.91**
1. Syria
ISBN 1617836397; 9781617836398
                                            LC 2012946084
This book by Dale Ewa Gelfant is part of the Countries
of the World series and looks at Syria. It "introduces Syria's
history, geography, culture, climate, government, economy,
and other significant features. Sidebars, maps, fact pages, a
glossary, a timeline, historic images and full-color photos"
are included. (Publisher's note)

956.94   Palestine; Israel

Armstrong, Karen
  Jerusalem; one city, three faiths. Knopf 1996
xxi, 471p il maps hardcover o.p. pa $17.95
Grades: 11 12 Adult   **956.94**
1. Jerusalem -- History
ISBN 0-679-43596-4; 0-345-39168-3 pa
                                            LC 96-75888
Armstrong's "overarching theme, that Jerusalem has
been central to the experience and 'sacred geography' of
Jews, Muslims and Christians and thus has led to deadly
struggles for dominance, is a familiar one, yet she brings
to her sweeping, profusely illustrated narrative a grasp of
sociopolitical conditions seldom found in other books."
Publ Wkly

Aronson, Marc
  ★ **Unsettled**; the problem of loving Israel. Gi-
nee Seo Books/Athaeneum Books for Young Readers
2008 184p il map $18.99
Grades: 9 10 11 12   **956.94**
1. Israel -- History
ISBN 978-1-4169-1261-3; 1-4169-1261-4
                                            LC 2008-300316
An exploration of the history of Israel, its relationships
with its neighboring countries, and questions about what Israel should be.
"This title gives a lot of information and forces readers to
think deeply about morality, bigotry, politics, and religion. It
is a fascinating look at a complicated country." SLJ
Includes bibliographical references

Frank, Mitch
  ★ **Understanding** the Holy Land; answering
questions about the Israeli-Palestinian Conflict. Vi-
king 2005 152p il map (paperback) $8.99
Grades: 6 7 8 9 10   **956.94**
1. Israel-Arab conflicts
ISBN 0670060437; 9780670060436
                                            LC 2004014973
The author "tackles the complex subject of the Israeli-
Palestinian conflict, making it comprehensible, if not any
less horrific. . . . He uses a simple yet wonderfully effective
technique to present the information: questions and answers.
. . . Evenhanded and honest." Booklist
Includes bibliographical references

Israel: opposing viewpoints; Myra Immell, book
editor. Greenhaven Press 2011 193p map (Opposing viewpoints series) $41.70; pa $28.90
Grades: 8 9 10 11 12   **956.94**
1. Israel-Arab conflicts
ISBN 978-0-7377-4974-8; 0-7377-4974-1; 978-0-
7377-4975-5 pa; 0-7377-4975-X pa
                                            LC 2010022999
Articles in this anthology discuss Israel's right to exist,
key issues in the conflict between Israel and Palestine, and
what U.S. policy should be regarding Israel.
Includes bibliographical references

Owings, Lisa
  Israel; by Lisa Owings. ABDO Pub. Co. 2013
144 p. (library) $35.64
Grades: 8 9 10 11 12   **956.94**
1. Israel
ISBN 1617836303; 9781617836305
                                            LC 2012946075
This book by Lisa Owings is part of the Countries of
the World series and looks at Israel. It "introduces Israel's
history, geography, culture, climate, government, economy,
and other significant features. Sidebars, maps, fact pages, a
glossary, a timeline, historic images and full-color photos,
and well-placed graphs and charts" are included. (Publisher's note)

Reich, Bernard
  ★ A **brief** history of Israel; 2nd ed; Facts On
File 2008 382p il map (Brief history) $45; pa
$19.95
Grades: 9 10 11 12 Adult   **956.94**
1. Israel -- History
ISBN 978-0-8160-7126-5; 978-0-8160-7127-2 pa
                                            LC 2008-3838
First published 2005
This book "explores Israel's history with an emphasis on
the period since its independence in 1948. The chronological
narration begins with the time of Abraham and the period of
the Israelite kingdoms and continues to World War II and the
United Nations Partition Plan. This . . . reference then examines the independent country of Israel, including the Arab–
Israeli conflict, domestic politics, Knesset election results,
the economy, and international relations." Publisher's note
Includes bibliographical references

956.940   Palestine, Israel - 1948

Pendergast, Tom
  The **Middle** East conflict. Primary sources; [by]
Tom and Sara Pendergast; [project editor] Ralph Zer-
bonia. UXL 2006 xlii, 238p il map (U-X-L Middle
East conflict reference library) $67
Grades: 9 10 11 12   **956.940**
1. Israel-Arab conflicts 2. Middle East -- History
ISBN 0-7876-9458-4; 978-0-7876-9458-6
                                            LC 2005-12551
This book "includes numerous declarations, personal ac-
counts, United Nations resolutions, and other primary docu-

ments relating to the conflict. Divided into seven chapters arranged by theme, this volume provides a good perspective of the regions troubled history, particularly through the first-person accounts." Ref & User Services Quarterly

Includes bibliographical references

958   Central Asia

Hanks, Reuel R.

★ **Central** Asia; a global studies handbook. ABC-CLIO 2005 xvii, 467p il map (Global studies) $55

Grades: 11 12 Adult   **958**
   1. Central Asia
   ISBN 1-85109-656-6

                           LC 2005-14716

"The superb text makes accessible, whether for reports or general reading, former Silk Road lands that may play increasingly important roles—think of oil-rich Kazakhstan—in the world's economy." SLJ

Includes bibliographical references

958.1   Afghanistan

Ansary, Mir Tamim

West of Kabul, East of New York; an Afghan American story. Farrar, Straus & Giroux 2002 292p hardcover o.p. pa $13

Grades: 11 12 Adult   **958.1**
   1. Islamic civilization 2. Afghanistan -- Social conditions
   ISBN 0-374-28757-0; 0-312-42151-6 pa

The author, an Afghan American, reflects on his dual heritage. In light of the events of September 11, he focuses particular attention on the relationship between Islam and the West.

"While Ansary's political insights can be detached or perhaps purposefully aloof his descriptions of having lived in and identified alternately with the West and the Islamic world are utterly compelling." Publ Wkly

Guibert, Emmanuel

The **photographer**; [by] Emmanuel Guibert, Didier Lefèvre and Frédéric Lemercier; translated by Alexis Siegel. First Second 2009 267p il map pa $29.95

Grades: 11 12 Adult   **958.1**
   1. Graphic novels 2. Photojournalism -- Graphic novels 3. Médecins Sans Frontières (Organization) -- Graphic novels 4. Afghanistan -- History -- Soviet occupation, 1979-1989 -- Graphic novels
   ISBN 978-1-59643-375-5; 1-59643-375-2

"Originally published as three volumes in France from 2003 to 2006, this graphic novel follows photojournalist Didier Lefèvre during his three months in Pakistan and Afghanistan in 1986 as he documented the medical missions of Doctors without Borders. . . . The graphic novel combines traditional comic art with some of the four thousand photographs Lefevre shot while in Afghanistan. . . . Many images

will stay with readers as both horrifying and glorious. The Afghan children being treated for burns, bullet wounds, and shrapnel are page by page next to the beauty of the Afghan mountainous landscapes. . . . [This book] has a powerful message and images of a part of the world that should be discussed more often." Voice Youth Advocates

Sadeed, Suraya

Forbidden lessons in a Kabul guesthouse; the true story of a woman who risked everything to bring hope to Afghanistan. [by] Suraya Sadeed with Damien Lewis. Voice/Hyperion 2011 280p il $24.99

Grades: 11 12 Adult   **958.1**
   1. Reformers 2. Child benefactors 3. Afghanistan -- Social conditions
   ISBN 978-1-4013-4131-2

                           LC 2010053485

"Sadeed provides insight into the traditional values which still sustain the culture, while making an eloquent appeal for understanding, compassion and aid for the people of Afghanistan, and for more schools in order to educate young people and break the cycle of violence." Kirkus

Wahab, Shaista

★ **A brief** history of Afghanistan; [by] Shaista Wahab and Barry Youngerman. 2nd ed; Facts on File 2010 354p il map (Brief history) $49.50; pa $19.95

Grades: 11 12 Adult   **958.1**
   1. Afghanistan -- History
   ISBN 978-0-8160-8218-6; 978-0-8160-8219-3 pa; 978-1-4381-0819-3 ebook

                           LC 2010-19656

First published 2006

This history of Afghanistan "examines this country's isolation and how it found itself involved in 30 years of war and anarchy. . . . [It] explores the culture and politics of the Pashtun tribes whose homeland extends across much of Afghanistan and northern Pakistan, as well as the Taliban insurgency and the relationship between local leaders and the central government in Kabul." Publisher's note

Includes bibliographical references

Whitehead, Kim

Afghanistan; Revised ed. Mason Crest 2009 112 p. il map (Major Muslim Nations) lib bdg $25.95

Grades: 7 8 9 10   **958.1**
   1. Islam 2. Taliban 3. Afghanistan
   ISBN 9781422214039

This "presents a cogent overview of [Afghanistan]. Excellent-quality photos and reproductions appear throughout." SLJ

958.104   Afghanistan--1919-

Wahab, Saima, 1974-

In my father's country; an Afghan woman defies her fate. Saima Wahab. 1st ed. Crown Publishers 2012 346 p. (hardcover) $25.00; (ebook) $75.00

Grades: 10 11 12 Adult **958.104**
1. Refugees 2. Afghan American women -- Biography 3. Postwar reconstruction -- Afghanistan 4. Women translators -- Afghanistan -- Biography 5. Afghanistan -- Social conditions -- 21st century
ISBN 9780307884947; 9780307884961
LC 2011039456
This is Pashtun refugee Saima Wahab's memoir. At age five, "Wahab began her life on the run after her father was taken from their Kabul home by KGB agents during the Soviet occupation of Afghanistan." Ultimately educated in America, Wahab "was hired by the U.S. military in 2004 to help coordinate efforts in Afghanistan." (Kirkus)

959 Southeast Asia

Phillips, Douglas A.
Southeast Asia; series consulting editor Charles F. Gritzner. Chelsea House Publishers 2006 129p (Modern world cultures) lib bdg $30
Grades: 7 8 9 10 **959**
1. Southeast Asia
ISBN 0-7910-8149-4
This describes the geography, history, people and cultures, politics, economics, and possible future of Southeast Asia.
This "accessible [title is] generously illustrated with colorful photos, maps, and clear charts, graphs, and other statistical data.... Phillips does an excellent job of organizing each topic by providing clear and outlined information. The research is well done, and information and statistics are up to date." SLJ

Southeast Asia; a historical encyclopedia from Angkor Wat to East Timor. edited by Ooi Keat Gin. ABC-CLIO 2004 3v il map set $285
Grades: 11 12 Adult **959**
1. Southeast Asia
ISBN 1-576-07770-5
LC 2004-4813
The countries covered in this book include "Myanmar (Burma), Thailand (Siam), Laos, Cambodia, Vietnam, Malaysia, Singapore, Brunei, the Philippines, Indonesia, and East Timor. This A-Z aims to help students and researchers grasp the fragmented region through 800 detailed articles on archaeology, politics, culture, economic transformation, and more." Libr J
Includes bibliographical references

959.6 Cambodia

Ung, Loung
First they killed my father; a daughter of Cambodia remembers. HarperCollins Pubs. 2000 240p il hardcover o.p. pa $13.95
Grades: 11 12 Adult **959.6**
1. Cambodia -- History -- 1975-
ISBN 0-06-019332-8; 0-06-085626-2 pa
LC 99-34707

The author's father was a "high-ranking government official in Phnom Penh. She was only five when the Khmer Rouge stormed the city and her family was forced to flee. They sought refuge in various camps, hiding their wealth and education, always on the move and ever fearful of being betrayed. After 20 months, Ung's father was taken away, never to be seen again. Her story of starvation, forced labor, beatings, attempted rape, separations, and the deaths of her family members is one of horror and brutality." SLJ

959.704 Vietnam--1945-

★ **America** in Vietnam; a documentary history. edited with commentaries by William Appleman Williams ... [et al.] Norton 1989 345p map pa $17.95
Grades: 11 12 Adult **959.704**
1. Vietnam War, 1961-1975
ISBN 0-393-30555-4
First published 1985 by Anchor Press/Doubleday
In this collection of original essays and documentary sources, historians try to explain the U.S.-Vietnamese War of 1963-75 within the greater context of two centuries of American involvement in Asia.
Includes bibliographical references

★ **Bloods:** an oral history of the Vietnam War by black veterans; [edited by] Wallace Terry. Random House 1984 311p il hardcover o.p. pa $6.99
Grades: 11 12 Adult **959.704**
1. African American soldiers 2. Vietnam War, 1961-1975 -- Personal narratives
ISBN 0-394-53028-4; 0-345-31197-3 pa
LC 83-42775
Black Vietnam War veterans discuss their experiences in battle and stateside.
This is "an intimate overview that often makes the reader stop, sit back, and think about this war that tore at America. . . . The accounts are moving, powerful and offer several views." Voice Youth Advocates
Includes bibliographical references

Everything we had; an oral history of the Vietnam War. by thirty-three American soldiers who fought it; [edited by] Al Santoli. Random House 1981 265p il hardcover o.p. pa $6.99
Grades: 9 10 11 12 **959.704**
1. Veterans 2. Vietnam War, 1961-1975 -- Personal narratives
ISBN 0-394-51269-3; 0-345-32279-7 pa
LC 80-5309
Interviews with 33 veterans assess the impact the Vietnam War has had on their lives.
Includes glossary

Isserman, Maurice
Vietnam War; John S. Bowman, general editor. Rev. ed.; Chelsea House 2010 210p il map (America at war) $45

811

Grades: 9 10 11 12	**959.704**
1. Vietnam War, 1961-1975
ISBN 978-0-8160-8187-5

LC 2009-39184

First published 1992

This history of the Vietnam War includes a "discussion of the roots of U.S. involvement in Indochina in the days just after World War II and goes on to explore the varied and complex motives behind America's effort to halt the spread of communism in Asia. . . . [It] also features a chapter focusing on the innovative military tactics and weaponry involved throughout the conflict." Publisher's note

Includes glossary and bibliographical references

Karnow, Stanley

★ **Vietnam**; a history. 2nd rev & updated ed; Penguin Bks. 1997 768p il maps pa $17.95
Grades: 11 12 Adult	**959.704**
1. Vietnam War, 1961-1975 2. Vietnam -- History
ISBN 0-14-026547-3
First published 1983

A summation "of over two centuries of conflict in Indochina. Chronicling a tragic history, Karnow presents a balanced and sympathetic view of Vietnamese aspirations and the mishaps that led to American involvement in a 'war nobody won.'" Voice Youth Advocates [review of 1983 edition]

Includes bibliographical references

Kovic, Ron

Born on the Fourth of July. Akashic Books 2005 216p pa $14.95
Grades: 9 10 11 12	**959.704**
1. Vietnam War, 1961-1975 -- Personal narratives
ISBN 978-1-88845-178-8; 1-88845-178-5

LC 2004-115734

First published 1976 by McGraw-Hill

The autobiography of a young marine who was physically and emotionally scarred by his experience in Vietnam.

Living through the Vietnam War; edited by Samuel Brenner. Greenhaven Press 2005 142p map (Living through the Cold War) lib bdg $32.45
Grades: 9 10 11 12	**959.704**
1. Vietnam War, 1961-1975 2. United States -- History -- 1961-1974
ISBN 0-7377-2308-4

LC 2003-62477

"This volume discusses how American life was changed and shaped by the longest war in American history. In separate chapters the volume presents the words of the U.S. government, the views of those against the war, the experiences of soldiers and veterans, and the ways in which Vietnam was portrayed in media and popular culture." Publisher's note

Includes bibliographical references

Murray, Stuart

Vietnam War; written by Stuart Murray. DK Pub. 2005 71p il (DK eyewitness books) $15.99; lib bdg $19.99

Grades: 7 8 9 10	**959.704**
1. Vietnam War, 1961-1975
ISBN 0-7566-1166-0; 978-0-7566-1166-8; 0-7566-1165-2 lib bdg; 978-0-7566-1165-1 lib bdg

LC 2004-24516

"Besides identifying major political and military figures from both sides of the conflict, photos and text also document supporters and protesters, as well as the medical workers and civilians caught in the crossfire. Pictures and descriptions of weaponry and machinery will please military buffs, while troubling descriptions of Napalm and Agent Orange expose the grim realities of warfare." Booklist

New York Vietnam Veterans Memorial Commission

★ **Dear** America: letters home from Vietnam; edited by Bernard Edelman for the New York Vietnam Veterans Memorial Commission. Norton 1985 316p il maps hardcover o.p. pa $13.95
Grades: 9 10 11 12	**959.704**
1. Vietnam War, 1961-1975 -- Personal narratives
ISBN 0-393-01998-5; 0-393-32304-8 pa

LC 85-273

"The letters have been intelligently organized to follow a typical tour of duty in Vietnam. . . . Readers will be struck by the variations in attitudes reflected in these letters of the combatants. . . . This is a wonderful book of raw data for the reader to sift through and interpret." Readings

Palmer, Laura

★ **Shrapnel** in the heart; letters and remembrances from the Vietnam Veterans Memorial. Random House 1987 xx, 243p il hardcover o.p. pa $13
Grades: 9 10 11 12	**959.704**
1. Vietnam Veterans Memorial (Washington, D.C.) 2. Vietnam War, 1961-1975 -- Personal narratives
ISBN 0-394-56027-2; 0-394-75988-5 pa

LC 87-42652

"A collection of letters and poems that have been left at the Vietnam Veterans Memorial, with background information on the deceased and the bereaved writers." Booklist

Senker, Cath

The **Vietnam** War; by Cath Senker. Heinemann Library 2012 80 p. ill. (some col.), col. maps (Living through) (library) $36.50; (paperback) $10.99
Grades: 6 7 8 9	**959.704**
1. Vietnam War, 1961-1975
ISBN 1432960008; 9781432960001; 9781432960094

LC 2011015928

In this book on the Vietnam War, part of the "Living Through" series, author "[Cath] Senker begins her story with the French colonization of Southeast Asia and ends it with an analysis of why the war ended the way it did. In between, Senker takes her readers back to a time in American history when policies went awry and the nation imposed terrible destruction on foreign lands and its own people." (Children's Literature)

Includes bibliographical references (p. 76-77) and index

Sheinkin, Steve

★ **Most** dangerous; Steve Sheinkin. Roaring Brook Press 2015 384 p. illustrations, map (hardback) $19.99

Grades: 7 8 9 10 11 12 **959.704**

1. Vietnam War, 1961-1975 2. Pentagon Papers 3. Rand Corporation -- Employees -- Biography

ISBN 1596439521; 9781596439528

LC 2014040761

National Book Award Finalist: Young People's Literature (2015)

Boston Globe Horn Book Nonfiction Award (2016)

YALSA Award for Excellence in Nonfiction for Young Adults (2016)

Author Steve Sheinkin presents this "exploration of . . . how Daniel Ellsberg transformed from obscure government analyst into 'the most dangerous man in America,' and risked everything to expose the government's deceit. [The] book . . . interrogates the meanings of patriotism, freedom, and integrity." (Publisher's note)

"In this thoroughly researched, thoughtfully produced, and beautifully written book, Sheinkin delves into the life of Daniel Ellsberg, former Pentagon consultant and a self-described "cold warrior," who gradually made an about-face with regard to America's presence in Vietnam. . . . A timely and extraordinary addition to every library." SLJ

Includes bibliographical references and index

The **Vietnam** War; Nick Treanor, book editor. Greenhaven Press 2004 234p il map (Interpreting primary documents) hardcover o.p. pa $23.70

Grades: 7 8 9 10 **959.704**

1. Vietnam War, 1961-1975

ISBN 0-7377-2262-2 lib bdg; 0-7377-2263-0 pa

LC 2003-49058

"This anthology presents primary documents tracing the development of American intervention in Southeast Asia from Ho Chi Mingh's 1945 declaration of Vietnamese independence through to the fall of Saigon." Publisher's note

Includes bibliographical references

Young, Marilyn Blatt

★ The **Vietnam** War: a history in documents; [by] Marilyn B. Young, John J. Fitzgerald, A. Tom Grunfeld. Oxford Univ. Press 2002 175p il maps (Pages from history) lib bdg $32.95; pa $19.95

Grades: 7 8 9 10 **959.704**

1. Vietnam War, 1961-1975

ISBN 0-19-512278-X lib bdg; 0-19-516635-3 pa

LC 2001-52338

"The documents are skillfully tied together by brief text that gives good background information. . . . The book is well balanced in showing both sides. . . . Good-quality, black-and-white photos and illustrations are plentiful and informative." SLJ

Includes glossary and bibliographical references

960 History of Africa

★ **Africa:** opposing viewpoints; David M. Haugen, book editor. Gale/Cengage Learning 2008 219p (Opposing viewpoints series) lib bdg $39.70; pa $27.50

Grades: 8 9 10 11 12 **960**

1. Africa -- Social conditions 2. Africa -- Economic conditions 3. Africa -- Politics and government

ISBN 978-0-7377-3988-6 lib bdg; 978-0-7377-3989-3 pa

LC 2008-811

Articles in this anthology discuss important issues facing Africa today, foreign aid and free trade, the status of democracy and human rights in Africa, and ways the United States and other western nations can help Africa.

Includes bibliographical references

Caplan, Gerald L.

The **betrayal** of Africa; [by] Gerald Caplan. Groundwood Books 2008 144p il map (Groundwork guides) $18.95; pa $10

Grades: 9 10 11 12 **960**

1. Africa -- Foreign relations 2. Africa -- Social conditions

ISBN 978-0-88899-824-8; 0-88899-824-4; 978-0-88899-825-5 pa; 0-88899-825-2 pa

LC 2008-411359

Argues that it is the policies of rich Western nations that are responsible for many of Africa's problems, discussing such issues as the large gap between rich and poor, women's rights, health, and education, and advocates change.

"This is ideal for classroom use, as a discussion-starter, or simply an eye-opening introduction to some of the world's greatest mass tragedies." Booklist

Includes bibliographical references

Encyclopedia of African history; Kevin Shillington, editor. Fitzroy Dearborn 2004 3v il map set $395

Grades: 11 12 Adult **960**

1. Reference books 2. Africa -- Encyclopedias

ISBN 1-579-58245-1

LC 2004-16779

"The scope of the coverage encompasses the entire continent, including North Africa, and features all historical periods, with special attention to recent events. Most entries are given 1000 words, though major topics, such as regional surveys, stretch to 3000-4000 words. Topics range from art to anthropology to economics, but emphasis is placed on biographies and country studies, both pre- and postcolonial. . . . Simply put, this is an essential reference resource for students of African history." Libr J

Includes bibliographical references

★ **Encyclopedia** of African history and culture; Willie F. Page, editor. rev ed; Facts on File 2005 5v il map set $425

Grades: 9 10 11 12 Adult **960**
1. Reference books 2. Africa -- Encyclopedias
ISBN 0-8160-5199-2

LC 2004-22929

First published 2001

This set "fulfills its information and education goals and is highly recommended for high-school, public, and academic libraries." Booklist

Includes bibliographical references

Falola, Toyin

Key events in African history; a reference guide. Greenwood Press 2002 xxiii, 347p il maps $64.95; pa $25

Grades: 11 12 Adult **960**
1. Africa -- History
ISBN 0-313-31323-7; 0-313-36122-3 pa

LC 2001-58644

"Falola surveys the . . . history of the African continent by focusing on 36 pivotal events that either caused or led to significant changes and developments in African social, political, and cultural life from around 40,000 B.C.E. to the collapse of apartheid in the 1990s. . . . Following a detailed time line of historical events, each topic is highlighted in an individual chapter including cross-references, historical and political maps, illustrations, a notes section, and a suggested list for further reading." Booklist

Includes bibliographical references

Gates, Henry Louis

Wonders of the African world; [by] Henry Louis Gates, Jr. Knopf 1999 275p il map hardcover o.p. pa $24.95

Grades: 11 12 Adult **960**
1. Africa -- Civilization
ISBN 0-375-40235-7; 0-375-70948-7 pa

LC 99-18496

"Gates writes with concentration and clarity, and anticipates the questions that arise in the wary reader's mind, delivering the answers at just the right time." N Y Times Book Rev

Includes bibliographical references

Habeeb, William Mark

Africa; Facts and Figures. by William Mark Habeeb. Mason Crest Publishers 2012 87 p. ill. (chiefly col.), col. map (The Evolution of Africa's Major Nations) (library) $22.95

Grades: 7 8 9 10 **960**
1. Africa -- History 2. Africa -- Social conditions 3. Africa -- Politics and government 4. Africa
ISBN 1422221768; 9781422221761

LC 2010048000

This book is "[t]he first of a new series, 'Continent in the Balance: Africa,' . . . introduces the continent in all its geographical and cultural diversity. . . . [H]istorian [William Mark] Habeeb discusses the huge contemporary problems in many countries, including poverty and AIDS, and exam-ines how colonialism carved up the continent with arbitrary borders that have resulted in devastating ethnic and religious conflicts that exist even today." (Booklist)

This is an "excellent, detailed overview. . . . The attractive, open design, with clear type, beautiful photos, maps, and lots of extras in lists and insets, manages to pack in an extraordinary amount of information." Booklist

Includes bibliographical references (p. 82-83) and index.

Lefkowitz, Mary R.

Not out of Africa; how Afrocentrism became an excuse to teach myth as history. [by] Mary Lefkowitz. Basic Bks. 1996 222p il map hardcover o.p. pa $19

Grades: 11 12 Adult **960**
1. Africa -- Historiography 2. History -- Study and teaching
ISBN 0-465-09837-1; 0-465-09838-X pa

LC 95-49109

"The book is a case study in historical methods, the value and limits of scholarship, and the preciousness of hard-bitten reason and objectivity. The book is also lucid and accessible." Christ Sci Monit

Includes bibliographical references

Reader, John

Africa: a biography of the continent. Knopf 1998 801p il maps hardcover o.p. pa $18

Grades: 11 12 Adult **960**
1. Africa -- History
ISBN 0-679-40979-3; 0-679-73869-X pa

LC 97-36892

First published 1997 in the United Kingdom

Reader "writes with sweeping historical perspective and an engaging familiarity with the continent and its people." Publ Wkly

Includes bibliographical references

Stewart, John

★ **African** states and rulers; 3rd ed.; McFarland & Co. 2006 423p $115

Grades: 9 10 11 12 **960**
1. Africa -- History
ISBN 0-7864-2562-8; 978-0-7864-2562-4

LC 2006-5823

First published 1989

Arranged alphabetically by the country's official name, each entry gives the country's location, capital, other names, a brief history, and a chronological listing of its rulers and their official titles. Coverage includes contemporary nation-states and ancient tribal kingdoms.

This volume offers "the most in-depth treatment of Africa's changing political boundaries and heads of state." Booklist

Includes bibliographical references

962   Egypt, Sudan, South Sudan

Goldschmidt, Arthur
★ A **brief** history of Egypt. Facts on File 2008 294p il map (Brief history) $45; pa $19.95
Grades: 9 10 11 12 Adult   **962**
1. Egypt -- History
ISBN 978-0-8160-6672-8; 0-8160-6672-8; 978-0-8160-7333-7 pa; 0-8160-7333-3 pa
LC 2007-7374
The author "explores Egypt's broad political, economic, social, and cultural developments, covering roughly 6,000 years of history." Publisher's note
Includes glossary and bibliographical references

962.4   Sudan and South Sudan

Childress, Diana
Omar al-Bashir's Sudan. Twenty-First Century Books 2010 160p il map (Dictatorships) lib bdg $38.60
Grades: 10 11 12   **962.4**
1. Generals 2. Heads of state 3. Sudan
ISBN 978-0-8225-9096-5
LC 2008-53931
"Bashir took control of Sudan in a 1989 coup and has been working to establish an Islamist state throughout the country, a movement that began in the late 1970s. The imposition of Sharia law onto the largely non-Muslim south escalated tensions, and the south waged a civil war that lasted until 2002. Altogether, this is a useful and up-to-date look at an ongoing dictatorship. . . . Photographs are well chosen, and sidebars give readers some background on issues such as Islamism, Sharia, and the Lost Boys of Sudan." SLJ
Includes glossary and bibliographical references

The **crisis** in Darfur; Jeff Hay, book editor. Greenhaven Press 2011 165p il map (Perspectives on modern world history) $39.70
Grades: 8 9 10 11 12   **962.4**
1. Sudan -- History -- Darfur conflict, 2003-
ISBN 978-0-7377-5257-1; 0-7377-5257-2
LC 2010033168
In discussing "the continuing human tragedy in Darfur, [this] well-organized [volume presents] a wealth of clearly written analyses from a rich variety of viewpoints. With the inclusion of historical background, firsthand experiences, and discussions of particular points of controversy, [it helps] to familiarize readers with the [topic] . . . and [serves] as [an exercise] in the development of analytical thinking skills." SLJ
Includes bibliographical references

Dau, John Bul
Lost boy, lost girl; escaping civil war in Sudan. by John Bul Dau and Martha Arual Akech; with Michael Sweeney and K. M. Kostyal. National Geographic 2010 159p il map $15.95; lib bdg $23.90
Grades: 7 8 9 10   **962.4**
1. Refugees 2. Sudan -- History -- Civil War, 1983-

2005
ISBN 978-1-4263-0708-9; 1-4263-0708-X; 978-1-4263-0709-6 lib bdg; 1-4263-0709-8 lib bdg
LC 2010-17960
"The tragic story of Sudan's Lost Boys and Lost [Girls] is told in simple language by two survivors. . . . In 1987, when Dau was 13 and Akech was 6, war came to their village. Both traveled hundreds of miles to a UN refugee camp in Ethiopia. After a few years of safety, the refugees were forced to move again. . . . Teens who know little about Sudan and its problems will be drawn into this moving, inspiration story." SLJ

Deng, Benson
They poured fire on us from the sky; the true story of three lost boys from Sudan. [by] Benson Deng, Alephonsion Deng, Benjamin Ajak; with Judy Bernstein. Public Affairs 2005 xxiii, 311p map hardcover o.p. pa $13.95
Grades: 11 12 Adult   **962.4**
1. Refugees 2. Sudan
ISBN 1-58648-269-6; 1-58648-388-9 pa
LC 2005-42566
"This collection is moving in its depictions of unbelievable courage." Publ Wkly

963   Ethiopia and Eritrea

Mezlekia, Nega
Notes from the Hyena's belly; an Ethiopian boyhood. Picador 2001 351p il map hardcover o.p. pa $14
Grades: 9 10 11 12   **963**
1. Ethiopia
ISBN 0-312-26988-9; 0-312-28914-6 pa
LC 00-50126
First published 2000 by Penguin
"Full of adventure, political struggle, and intrigue [this] memoir works as a coming-of-age story as well as a glimpse into a world of political corruption and change that Westerners rarely get to know so intimately." Libr J

965   Algeria

Wagner, Heather Lehr
The **Algerian** war; by Heather Lehr Wagner. Chelsea House 2012 120 p. (Milestones in modern world history) (hardcover) $35
Grades: 7 8 9 10 11 12   **965**
1. France -- Foreign relations -- Algeria 2. Algeria -- History -- 1954-1962, Revolution 3. France -- Colonies -- Africa -- History 4. National liberation movements -- Algeria
ISBN 1604139234; 9781604139235
LC 2011023060
This book, part of the Milestones in Modern World History series, "opens with a triumphant France celebrating its freedom at the end of WWII while citizens of its colony, Algeria, were denied their own equality and freedom. Fol-

lowing an overview of Algerian possession, the text outlines French injustices toward Algeria, most notably discrimination of its Muslim population and the rise of revolution." (Booklist)

Includes bibliographical references and index

966.3 Senegal

Molloy, Aimee

However Long the Night; One American Woman's Journey to Help Millions of African Women and Girls Triumph. Aimee Molloy. HarperCollins 2013 272 p. $25.99

Grades: 10 11 12   **966.3**
  1. Americans -- Africa 2. Humanitarians -- Biography 3. Human rights -- Africa 4. Community education -- Africa 5. Human rights workers -- Africa 6. Tostan (Organization: Senegal) 7. Non-governmental organizations -- Africa 8. Female circumcision -- Africa -- Prevention
  ISBN 0062132768; 9780062132765
                                              LC 2012048654
Amelia Bloomer Project (2014)

In this book, author "Aimee Molloy tells the unlikely and inspiring story of Molly Melching, an American woman whose experience as an exchange student in Senegal led her to found Tostan and dedicate almost four decades of her life to the girls and women of Africa. This moving biography details Melching's beginnings at the University of Dakar and follows her journey of 40 years in Africa, where she became a social entrepreneur." (Publisher's note)

"Molloy offers a moving account of one woman's struggle to empower African women and challenge tradition. Molly Melching, founder of the NGO Tostan in Senegal, went from a quiet life in small-town Illinois to running an educational organization that has had remarkable success in ending the practice of female genital cutting (FGC). ...Reading like a novel, this book demonstrates the power of education and grassroots organizing." (Publishers Weekly)

966.7 Ghana

Weatherly, Myra

Teens in Ghana. Compass Point Books 2008 96p il map (Global connections) lib bdg $33.26
Grades: 7 8 9 10   **966.7**
  1. Teenagers 2. Ghana
  ISBN 978-0-7565-3417-2; 0-7565-3417-8
                                              LC 2007-33086
Uncovers the challenges, pastimes, customs and culture of teens in Ghana

"Color photographs of native teens enliven the text and help reinforce the connection between reader and subject matter. . . . Religion is discussed, as well as technology, government, and social roles and expectations. . . . [This] would be a wonderful addition to any library." Voice Youth Advocates

Includes bibliographical references

966.9 Nigeria

Walker, Ida

  ★ **Nigeria**; Ida Walker. Mason Crest Publishers 2013 79 p. (hardcover: alk. paper) $22.95
Grades: 5 6 7 8 9 10 11   **966.9**
  1. Nigeria
  ISBN 1422222004; 9781422222003; 9781422222287; 9781422294406
                                              LC 2010047767
This book, by Ida Walker, focuses on the country of Nigeria. "With a population of more than 133 million people, Nigeria is Africa's most populous country. Military leaders have ruled Nigeria for much of its history as an independent country, and it was not until 1999 that a civilian government was restored. However, this has not ensured peace. . . . Although Nigeria controls great reserves of oil, and is one of the largest exporters of oil to the United States, most Nigerians are very poor." (Publisher's note)

"This series is a needed collection for high school media centers. It fills a void by supplying up-to-date books on African countries that incorporates both an historical and modern perspective. Each book covers the land, government, economy, culture, people, religion, holidays, and festivals... These books will be useful for researchers and browsers alike." (Library Media Connection)

Includes bibliographical references and index

967 Central Africa and offshore islands

Davidson, Basil

  ★ The **African** slave trade; rev and expanded ed; Little, Brown 1980 304p il maps hardcover o.p. pa $19.99
Grades: 11 12 Adult   **967**
  1. Slave trade 2. Central Africa -- History
  ISBN 0-316-17439-4; 0-316-17438-6 pa
                                              LC 81-65588
First published 1961 with title: Black mother

An account of the slave trade and its impact on West African society.

Includes bibliographical references

Oppong, Joseph R.

Africa South of the Sahara; series consulting editor Charles F. Gritzner. Chelsea House Publishers 2006 124p il map (Modern world cultures) lib bdg $30
Grades: 6 7 8 9 10   **967**
  1. Sub-Saharan Africa
  ISBN 0-7910-8146-X
This describes the physical and historical geography, population and settlement, cultures, politics, and economy of sub-Saharan Africa.

This "accessible [title is] generously illustrated with colorful photos, maps, and clear charts, graphs, and other statistical data." SLJ

967.571   Rwanda

Gourevitch, Philip

We wish to inform you that tomorrow we will be killed with our families; stories from Rwanda. Farrar, Straus & Giroux 1998 355p hardcover o.p. pa $15

Grades: 11 12 Adult   967.571

1. Genocide 2. Rwanda -- Politics and government
ISBN 0-374-28697-3; 0-312-24335-9 pa

LC 98-22132

This work is "readable and moving, Gourevitch is an impassioned and thoughtful observer. But this is not a work that gives much pleasure or comfort. Nor are its arguments fool-proof, its evidence complete, or its documentation thorough. . . . Still Gourevitch does struggle to come close to a great mystery of evil, and he makes us attend to great crimes." Commonweal

Hatzfeld, Jean

Machete season; the killers in Rwanda speak: a report. translated from the French by Linda Coverdale; preface by Susan Sontag. Farrar, Straus and Giroux 2005 253p il maps hardcover o.p. pa $14

Grades: 11 12 Adult   967.571

1. Genocide 2. Hutu (African people) 3. Tutsi (African people) 4. Rwanda
ISBN 0-374-28082-7; 0-312-42503-1 pa

LC 2004-61600

Original French edition, 2003

"Steering clear of politics, this important book succeeds in offering the reader some grasp of how such unspeakable acts unfolded." Publ Wkly

Kinzer, Stephen

A thousand hills; Rwanda's rebirth and the man who dreamed it. John Wiley & Sons 2008 380p il map $25.95

Grades: 11 12 Adult   967.571

1. Genocide 2. Guerrillas 3. Presidents 4. Rwanda 5. Revolutionaries 6. Political leaders 7. Presidents -- Rwanda
ISBN 978-0-470-12015-6

LC 2007041613

This book "is a balanced look at how one man's doctrine of self-reliance has made his impoverished, decimated country a potential model for the rest of Africa. . . . [The author] comes closer than any other journalist yet to capturing the energy, will, self-discipline—and anger—that brought Rwanda back to life." Washington Monthly

Includes bibliographical references

Nardo, Don

The Rwandan genocide; by Don Nardo. Lucent Books 2011 104 p. ill. (hardcover) $34.95

Grades: 6 7 8 9   967.571

1. Genocide 2. Ethnic relations 3. Rwanda -- History 4. Rwanda -- History -- Civil War, 1994
ISBN 142050567X; 9781420505672

LC 2010039533

This book by Don Nardo is part of the World History series and looks at the Rwandan Genocide. The series "examines the eras, events, civilizations, and movements that have shaped human history, providing readers with insight into the past and its many legacies." Photographs, timelines, sidebars, and annotated bibliographies are included. (Publisher's note)

Includes bibliographical references and index.

The Rwandan genocide; Alexander Cruden, book editor. Greenhaven Press 2010 227p il map (Perspectives on modern world history) $39.70

Grades: 9 10 11 12   967.571

1. Genocide 2. Rwanda
ISBN 978-0-7377-5007-2

LC 2010-10290

"Following an introduction to the subject, various articles, primary sources, speeches, and other documents provide perspectives on how this tragedy unfolded, who was affected, and what was done to either stop the genocide or allow it flourish. Students will find a wealth of information on what actually happened during this dark time in Rwanda, as well as how the genocide was treated by the international community and how people and organizations caught up in the event responded. . . . An informative addition to any collection." SLJ

Includes bibliographical references

967.62   Kenya

Lemasolai-Lekuton, Joseph

Facing the lion; growing up Maasai on the African savanna. by Joseph Lekuton with Herman Viola. National Geographic Soc. 2003 127p il map $15.95

Grades: 7 8 9 10 11 12   967.62

1. Masai (African people) 2. Kenya 3. Authors 4. Teachers 5. Memoirists
ISBN 0-7922-5125-3

LC 2003-750

A member of the Masai people describes his life as he grew up in a northern Kenya village, travelled to America to attend college, and became an elementary school teacher in Virginia

"Lekuton's story touches a universal chord, and shows readers the beauty of another culture from the inside. Simple and direct enough for reluctant readers, and written in a conversational and occasionally wryly humorous style, this book will be enjoyed by a wide range of readers." SLJ

968   Republic of South Africa and neighboring southern African countries

Downing, David

Apartheid in South Africa; [by] David Downing. Heinemann Library 2004 56p il $31.36

Grades: 7 8 9 10   968

1. Apartheid 2. South Africa -- Race relations
ISBN 1-4034-4870-1; 9780431170619

LC 2003-18235

"This dense volume is an excellent narrative overview of the apartheid struggle, drawing extensively on primary sources that provide depth, detail, drama, and authenticity." Booklist

Thompson, Leonard Monteath

A **history** of South Africa; {by} Leonard Thompson. 3rd ed; Yale Univ. Press 2001 xxiv, 358p il maps pa $17.95

Grades: 9 10 11 12   **968**

1. South Africa -- History 2. South Africa -- Race relations

ISBN 0-300-08776-4

LC 00-32101

First published 1990

This "exploration of South Africa's history—from the earliest known human settlement of the region to the present—focuses primarily on the experiences of its black inhabitants, rather than on those of its white minority." Publisher's note

Includes bibliographical references and index

968.06   South Africa--Period as Republic, 1961-

Biko, Stephen

I write what I like; selected writings. edited with a personal memoir by Aelred Stubbs; preface by Archbishop Desmond Tutu; introduction by Malusi and Thoko Mpumlwana; with a new foreword by Lewis R. Gordon. University of Chicago Press 2002 xxxiii, 216p pa $17

Grades: 9 10 11 12   **968.06**

1. South Africa -- Race relations 2. South Africa -- Politics and government

ISBN 0-226-04897-7

LC 2002-23951

First published 1978 in the United Kingdom

"Readers will find [Biko's] essential humaneness, intelligence, and lack of malice as impressive as his eloquence and compelling arguments." Libr J

Carlin, John

Playing the enemy; Nelson Mandela and the game that made a nation. Penguin 2008 274p il $24.95

Grades: 11 12 Adult   **968.06**

1. Presidents 2. Rugby football 3. Political prisoners 4. Political leaders 5. Human rights activists 6. Nobel laureates for peace

ISBN 978-1-59420-174-5; 1-59420-174-9

LC 2008-298721

"Deftly sketched characters make up both an audience for the big game and a gallery of South Africa, through which Carlin will recount the absorbing story of a country emerging from its cruelly absurd racist experiment." N Y Times Book Rev

Includes bibliographical references

Finnegan, William

Crossing the line; a year in the land of apartheid. Persea Books 2006 434p map pa $20

Grades: 9 10 11 12   **968.06**

1. Discrimination in education 2. High schools -- South Africa 3. South Africa -- Race relations

ISBN 0-89255-325-1

LC 2006-47648

First published 1986 by Harper & Row

The author, an American school teacher, recalls his experiences in the segregated black schools of South Africa.

Gaines, Ann

★ **Nelson** Mandela and apartheid in world history; {by} Ann Graham Gaines. Enslow Pubs. 2001 128p il maps (In world history) $20.95

Grades: 9 10 11 12   **968.06**

1. Presidents 2. Political prisoners 3. Political leaders 4. Human rights activists 5. Nobel laureates for peace 6. South Africa -- Race relations 7. South Africa -- Politics and government

ISBN 0-7660-1463-0

LC 00-10369

This biography of the Nobel Peace Prize laureate "does a fine job of integrating Mandela's personal story with an overview of early South African history and the rise and fall of apartheid." Booklist

Includes bibliographical references

Mandela, Nelson

★ **Mandela**; an illustrated autobiography. Little, Brown 1996 208p il map $29.95

Grades: 11 12 Adult   **968.06**

1. Presidents 2. Political prisoners 3. Political leaders 4. Human rights activists 5. Nobel laureates for peace 6. South Africa -- Race relations 7. South Africa -- Politics and government

ISBN 0-316-55038-8

LC 96-77497

"The photos, from a variety of archives and journalistic sources, ably illustrate Mandela and, even more so, the South Africa around him." Libr J

★ **Nelson** Mandela speaks; forging a democratic nonracial South Africa. Pathfinder Press 1993 296p il map hardcover o.p. pa $18.95

Grades: 11 12 Adult   **968.06**

1. Apartheid 2. African National Congress 3. South Africa -- Politics and government

ISBN 0-87348-775-3 lib bdg; 0-87348-774-5 pa

LC 93-85689

In this volume "the South African leader's significant speeches, letters, and interviews from the period since his February 1990 release from prison are brought together. . . . [The editor] provides a useful glossary and chronology of the 1990-93 period, and supplies a brief introduction to each entry." Booklist

Sonneborn, Liz

The **end** of apartheid in South Africa. Chelsea House Publishers 2010 120p il (Milestones in modern world history) lib bdg $35

Grades: 8 9 10 11 12   **968.06**

   1. Apartheid 2. Anti-apartheid movement 3. South Africa -- Race relations

   ISBN 978-1-60413-409-4; 1-60413-409-7

                    LC 2008-54805

This is "an excellent in-depth overview, one of the best on the subject, with chapters on the early history before the establishment of the apartheid regime and with profiles of many important leaders (not just Nelson Mandela), as well as clear discussion of present-day politics, the role of the Truth and Reconciliation Commission, and the ongoing inequality. Never simplistic, it is an outstanding overview for teens new to the subject; for those who know something of the history, it fills in the big picture with depth and detail about both leaders and ordinary people, what has changed, and how much still needs to be done." Booklist

Includes bibliographical references

968.91   Zimbabwe

Arnold, James R.

Robert Mugabe's Zimbabwe; by James R. Arnold and Roberta Wiener. Twenty-First Century Books 2008 160p (Dictatorships) lib bdg $38.60

Grades: 7 8 9 10   **968.91**

   1. Presidents 2. Prime ministers 3. Zimbabwe

   ISBN 978-0-8225-7283-1

                    LC 2006-100765

This history of Zimbabwe under the dictatorship of Robert Mugabe gives "students a glimpse into the repression and daily struggle for survival under [this] brutal [government]." SLJ

Includes glossary and bibliographical references

970.004   North American native peoples

Ball, Dewi Ioan

★ **Competing** voices from native America; [by] Dewi Ioan Ball and Joy Porter. Greenwood Press 2009 445p (Fighting words) $65

Grades: 10 11 12   **970.004**

   1. Reference books 2. Native Americans -- History

   ISBN 978-1-84645-016-7

                    LC 2008-45342

"This volume of 'competing voices' is not limited to commentary on Native first encounters with Europeans, removal, and Manifest Destiny. It also traces the dynamic courses of relations between Native Americans and both the state and federal governments to the present day. . . . Whether discussing Pontiac's Rebellion or the 1977 trial of Leonard Peltier, these documents are sure to inspire debate among advanced students." SLJ

Includes bibliographical references

Bowes, John P.

The **Trail** of Tears; removal in the south. Chelsea House 2007 128p il map (Landmark events in Native American history) $35

Grades: 7 8 9 10   **970.004**

   1. Cherokee Indians 2. Native Americans -- Relocation

   ISBN 978-0-7910-9345-0; 0-7910-9345-X

                    LC 2006-102274

"This volume brings a difficult viewpoint to this historical event—that of the Indians involved. This 13- to 17-page chapters thoroughly describe the background of the Trail of Tears, its legal aspects, the development of the Cherokee Nations, the treaties and their effects, the horrors of the Trail itself, and the aftermath for the Indians as a people and a nation. It is well written and readable for students." Libr Media Connect

Includes bibliographical references

Brown, Dee Alexander

★ **Bury** my heart at Wounded Knee; an Indian history of the American West. [by] Dee Brown. Thirtieth anniversary ed; Holt & Co. 2001 487p il hardcover o.p. pa $16

Grades: 8 9 10 11 12 Adult   **970.004**

   1. Generals 2. Indian chiefs 3. Civil engineers 4. Government officials 5. West (U.S.) -- History 6. Native Americans -- Wars 7. Native Americans -- West (U.S.)

   ISBN 0-8050-6634-9; 0-8050-6669-1 pa

                    LC 00-40958

First published 1970

This is an account of the experience of the American Indian during the white man's expansion westward.

Includes bibliographical references

Bruchac, Joseph

★ **Our** stories remember; American Indian history, culture, & values through storytelling. Fulcrum 2003 192p map pa $16.95

Grades: 11 12 Adult   **970.004**

   1. Storytelling 2. Native Americans -- History

   ISBN 1-555-91129-3

                    LC 2002-151236

"This important volume includes a wealth of traditional stories and solid information." SLJ

Includes bibliographical references

Crow Dog, Leonard

Crow Dog; four generations of Sioux medicine men. [by] Leonard Crow Dog and Richard Erdoes. HarperCollins Pubs. 1995 243p il hardcover o.p. pa $13

Grades: 11 12 Adult   **970.004**

   1. Dakota Indians 2. American Indian Movement

   ISBN 0-06-016861-7; 0-06-092682-1 pa

                    LC 94-40695

Erdoes has recorded Leonard Crow Dog's oral narrative of the history of his family and his people, the Lakota. Mr. Crow Dog discusses "the generations of his family who have carried the name Crow Dog since the American government told them it would be their family name. . . . He tells of his involvement as the spiritual leader of the American Indian Movement and the occupation of Wounded Knee in the early 1970's." Booklist

★ **Encyclopedia** of Native American wars and warfare; general editors, William B. Kessel, Robert Wooster. Facts on File 2005 398p il map $75; pa $21.95

Grades: 7 8 9 10   **970.004**

1. Reference books 2. Native Americans -- Wars -- Encyclopedias

ISBN 0-8160-3337-4; 0-8160-6430-X pa

LC 00-56200

"This encyclopedia offers readers a wide range of information about Native American history in North America after 1492." Choice

Includes bibliographical references

Frazier, Ian

On the rez. Farrar, Straus & Giroux 2000 311p il hardcover o.p. pa $14

Grades: 11 12 Adult   **970.004**

1. Oglala Indians 2. Pine Ridge Indian Reservation (S.D.)

ISBN 0-374-22638-5; 0-312-27859-4 pa

LC 99-28353

Frazier discusses the history of the Oglala Sioux and the Indians that he met on the Pine Ridge Reservation in South Dakota, including his friend Le War Lance

"As Frazier serendipitously shuttles his narrative between Pine Ridge visits and snippets of Indian history, a fascinating picture emerges of a people struggling with the consequences of old wrongs and human orneriness." Time

★ **From** the heart; voices of the American Indian. edited and with narrative by Lee Miller. Knopf 1995 405p il hardcover o.p. pa $16

Grades: 11 12 Adult   **970.004**

1. Native Americans

ISBN 0-679-43549-2; 0-679-76891-2 pa

LC 94-28492

An anthology of excerpts from speeches by Native Americans from the 16th to the 19th centuries.

"Arranged by region and chronology, these extraordinarily moving extracts are placed into appropriate historical context by Miller's descriptive narrative. In addition, pertinent quotations of non-Indian witnesses are also included. A haunting and eloquent anthology." Booklist

Includes bibliographical references

Jastrzembski, Joseph C.

The **Apache** wars; the final resistance. Chelsea House Publishers 2007 133p il map (Landmark events in Native American history) lib bdg $35

Grades: 7 8 9 10   **970.004**

1. Apache Indians

ISBN 978-0-7910-9343-6; 0-7910-9343-3

LC 2007-990

This account features "lively writing and direct quotes, and [is] enhanced by many color and black-and-white photos, drawings, and illustrations." SLJ

Includes bibliographical references

Johansen, Bruce E.

★ The **Native** peoples of North America; a history. Praeger 2005 2v il set $99.95

Grades: 11 12 Adult   **970.004**

1. Native Americans -- History

ISBN 0-275-98159-2

LC 2004-28732

This is a history of "cultures indigenous to North America from their earliest origins to the present. . . . Encompassing not only traditional historical records but also oral histories and biographical sketches, these two volumes will undoubtedly become an integral part of Native American history, an increasingly popular field." Booklist

Includes bibliographical references

Johnson, Michael

Encyclopedia of native tribes of North America; color plates by Richard Hook. 3rd ed; Firefly Books 2007 320p il map $49.95

Grades: 11 12 Adult   **970.004**

1. Reference books 2. Native Americans -- Encyclopedias

ISBN 978-1-55407-307-8; 1-55407-307-3

First published 1993 in the United Kingdom with title: The native tribes of North America

"The volume is organized into ten regionally based culture areas (Northwestern Woodlands, Southeastern Woodlands, Plains and Prairie, Plateau, Great Basin, California, Southwest, Northwest Coast, Subarctic, and Arctic); each area is introduced with general information on language, subsistence, religion, culture, and history. . . . The rich illustrations and supplemental sections make this volume worthwhile." Choice

Includes bibliographical references

Josephy, Alvin M.

America in 1492; the world of the Indian peoples before the arrival of Columbus. edited and with an introduction by Alvin Josephy, Jr.; developed by Frederick E. Hoxie. Knopf 1992 477p il maps hardcover o.p. pa $20

Grades: 11 12 Adult   **970.004**

1. America -- Antiquities 2. America -- Exploration 3. Native Americans -- History 4. Native Americans -- Antiquities

ISBN 0-394-56438-3; 0-679-74337-5 pa

LC 90-26222

These essays depict "the diverse lives of the approximately 75 million people living in the Americas around the turn of the fifteenth century. Geography guides the first section. . . . Another section focuses on languages, spiritual beliefs and customs, art, and 'systems of knowledge.'" Booklist

Includes bibliographical references

Keenan, Jerry

Encyclopedia of American Indian wars, 1492-1890. ABC-CLIO 1997 278p il $65

Grades: 11 12 Adult   **970.004**

1. Reference books 2. Native Americans -- Wars -- Encyclopedias

ISBN 0-87436-796-4

LC 97-13841

"In over 450 separate entries (people, places, battles, terms); Keenan gives . . . coverage of most of the major elements in the 400-year struggle between the native peoples of the United States and the invading immigrants." Book Rep

Nardo, Don

The Native Americans. Lucent Bks. 2003 112p il maps (History of weapons and warfare) $27.45

Grades: 7 8 9 10   **970.004**

1. Military art and science 2. Native Americans -- Wars

ISBN 1-59018-070-4

LC 2002-8589

Discusses the weapons used by Native Americans and their different means of warfare.

Includes glossary and bibliographical references

National Museum of the American Indian (U.S.)

Do all Indians live in tipis? questions and answers. from the National Museum of the American Indian; foreword by Rick West; introduction by Wilma Mankiller. Collins, in association with the National Museum of the American Indian, Smithsonian Institution 2007 239p il pa $14.95

Grades: 8 9 10 11 12   **970.004**

1. Native Americans

ISBN 978-0-06-115301-3; 0-06-115301-X

LC 2007-60874

"This highly accessible and informative book aims to dispel some of the major myths and stereotypes still surrounding Native people in the United States and Canada. . . . The straightforward questions were compiled from actual phone calls, emails, letters, and in-person visits to the George Gustav Heye Center in New York, a major branch of the National Museum of the American Indian. The Native American writers who answered them did so concisely with hints of humor and an abundance of research and experience. . . . This is a topnotch resource for both people just learning about Native American cultures and those who think they know the facts." SLJ

Native universe; voices of Indian America. Gerald McMaster and Clifford E. Trafzer, editors. National Geographic Society 2004 320p il hardcover o.p. pa $22

Grades: 9 10 11 12   **970.004**

1. Native Americans -- Social life and customs

ISBN 0-7922-5994-7; 1-4262-0335-7 pa

LC 2004-40221

"Published in conjunction with the fall 2004 opening of the Smithsonian's new National Museum of the American Indian, this . . . book is an overview of the diverse cultures of the American Indian. . . . The text is primarily essays, but also includes some poetry and even a scene from the screen-

play, 'Smoke Signals.' The book is organized in sections that reflect the opening exhibits of the museum: Our Universes (spiritual beliefs and rituals); Our Peoples (key events in the history of Native America); and Our Lives (views of contemporary Native American life). . . . The strength of this book lies in the over 300 beautiful color illustrations, most of which are artifacts from the museum's vast collection. . . . Readers will gain much from simply browsing." Libr Media Connect

Includes bibliographical references

Philip, Neil

The great circle; a history of the First Nations. foreword by Dennis Hastings. Clarion Books 2006 153p il map $25

Grades: 7 8 9 10 11 12 Adult   **970.004**

1. Native Americans

ISBN 978-0-618-15941-3; 0-618-15941-X

LC 2005032743

"Philip takes on a huge challenge here: to present a unified narrative that explains the complex and confrontational relationships between Native Americans and white settlers. . . . He pulls it off, however, thanks to solid research, an engaging writing style, and a talent for making individual stories serve the whole. . . . Top marks, too, for the volume's photographs and historical renderings, which so intensely illustrate the pages." Booklist

Includes bibliographical references

Roberts, David

In search of the old ones; exploring the Anasazi world of the Southwest. Simon & Schuster 1996 271p il map hardcover o.p. pa $14

Grades: 11 12 Adult   **970.004**

1. Pueblo Indians 2. Native Americans -- Antiquities

ISBN 0-684-81078-6; 0-684-83212-7 pa

LC 95-46218

Roberts "chronicles the search for clues to the mystery of the Anasazi's abandonment of their extraordinary cliff dwellings some 700 years ago. Roberts blends accounts of his hiking adventures in the glorious canyon country of the Southwest with a chronicle of Anglos of the nineteenth century who shared his passion for studying the elusive Anasazi, especially the cowboy-archaeologist Richard Wetherell." Booklist

Includes bibliographical references

Treuer, Anton

★ Indian nations of North America; [by] Anton Treuer ... [et al.]; foreword by Herman Viola. National Geographic 2010 384p il map $40

Grades: 9 10 11 12 Adult   **970.004**

1. Reference books 2. Native Americans

ISBN 978-1-4262-0664-1

LC 2010-26728

The authors "examine important historical events for Indian tribes, identify contributions made by tribal leaders, and summarize contemporary cultural activities for native cultures of North America north of the Mexican border. . . . With its extensive coverage of native tribes and outstanding graphics, this . . . title should appeal to individuals interested

in Native American history, anthropology, and ethnic relations." Libr J

Includes bibliographical references

★ **Voices** from the Trail of Tears; edited by Vicki
Rozema. Blair 2003 240p il maps (Real voices,
real history series) pa $11.95
Grades: 9 10 11 12   **970.004**
1. Cherokee Indians
ISBN 0-89587-271-4

LC 2002-15299

Rozema "uses a variety of primary sources, including
eyewitness accounts, to recount . . . [the Cherokees'] sad
fate, climaxed by a forced march to Oklahoma during which
thousands died. Missionaries write outraged letters describing the mistreatment of Cherokees by white opportunists and
government officials. Ordinary soldiers charged with roust-
ing families from their homes describe the suffering of victims. This compilation is often stunning and heartbreaking in
its impact." Booklist

Includes bibliographical references

Zimmerman, Larry J.

Exploring the life, myth, and art of Native Americans. Rosen Pub. 2009 144p il map (Civilizations
of the world) lib bdg $29.95
Grades: 7 8 9 10 11 12   **970.004**
1. Native Americans -- Art 2. Native Americans --
Religion
ISBN 978-1-4358-5614-1; 1-4358-5614-7

LC 2009-9268

This book describes the cultures, myths, and art of
Native Americans.

"This beautifully illustrated and well-written [title] . . .
is perfect for those assignments where students must look
at the culture of a civilization. Artwork and pictures blend
seamlessly with the information and the reader is taken on
a journey of discovery. Myths are used as the story of how
the people view themselves, blended with the discussion of
the reality of life. Everyday life is tied to the belief systems
and is explained in light of those beliefs. The pictures are
beautifully done and there is almost as much information
in the captions as there is in the text." Libr Media Connect

Includes glossary and bibliographical references

970.01   North America--Early history to 1599

Mann, Charles C.

1491; new revelations of the Americas before Co-
lumbus. Knopf 2005 465p il maps
Grades: 11 12 Adult   **970.01**
1. America -- Antiquities 2. Native Americans --
History
ISBN 1-4000-3205-9 pa; 1-4000-4006-X

LC 2005-42178

This is a portrait "of the Americas before the arrival of
the Europeans in 1492." (Publisher's note) Index.

"Mann navigates adroitly through the controversies. He
approaches each in the best scientific tradition, carefully sift-
ing the evidence, never jumping to hasty conclusions, giving
everyone a fair hearing—the experts and the amateurs; the

accounts of the Indians and their conquerors. And rarely is
he less than enthralling." N Y Times Book Rev

Includes bibliographical references

National Museum of Natural History (U.S.)

★ **Vikings**: the North Atlantic saga; edited by
William W. Fitzhugh and Elisabeth I. Ward. Smithsonian Institution Press 2000 432p il maps hardcover
o.p. pa $34.95
Grades: 11 12 Adult   **970.01**
1. Vikings 2. America -- Exploration
ISBN 1-56098-970-X; 1-56098-995-5 pa

LC 99-57983

This book is "well designed, heavily illustrated and almost encyclopedic in scope and detail." Publ Wkly

Includes bibliographical references

Owsley, Douglas W.

★ **Their** skeletons speak; Kennewick man and
the Paleoamerican world. by Sally M. Walker and
Douglas W. Owsley. Carolrhoda Books 2012 136 p.
(lib. bdg.: alk. paper) $22.95
Grades: 8 9 10 11 12   **970.01**
1. Kennewick Man 2. Paleo-Indians 3. Human remains
(Archeology)   4.   Washington (State) -- Antiquities
5. Paleo-Indians -- Washington (State) -- Origin 6.
Human remains (Archaeology) -- Washington (State) 7.
Paleo-Indians -- Anthropometry -- Washington (State)
8. Indians of North America -- Washington (State) --
Antiquities
ISBN 0761374574; 9780761374572

LC 2011051329

This book by Sally M. Walker and Douglas W. Owsley
presents a "detailed study of the discovery and forensic evaluation of the skeleton dubbed 'Kennewick Man.' . . . From
his accidental discovery in 1996 through multiple examinations by scientists with ever-improving forensic tools . . . an
actual human being emerges from a time long gone, speaking to us through his bones. . . . A final facial reconstruction leaves readers face-to-face with a real person." (School
Library Journal)

Includes bibliographical references and index.

970.1   North American native peoples

Ellis, Deborah

Looks Like Daylight; Voices of Indigenous Kids.
by Deborah Ellis, with a foreword by Loriene Roy.
Pgw 2013 256 p. $15.95
Grades: 6 7 8 9 10 11 12   **970.1**
1. Interviews 2. Native American children
ISBN 1554981204; 9781554981205

This book, by Deborah Ellis, "is a . . . collection of interviews with [native] children aged nine to eighteen. They
come from all over the continent, from Iqaluit to Texas,
Haida Gwaii to North Carolina. . . . Many of these children are living with the legacy of the residential schools;
many have lived through the cycle of foster care. Many others have found something in their roots that sustains them,

have found their place in the arts, the sciences, athletics." (Publisher's note)

"In this cultural undertaking, Ellis interviews Native American and aboriginal children and teens, ages nine to eighteen. Whether heartwrenching or uplifting, each first-person narrative is compelling, insightful, and incredibly moving. Introductory matter sheds painful light on the historically horrific treatment of North America's indigenous peoples, as well as the challenges they face still. An extensive list of charitable and informational organizations is appended." (Horn Book)

971 Canada

Riendeau, Roger E.

★ A **brief** history of Canada; [by] Roger Riendeau. 2nd ed; Facts on File 2007 444p il map (Brief history) $45

Grades: 11 12 Adult   **971**

   1. Canada -- History

   ISBN 978-0-8160-6335-2

            LC 2006-47130

First published 2000

This is a history of Canada "beginning with the exploration of the Northern American frontier and continuing through the rise and fall of the French and British empires to the foundations of Canadian nationhood and the present day." Publisher's note

Includes bibliographical references

972 Mexico, Central America, West Indies, Bermuda

Aguilar-Moreno, Manuel

Handbook to life in the Aztec world. Facts on File 2006 xxiii, 440p il (Facts on file library of world history) $70

Grades: 11 12 Adult   **972**

   1. Aztecs

   ISBN 978-0-8160-5673-6; 0-8160-5673-0

This book includes "coverage of Aztec history, geography, foods, trades, arts, games, wars, political systems, class structure, religious practices, trading networks, writings, architecture, science, and more." Publisher's note

Includes bibliographical references

Foster, Lynn V.

★ A **brief** history of Mexico; 4th ed; Facts On File 2009 324p il map (Brief history) $49.50; pa $19.95

Grades: 9 10 11 12 Adult   **972**

   1. Mexico -- History

   ISBN 978-0-8160-7405-1; 978-0-8160-7406-8 pa

            LC 2009-18298

First published 1997

An overview of Mexican history covering pre-Columbian civilizations and contemporary indigenous cultures. Language, art, religion, politics and economics are discussed. A chronology and bibliography are included.

Includes bibliographical references

Kirkwood, Burton

The **history** of Mexico; 2nd ed.; Greenwood Press/ABC-CLIO 2010 258p il map (Greenwood histories of the modern nations) $49.95

Grades: 11 12 Adult   **972**

   1. Mexico -- History

   ISBN 978-0-313-36601-7; 0-313-36601-2

            LC 2009036964

First published 2000

A historical survey of Mexico and its people from the arrival of the first humans in the Western Hemisphere to the first decade of the 21st century. Topics range from Mexico's cultural past to more current issues such as the war on drugs and the North American Free Trade Agreement.

Includes bibliographical references

Smith, Michael Ernest

The **Aztecs**; [by] Michael E. Smith. 2nd ed; Blackwell 2003 367p il maps (Peoples of America) hardcover o.p. pa $29.95

Grades: 11 12 Adult   **972**

   1. Aztecs 2. Mexico -- Antiquities

   ISBN 0-631-23015-7; 0-631-23016-5 pa

            LC 2001-6950

First published 1996

The author "summarizes the results of archaeological research conducted largely in the past 30 years into the everyday lives of ordinary people in the villages, hamlets, and farmsteads from many regions of central Mexico. His method permits a fresh view of such topics as agricultural methods, population size, market system, relations between city-states and the empire, and even human sacrifice. Smith carries his social account of these people through transformation under Spanish rule and their legacy in modern Mexico." Libr J [review of 1996 edition]

Includes bibliographical references

Stein, R. Conrad

The **Mexican** Revolution. Morgan Reynolds Pub. 2008 160p il map (The story of Mexico) lib bdg $27.95

Grades: 6 7 8 9 10   **972**

   1. Mexico -- History

   ISBN 978-1-59935-051-6; 1-59935-051-3

            LC 2007-22136

"Opening with Porfirio Díaz's presidency (beginning in 1876), [this book] explains how Indian land was expropriated and allotted to rich hacienda owners, describes resistance movements led by Emiliano Zapata and Pancho Villa, and details 10 years of political upheaval and violent uprisings (1910-1920), ending with Alvaro Obregó's election as president of Mexico. . . . [The book has] a lively narrative style. . . . Pertinent illustrations, including photographs, historical paintings, and maps are sprinkled throughout. . . . Well-written and well-researched." SLJ

Includes bibliographical references

Townsend, Richard F.

★ The **Aztecs**; 3rd ed; Thames & Hudson 2009 256p il map (Ancient peoples and places) pa $24.95 Grades: 11 12 Adult　　　　　**972**

1. Aztecs
ISBN 978-0-500-28791-0

　　　　　　　　　　　　　　LC 2008-908216
First published 1992

"Examines the history of these accomplished people through a review of the monuments and artifacts they left behind; exploring how their water-control projects worked, the purposes of their ceremonial centers, and the way they built their incredible ancient structures that still stand today." Publisher's note

Includes bibliographical references

972.8　Other parts of Middle America

Foster, Lynn V.

★ A **brief** history of Central America; 2nd ed; Facts on File 2007 338p il map (Brief history) $45 Grades: 9 10 11 12　　　　　**972.8**

1. Central America -- History
ISBN 978-0-8160-6671-1; 0-8160-6671-X

　　　　　　　　　　　　　　LC 2006-49760
First published 2000

This book "explores the history of the Central American isthmus from the pre-Columbian cultures to the contemporary nations that make up the region today: Belize, Costa Rica, El Salvador, Guatemala, Honduras, Nicaragua, and Panama." Publisher's note

Includes bibliographical references

972.81　Guatemala

Laughton, Timothy

Exploring the life, myth, and art of the Maya; Timothy Laughton. Rosen Pub. 2012 144 p. (Civilizations of the world)

Grades: 7 8 9 10 11　　　　　**972.81**

1. Mayan art 2. Mayas -- History 3. Mayas -- Folklore 4. Mayas -- Social life and customs 5. Maya art
ISBN 9781448848324

　　　　　　　　　　　　　　LC 2011009790

This book on the Maya "offers an informative overview of . . . political and social history as well as its art, architecture, and mythology, all bolstered with plenty of . . . details and narratives. . . . [T]he illustrations include artworks, documents, and handsome maps as well as photos of significant sites and artifacts. . . . In "Maya," [Timothy] Laughton shows how archaeology and scholarship have shifted accepted views on this culture over the last century." (Booklist) The book "put[s] the art . . . in context, explaining how a society's religious beliefs, legends, and cultural traditions manifest themselves through images and iconography. The . . . layout features full-color photographs of architecture, sculpture, and painting on every page, accompanied by informative captions." (School Libr J)

Includes bibliographical references (p. 138) and index

Sharer, Robert J.

Daily life in Maya civilization; 2nd ed.; Greenwood Press 2009 280p il map (Greenwood Press 'Daily life through history' series) $49.95

Grades: 9 10 11 12　　　　　**972.81**

1. Mayas
ISBN 978-0-313-35129-7

　　　　　　　　　　　　　　LC 2009-194
First published 1996

"The book's 13 chapters move through the Maya civilization's 13,000-year social, economic, and cultural development. Also offered is a thought-provoking consideration of Maya civilization and the lessons it can impart to contemporary Western society. An absorbing read." Libr J

Includes bibliographical references

972.85　Nicaragua

Kallen, Stuart A.

The **aftermath** of the Sandinista Revolution. Twenty-First Century Books 2009 160p il (Aftermath of history) lib bdg $38.60

Grades: 8 9 10 11 12　　　　　**972.85**

1. Nicaragua -- Politics and government
ISBN 978-0-8225-9091-0; 0-8225-9091-3

　　　　　　　　　　　　　　LC 2008-25356

"The 1979 overthrow of the corrupt Nicaraguan government by the Marxist Sandinistas brought change to one of the poorest countries in the Americas and instilled in the U.S. new fears about the spread of Communism. . . . Kallen offers a good overview of one of the Latin American theaters of the Cold War." SLJ

Includes glossary and bibliographical references

972.9　West Indies (Antilles) and Bermuda

Figueredo, Danilo H.

★ A **brief** history of the Caribbean; [by] D. H. Figueredo, Frank Argote-Freyre. Facts on File 2008 xxv, 310p il map (Brief history) $45

Grades: 9 10 11 12　　　　　**972.9**

1. West Indies -- History
ISBN 978-0-8160-7021-3; 0-8160-7021-0

　　　　　　　　　　　　　　LC 2007-8202
First published 1991

This "is an overview of the historical events that have taken place and shaped the islands of the Caribbean Sea." Publisher's note

Includes bibliographical references

972.91　Cuba

Markel, Rita J.

Fidel Castro's Cuba. Twenty-First Century Books 2008 160p il map (Dictatorships) lib bdg $38.60

Grades: 7 8 9 10　　　　　**972.91**

1. Presidents 2. Communist leaders 3. Cuba -- History

-- 1959-
ISBN 978-0-8225-7284-8; 0-8225-7284-2
LC 2007-1067
"Markel presents a compelling study of this complex man from his privileged childhood as the son of a wealthy farmer to his position as the controversial dictator of Cuba." Voice Youth Advocates
Includes glossary and bibliographical references

972.95   Puerto Rico

Worth, Richard
Puerto Rico in American history. Enslow Publishers 2008 128p il map (From many cultures, one history) lib bdg $23.95
Grades: 6 7 8 9 10   **972.95**
1. Puerto Rico
ISBN 978-0-7660-2836-4; 0-7660-2836-4
LC 2006-37087
This is a "book about the ties between Puerto Rico and the U.S. . . . Worth's overview will help to acclimate readers new to the island's history. . . . Writing in short, plain sentences, the author touches upon the commonwealth's ongoing struggle with poverty, migration, and language and the current conflicts about statehood and independence. The book's clean design is inviting, with lots of color-screened boxes, full-color photos, archival artwork, and maps." Booklist
Includes glossary and bibliographical references

973   United States

★ **100** key documents in American democracy; edited by Peter B. Levy; foreword by William E. Leuchtenburg. Greenwood Press 1994 502p il $59.95; pa $42.95
Grades: 11 12 Adult   **973**
1. United States -- History -- Sources
ISBN 0-313-28424-5; 0-275-96525-2 pa
LC 93-1137
"The work is arranged chronologically within sections, such as 'The Early Republic' and 'The Progressive Era.' Beginning with Powhatan's call for peace in his 1609 'Letter to John Smith' and concluding with Jesse Jackson's moving speech at the 1988 Democratic National Convention. . . . Each piece is prefaced by a short chronology that sets the historical context and a commentary on the document that often refers to other writings in the book. Shorter documents are reprinted in their entirety, while longer ones have been edited." Booklist

America in world history; general editor, Susan Crean; consulting editor, Tom Lansford. M.E. Sharpe 2010 4v il map set $299
Grades: 9 10 11 12 Adult   **973**
1. World history 2. Reference books 3. United States -- History
ISBN 978-0-7656-8171-3
LC 2009-15865

"The appealing, accessible format and the in-depth treatment of American history make this a good choice for school and public libraries." SLJ
Includes bibliographical references

The **American** experience; the history and culture of the United States through speeches, letters, essays, articles, poems, songs, and stories. edited by Erik Bruun and Jay Crosby. Black Dog & Leventhal Publishers 2012 894 p. $22.95
Grades: 11 12 Adult   **973**
1. Popular culture -- United States 2. United States -- History -- Sources
ISBN 1579129072; 9781579129071
This book presents "569 primary documents, organized chronologically, cover[ing] elements of American history from 1763 to the present. Originally published in hardcover as 'Our Nation's Archive: The History of the United States in Documents' (1999), this update cuts about one-third of the initial volume's documents but adds recent events, from the 9/11 terrorist attacks through the Obama administration, ending with the text of the bill repealing collective bargaining in Wisconsin." (Booklist)

The **American** presidency; edited by Alan Brinkley and Davis Dyer. Houghton Mifflin Co 2004 572p il pa $19.95
Grades: 11 12 Adult   **973**
1. Presidents -- United States 2. United States -- Politics and government
ISBN 0-618-38273-9
LC 2003-62513
An updated version of The reader's companion to the American presidency (2000)
This work assesses "how presidents shape and define culture and society and, at the same time, reflect them. . . . {This} can serve as a beginning point for research and should engage casual readers as well as students of the American presidency." Choice
Includes bibliographical references

Americans at war; society, culture, and the homefront. John P. Resch, Editor in Chief. Macmillan Reference USA 2005 4v il set $395
Grades: 11 12 Adult   **973**
1. War and civilization 2. United States -- Civilization 3. United States -- Military history
ISBN 0-02-865806-X
LC 2004-17314
This book "delivers well-written articles and would make an excellent addition to high-school, academic, and public libraries." Booklist
Includes bibliographical references

Ashby, Ruth
The **great** american documents; Volume 1, 1620-1830. Ruth Ashby; illustrated by Ernie Colón; editorial consultant Russell Motter. Hill and Wang 2014 160 p. col. ill. (hardcover) $40
Grades: 9 10 11 12 Adult   **973**
1. United States -- History -- Sources 2. United States

-- Politics and government -- Sources
ISBN 0809094606; 9780809094608

LC 2013956401

Written by Ruth Ashby and illustrated by Ernie Colón, "'The Great American Documents: Volume 1' introduces as series narrator none other than Uncle Sam, who walks us through twenty essential documents. Each document gets a chapter, in which Uncle Sam explains its key passages, its origins, how it came to be written, and its impact. This graphic primer is an indispensable resource for students and anyone else who wants the facts of American history close at hand." (Publisher's note)

"Colon uses well-designed, full-color panel layouts to eloquently blend charts and other informative graphics with straightforward images of events, clothing, and customs as well as clear, concise metaphors, all with an eye toward promoting a solid understanding of the basic facts and their impact." Booklist

Includes bibliographical references

Bracks, Lean'tin

African American almanac; 400 years of triumph, courage and excellence. Lean'tin Bracks. Visible Ink Press 2012 xiii, 543 p.p ill. (pbk.) $22.95
Grades: 10 11 12 Adult   973
1. Almanacs 2. African Americans -- History 3. African Americans -- Encyclopedias 4. African Americans -- Biography -- Encyclopedias 5. African Americans -- Biography 6. African Americans -- Intellectual life 7. African Americans -- Social life and customs
ISBN 1578593239; 9781578593231

LC 2011038636

This reference book by Lean'tin Bracks "chronicles the African American experience from the arrival of the first Africans to North America in the early 1600s to the present day," including an almanac of topics such as Civil Rights, politics, and music, as well as biographies of various notable African Americans. "Bracks also gives context to less documented areas of African American history." (Booklist)

"This mostly excellent overview of African American contributions to the United States will be a welcome addition to school, public, and community college libraries.—" LJ

Includes bibliographical references (p. 469-477) and index

★ **Conflicts** in American history; a documentary encyclopedia. Facts on File 2010 8v il map (Facts on File library of American history) set $720
Grades: 9 10 11 12   973
1. Reference books 2. United States -- History -- Encyclopedias
ISBN 978-0-8160-7093-0; 978-1-4381-3485-7 ebook

LC 2009-47715

"Each volume covers a distinct period from 1492 to the present and addresses a broad range of topics encompassing critical social, economic, political, religious, and military conflicts. An introduction to the era and an annotated chronology begin each volume, followed by articles and a dozen or so documents. . . . The scope, variety, and quality of

these primary and secondary resources make this a superior addition." SLJ

Includes bibliographical references

Cornelison, Pam

The **great** American history fact-finder; the who, what, where, when, and why of American history. [by] Pam Cornelison and Ted Yanak. 2nd ed, updated and expanded; Houghton Mifflin 2004 608p il, maps pa $14.95
Grades: 11 12 Adult   973
1. Reference books 2. United States -- History -- Dictionaries
ISBN 0-618-43941-2

LC 2004-47480

First published 1993 with authors' names in reverse order

This book provides "information about significant persons as well as political, legal, sporting, and cultural events in American history. Entries are alphabetically arranged, and related entries cross-referenced. . . . Besides an index, there are suggested readings and information on the states, presidents, vice presidents, population, Supreme Court, Articles of Confederation, Declaration of Independence, and US Constitution (with signers and nonsigners). This is a good quick reference." Choice

Daily life through American history in primary documents; Randall M. Miller, general editor. Greenwood 2012 1099 p.
Grades: 10 11 12 Adult   973
1. Archives -- United States 2. United States -- History -- Chronology 3. United States -- Social life and customs
ISBN 161069032X; 1610690338; 9781610690324; 9781610690331

LC 2011040023

In this history book, "four volumes are organized chronologically and then thematically and present the 'many small things that made up Americans' daily life.' Volumes are 'The Colonial Period through the American Revolution,' 'The American Revolution to the Civil War,' 'The Civil War to World War I,' and 'World War I to the Present.' Each volume begins with a time line of selected events and a lengthy historical-overview essay describing significant themes, events, and concerns of the period. This is followed by about 100 primary documents that illustrate daily life." (Booklist)

Includes bibliographical references and index

Delman, Carmit

Burnt bread & chutney; growing up between cultures; a memoir of an Indian Jewish girl. One World/Ballantine Bks. 2002 xxiv, 261p hardcover o.p. pa $13.95
Grades: 9 10 11 12   973
1. Culture conflict 2. Racially mixed people 3. East Indians 4. Jews -- Biography
ISBN 0-345-44593-7; 0-345-44594-5 pa

LC 2002-22855

The author's "mother is a direct descendant of the Bene Israel, a tiny, ancient community of Jews . . . of Western India. Her father is American, a Jewish man of Eastern European descent. They met while working the land of a nascent Israeli state. . . . They hardly took notice of the interracial aspect of their union. But their daughter, Carmit, growing up in America, was well aware of her uncommon heritage." Publisher's note

★ **Encyclopedia** of American historical documents; edited by Susan Rosenfeld. Facts on File 2004 3v (Facts on File library of American history) set $300

Grades: 11 12 Adult   **973**
1. United States -- History -- Sources
ISBN 0-8160-4995-5

LC 2003-51610

"Each section begins with an overview of the period and each document is introduced with commentary on when and why it was created and its significance, then and now. Entries include material 'with resonance for the 21st century' that represents turning points in U.S. history, and documents of a controversial nature. Students can read Supreme Court justices' opinions, presidential announcements and inaugural addresses, excerpts from noteworthy books that influenced American thought and action, and speeches of women and people of color. . . . Students and teachers will welcome this mammoth resource." SLJ

Includes bibliographical references

★ **Encyclopedia** of American history; Gary B. Nash, general editor. Rev. ed.; Facts on File 2010 11v il map (Facts on File library of American history) set $1,150

Grades: 11 12 Adult   **973**
1. Reference books 2. United States -- History -- Encyclopedias
ISBN 978-0-8160-7136-4

LC 2008-35422

First published 2003

This encyclopedia provides a "presentation of the political, social, economic, and cultural events that have shaped the land and the nation." Publisher's note

Includes bibliographical references

Encyclopedia of the new American nation; the emergence of the United States, 1754-1829. Paul Finkelman, editor in chief. Thomson Gale 2005 3v il map set $395

Grades: 11 12 Adult   **973**
1. Reference books 2. United States -- History -- 1783-1865 -- Encyclopedias 3. United States -- History -- 1775-1783, Revolution -- Encyclopedias 4. United States -- History -- 1600-1775, Colonial period -- Encyclopedias
ISBN 0-684-31346-4

LC 2005-17783

The editor and contributors "have produced a wonderful reference source." Ref & User Services Quarterly

Includes bibliographical references

Encyclopedia of U.S. political history. CQ Press 2009 7v il map set $1200

Grades: 10 11 12 Adult   **973**
1. Reference books 2. Political science -- Encyclopedias 3. United States -- Politics and government --

Encyclopedias
ISBN 978-0-87289-320-7

LC 2010-2253

"An impressive work remarkable for its breath and scope, this encyclopedia covers U.S. political history chronologically from the year 1500 to the present day. . . . Written in a vivid and accessible yet scholarly manner, this wonderful synthesis of history and political science will greatly benefit students, lovers of political history, and academics alike." Libr J

Includes bibliographical references

Encyclopedia of women and American politics; [edited by] Lynne E. Ford. Facts On File 2008 636p il (Facts on File library of American history) $85

Grades: 9 10 11 12   **973**
1. Reference books 2. Women in politics -- United States -- Encyclopedias 3. United States -- Politics and government -- Encyclopedias
ISBN 978-0-8160-5491-6

LC 2007-4331

This "A-to-Z volume contains more than 500 entries covering the people, events, and terms involved in the history of women and politics. . . . [This] encyclopedia also provides a biography for every woman who has served in the U.S. House of Representatives, the Senate, and the Supreme Court." Publisher's note

Includes bibliographical references

Eyewitness to America; 500 years of America in the words of those who saw it happen. edited by David Colbert. Pantheon Bks. 1997 xxx, 599p hardcover o.p. pa $16.95

Grades: 11 12 Adult   **973**
1. United States -- History -- Sources
ISBN 0-679-44224-3; 0-679-76724-X pa

LC 96-24150

This volume contains a "panorama of first-person accounts of moments in the country's story that stretch from an October 10, 1492, diary entry by one of Columbus's crewmen to a 1994 e-mail message from Bill Gates. The nearly 300 entries tend to be short, preceded by informative introductions. The result is a feeling for history that is both immediate and dramatic." Publ Wkly

Includes bibliographical references

Gale Group

Gale encyclopedia of U.S. history: government and politics. Gale 2008 2v il set $220

Grades: 9 10 11 12   **973**
1. Reference books 2. United States -- Politics and government -- Encyclopedias
ISBN 978-1-4144-3118-5; 1-4144-3118-X

LC 2007-34360

"The 11 chapters in Government cover the period between the 15th century and today. Chapters detail 'How They Were Governed,' discussing such entries as Jamestown and Ellis Island; biographies of key political figures; political parties and key issues; events and social movements that influenced American politics; and legislation and court cases that had a role in the formation of the government." SLJ

Includes bibliographical references

Hart, Elva Trevino

Barefoot heart; stories of a migrant child. Bilingual Press/Editorial Bilingüe 1999 236p pa $17

Grades: 9 10 11 12   **973**

1. Migrant labor 2. Agricultural laborers 3. Mexican Americans -- Biography

ISBN 0-927534-81-9

LC 99-11731

This is "a powerful collection of vignettes." Libr J

Lee, Helie

Still life with rice; a young American woman discovers the life and legacy of her Korean grandmother. Scribner 1996 320p hardcover o.p. pa $13

Grades: 11 12 Adult   **973**

1. Korean Americans 2. Alternative medicine practitioners

ISBN 0-684-82711-5 pa

LC 95-41921

"Written with great narrative power and attention to detail, a testament to the will to survive." Booklist

Lubar, Steven D.

Legacies; collecting America's history at the Smithsonian. {by} Steven Lubar and Kathleen M. Kendrick. Smithsonian Institution Press 2001 256p il $39.95

Grades: 9 10 11 12   **973**

1. United States -- Civilization 2. National Museum of American History (U.S.)

ISBN 1-56098-886-X

LC 2001-20399

An illustrated look at more than 200 representative objects from the Smithsonian's collection. "The eclectic collage of artifacts ranges from the curious (an 1860s phrenology model used to decipher personality and behavior) to the provocative (the uniform of a WWI woman contract-surgeon). Elegant acquisitions, such as first ladies' inaugural gowns, are preserved along with the mundane (the Veg-O-Matic) and popular culture (Archie and Edith Bunkers' chairs), as well as scientific and technological advances. In every case, stories are the key elements that transform each specimen into a legacy worth preserving." Publ Wkly

Includes bibliographical references

Milestone documents in American history; exploring the primary sources that shaped America. Paul Finkelman, editor in chief; Bruce A. Lesh, consulting editor. Schlager Group 2008 4v il (Milestone documents) set $385

Grades: 9 10 11 12 Adult   **973**

1. Reference books 2. United States -- History -- Sources

ISBN 978-0-9797758-0-2; 0-9797758-0-9

"This exceptional work will be essential to students needing assistance interpreting primary sources, and teachers will find it invaluable for incorporating those resources into their curriculums. The entries . . . examine 133 chronologically arranged documents beginning with the British crown's Proclamation Act of 1763 and ending with the 2003 Supreme Court decision Lawrence v. Texas." SLJ

Includes bibliographical references

Milestone documents of American leaders; exploring the primary sources of notable Americans. Paul Finkelman, editor in chief; James A. Percoco, consulting editor. Schlager Group 2009 4v il (Milestone documents) set $385

Grades: 10 11 12 Adult   **973**

1. United States -- History -- Sources

ISBN 978-0-9797758-5-7

This collection offers "transcribed primary documents and analysis covering the works of many prominent Americans. . . . The transcribed text of each document includes a concise overview of the life and career of the document's creator(s) written by experts on the chosen author or topic. Also included . . . is a time line indicating where these documents fit into the author's life/career, resources to help facilitate discussion about the author and documents, and additional primary and secondary resources on the author and topics covered." Choice

★ **Opposing** viewpoints in American history; William Dudley, volume editor; John C. Chalberg, consulting editor. Greenhaven Press 2007 2v v1 $59.95; v1 pa $39.95; v2 $59.95; v2 pa $39.95

Grades: 9 10 11 12   **973**

1. United States -- History -- Sources

ISBN 0-7377-3184-2 v1; 978-0-7377-3184-2 v1; 0-7377-3185-0 v1 pa; 978-0-7377-3185-9 v1 pa; 0737731869 v2; 978-0-7377-3186-6 v2; 0-7377-3187-7 v2 pa; 978-0-7377-3187-3 v2 pa

LC 2006-24673

First published 1996

"Topics range chronologically from 'Origins of English Settlement' to 'National Security, Terrorism, and Iraq.' Essays, speeches, and letters by such notables as Elizabeth Cady Stanton, Malcolm X, and Bill Clinton provide historical context for the debates. Articles are clustered under prefaced general categories, such as 'The Gilded Age,' 'Antebellum America,' and 'New Challenges after the Cold War.'" SLJ

Includes bibliographical references

★ The **Oxford** companion to United States history; editor in chief, Paul S. Boyer; editors, Melvyn Dubofsky {et al.} Oxford Univ. Press 2001 xliv, 940p il maps $75

Grades: 11 12 Adult   **973**

1. Reference books 2. United States -- History -- Dictionaries

ISBN 0-19-508209-5

LC 00-55801

First published 1966 under the authorship of Thomas A. Johnson with title: The Oxford companion to American history

This reference work contains 1,400 alphabetically arranged signed entries. See and see also references are provided. Coverage starts with the colonial period and examines notable men and women and major events in U.S. history

Includes bibliographical references

Panchyk, Richard

★ The **keys** to American history; understanding our most important historic documents. Chicago Review Press 2009 241p il map $24.95; pa $19.95

Grades: 7 8 9 10 11 12   **973**

1. United States -- History -- Sources

ISBN 978-1-55652-716-6; 1-55652-716-0; 978-1-55652-804-0 pa; 1-55652-804-3 pa

"This impressive collection is a valuable resource for gaining a greater appreciation for and understanding of our nation's dynamic history." SLJ

Includes bibliographical references

Savage, William W.

The **cowboy** hero; his image in American history & culture. by William W. Savage, Jr. University of Okla. Press 1979 179p il hardcover o.p. pa $19.95

Grades: 9 10 11 12   **973**

1. Cowhands

ISBN 0-8061-1587-4; 0-8061-1920-9 pa

LC 79-4730

The author's "research extends into all facets of Western history with emphasis on the popular glorification of the cowboy in books, movies, radio, and television. . . . Savage . . . appears to have a real affection for his subject." Libr J

Includes bibliographical references

United States. National Arcives and Records Administration

Our documents; 100 milestone documents from the National Archives. Oxford University Press 2003 256p il $40; pa $24.95

Grades: 9 10 11 12   **973**

1. United States -- History -- Sources

ISBN 0-19-517206-X; 0-19-530959-6 pa

LC 2003-15080

A collection of one hundred documents that were important in the development of the United States from its founding to 1965, including the Declaration of Independence, Constitution, and lesser-known writings.

"Photographs and facsimile reproductions of documents are a highlight of the book—they let readers see the actual items. The appealing, clean layout is defined by clear blue and red headings and plenty of white space. A useful addition." SLJ

Includes bibliographical references

Vowell, Sarah

Assassination vacation. Simon & Schuster 2005 258p il hardcover o.p. pa $14

Grades: 11 12 Adult   **973**

1. United States -- Local history 2. United States -- Description and travel 3. Presidents -- United States -- Assassination

ISBN 0-7432-6003-1; 0-7432-6004-X pa

LC 2004-59134

The author "takes readers on a pilgrimage of sorts to the sites and monuments that pay homage to Lincoln, Garfield and McKinley, visiting everything from grave sites and simple plaques (like the one in Buffalo that marks the place where McKinley was shot) to places like the National Mu-seum of Health and Medicine, where fragments of Lincoln's skull are on display." Publ Wkly

Walker, Rebecca, 1969-

Black, white and Jewish; autobiography of a shifting self. Riverhead Bks. 2001 320p hardcover o.p. pa $14

Grades: 11 12 Adult   **973**

1. Authors 2. Journalists 3. Racially mixed people 4. Feminists 5. African American women -- Biography 6. Daughters -- United States -- Biography 7. Jewish women -- United States -- Biography 8. Racially mixed people -- United States -- Biography 9. Racially mixed people -- Race identity -- United States

ISBN 1-57322-169-4; 1-57322-907-5 pa

LC 00-35292

This is an autobiography by "the daughter of the black writer Alice Walker and a white Jewish lawyer, Mel Leventhal. Rebecca Walker writes that her confusion about being biracial began when her parents divorced when she was 8 years old. From then on, every two years, Walker alternated coast-to-coast between them." (N Y Times Book Rev)

This is an "involving, honest, poignant memoir." Booklist

Wilkins, Roger W.

★ **Jefferson's** pillow; the founding fathers and the dilemma of Black patriotism. [by] Roger Wilkins. Beacon Press 2001 163p hardcover o.p. pa $14

Grades: 11 12 Adult   **973**

1. Generals 2. Statesmen 3. Architects 4. Presidents 5. Vice-presidents 6. Essayists 7. Colonial leaders 8. Plantation owners 9. Members of Congress 10. Secretaries of state 11. United States -- History 12. United States -- Race relations

ISBN 0-8070-0956-3; 0-8070-0957-1 pa

LC 2001-25117

"This is an important look at the essential and ongoing contradictions at the heart of American ideals of liberty and patriotism." Booklist

Includes bibliographical references

973.09   Presidents--United States

Chronology of the U.S. presidency; Mathew Manweller, editor. ABC-CLIO 2012 4 v. xxii, 1556 p.p (hbk.: acid-free paper) $399.00

Grades: 10 11 12 Adult   **973.09**

1. Cabinet officers 2. United States -- History 3. Presidents -- United States 4. Presidents -- United States -- Biography 5. Presidents -- United States -- History -- Chronology 6. United States -- Politics and government -- Chronology

ISBN 1598846450; 9781598846454; 9781598846461

LC 2011053314

This book looks at the 44 U.S. presidents. "Entries begin with a portrait of the president and contain a biographical sketch of both the man himself and the First Family, information on each member of the cabinet, a chronology of significant term events, and primary-source materials." (Library Journal)

Includes bibliographical references and index.

Nowlan, Robert A.

The **American** presidents, Washington to Tyler; what they did, what they said, what was said about them, with full source notes. Robert A. Nowlan. McFarland & Co. 2012 x, 450 p.p (softcover: alk. paper) $55

Grades: 9 10 11 12   **973.09**

1. Presidents -- United States 2. Presidents -- United States -- Biography 3. United States -- Politics and government -- 1789-1815 4. United States -- Politics and government -- 1815-1861

ISBN 0786463368; 9780786463367

LC 2011039072

This book is an "account of each of the first 10 men who held the highest office in the United States. Within each chapter is a thorough account of the man's term, including major events in foreign affairs, primary-source documents by and about him, and, in some cases, how he was viewed by his contemporaries and other presidents." (School Library Journal)

"This book—the first volume in what the author states will be a multivolume set on all the American presidents—covers the life of the first 10 presidents...each chapter is devoted to a president, covering his time in office, domestic policy and foreign policy, family background, family life, religious beliefs, his life before and after the presidency, and a "Miscellanea" section featuring trivia and interesting facts.Black-and-white illustrations are included. The chapter notes and the reference section at the end of the book provide exhaustive and comprehensive sources that the reader can use to find out more about each president. This book is suitable for advanced high-school students, academic libraries, and history buffs." (Booklist)

Includes bibliographical references (p. 388-439) and index

★ The **presidency** A to Z; Gerhard Peters, editor; John T. Woolley, editor. 5th ed. CQ Press 2012 xix, 715 p.p ill. (hardcover) $125

Grades: 8 9 10 11 12 Adult   **973.09**

1. Presidents -- United States -- Biography 2. Presidents -- United States -- Encyclopedias

ISBN 1608719081; 9781608719082

LC 2012023290

This book, by Gerhard Peters, presents a dictionary of the U.S. presidency. The book is a "tool for understanding the presidency, both historically and today and for appraising how it and the executive branch have responded to the challenges facing the nation. It provides readers with quick information and in-depth background on the presidency through a comprehensive encyclopedia of over 300 easy-to-read entries." (Publisher's note)

"At over 700 pages and also available online, this core title. . . provid[es] a comprehensive encyclopedic treatment of the U.S. presidency. . . . A recommended purchase for all libraries and a required one for those with earlier editions, which it supplants." LJ

Includes bibliographical references (p. 684-690) and index.

973.2   United States--Colonial period, 1607-1775

Carpenter, Roger M.

Term paper resource guide to colonial American history. Greenwood Press/ABC-CLIO 2009 268p $65

Grades: 9 10 11 12   **973.2**

1. Report writing 2. Reference books 3. United States -- History -- 1600-1775, Colonial period

ISBN 978-0-313-35544-8

LC 2009-9048

"This excellent resource is a clear, well-arranged guide for starting and developing reports. . . . Carpenter's work will serve as an essential guide for research papers and discussions on topics of interest to AP students of Colonial American history." SLJ

Includes bibliographical references

Copeland, David A.

★ **Debating** the issues in colonial newspapers; primary documents on events of the period. Greenwood Press 2000 397p il $59.95

Grades: 9 10 11 12   **973.2**

1. Newspapers -- United States 2. United States -- History -- 1600-1775, Colonial period -- Sources

ISBN 0-313-30982-5

LC 99-89070

"Primary-source material on 31 events and issues from 1690 to 1776 including abolition, inoculation, women's rights, censorship, and separation from England. The principal source of communication for people during this period was the newspaper, and political and social concerns were debated there at length. . . . Following the colonialists' pro or con opinions, a number of questions are posed for students." SLJ

Includes bibliographical references

Events that changed America through the seventeenth century; edited by John E. Findling and Frank W. Thackeray. Greenwood Press 2000 193p (Greenwood Press 'Events that changed America' series) $39.95

Grades: 11 12 Adult   **973.2**

1. America -- History 2. United States -- History -- 1600-1775, Colonial period

ISBN 0-313-29083-0

LC 00-20080

A look at ten of the most important events in what was to become the continental United States from the settlement of the earliest peoples to the close of the seventeenth century. Coronado's expedition, the founding of St. Augustine, and early European-Native American encounters are among the topics discussed

Includes bibliographical references and index

Gray, Edward G.

★ **Colonial** America; a history in documents. 2nd ed.; Oxford University Press 2011 211p il map (Pages from history) $39.95; pa $24.95

Grades: 7 8 9 10   **973.2**

1. United States -- History -- 1600-1775, Colonial

period -- Sources
ISBN 978-0-19-976594-2; 978-0-19-976595-9 pa
LC 2010038458
First published 2003
This collection of primary sources examines "the lives of the colonists through their own words—in diaries, letters, sermons, newspaper columns, and poems." Publisher's note
Includes bibliographical references

Grizzard, Frank E.
Jamestown Colony; a political, social, and cultural history. [by] Frank E. Grizzard, Jr., D. Boyd Smith. ABC-CLIO 2007 lvi, 448p il map $95
Grades: 7 8 9 10 11 12 Adult   **973.2**
1. Reference books 2. Jamestown (Va.) -- History -- Encyclopedias
ISBN 1-85109-637-X; 978-1-85109-637-4
LC 2006-37359
"This volume is well written and well researched, and belongs in all collections relating to Colonial America." Am Ref Books Annu, 2008
Includes bibliographical references

Hawke, David Freeman
★ **Everyday** life in early America. Harper & Row 1988 195p il (Everyday life in America) hardcover o.p. pa $13
Grades: 11 12 Adult   **973.2**
1. United States -- Social life and customs 2. United States -- History -- 1600-1775, Colonial period
ISBN 0-06-091251-0 pa
LC 87-17667
The author "provides enlightening and colorful descriptions of early Colonial Americans and debunks many widely held assumptions about 17th century settlers." Publ Wkly
Includes bibliographical references

Hofstadter, Richard
America at 1750; a social portrait. Knopf 1971 293p hardcover o.p. pa $11
Grades: 11 12 Adult   **973.2**
1. United States -- Social conditions 2. United States -- History -- 1600-1775, Colonial period
ISBN 0-394-71795-3 pa
"Using primarily secondary accounts, Hofstadter examines the ethnic composition of the colonies in 1750; traces the development of white servitude, the slave trade, and the slave system; sketches briefly the middle-class framework of early America; and dissects the colonial religious paradigm and the impact of the Great Awakening." Choice
Includes bibliographical references

Mandell, Daniel R.
King Philip's war; the conflict over New England. Chelsea House 2007 144p il map (Landmark events in Native American history) lib bdg $35
Grades: 7 8 9 10   **973.2**
1. Wampanoag Indians 2. King Philip's War, 1675-1676 3. New England -- History -- 1600-1775, Colonial

period
ISBN 978-0-7910-9346-7; 0-7910-9346-8
LC 2006-102258
This account features "lively writing and direct quotes, and [is] enhanced by many color and black-and-white photos, drawings, and illustrations." SLJ
Includes bibliographical references

Philbrick, Nathaniel
★ The **Mayflower** and the Pilgrims' New World. G.P. Putnam's Sons 2008 338p il map $19.99
Grades: 7 8 9 10 11 12   **973.2**
1. Farmers 2. Historians 3. Native Americans 4. Pilgrims (New England colonists) 5. Colonists 6. Carpenters 7. Army officers 8. Pilgrim fathers 9. Massachusetts -- History -- 1600-1775, Colonial period
ISBN 978-0-399-24795-8; 0-399-24795-5
LC 2007-30669
An adaptation of Mayflower: a story of community, courage, and war, published 2006 by Viking for adults
"This volume highlights both the Pilgrims' determination to find and settle a home where they could worship freely and the perilous journey that it took to make that happen. In accessible prose, the author shatters the American myth of the landing at Plymouth Rock and the first Thanksgiving. . . . The various maps, reproductions of historical documents, photographs of significant locations, and illustrations all come together with the text to help separate fact from legend and create a realistic, readable portrayal of the Pilgrims and their first 50 years in America." SLJ
Includes bibliographical references

Purvis, Thomas L.
Colonial America to 1763. Facts on File 1999 381p il (Almanacs of American life) $95
Grades: 11 12 Adult   **973.2**
1. United States -- History -- 1600-1775, Colonial period 2. United States -- Social life and customs -- 1600-1775, Colonial period
ISBN 0-8160-2527-4
LC 98-29007
This compendium is "divided into 19 chapters that cover such topics as 'Diet and Health,' 'Religion,' 'The Cities,' 'Science and Technology,' 'Crime and Violence,' and 'Popular Life and Recreation.' There are general details of Colonial life as well as obscure and difficult-to-find facts that students need and teachers always want. . . . Young adults will enjoy learning through all of the fascinating facts and curious bits of information, but the well-organized, complete, and accessible text will also provide an invaluable resource for research and term papers." SLJ
Includes bibliographical references

Wolf, Stephanie Grauman
★ **As** various as their land; the everyday lives of eighteenth-century Americans. University of Arkansas Press 2000 304p il map pa $16.95
Grades: 9 10 11 12 Adult   **973.2**
1. United States -- Social life and customs -- 1600-1775, Colonial period
ISBN 1-557-28599-3
LC 99-86042

First published 1993 by HarperCollins
"An excellent overview of the foundation of our society's successes and failures." Booklist
Includes bibliographical references

973.3   United States--Periods of Revolution and Confederation, 1775-1789

The **American** Revolution; Kirk D. Werner, book editor. Greenhaven Press 2000 224p (Turning points in world history) lib bdg $31.20
Grades: 9 10 11 12   **973.3**
1. United States -- History -- 1775-1783, Revolution
ISBN 0-7377-0239-7
        LC 99-38377
This volume "contains 16 essays by well-known historians that center on the background, politics, and effects of the [American Revolution]. . . . There is an extensive section of documents (Stamp Act resolutions, excerpts from first-person accounts, Articles of Confederation, etc.) An excellent resource for research." SLJ
Includes bibliographical references

★ The **American** Revolution: writings from the War of Independence. Library of Am. 2001 878p $40
Grades: 11 12 Adult   **973.3**
1. United States -- History -- 1775-1783, Revolution
ISBN 1-88301-191-4
        LC 00-45373
"This work will serve as a marvelous research tool for specialists, but general readers with an interest in American history will also find fascinating gems." Booklist
Includes bibliographical references

★ **American** Revolutionary War; a student encyclopedia. Gregory Fremont-Barnes, Richard Alan Ryerson, volume editors; James Arnold and Roberta Wiener, editors, documents volume; foreword by Jack P. Greene. ABC-CLIO 2007 5v il map set $485
Grades: 9 10 11 12   **973.3**
1. Reference books 2. United States -- History -- 1775-1783, Revolution -- Encyclopedias
ISBN 978-1-85109-839-2; 1-85109-839-9
        LC 2006-31100
"With over 800 entries and essays and a separate documents volume, . . . [this encyclopedia] covers every battle and campaign, every political debate and diplomatic encounter. It also introduces students to the broad spectrum of American culture at the time (day-to-day life, art, music) as well as the personal lives of all those caught up in the war." Publisher's note
Includes bibliographical references

Aronson, Marc
★ The **real** revolution; the global story of American independence. Clarion Books 2005 238p il map lib bdg $21

Grades: 7 8 9 10   **973.3**
1. United States -- History -- 1775-1783, Revolution
ISBN 0-618-18179-2
        LC 2005-1088
In this "volume, Aronson investigates the origins of the American Revolution and discovers some startling global connections. The colonies' quest for independence is tied to such seemingly unrelated incidents as Robert Clive's triumph over the French in India in 1750 and John Wilkes's accusations against the king in his newspaper, The North Briton, in the 1760s. . . . This outstanding work is highly compelling reading and belongs in every library." SLJ
Includes bibliographical references

Barnes, Ian
★ The **historical** atlas of the American Revolution; Charles Royster, consulting editor. Routledge 2000 223p il maps $50
Grades: 11 12 Adult   **973.3**
1. Reference books 2. United States -- Historical geography -- Maps 3. United States -- History -- 1775-1783, Revolution -- Maps
ISBN 0-415-92243-7
        LC 99-59920
"Although the emphasis is on the Revolution, the scope is much broader—from settlement to 1820. Chronologically arranged, each chapter opens with an overview, followed by readable double-page spreads on the time periods, specific battles, pertinent individuals or peoples, and other relevant issues. Maps are large enough to show troop movement. Legends are clear with dissimilar symbols. Portraits, illustrations, and other graphics are clearly identified. A concluding section provides brief biographical sketches. An excellent presentation of the era." SLJ
Includes bibliographical references

Bober, Natalie
★ **Countdown** to independence; a revolution of ideas in England and her American colonies: 1760-1776. by Natalie S. Bober. Atheneum Bks. for Young Readers 2000 xxv, 342p il hardcover o.p. pa $19.95
Grades: 9 10 11 12   **973.3**
1. Great Britain -- History -- 1714-1837 2. United States -- History -- 1775-1783, Revolution -- Causes 3. United States -- Politics and government -- 1775-1783, Revolution
ISBN 0-689-81329-5; 978-0-689-81329-0; 1-4169-6392-8 pa; 978-1-4169-6392-9 pa
        LC 99-27086
Examines the people and events both in the American colonies and in Great Britain between 1760 and 1776 that led to the American Revolution.
This "is a compelling, yet scholarly resource that places readers at the center of the action, encouraging them to learn about the historic events and people, care about them, and, perhaps, learn more by investigating the extensive bibliography." Booklist
Includes bibliographical references

Burg, David F.

★ The **American** Revolution; Updated ed; Facts on File 2007 470p il map (Eyewitness history) $75

Grades: 11 12 Adult 973.3

1. United States -- History -- 1775-1783, Revolution
ISBN 978-0-8160-6482-3

LC 2006-33096

First published 2001

"The book begins with a discussion of the 'Prelude to Revolt: 1756-1774,' and concludes with thoughts on 'An Improbable Triumph: 1781' and 'An Unpromising Outcome: 1782-1783.' Each chapter offers a lengthy introductory essay summarizing important themes, followed by a descriptive chronology of key events. Pages of documented excerpts from contemporary newspapers, diaries, letters, speeches, and memoirs discuss the events of the day and how they were perceived by those who lived through them. The lively selections, many written by well-known individuals, paint vivid pictures that will capture readers' imaginations." SLJ

Includes bibliographical references

Casey, Susan

Women heroes of the American Revolution; 20 stories of espionage, sabotage, defiance, and rescue. Susan Cascy. Chicago Rcvicw Prcss 2015 240 p. illustrations (Women of action) (hardback) $19.95

Grades: 7 8 9 10 973.3

1. Women -- United States -- History 2. United States -- History -- 1775-1783, Revolution 3. Women -- United States -- History -- 18th century 4. United States -- History -- Revolution, 1775-1783 -- Women
ISBN 1613745834; 9781613745830

LC 2014032760

Author Susan Casey's book on the American Revolution looks at how "women took action in many ways: as spies, soldiers, nurses, water carriers, fundraisers, writers, couriers, and more. Women Heroes of the American Revolution brings a fresh new perspective to their stories resulting from interviews with historians and with descendants of participants of the Revolution and features ample excerpts from primary source documents. Also included are contextualizing sidebars, images, source notes, and a bibliography." (Publisher's note)

"Extensive source notes are appended. The many black-and-white illustrations include reproductions of archival portraits, prints and drawings, letters, and newspaper advertisements. A fine, useful resource for students of American history." Booklist

Includes bibliographical references and index

Draper, Theodore

A **struggle** for power; the American Revolution. Times Bks. 1996 544p hardcover o.p. pa $13.56

Grades: 11 12 Adult 973.3

1. United States -- History -- 1775-1783, Revolution
ISBN 0-679-77642-7 pa

LC 95-11605

This is an "elegantly written, masterful study. . . . Drawing freely on period pamphlets, letters, petitions, travelogues and assembly minutes, [the author] vividly evokes the popu-

list discontent, intellectual gymnastics and mob violence that led to revolution." Publ Wkly

Includes bibliographical references

Driver, Stephanie Schwartz

Understanding the Declaration of Independence. Rosen Pub. 2010 128p il (Words that changed the world) lib bdg $31.95

Grades: 7 8 9 10 973.3

1. Architects 2. Presidents 3. Vice-presidents 4. Essayists 5. United States -- Declaration of Independence 6. United States -- Politics and government -- 1775-1783, Revolution
ISBN 978-1-4488-1669-9; 1-4488-1669-6

LC 2010-10371

This surveys The Declaration of Independence, considering the "document's 'Context and Creator,' 'Immediate Impact,' 'Legacy,' and 'Aftermath.' . . . Exploring the colonial crisis leading to America's formal separation from the British Empire, . . . [the] author provides a balance of deep context, expressive writing, and pertinent information. Scattered throughout the [text] are a good number of well-captioned, color illustrations and photos. [This book is a] valuable [resource] for teachers and students doing research projects across the curriculum." SLJ

Includes glossary and bibliographical references

Fischer, David Hackett

Washington's crossing. Oxford University Press 2004 564p il maps (Pivotal moments in American history) $35; pa $16.95

Grades: 11 12 Adult 973.3

1. Generals 2. Presidents 3. United States -- History -- 1775-1783, Revolution -- Campaigns
ISBN 0-19-517034-2; 0-19-518159-X pa

LC 2003-19858

The author describes how "Washington, his officers, and their men turn the early military defeats of Long Island and New York City into victory at Trenton and Princeton. The opening chapter is devoted to the painting Washington Crossing the Delaware. Then the author discusses the British, Hessian, and American military units that were involved in these campaigns and gives background on their officers. This is Fischer's strong suit: he tells stories and gives details that bring history alive. . . . In the hands of such a thorough researcher and talented writer, this is powerful stuff." SLJ

Includes bibliographical references

Freedman, Russell, 1929-

Give me liberty! the story of the Declaration of Independence. Holiday House 2000 90p il $24.95; pa $14.95

Grades: 5 6 7 8 9 10 973.3

1. United States 2. United States -- Declaration of Independence 3. United States -- Politics and government -- 1775-1783
ISBN 0-8234-1448-5; 0-8234-1753-0 pa

LC 99-57513

This book describes the events leading up to the Declaration of Independence as well as the personalities and politics behind its framing. Chronology. Annotated bibliography. Index. "Grades five to eight." (Bull Cent Child Books)

"Handsomely designed with a generous and thoughtful selection of period art, the book is dramatic and inspiring." Horn Book

Includes bibliographical references

Gaustad, Edwin Scott

Benjamin Franklin; [by] Edwin S. Gaustad. Oxford University Press 2005 143p il (Lives and legacies) $17.95

Grades: 11 12 Adult **973.3**
    1. Authors 2. Diplomats 3. Inventors 4. Statesmen 5. Scientists 6. Writers on science 7. Members of Congress 8. Statesmen -- United States
    ISBN 0-19-530535-3
                         LC 2005-22906
This is a biography of the American statesman and scientist.

"Only diehard detractors of Franklin's Enlightenment rationalism may deny that Gaustad has written an excellent introduction to this foremost founding father." Booklist

Includes bibliographical references

Gilje, Paul A.

Encyclopedia of revolutionary America; foreword by Gary B. Nash. Facts On File 2010 3v il map (Facts on File library of American history) set $250

Grades: 9 10 11 12 Adult **973.3**
    1. Reference books 2. United States -- History -- 1783-1809 -- Encyclopedias 3. United States -- History -- 1775-1783, Revolution -- Encyclopedias
    ISBN 978-0-8160-6505-9; 0-8160-6505-5
                         LC 2009-13596
"These volumes do not just cover the continental U.S. but the entire North American continent. Gilje relies on primary sources as much as possible in the alphabetically arranged entries. Covering the period from the French and Indian War, in 1754, to the end of the War of 1812 (1815), the encyclopedia contains the expected biographical entries on the Founding Fathers, prominent politicians, and popular military leaders, but a special effort has been made to include previously neglected groups in the study of this era, such as Native Americans, African Americans, women, and the lower classes. . . . This is an easy-to-use, helpful, and comprehensive resource that would be a valuable addition to the history collections of high-school, academic, and public libraries." Booklist

Includes bibliographical references

Irvin, Benjamin

★ **Samuel** Adams; son of liberty, father of revolution. [by] Benjamin H. Irvin. Oxford University Press 2002 176p il (Oxford portraits) $28

Grades: 7 8 9 10 **973.3**
    1. Statesmen 2. Members of Congress 3. Writers on politics 4. United States -- History -- 1775-1783, Revolution
    ISBN 0-19-513225-4
                         LC 2002-4283
Examines the life of Samuel Adams, a hero of the American Revolution who is credited by some with having fired the first shot at Lexington Green, the "shot heard 'round the world"

"Irvin's account of events is exciting and written in a compelling narrative style. He presents an unbiased assessment of Adams's actions and character." SLJ

Includes bibliographical references

Maier, Pauline

American scripture; making the Declaration of Independence. Knopf 1997 xxi, 304p hardcover o.p. pa $14

Grades: 11 12 Adult **973.3**
    1. United States -- Declaration of Independence 2. United States -- Politics and government -- 1775-1783, Revolution
    ISBN 0-679-77908-6 pa
                         LC 97-2769
"In the spring of 1776, with a British invasion fleet on its way, the Second Continental Congress appointed a committee to compose a statement explaining America's decision to seek independence. Thomas Jefferson was the principal drafter of the statement, but Maier makes it clear that his task was to express the sentiments of the Congress, not his personal views, and she shows that when the congressmen edited his draft they improved it greatly (rather than 'mangling' it, as Jefferson ever after maintained). The Declaration of Independence is, she argues, a profoundly collective document, both in its origins and in our still-evolving interpretation of its self-evident truths." New Yorker

Minks, Benton

Revolutionary war; [by] Benton Minks and Louise Minks; John S. Bowman, general editor. Rev. ed.; Chelsea House 2010 217p il map (America at war) $45

Grades: 9 10 11 12 **973.3**
    1. United States -- History -- 1775-1783, Revolution
    ISBN 978-0-8160-8196-7
                         LC 2009-44102
First published 1992

This is an "account of America's heroic seven-year struggle for independence, from the first shots at Lexington and Concord to the British surrender at Yorktown, Virginia." Publisher's note

Includes glossary and bibliographical references

Purvis, Thomas L.

★ **Revolutionary** America, 1763-1800. Facts on File 1995 383p il maps (Almanacs of American life) $95

Grades: 11 12 Adult **973.3**
    1. United States -- Social life and customs 2. United States -- History -- 1775-1783, Revolution
    ISBN 0-8160-2528-2
                         LC 93-38382
"Arranged thematically, sections such as 'Climate,' 'Economy,' 'Population,' 'Health,' 'Religion,' 'Architecture,' and 'Education' provide statistical charts, graphs, and other data to show what life was like in the various parts of the country. . . . The text, covering perhaps a third of the book, explains and elaborates on the tabular informa-

tion, pulling everything together in a relevant, interesting manner." SLJ

Includes bibliographical references

Raphael, Ray

★ A **people's** history of the American Revolution; how common people shaped the fight for independence. 1st Perennial ed; Perennial 2002 506p pa $13.95

Grades: 11 12 Adult   973.3
1. United States -- History -- 1775-1783, Revolution
ISBN 0-06-000440-1

LC 2002-16992

First published 2001 by New Press

"Moving from broad overviews to stories of small groups or individuals, Raphael's study is impressive in both its sweep and its attention to the particular." Publ Wkly

Includes bibliographical references

Voices of revolutionary America; Carol Sue Humphrey, editor. Greenwood 2011 xxii, 270p (Voices of an era) $75

Grades: 8 9 10 11 12   973.3
1. Reference books 2. United States -- History -- 1775-1783, Revolution -- Sources
ISBN 978-0-313-37732-7; 978-0-313-37733-4 ebook

LC 2010047815

This book "provides a glimpse, through primary sources, of the impact the American Revolution had on the daily lives of real people living in the colonies from 1775 to 1783. . . . Highly recommended as a logical selection for middle- and high-school history collections." Booklist

Includes bibliographical references

Wood, W. J.

Battles of the Revolutionary War, 1775-1781; [by] W.J. Wood; with an introduction by John S.D. Eisenhower. Da Capo 2003 xxxii, 315p il map (Major battles and campaigns) pa $18.95

Grades: 9 10 11 12   973.3
1. United States -- History -- 1775-1783, Revolution -- Campaigns
ISBN 0-306-81329-7

First published 1990 by Algonquin Bks.

"Wood focuses on 10 major battles and campaigns of the American Revolution that have unique military qualities. Maps and new insights about the leadership of both armies make this a worthy addition to military history collections." Booklist

Includes bibliographical references

973.4   United States--Constitutional period, 1789-1809

Ellis, Joseph J.

★ **Founding** brothers; the revolutionary generation. Knopf 2000 288p $26.95; pa $14

Grades: 11 12 Adult   973.4
1. United States -- Biography 2. Presidents -- United States 3. United States -- History -- 1783-1809 4.

United States -- Politics and government -- 1783-1809
ISBN 0-375-40544-5; 0-375-70524-4 pa

LC 99-59304

"Ellis' essays are angled, fascinating, and perfect for general-interest readers." Booklist

Includes bibliographical references

Heidler, David Stephen

★ **Daily** life in the early American republic, 1790-1820; [by] David S. Heidler and Jeanne T. Heidler. Greenwood Press 2004 xxxi, 236p map (Greenwood Press 'Daily life through history' series) $49.95

Grades: 9 10 11 12   973.4
1. United States -- Social life and customs
ISBN 0-313-32391-7

LC 2004-11771

The authors "discuss the people who lived during this critical time, and uncover the essential and unexpected realities of ordinary life in the early American republic." Publisher's note

Includes bibliographical references

Lanier, Shannon

Jefferson's children; the story of one American family. by Shannon Lanier and Jane Feldman; with photographs by Jane Feldman; and an introduction by Lucian K. Truscott IV. Random House 2000 144p il hardcover o.p. pa $16.95

Grades: 7 8 9 10   973.4
1. Slaves 2. Racially mixed people 3. African Americans -- Biography 4. United States -- Race relations
ISBN 0-375-80597-4; 0-375-82168-6 pa

LC 00-44551

This is an "anthology of personal meditations by a variety of Jefferson's living descendants. Edited by Shannon Lanier, a descendant through Sally's son Madison Hemings's line, the portraits that emerge are as generous and jumbled as America itself. The statements range from hostile to conciliatory to indifferent to eloquent." NY Times Book Rev

Includes bibliographical references

Purcell, Sarah J.

★ The **early** national period; [by] Sarah Purcell. Facts on File 2004 420p il map (Eyewitness history) $75

Grades: 11 12 Adult   973.4
1. United States -- History -- 1783-1865
ISBN 0-8160-4769-3

LC 2003-14969

"A serious history student will find this book invaluable." Libr Media Connect

Includes bibliographical references

Qaiser, Annie

How to analyze the works of George Washington; by Annie Qaiser. ABDO Pub. Co. 2013 112 p. (library) $34.22

Grades: 9 10 11 12   **973.4**
1. Criticism 2. Critical thinking
ISBN 1617836451; 9781617836459

                LC 2012946240

This book by Annie Qaiser is part of the Essential Critiques series and looks at how to analyze the works of former U.S. president George Washington. This entry "examines his inaugural address, will, and even a letter to his granddaughter about love and marriage." The series focuses on "the basics of critical theory." (Booklist)

Stefoff, Rebecca

American voices from the new republic, 1783-1830. Benchmark Books 2004 xxiii, 116p (American voices from--) lib bdg $34.21
Grades: 6 7 8 9 10   **973.4**
1. United States -- History -- 1783-1865
ISBN 0-7614-1695-1

                LC 2004-11391

Describes, through excerpts from diaries, speeches, newspaper articles, and other documents of the time, United States history from 1783 to 1830. Includes review questions.

973.5   United States--1809-1845

Collins, Gail

William Henry Harrison; Gail Collins. Times Books/Henry Holt and Co. 2012 xviii, 153 p.p
Grades: 9 10 11 12 Adult   **973.5**
1. War of 1812 2. Presidents -- United States -- Biography 3. Governors -- Indiana -- Biography 4. United States -- History -- 1783-1865 5. Presidents -- United States -- Election -- 1840 6. United States -- Politics and government -- 1841-1845
ISBN 9780805091182

                LC 2011018976

This book offers a biography of U.S. former president William Henry Harrison. "Despite the legendary 1840 campaign featuring a 'log cabin, hard cider' frontiersman with humble origins, Harrison was born on a Virginia plantation, built himself a mansion as governor of the rough Indiana frontier territory, and avoided alcohol. His fame rested on two victories: the 1811 battle of Tippecanoe against the Shawnee Indians, and the 1813 Battle of the Thames during the War of 1812, in which the Indian leader Tecumseh was killed. For decades afterward, he struggled as a farmer and Ohio politician; he lost the 1836 presidential election but won four years later." (Publishers Weekly)
Includes bibliographical references and index

Greenblatt, Miriam

★ **War** of 1812; John S. Bowman, general editor. Rev. ed.; Chelsea House 2010 176p il map (America at war) $45
Grades: 9 10 11 12   **973.5**
1. War of 1812
ISBN 978-0-8160-8194-3

                LC 2009-29531

First published 1994

An account of the events surrounding the War of 1812 between the newly established United States and Great Britain. Includes glossary and bibliographical references

Heidler, David Stephen

★ The **War** of 1812; [by] David S. Heidler and Jeanne T. Heidler. Greenwood Press 2002 xxiii, 217p il maps (Greenwood guides to historic events, 1500-1900) $44.95
Grades: 11 12 Adult   **973.5**
1. War of 1812
ISBN 0-313-31687-2

                LC 2001-50102

This book discusses "the causes, battles, and personalities that surrounded the war. . . . The authors describe all of the factors that led to some of the more ignominious defeats and unexpected victories. . . . The book includes brief biographies of some of the major participants and some primary-source documents." SLJ
Includes glossary and bibliographical references

Howes, Kelly King

War of 1812; Julie L. Carnagie, editor. U.X.L 2002 xxvi, 318p $67
Grades: 7 8 9 10   **973.5**
1. War of 1812
ISBN 0-7876-5574-0

                LC 2001-44240

A chronological overview of the events of the War of 1812, accompanied by fifteen biographies of individuals associated with the war.
Includes glossary and bibliographical references

Marker, Sherry

★ **Plains** Indian wars; John S. Bowman, general editor. Rev. ed.; Chelsea House 2010 185p il map (America at war) $45
Grades: 9 10 11 12   **973.5**
1. West (U.S.) -- History 2. Native Americans -- Wars 3. Native Americans -- Great Plains
ISBN 978-0-8160-8184-4

                LC 2009-42018

First published 1996

This is an account of the wars between Plains Indians and white settlers in the American West in the 19th century.
Includes glossary and bibliographical references

Wills, Garry

★ **James** Madison. Times Bks. 2002 xx, 184p (American presidents series) $20
Grades: 11 12 Adult   **973.5**
1. Presidents 2. Members of Congress 3. Secretaries of state 4. Presidents -- United States
ISBN 0-8050-6905-4

                LC 2002-19692

The author "maintains that Madison possessed qualities that served him well early in his career but proved to be a handicap during his Presidency. . . . Written with flair, this clear and balanced account is based on a sure handling of the material." Libr J
Includes bibliographical references

973.6   United States--1845-1861

DiConsiglio, John

The **Mexican**-American War; by John DiConsiglio. Heinemann Library 2012 80 p. ill. (some col.), col. maps (library) $36.50; (paperback) $10.99

Grades: 6 7 8 9   973.6

   1. Mexican War, 1846-1848

   ISBN 1432959980; 9781432959982; 9781432960070

                            LC 2011016817

This book on the Mexican-American War by John DiConsiglio is part of the "Living Through" series. It "provid[e]s . . . an overview of the causes, events, and leading personalities that shaped this 19th century conflict" as well as "snapshots of the daily life of soldiers and civilians. . . . Issues linked to the legitimacy of the American invasion of Mexico, the dictatorial leadership of Mexican commanders, and the shifting course of military fortunes all are presented." (Children's Literature)

   Includes bibliographical references (p. 76-77) and index.

Lincoln, Abraham

The **Lincoln**-Douglas Debates of 1858; edited by Robert W. Johannsen; foreword to the anniversary edition by James L. Huston. 150th anniversary ed., Special commemorative ed.; Oxford University Press 2008 xxxviii, 329p pa $24.95

Grades: 9 10 11 12 Adult   973.6

   1. Lincoln-Douglas debates, 1858 2. United States -- Politics and government -- 1815-1861

   ISBN 978-0-19-533942-0; 0-19-533942-8

                            LC 2007034288

This edition first published 1965

With introductions to give perspective, this "includes the seven debates of 1858 as well as Douglas's speech in Chicago that set the tone for the debates." Guide to Read in Am Hist

   Includes bibliographical references

Mills, Bronwyn

★ **U.S.**-Mexican War; [by] Bronwyn Mills; John S. Bowman, general editor. Rev. ed.; Chelsea House 2010 170p il map (America at war) $45

Grades: 9 10 11 12   973.6

   1. Mexican War, 1846-1848

   ISBN 978-0-8160-8195-0

                            LC 2009-46082

First published 1992 with title: Mexican War

This book "tells the full story of a long-ignored but critical passage in American military history that was soon overshadowed by the Civil War. . . . [It] features a chapter focusing on the innovative military tactics and weaponry involved throughout the conflict." Publisher's note

   Includes glossary and bibliographical references

973.7   Administration of Abraham Lincoln, 1861-1865

Allen, Roger MacBride

Mr. Lincoln's High-Tech War; how the North used the telegraph, railroads, surveillance balloons, ironclads, high-powered weapons, and more to win the Civil War. [by] Thomas B. Allen & Roger MacBride Allen. National Geographic Society 2009 144p il $18.95; lib bdg $25.90

Grades: 5 6 7 8 9 10   973.7

   1. Lawyers 2. United States -- History -- 1861-1865, Civil War 3. Presidents 4. State legislators 5. Members of Congress 6. Technology -- History

   ISBN 1-4263-0379-3; 1-4263-0380-7 lib bdg; 978-1-4263-0379-1; 978-1-4263-0380-7 lib bdg

                            LC 2008-24546

This book contends that "President Lincoln's appreciation for the power of technology played a critical role in the North's Civil War victory over the less developed South, and discusses the specific technologies used by the North in the war." (Publisher's note) Bibliography. Index. "Grades nine to twelve." (Publisher's note)

"Well researched and clearly written, the book discusses the course of the Civil War in terms of new technology, from the ironclad and the submarine to the rapid-fire, repeating rifle and the use of railroads to carry troops and supplies. . . . The many illustrations include captioned black-and-white reproductions of period prints, paintings, and photos as well as clearly labeled drawings. . . . [Readers] will gain a fascinating perspective on why the war progressed as it did and how it was ultimately won." Booklist

   Includes bibliographical references

★   **American** Civil War; the essential reference guide. James R. Arnold and Roberta Wiener, editors. ABC-CLIO 2011 xxii, 432p il map $85

Grades: 7 8 9 10 11 12 Adult   973.7

   1. Reference books 2. United States -- History -- 1861-1865, Civil War -- Encyclopedias

   ISBN 978-1-59884-905-9; 978-1-59884-906-6 ebook

                            LC 2011018004

"Libraries that need single-volume Civil War ready reference or report material will appreciate this work. It combines opening essays featuring analysis of the war's causes, consequences, and historical controversies; 100 encyclopedia entries; a selection of primary-source readings; and a highly detailed time line. . . . The primary-source readings include laws, speeches, and private letters that reflect contemporaneous public opinion and official reactions to the war." SLJ

   Includes bibliographical references

Anderson, Tanya

Tillie Pierce; teen eyewitness to the Battle of Gettysburg. by Tanya Anderson. Twenty-First Century Books 2013 96 p. ill., maps (library) $34.60

Grades: 9 10 11 12   973.7

   1. Gettysburg (Pa.), Battle of, 1863

   ISBN 1467706922; 9781467706926

                            LC 2012018072

This book, by Tanya Anderson, profiles how "in July 1863, . . . Tillie Pierce, a normal teenager . . . , became an unlikely heroine of the Civil War. . . . Tillie and other women and girls like her found themselves trapped during this critical three-day battle in southern Pennsylvania. Without training, but with enormous courage and compassion, Tillie and other Gettysburg citizens helped save the lives of countless wounded Union and Confederate soldiers." (Publisher's note)

Includes bibliographical references (p. 90-93) and index.

Armstrong, Jennifer

Photo by Brady; a picture of the Civil War. Atheneum Books For Young Readers 2005 160p il $18.95

Grades: 6 7 8 9 10   **973.7**

1. Photographers 2. Photography -- History 3. United States -- History -- 1861-1865, Civil War

ISBN 0-689-85785-3

LC 2004-8967

"Armstrong chronicles the Civil War from Lincoln's election to his death with both a storylike narrative of events and a photo-essay. . . . This book is also a look at early photographic techniques and offers a description of [Mathew] Brady's rare collection. . . . When readers remember that the pictures are more than 100 years old, they should recognize their exquisiteness, grandeur, and genius." SLJ

Includes bibliographical references

Barney, William L.

The **Civil** War and Reconstruction; a student companion. Oxford Univ. Press 2001 368p il maps (Oxford student companions to American history) $60

Grades: 7 8 9 10   **973.7**

1. Reconstruction (1865-1876) 2. United States -- History -- 1861-1865, Civil War

ISBN 0-19-511559-7

LC 00-57444

"The book is encyclopedic in format, with many useful access points, and bibliographic information is located both at the ends of the articles and in several appendixes that suggest books, historic sites and addresses, and Web sites." Voice Youth Advocates

Includes bibliographical references (p. 358-359) and index

Blount, Roy

★ **Robert** E. Lee; a Penguin life. [by] Roy Blount, Jr. Lipper/Viking Bk. 2003 210p (Penguin lives series) $19.95; pa $13

Grades: 11 12 Adult   **973.7**

1. Generals 2. College presidents 3. Confederate States of America -- Army 4. United States -- History -- 1861-1865, Civil War

ISBN 0-670-03220-4; 0-14-303866-4 pa

LC 2002-32423

This is a biography of "the famous Southern general admired for his military leadership but also scorned for defending the Confederacy. Blount's concise writing keeps his bi-ography trim and succinct, and his admiration for the subject allows for enjoyable reading." Booklist

Includes bibliographical references

Boatner, Mark Mayo

The **Civil** War dictionary; by Mark Mayo Boatner III; maps and diagrams by Allen C. Northrop and Lowell I. Miller. 1st Vintage Civil War Library ed.; Vintage Civil War Library 1991 974p il map pa $24

Grades: 11 12 Adult   **973.7**

1. Reference books 2. United States -- History -- 1861-1865, Civil War -- Encyclopedias

ISBN 0-679-73392-2; 978-0-679-73392-8

LC 91-50013

First published 1959 by McKay

"With more than 4,000 entries . . . this dictionary remains the most comprehensive and consistently accurate reference tool on the American Civil War. In addition to the biographical sketches there are entries relating to campaigns and battles, naval engagements, weapons, issues and incidents, military terms and definitions, politics, literature, and statistics." Choice

Includes bibliographical references

Bodden, Valerie

How to analyze the works of Frederick Douglass; by Valerie Bodden. ABDO Pub. Co. 2013 112 p. (library) $34.22

Grades: 9 10 11 12   **973.7**

1. Criticism 2. Critical thinking

ISBN 1617836443; 9781617836442

LC 2012946238

This book by Valerie Bodden is part of the Essential Critiques series and looks at how to analyze the works of former slave and abolitionist Frederick Douglass. This entry considers Douglass's biography as well as his letters and speeches. The series focuses on "the basics of critical theory." (Booklist)

Bolden, Tonya

★ **Cause**: Reconstruction America, 1863-1877. Knopf 2005 138p il $19.95; lib bdg $21.99

Grades: 7 8 9 10   **973.7**

1. Reconstruction (1865-1876) 2. United States -- History -- 1865-1898

ISBN 0-375-82795-1; 0-375-92795-6 lib bdg

"This examination of America during Reconstruction covers Lincoln's Proclamation of Amnesty and Reconstruction, the Civil Rights Act of 1866, the troubles of freed slaves, the expansion of the nation and the plight of Native Americans, the 15th Amendment, and the women's suffrage movement. While this is well-documented nonfiction, Bolden writes in the voice of a storyteller. The excellent graphics include archival photos, political cartoons, and primary resources." SLJ

Emancipation Proclamation; Lincoln and the dawn of liberty. Tonya Bolden. Abrams Books for Young Readers 2012 128 p. (alk. paper) $24.95

Grades: 6 7 8 9   **973.7**

1. Slaves -- Emancipation   2. Emancipation

Proclamation 3. United States -- History -- 1861-1865, Civil War 4. United States. President (1861-1865: Lincoln). Emancipation Proclamation

ISBN 1419703900; 9781419703904

LC 2012000845

This book offers a "depiction of the issues and tensions surrounding abolition and the development of [Abraham] Lincoln's responses to them as the United States plunged into the Civil War. . . . The author tracks rising tides of both rhetoric and violence, as well as the evolution of President Abraham Lincoln's determined efforts to forge a policy that would serve military, political and moral necessities alike." (Kirkus Reviews)

Includes bibliographical references and index

Browne, Ray Broadus

★ The **Civil** War and Reconstruction; [by] Ray B. Browne and Lawrence A. Kreiser, Jr. Greenwood Press 2003 215p il (American popular culture through history) $49.95

Grades: 9 10 11 12   **973.7**

1. Reconstruction (1865-1876) 2. Popular culture -- United States 3. United States -- History -- 1861-1865, Civil War

ISBN 0-313-31325-3

LC 2002-35206

"Browne and Kreiser begin with overview chapters on daily life for the general population, and then examine in detail 10 aspects of culture including advertising, clothing and fashion, food, leisure activities, travel and transportation, and several categories of performing and fine arts. The authors describe both the trends and important people that shaped popular culture and the impact of the war and its aftermath. For example, they relate how baseball became America's pastime when Civil War soldiers, who learned to play while in camps, carried the game home with them at the war's end. Each chapter is well documented. . . . This well-written and objective book deserves a place in all libraries." SLJ

Includes bibliographical references

Carlisle, Rodney P.

★ Civil War and Reconstruction. Facts on File 2008 452p il map (Eyewitness history) $75

Grades: 7 8 9 10   **973.7**

1. Reconstruction (1865-1876) 2. United States -- History -- 1861-1865, Civil War -- Sources

ISBN 978-0-8160-6347-5

LC 2006-35425

First published 1991 under the authorship of Joe H. Kirchberger

"This illustrated chronology of the Civil War contains over 100 black-and-white photographs (mostly from the Library of Congress Prints and Photographs Division), 16 maps, and biographies of 50 key figures in the era. Each period-based chapter offers a narrative that delves into deeper issues of the causation of war; a chronicle of events, detailed to the week; and eyewitness testimony, including diaries, journals, correspondence, editorials, and news accounts." Choice

Includes bibliographical references

★ The **Causes** of the Civil War; edited by Kenneth M. Stampp. 3rd rev ed; Simon & Schuster 1991 255p pa $14

Grades: 11 12 Adult   **973.7**

1. Nationalism 2. State rights 3. Slavery -- United States 4. Southern States -- Economic conditions 5. United States -- History -- 1861-1865, Civil War -- Causes 6. United States -- History -- 1861-1865, Civil War -- Sources

ISBN 0-671-75155-7

LC 91-36819

First published 1959 by Prentice-Hall

This book integrates the conclusions of various post-war historians with the thoughts of contemporary commentators like Jefferson Davis, Horace Greeley, and Lincoln. Political, cultural and economic aspects are emphasized

Includes bibliographical references

Center for the National Archives Experience

Discovering the Civil War; by the National Archives Experience's 'Discovering the Civil War' Exhibition Team with a message from David S. Ferriero, Archivist of the United States; foreword by Ken Burns. D. Giles Ltd. 2010 208p il map $44.95

Grades: 11 12 Adult   **973.7**

1. United States -- History -- 1861-1865, Civil War

ISBN 978-1-904832-91-1

LC 2010-27924

"Created to accompany the major National Archives Civil War exhibit that mined our national trove of photographs, manuscripts, maps, ephemera, realia, and more, this book is spectacular in its presentation of the wide array of seemingly mundane but surprisingly revealing sources from both the well known and the obscure. . . . The intelligent framing of issues (e.g., government controls, technological and scientific innovation) for each chapter will invite readers to consider many questions about war and society, war making, and the economy of war." Libr J

Includes bibliographical references

The **Civil** War; James Tackach, book editor. Greenhaven Press 2004 186 p. ill. (Turning points) (library) $42.15

Grades: 7 8 9 10   **973.7**

1. United States -- History -- 1861-1865, Civil War

ISBN 0737711140; 9780737711141

LC 2003064297

"Comprised of 17 essays, this book is divided into four chapters: 'A Nation Divides: The Causes of the Civil War,' 'Early Battlefield Victories and the Prospect of European Intervention Fuel the South's Hope for Independence,' 'The North Gains the Advantage,' and 'A Changed Nation.' Many of the most respected Civil War historians . . . are excerpted. . . . Outstanding features of the book are discussion questions and the appendix of documents that are sure to inspire additional research and assist classroom teachers." SLJ

Includes bibliographical references (p. 179-181) and index.

The **Civil** War: a visual history; [produced in association with the Smithsonian Institution] DK Publishing 2011 360p il map $40

Grades: 11 12 Adult	**973.7**
1. United States -- History -- 1861-1865, Civil War -- Pictorial works
ISBN 978-0-7566-7185-3

"Drawing on Smithsonian Institution collections, this fact-filled and richly illustrated history brings the war fully to life, along with time lines, sidebars on particular issues, chapter introductions, lengthy captions, and detailed maps. The emphasis throughout is on the military. Multiple examples of weapons, supplies, uniforms, camp life necessities, transport, and battle scenes dominate and show the variety, complexity, and prolixity of making war. Espionage, the home front, and politics get a nod, but this book is for those wanting to smell the sulfur and hear the thunder of guns." Libr J

Clinton, Catherine
★ **Harriet** Tubman: the road to freedom. Little, Brown 2004 272p hardcover o.p. pa $14.95

Grades: 11 12 Adult	**973.7**
1. Abolitionists 2. Underground railroad 3. African American women -- Biography
ISBN 0-316-14492-4; 0-316-15594-2 pa

LC 2003-56185

"Clinton turns sobriquets into meaningful descriptors of a unique person. In her hands, a familiar legend acquires human dimension with no diminution of its majesty and power." Publ Wkly

Includes bibliographical references

DeRamus, Betty
Forbidden fruit; love stories from the Underground Railroad. Atria Books 2005 269p il $25; pa $14

Grades: 11 12 Adult	**973.7**
1. Love 2. Underground railroad 3. Slavery -- United States
ISBN 0-7434-8263-8; 978-0-7434-8263-9; 0-7434-8264-6 pa; 978-0-7434-8264-6 pa

LC 2004-63414

This is an "uplifting and sometimes heartbreaking look at love during the U.S.'s slavery years." Publ Wkly

Includes bibliographical references

Detzer, David
★ **Allegiance**; Fort Sumter, Charleston, and the beginning of the Civil War. Harcourt 2001 367p $27

Grades: 11 12 Adult	**973.7**
1. Charleston (S.C.) -- History 2. Fort Sumter (Charleston, S.C.) 3. United States -- History -- 1861-1865, Civil War -- Causes
ISBN 0-15-100641-5

LC 00-50570

"The central figure in this drama is Maj. Robert Anderson, commander of the Union garrison in Charleston Harbor. . . . Detzer's writing style brings the reader into close contact

with soldiers, civilians and politicians as they struggle to solve the fate of Anderson and his men." Publ Wkly

Includes bibliographical references

Dissonance; between Fort Sumter and Bull Run in the turbulent first days of the Civil War. Harcourt 2006 xxv, 371p $27; pa $15

Grades: 9 10 11 12	**973.7**
1. United States -- History -- 1861-1865, Civil War
ISBN 978-0-15-101158-2; 0-15-101158-3; 978-0-15-603064-9 pa; 0-15-603064-0 pa

LC 2005-20991

The author "has written an engaging and comprehensive account of the early days of the Civil War that should have wide appeal." Publ Wkly

Includes bibliographical references

Encyclopedia of the American Civil War; a political, social, and military history. David S. Heidler and Jeanne T. Heidler, editors; foreword by James W. McPherson; David J. Coles, associate editor; Gary W. Gallagher, James M. McPherson, Mark E. Neely, Jr., editorial board. ABC-CLIO 2000 5v il maps set $425

Grades: 11 12 Adult	**973.7**
1. Reference books 2. United States -- History -- 1861-1865, Civil War -- Encyclopedias
ISBN 1-57607-066-2

LC 00-11195

ALA RUSA Dartmouth Medal honorable mention (2001)

"The editors have compiled a comprehensive source that provides a first-stop reference on broad areas or specific topics on the Civil War. The contemporary photographs and lithographs bring the human element into the encyclopedia, a type of reference known more for facts and figures than emotions. The primary-source-documents volume brings obscure resources together, which will further illumine the period for students."—"Outstanding Reference Sources." American Libraries, May 2001

Includes bibliographical references

Faust, Drew Gilpin
★ **Mothers** of invention; women of the slaveholding South in the American Civil War. University of N.C. Press 1996 326p il $37.50; pa $19.95

Grades: 11 12 Adult	**973.7**
1. Women -- Southern States 2. United States -- History -- 1861-1865, Civil War -- Women
ISBN 0-8078-2255-8; 0-8078-5573-1 pa

LC 95-8896

Based on journals, letters and memoirs, this is an "analysis of the impact of secession, invasion and conquest on Southern white women. Antebellum images based on helplessness and dependence were challenged as women assumed an increasing range of social and economic responsibilities. . . . Faust's provocative analysis of a complex subject merits a place in all collections of U.S. history." Publ Wkly

Includes bibliographical references

Fredriksen, John C.

Civil War almanac. Facts on File, Inc. 2007 858p il map (Almanacs of American wars) $85

Grades: 11 12 Adult **973.7**

1. United States -- History -- 1861-1865, Civil War

ISBN 0-8160-6459-8; 978-0-8160-6459-5

LC 2006-29985

First published 1983 under the editorship of John Stewart Bowman

This book contains a "day-by-day chronology of the events and people of this monumental war, along with an A-to-Z dictionary offering biographical information on leading military and political figures involved in the conflict." Publisher's note

Includes bibliographical references

Geary, Rick

★ The **murder** of Abraham Lincoln; a chronicle of 62 days in the life of the American Republic, March 4-May 4, 1865. written and illustrated by Rick Geary. NBM ComicsLit 2005 un il map (A treasury of Victorian murder) $15.95; pa $8.95

Grades: 7 8 9 10 11 12 **973.7**

1. Actors 2. Lawyers 3. Presidents 4. Graphic novels 5. Murderers 6. State legislators 7. Members of Congress

ISBN 978-1-56163-425-5; 1-56163-425-5; 978-1-56163-426-2 pa; 1-56163-426-3 pa

LC 2005-41468

This graphic novel "covers Lincoln's assassination, the events that led up to it, and the aftermath. Geary also makes a point of bringing up still-unanswered questions, like the whereabouts of the missing pages of John Wilkes Booth's journal. . . . Even teens who know nothing about the tragedy will find their heads chock-full of information when they're finished reading this book." SLJ

Includes bibliographical references

Gienapp, William E.

Abraham Lincoln and Civil War America; a biography. Oxford Univ. Press 2001 239p il maps hardcover o.p. pa $24.95

Grades: 11 12 Adult **973.7**

1. Lawyers 2. Presidents 3. State legislators 4. Members of Congress 5. Presidents -- United States 6. United States -- History -- 1861-1865, Civil War

ISBN 0-19-515099-6; 0-19-515100-3 pa

LC 2001-50056

This biography focuses on the American president's leadership during the Civil War.

"In spite of the book's size, its discriminating history of Lincoln's life is surprisingly rich, and the narrative of his presidency and the unfolding of the war is crisp and coherent." Bookmarks

Includes bibliographical references

Gourley, Catherine

The **horrors** of Andersonville; life and death inside a Civil War prison. Twenty-First Century Books 2010 193p il lib bdg $38.60

Grades: 8 9 10 11 12 **973.7**

1. War criminals 2. Prisoners of war 3. Army officers 4. Andersonville Prison 5. United States -- History -- 1861-1865, Civil War -- Prisoners and prisons

ISBN 978-0-7613-4212-0; 0-7613-4212-5

LC 2008-46595

"This well-researched book describes the notorious Confederate prison camp known as Andersonville, where more than 45,000 Union soldiers lived in deplorable conditions and some 13,000 died, beginning in 1864. . . . Illustrated with many captioned photos and prints and enlivened with quotes from firsthand accounts, this book provides a balanced, informative introduction to Andersonville." Booklist

Includes bibliographical references

Hargrove, Hondon B.

★ **Black** Union soldiers in the Civil War. McFarland & Co. 1988 250p il hardcover o.p. pa $35

Grades: 11 12 Adult **973.7**

1. African American soldiers 2. United States -- Army -- History 3. United States -- History -- 1861-1865, Civil War

ISBN 0-89950-337-3; 0-7864-1697-1 pa

LC 88-42511

This volume "discusses the participation of Blacks in the Union Army during the Civil War. The chronologically arranged narrative covers Black soldiers in each battle. Special features include an extensive bibliography and nine appendixes that reprint documents and include rosters and statistics." Nichols. Guide to Ref Books for Sch Media Cent. 4th edition

Harris, Laurie Lanzen

How to analyze the works of Abraham Lincoln; by Laurie Lanzen Harris. ABDO Pub. Co. 2013 112 p. (library) $34.22

Grades: 9 10 11 12 **973.7**

1. Criticism 2. Critical thinking

ISBN 1617836427; 9781617836428

LC 2012946248

This book by Laurie Lanzen Harris is part of the Essential Critiques series and looks at how to analyze the works of former U.S. president Abraham Lincoln, This entry "discusses Lincoln's speeches from a historical, rhetorical, political, and religious perspective." The series focuses on "the basics of critical theory." (Booklist)

Hillstrom, Kevin

American Civil War: biographies; [by] Kevin Hillstrom and Laurie Collier Hillstrom; Lawrence W. Baker, editor. U.X.L 2000 2v il (American Civil War reference library) set $110

Grades: 8 9 10 11 12 **973.7**

1. United States -- History -- 1861-1865, Civil War -- Biography

ISBN 0-7876-3820-X

LC 99-46920

This set "chronicles the lives of 60 famous and lesser-known men and women, including abolitionists, spies, commanders, and writers." SLJ

Includes bibliographical references

Hyslop, Stephen G.

Atlas of the Civil War; a comprehensive guide to the tactics and terrain of battle. edited by Neil Kagan; narrative by Stephen G. Hyslop; introduction by Harris J. Andrews. National Geographic Society 2009 255p il map $40

Grades: 11 12 Adult   **973.7**

1. Reference books 2. Historical atlases 3. United States -- History -- 1861-1865, Civil War -- Maps

ISBN 978-1-4262-0347-3

LC 2008-35066

"Arranged chronologically, this atlas combines period photographs and illustrations, rare period maps and modern cartography, with just enough narrative to explain the two-page spread devoted to each subject (the majority being about particular battles or campaigns). . . . The text also features numerous sidebars throughout, offering micro-timelines, biographies, and images showing the human side of the war. All of these special features make this large-format atlas a superior choice for Civil War buffs as well as those new to the subject." Libr J

Krowl, Michelle A.

★ **Women** of the Civil War. Library of Congress 2006 63p il (Women who dare) $12.95

Grades: 9 10 11 12   **973.7**

1. United States -- History -- 1861-1865, Civil War -- Women

ISBN 0-7649-3546-1; 978-0-7649-3546-6

LC 2005-40195

This book "celebrates women of both the North and the South whose courage and daring brought them into the fray, whether by donning men's clothes and fighting as soldiers, becoming spies, working as nurses in the bloody battlefields, or becoming propagandists for the cause." Publisher's note

Includes bibliographical references

Leonard, Elizabeth D.

All the daring of the soldier; women of the Civil War armies. Norton 1999 368p il hardcover o.p. pa $22.95

Grades: 11 12 Adult   **973.7**

1. Women soldiers 2. United States -- Army 3. Confederate States of America -- Army 4. United States -- History -- 1861-1865, Civil War

ISBN 978-0-393-04712-7; 0-393-04712-1; 978-0-393-33547-7 pa; 0-393-33547-X pa

LC 98-52304

The author presents "stories of dozens of women who served in both the Union and Confederacy during the Civil War. Some were spies, but many more adopted men's names, dressed in men's clothes and lived and fought and died alongside mostly unsuspecting men." Publ Wkly

Includes bibliographical references

Lincoln, Abraham

The **Lincoln** mailbag; America writes to the President, 1861-1865. edited by Harold Holzer. Southern Ill. Univ. Press 1998 xxxv, 236p il $32; pa $22.95

Grades: 9 10 11 12   **973.7**

1. Lawyers 2. Presidents 3. State legislators 4. Members of Congress 5. United States -- History -- 1861-1865, Civil War

ISBN 0-8093-2072-X; 0-8093-2685-X pa

LC 97-42164

This collection of letters to President Lincoln includes "death threats, requests for offices, requests for money, invitations to speak, unsolicited gifts, proposals for new weapons, and pesterings for favors from obscure relatives and impostors. . . . A revealing glimpse into how civil war and emancipation appeared from the White House, this browsable collection of epistles and replies enriches the body of Lincolniana." Booklist

★ The **portable** Abraham Lincoln; edited with an introduction by Andrew Delbanco. Bicentennial ed.; Penguin Books 2009 xxvii, 369p (Penguin classics) pa $18

Grades: Adult   **973.7**

1. United States -- Politics and government -- 1815-1861 2. United States -- Politics and government -- 1861-1865

ISBN 978-0-14-310564-0; 0-14-310564-7

LC 2008-32452

First published 1992

Material drawn from Speeches and writings, published by the Library of America (1989).

"This collection shows Lincoln at work in law, politics, and war. All the great Lincoln works are here, with the added bonus of several personal memos that show Lincoln's humor." Libr J

Marten, James

★ **Civil** War America; voices from the home front. ABC-CLIO 2003 346p il $85

Grades: 11 12 Adult   **973.7**

1. United States -- History -- 1861-1865, Civil War -- Personal narratives

ISBN 1-576-07237-1

LC 2002-154377

"Marten offers a view of the war through the eyes of diverse noncombatants. Four parts of this five-part work each deal with Southerners, Northerners, children, and African Americans . . . Part five, 'Aftermaths,' includes descriptions of the postwar lives of veterans, orphans, and ex-slaves, and concludes with a chapter on the Civil War stories by Ambrose Bierce. Readers will find Marten's overarching theme of change—both immediate and long-range—revelatory and instructional." SLJ

Includes bibliographical references

Masur, Louis P.

The **Civil** War: a concise history. Oxford University Press 2011 118p il $18.95

Grades: 11 12 Adult   **973.7**

1. United States -- History -- 1861-1865, Civil War

ISBN 978-0-19-974048-2

LC 2010-19460

The author provides "a concise but compelling narrative of the Civil War era, packing in the critical information to track the trajectory of secession, war, emancipation, and Reconstruction. He focuses on the political and the military,

with Lincoln, Jefferson Davis, and the generals especially getting their due." Libr J
Includes bibliographical references

McNeese, Tim

The **abolitionist** movement; ending slavery. Chelsea House 2007 142p il (Reform movements in American history) lib bdg $30

Grades: 8 9 10 11 12   973.7
   1. Abolitionists 2. Slavery -- United States
ISBN 978-0-7910-9502-7; 0-7910-9502-9

                      LC 2007-14766

"Complex, detailed, and yet very readable, this title . . . discusses the struggles and differences within the antislavery movement as well as the fight for emancipation and its crucial role in the Civil War. . . . The book offers a sound exploration of the topic." Booklist
Includes bibliographical references

McPherson, James M.

Abraham Lincoln and the second American Revolution. Oxford Univ. Press 1991 173p hardcover o.p. pa $16.95

Grades: 11 12 Adult   973.7
   1. Lawyers 2. Presidents 3. State legislators 4. Members of Congress 5. United States -- History -- 1861-1865, Civil War
ISBN 0-19-507606-0 pa

                      LC 90-6885

The author "examines Lincoln's role in the transformation wrought by the Civil War—the liberation of four million slaves, the overthrow of the social and political order of the South." Publ Wkly
Includes bibliographical references

Drawn with the sword; reflections on the American Civil War. Oxford Univ. Press 1996 258p $45; pa $18.95

Grades: 11 12 Adult   973.7
   1. Authors 2. Lawyers 3. Generals 4. Novelists 5. Statesmen 6. Presidents 7. Abolitionists 8. Vice-presidents 9. Orators 10. State legislators 11. Children's authors 12. Nonfiction writers 13. Secretaries of war 14. Members of Congress 15. Short story writers 16. Secretaries of state 17. Glory (Motion picture) 18. Emancipation Proclamation (1863) 19. United States -- History -- 1861-1865, Civil War
ISBN 0-19-509679-7; 0-19-511796-4 pa

                      LC 95-38107

"These pieces provide a lively reminder that the best scholarship is also often a pleasure to read." N Y Times Book Rev

For cause and comrades; why men fought in the Civil War. Oxford Univ. Press 1997 237p $25; pa $15.95

Grades: 11 12 Adult   973.7
   1. Soldiers -- United States 2. United States -- History -- 1861-1865, Civil War
ISBN 0-19-509023-3; 0-19-512499-5 pa

                      LC 96-24760

"Volumes have been written on the causes of the Civil War, but less has been written on what caused soldiers to risk their lives on the battlefield. McPherson . . . fills the gap. After studying thousands of letters and diaries, he discusses what really led soldiers to enlist, what kept them in the army, and what led them to the front lines." Libr J
Includes bibliographical references

Murphy, Jim

The **boys'** war; Confederate and Union soldiers talk about the Civil War. Clarion Bks. 1990 110p il hardcover o.p. pa $8.95

Grades: 5 6 7 8 9 10   973.7
   1. United States -- History -- 1861-1865, Civil War
ISBN 0-89919-893-7; 0-395-66412-8 pa

                      LC 89-23959

This book includes diary entries, personal letters, and archival photographs to describe the experiences of boys, sixteen years old or younger, who fought in the Civil War.

"An excellent selection of more than 45 sepia-toned contemporary photographs augment the text of this informative, moving work." SLJ
Includes bibliographical references

Netzley, Patricia D.

★ **Civil** War. Greenhaven Press 2004 336p il (Greenhaven encyclopedia of) lib bdg $74.95

Grades: 8 9 10 11 12   973.7
   1. Reference books 2. United States -- History -- 1861-1865, Civil War -- Encyclopedias
ISBN 0-7377-0438-1

                    LC 2003-11808

An alphabetical presentation of definitions and descriptions of terms, people, and events of the Civil War

"Basic, accurate information about many aspects of the war. . . . The well-written, objective entries are cross-referenced. . . . Netzley's solid volume will be helpful to students needing introductory research material." SLJ
Includes bibliographical references

Osborne, Linda Barrett

Traveling the freedom road; from slavery and the Civil War through Reconstruction. Abrams Books for Young Readers 2009 128p il map $24.95

Grades: 6 7 8 9 10   973.7
   1. Reconstruction (1865-1876) 2. Slavery -- United States 3. African Americans -- History 4. United States -- History -- 1861-1865, Civil War 5. United States -- Politics and government -- 1783-1865 6. United States -- Politics and government -- 1865-1898
ISBN 0-8109-8338-9; 978-0-8109-8338-0

                    LC 2008-22298

"This fascinating, well-designed volume offers an essential introduction to the experiences of African Americans between 1800 and 1877. . . . Osborne moves from . . . personal stories to broader historical milestones, and in highly accessible language, she provides basic background even as she challenges readers with philosophical questions. . . . This fluid exchange between political events and intimate, human stories creates a highly absorbing whole." Booklist

Rees, Bob

The **Civil** War; by Bob Rees. Heinemann Library 2012 80 p. ill. (some col.), col. maps (library) $36.50; (paperback) $10.99

Grades: 6 7 8 9   **973.7**

1. United States -- History -- 1861-1865, Civil War

ISBN 1432959964; 9781432959968; 9781432960056

LC 2011018258

This book by Bob Rees is part of the Living Through . . . series and looks at the U.S. Civil War. The "set summarizes events in major conflicts using brief first-person accounts, sidebars, short biographies, color and archival photos, maps, and other graphics." The authors include "views from multiple perspectives." (School Library Journal)

Includes bibliographical references (p. 76) and index.

Sears, Stephen W.

★ **Gettysburg**. Houghton Mifflin 2003 623p il map $30; pa $17

Grades: 11 12 Adult   **973.7**

1. Gettysburg (Pa.), Battle of, 1863

ISBN 0-395-86761-4; 0-618-48538-4 pa

LC 2002-191259

This is an "assessment of the battle of Gettysburg and the events leading up to it. . . . Sears examines several turning points during the battle's buildup and three-day duration. The resulting insights add to the excellent and dramatic narrative flow. . . . For all Civil War collections and academic libraries." Libr J

Includes bibliographical references

Seidman, Rachel Filene

The **Civil** war: a history in documents. Oxford University Press 2001 206p il map (Pages from history) lib bdg $39.95

Grades: 8 9 10 11 12   **973.7**

1. United States -- History -- 1861-1865, Civil War -- Sources

ISBN 978-0-19-511558-1; 0-19-511558-9

LC 00-37523

"Seidman's documents bookend the Civil War with the territorial expansion that preceded the conflict and with the Reconstruction that followed it. In this structure the documents, under the guidance of Seidman's linking narrative, all make a powerful impression of immediacy about ordinary people's experience of, and condemnation or defense of, slavery." Booklist

Includes bibliographical references

Snodgrass, Mary Ellen

★ The **Underground** Railroad; an encyclopedia of people, places, and operations. Sharpe Reference 2007 2v il map set $199

Grades: 7 8 9 10 11 12 Adult   **973.7**

1. Reference books 2. Underground railroad -- Encyclopedias 3. Slavery -- United States -- Encyclopedias

ISBN 978-0-7656-8093-8

LC 2007-9199

The author "has compiled an important and extensively researched encyclopedia of the Underground Railroad. Be-

ginning with a concise, informative general introduction, this ambitious two-volume set neatly identifies the key people, places, documents, organizations, and publications of the Underground Railroad movement, along with significant actions, events, and ideas underlying it in the US and Canada. Offering photographs, bookplates, sketches, and handbills, the set is visually attractive." Choice

Includes bibliographical references

Swanson, James L.

Chasing Lincoln's killer; the search for John Wilkes Booth. Scholastic Press 2009 194p il map $16.99

Grades: 7 8 9 10   **973.7**

1. Actors 2. Lawyers 3. Presidents 4. Murderers 5. State legislators 6. Members of Congress 7. United States -- History -- 1861-1865, Civil War

ISBN 978-0-439-90354-7; 0-439-90354-8

LC 2008-17994

"This volume is an adaptation of Swanson's Manhunt: The 12-Day Chase for Lincoln's Killer (HarperCollins, 2006). Divided into 14 chapters and an epilogue, the sentences are shorter and chapters are condensed from the original but the rich details and suspense are ever present. . . . Excellent black-and-white illustrations complement the text. . . . Readers will be engrossed by the almost hour-by-hour search and by the many people who encountered the killer as he tried to escape. It is a tale of intrigue and an engrossing mystery." SLJ

Swanson, Mark

Atlas of the Civil War, month by month; major battles and troop movements. maps by Mark Swanson, with Jacqueline D. Langley. University of Georgia Press 2004 141p il map $39.95

Grades: 11 12 Adult   **973.7**

1. Reference books 2. Historical atlases 3. United States -- History -- 1861-1865, Civil War -- Maps

ISBN 0-8203-2658-5

LC 2004-12264

This Civil War atlas depicts "multiple aspects of the war's action in a month-by-month sequence from April 1861 to June 1865. . . . An absolute must for Civil War studies." Univ Press Books for Public and Second Sch Libr, 2006

Includes bibliographical references

Tobin, Jacqueline

Hidden in plain view; the secret story of quilts and the underground railroad. [by] Jacqueline L. Tobin and Raymond G. Dobard. Doubleday 1999 208p il map hardcover o.p. pa $14

Grades: 11 12 Adult   **973.7**

1. Quilts 2. Ciphers 3. Underground railroad

ISBN 0-385-49137-9; 0-385-49767-9 pa

LC 98-49804

This is "a needed and valuable contribution to the literature of African American culture." Libr J

Includes bibliographical references

Walker, Sally M.

★ **Secrets** of a Civil War submarine; solving the mysteries of the H.L. Hunley. Carolrhoda Books 2005 112p il lib bdg $17.95

Grades: 7 8 9 10 **973.7**

1. Shipwrecks 2. Submarines 3. Underwater exploration 4. Hunley (Submarine) 5. United States -- History -- 1861-1865, Civil War -- Naval operations

ISBN 1-57505-830-8

LC 2004-19646

This discusses "the Confederate submarine H. L. Hunley. . . . Walker begins with the history of the Hunley's design and construction as well as its place in Civil War and naval history. She really hits her stride, though, in explaining the complex techniques and loving care used in raising the craft, recovering its contents, and even reconstructing models of the crewmembers' bodies. . . . Thoroughly researched, nicely designed, and well illustrated with clear, color photos." Booklist

Includes glossary and bibliographical references

Ward, Andrew

The **slaves'** war; the Civil War in the words of former slaves. Houghton Mifflin Co. 2008 386p il $28

Grades: 11 12 Adult **973.7**

1. Slavery -- United States 2. Freedmen -- United States 3. Slaves -- Southern States -- Biography 4. United States -- History -- Civil War, 1861-1865 -- Social aspects 5. United States -- History -- Civil War, 1861-1865 -- African Americans 6. United States -- History -- 1861-1865, Civil War -- Personal narratives 7. United States -- History -- Civil War, 1861-1865 -- Personal narratives

ISBN 0-618-63400-2; 978-0-618-63400-2

LC 2008-1532

Collected from "interviews, diaries, letters, and memoirs, here is the Civil War as seen from not only battlefields, capitals, and camps, but also slave quarters, kitchens, roadsides, farms, towns, and swamps." (Publisher's note) Index.

The author "has provided a . . . narrative that gives voice to the experiences and attitudes of slaves who endured the conflict. Ward utilizes testimonials, diaries, and letters, and organizes them in chronological order from the months before the commencement of hostilities to the aftermath of the surrender at Appomattox. . . . This is a work that will interest both scholars and general readers." Booklist

Includes bibliographical references

Williams, David

Bitterly divided; the South's inner Civil War. David Williams. New Press 2008 310p ill., ports. (hbk.) o.p.; (pbk.) $14; (hbk.) o.p.

Grades: 11 12 Adult **973.7**

1. Social conflict 2. Southern States -- History 3. Secession -- Southern States 4. Confederate States of America 5. United States -- History -- 1861-1865, Civil War 6. Social conflict -- Southern States -- History -- 19th century

ISBN 1-59558-108-1; 978-1595584755; 9781595581082

LC 2007045285

In this book, author and "historian David Williams lays bare the myth of a united confederacy, revealing that the South was in fact fighting two civil wars--an external one that we know so much about and an internal one about which there is scant literature and virtually no public awareness. . . . [The book] shows that from the Confederacy's very beginnings white Southerners were as likely to have opposed secession as supported it, and they undermined the Confederate war effort at nearly every turn. In just one of many telling examples in . . . narrative history, Williams shows that when planters grew too much cotton and tobacco and exempted themselves from the draft, plain folk called the conflict a 'rich man's war' and rioted. Many formed armed anti-Confederate bands. Southern blacks, in what W.E.B. DuBois called 'a general strike against the Confederacy,' resisted in increasingly overt ways, escaped by the thousands, and forced a change in the war's direction that led to emancipation." (Publisher's note)

Includes bibliographical references (p. [275]-291) and index

Women in the American Civil War; Lisa Tendrich Frank, editor. ABC-CLIO 2008 2v il set $195

Grades: 10 11 12 Adult **973.7**

1. Reference books 2. United States -- History -- 1861-1865, Civil War -- Women -- Encyclopedias

ISBN 978-1-85109-600-8

LC 2007-25822

"Frank's two-volume work emphasizes the role of women in the American Civil War. With its wealth of information and resources, this set will be a welcome addition to any reference collection. Fourteen contextual essays discuss the social and political issues of the era and the varied backgrounds of women affected by the war. Over 300 entries include biographical sketches, key military and political events, and the contributions of women during the war." Choice

Includes bibliographical references

Woodworth, Steven E.

★ **Atlas** of the Civil War; by Steven Woodworth and Kenneth J. Winkle; foreword by James M. McPherson. Oxford University Press 2004 400p il map $75

Grades: 11 12 Adult **973.7**

1. Reference books 2. Historical atlases 3. United States -- History -- 1861-1865, Civil War -- Maps

ISBN 0-19-522131-1

LC 2004-53112

"Richly illustrated, this publication will be wanted by all types of libraries. . . . The text entries are useful, while the maps and illustrations are both informative and eye-catching." Choice

★ **Cultures** in conflict: the American Civil War. Greenwood Press 2000 xx, 220p (Greenwood Press cultures in conflict series) $45

Grades: 11 12 Adult **973.7**

1. United States -- History -- 1861-1865, Civil War

ISBN 0-313-30651-6

LC 99-43165

"The history documents, including diary entries, letters, and photographs, provide a rich panorama of America's bloodiest conflict. Brief introductory paragraphs to each document or set of documents remind readers about the cultural differences that brought the country to the point of war and continued to flourish throughout this period and beyond." Voice Youth Advocates

Includes bibliographical references

973.8 United States--Reconstruction period, 1865-1901

American eras. Gale Res. 1997 8v il set $1235
Grades: 11 12 Adult **973.8**
1. Reference books 2. United States -- History 3. United States -- Civilization
ISBN 0-7876-1477-7

This reference set "provides information on U.S. history, including social history, prior to the twentieth century. Each era-specific volume includes an introductory essay describing the time period to provide context and an overview, 150 illustrations, an index of photographs, a bibliography, a subject index and a list of contributors." Publisher's note

Douglass, Frederick, 1818-1895
Autobiographies. Library of Am. 1994 1126p $35; pa $13.95

Grades: 11 12 Adult **973.8**
1. Slaves 2. Authors 3. Abolitionists 4. Memoirists 5. African Americans -- Biography
ISBN 0-940450-79-8; 1-883011-30-2 pa
LC 93-24168

"This one volume containing Douglass's seminal works is highly recommended for black history collections." Libr J
Includes bibliographical references

Encyclopedia of the Gilded Age and Progressive Era; edited by John D. Buenker and Joseph Buenker. M.E. Sharpe 2005 3v il set $299

Grades: 11 12 Adult **973.8**
1. Reference books 2. United States -- History -- 1865-1898 -- Encyclopedias 3. United States -- History -- 1898-1919 -- Encyclopedias
ISBN 0-7656-8051-3
LC 2003-24653

This set focuses "on a period between 1870 and 1920, when the United States emerged as an urban and industrial world power. Some 900 A-Z entries cover key individuals, events, and organizations of the times, and 17 essays discuss broad themes like the economy, politics, religion, and pop culture." Libr J
Includes bibliographical references

Foner, Eric
★ **Forever** free; the story of emancipation and Reconstruction. illustrations edited and with commentary by Joshua Brown. Knopf 2005 xxx, 268p il $27.50; pa $15

Grades: 11 12 Adult **973.8**
1. Reconstruction (1865-1876) 2. Slavery -- United States 3. United States -- Politics and government --

1865-1898
ISBN 0-375-40259-4; 978-0-375-40259-3; 0-375-70274-1 pa; 978-0-375-70274-7 pa
LC 2005-40706

This "is an invaluable and timely book about a subject central to U.S. history and still of obvious significance today—slavery, the Civil War, emancipation, Reconstruction, and both the immediate aftermath and longer-term consequences of those things." Rev Am Hist
Includes bibliographical references

The **Gilded** Age: a history in documents; [compiled by] Janette Thomas Greenwood. Oxford Univ. Press 2000 191p il map (Pages from history) $39.95; pa $24.95

Grades: 7 8 9 10 **973.8**
1. United States -- History -- 1865-1898
ISBN 978-0-19-510523-0; 0-19-510523-0; 978-0-19-516638-5 pa; 0-19-516638-8 pa
LC 99-98194

Uses a wide variety of documents to show how Americans dealt with an age of extremes from 1887 to 1900, including rapid industrialization, unemployment, unprecedented wealth, and immigration

"There's plenty to absorb and much to capture the imagination. . . . Greenwood presents the history as a seamless tapestry sewn by the people who lived it." Booklist
Includes bibliographical references

Golay, Michael
★ **Spanish**-American war; John S. Bowman, general editor. Rev. ed.; Chelsea House 2010 170p il map (America at war) $45

Grades: 9 10 11 12 **973.8**
1. Spanish-American War, 1898
ISBN 978-0-8160-8189-9
LC 2009-31795

First published 1995

This is an "account of the events leading to war and of the ensuing battles fought on land and sea, ending with a thought-provoking assessment of this important conflict from which the United States emerged as a major player on the world stage. . . . [It] also features a chapter devoted to the new military tactics and weapons used during the conflict." Publisher's note
Includes glossary and bibliographical references

Grumet, Bridget Hall
★ **Reconstruction** era: primary sources; Lawrence W. Baker, project editor. UXL 2004 xxv, 228p il (Reconstruction Era reference library) $60

Grades: 11 12 Adult **973.8**
1. Reconstruction (1865-1876)
ISBN 0-7876-9219-0
LC 2004-17309

This book "contains 19 complete or partial documents, such as the Fourteenth Amendment of the U.S. Constitution and Rutherford B. Hayes' inaugural address. Each document is accompanied by an introduction, keys to reading the document, a discussion of subsequent events related to the document, and other material." Booklist
Includes bibliographical references

Hansen, Joyce

★ **Bury** me not in a land of slaves; African-Americans in the time of Reconstruction. Watts 2000 160p il lib bdg $23

Grades: 7 8 9 10   **973.8**
   1. Reconstruction (1865-1876) 2. African Americans -- History 3. United States -- Race relations
   ISBN 0-531-11539-9

                      LC 99-30040

An account of African-American life in the period of Reconstruction following the Civil War, based on first-person narratives, contemporary documents, and other historical sources

"Readers of this balanced, well-written account will come away with a solid understanding of the period's events and how they contributed to the twentieth century's segregation and prejudice." Booklist

Includes bibliographical references

Hillstrom, Kevin

  American Indian removal and the trail to Wounded Knee; [by] Kevin Hillstrom and Laurie Collier Hillstrom. Omnigraphics 2010 250p il (Defining moments) lib bdg $55

Grades: 8 9 10 11 12   **973.8**
   1. Wounded Knee Creek, Battle of, 1890 2. Native Americans -- Relocation 3. Native Americans -- Great Plains
   ISBN 978-0-7808-1129-4; 0-7808-1129-1

                      LC 2010-4676

"This well-written volume effectively explores a topic of intense historical debate. Fascinating sidebars add significantly to the text." SLJ

Includes glossary and bibliographical references

★ **Reconstruction;** opposing viewpoints in world history. Laura K. Egendorf, book editor. Greenhaven Press 2004 224p il map (Opposing viewpoints in world history) lib bdg $34.95; pa $23.70

Grades: 9 10 11 12   **973.8**
   1. Reconstruction (1865-1876)
   ISBN 0-7377-1703-3 lib bdg; 0-7377-1704-1 pa

                    LC 2003-49016

"The book uses a pro/con format to present articles both from the time period, such as ones by Abraham Lincoln, Frederick Douglass, and W.E.B. Du Bois, and articles written retrospectively. . . . [This] should be available in every high school library and in every upper-level Social Studies and AP classroom." Libr Media Connect

Includes bibliographical references

Roosevelt, Theodore, 1858-1919

The **Rough** Riders; new introduction by Elting E. Morison. Da Capo Press 1990 298p il pa $16

Grades: 9 10 11 12   **973.8**
   1. Spanish-American War, 1898 2. United States -- Army -- Volunteer Cavalry, 1st -- History
   ISBN 0-306-80405-0

                    LC 90-38860

A reprint of the title first published 1899 by Scribner

This is a history of the First United States Volunteer Cavalry, which fought in the Spanish-American War under the command of Theodore Roosevelt

Sandoz, Mari

The **Battle** of the Little Bighorn. Lippincott 1966 191p maps (Great battles of history series) hardcover o.p. pa $12.95

Grades: 11 12 Adult   **973.8**
   1. Generals 2. Little Bighorn, Battle of the, 1876 3. Army officers
   ISBN 0-397-00410-9; 0-8032-9100-0 pa

"An account of the United States Army expedition against the Sioux Nation with emphasis on the political motives and ambitions of General Custer." Publ Wkly

Includes bibliographical references

Schlereth, Thomas J.

Victorian America; transformations in everyday life, 1876-1915. HarperCollins Pubs. 1991 363p (Everyday life in America) hardcover o.p. pa $15

Grades: 11 12 Adult   **973.8**
   1. United States -- Social life and customs
   ISBN 0-06-092160-9 pa

                    LC 89-46555

The author surveys the objects, events, experiences, products and tastes that comprised what he terms America's Victorian culture (1876-1915) and shows how its values shaped modern life.

"What a wonderful book. . . . Schlereth is no wry compiler of trivia. His analysis of social context reveals truly profound, intangible transformations in how and where Americans spent their time during four pivotal decades." Booklist

Includes bibliographical references

Shifflett, Crandall A.

★ **Victorian** America, 1876 to 1913; {by} Crandall Shifflett. Facts on File 1996 408p il maps (Almanacs of American life) $95

Grades: 11 12 Adult   **973.8**
   1. United States -- Social life and customs
   ISBN 0-8160-2531-2

                    LC 95-13553

This illustrated overview of 19th century America contains sections on: historical geography; native American life; government; popular culture; urban development; influential personalities; and arts and letters

Includes bibliographical references

Telgen, Diane

The **Gilded** Age; Diane Telgen. Omnigraphics 2012 xvi, 252 p.p ill. (hardcover: alk. paper) $16.99

Grades: 7 8 9 10 11 12   **973.8**
   1. United States -- History -- 1865-1898 2. United States -- History -- 1865-1921 -- Sources
   ISBN 0780812387; 9780780812383

                    LC 2011048642

This book by Diane Telgen "surveys America's rapid economic, social, demographic, and political changes from the end of the Civil War to the dawn of the twentieth century. . . . The volume also explains how various hallmarks of this era -- including rapid industrialization and urbanization, the economic divide between rich and poor, political corruption and reform, and social and religious activism -- laid the groundwork for the United States we live in today." (Publisher's note)

Includes bibliographical references (p. 237-242) and index

Viola, Herman J.

★ **It** is a good day to die; Indian eyewitnesses tell the story of the Battle of the Little Bighorn. [by] Herman J. Viola with Jan Shelton Danis. University of Nebraska Press 2001 101p il map pa $12.95

Grades: 5 6 7 8 9 10   **973.8**

1. Generals 2. Cheyenne Indians 3. Little Bighorn, Battle of the, 1876 4. Army officers 5. Dakota Indians -- Wars

ISBN 0-8032-9626-6

LC 2001-34669

First published 1998 by Crown

A series of eyewitness accounts of the 1876 Battle of Little Bighorn and the defeat of General Custer as told by Native American participants in the war.

"This is a thought-provoking, accessible compilation that will give new insight to the study of American history." Bull Cent Child Books

Includes bibliographical references

Welch, James

★ **Killing** Custer; the Battle of the Little Bighorn and the fate of the Plains Indians. by James Welch with Paul Stekler. Norton 1994 320p il hardcover o.p. pa $14.95

Grades: 11 12 Adult   **973.8**

1. Little Bighorn, Battle of the, 1876 2. Native Americans -- Wars

ISBN 0-393-32939-9 pa

LC 94-5617

"Welch produced this history of the Indian wars of the northern plains as a by-product of his work scripting a television documentary on the Battle of the Little Bighorn. In addition to military history, it contains long sections describing the life of the Plains Indians, accounts of contemporary Indian radical groups, and Welch's reactions while visiting the various historic sites in the area." Libr J

Includes bibliographical references

973.9 United States--1901-

American decades. Gale Res. 1994 11v set $1495

Grades: 11 12 Adult   **973.9**

1. United States -- Civilization 2. United States -- History -- 20th century

ISBN 0-7876-5076-5

"A series of volumes covering the twentieth century by decades. . . . Fun to browse, each volume is divided into 13 sections covering topics such as the arts, government and politics, lifestyles and social trends, medicine and health, and sports. Each section opens with a chronology and overview and closes with short biographies, deaths, and a bibliography of important books published in the decade. Sidebars highlight events and prominent individuals." Am Libr

American decades primary sources; Cynthia Rose, project editor. Gale 2004 10v il map set $1495

Grades: 11 12 Adult   **973.9**

1. United States -- Civilization 2. United States -- History -- 20th century -- Sources

ISBN 0-7876-6587-8

LC 2002-8155

Companion set to American decades published 1994-2000

"A treasure trove of more than 2,000 primary sources on U.S. history and culture, ranging from speeches and literary works to graphs and architectural drawings. Although many of the sources might be found on the Internet, they lack the organization and context provided here." Booklist

Gould, Lewis L.

The **modern** American presidency; foreword by Richard Norton Smith. 2nd ed., rev. and updated.; University Press of Kansas 2009 318p il $34.95; pa $17.95

Grades: 11 12 Adult   **973.9**

1. Presidents -- United States

ISBN 978-0-7006-1683-1; 0-7006-1683-7; 978-0-7006-1684-8 pa; 0-7006-1684-5 pa

LC 2009-20161

First published 2003

"Gould traces the decline of the party system, the increasing importance of the media and its role in creating the president-as-celebrity, and the growth of the White House staff and executive bureaucracy. He also shows us a succession of chief executives who increasingly have known less and less about the business of governing the country, observing that most would have had a better historical reputation if they had contented themselves with a single term." Publisher's note

Includes bibliographical references

The **Greenwood** guide to American popular culture; edited by M. Thomas Inge and Dennis Hall. Greenwood Press 2002 4v il set $399.95

Grades: 11 12 Adult   **973.9**

1. Popular culture -- United States

ISBN 0-313-30878-0

LC 2002-71291

Based on the Handbook of American popular culture and Handbook of American popular literature

"Students searching for help in locating resources specific to different aspects of popular culture will find these volumes an excellent starting point." Voice Youth Advocates

Includes bibliographical references

Lemann, Nicholas

★ The **promised** land; the great black migration and how it changed America. Knopf 1991 401p hardcover o.p. pa $16.95

Grades: 11 12 Adult   **973.9**

1. Internal migration 2. African Americans -- Social

conditions
ISBN 0-679-73347-7 pa

LC 90-52951

The author "describes why the war on poverty did not succeed and why the civil rights movement yielded only partial victories in trying to win improvements. While Lemann's interviews establish the human drama of this process, his assessment of the consequences of this great movement both for African Americans and for the entire country raises substantial questions of justice and equality that cut to the heart of the social situation of the impoverished and oppressed today." Booklist

Includes bibliographical references

973.91   United States--1901-1953

Allen, Frederick Lewis

★ **Only** yesterday; an informal history of the 1920's. Wiley 1997 285p (Wiley investment classics) $21.95

Grades: 11 12 Adult   **973.91**

1. United States -- Social conditions 2. United States -- History -- 1919-1933 3. United States -- Economic conditions -- 1919-1933
ISBN 0-471-18952-9

LC 97-19930

A reissue of the title first published 1931 by Harper and Brothers

"An account of the years from the spring of 1919 to . . . {1931}. It is a kaleidoscopic picture of American politics, society, manners, morals, and economic conditions." Booklist

Includes bibliographical references

Bix, Cynthia Overbeck

Fad Mania! a history of american crazes. by Cynthia Overbeck Bix. Twenty-First Century Books 2015 64 p. (lib. bdg.: alk. paper) $34.60

Grades: 5 6 7 8 9 10   **973.91**

1. Fads 2. Popular culture -- United States 3. Popular culture -- United States -- History -- 20th century
ISBN 1467710342; 9781467710343

LC 2013034669

This book, by Cynthia Overbeck Bix, describes the history of several popular culture fads in 20th-century America. "College students crammed into phone booths. Couples dancing until they drop. Daredevils swallowing one live goldfish after another. Streakers dashing naked down the street. Planking and flash mobs and robotic pets. These are just some of the crazy fads that have caught hold . . . over the last century." (Publisher's note)

"Don't be fooled by the size of this slim volume. Inside, readers will find a collection of fads from the last 100 years that fascinated before quickly fading from mainstream American culture. . . . Each chapter is filled with striking photographs as well as decade-specific sidebars that list the time period's milestones, further enhancing the connections between pop culture and history. The selected bibliography and list of additional information resources may inspire greater investigation. Don't expect to see this title linger on the shelf for long." SLJ

Includes bibliographical references and index

Burg, David F.

The **Great** Depression; updated ed; Facts on File 2005 xx, 444p il (Eyewitness history) $75

Grades: 8 9 10 11 12   **973.91**

1. Great Depression, 1929-1939 2. United States -- Economic conditions -- 1919-1933 3. United States -- Economic conditions -- 1933-1945
ISBN 0-8160-5709-5; 978-0-8160-5709-2

LC 2004-29126

First published 1996

"The book is divided into seven chapters, each covering a specific timeframe beginning with causative events preceding the crisis (1919-1928) and ending with the emerging Second World War (1939-1941.) Each chapter opens with a narrative summary and analysis of the period, followed by a chronological listing of significant events and then by primary-source contemporary quotations from private citizens, politicians, radio broadcasts, and more." Voice Youth Advocates

Includes bibliographical references

Encyclopedia of the Great Depression;   Robert McElvaine, editor in chief. Macmillan Reference USA 2004 2v set $265

Grades: 11 12 Adult   **973.91**

1. Reference books 2. New Deal, 1933-1939 -- Encyclopedias 3. Great Depression, 1929-1939 -- Encyclopedias 4. United States -- Economic conditions -- 1933-1945 -- Encyclopedias
ISBN 0-02-865686-5

LC 2003-10292

"This comprehensive, accessible set will serve as a useful supplement for research." SLJ

Includes bibliographical references

Encyclopedia of the Jazz Age; from the end of World War I to the great crash. edited by James Ciment. M.E. Sharpe 2008 2v il set $199

Grades: 9 10 11 12   **973.91**

1. Reference books 2. United States -- History -- 1919-1933 -- Encyclopedias
ISBN 978-0-7656-8078-5

LC 2007-23928

This encyclopedia contains "information on the politics, economics, society, and culture of the [pre-Great Depression] era. . . . Entries cover themes, personalities, institutions, ideas, events, trends, and more." Publisher's note

Includes bibliographical references

The **forties** in America; editor, Thomas Tandy Lewis. Salem Press 2010 3v il map set $364

Grades: 9 10 11 12 Adult   **973.91**

1. Reference books 2. United States -- History -- 1933-1945 -- Encyclopedias 3. United States -- History -- 1945-1953 -- Encyclopedias 4. United States -- Social life and customs -- Encyclopedias
ISBN 978-1-58765-659-0

This set features "entries covering the social scene ('Bobby-soxers'), literature ('Literature in the United States'), music ('Andrews Sisters'), law ('Cantwell v. Connecticut'), and many other contemporary topics." Libr J

Includes bibliographical references

Gordon, Lois G.

★ **American** chronicle; year by year through the twentieth century. {by} Lois Gordon and Alan Gordon; with an introduction by Roger Rosenblatt. Yale Univ. Press 1999 998p $49.95

Grades: 11 12 Adult   **973.91**
    1. United States -- Civilization
    ISBN 0-300-07587-1

                LC 99-24886

First published 1987 by Atheneum Pubs. with title: American chronicle; six decades in American life, 1920-1980; variant title: The Columbia chronicles of American life, 1910-1992

This volume presents in a year by year format the events, personalities, and elements of popular culture for each year of the period

The **Great** Depression and World War II, 1929 to 1949; Rodney P. Carlisle, general editor. Facts on File 2009 287p il map (Handbook to life in America) $50

Grades: 9 10 11 12   **973.91**
    1. World War, 1939-1945 2. Great Depression, 1929-1939 3. United States -- History -- 1919-1933 4. United States -- History -- 1933-1945
    ISBN 978-0-8160-7180-7; 0-8160-7180-2

"The work is prefaced by a lucid general introduction covering the history of the Great Depression, the New Deal, World War II, and American arts and culture of the time. Each signed chapter focuses on topics from the fabric of daily life such as social attitudes, religion, transportation, labor, and education and concludes with a valuable list of titles for further reading.... With a combination of excellent writing, manageable length, and compelling subject matter, it will be an indispensable resource for research papers and AP classes." SLJ

Includes bibliographical references

Kennedy, David M.

Freedom from fear; the American people in depression and war, 1929-1945. Oxford Univ. Press 1999 936p il maps (Oxford history of the United States) $39.95; pa $22.50

Grades: 11 12 Adult   **973.91**
    1. United States -- History -- 1919-1933 2. United States -- History -- 1933-1945
    ISBN 0-19-503834-7; 0-19-514403-1 pa

                LC 98-49580

This narrative history of the United States spans the period from the Great Depression to the end of the Second World War

"Rarely does a work of historical synthesis combine such trenchant analysis and elegant writing. For its scope, its insight and its purring narrative engine, Kennedy's book will stand for years to come as the definitive account of the critical decades of the American century." Publ Wkly

Includes bibliographical references

Lerner, Gerda

Fireweed; a political autobiography. Temple Univ. Press 2002 377p (Critical perspectives on the past) $34.50; pa $22.95

Grades: 11 12 Adult   **973.91**
    1. Authors 2. Feminism 3. Historians 4. College teachers 5. Nonfiction writers
    ISBN 1-56639-889-4; 1-59213-236-7 pa

                LC 2001-54248

"A fascinating memoir." Booklist

Includes bibliographical references

★ **Lifetimes:** the Great War to the stock market crash: American history through biography and primary documents; edited by Neil A. Hamilton; writers, Mark LaFlaur, James M. Manheim, Renée Miller. Greenwood Press 2002 328p il $74.95

Grades: 11 12 Adult   **973.91**
    1. World War, 1914-1918 2. Great Depression, 1929-1939 3. United States -- Biography 4. United States -- History -- 20th century
    ISBN 0-313-31799-2

                LC 2001-54700

"Each entry includes a one- to two-page biographical essay, complete with a black-and-white photo. Primary sources include autobiographical sketches, reviews of the subjects' works, commentary from contemporaneous journals, political cartoons, and other materials. The essays are accurate, readable, and objective." Libr J

Includes bibliographical references

McElvaine, Robert S., 1947-

★ The **Depression** and New Deal; a history in documents. Oxford Univ. Press 2000 192p il (Pages from history) hardcover o.p. pa $19.95

Grades: 7 8 9 10   **973.91**
    1. Great Depression, 1929-1939 2. United States -- Economic conditions -- 1933-1945
    ISBN 0-19-510493-5; 0-19-516636-1 pa

                LC 99-36644

"A vast assortment of diary entries, newspaper articles, campaign memos and speeches, political cartoons, songs, poetry, art, advertisements, photographs, and personal letters provide students with a political, economic, and social picture of this nation during the Depression. . . . [This] provides a balanced, inclusive picture of the period through the senses of the people who lived it." SLJ

Includes bibliographical references

Schwartz, Richard Alan

★ The **1950s**; [by] Richard A. Schwartz. Facts on File 2003 504p il maps (Eyewitness history) $75

Grades: 9 10 11 12   **973.91**
    1. United States -- Civilization 2. United States -- History -- 1945-1953 3. United States -- History -- 1953-1961
    ISBN 0-8160-4597-6

                LC 2002-1149

The chapters in this volume "describe each year of the decade with a narrative account of the most significant social, cultural, and political developments; a chronology of events; and eyewitness testimonies drawn from newspapers, memoirs of private and public figures, literature, and other sources." Publisher's note

Includes bibliographical references

Stone, Oliver, 1946-

The **untold** history of the United States; young readers edition. Oliver Stone and Peter Kuznick; adapted by Susan Campbell Bartoletti. First edition Atheneum Books for Young Readers 2014 400 p. illustrations (hardcover: alk. paper) $19.99

Grades: 8 9 10 11 12   973.91

1. United States -- History -- 20th century 2. United States -- History -- 21st century 3. United States -- Politics and government -- 20th century 4. United States -- Politics and government -- 21st century

ISBN 1481421735; 9781481421737; 9781481421775

LC 2014043045

This book "by Academy Award–winning director Oliver Stone and renowned historian Peter Kuznick, [the] first of four volumes, presents young readers with a . . . look at the past century of American imperialism. This . . . young readers' edition challenges prevailing orthodoxies to reveal the dark reality about the rise and fall of the American empire for curious, budding historians who are hungry for the truth." (Publisher's note)

"The first of a planned four-volume set, this has a more open page design than the original book for adults and some additional photos. A natural and notable companion for Joy Hakim's magisterial but sunnier History of US (2006)." Kirkus

Includes bibliographical references and index

Streissguth, Thomas

The **roaring** twenties; [by] Tom Streissguth. Rev ed; Facts on File 2007 500p il map (Eyewitness history) $75

Grades: 9 10 11 12   973.91

1. United States -- History -- 1919-1933

ISBN 0-8160-6423-7; 978-0-8160-6423-6

LC 2006-21723

First published 2001 as part of the Facts on File library of American history series

This book "provides hundreds of firsthand accounts of the period—from diary entries, letters, speeches, and newspaper accounts—that illustrate how historical events appeared to those who lived through them." Publisher's note

Includes bibliographical references

Terkel, Studs, 1912-2008

★ **Hard** times; an oral history of the great depression. Norton 2000 462p pa $14.95

Grades: 11 12 Adult   973.91

1. Great Depression, 1929-1939 2. United States -- Social conditions 3. United States -- Economic conditions -- 1919-1933 4. United States -- Economic conditions -- 1933-1945

ISBN 1-56584-656-7

LC 2003-389318

A reissue of the title first published 1970 by Pantheon Bks.

"Persons of all ages, occupations, and classes scattered across the U.S. remember what they experienced or were told about the economic crisis of the 1930's. The result is a social document of immense interest." Booklist

Watkins, T. H.

The **hungry** years; a narrative history of the Great Depression in America. Holt & Co. 1999 587p il hardcover o.p. pa $17

Grades: 11 12 Adult   973.91

1. Great Depression, 1929-1939 2. United States -- Economic conditions -- 1919-1933 3. United States -- Economic conditions -- 1933-1945

ISBN 0-8050-6506-7 pa

LC 99-10391

"The vignettes Watkins selects are gritty, visceral, and seamlessly sutured to the federal programs that rolled out in the course of the decade, making this a signal addition to the rich historiography of the Depression." Booklist

Includes bibliographical references

Young, William H.

World War II and the postwar years in America; a historical and cultural encyclopedia. [by] William H. Young and Nancy K. Young. ABC-CLIO 2010 2v il set $180

Grades: 10 11 12   973.91

1. Reference books 2. World War, 1939-1945 -- Encyclopedias 3. United States -- History -- 1933-1945 -- Encyclopedias 4. United States -- History -- 1945-1953 -- Encyclopedias

ISBN 978-0-313-35652-0; 978-0-313-35653-7 ebook

LC 2010-21470

This encyclopedia "contains over 175 articles describing everyday life on the American home front during World War II and the immediate postwar years. . . . The work covers a . . . range of everyday activities throughout the 1940s, including movies, radio programming, music, the birth of commercial television, advertising, art, bestsellers, and other . . . topics." Publisher's note

Includes bibliographical references

973.917 Administration of Franklin Delano Roosevelt, 1933-1945

The **Eleanor** Roosevelt encyclopedia; edited by Maurine H. Beasley, Holly C. Shulman, and Henry R. Beasley; foreword by Blanche Wiesen Cook; introduction by James McGregor Burns. Greenwood Press 2000 xxvi, 628p il $73.95

Grades: 11 12 Adult   973.917

1. Diplomats 2. Columnists 3. Humanitarians 4. Social activists 5. Spouses of presidents 6. United Nations officials 7. United States -- Politics and government -- 1933-1945

ISBN 0-313-30181-6

LC 00-23530

This reference work "examines the many roles of our foremost First Lady. Given Roosevelt's significance and appeal, this volume is an exception to the rule that encyclopedic treatments of single individuals belong only in larger collections." Booklist

Includes bibliographical references

Freedman, Russell

★ **Eleanor** Roosevelt; a life of discovery. Clarion Bks. 1993 198p il hardcover o.p. pa $11.95

Grades: 5 6 7 8 9 10   **973.917**

1. Diplomats 2. Columnists 3. Humanitarians 4. Social activists 5. Spouses of presidents 6. United Nations officials 7. Presidents' spouses -- United States
ISBN 0-89919-862-7; 0-395-84520-3 pa

LC 92-25024

A Newbery Medal honor book, 1994

"This impeccably researched, highly readable study of one of this country's greatest First Ladies is nonfiction at its best. . . . Approximately 140 well-chosen black-and-white photos amplify the text." Publ Wkly

Includes bibliographical references

★ **Franklin** Delano Roosevelt. Clarion Bks. 1990 200p il hardcover o.p. pa $9.95

Grades: 5 6 7 8 9 10   **973.917**

1. Governors 2. Presidents 3. People with disabilities 4. Philatelists 5. Presidents -- United States 6. United States -- Politics and government -- 1933-1945
ISBN 0-89919-379-X; 0-395-62978-0 pa

LC 89-34986

"The carefully researched, highly readable text and extremely effective coordination of black-and-white photographs chronicle Roosevelt's priviledged youth, his early influences, and his maturation. . . . Even students with little or no background in American history will find this an intriguing and inspirational human portrait." SLJ

Includes bibliographical references

Kesselring, Mari

How to analyze the works of Franklin D. Rroosevelt; by Mari Kesselring. ABDO Pub. Co. 2013 112 p. (library) $34.22

Grades: 9 10 11 12   **973.917**

1. Criticism
ISBN 1617836435; 9781617836435

LC 2012946247

This book by Mari Kesselring is part of the Essential Critiques series and looks at how to analyze the works of former U.S. president Franklin D. Roosevelt. This entry "looks at Roosevelt's compelling fireside speeches on drought, the Depression, and Pearl Harbor." The series focuses on "the basics of critical theory." (Booklist)

Marrin, Albert, 1936-

Freedom's champion; FDR and America's crisis. Albert Marrin. Alfred A. Knopf 2015 336 p. illustrations $24.99

Grades: 9 10 11 12   **973.917**

1. World War, 1939-1945 -- United States 2. United States -- Politics and government 3. Presidents -- United States -- Biography
ISBN 0385753594; 9780385753593; 9780385753609

LC 2013042351

This book, by Albert Marrin, is a "biography of president Franklin Delano Roosevelt for young adult readers. . . . Brought up in a privileged family, . . . he found a path in politics and quickly began to move into the public eye. That ascent seemed impossible when he contracted polio and lost the use of his legs. But with a will of steel he fought the disease -- and public perception of his disability -- to become president of the United States of America." (Publisher's note)

"This book far surpasses most extant titles about Roosevelt and provides a more nuanced evaluation of his life and presidency . . . [i]t will help readers better understand one of our most fascinating and influential presidents, and it deserves a place in all secondary collections." SLJ

Includes bibliographical references

Roosevelt, Eleanor

Courage in a dangerous world; the political writings of Eleanor Roosevelt. edited by Allida M. Black. Columbia Univ. Press 1999 362p il $34.50; pa $17.95

Grades: 11 12 Adult   **973.917**

1. United States -- Politics and government -- 1933-1945 2. United States -- Politics and government -- 1953-1961
ISBN 0-231-11180-0; 0-231-11181-9 pa

LC 98-33807

"This collection of columns, essays, speeches, and letters documents Eleanor Roosevelt's political transformation from self-effacing first lady to outspoken defender of democracy and human rights." Libr J

Includes bibliographical references

973.92   United States--1953-2001

Bok, Chip

A recent history of the United States in political cartoons; a look Bok! University of Akron Press 2005 291p il (Series on law, politics, and society) $26.95; pa $16.95

Grades: 9 10 11 12   **973.92**

1. United States -- Politics and government -- 1989- -- Cartoons and caricatures 2. United States -- Politics and government -- 1974-1989 -- Cartoons and caricatures
ISBN 1-931968-11-X; 1-931968-12-8 pa

LC 2005-41935

This is a collection of political cartoons satirizing the people and events of the late 20th and early 21st century.

Brill, Marlene Targ

America in the 1970s. Lerner 2009 144p il (The decades of twentieth-century America) lib bdg $38.60

Grades: 7 8 9 10   **973.92**

1. United States -- Social conditions 2. United States -- History -- 1961-1974 3. United States -- History -- 1974-1989
ISBN 978-0-8225-3438-9; 0-8225-3438-X

LC 2007-38570

This is "a tightly constructed, smoothly phrased overview of the tumultuous 1970s. . . . The serviceable text is bolstered by skillful connections between events and movements, well-chosen representative quotes . . . and occasional snappy headlines . . . while sidebars profiling individuals and historical turning points . . . and a well-edited selection of photos add more interest." Booklist

Frum, David
How we got here; the 70's: the decade that brought you modern life (for better or worse) Basic Bks. 2000 xxiv, 418p il hardcover o.p. pa $18.95
Grades: 11 12 Adult **973.92**
1. United States -- Civilization -- 1970-
ISBN 0-465-01496-5 pa
The author "aims 'to describe—and to judge' the transformation of American values during the '70s. Surveying politics, legal cases and opinion polls as well as popular culture, he links what he sees as America's loss of faith in government, the rise of 'sourness and cynicism' and the culture of licentiousness and divorce, among other social changes, to events in that decade." Publ Wkly
Includes bibliographical references

Gregory, Ross
★ Cold War America, 1946 to 1990; Richard Balkin, general editor. Facts on File 2003 670p il map (Almanacs of American life) $105
Grades: 11 12 Adult **973.92**
1. Cold war 2. United States -- History -- 1945- 3. United States -- Social conditions
ISBN 0-8160-3868-6
LC 2001-51136
"This is a treasure trove of statistical information documenting the enormous changes in American life from 1945 to 1990. . . . Found herein are data on everything from the population by sex . . . region, and race, business formations and failures, bull and bear markets, and operations of the postal service to the federal debt, high school seniors and drugs, executions by gender and race, and recipients of National Book Awards and Pulitzer Prizes. . . . Enhancing the work's appeal are photographs throughout the text and an exhaustive index." Am Ref Books Annu, 2003
Includes bibliographical references

Kort, Michael
The Columbia guide to the Cold War. Columbia Univ. Press 1998 366p (Columbia guides to American history and cultures) $60; pa $19.50
Grades: 11 12 Adult **973.92**
1. Cold war 2. United States -- History -- 1945- 3. United States -- Foreign relations
ISBN 0-231-10772-2; 0-231-10773-0 pa
LC 98-7154
The author begins "with a narrative survey of the Cold War which explains some of the historiographical debates that have occupied historians for more than 50 years. Following this section is a mini-encyclopedia consisting of one- or two-page essays on a wide range of Cold War topics. The book concludes with a concise chronology and a comprehensive bibliography of books, films, novels, journal articles, and archival sources. Finally . . . Kort points out

some of the relevant current websites and CD-ROM products." Libr J

McWilliams, John C.
★ The 1960s cultural revolution. Greenwood Press 2000 xxxvii, 187p (Greenwood Press guides to historic events of the twentieth century) $49.95
Grades: 11 12 Adult **973.92**
1. United States -- History -- 1961-1974
ISBN 0-31329-913-7
LC 99-58963
"The changes and challenges that manifested themselves in the 1960s did not begin and end in a neat 10-year package, so this book actually runs through to 1975 and the end of the Vietnam War. . . . The book has a lengthy chronology, a notable selection of primary documents, and an extensive annotated bibliography that includes videos and Web sites." SLJ
Includes bibliographical references

The nineties in America; editor, Milton Berman. Salem Press, Inc. 2009 3v il set $364
Grades: 9 10 11 12 Adult **973.92**
1. Reference books 2. United States -- History -- 1989- -- Encyclopedias
ISBN 978-1-58765-500-5; 1-58765-500-4
LC 2008-49939
"The 600-plus entries are arranged alphabetically and vary in length from half a page to six pages. The focus is not only on the significant people and events of the last decade but also on the impact of technology and other advances. . . . Each volume contains a table of contents for all three volumes, and at the end of Volume 3 are 16 appendixes covering everything from major films of the decade to time lines for each year." Libr J
Includes bibliographical references

Postwar America; an encyclopedia of social, political, cultural, and economic history. James Ciment, editor. M.E. Sharpe 2006 4v il set $399
Grades: 11 12 Adult **973.92**
1. Reference books 2. United States -- Civilization -- Encyclopedias
ISBN 0-7656-8067-X; 978-0-7656-8067-9
LC 2004-13120
"A-Z entries address specific persons, groups, concepts, events, geographical locations, organizations, and cultural and technological phenomena. Sidebars highlight primary source materials, items of special interest, statistical data, and other information; and Cultural Landmark entries chronologically detail the music, literature, arts, and cultural history of the era. Bibliographies covering literature from the postwar era and about the era are also included, as well as illustrations and specialized indexes." Publisher's note
Includes bibliographical references

Sitkoff, Harvard
Postwar America; a student companion. Oxford Univ. Press 2000 292p il $45
Grades: 11 12 Adult **973.92**
1. United States -- History -- 1945-
ISBN 0-19-510300-9
LC 98-34183

"The articles in this volume cover events, people, documents, legal cases, and social and political movements and groups that have had an impact on our country since the end of World War II. The alphabetical entries range from one paragraph to four pages." SLJ

Includes bibliographical references

The **Sixties** in America; editor, Carl Singleton; project editor, Rowena Wildin. Salem Press 1999 3v il set $315

Grades: 11 12 Adult   **973.92**
1. Reference books 2. United States -- Social life and customs 3. United States -- History -- 1961-1974 -- Encyclopedias
ISBN 0-89356-982-8

LC 98-49255

This set covers "the events, people, organizations, scientific advances, and popular culture of the sixties. The generally brief articles are alphabetically arranged and written chiefly by academic contributors.... Appendixes cover such topics as major legislation and important Supreme Court decisions and provide statistics and a time line of science and technology. An extensive, up-to-date bibliography and a mediagraphy listing electronic materials, videos, and Web sites conclude the set." SLJ

Woodger, Elin
The **1980s**; [by] Elin Woodger and David F. Burg. Facts on File 2006 508p il map (Eyewitness history) $75

Grades: 9 10 11 12   **973.92**
1. United States -- History -- 1974-1989 2. United States -- Politics and government -- 1974-1989
ISBN 0-8160-5809-1; 978-0-8160-5809-1

LC 2005-18732

This book provides a look at the 1980s, "illustrating how events appeared to those who lived through them. In addition to the firsthand accounts, each chapter provides an introductory essay and a chronology of events. The book also includes critical documents, as well as capsule biographies of key figures, a bibliography, an index, 92 black-and-white photographs and illustrations, and 13 maps and graphs." Publisher's note

Includes bibliographical references

973.922 Administration of John Fitzgerald Kennedy, 1961-1963

O'Reilly, Bill, 1949-
Kennedy's last days; the assassination that defined a generation. by Bill O'Reilly. 1st ed. Henry Holt and Co. 2013 336 p. (hardcover) $19.99

Grades: 6 7 8 9   **973.922**
1. Assassination
ISBN 080509802X; 9780805098020

LC 2013009026

This book by Bill O'Reilly "chronicles John F. Kennedy's course from PT-109 through a challenging presidency and positively harps on Lee Harvey Oswald's determined but doomed quest to become a 'great man.'... News photos

or snapshots on nearly every page provide views of the Kennedy and Oswald families over time, as well as important figures, places and major world events." (Kirkus Reviews)

Includes bibliographical references and index.

Swanson, James L.
★ The **President** Has Been Shot! The Assassination of John F. Kennedy. James L. Swanson. Scholastic Press 2013 336 p. (hbk.) $18.99

Grades: 6 7 8 9 10 11 12   **973.922**
1. Kennedy, John F. (John Fitzgerald), 1917-1963 -- Assassination
ISBN 0545490073; 9780545490078; 9780545496544

LC 2012041167

YALSA Award for Excellence in Nonfiction for Young Adults: Finalist (2014)

This book by James L. Swanson is a "young-adult book on the Kennedy assassination" in which the author "transport[s] readers back to one of the most shocking, sad, and terrifying events in American history. ... The book [is] illustrated with archival photos, ... diagrams, source notes, bibliography, places to visit, and index." (Publisher's note)

"Swanson's clear, concisely written, and riveting narrative highlights the key events of the Kennedy administration before focusing on the moment-by-moment details of JFK's assassination. Also included are an exploration of Lee Harvey Oswald's background, an aerial-view photograph of Dealey Plaza in Dallas, a detailed map of the motorcade route, and images of the Texas School Book Depository, where Oswald perched, rifle in hand." (Horn Book)

973.923 Administration of Lyndon Baines Johnson, 1963-1969

Benson, Harry
RFK: a photographer's journal; [edited by Gigi Benson and Manuela Soares] PowerHouse Books 2008 143p il $40.07

Grades: 9 10 11 12 Adult   **973.923**
1. Senators 2. Attorneys general 3. Siblings of presidents 4. Presidential candidates 5. United States -- History -- 1961-1974 -- Pictorial works
ISBN 978-1-57687-450-9; 1-57687-450-8

"From Saint Patrick's Day 1968, when Robert F. Kennedy announced his candidacy for president of the United States, until his funeral procession to Arlington Cemetery on June 6, ... Scottish photographer Benson sought to capture the hope and excitement of RFK's brief campaign. Arranged chronologically, this series of documentary photographs begins with an intimate family vacation on the Snake River near Boise, ID, and continues through the fast-paced, highly publicized campaign. ... This moving tribute is recommended for all libraries." Libr J

Maga, Timothy P.
★ The **1960s**. Facts on File 2003 xx, 396p il map (Eyewitness history) $75

Grades: 9 10 11 12   **973.923**
1. United States -- Civilization 2. United States --

History -- 1961-1974
ISBN 0-8160-4809-6

LC 2002-14119

This volume covers the 1960s "from the cold war days of the Cuban Missile Crisis to the assassinations of John F. Kennedy, Robert F. Kennedy, and Martin Luther King, Jr., to the Vietnam War; from the Beach Boys to the Beatles to the Rolling Stones; from Hippies and Yippies to race riots and Kent State. [These events are depicted] in the words of Americans who experienced the major events and issues of the decade." Publisher's note

Includes bibliographical references

Pendergast, Tom

The **sixties** in America. Almanac; [by] Tom Pendergast and Sara Pendergast. U.X.L. 2005 xxxviii, 229p il (U-X-L the sixties in America reference library) $63

Grades: 11 12 Adult **973.923**
1. United States -- History -- 1961-1974
ISBN 0-7876-9246-8

LC 2004-16601

This book provides "essays on social and political developments: the antiwar movement, civil rights, feminism and the sexual revolution, and sweeping cultural changes in popular entertainment, sports, and the arts." Booklist

Includes bibliographical references

★ The **sixties** in America. Primary sources; [by] Tom Pendergast and Sara Pendergast. U.X.L 2005 xxxviii, 240p il (U-X-L the sixties in America reference library) $60

Grades: 9 10 11 12 **973.923**
1. United States -- History -- 1961-1974
ISBN 0-7876-9248-4

LC 2004-16602

This "volume contains primary documents including including George Wallace's inaugural speech, an excerpt from 'The Ballot or The Bullet' by Malcolm X, and NOW's 'Bill of Rights for Women in 1968.' Chapters are followed by Where to Learn More and an index. Each except is accompanied by a glossary that defines terms, people, and ideas." Libr Media Connect

Includes bibliographical references

★ **Sixties** counterculture; Stuart A. Kallen, book editor. Greenhaven Press 2001 224p il (History firsthand) hardcover o.p. pa $19.95

Grades: 9 10 11 12 **973.923**
1. Radicalism 2. Counter culture 3. United States -- Social conditions 4. United States -- History -- 1961-1974
ISBN 0-7377-0407-1; 0-7377-0406-3 pa

LC 00-29377

"The overview is interesting reading, and some of the excerpts are excellent. A few selections include language that may be objectionable, though a more sanitized approach would not accurately represent the era." Booklist

Includes bibliographical references

973.924 Administration of Richard Milhous Nixon, 1969-1974

Bernstein, Carl

All the president's men; {by} Carl Bernstein, Bob Woodward. Simon & Schuster 1999 349p il hardcover o.p. pa $14

Grades: 11 12 Adult **973.924**
1. Watergate Affair, 1972-1974 2. Washington post
ISBN 0-684-86355-3; 0-671-89441-2 pa

LC 98-54773

A reissue of the title first published 1974

The two Washington Post reporters whose investigative journalism first revealed the Watergate scandal tell the way it happened from the first suspicions, through the trail of false leads, lies, secrecy, and high-level pressure, to the final moments when they were able to put the pieces of the puzzle together and write the series that won the Post a Pulitzer Prize

Genovese, Michael A.

The **Watergate** crisis. Greenwood Press 1999 xxix, 197p il (Greenwood Press guides to historic events of the twentieth century) $46.95

Grades: 11 12 Adult **973.924**
1. Presidents 2. Vice-presidents 3. Watergate Affair, 1972-1974 4. Senators 5. Nonfiction writers 6. Members of Congress
ISBN 0-313-29878-5

LC 99-17858

This book "provides a historical overview of the Watergate crisis, an account of the development of Nixon's political personality, a discussion of whether the president can ever act outside legal limits, a presentation of historical precedent for presidential corruption, an analysis of Nixon's relationships with the news media, and a conclusion about the Watergate legacy." SLJ

Includes glossary and bibliographical references

Olson, Keith W.

Watergate; the presidential scandal that shook America. University Press of Kansas 2003 220p il $35; pa $15.95

Grades: 11 12 Adult **973.924**
1. Watergate Affair, 1972-1974
ISBN 0-7006-1250-5; 0-7006-1251-3 pa

LC 2002-38058

The author describes "the White House-approved break-in at Democratic National Committee headquarters in Washington's Watergate complex and its aftermath—most importantly, the dramatic proceedings of the Senate Watergate Committee. . . . {This} book provides an excellent, compact narrative of a crucial moment in the history of the American presidency." Publ Wkly

Includes bibliographical references

Woodward, Bob

The **final** days; {by} Bob Woodward, Carl Bernstein. Simon & Schuster 1976 476p il hardcover o.p. pa $16

Grades: 11 12 Adult **973.924**
1. Presidents 2. Vice-presidents 3. Watergate Affair,

1972-1974 4. Senators 5. Nonfiction writers 6. Members of Congress 7. United States -- Politics and government -- 1961-1974
ISBN 0-7432-7406-7 pa

The title refers to the final days of the Nixon Presidency. The authors have "constructed a two-part narrative, the first half covering the period from April 30, 1973—the day John Dean was fired as White House counsel—until late July 1974, and the second half covering the last two weeks in detail." N Y Times Book Rev

973.926 Administration of Jimmy (James Earl) Carter, 1977-1981

Carter, Jimmy

An **hour** before daylight; memories of my rural boyhood. Simon & Schuster 2001 284p il hardcover o.p. pa $15

Grades: 11 12 Adult   **973.926**
1. Governors 2. Presidents 3. Nobel laureates for peace 4. Presidents -- United States 5. Georgia -- Social life and customs
ISBN 0-7432-1193-6; 0-7432-1199-5 pa
LC 00-48248

In this memoir, the thirty-ninth president of the United States remembers his childhood in rural Georgia.

This "is social and agricultural history as plain and honest as one of the tables the author makes in his workshop—an American classic." New Yorker

973.929 Administration of Bill Clinton, 1993-2001

Klein, Joe

The **natural**: the misunderstood presidency of Bill Clinton. Doubleday 2002 230p hardcover o.p. pa $14.99

Grades: 11 12 Adult   **973.929**
1. Governors 2. Presidents 3. United States -- Politics and government -- 1989-
ISBN 0-385-50619-8; 0-7679-1412-0 pa
LC 2001-47428

The author discusses Bill Clinton's character, the accomplishments and problems of his administration, the making of policy and the workings of the White House.

"This book is more readable than . . . others, dense but tight, funny, adroitly written and, in sum, the first savvy synthesis of the Clinton Age." N Y Times Book Rev

973.93 United States--2001-

★ **Does** the world hate the U.S.? Roman Espejo, book editor. Greenhaven Press 2009 120p (At issue. International politics) $33.70; pa $23.85

Grades: 9 10 11 12   **973.93**
1. United States -- Foreign opinion 2. United States

-- Foreign relations
ISBN 978-0-7377-4096-7; 0-7377-4096-5; 978-0-7377-4097-4 pa; 0-7377-4097-3 pa
LC 2008022301

Articles in this anthology discuss the causes of anti-American sentiment worldwide.

Includes bibliographical references

973.931 Administration of George W. Bush, 2001-2009

★ **America's** battle against terrorism; Andrea C. Nakaya, book editor. Greenhaven Press 2005 208p (Current controversies) lib bdg $34.95; pa $23.70

Grades: 9 10 11 12   **973.931**
1. Terrorism 2. War on terrorism 3. United States -- Foreign relations
ISBN 0-7377-2783-7 lib bdg; 0-7377-2784-5 pa
LC 2004-54122

"This volume explores the effectiveness of the tactics the United States uses against terrorists, the effect battling terrorism has on civil liberties in America, the impact of the war in Iraq, and whether the United States is prepared for another terrorist attack." Publisher's note

Includes bibliographical references

Bernstein, Richard

★ **Out** of the blue; the story of September 11, 2001, from Jihad to Ground Zero. {by} Richard Bernstein and the staff of the New York Times. Times Bks. 2002 287p il hardcover o.p. pa $15

Grades: 11 12 Adult   **973.931**
1. Terrorism 2. September 11 terrorist attacks, 2001
ISBN 0-8050-7240-3; 0-8050-7410-4 pa
LC 2002-20396

This account of the September 11, 2001 terrorist attacks focuses "on the personal—the victims, the perpetrators and heroes whose lives became tangled in catastrophe. . . . It uses these stories as a jumping-off point for a comprehensive look at the terror attacks—the reactions of New Yorkers, the nation and the world; the criticism of U.S. government agencies; the lingering effects of the tragedy. While some of this information has been published elsewhere, it has not been gathered so comprehensively—nor has it been written so well." Publ Wkly

Bruni, Frank

Ambling into history: the unlikely odyssey of George W. Bush. HarperCollins Pubs. 2002 278p hardcover o.p. pa $12.95

Grades: 11 12 Adult   **973.931**
1. Governors 2. Presidents 3. Baseball executives 4. Children of presidents 5. Energy industry executives 6. Presidents -- United States
ISBN 0-06-093782-3 pa

The author, who covered Bush's 2000 presidential campaign for the New York Times, focuses on Bush's personality and mannerisms as well as his basic interactions with family, friends, and the public.

"Given [Bruni's] familiarity with Bush, one would expect his book to contain revealing insights, and this superb, incisive, and surprising account does not disappoint." Booklist

Includes bibliographical references

Friedman, Thomas L.

Longitudes and attitudes; exploring the world after September 11. Farrar, Straus & Giroux 2002 383p $23

Grades: 11 12 Adult 973.931

1. Terrorism 2. September 11 terrorist attacks, 2001 3. United States -- Foreign relations 4. United States -- Politics and government -- 1989-

ISBN 0-374-19066-6

LC 2002-74321

"Unapologetically pro-American, Friedman's deliberation on what changed on September 11 outside of the U.S. ultimately centers on the strength of American society and our place in the world." Publ Wkly

Includes bibliographical references

Gerdes, Louise

9 /11; Louise I. Gerdes, book editor. Greenhaven Press 2010 227p il map (Perspectives on modern world history) lib bdg $39.70

Grades: 8 9 10 11 12 973.931

1. September 11 terrorist attacks, 2001 2. War on terrorism 3. United States -- Politics and government -- 2001-

ISBN 978-0-7377-4793-5

LC 2010-264

"This comprehensive book includes articles about the evolution of the attacks and their aftermath, the emotional changes in New York City, the response of the international community post-9/11, and the experiences of American Muslims. The texts of a speech by former President George W. Bush and a document including one 9/11 terrorist's instructions for future terrorists are also included. Articles address civil liberties, conspiracy theories, and environmental and health threats in an intelligent, well-researched, and evenhanded manner." SLJ

Includes bibliographical references

Hillstrom, Kevin

The **September** 11 terrorist attacks; by Kevin Hillstrom. Omnigraphics 2012 xv, 268 p.p (Defining moments) (hardcover: alk. paper) $55

Grades: 8 9 10 11 12 973.931

1. Qaida (Organization) 2. September 11 terrorist attacks, 2001 3. Terrorism -- United States 4. September 11 Terrorist Attacks, 2001

ISBN 0780812409; 9780780812406

LC 2011050673

This teen nonfiction reference book, by Kevin Hillstrom, is part of the "Defining Moments" series. It "opens with a lengthy overview that traces the origins and evolution of radical Islam, the birth and growth of Al Qaeda and its early attacks on the West, the events of September 11th, and the lasting . . . effects of the attack. The next section provides brief biographical sketches of eight terrorists and American . . . officials." (School Library Journal)

Includes bibliographical references and index

★ **A** Just response; the Nation on terrorism, democracy, and September 11, 2001. edited by Katrina van den Heuvel. Thunder's Mouth Press 2002 349p pa $14.95

Grades: 11 12 Adult 973.931

1. Terrorism 2. September 11 terrorist attacks, 2001 3. Nation (Periodical)

ISBN 1-56025-400-9

"Although the Nation's targets range from Defense Secretary Donald Rumsfeld to Bayer, the manufacturer of Cipro, the harshest criticism is reserved for the mainstream media. . . . Those who found the early coverage of America's 'War on Terror' to be monotonous will appreciate the Nation's radical point of view." Publ Wkly

National Commission on Terrorist Attacks Upon the United States

The **9** /11 Commission report; final report of the National Commission on Terrorist Attacks Upon the United States. Norton 2004 567p il $19.95; pa $10

Grades: 11 12 Adult 973.931

1. Terrorism 2. September 11 terrorist attacks, 2001 3. War on terrorism 4. Qaida (Organization) 5. National security -- United States

ISBN 0-393-06041-1; 0-393-32671-3 pa

LC 2004-57564

This work aims to describe how the terrorist attacks of September 11, 2001 occurred and to provide recommendations for the prevention of future attacks.

This book "reads like a Shakespearean drama. . . . This multi-author document produces an absolutely compelling narrative intelligence, one with clarity, a sense of shared mission and an overriding desire to do something about the situation." Publ Wkly

Includes bibliographical references

Spiegelman, Art

In the shadow of no towers. Pantheon Books 2004 il $19.95

Grades: 10 11 12 Adult 973.931

1. Graphic novels 2. September 11 terrorist attacks, 2001 -- Graphic novels

ISBN 0-375-42307-9

LC 2004-43870

The author "provides a hair-raising and wry account of his family's frantic efforts to locate one another on September 11 as well as a morbidly funny survey of his trademark sense of existential doom. . . . This is a powerful and quirky work of visual storytelling by a master comics artist." Publ Wkly

973.932 Administration of Barack Obama, 2009-

Berry, Mary Frances

Power in words; the stories behind Barack Obama's speeches, from the state house to the White House. [by] Mary Frances Berry, Josh Gottheimer; foreword by Ted Sorensen. Beacon Press 2010 xxxiii, 267p $24.95

Grades: 11 12 Adult   **973.932**
1. American speeches 2. Presidents -- United States
-- Election -- 2008 3. United States -- Politics and
government -- 2001-
ISBN 978-0-8070-0104-2
LC 2010004085
Collection of 18 of Obama's most memorable speeches
between 2002 and 2008, each introduced by Berry and Gottheimer with political analysis, historical context, and commentary from the speechwriters.
"A book to savor and return to for subsequent
readings." Kirkus
Includes bibliographical references

974.7   New York

Dwyer, Jim
★ **102** minutes; the untold story of the fight to
survive inside the Twin Towers. [by] Jim Dwyer and
Kevin Flynn. Times Books 2005 322p il $26; pa
$15
Grades: 11 12 Adult   **974.7**
1. September 11 terrorist attacks, 2001 2. World Trade
Center terrorist attack, 2001
ISBN 0-8050-7682-4; 0-8050-8032-5 pa
LC 2004-55321
Dwyer and Flynn have "given us a fitting tribute to the
people caught up in one of the great dramas of our time.
And for people still haunted by the events of that day, read-
ing '102 Minutes' provides a cathartic release." N Y Times
Book Rev

Getzinger, Donna
★ The **Triangle** Shirtwaist Factory fire. Morgan
Reynolds Pub. 2008 128p il map (American workers) $27.95
Grades: 7 8 9 10   **974.7**
1. New York (N.Y.) -- History 2. Labor -- Law and
legislation 3. Triangle Shirtwaist Company, Inc.
ISBN 978-1-59935-099-8; 1-59935-099-8
LC 2008-4077
"Beginning with a brief account of the disaster, a description of the popular shirtwaist and the fabric used to
make the blouse, the women who lost their lives, and the
impact of the lack of communication among the workers,
the first chapter is sure to hook readers. Successive chapters
look more closely at New York City's growth, the varied immigrant population at that time, overcrowded factory conditions, the failure to enforce building regulations, and the
many sweatshops developed from the desire of contractors
to make money. . . . Archival photos and diagrams with captions add to the meaning of this devastating and important
event in the history of labor." SLJ
Includes bibliographical references

Joseph, Jamal
Panther baby; by Jamal Joseph. Algonquin
Books of Chapel Hill 2012 280p.
Grades: 11 12   **974.7**
1. Autobiographies 2. Black nationalism 3. Political

activists 4. New York (N.Y.) -- Biography 5. African
Americans -- Biography 6. Black Panther Party --
Biography 7. Bronx (New York, N.Y.) -- Biography
8. New York (N.Y.) -- Race relations -- History -- 20th
century 9. Bronx (New York, N.Y.) -- Race relations
-- History -- 20th century 10. African American young
men -- New York (State) -- New York -- Biography
ISBN 9781565129504; 9781616201296
LC 2011032139
This book recounts the author's "personal odyssey --
from the streets of Harlem to Riker's Island and Leavenworth to the Halls of Columbia. . . . [In] the late 1960s in
Bronx's black ghetto . . . fifteen-year-old Eddie was introduced to the tenets of the Black Panther Party . . . [and] by
sixteen, his devotion to the cause landed him in prison . . .
charged with conspiracy as one of the Panther 21 in one of
the most emblematic criminal cases of the sixties. When exonerated, Eddie -- now called Jamal -- became the youngest
spokesperson and leader of the Panthers' New York chapter.
. . . Sentenced to more than twelve years in Leavenworth, he
earned three degrees there and found a new calling." (Publisher's note)

Khan, Yasmin Sabina
Enlightening the world; the creation of the Statue of Liberty. Cornell University Press 2010 231p
il $24.95
Grades: 11 12 Adult   **974.7**
1. Artists 2. Sculptors 3. National monuments 4.
Statue of Liberty (New York, N.Y.) 5. France -- Foreign
relations -- United States 6. United States -- Foreign
relations -- France
ISBN 978-0-8014-4851-5; 0-8014-4851-4
LC 2009035711
This is "a lucid account connecting France's widespread
grief over Abraham Lincoln's 1865 assassination with that
country's own struggles to establish a lasting democracy.
Khan shows how Édouard-René Lefebvre de Laboulaye, a
legal scholar and celebrant of French-American friendship,
led others to design and construct what was officially called
Liberty Enlightening the World. . . . An important book for
general audiences." Publ Wkly
Includes bibliographical references

Marsico, Katie
The **Triangle** Shirtwaist Factory fire; its legacy of labor rights. Marshall Cavendish Benchmark
2010 112p il (Perspectives on) lib bdg $27.95
Grades: 7 8 9 10   **974.7**
1. Fires 2. New York (N.Y.) -- History 3. Triangle
Shirtwaist Company, Inc.
ISBN 978-0-7614-4027-7; 0-7614-4027-5
LC 2008-23267
"This well-written title examines many of the details
preceding the 1911 disaster, the conditions that caused it,
and the impact the incident continues to have on labor and
businesses today. Historical accounts of the event, told
through numerous direct quotes and shown in black-and-
white photos of sweatshops and descriptions of tenement
living conditions, reveal that poor labor laws and factory

regulations were to blame. . . . Color photos and full-page sidebars provide additional information." SLJ

Includes bibliographical references

Stanton, Brandon
Humans of New York; Brandon Stanton. St. Martin's Press 2013 304 p. color illustrations (hardback) $29.99

Grades: 9 10 11 12 Adult 974.7
1. Photography 2. Street life 3. New York (N.Y.) 4. Photography, Artistic 5. New York (N.Y.) -- Pictorial works 6. Street photography -- New York (State) -- New York 7. City and town life -- New York (State) -- New York -- Hisotry -- 21st century -- Pictorial works
ISBN 9781250038814; 9781250038821; 1250038820
LC 2013027586

This book, by photographer Brandon Stanton, is "inspired by the blog [of the same name]. With four hundred color photos, including exclusive portraits and all-new stories, 'Humans of New York' is a stunning collection of images that showcases the outsized personalities of New York." (Publisher's note)

"There's the Yugoslavian janitor who studied for 12 years to earn his classics degree; Banana George, the world's oldest barefoot water-skier who's now in a wheelchair; Muslims in prayer; and shots of adorable kids, crazy fashionistas, and young lovers, all paired with a comment from Stanton or from the subjects themselves. There's no judgment, just observation and in many cases reverence, making for an inspiring reading and visual experience." Pub Wkly

Humans of New York: stories; Brandon Stanton. St. Martin's Press 2015 432 p. chiefly color illustrations (hardcover) $29.99

Grades: 9 10 11 12 Adult 974.7
1. New York (N.Y.) 2. Portrait photography 3. New York (N.Y.) -- Biography 4. Interviews -- New York (State) -- New York 5. New York (N.Y.) -- Biography -- Pictorial works 6. Street photography -- New York (State) -- New York 7. New York (N.Y.) -- Social life and customs -- Pictorial works 8. City and town life -- New York (State) -- New York -- Pictorial works
ISBN 9781250058904; 9781466886964; 1250058902
LC 2015025568

Alex Award (2016)

"In the summer of 2010, photographer Brandon Stanton began an ambitious project--to single-handedly create a photographic census of New York City. The photos he took and the accompanying interviews became the blog Humans of New York. Ever since Brandon began interviewing people on the streets of New York, the dialogue he's had with them has increasingly become as in-depth, intriguing and moving as the photos themselves." (Publisher's note)

"Photographer and author Stanton returns with a companion volume to Humans of New York (2013), this one with similarly affecting photographs of New Yorkers but also with some tales from his subjects' mouths. . . . A wondrous mix of races, ages, genders, and social classes, and on virtually every page is a surprise." Kirkus

974.8 Pennsylvania

Walker, Sally M.
★ **Boundaries**; how the Mason-Dixon line settled a family feud and divided a nation. Sally M Walker. Candlewick Press 2014 208 p. ill., maps. $24.99

Grades: 7 8 9 10 11 12 974.8
1. Mason-Dixon Line 2. Surveying -- United States -- History -- 18th century
ISBN 0763656127; 9780763656126
LC 2013946612

This book, by Sally M. Walker, details the "Mason-Dixon Line's history, replete with property disputes, persecution, and ideological conflicts. . . . Walker traces the tale of the Mason-Dixon Line through family feuds, brave exploration, scientific excellence, and the struggle to define a cohesive country. But above all, this [is a] . . . story of surveying, marking, and respecting lines of demarcation." (Publisher's note)

"This thoroughly researched account of the Mason—Dixon Line encompasses a broad span of time and place, from sixteenth-century England to twentieth-century America... Walker's latest book offers a good deal of pertinent information on the subject at hand, as well as some interesting sidelights on American history." (Booklist)

975.2 Maryland

Moore, Wes, 1978-
Discovering Wes Moore; Wes Moore. Delacorte Press 2012 160 p. (hardcover) $15.99

Grades: 7 8 9 10 11 12 975.2
1. Family life 2. Conduct of life 3. Blacks -- Biography 4. Youth -- Conduct of life 5. African American men -- Biography 6. Baltimore (Maryland) -- Biography 7. Bronx (New York, N.Y.) -- Biography 8. Soldiers -- United States -- Biography 9. Criminals -- Maryland -- Baltimore -- Biography 10. African Americans -- Maryland -- Baltimore -- Social conditions -- 20th century 11. African Americans -- Bronx (New York, N.Y.) -- Social conditions -- 20th century
ISBN 0385741677; 9780375986703; 9780375990182; 9780385741675
LC 2011049135

Author Wes Moore describes his experiences growing up. "After receiving poor grades and falling in with a bad crowd, his family pooled their limited finances to send him to Valley Forge Military Academy, where he found positive role models and became a Corps commander and star athlete. After earning an undergraduate degree, Wes attended Oxford as a Rhodes Scholar. When the author read about the conviction of another Wes Moore for armed robbery and killing a police officer, he wanted to find out how two youths . . . could take such divergent paths." (Kirkus)

975.6 North Carolina

Miller, Lee

Roanoke; solving the mystery of the Lost Colony. Penguin Books 2002 362p il map pa $16
Grades: 11 12 Adult 975.6
  1. Roanoke Island (N.C.) -- History
  ISBN 978-0-14-200228-5; 0-14-200228-3
  First published 2000 in the United Kingdom; first U.S. edition 2001 by Arcade Pub.
  The author "blames the colony's disappearance on treachery and murder she traces to the court of Elizabeth I. Conspiracy theorists should find much to savor in this convoluted story, which includes palace intrigues, cultural misunderstandings, and gray-eyed Native Americans. . . . This is an interesting, well-told tale." Libr J
  Includes bibliographical references

975.8 Georgia

★ **Foxfire** 40th anniversary book; faith, family, and the land. edited by Angie Cheek, Lacy Hunter Nix, and Foxfire students. Anchor Books 2006 xxxix, 512p il pa $17.95
Grades: 11 12 Adult 975.8
  1. Handicraft 2. Country life -- Georgia 3. Appalachian region -- Social life and customs
  ISBN 0-307-27551-5; 978-0-307-27551-6
                                        LC 2006-45311
  "Drawing on the magazine's published talks by local high school students with elderly rural inhabitants, the books have explored the crafts, cooking, music, gardening and stories that have been passed down through the generations. The focus in this anniversary volume is on devotion to religion, family and the land. Collecting pieces from 40 years' worth of the magazine, the book inevitably covers topics covered in previous Foxfire collections, including snake handling, childhood toys and recipes. But the spoken words remain captivating, eloquent if plainspoken." Publ Wkly

975.9 Florida

Schafer, Daniel L.

Anna Madgigine Jai Kingsley; African princess, Florida slave, plantation slaveowner. University Press of Fla. 2003 177p il map $24.95
Grades: 11 12 Adult 975.9
  1. Slaves 2. Plantation life 3. Slavery -- United States 4. African American women -- Biography
  ISBN 0-8130-2616-4
                                        LC 2002-33372
  "Schafer traces the history of Anna Madgigine Jai from her homeland of Senegal, where she was captured at about 13 years of age in 1806 and sold to Zephaniah Kingsley, a maritime merchant, slave trader, and later an abolitionist. Kingsley eventually married Anna, made her manager of his plantation, and fathered four children with her. . . . This is a fascinating look at an extraordinary woman and the complexities of slavery beyond the common image of slavery in the South." Booklist
  Includes bibliographical references

976.1 Alabama

McWhorter, Diane

Carry me home; Birmingham, Alabama: the climactic battle of the civil rights revolution. Simon & Schuster 2001 701p il hardcover o.p. pa $17
Grades: 11 12 Adult 976.1
  1. African Americans -- Civil rights 2. Birmingham (Ala.) -- Race relations
  ISBN 0-684-80747-5; 0-7432-1772-1 pa
                                        LC 00-53827
  McWhorter presents an account of the struggle for civil rights in Birmingham, Ala., both from a personal and societal perspective
  "A daughter of Birmingham's privileged elite, McWhorter weaves a personal narrative through this startling account of the history, events, and major players on both sides of the civil rights battle in that city." Booklist
  Includes bibliographical references

976.3 Louisiana

Dyson, Michael Eric

Come hell or high water; Hurricane Katrina and the color of disaster. Basic Civitas 2006 258p $23; pa $14.95
Grades: 11 12 Adult 976.3
  1. Disaster relief 2. Hurricane Katrina, 2005 3. African Americans -- Social conditions
  ISBN 978-0-465-01761-4; 0-465-01761-4; 978-0-465-01772-0 pa; 0-465-01772-X pa
                                        LC 2007-310210
  This book on Hurrican Katrina "not only chronicles what happened when, it also argues that the nation's failure to offer timely aid to Katrina's victims indicates deeper problems in race and class relations. . . . [The author's] contention that Katrina exposed a dominant culture pervaded not only by 'active malice' toward poor blacks but also by a long history of 'passive indifference' to their problems is both powerful and unsettling." Publ Wkly
  Includes bibliographical references

Van Heerden, Ivor Ll.

The storm; what went wrong and why during Hurricane Katrina. [by] Ivor van Heerden and Mike Bryan. Viking 2006 308p il map hardcover o.p. pa $15
Grades: 11 12 Adult 976.3
  1. Disaster relief 2. Hurricane Katrina, 2005
  ISBN 0-670-03781-8; 0-14-311213-9 pa
                                        LC 2006-44727
  This book focuses on public mismanagement relating to Hurricane Katrina.
  "This serious, scientific explanation of what exactly happened in the hours—and years—leading up to Hurricane

Katrina's devestation of New Orleans brings a fresh perspective to a tragedy that has generated remarkably similar news accounts over the past eight months." Publ Wkly

Includes bibliographical references

Voices rising; stories from the Katrina Narrative Project. edited by Rebeca Antoine; [afterword by Fredrick Barton] UNO Press 2008 244p pa $12.95

Grades: 9 10 11 12 Adult **976.3**
1. Hurricane Katrina, 2005 -- Personal narratives
ISBN 978-0-9728143-6-2; 0-9728143-6-I

In this "collection of personal narratives, readers come face-to-face with the stark reality wrought by Hurricane Katrina and the failure of the federal levees. . . . Every aspect of the post-Katrina New Orleans experience is present here, from areas as divergent as the I10 overpass, the French Quarter, and shelters across the South. The rescuers and rescued have equal voices and share memories poignant and startling. . . . Miles away from academic analysis, this is American social history from the ground up and staggering in its significance." Booklist

976.4 Texas

Roberts, Randy
A **line** in the sand; the Alamo in blood and memory. {by} Randy Roberts, James S. Olson. Free Press 2001 356p il map hardcover o.p. pa $14

Grades: 11 12 Adult **976.4**
1. Texas -- History 2. Alamo (San Antonio, Tex.)
ISBN 0-684-83544-4; 0-743-21233-9 pa

LC 00-48421

The Alamo "was attacked by the Mexican Army under Santa Anna in 1836; its defenders, American and Tejano rebels, were quickly overwhelmed. In death, though, they became American folk heroes, symbols of frontier bravery and the unquenchable thirst for liberty. Roberts and Olson do a commendable job of re-creating the murky circumstances of the battle itself, but the real strength of this enjoyable, innovative book lies in its final movement, when the authors turn their attention to cultural criticism." New Yorker

Includes bibliographical references and index

977.3 Illinois

Barnes, Harper
Never been a time; the 1917 race riot that sparked the civil rights movement. Walker & Co. 2008 293p il $25.99

Grades: 11 12 Adult **977.3**
1. East Saint Louis (Ill.) riot, 1917 2. Illinois -- Race relations 3. African Americans -- Civil rights 4. African Americans -- Social conditions
ISBN 978-0-8027-1575-3; 0-8027-1575-3

LC 2008-368

"Authoritative account of a criminally overlooked incident in American history." Kirkus

Includes bibliographical references

Morrison, Joan Wehlen
Home front girl; a diary of love, literature, and growing up in wartime America. Joan Wehlen Morrison; edited by Susan Signe Morrison. Chicago Review Press 2012 272 p. $19.95

Grades: 7 8 9 10 11 12 **977.3**
1. History -- Sources 2. World War, 1939-1945 -- United States 3. Chicago (Ill.) -- Biography 4. Schoolgirls -- Illinois -- Chicago -- Diaries 5. Chicago (Ill.) -- Social life and customs -- 20th century
ISBN 1613744579; 9781613744574

LC 2012027068

This book is a "collection of journal entries, poems, clippings, and sketches by the late [Joan Wehlen] Morrison, edited by her daughter, span[ing] the tumultuous years between 1937 and 1943, which took Morrison from age 14 to 20, and took the world from the Great Depression into WWII. . . . Morrison details her school day concerns and studies, exploring the city, her crushes on boys, attending the University of Chicago, and her thoughts on religion, books, films, and more." (Publishers Weekly)

Murphy, Jim
★ The **great** fire. Scholastic 1995 144p il maps $16.95; pa $12.99

Grades: 5 6 7 8 9 10 **977.3**
1. Fires -- Chicago (Ill.)
ISBN 0-590-47267-4; 0-439-20307-4 pa

LC 94-9963

Newbery honor book, 1996

"Firsthand descriptions by persons who lived through the 1871 Chicago fire are woven into a gripping account of this famous disaster. Murphy also examines the origins of the fire, the errors of judgment that delayed the effective response, the organizational problems of the city's firefighters, and the postfire efforts to rebuild the city. Newspaper lithographs and a few historical photographs convey the magnitude of human suffering and confusion." Horn Book Guide

Includes bibliographical references

Owens, L. L.
The **great** Chicago fire. ABDO Pub. 2008 112p il (Essential events) lib bdg $32.79

Grades: 8 9 10 11 12 **977.3**
1. Fires -- Chicago (Ill.) 2. Chicago (Ill.) -- History
ISBN 978-1-59928-851-2

LC 2007-12007

This book "relies on many primary source documents to tell the story [of the Chicago fire], including testimonials from the official study of the fire. . . . [It also] contains a list of essential events and sources." Libr Media Connect

Includes glossary and bibliographical references

978 Western United States

The **American** frontier; James D. Torr, book editor. Greenhaven Press 2002 240p il (Turning points in world history) lib bdg $34.95; pa $23.70

Grades: 7 8 9 10 **978**
1. West (U.S.) -- History 2. United States -- Territorial

expansion 3. Frontier and pioneer life -- West (U.S.)
ISBN 0-7377-0786-0 lib bdg; 0-7377-0785-2 pa

LC 2001-33514

This is a collection of essays about the American frontier, with an introduction and summaries

Includes bibliographical references

Bertozzi, Nick

Lewis & Clark. First Second 2011 136p il pa $16.99

Grades: 5 6 7 8   978

1. Explorers 2. Graphic novels 3. Lewis and Clark Expedition (1804-1806) 4. Territorial governors 5. United States -- History -- 1783-1865 -- Graphic novels
ISBN 978-1-59643-450-9 pa; 1-59643-450-3 pa

LC 2010-36255

"Bertozzi offers an innovative take on Meriwether Lewis and William Clark's epic journey in this oversized graphic offering. Portraying the arduous trek through rough terrain and encounters with often unwelcoming natives, sequential panels transport readers alongside the famous duo and their equally renowned translator, Sacagawea, as they travel from St. Louis to the Pacific coast. Within a fictional framework, the narrative weaves in facets of the characters' personalities, including Lewis's tempestuous melancholy, Charbonneau's inept bumbling and Sacagawea's ability to endure this voyage surrounded by her intensely masculine cohorts." (Kirkus)

Brown, Don

★ The **great** American dust bowl; by Don Brown. Houghton Mifflin Harcourt 2013 80 p. $18.99

Grades: 5 6 7 8 9   978

1. Dust storms -- Graphic novels 2. Dust Bowl Era, 1931-1939
ISBN 0547815506; 9780547815503

Author Don Brown presents a "graphic novel of one of America's most catastrophic natural events: the Dust Bowl. On a clear, warm Sunday, April 14, 1935, a wild wind whipped up millions upon millions of these specks of dust to form a duster, a savage storm on America's high southern plains." (Publisher's note)

"In this bleak yet compelling graphic-novel-style glimpse at the Dirty Thirties, Brown crisply paces the narrative with fascinating glimpses of the sociological and geological causes of the Dust Bowl. The color brown is a recurring theme here, as Brown relies, aptly, almost entirely on shades of brown throughout. Primary source material is used liberally, as characters speak directly to the reader, documentary-style." (Horn Book)

Egan, Timothy

★ The **worst** hard time; the untold story of those who survived the great American dust bowl. Timothy Egan. Houghton Mifflin Co. 2006 340p ill., map $28; $28

Grades: 11 12 Adult   978

1. Dust storms 2. Great Depression, 1929-1939 3. United States -- History -- 20th century 4. Great Plains -- History 5. Great Plains -- Social conditions -- 20th

century
ISBN 061834697X; 9780618346974

LC 2005-08057

National Book Awards: Nonfiction (2006), Oklahoma Book Awards: Nonfiction Category (2006), Western Heritage Award: Outstanding Nonfiction (2007)

This book presents an "account of how America's . . . plains turned to dust, and how the ferocious plains winds stirred up an endless series of 'black blizzards' . . . in what became known as the Dust Bowl. But the plague was man-made, as Egan shows: the plains weren't suited to farming, and plowing up the grass to plant wheat, along with a confluence of economic disaster—the Depression—and natural disaster—eight years of drought—resulted in an ecological and human catastrophe. . . . [The author] grounds his tale in portraits of the people who settled the plains: hardy Americans and immigrants desperate for a piece of land to call their own and lured by the lies of promoters who said the ground was arable." (Publishers Weekly)

Includes bibliographical references (p. 315-327) and index

Freedman, Russell

★ The **life** and death of Crazy Horse; drawings by Amos Bad Heart Bull. Holiday House 1996 166p il maps $22.95

Grades: 5 6 7 8 9 10   978

1. Oglala Indians 2. Indian chiefs 3. Native Americans -- Biography
ISBN 0-8234-1219-9

LC 95-33303

A biography of the Oglala Indian leader who relentlessly resisted the white man's attempt to take over Indian lands.

This is "a compelling biography that is based on primary source documents and illustrated with pictographs by a Sioux band historian." Voice Youth Advocates

Includes bibliographical references

Lewis, Meriwether

★ The **essential** Lewis and Clark; Landon Y. Jones, editor. Ecco Press 2000 xx, 203p hardcover o.p. pa $13.95

Grades: 11 12 Adult   978

1. Lewis and Clark Expedition (1804-1806) 2. West (U.S.) -- Exploration
ISBN 0-06-019600-9; 0-06-001159-9 pa

LC 99-86335

In this volume the editor presents excerpts from the journals of Lewis and Clark "that focus on the seminal junctures of the journey, including their reactions to the breathtaking physical majesty of the West, their initial encounters with various Native American tribes, and their fascinating accounts of the physical and moral courage of their fellow travelers." Booklist

Luchetti, Cathy

★ **Children** of the West; family life on the frontier. Norton 2001 253p il $39.95

Grades: 11 12 Adult   978

1. Children -- West (U.S.) 2. West (U.S.) -- Social life

and customs 3. Frontier and pioneer life -- West (U.S.)
ISBN 0-393-04913-2

LC 00-53287

"In the nineteenth and early twentieth centuries, the children who resided in the sparsely populated plains and prairies of the western U.S. were subject to a unique variety of hardships and joys. . . . Utilizing more than 100 vintage photographs and excerpts from letters, diaries, and journals, Luchetti examines aspects of childbearing, child rearing, childhood, and adolescence on the American frontier." Booklist

Includes bibliographical references

McKissack, Fredrick, 1939-2013

★ **Best** shot in the West; the adventures of Nat Love. by Patricia C. McKissack and Fredrick L. McKissack, Jr.; illustrated by Randy DuBurke. Chronicle Books 2012 129 p. $19.99

Grades: 7 8 9 **978**
1. Cowhands -- Graphic novels 2. Railroads -- United States 3. West (U.S.) -- History -- Graphic novels 4. African Americans -- Biography -- Graphic novels 5. Cartoons and comics 6. West (U.S.) -- Cartoons and comics 7. Cowboys -- West (U.S.) -- Cartoons and comics 8. African American cowboys -- West (U.S.) -- Cartoons and comics 9. African Americans -- West (U.S.) -- Biography -- Cartoons and comics
ISBN 0811857492; 9780811857499

LC 2007021419

In this graphic novel, "Nat Love's cattle-driving days are long over and America is a much tamer place when the black cowboy, now a Pullman porter, runs into 'Bugler,' a man he knew back in the day. Bugler's son is a publisher . . . of . . . stories from the Wild West, and Love is persuaded to contribute his memoirs. From this . . . story, . . . [Patricia C. and Frederick L.] McKissack . . . segue into Love's adventures, based on his autobiography." (Bulletin of the Center for Children's Books)

Miller, Brandon Marie

Women of the frontier; 16 tales of trailblazing homesteaders, entrepreneurs, and rabble-rousers. Brandon Marie Miller. Chicago Review Press 2013 256 p. (hardcover) $19.95

Grades: 7 8 9 10 11 12 **978**
1. Women -- United States 2. Frontier and pioneer life -- United States 3. West (U.S.) -- History -- Biography
ISBN 1883052971; 9781883052973

LC 2012035756

This book, part of the Women of Action series, is a collection of "tales of women's trials and triumphs during the years of settlement in the [U.S.] West. . . . [The section] 'Many a Weary Mile' describes the trip west by wagon; 'Oh Give Me a Home' explores early pioneering experiences. 'A Woman Can Work,' 'And Now the Fun Begins' and 'Great Expectations for the Future' all examine the careers of women who stepped out of typical female roles of the era." (Kirkus)

Includes bibliographical references and index

★ The **New** encyclopedia of the American West; edited by Howard R. Lamar. Yale Univ. Press 1998 1324p il maps $60

Grades: 11 12 Adult **978**
1. Reference books 2. Frontier and pioneer life -- West (U.S.) -- Encyclopedias
ISBN 0-300-07088-8

LC 98-6231

First published 1977 by Crowell with title: The Reader's encyclopedia of the American West

This reference work covers "the history, geography, culture, literature, art, and natural history of both the real and the imaginary West. . . . {Coverage spans} prehistory to the present, and . . . {includes} events in the history of the trans-Mississippi West . . . {as well as} the frontier or 'western' stage of all 50 American states. Entries range from important events in the expansion of the U.S. . . . to the first European and American discoverers, among them Coronado, LaSalle, and Lewis and Clark." Publisher's note

Includes bibliographical references

Original journals of the Lewis and Clark Expedition

The **journals** of Lewis and Clark; [by] Meriwether Lewis, William Clark; abridged by Anthony Brandt; with an afterword by Herman J. Viola. National Geographic Adventure Classics 2002 xxxiii, 445p il, maps (National Geographic adventure classics) pa $16

Grades: 11 12 Adult **978**
1. Lewis and Clark Expedition (1804-1806) 2. West (U.S.) -- Exploration 3. West (U.S.) -- Description and travel
ISBN 978-0-7922-6921-2; 0-7922-6921-7

LC 2002-32003

"The epic Lewis and Clark Expedition comes to life on a human scale in this engrossing abridgment of the explorers' journals. . . . The editor's assiduous untangling of the explorers' notoriously bad spelling, punctuation and grammar, helpful notes and maps and fluent synopses of the duller stretches of the narrative make the journals accessible to a general readership." Publ Wkly

Pendergast, Tom

★ **Westward** expansion: almanac; [by] Tom Pendergast and Sara Pendergast; Christine Slovey, editor. U.X.L 2000 xlvi, 254p il (Westward expansion reference library) $60

Grades: 8 9 10 11 12 **978**
1. Reference books 2. West (U.S.) -- History 3. Frontier and pioneer life -- West (U.S.)
ISBN 0-7876-4862-0

LC 00-36375

This almanac "documents the chronological events that created a romantic national mythology around the pioneers who blazed trails through the wilderness." Publisher's note

Includes bibliographical references

★ **Westward** expansion: primary sources; [by] Tom Pendergast and Sara Pendergast; Christine

Slovey, editor. U.X.L 2001 xxix, 260p (Westward expansion reference library) $60

Grades: 7 8 9 10   **978**

1. West (U.S.) -- History 2. United States -- Territorial expansion

ISBN 0-7876-4864-7

LC 00-107861

This volume provides "full text or excerpts from diaries, books, letters and many other documents." Publisher's note
Includes bibliographical references

Quay, Sara E.

Westward expansion. Greenwood Press 2002 xx, 301p il (American popular culture through history) $49.95

Grades: 11 12 Adult   **978**

1. West (U.S.) -- History 2. Popular culture -- United States 3. Frontier and pioneer life -- West (U.S.)

ISBN 0-313-31235-4

LC 2001-54546

"This excellent title belongs on the reference shelves, and all staff members who assist with student research should be aware of and familiar with it." Voice Youth Advocates
Includes bibliographical references

Schlissel, Lillian

★ **Women's** diaries of the westward journey; [collected by] Lillian Schlissel; foreword by Mary Clearman Blew. Schocken Books 2004 278p il pa $14.95

Grades: 9 10 11 12   **978**

1. Overland journeys to the Pacific 2. Women -- Social conditions 3. West (U.S.) -- Description and travel 4. Frontier and pioneer life -- West (U.S.)

ISBN 0-8052-1176-4

LC 2004-556208

First published 1982

This account of the experiences, attitudes and perceptions of some hundred women who migrated West is based on their reminiscences, diaries, and letters. The book concerns their daily lives as they travelled the Overland Trail from the midwest to California or Oregon between 1840 and 1870.

Includes bibliographical references

Tunis, Edwin

★ **Frontier** living; written and illustrated by Edwin Tunis. Lyons Press 2000 165p il map pa $18.95

Grades: 5 6 7 8 9 10   **978**

1. West (U.S.) -- History 2. Frontier and pioneer life -- West (U.S.)

ISBN 1-58574-137-X

LC 00-710694

First published 1961 by World Publishing Company

This volume "portrays the manners and customs of the frontiersman and his family from the beginning of the westward movement through the 19th century in . . . text and more than 200 drawings." Wis Libr Bull

978.004   Western United States--American native peoples

Langley, Andrew

The **Plains** Indian wars 1864-1890; by Andrew Langley. Heinemann Library 2012 80 p. ill. (some col.), col. maps (hardcover) $36.50; (paperback) $10.99

Grades: 6 7 8 9   **978.004**

1. United States -- Military history 2. Native Americans -- Wars

ISBN 1432959999; 9781432959999; 9781432960087

LC 2011015925

This book by Andrew Langley is part of the Living Through series and focuses on the Plains Indian Wars. "The Plains Indian Wars were not like most other wars. There were few large battles, and they took place across a huge but sparsely populated region over several decades. . . . The Living Through series relates the overall chronology of major wars and shows their impact on everyday lives." (Publisher's note)

Includes bibliographical references (p. 76-78) and index.

Sanford, William R.

Comanche Chief Quanah Parker; by William R. Sanford. Enslow Publishers 2013 48 p. ill., map (library) $21.26

Grades: 6 7 8 9   **978.004**

1. Parker, Quanah, 1845?-1911 2. Comanche Indians -- History 3. Comanche Indians -- Wars 4. Comanche Indians -- Kings and rulers -- Biography

ISBN 076604095X; 9780766040953

LC 2011048762

This book by William R. Sanford is part of the Native American Chiefs and Warriors series. It "tells how Quanah, the last Comanche chief, at first drew controversy for surrendering to the U.S. government and agreeing to live on a reservation. He later earned praise for effectively bridging both cultures." (Booklist)

Includes bibliographical references and index.

Oglala Lakota Chief Red Cloud; by William R. Sanford. Enslow Publishers 2013 48 p. (library) $21.26

Grades: 6 7 8 9   **978.004**

1. Oglala Indians -- Wars 2. Oglala Indians -- Kings and rulers -- Biography

ISBN 0766040968; 9780766040960

LC 2011048760

This book is part of the Native American Chiefs and Warriors series and looks at Oglala Lakota Chief Red Cloud. Each title "focuses on the U.S. government's infringement upon Native American land and how these leaders responded." This entry "recounts Red Cloud's fight to prevent whites from traveling along the Bozeman and Oregon Trails, his meeting with President Ulysses Grant, and his band's forced move to a reservation." (Booklist)

Includes bibliographical references and index.

Oglala Sioux Chief Crazy Horse; by William R. Sanford. Enslow Publishers 2013 48 p. (library) $21.26

Grades: 6 7 8 9   **978.004**

1. Little Bighorn, Battle of the, Mont., 1876 2. Oglala Indians -- Kings and rulers -- Biography
ISBN 0766040941; 9780766040946

         LC 2011048758

This book is part of the Native American Chiefs and Warriors series and looks at Oglala Sioux Chief Crazy Horse. Each title "focuses on the U.S. government's infringement upon Native American land and how these leaders responded." This entry "describes Crazy Horse's success as a chief and warrior, particularly during the Battle of the Little Bighorn, and the resulting jealousy among other Sioux leaders that led to his contentious death." (Booklist)

Includes bibliographical references (p. 46) and index.

978.7   Wyoming

Meyer, Judith L.

The **spirit** of Yellowstone; the cultural evolution of a national park. photographs by Vance Howard. Roberts Rinehart 2003 145p il pa $19.95

Grades: 11 12 Adult   **978.7**

1. Human influence on nature 2. Yellowstone National Park
ISBN 1-570-98395-X

         LC 2002-156320

First published 1996 by Rowman & Littlefield

The author "pays tribute to the park and all its glories, covering the park's history, its prime landmarks, and its prominence in art. The photographs are truly striking and not the typical landscape fare. Howard plays with light and texture to capture images that will amaze even those already familiar with the park's unprecedented beauty." Libr J

Includes bibliographical references

978.752   Yellowstone National Park

A **weird** and wild beauty; the story of Yellowstone, the world's first national park. Erin Peabody. Skyhorse Publishing, Inc. 2016 192 p. color illustrations (print) $14.99

Grades: 6 7 8 9 10   **978.752**

1. Yellowstone National Park -- History 2. National parks and reserves -- United States 3. Landscape protection -- United States -- History 4. Yellowstone National Park -- Environmental conditions 5. Yellowstone National Park -- Discovery and exploration 6. National parks and reserves -- United States -- History
ISBN 1634502043; 9781634502047

         LC 2015035831

This book, by Erin Peabody, "tells the story of one of the first scientific expeditions into the vast Western wilderness surrounding the Yellowstone River. In 1871, Ferdinand Hayden led an expedition of geologists, naturalists, artists, photographers, soldiers, and adventurers into a remote corner of what was then the Montana Territory. The expedi-

tion's documentation . . . ultimately culminated in the passage of the Yellowstone Park Bill." (School Library Journal)

Includes bibliographical references and index

978.9   New Mexico

★ **When** we were young in the West; true stories of childhood. edited with an introduction and conclusion by Richard Melzer. Sunstone Press 2003 345p il map pa $19.95

Grades: 11 12 Adult   **978.9**

1. Children -- West (U.S.) 2. New Mexico -- Social life and customs
ISBN 0-86534-338-1

         LC 2003-42572

Presents biographical sketches of New Mexican children from different cultures, races, and classes who represent the strength and diversity of this state's heritage

"A unique and vastly informative book. . . . The richness of detail tells us as much about the past as it does about childhood." Booklist

Includes bibliographical references

979   Great Basin and Pacific Slope region of United States

Scott, Robert Alan

Chief Joseph and the Nez Perces; [by] Robert A. Scott. Facts on File 1993 134p il map (Makers of America) lib bdg $25

Grades: 8 9 10 11 12   **979**

1. Indian chiefs 2. Nez Percé Indians 3. Native Americans -- Biography
ISBN 0-8160-2475-8

         LC 92-15885

A biography of the nineteenth-century Nez Percé chief, concentrating on his unending struggle to win peace and equality for his people

Includes bibliographical references

979.1   Arizona

Hernandez, Daniel

They call me a hero; a memoir of my youth. Daniel Hernandez and Susan Goldman Rubin. Simon & Schuster Books for Young Readers 2013 240 p. (hardcover) $17.99

Grades: 7 8 9 10 11 12   **979.1**

1. Courage 2. Interns -- United States -- Biography 3. Heroes -- Arizona -- Tucson -- Biography 4. Sexual minorities -- Civil rights -- Arizona -- Tucson
ISBN 1442462280; 9781442462281; 9781442462380

         LC 2012019829

This book, by Daniel Hernandez, with Susan Gldman Rubin, is a memoir about heroism. "Daniel Hernandez was . . . working as an intern for U.S. Representative Gabrielle Giffords. On January 8, 2011, . . . Giffords was shot. Daniel Hernandez's quick thinking saved Giffords's life. . . . But while that may have been his most well-known moment in the spotlight, Daniel Hernandez, Jr. . . . [had] already accomplished much in his young life, and is working to achieve much more." (Publisher's note)

Pyne, Stephen J.

How the Canyon became Grand; a short history. Viking 1998 199p il maps hardcover o.p. pa $15

Grades: 11 12 Adult   **979.1**

1. Grand Canyon (Ariz.)

ISBN 0-14-028056-1 pa

LC 98-20094

"To understand the canyon as a place and as a perspective, Pyne traces its history from the time of the Spanish conquistadors and later explorers like John Wesley Powell and Clarence Dutton to its status today as a natural wonder attracting more than five million visitors annually. He also explains how our attitude toward the canyon has changed." Libr J

Includes bibliographical references

979.4   California

Dumas, Firoozeh

Funny in Farsi; a memoir of growing up Iranian in America. Villard Bks. 2003 187p il hardcover o.p. pa $12.95

Grades: 9 10 11 12   **979.4**

1. Authors 2. Iranian Americans 3. Memoirists

ISBN 1-4000-6040-0; 0-8129-6837-9 pa

LC 2002-34921

"Dumas has a unique perspective on American culture, and she effortlessly balances the comedy of her family's misadventures with the more serious prejudices they face." Booklist

979.7   Washington

Kirkpatrick, Katherine

Mysterious bones; the story of Kennewick Man. by Katherine Kirkpatrick; illustrated by Emma Stevenson. Holiday House 2011 60p il map $17.95

Grades: 6 7 8 9   **979.7**

1. Skeleton 2. Kennewick Man 3. Native Americans 4. Washington (State) 5. North America -- Antiquities

ISBN 978-0-8234-2187-9; 0-8234-2187-2

LC 2009025575

Kennewick Man "was found in remarkable condition near the Columbia River in Washington . . . in 1996—one of the oldest and most complete skeletons found in America. Kirkpatrick addresses the controversy surrounding the treatment of his remains. . . . Excellent illustrations accompany the story, with crisp line-drawings of tools, skeletons, maps and possible facial reconstructions." Kirkus

Includes glossary and bibliographical references

Sone, Monica

Nisei daughter; Monica Sone; introduction to the 2014 edition by Marie Rose Wong; introduction to the

1979 edition by S. Frank Miyamoto; preface to the 1979 edition by the author. University of Washington Press 2014 238 p. (paperback: alkaline paper) $18.95

Grades: 11 12 Adult   **979.7**

1. World War, 1939-1945 -- United States 2. Japanese Americans -- Evacuation and relocation, 1942-1945 3. Seattle (Wash.) -- Biography 4. Puyallup Assembly Center (Puyallup, Wash.) 5. Japanese Americans -- Washington (State) -- Seattle -- Biography

ISBN 9780295993553

LC 2013036826

In this memoir, author Monica Sone "tells what it was like to grow up Japanese American on Seattle's waterfront in the 1930s and to be subjected to 'relocation' during World War II. Along with over one hundred thousand other persons of Japanese ancestry — most of whom were U.S. citizens — Sone and her family were uprooted from their home and imprisoned in a camp." (Publisher's note)

979.8   Alaska

Sandler, Martin W.

★ The **impossible** rescue; by Martin Sandler. Candlewick Press 2012 176 p. il

Grades: 5 6 7 8 9   **979.8**

1. Reindeer 2. Shipwrecks 3. Rescue work 4. Barrow (Alaska) 5. Bear (Ship) 6. Whaling -- History 7. Overland Relief Expedition (1897-1898)

ISBN 0763650803; 9780763650803

LC 2011018618

This book by Martin W. Sander "follows an 1897-98 rescue mounted by the U.S. Revenue Cutter Service . . . in the wake of news that eight whaling ships with almost 300 men had been trapped in winter ice near Alaska's Point Barrow. Dubbed the Overland Relief Expedition, the small crew of rescuers and native residents . . . traveled over 1,500 miles of rough ice and rock on dogsleds. . . . Upon arrival, the rescuers were saddled with keeping the ill, unruly sailors in line for three months until the ice broke up." (Booklist)

980   History of South America

Encyclopedia of Latin America; Thomas M. Leonard, general editor. Facts On File 2010 4v il map (Facts on File library of world history) set $360

Grades: 11 12 Adult   **980**

1. Reference books 2. Latin America -- Encyclopedias

ISBN 978-0-8160-7359-7

LC 2009-14594

"Articles range from a paragraph to several pages and cover individuals, nations, and more; and larger articles cover general topics such as trade, government, and family relations. One of the best features of the set is the selection of primary source materials in each volume, including conquistador memoirs, indigenous poetry in translation, native histories, royal orders, revolutionary proclamations, and many other items." Booklist

Includes glossary and bibliographical references

★ **Encyclopedia** of Latin American history and culture; Jay Kinsbruner, editor in chief; Erick D. Langer, senior editor. 2nd ed.; Gale 2008 6v il map set $695

Grades: 11 12 Adult **980**
1. Reference books 2. Latin America -- Encyclopedias
ISBN 978-0-684-31270-5

LC 2008-3461

First published 1996
"This reference set covers the Western Hemisphere from Mexico to the tip of South America. . . . [This is] an outstanding encyclopedia that will serve a wide range of users from high school students to Latin American scholars." Libr J
Includes bibliographical references

Gritzner, Charles F.
Latin America. Chelsea House Publishers 2006 120p il map (Modern world cultures) lib bdg $30

Grades: 7 8 9 10 **980**
1. Latin America
ISBN 0-7910-8142-7; 978-0-7910-8142-6

LC 2005-32686

This book "explores the diverse cultural, economic, political, and natural landscapes of this unique region." Publisher's note
Includes bibliographical references

981 Brazil

Meade, Teresa
A **brief** history of Brazil; [by] Teresa A. Meade. 2nd ed; Facts On File 2009 280p il (Brief history) $49.50; pa $19.95

Grades: 11 12 Adult **981**
1. Brazil -- History
ISBN 978-0-8160-7788-5; 0-8160-7788-6; 978-0-8160-7789-2 pa; 0-8160-7789-4 pa; 978-1-4381-2736-1 ebook

LC 2009-33853

First published 2003
An account of Brazil's political, economic, and cultural landscape.
Includes bibliographical references

982 Argentina

Brown, Jonathan C.
A **brief** history of Argentina; 2nd ed; Facts On File 2010 354p il map (Brief history) $49.50; pa $19.95

Grades: 11 12 Adult **982**
1. Argentina -- History
ISBN 978-0-8160-7796-0; 978-0-8160-8361-9 pa; 978-1-4381-3111-5 ebook

LC 2010004887

First published 2002
This book covers "Argentina's diverse geography and its varied natural resources; the origins of the deep-seated

practices of discrimination, which continue today; the effects of neoliberalism on Argentina's large working class and urban poor, culminating in the caserola movement, the piqueteros movement, and the birth of the cartoneros; the impact a changing global economy has had within Argentina's borders; [and] the rich culture of Argentina, which has created five Nobel laureates, vibrant cities that draw millions of tourists annually, and sports teams that have won multiple world championships." Publisher's note
Includes bibliographical references

Parrado, Nando
★ **Miracle** in the Andes; 72 days on the mountain and my long trek home. [by] Nando Parrado with Vince Rause. Crown Publishers 2006 291p il map hardcover o.p. pa $13.95

Grades: 11 12 Adult **982**
1. Survival after airplane accidents, shipwrecks, etc. 2. Andes
ISBN 1-4000-9767-3; 978-1-4000-9767-8; 1-4000-9769-X pa; 978-1-4000-9769-2 pa

LC 2005-21629

"In October 1972, a plane carrying an Uruguayan rugby team crashed in the Andes. Not immediately rescued, the survivors turned to cannibalism to survive and after 72 days were saved. Rugby team member Parrado has written a beautiful story of friendship, tragedy and perseverance." Publ Wkly

985 Peru

Bingham, Hiram
★ **Lost** city of the Incas; the story of Machu Picchu and its builders. with an introduction by Hugh Thomson; photographs by Hugh Thomson. Sterling 2002 274p il hardcover o.p. pa $12.95

Grades: 11 12 Adult **985**
1. Incas 2. Machu Picchu (Peru) 3. Peru -- Antiquities
ISBN 0-2976-0759-6; 1-84212-585-0 pa

LC 2002-483039

A reissue of the title first published 1948 by Duell
"In 1911 Bingham, an American explorer, found the Inca city of Machu Picchu, which had been lost for 300 years. In this volume he tells of its origin, how it came to be lost and how it was finally discovered." Libr J
Includes bibliographical references

Cohen Suarez, Ananda
Handbook to life in the Inca World; [by] Ananda Cohen Suarez, Jeremy James George. Facts On File 2011 330p il map (Facts on File library of world history) $70

Grades: 11 12 Adult **985**
1. Incas
ISBN 978-0-8160-7449-5; 978-1-4381-3615-8 ebook

LC 2010032027

This "examination of the Inca Empire, which stretched across the Andes Mountains in Peru from the 13th century until the invasion of the Spanish in the 16th century . . . [draws upon] archaeology, anthropology, art history, ethnography, and 16th-century Spanish chronicles . . . [to explain] how the Inca Empire became such an influential and powerful civilization." Publisher's note

Includes bibliographical references

Hunefeldt, Christine

A **brief** history of Peru; 2nd ed; Facts On File 2010 xx, 332p il map (Brief history) $49.50

Grades: 11 12 Adult   **985**

1. Peru -- History

ISBN 978-0-8160-8144-8; 978-1-4381-0828-5 ebook

LC 2010-20748

First published 2004

This is a history of Peru ranging "from its ancient peoples and the Inca Empire through . . . recent political, social, and economic developments." Publisher's note

Includes bibliographical references

Malpass, Michael

★ **Daily** life in the Inca empire; [by] Michael A. Malpass. 2nd ed.; Greenwood Press 2009 xxx, 176p il map (Greenwood Press 'Daily life through history' series) $49.95

Grades: 11 12 Adult   **985**

1. Incas

ISBN 978-0-313-35548-6

LC 2009-193

First published 1996

This book explores different "aspects of Inca culture, including politics and social hierarchy, the life cycle, agriculture, architecture, women's roles, dress and ornamentation, food and drink, festivals, religious rituals, the calendar, and the unique Inca form of taxation." Publisher's note

Includes glossary and bibliographical references

Masterson, Daniel M.

The **history** of Peru; [by] Daniel Masterson. Greenwood Press 2009 xxv, 246p il map (Greenwood histories of the modern nations) $45

Grades: 11 12 Adult   **985**

1. Peru -- History

ISBN 978-0-313-34072-7; 0-313-34072-2

LC 2009-10348

Covers social life and culture, political practices, economics, and international influence throughout the ages in Peru, from the earliest social groups dating as far back as 500 B.C. to life today in the 21st century.

Includes bibliographical references

Moseley, Michael Edward

The **Incas** and their ancestors; the archaeology of Peru. {by} Michael E. Moseley. Thames & Hudson 1992 272p il maps hardcover o.p. pa $31.95

Grades: 11 12 Adult   **985**

1. Incas 2. Peru -- Antiquities

ISBN 0-500-28277-3 pa

LC 91-65309

This account of Andean prehistory and archaeology takes us from the first settlement of 10,000 years ago to the Spanish conquest

"Clearly presented, with a generous ration of maps and illustrations, {the volume} is thoughtful and welcome." Times Lit Suppl

994   Australia

West, Barbara A.

A **brief** history of Australia; [by] Barbara A. West with Frances T. Murphy. Facts On File 2010 356p il map (Brief history) $49.50

Grades: 11 12 Adult   **994**

1. Australia -- History

ISBN 978-0-8160-7885-1; 978-1-4381-3112-2 ebook

LC 2009-31925

"Beginning with the peopling of the continent about 60,000 years ago, the volume examines the early history and culture of the Aboriginals. It continues with the first documented sighting of the landmass by a European in the 17th century, followed by a discussion of the colonial period in the 18th and 19th centuries. From the Federation of 1901 to the Liberal government of John Howard (1998–2007) and the Labor government of Kevin Rudd (2007–present), this . . . book explores Australia's relationship to the British Crown, national security and education policy, the role of sport and environmental issues, Aboriginal rights, women's history, and gay rights." Publisher's note

Includes glossary and bibliographical references

996   Polynesia and other Pacific Ocean islands

Alexander, Caroline

The **Bounty**: the true story of the mutiny on the Bounty. Viking 2003 491p il hardcover o.p. pa $17

Grades: 11 12 Adult   **996**

1. Admirals 2. Explorers 3. Oceania 4. Mutineers 5. Bounty (Ship) 6. Naval officers 7. Government officials 8. Colonial administrators

ISBN 978-0-670-03133-7; 0-670-03133-X; 978-0-14-200469-2 pa; 0-14-200469-3 pa

LC 2003-50158

"A rollicking sea adventure told with enormous confidence and style." Booklist

Includes bibliographical references

998   Arctic islands and Antarctica

Alexander, Caroline

The **Endurance**; Shackleton's legendary Antarctic expedition. Knopf 1998 211p il $29.95

Grades: 11 12 Adult   **998**

1. Explorers 2. Endurance (Ship) 3. Antarctica -- Exploration 4. Imperial Trans-Antarctic Expedition (1914-1917)

ISBN 0-375-40403-1

In 1914, Sir Ernest Shackleton "sailed to Antarctica with 27 men in hopes of being the first human to transverse the continent. But his ship, the Endurance, was trapped, then crushed, by ice in the Weddell Sea, propelling the party into a nightmare of cold and near starvation. Alexander, relying extensively on journals by crew members, some never published, as well as on myriad other sources, delivers a spellbinding story of human courage. . . . What makes this book especially exciting, however, are the 170 previously unpublished photos by the expedition's photographer, Frank Hurley." Publ Wkly

Bryant, John H.

Dangerous crossings; the first modern polar expedition, 1925. {by} John H. Bryant and Harold N. Cones. Naval Inst. Press 2000 206p il maps $28.95
Grades: 9 10 11 12   **998**
1. Admirals 2. Explorers 3. Air pilots 4. Memoirists 5. Travel writers 6. Broadcasting executives 7. Arctic regions -- Exploration
ISBN 1-55750-187-4
                                                LC 00-26344
This book recounts the expedition mounted by Donald B. MacMillan, a colleague of Robert Peary's, Eugene F. McDonald, founder of the Zenith Corporation; and Richard E. Byrd, a young naval aviator
"Perfect Storm-like moments, a lack of supplies, some conflict with Danish officials in Greenland, nascent corporate development and the extraordinary bravery of the personnel involved make this an unusually rich exploration narrative." Publ Wkly
Includes bibliographical references (p.   )

Johnson, Kristin

The **Endurance** expedition. ABDO Pub. Co. 2011 112p il map (Essential events) lib bdg $23.95
Grades: 7 8 9 10 11 12   **998**
1. Explorers 2. Endurance (Ship) 3. Antarctica -- Exploration
ISBN 978-1-61714-764-7; 1-61714-764-8
                                                LC 2010043851
This book "about the race to be the first to reach the South Pole, focuses on the incredible rescue story—a grim survival adventure. The spacious . . . design is inviting, with many color illustrations and screens, and the extensive back matter includes a detailed time line, glossary, bibliography and source notes." Booklist
Includes glossary and bibliographical references

Myers, Walter Dean, 1937-2014

★ **Antarctica**; journeys to the South Pole. Scholastic Press 2004 134p il maps $18.95
Grades: 6 7 8 9   **998**
1. Antarctica
ISBN 0-439-22001-7
                                                LC 2004-2501
This book tracks "the explorers of the South Pole—including James Cook, Ernest Shackleton, and Richard Evelyn Byrd—and the dangers they encountered there, as well as their contributions to science." (Publisher's note) Index. "Grades five to nine." (Bull Cent Child Books)
This is "a lucid, well-written text." SLJ

Walker, Sally M.

Frozen secrets; Antarctica revealed. Carolrhoda Books 2010 104p il map $20.95

Grades: 7 8 9 10   **998**
1. Antarctica
ISBN 978-1-58013-607-5; 1-58013-607-9
                                                LC 2009-34282
This is an "account of the rich scientific findings coming out of the planet's southernmost continent. . . . It's an excellent overview that manages to pack a lot of technical and scientific information into a small space, but it's sufficiently well structured conceptually and well laid out visually . . . that it all goes down pretty easily. The photographic images reveal the stunning beauty of the continent in shot after shot, but there are also illuminating views of the scientists at work, and diagrams and maps round out the view." Bull Cent Child Books

Fic   FICTION

Abdel-Fattah, Randa

★ **Does** my head look big in this? Orchard Books 2007 360p $16.99
Grades: 7 8 9 10 11 12   **Fic**
1. School stories 2. Muslims -- Fiction 3. Australia -- Fiction 4. Clothing and dress -- Fiction
ISBN 0-439-91947-9; 978-0-439-91947-0
                                                LC 2006-29117
Year Eleven at an exclusive prep school in the suburbs of Melbourne, Australia, would be tough enough, but it is further complicated for Amal when she decides to wear the hijab, the Muslim head scarf, full-time as a badge of her faith—without losing her identity or sense of style. "Grades seven to ten." (Bull Cent Child Books)
"While the novel deals with a number of serious issues, it is extremely funny and entertaining." SLJ

★ **Ten** things I hate about me. Orchard Books 2009 297p $16.99
Grades: 7 8 9 10   **Fic**
1. School stories 2. Muslims -- Fiction 3. Lebanese -- Fiction 4. Australia -- Fiction 5. Prejudices -- Fiction
ISBN 978-0-5450-5055-5; 0-5450-5055-3
                                                LC 2008-13667
This novel is set in Australia. Jamilia, known in school as Jamie, tries to hide her Muslim heritage from her classmates, until her conflicted feelings become too difficult for her to bear. "Grades six to nine." (Bull Cent Child Books)
A "message of the importance of self-disclosure to maintain loving relationships of all kinds plays itself out as Jamie learns to negotiate her roles as daughter, sister, and friend. Readers will also get an enlightening look at post-9/11 racial tensions outside the U.S. and the problems they pose for Muslim teens." Bull Cent Child Books

Abercrombie, Joe

Half a King; Joe Abercrombie. Random House Inc 2014 352 p. map (Shattered Sea) (hardcover) $26
Grades: 11 12 Adult   **Fic**
1. Fantasy fiction 2. Kings and rulers -- Fiction
ISBN 0804178321; 9780804178327
                                                LC 2014017107

In this fantasy novel, by Joe Abercrombie, "among the royalty of Gettland, only strong, fearless, cold-eyed warriors have value. So Prince Yarvi, born with a withered hand, had only one option: to train as a minister (counselor). After years studying . . . Yarvi is ready to take the ministry's test when news arrives that his father and elder brother have been treacherously murdered by [a] neighboring rival King." (Publisher's note)

"The world building here is complete and convincing, and the characters are arresting in their all-too-human nature." Booklist

Followed by: Half the World (2015)

Half a war; Joe Abercrombie. Del Rey 2015 384 p. (Shattered sea) $26

Grades: 11 12 Adult   **Fic**

1. Fantasy fiction 2. Kings and rulers -- Fiction 3. People with disabilities -- Fiction 4. Kings and rulers -- Succession -- Fiction

ISBN 0804178453; 9780804178457

LC 2015018064

In this fantasy novel, by Joe Abercrombie, the concluding volume of the "Shattered sea" series, "Princess Skara of Throvenland watches helplessly as Bright Yilling, the High King's war leader, callously kills her grandfather King Fynn, burns his halls, and lays waste to her homeland after what the king thought was an agreement turned out to be a betrayal. . . . The allies will need elf-weapons, hidden and deadly dangerous, designed to kill a god." (Kirkus Reviews)

"The narrative, well-sprinkled with gory action and impelled by characters at this stage not just familiar, but gratifying, moves along at a brisk clip. Best of all, the relentless intrigues, plots, and schemes bubble just below the surface." Kirkus

Half the world; Joe Abercrombie. Del Rey 2015 366 p. map (hardcover: acid-free paper) $26

Grades: 11 12 Adult   **Fic**

1. Fantasy fiction 2. Teenage girls -- Fiction 3. First loves -- Fiction

ISBN 0804178429; 9780804178426

LC 2014038766

Alex Award (2016)

"This stand-alone sequel to the author's popular Half a King (2014) features a new protagonist: 16-year-old Thorn, who finds herself pressed into service to Father Yarvi, the cunning minister to King Uthil of Gettland and his queen, Laithlin. Thorn will accompany Yarvi on a voyage designed to turn enemies into friends and allies as Gettland faces the possibility of war with the High King. Along the way, she will be trained in fighting by a woman named Skifr, whom some call a witch, and find her feelings for a boy named Brand changing." (Booklist)

"Abercrombie has a knack for building characters with pathos and wit. Both plot and setting are believable, and readers will easily immerse themselves in Thorn and Yarvi's world." Pub Wkly

Followed by: Half a War (2015)

Abouet, Marguerite

Aya; love in Yop City. by Marguerite Abouet and Clement Oubrerie; translatied by Helge Dascher. 1st

paperback ed. Drawn & Quarterly 2013 328 p. col. ill. (paperback) $24.95

Grades: 10 11 12 Adult   **Fic**

1. Nineteen seventies 2. Ivory Coast -- Graphic novels 3. Graphic novels -- Côte d'Ivoire 4. Côte d'Ivoire -- Comic books, strips, etc 5. Teenage girls -- Côte d'Ivoire -- Comic books, strips, etc

ISBN 1770460926; 9781770460928

LC 2012545664

This graphic novel, written by Marguerite Abouet and Clément Oubrerie, comprises the final three chapters of the 'Aya' story, . . . a lighthearted story about life in the Ivory Coast during the 1970s, a particularly thriving and wealthy time in the country's history. When a professor tries to take advantage of Aya, her plans to become a doctor are . . . shaken, and she vows to take revenge on [him]." The book includes "recipes, guides to understanding Ivorian slang, street sketches, and concluding remarks from Abouet explaining . . . social milieu." (Publisher's note)

Abrahams, Peter

Reality check. HarperTeen 2009 330p $16.99; lib bdg $17.89; pa $8.99

Grades: 7 8 9 10   **Fic**

1. School stories 2. Gambling -- Fiction 3. Social classes -- Fiction 4. Missing persons -- Fiction

ISBN 978-0-06-122766-0; 0-06-122766-8; 978-0-06-122767-7 lib bdg; 0-06-122767-6 lib bdg; 978-0-06-122768-4 pa; 0-06-122768-4 pa

LC 2008-22593

After a knee injury destroys sixteen-year-old Cody's college hopes, he drops out of high school and gets a job in his small Montana town, but when his ex-girlfriend disappears from her Vermont boarding school, Cody travels cross-country to join the search.

"Abrahams writes a fine thriller that is pitched to attract everyone from reluctant readers to sports fans to romantic idealists." Voice Youth Advocates

Abrams, Amir

Hollywood High. Dafina KTeen Books 2012 310 p. (prebind) $20.80; (paperback) $9.95

Grades: 9 10 11 12   **Fic**

1. School stories 2. Teenage pregnancy -- Fiction

ISBN 0606263780; 0758263171; 9780606263788; 9780758263179

LC 2012418660

This book is told by four high school narrators, all spoiled daughters of entertainment industry elites, "including ex-New Yorker London, tabloid queen Rich and . . . Spencer. Heather . . . supports her alcoholic mother with her own acting career and struggles with an Adderall addiction. Drama escalates practically within milliseconds. . . . Much of the drama involves competition over boys." (Kirkus)

Acosta, Marta

Dark companion; Marta Acosta. Tom Doherty Assoc. 2012 364 p. (hardcover) $17.99

Grades: 9 10 11 12   **Fic**

1. School stories 2. Orphans -- Fiction 3. Supernatural -- Fiction 4. Private schools -- Fiction 5. Schools --

Fiction 6. Boarding schools -- Fiction
ISBN 0765329646; 9780765329646; 9781429988292
LC 2012011656

This book tells the story of Jane Williams. "Orphaned at the age of six, [she] has grown up in a series of foster homes, learning to survive in the shadows of life. . . . [S]he manages to win a scholarship to the exclusive Birch Grove Academy. There, for the first time, Jane finds herself accepted by a group of friends. She even starts tutoring the headmistress's gorgeous son, Lucien." But, the "more she learns about Birch Grove's recent past, the more Jane comes to suspect that there is something sinister going on. . . . As Jane begins to piece together the answers to the puzzle, she must find out why she was brought to Birch Grove—and what she would risk to stay there." (Publisher's note)

Adams, Douglas

★ The **hitchhiker's** guide to the galaxy; 25th anniversary illustrated collector's ed.; Harmony Books 2004 271p il $35
Grades: 7 8 9 10 11 12 Adult   **Fic**
1. Science fiction
ISBN 1-4000-5293-9
LC 2004-558987

First published 1980
"Based on a BBC radio series, . . . this is the episodic story of Arthur Dent, a contemporary Englishman who discovers first that his unpretentious house is about to be demolished to make way for a bypass, and second that a good friend is actually an alien galactic hitchhiker who announces that Earth itself will soon be demolished to make way for an intergalactic speedway. A suitably bewildered Dent soon finds himself hitching . . . rides throughout space, aided by a . . . reference book, The Hitchhiker's Guide to the Galaxy, a compendium of 'facts,' philosophies, and wild advice." Libr J

Life, the universe, and everything. Harmony Bks. 1982 227p hardcover o.p. pa $12.95
Grades: 11 12 Adult   **Fic**
1. Science fiction
ISBN 0-517-54874-7; 0-345-41890-6 pa
LC 82-15470

Third volume in The hitchhiker's series
"Arthur Dent and his motley crew do tie up most of the loose ends and manage to prevent the destruction of the universe, but the first two novels . . . 'must' be read to understand the situation, and even then it's confusing." Libr J
Followed by So long, and thanks for all the fish

Mostly harmless. Harmony Bks. 1992 277p hardcover o.p. pa $12.95
Grades: 11 12 Adult   **Fic**
1. Science fiction
ISBN 0-517-57740-2; 0-345-37933-0 pa
LC 92-25457

"A Grebulon reconnaissance ship with faulty programming, a news reporter suffering from a bad case of missed opportunities, a fugitive from the new 'improved' offices of the Hitchhiker's Guide to the Galaxy, and a hitchhiker lost in a parallel universe come together in grand style in the fifth installment of Adams's best-selling 'trilogy.'" Libr J

The **restaurant** at the end of the universe. Harmony Bks. 1981 250p hardcover o.p. pa $12.95
Grades: 11 12 Adult   **Fic**
1. Satire 2. Wit and humor 3. Science fiction 4. Interplanetary voyages
ISBN 0-517-54535-7; 0-345-41892-1 pa
LC 81-6563

Second volume in The hitchhiker's series
First published 1980 in the United Kingdom
"Poor uprooted Arthur Dent finds himself swept along in the wake of Zaphod Beeblebrox, former President of the Galaxy, as Zaphod searches for the man who rules the Universe. They and their companions tumble from one scrape into another, with the erratic aid of Zaphod's dead great-grandfather and Marvin, their perpetually depressed robot. Adams's lively sense of the ridiculous has concocted many hilarious episodes, though the inspired lunacy of the first book has become rather uneven here. Still, this is one of the best pieces of sf humor available." Libr J
Followed by Life, the universe, and everything

So long, and thanks for all the fish. Harmony Bks. 1985 204p hardcover o.p. pa $7.99
Grades: 11 12 Adult   **Fic**
1. Satire 2. Wit and humor 3. Science fiction 4. Interplanetary voyages
ISBN 0-517-55439-9; 0-345-39183-4 pa
LC 84-19350

Fourth volume in The hitchhiker's series
Arthur Dent "returns to a supposedly destroyed Earth to build a hyperspace bypass. The night of his return, Arthur falls in love with a sedated girl (her brother says she's 'barking mad'), only to lose her, then accidentally find her twice more. She is Fenchurch, the girl who in . . . 'Guide' . . . discovered the secret of Earth's potential happiness moments before it was demolished. Her 'madness' stems from the time when Earth should have been destroyed, and wasn't, but when all the dolphins disappeared. . . . The humor is still off-the-wall, but less forced and more gentle than the other books. . . . The series seems to be winding down, but it is still an addictive commodity to its fans." SLJ
Followed by Mostly harmless

Adams, Richard
Watership Down; Scribner classics ed.; Scribner 1996 429p $30; pa $15
Grades: 6 7 8 9 10   **Fic**
1. Allegories 2. Rabbits -- Fiction
ISBN 0-684-83605-X; 0-7432-7770-8 pa

First published 1972 in the United Kingdom; first United States edition 1974 by Macmillan
"Faced with the annihilation of its warren, a small group of male rabbits sets out across the English downs in search of a new home. Internal struggles for power surface in this intricately woven, realistically told adult adventure when the protagonists must coordinate tactics in order to defeat an enemy rabbit fortress. It is clear that the author has done research on rabbit behavior, for this tale is truly authentic." Shapiro Fic for Youth. 3d edition

Adams, S. J.

Sparks; the epic, completely true blue, (almost) holy quest of Debbie. 1; Flux 2011 256p pa $9.95

Grades: 8 9 10 11 12   **Fic**

1. Iowa -- Fiction 2. Lesbians -- Fiction 3. Religion -- Fiction

ISBN 978-0-7387-2676-2; 0-7387-2676-1

LC 2011022913

Stonewall Honor Book (2013)

"Adams has an easy sense of humor . . . and Debbie and her offbeat cohorts are nuanced and authentic as they follow a circuitous path to greater self-awareness and self-reliance." Publ Wkly

Adichie, Chimamanda Ngozi

★ **Purple** hibiscus; a novel. Anchor Books 2004 307p pa $14.95

Grades: 11 12 Adult   **Fic**

1. Nigeria -- Fiction 2. Family life -- Fiction

ISBN 978-1-4000-7694-9; 1-4000-7694-3

LC 2004-51629

First published 2003 by Algonquin Bks.

"Quiet, chilling, and heart wrenching, this debut novel is both a superb portrait of an unfamiliar culture and an un-flinching depiction of the universal turmoil of adolescence." Voice Youth Advocates

Adlington, L. J.

★ The **diary** of Pelly D. Greenwillow Books 2005 282p hardcover o.p. pa $8.99

Grades: 7 8 9 10   **Fic**

1. Science fiction

ISBN 0-06-076615-8; 0-06-076617-4 pa

LC 2004-52258

"On the planet Home From Home, Toni V is a brute la-borer, a barely educated member of the Demolition Crew that is busy pulverizing the bombed-out remains of City Five's central plaza. Pelly D is a hip member of the swank elite who used to live in an exclusive apartment fronting the plaza. Their stories come together when Toni V uncov-ers Pelly D's diary in the debris. . . . Middle school, high school." (Horn Book)

"Adlington has crafted an original and disturbing dystopian fantasy told in a smart and sympathetic teen voice." Booklist

Aguirre, Ann

Enclave. Feiwel & Friends 2011 262p $16.99

Grades: 8 9 10   **Fic**

1. Horror fiction 2. Fantasy fiction 3. Dystopian fiction 4. Apocalyptic fiction 5. Zombies -- Fiction

ISBN 978-0-312-65008-7; 0-312-65008-6

LC 2010031039

In a post-apocalyptic future, fifteen-year-old Deuce, a loyal Huntress, brings back meat while avoiding the Freaks outside her enclave, but when she is partnered with the mys-terious outsider, Fade, she begins to see that the strict ways of the elders may be wrong—and dangerous. "Grades six to eight." (Bull Cent Child Books)

"In this skilled though violent postapocalyptic thriller, Deuce has newly earned the rank of Huntress. . . . It's her duty to provide meat for her loveless, draconian enclave,

deep beneath the streets of a ruined city, as well as to defend it against cannibalistic Freaks, who are gradually eliminat-ing the scattered human survivors of a vaguely remembered plague. . . . Aguirre . . . has created a gritty and highly com-petent heroine, an equally deadly sidekick/love interest, and a fascinating if unpleasant civilization." Publ Wkly

Horde; by Ann Aguirre. Feiwel & Friends 2013 422 p. $17.99

Grades: 8 9 10   **Fic**

1. Science fiction 2. Dystopian fiction 3. Monsters -- Fiction

ISBN 1250024633; 9781250024633

This book, by Ann Aguirre, is the conclusion to the Enclave trilogy. "Salvation is surrounded, monsters at the gates, and this time, they're not going away. When Deuce, Fade, Stalker and Tegan set out, the odds are against them. But the odds have been stacked against Deuce from the mo-ment she was born. She might not be a Huntress anymore, but she doesn't run. With her knives in hand and her com-panions at her side, she will not falter, whether fighting for her life or Fade's love." (Publisher's note)

"Deuce's skills from her Huntress days come in handy when a horde of mutant "Freaks" descends upon the humans of her post-apocalyptic world, but trusting some of the en-emy turns out to be a worthwhile risk. Relationships, includ-ing Deuce's romance with Fade, soften a bloody tale; as in previous compelling installments, readers should suspend disbelief for Deuce's background-belying vocabulary and emotional intelligence." (Horn Book)

Outpost; by Ann Aguirre. Feiwel & Friends 2012 320 p. $17.99

Grades: 8 9 10   **Fic**

1. Monsters -- Fiction 2. Teenagers -- Fiction 3. Survival skills -- Fiction 4. Science fiction 5. Survival -- Fiction 6. Teenage girls -- Fiction

ISBN 0312650094; 9780312650094

LC 2011287957

In this book by Ann Aguirre "months have passed since Deuce and her band of survivors joined Salvation, a forti-fied settlement in the middle of Freak-infested land. While Tegan, Fade, and Stalker find helpful community roles, Deuce struggles to adjust to life where, as a female, she is forbidden from fighting. When the Freaks evolve into more cunning foes, however, Deuce's superior combat skills are instrumental in establishing an outpost to protect the town." (Booklist)

"When this follow-up to Enclave (2011) begins, trained Huntress Deuce and fellow travelers Fade, Stalker and Tegan have lived two months amid the town of Salvation's affluence, strict gender roles and relative freedom from the putrid, slavering, mindless Freaks who plague their world... Overall, an engaging world and forward-moving plot with a resolution that promises new settings and challenges in Book 3." (Kirkus)

Ahdieh, Renée

The **wrath** and the dawn; Renée Ahdieh. Put-nam Juvenile 2015 416 p. illustrations (color), map (hardback) $17.99

Grades: 9 10 11 12 **Fic**
1. Fairy tales 2. Love -- Fiction 3. Magic -- Fiction 4. Murder -- Fiction 5. Kings and rulers -- Fiction
ISBN 0399171614; 9780399171611
LC 2014046249

In this book, by Renée Ahdieh, "the brave Shahrzad volunteers to marry the Caliph of Khorasan after her best friend is chosen as one of his virgin brides and is summarily murdered the next morning. She uses her storytelling skills, along with well-placed cliff-hangers, to keep herself alive while trying to discover a way to exact revenge on the Caliph. However, the longer she stays in the palace, the more she realizes there's more going on than just a murderous prince." (School Library Journal)

"It's not a completely faultless debut—the prose very occasionally turns purple, but that's a minor offense; the characters are redeemingly nuanced and well crafted. Even more impressive, Ahdieh is in complete control of her plot, tightly spooling out threads of the richly layered story just as surely as Shahrzad herself. The result is that the reader can't help but be absorbed by the time the crescendoing conclusion come—and in true Arabian Nights fashion, it's a cliff-hanger. Like the caliph, we will just have to wait for the rest."Booklist

Wrath and the dawn

Albertalli, Becky

★ **Simon** vs. the Homo Sapiens agenda; Becky Albertalli. Balzer + Bray, an imprint of HarperCollinsPublishers 2015 320 p. (hardback) $17.99
Grades: 9 10 11 12 **Fic**
1. School stories 2. Friendship -- Fiction 3. Gay teenagers -- Fiction 4. Gays -- Fiction 5. Schools -- Fiction 6. Secrets -- Fiction 7. Pen pals -- Fiction 8. Extortion -- Fiction 9. High schools -- Fiction
ISBN 0062348671; 9780062348678
LC 2014022536
Morris Award (2016)

In this novel by Becky Albertalli, "sixteen-year-old and not-so-openly gay Simon Spier prefers to save his drama for the school musical. But when an email falls into the wrong hands, his secret is at risk of being thrust into the spotlight. Now change-averse Simon has to find a way to step out of his comfort zone before he's pushed out--without alienating his friends, compromising himself, or fumbling a shot at happiness." (Publisher's note)

"While Simon is focused on Blue, other characters go on journeys of their own, and the author is careful not only to wrap up Simon's story, but to draw attention to the stories the romance plot might overshadow in lesser hands. Funny, moving and emotionally wise." Kirkus

Albin, Gennifer

Crewel; Gennifer Albin. by Gennifer Albin. Farrar Straus Giroux 2012 368 p. (hardcover) $17.99
Grades: 8 9 10 11 **Fic**
1. Spiritual gifts 2. Secrecy -- Fiction 3. Psychics -- Fiction 4. Science fiction
ISBN 0374316414; 9780374316419; 9780374316440
LC 2011043930

In author Gennifer Albin's book, "sixteen year-old Adelice Lewys has a secret: she wants to fail. Gifted with the ability to weave time with matter, she's exactly what the Guild is looking for, and in the world of Arras, being chosen as a Spinster is everything a girl could want. . . . It also means the power to embroider the very fabric of life . . . [and] Adelice isn't interested. Not that her feelings matter, because she slipped and wove a moment at testing, and they're coming for her--tonight. Now she has one hour . . . to escape." (genniferalbin.com)

Alegria, Malin

Estrella's quinceanera. Simon & Schuster Books for Young Readers 2006 272p $14.95
Grades: 7 8 9 10 **Fic**
1. Mexican Americans -- Fiction 2. Quinceañera (Social custom) -- Fiction
ISBN 0-689-87809-5

Estrella's mother and aunt are planning a gaudy, traditional quinceañera for her, even though it is the last thing she wants.

"Alegria writes about Mexican American culture, first love, family, and of moving between worlds with poignant, sharp-sighted humor and authentic dialogue." Booklist

Alender, Katie

Bad girls don't die. Hyperion Books 2009 352p $15.99
Grades: 7 8 9 10 **Fic**
1. School stories 2. Sisters -- Fiction 3. Demoniac possession -- Fiction
ISBN 978-1-4231-0876-4; 1-4231-0876-0
LC 2008-46179

When fifteen-year-old Lexi's younger sister Kasey begins behaving strangely and their old Victorian house seems to take on a life of its own, Lexi investigates and discovers some frightening facts about previous occupants of the house, leading her to believe that many lives are in danger.

This "novel is both a mystery and a trip into the paranormal. . . . With just enough violence, suspense, and romance to keep readers turning pages, this . . . will be a popular addition to any YA collection." Booklist

Followed by: From bad to cursed (2011)

The **dead** girls of Hysteria Hall; Katie Alender. Point, an imprint of Scholastic Inc. 2015 336 p. (jacketed hardcover) $18.99
Grades: 7 8 9 10 11 12 **Fic**
1. Ghost stories 2. Horror fiction 3. Secrets -- Fiction 4. Family life -- Fiction 5. Pennsylvania -- Fiction 6. Haunted houses -- Fiction 7. Psychiatric hospitals -- Fiction 8. Horror tales 9. Horror stories 10. Ghosts -- Fiction 11. Sisters -- Fiction
ISBN 9780545639996
LC 2014046681

In this book, by Katie Alender, "Delia's new house isn't just a house. Long ago, it was the Piven Institute for the Care and Correction of Troubled Females -- an insane asylum. . . . However, many of the inmates were not insane, just defiant and strong willed. Kind of like Delia herself. But the house still wants to keep "troubled" girls locked away. So, in the most horrifying way, Delia becomes trapped. And that's when she learns that the house is also haunted." (Publisher's note)

"Alender creates a fascinating, eerie world that turns on a nicely original use of time and features constantly interesting characters. Delia is likable and sympathetic even as she strikes out, and the house itself becomes a character, as readers wonder who or what is at the root of the evil that lurks there. The final confrontation will have readers curling their toes. A really scary and original ghost story, well told. Read it with the lights on." Kirkus

Alexander, Jill S.

The **sweetheart** of Prosper County. Feiwel and Friends 2009 212p $16.99

Grades: 7 8 9 10   **Fic**

1. Texas -- Fiction 2. Bullies -- Fiction 3. Bereavement -- Fiction 4. Mother-daughter relationship -- Fiction
ISBN 978-0-312-54856-8; 0-312-54856-7

LC 2008-34757

In a small East Texas town largely ruled by prejudices and bullies, fourteen-year-old Austin sets out to win a ride in the next parade and, in the process, grows in her understanding of friendship and helps her widowed mother through her mourning.

"This is a warm, humorous story. . . . A refreshing picture of teen angst, with realistic dialogue and memorable characters." SLJ

Alexander, Kwame

★ The **crossover**; by Kwame Alexander. Houghton Mifflin Harcourt 2014 240 p. hc $16.99

Grades: 6 7 8 9 10   **Fic**

1. Rap music 2. Brothers -- Fiction 3. Basketball -- Fiction 4. Novels in verse 5. Twins -- Fiction 6. Fathers and sons -- Fiction 7. African Americans -- Fiction
ISBN 0544107713; 9780544107717

LC 2013013810

Newbery Medal (2015)

Coretta Scott King Author Award Honor Book (2015)

In this novel, by Kwame Alexander, "12-year old Josh Bell . . . and his twin brother Jordan are awesome on the court. But Josh has more than basketball in his blood, he's got mad beats, too, that tell his family's story in verse. . . . Josh and Jordan must come to grips with growing up on and off the court to realize breaking the rules comes at a terrible price, as their story's . . . climax proves a game-changer for the entire family." (Publisher's note)

"Twins Josh and Jordan are junior high basketball stars, thanks in large part to the coaching of their dad, a former professional baller who was forced to quit playing for health reasons, and the firm, but loving support of their assistant-principal mom...Despite his immaturity, Josh is a likable, funny, and authentic character. Underscoring the sports and the fraternal tension is a portrait of a family that truly loves and supports one another. Alexander has crafted a story that vibrates with energy and heart and begs to be read aloud. A slam dunk." SLJ

He said, she said; by Kwame Alexander. Harper, an imprint of HarperCollinsPublishers 2013 336 p. (hardcover bdg.) $17.99

Grades: 9 10 11 12   **Fic**

1. High school students -- Fiction 2. Man-woman relationship -- Fiction 3. Love -- Fiction 4. Schools -- Fiction 5. High schools -- Fiction 6. African Americans -- Fiction 7. Protest movements -- Fiction
ISBN 006211896X; 9780062118967; 9780062118974

LC 2012043496

In this book, by Kwame Alexander, "a star high school quarterback bets he can get the attention of a girl who claims not to be interested by leading a protest for a cause she champions. Omar 'T-Diddy' Smalls has the swagger that comes with his exalted status. . . . he attracts the attention of every desirable girl at school, except for Claudia Clarke. . . . Omar never runs away from a challenge, and he bets his friends that Claudia will become his next conquest." (Kirkus Reviews)

"Claudia Clarke--sharp, opinionated, and Harvard-bound--is the only girl who isn't impressed by quarterback Omar "T-Diddy" Smalls. Omar takes a bet that he can win Claudia over, and when his usual seduction tactics fail, he applies his social clout to Claudia's cause du jour. His burgeoning social awareness and transformation from carefree jock to true campus leader are satisfying and convincing." (Horn Book)

Alexander, Shannon Lee

Love and other unknown variables; Shannon Lee Alexander. First edition October 2014 Entangled Teen 2014 329 p. $16.99

Grades: 9 10 11 12   **Fic**

1. Love -- Fiction 2. Terminally ill -- Fiction 3. Physics 4. Chemistry 5. Love stories
ISBN 1622664671; 9781622664672

This book by Shannon Lee Alexander "is told from the perspective of Charlie Hanson, a senior at Brighton School of Mathematics and Science. His life is planned out for him until he meets Charlotte Finch. She is ill, but this is a secret she does not immediately share. At Charlotte's urging and without knowing why, Charlie begins a prank campaign at Brighton in spite of the consequences to his future." (Library Media Connection)

"The characters' quirky affinities—Charlie's for math, Charlotte's for drawing, Ms. Finch's for literature—paint a world of passion and personality. A heartwarming YA story of love and entering the unknown territories of adulthood." Kirkus

Alexie, Sherman, 1966-

★ The **absolutely** true diary of a part-time Indian; art by Ellen Forney. Little, Brown 2007 229p il $18.99

Grades: 8 9 10   **Fic**

1. School stories 2. Friendship -- Fiction 3. Family life -- Fiction 4. Native Americans -- Fiction
ISBN 0316013684; 9780316013680

LC 2007-22799

Boston Globe-Horn Book Award: Fiction and Poetry (2008)

National Book Award for Young People's Literature (2007)

Budding cartoonist Junior leaves his troubled school on the Spokane Indian Reservation to attend an all-white farm town school where the only other Indian is the school mascot. "Grades seven to ten." (Bull Cent Child Books)

"The many characters, on and off the rez, with whom he has dealings are portrayed with compassion and verve. . . . Forney's simple pencil cartoons fit perfectly within the story and reflect the burgeoning artist within Junior." Booklist

Allen, Sarah Addison

The **girl** who chased the moon; a novel. Bantam Books 2010 269p $25; pa $15

Grades: 11 12 Adult **Fic**
1. Family life -- Fiction 2. Grandfathers -- Fiction 3. North Carolina -- Fiction
ISBN 978-0-553-80721-9; 0-553-80721-8; 978-0-553-38559-5 pa; 0-553-38559-3 pa
LC 2009-42254

Emily Benedict came to Mullaby, North Carolina, hoping to solve at least some of the riddles surrounding her mother's life. But the moment Emily enters the house where her mother grew up and meets the grandfather she never knew—a reclusive, real-life gentle giant—she realizes that mysteries aren't solved in Mullaby, they're a way of life.

"That it is never too late to change the future and that high school sins can be forgiven—these are wonderful messages, but Allen's warm characters and quirky setting are what will completely open readers' hearts to this story. Nothing in it disappoints." Libr J

Allende, Isabel

Daughter of fortune; a novel. translated from the Spanish by Margaret Sayers Peden. HarperCollins Pubs. 1999 399p hardcover o.p. pa $16.95

Grades: 11 12 Adult **Fic**
1. Love stories 2. Adventure fiction 3. California -- Gold discoveries -- Fiction
ISBN 0-06-019491-X; 0-06-156533-4 pa
LC 99-26021

Original Spanish edition, 1999

"This novel has pretensions, but they are overridden by Allende's riproaring girl's adventure story. . . . Throughout it all, Allende projects a woman's point of view with confidence, control and an expansive definition of romance as a fact of life." Time

Island beneath the sea; a novel. translated from the Spanish by Margaret Sayers Peden. Harper 2010 457p $26.99; pa $14.99

Grades: 11 12 Adult **Fic**
1. Haiti -- Fiction 2. Slavery -- Fiction 3. Plantation life -- Fiction 4. Caribbean region -- Fiction 5. Racially mixed people -- Fiction
ISBN 978-0-06-198824-0; 0-06-198824-3; 978-0-06-198825-7 pa; 0-06-198825-1 pa
LC 2009-46251

Original Spanish edition, 2009

"In a many-faceted plot, Allende animates irresistible characters authentic in their emotional turmoil and pragmatic adaptability. She also captures the racial, sexual, and entrepreneurial dynamics of each society in sensuous detail while masterfully dramatizing the psychic wounds of slavery. Sexually explicit, Allende is grace incarnate in her evocations of the spiritual energy that still sustains the beleaguered people of Haiti and New Orleans." Booklist

Zorro; a novel. translated from the Spanish by Margaret Sayers Peden. HarperCollins Publishers 2005 390p maps $25.95; pa $14.95

Grades: 11 12 Adult **Fic**
1. Adventure fiction 2. California -- Fiction
ISBN 0-06-077897-0; 0-06-077900-4 pa
LC 2005-46389

"Allende's lively retelling of the Zorro legend reads as effortlessly as the hero himself might slice his trademark 'Z' on the wall with a flash of his sword." Publ Wkly

Almond, David, 1951-

★ **Kit's** wilderness; 10th-anniversary edition; Delacorte Press 2009 229p $16.99

Grades: 6 7 8 9 10 **Fic**
1. Ghost stories 2. Great Britain -- Fiction 3. Coal mines and mining -- Fiction
ISBN 978-0-385-32665-0; 0-385-32665-3
First published 1999
Michael L. Printz Award, 2001

Thirteen-year-old Kit goes to live with his grandfather in the decaying coal mining town of Stoneygate, England, and finds both the old man and the town haunted by ghosts of the past

The author "explores the power of friendship and family, the importance of memory, and the role of magic in our lives. This is a highly satisfying literary experience." SLJ

★ **Skellig**; 10th anniversary ed.; Delacorte Press 2009 182p $16.99; pa $6.99

Grades: 5 6 7 8 9 10 **Fic**
1. Fantasy fiction
ISBN 978-0-385-32653-7; 0-385-32653-X; 978-0-440-41602-9 pa; 0-440-41602-7 pa
First published 1998 in the United Kingdom; first United States edition 1999
Michael L. Printz Award honor book

Unhappy about his baby sister's illness and the chaos of moving into a dilapidated old house, Michael retreats to the garage and finds a mysterious stranger who is something like a bird and something like an angel.

"The plot is beautifully paced and the characters are drawn with a graceful, careful hand. . . . A lovingly done, thought-provoking novel." SLJ

★ **A song** for Ella Grey; David Almond. Delacorte Press 2015 272 p. (hardcover) $16.99 **Fic**
1. Love stories 2. England -- Fiction 3. Orpheus (Greek mythology) -- Fiction 4. Love -- Fiction 5. Friendship -- Fiction 6. Mythology, Greek -- Fiction
ISBN 9780553533590; 9780553533606
LC 2014040181

This young adult novel, by David Almond, retells the story of Orpheus and Eurydice in contemporary England. It "is a tale of the joys, troubles, and desires of modern teens. It takes place in the ordinary streets of Tyneside and on the beautiful beaches of Northumberland. It's a story of first love, a love song that draws on ancient mythical forces. A love that leads Ella, Orpheus, and Claire to the gates of Death and beyond." (Publisher's note)

"Patient readers will likely be transfixed by this rhapsodic modern retelling of a classic tragedy." Booklist

★ The **tightrope** walkers; David Almond. Candlewick Press 2015 336 p. (hbk.) $17.99
Grades: 9 10 11 12   **Fic**
1. Bildungsromans 2. England -- Fiction 3. Teenagers -- Fiction 4. Love stories 5. Bullying -- Fiction 6. Shipbuilding -- Fiction
ISBN 0763673102; 9780763673109
LC 2014944915
In this book by David Almond, "Dominic Hall is the son of a shipbuilder, living in modest conditions in mid-20th century England. As he grows up, he finds himself torn between two influences--the dreamy intellectual artist girl next door and the brutal outcast boy who seems to cultivate a darker side of Dominic's nature. His coming-of-age is marked by the ramifications of his choices between the two." (School Library Journal)
"This brilliant novel follows Dom, a working-class boy in 1960s northern England, from ages five to seventeen. Dom forges his own values; succumbs to the lure of thug Vincent; falls in love with childhood pal Holly; discovers himself as a writer; and learns to walk a tightrope both literal and figurative. It's all unsettling emotion as Almond limns the nature of joy and rage." Horn Book

The **true** tale of the monster Billy Dean; David Almond. Viking 2011 255 p. $17.99
Grades: 9 10 11 12   **Fic**
1. Dystopian fiction 2. Children and war -- Fiction 3. Parent-child relationship -- Fiction 4. Dystopias -- Fiction
ISBN 0763663093; 9780763663094
LC 2012358384
This novel, by David Almond, is "about a hidden-away child who emerges into a broken world. Billy Dean is a secret child. . . . His father fills his mind and his dreams with mysterious tales and memories and dreadful warnings. But then his father disappears, and Billy's mother brings him out into the world at last. He learns the horrifying story of what was saved and what was destroyed on the day he was born, the day the bombers came to Blinkbonny." (Publisher's note)
"The opening scenes of this postapocalyptic, psychological novel describing the protagonist's confinement in a small, locked room is strongly reminiscent of Emma Donoghue's adult title Room (Little, Brown, 2010). Billy Dean's mother was seduced by an unethical priest, and young Billy is forced to suffer the consequences of their affair by being kept hidden. The compelling story is told from Billy's point of view and with the language and phonetic spelling of a child whose development has been stunted by his lifelong imprisonment... This challenging title demands to be read more than once, and even then it will leave questions unanswered.—" (School Library Journal)

Alonzo, Sandra
★ **Riding** invisible; written by Sandra Alonzo; illustrated by Nathan Huang. Hyperion 2010 234p il lib bdg $15.99
Grades: 7 8 9 10   **Fic**
1. Horses -- Fiction 2. Brothers -- Fiction 3. Family

life -- Fiction 4. Personality disorders -- Fiction
ISBN 978-1-4231-1898-5; 1-4231-1898-7
LC 2010-05041
After his older brother Will attacks his horse, Shy, Yancey runs away into the desert. Follow his adventures as he returns home to face life with a brother who has "conduct disorder."
"Written in a journal style and punctuated with sketches depicting Yancy's experiences, there's a lot here to engage readers." Horn Book Guide

Alpine, Rachele
Canary; By Rachele Alpine. Medallion Press 2013 400 p. $9.99
Grades: 9 10 11 12   **Fic**
1. Secrecy -- Fiction 2. Rape victims -- Fiction 3. Father-daughter relationship -- Fiction
ISBN 1605425877; 9781605425870
"In this debut novel . . . Kate Franklin's . . . . dad is hired to coach at Beacon Prep, home of one of the best basketball teams in the state. In a blog of prose and poetry, Kate chronicles her new world--dating a basketball player, being caught up in a world of idolatry and entitlement, and discovering the perks the inner circle enjoys. Then Kate's fragile life shatters once again when one of her boyfriend's teammates assaults her at a party." (Publisher's note)
"In an engrossing, carefully unfolding drama, sophomore Kate Franklin adjusts to a new school, a powerful set of friends and a family that is falling apart... Overall, a sophisticated, evocative portrait of a teen girl finding her place among peers and family." (Kirkus)

Alsaid, Adi
Let's Get Lost; Adi Alsaid. Harlequin Books 2014 352 p. $17.99
Grades: 9 10 11 12   **Fic**
1. Teenagers -- Fiction 2. Interpersonal relations 3. Automobile travel -- Fiction 4. Grief 5. Friendship 6. Adolescence 7. Bildungsromans
ISBN 0373211244; 9780373211241
In this novel by Adi Alsaid "four teens across the country have only one thing in common: a girl named Leila. She crashes into their lives in her absurdly red car at the moment they need someone the most. Hudson, Bree, Elliot and Sonia find a friend in Leila. And when Leila leaves them, their lives are forever changed. But it is during Leila's own 4,268-mile journey that she discovers the most important truth--sometimes, what you need most is right where you started." (Publisher's note)
"With romantic interludes, witty banter, some exhilarating minor law breaking, occasional drinking, an empowering message, and satisfying conclusions for everyone involved, this will likely be a popular summer hit, especially for older teens about to embark on their own journeys of self-discovery." Booklist

Never Always Sometimes; Adi Alsaid. Harlequin Books 2015 352 p. $17.99
Grades: 9 10 11 12   **Fic**
1. Love stories 2. Friendship -- Fiction 3. High school students -- Fiction
ISBN 0373211546; 9780373211548

In this book by Adi Alsaid, "before beginning high school, best friends Dave and Julia create a list of cliches they plan to avoid: never run for prom king, never hook up with a teacher, etc. But after they get accepted to college, a slump sets in, and they decide to mix things up by tackling items on the list." (Booklist)

"There is a kernel of truth in every cliché, and Alsaid cracks the teen-lit trope of friends becoming lovers wide open, exposing a beautiful truth inside. He also perfectly captures the golden glow of senioritis, a period when teens are bored and excited and wistful and nostalgic all at once. Everything is possible in this handful of weeks, including making up for squandered time. A good romance is hard to come by. This is a great one." Kirkus

Alvarez, Julia

★ **How** the Garcia girls lost their accents. Algonquin Bks. 1991 290p hardcover o.p. pa $13.95

Grades: 11 12 Adult **Fic**

1. Sisters -- Fiction 2. Family life -- Fiction 3. Culture conflict -- Fiction 4. Dominican Americans -- Fiction
ISBN 0-945575-57-2; 1-56512-975-X pa

LC 90-48575

"This is an account of parallel odysseys, as each of the four daughters adapts in her own way, and a large part of Alvarez's accomplishment is the complexity with which these vivid characters are rendered." Publ Wkly

Yo! Algonquin Bks. 1997 309p $18.95

Grades: 11 12 Adult **Fic**

1. Sisters -- Fiction 2. Dominican Americans -- Fiction
ISBN 1-56512-157-0

LC 96-24611

Sequel to How the Garcia girls lost their accents

"Yolanda Garcia's mother and sisters are furious at her for having plagiarized their lives in her all-too-celebrated novel. The balance of this novel is a rebuttal of sorts, narrated by her defenders. For everyone else who has come into contact with Yo and her storytelling prowess—from her repressed professor to her downtrodden landlady—life has changed for the better. These high-spirited accounts indulge the pleasing fantasy that we are the heroes not only of our own lives but of everyone else's as well." New Yorker

Amato, Mary

Get happy; Mary Amato. Egmont USA 2014 256 p. (hardback) $16.99

Grades: 6 7 8 9 **Fic**

1. Family -- Fiction 2. Musicians -- Fiction 3. Friendship -- Fiction 4. Father-daughter relationship -- Fiction 5. Families -- Fiction 6. Fathers and daughters -- Fiction
ISBN 1606845225; 9781606845226

LC 2014008736

"Minerva has been raised by her single mother after her father left them both. On her 17th birthday, she is shocked to discover that he has been trying to keep in touch, but her mother has been sabotaging his attempts. Furious at her mom, she begins to investigate her dad, a famous marine biologist, only to discover that he has a new family, including a beloved, and perfect, stepdaughter--a girl Minerva already knows and despises." (Publisher's note)

"Though the book explores a heavy, fraught situation, the prose is light and the ending optimistic. Some readers may be frustrated with the lack of closure, as quite a bit is left unresolved. Overall, however, this is a moving, charged tale of family and identity." SLJ

Anderson, Jessica Lee

Border crossing. Milkweed Editions 2009 174p $17; pa $8

Grades: 7 8 9 10 **Fic**

1. Alcoholism -- Fiction 2. Schizophrenia -- Fiction 3. Mental illness -- Fiction 4. Racially mixed people -- Fiction
ISBN 978-1-57131-689-9; 1-57131-689-2; 978-1-57131-691-2 pa; 1-57131-691-4 pa

LC 2008-49408

Manz, a troubled fifteen-year-old, ruminates over his Mexican father's death, his mother's drinking, and his still-born stepbrother until the voices he hears in his head take over and he cannot tell reality from delusion.

"A sad and thought-provoking exploration of mental illness." Kirkus

Anderson, Jodi Lynn

★ **Tiger** Lily; Jodi Lynn Anderson. HarperTeen 2012 304 p. (trade bdg.) $17.99

Grades: 8 9 10 11 **Fic**

1. Love stories 2. Jealousy -- Fiction 3. Fairy tales -- Fiction 4. Love -- Fiction 5. Magic -- Fiction 6. Fairies -- Fiction
ISBN 0062003259; 9780062003256

LC 2011032659

This is the story of Tiger Lily, the girl Peter Pan spurned for Wendy. "Told from the perspective of Tinker Bell, the novel explores how Tiger Lily meets and falls in love with Peter, despite being betrothed to another villager, a man Tiger Lily despises. Tiger Lily and Peter's complicated inner conflicts emerge as they sort out their feelings about freedom, power, loyalty, and responsibility. When a girl from England arrives, Tiger Lily" feels jealous for the first time. (Publishers Weekly)

The **vanishing** season; Jodi Lynn Anderson; [edited by] Kari Sutherland. First edition HarperTeen 2014 272 p. (hardcover) $17.99

Grades: 7 8 9 10 11 12 **Fic**

1. Homicide -- Fiction 2. Teenage girls -- Fiction 3. Teenage girls 4. Children's stories 5. Door County (Wis.)
ISBN 0062003275; 9780062003270

LC 2014934799

In this teen novel, by Jodi Lynn Anderson, edited by Kari Sutherland, "for Maggie Larsen . . . . what starts as an uneventful year suddenly changes. Someone is killing teen-aged girls, and the town reels from the tragedy. As Maggie's and Pauline's worlds collide and change around them, they will both experience love and loss. And by the end of the book, only one of them will survive." (Pubisher's note)

"For all the mythic overtones of Maggie and Pauline's friendship, Anderson still manages to give her characters authentic teen voices, striking an uneasy balance between naïveté and worldliness. The pace might be slow for some, but readers who like their romances tragic and dreamy should dive in." Booklist

Anderson, Katie D.

Kiss & Make Up. Amazon Childrens Pub 2012 307 p. (hardcover) $16.99

Grades: 7 8 9 10   **Fic**
   1. School stories 2. Paranormal fiction
   ISBN 076146316X; 9780761463160

This book focuses on Emerson Taylor, who "has a gift—or a curse. She can read a person's mind with the lightest of kisses. When her financially strapped aunt announces that Emerson will not be attending private school the following year if her grades don't improve, Emerson initializes Operation Liplock. She will begin study sessions with the geeky Ivys—those destined to attend Ivy League colleges—where she will kiss them, allowing their knowledge to transfer to her mind." (School Library Journal)

Anderson, Laurie Halse, 1961-
   ★ **Chains**; seeds of America. Simon & Schuster Books for Young Readers 2008 316p $17.99

Grades: 6 7 8 9 10   **Fic**
   1. Spies -- Fiction 2. Slavery -- Fiction 3. New York (N.Y.) -- Fiction 4. African Americans -- Fiction
   ISBN 1-4169-0585-5; 1-4169-0586-3 pa; 978-1-4169-0585-1; 978-1-4169-0586-8 pa

                       LC 2007-52139

After being sold to a cruel couple in New York City, a slave named Isabel spies for the rebels during the Revolutionary War. "Grades seven to ten." (Bull Cent Child Books)

"This gripping novel offers readers a startlingly provocative view of the Revolutionary War. . . . [Anderson's] solidly researched exploration of British and Patriot treatment of slaves during a war for freedom is nuanced and evenhanded, presented in service of a fast-moving, emotionally involving plot." Publ Wkly

   Followed by: Forge (2010)

Fever, 1793. Simon & Schuster Bks. for Young Readers 2000 251p $17.99; pa $6.99

Grades: 5 6 7 8 9   **Fic**
   1. Epidemics 2. Philadelphia (Pa.) 3. Epidemics -- Fiction 4. Yellow fever -- Fiction 5. Philadelphia (Pa.) -- Fiction 6. Pennsylvania -- History -- 1775-1865 7. Yellow fever -- Pennsylvania -- Philadelphia
   ISBN 0689838581; 0689848919 pa; 9780689838583; 9780689848919 pa

                       LC 00-32238
ALA YALSA Margaret A. Edwards Award (2009)

In 1793 Philadelphia, sixteen-year-old Matilda Cook, separated from her sick mother, learns about perseverance and self-reliance when she is forced to cope with the horrors of a yellow fever epidemic. 'Age ten and up' (N Y Times Book Rev)

"A vivid work, rich with well-drawn and believable characters. Unexpected events pepper the top-flight novel that combines accurate historical detail with a spellbinding story line." Voice Youth Advocates

Forge. Atheneum Books for Young Readers 2010 297p (Seeds of America) $16.99

Grades: 6 7 8 9 10   **Fic**
   1. Slavery -- Fiction 2. Soldiers -- Fiction 3. Pennsylvania -- Fiction 4. African Americans -- Fiction 5. United States -- History -- 1775-1783, Revolution -- Fiction
   ISBN 978-1-4169-6144-4; 1-4169-6144-5

                       LC 2010-15971
   Sequel to: Chains (2008)

Separated from his friend Isabel after their daring escape from slavery, fifteen-year-old Curzon serves as a free man in the Continental Army at Valley Forge until he and Isabel are thrown together again, as slaves once more.

"Weaving a huge amount of historical detail seamlessly into the story, Anderson creates a vivid setting, believable characters both good and despicable and a clear portrayal of the moral ambiguity of the Revolutionary age. Not only can this sequel stand alone, for many readers it will be one of the best novels they have ever read." Kirkus

   ★ The **impossible** knife of memory; Laurie Halse Anderson. Viking, published by Penguin Group 2014 400 p. (hardback) $18.99

Grades: 9 10 11 12   **Fic**
   1. Father-daughter relationship -- Fiction 2. Iraq War, 2003-2011 -- Veterans -- Drama 3. Post-traumatic stress disorder -- Fiction 4. Veterans -- Fiction 5. Family problems -- Fiction 6. Fathers and daughters -- Fiction
   ISBN 0670012092; 9780670012091

                       LC 2013031267
National Book Award Long List (2014)

In this book, by Laurie Halse Anderson, "Hayley Kincaid and her father, Andy, have been on the road, never staying long in one place as he struggles to escape the demons that have tortured him since his return from Iraq. Now they are back in the town where he grew up so Hayley can attend school. Perhaps, for the first time, Hayley can have a normal life. . . . Will being back home help Andy's PTSD, or will his terrible memories drag him to the edge of hell, and drugs push him over?" (Publisher's note)

"With powerful themes of loyalty and forgiveness, this tightly woven story is a forthright examination of the realities of war and its aftermath on soldiers and their families." SLJ

Prom; Laurie Halse Anderson. Viking 2005 215p $16.99; pa $8.99

Grades: 9 10 11 12   **Fic**
   1. School stories 2. Pennsylvania -- Fiction
   ISBN 0-670-05974-9; 0-14-240570-1 pa

                       LC 2004-14974

Eighteen-year-old Ash wants nothing to do with senior prom, but when disaster strikes and her desperate friend, Nat, needs her help to get it back on track, Ash's involvement transforms her life

"Whether or not readers have been infected by prom fever themselves, they will be enraptured and amused by Ashley's attitude-altering, life-changing commitment to a cause." Publ Wkly

   ★ **Speak;** 10th anniversary ed.; Speak 2009 197p pa $11.99

Grades: 7 8 9 10   **Fic**
1. School stories 2. Rape -- Fiction
ISBN 978-0-14-241473-6

LC 2009-502164

First published 1999

A traumatic event near the end of the summer has a devastating effect on Melinda's freshman year in high school.

The novel is "keenly aware of the corrosive details of outsiderhood and the gap between home and daily life at high school; kids whose exclusion may have less concrete cause than Melinda's will nonetheless find the picture recognizable. This is a gripping account of personal wounding and recovery." Bull Cent Child Books

Twisted. Viking 2007 250p $16.99
Grades: 9 10 11 12   **Fic**
1. School stories 2. Ohio -- Fiction 3. Family life -- Fiction
ISBN 978-0-670-06101-3

LC 2006-31297

After finally getting noticed by someone other than school bullies and his ever-angry father, seventeen-year-old Tyler enjoys his tough new reputation and the attentions of a popular girl, but when life starts to go bad again, he must choose between transforming himself or giving in to his destructive thoughts.

"This is a gripping exploration of what it takes to grow up, really grow up, against the wishes of people and circumstances conspiring to keep you the victim they need you to be." Bull Cent Child Books

★ **Wintergirls**. Viking 2009 288p $17.99
Grades: 8 9 10 11 12   **Fic**
1. Death -- Fiction 2. Friendship -- Fiction 3. Self-mutilation -- Fiction 4. Anorexia nervosa -- Fiction
ISBN 0-670-01110-X; 978-0-670-01110-0

LC 2008-37452

Eighteen-year-old Lia comes to terms with her best friend's death from anorexia as she struggles with the same disorder.

"As events play out, Lia's guilt, her need to be thin, and her fight for acceptance unravel in an almost poetic stream of consciousness in this startlingly crisp and pitch-perfect first-person narrative." SLJ

Anderson, M. T., 1968-

★ The **astonishing** life of Octavian Nothing, traitor to the nation; the pox party. taken from accounts by his own hand and other sundry sources; collected by M.T. Anderson of Boston. Candlewick Press 2006 351p $17.99
Grades: 9 10 11 12   **Fic**
1. Slavery -- Fiction 2. African Americans -- Fiction 3. United States -- History -- 1775-1783, Revolution -- Fiction
ISBN 0763624020; 9780763624026

LC 2006043170

Michael L. Printz Award honor book (2007), National Book Award for Young People's Literature (2006), Boston Globe-Horn Book Awards: Fiction and Poetry (2007)

This is the first of two volumes in The astonishing life of Octavian Nothing, traitor to the nation series. Various diaries, letters, and other manuscripts chronicle the experiences of Octavian, a young African American, from birth to age sixteen, as he is brought up as part of a science experiment in the years leading up to and during the Revolutionary War.

"Teens looking for a challenge will find plenty to sink into here. The questions raised about race and freedom are well developed and leave a different perspective on the Revolutionary War than most novels." Voice Youth Advocates

Followed by: The kingdom on the waves (2008)

The **astonishing** life of Octavian Nothing, traitor to the nation; v. #2 The kingdom on the waves. taken from accounts by his own hand and other sundry sources; collected by M.T. Anderson of Boston. Candlewick Press 2008 561p 2 maps (hardcover: alk. paper) $11.99
Grades: 9 10 11 12   **Fic**
1. Freedom -- Fiction 2. African Americans -- Fiction 3. Slavery -- United States -- Fiction 4. United States -- History -- 1775-1783, Revolution -- Fiction 5. Slavery -- Fiction
ISBN 0763646261; 9780763646264; 0763629502; 9780763629502

LC 2008929919

Sequel to: The astonishing life of Octavian Nothing, traitor to the nation: the pox party (2006)

In this book, a Michael L. Printz Honor Book of 2009, "[f]earing a death sentence, Octavian and his tutor, Dr. Trefusis, escape through rising tides and pouring rain to find shelter in British-occupied Boston. Sundered from all he knows -- the College of Lucidity, the rebel cause -- Octavian hopes to find safe harbor. Instead, he is soon to learn of Lord Dunmore's proclamation offering freedom to slaves who join the counterrevolutionary forces. . . . [Author] M. T. Anderson recounts Octavian's experiences as the Revolutionary War explodes around him, thrusting him into intense battles and tantalizing him with elusive visions of liberty." (Publisher's note)

"Elegantly crafted writing in an 18th-century voice, sensitive portrayals of primary and secondary characters and a fascinating author's note make this one of the few volumes to fully comprehend the paradoxes of the struggle for liberty in America." Kirkus

Burger Wuss; M.T. Anderson. Candlewick Press 1999 192p (pbk.) $7.99
Grades: 7 8 9 10 11 12   **Fic**
1. Teenagers -- Fiction 2. Conformity -- Fiction 3. Fast food restaurants -- Fiction
ISBN 0763606804; 9780763631789; 9781439530726

LC 99014257

In this book that is set "[i]n a world where every teenager works at one fast food chain or another and likes it, Anthony just doesn't fit in. His first real girlfriend has dumped him for a meathead named Turner who works at O'Dermott's, so Anthony plots revenge. He gets a job at the restaurant and embarks on a complicated plot to pit the kids from Burger Queen against the kids from O'Dermott's--and thereby draw the BQ wrath down on company-man Turner's head. . . . [T]his book is a burlesque of teenage angst and conformist

culture. . . . Anarchist vagabond Shunt is Anthony's partner
in his anti-conformity crimes." (Publishers Weekly)

★ **Feed**. Candlewick Press 2002 237p hardcover o.p. pa $7.99
Grades: 8 9 10 11 12　　　　　　　　　　**Fic**
　　1. Satire　2. Science fiction
　　ISBN 0-7636-1726-1;　0-7636-2259-1 pa
　　　　　　　　　　　　　　　LC 2002-23738
In a future where most people have computer implants
in their heads to control their environment, a boy meets an
unusual girl who is in serious trouble
　"An ingenious satire of corporate America and our present-day value system." Horn Book Guide

Anderson, R. J.
　Ultraviolet. Carolrhoda Lab 2011 306p $17.95
Grades: 7 8 9 10　　　　　　　　　　　　**Fic**
　　1. Science fiction　2. Synesthesia -- Fiction　3.
　　Extraterrestrial beings -- Fiction
　　ISBN 978-0-7613-7408-4;　0-7613-7408-6
　　　　　　　　　　　　　　　LC 2011000882
Almost seventeen-year-old Alison, who has synesthesia,
finds herself in a psychiatric facility accused of killing a
classmate whose body cannot be found.
　"Anderson keeps readers guessing throughout with sev-
eral twists, including a very unexpected divergence in the
last third of the book." Publ Wkly

Andreu, Maria E.
　The **secret** side of empty; Maria E. Andreu.
Running Press Teens 2014 336 p. $16.95
Grades: 9 10 11 12　　　　　　　　　　**Fic**
　　1. High school students　2. Teenage girls -- Fiction　3.
　　United States -- Immigration and emigration -- Fiction
　　4. Teenage girls　5. Emigration and immigration
　　ISBN 0762451920;　9780762451920
　　　　　　　　　　　　　　　LC 2013950819
This book, by Maria E. Andreu, asks "what's it like to
be undocumented? High school senior M.T. knows all too
well. . . . M.T. was born in Argentina and brought to America
as a baby without any official papers. And as questions of
college, work, and the future arise, M.T. will have to decide
what exactly she wants for herself, knowing someone she
loves will unavoidably pay the price for it. . . . What is it like
when the only country you've ever known says you don't
belong?" (Publisher's note)
　"An illegal immigrant, Monserrat Thalia has kept her
status a secret for years. Despite her achievements in high
school, now that she's a senior her future is uncertain and
she's fighting for survival. Andreu draws from personal experience, and M.T.'s struggles with first love, depression,
an abusive father, and the constant fear of deportation feel
wholly real. A compelling and timely story." Horn Book

Andrews, Jesse
　The **Haters**; a book about being in a band. Jesse
Andrews. Amulet Books 2016 336 p. (hardback)
$18.95
Grades: 10 11 12　　　　　　　　　　　　**Fic**
　　1. Humorous fiction　2. Musicians -- Fiction　3.

Friendship -- Fiction　4. Bands (Music) -- Fiction
ISBN 9781419720789
　　　　　　　　　　　　　　　LC 2015030408
In this book, by Jesse Andrews, "for Wes and his best
friend, Corey, jazz camp turns out to be lame. It's pretty
much all dudes talking in Jazz Voice. But then they jam with
Ash, a charismatic girl with an unusual sound, and the three
just click. It's three and a half hours of pure musical magic,
and Ash makes a decision: They need to hit the road. Because the road, not summer camp, is where bands get good."
(Publisher's note)
　"At a jazz camp of "mostly dudes," bass player Wes and
his drummer best friend Corey meet Ash, who has her own
unique musical style and refuses to play with the condescending guys. Frustrated, she leaves--and Wes and Corey
go with her. What follows is both a classic road-trip novel
and an inventive teen adventure that subtly addresses race,
family, and socioeconomics." Horn Book

Me & Earl & the dying girl;　by Jesse Andrews.
Amulet Books 2012 295 p. $16.95
Grades: 8 9 10　　　　　　　　　　　　**Fic**
　　1. Leukemia -- Fiction　2. Friendship -- Fiction　3.
　　Family life -- Fiction　4. Pittsburgh (Pa.) -- Fiction　5.
　　High school students -- Fiction　6. Humorous stories　7.
　　Schools -- Fiction　8. High schools -- Fiction　9. Jews --
　　United States -- Fiction　10. Family life -- Pennsylvania
　　-- Fiction
　　ISBN 9781419701764
　　　　　　　　　　　　　　　LC 2011031796
This book is a "confessional from a teen narrator who
won't be able to convince readers he's as unlikable as he
wants them to believe." It covers "[h]is filmmaking ambi-
tions . . . his unlikely friendship with the . . . Earl of the title.
And his unlikelier friendship with Rachel, the titular 'dying
girl'. . . . He chronicles his senior year, in which his mother
guilt-trips him into hanging out with Rachel, who has acute
myelogenous leukemia." (Kirkus Reviews)

Anhalt, Ariela
　Freefall. Harcourt 2010 250p $17
Grades: 9 10 11 12　　　　　　　　　　**Fic**
　　1. School stories　2. Death -- Fiction　3. Friendship
　　-- Fiction
　　ISBN 978-0-15-206567-6;　0-15-206567-9
　　　　　　　　　　　　　　　LC 2009-18936
Briar Academy senior Luke prefers avoiding conflict
and letting others make his decisions, but he is compelled
to choose whether or not to stand by the best friend whose
reckless behavior has endangered Luke and may have
caused another student's death.
　"The plot is straightforward, but the high stakes, complex character development, and realistic dialogue and interactions will keep readers riveted—and likely have them
imagining themselves in Luke's position." Publ Wky

Anthony, Jessica
　Chopsticks;　Jessica Anthony, Rodrigo Corral.
Penguin/Razorbill 2012 304 p.
Grades: 9 10 11 12　　　　　　　　　　**Fic**
　　1. Mystery fiction　2. Musicians -- Fiction　3. Piano
　　music -- Fiction　4. Mental illness -- Fiction　5. Missing

children -- Fiction

ISBN 9781595144355

This "mystery [book] reveals the events leading up to the disappearance of Glory, a teenaged piano prodigy who goes missing after her struggle with mental illness that causes her to play the children's waltz 'Chopsticks' obsessively. Photographs, ephemera, and instant-message screenshots weave together the details of a forbidden romance with Francisco, the boy next door. . . . The story requires . . . visual literacy. . . . An example of the emerging trend of transmedia storytelling, this book will also be available in a 'fully interactive electronic version.' The inclusion of links to online media requires Internet access and a willingness to type . . . URLs, but the content of the links can be gleaned from context." (School Libr J)

Antieau, Kim

Broken moon. Margaret K. McElderry Books 2007 183p $15.99

Grades: 7 8 9 10   **Fic**

1. Pakistan -- Fiction 2. Siblings -- Fiction 3. Kidnapping -- Fiction

ISBN 978-1-4169-1767-0; 1-4169-1767-5

LC 2006-03780

When her little brother is kidnapped and taken from Pakistan to race camels in the desert, eighteen-year-old Nadira overcomes her own past abuse and, dressed as a boy and armed with knowledge of the powerful storytelling of the legendary Scheherazade, is determined to find and rescue him.

The author "presents important issues without letting them overtake the narrative, and the classic plot and sympathetic characters add up to an absorbing read." Horn Book

Applegate, Katherine

Eve & Adam; by Michael Grant and Katherine Applegate. Feiwel and Friends 2012 291p. $17.99

Grades: 7 8 9 10   **Fic**

1. Medical genetics 2. Biomedical engineering 3. Mother-daughter relationship -- Fiction

ISBN 0312583516; 9780312583514

In this book by authors Michael Grant and Katherine Applegate, "a run-in with a streetcar left Evening Spiker's body seriously mangled . . . [H]er widowed mother, Terra, insists on moving her from the hospital to . . . [the] biotech company . . . Spiker Biopharmaceuticals. . . . Eve's healing is strangely swift [and] Terra drops a project . . . in her lap: Design a virtual human being from scratch. With help from her feisty, reckless friend Aislin, Eve takes up the challenge." (Kirkus Reviews)

Archer, E.

Geek fantasy novel. Scholastic Press 2011 310p $17.99

Grades: 7 8 9 10   **Fic**

1. Fantasy fiction 2. Aunts -- Fiction 3. Wishes -- Fiction 4. Cousins -- Fiction 5. Great Britain -- Fiction

ISBN 978-0-545-16040-7; 0-545-16040-5

"Fourteen-year-old Ralph Stevens escapes his humdrum life when he's invited to spend the summer with his British cousins, ostensibly to set up their wireless network. What he discovers is a family given to eccentricity. . . . Things get

seriously weird when their infamous aunt/fairy godmother Chessie of Cheshire turns up, ready to grant each child a wish." Publ Wkly

Archer, Jennifer

Through her eyes. HarperTeen 2011 377p $16.99

Grades: 7 8 9 10   **Fic**

1. School stories 2. Mystery fiction 3. Texas -- Fiction 4. Moving -- Fiction 5. Family life -- Fiction 6. Grandfathers -- Fiction 7. Supernatural -- Fiction

ISBN 978-0-06-183458-5; 0-06-183458-0

LC 2010-18440

Sixteen-year-old Tansy is used to moving every time her mother starts writing a new book, but in the small Texas town where her grandfather grew up, she is lured into the world of a troubled young man whose death sixty years earlier is shrouded in mystery.

"Archer's engrossing story gracefully weaves together the contemporary and historical into an eerie mystery, while examining relationships, reality, and the power of the mind." Publ Wkly

Arcos, Carrie

★ **Out** of reach; Carrie Arcos. Simon Pulse 2012 250 p. (alk. paper) $16.99

Grades: 9 10 11 12   **Fic**

1. Siblings -- Fiction 2. Drug abuse -- Fiction 3. Families of drug addicts -- Fiction 4. Runaways -- Fiction 5. Methamphetamine -- Fiction 6. Brothers and sisters -- Fiction 7. California, Southern -- Fiction

ISBN 1442440538; 9781442440531; 9781442440555

LC 2011044501

In this book by Carrie Arcos, "Rachel's older brother Micah is using crystal meth, and he is lying, stealing, and hurting those who love him in order to feed his addiction. . . . An anonymous e-mail warns Rachel that Micah is in serious trouble. So Rachel teams up with Micah's fellow band member . . . Tyler, to find her brother. . . . But, despite the heartache of the search, Rachel begins to see that her life isn't destroyed -- and that Tyler is surprisingly kind and caring." (Booklist)

There will come a time; Carrie Arcos. First Simon Pulse hardcover ed Simon Pulse 2014 315 p. $17.99

Grades: 9 10 11 12   **Fic**

1. Grief -- Fiction 2. Twins -- Fiction 3. Suicide -- Fiction 4. Death -- Fiction 5. Diaries -- Fiction 6. Filipino Americans -- Fiction 7. Brothers and sisters -- Fiction 8. Los Angeles (Calif.) -- Fiction 9. Family life -- California -- Los Angeles -- Fiction

ISBN 1442495855; 9781442495852

LC 2014002771

In this young adult novel by Carrie Arcos, "Mark knows grief. Ever since the accident that killed his twin sister, Grace, the only time he feels at peace is when he visits the bridge on which she died. Comfort is fleeting, but it's almost within reach when he's standing on the wrong side of the suicide bars. Almost. Grace's best friend, Hanna, says she understands what he's going through. . . . Hanna convinces

Mark to complete Grace's bucket list from her journal."
(Publisher's note)

" This nuanced story presents a close study on how different people react to loss while posing many thorny questions about relationships. Mark is Filipino American, and another character is Korean American, offering diversity for those wishing to widen their lists. Give this book to anyone who wants a rock-solid, character-driven story of finding one's footing after a life-changing event." Booklist

Armentrout, Jennifer L.

White Hot Kiss; by Jennifer L. Armentrout. Harlequin Books Teen 2014 400 p. $9.99

Grades: 9 10 11 12   **Fic**
1. Love stories 2. Gargoyles -- Fiction 3. Demonology -- Fiction 4. Supernatural -- Fiction
ISBN 0373211104; 9780373211104

In this book, "seventeen-year-old Layla just wants to be normal. But with a kiss that kills anything with a soul, she's anything but normal. Half demon, half gargoyle, Layla has abilities no one else possesses.Layla tries to fit in, but that means hiding her own dark side from those she loves the most. Especially Zayne, the . . . completely off-limits Warden she's crushed on since forever. Then she meets Roth--a tattooed, sinfully hot demon who claims to know all her secrets." (Publisher's note)

"With this first title in her new Dark Elements series, powerhouse author Armentrout delivers another action-packed, believably narrated ride through a paranormal world as seen by a teen... Intense, well plotted, and very readable, this title should fly into the hands of every paranormal reader out there." Booklist

Armistead, Cal

Being Henry David; by Cal Armistead. Albert Whitman 2013 312 p. (hardcover) $16.99

Grades: 8 9 10 11 12   **Fic**
1. Mystery fiction 2. Amnesia -- Fiction 3. Guilt -- Fiction 4. Runaways -- Fiction 5. Concord (Mass.) -- Fiction 6. Family problems -- Fiction 7. New York (N.Y.) -- Fiction 8. Street children -- Fiction
ISBN 080750615X; 9780807506158

           LC 2012017377

In this book, a "boy wakes up in Penn Station, remembering nothing. He guesses that he's about 17, he has a head injury, and he is carrying only 10 dollars. Near at hand is a copy of Walden, so for want of anything better he calls himself Henry David (Hank). He heads to Concord, Massachusetts, to find, he hopes, some clues at Walden Pond. As his memories slowly return, he remembers who he was; as he copes with the memories, he discovers who he is and can be." (School Library Journal)

Armstrong, Kelley

The **awakening**. HarperCollinsPublishers 2009 360p (Darkest powers) $17.99; lib bdg $18.89; pa $8.99

Grades: 7 8 9 10   **Fic**
1. Ghost stories 2. Supernatural -- Fiction
ISBN 978-0-06-166276-8; 0-06-166276-3; 978-0-06-166280-5 lib bdg; 0-06-166280-1 lib bdg; 978-0-06-145055-6 pa; 0-06-145055-3 pa

           LC 2008044030

Sequel to: The summoning (2008)

Fifteen-year-old necromancer Chloe, having escaped from Lyle House with Derek, Simon, and Rae, finds herself imprisoned in a laboratory run by a sinister organization determined to control her and her supernatural friends.

"Armstrong has some fun toying with supernatural teen thriller conventions, and the taut pacing should please fans of the exploding genre." Booklist

Followed by: The reckoning (2010)

The **reckoning**. Harper 2010 391p (Darkest powers) $17.99

Grades: 7 8 9 10   **Fic**
1. Ghost stories 2. Werewolves -- Fiction 3. Supernatural -- Fiction
ISBN 978-0-06-166283-6; 0-06-166283-6

Sequel to: The awakening (2009)

Fifteen-year-old Chloe, a necromancer, struggles to understand her feelings for werewolf Derek and his sorcerer brother, Simon, while seeking a way to enter the headquarters of the sinister Edison Group and rescue her aunt Lauren and friend Rachelle.

"Armstrong's story is full of action, romance, deception, and intrigue as well as complex characters and serious teenage issues." SLJ

The **summoning**. HarperCollinsPublishers 2008 390p (Darkest powers) $17.99; lib bdg $18.89

Grades: 7 8 9 10   **Fic**
1. Ghost stories 2. Supernatural -- Fiction
ISBN 978-0-06-166269-0; 0-06-166269-0; 978-0-06-166272-0 lib bdg; 0-06-166272-0 lib bdg

           LC 2008-14221

After fifteen-year-old Chloe starts seeing ghosts and is sent to Lyle House, a mysterious group home for mentally disturbed teenagers, she soon discovers that neither Lyle House nor its inhabitants are exactly what they seem, and that she and her new friends are in danger.

"Suspenseful, well-written, and engaging, this page-turning . . . [novel] will be a hit." Voice Youth Advocates

Other titles in this series are:
The awakening (2009)
The reckoning (2010)

Arnett, Mindee

Avalon; Mindee Arnett. Balzer + Bray, an imprint of HarperCollinsPublishers 2014 432 p. (hardcover) $17.99

Grades: 8 9 10 11 12   **Fic**
1. Science fiction 2. Freedom -- Fiction 3. Outer space -- Fiction 4. Mercenary soldiers -- Fiction 5. Space ships -- Fiction 6. Mercenary troops -- Fiction 7. Brothers and sisters -- Fiction 8. Life on other planets -- Fiction
ISBN 0062235591; 9780062235596

           LC 2013005155

This book, by Mindee Arnett, is "about a group of teenage mercenaries who stumble upon a conspiracy that threatens the entire galaxy. Jeth Seagrave and his crew have made their name stealing metatech: the devices that allow people to travel great distances faster than the speed of light. . . . When he finds himself in possession of information that both government and the crime bosses are willing to kill for, he's going to find there's no escaping his past anymore." (Publisher's note)

"Jeth has one last job to complete before he can buy back his parents' spaceship from a crime boss. But the ship he was sent to find carries a deadly cargo that everyone in the galaxy wants. The strong bond between Jeth and his humorously motley crew of teenage mercenaries outshines the predictable plot and will appeal to Firefly-esque space-opera fans." Horn Book

Arnold, David

★ **Mosquitoland**; David Arnold. Viking, published by Penguin Group 2015 352 p. (hardcover) $17.99

Grades: 9 10 11 12   **Fic**
1. Stepfamilies -- Fiction 2. Mental illness -- Fiction 3. Runaway teenagers -- Fiction 4. Voyages and travels -- Fiction 5. Mother-daughter relationship -- Fiction 6. Runaways -- Fiction 7. Mothers and daughters -- Fiction
ISBN 045147077X; 9780451470775
        LC 2014009137

In this book, by David Arnold, "[a]fter the sudden collapse of her family, Mim Malone is dragged from her home in northern Ohio to . . . Mississippi, where she lives in a medicated milieu with her dad and new stepmom. Before the dust has a chance to settle, she learns her mother is sick back in Cleveland. So she ditches her new life and hops aboard a northbound Greyhound bus to her real home and her real mother, meeting a quirky cast of fellow travelers along the way." (Publisher's note)

" As she so often claims, "I am Mary Iris Malone and I am not okay." For most of her 16 years, Mim has believed this to be the truth. But after her father and new stepmom conspire to keep her away from her mother, who is struggling to get well in Cleveland, Mim sets out on an odyssey from Mississippi...As Mim reaches Cleveland, and Walt and Beck follow the road to their own destinations, Arnold never lets up on the accelerator of life's hard lessons. In the words of one of Mim's Greyhound seatmates, this has pizzazz—lots and lots of it." Booklist

Arnold, Elana K.

Infandous; by Elana K. Arnold. Carolrhoda Lab 2015 189 p. (trade hard cover: alk. paper) $18.99

Grades: 9 10 11 12   **Fic**
1. Secrets -- Fiction 2. Mother-daughter relationship -- Fiction 3. Sex -- Fiction 4. Sculptors -- Fiction 5. Mothers and daughters -- Fiction 6. Single-parent families -- Fiction 7. Venice (Los Angeles, Calif.) -- Fiction
ISBN 1467738492; 9781467738491; 9781467761802; 9781467776738; 9781467776745; 9781467776752
        LC 2014008998

In this novel, by Elana K. Arnold, "Sephora Golding lives in the shadow of her unbelievably beautiful mother. Even though they scrape by in the seedier part of Venice Beach, she's always felt lucky. . . . But now, at sixteen, the fairy tale is less Disney and more Grimm. And she wants the story to be her own. Then she meets Felix, and the fairy tale takes a turn she never imagined. Sometimes, a story is just a way to hide the unspeakable in plain sight." (Publisher's note)

"Clocking in at just 200 pages, this is a story that packs no less of a punch for its brevity. Sephora's grim reimaginings of fairy tales are anti-Disney in the extreme (making this best suited for more mature readers). The strands are worked so surely into the narrative that they feel powerful instead of tired. Sephora herself is a narrator who defies convention, and her story, harsh and spare, is unforgettable." Booklist

Arntson, Steven

The **wrap**-up list; by Steven Arntson. Houghton Mifflin Harcourt 2013 240 p. (hardcover) $15.99

Grades: 7 8 9 10   **Fic**
1. Fantasy fiction 2. Death -- Fiction 3. Conduct of life -- Fiction 4. Hispanic Americans -- Fiction
ISBN 0547824106; 9780547824109
        LC 2012014035

This paranormal young adult novel, by Steven Arntson, is set in a "modern-day suburban town, [where] one percent of all fatalities come about in the most peculiar way. Deaths . . . send a letter . . . to whomever is chosen . . . , telling them to wrap up their lives and do the things they always wanted to do before they have to 'depart.' When sixteen-year-old Gabriela receives her notice, she is, of course devastated. Will she kiss her crush Sylvester before it's too late?" (Publisher's note)

Ashby, Amanda

Zombie queen of Newbury High. Speak 2009 199p pa $7.99

Grades: 7 8 9 10   **Fic**
1. School stories 2. Zombies -- Fiction
ISBN 978-0-14-241256-5; 0-14-241256-5
        LC 2008-41035

While trying to cast a love spell on her date on the eve of the senior prom, Mia inadvertently infects her entire high school class with a virus that will turn them all into zombies.

"Zombie Queen is light, fast-paced, and . . . will quench the thirst of the Christopher Pike and R. L. Stine set." SLJ

Asher, Jay

★ The **future** of us; [by] Jay Asher and Carolyn Mackler. Razorbill 2011 356p $18.99

Grades: 8 9 10 11 12   **Fic**
1. School stories 2. Computers -- Fiction 3. Supernatural -- Fiction
ISBN 978-1-59514-491-1; 1-59514-491-9

In this book by Jay Asher and Carolyn Mackler, "it's 1996, before Facebook's been invented. Yet Emma's first computer leads her to her Facebook page from fifteen years in the future. She tells only her friend and would-be boyfriend Josh, and they contemplate their futures with concern. Can their current actions change who they become?" (Voice of Youth Advocates)

"It's 1996, and Emma Nelson has just received her first computer. . . . When Emma powers up the computer, she discovers her own Facebook page (even though Facebook doesn't exist yet) and herself in an unhappy marriage—15 years in the future. Alternating chapters from Josh and Emma over the course of five days propel this riveting read, as Emma discovers she can alter her future by adjusting her present actions and intentions." Booklist

Thirteen reasons why; a novel. Razorbill 2007 288p $16.99

Grades: 8 9 10 11 12   **Fic**
1. School stories 2. Suicide -- Fiction
ISBN 9781595141712

LC 2007-03097

When high school student Clay Jenkins receives a box in the mail containing thirteen cassette tapes recorded by his classmate Hannah, who committed suicide, he spends a bewildering and heartbreaking night crisscrossing their town, listening to Hannah's voice recounting the events leading up to her death.

"Clay's pain is palpable and exquisitely drawn in gripping casually poetic prose. The complex and soulful characters expose astoundingly rich and singularly teenage inner lives." SLJ

Ashton, Brodi

Everbound; an Everneath novel. Brodi Ashton. Balzer + Bray 2013 368 p. (Everneath) (hardcover bdg: alk. paper) $17.99

Grades: 7 8 9 10   **Fic**
1. Love stories 2. Paranormal fiction 3. Future life -- Fiction 4. Hell -- Fiction 5. Love -- Fiction 6. Supernatural -- Fiction
ISBN 0062071165; 9780062071163

LC 2012028327

This young adult paranormal story, by Brodi Ashton, is the sequel to "Everneath." "Nikki Beckett could only watch as . . . Jack . . . sacrificed himself to save her, taking her place in the Tunnels of the Everneath for eternity. . . . Desperate for answers, Nikki turns to Cole, the immortal bad boy who wants to make her his queen. . . . But his heart has been touched by everything about Nikki, and he agrees to help in the only way he can: by taking her to the Everneath himself." (Publisher's note)

Everneath; Brodi Ashton. 1st ed; Balzer + Bray 2012 370p. $17.99

Grades: 7 8 9 10   **Fic**
1. Love stories 2. Fantasy fiction 3. Paranormal fiction
ISBN 9780062071132 (trade bdg.)

LC 2011022892

This book tells the story of "Nikki Beckett [who] vanished, sucked into an underworld known as the Everneath. Now she's returned—to her old life, her family, her boyfriend—before she's banished back to the underworld . . . this time forever. She has six months before the Everneath comes to claim her, six months for good-byes she can't find the words for, six months to find redemption, if it exists. Nikki longs to spend these precious months forgetting the Everneath and trying to reconnect with her boyfriend, Jack, the person most devastated by her disappearance—and the

one person she loves more than anything. But there's just one problem: Cole, the smoldering immortal who enticed her to the Everneath in the first place, has followed Nikki home. Cole wants to take over the throne in the underworld and is convinced Nikki is the key to making it happen." (Publisher's note)

Asimov, Isaac

★ **Fantastic** voyage. Bantam Bks. 1988 186p pa $7.99

Grades: 9 10 11 12   **Fic**
1. Science fiction
ISBN 0-553-27572-0

First published 1966 by Houghton Mifflin

"Five people are sent on a rescue mission in a submarine, but this is no ordinary submarine moving through an ordinary sea. The people and the submarine are miniaturized. They are moving through a man's blood vessels to reach and break up a blood clot in his brain. The miniaturization will not last—they have only 60 minutes to do the job and leave the man's body, before they return to ordinary size." Publ Wkly

★ **Foundation**. Bantam Books 2004 244p $24; pa $15

Grades: 9 10 11 12   **Fic**
1. Science fiction
ISBN 0-553-80371-9; 0-553-38257-8 pa

LC 2003-69137

A reissue of the title first published 1951 by Gnome Press

The first volume in the author's Foundation series narrating the fall of a great galactic empire and the efforts of the Foundations to combat the barbarism that follows

Other titles in the series are:
Forward the Foundation (1993)
Foundation and earth (1986)
Foundation and empire (1952)
Foundation's edge (1982)
Prelude to Foundation (1988)
Second Foundation (1986)

Atkins, Catherine

The **file** on Angelyn Stark; by Catherine Atkins. 1st ed; Alfred A. Knopf 2011 250p.

Grades: 9 10 11 12   **Fic**
1. Young women -- Fiction 2. Child sexual abuse -- Fiction 3. Teacher-student relationship -- Fiction
ISBN 9780375869068; 9780375969065 (lib. bdg.); 9780375899898 (ebook)

LC 2011016681

This book tells the story of "[f]ifteen-year-old Angelyn Stark [who] seems to relish her position as the head of a pack of bad girls, but her tough exterior covers a terrible secret. The summer she was 12, her stepfather, Danny, sexually molested her. The abuse stopped after a neighbor called police, but when her mom didn't believe her, Angelyn told investigators it never happened. . . . Angelyn's boyfriend, Steve, keeps pressuring her for sex, but she's only interested in her teacher, Mr. Rossi, the single adult in her life who encourages her. But Mr. Rossi is fighting demons of his own and rightly fears that a relationship with Angelyn will jeopardize his reputation." (Kirkus)

Atwater-Rhodes, Amelia

Persistence of memory. Delacorte Press 2008 212p $15.99; lib bdg $18.99; pa $8.99

Grades: 8 9 10 11 12   **Fic**

1. Witches -- Fiction 2. Vampires -- Fiction 3. Supernatural -- Fiction 4. Schizophrenia -- Fiction

ISBN 978-0-385-73437-0; 0-385-73437-9; 978-0-385-90443-8 lib bdg; 0-385-90443-6 lib bdg; 978-0-440-24004-4 pa; 0-440-24004-2 pa

LC 2008-16062

Diagnosed with schizophrenia as a child, sixteen-year-old Erin has spent half of her life in therapy and on drugs, but now must face the possibility of weird things in the real world, including shapeshifting friends and her "alter," a centuries-old vampire.

"What sets this novel apart . . . are the two narrators—Erin, grown used to, and even comfortable with, the idea that she is mentally ill; and Shevaun, willing to do anything to protect the family she's cobbled together. Secondary characters are equally compelling, and the world that Atwater-Rhodes has created is believable and intriguing." SLJ

Atwood, Margaret, 1939-

★ The **Handmaid's** tale; with an introduction by Valerie Martin. Everyman's Library 2006 xxxiii, 350p

Grades: 11 12 Adult   **Fic**

1. Allegories 2. Future 3. Fantasy fiction 4. Women -- Fiction 5. Fundamentalism -- Fiction 6. Women -- Social conditions

ISBN 0307264602

LC 2006042618

First published 1986 by Houghton Mifflin

This is a new edition of Atwood's 1986 novel with an introduction by Valerie Martin. The book is "set in the near future, in a fundamentalist Christian totalitarian state called the Republic of Gilead. . . . Because of environmental pollution, the number of fertile women is low and those who can still bear children are effectively prisoners of the government. When the Christian fundamentalists took power they removed fertile women from their husbands and children and sent them to live with government leaders—or 'Commanders'—and their infertile wives—so that they could conceive and bear children who would then be raised by the Commanders and their wives as their own. The novel is narrated by one of these fertile women, called Handmaids." (N Y Rev Books)

"A gripping suspense tale, The Handmaid's Tale is an allegory of what results from a politics based on misogyny, racism, and anti-Semitism." Ms

Augarde, Steve

X-Isle. David Fickling Books 2010 476p $17.99

Grades: 7 8 9 10   **Fic**

1. Science fiction 2. Islands -- Fiction

ISBN 978-0-385-75193-3; 0-385-75193-1

LC 2010-281037

Baz and Ray, survivors of an apocalyptic flood, win places on X-Isle, an island where life is rumored to be better than on the devastated mainland, but they find the island to be a violent place ruled by religious fanatic Preacher John, and they decide they must come up with a weapon to protect themselves from impending danger.

"Augarde's near-future apocalyptic world is gruesomely hardscrabble without being overly graphic. . . . A gripping tale of fighting for the slenderest chance of hope." Publ Wkly

Austen, Jane, 1775-1817

Pride and prejudice and zombies; the classic regency romance--now with ultraviolent zombie mayhem. by Jane Austen and Seth Grahame-Smith. Quirk Books 2009 319p. ill. (pbk.: alk. paper) $12.95

Grades: 11 12 Adult   **Fic**

1. Authors 2. Novelists 3. Love stories 4. Zombies -- Fiction 5. England -- Fiction 6. Sisters -- Fiction 7. Social classes -- Fiction 8. Young women -- England -- Fiction 9. Social classes -- England -- Fiction 10. Bennet, Elizabeth (Fictitious character) -- Fiction 11. Great Britain -- History -- 19th century -- Fiction 12. Darcy, Fitzwilliam (Fictitious character) -- Fiction

ISBN 978159474334; 9781594743351

LC 2008937609

This book "features the original text of Jane Austen's beloved novel with . . . scenes of . . . zombie action. As our story opens, a mysterious plague has fallen upon the quiet English village of Meryton-and the dead are returning to life! Feisty heroine Elizabeth Bennet is determined to wipe out the zombie menace, but she's soon distracted by the arrival of the haughty and arrogant Mr. Darcy. What ensues is . . . civilized sparring between the two young lovers-and . . . violent sparring on the blood-soaked battlefield as Elizabeth wages war against hordes of flesh-eating undead." (Publisher's note)

The author "has taken the merry world established by a 19th-century literary lady, added a scourge of reanimated corpses, and created . . . a pop culture phenomenon. . . . But, the greater achievement of the book may lie in the satisfying desire it awakens to read the remix and the original side by side." Entertainment Weekly

Avasthi, Swati

Chasing Shadows; by Swati Avasthi and illustrated by Craig Phillips. Random House Childrens Books 2013 320 p. $17.99

Grades: 9 10 11 12   **Fic**

1. Death -- Fiction 2. Teenage girls -- Fiction

ISBN 0375863427; 9780375863424

Author Swati Avasthi's book looks "at the impact of one random act of violence." The book offers a "portrait of two girls teetering on the edge of grief and insanity. Two girls who will find out just how many ways there are to lose a friend . . . and how many ways to be lost." Holly and Savitri cope with the death of their friend Corey as they look for Corey's killer. (Publisher's note)

"Savitri's boyfriend Corey is killed and her best friend, Holly (Corey's sister), is injured by a seemingly senseless shooting. With the killer at large, Holly teeters on the brink of sanity. The narrative alternates among Savitri's voice; a second-person narrator; and Holly's perspective, told through first-person text and dramatic graphic novel style interludes. Avasthi delves deeply into the pysche of both girls." (Horn Book)

★ **Split**. Alfred A. Knopf 2010 282p $16.99; lib bdg $19.99

Grades: 10 11 12   **Fic**

1. Brothers -- Fiction 2. Child abuse -- Fiction
ISBN 978-0-375-86340-0; 0-375-86340-0; 978-0-375-96340-7 lib bdg; 0-375-96340-5 lib bdg

LC 2009-22615

A teenaged boy thrown out of his house by his abusive father goes to live with his older brother, who ran away from home years ago to escape the abuse.

"Readers seeking sensational violence should look elsewhere; this taut, complex family drama depicts abuse unflinchingly but focuses on healing, growth and learning to take responsibility for one's own anger." Kirkus

Avery, Lara

The **memory** book; Lara Avery. Little, Brown & Co. 2016 368 p.

Grades: 9 10 11 12   **Fic**

1. Love -- Fiction 2. Memory -- Fiction 3. Friendship -- Fiction 4. Terminally ill -- Fiction 5. Genetic disorders -- Fiction
ISBN 9780316283748

LC 2015029157

"Resolving to graduate at the top of her class and leave her small town in spite of a rare genetic disorder that will eventually steal her memories and health, Sammie writes a journal to her future self so that she will recall her feelings of friendship, love and laughter. By the author of A Million Miles Away." (Publisher's note)

"When Sammie gets the diagnosis her senior year—that a genetic condition will rob her of her mind, the one thing she valued over everything else—it's just one more thing for her to overcome, with the help of her 'memory book,' a diary that will remind her future self of the Sammie she once was. But as the realities of her condition become more glaring, Sammie has to reevaluate everything she thought made her who she is. . . . Though there are moments recorded in Sammie's book that seem like they were captured at a very unlikely time to journal, each entry adds to a story of self-discovery that's hard to put down." Booklist

Avery, Tom

My brother's shadow; Tom Avery. First edition Schwartz & Wade books 2014 176 p. (hc) $16.99

Grades: 8 9 10 11 12   **Fic**

1. Suicide -- Fiction 2. Friendship 3. Bereavement 4. London (England) 5. Grief -- Fiction 6. Mutism -- Fiction
ISBN 0385384874; 9780385384872; 9780385384889

LC 2013030321

In this juvenile novel, by Tom Avery, "eleven-year-old Kaia, who has felt isolated since her older brother committed suicide more than a year before, befriends a wild boy who mysteriously appears at her London school. Though the boy is mute and can only communicate with a flash of his gray eyes, he might be the friend Kaia needs to bring her through her grief." (Publisher's note)

"Uncomplicated yet potent storytelling renders this an acutely heart-wrenching tale of despondency and renewal in a fresh manner. Readers who love stories of overcoming personal struggles and emotional strife will eat this up." Booklist

Aveyard, Victoria

Red queen; Victoria Aveyard. First edition HarperTeen, an imprint of HarperCollins Publishers 2015 388 p. (Red queen trilogy) $17.99

Grades: 8 9 10 11   **Fic**

1. Ability -- Fiction 2. Princesses -- Fiction 3. Teenage girls -- Fiction 4. Kings and rulers -- Fiction 5. Resistance to government -- Fiction 6. Blood 7. Ability 8. Princesses 9. Teenage girls 10. Government, Resistance to
ISBN 0062310631; 9780062310637

LC 2014952542

This book, by Victoria Aveyard, is the "sweeping tale of seventeen-year-old Mare, a common girl whose once-latent magical power draws her into the dangerous intrigue of the king's palace. Mare Barrow's world is divided by blood--those with common, Red blood serve the Silver- blooded elite, who are gifted with superhuman abilities. Mare is a Red, scraping by as a thief in a poor, rural village, until a twist of fate throws her in front of the Silver court." (Publisher's note)

"First-time author Aveyard has created a volatile world with a dynamic heroine, and while there are moments of romance, they refreshingly take a backseat to the action. Anticipation is already high for this debut, and with the movie rights already acquired and two sequels to come, it will likely only grow." Booklist

Axelrod, Kate

The **law** of loving others; a novel. by Kate Axelrod. Razorbill 2015 240 p. (hardback) $17.99

Grades: 9 10 11 12   **Fic**

1. Love stories 2. Bildungsromans 3. Mother-daughter relationship -- Fiction 4. Love -- Fiction 5. Coming of age -- Fiction 6. Schizophrenia -- Fiction 7. Mental illness -- Fiction 8. Mothers and daughters -- Fiction
ISBN 1595147896; 9781595147899

LC 2014032004

In this novel, by Kate Axelrod, "hours after Emma returns home from boarding school, she realizes that her mom is suffering from a schizophrenic break. Suddenly, Emma's entire childhood and identity is called into question. . . . In the span of just one winter break, Emma's relationships alter forever and she is forced to see the wisdom in a line from Anna Karenina: 'The law of loving others could not be discovered by reason, because it is unreasonable.'" (Publisher's note)

"In this candid, affecting portrait of a girl in crisis, debut author Axelrod nonjudgmentally and realistically captures the swirling ups and downs of anxiety, and the frantic, impotent grasp for control in the face of unpredictable, catastrophic change." Booklist

Ayarbe, Heidi

Compulsion. Balzer + Bray 2011 297p lib bdg $16.99

Grades: 10 11 12 **Fic**
1. School stories 2. Soccer -- Fiction 3. Obsessive-compulsive disorder -- Fiction
ISBN 978-0-06-199386-2

LC 2010027826

Poised to lead his high school soccer team to its third straight state championship, seventeen-year-old star player Jake Martin struggles to keep hidden his nearly debilitating obsessive-compulsive disorder.

"Ayarbe exercises both enormous skill and restraint getting to the root of just how debilitating OCD can become, juxtaposing descriptions of the ways the mind's compulsions can trip a trap of mental and physical anguish against a complex, credibly casted portrayal of teen social dynamics, which are treacherous enough on their own. A gripping, claustrophobic read." Booklist

Bacigalupi, Paolo

The **doubt** factory; a novel. by Paolo Bacigalupi. Little, Brown & Co. 2014 496 p. (hardback) $18
Grades: 9 10 11 12 **Fic**
1. Adventure fiction 2. Whistle blowing -- Fiction 3. Father-daughter relationship -- Fiction 4. Social action -- Fiction 5. Fathers and daughters -- Fiction 6. Corporations -- Corrupt practices -- Fiction
ISBN 0316220752; 9780316220750

LC 2014002543

This suspense novel, by Paolo Bacigalup, "explores the . . . issue of how public information is distorted for monetary gain, and how those who exploit it must be stopped. Everything Alix knows about her life is a lie. At least that's what a mysterious young man who's stalking her keeps saying. But then she begins investigating the disturbing claims he makes against her father." (Publisher's note)

"This openly didactic novel asks challenging questions about the immorality of the profit motive and capitalism, but does so within the context of a highly believable plot . . . and well-developed, multifaceted characters." Pub Wkly

★ The **drowned** cities; by Paolo Bacigalupi. Little, Brown and Company 2012 448p. paperback $11.00
Grades: 9 10 11 12 **Fic**
1. Science fiction 2. Apocalyptic fiction 3. Refugees -- Fiction 4. War -- Fiction 5. Orphans -- Fiction 6. Soldiers -- Fiction 7. Survival -- Fiction 8. Conduct of life -- Fiction 9. Genetic engineering -- Fiction
ISBN 9780316056243; 9780316056229 paperback
LC 2011031762

This book takes place "[i]n a dark future America where violence, terror, and grief touch everyone, young refugees Mahlia and Mouse have managed to leave behind the wartorn lands of the Drowned Cities by escaping into the jungle outskirts. But when they discover a wounded half-man--a bioengineered war beast named Tool--who is being hunted by a vengeful band of soldiers, their fragile existence quickly collapses." (Publisher's note)

★ **Ship** Breaker; Bacigalupi, Paolo. Little, Brown and Co. 2010 326p $17.99

Grades: 8 9 10 11 12 **Fic**
1. Science fiction 2. Recycling -- Fiction
ISBN 0316056219; 9780316056212

LC 2009-34424

Michael L. Printz Award, 2011

In a futuristic world, teenaged Nailer scavenges copper wiring from grounded oil tankers for a living, but when he finds a beached clipper ship with a girl in the wreckage, he has to decide if he should strip the ship for its wealth or rescue the girl.

"Bacigalupi's cast is ethnically and morally diverse, and the book's message never overshadows the storytelling, action-packed pacing, or intricate world-building. At its core, the novel is an exploration of Nailer's discovery of the nature of the world around him and his ability to transcend that world's expectations." Publ Wkly

Backes, M. Molly

The **princesses** of Iowa; M. Molly Backes. Candlewick Press 2012 442 p. $16.99
Grades: 9 10 11 12 **Fic**
1. Iowa -- Fiction 2. Schools -- Fiction 3. Popularity -- Fiction 4. High schools -- Fiction 5. Conduct of life -- Fiction
ISBN 0763653128; 9780763653125

LC 2011018622

This young adult novel follows "Paige Sheridan . . . she's pretty, rich, and popular, and her spot on the homecoming court is practically guaranteed. But when a night of partying ends in an it-could-have-been-so-much worse crash, everything changes. Her best friends start ignoring her, her boyfriend grows cold and distant. . . . A charismatic new teacher . . . encourages students to be true to themselves. But who is Paige, if not the homecoming princess everyone expects her to be?" (Publisher's note)

"Backes addresses guilt, deceit, homophobia, loyalty, and the burden of keeping up appearances in a brutally believable high school setting." Pub Wkly

Badoe, Adwoa

Between sisters. Groundwood Books/House of Anansi Press 2010 205p $16.95
Grades: 9 10 11 12 **Fic**
1. School stories 2. Poor -- Fiction 3. Ghana -- Fiction 4. Family life -- Fiction
ISBN 978-0-88899-996-2

"When sixteen-year-old Gloria fails thirteen out of fifteen subjects on her final exams, her future looks bleak indeed. Her family's resources are meager so the entire family is thrilled when a distant relative, Christine, offers to move Gloria north to Kumasi to look after her toddler son, Sam. In exchange, after two years, Christine will pay for Gloria to go to dressmaking school. Life in Kumasi is more grand than anything Gloria has ever experienced. . . . [But] Kumasi is also full of temptations." Publisher's note

Baer, Marianna

Frost; Marianna Baer. Balzer + Bray 2011 400p $17.99; ebook $9.99
Grades: 8 9 10 11 12 **Fic**
1. School stories 2. Houses -- Fiction 3. Supernatural

-- Fiction
ISBN 978-0-06-179949-5; 978-0-06-209331-8 ebook
LC 2011019308

When Leena Thomas gets her wish to live in an old Victorian house with her two closest friends during their senior year at boarding school, the unexpected arrival of another roommate—a confrontational and eccentric classmate—seems to bring up old anxieties and fears for Leena that may or may not be in her own mind.

"This nuanced blend of psychological suspense and boarding-school drama will tingle the spines of plenty of readers." Booklist

Bailey, Em

Shift; Em Bailey. Random House Distribution Childrens 2012 304 p. (hardcover) $16.99
Grades: 7 8 9 10 11 12   **Fic**
1. Human behavior -- Fiction 2. Female friendship -- Fiction 3. High school students -- Fiction 4. Orphans -- Fiction 5. Schools -- Fiction 6. Popularity -- Fiction 7. High school -- Fiction 8. Mental illness -- Fiction 9. Interpersonal relations -- Fiction
ISBN 1606843583; 9781606843581; 9781606843598
LC 2011034349

Author Em Bailey's character "Olive keeps it simple: take her meds, keep a low profile at school, stay away from the ocean (with its horrible memories), and try not to cause trouble since she's pretty sure her selfish, unruly behavior is what made her father take off six months ago. But then strange and mysterious Miranda Vaile shows up at her high school, and Olive's safeguards start to crumble. Miranda begins insinuating herself into the life of Olive's former best friend, Katie." (Publishers Weekly)

Bailey, Kristin

Legacy of the clockwork key; by Kristin Bailey. Simon Pulse 2013 416 p. (alk. paper) $17.99
Grades: 7 8 9 10   **Fic**
1. Inventions 2. Secret societies 3. Love -- Fiction 4. Science fiction 5. Orphans -- Fiction
ISBN 1442440260; 9781442440265
LC 2011049871

In this book, "a teen girl unravels the mysteries of a secret society and their most dangerous invention. . . . When a fire consumes Meg's home, killing her parents . . . all she has left is the tarnished pocket watch she rescued from the ashes. But this is no ordinary timepiece. The clock turns out to be a mechanical key--a key that only Meg can use--which unlocks a series of deadly secrets and intricate clues that Meg has no choice but to follow." (Publisher's note)

Other titles in the series include:
Rise of the Arcane Fire (2014)
Shadow of the War Machine (2015)

Baldwin, Kathleen

A **School** for Unusual Girls; A Stranje House Novel. Kathleen Baldwin. St. Martin's Press 2015 352 p. $17.99
Grades: 9 10 11 12   **Fic**
1. Spy stories 2. School stories 3. Historical fiction
ISBN 0765376008; 9780765376008
LC 2015012225

In this young adult novel by Kathleen Baldwin, "It's 1814. Napoleon is exiled on Elba. Europe is in shambles. Britain is at war on four fronts. And Stranje House, a School for Unusual Girls, has become one of Regency England's dark little secrets. The daughters of the beau monde who don't fit high society's constrictive mold are banished to Stranje House to be reformed into marriageable young ladies. Or so their parents think." (Publisher's note)

"The spunky, naive, and passsionate protagonist will resonate with readers, who will appreciate the lively, fast-paced narrative of personal discovery, maturing realizations, and understanding." SLJ

Ballard, J. G., 1930-2009

Empire of the Sun; a novel. Simon & Schuster 1984 279p hardcover o.p. pa $13
Grades: 9 10 11 12 Adult   **Fic**
1. Shanghai (China) -- Fiction 2. World War, 1939-1945 -- Fiction
ISBN 0-671-53051-8; 0-7432-6523-8 pa
LC 84-10630

"This novel is much more than the gritty story of a child's miraculous survival in the grimly familiar setting of World War II's concentration camps. There is no nostalgia for a good war here, no sentimentality for the human spirit at extremes. Mr. Ballard is more ambitious than romance usually allows. He aims to render a vision of the apocalypse, and succeeds so well that it can hurt to dwell upon his images." N Y Times Book Rev

Followed by The kindness of women (1991)

Balog, Cyn

Sleepless. Delacorte Press 2010 215p $16.99
Grades: 8 9 10 11 12   **Fic**
1. Love stories 2. Death -- Fiction 3. Dreams -- Fiction 4. Bereavement -- Fiction 5. Supernatural -- Fiction
ISBN 978-0-385-73848-4; 0-385-73848-X
LC 2010-00123

Eron, a supernatural being known as a Sandman whose purpose is to seduce humans to sleep, falls in love with a sad teenaged girl who is mourning her boyfriend's death.

"Suspense, believable characters and an imaginative twist on a ghost story/romance make for a lovely read." Kirkus

Banghart, Tracy E.

Shattered Veil; The Diatous Wars. Tracy E. Banghart. Createspace Independent Publishing Platform 2014 372 p. $15.99
Grades: 7 8 9 10 11 12   **Fic**
1. Love stories 2. Mystery fiction 3. Science fiction
ISBN 1493613200; 9781493613205

In this science fiction romance novel by Tracy E. Banghart, "War has invaded Atalanta's quiet villages and lush woodlands, igniting whispered worries in its glittering capitol. Far from the front lines, 18-year-old Aris Haan, a talented wingjet flyer, has little cause for concern. Until her beloved Calix is thrust into the fray, and a stranger makes her an impossible offer: the chance to join a secret army of women embedded within the all-male military." (Publisher's note)

"Part mystery, part romance, part sci-fi, Banghart's fast-paced exploration of loyalty, identity and commitment is entertaining and intriguing." (Kirkus)

Bao, Karen

Dove arising; Karen Bao. Viking Books for Young Readers 2015 324 p. (Dove Chronicles) hardcover $17.99

Grades: 7 8 9 10   **Fic**

1. Space colonies 2. Militia movements -- Fiction 3. Children of prisoners -- Fiction 4. Moon -- Fiction 5. Science fiction 6. Youths' writings 7. Space colonies -- Fiction 8. Government, Resistance to -- Fiction

ISBN 0451469011; 9780451469014; 9780451476289

LC 2013041198

In this novel by Karen Bao, "Phaet Theta has lived her whole life in a colony on the Moon. She's barely spoken since her father died in an accident nine years ago. She cultivates the plants in Greenhouse 22, lets her best friend talk for her, and stays off the government's radar. Then her mother is arrested. The only way to save her younger siblings from the degrading Shelter is by enlisting in the Militia, the faceless army that polices the Lunar bases and protects them from attacks by desperate Earth dwellers. Training is brutal, but it's where Phaet forms an uneasy but meaningful alliance with the preternaturally accomplished Wes, a fellow outsider. Rank high, save her siblings, free her mom: that's the plan. Until Phaet's logically ordered world begins to crumble..." (Publisher's note)

"Characters are well developed, especially strong-willed Phaet, and an even pace will keep teens turning pages. Fans of Orson Scott Card's Ender's Game (Tor, 1985), Veronica Roth's Divergent (HarperCollins, 2011) and Marie Lu's Legend (Putnam, 2011) should flock to this well-written debut effort by 19-year-old Bao." SLJ

Barakiva, Michael

One man guy; Michael Barakiva. First edition Farrar, Straus & Giroux 2014 272 p. (hardcover) $17.99

Grades: 9 10 11 12   **Fic**

1. Gay teenagers -- Fiction 2. Armenian Americans -- Fiction 3. Gays -- Fiction 4. Love -- Fiction 5. Coming out (Sexual orientation) -- Fiction

ISBN 0374356459; 9780374356453

LC 2013033518

In this book, by Michael Barakiva, "being forced to attend summer school becomes a blessing in disguise for 14-year-old Alek Khederian when it sparks a romance with an older boy named Ethan, who runs with a crowd of skateboarders and perceived burnouts. Alek's Armenian heritage is the ever-present frame for the boys' budding relationship in suburban New Jersey." (Publishers Weekly)

"[D]eftly draws strong parallels between homosexuality and ethnicity that will resonate with audiences. East Coast teens will see themselves; Midwesterners will feel a little envy." Kirkus

Baratz-Logsted, Lauren

Crazy beautiful. Houghton Mifflin Harcourt 2009 191p $16

Grades: 7 8 9 10   **Fic**

1. School stories 2. Bullies -- Fiction 3. Amputees -- Fiction 4. People with disabilities -- Fiction

ISBN 978-0-547-22307-0; 0-547-22307-2

LC 2008-40463

In this contemporary retelling of "Beauty and the Beast," a teenaged boy whose hands were amputated in an explosion and a gorgeous girl whose mother has recently died form an instant connection when they meet on their first day as new students.

"This romance transcends all of its potential pitfalls to create a powerful story about recovery and friendship." Kirkus

Twin's daughter. Bloomsbury 2010 390p $16.99

Grades: 7 8 9 10   **Fic**

1. Mystery fiction 2. Aunts -- Fiction 3. Twins -- Fiction 4. Homicide -- Fiction 5. London (England) -- Fiction 6. Great Britain -- History -- 19th century -- Fiction

ISBN 978-1-59990-513-6; 1-59990-513-2

LC 2010-08234

In Victorian London, thirteen-year-old Lucy's comfortable world with her loving parents begins slowly to unravel the day that a bedraggled woman who looks exactly like her mother appears at their door.

"Baratz-Logsted's gothic murder mystery is rife with twists and moves swiftly and elegantly. . . . The ending will intrigue and delight readers." Booklist

Bardugo, Leigh

Ruin and rising; Leigh Bardugo. Henry Holt and Co. 2014 432 p. (Grisha trilogy) (hardback) $18.99

Grades: 8 9 10 11 12   **Fic**

1. Fantasy fiction 2. Princes -- Fiction 3. Love stories

ISBN 080509461X; 9780805094619

LC 2013049306

In this young adult fantasy novel by Leigh Bardugo, part of the Grisha Trilogy, "Deep in an ancient network of tunnels and caverns, a weakened Alina must submit to the dubious protection of the Apparat and the zealots who worship her as a Saint. Yet her plans lie elsewhere, with the hunt for the elusive firebird and the hope that an outlaw prince still survives." (Publisher's note)

"Alina and company have only one hope: if they can kill the Firebird, its magical bones can be used to break the Darkling's chokehold on Ravka. In this concluding volume, Alina must rely on her childhood friend Mal's preternatural tracking ability. Bardugo's longstanding theme of "power corrupts" is developed organically; the magic she invents will surprise and delight readers." Horn Book

Shadow and bone; Leigh Bardugo. Henry Holt 2012 358 p. (Grisha trilogy) (hc) $17.99

Grades: 8 9 10 11   **Fic**

1. Fantasy fiction 2. Magic -- Fiction 3. Folklore -- Russia 4. Monsters -- Fiction 5. Slavic mythology 6. Fantasy 7. Ability -- Fiction 8. Orphans -- Fiction

ISBN 0805094598; 9780805094596

LC 2011034012

In this young adult novel, "[Leigh] Bardugo draws inspiration from Russian and Slavic myth and culture to kick off her 'Grisha' trilogy. In the nation of Ravka, Alina Starkov is a junior cartographer's assistant in the army, while her best friend Mai is an expert tracker. When a perilous mission into the magically created Shadow Fold goes wrong, Mai is gravely wounded and Alina manifests the rare ability to summon light. Immediately recruited into the order of the magic-using Grisha, Alina is taken under the wing of its intimidating and powerful leader, the Darkling, and heralded as the potential destroyer of the Shadow Fold. As she navigates Grisha politics and uncovers well-hidden secrets, she realizes that the fate of the nation rests on her shoulders and she may be in grave danger." (Publishers Weekly)

Siege and storm; Leigh Bardugo. 1st ed. Henry Holt and Co. 2013 448 p. (Grisha trilogy) (hardcover) $17.99

Grades: 8 9 10 11 12   **Fic**
    1. Fantasy fiction 2. Russia -- Fiction 3. Monsters -- Fiction 4. Fantasy 5. Magic -- Fiction 6. Orphans -- Fiction
ISBN 0805094601; 9780805094602

LC 2012046361

This fantasy novel, by Leigh Bardugo, is book 2 of the "Grisha Trilogy." "Alina must try to make a life with Mal in an unfamiliar land, all while keeping her identity as the Sun Summoner a secret. But she can't outrun her past or her destiny for long. The Darkling has emerged from the Shadow Fold with a terrifying new power and a dangerous plan that will test the very boundaries of the natural world." (Publisher's note)

★ **Six** of crows; Leigh Bardugo. Henry Holt & Co. 2015 480 p. illustrations, map (hardback) $18.99   **Fic**
    1. Theft -- Fiction 2. Criminals -- Fiction 3. Fantasy
ISBN 9781250076960; 9781627792127; 9781627795098

LC 2015005469

This book by Leigh Bardugo is set in the same universe as the author's Grisha Trilogy and is part of "a two-book story line called the Dregs. Six misfits and outcasts--a convict, a sharpshooter, a runaway, a spy, a magician, and a thief--join forces with criminal prodigy Kaz Brekker for a heist that could make them rich beyond imagination." (Booklist)

    "Cracking page-turner with a multiethnic band of misfits with differing sexual orientations who satisfyingly, believably jell into a family." Kirkus

Barnaby, Hannah

Wonder show; by Hannah Barnaby. Houghton Mifflin Books for Children 2012 viii, 274 p.p $16.99
Grades: 7 8 9 10 11 12   **Fic**
    1. Carnivals 2. Orphanages 3. Runaway children 4. Fathers -- Fiction 5. Runaways -- Fiction 6. Sideshows -- Fiction 7. Orphanages -- Fiction 8. Depressions -- 1929 -- United States -- Fiction
ISBN 0547599803; 9780547599809

LC 2011052426

William C. Morris Award Finalist (2013)

In this book by Hannah Barnaby, "Portia Remini, 13 . . . escapes . . . from the McGreavey Home for Wayward Girls to search for her father. . . . She joins a carnival. . . . On the lam from sinister 'Mister,' who runs McGreavey's, Portia

learns the stories of some of the carnival's strange troupe. . . . But . . . when Mister's dragnet closes in, Portia decides that to find the answers she seeks she must return to the horror of The Home." (School Library Journal)

Barnes, John

Losers in space; John Barnes. Viking 2012 433 p. ill. (hardcover) $18.99
Grades: 9 10 11 12   **Fic**
    1. Science fiction 2. Space vehicles -- Fiction 3. Runaway teenagers -- Fiction 4. Fame -- Fiction 5. Stowaways -- Fiction 6. Psychopaths -- Fiction
ISBN 0670061565; 9780670061563

LC 2011020579

This science fiction novel is "set in a celebrity-obsessed future. Susan Tervaille . . . is swept up in a crazy plot hatched by bad-boy Derlock. She and several friends stow away on a spacecraft headed to Mars, hoping they'll be broadcast . . . enough . . . on Earth to secure their status as up-and-coming superstars. What they don't realize is that Derlock is insane and hell-bent on snagging fame for himself -- even if it means lives are lost." (Publishers Weekly)

★ **Tales** of the Madman Underground; an historical romance 1973. Viking 2009 532p $18.99; pa $9.99
Grades: 10 11 12 Adult   **Fic**
    1. School stories 2. Ohio -- Fiction 3. Alcoholism -- Fiction 4. Friendship -- Fiction 5. Mother-son relationship -- Fiction
ISBN 978-0-670-06081-8; 0-670-06081-X; 978-0-14-241702-7 pa; 0-14-241702-5 pa

LC 2009-11072

ALA YALSA Printz Award Honor Book (2010)

In September 1973, as the school year begins in his depressed Ohio town, high school senior Kurt Shoemaker determines to be "normal," despite his chaotic home life with his volatile, alcoholic mother and the deep loyalty and affection he has for his friends in the therapy group dubbed the Madman Underground.

    "Teens initially turned off by Barnes's liberal use of profanities and the book's length will be captured by the sharp, funny dialogue and crisp personalities of the Madmen. Even minor characters are distinctive. . . . [This] is an excellent selection for book clubs of older teens that like sinking their teeth into longer stories with substance." Voice Youth Advocates

Barnholdt, Lauren

Through to you; Lauren Barnholdt. First Simon Pulse hardcover ed Simon Pulse 2014 278 p. (hbk.) $17.99
Grades: 9 10 11 12   **Fic**
    1. Love -- Fiction 2. Dating (Social customs) -- Fiction
ISBN 1442434635; 9781442434639

LC 2013048226

In this book, by Lauren Barnholdt, it "starts with a scribbled note in class: I like your sparkle. . . . Harper's surprised by Penn's attention—and so is Penn. The last thing he needs is a girlfriend. Or even a friend-with-benefits. The note is not supposed to lead to anything. Oh, but it does. . . . But Penn and Harper have very different ideas about what relationships look like, in no small part because of their very different family backgrounds." (Publisher's note)

"Chapters alternate between the two characters' vantage points, providing an insightful and humorous look into the complex connections among feelings, actions and words and how easily they can be misconstrued.An absorbing, skillfully written depiction of two teens caught in a vortex of doubt, insecurity and miscommunication." Kirkus

Barr, Nevada

Track of the cat. Putnam 1993 238p hardcover o.p. pa $7.99

Grades: 11 12 Adult   **Fic**
  1. Mystery fiction
  ISBN 0-399-13824-2; 0-425-19083-8 pa
                                                    LC 92-29694

In this first novel of the Anna Pigeon series, "Anna Pigeon has fled New York City after the accidental death of her husband, and she now works as a law enforcement ranger at Guadaloupe Mountains National Park. There she finds the remains of fellow ranger Sheila Drury, who apparently was clawed to death by a mountain lion. Although an autopsy confirms this judgment, Anna becomes convinced that the claw marks have been faked. Her superiors discourage her from probing further, but another supposedly accidental death goads her into investigating Sheila's activities before her death—her campaign to open up the park to the public and her relationships with a young divorcee and with a powerful rancher opposed to Park Service policies. . . . A park ranger herself, Barr develops a complex, credible and capable heroine who believes in truth and justice while remaining conscious of the ambiguities of human existence." Publ Wkly

Other titles in this series featuring Anna Pigeon are:
Blind descent (1998)
Blood lure (2001)
Borderline (2009)
Burn (2010)
Deep South (2000)
Endangered species (1997)
Firestorm (1996)
Flashback (2003)
Hard truth (2005)
High country (2004)
Hunting season (2002)
Ill wind (1995)
Liberty falling (1999)
A superior death (1994)
Winter study (2008)
The Rope (2012)
Destroyer Angel (2014)

Barrett, Tracy

Dark of the moon. Harcourt 2011 310p $16.99

Grades: 7 8 9 10   **Fic**
  1. Greece -- Fiction 2. Classical mythology -- Fiction
  3. Theseus (Greek Mythology) -- Fiction
  ISBN 978-0-547-58132-3; 0-547-58132-7
                                                   LC 2011009597

Retells the story of the minotaur through the eyes of his fifteen-year-old sister, Ariadne, a lonely girl destined to become a goddess of the moon, and her new friend, Theseus,

the son of Athens' king who was sent to Crete as a sacrifice to her misshapen brother.

"This retelling of the myth of the Minotaur is deft, dark, and enthralling. Barrett spares readers none of the gore and violence of the Kretan goddess-worship, which involves both human and animal sacrifice. Ariadne's beliefs, though alien to modern readers, are given sufficient context to make them comprehensible. . . . This thoughtful, well-written reimagining of a classic myth is a welcome addition to the genre." SLJ

King of Ithaka. Henry Holt and Company 2010 261p map $16.99

Grades: 7 8 9 10   **Fic**
  1. Classical mythology -- Fiction 2. Odysseus (Greek mythology) -- Fiction
  ISBN 978-0-8050-8969-1; 0-8050-8969-1
                                                   LC 2009-50770

Sixteen-year-old Telemachos and his two best friends leave their life of privilege to undertake a quest to find Telemachos's father Odysseus. "Grades six to ten." (Bull Cent Child Books)

"The exotic climes and vivid descriptions . . . give the story a sense of immediacy and color." Booklist

The **Stepsister's** Tale; by Tracy Barrett. Harlequin Books 2014 272 p. $16.99

Grades: 7 8 9 10   **Fic**
  1. Love stories 2. Stepsisters -- Fiction 3. Poor 4. Fantasy 5. Stepfamilies 6. Fantasy fiction 7. Poor -- Fiction
  ISBN 037321121X; 9780373211210

In this novel, by Tracy Barrett, "Jane Montjoy is tired of . . . pretending to live up to the standards of her mother's noble family--especially now that the family's wealth is gone. . . . When her stepfather suddenly dies, leaving nothing but debts and a bereaved daughter behind, it seems to Jane that her family is destined for eternal unhappiness. But a mysterious boy from the woods and an invitation to a royal ball are certain to change her fate." (Publisher's note)

"Sometimes it feels like fairy-tale retellings are a dime a dozen, and this is certainly not the first or the last account of a misunderstood antagonist. But, Barrett's comparably quiet account of a household of women working to survive together as a family, sometimes in spite of one another, shines with soft, bucolic realism...Overall, this is an enjoyable read. The inclusion of discussion questions in the back makes it a solid choice for book clubs." VOYA

Barry, Max

Lexicon; a novel. Max Barry. The Penguin Press 2013 400 p. (hardcover) $26.95

Grades: Adult   **Fic**
  1. Dystopian fiction 2. Paranormal fiction 3. Linguists -- Fiction 4. Secret societies -- Fiction 5. Persuasion (Psychology) -- Fiction
  ISBN 1594205388; 9781101604908; 9781594205385
                                                   LC 2012046980

Alex Award (2014)

In this novel, there is "a secret society of 'poets' who collect and wield special words to control others. Emily Ruff, a teenager living on the street, has been recruited by the organization but leaves in seeming disgrace. Years later, Wil Parke is caught in a firefight between the factions—over him. He is the only survivor of a horrifying event unleashed by an ultimate word of power. But there is a deeper connection between Wil and Emily and the organization that comes between them." (Library Journal)

Barwin, Steven

Hardball; Steven Barwin. Orca Book Publishers 2014 192 p. (Orca sports) (pbk.) $9.95

Grades: 7 8 9 10   **Fic**

1. Cousins -- Fiction 2. Baseball -- Fiction 3. School sports -- Fiction 4. Hazing 5. Cousins 6. Baseball players

ISBN 1459804414; 9781459804418; 9781459804425; 9781459804432

LC 2014935389

"Griffin has college in his sights and plans to land himself a baseball scholarship. His determination causes him to turn a blind eye to the hazing of new players by the team captain, Wade. But when Griffin senses that his cousin Carson is getting the brunt of Wade's aggression, Griffin finally stands up to him." (Publisher's note)

"Short, fast-paced chapters keep the narrative moving with a mix of baseball play-by-plays and sleuthing. A drug-dealing subplot adds a layer of suspense and raises the stakes well beyond troubles on the ball field. Ideal for reluctant readers, this book's gritty undertones will appeal to the intended high/low audience of sports fans." Booklist

Barzak, Christopher

★ **Wonders of the invisible world**; Christopher Barzak. Alfred A. Knopf 2015 339 p. (pbk.) $9.99

Grades: 9 10 11 12   **Fic**

1. Supernatural -- Fiction 2. Family secrets -- Fiction 3. Gays -- Fiction 4. Ohio -- Fiction 5. Death -- Fiction 6. Psychic ability -- Fiction 7. Farm life -- Ohio -- Fiction 8. Blessing and cursing -- Fiction

ISBN 0385392826; 9780385392792; 9780385392808; 9780385392822

LC 2014022809

Stonewall Book Award Honor Book, Youth (2016)

In this novel, by Christopher Barzak, winner of the Stonewall Honor award, "Aidan Lockwood lives in a sleepy farming town. . . . But . . . Aidan begins to see . . . a world that is haunted by the stories of his past. Visions from this invisible world come to him unbidden: a great-grandfather on the field of battle; his own father, . . . and a mysterious young boy, whose whispered words may be at the heart of the curse that holds Aidan's family in its grip." (Publisher's note)

"With leisurely pacing and simple, expressive language, Barzak expertly balances magical realism, historical flashbacks, and contemporary teen romance in Aiden's journey of self-discovery. Give this to teen readers who want a quieter paranormal tale or a sincere love story between two boys." Booklist

Bass, Karen, 1962-

Graffiti knight. Orca Book Publishers 2014 272 p. $14.95

Grades: 7 8 9 10   **Fic**

1. Graffiti -- Fiction 2. Family life -- Fiction 3. Communist countries -- Fiction 4. Resistance to government -- Fiction

ISBN 1927485533; 9781927485538

In this book, "after a childhood cut short by war and the harsh strictures of Nazi Germany, sixteen-year-old Wilm is finally tasting freedom. . . . It's dangerous, of course, to be sneaking out at night to leave messages on police buildings. But it's exciting, too, and Wilm feels justified, considering his family's suffering. Until one mission goes too far, and Wilm finds he's endangered the very people he most wants to protect." (Publisher's note)

"Just as Ruta Sepetys revealed a different perspective of the Holocaust in Between Shades of Gray (2011), Bass introduces another view of history unknown to many American readers...This eye-opening story shows that war's end is never tidy." (Booklist)

Summer of fire; [edited by Laura Peetoom] Coteau Books for Teens 2009 267p pa $10.95

Grades: 9 10 11 12   **Fic**

1. Germany -- Fiction 2. Sisters -- Fiction 3. Runaway teenagers -- Fiction 4. World War, 1939-1945 -- Fiction

ISBN 978-1-55050-415-6; 1-55050-415-0

"It is rare for a novel to offer a German civilian's viewpoint during Hitler's rise to power with such honesty. Alternating between Del's and Garda's voices, . . . the teen voices are immediate: Del's wry and self-aware; Garda's desperate and angry." Booklist

Bass, Ron

Lucid; Adrienne Stoltz, Ron Bass. Razorbill 2012 342 p. (hardback) $17.99

Grades: 9 10 11 12   **Fic**

1. Fantasy fiction 2. Dreams -- Fiction 3. Love -- Fiction 4. Schools -- Fiction 5. Friendship -- Fiction 6. High schools -- Fiction 7. Actors and actresses -- Fiction

ISBN 1595145192; 9781595145192

LC 2012014448

This young adult novel, by Adrienne Stoltz and Ron Bass, explores dreams and reality. "Sloane and Maggie have never met. . . . At night, they dream that they're each other. . . . Before long, Sloane and Maggie can no longer tell which life is real and which is just a dream. They realize that eventually they will have to choose one life to wake up to, or risk spiraling into insanity." (Publisher's note)

Bassoff, Leah

★ **Lost** Girl Found; by Leah Bassoff and Laura DeLuca. Pgw 2014 192 p. maps $16.95

Grades: 6 7 8 9 10   **Fic**

1. Refugees -- Fiction 2. Mother-daughter relationship -- Fiction 3. Sudan -- History -- Civil War, 1983-2005 -- Fiction

ISBN 1554984165; 9781554984169

LC bl2014008921

In this book, by Leah Bassoff and Laura DeLuca, "Poni . . . [lives in a] small village in southern Sudan. . . . Then the war comes and there is only one thing for Poni to do. Run. . . . [She is] driven by the sheer will to survive and the hope that she can . . . make it to the Kakuma refugee camp in Kenya. . . . In Kakuma she is almost overwhelmed by the misery that surrounds her. Poni realizes that she must leave the camp at any cost. Her destination is a compound in Nairobi." (Publisher's note)

"After her southern Sudan village is bombed, Poni arrives at a Kenyan refugee camp, where conditions are brutal. Poni wants to finish her education, and she has a chance to do so when she escapes the refugee camp. Poni is a fully realized and sympathetic character. This fast-paced novel covers a lot of ground and incorporates a good deal of historical background." Horn Book

Bastedo, Jamie

Cut Off; Jamie Bastedo. Red Deer Press 2015 320 p. $11.95

Grades: 7 8 9 10   **Fic**

1. Adventure fiction 2. Addiction -- Fiction 3. Internet and teenagers

ISBN 0889955115; 9780889955110

In this novel, by Jamie Bastedo, "fourteen-year-old Indio McCracken enjoys meteoric stardom as a guitar prodigy after his father posts a video of him playing. Things quickly go sour . Robbed of a normal childhood and already feeling alienated by his mixed Guatemalan-Canadian heritage, Indio desperately seeks escape online by creating a virtual identity. Facing school expulsion. . . unless he kicks his Internet habit, Indio is shipped off to a teen addictions rehab center." (Publisher's note)

"Indio's narration is completely believable throughout as he wrestles with identity and belonging. Bastedo gives readers who may be inclined to scoff at the addictive-cyberdevice premise the space to assess Indio's actions and reasoning and reach their own conclusions, all the while keeping the tension and pace high. A first-rate adventure with a powerful message." Kirkus

Bauer, Joan

★ Hope was here. Putnam 2000 186p $16.99; pa $7.99

Grades: 7 8 9 10   **Fic**

1. Aunts -- Fiction 2. Wisconsin -- Fiction 3. Restaurants -- Fiction

ISBN 0-399-23142-0; 0-14-240424-1 pa

LC 00-38232

A Newbery Medal honor book, 2001

When sixteen-year-old Hope and the aunt who has raised her move from Brooklyn to Mulhoney, Wisconsin, to work as waitress and cook in the Welcome Stairways diner, they become involved with G.T. Stoop, the diner owner, and his political campaign to oust the town's corrupt mayor. "Age twelve and up." (N Y Times Book Rev)

"Bauer manages to fill her heartfelt novel with gentle humor, quirky but appealing characters, and an engaging plot." Book Rep

★ Peeled. G.P. Putnam's Sons 2008 256p $16.99

Grades: 6 7 8 9 10   **Fic**

1. Ghost stories 2. School stories 3. Farm life -- Fiction 4. Journalism -- Fiction 5. New York (State) -- Fiction

ISBN 978-0-399-23475-0; 0-399-23475-6

LC 2007-42835

In an upstate New York farming community, high school reporter Hildy Biddle investigates a series of strange occurrences at a house rumored to be haunted.

This is "a warm and funny story full of likable, offbeat characters led by a strongly voiced, independently minded female protagonist on her way to genuine, well-earned maturity." SLJ

Bauman, Beth Ann

Jersey Angel; Beth Ann Bauman. Wendy Lamb Books 2012 201 p.

Grades: 9 10 11 12   **Fic**

1. Love stories 2. New Jersey -- Fiction 3. Female friendship -- Fiction 4. Dating (Social customs) -- Fiction 5. Girls -- Sexual behavior -- Fiction 6. Beaches -- Fiction 7. Italian Americans -- Fiction

ISBN 0385740204; 9780375899003; 9780385740203; 9780385740210; 9780385908283

LC 2011030915

This book follows "[s]ix months in the life of a proudly sex-positive 17-year-old from the Jersey Shore . . . . Angel Cassonetti's life is based on two things: her exquisite awareness of and facility at wielding her sex appeal, and her close, almost sisterly friendship with Inggy Olofsson. Pale and blond, studious and monogamous with her longtime boyfriend Cork, Inggy stands in sharp contrast to the easily tanned, curly brunette, scholastically blasé and sexually precocious Angel. When Angel's longtime on-again, off-again boyfriend Joey tells her he's done playing games . . . --she finds herself drifting through the summer before senior year. She begins a potentially explosive secret fling that she can't quite find a way out of". (Kirkus Reviews)

Rosie & Skate. Wendy Lamb Books 2009 217p $15.99; lib bdg $18.99

Grades: 9 10 11 12   **Fic**

1. Sisters -- Fiction 2. Alcoholism -- Fiction 3. New Jersey -- Fiction 4. Family life -- Fiction 5. Dating (Social customs) -- Fiction 6. Father-daughter relationship -- Fiction

ISBN 978-0-385-73735-7; 0-385-73735-1; 978-0-385-90660-9 lib bdg; 0-385-90660-9 lib bdg

LC 2009-10575

"Bauman's prose is lovely and real. Vivid descriptions bring her characters to life, and the dialogue is both believable and funny. . . . The novel expertly captures the ever-hopeful ache of adolescents longing for love, stability and certainty." Kirkus

Beagle, Peter S.

The last unicorn. Viking 1968 218p hardcover o.p. pa $14.95

Grades: 11 12 Adult   **Fic**

1. Allegories 2. Fantasy fiction 3. Unicorns -- Fiction

ISBN 0-670-41908-7; 0-451-45052-3 pa

"Beagle is a true magician with words, a master of prose and a deft practitioner in verse. He has been compared, not unreasonably, with Lewis Carroll and J. R. R. Tolkien, but he stands squarely and triumphantly on his own feet." Saturday Rev

Beah, Ishmael, 1980-

Radiance of tomorrow; a novel. Ishmael Beah. Sarah Crichton Books, Farrar, Straus and Giroux 2014 256 p. (hardback) $25

Grades: 11 12 Adult   **Fic**
1. Villages -- Fiction 2. Sierra Leone -- History -- Civil War, 1991- -- Fiction 3. Villages -- Sierra Leone -- Fiction 4. Sierra Leone -- History -- Civil War, 1991-2002 -- Fiction
ISBN 0374246025; 9780374246020

LC 2013036856

This novel, by Ishmael Beah, is "about postwar life in Sierra Leone. . . . Benjamin and Bockarie . . . return to their hometown, Imperi, after the civil war. . . . [They] try to forge a new community by taking up their former posts as teachers, but they're beset by obstacles . . . and the depredations of a foreign mining company. . . . As Benjamin and Bockarie search for a way to restore order, they're forced to reckon with the uncertainty of their past and future alike." (Publisher's note)

"The power of the story is in the close-up, heartbreaking detail of the struggle for survival, the cruelty, and also the kindness." Booklist

Beam, Cris

★ **I** am J. Little, Brown 2011 326p

Grades: 9 10 11 12   **Fic**
1. Transgender people -- Fiction 2. Friendship -- Fiction
ISBN 0-316-05361-9; 978-0-316-05361-7

LC 2010-08640

J, who feels like a boy mistakenly born as a girl, runs away from his best friend who has rejected him and the parents he thinks do not understand him when he finally decides that it is time to be who he really is.

"The book is a gift to transgender teens and an affecting story of self-discovery for all readers." Horn Book

Includes bibliographical references

Beaudoin, Sean

Wise Young Fool; by Sean Beaudoin. Little, Brown and Co. 2013 448 p. $18

Grades: 10 11 12   **Fic**
1. Juvenile delinquency 2. Teenagers -- Fiction 3. Bands (Music) -- Fiction 4. Musicians -- Fiction 5. Juvenile detention homes -- Fiction
ISBN 0316203793; 9780316203791

LC 2012032472

In this book by Sean Beaudoin, protagonist "Ritchie grabs readers by the throat before (politely) inviting them along for the (max-speed) ride. A battle of the bands looms. Dad split about five minutes before Mom's girlfriend moved in. There's the matter of trying to score with the dangerously hot Ravenna Woods while avoiding the dangerously huge Spence Proffer--not to mention just trying to forget what his sister, Beth, said the week before she died." (Publisher's note)

"This coming-of-age story is told in alternating story lines, leading up to Ritchie Sudden's arrest and his time in a juvenile detention center... There are a lot of messages about the importance of safe driving and staying away from drugs and alcohol without being preachy. This is not a typical rock band story; it is actually interesting. The author does a bril-liant job getting into the head of a troubled teen and does not shy away from racy topics.—" (School Library Journal)

★ **You** killed Wesley Payne. Little, Brown 2011 359p il $16.99

Grades: 9 10 11 12   **Fic**
1. School stories 2. Mystery fiction
ISBN 978-0-316-07742-2; 0-316-07742-9

LC 2010-08639

When hard-boiled, seventeen-year-old private investigator Dalton Rev transfers to Salt River High to solve the case of a dead student, he has his hands full trying to outwit the police, negotiate the school's social hierarchy, and get paid.

"This dark, cynical romp is full of clever references and red herrings, which will delight the adult noir fan and pique the curiosities of the observant outcast teen who's looking for a way to infiltrate the in-crowd." Kirkus

Beaufrand, M. J.

The **rise** and fall of the Gallivanters; M.J. Beaufrand. Harry N. Abrams, Inc. 2015 288 p. (hardcover: alk. paper) $16.95

Grades: 9 10 11 12   **Fic**
1. Punk rock music -- Fiction 2. Missing children -- Fiction 3. Sick -- Ficiton 4. Friendship -- Fiction 5. Bands (Music) -- Fiction 6. Family problems -- Fiction
ISBN 1419714953; 9781419714955

LC 2014013556

In this novel, by M. J. Beaufrand, "in Portland in 1983, girls are disappearing. Noah, a teen punk with a dark past, becomes obsessed with finding out where they've gone--and he's convinced their disappearance has something to do with the creepy German owners of a local brewery, the PfefferBrau Haus. . . . When the PfefferBrau Haus opens its doors for a battle of the bands, Noah pulls his band, the Gallivanters, back together in order to get to the bottom of the mystery." (Publisher's note)

"Beaufrand's masterful pace compels readers toward the satisfying though heartbreaking conclusion, prodding them to question throughout whether Noah's story takes place in reality or in a dissociative hellscape. A chilling yet poignant story about the suffering in front of us that we can't bear to see." Kirkus

Bechard, Margaret

Hanging on to Max. Simon Pulse 2003 204p pa $6.99

Grades: 7 8 9 10   **Fic**
1. Infants -- Fiction 2. Teenage fathers -- Fiction
ISBN 0-689-86268-7

First published 2002 by Roaring Brook Press

When his girlfriend decides to give their baby away, seventeen-year-old Sam is determined to keep him and raise him alone.

"An easy read filled with practical wisdom, this book is highly recommended as an important edition for any adolescent classroom collection." ALAN

Bedford, K. A.

Time machines repaired while-u-wait. EDGE Science Fiction and Fantasy Pub. 2008 324p pa $17.95

Grades: 10 11 12 Adult   **Fic**
1. Science fiction
ISBN 978-1-894063-42-5; 1-894063-42-2

"Al 'Spider' Webb is a time machine repairman who happens to detest time machines. On a routine call, he encounters a machine that seems about ready to blow. In order to repair it, he must work with Australian officials to create a small, alternate universe—to protect the rest of the world from the explosion, of course. The job becomes far from normal, though, when it becomes apparent that the explosive device is hiding both another machine and a dead body. The corpse sets off a series of events that sends Spider across alternate realities and puts everyone he cares about at risk." SLJ

Bedford, Martyn

Flip. Wendy Lamb Books 2011 261p $16.99; lib bdg $19.99; ebook $10.99
Grades: 8 9 10 11 12   **Fic**
1. Supernatural -- Fiction 2. Great Britain -- Fiction
ISBN 978-0-385-73990-0; 0-385-73990-7; 978-0-385-90808-5 lib bdg; 0-385-90808-3 lib bdg; 978-0-375-89855-6 ebook; 0-375-89855-7 ebook
LC 2010-13158

A teenager wakes up inside another boy's body and faces a life-or-death quest to return to his true self or be trapped forever in the wrong existence.

"Bedford packs so much exhilarating action and cleanly cut characterizations into his teen debut that readers will be catapulted head-first into Alex's strange new world." Kirkus

Never ending; by Martyn Bedford. Wendy Lamb Books 2014 304 p. (lib. bdg.) $19.99
Grades: 9 10 11 12   **Fic**
1. Grief -- Fiction 2. Guilt -- Fiction 3. Psychotherapy -- Fiction 4. Family problems -- Fiction
ISBN 0385908091; 9780375865534; 9780385739917; 9780385908092
LC 2012047731

In this book, by Martyn Bedford, "Shiv's best mate, her brother Declan, is dead. It's been all over the news. Consumed by grief and guilt, she agrees to become an inpatient at the Korsakoff Clinic. There she meets Mikey. Caron. The others. They share a similar torment. And there, subjected to the clinic's unconventional therapy, they must face what they can't bear to see. Shiv is flooded with memories of Nikos, the beautiful young man on the tour boat. It started there, with him." (Publisher's note)

In the wake of her brother Declan's death, Shiv and five other teens who feel responsible for the deaths of loved ones are inpatients in the new Korsakoff Clinic's first (unorthodox) therapy program. Shiv's activities in the clinic alternate with scenes flashing back toward revelation of what happened to Declan. Bedford writes with insight into and respect for adolescent grief and growth.

Beitia, Sara

The **last** good place of Lily Odilon. Flux 2010 301p pa $9.95
Grades: 8 9 10   **Fic**
1. Mystery fiction 2. Stepfathers -- Fiction 3. Runaway

teenagers -- Fiction 4. Child sexual abuse -- Fiction
ISBN 978-0-7387-2068-5; 0-7387-2068-2
LC 2010-19112

When seventeen-year-old Albert Morales's girlfriend Lily goes missing and he is the main suspect in her disappearance, he must deflect the worries of his angry parents, the suspicions of the police, and Lily's dangerous stepfather as Albert desperately tries to find her, with her sister as his only ally.

"This noir thriller hooks readers with realistic dialogue, fully fleshed characters and plenty of twists. Terrific to the last, good page." Kirkus

Bell, Alden

The **reapers** are the angels; a novel. Alden Bell. Henry Holt and Company 2010 225 p. pa $15
Grades: 10 11 12 Adult   **Fic**
1. Dystopian fiction 2. Zombies -- Fiction 3. Homicide -- Fiction 4. Young women -- Fiction 5. Life -- Fiction 6. Survival -- Fiction 7. Human beings -- Philosophy -- Fiction
ISBN 9780805092431; 0805092439
LC 2009048158

Alex Award (2011)

This book follows "15-year-old Temple," who was "[b]orn into a crumbling society plagued by zombies. . . . When she is assaulted at a safe house, she murders her human attacker, Abraham Todd, and runs from his vengeful brother, Moses. Temple soon acquires a traveling partner, a slow mute by the name of Maury, and begrudgingly takes responsibility for his care, remembering a young boy she swore to protect but couldn't save. Fleeing Moses, the 'meatskins,' and her own battered conscience, Temple still finds moments of simple joy in the brutal world." (Publishers Weekly)

Bell, Hilari

Traitor's son; by Hilari Bell. Houghton 2012 250 p. (The Raven duet) $16.99
Grades: 7 8 9 10 11 12   **Fic**
1. Science fiction 2. Magic -- Fiction 3. Bioterrorism -- Fiction 4. Environmental degradation -- Fiction 5. Native Americans -- Alaska -- Fiction 6. Alaska -- Fiction 7. Shapeshifting -- Fiction 8. Indians of North America -- Alaska -- Fiction
ISBN 9780547196213
LC 2011012241

This book offers a "companion to [the book] 'Trickster's Girl'" where protagonist "Raven works with a different human to try to fix the world's ecosystem." (School Libr J) Terrorists "have released a bioplague that, unchecked, will destroy the world's trees and humanity along with them. . . . Raven, the shape-shifter . . . must persuade the reluctant 16-year-old Jason to accept Atalhanes' quest or doom will follow." (Booklist) Author "[Hilari] Bell blends an advanced technological society with a traditional tribal one." (School Libr J)

Trickster's girl. Houghton Mifflin Harcourt 2011 281p (The Raven duet) $16
Grades: 7 8 9 10   **Fic**
1. Fantasy fiction 2. Magic -- Fiction 3. Bereavement

-- Fiction 4. Environmental degradation -- Fiction
ISBN 978-0-547-19620-6; 0-547-19620-2

LC 2010-06785

In the year 2098, grieving her father and angry with her mother, fifteen-year-old Kelsa joins the magical Raven on an epic journey from Utah to Alaska to heal the earth by restoring the flow of magic that humans have disrupted.

The "degree of nuance will sit especially well with readers who prefer their speculative fiction to be character-driven, and they'll appreciate the compelling exploration of the ways the hopeful can cope with uncertainty." Bull Cent Child Books

Bender, Aimee

The **particular** sadness of lemon cake; a novel Aimee Bender. 1st ed. Doubleday 2010 292 p. $25.95

Grades: 10 11 12 Adult   **Fic**
1. Girls 2. Taste 3. Emotions 4. Family life 5. Bildungsromans 6. Taste -- Fiction 7. Family secrets -- Fiction
ISBN 0385501129; 9780385501125

LC 2009032541

Alex Award (2011)

This book follows "young, needy Rose Edelstein, who can literally taste the emotions of whoever prepares her food, giving her unwanted insight into other people's secret emotional lives--including her mother's, whose lemon cake betrays a deep dissatisfaction." (Publishers Weekly) "When her mother begins an affair, Rose can taste that, too. Her brilliant older brother, Joseph, seems to have some type of autism spectrum disorder, though it is never named. Rose grows up and manages what she now considers her food skill, discerning not only the city of production but also the personality and temperament of the growers and pickers. She also draws closer to her father, finally understanding his prepossessions." (Library Journal)

"Nine-year-old Rose Edelstein bids adieu to normality after taking a bite of her mother's lemon cake. Immediately, she is overwhelmed by the emptiness of her mother's life. All food has this effect on her. She can taste emotions, particularly those that are hidden or repressed. . . . While the time period is never specified — the book appears to open in the 1970s — the setting is forever-sunny Los Angeles. Until the emergence of her super sense, Rose had been the unexceptional child of a supposedly unexceptional nuclear family. As we follow her into maturity, however, she discovers she has more in common with her father and her brother Joseph than previously thought. Each of them possesses a special ability as well." Miami Herald

Bennett Wealer, Sara

Rival. HarperTeen 2011 327p $16.99

Grades: 7 8 9 10   **Fic**
1. School stories 2. Singing -- Fiction 3. Contests -- Fiction 4. Friendship -- Fiction 5. Popularity -- Fiction
ISBN 978-0-06-182762-4

LC 2010-03092

Two high school rivals compete in a prestigious singing competition while reflecting on the events that turned them from close friends to enemies the year before.

"Through Kathryn and Brooke's experiences, teens will learn the important lesson that what you see is not always

what you get. This is a must-have addition to school and public libraries collections alike." Voice Youth Advocates

Bennett, Holly

Shapeshifter. Orca Book Publishers 2010 244p il pa $9.95

Grades: 7 8 9 10   **Fic**
1. Fantasy fiction
ISBN 978-1-55469-158-6; 1-55469-158-3

In order to escape the sorceror who wants to control her gift of song, Sive must transform herself into a deer, leave the Otherworld and find refuge in Eire, the land of mortals.

This is a "rich, slightly revisionist retelling of an ancient Irish legend. Basic human emotions—fear, love, greed—move the tale along, and short first-person narratives that personalize the action are interspersed throughout." Booklist

Benoit, Charles

You. HarperTeen 2010 223p $16.99

Grades: 8 9 10 11 12   **Fic**
1. School stories 2. Conduct of life -- Fiction
ISBN 978-0-06-194704-9; 0-06-194704-0

LC 2009-43990

Fifteen-year-old Kyle discovers the shattering ramifications of the decisions he makes, and does not make, about school, the girl he likes, and his future.

"The rapid pace is well suited to the narrative. . . . In the end, Benoit creates a fully realized world where choices have impact and the consequences of both action and inaction can be severe." SLJ

Benway, Robin

Also known as; by Robin Benway. Walker Books For Young Readers 2013 320 p. (hardcover) $16.99

Grades: 7 8 9 10   **Fic**
1. Spy stories 2. School stories 3. Spies -- Fiction 4. Schools -- Fiction 5. High schools -- Fiction 6. New York (N.Y.) -- Fiction 7. Adventure and adventurers -- Fiction
ISBN 0802733905; 9780802733900

LC 2012026254

In this book, "Maggie is a safecracking prodigy and the only child of parents who work as spies for an organization called the Collective. When the family relocates to New York City, 16-year-old Maggie lands her first assignment: befriending Jesse, a cute private school boy, to gain access to the e-mail belonging to his magazine editor father, who is suspected to be planning a revealing story about the Collective." (Publishers Weekly)

"While the framework requires more than a little suspension of disbelief, the absolutely delightful cast of characters and snappy dialogue transform this book into a huge success." SLJ

Audrey, wait! Razorbill 2008 313p

Grades: 9 10 11 12   **Fic**
1. Rock musicians -- Fiction 2. Dating (Social customs) -- Fiction
ISBN 9781595141910; 9781595141927

LC 2007-23912

While trying to score a date with her cute coworker at the Scooper Dooper, sixteen-year-old Audrey gains unwanted fame and celebrity status when her ex-boyfriend, a rock musician, records a breakup song about her that soars to the top of the Billboard charts.

"Audrey's narration is swift, self-aware, and contemporary in its touch of ironic distance as well as in its style. . . . Current, fresh, and funny, this will rocket up the charts." Bull Cent Child Books

Benwell, Sarah
★ The **last** leaves falling; by Sarah Benwell. SSBFYR 2015 368 p. (hardcover) $17.99
Grades: 7 8 9 10 11 12   **Fic**
1. Friendship -- Fiction 2. Terminally ill -- Fiction 3. Amyotrophic lateral sclerosis 4. Single-parent families -- Fiction 5. Mother-son relationship -- Fiction 6. Japan -- Fiction 7. Assisted suicide -- Fiction 8. Mothers and sons -- Fiction 9. Online chat groups -- Fiction 10. Amyotrophic lateral sclerosis -- Fiction
ISBN 9781481430654; 9781481430661
LC 2014022950

In this novel, by Sarah Benwell, is "infused with the haunting grace of samurai death poetry and the noble importance of friendship. Abe Sora is going to die, and he's only seventeen years old. Diagnosed with ALS (Lou Gehrig's disease), he's already lost the use of his legs, which means he can no longer attend school." (Publisher's note)

"References to samurai culture and snippets of poetry will leave readers at peace with the drifting ending. Benwell's gentle treatment of friendship and death with dignity will touch fans of John Green's The Fault in Our Stars (2012)." Kirkus

Berk, Josh
★ The **dark** days of Hamburger Halpin. Alfred A. Knopf 2010 250p $16.99; lib bdg $19.99
Grades: 8 9 10 11 12   **Fic**
1. School stories 2. Deaf -- Fiction
ISBN 978-0-375-85699-0; 0-375-85699-4; 978-0-375-95699-7 lib bdg; 0-375-95699-9 lib bdg
LC 2009-3118

"A coming-of-age mash-up of satire, realistic fiction, mystery, and ill-fated teen romance, The Dark Days of Hamburger Halpin is a genre-bending breakthrough that teens are going to love." SLJ

Guy Langman, crime scene procrastinator; Josh Berk. Alfred A. Knopf 2012 230 p. (lib. bdg.) $19.99
Grades: 7 8 9 10 11 12   **Fic**
1. Clubs -- Fiction 2. Teenagers -- Fiction 3. Bereavement -- Fiction 4. Forensic sciences -- Fiction 5. Father-son relationship -- Fiction 6. Death -- Fiction 7. Grief -- Fiction 8. Humorous stories 9. New Jersey -- Fiction 10. Fathers and sons -- Fiction 11. Mystery and detective stories
ISBN 037585701X; 9780375857010; 9780375897757; 9780375957017
LC 2011023864

This young adult presents "wisecracking humor, teenage insecurity, and the occasional corpse. When underachieving class clown Guy Langman joins his school's forensics club, it's both to help deal him with the death of his father

and to meet girls. Unfortunately, his plan to get closer to the lovely Raquel Flores fails when she falls for his best friend, Anoop. Guy throws himself into the lesson plan, mastering the art of fingerprinting and using his knowledge to pry into the mysteries of his father's checkered past. Then, during a forensics competition, he finds a real dead body. Convinced that recent events tie into one another, Guy tries to get to the heart of the matter, with help from the rest of the club." (Publishers Weekly)

Bernard, Romily
Find me; Romily Bernard. HarperTeen, an imprint of HarperCollinsPublishers 2013 320 p. (hardback) $17.99
Grades: 7 8 9 10 11 12   **Fic**
1. Foster children -- Fiction 2. Teenagers -- Suicide -- Fiction 3. Computer hackers -- Fiction 4. Foster home care -- Fiction 5. Mystery and detective stories
ISBN 0062229036; 9780062229038
LC 2013021519

In this book, "Tessa Waye was Wicket Tate's best friend until five years ago when Wick's drug-dealing father drove them apart. When Tessa commits suicide and her diary is left on the teen's front steps, Wick suspects there might be a dark reason she jumped to her death. Wick and her sister, Lily, are now free of their criminal father, living a shiny new life on the ritzy side of town with their foster parents. But Wick . . . fears her father will come back for them." (School Library Journal)

Berry, Julie
All the truth that's in me; by Julie Berry. Viking 2013 288 p. (hardcover: alk. paper) $17.99
Grades: 7 8 9 10 11 12   **Fic**
1. Truth -- Fiction 2. Kidnapping -- Fiction 3. Community life -- Fiction 4. War -- Fiction 5. Selective mutism -- Fiction
ISBN 0670786152; 9780670786152
LC 2012043218

In this book by Julie Berry, "sixteen-year-old Judith is still in love with Lucas, even after his father held her prisoner for two years and violently silenced her by cutting out part of her tongue. Another girl went missing at the same time and her body was found washed down a stream. Only Judith knows the truth of what happened to Lottie, but her muteness leaves her an outcast in the village, even from her own mother, and the truth stays bottled up inside her." (School Library Journal)

"Berry's novel is set in a claustrophobic village that seems to resemble an early American colonial settlement. Readers gradually learn "all the truth" from eighteen-year-old narrator Judith, who speaks directly (though only in her head) to her love, Lucas. Berry keeps readers on edge, tantalizing us with pieces of the puzzle right up until the gripping conclusion." (Horn Book)

★ The **passion** of Dolssa; by Julie Berry. Penguin Group 2016 496 p. (hardcover) $18.99
Grades: 7 8 9 10   **Fic**
1. Faith -- Fiction 2. France -- Fiction 3. Christian heresies 4. Friendship -- Fiction 5. Inquisition -- Fiction 6. F 7. Albigenses -- Fiction 8. Christian

heresies -- Fiction 9. France -- History -- Louis IX, 1226-1270 -- Fiction 10. Provence (France) -- History -- 13th century -- Fiction

ISBN 9780451469922

LC 2015020814

In this book, by Julie Berry, "Dolssa is an upper-crust city girl with a secret lover and an uncanny gift. Branded a heretic, she's on the run from the friar who condemned her mother to death by fire. . . . Botille is a matchmaker and a tavern-keeper, struggling to keep herself and her sisters on the right side of the law in their seaside town of Bajas. When their lives collide . . . Botille rescues a dying Dolssa and conceals her in the tavern." (Publisher's note)

"A (fictional) Catholic mystic, Dolssa de Stigata, escapes being burned as a heretic in 1241 France; mostly, this is the story of Botille, an enterprising young matchmaker from a tiny fishing village who rescues Dolssa. Botille's spirited character, the heart-rending suspense of events, and the terrifying context of the Inquisition in medieval Europe all render the novel irresistibly compelling." Horn Book

Includes bibliographical references

Berry, Nina

The **Notorious** Pagan Jones. Harlequin Books 2015 400 p. $17.99

Grades: 9 10 11 12   **Fic**

1. Cold war -- Fiction 2. Actresses -- Fiction 3. Juvenile delinquency -- Fiction 4. Berlin Wall (1961-1989) -- Fiction

ISBN 0373211430; 9780373211432

In this novel, by Nina Berry, "Pagan will be released from juvenile detention if she accepts a juicy role in a comedy directed by award-winning director Bennie Wexler. The shoot starts in West Berlin in just three days. If Pagan's going to do it, she has to decide fast--and she has to agree to a court-appointed 'guardian,' the handsome yet infuriating Devin, who's too young, too smooth and too sophisticated to be some studio flack." (Publisher's note)

"Scary in all the right places, with a strong setup for the sequel." Kirkus

Betts, A. J.

Zac and Mia; AJ. Betts. Houghton Mifflin Harcourt 2014 304 p. (hardback) $17.99

Grades: 9 10 11 12   **Fic**

1. Friendship -- Fiction 2. Cancer patients -- Fiction 3. Cancer -- Fiction

ISBN 0544331648; 9780544331648

LC 2013050126

In this young adult novel by A. J. Betts, "seventeen-year-old Zac is recovering from a bone marrow transplant when a loud new patient moves into the room next door. While Zac thinks he knows all there is to know about cancer . . . Mia's arrival proves that he does not know everything. The two develop a friendship and learn to see beyond their own sickness and circumstances." (School Library Journal)

"Above average in this burgeoning subgenre; it's the healing powers of friendship, love and family that make this funny-yet-philosophical tale of brutal teen illness stand out." Kirkus

Beyer, Kat

The **demon** catchers of Milan; by Kat Beyer. Egmont, USA 2012 288 p. (Demon catchers of Milan trilogy) (hardcover) $16.99

Grades: 7 8 9 10 11   **Fic**

1. Italy -- Fiction 2. Paranormal fiction 3. Demoniac possession -- Fiction 4. Demonology -- Fiction 5. Milan (Italy) -- Fiction 6. Americans -- Italy -- Fiction 7. Family life -- Italy -- Fiction

ISBN 1606843141; 9781606843147; 9781606843154

LC 2011034348

This book is "a tale of demonic possession and a centuries-old family trade in exorcism." Mia's life "is upended when a horrifying demon enters and nearly kills her. After Giuliano Della Torre and his grandson Emilio, long-estranged relatives from Milan, arrive and drive it out, they talk Mia's reluctant parents into letting her return to Italy with them." She shows a talent for the family business of exorcism. (Kirkus Reviews)

Bick, Ilsa J.

Ashes. Egmont USA 2011 465p $17.99; ebook $9.99

Grades: 8 9 10 11 12   **Fic**

1. Science fiction 2. Zombies -- Fiction 3. Wilderness survival -- Fiction

ISBN 978-1-60684-175-4; 978-1-60684-231-7 ebook

LC 2010-51825

Alex, a resourceful seventeen-year-old running from her incurable brain tumor, Tom, who has left the war in Afghanistan, and Ellie, an angry eight-year-old, join forces after an electromagnetic pulse sweeps through the sky and kills most of the world's population, turning some of those who remain into zombies and giving the others superhuman senses.

"Bick delivers an action-packed tale of an apocalypse unfolding. . . . [She] doesn't shy away from gore—one woman's guts 'boiled out in a dusky, desiccated tangle, like limp spaghetti'—but it doesn't derail the story's progress." Publ Wkly

Draw the dark. Carolrhoda Lab 2010 338p $16.95

Grades: 8 9 10 11 12   **Fic**

1. Jews -- Fiction 2. Crime -- Fiction 3. Artists -- Fiction 4. Wisconsin -- Fiction 5. Supernatural -- Fiction

ISBN 0-7613-5686-X; 978-0-7613-5686-8

LC 2009-51612

Seventeen-year-old Christian Cage lives with his uncle in Winter, Wisconsin, where his visions, dreams and unusual paintings draw him into a mystery involving German prisoners of war, a mysterious corpse, and Winter's last surviving Jew. "Grades eight to twelve." (Bull Cent Child Books)

"The novel brilliantly strikes a compelling balance between fantasy and contemporary fiction. Readers will be on the edge of their seats waiting to find out what happens next and will clamor for a sequel to follow Christian into the sideways place." SLJ

The **Sin** eater's confession; by Ilsa J. Bick. Carolrhoda Lab 2013 320 p. (trade hard cover: alk. paper) $17.95

Grades: 9 10 11 12 **Fic**
1. Hate crimes -- Fiction 2. Homosexuality -- Fiction
3. Conduct of life -- Fiction 4. Murder -- Fiction 5.
Wisconsin -- Fiction 6. Photography -- Fiction 7. Farm
life -- Wisconsin -- Fiction
ISBN 0761356878; 9780761356875
LC 2012015291
In this novel, by Isla J. Bick, "Ben . . . likes helping the
stern Mr. and Mrs. Lange and their 15-year-old son, Jimmy.
When Jimmy wins a national photography contest with sensual photographs of his own father and Ben . . . , rumors . . .
start circulating about Ben, who then distances himself from
Jimmy. When Ben witnesses a horrific crime and does noth-
ing, his life spins out of control; he begins to doubt himself,
his senses, his motives . . . even his connection to reality."
(Kirkus Reviews)

Bickle, Laura
The **hallowed** ones; Laura Bickle. Graphia
2012 311 p. (paperback) $8.99
Grades: 7 8 9 10 11 12 **Fic**
1. Horror stories 2. Amish -- Fiction 3. Terrorism
-- Fiction 4. Family life -- Fiction 5. Bioterrorism
-- Fiction 6. Coming of age -- Fiction 7. Christian life
-- Fiction 8. Communicable diseases -- Fiction
ISBN 0547859260; 9780547859262
LC 2012014800
This book follows "Katie [who] is [about] to taste the
freedom of rumspringa, [when] the elders close the gates
of her small Amish community. . . . Katie daringly ventures
Outside to find true horror: vampires have decimated a small
nearby town and apparently much of the world's population.
. . . Her situation is further complicated when she rescues
Alex, a handsome Outsider who may or may not be a carrier
of the contagion that seemingly caused the vampirism epidemic." (Bulletin of the Center for Children's Books)

The **outside**; Laura Bickle. Houghton Mifflin
Harcourt 2013 320 p. (hardcover) $16.99
Grades: 7 8 9 10 11 12 **Fic**
1. Horror fiction 2. Paranormal fiction 3. Vampires
-- Fiction 4. Horror stories 5. Amish -- Fiction 6.
Coming of age -- Fiction 7. Christian life -- Fiction
ISBN 0544000137; 9780544000131
LC 2012040065
Sequel to: The hallowed ones
This book is a sequel to Laura Bickle's "The Hallowed
Ones." Katie, an exile from an Amish community, travels
with "Alex and Ginger, the two outsiders she's befriended,
seeking other survivors of the vampire plague that's unmade
their world. . . . Discovering a group that's genetically engineered with immunity to vampires raises tension between
them, pitting science against religion: Are these vampires
aliens or mutants spawned in labs, rather than manifestations
of demonic evil?" (Kirkus Reviews)

Bigelow, Lisa Jenn
Starting from here; by Lisa Jenn Bigelow. Marshall Cavendish Children 2012 282 p. (hardcover)
$16.99
Grades: 8 9 10 11 12 **Fic**
1. School stories 2. Lesbians -- Fiction 3. Self-

realization -- Fiction 4. Dogs -- Fiction 5. Schools
-- Fiction 6. High schools -- Fiction 7. Fathers and
daughters -- Fiction 8. Dating (Social customs) --
Fiction
ISBN 0761462333; 9780761462330; 9780761462347
LC 2011040129
In this book by Lisa Jenn Bigelow, "Colby is about ready
to give up on people: her girlfriend Rachel dumps her and
immediately moves onto Colby's opposite (a nice Jewish
guy who does well in school), her mom is dead, and her dad
is a frequently absent truck driver to whom she still hasn't
come out. Only her best friend, Van, can bring her out of her
shell. Then she adopts Mo, a friendly but wary stray dog,
and life starts to move again." (Bulletin of the Center for
Children's Books)

Bilen, Tracy
What she left behind; Tracy Bilen. Simon Pulse
2012 237 p. $9.99
Grades: 9 10 11 12 **Fic**
1. Fathers -- Fiction 2. Missing persons -- Fiction 3.
Domestic violence -- Fiction 4. Family violence --
Fiction
ISBN 1442439513; 9781442439511
LC 2011028989
This book follows Sara, whose mother goes missing just
before their planned escape from her abusive father. "Sara
works to protect herself while trying to find her mother. Her
one lifeline in her increasingly isolated world is her friend
Zach, her brother's former best friend. Negotiating her father's abuse, her missing mother, and a burgeoning romantic
relationship with a new guy, Sara's juggling act takes all of
her strength and wits to survive." (School Library Journal)
"Sharp prose and an increasingly tense plot make this
debut a page-turner." Pub Wkly

Billingsley, Franny
★ **Chime**. Dial Books for Young Readers 2011
361p $17.99
Grades: 7 8 9 10 11 12 **Fic**
1. Guilt -- Fiction 2. Twins -- Fiction 3. Sisters --
Fiction 4. Stepmothers -- Fiction 5. Supernatural --
Fiction
ISBN 0-8037-3552-9; 978-0-8037-3552-1
LC 2010-12140
"Since her stepmother's recent death, 17-year-old Briony Larkin knows that if she can keep two secrets--that she
is a witch and that she is responsible for the accident that
left Rose, her identical twin, mentally compromised--and remember to hate herself always, no other harm will befall her
family in their Swampsea parsonage at the beginning of the
twentieth century. The arrival of Mr. Clayborne, a city engineer, and his university-dropout son, Eldric, makes Briony's
task difficult." (Booklist)
"Filled with eccentric characters—self-hating Briony
foremost—and oddly beautiful language, this is a darkly beguiling fantasy." Publ Wkly

Bingham, Kelly
Formerly shark girl; Kelly Bingham. Candlewick Press 2013 352 p. (reinforced) $16.99

Grades: 7 8 9 10   **Fic**
1. Artists -- Fiction 2. Shark attacks -- Fiction
ISBN 0763653624; 9780763653620

LC 2012952049

This book is the sequel to Kelly Bingham's "Shark Girl" and "chronicles Jane's recovery from her injuries." Jane struggles with boyfriends and with her future: Will she become a nurse or continue as an artist even though she has lost her drawing hand? Her artwork continues to improve, but she feels obligated to give back to others what she received from the doctors and nurses who saved her life when she lost her right arm to a shark." (Kirkus)

Shark girl. Candlewick Press 2007 276p $16.99; pa $8.99

Grades: 7 8 9 10   **Fic**
1. Novels in verse 2. Artists -- Fiction 3. Amputees -- Fiction
ISBN 978-0-7636-3207-6; 0-7636-3207-4; 978-0-7636-4627-1 pa; 0-7636-4627-X pa

LC 2006049120

After a shark attack causes the amputation of her right arm, fifteen-year-old Jane, an aspiring artist, struggles to come to terms with her loss and the changes it imposes on her day-to-day life and her plans for the future.

"In carefully constructed, sparsely crafted free verse, Bingham's debut novel offers a strong view of a teenager struggling to survive and learn to live again." Booklist

Birch, Carol

Jamrach's menagerie. Doubleday 2011 295 p. ill pa $15; $25.95

Grades: 11 12 Adult   **Fic**
1. Exotic animals 2. Dragons -- Fiction 3. Historical fiction 4. Sailors -- Fiction 5. Whaling -- Fiction 6. Friendship -- Fiction 7. Exotic animals -- Fiction
ISBN 9780307743176; 9780385534406; 0-385-53440-X

LC 2010038082

This is a novel by the author of Turn Again Home (2003) and Scapegallows (2007). "Following an incident with an escaped tiger, nineteenth-century London street urchin Jaffy Brown goes to work for Mr. Charles Jamrach, the famed importer of exotic animals, alongside Tim, a good but sometimes spitefully competitive boy. Mr. Jamrach recruits the two boys to capture a fabled dragon during the course of a three-year whaling expedition to the Dutch East Indies. They succeed in catching the reptilian beast, but when the ship's whaling venture falls short of expectations, the crew begins to regard the dragon—seething with feral power in its cage—as bad luck." (Publisher's note)

Bjorkman, Lauren

Miss Fortune Cookie; Lauren Bjorkman. Henry Holt and Co. 2012 279 p. (hardcover) $16.99

Grades: 9 10 11 12   **Fic**
1. School stories 2. Female friendship -- Fiction 3. Friendship -- Fiction 4. Advice columns -- Fiction 5. Chinese Americans -- Fiction 6. San Francisco (Calif.) -- Fiction 7. Interpersonal relations -- Fiction 8.

Chinatown (San Francisco, Calif.) -- Fiction
ISBN 0805089519; 9780805089516; 9780805096361

LC 2012006327

In this book, "Erin and her best friends, Linny and Mei, live in San Francisco's Chinatown and are" deciding where to go to college. Mei was accepted to Harvard, but "would rather attend Stanford in order to be near her secret boyfriend, Darren . . . . When Erin, who anonymously writes the advice blog Miss Fortune Cookie, answers a letter that she believes is from Mei and Mei seems to follow the advice by announcing her plan to elope with Darren, Erin is shocked." (School Library Journal)

My invented life. Henry Holt 2009 232p $17.99

Grades: 9 10 11 12   **Fic**
1. Poets 2. Authors 3. Dramatists 4. School stories 5. Sisters -- Fiction 6. Theater -- Fiction
ISBN 978-0-8050-8950-9; 0-8050-8950-0

LC 2008-50279

During rehearsals for Shakespeare's "As You Like It," sixteen-year-old Roz, jealous of her cheerleader sister's acting skills and heartthrob boyfriend, invents a new identity, with unexpected results.

"Narrator Roz is funny, well intentioned, and likable despite her cluelessness, and she is surrounded by a realistic cast of adult and teen characters representing a wide variety of viewpoints and sexual preferences. This is an enjoyable read that will be especially appealing to theater aficionados." SLJ

Black, Holly, 1971-

Black heart; Holly Black. Margaret K. McElderry Books 2012 296 p. (The curse workers) (hardcover) $17.99

Grades: 7 8 9 10   **Fic**
1. Love stories 2. Science fiction 3. Brothers -- Fiction 4. Organized crime -- Fiction 5. Love -- Fiction 6. Criminals -- Fiction
ISBN 9781442403468; 9781442403482

LC 2011028143

This book, the final volume of the Curse Workers trilogy, continues to follow "Cassel . . . [who has] figured out the truth about himself and signed on as a Fed-in-training, as has his charming and utterly unreliable older brother. But of course things don't go as planned; there are a lot of long cons Cassel has set in play or disrupted whose ripples are still being felt. And there's Lila, Cassel's best friend and the love of his life, who is also the rising head of a crime family" and who hates Cassel's guts." (Kirkus)

★ The **coldest** girl in Coldtown; by Holly Black. 1st ed. Little Brown & Co 2013 432 p. (hardcover) $19

Grades: 9 10 11 12   **Fic**
1. Paranormal fiction 2. Vampires -- Fiction 3. Love -- Fiction
ISBN 0316213101; 9780316213103

LC 2012043790

In this book by Holly Black, the vampires live in government-created ghettos called Coldtowns. "Seventeen-year-old Tana wakes up after a wild night of partying to discover that almost everyone in attendance has been killed by vampires. . . . Wandering through the carnage, she finds her infected ex-boyfriend, Aiden, and a mysterious, half-mad vampire named Gavriel chained in a bedroom. Escaping the massacre, Tana drives them to the nearest Coldtown," risking her life. (Publishers Weekly)

Red glove. Margaret K. McElderry Books 2011 325p (The curse workers) $17.99

Grades: 7 8 9 10   **Fic**

1. Science fiction 2. Magic -- Fiction 3. Brothers -- Fiction 4. Criminals -- Fiction

ISBN 1-4424-0339-X; 978-1-4424-0339-0

LC 2010-31884

Sequel to: White cat (2010)

When federal agents learn that seventeen-year-old Cassel Sharpe, a powerful transformation worker, may be of use to them, they offer him a deal to join them rather than the mobsters for whom his brothers work.

This offers "a sleek a stylish blend of urban fantasy and crime noir." Booklist

★ The **white** cat. Margaret K. McElderry Books 2010 310p (The curse workers) $17.99

Grades: 7 8 9 10   **Fic**

1. Science fiction 2. Memory -- Fiction 3. Brothers -- Fiction 4. Criminals -- Fiction 5. Swindlers and swindling -- Fiction

ISBN 978-1-416-96396-7; 1-416-96396-0

LC 2009-33979

When Cassel Sharpe discovers that his older brothers have used him to carry out their criminal schemes and then stolen his memories, he figures out a way to turn their evil machinations against them.

This "starts out with spine-tingling terror, and information is initially dispensed so sparingly, readers will be hooked." Booklist

Another title in this series is:

Red glove (2011)

Blagden, Scott

Dear Life, You Suck; Scott Blagden. Houghton Mifflin Harcourt 2013 320 p. $16.99

Grades: 9 10 11 12   **Fic**

1. Orphans -- Fiction 2. Church schools -- Fiction 3. Teenagers -- Conduct of life -- Fiction 4. Nuns -- Fiction 5. Maine -- Fiction 6. Bullies -- Fiction 7. Schools -- Fiction 8. Conduct of life -- Fiction 9. Catholic schools -- Fiction 10. Emotional problems -- Fiction

ISBN 0547904312; 9780547904313

LC 2013003903

This book portrays "a teen trying to figure out his place in the world and his sense of morality. . . . Cricket has lived in a Catholic church-run orphanage for years, and now that he's a senior, he's not sure if his future lies in being a drug dealer, a boxer, or in ending his own life. Other than sparring, Cricket is only motivated to watch old movies and watch out for the younger kids in the orphanage." (Publishers Weekly)

"With no plans for the future and an inability to comprehend a world in which he gets in trouble for standing up to bullies, delinquent orphan Cricket, almost eighteen, contemplates ending it all. However, he starts to reconsider when his longtime crush suddenly begins talking to him.

Alternately comedic and tragic, Cricket's profane but inventive narration crafts a heartrending portrait of the antihero." (Horn Book)

Blair, Jamie

Leap of Faith; Jamie Blair. Simon & Schuster 2013 240 p. (hardcover) $16.99

Grades: 9 10 11 12   **Fic**

1. Kidnapping -- Fiction 2. Children of drug addicts -- Fiction 3. Runaways -- Fiction 4. Parenting -- Fiction 5. Fugitives from justice -- Fiction

ISBN 1442447133; 1442447168; 9781442447134; 9781442447165

LC 2012043125

In this book, "17-year old Faith recounts her grim life with her abusive, drug-addicted mother and the circumstances that motivate her to flee. Although inured to her mother's frequent male visitors, Faith longs to save the baby her mother is carrying (for pay) for a guy that Faith considers 'drug-dealing scum.' Kidnapping the newborn from the hospital, Faith drives from Ohio to Florida, determined to start a new life with baby Addy." (Publishers Weekly)

Blankman, Anne

Conspiracy of blood and smoke; by Anne Blankman. Balzer + Bray, an imprint of HarperCollinsPublishers 2015 416 p. (hardcover) $17.99

Grades: 9 10 11 12   **Fic**

1. Love -- Fiction 2. Mystery fiction 3. National socialism -- Fiction 4. Germany -- History -- 1918-1933 -- Fiction 5. Nazis -- Fiction

ISBN 0062278843; 9780062278845

LC 2014038687

Sequel to: Prisoner of night and fog

In this book, by Anne Blankman, "Gretchen Whitestone has a secret: She used to be part of Adolf Hitler's inner circle. More than a year after she made an enemy of her old family friend and fled Munich, she lives in England, posing as an ordinary German immigrant, and is preparing to graduate from high school. Her love, Daniel, is a reporter in town. . . . But then Daniel gets a telegram that sends him back to Germany, and Gretchen's world turns upside down." (Publisher's note)

"Suspenseful and clever, intertwining historical truth with action-packed shootouts." Kirkus

Includes bibliographical references

Prisoner of night and fog; Anne Blankman. Balzer + Bray, an imprint of HarperCollinsPublishers 2014 416 p. (hardback) $17.99

Grades: 7 8 9 10 11 12   **Fic**

1. Love stories 2. National socialists -- Fiction 3. Germany -- History -- 1918-1933 -- Fiction 4. Love -- Fiction 5. Nazis -- Fiction 6. Jews -- Germany -- Fiction

ISBN 0062278819; 9780062278814

LC 2013043071

Sequel: Conspiracy of Blood and Smoke (2015)

This book, by Anne Blankman, is a "historical thriller set in 1930s Munich. . . . Gretchen Müller grew up in the National Socialist Party under the wing of her uncle Dolf, who has kept her family cherished and protected from the darker side of society ever since her father traded his life for Dolf's. But Uncle Dolf is none other than Adolf Hitler. And Gretchen follows his every command." (Publisher's note)

"It takes moxie to feature Adolf Hitler as a lead character, but that's just what debut author Blankman does, rejecting the safer route of hiding him offstage. It's a winning gamble, providing a fictionalized portrait of a man both approachably normal and chillingly unknowable...There is much to like here: the realistic changing of Gretchen's ingrained beliefs, the icy fright of her psychotic Nazi brother, side roles for everyone from Rudolf Hess to Eva Braun, and Blankman's exhaustive research. If it feels incomplete, that's because (thankfully) more is coming." Booklist

Bliss, Bryan

No parking at the end times; Bryan Bliss. First edition Greenwillow Books, an imprint of Harper-Collins Publishers 2015 272 p. (hardback) $17.99

Grades: 9 10 11 12   **Fic**

1. Faith -- Fiction 2. Twins -- Fiction 3. Swindlers and swindling -- Fiction 4. Family problems -- Fiction 5. Homeless persons -- Fiction 6. Brothers and sisters -- Fiction 7. San Francisco (Calif.) -- Fiction

ISBN 0062275410; 9780062275417

LC 2014037503

In this book by Bryan Bliss, "Abigail and her twin brother, Aaron, live in a van in San Francisco, begging for meals from local churches and waiting for the end of the world with their fervently religious father and dutiful mother. After their zealot preacher's prediction falls short, the teens approach their breaking points, desperate for some semblance of normalcy." (Publishers Weekly)

"Bliss's depiction of a middle-class, suburban family's transition to life on the inhospitable San Francisco streets is nuanced and character-driven; the tightly focused first-person narration centers the story squarely on Abigail as she gathers the courage to choose between her family and her future. Bliss's debut explores family, sacrifice, and the power of everyday faith with a deft and sensitive hand." Horn Book

Block, Francesca Lia

Dangerous angels; the Weetzie Bat books. Revised paperback ed.; HarperTeen 2010 478p pa $9.99

Grades: 9 10 11 12   **Fic**

1. Friendship -- Fiction 2. Los Angeles (Calif.) -- Fiction

ISBN 978-0-06-200740-7

This compilation first published 1998

This is an omnibus edition of five Weetzie Bat books.

The **island** of excess love; Francesca Lia Block. Henry Holt Books for Young Readers 2014 240 p. (hardback) $16.99

Grades: 8 9 10 11 12   **Fic**

1. Roman mythology 2. Adventure fiction 3. Love -- Fiction 4. Science fiction 5. Visions -- Fiction 6. Survival -- Fiction 7. Friendship -- Fiction 8. Los Angeles (Calif.) -- Fiction

ISBN 0805096310; 9780805096316

LC 2014005284

Companion to: Love in the Time of Global Warming

"Pen has lost her parents. She's lost her eye. But she has fought Kronen; she has won back her fragile friends and her beloved brother. Now Pen, Hex, Ash, Ez, and Venice are living in the pink house by the sea, getting by on hard work, companionship, and dreams. Until the day a foreboding ship appears in the harbor across from their home." (Publisher's note) The book is a companion to "Love in the Time of Global Warming."

"Just as Block's earlier novel was loosely based on The Odyssey, this is even more loosely based on The Aeneid. The result is a mesmerizing, magical, and mysterious tale of love and loss, stories and visions, and betrayal and redemption, all told in the author's signature lyrical voice." Booklist

★ **Love** in the time of global warming; Francesca Lia Block. Henry Holt and Co. 2013 240 p. (hardcover) $16.99

Grades: 8 9 10 11 12   **Fic**

1. Apocalyptic fiction 2. Voyages and travels -- Fiction 3. Love -- Fiction 4. Science fiction 5. Families -- Fiction 6. Survival -- Fiction 7. Earthquakes -- Fiction 8. Los Angeles (Calif.) -- Fiction

ISBN 0805096272; 9780805096279

LC 2012047808

Rainbow List (2014)

In this book, after "an earthquake and tidal wave destroy much of Los Angeles, Penelope—now going by Pen—sets out to find her family. In the course of a journey that explicitly parallels the one described in Homer's Odyssey, Pen navigates the blighted landscape with a crew of three other searchers. . . . Eventually they arrive in Las Vegas (the contemporary stand-in for the land of the dead) where Pen confronts the evil genius behind her world's destruction." (Publishers Weekly)

"In this Odyssey-inspired story, after the devastating Earth Shaker, Penelope sets out into the brutal Los Angeles landscape in search of her family. She meets an intriguing boy named Hex who joins her on her journey. Block's imagery is remarkable in this sophisticated melding of post-apocalyptic setting, re-imagined classic, and her signature magical realism." (Horn Book)

Missing Angel Juan. HarperCollins Pubs. 1993 138p hardcover o.p. pa $5.99

Grades: 9 10 11 12   **Fic**

1. Ghost stories 2. Friendship -- Fiction

ISBN 0-06-023004-5; 0-06-447120-9 pa

LC 92-38299

Sequel to Cherokee Bat and the Goat Guys

ALA YALSA Margaret A. Edwards Award (2005)

This novel "stands alone but really packs a wallop for readers who already know these characters. . . . 'Missing Angel Juan' is imaginative, mystical, and completely engaging. Highly recommended for readers looking for something different." Voice Youth Advocates

Followed by Necklace of kisses

Necklace of kisses; a novel. HarperCollins Pubs. 2005 227p $21.95; pa $12.95

Grades: 9 10 11 12   **Fic**
1. Friendship -- Fiction
ISBN 0-06-077751-6; 0-06-077752-4 pa

LC 2004-59651

Sequel to Missing Angel Juan
Final novel in the series about Weetzie Bat and her Los Angeles friends and lovers. Now 40, Weetzie is "facing a midlife crisis, and so is her boyfriend, Secret Agent Lover Man, who, since 9/11, just sits idly reading the newspaper. She leaves, hoping to find herself, but this time, rather than meditating in the wilderness, she remains in her beloved L.A., moving into the expensive and magical Pink Hotel, where she luxuriates in room service, gets her nails and toenails done, kisses a sushi-eating mermaid, chats to her father's ghost, and gets a necklace of gifts from a diva, an angel, a faun, and more. The self-parody is as wonderful as ever—Weetzie doesn't have to save the world; she can just go shopping—and, as always, the magic is in the detail." Booklist

★ **Teen** spirit; Francesca Lia Block. Harper-Teen, an imprint of HarperCollinsPublishers 2014 240 p. (hardcover bdg.) $17.99
Grades: 9 10 11 12   **Fic**
1. Spirits -- Fiction 2. Grandparent-grandchild relationship -- Fiction 3. Dead -- Fiction 4. Grandmothers -- Fiction 5. Supernatural -- Fiction 6. Beverly Hills (Calif.) -- Fiction 7. Single-parent families -- Fiction 8. Dating (Social customs) -- Fiction
ISBN 0062008099; 9780062008091

LC 2013008057

In this novel, by Francesca Lia Block, when Julie's grandmother Miriam dies, "Julie's entire world is beginning to unravel. . . . [Then] she meets sweetly eccentric Clark, who is also mourning a loss. . . . One night, the two use a Ouija board . . . , believing it's a chance to reach out to her grandmother. But when they get a response, it isn't from Miriam. And Julie discovers that while she has been eager to regain her past, Clark is haunted by his." (Publisher's Note)

"Told in Block's signature, flowing prose, Teen Spirit is a layered story that's more about grief than it is about ghosts. Julie's narration is fast paced and accessible; readers won't be bogged down by intricate plots or complex ghost mythology. This is just a story about two kids learning to deal with loss. Julie realizes she cannot cling to the dead; she must hold her grandmother in her heart as she tries to live her own life. A beautiful story from a legendary young adult author.—" (School Library Journal)

Weetzie Bat. Harper & Row 1989 88p hardcover o.p. pa $7.99
Grades: 9 10 11 12   **Fic**
1. Friendship -- Fiction
ISBN 0-06-020534-2; 0-06-073625-9 pa

LC 88-6214

ALA YALSA Margaret A. Edwards Award (2005)
Follows the wild adventures of Weetzie Bat and her Los Angeles punk friends, Dirk, Duck-Man, and Secret-Agent-Lover-Man

"A brief, off-beat tale that has great charm, poignancy, and touches of fantasy. . . . This creates the ambiance of Hol-lywood with no cynicism, from the viewpoint of denizens who treasure its unique qualities." SLJ

Other titles about Weetzie Bat and her friends are:
Baby be-bop (1995)
Cherokee Bat and the Goat Guys (1992)
Missing Angel Juan (1993)
Necklace of kisses (2005)
Pink smog (2012)
Witch baby (1991)

Bloor, Edward
A **plague** year. Alfred A. Knopf 2011 305p $15.99; lib bdg $10.99
Grades: 6 7 8 9 10   **Fic**
1. School stories 2. Drug abuse -- Fiction 3. Pennsylvania -- Fiction 4. Supermarkets -- Fiction 5. Coal mines and mining -- Fiction
ISBN 978-0-375-85681-5; 0-375-85681-1; 978-0-375-95681-2 lib bdg; 0-375-95681-6 lib bdg

LC 2010050651

A ninth-grader who works with his father in the local supermarket describes the plague of meth addiction that consumes many people in his Pennsylvania coal mining town from 9/11 and the nearby crash of United Flight 93 in Shanksville to the Quecreek Mine disaster in Somerset the following summer.

"The plot is message-heavy but goes down easily because Bloor excels at writing vivid scenes. Tom is a thoroughly sympathetic narrator as he grows to realize there is value in 'blooming where you are planted.'" Publ Wkly

Taken. Alfred A. Knopf 2007 247p $17; pa $8.99
Grades: 6 7 8 9 10   **Fic**
1. Science fiction 2. Kidnapping -- Fiction 3. Social classes -- Fiction
ISBN 978-0-375-83636-7; 0-375-83636-5; 978-0-440-42128-3 pa; 0-440-42128-4 pa

LC 2006-35561

In 2036 kidnapping rich children has become an industry, but when thirteen-year-old Charity Meyers is taken and held for ransom, she soon discovers that this particular kidnapping is not what it seems.

"Deftly constructed, this is as riveting as it is thought-provoking." Publ Wkly

Blume, Judy
Forever; a novel. Atheneum Books for Young Readers $17.99; pa $6.99
Grades: 9 10 11 12   **Fic**
1. Love stories 2. Sex -- Fiction 3. Families -- New Jersey -- Fiction
ISBN 0-689-84973-7; 0-671-69530-4 pa

A reissue of the title first published 1975 by Bradbury Press
ALA YALSA Margaret A. Edwards Award (1996)
The "story of a teenage senior-year love affair based primarily on physical attraction. Once Katherine Danziger and Michael Wagner meet at a party, they have eyes only for each other, and their romance progresses rapidly from kissing to heavy petting to lying together and finally to frequent sexual intercourse after Kath gets the Pill from a Planned

Parenthood officer. . . . Characters—including adults and friends of the protagonists—are well developed, dialog is natural, and the story is convincing; however, the explicit sex scenes will limit this to the mature reader." Booklist

Blumenthal, Deborah

Mafia girl; Deborah Blumenthal. Albert Whitman & Company 2014 256 p. (hardcover) $16.99

Grades: 8 9 10 11   Fic
1. Mafia -- Fiction 2. Family -- Fiction 3. Identity -- Fiction 4. Father-daughter relationship -- Fiction 5. Families -- Fiction
ISBN 0807549118; 9780807549117

LC 2013028440

In this book, by Deborah Blumenthal, "seventeen-year-old Gia is the most hated/loved girl in school. Why? Her father doesn't have a boss. He is the boss - the capo di tutti cappi, boss of all bosses. Not that Gia cares. But life gets complicated when she meets a cop she calls 'Officer Hottie' and feels a suprising chemistry. Then Vogue magazine wants to feature Gia in a fashion spread about real-life bad girls. On top of this, she's running for class president." (Publisher's note)

"Gia, the prized daughter of a New York Mafia boss, enjoys the carefree lifestyle her father's money and connections afford her. When the feds begin to close in on the family business, Gia must find an identity outside of Don's Daughter. Gia's voice is an entertaining, effervescent stream-of-consciousness, but the book's frantic pace muddles too many competing plot lines." Horn Book

Blundell, Judy

Strings attached. Scholastic Press 2011 310p $17.99

Grades: 7 8 9 10   Fic
1. Dance -- Fiction 2. Mafia -- Fiction 3. Homicide -- Fiction 4. New York (N.Y.) -- Fiction 5. Italian Americans -- Fiction
ISBN 978-0-545-22126-9; 0-545-22126-9

LC 2010-41078

Blundell "successfully constructs a complex web of intrigue that connects characters in unexpected ways. History and theater buffs will especially appreciate her attention to detail—Blundell again demonstrates she can turn out first-rate historical fiction." Publ Wkly

★ **What** I saw and how I lied. Scholastic Press 2008 284p $16.99

Grades: 8 9 10 11 12   Fic
1. Mystery fiction 2. Florida -- Fiction
ISBN 978-0-439-90346-2; 0-439-90346-7

LC 2008-08503

In 1947, with her jovial stepfather Joe back from the war and family life returning to normal, teenage Evie, smitten by the handsome young ex-GI who seems to have a secret hold on Joe, finds herself caught in a complicated web of lies whose devastating outcome change her life and that of her family forever.

"Using pitch-perfect dialogue and short sentences filled with meaning, Blundell has crafted a suspenseful, historical mystery." Booklist

Blythe, Carolita

Revenge of a not-so-pretty girl; Carolita Blythe. Delacorte Press 2013 336 p. (library) $19.99; (hardcover) $16.99

Grades: 7 8 9 10 11 12   Fic
1. African American youth -- Fiction 2. Teenagers -- Conduct of life -- Fiction 3. Old age -- Fiction 4. Schools -- Fiction 5. Conduct of life -- Fiction 6. Family problems -- Fiction 7. Catholic schools -- Fiction 8. African Americans -- Fiction 9. Mothers and daughters -- Fiction 10. Brooklyn (New York, N.Y.) -- Fiction
ISBN 037599081X; 9780307978455; 9780375990816; 9780385742863

LC 2012012735

This novel, by Carolita Blythe, follows "an African American girl living in 1980s Brooklyn. . . . Evelyn Ryder used to be a beautiful movie star--never mind that it was practically a lifetime ago. . . . So if you think I feel guilty about mugging her, think again. But for something that should have been so simple, it sure went horribly wrong. . . . That's why I'm returning to the scene of the crime. . . . To see if I might be able to turn my luck around." (Publisher's note)

Bobet, Leah

Above; by Leah Bobet. Arthur A. Levine Books 2012 363 p.

Grades: 9 10 11 12   Fic
1. Fantasy fiction 2. Adventure fiction 3. Storytelling -- Fiction 4. Fantasy
ISBN 0545296706; 9780545296700

LC 2011012955

In this fantasy novel, "Safe is an underground refuge for the sick, the broken, and the freaks, far from the prying eyes of Above. Narrator Matthew is the Teller, responsible for remembering and guarding the stories of his friends and surrogate family. . . . When the only person ever to be exiled from Safe returns at the head of an army of shadows. . . . the group navigates the treacherous world of Above as they seek to reclaim Safe and come to terms with long-hidden truths" (Publishers Weekly)

An **inheritance** of ashes; by Leah Bobet. Clarion Books 2015 400 p. map (hardback) $17.99

Grades: 7 8 9 10 11 12   Fic
1. War stories 2. Fantasy fiction 3. Secrets -- Fiction 4. Sisters -- Fiction 5. Monsters -- Fiction 6. Farm life -- Fiction 7. Fantasy 8. War -- Fiction
ISBN 9780544281110

LC 2015006823

In this book, by Leah Bobet, the "strange war down south—with its rumors of gods and monsters—is over. And while sixteen-year-old Hallie and her sister wait to see who will return from the distant battlefield, they struggle to maintain their family farm. When Hallie hires a veteran to help them, the war comes home in ways no one could have imagined, and soon Hallie is taking dangerous risks—and keeping desperate secrets." (Publisher's note)

"Bobet repeatedly emphasizes the importance family—of blood or of choice—plays in surviving calamity. The satisfying yet realistic ending will leave readers hoping for more." Booklist

Bock, Caroline

LIE. St. Martin's Griffin 2011 211p pa $9.99

Grades: 8 9 10 11 12 **Fic**

1. Homicide -- Fiction 2. Violence -- Fiction 3. Immigrants -- Fiction 4. Prejudices -- Fiction

ISBN 978-0-312-66832-7; 0-312-66832-5

LC 2011019824

Seventeen-year-old Skylar Thompson is being questioned by the police. Her boyfriend, Jimmy, stands accused of brutally assaulting two young El Salvadoran immigrants from a neighboring town, and she's the prime witness.

"This effective, character-driven, episodic story examines the consequences of a hate crime on the teens involved in it. . . . Realistic and devastatingly insightful, this novel can serve as a springboard to classroom and family discussions. Unusual and important." Kirkus

Bodeen, S. A.

The **Compound**. Feiwel and Friends 2008 248p $16.95; pa $8.99

Grades: 7 8 9 10 **Fic**

1. Twins -- Fiction 2. Fathers -- Fiction 3. Survival after airplane accidents, shipwrecks, etc. -- Fiction

ISBN 0-312-37015-6; 0-312-57860-1 pa; 978-0-312-37015-2; 978-0-312-57860-2 pa

LC 2007-36148

After his parents, two sisters, and he have spent six years in a vast underground compound built by his wealthy father to protect them from a nuclear holocaust, fifteen-year-old Eli, whose twin brother and grandmother were left behind, discovers that his father has perpetrated a monstrous hoax on them all.

"The audience will feel the pressure closing in on them as they, like the characters, race through hairpin turns in the plot toward a breathless climax." Publ Wkly

The **raft**; S.A. Bodeen. Feiwel and Friends 2012 231 p. $16.99

Grades: 7 8 9 10 **Fic**

1. Survival skills -- Fiction 2. Wilderness survival -- Fiction 3. Survival after airplane accidents, shipwrecks, etc. -- Fiction

ISBN 0312650108; 9780312650100

This novel, by S. A. Bodeen, is a plane crash survival story. "All systems are go until a storm hits during the flight. The only passenger, Robie doesn't panic until the engine suddenly cuts out and Max shouts at her to put on a life jacket. . . . And then . . . she's in the water. Fighting for her life. Max pulls her onto the raft. . . . They have no water. Their only food is a bag of Skittles. There are sharks. There is an island. But there's no sign of help on the way." (Publisher's note)

Bognanni, Peter

The **house** of tomorrow; Peter Bognanni. Amy Einhorn Books/G.P. Putnam's Sons 2010 354p o.p.; (pbk.) $15

Grades: 11 12 Adult **Fic**

1. Inventors -- Fiction 2. Architects -- Fiction 3. Rock music -- Fiction 4. Adolescence -- Fiction 5. Grandmothers -- Fiction

ISBN 0399156097; 9780425238882

LC 2009023542

Alex Award (2011)

This book follows teenager Sebastian Prendergast, who "lives in Iowa's first geodesic dome with his grandmother, a devout follower of futurist philosopher Buckminster R. Fuller. But when Nana has a stroke, Sebastian is thrown together with Janice and teenage Jared Whitcomb, who were touring the home when Nana was stricken. Soon, Sebastian and Jared form an unlikely bond via the great teenage tradition of punk rock, starting their own band despite the objections of everyone around them and Sebastian's lack of musical ability . . . And while Jared succeeds to some degree in socializing Sebastian—teaching him about music, smoking, and curse words—Sebastian ends up getting more than he bargained for when the two get caught up in Whitcomb family drama." (Publishers Weekly)

Bond, Gwenda

Fallout; by Gwenda Bond. Switch Press, a Capstone imprint 2015 304 p. (Lois Lane) (paper over board) $16.95

Grades: 9 10 11 12 **Fic**

1. School stories 2. Video games -- Fiction 3. Schools -- Fiction 4. Superheroes -- Fiction 5. High schools -- Fiction 6. Virtual reality -- Fiction

ISBN 1630790052; 9781630790059

LC 2014026793

Sequel: Double Down (2016)

In this book, by Gwenda Bond, "Lois Lane is starting a new life in Metropolis. . . . A group known as the Warheads is making life miserable for another girl at school. They're messing with her mind, somehow, via the high-tech immersive videogame they all play. . . . Lois has her sights set on solving this mystery. But sometimes it's all a bit much. Thank goodness for her maybe-more-than-a friend, a guy she knows only by his screenname, SmallvilleGuy." (Publisher's note)

"Once these elements have been set up, it's pretty clear what steps will lead to the happy ending, but to Bond's credit, the dry wit of the narrative and the satisfyingly coy online romance between Lois Lane and Smallville Guy make each of those steps delightful." Booklist

Boone, Martina

Compulsion; Martina Boone. First Simon Pulse Edition Simon Pulse 2014 433 p. (hardback) $17.99

Grades: 9 10 11 12 **Fic**

1. Aunts -- Fiction 2. Orphans -- Fiction 3. Spirits -- Fiction 4. Vendetta -- Fiction 5. Supernatural -- Fiction 6. South Carolina -- Fiction 7. Blessing and cursing -- Fiction 8. Islands -- South Carolina -- Fiction

ISBN 1481411225; 9781481411226; 9781481411240

LC 2014027787

Sequel: Persuasion (2015)

In this book, by Martina Boone, "Barrie Watson has been a virtual prisoner in the house where she lived with her shut-in mother. When her mother dies, Barrie promises to put some mileage on her stiletto heels. But she finds a new kind of prison at her aunt's South Carolina plantation instead--a prison guarded by an ancient spirit who long ago cursed one of the three founding families of Watson Island and gave the others magical gifts that became compulsions." (Publisher's note)

"Though the novel is grounded in the present day, there's an old-fashioned quality to Boone's dialogue and characters; she skillfully blends rich magic and folklore with adventure, sweeping romance, and hidden treasure, all while exploring the island and its accompanying legends. An impressive start to the Heirs of Watson Island series." Publishers Weekly

Booth, Coe
Bronxwood. Push 2011 328p $17.99
Grades: 10 11 12   **Fic**
1. Drug traffic -- Fiction 2. Foster home care -- Fiction 3. African Americans -- Fiction
ISBN 978-0-4399-2534-1
Sequel to Tyrell (2006)
"Action scenes combine with interpersonal exchanges to keep the pace moving forward at a lightning speed, but Booth never sacrifices the street-infused dialogue and emotional authenticity that characterize her works. She has created a compelling tale of a teen still trying to make the right choices despite the painful consequences." SLJ

Kendra. PUSH 2008 292p $16.99
Grades: 8 9 10 11 12   **Fic**
1. New York (N.Y.) -- Fiction 2. Teenage mothers -- Fiction 3. African Americans -- Fiction 4. Mother-daughter relationship -- Fiction
ISBN 978-0-439-92536-5; 0-439-92536-3
LC 2008-12819
High schooler Kendra longs to live with her mother who, unprepared for motherhood at age fourteen, left Kendra in the care of her grandmother.
"The convoluted but redeeming friendship between Kendra and her best friend and aunt, Adonna, resonates with heartbreak and honesty. Teens will appreciate Kendra's internal justification monologues, especially in relation to her Nana. . . . From Bronx blocks to Harlem hangouts, Booth delivers dynamic characters and an engaging story." SLJ

★ **Tyrell**. PUSH 2006 310p hardcover o.p. pa $7.99
Grades: 9 10 11 12   **Fic**
1. Poor -- Fiction 2. Homeless persons -- Fiction 3. African Americans -- Fiction 4. Bronx (New York, N.Y.) -- Fiction
ISBN 0-439-83879-7; 978-0-439-83879-5; 0-439-83880-0 pa; 978-0-439-83880-1 pa
LC 2005-37330
Fifteen-year-old Tyrell, who is living in a Bronx homeless shelter with his spaced-out mother and his younger brother, tries to avoid temptation so he does not end up in jail like his father.
"The immediate first-person narrative is pitch perfect: fast, funny, and anguished (there's also lots of use of the n-word, though the term is employed in the colloquial sense, not as an insult). Unlike many books reflecting the contemporary street scene, this one is more than just a pat situation with a glib resolution; it's filled with surprising twists and turns that continue to the end." Booklist
Followed by Bronxwood (2011)

Bosworth, Jennifer
Struck; Jennifer Bosworth. 1st ed. Farrar Straus Giroux 2012 376 p. (paperback) $9.99; (hardcover) $17.99
Grades: 9 10 11 12   **Fic**
1. Love stories 2. Cults -- Fiction 3. Lightning -- Fiction 4. Supernatural -- Fiction 5. Thunderstorms -- Fiction 6. Brothers and sisters -- Fiction 7. Los Angeles (Calif.) -- Fiction 8. Mothers and daughters -- Fiction
ISBN 9781250027405; 0374372837; 9780374372835; 9781429954709
LC 2011018298
In this book, "[d]oomsday cults play tug-of-war over a teenage girl who loves getting struck by lightning. . . . After lightning hits a fault line and causes a terrible earthquake in Los Angeles . . . Mia attracts attention from both [a] fundamentalist sect and a secret society that opposes them. . . . But mysterious, handsome Jeremy warns her from choosing either side and offers a very sudden relationship." (Kirkus Reviews)

Boulle, Pierre
Planet of the apes; translated by Xan Feilding. Ballantine 2001 268p pa $6.99
Grades: 11 12 Adult   **Fic**
1. Science fiction
ISBN 0-345-44798-0
First published 1963 by Vanguard Press; published in the United Kingdom with title: Monkey planet
"In this Swiftian fable Boulle gives full play to his not inconsiderable gift for irony and satire." Libr J

Bow, Erin
★ The **Scorpion** Rules; by Erin Bow. Simon & Schuster 2015 384 p. $17.99
Grades: 9 10 11 12   **Fic**
1. Fantasy fiction 2. Hostages -- Fiction 3. Princesses -- Fiction 4. Artificial intelligence -- Fiction
ISBN 1481442716; 9781481442718
In this book, by Erin Bow, "Greta is a Duchess and a Crown Princess. She is also a Child of Peace, a hostage held by the de facto ruler of the world, the great Artificial Intelligence, Talis. This is how the game is played: if you want to rule, you must give one of your children as a hostage. Start a war and your hostage dies. . . . Greta will be free if she can make it to her eighteenth birthday. . . . But everything changes when Elian arrives at the Precepture." (Publisher's note)
"Through Greta's conflicts, the author explores what it means to be human and gives readers a glimpse inside the mind of artificial intelligence." Booklist

★ **Sorrow's** knot; Erin Bow. Arthur A. Levine Books 2013 368 p. (hardcover: alk. paper) $17.99
Grades: 8 9 10 11 12   **Fic**
1. Dead 2. Magic 3. Knots and splices 4. Identity -- Fiction 5. Fate and fatalism -- Fiction
ISBN 0545166667; 9780545166669; 9780545166676; 9780545578004
LC 2013007855
In this book, by Erin Bow, "the dead do not rest easy. Every patch of shadow might be home to something hun-

gry, something deadly. Most of the people of this world live on the sunlit, treeless prairies. But a few carve out an uneasy living in the forest towns, keeping the dead at bay with wards made from magically knotted cords. The women who tie these knots are called binders. And Otter's mother, Willow, is one of the greatest binders her people have ever known." (Publisher's note)

"Sorrow's Knot is a dystopian novel that does not deal with the destruction of the broader world. Rather, it delves into the mythology of a group of people and how their prejudices and resistance to change came to be. Readers of suspense will love the dark tension of the story line, an ebb and flow that carries through to the very end.—" (School Library Journal)

Boyd, Maria

★ **Will.** Alfred A. Knopf 2010 300p $16.99; lib bdg $19.99

Grades: 8 9 10 11 12 **Fic**

1. School stories 2. Theater -- Fiction 3. Musicals -- Fiction 4. Australia -- Fiction 5. Homosexuality -- Fiction

ISBN 978-0-375-86209-0; 0-375-86209-9; 978-0-375-96209-7 lib bdg; 0-375-96209-3 lib bdg

LC 2009-39888

Seventeen-year-old Will's behavior has been getting him in trouble at his all-boys school in Sydney, Australia, but his latest punishment, playing in the band for a musical production, gives him new insights into his fellow students and helps him cope with an incident he has tried to forget.

"Readers should find it easy to sympathize with Will's vibrant, deadpan narration and his frequent use of slang, while recognizing that his jocular exterior hides a deeper vulnerability. . . . Boyd effectively handles Will's final outpouring of repressed emotions: the personal growth achieved by her realistic, likeable protagonist is abundantly clear." Publ Wkly

Bradbury, Jennifer

Shift. Atheneum Books for Young Readers 2008 245p $16.99

Grades: 7 8 9 10 11 12 **Fic**

1. Travel -- Fiction 2. Cycling -- Fiction 3. Friendship -- Fiction 4. Missing persons -- Fiction

ISBN 978-1-4169-4732-5; 1-4169-4732-9

LC 2007-23558

When best friends Chris and Win go on a cross country bicycle trek the summer after graduating and only one returns, the FBI wants to know what happened.

"Bradbury's keen details . . . . add wonderful texture to this exciting [novel.] . . . Best of all is the friendship story." Booklist

Bradbury, Ray

★ **Fahrenheit** 451. Ballantine Books 1996 179p pa $15

Grades: 9 10 11 12 Adult **Fic**

1. Science fiction 2. Books and reading -- Fiction

ISBN 978-0-345-41001-6; 0-345-41001-7

LC 96096738

First published 1953

Dystopian novel about a bookburner official in a future fascist state.

Something wicked this way comes. Avon Bks. 1999 293p $15.95; pa $7.99

Grades: 7 8 9 10 **Fic**

1. Horror fiction 2. Fantasy fiction

ISBN 0-380-97727-3; 0-380-72940-7 pa

A reissue of the title first published 1962 by Simon and Schuster

"We read here of the loss of innocence, the recognition of evil, the bond between generations, and the purely fantastic. These forces enter Green Town, Illinois, on the wheels of Cooger and Dark's Pandemonium Shadow Show. Will Halloway and Jim Nightshade, two 13-year-olds, explore the sinister carnival for excitement, which becomes desperation as the forces of the dark threaten to engulf them. Bradbury's gentle humanism and lyric style serve this fantasy well." Shapiro. Fic for Youth. 3d edition

Bradley, Alan

The **sweetness** at the bottom of the pie; Alan Bradley. Delacorte Press 2009 373p (pbk.) $15

Grades: 11 12 Adult **Fic**

1. Mystery fiction 2. Great Britain -- Fiction 3. Stamp collecting -- Fiction 4. England -- Fiction 5. Sisters -- Fiction 6. Poisoning -- Fiction 7. Detectives -- Fiction 8. Detective and mystery stories

ISBN 9780385343497; 9780385342308

LC 2008041787

Agatha Award: Best First Novel (2009)
Arthur Ellis Award: Best First Novel (2010)
Dilys Award (2010)
Macavity Award: Best First Mystery Novel (2010)

This book follows "11-year-old sleuth Flavia de Luce. . . . In an early 1950s English village, Flavia is preoccupied with retaliating against her lofty older sisters when a rude, redheaded stranger arrives to confront her eccentric father, a philatelic devotee. Equally adept at quoting 18th-century works, listening at keyholes and picking locks, Flavia learns that her father, Colonel de Luce, may be involved in the suicide of his long-ago schoolmaster and the theft of a priceless stamp. The sudden expiration of the stranger in a cucumber bed, wacky village characters with ties to the schoolmaster, and a sharp inspector with doubts about the colonel and his enterprising young detective daughter mean complications for Flavia." (Publishers Weekly)

"Mystery fans, Anglophiles, and science buffs will delight in this book and may come away with a slightly altered view of what is possible for a headstrong girl to achieve." SLJ

Other titles about Flavia de Luce are:
The weed that strings the hangman's bag (2010)
A red herring without mustard (2011)
I am half-sick of shadows (2011)
Speaking from among the bones (2013)
The dead in their vaulted arches (2014)
As chimney sweepers come to dust (2015)

Bradley, Marion Zimmer

★ The **mists** of Avalon. Ballantine Pub. Group 2000 876p $30; pa $16.95

Grades: 9 10 11 12 Adult   **Fic**
1. Fantasy fiction 2. Kings 3. Great Britain -- History
-- 0-1066 -- Fiction
ISBN 0-345-44118-4; 0-345-35049-9 pa

LC 00-712415
A reissue of the title first published 1982 by Knopf
This "retelling of the Arthurian legend is dominated by
the character of Morgan le Fay (here called Morgaine), the
powerful sorceress who symbolizes the historical clash between Christianity and the early pagan religions of the British Isles." Publ Wkly

Other novels in the Avalon series written with Diana L.
Paxson are: The forest house (1993); Lady of Avalon (1997);
Priestess of Avalon (2000). Following Bradley's death Pax-
son continued the series with: Ancestors of Avalon (2004);
Ravens of Avalon (2007); Sword of Avalon (2009)

Priestess of Avalon; {by} Marion Zimmer Bradley and Diana L. Paxson. Viking 2001 394p hardcover o.p. pa $15.95
Grades: 11 12 Adult   **Fic**
1. Saints 2. Fantasy fiction 3. Parents of prominent
persons 4. Great Britain -- History -- 0-1066 -- Fiction
ISBN 0-670-91023-6; 0-451-45862-1 pa

LC 00-51254
First published 2000 in the United Kingdom
"Bradley creates a powerful tale of magic and faith that
enlarges upon pagan and Christian traditions to express a
deeper truth. Though Bradley died before she finished the
novel, veteran fantasy author Paxson brings to completion
this last work of a master of the genre." Libr J

Brahmachari, Sita

Jasmine Skies; by Sita Brahmachari. Albert
Whitman & Company 2012 336 p. $16.99
Grades: 6 7 8 9   **Fic**
1. India -- Fiction 2. Family secrets -- Fiction 3.
Interpersonal relations -- Fiction 4. Secrecy 5. Families
-- India 6. Voyages and travels 7. Dysfunctional
families 8. Dating (social customs)
ISBN 0807537829; 1447205189; 9780807537824;
9781447205180

LC 2014013302
"Mira Levenson is excited to visit India for the first time.
But upon arriving she is hurled into new sights, sounds,
sweltering heat and deeply buried family secrets. From the
moment Mira meets Janu she feels an instant connection to
him. Nothing is as she imagined it--and suddenly home feels
a long way away. But Mira is determined to uncover the
truth about her family, and she must also make a decision
that will break someone's heart." (Publisher's note)
"Vivid descriptions of the exotic setting, an emotionally
honest (if naive and stubborn) narrator, and a sweet romance
should captivate readers." Booklist

Brande, Robin

Evolution, me, & other freaks of nature. Alfred
A. Knopf 2007 268p hardcover o.p. pa $7.99
Grades: 7 8 9 10   **Fic**
1. School stories 2. Evolution -- Fiction 3. Christian

life -- Fiction
ISBN 978-0-375-84349-5; 0-375-84349-3; 978-0-375-
94349-2 lib bdg; 0-375-94349-8 lib bdg; 978-0-440-
24030-3 pa; 0-440-24030-1 pa

LC 2006-34158
Following her conscience leads high school freshman
Mena to clash with her parents and former friends from
their conservative Christian church, but might result in better things when she stands up for a teacher who refuses to
include "Intelligent Design" in lessons on evolution.
"Readers will appreciate this vulnerable but ultimately
resilient protagonist who sees no conflict between science
and her own deeply rooted faith." Booklist

Brashares, Ann

Forever in blue; the fourth summer of the Sisterhood. Delacorte Press 2007 384p $18.99; lib bdg
$21.99
Grades: 9 10 11   **Fic**
1. Friendship -- Fiction
ISBN 978-0-385-72936-9; 0-385-72936-7; 978-0-385-
90413-1 lib bdg; 0-385-90413-4 lib bdg

LC 2006-18782
Fourth volume of the Traveling Pants books; Sequel to
Girls in pants (2005)
As their lives take them in different directions, Lena,
Tibby, Carmen, and Bridget discover many more things
about themselves and the importance of their relationship
with each other.
"This light read is a great ending to the series. Sisterhood
followers who are eagerly awaiting this final book will not
be disappointed." Voice Youth Advocates

Girls in pants; the third summer of the Sisterhood. Delacorte Press 2005 338p $16.95; lib bdg
$18.99; pa $8.95
Grades: 9 10 11 12   **Fic**
1. Friendship -- Fiction
ISBN 0-385-72935-9; 0-385-90919-5 lib bdg; 0-553-
37593-8 pa

LC 2004-15296
Third volume of the Traveling Pants books, previous
titles The sisterhood of the travelling pants and The second
summer of the sisterhood
"It's the summer before the Septembers go to college,
a summer in which old and new boyfriends appear, families grow and change, crises occur and are resolved, and
the pants continue their designated rounds. Despite their diverse schedules, the four friends . . . reunite one final weekend before they go off to four different colleges. Readers
of the other books won't be disappointed with these new
adventures." Booklist
Followed by Forever in blue (2007)

The **second** summer of the sisterhood. Delacorte
Press 2003 373p $15.95; lib bdg $17.99; pa $8.95
Grades: 9 10 11 12   **Fic**
1. Friendship -- Fiction
ISBN 0-385-72934-0; 0-385-90852-0 lib bdg; 0-385-
73105-1 pa

LC 2003-535308

"Brashares has done an outstanding job of showing the four teens growing up and giving readers a happy, ultimately hopeful book, easy to read and gentle in its important lessons." Booklist

Followed by Girls in pants (2005)

The **sisterhood** of the traveling pants. Delacorte Press 2001 294p $14.95; pa $8.95; pa $9.99
Grades: 8 9 10   Fic
1. Friendship -- Fiction
ISBN 0-385-72933-2; 0-385-73058-6 pa;
9780385730587 pa
LC 2002-282046

"Four teenagers—best friends since babyhood—have different destinations for the summer and are distressed about disbanding. When they find a pair of 'magic pants'— secondhand jeans that fit each girl perfectly, despite their different body types—they take a solemn vow that the Pants 'will travel to all the places we're going, and they will keep us together when we are apart.' . . . Middle school, high school." (Horn Book)

"Four lifelong high-school friends and a magical pair of jeans take summer journeys to discover love, disappointment, and self-realization." Booklist

Bray, Libba
★ **Beauty** queens. Scholastic Press 2011 396p $18.99
Grades: 8 9 10 11 12   Fic
1. Beauty contests -- Fiction 2. Survival after airplane accidents, shipwrecks, etc. -- Fiction
ISBN 978-0-439-89597-2; 0-439-89597-9
LC 2011-02321

In this book by Libba Bray, "on their way to the Miss Teen Dream competition, a planeload of beauty pageant contestants crashes on what appears to be a deserted island. While the surviving Teen Dreamers valiantly cope with the basics (finding food, water, and shelter; practicing their pageant skills), they become pawns in a massive global conspiracy involving a rogue former Miss Teen Dream winner; a megalomaniacal dictator; and a Big Brother-ish pageant sponsor, The Corporation." (Horn Book Magazine)

"A full-scale send-up of consumer culture, beauty pageants, and reality television: . . . it makes readers really examine their own values while they are laughing, and shaking their heads at the hyperbolic absurdity of those values gone seriously awry." Bull Cent Child Books

★ The **diviners**; by Libba Bray. Little, Brown 2012 608 p. (hardback) $19.99
Grades: 9 10 11 12   Fic
1. Mystery fiction 2. Historical fiction 3. Occultism -- Fiction 4. Murder -- Fiction 5. Uncles -- Fiction 6. Psychic ability -- Fiction 7. Mystery and detective stories
ISBN 031612611X; 9780316126113
LC 2012022868

In this book by Libba Bray, "Evie O'Neill has been exiled from her boring old hometown and shipped off to the bustling streets of New York City. . . . The only catch is Evie has to live with her Uncle Will, curator of The Museum of American Folklore, Superstition, and the Occult. . . . When

a rash of occult-based murders comes to light, Evie and her uncle are right in the thick of the investigation." (Publisher's note)

★ **Going** bovine. Delacorte Press 2009 480p $17.99; lib bdg $20.99
Grades: 9 10 11 12   Fic
1. Dwarfs -- Fiction 2. Automobile travel -- Fiction
ISBN 0-385-73397-6; 0-385-90411-8 lib bdg; 978-0-385-73397-7; 978-0-385-90411-7 lib bdg
LC 2008-43774
ALA YALSA Printz Award (2010)

In an attempt to find a cure after being diagnosed with Creutzfeldt-Jakob's (aka mad cow) disease, Cameron Smith, a disaffected sixteen-year-old boy, sets off on a road trip with a death-obsessed video gaming dwarf he meets in the hospital.

"Bray's wildly imagined novel, narrated in Cameron's sardonic, believable voice, is wholly unique, ambitious, tender, thought-provoking, and often fall-off-the-chair funny, even as she writes with powerful lyricism about the nature of existence, love, and death." Booklist

★ A **great** and terrible beauty. Delacorte Press 2004 403p $16.95
Grades: 9 10 11 12   Fic
1. Mystery fiction 2. Great Britain -- Fiction
ISBN 0-385-73028-4
LC 2003-9472

After the suspicious death of her mother in 1895, sixteen-year-old Gemma returns to England, after many years in India, to attend a finishing school where she becomes aware of her magical powers and ability to see into the spirit world.

"The reader will race to the end to discover the mysterious and realistic challenges of an exciting teenage gothic mystery." Libr Media Connect

Other titles featuring Gemma Doyle are:
Rebel angels (2005)
The sweet far thing (2007)

Lair of dreams; a Diviners novel. Libba Bray. Little Brown & Co. 2015 704 p. (hardback) $19
Grades: 9 10 11 12   Fic
1. Mystery fiction 2. Psychics -- Fiction 3. Supernatural -- Fiction 4. Sleep -- Fiction 5. Dreams -- Fiction 6. Psychic ability -- Fiction 7. Mystery and detective stories 8. New York (N.Y.) -- History -- 1898-1951 -- Fiction
ISBN 9780316126045
LC 2015010856

This book is the second in Libba Bray's Diviners series. "After a supernatural showdown with a serial killer, Evie O'Neill has outed herself as a Diviner. Now that the world knows of her ability to 'read' objects, and therefore, read the past, she has become a media darling, earning the title, 'America's Sweetheart Seer.' But not everyone is so accepting of the Diviners' abilities." (Publisher's note)

"A multilayered, character-driven, and richly rewarding installment to the paranormal historical fiction series." SLJ

Rebel angels. Delacorte Press 2005 548p $16.95; pa $9.99

Grades: 9 10 11 12   **Fic**
1. Mystery fiction 2. Magic -- Fiction 3. Great Britain -- Fiction
ISBN 0-385-73029-2; 0-385-73341-0 pa
LC 2005-3805
Sequel to A great and terrible beauty (2004)

Gemma and her friends from the Spence Academy return to the realms to defeat her foe, Circe, and to bind the magic that has been released.

"The writing never falters, and the revelations (such as Felicity's childhood of abuse, discreetly revealed) only strengthen the characters. Clever foreshadowing abounds, and clues to the mystery of Circe may have readers thinking they have figured everything out; they will still be surprised." SLJ

Followed by The sweet far thing (2007)

The **sweet** far thing. Delacorte Press 2007 819p $17.99; lib bdg $20.99
Grades: 9 10 11 12   **Fic**
1. Mystery fiction 2. Magic -- Fiction 3. Great Britain -- Fiction
ISBN 978-0-385-73030-3; 978-0-385-90295-3 lib bdg
LC 2007-31302
Sequel to Rebel angels (2005)

At Spence Academy, sixteen-year-old Gemma Doyle continues preparing for her London debut while struggling to determine how best to use magic to resolve a power struggle in the enchanted world of the realms, and to protect her own world and loved ones.

"The novel's fast-paced and exciting ending and Bray's lyrical descriptions of the decaying realms are sure to enchant readers who loved Gemma's previous exploits." SLJ

Brenna, Beverly

Waiting for no one. Red Deer 2011 187p pa $12.95
Grades: 7 8 9 10   **Fic**
1. Asperger's syndrome -- Fiction
ISBN 978-0-88995-437-3; 0-88995-437-2
Sequel to Wild orchid (2006)

Taylor Jane Smith is "taking a biology class at college and applying for a job at a local bookstore. Her Asperger's syndrome gives her an advantage in the class, but it's making the job-application process torture. . . . Taylor, with her flinty, exasperated approach to the world, remains a fascinating character and narrator." Bull Cent Child Books

Brennan, Sarah Rees

The **demon's** covenant. Margaret K. McElderry Books 2010 440p (The demon's lexicon trilogy) $17.99
Grades: 8 9 10 11 12   **Fic**
1. Magic -- Fiction 2. Brothers -- Fiction 3. Demonology -- Fiction
ISBN 978-1-4169-6381-3; 1-4169-6381-2
LC 2009-40798
Sequel to The demon's lexicon (2009)

Seventeen-year-old Mae feels that even though her world is out of control, she must find a way to protect the demon Nick from his brother Alan's betrayal.

"Plots thicken, characters deepen and snark is bantered with witty abandon in this dark fantasy sequel. . . . Not to be missed." Kirkus

The **demon's** lexicon. Margaret K. McElderry Books 2009 322p $17.99; pa $9.99
Grades: 9 10 11 12   **Fic**
1. Magic -- Fiction 2. Brothers -- Fiction 3. Demonology -- Fiction
ISBN 978-1-4169-6379-0; 1-4169-6379-0; 978-1-4169-6380-6 pa; 1-4169-6380-4 pa
LC 2008-39056
Sixteen-year-old Nick and his family have battled magicians and demons for most of his life, but when his brother, Alan, is marked for death while helping new friends Jamie and Mae, Nick's determination to save Alan leads him to uncover a devastating secret.

"A fresh voice dancing between wicked humor and crepuscular sumptuousness invigorates this urban fantasy. . . . The narrative peels back layers of revelation, deftly ratcheting up the tension and horror to a series of shattering climaxes." Kirkus

Other titles in this series are:
The demon's covenant (2010)
The demon's surrender (2011)

Unspoken; by Sarah Rees Brennan. Random House Books for Young Readers 2012 373 p. (The Lynburn legacy) (hardcover) $18.99
Grades: 7 8 9 10   **Fic**
1. Gothic novels 2. Fantasy fiction 3. Mystery fiction 4. Horror stories 5. Magic -- Fiction 6. England -- Fiction 7. Magicians -- Fiction
ISBN 9780375870415; 9780375970412
LC 2012001954

This juvenile gothic mystery, by Sarah Rees Brennan, starts The Lynburn Legacy series. "Kami Glass knows that she could be a great reporter. . . . The aristocratic, secretive Lynburns are coming home, . . . and Kami is determined . . . [to] get the scoop. Soon, two gorgeous, near-identical Lynburn cousins . . . join her journalistic team--not to mention Kami's imaginary best friend, . . . who turns out to be not quite so imaginary after all. And that's when the grisly murders start." (Kirkus Reviews)

Brewer, Heather

The **cemetery** boys; Heather Brewer. HarperTeen 2015 273 p. (hardback) $17.99
Grades: 9 10 11 12   **Fic**
1. Cults -- Fiction 2. Teenagers -- Fiction 3. Cemeteries -- Fiction 4. Horror stories 5. Twins -- Fiction 6. Supernatural -- Fiction 7. Peer pressure -- Fiction 8. Moving, Household -- Fiction 9. Brothers and sisters -- Fiction 10. Dating (Social customs) -- Fiction
ISBN 0062307886; 9780062307880
LC 2014027404

In this novel by Heather Brewer "Stephen's summer starts looking up when he meets punk girl Cara and her charismatic twin brother, Devon. With Cara, he feels safe and understood. In Devon and his group, he sees a chance at making real friends. Only, as the summer presses on, and harmless nights hanging out in the cemetery take a darker turn, Stephen starts to suspect that Devon is less a friend than a leader. And he might be leading them to a very sinister end." (Publisher's note)

"The novel's final pages will surely shock readers: The author takes great glee in not just presenting a great reveal toward the end, but also twisting the knife. Keen-eyed readers may spot the twist, but few will predict just how far it goes. A slick, spooky, chilling mystery." Kirkus

Brewster, Alicia Wright

Echo; Alicia Wright Brewster. Dragonfairy Press 2013 291 p. (paperback) $14.95

Grades: 7 8 9 10 11 12 **Fic**

1. Magic -- Fiction 2. End of the world -- Fiction
ISBN 0985023023; 9780985023027

LC 2012951596

In this book by Alicia Wright Brewster, "Earth-Two . . . will end in 10 days. Calling up all elemental practitioners to help, the Council elders have averted catastrophe only by repeatedly rewinding time back 10 days before the end. With each rewind, they become weakened echoes of their original selves. . . . Their efforts focus on eliminating the Mages--formerly human 'ether manipulators' whose elemental energies have consumed their humanity--causing the crisis." (Kirkus Reviews)

"Fully realized characters from Asha to the walk-ons lend their intense authenticity to the plot, which straddles the line between fantasy and science fiction, and deflect attention from the rubber science. This world has depth, mirroring the memorable characters who populate it." Kirkus

Brezenoff, Steve

Brooklyn, burning. Carolrhoda Lab 2011 202p $17.95

Grades: 8 9 10 11 **Fic**

1. Musicians -- Fiction 2. Runaway teenagers -- Fiction
3. Brooklyn (New York, N.Y.) -- Fiction
ISBN 978-0-7613-7526-5

LC 2010051447

"Homelessness, queerness and the rougher sides of living on the street are handled without a whiff of sensationalism, and the moments between Kid, the first-person narrator, and Scout, addressed as 'you,' are described in language so natural and vibrant that readers may not even notice that neither character's gender is ever specified. . . . Overall, the tone is as raw, down-to-earth and transcendent as the music Scout and Kid ultimately make together." Kirkus

Guy in real life; Steve Brezenoff. Balzer + Bray, an imprint of HarperCollinsPublishers 2014 400 p. (hardcover bdg.) $17.99

Grades: 9 10 11 12 **Fic**

1. Love -- Fiction 2. Minnesota -- Fiction 3. Video games -- Fiction 4. Fantasy games -- Fiction 5. Role playing -- Fiction
ISBN 0062266837; 9780062266835

LC 2013021584

"Sulky metal head boy meets artsy gamer girl. Awkward teenage love ensues. When Lesh's and Svetlana's worlds collide—literally—in Saint Paul, Minn., it precipitates a time-honored culture clash wherein magic happens, but that's where predictability ends. In a first-person narration

that alternates between the boy in black and the girl dungeon master, Brezenoff conjures a wry, wise and deeply sympathetic portrait of the exquisite, excruciating thrill of falling in love....(t)he realistic dialogue, internal and otherwise, captures the uncomfortably iterative process of adolescent self-discovery as Lesh and Svetlana struggle to figure out who they are and what they stand for." (Kirkus)

"The overall effect of the novel, then, is of marvelous fantasy sequences interspersed with the messiness of real-life romance. Lesh's predicament—that he loves becoming Svetlana as much as he loves Lana—is presented sweetly and believably. Like his easy evocation of gender-free characters in his Brooklyn, Burning (2011), Brezenoff deftly handles one teen's experience of gender dysphoria." -Booklist

Briant, Ed

I am (not) the walrus; Ed Briant. 1st ed. Flux 2012 280 p. (pbk.) $9.95

Grades: 8 9 10 11 **Fic**

1. Love stories 2. Rock music -- Fiction 3. Bands (Music) -- Fiction
ISBN 073873246X; 9780738732466

LC 2012004314

This novel, by Ed Briant, describes how "Toby and Zack's first gig could make or break their Beatles cover band, the Nowhere Men. But ever since getting dumped by his girlfriend, lead singer Toby can't quite pull off the Beatles' feel-good vibe. When Toby finds a note hidden inside his brother's bass claiming the instrument was stolen, he embarks on a quest to find the true owner--and hopes a girl named Michelle will help him recover his lost mojo along the way." (Publisher's note)

Brockenbrough, Martha

Devine intervention; Martha Brockenbrough. Arthur A. Levine Books 2012 297 p.

Grades: 7 8 9 10 11 **Fic**

1. Soul -- Fiction 2. Angels -- Fiction 3. Heaven -- Fiction 4. Future life -- Fiction 5. High school students -- Fiction 6. Dead -- Fiction 7. Guardian angels -- Fiction
ISBN 0545382130; 9780545382137; 9780545382144

LC 2011039768

This book follows "Jerome . . . A hell raiser when alive and killed by his cousin in eighth grade in an unfortunate archery accident, he has spent his afterlife in Soul Rehab assigned to Heidi in an attempt to win his way into Heaven. Not that he's very committed to the notion; he lost his 'Guardian Angel's Handbook' pretty much right away, but he sort of tries. Heidi has more or less enjoyed Jerome's company, though he could sometimes be annoying. When Heidi, having experienced unendurable humiliation in a high-school talent show, ventures onto thin ice and falls through, Jerome does his best to save her soul--as much for her own sake, he's surprised to find, as for his." (Kirkus Reviews)

The game of Love and Death; Martha Brockenbrough. First edition Arthur A. Levine Books, an imprint of Scholastic Inc. 2015 352 p. (hardcover) $17.99

Grades: 9 10 11 12   **Fic**
1. Love stories 2. Death -- Fiction 3. Race relations
-- Fiction 4. Love -- Fiction 5. African Americans --
Fiction 6. Man-woman relationships
ISBN 9780545668347; 0545668344

LC 2014033339

In this novel, by Martha Brockenbrough, "Flora and
Henry were born a few blocks from each other, innocent of
the forces that might keep a white boy and an African American girl apart; years later they meet again and their mutual
love of music sparks an even more powerful connection. But
what Flora and Henry don't know is that they are pawns in a
game played by the eternal adversaries Love and Death, here
. . . reimagined as two extremely sympathetic and fascinating characters." (Publisher's note)

"There is a deliberately archetypal quality to the story,
but the fully realized setting and characters make this more
than just a modern fairy tale. It's a poignant reminder of
how far we've come since the 1930s in terms of race, class,
and sexual orientation -- and how far we still have to go."
Horn Book

Brockmann, Suzanne
Night sky; Suzanne Brockmann and Melanie
Brockmann. Sourcebooks Fire 2014 484 p. (hc: alk.
paper) $16.99
Grades: 9 10 11 12   **Fic**
1. Adventure fiction 2. Psychics -- Fiction 3.
Kidnapping -- Fiction 4. Supernatural -- Fiction 5.
Psychic ability -- Fiction 6. Adventure and adventurers
-- Fiction
ISBN 1492601446; 9781492601449

LC 2014022430

In this book, by Suzanne and Melanie Brockmann, "Skylar Reid is shaken when Sasha, the little girl she babysits, is
kidnapped. Scared that the weird dreams she's been having
about Sasha are real–and even more afraid that Sasha is already dead. When a mysterious girl . . . roars into town on
a motorcycle and . . . stalks Skylar things get even weirder.
Supergirl Dana tells Sky that she also has abilities – that a
hormone in their blood makes them stronger, faster, smarter." (Publisher's note)

"With a little something for everyone and a hip sense
of humor, dialogue and teen angst, this is a gripping page-
turner from first to last." Kirkus

Brooks, Kevin
Black Rabbit summer. Scholastic 2008 488p
$17.99
Grades: 9 10 11 12   **Fic**
1. Mystery fiction 2. Drug abuse -- Fiction 3.
Homosexuality -- Fiction 4. Missing persons -- Fiction
ISBN 978-0-545-05752-3; 0-545-05752-3

LC 2007-035322

When two of sixteen-year-old Pete's childhood classmates disappear from a carnival the same night, he is a suspect, but his own investigation implicates other old friends
he was with that evening—and a tough, knife-wielding enemy determined to keep him quiet.

"This dark and complicated mystery tackles the nature of
friendships, loyalty and betrayal." KLIATT

The **bunker** diary; by Kevin Brooks. Carolrhoda Lab 2015 260 p. illustrations (trade hard cover:
alk. paper) $17.99
Grades: 9 10 11 12   **Fic**
1. Diaries -- Fiction 2. Torture -- Fiction 3. Kidnapping
-- Fiction 4. Conduct of life -- Fiction 5. Interpersonal
relations -- Fiction
ISBN 146775420X; 9781467754200

LC 2014026362

This book, by Kevin Brooks, is the winner of the 2014
Cilip Carnegie Medal. "Linus is a 16-year-old runaway living on the harsh English streets who wakes up one day in
an unfamiliar underground bunker with no water or food
while under constant surveillance by an unknown kidnapper. As each day passes, more people are kidnapped. . . .
When Linus and the rest try to escape, . . . they realize that .
. . they may have to resort to the ultimate horror to survive."
(School Library Journal)

"Brooks' latest is not an easy novel, but it's one that begs
for rereading to suss the intricacies of its construction of
plot, character development and insight into the human condition. Not for everyone, this heady novel is worthy of study
alongside existentialist works of the 20th century." Kirkus

IBoy. Chicken House 2011 288p il $17.99
Grades: 9 10 11 12   **Fic**
1. Science fiction 2. Gangs -- Fiction 3. Violence
-- Fiction 4. London (England) -- Fiction 5. Cellular
telephones -- Fiction
ISBN 978-0-54531-768-9

LC 2010054240

Sixteen-year-old Tom Harvey was an ordinary Londoner
until an attack that caused fragments of an iPhone to be embedded in his brain, giving him incredible knowledge and
power, but using that power against the gang that attacked
him and a friend could have deadly consequences.

"This classic superhero plot, at once cutting-edge science
fiction and moral fable, is guaranteed to keep even fiction-
averse, reluctant readers on the edge of their seats." Kirkus

Brooks, Martha
★ **Queen** of hearts. Farrar Straus Giroux 2011
224p $16.99
Grades: 7 8 9 10   **Fic**
1. Sick -- Fiction 2. Manitoba -- Fiction 3. Hospitals
-- Fiction 4. Family life -- Fiction 5. Tuberculosis
-- Fiction
ISBN 978-0-374-34229-6; 0-374-34229-6

LC 2010-52661

Shortly after her first kiss but before her sixteenth birthday in December, 1941, Marie Claire and her younger brother and sister are sent to a tuberculosis sanatorium near their
Manitoba farm.

"Readers will be held by the story's heartbreaking truths,
right to the end." Booklist

Brooks, Terry
Armageddon's children. Del Rey 2006 371p
(The genesis of Shannara) hardcover o.p. pa $7.99
Grades: 11 12 Adult   **Fic**
1. Fantasy fiction 2. Fantasies 3. Good and evil --

Fiction
ISBN 0-345-48408-8; 978-0-345-48408-6; 0-345-48410-X pa; 978-0-345-48410-9 pa

LC 2006-40423

"Characterizations are dynamic and multidimensional, the descriptions of the land as well as the ruined cities and small towns are compelling, the action and battles are mesmerizing, and, as is Brooks' wont, the ending is a cliffhanger that leaves readers salivating for the sequel." Booklist

Other titles in this series are:
The elves of Cintra (2007)
The gypsy morph (2008)

The **elves** of Cintra. Del Rey 2007 379p map (The genesis of Shannara) $26.95
Grades: 11 12 Adult   **Fic**
1. Fantasy fiction 2. Good and evil -- Fiction
ISBN 978-0-345-48411-6

LC 2007-15127

Sequel to Armageddon's children (2006)
"In a desolate post-apocalyptic earth, several diverse groups struggle to survive as demons stalk the countryside. Logan Tom, Knight of the Word, arrives too late to avert Hawk's and Tessa's executions but continues his mission to guide a ragtag collection of children southward. Thrown from the compound walls by their executioners, Hawk, a Gypsy Morph, and Tessa disappear in a flash of white light. They waken in the Gardens of Life, where Hawk's destiny, 'to lead his children to the Promised Land,' is revealed by the King of the Silver River." Voice Youth Advocates

Followed by The gypsy morph (2008)

The **gypsy** morph. Ballantine Books 2008 402p (The genesis of Shannara) $27
Grades: 11 12 Adult   **Fic**
1. Fantasy fiction 2. Good and evil -- Fiction
ISBN 978-0-345-48414-7

LC 2008-16680

Sequel to The elves of Cintra (2007)
"Civilization has collapsed, cities lie in ruins, and two Knights of the Word, Logan Tom and Angel Perez, continue their valiant battles against the demons and once-men to save the remnants of humanity and the newly discovered Elves, who have long hidden themselves from the world. . . . Strong storytelling and unforgettable characters make this a priority purchase for most libraries." Libr J

Jarka Ruus. Ballantine Bks. 2003 416p (High druid of Shannara) pa $13.95
Grades: 11 12 Adult   **Fic**
1. Fantasy fiction
ISBN 0-345-43573-7; 0-345-48389-8 pa
"As throughout the massive Shannara saga to date, Brooks proves himself a master at reworking and enriching the conventions of fantasy while maintaining the integrity of the characteristics of elves, dwarves, humans, and the other peoples of the saga that he set up at its very beginning." Booklist

★ The **sword** of Shannara; illustrated by the Brothers Hildebrandt. Ballantine Bks. 1991 726p il hardcover o.p. pa $7.99

Grades: 11 12 Adult   **Fic**
1. Fantasy fiction
ISBN 0-394-441333-4; 0-345-31425-5 pa

LC 90-43727

A reissue of the title first published 1977 by Random House
This is an "engrossing saga of hardship and adventure with well-maintained action that will keep readers captive right up to a nicely-wrought finish." SLJ

Other titles in this epic-fantasy are:
The druids of Shannara (1991)
The Elf queen of Shannara (1992)
The Elfstones of Shannara (1982)
First king of Shannara (1996)
The scions of Shannara (1990)
The talismans of Shannara (1993)
The wishsong of Shannara (1985)

Brothers, Meagan
Supergirl mixtapes; Meagan Brothers. Henry Holt 2012 248 p. (hc) $17.99
Grades: 9 10 11 12   **Fic**
1. Drug abuse -- Fiction 2. New York (N.Y.) -- Fiction 3. Mother-daughter relationship -- Fiction 4. Artists -- Fiction 5. Family problems -- Fiction 6. Mothers and daughters -- Fiction 7. Single-parent families -- Fiction 8. Lower East Side (New York, N.Y.) -- Fiction
ISBN 0805080813; 9780805080810

LC 2011025738

In this book by Meagan Brothers, "Maria is thrilled when her father finally allows her to visit her estranged artist mother in New York City. She's ready for adventure, and she soon finds herself immersed in a world of rock music and busy streets. . . . But just like her beloved New York City, Maria's life has a darker side. Behind her mother's carefree existence are shadowy secrets, and Maria must decide just where -- and with whom -- her loyalty lies." (Publisher's note)

Brouwer, Sigmund
Devil's pass; Sigmund Brouwer. Orca Book Publishers 2012 237 p. (pbk) $9.95
Grades: 6 7 8 9 10   **Fic**
1. Grandfathers -- Fiction 2. Voyages and travels -- Fiction 3. Grandparent-grandchild relationship -- Fiction 4. Canada -- Fiction 5. Street musicians -- Fiction 6. Canol Heritage Trail (N.W.T.) -- Fiction
ISBN 155469938X; 9781554699384

LC 2012938220

In author Sigmund Brouwer's book, "seventeen-year-old Webb's abusive stepfather has made it impossible for him to live at home, so Webb survives on the streets of Toronto. . . . When Webb's grandfather dies, his will stipulates that his grandsons fulfill specific requests. Webb's task takes him to the Canol Trail in Canada's Far North. . . . With a Native guide, two German tourists and his guitar for company, Webb is forced to confront terrible events in his grandfather's past and somehow deal with the pain and confusion of his own life." (Publisher's note)

Brown, Jaye Robin

Georgia peaches and other forbidden fruit; Jaye
Robin Brown; [edited by] Tara Weikum. HarperTeen
2016 432 p.

Grades: 9 10 11 12   **Fic**
1. Love stories 2. Lesbians -- Fiction 3. Father-
daughter relationship
ISBN 9780062270986

LC 2016936318

"Joanna has always been out as a lesbian to her minister
father, but now that he is remarrying and moving them from
tolerant Atlanta to a small Georgia town, he asks her to "lie
low." Initially, it doesn't seem so bad: it's only a year until
she graduates from high school, and it turns out that finding
friends who share her Christian faith is kind of great. Then
one of Jo's new friends reveals that she has feelings for her,
and that she isn't interested in hiding. . . . Faith matters in
this book, but so do family, friends, and being funny. The
dialogue is snappy—Joanna is sharp tongued and sometimes
bratty—and the characters aren't types. Rather, they're individuals navigating a complicated world, which makes for a
rich and satisfying read." PW

No place to fall; by Jaye Robin Brown. First
edition HarperTeen 2014 368 p. (harcover) $17.99
Grades: 9 10 11 12   **Fic**
1. Family -- Fiction 2. Singers -- Fiction 3. Friendship
-- Fiction 4. Schools -- Fiction 5. High schools --
Fiction 6. North Carolina -- Fiction 7. Family problems
-- Fiction 8. Dating (Social customs) -- Fiction
ISBN 0062270990; 9780062270993

LC 2013051284

In this novel by Jaye Robin Brown "Amber decides that
her dream--to sing on bigger stages--could also be her ticket
to a new life. Devon's older brother, Will, helps Amber prepare. The more time Will and Amber spend together, the
more complicated their relationship becomes. The bottom
drops out of her family's world--and Amber is faced with an
impossible choice between her promise as an artist and the
people she loves." (Publisher's note)

"Amber could be the best friend you had in high
school—she's funny and moody and truthful and absolutely
the real deal, and readers will clamor for another well-paced
story featuring her and her friends. Realistic treatment of social pot smoking, some drinking and (safe) sex make this
title appropriate for mature teens." SLJ

Brown, Jennifer

Bitter end. Little, Brown 2011 359p $17.99
Grades: 10 11 12   **Fic**
1. Friendship -- Fiction 2. Bereavement -- Fiction 3.
Abused women -- Fiction
ISBN 978-0-316-08695-0; 0-316-08695-9

LC 2010-34258

"Gritty and disturbing, this novel should be in all collections serving teens. It could be used in programs about
abuse, as well as in psychology or sociology classes." SLJ

Perfect escape; by Jennifer Brown. Little,
Brown 2012 364 p. $17.99
Grades: 9 10 11 12   **Fic**
1. Siblings -- Fiction 2. Voyages and travels -- Fiction

3. Cheating (Education) -- Fiction 4. Obsessive-
compulsive disorder -- Fiction 5. Automobile travel
-- Fiction 6. Brothers and sisters -- Fiction
ISBN 0316185574; 9780316185578

LC 2011027348

This book is a "road-trip drama" about brother and sister
Grayson and Kendra. Kendra "defines herself by two things:
her drive for academic and personal perfection, and her older
brother Grayson's severe obsessive-compulsive disorder. .
. . When a cheating scandal threatens to destroy Kendra's
academic standing, she snaps, dragging Grayson on a cross-
country trip from Missouri to California in an ill-defined attempt to 'fix' both their lives." (Publishers Weekly)

Brown, Pierce

Golden Son; Pierce Brown. First edition Del
Rey 2015 xii, 446 p.p $25
Grades: 11 12 Adult   **Fic**
1. Science fiction 2. Dystopian fiction 3. Resistance
to government -- Fiction 4. Government, Resistance to
-- Fiction
ISBN 0345539818; 9780345539816

LC 2014031015

This dystopian science fiction novel, by Pierce Brown,
book 2 of "The Red Rising Trilogy" series, "continues the .
. . saga of Darrow, a rebel forged by tragedy, battling to lead
his oppressed people to freedom. . . . Darrow sacrifices himself in the name of the greater good for which Eo, his true
love and inspiration, laid down her own life. He becomes a
Gold, infiltrating their privileged realm so that he can destroy it from within." (Publisher's note)

"The stakes are even higher than they were in Red Rising, and the twists and turns of the story are every bit as
exciting. The jaw-dropper of an ending will leave readers
hungry for the conclusion to Brown's wholly original, completely thrilling saga." Booklist

Morning Star; Pierce Brown. Del Rey 2016 544
p. ill (Red Rising trilogy) $27
Grades: Adult   **Fic**
1. War stories 2. Science fiction 3. Revenge -- Fiction
ISBN 0345539842; 9780345539847

LC 2015048261

"Darrow would have lived in peace, but his enemies
brought him war. The Gold overlords demanded his obedience, hanged his wife, and enslaved his people. But Darrow
is determined to fight back. Risking everything to transform
himself and breach Gold society, Darrow has battled to survive the cutthroat rivalries that breed Society's mightiest
warriors, climbed the ranks, and waited patiently to unleash
the revolution that will tear the hierarchy apart from within."
(Publisher's note)

"Brown's vivid, first-person prose puts the reader right at
the forefront of impassioned speeches, broken families, and
engaging battle scenes that don't shy away from the gore as
this intrastellar civil war comes to a most satisfying conclusion." Pub Wkly

Red Rising; Pierce Brown. Del Rey 2014 400
p. $25
Grades: 10 11 12 Adult   **Fic**
1. Dystopian fiction 2. Mars (Planet) -- Fiction 3.

Resistance to government -- Fiction 4. Government, Resistance to -- Fiction

ISBN 0345539788; 9780345539786

LC 2013020634

In this science fiction novel, by Pierce Brown, "Darrow is a Red, a member of the lowest caste in the . . . society of the future. . . . He works all day, believing that he and his people are making the surface of Mars livable for future generations. . . . Darrow sacrifices everything to infiltrate the legendary Institute, . . . where the next generation of humanity's overlords struggle for power. He will be forced to compete for his life and the very future of civilization." (Publisher's note)

"Brown's debut novel, the first volume in a planned trilogy, is reminiscent of both Suzanne Collins's The Hunger Games and William Goldman's The Lord of the Flies but has a dark and twisted power of its own that will captivate readers and leave them wanting more." LJ

Brown, Skila

★ **Caminar**; Skila Brown. Candlewick Press 2014 208 p. $15.99

Grades: 6 7 8 9   **Fic**

1. War stories 2. Guatemala -- Fiction 3. Novels in verse 4. Guatemala -- History -- Civil War, 1960-1996 -- fiction

ISBN 0763665169; 9780763665166

LC 2013946611

This book, by Skila Brown, is "set in 1981 Guatemala. . . . Carlos knows that when the soldiers arrive with warnings about the Communist rebels, it is time to be a man and defend the village, keep everyone safe. But Mama tells him not yet. . . . Numb and alone, he must join a band of guerillas as they trek to the top of the mountain where Carlos's abuela lives. Will he be in time, and brave enough, to warn them about the soldiers? What will he do then?" (Publisher's note)

"—Unlike many novels in verse, which can read like conventional narratives with line breaks, Caminarcontributes poetry that elevates the genre. In this story of a decimated Guatemalan village in 1981, readers will encounter a range of imagery, repetition, rhythms, and visual effects that bring to life the psychological experience of Carlos, a young boy caught in the violent clash between the government's army and the people's rebels...This is a much-needed addition to Latin American-themed middle grade fiction.—" (School Library Journal)

Bruchac, Joseph, 1942-

★ **Code** talker; a novel about the Navajo Marines of World War Two. Dial 2005 240p $16.99

Grades: 6 7 8 9 10   **Fic**

1. Navajo Indians -- Fiction 2. World War, 1939-1945 -- Fiction

ISBN 0-8037-2921-9

After being taught in a boarding school run by whites that Navajo is a useless language, Ned Begay and other Navajo men are recruited by the Marines to become Code Talkers, sending messages during World War II in their native tongue.

"Bruchac's gentle prose presents a clear historical picture of young men in wartime. . . . Nonsensational and accurate, Bruchac's tale is quietly inspiring." SLJ

Includes bibliographical references

Killer of enemies; Joseph Bruchac. Tu Books, an imprint of Lee & Low Books, Inc. 2013 400 p. (hardcover: alk. paper) $19.95

Grades: 7 8 9 10 11 12   **Fic**

1. Dystopian fiction 2. Heroes and heroines -- Fiction 3. Science fiction 4. Hunting -- Fiction 5. Hostages -- Fiction 6. Survival -- Fiction 7. Southwest, New -- Fiction 8. Chiricahua Indians -- Fiction 9. Genetic engineering -- Fiction 10. Extrasensory perception -- Fiction 11. Indians of North America -- Southwest, New -- Fiction

ISBN 1620141434; 9781620141434; 9781620141441

LC 2013023567

American Indian Youth Literature Award Winner (2014)

In this dystopian young adult novel by Joseph Bruchac, "seventeen year old Apache hunter Lozen and her family lives in a world of haves and have-nots. There were the Ones (people so augmented with technology and genetic enhancements that they were barely human) and there was everyone else who served the Ones. . . . She hunts monsters for the Ones who survived the apocalyptic events of the Cloud, which ensures the safety of her kidnapped family." (Publisher's note)

"A deadly assassin with extrasensory powers, Lozen (named for an Apache-Chiricahua warrior-woman forebear) takes out genetically modified superbeasts; her family is being held hostage to ensure her continued service. Bruchac devises ever-more-dangerous battles for his protagonist in the increasingly suspenseful story. What really makes the narrative vibrate is Lozen's sardonic voice, capturing both gallows humor and a very human vulnerability." (Horn Book)

Sacajawea; the story of Bird Woman and the Lewis and Clark Expedition. Silver Whistle Bks. 2000 199p $17; pa $6.99

Grades: 6 7 8 9 10   **Fic**

1. Explorers 2. Interpreters 3. Guides (Persons) 4. Territorial governors 5. Native Americans -- Fiction 6. Lewis and Clark Expedition (1804-1806) -- Fiction

ISBN 0-15-202234-1; 0-15-206455-9 pa

LC 99-47653

Sacajawea, a Shoshoni Indian interpreter, peacemaker, and guide, and William Clark alternate in describing their experiences on the Lewis and Clark Expedition to the Northwest

This is an "intelligent, elegantly written novel." SLJ

Includes bibliographical references

Walking two worlds; Joseph Bruchac; illustrated by David Fadden. 7th Generation 2015 120 p. (pbk.) $9.95

Grades: 5 6 7 8 9   **Fic**

1. Racism -- Fiction 2. Education -- Fiction 3. Seneca Indians -- Fiction 4. Native Americans -- Fiction 5. Indians of North America -- New York (State) -- Fiction

ISBN 9781939053107; 9781939053138

LC 2014046212

This book, by Joseph Bruchac, illustrated by David Fadden, and part of the Pathfinders series, is the "story of the early education of a famous Native American who gained greatness in the white man's world while staying true to his

Seneca people. Hasanoanda was his Indian name. But in mission school he became Ely. He encountered racism and deceit but, against all odds, did not give up on his quest to walk between two worlds." (Publisher's note)

"Though the book lacks formal resources and references, and the time frame of events, including Ely's birth date, is occasionally unclear, Ely's challenges and successes are supportively portrayed, and may inspire readers to learn more about his life and times. An afterword provides some information on his later years." Booklist

Bryant, Jennifer

Ringside, 1925; views from the Scopes trial, a novel. [by] Jen Bryant. Alfred A. Knopf 2008 228p $15.99; lib bdg $18.99

Grades: 8 9 10 11 12   **Fic**
1. Geologists 2. Novels in verse 3. Science teachers 4. Tennessee -- Fiction 5. Evolution -- Study and teaching -- Fiction
ISBN 978-0-375-84047-0; 0-375-84047-8; 978-0-375-94047-7 lib bdg; 0-375-94047-2 lib bdg
LC 2007-7177

Visitors, spectators, and residents of Dayton, Tennessee, in 1925 describe, in a series of free-verse poems, the Scopes 'monkey trial' and its effects on that small town and its citizens.

"Bryant offers readers a ringside seat in this compelling and well-researched novel. It is fast-paced, interesting, and relevant to many current first-amendment challenges." SLJ

Bryce, Celia

Anthem for Jackson Dawes; by Celia Bryce. Bloomsbury USA Childrens 2013 240 p. (hardback) $16.99

Grades: 7 8 9 10   **Fic**
1. Hospitals -- Fiction 2. Cancer patients -- Fiction 3. Cancer -- Fiction 4. Friendship -- Fiction 5. Family life -- Fiction 6. Medical care -- Fiction
ISBN 1599909758; 9781599909752
LC 2012024989

In this book, "after 13-year-old Megan Bright is diagnosed with a cancerous brain tumor, she's . . . determined to have everything remain as normal as possible during her time in the hospital. . . . Megan gets closer to the only other teenager there . . . and begins to acknowledge the emotions she's been keeping buried. Initially, Jackson rubs her the wrong way, but his positivity and determined interest in Megan teach her about optimism and taking control of what she can." (Publishers Weekly)

"Sensitive and honest, this novel addresses meaningful questions concerning mortality and soul searching, and its content is appropriate for younger teens." SLJ

Buckingham, Royce Scott

The **terminals**; Royce Scott Buckingham. First edition Thomas Dunne Books, St. Martin's Griffin 2014 288 p. (hardback) $18.99

Grades: 7 8 9 10   **Fic**
1. Spy stories 2. Adventure fiction 3. Terminally ill -- Fiction 4. Spies -- Fiction 5. Ability -- Fiction 6.

Adventure and adventurers -- Fiction
ISBN 1250011558; 9781250011558
LC 2014031142

This young adult adventure novel, by Royce Scott Buckingham, "tells the . . . story of a covert team of young, terminally ill teens who spend their last year alive running dangerous missions as super-spies. . . . Cam joins this extreme spy team, and . . . as his teammates fall around him, he starts to receive cryptic messages from a haggard survivor of last year's class hiding in the forest. She reveals that the program isn't what it claims to be." (Publisher's note)

"Buckingham's above-average writing and exotic settings are plenty appealing. Fans of Robert Muchamore's Cherub series will eat up this sf-tinged espionage thriller." Booklist

Buckley-Archer, Linda

The **many** lives of John Stone; Linda Buckley-Archer. SSBFYR 2015 544 p. illustrations (hardcover) $17.99

Grades: 8 9 10 11   **Fic**
1. England -- Fiction 2. Identity -- Fiction 3. Supernatural -- Fiction 4. Summer employment -- Fiction 5. Longevity -- Fiction
ISBN 9781481426374; 9781481426381
LC 2014035641

In this book, by Linda Buckley-Archer, "Stella Park (Spark for short) has found summer work cataloging historical archives in John Stone's remote and beautiful house in Suffolk, England. . . . [W]hat kind of people live in the twenty-first century without using electricity, telephones, or even a washing machine? Additionally, the notebooks she's organizing span centuries—they begin in the court of Louis XIV in Versailles—but are written in the same hand." (Publisher's note)

"Spark's contemporary coming-of-age story is brilliantly heightened by the reader's understanding of her secret connection to John Stone. Exceptionally well orchestrated and a simply magnificent story." Booklist

Budhos, Marina

Ask me no questions; [by] Marina Budhos. Atheneum Books for Young Readers 2006 162p $16.95; pa $8.99

Grades: 7 8 9 10   **Fic**
1. School stories 2. Family life -- Fiction 3. Asian Americans -- Fiction 4. New York (N.Y.) -- Fiction
ISBN 1-4169-0351-8; 1-4169-4920-8 pa
LC 2005-1831

Fourteen-year-old Nadira, her sister, and their parents leave Bangladesh for New York City, but the expiration of their visas and the events of September 11, 2001, bring frustration, sorrow, and terror for the whole family.

"Nadira and Aisha's strategies for surviving and succeeding in high school offer sharp insight into the narrow margins between belonging and not belonging." Horn Book Guide

Tell us we're home; [by] Marina Budhos. Atheneum 2010 297p $16.95

Grades: 6 7 8 9 10   **Fic**
1. Immigrants -- Fiction 2. New Jersey -- Fiction 3.

Social classes -- Fiction 4. Household employees --
Fiction 5. Mother-daughter relationship -- Fiction
ISBN 978-1-4169-0352-9; 1-4169-0352-6

LC 2009-27386

Three immigrant girls from different parts of the world
meet and become close friends in a small New Jersey town
where their mothers have found domestic work, but their relationships are tested when one girl's mother is accused of
stealing a precious heirloom.

"These fully realized heroines are full of heart, and their
passionate struggles against systemic injustice only make
them more inspiring. Keenly necessary." Kirkus

Watched. Random House 2016 272 p. hardcover $17.99

Grades: 9 10 11 12 **Fic**
1. Muslims -- Fiction 2. Undercover operations --
Fiction 3. Bangladeshi Americans -- Fiction
ISBN 9780553534184

LC 2015046828

"Moving quickly throughout his Queens immigrant
neighborhood to avoid the watchful eyes of his hardworking
Bangladeshi parents, their gossipy neighbors and surveillance cameras mounted everywhere, charismatic but troubled youth Naeem is offered a deal by the cops to become
a community protector in ways that challenge his sense of
identity." (Publisher's note)

"Naeem, a teenager living in an immigrant neighborhood in Queens, finds his grip on life slipping.With his
performance in school deteriorating, he feels unable to
deal with the disappointment of his hardworking and hopeful Bangladeshi parents—and then there are the inquisitive
eyes and mouths of their neighbors. Hoping to avoid them,
Naeem keeps himself constantly on the move. But he is always aware that he is always being watched, by cops and by
cameras placed all around. . . . Action takes second place to a
deeper message, and room is left for readers to speculate on
the fates of certain characters. While the absence of certainty
may frustrate some readers, it also speaks to the underlying
takeaway: you can never be sure what others' intentions are,
even if you have made it your job to study them." Kirkus

Buffie, Margaret

Winter shadows; a novel. Tundra Books 2010
327p $19.95

Grades: 7 8 9 10 **Fic**
1. Manitoba -- Fiction 2. Prejudices -- Fiction 3.
Family life -- Fiction 4. Stepmothers -- Fiction
ISBN 978-0-88776-968-9; 0-88776-968-3

"Hatred for their wicked stepmothers bonds two girls
living in a stone house in Manitoba, Canada, more than 150
years apart. Grieving for her dead mother, high-school senior Cass is furious that she has to share a room with the
daughter of her dad's new, harsh-tempered wife. Then she
finds the 1836 diary of Beatrice, who is part Cree and faces
vicious racism as a 'half-breed' in her mostly white community. . . . The alternating narratives are gripping, and the
characters are drawn with rich complexity." Booklist

Bullen, Alexandra

Wish; a novel. Point 2010 323p $17.99

Grades: 8 9 10 11 12 **Fic**
1. Fantasy fiction 2. Magic -- Fiction 3. Twins --
Fiction 4. Wishes -- Fiction 5. Sisters -- Fiction 6.
Bereavement -- Fiction 7. San Francisco (Calif.) --
Fiction
ISBN 978-0-545-13905-2; 0-545-13905-8

LC 2009-22730

After her vivacious twin sister dies, a shy teenaged girl
moves with her parents to San Francisco, where she meets a
magical seamstress who grants her one wish.

"The detailed descriptions of San Francisco and above
all the sisters' relationship provide solid grounding for a
touching, enjoyable read." Kirkus

Followed by: Wishful thinking (2011)

Bunce, Elizabeth C.

Liar's moon. Arthur A. Levine Books 2011
356p $17.99

Grades: 8 9 10 11 12 **Fic**
1. Fantasy fiction 2. Mystery fiction 3. Magic --
Fiction 4. Thieves -- Fiction 5. Homicide -- Fiction 6.
Social classes -- Fiction
ISBN 978-0-545-13608-2; 0-545-13608-3

LC 2011005071

"A solid fantasy sequel embroils its irresistible heroine in mystery, intrigue and romance. . . . A darn good
read." Kirkus

Burd, Nick

★ The **vast** fields of ordinary. Dial Books 2009
309p $16.99

Grades: 10 11 12 **Fic**
1. Iowa -- Fiction 2. Homosexuality -- Fiction 3.
Dating (Social customs) -- Fiction
ISBN 978-0-8037-3340-4; 0-8037-3340-2

LC 2008-46256

ALA GLBTRT Stonewall Book Award (2010)

The summer after graduating from an Iowa high school,
eighteen-year-old Dade Hamilton watches his parents' marriage disintegrate, ends his long-term, secret relationship,
comes out of the closet, and savors first love.

"A refreshingly honest, sometimes funny, and often tender novel." SLJ

Burgess, Melvin

The **hit**; Melvin Burgess. Chicken House/Scho-
lastic Inc. 2014 304 p. $17.99

Grades: 9 10 11 12 **Fic**
1. Death -- Fiction 2. Teenagers -- Drug use -- Fiction
3. Drugs -- Fiction 4. Manchester (England) -- Fiction
ISBN 0545556996; 9780545556996; 9780545557009

LC 2013013792

In this novel, by Melvin Burgess, "a new drug is on the
street. Everyone's buzzing about it. Take the hit. Live the
most intense week of your life. Then die. . . . Adam thinks it
over. He's poor, and doesn't see that changing. . . . His brother Jess is missing. And Manchester is in chaos, controlled by
drug dealers and besieged by a group of homegrown terrorists who call themselves the Zealots. . . . Adam downs one of
the Death pills." (Publisher's note)

"Burgess' dystopian novel posits a near-future world
in which the gap between rich and poor has grown to an

unbridgeable chasm. In their despair, many have-nots are taking a new drug called Death that offers seven days of euphoric bliss followed by the oblivion of death...the novel is viscerally exciting and emotionally engaging. Best of all, it is sure to excite both thoughtful analysis and heated discussion among its readers. A clear winner from Burgess." (Booklist)

Smack. Holt & Co. 1997 327p hardcover o.p. pa $8.99

Grades: 9 10 11 12   **Fic**
    1. Drug abuse -- Fiction 2. Great Britain -- Fiction 3. Runaway teenagers -- Fiction
    ISBN 0-8050-5801-X; 0-312-60862-4 pa
                                        LC 97-40629
First published 1996 in the United Kingdom with title: Junk

After running away from their troubled homes, two English teenagers move in with a group of squatters in the port city of Bristol and try to find ways to support their growing addiction to heroin

"Although the omnipresent British slang (most but not all of which is explained in a glossary) may put off some readers, lots of YAs will be drawn to this book because of the subject. Those who are will quickly find themselves absorbed in an honest, unpatronizing, unvarnished account of teen life on the skids." Booklist

Burgis, Stephanie
    Renegade Magic. Atheneum 2012 304p $16.99

Grades: 6 7 8 9 10   **Fic**
    1. Magic -- Fiction 2. Sisters -- Fiction 3. Great Britain -- History -- 1714-1837 -- Fiction
    ISBN 9781416994497
Twelve-year-old Kat tries to use her untrained magical powers to prevent use of the wild magic of Sulis Minerva found in Bath, England, where Stepmama has brought the family in hopes of finding Kat's sister a proper match.

"This combination of history and fantasy is sure to please." SLJ

Stolen magic; Stephanie Burgis. 1st ed. Atheneum Books for Young Readers 2013 400 p. (hardcover) $17.99

Grades: 6 7 8 9 10   **Fic**
    1. Magic -- Fiction 2. Nobility -- Fiction 3. Marriage -- Fiction 4. Witchcraft -- Fiction 5. Family problems -- Fiction 6. Brothers and sisters -- Fiction 7. Great Britain -- History -- George III, 1760-1820 -- Fiction
    ISBN 1416994513; 9781416994510; 9781416994527; 9781442433823
                                        LC 2011042347
In this book by Stephanie Burgis, "[w]ith just days to go before her sister Angeline's long-delayed wedding to Frederick Carlyle, the impetuous Kat Stephenson has resigned herself to good behavior. But Kat's initiation into the magical Order of the Guardians is fast approaching, and trouble seems to follow her everywhere," including "the arrival of the mysterious Marquise de Valmont, who bears suspicious resemblance to Kat's late mother." (Publisher's note)

"Though Kat's longing for the mother she never knew sounds a note of gravitas, the now-too-familiar characters

and predictable plotting call for freshening. A final plot twist that moves the series action beyond lives of the rich and titled could do the trick next time around. Kat's fans will want to hang on for Book 4." Kirkus

Butler, Octavia E.
    Fledgling; a novel. Seven Stories 2005 317p $24.95

Grades: 11 12 Adult   **Fic**
    1. Science fiction 2. Vampires -- Fiction
    ISBN 1-58322-690-7
                                        LC 2005-5664
"In the feisty Shori, Butler has created a new vampire paradigm—one that's more prone to sci-fi social commentary than gothic romance—and given a tired genre a much-needed shot in the arm." Publ Wkly

★ **Kindred**; 25th anniverary ed; Beacon Press 2003 287p (Black women writers series) pa $14

Grades: 11 12 Adult   **Fic**
    1. Science fiction 2. Slavery -- Fiction 3. Time travel -- Fiction
    ISBN 0-8070-8369-0
                                        LC 2003-62862
First published 1979 by Doubleday

"Dana, a well-educated contemporary African American woman, suddenly finds herself pulled into the past to save the life of a distant ancestor, an early-19th-century southern white boy named Rufus Weylin. Although she returns to the present moments later, she soon finds herself saving Rufus again and again. Although only a short time passes for her between each bout of time travel, years pass for Rufus, who gradually grows into adulthood and becomes a slave owner. This sometimes painful novel features superb character development." Anatomy of Wonder 5

Includes bibliographical references

★ **Parable** of the sower. Warner Books 2000 345p pa $13.99

Grades: 11 12 Adult   **Fic**
    1. Adventure fiction 2. California -- Fiction
    ISBN 0-446-67550-4
                                        LC 99-46567
First published 1993 by Four Walls Eight Windows

The author "infuses this tale with an allegorical quality that is part meditation, part warning. Simple, direct, and deeply felt, this should reach both mainstream and sf audiences." Libr J

Followed by Parable of the talents (1998)

Buzo, Laura
    Love and other perishable items; Laura Buzo. Alfred A. Knopf 2012 243 p. (trade) $17.99

Grades: 9 10 11 12   **Fic**
    1. Love -- Fiction 2. Work -- Fiction 3. Friendship -- Fiction 4. Australia -- Fiction 5. Maturation (Psychology) -- Fiction
    ISBN 0375870008; 9780307929747; 9780375870002; 9780375970009; 9780375986741
                                        LC 2011037579
Originally published as: Good oil. Crows Nest, N.S.W.: Allen & Unwin, 2010.

William C. Morris Award Finalist (2013)

In this book, Laura Buzo presents a love story centered on Amelia. "From the moment she sets eyes on Chris, she is a goner. Lost. Sunk. Head over heels infatuated with him. It's problematic, since Chris, 21, is a sophisticated university student, while Amelia, 15, is 15. . . . Working checkout together at the local supermarket, they strike up a friendship. . . . As time goes on, Amelia's crush doesn't seem so one-sided anymore." (Publisher's note)

Cabot, Meg

Airhead. Scholastic/Point 2008 340p $16.99

Grades: 7 8 9 10   Fic

1. Fashion models -- Fiction 2. New York (N.Y.) -- Fiction 3. Transplantation of organs, tissues, etc. -- Fiction

ISBN 978-0-545-04052-5; 0-545-04052-3

LC 2007-38269

Sixteen-year-old Emerson Watts, an advanced placement student with a disdain for fashion, is the recipient of a "whole body transplant"; and finds herself transformed into one of the world's most famous teen supermodels.

"Cabot's portrayal of Emerson is brilliant. . . . Pure fun, this first series installment will leave readers clamoring for the next." Publ Wkly

Other titles in this series are:

Being Nikki (2009)

Runaway (2010)

★ **All**-American girl. HarperCollins Pubs. 2002 247p hardcover o.p. pa $7.99

Grades: 7 8 9 10   Fic

1. Presidents -- Fiction

ISBN 0-06-029469-8; 0-06-029470-1 lib bdg; 0-06-147989-6 pa

LC 2002-19049

A sophomore girl stops a presidential assassination attempt, is appointed Teen Ambassador to the United Nations, and catches the eye of the very cute First Son. "Grades six to ten." (Bull Cent Child Books)

There's "surprising depth in the characters and plenty of authenticity in the cultural details and the teenage voices—particularly in Sam's poignant, laugh-out-loud narration." Booklist

Being Nikki. Point 2009 336p $16.99

Grades: 7 8 9 10   Fic

1. Fashion models -- Fiction 2. New York (N.Y.) -- Fiction 3. Transplantation of organs, tissues, etc. -- Fiction

ISBN 978-0-545-04056-3; 0-545-04056-6

LC 2008050746

Sequel to: Airhead (2008)

Studious, socially conscious Emerson Watts learns startling news about the family of Nikki Howard, the teen supermodel into whose body Emerson's brain was transplanted by the nefarious Stark corporation.

"Em's first-person narrative is as engaging as in the previous book." Booklist

Followed by: Runaway (2010)

Runaway. Point 2010 310p $16.99

Grades: 7 8 9 10   Fic

1. Fashion models -- Fiction 2. New York (N.Y.) -- Fiction 3. Transplantation of organs, tissues, etc. -- Fiction

ISBN 978-0-545-04060-0; 0-545-04060-4

LC 2009-46813

Sequel to: Being Nikki (2009)

When sixteen-year-old Emerson Watts learns the truth about Nikki, the teen supermodel into whose body Emerson's brain was transplanted, she finds that there is only one person to turn to for help—especially since her loved ones seem to be furious with her.

"Several romantic subplots with secondary characters provide humorous moments, as does the strong narrative voice." SLJ

Caine, Rachel

Ink and bone; the Great Library. Rachel Caine. New American Library 2015 355 p. (hardcover) $17.99

Grades: 8 9 10 11 12   Fic

1. Dystopian fiction 2. Libraries -- Fiction 3. Alternative histories 4. Alexandrian Library -- Fiction

ISBN 9780451472397; 045147239X

LC 2015001509

In this young adult alternative history novel, by Rachel Caine, "the Great Library [of Alexandria] is now a presence in every major city, governing the flow of knowledge to the masses. . . . When he inadvertently commits heresy by creating a device that could change the world, Jess discovers that those who control the Great Library believe that knowledge is more valuable than any human life--and soon both heretics and books will burn." (Publisher's note)

"Caine has created a Dickensian future with an odd mix of technologies and elements of sorcery. A strong cast of characters and nail-biting intensity make for a promising start to this new series." SLJ

Prince of Shadows; a novel of Romeo and Juliet. Rachel Caine. NAL, New American Library 2014 368 p. (hardback) $17.99

Grades: 7 8 9 10 11 12   Fic

1. Love -- Fiction 2. Italy -- Fiction 3. Family -- Fiction 4. Vendetta -- Fiction 5. Families -- Fiction 6. Italy -- History -- 1559-1789 -- Fiction 7. Verona (Italy) -- History -- 16th century -- Fiction

ISBN 0451414411; 9780451414410

LC 2013033482

This book, by Rachel Caine, is a "retelling of the star-crossed tale of Romeo and Juliet. . . . In the Houses of Montague and Capulet, there is only one goal: power. The boys are born to fight and die for honor. . . . Benvolio Montague, cousin to Romeo, knows all this. He expects to die . . . for his house, but a spark of rebellion still lives inside him. At night, he is the Prince of Shadows, the greatest thief in Verona--and he risks all as he steals from House Capulet." (Publisher's note)

"Choosing Romeo and Juliet as her base, Caine expands the story from the viewpoint of Benvolio, Romeo's Montague cousin. While Shakespeare's plot clearly anchors Caine's, the novel focuses on providing context for the well-known story rather than embellishing it. . . . Most impressive is the author's simulation of Shakespeare's language in her prose. Never too obscure for modern readers, it retains the flavor of Shakespearean dialogue throughout, lending an atmosphere of verisimilitude that's reinforced by the detailed city setting. Simply superb." Kirkus

Calame, Don

Beat the band; by Don Calame. 1st ed. Candlewick Press 2010 390 p. (reinforced) $16.99

Grades: 9 10 11 12   **Fic**

1. School stories 2. Humorous fiction 3. Popularity--Fiction 4. Rock music--Fiction

ISBN 0763646334; 9780763646332

LC 2010006607

Sequel to: Swim the fly.

This book, a sequel to "Swim the Fly," follows friends Coop, Matt, and Sean in tenth grade. "Right off the bat they are assigned partners for a semester-long health-class project. To his horror, Coop is paired with 'Hot Dog' Helen, the school outcast, and assigned to research contraceptives. Immediately dubbed 'Corn Dog Coop,' he is desperate for a way to salvage his social status. An upcoming Battle of the Bands presents the perfect opportunity for him to" do so. (School Library Journal)

"Creative sexual slang and bathroom humor begin on page one, but Coop is mostly just talk. Messages about bullying and consequences of teen sex (included via the health project) add just the right note of gravitas to this rockin' romp." SLJ

Call the shots; Don Calame. Candlewick Press 2012 457 p. $16.99

Grades: 9 10 11 12   **Fic**

1. Teenagers -- Fiction 2. Friendship -- Fiction 3. Man-woman relationship -- Fiction

ISBN 0763655562; 9780763655563

LC 2012938812

In the book by Don Calame, protagonist "Sean isn't initially swayed by his crazy friend Coop's idea to make himself, Sean and their third amigo Matt into millionaires by shooting a low-budget horror film. But after his parents announce that they are having another baby . . . Sean decides to sign on as screenwriter to avoid moving into his mean twin sister's room . . . also finds himself embroiled in a terrifying romantic four-way with his new . . . girlfriend Evelyn, his drama crush Leyna and his sister's best friend, the enigmatic Nessa." (Kirkus)

Swim the fly; by Don Calame. 1st ed. Candlewick Press 2009 345 p. (reinforced) $16.99; (paperback) $7.99

Grades: 9 10 11 12   **Fic**

1. Swimming -- Fiction 2. Adolescence -- Fiction

ISBN 076364157X; 0763647764; 9780763641573; 9780763647766

LC 2009920818

Sequel: Beat the Band

In this book, fifteen-year-old Matt Gratton and his two best friends, Coop and Sean, have set themselves a summer goal of seeing "a real-live naked girl for the first time—quite a challenge, given that none of the guys has the nerve to even ask a girl out on a date. But catching a girl in the buff

starts to look easy compared to Matt's other summertime aspiration: to swim the 100-yard butterfly . . . as a way to impress Kelly West, the sizzling new star of the swim team." (Publisher's note)

"Fifteen-year-old Matt has two summer goals: attract his crush Kelly's attention by learning to swim the fly and see a real girl naked. Matt and pals Cooper and Sean cook up several plots to catch a betty in the buff, but all attempts fail. . . . Fully realized secondary characters, realistically raunchy dialogue and the scatological subject matter assure that this boisterous and unexpectedly sweet read will be a word-of-mouth hit." Kirkus

Caletti, Deb

★ **Essential** maps for the lost; Deb Caletti. Simon Pulse 2016 336 p. (hardback) $17.99

Grades: 9 10 11 12   **Fic**

1. Books -- Fiction 2. Grief -- Fiction 3. Secrets -- Fiction 4. Love -- Fiction 5. Depression (Psychology) -- Fiction

ISBN 1481415166; 9781481415163

LC 2015024672

In this novel, by Deb Calettti, Mads "is trying her best to escape herself during one last summer away from a mother who needs more from her than she can give. The body Mads collides with in the middle of the water on a traumatic morning . . . changes everything. The son of the woman in the water, Billy . . . is struggling to find his way . . . in the shadow of grief. When three lives (and one special, shared book) collide, strange things happen." (Publisher's note)

"A moving story about rescuing yourself as well as finally being found." Booklist

The **fortunes** of Indigo Skye. Simon & Schuster Books for Young Readers 2008 304p pa $9.99

Grades: 9 10 11 12   **Fic**

1. Wealth -- Fiction 2. Family life -- Fiction 3. Restaurants -- Fiction 4. Washington (State) -- Fiction 5. Single parent family -- Fiction 6. Waiters and waitresses -- Fiction

ISBN pa; 978-1-4169-1008-4 pa

LC 2007-08744

Eighteen-year-old Indigo is looking forward to becoming a full-time waitress after high school graduation, but her life is turned upside down by a $2.5 million tip given to her by a customer. "Grades nine to twelve." (Bull Cent Child Books)

The author "builds characters with so much depth that readers will be invested in her story. . . . Caletti spins a network of relationships that feels real and enriching." Publ Wkly

★ The **last** forever; Deb Caletti. Simon Pulse 2014 336 p. (hardback) $17.99

Grades: 8 9 10 11 12   **Fic**

1. Love -- Fiction 2. Death -- Fiction 3. Grief -- Fiction 4. Father-daughter relationship -- Fiction 5. Friendship -- Fiction

ISBN 1442450002; 9781442450004

LC 2013031010

This book, by Deb Caletti, is a "novel of love and loss. . . . Nothing lasts forever, and no one gets that more than Tessa.

After her mother died, it's all she can do to keep her friends, her boyfriend, her happiness from slipping away. And then there's her dad. He's stuck in his own daze, and it's hard to feel like a family when their house no longer seems like a home. Her father's solution? An impromptu road trip that lands them in a small coastal town." (Publisher's note)

"After a trying bout with cancer, Tess's mother has died, but she's left behind a one-of-a-kind pixiebell plant. "My mother vowed that the last pixiebell would never die on her watch, and now that I have it, it isn't going to die on mine, either," Tess vows... Featuring sharp-witted first-person narration, some fascinating facts about plants and seeds, relatable characters, and evocative settings, Caletti's (The Story of Us) inspiring novel eloquently depicts the nature of mutability. As with her previous books, this love story reverberates with honesty and emotion." (Publishers Weekly)

The **secret** life of Prince Charming. Simon & Schuster Books for Young Readers 2009 322p $16.99; pa $9.99

Grades: 8 9 10 11 12   Fic
1. Divorce -- Fiction 2. Fathers -- Fiction
ISBN 978-1-4169-5940-3; 1-4169-5940-8; 978-1-4169-5941-0 pa; 1-4169-5941-6 pa
LC 2008-13014

Seventeen-year-old Quinn has heard all her life about how untrustworthy men are, so when she discovers that her charismatic but selfish father, with whom she has recently begun to have a tentative relationship, has stolen from the many women in his life, she decides she must avenge this wrong.

"This is a thoughtful, funny, and empowering spin on the classic road novel. . . . Because of its strong language and the mature themes, this is best suited to older teens, who will appreciate what it has to say about love, relationships, and getting what you need." SLJ

★ The **six** rules of maybe. Simon Pulse 2010 321p $16.99

Grades: 8 9 10 11 12   Fic
1. Oregon -- Fiction 2. Sisters -- Fiction 3. Pregnancy -- Fiction 4. Family life -- Fiction
ISBN 978-1-4169-7969-2; 1-4169-7969-7
LC 2009-22232

Scarlet, an introverted high school junior surrounded by outcasts who find her a good listener, learns to break old patterns and reach for hope when her pregnant sister moves home with her new husband, with whom Scarlet feels an instant connection.

"Reminiscent of the best of Sarah Dessen's work, this novel is beautifully written, deftly plotted, and movingly characterized." SLJ

Stay. Simon Pulse 2011 313p $16.99; ebook $9.99

Grades: 8 9 10 11 12   Fic
1. Islands -- Fiction 2. Washington (State) -- Fiction 3. Dating (Social customs) -- Fiction 4. Father-daughter relationship -- Fiction
ISBN 978-1-4424-0373-4; 1-4424-0373-X; 978-1-4424-0375-8 ebook; 1-4424-0375-6 ebook
LC 2010021804

"Clara has just graduated from high school, and her intense relationship with Christian is over, but he cannot accept that reality. The more he pushes and pleads, the more she pulls away. When Clara and her writer-father go to the coast for the summer without telling anyone, she begins to come to grips with Christian's obsession." (Booklist)

"Fear tinges this summer romance and underscores the issue of abusive and claustrophobic relationships among teens." SLJ

★ Calvin; Martine Leavitt. Farrar Straus Giroux 2015 192 p. (hardback) $17.99

Grades: 7 8 9 10 11 12   Fic
1. Teenagers -- Fiction 2. Schizophrenia -- Fiction 3. Hallucinations and illusions 4. Schools -- Fiction 5. High schools -- Fiction 6. Mental illness -- Fiction 7. Characters in literature -- Fiction
ISBN 0374380732; 9780374380731
LC 2015002574

In Martine Leavitt's novel "Calvin has always known his fate is linked to the comic book character from Calvin & Hobbes. He was born on the day the last strip was published. As a child Calvin played with the toy Hobbes. But now Calvin is a teenager who has been diagnosed with schizophrenia, Hobbes is back--as a delusion--and Calvin can't control him. Calvin decides that if he can convince Bill Watterson to draw one final comic strip, showing a normal teenaged Calvin, he will be cured." (Publisher's note)

"Funny, intellectual, and entertaining, it's a sensitive yet irreverent adventure about a serious subject. Ages 12–up." Pub Wkly

Cameron, Janet E

Cinnamon Toast and the End of the World; Janet E. Cameron. Hachette Books Ireland 2014 384 p. $12.95

Grades: 9 10 11 12   Fic
1. Bildungsromans 2. High school students -- Fiction 3. Interpersonal relations -- Fiction 4. Nova Scotia 5. Love stories 6. Interpersonal relations
ISBN 144474397X; 9781444743975
Rainbow List (2015)

This novel by Janet E. Cameron is set "the spring of 1987 and the world of Stephen Shulevitz who, with three months of high school to go . . . has just realized he's fallen in love--with exactly the wrong person. As Stephen navigates his last few months before college dealing with his overly dependent mother; his distant, pot-smoking father; and his dysfunctional best friends . . . he must decide between love and childhood friendship and between the person he is and the person he can be." (Publisher's note)

"Where this novel truly excels is in its ability to tackle several difficult subjects with clarity and conviction. From homophobia to bullying to parental abuse, Cameron doesn't shy away from the complexity of her material, and the effects are heart-wrenching. This stunning debut will surely appeal to both teenage readers and adults." Quill & Quire

Cameron, Peter

★ **Someday** this pain will be useful to you. Farrar, Straus and Giroux 2007 229p $16

Grades: 9 10 11 12   **Fic**
1. Conduct of life -- Fiction 2. New York (N.Y.) --
Fiction
ISBN 0-374-30989-2; 978-0-374-30989-3
                                          LC 2006-43747
Eighteen-year-old James, a gay teen living in New York
City with his older sister and divorced mother, struggles to
find a direction for his life.

"James makes a memorable protagonist, touching in his
inability to connect with the world but always entertaining
in his first-person account of his New York environment, his
fractured family, his disastrous trip to the nation's capital,
and his ongoing bouts with psychoanalysis. In the process
he dramatizes the ambivalences and uncertainties of adolescence in ways that both teen and adult readers will savor and
remember." Booklist

Cameron, Sharon
The **dark** unwinding; by Sharon Cameron.
Scholastic Press 2012 318 p. (jacketed hardcover)
$17.99
Grades: 6 7 8 9   **Fic**
1. Alternative histories 2. Fantasy fiction 3. Eccentrics
and eccentricities -- Fiction 4. Toys -- Fiction 5.
Uncles -- Fiction 6. Inventions -- Fiction 7. Inheritance
and succession -- Fiction 8. Great Britain -- History --
Victoria, 1837-1901 -- Fiction
ISBN 0545327865; 9780545327862
                                          LC 2011044431
This steampunk novel, by Sharon Cameron, begins
"when Katharine Tulman's inheritance is called into question by the rumor that her eccentric uncle is squandering
away the family fortune. . . . But . . . Katharine discovers . . .
[he is a] genius inventor with his own set of rules, who employs a village of . . . people rescued from the workhouses of
London. Katharine is now torn between protecting her own
inheritance and preserving the . . . community she grows to
care for deeply." (Publisher's note)

Campbell, Bonnie Jo, 1962-
Once upon a river; Bonnie Jo Campbell. W. W.
Norton & Co. 2011 348p. map $25.95
Grades: 11 12 Adult   **Fic**
1. Girls 2. Rivers 3. Adolescence 4. Voyages and
travels 5. Wilderness survival 6. Michigan 7. Teenage
girls -- Fiction 8. Fathers -- Death -- Fiction 9. Voyages
and travels -- Fiction 10. Wilderness survival -- Fiction
ISBN 978-0-393-07989-0; 0-393-07989-9;
9780393341775
                                          LC 201101499
'This novel, a National Book Award and National Book
Critics Circle Award finalist, tells the story of "Margo Crane,
a beauty whose unflinching gaze and uncanny ability with a
rifle have not made her life any easier. After the violent death
of her father, in which she is complicit, Margo takes to the
Stark River in her boat, with only a few supplies and a biography of Annie Oakley, in search of her vanished mother.
But the river . . . is a dangerous place for a young woman
traveling alone, and she must be strong to survive, using
her knowledge of the natural world and her ability to look
unsparingly into the hearts of those around her. Her river
odyssey through rural Michigan becomes a defining jour-

ney, one that leads her beyond self-preservation and to the
decision of what price she is willing to pay for her choices."
(Publisher's note)

Cann, Kate
Consumed. Point 2011 325p $16.99
Grades: 10 11 12   **Fic**
1. Supernatural -- Fiction 2. Good and evil -- Fiction 3.
Great Britain -- Fiction 4. Historic buildings -- Fiction
5. Household employees -- Fiction 6. Racially mixed
people -- Fiction 7. Dating (Social customs) -- Fiction
ISBN 978-0-545-26388-7
                                          LC 2010-20171
Sequel to Possessed (2010)
A new manager brings many changes to Morton's Keep,
capitalizing on its gothic atmosphere and history, but Rayne
sees ominous signs indicating that the one thing that has not
changed is the evil presence she had thought was destroyed.

"Eccentric characters are well-matched by absorbing
writing and a satisfactory ending. Cann effectively builds
both romantic and dramatic tension in a captivating gothic
atmosphere, as Rayne struggles to reconcile her modern sensibilities with myths and legends that refuse to be laid to
rest." Publ Wkly

Possessed. Point 2010 327p $16.99
Grades: 10 11 12   **Fic**
1. Supernatural -- Fiction 2. Good and evil -- Fiction 3.
Great Britain -- Fiction 4. Historic buildings -- Fiction
ISBN 978-0-545-12812-4; 0-545-12812-9
                                          LC 2009-20977
Sixteen-year-old Rayne escapes London, her mother,
and boyfriend for a job in the country at Morton's Keep,
where she is drawn to a mysterious clique and its leader, St.
John, but puzzles over whether the growing evil she senses
is from the manor house or her new friends.

"This atmospheric and deliciously chilling British import gets off to a quick start, and readers will empathize with
the very likable 16-year-old protagonist, who is clearly out
of her element. . . . With a minimum of actual bloodshed,
this supernatural delight can even be enjoyed by the faint of
heart." Booklist
Followed by Consumed (2011)

Cantor, Jillian
The **life** of glass. HarperTeen 2010 340p $16.99
Grades: 7 8 9 10 11 12   **Fic**
1. Fathers -- Fiction 2. Bereavement -- Fiction 3.
Family life -- Fiction
ISBN 978-0-06-168651-1; 0-06-168651-4
                                          LC 2009-1758
Throughout her freshman year of high school, fourteen-
year-old Melissa struggles to hold onto memories of her deceased father, cope with her mother's return to dating, get
along with her sister, and sort out her feelings about her best
friend, Ryan.

"Themes of memory, beauty, and secrets come together in this thoughtful, uplifting book that skillfully avoids
Cinderella-tale predictability. . . . A gentle portrait of a girl
growing through her grief." Booklist

The **September** sisters. HarperTeen 2009 361p $16.99

Grades: 7 8 9 10 11 12 **Fic**
1. Sisters -- Fiction 2. Family life -- Fiction 3. Missing persons -- Fiction
ISBN 978-0-06-168648-1; 0-06-168648-4
LC 2008-7120

A teenaged girl tries to keep her family and herself together after the disappearance of her younger sister.

"Cantor treats the shape of Abby's agony with poignant credibility. . . . This is a sensitive and perceptive account of the way tragedy unfolds both quickly and slowly and life reassembles itself around it." Bull Cent Child Books

Card, Orson Scott

Children of the mind. TOR Bks. 1996 349p (Ender's Game) hardcover o.p. pa $15.95; pa $8.99

Grades: 8 9 10 11 12 Adult **Fic**
1. Science fiction
ISBN 0-312-85395-5; 0-765-30474-0 pa; 9780812522396 pa
LC 95-53262

At the beginning of this fourth series title "Ender Wiggin has placed part of his consciousness and memory in two other bodies, one named after his brother Peter, the other after his sister Valentine. His own body is literally crumbling, and that is not the only problem. A human fleet is on the way to the planet of Lusitania to stop the deadly descolada virus by destroying the planet; meanwhile, the powers that be are also shutting down Ender's friend Jane, the sentient interstellar computer network who makes faster-than-light travel—and, therewith, discovery of the planet of origin of the descolada virus—possible." Booklist

Followed by Ender's shadow

Ender in exile. Tor 2008 380p $25.95; pa $7.99

Grades: 11 12 Adult **Fic**
1. Science fiction
ISBN 978-0-7653-0496-4; 0-7653-0496-1; 978-0-7653-4415-1 pa; 0-7653-4415-7 pa
LC 2008-34075

At the close of "Ender's Game," Andrew Wiggin—called Ender—is told that he can no longer live on Earth. The 12-year-old chooses to leave his home world and begins the long relativistic journey out to the colonies.

"For those who are familiar with Ender and his world, this is a wonderful treat to be devoured whole in a gulp and then returned to later to digest at leisure." SLJ

★ **Ender's** game. TOR Bks. 1991 xxi, 226p $24.95; pa $6.99

Grades: 7 8 9 10 11 12 Adult **Fic**
1. Science fiction 2. Interplanetary voyages -- Fiction
ISBN 0-312-93208-1; 0-8125-5070-6 pa

A reissue of the title first published 1985

ALA YALSA Margaret A. Edwards Award (2008)

"The key, of course, is Ender Wiggin himself. Mr. Card never makes the mistake of patronizing or sentimentalizing his hero. Alternately likable and insufferable, he is a convincing little Napoleon in short pants." N Y Times Book Rev

Other titles in the author's distant future series about Ender Wiggin include:
Children of the mind (1996)
Ender in exile (2008)
Ender's shadow (1999)
Shadow of the giant (2005)
Shadow of the Hegemon (2001)
Shadow of the giant (2005)
Shadow puppets (2002)
Speaker for the dead (1986)
A war of gifts (2007)
Xenocide (1991)

Pathfinder. Simon Pulse 2010 662p $18.99

Grades: 6 7 8 9 10 **Fic**
1. Science fiction 2. Time travel -- Fiction 3. Parapsychology -- Fiction 4. Space colonies -- Fiction 5. Interplanetary voyages -- Fiction
ISBN 978-1-4169-9176-2; 1-4169-9176-X
LC 2010-23243

Thirteen-year-old Rigg has a secret ability to see the paths of others' pasts, but revelations after his father's death set him on a dangerous quest that brings new threats from those who would either control his destiny or kill him.

"While Card delves deeply into his story's knotted twists and turns, readers should have no trouble following the philosophical and scientific mysteries, which the characters are parsing right along with them. An epic in the best sense, and not simply because the twin stories stretch across centuries." Publ Wkly

Seventh son. Doherty Assocs. 1987 241p (Tales of Alvin Maker) hardcover o.p. pa $6.99

Grades: 11 12 Adult **Fic**
1. Fantasy fiction
ISBN 0-312-93019-4; 0-812-53305-4 pa
LC 86-51490

"This beguiling book recalls Robert Penn Warren in its robust but reflective blend of folktale, history, parable and personal testimony, pioneer narrative." Publ Wkly

Other titles in this series about Alvin Maker are:
Alvin Journeyman (1995)
The crystal city (2003)
Heartfire (1998)
Prentice Alvin (1989)
Red prophet (1988)

Shadow of the giant. Tor 2005 384p $25.95; pa $7.99

Grades: 11 12 Adult **Fic**
1. Science fiction
ISBN 0-312-85758-6; 0-812-57139-8 pa
LC 2004-66083

"Bean has grown-up and become a power on Earth. Once the smallest boy at Battle School and Ender's right hand, he went on to serve the Hegemon as strategist and general in the terrible wars that followed the defeat of the alien empire attacking Earth. But now, his greatest wish is for a safe place to build a family—something he has never known—with his wife and fellow Battle School soldier, Petra. Yet there is nowhere on Earth that does not harbor his enemies, both old enemies from the days in Ender's Jeesh and new enemies from the wars on Earth. Bean knows that in order to find the security that he longs for, he must again follow in Ender's footsteps and leave the Earth behind." Publisher's note

Shadow of the Hegemon. TOR Bks. 2000 365p $25.95; pa $7.99

Grades: 11 12 Adult   **Fic**

1. Science fiction

ISBN 0-312-87651-3; 0-812-56595-9 pa

     LC 00-31678

Sequel to Ender's shadow

"The complexity and serious treatment of the book's young protagonists will attract many sophisticated YA readers, while Card's impeccable prose, fast pacing and political intrigue will appeal to adult fans of spy novels, thrillers and science fiction." Publ Wkly

Shadow puppets. TOR Bks. 2002 348p $25.95; pa $7.99

Grades: 11 12 Adult   **Fic**

1. Science fiction

ISBN 0-765-30017-6; 0-765-34005-4 pa

Sequel to: Shadow of the Hegemon

The seventh installment in the Ender Wiggins saga. "In the aftermath of the war against the alien insectoid Formics, the people of Earth experienced a period of unity under the benevolent rulership of the Hegemon Peter Wiggin, brother of war hero Ender Wiggin. As the fragile political peace erodes and internal wars threaten to erupt, the child-warriors of the Battle School—now young adults skilled in the arts of leadership and politics—struggle to bring about a new kind of peace despite the efforts of traitors in their midst." Libr J

Speaker for the Dead. TOR Bks. 1986 415p (Ender's Saga) $25.95; pa $7.99

Grades: 8 9 10 11 12 Adult   **Fic**

1. Science fiction

ISBN 0-312-93738-5; 9780812550757 pa

     LC 85-51765

In this second title in the series Ender Wiggin becomes "Speaker for the Dead out of remorse over his role in the unnecessary destruction of the Buggers. In his new identity, Wiggin plays a vital role in preventing war when a second nonhuman intelligent race—even more incomprehensible than the Buggers—is discovered. This book lacks the sheer dramatic power of Ender's transformation from child into warlord as portrayed in its predecessor. However, it benefits from increased dramatic unity, a well-developed background and supporting cast on the colony planet Lusitania, and the author's customarily stylish writing." Booklist

Followed by Xenocide

Xenocide. 1991 394p (Ender's Game) hardcover o.p. pa $15.95; pa $7.99

Grades: 8 9 10 11 12 Adult   **Fic**

1. Science fiction 2. Interplanetary wars

ISBN 0-312-93208-1; 0-312-86187-7 pa; 9780812509250 pa

     LC 90-27108

Third title in the author's distant future series about Ender Wiggin. "As an armed fleet from Starways Congress hurtles through space towards the rebellious planet Lu-

sitania, Ender Wiggin, his sister Valentine, and his family search for a miracle that will preserve the existence of three intelligent and vastly different species. As a storyteller, Card excels in portraying the quiet drama of wars fought not on battlefields but in the hearts and minds of his characters." Libr J

Followed by Children of the mind

Card, Orson Scott, 1951-

The **lost** gate; a novel of the Mither mages. Orson Scott Card. 1st ed. Tor 2011 384 p. (Novel of the Mither mages.) (hardcover) $24.99

Grades: 7 8 9 10 11 12   **Fic**

1. Magi -- Fiction 2. Magic -- Fiction 3. Family secrets -- Fiction

ISBN 0765326574; 9780765326577

     LC 2010043196

This book is the first installment of author Orson Scott Card's Mithermages series. Protagonist "Danny North . . . discovers that he is capable of creating gates between one place and another or between one world and another. This type of magic has been forbidden for centuries and is punishable by death. Striking out on his own, Danny flees the family compound and seeks to discover a way to live as the first Gate Mage in a thousand years." (Library Journal)

Ruins; by Orson Scott Card. Simon Pulse 2012 544 p. (hardback) $18.99

Grades: 7 8 9 10 11 12   **Fic**

1. Evolution -- Fiction 2. Time travel -- Fiction 3. Space colonies -- Fiction 4. Science fiction

ISBN 1416991778; 9781416991779

     LC 2011052745

Sequel to: Pathfinder

In this book by Orson Scott Card, part of the Pathfinders series, "three time-shifters discover that the secrets of the past threaten their world with imminent obliteration. Rigg, his sister, Param, and best friend, Umbo, have joined their abilities to slip through time . . . circumventing the invisible Wall that divides their planet into 19 independent evolutionary experiments." (Kirkus Reviews)

Cardi, Annie

The **Chance** you won't return; Annie Cardi. Candlewick Press 2014 352 p. $16.99

Grades: 9 10 11 12   **Fic**

1. Mentally ill -- Fiction 2. Mother-daughter relationship -- Fiction

ISBN 0763662925; 9780763662929

     LC 2013946619

In this book, protagonist Alex's "mother believes herself to be Amelia Earhart. As Alex's mother's delusion becomes more persistent, she is hospitalized, but Alex's father's insurance isn't enough, and the family has to take care of her at home. . . . When she realizes that her mother is working on a timeline that will eventually lead to her disappearance . . . her confession closes the distance she has been maintaining between herself and her friends." (Bulletin of the Center for Children's Books)

"The author creates nuanced characters and presents them with their flaws and strengths intact, including a character with a mental disorder who never loses her humanity or becomes a caricature.... This novel delivers something far more rare: a well-written, first-person narrative about negotiating life's curve balls that has a realistic ending. An honest, uncompromising story." - Kirkus

Carey, Edward

Heap House; The Iremonger Trilogy. by Edward Carey. Overlook Press 2014 416 p. illustrations $16.99

Grades: 5 6 7 8 9 10   **Fic**

1. Boys -- Fiction 2. Houses -- Fiction 3. London (England) -- Fiction 4. Great Britain -- History -- Victoria, 1837-1901 -- Fiction 5. Dwellings 6. London (England) 7. Orphans -- Fiction 8. Family secrets -- Fiction

ISBN 1468309536; 9781468309539

In this book, by Edward Carey, "Clod is an Iremonger. He lives in the Heaps, a vast sea of lost and discarded items collected from all over London. At the centre is Heap House, a puzzle of houses, castles, homes and mysteries reclaimed from the city and built into a living maze of staircases and scurrying rats. The Iremongers are a mean and cruel family, robust and hardworking, but Clod has an illness. He can hear the objects whispering." (Publisher's note)

"Living among sentient trash heaps, Clod Iremonger has always been able to hear the voices of the objects that his family members carry, but the arrival of serving girl Lucy imbues the objects with a new and dangerous energy. Descriptive prose and black-and-white portraits create a unique cast of characters in a bleak, dilapidated home. Fans of Joan Aiken will flock to this dark mystery." Horn Book

Other titles in this series are:
Foulsham (2015)
Lungdon (2015)

Carey, Janet Lee

Dragon's Keep. Harcourt 2007 302p $17

Grades: 7 8 9 10   **Fic**

1. Fantasy fiction 2. Dragons -- Fiction 3. Princesses -- Fiction 4. Mother-daughter relationship -- Fiction 5. Great Britain -- History -- 1066-1154, Norman period -- Fiction

ISBN 978-0-15-205926-2; 0-15-205926-1

LC 2006-24669

In 1145 A.D., as foretold by Merlin, fourteen-year-old Rosalind, who will be the twenty-first Pendragon Queen of Wilde Island, has much to accomplish to fulfill her destiny, while hiding from her people the dragon's claw she was born with that reflects only one of her mother's dark secrets.

This is told "in stunning, lyrical prose.... Carey smoothly blends many traditional fantasy tropes here, but her telling is fresh as well as thoroughly compelling." Booklist

In the time of dragon moon; by Janet Lee Carey. Kathy Dawson Books, an imprint of Penguin Group (USA) LLC 2015 472 p. (hardback) $17.99

Grades: 9 10 11 12   **Fic**

1. Fantasy fiction 2. Dragons -- Fiction 3. Healers -- Fiction 4. Fantasy 5. Fairies -- Fiction 6. Kidnapping -- Fiction 7. Racially mixed people -- Fiction 8. Kings, queens, rulers, etc. -- Fiction 9. British Isles -- History

-- 13th century -- Fiction

ISBN 0803738102; 9780803738102

LC 2014032216

In this medieval fantasy novel, by Janet Lee Carey, "Uma serves as her father's apprentice and dreams of succeeding him as Adan one day, but Euit tribal law forbids a woman as a healer. . . . When she becomes the queen's designated healer, Uma is soon embroiled in deadly court intrigues involving dragons and the fey folk. She also finds herself involved with Jackrun, a Pendragon prince who is part dragon and struggles to control the fire within him." (School Library Journal)

"The author's world-building is detailed and fascinating, and Uma is a strong, admirable heroine. This is a must-purchase for libraries owning the earlier installments and a great choice for where teen fantasy is popular." SLJ

★ **Stealing** death. Egmont USA 2009 354p map $16.99; lib bdg $19.99

Grades: 7 8 9 10   **Fic**

1. Fantasy fiction 2. Death -- Fiction 3. Siblings -- Fiction

ISBN 978-1-60684-009-2; 1-60684-009-6; 978-1-60684-045-0 lib bdg; 1-60684-045-2 lib bdg

LC 2009-16240

After losing his family, except for his younger sister Jilly, and their home in a tragic fire, seventeen-year-old Kipp Corwin, a poor farmer, must wrestle with death itself in order to save Jilly and the woman he loves.

"Carey's wonderful language weaves family, love, wise teachers, and petty villains together in a vast landscape. . . . This is quite simply fantasy at its best—original, beautiful, amazing, and deeply moving." SLJ

Carleson, J. C.

The **tyrant's** daughter; J.C. Carleson. Alfred A. Knopf 2014 304 p. (trade) $17.99

Grades: 8 9 10 11 12   **Fic**

1. Teenagers -- Fiction 2. Middle East -- Fiction 3. Kings and rulers -- Fiction 4. Exiles -- Fiction 5. Schools -- Fiction 6. Dictators -- Fiction 7. Immigrants -- Fiction 8. High schools -- Fiction 9. Middle East -- Politics and government -- Fiction

ISBN 0449809978; 9780449809976; 9780449809983; 9780449809990

LC 2013014783

In this book by J.C. Carleson, "when her father is killed in a coup, 15-year-old Laila flees from the war-torn middle east to a life of exile and anonymity in the U.S. She adjusts to a new school, new friends, and a new culture, but while Laila sees opportunity . . . her mother is focused on the past. She's conspiring with CIA operatives and rebel factions to regain the throne their family lost. Laila can't bear to stand still as an international crisis takes shape around her." (Publisher's note)

"Removed from her unnamed Middle Eastern country after her father is murdered during a coup, 15-year-old Laila is now living near Washington D. C. with her mother and brother...This is more than just Laila's story; rather, it is a story of context, beautifully written (by a former undercover CIA agent), and stirring in its questions and eloquent observations about our society and that of the Middle East." (Booklist)

Carlson, Melody

Premiere. Zondervan 2010 218p il (On the runway) pa $9.99

Grades: 7 8 9 10   **Fic**

1. Fashion -- Fiction 2. Sisters -- Fiction 3. Christian life -- Fiction 4. Television programs -- Fiction

ISBN 978-0-310-71786-7; 0-310-71786-8

LC 2009-48438

When two sisters get their own fashion-focused reality television show, vivacious Paige is excited, but Erin, a Christian who is more interested in being behind the camera than in front of it, has problems with some of the things they are asked to do

"This book is worth adding whether you have a demand for Christian novels or not. The fashion and reality-show fireworks are enough to keep even reluctant readers coming back for more." SLJ

Followed by Catwalk (2010)

Carriger, Gail

★ **Curtsies** & conspiracies; Gail Carriger. Little, Brown and Co. 2013 320 p. (Finishing school) $18

Grades: 7 8 9 10 11 12   **Fic**

1. Steampunk fiction 2. Espionage -- Fiction 3. Conspiracies -- Fiction 4. Science fiction 5. Robots -- Fiction 6. Schools -- Fiction 7. Etiquette -- Fiction 8. Boarding schools -- Fiction 9. Great Britain -- History -- George VI, 1936-1952 -- Fiction

ISBN 031619011X; 9780316190114

LC 2012048520

In this book, by Gail Carriger, "Sophronia's first year at Mademoiselle Geraldine's Finishing Academy for Young Ladies of Quality . . . is training her to be a spy. A conspiracy is afoot--one with dire implications for both supernaturals and humans. Sophronia must rely on her training to discover who is behind the dangerous plot-and survive the London Season with a full dance card." (Publisher's note)

"With the school's dirigible heading toward London for a liaison with an inventor studying aetherospheric travel, Sophronia (Etiquette & Espionage) is convinced that her professors are Up To Something. Is the academy affiliated with vampire hives, werewolf packs, the anti-supernatural Picklemen, or the Crown--all of whom would benefit from controlling aether technology? A witty and suspenseful steampunk romp." (Horn Book)

Curtsies and conspiracies

★ **Etiquette** & espionage; by Gail Carriger. Little, Brown 2013 320 p. (alk. paper) $17.99

Grades: 7 8 9 10 11 12   **Fic**

1. Spy stories 2. School stories 3. Assassins -- Fiction 4. Science fiction 5. Robots -- Fiction 6. Schools -- Fiction 7. Espionage -- Fiction 8. Etiquette -- Fiction 9. Boarding schools -- Fiction 10. Great Britain -- History -- George VI, 1936-1952 -- Fiction

ISBN 031619008X; 9780316190084

LC 2012005498

In this book, Sophronia's mother is "desperate for her daughter to become a proper lady. So she enrolls Sophronia in Mademoiselle Geraldine's Finishing Academy for Young Ladies of Quality. But Sophronia soon realizes the school is not quite what her mother might have hoped. At Mademoi-

selle Geraldine's, young ladies learn to finish . . . everything. Certainly, they learn the fine arts of dance, dress, and etiquette, but they also learn to deal out death, diversion, and espionage." (Publisher's note)

Carson, Rae

★ The **bitter** kingdom; by Rae Carson. Greenwillow Books 2013 448 p. (hardcover) $17.99

Grades: 8 9 10 11 12   **Fic**

1. Fantasy fiction 2. Magic -- Fiction 3. Queens -- Fiction 4. Love -- Fiction 5. Prophecies -- Fiction 6. Kings, queens, rulers, etc. -- Fiction

ISBN 0062026542; 9780062026545

LC 2013011912

Sequel to: The crown of embers

This is the final book in Rae Carson's Girl of Fire and Thorns trilogy. Here, "young Queen Elisa and her companions trek into enemy territory to rescue the man she loves, while a traitor back home attempts to overthrow her. Elisa's journeys take her to . . . Invierne, where she hopes to destroy the source of the Inviernos' magic and bargain for peace; to the Basajuan desert, where only her most audacious plans have any chance to stop the war; and home to try to regain her throne." (Publishers Weekly)

★ The **crown** of embers; by Rae Carson. Greenwillow Books 2012 410 p. (hardcover) $17.99

Grades: 8 9 10 11 12   **Fic**

1. Magic 2. Queens 3. Fantasy fiction 4. Adventure fiction 5. Love -- Fiction

ISBN 0062026518; 9780062026514

LC 2012014125

This young adult fantasy novel, by Rae Carson, is the sequel to the Morris, Cybils, and Andre Norton Award finalist book "The Girl of Fire and Thorns." "Elisa is a hero. . . . [But] to conquer the power she bears once and for all, Elisa must follow the trail of long-forgotten--and forbidden--clues from the deep, undiscovered catacombs of her own city to the treacherous seas. With her goes a one-eyed spy, a traitor, and the man who--despite everything--she is falling in love with." (Publisher's note)

★ The **girl** of fire and thorns. Greenwillow Books 2011 423p $17.99

Grades: 8 9 10 11 12   **Fic**

1. Fantasy fiction 2. Magic -- Fiction 3. Prophecies -- Fiction 4. Kings and rulers -- Fiction

ISBN 978-0-06-202648-4; 0-06-202648-8

LC 2010042021

Morris Award Finalist (2012)

"The first book in the acclaimed and award winning New York Times bestselling trilogy. The Girl of Fire and Thorns is a remarkable novel full of adventure, sorcery, heartbreak, and power...Once a century, one person is chosen for greatness. Elisa is the chosen one. But she is also the younger of two princesses. The one who has never done anything remarkable, and can't see how she ever will. Now, on her sixteenth birthday, she has become the secret wife of a handsome and worldly king...And he's not the only one who seeks her. Savage enemies, seething with dark magic, are hunting her. A daring, determined revolutionary thinks she could be his people's savior. Soon it is not just her life, but her very heart that is at stake." (Publisher's Note)

"This fast-moving and exciting novel is rife with political conspiracies and machinations." SLJ

Walk on Earth a Stranger; Rae Carson. Greenwillow books 2015 448 p. map $17.99
Grades: 7 8 9 10   Fic
   1. Magic -- Fiction 2. California -- Gold discoveries
   ISBN 0062242911; 9780062242914
                    LC 2015015751

In Rae Carson's novel "Lee Westfall has a secret. She can sense the presence of gold in the world around her. Veins deep beneath the earth, pebbles in the river, nuggets dug up from the forest floor. The buzz of gold means warmth and life and home--until everything is ripped away by a man who wants to control her. Lee disguises herself as a boy and takes to the trail across the country. Gold was discovered in California, and where else could such a magical girl find herself, find safety?" (Publisher's note)

"Carson's story is simply terrific—tense and exciting, while gently and honestly addressing the brutal hardships of the westward migration. Even minor characters are fully three-dimensional, but it's Leah who rightfully takes center stage as a smart, resourceful, determined, and realistic heroine who embodies the age-old philosophy that it isn't what happens to you, but how you react to it that matters. Ages 13–up." Pub Wkly

Carter, Ally
   Embassy row #1; all fall down. Ally Carter; [edited by] David Levithan. Scholastic Press 2015 320 p. $17.99
Grades: 7 8 9 10   Fic
   1. Murder -- Fiction 2. Revenge -- Fiction 3. Ambassadors -- Fiction 4. Mother-daughter relationship -- Fiction
   ISBN 0545654742; 9780545654746
                    LC 2014947739

In this book, by Ally Carter, "Grace Blakely is absolutely certain of three things: 1. She is not crazy. 2. Her mother was murdered. 3. Someday she is going to find the killer and make him pay. As certain as Grace is about these facts, nobody else believes her -- so there's no one she can completely trust. Not her grandfather, a powerful ambassador. Not her new friends, who all live on Embassy Row. . . . But they can't control Grace." (Publisher's note)

"This exciting first book in the Embassy Row series features sixteen-year-old Grace, who has moved into the United States Embassy on the coast of Adria with her ambassador grandfather. It is the first time in three years that she has been back to Adria, since her mother's tragic death in a fire... Her quest to find the truth is one that readers will love to follow, through the twists and turns of Embassy Row and with a diverse array of characters. Some help her, and some stand in her way . . . but Grace is a fighter, and she will stop at nothing to find out what happened to her mother. Readers will love this first book in what promises to be an exciting, thrilling mystery series from best-selling author Carter." VOYA

Perfect scoundrels; a Heist society novel. by Ally Carter. 1st ed. Disney/Hyperion Books 2013 328 p. (hardcover) $17.99
Grades: 7 8 9 10   Fic
   1. Crime -- Fiction 2. Theft -- Fiction 3. Wealth -- Fiction 4. Detective and mystery stories 5. Dating (Social customs) -- Fiction 6. Swindlers and swindling -- Fiction 7. Inheritance and succession -- Fiction
   ISBN 1423166000; 9781423166009
                    LC 2012032405

This book is an installment of Ally Carter's Heist Society series. "When Hale suddenly inherits his grandmother's billion-dollar company, it's pretty obvious that he and Kat can't be up to their old tricks anymore. But can Hale trust Kat not to dip her hand in the cookie jar and steal the company's fortune—even though he knows she's prepared to do the impossible?" (Dolly Magazine)

Carter, Caela
   Me, him, them, and it; by Caela Carter. Bloomsbury; Distributed to the trade by Macmillan 2013 320 p. (hardcover) $16.99
Grades: 9 10 11 12   Fic
   1. Teenage pregnancy -- Fiction 2. Dysfunctional families -- Fiction 3. Pregnancy -- Fiction 4. Family problems -- Fiction 5. Emotional problems -- Fiction
   ISBN 1599909588; 9781599909585
                    LC 2012014331

In this novel, by Caela Carter, "when Evelyn . . . [upset] her parents with a bad reputation, she wasn't planning to ruin her valedictorian status. She also wasn't planning to fall for Todd-the guy she was just using for sex. And she definitely wasn't planning on getting pregnant. When Todd turns his back on her, Evelyn's not sure where to go." (Publisher's note)

Casanova, Mary
   Frozen; Mary Casanova. University of Minnesota Press 2012 264 p. (hc/j: alk. paper) $16.95
Grades: 7 8 9 10   Fic
   1. Voice -- Fiction 2. Conduct of life -- Fiction 3. Mother-daughter relationship -- Fiction 4. Memory -- Fiction 5. Families -- Fiction 6. Identity -- Fiction 7. Selective mutism -- Fiction 8. Minnesota -- History -- 20th century -- Fiction
   ISBN 0816680566; 9780816680566; 9780816680573
                    LC 2012019376

Author Mary Casanova tells the story of a young girl's life after her mother dies. "Sixteen-year-old Sadie Rose hasn't spoken in eleven years—ever since she was found in a snowbank the night her mother died under strange circumstances . . . Like her voice, her memories of her mother and what happened that night were frozen . . . [The book] is a suspenseful, moving testimonial to the power of family and memory and the extraordinary strength of a young woman who has lost her voice in nearly every way, but is determined to find it again." (Publisher's note)

Includes bibliographical references (p.)

Casella, Jody
   Thin space; Jody Casella. Simon Pulse 2014 256 p. (hardcover: alk. paper) $16.99

Grades: 9 10 11 12 **Fic**
1. Fantasy fiction 2. Paranormal fiction 3. Dead
-- Fiction 4. Twins -- Fiction 5. Schools -- Fiction
6. Brothers -- Fiction 7. High schools -- Fiction 8.
Supernatural -- Fiction 9. Conduct of life -- Fiction 10.
Interpersonal relations -- Fiction
ISBN 158270435X; 9781582703923; 9781582704357
LC 2012045691

In this book, for "three months, high school junior Marsh
Windsor has been refusing to wear shoes, ignoring schoolwork and friends, and getting into fights. His parents and
teachers—even his former girlfriend—tolerate his bizarre
behavior as an inability to cope with the car wreck that
seriously injured Marsh and killed his twin, Austin. Only
the new girl, Maddie, knows that Marsh is seeking a 'thin
space,' a portal between the realms of the living and the
dead." (Kirkus Reviews)

Cashore, Kristin
★ **Bitterblue**; Kristin Cashore. Dial Books
2012 563 p.
Grades: 9 10 11 12 **Fic**
1. Fantasy fiction 2. Queens -- Fiction 3. Brainwashing
-- Fiction 4. Conspiracies -- Fiction 5. Fantasy
ISBN 0803734735; 9780803734739
LC 2011035026
"Sequel to Graceling, companion to Fire"-Jkt

This young adult fantasy novel "grapples with the messy
aftermath of destroying an evil overlord. Nine years after
Bitterblue took the crown, the young queen and her realm
are still struggling to come to terms with the monstrous
legacy of her father. . . . Bitterblue discovers that her people
have not healed as much as she has been told. . . . [She] must
draw upon all her courage, cleverness and ferocious compassion to reveal the truth -- and to care for those it shatters."
(Kirkus Reviews)

★ **Fire**; a novel. Dial Books 2009 461p map
$17.99
Grades: 9 10 11 12 **Fic**
1. Fantasy fiction
ISBN 978-0-8037-3461-6; 0-8037-3461-1
LC 2009-5187

In a kingdom called the Dells, Fire is the last human-
shaped monster, with unimaginable beauty and the ability to
control the minds of those around her, but even with these
gifts she cannot escape the strife that overcomes her world.

"Many twists propel the action . . . [and] Cashore's
conclusion satisfies, but readers will clamor for a sequel to
the prequel—a book bridging the gap between this one and
Graceling." Publ Wkly

★ **Graceling**. Harcourt 2008 471p map $17;
pa $9.99
Grades: 8 9 10 11 12 **Fic**
1. Fantasy fiction
ISBN 978-0-15-206396-2; 0-15-206396-X; 978-0-
547-25830-0 pa; 0-547-25830-5 pa
LC 2007045436
ALA YALSA Morris Award Finalist, 2009

In a world where some people are born with extreme
skills called Graces, Katsa struggles for redemption from

her own horrifying Grace, the Grace of killing. She teams up
with another young fighter to save their land from a corrupt
king. "Age fourteen and up." (N Y Times Book Rev)

"This is gorgeous storytelling: exciting, stirring, and accessible. Fantasy and romance readers will be thrilled." SLJ

Castan, Mike
Fighting for Dontae; Mike Castan. Holiday
House 2012 150 p. (hardcover) $16.95
Grades: 6 7 8 9 10 11 12 **Fic**
1. Gangs -- Fiction 2. Reading -- Fiction 3. Children
with disabilities -- Fiction 4. Schools -- Fiction 5.
California -- Fiction 6. Middle schools -- Fiction 7.
Conduct of life -- Fiction 8. Family problems -- Fiction
9. Mexican Americans -- Fiction 10. People with
disabilities -- Fiction 11. People with mental disabilities
-- Fiction
ISBN 0823423484; 9780823423484
LC 2011042115

This book is the story of seventh-grader Javier, who
"does not really want to be in a gang," but thinks he must
join the Playaz gang to be cool, which he desperately wants
to be. "When he is assigned to work with the special-ed class
at school, Javier knows that his days as a cool kid are officially over. He does not expect to enjoy it, but reading to
Dontae, a severely disabled boy, becomes the one thing Javier looks forward to." (Children's Literature)

Castellucci, Cecil
Beige. Candlewick Press 2007 307p $16.99;
pa $8.99
Grades: 7 8 9 10 **Fic**
1. Musicians -- Fiction 2. Punk rock music -- Fiction
3. Los Angeles (Calif.) -- Fiction 4. Father-daughter
relationship -- Fiction
ISBN 978-0-7636-3066-9; 0-7636-3066-7; 978-0-
7636-4232-7 pa; 0-7636-4232-0 pa
LC 2006-52458

Katy, a quiet French Canadian teenager, reluctantly
leaves Montréal to spend time with her estranged father, an
aging Los Angeles punk rock legend.

This a "a good read and an interesting look at the world
of punk and alternative rock." Kliatt

Boy proof. Candlewick Press 2005 203p
$15.99; pa $7.99
Grades: 7 8 9 10 **Fic**
1. Motion pictures -- Fiction 2. Los Angeles (Calif.)
-- Fiction
ISBN 0-7636-2333-4; 0-7636-2796-6 pa
LC 2004-50256

Feeling alienated from everyone around her, Los Angeles high school senior and cinephile Victoria Denton hides
behind the identity of a favorite movie character until an interesting new boy arrives at school and helps her realize that
there is more to life than just the movies.

This "novel's clipped, funny, first-person, present-tense
narrative will grab teens . . . with its romance and the screwball special effects, and with the story of an outsider's struggle both to belong and to be true to herself." Booklist

Rose sees red. Scholastic Press 2010 197p $17.99

Grades: 7 8 9 10 **Fic**

1. School stories 2. Ballet -- Fiction 3. Russians -- Fiction 4. Friendship -- Fiction 5. New York (N.Y.) -- Fiction

ISBN 978-0-545-06079-0; 0-545-06079-6

LC 2009-36850

In the 1980s, two teenaged ballet dancers—one American, one Russian—spend an unforgettable night in New York City, forming a lasting friendship despite their cultural and political differences.

"The protagonist is a complexly layered character who suffers from crippling sensitivity, and her difficulty feeling at home in her body will resonate with teens. She is honest, funny, and completely authentic. . . . The prose is poetic and rich." SLJ

Castle, Jennifer

You look different in real life; Jennifer Castle. HarperTeen, an imprint of HarperCollinsPublishers 2013 368 p. (hardback) $17.99

Grades: 7 8 9 10 **Fic**

1. School stories 2. Documentary films -- Fiction 3. Identity -- Fiction 4. Celebrities -- Fiction 5. New York (State) -- Fiction 6. Interpersonal relations -- Fiction 7. Family life -- New York (State) -- Fiction 8. Documentary films -- Production and direction -- Fiction

ISBN 0061985813; 9780061985812

LC 2012051743

This book follows five ordinary 16-year-olds who have been the subjects of two documentaries at ages 6 and 11. Now, many "changes have occurred since the last time they were filmed" so the "producers struggle to find usable footage and resort to staging some scenes, which in previous years was unnecessary." (School Library Journal)

Castor, H. M.

VIII; H.M. Castor. Simon & Schuster Books for Young Readers 2013 399 p. (hardcover) $17.99

Grades: 8 9 10 11 12 **Fic**

1. Great Britain -- History -- 1485-1603, Tudors 2. Kings, queens, rulers, etc. -- Fiction 3. Great Britain -- History -- Henry VII, 1485-1509 -- Fiction 4. Great Britain -- History -- Henry VIII, 1509-1547 -- Fiction

ISBN 1442474181; 9781442474185; 9781442474208

LC 2012021550

This book is a biography of Henry VIII of England. As a second son, Henry's youth is full of "fighting, jousting and gambling. When his elder brother, Arthur, unexpectedly dies, Hal realizes that . . . he now has a straight line to the throne. However . . . the difficulties of producing a royal heir, together with the thwarting of his overweening military ambition against the French by Spanish Catherine's family and his own . . . advisers cause Henry to become increasingly cynical and desperate." (Kirkus Reviews)

Catmull, Katherine

The **radiant** road; a novel. by Katherine Catmull. Dutton Books, an imprint of Penguin Random House LLC 2016 368 p. (hardcover) $17.99

Grades: 7 8 9 10 **Fic**

1. Magic -- Fiction 2. Fairies -- Fiction 3. Identity -- Fiction 4. Good and evil -- Fiction

ISBN 9780525953470

LC 2015020678

In this book, by Katherine Catmull, "Clare Macleod and her father are returning to Ireland, where they'll inhabit the house Clare was born in—a house built into a green hillside with a tree for a wall. For Clare, the house is not only full of memories of her mother, but also of a mysterious boy with raven-dark hair and dreamlike nights filled with stars and magic. Clare soon discovers that the boy is as real as the fairy-making magic." (Publisher's note)

"Catmull has created an eerily lovely story, writing with an old-fashioned style that at times sings like a lullaby. An excellent addition to either teen or juvenile collections of all sizes." Booklist

Chaltas, Thalia

Because I am furniture. Viking Children's Books 2009 352p $16.99

Grades: 8 9 10 11 **Fic**

1. School stories 2. Novels in verse 3. Guilt -- Fiction 4. Child abuse -- Fiction 5. Child sexual abuse -- Fiction

ISBN 978-0-670-06298-0; 0-670-06298-7

LC 2008-23235

The youngest of three siblings, fourteen-year-old Anke feels both relieved and neglected that her father abuses her brother and sister but ignores her, but when she catches him with one of her friends, she finally becomes angry enough to take action.

"Incendiary, devastating, yet—in total—offering empowerment and hope, Chaltas's poems leave an indelible mark." Publ Wkly

Chambers, Aidan

★ **Dying** to know you; Aidan Chambers. Amulet Books 2012 275 p.

Grades: 9 10 11 12 **Fic**

1. Authors -- Fiction 2. Dyslexia -- Fiction 3. Friendship -- Fiction 4. Elderly men -- Fiction 5. Self-perception -- Fiction 6. Self perception -- Fiction 7. Interpersonal relations -- Fiction

ISBN 1419701657; 9781419701658

LC 2012000843

This young adult novel is "a story told in . . . first-person voice by a 75-year-old man. . . . Karl approaches the older man, an author, with a request. His new girlfriend, Fiorella, has tasked him with providing a series of written answers to questions . . . so that she can find out more about him. But Karl, an 18-year-old plumber who's no longer in school, is dyslexic. . . . The friendship . . . form[s] as Karl gradually gains knowledge of himself that isn't based on the previous failures in his life." (Kirkus)

Chambers, Veronica

Fifteen candles. Hyperion 2010 187p (Amigas) pa $7.99

Grades: 6 7 8 9 10 **Fic**

1. Friendship -- Fiction 2. Cuban Americans -- Fiction 3. Business enterprises -- Fiction 4. Quinceañera

(Social custom) -- Fiction
ISBN 978-1-4231-2362-0; 1-4231-2362-X

"It's Alicia's quince años, and even though her thoroughly modern parents took her to Spain for her quinceañera, most of her friends are having elaborate parties to celebrate their entry into womanhood. When she realizes that a fellow intern in the mayor's office needs help in planning her quince, Alicia envisions a new business venture for her and her three best friends, Amigas Inc. . . . A warm celebration of Latin culture, especially the traditional quinceañera, this is the first in a series that is sure to draw a large audience." Booklist

Chandler, Kristen

Wolves, boys, & other things that might kill me. Viking 2010 371p $17.99; pa $8.99

Grades: 7 8 9 10 11 12   **Fic**

1. Wolves -- Fiction 2. Yellowstone National Park -- Fiction
ISBN 978-0-670-01142-1; 0-670-01142-8; 978-0-14-241883-3 pa; 0-14-241883-8 pa

LC 2009-30179

Two teenagers become close as the citizens of their town fight over the packs of wolves that have been reintroduced into the nearby Yellowstone National Park.

This "is a lively drama, saturated with multifaceted characters and an environmental undercurrent. She writes persuasively about the great outdoors, smalltown dynamics and politics, and young love." Publ Wkly

Charbonneau, Joelle

Graduation day; Joelle Charbonneau. Houghton Mifflin Harcourt 2014 304 p. (hardback) $17.99

Grades: 7 8 9 10 11 12   **Fic**

1. Dystopian fiction 2. Love -- Fiction 3. Loyalty -- Fiction 4. Survival -- Fiction 5. Adventure and adventurers -- Fiction 6. Government, Resistance to -- Fiction
ISBN 0547959214; 9780547959214

LC 2013034743

In this book, by Joelle Charbonneau, "The United Commonwealth teeters on the brink of all-out civil war. The rebel resistance plots against a government that rules with cruelty and cunning. Gifted student and Testing survivor, Cia Vale, vows to fight. . . . This is the chance to lead that Cia has trained for -- but who will follow? Plunging through layers of danger and deception, Cia must risk the lives of those she loves--and gamble on the loyalty of her lethal classmates." (Publisher's note)

"Charbonneau concludes her dystopian Testing trilogy with this action-packed finale, which sees Cia Vale secretly tasked by the President of the United Commonwealth to remove the officials behind the lethal Testing process that has claimed so many young lives...As in the previous books, Charbonneau remains focused on philosophical worries and moral tests over spectacle and bloodshed, with multiple layers and twists to keep readers forever guessing. Enough potential threads are left dangling to leave room for future stories." (Publishers Weekly)

Independent study; by Joelle Charbonneau. Houghton Mifflin, Houghton Mifflin Harcourt 2014 320 p. (The testing) (hardback) $17.99

Grades: 7 8 9 10 11 12   **Fic**

1. Love 2. College students 3. Resistance to government 4. Adventure and adventurers
ISBN 0547959206; 9780547959207

LC 2013004815

In this book, by Joelle Charbonneau, "sixteen-year-old Cia Vale was chosen by the United Commonwealth government as one of the best and brightest graduates of all the colonies. . . . [Now], Cia is a freshman at the University in Tosu City with her hometown sweetheart, Tomas—and though the government has tried to erase her memory of the brutal horrors of The Testing, Cia remembers. Her attempts to expose the ugly truth behind the government's murderous programs put her . . . in a world of danger." (Publisher's note)

"—In this sequel to The Testing (Houghton Harcourt, 2013), Cia is drawn deeper into the political machinations of Tosu City as she enters the University...Fans of The Testing will be thrilled with this new installment and will be anxiously waiting for the story's conclusion." (School Library Journal)

★ The **Testing**; by Joelle Charbonneau. Houghton Mifflin Harcourt 2013 344 p. (hardcover) $17.99

Grades: 7 8 9 10 11 12   **Fic**

1. Examinations -- Fiction 2. Survival skills -- Fiction 3. Schools -- Fiction 4. Missing persons -- Fiction 5. Graduation (School) -- Fiction 6. Universities and colleges -- Fiction
ISBN 0547959109; 9780547959108

LC 2012018090

In this book by Joelle Charbonneau, "Cia Vale is one of four teens chosen to represent her small colony at the annual Testing, an intensive mental and physical examination aimed at identifying the best and brightest, who will go on to the University and help rebuild their shattered world. Forewarned not to trust anyone, Cia nonetheless forms a tentative partnership with resourceful Tomas, with whom she shares an unexpected emotional connection." (Publishers Weekly)

Charlton-Trujillo, e. E.

★ **Fat** Angie; E. E. Charlton-Trujillo. Candlewick Press 2013 272 p. $16.99

Grades: 9 10 11 12   **Fic**

1. School stories 2. Obesity -- Fiction 3. Lesbians -- Fiction
ISBN 0763661198; 9780763661199

LC 2012942623

Stonewall Book Award-Mike Morgan and Larry Romans Children's & Young Adult Literature Award (2014)

Lambda Literary Awards Finalist (2014)

This teenage novel, by E. E. Charlton-Trujillo, follows Angie, an overweight high school student who is bullied and dealing with grief over her sister, a presumed dead prisoner of the Iraq War. After entering into a friendship and lesbian relationship with a gothic new girl named KC Romance, Angie comes to rediscover her self confidence.

Chayil, Eishes

Hush. Walker 2010 359p $16.99

Grades: 8 9 10 11 12   **Fic**
1. Judaism -- Fiction 2. Suicide -- Fiction 3. Conduct of life -- Fiction 4. Child sexual abuse -- Fiction 5. Jews -- New York (N.Y.) -- Fiction 6. Brooklyn (New York, N.Y.) -- Fiction
ISBN 978-0-8027-2088-7; 0-8027-2088-9
LC 2010-10329
"The author balances outrage at the routine cover-up of criminal acts with genuine understanding of the community's fear of assault on their traditions by censorious gentiles. Moreover, she delivers her central message in an engaging coming-of-age story in which tragedy is only one element in a gossipy milieu of school and career decisions and arranged marriages, designer shoes and tasteful cosmetics, and sneak peaks out from a world of restraint and devotion into the world of Oprah." Bull Cent Child Books

Chbosky, Stephen
★ The **perks** of being a wallflower; [by] Stephen Chbosky. Pocket Bks. 1999 213p pa $12
Grades: 9 10 11 12   **Fic**
1. School stories 2. Letters -- Fiction 3. Young men -- Social life and customs -- 20th century
ISBN 0-671-02734-4
LC 99-236288
This novel in letter form is narrated by Charlie, a high school freshman. "His favorite aunt passed away, and his best friend just committed suicide. The girl he loves wants him as a friend; a girl he does not love wants him as a lover. His 18-year-old sister is pregnant. The LSD he took is not sitting well. And he has a math quiz looming. . . . Young adult." (Time)
"Charlie, his friends, and family are palpably real. . . . This report on his life will engage teen readers for years to come." SLJ

Chee, Traci
★ The **Reader**; sea of ink and gold. Penguin 2016 464 p. hardcover $19.99
Grades: 9 10 11 12   **Fic**
1. Fantasy fiction 2. Adventure fiction 3. Murder -- Fiction 4. Kidnapping -- Fiction
ISBN 9780399176777
LC 2015039924
"Fleeing into the wilderness after her father's brutal murder, Sefia learns how to hunt, track and steal in order to survive before embarking on a quest to rescue the beloved aunt who is her mentor, an effort that is shaped by a magnificent book that is unheard of in her otherwise illiterate society. A first novel." (Publisher's note)
"In her debut for teens, Chee takes readers on a heart-racing adventure.In the land of Kelanna, Sefia and her aunt Nin have been on the run for years, avoiding detection and the people who murdered her father. But when Nin is kidnapped, Sefia knows what they want: the mysterious package she salvaged from the wreckage of her home all those years ago. Determined to stop running, Sefia opens the package and finds a book: a foreign object known to a dangerous few and possibly the key to her past and finding Nin. . . . This cleverly layered fantasy leaves more questions than it answers, but fortunately, it's only the first of what promises to be an enchanting series." Kirkus

Chen, Justina
Return to me; by Justina Chen. Little, Brown and Co. 2013 352 p. (hardcover) $17.99
Grades: 7 8 9 10   **Fic**
1. Moving -- Fiction 2. Family life -- Fiction 3. Clairvoyance -- Fiction 4. Love -- Fiction 5. Architecture -- Fiction 6. Family problems -- Fiction 7. Moving, Household -- Fiction 8. Self-actualization (Psychology) -- Fiction
ISBN 0316102555; 9780316102551
LC 2012001549
In this book, "moving away from her Washington home seems to be a logical part of Reb's life plan; after the summer, she'll start at Columbia University, studying to be a corporate architect in the family firm, while her family moves to New Jersey for her father's new job. All that unravels upon their arrival on the East Coast, when her father announces that he's leaving the family to be with another woman, forcing Reb to question everything." (Bulletin of the Center for Children's Books)

Chevalier, Tracy
Girl with a pearl earring. Dutton 2000 240p hardcover o.p. pa $16
Grades: 11 12 Adult   **Fic**
1. Artists 2. Painters 3. Artists -- Fiction 4. Netherlands -- Fiction 5. Social classes -- Fiction
ISBN 0-525-94527-X; 0-452-28702-2 pa
LC 99-32493
Chevalier examines the world of artist Johannes Vermeer and the city of Delft in the 17th century through the eyes of Griet, an illiterate 17-year-old. In this novel the fictional character of Griet, a servant in the Vermeer household, acts as the model for the artist's portrait Girl With a Pearl Earring.
The author "has done very well in creating the feel of a society with sharp divisions of status and creed. . . . Griet is a memorable character—reserved, wary, observant, and, although she does not know it, afflicted with a serious and ultimately dangerous crush on her employer. The situation makes a fine story, which is exceptionally well told." Atl Mon

Chibbaro, Julie
Deadly; illustrations by Jean-Marc Superville Sovak. Atheneum Books for Young Readers 2011 293 p. $16.99
Grades: 6 7 8 9 10   **Fic**
1. Sick 2. Domestics 3. Diaries -- Fiction 4. Diaries -- Fiction 5. Sex role -- Fiction 6. Epidemiology -- Fiction 7. Typhoid fever -- Fiction 8. New York (N.Y.) -- Fiction
ISBN 0689857381; 9780689857386; 978-0-689-85738-6; 0-689-85738-1
LC 2010002291
"Sixteen-year-old Prudence lives in a New York City tenement with her mother and attends a school where she feels like a misfit. Haunted by memories of her brother's painful dying and by unanswered questions about her father, who never returned from the Spanish-American War, she longs to fight death itself. Prudence takes a job with the health department, where she helps track down the source

of a typhoid outbreak, a healthy carrier now remembered as Typhoid Mary." (Booklist)

"A deeply personal coming-of-age story set in an era of tumultuous social change, this is topnotch historical fiction that highlights the struggle between rational science and popular opinion as shaped by a sensational, reactionary press." SLJ

Childs, Tera Lynn

Sweet venom. Katherine Tegen Books 2011 345p $17.99

Grades: 7 8 9 10   **Fic**

1. Sisters -- Fiction 2. Monsters -- Fiction 3. Fate and fatalism -- Fiction 4. Classical mythology -- Fiction 5. San Francisco (Calif.) -- Fiction 6. Medusa (Greek mythology) -- Fiction

ISBN 978-0-06-200181-8; 0-06-200181-7

LC 2010050525

As monsters walk the streets of San Francisco, unseen by humans, three teenaged descendants of Medusa, the once-beautiful gorgon maligned in Greek mythology, must reunite and embrace their fates.

"Childs clearly has a sequel (or more) in mind and uses this book to ably set up an appealing conflict, introduce quite likable characters, and get readers ready for intrigue in the romance and fate-of-the-world departments." Booklist

Chima, Cinda Williams

The **Crimson** Crown; a Seven Realms novel. Cinda Williams Chima. Hyperion 2012 598 p. (hardback) $18.99

Grades: 7 8 9 10 11 12   **Fic**

1. Fantasy fiction 2. Queens -- Fiction 3. Magicians -- Fiction 4. Fantasy 5. Wizards -- Fiction 6. Kings, queens, rulers, etc. -- Fiction

ISBN 1423144333; 9781423144335

LC 2011053079

In this fantasy novel by Cinda Williams Chima, book 4 of the Seven Realms series, "the Queendom of the Fells seems likely to shatter apart. For young queen Raisa . . ., maintaining peace even within her own castle walls is nearly impossible; tension between wizards and Clan has reached a fevered pitch. . . . Raisa's best hope is to unite her people against a common enemy. But that enemy might be the person with whom she's falling in love." (Publisher's note)

★ The **Demon** King; a Seven Realms novel. Disney Hyperion 2009 506p map (Seven Realms) $17.99

Grades: 7 8 9 10 11 12   **Fic**

1. Fantasy fiction 2. Princesses -- Fiction 3. Witchcraft -- Fiction

ISBN 978-1-4231-1823-7; 1-4231-1823-5

LC 2008-46178

Relates the intertwining fates of former street gang leader Han Alister and headstrong Princess Raisa as Han takes possession of an amulet that once belonged to an evil wizard and Raisa uncovers a conspiracy in the Grey Wolf Court.

"With full-blooded, endearing heroes, a well-developed supporting cast and a detail-rich setting, Chima explores the lives of two young adults, one at the top of the world and the other at the bottom, struggling to find their place and protect those they love." Publ Wkly

Other titles in this series are:

The exiled queen (2010)

The Gray Wolf Throne (2011)

The **enchanter** heir; by Cinda Williams Chima. Hyperion Books 2013 464 p. (The heir chronicles) $18.99

Grades: 7 8 9 10 11 12   **Fic**

1. Massacres 2. Magic -- Fiction 3. Wizards -- Fiction 4. Terrorism -- Fiction 5. Conspiracies -- Fiction

ISBN 1423144341; 9781423144342

LC 2013013816

In this book, by Cinda Williams Chima, "someone is killing wizards and framing Nightshade, the secret organization whose job it is to track down undead souls. Jonah, . . . is also on the trail of wizard killers, but for a different reason: he wants to know who was behind the Thorn Hill disaster, where thousands of adult sorcerers and nearly as many children died. Emma, in search of her sorcerer father, lands directly in Jonah's path. Can he save her from those who think she knows the secret to Thorn Hill?" (Publisher's note)

"Chima adds two new players to her magical underworld, both with a connection to a mysterious massacre that upset the balance of power among the magical guilds and to a new threat: ghost-like "shades." Tangled conflict lines, secret identities, besieged protagonists, and nonstop action make this a thrilling and thought-provoking Heir Chronicles volume..." (Horn Book)

The **exiled** queen. Disney/Hyperion 2010 586p (Seven Realms) $17.99; pa $9.99

Grades: 7 8 9 10 11 12   **Fic**

1. Fantasy fiction 2. Magic -- Fiction 3. Princesses -- Fiction

ISBN 978-1-4231-1824-4; 1-4231-1824-3; 978-1-4231-2137-4 pa; 1-4231-2137-6 pa

LC 2009-47749

Sequel to: The Demon King (2009)

Two teenagers, one fleeing from a forced marriage and the other from a dangerous family of wizards, cross paths and fall in love.

"The pacing of the story is pitch-perfect, with the focus shifting back and forth from Han to Raisa until their paths merge, making this an excellent choice for reluctant readers." Voice Youth Advocates

Followed by: The Gray Wolf Throne (2011)

The **Gray** Wolf Throne. Hyperion 2011 517p (Seven Realms) $17.99

Grades: 7 8 9 10 11 12   **Fic**

1. Fantasy fiction 2. Princesses -- Fiction 3. Witchcraft -- Fiction

ISBN 978-1-4231-1825-1; 1-4231-1825-1

LC 2011008663

Sequel to: The exiled queen (2010)

Thief-turned-wizard Han Alister joins forces with Raisa ana'Marianna, heir to the Queendom of the Fells, to defend her right to the Gray Wolf Throne.

"The eddy and flow of complex political and personal intrigues is riveting. . . . Every character is both likable and flawed, written with such clear-eyed compassion that it is impossible not to sympathize with all their competing goals." Kirkus

The **warrior** heir. Hyperion Books for Children 2006 426p hardcover o.p.

Grades: 7 8 9 10 11 12   **Fic**

    1. Fantasy fiction 2. Magic -- Fiction

ISBN 0-7868-3916-3; 0-7868-3917-1 pa; 978-0-7868-3916-2; 978-0-7868-3917-9 pa

LC 2005-52720

After learning about his magical ancestry and his own warrior powers, sixteen-year-old Jack embarks on a training program to fight enemy wizards. "Grades seven to ten." (Bull Cent Child Books)

"Twists and turns abound in this remarkable, nearly flawless debut novel that mixes a young man's coming-of-age with fantasy and adventure. Fast paced and brilliantly plotted." Voice Youth Advocates

    Other titles in this series are:

    The dragon heir (2008)

    The wizard heir (2007)

The **wizard** heir. Hyperion 2007 458p hardcover o.p. pa $8.99

Grades: 7 8 9 10 11 12   **Fic**

    1. Fantasy fiction 2. Magic -- Fiction

ISBN 978-1-4231-0487-2; 1-4231-0487-0; 978-1-4231-0488-9 pa; 1-4231-0488-9 pa

LC 2007-15262

Sequel to: The warrior heir

Sixteen-year-old Seph, a powerful wizard, gets caught up in a conflict between the Wizard Council, smaller groups with their own agendas, and a rogue politician—the Dragon—whose identity and whereabouts the others seek to know.

"Chima uses her pen like a wand and crafts a wonderfully rich web of magic." Voice Youth Advocates

    Followed by: The dragon heir

Chokshi, Roshani

The **star**-touched queen; Roshani Chokshi. St. Martin's Griffin 2016 352 p. (hardback) $18.99

    Grades: 9 10 11 12   **Fic**

    1. Fantasy fiction 2. Queens -- Fiction 3. Arranged marriage -- Fiction

ISBN 9781250085474

LC 2016001958

In this book, by Roshani Chokshi, "Maya is cursed. With a horoscope that promises a marriage of Death and Destruction, she has earned only the scorn and fear of her father's kingdom. Content to follow more scholarly pursuits, her whole world is torn apart when her father, the Raja, arranges a wedding of political convenience to quell outside rebellions. Soon Maya becomes the queen of Akaran and wife of Amar. Neither roles are what she expected." (Publisher's note)

"Mayavati, favored daughter of the raja, lacks a shadow, but is well supplied in knowledge and bad fortune. When her father calls in men from surrounding kingdoms in an attempt to find her a husband, Maya is disappointed, wanting more out of life than to sit bored in a harem. But on her wedding day, magic and adventure find her as her kingdom of Bharata falls to war. . . . A unique fantasy that is epic myth and beautiful fairy tale combined." Booklist

    Star touched queen

Chow, Cara

Bitter melon. Egmont USA 2011 309p $16.99; lib bdg $19.99

Grades: 8 9 10   **Fic**

    1. School stories 2. Child abuse -- Fiction 3. Chinese Americans -- Fiction 4. Mother-daughter relationship -- Fiction

ISBN 978-1-60684-126-6; 978-1-60684-204-1 lib bdg

LC 2010-36630

"Chow skillfully describes the widening gulf between mother and daughter and the disparity between the Chinese culture's expectation of filial duty and the American virtue of independence." SLJ

Christopher, Lucy

The **killing** woods; Lucy Christopher. Chicken House/Scholastic 2014 384 p. $17.99

Grades: 9 10 11 12   **Fic**

    1. Mystery fiction 2. Murder -- Fiction 3. Games -- Fiction 4. Mystery and detective stories

ISBN 0545461006; 9780545461009; 9780545461016; 9780545576710

LC 2013022566

In this young adult novel, by Lucy Christopher, winner of the Michael L. Printz Honour and ALA Best Fiction for Young Adults awards, "Ashlee Parker is dead, and Emily Shepherd's dad is accused of the crime. . . . What really happened that night? Before he's convicted, Emily must find out the truth. Mina and Joe . . . warn Emily against it, but she feels herself strongly drawn to Damon, Ashlee's charismatic boyfriend. Together they explore the dark woods." (Publisher's note)

"This taut, psychologically realistic murder mystery knits trauma, danger, tragedy and hope into one cohesive tale...Readers will be riveted by slow, potent reveals about the rough nature of the Game, Ashlee's insistence on danger and adrenaline, and what happened that night. The answers hurt, but they feel right and they make sense. A sprout of hope at the end is fragile and unforced. A gripping, heartbreaking, emotionally substantial look at war wounds and the allure of danger." (Kirkus)

Chu, Wesley

The **Lives** of Tao; Wesley Chu. Angry Robot 2013 464 p. $7.99

Grades: 9 10 11 12 Adult   **Fic**

    1. Science fiction 2. Extraterrestrial beings -- Fiction

ISBN 0857663291; 9780857663290

Alex Award (2014)

"When out-of-shape IT technician Roen woke up and started hearing voices in his head, he naturally assumed he was losing it. He wasn't. He now has a passenger in his brain - an ancient alien life-form called Tao, whose race crash-landed on Earth before the first fish crawled out of the oceans. Now split into two opposing factions - the peace-loving, but under-represented Prophus, and the savage, powerful Genjix - the aliens have been in a state of civil war for centuries. Both sides are searching for a way off-planet, and the Genjix will sacrifice the entire human race, if that's what it takes." (Publisher's note)

"Imagine humans are not Earth's dominant species, and aliens live among us in plain sight. This is the conceit of Chu's hip, wise-cracking military SF debut." Pub Wkly

Other titles in this series are:
The Deaths of Tao (2014)
The Rebirths of Tao (2015)

Chupeco, Rin

The **Girl** from the Well; Rin Chupeco. Sourcebooks Fire 2014 272 p. $16.99

Grades: 9 10 11 12   **Fic**
1. Horror fiction 2. Dead -- Fiction 3. Revenge 4. Ghost stories 5. Good and evil 6. Horror stories
ISBN 140229218X; 9781402292187

In this horror novel by Rin Chupeco, "Okiku is a lonely soul. She has wandered the world for centuries, freeing the spirits of the murdered-dead. Once a victim herself, she now takes the lives of killers with the vengeance they're due. But releasing innocent ghosts from their ethereal tethers does not bring Okiku peace. Still she drifts on. Such is her existence, until she meets Tark. Evil writhes beneath the moody teen's skin, trapped by a series of intricate tattoos." (Publisher's note)

"Told in a marvelously disjointed fashion from Okiku's numbers-obsessed point of view, this story unfolds with creepy imagery and an intimate appreciation for Japanese horror, myth, and legend. The tropes Chupeco invokes will be familiar to any fan of J-horror, but the execution is spine-tingling, relying more on cinematic cuts than outright gore." Publishers Weekly

Companion:
The Suffering (2015)

Cisneros, Sandra, 1954-

★ **Caramelo,** or, Puro cuento; a novel. Sandra Cisneros. Knopf 2002 443p (hbk.) o.p.; (pbk.) $15.95; o.p.

Grades: 11 12 Adult   **Fic**
1. Women -- Fiction 2. Family life -- Fiction 3. Grandmothers -- Fiction 4. Chicago (Ill.) -- Fiction 5. Mexican Americans -- Fiction 6. Women 7. Grandmothers 8. Girls -- Fiction 9. Mexican Americans 10. Women -- Mexico -- Fiction 11. Grandparent and child -- Fiction 12. Mexican American families -- Fiction
ISBN 9781400041503; 9780679742586; 0679435549
LC 2002025488

This book, shortlisted for the 2004 International IMPAC Dublin Literary Award, tells the story of "Celaya Reyes, [author Sandra] Cisneros's narrator and heroine, born in Chicago and on pilgrimage to Mexico City every summer of her young life, [who] extracts what's useful from both her worlds. Lala, as she's known, affirms those values (faith, loyalty, love, work) that both [Mexican and American] cultures claim to hold dear, all the while bearing . . . witness to the oppressions practiced in their names. 'Like all emigrants caught between here and there,' Lala has two tales to tell, a personal story of family and a political story of culture and power. . . . 'Caramelo' opens with a boisterous rendition of

the Reyes caravan -- traveling in a 'brand-new used white Cadillac,' a green Impala and a red Chevy station wagon -- from Chicago to Mexico City, with Lala and her six brothers making faces out the window to her cousins Elvis, Aristotle and Byron." (New York Times)

★ The **house** on Mango Street. Knopf 1994 134p $24

Grades: 7 8 9 10   **Fic**
1. Chicago (Ill.) -- Fiction 2. Mexican Americans -- Fiction
ISBN 0-679-43335-X
LC 93-43564

Originally published by Arte Público Press in 1984

In this book by Sandra Cisneros, "Esperanza Cordero, a girl coming of age in the Hispanic quarter of Chicago, uses poems and stories to express thoughts and emotions about her . . . environment." (Publishers Weekly) It is "told in a series of vignettes--sometimes heartbreaking, sometimes deeply joyous". (Publisher's note)

This is "a composite of evocative snapshots that manages to passionately recreate the milieu of the poor quarters of Chicago." Commonweal

Clare, Cassandra

City of bones. Margaret K. McElderry Books 2007 485p (The mortal instruments) $17.99; pa $9.99

Grades: 9 10 11 12   **Fic**
1. Horror fiction 2. Devil -- Fiction 3. Supernatural -- Fiction 4. New York (N.Y.) -- Fiction
ISBN 1-4169-1428-5; 1-4169-5507-0 pa; 978-1-4169-1428-0; 978-1-4169-5507-8 pa
LC 2006-08108

Suddenly able to see demons and the Darkhunters who are dedicated to returning them to their own dimension, fifteen-year-old Clary Fray is drawn into this bizzare world when her mother disappears and Clary herself is almost killed by a monster.

"This version of New York, full of Buffyesque teens who are trying to save the world, is entertaining and will have fantasy readers anxiously awaiting the next book in the series." SLJ

Other titles in the series include:
City of Ashes (2008)
City of Glass (2009)
City of Fallen Angels (2011)
City of Lost Souls (2012)
City of Heavenly Fire (2014)

Clockwork angel; by Cassandra Clare. Margaret K. McElderry Books 2010 479 p. (The infernal devices) hbk $24.99

Grades: 9 10 11 12   **Fic**
1. Fantasy fiction 2. Steampunk fiction 3. Fantasy graphic novels 4. Orphans -- Fiction 5. Demonology -- Fiction 6. Supernatural -- Fiction 7. London (England) -- Fiction 8. Secret societies -- Fiction
ISBN 1416975861; 9781416975861
LC 2012359456

"When sixteen-year-old Tessa Gray crosses the ocean to find her brother, her destination is England, the time is the reign of Queen Victoria, and something terrifying is waiting for her in London's Downworld, where vampires, warlocks and other supernatural folk stalk the gaslit streets. Only the Shadowhunters, warriors dedicated to ridding the world of demons, keep order amidst the chaos. . . . Tessa soon learns that she herself is a Downworlder with a rare ability: the power to transform, at will, into another person." (Publisher's note)

"Mysteries, misdirection, and riddles abound, and while there are some gruesome moments, they never feel gratuitous. Fans of the Mortal Instruments series and newcomers alike won't be disappointed." Publ Wkly

Other titles in this series are:
Clockwork prince (2011)
Clockwork princess (2013)

Clockwork prince; Cassandra Clare. 1st ed. Margaret K. McElderry Books 2011 528 p. (The infernal devices) (hardcover) $19.99

Grades: 6 7 8 9 10 11 12   **Fic**
1. Fantasy fiction 2. Orphans -- Fiction 3. Demonology -- Fiction 4. Supernatural -- Fiction 5. London (England) -- Fiction 6. Secret societies -- Fiction 7. Identity -- Fiction 8. London (England) -- History -- 19th century -- Fiction
ISBN 9781416975885; 9781442431348

LC 2011017869

In this book, a #1 New York Times Bestseller, set "[i]n the magical underworld of Victorian London, Tessa Gray has at last found safety with the Shadowhunters. But that safety proves fleeting when rogue forces in the Clave plot to see her protector, Charlotte, replaced as head of the Institute. If Charlotte loses her position, Tessa will be out on the street—and easy prey for the mysterious Magister, who wants to use Tessa's powers for his own dark ends. With the help of the handsome, self-destructive Will and the fiercely devoted Jem, Tessa discovers that the Magister's war on the Shadowhunters is deeply personal. . . . To unravel the secrets of the past, the trio journeys from mist-shrouded Yorkshire to a manor house that holds untold horrors, from the slums of London to an enchanted ballroom where Tessa discovers that the truth of her parentage is more sinister than she had imagined." (Publisher's note)

Clockwork princess; Cassandra Clare. 1st ed. Margaret K. McElderry Books 2013 592 p. (The infernal devices) (hardcover) $19.99

Grades: 6 7 8 9 10 11 12   **Fic**
1. Love stories 2. Fantasy fiction 3. Orphans -- Fiction 4. Demonology -- Fiction 5. Supernatural -- Fiction 6. Secret societies -- Fiction 7. London (England) -- History -- 19th century -- Fiction 8. Great Britain -- History -- Victoria, 1837-1901 -- Fiction
ISBN 141697590X; 9781416975908

LC 2012048910

This is the third installment of Cassandra Clare's The Infernal Devices trilogy. Here, "Tessa leads the fight against Mortmain (a.k.a. the Magister) and his army of clockwork automatons that threaten to wipe out the Shadowhunter race," automatons that are "reanimated with demon souls." Also of note are "Tessa's tangled relationships with her fiancé, Jem Carstairs, who has a terminal demon-related illness,

and Jem's blood brother, Will Herondale, who's also in love with her." (Entertainment Weekly)

The **Shadowhunter's** codex; being a record of the ways and laws of the Nephilim, the chosen of the Angel Raziel. as compiled by Cassandra Clare & Joshua Lewis. Margaret K. McElderry Books 2013 274 p. (hardcover: alk. paper) $19.99

Grades: 9 10 11 12   **Fic**
1. Fantasy fiction 2. Magic -- Fiction 3. Demonology -- Fiction 4. Supernatural -- Fiction
ISBN 1442416920; 9781442416925; 9781442496828

LC 2013008628

In this book, by Cassandra Clare and Joshua Lewis, is an "illustrated guide to the knowledge and lore of the Shadowhunter world.It is a "manual for Shadowhunters looking to brush up on their demon languages, learn proper stele use, and discover just what exactly a pyxis is. . . . The Codex contains images of the famous Shadowhunter homeland of Idris, as well as depictions of demons and other Downworlders." (Publisher's note)

"Intended as the ultimate resource for the young Shadowhunter in Clare's enormously successful Mortal Instruments and Infernal Devices series, this serves as a behind-the-scenes guide to heroine Clary's world, as it is supposed to be her personal copy of the Codex. Including chapters and sections titled Bestiaire Part I: Demonologie; Angelic Magic; and The Rise of Nephilim in the World, it also sports scribblings and notes taken by Clary and her two friends, Simon and Jace, who occasionally snatched away her Codex to add their own thoughts...An excellent addendum to the complex world Clare has built and meant for the serious fan." (Booklist)

Clark, Jay

Finding Mr. Brightside; Jay Clark. First edition Henry Holt Books for Young Readers 2015 224 p. (hardback) $16.99

Grades: 9 10 11 12   **Fic**
1. Love stories 2. Neighbors -- Fiction 3. Loss (Psychology) -- Fiction 4. Drug abuse -- Fiction 5. Neighborhoods -- Fiction 6. Single-parent families -- Fiction 7. Dating (Social customs) -- Fiction
ISBN 0805092579; 9780805092578; 9781250073655

LC 2014039994

In this novel by Jay Clark, "high school seniors and neighbors Abram Morgan and Juliette Flynn have each been hiding in their own ways since his father and her mother died in a car accident while having a secret affair. Abram takes too much Paxil, which has caused him to be lethargic, drop tennis, overeat, and avoid thinking about college. Juliette is hooked on Adderall, runs compulsively, and barely eats. One night . . they stop avoiding one another and are surprised by their easy chemistry." (Publisher's note)

"Though the problems the teens face are myriad, the story never bogs down. Instead, the uncomfortable silences, the awkward conversations, and the slow but gradual trust that connects both the teens and their surviving parents ground the novel in the stark reality that sometimes life is full of genuine surprises." Booklist

Finding Mister Brightside

Clark, Kristin Elizabeth

★ **Freakboy**; by Kristin Elizabeth Clark. Farrar, Straus and Giroux 2013 448 p. (hardcover) $18.99

Grades: 8 9 10 11 12   **Fic**

1. Gender role 2. Identity (Psychology) 3. Teenagers -- Sexual behavior 4. Novels in verse 5. Schools -- Fiction 6. Wrestling -- Fiction 7. Family life -- Fiction 8. High schools -- Fiction 9. Sexual orientation -- Fiction 10. Transgender people -- Fiction

ISBN 0374324727; 9780374324728

LC 2012050407

Rainbow List (2014)

In this book, by Kristin Elizabeth Clark, "Brendan . . . seems to have it pretty easy. He's a star wrestler . . . and a loving boyfriend to . . . Vanessa. But on the inside, Brendan struggles to understand why his body feels so wrong. Clark folds three narratives into one powerful story: Brendan trying to understand his sexual identity, Vanessa fighting to keep her and Brendan's relationship alive, and Angel struggling to confront her demons." (Publisher's note)

"High school wrestler Brendan likes girls "too much, / and not in / the same / way / everyone / else / does." Brendan's story weaves together with his girlfriend Vanessa's and that of transgender woman Angel in three-part verse-harmony. Each individual has a unique personality all his or her own in this sincere, profound rendering of sexuality, queerness, and identity." (Horn Book)

Clarke, Judith

One whole and perfect day. Front Street 2007 250p $16.95

Grades: 7 8 9 10   **Fic**

1. Australia -- Fiction 2. Family life -- Fiction 3. Grandfathers -- Fiction

ISBN 978-1-932425-95-6; 1-932425-95-0

LC 2006-20126

Michael L. Printz Award honor book, 2008

As her irritating family prepares to celebrate her grandfather's eightieth birthday, sixteen-year-old Lily yearns for just one whole perfect day together.

The author's "sharp, poetic prose evokes each character's inner life with rich and often amusing vibrancy." Horn Book

Cline, Ernest

Ready player one; [by] Ernest Cline. Crown Publishers 2011 374p. $24

Grades: 11 12 Adult   **Fic**

1. Puzzles 2. Fantasy fiction 3. Science fiction 4. Virtual reality 5. Future 6. Utopias -- Fiction 7. Virtual reality -- Fiction 8. Regression (Civilization) -- Fiction

ISBN 978-0-307-88743-6; 0-307-88743-X; 9780307887450; 9780307887443; 9780307887436

LC 2011015247

Alex Award (2012)

The events in this novel take place in 2044. Many of the students of 1980s trivia are interested in that particular time period "because a billionaire inventor, James Halliday, died and left behind a mischievous legacy. Whoever first cracks Halliday's series of '80s-related riddles, clues and puzzles that are included in a film called 'Anorak's Invitation' will inherit his fortune." (N Y Times (Late N Y Ed))

Clinton, Cathryn

★ **A stone** in my hand. Candlewick Press 2002 191p hardcover o.p. pa $6.99

Grades: 8 9 10 11   **Fic**

1. Family life -- Fiction 2. Palestinian Arabs -- Fiction

ISBN 0-7636-1388-6; 0-7636-4772-1 pa

LC 2001-58423

Eleven-year-old Malaak and her family are touched by the violence in Gaza between Jews and Palestinians when first her father disappears and then her older brother is drawn to the Islamic Jihad

"With a sharp eye for nuances of culture and the political situation in the Middle East, Clinton has created a rich, colorful cast of characters and created an emotionally charged novel." SLJ

Coates, Jan L.

A **hare** in the elephant's trunk; [by] Jan L. Coates. Red Deer Press 2010 291p il map pa $12.95

Grades: 8 9 10 11 12   **Fic**

1. Refugees 2. Refugees -- Fiction 3. Sudan -- History -- Civil War, 1983-2005 -- Fiction

ISBN 978-0-88995-451-9

Inspired by the real life experiences of a Sudanese boy, follows Jacob Akech Deng's journey as he flees his home under the threat of war, and, guided by the memory of his mother, tries to survive in a refugee camp.

"This novel, based on the life of the real Jacob Deng, provides insight into the struggles of the Sudan as well as a strong, clear voice. Coates gives an unflinching and poetic glimpse into the life of a boy who chose hope in the face of adversity." SLJ

Coats, J. Anderson

The **wicked** and the just; by Jillian Anderson Coats. Harcourt 2012 344 p. $16.99

Grades: 7 8 9 10 11 12   **Fic**

1. Daughters -- Fiction 2. Prejudices -- Fiction 3. Middle Ages -- Fiction 4. Wales -- History -- Fiction 5. Household employees -- Fiction 6. Wales -- History -- 1284-1536 -- Fiction

ISBN 0547688377; 9780547688374

LC 2011027315

In this young adult historical novel, "two girls of very different degree are brought together unwillingly by the English conquest of Wales. Cecily is in a pet at having to leave the home of her youth . . . and relocate to the Welsh frontier. . . . Cecily hates Caernarvon. She hates its weather, its primitive appointments and its natives, especially Gwinny, the servant girl who doesn't obey, and the young man who stares at her." (Kirkus Review)

Coben, Harlan

Shelter; a Mickey Bolitar novel. G. P. Putnam's Sons 2011 304p $18.99

Grades: 8 9 10 11 12   **Fic**

1. School stories 2. Mystery fiction 3. Moving -- Fiction 4. Uncles -- Fiction 5. Missing persons -- Fiction

ISBN 9780399256509

LC 2011009004

After tragic events tear Mickey Bolitar away from his parents, he is forced to live with his estranged Uncle Myron and switch high schools, where he finds both friends and enemies, but when his new girlfriend, Ashley, vanishes, he follows her trail into a seedy underworld that reveals she is not what she seems to be.

This is a "suspenseful, well-executed spin-off of [the author's] bestselling Myron Bolitar mystery series for adults. . . . Coben's semi-noir style translates well to YA, and the supporting cast is thoroughly entertaining." Publ Wkly

Coben, Harlan, 1962-

★ **Seconds** away; a Mickey Bolitar novel. Harlan Coben. G. P. Putnam's Sons 2012 352 p. (hardback) $18.99

Grades: 8 9 10 11 12   **Fic**

1. Mystery fiction 2. Adventure fiction 3. Murder -- Fiction 4. Uncles -- Fiction 5. Schools -- Fiction 6. High schools -- Fiction 7. Mystery and detective stories 8. Adventure and adventurers -- Fiction
ISBN 9780399256516; 0399256512

LC 2012026728

This young adult adventure novel, by Harlan Coben, is the second book in his Mickey Bolitar series. "Mickey . . . continues to hunt for clues about the Abeona Shelter and the mysterious death of his father--all while trying to navigate the challenges of a new high school. . . . Now, not only does Mickey need to keep himself and his friends safe from the Butcher of Lodz, but he needs to figure out who shot [his classmate] Rachel." (Publisher's note)

Cohen, Joshua C.

★ **Leverage.** Dutton Children's Books 2011 425p $17.99

Grades: 10 11 12   **Fic**

1. School stories 2. Bullies -- Fiction 3. Football -- Fiction 4. Violence -- Fiction 5. Gymnastics -- Fiction
ISBN 978-0-525-42306-5

LC 2010-13472

High school sophomore Danny excels at gymnastics but is bullied, like the rest of the gymnasts, by members of the football team, until an emotionally and physically scarred new student joins the football team and forms an unlikely friendship with Danny.

"Sports fans will love Cohen's style: direct, goal oriented, and filled with sensory detail. Characters and subplots are overly abundant yet add a deepness rarely found in comparable books. Drugs, rape, language, and violence make this book serious business, but those with experience will tell you that sports is serious business, too." Booklist

Cohen, Tish

Little black lies. Egmont USA 2009 305p $16.99; lib bdg $19.99

Grades: 7 8 9 10   **Fic**

1. School stories 2. Janitors -- Fiction 3. Popularity -- Fiction 4. Obsessive-compulsive disorder -- Fiction
ISBN 978-1-60684-033-7; 1-60684-033-9; 978-1-60684-046-7 lib bdg; 1-60684-046-0 lib bdg

LC 2009-14637

Starting her junior year at an ultra-elite Boston school, sixteen-year-old Sara, hoping to join the popular crowd,

hides that her father not only is the school janitor, but also has obsessive-compulsive disorder.

"The characters are real, and readers will feel as if they are right alongside Sara for the ride. Cohen skillfully keeps her readers fully engaged. They will find themselves cringing at the predicaments Sara enters and wonder whether she will completely sell out." Voice Youth Advocates

Cohn, Rachel

Cupcake. Simon & Schuster Books for Young Readers 2007 248p $15.99

Grades: 9 10 11 12   **Fic**

1. Stepfamilies -- Fiction 2. New York (N.Y.) -- Fiction
ISBN 978-1-4169-1217-0; 1-4169-1217-7

LC 2005-35934

Sequel to Shrimp (2005)

Former "bad girl" Cyd Charisse moves to New York City to live with her half-brother Danny while exploring career options and various relationships, including the one with Shrimp, who is surfing in New Zealand.

"Fans of the Cyd/Shrimp love story will not be disappointed with this thoroughly satisfying conclusion to the saga." SLJ

Gingerbread. Simon & Schuster Bks. for Young Readers 2002 172p $15.95

Grades: 9 10 11 12   **Fic**

1. Parent-child relationship -- Fiction
ISBN 0-689-84337-2

LC 00-52225

After being expelled from a fancy boarding school, Cyd Charisse's problems with her mother escalate after Cyd falls in love with a sensitive surfer and is subsequently sent from San Francisco to New York City to spend time with her biological father.

"Cohn works wonders with snappy dialogue, up-to-the-minute language, and funny repartee. Her contemporary voice is tempered with humor and deals with problems across two generations. Funny and irreverent reading with teen appeal that's right on target." SLJ

Other titles featuring Cyd Charisse are:
Cupcake (2007)
Shrimp (2005)

Shrimp. Simon & Schuster Books for Young Readers 2005 288p $15.95

Grades: 9 10 11 12   **Fic**

1. School stories
ISBN 0-689-86612-7

LC 2003-23992

Sequel to Gingerbread (2002)

Back in San Francisco for her senior year in high school, seventeen-year-old Cyd attempts to reconcile with her boyfriend, Shrimp, making some girlfriends and beginning to feel more a part of her family in the process.

"Cohn's humor is right on. . . . The joy of the book can be found in the familiar characters and meeting new ones, and this title leaves open the possibility for a third installment." SLJ

Followed by Cupcake (2007)

Cokal, Susann

★ The **Kingdom** of little wounds; Susann Cokal. Candlewick Press 2013 576 p. $22.99

Grades: 10 11 12 Adult   Fic

1. Queens -- Fiction 2. Princesses -- Fiction
ISBN 0763666947; 9780763666941

     LC 2013933162

Printz Honor Book (2014)

In this book, by Susann Cokal, it's "the eve of Princess Sophia's wedding [and] the Scandinavian city of Skyggehavn prepares to fete the occasion with a sumptuous display of riches. . . . Yet beneath the . . . celebration, a shiver of darkness creeps through the palace halls. . . . When [the] . . . prick of a needle sets off a series of events that will alter the course of history, the fates of seamstress Ava Bingen and mute nursemaid Midi Sorte become . . . intertwined with that of mad Queen Isabel." (Publisher's note)

"Despite the challenging content, the book's lyrical writing, enthralling characters, and compelling plot will give older readers lots to ponder." Booklist

Coker, Rachel, 1997-

Chasing Jupiter; Rachel Coker. Zondervan 2012 224 p. $15.99

Grades: 9 10   Fic

1. Faith -- Fiction 2. Autism -- Fiction 3. Brothers and sisters -- Fiction 4. Farm life -- Georgia -- Fiction 5. Moneymaking projects -- Fiction 6. Family life -- Georgia -- Fiction 7. Georgia -- History -- 20th century -- Fiction
ISBN 031073293X; 9780310732938

     LC 2012051600

In this book, "16-year-old Scarlett Blaine . . . struggles to be the perfect family member and caregiver for her autistic younger brother, Cliff. . . . When Cliff sees Neil Armstrong's Moon walk, he wants to fly to Jupiter and enlists Scarlett and Frank, the local peach farmer's son, to help build a rocket. Scarlett loves Frank, but his crush on her free-spirited, older sister and her parents' fighting leave the teen wondering how to cope with a world turned upside down." (School Library Journal)

"—In rural Georgia, in 1969, 16-year-old Scarlett Blaine is a people pleaser. She struggles to be the perfect family member and caregiver for her autistic younger brother, Cliff, and her mentally unbalanced grandfather...carlett puts her faith in God and family. This book is recommended for libraries looking to expand their Christian-fiction collections." (School Library Journal)

Colasanti, Susane

So much closer. Viking 2011 241p $17.99

Grades: 7 8 9 10   Fic

1. School stories 2. Moving -- Fiction 3. Divorce -- Fiction 4. New York (N.Y.) -- Fiction
ISBN 978-0-670-01224-4; 0-670-01224-6

     LC 2010-31962

Seventeen-year-old Brooke has a crush on Scott so big that when he heads for New York City, she moves into her estranged father's Greenwich Village apartment, but soon she begins to focus on knowing herself and finding her future path.

"Colasanti has once again formulated a teen romance that feels realistic, which will make this novel a hit with readers." SLJ

Something like fate. Viking 2010 268p il $17.99

Grades: 7 8 9 10   Fic

1. Love stories 2. School stories 3. Guilt -- Fiction 4. Friendship -- Fiction
ISBN 978-0-670-01146-9; 0-670-01146-0

Lani and Jason, who is her best friend's boyfriend, fall in love, causing Lani tremendous anguish and guilt.

"Colasanti provides credible and engaging character development for each cast member and interactions that spark just the right amount of tension to make this a romantic page-turner." Booklist

Cole, Kresley

Poison princess; Kresley Cole. 1st ed. Simon & Schuster Books For Young Readers 2012 369 p. (hardcover) $18.99

Grades: 9 10 11 12   Fic

1. Love stories 2. Paranormal fiction 3. Tarot -- Fiction 4. Ability -- Fiction 5. Prophecies -- Fiction 6. Supernatural -- Fiction
ISBN 9781442436640; 1442436646; 9781442436664

     LC 2012000919

This paranormal romance novel, by Kresley Cole, is book one in the "Arcana Chronicles" series. "When an apocalyptic event decimates her Louisiana hometown, Evie realizes her hallucinations were actually visions of the future--and they're still happening. . . . An ancient prophesy is being played out, and Evie is not the only one with special powers. A group of twenty-two teens has been chosen to reenact the ultimate battle between good and evil." (Publisher's note)

Coleman, Wim

Anna's world; [by] Wim Coleman and Pat Perrin. Chiron Books 2009 280p il pa $10.95

Grades: 8 9 10   Fic

1. Shakers -- Fiction 2. Family life -- Fiction
ISBN 978-1-935178-06-4

First published 2000 by Discovery Enterprises with title: Sister Anna

The United States of America in the late 1840s is a national torn by the crime of slavery and a war of conquest in Mexico. Fourteen-year-old Anna Coburn doesn't want to grapple with such terrible issues. Forced to live among the Shakers, then plunged into upper-class Boston life, Anna faces troubling responsibilities to herself, her loved ones and to her country.

"This story accurately portrays life in a Shaker community and the fabric of America during the 1840s. . . . An excellent ancillary choice for social-studies classes." SLJ

Collins, Brandilyn

Always watching; by Brandilyn and Amberly Collins. Zonderkidz 2009 224p (Rayne Tour series) pa $9.99

Grades: 10 11 12 Adult   Fic

1. Mystery fiction 2. Fame -- Fiction 3. Homicide -- Fiction 4. Rock music -- Fiction 5. Christian life

-- Fiction 6. Single parent family -- Fiction
ISBN 978-0-310-71539-9; 0-310-71539-3

LC 2008-39515

When a frightening murder occurs after one of her famous mother's rock concerts, sixteen-year-old Shayley tries to help the police find the killer and to determine whether her long-lost father has some connection to the crime.

"This solid teen mystery, the initial entry in a new series, will appeal to young girls and adults who enjoy a good yarn." Libr J

Collins, Pat Lowery

Hidden voices; the orphan musicians of Venice. Candlewick Press 2009 345p $17.99

Grades: 8 9 10 11 12 **Fic**

1. Composers 2. Violinists 3. Orphans -- Fiction 4. Musicians -- Fiction 5. Venice (Italy) -- Fiction
ISBN 978-0-7636-3917-4; 0-7636-3917-6

LC 2008-18762

Anetta, Rosalba, and Luisa, find their lives taking unexpected paths while growing up in eighteenth century Venice at the orphanage Ospedale della Pieta, where concerts are given to support the orphanage as well as expose the girls to potential suitors.

"Collins's descriptive prose makes Venice and a unique slice of history come alive as the three connecting narrative strains create a rich story of friendship and self-realization." SLJ

Collins, Suzanne, 1962-

Catching fire. Scholastic Press 2009 391p $17.99

Grades: 7 8 9 10 **Fic**

1. Science fiction
ISBN 978-0-439-02349-8; 0-439-02349-1

LC 2008-50493

Sequel to: Hunger Games (2008)

This dystopian young adult novel, volume 2 of the Hunger Games trilogy, takes place after a televised, state-sponsored duel known as the Hunger Games. "Katniss Everdeen has won . . . with fellow district tribute Peeta Mellark. But it was a victory won by defiance of the Capitol and their harsh rules. Katniss and Peeta should be happy. After all, they have just won for themselves and their families a life of safety and plenty. But there are rumors of rebellion among the subjects, and Katniss and Peeta, to their horror, are the faces of that rebellion." (Publisher's note)

"Beyond the expert world building, the acute social commentary and the large cast of fully realized characters, there's action, intrigue, romance and some amount of hope in a story readers will find completely engrossing." Kirkus

Followed by: Mockingjay (2010)

★ The **Hunger** Games. Scholastic Press 2008 374p $17.99; pa $8.99

Grades: 7 8 9 10 **Fic**

1. Science fiction
ISBN 978-0-439-02348-1; 0-439-02348-3; 978-0-439-02352-8 pa; 0-439-02352-1 pa

LC 2007-39987

In this dystopian young adult novel, "in the ruins of a place once known as North America lies the nation of Panem,
a shining Capitol surrounded by twelve outlaying districts. The Capitol . . . keeps the districts in line by forcing them all to send one girl and one boy between the ages of twelve and eighteen to participate in the annual Hunger Games, a fight to the death on live TV. Sixteen-year-old Katniss Everdeen . . . regards it as a death sentence when she is forced to represent her district in the Games." (Publisher's note)

"Collins's characters are completely realistic and sympathetic. . . . The plot is tense, dramatic, and engrossing." SLJ

Mockingjay. Scholastic Press 2010 390p (Hunger Games) $17.99

Grades: 7 8 9 10 **Fic**

1. Science fiction
ISBN 978-0-439-02351-1; 0-439-02351-3

LC 2008-50493

Sequel to: Catching fire (2009)

This dystopian novel, volume 3 of the Hunger Games trilogy, takes place after heroine Katniss Everdeen has "survived the Hunger Games twice. But now that she's made it out of the bloody arena alive, she's still not safe. . . . The Capitol wants revenge. Who do they think should pay for the unrest? Katniss. And what's worse, President Snow has made it clear that no one else is safe either. Not Katniss's family, not her friends, not the people of District 12." (Publisher's note)

"This concluding volume in Collins's Hunger Games trilogy accomplishes a rare feat, the last installment being the best yet, a beautifully orchestrated and intelligent novel that succeeds on every level." Publ Wkly

Combres, Elisabeth

Broken memory; a novel of Rwanda. translated by Shelley Tanaka. Groundwood Books/House of Anansi Press 2009 139p $17.95

Grades: 6 7 8 9 10 **Fic**

1. Rwanda -- Fiction 2. Orphans -- Fiction 3. Genocide -- Fiction 4. Hutu (African people) -- Fiction 5. Tutsi (African people) -- Fiction
ISBN 978-0-88899-892-7; 0-88899-892-9

Original French edition, 2007

"This is a quiet, reflective story; neither laden with detail nor full of historical descriptions, it is simply one girl's horrific tale of personal tragedy. . . . Combres' story offers readers intimate access to this chapter of history as well as considerable potential for discussion." Bull Cent Child Books

Combs, Sarah

Breakfast served anytime; Sarah Combs. Candlewick Press 2014 272 p. $16.99

Grades: 7 8 9 10 11 12 **Fic**

1. Bildungsromans 2. Camps -- Fiction 3. Kentucky -- Fiction 4. Gifted children -- Fiction
ISBN 0763667919; 9780763667917

LC 2013944002

In this book, by Sarah Combs, "when Gloria sets out to spend the summer before her senior year at a camp for gifted and talented students, she doesn't know quite what to expect. Fresh from the heartache of losing her grandmother and missing her best friend, Gloria resolves to make the best of her new circumstances. But some things are proving to be more challenging than she expected." (Publisher's note)

"At a summer college program in Kentucky, a classroom of gifted students studying "The Secrets of the Written Word" grapples with life's big questions. Mercurial, dreamy, and verbose, protagonist Gloria narrates with intellectual enthusiasm and attention to emotional detail. Although the plot meanders, Gloria's open, genuine voice carries this debut novel to the end of a life-changing summer." Horn Book

Conaghan, Brian

When Mr. Dog bites; Brian Conaghan. Bloomsbury 2014 368 p. (hardback) $17.99

Grades: 10 11 12   **Fic**
1. School stories 2. Family life -- Fiction 3. Terminally ill -- Fiction 4. Tourette syndrome -- Fiction 5. Interpersonal relations -- Fiction 6. England -- Fiction 7. Schools -- Fiction 8. Family life -- England -- Fiction
ISBN 1619633469; 9781619633469
                                         LC 2013044567

In this book, by Brian Conaghan, "[a]ll Dylan Mint has ever wanted is to keep his Tourette's in check and live life as a 'normal' teenager. The swearing, the tics, the howling 'dog' that escapes when things are at their worst. . . . But a routine hospital visit changes everything-- Dylan overhears that he's going to die. In an attempt to claim the life he's always wanted, he decides to grant himself parting wishes." (Publisher's note)

"Dylan's habitual use of Cockney slang may make for a tough reading experiencing for American teenagers, but Dylan is smart and caring, and beneath his realistically portrayed condition, he is a normal teenager with relatable concerns. As Dylan would say, this one is 'A-mayonnaise-ing.'" Booklist

Condie, Ally

Crossed; Ally Condie. Dutton Books 2011 367p map $17.99

Grades: 7 8 9 10   **Fic**
1. Fantasy fiction 2. Resistance to government -- Fiction
ISBN 978-0-525-42365-2; 0-525-42365-6
                                         LC 2011016442
Sequel to: Matched (2010)

Seventeen-year-old Cassia sacrifices everything and heads to the Outer Provinces in search of Ky, where she is confronted with shocking revelations about Society and the promise of rebellion.

"Newcomers will need to read the first book for background, but vivid, poetic writing will pull fans through as Condie immerses readers in her characters' yearnings and hopes." Publ Wkly

Matched; Ally Condie. Dutton Books 2010 369p $17.99

Grades: 7 8 9 10   **Fic**
1. Fantasy fiction
ISBN 978-0-525-42364-5; 0-525-42364-8

All her life, Cassia has never had a choice. The Society dictates everything: when and how to play, where to work, where to live, what to eat and wear, when to die, and most importantly to Cassia as she turns 17, who to marry. When she is Matched with her best friend Xander, things couldn't

be more perfect. But why did her neighbor Ky's face show up on her match disk as well?

"Condie's enthralling and twisty dystopian plot is well served by her intriguing characters and fine writing. While the ending is unresolved . . . , Cassia's metamorphosis is gripping and satisfying." Publ Wkly

Followed by: Crossed (2011)

Reached; Ally Condie. Dutton 2012 512 p. (Matched trilogy) (hardcover) $17.99

Grades: 7 8 9 10   **Fic**
1. Science fiction 2. Epidemics -- Fiction 3. Resistance to government -- Fiction 4. Fantasy 5. Government, Resistance to -- Fiction
ISBN 9780525423669; 0525423664
                                         LC 2012031916
Sequel to: Crossed

"This final story in the 'Matched' trilogy finds Cassia, Ky, and Xander all working for the Rising, but in different locations and for different reasons. The Rising has introduced a plague into the cities for which they have the cure. They are easily able to take control as they cure people. An unexpected mutation of the illness catches the Rising off guard, and the Pilot (the Rising's leader) realizes he could quickly lose all that has been gained." (Voice of Youth Advocates)

Connelly, Neil O.

★ The miracle stealer; [by] Neil Connelly. Arthur A. Levine Books 2010 230p $17.99

Grades: 8 9 10 11 12   **Fic**
1. Camps -- Fiction 2. Faith -- Fiction 3. Miracles -- Fiction 4. Siblings -- Fiction 5. Family life -- Fiction 6. Pennsylvania -- Fiction
ISBN 978-0-545-13195-7; 0-545-13195-2
                                         LC 2010-727

In small-town Pennsylvania, nineteen-year-old Andi Grant will do anything to protect her six-year-old brother Daniel from those who believe he has a God-given gift as a healer—including their own mother.

"Neil Connelly has written a deeply thought provoking novel. . . . Throughout this gripping novel the climax builds from a slow burn to a tension packed conclusion." Libr Media Connect

Connor, Leslie

The things you kiss goodbye; Leslie Connor. First edition Katherine Tegen Books, an imprint of HarperCollinsPublishers 2014 368 p. (hardback) $17.99

Grades: 9 10 11 12   **Fic**
1. Love stories 2. Abused women -- Fiction 3. Teenage girls -- Fiction 4. Love -- Fiction 5. Dating violence -- Fiction 6. Greek Americans -- Fiction
ISBN 0060890916; 9780060890919
                                         LC 2013043191

In this teen novel, by Leslie Connor, "Bettina falls in love . . . , but when school starts up again, Brady unexpectedly changes for the worse. Unable to give up on her first love just yet, she finds herself trapped in an abusive relationship. Then she meets . . . a smoldering older guy. . . . Yet he is everything Brady is not. . . . When tragedy strikes, Bettina must tell her family the truth--and kiss goodbye the things she thought she knew about herself and the men in her life." (Publisher's note)

" Connor lets the story, and Bettina's realization of the situation, play out slowly, a choice that adds multiple subplots but also deepens characterization and elevates the book above simple problem-novel territory. Bettina begins finding herself through her art; her ensuing pride in her work is convincingly portrayed. A melodramatic ending and tendency to tie up all plot threads are somewhat distracting, but Bettina's situation creates much food for thought." Horn Book

Cook, Eileen

The **education** of Hailey Kendrick. Simon Pulse 2011 256p $16.99

Grades: 7 8 9 10   **Fic**
1. School stories 2. Dating (Social customs) -- Fiction
ISBN 978-1-4424-1325-2
LC 2010-25608

Dating a popular boy and adhering to every rule ever written, a high school senior at an elite Vermont boarding school begins to shed her good girl identity after an angry incident with her distant father.

"Hailey is a likable character, and the events leading up to and away from her episode of vandalism are believable. Her emotions ring true as well. . . . The plot develops quickly, and readers will be madly flipping pages to find out what happens next." SLJ

Cook, Trish

Notes from the blender; [by] Trish Cook and Brendan Halpin. Egmont USA 2011 229p $16.99

Grades: 9 10 11 12   **Fic**
1. Stepfamilies -- Fiction 2. Homosexuality -- Fiction
3. Dating (Social customs) -- Fiction
ISBN 978-1-60684-140-2
LC 2010-11315

Two teenagers—a heavy-metal-music-loving boy who is still mourning the death of his mother years earlier, and a beautiful, popular girl whose parents divorced because her father is gay—try to negotiate the complications of family and peer relationships as they get to know each other after learning that their father and mother are marrying each other.

"This well developed story gives readers an opportunity to see teens 'taking the high road' as they deal with both peers and parents in a novel teens will not want to put down." Libr Media Connect

Cooney, Caroline B., 1947-

The **face** on the milk carton. Delacorte Press 2006 184p $15.95; pa $6.99

Grades: 7 8 9 10   **Fic**
1. Kidnapping -- Fiction
ISBN 978-0-385-32328-4; 0-385-32328-X; 978-0-440-22065-7 pa; 0-440-22065-3 pa

Cooney "demonstrates an excellent ear for dialogue and a gift for portraying responsible middle-class teenagers trying to come to terms with very real concerns." SLJ

If the witness lied. Delacorte Press 2009 213p $16.99; lib bdg $19.99

Grades: 6 7 8 9 10   **Fic**
1. Orphans -- Fiction 2. Siblings -- Fiction 3.

Bereavement -- Fiction 4. Connecticut -- Fiction
ISBN 978-0-385-73448-6; 0-385-73448-4; 978-0-385-90451-3 lib bdg; 0-385-90451-7 lib bdg
LC 2008-23959

Torn apart by tragedies and the publicity they brought, siblings Smithy, Jack, and Madison, aged fourteen to sixteen, tap into their parent's courage to pull together and protect their brother Tris, nearly three, from further media exploitation and a much more sinister threat.

"The pacing here is pure gold. Rotating through various perspectives to follow several plot strands . . . Cooney draws out the action, investing it with the slow-motion feel of an impending collision. . . . This family-drama-turned-thriller will have readers racing, heart in throat, to reach the conclusion." Horn Book

Janie face to face; Caroline B. Cooney. Delacorte Press 2013 352 p. (Janie Johnson) (ebk) $20.99; (trade hardcover) $17.99

Grades: 7 8 9 10   **Fic**
1. Love stories 2. Kidnapping -- Fiction 3. Family life -- Fiction 4. Love -- Fiction 5. Identity -- Fiction 6. Authorship -- Fiction 7. New York (N.Y.) -- Fiction 8. Universities and colleges -- Fiction
ISBN 0385742061; 9780375979972; 9780375990397; 9780385742061
LC 2012006145

This book, by Caroline B. Cooney, is the conclusion to the "Janie Johnson" series which begun in 1990. "All will be revealed as readers find out if Janie and Reeve's love has endured, and whether or not the person who brought Janie and her family so much emotional pain and suffering is brought to justice." (Publisher's note)

Cooper, Michelle

★ A **brief** history of Montmaray. Alfred A. Knopf 2009 296p $16.99; lib bdg $19.99

Grades: 7 8 9 10   **Fic**
1. Europe -- Fiction 2. Diaries -- Fiction 3. Islands -- Fiction 4. Princesses -- Fiction 5. Family life -- Fiction
ISBN 0-375-85864-4; 0-375-95864-9 lib bdg; 978-0-375-85864-2; 978-0-375-95864-9 lib bdg
LC 2008-49800

This book features "Sophie FitzOsborne [who] lives in a crumbling castle in the tiny island kingdom of Montmaray, along with her tomboy younger sister Henry, her beautiful, intellectual cousin Veronica, and Veronica's father, the completely mad King John. When Sophie receives a leather journal for her sixteenth birthday, she decides to write about her life on the island. But it is 1936 and bigger events are on the horizon." (Publisher's note)

"Cooper has crafted a sort of updated Gothic romance where sweeping adventure play equal with fluttering hearts." Booklist

Followed by: The FitzOsbornes in exile (2011)

The **FitzOsbornes** at war; Michelle Cooper. Alfred A. Knopf 2012 560 p. (hardcover) $17.99

Grades: 7 8 9 10   **Fic**
1. Exiles -- Fiction 2. Diaries -- Fiction 3. Historical fiction 4. World War, 1939-1945 -- Fiction 5. War -- Fiction 6. Family life -- England -- Fiction 7. World

War, 1939-1945 -- England -- Fiction 8. Great Britain -- History -- George VI, 1936-1952 -- Fiction
ISBN 0375870504; 9780307974044; 9780375870507; 9780375970504

LC 2012009094

In this historical novel, by Michelle Cooper, "Sophie FitzOsborne and the royal family of Montmaray escaped their remote island home when the Nazis attacked. But as war breaks out in England and around the world, nowhere is safe. Sophie fills her journal with tales of a life during wartime. . . . But even as bombs rain down on London, hope springs up, and love blooms for this most endearing princess." (Publisher's note)

The **FitzOsbornes** in exile. Alfred A. Knopf 2011 457p $17.99; lib bdg $20.99

Grades: 7 8 9 10   **Fic**

1. Diaries -- Fiction 2. Princesses -- Fiction 3. Family life -- Fiction 4. Great Britain -- Fiction
ISBN 0-375-85865-2; 0-375-95865-7 lib bdg; 978-0-375-85865-9; 978-0-375-89802-0 e-book; 978-0-375-95865-6 lib bdg

LC 2010-34706

Sequel to: A brief history of Montmaray (2009)

In this second volume of the Montmaray Journals series, "forced to leave their island kingdom, Sophie FitzOsborne and her eccentric family take shelter in England. . . . Aunt Charlotte is ruthless in her quest to see Sophie and Veronica married off by the end of the Season, Toby is as charming and lazy as ever, Henry is driving her governess to the brink of madness, and the battle of wills between Simon and Veronica continues." (Publisher's note)

"Readers who enjoy their history enriched by immersion into the social milieu of the time period will find this a fascinating, utterly absorbing venture into English society of the late '30s." Bull Cent Child Books

Cooper, T., 1972-

Changers book one; drew. T Cooper, Allison Glock. Akashic Books 2014 288 p. illustrations (Changers) (trade pbk.) $11.95

Grades: 7 8 9 10 11 12   **Fic**

1. Fantasy fiction 2. High school students 3. Identity (Psychology) 4. Science fiction
ISBN 1617751952; 9781617751950; 9781617752070; 9781617752117

LC 2013938807

Sequel: Oryon (2015)

This book, by T Cooper and Allison Glock, "opens on the eve of Ethan Miller's freshman year of high school in a brand-new town. . . . everything is looking up in life. Until the next morning. When Ethan awakens as a girl. Ethan is a Changer, a little-known, ancient race of humans who live out each of their four years of high school as a different person. After graduation, Changers choose which version of themselves they will be forever." (Publisher's note)

"Ethan wakes up on his first day of high school to discover that he is no longer the same person he was when he went to sleep—overnight he was transformed into a beautiful girl. His parents inform him that his father was a Changer and that this is the first of four transformations. He will experience each year of high school in a new body, and at the end of his senior year, he will get to choose which body he will live in for the rest of his life...By the end of this book, readers will be invested in this character and will want to know what Ethan's future holds and how he will physically and emotionally transform over the next installments." SLJ

Cormier, Robert

★ **After** the first death. Dell Publishing 1991 233p pa $6.50

Grades: 7 8 9 10   **Fic**

1. Terrorism -- Fiction
ISBN 0-440-20835-1
First published 1979 by Pantheon Bks.
ALA YALSA Margaret A. Edwards Award (1991)

"A busload of children is hijacked by a band of terrorists whose demands include the exposure of a military brainwashing project. The narrative line moves from the teenage terrorist Milo to Kate the bus driver and the involvement of Ben, whose father is the head of the military operation, in this confrontation. The conclusion has a shocking twist." Shapiro. Fic for Youth. 2d edition

Beyond the chocolate war; a novel. Dell 1986 278p pa $6.99

Grades: 9 10 11 12   **Fic**

1. School stories
ISBN 0-440-90580-X
First published 1985

Dark deeds continue at Trinity High School, climaxing in a public demonstration of one student's homemade guillotine. Sequel to "The Chocolate War."

★ The **chocolate** war; a novel. Pantheon Bks. 1974 253p rpt $8.99; $19.95

Grades: 7 8 9 10   **Fic**

1. School stories
ISBN 9780375829871 rpt; 0-394-82805-4
ALA YALSA Margaret A. Edwards Award (1991)

"In the Trinity School for Boys the environment is completely dominated by an underground gang, the Vigils. During a chocolate candy sale Brother Leon, the acting headmaster of the school, defers to the Vigils, who reign with terror in the school. Jerry Renault is first a pawn for the Vigils' evil deeds and finally their victim." Shapiro. Fic for Youth. 3d edition

Followed by Beyond the chocolate war (1985)

★ **I** am the cheese; a novel. Pantheon Bks. 1977 233p hardcover o.p. pa $6.50

Grades: 7 8 9 10 11 12 Adult   **Fic**

1. Intelligence service -- Fiction
ISBN 0-394-83462-3; 0-440-94060-5 pa

LC 76-55948

ALA YALSA Margaret A. Edwards Award (1991)

"The suspense builds relentlessly to an ending that, although shocking, is entirely plausible." Booklist

Cornwell, Autumn

Carpe diem. Feiwel & Friends 2007 360p $16.95; pa $8.99

Grades: 7 8 9 10   **Fic**

1. Artists -- Fiction 2. Authorship -- Fiction 3.

942

Grandmothers -- Fiction 4. Southeast Asia -- Fiction
ISBN 0-312-36792-9; 978-0-312-36792-3; 978-0-312-56129-1 pa; 0-312-56129-6 pa

LC 2006-32054

Sixteen-year-old Vassar Spore's detailed plans for the next twenty years of her life are derailed when her bohemian grandmother insists that she join her in Southeast Asia for the summer, but as she writes a novel about her experiences, Vassar discovers new possibilities.

"Suspenseful and wonderfully detailed, the well-crafted story maintains its page-turning pace while adding small doses of insight and humor." SLJ

Cornwell, Betsy

Tides; by Betsy Cornwell. Clarion Books 2013 304 p. (hardcover) $16.99

Grades: 7 8 9 10 11 12 **Fic**
1. Love stories 2. Selkies -- Fiction 3. Internship programs -- Fiction 4. Love -- Fiction 5. Isles of Shoals (Me. and N.H.) -- Fiction
ISBN 054792772X; 9780547927725

LC 2012022415

In this teen novel, by Betsy Cornwell, "high school senior Noah Gallagher and his adopted teenage sister, Lo, go to live with their grandmother in her island cottage for the summer. . . . Noah has landed a marine biology internship, and Lo wants to draw and paint, perhaps even to vanquish her struggles with bulimia. But then things take a dramatic turn for them both when Noah mistakenly tries to save a mysterious girl from drowning." (Publisher's note)

Corrigan, Eireann

Accomplice. Scholastic Press 2010 296p $17.99

Grades: 7 8 9 10 **Fic**
1. School stories 2. Fraud -- Fiction 3. Friendship -- Fiction 4. New Jersey -- Fiction
ISBN 978-0-545-05236-8; 0-545-05236-X

LC 2009-53869

High school juniors and best friends Finn and Chloe hatch a daring plot to fake Chloe's disappearance from their rural New Jersey town in order to have something compelling to put on their college applications, but unforeseen events complicate matters.

"Corrigan has crafted a complex, heart-wrenchingly plausible YA thriller. . . . A fascinating character study of individuals and an entire town, this tension-filled story will entice readers with a single booktalk." Booklist

Ordinary ghosts. Scholastic Press 2007 328p $16.99

Grades: 9 10 11 12 **Fic**
1. School stories
ISBN 978-0-439-83243-4; 0-439-83243-8

LC 2007-276078

Emil feels invisible at school and at home. When he finds a master key to his private school, he sneaks in to explore, and finds a reason to become visible.

"Corrigan is a superb storyteller, and her Salingeresque tale keenly depicts not only her troubled narrator's emotional struggles but also the emotional components to the physical landscapes he vividly inhabits: his home, foundered on the wreck of family tragedy, and his school, thick during

the day with manipulatable adults and heedless kids, . . . but transformed at night into a place of possibility that both entices and disappoints." Bull Cent Child Books

Cousins, Dave

Waiting for Gonzo; Dave Cousins. First U.S. edition Flux 2015 288 p. $9.99

Grades: 7 8 9 10 **Fic**
1. Moving -- Fiction 2. Family life -- Fiction 3. High schools -- Fiction 4. Practical jokes -- Fiction 5. Brothers and sisters -- Fiction 6. England -- Fiction 7. Schools -- Fiction 8. Pregnancy -- Fiction 9. Moving, Household -- Fiction 10. Family life -- England -- Fiction
ISBN 073874199X; 9780738741994

LC 2014031277

In this book, by Dave Cousins, "[t]hings could be going better for Oz. He's just moved miles from all his friends. A prank at his new school puts him in the crosshairs of 'Psycho' Isobel Skinner, a bully who also happens to be his mum's new best friend. And he's driven off the only other kid who will have anything to do with him: a Tolkien-obsessed boy in desperate need of a decent playlist." (Publisher's note)

"In a darkly comic story written as Marcus's monologue to his unborn nephew (whom he nicknames Gonzo), Cousins (15 Days Without a Head) offers a vibrant, highly visual account of teen angst and backfiring schemes. Marcus makes more than a few mistakes at school and at home, but readers will never doubt that his heart is in the right place." Publishers Weekly

Cowan, Jennifer

★ **Earthgirl**. Groundwood Books 2009 232p $17.95

Grades: 8 9 10 11 12 **Fic**
1. Weblogs -- Fiction 2. Environmental movement -- Fiction
ISBN 978-0-88899-889-7; 0-88899-889-9

Sabine Solomon undergoes a transformation when she joins the environmental movement and becomes involved with activist Vray Foret, but when his activities involve something that is potentially illegal, she begins to question her identity and values.

This "novel with enormous teen appeal will inspire readers to question Sabine's tactics and their own impact on the earth." Kirkus

Cox, Suzy

The **Dead** Girls Detective Agency; Suzy Cox. Harper 2012 355 p. (trade bdg.) $9.99

Grades: 7 8 9 10 **Fic**
1. Future life 2. Ghost stories 3. Mystery fiction 4. Dead -- Fiction 5. Murder -- Fiction 6. New York (N.Y.) -- Fiction 7. Mystery and detective stories
ISBN 0-06-202064-1; 9780062020642

LC 2012006567

This novel, by Suzy Cox, follows the ghost of a teenager seeking to solve her own murder. "Meet the Dead Girls Detective Agency: Nancy, Lorna, and Tess--not to mention Edison, the really cute if slightly hostile dead boy. Apparently, the only way out of this limbo is to figure out who killed me, or I'll have to spend eternity playing Nancy Drew. Considering I was fairly invisible in life, who could hate me enough to want me dead? And what if my murderer is someone I never would have suspected?" (Publisher's note)

Coy, John

★ **Crackback**. Scholastic 2005 201p $16.99

Grades: 7 8 9 10   **Fic**

1. School stories 2. Football -- Fiction 3. Drug abuse -- Fiction 4. Father-son relationship -- Fiction

ISBN 0-439-69733-6

LC 2004-30972

Miles barely recalls when football was fun after being sidelined by a new coach, constantly criticized by his father, and pressured by his best friend to take performance-enhancing drugs. "Grades seven to ten." (Bull Cent Child Books)

The author "writes a moving, nuanced portrait of a teen struggling with adults who demand, but don't always deserve, respect." Booklist

Coyle, Katie

Vivian Apple at the end of the world; by Katie Coyle. Houghton Mifflin Harcourt 2015 272 p. (hardback) $17.99

Grades: 9 10 11 12   **Fic**

1. Bildungsromans 2. Religion -- Fiction 3. End of the world -- Fiction 4. Christian fundamentalism -- Fiction 5. Coming of age -- Fiction 6. Fundamentalism -- Fiction

ISBN 0544340116; 9780544340114

LC 2013050206

In this book, "seventeen-year-old Vivian Apple never believed in the evangelical Church of America, unlike her recently devout parents. But when Vivian returns home the night after the supposed 'Rapture,' all that's left of her parents are two holes in the roof. Suddenly, she doesn't know who or what to believe. With her best friend Harp and a mysterious ally, Peter, Vivian embarks on a desperate cross-country roadtrip through a paranoid and panic-stricken America to find answers." (Publisher's note)

"Coyle's debut (first published in Great Britain in 2013) is a unique and unpredictable apocalypse story steeped in tension and creepy atmosphere, with intelligent commentary on Fundamentalism and corporate influence in America; it's also an empowering coming-of-age adventure starring a relatable protagonist who successfully becomes 'the hero of [her] own story.'" Horn Book

Vivian Apple needs a miracle; by Katie Coyle. Houghton Mifflin Harcourt 2015 304 p. (hardback) $17.99

Grades: 9 10 11 12   **Fic**

1. Bildungsromans 2. Religion -- Fiction 3. Missing persons -- Fiction 4. Revolutionaries -- Fiction 5. End of the world -- Fiction 6. Christian fundamentalism -- Fiction 7. Coming of age -- Fiction 8. Fundamentalism -- Fiction

ISBN 9780544390423

LC 2014046783

Sequel to: Vivian Apple at the end of the world

In this book, by Katie Coyle, the "predicted Rapture by Pastor Frick's Church of America has come and gone, and three thousand Believers are now missing or dead. Seven-

teen-year-old Vivian Apple and her best friend, Harpreet, are revolutionaries, determined to expose the Church's diabolical power grab . . . and to locate Viv's missing heartthrob, Peter Ivey." (Publisher's note)

"Coyle adeptly handles an exceptionally multifaceted plot, easily seguing from snarky social criticism to heart-pounding action to stomach-fluttering romance, creating a breathless whirlwind that keeps the pages flying until the very end. A distinctive, complex, and thoughtful page-turner certain to leave readers clamoring for more." Kirkus

Craig, Colleen

Afrika. Tundra Books 2008 233p pa $9.95

Grades: 7 8 9 10   **Fic**

1. Fathers -- Fiction 2. Mothers -- Fiction 3. South Africa -- Fiction

ISBN 978-0-88776-807-1; 0-88776-807-5

"Growing up in Canada with her white South African mother, Kim van der Merwe does not know who her father is. Now, at 13, she goes to Cape Town for the first time, shortly after independence in the mid-1990s, because her mother, a journalist, is going to report on the Truth and Reconciliation Commission. . . . Visiting and meeting her family for the first time, she decides that her mission will be to discover her father's identity. . . . . The realities of the society are carefully and skillfully portrayed, so that Kim's story is truly the emotional heart of the book, and not a vehicle for ideas." SLJ

Cranse, Pratima

All the major constellations; by Pratima Cranse. Viking 2015 336 p. (hardcover) $17.99

Grades: 9 10 11 12   **Fic**

1. Coma -- Fiction 2. Friendship -- Fiction 3. Christian life -- Fiction

ISBN 0670016454; 9780670016457

LC 2014044806

In this book, by Pratima Cranse, "Andrew is leaving high school behind and looking ahead to a fresh start at college and distance from his not-so-secret infatuation: Laura Lettel. But when a terrible accident leaves him without the companionship of his two best friends, Andrew is cast adrift and alone—until Laura unexpectedly offers him comfort, friendship, and the support of a youth group of true believers, fundamentalist Christians with problems and secrets of their own." (Publisher's note)

"Andrew is prepared to graduate from high school, work his summer job, and finally escape his alcoholic father. His plans are thrown for a loop when one of his best friends, Sara, is in a coma after a car accident and his other best friend, Marcia, becomes distant as she helps to care for Sara. The fact that Andrew's older, baseball-star, bully brother is coming home from college only makes his home life more unbearable. A note slipped to him from his longtime crush, Laura, leads Andrew to a fundamentalist Christian youth group. . . . Older fans of realistic fiction will enjoy riding along with Andrew." SLJ

Cremer, Andrea

Invisibility; Andrea Cremer and David Levithan. Philomel Books 2013 320 p. (hardcover) $18.99

Grades: 7 8 9 10 11 12   **Fic**
1. Love -- Fiction 2. Invisibility -- Fiction 3. Magic
-- Fiction 4. Charms -- Fiction 5. Friendship -- Fiction
6. Family problems -- Fiction 7. New York (N.Y.) --
Fiction
ISBN 0399257608; 9780399257605
                                      LC 2012024514
This book by Andrea Cremer and David Levithan chronicles the "romance between a boy cursed with invisibility and the one girl who can see him. . . . Stephen is used to invisibility. He was born that way. . . . Elizabeth sometimes wishes for invisibility. . . . To Stephen's amazement, she can see him. And to Elizabeth's amazement, she wants him to be able to see her--all of her. But as the two become closer, an invisible world gets in their way." (Publisher's note)

"hough it begins as a stumbling, near–coming-out story (for Stephen), the novel deftly switches gears to a fast-paced supernatural thriller that will surely leave readers wanting more." Kirkus

Crichton, Michael., 1942-2008
★ The **Andromeda** strain. Harper 2008 364p pa $9.99
Grades: 11 12 Adult   **Fic**
1. Science fiction
ISBN 978-0-06-170315-7
First published 1969 by Knopf
"In these days of interplanetary exploration, this tale of the world's first space-age biological emergency may seem uncomfortably believable. When a contaminated space capsule drops to earth in a small Nevada town and all the town's residents suddenly die, four American scientists gather at an underground laboratory of Project Wildfire to search frantically for an antidote to the threat of a worldwide epidemic." Shapiro. Fic for Youth. 3d edition
Includes bibliographical references

★ **Jurassic** Park; a novel. Knopf 1990 399p pa $7.99; $28.95
Grades: 7 8 9 10 11 12 Adult   **Fic**
1. Science fiction 2. Genetics 3. Dinosaurs 4. Scientists 5. Asexual reproduction 6. Dinosaurs -- Fiction 7. Scientists -- Fiction 8. Genetic engineering -- Fiction
ISBN 0-345-37077-5 pa; 0-394-58816-9
                                        LC 90-52960
This novel "tells of a modern-day scientist bringing to life a horde of prehistoric animals." (N Y Times Book Rev)
"Crichton is a master at blending technology with fiction. . . . Suspense, excitement, and good adventure pervade this book." SLJ
Followed by The lost world (1995)

Pirate latitudes; a novel. Harper 2009 312p map $27.99
Grades: 11 12 Adult   **Fic**
1. Sea stories 2. Adventure fiction 3. Pirates -- Fiction 4. Caribbean region -- Fiction
ISBN 978-0-06-192937-3; 0-06-192937-9
                                      LC 2009-49965
The Caribbean, 1665. Pirate captain Charles Hunter, with backing from a powerful ally, assembles a crew of ruf-

fians to take the Spanish galleon, "El Trinidad," guarded by the bloodthirsty Cazalla, a favorite commander of the Spanish king himself.
"Pirate fans will love the book for its flashy characters and historical authenticity. Crime fans will enjoy the caper-novel structure and the way the author keeps them on their toes." Booklist

Crockett, S. D.
After the snow; S. D. Crockett. Feiwel & Friends 2012 304 p. (hardback) $22.55
Grades: 6 7 8 9 10 11 12   **Fic**
1. Science fiction 2. Adventure fiction 3. Winter -- Fiction 4. Missing persons -- Fiction 5. Children and war -- Fiction 6. Survival -- Fiction 7. Voyages and travels -- Fiction 8. Adventure and adventurers -- Fiction
ISBN 9780312641696
                                      LC 2011036122
William C. Morris Award Finalist (2013)
In this book, "Willo's father can still remember what life was like in Great Britain before the country entered a new ice age. . . . When his father and the rest of his family mysteriously disappear, Willo leaves the scant safety of home to search for them. . . . [He] saves a . . . girl he encounters along the way, and together they find their way into the city, in which a long-dormant resistance movement is preparing for a final desperate exodus." (Bulletin of the Center for Children's Books)

One Crow Alone; by S.D. Crockett. Feiwel & Friends 2013 320 p. $16.99
Grades: 6 7 8 9 10 11 12   **Fic**
1. Evacuation of civilians 2. Mother-daughter relationship -- Fiction
ISBN 1250024250; 9781250024251
In this book, by S.D. Crockett, "living in an isolated Polish village with her grandmother, fifteen-year-old Magda Krol has no idea of the troubles sweeping across the planet. But when her village is evacuated without her, Magda must make her way alone across the frozen wilderness to Krakow, and then on to London, where she dreams of finding warmth and safety with her long-lost mother." (Publisher's note)

Croggon, Alison
Black spring; Alison Croggon. Candlewick Press 2013 288 p. $16.99
Grades: 9 10 11 12   **Fic**
1. Revenge -- Fiction 2. Witches -- Fiction 3. Social classes -- Fiction
ISBN 0763660094; 9780763660093
                                      LC 2012950560
This book by Alison Croggon is "an homage to 'Wuthering Heights,' trading the English moors of the original for the remote northern wilds of Elbasa, a land of powerful wizards and strict rules concerning vendetta. . . . . It's a fantasy setting, but Croggon maintains the north/south, high/low, and male/female class divisions Brontë explores; Lina, born a witch, takes the place of Catherine, while 'swarthy' Damek il Haran has his analogue in Heathcliff." (Publishers Weekly)

"Violet-eyed witch Lina, daughter of a powerful lord, is subject to the wrath of the wizards of the North, who seek to suppress any competing powers--especially those found in women. Seemingly cursed, Lina only finds strength once she sheds the control of domineering men, including her love, Damek. The magical slant of this poetic Wuthering Heights reimagining is compelling." (Horn Book)

Cronn-Mills, Kirstin

Beautiful Music for Ugly Children; Kirstin Cronn-Mills. Flux 2012 271 p. $9.99

Grades: 9 10 11 12   **Fic**
1. Transgender people 2. Disc jockeys -- Fiction 3. High schools -- Fiction 4. Schools -- Fiction 5. Transgender people -- Fiction
ISBN 9780738732510

                LC 2012019028

Stonewall Book Award-Mike Morgan and Larry Romans Children's & Young Adult Literature Award

In author Kirstin Cronn-Mills's book, "it is only after hearing Gabe's friend and neighbor John . . . use Gabe's birth name that readers learn that Gabe is transgender. Being trans, Gabe opines, is like being a 45 record with an A side and a B side. When the story opens, only a few people know about Gabe's B side; the rest see him as a girl. When Gabe's radio show becomes an underground hit, generating a . . . cadre of fans calling themselves the Ugly Children Brigade, Gabe's B side is pushed further into public view." (Kirkus Reviews)

Cross, Gillian, 1945-

Where I belong. Holiday House 2011 245p $17.95

Grades: 7 8 9 10   **Fic**
1. Somalia -- Fiction 2. Refugees -- Fiction 3. Kidnapping -- Fiction 4. London (England) -- Fiction 5. Fashion designers -- Fiction
ISBN 978-0-8234-2332-3; 0-8234-2332-8

                LC 2010-23671

This is a "fast-paced adventure. . . . The fashion element will engage readers who would otherwise not read this genre. . . . This broadly appealing title has an engaging cover and is a worthy addition to any collection." SLJ

Cross, Julie

Tempest; Julie Cross. St. Martin's Griffin 2012 339p. (hardback) $17.99

Grades: 8 9 10 11 12   **Fic**
1. Love stories 2. Science fiction 3. Suspense fiction 4. Young men -- Fiction 5. Time travel -- Fiction 6. Spies -- Fiction
ISBN 9780312568894

                LC 2011032799

This novel follows "[n]ineteen-year-old Jackson Meyer . . . [who is] able to jump a couple of hours back in time . . . [and decides to] keep his . . . skill set a secret from his over-protective father and his beloved girlfriend Holly. When two armed men attempt to kidnap Jackson, shooting and most likely killing Holly in the process, Jackson time-jumps in a panic and inexplicably finds himself in 2007, where he is stuck until he can figure out how to get back to the future and save Holly. In the meantime, Jackson discovers that the

man he has called Dad all these years is not in fact his father but rather a CIA agent and part of a shadowy government experiment called Tempest—an experiment that includes Jackson as one of its results." (Bulletin of the Center for Children's Books)

Cross, Sarah

Dull boy. Dutton Childrens Books 2009 308p $17.99

Grades: 7 8 9 10   **Fic**
1. Science fiction 2. Superheroes -- Fiction 3. Supernatural -- Fiction
ISBN 978-0-525-42133-7; 0-525-42133-5

                LC 2008-34208

Avery, a teenaged boy with frightening super powers that he is trying to hide, discovers other teenagers who also have strange powers and who are being sought by the icy and seductive Cherchette, but they do not know what she wants with them.

"Avery's narration, generously peppered with swear words, is hip, witty, funny, and sarcastic." SLJ

Crossan, Sarah

Breathe; Sarah Crossan. Greenwillow Books 2012 373 p. (hardback) $17.99

Grades: 7 8 9 10 11 12   **Fic**
1. Friendship -- Fiction 2. Dystopian juvenile fiction 3. Science fiction 4. Science fiction
ISBN 0062118692; 9780062118691

                LC 2012017496

In author Sarah Crossan's book, "Alina has been stealing for a long time . . . Quinn should be worried about Alina and a bit afraid for himself, too, but . . . it isn't every day that the girl of your dreams asks you to rescue her. Bea wants to tell him that none of this is fair; they'd planned a trip together, the two of them, and she'd hoped he'd discover her out here, not another girl. And as they walk into the Outlands with two days' worth of oxygen in their tanks, everything they believe will be shattered. Will they be able to make it back? Will they want to?" (Publisher's note)

One; by Sarah Crossan. Greenwillow Books, an imprint of HarperCollinsPublishers 2015 400 p. (trade ed.) $17.99

Grades: 8 9 10 11 12   **Fic**
1. Novels in verse 2. Conjoined twins -- Fiction 3. Twins -- Fiction 4. Schools -- Fiction 5. Sisters -- Fiction 6. High schools -- Fiction 7. Family problems -- Fiction
ISBN 9780062118752; 0062118757

                LC 2015004714

"Life for 16-year-old Grace and her sister Tippi hasn't been easy: they're conjoined twins--literally joined at the hip. They've spent their lives dealing with staring strangers and invasive questions, but the girls are happy together and wouldn't have it any other way. Grace and Tippi have been home-schooled until now, but when the state decides to pay for the girls to attend a private high school instead, they begin their junior year among peers. . . . When Grace is diagnosed with a bad heart, the twins have a difficult decision to make: risk the dangerous separation surgery so Grace can qualify for a transplant, or stay together and get sicker until they both die." (Kirkus)

"Crossan trusts her characters and her readers to find their better selves through her gently paced story." Booklist

Crossley-Holland, Kevin

★ **Crossing** to Paradise. Arthur A. Levine Books 2008 339p $17.99

Grades: 7 8 9 10   **Fic**

1. Kings 2. Singing -- Fiction 3. Literacy -- Fiction 4. Middle Ages -- Fiction 5. Christian life -- Fiction 6. Pilgrims and pilgrimages -- Fiction 7. Great Britain -- History -- 1154-1399, Plantagenets -- Fiction
ISBN 978-0-545-05866-7; 0-545-05866-X; 978-0-545-05868-1 pa; 0-545-05868-6 pa

LC 2007-51853

First published 2006 in the United Kingdom with title: Gatty's tale

Gatty, the field-girl who appeared in the author's trilogy about King Arthur, is now an orphan. When she is selected for a pilgrimage, she travels from her home on an English estate to London, Venice, and eventually Jerusalem. "Grades six to ten." (Bull Cent Child Books)

"Gatty, the irrepressible peasant girl first introduced in Crossley-Holland's 'Arthur' trilogy . . . comes into her own in this sweeping, vibrant story." SLJ

Crowder, Melanie

Audacity; Melanie Crowder. Philomel Books 2015 400 p. illustrations $17.99

Grades: 9 10 11 12   **Fic**

1. Labor movement -- Fiction 2. Russian Americans -- Fiction 3. Jews -- United States -- Fiction 4. Immigrants -- United States -- Fiction 5. Novels in verse 6. Immigrants -- Fiction 7. New York (N.Y.) -- History -- 1898-1951 -- Fiction 8. Women in the labor movement -- New York (State) -- New York
ISBN 0399168990; 9780399168994

LC 2014018466

This novel, by Melanie Crowder, "is inspired by the real-life story of Clara Lemlich, a spirited young woman who emigrated from Russia to New York at the turn of the twentieth century and fought tenaciously for equal rights. Bucking the norms of both her traditional Jewish family and societal conventions, Clara refuses to accept substandard working conditions in the factories on Manhattan's Lower East Side." (Publisher's note)

"Crowder breathes life into a world long past and provides insight into the achievements of one determined woman who knows she will 'give / without the thought / of ever getting back, / to ease the suffering of others. / That, / I think, / I will be doing / the rest of my life.' Compelling, powerful and unforgettable."

Includes bibliographical references

Crowe, Chris

Mississippi trial, 1955. Penguin Putnam 2002 231p pa $5.99; $17.99

Grades: 7 8 9 10   **Fic**

1. Children 2. Racism 3. Grandfathers 4. Murder victims 5. Fathers and sons 6. Racism -- Fiction 7. Grandfathers -- Fiction 8. Mississippi -- Race relations
ISBN 0-14-250192-1 pa; 0-8037-2745-3

LC 2001-40221

In Mississippi in 1955, a sixteen-year-old finds himself at odds with his grandfather over issues surrounding the kidnapping and murder of a fourteen-year-old African American from Chicago. "Grades seven to ten." (Bull Cent Child Books)

"By combining real events with their impact upon a single fictional character, Crowe makes the issues in this novel hard-hitting and personal. The characters are complex." Voice Youth Advocates

Crowley, Cath

A **little** wanting song. Knopf 2010 265p $16.99; lib bdg $19.99

Grades: 8 9 10 11 12   **Fic**

1. Shyness -- Fiction 2. Australia -- Fiction 3. Musicians -- Fiction 4. Friendship -- Fiction 5. Loneliness -- Fiction
ISBN 978-0-375-86096-6; 0-375-86096-7; 978-0-375-96096-3 lib bdg; 0-375-96096-1 lib bdg

LC 2009-20305

First published 2005 in Australia with title: Chasing Charlie Duskin

One Australian summer, two very different sixteen-year-old girls—Charlie, a talented but shy musician, and Rose, a confident student longing to escape her tiny town—are drawn into an unexpected friendship, as told in their alternating voices

"Crowley's prose is lyrical and lovely, her characters are beautifully crafted, and her portrayal of teen life in Australia is a delight. . . . Female readers especially will enjoy this upbeat tale." Voice Youth Advocates

Crutcher, Chris, 1946-

Period 8; by Chris Crutcher. Greenwillow Books 2013 288 p. (hardback) $17.99

Grades: 7 8 9   **Fic**

1. School stories 2. Missing persons -- Fiction 3. Clubs -- Fiction 4. Bullies -- Fiction 5. Schools -- Fiction 6. Kidnapping -- Fiction 7. High schools -- Fiction 8. Sexual abuse -- Fiction 9. Missing children -- Fiction 10. Mystery and detective stories
ISBN 0061914800; 9780061914805; 9780061914812

LC 2012046726

In this book, high school teacher "Bruce Logsdon's Period 8 session, held during the regular lunch period, is a place for Heller High School students to talk about their concerns and feelings. . . . When quiet, unassuming Mary Wells (called the 'Virgin Mary' by other students due to her outwardly prudish behavior) goes missing, Period 8 must grapple with the fact that their safe space has been compromised." (School Library Journal)

Running loose. Greenwillow Bks. 1983 190p hardcover o.p. pa $8.99; pa $6.99

Grades: 7 8 9 10   **Fic**

1. School stories
ISBN 9780060094911 pa; 0-688-02002-X; 0-06-009491-5 pa

LC 82-20935

ALA YALSA Margaret A. Edwards Award (2000)

"Louie Banks tells what happened to him in his senior year in a small town Idaho high school. Besides falling in love with Becky and losing her in a senseless accident, Louie takes a stand against the coach when he sets the team up to injure a black player on an opposing team, and learns that you can't be honorable with dishonorable men. . . . Grade seven and up." (Voice Youth Advocates)

"Louie Banks tells what happened to him in his senior year in a small town Idaho high school. Besides falling in love with Becky and losing her in a senseless accident, Louie takes a stand against the coach when he sets the team up to injure a black player on an opposing team, and learns that you can't be honorable with dishonorable men." Voice Youth Advocates

★ **Staying** fat for Sarah Byrnes. Greenwillow Bks. 1993 216p hardcover o.p. pa $6.99

Grades: 7 8 9 10 **Fic**

1. Obesity -- Fiction 2. Swimming -- Fiction 3. Friendship -- Fiction 4. Child abuse -- Fiction
ISBN 0-688-11552-7; 0-06-009489-3 pa
LC 91-40097

ALA YALSA Margaret A. Edwards Award (2000)

"An obese boy and a disfigured girl suffer the emotional scars of years of mockery at the hands of their peers. They share a hard-boiled view of the world until events in their senior year hurl them in very different directions. A story about a friendship with staying power, written with pathos and pointed humor." SLJ

Stotan! HarperTempest 2003 261p pa $6.99

Grades: 7 8 9 10 **Fic**

1. Swimming -- Fiction
ISBN 0-06-009492-3
LC 85-12712

First published 1986

ALA YALSA Margaret A. Edwards Award (2000)

A high school coach invites members of his swimming team to a memorable week of rigorous training that tests their moral fiber as well as their physical stamina.

"A subplot involving the boys' fight against local Neo-Nazi activists provides some immediate action, while the various characters' conflicts tighten the middle and ending. The pace lags through the story's introduction; nevertheless, this is a searching sports novel, with a tone varying from macho-tough to sensitive." Bull Cent Child Books

Culbertson, Kim

Instructions for a broken heart. Sourcebooks Fire 2011 295p pa $9.99

Grades: 8 9 10 11 12 **Fic**

1. Italy -- Fiction 2. Theater -- Fiction 3. Voyages and travels -- Fiction
ISBN 978-1-4022-4302-8; 1-4022-4302-2
LC 2011021860

While high school junior Jessa is on a Drama Academy trip to Italy with ex-boyfriend Sean and his new girlfriend, she opens her heart to change by following all of the outrageous instructions in her best friend's care package.

"Culbertson gives Jessa the room to be angry, mischievous, confused, and wounded without heading into over-

wrought angst, and she creates a well-developed character with the self-reflection and strength needed to pull herself out of a funk, with a little help from friends, of course." Booklist

Cummings, Priscilla

Blindsided. Dutton Children's Books 2010 226p $16.99

Grades: 7 8 9 10 **Fic**

1. School stories 2. Blind -- Fiction 3. Maryland -- Fiction
ISBN 978-0-525-42161-0; 0-525-42161-0
LC 2009-25092

"Natalie, 14, knows that her future is becoming dimmer as the loss of her eyesight is a nightmare she can't avoid. . . . Part of going from denial to acceptance is attending a boarding school for the blind. . . . Natalie is a credible character and her fear is palpable and painful. . . . Readers will enjoy the high drama and heroics." SLJ

Cypess, Leah

Death sworn; by Leah Cypess. Greenwillow Books, an imprint of HarperCollinsPublishers 2014 352 p. (hardback) $17.99

Grades: 7 8 9 10 11 12 **Fic**

1. Love stories 2. Fantasy fiction 3. Magic -- Fiction 4. Assassins -- Fiction 5. Fantasy 6. Love -- Fiction 7. Secrets -- Fiction
ISBN 0062221213; 9780062221216
LC 2013037379

Sequel: Death Marked (2015)

In this book, by Leah Cypress, "when a young sorceress is exiled to teach magic to a clan of assassins, she will find that secrets can be even deadlier than swords. . . . Ileni is losing her magic. And that means she's losing everything: her position as the rising star of her people, her purpose in life, and even the young man she loves. . . . Sent to the assassins' cave, . . . she'll find an ally in Sorin, the deadly young man who could be the assassins' next leader. . . . Sparks--magical and romantic--will fly." (Publisher's note)

"As seventeen-year-old Ileni's magic begins to fade, she's sent to the Black Mountain to tutor assassins in sorcery. With the help of Sorin, her student and assigned protector, she must discover who killed her predecessors before someone kills her. Ileni proves a compelling protagonist, and the blend of romance, assassins, magic, and murder-mystery consistently raises the stakes." Horn Book

Mistwood. Greenwillow Books 2010 304p $16.99

Grades: 7 8 9 10 **Fic**

1. Fantasy fiction 2. Magic -- Fiction 3. Kings and rulers -- Fiction
ISBN 978-0-06-195699-7; 0-06-195699-6
LC 2009-23051

Brought back from the Mistwood to protect the royal family, a girl who has no memory of being a shape-shifter encounters political and magical intrigue as she struggles with her growing feelings for the prince.

"A traditional premise is transformed into a graceful meditation on the ramifications of loyalty, duty and purpose. . . . Astonishing and inspiring." Kirkus

Nightspell. Greenwillow Books 2011 326p $16.99

Grades: 7 8 9 10   **Fic**

1. Ghost stories 2. Dead -- Fiction 3. Sisters -- Fiction 4. Kings and rulers -- Fiction

ISBN 978-0-06-195702-4; 0-06-195702-X

LC 2010012637

Sent by her father, the king of Raellia, who is trying to forge an empire out of warring tribes, Darri arrives in Ghost-land and discovers that her sister, whom she planned to res-cue, may not want to leave this land where the dead mingle freely with the living.

"Swordfights, blood, and double-dealing pack the pages as this action-filled story races to a surprising conclusion." Booklist

Dagg, Carole Estby

The **year** we were famous. Clarion Books 2011 250p $16.99

Grades: 6 7 8 9 10   **Fic**

1. Adventure fiction 2. Voyages and travels -- Fiction 3. Mother-daughter relationship -- Fiction

ISBN 978-0-618-99983-5; 0-618-99983-3

"Dagg writes a captivating story about the determina-tion of a mother and daughter, who in 1896 walked from Washington State to New York City. . . . Clara's free-spirited but unreliable mother suggests that they walk nearly 4,000 miles to save their farm from foreclosure (a publisher offers them a 10,000 advance if they make it in seven months) and bring attention to the suffragist movement. . . . The pages go by quickly. . . . The journey in itself is amazing, but Dagg's tender portrayal of a mother and daughter who learn to ap-preciate and forgive each other makes it unforgettable." Publ Wkly

Daley, James Ryan

Jesus Jackson; James Ryan Daley. First edition Poisoned Pencil Press 2014 viii, 267 p (trade pbk: alk. paper) $10.95

Grades: 8 9 10 11 12   **Fic**

1. Mystery fiction 2. Religion -- Fiction 3. High school students -- Fiction 4. Death 5. Faith 6. Teenage boys 7. Brothers -- Death 8. Brothers and sisters

ISBN 1929345062; 9781929345069

LC 2014938496

"Jonathan Stiles is a 14-year-old atheist who is coping with his first day of ninth grade at the fervently religious St. Soren's Academy when his idolized older brother Ryan is found dead at the bottom of a ravine behind the school. As his world crumbles, Jonathan meets an eccentric stranger who bears an uncanny resemblance to Jesus Christ (except for his white linen leisure suit and sparkling gold chains)." (Publisher's note)

"The book excels, sidestepping holier-than-thou rhetoric and addressing the pain of loss head-on as well as painting a wonderful depiction of a young man coming to terms with how he was raised and how he wants to lead his own life. The mystery element and minor romance are icing on the cake: well-executed and finely tuned, complementing the book's major themes in all the right ways.Smart and sweet, comforting and moving. " Kirkus

Damico, Gina

Croak; by Gina Damico. Houghton Mifflin Har-court 2012 311 p. $8.99

Grades: 7 8 9 10   **Fic**

1. Mystery fiction 2. Soul -- Fiction 3. Death -- Fiction 4. Justice -- Fiction 5. Future life -- Fiction

ISBN 9780547608327

LC 2011017125

This book tells the story of "sixteen-year-old bad girl Lex Bartleby [who] is shipped off to her uncle Mort's farm, supposedly to figure out her anger issues with the help of manual labor. Instead, she learns that "farmer" Mort is a reaper of another kind entirely and that, as mayor of Croak, a small collection of Grim Reapers, he will be teaching Lex the family business. Although she initially takes to ferrying souls into the Afterlife with aplomb, Lex begins to question the roles of Reapers as silent witnesses to the world's in-justices, especially when their knowledge of people's deaths would allow them to wreak karmic justice upon the murder-ers and rapists that otherwise get away with their crimes." (Bulletin of the Center for Children's Books)

Hellhole; by Gina Damico. Houghton Mifflin Harcourt 2014 368 p. illustrations

Grades: 9 10 11 12   **Fic**

1. Sick -- Fiction 2. Devil -- Fiction 3. Humorous stories 4. Conduct of life -- Fiction 5. Mothers and sons -- Fiction 6. Single-parent families -- Fiction 7. Interpersonal relations -- Fiction

ISBN 9780544307100

LC 2013042827

In this novel by Gina Damico "squeaky-clean Max Kilgore . . . accidentally unearths a devil. The big red guy has a penchant for couch surfing and junk food--and you should never underestimate evil on a sugar high. With the help of Lore, a former goth girl who knows a thing or two about the dark side, Max is racing against the clock to get rid of the houseguest." (Publisher's note)

"Damico's blend of bleak humor and harsh reality lends itself well to Max's social awkwardness and Lore's biting cynicism, while Burg is outrageously appalling (one mo-ment he's munching on a stick of butter half-naked, the next he's hurling a fireplace poker at Max's head). The ending is somewhat rushed and leaves a few loose ends, but this remains a wild and unpredictable cautionary tale about ill-considered bargains and bad decisions." Pub Wkly

Rogue; by Gina Damico. Graphia 2013 336 p. (paperback) $8.99

Grades: 8 9 10   **Fic**

1. Future life -- Fiction 2. Grim Reaper (Symbolic character) -- Fiction 3. Death -- Fiction 4. Humorous stories 5. Ghosts -- Fiction

ISBN 0544108841; 9780544108844

LC 2013004154

This book by Gina Damico follows a "band of surly teenage grim reapers risking everything on their mission to save the Afterlife. Uncle Mort's plan to save the Afterlife by enlisting Junior Grims to help destroy the portals that access it is full of risks, loopholes and secrets--and fiery-tempered, impulsive Lex is the plan's unstable lynchpin." (Kirkus Reviews)

Scorch; Gina Damico. Houghton Mifflin Harcourt 2012 332 p. (paperback) $8.99

Grades: 7 8 9 10   **Fic**

1. Fantasy fiction 2. Death -- Fiction 3. Humorous stories 4. Future life -- Fiction

ISBN 0547624573; 9780547624570

LC 2012014799

In this novel by Gina Damico "Lex is a full-time teenage grim reaper -- but now has the bizarre ability to Damn souls.... [S]he and her friends embark on a wild road trip to DeMyse. Though this sparkling desert oasis is full of luxuries and amusements, it feels like a prison to Lex. Her best chance at escape would be to stop all the senseless violence that she caused -- but how can she do that from DeMyse, where the Grims seem mysteriously oblivious to the bloodshed?" (Publisher's note)

Dana, Barbara

A **voice** of her own; becoming Emily Dickinson: a novel. HarperTeen 2009 346p $16.99

Grades: 7 8 9 10   **Fic**

1. Poets 2. Authors 3. Poets -- Fiction 4. Massachusetts -- Fiction

ISBN 978-0-06-028704-7; 0-06-028704-7

LC 2008-10289

A fictionalized first-person account of revered American poet Emily Dickinson's girlhood in mid-nineteenth-century Amherst, Massachusetts.

"An obvious choice for curriculum support, this heartfelt, exhaustively detailed portrait humanizes the reclusive literary figure and offers an intimate sense of how a poet draws from small moments, gathered on scraps, to create great works." Booklist

Includes bibliographical references

Danforth, Emily M.

★ The **miseducation** of Cameron Post; emily m. danforth. 1st ed. Balzer + Bray 2012 480p

Grades: 9 10 11 12   **Fic**

1. Bildungsromans 2. Lesbians -- Fiction 3. Christian fundamentalism -- Fiction 4. Gays -- Fiction 5. Montana -- Fiction 6. Orphans -- Fiction

ISBN 9780062020567 (trade bdg.)

LC 2011001947

William C. Morris Award Finalist (2013)

This book offers a story about "coming of age as a lesbian in Miles City, Montana, in the early '90s, and . . . [focuses on] teen life in a pray-away-the-gay camp. Adopted by her born-again aunt Ruth after her parents' deaths, Cameron finds her first sexual explorations result in a betrayal that lands her in a re-education program called God's Promise." Bulletin of the Center for Children's Books)

Danticat, Edwidge, 1969-

Untwine; a novel. Edwidge Danticat. Scholastic Press 2015 320 p. (jacketed hardcover: alk. paper) $16.99

Grades: 9 10 11 12   **Fic**

1. Grief -- Fiction 2. Twins -- Fiction 3. Sisters --

Fiction 4. Haitian Americans -- Fiction 5. Traffic accidents -- Fiction 6. Miami (Fla.) -- Fiction

ISBN 9780545423038

LC 2014046787

NAACP Image Award Nominee: Outstanding Literary Work- Youth/Teens (2016)

In this book, by Edwidge Danticat, "Giselle Boyer and her identical twin, Isabelle, are as close as sisters can be, even as their family seems to be unraveling. Then the Boyers have a tragic encounter that will shatter everyone's world forever. Giselle wakes up in the hospital, injured and unable to speak or move. Trapped in the prison of her own body, Giselle must revisit her past in order to understand how the people closest to her . . . have shaped and defined her." (Publisher's note)

"There's a lot quietly packed into this novel—Giselle's Haitian heritage, her parents' imminent separation, the complications and thrills of first love, music, and art—yet most interesting is Danticat's rendering of identical twins as unique individuals. This is a poignant story for thoughtful teens that explores what it means to be a twin and how to say good-bye without losing oneself." Booklist

Darnielle, John, 1967-

Wolf in white van; a novel. John Darnielle. First edition Farrar, Straus & Giroux 2014 224 p. (hardback) $24

Grades: 11 12 Adult   **Fic**

1. California -- Fiction 2. Role playing -- Fiction 3. People with disabilities -- Fiction 4. Eccentrics and eccentricities -- Fiction 5. Role playing -- fiction 6. Disfigured persons -- fiction 7. Alienation (Social psychology) -- fiction

ISBN 0374292086; 9780374292089

LC 2014015427

Alex Award (2015)

In this novel, by John Darnielle, "[i]solated by a disfiguring injury since the age of seventeen, Sean Phillips crafts imaginary worlds for strangers to play in. From his small apartment in southern California, he orchestrates fantastic adventures where possibilities, both dark and bright, open in the boundaries between the real and the imagined." (Publisher's note)

"Sean Phillips was an unremarkable, moody teenager until tragedy left him with a horrific injury, changing his life forever. Who or what drove him to his fate? Can anyone be blamed? Is there a lesson to be learned? These questions are explored but never fully answered in Darnielle's first full-length novel...As senseless as a car accident, and as hard to look away from, the inconclusiveness of this journey will either captivate or madden readers." Booklist

Dashner, James

The **kill** order; James Dashner. Delacorte Press 2012 329 p. $17.99

Grades: 7 8 9 10 11 12   **Fic**

1. Viruses -- Fiction 2. Survival skills -- Fiction 3. Natural disasters -- Fiction 4. Science fiction 5. Survival -- Fiction 6. Virus diseases -- Fiction

ISBN 9780307979117; 9780375990823; 9780385742887; 0385742886

LC 2012016790

In this book by James Dashner "sun flares hit the earth and mankind fell to disease. Mark and Trina were there when it happened, and they survived. But surviving the sun flares was easy compared to what came next. Now a disease of rage and lunacy races across the eastern United States, and there's something suspicious about its origin. Worse yet, it's mutating, and all evidence suggests that it will bring humanity to its knees." (Publisher's note)

The **maze** runner. Delacorte Press 2009 375p $16.99; lib bdg $19.99
Grades: 7 8 9 10 11 12   **Fic**
  1. Science fiction 2. Amnesia -- Fiction
ISBN 0-385-73794-7; 0-385-90702-8 lib bdg; 978-0-385-73794-4; 978-0-385-90702-6 lib bdg
                LC 2009-1345
Sixteen-year-old Thomas wakes up with no memory in the middle of a maze and realizes he must work with the community in which he finds himself if he is to escape.
"With a fast-paced narrative steadily answering the myriad questions that arise and an ever-increasing air of tension, Dashner's suspenseful adventure will keep readers guessing until the very end." Publ Wkly
  Other titles in this series are:
  The scorch trials (2010)
  The death cure (2011)

The **scorch** trials. Delacorte Press 2010 361p $17.99; lib bdg $20.99
Grades: 7 8 9 10 11 12   **Fic**
  1. Science fiction 2. Science -- Experiments -- Fiction
ISBN 978-0-385-73875-0; 0-385-73875-7; 978-0-385-90745-3 lib bdg; 0-385-90745-1 lib bdg
  Sequel to: The maze runner (2009)
After surviving horrific conditions in the Maze, Thomas is entrapped, along with nineteen other boys, in a scientific experiment designed to observe their responses and gather data believed to be essential for the survival of the human race.
"Taut and bleak, continually intriguing and surprising, this is a solid sequel that keeps both Thomas and readers wondering what is really going on. Hooked readers will hope they won't have to wait long for the answers that have been promised in the next installment." Kirkus

Davies, Anna
  Identity Theft. Point Horror 2013 250 p. $9.99
Grades: 9 10 11 12   **Fic**
  1. Mystery fiction 2. Identity theft -- Fiction
ISBN 0545477123; 1480613169; 9780545477123; 9781480613164
In this book, "Hayley Westin knows exactly what she wants from life. As an overachiever who is determined to land a prestigious college scholarship, the high school senior doesn't have time for friends, sports, dating, or social media. So when she discovers that a fake Facebook account has been created in her name, she's convinced that someone is out to ruin her chances for the scholarship." But things might be even more malicious than they first appear. (School Library Journal)

Davies, Jacqueline
  Lost. Marshall Cavendish 2009 242p $16.99
Grades: 7 8 9 10   **Fic**
  1. Sisters -- Fiction 2. Factories -- Fiction 3. Bereavement -- Fiction 4. New York (N.Y.) -- Fiction 5. Triangle Shirtwaist Company, Inc. -- Fiction
ISBN 978-0-7614-5535-6; 0-7614-5535-3
                LC 2008-40560
In 1911 New York, sixteen-year-old Essie Rosenfeld must stop taking care of her irrepressible six-year-old sister when she goes to work at the Triangle Waist Company, where she befriends a missing heiress who is in hiding from her family and who seems to understand the feelings of heartache and grief that Essie is trying desperately to escape.
The "unusual pacing adds depth and intrigue as the plot unfolds. There are many layers to this story, which will appeal to a variety of interests and age levels." SLJ

Davis, Lane
  I swear; Lane Davis. Simon & Schuster Books For Young Readers 2012 279 p. (hardcover) $16.99
Grades: 9 10 11 12   **Fic**
  1. Suicide -- Fiction 2. Litigation -- Fiction 3. Cyberbullying -- Fiction 4. Bullying -- Fiction
ISBN 1442435062; 9781442435063
                LC 2011046310
In this book by Lane Davis, "after years of abuse from her classmates, Leslie Gatlin decided she had no other options and took her own life. Now her abusers are dealing with the fallout. When Leslie's parents file a wrongful death lawsuit against their daughter's tormenters, the proceedings uncover the systematic cyber bullying and harassment that occurred. . . . Leslie may have taken her own life, but her bullies took everything else." (Publisher's note)

Davis, Tanita S.
  Happy families; by Tanita S. Davis. Alfred A. Knopf 2012 234 p. (hardcover) $16.99
Grades: 9 10 11 12   **Fic**
  1. Twins -- Fiction 2. Family -- Fiction 3. Transgender parents -- Fiction 4. Fathers -- Fiction 5. Transgender people -- Fiction 6. Brothers and sisters -- Fiction
ISBN 9780375869662; 9780375969669; 9780375984570
                LC 2011026546
In this book, "twins Ysabel and Justin struggle with the revelation that their father has begun living as a woman. . . . For spring break, Ysabel and Justin's parents arrange for the twins to stay with their father for the first time after the big news. Both the tension and the deep caring among Ysabel, Justin and Christine are palpable as the family . . . attends daily therapy sessions . . . and embarks on a guided rafting trip with other transgender parents and their children." (Kirkus Reviews)

A **la** carte. Alfred A. Knopf Books for Young Readers 2008 288p $15.99; lib bdg $18.99
Grades: 7 8 9 10   **Fic**
  1. Cooking -- Fiction 2. African Americans -- Fiction
ISBN 978-0-375-84815-5; 0-375-84815-0; 978-0-375-94815-2 lib bdg; 0-375-94815-5 lib bdg
                LC 2007-49656

Lainey, a high school senior and aspiring celebrity chef, is forced to question her priorities after her best friend (and secret crush) runs away from home.

"The relationships and characters in this book are authentic. The actions and dialogue seem true to those represented. Even though it is a quick read, the story is a meaningful one." Voice Youth Advocate

Mare's war. Alfred A. Knopf 2009 341p $16.99; lib bdg $19.99

Grades: 7 8 9 10   **Fic**
1. Alabama -- Fiction 2. Sisters -- Fiction 3. Grandmothers -- Fiction 4. African Americans -- Fiction 5. Automobile travel -- Fiction 6. World War, 1939-1945 -- Fiction 7. United States -- Army -- Women's Army Corps -- Fiction
ISBN 978-0-375-85714-0; 0-375-85714-1; 978-0-375-95714-7 lib bdg; 0-375-95714-6 lib bdg
                                    LC 2008-33744
ALA EMIERT Coretta Scott King Author Award Honor Book (2010)

Teens Octavia and Tali learn about strength, independence, and courage when they are forced to take a car trip with their grandmother, who tells about growing up Black in 1940s Alabama and serving in Europe during World War II as a member of the Women's Army Corps.

"The parallel travel narratives are masterfully managed, with postcards from Octavia and Tali to the folks back home in San Francisco signaling the shift between 'then' and 'now.' Absolutely essential reading." Kirkus

Dawn, Sasha

Oblivion; Sasha Dawn. Egmont USA 2014 400 p. (hardcover) $17.99 **Fic**
1. Mentally ill -- Fiction 2. Missing persons -- Fiction 3. Illinois -- Fiction 4. Mental illness -- Fiction 5. Foster home care -- Fiction 6. Recovered memory -- Fiction 7. Compulsive behavior -- Fiction 8. Dating (Social customs) -- Fiction
ISBN 1606844768; 9781606844762
                                    LC 2013018267
In this young adult novel by Sasha Dawn, "all [Callie] knows is that her father, the reverend at the Church of the Holy Promise, is missing, as is Hannah, a young girl from the parish. Their disappearances have to be connected and Callie knows that her father was not a righteous man. Since that fateful night, she's been plagued by graphomania--an unending and debilitating compulsion to write." (Publisher's note)

"The story works on two levels: as a psychological mystery and as a story of Callie's rocky relationships with her sister and boyfriends, always grounding her difficulties in reality. Thoroughly compelling." Kirkus

Dawson, Delilah S.

Servants of the storm; Delilah S. Dawson. First Simon Pulse hardcover ed Simon Pulse 2014 384 p. $17.99

Grades: 9 10 11 12   **Fic**
1. Ghost stories 2. Fantasy fiction 3. Savannah (Ga.) -- Fiction 4. Demonology -- Fiction 5. Supernatural

-- Fiction
ISBN 1442483784; 9781442483781
                                    LC 2013031587
In this Southern gothic fantasy novel by Delilah S. Dawson, "a year ago, Hurricane Josephine swept through Savannah, Georgia, ... taking the life of Dovey's best friend, Carly. Since that night, Dovey has been in a medicated haze, numb to everything around her. But recently she's started . . . seeing things that can't be real. . . . Determined to learn the truth, Dovey stops taking her pills. And the world that opens up to her is unlike anything she could have imagined." (Publisher's note)

"The plot here is deep and twisting, and the mystery that lurks beneath it all is eerie. Though the ending is a tad abrupt, Dawson's atmospheric southern gothic spook-fest still pleases." Boklist

De Fombelle, Timothée, 1973-

★ **Vango**; between sky and earth. Timothee de Fombelle. Candlewick Press 2014 432 p. illustrations hc $17.99

Grades: 9 10 11 12   **Fic**
1. Adventure fiction 2. Clergy -- Fiction 3. Historical fiction 4. Friendship -- Fiction 5. False accusation -- Fiction
ISBN 9780763671969; 0763671967
                                    LC 2013955696
In this book, by Timothée de Fombelle, translated by Sarah Ardizzone, "minutes from joining the priesthood in 1934, Vango, who was found washed ashore on a tiny Italian island as a toddler, must suddenly avoid both arrest and a simultaneous assassination attempt. Establishing his innocence while on the run across Europe requires untangling his mysterious past." (Kirkus Reviews)

"de Fombelle has written a brilliant, wonderfully exciting story of flight and pursuit, filled with colorful characters and head-scratching mystery. As the novel proceeds, the suspense is ratcheted up to breathtaking levels as the boy remains only one step ahead of his relentless pursuers." Booklist

De Goldi, Kate

The **10** p.m. question. Candlewick Press 2010 245p $15.99

Grades: 6 7 8 9 10   **Fic**
1. School stories 2. Worry -- Fiction 3. Agoraphobia -- Fiction 4. Family life -- Fiction 5. New Zealand -- Fiction 6. Eccentrics and eccentricities -- Fiction
ISBN 978-0-7636-4939-5; 0-7636-4939-2
                                    LC 2009-49726
First published 2008 in New Zealand

Twelve-year-old Frankie Parsons has a quirky family, a wonderful best friend, and a head full of worrying questions that he shares with his mother each night, but when free-spirited Sydney arrives at school with questions of her own, Frankie is forced to face the ultimate ten p.m. question.

"De Goldi's novel is an achingly poignant, wryly comic story of early adolescence. . . . Nearly every character . . . is a loving, talented, unforgettable eccentric whose dialogue, much like De Goldi's richly phrased narration, combines heart-stopping tenderness with perfectly timed, deliciously zany humor." Booklist

De Gramont, Nina

Every little thing in the world. Atheneum Books for Young Readers 2010 282p $16.99

Grades: 9 10 11 12   **Fic**

1. Camps -- Fiction 2. Pregnancy -- Fiction 3. Friendship -- Fiction 4. Wilderness areas -- Fiction

ISBN 978-1-4169-8013-1; 1-4169-8013-X

LC 2009-40335

Before she can decide what do about her newly discovered pregnancy, sixteen-year-old Sydney is punished for "borrowing" a car and shipped out, along with best friend Natalia, to a wilderness camp for the next six weeks.

"De Gramont's compelling coming-of-age story, often poetic, compassionately probes the dilemma of and complex choices surrounding Sydney's pregnancy. As told from Sydney's point of view in an authentic adolescent voice, her growing self-awareness of 'what's discovered after losing your way' is both moving and hopeful." Kirkus

De la Cruz, Melissa

★ Blue bloods. Hyperion 2006 302p hardcover o.p. pa $8.99

Grades: 9 10 11 12   **Fic**

1. Vampires -- Fiction 2. New York (N.Y.) -- Fiction

ISBN 978-0-7868-3892-9; 0-7868-3892-2; 978-1-4231-0126-0 pa; 1-4231-0126-X pa

LC 2005-44786

Select teenagers from some of New York City's wealthiest and most socially prominent families learn a startling secret about their bloodlines.

"History, mythology, and the contemporary New York prep-school and club scene blend seamlessly in this sexy and sophisticated riff on vampire lore that never collapses into camp." Bull Cent Child Books

Other titles in this series are:

Lost in time (2011)

Masquerade (2007)

Misguided angel (2010)

Revelations (2008)

The Van Alen legacy (2009)

Gates of Paradise; a Blue Bloods novel. Melissa de la Cruz. Hyperion 2013 355 p. (hardcover) $16.99

Grades: 9 10 11 12   **Fic**

1. Fantasy fiction 2. Angels -- Fiction 3. Paranormal fiction 4. Wealth -- Fiction 5. Vampires -- Fiction 6. New York (N.Y.) -- Fiction

ISBN 1423157419; 9781423157410

LC 2012032358

This is the ninth entry in Melissa de la Cruz's Blue Bloods series. Here, "Schuyler Van Alen is running out of time. The Dark Prince of Hell is storming the Gates of Paradise, intent on winning the heavenly throne for good. This time he has his greatest angels by his side, Abbadon and Azrael--Jack and Mimi Force, as they are known in the Coven. Or so he thinks. Even as Lucifer assigns Jack and Mimi the tasks of killing their true loves, the Force twins secretly vow to defeat the Dark Prince." (Publisher's note)

Lost in time; a Blue Bloods novel / Melissa de la Cruz. 1st ed. Hyperion 2011 342 p. (reinforced) $16.99

Grades: 9 10 11 12   **Fic**

1. Fantasy fiction 2. Paranormal fiction 3. Egypt -- Fiction 4. Wealth -- Fiction 5. Vampires -- Fiction 6. New York (N.Y.) -- Fiction

ISBN 1423121295; 9781423121299

LC 2011024414

This book is the eighth entry in Melissa de la Cruz's Blue Bloods series. "The stakes have never been higher for the young Blue Bloods of Manhattan. After their brief yet beautiful bonding ceremony in Italy, Schuyler Van Alen and Jack Force depart for Egypt, desperate to find the elusive Gate of Promise before Jack must face his twin, Mimi, for a blood trial. . . . But everything Schuyler thought she knew about the gate turns out to be a lie, and they soon find themselves ensnared in a deadly battle." (Publisher's note)

Masquerade; a Blue Bloods novel. Hyperion 2007 311p $15.99; pa $8.99

Grades: 9 10 11 12   **Fic**

1. Vampires -- Fiction 2. New York (N.Y.) -- Fiction

ISBN 978-0-7868-3893-6; 0-7868-3893-0; 978-1-4231-0127-7 pa; 1-4231-0127-8 pa

LC 2006-100446

Sequel to Blue bloods (2006)

Schuyler Van Alen, growing comfortable with her newfound vampire powers, seeks her grandfather in Italy, while back in New York plans are being completed for the fabulous Four Hundred Ball, to be followed by an elite, teens-only event at which masks hide a terrible secret.

Followed by Revelations (2008)

Misguided angel; a Blue Bloods novel. Hyperion 2010 265p (A Blue Bloods novel) $16.99; pa $8.99

Grades: 9 10 11 12   **Fic**

1. Vampires -- Fiction

ISBN 978-1-4231-2128-2; 1-4231-2128-7; 978-1-4231-2257-9 pa; 1-4231-2257-7 pa

LC 2010-23408

Sequel to The Van Alen legacy (2009)

While fleeing to Florence to find and protect the seven gates that guard earth from Lucifer, lord of the Silverbloods, Schuyler approaches a terrifying crossroads—and a choice that will determine the destiny of all vampires.

Followed by Lost in time (2011)

Revelations; a Blue Bloods novel. Hyperion 2008 264p $15.99; pa $8.99

Grades: 9 10 11 12   **Fic**

1. Brazil -- Fiction 2. Vampires -- Fiction

ISBN 978-1-4231-0228-1; 1-4231-0228-2; 978-1-4231-0229-8 pa; 1-4231-0229-0 pa

LC 2009-278505

Sequel to Masquerade (2007)

Schuyler Van Alen's blood legacy has just been called into question: Is the young woman in fact a Blue Blood, or is it the sinister Silver Blood that runs through her veins? When one of the Gates of Hell is breached by the Silver Bloods, the Blue Bloods will need Schuyler on their side.

Followed by The Van Alen legacy (2009)

The **Van** Alen legacy; a Blue Bloods novel. Disney/Hyperion 2009 368p (Blue Bloods) $16.99; pa $8.99

Grades: 9 10 11 12	**Fic**

1. Wealth -- Fiction 2. Vampires -- Fiction 3. New York (N.Y.) -- Fiction

ISBN 978-1-4231-0226-7; 978-1-4231-0227-4 pa

LC 2009-23816

Sequel to Revelations (2008)

Once left to live the glamorous life in New York City, the Blue Bloods—an ancient group of vampires—now find themselves in an epic battle for survival following the stunning revelation of a young socialite's true identity and the growing threat of the sinister Silver Bloods.

"There is plenty of adventure, romance, brand-name dropping, and even classical history in this installment; the Blue Bloods faithful will not be disappointed." Voice Youth Advocates

Followed by Misguided angel (2010)

De la Pena, Matt

Ball don't lie. Delacorte Press 2005 280p hardcover o.p. pa $7.99

Grades: 9 10 11 12	**Fic**

1. Basketball -- Fiction 2. Race relations -- Fiction 3. Foster home care -- Fiction 4. Los Angeles (Calif.) -- Fiction 5. Obsessive-compulsive disorder -- Fiction

ISBN 0-385-73232-5; 0-385-73425-5 pa

LC 2004-18057

Seventeen-year-old Sticky lives for basketball and plays at school and at the Lincoln Rec Center in Los Angeles but he is unaware of the many dangers—including his own past—that threaten his dream of playing professionally.

"The prose moves with the rhythm of a bouncing basketball and those who don't mind mixing their sports stories with some true grit may find themselves hypnotized by Sticky's grim saga." Publ Wkly

The **living**; Matt de la Peña. Delacorte Press 2013 320 p.

Grades: 8 9 10 11 12	**Fic**

1. Cruise ships -- Fiction 2. Natural disasters -- Fiction 3. Survival after airplane accidents, shipwrecks, etc. -- Fiction 4. Diseases -- Fiction 5. Survival -- Fiction 6. Mexican Americans -- Fiction

ISBN 9780375989919; 9780385741200

LC 2012050778

Pura Belpre Author Award (2014)

In this book, by Matt de la Peña, "Shy took [a] summer job to make some money. In a few months on a luxury cruise liner, he'll rake in the tips and be able to help his mom and sister out with the bills. . . . But everything changes when the Big One hits. Shy's only weeks out at sea when an earthquake more massive than ever before recorded hits California, and his life is forever changed. The earthquake is only the first disaster. Suddenly it's a fight to survive for those left living." (Publisher's note)

"Shy Espinoza's summer job on Paradise Cruise Lines is, literally, a disaster. A series of catastrophes befall the cruise and eventually threaten civilization as he knows it;

Shy finds himself on a life raft in the Pacific Ocean with a racist "spoiled-ass blond chick." Readers wanting a fast-paced survival story with plenty of action won't mind the over-the-top plot." (Horn Book)

Mexican whiteboy. Delacorte Press 2008 249p $15.99; lib bdg $18.99

Grades: 8 9 10 11 12	**Fic**

1. Cousins -- Fiction 2. California -- Fiction 3. Mexican Americans -- Fiction 4. Racially mixed people -- Fiction

ISBN 978-0-385-73310-6; 0-385-73310-0; 978-0-385-90329-5 lib bdg; 0-385-90329-4 lib bdg

LC 2007-32302

Sixteen-year-old Danny searches for his identity amidst the confusion of being half-Mexican and half-white while spending a summer with his cousin and new friends on the baseball fields and back alleys of San Diego County, California.

"The author juggles his many plotlines well, and the portrayal of Danny's friends and neighborhood is rich and lively." Booklist

We were here. Delacorte Press 2009 357p $17.99; lib bdg $20.99

Grades: 7 8 9 10 11 12	**Fic**

1. Brothers -- Fiction 2. California -- Fiction 3. Friendship -- Fiction 4. Runaway teenagers -- Fiction 5. Juvenile delinquency -- Fiction

ISBN 978-0-385-73667-1; 0-385-73667-3; 978-0-385-90622-7 lib bdg; 0-385-90622-6 lib bdg

LC 2008-44568

Haunted by the event that sentences him to time in a group home, Miguel breaks out with two unlikely companions and together they begin their journey down the California coast hoping to get to Mexico and a new life.

"The contemporary survival adventure will keep readers hooked, as will the tension that builds from the story's secrets." Booklist

De Lint, Charles

The **blue** girl; Charles de Lint. Viking 2004 368p hardcover o.p. pa $7.99

Grades: 7 8 9 10	**Fic**

1. Ghost stories 2. School stories 3. Fairies -- Fiction

ISBN 0-670-05924-2; 0-14-240545-0 pa

LC 2004-19051

New at her high school, Imogene enlists the help of her introverted friend Maxine and the ghost of a boy who haunts the school after receiving warnings through her dreams that soul-eaters are threatening her life

"The book combines the turmoil of high school intertwined with rich, detailed imagery drawn from traditional folklore and complex characters with realistic relationships. . . . This book is not just another ghost story, but a novel infused with the true sense of wonder and magic that is De Lint at his best. It is strongly recommended." Voice Youth Advocates

Dingo. Firebird 2008 213p $11.99

Grades: 9 10 11 12	**Fic**

1. Twins -- Fiction 2. Sisters -- Fiction 3. Wild dogs

-- Fiction 4. Supernatural -- Fiction 5. Space and time
-- Fiction
ISBN 978-0-14-240816-2; 0-14-240816-6
LC 2007-31716

Seventeen-year-old Miguel Schreiber and a long-term enemy are drawn into a strange dream world when they fall in love with shapeshifting sisters from Australia—twins hiding from a cursed ancestor who can only be freed with the girls' cooperation.

"The fated love angle will certainly draw in romance readers, and while they may be perfectly content with just following Miguel and Lainey's connection through to its expected happy ending, the intriguing details about shapeshifting, dingoes, and Aboriginal traditions may also lead them to dig a bit further into Australian myths and culture." Bull Cent Child Books

Deebs, Tracy

Tempest rising. Walker & Co. 2011 344p $16.99

Grades: 8 9 10 11 12   **Fic**
1. War stories 2. Mermaids and mermen -- Fiction
ISBN 978-0-8027-2231-7; 0-8027-2231-8
LC 2010-34339

On her seventeenth birthday, Tempest must decide whether to remain a human and live on land or submit to her mermaid half, like her mother before her, and enter into a long-running war under the sea.

"Tempest is a gutsy, independent heroine with more than enough agency to save herself from danger. . . . For readers wanting a solid, familiar, but slightly different paranormal romance." Booklist

Delaney, Joseph, 1945-

A **new** darkness; 1 Joseph Delaney. Greenwillow Books, an imprint of HarperCollinsPublishers 2014 352 p. 22 cm (Starblade Chronicles) (hardback) $17.99

Grades: 7 8 9 10   **Fic**
1. Horror fiction 2. Witches -- Fiction 3. Monsters -- Fiction 4. Apprentices -- Fiction 5. Supernatural -- Fiction 6. Horror stories
ISBN 0062334530; 9780062334534
LC 2014011963

"Tom Ward is the Spook, the one person who can defend the county from bloodthirsty creatures of the dark. But he's only seventeen, and his apprenticeship was cut short when his master died in battle. . . . [F]ifteen-year-old . . . Jenny . . . is a seventh daughter of a seventh daughter, and she wants to be Tom's first apprentice. . . . Together, Tom and Jenny will uncover the grave danger heading straight toward the county." (Publisher's note)

"A plethora of action involving ghastly creatures, sword fights, and magic coupled with just enough backstory and description make this novel engaging enough to keep even the most reluctant reader turning pages until the end. Tom's story has a doozy of a cliff-hanger that is sure to bring teens back for more." - SLJ Reviews

Dellaira, Ava

Love letters to the dead; Ava Dellaira. Farrar Straus & Giroux 2014 336 p. (hardback) $17.99

Grades: 7 8 9 10   **Fic**
1. Death -- Fiction 2. Grief -- Fiction 3. Letters -- Fiction 4. Sisters -- Fiction
ISBN 0374346674; 9780374346676
LC 2013029594

This book, by Ava Dellaira, "begins [with] an assignment for English class: Write a letter to a dead person. Laurel chooses Kurt Cobain because her sister, May, loved him. And he died young, just like May did. Soon, Laurel has a notebook full of letters to people. . . . She writes about starting high school, navigating new friendships, falling in love for the first time, . . . and, finally, about the abuse she suffered while May was supposed to be looking out for her." (Publisher's note)

Delsol, Wendy

Flock; Wendy Delsol. Candlewick Press 2012 384 p. (hardback) $16.99

Grades: 7 8 9 10   **Fic**
1. Infants -- Fiction 2. Paranormal fiction 3. Sisters -- Fiction 4. Schools -- Fiction 5. High schools -- Fiction 6. Supernatural -- Fiction 7. Students, Foreign -- Fiction 8. Interpersonal relations -- Fiction
ISBN 0763660108; 9780763660109
LC 2011048371

Sequel to: Frost

This book is the final in the "Stork" trilogy. Protagonist Katla has returned to her high school life after saving her boyfriend Jack in Iceland. But "her hopes of dodging unfinished business are dashed by the arrival of two Icelandic exchange students: Marik . . . and Jinky . . . . It seems Katla not only enraged the Snow Queen by rescuing . . . Jack, she also was tricked into promising her frail baby sister to the water queen — and Marik has come to collect. What's worse, Katla doesn't dare confide in anyone lest she endanger them, so even her soul mate, Jack, is growing suspicious. And now Katla's stork dreams, her guide for matching babies with mothers, have become strange and menacing as well. (Amazon.com)

Frost. Candlewick Press 2011 376p $15.99

Grades: 7 8 9 10   **Fic**
1. School stories 2. Snow -- Fiction 3. Supernatural -- Fiction 4. Arctic regions -- Fiction
ISBN 978-0-7636-5386-6; 0-7636-5386-1
LC 2010047656

Sequel to Stork (2010)

After her boyfriend Jack conjures up a record-breaking snow storm, sixteen-year-old Kat LeBlanc finds herself facing an unusual rival in the form of an environmental researcher from Greenland who is drawn to their small town of Norse Falls, Minnesota, by the storm.

"Well-paced narration will keep readers interested—a superior paranormal adventure." Kirkus

Stork. Candlewick Press 2010 357p $15.99; pa $8.99

Grades: 7 8 9 10   **Fic**
1. School stories 2. Minnesota -- Fiction 3.

Supernatural -- Fiction
ISBN 978-0-7636-4844-2; 0-7636-4844-2; 978-0-7636-5687-4 pa; 0-7636-5687-9 pa

LC 2009-51357

After her parents' divorce, Katla and her mother move from Los Angeles to Norse Falls, Minnesota, where Kat immediately alienates two boys at her high school and, improbably, discovers a kinship with a mysterious group of elderly women—the Icelandic Stork Society—who "deliver souls."

"This snappy, lighthearted supernatural romance blends Norse mythology and contemporary issues with an easy touch." Booklist

Followed by: Frost (2011)

Demetrios, Heather

Something real; Heather Demetrios. Henry Holt and Co. 2014 416 p. (hardback) $17.99

Grades: 9 10 11 12 **Fic**

1. Family -- Fiction 2. Reality television programs -- Fiction 3. Family life -- Fiction

ISBN 0805097945; 9780805097948

LC 2013030798

In this book, by Heather Demetrios, Bonnie "and her twelve siblings are the stars of one-time hit reality show Baker's Dozen. Since the show's cancellation, Bonnie has tried to live a normal life. But it's about to fall apart . . . because Baker's Dozen is going back on the air. Bonnie's mom and the show's producers won't let her quit and soon the life that she has so carefully built for herself, with real friends (and maybe even a real boyfriend), is in danger." (Publisher's note)

"It's been four years since the reality television show Baker's Dozen went off the air. Bonnie Baker, 17, feels lucky to have survived the tension and challenges from constantly being in the limelight with her 12 siblings... With likable protagonists and snappy dialogue, Something Real credibly zooms in on reality TV's impact on unwilling subjects-a shoo-in for teens drawn to contemporary romance and drama. It will especially attract those who liked the similarly compelling reality show fictional exposés Reality Boy by A. S. King (Little, Brown, 2013) and The Real Real by Emma McLaughlin and Nicola Kraus (HarperCollins, 2009)." (School Library Journal)

Dennard, Susan

Something strange and deadly; Susan Dennard. 1st ed. Harpercollins Childrens Books 2012 388 p. (hardback) $17.99; (paperback) $9.99

Grades: 7 8 9 10 11 12 **Fic**

1. Fairs 2. Ghost stories 3. Zombies -- Fiction 4. Horror stories 5. Dead -- Fiction 6. Magic -- fiction 7. Brothers and sisters -- Fiction 8. Philadelphia (Pa.) -- History -- 19th century -- Fiction

ISBN 0062083260; 9780062083265; 9780062083272

LC 2011042114

Author Susan Dennard's protagonist Eleanor Fitt "and her dear Mama have just about run out of funds, and she misses [her brother] Elijah terribly [while he is on a] . . . three-year odyssey abroad. So when . . . he's been detained, she is mightily distressed. The next day, the determined teen is off for some help from the Spirit-Hunters. . . . Her can-do attitude finds her at one point systematically disabling

a throng of zombies by smashing their kneecaps with her parasol." (Kirkus Reviews)

Followed by A Darkness Strange and Lovely (2013)

Truthwitch; by Susan Dennard. St. Martin's Press 2016 416 p. $18.99

Grades: 8 9 10 11 12 **Fic**

1. Fantasy fiction 2. Witches -- Fiction 3. Friendship -- Fiction

ISBN 0765379287; 9780765379283

LC 2015031484

In this book, by Susan Dennard, "Safiya is a Truthwitch, able to discern truth from lie. . . . Iseult, a Threadwitch, can see the invisible ties that bind and entangle the lives around her--but she cannot see the bonds that touch her own heart. Her unlikely friendship with Safi has taken her from life as an outcast into one of of reckless adventure, where she is a cool, wary balance to Safi's hotheaded impulsiveness." (Publisher's note)

"A great choice for fans of fantasy adventure and strong female characters." SLJ

Deriso, Christine Hurley

Then I met my sister. Flux 2011 269p pa $9.95

Grades: 8 9 10 11 12 **Fic**

1. Death -- Fiction 2. Diaries -- Fiction 3. Sisters -- Fiction

ISBN 978-0-7387-2581-9; 0-7387-2581-1

LC 2010-45239

Summer Stetson has always lived in the shadow of her dead sister, knowing she can never measure up in any way, but on her seventeenth birthday her aunt gives her Shannon's diary, which reveals painful but liberating truths about Summer's family and herself.

"The journey Summer goes on to 'meet' her sister is compelling, but equally interesting are her discoveries about herself and her relationships. . . . This is a book intriguing enough to read in one sitting." SLJ

Derting, Kimberly

The **body** finder. Harper 2009 329p $16.99

Grades: 7 8 9 10 11 12 **Fic**

1. Mystery fiction 2. Dead -- Fiction 3. Supernatural -- Fiction 4. Extrasensory perception -- Fiction

ISBN 978-0-06-177981-7; 0-06-177981-4

LC 2009-39675

"Violet Ambrose can find dead bodies. Their aura of sound, color, or even taste imprints itself on their murderers, and Violet's extrasensory perception picks up on those elements. . . . Derting has written a suspenseful mystery and sensual love story that will captivate readers who enjoy authentic high-school settings, snappy dialogue, sweet romance, and heart-stopping drama." Booklist

Followed by: Desires of the dead (2011)

Desires of the dead. HarperCollins 2011 358p $16.99

Grades: 7 8 9 10 **Fic**

1. School stories 2. Homicide -- Fiction 3. Friendship -- Fiction 4. Supernatural -- Fiction 5. Washington (State) -- Fiction 6. Extrasensory perception -- Fiction 7. United States -- Federal Bureau of Investigation --

Fiction
ISBN 978-0-06-177984-8; 0-06-177984-9

LC 2010017838

Sequel to: The body finder (2010)

Sixteen-year-old Violet Ambrose's ability to find murder victims and their killers draws the attention of the FBI just as her relationship with Jay, her best-friend-turned-boyfriend, heats up.

"The author paces the story beautifully, weaving together several story lines as she inches up to the final, desperate scene. . . . Imaginative, convincing and successful suspense." Kirkus

The **last** echo; Kimberly Derting. Harper 2012 360 p. (hbk.) $17.99

Grades: 7 8 9 10 11 12 **Fic**

1. Love stories 2. Parapsychology -- Fiction 3. Serial killers -- Fiction 4. Dead -- Fiction 5. Schools -- Fiction 6. Friendship -- Fiction 7. Best friends -- Fiction 8. High schools -- Fiction 9. Serial murders -- Fiction 10. Psychic ability -- Fiction 11. Washington (State) -- Fiction

ISBN 0062082191; 9780062082190

LC 2011044633

Sequel to: Desires of the dead (2011)

This book, "the third installment of the Body Finder series," begins with protagonist Violet "working for a secret agency that specializes in using paranormal powers to fight crime. . . . She still loves her normal boyfriend Jay, so she worries about the strong physical response she feels whenever she touches Rafe, a member of the team. Meanwhile, Violet doesn't know she's become the target of a terrifying serial killer." (Kirkus Reviews)

"As always, this author writes a gripping tale... Personalities come across quite strongly, as several of the characters tend toward the eccentric." Kirkus

Desai Hidier, Tanuja

★ **Born** confused. Scholastic Press 2002 413p hardcover o.p. pa $7.99

Grades: 8 9 10 11 12 **Fic**

1. Friendship -- Fiction 2. East Indian Americans -- Fiction

ISBN 0-439-35762-4; 0-439-51011-2 pa

LC 2002-4515

Seventeen-year-old Dimple, whose family is from India, discovers that she is not Indian enough for the Indians and not American enough for the Americans, as she sees her hypnotically beautiful, manipulative best friend taking possession of both her heritage and the boy she likes

"This involving story . . . will reward its readers. The family background and richness in cultural information add a new level to the familiar girl-meets-boy story." SLJ

Desir, C.

Bleed like me; Christa Desir. First Simon Pulse hardcover ed Simon Pulse 2014 288 p. $17.99

Grades: 9 10 11 12 **Fic**

1. Self-harm -- Fiction 2. Teenagers -- Fiction 3. Interpersonal relations -- Fiction 4. Love stories 5. Love -- Fiction 6. Dating (Social customs) 7. Cutting (Self-mutilation) 8. Emotional problems -- Fiction 9.

Emotional problems of teenagers
ISBN 1442498900; 9781442498907

LC 2013031611

In C. Desir's novel "Amelia starts . . . cutting herself to deal with the anger and feelings of abandonment. Michael Brooks has been in foster care since getting out of juvenile detention. He turns to drugs and various forms of physical pain to handle his own anger and fear. When the two teens meet, an obsessive relationship forms that sends both . . . spiraling deep into addiction and despair." (School Library Journal)

"Edgy, dark, and turbulent with passion, Desir's second novel offers a bleak yet compassionate rawness instead of a lecture. Be prepared to have your heart wrenched from your chest as Gannon struggles with her silent cries for help." Booklist

Dessen, Sarah

Along for the ride; a novel. Viking 2009 383p $19.99

Grades: 7 8 9 10 **Fic**

1. Divorce -- Fiction 2. Infants -- Fiction 3. Stepfamilies -- Fiction 4. Dating (Social customs) -- Fiction

ISBN 978-0-670-01194-0; 0-670-01194-0

LC 2009-5661

When Auden impulsively goes to stay with her father, stepmother, and new baby sister the summer before she starts college, all the trauma of her parents' divorce is revived, even as she is making new friends and having new experiences such as learning to ride a bike and dating.

"Dessen explores the dynamics of an extended family headed by two opposing, flawed personalities, revealing their parental failures with wicked precision yet still managing to create real, even sympathetic characters. . . . [This book] provides the interpersonal intricacies fans expect from a Dessen plot." Horn Book

★ **Just** listen; a novel. Viking 2006 371p $17.99

Grades: 9 10 11 12 **Fic**

1. School stories 2. Friendship -- Fiction 3. Family life -- Fiction

ISBN 0-670-06105-0; 978-0-670-06105-1

LC 2006-472

Isolated from friends who believe the worst because she has not been truthful with them, sixteen-year-old Annabel finds an ally in classmate Owen, whose honesty and passion for music help her to face and share what really happened at the end-of-the-year party that changed her life.

The author "weaves a sometimes funny, mostly emotional, and very satisfying story." Voice Youth Advocates

Lock and key; a novel. Viking Children's Books 2008 422p $18.99

Grades: 7 8 9 10 **Fic**

1. Child abuse -- Fiction 2. Family life -- Fiction 3. Abandoned children -- Fiction

ISBN 978-0-670-01088-2; 0-670-01088-X

LC 2007-25370

When she is abandoned by her alcoholic mother, high school senior Ruby winds up living with Cora, the sister she has not seen for ten years, and learns about Cora's new life, what makes a family, how to allow people to help her when she needs it, and that she too has something to offer others.

"The dialogue, especially between Ruby and Cora, is crisp, layered, and natural. The slow unfolding adds to an anticipatory mood. . . . Recommend this one to patient, sophisticated readers." SLJ

The **moon** and more; by Sarah Dessen. Viking 2013 384 p. (hardcover) $19.99

Grades: 7 8 9 10   **Fic**

1. Bildungsromans 2. Dating (Social customs) -- Fiction 3. Father-daughter relationship -- Fiction 4. Beaches -- Fiction 5. Resorts -- Fiction 6. Coming of age -- Fiction 7. Fathers and daughters -- Fiction 8. Family-owned business enterprises -- Fiction 9. Documentary films -- Production and direction -- Fiction
ISBN 0670785601; 9780670785605

LC 2012035720

In this novel, by Sarah Dessen, "Luke is the perfect boyfriend. . . . But now, in the summer before college, Emaline wonders if perfect is good enough. Enter Theo, a super-ambitious outsider. . . . Emaline's . . . father, too, thinks Emaline should have a bigger life. . . . Emaline is attracted to the bright future that Theo and her father promise. But she also clings to the deep roots of her loving mother, stepfather, and sisters." (Publisher's note)

"Dessen's characters behave as deliciously unpredictably as people do in real life, and just as in real life, they sometimes have to make difficult choices with not-so-predictable outcomes... Completely engaging." Kirkus

Dessen, Sarah, 1970-

Saint Anything; a novel. Sarah Dessen. Viking Juvenile 2015 432 p. (hardback) $19.99

Grades: 9 10 11 12   **Fic**

1. Family -- Fiction 2. Self-acceptance -- Fiction 3. Friendship -- Fiction 4. Family life -- Fiction 5. Family problems -- Fiction 6. Self-perception -- Fiction 7. Brothers and sisters -- Fiction 8. Dating (Social customs) -- Fiction
ISBN 0451474708; 9780451474704

LC 2014039813

In Sara Dessen's novel "Sydney has always felt invisible. She's grown accustomed to her brother, Peyton, being the focus of the family's attention. Now, after a drunk-driving accident that crippled a boy, Peyton's serving some serious jail time, and Sydney is on her own, questioning her place in the family and the world. Then she meets the Chatham family. Drawn into their warm, chaotic circle, Sydney experiences unquestioning acceptance for the first time." (Publisher's note)

"Once again, Dessen demonstrates her tremendous skill in evoking powerful emotions through careful, quiet prose, while delivering a satisfying romance. The author's many devotees are sure to enjoy this weighty addition to her canon." Pub Wkly

What happened to goodbye. Viking 2011 402p $19.99

Grades: 8 9 10 11 12   **Fic**

1. School stories 2. Divorce -- Fiction
ISBN 978-0-670-01294-7; 0-670-01294-7

LC 2010-41041

"The novel nimbly weaves together familiar story lines of divorce, high-school happiness and angst, and teen-identity struggles with likable, authentic adult and teen characters and intriguing yet credible situations." Booklist

DeStefano, Lauren

Fever; Lauren DeStefano. Simon & Schuster BFYR 2012 341 p. (The Chemical Garden trilogy)

Grades: 9 10 11 12   **Fic**

1. Science fiction 2. Dystopian fiction 3. Escapes -- Fiction 4. Viruses -- Fiction 5. Genetic engineering -- Fiction 6. Youths' writings 7. Orphans -- Fiction
ISBN 9781442409071

LC 2011016961

This young adult novel is the second installment in Lauren DeStefano's "Chemical Garden Trilogy." "Having recently escaped the compound where she was forced to marry, take on sister wives and ultimately become her evil father-in-law Vaughn's scientific experiment in the name of finding a cure for the virus that kills off men and women at a young age, Rhine, along with former servant and love interest Gabriel, finds herself in trouble again. Plotting another escape from a heartless "First Generation" who runs a brothel out of an abandoned carnival site, continuing to evade Vaughn, picking up a malformed and mute girl and trying to find Rhine's twin brother should be adventurous. And finally being able to communicate freely should bring out the intimacy between Rhine and Gabriel." (Kirkus)

Perfect ruin; by Lauren DeStefano and illustrated by Teagan White. Simon and Schuster Books for Young Readers 2013 368 p. (The Internment chronicles) (hardcover: alk. paper) $17.99

Grades: 7 8 9 10   **Fic**

1. Utopias 2. Imaginary places 3. Criminal investigation -- Fiction 4. Science fiction 5. Utopias -- Fiction
ISBN 1442480610; 9781442480612

LC 2013014392

Sequel: Burning Kingdoms (2015)

In this book by Lauren DeStefano "Morgan Stockhour knows getting too close to the edge of Internment, the floating city in the clouds where she lives, can lead to madness. Then a murder, the first in a generation, rocks the city. With whispers swirling and fear on the wind, Morgan can no longer stop herself from investigating, especially once she meets Judas. Betrothed to the victim, he is the boy being blamed for the murder, but Morgan is convinced of his innocence." (Publisher's note)

Sever; Lauren DeStefano. Simon & Schuster 2013 384 p. (The Chemical Garden trilogy) (hardcover: alk. paper) $17.99

Grades: 9 10 11 12   **Fic**

1. Love stories 2. Science fiction 3. Genetic engineering

-- Fiction 4. Orphans -- Fiction 5. Survival -- Fiction
ISBN 1442409096; 9781442409095; 9781442409101;
9781442409132

LC 2012015702

This young adult dystopian romance novel, by Lauren DeStefano, is the "conclusion to the New York Times bestselling Chemical Garden Trilogy. . . . While Gabriel haunts Rhine's memories, Cecily is determined to be at Rhine's side, even if Linden's feelings are still caught between them. Meanwhile, Rowan's growing involvement in an underground resistance compels Rhine to reach him before he does something that cannot be undone." (Publisher's note)

Wither. Simon & Schuster Books for Young Readers 2011 358p (The Chemical Garden trilogy) $17.99

Grades: 9 10 11 12   Fic
1. Science fiction 2. Orphans -- Fiction 3. Marriage -- Fiction 4. Kidnapping -- Fiction 5. Genetic engineering -- Fiction
ISBN 978-1-4424-0905-7

LC 2010-21347

After modern science turns every human into a genetic time bomb with men dying at age twenty-five and women dying at age twenty, girls are kidnapped and married off in order to repopulate the world.

"This beautifully-written . . . fantasy, with its intriguing world-building, well-developed characters and intricate plot involving flashbacks as well as edge-of-the-seat suspense, will keep teens riveted to the plight of Rhine and her sister wives. . . . This thought-provoking novel will also stimulate discussion in science and ethics classes." Voice Youth Advocates

Deuker, Carl

Gym candy. Houghton Mifflin Company 2007 313p $16

Grades: 7 8 9 10 11 12   Fic
1. School stories 2. Football -- Fiction 3. Steroids -- Fiction 4. Washington (State) -- Fiction 5. Father-son relationship -- Fiction
ISBN 978-0-618-77713-6; 0-618-77713-X

LC 2007-12749

Groomed by his father to be a star player, football is the only thing that has ever really mattered to Mick Johnson, who works hard for a spot on the varsity team his freshman year, then tries to hold onto his edge by using steroids, despite the consequences to his health and social life.

"Deuker skillfully complements a sobering message with plenty of exciting on-field action and locker-room drama, while depicting Mick's emotional struggles with loneliness and insecurity as sensitively and realistically as his physical ones." Booklist

Painting the black. Avon Books 1999 248p pa $5.99

Grades: 8 9 10 11 12   Fic
1. School stories 2. Baseball -- Fiction
ISBN 0-380-73104-5
First published 1997 by Houghton Mifflin
"After a disastrous fall from a tree, senior Ryan Ward wrote off baseball. But he is swept back into the game

when cocky, charismatic Josh Daniels—a star quarterback with the perfect spiral pass as well as a pitcher with a mean slider—moves into the neighborhood. . . . The well-written sports scenes—baseball and football—will draw reluctant readers, but it is Ryan's moral courage that will linger when the reading is done." Booklist

Runner. Houghton Mifflin 2005 216p $16; pa $7.99

Grades: 7 8 9 10   Fic
1. Smuggling -- Fiction 2. Terrorism -- Fiction 3. Alcoholism -- Fiction
ISBN 0-618-54298-1; 0-618-73505-4 pa

LC 2004-15781

Living with his alcoholic father on a broken-down sailboat on Puget Sound has been hard on seventeen-year-old Chance Taylor, but when his love of running leads to a high-paying job, he quickly learns that the money is not worth the risk

"Writing in a fast-paced, action-packed, but at the same time reflective style, Deuker . . . uses running as a hook to entice readers into a perceptive coming-of-age novel." SLJ

Swagger; Carl Deuker. Houghton Mifflin Harcourt 2013 304 p. $17.99

Grades: 7 8 9 10 11 12   Fic
1. Basketball -- Fiction 2. Child sexual abuse -- Fiction 3. Sexual abuse -- Fiction
ISBN 0547974590; 9780547974590

LC 2012045062

In this book, by Carl Deuker, "high school senior Jonas moves to Seattle [and] is glad to meet Levi, a nice, soft-spoken guy and fellow basketball player." Then, readers are introduced to "Ryan Hartwell, a charismatic basketball coach and sexual predator. When Levi reluctantly tells Jonas that Hartwell abused him, Jonas has to decide whether he should risk his future career to report the coach." (Publisher's note)

"When his family moves to Seattle, high school basketball star Jonas befriends new neighbor Levi, who plays power forward. Assistant coach Ryan Hartwell appreciates Jonas's fast-breaking style, but something about Hartwell feels wrong. Eventually his misdeeds lead to tragedy, and Jonas must find the courage to do what's right. Basketball fans will love the realistic hardwood action and the story's quick pacing." (Horn Book)

Devine, Eric

Press play; Eric Devine. Running Press Book Publishers 2014 368 p. $9.95

Grades: 9 10 11 12   Fic
1. Hazing 2. School stories 3. Documentary films 4. School sports -- Corrupt practices
ISBN 0762455128; 9780762455126

LC 2014937889

In this book by Eric Devine, "at nearly 400 pounds, Greg is determined to shed his excess weight while making a documentary of the process. One day, Greg and his friend, Quinn, witness the lacrosse team involved in brutal hazing rituals, which Greg captures on film. Quinn wants to go to the principal, who is also the coach, but Greg convinces his friend that they need to record more evidence." (School Library Journal)

"It's thrilling to watch Greg enter the lion's den him-self—the lacrosse team's Hell Week—for the bruising finale. A tough, smart look at weight issues, self-respect, and our intrinsic desire to belong at all costs." Booklist

Devoto, Pat Cunningham

The **summer** we got saved; Pat Cunningham Devoto. Warner Books 2005 411p msp hardcover o.p. o.p.; (pbk.) $21.99

Grades: 9 10 11 12 Adult   **Fic**
1. Alabama -- Fiction 2. Segregation -- Fiction 3. Civil rights demonstrations -- Fiction 4. African Americans -- Civil rights -- Fiction 5. Racism -- Fiction 6. Friendship -- Fiction 7. Race relations -- Fiction 8. Voter registration -- Fiction 9. Political campaigns -- Fiction 10. Civil rights movements -- Fiction 11. Highlander Folk School (Monteagle, Tenn.) -- Fiction
ISBN 0446576964; 9780446697156
                                                LC 2004010408

This book, "takes place in Alabama and Tennessee dur-ing the early 1960s. Tab is a junior high school girl, . . . her childhood friend, Maudie, is a black polio victim who wears a leg brace and recently survived a fire at the Tuskegee Polio Institute. Tab's father, Charles, is a hardworking farmer de-scended from one of the founders of the Ku Klux Klan. . . . When Tab and her older sister embark on a secret trip to the Highlander Folk School with their socially conscious aunt, they become unwilling participants in an interracial camp, living with Civil Rights activists. At the same time, Maudie is recruited to help prepare resistant African Americans for voter registration by teaching life skills and reading, and Charles is . . . supporting the candidate running against seg-regationist George Wallace. The stories converge when the main characters experience the tragic consequences of their involvement with integration." (School Library Journal)

"In 1960s Alabama, young Tab and her sister are intro-duced to nonviolent protests and the lies told by both white and black. Realistic, flawed characters, poignant humor, and provocative questions about social injustice combine in this compelling historical novel." Booklist

DeWoskin, Rachel

Big girl small; Rachel DeWoskin. Farrar, Straus and Giroux 2011 294p. $25

Grades: 11 12 Adult   **Fic**
1. Girls 2. Dwarfs 3. Adolescence 4. School life -- United States
ISBN 978-0-374-11257-8; 9781250002532; 9780374112578; 9781611731132
                                                LC 201033106
Alex Award (2012)

Blind; Rachel DeWoskin. Viking, published by Penguin Group 2014 394 p. (hardback) $17.99

Grades: 9 10 11 12   **Fic**
1. Blind -- Fiction 2. Teenagers -- Fiction 3. Schools -- Fiction 4. Family life -- Fiction 5. High schools -- Fiction 6. Interpersonal relations -- Fiction 7. People with disabilities -- Fiction
ISBN 0670785229; 9780670785223
                                                LC 2013041189

In this young adult novel by Rachel DeWoskin, "when Emma Sasha Silver loses her eyesight in a nightmare ac-cident, she must relearn everything from walking across the street to recognizing her own sisters to imagining colors. . . . Emma used to be the invisible kid, but now it seems ev-eryone is watching her. And just as she's about to start high school and try to recover her friendships and former life, one of her classmates is found dead in an apparent suicide." (Publisher's note)

"The life of a formerly sighted teen blossoms in Emma's strong voice as she explores the world, conquers fears, and attempts living everyday life again with her large, bustling, Jewish suburban family. A gracefully written, memorable, and enlightening novel." Booklist

Dickinson, Peter

★ **Eva**. Delacorte Press 1989 219p hardcover o.p. pa $6.50; pa $7.99

Grades: 7 8 9 10   **Fic**
1. Science fiction 2. Chimpanzees -- Fiction
ISBN 0-385-29702-5; 0-440-20766-5 pa; 9780440207665 pa
                                                LC 88-29435

"Eva wakes up from a deep coma that was the result of a terrible car accident and finds herself drastically altered. The accident leaves her so badly injured that her parents consent to a radical experiment to transplant her brain and memory into the body of a research chimpanzee. With the aid of a computer for communication, Eva slowly adjusts to her new existence while scientists monitor her progress, feelings, and insight into the animal world." Voice Youth Advocates

Diederich, Phililippe

Playing for the Devil's Fire; by Phillippe Died-erich. Cinco Puntos Press 2016 232 p. (hardback) $16.95

Grades: 7 8 9 10 11 12   **Fic**
1. Bildungsromans 2. Mexico -- Fiction 3. Organized crime -- Fiction 4. Criminals -- Fiction 5. Coming of age -- Fiction 6. Missing persons -- Fiction 7. Abandoned children -- Fiction 8. Mexico City (Mexico) -- Fiction
ISBN 9781941026298; 9781941026304
                                                LC 2015024951

In this young adult novel, by Phillippe Diederich, "noth-ing ever happens in the small Mexican town of Izayoc, where 13-year-old Boli spends his time playing marbles with his friends . . . and reading about the luchadores, who not only wrestle but fight crime, too. . . . When Boli's parents fail to return from their trip to request federal assistance, he sets out to discover the truth behind their disappearance with the help of washed-up wrestler El Chicano Estrada." (School Library Journal)

Diffenbaugh, Vanessa

The **language** of flowers; Vanessa Diffenbaugh. Ballantine Books 2011 322 p. $25

Grades: 11 12 Adult   **Fic**
1. Flowers 2. Love stories 3. Single women 4. Foster

children 5. Florists 6. California -- San Francisco
ISBN 978-0-345-52554-3; 0-345-52554-X;
9780345525567

LC 201051026

The book tells the story of orphan "Victoria [who] was placed with a woman named Elizabeth, on a picturesque Napa vineyard. . . . Unable to trust her turn of luck, the furious little girl tried to sabotage her new situation. . . . But Elizabeth refused to be baited, offering consequences but not ultimatums, making it clear that no matter what, Victoria was there to stay. . . . But something went terribly wrong. We meet the girl as she walks away from her last group home, only to unfurl her sleeping bag at a park on Potrero Hill, scrounge leftovers off cafe tables and begin a job search, with no diploma or work experience. . . . In chapters taking us back to the past, we learn that although Victoria failed at school, Elizabeth recognized that she was bright and curious, and taught her everything about the grapes and the flowers on her vineyard. . . . As an adult, Victoria . . . serendipitously find[s] work at an upscale flower shop." (SFGate)

Dinnison, Kris

You and me and him; by Kris Dinnison. Houghton Mifflin Harcourt 2015 288 p. (hardcover) $17.99
Grades: 9 10 11 12   **Fic**
1. School stories 2. Friendship -- Fiction 3. Gay teenagers -- Fiction 4. Gays -- Fiction 5. Love -- Fiction 6. Schools -- Fiction 7. High schools -- Fiction
ISBN 9780544301122

LC 2014011663

In this young adult novel, by Kris Dinnison, "Maggie and Nash are outsiders. She's overweight. He's out of the closet. The best of friends, they have seen each other through thick and thin, but when Tom moves to town at the start of the school year, they have something unexpected in common: feelings for the same guy." (Publisher's note)

"Stilted and sometimes clunkily expository dialogue also reveals little, making several of the book's many interpersonal conflicts more confusing than compelling. The (mostly) fat-positive message is important, but its delivery falters." Kirkus

Dixon, Heather

★ **Entwined**. Greenwillow Books 2011 472p
Grades: 7 8 9 10   **Fic**
1. Fantasy fiction 2. Dance -- Fiction 3. Death -- Fiction 4. Magic -- Fiction 5. Princesses -- Fiction 6. Kings and rulers -- Fiction 7. Young adult literature -- Works 8. Father-daughter relationship -- Fiction
ISBN 0-06-200103-5; 978-0-06-200103-0

LC 2010-11686

Confined to their dreary castle while mourning their mother's death, Princess Azalea and her eleven sisters join The Keeper, who is trapped in a magic passageway, in a nightly dance that soon becomes nightmarish.

"The story gracefully explores significant themes of grief and loss, mercy and love. Full of mystery, lush settings, and fully orbed characters, Dixon's debut is both suspenseful and rewarding." Booklist

Dixon, John

Phoenix Island; John Dixon. Gallery Books 2014 320 p. (hardback) $19.99
Grades: 9 10 11 12   **Fic**
1. Boxers (Sports) 2. Juvenile delinquents -- Fiction 3. Science fiction 4. Boxing -- Fiction 5. Orphans -- Fiction 6. Mercenary troops -- Fiction
ISBN 1476738637; 9781476738635; 9781476738659

LC 2013033616

"A champion boxer with a sharp hook and a short temper, sixteen-year-old Carl Freeman has been shuffled from foster home to foster home. He can't seem to stay out of trouble--using his fists to defend weaker classmates from bullies. His latest incident sends his opponent to the emergency room, and now the court is sending Carl to the worst place on earth: Phoenix Island," which "is ground zero for the future of combat intelligence." (Publisher's note)

"An unusual premise makes Dixon's thriller debut a welcome series kickoff. . . . There are some predictable elements--Carl falls for an attractive girl with a secret--but the pacing and smooth prose will have suspense fans waiting for the next book." Pub Wkly

Another title in this series is:
Devil's Pocket (2015)

Doctorow, Cory

For the win. Tor 2010 475p $17.99
Grades: 8 9 10 11 12   **Fic**
1. Science fiction 2. Internet games -- Fiction
ISBN 0-7653-2216-1; 978-0-7653-2216-6

LC 2010-18644

A group of teens from around the world find themselves drawn into an online revolution arranged by a mysterious young woman known as Big Sister Nor, who hopes to challenge the status quo and change the world using her virtual connections.

The author "has taken denigrated youth behavior (this time, gaming) and recast it into something heroic. He can't resist the occasional lecture--sometimes breaking away from the plot to do so--but thankfully his lessons are riveting. With its eye-opening humanity and revolutionary zeal, this ambitious epic is well worth the considerable challenge." Booklist

★ **Homeland**; Cory Doctorow. 1st ed. Tor Teen 2013 396 p. (hardcover) $17.99
Grades: 9 10 11 12   **Fic**
1. Adventure fiction 2. Hacktivism -- Fiction 3. Civil rights -- Fiction 4. Counterculture -- Fiction 5. Computer hackers -- Fiction 6. Politics, Practical -- Fiction 7. San Francisco (Calif.) -- Fiction 8. United States. Dept. of Homeland Security -- Fiction
ISBN 0765333694; 9780765333698

LC 2012037366

This is a follow-up to Cory Doctorow's "Little Brother." Here, California's economy collapses, but Marcus's hacktivist past lands him a job as webmaster for a crusading politician who promises reform. Soon his former nemesis Masha emerges from the political underground to gift him with a thumbdrive containing a Wikileaks-style cable-dump of hard evidence of corporate and governmental perfidy" and Marcus must choose whether to release it to the public. (Publisher's note)

★ **Little** brother. Tor Teen 2008 380p

Grades: 8 9 10 11 12   **Fic**

1. Computers -- Fiction 2. Terrorism -- Fiction 3. Civil rights -- Fiction 4. San Francisco (Calif.) -- Fiction 5. United States -- Dept. of Homeland Security -- Fiction

ISBN 0765319853; 9780765319852

LC 2008-1827

After being interrogated for days by the Department of Homeland Security in the aftermath of a terrorist attack on San Francisco, California, 17-year-old Marcus, released into what is now a police state, decides to use his expertise in computer hacking to set things right. "High school." (Horn Book)

"The author manages to explain naturally the necessary technical tools and scientific concepts in this fast-paced and well-written story. . . . The reader is privy to Marcus's gut-wrenching angst, frustration, and terror, thankfully offset by his self-awareness and humorous observations." Voice Youth Advocates

Makers. Tor 2009 416p $24.99

Grades: 11 12 Adult   **Fic**

1. Science fiction 2. Inventors -- Fiction 3. Businessmen -- Fiction

ISBN 978-0-7653-1279-2; 0-7653-1279-4

LC 2009-36212

"Perry Gibbons and Lester Banks, typical brilliant geeks in a garage, are trash-hackers who find inspiration in the growing pile of technical junk. Attracting the attention of suits and smart reporter Suzanne Church, the duo soon get involved with cheap and easy 3D printing, a cure for obesity and crowd-sourced theme parks. The result is bitingly realistic and miraculously avoids cliché or predictability. While dates and details occasionally contradict one another, Doctorow's combination of business strategy, brilliant product ideas and laugh-out-loud moments of insight will keep readers powering through this quick-moving tale." Publ Wkly

Pirate cinema; Cory Doctorow. 1st ed. Tor Teen 2012 384 p. (hardback) $19.99; (paperback) $9.99; (audiobook) $24.00

Grades: 7 8 9 10   **Fic**

1. Copyright 2. Runaway teenagers -- Fiction 3. Science fiction 4. England -- Fiction 5. Internet -- Fiction 6. Protest movements -- Fiction 7. Motion pictures -- Production and direction -- Fiction

ISBN 0765329085; 9780765329080; 9781429943185; 9780765329097; 9780307879585

LC 2012019871

In this book, author Cory Doctorow tells the story of Trent McCauley, a boy who "has an irrepressible drive to create . . . [films] through illegal downloading, and when he's caught, . . . [he] runs away to London, where he's taken under the wing of streetwise Jem Dodger. . . . He meets 26 and creates the persona Cecil B. DeVil. Pulled by 26 into the politics of copyright and the lobbyist money that purchases laws, Cecil becomes a creative figurehead for reform against escalating laws that aggressively jail kids." (Kirkus Reviews)

Dogar, Sharon

★ **Annexed**. Houghton Mifflin Harcourt 2010 333p $17

Grades: 8 9 10 11 12   **Fic**

1. Children 2. Diarists 3. Holocaust victims 4. Netherlands -- Fiction 5. Holocaust, 1933-1945 -- Fiction

ISBN 978-0-547-50195-6; 0-547-50195-1

LC 2010-282410

"On July 13, 1942, 15-year-old Peter van Pels and his parents entered the attic that became their home for two years. Peter is angry that he is hiding and not fighting Nazis. He is also not happy to be sharing cramped living quarters with the Franks, especially know-it-all Anne. In this novel, Dogar 'reimagines' what happened between the families who lived in the secret annex immortalized in Anne Frank's diary. In doing so, she creates a captivating historical novel and fully fleshes out the character of Peter, a boy whom teens will easily relate to." SLJ

Doig, Ivan

The **whistling** season. Harcourt 2006 345p hardcover o.p. pa $14.95

Grades: 11 12 Adult   **Fic**

1. Western stories 2. Montana -- Fiction 3. Siblings -- Fiction 4. Teachers -- Fiction 5. Household employees -- Fiction

ISBN 978-0-15-101237-4; 0-15-101237-7; 978-0-15-603164-6 pa; 0-15-603164-7 pa

LC 2005-25457

"Set in the early 1900s, this novel is a nostalgic, bittersweet story about a widower, his three sons, and the year these boys spend in a one-room country schoolhouse. The novel begins with the father, Oliver, hiring a widowed housekeeper named Rose from Minneapolis (her advertisement reads 'Can't Cook but Doesn't Bite'). She arrives with her unconventional brother, Morrie, in tow. Morrie is something of a scholar, and he soon finds himself pressed into service as a replacement teacher. During the course of the novel, these intriguing and unpredictable characters come together in surprising and uplifting ways. This is an affectionate, heartwarming tale that also celebrates a vanished way of life and laments its passing." Libr J

Doktorski, Jennifer Salvato

Famous last words; Jennifer Salvato Doktorski. Henry Holt and Company 2013 288 p. (hardcover) $17.99

Grades: 7 8 9 10   **Fic**

1. Women journalists -- Fiction 2. Internship programs -- Fiction 3. Journalism -- Fiction 4. Newspapers -- Fiction 5. Self-perception -- Fiction 6. Dating (Social customs) -- Fiction

ISBN 0805093672; 9780805093674

LC 2012046312

In this book, "aspiring reporter Sam D'Angelo, 16, is interning at her local New Jersey paper for the summer, stuck writing obituaries with her occasionally annoying, college-age fellow intern AJ. When she's not taking phone calls about dead people, Sam writes humorous imaginary obits (including one for herself); spends time with her grandmother; lusts after the 'incredibly hot' features intern, Tony

Roma; and covertly investigates the shady mayor with AJ." (Publishers Weekly)

"Something of a love note to print journalism, the story is nevertheless snappy and contemporary, furthered by Sam's wry, self-deprecating narration and convincingly colloquial dialogue. Cleverly titled, realistically written, and on the whole engaging and sympathetic, this story rings true." Kirkus

The **summer** after you and me; Jennifer Salvato Doktorski. Sourcebooks Fire 2015 304 p. (13: alk. paper) $9.99

Grades: 9 10 11 12   **Fic**
1. Summer -- Fiction 2. Resorts -- Fiction 3. New Jersey -- Fiction 4. Family life -- Fiction 5. Dating (Social customs) -- Fiction 6. Twins -- Fiction 7. Summer resorts -- Fiction 8. Family life -- New Jersey -- Fiction
ISBN 1492619035; 9781492619031
LC 2014044296

In this book, by Jennifer Salvato Doktorski, "[f]or Lucy, the Jersey Shore isn't just the perfect summer escape, it's home. As a local girl, she knows not to get attached to the tourists. . . . Still, she can't help but crush on charming Connor Malloy. . . . Then Superstorm Sandy sweeps up the coast, bringing Lucy and Connor together for a few intense hours. Except nothing is the same in the wake of the storm, and Lucy is left to pick up the pieces of her broken heart and her broken home." (Publisher's note)

"Doktorski has crafted a rich, multilayered novel with a strong sense of place and a good mix of characters and problems." Booklist

Dolamore, Jaclyn
Magic under glass. Bloomsbury Children's Books 2010 225p $16.99

Grades: 7 8 9 10 11 12   **Fic**
1. Fantasy fiction 2. Magic -- Fiction 3. Robots -- Fiction 4. Fairies -- Fiction 5. Singers -- Fiction
ISBN 978-1-59990-430-6; 1-59990-430-6
LC 2009-20944

A wealthy sorcerer's invitation to sing with his automaton leads seventeen-year-old Nimira, whose family's disgrace brought her from a palace to poverty, into political intrigue, enchantments, and a friendship with a fairy prince who needs her help.

"Delamore successfully juggles several elements that might have stymied even a more experienced writer: intriguing plot elements, sophisticated characterizations, and a subtle boost of girl power." Booklist

Dole, Mayra L.
★ **Down** to the bone; [by] Mayra Lazara Dole. HarperTeen 2008 384p $16.99; lib bdg $17.89

Grades: 8 9 10 11 12   **Fic**
1. Lesbians -- Fiction 2. Cuban Americans -- Fiction
ISBN 978-0-06-084310-6; 0-06-084310-1; 978-0-06-084311-3 lib bdg; 0-06-084311-X lib bdg
LC 2007-33270

Laura, a seventeen-year-old Cuban American girl, is thrown out of her house when her mother discovers she is a lesbian, but after trying to change her heart and hide from the truth, Laura finally comes to terms with who she is and learns to love and respect herself.

"Using Spanish colloquialisms and slang, this debut author pulls off the tricky task of dialect in a manner that feels authentic. As Dole tackles a tough and important topic, her protagonist will win over a range of teen audiences, gay and straight." Publ Wkly

Doller, Trish
The **devil** you know; by Trish Doller. Bloomsbury 2015 256 p. (hardcover) $17.99

Grades: 10 11 12   **Fic**
1. Murder -- Fiction 2. Camping -- Fiction 3. Florida -- Fiction 4. Single-parent families -- Fiction 5. Father-daughter relationship -- Fiction 6. Psychopaths -- Fiction 7. Fathers and daughters -- Fiction
ISBN 1619634163; 9781619634169
LC 2014023032

In this book, by Trish Doller, "[e]ighteen-year-old Arcadia wants adventure. Living in a tiny Florida town with her dad and four-year-old brother, Cadie spends most of her time working, going to school, and taking care of her family. So when she meets two handsome cousins at a campfire party, . . . [they] invite her . . . to join them on a road trip, and it's just the risk she's been craving. . . . But . . . she discovers that one of them is not at all who he claims to be." (Publisher's note)

"Cadie, 18, lives in a tiny Floridian town with her widowed dad and kid brother. She's spent the last couple years pining for an adventure to take her away from her boring home. When two cute cousins, Matt and Noah, show up at a campfire party, Cadie is so strongly attracted to Noah that it thrills and scares her. The next day, the guys invite her and her old friend to join them on their road trip. Even though they're not much more than strangers, Cadie just can't say no. What the teen thought was going to be a sexy and temporary getaway slowly turns out to be a dangerous, terrifying, and deadly experience. . . . . This dark thriller features a strong female lead and a heap of sexy; a must-buy for readers looking for a healthy dose of drama." SLJ

Something like normal; Trish Doller. Bloomsbury Pub. Children's Books 2012 216 p. (hardback) $16.99

Grades: 9 10 11 12   **Fic**
1. Love stories 2. Military personnel -- United States -- Fiction 3. Triangles (Interpersonal relations) -- Fiction 4. Love -- Fiction 5. Brothers -- Fiction 6. Veterans -- Fiction 7. Afghanistan -- Fiction 8. Family problems -- Fiction 9. Afghan War, 2001- -- Fiction 10. United States. Marine Corps -- Fiction 11. Post-traumatic stress disorder -- Fiction
ISBN 1599908441; 9781599908441
LC 2011035511

In this book, "Travis is home in southwest Florida, on leave from Afghanistan and dealing with the death of his best friend and fellow soldier Charlie, the breakup of his parents' marriage, and his girlfriend having left him for his brother. While processing all of this, he meets Harper, a girl whose reputation he destroyed years ago, and the two slowly start to connect." (Publishers Weekly)

Donnelly, Jennifer

A **northern** light. Harcourt 2003 389p $17; pa $8.95

Grades: 9 10 11 12 **Fic**

1. Farm life -- Fiction

ISBN 0-15-216705-6; 0-15-205310-7 pa

LC 2002-5098

Michael L. Printz Award honor book, 2004

In 1906, sixteen-year-old Mattie, determined to attend college and be a writer against the wishes of her father and fiance, takes a job at a summer inn where she discovers the truth about the death of a guest. Based on a true story.

"Donnelly's characters ring true to life, and the meticulously described setting forms a vivid backdrop to this finely crafted story. An outstanding choice for historical-fiction fans." SLJ

★ **Revolution**. Delacorte Press 2010 471p $18.99; lib bdg $21.99

Grades: 9 10 11 12 **Fic**

1. Princes 2. Diaries -- Fiction 3. Musicians -- Fiction 4. Bereavement -- Fiction 5. Family life -- Fiction 6. Paris (France) -- Fiction

ISBN 978-0-385-73763-0; 0-385-73763-7; 978-0-385-90678-4 lib bdg; 0-385-90678-1 lib bdg

LC 2010-08993

An angry, grieving seventeen-year-old musician facing expulsion from her prestigious Brooklyn private school travels to Paris to complete a school assignment and uncovers a diary written during the French revolution by a young actress attempting to help a tortured, imprisoned little boy—Louis Charles, the lost king of France.

"The ambitious story, narrated in Andi's grief-soaked, sardonic voice, will wholly capture patient readers with its sharply articulated, raw emotions and insights into science and art; ambition and love; history's ever-present influence; and music's immediate, astonishing power." Booklist

Includes bibliographical references

These shallow graves; Jennifer Donnelly. Delacorte Press 2015 496 p. (hc) $19.99

Grades: 7 8 9 10 **Fic**

1. Death -- Fiction 2. Gender role -- Fiction 3. Social classes -- Fiction 4. New York (N.Y.) -- History -- Fiction 5. Father-daughter relationship -- Fiction 6. Sex role -- Fiction 7. Fathers and daughters -- Fiction 8. New York (N.Y.) -- History -- 19th century -- Fiction

ISBN 9780385737654

LC 2014047825

In this book, by Jennifer Donnelly, "Jo Montfort . . . [will] graduate from finishing school and be married off to a wealthy bachelor. Which is the last thing she wants. Jo dreams of becoming a writer. . . . Wild aspirations aside, Jo's life seems perfect until tragedy strikes: her father is found dead. Charles Montfort shot himself while cleaning his pistol. One of New York City's wealthiest men . . . . Jo knows he was far too smart to clean a loaded gun." (Publisher's note)

"Melodrama and intrigue drive this fast-paced thriller with a Wharton-esque setting and a naïve young protagonist willing to be exposed to the shadier side of life—prostitutes, uncouth men, and abject poverty—on her way to solving a mystery and asserting her right to claim her future for her-

self. The author keeps the clues coming at a rate that allows readers to be one small step ahead of Jo as the story races to its surprising conclusion. Readers who love costume dramas will relish this one." Kirkus

Donoghue, Emma

★ **Room**; a novel. Emma Donoghue. Little, Brown and Co. 2010 321p

Grades: 10 11 12 Adult **Fic**

1. Rape -- Fiction 2. Kidnapping -- Fiction 3. Mother-son relationship -- Fiction 4. Escapes 5. Kidnapping 6. Boys -- Fiction 7. Mothers and sons 8. Suspense fiction 9. Psychological novels 10. Mother and child -- Fiction 11. Insane, Criminal and dangerous

ISBN 0316098337; 9780316098335

LC 2010006983

Alex Award (2011), CBA Libris Awards (Canadian Booksellers Association): Fiction Book of the Year (2011), Rogers Writers' Trust Fiction Prize (2010), Indies' Choice Book Awards: Adult Fiction (2011)

"The narrator of Emma Donoghue's 'Room' is a 5-year-old boy. . . . He and his mother have been trapped in the 11-by-11-foot room of the title since the day he was born." (N Y Times (Late N Y Ed))

Dooley, Sarah

Livvie Owen lived here. Feiwel and Friends 2010 229p $16.99

Grades: 6 7 8 9 10 **Fic**

1. School stories 2. Autism -- Fiction 3. Family life -- Fiction

ISBN 978-0-312-61253-5; 0-312-61253-2

LC 2010-13009

Fourteen-year-old Livvie Owen, who has autism, and her family have been forced to move frequently because of her outbursts, but when they face eviction again, Livvie is convinced she has a way to get back to a house where they were all happy, once.

"This novel is an interesting perspective of what a teenage girl with autism might experience, but also a heartwarming story of how a family binds together during emotional and financial turmoil." Libr Media Connect

Dorris, Michael

★ A **yellow** raft in blue water. Holt & Co. 1987 343p hardcover o.p. pa $14

Grades: 11 12 Adult **Fic**

1. Women -- Fiction 2. Family life -- Fiction 3. Native Americans -- Fiction 4. Mother-daughter relationship -- Fiction

ISBN 0-8050-0045-3; 0-312-42185-0 pa

LC 86-26947

"The bitter rifts and inevitable bonds between generations are highlighted as a teenaged daughter, mother, and grand matriarch of an American Indian family tell their life stories. Humorous and poignant, with unique characters." SLJ

Dos Santos, Steven

The **culling**; Steven Dos Santos. Flux 2013 432 p. (The torch keeper) $9.99

Grades: 9 10 11 12   **Fic**
1. Dystopian fiction 2. Homosexuality -- Fiction
3. Resistance to government -- Fiction 4. Science
fiction 5. Orphans -- Fiction 6. Contests -- Fiction 7.
Survival -- Fiction 8. Brothers and sisters -- Fiction 9.
Government, Resistance to -- Fiction
ISBN 073873537X; 9780738735375

LC 2012041699

Rainbow List (2014)

In this young adult dystopian novel, by Steven dos Santos, book one of "The Torch Keeper" series, "for Lucian . . . , Recruitment Day means the . . . totalitarian government will force him to . . . compet[e] to join the ruthless Imposer task force. Each Recruit participates in increasingly difficult and violent military training . . . , those who fail must choose . . . a family member to be brutally killed." (Publisher's note)

"The Establishment controls everyone and everything in this bleak future world. Sixteen-year-old Lucky and his four-year-old brother, Cole, live in a rundown building and have little to eat. Their parents are dead, and they have only a friendly (but sickly) neighbor to watch over them...This novel is similar to Suzanne Collins's The Hunger Games in its brutality, but it fails to provoke the same emotional attachment readers feel for the characters in Collins's blockbuster. In some ways, this dystopian vision seems even more unsettling; throughout the Trials, the Recruits' loved ones are killed in increasingly disturbing ways.—" (School Library Journal)

Dowd, Siobhan

★ **Bog** child. David Fickling Books 2008 321p
Grades: 8 9 10 11 12   **Fic**
1. Mummies -- Fiction 2. Prisoners -- Fiction
3. Terrorism -- Fiction 4. Family life -- Fiction 5.
Northern Ireland -- Fiction
ISBN 0-385-75170-2 lib bdg; 978-0-385-75169-8;
0-385-75169-9; 978-0-385-75170-4 lib bdg

LC 2008-2998

This novel is set in Northern Ireland in 1981. 18-year-old Fergus is distracted from his upcoming A-level exams by the discovery of a girl's body in a peat bog, his imprisoned brother's hunger strike, and the stress of being a courier for Sinn Fein. "Grades eight to twelve." (Bull Cent Child Books)

"Dowd raises questions about moral choices within a compelling plot that is full of surprises, powerfully bringing home the impact of political conflict on innocent bystanders." Publ Wkly

★ **Solace** of the road. David Fickling Books
2009 260p $17.99; lib bdg $20.99
Grades: 9 10 11 12   **Fic**
1. Great Britain -- Fiction 2. Foster home care -- Fiction
3. Runaway teenagers -- Fiction 4. Voyages and travels
-- Fiction
ISBN 978-0-375-84971-8; 0-375-84971-8; 978-0-375-
94971-5 lib bdg; 0-375-94971-2 lib bdg

LC 2008-44603

While running away from a London foster home just before her fifteenth birthday, Holly has ample time to consider her years of residential care and her early life with her Irish mother, whom she is now trying to reach.

"A compelling psychological portrait of a girl's journey from denial to facing the facts that will let her move beyond her troubled past. . . . Readers will root for her to find her balance and arrive safely at the right destination." Publ Wkly

A **swift** pure cry. David Fickling Books 2007
309p hardcover o.p. pa $8.99
Grades: 9 10 11 12   **Fic**
1. Fathers -- Fiction 2. Ireland -- Fiction 3. Pregnancy
-- Fiction 4. Family life -- Fiction
ISBN 978-0-385-75108-7; 0-385-75108-7; 978-0-440-
42218-1 pa; 0-440-42218-1 pa

LC 2006-14562

Coolbar, Ireland, is a village of secrets and Shell, caretaker to her younger brother and sister after the death of their mother and with the absence of their father, is not about to reveal hers until suspicion falls on the wrong person.

"This book, with its serious tone and inclusion of social issues, will have appeal for American readers desiring weightier material, and teachers might find it useful in the classroom." Voice Youth Advocates

Downes, Patrick

★ **Fell** of dark; a novel. Patrick Downes.
Philomel Books, an imprint of Penguin Group (USA)
2015 208 p. (hardback) $17.99
Grades: 9 10 11 12   **Fic**
1. Good and evil -- Fiction 2. Mental illness -- Fiction
3. Hallucinations and illusions -- Fiction
ISBN 0399172904; 9780399172908

LC 2014037606

In this young adult novel, by Patrick Downes, "Erik is often silenced by headaches and suffers from more mysterious afflictions including stigmatalike bleeding. . . . Thorn is plagued by demons and the voices that come from within. Eventually, the stories of these two deeply disturbed young men collide. . . . At the . . . end . . . Erik must stop Thorn from doing something terrible." (School Library Journal)

"This debut novel jumps between first-person narrators Erik (sexually abused after his father's death) and Thorn (blamed by his parents for his sister's death). The story reaches a crescendo when the teens finally meet--on opposite ends of a gun outside an elementary school. This unflinching exploration of loss, abuse, and mental illness occasionally stumbles under the weight of its stylistic techniques." Horn Book

Downham, Jenny

★ **Before** I die. David Fickling Books 2007
326p hardcover o.p. pa $9.99
Grades: 8 9 10 11 12   **Fic**
1. Death -- Fiction 2. Terminally ill -- Fiction
ISBN 978-0-385-75155-1; 978-0-385-75183-4 pa

LC 2007-20284

A terminally ill teenaged girl makes and carries out a list of things to do before she dies.

"Downham holds nothing back in her wrenchingly and exceptionally vibrant story." Publ Wkly

★ **Unbecoming;** by Jenny Downham. David
Fickling Books/Scholastic Inc. 2016 384 p. illustrations $17.99
Grades: 9 10 11 12   **Fic**
1. England -- Fiction 2. Family life -- Fiction 3.

Grandmothers -- Fiction 4. Family secrets -- Fiction 5. Alzheimer's disease -- Fiction 6. Brothers and sisters -- Fiction 7. Mother-daughter relationship -- Fiction 8. Secrets -- Fiction
ISBN 0545907179; 9780545907170

LC 2015036012

In this book, by Jenny Downham, "Katie's life is falling apart: her best friend thinks she's a freak, her mother, Caroline, controls every aspect of her life, and her estranged grandmother, Mary, appears as if out of nowhere. Mary has dementia and needs lots of care, and when Katie starts putting together Mary's life story, secrets and lies are uncovered: Mary's illegitimate baby, her zest for life and freedom and men; the . . . huge sacrifices along the way." (Publisher's note)

"Downham keenly weaves together musings, revelations, confrontations, and poignancy. Her prose gets right down inside human fragility, tenderness, fury, gusto, and strength—leaving sweet, sharp images that are impossible to forget. Exceptional. (Fiction. 14 & up)." Kirkus

★ **You** against me. David Fickling Books 2011 412p $16.99; lib bdg $19.99; ebook $10.99
Grades: 9 10 11 12   **Fic**
1. Rape -- Fiction 2. Guilt -- Fiction 3. Siblings -- Fiction 4. Great Britain -- Fiction 5. Social classes -- Fiction
ISBN 978-0-385-75160-5; 978-0-385-75161-2 lib bdg; 978-0-375-98938-4 ebook

LC 2010038226

"Crisp, revealing dialogue, measured pacing and candid, unaffected prose round out this illuminating novel in which any reader can find someone to root for or relate to." Kirkus

Dowswell, Paul
The **Auslander**. Bloomsbury Children's Books 2011 295p $16.99
Grades: 7 8 9 10   **Fic**
1. Orphans -- Fiction 2. Adoption -- Fiction 3. Insurgency -- Fiction 4. Berlin (Germany) -- Fiction 5. National socialism -- Fiction 6. World War, 1939-1945 -- Fiction 7. Germany -- History -- 1933-1945 -- Fiction
ISBN 1599906333; 9781599906331

LC 2010035626

First published 2009 in the United Kingdom
German soldiers take Peter from a Warsaw orphanage, and soon he is adopted by Professor Kaltenbach, a prominent Nazi, but Peter forms his own ideas about what he sees and hears and decides to take a risk that is most dangerous in 1942 Berlin.

"The characters are rich and nuanced; . . . the action is swift and suspenseful; and the juxtaposition of wartime nobility and wartime cruelty is timeless." Horn Book

Doyle, Marissa
Courtship and curses; Marissa Doyle. Henry Holt 2012 343 p. (hc) $17.99
Grades: 7 8 9 10   **Fic**
1. Regency novels 2. Mystery fiction 3. Magic -- Fiction 4. Witches -- Fiction 5. Self-acceptance -- Fiction 6. People with disabilities -- Fiction 7. Aristocracy (Social class) -- Fiction 8. Brussels (Belgium) -- History --

Fiction 9. Belgium -- History -- 1814-1830 -- Fiction 10. Great Britain -- History -- 1800-1837 -- Fiction
ISBN 0805091874; 9780805091878

LC 2011031999

This book tells the story of "Lady Sophronia Rosier (Sophie)," who is preparing "for her entrance into London society," despite a disability incurred from illness. She has help from "her new best friend, Parthenope" and "begins her procession into society." It soon becomes clear that someone is using magic to target her and her father. "Sophie and Parthenope begin to investigate while playing their roles in society, dreadfully aware that lives are at stake." (Voice of Youth Advocates)

Doyle, Roddy, 1958-
A **greyhound** of a girl; Roddy Doyle. Amulet Books 2012 208 p. (hbk.) $16.95
Grades: 7 8 9 10 11 12   **Fic**
1. Dog racing -- Fiction 2. Family life -- Fiction 3. Dublin (Ireland) -- Fiction 4. Women -- Ireland -- Fiction 5. Death -- Fiction 6. Ghosts -- Fiction 7. Ireland -- Fiction 8. Grandmothers -- Fiction 9. Voyages and travels -- Fiction 10. Mothers and daughters -- Fiction
ISBN 9781407129334 Marion Lloyd; 1407129333 Marion Lloyd; 9781419701689 Amulet; 1419701681 Amulet

LC 2011042200

This book tells the story of "Twelve-year-old Mary O'Hara," an Irish girl who "is surrounded by good-humored women . . . her mum at home, her mum's mum, who is dying in Dublin's Sacred Heart Hospital, and her mum's mum's mum, who has just materialized as a ghost on her street. . . . [Roddy] Doyle divides up the novel by character, giving readers first-hand glimpses into the nature of each woman through time." (Kirkus)

Draper, Sharon M. (Sharon Mills), 1948-
The **Battle** of Jericho. Atheneum Books for Young Readers 2003 297p $16.95; pa $6.99
Grades: 7 8 9 10   **Fic**
1. School stories 2. Clubs -- Fiction 3. Death -- Fiction 4. Cousins -- Fiction
ISBN 0-689-84232-5; 0-689-84233-3 pa

LC 2002-8612

"This title is a compelling read that drives home important lessons about making choices." SLJ

Other titles in this series are:
Just another hero (2009)
November blues (2007)

Copper sun; [by] Sharon Draper. Atheneum Books for Young Readers 2006 302p $16.95
Grades: 8 9 10 11 12   **Fic**
1. Slavery -- Fiction 2. African Americans -- Fiction
ISBN 0-689-82181-6

LC 2005-05540

Two fifteen-year-old girls—one a slave and the other an indentured servant—escape their Carolina plantation and try to make their way to Fort Moses, Florida, a Spanish colony that gives sanctuary to slaves.

"This action-packed, multifaceted, character-rich story describes the shocking realities of the slave trade and plantation life while portraying the perseverance, resourcefulness, and triumph of the human spirit." Booklist

Just another hero. Atheneum Books for Young Readers 2009 280p $16.99

Grades: 7 8 9 10   **Fic**

1. School stories 2. Violence -- Fiction 3. African Americans -- Fiction
ISBN 978-1-4169-0700-8; 1-4169-0700-9

LC 2008-30961

Sequel to November blues

As Kofi, Arielle, Dana, November, and Jericho face personal challenges during their last year of high school, a misunderstood student brings a gun to class and demands to be taken seriously.

"The author presents a timeless theme in a well-crafted, highly readable story." Voice Youth Advocates

November blues. Atheneum Books for Young Readers 2007 316p $16.99; pa $6.99

Grades: 8 9 10 11 12   **Fic**

1. School stories 2. Pregnancy -- Fiction 3. African Americans -- Fiction
ISBN 978-1-4169-0698-8; 1-4169-0698-3; 978-1-4169-0699-5 pa; 1-4169-0699-1 pa

LC 2006-101343

Sequel to The battle of Jericho (2003)

A teenaged boy's death in a hazing accident has lasting effects on his pregnant girlfriend and his guilt-ridden cousin, who gives up a promising music career to play football during his senior year in high school.

"Urban teens often ask, 'Where are the books about us, Miss?' and with this novel Draper has . . . given them something meaty and meaningful to read." SLJ

Followed by Just another hero (2009)

Panic; Sharon Draper. 1st ed. Atheneum Books for Young Readers 2013 272 p. (hardcover) $17.99

Grades: 9 10 11 12   **Fic**

1. Kidnapping -- Fiction 2. Ballet dancers -- Fiction 3. Dance -- Fiction 4. Sexual abuse -- Fiction 5. African Americans -- Fiction
ISBN 1442408960; 9781442408968; 9781442408982

LC 2012016339

In this book, "after teenage Diamond makes a disastrously foolish mistake, she is abducted and finds herself in terrible danger. Will she survive? Will her life ever be the same? Told from multiple points of view, 'Panic' is not only Diamond's story but also that of three of her friends, all of them students at the Crystal Pointe Dance Academy." (Booklist)

Tears of a tiger. Atheneum Pubs. 1994 162p $16.95; pa $5.99

Grades: 7 8 9 10   **Fic**

1. Death -- Fiction 2. Suicide -- Fiction 3. African Americans -- Fiction
ISBN 0-689-31878-2; 0-689-80698-1 pa

LC 94-10278

The death of African American high school basketball star Rob Washington in a drunk driving accident leads to the suicide of his friend Andy, who was driving the car

"The story emerges through newspaper articles, journal entries, homework assignments, letters, and conversations that give the book immediacy; the teenage conversational idiom is contemporary and well written. Andy's perceptions of the racism directed toward young black males . . . will be recognized by African American YAs." Booklist

Dray, Stephanie

Lily of the Nile; Berkley trade pbk. ed.; Berkley Books 2011 351p pa $15

Grades: 9 10 11 12   **Fic**

1. Queens 2. Emperors 3. Rome -- History -- Fiction
ISBN 978-0-425-23855-4

LC 2010-37153

This book focuses on "Cleopatra Selene, daughter of Antony and Cleopatra. The novel follows Selene's story from her parents' suicides, through the years that she and her brothers, Alexander and Philadelphus, were wards of Octavian, living in his sister's home until her betrothal to Juba II. . . . Dray imbues her work with meticulously researched details of Roman life, historical figures, and political upheaval. Add magical realism and controversial goddess-worship, and you have a novel that will appeal to readers on many levels." Libr J

Duane, Diane

So you want to be a wizard; Diane Duane. HMH Books for Young Readers 2001 400 p. (Young Wizards) (pbk.) $7.99; (hbk.) $14.95

Grades: 6 7 8 9 10   **Fic**

1. Wizards 2. Fantasy fiction 3. Fantasy 4. Bullies -- Fiction 5. Wizards -- Fiction
ISBN 015216250X; 0385293054; 9780152162504; 9780385293051

LC 83005216

Originally published 1983

"Kit, 12, and Nita, 13, turn to magic in desperation as a way to protect themselves from bullies who beat them up regularly. They and Fred, a white mole they called up, jump through a worldgate into an alternate Manhattan where malevolent machines attack them at every turn. Their task is to rescue The Book of Night with Moon, which the evil Starsnuffer has hidden." (Voice of Youth Advocates)

Other titles in this series are:
Deep wizardry (1985)
High wizardry (1990)
A wizard abroad (1997)
The wizard's dilemma (2001)
A wizard alone (2002)
Wizard's holiday (2003)
Wizards at war (2005)
A wizard of Mars (2010)
Games wizards play (2016)

Dubosarsky, Ursula

★ The **golden** day; by Ursula Dubosarsky. Candlewick 2013 160 p. $15.99

Grades: 7 8 9 10   **Fic**

1. Mystery fiction 2. Friendship -- Fiction 3. Missing persons -- Fiction
ISBN 0763663999; 9780763663995; 9781742374710

LC 2012452201

In this novel by Ursula Dubosarsky "eleven school-girls embrace their own chilling history when their teacher abruptly goes missing on a field trip. Who was the mysterious poet they had met in the Garden? What actually happened in the seaside cave that day? And most important — who can they tell about it?" (Publisher's note)

"Spare and well written, this slim novel covers the days following a teacher's disappearance during a class outing. Eleven girls must make their way back to school where they are determined to keep their teacher's rendezvous with the local park's gardener a secret. The book's chilling atmosphere and mature tone are best suited for older readers." (Horn Book)

Duncan, Lois

★ **Killing** Mr. Griffin. Dell 1990 223p hardcover o.p. pa $6.50

Grades: 7 8 9 10   **Fic**

1. School stories 2. Kidnapping -- Fiction

ISBN 0-440-94515-1 pa

First published 1978 by Little, Brown

ALA YALSA Margaret A. Edwards Award (1992)

The author's "skillful plotting builds layers of tension that draws readers into the eye of the conflict. The ending is nicely handled in a manner which provides relief without removing any of the chilling implications." SLJ

Dunlap, Susanne Emily

The **musician's** daughter; [by] Susanne Dunlap. Bloomsbury 2009 322p $16.99

Grades: 8 9 10 11 12   **Fic**

1. Composers 2. Mystery fiction 3. Gypsies -- Fiction 4. Homicide -- Fiction 5. Musicians -- Fiction 6. Vienna (Austria) -- Fiction

ISBN 978-1-59990-332-3; 1-59990-332-6

LC 2008-30307

In eighteenth-century Vienna, Austria, fifteen-year-old Theresa seeks a way to help her mother and brother financially while investigating the murder of her father, a renowned violinist in Haydn's orchestra at the court of Prince Esterhazy, after his body is found near a gypsy camp.

"Dunlap skillfully builds suspense until the final page. . . . Readers will root for courageous Theresa through the exciting intrigue even as they absorb deeper messages about music and art's power to lift souls and inspire change." Booklist

Durham, David Anthony

Gabriel's story. Doubleday 2001 291p hardcover o.p. pa $13.95

Grades: 11 12 Adult   **Fic**

1. Kansas -- Fiction 2. African Americans -- Fiction 3. Frontier and pioneer life -- Fiction

ISBN 0-385-49814-4; 0-385-72033-5 pa

LC 00-25291

Alex Award (2002)

In this "novel, set in the eighteen-seventies, Gabriel, a fifteen-year-old black boy from Baltimore, resents his new life on the Kansas plains when his widowed mother marries a homesteader. But then he falls in with a charismatic cowpunch and horse thief, and as they travel west to New Mexico a series of violent episodes brings Gabriel to swift maturity. The moral gravity of Durham's narrative is offset by his attentiveness to the primacy of nature in the Western landscape." New Yorker

Durst, Sarah Beth

Ice. Margaret K. McElderry Books 2009 308p $16.99

Grades: 7 8 9 10   **Fic**

1. Fairy tales 2. Polar bear -- Fiction 3. Scientists -- Fiction 4. Supernatural -- Fiction 5. Arctic regions -- Fiction

ISBN 978-1-4169-8643-0; 1-4169-8643-X

LC 2009-8618

A modern-day retelling of "East o' the Sun, West o' the Moon" in which eighteen-year-old Cassie learns that her grandmother's fairy tale is true when a Polar Bear King comes to claim her for his bride and she must decide whether to go with him and save her long-lost mother, or continue helping her father with his research

"Told in a descriptive style that perfectly captures the changing settings, Durst's novel is a page-turner that readers who enjoy adventure mixed with fairy-tale romance will find hard to put down." Booklist

Vessel; Sarah Beth Durst. Margaret K. McElderry Books 2012 424 p. (hardcover) $16.99

Grades: 7 8 9 10   **Fic**

1. Deserts -- Fiction 2. Fantasy fiction 3. Adventure fiction 4. Gods and goddesses 5. Fantasy 6. Survival -- Fiction 7. Goddesses -- Fiction 8. Fate and fatalism -- Fiction

ISBN 1442423765; 9781442423763; 9781442423787

LC 2011044691

In this book by Sarah Beth Durst, "Liyana has trained all her life to be the vessel for her desert tribe's goddess Bayla. . . . "Bayla never shows up, but the trickster god Korbyn appears in human form and gives Liyana some startling news: the gods have all been imprisoned in false vessels, and he and Liyana must retrieve the various tribes' unsuccessful vessels, figure out where the deities are being held, and rescue them." (Bulletin of the Center for Children's Books)

Duyvis, Corinne

★ **Otherbound**; by Corinne Duyvis. Amulet Books 2014 400 p. (alk. paper) $17.95

Grades: 9 10 11 12   **Fic**

1. Fantasy fiction 2. Mute persons -- Fiction 3. Fantasy 4. Shapeshifting -- Fiction 5. Household employees -- Fiction

ISBN 1419709283; 9781419709289

LC 2013029536

In this young adult novel by Corinne Duyvis, "Nolan doesn't see darkness when he closes his eyes. Instead, he's transported into the mind of Amara, a girl living in a different world. Nolan's life in his small Arizona town is full of history tests, family tension, and laundry; his parents think he has epilepsy, judging from his frequent blackouts. Amara's world is full of magic and danger--she's a mute servant girl who's tasked with protecting a renegade princess." (Publisher's note)

"Whenever seventeen-year-old Nolan closes his eyes, he's transported into the body of Amara, a mute slave girl on an alien world who acts as decoy against would-be assassins of a princess. After years of being a helpless witness, Nolan suddenly becomes a player in the action. Duyvis keeps tensions high in both Nolan's Arizona and Amara's Dunelands. A humdinger of an adventure." Horn Book

Easton, T. S.

Boys Don't Knit; T.S. Easton. Feiwel & Friends 2015 272 p. $16.99

Grades: 9 10 11 12   **Fic**

1. Knitting 2. Probation 3. Teenagers -- Fiction 4. England 5. Conduct of life 6. Humorous stories 7. Families -- England

ISBN 1250053315; 9781250053312

In this novel by T.S. Easton, "after an incident regarding a crossing guard and a bottle of Martini & Rossi (and his friends), 17-year-old worrier Ben Fletcher must develop his sense of social alignment, take up a hobby, and do some community service to avoid any further probation. He takes a knitting class . . . [that] helps ease his anxiety and worrying. The only challenge now is to keep it hidden from his friends, his crush, and his soccer-obsessed father." (Publisher's note)

"Despite some unnecessary Americanization of the text, this wonderfully funny novel is infused with British slang, including dozens of terms easily understood in context. Wacky characters, a farcical plot and a fledgling romance are all part of the fun in this novel that will appeal to fans of Angus, Thongs, and Full-Frontal Snogging." Kirkus

Edwards, Janet

★ **Earth** girl; by Janet Edwards. Pyr 2013 350 p. (Earth girl trilogy) hbk $17.95

Grades: 7 8 9 10   **Fic**

1. Science fiction 2. People with disabilities -- Fiction

ISBN 9781616147655; 1616147652

LC 2012044570

In this young adult novel set in the future, Jarra and other Handicapped are discriminated against by the Norms. "Jarra decides to show them that she is just as good as they are and applies to an off-world college conducting an archaeology dig on the abandoned buildings of New York. Reinventing herself as Jarra Military Kid, JMK watches vids and takes combat lessons. . . . Since she grew up on Earth and has been to the New York digs many times, her skills quickly allow her to shine." (School Library Journal)

"The future that Edwards constructs is creative and the dig descriptions are well thought out. . . . The 'person against nature' conflict with unstable dig conditions and solar flares makes a refreshing change." SLJ

★ **Earth** star; Janet Edwards. Pyr, an imprint of Prometheus Books 2014 360 p. (hardback) $17.99

Grades: 7 8 9 10 11 12   **Fic**

1. Children with disabilities -- Abuse of -- Fiction

ISBN 1616148977; 9781616148973

LC 2013040057

In this sequel to Janet Edwards's "Earth Girl," "it's 2789. People portal between planets in seconds, often many times per day--except the Handicapped, like Jarra, whose immune systems can survive only on Earth. . . . She plans to continue studying prehistory by excavating sites of long-dead cities. But before the next dig begins, Jarra and boyfriend Fian are

whisked off to a military base and inexplicably sworn in as officers. An unidentified alien sphere is hovering above Africa." (Kirkus Reviews)

"This far-future science-fiction sequel skips tired genre tropes to offer a fresh and thrilling adventure about hazardous archaeological excavation, a mystery in the sky and a potential threat to all of humanity...Nitty-gritty archaeology details are vivid, and easy slang creates color ("Twoing" is dating; "amaz" means amazing). Edwards shows that speculative fiction needn't be dystopic, conspiracy-filled or love-triangled to be riveting and satisfying. Amaz—simply amaz." (Kirkus)

Efaw, Amy

After. Viking 2009 350p $17.99

Grades: 7 8 9 10   **Fic**

1. School stories 2. Infants -- Fiction 3. Pregnancy -- Fiction 4. Abandoned children -- Fiction

ISBN 978-0-670-01183-4; 0-670-01183-5

LC 2010-275195

In complete denial that she is pregnant, straight-A student and star athlete Devon Davenport leaves her baby in the trash to die, and after the baby is discovered, Devon is accused of attempted murder.

"Authentic dialogue and pithy writing allow teens to feel every prick of panic, embarrassment and fear." Kirkus

Egan, Laury A.

The **Outcast** Oracle; Laury A. Egan. Humanist Press 2013 205 p. $13.46

Grades: 8 9 10 11 12   **Fic**

1. Fraud -- Fiction 2. Orphans -- Fiction 3. Grandfathers -- Fiction 4. Teenage girls -- Fiction 5. Grandparent and child -- Fiction 6. Swindlers and swindling -- Fiction

ISBN 0931779367; 9780931779367

In this book, by Laury A. Egan, "14-year-old Charlene Beth Whitestone has been deserted by her parents, leaving her in the custody of her grandfather, C.B. Although he loves Charlie, he is a charming con artist. . . . When C.B. suddenly dies, Charlie . . . must use her wits and resourcefulness to . . . [continue] her grandfather's schemes. When a . . . stranger, Blake, arrives, he . . . mounts a lucrative PR campaign, touting Charlie as an 'oracle' and arranging for her to perform miracles." (Publisher's note)

"In this brilliantly written novel, a girl who lives with her con-artist grandfather after her parents have gone wandering hopes to lead a more honest life but must scheme to get by when he dies suddenly...Hoping to avoid an orphanage, Charlie hides Grandpa's body and stashes the cash...Egan tells the story in Charlie's first-person countrified style, but with True Grit–style lofty grammar and sentence structure, in keeping with Charlie's abundant talent. It's this highly literary, easily accessible writing that lifts this story to the very top of the heap. Simply delicious fun from start to finish." (Kirkus)

Eggers, Dave, 1970-

What is the what; the autobiography of Valentino Achak Deng: a novel. Dave Eggers. McSweeney's 2006 475 p. map (pbk.) $16; $26

Grades: 11 12 Adult   **Fic**

1. Refugees 2. Students 3. Sudan -- History -- Civil

War, 1983-2005 4. Refugees -- Sudan -- Fiction 5. Refugees -- United States -- Fiction 6. Sudanese -- United States -- Fiction

ISBN 9780307385901; 1932416641; 9781932416640

LC 2007276445

This "novel's subtitle, 'The Autobiography of Valentino Achak Deng,' refers to a real-life Sudanese refugee who informs us in a brief preface that 'over the course of many years, I told my story orally to the author. He then concocted this novel, approximating my voice and using the basic events of my life as the foundation.'" The book presents the fictionalized story of Deng's "odyssey from his village in southern Sudan to temporary shelter in Ethiopia to a vast refugee camp in Kenya and finally to Atlanta." (New York Times)

Egloff, Z.

Leap. Bywater Books 2013 256 p. $14.95

Grades: 9 10 11 12 **Fic**

1. Summer -- Fiction 2. Teenagers -- Fiction 3. Family secrets -- Fiction 4. Life change events -- Fiction

ISBN 1612940234; 9781612940236

This novel, by Z. Egloff, is set in "Summer 1979. Rowan Marks is done with high school. Next comes college. And in between there's a yawning gulf--he last carefree summer vacation. . . . But Rowan's older brother Ben is smoking way too much pot. Her best friend Danny is in love with her. And Catherine, the new girl in their small Ohio town, rubs her the wrong way. . . . Catherine steals her heart, Danny falls out with her, and Ben crashes the family car, ripping the family secrets bare." (Publisher's note)

Ehrenberg, Pamela

Tillmon County fire. Eerdmans Books for Young Readers 2009 175p pa $9

Grades: 9 10 11 12 **Fic**

1. Arson -- Fiction 2. Hate crimes -- Fiction 3. West Virginia -- Fiction 4. Community life -- Fiction

ISBN 978-0-8028-5345-5; 0-8028-5345-5

LC 2008-22102

An act of arson commited as an anti-gay hate crime affects the lives of several teenagers from a small town.

"This cleverly plotted and well-crafted story of abuse and vengeance is told in pieces from the varying perspectives of a half-dozen teens, and Ehrenberg uses intertwining chapters to explore their motives and desires. . . . The vividly drawn setting, almost a character in itself, embraces an important message all readers need to hear." SLJ

Ehrenhaft, Daniel

Friend is not a verb; a novel. HarperTeen 2010 241p $16.99

Grades: 7 8 9 10 **Fic**

1. Siblings -- Fiction 2. Rock music -- Fiction 3. Family life -- Fiction 4. Bands (Music) -- Fiction 5. New York (N.Y.) -- Fiction

ISBN 978-0-06-113106-6; 0-06-113106-7

LC 2009-44006

While sixteen-year-old Hen's family and friends try to make his supposed dreams of becoming a rock star come true, he deals with the reality of being in a band with an ex-girlfriend, a friendship that may become love, and his older sister's mysterious disappearance and reappearance.

"Offbeat characters, an intriguing mystery, and a sweet romance make Ehrenhaft's . . . coming-of-age story stand out. . . . The mystery—and romance—wrap up rather neatly, but readers should be impressed by the clever surprise ending." Publ Wkly

Elkeles, Simone

How to ruin a summer vacation. Flux 2006 234p pa $9.95

Grades: 7 8 9 10 11 12 **Fic**

1. Jews -- Fiction 2. Israel -- Fiction 3. Family life -- Fiction 4. Father-daughter relationship -- Fiction

ISBN 978-0-7387-0961-1; 0-7387-0961-1

LC 2006-40592

When sixteen-year-old Amy, a spoiled American, goes to Israel for a three-month summer vacation with a father she barely knows, she is not prepared for his Jewish family and the changes they bring about in her life.

"Amy's feisty attitude and penchant for drama keep the reader engaged. With just a touch of spice to the romance, this [is a] fast read." Voice Youth Advocates

Followed by: How to ruin my teenage life (2007)

How to ruin my teenage life. Flux 2007 281p pa $8.95

Grades: 7 8 9 10 11 12 **Fic**

1. Jews -- Fiction 2. Israelis -- Fiction 3. Chicago (Ill.) -- Fiction 4. Father-daughter relationship -- Fiction

ISBN 978-0-7387-0961-1; 0-7387-1019-9

LC 2007005535

Living with her Israeli father in Chicago, seventeen-year-old Amy Nelson-Barak feels like a walking disaster, worried about her "non-boyfriend" in the Israeli army, her mother, new stepfather, and the baby they are expecting, a new boy named Nathan who has moved into her apartment building and goes to her school, and whether or not she really is the selfish snob that Nathan says she is.

"This book has laugh-out-loud moments. . . . Amy's thoughtfulness and depth raise this book above most of the chick-lit genre." Voice Youth Advocates

Other titles in this series are:

How to ruin a summer vacation (2006)

How to ruin your boyfriend's reputation (2009)

How to ruin your boyfriend's reputation. Flux 2009 257p pa $9.95

Grades: 7 8 9 10 11 12 **Fic**

1. Israel -- Fiction 2. Soldiers -- Fiction 3. Military bases -- Fiction

ISBN 978-0-7387-1879-8 pa; 0-7387-1879-3 pa

LC 2009-23853

Sequel to: How to ruin my teenage life (2007)

During the summer between her junior and senior year of high school, spoiled Chicagoan Amy Nelson-Barak volunteers for Israeli military boot camp when she learns that her boyfriend, a commando in the Israeli Defense Force, will be at the same military base

"Readers can't help but get drawn in by Amy's fun way of telling her story, and they learn a lot about Israeli teens' mandatory military service." SLJ

Perfect chemistry. Walker 2009 360p pa $9.99; $16.99

Grades: 9 10 11 12   **Fic**

1. School stories 2. Gangs -- Fiction 3. Social classes -- Fiction

ISBN 0-8027-9822-5 pa; 0-8027-9823-3; 978-0-8027-9822-0 pa; 978-0-8027-9823-7

LC 2008-13769

When wealthy, seemingly perfect Brittany and Alex Fuentes, a gang member from the other side of town, develop a relationship after Alex discovers that Brittany is not exactly who she seems to be, they must face the disapproval of their schoolmates—and others.

"Brittany's controlling parents and sister with cerebral palsy are well drawn, but it is Elkeles rendition of Alex and his life that is particularly vivid. Sprinkling his speech with Spanish, his gruff but tender interactions with his family and friends feel completely genuine. . . . This is a novel that could be embraced by male and female readers in equal measure." Booklist

Followed by Rules of attraction (2010)

Rules of attraction. Walker & Co. 2010 326p $16.99

Grades: 9 10 11 12   **Fic**

1. School stories 2. Drug traffic -- Fiction 3. Mexican Americans -- Fiction

ISBN 978-0-8027-2085-6

LC 2009-49235

Sequel to Perfect chemistry (2009)

Living on the University of Colorado-Boulder campus with his older brother Alex, a college student and ex-gang member, high school senior Carlos is not ready to give up his wild ways until he meets a shy classmate named Kiara and becomes unwillingly involved in a drug ring.

The author "delivers a steamy page-turner bound to make teens swoon." SLJ

Ellen, Laura

Blind spot; Laura Ellen. Houghton Mifflin Harcourt 2012 332 p. $16.99

Grades: 9 10 11 12   **Fic**

1. Mystery fiction 2. Homicide -- Fiction 3. Teenagers -- Fiction 4. Blind -- Fiction 5. Schools -- Fiction 6. High schools -- Fiction 7. Mystery and detective stories 8. People with disabilities -- Fiction

ISBN 0547763441; 9780547763446

LC 2012028976

Author Laura Ellen presents a murder mystery. "When AP student Roz discovers she's in a special ed class because of her visual 'disability,' she is furious. . . . Everything about Life Skills is awful, especially junkie Tricia, who, on the first day of school, somehow manages to get Roz to buy pot for her with the help of hottie Jonathan Webb. This isn't all bad, as soon Jonathan is . . . taking her to parties. Meanwhile, Roz . . . slowly comes to appreciate her fellow Life Skills classmates. And then Tricia goes missing after a calamitous party and is discovered dead months later." (Kirkus)

Elliott, Laura, 1957-

Across a war-tossed sea; L.M. Elliott. Disney-Hyperion Books 2014 256 p. (hardback) $16.99

Grades: 7 8 9 10   **Fic**

1. Brothers -- Fiction 2. Virginia -- Fiction 3. World War, 1939-1945 -- United States -- Fiction 4. World War, 1939-1945 -- Evacuation of civilians -- Fiction 5. British -- United States -- Fiction 6. Richmond (Va.) -- History -- 20th century -- Fiction

ISBN 1423157559; 9781423157557

LC 2013035303

In this book, by L.M. Elliott, "it's 1943, and World War II is raging. To escape the terror of the Blitz, ten-year-old Wesley and fourteen-year-old Charles were evacuated from England to America. After a few near misses with German U-boats and a treacherous ocean crossing, the brothers arrived in Virginia. The culture shock is intense as the London boys adjust to rural farm life and have to learn new sports, customs, and spellings, plus contend with racial segregation and bullying." (Publisher's note)

"Brothers Charles, fourteen, and Wesley, ten, are evacuated from London's 1943 Blitz and sent to live with a Virginian family. Adjusting to an American lifestyle and reconciling their misperceptions about it is stressful enough, but then they learn of Germans in a nearby POW camp. Evocative setting details and deft character portrayals make this a well-defined historical story. Includes an informative afterword." Horn Book

Elliott, Patricia

The **Pale** Assassin. Holiday House 2009 336p $17.95

Grades: 7 8 9 10   **Fic**

1. Adventure fiction 2. Siblings -- Fiction 3. France -- History -- 1789-1799, Revolution -- Fiction

ISBN 978-0-8234-2250-0; 0-8234-2250-X

LC 2009-7554

In early 1790s Paris, as the Revolution gains momentum, young and sheltered Eugenie de Boncoeur finds it difficult to tell friend from foe as she and the royalist brother she relies on become the focus of "le Fantome," the sinister spymaster with a long-held grudge against their family.

"The best aspect of this excellent work of historical fiction is Eugenie herself. Her gradual coming of age and growing political awareness provides resonant depth to what becomes a highly suspenseful survival tale." Booklist

Followed by: The traitor's smile (2011)

The **traitor's** smile. Holiday House 2011 304p $17.95

Grades: 7 8 9 10   **Fic**

1. Adventure fiction 2. Cousins -- Fiction 3. France -- History -- 1789-1799, Revolution -- Fiction

ISBN 978-0-8234-2361-3; 0-8234-2361-1

Sequel to: The Pale Assassin (2009)

First published 2010 in the United Kingdom

As the French Revolutin rages around her, wealthy and beautiful Eugenie de Boncoeur is no longer safe in her own country. She flees the bloody streeets of Paris for her cousin Hetta's house in England, narrowly excaping the clutches of the evil Pale Assassin, who is determined to force her to marry him.

Ellis, Deborah

★ No safe place. Groundwood Books/House of Anansi Press 2010 205p $16.95

Grades: 9 10 11 12   **Fic**

1. Iraq -- Fiction 2. France -- Fiction 3. Refugees -- Fiction 4. Great Britain -- Fiction

ISBN 978-0-88899-973-3

Fifteen-year-old Abdul, having lost everyone he loves, journeys from Baghdad to a migrant community in Calais where he sneaks aboard a boat bound for England, not knowing it carries a cargo of heroin, and when the vessel is involved in a skirmish and the pilot killed, it is up to Abdul and three other young stowaways to complete the journey.

"Ellis deftly uses flashbacks to fill in the backstories of each character, reminding readers of how they can never really know where people are coming from emotionally. Her writing is highly accessible, and yet understated. Orphans of the world and victims of human trafficking need all the press they can get, and this book does a great job of introducing the topic and allowing young people to see beyond the headlines of 'Another illegal accidentally dies in Chunnel.'" SLJ

Elston, Ashley

The **rules** for disappearing; Ashley Elston. 1st ed. Hyperion 2013 320 p. (reinforced) $16.99

Grades: 7 8 9 10 11 12   **Fic**

1. Witnesses -- Fiction 2. Friendship -- Fiction 3. Dysfunctional families -- Fiction 4. Schools -- Fiction 5. High schools -- Fiction 6. Moving, Household -- Fiction 7. Natchitoches (La.) -- Fiction

ISBN 1423168976; 9781423168973

LC 2012035122

In this book by Ashley Elston, "seventeen-year-old Meg Jones . . . and her family are in the witness protection program, and they've changed towns six times in less than a year. . . . Meg's mother is an alcoholic, her father is depressed and secretive, and her 11-year-old sister is having trouble coping with all of the change. Fed up, Meg wants out of the program and will do anything to save her family, including digging up what her father did to get them into this mess." (Publishers Weekly)

"The fresh first-person narration serves the story well, providing grounding in reality as events spin out of control. Though the plot may seem a bit far-fetched at times, the realistic setting, believable romance and spunky protagonist will make this one worth the trip for mystery and romance fans." Kirkus

Emond, Stephen

Bright lights, dark nights; Stephen Emond. Roaring Brook Press 2015 384 p. illustrations (hardback) $17.99

Grades: 7 8 9 10   **Fic**

1. Race relations -- Fiction 2. Dating (Social customs) -- Fiction 3. Schools -- Fiction 4. Friendship -- Fiction 5. Best friends -- Fiction 6. High schools -- Fiction 7. Fathers and sons -- Fiction 8. Single-parent families -- Fiction

ISBN 1626722064; 9781626722064

LC 2014047413

In this novel, by Stephen Emond, "Walter Wilcox has never been in love. That is, until he meets Naomi, and

sparks, and clever jokes, fly. But when his cop dad is caught in a racial profiling scandal, Walter and Naomi, who is African American, are called out at school, home, and online. Can their bond (and mutual love of the Foo Fighters) keep them together?" (Publisher's note)

"Readers coming to this story for romance may feel shortchanged, as the relationship here is more true-to-life and awkward than swooningly romantic, but that's what sets Emond's book apart. A real slice of contemporary teenage life that's painfully honest about the below-the-surface racism in today's America." Booklist

Happyface. Little, Brown and Co. 2010 307p il $16.99

Grades: 7 8 9 10   **Fic**

1. School stories 2. Diaries -- Fiction 3. Divorce -- Fiction 4. Dating (Social customs) -- Fiction

ISBN 978-0-316-04100-3; 0-316-04100-9

LC 2008-47386

After going through traumatic times, a troubled, socially awkward teenager moves to a new school where he tries to reinvent himself.

"The illustrations range from comics to more fleshed-out drawings. Just like Happyface's writing, they can be whimsical, thoughtful, boyishly sarcastic, off-the-cuff, or achingly beautiful." Publ Wkly

Engdahl, Sylvia Louise

★ **Enchantress** from the stars; foreword by Lois Lowry. Firebird 2003 288p pa $6.99

Grades: 7 8 9 10 11 12   **Fic**

1. Science fiction

ISBN 0-14-250037-2

A reissue of the title first published 1970 by Atheneum Pubs.

A Newbery Medal honor book, 1971

When young Elana unexpectedly joins the team leaving the spaceship to study the planet Andrecia, she becomes an integral part of an adventure involving three very different civilizations, each one centered on the third planet from the star in its own solar system

"Emphasis is on the intricate pattern of events rather than on characterization, and readers will find fascinating symbolism—and philosophical parallels to what they may have observed or thought. The book is completely absorbing and should have a wider appeal than much science fiction." Horn Book

Engle, Margarita

★ **Firefly** letters; a suffragette's journey to Cuba. Henry Holt & Co. 2010 151p $16.99

Grades: 7 8 9 10 11 12   **Fic**

1. Authors 2. Novelists 3. Novels in verse 4. Cuba -- Fiction 5. Slavery -- Fiction 6. Sex role -- Fiction

ISBN 978-0-8050-9082-6; 0-8050-9082-7

LC 2009-23445

"This engaging title documents 50-year-old Swedish suffragette and novelist Fredrika Bremer's three-month travels around Cuba in 1851. Based in the home of a wealthy sugar planter, Bremer journeys around the country with her host's teenaged slave Cecilia, who longs for her mother and home in the Congo. Elena, the planter's privileged 12-year-old daughter, begins to accompany them on their trips into the countryside. . . . Using elegant free verse and alternating among each character's point of view, Engle offers powerful glimpses into Cuban life at that time. Along the way, she comments on slavery, the rights of women, and the stark contrast between Cuba's rich and poor." SLJ

Hurricane dancers; the first Caribbean pirate shipwreck. Henry Holt and Co. 2011 145p $16.99
Grades: 6 7 8 9 10   **Fic**
1. Novels in verse 2. Pirates -- Fiction 3. Shipwrecks -- Fiction 4. Caribbean region -- Fiction 5. Native Americans -- West Indies -- Fiction
ISBN 978-0-8050-9240-0; 0-8050-9240-4
LC 2010-11690

This is an "accomplished historical novel in verse set in the Caribbean. . . . The son of a Taíno Indian mother and a Spanish father, [Quebrado] is taken in 1510 from his village on the island that is present-day Cuba and enslaved on a pirate's ship, where a brutal conquistador . . . is held captive for ransom. When a hurricane destroys the boat, Quebrado is pulled from the water by a fisherman, Naridó, whose village welcomes him, but escape from the past proves nearly impossible. . . . Engle fictionalizes historical fact in a powerful, original story. . . . Engle distills the emotion in each episode with potent rhythms, sounds, and original, unforgettable imagery." Booklist

★ The **Lightning** Dreamer; Cuba's Greatest Abolitionist. Margarita Engle. Houghton Mifflin Harcourt 2013 192 p. $16.99
Grades: 6 7 8 9 10   **Fic**
1. Historical fiction 2. Novels in verse 3. Authors -- Fiction 4. Feminists -- Fiction 5. Abolitionists -- Fiction 6. Cuba -- History -- 1810-1899 -- Fiction
ISBN 0547807430; 9780547807430
LC 2013003913
Pura Belpre Author Honor Book (2014)

This book is a "work of historical fiction about Cuban poet, author, antislavery activist and feminist Gertrudis Gómez de Avellaneda. Written in free verse, the story tells of how Tula, which was her childhood nickname, grows up in libraries, which she calls 'a safe place to heal/ and dream . . .,' influenced by the poetry of Jose Maria Heredia." (School Library Journal)

Includes bibliographical references.

Eulberg, Elizabeth

Revenge of the Girl With the Great Personality; Elizabeth Eulberg. Scholastic 2013 272 p. (hardcover) $17.99
Grades: 7 8 9 10   **Fic**
1. Sisters -- Fiction 2. Beauty contests -- Fiction
ISBN 9780545476997; 0545476992

"Everybody loves Lexi. She's popular, smart, funny . . . but she's never been one of . . . the pretty ones who get all the attention from guys. And on top of that, her seven-year-old sister, Mackenzie, is a terror in a tiara . . . . Lexi's sick of it. . . . The time has come for Lexi to step out from the sidelines. Girls without great personalities aren't going to know what hit them. Because Lexi's going to play the beauty game." (Publisher's note)

Evans, Richard Paul

Battle of the Ampere; 3 Richard Paul Evans. Mercury Ink/Simon Pulse 2013 307 p. $17.99
Grades: 6 7 8 9   **Fic**
1. Science fiction 2. Electricity -- Fiction 3. Friendship -- Fiction 4. Tourette syndrome -- Fiction
ISBN 1442475110; 9781442475113; 9781442475137
LC 2013026653

This young adult science fiction novel, by Richard Paul Evans, part three in the "Michael Vey" series, "Michael, Taylor, Ostin and the rest of the Electroclan have destroyed the largest of the Elgen Starxource plants, but now they're on the run. The Elgen have teamed up with the Peruvian army to capture them, and only Michael remains free. With his friends due to stand trial for terrorism . . . Michael will need all his wits and his abilities if he's to save them." (Publisher's note)

"Though the Electroclan's destruction of the Starxource plant was a major victory over the Elgen, the Peruvian government has branded it a terroristic act. Hunted by both the army and the Elgen fleet, Michael and friends must evade capture as they plan their next move against Dr. Hatch. Evans develops character relationships better in this third installment, which continues to be exciting." Horn Book

Other titles in the series include:
The Prisoner of Cell 25 (2011)
Rise of the Elgen (2012)
Hunt for Jade Drago (2014)

Michael Vey; rise of the Elgen. by Richard Paul Evans. Mercury Ink/Simon Pulse 2012 335 p. (hardcover) $17.99
Grades: 6 7 8 9   **Fic**
1. Fantasy fiction 2. Voyages and travels -- Fiction 3. Peru -- Fiction 4. Science fiction 5. Friendship -- Fiction 6. Electricity -- Fiction 7. Tourette syndrome -- Fiction
ISBN 1442454148; 9781442454149; 9781442454620; 9781442475106
LC 2012022717
Sequel to: Michael Vey, the prisoner of cell 25

This is the second book in Richard Paul Evans's Michael Vey series. Here, "after using their wits and powers to narrowly escape an Elgen trap, a mysterious voice leads the Electroclan to the jungles of Peru in search of Michael's mother. Once there, they discover that Dr. Hatch and the Elgen are far more powerful than anyone realizes. . . . Only the Electroclan and an anonymous voice now stand in the way of the Elgen's plan for global domination." (Publisher's note)

Extence, Gavin, 1982-

The **Universe** Versus Alex Woods; Gavin Extence. Little Brown & Co. 2014 320 p. $15
Grades: 9 10 11 12 Adult   **Fic**
1. Astrology -- Fiction 2. Astronomy -- Fiction 3. Supernatural -- Fiction 4. Curiosities and wonders -- Fiction
ISBN 031624659X; 9780316246590
Alex Awards Winner (2014)

In this book, by Gavin Extence, "a rare meteorite struck Alex Woods when he was ten years old, leaving scars and marking him for an extraordinary future. The son of a fortune teller, bookish, and an easy target for bullies, Alex hasn't had the easiest childhood. But when he meets curmudgeonly widower Mr. Peterson, he finds an unlikely friend. Someone who teaches him that that you only get one shot at life. That you have to make it count." (Publisher's note)

"Most teens think the universe is against them at some point. Seventeen-year-old Alex Woods has plenty of evidence for his case: a tarot-reading witch for a mother, his father a one-night Solstice stand long since forgotten, a chunk of meteorite crashing through the roof and smashing into him, the onset of epileptic seizures, and school bullies eager to target him...A bittersweet, cross-audience charmer, this debut novel will appeal to guys, YA readers, and Vonnegut and coming-of-age fiction fans.—" (Library Journal)

Falkner, Brian

Brain Jack. Random House 2010 349p $17.99; lib bdg $20.99

Grades: 7 8 9 10   **Fic**

1. Science fiction 2. Computers -- Fiction 3. New York (N.Y.) -- Fiction

ISBN 978-0-375-84366-2; 0-375-84366-3; 978-0-375-93924-2 lib bdg; 0-375-93924-5 lib bdg

LC 2008-43386

In a near-future New York City, fourteen-year-old computer genius Sam Wilson manages to hack into the AT&T network and sets off a chain of events that have a profound effect on human activity throughout the world.

"This fast-paced, cyber thriller is intelligent, well-written, and very intuitive to the possibilities and challenges we may face in our ever changing digital society." Libr Media Connect

The project. Random House 2011 275p $17.99

Grades: 6 7 8 9 10   **Fic**

1. Adventure fiction 2. Time travel -- Fiction 3. National socialism -- Fiction 4. World War, 1939-1945 -- Fiction

ISBN 978-0-375-96945-4; 0-375-96945-4

LC 2010033449

After discovering a terrible secret hidden in the most boring book in the world, Iowa fifteen-year-olds Luke and Tommy find out that members of a secret Nazi organization intend to use this information to rewrite history.

"The wacky unbelievability of this story in no way detracts from its enjoyment. It reads like an action movie, with plenty of chases, explosions, and by-a-hair escapes." SLJ

Falls, Kat

Inhuman; Kat Falls. Scholastic Press 2013 384 p. $17.99

Grades: 7 8 9 10   **Fic**

1. Dystopian fiction 2. Apocalyptic fiction 3. Survival 4. Dystopias 5. Science fiction 6. Survival -- Fiction 7. Quarantine -- Fiction 8. Virus diseases -- Fiction 9. Fathers and daughters -- Fiction

ISBN 054537099X; 9780545370998

LC 2013026360

In this dystopian novel by Kat Falls, "the United States east of the Mississippi has been abandoned. Now called the Feral Zone, a reference to the virus that turned millions of people into bloodthirsty savages, the entire area is off-limits.

. . . [Protagonist] Lane gets the shock of her life when she learns that someone close to her has crossed into the Feral Zone." (Publisher's note)

"Years ago, the U.S. was bisected by a pandemic (spread by biting) that causes humans to mutate into feral human-animal hybrids. When pampered teenager Lane is blackmailed into the Feral Zone, she joins the search for a cure and discovers the gray area between human and feral. While Lane and her love triangle are bland, the zombie-apocalypse-meets-wereanimals-gone-wild setup captures the imagination." (Horn Book)

Fantaskey, Beth

Buzz kill; by Beth Fantaskey. Houghton Mifflin Harcourt 2014 368 p. $17.99

Grades: 8 9 10 11 12   **Fic**

1. Murder -- Fiction 2. High schools -- Fiction 3. Football -- Coaching -- Fiction 4. Mystery and detective stories 5. Coaches (Athletics) -- Fiction 6. Dating (Social customs) -- Fiction

ISBN 0547393105; 9780547393100

LC 2013011423

In this book, by Beth Fantaskey, "when the widely disliked Honeywell Stingers football coach is found murdered, 17-year-old Millie is determined to investigate. She is chasing a lead for the school newspaper--and looking to clear her father, the assistant coach, and prime suspect. . . . Millie joins forces with her mysterious classmate Chase who seems to want to help her even while covering up secrets of his own." (Publisher's note)

"When the head football coach is killed, seventeen-year-old Millie, a school reporter obsessed with Nancy Drew, sets out to learn the truth and clear her assistant-coach father of any suspicion. She gets some unexpected help from dreamy quarterback Chase, who's hiding some secrets. This entertaining sleuth story is a good choice for teens now graduated from books featuring Millie's literary hero." Horn Book

Jessica's guide to dating on the dark side. Harcourt 2009 354p $17

Grades: 8 9 10 11 12   **Fic**

1. Vampires -- Fiction

ISBN 978-0-15-206384-9; 0-15-206384-6

LC 2007-49002

Seventeen-year-old Jessica, adopted and raised in Pennsylvania, learns that she is descended from a royal line of Romanian vampires and that she is betrothed to a vampire prince, who poses as a foreign exchange student while courting her.

"Fantaskey makes this premise work by playing up its absurdities without laughing at them. . . . The romance sizzles, the plot develops ingeniously and suspensefully, and the satire sings." Publ Wkly

Farinango, Maria Virginia

★ **The Queen** of Water. Delacorte Press 2011 352p $16.99; lib bdg $19.99

Grades: 8 9 10 11 12   **Fic**

1. Ecuador -- Fiction 2. Social classes -- Fiction

ISBN 978-0-385-73897-2; 0-385-73897-8; 978-0-385-90761-3 lib bdg; 0-385-90761-3 lib bdg

LC 2010-10512

"The complexities of class and ethnicity within Ecuadorian society are explained seamlessly within the context of the first-person narrative, and a glossary and pronunciation guide further help to plunge readers into the novel's world. By turns heartbreaking, infuriating and ultimately inspiring." Kirkus

Farish, Terry

★ The **good** braider; by Terry Farish. Marshall Cavendish 2012 221 p. (hardcover) $17.99

Grades: 9 10 11 12   **Fic**

1. Refugees -- Fiction 2. Sudanese Americans -- Fiction 3. Mother-daughter relationship -- Fiction 4. Immigrants -- Fiction 5. Portland (Me.) -- Fiction 6. Mothers and daughters -- Fiction 7. Sudan -- History -- Civil War, 1983-2005 -- Fiction

ISBN 0761462678; 9780761462675; 9780761462682

LC 2011033659

In this novel by Terry Farish, written "in . . . free verse," protagonist Viola tells "the story of her family's journey from war-torn Sudan, to Cairo, and finally to Portland, Maine. Here, in the sometimes too close embrace of the local Southern Sudanese Community, she dreams of South Sudan while she tries to navigate the strange world of America . . . a world that puts her into sharp conflict with her traditional mother." (Publisher's note)

Farizan, Sara

★ **If** you could be mine; a novel. Sara Farizan. Algonquin 2013 256 p. (hardcover) $16.95

Grades: 8 9 10 11 12   **Fic**

1. Sex reassignment surgery -- Fiction 2. Iran -- Social conditions -- Fiction 3. Iran -- Fiction 4. Love -- Fiction 5. Lesbians -- Fiction 6. Friendship -- Fiction 7. Best friends -- Fiction

ISBN 1616202513; 9781616202514

LC 2013008931

Rainbow List (2014)

Lambda Literary Awards Wiiner - LGBT Children's/YA (2014)

This novel, set in Iran, 17-year-old Sahar, who has wanted to marry her best friend Nasrin since they were six years old, dreams of living openly with her lover. Nasrin prefers to accept an arranged marriage, while intending to continue their illicit affair. Exposed to a world of sexual diversity by her gay cousin and made desperate by Nasrin's impending marriage, Sahar explores the one legal option for the two of them to be together: her own sex reassignment surgery." (Publishers Weekly)

"Rich with details of life in contemporary Iran, this is a GLBTQ story that we haven't seen before in YA fiction." SLJ

Tell me again how a crush should feel; Sara Farizan. Algonquin Young Readers 2014 304 p. hc $16.95

Grades: 9 10 11 12   **Fic**

1. Love -- Fiction 2. Lesbians -- Fiction 3. Friendship -- Fiction 4. High schools -- Fiction 5. Iranian Americans -- Fiction 6. Schools -- Fiction

ISBN 161620284X; 9781616202842

LC 2014021580

This book, by Sara Farizan, follows "sixteen-year-old Iranian American Leila Azadi. . . . Afraid to tell her best friends and her conservative family that she is gay, Leila finds herself in a secret relationship with Saskia, a gorgeous, sophisticated new girl with a decidedly wicked side. As Saskia reveals herself to be a master manipulator, Leila turns to an unexpected ally, Lisa, an old friend who recently lost her brother in a car accident." (Horn Book Magazine)

"Farizan fashions an empowering romance featuring a lovable, awkward protagonist who just needs a little nudge of confidence to totally claim her multifaceted identity." Booklist

Farmer, Nancy

★ The **Ear,** the Eye, and the Arm; a novel. Puffin Books 1995 311p pa $6.99

Grades: 6 7 8 9 10   **Fic**

1. Science fiction 2. Zimbabwe -- Fiction

ISBN 978-0-14-131109-8; 0-14-131109-6

LC 95019982

First published 1994 by Orchard Books

A Newbery Medal honor book, 1995

In 2194 in Zimbabwe, General Matsika's three children are kidnapped and put to work in a plastic mine while three mutant detectives use their special powers to search for them

"Throughout the story, it's the thrilling adventure that will grab readers, who will also like the comic, tender characterizations." Booklist

★ The **house** of the scorpion. Atheneum Bks. for Young Readers 2002 380p $17.95; pa $7.99

Grades: 7 8 9 10   **Fic**

1. Science fiction 2. Cloning -- Fiction

ISBN 0-689-85222-3; 0-689-85223-1 pa

LC 2001-56594

A Newbery Medal honor book, 2003

In a future where humans despise clones, Matt enjoys special status as the young clone of El Patrón, the 142-year-old leader of a corrupt drug empire nestled between Mexico and the United States. "Grades seven to ten." (Bull Cent Child Books)

"This is a powerful, ultimately hopeful, story that builds on today's sociopolitical, ethical, and scientific issues and prognosticates a compelling picture of what the future could bring." Booklist

★ The **lord** of Opium; Nancy Farmer. Atheneum Books for Young Readers 2013 432 p. (hardcover) $17.99

Grades: 7 8 9 10   **Fic**

1. Fantasy fiction 2. Drug traffic -- Fiction 3. Science fiction 4. Cloning -- Fiction 5. Environmental degradation -- Fiction

ISBN 1442482540; 9781442482548

LC 2012030418

Sequel to: House of the scorpion (2002)

This book is the sequel to Nancy Farmer's "The House of the Scorpion." Here, "Matt was a clone of El Patrón, drug lord of Opium, but with El Patrón dead, Matt is now considered by international law to be fully human and El Patrón's rightful heir. But it's a corrupt land . . . ruled over by drug lords and worked by armies of Illegals turned into 'eejits,' or zombies. Matt wants to bring reform." (Kirkus Reviews)

Farrey, Brian

With or without you. Simon Pulse 2011 348p pa $8.99; ebook $7.99

Grades: 9 10 11 12   **Fic**

1. Wisconsin -- Fiction 2. Friendship -- Fiction 3. Hate crimes -- Fiction 4. Homosexuality -- Fiction
ISBN 978-1-4424-0699-5 pa; 978-1-4424-0700-8 ebook

LC 2010-38722

When eighteen-year-old best friends Evan and Davis of Madison, Wisconsin, join a community center group called "chasers" to gain acceptance and knowledge of gay history, there may be fatal consequences.

"Farrey paces his story beautifully, covering many contemporary issues for teens about coming out, friendship, relationships, and following a dangerous crowd simply for a sense of belonging." SLJ

Federle, Tim

★ **The great** American whatever; Tim Federle. Simon & Schuster Books for Young Readers 2016 288 p. (hardback) $17.99

Grades: 9 10 11 12   **Fic**

1. Grief -- Fiction 2. Gay men -- Fiction 3. Screenwriters -- Fiction 4. Gays -- Fiction
ISBN 9781481404099; 9781481404105; 9781481404112

LC 2015015712

In this book, by Tim Federle, "Quinn Roberts is a sixteen-year-old smart aleck and Hollywood hopeful whose only worry used to be writing convincing dialogue for the movies he made with his sister Annabeth. Of course, that was all before—before Quinn stopped going to school, before his mom started sleeping on the sofa and before the car accident that changed everything. Enter: Geoff, Quinn's best friend who insists it's time that Quinn came out—at least from hibernation." (Publisher's note)

"It is cleverly plotted and smoothly written with many scenes presented in screenplay style. More important, while it has its serious aspects, it is whimsical, wry, and unfailingly funny—a refreshing change from the often dour nature of much LGBTQ literature. Bright

Fehlbaum, Beth

Big fat disaster; Beth Fehlbaum. Merit Press, an imprint of F+W Media, Inc. 2014 288 p. (pb) $17.99

Grades: 7 8 9 10   **Fic**

1. Moving -- Fiction 2. Family life -- Fiction 3. Eating disorders -- Fiction 4. Overweight teenagers -- Fiction 5. Texas -- Fiction 6. Schools -- Fiction 7. High schools -- Fiction 8. Moving, Household -- Fiction
ISBN 1440570485; 9781440570483

LC 2013044512

In this book, by Beth Fehlbaum, "insecure, shy, and way overweight, Colby hates the limelight as much as her pageant-pretty mom and sisters love it. It's her life: Dad's a superstar, running for office on a family values platform. Then suddenly, he ditches his marriage for a younger woman and gets caught stealing money from the campaign. Everyone hates Colby for finding out and blowing the whistle on him. From a mansion, they end up in a poor relative's trailer." (Publisher's note)

"Colby's life as the heavy daughter of a disapproving former Miss Texas beauty queen is difficult enough, but it gets worse very quickly once she discovers a photo of her politician father kissing another woman...Colby's experiences, while extreme, ring true, and the fast pace, lively and profane dialogue, and timely topic make it a quick and enjoyable read." (Kirkus)

Hope in Patience. WestSide Books 2010 312p $16.95

Grades: 10 11 12   **Fic**

1. School stories 2. Texas -- Fiction 3. Family life -- Fiction 4. Child sexual abuse -- Fiction 5. Post-traumatic stress disorder -- Fiction
ISBN 978-1-934813-41-6

LC 2010-31118

After years of sexual abuse by her stepfather, fifteen-year-old Ashley Asher starts a better life with her father and stepmother in Patience, Texas, but despite psychotherapy and new friends, she still suffers from Post Traumatic Stress Disorder.

"Teens who are attracted by . . . [Ashley's] honesty and her compelling story will come away with a deeper understanding of trauma and healing. This book will open hearts and might well save lives." SLJ

Feinstein, John

Foul trouble; by John Feinstein. Alfred A. Knopf 2013 400 p. (trade) $16.99

Grades: 8 9 10 11 12   **Fic**

1. College basketball -- Fiction 2. High school students -- Fiction 3. Basketball -- Fiction 4. African Americans -- Fiction
ISBN 0375869646; 9780375869648; 9780375871696; 9780375982460

LC 2012042982

In this basketball novel by John Feinstein, "Danny Wilcox is Terrell's best friend and teammate, and a top prospect himself, but these days it seems like everyone wants to get close to Terrell: the sneaker guys, the money managers, the college boosters. They show up offering fast cars, hot girls, and cold, hard cash. They say they just want to help, but their kind of help could get Terrell disqualified." (Publisher's note)

"Danny works to guide his friend and teammate, Terrell Jamerson, through the trials and temptations of the college recruiting process, as agents, boosters, and other "dudes" look to hitch a ride with the top recruit. Engaging characters (including real-life cameos), intense basketball action, and sports-writer Feinstein's behind-the-scenes background provide an authentic view of a system that can both promote and exploit young athletes." (Horn Book)

Feldman, Ruth Tenzer

Blue thread; Ruth Tenzer Feldman. Ooligan Press 2012 302 p. $12.95

Grades: 7 8 9 10   **Fic**

1. Historical fiction 2. Jewish women -- Fiction 3.

Women's rights -- Fiction
ISBN 1932010416; 9781932010411

LC 2011024382

This young adult novel focuses on Miriam, a young Jewish girl in 1912 Portland, Oregon. "While her mother plans their trip to New York City to find her a husband, Miriam gets caught up in the fight for women's suffrage. At first she's nervous about going against her parents' wishes, but curiosity gets the better of her . . . . However, after a mysterious girl named Serakh whisks Miriam back to biblical times, her desire to be a larger part of the movement becomes stronger." (School Library Journal)

Felin, M. Sindy

Touching snow. Atheneum Books for Young Readers 2007 234p $16.99

Grades: 9 10 11 12   **Fic**
1. Child abuse -- Fiction 2. Stepfathers -- Fiction 3. New York (N.Y.) -- Fiction 4. Haitian Americans -- Fiction
ISBN 978-1-4169-1795-3; 1-4169-1795-0

LC 2006-14794

After her stepfather is arrested for child abuse, thirteen-year-old Karina's home life improves but while the severity of her older sister's injuries and the urging of her younger sister, their uncle, and a friend tempt her to testify against him, her mother and other well-meaning adults persuade her to claim responsibility.

"Although the resolution is brutal, this story is a compelling read from an important and much-needed new voice. Readers will cheer for the young narrator." SLJ

Fforde, Jasper

The **Eye** of Zoltar; 2 by Jasper Fforde. Houghton Mifflin Harcourt 2014 416 p. (The Chronicles of Kazam) (hardback) $16.99

Grades: 7 8 9 10   **Fic**
1. Fantasy fiction 2. Magic -- Fiction 3. Orphans -- Fiction 4. Voyages and travels -- Fiction 5. Fantasy
ISBN 0547738498; 9780547738499

LC 2014001381

In this book, by Jasper Fforde, "although she's an orphan in indentured servitude, sixteen-year-old Jennifer Strange is pretty good at her job of managing the unpredictable crew at Kazam Mystical Arts Management. She already solved the Dragon Problem, avoided mass destruction by Quarkbeast, and helped save magic in the Ununited Kingdoms. Yet even Jennifer may be defeated when the long-absent Mighty Shandar makes an astonishing appearance and commands her to find the Eye of Zoltar." (Publisher's note)

"This installment is darker than the first two outings and contains a Grand Canyon–sized cliff-hanger of an ending. Fans of strong, brave, intelligent females will root for Jennifer and her gang, and wait impatiently for the next book." SLJ

The **Eyre** affair; a novel. Viking 2002 374p hardcover o.p. pa $14

Grades: 11 12 Adult   **Fic**
1. Fantasy fiction
ISBN 0-670-03064-3; 0-14-200180-5 pa

LC 2001-43775

First published 2001 in the United Kingdom
Alex Award (2003)

"It's 1985 in England, at least on the calendar; the Crimean War is in its hundred-and-thirty-first year; time travel is nothing new; Japanese tourists slip in and out of Victorian novels; and the literary branch of the special police, led gamely by the beguiling Thursday Next, are pursuing Acheron Hades, who has stolen the manuscript of 'Martin Chuzzlewit' and set his sights on kidnapping the character Jane Eyre, a theft that could have disastrous consequences for Brontë lovers who like their story straight. This rambunctious caper could be taken as a warning about what might happen if society considered literature really important—like, say, energy futures or accounting." New Yorker

Other titles featuring Thursday Next are:
Thursday Next in Lost in a good book (2003)
Thursday Next in Something rotten (2004)
Thursday Next in The well of lost plots (2004)

★ The **last** Dragonslayer; Jasper Fforde. Hodder & Stoughton 2010 281 p. (The Chronicles of Kazam) $16.99; (hbk.) $16.99

Grades: 7 8 9 10   **Fic**
1. Magic -- Fiction 2. Dragons -- Fiction 3. Employment agencies -- Fiction
ISBN 978-0547738475; 1444707175; 1444707191; 9781444707175; 9781444707199

LC 2010551874

In this book by Jasper Fforde, part of the Chronicles of Kazam series, "magic is fading. . . . Fifteen-year-old foundling Jennifer Strange runs Kazam, an employment agency for magicians -- but it's hard to stay in business when magic is drying up. And then the visions start, predicting the death of the world's last dragon at the hands of an unnamed Dragonslayer. If the visions are true, everything will change for Kazam -- and for Jennifer." (Publisher's note)

Lost in a good book; a Thursday Next novel. Viking 2003 399p il hardcover o.p. pa $15

Grades: 11 12 Adult   **Fic**
1. Books and reading 2. Fantasies
ISBN 0-670-03190-9; 0-14-200403-0 pa

LC 2002-71304

Companion volume to: The Eyre affair
First published 2002 in the United Kingdom with title: Lost in a good book

"Time flies—and leaps and zigzags—while reading this wickedly funny and clever fantasy. Would-be wordsmiths and mystery fans will find the surreal genre-buster irresistible." Publ Wkly

Something rotten; a Thursday Next novel. Viking 2004 383p $24.95

Grades: 11 12 Adult   **Fic**
1. Fantasy fiction 2. Books and reading 3. Fantasies 4. Books and reading -- Fiction
ISBN 0-670-03359-6

LC 2004-49497

Published in the United Kingdom with title: Something rotten

Thursday Next, "the literary detective is fed up with the bureaucracy and red tape of BookWorld, where the characters and plots of novels are alive and need constant governing. The Council of Genres refuses to accept her resignation as head of JurisFiction, but she returns to her home in the real world anyway—Swindon, England. Here she hopes to regroup, raise her two-year-old son, Friday, and find some way to uneradicate her husband, Landen Parke-Laine. But this may be Next's most complicated caper yet. Still facing unfinished disciplinary action from earlier outings, she must also sort out personality conflicts in Hamlet; protect Danish literature from a book-burning campaign; rescue the president from the realm of the semidead; and manage the underdog Swindon Mallets croquet team to victory in the SuperHoop." Booklist

The **song** of the Quarkbeast; Jasper Fforde. Houghton Mifflin Harcourt 2013 304 p. (The chronicles of Kazam) $16.99

Grades: 7 8 9 10   Fic
1. Magic 2. Fantasy fiction
ISBN 054773848X; 9780547738482

LC 2012047318

This is the second book in Jasper Fforde's Chronicles of Kazam series. Here, now "that magical power is on the rise again, the despotic King Snodd IV hopes to cash in, specifically by putting the wizards who work at Kazam Mystical Arts Management under his control by proposing they merge with iMagic, the rival house led by the Amazing Blix, a questionable character with a new royal appointment: Court Mystician." (Publishers Weekly)

Fichera, Liz
Hooked; Liz Fichera. Harlequin Books 2013 368 p. $9.99

Grades: 9 10 11 12   Fic
1. Love stories 2. Golf -- Fiction 3. School sports -- Fiction
ISBN 0373210728; 9780373210725

In this young adult romance story, by Liz Fichera, Fred Oday finds herself as the first girl on her school's golf team. She is worried about being assigned to the boys' team and what it will do to her popularity, but she also can't help noticing the attractive Ryan Berenger who she's been assigned to work with by the coach.

Fiedler, Lisa
Romeo's ex; Rosaline's story. Henry Holt 2006 246p $16.95

Grades: 8 9 10 11 12   Fic
1. Poets 2. Authors 3. Dramatists 4. Love stories
ISBN 978-0-8050-7500-7; 0-8050-7500-3

LC 2005-35692

In a story based on the Shakespeare play, sixteen-year-old Roseline, who is studying to be a healer, becomes romantically entangled with the Montague family even as her beloved young cousin, Juliet Capulet, defies the family feud to secretly marry Romeo.

"This novel manages to be both witty and multilayered, leaving readers with plenty to ponder." Publ Wkly

Fine, Sarah
Of Metal and Wishes; Sarah Fine. Margaret K. McElderry 2014 336 p. 22 cm $17.99

Grades: 9 10 11 12   Fic
1. Love stories 2. Ghost stories 3. China -- Fiction 4. Wishes 5. Prejudices 6. Steel-works 7. Teenage girls
ISBN 144248358X; 9781442483583
Sequel: Of Dreams and Rust (2015)

In this novel by Sarah Fine, "sixteen-year-old Wen assists her father in his medical clinic, housed in a slaughterhouse staffed by the Noor, men hired as cheap factory labor. Wen often hears . . . a ghost in the slaughterhouse, a ghost who grants wishes to those who need them most. And after one of the Noor humiliates Wen, the ghost grants an impulsive wish of hers--brutally. Guilt-ridden, Wen befriends the Noor, including the outspoken leader, a young man named Melik." (Publisher's note)

"Fine creates a memorable atmosphere of desperation, deftly weaving together numerous subplots that intersect in a grisly and satisfying climax." Publishers Weekly

Fink, Mark
The **summer** I got a life. WestSide 2009 196p $15.95

Grades: 7 8 9   Fic
1. Love stories 2. Wisconsin -- Fiction 3. People with disabilities -- Fiction
ISBN 978-1-934813-12-6; 1-934813-12-5

"Andy is pumped that his freshman year is over and his vacation is about to begin. Then his dad's promotion changes everything. Instead of Hawaii, Andy is spending two weeks on a farm in Wisconsin with his somewhat odd, but well-meaning, aunt and uncle. Once there, though, he finds that things aren't so bad particularly when he spots 'the most incredible-looking girl he has ever seen.' . . . Andy discovers that an accident at age four has left Laura confined to a wheelchair. . . . This is an engaging novel filled with life lessons, a little romance, humor, sports, and fraternal love." SLJ

Finneyfrock, Karen
Starbird Murphy and the world outside; by Karen Finneyfrock. Viking 2014 384 p. (hardcover) $17.99

Grades: 9 10 11 12   Fic
1. Cults -- Fiction 2. Communal living -- Fiction 3. Schools -- Fiction 4. High schools -- Fiction 5. Washington (State) -- Fiction 6. Waiters and waitresses -- Fiction
ISBN 0670012769; 9780670012763

LC 2013027007

This young adult novel by Karen Finneyfrock describes how "In her sixteen years of life, Starbird has . . . never been in a car. She's never used a cell phone. That's because Starbird has always lived on the Free Family Farm, a commune in the woods of Washington State. But all that is about to change. When Starbird gets her 'Calling' to be a waitress at the Free Family's restaurant in Seattle, she decides to leave behind the only home she's ever known." (Publisher's note)

""My breath caught in my throat. Io didn't believe in the Translations?" When Starbird leaves the Free Family Farm commune to work at the cult's cafe, she begins to uncover details about the life she shares with her Family that some members would rather remained hidden. An unwitting catalyst, Starbird's voice remains strong as her worldview begins to change." Horn Book

The **sweet** revenge of Celia Door; by Karen Finneyfrock. Viking 2013 272 p. (hardcover) $16.99

Grades: 7 8 9 10   **Fic**
  1. School stories 2. Revenge -- Fiction 3. Teenagers -- Fiction 4. Gays -- Fiction 5. Poetry -- Fiction 6. Schools -- Fiction 7. High schools -- Fiction 8. Hershey (Pa.) -- Fiction 9. Family life -- Pennsylvania -- Hershey -- Fiction
  ISBN 0670012750; 9780670012756
                        LC 2011047221
  In this teen novel, by Karen Finneyfrock, "Celia Door enters her freshman year . . . with giant boots, dark eyeliner, and a thirst for revenge against Sandy Firestone. . . . But then Celia meets Drake, the cool new kid from New York City who entrusts her with his deepest, darkest secret. When Celia's quest for justice threatens her relationship with Drake, she's forced to decide which is sweeter: revenge or friendship." (Publisher's note)

Fisher, Catherine
Darkwater; by Catherine Fisher. Penguin Group USA 2012 229p (hardcover) $16.99

Grades: 6 7 8 9 10 11 12   **Fic**
  1. Sin 2. Teenagers -- Fiction 3. Private schools -- Fiction 4. Soul -- Fiction 5. Twins -- Fiction 6. England -- Fiction 7. Schools -- Fiction 8. Brothers -- Fiction 9. Supernatural -- Fiction 10. Great Britain -- History -- Edward VII, 1901-1910 -- Fiction
  ISBN 9780803738188
                        LC 2011048063
  In author Catherine Fisher's book, "Sarah Trevelyan would give anything to regain the power and wealth her family has lost, so she makes a bargain with Azrael, Lord of Darkwater Hall. He gives her one hundred years and the means to accomplish her objective--in exchange for her soul. Fast-forward a hundred years to Tom, a fifteen-year-old boy who dreams of attending Darkwater Hall School but doesn't believe he has the talent. Until he meets a professor named Azrael, who offers him a bargain. Will Sarah be able to stop Tom from making the same mistake she did a century ago?" (Publisher's note)

The **door** in the moon; Catherine Fisher. Dial Books for Young Readers 2015 352 p. (Obsidian mirror) (hardback) $17.99

Grades: 9 10 11 12   **Fic**
  1. Fantasy fiction 2. Fairies -- Fiction 3. Time travel -- Fiction 4. Fantasy 5. Mirrors 6. Magic mirrors
  ISBN 0803739710; 9780803739710
                        LC 2014028161
  In this novel, by Catherine Fisher, the third volume in the Obsidian Mirror series "it's Midsummer Eve, and as Wintercombe Abbey is under siege by the Shee and their heartless faery queen, Jake and Sarah are snatched by a gang of time-traveling thieves and thrust into the chaos of the Reign of Terror. Meanwhile Janus, the tyrant of a dystopian future, is reaching back through the magical, inscrutable obsidian mirror to secure his power." (Kirkus Reviews)

"Fisher's genre mixing is as successful as ever, and while the labyrinthine story is challenging and a little crowded, it has lost none of its addictive appeal. Though readers might be flummoxed by the twisty plot, at this point they are likely in it for the long haul." Booklist

Incarceron. Dial Books 2010 442p $17.99

Grades: 7 8 9 10   **Fic**
  1. Fantasy fiction 2. Prisoners -- Fiction
  ISBN 978-0-8037-3396-1; 0-8037-3396-8
                        LC 2008-46254
  First published 2007 in the United Kingdom
  To free herself from an upcoming arranged marriage, Claudia, the daughter of the Warden of Incarceron, a futuristic prison with a mind of its own, decides to help a young prisoner escape.
  "Complex and inventive, with numerous and rewarding mysteries, this tale is certain to please." Publ Wkly
  Followed by Sapphique (2011)

Obsidian mirror; the slanted worlds. by Catherine Fisher. Dial Books, an imprint of Penguin Group (USA) Inc. 2014 368 p. (hardcover: alk. paper) $17.99

Grades: 7 8 9 10 11 12   **Fic**
  1. Fantasy fiction 2. Apocalyptic fiction 3. Time travel -- Fiction 4. Missing persons -- Fiction 5. Coins -- Fiction 6. Fathers -- Fiction
  ISBN 0803739702; 9780803739703
                        LC 2013018259
  This book, by Catherine Fisher, is a "genre-blend of time travel, dark fantasy and post-apocalyptic thriller. . . . It starts with a literal explosion, as most of the cast of teenagers, adventurers, schoolmasters, changelings, ghosts and duplicated cats hunker down at the crumbling Wintercombe Abbey, desperately trying to master the Chronoptika excepting Sarah, sent from a ravaged future to destroy the enigmatic device, and Jake, trapped in the London Blitz." (Kirkus Reviews)
  "This second in a projected trilogy provides a sumptuous genre-blend of time travel, dark fantasy and post-apocalyptic thriller, along with more complications than answers. . . . The fiendishly labyrinthine plot twists back and forth through perspectives and centuries, from England to medieval Florence to the dreamlike illusions of the Summerland, but elegant prose, deft characterization and an acute eye for telling details keep readers anchored. . . . Gorgeous, atmospheric, and addictive but ultimately frustrating; absolutely necessary wherever the first has fans." Kirkus
  Slanted worlds

The **obsidian** mirror; by Catherine Fisher. Dial Books 2013 384 p. (Obsidian Mirror) (hardcover) $17.99

Grades: 7 8 9 10 11 12   **Fic**
  1. Fantasy fiction 2. Science fiction 3. Fathers -- Fiction 4. Time travel -- Fiction 5. Missing persons -- Fiction
  ISBN 0803739699; 9780803739697
                        LC 2012019459
  This book is the first in a trilogy from Catherine Fisher. The "mirror of the title, a dangerous gateway to other time

periods, is being pursued by not one but three equally un-pleasant and obsessive mad scientists. One of them, Oberon Venn, is the master of spooky Wintercombe Abbey. . . . Jake Wilde, Venn's teenage godson and his equal in arrogance, has been expelled from boarding school and shipped off to Wintercombe, where the boy plans to accuse Venn of having murdered Jake's father." (Publishers Weekly)

Sapphique. Dial Books 2011 460p $17.99

Grades: 7 8 9 10   **Fic**
1. Fantasy fiction 2. Computers -- Fiction 3. Prisoners -- Fiction 4. Identity (Psychology) -- Fiction
ISBN 978-0-8037-3397-8; 0-8037-3397-6
                                              LC 2009-31479
Sequel to: Incarceron (2010)

After his escape from the sentient prison, Incarceron, Finn finds that the Realm is not at all what he expected, and he does not know whether he is to be its king, how to free his imprisoned friends, or how to stop Incarceron's quest to be free of its own nature.

"Fisher's superb world-building marks this title, effectively drawing the reader in to a place so rife with secrets even its inhabitants don't entirely understand the depth of its illusions." Bull Cent Child Books

Fishman, Seth

The **well's** end; Seth Fishman. G.P. Putnam's Sons, an imprint of Penguin Group (USA) Inc. 2014 352 p. (hardback) $17.99

Grades: 9 10 11 12   **Fic**
1. School stories 2. Science fiction 3. Adventure fiction 4. Colorado -- Fiction 5. Schools -- Fiction 6. Survival -- Fiction 7. Virus diseases -- Fiction 8. Boarding schools -- Fiction 9. Fathers and daughters -- Fiction 10. Single-parent families -- Fiction 11. Adventure and adventurers -- Fiction
ISBN 0399159908; 9780399159909
                                              LC 2013022716
Sequel: The Dark Water (2015)

In this book, by Seth Fishman, "a deadly virus and an impossible discovery unite. . . . Sixteen-year-old Mia Kish's small town of Fenton, Colorado is known for . . . one of the ritziest boarding schools in the country, Westbrook Academy. But when emergency sirens start blaring and Westbrook is put on lockdown, quarantined and surrounded by soldiers who shoot first and ask questions later, Mia realizes she's only just beginning to discover what makes Fenton special." (Publisher's note)

"When a bizarre disease that accelerates aging locks down her boarding school's campus, sixteen-year-old Mia and her friends stage a daring escape. If they can reach her father's secretive, subterranean office at mysterious Fenton Electronics, they will find a cure--and, hopefully, an explanation. This suspenseful sci-fi adventure ends with a cliffhanger that will leave readers eager for another installment." Horn Book

Fitzgerald, F. Scott

★ The **great** Gatsby; preface by Matthew J. Bruccoli. Scribner Classics 1996 170p

Grades: 11 12 Adult   **Fic**
1. Wealth 2. Success 3. Marriage problems 4. Wealth -- Fiction 5. Long Island (N.Y.) 6. New York (N.Y.) -- Manhattan 7. Long Island (N.Y.) -- Fiction 8. United States -- 20th century 9. New York (N.Y.) -- 20th century
ISBN 0684830426
                                              LC 96016596
First published 1925

"The mysterious Jay Gatsby lives in a luxurious mansion on the Long Island shore. . . . Nick Carraway, the narrator, lives next door to Gatsby, and Nick's cousin Daisy and her crude but wealthy husband Tom Buchanan live directly across the harbor. Gatsby reveals to Nick that he and Daisy had a brief affair before the war and her marriage to Tom. . . . He persuades Nick to bring him and Daisy together again but ultimately he is unable to win her away from Tom. Daisy, driving Gatsby's car, runs over and kills Tom's mistress Myrtle, unaware of her identity. Myrtle's husband traces the car and shoots Gatsby, who has remained silent in order to protect Daisy. Gatsby's friends and business associates have all deserted him, and only Gatsby's father, and one former guest attend the funeral." Reader's Ency. 4th edition

FitzGerald, Helen

Deviant; Helen FitzGerald. Soho Teen 2013 248 p. (hardcover) $17.99

Grades: 10 11 12   **Fic**
1. Mystery fiction 2. Orphans -- Fiction 3. Science fiction 4. Behavior -- Fiction 5. Families -- Fiction
ISBN 1616951397; 9781616951399
                                              LC 2012033455

In this book, "Abigail Thorn was given up by her mother as a newborn," so at 16, she's "surprised to learn that her birth mother has just died, leaving her a letter, a large sum of money, and a one-way plane ticket to Los Angeles to live with a family Abigail never knew existed. . . . Abigail gradually begins to let down her guard around her new older sister . . . , but she still senses that something is not right within her privileged new family." (Publishers Weekly)

"This thriller has great character development and will keep readers hooked until the cliff-hanger ending... There's quite a bit of crude language in this one, but overall it's a great action-filled mystery." SLJ

Fitzpatrick, Becca

Black ice; Becca Fitzpatrick. Simon & Schuster Books for Young Readers 2014 400 p. (hardback) $19.99

Grades: 9 10 11 12   **Fic**
1. Love -- Fiction 2. Hostages -- Fiction 3. Blizzards -- Fiction 4. Wilderness survival -- Fiction 5. Survival -- Fiction
ISBN 1442474262; 9781442474260; 9781442474277
                                              LC 2014004913

In this book, by Becca Fitzpatrick, "Britt Pheiffer has trained to backpack the Teton Range, but she isn't prepared when her ex-boyfriend, who still haunts her every thought, wants to join her. Before Britt can explore her feelings for Calvin, an unexpected blizzard forces her to seek shelter in a remote cabin, accepting the hospitality of its two very handsome occupants--but these men are fugitives, and they take her hostage." (Publisher's note)

"While the romance between Britt and one of her captors is soapy, it dovetails nicely with the murder mystery. With an action-packed conclusion, capped off with a fairy-tale ending, this finds a good intersection between romance and suspense." Booklist

Fitzpatrick, Huntley

My life next door; by Huntley Fitzpatrick. Dial Books 2012 394 p.

Grades: 9 10 11 12 **Fic**

1. Love stories 2. Teenagers -- Fiction 3. Family life -- Fiction 4. Love -- Fiction 5. Conduct of life -- Fiction 6. Politics, Practical -- Fiction

ISBN 0803736991; 9780803736993

LC 2011027166

This novel by Huntley Fitzpatrick is "about family, friendship, first romance, and how to be true to one person you love without betraying another . . . The Garretts are everything the Reeds are not. Loud, numerous, messy, affectionate. And every day from her balcony perch, seventeen-year-old Samantha Reed wishes she was one of them . . . until one summer evening, Jase Garrett climbs her terrace and changes everything. As the two fall fiercely in love, Jase's family makes Samantha one of their own. Then in an instant, the bottom drops out of her world and she is suddenly faced with an impossible decision." (Publisher's note)

What I thought was true; by Huntley Fitzpatrick. Dial 2014 416 p. (hardback) $17.99

Grades: 9 10 11 12 **Fic**

1. Love stories 2. Islands -- Fiction 3. Social classes -- Fiction 4. Dating (Social customs) -- Fiction 5. Old age -- Fiction 6. Connecticut -- Fiction 7. People with disabilities -- Fiction 8. Family life -- Connecticut -- Fiction

ISBN 0803739095; 9780803739093

LC 2013027029

This book, by Huntley Fitzpatrick, is a "love story [that] shows the clash between classes in a New England beach community. . . Gwen, whose mother is a house cleaner, has . . . [a poor] reputation among the members of the boys' swim team, including rich Cass. . . . After a humiliating run-in with him at a party, it's hard for Gwen to believe that he wants more from her than a quick fling, but over the course of the summer, he gradually wins her trust and her heart." (Publishers Weekly)

"A teenage girl struggles with class divisions, sex and the tricky art of communication. Gwen . . . is an islander, while Cass Somers is a rich boy . . . The two have had some romantic moments, but miscommunication, misinterpretation and fear keep them from moving forward. . . . What starts out as snappy chick-lit writing quickly becomes deeper and more complex . . . A late revelation will surprise readers as much as it does Gwen; natural dialogue and authentic characters abound. Much deeper than the pretty cover lets on." Kirkus

Fixmer, Elizabeth

Down from the mountain; by Elizabeth Fixmer. Albert Whitman & Co. 2015 272 p. (hardcover) $16.99

Grades: 9 10 11 12 **Fic**

1. Cults -- Fiction 2. Polygamy -- Fiction 3.

Fanaticism -- Fiction 4. Christian life -- Fiction 5. Mother-daughter relationship -- Fiction 6. Mothers and daughters -- Fiction

ISBN 0807583707; 9780807583708

LC 2014027714

In this book, by Elizabeth Fixmer, "Eva is mostly content with her life in Righteous Path, an isolated religious compound led by Ezekiel, a man who claims to speak directly with God. . . . Once she witnesses the kindness and generosity of the 'heathens' in the city, however, as well as Ezekiel's growing egomania and paranoid, misogynistic behavior, she starts to question whether he is as holy as he claims." (Booklist)

"Teen readers fascinated by religious cults will be drawn in by Eva's story." Booklist

Flack, Sophie

★ **Bunheads.** Poppy 2011 294p $17.99

Grades: 8 9 10 11 12 **Fic**

1. Ballet -- Fiction 2. New York (N.Y.) -- Fiction 3. Dating (Social customs) -- Fiction

ISBN 978-0-316-12653-3; 0-316-12653-5

LC 2011009715

Hannah Ward, nineteen, revels in the competition, intense rehearsals, and dazzling performances that come with being a member of Manhattan Ballet Company's corps de ballet, but after meeting handsome musician Jacob she begins to realize there could be more to her life.

"Readers, both dancers and 'pedestrians' (the corps' term for nondancers), will find Hannah's struggle a gripping read." Publ Wkly

Flake, Sharon G.

Bang! Jump at the Sun/Hyperion Books for Children 2005 298p hardcover o.p. pa $7.99

Grades: 8 9 10 11 12 **Fic**

1. Violence -- Fiction 2. Family life -- Fiction 3. African Americans -- Fiction

ISBN 0-7868-1844-1; 0-7868-4955-X pa

LC 2005-47434

A teenage boy must face the harsh realities of inner city life, a disintegrating family, and destructive temptations as he struggles to find his identity as a young man.

"This disturbing, thought-provoking novel will leave readers with plenty of food for thought and should fuel lively discussions." SLJ

Pinned; Sharon G. Flake. Scholastic Press 2012 228 p. $17.99

Grades: 9 10 11 12 **Fic**

1. Disabilities 2. Learning disabilities 3. People with disabilities 4. Schools -- Fiction 5. Friendship -- Fiction 6. Best friends -- Fiction 7. High schools -- Fiction 8. African Americans -- Fiction

ISBN 0545057183; 9780545057189; 9780545057332

LC 2012009239

This novel by Sharon G. Flake is "about a teen boy and girl, each tackling disabilities. Autumn is outgoing and has lots of friends. Adonis is shy and not so eager to connect with people. But even with their differences, the two have one thing in common--they're each dealing with a handicap. For Autumn, who has a learning disability, reading is a painful struggle that makes it hard to focus in class. . . . Adonis is confined to a wheelchair. But he's a strong reader who loves books." (Publisher's note)

Fleischman, Paul

Seek. Simon Pulse 2003 167p pa $7.99

Grades: 7 8 9 10   **Fic**
  1. Radio -- Fiction 2. Fathers -- Fiction
ISBN 0-689-85402-1
First published 2001 by Front St./Cricket Bks.

"Fleischman has orchestrated a symphony that is both joyful and poignant with this book designed for reader's theatre." Voice Youth Advocates

Fleming, Candace

On the day I died; stories from the grave. Candace Fleming. Schwartz & Wade Books 2012 199 p. $16.99

Grades: 6 7 8 9   **Fic**
  1. Short stories 2. Horror fiction 3. Teenagers -- Fiction 4. Ghosts -- Fiction 5. Illinois -- Fiction 6. Cemeteries -- Fiction
ISBN 0375867813; 9780375867811; 9780375967818
                                       LC 2011018661

This book is a collection of nine "tales told by dead teens." Author Candace Fleming "draws inspiration from several . . . horror shorts, monster movies and actual locales and incidents. . . . Ghostly young people regale [the narrator] with the ghastly circumstances of their demises. These range from being sucked into a magical mirror to being partially eaten by a mutant rubber ducky, from being brained by a falling stone gargoyle at an abandoned asylum to drowning in a car driven by a demonic hood ornament." (Kirkus Reviews)

Fletcher, Christine

★ **Ten** cents a dance. Bloomsbury U.S.A. Children's Books 2008 356p $16.95

Grades: 9 10 11 12   **Fic**
  1. Dancers -- Fiction 2. Poverty -- Fiction 3. Chicago (Ill.) -- Fiction 4. Conduct of life -- Fiction 5. World War, 1939-1945 -- Fiction
ISBN 978-1-59990-164-0; 1-59990-164-1
                                       LC 2007-50737

In 1940s Chicago, fifteen-year-old Ruby hopes to escape poverty by becoming a taxi dancer in a nightclub, but the work has unforeseen dangers and hiding the truth from her family and friends becomes increasingly difficult.

"The descriptions of nightlife are lively and engaging, and they bring to light race, class, and gender issues in 1940s Chicago, which are fodder for discussion. Leisure readers will enjoy this novel, but it will also be useful in the classroom as a historical snapshot." Voice Youth Advocates

Fletcher, Susan

Alphabet of dreams. Atheneum Books for Young Readers 2006 294p map $16.95

Grades: 6 7 8 9 10   **Fic**
  1. Iran -- Fiction 2. Dreams -- Fiction 3. Zoroastrianism -- Fiction
ISBN 0-689-85042-5

In this book by Susan Fletcher, "Mitra comes from Persian royalty, but now that her family is dead, she disguises herself as a boy, stealing food and sheltering in burial caves with her younger brother, Babak. A journey is set in motion when Babak dreams of a portentous star, and the siblings follow Melchior and his two magi companions as they seek the king it represents." (Booklist)

"The characters are vivid and whole, the plot compelling, and the setting vast." Voice Youth Advocates

Flinn, Alex

Breaking point; [by] Alex Flinn. HarperTempest 2002 241p hardcover o.p. pa $6.99

Grades: 9 10 11 12   **Fic**
  1. School stories 2. Friendship -- Fiction
ISBN 0-06-623847-1; 0-06-623848-X; 9780064473712 pa
                                       LC 2001-39504

"Gate-Brickell Christian is a toney private school attended by the rich and privileged—and a few despised offspring of the staff, like Paul Richmond. . . . Charlie, the magnetic class ringleader, becomes the center of Paul's world. . . . Paul's loyalty to Charlie takes him from vandalism (battering mailboxes) to cheating . . . to, finally, leaving a Charlie-made bomb in a classroom." Bull Cent Child Books

★ **Breathing** underwater. HarperCollins Pubs. 2001 263p hardcover o.p. pa $8.99

Grades: 9 10 11 12   **Fic**
  1. Domestic violence -- Fiction
ISBN 0-06-029198-2; 0-06-447257-4 pa
                                       LC 00-44933

Sent to counseling for hitting his girlfriend, Caitlin, and ordered to keep a journal, sixteen-year-old Nick recounts his relationship with Caitlin, examines his controlling behavior and anger, and describes living with his abusive father.

"This book attempts to understand the root of domestic violence. Flinn has created sympathetic characters who are struggling with their insecurities. While it is difficult at first to be sympathetic towards Nick, it becomes easier as he examines his life and relationships. This is a good book to use in discussion with teens who have anger issues." Book Rep

Followed by Diva (2006)

Floreen, Tim

Willful machines; Tim Floreen. Simon Pulse 2015 368 p. (hardcover) $17.99

Grades: 9 10 11 12   **Fic**
  1. Science fiction 2. Gay men -- Fiction 3. Terrorism -- Fiction 4. Presidents -- United States -- Fiction 5. Gays -- Fiction 6. Computer programs -- Fiction 7. Presidents -- Family -- Fiction
ISBN 9781481432771; 9781481432788
                                       LC 2014030181

In this book, by Tim Floreen, "scientists create what may be a new form of life: an artificial human named Charlotte. All goes well until Charlotte escapes, transfers her consciousness to the Internet, and begins terrorizing the American public. Charlotte's attacks have everyone on high alert—everyone except Lee Fisher, the closeted son of the US president. . . . But when attacks start happening at his school, Lee realizes he's Charlotte's next target." (Publisher's note)

"An excellent debut thriller that will reach a wide range of readers." SLJ

Flores-Scott, Patrick

Jumped in; Patrick Flores-Scott. Christy Ottaviano Books, Henry Holt and Company 2013 304 p. (hardback) $16.99

Grades: 8 9 10   **Fic**
> 1. Gangs 2. Friendship 3. Slam poetry 4. Poetry -- Fiction 5. Schools -- Fiction 6. High schools -- Fiction 7. Mexican Americans -- Fiction 8. Des Moines (Wash.) -- Fiction 9. Interpersonal relations -- Fiction 10. Family life -- Washington (State) -- Fiction
> ISBN 0805095144; 9780805095142
>   LC 2013018844

In this book, "grunge-rock devotee Sam has been trying to avoid the attention of teachers and other students ever since his mom left town two years earlier. Then the equally quiet Luis Cárdenas arrives in Sam's English class. . . . Sam doesn't see Luis' true colors until Ms. Cassidy announces that the class will have a poetry slam. Luis not only throws himself into creating a poem, he inspires Sam to do the same." (Kirkus Reviews)

Foer, Jonathan Safran

Extremely loud & incredibly close. Houghton Mifflin 2005 326p il $24.95; pa $13.95

Grades: 11 12 Adult   **Fic**
> 1. New York (N.Y.) -- Fiction 2. Father-son relationship -- Fiction 3. September 11 terrorist attacks, 2001 -- Fiction
> ISBN 0-618-32970-6; 0-618-71165-1 pa
>   LC 2004-65131

The author's "depiction of Oskar's reaction to phone messages left by his father as he awaited rescue in the burning World Trade Center, his description of Oskar's grandfather's love affair . . . and his experiences during the bombing of Dresden—these passages underscore Mr. Foer's ability to evoke, with enormous compassion and psychological acuity, his characters' emotional experiences, and to show how these private moments intersect with the great public events of history." N Y Times (Late N Y Ed)

Foley, Jessie Ann

★ **Carnival** at Bray; a novel. Jessie Ann Foley. First edition Elephant Rock Books 2014 235 p. $12.95

Grades: 9 10 11 12   **Fic**
> 1. Ireland 2. Teenage girls 3. Bildungsromans
> ISBN 0989515591; 9780989515597
>   LC 2014937608

Printz Honor Book (2015)

"This promising debut, set in the heyday of grunge, tells the story of Maggie Lynch, a displaced Chicagoan and grunge music fan, living in a quiet town (Bray) on the Irish Sea. Maggie was uprooted from her friends, her music scene, and her beloved Uncle Kevin when her romantically fickle mother married her latest boyfriend, resulting in a move to his hometown. During her time of difficult adjustment to Ireland, Maggie falls in love with Eion the very moment a devastating loss hits her family, leading to rebellion and a journey to Rome to see Nirvana and fulfill Uncle Kevin's

wish for her...Foley has also populated Bray with a host of quirky, loving, and memorable background characters, which enriches the story. Recommended for teens who enjoy travelogue romance stories or novels about rock music." SLJ

Follett, Ken

The **pillars** of the earth; Ken Follett. Morrow 1989 973p ill. (hbk.) $34.99

Grades: 11 12 Adult   **Fic**
> 1. Cathedrals -- Fiction 2. Middle Ages -- Fiction 3. Church architecture -- Fiction 4. Great Britain -- History -- 1154-1399, Plantagenets -- Fiction 5. Cathedrals -- Design and construction -- Fiction 6. Great Britain -- History -- Stephen, 1135-1154 -- Fiction
> ISBN 0688046592; 9780688046590
>   LC 89009405

This book takes place in "the twelfth century; the place—feudal England; and the subject—the building of a glorious cathedral. [Author Ken] Follett has re-created the . . . England of the Middle Ages. . . . The vast forests, the walled towns, the castles, and the monasteries become a familiar landscape. Against this . . . backdrop, filled with the ravages of war and the rhythms of daily life, the . . . storyteller draws the reader . . . into the intertwined lives of his characters—into their dreams, their labors, and their loves: Tom, the master builder; Aliena, the ravishingly beautiful noblewoman; Philip, the prior of Kingsbridge; Jack, the artist in stone; and Ellen, the woman of the forest who casts a terrifying curse." (Publisher's note)

Ford, John C.

★ The **morgue** and me. Viking 2009 313p $17.99

Grades: 8 9 10 11 12   **Fic**
> 1. Mystery fiction 2. Homicide -- Fiction 3. Michigan -- Fiction 4. Journalists -- Fiction 5. Criminal investigation -- Fiction
> ISBN 978-0-670-01096-7; 0-670-01096-0
>   LC 2009-1956

Eighteen-year-old Christopher, who plans to be a spy, learns of a murder cover-up through his summer job as a morgue assistant and teams up with Tina, a gorgeous newspaper reporter, to investigate, despite great danger.

"Ford spins a tale that's complex but not confusing, never whitewashing some of the harsher crimes people commit. The result is a story that holds its own as a mainstream mystery as well as a teen novel." Publ Wkly

Ford, Michael

The **poisoned** house. Albert Whitman 2011 319p $16.99

Grades: 6 7 8 9 10   **Fic**
> 1. Ghost stories 2. Supernatural -- Fiction 3. London (England) -- Fiction 4. Household employees -- Fiction 5. Great Britain -- History -- 19th century -- Fiction
> ISBN 978-0-8075-6589-6; 0-8075-6589-X
>   LC 2010048250

As the widowed master of an elegant house in Victorian-era London slips slowly into madness and his tyrannical housekeeper takes on more power, a ghostly presence distracts a teenaged maidservant with clues to a deadly secret.

"This ghost story is light fare, chilling, and suspenseful." SLJ

Ford, Michael Thomas

Suicide notes; a novel. HarperTeen 2008 295p $16.99; pa $8.99

Grades: 9 10 11 12 Adult **Fic**

1. Suicide -- Fiction 2. Homosexuality -- Fiction 3. Psychiatric hospitals -- Fiction

ISBN 978-0-06-073755-9; 0-06-073755-7; 978-0-06-073757-3 pa; 0-06-073757-3 pa

LC 2008-19199

Brimming with sarcasm, fifteen-year-old Jeff describes his stay in a psychiatric ward after attempting to commit suicide.

Ford's "characterizations run deep, and without too much contrivance the teens' interactions slowly dislodge clues about what triggered Jeff's suicide attempt." Publ Wkly

Z. HarperTeen 2010 276p $16.99; lib bdg $17.89

Grades: 7 8 9 10 **Fic**

1. Science fiction 2. Games -- Fiction 3. Zombies -- Fiction

ISBN 978-0-06-073758-0; 0-06-073758-1; 978-0-06-073759-7 lib bdg; 0-06-073759-X lib bdg

LC 2009-44005

In the year 2032, after a virus that turned people into zombies has been eradicated, Josh is invited to join an underground gaming society, where the gamers hunt zombies and the action is more dangerous than it seems.

"This book is a thriller, and the clever plot and characters will have readers hoping for more." SLJ

The **Forgetting**. Scholastic 2016 416 p. hardcover $18.99

Grades: 8 9 10 11 12 **Fic**

1. Science fiction 2. Memory -- Fiction 3. Amnesia -- Fiction 4. Friendship -- Fiction

ISBN 9780545945219

LC 2016007978

"In Canaan, your book is your truth and your identity, and Nadia knows exactly who hasn't written the truth. Because Nadia is the only person in Canaan who has never forgotten.

But when Nadia begins to use her memories to solve the mysteries of Canaan, she discovers truths about herself and Gray, the handsome glassblower, that will change her world forever. As the anarchy of the Forgetting approaches, Nadia and Gray must stop an unseen enemy that threatens both their city and their own existence - before the people can forget the truth. And before Gray can forget her." (Publisher's note)

"Every 12 years, the orderly city of Canaan undergoes the chaotic, bloody time known as the Forgetting. During these brief hours, people's memories are erased. If it were not for the books in which inhabitants are required by law to record the events of their lives, they would have no way of knowing what happened before the Forgetting, or even of knowing their names or who their families are. Nadia is different. She remembers. The next Forgetting is a few weeks away. The teen is determined to keep her family together and

away from the ensuing anarchy, but how? . . . This excellent work belongs in every collection." SLJ

Forman, Gayle

I was here; Gayle Forman. Viking 2015 288 p. (hardcover) $18.99

Grades: 9 10 11 12 **Fic**

1. Secrets -- Fiction 2. Female friendship -- Fiction 3. Grief -- Fiction 4. Suicide -- Fiction 5. Friendship -- Fiction 6. Mystery and detective stories 7. Washington (State) -- Fiction

ISBN 0451471474; 9780451471475

LC 2014011445

In this book by Gayle Forman, "Cody struggles to figure out why Meg took her own life and puzzles over a suspicious line in her friend's suicide email. The distraught but determined teen begins to encrypt files on Meg's laptop, which lead her to a suicide support group and posts from . . . a Pied Piper-type character who encourages suicide. As she goes further down the rabbit hole, Cody comes to the realization that she needs to forgive Meg, and, more importantly, herself." (School Library Journal)

"An engrossing and provocative look at the devastating finality of suicide, survivor's guilt, the complicated nature of responsibility and even the role of the Internet in life-and-death decisions." Kirkus

★ **If** I stay; a novel. Dutton Children's Books 2009 201p $16.99

Grades: 7 8 9 10 **Fic**

1. Coma -- Fiction 2. Death -- Fiction 3. Oregon -- Fiction 4. Medical care -- Fiction

ISBN 0-525-42103-3; 978-0-525-42103-0

LC 2008-23938

While in a coma following an automobile accident that killed her parents and younger brother, seventeen-year-old Mia, a gifted cellist, weights whether to live with her grief or join her family in death.

"Intensely moving, the novel will force readers to take stock of their lives and the people and things that make them worth living." Publ Wkly

Followed by: Where she went (2011)

Just one day; Gayle Forman. Dutton Books 2013 320 p. (hardcover: alk. paper) $17.99

Grades: 9 10 11 12 **Fic**

1. Love stories 2. Voyages and travels -- Fiction 3. Love -- Fiction 4. Europe -- Fiction 5. Actors and actresses -- Fiction 6. Self-actualization (Psychology) -- Fiction

ISBN 0525425918; 9780525425915

LC 2012030798

In this story, recent high school graduate Allyson meets Dutch actor Willem and "the two take an impulsive trip to Paris, but Willem disappears and Allyson is left stranded. Back in the U.S., Allyson is unable to wipe Willem from her mind, and her carefully planned future takes unexpected turns. . . . In college, Allyson breaks away from her mother's expectations, realizes her passion for theater and language, and tries to gather clues about Willem's whereabouts." (Publishers Weekly)

Where she went. Dutton Books 2011 264p
$16.99

Grades: 7 8 9 10 **Fic**

1. Musicians -- Fiction 2. Rock music -- Fiction 3.
Violoncellos -- Fiction 4. New York (N.Y.) -- Fiction
ISBN 978-0-525-42294-5; 0-525-42294-3

LC 2010-13474

"Both characters spring to life, and their pain-filled back
story and current realities provide depth and will hold readers fast." Kirkus

"Both characters spring to life, and their pain-filled back
story and current realities provide depth and will hold readers fast." Kirkus

Forster, Miriam

City of a Thousand Dolls; Miriam Forster. HarperTeen 2013 368 p. (hardcover) $17.99

Grades: 9 10 11 12 **Fic**

1. Fantasy fiction 2. Mystery fiction 3. Fantasy 4.
Orphans -- Fiction
ISBN 0062121308; 9780062121301

LC 2012004289

In this book, "Nisha has lived in the City of a Thousand Dolls for 10 years, ever since her parents abandoned
her there. Unlike the other girls there, she was never placed
in one of the city's Houses to be trained. Nisha's only status comes from her position as the assistant to the Matron,
a placement that allows her access to any house on the
grounds. When someone begins killing girls on the eve of
the Royal Prince's arrival to claim his bride, terror and chaos
ensue." (School Library Journal)

Fowley-Doyle, Moïra

★ The **accident** season; Moïra Fowley-Doyle.
Kathy Dawson Books 2015 304 p. (hardback)
$17.99 Fic

1. Love -- Fiction 2. Accidents -- Fiction 3. Family
secrets -- Fiction 4. Families -- Fiction 5. Supernatural
-- Fiction
ISBN 0525429484; 9780525429487

LC 2014047858

In this novel by Moïra Fowley-Doyle, "every October for Cara and her family is the accident season. Broken
bones, cuts, scrapes, and even death can occur during those
long thirty-one days. This year's accident season is coming
to a close, and it seems like a typical year . . . until they realize that it is not as normal as they thought. This year is bad,
and not all the injuries they accrue are surface level--some
are more than skin deep." (Voice of Youth Advocates)

"Beautifully crafted and atmospheric, the magic realism of this book gradually peels away to expose secrets and
reveal unexpected truths. Readers will be swept away by
Fowley-Doyle's lyrical writing and entrancing premise in
this tale of forbidden love and magic." Booklist

Foxlee, Karen

The **anatomy** of wings. Alfred A. Knopf 2009
361p $16.99; lib bdg $19.99

Grades: 8 9 10 11 12 **Fic**

1. Sisters -- Fiction 2. Suicide -- Fiction 3. Australia
-- Fiction 4. Bereavement -- Fiction 5. Family life

-- Fiction
ISBN 978-0-375-85643-3; 0-375-85643-9; 978-0-375-
95643-0 lib bdg; 0-375-95643-3 lib bdg

LC 2008-19373

First published 2007 in Australia

After the suicide of her troubled teenage sister,
eleven-year-old Jenny struggles to understand what
actually happened.

Jenny's "observations are . . . poetic and washed with
magic realism. . . . With heart-stopping accuracy and sly
symbolism, Foxlee captures the small ways that humans
reveal themselves, the mysterious intensity of female adolescence, and the surreal quiet of a grieving house, which
slowly and with astonishing resilience fills again with sound
and music." Booklist

The **midnight** dress; Karen Foxlee. Alfred A.
Knopf 2013 288 p. $16.99

Grades: 9 10 11 12 **Fic**

1. Magic -- Fiction 2. Female friendship -- Fiction 3.
Clothing and dress -- Fiction 4. Sewing -- Fiction 5.
Schools -- Fiction 6. Australia -- Fiction 7. Alcoholism
-- Fiction 8. Friendship -- Fiction 9. Mystery and
detective stories 10. Single-parent families -- Fiction
11. Eccentrics and eccentricities -- Fiction
ISBN 0375856455; 9780375856457; 9780375956454;
9780449818213

LC 2012029108

In this book by Karen Foxlee, "Rose doesn't expect to
fall in love with the . . . town of Leonora. Nor does she expect to become fast friends with . . . Pearl Kelly, organizer of
the high school float at the annual Harvest Festival parade.
Pearl convinces Rose to visit Edie Baker, once a renowned
dressmaker, now a rumored witch. Together Rose and Edie
hand-stitch [a dress] for Rose to wear at the Harvest Festi-
val--a dress that will have long-lasting consequences." (Publisher's note)

"After arriving in Australian beach town Leonora, self-
contained, morose Rose is befriended by outgoing Pearl.
Pearl tells Rose about the annual harvest festival and urges her to start thinking about a gown. Enter the enigmatic
Edie Baker, an old dressmaker. There are many story lines
within Foxlee's complex novel; they coalesce into a dreamlike, eerie whole told in mesmerizing, sensuous prose."
(Horn Book)

Frank, E. R.

Dime; E.R. Frank. Atheneum Books for Young
Readers 2015 336 p. (hardcover: alk. paper) $17.99

Grades: 9 10 11 12 **Fic**

1. Juvenile prostitution -- Fiction 2. African American
teenage girls -- Fiction 3. Families -- Fiction 4.
Prostitution -- Fiction 5. African Americans -- Fiction
ISBN 1481431609; 9781481431606; 9781481431613

LC 2014023579

In this novel, by E. R. Frank, "as a teen girl in Newark,
New Jersey, lost in the foster care system, Dime just wants
someone to care about her, to love her. A family. And that is
exactly what she gets--a daddy and two 'wifeys.' So what if
she has to go out and earn some coins to keep her place? It
seems a fair enough exchange for love. Dime never meant
to become a prostitute. It happened so gradually, she pretty

much didn't realize it was happening until it was too late." (Publisher's note)

"Dime's desire to save her friend transcends artifice and approaches heroism, making for a tremendously affecting novel." Kirkus

Life is funny; a novel. Puffin Books 2002 263p pa $7.99

Grades: 7 8 9 10 **Fic**

1. Family life -- Fiction 2. Brooklyn (New York, N.Y.) -- Fiction

ISBN 0-14-230083-7

LC 2001-48436

First published 2000 by DK Ink

The lives of a number of young people of different races, economic backgrounds, and family situations living in Brooklyn, New York, become intertwined over a seven year period.

"The voices ring true, and the talk is painful, vulgar, rough, sexy, funny, fearful, furious, gentle." Booklist

Frank, Lucy

Two girls staring at the ceiling; Lucy Frank. First edition Schwartz & Wade 2014 272 p. $16.99

Grades: 9 10 11 12 **Fic**

1. Novels in verse 2. Hospitals -- Fiction 3. Teenage girls -- Fiction 4. Friendship -- Fiction 5. Crohn's disease -- Fiction

ISBN 0307979741; 9780307979742; 9780307979759

LC 2013023236

A young adult novel by Lucy Frank, "This novel-in-verse--at once literary and emotionally gripping--follows the unfolding friendship between two very different teenage girls who share a hospital room and an illness. Chess, the narrator, is sick, but with what exactly, she isn't sure. And to make matters worse, she must share a hospital room with Shannon, her polar opposite. Where Chess is polite, Shannon is rude." (Publisher's note)

"Carefully rendered details (instead of magazines, Chess requests "running shoes, / a black bikini, a bottle of sriracha, / a kite, a Bernese mountain dog") characterize Chess and Shannon well beyond their shared diagnosis of Crohn's disease. A sympathetic and illuminating story of illness, friendship, and resilience." Horn Book

Franklin, Emily

The **half** life of planets; a novel. [by] Emily Franklin and Brendan Halpin. Disney Hyperion Books 2010 247p $16.99

Grades: 7 8 9 10 **Fic**

1. Astronomy -- Fiction 2. Rock music -- Fiction 3. Bereavement -- Fiction 4. Family life -- Fiction 5. Asperger's syndrome -- Fiction

ISBN 978-1-4231-2111-4; 1-4231-2111-2

LC 2010-4606

An unlikely romance develops between a science-minded girl who is determined to reclaim her reputation and a boy with Asperger's Syndrome.

"The discursive story favors dialogue and introspection over action and can border on melodrama, but the characters' candid perspectives ring true and the romance should have readers longing for connections as deeply felt." Publ Wkly

Frazier, Angie

The **Eternal** Sea. Scholastic Press 2011 362p $17.99

Grades: 8 9 10 11 12 **Fic**

1. Adventure fiction 2. Egypt -- Fiction 3. Supernatural -- Fiction

ISBN 978-0-545-11475-2; 0-545-11475-6

Sequel to: Everlasting (2010)

Realizing that the magic of Umandu, the stone that grants immortality, is not done, seventeen-year-old Camille accompanies Oscar, Ira, and Randall to Egypt, where all their lives are in grave danger.

"Readers who enjoy sea romances won't go wrong." SLJ

Everlasting. Scholastic Press 2010 329p $17.99

Grades: 8 9 10 11 12 **Fic**

1. Adventure fiction 2. Australia -- Fiction 3. Shipwrecks -- Fiction 4. Supernatural -- Fiction 5. Seafaring life -- Fiction 6. Father-daughter relationship -- Fiction

ISBN 978-0-545-11473-8; 0-545-11473-X

LC 2009-20519

In 1855, seventeen-year-old Camille sets out from San Francisco, California, on her last sea voyage before entering a loveless marriage, but when her father's ship is destroyed, she and a friend embark on a cross-Australian quest to find her long-lost mother who holds a map to a magical stone.

"Although this novel takes place in the nineteenth century, many of the themes are relevant for today's teens. The author does a nice job of developing strong and funny characters while keeping the plot moving at a readable pace." Voice Youth Advocates

Followed by: The eternal sea (2011)

Fredericks, Mariah

Crunch time. Atheneum Bks. for Young Readers 2006 317p $15.95

Grades: 9 10 11 12 **Fic**

1. School stories 2. Friendship -- Fiction

ISBN 0-689-86938-X

LC 2004-20008

Four students, who have formed a study group to prepare for the SAT exam, sustain each other through the emotional highs and lows of their junior year in high school. "Grades seven to ten." (Bull Cent Child Books)

"Fredericks writes about high school academics and social rules with sharp insight and spot-on humor." Booklist

The **girl** in the park; Mariah Fredericks. Schwartz & Wade Books 2012 217 p. $16.99

Grades: 10 11 12 **Fic**

1. Mystery fiction 2. Crime -- Fiction 3. Girls -- Fiction 4. New York (N.Y.) -- Fiction 5. Murder -- Fiction 6. Schools -- Fiction 7. High schools -- Fiction 8. Mystery and detective stories

ISBN 0375868437; 9780375868436; 9780375899072; 9780375968433

LC 2011012309

This young adult mystery novel by Mariah Frederick follows teenage social life in New York City. "When Wendy Geller's body is found in Central Park after the night of a rager, . . . Shy Rain, once Wendy's best friend, knows there was more to Wendy than just 'party girl.' As she struggles to separate the friend she knew from the tangle of gossip and headlines, Rain becomes determined to discover the truth about the murder." (Publisher's note)

Freitas, Donna

The **Survival** Kit. Farrar Straus Giroux 2011 351p $16.99

Grades: 7 8 9 10   **Fic**

1. Death -- Fiction 2. Bereavement -- Fiction
ISBN 978-0-374-39917-7; 0-374-39917-4

     LC 2010041294

"The premise of the survival kit, a real-life tradition from Freitas's own mother, begs to be discussed and glued-and-scissored with friends, students, teachers, and librarians. A copy of The Survival Kit would be a worthy addition for a teen coping with her own loss or struggling to help friends or family cope with theirs." Voice Youth Advocates

Friedman, Robin

Nothing. Flux 2008 232p pa $9.95

Grades: 7 8 9 10   **Fic**

1. Novels in verse 2. Jews -- Fiction 3. Bulimia -- Fiction 4. Family life -- Fiction
ISBN 978-0-7387-1304-5; 0-7387-1304-X

     LC 2008-08184

Despite his outward image of popular, attractive high-achiever bound for the Ivy League college of his father's dreams, high school senior Parker sees himself as a fat, unattractive failure and finds relief for his overwhelming anxieties in ever-increasing bouts of binging and purging.

"The novel does a good job of letting readers inside the head of someone who is suffering from an eating disorder. Compelling reading." SLJ

Friend, Natasha

For keeps. Viking 2010 267p $16.99

Grades: 8 9 10 11 12   **Fic**

1. School stories 2. Massachusetts -- Fiction 3. Father-daughter relationship -- Fiction 4. Mother-daughter relationship -- Fiction
ISBN 978-0-670-01190-2; 0-670-01190-8

     LC 2009-22472

Just as sixteen-year-old Josie and her mother finally begin trusting men enough to start dating seriously, the father Josie never knew comes back to town and shakes up what was already becoming a difficult mother-daughter relationship.

"The book discusses sex and abortion, and includes adult language and underage drinking. Many readers will be able to relate to this protagonist, whose strength and maturity set a positive example. Friend skillfully portrays the challenges of adolescence while telling an engaging story with unique and genuine characters." SLJ

Lush. Scholastic Press 2006 178p $16.99

Grades: 7 8 9 10   **Fic**

1. Fathers -- Fiction 2. Alcoholism -- Fiction
ISBN 0-439-85346-X

     LC 2005-031333

Unable to cope with her father's alcoholism, thirteen-year-old Sam corresponds with an older student, sharing her family problems and asking for advice.

"Friend adeptly takes a teen problem and turns it into a believable, sensitive, character-driven story, with realistic dialogue." Booklist

My life in black and white; by Natasha Friend. Penguin Group USA 2012 294 p. (hardcover) $17.99; (paperback) $8.99

Grades: 8 9 10 11   **Fic**

1. Sisters 2. Self-perception 3. Self-consciousness 4. Boxing -- Fiction 5. Friendship -- Fiction 6. Peer pressure -- Fiction 7. Self-acceptance -- Fiction 8. Beauty, Personal -- Fiction 9. Dating (Social customs) -- Fiction
ISBN 067001303X; 9780670013036; 9780670784943

     LC 2011021436

Author Natasha Friend tells the story of Lexi and her best friend Taylor. "After finding her boyfriend . . . and Taylor making out at a party, . . . an argument quickly escalates, leading to an accident that changes Lexi's life forever. . . . It isn't until her sister, Ruthie, and [friend] Theo . . . are honest with her that Lexi starts peeling away the plastic life she once had and discovers the real one underneath." (Kirkus Reviews)

Friesner, Esther

Spirit's princess; Esther Friesner. 1st ed. Random House Childrens Books 2012 449 p. (trade) $17.99; (paperback) $10.99; (ebook) $53.97; (lib bdg.) $20.99

Grades: 7 8 9 10   **Fic**

1. Family -- Fiction 2. Father-daughter relationship -- Fiction 3. Children with physical disabilities -- Fiction 4. Magic -- Fiction 5. Shamans -- Fiction 6. Spirits -- Fiction 7. Sex role -- Fiction 8. Japan -- History -- To 645 -- Fiction
ISBN 0375869077; 9780375869075; 9780375873140; 9780375873157; 9780375899904; 9780375969072

     LC 2011010468

In the book by Esther Friesner, "Himiko's chieftain father adores her, as do her older brother and her father's wives. Despite their love and affection, none of them takes Himiko seriously when she insists she is a shaman. Himiko herself isn't sure she can achieve her goal; with one leg lame since she was a child, she can't do a shaman's dances. Though the current shaman insists Himiko will be her heir, it can't happen until Himiko is ready to stand up to her father." (Kirkus Reviews)

Friesner, Esther M.

Nobody's princess; [by] Esther Friesner. Random House 2007 305p hardcover o.p. pa $7.99

Grades: 6 7 8 9 10   **Fic**

1. Adventure fiction 2. Sex role -- Fiction 3. Classical mythology -- Fiction 4. Helen of Troy (Legendary character) -- Fiction
ISBN 978-0-375-87528-1; 0-375-87528-X; 978-0-375-87529-8 pa; 0-375-87529-8 pa

     LC 2006-06515

Determined to fend for herself in a world where only men have real freedom, headstrong Helen, who will be called queen of Sparta and Helen of Troy one day, learns to fight, hunt, and ride horses while disguised as a boy, and goes on an adventure throughout the Mediterranean world.

This "is a fascinating portrait. . . . Along the way, Friesner skillfully exposes larger issues of women's rights, human bondage, and individual destiny. It's a rollicking good story." Booklist

Followed by: Nobody's prize (2008)

Sphinx's princess. Random House 2009 370p il map $17.99; lib bdg $20.99

Grades: 8 9 10 11 12   **Fic**
1. Queens 2. Queens -- Fiction 3. Egypt -- History -- Fiction
ISBN 978-0-375-85654-9; 0-375-85654-4; 978-0-375-95654-6 lib bdg; 0-375-95654-9 lib bdg
LC 2009-13719

Although she is a dutiful daughter, Nefertiti's dancing abilities, remarkable beauty, and intelligence garner attention near and far, so much so that her family is summoned to the Egyptian royal court, where Nefertiti becomes a pawn in the power play of her scheming aunt, Queen Tiye.

"Dramatic plot twists, a powerful female subject, and engrossing details of life in ancient Egypt make for lively historical fiction." Booklist

Followed by: Sphinx's queen (2010)

Sphinx's queen. Random House 2010 352p $17.99; lib bdg $29.99

Grades: 8 9 10 11 12   **Fic**
1. Queens 2. Queens -- Fiction 3. Egypt -- History -- Fiction
ISBN 978-0-375-85657-0; 0-375-85657-9; 978-0-375-95657-7 lib bdg; 0-375-95657-3 lib bdg
LC 2010-13769

Sequel to: Sphinx's princess (2009)

Chased after by the prince and his soldiers for a crime she did not commit, Nefertiti finds temporary refuge in the wild hills along the Nile's west bank before returning to the royal court to plead her case to the Pharaoh.

This is written "in fine prose that expresses the questioning of religion that most young people experience as they approach maturity. . . . This deeply moral book tells a good story; or, rather, this good story reveals deeply moral truths." SLJ

Threads and flames. Viking 2010 390p $17.99

Grades: 6 7 8 9 10   **Fic**
1. Jews -- Fiction 2. Fires -- Fiction 3. Immigrants -- Fiction 4. New York (N.Y.) -- Fiction 5. Polish Americans -- Fiction 6. Triangle Shirtwaist Company, Inc. -- Fiction
ISBN 978-0-670-01245-9; 0-670-01245-9

"Friesner's sparkling prose makes the immigrant experience in New York's Lower East Side come alive. . . . Readers will turn the pages with rapt attention to follow the characters' intrepid, risk-all adventures in building new lives." Booklist

Frost, Gregory

Lord Tophet; a Shadowbridge novel. by Gregory Frost. Del Rey/Ballantine Books 2008 222 p. (paperback) $14

Grades: 9 10 11 12   **Fic**
1. Fantasy fiction 2. Magic -- Fiction 3. Paranormal fiction 4. Puppeteers -- Fiction 5. Women storytellers -- Fiction
ISBN 0345497597; 9780345497598
LC 2008006642

This book is part of the Shadowbridge series by Gregory Frost. Here, "daughter of the legendary shadow-puppeteer Bardsham, Leodora has inherited her father's skills . . . and his enemies. Together with her manager—Soter, keeper of her father's darkest secrets, and a gifted young musician named Diverus, Leodora has traveled from span to span, her masked performances given under the stage name Jax, winning fame and fortune." (Publisher's note)

Shadowbridge; [by] Gregory Frost. Ballantine Books 2008 255p pa $14

Grades: 9 10 11 12   **Fic**
1. Fantasy fiction 2. Orphans -- Fiction
ISBN 978-0-345-49758-1 pa; 0-345-49758-9 pa
LC 2007033139

"Orphaned 16-year-old Leodora, a talented puppeteer and storyteller, is forced to hide her identity and gender as she travels the spans and tunnels of the ocean-crossing Shadowbridge in Frost's exciting first of a diptych. . . . Frost (Fitcher's Brides) draws richly detailed human characters and embellishes his multilayered stories with intriguing creatures—benevolent sea dragons, trickster foxes, death-eating snakes and capricious gods—that make this fantasy a sparkling gem of mythic invention and wonder." SLJ

Frost, Helen

★ The **braid**. Farrar, Straus and Giroux 2006 95p $16

Grades: 7 8 9 10   **Fic**
1. Novels in verse 2. Canada -- Fiction 3. Sisters -- Fiction 4. Scotland -- Fiction 5. Immigrants -- Fiction
ISBN 0-374-30962-0
LC 2005-40148

Two Scottish sisters, living on the western island of Barra in the 1850s, relate, in alternate voices and linked narrative poems, their experiences after their family is forcible evicted and separated with one sister accompanying their parents and younger siblings to Cape Breton, Canada, and the other staying behind with other family on the small island of Mingulay.

"The book will inspire both students and teachers to go back and study how the taut poetic lines manage to contain the powerful feelings." Booklist

★ **Crossing** stones. Farrar, Straus and Giroux 2009 184p $16.99

Grades: 6 7 8 9 10   **Fic**
1. War stories 2. Novels in verse 3. Soldiers -- Fiction 4. Family life -- Fiction 5. Women -- Suffrage -- Fiction 6. World War, 1914-1918 -- Fiction
ISBN 0-374-31653-8; 978-0-374-31653-2
LC 2008-20755

In their own voices, four young people, Muriel, Frank, Emma, and Ollie, tell of their experiences during the first World War, as the boys enlist and are sent overseas, Emma finishes school, and Muriel fights for peace and women's suffrage.

"Beautifully written in formally structured verse. . . . This [is a] beautifully written, gently told story." Voice Youth Advocates

Hidden. Farrar Straus Giroux 2011 147p $16.99

Grades: 6 7 8 9 10   **Fic**

1. Novels in verse 2. Camps -- Fiction 3. Friendship -- Fiction

ISBN 0-374-38221-2; 978-0-374-38221-6

LC 2010-24854

When Wren Abbott and Darra Monson are eight years old, Darra's father steals a minivan. He doesn't know that Wren is hiding in the back. Years later, in a chance encounter at camp, the girls face each other for the first time.

"This novel in verse stands out through its deliberate use of form to illuminate emotions and cleverly hide secrets in the text." Booklist

Keesha's house. Frances Foster Bks./Farrar, Straus & Giroux 2003 116p hardcover o.p. pa $8

Grades: 7 8 9 10   **Fic**

1. Home -- Fiction

ISBN 0-374-34064-1; 0-374-40012-1 pa

LC 2002-22698

Michael L. Printz Award honor book, 2004

Seven teens facing such problems as pregnancy, closeted homosexuality, and abuse each describe in poetic forms what caused them to leave home and where they found home again

"Spare, eloquent, and elegantly concise. . . . Public, private, or correctional educators and librarians should put this must-read on their shelves." Voice Youth Advocates

Fukuda, Andrew

The **Prey**; Andrew Fukuda. St Martins Press 2013 336 p. $18.99

Grades: 7 8 9 10 11 12   **Fic**

1. Horror fiction 2. Paranormal fiction 3. Survival skills -- Fiction

ISBN 1250005116; 9781250005113

LC 2013002667

This teen horror thriller, by Andrew Fukuda, is book 2 of the "Hunt" series. "With death only a heartbeat away, Gene and the remaining humans must find a way . . . to escape the hungry predators chasing them through the night. . . . Their escape takes them to a refuge of humans living high in the mountains. Gene and his friends think they're finally safe, but not everything here is as it seems." (Publisher's note)

Funke, Cornelia, 1958-

Fearless; Cornelia Funke. Little, Brown Books for Young Readers 2013 432 p. (hardcover) $19.99

Grades: 6 7 8 9   **Fic**

1. Fantasy fiction 2. Brothers -- Fiction 3. Blessing and cursing -- Fiction 4. Fantasy 5. Magic -- Fiction 6. Adventure and adventurers -- Fiction

ISBN 0316056103; 9780316056106

LC 2012028742

This fantasy novel, by Cornelia Funke, translated by Oliver Latsch, is part of the "Mirrorworld" series. "Jacob

Reckless has . . . tried everything to shake the Fairy curse that traded his life for his brother's. . . . But . . . they hear of one last possibility . . .: a crossbow that can kill thousands, or heal one, when shot through the heart. But a Goyl treasure hunter is also searching for the prized crossbow." (Publisher's note)

"Adroitly building on layers of European fairy tale, Funke's original, rapid-fire narrative fearlessly transports Jacob and a bevy of ominous, multifaceted fantastical characters through a dark, decaying landscape in which death waits and honor is rare. Provocative, harrowing, engrossing." Kirkus

Fusco, Kimberly Newton

Tending to Grace. Knopf 2004 167p $14.95

Grades: 7 8 9 10   **Fic**

1. Aunts -- Fiction 2. Mothers -- Fiction 3. Speech disorders -- Fiction

ISBN 0-375-82862-1

LC 2003-60406

When Cornelia's mother runs off with a boyfriend, leaving her with an eccentric aunt, Cornelia must finally confront the truth about herself and her mother.

"This quiet, beautiful first novel makes the search for home a searing drama." Booklist

Gagnon, Michelle

Don't let go; Michelle Gagnon. Harper, an imprint of HarperCollinsPublishers 2014 352 p. (hardback) $17.99

Grades: 7 8 9 10 11 12   **Fic**

1. Dystopian fiction 2. Experiments -- Fiction 3. Computer hackers -- Fiction 4. Foster home care -- Fiction 5. Abandoned children -- Fiction 6. Adventure and adventurers -- Fiction

ISBN 0062102966; 9780062102966

LC 2014001880

Sequel to: Don't look now

This novel by Michelle Gagnon is the "finale to the Don't Turn Around trilogy," in which "Noa Torson is out of options. On the run with Peter and the two remaining teens of Persephone's Army, and with quickly failing health, she is up against immeasurable odds. The group is outnumbered, outsmarted, and outrun. But they will not give up. They know they must return to where this all began." (Publisher's note)

"Noa and three friends are on the run. They are toting heavy backpacks loaded with hard drives that contain the encrypted information they need to bring to the authorities to prove what experiments Pike has been doing on live people...A look into a future marred by what powerful people will do to fulfill their needs and wants is a little scary. It is heartening to see that young people who discover the truth can band together and battle what seems like overwhelming odds to triumph in the end." VOYA

Don't Look Now; Michelle Gagnon. Harpercollins Childrens Books 2013 336 p. $17.99

Grades: 7 8 9 10 11 12   **Fic**

1. Computer hackers -- Fiction 2. Abandoned children -- Fiction 3. Experiments -- Fiction 4. Foster home

care -- Fiction
ISBN 0062102931; 9780062102935

LC 2013021823

In this book, by Michelle Gagnon, "Noa Torsen is on the run. Having outsmarted the sinister Project Persephone, Noa and her friend Zeke now move stealthily across the country . . . Back in Boston, Peter anxiously follows Noa's movements from his computer, using his hacker skills to feed her the information she needs to stay alive. . . . It will take everything Noa and Peter have to bring down the Project before it gets them first." (Publisher's note)

"Still suffering strange side effects from her stint as a human lab rat at Pike & Dolan, Noa (Don't Turn Around) leads a group of homeless teens bent on sabotaging the corporation. In Boston, her "hacktivist" friend Peter and his ex-girlfriend, Amanda, uncover new evidence that places them all in danger. This tense, suspenseful tech-thriller will engage readers from beginning to end." (Horn Book)

Don't turn around; by Michelle Gagnon. Harper 2012 320 p. (trade bdg.) $17.99
Grades: 7 8 9 10 11 12   **Fic**
1. Dystopian fiction 2. Teenagers -- Fiction 3. Conspiracies -- Fiction 4. Computer hackers -- Fiction 5. Experiments -- Fiction 6. Foster home care -- Fiction 7. Abandoned children -- Fiction
ISBN 0062102907; 9780062102904

LC 2012009691

This book tells the story of "[t]eenage hackers Noa and Peter." Orphan Noa escapes a hospital after waking up from an operation she has no memory of. After having his computer seized when he investigated his father's files, "Peter enlists his hacktivist group /ALLIANCE/ (of which Noa is a member) to" investigate and counterattack. "The attack only serves to dig the teens in deeper when they uncover a frightening conspiracy of human experimentation and corporate malfeasance." (Kirkus Reviews)

Strangelets; by Michelle Gagnon. Soho Teen 2013 1 p. (alk. paper) $17.99
Grades: 8 9 10 11 12   **Fic**
1. Horror fiction 2. Mystery fiction 3. Science fiction 4. Escapes -- Fiction 5. Survival -- Fiction 6. Near-death experiences -- Fiction
ISBN 1616951370; 9781616951375

LC 2012038333

This book by Michelle Gagnon shows the "horror endured by six teens trapped in a hospital-like bunker. They come from every point on the globe: cancer-stricken Sophie from California, petty thief Declan from Ireland, military trainee Anat from Israel, hiker Nico from Switzerland, shy Yosh from Japan, and studious Zain from India." They must figure out why they are there. (Publishers Weekly)

Gaiman, Neil
American gods; a novel. Morrow 2001 465p $26
Grades: 11 12 Adult   **Fic**
1. Fantasy fiction 2. Science fiction 3. Gods 4. Mythology 5. Widowers -- Fiction 6. Bodyguards -- Fiction 7. Ex-convicts -- Fiction 8. Spiritual warfare --

Fiction 9. National characteristics, American -- Fiction
ISBN 0-380-97365-0

LC 2001-30407

This is a "sci-fi road trip novel. . . . Early in 'American Gods' we are introduced to Shadow, a man who has been released from prison only to learn that his wife has died in a car crash. With nothing to return home to, Shadow accepts a job protecting Mr. Wednesday, an omniscient one-eyed grifter. . . . Soon the ex-convict finds himself in an alternate universe, where he is haunted by prophetic nightmares and visited by his dead wife." (N Y Times Book Rev)

"A noirish sci-fi road trip novel in which the melting pot of the United States extends not merely to mortals but to a motley assortment of disgruntled gods and deities. Early in 'American Gods' we are introduced to Shadow, a man who has been released from prison only to learn that his wife has died in a car crash. With nothing to return home to, Shadow accepts a job protecting Mr. Wednesday, an omniscient one-eyed grifter. . . . Soon the ex-convict finds himself in an alternate universe, where he is haunted by prophetic nightmares and visited by his dead wife." N Y Times Book Rev

★ **Anansi** boys. William Morrow 2005 336p il $26.95; pa $7.99
Grades: 11 12 Adult   **Fic**
1. Fantasy fiction 2. Fantasies
ISBN 978-0-06-051518-8; 0-06-051518-X; 978-0-06-051519-5 pa; 0-06-051519-8 pa

LC 2005-47176

"Fat Charlie's life is about to be spiced up—his estranged father dies in a karaoke bar, and the handsome brother he never knew he had shows up on his doorstep with a gleam in his eye. Next thing he knows, Fat Charlie is being investigated by the police, his fiancée's falling in love with the wrong brother, and he finds out that his father was the god Anansi, Trickster and Spider, and that the beast gods of folklore are plotting their own revenge upon his family bloodline. A fun book with a little of everything—horror, mystery, magic, comedy, song, romance, ghosts, scary birds, ancient grudges, and trademark British wit." Libr J

★ **The** **graveyard** book; with illustrations by Dave McKean. HarperCollins 2008 312p il $17.99; lib bdg $18.89
Grades: 5 6 7 8 9 10   **Fic**
1. Death -- Fiction 2. Cemeteries -- Fiction 3. Supernatural -- Fiction
ISBN 0-06-053092-8; 0-06-053093-6 lib bdg; 978-0-06-053092-1; 978-0-06-053093-8 lib bdg

LC 2008-13860

Awarded the Newbery Medal (2009)

Nobody Owens, nicknamed Bod, is a normal boy, except that he has been raised by in a graveyard by ghosts. "Grades five to nine." (Bull Cent Child Books)

"Gaiman writes with charm and humor, and again he has a real winner." Voice Youth Advocates

Interworld; [by] Neil Gaiman [and] Michael Reaves. Eos 2007 239p $16.99; lib bdg $17.89

Grades: 6 7 8 9 10 **Fic**
1. Science fiction 2. Space and time -- Fiction
ISBN 978-0-06-123896-3; 978-0-06-123897-0 lib bdg
LC 2007-08617

At nearly fifteen years of age, Joey Harker learns that he is able to travel between dimensions. Soon, he joins a team of different versions of himself, each from another dimension, to fight the evil forces striving to conquer all the worlds.

This offers "vivid, well-imagined settings and characters. . . . [A] rousing sf/fantasy hybrid." Booklist

★ The **Sleeper** and the Spindle; Neil Gaiman; illustrated by Chris Riddell. Harpercollins Childrens Books 2015 72 p. illustrations $19.99
Grades: 5 6 7 8 9 10 **Fic**
1. Fantasy fiction 2. Sleep -- Fiction 3. Fractured fairy tales
ISBN 0062398245; 9780062398246
LC 2015033123

"Three dwarves discover a realm in which everyone has fallen asleep, and they cross into the next country to warn its queen [Snow White] of the great plague that threatens her people. . . . Traveling to the cursed kingdom, the queen and dwarves encounter threatening zombie sleepers and more." (Publishers Weekly)

"Each page is packed with marvelous details--vines claustrophobically twist everywhere and expressions convey far more emotion than the words let on. Gaiman's narrative about strength, sacrifice, choice, and identity is no simple retelling; he sends readers down one path then deliciously sends the story veering off in an unexpected direction." SLJ

Stardust. Avon Bks. 1999 238p hardcover o.p. pa $13.95; $30.00
Grades: 8 9 10 11 12 Adult **Fic**
1. Fantasy fiction 2. Fantasies
ISBN 0-380-97728-1; 0-06-114202-6 pa; 9780062200396
LC 98-8773

"Young Tristran Thorn has grown up in the isolated village of Wall, on the edge of the realm of Faerie. When Tristran and the lovely Victoria see a falling star during the special market fair, Victoria impulsively offers him his heart's desire if he will retrieve the star for her. Tristran crosses the border into Faerie and encounters witches, unicorns, and other strange creatures." Libr J

Galante, Cecilia
The **sweetness** of salt. Bloomsbury 2010 311p $16.99
Grades: 9 10 11 12 **Fic**
1. Sisters -- Fiction 2. Vermont -- Fiction 3. Family life -- Fiction 4. Self-perception -- Fiction
ISBN 978-1-59990-512-9; 1-59990-512-4
LC 2010-03477

After graduating from high school, class valedictorian Julia travels to Poultney, Vermont, to visit her older sister, and while she is there she learns about long-held family secrets that have shaped her into the person she has grown up to be.

"What makes this novel great is its simplicity. It is poignant without becoming overbearing; it is quiet yet speaks volumes. It contains a realness that is almost uncomfortable to face at times. . . . This is an excellent novel, one that deserves to be read." Voice Youth Advocates

Gant, Gene
The **Thunder** in His Head. Lightning Source Inc 2012 200 p. (paperback) $14.99
Grades: 9 10 11 12 **Fic**
1. Divorce -- Fiction 2. Gay teenagers -- Fiction
ISBN 1613725728; 9781613725726

In this book, "Kyle Manning is a tall, strong, openly gay sixteen-year-old who makes decent grades and plays on his school's basketball team. He's a good kid who cares deeply about his family and friends. But his life has become a mess" due to his parents' divorce. "As Kyle struggles with his fear and frustration, he grows angrier and more erratic. Then he meets Dwight Varley, a buff, attractive athlete from another school." Will having Dwight make things better or worse? (Publisher's note)

Gantos, Jack
The **trouble** in me; Jack Gantos. Farrar, Straus & Giroux 2015 224 p. (hardback) $17.99
Grades: 6 7 8 9 10 **Fic**
1. Humorous fiction 2. Moving -- Fiction 3. Florida -- Fiction 4. Friendship -- Fiction 5. Juvenile delinquency -- Fiction 6. Humorous stories 7. Behavior -- Fiction 8. Moving, Household -- Fiction
ISBN 9780374379957
LC 2015013115

This autobiographical novel, by Jack Gantos, "opens with an explosive encounter in which Jack first meets his awesomely rebellious older neighbor, Gary Pagoda, just back from juvie for car theft. Instantly mesmerized, Jack decides he will do whatever it takes to be like Gary. As a follower, Jack is eager to leave his old self behind, and desperate for whatever crazy, hilarious, frightening thing might happen next. But he may not be as ready as he thinks." (Publisher's note)

"Gantos has won a Newbery Medal, Printz Honor, Sibert Honor, and countless hearts. Readers will want to know how he became one of a kind." Booklist

Garcia, Kami
Beautiful creatures; by Kami Garcia & Margie Stohl. Little, Brown and Co. 2010 563p $17.99
Grades: 7 8 9 10 **Fic**
1. Love stories 2. School stories 3. Supernatural -- Fiction 4. South Carolina -- Fiction
ISBN 0-316-04267-6; 978-0-316-04267-3
LC 2008-51306

ALA YALSA Morris Award Finalist, 2010

This novel is set in a small South Carolina town. Ethan is powerfully drawn to Lena, a new classmate with whom he shares a psychic connection and whose family hides a secret that my be revealed on her sixteenth birthday. "Grades eight to ten." (Bull Cent Child Books)

"The intensity of Ethan and Lena's need to be together is palpable, the detailed descriptions create a vivid, authentic world, and the allure of this story is the power of love.

The satisfying conclusion is sure to lead directly into a sequel." SLJ

Followed by Beautiful darkness (2010)

Beautiful darkness; by Kami Garcia & Margaret Stohl. Little, Brown 2010 503p $17.99; pa $9.99
Grades: 8 9 10 11 12   **Fic**
    1. Love stories 2. Supernatural -- Fiction 3. South Carolina -- Fiction 4. Extrasensory perception -- Fiction
    ISBN 978-0-316-07705-7; 0-316-07705-7; 978-0-316-07704-0 pa; 0-316-07704-6 pa
                                    LC 2010-7015
Sequel to: Beautiful creatures (2010)
    In a small southern town with a secret world hidden in plain sight, sixteen-year-old Lena, who possesses supernatural powers and faces a life-altering decision, draws away from her true love, Ethan, a mortal with frightening visions.
    "The southern gothic atmosphere, several new characters, and the surprising fate of one old favorite will keep readers going until the next book, which promises new surprises as '18 moons' approaches." Booklist

Unbreakable; by Kami Garcia. Little Brown & Co 2013 320 p. (international) $18
Grades: 7 8 9 10   **Fic**
    1. Paranormal fiction 2. Secret societies -- Fiction 3. Love -- Fiction 4. Demonology -- Fiction 5. Supernatural -- Fiction
    ISBN 9780316210171; 031621017X
                                    LC 2012048435
    In this young adult paranormal novel, by Kami Garcia, "when Kennedy Waters finds her mother dead, she doesn't realize that paranormal forces are responsible--not until mysterious identical twins Jared and Lukas Lockhart break into her room and destroy a deadly spirit sent to kill her. Kennedy learns that her mother's death was no accident, and now she has to take her place in the Legion of the Black Dove--a secret society whose five members were all murdered on the same night." (Publisher's note)
    "Readers are quickly drawn into the action, from the murder at the beginning to the cliff-hanger at the end. It's the horror aspect more than the fast-paced intrigue, however, that is the book's strong point. The Legion members must travel from one terrifying location to another, and Garcia describes these chilling locations with flawless detail." - SLJ reviews

García, Cristina, 1958-
Dreams of significant girls. Simon & Schuster Books for Young Readers 2011 238p $16.99
Grades: 9 10 11 12   **Fic**
    1. School stories 2. Summer -- Fiction 3. Friendship -- Fiction 4. Switzerland -- Fiction
    ISBN 978-1-4169-7920-3; 1-4169-7920-4
                                    LC 2010002585
    In the 1970s, a teenaged Iranian princess, a German-Canadian girl, and a Cuban-Jewish girl from New York City become friends when they spend three summers at a Swiss boarding school.
    "The girls' personal awakenings feel organic, and the narrative handles mature themes well, including abortion, family connections to Nazis, and sexual awakenings. Gar-

cía's boarding school setting feels vibrantly alive, an international home away from home that readers should find as magical as do the protagonists." Publ Wkly

Gardner, Sally
    ★ **Maggot** moon; Sally Gardner. Candlewick Press 2013 288 p. (reinforced) $16.99
Grades: 7 8 9 10 11 12   **Fic**
    1. Dystopian juvenile fiction 2. Alternative histories
    ISBN 0763665533; 9780763665531
                                    LC 2012947247
Costa Children's Book Award Winner 2012
Printz Honor Book (2014)
    In this dystopian novel, "Standish Treadwell, 15, has lost parents, neighbors, best friend: All disappeared from Zone Seven, a post-war occupied territory, into the hellish clutches of the Motherland. Now a new horror approaches. . . . Standish and [his friend] Hector spin fantasies about the far-off tantalizing consumer culture they glimpsed on television (now banned), but they lack a vision of the future beyond vague dreams of rescue." (Kirkus Reviews)

    ★ The **red** necklace; a story of the French Revolution. Dial Books 2008 378p $16.99
Grades: 8 9 10 11 12   **Fic**
    1. Adventure fiction 2. Gypsies -- Fiction 3. Orphans -- Fiction 4. Social classes -- Fiction 5. France -- History -- 1789-1799, Revolution -- Fiction
    ISBN 978-0-8037-3100-4; 0-8037-3100-0
                                    LC 2007-39813
    In the late eighteenth-century, Sido, the twelve-year-old daughter of a self-indulgent marquis, and Yann, a fourteen-year-old Gypsy orphan raised to perform in a magic show, face a common enemy at the start of the French Revolution.
    "Scores are waiting to be settled on every page; this is a heart-stopper." Booklist
    Followed by: The silver blade (2009)

The **Silver** Blade. Dial Books 2009 362p $16.99
Grades: 8 9 10 11 12   **Fic**
    1. Adventure fiction 2. Magic -- Fiction 3. France -- History -- 1789-1799, Revolution -- Fiction
    ISBN 978-0-8037-3377-0; 0-8037-3377-1
                                    LC 2009-9282
Sequel to: The red necklace (2008)
    As the Revolution descends into the ferocious Reign of Terror, Yann, now an extraordinary practioner of magic, uses his skills to confound his enemies and help spirit refugees out of France, but the question of his true identity and the kidnapping of his true love, Sido, expose him to dangers that threaten to destroy him.
    "A luscious melodrama, rich in sensuous detail from horrific to sublime, with an iridescent overlay of magic." Kirkus

Gardner, Scot
    ★ The **dead** I know; by Scot Gardner. Houghton Mifflin Harcourt 2015 201 p. $17.99
Grades: 9 10 11 12   **Fic**
    1. Sleepwalking -- Fiction 2. Senile dementia -- Fiction 3. Undertakers and undertaking -- Fiction 4. Dreams -- Fiction 5. Memories -- Fiction 6. Funeral homes

-- Fiction 7. Emotional problems -- Fiction
ISBN 0544232747; 9780544232747

LC 2013050162

In this book by Scot Gardner, "faced with recurring nightmares, uncontrollable sleepwalking, threats from gangs, and a mother suffering from dementia, Aaron Rowe becomes assistant to a funeral director. He retrieves and prepares bodies. John Barton, the funeral director, considers Aaron a valued member of his household and provides the teen with a strong, healthy environment. Extremely violent encounters require Aaron to make some difficult decisions." (Library Media Connection)

"Aaron has trouble connecting with people. He suffers from recurring nightmares—horrific memories of a dead woman—that have been locked away, and most nights he sleepwalks away from his home and into a caravan park where the majority of residents are drug addicts. When the teen gets a funeral director apprenticeship with Mr. Barton, it is not the dead bodies that make him nervous, but Mr. Barton's family and the grieving mourners instead...With humorous interactions and their unwavering belief that Aaron is worthwhile, Mr. Barton and his daughter, Skye, help him appreciate life in the midst of death and tragedy. A darkly funny book..." SLJ

Garner, Em

Contaminated; by Em Garner. Egmont USA 2013 336 p. (hardcover) $17.99; (ebook) $17.99
Grades: 7 8 9 10   Fic
1. Horror fiction 2. Dystopian fiction 3. Horror stories 4. Science fiction 5. Mothers -- Fiction
ISBN 1606843540; 9781606843543; 9781606843550

LC 2012024472

This book is set two years after "a diet drink with genetically modified ingredients transformed countless Americans into mindlessly violent animals" Now, "the Contaminated are controlled by electronic collars, and the unclaimed are housed in kennels like that in which Velvet Ellis, 17, finds her mother." Velvet and her sister's "shaky hold on normal life is finally upended when Velvet brings their mother home, facing anger and fear from neighbors and eviction from their landlord." (Kirkus Reviews)

Mercy mode; Em Garner. Egmont USA 2014 352 p. (Contaminated) (hardback) $17.99
Grades: 9 10 11 12   Fic
1. Dystopian fiction 2. Horror stories 3. Science fiction 4. Survival -- Fiction 5. Government -- Resistance to -- Fiction
ISBN 1606843567; 9781606843567

LC 2014007247

In this dystopian young adult novel by Em Garner, part of the Contaminated series, "seventeen-year-old Velvet, her little sister, Opal, their mom, who is recovering from the Contamination, and Velvet's sweet boyfriend, Dillon, are attempting to build a new life amid the rationing and regulations of the post-outbreak nation. But the outbreak isn't over: more people turning into 'Connies,' more madness erupting, more killings occurring." (Publisher's note)

"Velvet's complexity and thoughtfulness make her an especially interesting dystopian heroine, and the intense and horrifying plot comes to an exciting conclusion that satisfies

but provides some enticing threads to continue in the next installment." Horn Book

Garsee, Jeannine

Before, after, and somebody in between. Bloomsbury 2007 342p $16.95
Grades: 8 9 10 11 12   Fic
1. School stories 2. Poor -- Fiction 3. Alcoholism -- Fiction 4. Family life -- Fiction 5. Cleveland (Ohio) -- Fiction
ISBN 978-1-59990-022-3; 1-59990-022-X

LC 2006-27975

After dealing with an alcoholic mother and her abusive boyfriend, a school bully, and life on the wrong side of the tracks in Cleveland, Ohio, high school sophomore Martha Kowalski expects to be happy when she moves in with a rich family across town, but finds that the "rich life" has problems of its own.

"Readers who live in better conditions can experience the underside of life from her dead-on observations. Martha is just a hairsbreadth away from being sucked under like so many around her. Readers will be pulling for her to beat the odds." SLJ

Say the word. Bloomsbury Children's Books 2009 360p $16.99
Grades: 9 10 11 12   Fic
1. Ohio -- Fiction 2. Lesbians -- Fiction 3. Bereavement -- Fiction 4. Family life -- Fiction
ISBN 978-1-59990-333-0; 1-59990-333-4

LC 2008-16476

After the death of her estranged mother, who left Ohio years ago to live with her lesbian partner in New York City, seventeen-year-old Shawna Gallagher's life is transformed by revelations about her family, her best friend, and herself.

"This sensitive and heart-wrenching story slowly unfolds into a gripping read featuring realistically flawed characters who undergo genuine growth." Booklist

Garvey, Amy

Cold kiss. HarperTeen 2011 292p $17.99; ebook $9.99
Grades: 9 10 11 12   Fic
1. School stories 2. Dead -- Fiction 3. Future life -- Fiction 4. Parapsychology -- Fiction
ISBN 978-0-06-199622-1; 978-0-06-210335-2 ebook

LC 2010040421

When her boyfriend is killed in a car accident, high school student Wren Darby uses her hidden powers to bring him back from the dead, never imagining the consequences that will result from her decision.

"Garvey sidesteps zombie tropes by keeping the focus on Wren's emotional state and the consequences of her actions, painting a delicate portrait of first love, loss, and a 'girl who thought love came with ownership papers.'" Publ Wkly

Glass Heart; Amy Garvey. 1st ed. HarperTeen 2012 310 p. (hardcover) $17.99
Grades: 9 10 11 12   Fic
1. Horror fiction 2. Magic -- Fiction 3. Psychics --

Fiction 4. Horror stories 5. Psychic ability -- Fiction
ISBN 0061996246; 9780061996245

LC 2011052410

In this book by Amy Garvey, protagonist Wren has discovered "new magical abilities that include the power to
resurrect the dead. . . . Desperate to learn more . . . Wren
presses her mother for help. Unfortunately, secrecy, shame
and pain keep her from teaching Wren. . . . Looking to her
new friends, who have abilities of their own, Wren begins
leading a secret life full of spells and excitement. But while
Fiona seems mostly fun and frivolous, Bay is dark and dangerous." (Kirkus Reviews)

Gee, Maurice
Gool. Orca Book Publishers 2010 215p (The
Salt trilogy) lib bdg $18
Grades: 6 7 8 9 10   Fic
1. Fantasy fiction
ISBN 978-1-55469-214-9; 1-55469-214-8
Sequel to: Salt (2009)

Xantee and Lo set out to find the Dog King, Tarl, whose
help they will need if they are to have any hope of destroying the gool and ridding the world of its life-sucking force.

"The unexpected twists of this original fantasy adventure keep the pages turning. The fascinating buildup leads to
a thrilling climax." Kirkus

Followed by: The Limping Man (2011)

The **Limping** Man. Orca Book Publishers 2011
195p il (The Salt trilogy) lib bdg $18
Grades: 6 7 8 9 10   Fic
1. Fantasy fiction
ISBN 978-1-55469-216-3 ib bdg; 1-55469-216-4
lib bdg

LC 2010-413414

Sequel to: Gool (2010)

Hana narrowly escapes Blood Burrow after her mother
chooses to swallow poison rather than die in the great witch-
burning in People's Square. Deep in the forest she meets
Ben, son of Lo, and Hawk, who becomes her silent protector
and guide. But even in the forest there is no peace. When
they learn of the advancing armies that will wipe out all
those who have sought refuge in the wilderness, they realize
they have no choice but to return to the city and confront the
terrible power of the Limping Man head-on.

★ **Salt.** Orca Book Publishers 2009 252p map
(The Salt trilogy) $18; pa $12.95
Grades: 6 7 8 9 10   Fic
1. Fantasy fiction 2. Extrasensory perception -- Fiction
ISBN 978-1-55469-209-5; 1-55469-209-1; 978-1-
55469-369-6 pa; 1-55469-369-1 pa

"Hari lives in Blood Burrow, a hellacious, rat-infested
slum. . . . Pearl is a pampered daughter of Company, her only
purpose in life to be married off to cement one of her father's
political alliances. When both young people, who share rare
psychic gifts, revolt against their fates, they find themselves
on a desperate journey across a hostile landscape, with the
forces of Company at their heels. . . . A compelling tale of
anger and moral development that also powerfully explores
the evils of colonialism and racism." Publ Wkly

Other titles in this series are:

Gool (2010)
The Limping Man (2011)

Gelbwasser, Margie
Inconvenient. Flux 2010 305p pa $9.95
Grades: 7 8 9 10   Fic
1. School stories 2. Alcoholism -- Fiction 3. Immigrants
-- Fiction 4. Popularity -- Fiction 5. Russian Americans
-- Fiction 6. Jews -- United States -- Fiction
ISBN 978-0-7387-2148-4; 0-7387-2148-4

LC 2010025578

While fifteen-year-old Russian-Jewish immigrant Alyssa tries desperately to cope with her mother's increasingly
out-of-control alcoholism by covering for her and pretending things are normal, her best friend Lana attempts to fit in
with the popular crowd at their high school.

"This will be a hit with girls who like realistic fiction that
focuses on the complexity of human relationships." Voice
Youth Advocates

Gemini. Simon & Schuster Books for Young Readers
2016 326 pp. hardcover $17.99
Grades: 8 9 10 11 12   Fic
1. School stories 2. Sisters -- Fiction 3. Conjoined
twins -- Fiction
ISBN 9781481456777

LC 2015019774

"Seventeen-year-old conjoined twins, Clara and Hailey,
have lived in the same small town their entire lives—no one
stares at them anymore. But there are cracks in their quiet
existence and they're slowing becoming more apparent.
Clara and Hailey are at a crossroads. Clara wants to stay
close to home, avoid all attention, and study the night sky.
Hailey wants to travel the world, learn from great artists,
and dance with mysterious boys. As high school graduation
approaches, each twin must untangle her dreams from her
sister's, and figure out what it means to be her own person."
(Publisher's note)

"Even for sisters, Clara and Hailey are close. They have
to be—they're conjoined twins attached at the spine. They've
lived their whole lives in the small California town of Bear
Pass, where people are used to them, and they'll likely spend
college—and everything after—there as well. For Clara, shy
and quiet, with a love for astronomy, that's just fine, but
spirited and rebellious artist Hailey wants more. . . . With
references to famous conjoined twins such as Daisy and
Violet Hilton—and distinct shades of the Tony-nominated
Side Show—this debut is a well-researched and particularly
heartfelt account of a rare medical condition and the people
it affects. Though they share a body, Clara and Hailey are
two very different people with different dreams, and their
fight for a normal life will resonate with many." Booklist

Gensler, Sonia
The **revenant.** Alfred A. Knopf 2011 336p
$16.99; lib bdg $19.99
Grades: 7 8 9 10   Fic
1. Ghost stories 2. School stories 3. Oklahoma --
Fiction 4. Teachers -- Fiction 5. Cherokee Indians

-- Fiction

ISBN 978-0-375-86701-9; 0-375-86701-5; 978-0-375-96701-6 lib bdg; 0-375-96701-X lib bdg

LC 2010-28701

When seventeen-year-old Willemina Hammond fakes credentials to get a teaching position at a school for Cherokee girls in nineteenth-century Oklahoma, she is haunted by the ghost of a drowned student.

"Gensler makes a solid debut with an eerie and suspenseful work of historical fiction in which everyone is a murder suspect. . . . The layers of detail address the complex social structure of the period, and Gensler's characters and dialogue are believably crafted." Publ Wkly

George, Madeleine

The **difference** between you and me; by Madeleine George. Viking 2012 256 p. (hardcover) $16.99

Grades: 7 8 9 10 11 12   **Fic**

1. Secrecy -- Fiction 2. Lesbians -- Fiction 3. High school students -- Fiction 4. Schools -- Fiction 5. High schools -- Fiction 6. Protest movements -- Fiction

ISBN 9780670011285

LC 2011012192

This young adult novel uses a trio of alternating narrators to tell the story of "self-proclaimed misfit and outspoken manifesto-author Jesse [who] deals daily with the hazards of being out and proud in high school. She's also carrying on a secret affair with image-conscious Emily, the girlfriend of a popular boy at school. Meeting weekly in the bathroom of the local public library, the two experience an inexplicable chemistry, even though Emily will barely acknowledge Jesse at any other time. Switching perspective among Emily, Jesse and a third girl, Esther, this . . . tale . . . explor[es] . . . attraction and shame. Jesse hides her relationship from her warmly quirky and accepting parents not because it is with a girl, but because she knows they will disapprove of its secrecy." (Kirkus)

★ **Looks**. Viking 2008 240p $16.99; pa $7.99

Grades: 8 9 10 11 12   **Fic**

1. School stories 2. Obesity -- Fiction 3. Friendship -- Fiction 4. Anorexia nervosa -- Fiction

ISBN 978-0-670-06167-9; 0-670-06167-0; 978-0-14-241419-4 pa; 0-14-241419-0 pa

LC 2007-38218

"Meghan and Aimee are on opposite ends of the outcast spectrum. Meghan is extremely overweight. . . . Aimee, on the other hand, is classic anorexic. Both girls have been hurt by one of the popular girls at school. They join forces to bring Cara down in a stunning bit of public humiliation. . . . The story will make readers think about the various issues touched upon, and it is difficult to put down." SLJ

Geras, Adele

Ithaka. Harcourt 2006 360p $17; pa $6.95

Grades: 7 8 9 10   **Fic**

1. Trojan War -- Fiction 2. Classical mythology -- Fiction 3. Odysseus (Greek mythology) -- Fiction

ISBN 0-15-205603-3; 0-15-206104-5 pa

LC 2005-7569

Companion volume to: Troy

The island of Ithaka is overrun with uncouth suitors demanding that Penelope choose a new husband, as she patiently awaits the return of Odysseus from the Trojan War.

This book "can introduce young people to the power of story in Homer's epics as well as being a beautifully written story in its own right." Voice Youth Advocates

★ **Troy**. Harcourt 2001 340p hardcover o.p. pa $6.95

Grades: 7 8 9 10   **Fic**

1. Trojan War -- Fiction

ISBN 0-15-216492-8; 0-15-204570-8 pa

LC 00-57262

"Mythology buffs will savor the author's ability to embellish stories of old without diminishing their original flavor, while the uninitiated will find this a captivating introduction to a pivotal event in classic Greek literature." Publ Wkly

Gershow, Miriam

The **local** news. Spiegel & Grau 2009 360p $24.95

Grades: 11 12 Adult   **Fic**

1. Brothers -- Fiction 2. Bereavement -- Fiction 3. Missing persons -- Fiction

ISBN 978-0-385-52761-3; 0-385-52761-6

LC 2008-33391

Still haunted by the disappearance of her popular older brother when she was sixteen, Lydia Pasternak grows up dealing with her frantic parents and assisting the private investigator hired by her family to search for clues to his fate.

"Gershow's writing is fluid, her imagery of the mid '90s concise and compelling, and her story universal." SLJ

Gibney, Shannon

See no color; Shannon Gibney. Carolrhoda Lab 2015 186 p. (lb: alk. paper) $18.99

Grades: 7 8 9 10   **Fic**

1. Adopted children -- Fiction 2. Baseball players -- Fiction 3. Adoption -- Fiction 4. Baseball -- Fiction 5. Identity -- Fiction 6. Family life -- Fiction 7. Self-acceptance -- Fiction 8. African Americans -- Fiction

ISBN 1467776823; 9781467776820

LC 2015001619

In Shannon Gibey's novel "for as long as she can remember, sixteen-year-old Alex Kirtridge has known two things: 1. She has always been Little Kirtridge, a stellar baseball player, just like her father. 2. She's adopted. But now, things are changing: she meets Reggie, the first black guy who's wanted to get to know her; she discovers the letters from her biological father that her adoptive parents have kept from her; and her body starts to grow into a woman's, affecting her game." (Publisher's note)

"Recommended for purchase, particularly by libraries serving less diverse communities, where it will provide welcome education and support." SLJ

Gier, Kerstin

Emerald green; Kerstin Gier; translated by Anthea Bell. Henry Holt and Co 2013 464 p. (hardback) $17.99

Grades: 7 8 9 10   **Fic**
1. Love stories 2. Time travel -- Fiction 3. Secret
societies -- Fiction 4. Love -- Fiction 5. England --
Fiction 6. London (England) -- Fiction 7. Great Britain
-- History -- Fiction 8. Family life -- England -- London
-- Fiction
ISBN 0805092676; 9780805092677
                                        LC 2013017885
Sequel to: Sapphire blue
In the conclusion to author Kerstin Gier's Ruby Red trilogy, Gwen has "recently learned that she is the Ruby, the final member of the time-traveling Circle of Twelve, and since
then nothing has been going right. She suspects the founder
of the Circle, Count Saint-German, is up to something nefarious, but nobody will believe her. And she's just learned
that her charming time-traveling partner, Gideon, has probably been using her all along." (Publisher's note)

"The conclusion to the Ruby Red series has as many
twists as the two previous books in the trilogy. Gwen has
endured danger and flirted with romance throughout the two
weeks (!) since she learned she's the final member of the
time-traveling Circle of Twelve. Now, the questions aren't
resolved until the final few pages as she tries to counteract
the plans of the dastardly Count Saint-Germain. The best-
selling series has been blessed with a clever heroine, a hysterical gargoyle, and a guy as good looking as he is enigmatic. With loooong lives ahead of them, perhaps this not
the end after all. " (Booklist)

★ **Ruby** red; translated from the German by
Anthea Bell. Henry Holt 2011 330p $16.99
Grades: 7 8 9 10   **Fic**
1. Family life -- Fiction 2. Time travel -- Fiction 3.
London (England) -- Fiction 4. Secret societies --
Fiction
ISBN 978-0-8050-9252-3; 0-8050-9252-8
                                        LC 2010-49223
"Sixteen-year-old Gwyneth has known all her life that a
time-traveling gene runs in her family: her cousin, Charlotte,
has been trained as the carrier since birth. Gwyneth starts
to experience time traveling symptoms. When she suddenly
finds herself sent to different eras three times within forty-
eight hours, she begins to wonder whether her family made a
mistake about who was to inherit the gene." (VOYA)
"Adventure, humor, and mystery all have satisfying
roles here." Booklist

Sapphire blue; Kerstin Gier; translated from the
German by Anthea Bell. Henry Holt 2012 362 p.
(hc) $16.99
Grades: 7 8 9 10   **Fic**
1. Fantasy fiction 2. Time travel -- Fiction 3. Secret
societies -- Fiction 4. England -- Fiction 5. London
(England) -- Fiction 6. Great Britain -- History --
Fiction 7. Family life -- England -- London -- Fiction
ISBN 0805092668; 9780805092660
                                        LC 2011034011
Sequel to: Ruby red
In this young adult fantasy novel, by Kerstin Gier,
"16-year-old Gwen continues her time-traveling adventures
as the newest member of the Circle of Twelve. . . . Her life's
now controlled by . . . a secret society monitoring time trav-

el. . . . All 12 time travelers must be introduced into the chro-
nograph so the Circle can be closed, and the Guardians have
assigned Gwen and irresistible Gideon de Villiers the task
of locating four missing time travelers." (Kirkus Reviews)

Gilbert, Kelly Loy
Conviction; Kelly Loy Gilbert. Disney-Hyper-
ion 2015 352 p. (hardback) $17.99
Grades: 9 10 11 12   **Fic**
1. Trials (Homicide) -- Fiction 2. Father-son
relationship -- Fiction 3. Faith -- Fiction 4. Trials
(Murder) -- Fiction 5. Fathers and sons -- Fiction
ISBN 1423197380; 9781423197386
                                        LC 2014042087
William C. Morris Award Finalist (2016)
In this young adult novel by Kelly Loy Gilbert, "Braden
has always measured himself through baseball. . . . Now the
rules of the sport that has always been Braden's saving grace
are blurred in ways he never realized, and the prospect of
playing against Alex Reyes, the nephew of the police officer
his father is accused of killing, is haunting his every pitch."
(Publisher's note)

Giles, Gail
Dark song. Little, Brown 2010 292p $16.99
Grades: 8 9 10 11 12   **Fic**
1. Criminals -- Fiction 2. Family life -- Fiction
ISBN 978-0-316-06886-4; 0-316-06886-1
                                        LC 2010-06888
After her father loses his job and she finds out that her
parents have lied to her, fifteen-year-old Ames feels betrayed
enough to become involved with a criminal who will stop at
nothing to get what he wants.
"Suspense lovers will savor this fast-paced psychological thriller." Voice Youth Advocates

★ **Girls** like us; Gail Giles. Candlewick Press
2014 224 p. $16.99
Grades: 9 10 11 12   **Fic**
1. Roommates -- Fiction 2. Friendship -- Fiction 3.
People with disabilities -- Fiction
ISBN 0763662674; 9780763662677
                                        LC 2013944011
Schneider Family Book Award (Ages 13 - 18) (2015)
" In compelling, engaging, and raw voices, 18-year-olds
Biddy and Quincy, newly independent, intellectually disabled high-school graduates, narrate their growing friendship and uneasy transition into a life of jobs, real world
apartments, and facing cruel prejudice... Giles (Dark Song,
2010) offers a sensitive and affecting story of two young
women learning to thrive in spite of their hard circumstances." (Booklist)

Right behind you. Little, Brown 2007 292p
hardcover o.p. pa $7.99
Grades: 8 9 10 11 12   **Fic**
1. Homicide -- Fiction 2. Family life -- Fiction 3.
Psychotherapy -- Fiction
ISBN 978-0-316-16636-2; 0-316-16636-7; 978-0-316-
16637-9 pa; 0-316-16637-5 pa
                                        LC 2007-12336

After spending over four years in a mental institution for murdering a friend in Alaska, fourteen-year-old Kip begins a completely new life in Indiana with his father and stepmother under a different name, but not only has trouble fitting in, he finds there are still problems to deal with from his childhood.

"The story-behind-the-headlines flavor gives this a voyeuristic appeal, while the capable writing and sympathetic yet troubled protagonist will suck readers right into the action." Bull Cent Child Books

Shattering Glass. Simon Pulse 2003 215p pa $7.99
Grades: 7 8 9 10   Fic
1. School stories 2. Violence -- Fiction
ISBN 978-0-689-85800-0; 0-689-85800-0
First published 2002 by Roaring Brook Press
When Rob, the charismatic leader of the senior class, turns the school nerd into Prince Charming, his actions lead to unexpected violence.

"Tricky, surprising, and disquieting, this tension-filled story is a psychological thriller as well as a book about finding oneself and taking responsibility." Booklist

★ **What** happened to Cass McBride? a novel. Little, Brown and Company 2006 211p $16.99; pa $7.99
Grades: 11 12   Fic
1. Suicide -- Fiction 2. Kidnapping -- Fiction 3. Family life -- Fiction
ISBN 978-0-316-16638-6; 0-316-16638-3; 978-0-316-16639-3 pa; 0-316-16639-1 pa
LC 2005-37298
After his younger brother commits suicide, Kyle Kirby decides to exact revenge on the person he holds responsible.

"Often brutal, this outstanding psychological thriller is recommended for older teens." Voice Youth Advocates

Giles, Lamar
Fake ID; L.R. Giles. Amistad 2014 320 p. (hardback) $17.99
Grades: 8 9 10 11 12   Fic
1. Homicide -- Fiction 2. Witnesses -- Fiction 3. Conspiracies -- Fiction 4. African Americans -- Fiction 5. Mystery and detective stories 6. Witness protection programs -- Fiction
ISBN 0062121847; 9780062121844
LC 2013032149
In this novel by Lamar Giles, "Nick Pearson is hiding in plain sight. In fact, his name isn't really Nick Pearson. He shouldn't tell you his real name, his real hometown, or why his family just moved to Stepton, Virginia. And he definitely shouldn't tell you about his friend Eli Cruz and the major conspiracy Eli was uncovering when he died. About how Nick had to choose between solving Eli's murder with his . . . sister, Reya, and 'staying low-key' like the Program said to do." (Publisher's note)

"Nick Pearson's real name is Tony Bordeaux. A high schooler in Witness Protection, this is the fourth new identity and home for Nick in the last few years. It's all because his father keeps falling into his old criminal habits...Teen readers will especially relate to the likable everyman and

African American main character. His burgeoning relationship with Reya, despite being grounded in tragedy, is one of the more charming aspects of the plot. A twist reveal at the novel's climax will shock many and will leave fans of mystery and suspense books extremely satisfied.—" (School Library Journal)

Gill, David Macinnis
Black hole sun. Greenwillow Books 2010 340p $16.99
Grades: 8 9 10 11 12   Fic
1. Science fiction 2. Miners -- Fiction 3. Mars (Planet) -- Fiction
ISBN 0-06-167304-8; 978-0-06-167304-7
LC 2009-23050
"Now that life on Mars has evolved beyond mere survival, humans have increasingly brought their corruption and vices from Earth to the newly inhabited planet. As the story opens, Durango and his crew of teenage bounty hunters are working to liberate the daughter of a wealthy aristocrat from the clutches of a kidnapper. Their next assignment takes them to Mars's South Pole to defend poor miners against the attacks of savage cannibals. . . . High school." (Horn Book)

"Durango is the 16-year-old chief of a team of mercenaries who eke out a living on Mars by earning meager commissions for their dangerous work. Their current job, and the main thrust of this high-energy, action-filled, science-fiction romp, is to protect South Pole miners from the Dræu, a cannibalistic group who are after the miners' treasure. . . . Throughout the novel, the dialogue crackles with expertly delivered sarcastic wit and venom. . . . Readers will have a hard time turning the pages fast enough as the body count rises to the climactic, satisfying ending." Booklist

Invisible sun; by David Macinnis Gill. 1st ed. Greenwillow Books 2012 370 p. (Black Hole Sun Trilogy) (paperback) $9.99; (trade bdg.) $16.99
Grades: 8 9 10 11   Fic
1. Science fiction 2. Mars (Planet) -- Fiction 3. Adventure and adventurers -- Fiction
ISBN 9780062073334; 006207332X; 9780062073327
LC 2011002841
Sequel to Black Hole Sun.
This science fiction adventure story, by David Macinnis Gill, is the sequel to "Black Hole Sun," continuing to describe how "Martian freedom fighters Durango and Vienne infiltrate an evil government compound in search of missing data they hope will render the planet safe from future harm. This . . . novel is packed with . . . death-defying escapes, ambushes and . . . shootouts." (Kirkus)

Shadow on the sun; David Macinnis Gill. 1st ed. Greenwillow Books, an imprint of HarperCollins Publishers 2013 432 p. (Black Hole Sun Trilogy) (hardcover) $17.99
Grades: 8 9 10 11   Fic
1. Science fiction 2. Mars (Planet) -- Fiction
ISBN 0062073354; 9780062073358
LC 2013008361
This young adult science fiction novel, by David Macinnis Gill, is the sequel to "Invisible Sun." "Ex-Regulators Durango and Vienne are at it again in a race against time

on a dangerous Martian landscape. Shocked to have learned that his father heads up the enemy forces who captured him at the end of the previous book, wisecracking teen soldier Durango fights to escape the clutches of his evil dad and to reunite with his ex-assassin sidekick and love interest, Vienne." (Kirkus Reviews)

"This sequel doesn't stand alone, and Gill inserts just enough left turns and red herrings to keep seasoned series readers guessing. . . . A refreshingly nondystopic sci-fi adventure." Kirkus

Soul enchilada. Greenwillow Books 2009 368p $16.99; lib bdg $17.89

Grades: 7 8 9 10   **Fic**
1. Devil -- Fiction 2. Grandfathers -- Fiction 3. Racially mixed people -- Fiction
ISBN 978-0-06-167301-6; 0-06-167301-3; 978-0-06-167302-3 lib bdg; 0-06-167302-1 lib bdg
LC 2008-19486

When, after a demon appears to repossess her car, she discovers that both the car and her soul were given as collateral in a deal made with the Devil by her irrascible grandfather, eighteen-year-old Bug Smoot, given two-days' grace, tries to find ways to outsmart the Devil as she frantically searches for her conveniently absent relative.

"Bug is a refreshingly gutsy female protagonist with an attitude that will win over readers searching for something different." Booklist

Gilman, David

Blood sun. Delacorte Press 2011 (Danger zone) $17.99; lib bdg $20.99; e-book $10.00

Grades: 7 8 9 10 11 12   **Fic**
1. Mystery fiction 2. Adventure fiction 3. Rain forests -- Fiction 4. Great Britain -- Fiction 5. Central America -- Fiction 6. Wilderness survival -- Fiction 7. Environmental protection -- Fiction
ISBN 978-0-385-73562-9; 978-0-385-90548-0 lib bdg; 978-0-375-89809-9 e-book
LC 2010005169

Sequel to: Ice claw (2010)

Desperate to uncover the secret of his mother's death, fifteen-year-old Max Gordon, pursued by enemies, travels from the bleakness of Dartmoor to the rainforest of Central America, where the environmental devastation hides a sinister secret.

"Max Gordon is a likable character who faces tough challenges with determination, physical strength and a positive attitude. . . . This is . . . a solid read from start to breathless finish." Kirkus

The **devil's** breath. Delacorte Press 2008 391p (Danger zone) $15.99; lib bdg $18.99

Grades: 7 8 9 10 11 12   **Fic**
1. Adventure fiction 2. Namibia -- Fiction 3. Environmental protection -- Fiction
ISBN 978-0-385-73560-5; 978-0-385-90546-6 lib bdg
LC 2007-46744

When fifteen-year-old Max Gordon's environmentalist-adventurer father goes missing while working in Namibia and Max becomes the target of a would-be assassin at his

school in England, he decides he must follow his father to Africa and find him before they both are killed.

"The action is relentless. . . . Gilman has a flair for making the preposterous seem possible." Booklist

Other titles in this series are:
Ice claw (2010)
Blood sun (2011)

Ice claw. Delacorte Press 2010 439p (Danger zone) $15.99; lib bdg $18.99

Grades: 7 8 9 10 11 12   **Fic**
1. Mystery fiction 2. Adventure fiction
ISBN 978-0-385-73561-2; 0-385-73561-8; 978-0-385-90547-3 lib bdg; 0-385-90547-5 lib bdg
LC 2009-13228

Sequel to: The Devil's breath (2008)

High in the French Pyrenees, fifteen-year-old Max Gordon's race to win an extreme sports challenge becomes a race to survive when he is accused of causing the death of a mysterious Basque monk who has predicted a cataclysmic ecological disaster

"The omniscient point of view . . . does a lot for clarity, which is his strong suit—few authors are able to depict action scenes so lucidly. . . . But it's Max's humanity . . . that makes Gilman's research and storytelling come alive." Booklist

Followed by: Blood sun (2011)

Gleason, Colleen

The **clockwork** scarab; Colleen Gleason. Chronicle Books 2013 356 p. (Stoker & Holmes) (alk. paper) $17.99

Grades: 7 8 9 10   **Fic**
1. Mystery fiction 2. Historical fiction 3. Scarabs -- Fiction 4. Time travel -- Fiction 5. Secret societies -- Fiction 6. Detective and mystery stories
ISBN 1452110700; 9781452110707
LC 2012036578

This is the first book in Colleen Gleason's Stoker and Holmes series. The "narrative switches between two young women living in 1889 London: observant and cerebral Alvermina Holmes (she goes by Mina . . .), the niece of Sherlock Holmes; and Evaline Stoker, the headstrong (and physically strong) younger sister to Bram, and member of a proud line of vampire hunters." They "investigate the connection between the disappearance of a young woman and several recent murders." (Publishers Weekly)

Gleitzman, Morris

Now; Morris Gleitzman. Henry Holt 2012 184 p. (hc) $16.99

Grades: 7 8 9 10   **Fic**
1. Psychological fiction 2. Family life -- Fiction 3. Grandfathers -- Fiction 4. Holocaust survivors -- Fiction 5. Australia -- Fiction 6. Wildfires -- Fiction 7. Jews -- Australia -- Fiction 8. Separation (Psychology) -- Fiction
ISBN 0805093788; 9780805093780
LC 2011033496

Sequel to: Then

This novel by Morris Gleitzman is "[s]et in the current day, this is the final book in the series that began with Once, continued with Then and is . . . Now. . . . While her physician-parents are working in Africa, eleven-year-old Zelda is living with her grandfather, eighty-year-old Holocaust-survivor Felix Salinger, in Australia . . . He has achieved much in his life and is widely admired in the community. He has mostly buried the painful memories of his childhood . . . when a disaster leads them both to deal with unresolved feelings about the first Zelda, Felix's childhood friend." (Publisher's note)

Once. Henry Holt and Company 2010 163p $16.99

Grades: 7 8 9 10   **Fic**
1. Jews -- Poland -- Fiction 2. Holocaust, 1933-1945 -- Fiction
ISBN 978-0-8050-9026-0; 0-8050-9026-6
                                        LC 2009-24153
"The horror of the Holocaust is told here through the eyes of a Polish Jewish child, Felix, who loses his innocence as he witnesses Nazi-led roundups, shootings, and deportations. . . . Most moving is the lack of any idealization. . . . Felix escapes, but one and a half million Jewish children did not, and this gripping novel will make readers want to find out more about them." Booklist
Followed by: Then (2011)

Goeglein, T. M.
Cold fury; T.M. Goeglein. G.P. Putnam's Sons 2012 312 p. (hardcover) $17.99

Grades: 8 9 10 11 12   **Fic**
1. Mafia -- Fiction 2. Chicago (Ill.) -- Fiction 3. Missing persons -- Fiction 4. Violence -- Fiction 5. Secret societies -- Fiction 6. Mystery and detective stories
ISBN 0399257209; 9780399257209
                                        LC 2011025824
This book by T. M. Goeglein follows "Sara Jane Rispoli . . . a normal sixteen-year-old coping with school and a budding romance--until her parents and brother are kidnapped and she discovers her family is deeply embedded in the Chicago Outfit (aka the mob). Now on the run from a masked assassin, rogue cops and her turncoat uncle, Sara Jane is chased and attacked at every turn, fighting back with cold fury as she searches for her family." (Publisher's note)

Goelman, Ari
The **path** of names; by Ari Goelman. Arthur A. Levine Books 2013 352 p. (hard cover: alk. paper) $16.99

Grades: 7 8 9 10   **Fic**
1. Ghost stories 2. Mystery fiction 3. Camps -- Fiction 4. Magic -- Fiction 5. Cabala -- Fiction 6. Labyrinths -- Fiction 7. Magic tricks -- Fiction
ISBN 0545474302; 9780545474306; 9780545474313; 9780545540148
                                        LC 2012030554
This book features Dahlia whom "her parents have sent . . . to Camp Arava. . . . When Dahlia first sees two young girls disappear through the cabin wall, she's convinced it's a great magic trick, but soon she realizes that they're actually ghosts. . . . These strange phenomena begin to converge around a mysterious garden maze on the campgrounds, a maze that is rumored to be connected to the disappearance of children and that is ferociously guarded by the skulking camp caretaker." (Bulletin of the Center for Children's Books)
"Thirteen-year-old magic nerd Dahlia loathes her Jewish summer camp until she starts dreaming about a Jewish teen in 1940s New York City who seems to be connected to a pair of ghosts haunting the camp. Readers with an interest in Jewish mysticism will enjoy the book's paranormal elements and tweens will appreciate the realistic relationships among the campers." (Horn Book)

Going, K. L.
★ **Fat** kid rules the world. Putnam 2003 187p $17.99; pa $6.99

Grades: 7 8 9 10   **Fic**
1. Obesity -- Fiction 2. Musicians -- Fiction 3. Friendship -- Fiction
ISBN 0-399-23990-1; 0-14-240208-7 pa
                                        LC 2002-67956
Michael L. Printz Award honor book, 2004
Seventeen-year-old Troy, depressed, suicidal, and weighing nearly 300 pounds, gets a new perspective on life when a homeless teenager who is a genius on guitar wants Troy to be the drummer in his rock band
"Going has put together an amazing assortment of characters. . . . This is an impressive debut that offers hope for all kids." Booklist

★ **King** of the screwups. Houghton Mifflin Harcourt 2009 310p $17

Grades: 9 10 11 12   **Fic**
1. Uncles -- Fiction 2. Homosexuality -- Fiction 3. Father-son relationship -- Fiction
ISBN 978-0-15-206258-3; 0-15-206258-0
                                        LC 2008-25113
After getting in trouble yet again, popular high school senior Liam, who never seems to live up to his wealthy father's expectations, is sent to live in a trailer park with his gay "glam-rocker" uncle.
"Readers—screwups or not—will empathize as Liam, utterly likable despite his faults, learns to be himself." Publ Wkly

Saint Iggy. Harcourt 2006 260p $17

Grades: 9 10 11 12   **Fic**
1. Poor -- Fiction 2. Drug abuse -- Fiction 3. Family life -- Fiction
ISBN 0-15-205795-1; 978-0-15-205795-4
                                        LC 2005-34857
Iggy Corso, who lives in city public housing, is caught physically and spiritually between good and bad when he is kicked out of high school, goes searching for his missing mother, and causes his friend to get involved with the same dangerous drug dealer who deals to his parents.
"Teens will connect with Iggy's powerful sense that although he notices everything, he is not truly seen and accepted himself." Booklist

Goldberg, Myla
Bee season; a novel. Doubleday 2000 275p hardcover o.p. pa $13.95

Grades: 11 12 Adult   **Fic**
1. Family life -- Fiction 2. Jews -- United States --
Fiction
ISBN 0-385-49879-9; 0-385-49880-2 pa
                                    LC 99-47933
"Some of the events that unfold . . . seem a little con-
trived. But Goldberg engenders considerable suspense
around both Eliza's string of spelling successes and the fates
of the other Naumanns." Time

Golden, Arthur
    Memoirs of a geisha; a novel. Knopf 1997
434p il $26.95; pa $7.99
Grades: 11 12 Adult   **Fic**
1. Japan -- Fiction 2. Geishas -- Fiction
ISBN 0-375-40011-7; 1-4000-9689-8 pa
                                    LC 97-74747

"Rarely has a world so closed and foreign been evoked
with such natural assurance, from the aesthetics of the Kyoto
geisha's 'art'—to the fetishized sexuality of Gion in the thirties and forties, at once delicate and crude, repressed and
flagrant." New Yorker

Golden, Christopher
    The **sea** wolves; by Christopher Golden & Tim
Lebbon; with illustrations by Greg Ruth. Harper
2012 384 p. $16.99
Grades: 7 8 9 10   **Fic**
1. Sea stories 2. Adventure fiction 3. Monsters 4.
Supernatural 5. Pirates -- Fiction 6. Supernatural --
Fiction 7. Adventure and adventurers -- Fiction
ISBN 0061863203; 9780061863202; 9780061863219
                                    LC 2011010031
This young adult fantasy adventure novel by Christopher Golden and Tim Lebbon follows "Jack London . . . a
writer who lived his own real-life adventures. But . . . even
he couldn't set down [all his adventures] in writing. Terrifying, mysterious, bizarre, and magical. . . . Clinging to life
after he is captured in an attack by savage pirates, Jack is
unprepared for what he faces at the hands of the crew and
their charismatic, murderous captain, Ghost. For these mariners are not mortal men but hungry beasts chasing gold and
death across the North Pacific. Jack's only hope lies with
Sabine—a sad, sultry captive of Ghost's insatiable hunger.
But on these waters, nothing is as it seems, and Sabine may
be biding dangerous secrets of her own." (Publisher's note)

    The **wild**; by Christopher Golden & Tim Lebbon;
with illustrations by Greg Ruth. Harper 2011 348p
il (The secret journeys of Jack London) $15.99; lib
bdg $16.89
Grades: 7 8 9 10   **Fic**
1. Authors 2. Novelists 3. Adventure fiction 4. Wolves
-- Fiction 5. Short story writers 6. Supernatural --
Fiction 7. Wilderness survival -- Fiction 8. Gold mines
and mining -- Fiction 9. Yukon River valley (Yukon and
Alaska) -- Fiction
ISBN 978-0-06-186317-2; 0-06-186317-3; 978-0-06-
186318-9 lib bdg; 0-06-186318-1 lib bdg
                                    LC 2010-07475
Seventeen-year-old Jack London makes the arduous
journey to the Yukon's gold fields in 1893, becoming in-

creasingly uneasy about supernatural forces in the wilderness that seem to have taken a special interest in him.
    "Golden and Lebbon write with a gritty assurance that
brings the fantasy elements . . . down to earth. . . . Occasional
sketches add a bit of cinematic drama." Booklist

Goldman, Steven
    ★ **Two** parties, one tux, and a very short film
about the Grapes of Wrath. Bloomsbury Children's
Books 2008 307p $16.99
Grades: 7 8 9 10   **Fic**
1. School stories 2. Friendship -- Fiction 3.
Homosexuality -- Fiction 4. Dating (Social customs)
-- Fiction
ISBN 978-1-59990-271-5; 1-59990-271-0
                                    LC 2008-11587
Mitch, a shy and awkward high school junior, negotiates
the difficult social situations he encounters, both with girls
and with his best friend David, after David reveals to him
that he is gay.
    "With fitting touches of rough language and situations
and on-target characters, this witty and skillfully developed
story creates a compelling picture of high school life." Voice
Youth Advocates

Goodman, Alison
    The **Dark** Days Club; Alison Goodman. Viking
2016 496 p. (hardcover) $18.99
    Grades: 8 9 10 11 12   **Fic**
    1. Secrets -- Fiction 2. Conspiracies -- Fiction 3.
    Supernatural -- Fiction 4. London (England) -- Fiction
    5. Courts and courtiers -- Fiction 6. Great Britain
    -- History -- 1714-1837 -- Fiction 7. Great Britain --
    History -- 1800-1837 -- Fiction 8. London (England)
    -- History -- 19th century -- Fiction
    ISBN 9780670785476
                                    LC 2015006792
In this book, by Alison Goodman, "Lady Helen Wrexhall
is on the eve of her debut presentation at the royal court of
George III. Her life should revolve around gowns, dancing,
and securing a suitable marriage. Instead, when one of her
family's maids disappears, she is drawn into the shadows of
Regency London. There, she meets Lord Carlston, one of the
few able to stop the perpetrators: a cabal of demons that has
infiltrated all levels of society." (Publisher's note)
    "Readers willing to embrace the deep, deliberately paced
journey will find the pace and tension increasing until the
end leaves them eager for the next volume." Kirkus

    ★ **Eon**: Dragoneye reborn. Viking 2009 531p
$19.99
Grades: 7 8 9 10   **Fic**
    1. Fantasy fiction 2. Magic -- Fiction 3. Dragons --
    Fiction 4. Sex role -- Fiction 5. Apprentices -- Fiction
    ISBN 978-0-670-06227-0; 0-670-06227-8
                                    LC 2008-33223
Sixteen-year-old Eon hopes to become an apprentice to
one of the twelve energy dragons of good fortune and learn
to be its main interpreter, but to do so will require much,
including keeping secret that she is a girl.

"Entangled politics and fierce battle scenes provide a pulse-quickening pace, while the intriguing characters add interest and depth." Booklist

Followed by: Eona: The last Dragoneye (2011)

Eona: the last Dragoneye. Viking 2011 637p il $19.99

Grades: 7 8 9 10   **Fic**

1. Fantasy fiction 2. Magic -- Fiction 3. Dragons -- Fiction 4. Apprentices -- Fiction

ISBN 978-0-670-06311-6; 0-670-06311-8

LC 2011-02997

Sequel to: Eon: Dragoneye reborn (2009)

Eon has been revealed as Eona, the first female Dragoneye in hundreds of years. Along with fellow rebels Ryko and Lady Dela, she is on the run from High Lord Sethon's army. The renegades are on a quest for the black folio, stolen by the drug-riddled Dillon; they must also find Kygo, the young Pearl Emperor, who needs Eona's power and the black folio if he is to wrest back his throne from the self-styled "Emperor" Sethon.

"One of those rare and welcome fantasies that complicate black-and-white morality." Kirkus

Goodman, Shawn

Kindness for weakness; Shawn Goodman. 1st ed. Delacorte Press 2013 272 p. (ebook) $50.97; (library) $19.99; (hardcover) $16.99

Grades: 9 10 11 12   **Fic**

1. Gangs -- Fiction 2. Juvenile delinquency -- Fiction 3. Brothers -- Fiction 4. Self-esteem -- Fiction 5. Drug dealers -- Fiction

ISBN 0375991026; 9780307982070; 9780375991028; 9780385743242

LC 2012015772

In this book, Shawn Goodman "introduces 15-year-old James, who is caught running drugs for his older brother and sentenced to a year in juvie. Despite a rough initiation to the program, James—inspired by books recommended to him by his English teacher—does his best to stay out of trouble; however, his emotional and physical strength are tested time and again by corrupt, belligerent guards and boys who pressure him into joining a gang." (Publishers Weekly)

Something like hope. Delacorte Press 2011 193p $16.99; lib bdg $19.99

Grades: 9 10 11 12   **Fic**

1. African Americans -- Fiction 2. Juvenile delinquency -- Fiction

ISBN 978-0-385-73939-9; 978-0-385-90786-6 lib bdg

LC 2009-53657

"Smart, angry, and desperate, Shavonne, 17, is in juvenile detention again, and in her present-tense, first-person narrative, she describes the heartbreaking brutality that she suffered before she was locked up, as well as the harsh treatment, and sometimes the kindness, she encounters in juvie." (Booklist)

The author "delivers a gritty, frank tale that doesn't shrink from the harshness of the setting but that also provides a much-needed redemption for both Shavonne and readers." Kirkus

Gould, Sasha

Cross my heart; Sasha Gould. Delacorte Press 2011 263 p. (hc) $17.99

Grades: 9 10 11 12   **Fic**

1. Historical fiction 3. Secret societies 4. Love -- Fiction 5. Sex role -- Fiction

ISBN 0385741502; 9780375985409; 9780375990076; 9780385741507

LC 2011012357

This novel, by Sasha Goul, takes place in "Venice, 1585. When 16-year-old Laura della Scala['s] . . . older sister, Beatrice, . . . drown[s], she is given no time to grieve. Instead, Laura's father removes her from the convent where he forcibly sent her years earlier and orders her to marry Beatrice's fiance. . . . Panicked, Laura betrays a powerful man to earn her way into the Segreta, a shadowy society of women who deal in only one currency--secrets." (Publisher's note)

Grace, Amanda

In too deep; Amanda Grace. Flux 2012 228 p. $9.95

Grades: 7 8 9 10 11 12   **Fic**

1. Rape -- Fiction 2. Honesty -- Fiction 3. False accusation -- Fiction 4. High school students -- Fiction 5. Teenagers -- Conduct of life -- Fiction 6. Rumor -- Fiction 7. Schools -- Fiction 8. High schools -- Fiction 9. Conduct of life -- Fiction

ISBN 0738726001; 9780738726007

LC 2011028806

In this young adult novel, a "girl gets caught in a lie she didn't tell but doesn't have the courage to correct. . . . Samantha wants to spark some romantic interest from her best friend and secret heartthrob Nick, so she makes a play for popularity-magnet Carter. He rebuffs her, but someone sees her leaving his bedroom in tears and jumps to the false conclusion that Carter assaulted her. Sam doesn't hear about the resulting rumors until she returns to school. Soon she feels too overwhelmed by social pressure to deny them. Sam finds many opportunities to confess the truth, but she can't bring herself to exonerate Carter. . . . Complicating matters, Sam knows that because of the deception, she's likely to lose Nick, who finally has declared his love for her." (Kirkus)

Grant, Christopher

Teenie. Alfred A. Knopf 2010 264p $16.99; lib bdg $19.99; ebook $10.99

Grades: 9 10 11 12   **Fic**

1. School stories 2. Family life -- Fiction 3. African Americans -- Fiction 4. Dating (Social customs) -- Fiction 5. Brooklyn (New York, N.Y.) -- Fiction

ISBN 978-0-375-86191-8; 978-0-375-96191-5 lib bdg; 978-0-375-89779-5 ebook

LC 2010-35377

High school freshman Martine, longing to escape Brooklyn and her strict parents, is trying to get into a study-abroad program but when her long-time crush begins to pay attention to her and her best friend starts an online relationship, Teenie's mind is on anything but her grades.

"Realistic descriptions of teenage life and appealing characters make for an enjoyable reading experience." SLJ

Grant, Helen

The **glass** demon; Helen Grant. Bantam Books Trade Paperbacks 2010 305p. ill. pa $15

Grades: 11 12 Adult   **Fic**

1. Windows 2. Family life 3. Teenagers -- Fiction 4. Horror tales 5. Horror stories 6. Germany -- Fiction 7. Detective and mystery stories 8. Mystery and detective stories -- Germany

ISBN 978-0-385-34420-3; 0-385-34420-1; 9780345527585

LC 2011000738

First published 2010 in the United Kingdom.

This book tells the story of "Lin Fox, [who] finds herself in a falling-down castle deep in the woods of Germany while her father attempts to resuscitate his academic career. For generations, the village has lived with the legend of the Allerheiligen Glass–medieval stained glass windows that are said to have been cursed by a demon, bringing death to those who gaze upon them. . . . On Lin's first day, she meets Michel, a mysterious boy who eventually becomes her only ally. . . . What's unclear is if the escalating threats to her family and mounting village deaths are the result of Michel's mad father, or the Glass Demon himself. Combined with the mystery is the story of Lin's everyday teenage concerns: fitting in at school, pining over a crush, and worrying about family dynamics." (School Libr J)

The **vanishing** of Katharina Linden; a novel. Helen Grant. Delacorte Press 2010 287 p. (hbk.) $24; (pbk.) $15

Grades: 11 12 Adult   **Fic**

1. Girls -- Fiction 2. Kidnapping -- Fiction 3. Missing children -- Fiction 4. Alienation (Social psychology) -- Fiction 5. Missing persons -- Investigation -- Fiction

ISBN 9780385344173; 9780440339618; 9780385344180

LC 201003415

First published 2009 in the United Kingdom

Alex Award (2011)

This book follows "ten-year-old Pia Kolvenbach, [who] becomes known in her German hometown of Bad Münstereifel as 'The Girl Whose Grandmother Exploded.' Pia, whose mother is one of only three British citizens in the area, is already familiar with the peculiarities of this insular town, but the ostracism she now faces leaves her with only two confidantes: StinkStefan, a classmate and fellow outcast, and grouchy, secretive Herr Schiller, a source of town lore. Attention soon shifts from Pia when a local girl, Katharina Linden, becomes neither the first nor the last girl to go missing. Pia and Stefan, inspired . . . by Herr Schiller's gruesome stories, become determined to investigate the disappearances." (Library Journal)

Grant, K. M.

Blue flame; book one of the Perfect Fire trilogy. Walker & Co. 2008 246p (Perfect fire trilogy) $16.99

Grades: 7 8 9 10   **Fic**

1. Middle Ages -- Fiction 2. Knights and knighthood -- Fiction 3. France -- History -- 0-1328 -- Fiction

ISBN 0-8027-9694-X; 978-0-8027-9694-3

LC 2007-51384

This first volume in a projected trilogy is set in southern France (Occitan) in 1242 amidst the struggle between Cathars and Catholics. "Many years have passed since the Occitanian knights killed Richard the Lionheart in a courageous battle to keep the Blue Flame—sparked at the moment of Christ's death—from falling into the wrong hands. Now it is in danger once again, as enemies from the north draw near. . . . Lifelong friends Raimon, son of a Cathar weaver, and Yolanda, daughter of a Catholic Count, are falling in love. But a new religious crusade is about to begin, setting boy against girl, family against family, south against north." (Publisher's note) "Middle school, high school." (Horn Book)

"Characters are as complex as the moral issues they face, and Grant's nuanced, thought-provoking look at the religious conflicts they face will resonate today." Booklist

Other books in this series are Paradise red (2010)

White heat (2009)

Paradise red; by K.M. Grant. Walker & Co. 2010 279 p. (hardcover) $17.99

Grades: 7 8 9 10   **Fic**

1. Love stories 2. Fantasy fiction 3. Albigenses -- Fiction 4. Middle Ages -- Fiction 5. Knights and knighthood -- Fiction 6. France -- History -- Louis IX, 1226-1270 -- Fiction 7. Languedoc (France) -- History -- 13th century -- Fiction 8. Montségur (France) -- History -- 13th century -- Fiction

ISBN 0802796966; 9780802796967

LC 2009054214

This is the final book in K.M. Grant's Perfect Fire trilogy. The novel "concludes the story of Raimon's quest to save the mystical blue flame which is at the heart of his love for the land he grew up in. This runs alongside the complicated story of his relationship with Yolanda who has made a political marriage to one of the enemy." (School Librarian)

White heat. Walker & Co. 2009 260p (Perfect fire trilogy) $16.99

Grades: 7 8 9 10   **Fic**

1. Inquisition -- Fiction 2. Middle Ages -- Fiction 3. Knights and knighthood -- Fiction 4. France -- History -- 0-1328 -- Fiction

ISBN 978-0-8027-9695-0; 0-8027-9695-8

LC 2008-46984

Sequel to: Blue heat (2008)

As the conflict in Languedoc, also called Occitan, intensifies, Raimon, having escaped the pyre, suppresses his longing to find his beloved Yolanda and, together with Parsifal, carries the Blue Flame to the mountains where it serves to rally loyal Occitanians to organize against the formidable French forces set to invade their beloved country.

"With thorough scholarship and an immersion into medieval sights, sounds, and points of view, Grant invites readers on a thrilling trip back in time." Horn Book

Grant, Michael

Front Lines; Michael Grant; [edited by] Katherine Tegen. Harpercollins Childrens Books 2016 576 p. (hardcover) $18.99

Grades: 9 10 11 12   **Fic**
1. Alternative histories 2. Women soldiers -- Fiction
ISBN 9780062342157; 0062342150

LC 2015939082

This young adult novel, by Michael Grant, edited by Katherine Tegen, "reimagines World War II with girl soldiers fighting on the front lines. . . . [In] 1942, . . . three girls sign up to fight. . . . Each has her own reasons for volunteering: Rio fights to honor her sister; Frangie needs money for her family; Rainy wants to kill Germans. For the first time they leave behind their homes and families—to go to war." (Publisher's note)

"Bestselling science-fiction author Grant did his research (an extensive bibliography is provided), but the odd and likely unintended consequence of his premise is the erasure of thousands of military women who historically served and fought and died. Still, an engrossing portrayal of ordinary women in extraordinary circumstances." Kirkus

Messenger of Fear; Michael Grant. First edition Katherine Tegen Books 2014 272 p. (hardback) $17.99
Grades: 9 10 11 12   **Fic**
1. Fear -- Fiction 2. Good and evil -- Fiction 3. Games -- Fiction 4. Justice -- Fiction 5. Apprentices -- Fiction 6. Supernatural -- Fiction
ISBN 0062207407; 9780062207401

LC 2014013832

In this novel by Michael Grant "Mara Todd . . . can't remember who she is or anything about her past. Is it because of the boy that appears? He calls himself the Messenger of Fear. If the world does not bring justice to those who do evil, the Messenger will. He offers the wicked a game. If they win, they go free. If they lose, they will live their greatest fear. Why was Mara chosen to be the Messenger's apprentice?" (Publisher's note)

"Grant explores bullying, family problems, suicide, and more, and several painful passages will have readers cringing, even as they make them think about what they would do in the same situation. This is a solid beginning to a series that is likely to be quite popular with horror and paranormal fans." Booklist

Other titles in the series are:
The Tattooed Heart (2015)

Gratton, Tessa

The **blood** keeper; Tessa Gratton. Random House Books for Young Readers 2012 432 p. (hardback) $17.99
Grades: 9 10 11 12   **Fic**
1. Love stories 2. Magic -- Fiction 3. Supernatural -- Fiction
ISBN 0375867341; 9780375867347; 9780375897696; 9780375967344

LC 2011049532

This book follows "Mab Prowd, [for whom] the practice of blood magic is as natural as breathing. . . . Growing up on an isolated farm in Kansas with other practitioners may have kept her from making friends her own age, but it has also given her a sense of purpose -- she's connected to the land and protective of the magic. . . . But one morning . . . she

encounters Will, a local boy who is trying to exorcise some mundane personal demons." (Publisher's note)

"A perfect book for those who loved Wuthering Heights and are looking for an essentially American gothic." Kirkus

Gratz, Alan

★ The **Brooklyn** nine; a novel in nine innings. Dial Books 2009 299p $16.99
Grades: 5 6 7 8 9   **Fic**
1. Baseball -- Fiction 2. Family life -- Fiction 3. German Americans -- Fiction 4. United States -- History -- Fiction 5. Brooklyn (New York, N.Y.) -- Fiction
ISBN 978-0-8037-3224-7; 0-8037-3224-4

LC 2008-21263

This novel follows the fortunes of a German immigrant family through nine generations, beginning in 1845, as they experience American life and play baseball. "Grades five to nine." (Bull Cent Child Books)

Gratz "builds this novel upon a clever . . . conceit . . . and executes it with polish and precision." Booklist

★ **Samurai** shortstop. Dial Books 2006 280p hardcover o.p. pa $7.99
Grades: 7 8 9 10   **Fic**
1. School stories 2. Baseball -- Fiction 3. Tokyo (Japan) -- Fiction 4. Father-son relationship -- Fiction
ISBN 0-8037-3075-6; 978-0-8037-3075-5; 0-14-241099-3 pa; 978-0-14-24099-8 pa

LC 2005-22081

While obtaining a Western education at a prestigious Japanese boarding school in 1890, sixteen-year-old Toyo also receives traditional samurai training which has profound effects on both his baseball game and his relationship with his father. This book features some scenes of graphic violence.

"This is an intense read about a fascinating time and place in world history." Publ Wkly

Something rotten; a Horatio Wilkes mystery. Dial Books 2007 207p $16.99; pa $6.99
Grades: 8 9 10 11 12   **Fic**
1. Poets 2. Authors 3. Dramatists 4. Mystery fiction 5. Homicide -- Fiction 6. Tennessee -- Fiction
ISBN 978-0-8037-3216-2; 0-8037-3216-3; 978-0-14-241297-8 pa; 0-14-241297-X pa

LC 2006-38484

In a contemporary story based on Shakespeare's play, Hamlet, Horatio Wilkes seeks to solve the murder of his friend Hamilton Prince's father in Denmark, Tennessee.

"Readers will find this enjoyable as a pleasure read and surprisingly painless as a curricular entry." Bull Cent Child Books

Followed by: Something wicked (2008)

Graudin, Ryan

The **walled** city; by Ryan Graudin. Little, Brown & Co. 2014 448 p. illustrations (hardcover) $18
Grades: 9 10 11 12   **Fic**
1. Gangs -- Fiction 2. Sisters -- Fiction 3. Street life -- Fiction 4. Hong Kong (China) -- Fiction 5. Survival -- Fiction 6. Street children -- Fiction 7. Hong Kong

(China) -- History -- 20th century -- Fiction
ISBN 0316405051; 9780316405058

LC 2013044748

In this book, by Ryan Graudin, "Dai, trying to escape a haunting past, traffics drugs for the most ruthless kingpin in the Walled City.... Jin hides under the radar, afraid the wild street gangs will discover her biggest secret: Jin passes as a boy to stay safe. Still, every chance she gets, she searches for her lost sister.... Mei Yee has been trapped in a brothel for the past two years, dreaming of getting out while watching the girls who try fail one by one." (Publisher's note)

"Vivid descriptions add color and infuse the story with realism. While there are mature situations dealing with drugs, violence, and rape, they are skillfully relayed without being graphic. This complex, well-written novel is full of tension, twists, and turns, and teens will not be able to put it down." SLJ

Wolf by wolf; by Ryan Graudin. Little, Brown & Co. 2015 400 p. (hardcover) $18

Grades: 9 10 11 12 **Fic**

1. Resistance to government -- Fiction 2. Motorcycle racing -- Fiction 3. Government, Resistance to -- Fiction
ISBN 9780316405126

LC 2014044026

In this book, by Ryan Graudin, "the Axis powers of the Third Reich and Imperial Japan rule. To commemorate their Great Victory, they host the Axis Tour: an annual motorcycle race across their conjoined continents. The prize? An audience with the highly reclusive Adolf Hitler at the Victor's ball in Tokyo. Yael, a former death camp prisoner, has witnessed too much suffering. . . . The resistance has given Yael one goal: Win the race and kill Hitler." (Publisher's note)

"Alternate histories can be risky gambits, but in Graudin's capable hands, it pays off in spades. Yael is a compelling protagonist, both strong and flawed, and, even imbued as it is with sci-fi elements, seeing both WWII and the concentration camp experience through her eyes is a terrifying adventure." Booklist

Gray, Claudia

Evernight. HarperTeen 2008 327p (Evernight) $16.99; lib bdg $17.89; pa $8.99

Grades: 8 9 10 11 12 **Fic**

1. Horror fiction 2. School stories 3. Vampires -- Fiction
ISBN 978-0-06-128439-7; 0-06-128439-4; 978-0-06-128443-4 lib bdg; 0-06-128443-2 lib bdg; 978-0-06-128444-1 pa; 0-06-128444-0 pa

LC 2007-36733

Bianca has been "uprooted from her small hometown and enrolled at Evernight Academy, an eerie Gothic boarding school where the students are somehow too perfect. . . . Bianca knows she doesn't fit in. Then she meets Lucas. . . . Lucas ignores the rules, stands up to the snobs, and warns Bianca to be careful—even when it comes to caring about him. . . . But the connection between Bianca and Lucas can't be denied. Bianca will risk anything to be with Lucas, but dark secrets are fated to tear them apart." (Publisher's note)
"Grades eight to ten." (Bull Cent Child Books)

"Gray's writing hooks readers from the first page and reels them in with surprising plot twists and turns. . . . A must-have for fans of vampire stories." SLJ

Spellcaster; Claudia Gray. HarperTeen 2013 400 p. (hardback) $17.99

Grades: 8 9 10 11 12 **Fic**

1. Paranormal fiction 2. Witches -- Fiction 3. Love stories 4. Horror stories 5. Magic -- Fiction 6. Schools -- Fiction 7. High schools -- Fiction 8. Rhode Island -- Fiction 9. Blessing and cursing -- Fiction 10. Family life -- Rhode Island -- Fiction
ISBN 0061961205; 9780061961205

LC 2012025331

This young adult paranormal romance story, by Claudia Gray, follows a teenage girl with magical powers. "Descended from witches, Nadia can sense that a spell has been cast over the tiny Rhode Island town--a sickness infecting everyone and everything in it. The magic at work is darker and more powerful than anything she's come across and has sunk its claws most deeply into Mateo . . . her rescuer, her friend, and the guy she yearns to get closer to even as he pushes her away." (Publisher's note)

Steadfast; a Spellcaster novel. Claudia Gray. HarperTeen 2014 352 p. (hardcover bdg.) $17.99

Grades: 8 9 10 11 12 **Fic**

1. Imaginary places 2. Magic -- Fiction 3. Horror stories 4. Schools -- Fiction 5. Witches -- Fiction 6. High schools -- Fiction 7. Rhode Island -- Fiction 8. Blessing and cursing -- Fiction 9. Family life -- Rhode Island -- Fiction
ISBN 0061961221; 9780061961229

LC 2013015445

Sequel to: Spellcaster

In this book, by Claudia Gray, "Nadia, Mateo, and Verlaine saved Captive's Sound from the dark sorceress Elizabeth . . . or so they thought. But despite their best efforts, a crack opened and a new, greater evil seeped through. With Mateo as her Steadfast, Nadia's magic is magnified but her training is still incomplete. And a darker magic has begun to call Nadia. With her Steadfast, Mateo, and her best friend, Verlaine, Nadia must fight the black magic that tempts her and stop the One Beneath." (Publisher's note)

"The first barrier between our world and the evil entity known as The One Beneath has been breached and redemption is impossible - —unless untrained teen witch Nadia, along with her steadfast Mateo and friend Verlaine, can resist a seemingly invincible sorceress' power and a demon's meddling, all while remaining true to their friendship and ideals...Gray uses unique and lyrical free-verse spells, spoken by both Nadia and the dark sorceress Elizabeth, as inroads to sets of memories—a clever tactic that helps readers understand motivation while providing backstories that make it easy to bond with Nadia and her friends. The ending will provide terrific fodder for book discussions, so make sure you have enough copies to go around." (Booklist)

A thousand pieces of you; Claudia Gray. HarperTeen, an imprint of HarperCollinsPublishers 2014 368 p. (hardcover) $17.99

Grades: 8 9 10 11 **Fic**
1. Science fiction 2. Adventure fiction 3. Murder --
Fiction 4. Family life -- Fiction 5. Space and time
-- Fiction 6. Adventure and adventurers -- Fiction
ISBN 0062278967; 9780062278968

LC 2014001894

This book, by Claudia Gray, is "about a girl who must
chase her father's killer through multiple dimensions. Marguerite Caine's physicist parents are known for their groundbreaking achievements. Their most astonishing invention,
called the Firebird, allows users to jump into multiple universes. . . . But then Marguerite's father is murdered, and
the killer--her parent's handsome, enigmatic assistant Paul-
-escapes into another dimension before the law can touch
him." (Publisher's note)

"Readers will appreciate Marguerite's determination to
help her parents, even though she is a misfit, the lone artist in a family of scientific geniuses. The secondary players are equally well rounded, and their various incarnations
in each dimension make for intriguing character explorations. In resourceful Marguerite's first-person narration, the
story moves quickly, and the science is explained enough
to make the plot clear, but not so much as to bog things
down." Booklist

Gray, Keith

★ **Ostrich** boys. Random House 2010 297p
$17.99; lib bdg $20.99
Grades: 8 9 10 11 12 **Fic**
1. Death -- Fiction 2. Scotland -- Fiction 3. Friendship
-- Fiction 4. Great Britain -- Fiction
ISBN 978-0-375-85843-7; 0-375-85843-1; 978-0-375-
95843-4 lib bdg; 0-375-95843-6 lib bdg

LC 2008-21729

After their best friend Ross dies, English teenagers
Blake, Kenny, and Sim plan a proper memorial by taking
his ashes to Ross, Scotland, an adventure-filled journey that
tests their loyalty to each other and forces them to question
what friendship means.

"Gray's writing is cheeky, crisp, and realistic. He has
created funny, bright characters whom readers cannot help
but root for." SLJ

Green, John, 1977-

★ An **abundance** of Katherines. Dutton Books
2006 227p $16.99
Grades: 9 10 11 12 **Fic**
1. Mathematics -- Fiction
ISBN 0-525-47688-1; 978-0-525-47688-7

LC 2006-4191

Michael L. Printz Award honor book, 2007

Having been recently dumped for the nineteenth time by
a girl named Katherine, recent high school graduate and former prodigy Colin sets off on a road trip with his best friend
to try to find some new direction in life while also trying to
create a mathematical formula to explain his relationships.
"Grades seven to twelve." (Bull Cent Child Books)

This "is an enjoyable, thoughtful novel that will attract
readers interested in romance, math, or just good storytelling." Voice Youth Advocates

★ The **fault** in our stars; John Green. Dutton
Books 2012 318p.
Grades: 9 10 11 12 **Fic**
1. Love stories 2. Cancer patients -- Fiction 3.
Terminally ill children -- Fiction 4. Love -- Fiction 5.
Cancer -- Fiction 6. Terminally ill -- Fiction
ISBN 9780525478812

LC 2011045783

Odyssey Award Winner (2013)

This book tells the story of "Hazel Lancaster and Augustus Waters [who] are very different: She's a sensitive poetry aficionado; he's a hunky ex-basketball player. But their
paths (and stars) cross in a cancer support group for teens. .
. . Hazel yearns to travel to Amsterdam to meet her favorite
author, and Augustus leaps to help even as their respective
cancers threaten to derail her dream." (Washington Post)

★ **Looking** for Alaska. Dutton Books 2005
221p $15.99; pa $7.99
Grades: 9 10 11 12 **Fic**
1. School stories 2. Death -- Fiction 3. Birmingham
(Ala.) -- Fiction
ISBN 0-525-47506-0; 0-14-240251-6 pa

LC 2004-10827

Michael L. Printz Award, 2006

Sixteen-year-old Miles' first year at Culver Creek Preparatory School in Alabama includes good friends and great
pranks, but is defined by the search for answers about life
and death after a fatal car crash

"The language and sexual situations are aptly and realistically drawn, but sophisticated in nature. Miles's narration is alive with sweet, self-deprecating humor, and
his obvious struggle to tell the story truthfully adds to his
believability." SLJ

Paper towns. Dutton Books 2008 305p $17.99
Grades: 9 10 11 12 **Fic**
1. Mystery fiction 2. Florida -- Fiction 3. Missing
persons -- Fiction
ISBN 0-525-47818-3; 978-0-525-47818-8

LC 2007-52659

One month before graduating from his Central Florida
high school, Quentin "Q" Jacobsen has a pretty good life.
Then Margo Roth Spiegelman, Q's neighbor and classmate,
takes him on a midnight adventure after which she mysteriously disappears. "Grades nine to twelve." (Bull Cent
Child Books)

"The writing is . . . stellar, with deliciously intelligent
dialogue and plenty of mind-twisting insights. . . . Language
and sex issues might make this book more appropriate for
older teens, but it is still a powerfully great read." Voice
Youth Advocates

★ **Will** Grayson, Will Grayson; [by] John Green
& David Levithan. Dutton 2010 310p $17.99
Grades: 9 10 11 12 **Fic**
1. Obesity -- Fiction 2. Theater -- Fiction 3.
Homosexuality -- Fiction 4. Chicago (Ill.) -- Fiction 5.
Dating (Social customs) -- Fiction
ISBN 978-0-525-42158-0; 0-525-42158-0

LC 2008-48979

When two teens, one gay and one straight, meet accidentally and discover that they share the same name, their
lives become intertwined as one begins dating the other's
best friend, who produces a play revealing his relationship
with them both.

"Each character comes lovingly to life, especially Tiny
Cooper, whose linebacker-sized, heart-on-his-sleeve personality could win over the grouchiest of grouches. . . . Their
story, along with the rest of the cast's, will have readers simultaneously laughing, crying and singing at the top of their
lungs." Kirkus

Green, Sally

Half bad; Sally Green. Viking, published by the
Penguin Group 2014 416 p. (hardback) $18.99
Grades: 9 10 11 12   **Fic**
1. Witches -- Fiction 2. England -- Fiction 3. Prisoners
-- Fiction 4. Toleration -- Fiction 5. Good and evil
-- Fiction 6. Fathers and sons -- Fiction 7. Family life
-- England -- Fiction
ISBN 0670016780; 9780670016785

LC 2013041190

In this book, by Sally Green, "witches live alongside
humans: White witches, who are good; Black witches, who
are evil; and sixteen-year-old Nathan, who is both. Nathan's
father is the world's most powerful and cruel Black witch,
and his mother is dead. He is hunted from all sides. Trapped
in a cage, beaten and handcuffed, Nathan must escape before
his seventeenth birthday, at which point he will receive three
gifts from his father and come into his own as a witch--or
else he will die." (Publisher's note)

"In a world divided by two factions at war, Nathan is
caught in the middle, for he is neither a White Witch nor a
Black Witch, but a Half Code—-half White and half Black...
Told at times in first- and second-person, the story allows
unique insights into Nathan's perspectives, including the
fast-paced escapes and heart-wrenching torment. An interesting spin on the paranormal that runs adjacent to some important social issues, Half Bad leaves readers questioning if
the division between good and evil is ever as simple as black
and white." (VOYA)

Half wild; Sally Green. Viking 2015 432 p.
(The half bad trilogy) (hardback) $18.99
Grades: 9 10 11 12   **Fic**
1. England -- Fiction 2. Witches -- Fiction 3. Father-
son relationship -- Fiction 4. Fathers and sons -- Fiction
ISBN 0670017132; 9780670017133

LC 2014044805

This book, by Sally Green, takes place in "a modern-day
England where two warring factions of witches live amongst
humans. . . . Nathan is an abomination, the illegitimate son
of the world's most powerful and violent witch. Nathan is
hunted from all sides: nowhere is safe and no one can be
trusted. Now, Nathan has come into his own unique magical
Gift, and he's on the run--but the Hunters are close behind."
(Publisher's note)

"The blood and gore, the willingness to endure and
survive at any price, and the dichotomies between good
and bad, love and hate, wild and civilized—all haunt the
reader, climaxing in a tragic ending that portends the horror, violence, and possible relationships in the trilogy's final
installment." Booklist

Greenberg, Joanne

I never promised you a rose garden; a novel.
Henry Holt 2009 291p pa $15
Grades: 7 8 9 10 11 12 Adult   **Fic**
1. Mentally ill -- Fiction 2. Psychotherapy -- Fiction
ISBN 978-0-8050-8926-4; 0-8050-8926-8

LC 2010-275768

First published 1964

Chronicles the three-year battle of a mentally ill, but perceptive, teenage girl against a world of her own creation,
emphasizing her relationship with the doctor who gave her
the ammunition of self-understanding with which to destroy
that world of fantasy.

"The hospital world and Deborah's fantasy world are
strikingly portrayed, as is the girl's violent struggle between
sickness and health, a struggle given added poignancy by
youth, wit, and courage." Libr J

Grey, Melissa

The **girl** at midnight; Melissa Grey. First edition
Delacorte Press 2015 368 p. (hc) $17.99
Grades: 9 10 11 12   **Fic**
1. Fantasy fiction 2. Fantasy 3. War stories 4. Adopted
children
ISBN 038574465X; 9780375991790; 9780385744652

LC 2014008700

In this book, by Melissa Grey, "[b]eneath the streets of
New York City live the Avicen, an ancient race of people
with feathers for hair and magic running through their veins.
Age-old enchantments keep them hidden from humans. All
but one. Echo is a runaway pickpocket who survives by selling stolen treasures on the black market, and the Avicen are
the only family she's ever known." (Publisher's note)

"The well-built world, vivid characters, and perfect
blend of action and amour should have readers eagerly seeking the sequel." Kirkus

Griffin, Adele

★ **All** you never wanted; Adele Griffin. Alfred
A. Knopf 2012 225 p. (hard cover) $16.99
Grades: 9 10 11 12   **Fic**
1. Popularity -- Fiction 2. Self-destructive behavior
3. Sibling rivalry -- Fiction 4. Personal appearance --
Fiction 5. Wealth -- Fiction 6. Sisters -- Fiction
ISBN 9780307974662; 9780375870811;
9780375870828; 9780375970825

LC 2012020504

Author Adele Griffith tells a story of a sibling rivalry.
"Alex has it all--brains, beauty, popularity, and a dangerously hot boyfriend. Her little sister Thea wants it all, and
she's stepped up her game to get it. Even if it means spinning
the truth to win the attention she deserves. Even if it means
uncovering a shocking secret her older sister never wanted
to share. Even if it means crying wolf. (Publisher's note)

The **Julian** game. G.P. Putnam's Sons 2010
200p $16.99
Grades: 8 9 10 11 12   **Fic**
1. School stories 2. Bullies -- Fiction
ISBN 978-0-399-25460-4; 0-399-25460-9

LC 2010-2281

In an effort to improve her social status, a new scholarship student at an exclusive girls' school uses a fake online profile to help a popular girl get back at her ex-boyfriend, but the consequences are difficult to handle.

This is a "perceptive novel. . . . Canny use of details makes Griffin's characters fully realized and believable. . . . Strong pacing and a sympathetic protagonist ought to keep readers hooked." Publ Wkly

Tighter. Alfred A. Knopf 2011 216p $16.99; lib bdg $19.99; ebook $10.99
Grades: 9 10 11 12 Fic
1. Ghost stories 2. Death -- Fiction 3. Nannies -- Fiction 4. Rhode Island -- Fiction 5. Mental illness -- Fiction 6. Social classes -- Fiction
ISBN 978-0-375-86645-6; 978-0-375-96645-3 lib bdg; 978-0-375-89643-9 ebook
LC 2010-25301
Based on Henry James's "The Turn of the Screw," tells the story of Jamie Atkinson's summer spent as a nanny in a small Rhode Island beach town, where she begins to fear that the estate may be haunted, especially after she learns of two deaths that occurred there the previous summer.

"Griffin interweaves subtle commentary about social class, drug abuse and mental illness into this marvelous homage while winding the suspense knob all the way to 11. Whether or not the ghosts are real, Jamie's alienation and addiction are, and readers will feel her growing claustrophobia at each turn of the page." Kirkus

The **unfinished** life of Addison Stone; Adele Griffin. Soho Teen 2014 256 p. illustrations (chiefly color) (hardback) $17.99
Grades: 9 10 11 12 Fic
1. Artists -- Fiction 2. Celebrities -- Fiction 3. New York (N.Y.) -- Fiction 4. Mystery and detective stories
ISBN 1616953608; 9781616953607
LC 2014009576
In this young adult novel by Adele Griffin, "from the moment she stepped foot in NYC, Addison Stone's subversive street art made her someone to watch, and her violent drowning left her fans and critics craving to know more. [Griffin] conducted interviews with those who knew her best--including close friends, family, teachers, mentors, art dealers, boyfriends, and critics--and retraced the tumultuous path of Addison's life." (Publisher's note)

"This novel is . . . a terrific experiment, something fresh and hard to put down. It gives a sense of both the artistic temperament and the nature of madness—and the sometimes thin line in between." Booklist

Where I want to be. G.P. Putnam's Sons 2005 150p pa $6.99
Grades: 7 8 9 10 Fic
1. Death -- Fiction 2. Sisters -- Fiction 3. Rhode Island -- Fiction 4. Mental illness -- Fiction
ISBN 0-399-23783-6; 0-14-240948-0 pa
LC 2004-1887
Two teenaged sisters, separated by death but still connected, work through their feelings of loss over the closeness they shared as children that was later destroyed by one's mental illness, and finally make peace with each other

"Thoughtful, unique, and ultimately life-affirming, this is a fascinating take on the literary device of a main character speaking after death." SLJ

Griffin, Claire J.
Nowhere to run; Claire J. Griffin. 1st ed. Namelos llc 2013 118 p. (hardcover) $18.95
Grades: 7 8 9 10 Fic
1. School stories 2. Juvenile delinquency -- Fiction
ISBN 1608981444; 9781608981441; 9781608981458
LC 2012951212
In this novel, by Claire J. Griffin, "Calvin has Deej--and a coach who thinks Calvin can win the championship in the 100-meter dash, a little brother who looks up to him, a boss who trusts him with the keys to the car shop, and Momma, who made him promise to stay in school. And then there's Junior, the girlfriend of Calvin's dreams. . . . But when Calvin and Deej get suspended from school on a trumped-up charge, things start to fall apart." (Publisher's note)

Griffin, N.
★ The **whole** stupid way we are; N. Griffin. Atheneum Books for Young Readers 2013 368 p. (hardcover) $16.99
Grades: 9 10 11 12 Fic
1. Friendship -- Fiction 2. Dysfunctional families -- Fiction 3. Maine -- Fiction 4. Best friends -- Fiction 5. Family problems -- Fiction
ISBN 1442431555; 9781442431553; 9781442431584
LC 2012002595
In this young adult novel, by N. Griffin, "the friendship between optimistic Dinah Beach and depressed, nihilistic Skint Gilbert is tested. . . . Skint thinks constantly about human cruelty; Dinah wants playful distractions. Skint lives with a father suffering from dementia and a mother who is bitter, angry and occasionally violent; Dinah takes care not to bring up Skint's family . . . ," until one day when she decides to help. (Kirkus Reviews)

Griiffin, Paul
Adrift; Paul Griffin. Scholastic Press 2015 228 p. (hardcover) $17.99 Fic
1. Sea stories 2. Survival after airplane accidents, shipwrecks, etc. -- Fiction 3. Sailing 4. Survival
ISBN 9780545709392; 0545709393; 0545871956; 9780545871952
LC 2015506208
In this young adult novel, by Paul Griffin, "Matt and John are best friends working out in Montauk for the summer. When Driana, JoJo and Stef invite the boys to their Hamptons mansion, Matt and John find themselves in a sticky situation where temptation rivals sensibility. The newfound friends head out into the Atlantic after midnight in a stolen boat. None of them come back whole, and not all of them come back." (Publisher's note)

"Griffin keeps the pages turning; he has a gift for drawing out the suspense and immersing the reader in the story. At the same time, his characters are complex, unpredictable, and entirely authentic. Dispatches from rescue units heighten the suspense. It's a great summer read—as long as you stay on dry land."

Burning blue; by Paul Griffin. Dial Books 2012 288 p. (hardcover) $17.99

Grades: 9 10 11 12   **Fic**

1. Love stories 2. Accidents -- Fiction 3. Popularity -- Fiction 4. Beauty, Personal -- Fiction 5. Computer hackers -- Fiction 6. Disfigured persons -- Fiction 7. Mystery and detective stories

ISBN 0803738153; 9780803738157

LC 2012003578

Author Paul Griffin's protagonist "Nicole Castro, the most beautiful girl in her wealthy New Jersey high school, is splashed with acid on the left side of her perfect face, [and] the whole world takes notice. But quiet loner Jay Nazarro does more than that--he decides to find out who did it. Jay understands how it feels to be treated like an outsider, and he also has a secret: He's a brilliant hacker. But the deeper he digs, the more danger he's in--and the more he falls for Nicole. Too bad everyone is turning into a suspect, including Nicole herself." (paulgriffinstories.net)

★ The **Orange** Houses. Dial Books 2009 147p $16.99

Grades: 9 10 11 12   **Fic**

1. Veterans -- Fiction 2. Illegal aliens -- Fiction 3. Mental illness -- Fiction 4. Bronx (New York, N.Y.) -- Fiction 5. People with disabilities -- Fiction 6. Africans -- United States -- Fiction

ISBN 978-0-8037-3346-6; 0-8037-3346-1

LC 2008-46259

"Tamika, a fifteen-year-old hearing-impaired girl, Jimmi, an eighteen-year-old veteran who stopped taking his antipsychotic medication, and sixteen-year-old Fatima, an illegal immigrant from Africa, meet and connect in their Bronx, New York, neighborhood." (Publisher's note) "Grades eight to twelve." (Bull Cent Child Books)

"Griffin's . . . prose is gorgeous and resonant, and he packs the slim novel with defeats, triumphs, rare moments of beauty and a cast of credible, skillfully drawn characters. A moving story of friendship and hope under harsh conditions." Publ Wkly

★ **Stay** with me. Dial Books for Young Readers 2011 288p il $16.99

Grades: 10 11 12   **Fic**

1. Dogs -- Fiction 2. Family life -- Fiction 3. Restaurants -- Fiction

ISBN 978-0-8037-3448-7

LC 2011001287

Fifteen-year-olds Mack, a high school dropout but a genius with dogs, and Céce, who hopes to use her intelligence to avoid a life like her mother's, meet and fall in love at the restaurant where they both work, but when Mack lands in prison he pushes Céce away and only a one-eared pit-bull can keep them together.

"A stellar story, with genuine dialogue and drama, this is a book that will appeal greatly to teens, especially dog lovers." SLJ

Grimes, Nikki

★ **Bronx** masquerade. Dial Bks. 2002 167p $16.99; pa $5.99

Grades: 7 8 9 10   **Fic**

1. School stories 2. African Americans -- Fiction 3. Bronx (New York, N.Y.) -- Fiction

ISBN 0-8037-2569-8; 0-14-250189-1 pa

LC 00-31701

While studying the Harlem Renaissance, students at a Bronx high school read aloud poems they've written, revealing their innermost thoughts and fears to their formerly clueless classmates

"Funny and painful, awkward and abstract, the poems talk about race, abuse, parental love, neglect, death, and body image. . . . Readers will enjoy the lively, smart voices that talk bravely about real issues and secret fears. A fantastic choice for readers' theater." Booklist

Dark sons. Jump at the Sun 2005 216p $15.99

Grades: 6 7 8 9 10   **Fic**

1. Novels in verse 2. Stepfamilies -- Fiction 3. Father-son relationship -- Fiction

ISBN 0-7868-1888-3

LC 2004-54208

Alternating poems compare and contrast the conflicted feelings of Ishmael, son of the Biblical patriarch Abraham, and Sam, a teenager in New York City, as they try to come to terms with being abandoned by their fathers and with the love they feel for their younger stepbrothers.

"The simple words eloquently reveal what it's like to miss someone. . . . but even more moving is the struggle to forgive and the affection each boy feels for the baby that displaces him. The elemental connections and the hope . . . will speak to a wide audience." Booklist

A **girl** named Mister. Zondervan 2010 223p $15.99

Grades: 8 9 10 11   **Fic**

1. Saints 2. Novels in verse 3. Pregnancy -- Fiction 4. Christian life -- Fiction 5. African Americans -- Fiction

ISBN 978-0-310-72078-2; 0-310-72078-8

LC 2010-10830

A pregnant teenager finds support and forgiveness from God through a book of poetry presented from the Virgin Mary's perspective.

"Writing in lovely prose with lyrical, forthright language that avoids over-moralizing while driving home the big issues of teen pregnancy, award-winning Nikki Grimes just may help a few young women make different choices. At the same time, she effectively makes the case for parents and schools to continue to educate, educate, educate." Voice Youth Advocates

Grisham, John

The **client**. Doubleday 1993 422p $29.95; pa $7.99

Grades: 11 12 Adult   **Fic**

1. Boys 2. Mafia 3. Brothers 4. Legal stories 5. Boys -- Fiction 6. Law and lawyers 7. Suspense novels 8. Mafia -- Fiction 9. Suspense fiction 10. Lawyers -- Fiction

ISBN 0-385-42471-X; 0-440-21352-5 pa

LC 92-39079

This novel's "hero is 11-year-old Mark Sway, who, with his 8-year-old brother, witnesses a Mafia-defending {lawyer's} . . . suicide, unfortunately not before he's learned . . . a secret that one Barry the Blade in particular is not going to let the lawyer live with. Now that Mark knows it, he's in danger, too, and not only from the bad guys. A politically ambitious U.S. attorney . . . is hot on Barry's case, and he'll pull any string, ruin any life, to get ahead. So the cops and the FBI start coming down hard on Mark. But Mark . . . finds an attorney, Reggie Love, a . . . specialist in defending children." (Booklist)

"While sneaking into the woods to smoke forbidden cigarettes, preteen brothers Mark and Ricky find a lawyer committing suicide in his car. Mark tries to save the man but is instead grabbed by him and told the location of the body of a murdered U.S. senator—a murder for which the lawyer's Mafia-connected client is accused. Witnessing the successful suicide sends Ricky into shock and Mark into a web of lies, half-truths, and finally into refusal to tell the confided secret to the police. Mark accidentally but fortuitously hires a lawyer, Reggie Love, who steers him through a maze of FBI agents, legal proceedings, judges, ambitious lawyers, and hit men. . . . This thriller is unique in its theme and in its suspense mixed with humor. A sure 'all-night' read." SLJ

The **firm**. Doubleday 1991 421p hardcover o.p. pa $9.99

Grades: 11 12 Adult   **Fic**
1. Mafia -- Fiction 2. Lawyers -- Fiction 3. Memphis (Tenn.) -- Fiction
ISBN 0-385-41634-2; 0-440-24592-6 pa
     LC 90-3945
"The aphorism 'between a rock and a hard place' aptly describes the dilemma of a young attorney pressed by the FBI to reveal crime-related secrets of his firm, while also hounded by his employers to simply take his huge salary and zip his lip. No aphorism, though, can convey the suspense, wit, and polished writing of this laser-sharp candidate for the best recent updating of the David and Goliath story." Libr J

Grossman, Lev

The **magician** king; Lev Grossman. Viking 2011 400p. $26.95

Grades: 11 12 Adult   **Fic**
1. Magic 2. Fantasy fiction 3. Voyages and travels -- Fiction 4. Fantasies 5. Magic -- Fiction
ISBN 978-0-670-02231-1; 0-670-02231-4
     LC 2011019733
"After Quentin and his old friend Julia leave Fillory on a magical sailing ship, they end up back in Quentin's home in Chesterton, Massachusetts, and only Julia's dark magic can get them back to the realm they have grown to love." (Publisher's note)

★ The **magicians**; a novel. Viking 2009 402p $26.95; pa $16

Grades: 11 12 Adult   **Fic**
1. Fantasy fiction 2. Magic -- Fiction 3. College students -- Fiction
ISBN 978-0-670-02055-3; 0-670-02055-9; 978-0-452-29629-9 pa; 0-452-29629-3 pa
     LC 2008-55900
Alex Award (2010)

"Quentin Coldwater is a geeky high-school senior in Brooklyn who is convinced that happiness and 'the life he should be living' are elsewhere—for example, in the series of nineteen-thirties British adventure novels that he was obsessed with as a child. When Quentin stumbles on a portal that takes him to a college for magicians in upstate New York, he learns that the world depicted in these novels, known as Fillory, is real, and he is forced to square his youthful ideas with the realities that exist there, too—boredom, regret, shame, and despair. Quentin's journey becomes an unexpectedly moving coming-of-age story in which he learns that magical worlds are much like the real one." New Yorker

Grove, S. E.

★ The **glass** sentence; S.E. Grove. Viking, an imprint of Penguin Group (USA) 2014 512 p. (Mapmakers) (hardcover) $17.99

Grades: 6 7 8 9 10   **Fic**
1. Historical fiction 2. Kidnapping -- Fiction 3. Fantasy 4. Maps -- Fiction
ISBN 0670785024; 9780670785025
     LC 2013025832
In this young adult novel by S. E. Grove, part of The Mapmakers Trilogy, "Shadrack is kidnapped. And Sophia, who has rarely been outside of Boston, is the only one who can search for him. Together with Theo, a refugee from the West, she travels over rough terrain and uncharted ocean, encounters pirates and traders, and relies on a combination of Shadrack's maps, common sense, and her own slantwise powers of observation." (Publisher's note)

"In a world fractured into disparate eras during the Great Disruption, Sophia Tims is entrusted with the Tracing Glass (containing a memory thought to be the cause of the Disruption) when her uncle, the cartographer Shadrack Elli, is kidnapped. An intricate fantasy with a Gilded-Age feel, this solidly constructed quest features maps of all kinds and unusual steampunk-flavored elements." Horn Book

Guene, Faiza

Kiffe kiffe tomorrow; [translated from the French by Sarah Adams] Harcourt 2006 179p pa $13

Grades: 11 12 Adult   **Fic**
1. Poor -- Fiction 2. Muslim women -- Fiction 3. Paris (France) -- Fiction
ISBN 0-15-603048-9; 978-0-15-603048-9
     LC 2005-30456
Original French edition, 2004
"Doria, 15, a child of Muslim immigrants, describes her daily struggle in Paris' rough housing projects in a contemporary narrative that's touching, furious, and very funny." Booklist

Guibord, Maurissa

★ **Warped**. Delacorte Press 2011 339p $16.99; lib bdg $19.99

Grades: 7 8 9 10   **Fic**
1. Magic -- Fiction 2. Tapestry -- Fiction 3. Time travel -- Fiction 4. Great Britain -- History -- 1485-

1603, Tudors -- Fiction

ISBN 0-385-73891-9; 0-385-90758-3 lib bdg; 978-0-385-73891-0; 978-0-385-90758-3 lib bdg

LC 2009-53654

When seventeen-year-old Tessa Brody comes into possession of an ancient unicorn tapestry, she is thrust into sixteenth-century England, where her life is intertwined with that of a handsome nobleman. "Grades seven to ten." (Bull Cent Child Books)

"This has it all—fantasy, romance, witchcraft, life-threatening situations, detective work, chase scenes, and a smattering of violence. Imaginative and compelling, it's impossible to put down." SLJ

Guterson, David

★ **Snow** falling on cedars. Harcourt Brace & Co. 1994 345p $25

Grades: 11 12 Adult   **Fic**

1. Trials -- Fiction 2. Journalists -- Fiction 3. Japanese Americans -- Fiction 4. Washington (State) -- Fiction
ISBN 0-15-100100-6

LC 94-7535

"Japanese American Kabuo Miyomoto is arrested in 1954 for the murder of a fellow fisherman, Carl Heine. Miyomoto's trial, which provides a focal point to the novel, stirs memories of past relationships and events in the minds and hearts of the San Piedro Islanders. Through these memories, Guterson illuminates the grief of loss, the sting of prejudice triggered by World War II, and the imperatives of conscience. With mesmerizing clarity he conveys the voices of Kabuo's wife, Hatsue, and Ishmael Chambers, Hatsue's first love who, having suffered the loss of her love and the ravages of war, ages into a cynical journalist now covering Kabuo's trial." Libr J

Haas, Abigail

Dangerous girls; by Abigail Haas. Simon Pulse 2013 400 p. (hardback) $16.99

Grades: 10 11 12   **Fic**

1. Homicide -- Fiction 2. Female friendship -- Fiction 3. Teenagers -- Conduct of life -- Fiction 4. Aruba -- Fiction 5. Murder -- Fiction 6. Friendship -- Fiction 7. Best friends -- Fiction 8. Trials (Murder) -- Fiction 9. Mystery and detective stories
ISBN 1442486597; 9781442486591

LC 2013008216

In this book, "an American teen languishes in an Aruba jail, charged with the brutal murder of her best friend. When Anna Chevalier's on-the-rise father moves her . . . to tony Hillcrest Prep, she quickly makes friends with the charismatic Elise. . . .They and their posse of rich and beautiful teens party hard and often; the centerpiece of their senior year is their unsupervised trip to Aruba--where Elise's stabbing death brings their perpetual celebration to a grinding halt." (Kirkus Reviews)

"Anna's wild spring break ends abruptly when her best friend Elise is found murdered. Anna is the primary suspect--she narrates from an Aruban jail, awaiting her trial. Anna's flashbacks reveal additional suspects on the island, but also rivalries, romances, and betrayals among Anna, Elise, and their friends. Anna's riveting unreliable narration will keep readers guessing until the final page." (Horn Book)

Haddix, Margaret Peterson, 1964-

Full ride; Margaret Peterson Haddix. Simon & Schuster Books for Young Readers 2013 352 p. (hardcover) $16.99

Grades: 6 7 8 9 10 11 12   **Fic**

1. Scholarships -- Fiction 2. Family secrets 3. Ohio -- Fiction 4. Schools -- Fiction 5. Secrets -- Fiction 6. Criminals -- Fiction 7. High schools -- Fiction 8. Mothers and daughters -- Fiction
ISBN 1442442786; 9781442442788; 9781442442795; 9781442442801

LC 2012038146

In this book, by Margaret Peterson Haddix, "Becca's claim to fame is one she's been hiding from for the past three years: Her father is a notorious embezzler. . . . Three years after the trial and imprisonment that destroyed Becca's life, she and her mother have started over again and are living in a town where no one knows their secret. But as college--and its cost--looms large, Becca begins to wonder how they'll afford it. And how she can apply for financial aid without divulging her secret?" (Publisher's note)

"Her father in prison for embezzlement, fourteen-year-old Becca and her mother flee to an Ohio suburb to hide from the media and start new lives. Years later, a chain of events reveals layers of secrets behind Becca's father's crimes, his victims, and her mother's motivations. Haddix deftly emphasizes relatable issues: moving, losing faith in a parent, and falling out of economic comfort." (Horn Book)

Uprising. Simon & Schuster Books for Young Readers 2007 346p $16.99; pa $7.99

Grades: 6 7 8 9 10   **Fic**

1. Fires -- Fiction 2. Strikes -- Fiction 3. Triangle Shirtwaist Company, Inc. -- Fiction
ISBN 978-1-4169-1171-5; 1-4169-1171-5; 978-1-4169-1172-2 pa; 1-4169-1172-3 pa

LC 2006-34870

In 1927, at the urging of twenty-one-year-old Harriet, Mrs. Livingston reluctantly recalls her experiences at the Triangle Shirtwaist factory, including miserable working conditions that led to a strike, then the fire that took the lives of her two best friends, when Harriet, the boss's daughter, was only five years old. Includes historical notes.

"This deftly crafted historical novel unfolds dramatically with an absorbing story and well-drawn characters who readily evoke empathy and compassion." SLJ

Haddon, Mark

★ The **curious** incident of the dog in the night-time; Today Show Book Club ed; Doubleday 2003 226p il $24.95

Grades: 9 10 11 12   **Fic**

1. Autism -- Fiction 2. Great Britain -- Fiction 3. Parent-child relationship -- Fiction
ISBN 0-385-51210-4
Alex Award (2004)

Despite his overwhelming fear of interacting with people, Christopher, a mathematically-gifted, autistic fifteen-year-old boy, decides to investigate the murder of a neighbor's dog and uncovers secret information about his mother

"Unable to feel emotions himself, his story evokes emotions in readers—heartache and frustration for his well-meaning but clueless parents and deep empathy for the wonderfully honest, funny, and lovable protagonist. Readers will never view the behavior of an autistic person again without more compassion and understanding." SLJ

Hahn, Mary Downing, 1937-
Mister Death's blue-eyed girls; Mary Downing Hahn. Clarion Books 2012 330 p. $16.99
Grades: 8 9 10 11 12   **Fic**
1. Mystery fiction 2. Historical fiction 3. Homicide -- Fiction 4. Grief -- Fiction 5. Murder -- Fiction 6. Coming of age -- Fiction 7. Baltimore (Md.) -- History -- 20th century -- Fiction
ISBN 0547760620; 9780547760629
LC 2011025950
In this work of historical fiction, "[t]he high-school year is almost over, there's a party in the park and Mister Death will soon be there, rifle in hand. . . . Two girls, Cheryl and Bobbi Jo, never make it to school the next day, their bloody bodies found in the park where they were shot. [Mary Downing] Hahn's . . . story traces the effects of a crime on everyone involved, including Buddy Novak, accused of a crime he didn't commit." (Kirkus Reviews)

Hahn, Rebecca
A **creature** of moonlight; Rebecca Hahn. Houghton Mifflin Harcourt 2014 224 p. $17.99
Grades: 7 8 9 10 11 12   **Fic**
1. Fantasy fiction 2. Dragons -- Fiction 3. Fantasy 4. Magic -- Fiction 5. Flowers -- Fiction 6. Identity -- Fiction 7. Princesses -- Fiction 8. Forests and forestry -- Fiction
ISBN 054410935X; 9780544109353
LC 2013020188
In this novel, by Rebecca Hahn, "as the only heir to the throne, Marni should have been surrounded by wealth and privilege, not living in exile--but now the time has come when she must choose between claiming her birthright as princess of a realm whose king wants her dead, and life with the father she has never known: a wild dragon who is sending his magical woods to capture her." (Publisher's note)

"Marni lives in a shack at the edge of the woods with her Gramps, where she tends flowers, as she's done for most of her life. Yet change is afoot... This book's greatest strength lies in the vivid woodland scenes and the rich detail that describes the mystical pieces of Marni's tale." (School Library Journal)

★ The **shadow** behind the stars; Rebecca Hahn. Atheneum Books for Young Readers 2015 256 p. (hardcover) $17.99
Grades: 7 8 9 10 11 12   **Fic**
1. Oracles -- Fiction 2. Prophecies -- Fiction 3. Greek mythology -- Fiction 4. Fate and fatalism -- Fiction 5. Gods and goddesses -- Fiction 6. Goddesses, Greek -- Fiction 7. Mythology, Greek -- Fiction
ISBN 9781481435710; 9781481435727
LC 2014026428
In this book, by Rebecca Hahn, "Chloe is the youngest. . . . She and her sisters have been on their isolated Greek island for longer than any mortal can remember. . . . So when a beautiful girl named Aglaia shows up on their doorstep,

Chloe tries to make sure her sisters don't become attached. But in seeking to protect them, Chloe discovers the dark power of Aglaia's destiny." (Publisher's note)

"Hahn's lovingly crafted characters and the brief, unexpected pops of violence in an otherwise peaceful narrative enhance yet another explication of the tragedy of humankind, making this an obvious choice for mythology fans (plenty of those around) and teen philosophers alike." Booklist

Haig, Matt
The **Radleys**. Free Press 2010 371p $25
Grades: 11 12 Adult   **Fic**
1. Vampires -- Fiction 2. Family life -- Fiction
ISBN 978-1-4391-9401-0; 1-4391-9401-7
LC 2010-04459
Alex Award (2011)
Struggling with overwork and parenting angst, English village doctor Peter Radley endeavors to hide his family's vampire nature until their daughter's oddly satisfying act of violence reveals the truth, an event that is complicated by the arrival of a practicing vampire family member.

"Dark humor pervades Haig's . . . entertaining vampire family soap opera. . . . This witty novel offers a refreshing take on an oversaturated genre." Libr J

Haines, Kathryn Miller
★ The **girl** is murder. Roaring Brook Press 2011 352p $16.99
Grades: 7 8 9 10   **Fic**
1. Mystery fiction 2. Social classes -- Fiction 3. Missing persons -- Fiction 4. New York (N.Y.) -- Fiction
ISBN 978-1-59643-609-1; 1-59643-609-3
LC 2010-32935
In 1942 New York City, fifteen-year-old Iris grieves for her mother who committed suicide, and secretly helps her father with his detective business since he, having lost a leg at Pearl Harbor, struggles to make ends meet. "Grades six to ten." (Bull Cent Child Books)

This is "a smart offering that gives both mysteries and historical fiction a good name. . . . The mystery is solid, but what makes this such a standout is the cast. . . . The characters, young and old, leap off the pages." Booklist

Halaby, Laila
West of the Jordan; a novel. Beacon Press 2003 220p (Bluestreak) pa $13
Grades: 11 12 Adult   **Fic**
1. Cousins -- Fiction 2. Muslim women -- Fiction 3. Arab Americans -- Fiction
ISBN 0-8070-8359-3
LC 2002-154924
"Halaby's choice to alternate the narratives of the four young women offers real characterizations to latch onto, and her prose, often lyrical—particularly when the speakers relate other peoples' stories—deepens the complications of history and heritage. Contemplative and lush, this coming-of-age tale resonates with the challenges of cross-cultural life." Publ Wkly

Hale, Marian
The **goodbye** season. Henry Holt and Co. 2009 271p $16.99

Grades: 7 8 9 10   **Fic**
1. Texas -- Fiction 2. Bereavement -- Fiction 3. Family
life -- Fiction 4. Household employees -- Fiction 5.
Mother-daughter relationship -- Fiction
ISBN 978-0-8050-8855-7; 0-8050-8855-5
                                    LC 2008-50275
In Canton, Texas, seventeen-year-old Mercy's dreams
of a different life than her mother's are postponed by harsh
circumstances, including the influenza epidemic of 1918-19,
which forces her into doing domestic work for a loving, if
troubled, family.
This is a "compelling, tautly written novel." SLJ

Hale, Shannon
★ **Book** of a thousand days; illustrations by
James Noel Smith. Bloomsbury Children's Books
2007 305p il $17.95
Grades: 7 8 9 10   **Fic**
1. Love stories 2. Fantasy fiction
ISBN 978-1-59990-051-3; 1-59990-051-3
                                    LC 2006-36999
Fifteen-year-old Dashti, sworn to obey her sixteen-year-
old mistress, the Lady Saren, shares Saren's years of punishment locked in a tower, then brings her safely to the lands
of her true love, where both must hide who they are as they
work as kitchen maids.
This is a "captivating fantasy filled with romance, magic,
and strong female characters." Booklist

Haley, Alex
Mama Flora's family. Delta 1999 462p pa $23
Grades: 11 12 Adult   **Fic**
1. African Americans -- Fiction
ISBN 0-440-61409-0
First published 1998 by Scribner
In this multigenerational family saga, the "lives of
Mama Flora and her family provide a whirlwind survey of
the 20th-century black experience. As a young woman in a
small Tennessee town, Flora bears a son and sees his father
killed at the hands of white racists. She realizes that education is the only way out of poverty. Soon, her daughter becomes a social worker while her son dabbles in communism
and enlists to fight in World War II. As Flora lays dying, she
can look back on her family and their accomplishments with
pride." Libr J

Hallaway, Tate
Almost final curtain; a vampire princess novel.
New American Library 2011 273p pa $9.99
Grades: 9 10 11 12 Adult   **Fic**
1. Horror fiction 2. Witches -- Fiction 3. Vampires
-- Fiction
ISBN 978-0-451-23311-0
                                    LC 2011004453
Sequel to Almost to die for (2010)
"Raised as a witch, Anastasija Parker has always been
an outsider and led a secret life. Then, on her 16th birthday,
she discovers that she is a dhampir (half witch and half vampire). Now she is torn between two groups that are sworn
mortal enemies. . . . As Ana tries to balance these opposing
forces, she learns of a mystical talisman that was assumed
lost. Used against the vampires, it can render them slaves

to the witches for all eternity. . . . Ana is a true heroine who
makes her voice heard. She is not willing to take things at
face value and struggles to find a way to walk the fine line
between two worlds." SLJ

Almost to die for; a vampire princess novel.
New American Library 2010 241p pa $9.99
Grades: 11 12 Adult   **Fic**
1. Horror fiction 2. Witches -- Fiction 3. Vampires
-- Fiction
ISBN 978-0-451-23057-7
                                    LC 2010-10401
"Anastasija Ramses Parker is a modern-day witch's
daughter, fond of wearing 'black with black and black' but
hopelessly unable to perform actual magic. When she flunks
her coven's initiation ceremony, she learns that her father is
a vampire—and not just any vampire, but a vampire leader,
which makes her 'some kind of vampire princess.' Possibly
more important, Ana's best friend, Bea, has a crush on vampire hunter/punk rocker Nikolai, who's torn between kissing
and killing Ana, who thinks he's cute but wants to stay loyal
to Bea. Ana's narration is pitch-perfect and totally teen: half
calculated attitude, half wistful empathy." Publ Wkly
Followed by Almost final curtain (2011)

Halpern, Julie
Get well soon. Feiwel & Friends 2007 193p
$16.95; pa $8.99
Grades: 7 8 9 10   **Fic**
1. Mental illness -- Fiction 2. Psychiatric hospitals --
Fiction
ISBN 0-312-36795-3; 978-0-312-36795-4; 0-312-
58148-3 pa; 978-0-312-58148-0 pa
                                    LC 2006-32358
When her parents confine her to a mental hospital, Anna,
an overweight teenage girl who suffers from panic attacks,
describes her experiences in a series of letters to a friend.
"Halpern creates a narrative that reflects the changes in
Anna with each passing day that includes self-reflection and
a good dose of humor." Voice Youth Advocates

Have a nice day; Julie Halpern. Feiwel and
Friends 2012 325 p. $16.99
Grades: 7 8 9 10 11 12   **Fic**
1. Mental illness -- Fiction 2. Self-perception 3.
Parent-child relationship
ISBN 0312606605; 9780312606602
In author Julie Halpern's book, "Anna Bloom has just
come home from a three-week stay in a mental hospital. She
feels...okay. It's time to get back to some sort of normal life,
whatever that means. She has to go back to school, where
teachers and friends are dying to know what happened to
her, but are too afraid to ask. And Anna is dying to know
what's going on back at the hospital with her crush, Justin,
but is too afraid to ask. Meanwhile, Anna's parents are"t getting along, and she wonders if she's the cause of her family's
troubles." (Publisher's note)

Into the wild nerd yonder. Feiwel and Friends
2009 247p $16.99
Grades: 9 10 11 12   **Fic**
1. School stories 2. Siblings -- Fiction 3. Friendship --

Fiction 4. Popularity -- Fiction 5. Dungeons & dragons (Game) -- Fiction

ISBN 978-0-312-38252-0; 0-312-38252-9

LC 2008-34751

When high school sophomore Jessie's long-term best friend transforms herself into a punk and goes after Jessie's would-be boyfriend, Jessie decides to visit "the wild nerd yonder" and seek true friends among classmates who play Dungeons and Dragons.

"Descriptions of high school cliques . . . are hilarious and believable. . . . This novel is particularly strong in showing how teen friendships evolve and sometimes die away, and how adolescents redefine themselves." SLJ

Halpin, Brendan

A **really** awesome mess; Trish Cook and Brendan Halpin. Egmont USA 2013 288 p. (hardcover) $17.99

Grades: 9 10 11 12   **Fic**

1. Private schools -- Fiction 2. Chinese Americans -- Fiction 3. Schools -- Fiction 4. Psychotherapy -- Fiction 5. Boarding schools -- Fiction 6. Emotional problems-- Fiction

ISBN 160684363X; 9781606843635

LC 2012045978

In this book, "a group of teens at a live-in institution for troubled young people bond, pull off a caper and overcome their issues. . . . Emmy, adopted from China by white parents, feels out of place and unwanted in her family. She is sent to Heartland Academy after retaliating against a tormentor at school. . . . Justin, who resents his father's absence, comes to Heartland following a suicide attempt and after being caught receiving oral sex from a girl he met earlier that day." (Kirkus Reviews)

"Having found themselves at Heartland Academy, a reform school for troubled youth, Justin, Emmy, and a band of misfit teens attempt to sneak out for one really awesome night of fun and adventure. With Eleanor & Park-esque protagonists and a cast reminiscent of Girl, Interrupted, this is a satisfying story about trauma and laughter, and the power of friendship." (Horn Book)

Hambly, Barbara

A **free** man of color. Bantam Bks. 1997 311p hardcover o.p. pa $5.99

Grades: 11 12 Adult   **Fic**

1. Creoles -- Fiction 2. Homicide -- Fiction 3. Race relations -- Fiction

ISBN 0-553-10258-3; 0-553-57526-0 pa

LC 96-44942

"A few suspenseful moments not-withstanding, this isn't an action-packed or suspenseful whodunit. Rather, it's a richly detailed, telling portrait of an intricately structured racial hierarchy." Booklist

Hamill, Pete

Snow in August; a novel. Little, Brown 1997 327p hardcover o.p. pa $14

Grades: 11 12 Adult   **Fic**

1. Jews -- Fiction 2. Prejudices -- Fiction 3. Irish Americans -- Fiction 4. Brooklyn (New York, N.Y.) -- Fiction

ISBN 0-316-34094-4; 0-446-67525-3 pa

LC 96-36043

"Mr. Hamill is not a subtle writer, but his gift for sensual description and his tabloid muscularity . . . fit this page turner of a fable." N Y Times Book Rev

Hamilton, Alwyn

Rebel of the sands; by Alwyn Hamilton. Viking, published by Penguin Group 2016 320 p. (hardback) $18.99

Grades: 9 10 11 12   **Fic**

1. Fantasy fiction 2. Deserts -- Fiction 3. Shooters of firearms -- Fiction 4. Love stories 5. Fantasy 6. Love -- Fiction 7. Adventure and adventurers -- Fiction

ISBN 9780451477538

LC 2015026037

In this book, by Alwyn Hamilton, "Amani Al'Hiza is a gifted gunslinger with perfect aim, but she can't shoot her way out of Dustwalk, the back-country town where she's destined to wind up wed or dead. Then she meets Jin, a rakish foreigner, in a shooting contest, and sees him as the perfect escape route. But though she's spent years dreaming of leaving Dustwalk, she never imagined she'd gallop away on a mythical horse." (Publisher's note)

"A readable, middle-of-the-pack 'teens save the world' story. Consider for large collections." SLJ

Hamilton, Kersten

In the forests of the night; Kersten Hamilton. Clarion Books 2011 295 p. $16.99

Grades: 7 8 9 10   **Fic**

1. Fantasy fiction 2. Goblins -- Fiction 3. Zoos -- Fiction 4. Magic -- Fiction 5. Finn MacCool -- Fiction 6. Irish Americans -- Fiction 7. Imaginary creatures -- Fiction 8. People with mental disabilities -- Fiction

ISBN 0547435606; 9780547435602

LC 2011009846

This book is the second in Kersten Hamilton's Goblin Wars series. Here, "Teagan and her friends must cope with the aftermath of escaping from the Dark Man's forces as well as new dangers. As she picks up the pieces of her life, Teagan begins a tentative relationship with goblin hunter Finn and struggles with her newly revealed goblin heritage." (School Library Journal)

"In her second book, high schooler Teagan (who found out in Tyger, Tyger that she's half-goblin) is back safely from Mag Mell. While she, her little brother Aiden, and love interest Finn Mac Cumhaill (Finn MacCool from Irish folklore) regroup at home in Chicago, wicked forces track them. Well-incorporated folklore elements blend nicely with everyday concerns (e.g., Teagan's post-high-school plans; best friend/boyfriend rivalry)." (Horn Book)

Tyger tyger; by Kersten Hamilton. Clarion Books 2010 308p (Goblin wars) $17

Grades: 7 8 9 10   **Fic**

1. Fantasy fiction 2. Magic -- Fiction 3. Goblins -- Fiction 4. Irish Americans -- Fiction 5. Children with mental disabilities -- Fiction

ISBN 978-0-547-33008-2; 0-547-33008-1

LC 2010-01337

Soon after the mysterious and alluring Finn arrives at her family's home, sixteen-year-old Teagan Wylltson and her disabled brother are drawn into the battle Finn's family has fought since the thirteenth century, when Finn MacCumhaill angered the goblin king. "Grades eight to ten." (Bull Cent Child Books)

"Laced with humor, packed with surprises and driven by suspense, the plot grabs readers from the start using the stylistic tactics of the best fantasy writing. Major characters are beautifully drawn, and many of the secondary characters are equally distinct." Kirkus

Followed by: In the forests of the night (2011) and When the Stars Threw Down Their Spears (2013)

When the stars threw down their spears; by Kersten Hamilton. Clarion Books 2013 400 p. (hardback) $16.99

Grades: 7 8 9 10   Fic

1. Love stories 2. Magic -- Fiction 3. Goblins -- Fiction 4. Zoos -- Fiction 5. Horror & Ghost Stories 6. Finn MacCool -- Fiction 7. Chicago (Ill.) -- Fiction 8. Irish Americans -- Fiction 9. Imaginary creatures -- Fiction 10. People with mental disabilities -- Fiction

ISBN 0547739648; 9780547739649

LC 2012029195

In this novel by Kersten Hamilton "magical creatures are tumbling through mysterious portals from Mag Mell, the world-between-worlds, into the streets of Chicago. Meanwhile, the romance between seventeen-year-old Teagan, who is part goblin, and the alluring bad boy Finn Mac Cumhaill is heating up . . . which is awkward, to say the least, considering he is bound by a family curse to fight goblins his entire life." (Publisher's note)

"In this third book, Teagan and her friends deal with the evil creatures seeping out of Mag Mell and into the streets of Chicago. Teagan and Finn work together to fight the darkness while their love continues to grow, even though it's now forbidden. Fans of fast-paced adventures and Irish folklore will find the two components nicely intertwined." (Horn Book)

Hamilton, Steve

★ The **lock** artist; Steve Hamilton. Minotaur Books 2010 304 p. $24.99

Grades: 11 12 Adult   Fic

1. Locks and keys 2. Mute persons -- Fiction 3. Savants (Savant syndrome) 4. Criminals -- Fiction 5. Lock picking -- Fiction

ISBN 0312380429; 9780312380427

LC 2009034523

Dagger Awards: CWA Ian Fleming Steel Dagger (2011), Edgar Allan Poe Awards: Best Novel (2011), Alex Award (2011)

In this book, "traumatized at the age of eight, Michael, now eighteen, is no ordinary young man. Besides not uttering a single word in ten years, he discovers the one thing he can somehow do better than anyone else. Whether it's a locked door without a key, a padlock with no combination, or even an eight-hundred pound safe, . . . he can open them all. . . . [His] talent . . . will make young Michael a hot commodity with the wrong people and, whether he likes it or not, push him ever close to a life of crime. Until he finally sees his chance to escape, and with one desperate gamble risks

everything to come back home to the only person he ever loved, and to unlock the secret that has kept him silent for so long." (Publisher's note)

Han, Jenny

It's not summer without you; a summer novel. Simon & Schuster Books for Young Readers 2010 275p $16.99

Grades: 7 8 9 10   Fic

1. Summer -- Fiction 2. Beaches -- Fiction 3. Friendship -- Fiction

ISBN 978-1-4169-9555-5; 1-4169-9555-2

LC 2009-42180

Sequel to: The summer I turned pretty (2009)

Teenaged Isobel "Belly" Conklin, whose life revolves around spending the summer at her mother's best friend's beach house, reflects on the tragic events of the past year that changed her life forever

"Han artfully weaves together Belly's and Jeremiah's back stories, recent and long past, to create a solid fabric of relationship and longing. Flashes of humor, realistic (and often salty) dialogue and growing-up moments both painful and authentic create a convincing and poignant read." Publ Wkly

Followed by: We'll always have summer (2011)

The **summer** I turned pretty. Simon & Schuster Books for Young Readers 2009 276p $16.99

Grades: 7 8 9 10   Fic

1. Summer -- Fiction 2. Beaches -- Fiction 3. Vacations -- Fiction 4. Friendship -- Fiction

ISBN 978-1-4169-6823-8; 1-4169-6823-7

LC 2008-27070

Belly spends the summer she turns sixteen at the beach just like every other summer of her life, but this time things are very different.

"Romantic and heartbreakingly real. . . . The novel perfectly blends romance, family drama, and a coming-of-age tale, one that is substantially deeper than most." SLJ

Other titles in this series are:

It's not summer without you (2010)

We'll always have summer (2011)

To all the boys I've loved before; Jenny Han. Simon & Schuster BFYR 2014 368 p. (hardback) $17.99

Grades: 9 10 11 12   Fic

1. Love -- Fiction 2. Sisters -- Fiction 3. Dating (Social customs) -- Fiction

ISBN 1442426705; 9781442426702; 9781442426719

LC 2013022311

In this book, by Jenny Han, "Lara Jean Song keeps her love letters in a hatbox. . . . They aren't love letters that anyone else wrote for her; these are ones she's written. One for every boy she's ever loved--five in all. When she writes, she pours out her heart and soul and says all the things she would never say in real life, because her letters are for her eyes only. Until the day her secret letters are mailed, and suddenly, Lara Jean's love life goes from imaginary to out of control." (Publisher's note)

"Lara Jean writes letters to boys she's liked without thinking they'll ever be sent. When she discovers that the letters have been mailed, she pretends to date one of those boys to save face in front of another (who also dated her studying-abroad sister). What follows is a sweet, honest, and beautifully written story about sisterly bonds and true first love." Horn Book

To all the boys I have loved before

We'll always have summer; a Summer novel. Simon & Schuster Books for Young Readers 2011 291p $17.99

Grades: 7 8 9 10 **Fic**

1. Love stories 2. Summer -- Fiction 3. Beaches -- Fiction 4. Brothers -- Fiction 5. Vacations -- Fiction
ISBN 978-1-4169-9558-6; 1-4169-9558-7; 978-1-4169-9560-9 eBook

LC 2010046670

Sequel to: It's not summer without you (2010)

The summer after her first year of college, Isobel "Belly" Conklin is faced with a choice between Jeremiah and Conrad Fisher, brothers she has always loved, when Jeremiah proposes marriage and Conrad confesses that he still loves her.

"In Han's conclusion to the trilogy that began with The Summer I Turned Pretty, she both underscores the folly of getting engaged too young and vividly depicts the emotions of a girl on the brink of womanhood." Publ Wkly

Hand, Elizabeth

Illyria; a novel. Viking 2010 135p $15.99

Grades: 10 11 12 **Fic**

1. Poets 2. Authors 3. Dramatists 4. Acting -- Fiction 5. Incest -- Fiction 6. Cousins -- Fiction 7. Theater -- Fiction
ISBN 978-0-670-01212-1; 0-670-01212-2

First published 2007 in the United Kingdom

Teenage cousins Madeleine and Rogan, who share twin souls and a sexual relationship, are cast in a school production of Twelfth Night that forces them to confront their respective strengths and future prospects.

"The edgy subject matter, explicit but not gratuitous, relegates this novel to mature readers, but it's beautifully written, rich in theatrical detail and intensely realized characters." Publ Wkly

Handler, Daniel, 1970-

★ **Why** we broke up; art by Maira Kalman. Little, Brown 2012 354p il $19.99

Grades: 8 9 10 11 12 **Fic**

1. Man-woman relationship -- Fiction 2. Breaking up (Interpersonal relations) 3. Letters -- Fiction 4. Dating (Social customs) -- Fiction
ISBN 978-0-316-12725-7

LC 2011009714

Printz Honor Book (2012)

Sixteen-year-old Min Green writes a letter to Ed Slaterton in which she breaks up with him, documenting their relationship and how items in the accompanying box, from bottle caps to a cookbook, foretell the end.

Hardinge, Frances, 1973-

Cuckoo Song; Frances Hardinge. Amulet Books 2014 416 p. (hardback) $17.95

Grades: 9 10 11 12 **Fic**

1. Horror fiction 2. Identity (Psychology) -- Fiction 3. Memory 4. Fantasy 5. Identity 6. Magicians 7. Supernatural 8. Paranormal fiction 9. Families -- England 10. Identity (Psychology) 11. Family life -- England 12. Great Britain -- History -- George V, 1910-1936
ISBN 9781419714801; 9780330519731; 0330519735; 1419714805

LC 2014045264

In this suspense novel, by Frances Hardinge, "when Triss wakes up after an accident, she knows that something is very wrong. She is insatiably hungry; her sister seems scared of her and her parents whisper behind closed doors. She looks through her diary to try to remember, but the pages have been ripped out. Soon Triss discovers that what happened to her is more strange and terrible than she could ever have imagined, and that she is quite literally not herself." (Publisher's note)

"Nuanced and intense, this painstakingly created tale mimics the Escher-like constructions of its villainous Architect, fooling the eyes and entangling the emotions of readers willing and able to enter into a world like no other." Kirkus

★ The **Lie** Tree; Frances Hardinge. Amulet Books 2016 416 p. $17.95

Grades: 7 8 9 10 11 12 **Fic**

1. Murder -- Fiction 2. Secrets -- Fiction 3. Scientists -- Fiction
ISBN 1419718959; 9781419718953

LC 2015028326

Originally published in the United Kingdom by Macmillan Children's Books, 2015

Boston Globe-Horn Book Award: Fiction (2016)

"Faith Sunderly leads a double life. To most people, she is reliable, dull, trustworthy--a proper young lady who knows her place as inferior to men. But inside, Faith is full of questions and curiosity, and she cannot resist mysteries: an unattended envelope, an unlocked door. She knows secrets no one suspects her of knowing. She knows that her family moved to the close-knit island of Vane because her famous scientist father was fleeing a reputation-destroying scandal. And she knows, when her father is discovered dead shortly thereafter, that he was murdered. In pursuit of justice and revenge, Faith hunts through her father's possessions and discovers a strange tree. The tree bears fruit only when she whispers a lie to it. The fruit of the tree, when eaten, delivers a hidden truth. The tree might hold the key to her father's murder--or it may lure the murderer directly to Faith herself." (Publisher's note)

"Smart, feminist, and shadowy, Hardinge's talents are on full display here." SLJ

★ The **lost** conspiracy. Harper 2009 568p $16.99; lib bdg $17.89

Grades: 6 7 8 9 10 **Fic**

1. Fantasy fiction 2. Sisters -- Fiction
ISBN 978-0-06-088041-5; 0-06-088041-4; 978-0-06-088042-2 lib bdg; 0-06-088042-2 lib bdg

LC 2008-45380

Published in the United Kingdom with title: Gullstruck Island

When a lie is exposed and their tribe turns against them, Hathin must find a way to save her sister Arilou—once considered the tribe's oracle—and herself.

"A deeply imaginative story, with nuanced characters, intricate plotting, and an amazingly original setting. . . . A perfectly pitched, hopeful ending caps off this standout adventure." Booklist

Harland, Richard

Liberator; Richard Harland. 1st ed. Simon & Schuster Book for Young Readers 2012 487 p. maps (paperback) $9.99; (hardcover) $17.99

Grades: 6 7 8 9 10   Fic
1. Steampunk fiction 2. Revolutions -- Fiction 3. Social conflict -- Fiction 4. Fantasy 5. Social classes -- Fiction
ISBN 9781442423343; 1442423331; 9781442423336; 9781442423350

LC 2010050911

This is the "second of [Richard] Harland's steampunk series." Here, "[a]fter the Filthies revolted, Col Porpentine and his family were among the few swanks to stay aboard the juggernaut now called the 'Liberator.' But the new regime has troubles galore: A saboteur stalks the halls, an anti-Swank zealot joins the Revolutionary Council and people are disappearing. It's hard for Col to maintain a blossoming romance with revolutionary Filthy Riff in this atmosphere." (Kirkus Reviews)

Worldshaker. Simon & Schuster Books for Young Readers 2010 388p $16.99

Grades: 6 7 8 9 10   Fic
1. Fantasy fiction 2. Social classes -- Fiction
ISBN 978-1-4169-9552-4; 1-4169-9552-8

LC 2009-16924

Sixteen-year-old Col Porpentine is being groomed as the next Commander of Worldshaker, a juggernaut where elite families live on the upper decks while the Filthies toil below, but when he meets Riff, a Filthy girl on the run, he discovers how ignorant he is of his home and its residents.

"Harland's steampunk alternate history is filled with oppression, class struggle, and war, showing their devastation on a personal level through Col's privileged eyes. . . . The writing is sharp and the story fast-paced, demonstrating that, despite his elite status, Col may be just as trapped as any Filthy." Publ Wkly

Harmon, Michael

Under the bridge; by Michael Harmon. 1st ed. Alfred A. Knopf 2012 259 p. (paperback) $8.99; (hardcover) $16.99; (ebook) $50.97; (library) $19.99

Grades: 9 10 11 12   Fic
1. Urban fiction 2. Brothers -- Fiction 3. Skateboarding -- Fiction 4. Drug dealers -- Fiction 5. Spokane (Wash.) -- Fiction
ISBN 0375866469; 9780375859304; 9780375866463; 9780375896422; 9780375966460

LC 2011036368

In this teenage novel, by Michael Harmon, "Tate's younger brother Indy is probably the best skateboarder in Spokane. . . . But when Indy clashes with his father one too

many times and drops out of school, it's up to Tate to win his brother back from the seedier elements of Spokane." (Publisher's note)

Harrington, Hannah

Speechless; Hannah Harrington. Harlequin Teen 2012 268 p. (paperback) $9.99

Grades: 9 10 11 12   Fic
1. Gossip -- Fiction 2. Bullies -- Fiction 3. Hate crimes -- Fiction 4. Schools -- Fiction 5. Secrets -- Fiction 6. Bullying -- Fiction 7. High schools -- Fiction 8. Interpersonal relations -- Fiction
ISBN 0373210523; 9780373210527

LC 2012471034

"Chelsea Knot falls from the top of her high school's social ladder to hated loser in one night when she informs the police of an attack on a gay student by a couple of popular basketball players. It's partially her fault—she instigated the attack by gossiping about the teen and spreading his secret to the student body. Trapped between guilt and broken pride, Chelsea takes a vow of silence to keep herself from causing any more harm." (Booklist)

Harrington, Laura

Alice Bliss; Laura Harrington. Pamela Dorman Books/Viking 2011 306p. $25.95

Grades: 11 12 Adult   Fic
1. Girls 2. Sisters 3. Adolescence 4. Iraq War, 2003-2011 5. Iraq War, 2003- 6. Small town life 7. New York (State) 8. Fathers and daughters 9. Mothers and daughters 10. Soldiers -- United States
ISBN 978-0-670-02278-6; 0-670-02278-0; 9780143121114

LC 201049089

This book tells the story of a teenaged girl, Alice Bliss, who "learns that her father, Matt, is being deployed to Iraq. . . . Alice idolizes her father. . . . When he ships out, Alice is faced with finding a way to fill the emptiness he has left behind." (Publisher's note) "[Alice's mother] Angie, worried sick about Matt and the pressure of suddenly being a single parent, begins to crumble. It is up to Alice to fill the void left by both parents for not only herself but her quirky younger sister, Ellie. . . . [S]he discovers that when it counts, compassion comes from friends and neighbors, who reach out with comfort, advice, and encouragement." (us.penguingroup.com)

Harris, Robert

Pompeii; a novel. Random House 2003 278p map hardcover o.p. pa $13.95

Grades: 11 12 Adult   Fic
1. Adventure fiction 2. Volcanoes -- Fiction 3. Rome -- History -- Fiction
ISBN 0-679-42889-5; 0-8129-7461-1 pa

LC 2003-58446

"An upstanding Roman engineer rushes to repair an aqueduct in the shadow of Mount Vesuvius, which, in A.D. 79, is getting ready to blow its top. . . . Lively writing, convincing but economical period details and plenty of intrigue keep the pace quick." Publ Wkly

Harstad, Johan

★ **172** hours on the moon; Johan Harstad; translation by Tara F. Chace. Little, Brown and Company 2012 351 p. $17.99

Grades: 9 10 11 12   **Fic**

1. Horror fiction 2. Science fiction 3. Moon -- Fiction 4. Astronauts -- Fiction 5. Space flight to the moon -- Fiction 6. United States. National Aeronautics and Space Administration -- Fiction

ISBN 0316182885; 9780316182881

LC 2011025414

This novel by Johan Harstad tells of "three teenagers [who] join an expedition to the Moon in 2019 and find horror there. . . . [They are] Mia, a Norwegian punk rocker, Midori, a Japanese girl rebelling against her restrictive culture, and Antoine, a French boy devastated by a broken romance. . . . The group intends to shelter for a week in a previously secret lab that NASA had established on the Moon in the 1970s. As soon as the group arrives, however, things start to go horribly wrong." (Kirkus Reviews)

Hartinger, Brent

Geography Club. HarperTempest 2003 226p hardcover o.p. pa $8.99

Grades: 9 10 11 12   **Fic**

1. School stories 2. Clubs -- Fiction 3. Homosexuality -- Fiction

ISBN 0-06-001221-8; 0-06-001223-4 pa

LC 2001-51736

A group of gay and lesbian teenagers finds mutual support when they form the "Geography Club" at their high school.

"Hartinger grasps the melodrama and teen angst of high school well. . . . Frank language and the intimation of sexual activity might put off some readers." Voice Youth Advocates

Other titles in this series are:

The Order of the Poison Oak (2005)

Split screen (2007)

Hartman, Rachel

★ **Seraphina**; a novel. by Rachel Hartman. Random House 2012 465 p. (hardcover) $17.99

Grades: 7 8 9 10 11 12   **Fic**

1. Fantasy fiction 2. Dragons -- Fiction 3. Kings and rulers -- Fiction 4. Fantasy 5. Music -- Fiction 6. Secrets -- Fiction 7. Identity -- Fiction 8. Courts and courtiers -- Fiction 9. Self-actualization (Psychology) -- Fiction

ISBN 9780375866562; 9780375896583; 9780375966569; 0375866566

LC 2011003015

Boston Globe-Horn Book Honor: Fiction (2013).

William C. Morris Award (2013)

In this book, "[a]fter 40 years of peace between human and dragon kingdoms, their much-maligned treaty is on the verge of collapse. Tensions are already high with an influx of dragons, reluctantly shifted to human forms, arriving for their ruler Ardmagar Comonot's anniversary. But when Prince Rufus is found murdered in the fashion of dragons--that is, his head has been bitten off--things reach a fever pitch." (Booklist)

Followed by: Shadow Scale (2015)

★ **Shadow** scale; Rachel Hartman. Random House Books for Young Readers 2015 596 p. $21.99

Grades: 9 10 11 12   **Fic**

1. Magic -- Fiction 2. Dragons -- Fiction 3. War stories 4. Fantasy fiction 5. Courts and courtiers -- Fiction

ISBN 0375966579; 9780375866579; 9780375966576

Sequel to: Seraphina (2012)

In this sequel to her novel "Seraphina," author Rachel Hartman "continues the adventures of that book's eponymous half-dragon, who is now assigned with finding and uniting her fellow 'ityasaari' before the full-blooded dragons can resolve their civil war and mobilize to wipe out the southern human kingdoms. But some ityasaari don't want to be found, and one, who has the power to enter and control minds, would rather see them united for her own bitter purpose." (Publishers Weekly)

"With the dragon civil war closing in on Goredd, Seraphina (Seraphina, rev. 7/12) begins an uncertain mission: she and Abdo, a fellow half-dragon, embark on a journey to recruit other ityasaari like themselves, hoping that if they can learn to thread their minds together, they will be able to defend Goredd by forming a trap to stop a dragon in flight...From graceful language to high stakes to daring intrigue, this sequel shines with the same originality, invention, and engagement of feeling that captivated readers in Hartman's debut." Horn Book

Hartnett, Sonya, 1968-

Butterfly. Candlewick Press 2010 232p $16.99

Grades: 7 8 9 10 11 12   **Fic**

1. Australia -- Fiction 2. Family life -- Fiction

ISBN 0-7636-4760-8; 978-0-7636-4760-5

LC 2009046549

In 1980s Australia, nearly fourteen-year-old Ariella "Plum" Coyle fears the disapproval of her friends, feels inferior to her older brothers, and hates her awkward, adolescent body but when her glamorous neighbor befriends her, Plum starts to become what she wants to be—until she discovers her neighbor's ulterior motive.

"The deliberate pacing, insight into teen angst, and masterful word choice make this a captivating read to savor." SLJ

★ **The ghost's** child. Candlewick Press 2008 176p $16.99

Grades: 8 9 10 11 12   **Fic**

1. Ghost stories 2. Voyages and travels -- Fiction

ISBN 978-0-7636-3964-8; 0-7636-3964-8

LC 2008-30817

When a mysterious child appears in her living room one day, the elderly Maddy tells him the story of her love for the wild and free-spirited Feather, who tried but failed to live a conventional life with her, and her search for him on a fantastical voyage across the seas.

"Those who enjoy fables or magical realism will be spellbound by this redemptive story of a search for love, love lost and love (of a sort) found again. . . . [Written in] exquisite prose." Publ Wkly

Golden Boys; Sonya Hartnett. Candlewick Press 2016 256 p. (hardcover) $17.99

Grades: 10 11 12 Adult   **Fic**
1. Domestic fiction 2. Neighborhood -- Fiction 3.
Father-son relationship -- Fiction
ISBN 9780763679491; 0763679496

In this novel, by Sonya Hartnett, "Colt Jenson and his
younger brother . . . have moved to a new, working-class
suburb. . . . Their father, Rex, showers them with gifts . . .
and makes them the envy of the neighborhood. To the local
kids, the Jensons are a family out of a movie, and Rex a
hero. . . . But to Colt he's an impossible figure: unbearable,
suffocating. Has Colt got Rex wrong, or has he seen something in his father that will destroy their fragile new lives?"
(Publisher's note)

"The menacing dynamics present in so many of the relationships are persistently disquieting but also authentic, and
a tone of dread pervades, though in the end, events are understated. Sophisticated teen readers will be wowed by this
gorgeous, tension-filled novel, but its more natural audience
may be adults." Kirkus

★ **Surrender**. Candlewick Press 2006 248p
$16.99; pa $7.99
Grades: 9 10 11 12   **Fic**
1. Dogs -- Fiction 2. Brothers -- Fiction 3. Family
life -- Fiction
ISBN 0-7636-2768-2; 07636-3423-9 pa
                                    LC 2005-54259
Michael L. Printz Award honor book, 2007

As he is dying, a twenty-year-old man known as Gabriel
recounts his troubled childhood and his strange relationship
with a dangerous counterpart named Finnigan.

"From the gripping cover showing a raging inferno to
the blood-chilling revelation of the final chapter, this page-
turner is a blistering yet dense psychological thriller." Voice
Youth Advocates

Thursday's child. Candlewick Press 2002 261p
hardcover o.p. pa $7.99
Grades: 7 8 9 10   **Fic**
1. Poverty -- Fiction 2. Australia -- Fiction 3. Farm life
-- Fiction 4. Family life -- Fiction
ISBN 0-7636-1620-6; 0-7636-2203-6 pa
                                    LC 2001-25223
Harper Flute recounts her Australian farm family's poverty during the Depression, her father's cowardice, and her
younger brother Tin's obsession for digging tunnels and
living underground

"This coming-of-age story with allegorical overtones
will burrow into young people's deepest hopes and fears,
shining light in the darkest inner rooms." Booklist

Hartzler, Aaron
What we saw; Aaron Hartzler. HarperTeen
2015 336 p. (hardback) $17.99 **Fic**
1. Rape -- Fiction 2. Parties -- Fiction 3. Witnesses
-- Fiction
ISBN 9780062338747
                                    LC 2015005619
In this novel, by Aaron Hartzler, "inspired by the events
in the Steubenville rape case . . . , The party at John Doone's
last Saturday night is a bit of a blur. . . . But when a picture
of Stacey passed out over Deacon Mills's shoulder appears

online the next morning, [and] . . . Stacey levels charges
against four of Kate's classmates, the whole town erupts into
controversy." (Publisher's note)

"Even minor characters here are carefully conceived,
and every bit of dialogue and social media activity is chillingly note-perfect. Classroom scenes and conversations offer frameworks for understanding what has happened and
why, but the touch is so light and the narrative voice so
strong that even a two-page passage breaking down the sexism in Grease! avoids seeming didactic. A powerful tale of
betrayal and a vital primer on rape culture." Kirkus

Harvey, Alyxandra
Hearts at stake. Walker & Co. 2010 248p (The
Drake chronicles) $16.99; pa $9.99
Grades: 8 9 10 11 12   **Fic**
1. Siblings -- Fiction 2. Vampires -- Fiction 3.
Friendship -- Fiction
ISBN 978-0-8027-9840-4; 0-8027-9840-3; 978-0-
8027-2074-0 pa; 0-8027-2074-9 pa
                                    LC 2009-23156
As her momentous sixteenth birthday approaches, Sol-
ange Drake, the only born female vampire in 900 years, is
protected by her large family of brothers and her human best
friend Lucy from increasingly persistent attempts on her life
by the powerful vampire queen and her followers.

"Witty, sly, and never disappointing." Booklist
Other titles in this series are:
Blood feud (2010)
Out for blood (2011)

Harvey, Sarah N.
Plastic. Orca Book Publishers 2010 120p (Orca
soundings) pa $9.95
Grades: 7 8 9 10   **Fic**
1. Friendship -- Fiction 2. Plastic surgery -- Fiction
ISBN 978-1-55469-252-1; 1-55469-252-0
Trying to save his best friend from the horrors of plastic surgery, Jack ends up on the front line of a protest of
unscrupulous surgeons.

"This novel is characteristically fast paced and of high
interest. Information about both the pros and the cons of
plastic surgery is included without detracting from the plot.
Plastic does a good job of exploring an important societal
issue while telling a timely tale." SLJ

Hassan, Michael
★ **Crash** and Burn; by Michael Hassan. 1st ed.
Balzer + Bray 2013 544 p. (hardcover) $14.99
Grades: 9 10 11 12   **Fic**
1. School stories 2. School shootings -- Fiction 3.
Schools -- Fiction 4. Violence -- Fiction 5. High
schools -- Fiction 6. Emotional problems -- Fiction 7.
Interpersonal relations -- Fiction
ISBN 0062112929; 9780062112903
                                    LC 2012004280
In this book, "Steven 'Crash' Crashinsky becomes a hero
when he saves more than a thousand people at his high school
by confronting his armed and dangerous classmate, David
'Burn' Burnett, during a chilling hostage situation. Crash
signs a book deal to write about events leading up to the

crisis, his understanding of Burn, and the final secret Burn shared with him that horrible day." (School Library Journal)

Hattemer, Kate

The **vigilante** poets of Selwyn Academy; Kate Hattemer. Alfred A. Knopf 2014 336 p. $16.99

Grades: 8 9 10 11 12   Fic

1. School stories 2. Poetry -- Fiction 3. Arts -- Fiction 4. Schools -- Fiction 5. Minnesota -- Fiction 6. Friendship -- Fiction 7. Creative ability -- Fiction 8. Family life -- Minnesota -- Fiction 9. Reality television programs -- Fiction

ISBN 0385753780; 9780385753784; 9780385753791

LC 2013014325

"Witty, sarcastic Ethan and his three friends decide to take down the reality TV show, 'For Art's Sake,' that is being filmed at their high school, the esteemed Selwyn Arts Academy, where each student is more talented than the next. While studying Ezra Pound in English class, the friends are inspired to write a vigilante long poem and distribute it to the student body, detailing the evils of 'For Art's Sake.'" (Publisher's note)

"Relying on the passion and ideals that drive adolescence, this has a vibrancy and authenticity that will resonate with anyone who has fought for their beliefs--or who has loved a hamster." Booklist

Hautman, Pete

All-in. Simon & Schuster Books for Young Readers 2007 181p hardcover o.p. pa $5.99

Grades: 7 8 9 10   Fic

1. Poker -- Fiction 2. Gambling -- Fiction 3. Las Vegas (Nev.) -- Fiction

ISBN 978-1-4169-1325-2; 1-4169-1325-4; 978-1-4169-1326-9 pa; 1-4169-1326-9 pa

LC 2006-23871

Sequel to No limit (2005)

Having won thousands of dollars playing high-stakes poker in Las Vegas, seventeen-year-old Denn Doyle hits a losing streak after falling in love with a young casino card dealer named Cattie Hart.

"Skillfully using the multiple-voice approach, Hautman brings to life the intricacies of poker, crafting a thrilling story of loss, good versus evil, and redemption." Voice Youth Advocates

Blank confession. Simon & Schuster Books for Young Readers 2010 170p $16.99

Grades: 7 8 9 10   Fic

1. School stories 2. Bullies -- Fiction 3. Drug traffic -- Fiction

ISBN 978-1-4169-1327-6; 1-4169-1327-0

LC 2009-50169

A new and enigmatic student named Shayne appears at high school one day, befriends the smallest boy in the school, and takes on a notorious drug dealer before turning himself in to the police for killing someone.

"Masterfully written with simple prose, solid dialogue and memorable characters, the tale will grip readers from the start and keep the reading in one big gulp, in the hope

of seeing behind Shayne's mask. A sure hit with teen readers." Kirkus

★ **Invisible**. Simon & Schuster Books for Young Readers 2005 149p $15.95; pa $7.99

Grades: 7 8 9 10   Fic

1. Friendship -- Fiction 2. Mental illness -- Fiction

ISBN 0-689-86800-6; 0-689-86903-7 pa

LC 2004-2484

Doug and Andy are unlikely best friends—one a loner obsessed by his model trains, the other a popular student involved in football and theater—who grew up together and share a bond that nothing can sever

"With its excellent plot development and unforgettable, heartbreaking protagonist, this is a compelling novel of mental illness." SLJ

Hautman, Pete, 1952-

★ The **Cydonian** pyramid; Pete Hautman. Candlewick Press 2013 368 p. (The Klaatu Diskos) (reinforced) $16.99

Grades: 7 8 9 10 11 12   Fic

1. Science fiction 2. Time travel -- Fiction

ISBN 0763654043; 9780763654047

LC 2012942673

This novel, by Pete Hautman, is part of the "Klaatu Diskos" series. "More than half a millennium in the future, in the shadow of the looming Cydonian Pyramid, a pampered girl named Lah Lia has been raised for one purpose: to be sacrificed. . . . But just as she is about to be killed, a strange boy appears from the diskos, providing a cover of chaos that allows her to escape and launching her on a time-spinning journey in which her fate is irreversibly linked to his." (Publisher's note)

Eden West; Pete Hautman. First edition Candlewick Press 2015 320 p. $17.99

Grades: 9 10 11 12   Fic

1. Cults -- Fiction 2. Cults 3. Faith

ISBN 0763674184; 9780763674182

LC 2014945452

In this book, author Pete Hautman "explores a boy's unraveling allegiance to an insular cult. Twelve square miles of paradise, surrounded by an eight-foot-high chain-link fence: this is Nodd, the land of the Grace. Beyond the fence lies the World, a wicked, terrible place, doomed to destruction. When the Archangel Zerachiel descends from Heaven, only the Grace will be spared the horrors of the Apocalypse. But something is rotten in paradise." (Publisher's note)

"While projecting a unique and expressive voice in Jacob, Hautman sensitively and gracefully explores powerful ideas about faith and church communities, keeping a deft balance between criticism of religious fervor and deep respect for faith and belief. Thought-provoking and quietly captivating." Booklist

★ **Godless**. Simon & Schuster Books for Young Readers 2004 208p $15.95; pa $8.99

Grades: 7 8 9 10   **Fic**
1. Religion -- Fiction
ISBN 0-689-86278-4; 1-4169-0816-1 pa

                       LC 2003-10468
When sixteen-year-old Jason Bock and his friends create their own religion to worship the town's water tower, what started out as a joke begins to take on a power of its own. "Grades seven to twelve." (Bull Cent Child Books)

"The witty text and provocative subject will make this a supremely enjoyable discussion-starter as well as pleasurable read." Bull Cent Child Books

The **Klaatu** terminus; Pete Hautman. Candlewick Press 2014 368 p. (The Klaatu diskos) $16.99
Grades: 7 8 9 10 11 12   **Fic**
1. Science fiction 2. Dystopian fiction 3. Apocalyptic fiction
ISBN 0763654051; 9780763654054

                      LC 2013944132
In this series finale, Pete Hautman "weaves several diverging time streams into one . . . masterwork. . . . In a far distant future, Tucker Feye and . . . Lia find themselves atop a crumbling pyramid in an abandoned city. In present-day Hopewell, Tucker's uncle Kosh faces armed resistance . . . as he attempts to help a terrorized woman named Emma. . . . And on a train platform in 1997, a seventeen-year-old Kosh is given an instruction that will change his life." (Publisher's note)

"Tucker and Lia (The Obsidian Blade; The Cydonian Pyramid) join together in the end stage of their journey through the millennia and the final confrontation with the murderous Lah Sept; Tucker uncovers his own role in Lah Sept history. Pulling together elaborate strands of the first two books, this conclusion rewards readers with a surprising yet cogent and satisfying chronicle across time." Horn Book

★ The **obsidian** blade; Pete Hautman. Candlewick Press 2012 308 p. (Klaatu diskos)
Grades: 7 8 9 10 11 12   **Fic**
1. Science fiction 2. Uncles -- Fiction 3. Time travel -- Fiction 4. Missing persons -- Fiction 5. Supernatural
ISBN 9780763654030

                      LC 2011018617
In this book, which is the first in a series, "[o]ne day Tucker sees his father disappear through a strange disk in the air and then come back an hour later changed, . . . but offering no explanation. . . . Tucker . . . realizes that . . . the disks . . . appear to be portals to other times and places. The disks are unpredictable, though, and their passages seem to lead to sites where violent, traumatic events are occurring." (Bulletin of the Center for Children's Books)

What boys really want? Pete Hautman. Scholastic Press 2012 297 p. (hbk.) $17.99
Grades: 8 9 10 11   **Fic**
1. Friendship 2. High school students -- Fiction 3. Dating (Social customs) 4. Jealousy 5. Plagiarism
ISBN 0545113156; 9780545113151

                      LC 2011278706
In this book, "Lita has never told Adam that she is behind the snarky and irreverent teen advice blog 'Miz Fitz,' or that she has basically sabotaged all of his romantic rela-

tionships. . . . Adam hasn't confided the fact that he's getting most of his information for his . . . book on what boys want from girls . . . from the internet, specifically Miz Fitz's blog. As Adam barrels forward with his project, Lita . . . [is] jealous: writing is her territory, not his." (Bulletin of the Center for Children's Books)

"The book moves along at a snappy pace...This is fresh, realistic YA fiction at its best." SLJ

Hawkins, Rachel
Demonglass; a Hex Hall novel. Hyperion 2011 359p $16.99
Grades: 7 8 9 10   **Fic**
1. Ghost stories 2. Magic -- Fiction 3. Witches -- Fiction 4. Supernatural -- Fiction 5. Great Britain -- Fiction 6. Father-daughter relationship -- Fiction
ISBN 978-1-4231-2131-2; 1-4231-2131-7

                      LC 2010-10511
Sequel to: Hex Hall (2010)
After learning that she is capable of dangerous magic, Sophie Mercer goes to England with her father, friend Jenna, and Cal hoping to have her powers removed, but soon she learns that she is being hunted by the Eye—and haunted by Elodie.

"Narrator Sophie's delivery is . . . delightfully bold, and the many action scenes lend a cinematic feel." Booklist

Hex Hall. Disney/Hyperion Books 2010 323p $16.99
Grades: 7 8 9 10   **Fic**
1. School stories 2. Witches -- Fiction 3. Supernatural -- Fiction
ISBN 1423121309; 9781423121305
When Sophie attracts too much human attention for a prom-night spell gone horribly wrong, she is exiled to Hex Hall, an isolated reform school for witches, faeries, and shapeshifters. "Grades seven to ten." (Bull Cent Child Books)

"Sixteen-year-old Sophie Mercer, whose absentee father is a warlock, discovered both her heritage and her powers at age 13. While at her school prom, Sophie happens upon a miserable girl sobbing in the bathroom and tries to perform a love spell to help her out. It misfires, and Sophie finds herself at Hecate (aka Hex) Hall, a boarding school for delinquent Prodigium (witches, warlocks, faeries, shape-shifters, and the occasional vampire). What makes this fast-paced romp work is Hawkins' wry humor and sharp eye for teen dynamics." Booklist

Followed by: Demonglass (2011)

School spirits; Rachel Hawkins. Hyperion 2013 304 p. (hardcover) $17.99
Grades: 7 8 9 10   **Fic**
1. School stories 2. Paranormal fiction 3. Monsters -- Fiction 4. Magic -- Fiction 5. Schools -- Fiction 6. High schools -- Fiction 7. Supernatural -- Fiction
ISBN 1423148495; 9781423148494

                      LC 2012046402
This young adult paranormal novel, by Rachel Hawkins, is part of the "Hex Hall" series. "Izzy and her mom move to a new town, but . . . discover it's not as normal as it appears. A series of hauntings has been plaguing the local high

school, and Izzy is determined to . . . investigate. But assuming the guise of an average teenager is easier said than done. For a tough girl who's always been on her own, it's strange to suddenly make friends and maybe even have a crush." (Publisher's note)

Haydu, Corey Ann

★ **OCD** love story; Corey Ann Haydu. Simon Pulse 2013 352 p. (alk. paper) $17.99

Grades: 9 10 11 12 **Fic**

1. Love stories 2. Obsessive-compulsive disorder -- Fiction 3. Psychotherapy -- Fiction 4. Interpersonal relations -- Fiction

ISBN 1442457325; 9781442457324

LC 2012021545

In this book, when "Bea kisses a strange boy during a blackout at a school dance, it's clear she's a little eccentric, but it isn't until her therapist slips several pamphlets about OCD into Bea's hands that" her problem becomes clear. "Bea's need to perform certain rituals, even at the risk of alienating those she loves, becomes all-consuming. The one bright spot in Bea's life is a budding romance with Beck, the boy from the school dance, who resurfaces in Bea's group-therapy sessions." (Kirkus Reviews)

"Bea and Beck both have debilitating obsessive-compulsive disorder. As they begin dating, they must navigate their feelings for each other and the complications of their individual compulsions. Thanks to some leaps of faith and a lot of therapy, the teens get a happy ending. Haydu explores a sweet, unconventional romance in this compulsively readable novel." (Horn Book)

Headley, Justina Chen

★ **North** of beautiful. Little, Brown 2009 373p $16.99

Grades: 7 8 9 10 11 12 **Fic**

1. Aesthetics -- Fiction

ISBN 978-0-316-02505-8; 0-316-02505-4

LC 2008-09260

Headley's "finely crafted novel traces a teen's uncharted quest to find beauty. Two things block Terra's happiness: a port-wine stain on her face and her verbally abusive father. . . . A car accident brings her together with Jacob, an Asian-born adoptee with unconventional ideas. . . . The author confidently addresses very large, slippery questions about the meaning of art, travel, love and of course, beauty." Publ Wkly

Healey, Karen

Guardian of the dead. Little, Brown 2010 345p $17.99

Grades: 9 10 11 12 **Fic**

1. School stories 2. Magic -- Fiction 3. Maoris -- Fiction 4. Fairies -- Fiction 5. New Zealand -- Fiction

ISBN 978-0-316-04430-1

LC 2009-17949

Eighteen-year-old New Zealand boarding school student Ellie Spencer must use her rusty tae kwon do skills and new-found magic to try to stop a fairy-like race of creatures from Maori myth and legend that is plotting to kill millions of humans in order to regain their lost immortality.

"Fast-paced adventure and an unfamiliar, frightening enemy set a new scene for teen urban fantasy." Kirkus

The **shattering**. Little, Brown 2011 311p $17.99

Grades: 7 8 9 10 **Fic**

1. Mystery fiction 2. Suicide -- Fiction 3. Homicide -- Fiction 4. New Zealand -- Fiction 5. Supernatural -- Fiction

ISBN 978-0-316-12572-7; 0-316-12572-5

LC 2010047996

When a rash of suicides disturbs Summerton, an oddly perfect tourist town on the west coast of New Zealand, the younger siblings of the dead boys become suspicious and begin an investigation that reveals dark secrets and puts them in grave danger.

"Juggling multiple viewpoints, Healey skillfully keeps her characters on an emotional roller-coaster even as they deal with physical threats. The climax delivers a gut punch that only underscores the sensitivity of the subject matter (without lessening the thrill at all)." Publ Wkly

When we wake; Karen Healey. Little, Brown Books for Young Readers 2013 304 p. (hardcover) $17.99

Grades: 7 8 9 10 11 12 **Fic**

1. Science fiction 2. Dystopian fiction 3. Science Fiction 4. Australia -- Fiction

ISBN 031620076X; 9780316200769

LC 2012028739

"Sixteen-year-old Tegan is just like every other girl living in 2027--But on what should have been the best day of Tegan's life, she dies--and wakes up a hundred years in the future, locked in a government facility with no idea what happened. . . . But the future isn't all she hoped it would be, and when . . . secrets come to light, Tegan must make a choice: Does she keep her head down and survive, or fight for a better future?" (Publisher's note)

While we run; by Karen Healey. Little Brown & Co 2014 336 p. (hardcover) $18

Grades: 7 8 9 10 11 12 **Fic**

1. Cryonics 2. Science fiction 3. Cryonics -- Fiction 4. Australia -- Fiction

ISBN 031623382X; 9780316233828

LC 2013022281

Sequel to: When we wake

In this science fiction novel by Karen Healey, "Abdi Taalib thought he was moving to Australia for a music scholarship. But after meeting the beautiful and brazen Tegan Oglietti, his world was turned upside down. Tegan's no ordinary girl--she died in 2027, only to be frozen and brought back to life in Abdi's time, 100 years later." (Publisher's note)

"In When We Wake, Tegan and Abdi revealed the government's plan to populate a new planet with cryogenically frozen slaves. Abdi begins narrating six months after their capture by the government. Like its predecessor, Run succeeds simply as a sci-fi thriller, but it's elevated by its social commentary, emphasizing the importance of fighting for justice in a world that has little of it." Horn Book

Hearn, Julie

★ **Ivy**; a novel. Atheneum Books for Young Readers 2008 355p $17.99; pa $9.99

Grades: 8 9 10 11 12   **Fic**

1. Artists -- Fiction 2. Criminals -- Fiction 3. Drug abuse -- Fiction 4. London (England) -- Fiction 5. Great Britain -- History -- 19th century -- Fiction

ISBN 978-1-4169-2506-4; 1-4169-2506-6; 978-1-4169-2507-1 pa; 1-4169-2507-4 pa

LC 2007-045463

In mid-nineteenth-century London, young, mistreated, and destitute Ivy, whose main asset is her beautiful red hair, comes to the attention of an aspiring painter of the pre-Raphaelite school of artists who, with the connivance of Ivy's unsavory family, is determined to make her his model and muse.

"Quirky characters, darkly humorous situations, and quick action make this enjoyable historical fiction." SLJ

The **minister's** daughter. Atheneum Books for Young Readers 2005 263p hardcover o.p. pa $7.99

Grades: 7 8 9 10   **Fic**

1. Witchcraft -- Fiction 2. Supernatural -- Fiction 3. Salem (Mass.) -- Fiction 4. Great Britain -- History -- 1642-1660, Civil War and Commonwealth -- Fiction

ISBN 0-689-87690-4; 0-689-87691-2 pa

LC 2004-18324

In 1645 in England, the daughters of the town minister successfully accuse a local healer and her granddaughter of witchcraft to conceal an out-of-wedlock pregnancy, but years later during the 1692 Salem trials their lie has unexpected repercussions.

"With its thought-provoking perceptions about human nature, magic and persecution, this tale will surely cast a spell over readers." Publ Wkly

Hearn, Lian

Across the nightingale floor. Riverhead Bks. 2002 287p (Tales of the Otori) hardcover o.p. pa $15

Grades: 11 12 Adult   **Fic**

1. Japan -- Fiction

ISBN 1-57322-225-9; 1-57322-332-8 pa

LC 2002-22339

"In an imaginary country reminiscent of feudal Japan, Takeo is adopted by Lord Shigeru after his village is wiped out, and he learns that the lord may have acted out of more than compassion as he himself is heir to powerful, mysterious abilities. A riveting start to an imaginative trilogy." Booklist

Other available titles in this series are:

Grass for his pillow (2003)

Brilliance of the moon (2004)

Brilliance of the moon. Riverhead Books 2004 330p (Tales of the Otori) $24.95

Grades: 11 12 Adult   **Fic**

1. Japan -- Fiction

ISBN 1-573-22270-4

LC 2003-61777

This continues the adventures of Kaede and Takeo begun in Across the nightingale floor and Grass for his pillow

In this volume "Kaede and Takeo find themselves in danger after their hasty marriage. Lord Fujiwara is furious that Kaede chose to marry another man when he considered them betrothed, and the warlord Arai considers Takeo presumptuous. The Tribe is split over the decision to kill Takeo. The young lovers must find allies in unexpected places to claim the domains that are rightfully theirs." SLJ

Grass for his pillow. Riverhead Bks. 2003 292p (Tales of the Otori) $24.95

Grades: 11 12 Adult   **Fic**

1. Japan -- Fiction

ISBN 1-57322-251-8

LC 2003-43215

"The second installment in the Otori trilogy, set in ancient Japan, picks up where Across the Nightingale Floor . . . left off, with Otori Takeo leaving his love, Shirakawa Kaede, to join his ancestral tribe. The tribe, a stealthy group possessing mysterious powers, wants Takeo to devote his life to them, and he feels honor bound to do so. Kaede is heartbroken but understands that he needs to do his duty just as she needs to stake her claim on the inheritance her aunt left her. . . . Hearn maintains the epic scale of the first, and adds depth to the exotic world his characters inhabit." Booklist

Heath, Jack

The **Lab**. Scholastic Press 2008 311p $17.99

Grades: 7 8 9 10   **Fic**

1. Science fiction 2. Adventure fiction 3. Spies -- Fiction 4. Genetic engineering -- Fiction

ISBN 978-0-545-06860-4; 0-545-06860-6

"A gritty dystopic world exists under the iron rule of the mega-corporation Chao-Sonic, with only a few vigilante groups around to act as resistance. Six of Hearts is easily the best agent on one such group, the Deck, and he is fiercely dedicated to justice, using his extensive genetic modifications to his advantage. . . . The compelling and memorable protagonist stands out even against the intricately described and disturbing city whose vividness makes the place's questionable fate a suspenseful issue in its own right." Bull Cent Child Books

Followed by: Remote control (2010)

Money run; by Jack Heath. 1st American ed. Scholastic Press 2013 245 p. (hardcover) $17.99

Grades: 8 9 10   **Fic**

1. Crime -- Fiction 2. Adventure fiction 3. Stealing -- Fiction 4. Assassins -- Fiction 5. Theft

ISBN 0545512662; 9780545512664

LC 2013004005

In this book, "Ashley and Benjamin are two teen partners in crime--real crime, as in major heists--who rely on their youth to avoid suspicion. . . . Their prey today happens to be a billionaire businessman who has sponsored an essay contest with a prize of $10,000 (Ash has won with an essay ghostwritten by Benjamin), but that's peanuts compared to the $2 million they hope to loot." (Kirkus Reviews)

Remote control. Scholastic Press 2010 326p $17.99

Grades: 7 8 9 10   **Fic**

1. Science fiction 2. Adventure fiction 3. Spies --

Fiction 4. Genetic engineering -- Fiction
ISBN 978-0-545-07591-6; 0-545-07591-2
Sequel to: The Lab (2008)
First published 2007 in Australia

Agent Six of Hearts, 16-year-old superhuman, is on a mission. His brother Kyntak has been kidnapped. A strange and sinister new figure is rising in power. Six is suspected of being a double agent. The Deck has been put into lockdown by the Queen of Spades. A mysterious girl has appeared who acts as Six's guardian angel. Who can he trust?

"The technothriller begun in The Lab (2008) takes several intriguing twists . . . on its way to a satisfying, if temporary, resolution." Booklist

Heathfield, Lisa

Seed; Lisa Heathfield. Running Press Teens 2015 336 p. (hbk.) $16.95
Grades: 7 8 9 10   **Fic**
1. Hi-Lo books 2. Cults -- Fiction 3. Teenage girls -- Fiction 4. Communal living -- Fiction
ISBN 9780762456345
                                                    LC 2014949872
In this young adult novel, by Lisa Heathfield, "Seed is at the center of 15-year-old Pearl's life: it is the isolated family of which she is part . . . and . . . the remote patch of land . . . where she sows and gathers crops. . . . She does not often leave because . . . Seed is pure and leaving risks contact with poisoned Outsiders who may taint Pearl's spiritual core. . . . But when three Outsiders unexpectedly join the family, . . . Pearl's entire reality is challenged." (School Library Journal)

"Well-developed secondary characters and Heathfield's willingness to do serious damage to central ones make this novel a powerful read." Pub Wkly

Heinlein, Robert A.

★ The **moon** is a harsh mistress. Orb 1997 382p il pa $14.95
Grades: 11 12 Adult   **Fic**
1. Science fiction
ISBN 0-312-86355-1
First published 1966 by Putnam
"Colonists of the Moon declare independence from Earth, and contrive to win the ensuing battle with the aid of a sentient computer. Action-adventure with some exploration of new possibilities in social organization and fierce assertion of the motto 'There Ain't No Such Thing as a Free Lunch.'" Anatomy of Wonder 4

Stranger in a strange land. Putnam 1961 408p hardcover o.p. pa $16.95
Grades: 11 12 Adult   **Fic**
1. Science fiction
ISBN 0-441-78838-6 pa
"The hero is a human born of space travelers from earth and raised by Martians. He is brought to the totalitarian post-World War III world that is in many ways depicted as a satire of the U.S. in the 1960s, marked by repressiveness in sexual morality and religion. The plot, which tells how the heroic stranger creates a Utopian society in which people preserve their individuality but share a brotherhood of community, made Heinlein and his novel cult objects for young people

dedicated to a counterculture." Oxford Companion to Am Lit. 5th edition

Helig, Heidi

The **Girl** from Everywhere; Heidi Heilig. Harpercollins Childrens Books 2016 464 p. (hardback) $17.99
Grades: 9 10 11 12   **Fic**
1. Sea stories 2. Fantasy fiction 3. Time travel -- Fiction
ISBN 0062380753; 9780062380753
                                                    LC 2015035884
This young adult fantasy novel, by Heidi Heilig, "sweeps from modern-day New York City, to nineteenth-century Hawaii, to places of myth and legend. Sixteen-year-old Nix has sailed across the globe and through centuries aboard her time-traveling father's ship. But when he gambles with her very existence, it all may be about to end." (Publisher's note)

"With time travel, fantasy, Hawaiian history, mythology, cute animals, and a feisty protagonist, romance and fantasy readers will find much to enjoy in this quick read, which features a conclusion suggesting a sequel." Booklist

Heller, Joseph

★ **Catch**-22; with an introduction by Malcolm Bradbury. Knopf 1995 xxxix, 568p $20
Grades: 11 12 Adult   **Fic**
1. World War, 1939-1945 -- Fiction
ISBN 0-679-43722-3
                                                    LC 94-13984
A reissue of the title first published 1961 by Simon & Schuster

"By way of some of the funniest dialogue ever, Heller takes shots at the hypocrisy, meanness, and stupidities of our society." Shapiro. Fic for Youth. 3d edition
Followed by Closing time (1994)

Hemingway, Amanda

The **Greenstone** grail; Amanda Hemingway. Del Rey/Ballentine Books 2005 360p hardcover o.p. $16.95; $12.95
Grades: 11 12 Adult   **Fic**
1. Fantasy fiction 2. Immortality -- Fiction 3. Gifted children -- Fiction 4. Grail -- Fiction 5. England -- Fiction 6. Villages -- Fiction 7. Immortalism -- Fiction 8. Homeless women -- Fiction 9. Albinos and albinism -- Fiction
ISBN 0345460782; 9780345460790
                                                    LC 2004049396
First published 2004 in the United Kingdom.
This book follows Nathan Ward, who "is just your typical 11-year-old of supernatural parentage, until he stumbles on a hidden altar that gives him visions of a green stone cup filled with blood. Soon he begins dreaming of Eos, a world that needs the grail for a spell to ward off a terrible plague. As the dreams become astral excursions, the grail surfaces in Nathan's world, but then is stolen and sent to Eos, at the wrong time and into the wrong hands. While Nathan goes to the rescue, his mother and the venerable grail guardian, Bartlemy Goodman, fend off the village witch, an antiques trader, police and a malevolent river spirit." (Publishers Weekly)

"Nathan Ward is just your typical 11-year-old of supernatural parentage, until he stumbles on a hidden altar that gives him visions of a green stone cup filled with blood. Soon he begins dreaming of Eos, a world that needs the grail for a spell to ward off a terrible plague. As the dreams become astral excursions, the grail surfaces in Nathan's world, but then is stolen and sent to Eos, at the wrong time and into the wrong hands. . . . The book glows with a blend of ancient magic and wide-eyed wonder that should captivate audiences on both sides of the Atlantic, especially readers weary of more conventional Arthurian epics." Publ Wkly

The **poisoned** crown. Del Rey 2007 374p pa $12.95

Grades: 11 12 Adult   Fic
  1. Fantasy fiction
  ISBN 978-0-345-46082-0
                                       LC 2006-50823
Sequel to The sword of straw (2005)
"In the conclusion to the Sangreal Trilogy, young Nathan finds the crown of the title and faces the Grandir and his ultimate plan. . . . The climactic battle ranks with the best for power and terror." Booklist

The **sword** of straw. Del Rey 2005 320p pa $12.95

Grades: 11 12 Adult   Fic
  1. Fantasy fiction
  ISBN 0-345-46080-4; 978-0-345-46080-6
                                       LC 2005-48462
Sequel to The Greenstone grail (2005)
In this second volume of the Sangreal trilogy, Nathan Ward "is now a teenager at boarding school. Lately, his dreams have taken him to a ruined city, deserted by all save a disabled king and his daughter, Princess Nell. Nathan wants to help her, but he can only reach her in dreams; moreover, he can't control when or how he gets to the city. Hemingway does a superb job of blending British folklore, plot elements, and characters from the preceding book and an excellent portrayal of contemporary teenagers into a real page-turner likely to please a broad readership." Booklist
Followed by The poisoned crown (2007)

Hemmings, Kaui Hart

Juniors; Kaui Hart Hemmings. G.P. Putnam's Sons, an imprint of Penguin Group (USA) 2015 320 p. (hardcover) $18.99

Grades: 9 10 11 12   Fic
  1. School stories 2. Hawaii -- Fiction 3. Wealth -- Fiction 4. Schools -- Fiction 5. Friendship -- Fiction 6. High schools -- Fiction 7. Interpersonal relations -- Fiction
  ISBN 9780399173608
                                       LC 2014040377
In this novel, by Kaui Hart Hemmings, "Lea Lane . . . [is] part Hawaiian, part Mainlander. . . . Hanging in the shadow of her actress mother's spotlight. And now: new resident of the prominent West family's guest cottage. Bracing herself for the embarrassment of being her classmates' latest charity case, Lea is surprised when she starts becoming friends with Will and Whitney West insteador in the case of gorgeous,

unattainable Will, possibly even more than friends." (Publisher's note)
"Friendship and romance brush cheek to cheek in a story that deals frankly with race, class, and culture while also managing to wonderfully portray the luminous, dreamlike setting of Hawaii. A perfect complement to the shelves of readers who follow Jenny Han and E. Lockhart." Booklist

Hemphill, Helen

Long gone daddy. Front Street 2006 176p $16.95

Grades: 8 9 10 11 12   Fic
  1. Grandfathers -- Fiction 2. Christian life -- Fiction 3. Las Vegas (Nev.) -- Fiction 4. Father-son relationship -- Fiction
  ISBN 1-932425-38-1
                                       LC 2005-25105
Young Harlan Q. Stank gets a taste of life in the fast lane when he accompanies his preacher father on a road trip to Las Vegas to bury his grandfather and to fulfill the terms of the old man's will.
"Many teens will see their own questions about faith, worship, and independence in Harlan's heart-twisting feelings." Booklist

Hemphill, Stephanie

Hideous love; the story of the girl who wrote Frankenstein. Stephanie Hemphill. Balzer + Bray, an imprint of HarperCollinsPublishers 2013 320 p. (hardcover bdg.) $17.99

Grades: 9 10 11 12   Fic
  1. Novels in verse 2. Historical fiction 3. Love -- Fiction 4. Authorship -- Fiction
  ISBN 0061853313; 9780061853319
                                       LC 2013000237
This book is a "fictionalized verse biography of" author Mary Shelley. Stephanie Hemphill "explores the particular challenges facing a gifted female artist who allies herself with a renowned male poet. Central to the plot is the parentage of Mary Wollstonecraft Godwin Shelley, daughter of Mary Wollstonecraft, the pioneering feminist philosopher who died days after Mary was born, and William Godwin, a radical political philosopher who espoused free love for all but his daughters." (Kirkus Reviews)

Sisters of glass; Stephanie Hemphill. Alfred A. Knopf 2012 150 p. $16.99

Grades: 7 8 9 10   Fic
  1. Love stories 2. Novels in verse 3. Historical fiction 4. Families -- Fiction 5. Family life -- Fiction 6. Venice (Italy) -- Fiction
  ISBN 0375861092; 0375961097; 9780375861093; 9780375961090
                                       LC 2011277551
This book presents "[a] . . . tale of destiny, fidelity, and true love" set in "fourteenth-century Murano, Italy (of glass-making renown) and . . . told through verse. . . . Maria is disdainful of her training to be a society woman and yearns instead to spend her time with her art or in the family's furnaces with Luca, an employee whose skill with glass is the

marvel that leads Maria, who once aspired to be a glassblower, to fall in love with him." (Booklist)

★ **Wicked** girls; a novel of the Salem witch trials. Balzer + Bray 2010 408p il $17.99; lib bdg $17.89

Grades: 7 8 9 10 11 12   **Fic**

1. Novels in verse 2. Trials -- Fiction 3. Witchcraft -- Fiction 4. Salem (Mass.) -- Fiction

ISBN 0-06-185328-3; 0-06-185329-1 lib bdg; 978-0-06-185328-9; 978-0-06-185329-6 lib bdg

LC 2010-9593

This is "a fictionalized account of the Salem witch trials told from the perspectives of three of the real young women living in Salem in 1692. Ann Putnam Jr. plays the queen bee. When her father suggests that a spate of illnesses within the village is the result of witchcraft, Ann . . . puts in motion a chain of events that will change the lives of the people around her forever. Mercy Lewis, the beautiful servant in Ann's house, inspires adulation in some and envy in others. With a troubled past, she seizes her only chance at safety. Margaret Walcott, Ann's cousin, is desperately in love and consumed with fiery jealousy. She is torn between staying loyal to her friends and pursuing the life she dreams of with her betrothed." (Publisher's note) "Middle school, high school." (Horn Book)

"Hemphill's raw, intimate poetry probes behind the abstract facts and creates characters that pulse with complex emotion." Booklist

Includes bibliographical references

Henderson, Eleanor

Ten thousand saints; Eleanor Henderson. Ecco 2011 388p.

Grades: 11 12 Adult   **Fic**

1. Drugs 2. Adolescence 3. Vermont 4. Parent and child 5. Vermont -- Fiction 6. Musicians -- Fiction 7. Teenagers -- Fiction 8. New York (N.Y.) -- Fiction 9. Parent and child -- Fiction 10. New York (N.Y.) -- Greenwich Village

ISBN 0062021028; 9780062021021

LC 2011283405

This book is "a coming-of-age story set in the 1980s that departs from the genre's familiar tropes to find a panoramic view of how the imperfect escape from our parents' mistakes makes (equally imperfect) adults of us. Jude Keffy-Horn and Teddy McNicholas are drug-addled adolescents stuck in suburban Vermont and dreaming of an escape to New York City. But after Teddy dies of an overdose, Jude makes good on their dream and forms a de facto family with Teddy's straight-edge brother, Johnny; Jude's estranged pot-farmer father, Lester; and the troubled Eliza Urbanski, who may be carrying Teddy's child. What results is an odyssey encompassing the age of CBGB, Hare Krishnas, zincs, and the emergence of AIDS." (Publishers Weekly)

Henderson, Jason

The **Triumph** of Death; Jason Henderson. HarperTeen 2012 310 p.

Grades: 8 9 10 11 12   **Fic**

1. Vampires 2. Occult fiction 3. Adventure fiction 4. Horror stories 5. Witches -- Fiction 6. Vampires

-- Fiction 7. Supernatural -- Fiction

ISBN 9780061951039

LC 2012004297

This young adult paranormal adventure, by Jason Henderson, is book three of the "Alex Van Helsing" series. "There is a famous painting in Madrid that holds the key to an apocalypse only Alex Van Helsing can stop . . . [and] a newly risen vampire queen threatens the fate of the world. . . . Teaming up with a motorcycle-riding witch, Alex jets between Switzerland, the UK, and Spain in a frantic race to prevent the queen from . . . [plunging] the world into darkness." (Publisher's note)

Hensley, Joy N.

Rites of passage; Joy N. Hensley. First edition HarperTeen 2014 416 p. (hardback) $17.99

Grades: 7 8 9 10   **Fic**

1. School stories 2. Bullies -- Fiction 3. Secret societies -- Fiction 4. Schools -- Fiction 5. Bullying -- Fiction 6. Sex role -- Fiction 7. Military training -- Fiction 8. Blue Ridge Mountains -- Fiction

ISBN 0062295195; 9780062295194

LC 2014010022

In this novel by Joy N. Hensley, "sixteen-year-old Sam McKenna discovers that becoming one of the first girls to attend a revered military academy means living with a target on her back. As Sam struggles to prove herself, she learns that a decades-old secret society is alive and active . . . and determined to force her out." (Publisher's note)

"The narrative flows along terrifically as Sam courageously battles to make it even while the forces against her increase. The characters stand out as individual and real; readers will cheer Sam on throughout. Absolutely compelling." Kirkus

Heppermann, Christine

★ **Ask** Me How I Got Here; Christine Heppermann. Harpercollins Childrens Books 2016 240 p. $17.99

Grades: 9 10 11 12   **Fic**

1. Novels in verse 2. Abortion -- Fiction 3. Teenage pregnancy -- Fiction 4. Choice (Psychology) -- Fiction

ISBN 0062387952; 9780062387950

LC 2016004714

In this novel by Christine Heppermann, "Addie is a good student and the star of the cross-country team at her private Catholic school. When she discovers that she is pregnant, she gets an abortion with the support of her boyfriend and parents. Afterward, she struggles with what the pregnancy and her decision mean, both to her self-perception and those around her, leading Addie to discover more surprising things about herself." (School Library Journal)

"Addie has got a great boyfriend, a fantastic cross-country record at her all-girls Catholic high school, and a powerful talent for poetry. When she gets pregnant, she doesn't face terrible strife: her parents are supportive, her boyfriend isn't angry, and it's over in a flash. But in the aftermath, she finds herself reevaluating many of her choices, especially track, and, surprisingly, deeply drawn to a track-star alumna who is taking a break from both running and college. . . . This absorbing book would be an excellent choice for teen book groups." Booklist

Herbach, Geoff

Nothing special; Geoff Herbach. Sourcebooks Inc. 2012 290 p. (paperback) $9.99; (ebook) $9.99

Grades: 6 7 8 9 10   **Fic**

1. Friendship -- Fiction 2. Dysfunctional families -- Fiction 3. Teenagers -- Conduct of life -- Fiction

ISBN 1402265077; 9781402265075; 9781402265099

In this book, author Geoff Herbach tells the story of Felton, a football and track star who deals with his girlfriend Aleah abroad in Germany and "the possibility that his younger brother Andrew could be falling apart. Andrew has convinced their mother to let him go to band camp, but Felton discovers that Andrew, usually the sane member of the family, has in fact run away to Florida. An impromptu road trip with erstwhile best friend Gus turns up surprising reasons for Andrew's escape." (Kirkus Reviews)

Herbert, Brian

Dune: House Atreides; [by] Brian Herbert and Kevin J. Anderson. Bantam Bks. 1999 604p

Grades: 11 12 Adult   **Fic**

1. Science fiction

ISBN 0-553-11061-6

LC 99-17726

"Though the plot here is intricate, even readers new to the saga will be able to follow it easily." Publ Wkly

"Here is the rich and complex world that Frank Herbert created, in the time leading up to the momentous events of Dune. As Emperor Elrood's son plots a subtle regicide, young Leto Atreides leaves for a year's education on the mechanized world of Ix; a planetologist named Pardot Kynes seeks the secrets of Arrakis; and the eight-year-old slave Duncan Idaho is hunted by his cruel masters in a terrifying game from which he vows escape and vengeance. But none can envision the fate in store for them: one that will make them renegades—and shapers of history." (Publisher's note)

Herbert, Frank

★ **Dune**. Ace Bks. 1999 517p il $27.95

Grades: 11 12 Adult   **Fic**

1. Science fiction

ISBN 0-441-00590-X

First published 1965 by Chilton

"Herbert combines several classic elements: a Machiavellian world of political intrigue worthy of fourteenth-century Italy, a huge cast of characters, and a detailed picture of a culture. Duke Leto Atreides and his family are coerced into exchanging their rich lands for a barren planet, Dune, which produces a unique drug. Duke's son, Paul, becomes the leader of a group that leads the Fremen of Dune against the enemy. This is a science fiction story with sociological and ecological import." Shapiro. Fic for Youth. 3d edition

Other titles about Dune are:

Chapterhouse: Dune (1985)

Children of Dune (1976)

Dune messiah (1969)

God Emperor of Dune (1981)

Heretics of Dune (1984)

Herlong, Madaline

The **great** wide sea; [by] M. H. Herlong. Viking Children's Books 2008 283p pa $6.99; $16.99

Grades: 7 8 9 10   **Fic**

1. Sailing -- Fiction 2. Brothers -- Fiction 3. Bereavement -- Fiction

ISBN 0-14-241670-3 pa; 0-670-06330-4; 978-0-14-241670-9 pa; 978-0-670-06330-7

LC 2008-08384

Still mourning the death of their mother, three brothers go with their father on an extended sailing trip off the Florida Keys and have an adventure at sea. "Grades six to ten." (Bull Cent Child Books)

"Herlong makes the most of the three boys' characters, each exceptionally well developed here, to make this as much a novel of brotherhood as a sea story." Bull Cent Child Books

Hernandez, David

No more us for you. HarperTeen 2009 281p $16.99

Grades: 9 10 11 12   **Fic**

1. School stories 2. Death -- Fiction 3. California -- Fiction 4. Friendship -- Fiction 5. Bereavement -- Fiction

ISBN 978-0-06-117333-2; 0-06-117333-9

LC 2008-19203

Teenagers Isabel and Carlos find themselves growing closer after a car crash forces them to confront difficult issues. "Grades eight to twelve." (Bull Cent Child Books)

"Hernandez builds Isabel and Carlos into characters that readers come to root for and love." Voice Youth Advocates

★ **Suckerpunch**. HarperTeen 2008 217p $17.89

Grades: 9 10 11 12   **Fic**

1. Brothers -- Fiction 2. Drug abuse -- Fiction 3. Child abuse -- Fiction 4. Hispanic Americans -- Fiction 5. Father-son relationship -- Fiction

ISBN 978-0-06-117330-1; 0-06-117331-2

Accompanied by two friends, teenage brothers Marcus and Enrique head on a road trip to confront the abusive father who walked out on them a year earlier.

"The author's imagery, sometimes subtle, sometimes searing, invariably hits its mark." Publ Wkly

Herrick, Steven

By the river. Front Street 2006 238p $16.95

Grades: 8 9 10 11 12   **Fic**

1. Death -- Fiction 2. Brothers -- Fiction 3. Australia -- Fiction 4. Single parent family -- Fiction

ISBN 1-932425-72-1

LC 2005-23967

First published 2004 in the United Kingdom

A fourteen-year-old describes, through prose poems, his life in a small Australian town in 1962, where, since their mother's death, he and his brother have been mainly on their own to learn about life, death, and love.

"The poems are simple but potent in their simplicity, blending together in a compelling, evocative story of a gentle, intelligent boy growing up and learning to deal with a sometimes-ugly little world that he . . . will eventually escape." Voice Youth Advocates

Cold skin. Front Street 2009 279p $17.95
Grades: 8 9 10 11 12 **Fic**
1. Mystery fiction 2. Novels in verse 3. Homicide -- Fiction 4. Australia -- Fiction 5. Country life -- Fiction
ISBN 978-1-59078-572-0; 1-59078-572-X
LC 2008-18620
In a rural Australian coal mining town shortly after World War II, teenaged Eddie makes a startling discovery when he investigates the murder of a local high school girl.

"The strongest plot element is the mystery, which is well developed and has a surprising yet satisfying outcome. Some sexual scenarios make this most appropriate for older teens. Overall, a multilayered and affecting read." SLJ

The **wolf**. Front Street 2007 214p $17.95
Grades: 8 9 10 11 12 **Fic**
1. Novels in verse 2. Australia -- Fiction 3. Domestic violence -- Fiction 4. Father-daughter relationship -- Fiction
ISBN 978-1-932425-75-8; 1-932425-75-6
LC 2006-12072
Sixteen-year-old Lucy, living in the shadow of her violent father, experiences a night of tenderness, danger and revelation as she and Jake, her fifteen-year-old neighbor, search for a legendary wolf in the Australian outback.

"Herrick's verse style perfectly suits this emotionally taut survival story. . . . Readers will find this novel compelling, its fast-moving narrative rewarding." SLJ

Hesse, Karen
Safekeeping; Karen Hesse. Feiwel and Friends 2012 294 p. ill., map $17.99
Grades: 7 8 9 10 11 12 **Fic**
1. Alternative histories 2. Revolutions -- Fiction 3. Voyages and travels -- Fiction
ISBN 1250011345; 9781250011343
LC 2012288414
In this book, a "group of rebels called the American People's Party has taken control" in the U.S. "Radley, an American teenager returning home from doing volunteer work in Haiti, finds her parents gone and her Vermont home abandoned. Not knowing whom to trust or where she'll be safe, she sets out on foot to Canada, befriending a reticent girl along the way. The two form a tentative friendship and manage to cross into Canada." (Publishers Weekly)

Hesse, Monica
Girl in the blue coat; Monica Hesse. Little, Brown & Co. 2016 320 p. (hardback) $17.99
Grades: 9 10 11 12 **Fic**
1. Missing children -- Fiction 2. Netherlands -- History -- 1940-1945, German occupation -- Fiction 3. Black market -- Fiction 4. Mystery and detective stories 5. Jews -- Netherlands -- Fiction 6. Netherlands -- History -- German occupation, 1940-1945 -- Fiction 7. Holocaust, Jewish (1939-1945) -- Netherlands -- Amsterdam -- Fiction 8. World War, 1939-1945 --

Underground movements -- Netherlands -- Fiction
ISBN 9780316260602; 0316260606
LC 2015020565
In this novel by Monica Hesse, set "in Nazi-occupied Holland, Hanneke seems like an ordinary . . . [b]ut her Aryan features . . . allow her to work as a courier on the black market smuggling . . . items to paying customers. Her actions are a direct result of the loss of Bas, her boyfriend. When one of her best customers asks for her assistance in finding a Jewish girl she was hiding, Hanneke . . . is drawn into the mysterious disappearance of the girl." (School Library Journal)

"In 1943 Amsterdam, Hanneke nurses a broken heart--her boyfriend has died in the war--while delivering black market goods (foodstuffs, cigarettes, etc.) to her neighbors. One customer, Mrs. Janssen, implores Hanneke to find a missing girl whom the woman had been sheltering, leading to an engaging mystery that shakes Hanneke from her emotional stupor. An author's note includes useful information about the Dutch Resistance." Horn Book

Hiassen, Carl, 1953-
Skink--no surrender; Carl Hiaasen. Alfred A. Knopf 2014 288 p. (hardback) $18.99
Grades: 9 10 11 12 **Fic**
1. Mystery fiction 2. Missing persons -- Fiction 3. Florida -- Fiction 4. Missing children -- Fiction 5. Wilderness areas -- Fiction 6. Mystery and detective stories
ISBN 0375870512; 9780375870514; 9780375970511
LC 2014006036
In this young adult novel by Carl Hiaasen, "Classic Malley--to avoid being shipped off to boarding school, she takes off with some guy she met online. Poor Richard--he knows his cousin's in trouble before she does. Wild Skink--he's a ragged, one-eyed ex-governor of Florida, and enough of a renegade to think he can track Malley down. With Richard riding shotgun, the unlikely pair scour the state, undaunted by blinding storms, crazed pigs, flying bullets, and giant gators." (Publisher's note)

Hickam, Homer
Crescent; second in the Helium-3 series. by Homer Hickam. Thomas Nelson 2013 336 p. (A Helium-3 novel) (pbk.) $9.99
Grades: 7 8 9 10 11 12 **Fic**
1. Moon -- Fiction 2. Fugitives from justice -- Fiction 3. War -- Fiction 4. Science fiction 5. Prejudices -- Fiction 6. Prisoners of war -- Fiction
ISBN 1595546634; 9781595546630
LC 2012051410
This book is the sequel to author Homer Hickam's "Crater". "Weary of the war with the Unified Countries of the World . . . Crater Trueblood captures Crescent--a short, mouthy and thoroughly deadly genetically altered superwarrior from Earth. He is then faced with the tall task of keeping her from killing, or being killed by, the vengeful citizens of Moontown. Meanwhile, his estranged sweetheart, Maria, . . . barely blasts her way out of a UCW kidnap attempt." (Kirkus Reviews)

"Expertly blending space opera and hard sci-fi, romance, and even mystery (there's a detour for a nifty whodunit), this is fast paced, packed with intriguing ideas." Booklist

Hidier, Tanuja Desai

Bombay Blues; Tanuja Desai Hidier. Push 2014
560 p. illustrations $18.99

Grades: 9 10 11 12　　　　**Fic**

1. Bombay (India) -- Fiction 2. India 3. Families
4. Mumbai (India) 5. East Indian Americans 6.
Interpersonal Relations

ISBN 0545384788; 9780545384780

In this young adult novel, by Tanuja Desai Hidier,
"Dimple Lala thought that growing up would give her all
the answers, but instead she has more questions than ever. .
. . It's time for a change, and a change is just what Dimple
is going to get--of scenery, of cultures, of mind. She thinks
she's heading to Bombay for a family wedding--but really
she is plunging into the unexpected, the unmapped, and the
uncontrollable." (Publisher's note)

"The novel is closer in tone to Indian young adult fiction, which features savvy, stylish Indian youth already out
of high school. The pacing is rapid, with Hidier's snappy
dialogue and insider jokes propelling the reader through
more than 500 pages. This is highly recommended for older
teens with an interest in the Indian sub-continent." VOYA

Higgins, Joanna

Waiting for the queen; Joanna Higgins. Milkweed Editions 2013 256 p. (alk. paper) $16.95

Grades: 6 7 8 9 10　　　　**Fic**

1. Historical fiction 2. Immigrants -- United States 3.
Shakers -- Fiction 4. Slavery -- Fiction 5. Friendship
-- Fiction 6. Social classes -- Fiction 7. Pennsylvania --
History -- 1775-1865 -- Fiction 8. Frontier and pioneer
life -- Pennsylvania -- Fiction 9. France -- History --
Revolution, 1789-1799 -- Fiction

ISBN 1571317007; 9781571317001

LC 2012042167

In this book, "Eugenie, 15 and haunted by the horrors [of
the French Revolution] they've escaped, arrives unprepared
for the harshly primitive conditions they find [in America],
and she's annoyed by her unrealistic mother's matchmaking
with an unpleasant young noble. In alternating chapters, her
story is contrasted with that of Quaker Hannah, who . . . has
been hired to help the French out for a year but whose faith
keeps her from the subservience the noblemen demand."
(Kirkus Reviews)

Higgins, M. G.

Bi-Normal; M. G. Higgins. Saddleback Pub
2013 191 p. (paperback) $9.95

Grades: 7 8 9 10 11 12　　　　**Fic**

1. School stories 2. Gay teenagers -- Fiction

ISBN 1622500040; 9781622500048

In this book, "a teen football player with a girlfriend
discovers he has feelings for another boy. When Brett first
notices his attraction to Zach, a boy who sits next to him in
art class, he wants to push it away Brett and his friends are
the kind of guys who ogle girls' bodies and pick on boys they
perceive as gay. As his feelings intensify, however, Brett is
torn between acting on his attraction and acting out of his
denial." (Kirkus Reviews)

Higson, Charles

The dead; [by] Charlie Higson. Hyperion 2011
485p map $16.99

Grades: 8 9 10　　　　**Fic**

1. Horror fiction 2. Zombies -- Fiction

ISBN 978-1-4231-3412-1; 1-4231-3412-5

As a disease turns everyone over sixteen into brainless,
decomposing, flesh-eating creatures, a group of teenagers
head to London. Ed, Jack, Bam and the other students at
Rowhurst School learn more about the Disaster, and meet an
adult who seems to be immune to the disease.

"With the book's immense cast and substantial body
count, it doesn't pay to get too attached to any one character,
while the intense descriptions of violence and sickness will
get under readers' skin." Publ Wkly

★ The **enemy**. Hyperion/DBG 2010 440p
$16.99; pa $8.99

Grades: 9 10 11 12　　　　**Fic**

1. Horror fiction 2. Zombies -- Fiction 3. London
(England) -- Fiction

ISBN 978-1-4231-3175-5; 1-4231-3175-4; 978-1-
4231-3312-4 pa; 1-4231-3312-9 pa

First published 2009 in the United Kingdom

"Nearly two years ago, the world changed; everyone
over 16 became horrifically ill and began to crave fresh
meat. As supplies are exhausted and the vicious grown-ups
grow braver, Arrum and Maxie, along with their band of
refugees, must embark on a perilous journey across London
to reach the safest spot in the city: Buckingham Palace. .
. . Intrigue, betrayal and the basic heroic-teens-against-ma-
rauding-adults conflict give this work a high place on any
beach-reading list." Kirkus

Followed by: The dead (2011)

Hijuelos, Oscar

Dark Dude. Atheneum Books for Young Readers
2008 439p $16.99; pa $9.99

Grades: 7 8 9 10　　　　**Fic**

1. Wisconsin -- Fiction 2. Cuban Americans -- Fiction

ISBN 978-1-4169-4804-9; 1-4169-4804-X; 978-1-
4169-4945-9 pa; 1-4169-4945-3 pa

LC 2008-00959

In the 1960s, Rico Fuentes, a pale-skinned Cuban
American teenager, abandons drug-infested New York
City for the picket fence and apple pie world of Wisconsin, only to discover that he still feels like an outsider and
that violent and judgmental people can be found even in the
wholesome Midwest.

"Hijuelos weaves a compelling and insightful tale of one
outsider's coming-of-age. . . . The resolution is quick and
tidy, but the imagery is rich and the content sure to engage
teen readers." Voice Youth Advocates

Hill, C. J.

Erasing time; C. J. Hill. Katherine Tegen Books
2012 361 p. $17.99

Grades: 8 9 10 11　　　　**Fic**

1. Secrecy -- Fiction 2. Resistance to government
3. Future life 4. Science fiction 5. Twins -- Fiction
6. Sisters -- Fiction 7. Time travel -- Fiction 8.

Government, Resistance to -- Fiction
ISBN 0062123920; 9780062123923

LC 2011044624

"When twins Sheridan and Taylor wake up 400 years in the future, they find a changed world: domed cities, no animals, and a language that's so different, it barely sounds like English. And the worst news: They can't go back home.

The twenty-fifth-century government transported the girls to their city hoping to find a famous scientist to help perfect a devastating new weapon. The same government has implanted tracking devices in the citizens, limiting and examining everything they do. Taylor and Sheridan have to find a way out of the city before the government discovers their secrets." (Publisher's note)

Slayers; friends and traitors. by C. J. Hill. Feiwel & Friends 2013 390 p. $16.99
Grades: 7 8 9 10 11 12   Fic
1. Dragons -- Fiction 2. Teenagers -- Fiction
ISBN 1250024617; 9781250024619

In this book, by C. J. Hill, "Tori's got a problem. She thought she'd have one more summer to train as a dragon Slayer, but time has run out. When Tori hears the horrifying sound of dragon eggs hatching, she knows the Slayers are in trouble. In less than a year, the dragons will be fully grown and completely lethal. The Slayers are well-prepared, but their group is still not complete, and Tori is determined to track down Ryker--the mysterious missing Slayer." (Publisher's note)

"When Tori breaks the rules that keep the dragon slayers safe, all the slayers are endangered unless they can figure out which one of them is a traitor. A steamy love triangle takes center stage over the dragon-fighting in this installment; though many characters from the first book only show up fleetingly, fans of Slayers will find plenty to entertain them." (Horn Book)

Hill, Will
Department 19. Razorbill 2011 540p
Grades: 10 11 12   Fic
1. Horror fiction 2. Homicide -- Fiction 3. Vampires -- Fiction 4. Supernatural -- Fiction 5. Great Britain -- Fiction
ISBN 1595144064; 9781595144065

LC 2010-54252

After watching his father's murder, sixteen-year-old Jamie Carpenter joins Department 19, a secret government agency, where he learns of the existence of vampires and the history that ties him to the team destined to stop them. "Grades eight to ten." (Bull Cent Child Books)

"This is a nonstop thrill ride right up to the cliffhanger ending. This cinematic adrenaline rush has the makings of a surefire hit." Publ Wkly

The **rising**; Will Hill. Razorbill 2012 576 p.
Grades: 10 11 12   Fic
1. Vampires 2. Supernatural 3. Adventure fiction
ISBN 1595144072; 9781595144072

In this novel, by Will Hill, "Sixteen-year-old Jamie Carpenter's life was violently upended when he was brought into Department 19, a classified government agency of vampire hunters. . . . But being the new recruit at the Department isn't all weapons training and covert missions. Jamie's

own mother has been turned into a vampire--and now Jamie will stop at nothing to wreak revenge on her captors." (Publisher's note)

Hillerman, Tony
The **fallen** man. HarperCollins Pubs. 1996 294p
Grades: 11 12 Adult   Fic
1. Detectives 2. Navajo Indians 3. Mystery and detective stories -- United States
ISBN 9781442079335; 9780060547967; 9780061967771

LC 96029469

This is Hillerman's thirteenth mystery novel set on a Navajo reservation in the Southwest. "On Halloween a human skeleton is discovered near the peak of the 1700-foot-high Ship Rock, . . . a holy site to the Navajos. Could it be the body of Hal Breedlove, a rancher who went missing 11 years ago? Retired tribal police officer Joe Leaphorn, who had investigated the case, approaches newly promoted Lieutenant Jim Chee with his theory. But before they can close the case, an old Navajo guide who was the last man to see Breedlove alive is seriously wounded by a sniper, raising the possibility that Breedlove's death was murder." (Libr J)

"A skeleton is found on a high ledge of Ship Rock mountain, a place sacred to the Navahos. Tribal Police Lieutenant Chee and the now retired Leaphorn suspect correctly that it belongs to a wealthy rancher missing for 11 years, and Chee tries to discover if it is murder or an accidental death. Meanwhile, Leaphron is hired by a lawyer to look into the investigation for the rancher's Eastern family, who want to own his land legally so they can accept a lucrative bid for the mining rights." SLJ

Hills, Lia
★ The **beginner's** guide to living. Farrar, Straus and Giroux 2010 221p il $17.99
Grades: 9 10 11 12   Fic
1. School stories 2. Bereavement -- Fiction
ISBN 978-0-374-30659-5; 0-374-30659-1

LC 2009-19248

Struggling to cope with his mother's sudden death and growing feelings of isolation from his father and brother, seventeen-year-old Will turns to philosophy for answers to life's biggest questions, while finding some solace in a new love.

"Almost nothing escapes Will's notice (though his perceptiveness alone doesn't produce answers), and the mosaic of imagery and musings in his poetic, staccato narration offers thought-provoking ideas about grief and the universal drive to find a purpose. Although this novel begins with a death, it is a celebration of life, companionship, and love." Publ Wkly

Hinton, S. E.
★ The **outsiders**. Viking 1967 188p $17.99; pa $9.99
Grades: 7 8 9 10   Fic
1. Social classes -- Fiction 2. Juvenile delinquency -- Fiction
ISBN 0-670-53257-6; 0-14-038572-X pa
ALA YALSA Margaret A. Edwards Award (1988)

"This remarkable novel by a seventeen-year-old girl gives a moving, credible view of the outsiders from the inside—their loyalty to each other, their sensitivity under tough crusts, their understanding of self and society." Horn Book

Hitchcock, Bonnie-Sue

The **smell** of other people's houses; Bonnie-Sue Hitchcock. Wendy Lamb Books 2016 240 p. (trade) $17.99

Grades: 7 8 9 10   **Fic**
1. Alaska -- Fiction 2. Teenagers -- Fiction 3. Friendship -- Fiction 4. Alaska -- History -- 20th century -- Fiction
ISBN 9780553497786; 9780553497793; 9780553497816

LC 2015011309

This novel, by Bonnie-Sue Hitchcock, is set "In Alaska, 1970. . . . Ruth has a secret that she can't hide forever. Dora wonders if she can ever truly escape where she comes from, even when good luck strikes. Alyce is trying to reconcile her desire to dance, with the life she's always known on her family's fishing boat. Hank and his brothers decide it's safer to run away than to stay home—until one of them ends up in terrible danger." (Publisher's note)

"Less a narrative and more a series of portraits, this is an exquisitely drawn, deeply heartfelt look at a time and place not often addressed. Hitchcock's measured prose casts a gorgeous, almost otherworldly feel over the text, resulting in a quietly lovely look at the various sides of human nature and growing up in a difficult world." Booklist

Hoban, Russell, 1925-2011

Soonchild; Russell Hoban; illustrated by Alexis Deacon. Candlewick 2012 144 p. (hardback) $15.99

Grades: 9 10 11 12   **Fic**
1. Paranormal fiction 2. Shamans -- Fiction 3. Arctic regions -- Fiction 4. Inuit -- Fiction 5. Eskimos -- Fiction 6. Pregnancy -- Fiction 7. Supernatural -- Fiction 8. Father and child -- Fiction
ISBN 9780763659202

LC 2011048373

In this book, set "[s]omewhere in the Arctic Circle, Sixteen-Face John, a shaman, learns that his first child, a soonchild, cannot hear the World Songs from her mother's womb. The World Songs are what inspire all newborns to come out into the world, and John must find them for her. But how? The answer takes him through many lifetimes and many shape-shifts, as well as encounters with beasts, demons and a mysterious benevolent owl spirit, Ukpika." (Publisher's note)

Hobbs, Will

Beardance. Atheneum Pubs. 1993 197p il pa $5.99

Grades: 7 8 9 10   **Fic**
1. Bears -- Fiction 2. Ute Indians -- Fiction
ISBN 0-689-31867-7; 0-689-87072-8 pa

LC 92-44874

Sequel to Bearstone

While accompanying an elderly rancher on a trip into the San Juan Mountains, Cloyd, a Ute Indian boy, tries to

help two orphaned grizzly cubs survive the winter and, at the same time, completes his spirit mission.

"The story offers plenty of action and memorable characters, and the descriptions of Ute rituals and legends, the setting, and Cloyd's first experiences with spirit dreams are particularly well done." Horn Book Guide

Bearstone. Atheneum Pubs. 1989 154p hardcover o.p. pa $4.99

Grades: 7 8 9 10   **Fic**
1. Ute Indians -- Fiction
ISBN 0-689-87071-X pa

LC 89-6641

"The growth and maturity that Cloyd acquires as the summer progresses is juxtaposed poetically against the majestic Colorado landscape. Hobbs has creatively blended myth and reality as Cloyd forges a new identity for himself." Voice Youth Advocates

Followed by Beardance (1993)

★ The **maze**. Morrow Junior Bks. 1998 198p $15.99; pa $5.99

Grades: 7 8 9 10   **Fic**
1. Condors -- Fiction 2. Runaway teenagers -- Fiction
ISBN 0-688-15092-6; 0-380-72913-X pa

LC 98-10791

Rick, a fourteen-year-old foster child, escapes from a juvenile detention facility near Las Vegas and travels to Canyonlands National Park in Utah where he meets a bird biologist working on a project to reintroduce condors to the wild

"Hobbs spins an engrossing yarn, blending adventure with a strong theme, advocating the need for developing personal values." Horn Book Guide

Hockensmith, Steve

Pride and prejudice and zombies; dawn of the dreadfuls. by Steve Hockensmith; illustrations by Patrick Arrasmith. Quirk Books 2010 287p il (Quirk classics) pa $12.95

Grades: 11 12 Adult   **Fic**
1. Authors 2. Novelists 3. Zombies -- Fiction 4. Social classes -- Fiction 5. Great Britain -- History -- 19th century -- Fiction
ISBN 978-1-59474-454-9

LC 2009-943659

When a funeral at the local parish goes strangely and horribly awry and corpses suddenly spring from the soft earth, only one person can stop them. As the bodies pile up, Elizabeth Bennet evolves from a naive young teenager into a savage slayer of the undead in this prequel to Pride and Prejudice and Zombies.

"Hockensmith does not abandon Austen's original characters. Mrs. Bennett is the most true to the original, and even silly Kitty and Lydia are the same, only they fight instead of fuss over men. Elizabeth, from whose point of view significant elements of the story are told, is the most fully developed, and while she departs a little from the original, it's not so far as to make Austen fans cringe (given that they're OK with zombies, of course). This is a must-read for the growing legion of alternate-Austen fans." Booklist

Hocking, Amanda

Wake; Amanda Hocking. St. Martin's Griffin 2012 309 p. (hardback) $17.99

Grades: 7 8 9 10 **Fic**

1. Fantasy fiction 2. Paranormal fiction 3. Sirens (Mythology) -- Fiction 4. Love -- Fiction 5. Sisters -- Fiction 6. Supernatural -- Fiction 7. Seaside resorts -- Fiction

ISBN 1250008123; 9781250008121; 9781429956581
LC 2012014630

This is the first in Amanda Hocking's Watersong series. Here, "Gemma Fisher is happy—she's a star on the swim team, her family is loving and supportive, and the crushworthy boy next door returns her interest. The only downside: three gorgeous but creepy new girls who have her in their sights." These girls ultimately turn out to be Sirens who trick Gemma into drinking potion that turns her into a Siren as well. (Publishers Weekly)

Followed by Lullaby (2012) and Tidal (2013)

Hodge, Rosamund

Crimson bound; Rosamund Hodge. Balzer + Bray 2015 448 p. (hardback) $17.99

Grades: 9 10 11 12 **Fic**

1. Fantasy fiction 2. Magic -- Fiction 3. Kings and rulers -- Fiction 4. Fantasy

ISBN 9780062224767; 006222476X
LC 2014030890

In this novel by Rosamund Hodge "when Rachelle was fifteen she was good--apprenticed to her aunt and in training to protect her village from dark magic. Three years later, Rachelle has given her life to serving the realm, fighting deadly creatures in a vain effort to atone. When the king orders her to guard his son Armand--the man she hates most--Rachelle forces Armand to help her hunt for the legendary sword that might save their world." (Publisher's note)

"Though Rachelle's inner monologue is often bogged down by repetitive moments of self-loathing and doubt, Hodge's writing occasionally glimmers with flashes of brilliance: 'the neckline bared her shoulders and her collarbones like a declaration of war.' Plot twists and romance keep the pages turning in this grim and intricate take on the classic tale." Booklist

Cruel Beauty; Rosamund Hodge. Balzer + Bray, an imprint of HarperCollinsPublishers 2014 352 p. (hardcover) $17.99

Grades: 8 9 10 11 12 **Fic**

1. Love stories 2. Imaginary places 3. Magic -- Fiction 4. Fantasy

ISBN 0062224735; 9780062224736
LC 2013015418

In this book, by Rosamund Hodge, "betrothed to the evil ruler of her kingdom, Nyx has always known her fate was to marry him, kill him, and free her people from his tyranny. On her seventeenth birthday, when she moves into his castle high on the kingdom's mountaintop, nothing is as she expected. Nyx knows she must save her homeland at all costs, yet she can't resist the pull of her sworn enemy--who's gotten in her way by stealing her heart." (Publisher's note)

"Hodge's story infuses elements of Greek mythology and classic fairy tales. The plot moves quickly, and the char-

acters are well formed; their transgressions make them interesting and authentic. The complex relationship between Nyx and Ignifex is especially engaging. An entertaining read for teens who enjoy romantic fantasy.—" (School Library Journal)

Hodkin, Michelle

The **evolution** of Mara Dyer; Michelle Hodkin. Simon & Schuster Books for Young Readers 2012 527 p. (hardcover) $17.99

Grades: 7 8 9 10 11 12 **Fic**

1. Stalkers -- Fiction 2. Supernatural -- Fiction 3. Posttraumatic stress disorder -- Fiction 4. Love -- Fiction 5. Florida -- Fiction

ISBN 1442421797; 9781442421790; 9781442421813
LC 2012019195

Sequel to: The unbecoming of Mara Dyer

In this novel by Michelle Hodkin, part of the Mara Dyer Trilogy, "Mara continues her relationship with wealthy Noah. . . . Meanwhile, Mara insists that her supposedly dead former boyfriend, Jude, continues to stalk her. She is being treated as an outpatient for PTSD after causing (as she originally believed) the deaths of Jude and her friends. . . . Noah uses his wits and wealth to try to protect her and to investigate the possibility that Jude indeed survived." (Kirkus)

Hoffman, Alice

Blue diary. Putnam 2001 303p hardcover o.p. pa $14

Grades: 11 12 Adult **Fic**

1. Homicide -- Fiction 2. Family life -- Fiction 3. Massachusetts -- Fiction

ISBN 0-399-14802-7; 0-425-18494-3 pa
LC 2001-19517

Ethan Ford is "suddenly arrested on suspicion of the rape and murder of teenager Rachel Morris 15 years earlier in Maryland. Ethan confesses to the crime, but says that he is now 'a different man,' who has redeemed himself through exemplary behavior. What this revelation means to his beautiful wife of 13 years, Jorie {and} his 12-year-old son, Collie . . . allows the novel to investigate the themes of devotion, betrayal, guilt and forgiveness in trenchantly effective ways." Publ Wkly

★ **Incantation**. Little, Brown 2006 166p hardcover o.p. pa $8.99

Grades: 8 9 10 11 12 **Fic**

1. Spain -- Fiction 2. Prejudices -- Fiction 3. Inquisition -- Fiction 4. Jews -- Persecutions -- Fiction

ISBN 978-0-316-01019-1; 0-316-01019-7; 978-0-316-15428-4 pa; 0-316-15428-8 pa
LC 2005-37301

During the Spanish Inquisition, sixteen-year-old Estrella, brought up a Catholic, discovers her family's true Jewish identity, and when their secret is betrayed by Estrella's best friend, the consequences are tragic. Includes some scenes of graphic violence.

"Hoffman's lyrical prose and astute characterization blend to create a riveting, horrific tale that unites despair with elements of hope." SLJ

Hoffmeister, Peter Brown

This is the part where you laugh; Peter Brown Hoffmeister. Alfred A. Knopf 2016 336 p. (hardback) $17.99

Grades: 9 10 11 12   **Fic**
1. Poverty -- Fiction   2. Basketball -- Fiction   3. Friendship -- Fiction   4. Conduct of life -- Fiction   5. Sick -- Fiction   6. Family problems -- Fiction
ISBN 9780553538106; 9780553538113
LC 2015022147

In this book, by Peter Brown Hoffmeister, "Travis is perpetrator, victim, or both. He spends much of the narrative searching for the heroin-addicted mother who abandoned him, and he suffered the depredations of foster care and the juvenile justice system before being taken in by his caring but poverty-stricken grandparents. Basketball provides solace and purpose for his life, but even here his violent nature intrudes." (School Library Journal)

"In this tragicomic YA debut from adult author Hoffmeister (Let Them Be Eaten by Bears), a young man contends with anger, family troubles, and romance over a few increasingly chaotic months. Travis's summer goals are simple: improve his basketball skills, stay out of trouble, and try to cheer up his grandmother, who's dying from cancer. He also hangs out with his best friend Creature, spends time with a mercurial girl named Natalie, and searches for his drug-addicted mother in the homeless camps around the area. . . . The result is a raw, offbeat novel with an abundance of honesty and heart." PW

Holder, Nancy

Crusade; by Nancy Holder and Debbie Viguie. Simon Pulse 2010 470p $16.99

Grades: 7 8 9 10 11   **Fic**
1. Horror fiction   2. Sisters -- Fiction   3. Vampires -- Fiction   4. Supernatural -- Fiction
ISBN 978-1-4169-9802-0; 1-4169-9802-0
LC 2010-9094

An international team of six teenaged vampire hunters, trained in Salamanca, Spain, goes to New Orleans seeking to rescue team-member Jenn's younger sister as the vampires escalate their efforts to take over the Earth.

"The cinematic writing and apocalyptic scenario should find a ready audience." Publ Wkly

Followed by: Damned (2011)

Holub, Josef

An **innocent** soldier; translated by Michael Hofmann. Arthur A. Levine Books 2005 231p $16.99
Grades: 8 9 10 11 12   **Fic**
1. War stories   2. Russia -- Fiction   3. France -- History -- 1799-1815 -- Fiction
ISBN 0-439-62771-0

A sixteen-year-old farmhand is tricked into fighting in the Napoleonic Wars by the farmer for whom he works, who secretly substitutes him for the farmer's own son.

"This is a well-wrought psychological tale. . . . [It] has a lot to offer to those seeking to build a deep historical fiction collection." SLJ

Hooper, Mary

Fallen Grace. Bloomsbury 2011 309p $16.99
Grades: 7 8 9 10   **Fic**
1. People with mental disabilities -- Fiction   2. Orphans -- Fiction   3. Poverty -- Fiction   4. Sisters -- Fiction   5. London (England) -- Fiction   6. Swindlers and swindling -- Fiction   7. Funeral rites and ceremonies -- Fiction   8. Great Britain -- History -- 19th century -- Fiction
ISBN 978-1-59990-564-8; 1-59990-564-7
LC 2010-25498

In Victorian London, impoverished fifteen-year-old orphan Grace takes care of her older but mentally unfit sister Lily, and after enduring many harsh and painful experiences, the two become the victims of a fraud perpetrated by the wealthy owners of several funeral businesses.

Hooper "packs her brisk Dickensian fable with colorful characters and suspenseful, satisfying plot twists. The sobering realities of child poverty and exploitation are vividly conveyed, along with fascinating details of the Victorian funeral trade." Kirkus

Includes bibliographical references

Hopkins, Ellen

★ **Burned**. Margaret K. McElderry Books 2006 532p $16.95
Grades: 9 10 11 12   **Fic**
1. Novels in verse   2. Mormons -- Fiction   3. Sex role -- Fiction   4. Child abuse -- Fiction   5. Family life -- Fiction
ISBN 1-4169-0354-2; 978-1-4169-0354-3
LC 2005-32461

Seventeen-year-old Pattyn, the eldest daughter in a large Mormon family, is sent to her aunt's Nevada ranch for the summer, where she temporarily escapes her alcoholic, abusive father and finds love and acceptance, only to lose everything when she returns home.

"The free verses, many in the form of concrete poems, create a compressed and intense reading experience with no extraneous dialogue or description. . . . This book will appeal to teens favoring realistic fiction and dramatic interpersonal stories." Voice Youth Advocates

Identical. Margaret K. McElderry Books 2008 565p $17.99
Grades: 10 11 12   **Fic**
1. Novels in verse   2. Twins -- Fiction   3. Sisters -- Fiction   4. Child sexual abuse -- Fiction
ISBN 978-1-4169-5005-9; 1-4169-5005-2
LC 2007-32463

Sixteen-year-old identical twin daughters of a district court judge and a candidate for the United States House of Representatives, Kaeleigh and Raeanne Gardella desperately struggle with secrets that have already torn them and their family apart.

This book "tells the twins' story in intimate and often-graphic detail. Hopkins packs in multiple issues including eating disorders, drug abuse, date rape, alcoholism, sexual abuse, and self-mutilation as she examines a family that 'puts the dys in dysfunction.'. . . Gritty and compelling, this is not a comfortable read, but its keen insights make it hard to put down." SLJ

Rumble; Ellen Hopkins. Margaret K. McElderry Books 2014 560 p. (hardcover) $19.99

Grades: 8 9 10 11 12 **Fic**

1. Novels in verse 2. Grief -- Fiction 3. Suicide -- Fiction 4. Schools -- Fiction 5. High schools -- Fiction 6. Family problems -- Fiction

ISBN 1442482842; 9781442482845

LC 2013037681

In this young adult verse novel by Ellen Hopkins, "Matthew Turner doesn't have faith in anything. Not in family--his is a shambles after his younger brother was bullied into suicide. Not in so-called friends who turn their backs when things get tough. Not in some all-powerful creator who lets too much bad stuff happen. . . . No matter what his girlfriend Hayden says about faith and forgiveness, there's no way Matt's letting go of blame." (Publisher's note)

"Matt is a wonderfully faceted character that readers will alternately sympathize with and dislike. His actions are directly related to his emotional turmoil, and teens will understand his pain and admire his intellect, even while shaking their heads over his actions.." SLJ

Smoke; Ellen Hopkins. 1st ed. Margaret K. McElderry Books 2013 560 p. (hardcover) $19.99

Grades: 9 10 11 12 **Fic**

1. Rape -- Fiction 2. Homicide -- Fiction 3. Novels in verse 4. Grief -- Fiction 5. Mormons -- Fiction 6. Sisters -- Fiction 7. Runaways -- Fiction 8. Emotional problems -- Fiction

ISBN 9781416983286; 1416983287

LC 2012038452

Sequel to: Burned

In this sequel to Ellen Hopkins' "Burned," sisters Pattyn and Jackie "wrestle with guilt and fear after one kills the father who battered them." Pattyn stays with a family of farm workers while hiding from police. "Meanwhile, 15-year-old Jackie is stuck at home, narrating her own half of the story. Through free-verse poems . . . ., the shooting's details emerge. A schoolmate raped Jackie; blaming Jackie, Dad broke her ribs and loosened her teeth; Pattyn's gun stopped Dad forever." (Kirkus Reviews)

Tricks. Margaret K. McElderry Books 2009 627p $18.99

Grades: 10 11 12 **Fic**

1. Novels in verse 2. Family life -- Fiction 3. Prostitution -- Fiction

ISBN 978-1-4169-5007-3

LC 2009-20297

Five troubled teenagers fall into prostitution as they search for freedom, safety, community, family, and love.

"Hopkins's pithy free verse reveals shards of emotion and quick glimpses of physical detail. It doesn't matter that the first-person voices blur, because the stories are distinct and unmistakable. Graphic sex, rape, drugs, bitter loneliness, despair—and eventually, blessedly, glimmers of hope." Kirkus

Hopkinson, Nalo

The **Chaos**; Nalo Hopkinson. Margaret K. McElderry Books 2012 241p. (hardcover) $16.99

Grades: 7 8 9 10 11 12 **Fic**

1. Science fiction 2. Toronto (Ont.) -- Fiction 3. Siblings 4. Racially mixed people -- Fiction 5. Supernatural 6. Canada -- Fiction 7. Identity -- Fiction 8. Supernatural -- Fiction 9. Brothers and sisters -- Fiction 10. Family life -- Canada -- Fiction 11. Interpersonal relations -- Fiction

ISBN 1416954880; 9781416954880; 9781442409552

LC 2011018154

In this young adult science fiction novel, "Scotch's womanly build and mixed heritage (white Jamaican dad, black American mom) made her the target of small-town school bullies. Since moving to Toronto, she's found friends and status. . . . When a giant bubble appears at an open-mic event, Scotch dares her brother, Rich, to touch it. He disappears, a volcano rises from Lake Ontario and chaos ripples across city and world, transforming reality in ways bizarre." (Kirkus Reviews)

Hornby, Nick, 1957-

★ **Slam**. G.P. Putnam's Sons 2007 309p $19.99; (audiobook) $29.95

Grades: 8 9 10 11 12 **Fic**

1. Skateboarders 2. Skateboarding -- Fiction 3. Teenage fathers -- Fiction

ISBN 9780399250484; 0399250484; 9780143142836

LC 2007-14146

In this book by Nick Hornby, "for 16-year-old Sam, life is about to get extremely complicated. He and his girlfriend--make that ex-girlfriend--Alicia have gotten themselves into a bit of trouble." When she gets pregnant, "Sam is suddenly forced to grow up and struggle with the familiar fears and inclinations that haunt us all." (Publisher's note)

The author "pens a first novel for teens that is a sweet and funny story about mistakes and choices. . . . Recommend this delightful and poignant novel to older teens who will laugh and weep with Sam." Voice Youth Advocates

Hosler, Jay

Last of the sandwalkers; written and illustrated by Jay Hosler. First Second 2015 312 p. illustrations (paperback) $16.99

Grades: 5 6 7 8 9 10 **Fic**

1. Graphic novels 2. Science fiction 3. Adventure fiction 4. Beetles -- Fiction 5. Scientific expeditions -- Fiction

ISBN 162672024X; 9781626720244

LC 2014045542

This book, by Jay Hosler, is about a "civilization of beetles. In this bug's paradise, beetles write books, run restaurants, and even do scientific research. But not too much scientific research is allowed by the powerful elders, who guard a terrible secret about the world outside. . . . Lucy is not one to quietly cooperate, however. This tiny field scientist defies the law of her safe but authoritarian home and leads a team of researchers out into the desert." (Publisher's note)

"Hosler's cartooning is no less meticulous than his writing and similarly retains a sense of animated energy and humor, engaging readers with characters that are far from human, but filled with humanity." Booklist

Includes bibliographical references

Hosseini, Khaled, 1965-

★ The **kite** runner. Riverhead Bks. 2003 324p $24.95; pa $14

Grades: 11 12 Adult   **Fic**

1. Guilt 2. Authors 3. Friendship 4. Social classes 5. Afghanistan 6. Taliban -- Fiction 7. Friendship -- Fiction 8. Afghanistan -- Fiction 9. Social classes -- Fiction 10. Kabul (Afghanistan) -- Fiction

ISBN 1-57322-245-3; 1-59448-000-1 pa

LC 2003043106

The narrator, "a thirty-eight-year-old writer named Amir, recounts the odyssey of his life from Kabul to San Francisco via Peshwar, Pakistan. The protagonist was born into a wealthy family in Kabul. Raised by his father, . . . Amir lives a relatively happy life until the Soviet tanks roll into Afghanistan. Then he and his father flee to Pakistan and end up in America. In the United States, his father becomes a gas-station manager. . . . Amir meets Soraya, the daughter of a former Afghan general, and soon [marries]. . . . For fifteen years the young couple tries in vain to have children. Then Amir receives a call from Rahim Khan, a friend and former business partner of his now-deceased father. Amir flies to Peshwar to meet with him. Rahim Khan reveals that Hassan, Amir's childhood friend, the presumed son of the family servant Ali, was in reality Amir's half-brother, his father's illegitimate son with Ali's wife. Hassan and his wife were killed by the Taliban. Rahim Khan wants Amir to go to Kabul and bring Hassan's son to Peshwar." (World Lit Today)

"Khaled Hosseini gives us a vivid and engaging story that reminds us how long his people have been struggling to triumph over the forces of violence." N Y Times Book Rev

Houck, Colleen

Tiger's curse. Sterling 2011 402p $17.95

Grades: 8 9 10 11 12   **Fic**

1. India -- Fiction 2. Circus -- Fiction 3. Tigers -- Fiction 4. Orphans -- Fiction 5. Immortality -- Fiction

ISBN 978-1-4027-8403-3

LC 2010-33191

Seventeen-year-old Oregon teenager Kelsey forms a bond with a circus tiger who is actually one of two brothers, Indian princes Ren and Kishan, who were cursed to live as tigers for eternity, and she travels with him to India where the tiger's curse may be broken once and for all.

The author "tells a good story filled with chaste romance that will keep readers turning pages to the inconclusive ending." Booklist

Other titles in this series are:

Tiger's quest (2011)

Tiger's voyage (2011)

Tiger's quest. Sterling 2011 479p $17.95

Grades: 9 10 11 12   **Fic**

1. India -- Fiction 2. Oregon -- Fiction 3. Tigers -- Fiction 4. Orphans -- Fiction 5. Immortality -- Fiction 6. Colleges and universities -- Fiction

ISBN 978-1-4027-8404-0

LC 2010049270

Sequel to Tiger's curse (2011)

Kelsey returns home to Oregon, where Mr. Kadam has enrolled her in college, but danger sends her back to India to begin another quest, this time with Kishan, to try to break the curse that forces Kishan and his brother Ren to live as tigers.

"This series will appeal to teens who grew up on fairy tales and believe wholeheartedly that the most perfectly ordinary girl will find her handsome prince, have many wonderful adventures, and live happily ever after." SLJ

Followed by Tiger's voyage (2011)

Houston, Julian

New boy. Houghton Mifflin Co. 2005 282p $16

Grades: 8 9 10 11 12   **Fic**

1. School stories 2. Prejudices -- Fiction 3. African Americans -- Fiction

ISBN 0-618-43253-1

LC 2004-27207

"As the first black student in an elite Connecticut boarding school in the late 1950s, Rob Garrett, 16, knows he is making history. . . . When his friends in the South plan a sit-in against segregation, he knows he must be part of it. . . . The honest first-person narrative makes stirring drama. . . . This brings up much for discussion about then and now." Booklist

Howard, A. G.

Unhinged; a novel. by A. G. Howard. Amulet Books 2014 400 p. (hardback) $17.95

Grades: 9 10 11 12   **Fic**

1. Paranormal fiction 2. Mentally ill -- Fiction 3. Mother-daughter relationship -- Fiction 4. Supernatural -- Fiction 5. Mental illness -- Fiction 6. Mothers and daughters -- Fiction 7. Characters in literature -- Fiction

ISBN 1419709712; 9781419709715

LC 2013026395

Sequel to: Splintered

In this young adult novel, by A. G. Howard, book two in the "Splintered" series, "Alyssa Gardner has been down the rabbit hole. . . . Now all she has to do is graduate high school. That would be easier without her mother, freshly released from an asylum, acting overly protective and suspicious. It would be much simpler if the mysterious Morpheus didn't show up for school one day to tempt her with another dangerous quest in the dark, challenging Wonderland." (Publisher's note)

"Alyssa left Wonderland (in Splintered) a year ago, but now her dreams foreshadow new trouble there. When Wonderland's inhabitants enter the human realm, Alyssa's two worlds collide. Though a romantic triangle and Alyssa's identity struggle bog down this second installment, fans will be intrigued by the cliffhanger ending, which hints at future trips to Wonderland--and to "the looking-glass world, Any-Elsewhere." Horn Book

Howard, J. J.

That time I joined the circus; J.J. Howard. Point 2013 272 p. (hardcover) $17.99

Grades: 7 8 9 10   **Fic**

1. Circus -- Fiction 2. Absent mothers -- Fiction 3. Florida -- Fiction 4. Friendship -- Fiction 5. Best friends -- Fiction 6. New York (N.Y.) -- Fiction 7. Mothers and daughters -- Fiction 8. Single-parent families -- Fiction

ISBN 0545433819; 9780545433815

LC 2012016715

In this novel, 17-year-old Lexi lives with her father Gavin, a musician in New York City. Her "long-absent mother . . . has apparently joined the circus. When Gavin dies unexpectedly, leaving his daughter penniless, her only option is to track down her mother in Florida. Failing to find her, Lexi gratefully accepts work with the Circus Europa." (Publishers Weekly)

Howe, James, 1946-

The **misfits**; James Howe. Atheneum Books for Young Readers 2001 274 p. $17.99

Grades: 5 6 7 8   **Fic**

1. School stories 2. Bullies -- Fiction 3. Elections -- Fiction 4. Friendship -- Fiction 5. Teasing
ISBN 0689839553; 9780689839559

LC 0066390

This book, by James Howe, is "about junior high school politics and nasty name calling. . . . Bobby Goodspeed [is] an overweight seventh grader who belongs to the Gang of Five, which (ironically) is made up of four not five kids who consider themselves misfits. The student council elections are coming up, and [the Gang of Five] decide to run on the 'No-Name Party,' which promises to bring an end to all name calling in the school." (School Library Journal)

Howe, Katherine

Conversion; Katherine Howe. G. P. Putnam's Sons 2014 432 p. (hardback) $18.99

Grades: 7 8 9 10 11 12   **Fic**

1. School stories 2. Salem witch trials 3. Schools -- Fiction 4. Epidemics -- Fiction 5. Friendship -- Fiction 6. Massachusetts -- Fiction 7. Preparatory schools -- Fiction
ISBN 0399167773; 9780399167775

LC 2014000397

In this young adult novel by Katherine Howe, "It's senior year at St. Joan's Academy, and school is a pressure cooker. College applications, the battle for valedictorian, deciphering boys' texts: Through it all, Colleen Rowley and her friends are expected to keep it together. Until they can't. . . . Only Colleen--who's been reading 'The Crucible' for extra credit--comes to realize what nobody else has: Danvers was once Salem Village." (Publisher's note)

"St. Joan's Academy in Danvers, Massachusetts, a well-to-do private girl's school for the best and brightest, is usually only home to hysteria of the college-admissions kind. But when Clara starts convulsing in class, a media frenzy fixates on the St. Joan's mystery disease...A simmering blend of relatable high-school drama with a persistent pinprick of unearthliness in the background." Booklist

Howell, Simmone

Girl defective; Simmone Howell. First US edition Atheneum Books for Young Readers 2014 320 p. (hardcover) $17.99

Grades: 9 10 11 12   **Fic**

1. Record stores 2. Family life -- Fiction 3. Teenage girls -- Fiction 4. Australia -- Fiction 5. Friendship -- Fiction 6. Coming of age -- Fiction 7. Record stores -- Fiction 8. Mystery and detective stories 9. Saint Kilda

(Vic.) -- Fiction 10. Family life -- Australia -- Fiction
ISBN 1442497602; 9781442497603; 9781442497610

LC 2013032738

This young adult novel by Simmone Howell, with photography by Henry Beer, is "a story about Skylark Martin, who lives with her father and brother in a vintage record shop and is trying to find her place in the world. It's about ten-year-old Super Agent Gully and his case of a lifetime. And about beautiful, reckless, sharp-as-knives Nancy. It's about tragi-hot Luke, and just-plain-tragic Mia Casey. . . . It's about summer, and weirdness, and mystery, and music." (Publisher's note)

"Funny, observant, a relentless critic of the world's (and her own) flaws, Sky is original, thoroughly authentic and great company, decorating her astute, irreverent commentary with vivid Aussie references; chasing these down should provide foreign readers with hours of online fun." Kirkus

Howland, Leila

Nantucket blue; Leila Howland. 1st ed. Hyperion 2013 304 p. (reinforced) $16.99

Grades: 8 9 10 11 12   **Fic**

1. Summer -- Fiction 2. Female friendship -- Fiction 3. Interpersonal relations -- Fiction 4. Grief -- Fiction 5. Divorce -- Fiction 6. Friendship -- Fiction 7. Best friends -- Fiction 8. Grief
ISBN 1423160517; 9781423160519

LC 2012035121

This novel, by Leila Howland, follows a girl named "Cricket Thompson. . . . When Jules and her family suffer a devastating tragedy that forces the girls apart, Jules becomes a stranger whom Cricket wonders whether she ever really knew. . . . But it's the things Cricket hadn't counted on— most of all, falling hard for someone who should be completely off-limits—that turn her dreams into an exhilarating, bittersweet reality." (Publisher's note)

"Lacrosse-champ Cricket Thompson has always been welcomed by her best friend Jules's affluent family. But when Nina, Jules's mother, dies suddenly, big changes ensue. Expecting her usual warm reception, Cricket shows up at Jules's family home on Nantucket to find herself shunned. There's some emotional heaviness to the story, but it's also a breezy, beach-ready tale of self-awakening and first love." (Horn Book)

Howrey, Meg

Blind sight; Meg Howrey. Pantheon Books 2011 289p. $24.95

Grades: 11 12 Adult   **Fic**

1. Actors 2. Adolescence 3. Homosexuality 4. Domestic fiction 5. Fathers and sons 6. Mothers and sons 7. Teenagers -- Fiction 8. California -- Hollywood 9. Maturation (Psychology) -- Fiction
ISBN 978-0-307-37916-0; 0-307-37916-7; 9780307739292

LC 201012935

The book tells the story of a teenaged boy, "Luke Prescott, who has been brought up in a bohemian matriarchy by his divorced New Age mother, a religious grandmother, and two precocious half-sisters. . . . Luke is writing his college applications when his father -- a famous television star whom he never knew -- calls and invites him to Los Angeles for the summer. Luke accepts and is plunged into a world of location shooting, celebrity interviews, glamorous parties, and premieres. As he begins to know the difference between his father's public persona and his private one, Luke finds himself sorting through his own personal mythology." (Publisher's note)

Hrdlitschka, Shelley

Allegra; by Shelley Hrdlitschka. Orca Book Publishers 2013 280 p. (paperback) $12.95; (ebook) $12.99; (ebook) $12.99

Grades: 7 8 9 10   Fic
1. School stories 2. Teacher-student relationship -- Fiction 3. Performing arts high schools
ISBN 1459801970; 9781459801974; 9781459801998; 9781459801981

LC 2012952952

In this book, Allegra, daughter of two musicians, is thrilled to be at Deer Lake School for the Fine and Performing Arts. She "has her sights set on becoming a professional dancer. However, her excitement is dimmed by the school's requirement that she take a music-theory class. Despite her initial reluctance, Allegra soon begins to enjoy the class due to the charisma of its young and attractive teacher," Mr. Rocchelli. Is their relationship too close? (School Library Journal)

Sister wife. Orca 2008 269p pa $12.95

Grades: 8 9 10 11 12   Fic
1. Polygamy -- Fiction
ISBN 978-1-55143-927-3; 1-55143-927-1

In a remote polygamist community, Celeste struggles to accept her destiny while longing to be free to live her life her way.

"This compelling story combines with authentic characters to pique the interest of a wide array of teens and get them talking about faith and free will." Voice Youth Advocates

Hubbard, Amanda

But I love him; [by] Amanda Grace. Flux 2011 253p pa $9.95

Grades: 7 8 9 10   Fic
1. School stories 2. Abused women -- Fiction 3. Washington (State) -- Fiction 4. Dating (Social customs) -- Fiction
ISBN 978-0-7387-2594-9; 0-7387-2594-3

LC 2010-50131

Traces, through the course of a year, Ann's transformation from a happy A-student, track star, and popular senior to a solitary, abused woman whose love for the emotionally-scarred Connor has taken away everything—even herself.

"A great shared read for parents and teens." Voice Youth Advocates

Ripple; [by] Mandy Hubbard. Razorbill 2011 260p $16.99

Grades: 8 9 10 11 12   Fic
1. Love stories 2. Fantasy fiction 3. Sirens (Mythology)
ISBN 978-1-59514-423-2; 1-59514-423-4

"Lexi, 18, is responsible for the death of Steven, her friend Siena's brother and the only boy she ever loved. That was two years ago, right before discovering that she is a siren, cursed to swim each night and sing out haunting melodies that will lure men to their deaths in the water. She has been protecting herself and those around her by keeping everyone at a distance and swimming in an isolated lake where no one will hear her song. But as the new school year begins, Lexi finds herself pursued by two boys whom she can't ignore. . . . In this new twist on a supernatural romance, Hubbard expands the genre by including both a siren and a nix in among the high school drama. . . . Fans of girl dramas, mysteries, and fantasy romance will devour the story." SLJ

Hubbard, Jenny

★ **And** we stay; Jenny Hubbard. Delacorte Press 2014 240 p. (hc) $16.99

Grades: 9 10 11 12   Fic
1. High school students -- Fiction 2. Teenagers -- Suicide -- Fiction 3. Poetry -- Fiction 4. Schools -- Fiction 5. Suicide -- Fiction 6. High schools -- Fiction 7. Amherst (Mass.) -- Fiction 8. Boarding schools -- Fiction 9. Interpersonal relations -- Fiction
ISBN 0385740573; 9780375989551; 9780385740579

LC 2013002236

Printz Honor Book (2015)

In this book, by Jenny Hubbard "high school senior Paul Wagoner walks into his school library with a stolen gun, . . . threatens his girlfriend Emily Beam, then takes his own life. In the wake of the tragedy, an angry and guilt-ridden Emily is shipped off to boarding school in Amherst, Massachusetts, where she encounters a ghostly presence who shares her name. The spirit of Emily Dickinson and two quirky girls offer helping hands, but it is up to Emily to heal her own damaged self." (Publisher's note)

"Budding poets may particularly appreciate Emily's story, but there is certainly something for anyone looking for a good read with a strong, believable female lead who is working her hardest to overcome tragedy." SLJ

★ **Paper** covers rock. Delacorte Press 2011 183p audiobook $46.75; audiobook $46.75; audiobook $42.00; $16.99; lib bdg $19.99; ebook $10.99

Grades: 9 10 11 12   Fic
1. School stories 2. Death -- Fiction 3. North Carolina -- Fiction 4. Conduct of life -- Fiction
ISBN 9781464021572; 9781464021565; 9781464021657; 978-0-385-74055-5; 978-0-375-98954-4 lib bdg; 978-0-375-89942-3 ebook

LC 2010-23462

In this book, set at a "boys' boarding school, 16-year-old Alex is devastated when he fails to save a drowning friend. When questioned, Alex and his friend Glenn, who was also at the river, begin weaving their web of lies. . . . Caught in the web with Alex and Glenn is their English teacher, Miss Dovecott, fresh out of Princeton, who suspects there's more to what happened at the river when she perceives guilt in Alex's writing for class." (Booklist)

This is "a powerful story of how the truth can easily be manipulated, how actions can be misinterpreted, and how fragile adolescent friendships and alliances can be." Voice Youth Advocates

Try not to breathe; Jennifer R. Hubbard. Viking 2012 233 p. (hardcover) $16.99

Grades: 10 11 12 **Fic**
1. Friendship -- Fiction 2. Teenagers -- Suicide -- Fiction 3. Mentally ill -- Institutional care -- Fiction 4. Suicide -- Fiction 5. Interpersonal relations -- Fiction
ISBN 0670013900; 9780670013906

LC 2011012203

In this book, a "half-hearted suicide attempt lands Ryan at a facility for adolescents with emotional problems. He makes friends and recovers, but now that he's home again, he's not quite sure how to re-enter his life, especially when he meets a girl named Nicki, who keeps pressuring him to share his secrets. . . . He gradually realizes that he has the inner resources to cope with rejection and uncertainty." (Bulletin of the Center for Children's Books)

Hubbard, Kirsten
Like Mandarin. Delacorte Press 2011 308p $17.99; lib bdg $20.99
Grades: 8 9 10 11 12 **Fic**
1. School stories 2. Wyoming -- Fiction 3. Friendship -- Fiction 4. Family life -- Fiction
ISBN 978-0-385-73935-1; 0-385-73935-4; 978-0-385-90784-2 lib bdg; 0-385-90784-2 lib bdg

LC 2009-53653

When shy, awkward fourteen-year-old Grace Carpenter is paired with the beautiful and wild Mandarin on a school project, an unlikely, explosive friendship begins, but all too soon, Grace discovers that Mandarin is a very troubled, even dangerous, girl.

"With a flair for metaphors and character description, Hubbard's writing exposes the deep emotions and conflicts that have rippled through most of Grace and Mandarin's lives. These small-town girls could be found anywhere." Voice Youth Advocates

Wanderlove; Kirsten Hubbard. Delacorte Press 2012 338 p. (hc) $17.99
Grades: 10 11 12 **Fic**
1. Travel -- Fiction 2. Children -- Travel 3. Central America -- Fiction 4. Love -- Fiction 5. Artists -- Fiction
ISBN 0385739370; 9780375897511; 9780385739375; 9780385907859

LC 2011007435

In this book, "Bria decides to do the most un-Bria-like thing she can think of: she signs up alone for a tour to Central America. When she finds out her traveling companions are a group of middle-aged tourists rather than the young, carefree backpackers on the brochure, she's thoroughly disappointed. . . . She breaks from her tour group and joins a girl named Starling and her brother Rowan to pursue what she considers a more authentic traveling experience." (Bulletin of the Center for Children's Books)

"With an extraordinary setting, delicately rendered and well informed by Hubbard's years as a guide to Central American travel on About.com, this becomes a wonderful story of kindred souls in a land of beauty, illuminated by Hubbard's own drawings." Booklist

Hudson, Tara
Hereafter. HarperTeen 2011 407p $17.99

Grades: 8 9 10 11 12 **Fic**
1. Ghost stories 2. Oklahoma -- Fiction 3. Family life -- Fiction 4. Future life -- Fiction 5. Good and evil -- Fiction 6. Near-death experiences -- Fiction
ISBN 978-0-06-202677-4; 0-06-202677-1

LC 2010045622

Amelia, long a ghost, forms a strong bond with eighteen-year-old Joshua, who nearly drowned where she did and who awakens in her long-forgotten senses and memories even as Eli, a spirit, tries to draw her away.

"A must for collections given the genre's popularity." Booklist

Hughes, Dean
Search and destroy. Atheneum Books for Young Readers 2006 216p $16.95
Grades: 7 8 9 10 **Fic**
1. Vietnam War, 1961-1975 -- Fiction
ISBN 0-689-87023-X

LC 2005-11255

Recent high school graduate Rick Ward, undecided about his future and eager to escape his unhappy home life, joins the army and experiences the horrors of the war in Vietnam.

"This is a compelling, insightful story about the emotional, physical, and psychological scars that wars leave upon soldiers." Booklist

Huntley, Amy
The **everafter**. Balzer + Bray 2009 144p $16.99; lib bdg $17.89; pa $8.99
Grades: 7 8 9 10 **Fic**
1. Dead -- Fiction 2. Death -- Fiction 3. Friendship -- Fiction 4. Lost and found possessions -- Fiction
ISBN 978-0-06-177679-3; 0-06-177679-3; 978-0-06-177680-9 lib bdg; 0-06-177680-7 lib bdg; 978-0-06-177681-6 pa; 0-06-177681-5 pa

LC 2008-46149

ALA YALSA Morris Award Finalist, 2010

Madison Stanton doesn't know where she is or how she got there. But she does know this—she is dead. And alone in a vast, dark space. The only company Maddy has in this place are luminescent objects that turn out to be all the things she lost while she was alive. And soon she discovers that, with these artifacts, she can re-experience—and even—change moments from her life.

"This fresh take on a teen's journey of self-exploration is a compelling and highly enjoyable tale. Huntley expertly combines a coming-of-age story with a supernatural mystery that keeps readers engrossed until the climactic ending. This touching story will appeal to those looking for a ghost story, romance, or family drama." SLJ

Hurley, Tonya
★ **Ghostgirl**. Little, Brown 2008 328p $17.99
Grades: 7 8 9 10 **Fic**
1. Ghost stories 2. School stories 3. Death -- Fiction 4. Popularity -- Fiction
ISBN 978-0-316-11357-1; 0-316-11357-3

LC 2007-31541

After dying, high school senior Charlotte Usher is as invisible to nearly everyone as she always felt, but despite what she learns in a sort of alternative high school for dead teens, she clings to life while seeking a way to go to the Fall Ball with the boy of her dreams.

"Hurley combines afterlife antics, gothic gore, and high school hell to produce an original, hilarious satire. . . . Tim Burton and Edgar Allan Poe devotees will die for this fantastic, phantasmal read." SLJ

Other titles in this series are:
Ghostgirl: Homecoming (2009)
Ghostgirl: Lovesick (2010)

Hurston, Zora Neale

Their eyes were watching God; with a foreword by Edwidge Danticat. HarperCollins Pubs. 2000 xxii, 231p $22; pa $15.95

Grades: 9 10 11 12 Adult   **Fic**
1. Florida -- Fiction 2. African Americans -- Fiction
ISBN 0-06-019949-0; 0-06-112006-0 pa
LC 00-58186

First published 1937 by Lippincott

This novel "treats social problems from a racial and feminist perspective. Janie Crawford, raised by her grandmother in rural poverty, flees her old and dictatorial husband with Joe Starks, an ambitious man who becomes the mayor of Florida's first town run by African Americans. When Joe dies, Janie falls in love with the younger Teacake and follows him to the truck farming area of the Florida swamps. In the floods following a hurricane, he is bitten by a rabid dog and, crazed, attacks Janie. She shoots him, is charged with murder, and finally exonerated. When she returns to the town she and Joe built, she tells her story to a friend." HarperCollins Reader's Ency of Am Lit

Hurwin, Davida

Freaks and revelations; a novel. by Davida Wills Hurwin. Little, Brown and Co. 2009 234p $16.99

Grades: 10 11 12   **Fic**
1. California -- Fiction 2. Drug abuse -- Fiction 3. Prejudices -- Fiction 4. Homosexuality -- Fiction
ISBN 978-0-316-04996-2; 0-316-04996-4
LC 2008-47384

Tells, in two voices, of events leading up to a 1980 incident in which fourteen-year-old Jason, a gay youth surviving on the streets as a prostitute, and seventeen-year-old Doug, a hate-filled punk rocker, have a fateful meeting in a Los Angeles alley.

"Sympathetic to both characters without shying away from brutality—physical or emotional—the finely crafted story leads to a powerful climax of hope and redemption that will stay with readers." Publ Wkly

Huser, Glen

Stitches. Groundwood Books 2003 198p hardcover o.p. pa $6.95

Grades: 7 8 9 10   **Fic**
1. Canada -- Fiction 2. Bullies -- Fiction 3. Sex role -- Fiction 4. Puppets and puppet plays -- Fiction
ISBN 0-88899-553-9; 0-88899-578-4 pa
LC 2003-363167

"Teachers will use this book in their classrooms, but it will appeal to leisure readers as well." Voice Youth Advocates

Hutchinson, Shaun David

The **five** stages of Andrew Brawley; Shaun David Hutchinson; illustrations by Christine Larsen. Simon Pulse 2015 336 p. illustrations (hardback) $17.99

Grades: 9 10 11 12   **Fic**
1. Hospitals -- Fiction 2. Bereavement -- Fiction 3. Gay teenagers -- Fiction 4. Gays -- Fiction 5. Grief -- Fiction 6. Orphans -- Fiction 7. Runaways -- Fiction 8. Cartoons and comics -- Fiction
ISBN 1481403109; 9781481403108
LC 2014022200

In this novel, by Shaun David Hutchinson, with illustrations by Christine Larsen, offers "narrator Andrew is a 17-year-old survivor of a terrible car accident that killed his parents and younger sister. He blames himself . . . , hiding out in a half-finished wing of the hospital where they died. One night, Rusty, another boy his age, arrives in the ER. . . . The boys come to realize a powerful attraction for one another and Andrew begins to open up to love and forgiveness." (School Library Journal)

"Hutchinson's latest is an unflinching look at loss, grief, and recovery. Seventeen-year-old Drew Brawley has been hiding from death for months in the Florida hospital where the rest of his family died. He passes the time working at the cafeteria and making friends with teen patients in the oncology ward. . . . Dark and frequently grim situations are lightened by realistic dialogue and genuineness of feeling. The rapid-fire back-and-forth snark between Drew and his hospital "family" rings true, and the mystery of Drew's past will keep readers turning the pages. This is a heartbreaking yet ultimately hopeful work from a writer to watch." Booklist

★ **We** are the ants; Shaun David Hutchinson. Simon & Schuster 2016 464 p. (hardback) $17.99 **Fic**
1. Gay men -- Fiction 2. Psychological fiction 3. Alien abduction -- Fiction 4. Depression (Psychology) -- Fiction
ISBN 148144963X; 9781481449632; 9781481475204
LC 2015042594

In this science fiction novel, by Shaun David Hutchinson, "the world will end in 144 days, and all Henry has to do to stop it is push a big red button. . . . But Henry is a scientist first, and facing the question thoroughly and logically, he begins to look for pros and cons. . . . Weighing the pain and the joy that surrounds him, Henry is left with the ultimate choice: push the button and save the planet and everyone on it or let the world—and his pain—be destroyed forever." (Publisher's note)

"Hutchinson's excellent novel of ideas invites readers to wonder about their place in a world that often seems uncaring and meaningless. The novel is never didactic; on the contrary, it is unfailingly dramatic and crackling with characters who become real upon the page. Will Henry press the button? We all await his decision." Booklist

Hyde, Catherine Ryan

Jumpstart the world. Alfred A. Knopf 2010 186p $16.99; lib bdg $19.99

Grades: 9 10 11 12   **Fic**
1. School stories 2. Transgender people -- Fiction 3. Moving -- Fiction 4. Apartment houses -- Fiction 5.

Mother-daughter relationship -- Fiction
ISBN 978-0-375-86665-4; 978-0-375-96665-1 lib
bdg; 978-0-375-89677-4 ebook

LC 2010-02511

Sixteen-year-old Elle falls in love with Frank, the neighbor who helps her adjust to being on her own in a big city, but learning that he is transgendered turns her world upside-down.

"For a book loaded with issues—there is even treatment of mental illness—this is a plain good read. These characters are funny, complex, and engaging. . . . There are many teens today who need this book." Voice Youth Advocates

Ibbitson, John

The **Landing**; a novel. KCP Fiction 2008 160p
$17.95; pa $7.95
Grades: 7 8 9 10 **Fic**
1. Canada -- Fiction 2. Uncles -- Fiction 3. Violinists
-- Fiction
ISBN 978-1-55453-234-6; 1-55453-234-5; 978-1-
55453-238-4 pa; 1-55453-238-8 pa

Ben thinks he will always be stuck at Cook's Landing, barely making ends meet like his uncle. But when he meets a wealthy widow from New York City, he sees himself there too. When she hires him to play his violin, he realizes his gift could unlock the possibilities of the world. Then, during a stormy night on Lake Muskoka, everything changes.

"With lovely prose, Ibbitson brings to life the rugged beauty and the devastating poverty of the Lake Muskoka region. His characters are as strong and remote as their surroundings." Voice Youth Advocates

Irving, John

★ The **world** according to Garp. Modern Library 1998 688p $21.95
Grades: 11 12 Adult **Fic**
1. Family life -- Fiction 2. Mother-son relationship
-- Fiction
ISBN 0-679-60306-9

LC 97-39458

First published 1978 by Dutton

This "is a long family novel, spanning four generations and two continents, crammed with incidents, characters, feelings and craft. The components of black comedy and melodrama, pathos and tragedy, mesh effortlessly in a tale that can also be read as a commentary on art and the imagination." Time

Isbell, Tom

The **Prey**; Tom Isbell. Harperteen 2015 416
p. $17.99
Grades: 7 8 9 10 **Fic**
1. Science fiction 2. Dystopian fiction 3. Twins --
Fiction 4. Orphans -- Fiction 5. Survival -- Fiction
ISBN 0062216015; 9780062216014
Sequel: The Capture (2015)

In this young adult science fiction novel, by Tom Isbell, "orphaned teens, soon to be hunted for sport, must flee their resettlement camps in their fight for survival and a better life. For in the Republic of the True America, it's always hunting season. . . . As unlikely Book and fearless Hope lead their quest for freedom, these teens must find the best in themselves to fight the worst in their enemies." (Publisher's note)

"An electromagnetic pulse followed by radiation—they called it Omega, the end—destroyed civilization as it once existed. The survivors established the Republic of the True America. But the future still looks like a dead end for Book and Hope, two teens who find themselves in the camps that purport to be orphanages...Careful readers will appreciate the irony and subtle, deeper meanings in character and location names as Isbell shapes his own vision of a dark world..." Booklist

Ishiguro, Kazuo, 1954-

★ **Never** let me go. Knopf 2005 288p
Grades: 11 12 Adult **Fic**
1. School stories 2. Science fiction 3. Children 4.
England -- Fiction 5. Schools -- Fiction 6. Bioethics --
Fiction 7. Philosophical novels 8. Psychological novels
9. Friendship -- Fiction 10. School life -- England
ISBN 1400043395

LC 2004048966

This is a novel by the author of The Remains of the Day (1989). "Kathy, Ruth and Tommy were pupils at Hailsham—an idyllic establishment situated deep in the English countryside. The children there were tenderly sheltered from the outside world, brought up to believe they were special, and that their personal welfare was crucial. But for what reason were they really there? It is only years later that Kathy, now aged 31, finally allows herself to yield to the pull of memory. What unfolds is the . . . story of how Kathy, Ruth and Tommy slowly come to face the truth about their seemingly happy childhoods—and about their futures." (Publisher's note)

This novel is "set in late 1990s England, in a parallel universe in which humans are cloned and raised expressly to 'donate' their healthy organs and thus eradicate disease from the normal population." Publ Wkly

Jackson, Shirley

★ The **haunting** of Hill House. Viking 1959
246p hardcover o.p. pa $14
Grades: 11 12 Adult **Fic**
1. Ghost stories 2. Horror fiction
ISBN 0-14-303998-9 pa

"Dr. John Montague, an anthropologist, is interested in the analysis of supernatural manifestations. He rents Hill House, which is reported to be haunted, and plans to spend the summer there with research assistants. Eleanor Vance, one of the researchers, is at first repelled by the house but soon adjusts. Other people come and signs of psychic activity are rampant, many of them centered on Eleanor. When Dr. Montague insists that she leave to insure her safety, the house does not release her." Shapiro. Fic for Youth. 3d edition

★ The **lottery**. Creative Education 2008 32p il
(Creative short stories) $28.50
Grades: 9 10 11 12 **Fic**
1. Horror fiction
ISBN 978-1-58341-584-9

LC 2007-8487

This short story "portrays a small town that gathers to hold its yearly lottery, a barbaric game of chance. Each head of household draws a slip, and the family with the marked slip will lose a member to stoning by the townsfolk. The shocking story forces readers to grapple with issues of ritual and violence. . . . [This book also features] a section after the tale examining the background of the story's publication, providing initial reactions, and exploring themes and motivations. An author profile is also appended. These additions will help readers more thoroughly understand the story, its context, and the author." Voice Youth Advocates

Jacobs, John Hornor

The **Shibboleth**; by John Hornor Jacobs. Carolrhoda Lab 2014 393 p. (Book two in the twelve-fingered boy trilogy) (trade hard cover: alk. paper) $17.95

Grades: 9 10 11 12   **Fic**
   1. Memory -- Fiction   2. Ability -- Fiction   3. Supernatural -- Fiction   4. Psychiatric hospitals -- Fiction 5. Bullies -- Fiction
ISBN 0761390081; 9780761390084
                         LC 2013009535

This is the second book in the Twelve-Fingered Boy Trilogy, by John Hornor Jacobs. "Branded a 'candy' dealer for doling out drugs, Shreve is incarcerated in a juvenile detention center at first, but after he frightens a nurse there, he's sent to a mental hospital, where he's drugged for schizophrenia. What his keepers don't know is that he's not schizophrenic at all. Instead, he's a shibboleth, a being that can read minds and possess the bodies of others." (Kirkus Reviews)

"Polydactyl hero Shreve, now sixteen, escapes from Tulaville Psychiatric Hospital to seek Hiram Quincrux--the monster behind an insomnia epidemic causing mayhem in the U.S.--and pit his own "extranatural" powers, his shibboleth, against Quincrux's. The sheer weirdness of it all will captivate readers and involve them in a memorable second installment that nicely sets up what's sure to be a dramatic conclusion." Horn Book

★ The **twelve**-fingered boy; John Hornor Jacobs. Carolrhoda Lab. 2013 264 p. (The Twelve-Fingered Boy Trilogy) (reinforced) $17.95

Grades: 9 10 11 12   **Fic**
   1. Fantasy fiction 2. Teenagers -- Fiction 3. Ability -- Fiction 4. Bullies -- Fiction 5. Supernatural -- Fiction 6. Juvenile detention homes -- Fiction
ISBN 0761390073; 9780761390077
                         LC 2012015292

This is the first in a trilogy from John Hornor Jacobs about superhuman teens. "Fifteen-year-old Shreve Cannon is passing the time in Pulaski Juvenile Detention Center, . . . when he's assigned a new roommate: Jack Graves, a small, quiet 13-year old with 12 fingers and uncontrollable telekinetic abilities. When a stranger named Mr. Quincrux shows up, sporting nasty mental powers and an uncomfortable interest in Jack, the boys . . . break out of juvie and go on the run." (Publishers Weekly)

Jacobson, Jennifer

The **complete** history of why I hate her; [by] Jennifer Richard Jacobson. Atheneum Books for Young Readers 2010 181p $16.99

Grades: 7 8 9 10   **Fic**
   1. Maine -- Fiction 2. Cancer -- Fiction 3. Resorts -- Fiction 4. Sisters -- Fiction 5. Personality disorders -- Fiction
ISBN 978-0-689-87800-8; 0-689-87800-1
                         LC 2008-42959

Wanting a break from being known only for her sister's cancer, seventeen-year-old Nola leaves Boston for a waitressing job at a summer resort in Maine, but soon feels as if her new best friend is taking over her life.

"A compelling story of self-discovery with plenty of insights into the motivations that drive relationships." Booklist

Jaden, Denise

Losing Faith. Simon Pulse 2010 381p pa $9.99
Grades: 7 8 9 10 11 12   **Fic**
   1. School stories 2. Cults -- Fiction 3. Death -- Fiction 4. Sisters -- Fiction 5. Bereavement -- Fiction 6. Christian life -- Fiction
ISBN 978-1-4169-9609-5; 1-4169-9609-5
                         LC 2010-7296

Brie tries to cope with her grief over her older sister Faith's sudden death by trying to learn more about the religious "home group" Faith secretly joined and never talked about with Brie or her parents.

"With pitch-perfect portrayals of high school social life and a nuanced view into a variety of Christian experiences of faith, this first novel gives readers much to think about." SLJ

Never enough; Denise Jaden. 1st Simon Pulse paperback ed. Simon Pulse 2012 372 p. (paperback) $9.99

Grades: 9 10 11 12   **Fic**
   1. Personal appearance 2. High school students 3. Parent-child relationship 4. Sisters -- Fiction 5. Popularity -- Fiction 6. Photography -- Fiction 7. Family problems -- Fiction 8. Eating disorders -- Fiction 9. Self-realization -- Fiction
ISBN 1442429070; 9781442429079
                         LC 2011033407

Author Denise Jaden tells the story "from the perspective of high school junior Loann, who lives in the shadow of her more beautiful and gifted older sister, Claire. Loann's feelings of inadequacy and resentment are overtaken by fear when she discovers that her sister is going to extreme measures to remain thin . . . Loann's horror intensifies when she realizes her parents are incapable of handling Claire's eating disorder and finding a solution. While struggling to understand her sister, Loann is drawn to a boy at school with serious problems of his own." (Publishers Weekly)

Jaffe, Michele

Rosebush. Razorbill 2010 326p $16.99
Grades: 8 9 10 11 12   **Fic**
   1. Mystery fiction 2. Traffic accidents -- Fiction
ISBN 978-1-59514-353-2; 1-59514-353-X

Instead of celebrating Memorial Day weekend on the Jersey Shore, Jane is in the hospital surrounded by teddy bears, trying to piece together what happened last night. One minute she was at a party, wearing fairy wings and cuddling with her boyfriend. The next, she was lying near-dead in a rosebush after a hit-and-run.

"Compulsively readable, the novel bristles with red herrings, leading readers down one tempting plot branch after another, each one blooming with plausibility. The characters are skillfully cultivated through flashbacks, and the insecure, people-pleasing Jane grows believably as she takes on the mystery." Booklist

James, Henry

★ The **turn** of the screw; edited by Allan Lloyd Smith. J.M. Dent 1993 xxxii, 139p pa $8.95

Grades: 11 12 Adult   **Fic**

1. Horror fiction
ISBN 0-460-87299-0

LC 94-125860

First published 1898

This novella "is told from the viewpoint of the leading character, a governess in love with her employer, who goes to an isolated English estate to take charge of Miles and Flora, two attractive and precocious children. She gradually realizes that her young charges are under the evil influence of two ghosts, Peter Quint, the ex-steward, and Miss Jessel, their former governess. At the climax of the story, she enters into open conflict with the children, as a result of which Flora is alienated and Miles dies of fright." Reader's Ency. 4th edition

James, Rebecca

Beautiful malice; a novel. Bantam Books 2010 260p $25

Grades: 9 10 11 12   **Fic**

1. Australia -- Fiction 2. Friendship -- Fiction 3. Bereavement -- Fiction
ISBN 978-0-553-80805-6

LC 2010-6255

To escape the media attention generated by her sister's murder, a grieving seventeen-year-old Australian girl moves away and meets a vibrant new friend who harbors a dangerous secret.

This "novel will grab your attention on the first page, and you won't want to turn away even after the last page has been turned." Voice Youth Advocates

Jansen, Hanna

★ **Over** a thousand hills I walk with you; translated from the German by Elizabeth D. Crawford. Carolrhoda Books 2006 342p $16.95

Grades: 7 8 9 10   **Fic**

1. Rwanda -- Fiction
ISBN 1-57505-927-4; 978-1-57505-927-3

LC 2005-21123

Original German edition, 2002

"Eight-year-old Jeanne was the only one of her family to survive the 1994 Rwanda genocide. Then a German family adopted her, and her adoptive mother now tells Jeanne's story in a compelling fictionalized biography that stays true to the traumatized child's bewildered viewpoint." Booklist

Jarzab, Anna

All unquiet things. Delacorte Press 2010 339p $17.99

Grades: 8 9 10 11 12   **Fic**

1. School stories 2. Mystery fiction 3. Homicide -- Fiction 4. California -- Fiction 5. Social classes -- Fiction
ISBN 978-0-385-73835-4; 0-385-73835-8; 978-0-385-90723-1 lib bdg; 0-385-90723-0 lib bdg

LC 2009-11557

After the death of his ex-girlfriend Carly, northern California high school student Neily joins forces with Carly's cousin Audrey to try to solve her murder.

"A year after Carly's murder, friends Neily and Audrey team up to find her killer. Their investigation exposes unsettling secrets about her final months. Jarzab's deft construction of alternating narratives by Neily and Audrey reveals not only Carly's mysterious last days but also the girls' relationship with one another. The murder mystery, while suspenseful, is not as well developed as the fully realized characters." Horn Book

The **opposite** of hallelujah; Anna Jarzab. Delacorte Press 2012 452 p. (hc) $16.99

Grades: 7 8 9 10   **Fic**

1. Ex-nuns -- Fiction 2. Secrets -- Fiction 3. Sisters -- Fiction 4. Nuns -- Fiction 5. Guilt -- Fiction
ISBN 0385738366; 9780375894084; 9780385738361; 9780385907248

LC 2012010882

In this book by Anna Jarzab "Caro's parents drop the bombshell news that [her sister] Hannah is returning to live with them. . . . Unable to understand Hannah, Caro resorts to telling lies about her mysterious reappearance. . . . And as she unearths a clue from Hannah's past--one that could save Hannah from the dark secret that possesses her--Caro begins to see her sister in a whole new light." (Publisher's note)

Jaskulka, Marie

The **Lost** Marble Notebook of Forgotten Girl and Random Boy; Marie Jaskulka. Sky Pony Press 2015 272 p. (hardcover) $16.99

Grades: 9 10 11 12   **Fic**

1. Love stories 2. Poetry -- Fiction 3. Diaries -- Fiction 4. Divorce 5. Novels in verse 6. Poetry -- Authorship
ISBN 1632204266; 9781632204264

In this book, by Marie Jaskulka, "Forgotten Girl, a fifteen-year-old poet, is going through the most difficult time of her life--the breakup of her parents, and her mom's resulting depression--when she meets Random Boy, a hot guy who, like her, feels like an outcast and secretly writes poetry to deal with everything going on in his life." (Publisher's note)

"Jaskulka's narrative explores the hows and whys of an abusive teenage relationship with heartbreaking honesty, and her delicate touch renders the dark story even more powerful. Graceful. Searing. Haunting." Kirkus

Jayne, Hannah

Truly, madly, deadly; by Hannah Jayne. Sourcebooks Fire 2013 272 p. (paperback) $9.99

Grades: 9 10 11 12   **Fic**

1. School stories 2. Stalkers -- Fiction 3. Murder -- Fiction 4. Dating violence -- Fiction

ISBN 1402281218; 9781402281211

LC 2012046383

In this book, "high school junior Sawyer Dodd is still reeling from her boyfriend's death in a drunk driving accident when she receives a note from an 'admirer' that simply reads, 'You're welcome.' Meanwhile, Sawyer's former friend Maggie is making her life at school miserable, and her parents want her to attend therapy. When a second person is killed, Sawyer realizes that her admirer/stalker is closer than she suspected and knows everything about her life." (Publishers Weekly)

Jen, Gish

★ **Typical** American; a novel. 1st Vintage Contemporaries ed.; Vintage Contemporaries 2008 296p pa $15

Grades: 9 10 11 12 Adult   **Fic**

1. Chinese Americans -- Fiction

ISBN 978-0-307-38922-0

LC 2008270242

First published 1991 by Houghton Mifflin

"Yefing Chang becomes Ralph Chang in America and begins a hard struggle to achieve the American dream—a career, a family and a home of his own. In poverty, he succeeds finally to win a doctoral degree, a college position, a happy marriage to Helen, two delightful daughters and a close reunion with his older sister, Theresa. The dream becomes a nightmare when he meets Grover Ding whose corrupt influence over Ralph and Helen begins to unravel all that the Changs have managed to achieve. This is an honest novel that does not promise happy endings and recognizes the human weaknesses that can destroy a family's stability." Shapiro. Fic for Youth. 3d edition

Followed by Mona in the promised land (1996)

Jenkins, A. M.

Beating heart; a ghost story. HarperCollins Publishers 2006 244p $15.99; pa $8.99

Grades: 9 10 11 12   **Fic**

1. Ghost stories 2. Moving -- Fiction 3. Divorce -- Fiction

ISBN 0-06-054607-7; 0-06-054609-3 pa

LC 2005-05071

Following his parents' divorce, seventeen-year-old Evan moves with his mother and sister into an old house where the spirit of a teenager who died there awakens and mistakes him for her long-departed lover.

"Both accessible and substantive, this book will be an easy sell to teens." Booklist

Repossessed. HarperTeen 2007 218p $15.99

Grades: 7 8 9 10   **Fic**

1. School stories 2. Devil -- Fiction 3. Demoniac possession -- Fiction

ISBN 978-0-06-083568-2; 0-06-083568-0

LC 2007-09142

Michael L. Printz Award honor book, 2008

A fallen angel, tired of being unappreciated while doing his pointless, demeaning job, leaves Hell, enters the body of a seventeen-year-old boy, and tries to experience the full range of human feelings before being caught and punished, while the boy's family and friends puzzle over his changed behavior.

"Funny and clever. . . . It's a quick, quirky and entertaining read, with some meaty ideas in it, too." Kliatt

Jensen, Cordelia

Skyscraping; Cordelia Jensen. Philomel Books, an imprint of Penguin Group (USA) 2015 352 p. $17.99

Grades: 9 10 11 12   **Fic**

1. Adjustment (Psychology) 2. Family secrets -- Fiction 3. Father-daughter relationship -- Fiction 4. Novels in verse 5. Schools -- Fiction 6. Secrets -- Fiction 7. Gay fathers -- Fiction 8. High schools -- Fiction 9. Fathers and daughters -- Fiction 10. New York (N.Y.) -- History -- 20th century -- Fiction

ISBN 0399167714; 9780399167713

LC 2014035150

In Cordelia Jensen's novel "Mira is just beginning her senior year of high school when she discovers her father with his male lover. Unable to comprehend the lies . . . Mira distances herself from her sister and closest friends as a means of coping. A shocking health scare brings to light his battle with HIV. As Mira struggles to make sense of the many fractures in her family's fabric and redefine her wavering sense of self, she must find a way to reconnect with her dad." (Publisher's note)

"Small period details, from Keith Haring's artwork to the emergence of Starbucks to Kurt Cobain's death, layer in historical context naturally, but it's Jensen's stunning ability to bring the raw uncertainty of the AIDS crisis in the 1990s to vivid life that is so exceptional. Illuminating and deeply felt." Booklist

Jeschonek, Robert T.

My favorite band does not exist. Clarion Books 2011 327p $16.99

Grades: 8 9 10 11 12   **Fic**

1. Fantasy fiction

ISBN 978-0-547-37027-9; 0-547-37027-X

Sixteen-year-old Idea Deity, who believes that he is a character in a novel who will die in the sixty-fourth chapter, has created a fictional underground rock band on the internet which, it turns out, may actually exist, and whose members are wondering who is broadcasting all their personal information.

"Jeschonek has created a quirky, time and space-bending adventure that might just gather a cult following of its own. . . . Libraries looking for a strong addition to their science-fiction collections will want to invest in this sophisticated novel." SLJ

Jimenez, Francisco

★ **Reaching** out. Houghton Mifflin 2008 196p $16; pa $6.99

Grades: 7 8 9 10 11 12   **Fic**

1. California -- Fiction 2. Mexican Americans -- Fiction 3. Father-son relationship -- Fiction

ISBN 978-0-618-03851-0; 0-618-03851-5; 978-0-547-25030-4 pa; 0-547-25030-4 pa

Sequel to: Breaking through (2001)

A Pura Belpre Author Award honor book, 2009

"Papa's raging depression intensifies young Jiménez's personal guilt and conflict in the 1960s. . . . He is the first in his Mexican American migrant family to attend college in California. . . . Like his other fictionalized autobiographies, The Circuit (1997) and Breaking Through (2001), this sequel tells Jiménez's personal story in self-contained chapters that join together in a stirring narrative. . . . The spare episodes will draw readers with the quiet daily detail of work, anger, sorrow, and hope." Booklist

Jinks, Catherine

★ **Evil** genius. Harcourt 2007 486p $17

Grades: 7 8 9 10 **Fic**

1. School stories 2. Crime -- Fiction 3. Genius -- Fiction 4. Australia -- Fiction 5. Good and evil -- Fiction

ISBN 978-0-15-205988-0; 0-15-205988-1

LC 2006-14476

First published 2005 in Australia

Child prodigy Cadel Piggot, an antisocial computer hacker, discovers his true identity when he enrolls as a first-year student at an advanced crime academy.

"Cadel's turnabout is convincingly hampered by his difficulty recognizing appropriate outlets for rage, and Jinks' whiplash-inducing suspense writing will gratify fans of Anthony Horowitz's high-tech spy scenarios." Booklist

Other titles about Cadel Piggot are:

Genius squad (2008)

Genius wars (2010)

Genius squad. Harcourt 2008 436p $17

Grades: 7 8 9 10 **Fic**

1. Crime -- Fiction 2. Genius -- Fiction 3. Australia -- Fiction 4. Good and evil -- Fiction

ISBN 978-0-15-205985-9; 0-15-205985-7

After the Axis Institute is blown up, fifteen-year-old Cadell Piggot is unhappily stuck in foster care with constant police surveillance to protect him from the evil Prosper English until he gets an offer to join a mysterious group called Genius Squad.

"Readers who loved Evil Genius will find this sequel as gripping, devilish and wonderfully dark as its predecessor." Publ Wkly

The **genius** wars. Harcourt 2010 378p $17

Grades: 7 8 9 10 **Fic**

1. Science fiction 2. Crime -- Fiction 3. Genius -- Fiction 4. Australia -- Fiction 5. Good and evil -- Fiction

ISBN 978-0-15-206619-2; 0-15-206619-5

LC 2009-49979

Fifteen-year-old genius Cadel Piggot Greenaus sets aside his new, crime-free life when his best friend Sonja is attacked, and he crosses oceans and continents trying to track down his nemesis Prosper English, breaking whatever rules he must.

"The climax is taut, absorbing and tantalizingly ambiguous." Kirkus

Living hell. Harcourt 2010 256p $17

Grades: 7 8 9 10 **Fic**

1. Science fiction

ISBN 978-0-15-206193-7; 0-15-206193-2

LC 2009-18938

Chronicles the transformation of a spaceship into a living organism, as seventeen-year-old Cheney leads the hundreds of inhabitants in a fight for survival while machines turn on them, treating all humans as parasites.

"Jinks' well-thought-out environs and rational characters help ground this otherwise out-of-control interstellar thriller." Booklist

The **reformed** vampire support group. Houghton Mifflin Harcourt 2009 362p $17; pa $8.99

Grades: 8 9 10 11 12 **Fic**

1. Mystery fiction 2. Vampires -- Fiction

ISBN 978-0-15-206609-3; 0-15-206609-8; 978-0-547-41166-8 pa; 0-547-41166-9 pa

LC 2008-25115

Fifteen-year-old vampire Nina has been stuck for fifty-one years in a boring support group for vampires, and nothing exciting has ever happened to them—until one of them is murdered and the others must try to solve the crime.

"Those tired of torrid bloodsucker stories or looking for a comic riff on the trend will feel refreshed by the vomitous, guinea-pig-drinking accidental heroics of Nina and her pals." Kirkus

Followed by: The abused werewolf rescue group (2011)

Jocelyn, Marthe

Would you. Wendy Lamb Books 2008 165p $15.99; lib bdg $18.99; pa $6.50

Grades: 8 9 10 11 12 **Fic**

1. Coma -- Fiction 2. Sisters -- Fiction 3. Family life -- Fiction 4. Medical care -- Fiction 5. Traffic accidents -- Fiction

ISBN 978-0-375-83703-6; 0-375-83703-5; 978-0-375-93703-3 lib bdg; 0-375-93703-X lib bdg; 978-0-375-83704-3 pa; 0-375-83704-3 pa

LC 2007-18913

When her beloved sister, Claire, steps in front of a car and winds up in a coma, Nat's anticipated summer of working, hanging around with friends, and seeing Claire off to college is transformed into a nightmare of doctors, hospitals, and well-meaning neighbors.

"Jocelyn captures a teen's thoughts and reactions in a time of incredible anguish without making her overly dramatic. Readers will fly through the pages of this book, crying, laughing, and crying some more." SLJ

John, Antony

Five flavors of dumb. Dial Books 2010 337p $16.99

Grades: 7 8 9 10 **Fic**

1. Deaf -- Fiction 2. Rock musicians -- Fiction 3. Seattle (Wash.) -- Fiction

ISBN 978-0-8037-3433-3; 0-8037-3433-6

LC 2009-44449

Eighteen-year-old Piper is profoundly hearing impaired and resents her parent's decision raid her college fund to get cochlear implants for her baby sister. She becomes the manager for her classmates' popular rock band, called Dumb, giving her the chance to prove her capabilities to her parents and others, if only she can get the band members to get along.

"Readers interested in any of the narrative strands . . . will find a solid, satisfyingly complex story here." Bull Cent Child Books

Johnson, Alaya Dawn

★ The **summer** prince; Alaya Dawn Johnson. Arthur A. Levine Books 2013 304 p. (jacketed hardcover: alk. paper) $17.99

Grades: 9 10 11 12 **Fic**

1. Science fiction 2. Artists -- Fiction 3. Resistance to government -- Fiction 4. Love -- Fiction 5. Brazil -- Fiction 6. Government, Resistance to -- Fiction 7. Kings, queens, rulers, etc. -- Fiction

ISBN 0545417791; 9780545417792; 9780545417808; 9780545520775

LC 2012022236

Lambda Literary Awards Finalist (2014)

Rainbow List (2014)

This speculative fiction novel, by Alaya Dawn Johnson, takes place in "a futuristic Brazil. . . . In the midst of this vibrant metropolis, June Costa creates art that's sure to make her legendary. But her dreams of fame become something more when she meets Enki, the bold new Summer King. . . . Together, June and Enki will stage explosive, dramatic projects that Palmares Tres will never forget. They will add fuel to a growing rebellion against the government's strict limits on new tech." (Publisher's note)

Johnson, Angela, 1961-

★ A **certain** October; Angela Johnson. Simon & Schuster Books For Young Readers 2012 176 p. (hardback) $16.99

Grades: 7 8 9 10 11 12 **Fic**

1. Bildungsromans 2. Death -- Fiction 3. Guilt -- Fiction 4. Teenagers -- Fiction 5. Autism -- Fiction 6. Friendship -- Fiction 7. High schools -- Fiction

ISBN 9781442417267; 9780689865053; 9780689870651

LC 2012001595

In this book, "when a terrible accident occurs, Scotty feels responsible for the loss of someone she hardly knew, and the world goes wrong. She cannot tell what is a dream and what is real. Her friends are having a hard time getting through to her and her family is preoccupied with their own trauma. But the prospect of a boy, a dance, and the possibility that everything can fall back into place soon help Scotty realize that she is capable of adding her own flavor to life." (Publisher's note)

The **first** part last. Simon & Schuster Bks. for Young Readers 2003 131p $15.95

Grades: 7 8 9 10 **Fic**

1. Infants -- Fiction 2. Teenage fathers -- Fiction 3. African Americans -- Fiction

ISBN 0-689-84922-2

LC 2002-36512

Prequel to Heaven (1998)

Michael L. Printz Award, 2004

Bobby's carefree teenage life changes forever when he becomes a father and must care for his adored baby daughter. "Brief, poetic, and absolutely riveting." SLJ

Followed by: Sweet hereafter (2010)

Sweet, hereafter; Angela Johnson. 1st ed. Simon and Schuster Books for Young Readers 2010 118 p. (paperback) $7.99; (hardcover) $16.99

Grades: 7 8 9 10 **Fic**

1. Iraq War, 2003- -- Fiction 2. African Americans -- Fiction

ISBN 0689873859; 9780689873867; 9780689873850; 0689873867

LC 2009027618

"Grades seven to ten." (Bull Cent Child Books)

"Johnson concludes the trilogy that began with Heaven (1998) and The First Part Last (2003). . . . Johnson's stripped-down, poetic prose is filled with shattering emotional truths about war's incalculable devastation, love's mysteries, and the bewildering, necessary search for happiness." Booklist

"With heartfelt empathy, we share in Shoogy's personal loss and her need for a new direction. Characters from the two other titles reappear, and we get a glimpse of how their lives are moving forward. This book belongs in all junior and senior high school collections, especially those who already own the first two titles. . . . Johnson now has one more well-woven character development novel to her name." Libr Media Connect

Johnson, Christine

Claire de Lune. Simon Pulse 2010 336p $16.99

Grades: 7 8 9 10 **Fic**

1. Werewolves -- Fiction 2. Mother-daughter relationship -- Fiction

ISBN 978-1-4169-9182-3; 1-4169-9182-4

LC 2009-36269

On her sixteenth birthday Claire discovers strange things happening and when her mother reveals their family secret which explains the changes, Claire feels her world, as she has known it to be, slowly slipping away.

"Strong characters and major plot twists coupled with a new twist on werewolf mythology make this a fun and entertaining read that will satisfy fans of the genre." SLJ

Followed by Nocturne (2011)

Nocturne; a Claire de Lune novel. Simon Pulse 2011 355p $16.99

Grades: 7 8 9 10 **Fic**

1. School stories 2. Werewolves -- Fiction 3. Supernatural -- Fiction 4. Identity (Psychology) -- Fiction 5. Mother-daughter relationship -- Fiction

ISBN 978-1-4424-0776-3

LC 2010032068

Sequel to Claire de Lune (2010)

After the tragic events of the summer, Claire wants to worry about nothing but finding the perfect dress for the Autumn Ball, but her worst nightmares come true when someone learns that she is a werewolf, placing everyone she knows at risk.

Johnson, Harriet McBryde

★ **Accidents** of nature. Holt 2006 229p $16.95

Grades: 9 10 11 12   **Fic**

1. Camps -- Fiction 2. Cerebral palsy -- Fiction 3. People with disabilities -- Fiction

ISBN 0-8050-7634-4; 978-0-8050-7634-9

LC 2005-24598

Having always prided herself on blending in with "normal" people despite her cerebral palsy, seventeen-year-old Jean begins to question her role in the world while attending a summer camp for children with disabilities.

"This book is smart and honest, funny and eye-opening. A must-read." SLJ

Johnson, J. J.

★ The **theory** of everything; by Jen Wichman. Peachtree Publishers 2012 334 p. ill. (hardcover) $16.95

Grades: 7 8 9 10   **Fic**

1. Bereavement -- Fiction 2. Interpersonal relations -- Fiction 3. Grief -- Fiction 4. Friendship -- Fiction 5. Best friends -- Fiction 6. New York (State) -- Fiction 7. Loss (Psychology) -- Fiction 8. Family life -- New York (State) -- Fiction

ISBN 1561456233; 9781561456239

LC 2011020973

In this novel, by J. J. Johnson, "ever since Sarah Jones's best friend Jamie died in a freak accident, life has felt sort of . . . random. Sarah has always followed the rules. . . . Now what? . . . In a last ditch effort to pull it together, Sarah ends up working for Roy, a local eccentric who owns a Christmas tree farm, and who might also be trying to understand the rules, patterns, and connections in life." (Publisher's note)

Johnson, LouAnne

Muchacho. Alfred A. Knopf 2009 197p $15.99; lib bdg $18.99

Grades: 8 9 10   **Fic**

1. Bildungsromans 2. Teenagers -- Fiction 3. Mexican Americans -- Fiction 4. School stories 5. New Mexico -- Fiction

ISBN 978-0-375-86117-8; 0-375-86117-3; 978-0-375-96117-5 lib bdg; 0-375-96117-8 lib bdg

LC 2009-1768

Living in a neighborhood of drug dealers and gangs in New Mexico, high school junior Eddie Corazon, a juvenile delinquent-in-training, falls in love with a girl who inspires him to rethink his life and his choices.

"Eddie's first-person narration and street language will hold teenagers' interest. Set in New Mexico, one of the states with the highest dropout rates among Hispanics, this novel unveils the social pressures and struggles of teens living in inner cities." Kirkus

Johnson, Maureen

★ **13** little blue envelopes. HarperCollins Publishers 2005 317p $15.99; pa $8.99

Grades: 8 9 10 11 12   **Fic**

1. Aunts -- Fiction 2. Europe -- Fiction 3. Voyages and travels -- Fiction

ISBN 0-06-054141-5; 0-06-054143-1 pa

LC 2005-02658

When seventeen-year-old Ginny receives a packet of mysterious envelopes from her favorite aunt, she leaves New Jersey to criss-cross Europe on a sort of scavenger hunt that transforms her life.

"Equal parts poignant, funny and inspiring, this tale is sure to spark wanderlust." Publ Wkly

Followed by: The last little blue envelope (2011)

★ The **madness** underneath; Maureen Johnson. G. P. Putnam's Sons 2013 304 p. (Shades of London) (hardback) $17.99

Grades: 6 7 8 9 10   **Fic**

1. Ghost stories 2. Mystery fiction 3. Paranormal fiction 4. Ghosts -- Fiction 5. Murder -- Fiction 6. England -- Fiction 7. Schools -- Fiction 8. Boarding schools -- Fiction 9. London (England) -- Fiction

ISBN 039925661X; 9780399256615

LC 2012026755

This paranormal mystery novel, by Maureen Johnson, is book two of "The Shades of London Trilogy." "After her near-fatal run-in with the Jack the Ripper copycat, Rory Devereaux . . . [has] become a human terminus, with the power to eliminate ghosts on contact. . . . The Ripper may be gone, but now there is a string of new inexplicable deaths threatening London. Rory has evidence that the deaths are no coincidence. Something much more sinister is going on." (Publisher's note)

The **name** of the star. G. P. Putnam's Sons 2011 384p $16.99

Grades: 6 7 8 9 10   **Fic**

1. Ghost stories 2. School stories 3. Homicide -- Fiction 4. Witnesses -- Fiction 5. London (England) -- Fiction

ISBN 978-0-399-25660-8; 0-399-25660-1; 9780399256608; 0399256601

LC 2011009003

"Johnson's trademark sense of humor serves to counterbalance some grisly murders in this page-turner, which opens her Shades of London series. . . . As one mutilated body after another turns up, Johnson . . . amplifies the story's mysteries with smart use of and subtle commentary on modern media shenanigans and London's infamously extensive surveillance network. . . . Readers looking for nonstop fun, action, and a little gore have come to the right place." Publ Wkly

The **shadow** cabinet; Maureen Johnson. G. P. Putnam's Sons, an imprint of Penguin Group (USA) 2015 384 p. (Shades of London) (hardback) $17.99

Grades: 9 10 11 12   **Fic**

1. Ghost stories 2. London (England) -- Fiction 3. Ghosts -- Fiction 4. Murder -- Fiction 5. England -- Fiction 6. Schools -- Fiction 7. Boarding schools -- Fiction

ISBN 0399256628; 9780399256622

LC 2014031153

This supernatural novel, by Maureen Johnson, is book three in the "Shades of London" series, "Time is running out as Rory fights to find her friends and the ghost squad struggles to stop Jane from unleashing her spectral nightmare on the entire city. In the process, they'll discover the existence of an organization that underpins London itself . . . and Rory will learn that someone she trusts has been keeping a tremendous secret." (Publisher's note)

"The plot . . . is among Johnson's finest and incorporates creepy bits of backstory, fascinating historical asides, and truly ghoulish side characters—take, for example, a lumpen cemetery ghost that is 'just a glob of people pieces mixed together.' Lots of juicy setup here for the next outing." Booklist

Suite Scarlett. Scholastic Point 2008 353p $16.99

Grades: 6 7 8 9 10 **Fic**

1. Authorship -- Fiction 2. Family life -- Fiction 3. New York (N.Y.) -- Fiction 4. Hotels and motels -- Fiction

ISBN 978-0-439-89927-7; 0-439-89927-3

LC 2007-041903

Fifteen-year-old Scarlett Marvin is stuck in New York City for the summer working at her quirky family's historic hotel, but her brother's attractive new friend and a seasonal guest who offers her an intriguing and challenging writing project improve her outlook.

"Utterly winning, madcap Manhattan farce, crafted with a winking, urbane narrative and tight, wry dialogue." Booklist

Another title about Scarlett is:

Scarlett fever (2010)

Johnson, Varian

Saving Maddie. Delacorte Press 2010 231p $16.99; lib bdg $19.99

Grades: 9 10 11 12 **Fic**

1. Clergy -- Fiction 2. Religion -- Fiction 3. Family life -- Fiction 4. South Carolina -- Fiction

ISBN 978-0-385-73804-0; 0-385-73804-8; 978-0-385-90708-8 lib bdg; 0-385-90708-7 lib bdg

LC 2010-277721

"Joshua and Maddie, both preacher's kids, were best friends when they were younger, until Maddie's father moved the family to Norfolk. Now Maddie's back in town. Her father, having refused to pay her tuition at Brown, has sent her to an aunt's house to straighten up after years of too much boys and booze. Joshua, PK that he is, is sure he can save Maddie, but angry and hostile, she has resolved to stay the way she is." (Booklist)

Johnston, E. K.

★ **Exit,** pursued by a bear; E.K. Johnston. Dutton Books 2016 256 p. (hardcover) $17.99

Grades: 9 10 11 12 **Fic**

1. Date rape -- Fiction 2. Cheerleading -- Fiction 3. Teenage girls -- Fiction 4. Rape -- Fiction 5. Canada -- Fiction 6. Ontario -- Fiction 7. Schools -- Fiction 8. Friendship -- Fiction 9. Best friends -- Fiction 10. High schools -- Fiction

ISBN 9781101994580; 1101994584

LC 2015020645

In this novel, by E.K. Johnston, "when Hermione Winters arrives at Camp Manitouwabing for the final pre-season cheer camp of her high school career, she's prepared for intense competition and exhausting practices. Working with her fierce best friend Polly as co-captain, Hermione anticipates athletic challenges and triumphs--not being drugged

and raped at a camp dance. . . . When a pregnancy test two weeks later yields a positive result, Hermione knows she has a second chance at justice." (Kirkus)

"A beautifully written portrait of a young woman facing the unthinkable." SLJ

Prairie fire; E.K. Johnston. Carolrhoda Books 2015 304 p. (trade hard cover: alk. paper) $18.99

Grades: 7 8 9 10 11 12 **Fic**

1. Dragons -- Fiction 2. Friendship -- Fiction 3. Fame -- Fiction 4. High schools -- Fiction 5. Bards and bardism -- Fiction 6. Family life -- Canada -- Fiction 7. Adventure and adventurers -- Fiction

ISBN 146773909X; 9781467739092; 9781467761819; 9781467776790; 9781467776806; 9781467776813

LC 2014008995

Sequel to: The story of Owen

In this young adult novel by E. K. Johnston, the sequel to "The Story of Owen," "Every dragon slayer owes the Oil Watch a period of service, and young Owen was no exception. What made him different was that he did not enlist alone. His two closest friends stood with him shoulder to shoulder. . . . But the arc of history is long and hardened by dragon fire. Try as they might, Owen and his friends could not twist it to their will." (Publisher's note)

"A fantasy YA novel that steers clear of love triangles, teen angst, and a tidy ending is hard to come by; Prairie Fire and its prequel are must-haves." SLJ

The **story** of Owen; dragon slayer of Trondheim. E. K. Johnston. Carolrhoda Lab 2014 305 p. (hardcover) $17.95

Grades: 7 8 9 10 11 12 **Fic**

1. Adventure fiction 2. Canada -- Fiction 3. Dragons -- Fiction 4. Family life -- Fiction 5. Fame -- Fiction 6. Schools -- Fiction 7. High schools -- Fiction 8. Bards and bardism -- Fiction 9. Family life -- Canada -- Fiction 10. Adventure and adventurers -- Fiction

ISBN 9781467710664; 1467710660

LC 2013020492

William C. Morris Finalist (2015)

In this book, author E. K. Johnston, "envisions an Earth nearly identical to our own, with one key difference: dragons. . . . After 16-year-old Siobhan McQuaid agrees to become the bard for dragon-slayer-in-training Owen Thorskard, who has moved with his famous dragon-slaying family to her small Ontario town, she winds up at the center of a grassroots effort to understand an odd spike in dragon numbers." (Publishers Weekly)

"Humor, pathos and wry social commentary unite in a cleverly drawn, marvelously diverse world. Refreshingly, the focus is on the pair as friends and partners, not on potential romance." Kirkus

A **thousand** nights; E. K. Johnston. Disney-Hyperion 2015 336 p. (hardback) $18.99

Grades: 7 8 9 10 **Fic**

1. Magic -- Fiction 2. Adventure fiction 3. Kings and rulers -- Fiction 4. Fairy tales 5. Kings, queens, rulers, etc. -- Fiction

ISBN 9781484722275; 1484728475

LC 2014049058

This book, by E.K. Johnston, "explores the setting and central characters from the classic 'Arabian Nights: Tales from One Thousand and One Nights,' adding a mystical backstory for why the Prince kills his 300 wives but spares the Storyteller. In this retelling, the unnamed heroine sacrifices herself for her sister . . . when the Prince comes to claim a new bride. When her sister builds a shrine to make her a small god, the protagonist finds . . . her powers growing unexpectedly strong." (Publisher's note)

"Detailed and quiet, beautifully written with a literary rhythm that evokes a sense of oral tale-telling, this unexpected fantasy should not be missed." Kirkus

Jolin, Paula

In the name of God. Roaring Brook Press 2007 208p $16.95

Grades: 8 9 10 11 12   Fic

1. Syria -- Fiction 2. Muslims -- Fiction 3. Family life -- Fiction 4. Islamic fundamentalism -- Fiction

ISBN 978-1-59643-211-6; 1-59643-211-X

LC 2006-23834

Determined to follow the laws set down in the Qur'an, seventeen-year-old Nadia becomes involved in a violent revolutionary movement aimed at supporting Muslim rule in Syria and opposing the Western politics and materialism that increasingly affect her family.

"The well-written prose and short chapters give stories in the news a face and a character. Readers of this book will not be able to read or watch the news in the same way." Voice Youth Advocates

Jones, Allan Frewin

Destiny's path; [by] Frewin Jones. HarperTeen 2009 329p $16.99

Grades: 8 9 10 11 12   Fic

1. War stories 2. Magic -- Fiction 3. Wales -- Fiction 4. Princesses -- Fiction 5. Fate and fatalism -- Fiction

ISBN 978-0-06-087146-8; 0-06-087146-6

LC 2009-14587

Sequel to: Warrior princess (2009)

When fifteen-year-old Princess Branwen tries to turn away from her destiny as the one who will save Wales from the Saxons, the Shining Ones send an owl in the form of a young girl called Blodwedd to guide her and Rhodri on the right path.

"Branwen's compelling story leaves readers waiting for the sequel." Booklist

Followed by: The emerald flame (2010)

Jones, Edward, 1951-

★ The known world; Edward P. Jones. Amistad 2003 388 p. (acid-free paper) $14.95

Grades: 11 12 Adult   Fic

1. Historical fiction 2. Virginia -- Fiction 3. Plantation life -- Fiction 4. Slavery -- United States -- Fiction 5. Slaves -- Fiction 6. Slavery -- Fiction

ISBN 9780060557546; 0060557540

LC 2003040389

International IMPAC Dublin Literary Award (2005), National Book Critics Circle Award for Fiction (2003), Pultizer Prize for Fiction (2004)

This work of historical fiction explores "the world of blacks who owned blacks in the antebellum South." The book "starts with the dying 31-year-old Henry Townsend, a former slave -- now master of 33 slaves of his own and more than 50 acres of land . . . worried about the fate of his holdings upon his early death." (Publishers Weekly)

Jones, Lloyd

Mister Pip. Dial Press 2007 256p hardcover o.p. pa $15

Grades: 11 12 Adult   Fic

1. New Guinea -- Fiction 2. Storytelling -- Fiction 3. Books and reading -- Fiction

ISBN 978-0-385-34106-6; 0-385-34106-7; 978-0-385-34107-3 pa; 0-385-34107-5 pa

LC 2007-5224

First published 2006 in Australia

"The novel is a paean to the transformative power of literature, particularly its ability to occlude an unpleasant reality with a fictional alternative and to expand an individual's sense of possibility." N Y Sun

Jones, Patrick

★ Bridge; Patrick Jones. Darby Creek 2014 92 p. (The alternative) $7.95

Grades: 6 7 8 9 10 11 12   Fic

1. School stories 2. Family life -- Fiction 3. High schools -- Fiction 4. Hispanic Americans -- Fiction 5. Unauthorized immigrants -- Fiction 6. Work -- Fiction 7. Schools -- Fiction 8. Illegal aliens -- Fiction 9. Spanish language -- Fiction

ISBN 1467744824; 9781467739030; 9781467744829

LC 2013041390

"José can't keep up. As the only English speaker in a family of undocumented immigrants, he handles everything from taking family members to the doctor to bargaining with the landlord. Plus he works two jobs. With all this responsibility, he's missing a lot of school. . . . José knows he has to turn things around if he wants to graduate from Rondo Alternative High School. Can he raise his grades enough to have a shot at college and a better life?" (Publisher's note)

"The author's effective use of flashbacks and crisp portraits of positive adult characters add further emotional depth to this emotional glimpse at the high-pressure difficulties facing children in immigrant families. References to O'Brien's book will likely spark the interest of readers in that title as well." PW Reviews

Jordan, Hillary, 1963-

Mudbound; a novel. Algonquin Books of Chapel Hill 2008 328p hardcover o.p. pa $13.95

Grades: 11 12 Adult   Fic

1. Veterans -- Fiction 2. Farm life -- Fiction 3. Mississippi -- Fiction 4. Race relations -- Fiction 5. World War, 1939-1945 -- Fiction

ISBN 978-1-56512-569-8; 1-56512-569-X; 978-1-56512-677-0 pa; 1-56512-677-7 pa

LC 2007-44471

"In 1946, Laura McAllan, a college-educated Memphis schoolteacher, becomes a reluctant farmer's wife when her husband, Henry, buys a farm on the Mississippi Delta, a farm she aptly nicknames Mudbound. Laura has difficulty adjusting to life without electricity, indoor plumbing, read-ily accessible medical care for her two children and, worst of all, life with her live-in misogynous, racist, father-in-law. Her days become easier after Florence, the wife of Hap Jack-son, one of their black tenants, becomes more important to Laura as companion than as hired help. Catastrophe is in-evitable when two young WWII veterans, Henry's brother, Jamie, and the Jacksons' son, Ronsel, arrive, both battling nightmares from horrors they've seen, and both unable to bow to Mississippi rules after eye-opening years in Europe. . . . [This is] a superbly rendered depiction of the fury and terror wrought by racism." Publ Wkly

When she woke; a novel. Algonquin Books of Chapel Hill 2011 344p

Grades: 11 12 Adult   **Fic**

1. Clergy 2. Authors 3. Abortion 4. Novelists 5. Texas 6. Future 7. Love affairs 8. Short story writers 9. Women -- Social conditions 10. Prisoners -- Fiction
ISBN 1565126297; 9781565126299; 1-56512-629-7; 978-1-56512-629-9

LC 201122799

This book tells the story of "Hannah Payne . . . [whose] life has been devoted to church and family, but after her ar-rest, she awakens to a nightmare: she is lying on a table in a bare room, covered only by a paper gown, and cameras are broadcasting her every move to millions at home, for home observing new Chromes--criminals whose skin color has been genetically altered to match the class of their crime--is a new and sinister form of entertainment. Hannah is a Red; her crime is murder. The victim, says the state of Texas, was her unborn child, and Hannah is determined to protect the identity of the father—a public figure with whom she's shared a fierce and forbidden love." (Publisher's note)

Jordan, Robert

The **eye** of the world; Robert Jordan. Tor Books 1990 670p il maps (The Wheel of Time) pbk $8.99; hbk $34.99

Grades: 10 11 12 Adult   **Fic**

1. Fantasy fiction 2. Magic -- Fiction 3. Good and evil -- Fiction
ISBN 9780812511819; 9780312850098; 0812511816; 0312850093

"The peaceful villagers of Emond's Field pay little heed to rumors of war in the western lands until a savage attack by troll-like minions of the Dark One forces three young men to confront a destiny which has its origins in the time known as The Breaking of the World." (Library Journal)

Other titles in this series are:
The great hunt (1990)
The dragon reborn (1991)
The shadow rising (1992)
The fires of heaven (1993)
Lord of chaos (1994)
A crown of swords (1996)
The path of daggers (1998)
Winter's heart (2000)
Crossroads of twilight (2003)
Knife of dreams (2005)
The gathering storm (2009)
Towers of midnight (2010)
A memory of light (2013)

Joseph, Lynn

Flowers in the sky; by Lynn Joseph. HarperTeen 2013 240 p. (hardcover) $17.99

Grades: 8 9 10 11 12   **Fic**

1. Bildungsromans 2. New York (N.Y.) -- Fiction 3. Brothers and sisters -- Fiction 4. Love -- Fiction 5. Immigrants -- Fiction 6. Coming of age -- Fiction 7. Dominican Republic -- Fiction 8. Dominican Americans -- Fiction
ISBN 0060297948; 9780060297947

LC 2012038122

In this novel, by Lynn Joseph, "fifteen-year-old Nina Perez . . . must leave her . . . lush island home in Samana, Dominican Republic, when she's sent . . . to live with her brother, Darrio, in New York, to seek out a better life. . . . But then she meets . . . [a] tall, green-eyed boy . . . , who just might help her learn to see beauty in spite of tragedy." (Publisher's note)

Joyce, Graham, 1954-

The **exchange**. Viking 2008 241p $16.99

Grades: 7 8 9 10   **Fic**

1. Tattooing -- Fiction 2. Supernatural -- Fiction 3. Single parent family -- Fiction 4. Dating (Social customs) -- Fiction
ISBN 978-0-670-06207-2; 0-670-06207-3

LC 2007-32160

Cursed by the elderly recluse whose home she and a friend were creeping through late one night, fourteen-year-old Caz soon finds her life disintegrating and realizes she must find a way of lifting the curse—or at least understand-ing its power.

"Joyce has crafted a bizarre, magically realistic tale. . . . It's a wild ride with subtly moralistic undertones and a sur-prisingly happy ending that will stay with readers." Booklist

Juby, Susan

Another kind of cowboy. HarperTeen 2007 344p $16.99

Grades: 8 9 10 11 12   **Fic**

1. Horses -- Fiction 2. Friendship -- Fiction 3. Horsemanship -- Fiction 4. Homosexuality -- Fiction 5. British Columbia -- Fiction
ISBN 0-06-076517-8; 978-0-06-076517-0

LC 2006-36336

In Vancouver, British Columbia, two teenage dressage riders, one a spoiled rich girl and the other a closeted gay sixteen-year-old boy, come to terms with their identities and learn to accept themselves.

"Wry humor infuses this quiet story with a gentle warmth, and the secondary characters are well developed." Booklist

★ The **Truth** Commission; Susan Juby. Viking, an imprint of Penguin Group (USA) 2015 320 p. (hardcover) $18.99

Grades: 9 10 11 12   **Fic**

1. Truth -- Fiction 2. Artists -- Fiction 3. Sisters -- Fiction 4. High schools -- Fiction 5. Schools -- Fiction 6. Family problems -- Fiction
ISBN 0451468775; 9780451468772

LC 2014015259

In this book, by Susan Juby, "open secrets are the heart of gossip -- the obvious things that no one is brave or tactless enough to ask. Except for Normandy Pale and her friends. They are juniors at a high school for artists, and have no fear. They are the Truth Commission. Then, one of their truth targets says to Normandy: 'If you want to know about the truth, you might want to look a little closer to home.'" (Publisher's note)

"Best friends and art-school students Normandy (a girl), Dusk (a girl), and Neil (a boy, duh!) form a de facto truth commission: each week, each of them will ask someone to give them the straight truth. The experiment's results will constitute Normandy's creative nonfiction project. The novel, then, is presented as that project, complete with footnotes and the occasional piece of spot art...The problem, as Juby expertly shows, is that truth is messy and sometimes—like a hot potato—hard to handle. Though it comes dangerously close to melodrama by the end, the story is clever, the characters appealing, and the theme is thought-provoking." Horn Book

Jägerfeld, Jenny

Me on the Floor, Bleeding; Jenny Jägerfeld; translated by Susan Beard. Stockholm Text 2014 288 p. $14.95

Grades: 9 10 11 12   **Fic**
1. Bildungsromans 2. High school students -- Fiction 3. Identity 4. High school girls
ISBN 917547011X; 9789175470115

In this young adult novel by Jenny Jägerfeld, translated by Susan Beard, "High school outsider Maja would never hurt herself on purpose as her dad, teachers, and classmates seem to believe. . . . In this funny and clever coming-of-age novel, seventeen-year-old Maja describes each moment with such bare-bones honesty that one can't help but be drawn into her world." (Publisher's note)

"While the translation from Swedish may account in part for the plodding nature of the narration, Maja's life is plodding, a fact surely understood and appreciated by readers who will come to root for her in her search to understand her parents and thus herself." Booklist

Kade, Stacey

The **ghost** and the goth. Hyperion 2010 281p $16.99

Grades: 8 9 10 11 12   **Fic**
1. Ghost stories 2. School stories
ISBN 1-4231-2197-X; 978-1-4231-2197-8

LC 2010-8135

After being hit by a bus and killed, a high school homecoming queen gets stuck in the land of the living, with only a loser classmate—who happens to be able to see and hear ghosts—to help her.

"The tale is absorbing, and Kade successfully portrays a typical present-day high school. This novel will appeal to fans of romances and ghost stories alike." SLJ

Followed by: Queen of the dead (2011)

The **rules**; Stacey Kade. Hyperion 2013 416 p. $17.99

Grades: 7 8 9 10 11 12   **Fic**
1. Science fiction 2. Schools -- Fiction 3. Identity

-- Fiction 4. High schools -- Fiction 5. Genetic engineering -- Fiction 6. Fathers and daughters -- Fiction 7. Extraterrestrial beings -- Fiction 8. Interpersonal relations -- Fiction
ISBN 9781423153283

LC 2012033732

In this book, rescued "from a genetics lab by her adoptive father, Ariane Tucker has spent the last ten years hiding" that she's "a human-extraterrestrial hybrid, created by GenTex Labs as part of Project Paper Doll. She must follow 'the rules' set out by her father to avoid being detected by her classmates or GTX. Blend in, do not get noticed, trust no one, and never forget that they are searching for her." But Ariane breaks the rules when she catches the eye of Zane Bradshaw. (Voice of Youth Advocates)

Kagawa, Julie

The **Eternity** Cure; Julie Kagawa. Harlequin Books 2013 448 p. (hardcover) $16.99

Grades: 7 8 9 10 11 12   **Fic**
1. Science fiction 2. Vampires -- Fiction 3. Epidemics -- Fiction
ISBN 0373210698; 9780373210695

This vampire novel, by Julie Kagawa, is part of the "Blood of Eden" series. "Allie will follow the call of blood to save her creator, Kanin, from the psychotic vampire Sarren. But when the trail leads to Allie's birthplace in New Covington, what Allie finds there will change the world forever. . . . There's a new plague on the rise, a strain of the Red Lung virus that wiped out most of humanity generations ago--and this strain is deadly to humans and vampires alike." (Publisher's note)

The **forever** song; by Julie Kagawa. Harlequin Books 2014 416 p. (Blood of Eden) $16.99

Grades: 7 8 9 10 11 12   **Fic**
1. Vampires -- Fiction 2. Revenge 3. Vampires 4. Horror tales 5. Fantasy fiction
ISBN 0373211120; 9780373211128

In this novel, by Julie Kagawa, "Allie will embrace her cold vampire side to hunt down and end Sarren, the psychopathic vampire who murdered Zeke. But the trail is bloody and long, and Sarren has left many surprises for Allie and her companions--her creator, Kanin, and her blood brother, Jackal. The trail is leading straight to the one place they must protect at any cost--the last vampire-free zone on Earth, Eden. And Sarren has one final, brutal shock in store for Allie." (Publisher's note)

"Stomach-churning gore and heart-pounding action balance the (occasionally repetitive) romantic angst and moral inquiries into the nature of monsters. A bloody good way to end a trilogy."

★ The **immortal** rules; a legend begins. Julie Kagawa. Harlequin Teen 2012 504 p. (Blood of Eden) (hardcover) $18.99

Grades: 7 8 9 10 11 12   **Fic**
1. Love stories 2. Diseases -- Fiction 3. Vampires -- Fiction
ISBN 0373210515; 9780373210510

LC 2011279454

In this book, "[r]abids, vicious hybrid creatures born of the plague, prowl the land beyond the walled vampire cities. . . . When Allie is savagely attacked by a rabid, . . . a mysterious vampire offers her the choice of a human death or 'life' as a vampire. . . . Allie's determination to remain more human than monster is put to the test, particularly when she joins a band of humans on a desperate journey to safety on the island of Eden. Particularly when she falls in love." (Kirkus)

"Kagawa wraps excellent writing and skillful plotting around a well-developed concept and engaging characters, resulting in a fresh and imaginative thrill-ride that deserves a wide audience." Pub Wkly

Talon; by Julie Kagawa. Harlequin Books Teen 2014 464 p. $17.99

Grades: 8 9 10 11   **Fic**
  1. Fantasy fiction 2. Dragons -- Fiction 3. Brothers and sisters -- Fiction 4. Shapeshifting
  ISBN 0373211392; 9780373211395

In this book, by Julie Kagawa, "dragons were hunted to near extinction by the Order of St. George, a legendary society of dragon slayers. Hiding in human form and growing their numbers in secret, the dragons of Talon have become strong and cunning. . . . Ember and Dante Hill are the only sister and brother known to dragonkind. Trained to infiltrate society, Ember wants to live the teen experience and enjoy a summer of freedom before taking her destined place in Talon." (Publisher's note)

"Young love, sibling rivalry, rogue dragons, and plots for world domination create an intriguing mix in this new series." Horn Book

Kamata, Suzanne

Gadget Girl; the art of being invisible. Suzanne Kamata. GemmaMedia 2013 256 p. (pbk.) $14.95

Grades: 9 10 11 12   **Fic**
  1. Artists 2. Cerebral palsy -- Fiction 3. Mother-daughter relationship -- Fiction 4. France -- Fiction 5. Artists -- Fiction 6. Coming of age -- Fiction 7. Paris (France) -- Fiction 8. Cartoons and comics -- Fiction 9. Mothers and daughters -- Fiction 10. Single-parent families -- Fiction 11. People with disabilities -- Fiction
  ISBN 1936846381; 9781936846382
                    LC 2012051566

Asian/Pacific American Awards for Literature: Young Adult Literature Honor (2014)

In this book by Suzanne Kamata, "Aiko, who has cerebral palsy . . . is the 14-year-old secretive creator of a manga comic starring Lisa Cook as Gadget Girl. Aiko also serves as the reluctant muse to her midwestern American mother, an award-winning sculptor who has been invited to Paris, even as she longs for a connection to her birth father in Japan." (Booklist)

"For Aiko Cassidy, it's hard enough sitting at the "invisible" table and dealing with trespassing geeks. It's harder when her cerebral palsy makes guys notice her in all the wrong ways...Awkwardly and believably, this sensitive novel reveals an artistic teen adapting to family, disability and friendships in all their flawed beauty." (Kirkus)

Karp, Jesse

Those that wake. Harcourt 2011 329p

Grades: 9 10 11 12   **Fic**
  1. Science fiction 2. New York (N.Y.) -- Fiction 3. Identity (Psychology) -- Fiction
  ISBN 978-0-547-55311-5

"Things have been bleak in New York City ever since 'Big Black,' the explosion that destroyed Con Edison and the two-week aftermath of darkness, rioting, looting, and murder. Residents interact with their cell phones more than with one another. For four New Yorkers, though, things are much worse than bleak. One day Laura wakes to find that no one remembers her existence. Mal's brother is missing, and his only lead is that Tommy was running errands for someone in an empty office tower that doesn't seem to conform to the laws of physics. . . . With plenty of action, challenging ideas, and bizarre antagonists, this one should appeal to a broad section of teens." SLJ

Kaslik, Ibolya

Skinny; [by] Ibi Kaslik. Walker & Company 2006 244p $16.95

Grades: 11 12   **Fic**
  1. Sisters -- Fiction 2. Anorexia nervosa -- Fiction 3. Father-daughter relationship -- Fiction
  ISBN 978-0-8027-9608-0; 0-8027-9608-7
                    LC 2006-42140

First published 2004 in Canada

After the death of their father, two sisters struggle with various issues, including their family history, personal relationships, and an extreme eating disorder

"It's refreshing that Gigi's anorexia and briefly described lesbian romance are treated as only parts of a larger story, and the girls' grief following their father's death and the pressures they face growing up with immigrant parents add depth to the novel. . . . This is an ambitious, often moving offering, and older readers will likely connect with the raw emotions and intelligent insights into a family's secrets, pain, and enduring love." Booklist

Katcher, Brian

★ **Almost** perfect. Delacorte Press 2009 360p $17.99

Grades: 9 10 11 12   **Fic**
  1. School stories 2. Transgender people -- Fiction 3. Missouri -- Fiction 4. Single parent family -- Fiction 5. Dating (Social customs) -- Fiction
  ISBN 978-0-385-73664-0; 0-385-73664-9
                    LC 2008-37659

Stonewall Children's and Young Adult Literature Award, 2011

With his mother working long hours and in pain from a romantic break-up, eighteen-year-old Logan feels alone and unloved until a zany new student arrives at his small-town Missouri high school, keeping a big secret.

"The author tackles issues of homophobia, hate crimes and stereotyping with humor and grace in an accessible tone that will resonate with teens who may not have encountered the issue of transgender identity before." Kirkus

The **improbable** theory of Ana and Zak; Brian Katcher. Katherine Tegen Books, an imprint of HarperCollinsPublishers 2015 336 p. (hardcover) $17.99
Grades: 7 8 9 10 11 12   Fic
  1. Love -- Fiction 2. Teenagers -- Fiction 3. Brothers and sisters -- Fiction 4. High school students -- Fiction 5. Genius -- Fiction 6. Schools -- Fiction 7. Contests -- Fiction
  ISBN 0062272772; 9780062272775
                                              LC 2014030718
  This book, by Brian Katcher, is a "he said/she said romance about two teens discovering themselves. . . . When Ana Watson's brother ditches a high school trip to run wild at Washingcon, type-A Ana knows that she must find him. . . . In her desperation, she's forced to enlist the last person she'd ever want to spend time with—slacker Zak Duquette—to help find her brother before morning comes." (Publisher's note)
  "Type-A Ana and relaxed geek Zak take turns narrating as they spend a night searching for Ana's younger brother at a comic-book convention. The he said/she said romance has been done before, of course, but the unconventional setting, quirky convention-goers, and many over-the-top hijinks (e.g., multiple fights, a sci-fi-themed gay wedding, inadvertent drug-running) give this one a unique twist." Horn Book

Playing with matches. Delacorte Press 2008 294p $15.99; lib bdg $18.99
Grades: 8 9 10 11 12   Fic
  1. School stories 2. Missouri -- Fiction 3. Burns and scalds -- Fiction 4. Dating (Social customs) -- Fiction
  ISBN 978-0-385-73544-5; 0-385-73544-8; 978-0-385-90525-1 lib bdg; 0-385-90525-4 lib bdg
                                              LC 2007-27654
  While trying to find a girl who will date him, Missouri high school junior Leon Sanders befriends a lonely, disfigured female classmate.
  "This is a strong debut novel with a cast of quirky, multidimensional characters struggling with issues of acceptance, sexuality, identity, and self-worth." SLJ

Kearney, Meg
  The **girl** in the mirror; a novel in poems and journal entries. Meg Kearney. Persea Books 2012 168 p. (trade pbk.: alk. paper) $15
Grades: 9 10 11 12   Fic
  1. Novels in verse 2. Grief -- Fiction 3. Adoptees -- Fiction 4. Identity (Psychology) -- Fiction 5. Adoption -- Fiction
  ISBN 0892553855; 9780892553853
                                              LC 2011045052
  Sequel to: The secret of me
  This book, the sequel to "The Secret of Me," is "told in verse and journal entries." The protagonist's "father passed away on the same day that a letter with non-identifying information about her birth mother arrived from the adoption agency. . . . She . . . joins her older coworkers in late-night partying and drinking. . . . When her change in lifestyle results in losing close friends and a near rape, Lizzie realizes that she no longer recognizes the girl she sees in the mirror." (Kirkus Reviews)

"Kearney tenderly explores Lizzie's anger, sadness, and ambivalence about her identity as she grapples with whether to risk being hurt by the mother she never knew or to approach the future without first claiming her past." Pub Wkly
  Includes bibliographical references

Kehoe, Stasia Ward
  The **sound** of letting go; by Stasia Ward Kehoe. Viking, published by Penguin Group 2014 400 p. (hardcover) $17.99
Grades: 7 8 9 10 11 12   Fic
  1. Autism -- Fiction 2. Family life -- Fiction 3. High school students -- Fiction 4. Alienation (Social psychology) -- Fiction 5. Jazz -- Fiction 6. Novels in verse 7. Schools -- Fiction 8. Trumpet -- Fiction 9. High schools -- Fiction 10. Family problems -- Fiction
  ISBN 0670015539; 9780670015535
                                              LC 2013013098
  In this book, by Stasia Ward Kehoe, "for sixteen years, Daisy has been good. A good daughter, helping out with her autistic younger brother uncomplainingly. A good friend, even when her best friend makes her feel like a third wheel. When her parents announce they're sending her brother to an institution--without consulting her--Daisy's furious, and decides the best way to be a good sister is to start being bad. She quits jazz band and orchestra, slacks in school, and falls for bad-boy Dave." (Publisher's note)
  "Kehoe's second novel-in-verse, after 2011's Audition, movingly evokes the conflicting emotions of 17-year-old Daisy Meehan as her family teeters on the edge of falling apart due to her younger brother Steven's violent episodes. . . . This painfully honest portrait of a family in crisis raises questions about love, responsibility, and self-sacrifice as it moves gracefully to a difficult but realistic resolution." Pub Wkly

Kelly, Tara
  Harmonic feedback. Henry Holt and Company 2010 280p $16.99
Grades: 9 10 11 12   Fic
  1. Drug abuse -- Fiction 2. Rock music -- Fiction 3. Washington (State) -- Fiction 4. Asperger's syndrome -- Fiction
  ISBN 978-0-8050-9010-9; 0-8050-9010-X
                                              LC 2009-24150
  When Drea and her mother move in with her grandmother in Bellingham, Washington, the sixteen-year-old finds finds that she can have real friends, in spite of her Asperger's, and that even when you love someone it doesn't make life perfect.
  "The novel's strength lies in Drea's dynamic personality: a combination of surprising immaturity, childish wonder, and profound insight. Her search for stability and need to escape being labeled is poignant and convincing." Publ Wkly

Keneally, Thomas
  ★ **Schindler's** list. Simon & Schuster 1982 400p $25; pa $14
Grades: 11 12 Adult   Fic
  1. Humanitarians 2. Jews -- Fiction 3. Manufacturing executives 4. Holocaust, 1933-1945 -- Fiction 5. World

War, 1939-1945 -- Fiction
ISBN 0-671-51688-4; 0-671-88031-4 pa

LC 82-10489

"An actual occurrence during the Nazi regime in Germany forms the basis for this story. Oskar Schindler, a Catholic German industrialist, chose to act differently from those Germans who closed their eyes to what was happening to the Jews. By spending enormous sums on bribes to the SS and on food and drugs for the Jewish prisoners whom he housed in his own camp-factory in Cracow, he succeeded in sheltering thousands of Jews, finally transferring them to a safe place in Czechoslovakia. Fifty Schindler survivors from seven nations helped the author with information." Shapiro. Fic for Youth. 3d edition

Kenneally, Miranda

Racing Savannah; Miranda Kenneally. Sourcebooks Fire 2013 304 p. (tp: alk. paper) $9.99
Grades: 8 9 10 11 12   **Fic**
1. Horsemanship -- Fiction 2. Love 3. Horses
ISBN 1402284764; 9781402284762

LC 2013023322

In this book, by Miranda Kenneally, "Savannah has always been much more comfortable around horses than boys. Especially boys like Jack Goodwin. . . . She knows the rules: no mixing between the staff and the Goodwin family. But Jack has no such boundaries. With her dream of becoming a jockey, Savannah isn't exactly one to follow the rules either." (Publisher's note)

"Kenneally (Stealing Parker, 2012) again looks at sports through a female lens, this time tackling male-dominated horse racing, in this fourth Hundred Oaks novel. Savannah, her widowed horse-trainer father, and her father's pregnant girlfriend move to Tennessee's Cedar Hill, a farm that trains horses for races including the Kentucky Derby...The author's knack for weaving forbidden romance, breezy dialogue, and details of this lesser-known sports venue places it in the winner's circle for reluctant readers and chick-lit fans." (Booklist)

Kennedy, William

Ironweed. Viking 1983 227p hardcover o.p. pa $14
Grades: 11 12 Adult   **Fic**
1. Homeless persons -- Fiction 2. New York (State) -- Fiction 3. Great Depression, 1929-1939 -- Fiction
ISBN 0-14-007020-6 pa

LC 82-40370

With this "tale of skid-row life in the Depression, Kennedy adds another chapter to his 'Albany cycle'—a group of novels set in the Albany, New York, underworld from the 1920s onward. Following 'Legs' and 'Billy Phelan's Greatest Game,' 'Ironweed' tells the story of Francis Phelan, a 58-year-old bum with muscatel on his breath and hallucinations on his mind. Chief among the latter is a vision of his infant son, who died after falling out of Francis' arms. It is the desire to reconcile himself to the memory of his dead son that brings Francis home to Albany, ultimately opening the door to a possible reconciliation with his family." Booklist

Kephart, Beth

Dangerous neighbors; a novel. Egmont USA 2010 176p $16.99; lib bdg $19.99
Grades: 7 8 9 10   **Fic**
1. Death -- Fiction 2. Guilt -- Fiction 3. Twins -- Fiction 4. Sisters -- Fiction 5. Bereavement -- Fiction 6. Philadelphia (Pa.) -- Fiction 7. Centennial Exhibition (1876: Philadelphia, Pa.) -- Fiction
ISBN 978-1-60684-080-1; 1-60684-080-0; 978-1-60684-106-8 lib bdg; 1-60684-106-8 lib bdg

LC 2010-11249

Set against the backdrop of the 1876 Centennial Exhibition in Philadelphia, Katherine cannot forgive herself when her beloved twin sister dies, and she feels that her only course of action is to follow suit.

"Exceptionally graceful prose . . . and flashbacks are so realistically drawn and deftly integrated that readers will be as startled as Katherine to find themselves yanked out of morose memories and surrounded by noisy fairgoers." Bull Cent Child Books

Dr. Radway's Sarsaparilla Resolvent; by Beth Kephart; illustrated by William Sulit. Temple Univ Pr 2013 198 p. ill. (paperback) $15.95
Grades: 6 7 8 9   **Fic**
1. Grief -- Fiction 2. Police brutality -- Fiction
ISBN 0984042962; 9780984042968

This book by Beth Kephart follows 14-year-old protagonist William Quinn. "With his father in the Cherry Hill prison and his genially wayward older brother, Francis, recently beaten to death by a brutal policeman, his mother has ground herself into unbearable, paralyzing grief, and the boy has to find a way to save them both. . . . Gradually, William finds a way to make right some terrible wrongs." (Kirkus Reviews)

★ **Going** over; Beth Kephart. Chronicle Books 2014 262 p. map (alk. paper) $17.99
Grades: 8 9 10 11 12   **Fic**
1. Love -- Fiction 2. Family life -- Fiction 3. Berlin (Germany) -- Fiction 4. Berlin Wall (1961-1989) -- Fiction 5. Family life -- Germany -- Fiction 6. Germany -- History -- 1945-1990 -- Fiction 7. Berlin Wall, Berlin, Germany, 1961-1989 -- Fiction 8. Berlin (Germany) -- History -- 1945-1989 -- Fiction
ISBN 1452124574; 9781452124575

LC 2012046894

In this book, by Beth Kephart, "Ada lives among the rebels, punkers, and immigrants of Kreuzberg in West Berlin. Stefan lives in East Berlin, in a faceless apartment bunker of Friedrichshain. Bound by love and separated by circumstance, their only chance for a life together lies in a high-risk escape. But will Stefan find the courage to leap? Or will forces beyond his control stand in his way?" (Publisher's note)

"In a present-tense narration alternating between Ada's first-person and Stefan's second-person, the young lovers on opposite sides of the Berlin Wall in 1983 plan for Stefan's escape to the West. Kephart works romantic chemistry into a danger-packed plot with moving results in this captivating glimpse into an underrepresented era that will appeal

to older readers with a taste for literary historical fiction."
Horn Book

House of Dance. HarperTeen 2008 263p
$16.99; lib bdg $17.89; pa $10.99
Grades: 7 8 9 10   **Fic**
1. Death -- Fiction 2. Cancer -- Fiction 3. Dancers --
Fiction 4. Grandfathers -- Fiction 5. Mother-daughter
relationship -- Fiction
ISBN 978-0-06-142928-6; 0-06-142928-7; 978-0-06-
142929-3 lib bdg; 0-06-142929-5 lib bdg; 978-0-06-
142930-9 pa; 0-06-142930-9 pa
LC 2007-26011
During one of her daily visits across town to visit her
dying grandfather, fifteen-year-old Rosie discovers a
dance studio that helps her find a way to bring her family
members together.
This is "distinguished more by its sharp, eloquent prose
than by its plot. . . . Poetically expressed memories and moving dialogue both anchor and amplify the characters' emotions." Publ Wkly

Nothing but ghosts. HarperTeen 2009 278p
$17.95
Grades: 8 9 10 11 12   **Fic**
1. Art -- Fiction 2. Mothers -- Fiction 3. Gardening --
Fiction 4. Bereavement -- Fiction 5. Loss (Psychology)
-- Fiction
ISBN 978-0-06-166796-1; 0-06-166796-X
LC 2008-26024
After her mother's death, sixteen-year-old Katie copes
with her grief by working in the garden of an old estate,
where she becomes intrigued by the story of a reclusive millionaire, while her father, an art restorer, manages in his own
way to come to terms with the death of his wife.
"Kephart's evocative writing and gentle resolution offer
healing and hope as her characters come to terms with their
losses." Publ Wkly

One thing stolen; Beth Kephart. Chronicle
Books 2015 272 p. (alk. paper) $17.99
Grades: 9 10 11 12   **Fic**
1. Love stories 2. Theft -- Fiction 3. Psychology
-- Fiction 4. Italy -- Fiction 5. Dementia -- Fiction
6. Family life -- Fiction 7. Kleptomania -- Fiction 8.
Florence (Italy) -- Fiction
ISBN 9781452128313; 1452128316
LC 2014005286
In this novel by Beth Kephart, "something very bad is
happening to 17-year-old Nadia. Ever since her family relocated to Florence for her father's sabbatical, she's been
slipping out at night to steal random objects and then weave
them into bizarre nest-shaped forms she hides from her family, and she's losing her ability to speak." (Kirkus Reviews)
"Fans of Jandy Nelson's dense, unique narratives will
lose themselves in Kephart's enigmatic, atmospheric, and
beautifully written tale." Booklist

★ **Small** damages; Beth Kephart. Philomel
Books 2012 304 p. $17.99
Grades: 10 11 12   **Fic**
1. Spain -- Fiction 2. Adoption -- Fiction 3. Teenage

pregnancy -- Fiction 4. Cooking -- Fiction 5.
Pregnancy -- Fiction 6. Ranch life -- Spain -- Fiction 7.
Interpersonal relations -- Fiction
ISBN 0399257489; 9780399257483
LC 2011020947
As Beth Kephart's character is "provided by her mother
with only the barest of details about a couple that wishes to
adopt her baby, Kenzie finds herself an unofficial apprentice
in the kitchen of the home of a successful bull breeder connected to the prospective adoptive parents. . . . Her initially
strained relationship with terse Estela, the marvelous chef
charged with her safekeeping, eventually melts into a mutual
trust." (Kirkus Reviews)

This is the story of you; Beth Kephart. Chronicle
Books Llc 2016 264 p. $17.99
Grades: 7 8 9 10 11 12   **Fic**
1. Islands -- Fiction 2. Hurricanes -- Fiction 3. New
Jersey -- Fiction 4. Survival skills -- Fiction 5. Survival
-- Fiction
ISBN 9781452142845
LC 2015003765
In this book, by Beth Kephart, "on Haven, a six-mile
long, half-mile-wide stretch of barrier island, Mira Banul
and her Year-Rounder friends have proudly risen to every
challenge. But then a superstorm defies all predictions and
devastates the island, upending all logic and stranding Mira's mother and brother on the mainland. Nothing will ever
be the same." (Publisher's note)
"Six miles long and a half-mile wide. That's the size
of the barrier island of Haven, home to year-rounder Mira,
which comes under siege during a powerful hurricane that's
supposed to bypass the Jersey Shore. With her little brother,
Jasper Lee, afflicted by the rare Hunter syndrome and her
mother far away at the hospital, Mira's responsible for defending her home. The storm changes everything, fractur-
ing contact with the outside world and leaving Mira alone to
grapple with the fallout: her best friend Ava gone missing,
their belongings swept out to sea, and a stranger breaking
into her home. . . . At once an exploration of the unrelenting
power of nature and a reminder of the one thing in the world
that is irreplaceable: family." Booklist

Undercover. HarperTeen 2007 278p $16.99;
lib bdg $17.89; pa $8.99
Grades: 8 9 10 11 12   **Fic**
1. School stories 2. Poetry -- Fiction 3. Family life
-- Fiction
ISBN 978-0-06-123893-2; 0-06-123893-7; 978-0-06-
123894-9 lib bdg; 0-06-123894-5 lib bdg; 978-0-06-
123895-6 pa; 0-06-123895-3 pa
LC 2007-2981
High school sophomore Elisa is used to observing while
going unnoticed except when classmates ask her to write
love notes for them, but a teacher's recognition of her talent,
a "client's" desire for her friendship, a love of ice skating,
and her parent's marital problems draw her out of herself.
"Kephart tells a moving story. . . . Readers will fall easily
into the compelling premise and Elisa's memorable, graceful
voice." Booklist

You are my only; a novel. Egmont USA 2011 240p $16.99

Grades: 7 8 9 10　　　　　　　　　　　　**Fic**
1. Kidnapping -- Fiction　2. Home schooling -- Fiction　3. Mother-daughter relationship -- Fiction
ISBN 978-1-60684-272-0; 1-60684-272-2

LC 2010052662

Tells, in their separate voices and at a space of fourteen years, of Emmy, whose baby has been stolen, and Sophie, a teenager who defies her nomadic, controlling mother by making friends with a neighbor boy and his elderly aunts.

This is a "a psychologically taut novel. . . . Succinct, emotionally packed chapters capture similarities between mother and daughter, the depth of their despair, their common desire to be free, and their poetic vision of the world." Publ Wkly

Keplinger, Kody

A **midsummer's** nightmare; a novel. by Kody Keplinger. Poppy 2012 291 p. $17.99

Grades: 9 10 11 12　　　　　　　　　　　　**Fic**
1. Family life　2. Stepfamilies　3. Illinois -- Fiction　4. Remarriage -- Fiction　5. Conduct of life -- Fiction　6. Family problems -- Fiction　7. Fathers and daughters -- Fiction
ISBN 0316084220; 9780316084222

LC 2011026949

This young adult novel by Kody Keplinger tells how "Whitley Johnson's dream summer with her divorce dad has turned into a nightmare. She's just met his new fiancee and her kids. . . . Worse, she totally doesn't fit in with her dad's perfect new country-club family. So Whitley acts out. . . . It will take all [of her friends and step family] to help Whitley get through her anger and begin to put the pieces of her [life] together." (Publisher's note)

Kerouac, Jack

On the road; 50th anniversary ed.; Viking 2007 307p $25.95

Grades: 11 12 Adult　　　　　　　　　　　**Fic**
1. Friendship -- Fiction　2. Voyages and travels -- Fiction
ISBN 978-0-670-06326-0

LC 2007021285

First published 1957

"Sal Paradise (a self-portrait of Kerouac), a struggling author in his mid-twenties, tells of his meeting Dean Moriarty (based on Neal Cassady), a fast-living teenager just out of a New Mexico reform school, whose soul is 'wrapped up in a fast car, a coast to reach, and a woman at the end of the road.' During the next five years they travel coast to coast, either with each other or to each other. Five trips are described." Oxford Companion to Am Lit. 6th edition

Kessler, Jackie

Loss; Jackie Morse Kessler. Graphia 2012 258 p. pa $8.99

Grades: 8 9 10 11 12　　　　　　　　　　**Fic**
1. Fantasy fiction　2. Plague -- Fiction　3. Bullies -- Fiction　4. Apocalyptic fiction　5. Schools -- Fiction　6. Diseases -- Fiction　7. Self-esteem -- Fiction　8. Time travel -- Fiction　9. High schools -- Fiction　10. Four

Horsemen of the Apocalypse -- Fiction
ISBN 0547712154; 9780547712154

LC 2011031490

This young adult novel is part of Jackie Morse Kessler's Riders of the Apocalypse
series in which "[f]ifteen-year-old Billy Ballard is the kid that everyone picks on. But things change drastically when Death tells Billy he must stand in as Pestilence, the White Rider of the Apocalypse. Now armed with a Bow that allows him to strike with disease from a distance, Billy lashes out at his tormentors . . . and accidentally causes an outbreak of meningitis. Horrified by his actions, Billy begs Death to take back the Bow. For that to happen, says Death, Billy must track down the real White Rider, and stop him from unleashing something awful on humanity . . . that could make the Black Plague look like a summer cold. Does one bullied teenager have the strength to stand his ground—and the courage to save the world?" (Publisher's note)

Keyes, Daniel

Flowers for Algernon. Harcourt Brace & Co. 1995 286p $17

Grades: 9 10 11 12　　　　　　　　　　　**Fic**
1. Science fiction　2. People with mental disabilities
ISBN 0-15-100163-4

LC 95-148312

First published 1966

"Charlie Gordon, aged 32, is mentally retarded and enrolls in a class to 'become smart.' He keeps a journal of his progress after an experimental operation that increases his I.Q. Although Charlie becomes brilliant, he is unhappy because he cannot shed his former personality and is tormented by his memories. In the end he begins to lose the mental powers he has gained." Shapiro. Fic for Youth. 3d edition

Keyser, Amber J.

The **way** back from broken; by Amber J. Keyser. Carolrhoda Lab, a division of Lerner Publishing Group 2015 216 p. (lb: alk. paper) $18.99

Grades: 9 10 11 12　　　　　　　　　　　**Fic**
1. Death -- Fiction　2. Grief -- Fiction　3. Canada -- Fiction　4. Camping -- Fiction　5. Wilderness survival -- Fiction　6. Brothers and sisters -- Fiction　7. Survival -- Fiction　8. Racially mixed people -- Fiction
ISBN 9781467775908

LC 2015001617

In this book, by Amber J. Keyser, "Rakmen Cannon's life is turning out to be one sucker punch after another. His baby sister died in his arms, his parents are on the verge of divorce, and he's flunking out of high school. The only place he fits in is with the other art therapy kids stuck in the basement of Promise House. . . . When he's shipped off to the Canadian wilderness with ten-year-old Jacey, another member of the support group, and her mom, his summer goes from bad to worse." (Publisher's note)

"With a cast of diverse and well-rounded characters, poignant relationships that never become schmaltzy, and a compelling high-stakes adventure, this vivid, moving exploration of grief and recovery hits all the right notes." Booklist

Kidd, Sue Monk

The **invention** of wings; a novel. Sue Monk Kidd. Viking 2014 384 p. (hardback) $27.95

Grades: 11 12 Adult   **Fic**

1. Historical fiction 2. Slavery -- Fiction 3. Feminism -- Fiction 4. Women's rights. -- Fiction 5. Antislavery movements -- Fiction

ISBN 0670024783; 9780670024780

LC 2013028185

In this novel, by Sue Monk Kidd , "Hetty 'Handful' Grimke, an urban slave in early nineteenth century Charleston, yearns for life beyond the . . . Grimke household. The Grimke's daughter, Sarah, has known from an early age she is meant to do something large in the world, but she is hemmed in by the limits imposed on women. . . . On Sarah's eleventh birthday, . . . she is given ownership of ten year old Handful, who is to be her handmaid." (Publisher's note)

★ The **secret** life of bees. Viking 2002 301p hardcover o.p. pa $14

Grades: 11 12 Adult   **Fic**

1. Girls 2. Adolescence 3. South Carolina 4. African Americans 5. Teenage girls -- Fiction 6. Race relations -- Fiction 7. South Carolina -- Fiction 8. African Americans -- Fiction 9. Maternal deprivation -- Fiction 10. United States -- Race relations 11. African American women -- Fiction

ISBN 0-14-200174-0 pa; 0-670-89460-5

LC 2001-26310

"It is 1964, in small-town Georgia peach country. Lily . . . {is the} daughter of T. Ray, a man of implacable rage. . . . He mocks her, he beats her. . . . On the day of Lily's fourteenth birthday, . . . Lily and {her black housekeeper} Rosaleen take a fateful walk into town so that Lily can buy herself a present and Rosaleen can register to vote. . . . Rosaleen, challenged, gets herself jailed for spitting on a white man's shoes. . . . The feisty Lily springs her and, loosed from their assorted prisons, they take off. . . . {They find themselves at} the idosyncratic compound of three black women bee-keepers, May, June, and August {Boatwright}." (Women's Rev Books)

"Lily is a wonderfully petulant and self-absorbed adolescent, and Kidd deftly portrays her sense of injustice as it expands to accommodate broader social evils." N Y Times Book Rev

Kiely, Brendan

★ **All** American Boys; by Jason Reynolds and Brendan Kiely. Simon & Schuster 2015 320 p. $17.99

Grades: 9 10 11 12   **Fic**

1. Racism -- Fiction 2. Teenagers -- Fiction 3. Race relations -- Fiction 4. Police brutality -- Fiction

ISBN 1481463330; 9781481463331

Coretta Scott King Author Award, Honor Book (2016)

In this book, by Jason Reynolds and Brendan Kiely, "two teens—one black, one white—grapple with the repercussions of a single violent act that leaves their school, their community, and, ultimately, the country bitterly divided by racial tension. . . . [It] shares the alternating perspectives of Rashad and Quinn as the complications from that single violent moment, the type taken from the headlines, unfold

and reverberate to highlight an unwelcome truth." (Publisher's note)

★ The **gospel** of winter; Brendan Kiely. Simon & Schuster 2014 304 p. $17.99

Grades: 9 10 11 12   **Fic**

1. Priests -- Fiction 2. Child sexual abuse -- Fiction

ISBN 1442484896; 9781442484894

This book, by Brendan Kiely, is "about the restorative power of truth and love after the trauma of abuse. As sixteen-year-old Aidan Donovan's fractured family disintegrates around him, he searches for solace in a few bumps of Adderall, his father's wet bar, and the attentions of his local priest, Father Greg--the only adult who actually listens to him. When Christmas hits, Aidan's world collapses in a crisis of trust when he recognizes the darkness of Father Greg's affections." (Publisher's note)

Kiely's gutsy debut addresses abuse in the Catholic Church. The year is 2001, the events of 9/11 are only two months old, and 16-year-old Aidan's family is falling apart. Aidan finds comfort in snorting lines of Adderall, swiping drinks from his father's wet bar, and forming a friendship with Father Greg of Most Precious Blood, the town's Catholic church. The scandal among the Boston archdiocese in early 2002 gets Aidan's town's attention, and when it does, Aidan's feelings of rage and denial and fear come to a head. This is challenging, thought-provoking material, presented in beautiful prose that explores the ways in which acts rendered in the name of love can both destroy and heal." (Booklist)

Kiem, Elizabeth

Dancer, daughter, traitor, spy; by Elizabeth Kiem. Soho Teen 2013 288 p. (alk. paper) $17.99

Grades: 9 10 11 12   **Fic**

1. Clairvoyance -- Fiction 2. Russian Americans -- Fiction 3. Soviet Union -- Foreign relations -- United States -- Fiction 4. Spies -- Fiction 5. Soviet Union -- Relations -- United States -- Fiction 6. United States -- Relations -- Soviet Union -- Fiction 7. Brooklyn (New York, N.Y.) -- History -- 20th century -- Fiction

ISBN 1616952636; 9781616952631

LC 2013006502

This book by Elizabeth Kiem is set in "the 'Russia by the Sea' neighborhood of Brighton Beach, Brooklyn. Marina and her father escape there following the State Psychiatric Directorate's institutionalization of her mother, Sveta, a celebrated Bolshoi dancer, who had a vision of a terrible past event the regime must keep hidden. . . . Marina and her father cannot shake the suspicion and danger Sveta's vision put them under." (Publishers Weekly)

"The disappearance of a star ballerina in Soviet Russia shatters the life of her daughter. Bright, 17-year-old Marya is the daughter of the Bolshoi's star ballerina and her scientist husband, and she's a dancer herself...The pacing is somewhat uneven, but there are enough twists to surprise and engage readers to the end. A compelling portrait of a young woman on the verge of adulthood, caught up in the domestic secrets of her parents and the enmity of two countries." (Kirkus)

Hider, seeker, secret keeper; Elizabeth Kiem. Soho Teen 2014 272 p. illustrations (hardback) $17.99

Grades: 9 10 11 12   **Fic**
  1. Mystery fiction 2. Ballerinas -- Fiction 3. Ballet dancing -- Fiction 4. Mystery and detective stories 5. Bolshoi Ballet Company -- Fiction
  ISBN 1616954124; 9781616954123
                                     LC 2014009577
Sequel to: Dancer, daughter, traitor, spy
In this young adult novel by Elizabeth Kiem, "Lana Du-kovskaya has spent her life in her mother, Marina's, shadow, and nowhere more so than at Russia's world-famous Bolshoi ballet, where Marina danced years ago. But when Daniela, Lana's friend and chief rival, is brutally attacked on the eve of a New York tour, Lana is given her coveted solo--an un-likely stroke of luck that makes Lana the chief suspect in the attack." (Publisher's note)
"Kiem's prose is infused with a grim urgency, both cold and vividly alive as Lana navigates the minefields of unfold-ing secrets and danger, love and fear. While technically a se-quel, readers need not have read the first book (though they will find spoilers). Those looking for the thrill of a wrongly accused heroine, infused with the passion of a dancer's dedi-cation to her craft, will enjoy this taut mystery." Booklist

Kiernan, Celine
  Into the grey; Celine Kiernan. First U.S. edition Candlewick Press 2014 304 p. $16.99
Grades: 9 10 11 12   **Fic**
  1. Ghost stories 2. Twins -- Fiction 3. Brothers -- Fiction 4. Twins 5. Horror tales
  ISBN 0763670618; 9780763670610
                                     LC 2013952836
In this novel by Celine Kiernan, "after their nan acci-dentally burns their home down, twin brothers Pat and Dom must move with their parents and baby sister to the seaside cottage they've summered in, now made desolate by the winter wind. It's there that the ghost appears — a strange boy who cries black tears and fears a bad man, a soldier, who is chasing him . . . . With white-knuckle pacing and a deft portrayal of family relationships, Celine Kiernan offers a taut psychological thriller that is sure to haunt readers long after the last page is turned." (Publisher's note)
"At its best it is confident, pungent, and poetic. Fam-ily love, loyalty, and protectiveness are palpable in a well-drawn cast of characters, and the pace is frequently galva-nized with energetic drama and dialogue pierced with Irish dialect." Horn Book

Kinch, Michael P.
  The **blending** time; [by] Michael Kinch. Flux 2010 254p pa $9.95
Grades: 10 11 12   **Fic**
  1. Science fiction 2. Africa -- Fiction 3. Violence -- Fiction
  ISBN 978-0-7387-2067-8
                                     LC 2010-24149
In the harsh world of 2069, ravaged by plagues and en-vironmental disasters, friends Jaym, Reya, and D'Shay are chosen to help repopulate Africa as their mandatory Global Alliance work, but civil war and mercenaries opposed

to the Blending Program separate them and threaten their very lives.
"Determinedly multiethnic, fast-paced, and with plenti-ful gore and violence, the book will draw reluctant readers who enjoy action and adventure." Booklist

The **fires** of New SUN; a Blending time novel. Michael Kinch. Flux 2012 275 p. (Blending time) $9.95
Grades: 9 10 11 12   **Fic**
  1. Africa -- Fiction 2. Dystopian fiction 3. Deserts -- Fiction 4. Science fiction 5. Survival -- Fiction 6. Violence -- Fiction 7. Friendship -- Fiction
  ISBN 0738730769; 9780738730769
                                     LC 2011035527
This dystopian thriller novel, by Michael Kinch, is set "in the harsh African desert. . . . Jaym and D'Shay . . . have helped dozens of Nswibe refugees cross the African desert. . . . They've finally reunited with their friend, Reya, and found safe haven at a New SUN outpost, a cavern fortress hidden in the Blue Mountains. But their troubles are just beginning. . . . As a massive [renegade] attack looms, the three friends are quickly drawn into a deadly battle." (Publisher's note)

The **rebels** of New SUN; a Blending time novel. Michael Kinch. Flux 2013 288 p. (Blending time) $9.99
Grades: 9 10 11 12   **Fic**
  1. Africa -- Fiction 2. Dystopian fiction 3. Deserts -- Fiction 4. Science fiction 5. Survival -- Fiction 6. Violence -- Fiction 7. Friendship -- Fiction
  ISBN 073873151X; 9780738731513
                                     LC 2012028409
This dystopian thriller novel, by Michael Kinch, is book three of the "Blending Time" series. "Before the 'gades se-cure the savannah and wipe out the New SUN resistance, Reya, D'Shay, Jaym, and a handful of other rebels launch a daring mission to infiltrate . . . Chewena's capital city. . . . To free the country from GlobeTran's . . . control, they seek out allies and information that could help the resistance . . . return power to the people of Africa." (Publisher's note)

Kincy, Karen
  Other. Flux 2010 326p pa $9.95
Grades: 9 10 11 12   **Fic**
  1. Homicide -- Fiction 2. Supernatural -- Fiction 3. Self-acceptance -- Fiction 4. Washington (State) -- Fiction
  ISBN 978-0-7387-1919-1
                                     LC 2010-5297
Gwen Williams is like any seventeen-year-old except that she is a shapeshifter living in Klikamuks, Washing-ton, where not everyone tolerates "Others" like Gwen, but when someone begins killing Others she must try to em-brace her true self and find the killer before she becomes the next victim.
"The emotional turmoil of the characters is evident and will appeal to readers who have felt misunderstood or as if they don't belong—teenagers." SLJ

Kindl, Patrice

Keeping the castle; a tale of romance, riches, and real estate. by Patrice Kindl. Viking Childrens Books 2012 261 p. $16.99; (hardcover) $16.99

Grades: 7 8 9 10 11 **Fic**

1. Love stories 2. Regency novels 3. Marriage -- Fiction 4. Castles -- Fiction 5. Courtship -- Fiction 6. Social classes -- Fiction 7. Great Britain -- History -- 1789-1820 -- Fiction 8. England -- Social life and customs -- 19th century -- Fiction

ISBN 0670014389; 9780670014385

LC 2011033185

In this book, "[s]eventeen-year-old Althea Crawley is . . . on a quest to marry rich so that she may secure the family's only inheritance, a dilapidated castle on the edge of the North Sea. . . . Marriage prospects in tiny Lesser Hoo are slim, to say the least, until dashing and wealthy Lord Boring arrives on the scene. Matters are further complicated by a revolving cast of potential suitors, including Lord Boring's cousin, Mr. Fredericks." (Booklist)

A **school** for brides; a story of maidens, mystery, and matrimony. by Patrice Kindl. Viking, an imprint of Penguin Group (USA) LLC 2015 272 p. (hardcover) $17.99

Grades: 7 8 9 10 **Fic**

1. School stories 2. Marriage -- Fiction 3. Great Britain -- History -- 1714-1837 -- Fiction 4. Schools -- Fiction 5. Courtship -- Fiction 6. Boarding schools -- Fiction 7. Mystery and detective stories 8. Great Britain -- History -- 1789-1820 -- Fiction 9. England -- Social life and customs -- 19th century -- Fiction

ISBN 9780670786084

LC 2014028087

Sequel to: Keeping the castle

In this companion novel to "Keeping the Castle," also written by Patrice Kindl, "[t]he Winthrop Hopkins Female Academy of Lesser Hoo, Yorkshire, has one goal: to train its students in the feminine arts with an eye toward getting them married off. This year, there are five girls of marriageable age. There's only one problem: the school is in the middle of nowhere, and there are no men." (Publisher's note)

"This affectionate homage to the genre delivers what's missing: a witty, intelligent plot whose characters—complex, conniving, hypocritical, and hilarious—seek happiness within an ordered world. This airy soufflé of a tale, garnished with quirky charm, is an unmitigated delight from start to finish." Kirkus

King, A. S. (Amy Sarig), 1970-

★ **Ask** the passengers; a novel. by A.S. King. Little, Brown 2012 304 p. (hardcover) $17.99

Grades: 9 10 11 12 **Fic**

1. Moving -- Fiction 2. Identity -- Fiction 3. Love stories 4. Love -- Fiction 5. Gossip -- Fiction 6. Schools -- Fiction 7. Lesbians -- Fiction 8. Prejudices -- Fiction 9. High schools -- Fiction 10. Family problems -- Fiction

ISBN 0316194689; 9780316194686

LC 2011053207

This book by A.S. King follows teenage protagonist Astrid, "her closeted BFF, Kristina, and Dee, a star hockey player she met while working for a local catering company. Sparks fly between Astrid and Dee, causing Astrid to feel even more distanced and confused. . . . She's in love with Dee, but she's not sure if she's a lesbian. She's ignoring all of the labels and focusing on what she feels." (Kirkus Reviews)

★ **Everybody** sees the ants; by A.S. King. Little, Brown 2011 282p. $17.99; ebook $9.99

Grades: 9 10 11 12 **Fic**

1. Family -- Fiction 2. Domestic relations 3. Teenagers -- Fiction 4. Dreams -- Fiction 5. Arizona -- Fiction 6. Bullies -- Fiction 7. Family life -- Fiction 8. Grandfathers -- Fiction 9. Missing persons -- Fiction 10. Vietnam War, 1961-1975 -- Fiction

ISBN 978-0-316-12928-2; 978-0-316-19181-4 ebook; 9780316129275

LC 2010049434

Overburdened by his parents' bickering and a bully's attacks, fifteen-year-old Lucky Linderman begins dreaming of being with his grandfather, who went missing during the Vietnam War, but during a visit to Arizona, his aunt and uncle and their beautiful neighbor, Ginny, help him find a new perspective.

"Blending magic and realism, this is a subtly written, profoundly honest novel about a kid falling through the cracks and pulling himself back up." Booklist

★ **Glory** O'Brien's history of the future; a novel. by A.S. King. Little, Brown & Co. 2014 320 p. (hardcover) $18

Grades: 9 10 11 12 **Fic**

1. Fantasy fiction 2. Clairvoyance -- Fiction 3. Suicide -- Fiction 4. Friendship -- Fiction 5. Photography -- Fiction 6. Best friends -- Fiction 7. Fathers and daughters -- Fiction 8. Eccentrics and eccentricities -- Fiction

ISBN 0316222720; 9780316222723

LC 2013041670

In this novel, the main character Glory "begins to experience an astonishing new power to see a person's infinite past and future. From ancient ancestors to many generations forward, Glory is bombarded with visions--and what she sees ahead of her is terrifying. . . . Glory makes it her mission to record everything she sees, hoping her notes will somehow make a difference. . . . She'll do anything to make sure this one doesn't come to pass." (Publisher's note)

"Imbuing Glory's narrative with a graceful, sometimes dissonant combination of anger, ambivalence, and hopefulness that resists tidy resolution, award-winning King presents another powerful, moving, and compellingly complex coming-of-age story." Booklist

★ **I** crawl through it; by A.S. King. Little, Brown & Co. 2015 336 p. (hardcover) $18 **Fic**

1. Teenagers -- Fiction 2. Psychological fiction 3. Reality -- Fiction

ISBN 9780316334099

LC 2014036896

In this surrealist novel, by A. S. King, "four teenagers are on the verge of exploding. The anxieties they face at every turn have nearly pushed them to the point of surrender: senseless high-stakes testing, the lingering damage of past trauma, the buried grief and guilt of tragic loss. . . . So they will lie. They will split in two. They will turn inside out. They will even build an invisible helicopter to fly themselves far away . . . but nothing releases the pressure." (Publisher's note)

"Characters unfold like riddles before the reader, while King uses magical realism and a motif of standardized testing to emphasize the flaw in obtaining answers without confronting reality's hard questions. Beautiful prose, poetry, and surreal imagery combine for an utterly original story that urges readers to question, love, and believe—or risk explosion." Booklist

★ **Please** ignore Vera Dietz. Alfred A. Knopf 2010 326p $16.99; lib bdg $19.99; ebook $16.99
Grades: 9 10 11 12 **Fic**
1. Death -- Fiction 2. Friendship -- Fiction
ISBN 978-0-375-86586-2; 978-0-375-96586-9 lib bdg; 978-0-375-89617-0 ebook
LC 2010-12730
A Michael L. Printz honor book, 2011

When her best friend, whom she secretly loves, betrays her and then dies under mysterious circumstances, high school senior Vera Dietz struggles with secrets that could help clear his name.

This "is a gut-wrenching tale about family, friendship, destiny, the meaning of words, and self-discovery." Voice Youth Advocates

★ **Reality** Boy; A.S. King. Little, Brown and Co. 2013 368 p. $18
Grades: 10 11 12 **Fic**
1. Special education -- Fiction 2. Reality television programs -- Fiction 3. Fame -- Fiction 4. Family problems -- Fiction 5. Emotional problems -- Fiction 6. Dating (Social customs) -- Fiction 7. Self-actualization (Psychology) -- Fiction
ISBN 0316222704; 9780316222709
LC 2012048432
Author A. S. King's book looks at "a boy saddled with the nickname the Crapper because of his infamous behavior at age five on a reality show, Network Nanny. Now almost 17, Gerald Faust is ostracized by his peers, barely keeping his violent urges at bay, and grateful for his spot in special ed because" it is a safe place for him. Although "the Network Nanny episodes about Gerald's family framed him as the problem child among his siblings, the truth was more disturbing, as King shows in flashbacks." (Publishers Weekly)

"When Gerald was five, TV's Network Nanny came to his house to help solve his behavior problems. Now nearly seventeen, Gerald bears the emotional scars of having his deeply dysfunctional childhood nationally televised. When Gerald meets Hannah, he discovers he's not the only one with a messed-up family. As always, King's societal critique is spot-on and scathing." (Horn Book)

King, Laurie R.
The **beekeeper's** apprentice, or, on the segregation of the queen; Laurie R. King. Picador/Thomas Dunne Books 2007 xxi, 346p (Mary Russell and Sherlock Holmes mysteries) pa $14

Grades: 11 12 Adult **Fic**
1. Mystery fiction 2. Great Britain -- Fiction 3. Holmes, Sherlock (Fictional character)
ISBN 978-0-312-42736-8
First published 1994 by St. Martin's Press

Chance meeting with a Sussex beekeeper turns into a pivotal, personal transformation when fifteen-year-old Mary Russell discovers that the beekeeper is the reclusive, retired detective Sherlock Holmes, who soon takes on the role of mentor and teacher.

"A wonderfully original and entertaining story that is funny, heartwarming, and full of intrigue. . . . Holmes fans, history buffs, lovers of humor and adventure, and mystery devotees will all find King's book absorbing from beginning to end." Booklist
Other titles in this series are:
A monstrous regiment of women (1995)
A letter of Mary (1997)
The moor (1998)
O Jerusalem (1999)
Justice Hall (2002)
The game (2004)
Locked rooms (2005)
The language of bees (2009)
The god of the hive (2010)
Pirate king (2011)
Garment of shadows (2012)
Dreaming spies (2015)
The murder of Mary Russell (2016)

King, Stephen, 1947-
Carrie. Doubleday 1974 199p $32.50
Grades: 11 12 Adult **Fic**
1. Horror fiction 2. Maine -- Fiction 3. Psychokinesis -- Fiction
ISBN 0-385-08695-4
"A terrifying treat for both horror and parapsychology fans." SLJ

"An introverted girl with remarkable powers of telekinesis faces the horrors of teenage life and unleashes a few horrors of her own when she attends the high school prom." (Publisher's note)

Firestarter. Viking 1980 428p hardcover o.p. pa $7.99
Grades: Adult **Fic**
1. Horror fiction 2. Psychokinesis -- Fiction
ISBN 0-670-31541-9; 0-451-16780-5 pa
LC 80-14793
"This is your advanced post-Watergate cynical American thriller with some eerie parapsychological twists, and it's been done so distinctively well that we'd better talk about genius rather than genre." Quill Quire

The **girl** who loved Tom Gordon; a novel. Scribner 1999 224p $16.95
Grades: 11 12 Adult **Fic**
1. Fear 2. Bears 3. Girls 4. Wilderness survival 5. Wilderness survival -- Fiction
ISBN 0-684-86762-1
LC 99-13109

"Nine-year-old Trisha McFarland is hopelessly lost in the woods. Out for a morning hike with her bickering mother and brother, she runs off to relieve herself and discovers she can't find her way back to the path. . . . Trisha wanders for a week in the mosquito-infested forest with nothing but her wits, her Walkman and the pitching prowess of her hero, the dreamy Red Sox reliever Tom Gordon, to guide her. As Trisha fights to stay alive, King demonstrates his empathy for the inner lives of children and an outdoorsman's knowledge of the edible wild flora of Maine." N Y Times Book Rev

Kingsolver, Barbara

★ The **bean** trees; a novel. 10th anniversary ed; HarperFlamingo 1997 261p $19.95; pa $7.99
Grades: 11 12 Adult   Fic
1. Arizona -- Fiction
ISBN 0-06-017579-6; 0-06-109731-4 pa
LC 97-2691
A reissue of the title first published 1988
In this novel, "Taylor Greer, a poor, young woman, flees her Kentucky home and heads west. . . . While passing through Oklahoma, she becomes responsible for a two-year-old Cherokee girl. The two continue on the road. When they roll off the highway in Tucson, Taylor and the child, whom she has named Turtle, . . . meet Mattie, a widow who runs Jesus Is Lord Used Tires and is active in the sanctuary movement on the side." Ms
Followed by Pigs in heaven (1993)

★ The **poisonwood** Bible; a novel. HarperFlamingo 1998 546p $26; pa $16.99
Grades: 11 12 Adult   Fic
1. Congo (Republic) -- Fiction 2. Christian missionaries -- Fiction
ISBN 0-06-017540-0; 0-06-157707-3 pa
LC 98-19901
"Buttressing her suspenseful chronicle with authentic background detail, Kingsolver's narrative is at once a compelling family saga and an astute look at Western imperialism in Africa." Publ Wkly

Kinsella, Sophie

Finding Audrey; Sophie Kinsella. Delacorte Press 2015 288 p. (trade hardcover) $18.99
Grades: 9 10 11 12   Fic
1. Anxiety -- Fiction 2. Friendship -- Fiction 3. Anxiety disorders -- Fiction
ISBN 9780553536515; 0553536516
LC 2014048476
In this novel by Sophie Kinsella, "an anxiety disorder disrupts fourteen-year-old Audrey's daily life. She has been making slow but steady progress with Dr. Sarah, but when Audrey meets Linus, her brother's gaming teammate, she is energized. She connects with him. Audrey can talk through her fears with Linus in a way she's never been able to do with anyone before. As their friendship deepens and her recovery gains momentum, a sweet romantic connection develops." (Publishers Weekly)
"A deep and sensitive portrayal of a British teen's recovery from a traumatic experience. Expect requests!" SLJ

Kinsella, W. P.

Shoeless Joe. Houghton Mifflin 1982 265p hardcover o.p. pa $13.95
Grades: 9 10 11 12 Adult   Fic
1. Fantasy fiction 2. Baseball -- Fiction
ISBN 0-395-32047-X; 0-395-95773-7 pa
LC 81-19196
In this fantasy, Iowan farmer Ray Kinsella "hears a voice say 'If you build it, he will come,' and knows that 'it' refers to a baseball park and 'he' to Shoeless Joe Jackson. . . . Ray builds his magic stadium and while watching Shoeless Joe and others play ball, hears the voice again, this time saying, 'Ease his pain.' The mission clearly means kidnapping J. D. Salinger and taking him to Fenway Park for a Red Sox game. Ray succeeds and Salinger . . . joins Ray on a further quest. Their odyssey culminates back at home plate in Iowa." Quill Quire

Kirby, Jessi

Golden; Jessi Kirby. 1st ed. Simon & Schuster Books for Young Readers 2013 288 p. (hardcover) $16.99
Grades: 7 8 9 10 11 12   Fic
1. Love stories 2. Mystery fiction 3. Diaries -- Fiction 4. Love -- Fiction 5. Choice -- Fiction 6. Family problems -- Fiction 7. Mothers and daughters -- Fiction
ISBN 1442452161; 9781442452169; 9781442452183; 9781442452251
LC 2012042216
In this novel, by Jessi Kirby, "seventeen-year-old Parker Frost has never taken the road less traveled. . . . Julianna Farnetti and Shane Cruz are remembered as the golden couple of Summit Lakes High . . . but Julianna's journal tells . . . the secrets that were swept away with her the night that Shane's jeep plunged into an icy river. . . . Reading Julianna's journal gives Parker . . . reasons to question what really happened the night of the accident." (Publisher's note)
"Kirby's . . . third novel is inspirational and contemplative in its mood and tone. Multifaceted characters and dashes of mystery and romance come together in a successful mediation on the value of taking an active role in one's life." Pub Wkly

Moonglass. Simon & Schuster Books for Young Readers 2011 232p $16.99; ebook $9.99
Grades: 8 9 10 11 12   Fic
1. Guilt -- Fiction 2. Moving -- Fiction 3. Beaches -- Fiction 4. Suicide -- Fiction 5. California -- Fiction 6. Father-daughter relationship -- Fiction
ISBN 978-1-4424-1694-9; 1-4424-1694-7; 978-1-4424-1696-3 ebook; 1-4424-1696-3 ebook
LC 2010-37389
At age seven, Anna watched her mother walk into the surf and drown, but nine years later, when she moves with her father to the beach where her parents fell in love, she joins the cross-country team, makes new friends, and faces her guilt.
"Kirby creates a cast of sympathetic and credible characters, each imperfect but well intentioned. There's action as well as introspection here." Booklist

Kirkpatrick, Katherine

Between two worlds; by Katherine Kirkpatrick.
Wendy Lamb Books, an imprint of Random House
Children's Books 2014 304 p. (trade) $16.99

Grades: 10 11 12   **Fic**

1. Inuit -- Fiction 2. Arctic regions -- Exploration --
Fiction 3. Eskimos -- Fiction

ISBN 0385740476; 9780375872211; 9780375989476;
9780385740470

LC 2013014735

In this book, by Katherine Kirkpatrick, "on the treeless
shores of Itta, Greenland, as far north as humans can settle,
sixteen-year-old Inuit Billy Bah spots a ship far out among
the icebergs on the bay. . . . The ship carries provisions for
Robert E. Peary, who is making an expedition to the North
Pole. As a child, Billy Bah spent a year in America with
Peary's family. . . . Winter comes on fast, and when the
ship gets caught in the ice, Billy Bah sets out to find Peary."
(Publisher's note)

"In 1900, sixteen-year-old Greenland Inuit girl Billy Bah
sets out to rescue Lieutenant Peary, his ship stuck in the ice
during a polar expedition. Though torn between cultures,
having spent a year with Peary's family in America, Billy
Bah ultimately feels she must risk her life to find him. A
compelling tale with enthralling details of the stark, beautiful Greenland landscape."

Kittredge, Caitlin

The **Iron** Thorn. Delacorte Press 2011 493p
(Iron Codex) $17.99; lib bdg $20.99

Grades: 7 8 9 10   **Fic**

1. Fantasy fiction

ISBN 0-385-73829-3; 0-385-90720-6 lib bdg; 978-0-
385-73829-3; 978-0-385-90720-0 lib bdg

LC 2010-00972

In an alternate 1950s, mechanically gifted fifteen-year-
old Aoife Grayson, whose family has a history of going mad
at sixteen, must leave the totalitarian city of Lovecraft and
venture into the world of magic to solve the mystery of her
brother's disappearance and the mysteries surrounding her
father and the Land of Thorn.

"Steampunk fans will delight in this first title in the sure-
to-be-popular Iron Codex series. . . . There's plenty of tame
but satisfying romance, too, and plot twists galore. Aoife is a
caustic-tongued, feisty, and independent young woman, with
plenty of nerve and courage." Booklist

Kizer, Amber

A **matter** of days; Amber Kizer. 1st ed. Delacorte Press 2013 288 p. (ebook) $50.97; (hard-
cover) $16.99; (library) $19.99

Grades: 7 8 9 10   **Fic**

1. Apocalyptic fiction 2. Voyages and travels 3.
Science fiction 4. Survival -- Fiction 5. Epidemics
-- Fiction 6. Virus diseases -- Fiction 7. Brothers and
sisters -- Fiction

ISBN 0385908040; 9780375898259; 9780385739733;
9780385908047

LC 2012012200

In this book, "Nadia and Rabbit's military doctor uncle,
Bean, visited them and insisted on injecting them with a vaccine for a 'new bug.' Not long afterward, the disease XRD

TB . . . starts ravaging the world, and 16-year-old Nadia and
11-year-old Rabbit are the only survivors in their entire town.
With the assorted survival gear their uncle ordered for them,
they attempt to make their way from their Seattle suburb to
their grandfather in West Virginia." (Publishers Weekly)

"This post-apocalyptic tale is particularly frightening as
it doesn't take place in some distant, imagined future. A solid, realistically imagined survival tale with a strong female
protagonist." Kirkus

Klass, David

★ **You** don't know me; a novel. Foster Bks.
2001 262p $17

Grades: 7 8 9 10   **Fic**

1. School stories 2. Child abuse -- Fiction

ISBN 0-374-38706-0

LC 00-22709

Fourteen-year-old John creates alternative realities in his
mind as he tries to deal with his mother's abusive boyfriend,
his crush on a beautiful, but shallow classmate and other
problems at school

"Klass is effective with John's deliberately distanced
voice, his constant dancing with and away from reality, . . .
. and his brittle and even dorky defenses, and the rising tension is suspenseful." Bull Cent Child Books

Klass, Sheila Solomon

Soldier's secret; the story of Deborah Sampson.
Henry Holt 2009 215p $17.95

Grades: 6 7 8 9 10   **Fic**

1. Soldiers 2. Memoirists 3. Soldiers -- Fiction 4.
United States -- History -- 1775-1783, Revolution --
Fiction

ISBN 978-0-8050-8200-5; 0-8050-8200-X

LC 2008-36783

During the Revolutionary War, a young woman named
Deborah Sampson disguises herself as a man in order to
serve in the Continental Army.

In this novel, Sampson "is strong, brave, and witty. .
. . Klass doesn't shy away from the horrors of battle; she
also is blunt regarding details young readers will wonder
about, like how Sampson dealt with bathing, urination, and
menstruation. . . . Sampson's romantic yearnings for a fellow soldier . . . . is given just the right notes or restraint and
realism." Booklist

Klause, Annette Curtis

★ **Blood** and chocolate. Delacorte Press 1997
264p hardcover o.p. pa $6.50

Grades: 7 8 9 10   **Fic**

1. Horror fiction 2. Werewolves -- Fiction

ISBN 0-385-32305-0; 0-440-22668-6 pa

LC 96-35247

Having fallen for a human boy, a beautiful teenage
werewolf must battle both her packmates and the fear of the
townspeople to decide where she belongs and with whom

"Klause's imagery is magnetic, and her language fierce,
rich, and beautiful. . . . Passion and philosophy dovetail
superbly in this powerful, unforgettable novel for mature
teens." Booklist

★ The **silver** kiss. Delacorte Press 1990 198p hardcover o.p. pa $5.99
Grades: 8 9 10 11 12   **Fic**
    1. Death -- Fiction 2. Vampires -- Fiction
    ISBN 0-385-30160-X; 0-440-21346-0 pa
                                            LC 89-48880
"There's inherent romantic appeal in the vampire legend, and Klause weaves all the gory details into a poignant love story that becomes both sensuous and suspenseful." Booklist

Klavan, Andrew
    MindWar; a novel. Andrew Klavan. Thomas Nelson, Inc. 2014 352 p. (The MindWar Trilogy) (hardback) $15.99
Grades: 7 8 9 10   **Fic**
    1. Teenagers -- Fiction 2. Video games -- Fiction 3. Virtual reality -- Fiction 4. Video gamers -- Fiction 5. Undercover operations -- Fiction 6. Cyberterrorism -- Prevention -- Fiction
    ISBN 1401688926; 9781401688929
                                            LC 2013050887
In this novel by Andrew Klaven "high school football star Rick Dial . . . immerses himself in video games after a car accident leaves his legs painfully useless. The teen is recruited to fight real life baddies. . . a virtual reality world created by Kurodar, a terrorist out to destroy the free world. He must fight for his life, because what happens to you in this virtual world affects your body in real life." (School Library Journal)
    "Edgar Award–winning Klavan's well-orchestrated fantasy thriller features brisk but compelling character development, a touch of wry humor, Christian sensitivity that doesn't proselytize, and an imaginative mix of gaming action with real-life stakes. With just the right cliff-hanger ending, this trilogy opener shows promise." Booklist
    Mind War
    Other titles in this series are:
    Hostage Run (2015)

Klein, Lisa M.
    Cate of the Lost Colony; by Lisa Klein. Bloomsbury 2010 329p $16.99
Grades: 8 9 10 11 12   **Fic**
    1. Poets 2. Queens 3. Authors 4. Explorers 5. Historians 6. Courtiers 7. Travel writers 8. Orphans -- Fiction 9. Lumbee Indians -- Fiction 10. Roanoke Island (N.C.) -- History -- Fiction 11. Great Britain -- History -- 1485-1603, Tudors -- Fiction
    ISBN 978-1-59990-507-5; 1-59990-507-8
                                            LC 2010-8299
When her dalliance with Sir Walter Ralegh is discovered by Queen Elizabeth in 1587, lady-in-waiting Catherine Archer is banished to the struggling colony of Roanoke, where she and the other English settlers must rely on a Croatoan Indian for their survival. Includes author's note on the mystery surrounding the Lost Colony.
    "This robust, convincing portrait of the Elizabethan world with complex, rounded characters wraps an intriguingly plausible solution to the 'lost colony' mystery inside a compelling love story of subtle thematic depth." Kirkus
    Includes bibliographical references

Ophelia. Bloomsbury Children's Books 2006 328p $16.95
Grades: 9 10 11 12   **Fic**
    1. Poets 2. Authors 3. Dramatists 4. Princes -- Fiction 5. Homicide -- Fiction
    ISBN 978-1-58234-801-8; 1-58234-801-4
                                            LC 2005-32601
In a story based on Shakespeare's Hamlet, Ophelia tells of her life in the court at Elsinore, her love for Prince Hamlet, and her escape from the violence in Denmark.
    "Teens need not be familiar with Shakespeare's original to enjoy this fresh take—with the added romance and a strong heroine at its center." Publ Wkly

Kluger, Steve
    My most excellent year; a novel of love, Mary Poppins, & Fenway Park. Dial Books 2008 403p $16.99; pa $8.99
Grades: 8 9 10 11 12   **Fic**
    1. Friendship -- Fiction 2. Boston (Mass.) -- Fiction
    ISBN 978-0-8037-3227-8; 0-8037-3227-9; 978-0-14-241343-2 pa; 0-14-2413437 pa
                                            LC 2007-26651
"Three bright and funny Brookline, MA, eleventh graders look back on their most excellent year—ninth grade—for a school report. Told in alternating chapters by each of them, this enchanting, life-affirming coming-of-age story unfolds through instant messages, emails, memos, diary entries, and letters. . . . This is a rich and humorous novel for older readers." SLJ

Knowles, Jo
    Jumping off swings; [by] Jo Knowles. Candlewick Press 2009 230p $16.99
Grades: 10 11 12   **Fic**
    1. Pregnancy -- Fiction
    ISBN 0-7636-3949-4; 978-0-7636-3949-5
                                            LC 2009-4587
When Josh "leads Ellie to the back seat of his van after a party, Ellie gets pregnant and Josh reacts with shame and heartbreak, while their confidantes, Caleb and Corinne grapple with their own complex emotions." (Publisher's note) "Grades seven to ten." (Bull Cent Child Books)
    "With so many protagonists in the mix, it is no small feat that each character is fully developed and multidimensional—there are no villains or heroes here, only kids groping their way through a desperate situation. . . . [This is] a moving tale with a realistically unresolved ending." Kirkus

★ **Living** with Jackie Chan; by Jo Knowles. Candlewick Press 2013 384 p. $16.99
Grades: 10 11 12   **Fic**
    1. Teenage fathers 2. Guilt -- Fiction 3. Uncles -- Fiction
    ISBN 0763662801; 9780763662806
                                            LC 2012955157
In this book, by Jo Knowles, "after fathering a baby, a teenager moves in with his karate-loving uncle and tries to come to terms with his guilt — and find a way to forgive. Readers first met Josh in 'Jumping Off Swings' which told the story of four high school students and how one pregnancy changed all of their lives. In this companion book,

they follow Josh as he tries to come to terms with what happened." (Publisher's note)

"Overcome with guilt after getting Ellie pregnant (Jumping Off Swings), Josh moves in with his karate-obsessed, incessantly cheerful uncle. He starts senior year at a new school, attends his uncle's karate classes, and makes a new friend-who-might-be-more. Josh is a sensitive guy whose pain is palpable; readers will root for him as he--slowly--conquers the demons of his past." (Horn Book)

Read between the lines; Jo Knowles. Candlewick Press 2015 336 p. $16.99

Grades: 9 10 11 12   **Fic**
1. School stories 2. Teenagers -- Fiction 3. High schools 4. Cities and towns 5. High school students 6. High school teachers
ISBN 0763663875; 9780763663872
LC 2014944796

This novel by Jo Knowles "follows nine teens and one teacher through a seemingly ordinary day. Thanks to a bully in gym class, unpopular Nate suffers a broken finger. Claire envisions herself sitting in an artsy café, filling a journal, but fate has other plans. One cheerleader dates a closeted basketball star; another questions just how, as a 'big girl,' she fits in. These voices and others speak loud and clear about the complex dance that is life in a small town." (Publisher's note)

"Issues of absent parents, conflicted sexuality, eating disorders, and various forms of abuse are dealt with succinctly but tenderly, and some nuances are subtle enough that multiple levels of reading are possible, with a twist at the end so understated you may miss it. This is likely to speak to any teenager in a stage of transition." Booklist

See you at Harry's; Jo Knowles. 1st ed. Candlewick Press 2012 310 p. $16.99

Grades: 6 7 8 9 10 11   **Fic**
1. Siblings -- Fiction 2. Bereavement -- Fiction 3. Restaurants -- Fiction 4. Gay teenagers -- Fiction 5. Family 6. Grief -- Fiction 7. Family life -- Fiction 8. Homosexuality -- Fiction 9. Family problems -- Fiction 10. Brothers and sisters -- Fiction
ISBN 9780763654078
LC 2011018619

In this children's novel, "seventh grader Fern . . . relates the . . . tragedies of her family. Her high-school-freshman older brother Holden has come to the place in his life where he's acknowledged that he's gay. . . . Fern offers him support and love. . . . And then there's 3-year-old Charlie, always messy, often annoying, but deeply loved. Fern's busy, distracted parents leave all of the kids wanting for more attention--until a tragic accident tears the family apart." (Kirkus Reviews)

Knowles, John
★ A **separate** peace. Scribner Classics 1996 204p $20; pa $11

Grades: 11 12 Adult   **Fic**
1. School stories 2. Friendship -- Fiction
ISBN 0-684-83366-2; 0-7432-5397-3 pa
LC 96-25844
A reissue of the title published 1960 by Macmillan

"Gene Forrester looks back on his school days, spent in a New England town just before World War II. He both admires and envies his close friend and roommate, Finny, who is a natural athlete, in contrast to Gene's special competence as a scholar. When Finny suffers a crippling accident, Gene must face his own involvement in it." Shapiro. Fic for Youth. 3d edition

Knox, Elizabeth
Dreamhunter; book one of the Dreamhunter duet. Farrar, Straus & Giroux 2006 365p (Dreamhunter duet) $19; pa $8.99

Grades: 7 8 9 10   **Fic**
1. Fantasy fiction 2. Dreams -- Fiction
ISBN 0-374-31853-0; 0-312-53571-6 pa
LC 2005-46366
First published 2005 in the United Kingdom

In a world where select people can enter "The Place" and find dreams of every kind to share with others for a fee, a fifteen-year-old girl is training to be a dreamhunter when her father disappears, leaving her to carry on his mysterious mission. "Grades nine to twelve." (Bull Cent Child Books)

This first of a two-book series is "a highly original exploration of the idea of a collective unconscious, mixed with imagery from the raising of Lazarus and with the brave, dark qualities of the psyche of an adolescent female." Horn Book Guide

Followed by Dreamquake (2007)

Dreamquake; book two of the Dreamhunter duet. Farrar, Straus & Giroux 2007 449p map (Dreamhunter duet) $19

Grades: 7 8 9 10   **Fic**
1. Fantasy fiction 2. Dreams -- Fiction
ISBN 978-0-374-31854-3; 0-374-31854-9
LC 2006-48109
Sequel to Dreamhunter
Michael L. Printz Award honor book, 2008

Aided by her family and her creation, Nown, Laura investigates the powerful Regulatory Body's involvement in mysterious disappearances and activities and learns, in the process, the true nature of the Place in which dreams are found.

The author's "haunting, invigorating storytelling will leave readers eager to return to its puzzles—and to reap its rewards." Booklist

Mortal fire; by Elizabeth Knox. 1st ed. Frances Foster Books 2013 448 p. (hardcover) $17.99

Grades: 7 8 9 10 11   **Fic**
1. Fantasy fiction 2. Paranormal fiction 3. Magic -- Fiction 4. Identity -- Fiction 5. Stepbrothers -- Fiction 6. Islands of the Pacific -- Fiction
ISBN 0374388296; 9780374388294
LC 2012040872

This novel, set in a fictional area of New Zealand, stars Canny, a "16-year-old Ma'eu, taciturn, antisocial, and exceptionally gifted in math." She has what she calls "Extra," an "ethereal script that Canny alone can see, attached to plants, buildings, or nothing at all." When she and friends "come upon a valley dense with the Extra, Canny realizes that there is more to her visions than her own oddness—

there are people, the Zarenes, whose existence is interwoven with this magical language." (Publishers Weekly)

Knudsen, Michelle

Evil librarian; Michelle Knudsen. First edition Candlewick Press 2014 352 p. $16.99

Grades: 9 10 11   **Fic**

1. Fantasy fiction 2. Demonology -- Fiction 3. Friendship -- Fiction 4. Librarians -- Fiction 5. Schools -- Fiction 6. Best friends -- Fiction 7. High schools -- Fiction

ISBN 0763660388; 9780763660383

LC 2013957277

In this book, "when Cynthia Rothschild's best friend, Annie, falls head over heels for the new high-school librarian, Cyn can totally see why. He's really young and super cute and thinks Annie would make an excellent library monitor. But after meeting Mr. Gabriel, Cyn realizes something isn't quite right. Maybe it's the creepy look in the librarian's eyes, or the weird feeling Cyn gets whenever she's around him. Before long Cyn realizes that Mr. Gabriel is, in fact . . . a demon." (Publisher's note)

"There's plenty to like here: a budding will-they-won't-they romance, demonic possession, musical theater references, and more. Knudsen keeps the terror well-tempered with plenty of hilarious situational comedy and touches of the absurd." Booklist

Knutsson, Catherine

Shadows cast by stars; Catherine Knutsson. 1st ed. Atheneum Books for Young Readers 2012 456 p. (hardcover) $17.99; (paperback) $9.99

Grades: 7 8 9 10   **Fic**

1. Blood 2. Science fiction 3. Plague -- Fiction 4. Twins -- Fiction 5. Spirits -- Fiction 6. Family life -- Fiction 7. Brothers and sisters -- Fiction 8. Indians of North America -- Fiction

ISBN 1442401915; 9781442401914; 9781442401938; 9781442401921

LC 2011038419

Author Catherine Knutsson tells the story of Native American Cassandra Mercredi. The "sixteen-year-old . [may] be immune to Plague, but that doesn't mean she's safe--government forces are searching for those of aboriginal heritage to harvest their blood. When a search threatens Cassandra and her family, they flee to the Island: a mysterious and idyllic territory protected by the Band, a group of guerilla warriors--and by an enigmatic energy barrier that keeps outsiders out and the spirit world in." (Publisher's note)

Koertge, Ron

Lies, knives and girls in red dresses; Ron Koertge; illustrated by Andrea Dezso. Candlewick 2012 96 p. ill. (hardcover) $17.99

Grades: 9 10 11   **Fic**

1. Fairy tales 2. Orphans -- Fiction 3. Princesses -- Fiction 4. Novels in verse 5. Fairy tales -- Fiction 6. Characters in literature -- Fiction

ISBN 0763644064; 9780763644062

LC 2011047027

This illustrated poetry collection "retells 23 classic fairy tales in free verse, written from the perspectives of iconic characters like Little Red Riding Hood, as well as maligned or minor figures such as the Mole from Thumbelina and Cinderella's stepsisters. . . . Several stories trade happily ever after for disappointment and discontent, as with the danger-addicted queen in Rumpelstiltskin." (Publishers Weekly)

★ Margaux with an X; [by] Ron Koertge. Candlewick Press 2004 165p $15.99; pa $6.99

Grades: 7 8 9 10   **Fic**

1. Domestic violence -- Fiction

ISBN 0-7636-2401-2; 0-7636-2679-1 pa

LC 2003-65279

Margaux, known as a "tough chick" at her Los Angeles high school, makes a connection with Danny, who, like her, struggles with the emotional impact of family violence and abuse.

This book "excels in character development. It is an intriguing story that constantly provokes readers' curiosity. . . . [The author's] language at times is advanced, an accurate reflection of his characters' intellectual capacity." SLJ

Now playing; Stoner & Spaz II. [by] Ron Koertge. Candlewick Press 2011 208p $16.99

Grades: 8 9 10 11 12   **Fic**

1. School stories 2. Drug abuse -- Fiction 3. Cerebral palsy -- Fiction 4. Self-acceptance -- Fiction 5. Dating (Social customs) -- Fiction

ISBN 978-0-7636-5081-0; 0-7636-5081-1

LC 2010040151

Sequel to: Stoner & Spaz (2002)

High schooler Ben Bancroft, a budding filmmaker with cerebral palsy, struggles to understand his relationship with drug-addict Colleen while he explores a new friendship with A.J., who shares his obsession with movies and makes a good impression on Ben's grandmother.

"Koertge writes sharp dialogue and vivid scenes." Publ Wkly

Stoner & Spaz; [by] Ron Koertge. Candlewick Press 2002 169p hardcover o.p. pa $6.99

Grades: 8 9 10 11 12   **Fic**

1. School stories 2. Cerebral palsy -- Fiction

ISBN 0-7636-1608-7; 0-7636-2150-1 pa

LC 2001-43050

A troubled youth with cerebral palsy struggles toward self-acceptance with the help of a drug-addicted young woman

"Funny, touching, and surprising, it is a hopeful yet realistic view of things as they are and as they could be." Booklist

Followed by: Now Playing: Stoner & Spaz II (2011)

★ Strays; [by] Ron Koertge. Candlewick Press 2007 167p $16.99

Grades: 7 8 9 10 11 12   **Fic**

1. Orphans -- Fiction 2. Foster home care -- Fiction

ISBN 978-0-7636-2705-8; 0-7636-2705-4

LC 2007-24096

After his parents are killed in a car accident, high school senior Sam wonders whether he will ever feel again or if he will remain numbed by grief.

"Though Koertge never soft pedals the horrors faced by some foster children, this thoughtful novel about the lost and abandoned is a hopeful one." Booklist

Koja, Kathe

Buddha boy. Speak 2004 117p pa $5.99

Grades: 7 8 9 10   **Fic**

1. School stories 2. Artists -- Fiction 3. Buddhism -- Fiction 4. Conduct of life -- Fiction

ISBN 0-14-240209-5

LC 2004041669

First published 2003 by Farrar, Straus & Giroux

Justin spends time with Jinsen, the unusual and artistic new student whom the school bullies torment and call Buddha Boy, and ends up making choices that impact Jinsen, himself, and the entire school.

"A compelling introduction to Buddhism and a credible portrait of how true friendship brings out the best in people." Publ Wkly

Kissing the bee. Farrar, Straus and Giroux 2007 121p $16

Grades: 8 9 10 11 12   **Fic**

1. Love stories 2. School stories 3. Bees -- Fiction 4. Friendship -- Fiction

ISBN 978-0-374-39938-2; 0-374-39938-7

LC 2006-37378

While working on a bee project for her advanced biology class, quiet high school senior Dana reflects on her relationship with gorgeous best friend Avra and Avra's boyfriend Emil, whom Dana secretly loves.

The "understated, tightly focused language evokes vivid scenes and heady emotions." Publ Wkly

Konigsberg, Bill

★ **Openly** straight; Bill Konigsberg. Arthur A. Levine Books 2013 336 p. (hard cover: alk. paper) $17.99

Grades: 8 9 10 11   **Fic**

1. School stories 2. Gay teenagers -- Fiction 3. Schools -- Fiction 4. Identity -- Fiction 5. Homosexuality -- Fiction 6. Massachusetts -- Fiction 7. Preparatory schools -- Fiction

ISBN 0545509890; 9780545509893; 9780545509909

LC 2012030552

Lambda Literary Awards Finalist (2014)

In this book, "Coloradan Rafe Goldberg has always been the token gay kid. He's been out since eighth grade. His parents and community are totally supportive. . . . On the outside, Rafe seems fine, but on the inside, he's looking for change, which comes with the opportunity to reinvent himself at the prestigious Natick Academy in Massachusetts. There for his junior year, Rafe cloaks his gayness in order to be just like one of the other guys." All is well until he falls for a straight friend. (Kirkus Reviews)

"Rafe is sick of being the poster child for all things gay at his uber-liberal Colorado high school, so when he gets into a Massachusetts boarding school for his junior year, he decides to reboot himself as "openly straight." Konigsberg slyly demonstrates how thoroughly assumptions of straightness are embedded in everyday interactions. For a thought-provoking take on the coming-out story, look no further." (Horn Book)

★ The **porcupine** of truth; Bill Konigsberg. Arthur A. Levine Books, an imprint of Scholastic Inc. 2015 336 p. (alk. paper) $17.99

Grades: 9 10 11 12   **Fic**

1. Montana -- Fiction 2. Alcoholism -- Fiction 3. Friendship -- Fiction 4. Family secrets -- Fiction 5. Children of alcoholics -- Fiction 6. Dysfunctional families -- Fiction

ISBN 0545648939; 9780545648936; 9780545648943; 9780545754927

LC 2014027136

Stonewall Book Award, Young Adult (2016)

In this book, by Bill Konigsberg, "Carson Smith is resigned to spending his summer in Billings, Montana, helping his mom take care of his father, a dying alcoholic he doesn't really know. Then he meets Aisha Stinson, a beautiful girl who has run away from her difficult family, and Pastor John Logan, who's long held a secret regarding Carson's grandfather, who disappeared without warning or explanation thirty years before." (Publisher's note)

"Visiting small-town Montana to care for his long-absent alcoholic father, also the child of estranged parents, Carson becomes obsessed with discovering the reason for his grandfather's abandonment. New friend Aisha, homeless since coming out to her family, joins his cross-country scavenger hunt. Smart-alecky dialogue and quirky roadside characters lighten the commentary on religion, secrets, family, and forgiveness." Horn Book

Kontis, Alethea

Enchanted; Alethea Kontis. Harcourt 2012 308 p.

Grades: 9 10 11 12   **Fic**

1. Fantasy fiction 2. Frogs -- Fiction 3. Magic -- Fiction 4. Fractured fairy tales 5. Princes

ISBN 0547645708; 9780547645704

LC 2011027317

This young adult fantasy book presents the "fairy-tale mashup story of the adventures of a girl named Sunday Woodcutter and her six siblings. Sunday becomes friends with the enchanted frog Grumble and unwittingly helps him transform back into Prince Rumbold. Author Alethea Kontis has . . . woven just about every fairy character tale readers might half-remember into the fabric of her story: the beanstalk, the warrior maiden, Cinderella and Sleeping Beauty and some darker ones, too." (Kirkus)

Korman, Gordon

The **Juvie** three. Hyperion 2008 249p lib bdg $15.99

Grades: 7 8 9 10   **Fic**

1. Friendship -- Fiction 2. Juvenile delinquency -- Fiction

ISBN 978-1-4231-0158-1; 1-4231-0158-8

LC 2008-19087

Gecko, Arjay, and Terence, all in trouble with the law, must find a way to keep their halfway house open in order to stay out of juvenile detention.

"Korman keeps lots of balls in the air as he handles each boy's distinct voice and character—as well as the increasingly absurd situation—with humor and flashes of sadness." Booklist

Son of the mob. Hyperion Bks. for Children 2002 262p hardcover o.p. pa $7.99
Grades: 7 8 9 10   Fic
  1. Mafia -- Fiction
  ISBN 0-7868-0769-5; 0-7868-1593-0 pa
            LC 2002-68672

Seventeen-year-old Vince's life is constantly complicated by the fact that he is the son of a powerful Mafia boss, a relationship that threatens to destroy his romance with the daughter of an FBI agent

"The fast-paced, tightly focused story addresses the problems of being an honest kid in a family of outlaws—and loving them anyway. Korman doesn't ignore the seamier side of mob life, but even when the subject matter gets violent . . . he keeps things light by relating his tale in the first-person voice of a humorously sarcastic yet law-abiding wise guy." Horn Book

Another title about Vince is:
Son of the mob: Hollywood hustle (2004)

Son of the mob: Hollywood hustle. Hyperion 2004 268p $15.99
Grades: 9 10 11 12   Fic
  1. Mafia -- Fiction 2. California -- Fiction
  ISBN 0-7868-0918-3
            LC 2004-44181

Sequel to Son of the mob
Eighteen-year-old Vince Luca, son of mob boss Anthony Luca, goes away to college in southern California hoping to escape his past, but soon his brother and a series of "uncles" appear at his dorm, and before long he is caught up in criminal activity once again

"Teens will love this hilarious latest chapter of Vince's life. . . . {This} is a wonderful sauce filled with brilliant characterization, sneaky plot twists, and humor that will make teens fall off their chairs with laughter." Voice Youth Advocates

Kornher-Stace, Nicole

Archivist wasp; a novel. Nicole Kornher-Stace. Big Mouth House 2015 256 p. (paperback) $14
Grades: 9 10 11 12   Fic
  1. Ghost stories 2. Adventure fiction 3. Dystopian fiction 4. Fantasy 5. Ghosts -- Fiction
  ISBN 1618730975; 9781618730978
            LC 2014046381

In this young adult novel, by Nicole Kornher-Stace, "Wasp's job is simple. Hunt ghosts. And every year she has to fight to remain Archivist. Desperate and alone, she strikes a bargain with the ghost of a supersoldier. She will go with him on his underworld hunt for the long-long ghost of his partner and in exchange she will find out more about his pre-apocalyptic world than any Archivist before her." (Publisher's note)

"A must-have for dystopian fans who prefer to avoid love stories and pat endings." SLJ

Kostick, Conor

Edda. Viking 2011 440p il
Grades: 7 8 9 10   Fic
  1. War stories 2. Science fiction 3. Video games -- Fiction
  ISBN 0-670-01218-1; 978-0-670-01218-3
            LC 2011003000

Sequel to: Saga (2008)
In the virtual world of Edda, ruler Scanthax decides he wants to invade another virtual world, embroiling the universes of Edda, Saga, and Epic in war, with only three teenagers to try to restore peace.

"Humans, electronic beings and servers are separated by light years and metaphysics, but Kostick's action-filled series conclusion is immediate and relevant." Kirkus

★ **Epic**. Viking 2007 364p $17.99
Grades: 7 8 9 10   Fic
  1. Fantasy fiction 2. Video games -- Fiction
  ISBN 0-670-06179-4; 978-0-670-06179-2
            LC 2006-19958

On New Earth, a world based on a video role-playing game, fourteen-year-old Erik persuades his friends to aid him in some unusual gambits in order to save his father from exile and safeguard the futures of each of their families.

"There is intrigue and mystery throughout this captivating page-turner. Veins of moral and ethical social situations and decisions provide some great opportunities for discussion. Well written and engaging." SLJ

Other titles in this series are:
Edda (2011)
Saga (2008)

Saga. Viking 2008 367p $18.99
Grades: 7 8 9 10   Fic
  1. Fantasy fiction 2. Video games -- Fiction
  ISBN 978-0-6700-6280-5; 0-6700-6280-4
            LC 2007-32175

Sequel to Epic (2007)
On Saga, a world based on a video role-playing game, fifteen-year-old Ghost lives to break rules, but the Dark Queen who controls Saga plans to enslave its people and those of New Earth, and Ghost and her airboarding friends, along with Erik and his friends from Epic, try to stop her.

"The plot and pacing are near perfect in this tale of a world cramped by fear and tradition. . . . Compulsively readable and palpable (the descriptions of airboarding are a near-physical experience), it will appeal to SF fans across the board." Voice Youth Advocates

Kraus, Daniel

The **death** and life of Zebulon Finch; Volume one At the edge of empire. as prepared by the esteemed fictionist, Daniel Kraus. Simon & Schuster Books for Young Readers 2015 656 p. (hardcover: alk. paper) $18.99
Grades: 9 10 11 12   Fic
  1. Death -- Fiction 2. Murder -- Fiction 3. Dead -- Fiction
  ISBN 9781481411394; 9781481411400
            LC 2014039293

In this book, by Daniel Kraus, "Zebulon Finch is gunned down by the shores of Lake Michigan. But after mere minutes in the void, he is mysteriously resurrected. His second life will be nothing like his first. Zebulon's new existence begins as a sideshow attraction in a traveling medicine show. From there he will be poked and prodded by a scientist obsessed with mastering the secrets of death." (Publisher's note)

"A hefty volume for fans of historical fiction with an undead twist." SLJ

Rotters. Delacorte Press 2011 448p $16.99; lib bdg $19.99; ebook $10.99

Grades: 9 10 11 12 Fic

1. School stories 2. Iowa -- Fiction 3. Moving -- Fiction 4. Bullies -- Fiction 5. Grave robbing -- Fiction 6. Father-son relationship -- Fiction

ISBN 978-0-385-73857-6; 978-0-385-90737-8 lib bdg; 978-0-375-89558-6 ebook

LC 2010005174

Sixteen-year-old Joey's life takes a very strange turn when his mother's tragic death forces him to move from Chicago to rural Iowa with the father he has never known, and who is the town pariah.

"Disturbing characters and grotesque details make for a tale of death that ultimately exhumes truths about life." Horn Books Guide

Scowler; Daniel Kraus. Delacorte Press 2013 304 p. (glb) $19.99

Grades: 9 10 11 12 Fic

1. Horror fiction 2. Meteorites -- Fiction 3. Adult child abuse victims -- Fiction 4. Horror stories 5. Iowa -- Fiction 6. Violence -- Fiction 7. Mentally ill -- Fiction 8. Farm life -- Iowa -- Fiction 9. Family life -- Iowa -- Fiction

ISBN 0375990941; 9780307980878; 9780375990946; 9780385743099

LC 2012005363

Odyssey Award (2014)

"This literary horror novel[, by Daniel Kraus,] gives readers insight into the mind of a controlling homicidal man and the son who must stop him. . . . Nineteen-year-old Ry Burke . . . wishes for anything to distract him from the grim memories of his father's physical and emotional abuse. Then a meteorite falls from the sky, bringing with it not only a fragment from another world but also the arrival of a ruthless man intent on destroying the entire family." (Publisher's note)

"A Midwestern gothic family saga that will hook readers--or scare them away." Kirkus

Kriegman, Mitchell

Being Audrey Hepburn; a novel. Mitchell Kriegman. First edition St. Martin's Griffin 2014 336 p. (hardback) $18.99

Grades: 9 10 11 12 Fic

1. Bildungsromans 2. Teenage girls -- Fiction 3. New Jersey -- Fiction 4. Coming of age -- Fiction 5. Family problems -- Fiction 6. Self-actualization -- Fiction 7.

Single-parent families -- Fiction

ISBN 1250001463; 9781250001467

LC 2014027321

This novel by Mitchell Kriegman "tells the story of a 19-year-old girl from Jersey who finds herself thrust into the world of socialites after being seen in Audrey Hepburn's dress from the film 'Breakfast at Tiffany's.' . . . Obsessed with everything Audrey Hepburn, Lisbeth is transformed when she secretly tries on Audrey's iconic Givenchy. She becomes who she wants to be by pretending to be somebody she's not and living among the young and privileged Manhattan elite." (Publisher's note)

"A satisfying ending to this mixture of The Devil Wears Prada and Breakfast at Tiffany's reveals old family secrets and a promising future for the heroine. Probably a read for girls, this is a thoroughly entertaining romp through the world of runways and art openings with great dialogue and characterizations along the way." VOYA

Kristoff, Jay

★ **Illuminae;** Amie Kaufman; Jay Kristoff. Alfred A. Knopf 2015 608 p. illustrations (hardcover) $18.99

Grades: 8 9 10 11 12 Fic

1. Science fiction 2. Interplanetary voyages -- Fiction 3. Plague -- Fiction 4. Artificial intelligence -- Fiction

ISBN 9780553499117; 9780553499124; 9780553499148

LC 2014017908

In this young adult novel, by Amie Kaufman and Jay Kristoff, "the year is 2575, and two rival megacorporations are at war over a planet that's little more than an ice-covered speck at the edge of the universe. Too bad nobody thought to warn the people living on it. With enemy fire raining down on them, Kady and Ezra--who are barely even talking to each other--are forced to fight their way onto one of the evacuating fleet, with an enemy warship in hot pursuit." (Publisher's note)

"Kady Grant has typical problems: school, parents, and a boyfriend she just dumped. But life spirals out of control when Kady's planet, Kerenza, is attacked by an unknown enemy. As destruction unfolds around her, Kady manages to escape her planet on one of three ships. Kady is considered lucky, with her mother on one ship and her ex, Ezra, on another. As the convoy flees Kerenza with the enemy close behind, it is clear that the problems have just begun. A deadly virus is spreading through one of the ships; AIDEN, the onboard computer of the lead ship, has gone rogue; and the enemy is in close pursuit in an attempt to destroy the last witnesses of the Kerenza catastrophe. . . . A great recommendation for middle and high school science-fiction fans." SLJ

Krokos, Dan

False memory; Dan Krokos. Disney Press 2012 327 p. $17.99

Grades: 6 7 8 9 Fic

1. Secrecy -- Fiction 2. Teenagers -- Fiction 3. Genetic transformation 4. Science fiction 5. Memory -- Fiction 6. Genetic engineering -- Fiction

ISBN 1423149769; 9781423149767

LC 2011053532

In author Dan Krokos' book, "Miranda North wakes up alone on a park bench with no memory. In her panic, she releases a mysterious energy that incites pure terror in everyone around her . . . Miranda discovers she was trained to be a weapon and is part of an elite force of genetically-altered teens who possess flawless combat skills and powers strong enough to destroy a city . . . Then Miranda uncovers a dark truth that sets her team on the run. Suddenly her past doesn't seem to matter when there may not be a future." (Publisher's note)

Krovatin, Christopher

Heavy metal and you. Scholastic 2005 186p $16.95; pa $7.99

Grades: 9 10 11 12 **Fic**

1. School stories 2. Rock music -- Fiction 3. New York (N.Y.) -- Fiction

ISBN 0-439-73648-X; 0-439-74399-0 pa

LC 2004-23645

High schooler Sam begins losing himself when he falls for a preppy girl who wants him to give up getting wasted with his best friends and even his passion for heavy metal music in order to become a better person.

"From the terrific cover and portrait of selfish love to the clever CD player icons indicating narrative switches . . . this is an authentic portrayal of an obsession with music. Teens don't have to like heavy metal to appreciate this novel, which is guaranteed to attract readers looking for a book to reach their death-metal souls." Booklist

Kuehn, Stephanie

★ **Charm** & strange; by Stephanie Kuehn. 1st ed. St. Martin's Griffin 2013 224 p. (hardcover) $17.99

Grades: 9 10 11 12 **Fic**

1. School stories 2. Mystery fiction 3. Sexual abuse -- Fiction 4. Mental illness -- Fiction 5. Psychological abuse -- Fiction

ISBN 1250021944; 9781250021946

LC 2013003247

William C. Morris Award (2014)

This book follows Andrew Winston Winters, known as Win. Present-day "Win is smart, competitive and untrusting, estranged from his former roommate, Lex, his one ally and defender. The reasons for Win's self-loathing and keyed-up anxiety won't be fully revealed until story's end. What exactly does he expect to happen during the full moon? Why has he fallen out with Lex? Win's privileged childhood, when he was known as Drew, is another mystery." (Kirkus Reviews)

"Kuehn . . . keeps us on constant edge regarding exactly what genre of book it is that we're reading." Booklist

Complicit; Stephanie Kuehn. St. Martin's Griffin 2014 256 p. illustrations (hardback) $19.99

Grades: 8 9 10 11 12 **Fic**

1. Orphans -- Fiction 2. Mental illness -- Fiction 3. Private schools -- Fiction 4. Brothers and sisters -- Fiction 5. Amnesia -- Fiction 6. Schools -- Fiction

ISBN 1250044596; 9781250044594

LC 2014008117

"Cate is out of juvie. For her little brother, 17-year-old Jamie, that's bad. It's been two years since Cate horribly injured a rival by setting a barn on fire.This was the last in a long series of tempestuous, violent acts Cate committed since she and Jamie were adopted following the murder of their mother. With Cate locked up, Jamie is almost a whole being. . . . But Cate's return brings everything flooding back." (Booklist)

"...every page shows a firm, surprising choice, whether you like it or not. Cate, naturally, is the main event, the alternatingly irrational, gentle, explosive, and enigmatic center of this fast, black whirlpool of a novel." (Booklist)

Delicate Monsters; Stephanie Kuehn. St. Martin's Press 2015 240 p. (hardback) $19.99

Grades: 10 11 12 **Fic**

1. Secrets -- Fiction 2. Psychopaths -- Fiction

ISBN 9781250063847; 1250063841

LC 2015012473

In this novel, by Stephanie Kuehn, "centers on the convergence of the lives of Sadie, a damaged girl who enjoys causing others pain, and Emerson, a boy who's trying desperately to hide the dysfunction inside his family and himself. The novel follows Sadie as she arrives back in California . . . after being expelled from a series of . . . boarding schools. . . . When a life-or-death crisis occurs, both of them must finally face reality, along with their demons." (School Library Journal)

"Like her previous YA novels, Kuehn's latest benefits from tight construction, expert pacing, and voices that ring especially true for contemporary teenagers, particularly Sadie's entrancing, gleefully acerbic tone. Intelligent, compulsively readable literary fiction with a dark twist." Booklist

Kwok, Jean

Girl in translation; Jean Kwok. Riverhead Books 2010 293 p. $25.95

Grades: 11 12 Adult **Fic**

1. Women immigrants -- Fiction 2. Mothers and daughters -- Fiction 3. Chinese American teenagers -- Fiction 4. Chinese -- New York (State) -- New York -- Fiction

ISBN 9781594487569; 1594487561

LC 2009041041

Alex Award (2011)

Kyle, Aryn

The **god** of animals; a novel. Aryn Kyle. Scribner 2007 305p (hbk.) $25; (pbk.) $15

Grades: 11 12 Adult **Fic**

1. Girls 2. Ranch life 3. Adolescence 4. Family life 5. Ranches -- Fiction 6. Colorado -- Fiction

ISBN 9781416533245; 9781416533252

LC 200650605

Alex Award (2008), Spur Awards: Best Novel of the West (2008)

This book follows "12-year-old Alice Winston, whose father, Jody, knows more about horses than he does about running a successful business. After Alice's older sister Nona . . . runs off to marry a cowboy, Jody is reduced to stabling boarders. . . . Alice's mother Marian is a bed-ridden depressive; Alice herself is preoccupied by the drowning of her schoolmate Polly Cain, who was in the habit of making phone calls to her English teacher, Mr. Delmar. Alice

... starts to make secret calls to Delmar herself. .... Fearful expectations are ... realized as a sequence of disasters unfolds, starting with a horrific riding accident that leaves Jody's possible lover Patty Jo badly damaged. ... family argument brings about further cruelty, this time leading to the agonizing destruction of a horse." (Kirkus)

L'Engle, Madeleine

A **wrinkle** in time. Farrar, Straus & Giroux 1962 211p $17; pa $7.99

Grades: 5 6 7 8 9 10   **Fic**

1. Fantasy fiction
ISBN 0-374-38613-7; 0-312-36754-6 pa
Awarded The Newbery Medal, 1963
ALA YALSA Margaret A. Edwards Award (1998)

This book "makes unusual demands on the imagination and consequently gives great rewards." Horn Book

Other titles in this series are:
A swiftly tilting planet (1978)
A wind in the door (1973)

Laban, Elizabeth

The **Tragedy** Paper; Elizabeth LaBan. Alfred A. Knopf 2013 320 p. $17.99

Grades: 7 8 9 10 11 12   **Fic**

1. Love stories 2. School stories 3. Albinos and albinism -- Fiction 4. Schools -- Fiction 5. High schools -- Fiction 6. Boarding schools -- Fiction 7. Dating (Social customs) -- Fiction 8. Interpersonal relations -- Fiction
ISBN 0375870407; 9780375870408; 9780375970405; 9780375989124

LC 2012011294

This novel by Elizabeth Laban "follows the story of Tim Macbeth, a seventeen-year-old albino and a recent transfer to the prestigious Irving School. .... He finds himself falling for the quintessential 'It' girl, Vanessa Sheller. .... Vanessa is into him, too, but she can kiss her social status goodbye if anyone ever finds out. Tim and Vanessa begin a clandestine romance, but looming over them is the Tragedy Paper, Irving's version of a senior year thesis." (Publisher's note)

Lackey, Mercedes

The **outstretched** shadow; [by] Mercedes Lackey and James Mallory. Tor 2003 604p (Obsidian trilogy) hardcover o.p. pa $7.99

Grades: 9 10 11 12   **Fic**

1. Fantasy fiction
ISBN 0-7653-0219-5; 0-7653-4141-7 pa

LC 2003-55955

"Lackey and Mallory create a wide variety of multidimensional characters, especially Kellen who grows to manhood in realistic starts and stops, recognizing and accepting both his heritage and the consequences of his actions." Voice Youth Advocates

Other titles in this series are:
To light a candle (2004)
When darkness falls (2006)

The **phoenix** unchained; [by] Mercedes Lackey and James Mallory. Tor 2007 398p (Enduring flame) $27.95

Grades: 11 12 Adult   **Fic**

1. Fantasy fiction 2. Magic -- Fiction 3. Magicians -- Fiction
ISBN 978-0-7653-1593-9; 0-7653-1593-9

LC 2007-19647

This first book in the Enduring Flame series "takes place more than 1,000 years after events depicted in the Obsidian Trilogy. The city of Armethalieh is no longer ruled by mages, and High Magick itself is forgotten. .... Tiercel Rolfort, the scholarly son of lower nobility, rediscovers High Magick. Beset with visions and physically weakening, Tiercel decides his best hope is to take a journey to find a Wild Mage. Meanwhile, Wild Mage Bisochim has become convinced of his calling to set the balance aright by bringing darkness back into the world. .... This beguiling beginning promises a highly readable epic combining vivid characterization with an interesting exploration of how past heroics are twisted over centuries into something both more and less than they were." Publ Wkly

The **serpent's** shadow. DAW Bks. 2001 343p $24.95; pa $7.99

Grades: 11 12 Adult   **Fic**

1. Fantasy fiction
ISBN 0-88677-915-4; 0-7564-0061-9 pa

LC 2002-265143

"To an alternative Victorian London Dr. Maya Witherspoon, [daughter] of a Brahmin lady and an English physician, comes to practice. Besides standard Western medicine, Maya knows the magic of India, where she grew up. Maya's aunt Shivani has also come to England, but as a devotee of Kali, she hates her sister's marriage and is determined to wreak havoc on the English. Maya must seek the aid of British magical masters before the powers of Kali devastate London." Booklist

To light a candle; [by] Mercedes Lackey and James Mallory. Tor Books 2004 656p (Obsidian trilogy) hardcover o.p. pa $7.99

Grades: 9 10 11 12   **Fic**

1. Fantasy fiction
ISBN 0-7653-0220-9; 0-7653-4142-5 pa

LC 2004-49824

Sequel to The outstretched shadow (2003)

"Filled with magic, dragons, elves, and other mythical creatures, this title belongs in most fantasy collections." Libr J

Followed by When darkness falls (2006)

When darkness falls; [by] Mercedes Lackey and James Mallory. Tor 2006 496p (Obsidian trilogy) pa $7.99

Grades: 9 10 11 12   **Fic**

1. Fantasy fiction 2. Magic -- Fiction
ISBN 0-7653-0221-7; 978-0-7653-0221-2; 0-7653-4143-3 pa; 978-0-7653-4143-3 pa

LC 2005-34506

Sequel to To light a candle (2004)

"Knight-Mage Kennen, leader of the alliance of humans and elves, has his work cut out for him when the forces of demon queen Savilla go on the offensive. Fortunately, Kennen has a powerful ally in the half-breed healer Vestakia, who because she's half demon can read the mind of her demon father and provide priceless information on their enemies. The deft handling of the romance between Kennen and Vestakia helps heighten suspense as the struggle on both the physical and magical planes grows more intense." Publ Wkly

LaCour, Nina

★ The **Disenchantments**; Nina LaCour. Dutton Children's Books 2012 308 p. (hardcover) $16.99
Grades: 9 10 11 12   **Fic**
1. Bildungsromans 2. Teenagers -- Fiction 3. Friendship -- Fiction 4. Bands (Music) -- Fiction 5. Pacific Northwest -- Fiction 6. Artists -- Fiction 7. Secrets -- Fiction 8. Best friends -- Fiction 9. Automobile travel -- Fiction 10. Northwest, Pacific -- Fiction
ISBN 9780525422198
LC 2011021953

In this book, "[a]fter Colby graduates from high school, his . . . plans to spend a year traveling through Europe go up in smoke. . . . He . . . commit[s] himself to playing chauffeur for [his friend] Bev's . . . band . . . on their first . . . summer tour. Chronicling the band's road trip, . . .this . . . coming-of-age story expresses how a teen in limbo learns . . . lessons about disappointment, love, and the pursuit of dreams." (Publishers Weekly)

Everything leads to you; Nina LaCour. Dutton Books 2014 320 p. (hardback) $17.99
Grades: 9 10 11 12   **Fic**
1. Love -- Fiction 2. Summer -- Fiction 3. Secrets -- Fiction 4. Motion picture industry -- Fiction 5. Families -- Fiction 6. Lesbians -- Fiction 7. Set designers -- Fiction
ISBN 0525425888; 9780525425885
LC 2014004799

"Eighteen-year-old production design intern Emi is getting over her first love and trying to establish her place in the Los Angeles film industry...When she and her best friend Charlotte find a letter hidden in the possessions of a recently deceased Hollywood film legend at an estate sale, they begin searching for its intended recipient. Eventually that leads to Ava, a beautiful teen to whom Emi is immediately attracted. ..This one is highly enjoyable and highly recommended." (School Library Journal)

Hold still; with illustrations by Mia Nolting. Dutton 2009 229p il
Grades: 9 10 11 12   **Fic**
1. Suicide -- Fiction 2. Friendship -- Fiction 3. Bereavement -- Fiction
ISBN 0-525-42155-6; 978-0-525-42155-9
LC 2010-275162

Ingrid didn't leave a note. Three months after her best friend's suicide, Caitlin finds what she left instead: a journal, hidden under Caitlin's bed. "Grades seven to ten." (Bull Cent Child Books)

"Interspersed with drawings and journal entries, the story of Caitlin's journey through her grief is both heart-wrenching and realistic. . . . LaCour strikes a new path through a familiar story, leading readers with her confident writing and savvy sense of prose." Kirkus

LaFevers, Robin

★ **Dark** triumph; by Robin LaFevers. Houghton Mifflin Harcourt 2013 400 p. (His fair assassin) (hardcover) $17.99
Grades: 9 10 11 12   **Fic**
1. Fantasy fiction 2. Death -- Fiction 3. Assassins -- Fiction 4. Gods -- Fiction 5. Love -- Fiction 6. Brittany (France) -- History -- 1341-1532 -- Fiction 7. France -- History -- Charles VIII, 1483-1498 -- Fiction
ISBN 0547628382; 9780547628387
LC 2012033555

In this novel, by Robin LaFevers, book 2 of the "His Fair Assassin Trilogy," "Sybella's duty as Death's assassin in 15th-century France forces her return home to the personal hell that she had finally escaped. . . . While Sybella is a weapon of justice wrought by the god of Death himself, He must give her a reason to live. When she discovers an unexpected ally imprisoned in the dungeons, will a daughter of Death find something other than vengeance to live for?" (Publisher's note)

"LaFevers weaves the 'crazed, tangled web' of Sybella's life...with force, suspense and subtle tenderness. The prose's beauty inspires immediate re-reads of many a sentence, but its forward momentum is irresistible. An intricate, masterful page-turner about politics, treachery, religion, love and healing." Kirkus

★ **Grave** mercy; by Robin LaFevers. Houghton Mifflin 2012 549 p.
Grades: 9 10 11 12   **Fic**
1. Love stories 2. Historical fiction 3. Executions and executioners 4. Gods -- Fiction 5. Death -- Fiction 6. Assassins -- Fiction 7. Courts and courtiers -- Fiction 8. Brittany (France) -- History -- 1341-1532 -- Fiction 9. France -- History -- Charles VIII, 1483-1498 -- Fiction
ISBN 9780547628349
LC 2011039893

This book is a "historical romance with a . . . recreation of 15th-century Brittany. At its center is 17-year-old Ismae, . . . [who,] fleeing her thuggish husband, is taken in by the convent of St. Mortain. . . . Ismae is trained as an assassin. . . . [and] dispatched to the court of Anne of Brittany to keep track of Duval, the duchess's . . . older brother. Reluctantly, she falls in love with him, knowing . . . that she may someday be called upon to end his life." (Publishers Weekly)

★ **Mortal** heart; by Robin LaFevers. Houghton Mifflin Harcourt 2014 464 p. (His fair assassin) (hardback) $17.99
Grades: 9 10 11 12   **Fic**
1. Imaginary places 2. Magic -- Fiction 3. Assassins -- Fiction 4. Gods -- Fiction 5. Nuns -- Fiction 6. Death -- Fiction 7. Convents -- Fiction 8. Brittany (France) -- History -- 1341-1532 -- Fiction 9. France -- History -- Charles VIII, 1483-1498 -- Fiction
ISBN 0547628404; 9780547628400
LC 2014001877

In this book, the third in the "His Fair Assassin" series by Robin LaFevers, "Annith, overskilled and underused daughter of Mortain, god of Death, rebels against her abbess's decree that she remain immured in the convent as Mortain's seeress. Her rebellious escape to the world of politics, murder, and romance revolutionizes Annith's understanding of her nature and identity and brings about her sexual awakening." (Horn Book Magazine)

"This thrilling series conclusion narrates the fate of 17-year-old convent-raised Annith who impatiently awaits her assignment to serve as the god Mortain's Handmaiden of Death...The protagonists' sometimes-contradictory natures enrich their characters, and the intertwined relationships of realistic and Netherworld personages add depth to their personal stories. A plethora of strong females and their romantic relationships will have wide appeal for teens, making this a definite purchase where Grave Mercy (2012) and Dark Triumph (2013, both Houghton Harcourt) are popular and a strong story that can stand on its own." (SLJ)

Lahiri, Jhumpa

★ The **namesake**. Houghton Mifflin 2003 291p $24; pa $14

Grades: 11 12 Adult   **Fic**
1. Massachusetts -- Fiction 2. Culture conflict -- Fiction 3. East Indian Americans -- Fiction
ISBN 0-395-92721-8; 0-618-48522-8 pa
LC 2003-41718

"Its incorrigible mildness and its ungilded lilies aside, Lahiri's novel is unfailingly lovely in its treatment of Gogol's relationship with his father. This is the classic American parent-child bond." N Y Times Book Rev

Lake, Nick

Blood ninja II: the revenge of Lord Oda. Simon and Schuster Books for Young Readers 2010 377p $16.99

Grades: 7 8 9 10 11   **Fic**
1. Japan -- Fiction 2. Ninja -- Fiction 3. Vampires -- Fiction
ISBN 978-1-4169-8629-4; 1-4169-8629-4
LC 2010-10110

Sequel to: Blood ninja (2009)

In sixteenth-century Japan, Taro, a vampire like all ninja warriors, tries to protect his mother and defeat the power-hungry Lord Oda, who he believed was dead.

"Ghosts and Zen Buddhist philosophy add a surprising and sometimes effective depth to the story." Booklist

★ **Hostage** Three; by Nick Lake. Bloomsbury 2013 320 p. (hardback) $17.99

Grades: 9 10 11 12   **Fic**
1. Pirates -- Fiction 2. Hostages -- Fiction 3. Father-daughter relationship -- Fiction 4. Yachts -- Fiction 5. Survival -- Fiction 6. Fathers and daughters -- Fiction 7. Adventure and adventurers -- Fiction
ISBN 1619631237; 9781619631236
LC 2013002686

In this book, by Nick Lake, "Amy Fields is a privileged 17-year-old . . . Forced by her father and stepmother to accompany them on a round-the-world cruise in her father's posh yacht, she is at first withdrawn and surly. Then, in the Gulf of Aden, Somali pirates capture the yacht, and Amy begins to experience a bit of life outside the bubble as she and her family are held hostage. . . . Things are complicated further when Amy falls in love with one of the pirates and he with her." (Kirkus Reviews)

"The last way seventeen-year-old Amy wants to spend the summer after high school is sailing around the world with her father and new stepmother. When Somali pirates hijack the family's yacht, the sullen, entitled teen forms a surprising bond with one of their captors. Lake's sensitive character development and sophisticated storytelling (including alternate endings) helps elicit readers' sympathies for his complex characters." (Horn Book)

In darkness; Nick Lake. Bloomsbury 2012 341 p.

Grades: 8 9 10 11 12   **Fic**
1. Haiti -- Fiction 2. Earthquakes -- Fiction 3. Gangs -- Fiction 4. Survival -- Fiction 5. Violence -- Fiction 6. Haiti Earthquake, Haiti, 2010 -- Fiction
ISBN 9781599907437
LC 2011022350

Michael L. Printz Award (2013)

"This . . . novel, set in Haiti, alternates between the narration of a contemporary fifteen-year-old, trapped in the rubble following the 2010 earthquake, and the story of Toussaint L'Ouverture, the legendary eighteenth-century leader of Haiti's anti-colonial revolution. The two become aware of each other through dreams; Shorty experiences Toussaint's reality while Toussaint perceives the bewildering future setting in which Shorty lives. . . . [B]oth share graphic depictions of the cruelty and violence of the protagonists' lives. Shorty tells of his pre-earthquake life in quick allusions and references that eventually cohere into a complete story." (Bulletin of the Center for Children's Books)

Lalami, Laila

Secret son. Algonquin Books of Chapel Hill 2009 291p $23.95

Grades: 10 11 12 Adult   **Fic**
1. Morocco -- Fiction 2. Father-son relationship -- Fiction
ISBN 978-1-56512-494-3; 1-56512-494-4
LC 2008-52218

"A story brimming with insight into the complexities of life in contemporary Morocco." Booklist

"Raised by his mother in a one-room house in the slums of Casablanca, Youssef El Mekki has always had big dreams of living another life in another world. Suddenly his dreams are within reach when he discovers that his father—whom he'd been led to believe was dead—is very much alive. A wealthy businessman, he seems eager to give his son a new start. Youssef leaves his mother behind to live a life of luxury, until a reversal of fortune sends him back to the streets and his childhood friends. Trapped once again by his class and painfully aware of the limitations of his prospects, he becomes easy prey for a fringe Islamic group." (Publisher's note)

Lam, Laura

Pantomime; Laura Lam. Strange Chemistry 2013 394 p. (pbk.) $9.99

Grades: 9 10 11 12   **Fic**
1. Fantasy fiction 2. Magic -- Fiction 3. Circus -- Fiction 4. Fantasy 5. Love stories 6. Love -- Fiction

7. Runaways -- Fiction
ISBN 190884437X; 9781908844378; 9781908844385
LC 2012540335

In this book, R.H. Ragona's Circus of Magic is the greatest circus of Ellada. Nestled among the glowing blue Penglass -- remnants of a mysterious civilisation long gone -- are wonders beyond the wildest imagination. . . . Iphigenia Laurus, or Gene, the daughter of a noble family, is uncomfortable in corsets and crinoline, and prefers climbing trees to debutante balls. Micah Grey, a runaway living on the streets, joins the circus as an aerialist's apprentice and soon becomes the circus's rising star." (Publisher's note)

"At around page 90 in Lam's impressive debut fantasy novel, there's a reveal so stunning that it makes it difficult to discuss without spoilers... Using a flashback structure to show both why noble-born Iphigenia Laurus runs away and joins the circus and how she changes her identity to become trapeze-artist Micah Grey, Pantomime does feature standard YA elements such as parental estrangement and problematic romance—yet marvelously transfigures them... That said, Lam has more in store for us, as a hair-raising climax follows that recalls a classic Lon Chaney flick in terms of the operatic satisfaction it delivers." (Booklist)

Lanagan, Margo

★ The **brides** of Rollrock Island; Margo Lanagan. Alfred A. Knopf 2012 305 p. (hardback) $17.99

Grades: 9 10 11 12   **Fic**
1. Selkies -- Fiction 2. Magic 3. Fantasy fiction 4. Islands -- Fiction 5. Witches -- Fiction
ISBN 0375869190; 9780375869198; 9780375969195; 9780375989308
LC 2011047466

This novel, by Margo Lenagan, takes place around "remote Rollrock Island, [where] men go to sea to make their livings--and to catch their wives. The witch Misskaella knows the way of drawing a girl from the heart of a seal . . . [a]nd for a price a man may buy himself a lovely sea-wife. . . . But from his first look into [her] . . . eyes, he will be just as transformed as she. He will be equally ensnared. And the witch will have her true payment." (Publisher's note)

★ **Tender** morsels. Alfred A. Knopf 2008 436p $16.99; lib bdg $19.99

Grades: 10 11 12   **Fic**
1. Fantasy fiction
ISBN 978-0-375-84811-7; 0-375-84811-8; 978-0-375-94811-4 lib bdg; 0-375-94811-2 lib bdg
LC 2008-04155
Michael L. Printz Award honor book, 2009

A young woman who has endured unspeakable cruelties is magically granted a safe haven apart from the real world and allowed to raise her two daughters in this alternate reality, until the barrier between her world and the real one begins to break down.

The author "touches on nightmarish adult themes, including multiple rape scenarios and borderline human-animal sexual interactions, which reserve this for the most mature readers. . . . Drawing alternate worlds that blur the line between wonder and horror, and characters who traverse the nature of human and beast, this challenging, unforgettable work explores the ramifications of denying the most essential and often savage aspects of life." Booklist

Lancaster, Mike A.

The **future** we left behind; Mike A. Lancaster. Egmont USA 2012 367 p. (hardback) $16.99

Grades: 7 8 9 10   **Fic**
1. Science fiction 2. Cults -- Fiction 3. England -- Fiction 4. Computer programs -- Fiction 5. Family life -- England -- Fiction 6. Technological innovations -- Fiction
ISBN 1606844105; 9781606844106; 9781606844113
LC 2012003794

Sequel to: Human.4
This sequel to "Human.4" is set in the future. Here, "Peter is the son of the man who saved the world by inventing robot bees. Destined by his wealthy genius father for a future in science, Peter rebels against both by enrolling in a literature class and befriending Alpha, a girl in a wacky religious cult. Alpha is a Strakerite, following the ancient tapes of Kyle Straker. Kyle and his girlfriend Lilly believed humans are regularly upgraded by aliens. Skeptical at first, Peter is soon convinced." (Kirkus)

Lange, Erin Jade

Butter; Erin Jade Lange. Bloomsbury 2012 296 p. (hardback) $16.99

Grades: 8 9 10 11 12   **Fic**
1. Eating habits 2. Suicide -- Fiction 3. Teenagers -- Fiction 4. Obesity -- Fiction 5. Eating disorders -- Fiction
ISBN 1599907801; 9781599907802
LC 2011045509

In author Erin Jade Lange's book, a "lonely obese boy everyone calls 'Butter' is about to make history. He is going to eat himself to death-live on the Internet-and everyone is invited to watch. When he first makes the announcement online to his classmates, Butter expects pity, insults, and possibly sheer indifference. What he gets are morbid cheerleaders rallying around his deadly plan. Yet as their dark encouragement grows, it begins to feel a lot like popularity . . . But what happens when Butter reaches his suicide deadline?" (Publisher's note)

Larbalestier, Justine

★ **Liar**. Bloomsbury Children's Books 2009 376p $16.99

Grades: 9 10 11 12   **Fic**
1. Honesty -- Fiction 2. Werewolves -- Fiction
ISBN 978-1-59990-305-7; 1-59990-305-9
LC 2009-12581

Compulsive liar Micah promises to tell the truth after revealing that her boyfriend has been murdered.

"Micah's narrative is convincing, and in the end readers will delve into the psyche of a troubled teen and decide for themselves the truths and lies. This one is sure to generate discussion." SLJ

Razorhurst; Justine Larbalestier. Soho Teen 2015 309 p. map (hardback) $18.99

Grades: 9 10 11 12   **Fic**
1. Ghost stories 2. Criminals -- Fiction 3. Organized

crime -- Fiction 4. Sydney (Australia) -- Fiction 5. Ghost stories -- Fiction 6. Australia -- History -- 20th century -- Fiction 7. Sydney (N.S.W.) -- History -- 20th century -- Fiction
ISBN 1616955449; 9781616955441

LC 2014030128

This young adult historical suspense novel, by Justine Larbalestier, describes "Sydney's deadly Razorhurst neighborhood, 1932. Gloriana Nelson and Mr. Davidson, two ruthless mob bosses, have reached a fragile peace--one maintained by 'razor men.' Kelpie, orphaned and homeless, is blessed (and cursed) with the ability to see Razorhurst's many ghosts. They tell her secrets the living can't know about the cracks already forming in the mobs' truce." (Publisher's note)

"Larbalestier pulls no punches with the gruesome, gory details about the violence of poverty, and the result is a dark, unforgettable and blood-soaked tale of outlaws and masterminds." Kirkus

Lasky, Kathryn

★ **Ashes**. Viking 2010 318p $16.99
Grades: 6 7 8 9 10 11 12   **Fic**
1. Germany -- Fiction 2. National socialism -- Fiction
ISBN 978-0-670-01157-5; 0-670-01157-6

LC 2009-33127

In 1932 Berlin, thirteen-year-old Gaby Schramm witnesses the beginning of Hitler's rise to power, as soldiers become ubiquitous, her beloved literature teacher starts wearing a jewelled swastika pin, and the family's dear friend, Albert Einstein, leaves the country while Gaby's parents secretly bury his books and papers in their small yard.

"Gaby's questioning but assertive nature helps form a compelling, readable portrait of pre-WWII Germany." Publ Wkly

Latham, Jennifer

Scarlett undercover; Jennifer Latham. Little, Brown & Co. 2015 320 p. (hardcover) $18
Grades: 9 10 11 12   **Fic**
1. Murder -- Fiction 2. Paranormal fiction 3. Detectives -- Fiction 4. Genies -- Fiction 5. Secrets -- Fiction 6. Supernatural -- Fiction 7. Mystery and detective stories 8. Blessing and cursing -- Fiction 9. Private investigators -- Fiction
ISBN 0316283932; 9780316283939

LC 2014013252

In Jennifer Latham's novel readers "meet Scarlett, a smart, sarcastic fifteen-year-old, ready to take on crime in her hometown. When Scarlett agrees to investigate a local boy's suicide, she figures she's in for an easy case and a quick buck. But it doesn't take long for suicide to start looking a lot like murder. As Scarlett finds herself deep in a world of cults, curses, and the seemingly supernatural, she discovers that her own family secrets may have more to do with the situation than she thinks." (Publisher's note)

"This whip-smart, determined, black Muslim heroine brings a fresh hard-boiled tone to the field of teen mysteries." Kirkus

Lauren, Christina

Sublime; Christina Lauren. First edition Simon & Schuster 2014 336 p. (hardcover) $17.99
Grades: 10 11 12   **Fic**
1. Ghost stories 2. Dead -- Fiction 3. Love -- Fiction 4. Supernatural -- Fiction 5. Ghosts -- Fiction
ISBN 1481413686; 9781481413688; 9781481413695

LC 2013038763

This book, by Christina Lauren, presents a love story involving a ghost "who has appeared . . . 10 years after her murder. Lucy doesn't know why she has reappeared, but she quickly senses that it has to do with Colin, a daredevil student who lost both parents when his mother drove the family off a bridge. Lucy and Colin have a special connection, and as they fall for each other, he learns that if he brings himself to the edge of death, they can be together for real." (Publisher's note)

"The poetic writing and shared viewpoints of these two damaged souls seamlessly flow together in this spooky, sexy romance, dripping with heady sweetness." Booklist

Lawlor, Laurie

The **two** loves of Will Shakespeare. Holiday House 2006 278p $16.95
Grades: 9 10 11 12   **Fic**
1. Poets 2. Authors 3. Dramatists 4. Great Britain -- History -- 1485-1603, Tudors -- Fiction
ISBN 0-8234-1901-0; 978-0-8234-1901-2

LC 2005-52537

After falling in love, eighteen-year-old Will Shakespeare, a bored apprentice in his father's glove business and often in trouble for various misdeeds, vows to live an upstanding life and pursue his passion for writing.

"Quoting lines from Shakespeare's sonnets and highlighting the dismal treatment of women in that brutally repressive society, the author creates both a vivid setting and a feckless protagonist, equally credible as an adolescent and as a product of his times." Booklist

Le Guin, Ursula K.

Gifts. Harcourt 2004 274p $17; $17; pa $7.95
Grades: 7 8 9 10   **Fic**
1. Fantasy fiction
ISBN 9780152051235; 0-15-205123-6; 0-15-205124-4 pa

LC 2003-21449

"Brantors, or chiefs, of the various clans of the Uplands have powers passed down through generations, powers to call animals to the hunt, start fires, cast a wasting disease, or undo the very essence of a life or thing. The clans live isolated from the inhabitants of the Lowland cities in an uneasy truce, where each people's ambitions are kept at bay by fear of the other's vengeance. Two Upland teenagers, Gry and Orrec, have grown from childhood friendship into romance and also into a repudiation of their hereditary powers. . . . Rejecting traditions that bind them to roles unwanted and undesired, Gry and Orrec decide to leave their homes and seek a freer if less privileged life in the Lowlands. . . . Grades seven to twelve." (Bull Cent Child Books)

"Although intriguing as a coming-of-age allegory, Orrec's story is also rich in . . . earthy magic and intelligent plot twists." Booklist

The **lathe** of heaven; a novel. Scribner 2008 184p pa $15

Grades: 11 12 Adult   Fic

1. Science fiction 2. Dreams -- Fiction

ISBN 978-1-4165-5696-1; 1-4165-5696-6

LC 2007047222

First published 1971 by Scribner

"The author has done some profound research in psychology, cerebrophysiology and biochemistry. . . . In addition, her perceptions of such matters as geopolitics, race, socialized medicine and the patient/shrink relationship are razor-sharp and more than a little cutting." Natl Rev

★ The **left** hand of darkness. Ace Books 2000 304p pa $13.95

Grades: 9 10 11 12   Fic

1. Science fiction 2. Extrasensory perception -- Fiction

ISBN 0-441-00731-7

A reissue of the title first published 1969 by Walker & Company

ALA YALSA Margaret A. Edwards Award (2004)

"This is a tale of political intrigue and danger on the world of Gethen, the Winter planet. Genly Ai, high official of the Eukemen—the commonwealth of worlds—is on Gethen to convince the royalty to join the Federation. He soon becomes a pawn in Gethen's power struggles, set against the elaborate mores of the Gethenians, a unisex hermaphroditic people whose intricate sexual physiology plays a key role in the conflict. Allied with Estraven, fallen lord, Genly is forced to cross the savage and impassable Gobrin Ice." Shapiro. Fic for Youth. 3d edition

Powers. Harcourt 2007 502p map $17; pa $7.99

Grades: 7 8 9 10   Fic

1. Fantasy fiction

ISBN 978-0-15-205770-1; 0-15-205770-6; 978-0-15-206674-1 pa; 0-15-206674-8 pa

LC 2006-13549

Sequel to Voices (2006)

When young Gavir's sister is brutally killed, he escapes from slavery and sets out to explore the world and his own psychic abilities.

"Le Guin uses her own prodigious power as a writer to craft lyrical, precise sentences, evoking a palpable sense of place and believable characters." SLJ

Voices. Harcourt 2006 341p $17

Grades: 7 8 9 10   Fic

1. Fantasy fiction

ISBN 978-015-205678-0; 0-15-205678-5

LC 2005020753

Sequel to Gifts (2004)

Young Memer takes on a pivotal role in freeing her war-torn homeland from its oppressive captors.

"While her prose is simple and unadorned, Le Guin's superior narrative voice and storytelling power make even small moments ring with truth, and often with beauty." SLJ

Followed by Powers (2007)

Leavitt, Lindsey

Going vintage; by Lindsey Leavitt. 1st U.S. ed. Bloomsbury 2013 320 p. (hardcover) $16.99

Grades: 7 8 9 10   Fic

1. School stories 2. Sisters -- Fiction 3. Dating (Social customs) -- Fiction 4. Lists -- Fiction 5. Schools -- Fiction 6. California -- Fiction 7. High schools -- Fiction 8. Family life -- California -- Fiction

ISBN 1599907879; 9781599907871

LC 2012023269

In this book, "after discovering her boyfriend has a serious online relationship with another girl, Mallory very publicly dumps him on his social media site. She complicates the situation by deciding to try to fulfill a to-do list her grandmother crafted at the beginning of her junior year of high school in 1962, a time Mallory thinks must have been much simpler than today. . . . She's aided by her loyal younger sister, Ginnie, and the growing affection of her ex's cousin, charming Oliver." (Kirkus)

Sean Griswold's head. Bloomsbury 2011 276p $16.99

Grades: 7 8 9 10   Fic

1. School stories 2. Family life -- Fiction 3. Pennsylvania -- Fiction 4. Multiple sclerosis -- Fiction

ISBN 978-1-59990-498-6; 1-59990-498-5

LC 2010-06949

"Leavitt capably handles the issues of chronic illness with sensitivity, making this an insightful, humorous, and ultimately uplifting family drama." Bull Cent Child Books

Leavitt, Martine

My book of life by Angel; Martine Leavitt. Farrar, Straus and Giroux Books for Young Readers 2012 252 p. $17.99; (hardback) $17.99; (ebook) $12.95

Grades: 8 9 10 11   Fic

1. Novels in verse 2. Runaway teenagers -- Fiction 3. Juvenile prostitution -- Fiction 4. Runaways -- Fiction 5. Drug abuse -- Fiction 6. Prostitution -- Fiction 7. Vancouver (B.C.) -- Fiction

ISBN 0374351236; 9780374351236; 9781554983179

LC 2011044563

This "novel in verse tells the story of 16-year-old Angel, who has been working as a prostitute in Vancouver. . . . After Angel's friend Serena disappears, Angel decides to give up" the drugs her pimp Call feeds her "and try to return home. Angel's withdrawal is severe . . . but it's nothing compared to the pain she feels when Call brings home an 11-year-old girl, Melli, to follow in Angel's footsteps. Angel is determined to keep Melli safe, even while other women continue to disappear." (Publishers Weekly)

Lee, Harper

★ **To** kill a mockingbird; Harper Lee. 50th anniversary ed; Harper 2010 323p $25.00

Grades: 8 9 10 11 12 Adult   Fic

1. Alabama -- Fiction 2. Race relations -- Fiction

ISBN 9780061743528

A reissue of the title first published 1960 by Lippincott

"Scout, as Jean Louise is called, is a precocious child. She relates her impressions of the time when her lawyer father, Atticus Finch, is defending a black man accused of raping a white woman in a small Alabama town during the 1930's. Atticus's courageous act brings the violence and injustice that exists in their world sharply into focus as it intrudes into the lighthearted life that Scout and her brother Jem have enjoyed until that time." Shapiro. Fic for Youth. 3d edition

Lee, Stacey

Under a painted sky; Stacey Lee. G. P. Putnam's Sons, an imprint of Penguin Group (USA) 2015 374 p. $16.99

Grades: 9 10 11 12   **Fic**
1. Oregon Trail -- Fiction 2. Fugitive slaves -- Fiction 3. Chinese Americans -- Fiction 4. Slavery -- Fiction 5. Runaways -- Fiction 6. Sex role -- Fiction 7. African Americans -- Fiction 8. Adventure and adventurers -- Fiction 9. Oregon National Historic Trail -- Fiction 10. West (U.S.) -- History -- 1848-1860 -- Fiction
ISBN 0399168036; 9780399168031

LC 2014015976

In this book by Stacey Lee, "it's 1849 in Missouri and Chinese American Samantha is in trouble. Her father's shop burned down, he died in the blaze, and she is wanted for murder after killing a man who tried to rape her. Luckily, plucky Annamae, a slave, helps her escape. A runaway slave and a Chinese girl would stick out like a sore thumb on the Oregon Trail, so they disguise themselves as boys--Andy and Sammy--and try to lie low as they make their way to California." (Booklist)

"Debut author Lee packs the plot with plenty of peril and Wild West excitement, and Sammy's fixation on fate, luck, and the Chinese zodiac adds a unique flavor. A great fit for fans of historical adventure with a touch of romance." Booklist

Lee, Ying S.

The **body** at the tower. Candlewick Press 2010 337p (The Agency) $16.99

Grades: 8 9 10 11 12   **Fic**
1. Mystery fiction 2. Orphans -- Fiction 3. Great Britain -- History -- 19th century -- Fiction
ISBN 978-0-7636-4968-5; 0-7636-4968-6
Sequel to: A spy in the house (2010)

"Mary Quinn returns in another case for the Agency, a covert all-female detective agency in Victorian London. A man has recently fallen out of the soon-to-be-completed clock tower of the Houses of Parliament. Mary disguises herself as an errand boy and attempts to infiltrate the work site to discover potential suspects. . . . This second book is much stronger than the first, both in terms of character development and the central mystery." SLJ

Followed by: The traitor in the tunnel (2012)

A **spy** in the house. Candlewick Press 2010 335p (The Agency) $16.99

Grades: 8 9 10 11 12   **Fic**
1. Mystery fiction 2. Orphans -- Fiction 3. Household employees -- Fiction 4. Swindlers and swindling -- Fiction 5. Great Britain -- History -- 19th century --

Fiction
ISBN 978-0-7636-4067-5; 0-7636-4067-0

LC 2009-32736

Rescued from the gallows in 1850s London, young orphan and thief Mary Quinn is offered a place at Miss Scrimshaw's Academy for Girls where she is trained to be part of an all-female investigative unit called The Agency and, at age seventeen, she infiltrates a rich merchant's home in hopes of tracing his missing cargo ships.

"Lee fills the story with classic elements of Victorian mystery and melodrama. Class differences, love gone awry, racial discrimination, London's growing pains in the 1850s, and the status of women in society are all addressed. Historical details are woven seamlessly into the plot, and descriptive writing allows readers to be part of each scene." SLJ

Other titles in this series are:
The body at the tower (2010)
The traitor in the tunnel (2012)

LeFlore, Lyah

The **world** is mine; [by] Lyah B. LeFlore; with illustrations by DL Warfield. Simon Pulse 2009 269p il (Come up) pa $8.99

Grades: 7 8 9 10   **Fic**
1. School stories 2. Maryland -- Fiction 3. Family life -- Fiction 4. Music industry -- Fiction 5. African Americans -- Fiction
ISBN 978-1-4169-7963-0; 1-4169-7963-8

LC 2009-6900

Maryland high school juniors and best friends Blue Reynolds and Collin Andrews seem to have it all, and when they decide to become party promoters, anything can happen—including being pitted against parents, jealous girlfriends, and even one another.

"Teens, especially the hip-hop obsessed, will relate to the characters' stratospheric aspirations, their struggles to balance their passions with parental demands, as well as the sharp dialogue and narration." Publ Wkly

Lennon, Tom

When love comes to town; Tom Lennon. Albert Whitman 2013 304 p. (reinforced) $15.99

Grades: 8 9 10 11 12   **Fic**
1. Historical fiction 2. Gay teenagers -- Fiction 3. Gays -- Fiction 4. Ireland -- Fiction 5. Coming out (Sexual orientation) -- Fiction
ISBN 0807589160; 9780807589168

LC 2012020160

In this novel, by Tom Lennon, "the year is 1990, and in his hometown of Dublin, Ireland, Neil Byrne plays rugby, keeps up with the in-crowd at his school, and is just a regular guy. A guy who's gay. It's a secret he keeps from the wider world as he explores the city at night and struggles to figure out how to reveal his real self--and to whom." (Publisher's note)

Leroux, Gaston

The **phantom** of the opera; introduction by Anne Perry. Modern Library 2002 xxiii, 286p (The Modern Library Classics) pa $8.95

Grades: 9 10 11 12   **Fic**
  1. Paris (France) -- Fiction
ISBN 0-375-76113-6

LC 2002-67075

First published 1911 by The Bobbs-Merrill Company

This love story/thriller relates the tale of the mysterious masked terror who inhabits the cellars of the Paris Opera House

Les Becquets, Diane

Love, Cajun style. Bloomsbury 2005 296p $16.95; pa $7.95

Grades: 9 10 11 12   **Fic**
  1. Aunts -- Fiction 2. Louisiana -- Fiction 3. Friendship -- Fiction 4. Family life -- Fiction
ISBN 1-58234-674-7; 1-59990-030-0 pa

LC 2005-11948

Teenage Lucy learns about life and love with the help of her friends and saucy Tante Pearl over the course of one hot Louisiana summer before her senior year of high school.

"This is romantic, real, and lots of fun." Booklist

Lessing, Doris May

The **sweetest** dream; [by] Doris Lessing. HarperCollins Pubs. 2002 478p hardcover o.p. pa $13.95

Grades: 11 12 Adult   **Fic**
  1. Feminism -- Fiction 2. London (England) -- Fiction
ISBN 0-06-621334-7; 0-06-093755-6 pa

LC 2002-279950

"Lessing's understanding of relationships—both personal and political—has always been keen; now . . . it is unparalleled. This novel is warm and heartfelt, old-fashioned and ambitious in its historical sweep." New Statesman (1913)

Lester, Joan Steinau

Black, white, other. Zondervan 2011 222p $15.99

Grades: 7 8 9 10   **Fic**
  1. Divorce -- Fiction 2. Slavery -- Fiction 3. California -- Fiction 4. Family life -- Fiction 5. Grandmothers -- Fiction 6. Race relations -- Fiction 7. Racially mixed people -- Fiction
ISBN 978-0-310-72763-7; 0-310-72763-4

LC 2011015208

Twenty miles from Oakland, California, where fires have led to racial tension, multi-racial fifteen-year-old Nina faces the bigotry of long-time friends, her parents' divorce, and her brother's misbehavior, while learning about her great-great grandmother Sarah's escape from slavery.

"Lester . . . conjures a credible plot and complications; divorce is a fact of life and racially mixed heritage is conspicuously becoming one. The simple contrapuntal narrative of Sarah Armstrong's escaping slavery distinguishes the book emotionally and psychologically, raising it above other issue-oriented YA novels. Lester writes with social sensitivity and an ear for teen language and concerns. This is engaging treatment of a challenging subject that comes with little precedent." Publ Wkly

Includes bibliographical references

Lester, Julius

★ **Day** of tears; a novel in dialogue. Hyperion 2005 177p hardcover o.p. pa $7.99

Grades: 7 8 9 10   **Fic**
  1. Slavery -- Fiction 2. African Americans -- Fiction
ISBN 0-7868-0490-4; 1-42310-409-9 pa

Coretta Scott King Award for text

Emma has taken care of the Butler children since Sarah and Frances's mother, Fanny, left. Emma wants to raise the girls to have good hearts, as a rift over slavery has ripped the Butler household apart. Now, to pay off debts, Pierce Butler wants to cash in his slave "assets", possibly including Emma.

"The horror of the auction and its aftermath is unforgettable. . . . The racism is virulent (there's widespread use of the n-word). The personal voices make this a stirring text for group discussion." Booklist

★ **Guardian.** Amistad/HarperTeen 2008 129p $16.99; lib bdg $17.89

Grades: 7 8 9 10   **Fic**
  1. Lynching -- Fiction 2. Race relations -- Fiction 3. Southern States -- Fiction 4. African Americans -- Fiction
ISBN 978-0-06-155890-0; 0-06-155890-7; 978-0-06-155891-7 lib bdg; 0-06-155891-5 lib bdg

LC 2008-14251

In a rural southern town in 1946, a white man and his son witness the lynching of an innocent black man. Includes historical note on lynching.

"The author's understated, haunting prose is as compelling as it is dark; . . . [the story] leaves a deep impression." Publ Wkly

Includes bibliographical references

Time's memory. Farrar, Straus & Giroux 2006 230p $17

Grades: 8 9 10 11 12   **Fic**
  1. Slavery -- Fiction 2. African Americans -- Fiction
ISBN 0-374-37178-4; 978-0-374-37178-4

LC 2005-47716

Ekundayo, a Dogon spirit brought to America from Africa, inhabits the body of a young African American slave on a Virginia plantation, where he experiences loss, sorrow, and reconciliation in the months preceding the Civil War.

"More than a picture of slavery through the eyes of those enslaved or their captors, Lester's narrative evokes spiritual images of Mali's Dogon people." SLJ

Letting Ana go; Anonymous. Simon Pulse 2013 304 p. $17.99

Grades: 9 10 11 12   **Fic**
  1. Anorexia nervosa -- Fiction 2. Diet -- Fiction 3. Diaries -- Fiction 4. Food habits -- Fiction 5. Family problems -- Fiction 6. Self-perception -- Fiction 7. Anexoria nervosa -- Fiction
ISBN 1442472235; 9781442472235

LC 2012037458

This book provides an "account of one girl's battle with anorexia. . . . The unnamed narrator begins her story as a healthy, well-adjusted teen from a privileged family. Her overweight mother struggles with food issues on a daily basis and receives little emotional support from her husband. .

. . Witnessing the deterioration of her parents' marriage, the teen becomes overwhelmed by a flood of conflicting emotions and channels her need for order into restricting what she eats." (School Library Journal)

Levine, Ellen, 1939-2012

In trouble. Carolrhoda Lab 2011 200p $17.95
Grades: 7 8 9 10   **Fic**
1. Rape -- Fiction 2. Abortion -- Fiction 3. Pregnancy -- Fiction 4. Family life -- Fiction 5. New York (State) -- Fiction
ISBN 978-0-7613-6558-7; 0-7613-6558-3; 9780761365587; 0761365583
        LC 2010051448

In 1950s New York, sixteen-year-old Jamie's life is unsettled since her father returned from serving time in prison for refusing to name people as Communists, when her best friend turns to Jamie for help with an unplanned pregnancy.

"The author's notes and acknowledgments draw together the past and present, making the book a good choice for required reading in sociology or advanced American history classes. In Trouble should be available in every library serving young adults." SLJ

Levine, Gail Carson

Fairest. HarperCollins 2006 326p $16.99
Grades: 6 7 8 9   **Fic**
1. Fairy tales 2. Singing -- Fiction
ISBN 978-0-06-073408-4; 0-06-073408-6
        LC 2006-00337

In a land where beauty and singing are valued above all else, Aza eventually comes to reconcile her unconventional appearance and her magical voice, and learns to accept herself for who she truly is.

"The plot is fast-paced, and Aza's growth and maturity are well crafted and believable." SLJ

Levine, James A.

Bingo's Run; a novel. James A. Levine. First edition Spiegel & Grau 2013 287 p. (acid-free paper) $24

Grades: 11 12 Adult   **Fic**
1. Africa -- Fiction 2. Drug traffic -- Fiction 3. Art appreciation -- Fiction 4. Kibera (Kenya) -- Fiction 5. Drug traffic -- Kenya -- Fiction 6. Young men -- Conduct of life -- Fiction
ISBN 1400068835; 9781400068838
        LC 2013002647

Alex Award (2015)

This novel, by James A. Levine, is a story of "morality and the redemptive powers of art. . . . Meet Bingo, the greatest drug runner in the slums of Kibera, Nairobi, and maybe the world. A teenage grifter, often mistaken for a younger boy, he faithfully serves Wolf, the drug lord of Kibera. . . . Bingo earns his keep by running 'white' to a host of clients, including Thomas Hunsa, a reclusive artist whose paintings, rooted in African tradition, move him." (Publisher's note)

"As Bingo asserts many times throughout Levine's second novel (after The Blue Notebook), "I am the greatest runner in Kibera, Nairobi, and probably the world.".... Bingo is a fascinating and inimitably likable character. Levine, a Mayo clinic professor of medicine and well-known child advocate,

excels at telling his adventurous, comic, and realistically gritty story with humor but not with pathos, successfully addressing the harsh and sometimes tragic story of a child at risk." LJ

Levithan, David

Another day; David Levithan. Alfred A. Knopf 2015 336 p. (trade) $17.99 **Fic**
1. Hi-Lo books 2. Love stories 3. School stories 4. Identity -- Fiction 5. Love -- Fiction 6. Schools -- Fiction 7. High schools -- Fiction
ISBN 9780385756204; 9780385756211
        LC 2015005798

This novel, by David Levithan, is a companion to the author's previous novel "Every Day," told from another character's perspective. "Every day is the same for Rhiannon. . . . Then, one day, a stranger tells her that the Justin she spent that day with, the one who made her feel like a real person . . . wasn't Justin at all." (Publisher's note)

"...nothing really new or earth shattering is revealed other than Levithan's ability to tell the same story from a different perspective. A fast-paced, absorbing companion." Kirkus

Boy meets boy. Alfred A. Knopf 2003 208p hardcover o.p. pa $8.95
Grades: 9 10 11 12   **Fic**
1. Gay teenagers -- Fiction 2. Teenage boys -- Fiction
ISBN 0-375-82400-6; 0-375-83299-8 pa
        LC 2002-73154

"Somewhere on the eastern coast of the US that's home to Francesca Lia Block's Los Angeles is a town where six-foot-five drag queens play high-school football, kindergarten teachers write comments like "Definitely gay and has a very good sense of self" on student report cards, quiz-bowl teams are as important as football teams, and cheerleaders ride Harleys. Paul and his friends go to high school in this town. Paul meets Noah, falls for him, does something dumb, and loses him. The last half of the story is about Paul working to get Noah back." Kirkus

★ **Every** day; by David Levithan. Alfred A. Knopf 2012 336 p. (hard cover) $16.99
Grades: 9 10 11 12   **Fic**
1. Love stories 2. Paranormal fiction 3. Teenagers -- Fiction 4. Love -- Fiction 5. Interpersonal relations -- Fiction
ISBN 0307931889; 9780307931887; 9780307931894; 9780307975638; 9780375971112
        LC 2012004173

This book follows A, "who takes over the body of a different person each day at midnight. Right around A's 6,000th day on the planet, A meets Rhiannon—girlfriend of current host body Justin—and falls in love. A is careful not to disrupt the lives of the bodies he/she inhabits (A doesn't identify as male or female), but that starts to change as A pursues Rhiannon." (Publishers Weekly)

"Levithan's self-conscious, analytical style marries perfectly with the plot...Readers will devour his trademark poetic wordplay and cadences that feel as fresh as they were when he wrote Boy Meets Boy (2003)." Kirkus

Every you, every me; photographs by Jonathan Farmer. Alfred A. Knopf 2011 248p il $16.99; lib bdg $19.99; ebook $10.99

Grades: 9 10 11 12   **Fic**

1. School stories 2. Friendship -- Fiction 3. Mental illness -- Fiction

ISBN 978-0-375-86098-0; 978-0-375-96098-7 lib bdg; 978-0-375-89621-7 ebook

LC 2010048723

Evan is haunted by the loss of his best friend, but when mysterious photographs start appearing, he begins to fall apart as he starts to wonder if she has returned, seeking vengeance.

"The book is written for high school students who enjoy suspense but also for those who face depression in everyday life. Mental illness and loss touch all of us and this book shows what can happen to survivors self destructive behaviors." Voice Youth Advocates

★ **Hold** me closer; the Tiny Cooper story. by David Levithan. Dutton Books, an imprint of Penguin Group (USA) LLC 2015 208 p. (hardcover) $17.99

Grades: 9 10 11 12   **Fic**

1. Love -- Fiction 2. Musicals -- Fiction 3. Gay teenagers -- Fiction 4. Dating (Social customs) -- Fiction 5. Gays -- Fiction

ISBN 0525428844; 9780525428848

LC 2014039368

This book by David Levithan presents the "autobiographical musical extravaganza" composed by the character Tiny Cooper in the book "Will Grayson, Will Grayson". "The musical traces Tiny's life from birth through age sixteen. . . . Tiny . . . delivers extensive stage directions that tell some of the story behind the story, indicating tone, mood, and what other musicals he's channeling so that readers will be able to visualize the production." (Bulletin of the Center for Children's Books)

"Tiny Cooper, the memorable best friend from Levithan and John Green's Will Grayson, Will Grayson, gets his own star turn in this companion volume, which contains the script and lyrics of the autobiographical musical he wrote and staged in the original novel...hough billed as a "musical novel," there is no sheet music yet written for Tiny's magnum opus. Levithan is hoping for a crowd-sourced soundtrack, encouraging amateur and professional composers to put music to his words. Broadway, are you listening?" PW

Love is the higher law. Alfred A. Knopf 2009 167p $15.99; lib bdg $18.99

Grades: 8 9 10 11 12   **Fic**

1. Homosexuality -- Fiction 2. New York (N.Y.) -- Fiction 3. September 11 terrorist attacks, 2001 -- Fiction

ISBN 978-0-375-83468-4; 0-375-83468-0; 978-0-375-93468-1 lib bdg; 0-375-93468-5 lib bdg

LC 2008-40886

Three New York City teens express their reactions to the bombing of the World Trade Center on September 11, 2001, and its impact on their lives and the world.

"The author's prose has never been deeper in thought or feeling. His writing here is especially pure—unsentimental, restrained, and full of love for his characters and setting. . .

. Levithan captures the mood of post-9/11 New York exquisitely, slashed open to reveal a deep heart." SLJ

The **lover's** dictionary. Farrar, Straus, and Giroux 2011 240p. $18

Grades: 11 12 Adult   **Fic**

1. Love stories 2. Vocabulary -- Fiction

ISBN 978-0-374-19368-3

LC 201014392

Alex Award (2012)

"Written from the perspective of a man in an unnamed couple, each entry, from 'aberrant' to 'zenith,' defines a word within the context of their relationship. The entries follow the couple from their online meeting forward into cohabitation." Libr J

Marly's ghost; a remix of Charles Dickens' A Christmas Carol. with illustrations by Brian Selznick. Dial Books 2006 167p il hardcover o.p. pa $6.99

Grades: 7 8 9 10   **Fic**

1. Ghost stories 2. Valentine's Day -- Fiction

ISBN 0-8037-3063-2; 0-14-240912-X pa

LC 2005-16183

The spirit of Ben's girlfriend Marly returns with three other ghosts to haunt him with a painful journey though Valentine's Days past, present, and future.

"The magical realism is powerful throughout. . . . A solid story to mark the holiday." Booklist

★ **Two** boys kissing; by David Levithan. Alfred A. Knopf 2013 208 p. (hardcover library binding) $19.99

Grades: 8 9 10 11 12   **Fic**

1. School stories 2. Gay teenagers -- Fiction 3. Gays -- Fiction 4. Love -- Fiction 5. Homosexuality -- Fiction 6. Social change -- Fiction

ISBN 0307931900; 0375971122; 9780307931900; 9780307931917; 9780375971129

LC 2012047089

Lambda Literary Awards Winner - LGBT Children's/YA (2014)

Stonewall Honor Book: Children and Young Adult (2014)

In this book, students Craig and Henry are trying to set a world record for the longest kiss They "are no longer dating, throwing an element of uncertainty into an act that's romantic, political, and personal. Neil and Peter have been dating for a year and are beginning to wonder what's next. Avery, 'born a boy that the rest of the world saw as a girl,' and Ryan are caught up in the dizzying excitement of meeting someone new. And Cooper is rapidly losing himself into a digital oblivion." (Publishers Weekly)

"Craig and Harry attempt to break the world record for longest kiss, which, in turn, affects the lives of the people around them. Narrated by a ghostly chorus of past generations of gay men who died of AIDS, Levithan's latest novel weaves together an informed (sometimes melodramatic) perspective on the past with the present-day stories of seven boys constructing their own sexual identities." (Horn Book)

Lewis, Stewart

The **secret** ingredient; Stewart Lewis. Delacorte
Press 2013 256 p. (hc) $17.99

Grades: 7 8 9 10   **Fic**

1. Cooking -- Fiction 2. Mothers -- Fiction 3.
Interpersonal relations -- Fiction 4. Self-realization --
Fiction 5. Los Angeles (Calif.) -- Fiction

ISBN 0385743319; 9780375991066; 9780385743310

LC 2012027203

This novel by Stewart Lewis is a "journey of family,
food, romance, and self-discovery as Olivia, a teen chef living in L.A., finds a vintage cookbook and begins a search
for her birthmother that will change her life forever. A new
job leads Olivia to a gorgeous, mysterious boy named Theo.
And as Olivia cooks the recipes from a vintage cookbook
she stumbles upon, she begins to wonder if the mother she's
never known might be the secret ingredient she's been lacking." (Publisher's note)

"Adopted by two dads, Olivia begins to sense a void in
her life. Serendipitously, Olivia finds her supposedly "nameless" birth mother but quickly realizes that maybe the secret ingredient to a fulfilled life is appreciating what one
already has. Lewis's mature protagonist adapts remarkably
well to her nontraditional life in this story that limns themes
of adolescence, adoption, illness, and financial instability."
(Horn Book)

Lewis, Sylvia

Beautiful decay; Sylvia Lewis. Running Press
Teens 2013 303 p. $9.95

Grades: 7 8 9 10 11 12   **Fic**

1. Supernatural -- Fiction 2. Alienation (Social
psychology) -- Fiction

ISBN 0762446110; 9780762446117

LC 2012951788

This "paranormal horror novel" follows "17-year-old Ellie. . . . A touch of her bare skin can cause anyone or anything
to decay. No one wants to be near her, even though she wears
gloves to avoid contact with anyone. . . .Things at school
improve when Nate, the new guy, seems more curious than
grossed out by her. . . . Ellie finds the strength she didn't
know she had to break away from her lonely, 'bleached and
gloved' existence to help him." (School Library Journal)

"Ellie Miller lives a lonely life. Her parents are rarely
home when she is, her mother spends her time bleaching the
house, and her only friend, Mackenzie, lives two states away
and communicates via computer. Isolated by classmates due
to an "immunity disorder," she wears gloves and dares not
touch anything or anyone...Fans of paranormal will flock to
Lewis' fast-paced debut that offers a unique take on being
different. Many questions are left unanswered, laying the
groundwork for a sequel." (Booklist)

LeZotte, Ann Clare

T4; a novel in verse. written by Ann Clare
LeZotte. Houghton Mifflin Co. 2008 108p $14

Grades: 6 7 8 9 10   **Fic**

1. Novels in verse 2. Deaf -- Fiction 3. Euthanasia
-- Fiction 4. Germany -- History -- 1933-1945 -- Fiction

ISBN 978-0-547-04684-6; 0-547-04684-7

LC 2007-47737

When the Nazi party takes control of Germany, thirteen-
year-old Paula, who is deaf, finds her world-as-she-knows-it
turned upside down, as she is taken into hiding to protect her
from the new law nicknamed T4.

"This novel will have a lasting effect on readers, giving
insight into an often-forgotten aspect of the horrors of the
Third Reich." SLJ

Liberty, Anita

The **center** of the universe; yep, that would be
me. Simon Pulse 2008 291p il pa $9.99

Grades: 10 11 12   **Fic**

1. School stories 2. Girls -- Fiction

ISBN 978-1-4169-5789-8; 1-4169-5789-8

LC 2007-940383

An angst-ridden fictional memoir of Anita Liberty's last
two years in high school is presented through diary entries,
poems, sarcastic advice, scorecards of parental infractions,
and definitions of SAT vocabulary words.

"Female readers should laugh aloud throughout this fast,
entertaining read, and especially appreciate the interesting
epilogue continuing the author's post-high school experiences before ending with her present fulfilling circumstances." Voice Youth Advocates

Lieberman, Leanne

Off pointe; Leanne Lieberman. Orca Book Publishers 2015 128 p. (Orca limelights) (pbk.) $9.95

Grades: 6 7 8 9   **Fic**

1. Ballet -- Fiction 2. Dancers -- Fiction 3. Friendship
-- Fiction 4. Camps -- Fiction 5. Ballet dancers --
Fiction

ISBN 1459802802; 9781459802803; 9781459802810;
9781459802827

LC 2014935396

In this novel by Leanne Lieberman "Meg's summer ballet program is canceled and her ballet teacher suggests she
attend Camp Dance to learn new dance styles. At camp, Meg
struggles to learn contemporary dance. A girl named Logan,
who is jealous of Meg's ballet technique and her friendship
with Nio . . . makes Meg's life even more difficult. When
Meg, Nio and Logan have to work together to create a piece
for the final show, arguments threaten to ruin their dance. "
(Publisher's note)

"No dreadful swerves or lethal surprises here; the books
lead the reader to expect a happy ending and, after the requi-
site hardships, that is where they arrive. The journey may be
bittersweet, but the message is one of hope and encouragement: no success without failure, no learning without doing,
no joy without daring." Voya

Lindstrom, Eric

Not if I see you first; Eric Lindstrom. Little,
Brown & Co. 2016 320 p. (hardcover) $18

Grades: 9 10 11 12   **Fic**

1. School stories 2. Blind -- Fiction 3. Teenage girls
-- Fiction 4. Orphans -- Fiction 5. Schools -- Fiction
6. Friendship -- Fiction 7. High schools -- Fiction
8. Dating (Social customs) -- Fiction 9. People with
disabilities -- Fiction

ISBN 9780316259859

LC 2014037483

This novel, by Eric Lindstrom, follows a blind teenage girl. "Parker Grant doesn't need 20/20 vision to see right through you. . . . Just ask Scott Kilpatrick, the boy who broke her heart. When Scott suddenly reappears in her life after being gone for years, . . . avoiding her past quickly proves impossible, and the more Parker learns about what really happened--both with Scott, and her dad--the more she starts to question if things are always as they seem." (Publisher's Note)

"While Lindstrom's debut understandably contains plenty of melancholy, angst, and self-doubt, it also possesses crackling wit, intense teen drama, and a lively pace that pulls readers in, as do the everyday details of Parker's world: spoken-word texts, clever methods of finding her way, and a guide runner who helps Parker when she considers joining the school track team. This unique coming-of-age tale is off and running from the start." Booklist

Linn, Laurent

★ **Draw** the line; Laurent Linn. Margaret K. McElderry Books 2016 528 p. illustrations (hardback) $17.99

Grades: 9 10 11 12   Fic

1. Artists -- Fiction 2. Hate crimes -- Fiction 3. Gay teenagers -- Fiction 4. High school students 5. Gays -- Fiction 6. Schools -- Fiction 7. High schools -- Fiction

ISBN 9781481452809; 9781481452816; 1481452800

LC 2015029314

In this novel, by Laurent Linn, "Adrian Piper is used to blending into the background. He may be a talented artist, a sci-fi geek, and gay, but at his Texas high school those traits would only bring him the worst kind of attention. The only place he feels free . . . is at his drawing table, crafting a secret world through his own Renaissance-art-inspired superhero, Graphite. When a shocking hate crime flips his world upside down, Adrian must decide what kind of person he wants to be." (Publisher's note)

"At the risk of revealing his closeted sexuality and artistic talent, a Texas wallflower combats small minds. Adrian Piper dresses to hide. Innocuous palette, faded jeans, a hoodie: disappearing = safety at Rock Hollow High, where Bubbas with a penchant for pickups and longnecks are the dominant species. Adrian's escape from aggressive heteronormativity is "the feel of a 3B pencil skimming across the paper's surface." The result of said skimming: a gay superhero named Graphite with a flair for Renaissance couture and a longing for love. . . . A definite draw for comic-book fans, it will resonate with anyone struggling with a concealed or revealed identity. More defiant than its superhero's diaphanous costume portends. Bravo." Kirkus

Lippert-Martin, Kristen

Tabula rasa; Kristen Lippert-Martin. Egmont USA 2014 335 p. (hardcover) $17.99

Grades: 6 7 8 9   Fic

1. Science fiction 2. Adventure fiction 3. Memory -- Fiction 4. Hospitals -- Fiction 5. Adventure and adventurers -- Fiction

ISBN 1606845187; 9781606845189

LC 2013030315

In this book, by Kristen Lippert-Martin, "Sarah starts a crazy battle for her life within the walls of her hospital-turned-prison when a procedure to eliminate her memory goes awry and she starts to remember snatches of her past. Was she an urban terrorist or vigilante? Has the procedure been her salvation or her destruction? The answers lie trapped within her mind. To access them, she'll need the help of the teen computer hacker who's trying to bring the hospital down for his own reasons." (Publisher's note)

"Mysteries stack upon mysteries in this gripping, multifaceted thriller. A page-turning adventure that will leave readers hoping for a sequel." Horn Book

Lipsyte, Robert

★ The **contender**. Harper & Row 1967 182p hardcover o.p. pa $5.99

Grades: 7 8 9 10   Fic

1. Boxing -- Fiction 2. African Americans -- Fiction 3. Harlem (New York, N.Y.) -- Fiction

ISBN 0-06-447039-3

ALA YALSA Margaret A. Edwards Award (2001)

"After a street fight in which he is the chief target, Alfred wanders into a gym in his neighborhood. He decides not only to improve his physical condition but also to become a boxer. Because of this interest Alfred's life is completely changed. He assumes a more positive outlook on his immediate future, even within the confines of a black ghetto." Shapiro. Fic for Youth. 3d edition

Followed by The brave (1991) and The chief (1993)

One fat summer. Harper & Row 1977 152p hardcover o.p. pa $5.99

Grades: 7 8 9 10   Fic

1. Obesity -- Fiction 2. Weight loss -- Fiction

ISBN 0-06-023895-X; 0-06-447073-3 pa

LC 76-49746

ALA YALSA Margaret A. Edwards Award (2001)

"This is far superior to most of the summer-of-change stories; any change that takes place is logical and the protagonist learns by action and reaction to be both self-reliant and compassionate." Bull Cent Child Books

Followed by Summer rules (1981) and The summerboy (1982)

Littlefield, Sophie

Infected; Sophie Littlefield. First edition Delacorte Press 2015 256 p. (hc: alk. paper) $17.99

Grades: 7 8 9 10   Fic

1. Conspiracies -- Fiction 2. Family secrets -- Fiction 3. National security -- United States 4. Spies -- Fiction 5. Survival -- Fiction 6. Dating (Social customs) -- Fiction

ISBN 0385741065; 9780375989834; 9780385741064

LC 2013046923

"Carina's senior year is spiraling downward. Fast. Both her mother and her uncle, the only two family members she's ever known, are dead. Their deaths were accidents, unfortunate results of the highly confidential research they performed for a national security organization. The people Carina loved kept dangerous secrets. Secrets that make her question the life she's been living up to now." (Publisher's note)

"Nail-biting action with a scientifically and technologically involved plotline gives this novel an edge, and, more-

over, the character development is surprisingly rich given
the fast pace of the narrative. The weight of the themes also
keeps the story from reading like a movie script. Red herrings keep the reader guessing until the end. Hard to put
down." Booklist

Littman, Sarah Darer

Backlash; Sarah Darer Littman. First edition
Scholastic Press 2015 325 p. $17.99
Grades: 7 8 9　　　　　　　　　　　　　　　Fic
1. Bullies -- Fiction 2. Sisters -- Fiction 3. Suicide --
Fiction 4. Neighbors -- Fiction 5. Friendship -- Fiction
6. Family life -- Fiction 7. Cyberbullying -- Fiction 8.
Bullying -- Fiction
ISBN 0545651263; 9780545651264; 9780545651271;
9780545755023
　　　　　　　　　　　　　　　LC 2014020226
In this book, by Sarah Darer Littman, "Lara just got told
off on Facebook. She thought that Christian liked her, that
he was finally going to ask her to his school's homecoming dance. It's been a long time since Lara's felt this bad,
this depressed. . . . Bree used to be BBFs with overweight,
depressed Lara in middle school, but constantly listening
to Lara's problems got to be too much. Bree's secretly glad
that Christian's pointed out Lara's flaws to the world." (Publisher's note)
"The depression and bullying are handled realistically without sugarcoating, and fortunately, consequences are applied. An excellent choice for any antibullying
campaign." Booklist

Lloyd, Saci

★ The **carbon** diaries 2015. Holiday House
2009 330p il map $17.95
Grades: 8 9 10 11 12　　　　　　　　　　　　Fic
1. Science fiction 2. Family life -- Fiction 3. Great
Britain -- Fiction 4. Conservation of natural resources
-- Fiction
ISBN 978-0-8234-2190-9; 0-8234-2190-2
　　　　　　　　　　　　　　　LC 2008-19712
First published 2008 in the United Kingdom
In 2015, when England becomes the first nation to in-
troduce carbon dioxide rationing in a drastic bid to combat
climate change, sixteen-year-old Laura documents the first
year of rationing as her family spirals out of control.
"Deeply compulsive and urgently compulsory
reading." Booklist
Includes bibliographical references
Followed by The carbon diaries 2017 (2010)

The **carbon** diaries 2017. Holiday House 2010
326p il map $17.95
Grades: 8 9 10 11 12　　　　　　　　　　　　Fic
1. Science fiction 2. College students -- Fiction 3.
London (England) -- Fiction 4. Conservation of natural
resources -- Fiction
ISBN 978-0-8234-2260-9; 0-8234-2260-7
Sequel to: The carbon diaries 2015 (2009)
First published 2009 in the United Kingdom
Two years after England introduces carbon dioxide ra-
tioning to combat climatic change, eighteen-year-old Laura

chronicles her first year at a London university as natural
disasters and political upheaval disrupt her studies.
"The friction of living life in times of radical upheaval
remains potent, sobering, and awfully exciting." Booklist

Lloyd-Jones, Emily

Illusive; Emily Lloyd-Jones. Little, Brown & Co.
2014 416 p. (hardcover) $18
Grades: 7 8 9 10 11 12　　　　　　　　　　　Fic
1. Science fiction 2. Dystopian fiction 3. Vaccines --
Fiction 4. Superheroes -- Fiction 5. Organized crime --
Fiction 6. Robbers and outlaws -- Fiction 7. Adventure
and adventurers -- Fiction
ISBN 0316254568; 9780316254564
　　　　　　　　　　　　　　　LC 2013025295
Sequel: Deceptive (2015)
In this young adult science fiction novel by Emily Lloyd-
Jones, "When the MK virus swept across the planet, a vaccine was created to stop the epidemic, but it came with some
unexpected side effects. A small percentage of the population developed superhero-like powers. Seventeen-year-old
Ciere Giba has the handy ability to change her appearance
at will. She's what's known as an illusionist...She's also a
thief." (Publisher's note)
"Ciere, a teenage career criminal with the ability to create illusions, lives in a dystopian future where a vaccine
gone wrong created a feared minority of people with super-
powers. Her latest job pulls her and her Dickensian gang of
misfit allies into a power struggle involving the future of the
vaccine. Innovative world-building and a scrappy protagonist strengthen this high-stakes caper." Horn Book

Lo, Malinda

Adaptation; Malinda Lo. Little, Brown Books
for Young Readers 2012 400 p. (hardcover) $17.99
Grades: 9 10 11 12　　　　　　　　　　　　　Fic
1. Mystery fiction 2. Secrecy -- Fiction 3. Lesbians
-- Fiction 4. Love -- Fiction 5. Science fiction 6.
Conspiracies -- Fiction 7. Sexual orientation -- Fiction
8. Genetic engineering -- Fiction 9. Extraterrestrial
beings -- Fiction
ISBN 0316197963; 9780316197960
　　　　　　　　　　　　　　　LC 2012005489
Author Malinda Lo tells the story of "Reese and David,
traveling home after a disastrous debate tournament, [who]
are in a near-fatal car accident near a mysterious government facility. The tension is relentless until the teens make it
safely back to San Francisco, at which point romantic entan-
glements (Reese falls for Amber, but maybe she likes David
too) detract from the strange abilities Reese and David are
developing and the conspiracies they begin to unravel (with
lots of men in black after the)." (Kirkus)

Ash. Little, Brown and Co. 2009 264p $16.99;
pa $8.99
Grades: 8 9 10 11　　　　　　　　　　　　　Fic
1. Fairy tales 2. Love stories 3. Fairies -- Fiction 4.
Stepfamilies -- Fiction
ISBN 978-0-316-04009-9; 0-316-04009-6; 978-0-316-
04010-5 pa; 0-316-04010-X pa
　　　　　　　　　　　　　　　LC 2009-17471
ALA YALSA Morris Award Finalist, 2010

In this variation on the Cinderella story, Ash grows up believing in the fairy realm that the king and his philosophers have sought to suppress, until one day she must choose between a handsome fairy cursed to love her and the King's Huntress whom she loves.

"Part heart-pounding lesbian romance and part universal coming-of-age story, Lo's powerful tale is richly embroidered with folklore and glittering fairy magic that will draw fans of Sharon Shinn's earthy, herb-laced fantasies." Booklist

Followed by Huntress (2011)

Huntress. Little, Brown 2011 371p map $17.99
Grades: 9 10 11 12   **Fic**
1. Fairy tales 2. Love stories 3. Fairies -- Fiction 4. Lesbians -- Fiction 5. Voyages and travels -- Fiction
ISBN 978-0-316-04007-5; 0-316-04007-X
LC 2010-38827

"A 'Tam Lin'-inspired rendition of fairy society blends nicely with the author's Chinese and I Ching-inspired human society, creating a delicate, unusual setting; and although the expeditionary plot has an overly deliberate pace, the episodes are varied and emotional enough to retain interest. Most notably, the inclusion of gay characters in a young adult fantasy, and the natural unfolding of their relationship, comes as a refreshing change." Horn Book

Inheritance; by Malinda Lo. Little, Brown and Co. 2013 470 p. $18
Grades: 9 10 11 12   **Fic**
1. Love stories 2. Teenagers -- Fiction 3. Human-alien encounters -- Fiction 4. Love -- Fiction 5. Science fiction 6. Kidnapping -- Fiction 7. Conspiracies -- Fiction 8. Sexual orientation -- Fiction 9. Genetic engineering -- Fiction 10. Extraterrestrial beings -- Fiction
ISBN 0316198005; 9780316198004
LC 2012048433
Sequel to: Adaptation

In this book, by Malinda Lo, "after a car accident, mortally injured Reese and David are revived by an injection of alien DNA that has given the teens special abilities. They are kidnapped by brutal government forces. . . . Returned home, Reese and David are caught in a web of intrigue and lies. . . . The fate of the world seems to be at risk as the government, a secret faction of the government, and the aliens square off at the United Nations." (School Library Journal)

"Reese (Adaptation) juggles her discovery that the government has been working for decades with aliens called the Imria and her feelings for her Imrian ex and her new guy. When huge secrets are revealed, romantic alliances get back-burnered as Reese tries to understand what's next for Earth. Clever plot and strong world-building are this sequel's strengths." (Horn Book)

Lockhart, E.
The **boy** book; a study of habits and behaviors, plus techniques for taming them. Delacorte Press 2006 193p $15.95; lib bdg $17.99
Grades: 8 9 10 11 12   **Fic**
1. School stories 2. Friendship -- Fiction 3. Dating

(Social customs) -- Fiction
ISBN 978-0-385-73208-6; 0-385-73208-2; 978-0-385-90239-7 lib bdg; 0-385-90239-5 lib bdg
LC 2006-4601

A high school junior continues her quest for relevant data on the male species, while enjoying her freedom as a newly licensed driver and examining her friendship with a clean-living vegetarian classmate.

"Lockhart achieves the perfect balance of self-deprecating humor and self-pity in Ruby, and thus imbues her with such realism that she seems almost to fly off the page." Voice Youth Advocates

The **boyfriend** list; (15 guys, 11 shrink appointments, 4 ceramic frogs, and me, Ruby Oliver) Delacorte Press 2005 240p hardcover o.p. pa $8.95
Grades: 9 10 11 12   **Fic**
1. School stories 2. Washington (State) -- Fiction 3. Dating (Social customs) -- Fiction
ISBN 0-385-73206-6; 0-385-73207-4 pa
LC 2004-6691

A Seattle fifteen-year-old explains some of the reasons for her recent panic attacks, including breaking up with her boyfriend, losing all her girlfriends, tensions between her performance-artist mother and her father, and more.

"Readers will find many of Ruby's experiences familiar, and they'll appreciate the story as a lively, often entertaining read." Booklist

Other titles about Ruby Oliver are:
The boy book (2006)
Real live boyfriends (2010)
The treasure map of boys (2009)

★ The **disreputable** history of Frankie Landau-Banks. Hyperion 2008 352p $16.99; pa $8.99
Grades: 7 8 9 10 11 12   **Fic**
1. School stories
ISBN 0-7868-3818-3; 0-7868-3819-1 pa; 978-0-7868-3818-9; 978-0-7868-3819-6 pa
Michael L. Printz Award honor book, 2009

"Frankie Landau-Banks at age 14: Debate Club. Her father's 'bunny rabbit.' A mildly geeky girl attending a highly competitive boarding school. Frankie Landau-Banks at age 15: A knockout figure. A sharp tongue. A chip on her shoulder. And a gorgeous new senior boyfriend: . . . Matthew Livingston. Frankie Landau-Banks. No longer the kind of girl to take 'no' for an answer. Especially when 'no' means she's excluded from her boyfriend's all-male secret society. . . . Not when she knows she's smarter than any of them. When she knows Matthew's lying to her. . . . Frankie Banks at age 16: Possibly a criminal mastermind. This is the story of how she got that way." (Publisher's note) "Grades nine to twelve." (Bull Cent Child Books)

"On her return to Alabaster Prep . . . . [Frankie] attracts the attention of gorgeous Matthew . . . [who] is a member of the Loyal Order of the Basset Hounds, an all-male Alabaster secret society. . . . Frankie engineers her own guerilla membership by assuming a false online identity. . . . Lockhart creates a unique, indelible character. . . . Teens will be galvanized." Booklist

How to be bad; [by] E. Lockhart, Sarah Mlynowski [and] Lauren Myracle. HarperTeen 2008
325p $16.99; lib bdg $17.89

Grades: 9 10 11 12   **Fic**
1. Friendship -- Fiction 2. Automobile travel -- Fiction
ISBN 0-06-128422-X; 0-06-128423-8 lib bdg; 978-0-
06-128422-9; 978-0-06-128423-6 lib bdg

LC 2007-52946

Told in alternating voices, Jesse, Vicks, and Mel, hoping
to leave all their worries and woes behind, escape their small
town by taking a road trip to Miami.

"Whip-smart dialogue and a fast-moving, picaresque
plot that zooms from lump-in-the-throat moments to all-
out giddiness will keep readers going, and it's a testimony
to how real these girls seem that the final chapters are profoundly satisfying rather than tidy." Publ Wkly

Real live boyfriends; yes, boyfriends, plural,
if my life weren't complicated I wouldn't be Ruby
Oliver. Delacorte Press 2010 224p $16.99; lib bdg
$19.99

Grades: 8 9 10 11   **Fic**
1. School stories 2. Seattle (Wash.) -- Fiction 3. Dating
(Social customs) -- Fiction
ISBN 978-0-385-73428-8; 0-385-73428-X; 978-0-
385-90438-4 lib bdg; 0-385-90438-X lib bdg

LC 2009-41988

Now a senior at her Seattle prep school, Ruby continues her angst-filled days coping with the dilemmas of boyfriends, college applications, her parents' squabbling, and
realizing that her "deranged" persona may no longer apply.

The **treasure** map of boys; Noel, Jackson, Finn,
Hutch, Gideon--and me, Ruby Oliver. Delacorte
Press 2009 244p $15.99; lib bdg $18.99

Grades: 8 9 10 11 12   **Fic**
1. School stories 2. Friendship -- Fiction 3. Seattle
(Wash.) -- Fiction 4. Dating (Social customs) -- Fiction
ISBN 978-0-385-73426-4; 0-385-73426-3; 978-0-385-
90437-7 lib bdg; 0-385-90437-1 lib bdg

LC 2008-33062

A Seattle sixteen-year-old juggles therapy, running a
school bake sale, coping with her performance artist mother,
growing distant from an old friend, and conflicting feelings
about her ex-boyfriend and potential new boyfriends.

"Replete with wordplay, footnotes and . . . lots of laugh-
out-loud moments, this is a worthy follow-up." Kirkus

★ **We** were liars; E. Lockhart. Delacorte Press
2014 240 p. (hardback) $17.99

Grades: 7 8 9 10 11 12   **Fic**
1. Summer -- Fiction 2. Wealth -- Fiction 3. Love 4.
Family life 5. Love -- Fiction 6. Amnesia -- Fiction 7.
Families -- Fiction 8. Friendship -- Fiction
ISBN 038574126X; 9780375989940; 9780385741262

LC 2013042127

In this book, by E. Lockhart, "Cadence Sinclair East-
man is the oldest grandchild of a preeminent family. The
Sinclairs have . . . a private island off the coast of Massachusetts called Beechwood. Harris, the family patriarch, has
three daughters: Bess, Carrie, and Penny, who is Cadence's

mother. And then there is the next generation, 'the Liars':
Cadence, Johnny, . . . Mirren, . . . and outsider Gat, an Indian
boy and the nephew of Carrie's boyfriend." (Booklist)

"Cadence Sinclair Easton comes from an old-money
family, headed by a patriarch who owns a private island off
of Cape Cod. Each summer, the extended family gathers at
the various houses on the island, and Cadence, her cousins
Johnny and Mirren, and friend Gat (the four "Liars"), have
been inseparable since age eight....The story, while lightly
touching on issues of class and race, more fully focuses on
dysfunctional family drama, a heart-wrenching romance
between Cadence and Gat, and, ultimately, the suspense of
what happened during that fateful summer. The ending is
a stunner that will haunt readers for a long time to come."
(School Library Journal)

London, Alex

Guardian; Alex London. Philomel Books, an
imprint of Penguin Group (USA) Inc. 2014 352 p.
$17.99

Grades: 7 8 9   **Fic**
1. Science fiction 2. Dystopian fiction 3. Epidemics
-- Fiction 4. Social classes -- Fiction 5. Gays -- Fiction
ISBN 0399165762; 9780399165764

LC 2013025938

Sequel to: Proxy

"It's a grave new world when the revolution a reluctant
hero inspired could mean the death of everyone he tried to
save, including himself. In this sequel to Proxy (2013), radical groups form in the wake of the Jubilee. The Reconciliation staunchly endorses tech-free purity, while Machinists
demand a renaissance of the networks. Reluctant 16-year-
old hero Syd is paraded as a political puppet, labeled a savior by supporters and marked a target by the opposition. His
importance as a mascot for the Reconciliation necessitates a
bodyguard, 17-year-old Liam. Liam is strong (he has a killer
metal hand), silent (too shy for vocal eloquence) and will do
anything to remain near Syd for reasons other than professional integrity. Amid political upheaval, an illness begins to
spread, rendering victims' blue blood black and diminishing their mental faculties. Syd has been a hesitant political
figure but knows he is the only hope for ending the illness."
(Kirkus)

"Nonstop action and breakneck pace characterize this
exceptional thriller. London provides his audience with an
intricate plot, enriched by fine world-building and believable
characters. The ample backstory will enable readers to enjoy Guardian without having read Proxy, although most will
want to read these in sequence. This thought-provoking and
breathtaking novel belongs in all collections serving young
adults." VOYA

Long, Ruth Frances

The **treachery** of beautiful things; by Ruth
Frances Long. Dial Books 2012 363 p. (hardcover)
$17.99

Grades: 7 8 9 10 11 12   **Fic**
1. Fantasy fiction 2. Fairies -- Fiction 3. Forests and
forestry -- Fiction 4. Fantasy 5. Love -- Fiction 6.
Kings, queens, rulers, etc. -- Fiction
ISBN 0803735804; 9780803735804

LC 2011027165

In this book by Ruth Long, "the trees swallowed her brother whole, and Jenny was there to see it. Now seventeen, she revisits the woods where Tom was taken. . . . She's lured into the trees, where she finds strange and dangerous creatures. . . . Among them is Jack, mercurial and magnetic, with secrets of his own. Determined to find her brother, with or without Jack's help, Jenny struggles to navigate a faerie world where stunning beauty masks some of the most treacherous evils." (Publisher's note)

Longshore, Katherine

Brazen; by Katherine Longshore. Viking, published by Penguin Group 2014 528 p. $17.99

Grades: 9 10 11 12   Fic

1. Love stories 2. Courts and courtiers -- Fiction 3. Kings, queens, rulers, etc. -- Fiction 4. Great Britain -- History -- Henry VIII, 1509-1547
ISBN 067001401X; 9780670014019

LC 2013026557

In this young adult romance novel by Katherine Longshore, "Mary Howard has always lived in the shadow of her powerful family. But when she's married off to Henry Fitzroy, King Henry VIII's illegitimate son, she rockets into the Tudor court's inner circle. Mary and 'Fitz' join a tight clique of rebels who test the boundaries of court's strict rules with their games, dares, and flirtations." (Publisher's note)

"At age fourteen, Mary Howard and Henry FitzRoy (an illegitimate son of King Henry VIII) were married but forbidden to consummate the relationship. From this thin skein of historic fact, Longshore weaves a tale of love growing amid the corruption, ambition, and betrayals of the Tudor court. Detailed research and a deftly composed heroine make this hefty historical romance novel satisfying." Horn Book

Gilt; by Katherine Longshore. Viking 2012 406 p. $17.99; (hardcover) $17.99

Grades: 9 10 11 12   Fic

1. Historical fiction 2. Female friendship -- Fiction 3. Great Britain -- History -- 1485-1603, Tudors -- Fiction 4. Courts and courtiers -- Fiction 5. Kings, queens, rulers, etc. -- Fiction 6. Great Britain -- History -- Henry VIII, 1509-1547 -- Fiction
ISBN 0670013994; 9780670013999

LC 2011028214

This book is set in the court of English king Henry VIII. When "Kitty Tylney's best friend, Catherine Howard, worms her way into King Henry VIII's heart and brings Kitty to court, she's thrust into a world filled with fabulous gowns, sparkling jewels, and elegant parties. . . . But court is also full of secrets, lies, and sordid affairs, and as Kitty witnesses Cat's meteoric rise and fall as queen, she must figure out how to keep being a good friend." (Publisher's note)

Tarnish; by Katherine Longshore. Viking 2013 448 p. (hardcover) $17.99

Grades: 9 10 11 12   Fic

1. Historical fiction 2. Great Britain -- History -- 1485-1603, Tudors -- Fiction 3. Love -- Fiction 4. Sex role -- Fiction 5. Kings, queens, rulers, etc. -- Fiction 6. Great Britain -- History -- Henry VIII, 1509-1547 -- Fiction 7.

Great Britain -- History -- Henry VIII, 1509-1547
ISBN 0670014001; 9780670014002

LC 2012032988

This book is the companion to Katherine Longshore's novel "Gilt" and looks at the relationship between Anne Boleyn and Thomas Wyatt. Wyatt bets Anne that he can turn court favor to her side if she does as he asks. If the plan succeeds, he will have her in his bed because she will want to be there. After some thought she concedes and their game of courtly love begins. He pursues her and she encourages it. Soon she realizes that Wyatt's plan is working"—and that they're in love. (School Library Journal)

Lowitz, Leza

Jet Black and the ninja wind; Leza Lowitz, Shogo Oketani. Tuttle Publishing 2013 319 p. $17.99

Grades: 9 10 11 12   Fic

1. Ninja -- Fiction 2. Family secrets -- Fiction 3. Japan -- Fiction 4. Secrets -- Fiction 5. Buried treasure -- Fiction 6. Family life -- Japan -- Fiction 7. Adventure and adventurers -- Fiction
ISBN 480531284X; 9784805312841

LC 2013023578

Asian/Pacific American Awards for Literature: Young Adult Lit (2014)

In this book, by Leza Lowitz and Shogo Oketani, "Seventeen-year-old Jet Black is a ninja. There's only one problem—she doesn't know it. Others do, however, and they're scheming to capture her and uncover her secrets. When her mother dies, Jet knows only that she must go to Japan to protect a family treasure hidden in her ancestral land. . . . Stalked by bounty hunters and desperately in love with the man who's been sent to kill her, Jet must be strong enough to protect the treasure." (Publisher's note)

"At her mother's insistence, Rika Kuroi, nicknamed Jet Black, has spent her young life training in the art of combat and ninja techniques-with no idea why. Her mother dies before explaining, and when Jet travels to her family's village in Japan to lay her mother's ashes to rest, she is plunged into a complicated web of ancient mysteries and family secrets... Give this book to anime fans or anyone seeking an engaging and thought-provoking read.—" (School Library Journal)

Lowry, Lois, 1937-

★ **Son**; by Lois Lowry. Houghton Mifflin 2012 393 p. $17.99

Grades: 6 7 8 9 10 11 12   Fic

1. Science fiction 2. Dystopian fiction 3. Amnesia -- Fiction 4. Mothers -- Fiction 5. Secrecy -- Fiction 6. Identity -- Fiction 7. Mother-child relationship -- Fiction 8. Mother and child -- Fiction 9. Separation (Psychology) -- Fiction
ISBN 0547887205; 9780547887203

LC 2012014034

Author Lois Lowry tells the story of "14-year-old Claire, [who] has no contact with her baby Gabe until she surreptitiously bonds with him in the community Nurturing Center. . . . After living for years with Alys, a childless healer, Claire's memory returns. Intent on finding Gabe, she . . . encounters the sinister Trademaster and exchanges her youth for his help in finding her child, now living in the same village as middle-aged Jonas and his wife Kira. Elderly and failing,

Claire reveals her identity to Gabe, who must use his unique talent to save the village." (Kirkus Reviews)

Lu, Marie

★ **Champion**; a Legend novel. Marie Lu. G.P. Putnam's Sons, an imprint of Penguin Group (USA) 2013 384 p. (hardback) $18.99

Grades: 8 9 10 11 12　　　　　　　　　　**Fic**

1. Love -- Fiction 2. Dystopian fiction 3. Plague -- Fiction 4. Science fiction
ISBN 0399256776; 9780399256776

LC 2013028221

In this novel, by Marie Lu, "June and Day have sacrificed so much for the people of the Republic—and each other—and now their country is on the brink of a new existence. June is back in the good graces of the Republic, working within the government's elite circles as Princeps Elect while Day has been assigned a high level military position. But neither could have predicted the circumstances that will reunite them once again." (Publisher's note)

"Having been diagnosed with a terminal illness, Day (Legend; Prodigy) takes care of his brother, Eden, victim of the Republic's experiments in biological warfare. International diplomacy raises the stakes in this final volume of the trilogy, but readers will likely care more about whether Day and June (the Republic's prodigy) can repair their passionate romance. Lu's storytelling is compulsively readable." (Horn Book)

★ **Legend**. G. P. Putnam's Sons 2011 305p $17.99

Grades: 8 9 10 11 12　　　　　　　　　　**Fic**

1. War stories 2. Science fiction 3. Plague -- Fiction 4. Siblings -- Fiction 5. Soldiers -- Fiction 6. Criminals -- Fiction 7. Resistance to government -- Fiction
ISBN 978-0-399-25675-2; 0-399-25675-X

LC 2011002003

"The characters are likable, the plot moves at a good pace, and the adventure is solid." SLJ

★ **Prodigy**; a Legend novel. Marie Lu. G. P. Putnam's Sons 2012 384 p. (Legend) $17.99

Grades: 8 9 10 11 12　　　　　　　　　　**Fic**

1. Science fiction 2. Dystopian fiction 3. Fugitives from justice -- Fiction 4. Resistance to government -- Fiction 5. War -- Fiction 6. Soldiers -- Fiction 7. Criminals -- Fiction 8. Assassination -- Fiction 9. Government, Resistance to -- Fiction
ISBN 0399256768; 9780399256769

LC 2012003773

This young adult science fiction adventure novel, by Marie Lu, is the sequel to her novel "Legend." "Injured and on the run, it has been seven days since June and Day barely escaped Los Angeles and the Republic with their lives. Day is believed dead. . . . June is now the Republic's most wanted traitor. Desperate for help, they turn to the Patriots--a vigilante rebel group sworn to bring down the Republic. But can they trust them?" (Publisher's note)

"This is a well-molded mixture of intrigue, romance, and action, where things can change with almost any turn of the page, and frequently do." Booklist

The **Rose** Society; Marie Lu. Penguin Group USA 2015 416 p. map (hardcover) $18.99

Grades: 9 10 11 12　　　　　　　　　　**Fic**

1. Fantasy fiction 2. Revenge -- Fiction
ISBN 9780399167843; 0399167846

LC 2015954795

In this fantasy novel, by Marie Lu, book two of the "Young Elites" series, "Adelina Amouteru . . . , now known and feared as the White Wolf, . . . and her sister flee Kenettra to find other Young Elites in the hopes of building her own army of allies. Her goal: to strike down the Inquisition Axis, the white-cloaked soldiers who nearly killed her. But Adelina is no heroine. Her powers, fed only by fear and hate, have started to grow beyond her control." (Publisher's note)

"The Young Elites was both an instant best-seller and critically acclaimed, and the success is sure to hop to this even-stronger sequel." Booklist

The **Young** Elites; Marie Lu. Putnam Publishing Group 2014 368 p. map (hardback) $18.99

Grades: 8 9 10 11 12　　　　　　　　　　**Fic**

1. Fantasy fiction 2. Supernatural -- Fiction 3. Secret societies -- Fiction 4. Ability -- Fiction 5. Adventure and adventurers -- Fiction
ISBN 0399167838; 9780399167836

LC 2014025732

In this fantasy novel, by Marie Lu, "Adelina Amouteru is a survivor of the blood fever. . . . But some of the fever's survivors are rumored to possess . . . mysterious and powerful gifts, and though their identities remain secret, they have come to be called the Young Elites. . . . Teren Santoro . . . , as Leader of the Inquisition Axis, it is his job to seek out the Young Elites. . . . Enzo Valenciano is a member of . . . [a] secret sect of Young Elites [that] seeks out others like them before the Inquisition Axis can." (Publisher's note)

"In a gorgeously constructed world that somewhat resembles Renaissance Italy but with its own pantheon, geography and fauna, the multiethnic and multisexual Young Elites offer a cinematically perfect ensemble of gorgeous-but-unusual illusionists, animal speakers, fire summoners and wind callers. A must for fans of Kristin Cashore's Fire (2009) and other totally immersive fantasies." Kirkus

Lubar, David

★ **Character,** driven; David Lubar. Tor Teen 2016 304 p. (hardback) $17.99

Grades: 8 9 10 11 12　　　　　　　　　　**Fic**

1. Teenagers -- Fiction 2. High school students -- Fiction 3. Sex -- Fiction 4. Fathers and sons -- Fiction
ISBN 9780765316332; 0765316331

LC 2015032626

In this novel, by David Lubar, "with only one year left of high school, seventeen-year-old Cliff Sparks is desperate to find a girlfriend. But he's never had much luck with girls. At the same time, Cliff has to figure out what to do with the rest of his life, since he's pretty sure his unemployed father plans to kick him out of the house the minute he turns eighteen. Time is running out. Cliff is at the edge, on the verge, dangling--and holding on for dear life." (Publisher's note)

"With high-school graduation drawing near, Cliff stands at the precipice of his future, uncertain which way to jump. Yet he knows he has to do two things before the end of his senior year: lose his virginity and get Jillian, the new girl, to notice him. But that's not everything crowding his proverbial plate because life isn't that simple. His unemployed father threatens to kick him out when he turns 18 unless he contributes to the household, so Cliff works two part-time jobs and shelves the idea of college for the time being. His only havens are his closest friends, books, and art. However, one day he's forced to dial 911, and life as he knows it changes. . . . It wouldn't be fair to reveal whether he gets the girl, but readers will certainly fall for Cliff and find support in his trials and tribulations." Booklist

Includes bibliographical references and index

Sleeping freshmen never lie. Dutton Books 2005 279p $16.99; pa $6.99

Grades: 7 8 9 10   **Fic**

1. School stories 2. Authorship -- Fiction
ISBN 0-525-47311-4; 0-14-240780-1 pa

                          LC 2004-23067

While navigating his first year of high school and awaiting the birth of his new baby brother, Scott loses old friends and gains some unlikely new ones as he hones his skills as a writer

"The plot is framed by Scott's journal of advice for the unborn baby. The novel's absurd, comical mood is evident in its entries. . . . The author brings the protagonist to three-dimensional life by combining these introspective musings with active, hilarious narration." SLJ

Lucier, Makiia

A **death**-struck year; Makiia Lucier. Houghton Mifflin Harcourt 2014 288 p. (hardback) $17.99

Grades: 9 10 11 12   **Fic**

1. Nurses -- Fiction 2. Epidemics -- Fiction 3. Influenza -- Fiction 4. Portland (Or.) -- Fiction 5. Influenza Epidemic, 1918-1919 -- Fiction 6. Portland (Or.) -- History -- 20th century -- Fiction
ISBN 0544164504; 9780544164505

                          LC 2013037482

In this novel, by Makiia Lucier, "the Spanish influenza is devastating . . . Pacific Northwest. Schools, churches, and theaters are shut down. The entire city [of Portland, Oregon] is thrust into survival mode--and into a panic. Seventeen-year-old Cleo is told to stay put in her quarantine boarding school, but when the Red Cross pleads for volunteers, she cannot ignore the call for help." (Publisher's note)

"A teen girl struggles to survive the Spanish influenza pandemic of 1918...Readers will be swept up in the story as Cleo builds friendships and manages to find hope amid disease and death. A notable debut." (Kirkus)

Includes bibliographical references

Luedeke, Lisa

Smashed; Lisa Luedeke. Margaret K. McElderry Books 2012 323 p.

Grades: 9 10 11 12   **Fic**

1. Alcoholism -- Fiction 2. Field hockey players -- Fiction 3. Teenagers -- Alcohol use -- Fiction 4. Schools -- Fiction 5. High schools -- Fiction 6. Emotional problems -- Fiction
ISBN 1442427795; 9781442427792; 9781442427952

                          LC 2011030515

In this novel by Lisa Luedeke "Katie Martin is a field hockey star on the fast track to a college scholarship. Her relationship with alcohol has always been a little questionable, but things get bleak really quickly when she takes up with bad boy Alec Osborne. . . . On a rain-soaked, alcohol-drenched night, one impulsive decision threatens Katie's dreams, leaving her indebted to Alec in the worst possible way." (Author's note)

Lundgren, Jodi

Leap; [edited by Alison Kooistra] Second Story Press 2011 217p $11.95

Grades: 6 7 8 9 10   **Fic**

1. Dance -- Fiction 2. Friendship -- Fiction 3. Family life -- Fiction
ISBN 978-1-897187-85-2; 1-897187-85-8

Having just turned 15 and gone through her parents' divorce, Natalie and her best friend Sasha are going to be practicing with their dance team all summer, but her friendship with Sasha goes on the rocks, and her relationship with her boyfriend Kevin who is Sasha's brother goes too far.

"This novel, with its luminous descriptions of dance and frank discussions of sexuality and relationships, will captivate teens looking for a story they can relate to." SLJ

Luper, Eric

Seth Baumgartner's love manifesto. Balzer + Bray 2010 293p $16.99

Grades: 8 9 10 11 12   **Fic**

1. Golf -- Fiction 2. Love -- Fiction 3. Dating (Social customs) -- Fiction 4. Father-son relationship -- Fiction
ISBN 978-0-06-182753-2; 0-06-182753-3

                          LC 2009-29706

After his girlfriend breaks up with him and he sees his father out with another woman, high school senior Seth Baumgartner, who has a summer job at the country club and is preparing for a father-son golf tournament, launches a podcast in which he explores the mysteries of love.

"Luper weaves together many themes—trust and secrets, lies and truth, love, lust and, of course, golf—in a way that even the most introspection-hating male reader will eat with a spoon." Kirkus

Lurie, April

The **latent** powers of Dylan Fontaine. Delacorte Press 2008 208p $15.99; lib bdg $18.99

Grades: 8 9 10 11 12   **Fic**

1. Family life -- Fiction 2. New York (N.Y.) -- Fiction
ISBN 978-0-385-73125-6; 978-0-385-90153-6 lib bdg

                          LC 2007-32313

Fifteen-year-old Dylan's friend Angie is making a film about him while he is busy trying to keep his older brother from getting caught with drugs, to deal with his mother having left the family, and to figure out how to get Angie to think of him as more than just a friend.

"This is a story about guys, primarily . . . brothers; fathers and sons; lonely young men who are feeling somewhat lost. Any reader will care for each one of them. Lurie does a wonderful job of making them real." KLIATT

Lyga, Barry

★ The **astonishing** adventures of Fanboy &
Goth Girl. Houghton Mifflin 2006 311p $16.95

Grades: 8 9 10 11 12   **Fic**
1. School stories 2. Friendship -- Fiction 3. Cartoons
and caricatures -- Fiction
ISBN 0-618-72392-7

LC 2005-33259

A fifteen-year-old "geek" who keeps a list of the high
school jocks and others who torment him, and pours his energy into creating a great graphic novel, encounters Kyra,
Goth Girl, who helps change his outlook on almost everything, including himself.

"This engaging first novel has good characterization
with genuine voices. . . . The book is compulsively readable." Voice Youth Advocates

Followed by: Goth Girl rising (2009)

Blood of my blood; Barry Lyga. Little, Brown
& Co. 2014 472 p. (I hunt killers) (hardback) $18

Grades: 9 10 11 12   **Fic**
1. Mystery fiction 2. Serial killers -- Fiction 3. New
York (N.Y.) -- Fiction 4. Father-son relationship --
Fiction 5. Fathers and sons -- Fiction 6. Mystery and
detective stories
ISBN 0316198706; 9780316198707

LC 2014003643

In this book, by Barry Lyga, "Jazz Dent has been shot
and left to die in New York City. His girlfriend Connie is in
the clutches of Jazz's serial killer father, Billy. And his best
friend Howie is bleeding to death on the floor of Jazz's own
home in tiny Lobo's Nod. Somehow, these three must rise
above the horrors their lives have become and find a way to
come together in pursuit of Billy." (Publisher's note)

"You can't stop reading . . . Lyga's strength is a plot that
rockets with blood-slicked assurance and with the intercut
speed (and splatter) of Thomas Harris' The Silence of the
Lambs (1988). Will Jazz end up a Crow or just another
'prospect'? Here's hoping the Edgar Awards retroactively
present Lyga a trio of statuettes for his chilling three-book
answer." Booklist

Boy toy. Houghton Mifflin 2007 410p $16.95

Grades: 10 11 12   **Fic**
1. School stories 2. Child sexual abuse -- Fiction
ISBN 978-0-618-72393-5; 0-618-72393-5

LC 2006-39840

After five years of fighting his way past flickers of memory about the teacher who molested him and the incident that
brought the crime to light, eighteen-year-old Josh gets help
in coping with his molestor's release from prison when he
finally tells his best friends the whole truth.

The author "tackles this incredibly sensitive story
with boldness and confidence. He does not shy away from
graphic descriptions of Josh's past and even makes the audacious choice of showing young Josh enjoying the attention
. . . [Josh] works hard at healing himself and moving into
healthy adulthood, and by the end of this well-written, challenging novel, the reader has high hopes that he will make
it." Voice Youth Advocates

Game; by Barry Lyga. Little, Brown and Co.
2013 528 p. (hardcover) $17.99

Grades: 10 11 12   **Fic**
1. Mystery fiction 2. Serial killers -- Fiction 3. Murder
-- Fiction 4. Psychopaths -- Fiction 5. New York (N.Y.)
-- Fiction 6. Mystery and detective stories
ISBN 0316125873; 9780316125871

LC 2012040157

Sequel to: I hunt killers

This is Barry Lyga's follow-up to "Hunt Killers." It
"focuses on 17-year-old Jazz, the son of the world's most
prolific serial killer, but expands his world by fleshing out
previously minor characters. Jazz is called upon to help the
NYPD hunt Hat-Dog, a brutal killer who might be connected
to Jazz's now-escaped father, Billy Dent. Meanwhile, Jazz's
girlfriend, Connie, starts receiving mysterious information
about Jazz's past." (Publishers Weekly)

Goth girl rising. Houghton Mifflin Harcourt
2009 390p $17

Grades: 8 9 10 11 12   **Fic**
1. School stories 2. Psychotherapy -- Fiction
ISBN 978-0-547-07664-5; 0-547-07664-9

Sequel to: The astonishing adventures of Fanboy and
Goth Girl (2006)

"After six months in a mental hospital, Kyra, the newly
shaven-headed heroine of The Astonishing Adventures of
Fan Boy and Goth Girl (2006), has only one plan: to exact embarrassing revenge on sweet, loyal Fan Boy for not
contacting her while she was away. . . . Goth teens and fans
of the first novel will be drawn into the darkness that is her
life." Kirkus

★ **I** hunt killers; by Barry Lyga. Little, Brown
2012 359 p.

Grades: 10 11 12   **Fic**
1. Mystery fiction 2. Serial killers -- Fiction 3. Father-
son relationship -- Fiction 4. Teenagers -- Conduct of
life -- Fiction 5. Murder -- Fiction 6. Psychopaths --
Fiction 7. Conduct of life -- Fiction 8. Fathers and sons
-- Fiction 9. Mystery and detective stories
ISBN 9780316125840

LC 2011025418

This book tells the story of Jasper, a 17-year-old boy
whose father "is the most notorious serial killer of the 21st
century" and who has found that "having a normal life is
a struggle. . . . Now living with his Gramma, Jasper finds
himself investigating another serial killer with help from his
best friend Howie." (Kirkus Reviews)

Followed by: Game (2013)

Lynch, Chris

★ **Angry** young man. Simon & Schuster BFYR
2011 167p $16.99

Grades: 7 8 9 10   **Fic**
1. Brothers -- Fiction 2. Conduct of life -- Fiction 3.
Single parent family -- Fiction
ISBN 0-689-84790-4; 978-0-689-84790-5

LC 2009-52832

Eighteen-year-old Robert tries to help his half-brother
Xan, a seventeen-year-old misfit, to make better choices as

he becomes increasingly attracted to a variety of protesters, anarchists, and the like.

"For those who wonder about the roots of homegrown terror and extremism, . . . Lynch pushes the spotlight from the individual to society in a story that can be brutal and ugly, yet isn't devoid of hope." Publ Wkly

The **Big** Game of Everything. HarperTeen 2008 275p $16.99; lib bdg $17.89

Grades: 7 8 9 10   **Fic**

1. Golf -- Fiction 2. Family life -- Fiction 3. Grandfathers -- Fiction 4. Summer employment -- Fiction

ISBN 978-0-06-074034-4; 0-06-074034-5; 978-0-06-074035-1 lib bdg; 0-06-074035-3 lib bdg

LC 2007-49578

Jock and his eccentric family spend the summer working at Grampus's golf complex, where they end up learning the rules of "The Big Game of Everything."

"This Printz Honor-winning author offers up another touching and offbeat novel full of delightfully skewed humor." Voice Youth Advocates

Casualties of war; Chris Lynch. Scholastic Press 2013 192 p. (hc) $16.99

Grades: 8 9 10 11 12   **Fic**

1. War stories 2. Soldiers -- Fiction 3. Vietnam War, 1961-1975 -- Fiction 4. Airmen -- Fiction 5. Agent Orange -- Fiction

ISBN 0545270235; 9780545270236; 9780545270243

LC 2012014434

This book concludes "[Chris] Lynch's Vietnam War series . . . with the final narrative of four friends caught in the chaos of war. Morris, Ivan and Rudi have told their stories; it's Beck's turn. Beck, now in the Air Force, was always the smart one, the one bound for college. . . . And in Vietnam, Beck does feel as if he has 'just been handed the keys to the universe itself.' He is, literally, above it all, as he watches the war from on high in his C-123 aircraft." (Kirkus)

★ **Hothouse**. HarperTeen 2010 198p $16.99

Grades: 8 9 10 11 12   **Fic**

1. Death -- Fiction 2. Friendship -- Fiction 3. Bereavement -- Fiction 4. Fire fighters -- Fiction 5. Father-son relationship -- Fiction

ISBN 978-0-06-167379-5; 0-06-167379-X

LC 2010-3145

Teens D.J. and Russell, life-long friends and neighbors, had drifted apart but when their firefighter fathers are both killed, they try to help one another come to terms with the tragedy and its aftermath.

"Lynch fully commits to the first-person voice, giving into Russ' second-by-second conflicts and contradictions. The author also has a strong grasp of the garrulous slaps and punches that make up many male relationships. Russ' friendships are so real they hurt. The story hurts, too, but that's how it should be." Booklist

★ **Inexcusable**. Atheneum Books for Young Readers 2005 165p $16.95; pa $6.99

Grades: 8 9 10 11 12   **Fic**

1. School stories 2. Rape -- Fiction 3. Football --

Fiction

ISBN 0-689-84789-0; 1-416-93972-5 pa

LC 2004-30874

High school senior and football player Keir sets out to enjoy himself on graduation night, but when he attempts to comfort a friend whose date has left her stranded, things go terribly wrong

"This finely crafted and thought-provoking page-turner carefully conveys that it is simply inexcusable to whitewash wrongs, and that those responsible should (and hopefully will) pay the price." SLJ

Lynch, Chris, 1962-

Hit count; a novel. by Chris Lynch. Algonquin Young Readers 2015 368 p. $17.95

Grades: 8 9 10 11 12   **Fic**

1. Football -- Fiction 2. Wounds and injuries -- Fiction 3. High school students -- Fiction 4. Sports injuries -- Fiction

ISBN 1616202505; 9781616202507

LC 2014043009

In this young adult novel by Chris Lynch, "Arlo Brodie loves being at the heart of the action on the football field, getting hit hard and hitting back harder. . . . Arlo's girlfriend tries to make him see how dangerously he's playing; when that doesn't work, she calls time out on their relationship. Even Arlo's coaches begin to track his hit count, ready to pull him off the field when he nears the limit." (Publisher's note)

"This intense, timely story provides incredible insight into the reasons why knowledge of football's potential danger is not enough to keep young players from taking the field." Kirkus

Pieces; Chris Lynch. Simon & Schuster Books for Young Readers 2013 176 p. (hardcover) $16.99

Grades: 7 8 9 10 11 12   **Fic**

1. Brothers -- Fiction 2. Bereavement -- Fiction 3. Donation of organs, tissues, etc. -- Fiction 4. Death -- Fiction 5. Grief -- Fiction 6. Interpersonal relations -- Fiction

ISBN 1416927034; 9781416927037; 9781442453111

LC 2011042049

In this book, "a year after his 20-year-old brother Duane died in a diving accident, 18-year-old Eric still can't seem to move forward. In an attempt to keep the 'nothingness that is filling the Duane space' from taking hold, he reaches out to three of the donors who received his brother's 'pieces.' After meeting shy, redheaded Phil, brassy Barry and sweet single mom Melinda, Eric finds himself constantly asking the questions, 'Who are these people? Who are they, to me? Who am I, to them?'" (Kirkus Reviews)

Walking wounded; Chris Lynch. Scholastic Press 2014 208 p. (Vietnam) (alk. paper) $17.99

Grades: 9 10 11 12   **Fic**

1. Friendship -- Fiction 2. Vietnam War, 1961-1975 -- Fiction 3. War stories 4. Soldiers -- Fiction 5. Best friends -- Fiction

ISBN 054564013X; 9780545640138

LC 2014005197

In this novel by Chris Lynch "four best friends all sign up to fight during the Vietnam War. Though they promise to come home together, one friend doesn't survive and the remaining three must grapple with the truth about his death. The narrative switches among the various first person perspectives--even that of Rudi's ghost." (School Library Journal)

"While this series is accessible to reluctant readers, it is hard-hitting and accurate, making it appropriate for those familiar with Walter Dean Myers' Fallen Angels (1988) but not quite ready for Tim O'Brien's adult classic The Things They Carried (1990)." Booklist

Lynch, Janet Nichols

My beautiful hippie; Janet Nichols Lynch. Holiday House 2013 186 p. (hardcover) $16.95

Grades: 10 11 12   **Fic**

1. Bildungsromans 2. Hippies -- Fiction 3. Historical fiction 4. Feminism -- Fiction 5. Pianists -- Fiction 6. Coming of age -- Fiction 7. Vietnam War, 1961-1975 -- Fiction 8. Family life -- California -- Fiction 9. San Francisco (Calif.) -- History -- 20th century -- Fiction
ISBN 0823426033; 9780823426034

           LC 2012016563

In this novel, by Janet Nichols Lynch, "it's 1967 and Joanne's San Francisco neighborhood has become inundated with hippies . . . , which thrills her but appalls the rest of her family. In the midst of preparations for her sister's wedding, Joanne meets Martin . . . and begins to see him secretly. Over the course of the next year, Joanne discovers a world of drugs, anti-war demonstrations, and psychedelic dances that both fascinates and frightens her." (Publisher's note)

Lyne, Jennifer H.

Catch rider; by Jennifer H. Lyne. Clarion Books 2013 288 p. (hardcover) $16.99

Grades: 9 10 11 12   **Fic**

1. Poor -- Fiction 2. Horses -- Fiction 3. Uncles -- Fiction 4. Virginia -- Fiction 5. Horse shows -- Fiction 6. Horsemanship -- Fiction 7. Social classes -- Fiction 8. Single-parent families -- Fiction 9. Family life -- Virginia -- Fiction
ISBN 0547868715; 9780547868714

           LC 2012022616

In this book, "Sidney Criser might still be 14, but that doesn't stop her from driving the junk car her uncle gave her an hour over mountains to clean stalls at a rich woman's barn. Sid grew up tough, and she can ride anything, but times are desperate: Since her father's death, her mother has taken up with a no-good abuser who threatens to move them to California. Her mother's lost her job, and . . . her uncle Wayne, who's long been Sidney's mainstay, is just about to drink himself to death." (Kirkus)

Maas, Sarah J.

A court of thorns and roses; by Sarah J. Maas. Bloomsbury 2015 432 p. map (hardcover) $18.99

Grades: 9 10 11 12   **Fic**

1. Fantasy fiction 2. Fairies -- Fiction 3. Fantasy 4. Love -- Fiction 5. Blessing and cursing -- Fiction
ISBN 1619634449; 9781619634442

           LC 2014020071

In this fantasy novel, by Sarah J. Maas, "when nineteen-year-old huntress Feyre kills a wolf in the woods, a beast-like creature arrives to demand retribution for it. Dragged to a treacherous magical land she only knows about from legends, Feyre discovers that her captor is not an animal, but Tamlin--one of the lethal, immortal faeries who once ruled their world." (Publisher's note)

"A weak fantasy with strong romance elements. Good for fans of Maas's previous books looking for a more mature read." SLJ

Crown of midnight; by Sarah J. Maas. Bloomsbury 2013 432 p. (hardcover) $17.99

Grades: 9 10 11 12   **Fic**

1. Paranormal fiction 2. Assassins -- Fiction 3. Fantasy 4. Love -- Fiction 5. Courts and courtiers -- Fiction 6. Kings, queens, rulers, etc. -- Fiction
ISBN 1619630621; 9781619630628

           LC 2013009063

Sequel to: Throne of glass

This is the second book in Sarah J. Maas's Throne of Glass series. "After being named the King's Champion in 'Throne of Glass' (2012), Celaena Sardothien serves as the king of Adarlan's personal assassin—at least, she pretends to. . . . If the king catches Celaena disobeying his orders, he will execute her closest friends. However, she can't stomach advancing his agenda, especially if it means murdering innocents in cold blood." (Kirkus Reviews)

Throne of glass; Sarah J. Maas. Bloomsbury 2012 406 p. (hardback) $17.99

Grades: 10 11 12   **Fic**

1. Fantasy fiction 2. Contests -- Fiction 3. Assassins -- Fiction 4. Fantasy 5. Princes -- Fiction 6. Prisoners -- Fiction 7. Courts and courtiers -- Fiction
ISBN 1599906953; 9781599906959

           LC 2012011229

This book by Sarah J. Maas follows "17-year-old Celaena," an assassin whose work "has landed her in a slave-labor prison no one has ever survived. A year into her sentence, the Crown Prince offers to sponsor Celaena in a competition with 23 other criminals and murderers that, should she win, will result in her freedom. The only catch? She'll become the king's personal assassin for four years, the same dark-hearted king who sentenced her to imprisonment." (Kirkus Reviews)

Maberry, Jonathan

Dust & decay. Simon & Schuster 2011 519p $17.99; ebook $9.99

Grades: 8 9 10 11 12   **Fic**

1. Horror fiction 2. Zombies -- Fiction 3. Brothers -- Fiction
ISBN 978-1-4424-0235-5; 978-1-4424-0237-9 ebook

           LC 2010050305

Sequel to Rot & ruin (2010)

In post-apocalyptic America, fifteen-year-old Benny Imura and his friends set out into the great Rot & Ruin hoping to find a better future but are soon pitted against zombies, wild animals, insane murderers, and the horrors of Gameland.

"The language is easy to comprehend, the characters are relatable, and the action-filled plot keeps the story moving. The western elements, seldom seen in teen fiction, are a welcome addition." Voice Youth Advocates

Fire & ash; Jonathan Maberry. Simon & Schuster Books for Young Readers 2013 544 p. (Rot & ruin) (hardcover: alk. paper) $18.99
Grades: 8 9 10 11 12   **Fic**
1. Zombies -- Fiction 2. Survival skills -- Fiction 3. Survival -- Fiction
ISBN 1442439920; 9781442439924
                                        LC 2012047976
Sequel to: Flesh & bone (2012)
This is the final book in author Jonathan Maberry's "Rot & Ruin" series. It "picks up three weeks after Benny and his teen allies discovered the elusive jet that guided much of the series' story arc. Now bunkered in a monastery that also serves as a government laboratory, they await the fate of their friend Chong, who was bitten by a zombie at the end of the third novel." (Kirkus Reviews)

Flesh & bone; Jonathan Maberry. Simon & Schuster Books For Young Readers 2012 469 p.
Grades: 8 9 10 11 12   **Fic**
1. Wilderness areas -- Fiction 2. Future life 3. Science fiction 4. Zombies -- Fiction 5. Brothers -- Fiction 6. Survival -- Fiction 7. Bounty hunters -- Fiction
ISBN 1442439890; 9781442439894; 9781442439917
                                        LC 2012000178
Sequel to: Dust & decay (2011)
In author Jonathan Maberry's book, characters "Benny Imura and his friends plunge deep into the zombie-infested wastelands of the great Rot & Ruin. Benny, Nix, Lilah, and Chong journey through a fierce wilderness that was once America . . . But the Ruin is far more dangerous than any of them can imagine. Fierce animals hunt them. They come face to face with a death cult. And then there's the zombies--swarms of them coming from the east, devouring everything in their paths." (Publisher's note)

★ **Rot** & ruin. Simon & Schuster Books for Young Readers 2010 458p $17.99
Grades: 9 10 11 12   **Fic**
1. Horror fiction 2. Zombies -- Fiction 3. Brothers -- Fiction
ISBN 1-4424-0232-6; 978-1-4424-0232-4
                                        LC 2009-46041
In a post-apocalyptic world where fences and border patrols guard the few people left from the zombies that have overtaken civilization, fifteen-year-old Benny Imura is finally convinced that he must follow in his older brother's footsteps and become a bounty hunter.
"In turns mythic and down-to-earth, this intense novel combines adventure and philosophy to tell a truly memorable zombie story." Publ Wkly
Other titles in this series are:
Dust & decay (2011)
Flesh & bone (2012)
Fire & ash (2013)
Bits & pieces (2015)

MacColl, Michaela
Nobody's secret; by Michaela MacColl. Chronicle Books 2013 288 p. (reinforced) $16.99
Grades: 7 8 9 10   **Fic**
1. Mystery fiction 2. Historical fiction 3. Poets -- Fiction 4. Mystery and detective stories 5. Women poets, American -- 19th century -- Fiction 6. Amherst (Mass.) -- History -- 19th century -- Fiction
ISBN 1452108609; 9781452108605
                                        LC 2012030364
In this book, when "15-year-old Emily Dickinson meets and flirts with a handsome stranger, she feels the first flicker of romance. Then the young man is found dead in her family's pond, and the budding poet is sure that he was a victim of foul play. Determined to see that justice is done, she and her younger sister, Vinnie, investigate and discover that he is James Wentworth, heir to a fortune from which his aunt and uncle have defrauded him. Suspecting murder, Emily sets out to solve the case." (School Library Journal)

MacCullough, Carolyn
Once a witch. Clarion Books 2009 292p $16
Grades: 8 9 10 11 12   **Fic**
1. Sisters -- Fiction 2. Witches -- Fiction 3. Time travel -- Fiction 4. Good and evil -- Fiction 5. New York (N.Y.) -- Fiction
ISBN 978-0-547-22399-5; 0-547-22399-4
                                        LC 2008-49234
Born into a family of witches, seventeen-year-old Tamsin is raised believing that she alone lacks a magical "Talent," but when her beautiful and powerful sister is taken by an age-old rival of the family in an attempt to change the balance of power, Tamsin discovers her true destiny.
"The book will appeal to teen readers who enjoy stories with romance, magic, or time travel, along with hardcore fantasy aficionados, and it is appropriate for all young adult collections." Voice Youth Advocates
Followed by: Always a witch (2011)

Macdonald, Maryann, 1947-
Odette's secrets; by Maryann Macdonald. Bloomsbury 2013 240 p. (hardback) $16.99
Grades: 6 7 8 9   **Fic**
1. Novels in verse 2. Hidden children (Holocaust) 3. France -- History -- 1940-1945, German occupation -- Fiction 4. Identity -- Fiction 5. Jews -- France -- Fiction 6. Holocaust, Jewish (1939-1945) -- Fiction 7. World War, 1939-1945 -- France -- Fiction 8. France -- History -- German occupation, 1940-1945 -- Fiction
ISBN 159990750X; 9781599907505
                                        LC 2012015549
This biographical story-in-verse, by Maryann Macdonald, takes place in Nazi-occupied France. "Odette is a young Jewish girl living in Paris during a dangerous time. . . . After Odette's father enlists in the French army and her mother joins the Resistance, Odette is sent to the countryside until it is safe to return. On the surface, she leads the life of a regular girl . . . but inside, she is burning with secrets about the life she left behind and her true identity." (Publisher's note)

MacHale, D. J.

Storm; D.J. MacHale. Razorbill, a division of Penguin Young Readers Group 2014 496 p. (hardback) $17.99

Grades: 5 6 7 8   **Fic**
    1. War stories 2. Science fiction 3. Apocalyptic fiction 4. War -- Fiction 5. Survival -- Fiction 6. Conspiracies -- Fiction 7. Adventure and adventurers -- Fiction
    ISBN 1595146679; 9781595146670
                                            LC 2013047604
In this science fiction novel, by D.J. MacHale, "Tucker and his friends Tori, Kent and Olivia escaped from Pemberwick Island and the air-and-sea battle that raged around it to land in Portland. . . . Taking refuge in a hospital, the teens find a few other survivors but not a lot of additional information. A looping radio transmission encourages survivors to go west, where a force is gathering to fight back. Division threatens, as the teens argue about what to do: join this resistance or find refuge." (Kirkus)

"After escaping from the SYLO quarantine of Pemberwick Island, Tucker and friends head to the mainland only to discover that most of humanity has been wiped out by the mysterious Air Force planes. They embark on a road trip to seek out other survivors and the possibility of revenge. Though there's plenty of action, the story is bogged down by superfluous exposition." Horn Book

SYLO; by D.J. MacHale. Penguin Group USA 2013 416 p. (hardcover) $17.99

Grades: 5 6 7 8 9   **Fic**
    1. Dystopian juvenile fiction 2. Adventure fiction
    ISBN 1595146652; 9781595146656
This is the first book in a proposed trilogy from D.J. MacHale. Here, Tucker Pierce has a small but satisfying life on a small island. But when the island is quarantined by the U.S. Navy, things start to fall apart. . . . People start dying. The girl he wants to get to know a whole lot better, Tori, is captured along with Tucker and imprisoned behind barbed wire." They must escape to the mainland and try to figure out what this SYLO organization that is imprisoning them is. (Kirkus Reviews)

Maciel, Amanda

Tease; Amanda Maciel. Balzer + Bray, an imprint of HarperCollinsPublishers 2014 336 p. (hardback) $17.99

Grades: 9 10 11 12   **Fic**
    1. Bullies -- Fiction 2. High schools -- Fiction 3. High school students -- Fiction 4. Teenagers -- Suicide -- Fiction 5. Schools -- Fiction 6. Bullying -- Fiction
    ISBN 0062305301; 9780062305305
                                            LC 2013043067
This book, by Amanda Maciel, is "about a teenage girl who faces criminal charges for bullying after a classmate commits suicide. Emma Putnam is dead, and it's all Sara Wharton's fault. At least, that's what everyone seems to think. . . . Now Sara is the one who's ostracized, already guilty according to her peers, the community, and the media. In the summer before her senior year . . . Sara is forced to reflect on the events that brought her to this moment." (Publisher's note)

"Sara is climbing the high school social ladder when a new girl, Emma, steals her spotlight. Sara and her friends retaliate with pranks, rumors, and social media warfare, but all are shocked when Emma commits suicide. Sara is a fragile, conflicted narrator struggling to understand her role in Emma's death. A complex and thought-provoking examination of modern teen bullying." Horn Book

Mackler, Carolyn

★ The **earth**, my butt, and other big, round things. Candlewick Press 2003 246p $15.99; pa $8.99

Grades: 7 8 9 10   **Fic**
    1. School stories 2. Obesity -- Fiction 3. Family life -- Fiction 4. New York (N.Y.) -- Fiction
    ISBN 0-7636-1958-2; 0-7636-2091-2 pa
                                            LC 2002-73921
Michael L. Printz Award honor book, 2004
Feeling like she does not fit in with the other members of her family, who are all thin, brilliant, and good-looking, fifteen-year-old Virginia tries to deal with her self-image, her first physical relationship, and her disillusionment with some of the people closest to her

"The e-mails [Virginia] exchanges . . . and the lists she makes (e.g., 'The Fat Girl Code of Conduct') add both realism and insight to her character. The heroine's transformation into someone who finds her own style and speaks her own mind is believable—and worthy of applause." Publ Wkly

Guyaholic; a story of finding, flirting, forgetting . . . and the boy who changes everything. Candlewick Press 2007 176p $16.99; pa $7.99

Grades: 9 10 11 12   **Fic**
    1. Dating (Social customs) -- Fiction
    ISBN 978-0-7636-2537-5; 0-7636-2537-X; 978-0-7636-280107 pa; 0-7636-2801-8 pa
                                            LC 2007-24098
Sequel to Vegan virgin Valentine (2004)
V is "still living with her grandparents and still sleeping around. Then a hockey puck hits her in the head, and she literally falls into the arms of Sam Almond. . . . V comes across as an engaging character whose struggles seem very real. The details of her road trip are written with humor and verve, and the sex, while prevelant, is not graphic. There's also a sweetness here that makes V and Sam worth rooting for." Booklist

★ **Infinite** in Between; Carolyn Mackler. Harpercollins Childrens Books 2015 480 p. (hardcover) $17.99

Grades: 9 10 11 12   **Fic**
    1. School stories 2. High school students -- Fiction
    ISBN 0061731072; 9780061731075
This novel, by Carolyn Mackler, "chronicles the lives of five teenagers through the thrills, heartbreaks, and joys of their four years in high school. . . . Zoe, Jake, Mia, Gregor, and Whitney meet at freshman orientation. At the end of that first day, they make a promise to reunite after graduation. So much can happen in those in-between years." (Publisher's note)

"Things happen, for the most part, no more dramatically than they do in high schools every day. A clear, true portrait of life as it is for many teenagers." Booklist

Vegan virgin Valentine. Candlewick Press 2004 228p $16.99; pa $8.99

Grades: 9 10 11 12   **Fic**

1. School stories 2. Aunts 3. Nieces 4. Schools 5. High schools 6. Aunts -- Fiction
ISBN 0-7636-2155-2; 0-7636-2613-9 pa

LC 2004-45774

Mara's niece, who is only one-year-younger, moves in bringing conflict between the two teenagers because of their opposite personalities

"Racily narrated by likeable Mara, this fast-paced coming-of-age story is charged with sarcasm, angst, honesty, and hope. Many teen girls will recognize parts of themselves within its pages." Voice Youth Advocates

Followed by Guyaholic (2007)

MacLean, Jill

Nix Minus One; by Jill Maclean. Pajama Press 2013 296 p. (hardcover) $21.95

Grades: 7 8 9 10   **Fic**

1. School stories 2. Novels in verse
ISBN 192748524X; 9781927485248

This novel in verse focuses on 15-year-old Nix. "Formerly known as 'Fatty Humbolt,' he is struggling with his crush on Loren Cody, the girlfriend of the best player on the hockey team, and his love-hate relationship with his older sister, Roxy." Nix is shy while Roxy is the opposite. "Then Roxy falls for Bryan Sykes, a popular but notorious cad and politician's son, and Nix is forced to come out of his shell and find his voice." (School Library Journal)

Madigan, L. K.

★ **Flash** burnout; a novel. Houghton Mifflin 2009 332p $16

Grades: 9 10 11 12   **Fic**

1. School stories 2. Friendship -- Fiction 3. Photographers -- Fiction 4. Dating (Social customs) -- Fiction
ISBN 978-0-547-19489-9; 0-547-19489-7

LC 2010-278252

ALA YALSA The William C. Morris YA Debut Award (2010)

"This rich romance explores the complexities of friendship and love, and the all-too-human limitations of both. It's a sobering, compelling, and satisfying read for teens." Booklist

Madison, Bennett

★ **September** Girls; Bennett Madison. Harpercollins Childrens Books 2013 352 p. (hardcover) $17.99

Grades: 9 10 11 12   **Fic**

1. Love stories 2. Summer -- Fiction 3. Mermaids and mermen -- Fiction
ISBN 0061255637; 9780061255632

In this young adult, magical realist novel, by Bennett Madison, "Sam is spending the summer in a beach town filled with beautiful blond girls. . . . Sam finds himself in an unexpected summer romance when he falls for one of the Girls, DeeDee. But as they get closer, she pulls away without explanation. Sam knows that if he is going to win her back, he'll have to learn the Girls' secret." (Publisher's note)

Maetani, Valynne E.

Ink & ashes; Valynne E. Maetani. Tu Books, an imprint of Lee & Low Books, Inc. 2015 368 p. (hardback) $19.95

Grades: 7 8 9 10   **Fic**

1. Mystery fiction 2. Organized crime -- Fiction 3. Japanese Americans -- Fiction 4. Love -- Fiction 5. Fathers -- Fiction 6. Mystery and detective stories
ISBN 9781620142110

LC 2015006632

In this mystery novel by Valynne E. Maetani, "Claire Takata has never known much about her father. . . . But on the anniversary of his death, she finds a letter from her deceased father to her stepfather. . . . Struggling to understand why her parents kept this surprising history hidden, Claire combs through anything that might give her information about her father . . . until she discovers that he was a member of the yakuza, a Japanese organized crime syndicate." (Publisher's note)

"Maetani's fast-paced debut will appeal to readers who like their intrigue with a generous helping of romance." Booklist

Ink and ashes

Magoon, Kekla

37 things I love (in no particular order) Kekla Magoon. Henry Holt 2012 218 p. (hc) $16.99

Grades: 9 10 11 12   **Fic**

1. Girls 2. Grief 3. Family life 4. Coma -- Fiction
ISBN 0805094652; 9780805094657

LC 2011031998

This young adult novel by Kekla Magoon follows Ellis, who "only has four days of her sophomore year left. . . . Her father has been in a coma for years, . . . and her already-fragile relationship with her mother is strained over whether or not to remove him from life support. Her best friend fails even to notice that anything is wrong and Ellis feels like her world is falling apart. But when all seems bleak, Ellis finds comfort in the most unexpected places." (Publisher's note)

Fire in the streets; by Kekla Magoon. 1st Aladdin hardcover ed. Aladdin 2012 336 p. $15.99

Grades: 7 8 9 10   **Fic**

1. Historical fiction 2. Black nationalism -- Fiction 3. African Americans -- Civil rights -- Fiction 4. Racism -- Fiction 5. African Americans -- Fiction 6. Black Panther Party -- Fiction 7. Brothers and sisters -- Fiction 8. Civil rights movements -- Fiction
ISBN 1442422300; 9781442422308

LC 2011039129

Sequel to: The rock and the river

This historical novel by Kekla Magoon, is set "in the sweltering Chicago summer of 1968. [Maxie] is a Black Panther--or at least she wants to be one. . . . At fourteen, she's allowed to help out in the office, but she certainly can't help patrol the streets. Then Maxie realizes that there is a traitor in their midst, and if she can figure out who it is, it may be her ticket to becoming a real Panther. But when she learns the truth, the knowledge threatens to destroy her world." (Publisher's note)

★ **How** it went down; Kekla Magoon. First edition Henry Holt & Co. 2014 336 p. (hardback) $17.99

Grades: 9 10 11 12   **Fic**
1. Murder -- Fiction 2. United States -- Race relations 3. Death -- Fiction 4. Witnesses -- Fiction 5. Race relations -- Fiction 6. African Americans -- Fiction
ISBN 0805098690; 9780805098693; 9781250068231
                                        LC 2014027402
Coretta Scott King Author Award Honor Book (2015)

In this novel by Kekla Magoon "when sixteen-year-old Tariq Johnson dies from two gunshot wounds, his community is thrown into an uproar. Tariq was black. The shooter, Jack Franklin, is white. In the aftermath of Tariq's death, everyone has something to say, but no two accounts of the events line up. Day by day, new twists further obscure the truth." (Publisher's note)

"When 16-year-old Tariq, a black teen, is shot and killed by a white man, every witness has a slightly different perception of the chain of events leading up to the murder. Family, friends, gang members, neighbors, and a well-meaning but self-serving minster make up the broad cast of characters...With a great hook and relatable characters, this will be popular for fans of realistic fiction. The unique storytelling style and thematic relevance will make it a potentially intriguing pick for classroom discussion." SLJ

The **rock** and the river. Aladdin 2009 290p $15.99

Grades: 7 8 9 10   **Fic**
1. Brothers -- Fiction 2. Chicago (Ill.) -- Fiction 3. African Americans -- Fiction 4. Black Panther Party -- Fiction
ISBN 978-1-4169-7582-3; 1-4169-7582-9
                                        LC 2008-29170
ALA EMIERT Coretta Scott King John Steptoe New Talent Award (2010)

In 1968 Chicago, fourteen-year-old Sam Childs is caught in a conflict between his father's nonviolent approach to seeking civil rights for African Americans and his older brother, who has joined the Black Panther Party.

This "novel will make readers feel what it was like to be young, black, and militant 40 years ago, including the seething fury and desperation over the daily discrimination that drove the oppressed to fight back." Booklist

Maguire, Gregory, 1954-
★ **Egg** & spoon; a novel by Gregory Maguire. Candlewick Press 2014 475 p. hbk $17.99
Grades: 7 8 9 10 11 12   **Fic**
1. Poor -- Fiction 2. Girls -- Fiction 3. Russia -- Fiction 4. Monks 5. Princes 6. Mistaken identity 7. Baba Yaga (Legendary Character)
ISBN 0763672203; 9780763672201
                                        LC 2014931834
Boston Globe-Horn Book Honor: Fiction (2015)

In this young adult novel by Gregory Maguire, "Elena Rudina lives in the impoverished Russian countryside. Her

father has been dead for years. . . . Her mother is dying, slowly, in their tiny cabin. And there is no food. But then a train arrives in the village, a train carrying untold wealth, a cornucopia of food, and a noble family destined to visit the Tsar in Saint Petersburg." (Publisher's note)

"With one brother conscripted into the Tsar's army and another bound to serve a local landowner, Elena is left alone to care for her widowed and ailing mother in early 20th-century Russia. When an elegant train bearing a noble her age rolls through their barren village, Elena and her counterpart, Cat, accidentally swap places. . . . The author weaves a lyrical tale full of magic and promise, yet checkered with the desperation of poverty and the treacherous prospect of a world gone completely awry. Egg and Spoon is a beautiful reminder that fairy tales are at their best when they illuminate the precarious balance between lighthearted childhood and the darkness and danger of adulthood." SLJ

Son of a witch; a novel. ReganBooks 2005 337p il $26.95
Grades: 11 12 Adult   **Fic**
1. Satire 2. Authors 3. Dramatists 4. Journalists 5. Fantasy fiction 6. Mother-son relationship 7. Fantasies 8. Children's authors 9. Mother-son relationship -- Fiction
ISBN 0-06-054893-2
                                        LC 2005-46232
"The Wicked Years continue in Gregory Maguire'sSon of a Witch—the heroic saga of the hapless yet determined young man who may or may not be the offspring of the fabled Wicked Witch of the West. ANew York Timesbestseller like its predecessor, the remarkable Wicked, Son of a Witch follows the boy Liir on his dark odyssey across an ingeniously re-imagined and nearly unrecognizable Land of Oz—a journey that will take him deep into the bowels of the Emerald City, lately abandoned by the Wizard, and into the jaws of dragons. At once a grim fairy tale and an uplifting adventure, Son of a Witchis a true wonder." (Publisher's note)

Wicked; the life and times of the wicked witch of the West: a novel. Gregory Maguire; illustrations by Douglas Smith. ReganBooks 1995 406 p. ill. $26.99
Grades: 11 12 Adult   **Fic**
1. Fantasy fiction 2. Political satire 3. Witches -- Fiction 4. Oz (Imaginary place) -- Fiction
ISBN 0060391448
                                        LC 950669
This book tells the story of "Elphaba, the future Wicked Witch of the West. . . . Her mother is embarrassed and repulsed by her bright-green baby with shark's teeth and an aversion to water. At college, the coed experiences disapproval and rejection by her roommate, Glinda, a silly girl interested only in clothes, money, and popularity. Elphaba is a serious and inquisitive student. When she learns that the Wizard of Oz is politically corrupt and causing economic ruin, Elphaba finds a sense of purpose to her life -- to stop him and to restore harmony and prosperity to the land. . . . The conclusion, however, is the same as L. Frank Baum's." (School Library Journal)

Maizel, Rebecca

Infinite days; a vampire queen novel. St. Martin's Griffin 2010 325p (Vampire queen) pa $9.99

Grades: 7 8 9 10 **Fic**

1. School stories 2. Vampires -- Fiction 3. Supernatural -- Fiction

ISBN 978-0-312-64991-3; 0-312-64991-6

At a New England boarding school, Lenah Beaudonte tries to act like a normal sixteen-year-old although she was, before a hundred-year hibernation, a centuries-old vampire queen whose bloodthirsty, abandoned coven is seeking her.

"The story is filled with action, romance, longing, deception, and sacrifice. It will leave vampire fans thirsting for more." SLJ

Stolen nights; a Vampire queen novel. Rebecca Maizel. St. Martin's Griffin 2013 303 p. (paperback) $9.99

Grades: 7 8 9 10 **Fic**

1. Love -- Fiction 2. Vampires -- Fiction 3. Supernatural -- Fiction 4. Schools -- Fiction 5. Boarding schools -- Fiction

ISBN 0312649924; 9780312649920

LC 2012038339

This book, the second in author Rebecca Maizel's Vampire Queen series, follows Lenah Beaudonte . . . a vampire who has just become human again. . . . Lenah and her lover, Rhode, are now both human teens. . . . [T]hey are confronted . . . by the Aeris, a sort of supernatural communion of the elements, who . . . give them a choice: they can either go back to their original times . . . or stay in the present day with the caveat of not being able to be romantically linked to each other." (VOYA)

"At first, this novel seems to lack luster in its genre, but timeless themes of love and the search for identity, in addition to the cliff-hanger ending, leave readers pondering Lenah's choices and keenly anticipating the next installment." SLJ

Malley, Gemma

The **Declaration**. Bloomsbury 2007 300p $16.95

Grades: 7 8 9 10 **Fic**

1. Science fiction 2. Immortality -- Fiction 3. Great Britain -- Fiction

ISBN 978-1-59990-119-0; 1-59990-119-6

LC 2006-102138

In 2140 England, where drugs enable people to live forever and children are illegal, teenaged Anna, an obedient "Surplus" training to become a house servant, discovers that her birth parents are trying to find her.

This is "gripping. . . . The indoctrinated teen's awakening to massive injustice makes compulsive reading." Booklist

Other titles in this series are:

The legacy (2011)

The resistance (2008)

The **resistance**. Bloomsbury Children's Books 2008 323p $16.99

Grades: 7 8 9 10 **Fic**

1. Science fiction 2. Immortality -- Fiction 3. Great

Britain -- Fiction

ISBN 978-1-59990-302-6

LC 2008-10310

Sequel to The declaration (2007)

In a future England where young people, or "Surpluses," are heavily regulated and everyone takes a drug called Longevity, a member of the Underground infiltrates the Pincent Pharma manufacturing plant, and uncovers horrific acts being committed in an attempt to create eternal youth.

"The novel is well written and will be enjoyed by readers who liked the first book." Voice Youth Advocates

Followed by: The legacy (2011)

Mancusi, Mari

Scorched; Mari Mancusi. Sourcebooks Fire 2013 352 p. (hc: alk. paper) $16.99

Grades: 9 10 11 12 **Fic**

1. Fantasy fiction 2. Paranormal fiction 3. Eggs -- Fiction 4. Dragons -- Fiction 5. Grandfathers -- Fiction 6. Supernatural -- Fiction 7. Adventure and adventurers -- Fiction

ISBN 1402284586; 9781402284588

LC 2013011799

In this book, Trinity's kooky grandfather impulsively buys a "supposed dragon egg. Before she can determine how to rescue both their home and the once-reputable West Texas museum they run from foreclosure, twin brothers . . . appear from the future. Both brothers are there to collect Trinity. Both want possession of the egg. Both want to save the world from an apocalyptic future via starkly different but equally menacing means. Whom can Trinity trust?" (Kirkus Reviews)

Other titles in the series are:

Shattered (2014)

Smoked (2015)

Mangum, Lisa

After hello; Lisa Mangum. Shadow Mountain 2012 272 p. (hardbound: alk. paper) $17.99

Grades: 7 8 9 10 **Fic**

1. Friendship -- Fiction 2. Photographers -- Fiction 3. Man-woman relationship -- Fiction 4. Trust -- Fiction 5. New York (N.Y.) -- Fiction 6. Dating (Social customs) -- Fiction 7. Interpersonal relations -- Fiction

ISBN 1609070100; 9781609070106

LC 2012017735

Author Lisa Mangum focuses on Sara, a girl whose "first trip to New York City . . . turns into 24 hours she will never forget. An amateur photographer, Sara walks around the city taking pictures; when a boy named Sam wanders into her lens, she is intrigued by him and follows him on his missions to find and trade things for people . . . As Sam and Sara travel from St. John the Divine Cathedral to Central Park and Times Square, they meet a string of artists and musicians and reluctantly discuss their turbulent pasts." (Barnes & Noble)

Mantchev, Lisa

Eyes like stars. Feiwel and Friends 2009 356p $16.99

Grades: 8 9 10 11 12 **Fic**

1. Magic -- Fiction 2. Actors -- Fiction 3. Orphans -- Fiction 4. Theater -- Fiction 5. Books and reading

-- Fiction
ISBN 978-0-312-38096-0; 0-312-38096-8
LC 2008-15317

Thirteen-year-old Bertie strives to save Theater Illumi-nata, the only home she has ever known, but is hindered by the Players who magically live on there, especially Ariel, who is willing to destroy the Book at the center of the magic in order to escape into the outside world.

"The story contains enough mystery and mayhem to keep readers engaged, even as they analyze." Voice Youth Advocates

Other titles in this series include:
Perchance to dream (2010)
So silver bright (2011)

Perchance to dream. Feiwel and Friends 2010 337p $16.99; pa $9.99
Grades: 8 9 10 11 12   **Fic**
1. Magic -- Fiction 2. Fairies -- Fiction 3. Orphans -- Fiction 4. Theater -- Fiction
ISBN 978-0-312-38097-7; 0-312-38097-6; 978-0-312-67510-3 pa; 0-312-67510-0 pa
Sequel to Eyes like stars (2009)

Bertie, who is blessed with word magic, and her fairy sidekicks seek to save Nate, who has been kidnapped by the Sea Witch, but Bertie is torn between Nate and Ariel, an air spirit who loves Bertie enough to die for her.

"The pace is fast and furious . . . but it's Mantchev's fresh, intelligent style that delights most. . . . This fantasti-cal romp—an absolute must for theater buffs—might stand alone, but it'd be a pity not to start with the first." Kirkus
Followed by So silver bright (2011)

Manzano, Sonia
★ The **revolution** of Evelyn Serrano; Sonia Manzano. Scholastic 2012 205 p. $17.99
Grades: 6 7 8 9 10   **Fic**
1. Historical fiction 2. Puerto Ricans -- Fiction 3. Puerto Ricans -- New York (N.Y.) 4. Identity -- Fiction 5. Grandmothers -- Fiction 6. Protest movements -- Fiction
ISBN 0545325056; 9780545325059; 9780545325066
LC 2012009240
Pura Belpré Author Honor Book (2013)

This novel, by Sonia Manzano, is set "in New York's El Barrio in 1969. . . . The Young Lords, a Puerto Rican activist group, dump garbage in the street and set it on fire, ignit-ing a powerful protest. When Abuela steps in to take charge, Evelyn is thrust into the action. . . . Evelyn learns important truths about her Latino heritage and the history makers who shaped a nation." (Publisher's note)
Includes bibliographical references

Marchetta, Melina
★ **Finnikin** of the rock. Candlewick Press 2010 399p map $18.99
Grades: 8 9 10 11 12   **Fic**
1. Fantasy fiction
ISBN 0-7636-4361-0; 978-0-7636-4361-4
LC 2009-28046

In this fantasy novel, "Finnikin was only a child during the five days of the unspeakable, when the royal family of

Lumatere were brutally murdered, and an imposter seized the throne. . . . Finnikin, now on the cusp of manhood, is compelled to join forces with an arrogant and enigmatic young novice named Evanjalin, who claims that her dark dreams will lead the exiles to a surviving royal child and a way to pierce the cursed barrier and regain the land of Luma-tere." (Publisher's note)

"The skillful world building includes just enough de-tail to create a vivid sense of place, and Marchetta main-tains suspense with unexpected story arcs. It is the achingly real characters, though, and the relationships that emerge through the captivating dialogue that drive the story. Filled with questions about the impact of exile and the human need to belong, this standout fantasy quickly reveals that its real magic lies in its accomplished writing." Booklist

★ **Froi** of the exiles. Candlewick 2012 608 p.
Grades: 8 9 10 11 12   **Fic**
1. Exiles 2. War stories 3. Fantasy fiction
ISBN 9780763647599

In this fantasy book, "Froi, a former street thief who has started a new life in Lumatere, is sent to Charyn in disguise to assassinate its king, but his worldview is shaken by rev-elations about his own unknown past. Tensions between the two kingdoms ratchet up, and Froi's loyalties are tested as he becomes entrenched in the chaotic political situation in Charyn and is drawn to its unpredictable princess, Quin-tana, who has been horribly abused in an attempt to break Charyn's curse." (Publishers Weekly)

★ **Jellicoe** Road. HarperTeen 2008 419p $17.99; lib bdg $18.89
Grades: 9 10 11 12   **Fic**
1. School stories 2. Australia -- Fiction 3. Abandoned children -- Fiction 4. Identity (Psychology) -- Fiction
ISBN 978-0-06-143183-8; 0-06-143183-4; 978-0-06-143184-5 lib bdg; 0-06-143184-2 lib bdg
LC 2008-00760

First published 2006 in Australia with title: On the Jellicoe Road
Michael L. Printz Award, 2009

Abandoned by her drug-addicted mother at the age of eleven, high school student Taylor Markham struggles with her identity and family history at a boarding school in Australia.

"Readers may feel dizzied and disoriented, but as they puzzle out exactly how Hannah's narrative connects with Taylor's current reality, they will find themselves ensnared in the story's fascinating, intricate structure. A beautifully rendered mystery." Kirkus

★ **Quintana** of Charyn; Melina Marchetta. Candlewick Press 2013 528 p. (Lumatere chroni-cles) $18.99
Grades: 8 9 10 11 12   **Fic**
1. War stories 2. Fantasy fiction
ISBN 0763658359; 9780763658359
LC 2012955120

This is the conclusion of Melina Marchetta's trilogy which began with "Finnikin of the Rock." Here, "the king-doms of Lumatere and Charyn attempt to bridge past atroci-ties through a new generation of leaders. Although tragedies arise, unity and healing are core themes, compared to the horrors of the previous books. As the title suggests, Quintana--the rightful ruler of Charyn, hidden following the uprising in the kingdom in Froi of the Exiles--is at the center of this final book." (Publishers Weekly)

Marillier, Juliet

Child of the prophecy. TOR Bks. 2002 528p il map (Sevenwaters trilogy) $26.95; pa $15.95

Grades: 11 12 Adult   **Fic**

1. Fantasy fiction

ISBN 0-312-84881-1; 0-312-87036-1 pa

LC 2001-57480

Sequel to Son of the shadows (2001)

"As the daughter of Niamh of the Sevenwaters Clan, Fainne possesses a magic born of the land itself. Instructed by her grandmother, the sorceress Oonagh, Fainne believes she has a destiny to bring about a terrible change in the world.... The author captures the feel of myth in this Celtic-laced saga that belongs in most fantasy collections." Libr J

Daughter of the forest. TOR Bks. 2000 400p (Sevenwaters trilogy) hardcover o.p. pa $15.95

Grades: 11 12 Adult   **Fic**

1. Fantasy fiction

ISBN 0-312-84879-X; 0-312-87530-4 pa

LC 00-25216

"As the only daughter and youngest child of Lord Colum of Sevenwaters, Sorcha grows up protected and pampered by her six older brothers. When a sorceress's evil magic ensorcels Colum's sons, transforming them into swans, only Sorcha's efforts can break the curse.... The author's keen understanding of Celtic paganism and early Irish Christianity adds texture to a rich and vibrant novel that belongs in most fantasy collections." Libr J

Other titles in the Sevenwaters trilogy are:

Child of the prophecy (2002)

Son of the shadows (2001)

Raven flight; a Shadowfell novel. Juliet Marillier. Alfred A. Knopf 2013 416 p.

Grades: 7 8 9 10   **Fic**

1. Fantasy fiction 2. Paranormal fiction 3. Fantasy 4. Magic -- Fiction 5. Orphans -- Fiction 6. Insurgency -- Fiction 7. Voyages and travels -- Fiction

ISBN 9780375869556; 9780375969553

LC 2012039483

This is the second volume of Juliet Marillier's Shadowfell series. Here, "Neryn's time among the rebels has left her stronger and healthier but no closer to grasping her power and becoming a true Caller. When a potential ally sets a time limit for rebelling against tyrannical King Keldec, Neryn can no longer hide and sets off to find the Hag of the Isles and the Lord of the North." (Kirkus Reviews)

Shadowfell; Juliet Marillier. Alfred A. Knopf 2012 410 p. map (trade) $16.99

Grades: 7 8 9 10 11 12   **Fic**

1. Fantasy fiction 2. Magic -- Fiction 3. Adventure fiction 4. Fantasy 5. Orphans -- Fiction 6. Insurgency -- Fiction 7. Voyages and travels -- Fiction

ISBN 0375869549; 9780375869549; 9780375969546; 9780375983665

LC 2011041050

Originally published: Sydney, N.S.W.: Pan Macmillan, 2012.

In this novel by Juliet Marillier "Fifteen-year-old Neryn is alone in the land of Alban, where the oppressive king has ordered anyone with magical strengths captured and brought before him. Eager to hide her own canny skill--a uniquely powerful ability to communicate with the fairy-like Good Folk--Neryn sets out for the legendary Shadowfell, a home and training ground for a secret rebel group determined to overthrow the evil King Keldec." (Publisher's note)

Son of the shadows. TOR Bks. 2001 462p (Sevenwaters trilogy) $25.95; pa $14.95

Grades: 11 12 Adult   **Fic**

1. Fantasy fiction

ISBN 0-312-84880-3; 0-312-87529-0 pa

LC 2001-17387

Sequel to Daughter of the forest (2000)

"Sorcha has brought her British husband home and raised her children, including the gorgeous Niamh and her darker sister, Liadan, in peace. But evil stalks the land again when a tattooed outlaw appears to unsettle the alliances that keep Sevenwaters safe. And with whom but that Painted Man will our heroine—Liadan—fall passionately in love? Marillier's virtuosic pacing and vivid, filmic style make this an engaging continuation of one of last year's best fantasies." Booklist

Followed by Child of the prophecy (2002)

Marquardt, Marie F., 1972-

Dream Things True; Marie Marquardt. St. Martin's Press 2015 352 p. $18.99

Grades: 9 10 11 12   **Fic**

1. Love -- Fiction 2. Unauthorized immigrants -- Fiction

ISBN 1250070457; 9781250070456

LC 2015019022

In this novel, by Marie Marquardt, "the nephew of a senator, Evan seems to have it all - except a functional family. Alma has lived in Georgia since she was two, surrounded by a large (sometimes smothering) Mexican family. They both want out of this town. When they fall in love, they fall hard, trying to ignore their differences. Then Immigration and Customs Enforcement begins raids in their town, and Alma knows that she needs to share her secret. But how will she tell her country-club boyfriend that she and almost everyone she's close to are undocumented immigrants?" (Publisher's note)

"A debut romance for libraries looking to diversify their offerings." SLJ

Marr, Melissa

Darkest mercy. Harper 2011 327p $16.99; lib bdg $17.89

Grades: 8 9 10 11 12   **Fic**
1. Fantasy fiction 2. Fairies -- Fiction
ISBN 978-0-06-165925-6; 0-06-165925-8; 978-0-06-
165926-3 lib bdg; 0-06-165926-6 lib bdg
                                   LC 2010-33584
Sequel to: Radiant shadows (2010)
The political and romantic tensions that began when Ais-
lin became Summer Queen threaten to boil over as the Faerie
Courts brace against the threat of all-out war.

Fragile eternity. Bowen Press 2009 389p
$16.99; lib bdg $17.89
Grades: 8 9 10 11 12   **Fic**
1. Fantasy fiction 2. Fairies -- Fiction
ISBN 978-0-06-121471-4; 0-06-121471-X; 978-0-06-
121472-1 lib bdg; 0-06-121472-8 lib bdg
                                   LC 2008-34420
Sequel to: Ink exchange (2008)
Aislinn and Seth struggle with the unforeseen consequences of Aislinn's transformation from mortal
girl to faery queen as the world teeters on the brink of
cataclysmic violence.
Followed by: Radiant shadows (2010)

Ink exchange. HarperTeen 2008 325p il lib bdg
$17.89; $16.99
Grades: 8 9 10 11 12   **Fic**
1. Fantasy fiction 2. Fairies -- Fiction 3. Tattooing
-- Fiction 4. Kings and rulers -- Fiction
ISBN 978-0-06-121469-1 lib bdg; 0-06-121469-8 lib
bdg; 978-0-06-121468-4; 0-06-121468-X
                                   LC 2007-40106
Sequel to: Wicked lovely (2007)
Seventeen-year-old Leslie wants a tattoo as a way of
reclaiming control of herself and her body, but the eerie
image she selects pulls her into the dangerous Dark Court
of the faeries, where she draws on inner strength to make a
horrible choice.
"Readers will be drawn in by Marr's darkly poetic imagery and language, her vivid portrayal of the art of tattooing,
and her shadowy love triangle. This is indeed a delicious,
smoky delight." Bull Cent Child Books
Followed by Fragile eternity (2009)

Radiant shadows. HarperCollins 2010 340p
$16.99; lib bdg $17.89
Grades: 8 9 10 11 12   **Fic**
1. Fantasy fiction 2. Fairies -- Fiction
ISBN 978-0-06-165922-5; 0-06-165922-3; 978-0-06-
165923-2 lib bdg; 0-06-165923-1 lib bdg
                                   LC 2009-53458
Sequel to: Fragile eternity (2009)
Ani, a half-mortal driven by her hungers, and Devlin,
faery assassin and brother to the High Queen, have reason
to fear one another even as they are drawn together to save
all of Faerie.
"This is a worthy addition to a fine series. Readers who
have enjoyed the early books will find this a satisfying
read." SLJ
Followed by: Darkest mercy (2011)

Wicked lovely. HarperTeen 2007 328p il
$16.99; lib bdg $17.89
Grades: 8 9 10 11 12   **Fic**
1. Fantasy fiction 2. Fairies -- Fiction 3. Kings and
rulers -- Fiction
ISBN 978-0-06-121465-3; 0-06-121465-5; 978-0-06-
121466-0 lib bdg; 0-06-121466-3 lib bdg
                                   LC 2007-09143
Seventeen-year-old Aislinn, who has the rare ability to
see faeries, is drawn against her will into a centuries-old
battle between the Summer King and the Winter Queen, and
the survival of her life, her love, and summer all hang in
the balance.
"This story explores the themes of love, commitment,
and what it really means to give of oneself for the greater
good to save everyone else. It is the unusual combination of
past legends and modern-day life that gives a unique twist to
this 'fairy' tale." SLJ
Other titles in this series are:
Darkest mercy (2011)
Fragile eternity (2009)
Ink exchange (2008)
Radiant shadows (2010)

Marsden, Carolyn, 1950-
My Own Revolution; Carolyn Marsden. Candle-
wick Press 2012 174 p. $16.99
Grades: 7 8 9 10 11 12   **Fic**
1. Czechoslovakia -- Fiction 2. Communist countries
-- Fiction 3. Resistance to government -- Fiction
ISBN 0763653950; 9780763653958
                                   LC 2012942296
This young adult novel, by Carolyn Marsden, takes place
"in 1960s Czechoslovakia, [where] . . . fourteen-year-old
Patrik rebels against the communist regime in small ways
whenever he gets the chance. . . . But anti-Party sentiment
is risky, and when party interference cuts a little too close
to home, Patrik and his family find themselves faced with a
decision . . . that will change everything." (Publisher's note)

Marsden, John, 1950-
Hamlet: a novel. Candlewick Press 2009 229p
$16.99
Grades: 10 11 12   **Fic**
1. Poets 2. Authors 3. Dramatists 4. Denmark --
Fiction 5. Princes -- Fiction 6. Homicide -- Fiction
ISBN 978-0-7636-4451-2; 0-7636-4451-X
                                   LC 2009-7331
This is a retelling of Shakespeare's play. Grieving for the
recent death of his beloved father and appalled by his mother's quick remarriage to his uncle, Hamlet, heir to the Danish throne, struggles with conflicting emotions, particularly
after his father's ghost appeals to him to avenge his death.
"The setting is contemporary, but feels timeless. Marsden stays true to Shakespeare's text, while modernizing the
dialogue. He makes the prince a sympathetic teen who is
struggling with his hormones, his grief, and the fact that his
uncle is now his stepfather. . . . This is a wonderful treatment
of the play: engaging, gripping, dark, and lovely." SLJ

Incurable. Scholastic 2008 245p (The Ellie
chronicles) pa $7.99

Grades: 7 8 9 10 **Fic**
1. War stories 2. Australia -- Fiction
ISBN 978-0-439-78322-4 pa; 0-439-78322-4 pa
First published 2005 in Australia

Ellie has struggled to put the war behind her and lead a normal life. Although what's normal about your parents having been murdered; trying to run a farm and go to school; and bringing up a young boy who's hiding terrible secrets about his past?

The **other** side of dawn. Scholastic 2007 319p pa $8.99
Grades: 7 8 9 10 **Fic**
1. War stories 2. Australia -- Fiction
ISBN 978-0-439-85805-2

Sequel to The night is for hunting. Another title in the author's series which began with Tomorrow, when the war began

First published 1999 in Australia

Ellie and her friends, five Australian teenagers who survived the enemy invasion of their country, use guerrilla tactics to support a major counterattack by New Zealand troops.

"As were the previous titles, this final book is chock-ful of action sequences that are undeniably gripping if not always completely believable. The characters, on the other hand, feel quite real." Horn Book

Tomorrow, when the war began. Houghton Mifflin 1995 286p pa $9.99
Grades: 7 8 9 10 **Fic**
1. War stories 2. Australia -- Fiction
ISBN 9780439829106; 0395706734
LC 94-29299
First published 1993 in Australia

"Australian teenager Ellie and six of her friends return from a winter break camping trip to find their homes burned or deserted, their families imprisoned, and their country occupied by a foreign military force in league with a band of disaffected Australians. As their shock wears off, the seven decide they must stick together if they are to survive. After a life-threatening skirmish with the occupiers, the teens retreat to their isolated campsite in the bush country and make plans to fight a guerilla war against the invaders." (School Library Journal)

"The novel is a riveting adventure through which Marsden explores the capacity for evil and the necessity of working together to oppose it." Horn Book

While I live. Scholastic 2007 299p (The Ellie chronicles) $16.99
Grades: 7 8 9 10 **Fic**
1. War stories 2. Australia -- Fiction
ISBN 978-0-439-78318-7; 0-439-78318-6

Officially the war is over, but Ellie can not seem to escape it and resume a normal life especially after her parents are murdered and she becomes the ward of an unscrupulous lawyer who wants to acquire her family's property.

"Fans of 16-year-old Ellie Linton . . . will be overjoyed that she's back in an exciting series of her own. The realistic and shocking war-related violence that characterized the earlier titles is just as prevalent here." SLJ

Other titles about Ellie Linton are:

Circle of flight (2009)
Incurable (2008)

Martin, C. K. Kelly
The **lighter** side of life and death. Random House Children's Books 2010 231p $16.99; lib bdg $19.99
Grades: 9 10 11 12 **Fic**
1. School stories 2. Theater -- Fiction 3. Remarriage -- Fiction
ISBN 978-0-375-84588-8; 0-375-84588-7; 978-0-375-95588-4 lib bdg; 0-375-95588-7 lib bdg
LC 2009-15608

After the last, triumphant night of the school play, fifteen-year-old Mason loses his virginity to his good friend and secret crush, Kat Medina, which leads to enormous complications at school just as his home life is thrown into turmoil by his father's marriage to a woman with two children.

"This is not your ordinary teen romance. It's heavy on the sex but carefully nuanced. . . . The layers of emotion, so rarely evoked by young men in YA novels, give a depth and authenticity to Mason's personality that expose his naïveté and occasional bewilderment. The book's other characters are equally complex. . . . A more genuine representation of teen life would be hard to find." Booklist

Yesterday; C.K. Kelly Martin. Random House 2012 368 p. (hardcover library binding) $19.99
Grades: 9 10 11 12 **Fic**
1. Mystery fiction 2. Paranormal fiction 3. Interpersonal relations -- Fiction 4. Science fiction 5. Memory -- Fiction 6. Schools -- Fiction 7. Identity -- Fiction 8. High schools -- Fiction 9. Family life -- Canada -- Fiction 10. Canada -- History -- 20th century -- Fiction
ISBN 0375866507; 0375966501; 9780375866500; 9780375896446; 9780375966507
LC 2011023994

In this book, "[h]er father's recent death and the move from New Zealand to Toronto with her mother and sister in 1985 have left Freya Kallas seriously disoriented and plagued by headaches. Worse, her memories have puzzling gaps. . . . What do Freya's dreams of living another life mean? . . . Freya is sure the boy she spots on a school field trip has the answers she needs. Though she doesn't know his name and he doesn't recognize her, Freya, increasingly desperate, can't let him go." (Kirkus)

Martin, T. Michael
The **end** games; T. Michael Martin. Balzer + Bray 2013 384 p. (hardcover) $17.99
Grades: 9 10 11 12 **Fic**
1. Science fiction 2. Zombies -- Fiction 3. Brothers -- Fiction 4. Survival -- Fiction 5. West Virginia -- Fiction
ISBN 0062201808; 9780062201805
LC 2012038108

This novel, by T. Michael Martin, "takes place in rural West Virginia after a zombie apocalypse. Seventeen-year-old Michael and his baby brother . . . have managed to stay alive by following the Instructions of a mysterious Games Master. They spend their nights fighting the Bellows, grotesque, flesh-eating creatures. But the brothers may not survive much longer. The Bellows are evolving. And the others in The Game don't always follow the rules." (Publisher's note)

Martinez, Claudia Guadalupe

Pig Park; by Claudia Guadalupe Martinez. First edition Cinco Puntos Press 2014 248 p. illustrations (hardback) $15.95

Grades: 8 9 10 11 **Fic**
1. Ghost towns 2. Community life 3. Building -- Fiction 4. Neighborhoods -- Fiction 5. Hispanic Americans -- Fiction 6. Bakers and bakeries -- Fiction 7. Family life -- Illinois -- Chicago -- Fiction
ISBN 1935955764; 9781935955764; 9781935955771
LC 2013040645

In this novel by Claudia Guadalupe Martinez "Masi Burciaga hauls bricks to help build a giant pyramid in her neighborhood park. Her neighborhood is becoming more of a ghost town each day since the lard company moved away. As a last resort, the neighborhood grown-ups enlist all the remaining able-bodied boys and girls into this scheme in hopes of luring visitors. But something's not right about the entrepreneur behind it all." (Publisher's note)

"Martinez uses nicely specific physical details to relate Masi's experiences, and the moments in the bakery seem particularly authentic and are suffused with love.The warm, diverse community setting and the realistic family interactions help overcome the somewhat jumbled plotlines." Kirkus

Martinez, Jessica

Kiss kill vanish; by Jessica Martinez. First edition Katherine Tegen Books, an imprint of HarperCollinsPublishers 2014 432 p. (hardcover) $17.99

Grades: 9 10 11 12 **Fic**
1. Family secrets -- Fiction 2. Runaway children -- Fiction 3. Organized crime -- Fiction
ISBN 006227449X; 9780062274496
LC 2013043192

In this novel by Jessica Martinez "Valentina is living a charmed, glittering life in Miami . . . . when one shocking moment shatters everything she thought she knew about herself, her boyfriend, and her world. With no one left to trust, Valentina sheds her identity and flees to Montreal. [Her] new life comes crashing down when someone from her past resurfaces, putting her safety in question and her heart on the line." (Publisher's note)

"Valentina's decision making is sometimes opaque, but her strong voice, full of sensory imagery, and her exquisitely drawn relationships with Emilio, Marcel, and her father make this a memorable thriller." Publishers Weekly

Virtuosity. Simon Pulse 2011 294p $16.99
Grades: 8 9 10 11 12 **Fic**
1. Musicians -- Fiction 2. Drug abuse -- Fiction 3. Violinists -- Fiction 4. Chicago (Ill.) -- Fiction 5. Mother-daughter relationship -- Fiction
ISBN 978-1-4424-2052-6; 1-4424-2052-9
LC 2010042513

This is a "riveting novel. . . . The portrayal of Carmen's world . . . is unique and convincing. . . . Even readers without much interest in music will enjoy this exceptional novel." SLJ

Martinez, Victor

★ **Parrot** in the oven; a novel. Cotler Bks. 1996 216p $19.99; pa $5.99

Grades: 7 8 9 10 **Fic**
1. Family life -- Fiction 2. Mexican Americans -- Fiction
ISBN 0-06-026704-6; 0-06-447186-1 pa
LC 96-2119

Manny relates his coming of age experiences as a member of a poor Mexican American family in which the alcoholic father only adds to everyone's struggle

The author "maintains the authenticity of his setting and characterizations through a razor-sharp combination of tense dialogue, coursing narrative and startlingly elegant imagery." Publ Wkly

Mason, Bobbie Ann

★ **In** country; a novel. Harper Perennial 2005 245, 16p pa $14.99

Grades: 11 12 Adult **Fic**
1. Kentucky -- Fiction 2. Veterans -- Fiction 3. Vietnam War, 1961-1975 -- Fiction
ISBN 978-0-06-083517-0; 0-06-083517-6
LC 2006-273518

First published 1985

"Sam, 17, is obsessed with the Vietnam War and the effect it has had on her life—losing a father she never knew and now living with Uncle Emmett, who seems to be suffering from the effects of Agent Orange. In her own forthright way, she tries to sort out why and how Vietnam has altered the lives of the vets of Hopewell, Kentucky. . . . A harshly realistic, well-written look at the Vietnam War as well as the story of a young woman maturing." SLJ

Massey, David

Torn; David Massey. Scholastic 2013 288 p. $17.99

Grades: 9 10 11 12 **Fic**
1. Missing children -- Fiction 2. Afghan War, 2001- -- Fiction 3. War -- Fiction 4. Soldiers -- Fiction 5. Afghanistan -- Fiction 6. Medical care -- Fiction
ISBN 0545496454; 9780545496452
LC 2012024405

In this novel by David Massey, set "in war-torn Afghanistan, a girl walks right into a hail of bullets: Elinor watches it with her own eyes. The young British army medic risks the line of fire to rescue her, only to realize the girl is gone. To find the missing, mysterious child, Elinor enlists the help of an American Navy SEAL. But in all the confusion, with coalition troops fighting every day to maintain a fragile peace, does Ben have something to hide?" (Publisher's note)

"Nineteen-year-old Elinor is sent to Afghanistan as a medic in the British military. There she befriends an American Navy SEAL and repeatedly encounters a mysteriously elusive Afghan girl. Massey, a former counter-terrorism consultant, brings an air of authenticity to this intense novel that explores the power of friendships formed in combat as well as war's effect on one young woman's idealism." (Horn Book)

Matson, Morgan

Amy & Roger's epic detour. Simon and Schuster Books for Young Readers 2010 343p il $16.99

Grades: 9 10 11 12 **Fic**

1. Death -- Fiction 2. Guilt -- Fiction 3. Fathers -- Fiction 4. Bereavement -- Fiction 5. Automobile travel -- Fiction

ISBN 978-1-4169-9065-9; 1-4169-9065-8

LC 2009-49988

After the death of her father, Amy, a high school student, and Roger, a college freshman, set out on a carefully planned road trip from California to Connecticut. "Grades eight to twelve." (Bull Cent Child Books)

"This entertaining and thoughtful summertime road trip serves up slices of America with a big scoop of romance on the side." Kirkus

★ **Second** chance summer; Morgan Matson. Simon & Schuster Books For Young Readers 2012 468 p. (hardback) $16.99

Grades: 9 10 11 12 **Fic**

1. Cancer -- Fiction 2. Family -- Fiction 3. Vacations -- Fiction 4. Love -- Fiction 5. Terminally ill -- Fiction 6. Pocono Mountains (Pa.) -- Fiction 7. Interpersonal relations -- Fiction 8. Family life -- Pennsylvania -- Fiction

ISBN 1416990674; 9781416990673; 9781416990680; 9781439157527

LC 2011052241

In this young adult novel, Taylor and her parents and older brother and younger sister are headed to their lake house in the Poconos for the summer so her father, who is dying of cancer, can spend his last summer there. "Returning to their lake house after a five-year absence fills [Taylor] with dread: she'll have to face her estranged best friend as well as the boy she left without saying goodbye." (Publishers Weekly)

Since you've been gone; Morgan Matson. Simon & Schuster Books for Young Readers 2014 464 p. (hardback) $17.99

Grades: 7 8 9 10 **Fic**

1. Friendship -- Fiction 2. Family life -- Fiction 3. Self-reliance -- Fiction 4. Dating (Social customs) -- Fiction 5. Connecticut -- Fiction 6. Best friends -- Fiction 7. Family life -- Connecticut -- Fiction

ISBN 1442435003; 9781442435001; 9781442435018

LC 2013041617

In this book, by Morgan Matson, "Emily is about to take some risks and have the most unexpected summer ever. . . . Before Sloane, Emily didn't go to parties, she barely talked to guys, and she didn't do anything crazy. Enter Sloane, social tornado and the best kind of best friend—someone who yanks you out of your shell. But right before what should have been an epic summer, Sloane just disappears. . . . There's just a random to-do list with thirteen bizarre tasks that Emily would never try." (Publisher's note)

"Emily feels lost when her best friend, Sloane, disappears without explanation. But Sloane left Emily a daunting to-do list (with items like 'kiss a stranger'), and Emily bravely takes on each task, finding new friends, confidence, and a crush along the way. A perfectly awkward protagonist; well-rounded, quirky supporting characters; and spot-

on dialogue make this novel of self-discovery stand out." Horn Book

Mattison, Booker T.

Unsigned hype; a novel. Revell 2009 207p pa $9.99

Grades: 7 8 9 10 **Fic**

1. Rap music -- Fiction 2. Christian life -- Fiction 3. African Americans -- Fiction

ISBN 978-0-8007-3380-3; 0-8007-3380-0

LC 2008-54966

Fifteen-year-old Tory Tyson dreams of producing hip hop records, and as he rapidly begins to experience success doing just that, he finds that he must make choices between the way he has been raised by his single, God-fearing mother and the folks he meets in the music world.

This "novel has an authentic voice, taking readers into the world of New York City hip-hop through the wide eyes of a kid who's still refreshingly innocent." Publ Wkly

May, Kyla

Kiki; my stylish life. by Kyla May. Scholastic Inc. 2013 96 p.

Grades: 7 8 9 10 11 12 **Fic**

1. Diaries -- Fiction 2. Friendship -- Fiction 3. Clubs 4. Fashion -- Fiction 5. Schools -- Fiction 6. Popularity -- Fiction 7. Best friends -- Fiction 8. Elementary schools -- Fiction

ISBN 9780545445122; 9780545496131; 9780545496803; 0545496136

LC 2012034246

In this book by Kyla May, "Kiki, Coco, and Lulu are the BEST of friends. They even have their very own club! But Mika, the new girl, is shaking things up on Lotus Lane. This first book is written as Kiki's diary--with illustrations and doodles throughout. Kiki LOVES creating cool outfits, hanging out with friends, and collecting fun facts." (Publisher's note)

Mayhew, Julie

Red ink; Julie Mayhew. Candlewick Press 2015 297 p. $16.99

Grades: 9 10 11 12 **Fic**

1. Grief -- Fiction 2. London (England) -- Fiction 3. Mother-daughter relationship -- Fiction

ISBN 0763677310; 9780763677312

LC 2014957107

In this book, by Julie Mayhew, "when her mother is knocked down and killed by a London bus, fifteen-year-old Melon Fouraki is left with no family worth mentioning. Her mother, Maria, never did introduce her to a living, breathing father. The indomitable Auntie Aphrodite, meanwhile, is hundreds of miles away on a farm in Crete, and she is not likely to jump on a plane to come to East Finchley anytime soon. But at least Melon has . . . the Fouraki family fairy tale." (Publisher's note)

"Melon got many things from her mother, Maria: Greek heritage, an oft-told family fairy tale, and a ridiculous name. Maria claims that the name is a reminder of her happy childhood on a melon farm in Crete, but Melon, who, like many 15-year-olds, is stuck in the phase of hating her mom, just sees it as another thing that makes her different.

But everything upends when Maria is killed by a London bus, leaving Melon, who has never known her father, alone and questioning everything she thought she knew about her mother's past. . . . Melon tells her own story interspersed with her mother's in fractured, chaotic vignettes that circle the day of the accident: 17 days since, 3 days since, 6 years before. As a narrator, she is harsh and abrasive but always sympathetic. Gritty and sad as this may be, it certainly rings true." Booklist

Mazer, Harry

The **last** mission. Dell 1981 188p pa $5.99

Grades: 7 8 9 10   **Fic**

1. Jews -- Fiction 2. Prisoners of war -- Fiction 3. World War, 1939-1945 -- Fiction

ISBN 0-440-94797-9

First published 1979 by Delacorte Press

In 1944 a 15-year-old Jewish boy tells his family he will travel in the West but instead, enlists in the United States Air Corps and is subsequently taken prisoner by the Germans.

"Told in a rapid journalistic style, occasionally peppered with barrack-room vulgarities, the story is a vivid and moving account of a boy's experience during World War II as well as a skillful, convincing portrayal of his misgivings as a Jew on enemy soil and of his ability to size up—in mature human fashion—the misery around him." Horn Book

Somebody, please tell me who I am; Harry Mazer and Peter Lerangis. 1st ed; Simon & Schuster Books for Young Readers 2012 148p. $15.99

Grades: 6 7 8 9 10 11 12   **Fic**

1. Family -- Fiction 2. Amnesia -- Fiction 3. Veterans -- Fiction

ISBN 9781416938958 (hardcover)

LC 2011006010

Schneider Family Book Award (2013)

In this book, "[i]n May, Ben tells his family and friends he's joining the army after graduation; in June, he goes off to basic training; in July, he's deployed to Iraq; in September, . . . [he] return[s] stateside with a traumatic brain injury. His girlfriend, his best friend, and his family, all sick with grief and worry, come together to support Ben as he struggles to recover and communicate." (Bulletin of the Center for Children's Books)

Mazer, Norma Fox

★ The **missing** girl. HarperTeen 2008 288p $16.99; lib bdg $17.89

Grades: 7 8 9 10   **Fic**

1. Sisters -- Fiction 2. Kidnapping -- Fiction 3. New York (State) -- Fiction 4. Child sexual abuse -- Fiction

ISBN 978-0-06-623776-3; 978-0-06-623777-0 lib bdg

LC 2007-09136

In Mallory, New York, as five sisters, aged eleven to seventeen, deal with assorted problems, conflicts, fears, and yearnings, a mysterious middle-aged man watches them, fascinated, deciding which one he likes the best.

"Fans of . . . classic tales of high-tension peril will appreciate the way this successfully plays on their deepest fears." Bull Cent Child Books

McBride, Lish

Hold me closer, necromancer. Henry Holt 2010 342p $16.99

Grades: 9 10 11 12   **Fic**

1. Dead -- Fiction 2. Magic -- Fiction 3. Werewolves -- Fiction 4. Supernatural -- Fiction 5. Seattle (Wash.) -- Fiction

ISBN 978-0-8050-9098-7; 0-8050-9098-3

LC 2009-50768

Sam LaCroix, a Seattle fast-food worker and college dropout, discovers that he is a necromancer, part of a world of harbingers, werewolves, satyrs, and one particular necromancer who sees Sam as a threat to his lucrative business of raising the dead.

"With fine writing, tight plotting, a unique and uniquely odd cast of teens, adults, and children, and a pace that smashes through any curtain of disbelief, this sardonic and outrageous story's only problem is that it must, like all good things, come to an end." Booklist

McCafferty, Megan

Bumped. Balzer + Bray 2011 323p $16.99

Grades: 9 10 11 12   **Fic**

1. Twins -- Fiction 2. Sisters -- Fiction 3. Viruses -- Fiction 4. Pregnancy -- Fiction 5. New Jersey -- Fiction

ISBN 978-0-06-196274-5; 0-06-196274-0

LC 2010-30704

In 2036 New Jersey, when teens are expected to become fanatically religious wives and mothers or high-priced Surrogettes for couples made infertile by a widespread virus, sixteen-year-old identical twins Melody and Harmony find in one another the courage to believe they have choices.

"The book's carefree sexuality and exploitation makes it uncomfortable, scandalous, and not easily forgotten—there's little doubt that's exactly what McCafferty is going for." Publ Wkly

Thumped; Megan McCafferty. Balzer + Bray 2012 290 p. (hardback) $17.99

Grades: 9 10 11 12   **Fic**

1. Science fiction 2. Dystopian fiction 3. Teenage mothers -- Fiction 4. Teenage pregnancy -- Fiction 5. Twins -- Fiction 6. Honesty -- Fiction 7. Sisters -- Fiction 8. Pregnancy -- Fiction 9. Infertility -- Fiction 10. Virus diseases -- Fiction

ISBN 0061962767; 9780061962769

LC 2011042149

This book is the sequel to Megan McCafferty's science fiction novel 'Bumped' about the pregnancies of teenage twin girls twins Melody and Harmony in a future dystopian United States. "After a virus destroyed the ability of anyone over the age of 18 to reproduce, teen pregnancy became big business. . . . [T]his book . . . makes the deliberate point that teenage pregnancy and sex without love can seriously damage both the teens and society." (Kirkus Reviews)

"The well-paced plot and the twins' alternating narratives will keep readers engaged... A worthwhile read for teens beginning to think about their personal reproductive choices." LJ

McCaffrey, Anne

Dragon's kin; {by} Anne McCaffrey, Todd McCaffrey. Del Rey 2003 304p $24.95

Grades: 9 10 11 12   Fic
1. Fantasy fiction
ISBN 0-345-46198-3

"On the planet Pern, the colonists prepare for the return of the Red Star and the deadly fall of Thread, which consumes any organic matter it touches. When the mines that provide the planet with minerals for metalworking and coal for heat play out, a pair of young people discover a heretofore hidden power of the watchwhers, the lowly kin of dragonkind, and learn a new way to provide assistance for the people of Pern. . . . Personable characters and superb storytelling make this an excellent choice for sf collections and essential for Pern fans of all ages. Highly recommended." Libr J

Dragonflight; volume 1 of The Dragonriders of Pern. Ballantine Bks. 1978 337p il (Dragonriders of Pern) hardcover o.p. pa $12.95

Grades: 8 9 10 11 12 Adult   Fic
1. Fantasy fiction 2. Science fiction 3. Dragons -- Fiction
ISBN 0-345-27749-X; 0-345-48426-6 pa
LC 78-16707

First published 1968 in paperback. Based on two award winning stories entitled: Weyr search and Dragonrider. Many titles co-written by Todd McCaffrey

ALA YALSA Margaret A. Edwards Award (1999)

The planet Pern, originally colonized from Earth but long out of contact with it, has been periodically threatened by the deadly silver Threads which fall from the wandering Red Star. To combat them a life form on the planet was developed into winged, fire-breathing dragons. Humans with a high degree of empathy and telepathic power are needed to train and preserve these creatures. As the story begins, Pern has fallen into decay, the threat of the Red Star has been forgotten, the Dragonriders and dragons are reduced in number and in disrepute, and the evil Lord Fax has begun conquering neighboring holds.

Fantasy titles set on Pern include:
All the Weyrs of Pern (1991)
The chronicles of Pern: first fall (1993)
Dragon Harper (2007)
Dragon's fire (2006)
Dragon's kin (2003)
Dragon's time (2011)
Dragondrums (1979)
Dragonquest (1971)
Dragonsdawn (1988)
Dragonseye (1997)
Dragonsinger (1977)
Dragonsong (1976)
The masterharper of Pern (1998)
Morets: Dragonlady of Pern (1983)
Nerilka's story (1986)
The Renegades of Pern (1989)
The skies of Pern (2001)
White dragon (1978)

McCaffrey, Todd J.

Dragongirl; [by] Todd McCaffrey. Del Rey-Ballantine Books 2010 482p map (Dragonriders of Pern) $26; ebook $26

Grades: 9 10 11 12 Adult   Fic
1. Fantasy fiction 2. Dragons -- Fiction
ISBN 978-0-345-49116-9; 978-0-345-52191-0 ebook
LC 2010-14672

Sequel to Dragonheart (2008)

"Once again, the Red Star appears in the skies over Pern, triggering the fall of Thread, a corrosive and deadly space-born spore that comes in Passes that last approximately 50 years. This time, however, the dragons bred by the colonists of Pern to fight Thread are dying from a mysterious plague, and the population of Pern faces extinction. While gold-dragon rider Fiona concentrates on learning to heal sick and injured dragons and their riders, the harper Kindan and ex-dragon rider Lorana search for a cure." Libr J

McCahan, Erin

Love and other foreign words; by Erin McCahan. Dial Books, an imprint of Penguin Group (USA) Inc. 2014 336 p. (hardcover) $17.99

Grades: 8 9 10 11 12   Fic
1. Love stories 2. Love -- Fiction 3. Sisters -- Fiction 4. Friendship -- Fiction 5. Interpersonal relations -- Fiction 6. Best friends -- Fiction 7. Interpersonal communication -- Fiction
ISBN 0803740514; 9780803740518
LC 2013027095

In this book, by Erin McCahan, "[s]ixteen-year-old Josie lives her life in translation. She speaks High School, College, Friends, Boyfriends, Break-ups, and even the language of Beautiful Girls. But none of these is her native tongue-- the only people who speak that are her best friend Stu and her sister Kate. So when Kate gets engaged to an epically insufferable guy, how can Josie see it as anything but the mistake of a lifetime?" (Publisher's note)

"Josie doesn't like change. So when her sister Kate announces she's going to marry Geoff, Josie immediately tries everything to alienate him. But she also becomes curious about the nature of love and, with the help of her friends and family, tries to understand it. The highlight of this effectively drawn, often funny novel is its smart, precocious, and irrepressibly inquisitive protagonist." Horn Book

Mccall, Guadalupe Garcia

★ **Under** the mesquite. Lee & Low Books 2011 224p $17.95

Grades: 7 8 9 10 11 12   Fic
1. Texas -- Fiction 2. Cancer -- Fiction 3. Family life -- Fiction 4. Mexican Americans -- Fiction
ISBN 978-1-60060-429-4; 1-60060-429-3; 978-1-60060-875-9 ebook
LC 2010052567

"With poignant imagery and well-placed Spanish, the author effectively captures the complex lives of teenagers in many Latino and/or immigrant families." Kirkus

McCarry, Sarah

About a girl; Sarah McCarry. St. Martin's Griffin 2015 260 p. (hardback) $21.99 **Fic**

1. Bisexuality -- Fiction 2. Supernatural -- Fiction 3. Teenage girls -- Fiction 4. Love -- Fiction 5. Identity -- Fiction

ISBN 1250068622; 9781250068620

LC 2015016090

Sequel to: All our pretty songs

In this young adult novel, by Sarah McCarry, "eighteen-year-old Tally is . . . sure of everything. . . . There's no room in her tidy world for . . . the . . . mother who abandoned her soon after she was born. But when a sudden discovery upends her fiercely ordered world, Tally sets out on an unexpected quest to seek out the reclusive musician who may hold the key to her past—and instead finds Maddy, an enigmatic and beautiful girl who will unlock the door to her future." (Publisher's note)

"As in other books in the trilogy, McCarry inflects the Pacific Northwest setting with Greek mythology, weaving ancient magic throughout Tally's story and adding an enchanting dose of magic realism. Tally's imagistic, melodic narrative roils with urgent emotion, and readers who loved the first two installments in the series will be richly rewarded by this series ender." Booklist

All our pretty songs; by Sarah McCarry. 1st ed. St. Martin's Griffin 2013 234 p. (paperback) $9.99; (hardcover) $18.99

Grades: 9 10 11 12 **Fic**

1. Music -- Fiction 2. Supernatural -- Fiction 3. Triangles (Interpersonal relations) -- Fiction 4. Love -- Fiction 5. Musicians -- Fiction 6. Friendship -- Fiction 7. Best friends -- Fiction

ISBN 1250040884; 9781250027085; 9781250040886

LC 2013003451

This novel by Sarah McCarry is about "two best friends who grew up like sisters: charismatic, mercurial, and beautiful Aurora, and the devoted, watchful narrator. Their unbreakable bond is challenged when a mysterious and gifted musician named Jack comes between them. They're not the only ones who have noticed Jack's gift; his music has awakened an ancient evil--and a world both above and below which may not be mythical at all." (Publisher's note)

"—Art and music run rampant through an unnamed narrator's journey with her best friend, strikingly beautiful Aurora, as frightening and elusive strangers promise drugs, fame, and love. The writing is rich and lush, yet conveys immediacy and is comprehensible even when the events are not...The descent into the underworld is riveting as the heroine tries to fight for her loved ones' fates. Raw sex and foul language accompany the shadow world that promises fame and one's heart's desire, and only faith in the narrator makes the journey endurable. Brilliant in concept and execution." (School Library Journal)

Dirty wings; Sarah McCarry. St. Martin's Griffin 2014 288 p. (hardback) $19.99

Grades: 9 10 11 12 **Fic**

1. Musicians -- Fiction 2. Teenage girls -- Fiction 3. Love -- Fiction 4. Friendship -- Fiction 5. Supernatural -- Fiction

ISBN 1250049385; 9781250049384

LC 2014000136

"In 'Dirty Wings' by Sarah McCarry, Maia is a teenage piano prodigy and dutiful daughter, imprisoned in the oppressive silence of her adoptive parents' house like a princess in an ivory tower. Cass is a street rat, witch, and runaway, scraping by with her wits and her knack for a five-fingered discount. When a chance encounter brings the two girls together, an unlikely friendship blossoms that will soon change the course of both their lives." (Publisher's note)

"The mothers of the girls featured in All Our Pretty Songs (2013) receive their own girlhood story in this beautifully constructed and grim tale...Identity, musical talent, and poisonous relationships between parents and children are depicted in a bravura retelling of a classic myth." Booklist

McCarthy, Maureen

Rose by any other name. Roaring Brook Press 2008 336p $17.95

Grades: 9 10 11 12 **Fic**

1. Australia -- Fiction 2. Family life -- Fiction 3. Automobile travel -- Fiction

ISBN 978-1-59643-372-4; 1-59643-372-8

LC 2007-18406

First published 2006 in Australia

During a road trip with her mother from Melbourne to Fairy Point, Australia, to see her dying grandmother, nineteen-year-old Rose gains a new perspective on events of the previous year, when family problems, the end of a long-term friendship, and bad personal choices dramatically transformed her near-perfect life.

"This complex coming-of-age novel, which explores both universal self-destructive tendencies and resilience, will resonate with teen readers as well as many adults." Booklist

McCaughrean, Geraldine

The white darkness. HarperTempest 2007 384p hardcover o.p. pa $8.99

Grades: 8 9 10 11 12 **Fic**

1. Antarctica -- Fiction 2. Wilderness survival -- Fiction

ISBN 978-0-06-089035-3; 0-06-089035-5; 978-0-06-089037-7 pa; 0-06-089037-1 pa

LC 2006-02503

First published 2005 in the United Kingdom

Michael L. Printz Award, 2008

Taken to Antarctica by the man she thinks of as her uncle for what she believes to be a vacation, Symone—a troubled fourteen year old—discovers that he is dangerously obsessed with seeking Symme's Hole, an opening that supposedly leads into the center of a hollow Earth.

"McCaughrean's lyrical language actively engages the senses, plunging readers into a captivating landscape that challenges the boundaries of reality." Booklist

McClintock, Norah

About that night; Norah McClintock. Orca Book Publishers 2014 248 p. (pbk.) $12.95

Grades: 7 8 9 10 **Fic**

1. Murder -- Fiction 2. Missing persons -- Fiction 3. High school students -- Fiction 4. Triangles (Interpersonal relations) -- Fiction 5. Missing persons

6. Detective and mystery stories
ISBN 1459805941; 9781459805941; 9781459805958; 9781459805965

LC 2014935377

"Derek is staying with his new girlfriend and her parents while his family is out of town. He can't believe his luck--Jordie is the hottest girl in school, and he's going out with her. When Ronan, school bad boy and Jordie's ex-boyfriend, shows up, Jordie decides that maybe Derek isn't the one after all. But before she can end it with him, Derek disappears. Did he run away? Or did something happen to him?" (Publisher's note)

"Mystery fans will appreciate the thoughtful plotting, the complex characters, and an ambiguous ending that guarantees readers will be mulling over the story long after they finish. Of special note are the descriptions of landscape and weather: cold, forbidding, and characters in themselves, with their own secrets and dangers." Booklist

Masked; written by Norah McClintock. Orca Book Publishers 2010 108p (Orca soundings) pa $9.95
Grades: 7 8 9 10   Fic
1. Mystery fiction
ISBN 978-1-55469-364-1; 1-55469-364-0

Rosie walks in on an armed robbery in her father's convenience store. Who is that masked man? And why is the loser from school there?

"Tight plotting, swift pacing, and tension that intensifies with each page mark this entry in the always-reliable Orca Soundings series for reluctant readers." Booklist

McCormick, Patricia, 1956-
★ **Cut**. Front St. 2000 168p $16.95
Grades: 7 8 9 10   Fic
1. Family problems 2. Self-mutilation 3. Emotional problems 4. Psychiatric hospitals 5. Self-mutilation -- Fiction 6. Psychiatric hospitals -- Fiction
ISBN 1-88691-061-8

LC 00-34840

While confined to a mental hospital, thirteen-year-old Callie slowly comes to understand some of the reasons behind her self-mutilation, and gradually starts to get better. "Age twelve and up." (N Y Times Book Rev)

"Realistic, sensitive, and heartfelt." Voice Youth Advocates

Never fall down; a novel. Patricia McCormick. Balzer + Bray 2012 216 p.
Grades: 9 10 11 12   Fic
1. Genocide -- Fiction 2. Musicians -- Fiction 3. Human rights -- Fiction 4. Cambodian refugees -- Fiction 5. Cambodia -- History -- 1975- -- Fiction 6. Soldiers -- Fiction 7. Party of Democratic Kampuchea -- Fiction 8. Cambodia -- History -- 1975-1979 -- Fiction
ISBN 0061730939; 9780061730931

LC 2011052211

In this book, "drawing on hundreds of hours of interviews with Arn Chorn-Pond, who was eleven in 1975 when the Khmer Rouge gained control of Cambodia, [author Patricia] McCormick creates a . . . portrait of genocide as seen through a boy's eyes. . . . He becomes a motivating force for

fellow prisoners such as Mek, the music teacher enlisted to teach the boys how to play patriotic songs on traditional instruments. . . . Mek wants to die, too, but Arn won't let him." (Horn Book Magazine)
Includes bibliographical references and index

Purple Heart. Balzer + Bray 2009 198p $16.99; lib bdg $17.89; pa $8.99
Grades: 7 8 9 10   Fic
1. Memory -- Fiction 2. Soldiers -- Fiction 3. Hospitals -- Fiction 4. Iraq War, 2003- -- Fiction 5. Brain -- Wounds and injuries -- Fiction
ISBN 978-0-06-173090-0; 0-06-173090-4; 978-0-06-173091-7 lib bdg; 0-06-173091-2 lib bdg; 978-0-06-173092-4 pa; 0-06-173092-0 pa

LC 2009-1757

While recuperating in a Baghdad hospital from a traumatic brain injury sustained during the Iraq War, eighteen-year-old soldier Matt Duffy struggles to recall what happened to him and how it relates to his ten-year-old friend, Ali.

"Strong characters heighten the drama. . . . McCormick raises moral questions without judgment and will have readers examining not only this conflict but the nature of heroism and war." Publ Wkly

★ **Sold**. Hyperion 2006 263p $15.99
Grades: 9 10 11 12   Fic
1. Nepal -- Fiction 2. Slavery -- Fiction 3. Prostitution -- Fiction
ISBN 0-7868-5171-6; 978-0-7868-5171-3

LC 2006-49594

Thirteen-year-old Lakshmi leaves her poor mountain home in Nepal thinking that she is to work in the city as a maid only to find that she has been sold into the sex slave trade in India and that there is no hope of escape.

"In beautiful clear prose and free verse that remains true to the child's viewpoint, first-person, present-tense vignettes fill in Lakshmi's story. The brutality and cruelty are ever present ('I have been beaten here, / locked away, / violated a hundred times / and a hundred times more'), but not sensationalized. . . . An unforgettable account of sexual slavery as it exists now." Booklist

McCoy, Chris
The **prom** goer's interstellar excursion; by Chris McCoy. Alfred A. Knopf 2015 304 p. $17.99
Grades: 8 9 10 11 12   Fic
1. Science fiction 2. Adventure fiction 3. Interplanetary voyages -- Fiction 4. Dating (Social customs) -- Fiction 5. Extraterrestrial beings -- Fiction 6. Humorous stories 7. Bands (Music) -- Fiction 8. Alien abduction -- Fiction 9. Adventure and adventurers -- Fiction
ISBN 9780375855993; 9780375955990

LC 2013045875

In this book, by Chris McCoy, "Bennett pulls off something he never imagined possible: his dream girl, Sophie, agrees to be his date [to the prom]. Moments afterward, however, he watches Sophie get abducted by aliens in the middle of the New Mexico desert. Faced with a dateless prom (and likely kidnapping charges), Bennett does the only thing he can think of: he catches a ride into outer space with a band of extraterrestrial musicians to bring her back." (Publisher's note)

"Readers will root for Bennett to get the girl and even for crusty band member Skark to accomplish his dream of becoming better than the one billionth and sixteenth band in the universe. The book's ending is a nicely placed, realistic surprise. Witty and action-packed, the plot boldly glazes over science-fiction details in favor of well-wrought characters." SLJ

McCullers, Carson

★ The **heart** is a lonely hunter. Modern Lib. 1993 430p $14.95

Grades: 9 10 11 12   **Fic**
1. Deaf -- Fiction 2. Southern States -- Fiction
ISBN 0-679-42474-1

LC 92-51062

A reissue of the title first published 1940 by Houghton Mifflin

"After his friend is committed to a hospital for the insane, John Singer, a deaf mute, finds himself alone. He becomes the pivotal figure in a strange circle of four other lonely individuals: Biff Brannon, the owner of a cafe; Mick Kelly, a young girl; Jake Blount, a radical; and Benedict Copeland, the town's black doctor. Although Singer provides companionship for others, he remains outside the warmth of close relationships." Shapiro. Fic for Youth. 3d edition

McDonald, Abby

The **anti-**prom. Candlewick Press 2011 280p $16.99

Grades: 8 9 10 11   **Fic**
1. School stories
ISBN 978-0-7636-4956-2; 0-7636-4956-2

LC 2010-39170

On prom night, Bliss, Jolene, and Meg, students from the same high school who barely know one another, band together to get revenge against Bliss's boyfriend and her best friend, whom she caught together in the limousine they rented.

"McDonald instills more intelligence than you'd expect from such a plot while not skimping on the simple pleasures, either." Booklist

McDonald, Ian

Be my enemy; by Ian McDonald. Pyr 2012 280 p. (hardcover) $16.95

Grades: 7 8 9 10   **Fic**
1. Science fiction 2. Kidnapping -- Fiction 3. Technology -- Fiction 4. Father-son relationship -- Fiction
ISBN 1616146788; 9781616146788

LC 2012018572

Sequel to: Planesrunner (2011)

This book by Ian McDonald is the second in the Everness Series. "Everett Singh has escaped with the Infundibulum from the clutches of Charlotte Villiers and the Order, but at a terrible price. His father is missing, banished to one of the billions of parallel universes of the Panoply of All Worlds, and Everett and the crew of the airship Everness

have taken a wild Heisenberg jump to a random parallel plane." (Publisher's note)

Empress of the sun; by Ian McDonald. Pyr 2014 290 p. (Everness) (hardback) $17.99

Grades: 7 8 9 10   **Fic**
1. War stories 2. Airships -- Fiction 3. Human-alien encounters -- Fiction 4. Science fiction 5. Adventure and adventurers -- Fiction
ISBN 1616148659; 9781616148652

LC 2013036315

In this book by Ian McDonald, "the The airship Everness [enters an] . . . alternate Earth unlike any her crew has ever seen. Everett, Sen, and the crew find themselves above a plain that goes on forever in every direction without any horizon. There they find an Alderson Disc, an astronomical megastructure of incredibly strong material. Then they meet the Jiju, the dominant species on a plane where the dinosaurs didn't die out. War between their kingdoms is inevitable, total and terrible." (Publisher's note)

"The marvelous Everness series takes readers to a world with highly evolved dinosaurs in this third voyage through parallel universes...Fans might wish for more focus on the original Everett, but eventually, the three storylines weave themselves together nicely, setting up another sequel with hints of forthcoming romance. Endlessly fascinating and fun." (Kirkus)

McDonald, Janet

Harlem Hustle. Frances Foster Books 2006 182p $16

Grades: 8 9 10 11   **Fic**
1. Rap music -- Fiction 2. African Americans -- Fiction 3. Harlem (New York, N.Y.) -- Fiction
ISBN 978-0-374-37184-5; 0-374-37184-9

LC 2005-52108

Eric "Hustle" Samson, a smart and streetwise seventeen-year-old dropout from Harlem, aspires to rap stardom, a dream he naively believes is about to come true.

"The author nails the hip-hop lingo and the street slang, and her characters strike just the right attitude. . . . Young adults will love this book." SLJ

Off-color. Farrar, Straus and Giroux 2007 163p $16

Grades: 7 8 9 10 11 12   **Fic**
1. Single parent family -- Fiction 2. Racially mixed people -- Fiction 3. Brooklyn (New York, N.Y.) -- Fiction 4. Mother-daughter relationship -- Fiction
ISBN 0-374-37196-2

LC 2006-47334

Fifteen-year-old Cameron living with her single mother in Brooklyn finds her search for identity further challenged when she discovers that she is the product of a biracial relationship.

"McDonald dramatizes the big issues from the inside, showing the hard times and the joy in fast-talking dialogue that is honest, insulting, angry, tender, and very funny." Booklist

McEntire, Myra

Hourglass. Egmont USA 2011 390p $17.99

Grades: 7 8 9 10 **Fic**
1. Science fiction 2. Orphans -- Fiction 3. Homicide -- Fiction 4. Siblings -- Fiction 5. Parapsychology -- Fiction 6. Space and time -- Fiction
ISBN 1-60684-144-0; 978-1-60684-144-0

LC 2010-43618

Seventeen-year-old Emerson uses her power to manipulate time to help Michael, a consultant hired by her brother, to prevent a murder that happened six months ago. "Grades seven to ten." (Bull Cent Child Books)

"Em is an entertainingly cheeky narrator and appealingly resilient heroine. . . . McEntire deftly juggles plot, characters and dialogue; her portrait of grief is particularly poignant." Kirkus

McGarry, Katie

★ **Dare** You to; by Katie McGarry. Harlequin Books 2013 480 p. (hardcover) $17.99
Grades: 9 10 11 12 **Fic**
1. Love stories 2. Dysfunctional families -- Fiction 3. Man-woman relationship -- Fiction
ISBN 0373210639; 9780373210633

This book is a "coming-of-age love story" which follows "tattooed, pierced 'skater girl' Beth and high school baseball star Ryan. . . . Raised on opposite sides of the tracks, both teens contend with selfish, manipulative parents who use their children to satisfy their own desires; both also have mentors and family members offering guidance and support. . . . Beth's compulsive efforts to rescue her drug-addicted mother . . . captures their greatest obstacle." (Publishers Weekly)

Pushing the limits. Harlequin Teen 2012 403 p.
Grades: 9 10 11 12 **Fic**
1. Love stories
ISBN 0373210493; 9780373210497

LC 2011287989

In this young adult novel by Katie McGarry "[n]o one knows what happened the night Echo Emerson went from popular girl with jock boyfriend to gossiped-about outsider with 'freaky' scars on her arms. . . . [W]hen Noah Hutchins, the smoking-hot, girl-using loner in the black leather jacket, explodes into her life with his tough attitude and surprising understanding, Echo's world shifts in ways she could never have imagined." (Author's note)

McGinnis, Mindy

A **madness** so discreet; Mindy McGinni. Katherine Tegen Books, an imprint of HarperCollins Publishers 2015 384 p. (hardcover) $17.99
Grades: 11 **Fic**
1. Mystery fiction 2. Mentally ill -- Fiction 3. Criminal investigation -- Fiction 4. Physicians -- Fiction 5. Ohio -- History -- 19th century -- Fiction
ISBN 9780062320865

LC 2014041255

In this novel, by Mindy McGinni, "Grace Mae is already familiar with madness when family secrets and the bulge in her belly send her to an insane asylum--but . . . when a visiting doctor interested in criminal psychology recognizes Grace's brilliant mind beneath her rage, he recruits her as his assistant. Continuing to operate under the cloak of madness

at crime scenes allows her to gather clues from bystanders who believe her less than human." (Publisher's note)

"Readers will wish they could watch her and Thornhollow solve murders for pages and pages more. A dark study of the effects of power in the wrong hands, buoyed by a tenacious heroine and her colorful companions." Kirkus

McGovern, Cammie

Say what you will; Cammie McGovern; [edited by] Tara Weikum. HarperTeen 2014 352 p. (hardcover) $17.99
Grades: 9 10 11 12 **Fic**
1. Teenagers with disabilities -- Fiction 2. Cerebral palsy 3. Obsessive-compulsive disorder
ISBN 0062271105; 9780062271105

LC 2013958343

In this young adult novel by Cammie McGovern, "Born with cerebral palsy, Amy can't walk without a walker, talk without a voice box, or even fully control her facial expressions. Plagued by obsessive-compulsive disorder, Matthew is consumed with repeated thoughts, neurotic rituals, and crippling fear. Both in desperate need of someone to help them reach out to the world, Amy and Matthew are more alike than either ever realized." (Publisher's note)

"Amy, who has cerebral palsy, convinces her parents to hire a peer helper, Matthew (who has a severe anxiety disorder), so she can learn to socialize before college. The two develop a significant friendship--and a confusing mutual attraction. This book moves beyond the typical concerns people with disabilities encounter to present an honest portrayal of the lives of these particular characters." Horn Book

★ A **step** toward falling; Cammie McGovern; [edited by] Tara Weikum. HarperTeen 2015 384 p. (hardcover) $17.99 **Fic**
1. People with disabilities -- Fiction 2. Teenagers -- Conduct of life -- Fiction
ISBN 9780062271136

LC 2015946375

In this novel, by Cammie McGovern, edited by Tara Weikum, "Emily has always been the kind of girl who tries to do the right thing—until one night when she . . . sees Belinda, a classmate with developmental disabilities, being attacked. Inexplicably, she does nothing at all. . . . When their high school finds out what happened, Emily and Lucas, a football player who was also there that night, are required to perform community service at a center for disabled people." (Publisher's note)

"No mere empathy builder for Emily and Lucas, Belinda is a fully developed character--good at some things (better than Emily and Lucas, in fact), bad at others. Without evading or sugarcoating difficult topics, McGovern . . . shows that disabled and able aren't binary states but part of a continuum--a human one." Pub Wkly

McGuigan, Mary Ann

Morning in a different place. Front Street 2009 195p $17.95
Grades: 7 8 9 10 **Fic**
1. Friendship -- Fiction 2. Race relations -- Fiction 3. African Americans -- Fiction 4. Bronx (New York,

N.Y.) -- Fiction
ISBN 978-1-59078-551-5; 1-59078-551-7
LC 2007-17547

In 1963 in the Bronx, New York, eighth-graders Fiona and Yolanda help one another face hard decisions at home despite family and social opposition to their interracial friendship, but Fiona is on her own when popular classmates start paying attention to her and give her a glimpse of both a different way of life and a new kind of hatefulness.

This book is "never didactic. McGuigan's writing is spare and low-key, and her metaphors are acute." Booklist

McKay, Sharon E.

Enemy territory; Sharon McKay. Annick Press 2012 184 p. $21.95
Grades: 6 7 8 9 10 11 12   Fic
1. Toleration -- Fiction 2. Friendship 3. Israel-Arab conflicts -- Fiction
ISBN 1554514312; 9781554514311

In author Sharon E. McKay's book, "Sam, an Israeli teen whose leg may have to be amputated, and Yusuf, a Palestinian teen who has lost his left eye, find themselves uneasy roommates in a Jerusalem hospital. One night, the boys decide to slip away while the nurses aren't looking and go on an adventure to the Old City. . . . They band together to find their way home and to defend themselves against unfriendly locals, arrest by the military police, and an encounter with a deadly desert snake." (Publisher's note)

Thunder over Kandahar; photographs by Rafal Gerszak. Annick Press 2010 260p il $21.95; pa $12.95
Grades: 7 8 9 10 11 12   Fic
1. Afghanistan -- Fiction 2. Afghan War, 2001- -- Fiction
ISBN 978-1-55451-267-6; 1-55451-267-0; 978-1-55451-266-9 pa; 1-55451-266-2 pa

"When her British and American-educated parents' return to Afghanistan is cut short by a terrible attack, 14-year-old Yasmine is sent to Kandahar for safety. Instead, the driver abandons her and her friend Tamanna along the way, and they must travel on their own through Taliban-controlled mountains. . . . In spite of unrelenting violence, along with grinding poverty, restrictive customs, and the horrors of war, what shines through this sad narrative is the love Afghans have for their country. . . . [The author] traveled to Afghanistan and provides numerous credits for this gripping tale." SLJ

McKenzie, Nancy

Grail prince; {by} Nancy Affleck McKenzie. Del Rey 2003 510p pa $14.95
Grades: 9 10 11 12   Fic
1. Great Britain -- History -- 0-1066 -- Fiction
ISBN 0-345-45648-3
LC 2002-94133

"Brimming with romance, myth, and magic, this intriguing retelling of an ever-appealing fable will appease fans eager for new twists and turns in the lives and times of King Arthur and the knights of the Round Table." Booklist

Guinevere's gamble. Alfred A. Knopf 2009 361p (The Chrysalis Queen quartet) $16.99; lib bdg $19.99
Grades: 7 8 9 10   Fic
1. Kings 2. Merlin (Legendary character) -- Fiction 3. Guinevere (Legendary character) -- Fiction 4. Great Britain -- History -- 0-1066 -- Fiction 5. Morgan le Fay (Legendary character) -- Fiction
ISBN 978-0-375-84346-4; 0-375-84346-9; 978-0-375-94346-1 lib bdg; 0-375-94346-3 lib bdg
LC 2008-50617

Sequel to: Guinevere's gift (2008)

Thirteen-year-old Guinevere learns more about her destiny when she accompanies her aunt and uncle to an important council of Welsh kings and finds that she has a powerful enemy in the High King's sister Morgan.

"Readers who are familiar with Arthurian legends as well as those who are not will find this continuing story enjoyable." SLJ

Guinevere's gift. Alfred A. Knopf 2008 327p (The Chrysalis Queen quartet) $15.99; lib bdg $18.99
Grades: 7 8 9 10   Fic
1. Cousins -- Fiction 2. Guinevere (Legendary character) -- Fiction 3. Great Britain -- History -- 0-1066 -- Fiction
ISBN 978-0-375-84345-7; 0-375-84345-0; 978-0-375-94345-4 lib bdg; 0-375-94345-5 lib bdg
LC 2007-28782

When the orphaned Guinevere is twelve years old, living with Queen Alyse and King Pellinore of Gwynedd, she fearlessly helps rescue her cousin from kidnappers who are plotting to seize the palace and overthrow the king, even as the queen despairs of Guinevere's rebellious nature.

"Adventure seekers can be content with this tale of a heroine and her castle while dedicated legend fans will appreciate where it fits in the overall tapestry." Bull Cent Child Books

Another title in this series is:
Guinevere's gamble (2009)

McKinley, Robin

Pegasus. G.P. Putnam's Sons 2010 404p $18.99
Grades: 8 9 10 11 12   Fic
1. Fantasy fiction 2. Magic -- Fiction 3. Princesses -- Fiction 4. Pegasus (Greek mythology) -- Fiction
ISBN 0-399-24677-0; 978-0-399-24677-7
LC 2010-2279

Because of a thousand-year-old alliance between humans and pegasi, Princess Sylvi is ceremonially bound to Ebon, her own pegasus, on her twelfth birthday, but the closeness of their bond becomes a threat to the status quo and possibly to the safety of their two nations.

"McKinley's storytelling is to be savored. She lavishes page after page upon rituals and ceremonies, basks in the awe of her intricately constructed world, and displays a masterful sense of pegasi physicality and mannerisms." Booklist

McKinney-Whitaker, Courtney

The **last** sister; Courtney McKinney-Whitaker. University of South Carolina Press 2014 232 p. (Young Palmetto books) (hardback) $39.95

Grades: 7 8 9 10   **Fic**

1. Historical fiction 2. Native Americans -- Wars -- Fiction 3. Frontier and pioneer life -- Fiction 4. Cherokee Indians -- Wars, 1759-1761 -- Fiction 5. South Carolina -- History -- 1775-1865 -- Fiction 6. Frontier and pioneer life -- South Carolina -- Fiction
ISBN 1611174295; 9781611174298; 9781611174304
LC 2014011484

This young adult historical novel, by Courtney McKinney-Whitaker, "set during the Anglo-Cherokee War (1758-61), . . . traces a young woman's journey through grief, vengeance, guilt, and love in the unpredictable world of the early American frontier. After a band of fellow settlers fakes a Cherokee raid to conceal their murder of her family, seventeen-year-old Catriona 'Catie' Blair embarks on a quest to report the crime and bring the murderers to justice." (Publisher's note)

"This historical novel is set in the Carolinas during the Cherokee Wars, concurrent with Thomas Jefferson and John Adams writing the Declaration of Independence and George Washington navigating the Delaware River. Seventeen-year-old Catie Blair is forced to conjure up maturity and responsibility when tragedy strikes her family . . . A unique historical fiction title with a compelling plot and unique backdrop, taking place during a little-known skirmish in a pivotal time of American history." SLJ

McKissack, Fredrick

Shooting star. Atheneum Books for Young Readers 2009 273p $16.99

Grades: 8 9 10 11 12   **Fic**

1. School stories 2. Football -- Fiction 3. Steroids -- Fiction 4. African Americans -- Fiction
ISBN 978-1-4169-4745-5; 1-4169-4745-0
LC 2008-55525

Jomo Rogers, a naturally talented athlete, starts taking performance enhancing drugs in order to be an even better high school football player, but finds his life spinning out of control as his game improves.

"Profane and scatological language abounds, but it is not outside the realm of what one could hear any day in a school locker room. Top-notch sports fiction." SLJ

McLemore, Anna-Marie

The **weight** of feathers; Anna-Marie McLemore. St. Martin's Press 2015 320 p. (hardcover) $18.99

Grades: 9 10 11 12   **Fic**

1. Love stories 2. Vendetta -- Fiction 3. Performing arts -- Fiction
ISBN 1250058651; 9781250058652
LC 2015019216

William C. Morris Award Finalist (2016)

"Lace Paloma may be new to her family's show, but she knows as well as anyone that the Corbeaus are pure magia negra, black magic from the devil himself . . . and she's been taught from birth to keep away. But when disaster strikes the small town where both families are performing, it's a Corbeau boy, Cluck, who saves Lace's life." (Publisher's note)

McLoughlin, Jane

At Yellow Lake. Frances Lincoln Children's Books 2012 358 p. (paperback) $8.99

Grades: 7 8 9 10   **Fic**

1. Mystery fiction 2. Teenagers -- Fiction 3. Native Americans -- Fiction
ISBN 1847802877; 9781847802873

In this book by Jane McLoughlin, "Etta, Peter and Jonah all find themselves at a cabin by the shore of Yellow Lake. . . . Jonah has come to Yellow Lake to try to get in touch with his Ojibwe roots. Peter is there to bury a lock of his mother's hair -- her final request. Etta is on the run from her mother's creepy boyfriend. . . . But as the three take shelter in the cabin . . . they soon realise that they have inadvertently stumbled onto the scene of a horrifying crime." (Publisher's note)

McMann, Lisa

Fade. Simon Pulse 2009 248p $15.99

Grades: 8 9 10 11   **Fic**

1. School stories 2. Rape -- Fiction 3. Dreams -- Fiction
ISBN 978-1-4169-5358-6; 1-4169-5358-2
LC 2008-15201

Sequel to: Wake (2008)

Using her ability to tap into other people's dreams, eighteen-year-old Janie investigates an alleged sex ring at her high school that involves teachers using the date rape drug on students.

"A great blend of mystery, romance, and supernatural elements, and featuring a strong but vulnerable female protagonist." Booklist

Followed by: Gone (2010)

Wake. Simon Pulse 2008 210p $15.99; pa $8.99

Grades: 7 8 9 10   **Fic**

1. School stories 2. Dreams -- Fiction
ISBN 978-1-4169-5357-9; 1-4169-5357-4; 978-1-4169-7447-5 pa; 1-4169-7447-4 pa
LC 2007036267

Ever since she was eight years old, high school student Janie Hannagan has been uncontrollably drawn into other people's dreams, but it is not until she befriends an elderly nursing home patient and becomes involved with an enigmatic fellow-student that she discovers her true power.

"A fast pace, a great mix of teen angst and supernatural experiences, and an eerie, attention-grabbing cover will make this a hit." Booklist

Other titles in this series are:
Fade (2009)
Gone (2010)

McNamee, Graham

Beyond; a ghost story. by Graham McNamee. Wendy Lamb Books 2012 226 p. (trade) $15.99

Grades: 9 10 11 12   **Fic**

1. Supernatural -- Fiction 2. Shades and shadows -- Fiction 3. Near-death experiences -- Fiction 4. Ghosts -- Fiction
ISBN 0385737750; 9780375851650; 9780375897597; 9780385737753; 9780385906876
LC 2011043610

This book by Graham McNamee follows "Jane, [who is] no stranger to near-death experiences. Her shadow has forced her to drink drain cleaner and held her down on a train track as a speeding train approached. After a recent nail-gun 'accident' to the skull causes her to flat-line, Jane returns to the living with her shadow even more determined to kill her." (Kirkus Reviews)

McNeal, Laura

The **decoding** of Lana Morris; [by] Laura & Tom McNeal. Alfred A. Knopf 2007 289p $15.99

Grades: 7 8 9 10 11 12　　　　　　　　　　Fic
1. Drawing -- Fiction 2. Nebraska -- Fiction 3. Supernatural -- Fiction 4. Foster home care -- Fiction 5. People with disabilities -- Fiction
ISBN 0-375-83106-1; 978-0-375-83106-5
　　　　　　　　　　　　　　　LC 2006-23950

For sixteen-year-old Lana life is often difficult, with a flirtatious foster father, an ice queen foster mother, a houseful of special needs children to care for, and bullies harrassing her, until the day she ventures into an antique shop and buys a drawing set that may change her life.

This is "a colorful character drama with genuine spice and impact." Bull Cent Child Books

McNeal, Tom

★ **Far** far away; by Tom McNeal. 1st ed. Alfred A. Knopf Books for Young Readers 2013 371 p. (hardcover) $17.99; (ebook) $53.97; (library) $20.99

Grades: 7 8 9 10　　　　　　　　　　　　Fic
1. Fantasy fiction 2. Paranormal fiction 3. Ghosts -- Fiction 4. Friendship -- Fiction 5. Supernatural -- Fiction 6. Missing persons -- Fiction
ISBN 0375849726; 9780375849725; 9780375896989; 9780375949722
　　　　　　　　　　　　　　　LC 2012020603

Parents' Choice: Gold Medal Fiction (2013)

This book "is narrated by the ghost of Jacob Grimm . . . , unhappily caught in the Zwischenraum (a plane of existence between life and death). For now, he is the nearly constant companion of Jeremy Johnson," who hears voices. This ability "has made him an object of derision for many in his little town, though—thrillingly—not to the electrifyingly vibrant Ginger Boultinghouse, who is more than happy to lure Jeremy into more trouble than he's ever encountered." (School Library Journal)

McNish, Cliff

Angel. Carolrhoda Books 2008 312p $16.95

Grades: 7 8 9 10　　　　　　　　　　　　Fic
1. School stories 2. Angels -- Fiction 3. Bullies -- Fiction 4. Popularity -- Fiction 5. Mental illness -- Fiction
ISBN 978-0-8225-8900-6; 0-8225-8900-1
　　　　　　　　　　　　　　　LC 2007-9664

An unlikely friendship develops between fourteen-year-olds Stephanie, an angel-obsessed social outcast, and Freya, a popular student whose visions of angels sent her to a mental institution and who is now seeing a dark angel at every turn.

"The author beautifuly melds a tale of the fantastic and the mundane." Voice Youth Advocates

McQuein, Josin L.

Arclight; Josin L. McQuein. 1st ed. Greenwillow Books, an imprint of HarperCollins Publishers 2013 416 p. (hardcover) $17.99

Grades: 8 9 10 11 12　　　　　　　　　　Fic
1. Orphans 2. Fantasy fiction 3. Science fiction 4. Amnesia -- Fiction 5. Identity -- Fiction
ISBN 0062130145; 9780062130143
　　　　　　　　　　　　　　　LC 2013002929

In this book, "Marina was pulled from the Dark at the cost of nine lives, and she is paying the price. Ostracized and abused by those whose parents died for her sake, Marina is all but alone in the Arclight, a safe zone where it is never dark. The Fade live in the Dark—chameleons, they steal humans from the light to an unknown fate. Marina dreams of their voices and frets that she has no memory of her life before her rescue." She seeks answers about her past. (Publishers Weekly)

McQuerry, Maureen Doyle

The **Peculiars**; a novel. Maureen Doyle McQuerry. Amulet Books 2012 359 p. (hardback) $16.95

Grades: 7 8 9 10 11 12　　　　　　　　　Fic
1. Fantasy fiction 2. Voyages and travels -- Fiction 3. Father-daughter relationship -- Fiction 4. Goblins -- Fiction 5. Identity -- Fiction 6. Abnormalities, Human -- Fiction 7. Adventure and adventurers -- Fiction
ISBN 1419701789; 9781419701788
　　　　　　　　　　　　　　　LC 2012000844

This is the story of Lena Mattacascar, who at age 18 "travel[s] to Scree, an uncharted wilderness of 'indigenous folks' and deported convicts," sitting on the train with young librarian "Jimson Quiggley," with "marshal Thomas Saltre" watching them. "Lena cannot stop thinking about her mysterious father" or the possibility that she's part Peculiar (goblin). "Scree is the place where Lena's questions might be answered, but arriving there just multiplies them." (Publishers Weekly)

McStay, Moriah

Everything that makes you; Moriah McStay. First edition Katherine Tegen Books, an imprint of HarperCollins Children's Books 2015 346 p. 22 cm (hardcover) $17.99

Grades: 8 9 10 11　　　　　　　　　　　Fic
1. Accidents -- Fiction 2. Family life -- Fiction 3. Self-confidence -- Fiction 4. Interpersonal relations -- Fiction 5. Disfigured persons -- Fiction
ISBN 0062295489; 9780062295484
　　　　　　　　　　　　　　　LC 2014005864

In this book, by Moriah McStay, "Fiona Doyle's face was horribly scarred as a child. She writes about her frustrations and dreams in notebooks, penning song lyrics. But she'd never be brave enough to sing those songs in public. Fi Doyle . . . [is] the best lacrosse player in the state and can't be distracted by her friend who wants to be more than that. But then her luck on the field goes south. Alternating chapters between Fiona and Fi tell two stories about the same girl." (Publisher's note)

"Entertaining and intellectually stimulating, the novel invites discussion about how much of a person's life is determined by events and whether some tendencies are inborn." Publishers Weekly

McVoy, Terra Elan

After the kiss. Simon Pulse 2010 382p $16.99

Grades: 9 10 11 12 **Fic**

1. School stories 2. Novels in verse 3. Moving -- Fiction 4. Atlanta (Ga.) -- Fiction

ISBN 978-1-4424-0211-9

LC 2009-44220

In alternating chapters, two high school senior girls in Atlanta reveal their thoughts and frustrations as they go through their final semester of high school.

This is "a poignant tale of two girls on the brink of adulthood faced with real decisions about their future, who they want to be, and what role boys will play in their decisions." SLJ

Pure. Simon Pulse 2009 330p $16.99

Grades: 8 9 10 11 12 **Fic**

1. Friendship -- Fiction 2. Christian life -- Fiction 3. Dating (Social customs) -- Fiction

ISBN 978-1-4169-7872-5; 1-4169-7872-0

LC 2008-33404

Fifteen-year-old Tabitha and her four best friends all wear purity rings to symbolize their pledge to remain virgins until they marry, but when one admits that she has broken the pledge each girl must reexamine her faith, friendships, and what it means to be pure.

"Tabitha's blooming romance with Jake and her positive relationship with her supportive, if somewhat quirky, parents add pleasant undercurrents to a book that girls of a spiritual bent will enjoy." SLJ

Mecum, Ryan

Zombie haiku; Ryan Mecum. HOW Books 2008 139 p. ill. (some col.) (pbk.) $9.99

Grades: 9 10 11 12 **Fic**

1. Haiku 2. Zombies -- Fiction 3. Poetry -- Collections 4. Humorous poetry -- Collections 5. Haiku -- Humor 6. Zombies -- Humor 7. Zombies -- Poetry

ISBN 1600610706; 9781600610707

LC 2008008678

This book is a collection of haikus written from the perspective of an author who "managed to chronicle his change from artist to [zombie] . . . after being attacked by an undead mob." (booklistforworms.blogspot.com) In this book, "you'll find . . . three-line poems (all in the classic 5-7-5 syllable structure), and follow the undead poet on a journey through deserted streets and barricaded doors. Experience every . . . moment of the eventual downfall of the human race from the point of view of a zombie, and gain insight to help you survive." (firestormcafe.com)

Medina, Meg

★ **Burn** Baby Burn; Meg Medina. Candlewick Press 2016 320 p. $17.99

Grades: 9 10 11 12 **Fic**

1. Bildungsromans 2. Teenage girls -- Fiction 3. New York (N.Y.) -- Fiction

ISBN 0763674672; 9780763674670

LC 2015954454

In this novel, by Meg Medina, "Nora Lopez is seventeen during the infamous New York summer of 1977, when the city is besieged by arson, a massive blackout, and a serial killer named Son of Sam who shoots young women on the streets. Nora's family life isn't going so well either. All Nora wants is to turn eighteen and be on her own. And while there is a cute new guy who started working with her at the deli, is dating even worth the risk when the killer likes picking off couples who stay out too late? " (Publisher's note)

"Powerfully moving, this stellar piece of historical fiction emphasizes the timeless concerns of family loyalty and personal strength while highlighting important issues that still resonate today." Booklist

★ **Yaqui** Delgado wants to kick your ass; Meg Medina. Candlewick Press 2013 272 p. (reinforced) $16.99

Grades: 9 10 11 12 **Fic**

1. School stories 2. Bullies -- Fiction

ISBN 0763658596; 9780763658595

LC 2012943645

Pura Belpre Author Award (2014)

In this novel, by Meg Medina, "a Latina teen is targeted by a bully at her new school--and must discover resources she never knew she had. One morning before school, some girl tells Piddy Sanchez that Yaqui Delgado hates her and wants to . . . [beat her up.] . . . As the harassment escalates, avoiding Yaqui and her gang starts to take over Piddy's life. Is there any way for Piddy to survive without closing herself off or running away?" (Publisher's note)

Meehl, Brian

Suck it up. Delacorte Press 2008 323p $15.99; pa $8.99

Grades: 8 9 10 11 **Fic**

1. Vampires -- Fiction

ISBN 978-0-385-73300-7; 0-385-73300-3; 978-0-440-42091-0 pa; 0-440-42091-1 pa

LC 2007-27995

After graduating from the International Vampire League, a scrawny, teenaged vampire named Morning is given the chance to fulfill his childhood dream of becoming a superhero when he embarks on a League mission to become the first vampire to reveal his identity to humans and to demonstrate how peacefully-evolved, blood-substitute-drinking vampires can use their powers to help humanity.

This "an original and light variation on the current trend in brooding teen vampire protagonists. . . . Puns abound in this lengthy, complicated romp. . . . Teens will find it delightful." Booklist

You don't know about me. Delacorte Press 2011 406p $17.99; ebook $10.99; lib bdg $20.99

Grades: 9 10 11 12 **Fic**

1. Homosexuality -- Fiction 2. Christian life -- Fiction 3. Automobile travel -- Fiction 5. Father-son relationship

-- Fiction 6. Mother-son relationship -- Fiction
ISBN 978-0-385-73909-2; 978-0-375-89715-3 ebook;
978-0-385-90771-2 lib bdg

LC 2010-17101

Billy has spent his almost-sixteen years with four cardinal points—Mother, Christ, Bible, and Home-school—but when he sets off on a wild road trip to find the father he thought was dead, he learns much about himself and life.

"The humor, action, and edgy social commentary make this a book a mature reader, with knowledge and interest of the works of Mark Twain, might enjoy." Voice Youth Advocates

Meldrum, Christina

★ **Madapple**. Alfred A. Knopf 2008 410p il $16.99; lib bdg $19.99

Grades: 9 10 11 12   **Fic**

1. Trials -- Fiction 2. Miracles -- Fiction 3. Mother-daughter relationship -- Fiction
ISBN 978-0-375-85176-6; 978-0-375-95176-3 lib bdg

LC 2007-49653

ALA YALSA Morris Award finalist, 2009

A girl who has been brought up in near isolation is thrown into a twisted web of family secrets and religious fundamentalism when her mother dies and she goes to live with relatives she never knew she had.

"A markedly intelligent offering mixing lush descriptions of plants, history, science and religion, this should surely spark interest among a wide array of readers." Kirkus

Include bibliographical references

Melling, O. R.

The **book** of dreams. Amulet Books 2009 698p map (Chronicles of Faerie) $19.95

Grades: 7 8 9 10   **Fic**

1. Magic -- Fiction 2. Canada -- Fiction 3. Fairies -- Fiction 4. Native Americans -- Fiction 5. Voyages and travels -- Fiction
ISBN 978-0-8109-8346-5; 0-8109-8346-X

LC 2008-24689

Sequel to The Light-Bearer's daughter (2007)

Now thirteen and depressed, Dana has been living with her father and his new wife in Canada for two years, and when she finds that her gateway to the land of Faerie has been mysteriously shattered, she must travel the length and breadth of Canada to find the secret that will re-open the Faerie world.

"The author's exploration of folk traditions across cultures makes the book unique." Voice Youth Advocates

The **Hunter's** Moon. Amulet Books 2005 284p (Chronicles of Faerie) $16.95; pa $7.95

Grades: 7 8 9 10   **Fic**

1. Magic -- Fiction 2. Ireland -- Fiction
ISBN 0-8109-5857-0; 0-8109-9214-0 pa

LC 2004-22216

First published 1992 in Ireland

Two teenage cousins, one Irish, the other from the United States, set out to find a magic doorway to the Faraway Country, where humans must bow to the little people.

"This novel is a compelling blend of Irish mythology and geography. Characters that breathe and connect with readers, and a picturesque landscape that shifts between the present and the past, bring readers into the experience." SLJ

Other available titles in this series are:
The book of dreams (2009)
The Light-Bearer's daughter (2007)
The Summer King (2006)

The **Light-**Bearer's daughter. Amulet Books 2007 348p map (Chronicles of Faerie) hardcover o.p. pa $7.95

Grades: 7 8 9 10 11   **Fic**

1. Magic -- Fiction 2. Ireland -- Fiction
ISBN 978-0-8109-0781-2; 0-8109-0781-X; 978-0-8109-7123-3 pa; 0-8109-7123-2 pa

LC 2006-33517

Sequel to The Summer King (2006)

In exchange for the granting of her heart's desire, twelve-year-old Dana agrees to make an arduous journey to Lugnaquillia through the land of Faerie in order to warn King Lugh, second in command to the High King, that an evil destroyer has entered the Mountain Kingdom.

"The richly integrated, vivid fantasy scenes balance the strident calls for environmental protection and world peace, and the characters' private passages through 'layers of storied memory' will bring the issues home for readers." Booklist

Followed by The book of dreams (2009)

The **Summer** King. Amulet Books 2006 359p map (Chronicles of Faerie) $16.95

Grades: 7 8 9 10   **Fic**

1. Magic -- Fiction 2. Ireland -- Fiction
ISBN 0-8109-5969-0

LC 2005-15083

Seventeen-year-old Laurel returns to her grandparents' home in Ireland, where she encounters the roly-poly man, a cluricaun who sets Laurel on a quest to free her twin sister, thought to be dead, to live with her lover in the legendary world of Faerie.

"Fans of Melling's first title in the Chronicles of Faerie, The Hunter's Moon (2005), will recognize similarly thrilling action, fascinating Irish mythology, and magnificently detailed magic." Booklist

Meloy, Maile

The **apprentices**; by Maile Meloy; illustrated by Ian Schoenherr. G.P. Putnam's Sons, an imprint of Penguin Group (USA) Inc. 2013 432 p. (hardcover) $16.99

Grades: 6 7 8 9   **Fic**

1. Magic -- Fiction 2. Alchemy -- Fiction 3. Voyages and travels -- Fiction 4. Adventure and adventurers -- Fiction 5. Southeast Asia -- History -- 1945- -- Fiction
ISBN 9780399162459

LC 2012048715

In this book by Maile Meloy is the sequel to "The Apothecary". "Janie, now 16, is alone at an elite American boarding school, unaware of the whereabouts of her first boyfriend, Benjamin, and his apothecary father. After she is wrongly expelled, she realizes she is the victim of a nefarious scheme, which again poses a threat to world peace. The . . . plot spans the globe as the heroes find their way back to each other." (Publishers Weekly)

Meminger, Neesha

Shine, coconut moon. Margaret K. McElderry Books 2009 256p $16.99; pa $8.99

Grades: 7 8 9 10   **Fic**

1. School stories 2. Prejudices -- Fiction 3. East Indian Americans -- Fiction 4. September 11 terrorist attacks, 2001 -- Fiction

ISBN 978-1-4169-5495-8; 1-4169-5495-3; 978-1-4424-0305-5 pa; 1-4424-0305-5 pa

LC 2008-9836

In the days and weeks following the terrorist attacks on September 11, 2001, Samar, who is of Punjabi heritage but has been raised with no knowledge of her past by her single mother, wants to learn about her family's history and to get in touch with the grandparents her mother shuns.

"Meminger's debut book is a beautiful and sensitive portrait of a young woman's journey from self-absorbed navet to selfless, unified awareness." SLJ

Merullo, Roland

The talk-funny girl; Roland Merullo. Crown Publishers 2011 x, 304p.p

Grades: 11 12 Adult   **Fic**

1. Bildungsromans 2. Cults -- Fiction 3. Girls -- Fiction 4. Domestic relations

ISBN 9780307452924; 0307452921

LC 2011003328

Alex Award (2012)

This book tells the story of "seventeen-year-old- Marjorie Richards . . . [who] has been raised by parents so intentionally isolated from normal society that they have developed their own dialect . . . as the nearby factory town sinks deeper into economic ruin and as her parents fall more completely under the influence of a sadistic cult leader, her options for escape dwindle. But then, thanks to a loving aunt, Marjorie is hired by a man . . . who is building what he calls 'a cathedral,' right in the center of town. . . . Gradually, through exposure to the world beyond her parents' wood cabin thanks to the kindness of her aunt and her boss, and an almost superhuman determination, she discovers what is loveable within herself." (Publisher's note)

Mesrobian, Carrie

Cut both ways; Carrie Mesrobian. HarperTeen 2015 352 p. (hardback) $17.99 **Fic**

1. School stories 2. Bisexuality -- Fiction 3. Sex -- Fiction 4. Gays -- Fiction 5. Friendship -- Fiction 6. Interpersonal relations -- Fiction

ISBN 9780062349880

LC 2014047809

This novel, by Carrie Mesrobian, follows "a high school senior who must come to terms with his attraction to both his girlfriend and his male best friend. It took Will Caynes seventeen years to have his first kiss. He should be ecstatic . . . except that it was shared with his best friend, Angus, while they were both drunk and stoned." (Publisher's note)

"A great addition for most libraries, and perfect for older teens looking for nuanced realistic fiction." SLJ

Perfectly good white boy; by Carrie Mesrobian. Carolrhoda Lab 2014 296 p. (trade hard cover: alk. paper) $17.95

Grades: 8 9 10 11 12   **Fic**

1. Sex -- Fiction 2. Interpersonal relations -- Fiction 3. United States. Marine Corps -- Fiction

ISBN 1467734802; 9781467734806

LC 2013036749

In this book, by Carrie Mesrobian, "Sean Norwhalt can read between the lines. He knows Hallie's just dumped him. He was a perfectly good summer boyfriend, but now she's off to college, and he's still got another year to go. . . . The only hopeful possibilities in Sean's life are the Marine Corps, where no one expected he'd go, and Neecie Albertson, whom he never expected to care about." (Publisher's note)

"Engaging, perceptive, witty and at times gut-wrenchingly sad—this is an extraordinary addition to fiction for teens and adults alike." Kirkus

Sex and violence; by Carrie Mesrobian. Carolrhoda Lab 2013 304 p. (reinforced) $17.95

Grades: 10 11 12   **Fic**

1. School stories 2. Violence -- Fiction 3. Sex -- Fiction 4. Psychotherapy -- Fiction 5. Emotional problems -- Fiction 6. Interpersonal relations -- Fiction

ISBN 1467705977; 9781467705974

LC 2012047181

William C. Morris Honor Book (2014)

In this book, a teen boy "is brutally beaten in a communal shower by two classmates after he hooks up with one of their former girlfriends, setting the stage for a difficult recovery. After the assault that leaves Evan in the hospital, his father whisks him off to his own boyhood home in Minnesota, where he's uneasily sucked into a tightknit group spending their last summer at home getting high and hanging out before going off to college." (Kirkus Reviews)

"The absence of sentimentality and melodrama in favor of frank dialogue and bruising honesty is a gasp of fresh air." Booklist

Metzger, Lois

A trick of the light; by Lois Metzger. 1st ed. Balzer + Bray 2013 208 p. (hardcover) $17.99

Grades: 9 10 11 12   **Fic**

1. Family life -- Fiction 2. Anorexia nervosa -- Fiction 3. Schools -- Fiction 4. High schools -- Fiction 5. Family problems -- Fiction 6. Eating disorders -- Fiction

ISBN 006213308X; 9780062133083

LC 2012019039

In this book by Lois Metzger, "[t]he story of 15-year-old Mike Welles's descent into anorexia is narrated by the disease itself, the insidious voice inside his head preying on his every vulnerability. The voice waits patiently for an opening, which comes in the form of Mike's parents' marital crisis and his insecurity around a new crush, pushing Mike to exercise, coaching him to subsist on next to nothing, and encouraging a friendship with Amber, who is also anorexic." (Publishers Weekly)

"This is a somewhat familiar story told in a new way. . . . A chilling, straightforward novel written with depth and understanding." SLJ

Meyer, Carolyn

Duchessina; a novel of Catherine de' Medici. Harcourt 2007 261p (Young royals) $17

Grades: 7 8 9 10 **Fic**
1. Queens 2. Regents 3. Italy -- Fiction 4. Queens -- Fiction 5. Orphans -- Fiction
ISBN 978-0-15-205588-2; 0-15-205588-6
LC 2006028876

While her tyrannical family is out of favor in Italy, young Catherine de Medici is raised in convents, then in 1533, when she is fourteen, her uncle, Pope Clement VII, arranges for her marriage to prince Henri of France, who is destined to become king.

"With meticulous historical detail, sensitive characterizations, and Catherine's strong narration, Meyer's memorable story of a fascinating young woman who relies on her intelligence, rather than her beauty, will hit home with many teens." Booklist

Meyer, L. A.

Bloody Jack; being an account of the curious adventures of Mary Jacky Faber, ship's boy. Harcourt 2002 278p hardcover o.p. pa $6.95
Grades: 7 8 9 10 **Fic**
1. Adventure fiction 2. Orphans -- Fiction 3. Pirates -- Fiction 4. Sex role -- Fiction 5. Seafaring life -- Fiction
ISBN 0-15-216731-5; 0-15-205085-X pa
LC 2002-759

Reduced to begging and thievery in the streets of 18th-century London, a thirteen-year-old orphan disguises herself as a boy and connives her way onto a British warship set for high sea adventure in search of pirates

"From shooting a pirate in battle to foiling a shipmate's sexual attack to surviving when stranded alone on a Caribbean island, the action in Jacky's tale will entertain readers with a taste for adventure." Booklist

Other titles in this series are:
Curse of the blue tattoo (2004)
In the belly of The Bloodhound (2006)
The mark of the golden dragon (2011)
Mississippi Jack (2007)
My bonny light horseman (2008)
Rapture of the deep (2009)
Under the Jolly Roger (2005)
The wake of the Lorelei Lee (2010)

Curse of the blue tattoo; being an account of the misadventures of Jacky Faber, midshipman and fine lady. Harcourt 2004 488p $17
Grades: 7 8 9 10 **Fic**
1. Orphans -- Fiction 2. Sex role -- Fiction 3. Boston (Mass.) -- Fiction
ISBN 0-15-205115-5
LC 2003-19032

Sequel to Bloody Jack

In 1803, after being exposed as a girl and forced to leave her ship, Jacky Faber finds herself attending school in Boston, where, instead of learning to be a lady, she battles her snobbish classmates, roams the city in search of adventure, and learns to ride a horse.

"Meyer does an excellent job of conveying life in Boston in 1803, particularly the rights, or lack thereof, of women. . . . The narrative is full of lecherous men, and Jacky herself is free in her ways. This fact and the sometimes-

strong language make this book more appropriate for older readers." SLJ

In the belly of The Bloodhound; being an account of a particularly peculiar adventure in the life of Jacky Faber. [by] L. A. Meyer. 1st ed.; Harcourt 2006 515p $17
Grades: 7 8 9 10 **Fic**
1. Orphans -- Fiction 2. Kidnapping -- Fiction 3. Seafaring life -- Fiction
ISBN 978-0-15-205557-8; 0-15-205557-6
LC 2005033562

Sequel to: Under the Jolly Roger

Jacky Faber and her classmates at the Lawson Peabody School for Young Girls in Boston are kidnapped while on a school outing and transported in the hold of a slave ship bound for the slave markets of North Africa.

"This plot-driven novel . . . is one more fabulous adventure for Jacky and friends and a thoroughly delightful story." Voice Youth Advocates

Followed by: Mississippi Jack

The **mark** of the golden dragon; being an account of the further adventures of Jacky Faber, jewel of the East, vexation of the West, and pearl of the South China Sea. Harcourt 2011 378p $16.99
Grades: 7 8 9 10 **Fic**
1. Thieves -- Fiction 2. Indonesia -- Fiction 3. Seafaring life -- Fiction 4. London (England) -- Fiction
ISBN 978-0-547-51764-3; 0-547-51764-5
LC 2011009598

In 1807, having survived a typhoon in the East Indies, Jacky Faber makes her way to London to seek a pardon for herself and her betrothed, Jaimy Fletcher, who, posing as a highwayman, is trying to avenge her supposed death.

"The writing style is simple yet entertaining. The multiple viewpoints, including the thoughts of various characters, add interest to the story. Meyer also adds a little spice without being explicit, although a few words could be offensive to younger readers, so this selection is better suited to young adults, but all in all it is a very enjoyable read." Voice Youth Advocates

Mississippi Jack; being an account of the further waterborne adventures of Jacky Faber, midshipman, fine lady, and the Lily of the West. [by] L.A. Meyer. 1st ed.; Harcourt 2007 611p $17; pa $7.99
Grades: 7 8 9 10 **Fic**
1. Orphans -- Fiction 2. Mississippi River -- Fiction 3. Voyages and travels -- Fiction
ISBN 978-0-15-206003-9; 978-0-15-206632-1 pa
LC 2006034709

Sequel to: In the belly of The Bloodhound (2006)

In 1806, the exploits of Jacky Faber continue as she heads west to avoid capture by the British and discovers adventure aboard a keelboat on the mighty Mississippi River.

"The descriptions of the new frontier, river life, and the social climate of early nineteenth-century America seem right on. Jacky continues to amaze readers with her clever plots, narrow escapes, and the uncanny ability to outwit

thieves and bureaucrats, make money, and have some fun."
Voice Youth Advocates

My bonny light horseman; being an account of the further adventures of Jacky Faber, in love and war. Harcourt 2008 436p $17

Grades: 7 8 9 10   **Fic**
1. Adventure fiction 2. Spies -- Fiction 3. Orphans -- Fiction 4. France -- History -- 1799-1815 -- Fiction
ISBN 978-0-15-206187-6; 0-15-206187-8
                                                    LC 2007049582
Sequel to: Mississippi Jack (2007)
While trying to run a respectable shipping business in 1806, teenaged Jacky Faber finds herself in France, spying for the British Crown in order to save her friends.
"Jacky's wit and lots of action make it an engaging read." Voice Youth Advocates
Followed by: Rapture of the deep (2009)

Rapture of the deep; being an account of the further adventures of Jacky Faber, soldier, sailor, mermaid, spy. Harcourt 2009 454p $17

Grades: 7 8 9 10   **Fic**
1. Adventure fiction 2. Spies -- Fiction 3. Orphans -- Fiction 4. Kidnapping -- Fiction 5. Seafaring life -- Fiction 6. Buried treasure -- Fiction 7. Caribbean region -- Fiction
ISBN 978-0-15-206501-0; 0-15-206501-6
                                                    LC 2009-19494
Sequel to: My bonny light horseman (2008)
In 1806, star-crossed lovers Jacky Faber and Jaimy Fletcher are kidnapped by British Naval Intelligence and forced to embark on yet another daring mission—this time to search for sunken Spanish gold off the Florida coast.
"Meyer weaves details of nineteenth-century history, lore, and ballads into a fast-paced and often amusing swashbuckler." Booklist
Followed by: The wake of the Lorelei Lee (2010)

Under the Jolly Roger; being an account of the further nautical adventures of Jacky Faber. Harcourt 2005 518p $17

Grades: 7 8 9 10   **Fic**
1. Orphans -- Fiction 2. Pirates -- Fiction 3. Sex role -- Fiction 4. Seafaring life -- Fiction
ISBN 0-15-205345-X
                                                    LC 2004-22463
Sequel to: Curse of the blue tattoo
In 1804, fifteen-year-old Jacky Faber heads back to sea where she gains control of a British warship and eventually becomes a privateer.
"Readers will root for resilient Jacky and her memorable friends as she cannily makes the best of even the least-promising situations. A swashbuckling saga with a decidedly unconventional heroine." Booklist
Followed by: In the belly of The Bloodhound

Viva Jacquelina! being an account of the further adventures of Jacky Faber, over the hills and far away. written by L.A. Meyer. Harcourt 2012 p. cm. $16.99

Grades: 7 8 9 10   **Fic**
1. Spies 2. Spain -- History -- Fiction 3. Adventure fiction 4. Historical fiction
ISBN 9780547763507
                                                    LC 2011041931
This young adult adventure novel, by L. A. Meyer, continues the "Bloody Jack Adventures" series. "Once again under the thumb of British Intelligence, Jacky is sent to Spain to spy for the Crown during the early days of the nineteenth-century Peninsular War. She finds herself in the company of guerilla freedom fighters, poses for the famous artist Goya, runs with the bulls, is kidnapped by the Spanish Inquisition, and travels with a caravan of gypsies." (Publisher's note)

The wake of the Lorelei Lee; being an account of the adventures of Jacky Faber on her way to Botany Bay. Harcourt 2010 554p $17

Grades: 7 8 9 10   **Fic**
1. Sea stories 2. Orphans -- Fiction 3. Sex role -- Fiction 4. Australia -- Fiction 5. Prisoners -- Fiction 6. Seafaring life -- Fiction
ISBN 978-0-547-32768-6; 0-547-32768-4
                                                    LC 2010-8686
Sequel to: Rapture of the deep (2009)
Now rich, Jacky Faber has purchased the Lorelei Lee to carry passengers across the Atlantic, and believing she has been absolved of past sins against the Crown, she docks in London, where she is arrested and sentenced to life in the newly formed penal colony in Australia.
"L. A. Meyer's writing style is easy to read and entertaining. The story moves along at a brisk pace, with new turns in the plot keeping the reader's attention throughout." Voice Youth Advocates

Meyer, Marissa, 1984-
★ **Cinder**; Marissa Meyer. Feiwel & Friends 2012 320 p. $17.99

Grades: 7 8 9 10 11 12   **Fic**
1. Fairy tales 2. Science fiction 3. Robots -- Fiction
ISBN 9780312641894
                                                    LC 2011036123
In this book, "as plague ravages the overcrowded Earth, observed by a ruthless lunar people, Cinder, a gifted mechanic and cyborg, becomes involved with handsome Prince Kai and must uncover secrets about her past in order to protect the world in this futuristic take on the Cinderella story." (Publisher's note)
Followed by: Scarlet (2013)

★ **Cress**; Marissa Meyer. Feiwel & Friends 2014 560 p. $18.99

Grades: 7 8 9 10 11 12   **Fic**
1. Fugitives from justice -- Fiction 2. Human-alien encounters -- Fiction
ISBN 0312642970; 9780312642976
In this book by Marissa Meyer, third in her Lunar Chronicles series, "Cinder and Captain Thorne are fugitives on the run, now with Scarlet and Wolf in tow. Together, they're plotting to overthrow Queen Levana and prevent her army from invading Earth. Their best hope lies with Cress, a girl trapped on a satellite since childhood. When a daring rescue of Cress goes awry, the group is splintered. Meanwhile,

Queen Levana will let nothing prevent her marriage to Emperor Kai." (Publisher's note)

"—Cress is locked away in a floating satellite. She dreams of visiting Earth, the planet she has been forced to spy on, and meeting Carswell Thorne, the handsome ship captain who teamed up with Cinder in Scarlet (Feiwel & Friends, 2013)....Cress fills in more historical details about Earth and Luna's relationship—most of which will be of no surprise to the reader—and Cinder's rebirth as a cyborg. Fans of Scarlet and Wolf may be disappointed that their relationship takes a backseat to the newly introduced pairing. As always, Meyer excels at interweaving new characters that extend beyond the archetypes of their fairy tale into the main story. Readers will eagerly await the final installment of this highly appealing and well-constructed series." (School Library Journal)

★ **Scarlet**; Marissa Meyer. Feiwel and Friends 2013 464 p. $17.99

Grades: 7 8 9 10 11 12   **Fic**
   1. Science fiction 2. Fractured fairy tales 3. Cyborgs -- Fiction 4. Missing persons -- Fiction 5. Extraterrestrial beings -- Fiction
   ISBN 0312642962; 9780312642969
                                          LC 2012034060
This novel, by Marissa Meyer, is the second book of the "Lunar Chronicles" series. "Cinder, the cyborg mechanic, . . . [is] trying to break out of prison. . . . [Meanwhile,] Scarlet Benoit's grandmother is missing. . . . When Scarlet encounters Wolf, a street fighter who may have information . . . , she is loath to trust this stranger. . . . As Scarlet and Wolf unravel one mystery, they encounter another when they meet Cinder." (Publisher's note)

★ **Winter**; Marissa Meyer. Feiwel & Friends 2015 827 p. $22.99

   Grades: 7 8 9 10 11 12   **Fic**
   1. Love stories 2. Princesses -- Fiction 3. Revolutions -- Fiction
   ISBN 0312642989; 9780312642983
In this novel by Marissa Meyer "Winter despises her stepmother, and knows Levana won't approve of her feelings for her childhood friend--the handsome palace guard, Jacin. But Winter isn't as weak as Levana believes her to be and she's been undermining her stepmother's wishes for years. Together with the cyborg mechanic, Cinder, and her allies, Winter might even have the power to launch a revolution and win a war that's been raging for far too long." (Publisher's note)

"Meyer's series has sold well and achieved a degree of acclaim. This conclusion's cinder-block size should only drum up further interest." Booklist

Meyer, Stephenie

Breaking dawn; [by] Stephenie Meyer. Little, Brown 2008 756p $22.99

Grades: 8 9 10 11 12   **Fic**
   1. Marriage -- Fiction 2. Vampires -- Fiction 3. Werewolves -- Fiction
   ISBN 978-0-316-06792-8; 0-316-06792-X
   Sequel to: Eclipse (2007)

Although eighteen-year-old Bella joins the dark but seductive world of the immortals by marrying Edward the vampire, her connection to the powerful werewolf Jacob remains unsevered.

"For those who find it hard to say farewell to Bella and company, take heart: it may not be goodbye." Booklist

Eclipse. Little, Brown 2007 629p $18.99

Grades: 8 9 10 11 12   **Fic**
   1. School stories 2. Vampires -- Fiction 3. Werewolves -- Fiction 4. Washington (State) -- Fiction
   ISBN 978-0-316-16020-9; 0-316-16020-2
                                          LC 2007-12325
Sequel to: New moon (2006)
Bella must choose between her friendship with Jacob, a werewolf, and her relationship with Edward, a vampire, but when Seattle is ravaged by a mysterious string of killings, the three of them need to decide whether their personal lives are more important than the well-being of an entire city.

"Meyer knows what her fans want: thrills, chills, and a lot of romance, and she delivers on all counts." SLJ

New moon. Little, Brown and Co. 2006 563p $17.99

Grades: 8 9 10 11 12   **Fic**
   1. School stories 2. Vampires -- Fiction 3. Washington (State) -- Fiction
   ISBN 978-0-316-16019-3; 0-316-16019-9
                                          LC 2006012309
Sequel to Twilight (2005)
When the Cullens, including her beloved Edward, leave Forks rather than risk revealing that they are vampires, it is almost too much for eighteen-year-old Bella to bear, but she finds solace in her friend Jacob until he is drawn into a "cult" and changes in terrible ways.

"Vampire aficionados will voraciously consume this mighty tome in one sitting, then flip back and read it once more. It maintains a brisk pace and near-genius balance of breathtaking romance and action." Voice Youth Advocates
Followed by Eclipse (2007)

★ **Twilight**. Little, Brown and Co. 2005 498p $17.99; pa $8.99

Grades: 8 9 10 11 12   **Fic**
   1. School stories 2. Vampires -- Fiction 3. Washington (State) -- Fiction
   ISBN 0-316-16017-2; 0-316-01584-9 pa
                                          LC 2004-24730
When seventeen-year-old Bella leaves Phoenix to live with her father in Forks, Washington, she meets an exquisitely handsome boy at school for whom she feels an overwhelming attraction and who she comes to realize is not wholly human.

"Realistic, subtle, succinct, and easy to follow, . . . [this book] will have readers dying to sink their teeth into it." SLJ
Other titles in this series are:
   Breaking dawn (2008)
   Eclipse (2007)
   New moon (2006)

Mezrich, Ben

Bringing down the mouse; Ben Mezrich. Simon & Schuster Books for Young Readers 2014 336 p. (hardcover) $16.99

Grades: 5 6 7 8   Fic

1. Genius -- Fiction 2. Amusement parks -- Fiction 3. Conduct of life -- Fiction 4. Mathematics -- Competitions -- Fiction 5. Mathematics -- Fiction
ISBN 9781442496262; 1442496266

LC 2013027538

In this middle grades book, by Ben Mezrich, "Charlie Lewis is . . . really good at math. So good that he's recruited by a group of kids determined to game the system at the biggest theme park in the world . . . and win the grand prize. Soon Charlie is caught up in the excitement and thrill of using his math skills for awesomeness . . . but what's at stake may be more than he's willing to risk. How far will Charlie go for a chance at the ultimate reward?" (Publisher's note)

"The pacing is well developed, building tension to almost a fever pitch as the Carnival Killers perfect their skills and arrive at Incredo Land to take on the biggest scam of all. The mystery of who is truly behind the schemes adds another dimension to the adventure. The plot has several unexpected and well-placed twists, and keeps readers guessing until the very end." SLJ

Michaelis, Antonia

Tiger moon; translated from the German by Anthea Bell. Amulet Books 2008 453p pa $9.95; $19.95

Grades: 8 9 10 11 12   Fic

1. India -- Fiction 2. Tigers -- Fiction 3. Thieves -- Fiction 4. Princesses -- Fiction 5. Storytelling -- Fiction
ISBN 0-8109-4499-5 pa; 0-8109-9481-X; 978-0-8109-4499-2 pa; 978-0-8109-9481-2

LC 2007-22823

Sold to be the eighth wife of a rich and cruel merchant, Safia, also called Raka, tries to escape her fate by telling stories of Farhad the thief, his companion Nitish the white tiger, and their travels across India to retrieve a famous jewel that will save a kidnapped princess from becoming the bride of a demon king. "Grades eight to ten." (Bull Cent Child Books)

"The plot is fast paced and exciting, and the story gives an excellent overview of the conflicts of India at the time of British occupation, and of Hindu religious beliefs." SLJ

Milford, Kate

The **Boneshaker**; [illustrations by Andrea Offermann] Clarion Books 2010 372p il $17

Grades: 5 6 7 8 9   Fic

1. Bicycles -- Fiction 2. Missouri -- Fiction 3. Demonology -- Fiction 4. Supernatural -- Fiction
ISBN 978-0-547-24187-6; 0-547-24187-9

LC 2009-45350

"Natalie is a well-drawn protagonist with sturdy supporting characters around her. The tension built into the solidly constructed plot is complemented by themes that explore the literal and metaphorical role of crossroads and that thin line between good and evil." Kirkus

The **Broken** Lands; by Kate Milford; with illustrations by Andrea Offermann. Clarion Books 2012 455 p. ill. (hardback) $16.99

Grades: 5 6 7 8 9 10   Fic

1. Bridges -- Fiction 2. Supernatural -- Fiction 3. New York (N.Y.) -- Fiction 4. Orphans -- Fiction 5. Demonology -- Fiction 6. Good and evil -- Fiction 7. New York (N.Y.) -- History -- 1865-1898 -- Fiction 8. Coney Island (New York, N.Y.) -- History -- 19th century -- Fiction
ISBN 0547739664; 9780547739663

LC 2011049466

This book, a prequel to "Kate Milford's 'The Boneshaker,' [is] set in . . . nineteenth-century Coney Island and New York City. Few crossroads compare to the one being formed by the Brooklyn Bridge and the East River, and as the bridge's construction progresses, forces of unimaginable evil seek to bend that power to their advantage. . . . Can the teenagers Sam, a card sharp, and Jin, a fireworks expert, stop them before it's too late?" (Publisher's note)

Millay, Katja

The **Sea** of Tranquility; a novel. by Katja Millay. Atria Books 2013 448 p. $15

Grades: 10 11 12 Adult   Fic

1. Love stories 2. Secrets -- Fiction
ISBN 1476730946; 9781476730943

LC 2013012207

Alex Award Winner (2014)

"Two and a half years after an unspeakable tragedy left her a shadow of the girl she once was, Nastya Kashnikov moves to a new town determined to keep her dark past hidden and hold everyone at a distance. But her plans only last so long before she finds herself inexplicably drawn to the one person as isolated as herself: Josh Bennett. Josh's story is no secret. Every person he loves has been taken from his life until, at seventeen years old, there is no one left. . . . [A]s the undeniable pull between them intensifies, he starts to wonder if he will ever learn the secrets she's been hiding--or if he even wants to." (Publisher's note)

"[F]ans of character-driven fiction will find much to admire in this deeply felt novel that is an excellent example of crossover fiction." LJ

Miller, Kirsten

The **eternal** ones. Razorbill 2010 411p $17.99

Grades: 6 7 8 9 10   Fic

1. Love stories 2. Faith -- Fiction 3. Tennessee -- Fiction 4. Reincarnation -- Fiction 5. New York (N.Y.) -- Fiction 6. Fate and fatalism -- Fiction
ISBN 978-1-59514-308-2; 1-59514-308-4

LC 2010-22775

Seventeen-year-old Haven Moore leaves East Tennessee to attend the Fashion Institute of Technology in New York City, where she meets playboy Iain Morrow, whose fate may be tied to hers through a series of past lives.

"Miller's writing elevates the supernatural romance well beyond typical fare, and Haven's mix of naïveté and determination makes her a solid, credible heroine." Publ Wkly

Followed by: All you desire (2011)

How to lead a life of crime; Kirsten Miller. Razorbill 2013 358 p. (hardcover) $18.99

Grades: 9 10 11 12   **Fic**
1. School stories 2. Criminals -- Fiction 3. Ghosts -- Fiction 4. Schools -- Fiction 5. Survival -- Fiction
ISBN 1595145184; 9781595145185

LC 2012031576

In this young adult novel, by Kirsten Miller, "the Mandel Academy . . . has been training young criminals for over a century. Only the most ruthless . . . graduate. The rest disappear. Flick . . . has risen to the top of his class. But then Mandel recruits a fierce new competitor who also happens to be Flick's old flame. They've been told only one of them will make it out of the Mandel Academy. Will they find a way to save each other--or will the school destroy them both?" (Publisher's note)

Miller, Sarah

The **lost** crown. Atheneum Books for Young Readers 2011 412p $17.99

Grades: 8 9 10 11 12   **Fic**
1. Emperors 2. Sisters -- Fiction 3. Kings and rulers -- Fiction 4. World War, 1914-1918 -- Fiction 5. Russia -- History -- 1905, Revolution -- Fiction
ISBN 978-1-4169-8340-8; 1-4169-8340-6

LC 2010037001

In alternating chapters, Grand Duchesses Olga, Tatiana, Maria, and Anastasia tell how their privileged lives as the daughters of the tsar in early twentieth-century Russia are transformed by world war and revolution.

"Each Grand Duchess comes across as a unique personality. . . . Like the best historical novels, this allows modern-day teens to see themselves in very different people." Booklist

Miss Spitfire; reaching Helen Keller. Atheneum Books for Young Readers 2007 208p $16.99

Grades: 7 8 9 10 11   **Fic**
1. Deaf 2. Blind 3. Authors 4. Memoirists 5. Humanitarians 6. Deaf -- Fiction 7. Blind -- Fiction 8. Teachers -- Fiction 9. Teachers of the deaf 10. Inspirational writers 11. Teachers of the blind 12. Social welfare leaders
ISBN 978-1-4169-2542-2; 1-4169-2542-2

LC 2006014738

At age twenty-one, partially-blind, lonely but spirited Annie Sullivan travels from Massachusetts to Alabama to try and teach six-year-old Helen Keller, deaf and blind since age two, self-discipline and communication skills. Includes historical notes and timeline.

"This excellent novel is compelling reading even for those familiar with the Keller/Sullivan experience." SLJ

Includes bibliographical references

Miller, Walter M.

★ A **canticle** for Leibowitz; a novel. by Walter M. Miller, Jr. Lippincott 1960 320p hardcover o.p. pa $13.95

Grades: 9 10 11 12 Adult   **Fic**
1. Science fiction
ISBN 0-06-089299-4

"Here is science fiction of the highest literary excellence and thematic intelligence. A monastery founded by the scientist Leibowitz is discovered decades after an atomic war. In the first part of the book a young novice in the monastery is the protagonist; in the second part we see scholars in a new period of enlightenment; and in the final section we observe man's proclivity for repeating mistakes and the apparent inevitability of history's repeating itself." Shapiro. Fic for Youth. 3d edition

Miller-Lachmann, Lyn

Gringolandia; a novel. Curbstone Press 2009 279p $16.95

Grades: 9 10 11 12   **Fic**
1. Chile -- Fiction 2. Wisconsin -- Fiction 3. Political activists -- Fiction 4. Father-son relationship -- Fiction 5. Post-traumatic stress disorder -- Fiction
ISBN 978-1-931896-49-8; 1-931896-49-6

LC 2008-36990

In 1986, when seventeen-year-old Daniel's father arrives in Madison, Wisconsin, after five years of torture as a political prisoner in Chile, Daniel and his eighteen-year-old "gringa" girlfriend, Courtney, use different methods to help this bitter, self-destructive stranger who yearns to return home and continue his work.

"This poignant, often surprising and essential novel illuminates too-often ignored political aspects of many South Americans' migration to the United States." Kirkus

Minato, Kanae

Confessions; a novel. Kanae Minato, Stephen Snyder. First edition Little, Brown & Co. 2014 240 p. $15

Grades: 11 12 Adult   **Fic**
1. Japanese fiction 2. Murder -- Fiction 3. Bullies -- Fiction 4. Revenge -- fiction 5. Accidents -- fiction
ISBN 0316200921; 9780316200929

LC 2014937563

Alex Award (2015)

In this novel by Minato Kanai, "All Yuko Moriguchi had to live for was her four-year-old child, Manami. Now, after a heartbreaking accident on the grounds of the middle school where she teaches, Yuko has given up and tendered her resignation. But first, she has one last lecture to deliver. She tells a story that will upend everything her students ever thought they knew about two of their peers, and sets in motion a maniacal plot for revenge." (Publisher's note)

"Yuko Moriguchi leads a relatively simple life, teaching middle school and raising her four-year-old daughter, Manami, on her own. But when Manami is murdered in a sick act of hatred, Yuko decides the legal system is unreliable and plans her own revenge...This award-winning debut novel is a creepy and mesmerizing psychological thriller that challenges the conventions of right vs. wrong, good vs. evil, and law vs. justice. There are no happy endings here, but Minato has pieced together an intriguing puzzle that will keep readers glued to their seats." LJ

Minchin, Adele

★ The **beat** goes on. Simon & Schuster Books for Young Readers 2004 212p hardcover o.p. pa $11.95

Grades: 9 10 11 12 **Fic**
1. Cousins -- Fiction 2. Great Britain -- Fiction 3. AIDS (Disease) -- Fiction
ISBN 0-689-86611-9; 1-4169-6755-9 pa
First published 2001 in the United Kingdom
"Fifteen-year-old Leyla must keep her cousin's secret: Emma is HIV positive, and only her mother and Leyla know. The secret becomes a burden, especially when Leyla must lie to her parents in order to work with Emma's support group on their special project—to teach other HIV-positive teens how to play the drums. In spite of its heavy Briticisms and a didactic tone, this is one of the better YA books about HIV. The facts of transmission and symptoms are clearly presented, as are Emma's struggles to lead a normal, healthy life. . . . Minchin educates young readers while telling a gripping story that will keep personal tragedy aficionados turning the pages to the hopeful yet realistic conclusion." Booklist

Miranda, Megan
Hysteria; by Megan Miranda. Walker 2013 336 p. (hardback) $17.99
Grades: 9 10 11 12 **Fic**
1. School stories 2. Memory -- Fiction 3. Homicide -- Fiction 4. Death -- Fiction 5. Schools -- Fiction 6. Boarding schools -- Fiction
ISBN 0802723101; 9780802723109
LC 2012015780
In this novel, by Megan Miranda, "Mallory killed her boyfriend, Brian. She can't remember the details . . . but everyone knows it was self-defense, so she isn't charged. . . . In desperate need of a fresh start, Mallory is sent to . . . a fancy prep school where no one knows her. . . . Then, one of her new classmates turns up dead. As suspicion falls on Mallory, she must find a way to remember the details of both deadly nights so she can prove her innocence." (Publisher's note)

Soulprint; by Megan Miranda. Bloomsbury/ Walker 2015 368 p. (hardcover) $17.99
Grades: 7 8 9 10 **Fic**
1. Science fiction 2. Reincarnation -- Fiction 3. Fugitives from justice -- Fiction 4. Soul -- Fiction 5. Guilt -- Fiction 6. Prisoners -- Fiction 7. Conduct of life -- Fiction
ISBN 0802737749; 9780802737748
LC 2014009921
This novel by Megan Miranda is set "in a future where reincarnation can be scientifically tracked. . . .17-year-old half-Hispanic Alina Chase has spent her life isolated, allegedly for her own protection. She carries within her the soul of a charismatic and destructive whistleblower turned blackmailer, June Calahan. Broken out of confinement by a daring trio barely older than she is, Alina finds she still cannot escape June's shadow." (Publishers Weekly)
"A unique spin on recent dystopian reads featuring genetic heritability . . . [Soulprint] will fascinate teens already enthralled with questions about what they might do with their lives. A surprising new sf thriller with just enough of a touch of romance." Booklist

Miéville, China, 1972-
★ **Railsea**; China Mieville. Del Rey/Ballantine Books 2012 424 p. ill. (hbk.: alk. paper) $18.00

Grades: 7 8 9 10 **Fic**
1. Adventure fiction 2. Steampunk fiction 3. Railroads -- Fiction 4. Imaginary places -- Fiction
ISBN 0345524527; 9780345524522; 9780345524546
LC 2012009516
This book presents "a steampunk spin on 'Moby-Dick' . . . . Instead of chasing whales on the sea, the crew of the diesel train Medes hunt moldywarpes—enormous, man-eating, molelike creatures who are only one of the countless menacing species who burrow in the perilous earth beneath a tangled ocean of train tracks. And it is one moldywarpe in particular, the great Mocker-Jack, that Captain Naphi is after—it's trendy for any captain worth her iron to have such a defining obsession, and she is fully aware that they hunt metaphor in beast form. Aboard for the grand adventure is your hero, young Sham (don't call him Ishmael)." (Booklist)

Mlawski, Shana
Hammer of witches; by Shana Mlawski. Tu Books 2013 400 p. (reinforced) $18.95
Grades: 6 7 8 9 **Fic**
1. Fantasy fiction 2. Storytelling -- Fiction 3. America -- Exploration -- Fiction 4. Magic -- Fiction 5. Wizards -- Fiction 6. Explorers -- Fiction 7. America -- Discovery and exploration -- Spanish -- Fiction
ISBN 1600609872; 9781600609879
LC 2012048627
In this novel, by Shana Mlawski, "Baltasar Infante . . . encounters a monster straight out of stories one night . . . . Captured by . . . a mysterious witch-hunting arm of the Spanish Inquisition, . . . the Inquisitor demands he reveal the whereabouts of Amir al-Katib, a legendary Moorish sorcerer who can bring myths and the creatures within them to life. Now Baltasar must escape, find al-Katib, and defeat a dreadful power that may destroy the world." (Publisher's note)
"Newcomer Mlawski delivers a fast-paced coming-of-age adventure, respectfully evoking the complexities and cultural landscape of the period. She draws from a variety of sources, including Jewish and Biblical myth, offering an accessible, attention-grabbing story that seamlessly inserts its magical elements into historical fact." Pub Wkly

Mlynowski, Sarah
Don't even think about it; Sarah Mlynowski. Delacorte Press 2014 336 p. (hc: alk. paper) $17.99
Grades: 7 8 9 10 **Fic**
1. Telepathy -- Fiction 2. Extrasensory perception -- Fiction 3. Schools -- Fiction 4. High schools -- Fiction 5. New York (N.Y.) -- Fiction 6. TriBeCa (New York, N.Y.) -- Fiction
ISBN 0385737386; 9780385737388; 9780385906623
LC 2012050777
This book, by Sarah Mlynowski, follows three girls who "used to be average New York City high school sophomores" but develop "telepathic powers." The girls use their powers to find about "romance, secrets, [and] scandals" involving their friends, boyfriends and students at their high school. (Publisher's note)
"When a group of Manhattan 10th graders inadvertently receives telepathic abilities from tainted flu shots, things rapidly get chaotic (and noisy). Finding out too much information dramatically upends family relationships, friendships,

and romances. . . . Filled with heartbreak, hilarity, and some brutal truths, Mlynowski's novel will leave readers thinking about the gaps between our private and public selves and the lies we tell others and ourselves." Pub Wkly

Do not even think about it

Ten things we did (and probably shouldn't have) HarperTeen 2011 357p $16.99; ebook $9.99

Grades: 7 8 9 10   **Fic**

1. Friendship -- Fiction 2. Connecticut -- Fiction
ISBN 978-0-06-170124-5; 0-06-170124-6; 978-0-06-208461-3 ebook; 0-06-208461-5 ebook

LC 2010-45556

Sixteen-year-old April, a high school junior, and her friend Vi, a senior, get a crash course in reality as the list of things they should not do becomes a list of things they did while living parent-free in Westport, Connecticut, for the semester.

"With wit, energy, and an uncanny understanding of teenage logic, Mlynowski . . . weighs the pros and cons of independence in this modern cautionary tale. . . . Mlynowski avoids sermonizing, offering 10 madcap and remarkably tense escapades that will have readers laughing, cringing, and guessing how April will get out of the next pickle." Publ Wkly

Monaghan, Annabel

A **girl** named Digit; by Annabel Monaghan. Houghton Mifflin Harcourt 2012 187 p. $16.99; $16.99

Grades: 7 8 9   **Fic**

1. School stories 2. Terrorism -- Fiction 3. Cryptography -- Fiction 4. Kidnapping -- Fiction 5. Interpersonal relations -- Fiction 6. Adventure and adventurers -- Fiction
ISBN 054766852X; 9780547668529; 9780544022485

LC 2011012239

In this book, "saddled with the nickname Digit, Farrah resolved to fit in once she reached high school by hiding her math skills. Then Farrah stumbles upon an eco-terrorist organization after their suicide bomb attack on JFK Airport, and the terrorists want her dead. . . . Farrah's FBI protector, the cute, young rookie agent John Bennett, . . . works with Farrah to uncover a blackmail scheme involving the attack's bomber." (Kirkus Reviews)

Monninger, Joseph

Whippoorwill; by Joseph Monninger. Houghton Mifflin Harcourt 2015 288 p. (hardback) $17.99

Grades: 7 8 9 10   **Fic**

1. Dogs -- Fiction 2. Neighbors -- Fiction 3. Single-parent families -- Fiction 4. Dating (Social customs) -- Fiction 5. Father-daughter relationship -- Fiction 6. Neighborhoods -- Fiction 7. Dogs -- Training -- Fiction 8. Labrador retriever -- Fiction 9. Animals -- Treatment -- Fiction 10. Fathers and daughters -- Fiction
ISBN 9780544531239

LC 2014046833

In this young adult novel, by Joseph Monninger, "Sixteen-year-old Clair Taylor has neighbors who are what locals call whippoorwills, the kind of people who fill their yards with rusty junk. Clair tries to ignore her surroundings,

choosing instead to dream of a future beyond her rural New Hampshire town. But, when a black dog named Wally is chained up to a pole next door, Clair can't look the other way." (Publisher's note)

"Monninger revitalizes the boy-and-his-dog trope in this sweet novel." SLJ

Mont, Eve Marie

A **breath** of Eyre. Kensington/Kteen 2012 342 p.

Grades: 9 10 11 12   **Fic**

1. Love stories 2. Fantasy fiction 3. Supernatural -- Fiction 4. Books and reading
ISBN 9780758269485

In this book, "Emma Townsend has always believed in stories. . . . Perhaps it's because she feels like an outsider at her . . . school, or because her stepmother doesn't come close to filling the void left by her mother's death. And her only romantic prospect . . . is . . . a long-time friend who just adds to Emma's confusion. But escape soon arrives in a . . . copy of "Jane Eyre." . . . Reading of Jane's isolation sparks a deep sense of kinship. Then . . . a lightning storm catapults Emma right into Jane's body and her nineteenth-century world. . . . Emma has a sense of belonging she's never known"and an attraction to the brooding Mr. Rochester. Now, moving between her two realities and uncovering secrets in both, Emma must decide . . . [where] her destiny lies." (Publisher's note)

Moore, Carley

The **stalker** chronicles; Carley Moore. Farrar Straus Giroux 2012 230 p. (hardcover) $16.99

Grades: 8 9 10 11 12   **Fic**

1. School stories 2. Divorce -- Fiction 3. Interpersonal relations -- Fiction 4. Schools -- Fiction 5. Friendship -- Fiction 6. Best friends -- Fiction 7. High schools -- Fiction 8. New York (State) -- Fiction 9. Family life -- New York (State) -- Fiction
ISBN 9780374371807; 9781429961752

LC 2011013093

This book features "Cammie, a high-school sophomore, whose history has involved such intense interest in guys . . . that she's now known around school as a stalker. When cute new guy Toby turns up in her small town, Cammie's determined that she'll change her ways, . . . and finally get the relationship she's been longing for. . . . The dissolution of Cammie's parents' marriage . . . brings her dysfunctional patterns into sharp relief." (Bulletin of the Center for Children's Books)

Moore, Kelly

★ **Amber** House; by Kelly Moore, Tucker Reed, and Larkin Reed. Arthur A. Levine Books 2012 349 p. (hardback) $17.99

Grades: 9 10 11 12   **Fic**

1. Death -- Fiction 2. Friendship -- Fiction 3. Grandmothers -- Fiction 4. Family secrets -- Fiction 5. Haunted houses -- Fiction 6. Visions -- Fiction 7. Maryland -- Fiction 8. Psychic ability -- Fiction 9. Mystery and detective stories 10. Brothers and sisters

-- Fiction
ISBN 0545434165; 9780545434164; 9780545434171; 9780545469739

LC 2012014729

In this gothic fiction book, protagonist "Sarah Parsons has never seen Amber House, the grand Maryland estate that's been in her family for three centuries. She's never walked its hedge maze nor found its secret chambers; she's never glimpsed the shades that haunt it, nor hunted for lost diamonds in its walls. But all of that is about to change. After her grandmother passes away, Sarah and her friend Jackson decide to search for the diamonds, and the house comes alive." (Publisher's note)

Neverwas; by Kelly Moore, Tucker Reed, and Larkin Reed. Arthur A. Levine Books 2014 320 p. (Amber House trilogy) (hardback) $17.99

Grades: 9 10 11 12   Fic
1. Historical fiction 2. Alternative histories 3. Love -- Fiction 4. Visions -- Fiction 5. Maryland -- Fiction 6. Dwellings -- Fiction 7. Supernatural -- Fiction 8. Psychic ability -- Fiction 9. Family life -- Maryland -- Fiction
ISBN 0545434181; 9780545434188; 9780545434195

LC 2013020546

In this book by Kelly Moore, Tucker Reed, and Larkin Reed, "Sarah Parsons has settled in at . . . the stately Maryland home that's been in her family for generations. But the world surrounding the House feels deeply wrong to Sarah. It's a place where the colonists lost the 1776 Insurrection, where the American Confederation of States still struggles with segregation, and where Sarah is haunted by echoes of a better world." (Publisher's note)

"This installment presents a stark departure from the preceding volume; gone are the creepy ghost children and specters in mirrors, now replaced by Sarah's confident knowledge that these ghosts are there to guide her. The authors' vision of this alternate, broken United States slowly comes into focus, rather as a ghost might materialize in the background. Sure, ghosts are scary, but a world where the Holocaust lasted for 75 years and may continue? That's inconceivably frightening. A wild ride that leaves its readers breathless for the final installment." (Kirkus)

Moore, Lisa

★ **Flannery;** Lisa Moore. Groundwood Books 2016 256 p. $16.95

Grades: 9 10 11 12   Fic
1. Love stories 2. Love -- Fiction 3. High school students -- Fiction 4. Teenage girls -- Fiction
ISBN 1554980763; 9781554980765

LC 20159046068

In this novel, by Lisa Moore, Flannery is "in love with Tyrone O'Rourke. Tyrone has grown from a dorky kid into an outlaw graffiti artist. Which is a problem, since he and Flannery are partners for the entrepreneurship class that she needs to graduate. And Tyrone's vanishing act may have darker causes than she realizes. When Flannery decides to make a love potion for her entrepreneurship project, rumors that it actually works go viral, and she suddenly has a hot commodity on her hands." (Publisher's note)

"Sixteen-year-old Flannery Malone has a loving but flaky mother, a charming but slightly spoiled younger brother, and a lifelong love for bad boy Tyrone O'Rourke. Life isn't easy for the teen. Her artist mother doesn't earn enough money to buy Flannery's biology book, her father doesn't know she exists, and her best friend is obsessed with a new, abusive boyfriend. Flannery hopes things might take a turn for the better when she is paired with Tyrone in entrepreneurship class, and the duo plan to market a love potion. . . . An engaging story and strong purchase with some valuable lessons about love, friendship, and growing up." SLJ

Moore, Peter

V is for villain; Peter Moore. Hyperion 2014 336 p. $17.99

Grades: 7 8 9 10   Fic
1. Adventure fiction 2. Ability -- Fiction 4. Brothers -- Fiction 5. Superheroes -- Fiction 6. Good and evil -- Fiction
ISBN 1423157494; 9781423157496

LC 2013026304

"When Brad makes friends who are more into political action than weight lifting, he's happy to join a new crew-especially since it means spending more time with Layla, a girl who may or may not have a totally illegal, totally secret super-power. And with her help, Brad begins to hone a dangerous new power of his own." (Publisher's note)

"Well-crafted characters, moral nuance, and a tale with nice, believable twists make this a great addition to the teen-superhero genre." Kirkus

Moracho, Cristina

Althea and Oliver; Cristina Moracho. Viking, an imprint of Penguin Group (USA) 2014 384 p. (hardcover) $17.99

Grades: 9 10 11 12   Fic
1. Friendship -- Fiction 3. Sleep disorders -- Fiction 4. Schools -- Fiction 5. Best friends -- Fiction 6. High schools -- Fiction 7. Coming of age -- Fiction 8. Single-parent families -- Fiction
ISBN 0670785393; 9780670785391

LC 2013041135

In this young adult novel by Cristina Moracho, "Althea Carter and Oliver McKinley have been best friends since they were six. . . . Their journey will take them from . . . their North Carolina hometown to . . . New York City before they once more stand together and face their chances. Set in the DIY, mix tape, and zine culture of the mid-1990s, Cristina Moracho's . . . debut is [a] story about identity, illness, and love--and why bad decisions sometimes feel so good." (Publisher's note)

"Prickly teenager Althea's more passive best friend Oliver develops a sleeping disorder. While she desires a romantic relationship with him, Oliver just wants everything to return to normal. This culturally rich novel set in mid-1990s North Carolina and New York City explores the duo's complex coming-of-age--full of bad decisions and secrets--and the undoing of their friendship. An ambitious, noteworthy, well-written debut." Horn Book

Moran, Katy

Bloodline. Candlewick Press 2009 297p il map $16.99

Grades: 7 8 9 10   **Fic**
1. War stories 2. Adventure fiction 3. Middle Ages
-- Fiction 4. Great Britain -- History -- 0-1066 -- Fiction
ISBN 978-07636-4083-5; 0-7636-4083-2

       LC 2008-21413

While traveling through early seventh-century Britain
trying to stop an impending war, Essa, who bears the blood
of native British tribes and of the invading Anglish, makes
discoveries that divide his loyalties.

"Essa is a complex, sympathetic protagonist: prickly
and quick of temper, but also clever, determined and of
unflinching integrity. If his struggle is authentically gory
and ultimately tragic, it is not without glimpses of love and
hope." Kirkus

Followed by: Bloodline rising (2011)

Bloodline rising. Candlewick Press 2011 328p
map $16.99

Grades: 7 8 9 10   **Fic**
1. Slaves -- Fiction 2. Criminals -- Fiction 3. Middle
Ages -- Fiction 5. Great Britain -- History -- 0-1066
-- Fiction
ISBN 978-0-7636-4508-3; 0-7636-4508-7

       LC 2010-46692

Sequel to: Bloodline (2009)

Cai, a thief in seventh-century Constantinople, finds
himself held captive on a trading ship bound for Britain—
the home his father, a ruthless barbarian assassin, fled long
ago—where he discovers that his Anglish captors know
more about the secrets of his family than he does.

"At its heart, this is the story of a boy's turbulent relationship with his father, torn between resentment and admiration, rivalry and respect, which renders the tale both as
intimate as heartbreak and universal as hope. Grim, lyrical
and unforgettable." Kirkus

Morgan, Page

The **beautiful** and the cursed; by Page Morgan. 1st ed. Delacorte Press 2013 352 p. (library)
$21.99; (hardcover) $18.99

Grades: 7 8 9 10 11 12   **Fic**
1. Love stories 2. Gargoyles -- Fiction 3. Brothers and
sisters -- Fiction 4. Sisters -- Fiction 5. Supernatural
-- Fiction 6. Paris (France) -- History -- 1870-1940 --
Fiction 7. France -- History -- Third Republic, 1870-
1940 -- Fiction
ISBN 0385743114; 9780375990953; 9780385743112

       LC 2012022378

In this book by Page Morgan, "Ingrid, her sister Gabby,
and their mom arrive at the abandoned abbey that they plan
to turn into an art gallery. Grayson, Ingrid's twin brother,
had procured the place and was supposed to meet them
there. Grayson, however, does not show up and the girls
are surprised to learn that he has actually been missing for
several days. . . . [Ingrid] and Gabby . . .discover a world
of living gargoyles that can transform into humans." (Children's Literature)

Other titles in the series are:
The Lovely and the Lost (2014)
The Wondrous and the Wicked (2015)

Morgenstern, Erin
★ The **night** circus. Doubleday 2010 387 p.
$26.95

Grades: 11 12 Adult   **Fic**
1. Circus -- Fiction 2. Historical fiction 3. Magicians
-- Fiction 4. Circus performers -- Fiction
ISBN 978-0-385-53463-5; 0-385-53463-9;
9780385534635

       LC 2010050546

Alex Award (2012), RUSA Reading List: Fantasy (2012)

In this book "two magicians of indefinite but certainly
magically long lifespan - one a public performer named
Prospero the Enchanter, aka Hector Bowen; the other known
only as 'the man in the grey suit' or 'Mr. A. H---' - are engaged in a profound rivalry, played out over many generations by appointed pupils. In the late 19th century, Bowen
elects his six-year-old daughter Celia, while his counterpart
chooses a nameless nine-year-old orphan who will be called
Marco Alisdair. These two are bound into a lifelong challenge, the parameters of which are never fully explained
to them; and for years they do not know their adversaries.
The circus . . . is also the creation of Marco and Celia, both
of who, over the years, become passionately embroiled in
its performances and acts, as well as, inevitably, with each
other." (The Guardian)

Moriarty, Jaclyn
★ A **corner** of white; Jaclyn Moriarty. Arthur
A. Levine Books 2013 384 p. (Colors of Madeleine
trilogy) (hardcover) $17.99

Grades: 7 8 9 10 11 12   **Fic**
1. Fantasy fiction 2. Epistolary fiction 3. Color --
Fiction 4. Magic -- Fiction 5. England -- Fiction 6.
Princesses -- Fiction 7. Missing persons -- Fiction
8. Cambridge (England) -- Fiction 9. Interpersonal
relations -- Fiction
ISBN 0545397367; 9780545397360

       LC 2012016582

Boston Globe-Horn Book Honor: Fiction (2013).

This opening volume of a fantasy series from Jaclyn
Moriarty focuses on 14-year-old Madeleine, who "lives
in Cambridge, England, with her zany mother in uncertain circumstances, having run away from their fabulously
privileged international existence. Meanwhile, Elliot lives in
Bonfire, The Farms, Cello, a parallel reality. . . . Through a
crack between their worlds, they begin exchanging letters."
(Kirkus Reviews)

"Australian writer Moriarty's marvelously original fantasy is quirky and clever... [she] captures the proud iconoclasm of many homeschoolers and does not shy away from
tenderness and poignancy." BookList

★ The **cracks** in the kingdom; Jaclyn Moriarty.
Arthur A. Levine Books, an imprint of Scholastic Inc.
2014 480 p. (The colors of Madeleine) (hardcover:
alk. paper) $18.99

Grades: 7 8 9 10 11 12   **Fic**
1. Fantasy fiction 2. Princesses -- Fiction 3. Missing
persons -- Fiction 4. Color -- Fiction 5. Magic --
Fiction 6. England -- Fiction 7. Cambridge (England)

-- Fiction 8. Interpersonal relations -- Fiction

ISBN 0545397383; 9780545397384; 9780545397391

LC 2013022827

In this book, by Jaclyn Moriarty, "Princess Ko's been bluffing about the mysterious absence of her father. . . . If she can't get him back in a matter of weeks, the consequence may be a devastating war. So under the guise of a publicity stunt she gathers a group of teens - each with a special ability - from across the kingdom to crack the unsolvable case of the missing royals of Cello." (Publisher's note)

"In this lively follow-up to A Corner of White (Scholastic, 2013), Moriarty chronicles the ever-intertwining lives of Cambridge resident Madeline Tully and her secret correspondent Elliot Baranski, a quick-witted farm boy from the Kingdom of Cello...The RYA's work around Cello expands an already complex and intricately drawn world. Readers will be clamoring for the next title after the thrilling yet satisfying conclusion.—" (School Library Journal)

A **tangle** of gold; Jaclyn Moriarty. Arthur A. Levine Books, an imprint of Scholastic Inc. 2016 480 p. (Colors of Madeleine) (hardcover: alk. paper) $18.99

Grades: 9 10 11 12   **Fic**

1. Color -- Fiction 2. Magic -- Fiction 3. England -- Fiction 4. Missing persons -- Fiction 5. Kings and rulers -- Fiction 6. Interpersonal relations -- Fiction

ISBN 9780545397407

LC 2015027754

In this book, by Jaclyn Moriarty, "Cello is in crisis. Princess Ko's deception of her people has emerged and the Kingdom is outraged; the Jagged Edge Elite have taken control, placing the Princess and two members of the Royal Youth Alliance under arrest and ordering their execution; the King's attempts to negotiate their release have failed; Color storms are rampant; and nobody has heard the Cello wind blowing in months." (Publisher's note)

"Readers may find themselves slowing down to savor Moriarty's distinctive language and humor in this final outing. This remains a series unlike any other, with frequent pockets of beautiful imagery and a unique rhythm all its own." Booklist

The **year** of secret assignments. Arthur A. Levine Books 2004 340p $16.95; pa $7.99

Grades: 8 9 10 11 12   **Fic**

1. School stories 2. Australia -- Fiction 3. Friendship -- Fiction

ISBN 0-439-49881-3; 0-439-49882-1 pa

LC 2003-14278

Three female students from Ashbury High write to three male students from rival Brookfield High as part of a pen pal program, leading to romance, humiliation, revenge plots, and war between the schools

"There are a few coarse moments—a reference to a blow job and some caustic outbursts. . . . This is an unusual novel with an exhilarating pace, irrepressible characters, and a screwball humor that will easily attract teens." Booklist

Other titles set at Ashbury High are:

The ghosts of Ashbury High (2010)

The murder of Bindy Mackenzie (2006)

Morpurgo, Michael

Listen to the Moon; by Michael Morpurgo. Feiwel & Friends 2015 352 p. $16.99

Grades: 5 6 7 8 9   **Fic**

1. England -- Fiction 2. Girls 3. World War, 1914-1918 4. Father-son relationship

ISBN 1250042046; 9781250042040

"In May 1915 a fisherman and his son, Alfie, from the Scilly Isles west of Great Britain, find a little girl near death on a deserted island, take her home, and care for her. She does not speak but clings to a teddy bear and a blanket with a German name sewn on it. Naming her Lucy Lost, Alfie and his parents and a kindly and wise doctor nurture her with love, music from a gramophone, and drawing material. Months go by, and still no one can uncover any details about her life. But World War I is raging, the British harbor fierce anti-German sentiments, and when news of the name on her blanket spreads, the family is shunned." (Kirkus)

"A framing device, built around the research of Lucy's future grandson, allows Morpurgo to shift among multiple narrators as he unspools the mystery of where she came from. Along the way, Morpurgo offers powerful descriptions of shipwreck, mass drowning, and devastation, as well as healing and growth." Pub Wkly

★ **Private** Peaceful. Scholastic Press 2004 202p $16.95; pa $5.99

Grades: 7 8 9 10   **Fic**

1. Great Britain -- Fiction 2. World War, 1914-1918 -- Fiction

ISBN 0-439-63648-5; 0-439-63653-1 pa

LC 2003-65347

First published 2003 in the United Kingdom

When Thomas Peaceful's older brother is forced to join the British Army, Thomas decides to sign up as well, although he is only fourteen years old, to prove himself to his country, his family, his childhood love, Molly, and himself

"In this World War I story, the terse and beautiful narrative of a young English soldier is as compelling about the world left behind as about the horrific daily details of trench warfare. . . . Suspense builds right to the end, which is shocking, honest, and unforgettable." Booklist

Morrison, Toni, 1931-

★ **Beloved**; a novel. by Toni Morrison; [with a new foreword by the author] Vintage International 2004 xix, 321 p.p

Grades: 9 10 11 12 Adult   **Fic**

1. Symbolism -- Fiction 2. African American women -- Fiction 3. Slavery -- United States -- Fiction 4. Mother-daughter relationship -- Fiction 5. Ohio -- Fiction 6. Infanticide -- Fiction 7. Women slaves -- Fiction

ISBN 1400033411; 9781400033416

LC 2004555136

Pulitzer Prize for Fiction (1988)

This novel takes place in "post-Civil War Ohio. [Toni] Morrison . . . has created [a] . . . world in this novel about ex-slaves haunted by violent memories. Before the war, Sethe, pregnant, sent her children away to their grandmother in Ohio, whose freedom had been paid for by their father. Sethe runs too, but when her 'owners' come to recapture her, she attempts to murder the children, succeeding with one, named

Beloved. This murder will (literally) haunt Sethe for the rest of her life and affect everyone around her." (Booklist)

This novel, "set in the third quarter of the 19th century, focuses on the life of the runaway slave woman Sethe and her struggle with the unspeakable pain of her past. Like Morrison's earlier novels, Beloved is marked by rich and lyrical language, narratives shot through with exotic and magical elements, and a fragmented structure that requires readers to participate in the telling." Benet's Reader's Ency of Am Lit

★ The **bluest** eye; with a new afterword by the author. Knopf 2005 215p $19.95

Grades: 11 12 Adult   **Fic**
 1. Ohio -- Fiction 2. African Americans -- Fiction
 ISBN 0-375-41155-0
          LC 93-43124

A reissue of the title first published 1970 by Holt, Rinehart & Winston

"This tragic study of a black adolescent girl's struggle to achieve white ideals of beauty and her consequent descent into madness was acclaimed as an eloquent indictment of some of the more subtle forms of racism in American society. Pecola Breedlove longs to have 'the bluest eye' and thus to be acceptable to her family, schoolmates, and neighbors, all of whom have convinced her that she is ugly."

"This tragic study of a black adolescent girl's struggle to achieve white ideals of beauty and her consequent descent into madness was acclaimed as an eloquent indictment of some of the more subtle forms of racism in American society. Pecola Breedlove longs to have 'the bluest eye' and thus to be acceptable to her family, schoolmates, and neighbors, all of whom have convinced her that she is ugly." Merriam-Webster's Ency of Lit

Sula. Knopf 1974 174p hardcover o.p. pa $14
Grades: 11 12 Adult   **Fic**
 1. Ohio -- Fiction 2. Poverty -- Fiction 3. Friendship -- Fiction 4. African Americans -- Fiction
 ISBN 0-394-48044-9; 1-4000-3343-8 pa

This "is the story of two black women friends and of their community of Medallion, Ohio. The community has been stunted and turned inward by the racism of the larger society. The rage and disordered lives of the townspeople are seen as a reaction to their stifled hopes. The novel follows the lives of Sula and Nel from childhood to maturity to death." Merriam-Webster's Ency of Lit

Moskowitz, Hannah

Gone, gone, gone. Pulse/Simon & Schuster 2012 251 p. (hardcover) $16.99
Grades: 9 10 11 12   **Fic**
 1. Grief -- Fiction 2. Bereavement -- Fiction 3. Gay teenagers -- Fiction 4. September 11 terrorist attacks, 2001 -- Fiction 5. Love stories 6. September 11 Terrorist Attacks, 2001 -- Fiction
 ISBN 9781442453128; 1442453125; 9781442407534
         LC 2011935726
Stonewall Honor Book (2013)

This book presents the story of the relationship between two 15-year-old boys, Craig and Lio, as they search for Craig's missing pets in the fall of 2002. Craig and Lio explore their feelings about the 2011 World Trade Center and Pentagon terrorist attacks and other current events as they look for the animals, relating these tragedies to losses in their own lives. "The Beltway sniper shootings and the attacks of 9/11 become the crucible for this exploration of teenage grief and love." (Kirkus Reviews)

"Craig is "unavailable" because he's hung up on his first boyfriend, who went nuts after 9/11. Lio is a survivor of childhood leukemia that killed his twin brother. Craig and Lio are powerfully drawn to each other, but can they overcome past hurts and move on? First-person narratives alternate in this raw, immediate love story set outside DC during the 2002 Beltway sniper attacks." Horn Book

★ **Teeth**; Hannah Moskowitz. Simon Pulse 2013 242 p. $17.99
Grades: 9 10 11 12   **Fic**
 1. Fantasy fiction 2. Mermaids and mermen -- Fiction 3. Mermen -- Fiction 4. Islands -- Fiction 5. Brothers -- Fiction 6. Loneliness -- Fiction 7. Supernatural -- Fiction 8. Cystic fibrosis -- Fiction
 ISBN 1442465328; 9781442449466; 9781442465329
         LC 2012019114

This novel, by Hannah Moskowitz, offers a "gritty, romantic modern fairy tale. . . . Rudy's . . . family moves to a remote island in a last attempt to save his sick younger brother. . . . Then he meets Diana, who makes him wonder what he even knows about love, and Teeth, who makes him question what he knows about anything. . . . He soon learns that Teeth has terrible secrets . . . that will force Rudy to choose between his own happiness and his brother's life." (Publisher's note)

Moulton, Courtney Allison

Angelfire; 1st ed. Katherine Tegen Books 2011 453 p. (trade bdg.) $17.99
Grades: 7 8 9 10   **Fic**
 1. Horror fiction 2. Horror stories 3. Souls -- Fiction 4. Youths' writings 5. Angels -- Fiction 6. Monsters -- Fiction 7. Reincarnation -- Fiction
 ISBN 9780062002327; 9780062002341
         LC 2010012821

A seventeen-year-old girl discovers that she has the reincarnated soul of an ancient warrior destined to battle the reapers --creatures who devour humans and send their souls to Hell. --Grades nine to twelve. -- (Bull Cent Child Books)

"The author has introduced a dark and compelling world of action and intrigue, albeit with enough 'normal' drama and humor sprinkled throughout to lighten it. . . . Older junior and senior high school readers will find themselves engrossed in the story until its powerful conclusion— then anxiously awaiting the second installment." Voice Youth Advocates

Mowll, Joshua

Operation Red Jericho; [illustrated by Benjamin Mowll, Julek Heller, Niroot Puttapipat] Candlewick Press 2005 271p il map (The Guild of Specialists) hardcover o.p. pa $8.99
Grades: 9 10 11 12   **Fic**
 1. Adventure fiction 2. Uncles -- Fiction 3. Siblings

-- Fiction
ISBN 0-7636-2634-1; 0-7636-3475-1 pa
LC 2005-45382

The posthumous papers of Rebecca MacKenzie document her adventures, along with her brother Doug, in 1920s China as the teenaged siblings are sent to live aboard their uncle's ship where they become involved in the dangerous activities of a mysterious secret society called the Honourable Guild of Specialists.

"Some readers may pore over the details in this novel; others will simply appreciate the comic adventure." SLJ

Includes bibliographical references
Other titles about Becca and Doug are:
Operation Storm City (2009)
Operation Typhoon Shore (2006)

Operation Storm City. Candlewick Press 2009 273p il (The Guild of Specialists) $16.99
Grades: 7 8 9 10　　　　　　　　　　Fic
1. Adventure fiction 2. China -- Fiction 3. Siblings -- Fiction
ISBN 978-0-7636-4224-2; 0-7636-4224-X
LC 2008-19703

Siblings Becca and Doug discover important clues to their missing parents' expedition route and the location of Ur-Can, the fabled Storm City, and they embark on a perilous journey to the Takla Makan desert, racing against their Guild enemies by steam train, riverboat, and airship across the Himalayas, trying to save not only their parents, but the entire planet.

"For readers who love adventure stories and can handle a greater level of complexity, this whirlwind of travel, fighting, and impending disaster is a great trip." Voice Youth Advocates

Operation typhoon shore. Candlewick Press 2006 272p il map (The Guild of Specialists) $15.99
Grades: 7 8 9 10　　　　　　　　　　Fic
1. Adventure fiction 2. China -- Fiction 3. Ships -- Fiction 4. Uncles -- Fiction 5. Siblings -- Fiction
ISBN 978-0-7636-3122-2; 0-7636-3122-1
LC 2006-47481

Sequel to Operation Red Jericho (2005)

In the spring of 1920, teenaged siblings Rebecca and Doug MacKenzie continue their adventures on their uncle's ship, sailing through a typhoon into the Celebes Sea in pursuit of a missing "gyrolabe" which may be connected to the disappearance of their parents.

"This book rolls along with plenty of action and fun. Readers will be captivated by the story line, but also will be intrigued by all of the sketches, photographs, newspaper clippings, and foldout information on technology." SLJ

Mullin, Mike
Ashfall. Tanglewood 2011 466p $16.99
Grades: 9 10 11 12　　　　　　　　　Fic
1. Science fiction 2. Volcanoes -- Fiction 3. Wilderness survival -- Fiction
ISBN 978-1-933718-55-2
LC 2011007133

"Mullin puts his characters through hell, depicting numerous deaths in detail. . . . There's also cannibalism and

a rape before the novel comes to a believable ending. . . . The book is well written and its protagonists are well-drawn, particularly the nontraditional and mechanically inclined Darla. Although more appropriate for older teens due to its violence, this is a riveting tale of survival." Publ Wkly

Sunrise; 3 Mike Mullin. Tanglewood Publishing 2014 546 p. (Ashfall Trilogy) (hardback) $17.99
Grades: 9 10 11 12　　　　　　　　　Fic
1. Dystopian fiction 2. Natural disasters -- Fiction 3. Science fiction 4. Survival -- Fiction 5. Volcanoes -- Fiction
ISBN 1939100011; 9781939100016
LC 2013050876

In this novel by Mike Mullin, the final book of the Ashfall Trilogy, "the Yellowstone supervolcano nearly wiped out the human race. Now, almost a year after the eruption, the survivors seem determined to finish the job. Communities wage war on each other, gangs of cannibals roam the countryside, and what little government survived the eruption has collapsed completely. The ham radio has gone silent. Sickness, cold, and starvation are the survivors' constant companions." (Publisher's note)

"The writing, even in transitory moments of peace, never lets readers forget that potential catastrophe lurks around every corner. A story about how hope is earned, as heartpounding as it is heart-wrenching." - Kirkus

Murdock, Catherine Gilbert
★ **Dairy** Queen; a novel. Houghton Mifflin 2006 275p $16
Grades: 7 8 9 10　　　　　　　　　　Fic
1. Football -- Fiction 2. Farm life -- Fiction
ISBN 0-618-68307-0
LC 2005-19077

After spending her summer running the family farm and training the quarterback for her school's rival football team, sixteen-year-old D.J. decides to go out for the sport herself, not anticipating the reactions of those around her.

"D. J.'s voice is funny, frank, and intelligent, and her story is not easily pigeonholed." Voice Youth Advocates

Other titles about D.J. Schwenk are:
Front and center (2009)
The off season (2007)

Front and center. Houghton Mifflin 2009 256p (The dairy queen trilogy) $16
Grades: 7 8 9 10　　　　　　　　　　Fic
1. Farm life -- Fiction 2. Basketball -- Fiction
ISBN 978-0-618-95982-2; 0-618-95982-3
LC 2009-24167

Sequel to: The off season (2007)

"In the third and final book . . . about farm girl, linebacker, and basketball star D.J. Schwenk, the self-aggrandizing heroine must decide her future: is she up to playing basketball for the Big Ten schools that are starting to recruit her, or should she choose a smaller college, where the game is less brutal but also less challenging? . . . D.J.'s voice is intimate and compelling, her story both universal and unique, familiar and eye-opening." Horn Book

The **off** season. Houghton Mifflin 2007 277p
$16

Grades: 7 8 9 10   **Fic**
   1. Football -- Fiction 2. Farm life -- Fiction
   ISBN 978-0-618-68695-7; 0-618-68695-9
                                        LC 2006029278
   Sequel to: Dairy Queen (2006)
   High school junior D.J. staggers under the weight of caring for her badly injured brother, her responsibilities on the
dairy farm, a changing relationship with her friend Brian,
and her own athletic aspirations.
   This "depicts a believably maturing D.J., a young woman whose character shines through even as she struggles to
find her voice. Readers will root for her at every tragicomic
turn." SLJ
   Followed by: Front and center (2009)

   Wisdom's kiss; a thrilling and romantic adventure, incorporating magic, villany and a cat. written
by Catherine Gilbert Murdock. Houghton Mifflin
2011 284p $16.99

Grades: 7 8 9 10   **Fic**
   1. Fairy tales 2. Cats -- Fiction 3. Orphans -- Fiction
   4. Soldiers -- Fiction 5. Princesses -- Fiction 6.
   Supernatural -- Fiction 7. Household employees --
   Fiction
   ISBN 978-0-547-56687-0; 0-547-56687-5
                                        LC 2011003708
   Princess Wisdom, who yearns for a life of adventure
beyond the kingdom of Montagne, Tips, a soldier keeping
his true life secret from his family, Fortitude, an orphaned
maid who longs for Tips, and Magic the cat form an uneasy
alliance as they try to save the kingdom from certain destruction. Told through diaries, memoirs, encyclopedia entries,
letters, biographies, and a stage play.
   "Packed with double entendres, humorous dialogue
and situations, and a black cat that will capture the reader's
imagination, this is a joyful, timeless fantasy that teens will
savor." Booklist

Murphy, Julie
   Dumplin' Julie Murphy. Balzer + Bray, an im-
print of HarperCollins Publishers 2015 384 p. (hardcover) $17.99 **Fic**
   1. Beauty contests -- Fiction 2. Overweight persons
   -- Fiction 3. Texas -- Fiction 4. Friendship -- Fiction
   5. Self-esteem -- Fiction 6. Dating (Social customs)
   -- Fiction
   ISBN 9780062327185
                                        LC 2014041047
   This novel, by Julie Murphy, follows an overweight teen
girl. "Dubbed 'Dumplin'' by her former beauty queen mom,
Willowdean has always been at home in her own skin . . .
until she meets Private School Bo, a hot former jock. . . .
Instead of finding new heights of self-assurance in her re-
lationship with Bo, Will starts to doubt herself. So she sets
out to take back her confidence by doing the most horrifying
thing she can imagine: entering the Miss Teen Blue Bonnet
Pageant." (Publisher's note)
   "Unfortunately, Murphy loses her step and undermines
her main point in the mournful, cringeworthy details of
Lucy's death and life, which are blamed on extreme fatness

rather than unfairness. In the end, it's more liberating than
oppressive, with bits of humor and a jubilant pageant take-
over by beauty rebels to crown this unusual book about a fat
character." Kirkus

Murray, Yxta Maya
   The **good** girl's guide to getting kidnapped. Ra-
zorbill 2010 251p $16.99; pa $9.99
Grades: 9 10 11 12   **Fic**
   1. Gangs -- Fiction 2. California -- Fiction 3.
   Kidnapping -- Fiction 4. Foster home care -- Fiction 5.
   Mexican Americans -- Fiction
   ISBN 978-1-59514-272-6; 1-59514-272-X; 978-1-
   59514-341-9 pa; 1-59514-341-6 pa
                                        LC 2009-21091
   Fifteen-year-old Michelle Pena, born into a powerful Mexican American gang family, tries to reconcile her
gangster legacy with the girl she has become—a nationally
ranked runner and academic superstar.
   This book "is action-packed, as it raises relevant questions of identity and loyalty. This fast-paced story, heavy
with street dialogue and slang, should have ample teen appeal." Publ Wkly

Mussi, Sarah
   ★ The **door** of no return. Margaret K. McElder-
ry Books 2008 394p $17.99; pa $8.99
Grades: 8 9 10 11 12   **Fic**
   1. Adventure fiction 2. Ghana -- Fiction 3. Blacks
   -- Fiction 4. Homicide -- Fiction 5. Great Britain --
   Fiction 6. Buried treasure -- Fiction
   ISBN 978-1-4169-1550-8; 1-4169-1550-8; 978-1-
   4169-6825-2 pa; 1-4169-6825-3 pa
                                        LC 2007-18670
   Sixteen-year-old Zac never believed his grandfather's
tales about their enslaved ancestors being descended from an
African king, but when his grandfather is murdered and the
villains come after Zac, he sets out for Ghana to find King
Baktu's long-lost treasure before the murderers do.
   "This exciting narrative takes place in England and Africa; in jungles, dark caves, and on the sea. . . . Overall, this
is a complex, masterful story for confident readers." SLJ

Myers, Walter Dean, 1937-2014
   All the right stuff; by Walter Dean Myers. Harp-
erTeen 2012 213 p.
Grades: 8 9 10 11 12   **Fic**
   1. Bildungsromans 2. Mentoring -- Fiction 3. Soup
   kitchens -- Fiction 4. Social contract -- Fiction 5.
   African Americans -- Harlem (New York, N.Y.) --
   Fiction 6. Coming of age -- Fiction 7. Conduct of life
   -- Fiction 8. African Americans -- Fiction 9. Harlem
   (New York, N.Y.) -- Fiction
   ISBN 9780061960871; 9780061960888
                                        LC 2011024251
   This novel tells the story of Paul DuPree, a 16-year-old
boy who "has taken on two jobs: work in a soup kitchen
and the required mentoring of a young basketball player. At
the soup kitchen, he meets Elijah Jones, the project's driving
force and resident philosopher," who helps Paul understand
"how one person's decisions and actions might affect the en-

tire community" as he mentors teenage mother Keisha and comes to terms with the death of his father." (Kirkus)

★ **Darius** & Twig; Walter Dean Myers. 1st ed. Harper, an imprint of HarperCollinsPublishers 2013 208 p. (hardcover) $17.99
Grades: 8 9 10 11 12   Fic
1. Friendship -- Fiction 2. Harlem (New York, N.Y.) -- Fiction 3. Running -- Fiction 4. Authorship -- Fiction 5. Best friends -- Fiction 6. New York (N.Y.) -- Fiction 7. African Americans -- Fiction 8. Dominican Americans -- Fiction
ISBN 0061728233; 9780061728235; 9780061728242
                                          LC 2012050678
Coretta Scott King Honor Book: Author (2014)
In this book by Walter Dean Myers, "Harlem teenager Darius, a writer, wants to get out of his neighborhood and make it to college, but his grades aren't good enough. He's hoping that if he can get a story published, he might nab a college scholarship. His best friend Twig is a track star, and sees athletics as his escape. Both are skeptical of the hype they are fed about how hard work pays off, and they face obstacles ranging from school bullies . . . to indifferent educators." (Publishers Weekly)
"This encouraging text may inspire teens who feel trapped by their surroundings...Told in Darius's voice, the prose is poetic but concise. This would be a worthwhile addition to any middle or high school media center or public library shelf and would make a valuable book for discussion in a middle school classroom.—" VOYA

Dope sick. HarperTeen/Amistad 2009 186p $16.99; lib bdg $17.89
Grades: 8 9 10 11 12   Fic
1. Drug abuse -- Fiction 2. Supernatural -- Fiction 3. African Americans -- Fiction 4. Harlem (New York, N.Y.) -- Fiction
ISBN 978-0-06-121477-6; 0-06-121477-9; 978-0-06-121478-3 lib bdg; 0-06-121478-7 lib bdg
                                          LC 2008-10568
Seeing no way out of his difficult life in Harlem, seventeen-year-old Jeremy "Lil J" Dance flees into a house after a drug deal goes awry and meets a weird man who shows different turning points in Lil J's life when he could have made better choices.
"Myers uses street-style lingo to cover Lil J's sorry history of drug use, jail time, irresponsible fatherhood and his own childhood grief. A didn't-see-that-coming ending wraps up the story on a note of well-earned hope and will leave readers with plenty to think about." Publ Wkly

★ **Fallen** angels; Walter Dean Myers. Scholastic Paperbacks 2008 336 p. hardcover o.p. (pbk.) $7.99
Grades: 8 9 10 11 12 Adult   Fic
1. Vietnam War, 1961-1975 -- Fiction 2. African American soldiers -- Fiction
ISBN 9780545055765; 0545055768
First published 1988
ALA YALSA Margaret A. Edwards Award (1994)
"Black, seventeen, perceptive and sensitive, Richie (the narrator) has enlisted and been sent to Vietnam; in telling the story of his year of active service, Richie is candid about the horror of killing and the fear of being killed, the fear and bravery and confusion and tragedy of the war." Bull Cent Child Books
"Except for occasional outbursts, the narration is remarkably direct and understated; and the dialogue, with morbid humor sometimes adding comic relief, is steeped in natural vulgarity, without which verisimilitude would be unthinkable. In fact, the foul talk, which serves as the story's linguistic setting, is not nearly as obscene as the events." Horn Book

Game. HarperTeen 2008 218p $16.99; lib bdg $17.89
Grades: 8 9 10 11 12   Fic
1. School stories 2. Basketball -- Fiction 3. Czech Americans -- Fiction 4. African Americans -- Fiction 5. Harlem (New York, N.Y.) -- Fiction
ISBN 978-0-06-058294-4; 978-0-06-058295-1 lib bdg
                                          LC 2007-18370
If Harlem high school senior Drew Lawson is going to realize his dream of playing college, then professional, basketball, he will have to improve at being coached and being a team player, especially after a new—white—student threatens to take the scouts' attention away from him.
"Basketball fans will love the long passages of detailed court action. . . . The authentic thoughts of a strong, likable, African American teen whose anxieties, sharp insights, and belief in his own abilities will captivate readers of all backgrounds." Booklist

Invasion! Walter Dean Myers. Scholastic Press 2013 224 p. $17.99
Grades: 7 8 9 10   Fic
1. Friendship 2. African American soldiers 3. Normandy (France), Attack on, 1944 4. War -- Fiction 5. Soldiers -- Fiction 6. African American soldiers -- Fiction 7. France -- History -- 20th century -- Fiction 8. Normandy (France) -- History 9. Normandy (France) -- History -- 20th century -- Fiction 10. Segregation -- United States -- History -- 20th century -- Fiction 11. World War, 1939-1945 -- Campaigns -- France -- Normandy -- Fiction 12. Segregation -- United States -- History -- 20th century 13. World War, 1939-1945 -- Campaigns -- France -- Normandy 14. World War, 1939-1945 -- Participation, African American 15. United States -- Armed Forces -- African Americans -- History -- 20th century
ISBN 0545384281; 9780545384285; 9780545384292; 9780545576598

                                          LC 2013005595
In this book by Walter Dean Myers, "old friends Josiah 'Woody' Wedgewood and Marcus Perry see each other in England prior to the invasion of Normandy. Woody is with the 29th Infantry, and Marcus, who's black, is with the Transportation Corps, the segregation of their Virginia hometown following them right into wartime. Their friendship frames the story, as the two occasionally encounter each other in the horrific days ahead." (Kirkus Reviews)
"Myers eloquently conveys how exhausting war is physically and emotionally. . . . [T]his novel can be hard to read, but it is also hard to put down." SLJ

Juba! Walter Dean Myers. HarperTeen 2015 208 p. illustrations (hardback) $17.99

Grades: 6 7 8 9   **Fic**

1. African American dancers 2. Dancers -- Fiction 3. Prejudices -- Fiction 4. New York (N.Y.) -- History -- 19th century -- Fiction 5. London (England) -- History -- 19th century -- Fiction 6. Great Britain -- History -- Victoria, 1837-1901 -- Fiction 7. African Americans -- New York (State) -- New York -- Fiction 8. Five Points (New York, N.Y.) -- History -- 19th century -- Fiction

ISBN 9780062112712; 0062112716

LC 2014042527

This historical novel by Walter Dean Myers "is based on the true story of the meteoric rise of an immensely talented young black dancer, William Henry Lane, who influenced today's tap, jazz, and step dancing. . . . The novel includes photographs, maps, and other images from Juba's time and an afterword from Walter Dean Myers's wife about the writing process." (Publisher's note)

"Juba is presented as a thoughtful, proud young man who means well and works hard; Myers gives him a direct and sympathetic voice, depicting the struggles and successes of his short life in the Five Points neighborhood of New York City, and later in London, with warmth and convincing detail." Pub Wkly

Kick; [by] Walter Dean Myers and Ross Workman. HarperTeen 2011 197p $16.99; lib bdg $17.89

Grades: 7 8 9 10   **Fic**

1. Police -- Fiction 2. Soccer -- Fiction 3. Mentoring -- Fiction 4. New Jersey -- Fiction 5. Family life -- Fiction

ISBN 978-0-06-200489-5; 0-06-200489-1; 978-0-06-200490-1 lib bdg; 0-06-200490-5 lib bdg

LC 2010-18441

Told in their separate voices, thirteen-year-old soccer star Kevin and police sergeant Brown, who knew his father, try to keep Kevin out of juvenile hall after he is arrested on very serious charges.

"Workman is a genuine talent, writing short, declarative sentences that move that narrative forward with assurance and a page-turning tempo. Myers, of course, is a master. . . . The respective voices and characters play off each other as successfully as a high-stakes soccer match." Booklist

Lockdown. Amistad 2010 247p $16.99; lib bdg $17.89

Grades: 8 9 10 11 12   **Fic**

1. Old age -- Fiction 2. Friendship -- Fiction 3. African Americans -- Fiction 4. Juvenile delinquency -- Fiction

ISBN 978-0-06-121480-6; 0-06-121480-9; 978-0-06-121481-3 lib bdg; 0-06-121481-7 lib bdg

LC 2009-7287

Coretta Scott King Author Award honor book, 2011

Teenage Reese, serving time at a juvenile detention facility, gets a lesson in making it through hard times from an unlikely friend with a harrowing past.

"Reese's first-person narration rings with authenticity. . . . Myers' storytelling skills ensure that the messages he offers are never heavy-handed." Booklist

★ **Monster**; illustrations by Christopher Myers. HarperCollins Pubs. 1999 281p il $14.95; lib bdg $14.89; pa $8.99

Grades: 7 8 9 10   **Fic**

1. Trials -- Fiction 2. African Americans -- Fiction

ISBN 0-06-028077-8; 0-06-028078-6 lib bdg; 0-06-440731-4 pa

LC 98-40958

Michael L. Printz Award, 2000

While on trial as an accomplice to a murder, sixteen-year-old Steve Harmon records his experiences in prison and in the courtroom in the form of a film script as he tries to come to terms with the course his life has taken.

"Balancing courtroom drama and a sordid jailhouse setting with flashbacks to the crime, Myers adeptly allows each character to speak for him or herself, leaving readers to judge for themselves the truthfulness of the defendants, witnesses, lawyers, and, most compellingly, Steve himself." Horn Book Guide

Oh, Snap! by Walter Dean Myers. Scholastic 2013 128 p. (hardcover) $17.99

Grades: 6 7 8 9   **Fic**

1. Theft 2. Journalists

ISBN 0439916291; 9780439916295

This is the fourth book in Walter Dean Myers's Cruisers series. Here, the "four budding urban journalists are psyched that their underground publication, 'The Cruiser,' was named the third-best school newspaper in the city, an honor that doesn't sit well with the official school newspaper, which ups its game. This pushes narrator Zander to hastily get involved with the case of Phat Tony, a wannabe rapper classmate who may be involved in a robbery." (Booklist)

On a clear day; Walter Dean Myers. First edition Crown Books for Young Readers, an imprint of Random House Children's Books 2014 256 p. (hardcover) $17.99

Grades: 6 7 8 9 10   **Fic**

1. Science fiction 2. Dystopian fiction 3. Teenagers -- Fiction 4. Social action -- Fiction 5. Interpersonal relations -- Fiction 6. England -- Fiction

ISBN 0385387539; 9780385387538; 9780385387545

LC 2013046708

In this book, by Walter Dean Myers, "[y]oung heroes decide that they are not too young or too powerless to change their world. . . . It is 2035. Teens, armed only with their ideals, must wage war on the power elite. Dahlia is a Low Gater. . . . The Gaters live in closed safe communities, protected from the Sturmers, mercenary thugs. And the C-8, a consortium of giant companies, control global access to finance, media, food, water, and energy resources." (Publisher's note)

"Readers are left to question what actions are possible, what actions are needed and what actions are right in a world where inaction is an impossibility. A clarion call from a beloved, much-missed master." Kirkus

A star is born; Walter Dean Myers. Scholastic 2012 176 p. (Cruisers) (ebook) $17.99; (hardcover) $17.99

Grades: 6 7 8 9   **Fic**
1. School stories 2. Autism -- Fiction 3. Siblings
-- Fiction 4. Gifted children -- Fiction 5. Schools
-- Fiction 6. Theater -- Fiction 7. Middle schools --
Fiction 8. African Americans -- Fiction 9. Brothers and
sisters -- Fiction 10. Harlem (New York, N.Y.) -- Fiction
ISBN 9780545512688; 9780439916288
                                        LC 2011030333
This book is the third in the Cruisers series. "For 14-year-
old LaShonda Powell, real life is a lot tougher than solving
for x and y in algebra class. She's been offered a full scholarship to the Virginia Woolf Society Program for Young Ladies, thanks to her costume designs for the recent class play,
and if she completes the program, she'll qualify for future
college scholarships. The problem is that LaShonda lives in
a group home with her autistic brother, Chris, and the two
are inseparable." (Kirkus)

★ **Sunrise** over Fallujah. Scholastic Press 2008
290p $17.99
Grades: 8 9 10 11 12   **Fic**
1. Iraq War, 2003- -- Fiction 2. African Americans --
Fiction
ISBN 978-0-439-91624-0; 0-439-91624-0
                                        LC 2007-25444
"Instead of heading to college as his father wishes, Robin leaves Harlem and joins the army to stand up for his country after 9/11. While stationed in Iraq with a war looming
that he hopes will be averted, he begins writing letters home
to his parents and to his Uncle Richie. . . . Myers brilliantly
freeze-frames the opening months of the current Iraq War by
realistically capturing its pivotal moments in 2003 and creating a vivid setting. Memorable characters share instances of
wry levity that balance the story without deflecting its serious tone." SLJ

Myracle, Lauren, 1969-
★ **Bliss.** Amulet Books 2008 444p $16.95
Grades: 9 10 11 12   **Fic**
1. Horror fiction 2. School stories 3. Occultism --
Fiction 4. Atlanta (Ga.) -- Fiction
ISBN 978-0-8109-7071-7; 0-8109-7071-6
                                        LC 2007-50036
Having grown up in a California commune, Bliss sees
her aloof grandmother's Atlanta world as a foreign country,
but she is determined to be nice as a freshman at an elite high
school, which makes her the perfect target for Sandy, a girl
obsessed with the occult.
"Catering to teens with a taste for horror, this carefully
plotted occult thriller set in 1969-1970 combines genre staples with creepy period particulars." Publ Wkly

The **infinite** moment of us; by Lauren Myracle.
Amulet Books 2013 336 p. (hardback) $17.95
Grades: 9 10 11 12   **Fic**
1. Love stories 2. Foster children -- Fiction 3. Love
-- Fiction 4. Atlanta (Ga.) -- Fiction 5. Family life --
Georgia -- Fiction 6. Dating (Social customs) -- Fiction
7. Assertiveness (Psychology) -- Fiction
ISBN 1419707930; 9781419707933
                                        LC 2013017135

This book is a love story between two high school graduates. "Poised and accomplished, Wren has always done what
her parents have expected of her, while Charlie is a foster
child, self-conscious about his often unpleasant upbringing,
but fiercely protective of his current family." The story is an
"account of two young people whose insecurities and personal histories weigh on the romance they work to build with
each other." (Publishers Weekly)

Peace, love, and baby ducks. Dutton Children's
Books 2009 292p $16.99; pa $8.99
Grades: 8 9 10 11 12   **Fic**
1. Sisters -- Fiction 2. Atlanta (Ga.) -- Fiction
ISBN 978-0-525-47743-3; 0-525-47743-8; 978-0-14-
241527-6 pa; 0-14-241527-8 pa
                                        LC 2008-34221
Fifteen-year-old Carly's summer volunteer experience makes her feel more real than her life of privilege in
Atlanta ever did, but her younger sister starts high school
pretending to be what she is not, and both find their
relationships suffering.
"Myracle empathetically explores issues of socioeconomic class, sibling rivalry, and parental influence in a story
that is deeper and more nuanced than the title and cutesy
cover." Booklist

Shine. Amulet Books 2011 359p $16.95
Grades: 10 11 12   **Fic**
1. Friendship -- Fiction 2. Hate crimes -- Fiction 3.
Homosexuality -- Fiction 4. North Carolina -- Fiction
ISBN 0-8109-8417-2; 978-0-8109-8417-2
                                        LC 2010-45017
When her best friend falls victim to a vicious hate crime,
sixteen-year-old Cat sets out to discover the culprits in her
small North Carolina town.
"Readers will find themselves thinking about Cat's complicated rural community long after the mystery has been
solved." Publ Wkly

Ttyl; by Lauren Myracle. Amulet Books 2014
182 p. (pbk.) $8.95
Grades: 9 10 11 12   **Fic**
1. School stories 2. Female friendship -- Fiction 3.
Schools -- Fiction 4. Friendship -- Fiction 5. High
schools -- Fiction 6. Instant messaging -- Fiction 7.
Interpersonal relations -- Fiction
ISBN 1419711423; 9781419711428
                                        LC 2013043345
Sequel: ttfn
This novel by Lauren Myracle "and its sequels follow
the ups and downs of high school for the winsome threesome, three very different but very close friends: wild Maddie (mad maddie), bubbly Angela (SnowAngel), and reserved Zoe (zoegirl). Through teacher crushes, cross-country moves, bossy Queen Bees, incriminating party pics, and
other bumps along the way, author Lauren Myracle explores
the many potholes of teenagedom." (Publisher's note)

Yolo; Lauren Myracle. Amulet Books 2014 208
p. (Internet girls, the) (hardback) $16.95
Grades: 9 10 11 12   **Fic**
1. Friendship -- Fiction 2. Teenage girls -- Fiction 3.

Best friends -- Fiction 4. Instant messaging -- Fiction 5. Interpersonal relations -- Fiction 6. Colleges and universities -- Fiction

ISBN 1419708716; 9781419708718

LC 2014014986

Sequel to: Ttfn

In this young adult novel by Lauren Myracle, part of The Internet Girls series, "it's freshman year of college for the winsome threesome, and *everything* is different. For one, the best friends are facing their first semester apart. Way, way apart. Maddie's in California, Zoe's in Ohio, and Angela's back in Georgia." (Publisher's note)

"The story, which can stand independently from the rest of the Internet Girls series, offers readers realistic, engaging, and provocative perspectives on scary first semesters away from home and sage advice about drinking, partying, and shutting down socially, all without ever leaving the perfectly crafted text-message flow." Booklist

Na, An

★ **A step** from heaven. Front St. 2000 156p $15.95

Grades: 7 8 9 10   **Fic**

1. Family life 2. Korean Americans 3. Family life -- Fiction 4. Emigration and immigration 5. Korean Americans -- Fiction

ISBN 1-88691-058-8

LC 00-41083

Michael L. Printz Award, 2002

A young Korean girl and her family find it difficult to learn English and adjust to life in America. "Age ten and up." (N Y Times Book Rev)

"This isn't a quick read, especially at the beginning when the child is trying to decipher American words and customs, but the coming-of-age drama will grab teens and make them think of their own conflicts between home and outside. As in the best writing, the particulars make the story universal." Booklist

★ **Wait** for me. Putnam 2006 169p hardcover o.p. pa $7.99

Grades: 8 9 10 11 12   **Fic**

1. Deaf -- Fiction 2. Sisters -- Fiction 3. Korean Americans -- Fiction 4. Mother-daughter relationship -- Fiction

ISBN 0-399-24275-9; 0-14-240918-9 pa

LC 2005-30931

As her senior year in high school approaches, Mina yearns to find her own path in life but working at the family business, taking care of her little sister, and dealing with her mother's impossible expectations are as stifling as the southern California heat, until she falls in love with a man who offers a way out.

"This is a well-crafted tale, sensitively told. . . . The mother-daughter conflict will resonate with teens of any culture who have wrestled parents for the right to choose their own paths." Bull Cent Child Books

Nadol, Jen

The **mark**. Bloomsbury 2010 228p $16.99

Grades: 9 10 11 12   **Fic**

1. Death -- Fiction 2. Kansas -- Fiction 3. Orphans --

Fiction 4. Clairvoyance -- Fiction 5. Fate and fatalism -- Fiction

ISBN 978-1-59990-431-3; 1-59990-431-4

LC 2009-16974

While in Kansas living with an aunt she never knew existed and taking a course in philosophy, sixteen-year-old Cass struggles to learn what, if anything, she should do with her ability to see people marked to die within a day's time.

"Nadol's story is more than a modern take on the Cassandra story of Greek myth, and the author uses her protagonist's moral torment (and a philosophy course she takes) to touch on schools of philosophical thought, from Aristotle to Plato. As in life, there are no tidy endings, but the engrossing narration and realistic characters create a deep, lingering story." Publ Wkly

Followed by The vision (2011)

The **vision**. Bloomsbury Children's Books 2011 232p $16.99

Grades: 9 10 11 12   **Fic**

1. Death -- Fiction 2. Orphans -- Fiction 3. Illinois -- Fiction 4. Clairvoyance -- Fiction 5. Fate and fatalism -- Fiction 6. Undertakers and undertaking -- Fiction

ISBN 978-1-59990-597-6

LC 2011004927

Sequel to The mark (2010)

Seventeen-year-old Cassie, now working in a funeral home on the outskirts of Chicago, continues to try to learn about death and her ability to identify people who will soon die, but her efforts to get help from others like herself only prove that she is on her own.

"For those willing to ponder difficult questions and appreciate the opportunity to come to their own conclusions, Cassie's visions will resonate long after the last page is turned." Kirkus

Naidoo, Beverley

★ **Burn** my heart. HarperCollins 2009 209p $15.99; lib bdg $16.89

Grades: 7 8 9 10 11 12   **Fic**

1. Kenya -- Fiction 2. Friendship -- Fiction 3. Race relations -- Fiction

ISBN 978-0-06-143297-2; 0-06-143297-0; 978-0-06-143298-9 lib bdg; 0-06-143298-9 lib bdg

LC 2008-928322

First published 2007 in the United Kingdom

This "is an interesting story of which few people will be aware but might wish to know more. This solid novel would be a good multicultural addition to a teen collection." Voice Youth Advocates

Nance, Andrew

Return to Daemon Hall: evil roots; with illustrations by Coleman Polhemus. Henry Holt 2011 240p il $16.99

Grades: 7 8 9 10   **Fic**

1. Horror fiction 2. Authors -- Fiction 3. Contests -- Fiction 4. Authorship -- Fiction 5. Storytelling -- Fiction

ISBN 978-0-8050-8748-2; 0-8050-8748-6

LC 2010048609

Sequel to: Daemon Hall (2007)

Wade and Demarius go to author Ian Tremblin's home as judges of the second writing contest but soon are mysteriously transported to Daemon Hall, where they and the three finalists must tell—and act out—the stories each has written.

"Polhemus' stark artwork builds the mood, with heavy lines and crosshatching complementing the campfire nature of the tales." Kirkus

Napoli, Donna Jo, 1948-

Beast. Atheneum Bks. for Young Readers 2000 260p hardcover o.p. pa $8

Grades: 7 8 9 10   **Fic**
  1. Fairy tales 2. Iran -- Fiction
  ISBN 0-689-83589-2; 0-689-87005-1 pa
                    LC 99-89923

"The reader is immersed in the imagery and spirituality of ancient Persia. . . . Although Napoli uses Farsi (Persian) and Arabic words in the text (there is a glossary), this only adds to the texture and richness of her remarkable piece of writing." Book Rep

The **magic** circle. Dutton Children's Bks. 1993 118p hardcover o.p. pa $4.99

Grades: 9 10 11 12   **Fic**
  1. Fairy tales 2. Witchcraft -- Fiction
  ISBN 0-525-45127-7; 0-14-037439-6 pa
                  LC 92-27008

After learning sorcery to become a healer, a good-hearted woman is turned into a witch by evil spirits and she fights their power until her encounter with Hansel and Gretel years later

"The strength of Napoli's writing and the clarity of her vision make this story fresh and absorbing. A brilliantly conceived and beautifully executed novel that is sure to be appreciated by thoughtful readers." SLJ

Storm; Donna Jo Napoli. Simon & Schuster 2014 350 p. (hardback) $17.99

Grades: 8 9 10 11 12   **Fic**
  1. Noah's ark -- Fiction 2. Survival after airplane accidents, shipwrecks, etc. -- Fiction 3. Deluge -- Fiction 4. Animals -- Fiction 5. Survival -- Fiction
  ISBN 1481403028; 9781481403023
              LC 2013026808

National Jewish Book Award: Children's and Young Adult (2014)

This young adult novel, by Donna Jo Napoli, is a reimagining of the Noah flood myth. "After days of downpour, her family lost, Sebah . . . is tempted just to die in the flames rather than succumb to a slow, watery death. Instead, she and Aban build a raft. What they find on the stormy seas is beyond imagining: a gigantic ark. But Sebah does not know what she'll find on board, and Aban is too weak to leave their raft." (Publisher's note)

"Sixteen-year-old Sebah, a Canaanite girl, survives a massive flood that kills her family. As the rains continue, she encounters a giant boat--Noah's ark. Exhausted and grief-stricken, Sebah finds herself in a cage with a pair of bonobos, with whom she soon bonds. The characters that Napoli creates to flesh out her retelling of the classic story add depth." Horn Book

Nayeri, Daniel

Another Faust; [by] Daniel & Dina Nayeri. Candlewick Press 2009 387p $16.99

Grades: 9 10 11 12   **Fic**
  1. School stories 2. Devil -- Fiction 3. Supernatural -- Fiction 4. New York (N.Y.) -- Fiction
  ISBN 978-0-7636-3707-1; 0-7636-3707-6
             LC 2008-940873

Years after vanishing, five teens reappear with a strange governess, and when they enter New York City's most prestigious high school, they soar to suspicious heights with the help of their benefactor's extraordinary "gifts."

"The writing is clever and stylish . . . It's an absorbing, imaginative read, with a tense climax." Publ Wkly

Followed by Another Pan (2010)

Another Pan; [by] Daniel & Dina Nayeri. Candlewick Press 2010 393p $16.99

Grades: 9 10 11 12   **Fic**
  1. Fantasy fiction 2. Peter Pan (Fictional character)
  ISBN 978-0-7636-3712-5
             LC 2010-6606

Companion volume to Another Faust (2009)

While attending an elite prep school where their father is a professor, Wendy and John Darling discover a book which opens the door to other worlds, to Egyptian myths long thought impossible, and to the home of an age-old darkness.

"Teens who like their fantasy layered and with multifaceted characters will enjoy this thought-provoking read." SLJ

Naylor, Phyllis Reynolds

Intensely Alice. Atheneum Books for Young Readers 2009 269p $16.99; pa $6.99

Grades: 7 8 9 10   **Fic**
  1. Summer -- Fiction 2. Maryland -- Fiction
  ISBN 978-1-4169-7551-9; 1-4169-7551-9; 978-1-4169-7554-0 pa; 1-4169-7554-3 pa
             LC 2008-49047

During the summer between her junior and senior years of high school, Maryland teenager Alice McKinley volunteers at a local soup kitchen, tries to do "something wild" without getting arrested, and wonders if her trip to Chicago to visit boyfriend Patrick will result in a sleepover.

"As candid, funny, and touching as the rest of the series." Booklist

Neely, Cynthia

Unearthly; [by] Cynthia Hand. HarperTeen 2011 435p $17.99

Grades: 7 8 9 10   **Fic**
  1. School stories 2. Angels -- Fiction 3. Moving -- Fiction 4. Wyoming -- Fiction 5. Supernatural -- Fiction
  ISBN 978-0-06-199616-0; 0-06-199616-5
             LC 2010-17849

Sixteen-year-old Clara Gardner's purpose as an angel-blood begins to manifest itself, forcing her family to pull up stakes and move to Jackson, Wyoming, where she learns that danger and heartbreak come with her powers.

"Hand avoids overt discussion of religion while telling an engaging and romantic tale with a solid backstory. Her characters deal realistically with the uncertainty of being on

the cusp of maturity without wrapping themselves in angst."
Publ Wkly

Nelson, Blake

Recovery Road. Scholastic Press 2011 310p
$17.99

Grades: 9 10 11 12   **Fic**
1. Alcoholism -- Fiction 2. Drug abuse -- Fiction 3.
Drug addicts -- Rehabilitation -- Fiction
ISBN 978-0-545-10729-7; 0-545-10729-6
LC 2010-31288

"Madeline is sent away to Spring Meadows to help with
a drinking and rage problem she has. It's a pretty intense
place, but there is the weekly movie night in town--where
Madeline meets Stewart, who's at another rehab place nearby. They fall for each other during a really crazy time in their
lives. Madeline gets out and tries to get back on her feet,
waiting for Stewart to join her. When he does, though, it's
not the ideal recovery world Madeline dreamed of." (Publisher's note)

The author "gives a hard, honest appraisal of addiction,
its often-fatal consequences, and the high probability of
relapse. This is an important story that pulls no punches."
Publ Wkly

Nelson, Jandy

★ **I'll** give you the sun; by Jandy Nelson. Dial
Books for Young Readers 2014 384 p. (hardcover)
$17.99

Grades: 9 10 11 12   **Fic**
1. Love stories 2. Twins -- Fiction 3. Gays -- Fiction
4. Death -- Fiction 5. Grief -- Fiction 6. Artists --
Fiction 7. California -- Fiction
ISBN 0803734964; 9780803734968
LC 2014001596

Michael L. Printz Award (2015)

Stonewall Honor Book: Children's & Young Adult Literature (2015)

In this novel by Jandy Nelson, "Jude and her twin brother, Noah, are incredibly close. At thirteen, isolated Noah
draws constantly and is falling in love with the charismatic
boy next door, while daredevil Jude cliff-dives and wears
red-red lipstick and does the talking for both of them. But
three years later, Jude and Noah are barely speaking. Something has happened to wreck the twins in different and dramatic ways." (Publisher's note)

Nelson, Marilyn, 1946-

American ace; Marilyn Nelson. Dial Books
2016 128 p. illustrations (hardcover) $17.99

Grades: 8 9 10 11 12   **Fic**
1. Fathers -- Fiction 2. Family secrets -- Fiction 3.
Novels in verse 4. Identity -- Fiction 5. Family life --
Fiction 6. Fathers and sons -- Fiction 7. Racially mixed
people -- Fiction 8. United States. Army Air Forces.
Bombardment Group, 477th -- Fiction
ISBN 9780803733053; 0803733054
LC 2015000851

In this novel, by Marilyn Nelson, "Connor's grandmother leaves his dad a letter when she dies, and the letter's
confession shakes their tight-knit Italian-American family:
The man who raised Dad is not his birth father. But the only

clues to this birth father's identity are a class ring and a pair
of pilot's wings. And so Connor takes it upon himself to
investigate. What Connor discovers will lead him and his
father to a new, richer understanding of race, identity, and
each other." (Publisher's note)

"The author's meticulous verse is the perfect vehicle to
convey the devastating fragility of racial and familial identity
in an America where interracial love is still divided through
the problem of the color line. Readers will join Nelson's protagonist in quietly hoping for that healing, too." Kirkus

Nelson, Vaunda Micheaux

No crystal stair; a documentary novel of the life
and work of Lewis Michaux, Harlem bookseller. by
Vaunda Micheaux Nelson; art work by R. Gregory
Christie. Carolrhoda Lab 2012 188p. ill.

Grades: 6 7 8 9 10 11 12   **Fic**
1. Harlem (New York, N.Y.) 2. African American
authors 3. Booksellers and bookselling 4. Harlem
(New York, N.Y.) 5. African Americans -- Books and
reading
ISBN 9780761361695
LC 2011021251

Coretta Scott King Author Honor Book (2013)

This "biographical novel presents the life and work of a
man whose Harlem bookstore became an intellectual, literary haven for African Americans from 1939 until 1975. [The
book proceeds t]hrough alternating voices of actual family
members, acquaintances, journalists, and the subject himself, [Lewis] Michaux. . . . Influenced by the nationalism of
Marcus Garvey and the intellect of Frederick Douglass, he
believed that black people needed to educate themselves . . .
[and h]e opened the National Memorial African Bookstore.
. . . He accumulated works by black writers and talked to
customers and passersby about cultural awareness and self-
improvement. His bookstore attracted Harlem residents;
civil-rights activists, including Malcolm X and Muhammad
Ali; and political attention." (School Libr J)

Neri, G.

Knockout Games; by G. Neri. Carolrhoda Lab
2014 304 p. (trade hard cover: alk. paper) $17.95

Grades: 7 8 9 10   **Fic**
1. Violence -- Fiction 2. Teenagers -- Fiction 3. Gangs
-- Fiction
ISBN 1467732699; 9781467732697
LC 2013036855

In this young adult novel by G. Neri, "for Kalvin Barnes,
the only thing that comes close to the rush of playing the
knockout game is watching videos of the knockout game . .
. For a while, Kalvin's knockouts are strangers. For a while,
Erica can ignore their suffering in the rush of creativity and
Kalvin's attention. Then comes the KO that forces her eyes
open, that makes her see what's really happening. No one
wins the knockout game." (Publisher's note)

"Kalvin may seem like every parent's worst nightmare
for their daughter, but the author draws him with a complexity that helps illustrate the larger themes being explored. Neri's main concern is the 'post-racial' urban landscape, raising many talking points while letting readers come to their
own conclusions. Harsh and relentless, a tough but worthy
read." Kirkus

Ness, Patrick 1971-

The **Ask** and the Answer; a novel. Candlewick Press 2009 519p (Chaos walking) $18.99

Grades: 8 9 10 11 12 **Fic**
1. Science fiction 2. Telepathy -- Fiction 3. Space colonies -- Fiction 4. Social problems -- Fiction
ISBN 978-0-7636-4490-1; 0-7636-4490-0
LC 2009-7329
Sequel to: The knife of never letting go (2008)

Alternate chapters follow teenagers Todd and Viola, who become separated as the Mayor's oppressive new regime takes power in New Prentisstown, a space colony where residents can hear each other's thoughts.

"Provocative questions about gender bias, racism, the meaning of war and the price of peace are thoughtfully threaded throughout a breathless, often violent plot peopled with heartbreakingly real characters." Kirkus

Followed by: Monsters of men (2010)

★ The **knife** of never letting go. Candlewick Press 2008 479p (Chaos walking) $18.99

Grades: 8 9 10 11 12 **Fic**
1. Boys -- Fiction 2. Science fiction 3. Dystopian fiction 4. Psychics -- Fiction 5. Telepathy -- Fiction 6. Space colonies -- Fiction
ISBN 978-0-7636-3931-0; 0-7636-3931-1
LC 2007-52334

Pursued by power-hungry Prentiss and mad minister Aaron, young Todd and Viola set out across New World searching for answers about his colony's true past and seeking a way to warn the ship bringing hopeful settlers from Old World.

"This troubling, unforgettable opener to the Chaos Walking trilogy is a penetrating look at the ways in which we reveal ourselves to one another, and what it takes to be a man in a society gone horribly wrong." Booklist

★ A **monster** calls; a novel. inspired by an idea from Siobhan Dowd; illustrations by Jim Kay. Candlewick Press 2011 204p il $15.99

Grades: 6 7 8 9 10 **Fic**
1. School stories 2. Cancer -- Fiction 3. Monsters -- Fiction 4. Great Britain -- Fiction 5. Loss (Psychology) -- Fiction 6. Mother-son relationship -- Fiction
ISBN 978-0-7636-5559-4; 0-7636-5559-7
LC 2010040741

"Conor O'Malley is struggling with his mother's illness and terrorized by nightmares which seem to come to life. The monster who visits him tells Conor three allegorical stories, each time instructing Conor that he will have to tell his own truth in the fourth and final story. Conor's daily life and 'truth' are even more haunting than the monster." (Library Media Connection)

This is a "profoundly moving, expertly crafted tale of unaccountable loss. . . . A singular masterpiece, exceptionally well-served by Kay's atmospheric and ominous illustrations." Publ Wkly

More than this; Patrick Ness. Candlewick Press 2013 480 p. $19.99

Grades: 9 10 11 12 **Fic**
1. Death -- Fiction 2. Dystopian fiction
ISBN 0763662585; 9780763662585
LC 2013943065

In this book, "teenage Seth is experiencing his own death in painful detail. In the next chapter, he wakes up physically weak, covered in bandages and strange wounds, and wonders if he is in Hell or the future or somewhere else entirely. . . . He is plagued by intense flashbacks of his life before he died. . . . Upon discovering two other young people . . . . Seth begins to learn the Matrix-like truth about what has happened to the rest of humanity." (School Library Journal)

★ The **rest** of us just live here; Patrick Ness. HarperTeen 2015 336 p. (hardcover) $17.99

Grades: 9 10 11 12 **Fic**
1. Zombies -- Fiction 2. Teenagers -- Fiction 3. High schools -- Fiction
ISBN 0062403168; 9780062403162
LC 2014959934

This young adult novel, by Patrick Ness, "reminds us that there are many different types of remarkable. What if you aren't the Chosen One? The one who's supposed to fight the zombies, or the soul-eating ghosts, or whatever the heck this new thing is, with the blue lights and the death? What if you're like Mikey? Who just wants to graduate and go to prom and maybe finally work up the courage to ask Henna out before someone goes and blows up the high school." (Publisher's note)

"The diverse cast of characters is multidimensional and memorable, and the depiction of teen sexuality is refreshingly m atter-of-fact. Magical pillars of light and zombie deer may occasionally drive the action here, but ultimately this novel celebrates the everyday heroism of teens doing the hard work of growing up." Kirkus

Neumeier, Rachel

The **keeper** of the mist; Rachel Neumeier. Alfred A. Knopf 2016 400 p. (lib. bdg.) $20.99

Grades: 7 8 9 10 11 12 **Fic**
1. Fantasy fiction 2. Magic -- Fiction 3. Kings and rulers -- Fiction 4. Fantasy 5. Kings, queens, rulers, etc. -- Fiction
ISBN 9780553509281; 9780553509298
LC 2015000547

In this book, by Rachel Neumeier, "Keri has been struggling to run her family bakery since her mother passed away. Now the father she barely knew—the Lord of Nimmira—has died, and ancient magic has decreed that she will take his place as the new Lady. The position has never been so dangerous: the mists that hide Nimmira from its vicious, land-hungry neighbors have failed, and Keri's people are visible to strangers for the first time since the mists were put in place generations ago." (Publisher's note)

"This is a beautifully written story that emphasizes intelligence and diplomacy. Recommend to fans of Patricia Wrede and Tamora Pierce, as well as lovers of traditional fantasy." SLJ

Newman, Leslea

October mourning; a song for Matthew Shepard. Leslea Newman. Candlewick 2012 xi, 111 p.p

Grades: 10 11 12 **Fic**
1. Poetry -- Collections 2. Gays -- Fiction 3. Novels in verse 4. Murder -- Fiction 5. Hate crimes -- Fiction 6. Laramie (Wyo.) -- Fiction
ISBN 0763658073; 9780763658076
LC 2011048358
Stonewall Honor Book (2013)
In this book "lesbian literary icon [Lesléa] Newman offers a 68-poem tribute to Matthew Shepard, . . . [who] was lured from a bar by two men who drove him to the outskirts of town, beat him mercilessly, tied him to a fence and left him to die. This cycle of poems, meant to be read sequentially as a whole, incorporates Newman's reflections on Shepard's killing and its aftermath, using a number of . . . literary devices to portray. . . that fateful night and the trial that followed." (Kirkus Reviews)
Includes bibliographical references.

Nicholson, William
Jango. Harcourt 2007 409p (Noble warriors) $17.
Grades: 7 8 9 10 **Fic**
1. Fantasy fiction
ISBN 978-0-15-206011-4; 0-15-206011-1
LC 2006-19971
Sequel to: Seeker (2006)
Seeker, the Wildman, and Morning Star discover that the mysterious warrior sect they had been so desperate to join is not quite what it appears from the outside.
"Nicholson . . . knows how to entertain. . . . Well plotted and paced." Booklist
Followed by: Noman (2008)

Noman; [by] William Nicholson. 1st ed.; Harcourt 2008 362p (Noble warriors) $17; pa $7.99
Grades: 7 8 9 10 **Fic**
1. Fantasy fiction
ISBN 978-0-15-206005-3; 0-15-206005-7; 978-0-15-206656-7 pa; 0-15-206656-X pa
LC 2007011209
Sequel to: Jango (2007)
Seeker, who is obsessed with his increasingly perilous quest to kill the last of the Old Ones, finds that his mission has placed him at odds with a new leader who preaches peace and joy.
"Returning readers in the midst of their own, spiritual questioning will likely be most receptive to this unusually contemplative series closer." Booklist

Seeker. Harcourt 2006 413p (Noble warriors) $17; pa $7.95
Grades: 7 8 9 10 **Fic**
1. Fantasy fiction
ISBN 978-0-15-205768-8; 0-15-205768-4; 978-0-15-205866-1 pa; 0-15-205866-4 pa
LC 2005-17171
"The classic coming-of-age tale is combined with a rich setting of cold villains, strange powers, and disturbing warriors." Voice Youth Advocates
Other titles in this series are:
Jango (2007)
Noman (2008)

Nielsen, Susin
We are all made of molecules; by Susin Nielsen. Wendy Lamb Books, an imprint of Random House Children's Books 2015 256 p. (lib. bdg.) $19.99
Grades: 9 10 11 12 **Fic**
1. Moving -- Fiction 2. Family life -- Fiction 3. High schools -- Fiction 4. Children of gay parents -- Fiction 5. Interpersonal relations -- Fiction 6. Bullies -- Fiction 7. Schools -- Fiction 8. Gay fathers -- Fiction 9. Family problems -- Fiction 10. Moving, Household -- Fiction 11. Dating (Social customs) -- Fiction
ISBN 0553496875; 9780553496864; 9780553496871; 9780553496895
LC 2014017652
In this book, by Susin Nielsen, "Stewart and Ashley are having a tough time adjusting to their new, blended family. Stewart is a highly gifted, socially awkward geek, whereas Ashley deems herself a fashion-conscious, popular girl. . . . Their comfortable lives are thrust together after the death of Stewart's mother and the coming out of Ashley's gay father. All of a sudden, Stewart and his dad must get used to sharing space with Ashley and her mother." (Voice of Youth Advocates)
"This work of realistic fiction should find a place in most libraries serving teens." SLJ

Niven, Jennifer
All the bright places; Jennifer Niven. Alfred A. Knopf 2015 400 p. (hard cover) $17.99
Grades: 9 10 11 12 **Fic**
1. Indiana -- Fiction 2. Suicide -- Fiction 3. Emotions -- Fiction 4. Friendship -- Fiction 5. Emotional problems -- Fiction
ISBN 0385755880; 9780385755887; 9780385755894
LC 2014002238
In this book, by Jennifer Niven, "Theodore Finch is fascinated by death, and he constantly thinks of ways he might kill himself. But each time, something good, no matter how small, stops him. Violet Markey lives for the future, counting the days until graduation, when she can escape her Indiana town and her aching grief in the wake of her sister's recent death. When Finch and Violet meet on the ledge of the bell tower at school, it's unclear who saves whom." (Publisher's note)
"Niven's first novel for teens tackles a big topic with sensitivity (suicide-prevention resources are included), and teens will likely swoon over Finch and Violet's doomed oddball romance . . . [w]ith an author tour, a major promotional campaign, and a film adaptation already in the works, publishers are banking on Niven's YA debut to be a hit." Booklist
Includes bibliographical references

Nix, Garth, 1963-
Abhorsen. HarperCollins Pubs. 2003 358p $17.99; lib bdg $18.89; pa $7.99
Grades: 7 8 9 10 **Fic**
1. Fantasy fiction
ISBN 0-06-027825-0; 0-06-027826-9 lib bdg; 0-06-052873-7 pa
LC 2002-3151
Sequel to Lirael, daughter of Clayr

Abhorsen-In-Waiting Lirael and Prince Sameth, a Wall-maker, must confront and bind the evil spirit Oranis before it can destroy all life

"The tension throughout the story is palatable, and despite a solid, satisfying conclusion, Nix leaves himself a bit of room to revisit his intricately designed universe." Booklist

★ Clariel; the lost Abhorsen. Garth Nix. HarperCollins 2014 400 p. maps (hardcover) $18.99
Grades: 7 8 9 10　　　　　　　　　　　　　　Fic
1. Fantasy fiction 2. Magic -- Fiction
ISBN 006156155X; 9780061561559

LC 2013047958

In this fantasy novel by Garth Nix, part of the Old Kingdom series, "Clariel is the daughter of one of the most notable families in the Old Kingdom, with blood relations to the Abhorsen and, most important, to the King. She dreams of living a simple life but discovers this is hard to achieve when a dangerous Free Magic creature is loose in the city, her parents want to marry her off to a killer, and there is a plot brewing against the old and withdrawn King Orrikan." (Publisher's note)

"Nix's intricate world building reveals more Old Kingdom history and its ever-shifting alliance between the political and magical. Themes of freedom and destiny underpin Clariel's harrowing, bittersweet story, and readers will delight in the telling." Booklist

A confusion of princes; by Garth Nix. HarperTeen 2012 337 p.
Grades: 8 9 10 11 12　　　　　　　　　　　　Fic
1. Science fiction 2. Princes 3. Adventure fiction 4. Inheritance and succession -- Fiction 5. Princes -- Fiction 6. Adventure and adventurers -- Fiction
ISBN 9780060096946; 9780060096953

LC 2011042308

This book tells the story of "a vast empire of 10 million biologically and mechanically augmented princes," where prince "Khemri discovers that--assassination attempts and imperial interference aside--royal life isn't what he'd been led to believe. While on a secret mission, he meets Raine, a young woman who changes his perspective and Khemri begins trying to fulfill his true potential. Aurealis Award-winning author [Garth] Nix develops an empire . . . with an emphasis on house loyalty and political machinations." (Booklist)

Lirael, daughter of the Clayr. HarperCollins Pubs. 2001 487p $17.99; lib bdg $18.89; pa $7.99
Grades: 7 8 9 10　　　　　　　　　　　　　　Fic
1. Fantasy fiction
ISBN 0-06-027823-4; 0-06-027824-2 lib bdg; 0-06-000542-4 pa

LC 00-59707

Sequel to Sabriel

"Sound world-building, swift plotting, and superb characterization, including some of the strongest animal characters in recent fantasy, make this sequel must reading for those who have read the first volume and a brisk, involving experience for those who have not." Voice Youth Advocates

★ Sabriel. HarperCollins Pubs. 1996 292p hardcover o.p. pa $7.99
Grades: 7 8 9 10　　　　　　　　　　　　　　Fic
1. Fantasy fiction
ISBN 0-06-027322-4; 0-06-447183-7 pa

LC 96-1295

First published 1995 in Australia

Sabriel, daughter of the necromancer Abhorsen, must journey into the mysterious and magical Old Kingdom to rescue her father from the Land of the Dead.

"The final battle is gripping, and the bloody cost of combat is forcefully presented. The story is remarkable for the level of originality of the fantastic elements . . . and for the subtle presentation, which leaves readers to explore for themselves the complex structure and significance of the magic elements." Horn Book

Other titles in this series are:
Abhorsen (2003)
Across the wall (2005)
Clariel (2014)
Lirael, daughter of the Clayr (2001)

★ To Hold the Bridge; by Garth Nix. Harpercollins Childrens Books 2015 416 p. $17.99
Grades: 6 7 8 9 10 11 12 Adult　　　　　　　Fic
1. Spirits -- Fiction 2. Vampires -- Fiction 3. Detectives -- Fiction 4. Short stories -- Collections 5. Fantasy fiction
ISBN 0062292528; 9780062292520

This book, by Garth Nix, "offers nineteen short stories from every genre of literature including science fiction, paranormal, realistic fiction, mystery, and adventure. Whether writing about vampires, detectives, ancient spirits, or odd jobs, Garth Nix's ability to pull his readers into new worlds is extraordinary." (Publisher's note)

"This anthology's titular novella is a suspenseful prequel to The Old Kingdom Chronicles. Eighteen other tales are organized by theme, with a satisfying variety of genres and tones. Some pay homage to famous speculative fiction (Hellboy; John Carter of Mars), others are companion pieces to Nix's own work; the majority stand alone. Nix's superb world-building and tight plotting are evident here." Horn Book

North, Pearl

The boy from Ilysies. Tor 2010 316p $17.99
Grades: 7 8 9 10　　　　　　　　　　　　　　Fic
1. Fantasy fiction 2. Books and reading -- Fiction
ISBN 978-0-7653-2097-1; 0-7653-2097-5

LC 2010-36676

Sequel to Libyrinth (2009)

Cast out of the Libyrinth after being tricked into committing a crime, young Po may return only if he completes a dangerous mission to retrieve a legendary artifact that could either be the answer to all of the Libyrinth's problems, or could destroy the world.

"North has created that rare thing: a second book in a series that is stronger than the first." SLJ

Libyrinth. Tor Teen 2009 332p $17.95

Grades: 7 8 9 10   **Fic**
1. Fantasy fiction 2. Books and reading -- Fiction
ISBN 978-0-7653-2096-4; 0-7653-2096-7
                                        LC 2009-1514
In a distant future where Libyrarians preserve and protect the ancient books that are housed in the fortress-like
Libyrinth, Haly is imprisoned by Eradicants, who believe
that the written word is evil, and she must try to mend the
rift between the two groups before their war for knowledge
destroys them all.

"Among this novel's pleasures are the many anonymous
quotations scattered throughout, snatches of prose that Haly
hears as she goes about her chores . . . all of which are carefully identified at the end. The complex moral issues posed
by this thoughtful and exciting tale are just as fascinating."
Publ Wkly

Followed by: The boy from Ilysies (2010)

North, Phoebe
Starglass; by Phoebe North. 1st ed. Simon &
Schuster Books for Young Readers 2013 448 p.
(hardcover) $17.99
Grades: 7 8 9 10   **Fic**
1. Jews -- Fiction 2. Underground movements -- Fiction
3. Interplanetary voyages -- Fiction 4. Science fiction
5. Insurgency -- Fiction 6. Fathers and daughters --
Fiction
ISBN 1442459530; 9781442459533; 9781442459557
                                        LC 2012021171
In this book by Phoebe North, "[o]n a generation ship
that left Earth 500 years ago, a teenager grapples with disillusionment and emotional isolation as her society nears the
planet it intends to land on. Terra lives with her harsh, alcoholic father and awaits her adult job assignment . . . from
the strict ruling Council." She "discovers a secret rebellion
aboard the Asherah." (Kirkus Reviews)

Nović, Sara
Girl at war; a novel. Sara Nović. Random House
Inc 2015 336 p. maps $26
Grades: 11 12 Adult   **Fic**
1. Children and war -- Fiction 2. Yugoslav War, 1991-
1995 -- Fiction 3. Croatia -- History -- 1990- -- Fiction
ISBN 9780812996340; 0812996348
                                        LC 2014027466
Alex Award (2016)
Author Sara Nović presents this "novel about a girl's
coming of age--and how her sense of family, friendship,
love, and belonging is profoundly shaped by war. Zagreb,
1991. Ana Jurić is a carefree ten-year-old. But that year, civil
war breaks out across Yugoslavia. Ana must find her way in
a dangerous world. New York, 2001. Ana is now a college
student. She can't escape her memories of war. Haunted by
the events that forever changed her family, Ana returns to
Croatia after a decade away." (Publisher's note)

"Elegiac, and understandably if unrelievedly so, with a
matter-of-factness about death and uprootedness. A promising start." Kirkus

Nowlin, Laura
If he had been with me; Laura Nowlin. Sourcebooks Fire 2013 336 p. (tp: alk. paper) $9.99

Grades: 9 10 11 12   **Fic**
1. Love stories 2. Friendship -- Fiction 3. Love --
Fiction
ISBN 1402277822; 9781402277825
                                        LC 2012041338
In this book by Laura Nowlin, "in eighth grade, Autumn
and Finny stop being friends due to an unexpected kiss. They
drift apart and find new friends, but their friendship keeps
asserting itself at parties, shared holiday gatherings and random encounters. In the summer after graduation, Autumn
and Finny reconnect and are finally ready to be more than
friends. But on August 8, everything changes, and Autumn
has to rely on all her strength to move on." (Kirkus Reviews)

Nussbaum, Susan
★ **Good** kings bad kings; a novel. by Susan
Nussbaum. Algonquin Books of Chapel Hill 2013
336 p. $23.95
Grades: 10 11 12 Adult   **Fic**
1. Youth with disabilities -- Fiction 2. People with
disabilities -- Institutional care -- Fiction 3. Institutional
care -- Employees -- Fiction 4. Children with disabilities
-- Institutional care -- Fiction
ISBN 1616202637; 9781616202637
                                        LC 2013001350
PEN/Bellwether Prize for Socially Engaged Fiction
(2012)
This book by Susan Nussbaum "takes readers behind the
scenes at a facility for disabled teens." It is "woven from
short individual chapters in first-person narrative. . . . As the
book progresses . . . the darker side of the facility's management and desire for profit emerges." Characters include
"Yessenia (transferred from Juvie) . . . Mia (keeping a horrifying secret) . . . [and] Michelle (working for the management company and slowly growing aware of what her job
entails)." (Publishers Weekly)

Nussbaum charms, outrages, and enlightens readers as
she cycles among these and other characters, boldly contrasting the transcendence of love with the harsh realities of
a negligent for-profit nursing home. This is unquestionably
an authentic, galvanizing, and righteous novel." (Booklist)

O'Brien, Caragh M.
The **vault** of dreamers; Caragh M. O'Brien.
First edition Roaring Brook Press 2014 432 p. il-
lustrations (hardback) $17.99
Grades: 8 9 10 11   **Fic**
1. Science fiction 2. Dreams -- Fiction 3. High schools
-- Fiction 4. Schools -- Fiction 5. Reality television
programs -- Fiction
ISBN 1596439386; 9781596439382; 9781596439399
                                        LC 2014013322
In this novel, by Caragh M. O'Brien, "the Forge School
is the most prestigious arts school in the country. The secret
to its success: every moment of the students' lives is televised as part of the insanely popular Forge Show, and the
students' schedule includes twelve hours of induced sleep
meant to enhance creativity. But when first year student
Rosie Sinclair skips her sleeping pill, she discovers there is
something off about Forge." (Publisher's note)

"Like O'Brien's Birthmarked trilogy, this dystopian,
sci-fi, psychological-thriller hybrid raises ethical and moral

questions about science. This might have been a difficult story to pull off, given the environment, but with a likable narrator who is thoroughly unimpressed with herself, it works. The end is abrupt, hinting at a sequel, and there is a good measure of predictability." Booklist

O'Connor, Heather M.

Betting Game; Heather M. O'Connor. Orca Book Publishers 2015 216 p. $9.95

Grades: 7 8 9 10   **Fic**

1. Sports betting 2. Soccer -- Fiction 3. Brothers -- Fiction

ISBN 1459809300; 9781459809307

                          LC 2015935527

In this novel, by Heather O'Connor, "Jack's a star player on an elite soccer team along with his brother. The Lancers are . . . favored to win the National Championship. A slick bookie wins Jack's friendship and introduces him to illegal betting. Before long, Jack is hooked. An ever-widening rift is forming between the two brothers. Suddenly, Jack's . . . luck runs out. When he can't pay, the bookie gives Jack one way out. But can he betray his brother, his team and himself?" (Publisher's note)

"The fast-paced writing has enough soccer action to keep reluctant readers turning the pages, and the gambling intrigue, along with a side plot involving a new player on Jack's team, adds to the increasing conflict. Though Jack's naivety about the dangers of gambling is sometimes unconvincing and the Canadian phrases may confuse some readers, the tone, dialogue, and emotional stakes ring true. A solid pick for high/low sports fiction." Booklist

O'Rourke, Erica

Tangled; Erica O'Rourke. KTeen/Kensington 2012 ix, 326 p.p (trade pbk.) $9.95

Grades: 7 8 9 10   **Fic**

1. Magic -- Fiction 2. Paranormal fiction 3. Interpersonal relations -- Fiction 4. Secrets -- Fiction 5. Friendship -- Fiction

ISBN 0758267053; 9780758267054

                          LC 2011277358

Sequel to: Torn.

This is the second in the "Torn" trilogy. To help her dead friend's sister, Mo must "summon Luc for help. But help for Constance comes with a price—the Quartoren, leaders of the Arcs, want Mo to repair the ley lines from which they draw their power." Several others require her attention as well, pulling Mo in several directions and exacerbating her struggle of living in both the human and magical worlds. (Kirkus)

Oakes, Stephanie

★ The **sacred** lies of Minnow Bly; by Stephanie Oakes. Dial Books 2015 400 p. (hardcover) $17.99 **Fic**

1. Cults -- Fiction 2. Amputees -- Fiction 3. Murder -- Fiction 4. African Americans -- Fiction 5. Juvenile detention homes -- Fiction 6. People with disabilities -- Fiction

ISBN 9780803740709; 0803740700

                          LC 2014033187

William C. Morris Award Finalist (2016)

In this novel, by Stephanie Oakes, "Minnow Bly survives when her hands are chopped off as punishment for refusing to wed the self-proclaimed 'Kevinian' Prophet, leader of an oppressive, polygamous Montana wilderness cult in which she was raised. . . . Furious, frightened, and heartbroken, she lashes out and commits a hideous random assault, Imprisoned for this crime in a juvenile detention facility until age 18, Minnow is coaxed to reveal the truth about the demise of the Community." (School Library Journal)

"Dark and not just a little sensational but hugely involving nevertheless." Kirkus

Oates, Joyce Carol, 1938-

★ **Freaky** green eyes. Harper Tempest 2003 341p hardcover o.p. pa $6.99

Grades: 7 8 9 10   **Fic**

1. Domestic violence -- Fiction

ISBN 0-06-623757-2 lib bdg; 0-06-447348-1 pa

                          LC 2002-32868

Fifteen-year-old Frankie relates the events of the year leading up to her mother's mysterious disappearance and her own struggle to discover and accept the truth about her parents' relationship.

"Oates pulls readers into a fast-paced, first-person thriller. . . . An absorbing page-turner." Booklist

Two or three things I forgot to tell you; Joyce Carol Oates. HarperTeen 2012 277 p. (trade bdg.) $17.99

Grades: 9 10 11 12   **Fic**

1. School stories 2. Secrecy -- Fiction 3. Friendship 4. Teenagers -- Suicide -- Fiction 5. Schools -- Fiction 6. Secrets -- Fiction 7. Friendship -- Fiction 8. Self-esteem -- Fiction 9. Preparatory schools -- Fiction 10. Cutting (Self-mutilation) -- Fiction

ISBN 0062110470; 9780062110473

                          LC 2012009699

This novel, by Joyce Carol Oates, tells a "story of three teenage girls in crisis. . . . In part one, Merissa . . . secretly embraces cutting. Part two flashes back to 15 months earlier, when . . . Tink, a former child star, transfers into their junior class and changes everything. Part three picks back up in the winter of their senior year and focuses on Nadia, who falls prey to sexts and cyberbullying." (Kirkus)

Ockler, Sarah

The **Book** of Broken Hearts; by Sarah Ockler. 1st Simon Pulse hardcover ed. Simon Pulse 2013 368 p. (hardcover) $16.99

Grades: 9 10 11 12   **Fic**

1. Love stories 2. Family life -- Fiction 3. Argentine Americans -- Fiction 4. Love -- Fiction

ISBN 1442430389; 9781442430389

                          LC 2012033041

In this romance novel, by Sarah Ockler, "Jude has learned a lot from her older sisters, but the most important thing is this: The Vargas brothers are notorious heartbreakers. . . . Now Jude is the only sister still living at home, and she's spending the summer helping her ailing father restore his vintage motorcycle--which means hiring a mechanic to help out. Is it Jude's fault he happens to be cute? And surprisingly sweet? And a Vargas?" (Publisher's note)

Okorafor, Nnedi

Who fears death; Nnedi Okorafor. Daw Books
Inc. 2010 386 p. $24.95

Grades: 11 12 Adult   **Fic**
1. Magic -- Fiction 2. Africa -- Fiction 3. Dystopian
fiction 4. Genocide -- Fiction
ISBN 9780756406172

LC 2011389634

Romantic Times Reviewers' Choice Award: Best Science Fiction & Fantasy (2010), World Fantasy Awards:
Novel (2011)

This book is set in "a desolate, postapocalyptic Africa of
endless desert, failing technology, superstition, and magic. .
. . Prophesy speaks of a sorcerer who will change the future,
end the wars and slavery, and reunite the people. Onyesonwu is a child of rare talent. Conceived by rape, physically
different from her peers, Onyesonwu has the light skin, fair
hair, and freckles that traditionally mark her as unworthy,
frightening, ugly, and evil. But rather than accepting her
outcast role, a defiant Onyesonwu uses her magic to prove
herself, avenge her mother's rape, and lead her people."
(Library Journal)

Okorafor, Nnedimma

The shadow speaker; [by] Nnedi Okorafor-Mbachu. Jump at the Sun/Hyperion Books for Children
2007 336p hardcover o.p. pa $8.99

Grades: 7 8 9 10   **Fic**
1. Fantasy fiction 2. Science fiction 3. West Africa
-- Fiction 4. Sahara Desert -- Fiction
ISBN 978-1-4231-0033-1; 1-4231-0033-6; 978-1-
4231-0036-2 pa; 1-4231-0036-0 pa

LC 2007-13313

In West Africa in 2070, after fifteen-year-old "shadow
speaker" Ejii witnesses her father's beheading, she embarks
on a dangerous journey across the Sahara to find Jaa, her
father's killer, and upon finding her, she also discovers
a greater purpose to her life and to the mystical powers
she possesses.

"Okorafor-Mbachu does an excellent job of combining
both science fiction and fantasy elements into this novel. .
. . The action moves along at a quick pace and will keep
most readers on their toes and wanting more at the end of the
novel." Voice Youth Advocates

Older, Daniel José

★ Shadowshaper; Daniel Jose Older. Arthur
A. Levine Books, an imprint of Scholastic Inc. 2015
304 p. (alk. paper) $17.99

Grades: 9 10 11 12   **Fic**
1. Art -- Fiction 2. Magic -- Fiction 3. Family secrets
-- Fiction 4. Paranormal fiction
ISBN 0545591619; 9780545591614

LC 2014032311

In this book by Daniel José Older, "Sierra finally learns
the truth: her grandfather was a powerful shadowshaper,
able to animate art with the spirit of a departed soul, and
now an interloper, anthropologist Dr. Wick, is trying to steal
these powers for himself. As Sierra investigates the shadow-
shapers, she discovers her own shockingly powerful role in
the disappearing community." (Booklist)

"Summer has just started, and Sierra plans to enjoy it,
hanging out with her friends in their Brooklyn neighborhood
and painting a mural at the local junklot. Then things start
to get weird. While she is talking to fellow artist Robbie at
the first party of the summer, a zombielike creature disrupts
things, Robbie disappears, and she is left to discover that
she lives in a world full of magic that she knows nothing
about. . . . . Excellent diverse genre fiction in an appealing
package." SLJ

Oliver, Jana

Soul thief; [by] Jana Oliver. St. Martin's Griffin
2011 339p (A demon trappers novel) pa $9.99

Grades: 7 8 9 10   **Fic**
1. Orphans -- Fiction 2. Demonology -- Fiction 3.
Apprentices -- Fiction 4. Supernatural -- Fiction 5.
Atlanta (Ga.) -- Fiction
ISBN 978-0-312-61479-9

LC 2011019930

Sequel to The demon trapper's daughter (2011)

In 2018 Atlanta, Georgia, seventeen-year-old apprentice
Demon Trapper Riley Blackthorne must deal with unwanted
fame, an unofficial bodyguard, an overprotective friend, the
Vatican's own Demon Trappers, and an extremely powerful
Grade Five demon who is stalking her.

Oliver, Jana G.

The demon trapper's daughter; a demon trapper
novel. [by] Jana Oliver. St. Martin's Griffin 2011
355p pa $9.99

Grades: 7 8 9 10   **Fic**
1. Demonology -- Fiction 2. Apprentices -- Fiction 3.
Supernatural -- Fiction 4. Atlanta (Ga.) -- Fiction 5.
Father-daughter relationship -- Fiction
ISBN 978-0-312-61478-2; 0-312-61478-0

LC 2010-38860

In 2018 Atlanta, Georgia, after a demon threatens seventeen-year-old Riley Blackthorne's life and murders her
father, a legendary demon trapper to whom she was ap-
prenticed, her father's partner, Beck, steps in to care for her,
knowing she hates him.

"With a strong female heroine, a fascinating setting, and
a complex, thrill-soaked story, this series is off to a strong
start." Publ Wkly

Followed by Soul thief (2011)

Oliver, Lauren

Before I fall. The Bowen Press 2010 470p
$17.99

Grades: 9 10 11 12   **Fic**
1. School stories 2. Dead -- Fiction 3. Popularity --
Fiction 4. Self-perception -- Fiction
ISBN 006172680X; 9780061726804; 978-0-06-
172680-4; 0-06-172680-X

LC 2009-7288

After she dies in a car crash, teenage Samantha relives
the day of her death over and over again until, on the seventh
day, she finally discovers a way to save herself.

"This is a compelling book with a powerful message that
will strike a chord with many teens." Booklist

★ Delirium. HarperCollins 2011 441p $17.99

Grades: 8 9 10 11 **Fic**
1. Science fiction 2. Love -- Fiction 3. Maine -- Fiction
4. Resistance to government -- Fiction
ISBN 978-0-06-172682-8; 0-06-172682-6

LC 2010-17839

This book is a "deft blend of realism and fantasy.... The story bogs down as it revels in romance—Alex is standard-issue perfection—but the book never loses its A Clockwork Orange–style bite regarding safety versus choice." Booklist

Pandemonium; Lauren Oliver. 1st ed.; Harper-CollinsPublishers 2012 375p $17.99
Grades: 8 9 10 11 **Fic**
1. Science fiction 2. Love -- Fiction 3. Resistance to government -- Fiction
ISBN 978-0-06-197806-7

LC 2011024241

Sequel to Delirium (2011)

After falling in love, Lena and Alex flee their oppressive society where love is outlawed and everyone must receive "the cure"—an operation that makes them immune to the delirium of love—but Lena alone manages to find her way to a community of resistance fighters, and although she is bereft without the boy she loves, her struggles seem to be leading her toward a new love.

Panic; Lauren Oliver. Harper, an imprint of HarperCollinsPublishers 2014 416 p. (hardcover bdg.) $17.99
Grades: 9 10 11 12 **Fic**
1. City and town life -- Fiction 2. Games -- Fiction 3. Risk-taking (Psychology) -- Fiction
ISBN 0062014552; 9780062014559

LC 2013008472

Written by Lauren Oliver, this young adult novel describes how "Heather never thought she would compete in Panic, a legendary game played by graduating seniors, where the stakes are high and the payoff is even higher.... Dodge has never been afraid of Panic.... For Heather and Dodge, the game will bring new alliances, unexpected revelations, and the possibility of first love for each of them." (Publisher's note)

"There's not much to do in tiny Carp, New York, so a group of teenagers take it upon themselves to create their own excitement through Panic, a risky game with potentially deadly sets of challenges... The bleak setting, tenacious characters, and anxiety-filled atmosphere will draw readers right into this unique story. Oliver's powerful return to a contemporary realistic setting will find wide a readership with this fast-paced and captivating book." (School Library Journal)

Requiem; Lauren Oliver. Harper 2013 432 p. (hardcover) $18.99
Grades: 8 9 10 11 12 **Fic**
1. Science fiction 2. Resistance to government -- Fiction 3. Love -- Fiction 4. Maine -- Fiction 5. Marriage -- Fiction 6. Friendship -- Fiction 7. Best friends -- Fiction 8. Government, Resistance to -- Fiction
ISBN 0062014536; 9780062014535

LC 2012030236

Sequel to; Pandemonium

This young adult novel, by Lauren Oliver, is the conclusion to the "Delirium" trilogy. "The nascent rebellion . . . has ignited into an all-out revolution . . . , and Lena is at the center of the fight. After rescuing Julian from a death sentence, Lena and her friends fled to the Wilds. But the Wilds are no longer a safe haven. . . . As Lena navigates the increasingly dangerous terrain of the Wilds, her best friend, Hana, lives a safe, loveless life in Portland." (Publisher's note)

Vanishing girls; by Lauren Oliver. Harper 2015 357 p. illustrations (hardback) $18.99
Grades: 9 10 11 12 **Fic**
1. Sisters -- Fiction 2. Accidents -- Fiction 3. Missing children -- Fiction 4. Dissociative disorders -- Fiction
ISBN 0062224107; 9780062224101

LC 2014028437

In this book, by Lauren Oliver, "Dara and Nick used to be inseparable, but that was before the accident that left Dara's beautiful face scarred and the two sisters totally estranged. When Dara vanishes on her birthday, Nick thinks Dara is just playing around. But another girl, nine-year-old Madeline Snow, has vanished, too, and Nick becomes increasingly convinced that the two disappearances are linked. Now Nick has to find her sister, before it's too late." (Publisher's note)

"Perfect for readers who devoured We Were Liars, it's the sort of novel that readers will race to finish, then return to the beginning to marvel at how it was constructed—and at everything they missed." Publishers Weekly

Olsen, Sylvia
★ **White** girl. Sono Nis Press 2004 235p pa $8.95
Grades: 7 8 9 10 **Fic**
1. Prejudices -- Fiction 2. Native Americans -- Fiction
ISBN 1-5503-9147-X

"The talk is contemporary and relaxed, and the characters will hold readers as much as the novel's extraordinary sense of place." Booklist

Oppegaard, David
The **Firebug** of Balrog County; by David Oppegaard. Llewellyn Worldwide Ltd 2015 312 p. $11.99
Grades: 9 10 11 12 **Fic**
1. Pyromania 2. Country life -- Fiction 3. High school students -- Fiction
ISBN 073874543X; 9780738745435

LC 2015014186

In this book, by David Oppegaard, "Dark times have fallen on remote Balrog County, and Mack Druneswald, a high school senior with a love of arson, is doing his best to deal. While his family is haunted by his mother's recent death, Mack spends his nights roaming the countryside, looking for something new to burn. When he encounters Katrina, a college girl with her own baggage, Mack sets out on a path of pyromania the likes of which sleepy Balrog County has never seen before." (Publisher's note)

"Drinking, F-bombs, and humor abound, but so does a genuine sense of mourning and growth, even if Mack's narrative sometimes smacks of adult understanding. An unusual coming of age, sparking a hot if not quite perfect conflagration." Kirkus

Oppel, Kenneth

Such wicked intent; Kenneth Oppel. Simon & Schuster Books For Young Readers 2012 320 p. (hardback) $16.99; (paperback) $9.99

Grades: 7 8 9 10 **Fic**
1. Love stories 2. Death -- Fiction 3. Friendship -- Fiction 4. Horror stories 5. Dead -- Fiction 6. Twins -- Fiction 7. Alchemy -- Fiction 8. Brothers -- Fiction 9. Supernatural -- Fiction 10. Geneva (Republic) -- History -- 18th century -- Fiction
ISBN 1442403187; 9781442403185; 9781442403208; 9781442403192

LC 2011042843

This book by Kenneth Oppel is part of the "Apprenticeship of Victor Frankenstein" series. "[T]hree weeks after [his twin] Konrad's death, Victor plucks a mysterious box from the still-warm ashes of the books of the Dark Library. Demonstrating tremendous hubris, Victor aims to return Konrad to the living world and still win Elizabeth, Konrad's grief-stricken love and the boys' childhood friend." (Kirkus Reviews)

This dark endeavor; the apprenticeship of Victor Frankenstein. Simon & Schuster Books for Young Readers 2011 298p $17.99

Grades: 7 8 9 10 **Fic**
1. Horror fiction 2. Twins -- Fiction 3. Alchemy -- Fiction 4. Brothers -- Fiction
ISBN 1-4424-0315-2; 1-4424-0317-9 ebook; 978-1-4424-0315-4; 978-1-4424-0317-8 ebook

LC 2011016974

When his twin brother falls ill in the family's chateau in the independent republic of Geneva in the eighteenth century, sixteen-year-old Victor Frankenstein embarks on a dangerous and uncertain quest to create the forbidden Elixir of Life described in an ancient text in the family's secret Biblioteka Obscura.

"Written in a readable approximation of early 19th-century style, Oppel's . . . tale is melodramatic, exciting, disquieting, and intentionally over the top." Publ Wkly

Oron, Judie

Cry of the giraffe; based on a true story. Annick Press 2010 193p map $21.95; pa $12.95

Grades: 8 9 10 11 12 **Fic**
1. Jews -- Ethiopia -- Fiction 2. Jews -- Persecutions -- Fiction
ISBN 978-1-55451-272-0; 978-1-55451-271-3 pa

Labeled outcasts by their Ethiopian neighbors because of their Jewish faith, 13-year-old Wuditu and her family make the arduous trek on foot to Sudan in the hope of being transported to Yerusalem and its promise of a better life. Based on real events.

"Oron's novel shows with brutal, unflinching detail the horrors of refugee life and child slavery and the shocking vulnerability of young females in the developing world, and she offers a sobering introduction to a community and historical episodes rarely covered in books for youth." Booklist

Oseman, Aice

Solitaire; Alice Oseman. HarperTeen 2015 357 p. (hardback) $17.99

Grades: 9 10 11 12 **Fic**
1. Friendship -- Fiction 2. High school students -- Fiction 3. Love -- Fiction 4. Schools -- Fiction 5. High schools -- Fiction 6. Practical jokes -- Fiction
ISBN 0062335685; 9780062335685

LC 2014026695

In this novel by Alice Oseman "sixteen-year-old Victoria 'Tori' Spring is the personification of angst. Her best friend has become preoccupied with boys; her brother, Charlie, is recovering from an episode of mental illness and attempted suicide; a former childhood friend has suddenly resurfaced with expectations that she can't fulfill. Then, there's Michael Holden, the crazy new student. He forces himself into her life at the same time as a bizarre prank is unleashed to instigate rebellion among the students at Higgs." (School Library Journal)

"The obvious nod to The Catcher in the Rye provides another pull to readers who will enjoy parsing the parallels." Booklist

Osterlund, Anne

Aurelia. Speak 2008 246p pa $8.99

Grades: 8 9 10 11 **Fic**
1. Mystery fiction 2. Princesses -- Fiction
ISBN 978-0-14-240579-6; 0-14-240579-5

LC 2007-36074

The king sends for Robert, whose father was a trusted spy, when someone tries to assassinate Aurelia, the stubborn and feisty crown princess of Tyralt.

"Osterlund's characters are both believable, relatable, and enviable, which makes this book enjoyable to read. Even though the book might seem to fit the mold of a quintessential princess fairy tale, Aurelia's spitfire attitude and her resulting actions lend the story a unique twist." Voice Youth Advocates

Followed by: Exile (2011)

Exile. Speak 2011 295p pa $8.99

Grades: 8 9 10 11 **Fic**
1. Princesses -- Fiction 2. Voyages and travels -- Fiction
ISBN 978-0-14-241739-3; 0-14-241739-4

LC 2010009645

Sequel to Aurelia (2008)

In exile, Princess Aurelia is free of responsibilities, able to travel the country and meet the people of Tyralt, but when her journey erupts in a fiery conflagration that puts the fate of the kingdom in peril, she and her companion Robert must determine whether they have the strength and the will to complete their mission.

Ostow, Micol

The **devil** and Winnie Flynn; by Micol Ostow and David Ostow. Soho Teen 2015 336 p. illustrations (hardback) $18.99

Grades: 9 10 11 12 **Fic**
1. Mystery fiction 2. Supernatural -- Fiction 3. Television programs -- Fiction 4. Psychic ability -- Fiction 5. Mystery and detective stories 6. Television

programs -- Production and direction -- Fiction
ISBN 9781616955977

LC 2015009878

In this book, by Micol Ostow and David Ostow, Winnie Flynn doesn't believe in ghosts. . . . When her mysterious aunt Maggie . . . recruits Winnie to spend a summer working as a production assistant on her current reality hit, Fantastic, Fearsome, she suddenly finds herself in . . . New Jersey. New Jersey's famous Devil makes perfect fodder for Maggie's show. But as the filming progresses, Winnie sees and hears things that make her think that the Devil might not be totally fake." (Publisher's note)

"This stylish novel is both a celebration of horror as a genre and chilling in its own right." Kirkus

★ **So** punk rock (and other ways to disappoint your mother) a novel. with art by David Ostow. Flux 2009 246p il pa $9.95

Grades: 8 9 10 11 12 **Fic**

1. School stories 2. New Jersey -- Fiction 3. Rock music -- Fiction 4. Bands (Music) -- Fiction 5. Jews -- United States -- Fiction

ISBN 978-0-7387-1471-4; 0-7387-1471-2

LC 2009-8216

Four suburban New Jersey students from the Leo R. Gittleman Jewish Day School form a rock band that becomes inexplicably popular, creating exhiliration, friction, confrontation, and soul-searching among its members.

The "comic-strip-style illustrations are true show-stoppers. . . . A rollicking, witty, and ultra-contemporary book that drums on the funny bone and reverberates through the heart." Booklist

Ostrovski, Emil

Away we go; by Emil Ostrovski. Harpercollins Childrens Books 2016 288 p. (hardback) $17.99

Grades: 9 10 11 12 **Fic**

1. School stories 2. Death -- Fiction
ISBN 9780062238559; 0062238558

LC 2015035883

In this novel, by Emil Ostrovski, "Westing is not your typical school. For starters, you have to have one very important quality in order to be admitted—you have to be dying. Every student at Westing has been diagnosed with PPV, or the Peter Pan Virus, and no one is expected to live to graduation. What do you do when you go to a high school where no one has a future or any clue how to find meaning in their remaining days?" (Publisher's note)

"Noah's snarky repartee and constant jokes belie the depth of his struggle, and the oscillation between his heartfelt interior thoughts and sometimes careless actions and words is both moving and infuriating—in other words, vividly human. An intelligent, thought-provoking exploration of living in spite of futility." Booklist

Palmer, Robin

The **Corner** of Bitter and Sweet; by Robin Palmer. Penguin Group USA 2013 400 p. $9.99

Grades: 7 8 9 10 11 12 **Fic**

1. Children of alcoholics -- Fiction 2. Television personalities -- Fiction 3. Mother-daughter relationship

-- Fiction
ISBN 0142412503; 9780142412503

In this book by Robin Palmer, "a teenage girl and her showbiz mom are forced to re-evaluate their relationship after rehab. . . . To learn how to cope, Annabelle joins Alateen. But when Janie scores a role in a new movie with hot young superstar Billy Barrett, Annabelle frets that if anything goes wrong, it could put her mom right back on the bottle. Fortunately she's distracted by her own crush on small-town boy Matt and the lure of a college photography fellowship." (Kirkus Reviews)

Paolini, Christopher

Brisingr; or, The seven promises of Eragon Shadeslayer and Saphira Bjartskular. Alfred A. Knopf 2008 759p (Inheritance) $27.50; lib bdg $30.50

Grades: 7 8 9 10 **Fic**

1. Fantasy fiction 2. Dragons -- Fiction
ISBN 978-0-375-82672-6; 0-375-82672-6; 978-0-375-92672-3 lib bdg; 0-375-92672-0 lib bdg

LC 2008-24489

Sequel to Eldest (2005)

The further adventures of Eragon and his dragon Saphira as they continue to aid the Varden in the struggle against the evil king, Galbatorix.

"Most of the combat—and it's brutal, gory stuff—belongs to Roran as he becomes a legendary warrior; Eragon's struggles are more cerebral and involve magic, a difficult thing to dramatize but something Paolini pulls off admirably." Booklist

Eldest. Alfred A. Knopf 2005 681p (Inheritance) $21; lib bdg $24.99; pa $12.99

Grades: 7 8 9 10 **Fic**

1. Fantasy fiction 2. Dragons -- Fiction
ISBN 978-0-375-82670-2; 0-375-82670-X; 978-0-375-92670-9 lib bdg; 0-375-92670-4 lib bdg; 978-0-375-84040-1 pa; 0-375-84040-0 pa

Sequel to Eragon (2003)

After successfully evading an Urgals ambush, Eragon is adopted into the Ingeitum clan and sent to finish his training so he can further help the Varden in their struggle against the Empire.

"The momentum of the narrative is steady and consistent. . . . Eragon's journey to maturity is well handled." SLJ

Followed by Brisingr (2008)

★ **Eragon.** Knopf 2003 509p (Inheritance) $18.95; lib bdg $20.99; pa $6.99

Grades: 7 8 9 10 **Fic**

1. Fantasy fiction 2. Dragons -- Fiction
ISBN 0-375-82668-8; 0-375-92668-2 lib bdg; 0-440-23848-X pa

LC 2003-47481

First published 2002 in different form by Paolini International

In Aagaesia, a fifteen-year-old boy of unknown lineage called Eragon finds a mysterious stone that weaves his life into an intricate tapestry of destiny, magic, and power, peopled with dragons, elves, and monsters

"This unusual, powerful tale . . . is the first book in the planned Inheritance trilogy. . . . The telling remains constantly fresh and fluid, and [the author] has done a fine job of creating an appealing and convincing relationship between the youth and the dragon." Booklist

Other titles in this series are:
Brisingr (2008)
Eldest (2005)

Papademetriou, Lisa

Homeroom diaries; by James Patterson and Lisa Papademetriou; illustrated by Keino. First Edition Little, Brown and Co. 2014 272 p. illustrations (hardcover) $18

Grades: 7 8 9 10   **Fic**
1. School stories 2. Teenage girls -- Fiction 3. Diaries -- Fiction 4. Friendship -- Fiction 5. High schools -- Fiction 6. Foster home care -- Fiction 7. Interpersonal relations -- Fiction
ISBN 0316207624; 9780316207621
           LC 2013016061

In this young adult novel by James Patterson and Lisa Papademetriou, illustrated by Keino, "Margaret 'Cuckoo' Clarke recently had a brief stay in a mental institution following an emotional breakdown, but she's turning over a new leaf with her 'Operation Happiness.' She's determined to beat down the bad vibes of the Haters, the Terror Teachers, and all of the trials and tribulations of high school by writing and drawing in her diary." (Publisher's note)

"Despite the fact that serious issues (a negligent mother, an attempted sexual assault, and an incident of cyberbullying) are at play, the lighthearted tone adds levity to the work. The novel is fully illustrated with humorous artwork that contributes to the story in a meaningful way. Fans of the popular "diary fiction" genre (as well as those simply looking for an approachable and quick read) will find much to enjoy here." SLJ

Park, Linda Sue, 1960-

A **long** walk to water; based on a true story. Clarion Books 2010 121p map $16

Grades: 6 7 8 9 10   **Fic**
1. Refugees 2. Relief workers 3. Water -- Fiction 4. Africans -- Fiction 5. Refugees -- Fiction 6. Sudan -- History -- Civil War, 1983-2005 -- Fiction
ISBN 0-547-25127-0; 978-0-547-25127-1
           LC 2009-48857

When the Sudanese civil war reaches his village in 1985, eleven-year-old Salva becomes separated from his family and must walk with other Dinka tribe members through southern Sudan, Ethiopia, and Kenya in search of safe haven. Based on the life of Salva Dut, who, after emigrating to America in 1996, began a project to dig water wells in Sudan.

This is a "spare, immediate account. . . . Young readers will be stunned by the triumphant climax of the former refugee who makes a difference." Booklist

Parker, Amy Christine

Astray; Amy Christine Parker. Random House 2014 343 p. (trade) $17.99
Grades: 9 10 11 12   **Fic**
1. Utopian fiction 2. Cults -- Fiction 3. Brainwashing -- Fiction 4. Religious life -- Fiction 5. Survival skills

-- Fiction 6. Utopias -- Fiction 7. Survival -- Fiction 8. Religious leaders -- Fiction
ISBN 0449816028; 9780449816028; 9780449816035
           LC 2013034047

Sequel to: Gated (2013)

This book, by Amy Christine Parker, is a "contemporary young adult thriller. . . . Lyla Hamilton almost died escaping the Community. In her new life, the outsiders call the Community a cult. . . . The Community is willing to do terrible things to bring her back to the fold. The members are still preaching Pioneer's twisted message that the end of the world is near. Pulled in two directions and unsure which way to turn, Lyla risks everything to follow her heart." (Publisher's note)

"Having escaped from Pioneer and his Community (Gated), Lyla must now adapt to life with the Outsiders--high school, dating--while surviving the Community's rage over her betrayal. As a brainwashed teen, Lyla's first-person narration is unreliable and emotional, scared yet resilient. This is a creepy, compelling, and enjoyable read." Horn Book

★ **Gated**; by Amy Christine Parker. 1st ed. Random House Inc 2013 339 p. (hardcover) $17.99; (library) $20.99

Grades: 9 10 11 12   **Fic**
1. Love stories 2. Cults -- Fiction 3. Utopias -- Fiction 4. Survival -- Fiction 5. Religious leaders -- Fiction
ISBN 0449815978; 9780449815977; 9780449815984
           LC 2012048123

In this book, 17-year-old "Lyla is part of the Community, a group of families led by the charismatic Pioneer, who has secluded them from the outside world in anticipation of the imminent apocalypse. With Pioneer's prophesied deadline fast approaching, Lyla struggles with her faith and resolve. A chance encounter with Cody, a boy from the outside, further tempts her away from the way of the Community, but when events escalate," she may have to make a difficult choice. (Publishers Weekly)

"Part of a select few who will survive the end of the world, Lyla and her family live in the Community, led by prophet Pioneer, and she can barely remember her old life. Then an outsider raises questions she shouldn't be asking, and Pioneer does not appreciate questions. Slowly mounting action builds suspense in this coming-of-age story and examination of cult mentality." (Horn Book)

Parker, Robert B.

Chasing the bear; a young Spenser novel. Philomel Books 2009 169p $14.99
Grades: 7 8 9 10   **Fic**
1. Bullies -- Fiction 2. Friendship -- Fiction 3. Kidnapping -- Fiction 4. Child abuse -- Fiction
ISBN 978-0-399-24776-7; 0-399-24776-9
           LC 2008-52725

Spenser reflects back to when he was fourteen-years-old and how he helped his best friend Jeannie when she was abducted by her abusive father.

"A clean, sharp jab of a read." Booklist

Parkinson, Siobhán

Long story short. Roaring Brook Press 2011 160p $16.99

Grades: 6 7 8 9 10 **Fic**
1. Ireland -- Fiction 2. Siblings -- Fiction 3. Runaway children -- Fiction
ISBN 978-1-59643-647-3; 1-59643-647-6
LC 2010-29023

Fourteen-year-old Jono and his eight-year-old sister Julie run away when, soon after their grandmother's death, their alcoholic mother hits Julie, but when the police find them in Galway, Jono learns he is in big trouble.

"A deeply affecting story about what can go wrong when adults fail children and the choices available to them are all bad." Publ Wkly

Patrick, Cat
The **Originals**; Cat Patrick. 1st ed. Little, Brown and Co. 2013 304 p. (hardcover) $18
Grades: 8 9 10 11 12 **Fic**
1. Sisters -- Fiction 2. Human cloning -- Fiction 3. Dating (Social customs) -- Fiction 4. Cloning -- Fiction 5. Individuality -- Fiction 6. Single-parent families -- Fiction
ISBN 0316219436; 9780316219433
LC 2012029853

In this novel, by Cat Patrick, "17-year-olds Lizzie, Ella, and Betsey Best grew up as identical triplets . . . until they discovered a shocking family secret. They're actually closer than sisters, they're clones . . . , hiding from a government agency that would expose them. . . . Then Lizzie meets Sean Kelly. . . . As their relationship develops, Lizzie realizes that she's not a carbon copy of her sisters; she's an individual with unique dreams and desires." (Publisher's note)

Revived; by Cat Patrick. 1st ed. Little, Brown & Co. 2012 336 p. (hardcover) $17.99; (paperback) $8.99
Grades: 7 8 9 10 11 12 **Fic**
1. Drugs -- Testing 2. Secrecy -- Fiction 3. Science -- Experiments -- Fiction 4. Death -- Fiction 5. Drugs -- Fiction 6. Schools -- Fiction 7. High schools -- Fiction 8. Moving, Household -- Fiction
ISBN 0316094625; 9780316094627; 9780316094634
LC 2011026950

This book, by Cat Patrick, follows Daisy, who since the age of five has been "part of a top-secret clinical trial for a drug called Revive that can bring the deceased back to life. . . . Daisy uncovers some secrets within the program: a mysterious extra case file, a new test batch of Revive, some unexplained car crashes, and the erratic behavior of the mysterious man at the top, nicknamed God." (Bulletin of the Center for Children's Books)

Patron, Susan
Behind the masks; the diary of Angeline Reddy. Susan Patron. Scholastic 2012 293 p. ill., map (paper-over-board) $12.99
Grades: 5 6 7 8 9 **Fic**
1. Mystery fiction 2. Diaries -- Fiction 3. Thieves -- Fiction 4. Gold mines and mining -- Fiction 5. Frontier and pioneer life -- California -- Fiction 6. Lawyers -- Fiction 7. Mystery and detective stories 8. Robbers and outlaws -- Fiction 9. California -- History -- 19th century -- Fiction
ISBN 9780545304375
LC 2011023826

"[T]his Dear America series title [is] set in Bodie, California, in 1880. Fourteen-year-old diarist and would-be dramatist Angeline Reddy does not believe her father, criminal lawyer Patrick Reddy, has been murdered. Convinced his disappearance is purposeful, Angie investigates his 'demise' and tries to bring him back to their rough-and-tumble mining community. Assisted by friends, a dashing young Wells Fargo clerk, and the members of a local theater troupe, . . . Angie offers a revealing look at frontier life "especially preoccupations with thespian entertainments, racial and social prejudices, and vigilante justice."(Booklist)

Pattou, Edith
Ghosting; Edith Pattou. Skyscape 2014 423 p. (trade hardcover: alk. paper) $16.99
Grades: 9 10 11 12 **Fic**
1. Violence -- Fiction 2. Practical jokes -- Fiction 3. Teenagers 4. Practical jokes 5. Firearms accidents
ISBN 147784774X; 9781477847749; 9781477847893
LC 2014933207

In this young adult novel by Edith Pattou, "on a hot summer night in a midwestern town, a high school teenage prank goes horrifically awry. Alcohol, guns, and a dare. Within minutes, as events collide, innocents becomes victims--with tragic outcomes altering lives forever, a grisly and unfortunate scenario all too familiar from current real-life headlines. But victims can also become survivors, and . . . we see how . . . they can reach out to one another . . . and survive." (Publisher's note)

"Pattou's deliberate attentiveness to character maturation, along with familial ties that bind and strain, strengthen this skillful portrayal of teen wrongheadedness at a most vulnerable moment." Booklist

Pauley, Kimberly
Cat Girl's day off; Kimberly Pauley. Tu Books 2012 334 p. (hardcover: alk. paper) $17.95
Grades: 6 7 8 9 10 **Fic**
1. Cats -- Fiction 2. Mystery fiction 3. Adventure fiction 4. High school students -- Fiction 5. Parapsychology 6. Schools -- Fiction 7. High schools -- Fiction 8. Chicago (Ill.) -- Fiction
ISBN 1600608833; 9781600608834; 9781600608841
LC 2011042997

In this young adult novel, "High school sophomore Natalie 'Nat' Ng has a 'Talent' she's not proud of: the ability to talk to cats. Her younger sister is a 'supergenius' with chameleonlike abilities; her older sister is proficient in truth divination and levitation, and has X-ray vision; and her parents work for the Bureau of Extrasensory Regulation and Management. When a film crew comes to Nat's Chicago high school to shoot a takeoff of 'Ferris Bueller's Day Off' things get fishy: the female star isn't acting like herself, and Nat learns from a cat that celebrity blogger Easton West may not be who she claims to be. Along with her friends Oscar and Melly, Nat gets dragged into a whirlwind adventure to find out what happened to the real Easton." (Publishers Weekly)

Paulsen, Gary

★ **Soldier's** heart; a novel of the Civil War. Delacorte Press 1998 106p $15.95; pa $5.99

Grades: 7 8 9 10 **Fic**

1. Post-traumatic stress disorder -- Fiction 2. United States -- History -- 1861-1865, Civil War -- Fiction
ISBN 0-385-32498-7; 0-440-22838-7 pa

LC 98-10038

"This compelling and realistic depiction of war is based on a true story. . . . Paulsen's writing is crisp and fast-paced, and this soldier's story will haunt readers long after they finish reading the novel." Book Rep

Peacock, Shane

Death in the air. Tundra Books 2008 254p (The boy Sherlock Holmes) pa $11.99; $12.50; lib bdg $19.95

Grades: 6 7 8 9 10 **Fic**

1. Mystery fiction 2. Great Britain -- Fiction
ISBN 978-0-88776-928-3 pa; 0-88776-928-4 pa; 978-0-88776-897-2; 0-88776-897-0; 978-0-88776-851-4 lib bdg; 0-88776-851-2 lib bdg

"While visiting his father at the magnificent Crystal Palace, Sherlock stops to watch a remarkable and dangerous trapeze performance high above, framed by the stunning glass ceiling of the legendary building. Suddenly, the troupe's star is dropping, screaming and flailing, toward the floor." Publisher's note

The dragon turn. Tundra Books 2011 220p (The boy Sherlock Holmes) $19.95

Grades: 6 7 8 9 10 **Fic**

1. Mystery fiction 2. Great Britain -- History -- 19th century -- Fiction
ISBN 978-1-77049-231-8; 1-77049-231-3

Summer 1869, and Sherlock Holmes and his friend Irene celebrate her sixteenth birthday by attending the theater to watch a celebrated magician make a real dragon appear on stage. It is the London sensation. Sherlock and Irene meet the magician, Alistair Hemsworth—just as he is arrested for the murder of his rival, The Wizard of Nottingham.

Eye of the crow. Tundra Books 2007 264p (The boy Sherlock Holmes) $24.99; pa $9.95

Grades: 6 7 8 9 10 **Fic**

1. Mystery fiction 2. Great Britain -- History -- 19th century -- Fiction
ISBN 978-0-88776-850-7; 0-88776-850-4; 978-0-88776-919-1 pa; 0-88776-919-5 pa

"A young woman is brutally murdered in a dark back street of Whitechapel; a young Arab is discovered with the bloody murder weapon; and a thirteen-year-old Sherlock Holmes, who was seen speaking with the alleged killer as he was hauled into jail, is suspected to be his accomplice. . . . Although imaginative reconstruction of Holmes childhood has been the subject of literary and cinematic endeavors, Peacock's take ranks among the most successful." Bull Cent Child Books

Other titles in this series are:
Death in the air (2008)
The dragon turn (2011)
The secret fiend (2010)

Vanishing girl (2009)

The **secret** fiend. Tundra Books 2010 244p (The boy Sherlock Holmes) $19.95

Grades: 6 7 8 9 10 **Fic**

1. Mystery fiction 2. Great Britain -- History -- 19th century -- Fiction
ISBN 978-0-88776-853-8; 0-88776-853-9

It is 1868, the week that Benjamin Disraeli becomes Prime Minister of the Empire. Sherlock's beautiful but poor admirer, Beatrice, the hatter's daughter, appears at the door late at night. She is terrified, claiming that she and her friend have just been attacked by the Spring Heeled Jack on Westminster Bridge and the fiend has made off with her friend.

Vanishing girl. Tundra Books 2009 307p (The boy Sherlock Holmes) $19.95

Grades: 6 7 8 9 10 **Fic**

1. Mystery fiction 2. Great Britain -- History -- 19th century -- Fiction
ISBN 978-0-88776-8521; 0-88776-852-0

When a wealthy young girl vanishes as if by magic in Hyde Park, Sherlock is once again driven to prove himself.

Pearce, Jackson

Sisters red. Little, Brown 2010 328p $16.99

Grades: 9 10 11 12 **Fic**

1. Sisters -- Fiction 2. Werewolves -- Fiction 3. Supernatural -- Fiction
ISBN 978-0-316-06868-0

LC 2009-44734

After a Fenris, or werewolf, killed their grandmother and almost killed them, sisters Scarlett and Rosie March devote themselves to hunting and killing the beasts that prey on teenaged girls, learning how to lure them with red cloaks and occasionally using the help of their old friend, Silas, the woodsman's son.

"Told by the sisters in alternating chapters, this well-written, high-action adventure grabs readers and never lets go." SLJ

Pearson, Mary

★ The **adoration** of Jenna Fox; [by] Mary E. Pearson. Henry Holt and Co. 2008 272p $16.95; pa $8.99

Grades: 7 8 9 10 11 12 **Fic**

1. Science fiction 2. Bioethics -- Fiction
ISBN 978-0-8050-7668-4; 0-8050-7668-9; 978-0-312-59441-1 pa; 0-312-59441-0 pa

LC 2007-27314

In the not-too-distant future, when biotechnological advances have made synthetic bodies and brains possible but illegal, a seventeen-year-old girl, recovering from a serious accident and suffering from memory lapses, learns a startling secret about her existence.

"The science . . . and the science fiction are fascinating, but what will hold readers most are the moral issues of betrayal, loyalty, sacrifice, and survival." Booklist

Followed by The Fox inheritance (2011)

Fox forever; Mary E. Pearson. Henry Holt and Company 2013 304 p. (hardcover) $17.99

Grades: 7 8 9 10 11 12 **Fic**
1. Science fiction 2. Dystopian fiction 3. Bioethics --
Fiction 4. Biotechnology -- Fiction 5. Medical ethics
-- Fiction 6. Government, resistance to -- Fiction
ISBN 0805094342; 9780805094343
LC 2012027677

This young adult novel, by Mary E. Pearson, is the conclusion to the "Jenna Fox Chronicles." "After . . . 260 years
as a disembodied mind in a little black box, [Lock Jenkins]
has a . . . body. But . . . he'll have to return the Favor he accepted from the . . . Network. Locke must infiltrate the home
of a government official by gaining the trust of his daughter,
seventeen-year-old Raine, and he soon finds himself pulled
deep into the world of the resistance--and into Raine's life."
(Publisher's note)

The **Fox** Inheritance; [by] Mary E. Pearson.
Henry Holt 2011 384p $16.99
Grades: 7 8 9 10 11 12 **Fic**
1. Science fiction 2. Bioethics -- Fiction
ISBN 0805088296; 9780805088298
LC 2011004800
Sequel to: The adoration of Jenna Fox (2008)

Two-hundred-sixty years after a terrible accident destroyed their bodies, sixteen-year-old Locke and seventeen-
year-old Kara have been brought back to life in newly bioengineered bodies, with many questions about the world they
find themselves in and more than two centuries of horrible
memories of being trapped in a digital netherworld wondering what would become of them.

"Pearson delivers another spellbinding thriller. . . . A
dazzling blend of science fiction, mystery, and teen friendship drama." Publ Wkly

The **kiss** of deception; Mary E. Pearson. First
edition Henry Holt Books for Young Readers 2014
496 p. (The Remnant Chronicles) (hardback) $17.99
Grades: 9 10 11 12 **Fic**
1. Fantasy 2. Love -- Fiction 3. Deception -- Fiction
4. Princesses -- Fiction
ISBN 0805099239; 9780805099232
LC 2014005163

In this novel by Mary E. Pearson, "Princess Lia's life
follows a preordained course. As First Daughter, she is expected to have the revered gift of sight--but she doesn't--and
she knows her parents are perpetrating a sham when they
arrange her marriage to secure an alliance with a neighboring kingdom--to a prince she has never met. On the morning of her wedding, Lia flees to a distant village. She settles
into a new life, hopeful when two mysterious and handsome
strangers arrive--and unaware that one is the jilted prince and
the other an assassin sent to kill her. Deception abounds, and
Lia finds herself on the brink of unlocking perilous secrets-
-even as she finds herself falling in love." (Publisher's note)

"This has the sweep of an epic tale, told with some
twists; it's a book that almost doesn't need a sequel, but
readers will be thrilled that it continues on." Booklist

Other titles in the series are:
The Heart of Betrayal (2015)

Peck, Richard
★ The **river** between us. Dial Bks. 2003 164p
$16.99; pa $6.99
Grades: 7 8 9 10 **Fic**
1. Race relations -- Fiction 2. Racially mixed people
-- Fiction 3. United States -- History -- 1861-1865, Civil
War -- Fiction
ISBN 0-8037-2735-6; 0-14-240310-5 pa
LC 2002-34815

During the early days of the Civil War, the Pruitt family
takes in two mysterious young ladies who have fled New
Orleans to come north to Illinois

"The harsh realities of war are brutally related in a complex, always surprising plot that resonates on mutiple levels." Horn Book Guide

Peet, Mal, 1947-2015
★ **Life**; an exploded diagram. Candlewick Press
2011 385p il $17.99
Grades: 9 10 11 12 **Fic**
1. War stories 2. Family life -- Fiction 3. Great Britain
-- Fiction 4. Social classes -- Fiction
ISBN 978-0-7636-5227-2; 978-0-7636-5631-7 ebook
LC 2010042742

In 1960s Norfolk, England, seventeen-year-old Clem
Ackroyd lives with his mother and grandmother in a tiny
cottage, but his life is transformed when he falls in love with
the daughter of a wealthy farmer in this tale that flashes back
through the stories of three generations.

"This [book] is mesmerizing through the sheer force and
liveliness of its prose, as well as its unpredictable, inexora-
ble plot. . . . Peet's subtle, literary play with narrative voice,
style, and chronology make this a satisfyingly sophisticated
teen novel. Outstanding." Horn Book

Peevyhouse, Parker
Where futures end; Parker Peevyhouse. Kathy
Dawson Books 2016 304 p. (hardback) $17.99
Grades: 9 10 11 12 **Fic**
1. Short stories 2. Science fiction
ISBN 9780803741607
LC 2015022984

This book, by Parker Peevyhouse, "is a collection of
five time-spanning, interconnected novellas that weave a
subtly science-fictional web stretching out from the present
into the future, presenting eerily plausible possibilities for
social media, corporate sponsorship, and humanity, as our
world collides with a mysterious alternate universe." (Publisher's note)

"Each story connects loosely with the one before, but
the novel's sprawling scope keeps the narratives relatively
thin. Still, Peevyhouse's ambitious debut offers readers
plenty to ponder and will hold appeal for Marcus Sedgwick
fans." Booklist

Perera, Anna
★ **Guantanamo** boy. Albert Whitman 2011
339p $17.99
Grades: 7 8 9 10 11 12 **Fic**
1. Cousins -- Fiction 2. Muslims -- Fiction 3. Torture
-- Fiction 4. Prisoners -- Fiction 5. Prejudices -- Fiction
6. Guantanamo Bay Naval Base (Cuba) -- Detention

Camp -- Fiction
ISBN 978-0-8075-3077-1; 0-8075-3077-8

LC 2010048016

"Readers will feel every ounce of Khalid's terror, frustration, and helplessness in this disturbing look at a sad, ongoing chapter in contemporary history." Publ Wkly

Perez, Ashley Hope

★ **Out** of darkness; by Ashley Hope Perez. Carolrhoda Lab 2015 408 p. illustrations (trade hard cover: alk. paper) $18.99

Grades: 9 10 11 12   **Fic**

1. School stories 2. Historical fiction 3. Race relations -- Fiction 4. Mexican Americans -- Fiction 5. Schools -- Fiction 6. Explosions -- Fiction 7. African Americans -- Fiction 8. New London (Tex.) -- History -- 20th century -- Fiction
ISBN 9781467742023; 9781467761796; 9781467776769; 9781467776776; 978146777678-3

LC 2014023837

Printz Award Honor Book (2016)

In this book, author "Ashley Hope Perez takes the facts of the 1937 New London school explosion the worst school disaster in American history as a backdrop for a . . . novel about segregation, love, family, and the forces that destroy people. . . . Naomi Vargas and Wash Fuller know about the lines in East Texas as well as anyone. . . . But sometimes the attraction between two people is so powerful it breaks through even the most entrenched color lines." (Publisher's note)

"Pérez's latest—following The Knife and the Butterfly (2012)—is a powerful work of historical fiction set in New London, Texas, that revolves around events leading up to the horrific 1937 school explosion that killed close to 300 people. This gripping story centers on high-school senior Naomi, a Mexican American girl who recently arrived from San Antonio with her half siblings, twins Beto and Cari, and their father, oil-field worker Henry. . . . Elegant prose and gently escalating action will leave readers gasping for breath at the tragic climax and moving conclusion." Booklist

Perez, Marlene

Dead is a battlefield; Marlene Perez. Graphia 2012 227 p.

Grades: 7 8 9 10   **Fic**

1. Zombies -- Fiction 2. Perfumes -- Fiction 3. Supernatural -- Fiction 4. Female friendship -- Fiction 5. High school students -- Fiction 6. Schools -- Fiction 7. High schools -- Fiction 8. Interpersonal relations -- Fiction
ISBN 0547607342; 9780547607344

LC 2011031489

In this young adult novel, a "high-school freshman learns that she's one of a group of women who fight evil beasties in her supernatural town of Nightshade, Calif. In this sixth installment of the "Dead Is . . ." series, Jessica discovers to her dismay that she's a "virago," a woman warrior destined to fight paranormal baddies. Jessica worries, too, about her very best friend in the whole world, Eva, who's been acting strangely since she discovered a new perfume. . . . Jessica also finds herself attracted to Dominic . . . while she's juggling dates with Connor. . . . Meanwhile, Eva joins

the groupies hanging around creepy Edgar and becomes ever more hostile toward Jessica, even trying to bite her. It seems that Edgar's perfume turns girls into zombies. Now Jessica has to find a cure and drive Edgar out of town." (Kirkus)

Dead is a killer tune; Marlene Perez. Graphia 2012 204 p. (paperback) $7.99

Grades: 8 9 10 11 12   **Fic**

1. Accidents -- Fiction 2. Bands (Music) -- Fiction 3. Mystery fiction 4. Music -- Fiction 5. Schools -- Fiction 6. High schools -- Fiction 7. Supernatural -- Fiction 8. Interpersonal relations -- Fiction
ISBN 0547608349; 9780547608341

LC 2012014798

Author Marlene Perez tells the story of a Battle of the Bands competition. "Jessica's romance with Dominic hasn't exactly progressed smoothly . . . Dominic's band, Side Effects May Vary, finds competition in an out-of-town act followed by a large entourage of obsessed fans--Hamlin, fronted by Brett Piper. When the most competitive bands start losing members to recklessness and bizarre accidents, Jessica must not only get to the bottom of the mystery, but also step into the spotlight as a musician herself." (Kirkus)

Dead is just a dream; by Marlene Perez. Houghton Mifflin Harcourt 2013 164 p. (Dead is) (hardback) $16.99

Grades: 8 9 10   **Fic**

1. Fantasy fiction 2. Clowns -- Fiction 3. Homicide -- Fiction 4. Murder -- Fiction 5. Schools -- Fiction 6. Nightmares -- Fiction 7. High schools -- Fiction 8. Supernatural -- Fiction 9. Psychic ability -- Fiction 10. Interpersonal relations -- Fiction
ISBN 0544102622; 9780544102620

LC 2013003883

In this book, by Marlene Perez "Jessica and her virago friends are . . . in the midst of four murders, all seemingly connected to creepy paintings being installed in the homes of Nightshade's most influential citizens. Just when the girls think they've solved the mystery, a bloody clown begins to stalk Jessica, confounding their original suspicions. Jessica and Dominic's status as a happy couple is also threatened when Dominic announces he will be touring with his band during part of their senior year." (Booklist)

"Jessica and her virago friends are back in this latest Dead Is series entry. This time they're in the midst of four murders, all seemingly connected to creepy paintings being installed in the homes of Nightshade's most influential citizens. Just when the girls think they've solved the mystery, a bloody clown begins to stalk Jessica, confounding their original suspicions...Girl drama, sweet romance, and murder—what more could young teens want in a breezy read?" Booklist

Perkins, Lynne Rae

★ **As** easy as falling off the face of the earth. Greenwillow Books 2010 352p il $16.99

Grades: 8 9 10 11 12   **Fic**

1. Adventure fiction 2. Chance -- Fiction 3. Accidents -- Fiction
ISBN 978-0-06-187090-3; 0-06-187090-0

LC 2009-42524

A teenaged boy encounters one comedic calamity after another when his train strands him in the middle of nowhere, and everything comes down to luck.

"The real pleasure is Perkins' relentlessly entertaining writing. . . . Wallowing in the wry humor, small but potent truths, and cheerful implausibility is an absolute delight." Booklist

Perkins, Mitali

Secret keeper. Delacorte Press 2009 225p $16.99; lib bdg $19.99

Grades: 7 8 9 10 **Fic**

1. India -- Fiction 2. Sisters -- Fiction 3. Family life -- Fiction

ISBN 978-0-385-73340-3; 0-385-73340-2; 978-0-385-90356-1 lib bdg; 0-385-90356-1 lib bdg

LC 2008-21475

In 1974 when her father leaves New Delhi, India, to seek a job in New York, Ashi, a tomboy at the advanced age of sixteen, feels thwarted in the home of her extended family in Calcutta where she, her mother, and sister must stay, and when her father dies before he can send for them, they must remain with their relatives and observe the old-fashioned traditions that Ashi hates.

"The plot is full of surprising secrets rooted in the characters' conflicts and deep connections with each other. The two sisters and their mutual sacrifices are both heartbreaking and hopeful." Booklist

Perkins, Stephanie

Isla and the happily ever after; a novel. Stephanie Perkins. Dutton Books 2014 352 p. (hardback) $17.99

Grades: 9 10 11 12 **Fic**

1. Love stories 2. Americans -- France -- Fiction 3. Love -- Fiction 4. France -- Fiction 5. Schools -- Fiction 6. Foreign study -- Fiction 7. Paris (France) -- Fiction 8. Boarding schools -- Fiction

ISBN 0525425632; 9780525425632

LC 2014020689

In this novel by Stephanie Perkins "Isla has had a crush on . . . Josh since their first year at the School of America in Paris. And after a chance encounter in Manhattan over the summer, romance might be closer than Isla imagined. But as they begin their senior year back in France, Isla and Josh are forced to confront the challenges every young couple must face, including family drama, uncertainty about their college futures, and the very real possibility of being apart." (Publisher's note)

"These choppy waters of neurosis will snag the soaring hearts of readers who have been there (and who hasn't?), and they'll ache upon Isla and Josh's rite-of-passage first doubts about their relationship. Fans of literary heart flutters will love it." Booklist

Lola and the boy next door. Dutton Books 2011 338p $16.99

Grades: 9 10 11 12 **Fic**

1. Costume -- Fiction 2. San Francisco (Calif.) -- Fiction 3. Dating (Social customs) -- Fiction 4. Father-

daughter relationship -- Fiction

ISBN 978-0-525-42328-7

LC 2011015533

"Perkins's novel goes a bit deeper than standard chick-lit fare, and Lola is a sympathetic protagonist even when readers disagree with her decisions. . . . Step back—it's going to fly off the shelves." SLJ

Perkins-Valdez, Dolen

Wench; a novel. Dolen Perkins-Valdez. 1st ed.; Amistad 2010 293 p. $24.99

Grades: 11 12 Adult **Fic**

1. Ohio -- Fiction 2. Slaves -- Fiction 3. Fugitive slaves -- Fiction 4. United States -- History -- 1783-1865 -- Fiction 5. Ohio -- History -- 1787-1865 -- Fiction 6. Resorts -- Ohio -- 19th century -- Fiction 7. Women slaves -- Ohio -- Social conditions -- Fiction

ISBN 006170654X; 9780061706547

LC 2010277174

This book, by Dolen Perkins-Valdez, chronicles "the lives of four slave women—Lizzie, Reenie, Sweet and Mawu—who are their masters' mistresses. The women meet when their owners vacation at the same summer resort in Ohio. There, they see free blacks for the first time and hear rumors of abolition, sparking their own desires to be free. For everyone but Lizzie, that is, who believes she is really in love with her master, and he with her." (Publishers Weekly)

"Readers of historical fiction centering on Southern women's stories like Lalita Tademy's Cane River or Lee Smith's On Agate Hill will be moved by the skillful portrayal of Lizzie's precarious situation and the tragic stories of her fellow slaves." LJ

Peterfreund, Diana

Across a star-swept sea; Diana Peterfreund. Balzer + Bray, an imprint of HarperCollinsPublishers 2013 464 p. (hardcover bdg.) $17.99

Grades: 9 10 11 12 **Fic**

1. Spy stories 2. Science fiction 3. Spies -- Fiction 4. Social classes -- Fiction 5. Government, Resistance to -- Fiction

ISBN 0062006169; 9780062006165

LC 2013003082

This book, a retelling of "The Scarlet Pimpernel," is a follow-up to Diana Peterfreund's "For Darkness Shows the Stars." Here, on "a Pacific island in a high-tech future, 16-year-old Persis Blake seems the epitome of a lady: beautiful, charming, stylish . . . shallow and stupid. The Wild Poppy, her alter ego, is clever, courageous and noble, crossing the sea to rescue aristos imprisoned by the tyrannical revolution." (Kirkus Reviews)

For darkness shows the stars; by Diana Peterfreund. Balzer + Bray 2012 407 p. (hardback) $17.99

Grades: 9 10 11 12 **Fic**

1. Science fiction 2. Farmers -- Fiction 3. Apocalyptic fiction 4. Man-woman relationship -- Fiction 5. Love -- Fiction 6. Social classes -- Fiction 7. Family problems -- Fiction

ISBN 0062006142; 9780062006141

LC 2011042126

Elliot North fights to save her family's land and her own heart in this post-apocalyptic reimaging of Jane Austen's 'Persuasion.'

"The story stands on its own, a richly envisioned portrait of a society in flux, a steely yet vulnerable heroine, and a young man who does some growing up." Publ Wkly

Peters, Julie Anne, 1952-

★ **Luna**; a novel. Little, Brown 2003 248p hardcover o.p. pa $7.99

Grades: 9 10 11 12   Fic
1. Siblings -- Fiction 2. Transgender people - Fiction
ISBN 0-316-73369-5; 0-316-01127-4 pa

LC 2003-58913

"Regan's brother Liam can't stand the person he is during the day... His true self, Luna, only reveals herself at night. In the secrecy of his basement bedroom Liam transforms himself into the beautiful girl he longs to be, with help from his sister's clothes and makeup...But are Liam's family and friends ready to welcome Luna into their lives? Compelling and provocative, this is an unforgettable novel about a transgender teen's struggle for self-identity and acceptance." (Publisher's Note)

"The author gradually reveals the issues facing a transgender teen, educating readers without feeling too instructional (Luna and Regan discuss lingo, hormones and even sex change operations). Flashbacks throughout help round out the story, explaining Liam/Luna's longtime struggle with a dual existence, and funny, sarcastic-but-strong Regan narrates with an authentic voice that will draw readers into this new territory." Publ Wkly

She loves you, she loves you not-- Little, Brown 2011 278p $17.99

Grades: 9 10 11 12   Fic
1. Mothers -- Fiction 2. Colorado -- Fiction 3. Lesbians -- Fiction 4. Family life -- Fiction
ISBN 978-0-316-07874-0; 0-316-07874-3

LC 2010-22853

The author "skillfully depicts the self-obsessed, tumultuous life of a heartbroken teenager, adding just enough action to draw along a plot that might otherwise be tepid. While the book alludes to the girls' sexual relations, the descriptions are not graphic and should not deter high school libraries from adding this title to their LGBTQ collection." Libr Media Connect

Petty, Heather W.

Lock & Mori; Heather Petty. SSBFYR Teen 2015 256 p. (hardcover: alk. paper) $17.99

Grades: 9 10 11 12   Fic
1. Mystery fiction 2. Love -- Fiction 3. England -- Fiction 4. Family problems -- Fiction 5. London (England) -- Fiction 6. Mystery and detective stories 7. Characters in literature -- Fiction
ISBN 9781481423038; 9781481423045

LC 2014028105

"In modern-day London, two brilliant high school students--one Sherlock Holmes and a Miss James 'Mori' Moriarty--meet. A murder will bring them together. The truth very well might drive them apart. . . . [They] should be hitting the books on a school night. Instead, they are out crashing a crime scene. . . . Lock has challenged Mori to solve the case before he does." (Publisher's note)

"A definite purchase where mysteries are loved and Sherlock fandom is celebrated." SLJ

Pfeffer, Susan Beth

Blood wounds. Harcourt 2011 248p $16.99

Grades: 7 8 9 10   Fic
1. Homicide -- Fiction 2. Family life -- Fiction 3. Stepfamilies -- Fiction 4. Self-mutilation -- Fiction
ISBN 978-0-547-49638-2

LC 2011009602

Willa seems to have a perfect life as a member of a loving blended family until the estranged father she barely remembers murders his wife and children, then heads toward Willa and her mother.

"This intense psychological drama, showing the brightest and darkest sides of humanity, offers remarkable acts of courage and disturbing images of domestic violence. Willa's frankly portrayed grief, confusion, and uncertainties will have a strong impact on readers." Publ Wkly

Life as we knew it. Harcourt 2006 337p $17

Grades: 7 8 9 10   Fic
1. Science fiction 2. Family life -- Fiction 3. Natural disasters -- Fiction
ISBN 0-15-205826-5; 978-0-15-205826-5

LC 2005-36321

Through journal entries sixteen-year-old Miranda describes her family's struggle to survive after a meteor hits the moon, causing worldwide tsunamis, earthquakes, and volcanic eruptions.

"Each page is filled with events both wearying and terrifying and infused with honest emotions. Pfeffer brings cataclysmic tragedy very close." Booklist

Other titles in this series are:
The dead & gone (2008)
This world we live in (2010)

Philbrick, W. R.

★ The **last** book in the universe; by Rodman Philbrick. Blue Sky Press (NY) 2001 223p hardcover o.p. pa $5.99

Grades: 9 10 11 12   Fic
1. Science fiction 2. Epilepsy -- Fiction
ISBN 0-439-08758-9; 0-439-08759-7 pa

LC 99-59878

Expanded from a short story in Tomorrowland edited by Michael Cart, published 1999 by Scholastic Press

After an earthquake has destroyed much of the planet, an epileptic teenager nicknamed Spaz begins the heroic fight to bring human intelligence back to the Earth of a distant future

"Enthralling, thought-provoking, and unsettling." Voice Youth Advocates

Philpot, Chelsey

Even in paradise; Chelsey Philpot. First edition HarperCollins Childrens Books 2014 368 p. (hardcover) $17.99

Grades: 9 10 11 12   Fic
1. School stories 2. Artists -- Fiction 3. Friendship -- Fiction 4. Private schools -- Fiction 5. Schools --

Fiction 6. Boarding schools -- Fiction
ISBN 0062293699; 9780062293695

LC 2013047956

In this book, by Chelsey Philpot, "Julia Buchanan enrolls at St. Anne's . . . [and] Charlotte Ryder already knows all about her. . . . Charlotte certainly never expects she'll be Julia's friend. But almost immediately, she dives headfirst into the larger-than-life new girl's world . . . a world of midnight rendezvous, dazzling parties, palatial vacation homes, and fizzy champagne cocktails. And then Charlotte meets, and begins falling for, Julia's handsome older brother, Sebastian." (Publisher's note)

"There is nothing in this Gatsbyesque world we haven't seen before, but Philpot knows that and happily hands over the tragic goods: disaffected, charming, well-drawn characters; gauzy tuxedo-and-gown parties; and a wistful, melancholy tone that makes it all seem achingly fleeting." Booklist

Picoult, Jodi, 1966-

★ **My** sister's keeper; a novel. Atria 2004 423p $25; pa $15

Grades: 11 12 Adult   **Fic**
1. Girls 2. Trials 3. Sisters 4. Leukemia 5. Family life 6. Medical ethics 7. Law and lawyers 8. Sisters -- Fiction 9. Bioethics -- Fiction 10. Mother-daughter relationship -- Fiction 11. Transplantation of organs, tissues, etc.
ISBN 0-7434-5452-9; 0-7434-5453-7 pa

LC 2004-300043

"Picoult's timely and compelling novel will appeal to anyone who has thought about the morality of medical decision making and any parent who must balance the needs of different children." Libr J

Pierce, Tamora, 1954-

Alanna: the first adventure; Tamora Pierce. Atheneum Pubs. 1983 241p $12.95

Grades: 7 8 9 10   **Fic**
1. Fantasy fiction 2. Gender role -- Fiction 3. Knights and knighthood -- Fiction
ISBN 0-689-30994-5

LC 83-2595

"Neither Alanna nor her twin brother Thom were happy with their father's decision to send Alanna to a convent and Thom to court. The two decide to switch places and Alanna posing as 'Alan' becomes a page at court while Tom goes to the convent to learn sorcery. Alanna finds life as a page hard, particularly as she is lighter and smaller than the other pages, but she struggles hard to overcome these disadvantages. She makes many friends at court, including . . . Prince Jonathan whose life she saves using her magical gift of healing." (Voice Youth Advocates)

Other titles in this series are:
In the hand of the goddess
The woman who rides like a man
Lioness rampant

Bloodhound. Random House 2009 551p il (Beka Cooper) $18.99; lib bdg $21.99; pa $10.99

Grades: 7 8 9 10   **Fic**
1. Fantasy fiction 2. Police -- Fiction 3. Counterfeits

and counterfeiting -- Fiction
ISBN 978-0-375-81469-3; 0-375-81469-8; 978-0-375-91469-0 lib bdg; 0-375-91469-2 lib bdg; 978-0-375-83817-0 pa; 0-375-83817-1 pa

LC 2008025838

Sequel to Terrier (2006)

Having been promoted from "Puppy" to "Dog," Beka, now a full-fledged member of the Provost's Guard, and her former partner head to a neighboring port city to investigate a case of counterfeit coins.

"Quirky, endearing characters save the story." Booklist
Followed by Mastiff (2011)

Mastiff. Random House 2011 593p (Beka Cooper) $18.99; lib bdg $21.99; e-book $10.99

Grades: 7 8 9 10   **Fic**
1. Fantasy fiction 2. Police -- Fiction 3. Kidnapping -- Fiction 4. Kings and rulers -- Fiction
ISBN 978-0-375-81470-9; 978-0-375-91470-6 lib bdg; 978-0-375-89328-5 e-book

LC 2011024152

Sequel to Bloodhound (2009)

Beka, having just lost her fiance in a slaver's raid, is able to distract herself by going with her team on an important hunt at the queen's request, unaware that the throne of Tortall depends on their success.

"This novel provides both crackerjack storytelling and an endearingly complex protagonist." Kirkus

Terrier. Random House 2006 581p il map (Beka Cooper) hardcover o.p. pa $9.99

Grades: 7 8 9 10   **Fic**
1. Fantasy fiction 2. Magic -- Fiction 3. Police -- Fiction
ISBN 0-375-81468-X; 0-375-83816-3 pa; 978-0-375-81468-6; 978-0-375-83816-3 pa

LC 2006-14834

When sixteen-year-old Beka becomes "Puppy" to a pair of "Dogs," as the Provost's Guards are called, she uses her police training, natural abilities, and a touch of magic to help them solve the case of a murdered baby in Tortall's Lower City. "Grades seven to ten." (Bull Cent Child Books)

"Pierce deftly handles the novel's journal structure, and her clear homage to the police-procedural genre applies a welcome twist to the girl-legend-in-the-making story line." Booklist

Other titles featuring Beka Cooper are:
Bloodhound (2009)
Mastiff (2011)

The **will** of the empress. Scholastic Press 2005 550p $17.99; pa $8.99

Grades: 8 9 10 11 12   **Fic**
1. Fantasy fiction
ISBN 0-439-44171-4; 0-439-44172-2 pa

LC 2005-02874

On visit to Namorn to visit her vast landholdings and her devious cousin, Empress Berenene, eighteen-year-old Sandry must rely on her childhood friends and fellow mages, Daja, Tris, and Briar, despite the distance that has grown between them

"This novel begins two years after the Circle of Magic and The Circle Opens series. . . . Readers will enjoy being reacquainted with these older but still very well-developed characters." SLJ

Pierson, D. C.

The **boy** who couldn't sleep and never had to; a novel. DC Pierson. Vintage Books 2010 226 p. ill. $14.95

Grades: 11 12 Adult　　　　　　　　　　**Fic**

1. Science fiction 2. Teenagers -- Fiction 3. Friendship -- Fiction 4. Sleep disorders -- Fiction 5. Sleep -- Fiction 6. Schools -- Fiction 7. High schools -- Fiction 8. Cartoons and comics -- Fiction

ISBN 9780307474612

LC 2009021984

Alex Award (2011)

In this book, the recipient of a 2010 ALA Alex Award, "[w]hen [high-school student] Darren Bennett meets [classmate] Eric Lederer, there's an instant connection. They share a love of drawing, the bottom rung on the cruel high school social ladder and a pathological fear of girls. Then Eric reveals a secret: He doesn't sleep. Ever. When word leaks out about Eric's condition, he and Darren find themselves on the run. Is it the government trying to tap into Eric's mind, or something far darker? It could be that not sleeping is only part of what Eric's capable of, and the truth is both better and worse than they could ever imagine." (Publisher's note)

Crap kingdom; by DC Pierson. Viking 2013 368 p. (hardcover) $17.99

Grades: 7 8 9 10 11 12　　　　　　　**Fic**

1. Fantasy fiction 2. Humorous fiction 3. Fantasy 4. Heroes -- Fiction

ISBN 067001432X; 9780670014323

LC 2012015578

In this comic novel, by D. C. Pierson, "with [a] . . . mysterious yet oddly ordinary-looking prophecy, Tom's fate is sealed: he's . . . whisked away to a magical kingdom to be its Chosen One. There's just one problem: The kingdom is mostly made of garbage from Earth. . . . When Tom turns down the job of Chosen One, he thinks he's making a smart decision. But when Tom discovers he's been replaced by his best friend Kyle, . . . Tom wants Crap Kingdom back--at any cost." (Publisher's note)

Pike, Aprilynne

Earthbound. Penguin Group USA 2013 352 p. $17.99

Grades: 7 8 9 10　　　　　　　　　　**Fic**

1. Science fiction 2. Paranormal fiction

ISBN 1595146504; 9781595146502

This is the first book in a series from Aprilynne Pike. Here, plane crash survivor Tavia "is in rehab and finishing her senior year online. She has time to look at the world with attentive eyes, and what she sees is often unnerving: glowing triangles on the historic houses of Portsmouth, N.H., or pedestrians who flicker. She tries to attribute these visions to the brain injury she sustained in the crash, but she can't dismiss the stalker with a blond ponytail so easily." (Publishers Weekly)

"The characters are well developed and the narrative is easy to follow... Pike does take a while to get to the heart of the matter, but overall the story is compelling. Readers of supernatural romances will be clamoring." SLJ

Illusions. HarperTeen 2011 375p $16.99

Grades: 7 8 9 10　　　　　　　　　　**Fic**

1. School stories 2. Fantasy fiction 3. Trolls -- Fiction 4. Fairies -- Fiction

ISBN 978-0-06-166809-8; 0-06-166809-5

LC 2010040320

Sequel to: Spells (2010)

As her senior year of high school starts, Laurel is just beginning to adjust to Tamani's absence when he suddenly reappears, telling her he must guard her against the returning threat of the trolls that pose a danger both to her and to Avalon.

"Fans will revel in the idealized characterizations, breathless abstinence romance, lurking danger and newly explicit Arthurian parallels." Kirkus

Spells. HarperTeen 2010 359p $16.99

Grades: 7 8 9 10　　　　　　　　　　**Fic**

1. Fantasy fiction 2. Trolls -- Fiction 3. Fairies -- Fiction

ISBN 978-0-06-166806-7; 0-06-166806-0

LC 2009-24072

Sequel to: Wings (2009)

"Laurel, who recently discovered she is a faerie, finds herself completely immersed in her new world when she begins studies at the Academy of Avalon. . . . But the action really begins when she returns home. The trolls what stalked her in the previous book are more dangerous than ever, and this time Laurel is not the only one being targeted. Pike astutely mixes these breathtaking events with the real meat of the story: the angst and uncertainty Laurel feels as she tries to combine—and sometimes keep separate—her two lives." Booklist

Pike, Christopher

Strange girl; by Christopher Pike. Simon Pulse 2015 432 p. (hardback) $19.99

Grades: 7 8 9 10　　　　　　　　　　**Fic**

1. Supernatural -- Fiction 2. African American teenage girls -- Fiction 3. Love -- Fiction 4. Healers -- Fiction 5. Goddesses -- Fiction

ISBN 9781481450584; 9781481450591

LC 2015012476

In this novel, by Christopher Pike, "from the moment Fred met Aja, he knew she was different. And she was. . . . After a shocking sequence of events, Fred must look back at their relationship, and piece together all of their shared moments, so he can finally understand Aja's precious gift . . . and its devastating repercussions." (Publisher's note)

"On the issue of race, the book is regressive and falls back on negative tropes by turning a significant black character into the Magical Negro. Pensive teen readers might appreciate the book's philosophical questions about the concept of advaita, the recognition of one's 'true self,' but this work better suits Pike's original fans—fans who are far removed from the teenage experience." Kirkus

Pitcher, Annabel

★ **Ketchup** clouds; a novel. by Annabel Pitcher. Little, Brown and Company 2013 272 p. $18

Grades: 8 9 10 11 12 **Fic**
1. Grief -- Fiction 2. Guilt -- Fiction 3. Secrets -- Fiction 4. England -- Fiction 5. Epistolary fiction 6. Letters -- Fiction 7. Bath (England) -- Fiction
ISBN 031624676X; 9780316246767
LC 2012044116

In this book, by Annabel Pitcher, "Zoe has an unconventional pen pal-Mr. Stuart Harris, a Texas Death Row inmate and convicted murderer. But then again, Zoe has an unconventional story to tell. A story about how she fell for two boys, betrayed one of them, and killed the other." (Publisher's note)

"Guilt-ridden British teen Zoe feels responsible for the fates of two brothers--Max, the hot guy with whom she's been making out; and Aaron, with whom she's in love. Zoe's original turns of phrase and sprightly narrative style give her story quick, light momentum and moments of lyricism. Sharp, articulate perceptions and a measure of suspense make this an engaging read." (Horn Book)

My sister lives on the mantelpiece; a novel. Annabel Pitcher. 1st US ed. Little, Brown & Co. 2012 214 p. (hardcover) $17.99

Grades: 6 7 8 9 10 **Fic**
1. Bullies 2. Religions 3. Prejudices 4. Grief -- Fiction 5. England -- Fiction 6. Family problems -- Fiction
ISBN 0316176907; 9780316176903
LC 2011027350

In this book, Annabel Pitcher tells a story about "grief, prejudice, religion, bullying, and familial instability. . . . Jamie and his family are still dealing with his sister Rose's death in a terrorist bombing five years earlier. . . . The family falls apart--their mother runs off with another man, and their alcoholic father moves from London to the Lake District with the children, where he lavishes attention on Rose's urn. . . . Jamie's pivotal friendship with a Muslim girl, Sunya, is a standout." (Publishers Weekly)

Plath, Sylvia

★ The **bell** jar; foreword by Frances McCullough; biographical note by Lois Ames; drawings by Sylvia Plath. 25th anniversary ed; HarperCollins Publishers 1996 296p il $20; pa $16.95 **Fic**
1. Mental illness -- Fiction
ISBN 0-06-017490-0; 0-06-114851-2 pa
LC 96-211742

First published 1963 in the United Kingdom; first United States edition published 1971

"Esther Greenwood, having spent what should have been a glorious summer as guest editor for a young woman's magazine, came home from New York, had a nervous breakdown, and tried to commit suicide. Through months of therapy, Esther kept her rationality, if not her sanity. In telling the story of Esther Plath thinly disguised her own experience with attempted suicide and time spent in an institution." Shapiro. Fic for Youth. 3d edition

Polonsky, Ami

Gracefully Grayson; Ami Polonsky. Hyperion 2014 256 p. $16.99

Grades: 6 7 8 9 **Fic**
1. School stories 2. Transgender teenagers 3. Teacher-student relationship -- Fiction 4. Orphans -- Fiction 5. Theater -- Fiction 6. Family life -- Fiction 7. Middle schools -- Fiction 8. Self-acceptance -- Fiction 9. Transgender people -- Fiction
ISBN 1423185277; 9781423185277
LC 2014010155

In this novel by Ami Polonsky "Grayson Sender has been holding onto a secret for what seems like forever: 'he' is a girl on the inside, stuck in the wrong gender's body. The weight of this secret is crushing, but sharing it would mean facing ridicule, scorn, rejection, or worse. Despite the risks, Grayson's true self itches to break free. Will new strength from an unexpected friendship and a caring teacher's wisdom be enough to help Grayson?" (Publisher's note)

"Sixth grader Grayson daydreams about being a girl, despite being seen by everyone as male. Grayson keeps people at a distance until Amelia moves to town. After landing the (female) lead in a play, Grayson fights for the right to present her truest self to others--both on and off stage. Polonsky captures her protagonist's loneliness, then courage, in an immediate and intimate narrative." Horn Book

Pon, Cindy, 1973-

Fury of the phoenix. Greenwillow Books 2011 362p $17.99

Grades: 9 10 11 12 **Fic**
1. China -- Fiction 2. Supernatural -- Fiction 3. Voyages and travels -- Fiction 4. Father-son relationship -- Fiction
ISBN 978-0-06-173025-2
LC 2010-11700

Sequel to Silver phoenix (2009)

When Ai Ling leaves her home and family to accompany Chen Yong on his quest to find his father, haunted by the ancient evil she thought she had banished to the underworld, she must use her growing supernatural powers to save Chen Yong from the curses that follow her.

Serpentine; Cindy Pon. Month9Books, LLC 2015 300 p. $14.99

Grades: 9 10 11 12 **Fic**
1. Bildungsromans 2. Self-acceptance 3. China -- History -- Fiction
ISBN 1942664338; 9781942664338

This novel by Cindy Pon is "set in the ancient Kingdom of Xia and tells the coming of age story of Skybright, a young girl who worries about her growing otherness. As she turns 16, Skybright notices troubling changes. By day, she is a companion and handmaid to the youngest daughter of a very wealthy family. But nighttime brings with it a darkness. Skybright learns that despite a dark destiny, she must struggle to retain her sense of self— even as she falls in love for the first time." (Publisher's note)

"A fast-paced and engrossing read for anyone weary of the same old hackneyed storylines." Kirkus

★ **Silver** phoenix; beyond the kingdom of Xia. Greenwillow Books 2009 338p $17.99; lib bdg $18.89; pa $8.99

Grades: 9 10 11 12   **Fic**
    1. China -- Fiction 2. Supernatural -- Fiction 3. Voyages and travels -- Fiction 4. Father-daughter relationship -- Fiction
    ISBN 978-0-06-173021-4; 0-06-173021-1; 978-0-06-178033-2 lib bdg; 0-06-178033-2 lib bdg; 978-0-06-173024-5 pa; 0-06-173024-6 pa
                                           LC 2008-29149

With her father long overdue from his journey and a lecherous merchant blackmailing her into marriage, seventeen-year-old Ai Ling becomes aware of a strange power within her as she goes in search of her parent.

"Pon's writing, both fluid and exhilarating, shines whether she's describing a dinner delicacy or what it feels like to stab an evil spirit in the gut. There's a bit of sex here, including a near rape, but it's all integral to a saga that spins and slashes as its heroine tries to find her way home." Booklist

Followed by Fury of the phoenix (2011)

Portes, Andrea
    Anatomy of a misfit; Andrea Portes. First edition HarperTeen, an imprint of HarperCollinsPublishers 2014 336 p. (hardback) $17.99

Grades: 9 10 11 12   **Fic**
    1. School stories 2. Schools -- Fiction 3. Popularity -- Fiction 4. High schools -- Fiction 5. Dating (Social customs) -- Fiction
    ISBN 0062313649; 9780062313645
                                           LC 2014008722

In this young adult novel by Andrea Portes, "narrator Anika Dragomir is the third most popular girl at Pound High School. But inside, she knows she's a freak; she can't stop thinking about former loner Logan McDonough, who showed up on the first day of tenth grade hotter, bolder, and more mysterious than ever. . . . So Anika must choose--ignore her feelings and keep her social status? Or follow her heart and risk becoming a pariah." (Publisher's note)

"Anika Dragomir looks like the All-American girl-next-door, but 'nobody knows that on the inside I am spider soup.' 'Nerd-ball turned goth romance hero' Logan McDonough and God's-gift-to-Nebraska, Jared Kline, vie for her affections. A dramatic climax is foreshadowed by sections in italics that hint at tragedy. Anika's observations are razor-sharp, especially when she's describing other people (and especially when she's ragging on her family)." Horn Book

Portman, Frank
    Andromeda Klein. Delacorte Press 2009 424p $17.99; lib bdg $20.99

Grades: 8 9 10 11 12   **Fic**
    1. Deaf -- Fiction 2. Tarot -- Fiction 3. Libraries -- Fiction 4. Occultism -- Fiction 5. Books and reading -- Fiction 6. People with disabilities -- Fiction
    ISBN 978-0-385-73525-4; 0-385-73525-1; 978-0-385-90512-1 lib bdg; 0-385-90512-2 lib bdg
                                           LC 2009-15879

High school sophomore Andromeda, an outcast because she studies the occult and has a hearing impairment and other disabilities, overcomes grief over terrible losses by enlisting others' help in her plan to save library books—and finds a kindred spirit along the way.

"Andromeda is a compelling character, whose reclaiming of misheard words and misspelled text messages gives her unique and likable flavor. . . . For readers who are occult fans, this quirky text will be a self-satisfied joy." Kirkus

King Dork Approximately; Frank Portman. First edition Delacorte Press 2014 368 p. illustrations (hc) $17.99

Grades: 9 10 11 12   **Fic**
    1. Interpersonal relations 2. High school students -- Fiction 3. Schools -- Fiction 4. High schools -- Fiction 5. Interpersonal relations -- Fiction
    ISBN 0385736185; 9780385736183; 9780385905916
                                           LC 2013042885

Sequel to: King Dork

In Frank Portman's novel "high school sophomore, aspiring rock star, and self-proclaimed outsider Tom Henderson is back in the [sequel] to 'King Dork.' The book opens with Tom being sent to a new school in the wake of the shutdown of his old school. New horizons provide more humorous opportunities for Tom to cast a snarky eye over all he sees." (School Library Journal)

"Because the novel is packed with music, book, and movie references, readers' cultural literacy will get a definite boost. Utterly enjoyable, this book's culture-meets-romantic-confusion focus makes it a teen take on Nick Hornby's High Fidelity (1995), and it should hit home with social misfits and 'subnormals.'" Booklist

Potter, Ryan
    Exit strategy. Flux 2010 303p pa $9.95

Grades: 8 9 10 11 12   **Fic**
    1. Summer -- Fiction 2. Michigan -- Fiction 3. Steroids -- Fiction 4. Friendship -- Fiction
    ISBN 978-0-7387-1573-5; 0-7387-1573-5
                                           LC 2009-27697

Seventeen-year-old Zach, his best friend (and state wrestling champion) Tank, and Tank's twin sister Sarah, an Ivy League-bound scholar, are desperate to leave their depressing hometown of Blaine, Michigan, after next year's graduation, but plans go awry when Zach uncovers a steroid scandal and falls in love with Sarah.

"Packed with suspense and drama, with some romance and a fight, this book is bound to be popular among the male crowd. Just make sure you get it into the right hands; mature themes exist, including extramarital affairs, underage drinking, and anger management." Libr Media Connect

Powell, Laura
    Burn mark; by Laura Powell. Bloomsbury Children's Books 2012 403p. (hardback) $17.99

Grades: 7 8 9 10 11 12   **Fic**
    1. Paranormal fiction 2. Witches -- Fiction 3. Supernatural -- Fiction 4. England -- Fiction 5. London (England) -- Fiction
    ISBN 1599908433; 9781599908434
                                           LC 2011034464

This young adult fantasy, by Laura Powell, is set "in a modern world where witches are hunted down and burned at the stake. . . . Glory is from a family of witches, and is desperate to develop her 'Fae' powers. . . . Lucas is the son of the Chief Prosecutor for the Inquisition with a privileged life very different from the witches he is being trained to prosecute. And then one day, both Glory and Lucas develop the Fae . . . [and] their lives are inextricably bound together." (Publisher's note)

The **game** of triumphs. Alfred A. Knopf 2011 269p $16.99; lib bdg $19.99; ebook $10.99
Grades: 7 8 9 10   Fic
1. Games -- Fiction 2. Tarot -- Fiction 3. Supernatural -- Fiction 4. Space and time -- Fiction 5. London (England) -- Fiction
ISBN 978-0-375-86587-9; 0-375-86587-X; 978-0-375-96587-6 lib bdg; 0-375-96587-4 lib bdg; 978-0-375-89774-0 ebook
                                          LC 2010021813
Fifteen-year-old Cat and three other London teens are drawn into a dangerous game in which Tarot cards open doorways into a different dimension and while there is everything to win, losing can be fatal.
"Original and engrossing." Kirkus

The **Master** of Misrule; Laura Powell. Alfred A. Knopf 2012 363 p. (trade hardcover) $16.99
Grades: 7 8 9 10 11 12   Fic
1. Games -- Fiction 2. Tarot -- Fiction 3. Supernatural -- Fiction 4. England -- Fiction 5. Role playing -- Fiction 6. Space and time -- Fiction 7. London (England) -- Fiction
ISBN 0375865888; 9780375865664; 9780375865886; 9780375897849; 9780375965883
                                          LC 2011021135
Sequel to: The Game of Triumphs
In this book, "despite holding the Triumphs that promise answers to their various back stories (including the murder of Cat's parents, Blaine's abusive stepfather and Flora's comatose sister, all related to the Game of Triumphs), resolution eludes Cat and her friends. They must fight the Fool, now the Master of Misrule, whom they released in the first volume, not only for their own success, but to save the world." (Kirkus Reviews)
"This fast-paced novel mixes fantasy and reality in an intricately described setting... Packed with mystery, action, and even a hint of romance, The Master of Misrule will appeal to fans of role-playing games or anyone seeking an adventurous read.—" VOYA

Powell, William Campbell
Expiration day; William Campbell Powell. Tor Teen 2014 336 p. (hardback) $17.99
Grades: 8 9 10 11 12   Fic
1. Bildungsromans 2. Science fiction 3. Robots -- Fiction 4. Diaries -- Fiction 5. England -- Fiction 6. Coming of age -- Fiction
ISBN 0765338289; 9780765338280
                                          LC 2013025453
In this book, by William Campbell Powell, "it is the year 2049, and humanity is on the brink of extinction. . . . Tania Deeley has always been told that she's a rarity: a human child in a world where most children are sophisticated androids manufactured by Oxted Corporation. . . . Though she

has always been aware of the existence of teknoids, it is not until her first day at The Lady Maud High School for Girls that Tania realizes that her best friend, Siân, may be one." (Publisher's note)
"In this coming-of-age diary, a girl navigates life in a dystopic near-future. By the year 2049, the world has become a rather unfriendly place for humans and robots alike. England is divided into color-coded zones, parts of the African continent are shadowed in mystery, and very few humans are still able to procreate....The author pays homage to the genre's giants while combining realistic characters (both human and android) and detailed worldbuilding with an unpredictably optimistic conclusion. In the end, the thoughtful balance of narrative and description and the well-paced plot are marred only by a mildly distracting subplot that unreels in interstitial "Intervals." An auspicious debut. " (Kirkus)

Pratchett, Terry, 1948-2015
★ **Dodger**; by Terry Pratchett. HarperCollins 2012 360 p. (hardback) $17.99
Grades: 7 8 9 10   Fic
1. Lifesaving 2. Love stories 3. Historical fiction 4. Love -- Fiction 5. Humorous stories 6. Conduct of life -- Fiction 7. Adventure and adventurers -- Fiction 8. Todd, Sweeney (Legendary character) -- Fiction 9. London (England) -- History -- 19th century -- Fiction 10. Great Britain -- History -- Victoria, 1837-1901 -- Fiction
ISBN 0062009494; 9780062009494; 9780062009500
                                          LC 2012022155
Michael L. Printz Honor Book (2013)
Author Terry Pratchett presents a story of historical fiction. "Dodger is a guttersnipe and a tosher . . . [and] a petty criminal but also (generally) one of the good guys. One night he rescues a beautiful young woman and finds himself hobnobbing quite literally with the likes of Charlie Dickens . . . and Ben Disraeli . . . And when he attempts to smarten himself up to impress the damsel in distress, he unexpectedly comes face to face with . . . Sweeney Todd." (Kirkus)

I shall wear midnight. Harper 2010 355p $16.99
Grades: 7 8 9 10   Fic
1. Ghost stories 2. Fantasy fiction 3. Fairies -- Fiction 4. Witches -- Fiction
ISBN 978-0-06-143304-7; 0-06-143304-7
                                          LC 2010-24442
Sequel to: Wintersmith (2006)
Fifteen-year-old Tiffany Aching, the witch of the Chalk, seeks her place amid a troublesome populace and tries to control the ill-behaved, six-inch-high Wee Free Men who follow her as she faces an ancient evil that agitates against witches.
"The final adventure in Pratchett's Tiffany Aching series brings this subset of Discworld novels to a moving and highly satisfactory conclusion." Publ Wkly

★ **Nation.** HarperCollins 2008 367p $16.99; lib bdg $17.89; pa $8.99
Grades: 7 8 9 10 11 12   Fic
1. Islands -- Fiction 2. Tsunamis -- Fiction 3. Survival

after airplane accidents, shipwrecks, etc. -- Fiction
ISBN 978-0-06-143301-6; 0-06-143301-2; 978-0-06-143302-3 lib bdg; 0-06-143302-0 lib bdg; 978-0-06-143303-0 pa; 0-06-143303-9 pa

LC 2008-20211

Boston Globe-Horn Book Award: Fiction (2009)

After a devastating tsunami destroys all that they have ever known, Mau, an island boy, and Daphne, an aristocratic English girl, together with a small band of refugees, set about rebuilding their community and all the things that are important in their lives.

"Quirky wit and broad vision make this a fascinating survival story on many levels." Booklist

The **shepherd's** crown; Terry Pratchett; [edited by] Kathrine Tegen. HarperCollins 2015 276 p. (Discworld series) (hardcover) $18.99

Grades: 6 7 8 9 10 **Fic**

1. Fantasy fiction 2. Fairies -- Fiction 3. Witches -- Fiction

ISBN 9780062429971; 9780062430557

LC 2015943558

In this book, by Terry Pratchett, "Deep in the Chalk, something is stirring. The owls and the foxes can sense it, and Tiffany Aching feels it in her boots. An old enemy is gathering strength. This is a time of endings and beginnings, old friends and new, a blurring of edges and a shifting of power. Now Tiffany stands between the light and the dark, the good and the bad. As the fairy horde prepares for invasion, Tiffany must summon all the witches to stand with her." (Publisher's Note)

"Readers young and old will savor this tale that emphasizes the values of hard work and standing firm in the face of evil. An exceptionally crafted finale from one of the greats." SLJ

Snuff; a novel of Discworld. Terry Pratchett. Harper 2011 398 p. (Discworld series) $25.99; ebook $12.99

Grades: 9 10 11 12 Adult **Fic**

1. Fantasy fiction 2. Criminal investigation -- Fiction 3. Discworld (Imaginary place) -- Fiction

ISBN 978-0-06-201184-8; 0-06-201184-7; 978-0-06-209786-6 ebook; 0-06-209786-5 ebook; 0062097865; 9780062011848; 9780062097866; 0062011847

LC 2011033117

Lady Sybil, wife of Sam Vimes, convinces him to travel to the countryside for a vacation. Out of his element, Sam soon finds various crimes to investigate. But he is out of his element and must rely on his instincts to bring the culprits to justice.

"Pratchett's fun, irreverent-seeming story line masks a larger discussion of social inequalities and the courage it takes to stand up for the voiceless." Libr J

★ The **Wee** Free Men. HarperCollins Pubs. 2003 263p hardcover o.p. pa $9.99

Grades: 7 8 9 10 **Fic**

1. Fantasy fiction 2. Witches -- Fiction

ISBN 0-06-001236-6; 0-06-201217-7 pa

LC 2002-15396

A young witch-to-be named Tiffany teams up with the Wee Free Men, a clan of six-inch-high blue men, to rescue her baby brother and ward off a sinister invasion from Fairyland. "Grades six to ten." (Bull Cent Child Books)

"Pratchett invites readers into his well-established realm of Discworld where action, magic, and characters are firmly rooted in literary reality. Humor ripples throughout, making tense, dangerous moments stand out in stark contrast." Bull Cent Child Books

Other titles about Tiffany are:

A hat full of sky (2004)
Wintersmith (2006)
I shall wear midnight (2010)
The Shepherd's crown (2015)

Preston, Caroline

The **scrapbook** of Frankie Pratt; Caroline Preston. Ecco Press 2011 228p. ill. (some col.)

Grades: 11 12 Adult **Fic**

1. Love stories 2. Historical fiction 3. Women authors -- Fiction 4. Voyages and travels -- Fiction

ISBN 0061966908; 9780061966903

LC 2012372952

Alex Award (2012)

In this book, "Frankie receives a blank scrapbook and her deceased father's typewriter as high-school graduation gifts and begins to record her adventures with the keepsakes she collects. Although Vassar offers Frankie a scholarship, Frankie still can't afford to attend college. Instead she takes a job caring for elderly Mrs. Pingree. . . . The dowager's visiting nephew Jamie, a dashing, emotionally damaged World War I vet in his 30s, emotionally seduces 17-year-old Frankie. . . . When the not-yet-sexual affair is discovered, Mrs. Pingree gives Frankie a $1,000 check. . . . Soon Frankie heads off to Vassar. . . . After graduation, Frankie moves to Greenwich Village and finds a job at 'True Story.' . . . When Frankie realizes why [her boyfriend doesn't propose], she goes to Paris, . . . where the past catches up with her and a whole new chapter of life starts." (Kirkus)

Preus, Margi

Enchantment Lake; a Northwoods mystery. by Margi Preus. University of Minnesota Press 2015 200 p. (hardback) $16.95

Grades: 6 7 8 9 10 **Fic**

1. Mystery fiction 2. Aunts -- Fiction 3. Lakes -- Fiction 4. Minnesota -- Fiction 5. Great-aunts -- Fiction 6. Buried treasure -- Fiction 7. Mystery and detective stories 8. Swindlers and swindling -- Fiction

ISBN 0816683026; 9780816683024

LC 2014042651

In this book, by Margi Preus, a "call from her great aunts Astrid and Jeannette sends seventeen-year-old Francie far from her new home in New York into a tangle of mysteries. Ditching an audition in a Manhattan theater, Francie travels to . . . the shores of Enchantment Lake in the woods of northern Minnesota, [where] something ominous is afoot, and as Francie begins to investigate, the mysteries multiply." (Publisher's note)

"Preus, whose Heart of a Samurai (2010) was a Newbery Honor Book, offers intriguing characters, suspenseful moments, and a love interest—plenty to keep readers involved." Booklist

Shadow on the mountain; a novel inspired by the true adventures of a wartime spy. by Margi Preus. Amulet Books 2012 286 p. (alk. paper) $16.95

Grades: 6 7 8 9   Fic

1. Spies 2. Adventure fiction 3. Historical fiction 4. World War, 1939-1945 5. Spies -- Fiction 6. Norway -- History -- German occupation, 1940-1945 -- Fiction 7. World War, 1939-1945 -- Underground movements -- Norway -- Fiction

ISBN 1419704249; 9781419704246

LC 2012015623

This juvenile historical fiction novel, by Margi Preus, "recounts the adventures of a 14-year-old Norwegian boy named Espen during World War II. After Nazi Germany invades and occupies Norway, Espen and his friends are swept up in the Norwegian resistance movement. Espen gets his start by delivering illegal newspapers, then graduates to the role of courier and finally becomes a spy, dodging the Gestapo along the way." (Publisher's note)

Includes bibliographical references.

Price, Charlie

The **interrogation** of Gabriel James. Farrar Straus Giroux 2010 170p $16.99

Grades: 9 10 11 12   Fic

1. Montana -- Fiction 2. Homicide -- Fiction 3. Criminal investigation -- Fiction

ISBN 978-0-374-33545-8; 0-374-33545-1

LC 2009-37309

As an eyewitness to two murders, a Montana teenager relates the shocking story behind the crimes in a police interrogation interspersed with flashbacks.

"The author writes intriguing and believable characters and keeps a stream of realism moving through the story even when neither readers nor Gabriel are really sure what's going on. Patience from readers won't be required, though, as plenty of action keeps the narrative moving while the plot details unfold. The result is not only suspense but a memorable and believable characterization. Top notch." Kirkus

Price, Lissa

Enders; by Lissa Price. Delacorte Press 2014 288 p. (hc: alk. paper) $17.99

Grades: 7 8 9 10   Fic

1. Brainwashing 2. Teenagers -- Fiction 3. Science -- Experiments -- Fiction 4. Science fiction

ISBN 0385742495; 9780375990618; 9780385742498

LC 2013011679

Sequel to: Starters

In this book by Lissa Price, the conclusion to her Starters series, "someone is after Starters like Callie and Michael--teens with chips in their brains. They want to experiment on anyone left over from Prime Destinations--Starters who can be controlled and manipulated. With the body bank destroyed, Callie no longer has to rent herself out to creepy Enders. But Enders can still get inside her mind and make her do things she doesn't want to do." (Publisher's note)

"Some glossed-over twists stretch believability, though the threat (and villain's secret plan), smaller-scale than in

Starters, is personal in a creepy way. Metals can be controlled remotely, and Callie's modified chip keeps her awake and aware, leading to a delightfully disturbing climax. It's not as intense as Starters, but it offers some answers and a solid conclusion that will repay readers." (Kirkus)

Starters; Lissa Price. Delacorte Press 2012 336 p. (paperback) $9.99; (ebook) $53.97; (glb) $20.99; (hardcover) $17.99

Grades: 7 8 9 10   Fic

1. Science fiction 2. Orphans -- Fiction 3. Intergenerational relations -- Fiction 4. Brothers and sisters -- Fiction

ISBN 9780385742481; 0385742371; 9780307975232; 9780375990601; 9780385742375

LC 2011040820

In this book, "[w]hen a deadly virus wipes out the entire population of the U.S. save the elderly and the young, . . . the result is a dysfunctional society polarized between young 'Starters' and the increasingly long-lived 'Enders.' Children who are unclaimed by surviving relatives are institutionalized, and many -- like Callie and her little brother, Tyler -- learn to fend for themselves in virtual hiding from the law to escape that fate." (Bulletin of the Center for Children's Books)

Price, Nora

Zoe letting go; Nora Price. Razorbill 2012 279 p. $17.99

Grades: 8 9 10 11 12   Fic

1. Rehabilitation -- Fiction 2. Eating disorders -- Fiction 3. Diaries -- Fiction 4. Letters -- Fiction 5. Friendship -- Fiction 6. Anorexia nervosa -- Fiction 7. Emotional problems -- Fiction

ISBN 1595144668; 9781595144669

LC 2012012257

This book tells the story of 16-year-old Zoe, who "finds herself in a small rehabilitation center for girls with eating disorders," which she feels "must be some kind of mistake" because "she feels in control of her cautious dietary habits. Through letters to her mysteriously silent best friend, Elise, as well as a personal journal," it becomes clear that Zoe is in denial and "that she is, in fact, a girl with a disorder that is spiraling out of control." (School Library Journal)

Priest, Cherie

★ **I** Am Princess X; Cherie Priest; with comic art by Kali Ciesemier. Scholastic Inc. 2015 240 p. $18.99

Grades: 7 8 9 10 11 12   Fic

1. Female friendship -- Fiction 2. Comic books, strips, etc. -- Fiction 3. Webcomics -- Fiction 4. Best friends -- Fiction 5. Missing children -- Fiction

ISBN 0545620856; 9780545620857

LC 2015003694

In this novel, by Cherie Priest, with comic art by Kali Ciesemier, "two best friends created a princess together . . . and their heroine, Princess X, slayed all the dragons and scaled all the mountains their imaginations could conjure. Once upon a few years later, . . . Libby passed away, and Princess X died with her. Once upon a now: May is sixteen and lonely, wandering the streets of Seattle, when she sees a sticker slapped in a corner window. Princess X?" (Publisher's note)

"May and Libby created Princess X on the day they met in fifth grade. That was before Libby and her mother died in a car crash. Now May is 16 and looking at another long, lonely summer in Seattle when she spots a Princess X sticker on the corner of a store window. Suddenly she starts seeing Princess X everywhere, including in a webcomic at IAmPrincessX.com, where the princess story is eerily similar to Libby's. . . . An excellent book with loads of cross-genre and cross-format appeal. Highly recommended." SLJ

Prose, Francine

The **turning**; by Francine Prose. HarperTeen 2012 256 p. (hardcover) $17.99

Grades: 7 8 9 10   **Fic**

1. Ghost stories 2. Horror fiction 3. Babysitters -- Fiction 4. Ghosts -- Fiction
ISBN 0061999660; 9780061999666
LC 2012019090

This book by Francine Prose is an "epistolary retelling of Henry James's 'The Turn of the Screw' [which] traces a contemporary babysitter's supernatural encounters. The protagonist, Jack, is hoping to earn some money for college when he agrees to care for orphan siblings on Crackstone's Landing, a remote island without phones, Internet, or TV. . . . Jack is spooked by two ethereal figures, perhaps the ghosts of the children's former governess and her beau." (Publishers Weekly)

Provoost, Anne

In the shadow of the ark; translated by John Nieuwenhuizen. Arthur A. Levine Books 2004 368p $17.95

Grades: 9 10 11 12   **Fic**

1. Noah's ark -- Fiction
ISBN 0-439-44234-6
LC 2003-9622

Original Dutch edition, 2001

This is a "story of the biblical Flood, recounted by Re Jana, whose family leaves the marshes to find the ark. The passion Re Jana finds with Ham, son of the Builder, leads to a place on the ark, but this 'safe haven,' with the stink and sounds of the animals, starvation, and repeated (if not lustful) rapes by Ham's brothers, tests her in every way, even as she carries new life into the New World. Exquisitely detailed and intelligently written, this is a YA novel only in the broadest sense; no one would blink if it appeared on an adult list." Booklist

Pullman, Philip, 1946-

The **amber** spyglass; His Dark Materials book III. [appendix illustrations by Ian Beck] Deluxe ed.; Alfred A. Knopf 2007 518p il $22.99; lib bdg $25.99

Grades: 7 8 9 10 11 12   **Fic**

1. Fantasy fiction
ISBN 978-0-375-84673-1; 978-0-375-94673-8 lib bdg
LC 2006-48865

Sequel to: The subtle knife
First published 2000

Third volume in His Dark Materials trilogy "starts where The Subtle Knife . . . left off. Lyra has been hidden away by her mother, and Will is determined to find her. Meanwhile, Lord Asriel is preparing to fight the forces of the Church's Consistorial Court, as well as the God-like Authority's Lieutenant, Metatron, who hungers for ultimate power over all worlds. At the heart of this discord is Dust, the mysterious substance that is linked irrevocably to consciousness; it is streaming away at an increasing rate, causing havoc in its wake. It is Lyra and Will's destiny to determine the outcome of this situation." SLJ

★ The **golden** compass; his dark materials book I. [appendix illustrations by Ian Beck] Deluxe 10th anniversary ed.; Alfred A. Knopf 2006 399p il $22.95

Grades: 7 8 9 10 11 12   **Fic**

1. Fantasy fiction
ISBN 978-0-375-83830-9; 0-375-83830-9
LC 2005-32556

First published 1995 in the United Kingdom with title: Northern lights

This first title in a fantasy trilogy "introduces the characters and sets up the basic conflict, namely, a race to unlock the mystery of a newly discovered type of charged particles simply called 'dust' that may be a bridge to an alternate universe. The action follows 11-year-old protagonist Lyra Belacqua from her home at Oxford University to the frozen wastes of the North on a quest to save dozens of kidnapped children from the evil 'Gobblers,' who are using them as part of a sinister experiment involving dust." Libr J [review of 1996 edition]

Other titles in the His dark materials series are:
The amber spyglass (2000)
The subtle knife (1997)

Once upon a time in the North; illustrated by John Lawrence. Knopf 2008 95p il $12.99

Grades: 7 8 9 10 11 12   **Fic**

1. Fantasy fiction
ISBN 978-0-375-84510-9; 0-375-84510-0
LC 2007-43993

Prequel to: The golden compass

In a time before Lyra Silvertongue was born, the tough American balloonist Lee Scoresby and the great armoured bear Iorek Byrnison meet when Lee and his hare daemon Hester crash-land their trading balloon onto a port in the far Arctic North and find themselves right in the middle of a political powder keg.

"The precise narrative prose is spiced up with Lee's flights of 'oratorical flamboyancy,' and the sardonic banter between Lee and his daemon Hester is as amusing as ever. [Illustrated with] engraved spot illustrations and 'reproduced' documents." Horn Book

The **subtle** knife; His Dark Materials book II. [appendix illustrations by Ian Beck] Deluxe 10th anniversary ed.; Alfred A. Knopf 2007 326p il $22.99; lib bdg $25.99

Grades: 7 8 9 10 11 12   **Fic**

1. Fantasy fiction

ISBN 978-0-375-84672-4; 978-0-375-94672-1 lib bdg

LC 2006-48866

Sequel to: The golden compass

First published 1997

In the second volume of His dark materials trilogy the boundaries between worlds begin to dissolve. Lyra and her daemon help Will Parry in his search for his father and for a powerful, magical knife.

"More than fulfilling the promise of The Golden Compass, this second volume in the His Dark Materials trilogy starts off at a heart-thumping pace and never slows down." Publ Wkly

Followed by: The amber spyglass

Purcell, Kim

  Trafficked; by Kim Purcell. Viking 2012 384 p.

Grades: 9 10 11 12   **Fic**

1. Slavery -- Fiction 2. Immigrants -- United States -- Fiction 3. Juvenile prostitution 4. Human trafficking -- Fiction 5. Los Angeles (Calif.) -- Fiction 6. Moldovans -- United States -- Fiction

ISBN 0670012807; 9780670012800

LC 2011011530

In this young adult novel by Kim Purcell, "[w]hen Hannah's parents are killed in an explosion in a café in the breakaway republic of Transnistria, she and her grandmother are hard pressed to make ends meet in their Moldovan home. . . . Hannah decides to take an offer to go to America as a nanny for a Russian family. . . . What she finds in America is a harsh reality check; yes, she is a nanny to a reasonably wealthy family, but the family confiscates her return ticket, she is forbidden to leave the house or even speak English, and no money is forthcoming. She is also under threat from a family friend to . . . [who] imports Russian girls as prostitutes. . . . Hannah is constantly worried about what will happen to her." (Bulletin of the Center for Children's Books)

Quick, Matthew

  Boy21; by Matthew Quick. Little, Brown and Co. 2012 250 p.

Grades: 8 9 10 11 12   **Fic**

1. Basketball -- Fiction 2. Friendship -- Fiction 3. Race relations -- Fiction 4. Boys -- Psychology -- Fiction 5. High school students -- Fiction 6. Violence -- Fiction 7. High schools -- Fiction 8. Pennsylvania -- Fiction 9. African Americans -- Fiction

ISBN 0316127973; 9780316127974

LC 2010047995

In this book, high school basketball player "Finley . . . take[s] under his wing Russell Washington, the . . . son of a family friend. Boy21, as Russell now calls himself, was a phenom . . . until his parents were killed and he withdrew into an outer-space obsession and refused to play ball. . . . Just as Boy21 begins to get his life back together, Finley's goes into a tailspin when [his girlfriend] Erin is run down by an enemy of her brother." (Bulletin of the Center for Children's Books)

  Forgive me, Leonard Peacock; by Matthew Quick. Little, Brown and Co. 2013 288 p. $18

Grades: 9 10 11 12   **Fic**

1. School stories 2. Suicide -- Fiction 3. School shootings -- Fiction

ISBN 0316221333; 9780316221337

LC 2012031410

This book by Matthew Quick follows "Leonard Peacock . . . a teenager who feels let down by adults and out of step with his sheeplike classmates. Foreseeing only more unhappiness and disappointment in life (and harboring a secret that's destroying him), Leonard packs up his grandfather's WWII handgun and heads to school, intending to kill his former best friend and then himself. First, though, he will visit the important people in his life." (Publishers Weekly)

"Eighteen-year-old Leonard Peacock is packing a handgun and planning to kill his former best friend, then himself. Over the course of one intense day (with flashbacks), Leonard's existential crisis is delineated through an engaging first-person narrative supplemented with letters from the future that urge Leonard to believe in a "life beyond the |bermorons" at school. Complicated characters and ideas mark this memorable story." (Horn Book)

Quintero, Isabel

  ★ **Gabi,** a girl in pieces; by Isabel Quintero. Cinco Puntos Press 2014 208 p. illustrations (hardback: alk. paper) $17.95

Grades: 9 10 11 12   **Fic**

1. Gay youth -- Fiction 2. Pregnancy -- Fiction 3. High schools -- Fiction 4. Mexican Americans -- Fiction 5. Gays -- Fiction 6. Family problems -- Fiction

ISBN 1935955942; 9781935955948; 9781935955955

LC 2014007658

William C. Morris Award (2015)

In this book, by Isabel Quintero, "Gabi Hernandez chronicles her last year in high school in her diary: Cindy's pregnancy, Sebastian's coming out, the cute boys, her father's meth habit, and the food she craves. And best of all, the poetry that helps forge her identity." (Publisher's note)

"Gabi's voice, as expressed in her diary through poetry, prose, lists, and overheard conversations, is funny, smart, full of wonder, and brutally honest." VOYA

Rabb, Margo

  ★ **Kissing** in America; Margo Rabb. Harpercollins Childrens Books 2015 400 p. $17.99

Grades: 9 10 11 12   **Fic**

1. Love stories 2. Grief -- Fiction 3. Travel -- Fiction 4. Best friends -- Fiction 5. Teenage girls -- Fiction 6. Automobile travel -- Fiction

ISBN 0062322370; 9780062322371

In Margo Robb's novel "in the two years since her father died, sixteen-year-old Eva has found comfort in reading romance novels. Her romantic fantasies become a reality when she meets Will, who understands Eva's grief. Unfortunately . . . he picks up and moves to California without any warning. Not wanting to lose the only person who has been able to pull her out of sadness . . . Eva and her best friend, Annie, concoct a plan to travel to the West Coast to see Will again." (Publisher's note)

"When Eva's boyfriend Will moves to Los Angeles, Eva ropes best friend Annie into a cross-country bus trip to compete on Smartest Girl in America. (Eva's mother thinks the game show, not Will, is the motivation for the trip.) A lineup of friends and meddling relatives adds humor and depth beyond the romance plot, giving Eva a chance to repair her relationships." Horn Book

Raf, Mindy

The **symptoms** of my insanity; Mindy Raf. Dial 2013 384 p. (hardcover) $17.99

Grades: 8 9 10 11 12   **Fic**

1. School stories 2. Puberty -- Fiction 3. Teenage girls -- Fiction 4. Mothers -- Fiction 5. High schools -- Fiction 6. Hypochondria -- Fiction

ISBN 0803732414; 9780803732414

LC 2012024708

In this novel, by Mindy Raf, "a teenage hypochondriac with large breasts learns to deal with life's pressure and find self-acceptance." Izzy's "ever-expanding chest is the brunt of ogling and inappropriate jokes." She is then pranked by a basketball player, exposing a picture of her on the Internet. "Her internal questioning of the incident exemplifies what many teenage girls feel about sexual expectations and misguided culpability in sexual assaults." (Kirkus Reviews)

"While the plot is predictable . . . Izzy's self-deprecating humor and wry observations bring fresh air to tired tropes. Raf's background in comedy serves her well and gives her protagonist an authenticity that will make readers feel invested in her story. A fairly standard contribution to the genre, but a solid one." SLJ

Rainfield, Cheryl

Stained; by Cheryl Rainfield. Harcourt, Houghton Mifflin Harcourt 2013 304 p. $16.99

Grades: 9 10 11 12   **Fic**

1. Kidnapping -- Fiction 2. Survival skills -- Fiction 3. Survival -- Fiction 4. Birthmarks -- Fiction 5. Body image -- Fiction 6. Psychopaths -- Fiction 7. Sexual abuse -- Fiction 8. Beauty, Personal -- Fiction

ISBN 0547942087; 9780547942087

LC 2012047540

In this book by Cheryl Rainfield, "Sarah Meadows longs for 'normal.' Born with a port wine stain covering half her face, all her life she's been plagued by stares, giggles, bullying, and disgust. But when she's abducted on the way home from school, Sarah is forced to uncover the courage she never knew she had, become a hero rather than a victim, and learn to look beyond her face to find the beauty and strength she has inside. It's that—or succumb to a killer." (Publisher's note)

Randall, Thomas

Dreams of the dead. Bloomsbury Children's Books 2009 276p (The waking) pa $8.99

Grades: 8 9 10 11 12   **Fic**

1. School stories 2. Death -- Fiction 3. Japan -- Fiction 4. Supernatural -- Fiction

ISBN 978-1-59990-250-0; 1-59990-250-8

LC 2008-30844

After her mother dies, sixteen-year-old Kara and her father move to Japan, where he teaches and she attends school, but she is haunted by a series of frightening nightmares and deaths that might be revenge—or something worse

"The story has suspense, mystery, and horror. It will be a great hit with fans of manga, anime, or Japanese culture." SLJ

Followed by: Spirits of the Noh (2011)

Rapp, Adam

★ **Punkzilla**. Candlewick Press 2009 244p $16.99

Grades: 10 11 12   **Fic**

1. Brothers -- Fiction 2. Drug abuse -- Fiction 3. Runaway teenagers -- Fiction

ISBN 978-0-7636-3031-7; 0-7636-3031-4

LC 2008-935655

ALA YALSA Printz Award Honor Book (2010)

"Punkzilla" is on a mission to see his older brother "P", before "P" dies of cancer. Still buzzing from his last hit of meth, he embarks on a days-long trip from Portland, Ore. to Memphis, Tenn., writing letters to his family and friends. Along the way, he sees a sketchier side of America and worries if he will make it to see his brother in time.

"Jamie, who has ADD, details every step (being taken advantage of sexually, getting jumped, befriending a female-to-male transsexual, losing his virginity) in expletive-filled, stream-of-consciousness narration with insights into seedy roadside America . . . and his own situation. . . . The teenager's singular voice and observations make for an immersive reading experience." Publ Wkly

★ **Under** the wolf, under the dog. Candlewick Press 2004 310p $16.99

Grades: 9 10 11 12   **Fic**

1. Suicide -- Fiction 2. Illinois -- Fiction 3. Family life -- Fiction

ISBN 0-7636-1818-7

LC 2004-50255

"Steve currently resides in a facility for troubled youth, but most are here for drug abuse or suicidal tendencies, and he doesn't really fit in either category. What's led him here, as he describes in his journal, is a series of life depredations that have sent him reeling into irrationality: his mother's long, horrible, and unsuccessful bout with cancer, his father's concomitant catatonic depression, his brother's drug-induced haze and subsequent suicide, and his own unintentional self-woundings along the way, from a lacerated leg to an injury that eventually results in blindness in one eye." Bull Cent Child Books

Reed, Amy

Over you; by Amy Reed. 1st Simon Pulse hardcover ed. Simon Pulse 2013 299 p. (hardcover) $16.99

Grades: 9 10 11 12   **Fic**

1. Communal living -- Fiction 2. Female friendship -- Fiction 3. Nebraska -- Fiction 4. Friendship -- Fiction 5. Family problems -- Fiction 6. Farm life -- Nebraska -- Fiction 7. Mothers and daughters -- Fiction

ISBN 1442456965; 9781442456969

LC 2012023492

In this book, 17-year-old friends Max and Sadie spend a summer on a communal farm. "Max welcomes the hippie residents (which include Sadie's absentee mother), yurts, and grueling farm work, but Sadie--volatile, self-absorbed, and always the center of attention--quickly grows bored and irate. After Sadie is quarantined with mono, Max has even more freedom to explore her own thoughts, interests, and desires--including a love/hate crush on a surly older boy that surprises even Max." (Publishers Weekly)

Reed, Jaime

Living violet; the Cambion chronicles. Jaime Reed. Dafina KTeen Books 2012 311 p. (paperback) $9.95

Grades: 9 10 11 12   **Fic**

1. Love stories 2. Supernatural -- Fiction 3. High school students -- Fiction 4. Paranormal fiction 5. Teenagers

ISBN 0758269242; 9780758269249

LC 2011275889

This book is a "supernatural boy-meets-girl romance. Samara doesn't understand" women's attraction to "her co-worker, Caleb . . . . When Caleb kills a would-be date-rapist in front of Samara to protect her friend, he's forced to reveal his nature to her. He's a Cambion, meaning he shares his body with an extra soul, that of a seductive incubus that draws the women to him to fulfill its life-sucking nutritional needs." (Kirkus Reviews)

Reese, James

The **strange** case of Doctor Jekyll and Mademoiselle Odile; James Reese. Roaring Brook Press 2012 357 p.

Grades: 9 10 11 12   **Fic**

1. Fantasy fiction 2. Historical fiction 3. Paranormal fiction 4. Witchcraft -- Fiction 5. Orphans -- Fiction 6. Shapeshifting -- Fiction 7. Characters in literature -- Fiction 8. Paris (France) -- History -- Siege, 1870-1871 -- Fiction 9. France -- History -- Occupation and evacuation, 1871-1873 -- Fiction

ISBN 1596436840; 9781596436848

LC 2010053366

In this novel, by James Reese, "desperate to find a cure for her brother Grel's mysterious progressive disease . . . Odile has gone to test some magicked salts on the monkeys, with horrific results. . . . She also runs into a young doctor named Jekyll. . . . Little does she know that Jekyll has been spying on her, so that when she does heal Grel, and in the process transforms him into a powerful, hulking, amoral male, Jekyll is watching." (Bulletin of the Center for Children's Books)

Reeve, Philip, 1966-

★ **Fever** Crumb. Scholastic Press 2010 325p $17.99

Grades: 6 7 8 9 10   **Fic**

1. Science fiction 2. Orphans -- Fiction 3. Sex role -- Fiction 4. London (England) -- Fiction

ISBN 978-0-545-20719-5; 0-545-20719-3

LC 2009-15457

Prequel to: The Hungry City Chronicles series

Foundling Fever Crumb has been raised as an engineer although females in the future London, England, are not believed capable of rational thought, but at age fourteen she leaves her sheltered world and begins to learn startling truths about her past while facing danger in the present.

"Reeve's captivating flights of imagination play as vital a role in the story as his endearing heroine, hiss-worthy villains, and nifty array of supporting characters." Booklist

Followed by A web of air (2011)

★ **Here** lies Arthur. Scholastic Press 2008 339p $16.99

Grades: 7 8 9 10   **Fic**

1. Kings 2. Magic -- Fiction 3. Great Britain -- History -- 0-1066 -- Fiction

ISBN 978-0-545-09334-7; 0-545-09334-1

LC 2008-05787

When her village is attacked and burned, Gwyna seeks protection from the bard Myrddin, who uses Gwyna in his plan to transform young Arthur into the heroic King Arthur.

"Powerfully inventive. . . . Events rush headlong toward the inevitable ending, but Gwyna's observations illuminate them in a new way." Booklist

Scrivener's moon; the third book in the Fever Crumb series. Philip Reeve. Scholastic Press 2012 341 p. (Fever Crumb series) (hardcover) $17.99

Grades: 6 7 8 9 10   **Fic**

1. Steampunk fiction 2. Technology -- Fiction 3. Science fiction 4. England -- Fiction 5. Identity -- Fiction

ISBN 0545222184; 9780545222181

LC 2012008124

This young adult steampunk adventure novel, by Philip Reeve, is the conclusion to the "Fever Crumb" trilogy. "The Scriven people are brilliant, mad--and dead. All except one, whose monstrous creation is nearly complete--a giant city on wheels. New London terrifies the rest of the world, and an army of mammoth-riders gathers to fight it. Meanwhile, young Fever Crumb begins a hunt for Ancient technology in the icy strongholds of the north." (Publisher's note)

A **Web** of Air. Scholastic Press 2011 293p $17.99

Grades: 6 7 8 9 10   **Fic**

1. Science fiction 2. Flight -- Fiction 3. Orphans -- Fiction

ISBN 0-545-22216-8; 978-0-545-22216-7

LC 2010043341

Sequel to: Fever Crumb (2010)

Two years ago, Fever Crumb escaped the wartorn city of London in a traveling theater. Now, she arrives in the extraordinary city of Mayda, where buildings ascend the cliffs on funicular rails, and a mysterious recluse is building a machine that can fly.

"It's clear that Reeve . . . is building toward an epic, and his remarkable storytelling gifts, coupled with a trenchant understanding of human nature, make these projected volumes worth the wait." Horn Book

Reichs, Kathleen J.

Virals; [by] Kathy Reichs. Penguin/Razorbill 2010 454p map $17.99

Grades: 6 7 8 9 10   **Fic**

1. Mystery fiction 2. Viruses -- Fiction 3. Missing

persons -- Fiction
ISBN 978-1-59514-342-6; 1-59514-342-4
                                              LC 2010-42384
Tory Brennan is the leader of a band of teenage "sci-philes" who live on an island off the coast of South Carolina and when the group rescues a dog caged for medical testing, they are exposed to an experimental strain of canine parvo-virus that changes their lives forever.

"From the opening sentence to the last word, readers will be absorbed in Tory Brennan's world. . . . Reichs has found a pitch-perfect voice for Tory that will ring true with today's teens, capturing and entirely new audience." Kirkus

Followed by: Seizure (2011)

Reinhardt, Dana

Harmless. Wendy Lamb Books 2007 229p hardcover o.p. pa $8.99
Grades: 7 8 9 10   **Fic**
1. Truthfulness and falsehood -- Fiction
ISBN 0-385-74699-7; 978-0-385-74699-1; 0-553-49497-X pa; 978-0-553-49497-6 pa
When Anna, Emma, and Mariah concoct a story about why they are late getting home one Friday night, their lie has unimaginable consequences for the girls, their families, and the community.

"Reinhardt's thought-provoking story avoids preachiness in part because of the girls' strong, complex characterizations." Booklist

★ The **things** a brother knows. Wendy Lamb Books 2010 245p $16.99; lib bdg $19.99
Grades: 7 8 9 10 11 12   **Fic**
1. Brothers -- Fiction 2. Soldiers -- Fiction 3. Family life -- Fiction 4. Boston (Mass.) -- Fiction 5. Jews -- United States -- Fiction
ISBN 978-0-375-84455-3; 0-375-84455-4; 978-0-375-94455-9 lib bdg; 0-375-94455-9 lib bdg
Although they have never gotten along well, seventeen-year-old Levi follows his older brother Boaz, an ex-Marine, on a walking trip from Boston to Washington, D.C. in hopes of learning why Boaz is completely withdrawn.

"Reinhardt's poignant story of a soldier coping with survivor's guilt and trauma, and his Israeli American family's struggle to understand and help, is timely and honest." Booklist

We are the Goldens; by Dana Reinhardt. Wendy Lamb Books, an imprint of Random House Children's Books 2014 208 p. (trade) $16.99
Grades: 9 10 11 12   **Fic**
1. Sisters -- Fiction 2. High schools -- Fiction 3. Child sexual abuse -- Fiction 4. Teacher-student relationship -- Fiction 5. Divorce -- Fiction 6. Schools -- Fiction 7. Sexual abuse -- Fiction 8. Teacher-student relationships -- Fiction
ISBN 0385742576; 9780375990656; 9780385742573; 9780385742580
                                              LC 2013023351
In this book, by Dana Reinhardt, 'Nell worships her older sister, Layla. They're one unit, intertwined: Nellayla. As Nell and her best friend, Felix, start their freshman year in high school, on Layla's turf, there's so much Nell looks

forward to: Joining Layla on the varsity soccer team. Parties. Boys. Adventures. But the year takes a very different turn. Layla is . . . hiding something, and when Nell discovers what it is, and the consequences it might have, she struggles." (Publisher's note)

"Reinhardt plunges into the dilemmas of sibling affection and loyalty. High schooler Nell's equilibrium shatters when she realizes her sister Layla is having an affair with a teacher. Nell's narrative (directly addressed to Layla as "you") explains how she arrived at the difficult decision to tell their parents. Nell's voice is engaging, clever, and colloquial, making this a speedy, engrossing read." Horn Book

Renn, Diana

Latitude zero; by Diana Renn. Viking, published by Penguin Group 2014 448 p. (hardback) $17.99
Grades: 7 8 9 10   **Fic**
1. Mystery fiction 2. Murder -- Fiction 3. Bicycles -- Fiction 4. Journalists -- Fiction 5. Organized crime -- Fiction 6. Ecuador -- Fiction 7. Bicycle racing -- Fiction 8. Mystery and detective stories 9. Investigative journalists -- Fiction
ISBN 067001558X; 9780670015580
                                              LC 2013043837
In this book, by Diana Renn, "[w]hen star cyclist Juan Carlos Macias-Leon is murdered during the course of a charity bicycle race, Tess, one of the last to see him alive, finds herself involved and, as she begins to investigate, in jeopardy. Determined, nevertheless, to find the truth, she travels to Juan Carlos' native country, Ecuador (the latitude zero of the title). There, she discovers that danger has pursued her, and the more she investigates, the more questions she has." (Booklist)

"Renn has constructed a salient "Whodunit" totally upon the sport of professional bike racing, injecting the plot with adrenaline at every twist, and throwing the reader in tandem with the characters. Furthermore, this diverse array of talented teen characters makes Latitude Zero an inspiring read for the adolescent reader." VOYA

Tokyo heist; by Diana Renn. Viking 2012 373 p. (hardcover) $17.99
Grades: 7 8 9 10 11 12   **Fic**
1. Mystery fiction 2. Art thefts -- Fiction 3. Tokyo (Japan) -- Fiction 4. Seattle (Wash.) -- Fiction 5. Mystery and detective stories 6. Fathers and daughters -- Fiction
ISBN 0670013323; 9780670013326
                                              LC 2011043364
In this book "when sixteen-year-old Violet agrees to spend the summer with her father, an up-and-coming artist in Seattle, she has no idea what she's walking into. Her father's newest clients, the Yamada family, are the victims of a high-profile art robbery: van Gogh sketches have been stolen from their home, and, until they can produce the corresponding painting, everyone's lives are in danger." (Publisher's note)

"The plot has lots of twists and turns, leaving readers on edge, and a hint of romance... Teens will learn about Japanese culture, and fans of manga and art students will rejoice that they can relate to the protagonist and story." LJ

Rennison, Louise

★ **Angus,** thongs and full-frontal snogging; confessions of Georgia Nicolson. HarperCollins Pubs. 2000 247p hardcover o.p. pa $6.95

Grades: 7 8 9 10 **Fic**

1. Great Britain -- Fiction
ISBN 0-06-028814-0; 0-06-447227-2 pa

LC 99-40591

First published 1999 in the United Kingdom
Michael L. Printz Award honor book, 2001

Presents the humorous journal of a year in the life of Georgia, a fourteen-year-old British girl who tries to reduce the size of her nose, stop her mad cat from terrorizing the neighborhood animals, and win the love of handsome hunk Robbie.

"Georgia is a wonderful character whose misadventures are not only hysterically funny but universally recognizable." Booklist

Other titles about Georgia are:

Are these my basoomas I see before me? (2009)

Away laughing on a fast camel (2004)

Dancing in my nuddy-pants (2003)

Knocked out by my nunga-nungas (2002)

Love is a many trousered thing (2007)

On the bright side, I'm now the girlfriend of a sex god (2001)

Startled by his furry shorts (2006)

Stop in the name of pants (2008)

Then he ate my boy entrancers (2005)

Are these my basoomas I see before me? final confessions of Georgia Nicolson. HarperTeen 2009 310p $16.99; lib bdg $17.89

Grades: 7 8 9 10 **Fic**

1. Diaries -- Fiction 2. Theater -- Fiction 3. Great Britain -- Fiction 4. Dating (Social customs) -- Fiction
ISBN 978-0-06-145935-1; 0-06-145935-6; 978-0-06-145936-8 lib bdg; 0-06-145936-4 lib bdg

LC 2009-25449

British teenager Georgia Nicolson's humorous diary entries reveal the results as she finally chooses between potential boyfriends, but then becomes involved in a play with the one not chosen, further complicating her love life.

Stop in the name of pants! HarperTeen 2008 310p $16.99; lib bdg $17.89

Grades: 7 8 9 10 **Fic**

1. Diaries -- Fiction 2. Great Britain -- Fiction 3. Dating (Social customs) -- Fiction
ISBN 978-0-06-145932-0; 0-06-145932-1; 978-0-06-145933-7 lib bdg; 0-06-145933-X lib bdg

LC 2008-14686

In a series of humorous diary entries, British teenager Georgia Nicolson tries to decide between two potential boyfriends—Masimo from Pizzagogoland (Italy) or local boy Dave the Laugh.

The taming of the tights; Louise Rennison. HarperTeen 2013 306 p. (trade bdg.) $17.99

Grades: 7 8 9 10 11 12 **Fic**

1. Love stories 2. School stories 3. Actresses -- Fiction 4. Teenagers -- Fiction 5. Humorous stories

6. England -- Fiction 7. Schools -- Fiction 8. High schools -- Fiction 9. Performing arts -- Fiction 10. Yorkshire (England) -- Fiction 11. Dating (Social customs) -- Fiction
ISBN 0062226207; 9780062226204

LC 2013021359

Sequel to: A midsummer tights dream

In this book, by Louise Rennison, "Tallulah and her mates are back to finish their winter term at the Dother Hall performing arts program. And Tallulah is determined to finally show the world she's a true star of the stage! She's distracted by bad-boy Cain and trying her best to keep her accidental snog-session with him a secret. And although she is slowly beginning to think that maybe he's not so bad after all, she also continues to wonder about unavailable Charlie and dreamy Alex." (Publisher's note)

"Tallulah (A Midsummer Tights Dream) and the Tree Sisters are back for another term at performing arts college where they comically reinterpret another Shakespeare play. But drama follows Tallulah offstage as she debates who is better boyfriend material: Cain or Charlie. Though the book is light on plot, readers will welcome the return of Tallulah's humorous musings and this distinctly British, quirky cast of characters." (Horn Book)

Resau, Laura

The **indigo** notebook. Delacorte Press 2009 324p $16.99; lib bdg $19.99; pa $9.99

Grades: 7 8 9 10 11 12 **Fic**

1. Ecuador -- Fiction 2. Fathers -- Fiction 3. Single parent family -- Fiction 4. Mother-daughter relationship -- Fiction
ISBN 978-0-385-73652-7; 0-385-73652-5; 978-0-385-90614-2 lib bdg; 0-385-90614-5 lib bdg; 978-0-375-84524-6 pa; 0-375-84524-0 pa

LC 2008-40519

Fifteen-year-old Zeeta comes to terms with her flighty mother and their itinerant life when, soon after moving to Ecuador, she helps an American teenager find his birth father in a nearby village

"Observant, aware, and occasionally wry, Zeeta's first-person narration will attract readers and hold them." Booklist

Followed by: The ruby notebook (2010)

The **jade** notebook; Laura Resau. Delacorte Press 2012 365 p. (hc) $16.99

Grades: 9 10 11 12 **Fic**

1. Mexico -- Fiction 2. Fathers -- Fiction 3. Missing persons -- Fiction 4. Mother-daughter relationship -- Fiction 5. Secrets -- Fiction 6. Mazunte (Mexico) -- Fiction 7. Mothers and daughters -- Fiction 8. Single-parent families -- Fiction
ISBN 0385740530; 9780375899416; 9780375989537; 9780385740531

LC 2011034861

Sequel to: The ruby notebook

This book is the "third in a series of novels focusing on Zeeta and her wanderlust-stricken mother. . . . Zeeta's decision to find her mom a job in Mazunte was no accident. Newly armed with a slew of hints about her father's background . . . she is madly hoping that it might be his hometown. . . . With her boyfriend, Wendell, by her side, she begins to fit together the pieces of the puzzle. Yet each answer uncovered seems to create more questions about her father's complex past." (Kirkus Reviews)

"The lush descriptions, intermittent action sequences, and sprinkling of fantasy all come together to form an engaging reading experience that will delight teens looking for a more mature story.—" SLJ

Red glass. Delacorte Press 2007 275p $15.99; lib bdg $18.99

Grades: 7 8 9 10   Fic
1. Mexico -- Fiction 2. Orphans -- Fiction 3. Guatemala -- Fiction 4. Family life -- Fiction 5. Automobile travel -- Fiction
ISBN 978-0-385-73466-0; 0-385-73466-2; 978-0-385-90464-3 lib bdg; 0-385-90464-9 lib bdg
                                    LC 2007-02408

Sixteen-year-old Sophie has been frail and delicate since her premature birth, but discovers her true strength during a journey through Mexico, where the six-year-old orphan her family hopes to adopt was born, and to Guatemala, where her would-be boyfriend hopes to find his mother and plans to remain.

"The vivid characters, the fine imagery, and the satisfying story arc make this a rewarding novel." Booklist

The **ruby** notebook. Delacorte Press 2010 373p $16.99; lib bdg $19.99

Grades: 7 8 9 10   Fic
1. France -- Fiction 2. Single parent family -- Fiction 3. Mother-daughter relationship -- Fiction
ISBN 978-0-385-73653-4; 0-385-73653-3; 978-0-385-90615-9 lib bdg; 0-385-90615-3 lib bdg
                                    LC 2009-51965

Sequel to: The indigo notebook (2009)

When sixteen-year-old Zeeta and her itinerant mother move to Aix-en-Provence, France, Zeeta is haunted by a mysterious admirer who keeps leaving mementoes for her, and when her Ecuadorian boyfriend comes to visit, their relationship seems to have changed.

"Weaving bits of magic, city lore and bittersweet romance into each of the many plot lines, Resau has again crafted a complex and satisfying novel. . . . Characters are rich and vibrant." Kirkus

Revis, Beth

Across the universe. Razorbill 2011 398p $17.99

Grades: 7 8 9 10   Fic
1. Science fiction 2. Dictators -- Fiction 3. Space vehicles -- Fiction
ISBN 978-1-59514-397-6; 1-59514-397-1
                                    LC 2010-51834

Amy, a cryogenically frozen passenger aboard the vast spaceship Godspeed, is nearly killed when her cyro chamber is unplugged fifty years before Godspeed's scheduled landing. All she knows is that she must race to unlock Godspeed's hidden secrets before whoever woke her tries to kill again—and she doesn't know who she can trust on a ship ruled by a tyrant.

"Revis's tale hits all of the standard dystopian notes, while presenting a believable romance and a series of tantalizing mysteries that will hold readers' attention." Publ Wkly

A **million** suns. Razorbill 2012 400 p.

Grades: 9 10 11 12   Fic
1. Science fiction 2. Homicide -- Fiction 3. Space flight -- Fiction 4. Interplanetary voyages -- Fiction
ISBN 9781101552247; 9781595143983; 9781595145376

This book follows a girl named Amy, who has been cryogenically frozen and placed "aboard the spaceship Godspeed" along with over two-thousand others. She and "16-year-old leader Elder . . . deal with two puzzles: who is killing members of the ship, and where are the hidden clues left behind by the murderer Orion leading?" (Booklist) "Since Elder demanded that the tranquilizing drug Phydus be removed from the water supply, people have awakened to their real emotions, and many are violent, angry, or depressed. Elder is faced with the very real possibility of rebellion, which he doesn't have time for because he's desperately trying to figure out what has gone wrong with the ship's engines. Also, food supplies are running low and the ship is beginning to break down." (School Libr J)

Shades of Earth; An Across the Universe Novel. Beth Revis. Penguin Group USA 2013 400 p. $18.99

Grades: 9 10 11 12   Fic
1. Science fiction 2. Space colonies -- Fiction 3. Life on other planets -- Fiction
ISBN 1595143998; 9781595143990

This young adult science fiction adventure story, by Beth Revis, is the conclusion to the "Across the Universe" trilogy. "Amy and Elder have finally left the oppressive walls of the spaceship Godspeed behind. They're ready to start life afresh . . . on Centauri-Earth, the planet that Amy has traveled 25 trillion miles across the universe to experience. But this new Earth isn't the paradise Amy had been hoping for. . . . And if they're going to stay, they'll have to fight." (Publisher's note)

Rex, Adam

Fat vampire; a never coming of age story. Balzer + Bray 2010 324p $16.99

Grades: 9 10 11 12   Fic
1. School stories 2. Obesity -- Fiction 3. Vampires -- Fiction 4. Television programs -- Fiction
ISBN 978-0-06-192090-5
                                    LC 2010-9616

After being bitten by a vampire, not only is fifteen-year-old Doug doomed eternally to be fat, but now he must also save himself from the desperate host of a public-access-cable vampire-hunting television show that is on the verge of cancellation.

"Rex successfully sustains the wonderfully dry humor and calculated silliness and then surprises the reader with a thoughtful, poignant, ambiguous ending that is bound to inspire discussion." Booklist

Reynolds, Jason

★ **Boy** in the black suit; Jason Reynolds. Atheneum Books for Young Readers 2015 272 p. (hardcover) $17.99

Grades: 7 8 9 10   **Fic**
1. Grief -- Fiction 2. African Americans -- Fiction 3. Undertakers and undertaking -- Fiction 4. Funeral homes -- Fiction 5. Brooklyn (New York, N.Y.) -- Fiction 6. Funeral rites and ceremonies -- Fiction 7. Family life -- New York (State) -- Brooklyn -- Fiction
ISBN 1442459506; 9781442459502; 9781442459519
      LC 2014001493

Coretta Scott King Author Award, Honor Book (2016)

In this teen novel, by Jason Reynolds, "with his mother newly dead, a job in a funeral home somehow becomes the perfect way for Matthew to deal with his crushing grief. Initially skeptical, he plans to use his early-release senior year program to work at a fried-chicken joint that's staffed by an entrancing girl with whom he eventually develops a . . . relationship. But the funerals intrigue him and then become deeply satisfying; Matthew finds solace in seeing others experiencing his pain." (Kirkus Reviews)

"High-school senior Matt has a job at Mr. Ray's funeral home, but he's also in mourning, for his mother who died and his long-on-the-wagon father who's returned to drink. While all this sounds like heavy problem-novel territory, it isn't. Reynolds writes about urban African American kids in a warm and empathetic way that the late Walter Dean Myers would have applauded." Horn Book

★ **When** I was the greatest; Jason Reynolds. Atheneum Books for Young Readers 2014 240 p. (hardcover) $17.99

Grades: 9 10 11 12   **Fic**
1. Street life 2. Teenagers -- Fiction 3. Violence -- Fiction 4. Neighborhoods -- Fiction 5. Conduct of life -- Fiction 6. African Americans -- Fiction 7. Brothers and sisters -- Fiction 8. Brooklyn (New York, N.Y.) -- Fiction 9. Family life -- New York (State) -- Brooklyn -- Fiction
ISBN 1442459476; 9781442459472
      LC 2012045734

Steptoe New Talent Author Award (2015)

In this book by Jason Reynolds "Ali lives . . . in the Bed-Stuy neighborhood of Brooklyn and spends all of his free time with best friends Noodles and Needles. Needles was born with Tourette's syndrome . . . [and the] teens hang out on the stoop and streets, living life and getting in just a touch of mischief. When their friend Tasha gets them into a party-and not just any party, an exclusive, adults-only party-trouble escalates." (School Library Journal)

"Sixteen-year-old Ali is a walking contradiction. He's a lauded boxer-in-training who's afraid of stepping into the ring; a straight-laced, head-down kind of kid on a bad block in Bed-Stuy, a neighborhood rife with drugs and violence... With fresh, fast-paced dialogue, Reynolds' debut novel chronicles Ali's friendship with next-door brothers Needles and Noodles, flawed but unforgettable characters all their own, as the three prepare for the party of a lifetime—and pay the consequences for thrusting themselves into a more sordid encounter than any of them could have envisioned. When I Was the Greatest is urban fiction with heart, a medi-

tation on the meaning of family, the power of friendship, and the value of loyalty." (Booklist)

Rice-Gonzalez, Charles

Chulito; Charles Rice-González. 1st Magnus Books ed. Magnus Books 2011 317 p. (paperback) $14.95

Grades: 10 11 12   **Fic**
1. School stories 2. Gay teenagers -- Fiction 3. Gay youth -- Fiction 4. Bronx (New York, N.Y.) -- Fiction 5. Coming out (Sexual orientation) -- Fiction 6. Latin Americans -- New York (State) -- New York -- Fiction
ISBN 1936833034; 9781936833030
      LC 2011279750

In this book, "Chulito is a 15-year-old Puerto Rican high school dropout, who is right at home among the hip-hop-loving, macho, 'anything to survive' neighbors in a tough section of the Bronx. Growing up, he is close to Carlos, who—like Chulito—lived with a single mother in the same building. But the boys grow apart when Carlos finishes high school and goes to Long Island to attend college—primarily because he is perceived as being gay." Chulito falls in love with Carlos. (Echo Magazine)

Rich, Naomi

Alis. Viking Children's Books 2009 274p $17.99

Grades: 7 8 9 10   **Fic**
1. Marriage -- Fiction 2. Religion -- Fiction 3. Runaway teenagers -- Fiction
ISBN 978-0-670-01125-4; 0-670-01125-8
      LC 2008-23234

Raised within the strict religious confines of the Community of the Book, Alis flees from an arranged marriage to the much older Minister of her town and her life takes a series of unexpected twists before she returns to accept her fate.

"Rich's sympathetic portrayal of Alis and her desperate struggle to exercise free will in a theocracy will have audiences firmly gripped." Publ Wkly

Rich, Simon

Elliot Allagash; a novel. Random House 2010 227p $23

Grades: 11 12 Adult   **Fic**
1. School stories 2. Money -- Fiction 3. Wealth -- Fiction 4. Friendship -- Fiction
ISBN 978-1-4000-6835-7
      LC 2009-43885

"The book follows the trial by fire of the narrator, Seymour, an obese but grudgingly docile eighth-grader at a posh Manhattan private school. He's the sort of kid who puts up with the school's arcane policy of putting any student involved in a scrap in detention—which means Seymour is in detention every week just for getting beaten up. His life changes dramatically when another character, an arrogant little bastard who stands to inherit an unimaginable fortune, takes an interest in Seymour's future. . . . Before long Seymour is stealing test answers; accepting a devilish bargain to sneak into Harvard; and corrupting the simplistic social systems of school to rise to the top of its hierarchy, no matter what it costs. . . . Rich is always funny, and he nails the bogus solemnity of high-school social politics. A high-school romp that John Hughes should be so lucky to direct." Kirkus

Richards, Jame

Three rivers rising; a novel of the Johnstown flood. Alfred A. Knopf 2010 293p $16.99; lib bdg $19.99

Grades: 6 7 8 9 10   **Fic**

1. Novels in verse 2. Floods -- Fiction 3. Pennsylvania -- Fiction 4. Social classes -- Fiction

ISBN 978-0-375-85885-7; 0-375-85885-7; 978-0-375-95885-4 lib bdg; 0-375-95885-1 lib bdg

LC 2009-4251

Sixteen-year-old Celestia is a wealthy member of the South Fork Fishing and Hunting Club, where she meets and falls in love with Peter, a hired hand who lives in the valley below, and by the time of the torrential rains that lead to the disastrous Johnstown flood of 1889, she has been disowned by her family and is staying with him in Johnstown. Includes an author's note and historical timeline.

This is a "striking novel in verse. . . . Richards builds strong characters with few words and artfully interweaves the lives of these independent thinkers." Publ Wkly

Includes bibliographical references

Richards, Natalie D.

Six months later; by Natalie D. Richards. Sourcebooks Fire 2013 336 p. (tp: alk. paper) $9.99

Grades: 9 10 11 12   **Fic**

1. School stories 2. Memory -- Fiction 3. Secrets -- Fiction 4. Schools -- Fiction 5. High schools -- Fiction

ISBN 1402285515; 9781402285516

LC 2013012470

In this book, by Natalie Richards, "Chloe, an average student with a bit of a rebellious streak, wakes up in study hall one day not remembering the past six months. But suddenly she's popular, dating her longtime crush, being recruited by Ivy League colleges because of top SAT scores, and her best friend is no longer speaking to her. As Chloe tries to unravel her memories, she begins to uncover secrets more dangerous than she ever thought possible." (Publisher's note)

Richmond, Michelle

No one you know; a novel. Delacorte Press 2008 306p pa $15

Grades: 10 11 12 Adult   **Fic**

1. Mystery fiction 2. Sisters -- Fiction 3. Homicide -- Fiction

ISBN 978-0-385-34013-7; 0-385-34013-3; 978-0-385-34014-4 pa; 0-385-34014-1 pa

LC 2008-13508

"As complex and beautiful as a mathematical proof, this gripping, thought-provoking novel will keep you thinking long after the last page has been turned." Family Circle

Richmond, Peter

Always a catch; Peter Richmond. Philomel Books, An Imprint of Penguin Group (USA) 2014 288 p. $17.99

Grades: 9 10 11 12   **Fic**

1. Football -- Fiction 2. High school students -- Fiction

3. Schools -- Fiction 4. Pianists -- Fiction 5. Boarding schools -- Fiction 6. Self-realization -- Fiction

ISBN 0399250557; 9780399250552

LC 2013045424

In this young adult novel by Peter Richmond, "Oakhurst is more than an escape--it's a chance for Jack to do something new, to try out for the football team. Once Jack makes the team, he's thrust into a foreign world--one of intense hazing, vitamin supplements, monkey hormones and steroids. Jack has to decide how far he's willing to go to fit in--and how much he's willing to compromise himself to be the man his team wants him to be." (Publisher's note)

"After transferring to boarding school Oakhurst Hall, Jack, a skilled pianist, joins the football team and finds himself facing an unknown world of hazing and performance-enhancing drugs. Jack treads the line between letting down his team and being honest with himself in a way that feels honest and tense without a false note of hope tacked on." Horn Book

Riggs, Ransom

Library of souls; Ransom Riggs. Random House Distribution Childrens 2015 458 p. illustrations, portraits (hardcover) $18.99

Grades: 9 10 11 12 Adult   **Fic**

1. Paranormal fiction 2. Rescue work -- Fiction

ISBN 9781594747588; 159474758X

LC 2015939051

In this young adult novel, by Ransom Riggs, book three of the "Miss Peregrine's peculiar children" series, "Time is running out for the Peculiar Children. With a dangerous madman on the loose and their beloved Miss Peregrine still in danger, Jacob Portman and Emma Bloom are forced to stage the most daring of rescue missions. They'll travel through a war-torn landscape, meet new allies, and face greater dangers than ever." (Publisher's Note)

"This YA series has strong crossover appeal; this latest volume is a must-purchase where fans have embraced the first two." SLJ

Riordan, James

The **sniper**. Frances Lincoln Children's Books 2009 229p il pa $8.95

Grades: 9 10 11 12   **Fic**

1. War stories 2. Stalingrad, Battle of, 1942-1943 -- Fiction

ISBN 978-1-84507-885-0

This is the story of a teenage sniper recruited in 1942 to seek out and shoot German officers. At first Tania finds it impossible to kill, but after a shocking discovery goes on to kill as many as 84 Germans.

"There is a deep poignancy and a moral tone here, along with exciting action, heroism and anguish. . . . This fine volume will appeal to many readers." Kirkus

Ritter, William

Beastly bones; a Jackaby novel. William Ritter. Algonquin Young Readers 2015 304 p. $17.95

Grades: 7 8 9 10   **Fic**

1. Supernatural -- Fiction 2. Private investigators -- Fiction 3. Monsters -- Fiction 4. Mystery and detective stories 5. Imaginary creatures -- Fiction 6. New

England -- History -- 19th century -- Fiction
ISBN 1616203544; 9781616203542

LC 2015010990

Sequel to Jackaby

In this novel by William Ritter, set "in 1892, New Fiddleham, New England, things are never quite what they seem, especially when Abigail Rook and her eccentric employer, R. F. Jackaby, are called upon to investigate the supernatural. Policeman Charlie Cane, exiled from New Fiddleham to the valley, calls on Abigail for help, and soon Abigail and Jackaby are on the hunt for a thief, a monster, and a murderer." (Publisher's note)

"With one case closed but two unsolved, the well-matched, well-written duo will undoubtedly return to fight a more fearsome foe. A witty and weird adventure equal parts Sherlock and Three Stooges." Kirkus

Robert, Na'ima B.

Boy vs. girl. Frances Lincoln Children's 2011
260p $15.95
Grades: 6 7 8 9 10 **Fic**
1. Twins -- Fiction 2. Muslims -- Fiction 3. Ramadan -- Fiction 4. Siblings -- Fiction 5. Great Britain -- Fiction 6. Pakistanis -- Great Britain -- Fiction
ISBN 978-1-84780-150-0; 1-84780-150-1

"Twins Farhana and Faraz determine to fast during Ramadan now that they are 16. . . . As first-generation Brits, they must respond to the demands of their Pakistani family, their secular schools, and their friends. . . . The characters are realistic. . . . A well-balanced chord is struck here between storytelling and exploring the complex and sometimes conflicting pulls of tradition, family, friends, and lifestyle." Booklist

She wore red trainers; A Muslim Love Story. by Na'ima B. Robert. Kube Publishing Ltd 2014 261 p. $12.95
Grades: 9 10 11 12 **Fic**
1. Love -- Fiction 2. Muslims -- Fiction 3. Marriage -- Fiction 4. Loss (Psychology) -- Fiction 5. Courtship 6. Dating (Social customs) -- Religious aspects
ISBN 1847740650; 9781847740656

In this book, by Na'ima B. Robert, "[w]hen Ali first meets Amirah, he notices everything about her—her hijab, her long eyelashes and her red trainers—in the time it takes to have one look, before lowering his gaze. And, although Ali is still coming to terms with the loss of his mother and exploring his identity as a Muslim, and although Amirah has sworn never to get married, they can't stop thinking about each other. Can Ali and Amirah ever have a halal 'happily ever after'?" (Publisher's note)

"Eighteen-year-old Muslim neighbors Ali and Amirah surprise themselves and each other by falling in love at first sight. . . . Alternating between Amirah and Ali's perspectives, Robert (Black Sheep) teases out the subtleties of young romance and the confounding pull of mutual attraction. While the story takes some melodramatic turns, it speaks vividly to conflicts of freedom, temptation, and faith." PW

Roberts, Jeyn

Dark inside. Simon & Schuster Books for Young Readers 2011 327p $17.99
Grades: 7 8 9 10 **Fic**
1. Science fiction 2. Monsters -- Fiction 3. Good and evil -- Fiction
ISBN 978-1-4424-2351-0; 1-4424-2351-X

LC 2011008642

After tremendous earthquakes destroy the Earth's major cities, an ancient evil emerges, turning ordinary people into hunters, killers, and insane monsters but a small group of teens comes together in a fight for survival and safety.

"Well-balanced, realistic suspense." Kirkus

Rage within; Jeyn Roberts. Simon & Schuster Books for Young Readers 2012 357 p. (hardcover) $17.99
Grades: 7 8 9 10 **Fic**
1. Science fiction 2. Apocalyptic fiction 3. Monsters -- Fiction 4. Survival -- Fiction 5. Good and evil -- Fiction
ISBN 1442423544; 9781442423541; 9781442423565

LC 2011047396

Sequel to: Dark inside

In author Jeyn Roberts' "apocalyptic sequel to 'Dark Inside' . . . Aries, Clementine, Michael, and Mason have survived the first wave of the apocalypse that wiped out most of the world's population and turned many of the rest into murderous Baggers. Now they're hiding out in an abandoned house . . . trying to figure out their next move. As the Baggers begin to create a new world order, these four teens will have to trust and rely on each other in order to survive." (Publisher's note)

Robinson, Kim Stanley

Fifty degrees below. Bantam Books 2005 405p $25
Grades: 9 10 11 12 **Fic**
1. Science fiction 2. Washington (D.C.) -- Fiction
ISBN 0-553-80312-3

LC 2005-48074

Sequel to Forty signs of rain

This book "provides perhaps the most realistic portrayal ever created of the environmental changes that are already occurring on our planet." Publ Wkly

Forty signs of rain. Bantam Books 2004 358p hardcover o.p. pa $7.99
Grades: 9 10 11 12 **Fic**
1. Science fiction 2. Washington (D.C.) -- Fiction
ISBN 0-553-80311-5; 0-553-58580-0 pa

LC 2003-63683

The author's "portrayal of how actual scientists would deal with this disaster-in-the-making is utterly convincing. Robinson clearly cares deeply about our planet's future, and he makes the reader care as well." Publ Wkly

Other titles in this series are:
Fifty degrees below (2005)
Sixty days and counting (2007)

Rocco, John

Swim that rock; John Rocco, Jay Primiano. Candlewick Press 2014 304 p. ill., map $16.99
Grades: 7 8 9 10 **Fic**
1. Bildungsromans 2. Fishing -- Fiction 3. Family life

-- Fiction 4. Rhode Island -- Fiction
ISBN 0763669059; 9780763669058

LC 2013952797

In this book, by John Rocco and Jay Primiano, "a young working-class teen fights to save his family's diner after his father is lost in a fishing-boat accident. . . . In Narragansett Bay, scrabbling out a living as a quahogger isn't easy, but with the help of some local clammers, Jake is determined to work hard and earn enough money to ensure his family's security and save the diner in time." (Publisher's note)

"When his fisherman father went missing, Jake and his mother lost their house, and now the family diner is in danger of being repossessed. A mysterious character named Captain and seasoned fisherman Gene Hassard help Jake earn money by learning the ways of the bay. With a lushly detailed sense of place and character, the story examines a boy coming to terms with his situation." Horn Book

Roecker, Laura

The **Liar** Society; by Lisa and Laura Roecker. Sourcebooks Fire 2011 361p pa $9.99

Grades: 7 8 9 10 **Fic**
1. School stories 2. Mystery fiction 3. Secret societies -- Fiction
ISBN 978-1-4022-5633-2; 1-4022-5633-7

When Kate receives a mysterious e-mail from her dead friend Grace, she must prove that Grace's death was not an accident, but finds that her elite private school holds secrets so big people are willing to kill to protect them.

This is a "smartly paced and plotted first novel, full of twists, clues, and sleuthing. Add this to your go-to list of mysteries." Booklist

The **lies** that bind; Lisa and Laura Roecker. Sourcebooks Fire 2012 314 p. (The Liar Society) (tp: alk. paper) $9.99

Grades: 7 8 9 10 **Fic**
1. School stories 2. Missing persons -- Fiction 3. Secret societies -- Fiction 4. Schools -- Fiction 5. High schools -- Fiction
ISBN 1402270240; 9781402270246

LC 2012035855

This young adult school mystery, by Lisa and Laura Roecker, is part of "The Liar Society" series. "Kate has heard of messages from beyond the grave, but she never expected to find one in a fortune cookie. Especially from her best friend, Grace--who's supposed to be dead. At the elite Pemberly Brown Academy, . . . a popular girl has gone missing, and Kate owes it to Grace's memory to find out what happened. But in a school ruled by secret societies, who can she trust?" (Publisher's note)

Roecker, Lisa

The **third** lie's the charm; Third lie is the charm. Lisa & Laura Roecker. Sourcebooks Fire 2013 288 p. (The Liar Society) (tp: alk. paper) $9.99

Grades: 7 8 9 10 **Fic**
1. School stories 2. Mystery fiction 3. Schools -- Fiction 4. High schools -- Fiction 5. Secret societies -- Fiction
ISBN 1402285930; 9781402285936

LC 2013023321

In this young adult mystery by Lisa Roecker and Laura Roecker, part of The Liar Society series, "Katie Lowry knows she could've stopped Alistair from doing something stupid if only she'd picked up the phone. Now she has to live with the guilt. She's sick of the lies, sick of the secret societies that rule life at Pemberly Brown Academy." (Publisher's note)

Third lie is the charm

Roesch, Mattox

Sometimes we're always real same-same. Unbridled Books 2009 317p pa $15.95

Grades: 11 12 Adult **Fic**
1. Inuit -- Fiction 2. Alaska -- Fiction 3. Cousins -- Fiction 4. Country life -- Fiction
ISBN 978-1-9329618-74; 1-9329618-79

LC 2009-17497

Troubled Cesar is stuck in nowhere Alaska because his Eskimo mother has moved home where she hopes both of them can carve out a fresh start. He's just biding his time until he can return to L.A., but his offbeat cousin Go-boy is convinced Cesar will stay, so they make a wager. If Cesar is still in Unalakleet in a year, he has to get a copy of Go-Boy's Eskimo Jesus tattoo. Gradually Cesar discovers the power of friendship and the potential positive strength that springs from a tight-knit community.

"Roesch's compelling story, exotic setting and eccentric characters make this coming-of-age tale a fresh, welcome read." Publ Wkly

Rorby, Ginny

The **outside** of a horse; a novel. Dial Books for Young Readers 2010 343p $16.99

Grades: 7 8 9 10 **Fic**
1. Horses -- Fiction 2. Amputees -- Fiction 3. Veterans -- Fiction 4. Father-daughter relationship -- Fiction
ISBN 978-0-8037-3478-4; 0-8037-3478-6

LC 2009-25101

When her father returns from the Iraq War as an amputee with post-traumatic stress disorder, Hannah escapes by volunteering to work with rescued horses, never thinking that the abused horses could also help her father recover.

Hannah "comes across as a believable teen. As a backdrop to the story, Rorby has interwoven a good deal of disturbing information about animal cruelty. Horse lovers and most others will saddle up right away with this poignant tale." Booklist

Rosen, Renee

★ **Every** crooked pot. St. Martin's Griffin 2007 227p pa $8.95

Grades: 7 8 9 10 **Fic**
1. Birth defects -- Fiction 2. Father-daughter relationship -- Fiction
ISBN 978-0-312-36543-1; 0-312-36543-8

LC 2007-10457

"Rosen looks back at the life of Nina Goldman, whose growing up is tied to two pillars: a port-wine stain around her eye and her inimitable father, Artie. The birthmark, she hates; her father, she loves. Both shape her in ways that merit Rosen's minute investigation. . . . There's real power in the writing." Booklist

Rosenfield, Kat

Amelia Anne is dead and gone; Kat Rosenfield. Dutton Books 2012 304 p. (hardcover) $17.99

Grades: 9 10 11 12 **Fic**

1. Mystery fiction 2. Homicide -- Fiction 3. Young women -- Fiction 4. Murder -- Fiction 5. Community life -- Fiction 6. Summer resorts -- Fiction 7. Dating violence -- Fiction 8. Mystery and detective stories 9. Dating (Social customs) -- Fiction

ISBN 9780525423898

LC 2011029958

In this book, "[t]he lives of two girls on the cusp of something bigger intertwine on a dusty road in a small, dead-end New England town. Amelia has just finished college and is on her way to a summer beach rental with her boyfriend before going to acting school. Becca, just graduated from high school, is looking forward to college. . . . Just hours before Amelia is beaten and left for dead, Becca's boyfriend breaks up with her--right after they have sex in the bed of his pickup." (Kirkus Reivews)

Inland; by Kat Rosenfield. Dutton Books 2014 400 p. (hardback) $17.99

Grades: 9 10 11 12 **Fic**

1. Ocean -- Fiction 2. Psychological fiction 3. Secrets -- Fiction 4. Families -- Fiction 5. Supernatural -- Fiction 6. Psychic trauma -- Fiction 7. Single-parent families -- Fiction

ISBN 0525426485; 9780525426486

LC 2014004800

In this young adult novel by Kat Rosenfield, "Callie Morgan has long lived choked by the failure of her own lungs, the result of an elusive pulmonary illness that has plagued her since childhood. A childhood marked early by the drowning death of her mother--a death to which Callie was the sole witness. Her father has moved them inland, away from the memories of the California coast her mother loved so much and toward promises of recovery . . . in arid, landlocked air." (Publisher's note)

" The delicious confusion between fantasy and madness finds perfect expression in Rosenfield's hypnotic prose and upside-down chapter construction; which direction is up is never clear. Combine Margo Lanagan's The Brides of Rollrock Island (2012) with Hannah Moskowitz's Teeth (2013), chum it with the remains of John Ajvide Lindqvist's Let Me In (2007), and you'll get something close to this sinister, salt-water sonata." Booklist

Roskos, Evan

★ **Dr.** Bird's advice for sad poets; Evan Roskos. Houghton Mifflin Harcourt 2013 320 p. $16.99

Grades: 9 10 11 12 **Fic**

1. Poetry -- Fiction 2. Siblings -- Fiction 3. Depression (Psychology) -- Fiction 4. Family problems -- Fiction 5. Depression, Mental -- Fiction

ISBN 054792853X; 9780547928531

LC 2012033315

William C. Morris Honor Book (2014)

This novel "portrays the struggle of 16-year-old James Whitman to overcome anxiety and depression. James blames himself for his older sister's expulsion from their home and estrangement from their bullying parents. [Evan]

Roskos . . . sketches James as a boy who is far more comfortable inside his own head than in connecting with others (case in point, he hugs trees to make himself feel better and seeks advice from Dr. Bird, an imaginary pigeon therapist)." (Publishers Weekly)

"Author Roskos's strength lies in his refusal to tidy up the mess in James's life and in his relentless honesty about surviving with depression and anxiety." Horn Book

Rosoff, Meg

★ **How** I live now. Wendy Lamb Books 2004 194p $16.95; lib bdg $18.99; pa $7.99

Grades: 7 8 9 10 **Fic**

1. War stories 2. Cousins -- Fiction 3. Great Britain -- Fiction

ISBN 0385746776; 038590908X; 0553376055

LC 2004-6443

Michael L. Printz Award, 2005

To get away from her pregnant stepmother in New York City, fifteen-year-old Daisy goes to England to stay with her aunt and cousins, with whom she instantly bonds, but soon war breaks out and rips apart the family while devastating the land

"Teens may feel that they have experienced a war themselves as they vicariously witness Daisy's worst nightmares. Like the heroine, readers will emerge from the rubble much shaken, a little wiser and with perhaps a greater sense of humanity." Publ Wkly

★ **Picture** me gone; by Meg Rosoff. G.P. Putnam's Sons 2013 256 p. $17.99

Grades: 7 8 9 **Fic**

1. Missing persons -- Fiction 2. Parent-child relationship -- Fiction 3. Coming of age -- Fiction 4. Mystery and detective stories 5. Fathers and daughters -- Fiction

ISBN 0399257659; 9780399257650

LC 2012048974

This book by Meg Rosoff is a story "about the relationship between parents and children, love and loss. Mila has an exceptional talent for reading a room—sensing hidden facts and unspoken emotions from clues that others overlook. So when her father's best friend, Matthew, goes missing from his upstate New York home, Mila and her beloved father travel from London to find him. Just when she's closest to solving the mystery, a shocking betrayal calls into question her trust." (Publisher's note)

"Sensitive Londoner Mila, twelve, travels with her father, Gil, to upstate New York to search for Gil's boyhood friend, who has inexplicably disappeared. The subject of this road-trip novel--how much guilt and tragedy can a person bear before he gives up on life?--is adult, but the writing is up to Rosoff's usual standards of originality, depth, wit, and insight." (Horn Book)

Ross, Elizabeth

Belle epoque; Elizabeth Ross. Delacorte Press 2013 336 p. (ebook) $53.97; (library) $20.99; (hardcover) $17.99

Grades: 7 8 9 10 11 12 **Fic**

1. Love stories 2. Historical fiction 3. Female friendship -- Fiction 4. Runaways -- Fiction 5. Social classes -- Fiction 6. Conduct of life -- Fiction 7. Beauty, Personal

-- Fiction 8. Interpersonal relations -- Fiction 9. Paris (France) -- History -- 1870-1940 -- Fiction 10. France -- History -- Third Republic, 1870-1940 -- Fiction
ISBN 0375990054; 9780375985270; 9780375990052; 9780385741460

LC 2012034694

William C. Morris Honor Book (2014)

In this book, "sixteen-year-old runaway Maude Pichon is ugly—so much so that she lands a job as a 'repoussoir,' an unattractive girl paid to be seen with a lovelier girl to make her appear even more beautiful by comparison . . . . Maude is humiliated by the idea, but her poverty leaves her few options." Then "chance sends a dashing composer Maude's way, and a countess hires her to befriend her independent-minded daughter, Isabelle." (Publishers Weekly)

"Ross models her plot on an 1866 story by Zola, "Les Repoussoirs," expanding its focus to highlight Maude's plight and using that to illuminate the chasm that existed between the wealthy and the poor... A refreshingly relevant and inspiring historical venture." Kirkus

Rossetti, Rinsai

The **girl** with borrowed wings; by Rinsai Rossetti. Dial Books 2012 300 p. (hardcover) $17.99

Grades: 7 8 9 10 11 12   Fic

1. Cats -- Fiction 2. Voyages and travels -- Fiction 3. Father-daughter relationship -- Fiction 4. Love -- Fiction 5. Flying -- Fiction 6. Deserts -- Fiction 7. Shapeshifting -- Fiction
ISBN 0803735669; 9780803735668

LC 2011027164

This is Rinsai Rossetti's debut, a coming-of-age novel. Of "Thai descent, 17-year-old Frenenqer Paje has grown up" with "her coldly overbearing father . . . . [S]he disobeys her father by rescuing a mistreated cat" who "is actually a shapeshifting 'Free person' named Sangris . . . . By night, he flies Frenenqer around the world to places both real and magical, slowly chipping away at the defenses she has built up to withstand her father's callous cruelty." (Publishers Weekly)

Rossi, Veronica

Under the never sky; Veronica Rossi. HarperCollins 2012 376 p. (hardback) $17.99

Grades: 6 7 8 9 10 11 12   Fic

1. Science fiction 2. Apocalyptic fiction 3. Cannibalism -- Fiction 4. Man-woman relationship -- Fiction
ISBN 9780062072030

LC 2011044631

This book tells the story of "Aria [who] knows her chances of surviving in the outer wasteland--known as The Death Shop--are slim. . . . Then Aria meets an Outsider named Perry. He's wild--a savage--and her only hope of staying alive. A hunter for his tribe in a merciless landscape, Perry views Aria as sheltered and fragile--everything he would expect from a Dweller. . . . Opposites in nearly every way, Aria and Perry must accept each other to survive." (Publisher's note)

Roth, Veronica

Allegiant; Veronica Roth; [edited by] Molly O'Neill. Katherine Tegen Books 2013 544 p. (hardcover bdg.) $19.99

Grades: 9 10 11 12   Fic

1. Love stories 2. Dystopian fiction 3. Science fiction 4. Loyalty -- Fiction 5. Dystopias -- Fiction 6. Social classes -- Fiction 7. Courage
ISBN 006202406X; 9780062024060

LC 2013941315

Author Veronica Roth presents the conclusion to her dystopian Divergent trilogy. "Tris and Tobias conarrate their adventures and attempt to understand their surroundings. As their true love relationship plays out, they venture beyond war-torn Chicago, only to uncover a new network of conspiracies and key revelations about eugenics, authority, and social duty." (Bookmarks)

"Roth shakes up her storytelling (and will do the same to some readers) in this highly anticipated, largely satisfying wrap-up to the Divergent trilogy...for those who have faithfully followed these five factions, and especially the Dauntless duo who stole hearts two books ago, this final installment will capture and hold attention until the divisive final battle has been waged." (Publishers Weekly)

★ **Divergent**. Katherine Tegen Books 2011 487p $17.99; ebook $9.99

Grades: 9 10 11 12   Fic

1. Science fiction 2. Courage -- Fiction 3. Family life -- Fiction 4. Social classes -- Fiction 5. Identity (Psychology) -- Fiction
ISBN 978-0-06-202402-2; 0-06-202402-7; 978-0-06-207701-1 ebook; 0-06-207701-5 ebook

LC 2010-40579

"Roth's nonstop action, excellent voice, and simple yet accessible writing style will draw in many new readers to the genre. The themes are particularly poignant for young adults trying to identify their place in the world—having the choice to follow in your parents' footsteps or do something new. . . . This is a fast-paced and fun read." Voice Youth Advocates

Insurgent; Veronica Roth. Katherine Tegen Books 2012 525 p.

Grades: 9 10 11 12   Fic

1. Science fiction 2. Courage -- Fiction 3. Apocalyptic fiction 4. Personality -- Fiction 5. Social classes -- Fiction 6. Families -- Fiction 7. Identity -- Fiction
ISBN 0062024043; 9780062024046

LC 2011053287

Sequel to: Divergent

In this "sequel to . . . 'Divergent' . . . a bleak post-apocalyptic Chicago ruled by 'factions' exemplifying different personality traits collapses into all-out civil war. With both the Dauntless and Abnegation factions shattered by the Erudite attack, Tris and her companions seek refuge with Amity and Candor, and even among the factionless. But the Erudite search for 'Divergents' continues relentlessly." (Kirkus Reviews)

Rothenberg, Jess

The **catastrophic** history of you & me; Jess Rothenberg. Dial Books 2012 375 p. (hardcover: alk. paper) $17.99

Grades: 9 10 11 12   Fic

1. Grief -- Fiction 2. Future life -- Fiction 3. Love

stories 4. Love -- Fiction 5. Death -- Fiction
ISBN 0803737203; 9780803737204

LC 2011021631

This book, by Jess Rothenberg, begins "when her boy-friend Jacob tells her that he no longer loves her, [and] Brie's heart spontaneously tears in two and she dies. . . . [She] finds herself in the heavenly version of her favorite pizza joint, where she meets Patrick, resident Lost Soul and guide to all things post-mortem. He informs her that she will have to work her way through the five stages of grief with a series of visits to her old life." (Bulletin of the Center for Children's Books)

Rowell, Rainbow, 1973-

★ **Carry** on; a novel. by Rainbow Rowell. St. Martin's Griffin 2015 528 p. illustrations (hardback) $19.99

Grades: 9 10 11 12   **Fic**
1. Magic -- Fiction 2. Monsters -- Fiction 3. Private schools -- Fiction 4. Dating (Social customs) -- Fiction 5. Schools -- Fiction 6. Boarding schools -- Fiction
ISBN 9781250049551

LC 2015029653

This book, by Rainbow Rowell, "Simon Snow is the worst Chosen One who's ever been chosen. That's what his roommate, Baz, says. And Baz might be evil and a vampire and a complete git, but he's probably right. Half the time, Simon can't even make his wand work, and the other half, he starts something on fire. His mentor's avoiding him, his girl-friend broke up with him, and there's a magic-eating monster running around, wearing Simon's face." (Publisher's note)

"The novel playfully twists genre conventions—there are plenty of wink-wink, nudge-nudge moments to satisfy faithful fantasy readers—but it also stands alone as a modern bildungsroman. Carry on, Simon Snow." Kirkus

★ **Eleanor** & Park; Rainbow Rowell. St. Martin's Griffin 2013 320 p. (hardcover) $18.99

Grades: 9 10 11 12 Adult   **Fic**
1. Love stories 2. School stories 3. Bullies -- Fiction 4. Love -- Fiction 5. Schools -- Fiction 6. High schools -- Fiction 7. Dating (Social customs) -- Fiction
ISBN 1250012570; 9781250012579; 9781250031211

LC 2012042136

Odyssey Honor Recording (2014)
Printz Honor Book (2014)
Boston Globe-Horn Book Award: Fiction (2013).

This book tells the story of the friendship between half-Korean sophomore Park Sheridan and the new girl Eleanor. "Tall, with bright red hair and a dress code all her own, [Eleanor is] an instant target. Too nice not to let her sit next to him, Park is alternately resentful and guilty for not being kinder to her. When he realizes she's reading his comics over his shoulder, a silent friendship is born" that will become something more. (Publishers Weekly)

"Through Eleanor and Park's alternating voices, readers glimpse the swoon-inducing, often hilarious aspects of first love... Funny, hopeful, foulmouthed, sexy and tear-jerking, this winning romance will captivate teen and adult readers alike." Kirkus

★ **Fangirl**; by Rainbow Rowell. St. Martin's Griffin 2013 448 p. (hardcover) $18.99

Grades: 9 10 11 12   **Fic**
1. Fan fiction 2. School stories 3. Characters and characteristics in literature
ISBN 1250030951; 9781250030955

LC 2013013842

This book "tells the story of a painfully shy teen who prefers the fantasy world of fanfiction to reality. Cath expected to survive her first year of college with the help of her twin sister. Wren, however, is taking full advantage of her newfound freedom from parental supervision, spending" her time partying rather than with Cath. "Feeling lost and alone, Cath scurries from class to class, hiding in her room and working on her Simon Snow fanfiction omnibus." (School Library Journal)

"Change-resistant college freshman Cather holes up in her dorm room, writing fantasy fanfiction. But as the year progresses, she is pushed outside her comfort zone by her snarky roommate, Reagan; by Levi, Reagan's ex-boyfriend (and eventually Cath's first love interest); and by her manic but well-meaning father. Rowell transitions seamlessly between Cath's strong interior voice and clever dialogue in this sophisticated coming-of-age novel." (Horn Book)

Rowling, J. K., 1965-

Harry Potter and the Chamber of Secrets; by J.K. Rowling; illustrations by Mary Grandpré. Arthur A. Levine Bks. 1999 341p il $22.99; pa $8.99

Grades: 4 5 6 7 8 9 10   **Fic**
1. Fantasy fiction 2. Witches -- Fiction
ISBN 0-439-06486-4; 0-439-06487-2 pa

LC 98-46370

Sequel to Harry Potter and the Sorcerer's Stone
When the Chamber of Secrets is opened again at the Hogswart School for Witchcraft and Wizardry, second-year student Harry Potter finds himself in danger from a dark power that has once more been released on the school
Followed by Harry Potter and the prisoner of Azkaban

Harry Potter and the deathly hallows; illustrations by Mary Grandpré. Arthur A. Levine Books 2007 759p il $34.99; pa $14.99

Grades: 4 5 6 7 8 9 10   **Fic**
1. Fantasy fiction 2. Witches -- Fiction
ISBN 978-0-545-01022-1; 0-545-01022-5; 978-0-545-13970-0 pa; 0-545-13970-8 pa
Sequel to: Harry Potter and the Half-blood Prince (2005)
This book is the final installment of J. K. Rowling's Harry Potter series. "With the Dark Lord in control of the Ministry of Magic, the trio uses their combined wizardly talents to stay hidden as they follow [Albus] Dumbledore's assignment to destroy the dangerous horcruxes. Finding those fragmented pieces of their enemy's soul lead the friends to angry arguments, near fatal encounters and, occasionally, humorous episodes." (School Library Journal)

Harry Potter and the Goblet of Fire; illustrations by Mary Grandpré. Arthur A. Levine Bks. 2000 734p il $29.99; pa $9.99

Grades: 4 5 6 7 8 9 10   **Fic**
1. Fantasy fiction 2. Witches -- Fiction
ISBN 0-439-13959-7; 0-439-13960-0 pa
LC 00-131084
Sequel to Harry Potter and the prisoner of Azkaban
Harry Potter, a fourth-year student at Hogwarts School of Witchcraft and Wizardry, longs to escape his hateful relatives, the Dursleys, and live as a normal fourteen-year-old wizard, but what Harry does not yet realize is that he is not a normal wizard, and in his case, different can be deadly.
Followed by Harry Potter and the Order of the Phoenix

Harry Potter and the Half-blood Prince; illustrations by Mary Grandpré. Arthur A. Levine 2005 652p il $29.99; pa $9.99
Grades: 4 5 6 7 8 9 10   **Fic**
1. Fantasy fiction 2. Witches -- Fiction
ISBN 0-439-78454-9; 0-439-78596-0 pa
Sequel to Harry Potter and the Half-blood Prince
Sixth-year Hogwarts student Harry Potter gains valuable insights into the boy Voldemort once was, even as his own world is transformed by maturing friendships, schoolwork assistance from an unexpected source, and devastating losses.
Followed by Harry Potter and the Deathly Hallows

Harry Potter and the Order of the Phoenix; illustrations by Mary Grandpre. Levine Bks. 2003 870p il $29.99; pa $9.99
Grades: 4 5 6 7 8 9 10   **Fic**
1. Fantasy fiction 2. Witches -- Fiction
ISBN 0-439-35806-X; 0-439-35807-8 pa
LC 2003-102525
Sequel to Harry Potter and the Goblet of Fire
When the government of the magic world and authorities at Hogwarts School of Witchcraft and Wizardry refuse to believe in the growing threat of a freshly revived Lord Voldemort, fifteen-year-old Harry Potter finds support from his loyal friends in facing the evil wizard and other new terrors
Followed by Harry Potter and the Half-blood Prince

Harry Potter and the prisoner of Azkaban; illustrations by Mary Grandpré. Arthur A. Levine Bks. 1999 435p il $22.99; pa $8.99
Grades: 4 5 6 7 8 9 10   **Fic**
1. Fantasy fiction 2. Witches -- Fiction
ISBN 0-439-13635-0; 0-439-13636-9 pa
LC 99-23982
Sequel to Harry Potter and the Chamber of Secrets
During his third year at Hogwarts School for Witchcraft and Wizardry, Harry Potter must confront the devious and dangerous wizard responsible for his parents' deaths
Followed by Harry Potter and the Goblet of Fire

★ **Harry** Potter and the Sorcerer's Stone; illustrations by Mary Grandpré. Arthur A. Levine Bks. 1998 309p il $22.99; pa $8.99
Grades: 4 5 6 7 8 9 10   **Fic**
1. Fantasy fiction 2. Witches -- Fiction
ISBN 0-590-35340-3; 0-590-35342-X pa
LC 97-39059

First published 1997 in the United Kingdom with title: Harry Potter and the Philosopher's Stone
Rescued from the outrageous neglect of his aunt and uncle, a young boy with a great destiny proves his worth while attending Hogwarts School for Witchcraft and Wizardry.
This "is a brilliantly imagined and beautifully written fantasy." Booklist
Other titles in this series are:
Harry Potter and the Chamber of Secrets (1999)
Harry Potter and the Prisoner of Azkaban (1999)
Harry Potter and Goblet of Fire (2000)
Harry Potter and the Order of the Phoenix (2003)
Harry Potter and the Half-Blood Prince (2005)
Harry Potter and the Deathly Hallows (2007)

Roy, Arundhati
★ The **god** of small things. Random House Trade Paperbacks 2008 333p (Telling stories!) pa $16
Grades: 11 12 Adult   **Fic**
1. India -- Fiction 2. Twins -- Fiction 3. Family life -- Fiction
ISBN 978-0-8129-7965-7
First published 1997
"If the symbolism is a trifle overdone, the lush local color and the incisive characterizations give the narrative power and drama." Publ Wkly

Roy, Jennifer Rozines
★ **Mindblind**; [by] Jennifer Roy. Marshall Cavendish 2010 248p il $15.99
Grades: 7 8 9 10 11   **Fic**
1. Genius -- Fiction 2. Bands (Music) -- Fiction 3. Asperger's syndrome -- Fiction
ISBN 978-0-7614-5716-9; 0-7614-5716-X
LC 2010-6966
Fourteen-year-old Nathaniel Clark, who has Asperger's Syndrome, tries to prove that he is a genius by writing songs for his rock band, so that he can become a member of the prestigious Aldus Institute, the premier organization for the profoundly gifted.
"Mature readers will empathize with Nathaniel as his friends, Jessa and Cooper, do. This book is for teens who appreciate a story about self-discovery, dreams, and friendship." Voice Youth Advocates

Rubens, Michael
Sons of the 613; Mike Rubens. Clarion Books 2012 305 p. (hardcover) $16.99
Grades: 7 8 9 10   **Fic**
1. Brothers -- Fiction 2. Bar mitzvah -- Fiction 3. Masculinity -- Fiction 4. Schools -- Fiction 5. Minnesota -- Fiction 6. Coming of age -- Fiction 7. Junior high schools -- Fiction 8. Jews -- United States -- Fiction 9. Family life -- Minnesota -- Fiction
ISBN 0547612168; 9780547612164
LC 2011044352
In this book by Michael Rubens, "Isaac's parents have abandoned him for a trip to Italy in the final days before his bar mitzvah. And even worse, his hotheaded older brother, Josh, has been left in charge. . . . When Josh declares that there is more to becoming a man than memorization, the

mad 'quest' begins for Isaac. . . . But when Isaac begins to fall for Josh's girlfriend, Leslie, the challenges escalate from bad to worse." (Publisher's note)

Rubin, Lance

Denton Little's deathdate; a novel. by Lance Rubin. Alfred A. Knopf 2015 352 p. (trade) $17.99 Grades: 9 10 11 12 Adult **Fic**
1. Science fiction 2. Death -- Fiction 3. Identity -- Fiction
ISBN 0553496964; 9780553496963; 9780553496970; 9780553496994

LC 2014008677

This book, by Lance Rubin, "takes place in a world exactly like our own except that everyone knows the day on which they will die. For Denton, that's in just two days—the day of his senior prom. Despite his early deathdate, Denton has always wanted to live a normal life, but his final days are filled with dramatic firsts. First hangover. First sex. First love triangle—as the first sex seems to have happened not with his adoring girlfriend, but with his best friend's hostile sister." (Publisher's note)

"Though some readers might be rankled by the one-dimensional women characters and the uneven pacing of this debut novel, they will likely still be intrigued by Denton's charmingly glib first-person narrative and sarcastic, irreverent gallows humor." Booklist

Ruby, Laura

★ Bad apple. HarperTeen 2009 247p $16.99; pa $8.99
Grades: 8 9 10 11 12 **Fic**
1. School stories 2. Bullies -- Fiction 3. Divorce -- Fiction 4. Teacher-student relationship -- Fiction
ISBN 978-0-06-124330-1; 0-06-124330-2; 978-0-06-124333-2 pa; 0-06-124333-7 pa

LC 2009-1409

Tola Riley, a high school junior, struggles to tell the truth when she and her art teacher are accused of having an affair.

"Tola and her family are fascinating, quirky-yet-believable, and wholly likable. Ruby works in traditional fairy-tale elements . . . with wry humor." Booklist

★ Bone Gap; Laura Ruby. Balzer + Bray, an imprint of HarperCollinsPublishers 2015 345 p. (hardcover) $17.99
Grades: 9 10 11 12 **Fic**
1. Brothers -- Fiction 2. Kidnapping -- Fiction 3. Bullying -- Fiction 4. Face perception -- Fiction 5. Interpersonal relations -- Fiction
ISBN 0062317601; 9780062317605

LC 2014013676

Printz Award (2016)

National Book Award Finalist: Young People's Literature (2015)

In this book by Laura Ruby, "Bone Gap is the small Illinois town where seventeen-year-old Finn has lived with his older brother, Sean, since their mother left them for a brand-new life with her brand-new husband two years ago. Now Finn's devastated by a new loss: Roza, the beautiful young Polish woman who turned up on Finn and Sean's farm from out of nowhere . . . was abducted one night, but nobody

believes Finn's account of her departure." (Bulletin of the Center for Children's Books)

"In Ruby's refined and delicately crafty hand, reality and fantasy don't fall neatly into place. She compellingly muddles the two together right through to the end. Even then, after she reveals many secrets, magic still seems to linger in the real parts of Bone Gap, and the magical elements retain their frightening reality. Wonder, beauty, imperfection, cruelty, love, and pain are all inextricably linked but bewitchingly so." Booklist

Ruditis, Paul

The four Dorothys. Simon Pulse 2007 236p (Drama!) pa $8.99
Grades: 7 8 9 10 **Fic**
1. School stories 2. Theater -- Fiction 3. Musicals -- Fiction
ISBN 978-1-4169-3391-5

LC 2006-928449

The students at the Orion Academy put on a musical based on the Wizard of Oz. Due to their egotism, four of them have the part of Dorothy, but as opening night approaches, the Dorothys drop out of the show one-by-one. Bryan Stark must find out why in order to keep the musical from being cancelled.

"Swift pacing and tightly layered subplots keep pages turning through this refreshing take on some familiar high school dramas." SLJ

Rudnick, Paul, 1957-

Gorgeous; by Paul Rudnick. 1st ed. Scholastic 2013 336 p. (hardcover) $18.99
Grades: 9 10 11 12 **Fic**
1. Fame -- Fiction 2. Magic -- Fiction 3. Princes -- Fiction 4. Identity -- Fiction 5. Beauty, Personal -- Fiction
ISBN 0545464269; 9780545464260

LC 2012046062

In this satirical modern fairy tale, Becky, a teenage girl from a trailer park, "receives three dresses from reclusive super-designer Tom Kelly, who knew Becky's late mother. The ensembles transform Becky into nothing less than the most beautiful woman in the world . . . with a couple catches." Suddenly she's "on the cover of 'Vogue,' dating a Hollywood hunk, and possibly in line to be the next queen of England." (Publishers Weekly)

It's all your fault; Paul Rudnick. Scholastic Press 2016 304 p. (jacketed hardcover) $19.99
Grades: 9 10 11 12 **Fic**
1. Cousins 2. Singers 3. Actresses 4. Child actors 5. Humorous stories
ISBN 9780545464284

LC 2015015697

In this book, by author Paul Rudnick, "Seventeen-year-old Caitlin Singleberry is a proper Christian teenager and member of a family singing group, but today she has been given a truly impossible assignment--keep her cousin Heller Harrigan, Hollywood wild child, out of trouble for the last weekend before her first big movie debuts." (Library of Congress)

"With its too outrageous to be true characters, caps lock style, absurd plot, and potentially problematic treatment of mental health, this title is not a good fit for library collections." SLJ

It is all your fault

Ruiz Zafon, Carlos, 1964-

Marina; Carlos Ruiz Zafon; translated by Lucia Graves. Little, Brown & Co. 2014 336 p. (hardcover) $19

Grades: 8 9 10 11 12   **Fic**
1. Suspense fiction 2. Barcelona (Spain) -- Fiction 3. Love -- Fiction 4. Supernatural -- Fiction 5. Mystery and detective stories 6. Spain -- History -- 20th century -- Fiction

ISBN 0316044717; 9780316044714
                                        LC 2013016666

In this novel by Carlos Ruiz Zafón, "15-year-old Oscar Drai suddenly vanishes from his boarding school in the old quarter of Barcelona. For seven days and nights no one knows his whereabouts. . . . His story begins in the heart of old Barcelona when he meets Marina and her father German Blau, a portrait painter." (Publisher's note)

"Set in Barcelona, Spain from late 1979 to May 1980, this gothic novel centers around 15-year-old boarding school student Oscar Drai. Instead of studying during his free time, the teen explores the city, and one day ends up in an area that seems deserted. Drawn in by music coming from an old dilapidated house, Oscar is given a scare by the owner, an eccentric and haunted German artist...With elements of romance, mystery, and horror, none of them overwhelming the other, this complex volume that hints at Mary Shelley's Frankenstein manages to weave together three separate stories for a cohesive and eerie result." SLJ

The **Prince** of Mist; translated by Lucia Graves. Little, Brown 2010 320p $17.99

Grades: 6 7 8 9 10   **Fic**
1. Dead -- Fiction 2. Magic -- Fiction 3. Siblings -- Fiction 4. Shipwrecks -- Fiction 5. Supernatural -- Fiction 6. Europe -- History -- 1918-1945 -- Fiction

ISBN 978-0-316-04477-6; 0-316-04477-6
                                        LC 2009-51256

In 1943, in a seaside town where their family has gone to be safe from war, thirteen-year-old Max Carver and sister, fifteen-year-old Alicia, with new friend Roland, face off against an evil magician who is striving to complete a bargain made before he died.

"Zafon is a master storyteller. From the first page, the reader is drawn into the mystery and suspense that the young people encounter when they move into the Fleischmann house. . . . This book can be read and enjoyed by every level of reader." Voice Youth Advocates

Runyon, Brent

Surface tension; a novel in four summers. Alfred A. Knopf 2009 197p $16.99; lib bdg $19.99

Grades: 8 9 10 11   **Fic**
1. Vacations -- Fiction 2. Family life -- Fiction 3. New

York (State) -- Fiction
ISBN 978-0-375-84446-1; 0-375-84446-5; 978-0-375-94446-8 lib bdg; 0-375-94446-X lib bdg
                                        LC 2008-9193

During the summer vacations of his thirteenth through his sixteenth year at the family's lake cottage, Luke realizes that although some things stay the same over the years that many more change.

"With sensitivity and candor, Runyon reveals how life changes us all and how these unavoidable changes can be full of both turmoil and wonder." Kirkus

Rush, Jennifer

Altered; by Jennifer Rush. 1st ed. Little, Brown and Co. 2013 336 p. (hardcover) $17.99

Grades: 7 8 9 10 11 12   **Fic**
1. Science fiction 2. Runaway teenagers -- Fiction 3. Memory -- Fiction 4. Identity -- Fiction 5. Runaways -- Fiction 6. Genetic engineering -- Fiction 7. Fathers and daughters -- Fiction

ISBN 0316197084; 9780316197083
                                        LC 2012007545

This is the debut novel in a series from Jennifer Rush. Here, "homeschooled 18-year-old Anna Mason has a life ruled by secrecy. Her widower father works for a clandestine organization called the Branch, and four gorgeous genetically altered teenage boys live in the basement laboratory of their New York State farmhouse. . . . When the Branch tries to collect 'the units,' chaos erupts, and Sam, Anna, and the others take off on the run." (Publishers Weekly)

"[T]his debut's strengths--pacing and plot twists, especially--outweigh the deficits. Riveting." Kirkus

Russell, Karen

★ **Swamplandia!** Karen Russell. Alfred A. Knopf 2011 315p. $24.95

Grades: 11 12 Adult   **Fic**
1. Girls 2. Alligators 3. Amusement parks 4. Girls -- Fiction 5. Alligators -- Fiction 6. Amusement parks -- Fiction 7. Everglades (Fla.) -- Fiction

ISBN 0307263991; 9780307263995
                                        LC 201036708

This book tells the story of "Swamplandia!, [which] is a shabby tourist attraction deep in the Everglades, owned by the Bigtree clan of alligator wrestlers. When Hilola, their star performer, dies, her husband and children lose their moorings, and Swamplandia! itself is endangered as audiences dwindle. The Chief leaves. Brother Kiwi, 17, sneaks off to work at the World of Darkness, a new mainland amusement park featuring the 'rings of hell.' Otherworldly sister Osceola, 16, vanishes after falling in love with the ghost of a young man who died while working for the ill-fated Dredge and Fill Campaign in the 1930s. It's up to Ava, 13, to find her sister." (Booklist)

Russell, Randy

Dead rules. HarperTeen 2011 376p $16.99

Grades: 7 8 9 10   **Fic**
1. School stories 2. Dead -- Fiction 3. Future life -- Fiction 4. Supernatural -- Fiction

ISBN 978-0-06-19867-03; 0-06-19867-04
                                        LC 2010032452

When high school junior Jana Webster dies suddenly, she finds herself in Dead School, where she faces choices that will determine when she, a Riser, will move on, but she strives to become a Slider instead, for the chance to be with the love of her life—even if it means killing him.

"Sarcastic quips and double entendres drive the story's humor, but it's the sensitivity of the supporting characters . . . that allows Jana (and readers) to see laughter within tragedy." Kirkus

Russo, Meredith
If I Was Your Girl; Meredith Russo. St. Martin's Press 2016 288 p. (hardback) $17.99

Grades: 9 10 11 12   **Fic**
1. Love stories 2. Gender identity -- Fiction 3. Transgender people -- Fiction
ISBN 1250078407; 9781250078407

LC 2016001596

In this young adult novel, by Meredith Russo, "Amanda Hardy is the new girl in school. . . . But when she meets sweet, easygoing Grant, Amanda can't help but start to let him into her life. . . . She finds herself yearning to share with Grant everything about herself, including her past. But Amanda's terrified that once she tells him the truth, . . . that at her old school, she used to be Andrew . . . , the truth cost Amanda her new life, and her new love." (Publisher's note)

"Though she's determined to lie low while finishing high school, she finds unexpected friendships with a trio of churchgoing Baptist girls and with art classmate Bee, a bisexual girl secretly in a relationship with one of them. Even more unexpected is her blossoming relationship with tender and respectful Grant, who has a complicated past of his own. . . . Flashbacks to Amanda's life pre-, during, and post-suicide attempt and subsequent transition are interspersed throughout the narrative. There is no gratuitous trauma, and Amanda's story is neither overly sentimental nor didactic. Russo, herself a trans woman living in Tennessee, crafts a thoughtful, truthful, and much needed coming-of-age tale." Horn Book

Russon, Penni
Breathe. Greenwillow Books 2007 356p $16.99; lib bdg $17.89

Grades: 8 9 10 11 12   **Fic**
1. Magic -- Fiction 2. Greece -- Fiction 3. Australia -- Fiction
ISBN 978-0-06-079393-7; 0-06-079393-7; 978-0-06-079394-4 lib bdg; 0-06-079394-5 lib bdg

LC 2006000944

Sequel to Undine
First published 2005 in Australia
Although Undine is excited about leaving Tasmania for a trip to see her father in Greece, she is also conflicted about using the magic that wells up inside her and confused about her personal relationships, including the one with her best friend Trout.

"Russon's bracing, poetic voice and earthy, likable characters ground the story's esoteric symbolism, and many readers will find their own fear and love reflected in the beautiful, open-ended metaphors." Booklist

Rutkoski, Marie
The **shadow** society; Marie Rutkoski. Farrar, Straus and Giroux 2012 408 p. $17.99

Grades: 7 8 9 10 11 12   **Fic**
1. Science fiction 2. Alternative histories 3. Supernatural -- Fiction 4. Schools -- Fiction 5. Identity -- Fiction 6. Illinois -- Fiction 7. High schools -- Fiction 8. Foster home care -- Fiction
ISBN 0374349053; 9780374349059

LC 2011033158

In this novel by Marie Rutkoski "Darcy Jones doesn't remember anything before the day she was abandoned as a child outside a Chicago firehouse. . . . But she couldn't have guessed that she comes from an alternate world where the Great Chicago Fire didn't happen and deadly creatures called Shades terrorize the human population. Memories begin to haunt Darcy when a new boy arrives at her high school, and he makes her feel both desire and desired in a way she hadn't thought possible." (Publisher's note)

The **winner's** crime; Marie Rutkoski. First edition Farrar Straus & Giroux 2015 416 p. (The winner's trilogy) (hardback) $17.99

Grades: 9 10 11 12   **Fic**
1. Love stories 2. Fantasy fiction 3. Secrets -- Fiction 4. Weddings -- Fiction 5. Love -- Fiction 6. Fantasy -- Fiction
ISBN 0374384703; 9780374384708

LC 2014025185

In this book, part of Marie Rutkoski's Winner's Trilogy, "Lady Kestrel has successfully bargained for limited independence for the Herrani people, but only at the price of her own freedom. Now betrothed to the feckless Imperial heir, she risks even more as a spy, while managing to convince everyone--most particularly Arin, once her slave, then her captor, now governor of Herran--of her ruthless devotion to tyrannical Valorian dominion." (Kirkus Reviews)

"A rich and complex story of political intrigue, missed opportunities, and thwarted trust fill the pages of this sequel to The Winner's Curse (2014). Rutkoski's world is splendid in its cruelty and beauty, with characters that continue to claim our hearts and leave us impatient for the trilogy's conclusion." Booklist

Ryan, Amy Kathleen
Flame; a Sky Chasers novel. Amy Kathleen Ryan. St. Martin's Griffin 2014 336 p. (Sky Chasers) (hardback) $18.99

Grades: 8 9 10 11 12   **Fic**
1. War stories 2. Airships -- Fiction 3. Science fiction
ISBN 0312621361; 9780312621360

LC 2013039416

In this novel, the conclusion to author Amy Kathleen Ryan's Sky Chasers series, "Waverly and the other members of the Empyrean have been scattered, and their home ship destroyed. Their mission to rescue their parents didn't go as planned, and now they're at an even greater disadvantage: trapped with their enemies on the New Horizon. Seth's situation is even worse. After setting out from the Empyrean on his own, with only a vague strategy to guide him, he is a fugitive aboard the New Horizon." (Publisher's note)

"When this meaty, harrowing conclusion to the Sky Chasers series opens, the inhabitants of the vessel Empyrean are fleeing their destroyed spacecraft to join their former enemies on board the New Horizon. Action begins immediately, and the story shifts mainly among the points of view of Waverly, Kieran and Seth...The pace is at times methodical, and much of the suspense comes from characters' and readers' uncertainty as to whom to trust. Stakes are high, however, and readers witness graphic (though generally not gory) violence and bodily harm as the three teens work to both overthrow and defend Pastor Anne Mather, the New Horizon's leader. It all comes to a head in a climax that is tense and viscerally frightening. Detailed and gripping, with a thorough and satisfying resolution." (Kirkus)

Glow. St. Martin's Griffin 2011 307p (Sky chasers) $17.99

Grades: 8 9 10 11 12   Fic
1. Science fiction
ISBN 978-0-312-59056-7; 0-312-59056-3
LC 2011020385
Part of the first generation to be conceived in deep space, fifteen-year-old Waverly is expected to marry young and have children to populate a new planet, but a violent betrayal by the dogmatic leader of their sister ship could have devastating consequences.

"The themes of survival, morality, religion, and power are well developed, and the characters are equally complex. The author has also created a unique and vivid outer-space setting that is exciting and easy to imagine." SLJ

Spark; a Sky chasers novel. Amy Kathleen Ryan. 1st ed. St. Martin's Press 2012 309 p. (hardcover) $17.99; (paperback) $9.99

Grades: 8 9 10 11 12   Fic
1. Mystery fiction 2. Friendship -- Fiction 3. Parent-child relationship -- Fiction 4. Science fiction
ISBN 0312621353; 9780312621353; 9781250014160; 9781250031952
LC 2012004631
Author Amy Kathleen Ryan's character "Waverly Marshall has endured and committed terrible acts aboard the 'New Horizon.' . . . [Kieran] delivers sermons designed to promote both unity and loyalty. . . . Meanwhile, Seth . . . escapes the brig under mysterious circumstances and discovers a major threat to the ship. As Waverly, Kieran, [and] Seth . . . work . . . to keep the peace, secure the ship and rescue their parents from the 'New Horizon,' . . . political and moral questions arise." (Kirkus Reviews)

Zen & Xander undone. Houghton Mifflin Harcourt 2010 212p $16

Grades: 8 9 10 11 12   Fic
1. Death -- Fiction 2. Sisters -- Fiction 3. Bereavement -- Fiction 4. Family life -- Fiction
ISBN 978-0-547-06248-8; 0-547-06248-6
Two teenaged sisters try to come to terms with the death of their mother in very different ways.

"Literate, believable, funny, and sometimes profound, this book has broad appeal." Voice Youth Advocates

Ryan, Carrie
The **dark** and hollow places. Delacorte Press 2011 376p $17.99; lib bdg $20.99

Grades: 9 10 11 12   Fic
1. Horror fiction 2. Zombies -- Fiction
ISBN 978-0-385-73859-0; 978-0-385-90738-5 lib bdg
LC 2010-45776
Sequel to The dead-tossed waves (2010)
Alone and listening to the moaning of the Dark City dying around her, Annah wants to find her way back home, to her sister and family and their village in the Forest of Hands and Teeth.

The **dead**-tossed waves. Delacorte Press 2010 407p $17.99

Grades: 9 10 11 12   Fic
1. Horror fiction 2. Zombies -- Fiction
ISBN 978-0-385-73684-8
LC 2009-30113
Sequel to The Forest of Hands and Teeth (2009)
Gabry lives a quiet life in a town trapped between a forest and the ocean, hemmed in by the dead who hunger for the living, but her mother Mary's secrets, a cult of religious zealots who worship the dead, and a stranger from the forest who seems to know Gabry threaten to destroy her world.

"Like its predecessor, this book features a breach of the town, an escape into the Forest, a love triangle, the ever-present and inexhaustible Mudo, and an extraordinarily bleak mood. But it also offers an expansion of postapocalyptic detail . . . and a few inspired surprises. . . . Readers are sure to be hooked." Publ Wkly
Followed by The dark and hollow places (2011)

★ The **Forest** of Hands and Teeth. Delacorte Press 2009 310p

Grades: 9 10 11 12   Fic
1. Horror fiction 2. Orphans -- Fiction 3. Zombies -- Fiction
ISBN 978-0-385-73681-7; 978-0-385-90631-9 lib bdg
LC 2008-06494
Through twists and turns of fate, orphaned Mary seeks knowledge of life, love, and especially what lies beyond her walled village and the surrounding forest, where dwell the Unconsecrated, aggressive flesh-eating people who were once dead.

"Mary's observant, careful narration pulls readers into a bleak but gripping story of survival and the endless capacity of humanity to persevere. . . . Fresh and riveting." Publ Wkly
Other titles in this series are:
The dark and hollow places (2011)
The dead-tossed waves (2010)

Ryan, Patrick
Gemini bites. Scholastic Press 2011 231p $17.99

Grades: 8 9 10 11 12   Fic
1. Twins -- Fiction 2. Vampires -- Fiction 3. Homosexuality -- Fiction 4. Dating (Social customs) -- Fiction
ISBN 978-0-545-22128-3; 0-545-22128-5
"Writing with humor and empathy in equal measure, Ryan . . . presents a touching gay romance as well as a pair

of well-rounded and entertaining narrators who come to re-spect each other." Publ Wkly

In Mike we trust; [by] P. E. Ryan. HarperTeen 2009 321p $16.99

Grades: 8 9 10 11 12 **Fic**

1. Uncles -- Fiction 2. Homosexuality -- Fiction 3. Swindlers and swindling -- Fiction

ISBN 978-0-06-085813-1; 0-06-085813-3

LC 2008-11722

As fifteen-year-old Garth is wrestling with the promise he made his mother to wait a while before coming out, his somewhat secretive uncle shows up unexpectedly for an extended visit.

"The author's use of language, at times brilliantly translucent, provides insightful dialogue. This contempo-rary coming-of-age story set in Richmond, VA, subtly and clearly provides a fresh perspective on teenage sexual iden-tity by imbedding it into the context of the bigger issue of truth." SLJ

Ryan, Sara

Empress of the world; Sara Ryan. Speak 2003 213 p. $8.99

Grades: 9 10 11 12 **Fic**

1. Camps 2. Lesbians 3. LGBT youth 4. Love stories 5. Teenagers -- Fiction 6. Bisexuality 7. Homosexuality
ISBN 0142500593; 9780142500590

LC 0052758

Lambda Literary Awards Children's and Teen Finalist (2002)

While attending a summer institute, fifteen-year-old Nic meets another girl named Battle, falls in love with her, and finds the relationship to be difficult and confusing. "Grades seven to twelve." (Bull Cent Child Books)

"At a summer institute for gifted high-school students, Nicola finds herself attracted to another girl. Nic's uncer-tainty about whether she's either lesbian or bisexual is be-lievably conveyed, and the dialogue is convincingly realis-tic. Despite a flimsily constructed conflict, YA readers are sure to embrace the believable passions in this summer ro-mance." (Horn Book)

Ryan, Tom

Way to go; Tom Ryan. Orca Book Publishers 2012 214 p. (paperback) $12.95; (ebook) $12.99

Grades: 9 10 11 12 **Fic**

1. Cooks -- Fiction 2. Gay teenagers -- Fiction
ISBN 145980077X; 9781459800779; 9781459800786 pdf; 9781459800793 epub

LC 2011943726

In this book, "as summer vacation begins on the island of Cape Breton in Nova Scotia, 17-year-old Danny feels lost, with no career aspirations and the burden of hiding that he's gay. . . . When Danny starts working at a new restaurant as a dishwasher, he discovers a passion for cooking, becomes sous chef at the restaurant, and bonds with Lisa, a hip and sophisticated waitress from New York City with troubles of her own." (Publishers Weekly)

Sachar, Louis

The **cardturner**; a novel about a king, a queen, and a joker. Delacorte Press 2010 336p $17.99; lib bdg $20.99

Grades: 8 9 10 11 12 **Fic**

1. Uncles -- Fiction 2. Family life -- Fiction 3. Bridge (Game) -- Fiction

ISBN 978-0-385-73662-6; 0-385-73662-2; 978-0-385-90619-7 lib bdg; 0-385-90619-6 lib bdg

LC 2009-27585

"Alton gets roped into serving as a card turner for his great-uncle, Lester Trapp, a bridge whizz who recently lost his eyesight. . . . To Alton's surprise, he becomes enamored of the game and begins to bond with his crusty uncle. . . . With dry, understated humor, Alton makes the intricacies of bridge accessible, while his relationships with and observa-tions about family members and friends . . . form a portrait of a reflective teenager whose life is infinitely enriched by connections he never expected to make." Publ Wkly

Saeed, Aisha

Written in the stars; by Aisha Saeed. Nancy Paulsen Books 2015 284 p. $17.99

Grades: 9 10 11 12 **Fic**

1. Love -- Fiction 2. Pakistan -- Fiction 3. Arranged marriage -- Fiction 4. Pakistani Americans -- Fiction 5. Dating (Social customs) -- Fiction 6. Forced marriage -- Fiction 7. Pakistani American teenage girls

ISBN 0399171703; 9780399171703

LC 2014019860

In this book, by Aisha Saeed, "Naila's conservative im-migrant parents have always said the same thing: She may choose what to study, how to wear her hair, and what to be when she grows up--but they will choose her husband. . . . And until then, dating--even friendship with a boy--is for-bidden. When Naila breaks their rule by falling in love with Saif, her parents are livid. Convinced she has forgotten who she truly is, they travel to Pakistan to visit relatives and ex-plore their roots." (Publisher's note)

"Naila's harrowing story is compellingly told, and Saeed includes an afterword about the problem of forced marriages not only in Pakistan but among immigrant communities in the U.S. Stirring, haunting, and ultimately hopeful." Booklist
Includes bibliographical references

Saenz, Benjamin Alire

He forgot to say good-bye. Simon & Schuster 2008 321p $16.99

Grades: 8 9 10 11 **Fic**

1. Drug abuse -- Fiction 2. Mexican Americans -- Fiction

ISBN 978-1-4169-4963-3; 1-4169-4963-1

LC 2007-21959

Two teenaged boys with very different lives find that they share a common bond—fathers they have never met who left when they were small boys—and in spite of their differences, they become close when they each need some-one who understands.

"The affirming and hopeful ending is well-earned for the characters and a great payoff for the reader. . . . Characters are well-developed and complex. . . . Overall it is a strong novel with broad teenage appeal." Voice Youth Advocates

★ **Sammy** and Juliana in Hollywood; by Benjamin Alire Saenz. Cinco Puntos Press 2004 294p hardcover o.p. pa $11.95

Grades: 9 10 11 12　　　　　　　　　　**Fic**
　1. Violence -- Fiction 2. New Mexico -- Fiction 3. Mexican Americans -- Fiction
　ISBN 0-938317-81-4; 1-933693-99-1 pa
　　　　　　　　　　　　　　　　LC 2004-2414
As a Chicano boy living in the unglamorous town of Hollywood, New Mexico, and a member of the graduating class of 1969, Sammy Santos faces the challenges of "gringo" racism, unpopular dress codes, the Vietnam War, barrio violence, and poverty

Saint-Exupery, Antoine de
The **little** prince; written and illustrated by Antoine de Saint-Exupery; translated from the French by Richard Howard. Harcourt 2000 83p il $18; pa $12

Grades: 4 5 6 7 8 9 10 11 12 Adult　　　　**Fic**
　1. Fantasy fiction 2. Princes -- Fiction 3. Air pilots -- Fiction 4. Extraterrestrial beings -- Fiction
　ISBN 0-15-202398-4; 0-15-601219-7 pa
　　　　　　　　　　　　　　　　LC 99-50439
A new translation of the title first published 1943 by Reynal & Hitchcock
"This many-dimensional fable of an airplane pilot who has crashed in the desert is for readers of all ages. The pilot comes upon the little prince soon after the crash. The prince tells of his adventures on different planets and on Earth as he attempts to learn about the universe in order to live peacefully on his own small planet. A spiritual quality enhances the seemingly simple observations of the little prince." Shapiro. Fic for Youth. 3d edition

Saldaña, René
Dancing with the devil and other tales from beyond; = Bailando con el diablo y otros cuentos del más allá. by = por René Saldaña, Jr.; Spanish translation by = traducción al español de Gabriela Baeza Ventura. Piñata Books 2012 81 p. (alk. paper) $9.95

Grades: 5 6 7 8 9　　　　　　　　　　**Fic**
　1. Short stories 2. Mexican Americans -- Fiction
　ISBN 1558857443; 9781558857445
　　　　　　　　　　　　　　　LC 2012008729
Author Rene Saldaña Jr. presents a book of short stories. "Lauro and Miguel run for their lives--with La Llorona's cold breath on their necks-- after being caught smoking cigarettes down by the river. There's Felipe, who's so determined to win back the Peñitas Grand Master Marble Champion title that he's willing to make a deal for a shooter with a supernatural edge. And when Louie's leg swells up after he cuts his toe playing with a knife, he can't help but wonder if his mom's warning could be true." (Publisher's note)

A **good** long way; by Rene Saldana, Jr. Piñata Books 2010 103p pa $10.95

Grades: 8 9 10 11　　　　　　　　　　　**Fic**
　1. School stories 2. Texas -- Fiction 3. Brothers -- Fiction 4. Mexican Americans -- Fiction 5. Runaway teenagers -- Fiction
　ISBN 978-1-55885-607-3; 1-55885-607-2
　　　　　　　　　　　　　　　LC 2010-32989
Three Mexican American teenagers in a small-town in Texas struggle with difficulties at home and at school as they try to attain the elusive status of adulthood.
"This fast-paced novel will make readers think about their own lives and responsibilities." SLJ

Sales, Leila
Mostly good girls. Simon Pulse 2010 347p $16.99

Grades: 9 10 11 12　　　　　　　　　　**Fic**
　1. School stories 2. Ability -- Fiction 3. Authorship -- Fiction 4. Friendship -- Fiction 5. Massachusetts -- Fiction
　ISBN 978-1-4424-0679-7
　　　　　　　　　　　　　　　LC 2010-7190
Sixteen-year-olds Violet and Katie, best friends since seventh grade despite differences in their family backgrounds and abilities, are pulled apart during their junior year at Massachusetts' exclusive Westfield School.
"This exploration of growing up, personal change and angst is well-written." Voice of Youth Advocates

Past perfect. Simon Pulse 2011 306p $16.99
Grades: 7 8 9 10　　　　　　　　　　　**Fic**
　1. New England -- Fiction 2. Summer employment -- Fiction 3. Dating (Social customs) -- Fiction
　ISBN 978-1-4424-0682-7; 1-4424-0682-8
　　　　　　　　　　　　　　　LC 2011025811
"Chelsea is an appealing narrator with a sharp sense of humor, and readers will tear through this novel to find out whether she reunites with Ezra or gets together with Dan from the rival museum. . . . This is a satisfying and fun read." SLJ

This song will save your life; Leila Sales. Farrar Straus & Giroux 2013 288 p. (hard) $17.99
Grades: 8 9 10 11 12　　　　　　　　　**Fic**
　1. Bullies -- Fiction 2. Disc jockeys -- Fiction 3. Schools -- Fiction 4. Suicide -- Fiction 5. Popularity -- Fiction 6. High schools -- Fiction 7. Interpersonal relations -- Fiction
　ISBN 0374351384; 9780374351380
　　　　　　　　　　　　　　　LC 2012050408
In this book, "Elise has endured a lifetime of social isolation and bullying at school. Walking alone one night soon after a halfhearted suicide attempt, the 16-year-old inadvertently ends up at an underground nightclub. There, an aspiring musician befriends her, and she catches the eye of Char, a cute DJ who agrees to teach her to mix music. But as talented, driven Elise spends more nights sneaking out to learn how to DJ (and kiss Char), her double life spins out of control." (Publishers Weekly)

Tonight the streets are ours; Leila Sales. Farrar, Straus & Giroux 2015 352 p. (hardback) $17.99 **Fic**
　1. New York (N.Y.) -- Fiction 2. Self-realization

-- Fiction 3. Blogs -- Fiction 4. Authors -- Fiction 5. Schools -- Fiction 6. High schools -- Fiction 7. Conduct of life -- Fiction 8. Family problems -- Fiction 9. Interpersonal relations -- Fiction
ISBN 9780374376659

LC 2015003571

In this novel, by Leila Sales, "lately [Arden's] . . . grown resentful of everyone . . . taking her loyalty for granted. Then Arden stumbles upon a website called Tonight the Streets Are Ours, the musings of a young New York City writer named Peter. . . . During one crazy night out in New York City filled with parties, dancing, and music . . . Arden discovers that Peter isn't exactly who she thought he was. And maybe she isn't exactly who she thought she was, either." (Publisher's note)

"This romantic adventure will grab fans of Rachel Cohen and David Levithan's Nick and Norah's Infinite Playlist (2006) and of Sarah Dessen, particularly with Arden's desire to flirt with danger." Booklist

Salinger, J. D.
★ The **catcher** in the rye. Little, Brown 1951 277p $24.95; pa $5.99
Grades: 11 12 Adult   Fic
1. New York (N.Y.) -- Fiction
ISBN 0-316-76953-3; 0-316-76948-7 pa

"The story of adolescent Holden Caulfield who runs away from boarding-school in Pennsylvania to New York where he preserves his innocence despite various attempts to lose it. The colloquial, lively, first-person narration, with its attacks on the 'phoniness' of the adult world and its clinging to family sentiment in the form of Holden's affection for his sister Phoebe, made the novel accessible to and popular with a wide readership, particularly with the young." Oxford Companion to Engl Lit. 5th edition

Salisbury, Graham
★ **Eyes** of the emperor. Wendy Lamb Books 2005 228p hardcover o.p. pa $6.99
Grades: 7 8 9 10   Fic
1. Japanese Americans -- Fiction 2. World War, 1939-1945 -- Fiction
ISBN 0-385-72971-5; 0-440-22956-1 pa

LC 2004-15142

Following orders from the United States Army, several young Japanese American men train K-9 units to hunt Asians during World War II.

"Based on the experiences of 26 Hawaiian-Americans of Japanese ancestry, this novel tells an uncomfortable story. Yet it tells of belief in honor, respect, and love of country." Libr Media Connect

Salisbury, Melinda
The **Sin** Eater's daughter; Melinda Salisbury. Scholastic Press, an imprint of Scholastic Inc. 2015 320 p. (alk. paper) $17.99
Grades: 9 10 11 12   Fic
1. Love stories 2. Fantasy fiction 3. Queens -- Fiction 4. Love -- Fiction 5. Death -- Fiction 6. Princes -- Fiction 7. Goddesses -- Fiction
ISBN 0545810620; 9780545810623

LC 2014038970

In this book by Melinda Salisbury, "seventeen-year-old Twylla has a gift and a curse as the embodiment of a goddess on Earth: she is worshipped and she can kill men in seconds with the briefest of touches. Twylla's mother is a Sin Eater, one who eats symbolic foods of the deceased person's sins at their grave site; Twylla is set to pursue this path until the Queen of Lormere takes her from her home to become the goddess Daunen Embodied." (School Library Journal)

"Seventeen-year-old Twylla has a gift and a curse as the embodiment of a goddess on Earth: she is worshipped and she can kill men in seconds with the briefest of touches. Twylla's mother is a Sin Eater, one who eats symbolic foods of the deceased person's sins at their grave site; Twylla is set to pursue this path until the Queen of Lormere takes her from her home to become the goddess Daunen Embodied... Twylla is strong and sensible, and teen fans of royal intrigue titles will be rooting for her." SLJ

Salomon, Peter Adam
All those broken angels; Peter Adam Salomon. Flux 2014 240 p. $9.99
Grades: 9 10 11 12   Fic
1. Ghost stories 2. Mystery fiction 3. Friendship -- Fiction 4. Savannah (Ga.) -- Fiction 5. Missing children -- Fiction 6. Ghosts -- Fiction 7. Best friends -- Fiction 8. Mystery and detective stories
ISBN 0738740799; 9780738740799

LC 2014014104

In this book, by Peter Adam Salomon, "Richard Harrison was the last person to see his friend Melanie alive. She vanished when they were six, and while the police never found her, a part of her remained - a living shadow that became Richard's closest friend. For ten years, Richard has never questioned the shadow that keeps him company . . . until a new girl moves to town, claiming to be Melanie." (Publisher's note)

"It has been 10 years since Richard's best friend, Melanie, vanished during their game of hide-and-seek, but over the subsequent decade, he has been comforted by the presence of her ghost: a silent, willful shadow figure, the single strong constant in his otherwise cowering life...An overly rationalized climax undercuts this accomplishment a bit, but that doesn't erase the effect of the book's dreadful, inching progress; startling, evolving relationships; and pervading sense of shuddery doom." Booklist

Salter, Sydney
Swoon at your own risk. Graphia 2010 356p pa $8.99
Grades: 9 10 11 12   Fic
1. Grandmothers -- Fiction 2. Summer employment -- Fiction 3. Dating (Social customs) -- Fiction
ISBN 978-0-15-206649-9; 0-15-206649-7

After a junior hear of dating disasters, Polly—the granddaughter of a famous advice columnist—swears off boys. But when her grandmother moves in for the summer, Polly mistakenly believes she'll be getting great advice when in reality, she discovers that her grandmother is a man-crazed sexagenarian.

"This book is a light read with an emotional awakening and enough romance to keep fans of the genre interested." SLJ

Samms, Olivia

Sketchy; Olivia Samms. Amazon Childrens Pub
2013 256 p. (hardcover) $16.99

Grades: 9 10 11 12   **Fic**

1. Mystery fiction 2. Paranormal fiction

ISBN 147781650X; 9781477816509

This novel, by Olivia Samms, is book one in "The Bea
Catcher Chronicles." "Bea is starting over at Packard High
School, in a city shaken from two assaults on young women.
The latest victim, Willa Pressman-the one who survived-
doesn't remember a thing. But Bea has a disturbing new
'skill': she can see-and then draw-images from other people's minds. And when she looks at Willa, Bea is shocked by
what she sketches." (Publisher's note)

Sanchez, Alex

Bait. Simon & Schuster Books for Young Readers
2009 239p $16.99

Grades: 7 8 9 10   **Fic**

1. Stepfathers -- Fiction 2. Mexican Americans --
Fiction 3. Child sexual abuse -- Fiction

ISBN 978-1-4169-3772-2; 1-4169-3772-2

LC 2008-38815

Diego keeps getting into trouble because of his explosive
temper until he finally finds a probation officer who helps
him get to the root of his anger so that he can stop running
from his past.

"This groundbreaking novel brings to life an appealing
young man who is neither totally a victim nor a victimizer,
one who struggles to handle conflicts that derail many young
lives. . . . High interest and accessible, this coming-of-age
story belongs in every collection." SLJ

Getting it. Simon & Schuster 2006 210p
$16.95; pa $8.99

Grades: 9 10 11 12   **Fic**

1. School stories 2. Friendship -- Fiction 3.
Homosexuality -- Fiction 4. Mexican Americans --
Fiction

ISBN 978-1-4169-0896-8; 1-4169-0896-X; 978-1-
4169-0898-2 pa; 1-4169-0898-6 pa

LC 2005-29905

Hoping to impress a sexy female classmate, fifteen-year-
old Carlos secretly hires gay student Sal to give him an image makeover, in exchange for Carlos's help in forming a
Gay-Straight Alliance at their Texas high school.

"This title's sexual frankness may make it a controversial choice, particularly for school libraries in more conservative communities, but its themes, appeal, and readability
make it a nearly essential purchase." Voice Youth Advocates

Rainbow boys. Simon & Schuster 2001 233p
hardcover o.p. pa $8.99

Grades: 10 11 12   **Fic**

1. School stories 2. Homosexuality -- Fiction

ISBN 0-689-84100-0; 0-689-85770-5 pa

LC 2001-20952

Three high school seniors, a jock with a girlfriend and an
alcoholic father, a closeted gay, and a flamboyant gay rights
advocate, struggle with family issues, gay bashers, first sex,
and conflicting feelings about each other.

"Some of the language and sexual situations may be too
mature for some readers, but overall there's enough conflict,
humor and tenderness to make this story believable—and
touching." Publ Wkly

Other titles featuring Nelson, Kyle, and Jason are:
Rainbow High (2004)
Rainbow road (2005)

Rainbow High. Simon & Schuster Books for
Young Readers 2004 247p $16.95; pa $8.99

Grades: 10 11 12   **Fic**

1. School stories 2. Homosexuality -- Fiction

ISBN 0-689-85477-3; 0-689-85478-1 pa

LC 2003-8252

Sequel to Rainbow boys (2001)

Follows three gay high school seniors as they struggle
with issues of coming out, safe sex, homophobia, being in
love, and college choices.

Followed by Rainbow road (2005)

Rainbow road. Simon & Schuster 2005 243p
$16.95; pa $8.99

Grades: 10 11 12   **Fic**

1. Homosexuality -- Fiction 2. Automobile travel --
Fiction

ISBN 0-689-86565-1; 1-4169-1191-X pa

LC 2004-25980

Sequel to Rainbow high (2003)

While driving across the United States during the summer after high school graduation, three young gay men encounter various bisexual and homosexual people and make
some decisions about their own relationships and lives.

"Some mature romance scenes, occasional frank language, and an inclusion of transgender/transsexual/bisexual
story lines translate into a tender book that will likely be appreciated and embraced by young adult readers." SLJ

Sandell, Lisa Ann

★ Song of the sparrow. Scholastic Press 2007
394p $16.99; pa $8.99

Grades: 8 9 10 11 12   **Fic**

1. War stories 2. Knights and knighthood -- Fiction 3.
Great Britain -- History -- 0-1066 -- Fiction

ISBN 978-0-439-91848-0; 0-439-91848-0; 978-0-439-
91849-7 pa; 0-439-91849-9 pa

LC 2007-00016

In fifth-century Britain, nine years after the destruction
of their home on the island of Shalott brings her to live with
her father and brothers in the military encampments of Arthur's army, seventeen-year-old Elaine describes her changing perceptions of war and the people around her as she becomes increasingly involved in the bitter struggle against the
invading Saxons.

The author "invents a unique and eloquently wrought addition to Arthurian lore in 44 verses. . . . The poetic narrative
. . . evokes a remarkable range (and natural progression) of
emotions." Publ Wkly

Sanders, Scott Loring

Gray baby; a novel. Houghton Mifflin Harcourt
2009 321p $17

Grades: 7 8 9 10 **Fic**
1. Homicide -- Fiction 2. Virginia -- Fiction 3. Alcoholism -- Fiction 4. Country life -- Fiction 5. Single parent family -- Fiction 6. Racially mixed people -- Fiction
ISBN 978-0-547-07661-4; 0-547-07661-4
LC 2008-36810
Clifton has grown up in rural Virginia with the memory of his African American father being beaten to death by policemen, causing his white mother to slip into alcoholism and depression, but after befriending an old man who listens to his problems, Clifton finally feels less alone in the world.
"Unflinching and raw, the story, set in the late 1980s, explores the destructiveness of racism." Horn Book Guide

The **Hanging** Woods; a novel. Houghton Mifflin 2008 326p $16
Grades: 10 11 12 **Fic**
1. Alabama -- Fiction 2. Homicide -- Fiction 3. Friendship -- Fiction 4. Country life -- Fiction
ISBN 978-0-618-88125-3
LC 2007-25773
In rural Alabama during the summer of 1975, three teen-aged boys build a treehouse, try to keep a headless turkey alive, and become involved in a murder mystery.
This is a "compelling, but disturbing story, which features mature subject matter and language." Kirkus

Sanders, Shelly
Rachel's secret. Second Story Press 2012 248 p. $12.95
Grades: 6 7 8 9 10 **Fic**
1. Historical fiction 2. Antisemitism -- Fiction 3. Judaism -- Relations -- Christianity -- Fiction
ISBN 1926920376; 9781926920375
This book follows "14-year-old Rachel . . . living under Russian rule in Kishinev in 1903, [she] was one of the last people to see her Christian friend Mikhail alive when she witnessed his murder at the hands of disgruntled relatives who stood to lose out on an inheritance. His death is blamed on Jews, however, and a vicious pogrom is unleashed on the city. Rachel's anguish about knowing what happened stems from a justified fear of not being believed if she comes forward, thus evoking more turmoil. She also harbors guilt that her somewhat risky friendship with a non-Jewish boy somehow triggered the calamity. . . . [W]hile Rachel does act courageously and courtroom justice is meted out, virulent anti-Semitism still rules the day." (Booklist)

Sanderson, Brandon
The **Rithmatist**; Brandon Sanderson. Tor Teen 2013 384 p. ill. (hardcover) $17.99
Grades: 7 8 9 10 **Fic**
1. Fantasy fiction 2. Magic -- Fiction 3. Fantasy
ISBN 0765320320; 9780765320322
LC 2012043417
In this young adult fantasy novel, by Brandon Sanderson, "Joel wants to be a Rithmatist. Chosen by the Master in a mysterious inception ceremony, Rithmatists have the power to infuse life into two-dimensional figures known as Chalklings. Rithmatists are humanity's only defense against the Wild Chalklings--merciless creatures that leave mangled

corpses in their wake. Having nearly overrun the territory of Nebrask, the Wild Chalklings now threaten all of the American Isles." (Publisher's note)

Sandler, Karen
Rebellion; Karen Sandler. First edition Tu Books 2014 396 p. map (Tankborn) (hardcover) $19.95
Grades: 7 8 9 10 **Fic**
1. Science fiction 2. Terrorism -- Fiction 3. Genetic engineering -- Fiction 4. Kidnapping -- Fiction
ISBN 9781600609848; 1600609848
LC 2014002775
Sequel to: Awakening
In this young adult science fiction novel by Karen Sandler, part of the Tankborn Trilogy series, "Kayla is a GEN--a genetically engineered nonhuman--in a world torn apart by castes separating GENs from 'real' humans. In the wake of a devastating bomb blast, Kayla finds herself at the headquarters of the organization that planted the bomb--and many others like it in GEN food warehouses and homes." (Publisher's note)
"Sandler tackles caste systems, slavery and terrorism (including its muddled logic) head-on. . . . With rebellions, ideological questions and a nonwhite, not-entirely-heterosexual cast, this series is a strong addition to the genre." Kirkus

Tankborn. Tu Books 2011 373p map $17.95
Grades: 7 8 9 10 **Fic**
1. Science fiction 2. Genetic engineering -- Fiction
ISBN 978-1-60060-662-5; 1-60060-662-8
LC 2011014589
Kayla and Mishalla, two genetically engineered non-human slaves (GENs), fall in love with higher-status boys, discover deep secrets about the creation of GENs, and in the process find out what it means to be human.
"Sandler has created a fascinating dystopian world. . . . The author's speculative vision of the darker side of future possibilities in genetic engineering and mind control is both chilling and thought-provoking." SLJ

Sax, Aline
★ The **war** within these walls; by Aline Sax; illustrated by Caryl Strzelecki; translated from the Dutch by Laura Watkinson. Eerdmans Books for Young Readers 2013 176 p. $17
Grades: 9 10 11 12 **Fic**
1. Jewish ghettos 2. World War, 1939-1945 -- Fiction 3. Jews -- Poland -- Fiction 4. Holocaust, Jewish (1939-1945) -- Poland -- Fiction 5. Poland -- History -- Occupation, 1939-1945 -- Fiction
ISBN 0802854281; 9780802854285
LC 2013005663
Mildred L. Batchelder Honor Book (2014)
National Jewish Book Award: Winner, Children's and Young Adult (2013)
In this book by Aline Sax and illustrated by Caryl Strzelecki "it's World War II, and Misha's family, like the rest of the Jews living in Warsaw, has been moved by the Nazis into a single crowded ghetto. Misha does his best to help his family survive, even crawling through the sewers to smuggle food. When conditions worsen, Misha joins a hand-

ful of other Jews who decide to make a final, desperate stand against the Nazis." (Publisher's note)

"The narrator lives with his parents and sister in what becomes the Warsaw Ghetto. He finds a secret escape from the ghetto and begins smuggling food, eventually joining with Mordechai Anielewicz's organized Resistance. The prose is spare; the book's format, with text on black or white pages and plentiful ink and wash illustrations, is dramatic and will grab young readers." (Horn Book)

Sayed, Kashua

Let it be morning; translated from Hebrew by Miriam Shlesinger. Black Cat 2006 271p pa $13

Grades: 11 12 Adult   **Fic**

1. Journalists -- Fiction 2. Israel-Arab conflicts -- Fiction

ISBN 0-8021-7021-8; 978-0-8021-7021-7

LC 2005-46768

Original Hebrew edition, 2004

"A young Arab-Israeli journalist moves from Tel Aviv back to his childhood village with his wife and baby daughter just in time to be caught up in a series of harrowing, dramatic events. In response to Israel's military presence in the village, neighbors and relatives find themselves fighting one another in order to survive. . . . The short chapters and fast pace, combined with the memories of youth that his return home elicits, make for an easy fit for older teens with an interest in other cultures or current events." SLJ

Scarrow, Alex

Day of the predator. Walker Books for Young Readers 2011 404p (TimeRiders) $16.99

Grades: 7 8 9 10   **Fic**

1. Science fiction 2. Time travel -- Fiction

ISBN 978-0-8027-2296-6; 0-8027-2296-2

LC 2010040987

Sequel to: TimeRiders (2010)

With teens Maddy, Liam, and Sal on their first solo assignment for a secret agency, Liam is sent back in time to prevent the murder of the father of time travel by a terrorist group, but due to a nuclear accident, he ends up in the late cretaceous period where the biggest threat is not from the legendary tyrannosaur.

"Readers will be intrigued, puzzled—and ready for the next one." Kirkus

Scelsa, Kate

Fans of the impossible life; Kate Scelsa. Balzer + Bray, an imprint of HarperCollins Publishers 2015 368 p. (hardback) $17.99 **Fic**

1. School stories 2. Friendship -- Fiction 3. Mental illness -- Fiction 4. Gays -- Fiction 5. Bullying -- Fiction 6. Best friends -- Fiction 7. Family problems -- Fiction 8. Foster home care -- Fiction

ISBN 9780062331755

LC 2015005754

In this novel, by Kate Scelsa, "Mira is starting over at Saint Francis Prep. . . . Jeremy is the painfully shy art nerd at Saint Francis who's been in self-imposed isolation after an incident that ruined his last year of school. . . . Sebby, Mira's gay best friend, is a boy who seems to carry sunlight around with him. . . . As Jeremy finds himself drawn into Sebby and

Mira's world, he begins to understand the secrets that they hide in order to protect themselves." (Publisher's note)

"So much more than a love triangle novel, Scelsa's debut is filled with teens discovering how to handle life's situations." SLJ

Schantz, Sarah Elizabeth

Fig; Sarah Elizabeth Schantz. Margaret K. McElderry Books 2015 352 p. (hardback) $17.99

Grades: 9 10 11 12   **Fic**

1. Schizophrenia -- Fiction 2. Mental illness -- Fiction 3. Mother-daughter relationship -- Fiction 4. Schools -- Fiction 5. Farm life -- Kansas -- Fiction 6. Family life -- Kansas -- Fiction 7. Mothers and daughters -- Fiction 8. Self-destructive behavior -- Fiction 9. Kansas -- History -- 20th century -- Fiction

ISBN 1481423584; 9781481423588; 9781481423595

LC 2014025394

In this novel, by Sarah Elizabeth Schantz, "love and sacrifice intertwine in this . . . [story] about a girl dealing with her mother's schizophrenia and her own mental illness. . . . Spanning the course of Fig's childhood from age six to nineteen, this . . . novel is more than a portrait of a mother, a daughter, and the struggle that comes with all-consuming love. It is an acutely honest and often painful portrayal of life with mental illness." (Publisher's note)

"Though some readers may be frustrated by the meandering pace of Fig's story, patient readers who appreciate melancholic, lyrical narratives will likely be moved by Fig's heartbreaking tale." Booklist

Scheibe, Lindsey

Riptide; one summer, endless possibilities. Lindsey Scheibe. 1st ed. Flux 2013 277 p. (paperback) $9.99

Grades: 7 8 9 10 11 12   **Fic**

1. Surfing -- Fiction 2. Teenage girls -- Fiction 3. Friendship -- Fiction 4. Child abuse -- Fiction 5. Best friends -- Fiction 6. San Diego (Calif.) -- Fiction 7. Dating (Social customs) -- Fiction

ISBN 0738735949; 9780738735948

LC 2012048951

In this novel, by Lindsey Scheibe, "signing up for her first surf competition, Grace has just one summer to train and impress the university scouts who will be judging the comp. But summer is about more than just big waves. As romances ignite and her feelings for Ford threaten to reach the point of no return, Grace must face the biggest challenges of her life." (Publisher's note)

Scheidt, Erica Lorraine

★ **Uses** for boys; Erica Lorraine Scheidt. St. Martin's Press 2013 240 p. $9.99

Grades: 9 10 11 12   **Fic**

1. Love stories 2. Dating (Social customs) -- Fiction 3. Teenagers -- Conduct of life -- Fiction

ISBN 1250007119; 9781250007117

In this novel by Erica Lorraine Scheidt "Anna learns that if you give boys what they want, you can get what you need. But the price is high--the other kids make fun of her; the girls call her a slut. . . . Then comes Sam. When Anna actually meets a boy who is more than just useful, whose family eats dinner together, laughs, and tells stories, the truth about love becomes clear. And she finally learns how it feels to have something to lose--and something to offer." (Publisher's note)

Schindler, Holly

★ **A blue** so dark. Flux 2010 277p pa $9.95
Grades: 8 9 10 11 12   **Fic**
1. School stories 2. Artists -- Fiction 3. Schizophrenia -- Fiction 4. Mental illness -- Fiction 5. Mother-daughter relationship -- Fiction
ISBN 978-0-7387-1926-9

LC 2009-31360

As Missouri fifteen-year-old Aura struggles alone to cope with the increasingly severe symptoms of her mother's schizophrenia, she wishes only for a normal life, but fears that her artistic ability and genes will one day result in her own insanity.

"A haunting, realistic view of the melding of art, creativity, and mental illness and their collective impact on a young person's life." Booklist

Playing hurt. Flux 2011 303p pa $9.95
Grades: 7 8 9 10   **Fic**
1. Love stories 2. Resorts -- Fiction 3. Minnesota -- Fiction 4. Loss (Psychology) -- Fiction
ISBN 978-0-7387-2287-0; 0-7387-2287-1

LC 2010-44173

Chelsea Keyes, a high school basketball star whose promising career has been cut short by a terrible accident on the court, and Clint Morgan, a nineteen-year-old ex-hockey player who gave up his sport following a game-related tragedy, meet at a Minnesota lake resort and find themselves drawn together by the losses they have suffered.

"Both heartbreaking and thrilling, the emotional journey that Clint and Chelsea embark on together is more than a heady romance; the characters are realistically drawn, and the book does not shy away from the reality of the characters' experiences: anger and grief mixed with desire and yearning. The book speaks to personal struggles and triumphs and the ability of the human spirit to heal." Voice Youth Advocates

Schlitz, Laura Amy

★ The **hired** girl; Laura Amy Schlitz. Candlewick Press 2015 400 p. $17.99
Grades: 7 8 9 10   **Fic**
1. Diaries -- Fiction 2. Young women -- Fiction 3. Household employees -- Fiction
ISBN 9780763678180

LC 2014955411

Boston Globe Horn Book Fiction Honor Book (2016)

In this book, by Laura Amy Schlitz, "Joan Skraggs . . . yearns for real life and true love. But what hope is there for adventure, beauty, or art on a hardscrabble farm in Pennsylvania where the work never ends? Over the summer of 1911, Joan pours her heart out into her diary as she seeks a new, better life for herself—because maybe, just maybe, a hired girl cleaning and cooking for six dollars a week can become what a farm girl could only dream of—a woman with a future." (Publisher's note)

"A wonderful look into the life of strong girl who learns that she needs the love of others to truly grow up." SLJ

Schmatz, Pat

Lizard radio; Pat Schmatz. Candlewick Press 2015 288 p. $16.99 **Fic**
1. Future life -- Fiction 2. Gender role -- Fiction
ISBN 0763676357; 9780763676353

LC 2014960012

In this novel, by Pat Schmatz, "fifteen-year-old bender Kivali has had a rough time in a gender-rigid culture. Abandoned as a baby . . . Kivali has always been surrounded by uncertainty. Where did she come from? Now she's in Crop-Camp, with all of its schedules and regs, and the first real friends she's ever had. Strange occurrences and complicated relationships raise questions. But she has . . . the power to enter a trancelike state to harness the 'knowings' inside her." (Publisher's note)

"An entertaining and thought-provoking read, this title will be a big hit for those who want something deeper from their dystopian fiction." SLJ

Schmidt, Gary D.

★ **Orbiting** Jupiter; Gary D. Schmidt. Clarion Books, Houghton Mifflin Harcourt 2015 192 p. (hardback) $17.99
Grades: 6 7 8 9   **Fic**
1. Teenage fathers -- Fiction 2. Foster home care -- Fiction 3. Friendship -- Fiction 4. Child abuse -- Fiction 5. Emotional problems -- Fiction
ISBN 9780544462229

LC 2015001338

This young adult novel, by Gary D. Schmidt, tells the "story of Joseph, 14, who joins his family as a foster child. Damaged in prison, Joseph wants nothing more than to find his baby daughter, Jupiter, whom he has never seen. When Joseph has begun to believe he'll have a future, he is confronted by demons from his past that force a tragic sacrifice." (Publisher's note)

"The matter-of-fact narrative voice ensures that the tragic plot never overwhelms this wrenching tale of growth and loss." SLJ

Schneider, Robyn

★ The **beginning** of everything; by Robyn Schneider. 1st ed. Katherine Tegen Books 2013 336 p. (hardcover) $17.99
Grades: 9 10 11 12   **Fic**
1. School stories 2. Popularity -- Fiction 3. Schools -- Fiction 4. California -- Fiction 5. High schools -- Fiction 6. Debates and debating -- Fiction 7. Interpersonal relations -- Fiction 8. People with disabilities -- Fiction 9. Family life -- California -- Fiction
ISBN 0062217135; 9780062217134

LC 2012030976

In this book, after "finding his vapid girlfriend going down on another guy, Ezra Faulkner is seriously injured in a hit-and-run accident, leaving him out of the loop with the jock-and-cheerleader set. When senior year begins, he gravitates toward his old friend Toby, no stranger to tragedy himself. Toby and his debate team welcome Ezra to their lunch table when they find out that the prom king is as smart and funny as they are." (Kirkus Reviews)

Schreck, Karen Halvorsen, 1962-

While he was away; Karen Schreck. Sourcebooks Fire 2012 249 p. $8.99

Grades: 7 8 9 10   **Fic**

1. Love stories 2. Loneliness -- Fiction 3. Iraq War, 2003-2011 -- Fiction

ISBN 140226402X; 9781402264023

This book follows a couple, Penna and David, as David "leaves for a stint in Iraq. . . . Penna is anxious and devastated, but eventually she finds ways to cope. . . . In Iraq, David struggles with the mind-numbing work of patrols and the terror that interrupts it, and he focuses on an orphanage for Iraqi refugee children as a way to be useful. . . . Paralleling Penna's story is her discovery of a grandmother who lost her first husband in World War II." (Kirkus Reviews)

"With realistic characters and interesting dialogue, While He Was Away is both insightful and tragic." VOYA

Schrefer, Eliot

The **deadly** sister. Scholastic Press 2010 310p $17.99

Grades: 8 9 10 11 12   **Fic**

1. Mystery fiction 2. Sisters -- Fiction 3. Homicide -- Fiction

ISBN 978-0-545-16574-7; 0-545-16574-1

LC 2010-281733

Abby Goodwin has always covered for her sister, Maya, but now Maya has been accused of murder, and Abby's not sure she'll be able to cover for her sister anymore. Abby helps Maya escape. But when Abby begins investigating the death, she find that you can't trust anyone, not even the people you think you know.

"Well-drawn characters, realistic dialogue, and suspenseful twists and turns add to the appeal. Teens crave mystery, and this book will suit them just fine." SLJ

★ **Endangered**; Eliot Schrefer. Scholastic Press 2012 264 p. (reinforced) $17.99

Grades: 7 8 9 10 11 12   **Fic**

1. Animal sanctuaries -- Fiction 2. Wildlife conservation -- Fiction 3. Congo (Democratic Republic) -- Fiction 4. Apes -- Fiction 5. Bonobo -- Fiction 6. Divorce -- Fiction

ISBN 0545165768; 9780545165761

LC 2012030877

This book by Eliot Schrefer was a 2012 National Book Award Finalist for Young People's Literature. "When one girl has to follow her mother to her sanctuary for bonobos, she's not thrilled to be there. It's her mother's passion, and she'd rather have nothing to do with it. But when revolution breaks out and their sanctuary is attacked, she must rescue the bonobos and hide in the jungle. Together, they will fight to keep safe, to eat, and to survive." (Publisher's note)

★ **Threatened**; Eliot Schrefer. Scholastic Press 2014 288 p. map (jacketed hardcover) $17.99

Grades: 7 8 9 10 11 12   **Fic**

1. Orphans -- Fiction 2. Chimpanzees -- Fiction 3. Animal rescue -- Fiction 4. Gabon -- Fiction 5.

Adventure stories 6. Wildlife rescue -- Fiction 7. Orphans -- Gabon -- Fiction

ISBN 0545551439; 9780545551434

LC 2013018599

National Book Award Shortlist: Young People's Literature (2014)

In this juvenile story, by Eliot Schrefer, "Luc and Prof head into the rough, dangerous jungle in order to study the elusive chimpanzees. There, Luc finally finds a new family--and must act when that family comes under attack. . . . [It] is the story of a boy fleeing his present, a man fleeing his past, and a trio of chimpanzees who are struggling not to flee at all." (Publisher's note)

"After the death of his mother and sister, Luc is left in the hands of a moneylender, Monsieur Tatagani. One of many orphans forced to do Tatagani's bidding, Luc has found a way to be useful and earn a few coins wiping glasses in a bar in Gabon...There are times when Luc's voice as an uneducated orphan adolescent seems vivid and real, at other times less so. Still, the valor and soul of Luc is captivating. Fascinating and sure to lead to discussion." (School Library Journal)

Schreiber, Joe

Au revoir, crazy European chick. Houghton Mifflin 2011 190p $16.99

Grades: 9 10 11 12   **Fic**

1. Adventure fiction 2. New York (N.Y.) -- Fiction

ISBN 978-0-547-57738-8

LC 2011009845

Perry's parents insist that he take Gobi, their quiet, Lithuanian exchange student, to senior prom but after an incident at the dance he learns that Gobi is actually a trained assassin who needs him as a henchman, behind the wheel of his father's precious Jaguar, on a mission in Manhattan.

"Perfect for action adventure junkies who will enjoy the car chases, thugs, graphic killing scenes, explosions, and a random bear fight, Schreiber's debut novel also contains enough humor, sexual tension, distinctive language, and character development to make this more than just a quick thrill read." Horn Book

★ **Perry's** killer playlist; by Joe Schreiber. Houghton Mifflin 2012 209 p. $16.99

Grades: 9 10 11 12   **Fic**

1. Adventure fiction 2. Europe -- Fiction 3. Assassins -- Fiction 4. Adventure and adventurers -- Fiction

ISBN 0547601174; 9780547601175

LC 2011041392

Sequel to: Au revoir, crazy European chick

This novel, by Joe Schreiber, is the sequel to the young adult adventure "Au Revoir, Crazy European Chick." "The last time [Perry] saw Gobi, five people were assassinated one crazy night in New York City. Well . . . Gobi shows up, and once again Perry is roped into a wild, nonstop thrill ride with a body count. Double crossings, kidnappings, CIA agents, arms dealers, boat chases in Venetian canals, and a shootout in the middle of a Santa Claus convention ensue." (Publisher's note)

Schroeder, Lisa

Far from you. Simon Pulse 2009 355p $15.99

Grades: 7 8 9 10   **Fic**
1. Novels in verse 2. Snow -- Fiction 3. Stepfamilies
-- Fiction
ISBN 978-1-4169-7506-9; 1-4169-7506-3
           LC 2008-25268
A novel-in-verse about sixteen-year-old Ali's reluctant road trip with her stepmother and new baby sister, and the terror that ensues after they end up lost in the snow-covered woods.

"Schroeder weaves Alice in Wonderland . . . references throughout the book to echo the topsy-turvy nature of her protagonist's life. It is this roller coaster of emotions to which many teen readers will relate. A quick, yet satisfying, novel in verse." SLJ

Schröder, Monika
My brother's shadow. Farrar Straus Giroux 2011 217p $16.99
Grades: 6 7 8 9 10   **Fic**
1. Germany -- Fiction 2. Journalism -- Fiction 3. Family life -- Fiction 4. Political activists -- Fiction 5. World War, 1914-1918 -- Fiction
ISBN 978-0-374-35122-9; 0-374-35122-8
           LC 2010033107
In 1918 Berlin, Germany, sixteen-year-old Moritz struggles to do what is right on his newspaper job, in his relationship with his mother and sister who are outspoken socialists, and with his brother, who returns from the war physically and emotionally scarred.

"In this nuanced and realistic work of historical fiction, Schröder . . . immerses readers in her setting with meticulous details and dynamic characters that contribute to a palpable sense of tension." Publ Wkly

Schumacher, Julie
★ **Black** box; a novel. Delacorte Press 2008 168p $15.99; lib bdg $18.99
Grades: 8 9 10 11 12   **Fic**
1. School stories 2. Sisters -- Fiction 3. Family life -- Fiction 4. Depression (Psychology) -- Fiction
ISBN 978-0-385-73542-1; 0-385-73542-1; 978-0-385-90523-7 lib bdg; 0-385-90523-8 lib bdg
           LC 2007-45774
When her sixteen-year-old sister is hospitalized for depression and her parents want to keep it a secret, fourteen-year-old Elena tries to cope with her own anxiety and feelings of guilt that she is determined to conceal from outsiders.

"The writing is spare, direct, and honest. Written in the first person, this is a readable, ultimately uplifting book about a difficult subject." SLJ

Schutt, Christine
★ **All** souls. Harcourt 2008 223p hardcover o.p. pa $13.95
Grades: 11 12 Adult   **Fic**
1. School stories 2. Friendship -- Fiction 3. New York (N.Y.) -- Fiction
ISBN 978-0-15-101449-1; 0-15-101449-3; 978-0-15-603338-1 pa; 0-15-603338-0 pa
           LC 2007-32814
This "is a bold, sharp story about teenage girls, class and illness, about those moment when we achieve the miracle of human connection—and those when we don't." N Y Times Book Rev

Scieszka, Jon, 1954-
Who done it? an investigation of murder most foul. conducted by Jon Scieszka and you, the reader. Soho Teen, an imprint of Soho Press, Inc. 2013 373 p. (hardcover) $17.99
Grades: 9 10 11 12   **Fic**
1. Mystery fiction 2. Humorous fiction 3. Authors -- Fiction 4. Humorous stories 5. Authorship -- Fiction
ISBN 1616951524; 9781616951528
           LC 2012033468
In this juvenile mystery, by Jon Scieszka, "the most cantankerous book editor alive . . . is Herman Mildew. The anthology opens with an invitation to a party, care of this . . . monster, where more than 80 of the most . . . recognizable names in . . . fiction learn that they are suspects in his murder. All must provide alibis in brief first-person entries. The problem is that all of them are liars, all of them are fabulists, and all have something to hide." (Publisher's note)

Scott, Elizabeth
Between here and forever. Simon Pulse 2011 250p $16.99; ebook $9.99
Grades: 9 10 11 12   **Fic**
1. Coma -- Fiction 2. Sisters -- Fiction
ISBN 978-1-4169-9484-8; 978-1-4169-9486-2 ebook
           LC 2010051366
When her older, "perfect" sister Tess has a car accident that puts her in a coma, seventeen-year-old Abby, who has always felt unseen in Tess's shadow, plans to bring her back with the help of Eli, a gorgeous boy she has met at the hospital, but her plans go awry when she learns some secrets about both Tess and Eli, enabling her to make some decisions about her own life.

"Abby's emotional growth from her experiences, conversations and introspection emerges ever so slowly but will satisfy many teen readers. Leisurely but gratifying." Kirkus

Grace. Dutton Books 2010 200p $16.99
Grades: 8 9 10 11 12   **Fic**
1. Fantasy fiction 2. Despotism -- Fiction 3. Insurgency -- Fiction
ISBN 978-0-525-42206-8; 0-525-42206-4
           LC 2009-53285
Sixteen-year-old Grace travels on a decrepit train toward a border that may not exist, recalling events that brought her to choose life over being a suicide bomber, and dreaming of freedom from the extremist religion-based government of Keran Berj

"Moody and compelling, without the easy moralizing so common in dystopian settings." Kirkus

★ **Living** dead girl. Simon Pulse 2008 170p $16.99; pa $8.99
Grades: 9 10 11 12   **Fic**
1. Kidnapping -- Fiction 2. Child sexual abuse -- Fiction
ISBN 978-1-4169-6059-1; 1-4169-6059-7; 978-1-4169-6060-7 pa; 1-4169-6060-0 pa
           LC 2007-943736

A novel about a 15-year-old girl who has spent the last five years being abused by a kidnapper named Ray and is kept powerless by Ray's promise to harm her family if she makes one false move.

"Scott's prose is spare and damning, relying on suggestive details and their impact on Alice to convey the unimaginable violence she repeatedly experiences. Disturbing but fascinating, the book exerts an inescapable grip on readers—like Alice, they have virtually no choice but to continue until the conclusion sets them free." Publ Wkly

Love you hate you miss you. HarperTeen 2009 276p $16.99; lib bdg $17.89; pa $8.99

Grades: 9 10 11 12   **Fic**
1. School stories 2. Death -- Fiction 3. Guilt -- Fiction 4. Alcoholism -- Fiction 5. Friendship -- Fiction
ISBN 978-0-06-112283-5; 0-06-112283-1; 978-0-06-112284-2 lib bdg; 0-06-112284-X lib bdg; 978-0-06-112285-9 pa; 0-06-112285-8 pa

LC 2008-31420

After coming out of alcohol rehabilitation, sixteen-year-old Amy sorts out conflicting emotions about her best friend Julia's death in a car accident for which she feels responsible.

"The pain, confusion, insights, and hope Amy expresses will speak to teen readers. The issue of binge drinking is handled clearly and bluntly, and without preaching: readers understand why Amy drinks and why she stops." Voice Youth Advocates

Miracle; Elizabeth Scott. Simon Pulse 2012 217 p. (hbk.) $16.99

Grades: 9 10 11 12   **Fic**
1. Aircraft accidents -- Fiction 2. Interpersonal relations -- Fiction 3. Post-traumatic stress disorder -- Fiction 4. Schools -- Fiction 5. Survival -- Fiction 6. Family life -- Fiction
ISBN 1442417064; 9781442417069

LC 2011008655

This book's main character, Megan, is the sole survivor of a plane crash, and is hailed as a miracle. "However, when Megan returns to her small, rural hometown, she feels overwhelmed by both the onslaught of well-wishers and the slowly returning memories of the crash and its victims. Megan is most challenged by her parents, who are unable to see beyond her miraculous escape and fail to recognize that she is suffering from post-traumatic stress disorder (PTSD) and seriously needs help." (Kirkus Reviews)

Stealing Heaven. HarperTeen 2008 307p $16.99; lib bdg $17.89; pa $8.99

Grades: 7 8 9 10   **Fic**
1. Thieves -- Fiction 2. Mother-daughter relationship -- Fiction
ISBN 978-0-06-112280-4; 0-06-112280-7; 978-0-06-112281-1 lib bdg; 0-06-112281-5 lib bdg; 978-0-06-112282-8 pa; 0-06-112282-3 pa

Eighteen-year-old Dani grows weary of her life as a thief when she and her mother move to a town where Dani feels like she can put down roots.

"Witty dialogue gives a new perspective full of hope to YAs who feel trapped between family and friends." KLIATT

Scott, Kieran, 1974-

Geek magnet; a novel in five acts. G.P. Putnam's Sons 2008 308p $16.99

Grades: 7 8 9 10   **Fic**
1. School stories 2. Theater -- Fiction 3. Dating (Social customs) -- Fiction
ISBN 978-0-399-24760-6; 0-399-24760-2

LC 2007-28707

Seventeen-year-old KJ Miller is determined to lose the label of "geek magnet" and get the guy of her dreams, all while stage managing the high school musical, with the help of the most popular girl in school.

"An enjoyable, touching read about self-discovery with a hopeful ending that avoids too-neat resolutions." Booklist

He's So Not Worth It; Kieran Scott. Simon & Schuster Books for Young Readers 2011 360 p. $17.99

Grades: 7 8 9 10   **Fic**
1. Beaches -- Fiction 2. New Jersey -- Fiction 3. Family life -- Fiction 4. Social classes -- Fiction 5. Dating (Social customs) -- Fiction
ISBN 1416999531; 9781416999539

LC 2010046494

Sequel to: She's so dead to us (2010)

Part of the He's So/She's So trilogy, this young adult novel by Kieran Scott describes how " when Ally has to choose where to spend the summer, she opts to put up with her mom's new boyfriend and hang out at the Jersey Shore instead of sticking around Orchard Hill, where Jake has decided to stay. Summer at the beach isn't all bad, especially when Ally gets involved with a local bad boy." (Publisher's note)

"... teens seeking a quick, escapist read set at the Jersey Shore will find one here. A worthwhile purchase for libraries that have gotten mileage out of the first book." - VOYA

He is so not worth it

She's so dead to us. Simon & Schuster 2010 278p $16.99

Grades: 8 9 10 11 12   **Fic**
1. School stories 2. Friendship -- Fiction 3. New Jersey -- Fiction 4. Social classes -- Fiction
ISBN 978-1-4169-9951-5; 1-4169-9951-5

LC 2009-46739

Told in two voices, high school juniors Allie, who now lives on the poor side of town, and Jake, the "Crestie" whose family bought her house, develop feelings for one another that are complicated by her former friends, his current ones, who refuse to forgive her for her father's bad investment that cost them all.

"In this successful blend of class struggle, betrayal, and forbidden romance, Scott creates an unpredictable and timely story." Horn Book Guide

Followed by He's so not worth it (2011)

This is so not happening; Kieran Scott. Simon & Schuster BFYR. 2012 315 p. (hardcover) $16.99

Grades: 7 8 9 10   **Fic**
1. Love stories 2. Teenage parents -- Fiction 3. Dating (Social customs) -- Fiction 4. Babies -- Fiction 5. Schools -- Fiction 6. New Jersey -- Fiction 7. High

schools -- Fiction 8. Social classes -- Fiction 9. Teenage fathers -- Fiction 10. Teenage mothers -- Fiction 11. Family life -- New Jersey -- Fiction
ISBN 1416999558; 9781416999553

LC 2011041612

In this book, the third in a series, "constantly thwarted lovers Ally and Jake finally establish a firm boyfriend-girl-friend relationship during their senior year in high school. . . . Ally learns that her former best friend Chloe is pregnant and saying that Jake is the father. Because the brief encounter between the two occurred outside of their formal relationship, Ally decides to forgive Jake and stick with him, even as he becomes ever more obsessed with the baby." (Kirkus Reviews)

Scott, Michael

The **enchantress**; Michael Scott. Delacorte Press 2012 517 p. $18.99

Grades: 7 8 9 10   **Fic**

1. Atlantis -- Fiction 2. Monsters -- Fiction 3. Time travel -- Fiction 4. Flamel, Nicolas, d. 1418 -- Fiction 5. Magic -- Fiction 6. Twins -- Fiction 7. Alchemists -- Fiction 8. Supernatural -- Fiction 9. Brothers and sisters -- Fiction
ISBN 0385735359; 9780385735353

LC 2012006497

In this book, the final installment of the "Secrets of the Immortal Nicholas Flamel" series, "Nicholas Flamel and his beloved wife, Perenelle, are making a final stand to save San Francisco from an attack of monsters large and small, launched from Alcatraz Island by Quetzalcoatl. Twins Josh (Gold) and Sophie (Silver) are being staged to take power from Aten and become rulers of an overthrown Danu Talis 10,000 years earlier." (Booklist)

"[Scott] fully fleshes out his main characters in their final roles, realistically and sometimes surprisingly melding their lives, their deaths, and their futures. This is a powerful and tidy conclusion to [the] series." Booklist

Scott, Mindi

Freefall. Simon Pulse 2010 315p pa $7.99

Grades: 8 9 10 11 12   **Fic**

1. Alcoholism -- Fiction 2. Bereavement -- Fiction 3. Rock musicians -- Fiction
ISBN 978-1-4424-0278-2; 1-4424-0278-4

LC 2010-12663

Seth, a bass guitar player in a teen rock band, deals with alcoholism, his best friend's death, and first love.

"Seth's character arc is fully realized, without the burden of too much introspection or weighty insight to bog down the pace of the narrative. . . . This is a solid exploration of what you can and can't do to help your friends, built on top of an engaging story of boy meets girl." Bull Cent Child Books

Live through this; Mindi Scott. Simon Pulse 2012 289 p. (hc) $16.99

Grades: 9 10 11 12   **Fic**

1. Stepfamilies -- Fiction 2. Family secrets -- Fiction 3. Child sexual abuse -- Fiction 4. Incest -- Fiction 5. Secrets -- Fiction 6. Sexual abuse -- Fiction 7. Family

life -- Washington (State) -- Fiction
ISBN 1442440597; 9781442440593; 9781442440609; 9781442440616

LC 2012006006

In this young adult novel, by Mindi Scott, "Coley Sterling's . . . stepdad is a successful attorney who gives Coley and her siblings everything, and her mother . . . escaped ten years ago from the abuse of Coley's real father. But Coley is keeping a lot of secrets. She won't admit . . . that her almost-perfect life is her own carefully crafted façade. Now, Coley and Reece are getting closer, and a decade's worth of Coley's lies are on the verge of unraveling." (Publisher's note)

Includes bibliographical references

Seamon, Hollis

★ **Somebody** up there hates you; a novel. by Hollis Seamon. 1st ed. Algonquin 2013 256 p. (hardcover) $16.95

Grades: 9 10 11 12   **Fic**

1. Cancer -- Fiction 2. Parties -- Fiction 3. Terminally ill children -- Fiction 4. Terminally ill -- Fiction 5. Hospices (Terminal care) -- Fiction
ISBN 1616202602; 9781616202606

LC 2013008476

This book follows Richie, a 17-year-old with terminal cancer. "Richie's uncle takes him out for a night of partying; girls start paying attention to him (and not just Sylvie, the 15-year-old across the hall); there are pranks and fistfights; and Richie gets a chance to be a normal teenager—or as normal as possible, given that he's surrounded by nurses, never knows how he'll feel next, and the annoying harpist in the lobby just keeps playing." (Publishers Weekly)

Sebold, Alice

★ The **lovely** bones. Little, Brown 2002 328p $21.95; pa $13.95

Grades: 11 12 Adult   **Fic**

1. Homicide -- Fiction 2. Family life -- Fiction
ISBN 0-316-66634-3; 0-316-16881-5 pa

LC 2001-50622

"As pleasant as Susie's heaven is, there's no God there, and certainly no Jesus. This is spirituality for an age that's ecumenical to a fault. But emotionally, it's faultless. Sebold never slips as she follows this family. The risks she walks are enough to give you vertigo." Christ Sci Monit

Sedgwick, Marcus

★ **Revolver**. Roaring Brook Press 2010 204p $16.99

Grades: 7 8 9 10   **Fic**

1. Death -- Fiction 2. Siblings -- Fiction 3. Arctic regions -- Fiction
ISBN 978-1-59643-592-6; 1-59643-592-5

First published 2009 in the United Kingdom
A Michael L. Printz honor book, 2011

In an isolated cabin, fourteen-year-old Sig is alone with a corpse: his father, who has fallen through the ice and frozen to death only hours earlier. Then comes a stranger claiming that Sig's father owes him a share of a horde of stolen gold. Sig's only protection is a loaded Colt revolver hidden in the cabin's storeroom.

"Tight plotting and a wealth of moral concerns—good versus evil; faith, love, and hope; the presence of God; survival in a bleak landscape; trusting the lessons parents teach—make this a memorable tale." Horn Book

★ **She** is not invisible; Marcus Sedgwick. Roaring Brook Press 2014 224 p. (hardback) $16.99
Grades: 7 8 9 10 11 12　　　　　　**Fic**
1. Mystery fiction 2. Blind -- Fiction 3. Missing persons -- Fiction 4. Brothers and sisters -- Fiction 5. Fathers -- Fiction 6. Mystery and detective stories 7. People with disabilities -- Fiction
ISBN 1596438010; 9781596438019
　　　　　　　　　　　　　　LC 2013029561
In this book, by Marcus Sedgwick, "Laureth Peak's father has taught her to look for recurring events, patterns, and numbers - a skill at which she's remarkably talented. Her secret: She is blind. But when her father goes missing, Laureth and her 7-year-old brother Benjamin are thrust into a mystery that takes them to New York City where surviving will take all her skill at spotting the amazing, shocking, and sometimes dangerous connections in a world full of darkness." (Publisher's note)
"Laureth is sixteen, smart, self-doubting, and blind. She is also desperate to find her missing famous writer father -- desperate enough to boost her mother's credit card to buy two plane tickets from London to New York City, forge travel documents, and "abduct" her beloved seven-year-old brother in order to disguise her blindness... Laureth herself is worth the journey. The tricks she uses to negotiate in a sighted world.. her determination to fight the tendency of sighted people to treat blind people as stupid or deaf or, most insidiously, invisible -- all are presented matter-of-factly and sympathetically. Readers will applaud Laureth's believable evolution into a more confident -- and definitely more visible -- young woman." (Horn Book)

★ **White** crow. Roaring Brook Press 2011 234p $15.99
Grades: 8 9 10 11 12　　　　　　**Fic**
1. Horror fiction 2. Villages -- Fiction 3. Friendship -- Fiction 4. Good and evil -- Fiction 5. Great Britain -- Fiction
ISBN 978-1-59643-594-0; 1-59643-594-1
　　　　　　　　　　　　　　LC 2010034053
"Sixteen-year-old Rebecca moves with her father from London to a small, seaside village, where she befriends another motherless girl and they spend the summer together exploring the village's sinister history." (Publisher's Note)
"Showing his customary skill with a gothic setting and morally troubled characters, Sedgwick keeps readers guessing to the very end." Publ Wkly

Seigel, Andrea
The **kid** table. Bloomsbury Children's Books 2010 306p $16.99
Grades: 10 11 12　　　　　　**Fic**
1. Cousins -- Fiction 2. Family life -- Fiction
ISBN 978-1-59990-480-1
　　　　　　　　　　　　　　LC 2010-4540
"Laugh-out-loud humor punctuates . . . [Ingrid's] clear-eyed musings about family and relationships, narrated in a

perceptive, analytical, with-it voice. . . . Teen girls in particular will enjoy this unusual coming-of-age novel." Voice Youth Advocates

Like the red panda. Harcourt 2004 280p pa $13
Grades: 9 10 11 12　　　　　　**Fic**
1. School stories 2. Orphans -- Fiction 3. Suicide -- Fiction 4. California -- Fiction
ISBN 0-15-603024-1
　　　　　　　　　　　　　　LC 2003-17164
"Seigel's novel is a keen portrait of young American angst and all its ironic posturing. The result veers between an earnest critique of the Columbine era and Heathers-like parody, which leaves its conclusion half tragedy, half punch line." Publ Wkly

Selfors, Suzanne
Mad love. Walker Books for Young Readers 2011 323p $16.99
Grades: 7 8 9 10　　　　　　**Fic**
1. Love stories 2. Authorship -- Fiction 3. Eros (Greek deity) -- Fiction 4. Manic-depressive illness -- Fiction 5. Mother-daughter relationship -- Fiction
ISBN 978-0-8027-8450-6; 0-8027-8450-X
　　　　　　　　　　　　　　LC 2010-23261
When her famous romance-novelist mother is secretly hospitalized in an expensive mental facility, sixteen-year-old Alice tries to fulfill her mother's contract with her publisher by writing a love story—with the help of Cupid.
"There's a bit of mythology, a bit of romance, a bit of the paranormal, and some real-life problems, but Selfors juggles them all assuredly. Serious ideas are handled carefully, while real humor is spread throughout the whole book. This book has real charm with great depth." Voice Youth Advocates

The **sweetest** spell; Suzanne Selfors. Walker & Co. 2012 404 p. (hardback) $16.99
Grades: 7 8 9 10 11 12　　　　　　**Fic**
1. Love stories 2. Fantasy fiction 3. People with physical disabilities -- Fiction 4. Fantasy 5. Magic -- Fiction 6. Chocolate -- Fiction 7. Prejudices -- Fiction 8. People with disabilities -- Fiction
ISBN 0802723764; 9780802723765
　　　　　　　　　　　　　　LC 2011034591
This book follows "Emmeline . . . an outcast among her people, the Kell. When the king enslaves the men and her village is destroyed in a flood, Emmeline is taken in by Owen Oak and his family. She discovers that she can churn butter into chocolate -- a food that's been lost for years in the land of Anglund. Romance blossoms, but the two are separated when the girl is kidnapped for her magical abilities." (School Library Journal)
"Selfors's story line initially comes across as chaotic, but the pacing is strong, and the elements of her tale fall into place in a logical and entirely satisfying manner. An exhilarating, romantic, and frequently funny story of self-discovery." Pub Wkly

Selzer, Adam
I kissed a zombie, and I liked it. Delacorte Press 2010 177p lib bdg $12.99; pa $7.99

Grades: 7 8 9 10   **Fic**
1. Zombies -- Fiction 2. Vampires -- Fiction 3. Dating (Social customs) -- Fiction
ISBN 978-0-385-90497-1 lib bdg; 0-385-90497-5 lib bdg; 978-0-385-73503-2 pa; 0-385-73503-0 pa
LC 2009-24052

Living in the post-human era when the undead are part of everyday life, high schooler Alley breaks her no-dating rule when Doug catches her eye, but classmate Will demands to turn her into a vampire and her zombie boyfriend may be unable to stop him.

"With snappy dialogue and a light, funny touch, Selzer creates a readable examination of love, self-sacrifice, and where to draw the line before you lose yourself." Publ Wkly

Senna, Danzy
★ **Caucasia**. Riverhead Bks. 1998 353p hardcover o.p. pa $14
Grades: 11 12 Adult   **Fic**
1. Interracial marriage -- Fiction
ISBN 1-57322-091-4; 1-57322-716-1 pa
LC 97-28911

Birdie's "struggles to fit in anywhere, to pass as anything, are vivid. . . . She tells this coming-of-age tale with impressive beauty and power." Newsweek

Sepetys, Ruta
★ **Between** shades of gray; Ruta Sepetys. Philomel Books 2011 344p map $17.99
Grades: 8 9 10 11 12   **Fic**
1. Lithuania -- Fiction 2. Soviet Union -- Fiction
ISBN 978-0-399-25412-3; 0-399-25412-9
LC 2009-50092

In this novel by Ruta Sepetys, "Fifteen-year-old Lina is a Lithuanian girl living an ordinary life--until Soviet officers invade her home and tear her family apart. Separated from her father and forced onto a crowded train, Lina, her mother, and her young brother make their way to a Siberian work camp, where they are forced to fight for their lives." (Publisher's note)

"A harrowing page-turner, made all the more so for its basis in historical fact, the novel illuminates the persecution suffered by Stalin's victims (20 million were killed), while presenting memorable characters who retain their will to survive even after more than a decade in exile." Publ Wkly

★ **Out** of the Easy; Ruta Sepetys. Philomel Books 2013 352 p. $17.99
Grades: 9 10 11 12   **Fic**
1. Mystery fiction 2. Historical fiction 3. Prostitution -- Fiction 4. New Orleans (La.) -- Fiction 5. Murder -- Fiction 6. Prostitition -- Fiction 7. Conduct of life -- Fiction 8. Mystery and detective stories 9. Mothers and daughters -- Fiction 10. New Orleans (La.) -- History -- 20th century -- Fiction
ISBN 039925692X; 9780399256929
LC 2012016062

This book, by Ruta Sepetys, is set in "1950 [in] . . . the French Quarter of New Orleans. . . . Known among locals as the daughter of a brothel prostitute, Josie Moraine wants more out of life than the Big Easy has to offer. She devises a plan get out, but a mysterious death in the Quarter leaves Josie tangled in an investigation that will challenge her allegiance to her mother, her conscience, and Willie Woodley, the brusque madam on Conti Street." (Publisher's note)

★ **Salt** to the sea; a novel. Ruta Sepetys. Philomel Books 2016 400 p. maps $18.99
Grades: 8 9 10 11 12   **Fic**
1. Prussia 2. Refugees -- Fiction 3. World War, 1939-1945 -- Fiction
ISBN 0399160302; 9780399160301
LC 2015009057

In this novel, by Ruta Sepetys, "World War II is drawing to a close in East Prussia and thousands of refugees are on a desperate trek toward freedom, many with something to hide. Among them are Joana, Emilia, and Florian, whose paths converge en route to the ship that promises salvation, the Wilhelm Gustloff. Forced by circumstance to unite, the three find their strength, courage, and trust in each other tested with each step closer to safety." (Publisher's note)

"YA author Sepetys (Between Shades of Gray; Out of the Easy) describes an almost unknown maritime disaster whose nearly 9,000 casualties dwarfed those of both the Titanic and the Lusitania. Told alternately from the perspective of each of the main characters, the novel also highlights the struggle and sacrifices that ordinary people—children—were forced to make. At once beautiful and heart-wrenching, this title will remind readers that there are far more casualties of war than are recorded in history books. Sure to have crossover appeal for adult readers." LJ

Shaara, Michael
★ The **killer** angels; a novel of the Civil War. Modern Library 2004 xx, 337p map $22.95
Grades: 9 10 11 12   **Fic**
1. Gettysburg (Pa.), Battle of, 1863 -- Fiction
ISBN 0-679-64324-9
LC 2004-46877

A reissue of the title first published 1974 by David McKay

This is a fictionalized account of four days in July, 1863 at the Battle of Gettysburg. The point of view of the Southern forces is represented by Generals Robert E. Lee and James Longstreet, while Colonel Joshua Chamberlain and General John Buford are the focus for the North

"Shaara's version of private reflections and conversations are based on his reading of documents and letters. Although some of his judgments are not necessarily substantiated by historians, he demonstrates a knowledge of both the battle and the area. The writing is vivid and fast moving." Libr J

Shabazz, Ilyasah
★ **X**; a novel. Ilyasah Shabazz, Kekla Magoon. Candlewick Press 2015 384 p. $16.99
Grades: 8 9 10 11 12   **Fic**
1. African Americans -- Biography 2. Poor 3. Racism 4. Black muslims
ISBN 0763669679; 9780763669676
LC 2014931838

NAACP Image Award: Outstanding Literary Work-Youth/Teens (2016)

Coretta Scott King Author Award, Honor Book (2016)

This novel, by Ilyasah Shabazz and Kekla Magoon, "follows the formative years of [Malcolm X]. . . . Malcolm Little's parents have always told him that he can achieve anything, but from what he can tell, that's a pack of lies—after all, his father's been murdered, his mother's been taken away, and his dreams of becoming a lawyer have gotten him laughed out of school." (Publisher's note)

"Malcolm X was born Malcolm Little. The story opens with his departure from Michigan as a teen, though there are flashbacks to his younger years. It follows Malcolm through his time in Boston and Harlem, culminating with his conversion to Islam and his decision to change his name while in prison in 1948...The author's honesty about his early troubles serves to convey that it is possible to rise through adversity to make a positive difference in this world. A worthwhile addition to any collection." SLJ

Shan, Darren

The **thin** executioner. Little, Brown 2010 483p map $17.99

Grades: 10 11 12   **Fic**

1. Slavery -- Fiction 2. Conduct of life -- Fiction 3. Capital punishment -- Fiction 4. Voyages and travels -- Fiction

ISBN 978-0-316-07865-8; 0-316-07865-4

LC 2009-45606

In a nation of warriors where weakness is shunned and all crimes, no matter how minor, are punishable by beheading, young Jebel Rum, along with a slave who is fated to be sacrificed, sets forth on a quest to petition the Fire God for invincibility, but when the long and arduous journey is over, Jebel has learned much about fairness and the value of life.

"Readers will hate the villains, feel sorry for the innocent, and root for Tel Hesani and Jebel to complete their mission. This is a must-read for thrill seekers with a strong stomach looking for an action-packed adventure with a host of fantastical creatures." Voice Youth Advocates

Sharenow, Robert

The **Berlin** Boxing Club. HarperTeen 2011 404p il $17.99

Grades: 7 8 9 10   **Fic**

1. Boxers (Persons) 2. Boxing -- Fiction 3. Family life -- Fiction 4. Jews -- Germany -- Fiction 5. Berlin (Germany) -- Fiction 6. National socialism -- Fiction 7. Holocaust, 1933-1945 -- Fiction

ISBN 978-0-06-157968-4; 0-06-157968-8

LC 2010024446

"Readers will be drawn by the sports detail and by the close-up narrative of the daily oppression." Booklist

Sharpe, Tess

Far from you; Tess Sharpe. Hyperion Books 2014 352 p. (hardback) $17.99

Grades: 9 10 11 12   **Fic**

1. Murder -- Fiction 2. Bisexuals -- Fiction 3. Drug abuse -- Fiction 4. Friendship -- Fiction 5. Best friends -- Fiction 6. Mystery and detective stories

ISBN 1423184629; 9781423184621

LC 2013037960

In this young adult novel by Tess Sharpe, "Sophie Winters nearly died. Twice. The first time, she's fourteen, and

escapes a near-fatal car accident with . . . an addiction to Oxy that'll take years to kick. The second time, she's seventeen, and . . . Sophie and her best friend Mina are confronted by a masked man in the woods. Sophie survives, but Mina is not so lucky. . . . No one is looking in the right places and Sophie must search for Mina's murderer on her own." (Publisher's note)

"Sophie was there when her best friend, Mina, was murdered, but she doesn't know by whom, or why. So Sophie launches her own investigation, knowing that Mina's death isn't related to Sophie's painkiller addiction, as everyone else seems to think. This tense, tragic page-turner has plenty of chills, but just as compelling is the depth of Sophie's physical and emotional pain." Horn Book

Shaw, Susan

Safe. Dutton Books 2007 168p $16.99

Grades: 7 8 9 10   **Fic**

1. Rape -- Fiction 2. Mothers -- Fiction

ISBN 978-0-525-47829-4; 0-525-47829-9

LC 2006-36428

When thirteen-year-old Tracy, whose mother died when she was three years old, is raped and beaten on the last day of school, all her feelings of security disappear and she does not know how to cope with the fear and dread that engulf her.

This is an "extraordinarily tender novel. . . . Intimate, first-person narrative honestly expresses Tracy's full range of emotions." Publ Wkly

Shea, John

A **kid** from Southie; [by] John 'Red' Shea and Michael Harmon. WestSide Books 2011 239p $16.95

Grades: 9 10 11 12   **Fic**

1. Boxing -- Fiction 2. Boston (Mass.) -- Fiction 3. Conduct of life -- Fiction 4. Organized crime -- Fiction 5. Mother-son relationship -- Fiction

ISBN 978-1-934813-53-9

LC 2010054022

Desperate to help his unemployed mother, seventeen-year-old Aiden O'Connor reluctantly begins working for the Irish mob in tough South Boston, despite his coach's efforts to convince him he could be a professional boxer.

"With lots of action, short chapters, and realistic but raw language, this one's a winner. The great cover will attract reluctant readers and the content will keep them turning the pages." SLJ

Shecter, Vicky Alvear

Cleopatra's moon. Arthur A. Levine Books 2011 353p $18.99

Grades: 8 9 10 11 12   **Fic**

1. Queens 2. Generals 3. Statesmen 4. Orators 5. Egypt -- Fiction 6. Princesses -- Fiction 7. Rome -- History -- Fiction

ISBN 978-0-545-22130-6; 0-545-22130-7

LC 2010028818

Cleopatra Selene, the only surviving daughter of Cleopatra and Marc Antony, recalls her life of pomp and splendor in Egypt and, after her parents' deaths, captivity and treachery in Rome.

"This novel has romance, drama, heartbreak, and adventure, all rooted in an accurate and descriptive historical setting. Shecter writes about the world of ancient Egypt and Rome with wonderful detail. . . . Her characters are skillfully fictionalized." SLJ

Shen, Prudence

Nothing Can Possibly Go Wrong; by Prudence Shen, illustrated by Faith Erin Hicks. First Second 2013 288 p. (paperback) $16.99

Grades: 7 8 9 10 **Fic**

1. Robots 2. Cheerleading 3. School stories -- Graphic novels

ISBN 159643659X; 9781596436596

"You wouldn't expect Nate and Charlie to be friends. Charlie's the laid-back captain of the basketball team, and Nate is the neurotic, scheming president of the robotics club. But they are friends, however unlikely--until Nate declares war on the cheerleaders. At stake is funding that will either cover a robotics competition or new cheerleading uniforms--but not both." (Publisher's note)

"Shen's plot ably balances drama, humor, angst, and robotic geekery, giving the book an immediate YA appeal, but one that's broad enough to be enjoyable to older readers, as well. Visually, Hicks's wide-eyed, inky b&w panels infuse the characters with real emotion and personality, capturing the book's heartfelt youthfulness." Pub Wkly

Shepard, Jim

★ **Project** X; a novel. Alfred A. Knopf 2004 163p hardcover o.p. pa $12

Grades: 9 10 11 12 **Fic**

1. School stories 2. School violence -- Fiction

ISBN 1-4000-4071-X; 1-4000-3348-9 pa

LC 2003-47575

"Flake and Edwin are often bullied; at other times, they have the horrible feeling of being completely invisible to their classmates. Flake is even more alienated than Edwin and hatches a revenge plan involving guns that they call 'project x.' Disaster looms. . . . The vivid dialogue is sprinkled with profanity and is movingly expressive. This heartbreaking and wrenching novel will leave teens with plenty of questions and, hopefully, some answers." SLJ

Shepard, Sara

The **lying** game. HarperTeen 2010 307p $16.99

Grades: 9 10 11 12 **Fic**

1. Mystery fiction 2. Dead -- Fiction 3. Twins -- Fiction 4. Sisters -- Fiction 5. Homicide -- Fiction

ISBN 978-0-06-186970-9; 0-06-186970-8

LC 2010-40332

Seventeen-year-old Emma Paxton steps into the life of her long-lost twin Sutton to solve her murder, while Sutton looks on from her afterlife.

"Shepard keeps the action rolling and the clues confusing as she spends this installment uncovering the twins' characters but not solving the murder yet. Naturally, boys and fashion also figure into the story, fleshing out a distinctive scenario that should appeal to many teen girls." Kirkus

Shepherd, Megan

Her Dark Curiosity. Harpercollins Childrens Books 2014 432 p. $17.99

Grades: 9 10 11 12 **Fic**

1. Murder -- Fiction 2. Father-daughter relationship -- Fiction

ISBN 0062128051; 9780062128058

This book, by Megan Shepherd, "explores the hidden natures of those we love and how far we'll go to save them from themselves. . . . after her trip to Dr. Moreau's horrific island, Juliet is rebuilding the life she once knew and trying to forget her father's legacy. But soon . . . people close to Juliet start falling victim to a murderer who leaves a macabre calling card of three clawlike slashes. Has one of her father's creations also escaped the island?" (Publisher's note)

"Megan Shepherd's deliciously dark and exciting sequel to The Madman's Daughter (HarperCollins, 2013) continues with Juliet's return to London after her escape from her father's island. Life is somewhat easier for Juliet now that she is back—a former colleague of her father's has taken her under his wing so that she does not want for anything, she has a job developing grafted rose bushes, and her friend Lucy has welcomed her with open arms. But not all is well...While the novel can be read independently of the first title, as enough of the backstory is given to make what is happening clear, readers will have a more satisfying experience if familiar with the previous installment. The psychological questions that Prince/Jekyll raises as to evil, desire, and nature vs. nurture add a depth of richness not often seen in young adult literature." (School Library Journal)

The **madman's** daughter; Megan Shepherd. Balzer + Bray 2013 432 p. (trade bdg.) $17.99

Grades: 9 10 11 12 **Fic**

1. Mental illness -- Fiction 2. Science -- Experiments -- Fiction 3. Father-daughter relationship -- Fiction 4. Science fiction 5. Fathers and daughters -- Fiction 6. Characters in literature -- Fiction

ISBN 0062128027; 9780062128027

LC 2012004281

This book by Megan Shepherd follows the events of "H.G. Wells' 'The Island of Doctor Moreau,' as seen through the eyes of the doctor's daughter. . . . When she learns that her father inhabits an island far, far away, where he performs horrific experiments on animals via vivisection, Juliet makes her way there along with Montgomery, her father's assistant, and Edward Prince, a castaway they meet along the way." (Kirkus Reviews)

Sherrill, Martha

The **Ruins** of California. Penguin Press 2006 318p hardcover o.p. pa $14

Grades: 11 12 Adult **Fic**

1. Divorce -- Fiction 2. California -- Fiction 3. Family life -- Fiction

ISBN 1-59420-080-7; 978-1-59420-080-9; 1-59448-231-4 pa; 978-1-59448-231-1 pa

LC 2005-49343

"Set in California in the 1970s, this beautifully written novel tells the story of a girl, trapped in a theatrical family, who manages to transform herself from an observer into the star of her own life." Booklist

Sheth, Kashmira

Keeping corner. Hyperion 2007 281p hardcover o.p. pa $5.99

Grades: 7 8 9 10 11 12   **Fic**
1. Authors 2. Journalists 3. Essayists 4. Pacifists 5. Memoirists 6. India -- Fiction 7. Political leaders 8. Widows -- Fiction 9. Writers on politics 10. Women's rights -- Fiction

ISBN 978-0-7868-3859-2; 0-7868-3859-0; 978-0-7868-3860-8 pa; 0-7868-3860-4 pa
LC 2007-15314

In India in the 1940s, twelve-year-old Leela's happy, spoiled childhood ends when her husband since age nine, whom she barely knows, dies, leaving her a widow whose only hope of happiness could come from Mahatma Ghandi's social and political reforms.

Sheth "sets up a thrilling premise in which politics become achingly personal." Booklist

Shinn, Sharon

Gateway. Viking 2009 280p $17.99

Grades: 6 7 8 9 10   **Fic**
1. Space and time -- Fiction 2. Chinese Americans -- Fiction

ISBN 978-0-670-01178-0; 0-670-01178-9
LC 2009-14002

While passing through the Arch in St. Louis, Missouri, a Chinese American teenager is transported to a parallel world where she is given a dangerous assignment.

The author's "fantasy finds the right balance between adventure and romance, while illuminating how seductive evil can be and that sometimes the best weapon one can possess is a skeptical mind." Publ Wkly

Shirvington, Jessica

Emblaze; Jessica Shirvington. Sourcebooks Fire 2013 464 p. (hardcover) $16.99

Grades: 10 11 12   **Fic**
1. Fantasy fiction 2. Paranormal fiction 3. Angels -- Fiction 4. Supernatural -- Fiction 5. Good and evil -- Fiction

ISBN 1402268467; 9781402268465
LC 2012037497

This book is the third installment of Jessica Shrivington's Embrace series. Here, "Violet and her Grigori brethren prepare for a battle of apocalyptic proportions. . . . Finding the time to focus and gain control over [her angel powers] is no easy feat with a father who has decided to finally show up and parent, the temptation of a partner who is also a forbidden soul mate, and an ex who plans to use her to help him open up the gates of hell." (Kirkus)

Embrace. Sourcebooks, Inc. 2012 397p

Grades: 10 11 12   **Fic**
1. Fantasy fiction 2. Angels -- Fiction 3. Teenagers -- Fiction

ISBN 9781402271250; 9781402268403

This book follows "seventeen-year-old Violet Eden, [whose] mother died in childbirth, leaving her to be raised by her detached, workaholic father. If it weren't for her best friend Steph and her trainer (and secret love) Lincoln, Violet would be very much alone. But on her 17th birthday, every-

thing changes. Though finally being kissed by Lincoln is a dream come true, Violet learns that their romantic involvement is forbidden because he and Violet are both Grigori--half angel and half human. They're destined to be eternal partners in the battle against exiled angels on Earth, and romance would make things far too complicated. Furious with Lincoln for keeping this secret, Violet pushes him away, making room for the dark and seductive Phoenix to take hold of her heart." (Kirkus)

Entice; Jessica Shirvington. Sourcebooks Fire 2013 464 p.

Grades: 10 11 12   **Fic**
1. Love stories 2. Angels -- Fiction 3. Supernatural -- Fiction 4. Good and evil -- Fiction

ISBN 1402268432; 9781402268434; 9781402271281
LC 2012037496

"Seventeen-year-old Violet Eden's whole life changed when she discovered she is Grigori • part angel, part human. Her destiny is to protect humans from the vengeance of exiled angels. Knowing who to trust is key, but when Grigori reinforcements arrive, it becomes clear everyone is hiding something - even her partner, Lincoln. And now Violet has to learn to live with her feelings for him while they work together to stay alive and stop the exiles from discovering the key to destroy all Grigori." (Publisher's note)

Shoemaker, Tim

Back before dark; Timothy Shoemaker. Zondervan 2013 384 p. (hardcover) $14.99

Grades: 7 8 9 10   **Fic**
1. Friendship -- Fiction 2. Kidnapping -- Fiction 3. Best friends -- Fiction 4. Christian life -- Fiction 5. Conduct of life -- Fiction 6. Mystery and detective stories

ISBN 0310734991; 9780310734994
LC 2012049855

"Every kid's worst nightmare, a ride through the park gets Gordy abducted. The kids find themselves in the wrong place at the wrong time. It's every kid's worst nightmare, when a ride through the park gets Gordy abducted. Their powers of observation are put to the test like never before, as they fight the clock to find their friend. In the dark, things are never what they seem." (Publisher's Note)

"In this sequel to Code of Silence, Gordy is kidnapped and his friends Hiro, Cooper, and Lunk decide to take his rescue into their own hands. While the suspense is vitiated by an excess of description and a slow pace, Shoemaker raises interesting questions about law and morality as the friends find themselves resorting to dubious means to catch the criminal." Horn Book

Code of silence; Tim Shoemaker. Zondervan 2012 331 p. (hardcover) $14.99

Grades: 7 8 9 10   **Fic**
1. Youth -- Fiction 2. Secrecy -- Fiction 3. Deception -- Fiction 4. Witnesses -- Fiction 5. Christian life -- Fiction 6. Conduct of life -- Fiction 7. Robbers and outlaws -- Fiction

ISBN 9780310726531
LC 2011048880

In this crime novel for young adults by Tim Shoemaker, "thirteen-year-olds Cooper, Gordy, and Hiro are snacking at their favorite burger joint, Frank 'n Stein's, when they witness a brutal robbery. Two men, masked as a clown and Elvis, savagely beat the owner and steal his considerable stash of cash. The kids manage to escape, and with the security camera hard drive to boot, but Clown gets a good look at Cooper and swears he'll find him. Afraid to go to the police (the robbers were wearing cop pants), Cooper convinces his friends to enact a code of silence. As the maybe-crooked police and other possible suspects get closer to identifying the witnesses, the kids' lies to their parents, their teachers, and one another set off increasingly desperate maneuvers and dangerous infighting" (Booklist)

Shraya, Vivek

God loves hair; by Vivek Shraya; illustrations by Juliana Neufeld. First Arsenal Pulp Pr edition Arsenal Pulp Press 2014 92 p. color illustrations $18.95
Grades: 9 10 11 12   **Fic**
   1. Religion 2. Gender role 3. Self-acceptance 4. Sex -- Psychological aspects 5. India 6. Youth 7. Bildungsromans
   ISBN 1551525437; 9781551525433
   Lambda Literary Award Children's/Young Adult Finalist (2011)
   This book, by Vivek Shraya, "is a collection of twenty-one short stories following a tender, intellectual, and curious child of Indian origin as he navigates the complex realms of sexuality, gender, racial politics, religion, and belonging." It is a "portrait of youth that celebrates diversity in all shapes, sizes, and colors." (Publisher's note)
   "Like the unnamed narrator of these evocative stories, the author grew up genderqueer in Canada. A book for all ages, this will be especially welcomed by contemporary genderqueer youth and twentysomethings, who will see themselves in these vividly realized pages." Booklist

Shukert, Rachel, 1980-

Love me; Rachel Shukert. Delacorte Press 2014 325 p. (hardcover: alk. paper) $17.99
Grades: 9 10 11 12   **Fic**
   1. Fame -- Fiction 2. Historical fiction 3. Actresses -- Fiction 4. Conduct of life -- Fiction 5. Actors and actresses -- Fiction 6. Hollywood (Los Angeles, Calif.) -- History -- 20th century -- Fiction
   ISBN 0385741103; 9780375989858; 9780385741101
                                                        LC 2012047071
   Sequel to: Starstruck
   In this historical novel, by Rachel Shukert, sequel to "Starstruck," "Amanda is heartbroken. She's tried, but she can't get over her breakup with hotshot writer Harry Gordon. . . . Margo has to pinch herself: there's talk of her getting an Oscar nom for her first film role, and she's living with the Dane Forrest, the gorgeous movie star. . . . [And] Gabby's drinking is out of control, but who cares? She's bored and depressed." (Publisher's note)
   "Actresses Margo, Gabby, and Amanda return for another soap about making it big--and staying big--in late-1930s Tinseltown. Much of the focus is on each girl's heartache at the hands of the domineering men in their lives, both lovers and movie-studio bigwigs. This sequel to Starstruck is rife

with far-fetched coincidences and melodrama, but it's all deliciously entertaining." Horn Book

Starstruck; by Rachel Shukert. Delacorte Press 2013 352 p. (ebook) $53.97; (library) $20.99; (hardcover) $17.99; (paperback) $9.99
Grades: 9 10 11 12   **Fic**
   1. Fame -- Fiction 2. Actresses -- Fiction 3. Actors and actresses -- Fiction 4. Hollywood (Los Angeles, Calif.) -- History -- 20th century -- Fiction
   ISBN 0375989846; 9780375984259; 9780375989841; 9780385741088; 9780385741095
                                                        LC 2012015771
   This novel, by Rachel Shukert, follows a girl trying to become a star. When "Margaret . . . [is] discovered by a powerful agent, she can barely believe her luck. She's more than ready to escape her snobby private school and conservative Pasadena family for a chance to light up the silver screen. . . . Set in Old Hollywood, [the story] follows the lives of three teen girls as they live, love, and claw their way to the top in a world where being a star is all that matters." (Publisher's note)

Shulman, Mark

Scrawl. Roaring Brook Press 2010 234p $16.99
Grades: 6 7 8 9 10   **Fic**
   1. School stories 2. Bullies -- Fiction 3. Diaries -- Fiction 4. Poverty -- Fiction 5. Self-perception -- Fiction
   ISBN 978-1-59643-417-2; 1-59643-417-1
                                                        LC 2010-10521
   When eighth-grade school bully Tod and his friends get caught committing a crime on school property, his penalty—staying after school and writing in a journal under the eye of the school guidance counsellor—reveals aspects of himself that he prefers to keep hidden.
   "Blackmail, cliques, and a sense of hopelessness from both students and teachers sets up an unexpected ending that will leave readers with a new appreciation for how difficult high school can be. With the potential to occupy the rarified air of titles like S.E. Hinton's The Outsiders and Chris Crutcher's Staying Fat for Sarah Byrnes . . ., Scrawl paints the stereotypical school bully in a different, poignant light." Voice Youth Advocates

Shusterman, Neal

Bruiser. HarperTeen 2010 328p $16.99; lib bdg $17.89
Grades: 8 9 10 11 12   **Fic**
   1. Twins -- Fiction 2. Siblings -- Fiction 3. Child abuse -- Fiction 4. Supernatural -- Fiction
   ISBN 978-0-06-113408-1; 0-06-113408-2; 978-0-06-113409-8 lib bdg; 0-06-113409-0 lib bdg
                                                        LC 2009-30930
   Inexplicable events start to occur when sixteen-year-old twins Tennyson and Bronte befriend a troubled and misunderstood outcast, aptly nicknamed Bruiser, and his little brother, Cody.
   "Narrated in turns by Tennyson, Bronte, Bruiser, and Bruiser's little brother, Cody, the story is a fascinating study in the art of self-deception and the way our best intentions for others are often based in the selfish desires of our deep-

est selves. . . . This eloquent and thoughtful story will most certainly leave its mark." Bull Cent Child Books

★ **Challenger** deep; Neal Shusterman. HarperCollins 2015 320 p. illustrations (hardcover) $17.99

Grades: 9 10 11 12   **Fic**
  1. Schizophrenia -- Fiction
  ISBN 0061134112; 9780061134111

               LC 2014009664

National Book Award: Young People's Literature (2015)
Boston Globe-Horn Book Honor: Fiction (2015)

In this novel about a schizophrenic teenager by Neal Shusterman, illustrated by Brendan Shusterman, "Caden Bosch is a brilliant high school student whose friends are starting to notice his odd behavior. . . . Caden Bosch pretends to join the school track team but spends his days walking for miles, absorbed by the thoughts in his head." (Publisher's note)

"This novel is a challenge to the reader from its first lines: author Shusterman takes us into the seemingly random, rambling, and surreal fantasies of fifteen-year-old Caden Bosch (yes, it makes sense to associate him with artist Hieronymus) as mental illness increasingly governs his consciousness. . . . Clearly written with love, the novel is moving; but it's also funny, with dry, insightful humor. Illustrations by the author's son Brendan, drawn during his own time in the depths of mental illness, haunt the story with scrambling, rambling lines, tremulousness, and intensity." Horn Book

Downsiders. Simon & Schuster Bks. for Young Readers 1999 246p hardcover o.p. pa $8.99

Grades: 9 10 11 12   **Fic**
  1. Subways -- Fiction 2. New York (N.Y.) -- Fiction
  ISBN 0-689-80375-3; 1-4169-9747-4 pa

             LC 98-38555

When fourteen-year-old Lindsay meets Talon and discovers the Downsiders world which had evolved from the subway built in New York in 1867 by Alfred Ely Beach, she and her new friend experience the clash of their two cultures.

"Shusterman has invented an alternate world in the Downside that is both original and humorous." Voice Youth Advocates

Everwild. Simon & Schuster Books for Young Readers 2009 424p (The Skinjacker trilogy) $16.99
Grades: 8 9 10 11 12   **Fic**
  1. Dead -- Fiction 2. Future life -- Fiction
  ISBN 978-1-4169-5863-5; 1-4169-5863-0

             LC 2008-51348

Sequel to: Everlost (2006)

Nick, known as the dreaded "chocolate ogre," is trying to find all the children in Everlost and release them from the limbo they are in, while Mikey and Allie have joined a band of skinjackers and are putting themselves in danger by visiting the world of the living.

"A fascinating read penned by an expert hand." Kirkus

Followed by: Everfound (2011)

UnDivided; Neal Shusterman. Simon & Schuster Books for Young Readers 2014 384 p. (Unwind dystology) (hardback) $18.99 **Fic**
  1. Science fiction 2. Fugitives from justice -- Fiction 3. Revolutionaries -- Fiction
  ISBN 1481409751; 9781481409759

             LC 2014003060

In this novel, by Neal Shusterman, "Proactive Citizenry, the company that created Cam from the parts of unwound teens, has a plan: to mass produce rewound teens like Cam for military purposes. And . . . Proactive Citizenry has been suppressing technology that could make unwinding completely unnecessary. As Conner, Risa, and Lev uncover these startling secrets, enraged teens begin to march on Washington to demand justice and a better future." (Publisher's note)

UnSouled; Neal Shusterman. Simon & Schuster Books for Young Readers 2013 416 p. (Unwind trilogy) (hardback) $17.99
Grades: 6 7 8 9 10 11 12   **Fic**
  1. Science fiction 2. Traffic accidents 3. Travel -- Fiction 4. Identity -- Fiction 5. Survival -- Fiction 6. Revolutionaries -- Fiction 7. Fugitives from justice -- Fiction
  ISBN 1442423692; 9781442423695

             LC 2013022703

In this book, the third in author Neal Shusterman's Un-Wholly series, "Lev and Connor are on the road again. Their destination is back to Ohio where Sonia, an antiques dealer with an important past, will help them end Unwinding once and for all. After a bizarre car accident . . . they wind up on a Native American reservation. Here, readers learn a lot more about Lev's past, and Connor meets up with Cam, the one and only Rewind." (School Library Journal)

"In the third of his projected four-volume Unwind "dystology" Shusterman brings most of his central cast of teenage fugitives together and introduces an important new character, who is exempt from being unwound (legally disassembled for body parts) because she has a mild spectrum disorder. Frequent references to events in previous episodes slow the pace somewhat but the present-tense tale remains suspenseful, the overall premise is as hauntingly plausible as ever, and an electrifying revelation at the end points the way to a possible resolution." (Booklist)

UnWholly; Neal Shusterman. Simon & Schuster Books For Young Readers 2012 402 p. (hardback) $17.99
Grades: 6 7 8 9 10 11 12   **Fic**
  1. Science fiction 2. Identity -- Fiction 3. Survival skills -- Fiction 4. Survival -- Fiction 5. Revolutionaries -- Fiction 6. Fugitives from justice -- Fiction
  ISBN 1442423668; 9781442423664; 9781442423688

             LC 2012002729

Sequel to: Unwind

This sequel to Neal Shusterman's book "Unwind" follows "Cam . . . a product of unwinding; made entirely out of the parts of other unwinds, he is a teen who does not technically exist. A futuristic Frankenstein, Cam struggles with a search for identity and meaning. . . . And when the actions of a sadistic bounty hunter cause Cam's fate to become inextricably bound with the fates of Connor, Risa, and Lev, he'll have to question humanity itself." (Publisher's note)

Unwind. Simon & Schuster Books for Young Readers 2007 335p $17.99

Grades: 6 7 8 9 10 11 12   **Fic**

1. Science fiction

ISBN 1-4169-1204-5; 1-4169-1205-3 pa; 978-1-4169-1204-0; 978-1-4169-1205-7 pa

LC 2006032689

In a future world where those between the ages of thirteen and eighteen can have their lives "unwound" and their body parts harvested for use by others, three teens go to extreme lengths to uphold their beliefs—and, perhaps, save their own lives. "Grades eight to ten." (Bull Cent Child Books)

"Poignant, compelling, and ultimately terrifying." Voice Youth Advocates

Other titles in this series are:

UnWholly (2012)

UnSouled (2013)

UnDivided (2014)

UnBound (2015)

Shute, Nevil

On the beach. Vintage International 2010 312p pa $15

Grades: 9 10 11 12 Adult   **Fic**

1. Science fiction 2. Australia -- Fiction 3. Nuclear warfare -- Fiction

ISBN 978-0-307-47399-8

First published 1957 by Morrow

"A nuclear war annihilates the world's Northern Hemisphere, and as atomic wastes are spreading southward, residents of Australia try to come to grips with their mortality. In spite of the inevitability of death, these people face their end with courage and live from day to day. They even plant trees they may never see mature." Shapiro. Fic for Youth. 3d edition

Silence is goldfish; a novel. by Annabel Pitcher. Little, Brown & Co. 2016 352 p. (hardback) $17.99

Grades: 6 7 8 9 10   **Fic**

1. Selective mutism -- Fiction 2. Identity (Psychology) -- Fiction 3. England -- Fiction 4. Fathers -- Fiction 5. Identity -- Fiction 6. Manchester (England) -- Ficition

ISBN 9780316370752

LC 2015024312

In this young adult novel, by Annabel Pitcher, "fifteen-year-old Tess doesn't mean to become mute. At first, she's just too shocked to speak. . . . Reeling from her family's betrayal, Tess sets out to discover the identity of her real father. . . . Tess continues to investigate, uncovering a secret that could ruin multiple lives. It all may be too much for Tess to handle, but how can she ask for help when she's forgotten how to use her voice?" (Publisher's note)

"Tess, fifteen, is an offbeat English introvert with a highly involved dad. After she discovers his startling blog post recounting her own birth ("It wasn't my daughter. It was... some sperm donor's"), her anger emboldens her to stand up against Dad's expectations. Her rebellion of choice is si-

lence, but her narrative voice speaks loudly--Tess is a witty and appealing protagonist." Horn Book

Silver, Eve

Rush; Eve Silver. Katherine Tegen Books 2013 368 p. (The game) (hardcover) $17.99

Grades: 9 10 11 12   **Fic**

1. Science fiction 2. Violence -- Fiction 3. Extraterrestrial beings -- Fiction 4. Combat -- Fiction 5. Interpersonal relations -- Fiction

ISBN 0062192132; 9780062192134

LC 2012025496

This young adult novel, by Eve Silver, is the first entry in "The Game" series. "Seventeen-year-old Miki Jones . . . wakes up . . . in a place called the lobby--pulled from her life, pulled through time and space into some kind of game in which she and a team of other teens are sent on missions to eliminate the Drau, terrifying and beautiful alien creatures." (Publisher's note)

Silvera, Adam

★ **More** happy than not; Adam Silvera. Soho Teen 2015 304 p. illustration (hardback) $18.99

Grades: 9 10 11 12   **Fic**

1. Grief -- Fiction 2. Gay teenagers -- Fiction 3. Gays -- Fiction 4. Youths' writings 5. Memory -- Fiction 6. New York (N.Y.) -- Fiction 7. Bronx (New York, N.Y.) -- Fiction 8. Single-parent families -- Fiction 9. Dating (Social customs) -- Fiction 10. Coming out (Sexual orientation) -- Fiction

ISBN 9781616955601

LC 2014044586

In this novel, by Adam Silvera, "Aaron struggles to find happiness despite the presence of his mother, older brother, and girlfriend, as well as a set of childhood buddies and a new, intriguing friend, Thomas. He is haunted by painful physical and emotional scars: the memory of his father's suicide in their home, his own similar failed attempt with its resulting smiley face scar, not to mention his family's poverty and his personal angst at an increasingly strong attraction for Thomas." (School Library Journal)

"Thought-provoking and imaginative, Silvera's voice is a welcome addition to the YA scene." Booklist

Silvey, Craig

★ **Jasper** Jones; a novel. Alfred A. Knopf 2011 312p $16.99

Grades: 6 7 8 9 10   **Fic**

1. Mystery fiction 2. Homicide -- Fiction 3. Australia -- Fiction 4. Family life -- Fiction

ISBN 0-375-86666-3; 0-375-96666-8 lib bdg; 978-0-375-86666-1; 978-0-375-96666-8 lib bdg

LC 2010-9364

In small-town Australia, teens Jasper and Charlie form an unlikely friendship when one asks the other to help him cover up a murder until they can prove who is responsible.

"Silvey infuses his prose with a musician's sensibility—Charlie's pounding heart is echoed in the terse staccato sentences of the opening scenes, alternating with legato phrases laden with meaning. The author's keen ear for dialogue is evident in the humorous verbal sparring between Charlie and Jeffrey, typical of smart 13-year-old boys. . . . A richly rewarding exploration of truth and lies by a masterful storyteller." Kirkus

Simmons, Kristen

Article 5; Kristen Simmons. Tor Teen 2012 364 p.

Grades: 9 10 11   **Fic**
1. Science fiction 2. Soldiers -- Fiction 3. Mothers and daughters -- Fiction 4. Government, Resistance to -- Fiction
ISBN 0765329581; 9780765329585
                                          LC 2011035411
This young adult dystopian novel, by Kristen Simmons, is set where "The Bill of Rights has been revoked, and replaced with the Moral Statutes. There are no more police--instead, there are soldiers. . . . Ember Miller . . . has perfected the art of keeping a low profile. . . . That is, until her mother is arrested for noncompliance with Article 5 of the Moral Statutes. And one of the arresting officers is none other than Chase Jennings . . . the only boy Ember has ever loved." (Publisher's note)

Three; Kristen Simmons. Tor 2014 382 p. (hardback) $17.99

Grades: 9 10 11 12   **Fic**
1. Science fiction 2. Dystopian fiction 3. Fugitives from justice -- Fiction 4. Resistance to government -- Fiction
ISBN 0765329603; 9780765329608; 9781429948036
                                          LC 2013026344
In this book, by Kristen Simmons, "Ember Miller and Chase Jennings are ready to stop running. After weeks spent in hiding as two of the Bureau of Reformation's most wanted criminals, . . . they search for . . . a settlement a few of them have heard about a settlement that is rumored to house the nebulous organization known as Three. . . . Three is responsible for the huge network of underground safe houses and resistance groups across the country." (Publisher's note)
"Teen activists Ember and Chase (Article 5; Breaking Point) are on the run from a dangerous government bureau and find their safe house in ruins. With only a few clues to go on, they search for Three, a mysterious organization they hope will take them in. Despite clumsy exposition, romance, dystopia, and suspense mingle to create a gripping conclusion to the trilogy." Horn Book

Other titles include:
Article 5 (2012)
Breaking Point (2013)

Simner, Janni Lee

Faerie after; Janni Lee Simner. Random House Inc. 2013 272 p. (ebook) $50.97; (hardcover) $16.99; (library) $19.99

Grades: 7 8 9 10   **Fic**
1. Fantasy fiction 2. Fairies -- Fiction 3. Paranormal fiction 4. Magic -- Fiction 5. Coming of age -- Fiction
ISBN 0375870695; 9780307974556; 9780375870699; 9780375970696
                                          LC 2012006430
Sequel to: Faerie winter
This is the third book in Janni Lee's Bones of Faerie trilogy. "Relative peace has descended upon Liza's town,

where she practices her summoner magic and waits for her half-faerie baby sister to be born. But the forest is showing new dangers, though subtle ones," particularly a strange dust. "Liza's quest to find out what's wrong reveals fresh disasters." (Kirkus)

Thief eyes. Random House 2010 272p $16.99

Grades: 7 8 9 10   **Fic**
1. Fantasy fiction 2. Magic -- Fiction 3. Iceland -- Fiction 4. Missing persons -- Fiction
ISBN 978-0-375-86670-8; 0-375-86670-1
                                          LC 2009-18166
Haley's mother disappeared while on a trip to Iceland, and a year later, when her father takes her there to find out what happened, Haley finds herself deeply involved in an ancient saga that began with her Nordic ancestors.
"Simner skillfully weaves Haley and Ari's modern emotional struggles into the ancient saga and enlivens the story with an intriguing cast of characters from the original tale." Booklist

Simone, Ni-Ni

Upgrade U; Ni-Ni Simone. Dafina Books 2011 viii, 276 p.p $9.95

Grades: 10 11 12   **Fic**
1. Love stories 2. Friendship -- Fiction 3. College students -- Fiction 4. College basketball -- Fiction 5. African Americans -- Fiction 6. Basketball players -- Fiction 7. Dating (Social customs) -- Fiction 8. Interpersonal relations -- Fiction
ISBN 0758241917; 9780758241917
                                          LC 2011282065
In this novel, "Seven McKnight, introduced in 'Shortie Like Mine' (2008), moves from Newark, N.J., to New Orleans, La., to join her best friend Shae and boyfriend Josiah at Stiles University. . . . Problem is, Josiah hasn't returned any of Seven's many texts or phone calls, and Seven is afraid. . . . As Seven and Josiah cycle through fighting and making up, Seven finds support in her band of new and old friends: insightful Shae; bold, flirtatious and social-networking-obsessed Khya and boa-clad next-door neighbor Courtney, who inserts himself into practically every conversation and outing. When Seven meets Zaire, a seemingly forthright, sophisticated New Orleans native, a love triangle develops--or is that a love quadrangle?" (Kirkus)

Simukka, Salla

As Red As Blood; Salla Simukka, translated by Owen Witesman. Skyscape 2014 272 p. $9.99

Grades: 9 10 11 12   **Fic**
1. Mystery fiction 2. Crime -- Fiction 3. Murder -- Fiction 4. Suspense fiction 5. Young adult fiction 6. Art students -- Finland
ISBN 1477847715; 9781477847718
In this crime novel by Salla Simukka, illustrated by Owen Witesman, part of the Snow White Trilogy, "seventeen-year-old Lumikki Andersson walks into her school's dark room and finds a stash of wet, crimson-colored money. Thousands of Euros left to dry--splattered with someone's blood. . . . Suddenly, Lumikki is swept into a whirlpool of events as she finds herself helping to trace the origins of the money." (Publisher's note)

"The starkly powerful opening paragraph of the Grimms' "Snow White" provides the narrative frame, and it's no flimsy high concept—rather, Simukka's onto something: Fairy tales, like mysteries, present uncompromising moral imperatives—no soft, comforting shades of gray for even the youngest readers.Limned in stark red, white and black, this cold, delicate snowflake of a tale sparkles with icy magic." Kirkus

Other titles in the series are:
As White as Snow (2015)
As Black as Ebony (2015)

Singleton, Linda Joy

Dead girl in love; Linda Joy Singleton. Flux 2009 283 p. $9.95

Grades: 8 9 10 11 12   Fic
1. Fantasy fiction 2. Supernatural -- Fiction 3. Female friendship -- Fiction 4. Identity -- Fiction 5. Friendship -- Fiction 6. Future life -- Fiction 7. Best friends -- Fiction 8. Grandmothers -- Fiction 9. Mothers and daughters -- Fiction
ISBN 0738714070; 9780738714073
LC 2009009049

This paranormal young adult book, the third book in Linda Joy Singleton's "Dead Girl" series after "Dead Girl Dancing," continues the story of Amber, whose "dead grandmother keeps finding people who have big problems and then [Amber has] the freaky experience of stepping into their life—and their body!—to provide help. This time, [she's] in the body of [her] BFF, Alyce. Since Alyce and [Amber] know everything about each other," Amber thinks she "won't have to do a lot of detective work" with this case. However, she's alarmed to discover that a question she does have to answer is why Alyce's body is in a coffin. (Publisher's note)

Sitomer, Alan Lawrence

The **secret** story of Sonia Rodriguez. Jump at the Sun/Hyperion Books For Children 2008 312p lib bdg $17.99

Grades: 7 8 9 10   Fic
1. Family life -- Fiction 2. Mexican Americans -- Fiction
ISBN 978-1-4231-1072-9; 1-4231-1072-2
LC 2007-45265

Tenth-grader Sonia reveals secrets about her life and her Hispanic family as she studies hard to become the first Rodriguez to finish high school.

"Sonia's immediate voice will hold teens with its mix of anger, sorrow, tenderness, and humor." Booklist

Skilton, Sarah

Bruised; by Sarah Skilton. Amulet Books 2013 288 p. $16.95

Grades: 9 10 11 12   Fic
1. Bildungsromans 2. Martial arts -- Fiction 3. Tae kwon do -- Fiction 4. Self-perception -- Fiction
ISBN 1419703870; 9781419703874
LC 2012042801

This book follows sixteen-year-old Imogen, a martial artist who "can break boards with her feet and toss a man twice her size, but when her skills are tested during a diner holdup, she cowers rather than acts, and a man dies. Having lost her confidence and her pride, Imogen is ready to give up martial arts until Ricky—another witness of the holdup—asks her to teach him how to throw a punch. While working with Ricky, Imogen makes discoveries about her passions and fears." (Publishers Weekly)

Skovron, Jon

Misfit. Amulet Books 2011 362p $16.95

Grades: 7 8 9 10   Fic
1. School stories 2. Demonology -- Fiction 3. Supernatural -- Fiction 4. Seattle (Wash.) -- Fiction 5. Single parent family -- Fiction
ISBN 978-1-4197-0021-7; 1-4197-0021-9
LC 2010048691

Seattle sixteen-year-old Jael must negotiate normal life in Catholic school while learning to control the abilities she inherited from her mother, a demon, and protect those she loves from Belial, the Duke of Hell.

This book features "a believable magical world that incorporates dry humor, mythological and biblical references, voodoo practices, exorcism, and romance. Although the supernatural element drives the plot, it is Jael's feeling of isolation and her search for family—even if her demonic maternal uncle smells like rotting fish—that motivates her courageous actions. She is an unlikely but wholly delightful heroine" Booklist

Skrypuch, Marsha Forchuk

Daughter of war. Fitzhenry & Whiteside 2008 210p pa $14.95

Grades: 9 10 11 12   Fic
1. Turkey -- Fiction 2. Armenian massacres, 1915-1923 -- Fiction
ISBN 978-1-55455-044-9; 1-55455-044-0

"In this powerful story of the Armenian genocide, Kevork witnesses the brutal suffering of his people as he travels, disguised as an Arab, through Turkey and Syria in search of his love, Marta. Upon their reunion, Kevork learns that Marta has escaped from a forced Turkish marriage and borne a child." SLJ

Skuse, C. J.

Rockoholic; C.J. Skuse. Scholastic 2012 358 p. (reinforced) $18.99

Grades: 9 10 11 12   Fic
1. Teenagers -- Fiction 2. Kidnapping -- Fiction 3. Rock musicians -- Fiction 4. Fame -- Fiction 5. Wales -- Fiction 6. Musicians -- Fiction 7. Friendship -- Fiction 8. Rock music -- Fiction 9. Best friends -- Fiction
ISBN 0545429609; 9780545429603
LC 2011046582

In this young adult novel, by C. J. Skuse, "Jody's addicted to Jackson Gatlin, frontman of The Regulators, and . . . she's front and center at his sold-out concert. But when she gets mashed in the moshpit . . . and bodysurfs backstage, she ends up with more than a mild concussion to deal with. By the next morning, the strung-out rock star is coming down in her garage. Jody . . . kind of kidnapped him. By accident. And now he doesn't want to leave." (Publisher's note)

Slade, Arthur G.

The **dark** deeps. Wendy Lamb Books 2010
310p (The hunchback assignments) $16.99; lib bdg
$19.99

Grades: 7 8 9 10   **Fic**

1. Science fiction 2. Spies -- Fiction 3. Shipwrecks --
Fiction 4. Supernatural -- Fiction 5. London (England)
-- Fiction 6. People with physical disabilities -- Fiction
7. Great Britain -- History -- 19th century -- Fiction
ISBN 978-0-385-73785-2; 0-385-73785-8; 978-0-385-
90695-1 lib bdg; 0-385-90695-1 lib bdg

          LC 2009052117

Sequel to: The hunchback assignments (2009)

Fourteen-year-old Modo, a shape-changing hunchback,
and Octavia take on another mission as secret agents for
the Permanent Association in Victorian London, investigating the cause behind the sinking of several ships in the
same place.

"The pacing and plotting are as tight and engaging as
in the opener. Slade does an excellent job of catching new
readers up to speed without pedantic reportage that would
bore those who have already read the first volume." Booklist

Empire of ruins; by Arthur Slade. Wendy Lamb
Books 2011 293p (The hunchback assignments)
$15.99; lib bdg $18.99

Grades: 7 8 9 10   **Fic**

1. Science fiction 2. Spies -- Fiction 3. Australia
-- Fiction 4. Great Britain -- Fiction 5. People with
Physical Disabilities -- Fiction
ISBN 978-0-385-73786-9; 0-385-73786-6; 978-0-385-
90696-8 lib bdg; 0-385-90696-X lib bdg

          LC 2010053419

While on an assignment in Queensland, Australia, to discover the truth behind a powerful weapon known as the God
Face, Modo, a teenaged, shape-changing hunchback living
in Victorian London, battles the evil machinations of the
Clockwork Guild and makes an astounding discovery—one
that hinges on Modo's true appearance.

"Another fun outing, sure to please series fans." Kirkus

Slouka, Mark

Brewster; a novel. Mark Slouka. W.W. Norton
& Co. Inc. 2013 256 p. (hardcover) $25.95

Grades: 11 12 Adult   **Fic**

1. Boys -- Fiction 2. Life change events -- Fiction 3.
Teenage boys -- Fiction 4. Vietnam War, 1961-1975
-- Fiction
ISBN 0393239756; 9780393239751

          LC 2013009415

Alex Award winner (2014)

Author Mark Slouka's book takes place in "1968, a year
after the summer of love and the peak of the Vietnam War.
The world is changing, and sixteen-year-old Jon Mosher is
determined to change with it. Racked by guilt over his older
brother's childhood death, Jon turns his rage into victories
running track. When he meets Ray Cappicciano, a local legend in the making, a rebel as gifted with his fists as Jon is
with his feet, he recognizes a friendship with the potential to
save him." (Publisher's note)

"The setup is familiar: bright Jewish track star Jon is
befriended by long-coat, wrong-side-of-the-tracks loner Ray

as they both fall for smart, empathetic beauty Karen, but
she loves only one of them (guess which?). What separates
Slouka's coming-of-age story from most others are dead-on
characters, the small-town setting in downstate New York,
and the 1968–71 time frame." (Library Journal)

Smelcer, John

Edge of nowhere; John Smelcer. First edition
Leapfrog Press 2012 193 p. $9.99

Grades: 8 9 10 11 12   **Fic**

1. Wilderness survival -- Fiction 2. Father-son
relationship -- Fiction 3. Alaska 4. Solitude 5.
Survival 6. Shipwrecks 7. Bildungsromans 8. Fathers
and sons 9. Adventure stories 10. Young adult fiction
ISBN 1849391963; 193524857X; 9781849391962;
9781935248576

In this young adult novel, by John Smelcer, based on
a true story, "sixteen-year-old Seth and his dog fall off his
father's commercial fishing boat in Prince William Sound.
They struggle to survive off land and sea as they work their
way home from island to island in a three-month journey.
The isolation allows Seth to understand his father's love, accept his Native Alaskan heritage, and accept his grief over
his mother's death." (Publisher's note)

"This is an example of authentic Native Alaskan storytelling at its best. Readers are drawn immediately into
this realistic modern-day vision-quest scenario and easily
identify and empathize with the characters. The excitement
and fast pace of the action are reminiscent of Jack London
stories. This novel would make a versatile addition to any
secondary English or multicultural curriculum. Not to be
missed." SLJ

Smibert, Angie

Memento Nora. Marshall Cavendish 2011 184p
$16.99

Grades: 8 9 10 11 12   **Fic**

1. Science fiction 2. Memory -- Fiction 3. Terrorism
-- Fiction 4. Cartoons and caricatures -- Fiction 5.
Resistance to government -- Fiction
ISBN 0-7614-5829-8; 978-0-7614-5829-6

          LC 2010011816

In a near future in which terrorism is commonplace but
memories of horrors witnessed can be obliterated by a pill,
teens Nora, Winter, and Micah, create an underground comic to share with their classmates the experiences they want
to remember.

This offers "a multi-threaded plot that manages to be
both complex and comfortably easy to follow. . . . The fast
pace encourages readers to fall headfirst into a gripping sus-
pense-adventure ride." Bull Cent Child Books

Smith, Alexander Gordon

Death sentence. Farrar Straus Giroux 2011 272p
(Escape from Furnace) $15.99

Grades: 7 8 9 10   **Fic**

1. Horror fiction 2. Science fiction 3. Prisoners --
Fiction
ISBN 978-0-374-32494-0; 0-374-32494-8

          LC 2010010938

After his failed attempt to escape from Furnace Penitentiary, Alex struggles to survive the bloodstained laboratories

beneath where monsters are manufactured, with a death sentence—or worse—hanging over his head.

"Smith strikes the ideal balance between action and introspection. Readers will feel genuine sympathy for antihero Alex." Kirkus

The **Devil's** engine; Hellraisers. Alexander Gordon Smith. Farrar, Straus & Giroux 2015 352 p. (hardcover) $17.99

Grades: 9 10 11 12 **Fic**
1. Adventure fiction 2. Paranormal fiction 3. Science fiction 4. Adventure stories 5. Schools -- Fiction 6. Monsters -- Fiction 7. Demonology -- Fiction 8. High schools -- Fiction 9. New York (N.Y.) -- Fiction
ISBN 9780374301699
LC 2015007190

In this novel, by Alexander Gordon Smith, "when a sixteen-year-old troublemaker named Marlow Green is trapped in a surreal firefight against nightmarish creatures in . . . New York City neighborhood, he unwittingly finds himself amid a squad of secret soldiers dedicated to battling the legions of the devil himself. Powering this army of young misfits is . . . the devil's engine, it can make any wish come true-as long as you are willing to put your life on the line." (Publisher's note)

"Marlow is a likable, flawed underdog of a hero, and his many comrades in arms gradually gain dimension as the plot progresses. First in a planned trilogy, Smith's latest is largely going to appeal to readers in it for the gritty action and horror." Booklist

Lockdown. Farrar, Straus and Giroux 2009 273p (Escape from Furnace) $14.99

Grades: 7 8 9 10 **Fic**
1. Science fiction 2. Escapes -- Fiction 3. Prisoners -- Fiction
ISBN 978-0-374-32491-9; 0-374-32491-3
LC 2008-43439

When fourteen-year-old Alex is framed for murder, he becomes an inmate in the Furnace Penitentiary, where brutal inmates and sadistic guards reign, boys who disappear in the middle of the night sometimes return weirdly altered, and escape might just be possible.

"Once a plot is hatched, readers will be turning pages without pause, and the cliffhanger ending will have them anticipating the next installment. Most appealing is Smith's flowing writing style, filled with kid-speak, colorful adjectives, and amusing analogies." SLJ

Other titles in this series are:
Death sentence (2011)
Solitary (2010)

Solitary. Farrar Straus Giroux 2010 232p (Escape from Furnace) $14.99

Grades: 7 8 9 10 **Fic**
1. Horror fiction 2. Science fiction 3. Prisoners -- Fiction
ISBN 978-0-374-32492-6; 0-374-32492-1
LC 2009-30843

Sequel to: Lockdown (2009)

Imprisoned for a murder he did not commit, fourteen-year-old Alex Sawyer thinks that he has escaped the hell-ish Furnace Penitentiary, but instead he winds up in solitary confinement, where new horrors await him.

"The author knows what keeps his readers locked to the page and delivers it soundly." Kirkus

Followed by: Death sentence (2011)

Smith, Andrew (Andrew Anselmo), 1959-
★ **100** sideways miles; Andrew Smith. Simon & Schuster Books for Young Readers 2014 288 p. (hardcover) $17.99

Grades: 9 10 11 12 **Fic**
1. Boys -- Fiction 2. Friendship -- Fiction 3. Authors -- Fiction 4. Epilepsy -- Fiction 5. California -- Fiction 6. Best friends -- Fiction 7. Fathers and sons -- Fiction 8. Dating (Social customs) -- Fiction
ISBN 1442444959; 9781442444959
LC 2013030326

In this young adult novel by Andrew Smith, "Finn Easton sees the world through miles instead of minutes. It's how he makes sense of the world, and how he tries to convince himself that he's a real boy and not just a character in his father's bestselling cult-classic book. Finn has two things going for him: his best friend, the possibly-insane-but-definitely-excellent Cade Hernandez, and Julia Bishop, the first girl he's ever loved." (Publisher's note)

"Leavened with humor and high-school high jinks, this unpredictable story of love and friendship is close to perfect." Booklist

★ The **Alex** crow; a novel. by Andrew Smith. Dutton Books, an imprint of Penguin Group (USA) LLC 2015 304 p. (hardcover) $18.99

Grades: 9 10 11 12 **Fic**
1. Science fiction 2. Death -- Fiction 3. Adoption -- Fiction
ISBN 0525426531; 9780525426530
LC 2014039366

In this novel, author Andrew Smith "chronicles the story of Ariel, a refugee who is the sole survivor of an attack on his small village. Now living with an adoptive family in Sunday, West Virginia, Ariel's story is juxtaposed against those of a schizophrenic bomber and the diaries of a failed arctic expedition from the late nineteenth century . . . and a depressed, bionic reincarnated crow." (Publisher's note)

"The author weaves several odd yet connected story threads: the 19th-century Arctic exploration aboard the ill-fated Alex Crow ship; a madman's bizarre U-Haul road trip; and the Merrie-Seymour Research Group and its de-extinction program. But the most compelling narrative is that of Ariel, a teenage refugee of an unnamed country, who is adopted into an American family...Smith follows up his enthralling, boundary-pushing Grasshopper Jungle (Dutton, 2014) with this more cohesive and brilliant work...A must-have for all YA collections." SLJ

★ **Grasshopper** jungle; by Andrew Smith. Dutton Juvenile 2014 432 p. (hardback) $18.99

Grades: 9 10 11 12 **Fic**
1. Praying mantis 2. Apocalyptic fiction 3. Iowa -- Fiction 4. Science fiction 5. Humorous stories 6. Insects -- Fiction 7. Survival -- Fiction 8. Friendship -- Fiction 9. Gender identity -- Fiction 10. Family life

-- Iowa -- Fiction
ISBN 0525426035; 9780525426035

LC 2013030265

Printz Honor Book (2015)

Boston Globe-Horn Book Award: Fiction (2014)

Author Andrew Smith presents a "novel of the apocalypse [featuring] a (dead) mad scientist, a fabulous underground bunker, voracious giant praying mantises and gobs of messy violence. Narrated by hapless Polish-Iowan sophomore Austin Szerba, [it describes] the dead-end town of Ealing, Iowa; his girlfriend, Shann Collins, . . . and most importantly, his gay best friend, Robby Brees, to whom he finds himself as attracted as he is to Shann." (Kirkus)

"Award-winning author Smith has cleverly used a B movie science fiction plot to explore the intricacies of teenage sexuality, love, and friendship. Austin's desires might garner buzz and controversy among adults but not among the teenage boys who can identify with his internal struggles. This novel is proof that when an author creates solely for himself-as Smith notes in the acknowledgments section-the result is an original, honest, and extraordinary work that speaks directly to teens as it pushes the boundaries of young adult literature." (School Library Journal)

In the path of falling objects. Feiwel and Friends 2009 326p $17.99

Grades: 10 11 12 Adult   **Fic**

1. Brothers -- Fiction 2. Vietnam War, 1961-1975 -- Fiction

ISBN 978-0-312-37558-4; 0-312-37558-1

LC 2008-34755

In 1970, after their older brother is shipped off to Vietnam, sixteen-year-old Jonah and his younger brother Simon leave home to find their father, who is being released from an Arizona prison, but soon find themselves hitching a ride with a violent killer.

"Powerful imagery and symbolism are threaded throughout the narrative along with Bible references, a map that Jonah is drawing, a meteorite that Simon takes along as a talisman, and references to gravity and its relentless pull. The intensity will suit serious readers who don't mind a little blood and gore." SLJ

The **Marbury** lens. Feiwel and Friends 2010 358p $17.99

Grades: 10 11 12   **Fic**

1. Horror fiction 2. Kidnapping -- Fiction 3. London (England) -- Fiction

ISBN 978-0-312-61342-6; 0-312-61342-3

LC 2010-13007

After being kidnapped and barely escaping, sixteen-year-old Jack goes to London with his best friend Connor, where someone gives him a pair of glasses that send him to an alternate universe where war is raging, he is responsible for the survival of two younger boys, and Connor is trying to kill them all.

"This bloody and genuinely upsetting book packs an enormous emotional punch. Smith's characters are very well developed and the ruined alternate universe they travel through is both surreal and believable." Publ Wkly

★ **Passenger**; Andrew Smith. Feiwel and Friends 2012 465 p. $17.99

Grades: 9 10 11 12   **Fic**

1. Horror fiction 2. Fantasy fiction 3. Paranormal fiction 4. Horror stories 5. Survival -- Fiction 6. Kidnapping -- Fiction 7. London (England) -- Fiction

ISBN 125000487X; 9781250004871

LC 2012288522

This horror fantasy novel, by Andrew Smith, is the sequel to "The Marbury Lens." "Best friends Jack and Conner can't stay away from Marbury. It's partly because of their obsession with this alternate world and the unresolved war that still wages there. . . . The boys try to destroy the lens that transports them to Marbury. But that dark world is not so easily reckoned with." (Publisher's note)

★ **Stand**-off; Andrew Smith. Simon & Schuster Books for Young Readers 2015 416 p. illustrations (hardback) $17.99

Grades: 9 10 11 12   **Fic**

1. School stories 2. Rugby football -- Fiction 3. Private schools -- Fiction 4. Schools -- Fiction 5. High schools -- Fiction 6. Boarding schools -- Fiction 7. Interpersonal relations -- Fiction

ISBN 9781481418294; 9781481418300

LC 2015002163

In this novel, by Andrew Smith, "it's his last year at Pine Mountain, and Ryan Dean should be focused on his future, but instead, he's haunted by his past. His rugby coach expects him to fill the roles once played by his lost friend, Joey, as the rugby team's stand-off and new captain. And somehow he's stuck rooming with twelve-year-old freshman Sam Abernathy, a cooking whiz with extreme claustrophobia and a serious crush on Annie Altman—aka Ryan Dean's girlfriend, for now, anyway." (Publisher's note)

"A brave, wickedly funny novel about grief and finding a way to live with it, with sweetly realistic first sexual experiences." Kirkus

sequel to Winger

★ **Stick**. Feiwel and Friends 2011 292p $17.99; ebook $9.99

Grades: 9 10 11 12   **Fic**

1. Brothers -- Fiction 2. Child abuse -- Fiction 3. Birth defects -- Fiction 4. Homosexuality -- Fiction 5. Runaway teenagers -- Fiction

ISBN 978-0-312-61341-9; 978-1-4299-9537-5 ebook

LC 2011023541

"Thirteen-year-old Stick was born with only one ear and secretly sadistic parents; for the slightest infraction, Stick s father will beat him and his older brother Bosten. After Dad finds out Bosten is gay, both boys, separately, run away." (Horn Book)

"Dark, painful, but ultimately hopeful, this is not a book for everyone, but in the right reader's hands, it will be treasured." Voice Youth Advocates

★ **Winger**; Andrew Smith. 1st ed. Simon & Schuster Books for Young Readers 2013 448 p. (hardcover) $16.99

Grades: 9 10 11 12   **Fic**

1. School stories 2. Rugby football -- Fiction 3.

Schools -- Fiction 4. High schools -- Fiction 5. Boarding schools -- Fiction 6. Interpersonal relations -- Fiction

ISBN 1442444924; 9781442444928; 9781442444942

LC 2011052750

Sequel: Stand-off (2015)

In this novel, by Andrew Smith, "Ryan Dean West is a fourteen-year-old junior at a boarding school for rich kids. He's living in . . . the dorm for troublemakers, and rooming with the biggest bully on the rugby team. And he's madly in love with his best friend Annie, who thinks of him as a little boy. With the help of his . . . humor, rugby buddies, and his penchant for doodling comics, Ryan Dean manages to survive life's complications and even find some happiness along the way." (Publisher's note)

"Smith deftly builds characters--readers will suddenly realize they've effortlessly fallen in love with them--and he laces meaning and poignantly real dialogue into uproariously funny scatological and hormonally charged humor, somehow creating a balance between the two that seems to intensify both extremes. Bawdily comic but ultimately devastating, this is unforgettable." Kirkus

Smith, Cynthia Leitich

Blessed. Candlewick Press 2011 462p $17.99

Grades: 9 10 11 12 **Fic**

1. Texas -- Fiction 2. Orphans -- Fiction 3. Vampires -- Fiction 4. Werewolves -- Fiction 5. Restaurants -- Fiction 6. Supernatural -- Fiction

ISBN 978-0-7636-4326-3

LC 2010-38697

Even as teenaged Quincie Morris adjusts to her appetites as a neophyte vampire, she must clear her true love, the hybrid-werewolf Kieren, of murder charges; thwart the apocalyptic ambitions of Bradley Sanguini, the vampire-chef who "blessed" her; and keep her dead parents' restaurant up and running before she loses her own soul.

"A satisfying blend of excitement and intrigue, Blessed provides a fun and entertaining read. Appealing to high schoolers with a flair for fantasy, this book provides a twist on life as an 'eternal.'" Voice Youth Advocates

Eternal. Candlewick Press 2009 307p $17.99

Grades: 8 9 10 11 **Fic**

1. Angels -- Fiction 2. Vampires -- Fiction

ISBN 978-0-7636-3573-2

LC 2008-27658

When Miranda's guardian angel Zachary recklessly saves her from falling into an open grave and dying, the result is that she turns into a vampire and he is left to try to reinstate his reputation by finally doing the right thing.

"Readers should be hooked by this fully formed world, up through the action-packed finale." Publ Wkly

Feral curse; Cynthia Leitich Smith. Candlewick Press 2014 272 p. $17.99

Grades: 9 10 11 12 **Fic**

1. Fantasy fiction 2. Mystery fiction 3. Curses -- Fiction 4. Shapeshifting -- Fiction 5. Adopted children -- Fiction

ISBN 076365910X; 9780763659103

LC 2013946609

This book, by Cynthia Leitich Smith, is the second book in the Feral series. "The adopted daughter of two respectable human parents, Kayla is a werecat in the closet. All she knows is the human world. When she comes out to her boyfriend, tragedy ensues, and her determination to know and embrace her heritage grows. Help appears in the lithe form of . . . male werecat Yoshi, backed up by Aimee and Clyde, as the four set out to solve [a] mystery." (Publisher's note)

"After touching the carousel-animal cougar in his Grams's antique store, Yoshi (Feral Nights) is transported to Pine Ridge, home of secret werecat Kayla. Within a few days, more Shifters show up, all inexplicably drawn to her. Debut character Kayla--level-headed, religious, but also quietly proud of her shifter nature--holds her own. Witty banter keeps the tone light even as the stakes ramp up." Horn Book

Feral nights; Cynthia Leitich Smith. Candlewick Press 2013 304 p. $17.99

Grades: 9 10 11 12 **Fic**

1. Paranormal fiction 2. Monsters -- Fiction

ISBN 0763659096; 9780763659097

LC 2012942377

This young adult paranormal fantasy story, by Cynthia Leitich Smith, is the first entry in the series "Feral." "When sexy, free-spirited werecat Yoshi tracks his sister, Ruby, to Austin, he discovers that she is not only MIA, but also the key suspect in a murder investigation. Meanwhile, werepossum Clyde and human Aimee have set out to do a little detective work of their own, sworn to avenge the brutal killing of werearmadillo pal Travis." (Publisher's note)

Tantalize. Candlewick Press 2007 310p $16.99; pa $8.99

Grades: 9 10 11 12 **Fic**

1. Texas -- Fiction 2. Vampires -- Fiction 3. Werewolves -- Fiction 4. Restaurants -- Fiction 5. Supernatural -- Fiction

ISBN 0-7636-2791-7; 978-0-7636-2791-1; 0-7636-4059-X pa; 978-0-7636-4059-0 pa

LC 2005-58124

When multiple murders in Austin, Texas, threaten the grand reopening of her family's vampire-themed restaurant, seventeen-year-old, orphaned Quincie worries that her best friend-turned-love interest, Kieren, a werewolf-in-training, may be the prime suspect.

"Horror fans will be hooked by Kieren's quiet, hirsute hunkiness, and Texans by the premise that nearly everybody in their capitol is a shapeshifter." Publ Wkly

Followed by Blessed (2011)

Smith, Emily Wing

Back when you were easier to love. Dutton Books 2011 296p $16.99

Grades: 8 9 10 11 12 **Fic**

1. Love stories 2. Mormons -- Fiction 3. Automobile travel -- Fiction

ISBN 978-0-525-42199-3; 0-525-42199-8

LC 2010-13469

When her boyfriend Zan leaves high school in Utah a year early to attend Pitzer College, a broken-hearted Joy and Zan's best friend Noah take off on a road trip to California seeking "closure."

Smith "effectively reconstructs Zan and Joy's relationship. . . . Joy's voice is sturdy, and her articulations about loss and belief are thoughtful and often moving. Self-acceptance and both the comforts and restrictions of the Mormon religion and identity are central themes in this sweet story." Publ Wkly

Smith, Hilary T.

A **Sense** of the Infinite; Hilary T. Smith. Katherine Tegen Books 2015 400 p. $17.99

Grades: 9 10 11 12   **Fic**
1. Bildungsromans 2. School stories 3. Female friendship -- Fiction
ISBN 0062184717; 9780062184719
LC 2014952736

In this coming of age novel by Hilary T. Smith, "it's senior year of high school, and Annabeth is ready--ready for everything she and her best friend, Noe, have been planning and dreaming. But there are some things Annabeth isn't prepared for, like the constant presence of Noe's new boyfriend. Like how her relationship with her mom is wearing and fraying. And like the way the secret she's been keeping hidden deep inside her for years has started clawing at her insides." (Publisher's note)

"Smith's prose is knock-down gorgeous. A fearless writer ably tackles a difficult story." Kirkus

Wild awake; Hilary T. Smith. 1st ed. Katherine Tegen Books, an imprint of HarperCollinsPublishers 2013 375 p. (hardcover) $17.99

Grades: 9 10 11 12   **Fic**
1. Bereavement -- Fiction 2. Dating (Social customs) -- Fiction 3. Secrets -- Fiction 4. Sisters -- Fiction 5. Mental illness -- Fiction
ISBN 0062184687; 9780062184689
LC 2012045524

In this young adult novel, by Hilary T. Smith, "Kiri Byrd . . . intends to devote herself to her music and win the Battle of the Bands with her bandmate and best friend, Lukas. Perhaps then . . . he will finally realize she's the girl of his dreams. But a phone call from a stranger shatters Kiri's plans. He says he has her sister Suki's stuff--her sister Suki, who died five years ago. This call throws Kiri into a spiral of chaos that opens old wounds and new mysteries." (Publisher's note)

Smith, Icy

Three years and eight months; written by Icy Smith; illustrated by Jennifer Kindert. East West Discovery Press 2013 44 p. color illustrations, maps (hardcover: alk. paper) $20.95

Grades: 9 10 11 12   **Fic**
1. Spies -- Fiction 2. China -- History -- Fiction 3. Hong Kong (China) -- Fiction 4. World War, 1939-1945 -- China 5. Sino-Japanese Conflict, 1937-1945 -- Fiction 6. China -- History -- 1937-1945 -- Fiction 7. World War, 1939-1945 -- China -- Fiction
ISBN 0985623780; 9780985623784
LC 2012040668

This book, written by Icy Smith and illustrated by Jennifer Kindert, "tells a compelling journey of hardships and human endurance of ordinary people in Hong Kong during the

Japanese occupation. A 10-year-old Chinese American boy secretly joins the Chinese war resistance group to help save the lives of thousands of prisoners of war, as well as allied American, British, and Canadian forces." (Publisher's note)

"Acknowledging that war may put soldiers in impossible positions too, Smith portrays Choi's supervisor-captor with compassion. On occasion, the text is repetitive, and a bibliography would have been helpful, but this does not detract from the power of this important story." Booklist

Includes bibliographical references (p.)

Smith, Jennifer E.

The **geography** of you and me; Jennifer E. Smith. Little, Brown & Co. 2014 352 p. (hardcover) $18

Grades: 7 8 9 10 11 12   **Fic**
1. Love -- Fiction 2. Social classes -- Fiction 3. Voyages and travels -- Fiction 4. Electric power failures -- Fiction 5. New York (N.Y.) -- Fiction
ISBN 0316254770; 9780316254779
LC 2013022845

In this book, by Jennifer E. Smith, "Lucy lives on the 24th floor. Owen lives in the basement. It's fitting, then, that they meet in the middle--stuck between two floors of a New York City apartment building, on an elevator rendered useless by a citywide blackout. After they're rescued, Lucy and Owen spend the night wandering the darkened streets. . . . But once the power is back, so is reality. Lucy soon moves abroad with her parents, while Owen heads out west with his father." (Publisher's note)

"Owen and Lucy meet during a citywide blackout in New York and spend a memorable (chaste) night together. Soon afterward, Lucy's parents take her to Europe, and Owen and his dad move to San Francisco, but even on opposite sides of the world, they think about each other. Smith's fans will recognize the alternating narration; reflective, deliberate writing style; and serendipitous coincidences." Horn Book

Hello, goodbye, and everything in between; Jennifer E. Smith. Little, Brown & Co. 2015 256 p. (hardcover) $18

Grades: 9 10 11 12   **Fic**
1. Dating (Social customs) -- Fiction 2. Breaking up (Interpersonal relations) -- Fiction 3. Love -- Fiction
ISBN 9780316334426
LC 2014043210

In this young adult novel, by Jennifer E. Smith, "on the night before they leave for college, Clare and Aidan only have one thing left to do: figure out whether they should stay together or break up. Over the course of twelve hours, they'll retrace the steps of their relationship, trying to find something in their past that might help them decide what their future should be." (Publisher's note)

"Students approaching the college transition, those who have already experienced it, and fans of romantic, realistic fiction will most enjoy this relatable, emotive story." SLJ

The **statistical** probability of love at first sight; Jennifer E. Smith. 1st ed. Little, Brown 2012 236 p.

Grades: 9 10 11 12   **Fic**
1. Love stories 2. Weddings -- Fiction 3. Air travel -- Fiction 4. Love -- Fiction 5. England -- Fiction 6.

Remarriage -- Fiction 7. London (England) -- Fiction 8. Fate and fatalism -- Fiction 9. Funeral rites and ceremonies -- Fiction
ISBN 9780316122382

LC 2010048704

In this book, "[a]lthough her mother has made peace with the situation, Hadley is still angry and hurt that her father left them for an Englishwoman. Rebooked on the next flight after missing her plane to London, where she's to be a bridesmaid in their wedding, Hadley is seated next to the English boy who helped her in the terminal. He comes to her rescue again after she confesses she suffers from claustrophobia. A good-looking Yale student, Oliver is smart, funny and thoughtful, though evasive about the purpose of his trip. Their mutual attraction is heightened by the limbo of air travel, but on arrival, they're separated. With just minutes to get to the wedding, Hadley . . . makes her way to the church and the father she's avoided seeing for a year." (Kirkus)

This is what happy looks like; Jennifer E. Smith. 1st ed. Poppy 2013 416 p. (hardcover) $17.99
Grades: 9 10 11 **Fic**
1. Love stories 2. Online dating -- Fiction 3. Teenage girls -- Fiction 4. Love -- Fiction 5. Maine -- Fiction 6. Actors and actresses -- Fiction
ISBN 0316212822; 9780316212823

LC 2012028755

In this novel, by Jennifer E. Smith, "when teenage movie star Graham Larkin accidentally sends small town girl Ellie O'Neill an email about his pet pig, the two seventeen-year-olds strike up a witty and unforgettable correspondence, discussing everything . . . except for their names or backgrounds. Then Graham finds out that Ellie's Maine hometown is the perfect location for his latest film, and he decides to take their relationship from online to in-person." (Publisher's note)

Smith, Lindsay

Dreamstrider; Lindsay Smith. Roaring Brook Press 2015 400 p. map (hardback) $17.99
Grades: 9 10 11 12 **Fic**
1. Spy stories 2. Dreams -- Fiction 3. Fantasy
ISBN 1626720428; 9781626720428

LC 2015011848

In this novel, by Lindsay Smith, "Livia . . . can inhabit a subject's body while they are sleeping and, for a short time, move around in their skin. She uses her talent to work as a spy for the Barstadt Empire. But her partner, Brandt, has lately become distant, and when Marez comes to join their team from a neighboring kingdom, he offers Livia the option of a life she had never dared to imagine. So only she understands the stakes when a plot against the Empire emerges that threatens to consume both the dreaming world and the waking one." (Publisher's note)

"An engaging stand-alone fantasy spy thriller." SLJ

Sekret; Lindsay Smith. Roaring Brook Press 2014 345 p. (hardback) $17.99
Grades: 8 9 10 11 12 **Fic**
1. Spies -- Fiction 2. Psychics -- Fiction 3. Soviet Union -- Fiction 4. Russia -- History -- 1917-1991, Soviet Union -- Fiction 5. KGB -- Fiction 6. Psychic

ability -- Fiction 7. Soviet Union -- History -- 1953-1985 -- Fiction
ISBN 1596438924; 9781596438927

LC 2013027913

Sequel: Skandal (2015)

In this book, by Lindsay Smith, "Yulia's father always taught her to hide her thoughts and control her emotions to survive the harsh realities of Soviet Russia. But when she's captured by the KGB and forced to work as a psychic spy with a mission to undermine the U.S. space program, she's thrust into a world of suspicion, deceit, and horrifying power." (Publisher's note)

"We the Living meets Genius Squad, this novel follows the misfortunes of Yulia, one of a group of psychic teens pressed into the service of the 1960s KGB. The concept is ambitious and the heroine fiery, but there is a surfeit of plot elements (including a hokey love triangle) and the writing is frequently turgid." Horn Book

Smith, Roland

The **edge**; by Roland Smith. Houghton Mifflin Harcourt 2015 240 p. $17.99
Grades: 6 7 8 9 10 **Fic**
1. Snow leopard -- Fiction 2. Mountaineering -- Fiction 3. Wilderness survival -- Fiction 4. Leopard -- Fiction 5. Survival -- Fiction
ISBN 9780544341227

LC 2014044086

Sequel to: Peak

In this book, by Ronald Smith, "The International Peace Ascent is the brainchild of billionaire Sebastian Plank: Recruit a global team of young climbers and film an inspiring, world-uniting documentary. The adventure begins when fifteen-year-old Peak Marcello and his mountaineer mother are helicoptered to . . . the Hindu Kush Mountains on the Afghanistan-Pakistan border. When the camp is attacked and his mother taken, Peak has no choice but to track down the perpetrators." (Publisher's note)

"While the climbing details are interesting and the setting in Afghanistan is a suitably dangerous and stark backdrop, the story is far from riveting. Awkward pacing, one-dimensional characters, and long stretches of exposition designed to educate readers in climbing minutiae and Afghan history further slow the action. Fails to summit." Kirkus

Smith, Sarah

The **other** side of dark. Atheneum Books for Young Readers 2010 312p $16.99
Grades: 6 7 8 9 10 **Fic**
1. Ghost stories 2. Orphans -- Fiction 3. Supernatural -- Fiction 4. Boston (Mass.) -- Fiction 5. Race relations -- Fiction 6. African Americans -- Fiction
ISBN 978-1-4424-0280-5; 1-4424-0280-6

LC 2010-14690

Since losing both of her parents, fifteen-year-old Katie can see and talk to ghosts, which makes her a loner until fellow student Law sees her drawing of a historic house and together they seek a treasure rumored to be hidden there by illegal slave-traders.

The author "weaves complicated racial issues into a romantic, mysterious novel." Booklist

Smith, Sherri L.

Orleans; Sherri L. Smith. G.P. Putnam's Sons 2013 324 p. (hardcover) $17.99

Grades: 9 10 11 12   **Fic**
1. Science fiction 2. Viruses -- Fiction 3. New Orleans (La.) -- Fiction 4. Virus diseases -- Fiction
ISBN 0399252940; 9780399252945

LC 2012009634

This novel, by Sherri L. Smith, describes a dystopian New Orleans. "After a . . . severe outbreak of Delta Fever, the Gulf Coast has been quarantined. Years later, residents of the Outer States are under the assumption that life in the Delta is all but extinct . . . but in reality, a new primitive society has been born. Fen de la Guerre . . . , left with her tribe leader's newborn, . . . is determined to get the baby to a better life over the wall." (Publisher's note)

Smith-Ready, Jeri

Shade. Simon Pulse 2010 309p $17.99

Grades: 9 10 11 12   **Fic**
1. Ghost stories 2. Trials -- Fiction 3. Musicians -- Fiction 4. Supernatural -- Fiction 5. Baltimore (Md.) -- Fiction
ISBN 978-1-4169-9406-0

LC 2009-39487

Sixteen-year-old Aura of Baltimore, Maryland, reluctantly works at her aunt's law firm helping ghosts with wrongful death cases file suits in hopes of moving on, but it becomes personal when her boyfriend, a promising musician, dies and persistently haunts her.

Although "Smith-Ready's occasionally racy . . . [book] resolves almost none of the issues surrounding the Shift, leaving the door open for future books, it is a fully satisfying read on its own, with well-developed, believable characters. . . . Perhaps even more impressive is the understatement of the paranormal premise—Smith-Ready changes the world completely by simply changing our ability to see." Publ Wkly

Followed by Shift (2011)

Shift. Simon Pulse 2011 367p $17.99

Grades: 9 10 11 12   **Fic**
1. Ghost stories 2. Musicians -- Fiction 3. Supernatural -- Fiction 4. Baltimore (Md.) -- Fiction
ISBN 978-1-4169-9408-4

LC 2010036784

Sequel to Shade (2011)

Logan returns as a ghost, complicating sixteen-year-old Aura's budding relationship with Zachary, especially when they discover that Logan might be able to become solid again.

"Smith-Ready's strengths are well-developed core characters, dialogue, and the clever narrative tone. Mature language and content make this better suited for older teens." SLJ

This side of salvation; Jeri Smith-Ready. Simon Pulse 2014 384 p. (hardcover) $17.99

Grades: 9 10 11 12   **Fic**
1. Cults -- Fiction 2. Family life -- Fiction 3. Missing persons -- Fiction 4. End of the world -- Fiction 5.

Grief -- Fiction 6. Schools -- Fiction
ISBN 1442439483; 9781442439481

LC 2013019948

In this book, by Jeri Smith-Ready, "when his older brother was killed, David got angry. . . . But his parents . . . got religious. David's still figuring out his relationship with a higher power, but there's one thing he does know for sure: The closer he gets to new-girl Bailey, the better . . . he feels. Then his parents start cutting all their worldly ties in to prepare for the Rush, the divine moment when the faithful will be whisked off to Heaven...and they want David to do the same." (Publisher's note)

"Following the death of his soldier brother, David's grief-stricken parents have turned to religion--specifically a fundamentalist cult--for solace. His recovering-alcoholic father speaks only in Bible verses; his mother is fixated on the upcoming Rapture, or Rush. When his parents disappear, David must untangle the mystery. Chapter flashbacks to "Before the Rush" alternate with "Now" in this nuanced study of relationships, religion, and faith." Horn Book

Solomon, Anna

The **little** bride; Anna Solomon. 1st Riverhead trade pbk. ed. Riverhead Books 2011 314p. pa $15

Grades: 11 12 Adult   **Fic**
1. Marriage 2. Immigrants 3. Jewish women 4. Frontier and pioneer life in literature 5. Jews 6. South Dakota 7. Russians -- United States
ISBN 978-1-59448-535-0; 1-59448-535-6

LC 201054194

This book tells the story of "Minna Losk, [who] flees an unhappy life as a servant in Odessa to become the mail-order bride of a Jewish man in South Dakota in the late nineteenth century. . . . [S]he's disappointed to discover that her intended, Max, is 40 years old and has two teenage sons, one of them older than Minna. It is this older son, Samuel, who captures Minna's attention and awakens desires in her that his father is incapable of stirring. An unfulfilling marriage is hardly the only challenge Minna faces. Frontier life is difficult and isolating, and Minna's inability to become pregnant weighs on her. A neighbor's carelessness costs Minna and her family their house, and as soon as the house is rebuilt, South Dakota is hit with a brutal winter that puts them in jeopardy again." (Booklist)

Sones, Sonya

One of those hideous books where the mother dies. Simon & Schuster Books for Young Readers 2004 268p $15.95; pa $6.99

Grades: 7 8 9 10   **Fic**
1. Actors -- Fiction 2. Bereavement -- Fiction 3. Father-daughter relationship -- Fiction
ISBN 0-689-85820-5; 1-416-90788-2 pa

LC 2003-9355

Fifteen-year-old Ruby Milliken leaves her best friend, her boyfriend, her aunt, and her mother's grave in Boston and reluctantly flies to Los Angeles to live with her father, a famous movie star who divorced her mother before Ruby was born

"Ruby's affable personality is evident in her humorous quips and clever wordplays. Her depth of character is revealed through her honest admissions, poignant revelations, and sensitive insights. . . . Ruby's story is gripping, enjoyable, and memorable." SLJ

What my girlfriend doesn't know. Simon & Schuster Books for Young Readers 2007 291p $16.99

Grades: 7 8 9 10 **Fic**

1. School stories 2. Artists -- Fiction 3. Boston (Mass.) -- Fiction 4. Dating (Social customs) -- Fiction

ISBN 978-0-689-87602-8; 0-689-87602-5

LC 2006-14682

Sequel to What my mother doesn't know (2001)

Fourteen-year-old Robin Murphy is so unpopular at high school that his name is slang for "loser," and so when he begins dating the beautiful and popular Sophie her reputation plummets, but he finds acceptance as a student in a drawing class at Harvard.

"Robin's believable voice is distinctive, and Sones uses her spare words (and a few drawings) to expert effect." Booklist

Sonnenblick, Jordan

Notes from the midnight driver. Scholastic Press 2006 265p $16.99

Grades: 8 9 10 11 12 **Fic**

1. Old age -- Fiction 2. Musicians -- Fiction 3. Friendship -- Fiction

ISBN 0-439-75779-7

LC 2005-27972

After being assigned to perform community service at a nursing home, sixteen-year-old Alex befriends a cantankerous old man who has some lessons to impart about jazz guitar playing, love, and forgiveness.

The author "deftly infiltrates the teenage mind to produce a first-person narrative riddled with enough hapless confusion, mulish equivocation, and beleaguered deadpan humor to have readers nodding with recognition, sighing with sympathy, and gasping with laughter—often on the same page." Horn Book

Sorrells, Walter

★ **First** shot. Dutton Children's Books 2007 279p hardcover o.p. pa $7.99

Grades: 7 8 9 10 11 12 **Fic**

1. Mystery fiction 2. Homicide -- Fiction 3. Father-son relationship -- Fiction

ISBN 978-0-525-47801-0; 0-525-47801-9; 978-0-14-241421-7 pa; 0-14-241421-2 pa

As David enters his senior year of high school, a family secret emerges that could solve the mystery of why his mother was murdered two years ago.

"David's first person narration pulls readers into the young man's torment. . . . This is a fast-paced, intriguing read." Booklist

Whiteout. Dutton Children's Books 2009 312p (Hunted) $15.99

Grades: 7 8 9 10 **Fic**

1. Mystery fiction 2. Homicide -- Fiction 3. Blizzards -- Fiction 4. Minnesota -- Fiction 5. Mother-daughter relationship -- Fiction

ISBN 978-0-525-42141-2; 0-525-42141-6

Sixteen-year-old Chass makes her way through a Minnesota blizzard, seeking not only the murderer of a beloved music teacher, but also something belonging to the killer who has been chasing her mother and herself around the country.

"There is . . . plenty of suspense to propel even a reluctant reader, and a number of false turns to keep the reader guessing." Voice Youth Advocates

Southgate, Martha

★ The **fall** of Rome; a novel. Scribner 2002 223p hardcover o.p. pa $13

Grades: 11 12 Adult **Fic**

1. School stories 2. Teachers -- Fiction 3. African Americans -- Fiction

ISBN 0-684-86500-9; 0-7432-2721-2 pa

LC 2001-34225

The author "delves deeply into the social and emotional elements that unite and divide us. Issues of race, identity, and integrity are intensely explored through a tragic human triangle." Booklist

Spears, Kat

Breakaway; a novel. Kat Spears. St. Martin's Griffin 2015 304 p. (hardcover) $18.99

Grades: 10 11 12 **Fic**

1. Love -- Fiction 2. Grief -- Fiction 3. Friendship -- Fiction

ISBN 9781250065513

LC 2015019024

In this novel, by Kat Spears, "[w]hen Jason Marshall's younger sister passes away, he knows he can count on his three best friends and soccer teammates—Mario, Jordie, and Chick—to be there for him. With a grief-crippled mother and a father who's not in the picture, he needs them more than ever. . . . Then Jason meets Raine, a girl he thinks is out of his league but who sees him for everything he wants to be." (Publisher's note)

"Readers will be hard-pressed to find a more realistic portrait of friends finding themselves while losing one another. A rare study of growing pains that gives equal weight to humor and hardship." Kirkus

Sway; by Kat Spears. First edition: September 2014 St. Martin's Press 2014 320 p. $18.99

Grades: 9 10 11 12 **Fic**

1. Teenagers -- Fiction 2. High schools -- Fiction 3. Interpersonal relations -- Fiction 4. Love stories 5. High school students 6. Interpersonal relations

ISBN 1250051436; 9781250051431

In this book, by Kat Spears, "high school senior Jesse Alderman, or 'Sway,' as he's known, . . . specializes in getting things people want---term papers, a date with the prom queen, fake IDs. . . . But when Ken Foster, captain of the football team, leading candidate for homecoming king, and all-around jerk, hires Jesse to help him win the heart of the angelic Bridget Smalley, Jesse finds himself feeling all sorts of things." (Publisher's note)

"Spears develops Jesse's character so thoroughly readers will believe they know him. Despite his ill egality and immorality, he remains sympathetic, revealing his hidden emotions as he forms real friendships with Pete and with an elderly man he meets while spying on Bridget. A compelling debut told with swagger and real depth." Kirkus

Spillebeen, Geert

Kipling's choice; written by Geert Spillebeen; translated by Terese Edelstein. Houghton Mifflin Co 2005 147p $16; pa $7.99

Grades: 7 8 9 10   **Fic**

1. Army officers 2. France -- Fiction 3. Children of prominent persons 4. World War, 1914-1918 -- Fiction
ISBN 0-618-43124-1; 0-618-80035-2 pa

LC 2004-20856

In 1915, mortally wounded in Loos, France, eighteen-year-old John Kipling, son of writer Rudyard Kipling, remembers his boyhood and the events leading to what is to be his first and last World War I battle.

"This well-written novel combines facts with speculation about John Kipling's short life and gruesome death. A riveting account of World War I." SLJ

Springer, Nancy

★ **I** am Mordred; a tale from Camelot. Philomel Bks. 1998 184p hardcover o.p. pa $6.99

Grades: 7 8 9 10   **Fic**

1. Kings 2. Mordred (Legendary character) -- Fiction 3. Great Britain -- History -- 0-1066 -- Fiction
ISBN 0-399-23143-9; 0-698-11841-3 pa

LC 97-39740

"Springer humanizes Arthurian archvillain Mordred in a thoroughly captivating and poignant tale." Booklist

I am Morgan le Fay; a tale from Camelot. Philomel Bks. 2001 227p hardcover o.p. pa $5.99

Grades: 7 8 9 10   **Fic**

1. Kings 2. Great Britain -- History -- 0-1066 -- Fiction 3. Morgan le Fay (Legendary character) -- Fiction
ISBN 0-399-23451-9; 0-698-11974-6 pa

LC 99-52847

In a war-torn England where her half-brother Arthur will eventually become king, the young Morgan le Fay comes to realize that she has magic powers and links to the faerie world

"Introspective, yet threaded with intrigue and adventure, this compelling study of the legendary villainess explores the ways that love, hate, jealousy, and the desire for power shape one young woman's fate and affect the destiny of others." Horn Book

St. Crow, Lili

Strange angels. Razorbill 2009 293p pa $9.99

Grades: 8 9 10 11 12   **Fic**

1. Orphans -- Fiction 2. Vampires -- Fiction 3. Werewolves -- Fiction 4. Supernatural -- Fiction 5. Extrasensory perception -- Fiction
ISBN 978-1-59514-251-1; 1-59514-251-7

LC 2008-39720

Sixteen-year-old Dru's psychic abilities helped her father battle zombies and other creatures of the "Real World," but now she must rely on herself, a "werwulf"-bitten friend, and a half-human vampire hunter to learn who murdered her parents, and why.

"The book grabs readers by the throat, sets hearts beating loudly and never lets go." Kirkus
Other titles in this series are:
Betrayals (2009)
Defiance (2011)
Jealousy (2010)

St. James, James

Freak show. Dutton Children's Books 2007 297p $18.99

Grades: 8 9 10 11 12   **Fic**

1. School stories 2. Florida -- Fiction 3. Prejudices -- Fiction 4. Homosexuality -- Fiction 5. Female impersonators -- Fiction
ISBN 978-0-525-47799-0; 0-525-47799-3

LC 2006-29716

Having faced teasing that turned into a brutal attack, Christianity expressed as persecution, and the loss of his only real friend when he could no longer keep his crush under wraps, seventeen-year-old Billy Bloom, a drag queen, decides the only to become fabulous again is to run for Homecoming Queen at his elite, private school near Fort Lauderdale, Florida.

"Though the subject matter and language will likely prove controversial, it's nearly impossible to remain untouched after walking a mile in the stilettos of someone so unfailingly true to himself and so blisteringly funny." Publ Wkly

Standiford, Natalie

★ The **boy** on the bridge; Natalie Standiford. Scholastic Press 2013 256 p. (hardcover) $17.99

Grades: 9 10 11 12   **Fic**

1. Love stories 2. School stories 3. Dissenters -- Fiction 4. Foreign study -- Fiction 5. Soviet Union -- History -- 1953-1985 -- Fiction 6. American students -- Soviet Union
ISBN 0545334810; 9780545334815

LC 2012033037

In this book, "Laura, an American college student studying in Lenigrad, is homesick. . . . That's before she meets Alyosha, a handsome young Russian artist who appears on a bridge just in time to save her from two aggressive gypsy women. Although Laura has been warned not to 'fall' for Russian men, who might have ulterior motives, she is drawn to her mysterious rescuer and arranges to meet with him secretly. Their rendezvous become increasingly frequent and intense, and . . . dangerous." (Publishers Weekly)

"In 1982, college student Laura travels to Russia to study but becomes involved in a romance with a young Russian man. Laura struggles to decide if he really loves her, or if he's using her to escape the oppressive Communist regime--as she and her fellow American students have been warned. The story's premise and unusual setting helps offset the occasionally flat writing." (Horn Book)

★ **Confessions** of the Sullivan sisters. Scholastic Press 2010 313p

Grades: 9 10 11 12   **Fic**

1. Sisters -- Fiction 2. Family life -- Fiction 3. Grandmothers -- Fiction 4. Baltimore (Md.) -- Fiction 5. Conduct of life -- Fiction 6. Inheritance and

succession -- Fiction
ISBN 9780545107105

LC 2010014512

Upon learning on Christmas Day that their rich and imperious grandmother may soon die and disown the family unless the one who offended her deeply will confess, each of the three Sullivan sisters sets down her offenses on paper. "High school." (Horn Book)

"A step above most books about rich girls, their boys, and their toys in both style and substance." Booklist

★ **How** to say goodbye in Robot. Scholastic 2009 276p $17.99; pa $8.99
Grades: 9 10 11 12   Fic
1. Death -- Fiction 2. Friendship -- Fiction 3. Family life -- Fiction 4. Baltimore (Md.) -- Fiction
ISBN 978-0-545-10708-2; 0-545-10708-3; 978-0-545-10709-9 pa; 0-545-10709-1 pa

LC 2009-5256

After moving to Baltimore and enrolling in a private school, high school senior Beatrice befriends a quiet loner with a troubled family history.

"This is an honest and complex depiction of a meaningful platonic friendship and doesn't gloss over troubling issues. The minor characters, particularly the talk-show regulars, are quirky and depicted with sly humor. . . . An outstanding choice for a book discussion group." SLJ

Staples, Suzanne Fisher

Haveli. Knopf 1993 259p pa $6.50
Grades: 8 9 10 11 12   Fic
1. Pakistan -- Fiction 2. Sex role -- Fiction
ISBN 0-679-84157-1; 0-679-86569-1 pa

LC 92-29054

Sequel to: Shabanu, daughter of the wind

Having relented to the ways of her people in Pakistan and married the rich older man to whom she was pledged against her will, Shabanu is now the victim of his family's blood feud and the malice of his other wives.

"Staples brews a potent mix here: the issue of a woman's role in a traditional society, page-turning intrigue, tough women characters, and a fluidity of writing that blends it all together." Booklist

Followed by: The house of djinn

★ **Shabanu**; daughter of the wind. Knopf 1989 240p hardcover o.p. pa $6.50
Grades: 8 9 10 11 12   Fic
1. Pakistan -- Fiction 2. Sex role -- Fiction
ISBN 0-394-84815-2; 0-440-23856-0 pa

LC 89-2714

A Newbery Medal honor book, 1990

When eleven-year-old Shabanu, the daughter of a nomad in the Cholistan Desert of present-day Pakistan, is pledged in marriage to an older man whose money will bring prestige to the family, she must either accept the decision, as is the custom, or risk the consequences of defying her father's wishes

"Interspersing native words throughout adds realism, but may trip up readers, who must be patient enough to find meaning through context. This use of language is, however, an important element in helping Staples paint an evocative

picture of life in the desert that includes references to the hard facts of reality." Booklist

Other titles in this series are:
Haveli (1993)
The house of djinn (2008)

Staunton, Ted

Acting up. Red Deer Press 2010 263p pa $12.95
Grades: 9 10 11 12   Fic
1. School stories 2. Canada -- Fiction 3. Family life -- Fiction 4. Conduct of life -- Fiction
ISBN 0-88995-441-0; 978-0-88995-441-0
Sequel to Sounding off (2004)

"Sam Foster, a normal teenager and drummer in the band ADHD, has maturity as his latest goal. Achieving this goal will put him well on the way to a parent-free weekend over spring break and getting his learner's permit. But as with most teenagers, circumstances have a way of preventing even the most enthusiastic teen from success. . . . Staunton has written a fast-paced coming-of-age novel that flows well. Teens will easily identify with the main characters and the hilarious antics that take place as he achieves maturity. There is mention of the effects of drinking alcohol and references to drug taking, but it is within the context of the story." Voice Youth Advocates

Steele, Allen

Apollo's outcasts; by Allen Steele. Pyr 2012 311 p. (hardcover) $16.99
Grades: 7 8 9 10   Fic
1. Science fiction 2. People with disabilities 3. United States -- Fiction 4. Space colonies -- Fiction 5. Coups d'état -- Fiction 6. Regression (Civilization) -- Fiction 7. Children with disabilities -- Fiction
ISBN 1616146869; 9781616146863

LC 2012023582

This book from Hugo Award-winning author Allen Steele sends "a handful of kids to the Moon in the wake of a political coup in America. Jamey Barlowe, 16, was born on the Moon but raised on Earth; as a result of a low-gravity infancy, Jamey uses a multifunctional 'mobil' chair to get around. . . . Anxious to do something productive upon arriving in Apollo (and able to walk for the first time), Jamey joins the elite Lunar Search and Rescue, just in time to end up on the front lines." (Publishers Weekly)

Stein, Tammar

High dive. Alfred A. Knopf 2008 201p $15.99; lib bdg $18.99
Grades: 7 8 9 10   Fic
1. Europe -- Fiction 2. Vacations -- Fiction 3. Friendship -- Fiction 4. Loss (Psychology) -- Fiction 5. Single parent family -- Fiction
ISBN 978-0-375-83024-2; 0-375-83024-3; 978-0-375-93024-9 lib bdg; 0-375-93024-8 lib bdg

LC 2007049657

With her mother stationed in Iraq as an Army nurse, Vanderbilt University student Arden Vogel, whose father was killed in a traffic accident a few years earlier, impulsively ends up on a tour of Europe with a group of college girls she meets on her way to attend to some family business in Sardinia.

"Ideal for the thoughtful armchair traveler, this story is engaging enough for readers on the long flight to the enduring wonders of Europe and emerging adulthood." SLJ

Light years; a novel. Knopf 2005 263p hardcover o.p. pa $6.99

Grades: 7 8 9 10   Fic
1. Bereavement -- Fiction 2. Israel-Arab conflicts -- Fiction
ISBN 0-375-83023-5; 0-440-23902-8 pa
LC 2004-7776

Maya Laor leaves her home in Israel to study astronomy at the University of Virginia after the tragic death of her boyfriend in a suicide bombing.

"This well-paced first novel, a moving study of grief and recovery, is also a love story that should appeal particularly to students interested in other ways of seeing the world." SLJ

Includes bibliographical references

Steinmetz, Karen

The **mourning** wars. Roaring Brook Press 2010 232p $17.99

Grades: 7 8 9 10   Fic
1. Mohawk Indians -- Fiction 2. United States -- History -- 1702-1713, Queen Anne's War -- Fiction
ISBN 978-1-59643-290-1; 1-59643-290-X
LC 2010-11735

In 1704, Mohawk Indians attack the frontier village of Deerfield, Massachusetts, kidnapping over 100 residents, including seven-year-old Eunice Williams. Based on a true story.

"Eunice's largely imagined life makes a fascinating story with a setting that is vividly and dramatically evoked. The book will be especially useful in the classroom." Booklist

Includes bibliographical references

Stevenson, Robin

★ A **thousand** shades of blue; [by] Robin Stevenson. Orca Book Publishers 2008 231p

Grades: 7 8 9 10   Fic
1. Bahamas -- Fiction 2. Sailing -- Fiction 3. Family life -- Fiction
ISBN 1551439212; 9781551439211

A yearlong sailing trip to the Bahamas reveals deep wounds in Rachel's family and brings out the worst in Rachel.

"The author does a fantastic job of making each character relatable to teens and creates some major drama between Rachel's mother and one of the locals that keeps the reader interested. . . . The book flows very smoothly, making it an easy read for teens." Voice Youth Advocates

Stevenson, Sarah Jamila

The **Latte** Rebellion. Flux 2011 328p pa $9.95

Grades: 8 9 10 11 12   Fic
1. School stories 2. Clubs -- Fiction 3. California -- Fiction 4. Family life -- Fiction 5. Racially mixed people -- Fiction
ISBN 978-0-7387-2278-8; 0-7387-2278-2
LC 2010-35002

When high school senior Asha Jamison is called a "towel head" at a pool party, she and her best friend Carey start a club to raise awareness of mixed-race students that soon sweeps the country, but the hubbub puts her Ivy League dreams, friendship, and beliefs to the test.

"The novel speaks directly to teenagers who are beginning to find their place in their world and figuring out how to make the world a better place for others. . . . This coming-of-age story is craftily written, fast paced and delivers a message of doing the right thing under difficult circumstances." Voice Youth Advocates

Stewart, Alex

Dragonwood; Alex Stewart. Evans 2010 56 p. pa $7.99

Grades: 7 8 9 10   Fic
1. Fantasy fiction 2. Mystery fiction 3. Elves -- Fiction 4. Criminals -- Fiction
ISBN 0237541351; 145174465X; 9780237541354; 9781451744651
LC 2011287528

This book is part of "the Shades series . . . from Britain" and "presents a fantasy story that dispenses with the massive casting and large chunks of world building" found in other fantasy stories. The story "follows a Halfling bounty hunter, Pip, who has been paid by an elven prince to track down and return the head of an orcish outlaw, who is rumored to have slain the prince's sister. He soon enough finds reason to doubt his employer's word, but Pip is sworn to carry out his mission one way or another." Author Alex Stewart offers "a conflicted-private-eye story in a fantasy setting." (Booklist)

Stewart, Mary

★ **Mary** Stewart's Merlin trilogy. Morrow 1980 919p maps $29.95

Grades: 11 12 Adult   Fic
1. Kings 2. Merlin (Legendary character) -- Fiction 3. Great Britain -- History -- 0-1066 -- Fiction
ISBN 0-688-00347-8
LC 80-21019

The first novel in this trilogy based on Arthurian legends concerns the difficult childhood and youth of the magician Merlin who grows up as a bastard at the court of the King of Wales where he is believed to be the offspring of the King's daughter and the devil. He gains much knowledge from a learned wizard and escapes to "Less Britain" where he becomes involved in efforts to unite all of Britain. The second novel tells of Merlin's involvement with the childhood of Arthur and Arthur's search for the magical sword, Caliburn. The last novel deals with Merlin's death and Arthur's turbulent reign.

The author's "skill in creating colorful characters, suspense, and a brooding atmosphere serves her well in portraying England's Dark Ages, where witches, sorcerers, and tragic kings moved heroically through an enchanted land. Though Arthur's rise to power is the subject, the true star and narrator of the tale is Merlin the magician." Husband, Sequels

Includes bibliographical references

Stiefvater, Maggie

Ballad; a gathering of faerie. Flux 2009 353p pa $9.95

Grades: 8 9 10 11 12   **Fic**
1. School stories 2. Magic -- Fiction 3. Fairies -- Fiction 4. Musicians -- Fiction 5. Supernatural -- Fiction
ISBN 978-0-7387-1484-4 pa; 0-7387-1484-4 pa
    LC 2009-19393
Sequel to: Lament: the faerie queen's deception (2008)
When music prodigy James Morgan and his best friend, Deirdre, join a private conservatory for musicians, his talent attracts Nuala, a faerie muse who fosters and feeds on creative energies, but soon he finds himself battling the Queen of the Fey for the very lives of Deirdre and Nuala.
"The themes of music, faerie, and romance combined with a smart male voice wil satisfy realistic fantasy readers as well as existing and new readers of the series." Libr Media Connect

★ **Blue** Lily, Lily Blue; Maggie Stiefvater; [edited by] David Levithan. Scholastic Press 2014 400 p. (The raven cycle) hc $18.99
Grades: 9 10 11 12   **Fic**
1. Magic -- Fiction 2. Mothers -- Fiction 3. Friendship -- Fiction
ISBN 9780545424967; 0545424968
    LC 2014947741
In this book, by Maggie Stiefvater, "Blue Sargent has found things. For the first time in her life, she has friends she can trust, a group to which she can belong. The Raven Boys have taken her in as one of their own. Their problems have become hers, and her problems have become theirs. The trick with found things, though, is how easily they can be lost. Friends can betray. Mothers can disappear. Visions can mislead. Certainties can unravel." (Publisher's note)
"This atmospheric fantasy is far more character driven than the former book, with increased and especially satisfying interactions among players. . . . The book's luminous and lively prose takes unanticipated paths, some new and surprising, with others connecting to previous events, demonstrating meticulous plot design." VOYA

★ The **dream** thieves; Maggie Stiefvater. Scholastic 2013 416 p. (Raven cycle) (jacketed hardcover) $18.99
Grades: 8 9 10 11 12   **Fic**
1. Fantasy fiction 2. Paranormal fiction 3. Magic -- Fiction 4. Dreams -- Fiction 5. Secrets -- Fiction 6. Occultism -- Fiction
ISBN 0545424941; 9780545424943
    LC 2013018731
This is the second book in Maggie Stiefvater's Raven Cycle series. Here, after "the transformative events at Cabeswater . . . , the context in which Gansey, Blue, Adam, Ronan, and Noah operate is further altered by the arrival of the Gray Man, a self-described hit man. . . . The Gray Man brings with him the machinations of larger, previously unknown forces as he takes orders from a voice on the phone to hunt the Greywaren, the identity of which is revealed early on." (Publishers Weekly)
"In this darker second book (The Raven Boys), Gansey, Blue, and the search for Glendower take a backseat to the exploration of Ronan's and Adam's tortured personalities. Stiefvater's descriptive prose reveals a complicated plot,

multiple viewpoints, and detailed backstories. Many mysteries remain, but the cliffhanger ending makes it clear that Glendower will resurface as the main focus of book three." (Horn Book)

Forever. Scholastic Press 2011 390p $17.99
Grades: 9 10 11 12   **Fic**
1. Love stories 2. Werewolves -- Fiction 3. Supernatural -- Fiction
ISBN 978-0-545-25908-8
    LC 2011023889
Sequel to Linger (2010)
A human girl and her werewolf boyfriend must fight for their love as death comes closing in.
"Stiefvater's emotional prose is rich without being melodramatic, and she clearly shares her fans' love of these characters." Booklist

Linger. Scholastic 2010 362p $17.99
Grades: 8 9 10 11 12   **Fic**
1. Werewolves -- Fiction 2. Supernatural -- Fiction
ISBN 978-0-545-12328-0; 0-545-12328-3
    LC 2009-39500
Sequel to Shiver (2009)
As Grace hides the vast depth of her love for Sam from her parents and Sam struggles to release his werewolf past and claim a human future, a new wolf named Cole wins Isabel's heart but his own past threatens to destroy the whole pack.
"This riveting narrative, impossible to put down, is not only an excellent addition to the current fangs and fur craze but is also a beautifully written romance that, along with Shiver, will have teens clamoring for the third and final entry." Voice Youth Advocates
Followed by Forever (2011)

★ The **raven** boys; Maggie Stiefvater. Scholastic Press 2012 409 p. (Raven Cycle) (hardcover) $18.99
Grades: 8 9 10 11 12   **Fic**
1. Magic -- Fiction 2. Supernatural -- Fiction 3. Private schools -- Fiction 4. Paranormal fiction 5. Occultism -- Fiction 6. Clairvoyance -- Fiction
ISBN 0545424925; 9780545424929
    LC 2012030880
This book is the first in Maggie Stiefvater's series the "Raven Cycle". It follows "16-year-old Blue Sargent, daughter of a small-town psychic, [who] has lived her whole life under a prophecy: If she kisses her true love, he will die. . . . She sees a vision of a dying Raven boy named Gansey. The Raven Boys--students at Aglionby, a nearby prep school, so-called because of the ravens on their school crest--soon encounter Blue in person." (Kirkus Reviews)
Other titles in the Raven Cycle are:
The dream thieves (2013)
Blue lily, lily blue (2014)
The raven king (2016)

★ The **Raven** King; by Maggie Stiefvater. Scholastic Inc. 2016 400 p. (Raven Cycle) $18.99
Grades: 8 9 10 11 12   **Fic**
1. Bildungsromans 2. Love -- Fiction 3. Magic --

Fiction 4. Teenagers -- Fiction
ISBN 0545424984; 9780545424981

"This [final] installment finds the world of the Raven Boys (Gansey, Ronan, Adam, and Noah) and their best friend Blue in considerable and dangerous disarray. As strange, increasingly sinister things begin happening in Henrietta and the magic forest of Cabeswater, the search for sleeping king Owen Glendower becomes more imperative, as it becomes apparent that something wicked this way comes." (Booklist)

"Stiefvater excels at building an intricately layered narrative with twisting, unpredictable turns, and her ability to introduce new, complex characters and storylines while also tying up previous loose ends is remarkable." VOYA

★ The **Scorpio** Races. Scholastic Press 2011 409p $17.99

Grades: 8 9 10 11 12   **Fic**
1. Love stories 2. Fantasy fiction 3. Horses -- Fiction 4. Racing -- Fiction 5. Orphans -- Fiction
ISBN 978-0-545-22490-1; 0-545-22490-X

         LC 2011015775

"Stiefvater's narration is as much about atmospherics as it is about event, and the water horses are the environment in which Sean and Puck move, allies and rivals to the end. It's not a feel-good story—dread, loss, and hard choices are the islanders' lot. As a study of courage and loyalty tested, however, it is an utterly compelling read." Publ Wkly

★ **Shiver**. Scholastic 2009 392p $17.99; pa $8.99

Grades: 9 10 11 12   **Fic**
1. Werewolves -- Fiction 2. Supernatural -- Fiction
ISBN 978-0-545-12326-6; 0-545-12326-7; 978-0-545-12327-3 pa; 0-545-12327-5 pa

         LC 2009-5257

In all the years she has watched the wolves in the woods behind her house, Grace has been particularly drawn to an unusual yellow-eyed wolf who, in his turn, has been watching her with increasing intensity.

"Stiefvater skillfully increases the tension throughout; her take on werewolves is interesting and original while her characters are refreshingly willing to use their brains to deal with the challenges they face." Publ Wkly

Other titles featuring the wolves of Mercy Falls are:
Forever (2011)
Linger (2010)

Sinner; Maggie Stiefvater. Scholastic Press 2014 368 p. (jacketed hardcover) $18.99
Grades: 9 10 11 12   **Fic**
1. Love stories 2. Los Angeles (Calif.) -- Fiction 3. Wolves 4. California 5. Metamorphosis 6. Paranormal Fiction 7. Human-animal relationships
ISBN 0545654572; 9780545654579

         LC 2014937299

In this young adult novel by Maggie Stiefvater, part of the Shiver series, "Cole St. Clair has come to California for one reason: to get back Isabel Culpeper. She fled from his damaged, drained life, and damaged and drained it even more. He doesn't just want her. He needs her. . . . Cole and Isabel share a past that never seemed to have a future. They

have the power to love each other and the power to tear each other apart." (Publisher's note)

"The relationship between the richly drawn characters is the heart of the book—it is light on paranormal and wolf action. Cole and Isabel are both jerks, but they are jerks with hearts, and they keep up with each other's witty banter. The ending wraps up a bit too neatly, but getting there is an absolute delight.A spectacularly messy, emotionally oh-so-human romance." Kirkus

Stirling, Tricia

When my heart was wicked; Tricia Stirling. First edition Scholastic Press 2015 192 p. $17.99

Grades: 9 10 11 12   **Fic**
1. Botany 2. Magic -- Fiction 3. Mother-daughter relationship -- Fiction 4. Choice -- Fiction 5. Stepmothers -- Fiction
ISBN 0545695732; 9780545695732

         LC 2014021741

In this book, by Tricia Stirling, "after a childhood bouncing between her mother, possibly a witch and probably unstable, and her father, whose presence made it possible for Lacy to see magic and beauty everywhere, Lacy's mother, Cheyenne, disappeared. Her mother's influence gone, Lacy's darkness blossomed into light and kindness. But her father has died, and although stepmother Anna wants to keep her, Cheyenne returns to drag Lacy back to Sacramento." (Kirkus Reviews)

"Stirling does a wonderful job of making the reader care for Lacy, who is not beyond casting spells herself. Her Northern California world of idiosyncratic personalities and oddball beauty is memorable and will be sure to appeal to teens who like their realism tempered with the otherworldly." Booklist

Stockett, Kathryn

The **help**. Amy Einhorn Books 2009 451p $24.95

Grades: 11 12 Adult   **Fic**
1. Authors -- Fiction 2. African American women 3. Mississippi -- Jackson 4. African Americans -- Civil rights 5. African American domestics -- Fiction 6. Mississippi -- Race relations -- Fiction
ISBN 0-399-15534-1; 978-0-399-15534-5

         LC 2008-30185

Twenty-two-year-old Skeeter has just returned home after graduating from Ole Miss. She may have a degree, but it is 1962, Mississippi, and her mother will not be happy till Skeeter has a ring on her finger. Skeeter would normally find solace with her beloved maid Constantine, the woman who raised her, but Constantine has disappeared and no one will tell Skeeter where she has gone.

Stohl, Margaret

Black Widow; forever red. by Margaret Stohl. Marvel 2015 416 p. $17.99

Grades: 7 8 9 10 11 12   **Fic**
1. Assassins -- Fiction 2. Superheroes -- Fiction 3. Secret societies -- Fiction 4. Avengers (Fictional characters) 5. Adventure stories
ISBN 9781484726433; 148472643X

         LC 2015020692

This is a prose novel about the Marvel character. "Natasha Romanoff is one of the world's most lethal assassins. . . . Natasha was given the title of Black Widow by Ivan Somodorov, her brutal teacher at the Red Room, Moscow's infamous academy for operatives. Ava Orlova is just trying to fit in as an average Brooklyn teenager. . . . The daughter of a missing Russian quantum physicist, Ava was once subjected to a series of ruthless military experiments-until she was rescued by Black Widow." (Publisher's note)

"Great fight sequences, plenty of action, twists in the plot, and characters motivated by strong emotions will keep readers engaged and entertained." SLJ

Stoker, Bram

★ **Dracula**; edited with an introduction and notes by Maurice Hindle; preface by Christopher Frayling. Penguin Books 2003 xlvii, 454p pa $11

Grades: 11 12 Adult Fic

1. Horror fiction 2. Vampires -- Fiction
ISBN 0-14-143984-X

LC 2003-269578

First published 1897

"Count Dracula, an 'undead' villain from Transylvania, uses his supernatural powers to lure and prey upon innocent victims from whom he gains the blood on which he lives. The novel is written chiefly in the form of journals kept by the principal characters—Jonathan Harker, who contacts the vampire in his Transylvanian castle; Harker's fiancée (later his wife), Mina, adored by the Count; the well-meaning Dr. Seward; and Lucy Westenra, a victim who herself becomes a vampire. The doctor and friends destroy Dracula in the end, but only after they drive a stake through Lucy's heart to save her soul." Merriam-Webster's Ency of Lit

Stone, Mary Hanlon

Invisible girl. Philomel Books 2010 279p $16.99

Grades: 7 8 9 10 Fic

1. California -- Fiction 2. Popularity -- Fiction 3. Child abuse -- Fiction
ISBN 978-0-399-25249-5; 0-399-25249-5

LC 2009-27255

Thirteen-year-old Stephanie, whisked from Boston to Encino, California, to stay with family friends after her abusive, alcoholic mother abandons her, tries desperately to fit in with her "cousin's" popular group even as she sees how much easier it would be to remain invisible.

"This edgy fish-out-of-water story features a strong and sympathetic protagonist." Horn Book Guide

Stone, Tamara Ireland

Time between us; Tamara Ireland Stone. Hyperion 2012 384 p. (hardcover) $17.99

Grades: 7 8 9 10 Fic

1. Love stories 2. Time travel -- Fiction 3. Love -- Fiction 4. Schools -- Fiction 5. Illinois -- Fiction 6. High schools -- Fiction 7. Space and time -- Fiction 8. Family life -- Illinois -- Fiction
ISBN 142315956X; 9781423159568

LC 2011053368

This book by Tamara Ireland Stone follows "Anna and Bennett," a couple who "were never supposed to meet: she lives in 1995 Chicago and he lives in 2012 San Francisco. But Bennett's unique ability to travel through time and space brings him into Anna's life, and with him, a new world of adventure and possibility. As their relationship deepens, they face the reality that time might knock Bennett back where he belongs." (Publisher's note)

Stork, Francisco X.

★ The **last** summer of the death warriors. Arthur A. Levine Books 2010 344p $17.99

Grades: 8 9 10 11 12 Fic

1. Death -- Fiction 2. Orphans -- Fiction 3. New Mexico -- Fiction 4. Mexican Americans -- Fiction
ISBN 978-0-545-15133-7; 0-545-15133-3

LC 2009-19853

"This novel, in the way of the best literary fiction, is an invitation to careful reading that rewards serious analysis and discussion. Thoughtful readers will be delighted by both the challenge and Stork's respect for their abilities." Booklist

★ **Marcelo** in the real world. Arthur A. Levine Books 2009 312p $17.99

Grades: 8 9 10 11 12 Fic

1. Autism -- Fiction 2. Asperger's syndrome -- Fiction
ISBN 0-545-05474-5; 978-0-545-05474-4

LC 2008-14729

ALA Schneider Family Book Award Honor Book (2010)

This book features "Marcelo Sandoval [who] is a 17-year-old looking forward to his senior year in high school. Living with something akin to Asperger's syndrome, Marcelo has spent his life learning step by step how to do things that many people learn intuitively. . . . Marcelo's father makes a deal with him: if he will spend the summer working at his father's law firm and successfully follow the rules of the real world, he can choose where he will spend his senior year." (Christian Century)

"Stork introduces ethical dilemmas, the possibility of love, and other 'real world' conflicts, all the while preserving the integrity of his characterizations and intensifying the novel's psychological and emotional stakes." Publ Wkly

★ The **memory** of light; Francisco X. Stork. Arthur A. Levine Books, an imprint of Scholastic Inc. 2016 325 p. (hbk.) $17.99

Grades: 9 10 11 12 Fic

1. Suicide -- Fiction 2. Friendship -- Fiction 3. Psychotherapy -- Fiction 4. Mexican Americans -- Fiction 5. Depression (Psychology) -- Fiction 6. Texas -- Fiction
ISBN 0545474329; 0545474337; 9780545474320

LC 2014044136

In this book, by Francisco X. Stork, "When Vicky Cruz wakes up in the Lakeview Hospital Mental Disorders ward, she knows one thing: She can't even commit suicide right. But there she meets Mona, the live wire; Gabriel, the saint; E.M., always angry; and Dr. Desai, a quiet force. With stories and honesty, kindness and hard work, they push her to reconsider her life before Lakeview, and offer her an acceptance she's never had." (Publisher's note)

"...From her darkest moments to welcome comedic respites to Emily Dickinson's poetry, Stork remains loyal to his characters, their moments of weakness, and their pragmatic views, and he does not shy away from such topics as domestic violence, social-class struggles, theology, and philosophy. Following Schneider Award-winning Marcelo in the Real World (2009), Stork further marks himself as a major voice in teen literature by delivering one of his richest and most emotionally charged novels yet." Kirkus

Strasser, Todd

Famous. Simon & Schuster Books for Young Readers 2011 257p $15.99

Grades: 7 8 9 10   **Fic**

1. Fame -- Fiction 2. Actors -- Fiction 3. Celebrities -- Fiction 4. Hollywood (Calif.) -- Fiction

ISBN 978-1-4169-7511-3; 1-4169-7511-X

LC 2009-48163

Sixteen-year-old Jamie Gordon had a taste of praise and recognition at age fourteen when her unflattering photograph of an actress was published, but as she pursues her dream of being a celebrity photographer, she becomes immersed in the dark side of fame.

"The book makes some astute observations about America's reality-television culture and its obsession with fame. . . . This well-crafted novel clearly belongs in all public, junior high, and high school libraries." Voice Youth Advocates

Give a boy a gun. Simon & Schuster Bks. for Young Readers 2000 146p hardcover o.p. pa $5.99

Grades: 9 10 11 12   **Fic**

1. School stories 2. Violence -- Fiction

ISBN 0-689-81112-8; 0-689-84893-5 pa

"Statistics, quotes, and facts related to actual incidents of school violence appear in dark print at the bottom of the pages. An appendix includes a chronology of school shootings in the United States, the author's own treatise on gun control, and places to get more information." SLJ

No place; Todd Strasser. Simon & Schuster Books for Young Readers 2014 272 p. (hardcover) $17.99

Grades: 7 8 9 10   **Fic**

1. Homelessness 2. Homeless persons -- Fiction 3. Poverty -- Fiction

ISBN 144245721X; 9781442457218

LC 2012043701

In this novel, by Todd Strasser, "It seems like Dan has it all. . . . Then his family loses their home. Forced to move into the town's Tent City, Dan feels his world shifting. . . . As Dan struggles to adjust to his new life, he gets involved with the people who are fighting for better conditions and services for the residents of Tent City. But someone wants Tent City gone, and will stop at nothing until it's destroyed." (Publisher's note)

"Coping with their personal financial catastrophe, wanting to stay in their familiar town, finding work, accepting charity, and maintaining self-respect are issues that weigh heavily on Dan and his parents. Readers will be drawn into this contemporary story." SLJ

Wish you were dead. Egmont USA 2009 236p

Grades: 8 9 10 11 12   **Fic**

1. School stories 2. Weblogs -- Fiction 3. Kidnapping -- Fiction 4. Missing persons -- Fiction 5. New York

(State) -- Fiction

ISBN 160684007X; 1606840495; 9781606840078; 9781606840498

LC 2009-14641

Madison, a senior at a suburban New York high school, tries to uncover who is responsible for the disappearance of her friends, popular students mentioned in the posts of an anonymous blogger, while she, herself, is being stalked online and in-person.

"The themes of bullying, tolerance, and friendship are issues to which readers can relate, as well as the inclusion of the IMing, blogging, texting, and social networking. This thriller will be popular and passed from one reader to another." Voice Youth Advocates

Stratton, Allan

★ **Borderline**. HarperTeen 2010 298p $16.99; lib bdg $17.89

Grades: 6 7 8 9 10   **Fic**

1. Muslims -- Fiction 2. Terrorism -- Fiction 3. Friendship -- Fiction 4. Prejudices -- Fiction 5. Father-son relationship -- Fiction

ISBN 978-0-06-145111-9; 0-06-145111-8; 978-0-06-145112-6 lib bdg; 0-06-145112-6 lib bdg

LC 2009-5241

Despite the strained relationship between them, teenaged Sami Sabiri risks his life to uncover the truth when his father is implicated in a terrorist plot.

This is "a powerful story and excellent resource for teaching tolerance, with a message that extends well beyond the timely subject matter." Publ Wkly

★ **Chanda's** secrets. Annick Press 2004 193p $19.95; pa $8.95

Grades: 7 8 9 10   **Fic**

1. Africa -- Fiction 2. AIDS (Disease) -- Fiction

ISBN 1-55037-835-X; 1-55037-834-1 pa

Michael L. Printz Award honor book, 2005

"The details of sub-Saharan African life are convincing and smoothly woven into this moving story of poverty and courage, but the real insight for readers will be the appalling treatment of the AIDS victims. Strong language and frank description are appropriate to the subject matter." SLJ

Another title about Chanda is:

Chanda's war (2007)

Chanda's wars; with an afterword by Roméo Dallaire. HarperCollinsPublishers 2008 384p $17.99; lib bdg $18.89; pa $8.99

Grades: 8 9 10 11 12   **Fic**

1. War stories 2. Africa -- Fiction 3. Orphans -- Fiction 4. Kidnapping -- Fiction

ISBN 978-0-06-087262-5; 0-06-087262-4; 978-0-06-087264-9 lib bdg; 0-06-087264-0 lib bdg; 978-0-06-087265-6 pa; 0-06-087265-9 pa

LC 2007-10829

Sequel to: Chanda's secrets (2004)

Chanda Kabelo, a teenaged African girl, must save her younger siblings after they are kidnapped and forced to serve as child soldiers in General Mandiki's rebel army.

"The characters are drawn without sentimentality, and the story is a moving portrayal of betrayal and love. The army's brutality and the traumas of the child soldiers are graphic and disturbing." Booklist

Strauss, Victoria

Passion blue; by Victoria Strauss. Marshall Cavendish Children 2012 346 p. (hardcover) $17.99

Grades: 7 8 9 10 11 12   **Fic**

1. Historical fiction 2. Convents -- Fiction 3. Women artists -- Fiction 4. Self-realization -- Fiction 5. Nuns -- Fiction 6. Magic -- Fiction 7. Artists -- Fiction 8. Talismans -- Fiction 9. Italy -- History -- 15th century -- Fiction

ISBN 0761462309; 9780761462309; 9780761462316

LC 2011040133

In this book by Victoria Strauss, when "Giulia is forced into a convent . . . she is surprised to learn of the beauty within, and that nuns and novices have vocations. . . . Her world expands as she learns the tools, materials, and techniques of great Renaissance painters. By chance, she meets a young male artisan repairing a convent masterpiece. They begin a clandestine romance. Her two desires -- painting and a husband -- war within as she contemplates her future." (School Library Journal)

Strohmeyer, Sarah

How Zoe made her dreams (mostly) come true; Sarah Strohmeyer. Balzer + Bray 2013 320 p. (pbk. bdg.) $9.99

Grades: 7 8 9 10   **Fic**

1. Amusement parks -- Fiction 2. Summer employment -- Fiction 3. Internship programs -- Fiction 4. Cousins -- Fiction 5. New Jersey -- Fiction

ISBN 0062187457; 9780062187451

LC 2012038163

In this book, "Zoe Kiefer, 17, and her cousin, Jess, are interns at Fairyland Kingdom, an over-the-top theme park in New Jersey. These internships are coveted. . . . Jess gets cast as a Little Red Riding Hood and Zoe is tasked with being the demanding Queen's personal assistant (aka slave). Zoe worries that these subpar positions won't put them in the running for the Dream and Do grant, a $25,000 prize that both girls desperately need." (School Library Journal)

Smart girls get what they want; by Sarah Strohmeyer. 1st ed. Harpercollins Childrens Books 2012 348 p. (tr. bdg.) $17.99; (paperback) $9.99

Grades: 7 8 9 10 11 12   **Fic**

1. Female friendship -- Fiction 2. Grading and marking (Education) 3. High school students -- Fiction 4. Schools -- Fiction 5. Friendship -- Fiction 6. Best friends -- Fiction 7. High schools -- Fiction 8. Interpersonal relations -- Fiction

ISBN 0061953407; 9780061953408; 9780061953415

LC 2011026094

Author Sarah Strohmeyer tells the story of Gigi, Neerja, and Bea, three friends who "stumble upon . . . [Neerja's sister] Parad's signature-less yearbook, making them think that maybe studying isn't everything. . . . When Gigi is accused of cheating on the AP Chemistry midterm along with Mike, a Man Clan wannabe who calls her 'Einstein,' the girls launch into action. Gigi finds herself running for student rep against Will, the new guy from California. . . . Neerja tries out for

the lead in Romeo and Juliet and Bea convinces Gigi to join the ski team with her." (Kirkus Reviews)

Stroud, Jonathan

The **Amulet** of Samarkand. Hyperion Bks. for Children 2003 462p (Bartimaeus trilogy) $17.95; pa $7.99

Grades: 7 8 9 10   **Fic**

1. Fantasy fiction

ISBN 0-7868-1859-X; 0-7868-5255-0 pa

LC 2003-49904

Nathaniel, a magician's apprentice, summons up the djinni Bartimaeus and instructs him to steal the Amulet of Samarkand from the powerful magician Simon Lovelace.

"There is plenty of action, mystery, and humor to keep readers turning the pages. This title, the first in a trilogy, is a must for fantasy fans." SLJ

Other titles in this series are:

The golem's eye (2004)

Ptolemy's gate (2006)

The **golem's** eye. Hyperion Books for Children 2004 562p (Bartimaeus trilogy) $17.95; pa $7.99

Grades: 7 8 9 10   **Fic**

1. Fantasy fiction

ISBN 0-7868-1860-3; 0-7868-3654-7 pa

Sequel to The amulet of Samarkand (2003)

In their continuing adventures, magician's apprentice Nathaniel, now fourteen years old, and the djinni Bartimaeus travel to Prague to locate the source of a golem's power before it destroys London.

"The characters are well developed and the action never lets up. A must-purchase for all fantasy collections." SLJ

Followed by Ptolemy's gate (2006)

★ **Heroes** of the valley. Hyperion Books for Children 2009 483p $17.99

Grades: 7 8 9 10   **Fic**

1. Adventure fiction 2. Middle Ages -- Fiction

ISBN 978-1-4231-0966-2; 1-4231-0966-X

"Twelve Houses control sections of a valley. Halli Sveinsson—at 15, the youngest child of the rulers of the House of Svein—goes against tradition when he sets out to avenge the death of his murdered uncle, and his actions result in warfare among Houses for the first time in generations. . . . Smart, funny dialogue and prose, revealing passages about the exploits of the hero Svein, bouts of action and a touch of romance briskly move the story along." Publ Wkly

Ptolemy's gate. Hyperion Books For Children 2006 501p (Bartimaeus trilogy) $17.95; pa $8.99

Grades: 7 8 9 10   **Fic**

1. Fantasy fiction

ISBN 0-7868-1861-1; 978-0-7868-1861-7; 0-7868-3868-X pa; 978-0-7868-3868-4 pa

LC 2005-52655

Sequel to The golem's eye (2004)

Dangerous adventures continue for the djinni Bartimaeus and his master, seventeen-year-old Nathaniel, a powerful magician who is serving as England's minister of information.

This "is an exciting and eminently satisfying conclusion to the trilogy. . . . literate, entertaining, and exciting." SLJ

The **ring** of Solomon; a Bartimaeus novel. Disney/Hyperion Books 2010 398p $17.99
Grades: 7 8 9 10   **Fic**
1. Fantasy fiction 2. Kings 3. Magic -- Fiction 4. Jerusalem -- Fiction 5. Witchcraft -- Fiction
ISBN 978-1-4231-2372-9; 1-4231-2372-7
LC 2010015468
Wise-cracking djinni Bartimaeus finds himself at the court of King Solomon with an unpleasant master, a sinister servant, and King Solomon's magic ring.

"In this exciting prequel set in ancient Israel, Stroud presents an early adventure of his sharp-tongued djinn, Bartimaeus. . . . This is a superior fantasy that should have fans racing back to those books." Publ Wkly

Sullivan, Tara
★ The **Bitter** Side of Sweet; Tara Sullivan. Penguin Group USA 2016 320 p. (hardback) $17.99
Grades: 9 10 11 12   **Fic**
1. Slavery -- Fiction 2. Child labor -- Fiction
ISBN 9780399173073; 0399173072
LC 2015038251
In this novel, by Tara Sullivan, "two young boys must escape a life of slavery in modern-day Ivory Coast. . . . The boys only wanted to make some money during the dry season to help their impoverished family. Instead they were tricked into forced labor on a plantation in the Ivory Coast; they spend day after day living on little food and harvesting beans in the hot sun—dangerous, backbreaking work." (Publisher's note)

"There are so few stories for teenagers that provide a glimpse into the complex global systems, such as cocoa production, that they unwittingly participate in every day and likely take for granted. An author's note, glossary, and source material provide further context to engage readers and teachers. Absorbing and important." Booklist

Golden boy; Tara Sullivan. G.P. Putnam's Sons, an imprint of Penguin Group (USA) Inc. 2013 368 p. (hardcover) $16.99
Grades: 7 8 9 10 11 12   **Fic**
1. Voyages and travels -- Fiction 2. Albinos and albinism -- Fiction 3. Survival -- Fiction 4. Tanzania -- Fiction 5. Human rights -- Fiction 6. Human skin color -- Fiction
ISBN 0399161120; 9780399161124
LC 2012043310
In this book, an albino boy named Habo does not fit in with his Tanzanian family, who shun him. "Only Habo's sister, Asu, protects and nurtures him. Poverty forces the family from their rural home near Arusha to Mwanza, hundreds of miles away, to stay with relatives. After their bus fare runs out, they hitch a ride across the Serengeti with an ivory poacher who sees opportunity in Habo. Forced to flee for his life, the boy eventually becomes an apprentice to Kweli, a wise, blind carver." (Kirkus)

Sullivan, Tricia
Shadowboxer; Tricia Sullivan. Ravenstone 2014 288 p. $9.99
Grades: 9 10 11 12   **Fic**
1. Immortality -- Fiction 2. Boxers (Sports) -- Fiction 3. Thailand 4. Mixed martial arts 5. Paranormal fiction
ISBN 1781082820; 9781781082829
In Tricia Sullivan's novel "after she has a confrontation with a Hollywood martial arts star that threatens her gym's reputation, Jade's coach sends her to a training camp in Thailand for an attitude adjustment. Hoping to discover herself, she instead uncovers a shocking conspiracy. In a world just beyond our own, a man is stealing the souls of children to try and live forever." (Publisher's note)

"SF author Sullivan (Lightborn) spins a kinetic, violent, and magical tale that makes excellent use of Jade's hard-edged voice. Sullivan brings to life the beauty of Thailand and the sweat and blood of the gym, infusing them with magic and danger. The mystical and realistic aspects of the plot don't always mesh, but it remains a strong showing." Publishers Weekly

Suma, Nova Ren
17 & gone; Nova Ren Suma. 1st ed. Dutton 2013 320 p. (hardcover) $17.99
Grades: 9 10 11 12   **Fic**
1. Paranormal fiction 2. Schizophrenia -- Fiction 3. Missing persons -- Fiction 4. Supernatural -- Fiction 5. Mental illness -- Fiction 6. Missing children -- Fiction 7. Psychiatric hospitals -- Fiction
ISBN 0525423400; 9780525423409
LC 2012029324
In this novel, by Nova Ren Suma, "seventeen-year-old Lauren is having visions of girls who have gone missing. And all these girls have just one thing in common--they are 17 and gone without a trace. As Lauren struggles to shake these waking nightmares, impossible questions demand urgent answers: Why are the girls speaking to Lauren? How can she help them? And . . . is she next?" (Publisher's note)

"Mature without being graphic, with a complex and intriguing plot, this novel should have no trouble finding readers." SLJ

Imaginary girls. Dutton 2011 348p $17.99
Grades: 9 10 11 12   **Fic**
1. Dead -- Fiction 2. Sisters -- Fiction 3. Supernatural -- Fiction 4. New York (State) -- Fiction
ISBN 978-0-525-42338-6; 0-525-42338-9
LC 2010-42758
Two years after sixteen-year-old Chloe discovered classmate London's dead body floating in a Hudson Valley reservoir, she returns home to be with her devoted older sister Ruby, a town favorite, and finds that London is alive and well, and that Ruby may somehow have brought her back to life and persuaded everyone that nothing is amiss.

The author "uses the story's supernatural, horror movie-ready elements in the best of ways; beneath all the strangeness lies beauty, along with a powerful statement about the devotion between sisters. Not your average paranormal novel." Publ Wkly

★ The **walls** around us; a novel. by Nova Ren Suma. Algonquin Young Readers 2015 336 p. $17.95

Grades: 9 10 11 12 **Fic**
1. Murder -- Fiction 2. Supernatural -- Fiction 3. Ballet dancers -- Fiction 4. Juvenile delinquency -- Fiction 5. Juvenile detention homes -- Fiction
ISBN 1616203722; 9781616203726
LC 2014031972

In this novel, by Nova Ren Suma, "Orianna and Violet are ballet dancers and best friends, but when the ballerinas who have been harassing Violet are murdered, Orianna is accused of the crime and sent to a juvenile detention center where she meets Amber and they experience supernatural events linking the girls together." (Publisher's note)

"This haunting and evocative tale of magical realism immerses readers in two settings that seem worlds apart. The book is told in alternating first-person voices from the perspective of two teenagers: lonely Amber, who at age 13 was convicted of murdering her abusive stepfather and sent to Aurora Hills, a juvenile detention facility, and Vee, an insecure yet ruthlessly ambitious Julliard-bound ballerina...A powerful story that will linger with readers." SLJ

Summers, Courtney

All the rage; by Courtney Summers. First edition St. Martin's Griffin 2015 336 p. (hardback) $18.99
Grades: 9 10 11 12 **Fic**
1. Rape -- Fiction 2. Missing persons -- Fiction 3. Bullying -- Fiction 4. Conduct of life -- Fiction 5. Interpersonal relations -- Fiction
ISBN 125002191X; 9781250021915
LC 2014040846

In this novel, by Courtney Summers, "the sheriff's son, Kellan Turner, is not the golden boy everyone thinks he is, and Romy Grey knows that for a fact. . . . But when a girl with ties to both Romy and Kellan goes missing after a party, and news of him assaulting another girl in a town close by gets out, Romy must decide whether she wants to fight or carry the burden of knowing more girls could get hurt if she doesn't speak up." (Publisher's note)

" Summers takes victim-shaming to task in this timely story, and the cruelties not only of Romy's classmates but also the adults she should be able to trust come heartbreakingly to the fore. Romy's breathy internal monologue is filled with bitter indignation, and while the narrative style may require some patience, older teens who like gritty realism will find plenty to ponder." Booklist

Fall for anything. St. Martin's Griffin 2011 230p pa $9.99
Grades: 9 10 11 12 **Fic**
1. Mystery fiction 2. Suicide -- Fiction 3. Bereavement -- Fiction 4. Father-daughter relationship -- Fiction
ISBN 978-0-312-65673-7
LC 2010-37873

As she searches for clues that would explain the suicide of her successful photographer father, Eddie Reeves meets the strangely compelling Culler Evans who seems to know a great deal about her father and could hold the key to the mystery surrounding his death.

"Readers may find the book fascinating or mesmerizingly melancholy depending on their moods, but there is no denying that Summers has brought Eddie's intense experience into the world of her readers. An unusual, bold effort that deserves attention." Kirkus

Some girls are. St. Martin's Griffin 2010 245p pa $9.99
Grades: 9 10 11 12 **Fic**
1. School stories 2. Bullies -- Fiction
ISBN 978-0-312-57380-5
LC 2009-33859

Regina, a high school senior in the popular—and feared—crowd, suddenly falls out of favor and becomes the object of the same sort of vicious bullying that she used to inflict on others, until she finds solace with one of her former victims.

"Regina's every emotion is palpable, and it's impossible not to feel every punch—physical or emotional—she takes." Publ Wkly

This is not a test; Courtney Summers. St. Martin's Griffin 2012 336 p. $9.99; (pbk.) $9.99
Grades: 7 8 9 10 11 12 **Fic**
1. Adventure fiction 2. Zombies -- Fiction 3. Child abuse -- Fiction 4. Horror stories 5. Schools -- Fiction 6. Survival -- Fiction 7. High schools -- Fiction 8. Family problems -- Fiction
ISBN 0312656742; 9780312656744; 9781250011817
LC 2012004633

In this book, "six teens who barely know or like each other seek refuge in their high school while the undead hordes lurk outside. . . . The end of the world unfolds through the eyes of high school junior Sloane Price, who has been contemplating suicide since her older sister ran away six months earlier, leaving Sloane with their physically abusive father. But these worries are pushed aside as Sloane tries to keep her fellow students alive." (Publishers Weekly)

Sun, Amanda

Ink; Amanda Sun. Harlequin Books 2013 304 p. (paperback) $9.99
Grades: 7 8 9 10 11 12 **Fic**
1. Love stories 2. Fantasy fiction 3. Japan -- Fiction
ISBN 037321071X; 9780373210718

In this teen romance novel, by Amanda Sun, part of "The Paper Gods" series, "Katie Greene must move halfway across the world. Stuck with her aunt in Shizuoka, Japan, Katie feels lost. Alone. . . . When Katie meets aloof but gorgeous Tomohiro, the star of the school's kendo team, she is intrigued by him. . . . Somehow Tomo is connected to the kami, powerful ancient beings who once ruled Japan--and as feelings develop between Katie and Tomo, things begin to spiral out of control." (Publisher's note)

"Katie's tendency to jump to conclusions, cry, and act before she thinks is frustrating, but it leaves plenty of room for growth. The descriptions of life in Japan—particularly teen life— create a strong sense of place, and set a vivid backdrop for this intriguing series opener by a debut author." BookList

Supplee, Suzanne

Somebody everybody listens to. Dutton 2010 245p $16.99

Grades: 7 8 9 10 11 12   **Fic**

1. Singers -- Fiction 2. Country music -- Fiction 3. Nashville (Tenn.) -- Fiction

ISBN 978-0-525-42242-6; 0-525-42242-0

         LC 2009-25089

Retta Lee Jones is blessed with a beautiful voice and has big dreams of leaving her tiny Tennessee hometown. With a beaten down car, a pocketful of hard-earned waitressing money, and stars in her eyes, Retta sets out to make it big in Nashville.

"While a must read for country music lovers, . . . [this book] will appeal to a wide audience, especially those who long to pursue a dream against the odds." Publ Wkly

Sutcliff, Rosemary

★ The **Shining** Company. Farrar, Straus & Giroux 1990 295p hardcover o.p. pa $7.95

Grades: 9 10 11 12   **Fic**

1. Great Britain -- History -- 0-1066 -- Fiction

ISBN 0-374-36807-4; 0-374-46616-5 pa

         LC 89-46142

"The realistic telling of the tale makes Sutcliff's story interesting. She creates a setting so genuine that readers will find themselves transposed into another time and place. Her language, reinforced by the Germanic influence of Old English, adds not only authenticity to the story but also a sense of poetry. This book will be cherished by the lover of history, the lover of literature, and the lover of adventure." Voice Youth Advocates

Sutton, Kelsey

Some quiet place; by Kelsey Sutton. 1st ed. Flux 2013 336 p. (paperback) $9.99

Grades: 7 8 9 10   **Fic**

1. Emotions 2. Occult fiction 3. School stories 4. Fear -- Fiction 5. Schools -- Fiction

ISBN 0738736430; 9780738736433

         LC 2013005021

In this book, "Elizabeth Caldwell's best friend is dying of cancer, one of the cutest boys in school loves her, and her alcoholic father beats her—but Elizabeth doesn't care about any of it. Her only meaningful interactions are with the Emotions, immortal personifications of the feelings she can't experience. With them, she does not have to pretend, as she must when she tries to muster believable social responses." The book explores the reasons behind Elizabeth's coldness. (Publishers Weekly)

"Haunting, chilling and achingly romantic, Sutton's debut novel for teens will keep readers up until the wee hours, unable to tear themselves away from this strange and beautifully crafted story. Elizabeth Caldwell can't feel emotions, yet she sees them everywhere, human in appearance, standing alongside their "summons.""...Chills and goose bumps of the very best kind accompany this haunting, memorable achievement." (Kirkus)

Swanwick, Michael

★ The **dragons** of Babel. Tor 2008 318p pa $15.99

Grades: 11 12 Adult   **Fic**

1. Fantasy fiction 2. Dragons -- Fiction

ISBN 978-0-7653-1950-0; 0-7653-1950-0; 978-0-7653-3114-4 pa; 0-7653-3114-4 pa

         LC 2007-34918

Sequel to: The iron dragon's daughter (2004)

Enslaved by a war-dragon of Babel, young Will evacuates to the Tower of Babel where he meets the confidence trickster, Nat Whilk, and becomes a hero to the homeless living in the tunnels under the city. As he rises from an underling to a politician, Will falls in love with a high-elven woman he dare not aspire to.

"Earthy, bawdy, and often brutal, . . . [this is] a story that will keep science fiction/fantasy fans involved till the end." SLJ

Sweeney, Diana

The **minnow**; Diana Sweeney. Text Publishing Co. 2015 263 p. $9.95

Grades: 8 9 10 11 12   **Fic**

1. Grief -- Fiction 2. Teenage mothers -- Fiction 3. Loss (Psychology) -- Fiction 4. Teenage pregnancy -- Fiction 5. Bildungsromans 6. Young adult fiction 7. Coming of age -- Fiction

ISBN 192218201X; 9781922182012

         LC 2015376822

Winner of the 2013 Text Prize for Young Adult and Children's Writing

In this book, by Diana Sweeney, "Tom survived a devastating flood that claimed the lives of her sister and parents. Now she lives with Bill in his old shed by the lake. But it's time to move out--Tom is pregnant. . . . In her longing for what is lost, Tom talks to fish: Oscar the carp in the pet shop, little Sarah catfish who might be her sister, an unhelpful turtle in a tank at the maternity ward. And the Minnow." (Publisher's note)

"Readers who can accept the ambiguous chronology and Tom's glib ability to communicate beyond worlds will be rewarded: the universe into which Minnow is born and will undoubtedly thrive is engaging and extraordinary. A promising and welcome debut." Booklist

Sweeney, Joyce

The **guardian**. Henry Holt and Co. 2009 177p $16.95

Grades: 7 8 9 10   **Fic**

1. School stories 2. Bullies -- Fiction 3. Siblings -- Fiction 4. Foster home care -- Fiction 5. Father-son relationship -- Fiction

ISBN 978-0-8050-8019-3; 0-8050-8019-8

         LC 2008-40602

When thirteen-year-old Hunter, struggling to deal with a harsh, money-grubbing foster mother, three challenging foster sisters, and a school bully, returns to his childhood faith and prays to St. Gabriel, he instantly becomes aware that he does, indeed, have a guardian.

"Sweeney's prose is insightful and realistic, with cleverly delivered descriptions. The peripheral characters are believable, and the religious undercurrent supports the plot. Well-paced, and with a satisfying conclusion." SLJ

Sáenz, Benjamin Alire, 1954-

★ **Aristotle** and Dante discover the secrets of the universe; Benjamin Alire Sáenz. Simon & Schuster Books for Young Readers 2012 359 p. (hardcover) $16.99

Grades: 9 10 11 12   **Fic**
1. Bildungsromans 2. Friendship -- Fiction 3. Gay teenagers -- Fiction 4. Mexican Americans -- Fiction 5. Families -- Fiction 6. Coming of age -- Fiction 7. Homosexuality -- Fiction 8. Mexican-Americans -- Fiction
ISBN 1442408928; 9781442408920
LC 2010033649
Michael L. Printz Honor Book (2013)
This book follows "fifteen-year-old Ari [who] is restless and bored when a boy named Dante offers to teach him to swim. . . . When Dante is almost hit by a car, Ari risks his life to save him and then pulls back emotionally from Dante's effusive gratitude, but it isn't until Dante moves away for the school year and begins experimenting with his sexuality . . . that Ari really has to confront the secrets of his own universe." (Bulletin of the Center for Children's Books)

★ **Last** night I sang to the monster; a novel. Cinco Puntos Press 2009 239p $16.95

Grades: 9 10 11 12   **Fic**
1. Alcoholism -- Fiction 2. Family life -- Fiction 3. Psychotherapy -- Fiction
ISBN 978-1-933693-58-3; 1-933693-58-4
LC 2009-15833
Eighteen-year-old Zach does not remember how he came to be in a treatment center for alcoholics. Through therapy and and the help of friends such as Rafael, his amnesia fades and he begins to heal. "Grades nine to twelve." (Bull Cent Child Books)
"Saenz' poetic narrative will captivate readers from the first sentence to the last paragraph of this beautifully written novel, which explores the painful journey of an adolescent through the labyrinth of addiction and alcoholism. It is also a celebration of life and a song of hope in celebration of family and friendship, one that will resonate loud and long with teens." Kirkus

Tahir, Sabaa

An **ember** in the ashes; a novel. by Sabaa Tahir. Razorbill 2015 464 p. (hardback) $19.95

Grades: 9 10 11 12   **Fic**
1. Fantasy fiction 2. Love -- Fiction 3. Slaves -- Fiction 4. Fantasy 5. Brothers and sisters -- Fiction 6. Undercover operations -- Fiction
ISBN 1595148035; 9781595148032
LC 2014029687
Sequel: A Torch Against the Night (2016)
In this book, by Sabaa Tahir, "Laia is a member of the conquered Scholars, who have lived under the rule of the oppressive Martial Empire for 500 years. Elias is on the winning side, close to graduating from a harsh program that produces Masks . . . a fate he feels trapped by. The two stumble into each other because Laia, a slave in the household, is attempting to spy on the Commandant, Elias' mother." (Bulletin of the Center for Children's Books)

"This epic debut, set in a fantasy empire with nods to ancient Rome and Egypt, relates the intersecting struggles of Elias, an elite enforcer, and Laia, a Resistance spy. Nuanced, multileveled world-building provides a dynamic backdrop for an often brutal exploration of moral ambiguity and the power of empathy. A compelling emergent romance is only one reason among many to anticipate the sequel." Horn Book

A **Torch** Against the Night. Penguin Group USA 2016 464 pp. hardcover $19.95

Grades: 9 10 11 12   **Fic**
1. Fantasy fiction 2. Brothers and sisters -- Fiction 3. Fugitives from justice -- Fiction
ISBN 9781101998878
"The sequel to Tahir's best-selling An Ember in the Ashes (2015) finds Elias and Laia on the run from Elias' mother—aka the unspeakably evil Commandant—and the vapid but vicious Emperor Marcus. Their destination: the Kauf Prison, where they hope to free Laia's brother, who knows the secret of serric steel, which just might save Laia's people, the Scholars, from extinction by the Empire. But Elias has been poisoned and his strength is ebbing, and their quest is further complicated by the presence of the rebel Keenan, who is Elias' rival for Laia's love. In the face of all this, how can they possibly succeed? . . . Infusing her story with magic, Tahir proves to be a master of suspense and a canny practitioner of the cliff-hanger, riveting readers' attention throughout." Booklist
Other titles in the series are:
An Ember in the Ashes (2015)

Tahmaseb, Charity

The **geek** girl's guide to cheerleading; [by] Charity Tahmaseb and Darcy Vance. Simon Pulse 2009 324p pa $8.99

Grades: 7 8 9 10   **Fic**
1. Friendship -- Fiction 2. Cheerleading -- Fiction 3. Dating (Social customs) -- Fiction
ISBN 978-1-4169-7834-3; 1-4169-7834-8
"Self-professed 'geek girl' Bethany has a crush on an unattainable jock, Jack. On a lark, she tries out for and makes the cheerleading squad and draws Jack's attention. But as her relationship with Jack blooms, complications arise that impact both her friendships and her romance. . . . The diverse characters and Bethany's introspective commentary on teen life creates an engaging and entertaining read." Booklist

Takoudes, Greg

When we wuz famous; Greg Takoudes. 1st ed. Christy Ottaviano Books 2013 320 p. (hardcover) $16.99

Grades: 9 10 11 12   **Fic**
1. School stories 2. Teenagers -- Fiction
ISBN 0805094520; 9780805094527
LC 2012027733
This novel "follows three teenagers in . . . Harlem, struggling to survive inside and outside the neighborhood. Francisco has been given the chance of a lifetime with a senior-year scholarship to a prestigious boarding school upstate. . . . While Francisco suffers bouts of homesickness, his cousin Vincent flounders back in N.Y.C. without Francisco to bail

him out of trouble, and Francisco's girlfriend, Reignbow, has her hands full trying to take care of her wheelchair-bound mother." (Publishers Weekly)

Tal, Eve

Cursing Columbus. Cinco Puntos Press 2009 248p $17.95

Grades: 7 8 9 10   **Fic**

1. Jews -- Fiction 2. Immigrants -- Fiction 3. Family life -- Fiction 4. New York (N.Y.) -- Fiction 5. Russian Americans -- Fiction

ISBN 978-1-933693-59-0; 1-933693-59-2

LC 2009-15834

Sequel to: Double crossing (2005)

In 1907, fourteen-year-old Raizel, who has lived in New York City for three years, and her brother Lemmel, newly-arrived, respond very differently to the challenges of living as Ukrainian Jews in the Lower East Side as Raizel works toward fitting in and getting ahead, while Lemmel joins a gang and lives on the streets

"The story offers a realistic and poignant picture of a bygone time." SLJ

Double crossing. Cinco Puntos Press 2005 261p $16.95

Grades: 7 8 9 10   **Fic**

1. Jews -- Fiction 2. Immigrants -- Fiction

ISBN 0-938317-94-6

LC 2005-8188

In 1905, as life becomes increasingly difficult for Jews in Ukraine, eleven-year-old Raizel and her father flee to America in hopes of earning money to bring the rest of the family there, but her father's health and Orthodox faith become barriers.

"Tal's fictionalized account of her grandfather's journey to America is fast paced, full of suspense, and highly readable." SLJ

Followed by: Cursing Columbus (2009)

Talley, Robin

What We Left Behind; by Robin Talley. Harlequin Books 2015 416 p. $18.99

Grades: 9 10 11 12   **Fic**

1. LGBT people -- Fiction 2. Gender identity -- Fiction 3. College students -- Fiction 4. Transgender people -- Fiction 5. Dating (Social customs) -- Fiction 6. Self realization -- Fiction 7. Lesbian teenagers -- Fiction

ISBN 0373211759; 9780373211753

LC 2016297369

In this book, by Robin Talley, "Toni and Gretchen are the couple everyone envied in high school. They've been together forever. They never fight. They're deeply, hopelessly in love. When they separate for their first year at college—Toni to Harvard and Gretchen to NYU—they're sure they'll be fine. Where other long-distance relationships have fallen apart, theirs is bound to stay rock-solid. The reality of being apart, though, is very different than they expected." (Publisher's note)

"High school's perfect queer couple, Toni and Gretchen, navigate changes in their relationship freshman year as they attend separate colleges and form new friendships. A group of transgender upperclassmen at Harvard befriend Toni, who

identifies as genderqueer, and offer support to explore questions of gender identity despite roommate drama and family strife. At NYU, Gretchen quickly forms a close friendship with Carroll, a freshman eager to experience gay life in the big city. . . . Recommended for all collections trying to fill a gap in the representation of transgender voices in teen fiction." SLJ

Tanner, Mike

★ **Resurrection** blues. Annick Press 2005 246p $19.95; pa $9.95

Grades: 9 10 11 12   **Fic**

1. Musicians -- Fiction 2. Rock music -- Fiction

ISBN 1-55037-897-X; 1-55037-896-1 pa

"In the middle of his senior year, 18-year-old Flynn Robinson drops out of high school to join a traveling bar band and chase his dream of being a professional musician like his uncle Ray. . . Flynn describes his six months on the road with the Sawyers band: the thrill of performing; his unease with his bandmates' adventures with drugs and sex; and ambivalence about his future, particularly his relationship with his high-school girlfriend. . . . Many readers, particularly teens who share his lyrically described musical passion, will easily connect with his questions, restlessness, and driving need for independence and expression." Booklist

Tarttelin, Abigail

★ **Golden** boy; a novel. by Abigail Tarttelin. Atria Books 2013 352 p. (hardcover) $24.99; (pbk.) $16

Grades: 11 12 Adult   **Fic**

1. Family secrets -- Fiction 2. Intersex people -- Fiction 3. Brothers -- Fiction 4. Families -- Fiction 5. Intersexuality -- Fiction 6. Gender identity -- Fiction

ISBN 1476705801; 9781476705804; 9781476705811

LC 2012049192

Alex Award Winner (2014)

Lambda Literary Awards Finalist (2014)

This book, by Abigail Tarttelin, is about "sixteen-year-old Max . . . the son of wealthy parents. But he also has a closely guarded secret that only his family knows. He is intersex. Max is comfortable with his circumstance, though, until something unthinkable happens, and his and his family's lives begin to unravel; for the first time, Max begins to regard himself as freakish." (Booklist)

Taub, Melinda

Still star-crossed; by Melinda Taub. 1st ed. Random House Childrens Books 2013 352 p. (library) $19.99; (hardcover) $16.99

Grades: 7 8 9 10 11 12   **Fic**

1. Love stories 2. Historical fiction 3. Love -- Fiction 4. Families -- Fiction 5. Vendetta -- Fiction 6. Characters in literature -- Fiction 7. Italy -- History -- 1559-1789 -- Fiction 8. Verona (Italy) -- History -- 16th century -- Fiction

ISBN 0385743505; 9780375991189; 9780385743501

LC 2012032626

This young adult novel is a sequel to the events of the play "Romeo and Juliet." The "peace purchased with Romeo's and Juliet's deaths lasts two weeks before the Capulets and Montagues renew their fight in the streets of Verona.

. . . Prince Escalus attempts to force the feuding families into concord by arranging a marriage between Rosaline and Benvolio." (Kirkus Reviews)

Tayleur, Karen
    Chasing boys. Walker & Co. 2009 244p $16.99
Grades: 7 8 9 10 11   **Fic**
    1. School stories 2. Fathers -- Fiction
    ISBN 978-0-8027-9830-5; 0-8027-9830-6
                                        LC 2008-23241
First published 2007 by Black Dog Books
With her father gone and her family dealing with financial problems, El transfers to a new school, where she falls for one of the popular boys and then must decide whether to remain true to herself or become like the girls she scorns.
    "All the ingredients of El's life are blended seamlessly, never downplaying the audience's intelligence, as Tayleur captures the all-consuming nature of a teenage crush without making El ridiculous. Moody, poetic, and intimate, this book is billed as the 'romance for girls who don't like pink,' but is much more than that." Booklist

Taylor, Laini
    ★ **Daughter** of smoke and bone. Little, Brown 2011 418p $18.99
Grades: 8 9 10 11 12   **Fic**
    1. Love stories 2. Fantasy fiction 3. Paranormal fiction 4. School stories 5. Angels -- Fiction 6. Artists -- Fiction 7. Supernatural -- Fiction 8. Classical mythology -- Fiction
    ISBN 978-0-316-13402-6; 0-316-13402-3;
    9780316196192
                                        LC 2010045802
Seventeen-year-old Karou, a lovely, enigmatic art student in a Prague boarding school, carries a sketchbook of hideous, frightening monsters—the chimaerae who form the only family she has ever known.
    Taylor "again weaves a masterful mix of reality and fantasy with cross-genre appeal. Exquisitely written and beautifully paced." Publ Wkly

    ★ **Days** of blood & starlight; Laini Taylor. 1st ed. Little, Brown Books for Young Readers 2012 528 p. maps (Daughter of smoke and bone trilogy) (hardcover) $18.99
Grades: 9 10 11 12   **Fic**
    1. Occult fiction 2. Fantasy fiction 3. Angels -- Fiction 4. Demonology -- Fiction 5. Supernatural -- Fiction 6. Czech Republic -- Fiction 7. Mythology, Greek -- Fiction 8. Prague (Czech Republic) -- Fiction 9. Chimera (Greek mythology) -- Fiction
    ISBN 0316133973; 9780316133975
                                        LC 2012028752
Sequel to: Daughter of smoke and bone
In this fantasy sequel to "Daughter of Smoke and Bone," "Karou . . . has taken up the resurrection work . . . under the direction of the dangerous chimaera leader, Thiago. . . . The angel army is menacing the countryside in an attempt to kill the remaining chimaera, so she is designing and resurrecting stronger, more effective winged warriors to protect her people." (Bulletin of the Center for Children's Books)

Dreams of gods & monsters; by Laini Taylor. Little, Brown and Co. 2014 624 p. (hardback) $19
Grades: 8 9 10 11 12   **Fic**
    1. Angels -- Fiction 2. Supernatural -- Fiction 3. Good and evil -- Fiction 4. Greek mythology -- Fiction 5. Fantasy 6. Demonology -- Fiction 7. Mythology, Greek -- Fiction 8. Chimera (Greek mythology) -- Fiction
    ISBN 0316134074; 9780316134071
                                        LC 2014003645
"In Taylor's third and final installment in her Daughter of Smoke and Bone trilogy, Karou and Akiva's dream of peace and a life together comes tantalizingly close, only to be repeatedly thwarted by their peoples' separate and conflicting histories, both mystical and real. Joined by angels and chimaera, Karou and Akiva lead their armies and fight side by side to prevent the apocalypse by banishing Jael, captain of the Dominion of Seraphim, from the earth he is determined to destroy." (Booklist)
    "Eliza Jones, a research fellow at Smithsonian's National Museum of Natural History, wakes from a recurring nightmare to the discovery that angels have appeared in the sky above Uzbekistan. Unbeknownst to Eliza, she is the linchpin upon which the salvation of worlds depends. The battle is well and truly on in this finale to the "Daughter of Smoke and Bone" trilogy (Little, Brown)... The conclusion promises resurrection, renewal, and long-postponed love happily resolved, and that should satisfy even the most meticulous fans." (School Library Journal)

Taylor, Mildred D.
    ★ The **land**. Phyllis Fogelman Bks. 2001 375p $17.99; pa $6.99
Grades: 7 8 9 10   **Fic**
    1. Race relations -- Fiction 2. African Americans -- Fiction 3. Racially mixed people -- Fiction
    ISBN 0-8037-1950-7; 0-14-250146-8 pa
                                        LC 00-39329
Prequel to Roll of Thunder, Hear My Cry
Coretta Scott King Award for text
After the Civil War Paul-Edward Logan, the son of a white father and a black mother, finds himself caught between the two worlds of colored folks and white folks as he pursues his dream of owning land of his own.
    "Taylor masterfully uses harsh historical realities to frame a powerful coming-of-age story that stands on its own merits." Horn Book Guide

Roll of thunder, hear my cry; 25th anniversary ed; Phyllis Fogelman Books 2001 276p $17.99; pa $7.99
Grades: 4 5 6 7 8 9   **Fic**
    1. Mississippi -- Fiction 2. African Americans -- Fiction
    ISBN 0-8037-2647-3; 0-14-240112-9 pa
                                        LC 00-39378
First published 1976 by Dial Press
Awarded the Newbery Medal, 1977
"The time is 1933. The place is Spokane, Mississippi where the Logans, the only black family who own their own land, wage a courageous struggle to remain independent, displeasing a white plantation owner bent on taking their land. But this suspenseful tale is also about the story's young narrator, Cassie, and her three brothers who decide to wage

their own personal battles to maintain the self-dignity and pride with which they were raised. .... Ms. Taylor's richly textured novel shows a strong, proud black family . . . resisting rather than succumbing to oppression." Child Book Rev Serv

Teller, Janne

★ **Nothing**; translated from the Danish by Martin Aitken. Atheneum Books for Young Readers 2010 227p $16.99

Grades: 7 8 9 10 11 12   **Fic**

1. School stories 2. Meaning (Philosophy) -- Fiction
ISBN 978-1-4169-8579-2; 1-4169-8579-4

LC 2009-19784

Michael J. Printz honor book, 2011

When thirteen-year-old Pierre Anthon leaves school to sit in a plum tree and train for becoming part of nothing, his seventh grade classmates set out on a desperate quest for the meaning of life.

"Indelible, elusive, and timeless, this uncompromising novel has all the marks of a classic." Booklist

Templeman, McCormick

The **glass** casket; McCormick Templeman. Delacorte Press 2014 352 p. (hc) $17.99

Grades: 9 10 11 12   **Fic**

1. Villages -- Fiction 2. Supernatural -- Fiction 3. Fairy tales 4. Love -- Fiction 5. Murder -- Fiction 6. Witches -- Fiction 7. Community life -- Fiction
ISBN 0385743459; 9780375991134; 9780385743457

LC 2013001970

In this young adult fantasy novel, by McCormick Templeman, "one bleak morning, . . . five horses and their riders thunder into [Rowan's] village and through the forest, disappearing into the hills. Days later, the riders' bodies are found. . . . Something has followed the path those riders made and has come down from the hills, through the forest, and into the village. Beast or man, it has brought death to Rowan's door." (Publisher's note)

"Templeman pulls a 180 from her incisive contemporary debut, The Little Woods (2012), with a fantasy involving witches, magic, and monsters...The story doesn't always fire, but, in fact, Templeman is at her best when leaving plot behind, as when one character's death acts as a sort of forbidden fruit leading to unleashed sexual passion—it's challenging, dizzying material. The legion of Maggie Stiefvater fans out there ought to look this way." (Booklist)

Teran, Andi

Ana of California; a novel. Andi Teran. Penguin Books 2015 368 p. (paperback) $16

Grades: 11 12 Adult   **Fic**

1. Farms -- Fiction 2. Foster children -- Fiction 3. California -- Fiction 4. Teenage girls -- Family relationships -- Fiction
ISBN 0143126490; 9780143126492

LC 2014042525

"Fifteen-year-old orphan Ana Cortez has just blown her last chance with a foster family. She agrees to leave East Los Angeles for a farm trainee program in Northern California. Emmett Garber is skeptical that this slight city girl can be any help on his farm. His sister Abbie, however, thinks

Ana might be just what they need. Ana comes to love Garber Farm. But when she inadvertently stirs up trouble in town, Ana is afraid she might have ruined her last chance." (Publisher's note)

"Teran presents a modern riff on the beloved classic Anne of Green Gables . . . [and] populates her novel with modern bugbears--drugs, gang violence, and hipsters. Newcomers will find a smart-mouthed heroine, a small town populated by a cast of lovable characters, and zippy dialogue that keeps the plot trotting along." Kirkus

Terrill, Cristin

All our yesterdays; Cristin Terrill. Hyperion 2013 368 p. (hardback) $17.99

Grades: 7 8 9 10 11 12   **Fic**

1. Science fiction 2. Time travel -- Fiction 3. Love -- Fiction 4. Murder -- Fiction
ISBN 1423176375; 9781423176374

LC 2013008007

In this book, narrator "Em and her boyfriend, Finn, escape from their totalitarian future, time traveling back four years to commit a heart-wrenching assassination of a loved one in order to prevent time travel from being invented and the future from turning so wrong. . . . The other side of the storyline, taking place in the past that Em and Finn travel to and starring their past selves, is narrated by Marina" and talks about her best friend and crush, James. (Kirkus Reviews)

Terry, Chris L.

Zero fade; Chris L Terry. Curbside Splendor Publishing 2013 294 p. $12

Grades: 7 8 9 10   **Fic**

1. School stories 2. Bullies -- Fiction 3. Historical fiction
ISBN 0988480433; 9780988480438

LC 2013944486

This book focuses on Kevin Phifer, "a black seventh-grader in 1990s Richmond, Va." He "wants a fade, thinking the stylish haircut will bolster his shaky standing in the cut-throat world of middle school, where he's just one friend away from eating lunch alone. But his mother, a church secretary and solo parent studying for a nursing degree at night, won't even try. Expressing his frustration leads to a week's grounding. Tyrell and his entourage of bullies make Kevin's life miserable at school." (Kirkus Reviews)

"Original, hilarious, thought-provoking and wicked smart: not to be missed." (Kirkus)

Terry, Teri

Fractured; Teri Terry. Nancy Paulsen Books 2013 336 p. (Slated trilogy) $17.99

Grades: 7 8 9 10   **Fic**

1. Dystopian fiction 2. Memory -- Fiction 3. Science fiction 4. England -- Fiction 5. Schools -- Fiction 6. Identity -- Fiction 7. Terrorism -- Fiction 8. High schools -- Fiction
ISBN 0399161732; 9780399161735

LC 2012044317

Author Teri Terry presents the "second installment of the Slated trilogy . . . set in a future where violent teens have their memory erased as an alternative to jail. Kyla has been Slated--her personality wiped blank, her memories lost to her forever. Or so she thought. When a mysterious man from her past comes back into her life and wants her help, she thinks she's on her way to finding the truth." (Publisher's note)

"Kyla's memories, wiped by the government in Slated, are slowly returning; she's been found by an anti-government group that claims she's a member and wants her to complete one last mission. Kyla's struggles to uncover her identity and think through the consequences of her actions are realistic and add an emotional backbone to this fast-paced middle volume of the trilogy." (Horn Book)

Slated; Teri Terry. Nancy Paulsen Books 2013 346 p. (hardcover) $17.99

Grades: 7 8 9 10   **Fic**
1. Science fiction 2. Memory -- Fiction 3. Identity -- Fiction 4. Schools -- Fiction 5. High schools -- Fiction 6. Family life -- England -- Fiction
ISBN 0399161724; 9780399161728
    LC 2012020873
In this novel, by Teri Terry, "Kyla has been Slated--her memory and personality erased as punishment for committing a crime she can't remember. The government has taught her how to walk and talk again, given her a new identity and a new family, and told her to be grateful for this second chance that she doesn't deserve. It's also her last chance--because they'll be watching to make sure she plays by their rules." (Publisher's note)

Testa, Dom

The **Cassini** code. Tor Teen 2010 283p (Galahad) pa $8.99

Grades: 7 8 9 10 11 12   **Fic**
1. Science fiction 2. Interplanetary voyages -- Fiction
ISBN 978-0-7653-6079-3; 0-7653-6079-9
First published 2008 by Profound Impact Group with title: Galahad 3
"The teen crew members of the starship Galahad find themselves navigating the treacherous asteroid field known as the Kuiper Belt with only their onboard computer, Roc, to guide them. Simultaneously, one crew member needs an emergency operation, while a boy named Merit begins leading a mutinous movement known as R.T.E. (Return to Earth). As before, Testa relies on interpersonal dynamics more than action, but his pacing has never been finer, making this the most satisfying entry yet." Booklist

The **comet's** curse. Tor Teen 2009 236p (Galahad) $16.95

Grades: 7 8 9 10 11 12   **Fic**
1. Science fiction 2. Interplanetary voyages -- Fiction
ISBN 978-0-7653-2107-7; 0-7653-2107-6
    LC 2008-35620
First published 2005 by Profound Impact Group
Desperate to save the human race after a comet's deadly particles devastate the adult population, scientists create a ship that will carry a crew of 251 teenagers to a home in a distant solar system.

This book is "both a mystery and an adventure, combining a solid cast of characters with humor, pathos, growing pains and just a hint of romance." Kirkus

Other titles in this series are:
The Cassini code (2010)

Cosmic storm (2011)
The dark zone (2011)
The web of Titan (2009)

Cosmic storm. Tor Teen 2011 267p (Galahad) $16.99

Grades: 7 8 9 10   **Fic**
1. Science fiction 2. Interplanetary voyages -- Fiction
ISBN 978-0-7653-2111-4; 0-7653-2111-4
    LC 2011021556
One year into their mission, as the teenaged crew of the Galahad is faced with waves of radiation that threaten the survival of their ship, Council leader Triana disappears and the crew must decide how to deal with assaults from both the outside and within their ranks.

Testa's "got his act down so well that it remains highly pleasurable." Booklist

The **dark** zone; a Galahad book. Tor 2011 284p (Galahad) $16.99

Grades: 7 8 9 10   **Fic**
1. Science fiction 2. Interplanetary voyages -- Fiction
ISBN 978-0-7653-2110-7; 0-7653-2110-6
    LC 2010052388
After navigating safely through the minefield of the Kuiper Belt, the teenaged crew of Galahad, led by Triana, decides to push forward through a group of incredibly fast and maneuverable organisms, setting off a cataclysmic series of events.

"Testa's teens remain refreshingly grounded, perceptive, and intelligent." Booklist

The **web** of Titan. Tor Teen 2010 255p (Galahad) pa $8.99

Grades: 7 8 9 10   **Fic**
1. Science fiction 2. Interplanetary voyages -- Fiction
ISBN 978-0-7653-6078-6; 0-7653-6078-0
Sequel to: The comet's curse (2009)
First published 2006 by Profound Impact Group
As the spaceship Galahad passes Titan, one of Saturn's moons, the teenage crew discovers a strange pod orbiting the moon, and when they investigate they face a crippling illness that is affecting the crew.

Followed by: The Cassini code (2010)

Tharp, Tim

Badd. Alfred A. Knopf 2011 308p $16.99; lib bdg $19.99; ebook $10.99

Grades: 9 10 11 12   **Fic**
1. Siblings -- Fiction 2. Iraq War, 2003- -- Fiction 3. Post-traumatic stress disorder -- Fiction
ISBN 978-0-375-86444-5; 978-0-375-96444-2 lib bdg; 978-0-375-89579-1 ebook
    LC 2010-12732
A teenaged girl's beloved brother returns home from the Iraq War completely unlike the person she remembers.

"With convincing three-dimensional characters, Tharp paints a sympathetic portrait of the constraints of small town life, the struggles of PTSD, and the challenges of faith." Publ Wkly

Knights of the hill country. Alfred A. Knopf 2006 233p hardcover o.p. pa $6.99

Grades: 8 9 10 11 12   **Fic**
1. School stories 2. Football -- Fiction 3. Oklahoma -- Fiction

ISBN 978-0-375-83653-4; 0-375-83653-5; 978-0-553-49513-3 pa; 0-553-49513-5 pa

LC 2005-33279

In his senior year, high school star linebacker Hampton Greene finally begins to think for himself and discovers that he might be interested in more than just football.

"Taut scenes on the football field and the dilemmas about choosing what feels right over what's expected are all made memorable by Hamp's unforgettable, colloquial voice." Booklist

★ The **spectacular** now. Alfred A. Knopf 2008 294p $16.99; lib bdg $19.99

Grades: 9 10 11 12   **Fic**
1. School stories 2. Oklahoma -- Fiction 3. Alcoholism -- Fiction 4. Stepfamilies -- Fiction 5. Dating (Social customs) -- Fiction

ISBN 978-0-375-85179-7; 978-0-375-95179-4 lib bdg; 0-375-95179-2 lib bdg

LC 2008-03544

In the last months of high school, charismatic eighteen-year-old Sutter Keely lives in the present, staying drunk or high most of the time, but that could change when he starts working to boost the self-confidence of a classmate, Aimee.

"Tharp offers a poignant, funny book about a teen who sees his life as livable only when his senses are dulled by drink . . . . Sutter is an authentic character [who] . . . will strike a chord with teen readers." Booklist

Thomas, Kara

The **darkest** corners; Kara Thomas. Delacorte Press 2016 336 p. (hc) $17.99

Grades: 9 10 11 12   **Fic**
1. Mystery fiction 2. Murder -- Fiction 3. Secrets -- Fiction 4. Sisters -- Fiction 5. Friendship -- Fiction 6. Pennsylvania -- Fiction 7. Youths' writings 8. Serial murderers -- Fiction 9. Detective and mystery stories 10. Mystery and detective stories

ISBN 9780553521450; 9780553521467

LC 2015004181

In this book, by Kara Thomas, "there are secrets around every corner in Fayette, Pennsylvania. Tessa left when she was nine and has been trying ever since not to think about what happened there that last summer. She and her childhood best friend Callie never talked about what they saw. Not before the trial. And certainly not after. But ever since she left, Tessa has had questions. Things have never quite added up." (Publisher's note)

"On the heels of TV documentaries Making a Murderer and The Jinx comes a psychological thriller strongly rooted in the true-crime tradition. Ten years ago, Tessa provided an eyewitness statement in the case of the Ohio River Monster, a serial killer whose last target was her best friend's cousin, Lori. Returning to Fayette, Pennsylvania, to say good-bye to her dying convict father, Tessa is stunned by the murder of another childhood friend in circumstances mirroring those of the murders 10 years ago. . . . Equally concerned with a

quest for the truth and the powerful motivation of guilt, this compelling novel won't linger on the shelf." Booklist

Thomas, Lex

Quarantine; 2 the Saints. by Lex Thomas. Egmont USA 2013 400 p. (Quarantine)

Grades: 9 10 11 12   **Fic**
1. Gangs -- Fiction 2. Diseases -- Fiction 3. High schools -- Fiction 4. Science fiction 5. Schools -- Fiction 6. Survival -- Fiction 7. Virus diseases -- Fiction 8. Interpersonal relations -- Fiction

ISBN 1606843362; 9781606843369

LC 2013008605

In this novel by Lex Thomas "McKinley High has been a battle ground . . . since a virus outbreak led to a military quarantine. When the doors finally open . . . a new group of teens enters the school and gains popularity. An epic party . . . where kids hookup and actually interact with members of other gangs seemed to signal a new, easier existence. But soon after, the world inside McKinley takes a startling turn for the worse, and Will and Lucy will have to fight harder than ever to survive." (Publisher's note)

Followed by The Burnouts

Quarantine 3: The Burnouts; Lex Thomas. Egmont USA 2014 272 p. (Quarantine) (hardback) $17.99

Grades: 9 10 11 12   **Fic**
1. Dystopias 2. Science fiction 3. Schools -- Fiction 4. Survival -- Fiction 5. Quarantine -- Fiction 6. High schools -- Fiction

ISBN 1606843389; 9781606843383

LC 2014003027

"In the third and final Quarantine book [by Lex Thomas], David and Will are alive . . . but on the outside of McKinley High. Lucy is the last of the trinity left inside, where Hilary will exact a deadly revenge before taking over McKinley and bringing one final reign of terror to the school before the doors open for good. But the outside world is just as dangerous for carriers of the virus." (Publisher's note)

"Even if someone tried to put a parental guidance sticker on this title, it would blister right off from the toxic rot inside. Two years after the escaped virus that got McKinley High sealed off from the world in Quarantine: The Loners (2012), the school has become a thunderdome of thuggery, violence, prostitution, and drugs...This trilogy-ender is the hastiest of the three—important moments are rushed through with regularity—but as a capper to this undersung "psycho soap opera," it sure does its dirty job. One character's last words sum up the whole mad series: "Peace, fuck, barf, love." Booklist

Thomas, Rob

Rats saw God. Simon & Schuster Bks. for Young Readers 1996 219p hardcover o.p. pa $6.99

Grades: 7 8 9 10   **Fic**
1. School stories 2. Father-son relationship -- Fiction

ISBN 0-689-80207-2; 1-4169-3897-4 pa

LC 95-43548

"The sharp descriptions of cliques, clubs and annoying authority figures will strike a familiar chord. The dialogue is fresh and Steve's intelligent banter and introspective musings never sound wiser than his years." Publ Wkly

Thomas, Sherry

The **burning** sky; by Sherry Thomas. Balzer + Bray 2013 480 p. (hardcover bdg.) $17.99

Grades: 7 8 9 10 11 12   **Fic**

1. Fantasy fiction 2. Magic -- Fiction 3. Fantasy
ISBN 0062207296; 9780062207296

LC 2013014504

This book, by author Sherry Thomas presents "the story of a girl who fooled a thousand boys, a boy who fooled an entire country, a partnership that would change the fate of realms, and a power to challenge the greatest tyrant the world had ever known." (Publisher's note)

"When sixteen-year-old elemental mage Iolanthe summons a lightning bolt, she draws the unwelcome attention of the Inquisitor of Atlantis. She also draws the eye of resistance fighter Prince Titus, who rescues her and disguises her as a boy. Heightened action combined with Scarlet Pimpernel-esque cleverness will keep readers eagerly turning pages, while the romantic tension adds juiciness to the fantasy plot." (Horn Book)

Other titles in the series are:
The Perilous Sea (2014)
The Immortal Heights (2015)

Thompson, Holly

The **language** inside; Holly Thompson. 1st ed. Delacorte Press 2013 528 p. (hardcover) $17.99

Grades: 7 8 9 10 11 12   **Fic**

1. Novels in verse 2. Moving -- Fiction 3. Interpersonal relations -- Fiction 4. Japan -- Fiction 5. Cancer -- Fiction 6. Tsunamis -- Fiction 7. Massachusetts -- Fiction 8. Moving, Household -- Fiction 9. Family life -- Massachusetts -- Fiction
ISBN 0385739796; 9780375898358; 9780385739795; 9780385908078

LC 2012030596

In this novel in verse, by Holly Thompson, "Emma's family moves to a town outside Lowell, Massachusetts, to stay with Emma's grandmother while her mom undergoes treatment. Emma feels out of place in the United States. She begins to have migraines, and longs to be back in Japan. At her grandmother's urging, she volunteers in a long-term care center to help Zena, a patient with locked-in syndrome, write down her poems." (Publisher's note)

Includes bibliographical references (p. 520).

Orchards; Holly Thompson; illustrations by Grady McFerrin. Delacorte Press 2011 327p il $17.99; lib bdg $20.99

Grades: 7 8 9 10   **Fic**

1. Novels in verse 2. Japan -- Fiction 3. Suicide -- Fiction 4. Bereavement -- Fiction 5. Family life -- Fiction 6. Racially mixed people -- Fiction
ISBN 978-0-385-73977-1; 0-385-73977-X; 978-0-385-90806-1 lib bdg; 0-385-90806-7 lib bdg

LC 2010-23724

"After a classmate commits suicide, Kana, a half-Japanese, half-Jewish American eighth grader, is sent to her maternal grandmother's farm in rural Japan for personal reflec-

tion. Kana tells her story in poignantly straightforward verse directed at the deceased classmate as she struggles with blame and regret, wondering if she and her friends are responsible because they took part in ostracizing the girl. She struggles, too, with her biracial, bicultural identity, feeling isolated in her new surroundings." (School Library Journal)

"Kanako's urgent teen voice, written in rapid free verse and illustrated with occasional black-and-white sketches, will hold readers with its nonreverential family story." Booklist

Thompson, Kate

Creature of the night. Roaring Brook Press 2008 250p $17.95

Grades: 9 10 11 12   **Fic**

1. Ireland -- Fiction 2. Homicide -- Fiction 3. Juvenile delinquency -- Fiction
ISBN 978-1-59643-511-7; 1-59643-511-9

Bobby lives a reckless life smoking, drinking, and stealing cars in Dublin. So his mother moves the family to the country. But Bobby suspects their cottage might not be as quaint as it seems. And spooky details of the history of their little cottage gradually turn Bobby into a detective of night creatures real and imagined.

"A unique blend of subtlety and brashness, this is an honest coming-of-age novel in the guise of a gripping YA thriller." Booklist

The **last** of the High Kings. Greenwillow Books 2008 323p hardcover o.p. pa $8.99

Grades: 7 8 9 10   **Fic**

1. Fantasy fiction 2. Fairies -- Fiction 3. Ireland -- Fiction 4. Musicians -- Fiction 5. Family life -- Fiction 6. Mythical animals -- Fiction
ISBN 978-0-06-117595-4; 0-06-117595-1; 978-0-06-117597-8 pa; 0-06-117597-8 pa

LC 2007-37467

Sequel to: The new policeman (2007)

When eleven-year-old Jenny Liddy, in turmoil over learning that she is a changeling, makes a deal with a devil creature, she endangers the human race but her own cleverness, her human and fairy fathers, and the last of Ireland's High Kings help to make things right.

"Resonantly Irish, Thompson's storytelling still easily leaps geographical and cultural boundries." Horn Book

Followed by: The white horse trick (2010)

The **new** policeman. Greenwillow Books 2007 442p hardcover o.p. pa $8.99

Grades: 7 8 9 10   **Fic**

1. Fantasy fiction 2. Music -- Fiction 3. Fairies -- Fiction 4. Ireland -- Fiction 5. Space and time -- Fiction
ISBN 978-0-06-117427-8; 0-06-117427-0; 978-0-06-117429-2 pa; 0-06-117429-7 pa

LC 2006-8246

First published 2005 in the United Kingdom

Irish teenager JJ Liddy discovers that time is leaking from his world into Tir na nOg, the land of the fairies, and when he attempts to stop the leak he finds out a lot about his family history, the music that he loves, and a crime his great-grandfather may or may not have committed.

"Mesmerizing and captivating, this book is guaranteed to charm fantasy fans." Voice Youth Advocates

Other titles in this series are:
The last of the High Kings (2008)
The white horse trick (2010)

The **white** horse trick. Greenwillow Books 2010 405p

Grades: 7 8 9 10   **Fic**
1. Fantasy fiction 2. Fairies -- Fiction 3. Ireland -- Fiction 4. Refugees -- Fiction 5. Family life -- Fiction
ISBN 0-06-200416-6; 0-06-200417-4 lib bdg; 978-0-06-200416-1; 978-0-06-200417-8 lib bdg
                                        LC 2010-10287

Sequel to: The last of the High Kings (2008)
First published 2009 in the United Kingdom

This is the "final volume of a trilogy that began with The New Policeman [2007] and continued with The Last of the High Kings [2008]. Former protagonist J.J. Liddy, now an old man, has retired to the fairy world, but his sons, Aidan and Donal, are wreaking havoc in the human realm. They have become warlords in a world ravaged beyond repair by global warming. . . . Middle school, high school." (Horn Book)

The author "offers readers a taste of genre-bending that is both challenging and successful." Booklist

Thompson, Ricki

City of cannibals. Front Street 2010 269p $18.95

Grades: 8 9 10 11 12   **Fic**
1. Monks -- Fiction 2. Persecution -- Fiction 3. Runaway teenagers -- Fiction 4. Great Britain -- History -- 1485-1603, Tudors -- Fiction
ISBN 978-1-59078-623-9; 1-59078-623-8
                                        LC 2010-2105

In 1536 England, sixteen-year-old Dell runs away from her brutal father and life in a cave carrying only a handmade puppet to travel to London, where she learns truths about her mother's death and the conflict between King Henry VIII and the Catholic Church.

"Thompson's England is authentically vulgar, and her grasp of period slang—as well as Dell's burgeoning sexual desires—is expert. Packed with rich metaphor, this is a challenging but rewarding read." Booklist

Thor, Annika

Deep sea; Annika Thor; translated from the Swedish by Linda Schenck. First American edition Delacorte Press 2015 240 p. (hc) $17.99

Grades: 7 8 9 10 11 12   **Fic**
1. Jews -- Fiction 2. Sweden -- Fiction 3. Sisters -- Fiction 4. Refugees -- Fiction 5. Friendship -- Fiction 6. World War, 1939-1945 -- Refugees -- Fiction 7. Schools -- Fiction 8. Jews -- Sweden -- Fiction 9. Sweden -- History -- Gustav V, 1907-1950 -- Fiction
ISBN 0385743858; 9780375991325; 9780385743853
                                        LC 2014005586

Sequel to The Lily Pond

In this book, by Annika Thor, "Stephie and her younger sister, Nellie, escaped the Nazis in Vienna and fled to an island in Sweden, where they were taken in by different

families. . . . Nellie wants to be adopted by her foster family. Stephie, on the other hand, can't stop thinking about her parents, who are in a Nazi camp in Austria." (Publisher's note)

"This novel about coming of age during a complicated, tragic time in history is both delicate and poignant, as when Stephie and Nellie sit on the dock, remembering a lullaby their mother sang. Thor's novel capably demonstrates the loneliness, powerlessness, and prejudice Stephie faces, as well as her growing inner strength." PW Annex

Tingle, Tim

House of purple cedar; by Tim Tingle. Cinco Puntos Press 2014 192 p. $16.95

Grades: 10 11 12   **Fic**
1. Oklahoma -- Fiction 2. Choctaw Indians -- Fiction 3. Choctaw Indians -- Oklahoma -- Fiction 4. Oklahoma -- History -- Land Rush, 1893 -- Fiction
ISBN 1935955241; 9781935955245; 9781935955696
                                        LC 2013010570

This book, by Tim Tingle, is "Rose Goode's story of . . . growing up in Indian Territory in pre-statehood Oklahoma. Skullyville, a once-thriving Choctaw community, was destroyed by land-grabbers, culminating in the arson on New Year's Eve, 1896, of New Hope Academy for Girls. Twenty Choctaw girls died, but Rose escaped. She is blessed by the presence of her grandmother Pokoni and her grandfather Amafo, both respected elders who understand the old ways." (Publisher's note)

"In 1896, as white settlers hungry for land flooded into Indian territory in what is now Oklahoma, a boarding school for Indian girls called the New Hope Academy was burned to the ground with a severe loss of life. It presaged the destruction of the Choctaw community, related here by fire survivor Rose Goode in measured but heartfelt language. VERDICT Tingle, who began interviewing Choctaw trible elders in the early 1990s, effectively recaptures a piece of buried history." LJ

Tolkien, J. R. R. (John Ronald Reuel), 1892-1973

★ The **hobbit,** or, There and back again. Houghton Mifflin 2001 330p il $18; pa $10

Grades: 5 6 7 8 9 10 11 12 Adult   **Fic**
1. Magic 2. Satire 3. Allegories 4. Fantasy fiction 5. Fantasies 6. Imaginary kingdoms
ISBN 0-618-16221-6; 0-618-26030-7 pa
                                        LC 2001276594

A reissue of the title first published 1938

"Bilbo Baggins is a hobbit who enjoys a comfortable, unambitious life, rarely traveling any farther than his pantry or cellar. But his contentment is disturbed when the wizard Gandalf and a company of dwarves arrive on his doorstep one day to whisk him away on an adventure. They have launched a plot to raid the treasure hoard guarded by Smaug the Magnificent, a large and very dangerous dragon. Bilbo reluctantly joins their quest, unaware that on his journey to the Lonely Mountain he will encounter both a magic ring and a frightening creature known as Gollum." (Publisher's note)

"This fantasy features the adventures of hobbit Bilbo Baggins, who joins a band of dwarves led by Gandalf the Wizard. Together they seek to recover the stolen treasure that is hidden in Lonely Mountain and guarded by Smaug the Dragon. This book precedes the Lord of the Rings trilogy." Shapiro. Fic for Youth. 3d edition

Followed by: The lord of the rings trilogy: The fellowship of the ring; The two towers; The return of the king

★ The **lord** of the rings; 50th Anniversary ed; Houghton Mifflin 2004 xxv, 1157p il map slip case $100

Grades: 7 8 9 10 11 12 Adult   **Fic**
1. Fantasy fiction
ISBN 0-618-51765-0

LC 2004-275215

First published 1954 in the United Kingdom

"This is a tale of imaginary gnomelike creatures who battle against evil. Led by Frodo, the hobbits embark on a journey to prevent a magic ring from falling into the grasp of the powers of darkness. The forces of good succeed in their fight against the Dark Lord of evil, and Frodo and Sam bring the Ring to Mount Doom, where it is destroyed." Shapiro. Fic for Youth. 3d edition

Tomlinson, Heather
Toads and diamonds. Henry Holt 2010 278p $16.99

Grades: 8 9 10 11 12   **Fic**
1. Fairy tales 2. India -- Fiction
ISBN 978-0-8050-8968-4; 0-8050-8968-3

LC 2009-23448

A retelling of the Perrault fairy tale set in pre-colonial India, in which two stepsisters receive gifts from a goddess and each walks her own path to find her gift's purpose, discovering romance along the way.

The author "creates a vivid setting. Lavish details starkly contrast the two girls' lives and personalities. . . . The complexities of the cultural backstory pose a challenge to readers, but this beautifully embroidered adventure is well worth the effort." Booklist

Torres Sanchez, Jenny
Death, Dickinson, and the demented life of Frenchie Garcia; by Jenny Torres Sanchez. Running Press 2013 272 p. (paperback) $9.95

Grades: 9 10 11 12   **Fic**
1. Grief -- Fiction 2. Suicide -- Fiction
ISBN 0762446803; 9780762446803

LC 2013934992

In this book, "Frenchie is in the limbo of what-comes-next. She's finished high school but has been rejected by art school. She is sullen and anxious and can't seem to get her life moving. Gradually, what happened that night with Andy and its lingering impact on Frenchie are revealed. It was the same night that Andy ended his own life. No one even knows that she liked Andy, let alone about the time they spent together, so Frenchie keeps her guilt and confusion to herself." (Kirkus Reviews)

Toten, Teresa
The **Unlikely** Hero of Room 13B; By Teresa Toten. Delacorte Press 2013 272 p. $17.99

Grades: 9 10 11 12   **Fic**
1. Love -- Fiction 2. Youth -- Fiction 3. Divorce -- Fiction 4. Obsessive-compulsive disorder -- Fiction 5. Schools 6. High schools 7. Dysfunctional families 8. Dating (Social customs) 9. Obsessive-compulsive

disorder 10. Emotional problems of teenagers
ISBN 0385678347; 0553507869; 9780385678346; 9780553507867

Schneider Family Book Award, Teen (2016)

In this young adult novel, by Teresa Toten, "when Adam meets Robyn at a support group for kids coping with obsessive-compulsive disorder, he is drawn to her almost before he can take a breath. . . . But when you're fourteen and the everyday problems of dealing with divorced parents and step-siblings are supplemented by the challenges of OCD, it's hard to imagine yourself falling in love." (Publisher's note)

"Fifteen-year-old Adam falls for Robyn in his teen OCD therapy group. Adam's insightful, steadfast support helps Robyn (and several other groupmates) improve--but Adam actually seems to get worse. While the tone is light overall (superhero group names!), there are plenty of touching, even wrenching, moments as Adam struggles to accept his own limitations and those of his loved ones." Horn Book

Treichel, Eliot
A **series** of small maneuvers; Eliot Treichel. Ooligan Press 2015 300 p. (trade paper: alk. paper) $14.95

Grades: 8 9 10 11   **Fic**
1. Grief -- Fiction 2. Father-daughter relationship -- Fiction 3. Fathers and daughters -- Fiction
ISBN 9781932010794

LC 2015020922

In this book, by Eliot Treichel, "Emma's growing up and feels isolated from her friends and family. Things go from bad to unfathomably worse when Emma inadvertently causes an accident that kills her increasingly distant father on a spring break canoe trip meant to bring them closer together. Suddenly, Emma's efforts to reconcile with her father as a parent and a person have to happen without him, and she must confront her guilt and her grief to begin moving forward." (Publisher's note)

"Dad's overbearing manner and the heavy factual overlay about rivers, canoeing, and all things outdoorsy may put some readers off, but this is a strong, coming-of-age tale, especially for those teens who would rather be adventuring in the great outdoors than doing anything else." Booklist

Trice, Dawn Turner
Only twice I've wished for heaven; a novel. Crown 1997 304p hardcover o.p. pa $13.50; pa 13.50

Grades: 11 12 Adult   **Fic**
1. Chicago (Ill.) -- Fiction 2. African Americans -- Fiction
ISBN 0-517-70428-5; 0-385-49123-9 pa; 9780385491235

LC 97-22164

"Trice creates vibrant characters via the counterpointed voices of Temmie and Jonetta. As each interprets events within the range of her knowledge and expectations, Trice obliquely provides insight into the crucial social issues that help shape the lives of African Americans." Publ Wkly

Tripp, Ben

The **accidental** highwayman; being the tale of Kit Bristol, his horse Midnight, a mysterious princess, and sundry magical persons besides. Ben Tripp. Tor Teen 2014 304 p. illustrations (hardback) $17.99

Grades: 7 8 9 10   **Fic**

1. Magic -- Fiction 2. Adventure fiction 3. Fairies -- Fiction 4. Princesses -- Fiction 5. Great Britain -- Fiction 6. Fate and fatalism -- Fiction 7. Robbers and outlaws -- Fiction 8. Adventure and adventurers -- Fiction 9. Great Britain -- History -- George III, 1760-1820 -- Fiction

ISBN 0765335492; 9780765335494

LC 2014033724

In this book, by Ben Tripp, "Christopher 'Kit' Bristol is the unwitting servant of notorious highwayman Whistling Jack. One dark night, Kit finds his master bleeding from a mortal wound, dons the man's riding cloak to seek help, and changes the course of his life forever. Mistaken for Whistling Jack and on the run from redcoats, . . . Kit takes up his master's quest to rescue a rebellious fairy princess from an arranged marriage to King George III of England." (Publisher's note)

"Readers will root for star-crossed lovers, Kit and Morgana, and delight in their 'opposites attract' romance, drawn onward by a rollicking plot . . . Fantasy readers, especially fans of Cathrynne Valente's work, will enjoy the author's elegant turns of phrase. A first purchase for all fantasy collections." SLJ

Tromly, Stephanie

Trouble is a friend of mine; by Stephanie Tromly. Kathy Dawson Books, an imprint of Penguin Group (USA) LLC 2015 336 p. (hardback) $17.99

Grades: 9 10 11 12   **Fic**

1. Mystery fiction 2. Moving -- Fiction 3. Divorce -- Fiction 4. High schools -- Fiction 5. Missing children -- Fiction 6. Schools -- Fiction 7. Moving, Household -- Fiction 8. Mystery and detective stories

ISBN 9780525428404

LC 2014040605

In this book, by Stephanie Tromly, "when Philip Digby first shows up on her doorstep, Zoe Webster is not impressed. He's rude and he treats her like a book he's already read and knows the ending to. But before she knows it, Digby--annoying, brilliant and somehow attractive?--has dragged her into a series of hilarious and dangerous situations all related to an investigation into the kidnapping of a local teenage girl." (Publisher's note)

"Zoe's sarcastic first-person narr ation is fresh and funny, and the zippy dialogue makes it easy to forgive a few moments when the action-packed plot strains readers' credulity. The highly stereotypical depiction of Felix, an Asian-American supporting character, is a notable exception to the generally solid characterization. Despite some flaws, an offbeat and entertaining caper." Kirkus

Trottier, Maxine

Three songs for courage. Tundra Books 2006 324p $16.95

Grades: 9 10 11 12   **Fic**

1. Canada -- Fiction 2. Bullies -- Fiction 3. Brothers -- Fiction 4. Homicide -- Fiction

ISBN 978-0-88776-745-6; 0-88776-745-1

LC 2005-927011

"From native wisdom to flatulence humor and from sexual assault to pigs in dresses, Trottier handles the serious with poignancy and lighter moments with flair. . . . This coming-of-age novel is rich, readable, and substantive." Voice Youth Advocates

Trueman, Terry

7 days at the hot corner. HarperTempest 2007 160p $15.99

Grades: 7 8 9 10   **Fic**

1. Baseball -- Fiction 2. Friendship -- Fiction 3. Homosexuality -- Fiction

ISBN 978-0-06-057494-9; 0-06-057494-1

LC 2006-03706

Varsity baseball player Scott Latimer struggles with his own prejudices and those of others when his best friend reveals that he is gay.

This "suspenseful story is enhanced by some late-inning surprises, the gay subplot is treated with honesty and integrity, and Scott and Travis are believable, sympathetic characters." Booklist

Life happens next; a novel. Terry Trueman. HarperTeen 2012 132 p. (trade bdg.) $17.99

Grades: 7 8 9 10   **Fic**

1. Love stories 2. Down syndrome -- Fiction 3. Cerebral palsy -- Fiction 4. Dogs -- Fiction 5. Communication -- Fiction 6. Seattle (Wash.) -- Fiction 7. Special education -- Fiction 8. People with disabilities -- Fiction 9. Family life -- Washington (State) -- Seattle -- Fiction

ISBN 0062028030; 9780062028037; 9780062028051

LC 2011044627

Sequel to: Stuck in neutral

This book is the sequel to author Terry Trueman's "Stuck in Neutral." Here, Shawn McDaniel, who has cerebral palsy, "fantasizes about his sister's best friend, Ally, and what it would be like if he ever got up the courage to tell her how he felt about her." He is also dealing with "Debi, [who] moves in with them. . . . Debi has Down's syndrome and is often disruptive, but . . . she becomes the first person to connect with Shawn on more than a surface level." (Voice of Youth Advocates)

Stuck in neutral. HarperCollins Pubs. 2000 114p $14.95; lib bdg $16.89; pa $6.99

Grades: 7 8 9 10   **Fic**

1. Euthanasia -- Fiction 2. Cerebral palsy -- Fiction 3. Father-son relationship -- Fiction

ISBN 0-06-028519-2; 0-06-028518-4 lib bdg; 0-06-447213-2 pa

LC 99-37098

"Shawn McDaniel thinks his father is considering killing him. Of course, no one knows that Shawn is able to think at all because the 14-year-old, who has cerebral palsy, can't speak, interact, or control his movements and bodily functions. But Shawn is also a genius; he remembers everything that he hears and is even able to read." (Publisher's note)

Tucholke, April Genevieve

Between the devil and the deep blue sea; by April Genevieve Tucholke. Dial Books 2013 368 p. (hardcover) $17.99

Grades: 7 8 9 10 **Fic**
1. Horror fiction 2. Mystery fiction
ISBN 0803738897; 9780803738898

LC 2012035586

In this horror novel, "Violet White and her 17-year-old twin brother are living in the dilapidated glory of their family's coastal estate while their parents traipse Europe. To help pay the bills, Violet places an ad for a boarder for their guesthouse; it's quickly answered by River West, a mysterious boy who cannily avoids giving straight answers about his past. Violet doesn't typically pay boys much mind, but she's soon spending the night with River, both drawn to and wary of him." (Publishers Weekly)

"It's no coincidence that when the alluring River West shows up to rent the guesthouse of Violet's dilapidated seaside mansion, eerie and brutal things begin to happen in town. Yet love-struck Violet finds herself powerless to act, or really care. A highly atmospheric and unreliable narrative wends its way between scenes alternately homey and macabre to a twisty ending." (Horn Book)

Followed by Between the Spark and the Burn

Between the spark and the burn; April Genevieve Tucholke. Dial Books 2014 368 p. (hardback) $17.99

Grades: 7 8 9 10 **Fic**
1. Gothic romances 2. Adventure fiction 3. Love -- Fiction 4. Trust -- Fiction 5. Good and evil -- Fiction
ISBN 0803740476; 9780803740471

LC 2013048697

Sequel to: Between the devil and the deep blue sea

In this gothic thriller young adult romance novel by April Genevieve Tucholke, "The crooked-smiling liar River West Redding, who drove into Violet's life one summer day and shook her world to pieces, is gone. Violet and Neely, River's other brother, are left to worry--until they catch a two a.m. radio program about strange events in a distant mountain town." (Publisher's note)

"The faded opulence of the setting is an ideal backdrop for this lushly atmospheric gothic thriller, which, happily, comes with a satisfying conclusion.Darkly romantic and evocative." Kirkus

Tucker, Todd

★ **Over** and under. Thomas Dunne Books/St. Martin's Press 2008 275p $23.95

Grades: 10 11 12 Adult **Fic**
1. Indiana -- Fiction 2. Friendship -- Fiction 3. Labor disputes -- Fiction 4. City and town life -- Fiction
ISBN 978-0-312-37990-2; 0-312-37990-0

LC 2008-12472

"A bitter 1979 labor strike at southern Indiana's Borden Casket Company serves as the volatile backdrop for this haunting coming-of-age novel. . . . With their fathers on opposite sides of the dispute, Andrew Jackson Gray and Thomas Jefferson Kruer, both 14, learn there is more to life than exploring caves, shooting targets with their prized M-6 Scout rifles and sneaking out on starry nights to run through

the woods. . . . Tucker convincingly makes Andy's voice at once eloquent and gritty, and makes the rural Indiana landscape palpable." Publ Wkly

Turner, Megan Whalen

A **conspiracy** of kings. Greenwillow Books 2010 316p $16.99; lib bdg $17.89

Grades: 7 8 9 10 **Fic**
1. Adventure fiction 2. Princes -- Fiction 3. Kidnapping -- Fiction 4. Kings and rulers -- Fiction
ISBN 978-0-06-187093-4; 0-06-187093-5; 978-0-06-187094-1 lib bdg; 0-06-187094-3 lib bdg

LC 2009-23052

Boston Globe-Horn Book Honor: Fiction (2010)

Kidnapped and sold into slavery, Sophos, an unwilling prince, tries to save his country from being destroyed by rebellion and exploited by the conniving Mede empire.

"Given the complexity of Turner's plot, readers should reread the first three books before beginning this one, which derives its power from the intricate construction of Turner's imagined world, a realm in which her founding mythology is as impressive as her descriptions of the land itself. . . . Strong evidence emerges that the story doesn't end here, and fans will savor this while they wait for more." Publ Wkly

The **King** of Attolia. Greenwillow Books 2006 387p lib bdg $17.89; paperback 9.99; $16.99

Grades: 7 8 9 10 **Fic**
1. Adventure fiction
ISBN 0-06-083578-8 lib bdg; 9780062642981; 0-06-083577-X

LC 2005-40303

Eugenides, still known as a Thief of Eddis, faces palace intrigue and assassins as he strives to prove himself both to the people of Attolia and to his new bride, their queen.

"Fans who've been waiting . . . for the sequel to The Queen of Attolia (2000) and The Thief (1996. . .) can finally rejoice. . . . To appreciate the amazingly charismatic and beguiling character of Eugenides fully, its best to read the titles in order." SLJ

The **Queen** of Attolia. Greenwillow Bks. 2000 279p pa $9.99

Grades: 6 7 8 9 **Fic**
1. Adventure fiction 2. Thieves -- Fiction
ISBN 0-688-17423-X; 0-06-084182-6 pa; 9780062642974 pa

LC 99-26916

"In this intense, intelligent sequel to The Thief . . . , war breaks out among three Balkanesque countries, engendering a series of crafty maneuvers and terrifying, high-stakes gambles. The uneasy balance between mountainous Eddis and larger neighbors Attolia and Sounis tips when Eugenides, the Queen of Eddis's official Thief, is captured by the ruthless young Queen of Attolia, and has his right hand struck off. Reprisals escalate, until Eddis is attacked on two sides and, ominously, troop ships from the huge Mede Empire approach. Turner creates a complex web of intrigue, hidden motives, feints, and counterfeints." (Kirkus)

★ The **thief.** Greenwillow Bks. 1996 219p $17.99; pa $6.99; 9.99

Grades: 7 8 9 10   **Fic**
1. Adventure fiction 2. Thieves -- Fiction
ISBN 0-688-14627-9; 0-06-082497-2 pa;
9780062642967

LC 95-41040

A Newbery Medal honor book, 1997
"A tantalizing, suspenseful, exceptionally clever novel.
. . . The author's characterization of Gen is simply superb."
Horn Book

Other titles in this series are:
A conspiracy of kings (2010)
The King of Attolia (2006)
The Queen of Attolia (2000)

Unsworth, Tania
The **one** safe place; a novel. by Tania Unsworth.
Algonquin Young Readers 2014 304 p. $15.95
Grades: 6 7 8 9 10   **Fic**
1. Dystopian fiction 2. Orphans -- Fiction 3. Survival
skills -- Fiction 4. Abandoned children -- Fiction 5.
Science fiction 6. Survival -- Fiction
ISBN 1616203293; 9781616203290

LC 2013043145

This book, by Tania Unsworth, is a "near-future dystopia. . . . Devin doesn't remember life before the world got
hot; he has grown up farming the scorched earth with his
grandfather in their remote valley. When his grandfather
dies, Devin heads for the city. Once there, among the stark
glass buildings, he finds scores of children, just like him,
living alone on the streets. They tell him rumors of a place
for abandoned children, . . . but only the luckiest get there."
(Publisher's note)

"Orphaned twelve-year-old Devin is invited to live at
the paradisaical Home for Childhood, but something terrifying is happening to the children there. Devin's synesthesia, which makes him interesting to the Home's sinister
Administrator, may provide the key to their escape. Set in
a world of post climate change desperation, Unsworth's
story thoughtfully explores the theme of adults' nostalgia for
childhood." Horn Book

Valentine, Jenny
Broken soup. HarperTeen 2009 216p $16.99
Grades: 7 8 9 10   **Fic**
1. Bereavement -- Fiction 2. Family life -- Fiction 3.
London (England) -- Fiction
ISBN 978-0-06-085071-5; 0-06-085071-X

LC 2008-11719

A photographic negative and two surprising new friends
become the catalyst for healing as fifteen-year-old Rowan
struggles to keep her family and her life together after her
brother's death.

"The mystery Valentine sets in motion is quickly paced
and packed with revelations. . . . The main appeal of the
book, however, is her beautifully modulated tone. . . . Insightful details abound." Booklist

★ **Me,** the missing, and the dead. HarperTeen
2008 201p paper $8.99
Grades: 8 9 10 11   **Fic**
1. Death -- Fiction 2. Fathers -- Fiction 3. Missing
persons -- Fiction 4. London (England) -- Fiction 5.

Single parent family -- Fiction
ISBN 978-0-06-085068-5; 0-06-085068-X; 978-
0-06-085069-2 lib bdg; 0-06-085069-8 lib bdg;
9780060850708

LC 2007-14476

First published 2007 in the United Kingdom with title:
Finding Violet Park
ALA YALSA Morris Award finalist, 2009
When a series of chance events leaves him in possession of an urn with ashes, sixteen-year-old Londoner Lucas
Swain becomes convinced that its occupant, Violet Park, is
communicating with him, initiating a voyage of self-discovery that forces him to finally confront the events surrounding
his father's sudden disappearance.

"Part mystery, part magical realism, part story of personal growth, and in large part simply about a funny teenager
making light of his and his family's pain, this short novel is
engaging from start to finish." SLJ

Van de Ruit, John
Spud. Razorbill 2007 331p hardcover o.p. pa
$16.99
Grades: 6 7 8 9 10   **Fic**
1. School stories 2. South Africa -- Fiction
ISBN 978-1-59514-170-5; 0-14-302484-1; 978-1-
59514-187-3 pa; 1-59514-187-1 pa; 9781595141873

LC 2007-6065

In 1990, thirteen-year-old John "Spud" Milton, a prepu-
bescent choirboy, keeps a diary of his first year at an elite,
boys-only boarding school in South Africa.

"This raucous autobiographical novel about a scholarship boy in an elite boys' boarding school in 1990 is mainly
farce but also part coming-of-age tale." Booklist

Followed by Spud—the madness continues... (2008)

Van Diepen, Allison
Takedown; Allison van Diepen. Simon Pulse
2013 288 p. (hardcover edition: alk. paper) $16.99
Grades: 9 10 11 12   **Fic**
1. Hostages 2. Adventure fiction 3. Vendetta -- Fiction
4. Drug traffic -- Fiction 5. African Americans --
Fiction 6. Criminal investigation -- Fiction
ISBN 1442463112; 9781442463110; 9781442463127

LC 2012039237

In this book, "Joe is hosting a party in honor of his
favorite weekly wrestling show when a college student-
turned-murderer crashes the get-together and holds the
13-year-olds hostage. As the terrifying ordeal continues, Joe
thinks back about how he met each friend, their history together, and problems they are facing in their lives." (School
Library Journal)

Van Draanen, Wendelin
The **running** dream. Alfred A. Knopf 2011
336p $16.99; lib bdg $19.99
Grades: 7 8 9 10 11 12   **Fic**
1. School stories 2. Running -- Fiction 3. Amputees
-- Fiction 4. People with Disabilities -- Fiction
ISBN 978-0-375-86667-8; 0-375-86667-1; 978-0-375-
96667-5 lib bdg; 0-375-96667-6 lib bdg

LC 2010-07072

"It's a classic problem novel in a lot of ways. . . . Overall, though, this is a tremendously upbeat book. . . . Van Draanen's extensive research into both running and amputees pays dividends." Booklist

Vande Velde, Vivian

The **book** of Mordred; [illustrations by Justin Gerard] Houghton Mifflin 2005 342p hardcover o.p. pa $8.99

Grades: 8 9 10 11 12   **Fic**
1. Kings 2. Knights and knighthood -- Fiction 3. Mordred (Legendary character) -- Fiction 4. Great Britain -- History -- 0-1066 -- Fiction
ISBN 0-618-50754-X; 0-618-80916-3 pa
           LC 2004-28223

As the peaceful King Arthur reigns, the five-year-old daughter of Lady Alayna, newly widowed of the village-wizard Toland, is abducted by knights who leave their barn burning and their only servant dead.

"All of the characters are well developed and have a strong presence throughout. . . . [This] provides an intriguing counterpoint to anyone who is interested in Arthurian legend." SLJ

Remembering Raquel. Harcourt 2007 160p $16

Grades: 7 8 9 10 11   **Fic**
1. School stories 2. Death -- Fiction 3. Obesity -- Fiction
ISBN 978-0-15-205976-7
           LC 2006-35769

Various people recall aspects of the life of Raquel Falcone, an unpopular, overweight freshman at Quail Run High School, including classmates, her parents, and the driver who struck and killed her as she was walking home from an animated film festival.

"Easily booktalked and deeper than it initially seems, this will be popular with reluctant readers." Booklist

Vanhee, Jason

Engines of the broken world; Jason Vanhee. Henry Holt and Company 2013 272 p. (hardcover) $16.99

Grades: 8 9 10 11 12   **Fic**
1. Supernatural -- Fiction 2. Brothers and sisters -- Fiction 3. Science fiction
ISBN 0805096299; 9780805096293
           LC 2013026768

In this book, by Jason Vanhee, "Merciful Truth and her brother, Gospel, have just pulled their dead mother into the kitchen and stowed her under the table. It was a long illness, and they wanted to bury her--they did--but it's far too cold outside, and they know they won't be able to dig into the frozen ground. The Minister who lives with them, who preaches through his animal form, doesn't make them feel any better about what they've done." (Publisher's note)

"Unlike most action-packed dystopias, the story's slower pace . . . allows readers to feel the fog encroaching on Merciful and Gospel's rustic home, and hear every scratch of their dead mother's awkward movements upon the cellar stairs." Booklist

Vasey, Paul

A **troublesome** boy; by Paul Vasey. Groundwood Books/House of Anansi Press 2012 225 p.

Grades: 9 10 11 12   **Fic**
1. Priests -- Fiction 2. Friendship -- Fiction 3. Private schools -- Fiction
ISBN 1554981549; 9781554981540

In this novel, "14-year-old Teddy's . . . despised stepfather sends him off to St. Ignatius Academy for Boys, an isolated Roman Catholic boarding school. St. Iggy's is run by priests who ruthlessly enforce discipline through intimidation and abuse. . . . The boys use their wits and humor to cope, but the endless beatings and humiliations take their toll, especially on the fragile Cooper. He reaches his breaking point when he becomes the victim of Father Prince, a pedophile." (Kirkus Reviews)

Vaught, Susan

Big fat manifesto. Bloomsbury 2008 308p $16.95

Grades: 9 10 11 12   **Fic**
1. School stories 2. Obesity -- Fiction 3. Prejudices -- Fiction
ISBN 978-1-59990-206-7; 1-59990-206-0
           LC 2007-23550

Overweight, self-assured, high school senior Jamie Carcaterra writes in the school newspaper about her own attitude to being fat, her boyfriend's bariatric surgery, and her struggles to be taken seriously in a very thin world

"Jamie's forcefully articulated perspectives about body image and her well-justified anger provoke soul-searching at every turn. . . . Readers will not only be challenged but also changed by meeting Jamie." Bull Cent Child Books

Freaks like us; by Susan Vaught. Bloomsbury 2012 240 p. (hardcover) $16.99

Grades: 7 8 9 10 11 12   **Fic**
1. Friendship -- Fiction 2. Schizophrenia -- Fiction 3. Mental illness -- Fiction 4. Missing persons -- Fiction 5. Love -- Fiction 6. Missing children -- Fiction 7. Mystery and detective stories
ISBN 1599908727; 9781599908724
           LC 2012004227

This is the story of Jason, whose selectively mute friend Sunshine has "vanished, and Jason, whose schizophrenia has shaped his life, is a suspect in her disappearance. Seniors Jason, Drip and Sunshine have ridden the short bus and gone through school labeled SED--that's 'Severely Emotionally Disturbed.' Bullying at the hands of kids with behavioral disabilities goes unreported and unpunished, but the trio's alliance made life bearable in their catchall special ed program . . . . As the FBI investigates, Jason's always-shaky world threatens to come apart. Not taking "fuzzy pills" keeps his brain sharp, but the voices plaguing him grow louder. Jason carries Sunshine's secrets--should he break his promise not to tell?" (Kirkus)

Venkatraman, Padma

★ **Climbing** the stairs. G.P. Putnam's Sons 2008 247p $16.99

Grades: 6 7 8 9 10   **Fic**
1. Prejudices -- Fiction 2. Family life -- Fiction 3.

Brain -- Wounds and injuries -- Fiction 4. India -- History -- 1765-1947, British occupation -- Fiction
ISBN 978-0-399-24746-0; 0-399-24746-7

LC 2007-21757

In India, in 1941, when her father becomes brain-damaged in a non-violent protest march, fifteen-year-old Vidya and her family are forced to move in with her father's extended family and become accustomed to a totally different way of life.

"Venkatraman paints an intricate and convincing backdrop of a conservative Brahmin home in a time of change. . . . The striking cover art . . . will draw readers to this vividly told story." Booklist

★ A **time** to dance; Padma Venkatraman. Nancy Paulsen Books, an imprint of Penguin Group (USA) Inc. 2014 320 p. $17.99

Grades: 8 9 10 11 12   **Fic**
1. Novels in verse 2. Dance -- Fiction 3. India -- Fiction 4. Amputees -- Fiction 5. People with disabilities -- Fiction
ISBN 0399257101; 9780399257100

LC 2013024244

Author Padma Venkatraman's "story of a young girl's struggle to regain her passion and find a new peace is told lyrically through verse that captures the beauty and mystery of India and the ancient bharatanatyam dance form. . . . Veda, a classical dance prodigy in India, lives and breathes dance - so when an accident leaves her a below-knee amputee, her dreams are shattered. . . . But Veda refuses to let her disability rob her of her dreams, and she starts all over again." (Publisher's note)

"This free-verse novel set in contemporary India stars Veda, a teenage Bharatanatyam dancer. After a tragic accident, one of Veda's legs must be amputated below the knee. Veda tries a series of customized prosthetic legs, determined to return to dancing as soon as possible. Brief lines, powerful images, and motifs of sound communicate Veda's struggle to accept her changed body." Horn Book

Verdelle, A. J.

The **good** negress. Algonquin Bks. 1995 298p
H $19.95; pa $15.95

Grades: 11 12 Adult   **Fic**
1. Detroit (Mich.) -- Fiction 2. African Americans -- Fiction
ISBN 1-56512-085-X; 9781565120853; 9781616205270

LC 94-40889

"Verdelle's truly fine debut novel belongs in the ranks of other classics in African American folk vernacular." Choice

Vigan, Delphine de

No and me; translated by George Miller. Blooms-bury Children's Books 2010 244p $16.99

Grades: 9 10 11 12   **Fic**
1. Family life -- Fiction 2. Paris (France) -- Fiction 3. Gifted children -- Fiction 4. Homeless persons -- Fiction
ISBN 978-1-59990-479-5

LC 2009-36897

Original French edition, 2007

Precocious thirteen-year-old Lou meets a homeless eighteen-year-old girl on the streets of Paris and Lou's life is forever changed.

"Subtle, authentic details; memorable characters . . . and realistic ambiguities in each scene ground the story's weighty themes, and teens will easily recognize Lou's fragile shifts between heartbreak, bitter disillusionment, and quiet, miraculous hope." Booklist

Villareal, Ray

Body slammed! by Ray Villareal. Piñata Books 2012 194 p. (alk. paper) $11.95

Grades: 7 8 9 10   **Fic**
1. Wrestling -- Fiction 2. Father-son relationship 3. Choice -- Fiction 4. Schools -- Fiction 5. High schools -- Fiction 6. Fathers and sons -- Fiction 7. Mexican Americans -- Fiction 8. San Antonio (Tex.) -- Fiction
ISBN 1558857494; 9781558857490

LC 2012003181

Sequel to: My father, the Angel of Death

This novel, by Ray Villareal, follows "[s]ixteen-year-old Jesse Baron . . . [who] is fed up with being cut down and dismissed, whether by the coach or his friends. . . . But it's through his dad that Jesse meets TJ Masters, a brash, new wrestling talent who's over 21, . . . TJ makes Jesse feel tough and confident. . . . But will Jesse listen to his family and friends when they warn him about hanging out with someone who's often reckless and irresponsible?" (Publisher's note)

Violi, Jen

Putting makeup on dead people. Hyperion 2011 326p il $16.99

Grades: 8 9 10 11 12   **Fic**
1. School stories 2. Bereavement -- Fiction 3. Risk-taking (Psychology) -- Fiction
ISBN 978-1-4231-3481-7; 1-4231-3481-8

Donna's discovery, that she wants to be a mortician, helps her come into her own and finally understand that moving forward doesn't mean forgetting someone you love.

This book "grabs the reader in the first few pages and does not let go. Donna transforms from a girl going through the motions in life to figuring out her dreams and to finally standing up for her future. . . . It discusses her sexual experimentation, the same that many women her age experience. . . . This is a great read for teens searching to find themselves." Voice Youth Advocates

Vivian, Siobhan

The **list**; Siobhan Vivian. Scholastic 2012 333 p. (hardcover: alk. paper) $17.99

Grades: 7 8 9 10 11 12   **Fic**
1. Female friendship 2. Self-perception -- Fiction 3. Personal appearance -- Fiction 4. High school students -- Fiction 5. Identity (Psychology) -- Fiction 6. Friendship -- Fiction 7. Self-esteem -- Fiction 8. High schools -- Fiction
ISBN 0545169178; 9780545169172

LC 2012004248

This young adult novel presents an "exploration of physical appearance and the status it confers. . . . Every year during homecoming week, a list is posted anonymously at Mount Washington High naming the prettiest and ugliest girls in each class. . . . The list confers instant status, transforming formerly homeschooled sophomore Lauren from geeky to hot while consigning her counterpart . . . Candace, to pariah. But what the label mainly confers is anxiety. Prettiest junior Bridget despairs that she'll ever be thin enough to merit her title. . . . Jennifer, four-time 'ugliest' winner, tries to relish the notoriety. . . . Whether clued in or clueless to the intricate social complexities, boyfriends reinforce the status quo, while moms carry scars of their own past physical insecurities." (Kirkus)

Not that kind of girl. PUSH/Scholastic 2010 322p $17.99
Grades: 9 10 11 12   Fic
   1. School stories 2. Dating (Social customs) -- Fiction
   ISBN 978-0-545-16915-8; 0-545-16915-1
                      LC 2010-13806
High school senior and student body president, Natalie likes to have everything under control, but when she becomes attracted to one of the senior boys and her best friend starts keeping secrets from her, Natalie does not know how to act.
The author "challenges the assumptions about sex being rampant in high school and sends a positive message about acceptance, forgiveness, and love." Booklist

Vizzini, Ned, 1981-2013
It's kind of a funny story. Miramax Books/Hyperion Books For Children 2006 444p hardcover o.p., pa $9.99; pa $9.99
Grades: 9 10 11 12   Fic
   1. New York (N.Y.) -- Fiction 2. Psychiatric hospitals -- Fiction 3. Depression (Psychology) -- Fiction
   ISBN 0-7868-5196-1; 1-4231-4191-1 pa; 9780786851973
                      LC 2005-52670
A humorous account of a New York City teenager's battle with depression and his time spent in a psychiatric hospital.
"What's terrific about the book is Craig's voice—intimate, real, funny, ironic, and one kids will come closer to hear." Booklist

Vlahos, Len
The **Scar** Boys; a novel. Len Vlahos. Egmont USA 2014 256 p. (hardcover) $17.99
Grades: 9 10 11 12   Fic
   1. Bullies -- Fiction 2. Friendship -- Fiction 3. Family life -- Fiction 4. Bands (Music) -- Fiction 5. New York (State) -- Fiction 6. Disfigured persons -- Fiction 7. Near-death experiences -- Fiction
   ISBN 9781606844397; 1606844393
                      LC 2013018265
William C. Morris Finalist (2015)
In this book, by Len Vlahos, "Harry is used to making people squirm. When others see his badly scarred face, there is an inevitable reaction that ranges from forced kindness to primal cruelty. In this first-person tale written as an extended college entrance essay, . . . he recounts the trauma of his young life spent recuperating from the act of childhood bullying that left him a burn victim. In middle school, he meets Johnny McKenna, the first person to seem to offer him genuine friendship." (Kirkus Reviews)

"Harry's obsession with punk music will appeal to music lovers, while his journey to accept himself for who he is-- scarred face and all--is one that will likely resonate with any teen trying to find his way in the world." Booklist

Volponi, Paul
The **Final** Four; by Paul Volponi. Viking 2012 244 p.
Grades: 9 10 11 12   Fic
   1. Athletes -- Conduct of life 2. College basketball -- Fiction 3. Sports tournaments -- Fiction 4. African American youth -- Fiction 5. Immigrants -- United States -- Fiction 6. Basketball -- Fiction 7. Conduct of life -- Fiction 8. African Americans -- Fiction
   ISBN 9780670012640
                      LC 2011011587
In this book by Paul "Volponi, . . . basketball's March Madness draws down toward the championship game with a match-up between the Michigan State Spartans and the Troy University (Alabama) Trojans, to see who will take on Duke or North Carolina for the national title. Spartans are led by Malcolm McBride, a . . . freshman who's headed directly to the NBA and is more than willing to spout his views to sports reporters concerning the inequity of unpaid college athletics. The Trojans boast Roko Bacic, a towering immigrant from war-torn Croatia who treasures his opportunity to play the game he loves and get a free college education into the bargain." (Bulletin of the Center for Children's Books)

★ The **hand** you're dealt. Atheneum Books for Young Readers 2008 176p $16.99
Grades: 8 9 10 11   Fic
   1. School stories 2. Poker -- Fiction 3. Teachers -- Fiction
   ISBN 978-1-4169-3989-4; 1-4169-3989-X
                      LC 2007-22988
When seventeen-year-old Huck's vindictive math teacher wins the town poker tournament and takes the winner's watch away from Huck's father while he is in a coma, Huck vows to get even with him no matter what it takes.
"The varied characters are unique and add to the book's interest quotient." Voice Youth Advocates

★ **Hurricane** song; a novel of New Orleans. Viking Childrens Books 2008 144p $15.99
Grades: 7 8 9 10 11 12   Fic
   1. Jazz music -- Fiction 2. New Orleans (La.) -- Fiction 3. Father-son relationship -- Fiction 4. Hurricane Katrina, 2005 -- Fiction
   ISBN 978-0-670-06160-0; 0-670-06160-3
                      LC 2007-38215
Twelve-year-old Miles Shaw goes to live with his father, a jazz musician, in New Orleans, and together they survive the horrors of Hurricane Katrina in the Superdome, learning about each other and growing closer through their painful experiences.
"A brilliant blend of reality and fiction, this novel hits every chord just right." Voice Youth Advocates

Voorhees, Coert
★ The **brothers** Torres. Hyperion Books for Children 2008 316p hardcover o.p. pa $8.99

Grades: 9 10 11 12   **Fic**
1. School stories 2. Gangs -- Fiction 3. Brothers --
Fiction 4. Racially mixed people -- Fiction 5. Dating
(Social customs) -- Fiction
ISBN 978-1-4231-0304-2; 1-4231-0304-1; 978-1-
4231-0306-6 pa; 1-4231-0306-8 pa
                                      LC 2007-15152
Sophomore Frankie finally finds the courage to ask
his long-term friend, Julianne, to the Homecoming dance,
which ultimately leads to a face-off between a tough senior whose family owns most of their small, New Mexico
town, and Frankie's soccer-star older brother and his gang-
member friends.

This "novel is solidly plotted and exceptionally well
paced; escalating tension keeps the pages flying, while narrator Frankie's self-deprecating humor prevents the action
from devolving into Southwestside Story melodrama." Bull
Cent Child Books

Lucky fools; Coert Voorhees. Hyperion Books
2012 293 p. $16.99
Grades: 8 9 10 11 12   **Fic**
1. College choice 2. Theater -- Fiction 3. Dating
(Social customs) -- Fiction 4. Schools -- Fiction 5.
College choice -- Fiction 6. Palo Alto (Calif.) -- Fiction
7. Preparatory schools -- Fiction
ISBN 1423123980; 9781423123989
                                      LC 2011026252
Author Coert Voorhees presents a story about an aspiring
high school actor. "For the seniors at prestigious Oak Fields
Prep, the pressure is on to get into an Ivy League school. .
. . But David Ellison, star of the school play . . . wants to
go to Juilliard instead. As David's Juilliard audition and the
play's opening night approach, he is plagued with doubts
about his acting ability and his relationships with two girls."
(Publishers Weekly)

Vrettos, Adrienne Maria
Burnout. Margaret K. McElderry Books 2011
193p $16.99
Grades: 7 8 9 10   **Fic**
1. Alcoholism -- Fiction 2. Drug abuse -- Fiction 3.
New York (N.Y.) -- Fiction
ISBN 978-1-4169-9469-5; 1-4169-9469-6
                                      LC 2010051617
Months after coming out of alcohol and drug rehab, high
school student Nan wakes up on the subway the day after
Halloween wearing a torn Halloween costume, her long hair
cut, and "HELP ME" scrawled across her chest, feeling sick
and having no idea how she got there.

"The gritty and biting story, coupled with its detective novel underpinnings, also has the potential to draw
new fans, perhaps even some reluctant readers." Voice
Youth Advocates

★ **Skin**. Margaret K. McElderry Books 2006
227p $16.95
Grades: 7 8 9 10   **Fic**
1. Siblings -- Fiction 2. Anorexia nervosa -- Fiction
ISBN 1-4169-0655-X
                                      LC 2005001119

When his parents decide to separate, eighth-grader
Donnie watches with horror as the physical condition of
his sixteen-year old sister, Karen, deteriorates due to an
eating disorder.

"The overwhelming alienation Donnie endures will
speak to many teens, while his honest perspective will be
welcomed by boys." Booklist

Wagner, Laura Rose
Hold tight, don't let go; by Laura Rose Wagner.
Amulet Books 2015 272 p. (hardback) $17.95
Grades: 9 10 11 12   **Fic**
1. Refugees 2. Haiti Earthquake, Haiti, 2010 3. Haiti --
Fiction 4. Cousins -- Fiction 5. Earthquakes -- Fiction
6. Refugee camps -- Fiction 7. Port-au-Prince (Haiti) --
Fiction 8. Separation (Psychology) -- Fiction 9. Haiti
Earthquake, Haiti, 2010 -- Fiction
ISBN 1419712047; 9781419712043
                                      LC 2014019622
Author Laura Rose Wagner's novel "follows the vivid
story of two teenage cousins, raised as sisters, who survive
the devastating 2010 earthquake in Haiti. After losing the
woman who raised them in the tragedy, Magdalie and Nadine must fend for themselves in the aftermath of the quake.
The girls are inseparable . . . until Nadine, whose father lives
in Miami, sends for her but not Magdalie." (Publisher's note)

"Wagner breaks away from stereotypes of an abject
Haiti, giving us complex characters who connect with and
care for one another, economies that rebuild, and environments that recover. By the end, readers will be buoyed by
the hopeful future the author imagines for Magdalie and for
Haiti." Booklist

Hold tight, do not let go

Wakefield, Vikki
Friday never leaving; Vikki Wakefield. Simon
& Schuster Books for Young Readers 2013 336 p.
(hardcover) $16.99
Grades: 9 10 11 12   **Fic**
1. Runaway teenagers -- Fiction 2. Teenagers --
Conduct of life 3. Australia -- Fiction 4. Coming of
age -- Fiction
ISBN 144248652X; 9781442486522; 9781442486539
                                      LC 2012036386
This book by Vikki Wakefield follows "Friday Brown,
[who] has never had a home. She and her mother live on
the road, running away from the past. . . . So when her mom
succumbs to cancer, the only thing Friday can do is keep
moving. Her journey takes her to an abandoned house where
a bunch of street kids are squatting, and an intimidating
girl named Arden holds court. Friday gets initiated into the
group, but her relationship with Arden is precarious." (Publisher's note)

Waldorf, Heather
Tripping. Red Deer Press 2008 342p pa $12.95
Grades: 8 9 10 11 12   **Fic**
1. Canada -- Fiction 2. Amputees -- Fiction 3. Voyages
and travels -- Fiction 4. Wilderness survival -- Fiction
ISBN 978-0-88995-426-7; 0-88995-426-7
"Rainey and five other teens begin an eight-week school-
sponsored educational/survival trek across Canada. . . .

Rainey's challenge is heightened because she has an artificial leg and she learns that her mother, who abandoned her as a baby, lives near one of their stops and wants to meet her. As the trip progresses, the individuals bond and become part of a team.... Waldorf has written a unique story in which six very different young people are united in a common cause. Told with wit and humor, this fast-paced novel has character development that is extraordinary." SLJ

Walker, Alice

★ The **color** purple; 10th anniversary ed; Harcourt Brace Jovanovich 1992 290p il $24; pa $14
Grades: 11 12 Adult   **Fic**
1. Sisters -- Fiction 2. Southern States -- Fiction 3. African Americans -- Fiction
ISBN 0-15-119154-9; 0-15-602835-2 pa
                LC 91-47202
A reissue of the title first published 1982
"A feminist novel about an abused and uneducated black woman's struggle for empowerment, the novel was praised for the depth of its female characters and for its eloquent use of black English vernacular." Merriam-Webster's Ency of Lit

Walker, Brian F.

Black boy/white school; Brian F. Walker. HarpercrTeen 2012 246p (trade bdg.) $17.99
Grades: 9 10 11 12   **Fic**
1. Scholarships 2. Private schools -- Fiction 3. High school students -- Fiction 4. Maine -- Fiction 5. Schools -- Fiction 6. Identity -- Fiction 7. High schools -- Fiction 8. Race relations -- Fiction 9. African Americans -- Fiction 10. Preparatory schools -- Fiction
ISBN 9780061914836; 9780061914843
                LC 2011016608
This book tells the story of "Anthony 'Ant' Jones [who] has never been outside his rough East Cleveland neighborhood when he's given a scholarship to Belton Academy, an elite prep school in Maine. But at Belton things are far from perfect. Everyone calls him 'Tony,' assumes he's from Brooklyn, expects him to play basketball, and yet acts shocked when he fights back. As Anthony tries to adapt to a world that will never fully accept him, he's in for a rude awakening: Home is becoming a place where he no longer belongs." (Publisher's note)

Walker, Kristin

7clues to winning you; Kristin Walker. Razorbill 2012 317 p. (glb) $18.99; (trade pbk) $9.99
Grades: 8 9 10 11   **Fic**
1. Love stories 2. High school students -- Fiction 3. Treasure hunt (Game) -- Fiction
ISBN 9781451759150; 1595144145; 9781595144140
                LC 2011279962
In this young adult romance novel, "[w]hen a humiliating picture of Blythe goes viral, she's instantly the target of ridicule at her new school. To salvage her reputation, Blythe teams up with Luke to win the Senior Scramble scavenger hunt.... Perhaps it's his Shakespearean witticisms that reel Blythe in despite her better judgment.... But as the hunt progresses, their relationship heats up. Soon their madcap mischief spirals out of control." (Publisher's note)

Wallace, Jason

Out of shadows. Holiday House 2011 282p $17.95
Grades: 7 8 9 10 11 12   **Fic**
1. School stories 2. Bullies -- Fiction 3. Zimbabwe -- Fiction 4. Race relations -- Fiction
ISBN 978-0-8234-2342-2; 0-8234-2342-5
                LC 2010-24372
In 1983, at an elite boys' boarding school in Zimbabwe, thirteen-year-old English lad Robert Jacklin finds himself torn between his black roommate and the white bullies still bitter over losing power through the recent civil war.
"This thought-provoking narrative offers teens a window into a distinctive time and place in history that is likely to be unfamiliar to most of them. A first purchase for high schools, especially those with a strong world cultures curriculum." SLJ

Wallace, Rich

One good punch. Alfred A. Knopf 2007 114p $15.99
Grades: 7 8 9 10 11 12   **Fic**
1. School stories 2. Journalism -- Fiction 3. Pennsylvania -- Fiction 4. Track athletics -- Fiction
ISBN 978-0-375-81352-8; 0-375-81352-7
                LC 2006-33270
Eighteen-year-old Michael Kerrigan, writer of obituaries for the Scranton Observer and captain of the track team, is ready for the most important season of his life—until the police find four joints in his school locker, and he is faced with a choice that could change everything.
"This novel's success is in creating a multidimensional male character in a format that will appeal to all readers. The moral dilemma . . . makes this novel ripe for ethical discussions." Voice Youth Advocates

Perpetual check. Alfred A. Knopf 2009 112p $15.99; lib bdg $18.99
Grades: 8 9 10 11   **Fic**
1. Chess -- Fiction 2. Brothers -- Fiction 3. Father-son relationship -- Fiction
ISBN 978-0-375-84058-6; 0-375-84058-3; 978-0-375-94058-3 lib bdg; 0-375-94058-8 lib bdg
                LC 2008-04159
Brothers Zeke and Randy participate in an important chess tournament, playing against each other while also trying to deal with their father's intensely competitive tendencies.
"Wallace cleverly positions Randy and Zeke for a win-win conclusion in this satisfying, engaging, and deceptively simple story." SLJ

★ **Wrestling** Sturbridge. Knopf 1996 135p hardcover o.p. pa $4.99
Grades: 7 8 9 10   **Fic**
1. Wrestling -- Fiction 2. Friendship -- Fiction
ISBN 0-679-87803-3; 0-679-88555-2 pa
                LC 95-20468
"The wresting scenes are thrilling. . . . Like Ben, whose voice is so strong and clear here, Wallace weighs his words carefully, making every one count in this excellent, understated first novel." Booklist

Wallace, Sandra Neil

Muckers; Sandra Neil Wallace. Alfred A. Knopf 2013 288 p. (hardback) $16.99

Grades: 7 8 9 10　　　　　　　　　　　　**Fic**

1. Football 2. Historical fiction 3. Grief -- Fiction 4. Schools -- Fiction

ISBN 0375867546; 9780375867545; 9780375967542

LC 2013003537

In this book, "Felix 'Red' O'Sullivan is the best hope to lead his team to a statewide football championship. Unlike other teams in 1950 in Arizona, whites and Latinos play together on the Hartley Muckers. Nevertheless, both groups are aware of the dividing lines." Red must also deal with an alcoholic father and a mother grieving for Red's older brother, killed in World War II. "For Red, this season will be his last chance to return glory to 'Bobby's school.'" (Kirkus Reviews)

Wallach, Tommy

Thanks for the trouble; Tommy Wallach. Simon & Schuster Books for Young Readers 2016 288 p. (hardback) $17.99

　Grades: 9 10 11 12　　　　　　　　　　**Fic**

　1. Love stories 2. Selective mutism -- Fiction 3. Love -- Fiction 4. Death -- Fiction

　ISBN 9781481418805; 9781481418812

LC 2015013388

This novel, by Tommy Wallach, "Parker Santé hasn't spoken a word in five years. While his classmates plan for bright futures, he skips school to hang out in hotels, killing time by watching the guests. But when he meets a silver-haired girl named Zelda Toth, a girl who claims to be quite a bit older than she looks, he'll discover there just might be a few things left worth living for." (Publisher's note)

"Bittersweet moments intersect with the intricate fairy tales Parker writes, compelling readers to judge what is real and what is make-believe." Pub Wkly

We all looked up; Tommy Wallach. First edition Simon & Schuster Books for Young Readers 2015 384 p. (hardcover: alk. paper) $17.99

Grades: 9 10 11 12　　　　　　　　　　**Fic**

1. Meteors -- Fiction 2. Friendship -- Fiction 3. High schools -- Fiction 4. Self-realization -- Fiction 5. High school students -- Fiction 6. Schools -- Fiction

ISBN 1481418777; 9781481418775; 9781481418782

LC 2014004565

In this book, by Tommy Wallach, "[f]our high school seniors put their hopes, hearts, and humanity on the line as an asteroid hurtles toward Earth. . . . As these four seniors--along with the rest of the planet--wait to see what damage an asteroid will cause, they must abandon all thoughts of the future and decide how they're going to spend what remains of the present." (Publisher's note)

"Debut novelist Wallach increases the tension among characters throughout, ending in a shocking climax that resonates with religious symbolism. Stark scenes alternating between anarchy and police states are counterbalanced by deepening emotional ties and ethical dilemmas, creating a novel that asks far bigger questions than it answers." Publishers Weekly

Wallenfels, Stephen

POD. Namelos 2009 212p $18.95; pa $9.95

Grades: 7 8 9 10　　　　　　　　　　　　**Fic**

1. Science fiction 2. Extraterrestrial beings -- Fiction

ISBN 978-1-60898-011-6; 1-60898-011-1; 978-1-60898-010-9 pa; 1-60898-010-3 pa

LC 2008-29721

As alien spacecrafts fill the sky and zap up any human being who dares to go outside, fifteen-year-old Josh and twelve-year-old Megs, living in different cities, describe what could be their last days on Earth.

"The dire circumstances don't negate the humor, the hormones, or the humanity found in the young narrators. This is solid, straightforward sci-fi." Booklist

Waller, Sharon Biggs

The Forbidden Orchid; by Sharon Biggs Waller. Penguin Group USA 2016 416 p. map (hardcover) $18.99

　　　　　　　　　　　　　　　　　　　Fic

1. Historical fiction 2. Father-daughter relationship -- Fiction

ISBN 9780451474117; 0451474112

LC 2015039617

In this novel, by Sharon Biggs Waller, "Elodie Buchanan is the eldest of ten sisters growing up in a small English market town in 1861. The girls barely know their father, a plant hunter usually off adventuring through China. . . . Then disaster strikes: Mr. Buchanan reneges on his contract to collect an extremely rare and valuable orchid. . . . Elodie can't stand by and see her family destroyed, so she persuades her father to return to China once more to try to hunt down the flower." (Publisher's note)

"Historical details, including the liberal prescription of morphine and Britain's patriarchal economy, lend rich, textural background. Well-researched and filled with adventure, romance, and lots of tension—this work of historical fiction has all the elements of an intriguing read." Kirkus

A mad, wicked folly; Sharon Biggs Waller. Viking, published by the Penguin Group 2014 448 p. map (hardback) $17.99

Grades: 8 9 10 11 12　　　　　　　　　　**Fic**

1. Love -- Fiction 2. Gender role -- Fiction 3. London (England) -- Fiction 4. Great Britain -- History -- Edward VII, 1901-1910 -- Fiction 5. Artists -- Fiction 6. Sex role -- Fiction 7. London (England) -- History -- 20th century -- Fiction

ISBN 0670014680; 9780670014682

LC 2013029858

This book, by Sharon Biggs Waller, is "about a young English woman who is talented, beautiful, passionate, and wealthy. Despite these advantages, Victoria Darling struggles with the harsh limitations imposed upon women prior to and during the Edwardian era of 1901-1910, which curtail her attempts to attend art school. While Victoria does not initially associate with the Suffragette Movement, she ultimately discovers that her fate is intertwined with the cause." (School Library Journal)

"Victoria's dream of becoming an artist leads her naively into scandals, tempts her into a convenient marriage, and drives her to join the Women's Social and Political Union.

Persistence eventually triumphs, and friendships, love, and art lessons are her rewards. Sound historical research provides the backbone for this warm novel about the development of women's opportunities in Edwardian London." Horn Book

Includes bibliographical references

Walsh, Alice

A **Long** Way from Home. Orca Book Pub 2012 232 p. (paperback) $11.95

Grades: 7 8 9 10   **Fic**

1. Immigrants -- Fiction 2. Prejudices -- Fiction 3. September 11 terrorist attacks, 2001 -- Fiction

ISBN 1926920791; 9781926920795

In this book by Alice Walsh, "thirteen-year-old Rabia, along with her mother and younger brother, flees Afghanistan. . . . They take part in a program that is relocating refugee widows and orphans to America. . . . After the terrorist attack on the World Trade Center in New York City, their plane is diverted to Gander, Newfoundland. Also on the plane is a boy named Colin, who struggles with his prejudices against Rabia and her family." (Publisher's note)

Walter, Jon

My name is not Friday; by Jon Walter. David Fickling Books/Scholastic Inc. 2016 384 p. (hardcover) $18.99

Grades: 7 8 9 10   **Fic**

1. African Americans 2. Slavery -- United States 3. Orphans -- Fiction 4. Slavery -- Fiction 5. Brothers -- Fiction

ISBN 9780545855228

LC 2015035464

In this novel, by Jon Walter, "well-mannered Samuel and his mischievous younger brother Joshua are free black boys living in an orphanage during the end of the Civil War. Samuel takes the blame for Joshua's latest prank, and the consequence is worse than he could ever imagine. He's taken from the orphanage to the South, given a new name -- Friday -- and sold into slavery." (Publisher's note)

"While readers on the young end of the age range and those unfamiliar with religious concepts may find the opening chapters somewhat confusing, Samuel's endearing, immersive narration makes the novel a fascinating and unforgettable account of a brutal and shameful chapter in America's history. A heartbreaking story about family, justice, and the resilience of the human spirit." Kirkus

Walters, Eric

In a flash. Orca 2008 108p (Orca currents) $16.95; pa $9.95

Grades: 7 8 9 10   **Fic**

1. School stories

ISBN 978-1-55469-035-0; 1-55469-035-8; 978-1-55469-034-3 pa; 1-55469-034-X pa

"Snappy, realistic dialogue; multidimensional characters; and an unpredictable plot (not to mention a hip, contemporary phenomenon) will have both reluctant and struggling readers madly flipping the pages." SLJ

Splat! written by Eric Walters. Orca Book Publishers 2008 112p $16.95; pa $9.95

Grades: 7 8 9 10   **Fic**

1. Canada -- Fiction 2. Tomatoes -- Fiction 3. Friendship -- Fiction

ISBN 978-1-55143-988-4; 1-55143-988-3; 978-1-55143-986-0 pa; 1-55143-986-7 pa

"The relationship between Keegan and narrator Alex, with their relentless and often quite funny smartassed exchanges, is the core of this speedy and readable novel." Bull Cent Child Books

Waltman, Kevin

Next; by Kevin Waltman. First edition Cinco Puntos Press 2013 287 p. (paperback) $11.95

Grades: 9 10 11 12   **Fic**

1. School stories 2. Basketball -- Fiction 3. African American athletes -- Fiction 4. Schools -- Fiction 5. High schools -- Fiction 6. African Americans -- Fiction

ISBN 1935955659; 9781935955641; 9781935955658

LC 2013026452

In this novel by Kevin Waltman, set "in Indiana, basketball is the next thing to religion. Especially for inner-city black kids like Derrick Bowen. . . . He wants to start at point guard for Marion High, but senior Nick Starks has that nailed down. Besides, the coach . . . thinks D-Bow needs to work on his game, his shot, and his attitude. That means bench time. And that's when Hamilton Academy, the elite school in the suburbs, comes sniffing around." (Publisher's note)

"The blend of sports action and relationships holds tremendous appeal for basketball fans and reluctant readers, although those who are not familiar with the game may have trouble understanding the jargon. A solid choice for fans of Paul Volponi and Walter Dean Myers." SLJ

Slump; by Kevin Waltman. First edition Cinco Puntos Press 2014 216 p. (D-Bow's high school hoops) (hardback) $16.95

Grades: 9 10 11 12   **Fic**

1. School stories 2. Basketball -- Fiction 3. High schools -- Fiction 4. African Americans -- Fiction 5. Schools -- Fiction

ISBN 1941026001; 9781941026007; 9781941026014

LC 2014007657

In this book, by Kevin Waltman, "Derrick Bowen's sophomore year is a grind. He's been looking forward to the basketball season all summer, but his girlfriend Jasmine leaves him for putting too much focus on basketball. The promise his Marion East basketball team showed at the end of last season isn't materializing. . . . When Derrick's father is severely injured in a car crash, Derrick is faced with a new reality where basketball can't be his only priority." (Publisher's note)

"All-star point guard Derrick "D-Bow" Bowen's (Next) sophomore year isn't turning out how he expected. He's having problems with his girlfriend, his team is struggling to click, and then an accident leaves his father injured and his family straining to make ends meet. Once again, Waltman skillfully blends play-by-play basketball action and strong character development; readers are left anticipating another book." Horn Book

Walton, K. M.

Empty; K.M. Walton. Simon Pulse 2013 256 p. (hardcover) $16.99

Grades: 9 10 11 12   **Fic**

1. Bullies -- Fiction 2. Overweight teenagers -- Fiction 3. Rape -- Fiction 4. Obesity -- Fiction 5. Schools -- Fiction 6. Self-esteem -- Fiction 7. High schools -- Fiction 8. Family problems -- Fiction 9. Emotional problems -- Fiction

ISBN 1442453591; 9781442453593

LC 2012011562

In this book, "seventeen-year-old Dell is overweight, and she eats to deal with a series of letdowns, beginning when her father left the family. . . . She hides behind her weight and self-deprecating jokes. Her classmates" bully her. "The bullying turns vicious at a party; she drinks too much and is raped by one of the bullies, on whom she happens to have had a crush. She has no one to turn to, and rumors start that she attacked him." (School Library Journal)

Walton, Leslye

The **strange** and beautiful sorrows of Ava Lavender; Leslye Walton. Candlewick Press 2014 320 p. illustrations $17.99

Grades: 9 10 11 12 Adult   **Fic**

1. Love stories 2. Teenagers -- Fiction 3. Supernatural -- Fiction

ISBN 0763665665; 9780763665661

LC 2013946615

William C. Morris Finalist (2015)

In this book, by Leslye Walton, "Ava--in all other ways a normal girl--is born with the wings of a bird. . . . Sixteen-year old Ava ventures into the wider world, ill-prepared for what she might discover and naive to the twisted motives of others. Others like the pious Nathaniel Sorrows, who mistakes Ava for an angel and whose obsession with her grows until the night of the summer solstice celebration." (Publisher's note)

"[T]here are many sorrows in Walton's debut, and most of them are Ava's through inheritance. Readers should prepare themselves for a tale where myth and reality, lust and love, the corporal and the ghostly, are interchangeable and surprising." (Booklist)

Ward, Jesmyn

★ **Salvage** the bones; Jesmyn Ward. Bloomsbury USA 2011 261p. $24

Grades: 11 12 Adult   **Fic**

1. Dogs 2. Poverty 3. Widowers 4. Pregnancy 5. Adolescence 6. Family life 7. Hurricane Katrina, 2005 8. Brothers and sisters 9. African Americans -- Mississippi

ISBN 978-1-608-19522-0; 1-608-19522-8; 9781608196265

LC 201053025

Alex Award (2012)

National Book Award: Fiction (2011)

This book, a winner of the 2011 National Book Award, chronicles a family's experiences when a hurricane threatens their town.

"Ward uses fearless, toughly lyrical language to convey this family's close-knit tenderness [and] the sheer bloody-minded difficulty of rural African American life... It's an eye-opening heartbreaker that ends in hope You owe it to yourself to read this book." Library Journal

Ward, Rachel

The **Chaos**. Chicken House 2011 339p $17.99

Grades: 8 9 10 11 12   **Fic**

1. Science fiction 2. Death -- Fiction 3. Orphans -- Fiction 4. London (England) -- Fiction 5. Blacks -- Great Britain -- Fiction 6. Extrasensory perception -- Fiction

ISBN 978-0-545-24269-1; 0-545-24269-X

Sequel to: Numbers (2010)

When rising flood waters force him and his grandmother to evacuate their coastal home and return to London, sixteen-year-old Adam, who has inherited his mother's curse of being able to see the day that someone will die when he looks into their eyes, becomes disturbed when he begins to see January 1, 2027, a date six months into the future, in nearly everyone around him.

"In this sequel to Numbers a fascinating premise is again worked out through gripping episodes and a lightly handled metaphysical dilemma." Horn Book

Infinity; Rachel Ward. Chicken House/Scholastic 2012 249 p. (Numbers) $17.99

Grades: 8 9 10 11 12   **Fic**

1. Death -- Fiction 2. England -- Fiction 3. Psychic ability -- Fiction 4. London (England) -- Fiction 5. Interpersonal relations -- Fiction 6. Blacks -- England -- London -- Fiction

ISBN 0545350921; 9780545350921; 9780545381918

LC 2011032709

This novel, by Rachel Ward, is the conclusion to the "Numbers" trilogy. "Sarah loves Adam, but can't bear the thought that every time he looks in her eyes, he can see her dying; can see her last day. It's 2029. Two years since the Chaos. . . . Little Mia was supposed to die that New Year's Day. The numbers don't lie. But somehow she changed her date. Mia's just a baby, oblivious to her special power. But ruthless people are hunting her down, determined to steal her secret." (Publisher's note)

Numbers. Chicken House/Scholastic 2010 325p $17.99

Grades: 8 9 10 11 12   **Fic**

1. Science fiction 2. Death -- Fiction 3. Runaway teenagers -- Fiction 4. Blacks -- Great Britain -- Fiction 5. Extrasensory perception -- Fiction

ISBN 978-0-545-14299-1; 0-545-14299-7

LC 2008-55440

"Ward's debut novel is gritty, bold, and utterly unique. Jem's isolation and pain, hidden beneath a veneer of toughness, are palpable, and the ending is a real shocker." SLJ

Followed by: The Chaos (2011)

Warman, Jessica

Between. Walker 2011 454p $17.99

Grades: 10 11 12   **Fic**

1. Dead -- Fiction 2. Family life -- Fiction 3. Future

life -- Fiction
ISBN 978-0-8027-2182-2

LC 2010-40986

"Liz runs the gamut of strong emotion throughout this compelling backtrack of a short life punctuated by early grief, parental failings, and honest, flawed love; her journey offers insight into the effects all of these things can have on an ordinary life." Bull Cent Child Books

★ **Breathless**. Walker 2009 311p $16.99
Grades: 9 10 11 12   **Fic**
1. School stories 2. Siblings -- Fiction 3. Swimming -- Fiction 4. Schizophrenia -- Fiction 5. Mental illness -- Fiction
ISBN 978-0-8027-9849-7; 0-8027-9849-7

LC 2008-42555

At boarding school, Katie tries to focus on swimming and becoming popular instead of the painful memories of her institutionalized schizophrenic older brother.

"Warman draws out Katie's emotions and her complex life and family with immediacy. Readers who dive in will surface with more awareness of the devastating effects of mental illness." Kirkus

Where the truth lies. Walker & Co. 2010 308p $16.99
Grades: 9 10 11 12   **Fic**
1. School stories 2. Dreams -- Fiction 3. Memory -- Fiction 4. Connecticut -- Fiction 5. Family life -- Fiction 6. Dating (Social customs) -- Fiction
ISBN 978-0-8027-2078-8; 0-8027-2078-1

LC 2010-00782

Emily, whose father is headmaster of a Connecticut boarding school, suffers from nightmares, and when she meets and falls in love with the handsome Del Sugar, pieces of her traumatic past start falling into place.

"Emily's unflinching, multilayered narration and realistic dialogue capture the wishes and fears that drive teens. A page-turner to the bittersweet ending." Kirkus

Wasserman, Robin

Crashed. Simon Pulse 2009 440p $16.99; pa $9.99
Grades: 9 10 11 12   **Fic**
1. Science fiction 2. Bioethics -- Fiction
ISBN 978-1-4169-7453-6; 1-4169-7453-9; 978-1-4169-3635-0 pa; 1-4169-3635-1 pa

LC 2009-3271

Sequel to Skinned (2008)

Living with other "mechs" since her wealthy parents transplanted her brain into a mechanical body to prevent her from dying in a horrible accident, Lia becomes a pawn in a religious leader's movement to outlaw "mech" technology and eradicate machines such as Lia.

"A thought-provoking bioethical conundrum that raises difficult questions about the definition of life, this text will intrigue and entertain readers." Kirkus

Followed by Wired (2010)

Hacking Harvard; a novel. Simon Pulse 2007 320p pa $8.99

Grades: 9 10 11 12   **Fic**
1. School stories 2. Computer crimes -- Fiction 3. Harvard University -- Fiction
ISBN 978-1-4169-3633-6; 1-4169-3633-5

When three brilliant nerds—Max Kim, Eric Roth, and Isaac "The Professor" Schwarzbaum—bet $20,000 that they can get anyone into Harvard, they take on the Ivy League in their quest for popularity, money, and the love of a beauty queen valedictorian.

"There is enough action, computers, electronics, and shenanigans to entice girls and boys, geeks and non-geeks to this thought-provoking, enjoyable read." Voice Youth Advocates

Skinned. Simon Pulse 2008 361p $15.99; pa $9.99
Grades: 9 10 11 12   **Fic**
1. Science fiction 2. Bioethics -- Fiction
ISBN 978-1-4169-3634-3; 1-4169-3634-3; 978-1-4169-7449-9 pa; 1-4169-7449-0 pa

LC 2008-15306

To save her from dying in a horrible accident, Lia's wealthy parents transplant her brain into a mechanical body.

"This is a captivating story that brings up many questions for teens, including how they fit in with their peers and what is their role in larger society. There are underlying themes as well such as suicide, free will, and what makes someone human." Libr Media Connect

Other titles in this series are:
Crashed (2009)
Wired (2010)

The **waking** dark; Robin Wasserman. Alfred A. Knopf 2013 464 p. $17.99
Grades: 9 10 11 12   **Fic**
1. Horror fiction 2. Homicide -- Fiction 3. Science fiction 4. Death -- Fiction 5. Kansas -- Fiction 6. Murder -- Fiction 7. City and town life -- Kansas -- Fiction
ISBN 0375868771; 9780375868771; 9780375968778

LC 2012032802

In this horror novel set in a small Kansas town, "five people suddenly go on murder sprees, with four of them committing suicide. A year later, five survivors are united when a storm (and later, soldiers) isolate the town: loner Daniel, closeted jock West, newly evangelical Ellie, outcast Jule, and Cassie—the one remaining murderer, who has no recollection of what she did or why. As the days pass, the five grow increasingly aware that everyone else in Oleander is starting to act strange." (Publishers Weekly)

Wired. Simon Pulse 2010 383p $15.99
Grades: 9 10 11 12   **Fic**
1. Science fiction 2. Bioethics -- Fiction
ISBN 978-1-4169-7454-3

LC 2010-10237

Sequel to Crashed (2009)

Lia is back at home, pretending to be the perfect daughter, but she has become the public face of the mechs, devoting her life to convincing the world that she and others like her deserve to exist, until shocking truths are revealed, forcing her to make a life-changing decision.

"Wasserman creates a convincing and imaginative dystopia that her characters fill with action and a wide range of human emotion. Harsh language makes this appropriate for older teens, who will also appreciate the overt and underlying ethical dilemmas throughout." Kirkus

Waters, Daniel

Break my heart 1,000 times; Daniel Waters. Hyperion 2012 342 p. (hardback) $16.99

Grades: 7 8 9 10 11 12   **Fic**

1. Homicide -- Fiction 2. Teenagers -- Fiction 3. Friendship -- Fiction 4. Supernatural -- Fiction 5. Ghosts -- Fiction 6. Schools -- Fiction 7. Teachers -- Fiction 8. High schools -- Fiction 9. Serial murders -- Fiction

ISBN 1423121988; 9781423121985

LC 2012009395

Author Daniel Waters presents a "supernatural thriller. Six years after the Event . . . ghosts . . . continue to inundate Jewell City. Teen Veronica Calder, born on leap day, sees many of these ghosts. . . . Hoping to capture Veronica's attention, classmate Kirk begins an independent study on the city's ghosts. Also vying for her attention is serial killer and . . . teacher August Bittner, whose daughter died on leap day" and who "plans to kill Veronica in an effort to bring back his daughter's spirit." (Kirkus Reviews)

Generation dead. Hyperion 2008 382p $16.99

Grades: 7 8 9 10   **Fic**

1. School stories 2. Death -- Fiction 3. Zombies -- Fiction 4. Prejudices -- Fiction

ISBN 978-1-4231-0921-1; 1-4231-0921-X

LC 2007-36361

When dead teenagers who have come back to life start showing up at her high school, Phoebe, a goth girl, becomes interested in the phenomenon, and when she starts dating a "living impaired" boy, they encounter prejudice, fear, and hatred.

This "is a classic desegregation story that also skewers adult attempts to make teenagers play nice. . . . Motivational speakers, politically correct speech and encounter groups come in for special ridicule." N Y Times Book Rev

Followed by: Kiss of life (2009)

Watkins, Steve

Great Falls; Steve Watkins. Candlewick Press 2016 256 p. $17.99

Grades: 8 9 10 11   **Fic**

1. Brothers -- Fiction 2. Veterans -- Fiction 3. Post-traumatic stress disorder -- Fiction

ISBN 076367155X; 9780763671556

In this novel, by Steve Watkins, "Shane has always worshiped his big brother, Jeremy. But three tours in Iraq and Afghanistan have taken their toll, and the easy-go-lucky brother Shane knew has been replaced by a surly drunk. When Jeremy . . . offers to take him to the family cabin overnight, Shane goes along. But as the camping trip turns into a days-long canoe trip . . . Shane realizes he . . . has no idea how to persuade Jeremy to return home and get the help he needs." (Publisher's note)

"Watkins (Juvie) delivers a powerful, emotionally raw tale, heartbreaking in its portrayal of damaged veterans, the

price some pay to serve, and the toll it takes on their friends and family. It's also a raw coming-of-age journey for Shane as he struggles with his own feelings, especially toward "the Colonel," the brothers' emotionally abusive, micromanaging, ex-military stepfather." PW

Juvie; by Steve Watkins. Candlewick Press 2013 320 p. $17.99

Grades: 9 10 11 12   **Fic**

1. Sisters -- Fiction 2. Juvenile delinquency

ISBN 0763655090; 9780763655099

LC 2012955219

This book, by Steve Watkins, "tells the story of two sisters grappling with accountability [and] sacrifice. Sadie Windas has always been the responsible one . . . not like her older sister, Carla, who leaves her three-year-old daughter, Lulu, with Aunt Sadie while she parties and gets high. But when both sisters are caught up in a drug deal — wrong place, wrong time — it falls to Sadie to confess to a crime she didn't commit to keep Carla out of jail and Lulu out of foster care." (Publisher's note)

"When seventeen-year-old Sadie and her sister, Carla, are caught participating (unintentionally) in a drug deal, Sadie takes the blame to protect her family; her punishment is a six-month sentence in a juvenile corrections facility. The novel is bleak and brutal--which, of course, is the point--making Sadie's loyalty to Carla and resolve to survive all the more powerful." (Horn Book)

What comes after. Candlewick Press 2011 334p $16.99

Grades: 8 9 10 11 12   **Fic**

1. Moving -- Fiction 2. Farm life -- Fiction 3. Bereavement -- Fiction 4. Child abuse -- Fiction 5. North Carolina -- Fiction 6. Domestic animals -- Fiction

ISBN 0-7636-4250-9; 978-0-7636-4250-1

LC 2010-38711

When her veterinarian father dies, sixteen-year-old Iris Wight must move from Maine to North Carolina where her Aunt Sue spends Iris's small inheritance while abusing her physically and emotionally, but the hardest to take is her mistreatment of the farm animals.

"This is the kind of book where readers will likely literally sigh with relief when Iris finally catches a break—while there is no rainbows-and-clouds-parting happy ending for a life this hard, it is enough that she is, for the moment, loved by a few fiercely loyal allies, beginning to face her demons, and wielding a bit more control over her own life." Bull Cent Child Books

Watson, Larry

★ **Montana** 1948; a novel. Milkweed Editions 2007 169p pa $14

Grades: 11 12 Adult   **Fic**

1. Montana -- Fiction 2. Family life -- Fiction

ISBN 978-1-57131-061-3

First published 1993

"The moral issues, and the consequences of following one's conscience, are made painfully evident here. Watson is to be congratulated for the honesty of his writing and the purity of his prose." Libr J

Watson, Renée

This side of home; by Renée Watson. Bloomsbury 2015 326 p. (hardcover) $17.99

Grades: 9 10 11 12   **Fic**

1. Twins -- Fiction 2. Sisters -- Fiction 3. Neighborhood
-- Fiction 4. Friendship -- Fiction 5. Best friends --
Fiction 6. Neighborhoods -- Fiction 7. Urban renewal
-- Fiction 8. Portland (Ore.) -- Fiction 9. Dating (Social
customs) -- Fiction
ISBN 1599906686; 9781599906683

LC 2014013743

In this novel, by Renée Watson, "identical twins Nikki
and Maya have been on the same page for everything. . . .
But as their neighborhood goes from rough-and-tumble to
up-and-coming, . . . Nikki is thrilled while Maya feels like
their home is slipping away. Suddenly, the sisters . . . must
confront their dissenting feelings on the importance of their
ethnic and cultural identities and, in the process, learn to
separate themselves from the long shadow of their identity
as twins." (Publisher's note)

"Readers may be surprised to find this multicultural story set in Portland, Oregon, but that just adds to its distinctive
appeal. Here's hoping Watson's teen debut will be followed
by many more." Kirkus

Weatherford, Carole Boston

★ **Becoming** Billie Holiday; art by Floyd Cooper. Wordsong 2008 116p il $19.95

Grades: 7 8 9 10   **Fic**

1. Singers 2. Blues musicians 3. Novels in verse 4.
Singers -- Fiction 5. Jazz music -- Fiction 6. African
Americans -- Fiction
ISBN 978-1-59078-507-2; 1-59078-507-X

LC 2007-51214

Coretta Scott King honor book for text, 2009

Jazz vocalist Billie Holiday looks back on her early
years in this fictional memoir written in verse.

"This captivating title places readers solidly into Holiday's world, and is suitable for independent reading as well
as a variety of classroom uses." SLJ

Includes bibliographical references

Weaver, Will

Checkered flag cheater. Farrar, Straus Giroux
2010 198p $16.99

Grades: 8 9 10 11 12   **Fic**

1. Minnesota -- Fiction 2. Automobile racing -- Fiction
ISBN 978-0-374-35062-8; 0-374-35062-0

LC 2009-13600

Sequel to Super stock rookie (2009)

Trace Bonham, a teenaged professional stock car racer,
blows away the competition wherever he races, but with every victory Trace is increasingly aware that his winning is
due to more than just his driving skills.

"This is a good choice for car-mad reluctant readers, although a couple of non-graphic sex scenes may limit it to a
slightly older audience than that for previous books in the
series." SLJ

Defect. Farrar, Straus and Giroux 2007 199p
$16

Grades: 7 8 9 10 11 12   **Fic**

1. School stories 2. Minnesota -- Fiction 3. Birth
defects -- Fiction 4. Foster home care -- Fiction
ISBN 0-374-31725-9; 978-0-374-31725-6

LC 2006-49152

After spending most of his life in Minnesota foster
homes hiding a bizarre physical abnormality, fifteen-year-
old David is offered a chance at normalcy, but must decide
if giving up what makes him special is the right thing to do.

The author "skillfully interweaves the improbable
with twenty-first-century realities in this provocative novel of the ultimate cost of being so, so different." Voice
Youth Advocates

Full service. Farrar, Straus & Giroux 2005 231p
hardcover o.p. pa $8.99

Grades: 7 8 9 10   **Fic**

1. Farm life -- Fiction 2. Minnesota -- Fiction 3.
Service stations -- Fiction
ISBN 0-374-32485-9; 0-374-40022-9 pa

LC 2004-57671

In the summer of 1965, teenager Paul Sutton, a northern
Minnesota farm boy, takes a job at a gas station in town,
where his strict religious upbringing is challenged by new
people and experiences.

"Weaver is a wonderful stylist and his beautifully chosen
words put such a shine on his deeply felt story that most
teens will be able to find their own faces reflected in its
pages." Booklist

Saturday night dirt. Farrar, Straus and Giroux
2008 163p $14.95; pa $7.99

Grades: 8 9 10 11   **Fic**

1. Minnesota -- Fiction 2. Automobile racing -- Fiction
ISBN 978-0-374-35060-4; 0-374-35060-4; 978-0-312-
56131-4 pa; 0-312-56131-8 pa

LC 2007-6988

In a small town in northern Minnesota, the much-antici-
pated Saturday night dirt-track race at the old-fashioned,
barely viable, Headwaters Speedway becomes, in many
ways, an important life-changing event for all the participants on and off the track.

"Weaver presents compelling character studies.
. . . Young racing fans . . . will find much that rings true
here." Booklist

Other titles in this series are Checkered flag cheater
(2010)

Super stock rookie (2009)

Super stock rookie. Farrar, Straus and Giroux
2009 199p $14.95

Grades: 8 9 10 11 12   **Fic**

1. Minnesota -- Fiction 2. Automobile racing -- Fiction
ISBN 978-0-374-35061-1; 0-374-35061-2

LC 2008-810

Trace Bonham knows he is fortunate to be offered a
chance at being a paid super stock driver when he is still in
high school, but regrets that he must leave his friends and
home track and wonders if the sponsor is legitimate.

"Weaver offers outstanding descriptions of the races,
putting readers in the center of the action." Booklist

The **survivors**; Will Weaver. 1st ed. Harper 2012 307p.

Grades: 7 8 9 10 **Fic**

1. Dystopian fiction 2. Amnesia -- Fiction 3. Wilderness survival -- Fiction

ISBN 9780060094768; 9780060094775

LC 2011002087

Sequel to: Memory boy

This book takes place after "[t]he volcanoes had erupted. . . . For Miles and his sister, Sarah, the real disaster started in the violent aftermath--when they were forced to leave their cushy suburban home and flee to the north woods for safety. Miles got them to a cabin, but now winter is setting in. All they have to get them through is the milk from Sarah's prized possession--her goat--and Miles's memory of wilderness survival skills. . . . And when a horrific twist of fate robs Miles of his memory, he discovers the heart of his true identity. They knew the volcanoes would change the world. Now, in order to survive, they must change with it." (Publisher's note)

Weber, Lori

If you live like me. Lobster Press 2009 331p pa $14.95

Grades: 7 8 9 10 **Fic**

1. Family life -- Fiction 2. Newfoundland -- Fiction

ISBN 1-897550-12-X; 978-1-897550-12-0

Cheryl's unhappiness builds with each move as her family travels across Canada while her father does research for a book, and by the time they reach Newfoundland, she is planning her escape, but events cause her to re-examine her feelings

"Weber's depiction of Cheryl is true to life, an accurate account of an independent and intelligent teenager struggling with loneliness, acceptance of change, and her own approaching adulthood." SLJ

Weil, Cynthia

I'm glad I did; Cynthia Weil. Soho Teen 2015 272 p. (hardback) $18.99

Grades: 8 9 10 11 12 **Fic**

1. Nineteen sixties 2. Rock music -- Fiction 3. Songwriters and songwriting 4. Love -- Fiction 5. Secrets -- Fiction 6. Composers -- Fiction 7. Popular music -- Fiction

ISBN 161695356X; 9781616953560

LC 2014025047

In this novel by Cynthia Weil "it's the summer of 1963 and JJ Green is a born songwriter . . . [and] she takes an internship at the Brill Building, the epicenter of a new sound called rock and roll. She even finds herself a writing partner in Luke Silver, a boy . . . who seems to connect instantly with her music. Best of all, they'll be cutting their first demo with legendary singer Dulcie Brown. But Dulcie's past is a tangle of secrets." (Publisher's note)

"Grammy-winning songwriter Weil makes an impressive YA debut with this period novel set against the rapidly changing music industry of the early 1960s. . . [s]howing both the bright and the dark sides of the music business, Weil crafts an enticing tale of a sheltered teenager's induction into a world where ambitions and morals are repeatedly tested." PW

Wein, Elizabeth

★ **Black** dove, white raven; Elizabeth Wein. Disney-Hyperion 2015 368 p. (hardback) $17.99

Grades: 8 9 10 11 12 **Fic**

1. Adoption -- Fiction 2. Air pilots -- Fiction 3. Race relations -- Fiction 4. Brothers and sisters -- Fiction 5. Italo-Ethiopian War, 1935-1936 -- Fiction 6. Americans -- Ethiopia -- Fiction 7. Adventure and adventurers -- Fiction 8. Ethiopia -- History -- 1889-1974 -- Fiction

ISBN 142318310X; 9781423183105

LC 2014044446

In this book, by Elizabeth Wein, "Emilia and Teo's lives changed in a fiery, terrifying instant when a bird strike brought down the plane their stunt pilot mothers were flying. Teo's mother died immediately, but Em's survived, determined to raise Teo according to his late mother's wishes. . . . But in 1930s America, a white woman raising a black adoptive son alongside a white daughter is too often seen as a threat." (Publisher's note)

"Em (white) and Teo (black) have grown up together, their mothers American stunt-pilots who met after World War I. After Teo's mother Delia dies in a crash, Em's mother moves the family to Ethiopia -- in part, to fulfill Delia's dream for her son to live in the land of his father, where his skin color won't bring discrimination...The intellectual, psychological, and emotional substance of this story is formidable, and Wein makes it all approachable and engaging." Horn Book

★ **Code** name Verity; Elizabeth Wein. Hyperion Books 2012 343 p. $16.99

Grades: 9 10 11 12 Adult **Fic**

1. Historical fiction 2. Prisoners of war -- Fiction 3. Women air pilots -- Fiction 4. Female friendship -- Fiction 5. France -- History -- 1940-1945, German occupation -- Fiction 6. Nazis -- Fiction 7. Espionage -- Fiction 8. Air pilots -- Fiction 9. Friendship -- Fiction 10. Insurgency -- Fiction 11. World War, 1939-1945 -- Fiction 12. Great Britain -- History -- 1936-1945 -- Fiction 13. France -- History -- German occupation, 1940-1945 -- Fiction

ISBN 9781423152194; 1423152190

LC 2011024857

Michael L. Printz Honor Book (2013)

This young adult historical fiction novel presents a "tale of friendship during World War II. In a cell in Nazi-occupied France, a young woman writes. Like Scheherezade, to whom she is compared by the SS officer in charge of her case, she dribbles out information . . . in exchange for time and a reprieve from torture. . . . [S]he describes her friendship with Maddie, the pilot who flew them to France. . . . She also describes . . . her unbearable current situation." (Kirkus Reviews)

"Wein balances the horrors of war against genuine heroics, delivering a well-researched and expertly crafted adventure." Pub Wkly

★ **Rose** under fire; by Elizabeth Wein. 1st ed. Hyperion 2013 368 p. (hardcover) $17.99

Grades: 9 10 11 12 **Fic**

1. Historical fiction 2. World War, 1939-1945 -- Fiction 3. Diaries -- Fiction 4. Air pilots -- Fiction 5. Prisoners

of war -- Fiction 6. Ravensbruck (Concentration camp) -- Fiction 7. World War, 1939-1945 -- Prisoners and prisons, German -- Fiction
ISBN 1423183096; 9781423183099

LC 2013010337

Schneider Family Book Award: Teen (2014)

Boston Globe-Horn Book Honor: Fiction (2014)

This historical novel chronicles the experiences of American pilot Rose in a Polish concentration camp. "After being brutally punished for her refusal to make fuses for flying bombs . . . , Rose is befriended by Polish 'Rabbits,' victims of horrific medical experimentation. She uses 'counting-out rhymes' to preserve her sanity and as a way to memorize the names of the Rabbits. Rose's poetry . . . is at the heart of the story, revealing her growing understanding of what's happening around her." (Kirkus Reviews)

"Wein excels at weaving research seamlessly into narrative and has crafted another indelible story about friendship borne out of unimaginable adversity." (Pub Wkly)

Weingarten, Lynn

Wherever Nina lies. Point 2009 316p $16.99

Grades: 8 9 10 11 12   Fic

1. Sisters -- Fiction 2. Missing persons -- Fiction
ISBN 978-0-545-06631-0; 0-545-06631-X

LC 2008-21527

"Sixteen-year-old Ellie Wrigley is desperate to find her unconventional, beloved older sister, Nina, who disappeared two years ago, seemingly without a trace. When Ellie uncovers a clue in a local secondhand shop . . . she is determined to investigate. . . . Ellie sets off on a cross-country chase with her new crush, Sean, who has also lost a sibling. . . . Weingarten's fast-paced, chatty style will keep readers tuned in." Publ Wkly

Weis, Margaret

Guardians of the lost; [by] Margaret Weis and Tracy Hickman. HarperCollins Pubs. 2001 592p hardcover o.p. pa $7.99

Grades: 11 12 Adult   Fic

1. Fantasy fiction
ISBN 0-06-105179-9; 0-06-102058-3 pa

LC 2001-40770

Sequel to Well of darkness

In this sequel the authors "again demonstrate their uncanny ability to create meticulously detailed imaginary worlds peopled with complex and vital characters." Libr J

Mistress of dragons. TOR Bks. 2003 381p hardcover o.p. pa $7.99

Grades: 11 12 Adult   Fic

1. Fantasy fiction 2. Dragons -- Fiction
ISBN 0-7653-0468-6; 0-7653-4390-8 pa

LC 2003-42618

When the Amazonian order of priestesses, who have kept dragons from interfering with humans, is violated by men, a wild and magical conflict ensues, revealing a secret lineage and dark truth about the Parliament of Dragons.

"Full of intrigue, magic, and violence, this first book of Dragonvarld—a projected trilogy chronicling the battle to preserve the uneasy relationship between dragons and humans—launches the project powerfully. Weis has bril-

liantly conceived a world viable for both dragons and humans." Booklist

Other titles in the Dragonvarld series are:

The dragon's son (2004)

Master of the dragons (2005)

Weisberg, Joseph

10th grade; a novel. Random House 2002 259p hardcover o.p. pa $13.95

Grades: 11 12 Adult   Fic

1. School stories
ISBN 0-375-50584-9; 0-8129-6662-7 pa

LC 2001-41916

This "novel is the journal of Jeremy Reskin, a tenth-grader with atrocious grammar who does not believe in the utility of commas and will stretch sentences across many lines because his writing teacher has told him to express himself. . . . The book is in fact quite charming and proves surprisingly readable. . . . Weisberg admirably captures the inarticulate voice of a suburban tenth-grader." Booklist

Wells, Dan

Bluescreen; Dan Wells. Balzer + Bray 2016 352 p. $17.99

Grades: 7 8 9 10   Fic

1. Drugs -- Fiction 2. Future life -- Fiction 3. Internet industry -- Fiction
ISBN 006234787X; 9780062347879

LC 2015943608

In this novel, by Dan Wells, "Los Angeles in 2050 is a city of open doors, as long as you have the right connections. That connection is a djinni--a smart device implanted right in a person's head. In a world where virtually everyone is online twenty-four hours a day. Anja . . . gets her hands on . . . a virtual drug that plugs right into a person's djinni and delivers a . . . safe high. But . . . Mari and her friends soon find themselves in the middle of a conspiracy." (Publisher's note)

"Wells' thrilling tale makes great use of its setting, and its diverse cast of characters is well suited for the futuristic L.A. demographic. Though it might hold special appeal for gamers, this is a great fit for readers who fancy noir thrillers and realistically flawed characters." Booklist

Fragments; Dan Wells. Balzer + Bray 2013 576 p. (hardcover bdg.) $17.99

Grades: 9 10 11 12   Fic

1. Survival skills -- Fiction 2. Genetic engineering -- Fiction 3. Identity (Psychology) -- Fiction 4. Science fiction 5. Robots -- Fiction 6. Identity -- Fiction 7. Survival -- Fiction 8. Medical care -- Fiction
ISBN 0062071076; 9780062071071

LC 2012038107

"In this second book in the saga, set in a postapocalyptic U.S. in 2076, Kira is struggling to accept the fact that she is a genetically enhanced human known as a Partial. She makes her way on foot from East Meadow, New York, to the company headquarters of ParaGen in Manhattan in search of a way to cure the RM virus that kills newborns and to stop the expiration of Partials at age 20. Kira allies herself with the last human in Manhattan . . . who may be able to help her." (School Library Journal)

Partials; Dan Wells. 1st ed. Balzer + Bray 2012 470 p. (paperback) $9.99; (hbk: trade bdg.) $17.99
Grades: 9 10 11 12   **Fic**
 1. Science fiction 2. Genetic engineering -- Fiction 3. Communicable diseases -- Fiction 4. Robots -- Fiction 5. Diseases -- Fiction 6. Survival -- Fiction 7. Medical care -- Fiction 8. Medicine -- Research -- Fiction
 ISBN 9780062071057; 0062071041; 9780062071040; 9780062135698
         LC 2011042146
 In this work of speculative fiction by Dan Wells, "after a virus released by the Partials (genetically engineered supersoldiers) . . . topples human civilization . . . [the] government . . . mandates pregnancy for every woman older than eighteen. . . . Kira Walker . . . has an alternative plan: since the Partials were immune to the virus, why not leave the safety of the island, capture a Partial, and bring it back to be studied?" (Bulletin of the Center for Children's Books)

Ruins; Dan Wells; [edited by] Jordan Brown. Balzer + Bray 2014 464 p. (hardcover) $17.99
Grades: 9 10 11 12   **Fic**
 1. Science fiction 2. Robots -- Fiction 3. Apocalyptic fiction
 ISBN 0062071106; 9780062071101
         LC 2013953788
 This young adult science fiction novel, by Dan Wells, is book three in "The Partial Sequence" trilogy. "As the clock ticks closer and closer to the final Partial expiration date, humans and Partials stand on the brink of war. Caught in the middle . . . are Samm and Kira: Samm, who is trapped on the far side of the continent beyond the vast toxic wasteland of the American Midwest; and Kira, now in the hands of Dr. Morgan, who is hell-bent on saving what's left of the Partials." (Publisher's note)
 "In the wake of one apocalypse, can humans and Partials, cloned supersoldiers, live together, or will the world end again? Kira Walker found a cure for the RM plague... Wells concludes his post-apocalyptic, action-packed trilogy with a literal bang and a lot of blood. Believable characters face tough moral choices, and though the end is tidy, the twists and treachery that get readers there are all the fun. It's enjoyable alone but best read after the first two. Science (fiction) at the end of the world done right." (Kirkus)

Wells, Martha
 Emilie & the hollow world; by Martha Wells. Strange Chemistry 2013 301 p. (paperback) $9.99
Grades: 9 10 11 12   **Fic**
 1. Fantasy fiction 2. Runaway teenagers -- Fiction 3. Missing persons -- Fiction 4. Runaway children -- Fiction
 ISBN 1908844493; 9781908844491
         LC 2012277394
 In this book, Emilie is trying to run away. "After spending too much on snacks, [she] can't afford the ferry ticket to reach her cousin's home. There's only one logical thing to do: jump off the docks, swim to the nearest boat and hope for the best. After boarding what she hopes is the right ship, she witnesses a pirate attack, saves a scaled man and watches as a merging of magic and science transports the ship to a legendary world within a world." (Kirkus Reviews)

Wells, Robison
 Feedback; Robison Wells. HarperTeen 2012 312 p. (hardback) $17.99
Grades: 7 8 9 10   **Fic**
 1. Private schools -- Fiction 2. School stories 3. Mystery fiction 4. Science fiction 5. Robots -- Fiction 6. Survival -- Fiction
 ISBN 0062026100; 9780062026101; 9780062228307
         LC 2012004296
 Sequel to: Variant
 In author Robison Wells' story, "Benson Fisher escaped from Maxfield Academy's deadly rules and brutal gangs. The worst was over. Or so he thought. But now he's trapped on the other side of the wall, in a different kind of prison. . . . [His friends] are all pawns in the school's twisted experiment, held captive and controlled by an unseen force. And while Benson struggles to figure out who, if anyone, can be trusted, he discovers that Maxfield Academy's plans are darker than anything he imagined--and they may be impossible to stop." (Publisher's note)

 Variant. HarperTeen 2011 376p $17.99
Grades: 7 8 9 10   **Fic**
 1. School stories 2. Science fiction
 ISBN 978-0-06-202608-8; 0-06-202608-9
         LC 2010042661
 After years in foster homes, seventeen-year-old Benson Fisher applies to New Mexico's Maxfield Academy in hopes of securing a brighter future, but instead he finds that the school is a prison and no one is what he or she seems.
 "Hard to put down from the very first page, this fast-paced novel with Stepford overtones answers only some of the questions it poses, holding some of the most tantalizing open for the next installment in a series that is anything but ordinary." Kirkus

Wells, Rosemary
 ★ **Red** moon at Sharpsburg. Viking 2007 236p $16.99; pa $7.99
Grades: 6 7 8 9 10   **Fic**
 1. United States -- History -- 1861-1865, Civil War -- Fiction
 ISBN 0-670-03638-2; 978-0-670-03638-7; 0-14-241205-8 pa; 978-0-14-241205-3 pa
 As the Civil War breaks out, India, a young Southern girl, summons her sharp intelligence and the courage she didn't know she had to survive the war that threatens to destroy her family, her Virginia home and the only life she has ever known.
 "This powerful novel is unflinching in its depiction of war and the devastation it causes, yet shows the resilience and hope that can follow such a tragedy. India is a memorable, thoroughly believable character." SLJ

Wemmlinger, Raymond
 Booth's daughter. Calkins Creek 2007 210p $17.95
Grades: 7 8 9 10   **Fic**
 1. Actors -- Fiction 2. New York (N.Y.) -- Fiction 3. Father-daughter relationship -- Fiction
 ISBN 978-1-932425-86-4; 1-932425-86-1
         LC 2006-12073

In nineteenth-century New York City, Edwina, daughter of the famous actor Edwin Booth and niece of John Wilkes Booth, finds it difficult to escape the family tragedy and to meet the needs of a demanding father while maintaining her independence.

"Elements reminiscent of an Edith Wharton novel—the mannered social interactions, Gilded Age settings, and matrimony-bound momentum—will draw many romantically inclined readers." Booklist

Wendig, Chuck

Under the Empyrean Sky. Amazon Childrens Pub 2013 368 p. $17.99

Grades: 7 8 9 10   **Fic**

1. Science fiction 2. Apocalyptic fiction
ISBN 1477817204; 9781477817209

In this first book in Chuck Wendig's Heartland Trilogy, "the haves hover above ruined Earth in luxurious flotillas and the have-nots toil below in the Heartland, [are] told whom to marry and what to grow. . . . When Cael and his friends discover a trail of precious, prohibited vegetables growing deep in the corn, they stumble on a secret that may save them—or get them killed." (Kirkus Reviews)

Werlin, Nancy

★ **Double** helix. Dial Books 2004 252p hardcover o.p. pa $6.99

Grades: 7 8 9 10   **Fic**

1. Science fiction 2. Bioethics -- Fiction 3. Genetic engineering -- Fiction
ISBN 0-8037-2606-6; 0-14-240327-X pa

LC 2003-12269

Eighteen-year-old Eli discovers a shocking secret about his life and his family while working for a Nobel Prizewinning scientist whose specialty is genetic engineering.

"Werlin clearly and dramatically raises fundamental bioethical issues for teens to ponder. She also creates a riveting story with sharply etched characters and complex relationships that will stick with readers long after the book is closed." SLJ

Impossible; a novel. Dial Books 2008 376p $17.99

Grades: 7 8 9 10   **Fic**

1. Magic -- Fiction 2. Pregnancy -- Fiction 3. Teenage mothers -- Fiction
ISBN 978-0-8037-3002-1; 0-8037-3002-0

LC 2008-06633

When seventeen-year-old Lucy discovers her family is under an ancient curse by an evil Elfin Knight, she realizes to break the curse she must perform three impossible tasks before her daughter is born in order to save them both.

"Werlin earns high marks for the tale's graceful interplay between wild magic and contemporary reality." Booklist

★ The **rules** of survival. Dial Books 2006 259p $16.99

Grades: 8 9 10 11 12   **Fic**

1. Siblings -- Fiction 2. Child abuse -- Fiction
ISBN 0-8037-3001-2

LC 2006-1675

Seventeen-year-old Matthew recounts his attempts, starting at a young age, to free himself and his sisters from the grip of their emotionally and physically abusive mother.

The author "tackles the topic of child abuse with grace and insight. . . . Teens will empathize with these siblings and the secrets they keep in this psychological horror story." SLJ

Wesselhoeft, Conrad

Adios, nirvana. Houghton Mifflin Harcourt 2010 235p $16

Grades: 10 11 12   **Fic**

1. School stories 2. Death -- Fiction 3. Musicians -- Fiction 4. Friendship -- Fiction 5. Bereavement -- Fiction 6. Seattle (Wash.) -- Fiction
ISBN 978-0-547-36895-5; 0-547-36895-X

LC 2010-06759

As Seattle sixteen-year-old Jonathan helps a dying man come to terms with a tragic event he experienced during World War II, Jonathan begins facing his own demons, especially the death of his twin brother, helped by an assortment of friends, old and new.

"The author gives the reader a wonderful blend of contemporary, historical, and literary fiction. His use of figurative language makes each page dance with images of raw realism. Wesselhoeft guides the reader down an open portal of teen suicide and grief issues. This is a poignant piece for older teens." Voice Youth Advocates

West, Kasie

Pivot point; Kasie West. HarperTeen 2013 352 p. (hardback) $17.99

Grades: 7 8 9 10   **Fic**

1. Love stories 2. Divorce -- Fiction 3. Paranormal fiction 4. Love -- Fiction 5. Schools -- Fiction 6. High schools -- Fiction 7. Choice (Psychology) -- Fiction
ISBN 0062117378; 9780062117373

LC 2012019089

This book tells the story of Addie Coleman, who has the ability to see into the future and choose between the better of two options. "She is a Searcher living in the Compound, the southern Texas home of the most gifted individuals in the county. When her parents decide to divorce, with her mother staying in the Compound, and her father opting to live in the normal world, she decides to use her ability to help her chose with whom to live." (Booklist)

Split second; Kasie West. HarperTeen, an imprint of HarperCollinsPublishers 2014 368 p. (hardcover bdg.) $17.99

Grades: 7 8 9 10   **Fic**

1. Love stories 2. Memory -- Fiction 3. Psychics -- Fiction 4. Love -- Fiction 5. Schools -- Fiction 6. Family life -- Fiction 7. High schools -- Fiction 8. Psychic ability -- Fiction 9. Choice (Psychology) -- Fiction
ISBN 0062117386; 9780062117380

LC 2013008053

In this young adult novel, by Kasie West, Addie has lost her memories, so "when Addie's dad invites her to spend her winter break with him in the Norm world, she jumps at the chance. There she meets the handsome and achingly familiar Trevor. . . . But after witnessing secrets that were supposed to stay hidden, Trevor quickly seems more suspicious of Addie than interested in her. She wants to change that." (Publisher's note)

"In this follow-up to Pivot Point (HarperCollins, 2013), Addie leaves the Compound after a bad breakup. As a Searcher, Addie can see two possible futures, and she finds it hard to believe this is the one she chose, the one in which she is betrayed by her best friend and her boyfriend... In this fast-paced fantasy, the plot is slow to begin but takes off after the first few chapters. Recommended for readers who love dystopian stories with a bit of romance." (School Library Journal)

Westerfeld, Scott

★ **Afterworlds**; by Scott Westerfeld. 1st edition Simon Pulse 2014 608 p. (hardback) $19.99

Grades: 9 10 11 12 **Fic**
1. Authors -- Fiction 2. New York (N.Y.) -- Fiction 3. Dead -- Fiction 4. Love -- Fiction 5. Ghosts -- Fiction 6. Lesbians -- Fiction 7. East Indian Americans -- Fiction
ISBN 1481422340; 9781481422345

LC 2014006852

"Eighteen-year-old Darcy drops her college plans and moves to New York to revise her soon-to-be-published novel and start the second one. Meanwhile, in chapters that alternate with Darcy's NYC adventures, her fictional protagonist, Lizzie, survives a near-death experience to find she has become a psychopomp, responsible for guiding souls to the afterlife." (Booklist)

"Readers who pay attention will see how Darcy's learning curve plays out and how she incorporates and transmutes her real-world experiences into her novel. Watching Darcy's story play off Darcy's novel will fascinate readers as well as writers." Kirkus

Behemoth; written by Scott Westerfeld; illustrated by Keith Thompson. Simon Pulse 2010 485p il

Grades: 7 8 9 10 **Fic**
1. War stories 2. Science fiction 3. Princes -- Fiction 4. Mythical animals -- Fiction 5. Genetic engineering -- Fiction
ISBN 1-4169-7175-0; 978-1-4169-7175-7

LC 2010-9755

Sequel to: Leviathan (2009)

Continues the story of Austrian Prince Alek who, in an alternate 1914 Europe, eludes the Germans by traveling in the Leviathan to Constantinople, where he faces a whole new kind of genetically-engineered warships.

"This exciting and inventive tale of military conflict and wildly reimagined history should captivate a wide range of readers. Thompson's evocative and detailed spot art (as well as the luridly gorgeous endpapers) only sweetens the deal." Publ Wkly

Followed by: Goliath (2011)

Extras. Simon Pulse 2011 399p $17.99; pa $9.99

Grades: 7 8 9 10 **Fic**
1. Science fiction
ISBN 978-1-4424-3007-5; 978-1-4424-1978-0 pa
Sequel to Specials (2006)

First published 2007

Aya is "an 'extra' (face rank stuck in the mid-400,000s) in a city run on a 'reputation economy.' If Aya can win fame as a 'kicker,' reporting with her trusty hovercam on a story that captures the city's imagination, her face rank will soar. . . . Westerfeld shows he has a finger on the pulse of our reputation economy, alchemizing the cult of celebrity, advertising's constant competition for consumer attention." Horn Book

Goliath; written by Scott Westerfeld; illustrated by Keith Thompson. Simon Pulse 2011 543p il $19.99

Grades: 7 8 9 10 **Fic**
1. War stories 2. Science fiction 3. Princes -- Fiction 4. Mythical animals -- Fiction 5. Genetic engineering -- Fiction
ISBN 978-1-4169-7177-1; 1-4169-7177-7

LC 2011015892

Sequel to: Behemoth (2010)

Alek and Deryn encounter obstacles on the last leg of their round-the-world quest to end World War I, reclaim Alek's throne as prince of Austria, and finally fall in love.

"The alternative-history steampunk extravaganza that began with Leviathan (2009) ends with this third volume, and it does not disappoint. Westerfeld propels the story to a satisfying close. . . . Once again, Thompson's evocative art enlivens the narrative." Booklist

The **killing** of worlds. TOR Bks. 2003 336p (Succession) hardcover o.p. pa $14.95

Grades: 11 12 Adult **Fic**
1. Science fiction
ISBN 0-7653-0850-9; 0-7653-2052-5 pa

LC 2003-56304

Sequel to The risen empire

"Captain Laurent Zai demonstrates his strategic cleverness as well as an unusual amount of luck, when he unexpectedly defeats the Rix ship he was sent to destroy—an assignment intended to be a suicide mission. Meanwhile, in the imperial senate, Nara Oxham walks a fine line between treason and her party's agenda as she fights the emperor himself. . . . [This is] a rip-roaring space opera, with its strength residing in the characters, all of them involved in believable dilemmas." Booklist

★ **Leviathan**; written by Scott Westerfeld; illustrated by Keith Thompson. Simon Pulse 2009 440p il map $19.99; pa $9.99

Grades: 7 8 9 10 **Fic**
1. War stories 2. Science fiction 3. Princes -- Fiction 4. Mythical animals -- Fiction 5. Genetic engineering -- Fiction
ISBN 978-1-4169-7173-3; 1-4169-7173-4; 978-1-4169-7174-0 pa; 1-4169-7174-2 pa

LC 2009-881

In an alternate 1914 Europe, fifteen-year-old Austrian Prince Alek, on the run from the Clanker Powers who are attempting to take over the globe using mechanical machinery, forms an uneasy alliance with Deryn who, disguised as a boy to join the British Air Service, is learning to fly genetically-engineered beasts.

"The protagonists' stories are equally gripping and keep the story moving, and Thompson's detail-rich panels bring Westerfeld's unusual creations to life." Publ Wkly

Other titles in this series are:
Behemoth (2010)
Goliath (2011)

★ **Peeps**. Razorbill 2005 312p hardcover o.p. pa $8.99

Grades: 9 10 11 12   **Fic**
1. Vampires -- Fiction
ISBN 1-59514-031-X; 1-59514-083-2 pa
                                        LC 2005-8151
Cal Thompson is a carrier of a parasite that causes vampirism, and must hunt down all of the girlfriends he has unknowingly infected.

"This innovative and original vampire story, full of engaging characters and just enough horror without any gore, will appeal to a wide audience." SLJ

Followed by The last days (2006)

Pretties. Simon Pulse 2011 348p $17.99; pa $9.99

Grades: 7 8 9 10   **Fic**
1. Science fiction
ISBN 978-1-4169-3639-8; 978-1-4424-1980-3 pa
Sequel to Uglies
First published 2005
Tally's transformation to perfect and popular including her totally hot boyfriend is everything she always wanted. But beneath the fun and freedom something is wrong and now Tally has to fight for her life because what she knows has put her in danger with the authorities.

"Riveting and compulsively readable, this action-packed sequel does not disappoint." Booklist

Followed by Specials

Specials. Simon Pulse 2011 350p $17.99; pa $9.99

Grades: 7 8 9 10   **Fic**
1. Science fiction
ISBN 978-1-4424-3008-2; 978-1-4424-1979-7 pa
Sequel to Pretties
First published 2006
Tally has been transformed from a repellent ugly to supermodel pretty. Now she's a super-amped fighting machine. Her mission is to keep the uglies down and the pretties stupid. But Tally's never been good at playing by the rules.

"Readers who enjoyed Uglies and Pretties . . . will not want to miss Specials. . . . Westerfeld's themes include vanity, environmental conservation, Utopian idealism, fascism, violence, and love." SLJ

Followed by Extras

Uglies. Simon Pulse 2005 425p rpt $17.99
Grades: 7 8 9 10   **Fic**
1. Science fiction
ISBN 9781416936381
"Tally is an ugly, waiting eagerly for her sixteenth birthday, when surgery will make her into a Pretty and she can join her old friend Peris in the life of the beautiful in New Pretty Town. In the meantime, she revels in hoverboard-

ing and pulling tricks with her rebellious friend, Shay, who doesn't share Tally's anticipation for joining the Pretty world. When Shay runs away to join dissidents outside the city, Tally is blackmailed by the city's Special Circumstances unit into following Shay and uncovering the location of the anti-establishment rebels, a task that becomes more difficult when Tally's sympathies begin to skew toward the rebels, especially their charismatic leader, David. . . . Grades six to ten." (Bull Cent Child Books)

"Fifteen-year-old Tally's eerily harmonious, postapocalyptic society gives extreme makeovers to teens on their sixteenth birthdays. . . . When a top-secret agency threatens to leave Tally ugly forever unless she spies on runaway teens, she agrees to infiltrate the Smoke, a shadowy colony of refugees from the 'tyranny of physical perfection.'" Booklist

Zeroes; by Scott Westerfeld, Margo Lanagan, and Deborah Biancotti. Simon Pulse 2015 hardcover $19.99

Grades: 8 9 10 11   **Fic**
1. Teenagers -- Fiction 2. California -- Fiction 3. Superheroes -- Fiction
ISBN 9781481443364
                                        LC 2015001667
In this book, "X-Men meets Heroes when New York Times bestselling author Scott Westerfeld teams up with award-winning authors Margo Lanagan and Deborah Biancotti to create a sizzling new series filled with action and adventure. Don't call them heroes. But these six Californian teens have powers that set them apart." (Publisher's note)

"A powerful tale with an emotional rawness that will resonate with readers." Booklist

Weston, Robert Paul

Blues for Zoey; Robert Paul Weston. Flux 2015 304 p. $9.99

Grades: 9 10 11 12   **Fic**
1. Love stories 2. Musicians -- Fiction 3. Bildungsromans 4. Fund-raising -- Fiction 5. Coming of age -- Fiction 6. Racially mixed people -- Fiction
ISBN 0738743402; 9780738743400
                                        LC 2014037101
In this book by Robert Paul Weston, "from his first glimpse, 16-year-old Kaz Barrett is hypnotized by Zoey, a mysterious street performer with pink dreadlocks and an enormous crucifix-shaped musical instrument. While they explore their frenetic romantic connection, Kaz is also preoccupied with his mother's immobilizing sleep disorder, a job at the local Laundromat, and untangling the lies and deceptions of the con artists and vagrants he tends to associate with." (Publishers Weekly)

"Music and mystery twist together in Robert Paul Weston's latest YA novel, which features Kaz Barrett, a 16-year-old boy who's as focused on building his bank account as he is on getting a girlfriend. But contrary to what everyone thinks, Kaz isn't desperately saving for college. Every dollar he earns working at the local laundromat goes toward sending his mother to an expensive clinic in New York in an attempt to cure the rare neurological disease that causes her to fall asleep for days at a time. . . . Weston effectively drops hints about Zoey's mysterious past, and it won't be too difficult for astute readers to put the pieces together a step or two ahead of Kaz. This isn't necessarily a criticism;

rather, it's entirely believable that Kaz's obsessive love for Zoey would blind him to the truth. Fortunately, the novel's journey is suitably winding to keep the reader intrigued." Quill & Quire

Dust city; a novel. by Robert Weston. Razorbill 2010 299p $16.99

Grades: 7 8 9 10　　　　　　　　　　　　　　**Fic**
1. Magic -- Fiction 2. Wolves -- Fiction 3. Fairies -- Fiction 4. Father-son relationship -- Fiction
ISBN 978-1-59514-296-2; 1-59514-296-7
　　　　　　　　　　　　　　　LC 2010-36067

Henry Whelp, son of the Big Bad Wolf, investigates what happened to the fairies that used to protect humans and animalia, and what role the corporation that manufactures synthetic fairy dust played in his father's crime.

"The premise is fractured fairy tale, but the play is pure noir. . . . The clever setup and gutting of fairy-tale tropes will garner plenty of enthusiasm." Booklist

Wettersten, Laura

My faire lady; Laura Wettersten. First edition Simon & Schuster 2014 352 p. (hardcover) $17.99

Grades: 7 8 9 10 11 12　　　　　　　　　　**Fic**
1. Historical reenactments 2. Teenage girls -- Fiction 3. Love -- Fiction 4. Renaissance fairs -- Fiction 5. Summer employment -- Fiction 6. Dating (Social customs) -- Fiction
ISBN 1442489332; 9781442489332
　　　　　　　　　　　　　　　LC 2013021542

In this young adult novel by Laura Wettersten, "Rowena Duncan is a thoroughly modern girl with big plans for her summer . . . until she catches her boyfriend making out with another girl. Heartbroken, she applies to an out-of-town job posting and finds herself somewhere she never expected: the Renaissance Faire. As a face-painter doubling as a serving wench, Ro is thrown headfirst into a vibrant community of artists and performers." (Publisher's note)

"Sharp, funny dialogue is mixed with thoughtful resolutions of relevant teenage topics—love and lust, admitting fault, the mettle it takes to pursue a passion. The rich backdrop of the fair, with its vivid description and appealing characters, is icing on the cake. Verily, fine fare." Kirkus

My fair lady

Weyn, Suzanne

Distant waves; a novel of the Titanic. Scholastic Press 2009 330p $17.99

Grades: 8 9 10 11　　　　　　　　　　　　　**Fic**
1. Inventors 2. Journalists 3. Financiers 4. Fur traders 5. Sisters -- Fiction 6. Electrical engineers 7. Inventors -- Fiction 8. Spiritualism -- Fiction 9. Titanic (Steamship) -- Fiction 10. Mother-daughter relationship -- Fiction
ISBN 978-0-545-08572-4; 0-545-08572-1
　　　　　　　　　　　　　　　LC 2008-40708

In the early twentieth century, four sisters and their widowed mother, a famed spiritualist, travel from New York to London, and as the Titanic conveys them and their acquaintances, journalist W.T. Stead, scientist Nikola Tesla, and industrialist John Jacob Astor, home, Tesla's inventions will either doom or save them all.

"The interplay of science, spirituality, history and romance will satisfy." Publ Wkly

Dr. Frankenstein's daughters; by Suzanne Weyn. Scholastic Press 2013 320 p. (hardcover) $17.99

Grades: 9 10 11　　　　　　　　　　　　　　**Fic**
1. Gothic novels 2. Human experimentation in medicine 3. Horror tales 4. Horror stories 5. Twins -- Fiction 6. Diaries -- Fiction 7. Sisters -- Fiction 8. Monsters -- Fiction
ISBN 0545425336; 9780545425339
　　　　　　　　　　　　　　　LC 2012033039

In this book, "twin teen sisters Giselle and Ingrid discover that they've inherited a castle in the Orkneys from their father, Victor. For giddy Giselle, it's a . . . chance to throw a huge party. . . . For the more studious Ingrid, her father's old journals . . . provide not only exciting insights into her father's work, but also the tools with which to outfit Walter, the moody and disabled ex-soldier to whom she's given her heart, with a new arm and leg." (Kirkus Reviews)

"Seventeen-year-old twins tell their story in alternating diary entries as they journey to claim an inherited castle and learn about their father, Dr. Victor Frankenstein. Giselle longs for social grace; Ingrid strives for education. But both are haunted by strange dangers and a series of murders. This curious takeoff on Shelley's classic is ornamented with absorbing gothic elements and a brooding romance." (Horn Book)

Empty. Scholastic Press 2010 183p $17.99

Grades: 7 8 9 10　　　　　　　　　　　　　**Fic**
1. Science fiction 2. Ecology -- Fiction 3. Hurricanes -- Fiction 4. Energy resources -- Fiction 5. Environmental degradation -- Fiction
ISBN 978-0-545-17278-3; 0-545-17278-0
　　　　　　　　　　　　　　　LC 2010-16743

When, just ten years in the future, oil supplies run out and global warming leads to devastating storms, senior high school classmates Tom, Niki, Gwen, Hector, and Brock realize that the world as they know it is ending and lead the way to a more environmentally-friendly society.

"The realistic and thought-provoking scenario is packaged into a speedy read, and given the popularity of dystopian fiction, it should find an audience." Booklist

Whaley, John Corey

Noggin; by John Corey Whaley. Atheneum Books for Young Readers 2014 352 p. (hardback) $17.99

Grades: 9 10 11 12　　　　　　　　　　　　**Fic**
1. Cryonics 2. Medical novels 3. Teenagers -- Fiction 4. Science fiction 5. Death -- Fiction 6. Identity -- Fiction 7. Family life -- Fiction 8. Interpersonal relations -- Fiction 9. Transplantation of organs, tissues, etc. -- Fiction
ISBN 1442458720; 9781442458727; 9781442458734
　　　　　　　　　　　　　　　LC 2013020137

National Book Award Shortlist: Young People's Literature (2014)

In this book by John Corey Whaley, "Travis Coates has his head surgically removed and cryogenically frozen after he dies. Five years after his death, technological advances allow doctors to attach his head to a donor body that's taller and more muscular than the original." The book focuses on "Travis's comic determination to turn back the hands of time." (Publishers Weekly)

"Whaley's sophomore effort eschews the complicated narrative structure of Where Things Come Back for a more straightforward one; and the premise isn't the most original, with variations ranging from Peter Dickinson's classic Eva (rev. 7/89) to Mary Pearson's recent Jenna Fox trilogy. But readers will find it easy to become invested in Travis's second coming-of age -- brimming with humor, pathos, and angst -- and root for him to make peace with his new life." (Horn Book)

★ **Where** things come back. Atheneum Books for Young Readers 2011 228p. $16.99
Grades: 9 10 11 12   **Fic**
1. Birds -- Fiction 2. Arkansas -- Fiction 3. Friendship -- Fiction 4. Family life -- Fiction 5. Missing persons -- Fiction
ISBN 978-1-4424-1333-7; 1-4424-1333-6
     LC 201024836
Michael L. Printz Award (2012)
William C. Morris YA Debut Award (2012)
Seventeen-year-old Cullen's summer in Lily, Arkansas, is marked by his cousin's death by overdose, an alleged spotting of a woodpecker thought to be extinct, failed romances, and his younger brother's sudden disappearance.

"The realistic characters and fascinating mix of mundane with life changing and tragic events create a memorable story most young adult readers will connect to." Libr Media Connect

Whelan, Gloria
All my noble dreams and then what happens; Gloria Whelan. 1st ed. Simon & Schuster Books for Young Readers 2013 272 p. (hardcover) $15.99
Grades: 6 7 8 9 10   **Fic**
1. India -- History 2. Historical fiction 3. Aunts -- Fiction 4. Insurgency -- Fiction 5. Family life -- India -- Fiction 6. Great Britain -- History -- George V, 1910-1936 -- Fiction 7. India -- History -- British occupation, 1765-1947 -- Fiction 8. India -- History -- British occupation, 1765-1947
ISBN 1442449764; 9781442449763; 9781442449770
     LC 2012018599
Sequel to: Small acts of amazing courage
This novel is a sequel to Gloria Whelan's "Small Acts of Amazing Courage." Set "in India in the year 1921," here British-born protagonist Rosy has returned to "India, the land she considers home, after an extended stay in England. The household . . . is bustling with preparations for a visit by the Prince of Wales. Rosy has promised to deliver a letter written by Mahatma Gandhi, an appeal to Great Britain to give India its freedom." (Publishers Weekly)

The **Disappeared**. Dial Books 2008 136p $16.99; pa $6.99

Grades: 8 9 10 11 12   **Fic**
1. Siblings -- Fiction 2. Argentina -- Fiction
ISBN 978-0-8037-3275-9; 0-8037-3275-9; 978-0-14-241540-5 pa; 0-14-241540-5 pa
     LC 2007-43750
Teenaged Silvia tries to save her brother, Eduardo, after he is captured by the military government in 1970s Argentina

"The deftly handled voices of Silvia and Eduardo follow the well-intentioned, but often grievous, mistakes of youth. Their compelling tale is a chilling account of the manipulative power of corruption." SLJ
Includes bibliographical references

★ **Homeless** bird. HarperCollins Pubs. 2000 216p hardcover o.p. pa $5.99
Grades: 6 7 8 9 10   **Fic**
1. India -- Fiction 2. Women -- India -- Fiction
ISBN 0-06-028454-4; 0-06-440819-1 pa
     LC 99-33241
When thirteen-year-old Koly enters into an ill-fated arranged marriage, she must either suffer a destiny dictated by India's tradition or find the courage to oppose it.

"This beautifully told, inspiring story takes readers on a fascinating journey through modern India and the universal intricacies of a young woman's heart." Booklist

See what I see. HarperTeen 2011 199p $16.99
Grades: 7 8 9 10 11 12   **Fic**
1. Sick -- Fiction 2. Artists -- Fiction 3. Detroit (Mich.) -- Fiction 4. Father-daughter relationship -- Fiction
ISBN 978-0-06-125545-8; 0-06-125545-9
     LC 2010-03094
When eighteen-year-old Kate arrives on the Detroit doorstep of her long-estranged father, a famous painter, she is shocked to learn that he is dying and does not want to support her efforts to attend the local art school.

"With elegant prose, Whelan portrays a gradually developing and complex relationship built on guilt, curiosity, love, and a passion for art." Booklist

Whipple, Natalie
House of ivy and sorrow; Natalie Whipple. HarperTeen, an imprint of HarperCollinsPublishers 2014 368 p. (pbk. bdg.) $9.99
Grades: 8 9 10 11 12   **Fic**
1. Love stories 2. Fantasy fiction 3. Friendship -- Fiction 4. Witchcraft -- Fiction 5. Grandmothers -- Fiction 6. Blessing and cursing -- Fiction 7. Fathers and daughters -- Fiction 8. Dating (Social customs) -- Fiction
ISBN 0062120182; 9780062120182
     LC 2013008052
In this young adult fantasy romance novel by Natalie Whipple, "Jo Hemlock is not your typical witch. Outside the walls of her grandmother's ivy-covered house, she's kept her magical life completely separate from her life in high school. But when the Curse that killed her mother resurfaces, it threatens to destroy not only her life but her grandmother's too--and keeping her secret may no longer be an option." (Publisher's note)

"Josephine, 17, lives with her grandmother in a house under the interstate where it's rumored that an old witch can make someone love you if you're willing to give her your pinkie finger. Jo knows that the rumors are true, because her grandmother is that witch...This is a fast-paced fantasy, with just the right amount of romance and realism. Readers will relate to Jo's relationships with her family, crush, and two best friends. Despite the current glut of supernatural and urban fantasy, this tale will stand out." SLJ

Whitaker, Alecia

Wildflower; by Alecia Whitaker. First edition Little, Brown and Co. 2014 320 p. illustrations (hardcover) $18

Grades: 7 8 9 10　　　　　　　　　　　　　**Fic**
1. Women musicians 2. Country music -- Fiction 3. Fame -- Fiction 4. Musicians -- Fiction 5. Family life -- Fiction 6. Nashville (Tenn.) -- Fiction 7. Dating (Social customs) -- Fiction
ISBN 0316251380; 9780316251365; 9780316251389
LC 2013023693

In this young adult novel by Alecia Whitaker, "Bird Barrett has grown up on the road, singing backup in her family's bluegrass band and playing everywhere from Nashville, Tennessee, to Nowhere, Oklahoma. But one fateful night, when Bird fills in for her dad by singing lead, a scout in the audience offers her a spotlight all her own. . . . With Bird's star on the rise, though, the rest of her life falls into chaos as tradition and ambition collide." (Publisher's note)

"Genuine dialogue, a quick pace and a plot that strikes the right balance between realistic and fantastic make for an engaging read. The lyrics and sheet music for one of Bird's songs are appended.This tender introduction to a newly minted country superstar sets the stage for a compelling series." Kirkus

Whitcomb, Laura

A **certain** slant of light. Graphia 2005 282p $8.99

Grades: 9 10 11 12　　　　　　　　　　　　**Fic**
1. Ghost stories 2. Future life -- Fiction
ISBN 0-618-58532-X pa
LC 2004-27208

After benignly haunting a series of people for 130 years, Helen meets a teenage boy who can see her and together they unlock the mysteries of their pasts.

The author "creatively pulls together a dramatic and compelling plot that cleverly grants rebellious teen romance a timeless grandeur." Bull Cent Child Books

The **Fetch**; a novel. Houghton Mifflin Harcourt 2009 379p il $17

Grades: 9 10 11 12　　　　　　　　　　　　**Fic**
1. Monks 2. Princes 3. Princesses 4. Courtiers 5. Death -- Fiction 6. Soviet Union -- History -- 1917-1921, Revolution -- Fiction
ISBN 978-0-618-89131-3; 0-618-89131-5
LC 2008-13307

After 350 years as a Fetch, or death escort, Calder breaks his vows and enters the body of Rasputin, whose spirit causes rebellion in the Land of Lost Souls while Calder struggles to convey Ana and Alexis, orphaned in the Russian Revolution, to Heaven.

"The rich descriptions, particularly of the exquisitely imagined afterlife, are exceptionally drawn, as are the sympathetic characters and the unusual premise. A challenging book with an intriguing conclusion, this will lead thoughtful readers to spirited discussions." Booklist

White, Andrea

Surviving Antarctica; reality TV 2083. HarperCollins Publishers 2005 327p hardcover o.p. pa $6.99

Grades: 7 8 9 10　　　　　　　　　　　　　**Fic**
1. Science fiction 2. Antarctica -- Fiction
ISBN 0-06-055454-1; 0-06-055456-8 pa
LC 2004-6249

In the year 2083, five fourteen-year-olds who were deprived by chance of the opportunity to continue their educations reenact Scott's 1910-1913 expedition to the South Pole as contestants on a reality television show, secretly aided by a Department of Entertainment employee

"A real page-turner, this novel will give readers pause as they ponder the ethics of teens risking their lives in adult-contrived situations for the entertainment of the masses." Booklist

White, Ellen Emerson

Long may she reign. Feiwel and Friends 2007 708p $15.95

Grades: 6 7 8 9 10　　　　　　　　　　　　**Fic**
1. School stories 2. Presidents -- Fiction 3. Post-traumatic stress disorder -- Fiction
ISBN 978-0-312-36767-1; 0-312-36767-8
LC 2007-32635

Meg Powers, daughter of the president of the United States, is recovering from a brutal kidnapping, and in an effort to deal with her horrific experience and her anger at her mother—the president—for not negotiating for her release, Meg decides to go away for her second semester of college, where she encounters even more challenges.

"The hip dialogue will hook teens. . . . Beneath its chick-lit veneer, this book is a thought-provoking read." Voice Youth Advocates

The **President's** daughter. Feiwel and Friends 2008 304p pa $9.99

Grades: 7 8 9 10　　　　　　　　　　　　　**Fic**
1. Moving -- Fiction 2. Politics -- Fiction 3. Washington (D.C.) -- Fiction 4. Mother-daughter relationship -- Fiction
ISBN 0-312-37488-7; 978-0-312-37488-4
LC 2008-6888

First published 1984

Sixteen-year-old Meghan Powers' happy life in Massachusetts changes drastically when her mother, one of the most prestigious senators in the country, becomes the front-runner in the race for United States President.

"Besides offering a solid look at the political system, this [book] has very strong characterizations." Booklist

Other titles about Meg are:
White House autumn (2008)
Long live the queen (2008)
Long may she reign (2007)

White, Kiersten

Perfect lies; Kiersten White. HarperTeen, an imprint of HarperCollinsPublishers 2014 240 p. (Mind games) (hardcover bdg.) $17.99 **Fic**

1. Sisters -- Fiction 2. Psychic ability -- Fiction
ISBN 0062135848; 9780062135841

LC 2013008056

Written by Kiersten White, this novel is a "sequel to "Mind Games'," describing how "For years, Annie and Fia have been in an endless battle for survival against the Keane Foundation. Now the sisters have found allies who can help them escape. But Annie's visions of the future and Fia's flawless instincts can't always tell them who to trust." (Publisher's note)

"Fia and Annie, sisters with paranormal powers, plot to take down the ruthless Keane Foundation that has controlled them in this breathless sequel to Mind Games (2013)...Suspenseful and smart, this ties up the main story lines while leaving the greater world-building details to the imagination." (Booklist)

White, T. H.

★ The **once** and future king. Putnam 1958 677p $25.95

Grades: 8 9 10 11 12 Adult **Fic**

1. Fantasy fiction 2. Kings 3. Knights and knighthood -- Fiction 4. Great Britain -- History -- 0-1066 -- Fiction
ISBN 0-399-10597-2

LC 58-10760

An omnibus edition of four novels; The sword in the stone (1939), The witch in the wood (1939, now called The Queen of Air and Darkness) and The ill-made knight (1940). A number of alterations have been made in the earlier books. Previously unpublished, The candle in the wind "deals with the plotting of Mordred and his kinsmen of the house of Orkney, and their undying enmity to King Arthur." Times Lit Suppl

Whitehead, Colson

Sag Harbor; a novel. Doubleday 2009 288p $24.95

Grades: 11 12 Adult **Fic**

1. Brothers -- Fiction 2. Adolescence -- Fiction 3. African Americans -- Fiction 4. Long Island (N.Y.) -- Fiction
ISBN 978-0-385-52765-1; 0-385-52765-9

LC 2008-13510

Benji, one of the only black kids at an elite prep school in Manhattan, tries desperately to fit in, but every summer, he and his brother, Reggie, escape to the East End of Sag Harbor, where a small community of African American professionals has built a world of its own.

The author "serves up whole sundaes worth of riffs on the quotidian, all hung on the skinny frame of a 15-year-old everyman virgin and his marginally less distinct friends, give or take a repressive father and a particularly evocative shoreline landscape." Village Voice

Whitley, David

The **children** of the lost. Roaring Brook Press 2011 357p $16.99

Grades: 7 8 9 10 **Fic**

1. Fantasy fiction
ISBN 978-1-59643-614-5; 1-59643-614-X

LC 2010-28112

Sequel to: Midnight charter (2009)

Banished from Agora, the ancient city-state where absolutely everything must be bartered, Mark and Lily are happy to find the apparently perfect land of Giseth except that the inhabitants seem fearful, something strange lurks in the surrounding forest, and a mysterious woman keeps appearing in their dreams urging them to find the children of the lost.

This "explores tantalizing new territory and solidifies the Agora Trilogy as one of the more literary ambitious and complex fantasies going." Booklist

Midnight charter. Roaring Brook Press 2009 319p $17.99

Grades: 7 8 9 10 **Fic**

1. Science fiction
ISBN 978-1-59643-381-6; 1-59643-381-7

"Deft world-building and crafty plotting combine for a zinger of an ending that will leave readers poised for book two. Surprisingly sophisticated upper-middle-grade fare, with enough meat to satisfy older readers as well." Kirkus

Followed by: The children of the lost (2011)

Whitman, Emily

Wildwing. Greenwillow Books 2010 359p $16.99

Grades: 7 8 9 10 **Fic**

1. Falcons -- Fiction 2. Time travel -- Fiction 3. Social classes -- Fiction 4. Great Britain -- History -- 1066-1154, Norman period -- Fiction
ISBN 978-0-06-172452-7; 0-06-172452-1

LC 2009-44189

In 1913 London, fifteen-year-old Addy is a lowly servant, but when she gets inside an elevator car in her employer's study, she is suddenly transported to a castle in 1240 and discovers that she is mistaken for the lord's intended bride.

"Whitman populates both of her worlds with vivid, believable characters. . . . This historical novel with a time-travel twist of sci-fi will find an avid readership." SLJ

Whitman, Sylvia

The **milk** of birds; by Sylvia Whitman. 1st ed. Atheneum Books for Young Readers 2013 384 p. (hardcover) $16.99; (paperback) $9.99

Grades: 9 10 11 12 **Fic**

1. Pen pals -- Fiction 2. Friendship -- Fiction 3. Sudan -- History -- Darfur conflict, 2003- -- Fiction 4. Sudan -- Fiction 5. Letters -- Fiction 6. Genocide -- Fiction 7. Refugees -- Fiction 8. Darfur (Sudan) -- Fiction
ISBN 144244682X; 9781442446823; 9781442446830; 9781442446847

LC 2012005594

In this book, "an American teen from Richmond, Va., and a Sudanese teen in Darfur exchange letters. . . . Fourteen-year-old Nawra has been raped, her family murdered and her village burned in Darfur's genocidal war. . . . Nonprofit Save the Girls matches Nawra with American pen pal K.C. Cannelli, an unconventional 14-year-old with an undiagnosed learning disability. . . . As K.C. discovers everything Nawra has endured, she becomes an advocate and fundraiser for Darfur's refugees." (Kirkus Reviews)

Whitney, Daisy

The **Mockingbirds**. Little, Brown 2010 339p $16.99

Grades: 10 11 12   **Fic**

1. School stories 2. Rape -- Fiction 3. Sisters -- Fiction 4. Secret societies -- Fiction

ISBN 978-0-316-09053-7; 0-316-09053-0

LC 2009-51257

When Alex, a junior at an elite preparatory school, realizes that she may have been the victim of date rape, she confides in her roommates and sister who convince her to seek help from a secret society, the Mockingbirds.

"Authentic and illuminating, this strong . . . [title] explores vital teen topics of sex and violence; crime and punishment; ineffectual authority; and the immeasurable, healing influence of friendship and love." Booklist

The **rivals**; by Daisy Whitney. Little, Brown and Co. 2012 346 p. $17.99

Grades: 9 10 11 12   **Fic**

1. Private schools -- Fiction 2. Medication abuse -- Fiction 3. Secret societies -- Fiction 4. Cheating (Education) -- Fiction 5. Teenagers -- Conduct of life -- Fiction 6. Schools -- Fiction 7. Cheating -- Fiction 8. Conduct of life -- Fiction 9. Boarding schools -- Fiction

ISBN 9780316090575

LC 2011019227

This book provides a sequel to Daisy Whitney's 2010 book "The Mockingbirds." Here, "Alex is now the leader of the underground student-run justice system at Themis Academy, a boarding school where adults ignore bullying and reputation is more important than ethics. Themes of truth, power, leadership, and personal responsibility are echoed in the students' reading assignments . . . as the Mockingbirds investigate the source of illegal ADHD drugs on campus, and Alex finds a caring relationship." (Booklist)

When you were here; by Daisy Whitney. Little, Brown and Co. 2013 272 p. $18

Grades: 7 8 9 10   **Fic**

1. Cancer -- Fiction 2. Tokyo (Japan) -- Fiction 3. Mother-son relationship -- Fiction 4. Grief -- Fiction 5. Japan -- Fiction 6. Mothers and sons -- Fiction

ISBN 0316209740; 9780316209748

LC 2012031409

In this novel by Daisy Whitney "when he gets a letter from his [deceased] mom's property manager in Tokyo, where she had been going for [cancer] treatment, it shows . . . a side of his mother he never knew.Danny travels to Tokyo to connect with his mother's memory and make sense of her final months. Among the cherry blossoms, temples, and crowds, and with the help of a . . . girl, he begins to see how it may not have been ancient magic or mystical treatment that kept his mother going." (Publisher's note)

"Danny's mother has recently died from cancer, his father died years ago, his estranged sister lives in China, and he and Holland, the love of his life, have broken up. A trip to Japan is enlightening and helps him handle a shocking secret he learns about Holland. The extent of Danny's prob-

lems stretches credulity, but readers will be caught up in the drama." (Horn Book)

Whitney, Kim Ablon

The **perfect** distance. Knopf 2005 256p hardcover o.p. pa $5.99

Grades: 9 10 11 12   **Fic**

1. Horsemanship -- Fiction 2. Mexican Americans -- Fiction

ISBN 0-375-83243-2; 0-553-49467-8 pa

LC 2005-40726

While competing in the three junior national equitation championships, seventeen-year-old Francie Martinez learns to believe in herself and makes some decisions about the type of person she wants to be

The author "inhabits Francie's character wholly and convincingly and gets the universals of serious competition just right—any athlete will recognize the imperious, unfeeling coach; the snotty front-runner; and the unparalleled thrill of hitting the zone." Booklist

Whittenberg, Allison

Life is fine. Delacorte Press 2008 181p $15.99; lib bdg $18.99

Grades: 8 9 10 11 12   **Fic**

1. Child abuse -- Fiction 2. African Americans -- Fiction 3. Mother-daughter relationship -- Fiction

ISBN 978-0-385-73480-6; 978-0-385-90478-0 lib bdg

LC 2007-27604

With a neglectful mother who has an abusive, live-in boyfriend, life for fifteen-year-old Samara is not fine, but when a substitute teacher walks into class one day and introduces her to poetry, she starts to view life from a different perspective.

"Samara's voice is sharp and convincing." Publ Wkly

Whyman, Matt

Goldstrike; a thriller. Atheneum Books for Young Readers 2010 262p $16.99

Grades: 7 8 9 10   **Fic**

1. Computer crimes -- Fiction 2. London (England) -- Fiction 3. United States -- Central Intelligence Agency -- Fiction

ISBN 978-1-4169-9510-4; 1-4169-9510-2

LC 2009-17830

Sequel to: Icecore (2007)

After escaping Camp Twilight, eighteen-year-old Carl Hobbes and Beth, his girlfriend, begin a new life in London, England, where he attempts to program Sphynx Cargo's highly intelligent supercomputer to help protect them from the CIA and assassins.

"The action sequences are believable and often realistically brutal, and the climactic battle is intense and entertaining." Publ Wkly

Icecore; a Carl Hobbes thriller. Atheneum Books for Young Readers 2007 307p $16.99; pa $8.99

Grades: 7 8 9 10   **Fic**

1. Torture -- Fiction 2. Prisoners -- Fiction 3. Arctic regions -- Fiction 4. Military bases -- Fiction 5.

Computer crimes -- Fiction

ISBN 978-1-4169-4907-7; 1-4169-4907-0; 978-1-4169-8960-8 pa; 1-4169-8960-9 pa

LC 2007-02674

Seventeen-year-old Englishman Carl Hobbes meant no harm when he hacked into Fort Knox's security system, but at Camp Twilight in the Arctic Circle, known as the Guantanamo Bay of the north, he is tortured to reveal information about a conspiracy of which he was never a part.

"Powered by a fast-paced narrative, this exploration of numerous timely themes . . . gives the eminently readable adventure a degree of depth." Publ Wkly

Followed by: Goldstrike (2010)

Wiggins, Bethany

Cured; by Bethany Wiggins. Bloomsbury/Walker 2014 320 p. (hardback) $17.99

Grades: 7 8 9 10 11 12   **Fic**

1. Science fiction 2. Apocalyptic fiction 3. Twins -- Fiction 4. Survival -- Fiction 5. Voyages and travels -- Fiction 6. Brothers and sisters -- Fiction

ISBN 0802734200; 9780802734204

LC 2013024935

Sequel to: Stung

In this book, by Bethany Wiggins, is a "reimagining of our world after an environmental catastrophe. . . . Now that Fiona Tarsis and her twin brother, Jonah, are no longer beasts, they set out to find their mother. . . . Heading for a safe settlement rumored to be in Wyoming . . . they are attacked by raiders. Luckily, they find a new ally in Kevin, who saves them and leads them to safety in his underground shelter. But the more they get to know Kevin, the more they suspect he has ties to the raiders." (Publisher's note)

"Jacqui lives as Jack in a dangerous zombie-ish dystopia caused by a vaccine's unforeseen effects. Searching for her missing older brother, Jacqui joins forces with Fiona Tarsis (Stung), who has the cure for the rabid vaccine recipients, but they are sidetracked by raiders. Mysterious romance and eleventh-hour reveals do not rescue this sequel from its meandering plot and clunky gender politics." Horn Book

Stung; Bethany Wiggins. Walker & Company 2013 304 p. (hardcover) $17.99

Grades: 7 8 9 10 11 12   **Fic**

1. Science fiction 2. Epidemics -- Fiction 3. Survival -- Fiction

ISBN 0802734189; 9780802734181

LC 2012027183

In this novel, by Bethany Wiggins, "a worldwide pandemic occurred and the government tried to bio-engineer a cure. Only the solution was deadlier than the original problem-the vaccination turned people into ferocious, deadly beasts who were branded as a warning to un-vaccinated survivors. Key people needed to rebuild society are protected from disease and beasts inside a fortress-like wall. But Fiona has awakened branded, alone-and on the wrong side of the wall." (Publisher's note)

"Wiggins. . . muses on the dangers of science and medicine and deftly maps out the chain of events that has led to catastrophe, creating a violent world vastly different from ours but still recognizable. With a stirring conclusion and space for a sequel, it's an altogether captivating story." Kirkus

Wignall, K. J.

Blood; [by] K. J. Wignall. Egmont USA 2011 264p (Mercian triology) $16.99; ebook $16.99

Grades: 7 8 9 10 11 12   **Fic**

1. Vampires -- Fiction 2. Good and evil -- Fiction

ISBN 978-1-60684-220-1; 1-60684-220-X; 978-1-60684-258-4 ebook; 1-60684-258-7 ebook

LC 2011005899

A centuries-old vampire wakes up in the modern day to find he is being hunted by an unknown enemy, and begins to uncover the secrets of his origin and the path of his destiny.

Wignall "develops what could have been yet another vampire story into a promising series opener with a sophisticated plot and elegant prose." Booklist

Wild, K.

Fight game; [by] Kate Wild. Chicken House/Scholastic 2007 279p $16.99

Grades: 7 8 9 10   **Fic**

1. Science fiction 2. Spies -- Fiction 3. Martial arts -- Fiction 4. Genetic engineering -- Fiction

ISBN 978-0-439-87175-4; 0-439-87175-1

LC 2006-32889

Fifteen-year-old Freedom Smith is a fighter, just like all of his relatives who have the "Hercules gene," which leads him to a choice between being jailed for attempted murder or working with a covert law enforcement agency to break up a mysterious, illegal fight ring.

"Intriguing supporting characters pepper Wild's debut novel and bolster an already strong portagonist. . . . Wild's story pulsates with raw energy." Voice Youth Advocates

Wilhelm, Doug

Falling. Farrar, Straus and Giroux 2007 241p $17

Grades: 8 9 10 11 12   **Fic**

1. School stories 2. Vermont -- Fiction 3. Basketball -- Fiction 4. Drug abuse -- Fiction 5. Family life -- Fiction

ISBN 978-0-374-32251-9; 0-374-32251-1

LC 2006-45293

Fifteen-year-old Matt's life has been turned upside-down, first when the brother he idolizes turns to drugs, then when a visit to a chat room leads him to a classmate, Katie, who he likes very much but cannot trust with his family secret.

"The addiction scenes are stark, and the story holds surprises to the end." Booklist

Wilkins, Ebony Joy

Sellout. Scholastic Press 2010 267p $17.99

Grades: 7 8 9 10   **Fic**

1. Social classes -- Fiction 2. African Americans -- Fiction

ISBN 978-0-545-10928-4; 0-545-10928-0

NaTasha loves her life of affluence in Park Adams, but her grandmother fears she has lost touch with her roots and whisks her off to Harlem, where NaTasha meets rough, streetwise girls at a crisis center and finds the courage to hold her own against them.

"Some elements of the story tie up too easily—NaTasha's greatest tormentors warm up to her a bit too quickly to be believed—but the message of staying true to oneself shines through." SLJ

Wilkinson, Lili

Pink. HarperTeen 2011 310p $16.99

Grades: 7 8 9 10 11 12   **Fic**

1. School stories 2. Theater -- Fiction 3. Australia -- Fiction 4. Homosexuality -- Fiction 5. Identity (Psychology) -- Fiction

ISBN 978-0-06-192653-2; 0-06-192653-1

LC 2010-9389

Sixteen-year-old Ava does not know who she is or where she belongs, but when she tries out a new personality—and sexual orientation—at a different school, her edgy girlfriend, potential boyfriend, and others are hurt by her lack of honesty.

"The novel is in turn laugh-out-loud funny, endearing, and heartbreaking as Ava repeatedly steps into teenage social land mines—with unexpected results. Because Wilkinson doesn't rely on stereotypes, the characters are well-developed, and interactions between them feel genuine." Voice Youth Advocates

Wilkinson, Sheena

Grounded; Sheena Wilkinson. Little Island 2012 287 p. $12.95

Grades: 7 8 9 10 11 12   **Fic**

1. Horsemanship -- Fiction 2. Northern Ireland -- Fiction 3. Show jumping -- Fiction 4. Inner cities -- Northern Ireland -- Belfast -- Fiction

ISBN 1554553296; 1908195177; 9781554553297; 9781908195173

LC 2012427287

In this book, by Sheena Wilkinson, "Declan loves Seaneen, but his ambition to work at a top showjumping yard is stronger than anything he's ever felt before. So when Declan is offered his dream job in Germany, he should be thrilled. There's nothing for him at home but dark history he'd rather forget. But he's terrified: leaving Seaneen's harder than he expected." (Publisher's note)

"Wilkinson portrays complicated situations with nuanced truth and spare elegance. A talented writer and a fantastic story." Kirkus

Taking Flight; by Sheena Wilkinson. Midpoint Trade Books Inc 2014 310 p. $12.95

Grades: 7 8 9 10 11 12   **Fic**

1. Courage -- Fiction 2. Horsemanship -- Fiction 3. Belfast (Northern Ireland) -- Fiction

ISBN 1554553288; 9781554553280

Children's Books Ireland: Book of the Year (2014)

This book, by Sheena Wilkinson, "is a . . . story of courage overcoming jealousy. The only riding fifteen-year-old Declan has ever done is joyriding. When he's forced to stay with his snobby cousin 'Princess' Vicky, he's shocked to find himself falling in love with horses. Vicky would do anything to keep this grubby hood away from her precious showjumper." (Publisher's note)

"Recommended for general purchase, this title should appeal to fans of horse stories." SLJ

Willey, Margaret

Beetle Boy; by Margaret Willey. Carolrhoda Lab 2014 208 p. hbk $17.95

Grades: 8 9 10 11   **Fic**

1. Child authors -- Fiction 2. Father-son relationship -- Fiction 3. Family problems -- Fiction 4. Emotional problems -- Fiction 5. Dating (Social customs) -- Fiction

ISBN 1467726397; 9781467726399

LC 2013036853

"When he was seven, Charlie Porter never intended to become the world's youngest published author. . . . But Charlie's story not only made his father stop crying. It made him start planning. The story became a book, and then it became school events and book festivals, and a beetle costume, and a catchphrase--'I was born to write!' . . . Beetle Boy is a novel of a broken family, the long shadow of neglect, and the light of small kindnesses." (Publisher's note)

"Willey takes readers along on Charlie's painful journey back to physical and emotional health via a meandering timeline of flashbacks, dreams and wrenching conversations, skillfully weaving together the bits and pieces of his life. Innovative use of type brings an immediacy to Charlie's struggles as he slowly looks the truth--and his brother--squarely in the face." Kirkus

A **summer** of silk moths. Flux 2009 246p il map pa $9.95

Grades: 7 8 9 10   **Fic**

1. Moths -- Fiction 2. Uncles -- Fiction 3. Fathers -- Fiction 4. Michigan -- Fiction

ISBN 978-0-73871-540-7; 0-73871-540-9

LC 2009-19681

A seventeen-year-old boy and girl learn long-held secrets about their pasts as they overcome their initial antipathy toward one another on a Michigan nature preserve dedicated to her dead father.

"A thoughtful, complex and moving story about loss and discovery of identity, love and the ability to change and the restorative powers of nature. . . . The believable characters and the insights into their awakening emotional lives will carry readers along." Kirkus

Williams, Carol Lynch

The **chosen** one. St. Martin's Griffin 2009 213p $16.95

Grades: 7 8 9 10   **Fic**

1. Cults -- Fiction 2. Polygamy -- Fiction 3. Family life -- Fiction

ISBN 978-0-312-55511-5; 0-312-55511-3

LC 2009-4800

In a polygamous cult in the desert, Kyra, not yet fourteen, sees being chosen to be the seventh wife of her uncle as just punishment for having read books and kissed a boy, in violation of Prophet Childs' teachings, and is torn between facing her fate and running away from all that she knows and loves.

"This book is a highly emotional, terrifying read. It is not measured or objective. Physical abuse, fear, and even murder are constants. It is a girl-in-peril story, and as such, it is impossible to put down and holds tremendous teen appeal." Voice Youth Advocates

Glimpse. Simon & Schuster Books for Young Readers 2010 484p $16.99

Grades: 7 8 9 10   **Fic**

1. Novels in verse 2. Sisters -- Fiction 3. Suicide -- Fiction 4. Child sexual abuse -- Fiction 5. Mother-daughter relationship -- Fiction

ISBN 978-1-4169-9730-6; 1-4169-9730-X

LC 2009-41147

Living with their mother who earns money as a prostitute, two sisters take care of each other and when the older one attempts suicide, the younger one tries to uncover the reason.

"Williams leans hard on her free-verse line breaks for drama . . . and it works. A page-turner for Ellen Hopkins fans." Kirkus

Miles from ordinary; a novel. St. Martin's Press 2011 197p $16.99

Grades: 7 8 9 10   **Fic**

1. Family life -- Fiction 2. Mental illness -- Fiction 3. Mother-daughter relationship -- Fiction

ISBN 978-0-312-55512-2; 0-312-55512-1

LC 2010-40324

"Thirteen-year-old Lacey hopes that this summer day will be a new start. She has gotten her mother a job at Winn-Dixie because they desperately need the money, and Lacey will be following in her aunt Linda's footsteps by working at the public library. Lacey craves an opportunity to be "normal," to flirt with her neighbor Aaron and not have to watch over Momma, who seems so much better these days. But the day quickly spins out of control when Momma disappears." (Booklist)

"The author has crafted both a riveting, unusual suspense tale and an absolutely convincing character in Lacey. The book truly is miles from ordinary, in the very best way. Outstanding." Kirkus

Waiting; Carol Lynch Williams. Simon and Schuster Books For Young Readers 2012 335 p.

Grades: 9 10 11 12   **Fic**

1. Siblings -- Fiction 2. Bereavement -- Fiction 3. Grief -- Fiction 4. Family problems -- Fiction 5. Brothers and sisters -- Fiction

ISBN 1442443537; 9781442443532; 9781442443556

LC 2011043898

This young adult novel by Carol Lynch Williams portrays "a teen [who] struggles to rediscover love and find redemption . . . [a]fter her brother's death. . . . Growing up, London and Zach were as close as could be. And then Zach dies, and the family is gutted. London's father is distant. Her mother won't speak. The days are filled with what-ifs and whispers: Was it London's fault? Alone and adrift, London finds herself torn between her brother's best friend and the handsome new boy in town as she struggles to find herself—and ultimately redemption." (Publisher's note)

Williams, Gabrielle

★ **Beatle** meets Destiny. Marshall Cavendish 2010 342p $17.99

Grades: 8 9 10 11 12   **Fic**

1. Love stories 2. Twins -- Fiction 3. Siblings -- Fiction 4. Australia -- Fiction 5. Family life -- Fiction

6. Dating (Social customs) -- Fiction

ISBN 978-0-7614-5723-7

When superstitious eighteen-year-old John "Beatle" Lennon, who is dating the best friend of his twin sister, meets Destiny McCartney, their instant rapport and shared quirkiness make it seem that their fate is written in the stars.

"Clever, amusing, yet surprisingly thoughtful, the book will appeal to readers looking for something a little different." Publ Wkly

Williams, Kathryn

Pizza, love, and other stuff that made me famous; Kathryn Williams. Henry Holt 2012 231 p. (hc) $16.99

Grades: 7 8 9 10   **Fic**

1. Cooking -- Fiction 2. Reality television programs -- Fiction 3. Restaurants -- Fiction 4. Interpersonal relations -- Fiction 5. Competition (Psychology) -- Fiction 6. Television -- Production and direction -- Fiction

ISBN 0805092854; 9780805092851

LC 2011034053

"Sixteen-year-old Sophie Nicolaides was practically raised in the kitchen of her family's Italian-Greek restaurant, Taverna Ristorante. When her best friend, Alex, tries to persuade her to audition for a new reality show, 'Teen Test Kitchen,' Sophie is reluctant. But the prize includes a full scholarship to one of America's finest culinary schools and a summer in Napa, California, not to mention fame. Once on set, Sophie immediately finds herself in the thick of the drama -- including a secret burn book, cutthroat celebrity judges, and a very cute French chef." (Publisher's note)

Williams, Katie

Absent; by Katie Williams. Chronicle Books 2013 288 p. (hardcover) $16.99

Grades: 9 10 11 12   **Fic**

1. Ghost stories 2. Suicide -- Fiction 3. High school students -- Fiction 4. Schools -- Fiction 5. Drug abuse -- Fiction 6. High schools -- Fiction

ISBN 0811871509; 9780811871501

LC 2012033600

In this novel, by Katie Williams, "when seventeen-year-old Paige dies in a freak fall from the roof . . . , her spirit is bound to the grounds of her high school. . . . But when Paige hears the rumor that her death wasn't an accident--that she supposedly jumped on purpose--she can't bear it. Then Paige discovers . . . she can possess living people when they think of her. . . . Maybe . . . she can get to the most popular girl in school and stop the rumors once and for all." (Publisher's note)

"The mystery is solid, but it is complicated; funny Paige herself sets the story apart." Booklist

The **space** between trees. Chronicle Books 2010 274p $17.99

Grades: 8 9 10 11 12   **Fic**

1. School stories 2. Homicide -- Fiction

ISBN 978-0-8118-7175-4; 0-8118-7175-4

LC 2009-48561

When the body of a classmate is discovered in the woods, sixteen-year-old Evie's lies wind up involving her with the girl's best friend, trying to track down the killer.

"Evie's raw honesty and the choices she makes make for difficult reading, but also a darkly beautiful, emotionally honest story of personal growth." Publ Wkly

Williams, Lori Aurelia

★ **When** Kambia Elaine flew in from Neptune. Simon & Schuster 2000 246p hardcover o.p. pa $10

Grades: 7 8 9 10   **Fic**
1. Houston (Tex.) -- Fiction 2. African Americans -- Fiction
ISBN 0-689-82468-8; 0-689-84593-6 pa
                                            LC 99-65154
"This is a strong and disturbing novel, told in beautiful language. Teens will find it engrossing." SLJ

Williams, Michael

Diamond boy; Michael Williams. First edition Little, Brown & Co. 2014 400 p. maps (hardcover) $18

Grades: 7 8 9 10   **Fic**
1. Blacks -- Fiction 2. Zimbabwe -- Fiction 3. Survival skills -- Fiction 4. Mines and mineral resources -- Fiction 5. Survival -- Fiction 6. Blacks -- Zimbabwe -- Fiction 7. Shona (African people) -- Fiction 8. Diamond mines and mining -- Fiction
ISBN 0316320692; 9780316320672; 9780316320696
                                            LC 2013042071
"Patson Moyo's life is perfectly ordinary. . . . His father, a teacher, is often a little dreamy but a wonderful storyteller. . . . Patson never would have guessed that his smart, university-graduate father . . . can barely make ends meet, due to government corruption and the massive devaluation of the Zimbabwean dollar. Egged on by Patson's stepmother, Sylvia, the Moyos decide to improve their situation by traveling to Marage." (School Library Journal)

"Written in diary format, the story brings the reader into the mind and soul of a young refugee suffering in a hell created by the greed and violence of powerful adults. More than simply a good read, Diamond Boy is a multilayered, teachable novel with a variety of approaches and is highly recommended for middle and high school collections." VOYA

Now is the time for running. Little, Brown 2011 233p $17.99

Grades: 6 7 8 9 10   **Fic**
1. Soccer -- Fiction 2. Brothers -- Fiction 3. Refugees -- Fiction 4. Zimbabwe -- Fiction 5. Homeless persons -- Fiction
ISBN 978-0-316-07790-3; 0-316-07790-9
                                            LC 2010043460
"There is plenty of material to captivate readers: fast-paced soccer matches every bit as tough as the players; the determination of Deo and his fellow refugees to survive unthinkably harsh conditions; and raw depictions of violence. . . . But it's the tender relationship between Deo and Innocent, along with some heartbreaking twists of fate, that will endure in readers' minds." Publ Wkly

Williams, Sean

Twinmaker; by Sean Williams. HarperCollins 2013 352 p. (hardcover bdg.) $17.99

Grades: 9 10 11 12   **Fic**
1. Fantasy fiction 2. Conspiracies -- Fiction 3. Teleportation -- Fiction 4. Science fiction 5. Friendship -- Fiction 6. Best friends -- Fiction 7. Space and time -- Fiction
ISBN 0062203215; 9780062203212
                                            LC 2012043498
In this book, "thanks to D-mat technology, teen Clair" and her friends "can jump around the globe in a matter of minutes simply by entering a booth. . . . They initially dismiss Improvement, a way to transform yourself through a series of jumps, but then Libby uses Improvement to remove her permanent birthmark, and as the disturbing consequences roll out, Clair digs for answers." (Booklist)

Other titles in this series include:
Crashland (2014)

Williams-Garcia, Rita

★ **Jumped**. HarperTeen 2009 169p $16.99; lib bdg $17.89

Grades: 8 9 10 11 12   **Fic**
1. School stories 2. Bullies -- Fiction
ISBN 978-0-06-076091-5; 0-06-076091-5; 978-0-06-076092-2 lib bdg; 0-06-076092-3 lib bdg
                                            LC 2008-22381
The lives of Leticia, Dominique, and Trina are irrevocably intertwined through the course of one day in an urban high school after Leticia overhears Dominique's plans to beat up Trina and must decide whether or not to get involved.

"In alternating chapters narrated by Leticia, Trina, and Dominique, Williams-Garcia has given her characters strong, individual voices that ring true to teenage speech, and she lets them make their choices without judgment or moralizing." SLJ

★ **Like** sisters on the homefront. Lodestar Bks. 1995 165p hardcover o.p. pa $5.99

Grades: 7 8 9 10   **Fic**
1. Family life -- Fiction 2. Teenage mothers -- Fiction 3. African Americans -- Fiction
ISBN 0-525-67465-9; 0-14-038561-4 pa
                                            LC 95-3690
"Beautifully written, the text captures the cadence and rhythm of New York street talk and the dilemma of being poor, black, and uneducated. This is a gritty, realistic, well-told story." SLJ

Williamson, Jill

Captives. Zondervan 2013 415 p. $9.99

Grades: 9 10 11 12   **Fic**
1. Dystopian fiction 2. Kidnapping -- Fiction
ISBN 0310724228; 1480604100; 9780310724223; 9781480604100
In this dystopian novel, a pandemic decades earlier in the Safe Lands "has made reproduction problematic. Consequently, the state abducts uninfected young outsiders for breeding purposes." One such kidnapped is Jem, fiancée of eighteen-year-old Levi, who plans to risk everything to rescue her. (Booklist)

"...Well-observed details skewer today's materialistic and superficial values. ...The biblical references can be too explicit—, but that's not a knock on the message, which is important and worth discussing. Ultimately, the multilayered, futuristic narrative should intrigue fans of sf." Booklist

Willis, Connie

To say nothing of the dog; or, How we found the bishop's bird stump at last. Bantam Bks. 1998 434p hardcover o.p. pa $7.99

Grades: 11 12 Adult   **Fic**
    1. Science fiction
    ISBN 0-553-09995-7; 0-553-57538-4 pa
                 LC 97-16002

"No one mixes scientific mumbo jumbo and comedy of manners with more panache than Willis." N Y Times Book Rev

Wilson, Daniel H.

Robopocalypse; Daniel H. Wilson. Doubleday 2011 347p. $25

Grades: 11 12 Adult   **Fic**
    1. Robots 2. Science fiction 3. Artificial intelligence 4. Future
    ISBN 978-0-385-53385-0; 0-385-53385-3
                 LC 201043134

Alex Award (2012)

In this book by Daniel H. Wilson, Archos, a robot with "infinite processing power and cognitive power" kills his creator and "uses 'smart' toys, battlefield 'pacification' units, and pleasure dolls to evoke his dominion over the human world. What he doesn't plan for are the small pockets of human resistors." (Voice of Youth Advocates)

Wilson, Diane L.

Firehorse. Margaret K. McElderry Books 2006 325p $16.95

Grades: 7 8 9 10   **Fic**
    1. Arson -- Fiction 2. Horses -- Fiction 3. Sex role -- Fiction 4. Family life -- Fiction 5. Boston (Mass.) -- Fiction 6. Veterinary medicine -- Fiction
    ISBN 1-4169-1551-6; 978-1-4169-1551-5
                 LC 2005-30785

Spirited fifteen-year-old horse lover Rachel Selby determines to become a veterinarian, despite the opposition of her rigid father, her proper mother, and the norms of Boston in 1872, while that city faces a serial arsonist and an epidemic spreading through its firehorse population.

"Wilson paces the story well, with tension building. . . The novel's finest achievement, though, is the convincing depiction of family dynamics in an era when men ruled the household and and women, who had few opportunities, folded their dreams and put them away with the linens they embroidered." Booklist

Wilson, John

Victorio's war; John Wilson. Orca Book Publishers 2012 157p (paperback) $12.95

Grades: 6 7 8 9   **Fic**
    1. Western stories 2. Historical fiction 3. Biographical fiction
    ISBN 9781554698820 pa; 9781554698837 (pdf); 9781554698844 (epub)
                 LC 2011942580

In this historical novel, by John Wilson, after "taking up a new job scouting for a troop of Buffalo Soldiers, Jim Doolen finds himself caught between friends in the military and friends riding with the Apaches they are chasing. . . . He is saved by his mystic old mentor Too-ah-yay-say from being killed . . . and held captive until a final massacre by Mexican soldiers." (Kirkus)

Wilson, Martin

★ **What** they always tell us. Delacorte Press 2008 293p $15.99; lib bdg $18.99

Grades: 9 10 11 12   **Fic**
    1. School stories 2. Alabama -- Fiction 3. Brothers -- Fiction 4. Homosexuality -- Fiction
    ISBN 978-0-385-73507-0; 0-385-73507-3; 978-0-385-90500-8 lib bdg; 0-385-90500-9 lib bdg
                 LC 2007-30269

Sixteen-year-old Alex feels so disconnected from his friends that he starts his junior year at a Tuscaloosa, Alabama, high school by attempting suicide, but soon, a friend of his older brother draws him into cross-country running and a new understanding of himself.

This "novel does an excellent job of showing the tension with which siblings deal on a daily basis. He also does a great job of exploring controversial issues, such as suicide and homosexuality. . . . Public and school libraries should seriously consider adding this book to their shelves." Voice Youth Advocates

Winspear, Jacqueline

Among the mad; a Maisie Dobbs novel. Henry Holt and Company 2009 303p $25

Grades: 11 12 Adult   **Fic**
    1. Detectives 2. Mystery fiction 3. Great Britain -- Fiction 4. Mystery and detective stories -- England
    ISBN 978-0-8050-8216-6; 0-8050-8216-6
                 LC 2008-32576

Sequel to: An incomplete revenge (2008)

"The lamentation over economic crisis, terrorism and traumatized veterans feels both true to its setting and disquietingly contemporary. Well-crafted and well worth reading." Kirkus

Followed by The mapping of love and death (2010)

Birds of a feather; a novel. Soho Press 2004 311p $25

Grades: 11 12 Adult   **Fic**
    1. Mystery fiction 2. Missing persons -- Fiction 3. London (England) -- Fiction
    ISBN 1-569-47368-4
                 LC 2003-25732

Sequel to Maisie Dobbs (2003)

"Having been trained by a master detective, the former serving girl now a Cambridge graduate is hired by grocery magnate Joseph Waite to find his wayward daughter, Charlotte. What begins as a simple missing-person case evolves into the investigation of three murders, all of young women who were friends during the [first world] war. Charlotte may be the next target. . . . This is an utterly enjoyable and painless history lesson and a well-plotted and consistent mystery that will appeal to teens looking for more than just historical fiction." SLJ

Followed by Pardonable lies (2005)

An **incomplete** revenge; a Maisie Dobbs novel. H. Holt 2008 306p $24; pa $14

Grades: 11 12 Adult   **Fic**

1. Mystery fiction 2. London (England) -- Fiction
ISBN 978-0-8050-8215-9; 0-8050-8215-8; 978-0-312-42818-1 pa; 0-312-42818-9 pa

LC 2007-40639

Sequel to Messenger of truth (2006)

Maisie Dobbs, the extraordinary psychologist and investigator, delves into a strange series of crimes in a small rural community involving mysterious fires, petty crimes, and the legacy of a wartime Zeppelin raid.

"Maisie is absolutely compelling not only as an investigator but also as a psychologist while she probes the hearts and minds of those she meets." Libr J

Followed by Among the mad (2009)

A **lesson** in secrets; a Maisie Dobbs novel. Harper 2011 323p $25.99

Grades: 11 12 Adult   **Fic**

1. Mystery fiction 2. Great Britain -- Fiction
ISBN 978-0-06-172767-2

Sequel to The mapping of love and death (2010)

"Winspear strikes the right balance between cozy mystery setting and her intelligent, street-savvy PI. The story adroitly presents a post-World War I world while foreshadowing the next global conflict." Libr J

★ **Maisie** Dobbs; a novel. Penguin Books 2004 294p pa $15

Grades: 11 12 Adult   **Fic**

1. Mystery fiction 2. Great Britain -- Fiction 3. World War, 1914-1918 -- Fiction
ISBN 978-0-14-200433-3; 0-14-200433-2

First published 2003 by Soho Press

"For a clever and resourceful young woman who has just set herself up in business as a private investigator, Maisie seems a bit too sober and much too sad. Romantic readers sensing a story-within-a-story won't be disappointed. But first, they must prepare to be astonished at the sensitivity and wisdom with which Maisie resolves her first professional assignment." N Y Times Book Rev

Other titles about Maisie Dobbs are:
Among the mad (2009)
Birds of a feather (2004)
An incomplete revenge (2008)
A lesson in secrets (2011)
The mapping of love and death (2010)
Messenger of truth (2006)
Pardonable lies (2005)

The **mapping** of love and death; a Maisie Dobbs novel. Harper 2010 338p $25.99; pa $14.99

Grades: 11 12 Adult   **Fic**

1. Mystery fiction 2. Great Britain -- Fiction 3. World

War, 1914-1918 -- Fiction
ISBN 978-0-06-172766-5; 0-06-172766-0; 978-0-06-172768-9 pa; 0-06-172768-7 pa

LC 2009-49970

Sequel to Among the mad (2009)

London investigator Maisie Dobbs must unravel a case of wartime love and death—an investigation that leads her to a doomed affair between a young cartographer, listed as missing in action when World War I ends, and a mysterious nurse.

"An engaging plot coupled with captivating characters makes this the best Dobbs novel to date. Highly recommended for historical mystery aficionados who enjoy intriguing whodunits wrapped in a wartime love story." Libr J

Followed by A lesson in secrets (2011)

Messenger of truth; a Maisie Dobbs novel. H. Holt 2006 322p $24; pa $14

Grades: 11 12 Adult   **Fic**

1. Mystery fiction 2. London (England) -- Fiction
ISBN 978-0-8050-7898-5; 0-8050-7898-3; 978-0-312-42685-9 pa; 0-312-42685-2 pa

LC 2006-43626

Sequel to Pardonable lies (2005)

This installment in the historical mystery series "finds our fearless psychologist/inquiry agent investigating the death of artist Nick Bassington-Hope. According to Detective Inspector Stratton, Nick's fall from a set of scaffolding was merely a tragic accident. Nick's twin sister, Georgina, however, insists he was murdered and hires Maisie to discover the truth. . . . The mystery itself is rather transparent, but what makes this book delightful is how Winspear shows Maisie's emotional development amid the bitter legacy of the Great War." Libr J

Followed by An incomplete revenge (2008)

Pardonable lies; a Maisie Dobbs novel. Henry Holt 2005 342p hardcover o.p. pa $15

Grades: 11 12 Adult   **Fic**

1. Detectives 2. Mystery fiction 3. London (England) -- Fiction 4. Mystery and detective stories -- England
ISBN 0-8050-7897-5; 0-312-42621-6 pa

LC 2005-46388

Sequel to Birds of a feather (2004)

"In late 1930, the London 'psychologist and investigator' gets involved in three cases: proving the innocence of a 13-year-old farm girl, Avril Jarvis, accused of murder; undertaking a search for Sir Cecil Lawton's only son, a pilot shot down behind enemy lines in WWI, whose body was never recovered; and looking into the circumstances of the death of her university friend Priscilla Evernden Partridge's brother in France during the war. . . . Winspear writes seamlessly, enriching the whole with vivid details of English life on a variety of social levels." Publ Wkly

Followed by Messenger of truth (2006)

Winston, Sherri

The **Kayla** chronicles; a novel. Little, Brown 2007 188p hardcover o.p. pa $7.99

Grades: 6 7 8 9 10   **Fic**

1. School stories 2. Dancers -- Fiction 3. Journalism

-- Fiction 4. African Americans -- Fiction
ISBN 978-0-316-11430-1; 0-316-11430-8; 978-0-316-11431-8 pa; 0-316-11431-6 pa

LC 2006-933219

Kayla transforms herself from mild-mannered journalist to hot-trotting dance diva in order to properly investigate her high school's dance team, and has a hard time remaining true to her real self while in the role.

"Few recent novels for younger YAs mesh levity and substance this successfully." Booklist

Winters, Cat

★ **In** the shadow of blackbirds; Cat Winters. Amulet Books 2013 400 p. $16.95

Grades: 8 9 10 11 12   Fic

1. Historical fiction 2. Paranormal fiction 3. Ghosts -- Fiction 4. Spiritualism -- Fiction 5. World War, 1914-1918 -- Fiction 6. Influenza Epidemic, 1918-1919 -- Fiction 7. San Diego (Calif.) -- History -- 20th century -- Fiction
ISBN 141970530X; 9781419705304

LC 2012039262

William C. Morris Honor Book (2014)

In this book, sixteen-year-old Mary Shelley Black lives in 1918. "With WWI raging on and Mary's father on trial for treason, she goes to live with her Aunt Eva in San Diego, Calif. . . . Grieving for her childhood beau Stephen, who died while fighting overseas with the Army, Mary goes outside during a thunderstorm and is struck dead by lightning—for a few minutes. When Mary comes to, she discovers she can communicate with the dead, including Stephen." (Publishers Weekly)

"Winters strikes just the right balance between history and ghost story . . . . Vintage photographs contribute to the authenticity of the atmospheric and nicely paced storytelling." Kirkus

★ The **steep** and thorny way; by Cat Winters. Amulet Books 2016 352 p. (hardback) $17.95

Grades: 8 9 10 11 12   Fic

1. Murder -- Fiction 2. Historical fiction 3. Racially mixed people -- Fiction 4. Ghosts -- Fiction 5. Prejudices -- Fiction 6. Oregon -- History -- 20th century -- Fiction
ISBN 9781419719158

LC 2015022705

This novel, by Cat Winters, is a re-setting of William Shakespeare's Hamlet in 1920s Oregon. "Hanalee [Denney's] . . . father, Hank Denney, died a year ago, hit by a drunk-driving teenager. Now her father's killer is out of jail and back in town, and he claims that Hanalee's father wasn't killed by the accident at all but, instead, was poisoned by the doctor who looked after him—who happens to be Hanalee's new stepfather." (Publisher's Note)

"A fast-paced read with multiple twists, the novel delivers a history lesson wrapped inside a murder mystery and ghost story. Winters deftly captures the many injustices faced by marginalized people in the years following World War I as well as a glimmer of hope for the better America to come. A riveting story of survival, determination, love, and friendship." Kirkus

Wise, Tama

Street dreams. Bold Strokes Books 2012 264 p. $13.95

Grades: 9 10 11 12   Fic
ISBN 1602826501; 9781602826502

LC 2011279902

In this novel by Tama Wise "Tyson Rua has more than his fair share of problems growing up in South Auckland. . . . Now Tyson's fallen in love at first sight. Only thing is, it's another guy. Living life on the sidelines of the local hip-hop scene, Tyson finds that to succeed in becoming a local graffiti artist or in getting the man of his dreams, he's going to have to get a whole lot more involved. And that means more problems." (Publisher's note)

Wiseman, Eva

Puppet; a novel. Tundra Books 2009 243p $17.95

Grades: 7 8 9 10 11 12   Fic
1. Prejudices -- Fiction 2. Jews -- Hungary -- Fiction
ISBN 0-88776-828-8; 978-0-88776-828-6

"The year is 1882. A young servant girl named Esther disappears from a small Hungarian village. Several Jewish men from the village of Tisza Eszvar face the 'blood libel'—the centuries-old calumny that Jews murder Christian children for their blood. A fourteen-year-old Jewish boy named Morris Scharf becomes the star witness of corrupt authorities who coerce him into testifying against his fellow Jews, including his own father, at the trial. This . . . fictionalized account of one of the last blood libel trials in Europe is told through the eyes of Julie, a friend of the murdered Esther, and a servant at the jail where Morris is imprisoned." (Publisher's note) "Age eleven and up." (Quill Quire)

"Times are hard in Julie Vamosi's Hungarian village in the late nineteenth-century, and the townspeople . . . blame the Jews. After Julie's best friend, Esther, . . . disappears, the rumor spreads that the Jews cut her throat and drained her blood to drink with their Passover matzos. . . . Based on the records of a trial in 1883, this searing novel dramatizes virulent anti-Semitism from the viewpoint of a Christian child. . . . The climax is electrifying." Booklist

Withers, Pam

Andreo's race; Pam Withers. Tundra Books of Northern New York 2015 224 p. (pbk.) $12.99

Grades: 9 10 11 12   Fic
1. Contests 2. Adopted children -- Fiction 3. Human trafficking -- Fiction
ISBN 1770497668; 9781770497665; 9781770497672

LC 2014934267

In Pam Wither's novel "just as sixteen-year-old Andreo, skilled in death-defying ironman events in wilderness regions, is about to compete in rugged Bolivia, he and his friend Raul (another Bolivian adoptee) begin to suspect that their adoptive parents have unwittingly acquired them illegally. Plotting to use the upcoming race to pursue the truth, they veer on an epic journey to locate Andreo's birth parents, only to find themselves hazardously entangled with a gang of baby traffickers." (Publisher's note)

"The simple, straightforward language, surprise twist, and nonstop action will appeal to reluctant readers looking for a thrilling novel." SLJ

First descent. Tundra Books 2011 265p $17.95
Grades: 7 8 9 10   **Fic**
1. Colombia -- Fiction 2. Kayaks and kayaking -- Fiction
ISBN 978-1-77049-257-8; 1-77049-257-7
"Seventeen-year-old champion slalom kayaker Rex Scruggs is determined to kayak Colombia's Furioso River, when he meets a young woman, an Andean indigena, who both aids Rex in his quest and puts him in the crosshairs of Colombia's battling guerrillas and paramilitaries. . . . Withers flings the reader from one perilous adventure to another." Booklist

Wittlinger, Ellen
Hard love. Simon & Schuster Bks. for Young Readers 1999 224p hardcover o.p. pa $8.99
Grades: 7 8 9 10   **Fic**
1. Lesbians -- Fiction 2. Authorship -- Fiction
ISBN 0-689-82134-4; 0-689-84154-X pa
LC 98-6668
Michael L. Printz Award honor book, 2000
"John, cynical yet vulnerable, thinks he's immune to emotion until he meets bright, brittle Marisol, the author of his favorite zine. He falls in love, but Marisol, a lesbian, just wants to be friends. A love story of a different sort—funny, poignant, and thoughtful." Booklist
Followed by: Love & lies: Marisol's story (2008)

Love & lies; Marisol's story. Simon & Schuster Books for Young Readers 2008 245p $16.99
Grades: 7 8 9 10   **Fic**
1. Lesbians -- Fiction 2. Authorship -- Fiction 3. Massachusetts -- Fiction
ISBN 978-1-4169-1623-9; 1-4169-1623-7
LC 2007-18330
When Marisol, a self-confident eighteen-year-old lesbian, moves to Cambridge, Massachusetts to work and try to write a novel, she falls under the spell of her beautiful but deceitful writing teacher, while also befriending a shy, vulnerable girl from Indiana.
"The emotional morass of Marisol's life . . . is complex and realistic; it will draw in both fans of the earlier novel . . . and realistic-fiction readers seeking a love story with depth." Bull Cent Child Books

★ **Parrotfish**. Simon & Schuster Books for Young Readers 2007 294p $16.99
Grades: 7 8 9 10   **Fic**
1. School stories 2. Transgender people -- Fiction 3. Family life -- Fiction
ISBN 978-1-4169-1622-2; 1-4169-1622-9
LC 2006-9689
Grady, a transgendered high school student, yearns for acceptance by his classmates and family as he struggles to adjust to his new identity as a male.

"The author demonstrates well the complexity faced by transgendered people and makes the teen's frustration with having to fit into a category fully apparent." Publ Wkly

★ **Sandpiper**. Simon & Schuster Books for Young Readers 2005 227p hardcover o.p. pa $6.99
Grades: 9 10 11 12   **Fic**
1. Dating (Social customs) -- Fiction
ISBN 0-689-86802-2; 1-4169-3651-3 pa
LC 2004-7576
When The Walker, a mysterious boy who walks constantly, intervenes in an argument between Sandpiper and a boy she used to see, their lives become entwined in ways that change them both.
"While heavy on message and mature in subject matter, the novel is notable for the bold look it takes at relationships and at the myth that oral sex is not really sex." SLJ

Wizner, Jake
Spanking Shakespeare. Random House Children's Books 2007 287p $15.99; lib bdg $18.99
Grades: 8 9 10   **Fic**
1. School stories 2. Authorship -- Fiction
ISBN 978-0-375-84085-2; 978-0-375-94085-9 lib bdg
LC 2006-27035
Shakespeare Shapiro navigates a senior year fraught with feelings of insecurity while writing the memoir of his embarrassing life, worrying about his younger brother being cooler than he is, and having no prospects of ever getting a girlfriend.
"Raw, sexual, cynical, and honest, this book belongs on library shelves and gift lists." Voice Youth Advocates

Wolf, Allan
★ The **watch** that ends the night; voices from the Titanic. Candlewick Press 2011 466p $21.99
Grades: 7 8 9 10   **Fic**
1. Novels in verse 2. Shipwrecks -- Fiction 3. Titanic (Steamship) -- Fiction
ISBN 978-0-7636-3703-3
LC 2010040150
"Millionaire John Jacob Astor hopes to bring home his pregnant teen bride with a minimum of media scandal. A beautiful Lebanese refugee, on her way to family in Florida, discovers the first stirrings of love. And an ancient iceberg glides south, anticipating its fateful encounter. The voices in this remarkable re-creation of the Titanic disaster span classes and stations, from Margaret ('the unsinkable Molly') Brown to the captain who went down with his ship; from the lookout and wireless men to a young boy in search of dragons and a gambler in search of marks." (Publisher's note)
"A lyrical, monumental work of fact and imagination that reads like an oral history revved up by the drama of the event." Kirkus

Zane's trace. Candlewick Press 2007 177p $16.99
Grades: 7 8 9 10 11 12   **Fic**
1. Novels in verse 2. Death -- Fiction 3. Orphans -- Fiction 4. Epilepsy -- Fiction 5. Automobile travel

-- Fiction 6. Racially mixed people -- Fiction
ISBN 978-0-7636-2858-1; 0-7636-2858-1

LC 2007-24187

Believing he has killed his grandfather, Zane Guesswind heads for his mother's Zanesville, Ohio, grave to kill himself, driving the 1969 Plymouth Barracuda his long-gone father left behind, and meeting along the way assorted characters who help him discover who he really is.

"This novel manages to be suspenseful, funny, and deeply moving at the same time." Voice Youth Advocates

Wolf, Jennifer Shaw

Breaking beautiful; Jennifer Shaw Wolf. Walker 2012 356 p. (hardcover) $16.99

Grades: 9 10 11 12 **Fic**

1. Siblings -- Fiction 2. Date rape -- Fiction 3. Traffic accidents -- Fiction 4. Twins -- Fiction 5. Memory -- Fiction 6. Dating violence -- Fiction 7. Mystery and detective stories 8. Brothers and sisters -- Fiction 9. Dating (Social customs) -- Fiction
ISBN 0802723527; 9780802723529

LC 2011010944

This novel, by Jennifer Shaw Wolf, follows "Allie[, who] lost everything the night her boyfriend, Trip, died in a horrible car accident—including her memory of the event. As their small town mourns his death, Allie is afraid to remember because doing so means delving into what she's kept hidden for so long: the horrible reality of their abusive relationship. . . . Can she reach deep enough to remember that night so she can finally break free?" (Publisher's note)

Wolff, Tobias

Old school; a novel. Knopf 2003 195p $22; pa $12

Grades: 9 10 11 12 **Fic**

1. School stories 2. Authors -- Fiction 3. New England -- Fiction
ISBN 0-375-40146-6; 0-375-70149-4 pa

LC 2003-52930

"The unnamed narrator of this coming-of-age story set in 1960 is a scholarship student at a prestigious New England prep school that has a tradition of inviting literary stars to the campus. Prior to the visit, the seniors are requested to write a piece to be 'judged' by the guest. The winner is given a private meeting with the literary luminary and the story is published in the school paper. . . . In his fervent desire to be chosen, the narrator 'borrows' an idea and reveals a secret about his heritage that he has carefully hidden. He wins, but the results of his story's publication are disastrous and his life is forever changed. The events and ideas in this thoughtful and thought-provoking novel remain with readers after the story is over and could provide meat for discussion." SLJ

Wolff, Virginia Euwer

★ **Make** lemonade. Holt & Co. 1993 200p $17.95; pa $7.95

Grades: 8 9 10 11 12 **Fic**

1. Novels in verse 2. Poverty -- Fiction 3. Babysitters -- Fiction 4. Teenage mothers -- Fiction
ISBN 978-0-8050-2228-5; 0-8050-2228-7; 978-0-8050-8070-4 pa; 0-8050-8070-8 pa

LC 92-41182

"Fourteen-year-old LaVaughn accepts the job of babysitting Jolly's two small children but quickly realizes that the young woman, a seventeen-year-old single mother, needs as much help and nurturing as her two neglected children. The four become something akin to a temporary family, and through their relationship each makes progress toward a better life. Sixty-six brief chapters, with words arranged on the page like poetry, perfectly echo the patterns of teenage speech." Horn Book Guide

Other titles in this trilogy are:
This full house (2009)
True believer (2001)

This full house. Bowen Press 2009 476p $17.99; lib bdg $18.89

Grades: 8 9 10 11 12 **Fic**

1. School stories 2. Novels in verse 3. Friendship -- Fiction
ISBN 978-0-06-158304-9; 0-06-158304-9; 978-0-06-158305-6 lib bdg; 0-06-158305-7 lib bdg

LC 2008-20157

Sequel to: True believer (2001)

High-school-senior LaVaughn's perceptions and expectations of her life begin to change as she learns about the many unexpected connections between the people she loves best.

"LaVaughn's ferocious determination and intelligence will wholly captivate readers, as will her beautifully articulated, elemental questions about integrity, faith, and how best to build a life." Booklist

True believer. Atheneum Bks. for Young Readers 2001 264p $17; pa $7.99

Grades: 8 9 10 11 12 **Fic**

1. Novels in verse 2. Poverty -- Fiction 3. Single parent family -- Fiction
ISBN 0-689-82827-6; 0-689-85288-6 pa

LC 00-32792

Sequel to: Make lemonade (1993)

Michael L. Printz Award honor book, 2002

Living in the inner city amidst guns and poverty, fifteen-year-old LaVaughn learns from old and new friends, and inspiring mentors, that life is what you make it—an occasion to rise to

"LaVaughn tells her own story in heart-stopping stream-of-consciousness that reveals her convincing naiveté and her blazing determination, intelligence, and growth. . . . Transcendent, raw, and fiercely optimistic, the novel answers some of its own questions about overcoming adversity." Booklist

Followed by: This full house (2009)

Wolfson, Jill

Cold hands, warm heart. Henry Holt and Co. 2009 245p

Grades: 7 8 9 10 **Fic**

1. Death -- Fiction 2. Siblings -- Fiction 3. Hospitals -- Fiction 4. Jews -- United States -- Fiction 5. Transplantation of organs, tissues, etc. -- Fiction
ISBN 0-8050-8282-4; 978-0-8050-8282-1

LC 2008040594

After sixteen-year-old Tyler convinces his parents to donate the organs of his fourteen-year-old sister, who died during a gymnastics meet, he writes letters to the recipients, including Dani, who finally has a chance at normalcy after living fifteen years with a congenital heart defect.

"Detailed, accurate descriptions of medical procedures are leavened with humor and sincerity, providing a powerful, multifaceted exploration of ethics, love and the celebration." Kirkus

★ **Furious**; by Jill Wolfson. 1st ed. Henry Holt and Co. 2013 336 p. (hardcover) $17.99

Grades: 9 10 11 12   **Fic**
1. Revenge -- Fiction 2. Erinyes (Greek mythology) -- Fiction 3. Schools -- Fiction 4. High schools -- Fiction 5. Mythology, Greek -- Fiction
ISBN 0805082832; 9780805082838
LC 2012027653

This book presents "a cautionary tale of bullying and retribution, featuring three righteously angry 10th-grade girls. Meg, a neglected and abused foster kid . . . Alix . . . [who] has a soft spot for her developmentally disabled big brother; and Stephanie . . . an environmental activist. . . . After each girl comes undone by her rage, cool, popular classmate Ambrosia explains to them that they are 'Furies' and then manipulates them into . . . embrac[ing] a vindictive twisted justice." (School Library Journal)

"For readers moving beyond Percy Jackson into the more complex realm of teen angst, this is an enthralling and chilling tale that uses Greek mythology to create a timely fable." Kirkus

Wolitzer, Meg

★ **Belzhar**; Meg Wolitzer. Dutton Juvenile 2014 272 p. (hardback) $17.99

Grades: 9 10 11 12   **Fic**
1. Private schools -- Fiction 2. Schools -- Fiction 3. Friendship -- Fiction 4. Boarding schools -- Fiction 5. Emotional problems -- Fiction 6. Dating (Social customs) -- Fiction
ISBN 0525423052; 9780525423058
LC 2014010747

In this young adult novel by Meg Wolitzer, "If life were fair, Jam Gallahue would still be at home in New Jersey with her sweet British boyfriend, Reeve Maxfield. . . . But life isn't fair, and Reeve Maxfield is dead. Until a journal-writing assignment leads Jam to Belzhar, where the untainted past is restored, and Jam can feel Reeve's arms around her once again. But there are hidden truths on Jam's path to reclaim her loss." (Publisher's note)

"When Jam suffers a terrible trauma and feels isolated by grief, her parents send her to the Wooden Barn, a boarding school for "highly intelligent, emotionally fragile" teens. Once there she is enrolled in a class with only five specially selected students where they exclusively read Sylvia Plath... While the conclusion is a touch heavy-handed, older teen readers, especially rabid Plath fans, will relish Wolitzer's deeply respectful treatment of Jam's realistic emotional struggle." (Booklist)

Wong, David

Futuristic Violence and Fancy Suits; by David Wong. St. Martin's Press 2015 384 p. $26.99

Grades: 11 12 Adult   **Fic**
1. Cats -- Fiction 2. Science fiction
ISBN 1250040191; 9781250040190
LC 2015025817

Alex Award (2016)

This novel by David Wong, takes place in "a world in which . . . human achievement soars to new heights while its depravity plunges to the blackest depths. . . . This is the world in which Zoey Ashe finds herself, navigating a futuristic city in which one can find elements of the fantastic, nightmarish and ridiculous on any street corner. Her only trusted advisor is . . . [a] cat, but even in the future, cats cannot give advice. At least not any that you'd want to follow." (Publisher's note)

"Well-timed humor and explosive thrills, a smart backbone, and witty wordsmithing make this new release by Cracked.com's pseudonym-wielding Jason Pargin (John Dies at the End, 2009) as fun as it gets. Steer this one toward readers of sf with a sense of humor, and fans of Max Barry's satirical futuristic novels." Booklist

Wood, Maryrose

The **poison** diaries; based on a concept by the Duchess of Northumberland. Balzer + Bray 2010 278p $16.99

Grades: 8 9 10 11   **Fic**
1. Plants -- Fiction 2. Supernatural -- Fiction 3. Great Britain -- Fiction 4. Poisons and poisoning -- Fiction 5. Father-daughter relationship -- Fiction
ISBN 978-0-06-180236-2; 0-06-180236-0
LC 2009-54427

In late eighteenth-century Northumberland, England, sixteen-year-old Jessamine Luxton and the mysterious Weed uncover the horrible secrets of poisons growing in Thomas Luxton's apothecary garden.

"This intriguing fantasy has many tendrils to wrap around teen hearts. . . . The haunting ending will leave readers wanting to talk about the themes of cruelty, honesty, and loyalty." Booklist

Another title in this series is:
Nightshade (2011)

Wooding, Chris

The **haunting** of Alaizabel Cray. Orchard Bks. 2004 292p $16.95; pa $7.99

Grades: 7 8 9 10   **Fic**
1. Horror fiction 2. Supernatural -- Fiction 3. London (England) -- Fiction
ISBN 0-439-54656-7; 0-439-59851-6 pa
LC 2003-69108

First published 2001 in the United Kingdom

In a world similar to Victorian London, Thaniel, a seventeen-year-old hunter of deadly, demonic creatures called the wych-kin, takes in a lost, possessed girl, and becomes embroiled in a plot to unleash evil on the world

"Eerie and exhilarating. . . . [The author] fuses together his best storytelling skills . . . to create a fabulously horrific and ultimately timeless underworld." SLJ

Poison. Orchard Bks. 2005 273p $16.99; pa $7.99

Grades: 7 8 9 10   Fic

1. Fantasy fiction 2. Fairies -- Fiction 3. Storytelling -- Fiction

ISBN 0-439-75570-0; 0-439-75571-9 pa

LC 2005-02174

First published 2003 in the United Kingdom

When Poison leaves her home in the marshes of Gull to retrieve the infant sister who was snatched by the fairies, she and a group of unusual friends survive encounters with the inhabitants of various Realms, and Poison herself confronts a surprising destiny.

"Poison's story should please crowds of horror fans who like their books fast-paced, darkly atmospheric, and melodramatic." SLJ

Retribution falls; Chris Wooding. Ballantine Books 2011 461p. (pbk.: alk. paper) $16

Grades: 11 12 Adult   Fic

1. Fantasy fiction 2. Adventure fiction 3. Pirates -- Fiction

ISBN 0345522516; 0345522583; 9780345522511; 9780345522580

LC 2010047793

In this book, "Dorian Frey's Ketty Jay is a hugely battered old freighter which just about runs. Frey keeps accepting jobs for himself and his crew in the hope of a big pay cheque. His current job turns out to be too good to be true. Suddenly Frey and his crew are running from the Navy Coalition and hired bounty hunters, as he is set up to take the fall after a freighter he is chasing explodes. Dorian Frey must outwit them all to prove his innocence and catch the real culprits." (Fantasy Book Review)

Silver; Chris Wooding. Scholastic Press 2014 320 p. (hc) $17.99

Grades: 7 8 9 10 11 12   Fic

1. Horror fiction 2. School stories 3. Schools -- Fiction 4. Survival -- Fiction 5. Boarding schools -- Fiction 6. Survival 7. Communicable diseases -- Fiction 8. Boarding schools 9. Communicable diseases 10. Boarding school students

ISBN 0545603927; 9780545603928

LC 2013014037

In this young adult science fiction horror novel, by Chris Wooding, "without warning, a horrifying infection will spread across the school grounds [of Mortingham Boarding Academy], and a group of students with little in common will find themselves barricaded in a classroom, fighting for their lives. Some will live. Some will die. And then it will get even worse." (Publisher's note)

"When strange insects assault a remote boarding school in England, the kids try to save the day in this tense page-turner...Skillfully managed subplots keep the pages flying. It looks like the end of the world is nigh.... It's just all kinds of white-knuckle fun." (Kirkus)

The **storm** thief. Orchard Books 2006 310p $16.99

Grades: 6 7 8 9 10   Fic

1. Science fiction

ISBN 0-439-86513-1

LC 2005-35993

With the help of a golem, two teenaged thieves try to survive on the city island of Orokos, where unpredictable probability storms continually change both the landscape and the inhabitants.

The author "delivers memorable characters, such as Vago, whose plight—Who am I and where do I belong in the world?—will be understood by many teens. Wooding also creates a unique world for his characters to explore, and the setting serves as an excellent backdrop for the author to develop his theme of order versus chaos and the need for balance between the two." Voice Youth Advocates

Woodrell, Daniel

Winter's bone; a novel. Little, Brown and Co. 2006 193p hardcover o.p. pa $13.99

Grades: 11 12 Adult   Fic

1. Criminals -- Fiction 2. Mountain life -- Fiction 3. Ozark Mountains -- Fiction 4. Father-daughter relationship -- Fiction

ISBN 0-316-05755-X; 978-0-316-05755-4; 0-316-06641-9 pa; 978-0-316-06641-9 pa

LC 2005-17349

"This lyrical and haunting story exposes the dark underside of its scenic setting. . . . But the book is not for the young or the faint-of-heart; Ree is not a saint, and this gritty story requires maturity to appreciate." Voice Youth Advocates

Woods, Elizabeth Emma

Choker; [by] Elizabeth Woods. Simon & Schuster Books for Young Readers 2011 233p $16.99

Grades: 9 10 11 12   Fic

1. School stories 2. Friendship -- Fiction 3. Mental illness -- Fiction

ISBN 978-1-4424-1233-0

LC 2010-34672

Teenaged Cara, solitary and bullied in high school, is delighted to reconnect with her childhood best friend Zoe whose support and friendship help Cara gain self-confidence, even as her classmates start dying.

"Terrific pacing and mounting suspense lead to a resolution that may not surprise savvy readers but is nonetheless chilling." Booklist

Woodson, Jacqueline

Behind you. Putnam 2004 118p $15.99; pa $7.99

Grades: 7 8 9 10   Fic

1. Death -- Fiction 2. New York (N.Y.) -- Fiction 3. African Americans -- Fiction

ISBN 978-0-399-23988-5; 0-399-23988-X; 978-0-14-241554-2 pa; 0-14-241554-5 pa

Sequel to: If you come softly

After fifteen-year-old Jeremiah is mistakenly shot by police, the people who love him struggle to cope with their loss as they recall his life and death, unaware that 'Miah is watching over them.

"Woodson writes with impressive poetry about race, love, death, and what grief feels like—the things that 'snap the heart' and her characters' open strength and wary optimism will resonate with many teens." Booklist

★ **Beneath** a meth moon; Jacqueline Woodson. Nancy Paulsen Books　2012　181p
Grades: 9 10 11 12　　　　　　　　　　**Fic**
　　1. Methamphetamine　2. Teenagers -- Drug use -- Fiction　3. Hurricane Katrina, 2005 -- Fiction　4. Iowa -- Fiction　5. Grief -- Fiction　6. Runaways -- Fiction　7. Drug abuse -- Fiction　8. Methamphetamine -- Fiction　9. Pass Christian (Miss.) -- Fiction
　　ISBN 9780399252501
　　　　　　　　　　　　　　　　　　LC 2011046799
In this novel, "Laurel, her father, and her little brother are reeling from the deaths of her mother and grandmother, who refused to leave their home in Pass Christian, Mississippi, during Hurricane Katrina. As they try to start life over in a new town, things look better for Laurel: she meets a sympathetic new friend named Kaylee, becomes a cheerleader, and starts dating T-Boom. Their first night together, though, T-Boom introduces her to meth, and she becomes instantly addicted. Her addiction progresses quickly, and when Kaylee confronts her and her father finds her stash, she runs away and lives on the streets, begging for money and trying desperately to stay high." (Bulletin of the Center for Children's Books)

If you come softly. Putnam　1998　181p $15.99; pa $5.99
Grades: 7 8 9 10　　　　　　　　　　　**Fic**
　　1. Race relations -- Fiction　2. New York (N.Y.) -- Fiction　3. African Americans -- Fiction
　　ISBN 0-399-23112-9; 0-698-11862-6 pa
　　　　　　　　　　　　　　　　　　LC 97-32212
ALA YALSA Margaret A. Edwards Award (2006)
After meeting at their private school in New York, fifteen-year-old Jeremiah, who is black and whose parents are separated, and Ellie, who is white and whose mother has twice abandoned her, fall in love and then try to cope with people's reactions
"The gentle and melancholy tone of this book makes it ideal for thoughtful readers and fans of romance." Voice Youth Advocates
Another title about Jeremiah is:
Behind you (2004)

Miracle's boys. Putnam　2000　133p $15.99; pa $5.99
Grades: 9 10 11 12　　　　　　　　　　**Fic**
　　1. Orphans -- Fiction　2. Brothers -- Fiction　3. New York (N.Y.) -- Fiction　4. African Americans -- Fiction
　　ISBN 0-399-23113-7; 0-698-11916-9 pa
　　　　　　　　　　　　　　　　　　LC 99-40050
ALA YALSA Margaret A. Edwards Award (2006)
Twelve-year-old Lafayette's close relationship with his older brother Charlie changes after Charlie is released from a detention home and blames Lafayette for the death of their mother
"The fast-paced narrative is physically immediate, and the dialogue is alive with anger and heartbreak." Booklist

Woolston, Blythe
　★ **Black** helicopters; Blythe Woolston. Candlewick Press　2013　176 p.　$15.99
Grades: 9 10 11 12　　　　　　　　　　**Fic**
　　1. Dystopias　2. Adventure fiction　3. Survivalism -- Fiction
　　ISBN 0763661465; 9780763661465
　　　　　　　　　　　　　　　　　　LC 2012942619
This young adult suspense novel, by Blythe Woolston, follows "a teenage girl. A survivalist childhood. And now a bomb strapped to her chest. . . . With Da unexpectedly gone and no home to return to, [the] teenage . . . Valkyrie . . . and her big brother must bring their message to the outside world--a not-so-smart place where little boys wear their names on their backpacks and young men don't pat down strangers before offering a lift." (Publisher's note)

　Catch & release; Blythe Woolston. Carolrhoda Lab　2012　210 p.
Grades: 9 10 11 12　　　　　　　　　　**Fic**
　　1. Fishing -- Fiction　2. Friendship -- Fiction　3. Automobile travel -- Fiction　4. Communicable diseases -- Fiction　5. People with disabilities -- Fiction　6. Trout -- Fiction　7. West (U.S.) -- Fiction　8. Disfigured persons -- Fiction
　　ISBN 0761377557; 9780761377559
　　　　　　　　　　　　　　　　　　LC 2011009630
In this book, "[e]ighteen-year-old Polly recounts her road trip with Odd, a fellow survivor of the disease that killed five others from their small town, in D'Elegance, his Gramma's old baby-blue Cadillac. Fishing is ostensibly the purpose of their outing, and it symbolically charts the way the two teens process their disabilities. . . . Polly once had a boyfriend and a sense of a normal future. . . . Odd Estes lost a foot as well as some football buddies, and although the two barely knew each other before, they both now struggle to accommodate their good fortune in surviving and their misfortune of disability. . . . Odd and Polly move from isolation to a mutual connection that helps them deal with their pain." (Kirkus)

　★ The **Freak** Observer. Carolrhoda Lab　2010　202p $16.95
Grades: 8 9 10 11 12　　　　　　　　　**Fic**
　　1. Post-traumatic stress disorder -- Fiction
　　ISBN 978-0-7613-6212-8; 0-7613-6212-6
　　　　　　　　　　　　　　　　　　LC 2010-989
Suffering from a crippling case of post-traumatic stress disorder, sixteen-year-old Loa Lindgren tries to use her problem solving skills, sharpened in physics and computer programming, to cure herself.
"Woolston's talent for dialogue and her unique approach to scenes make what sounds standard about this story feel fresh and vital. . . . A strong . . . [novel] about learning to see yourself apart from the reflection you cast off others." Booklist

　★ **Martians**; Blythe Woolston. Candlewick Press　2015　224 p. (hardcover) $16.99
Grades: 9 10 11 12　　　　　　　　　　**Fic**
　　1. Science fiction　2. Consumption (Economics) --

Fiction
ISBN 9780763677565; 0763677566

LC 2015931430

In this novel, by Blythe Woolston, set "in a near-future world of exurban decay studded with big box stores, daily routine revolves around shopping—for those who can. For Zoë, the mission is simpler: live. . . . With a handful of other disaffected, forgotten kids, Zoë must find her place in a world that has consumed itself beyond redemption." (Publisher's note)

"Imagination shines through the bleak but poetic prose, love and kindness prove hearty, and once again, life proves that roses not only do, but always will, grow in concrete. Dystopian aficionados, budding social pundits, and readers who enjoy quirky characters, settings, and challenges will find a lot to love here." VOYA

Woon, Yvonne

Life eternal; a Dead beautiful novel. Yvonne Woon. 1st ed. Hyperion 2012 393 p. (paperback) $9.99; (hardcover) $16.99

Grades: 9 10 11 12   **Fic**
1. Love stories 2. Suspense fiction 3. Supernatural -- Fiction 4. Canada -- Fiction 5. Schools -- Fiction 6. Immortality -- Fiction 7. Boarding schools -- Fiction 8. Montreal (Quebec) -- Fiction
ISBN 9781423137627; 1423119576; 9781423119579

LC 2011018257

This book is a sequel to "Dead Beautiful." Having "been saved by [her Undead soul mate] Dante . . . Renée is left to wonder whether she too is now one of the Undead." She is transferred to a new school, away from Dante. "Knowing that Dante only has five more years of animation before he will need to either take a life or die a second time, Renée searches the school's library and mystical texts for a solution." (Kirkus)

Wray, John

★ Lowboy. Farrar, Straus and Giroux 2009 258p $25

Grades: 11 12 Adult   **Fic**
1. Subways -- Fiction 2. Schizophrenia -- Fiction 3. New York (N.Y.) -- Fiction
ISBN 978-0-374-19416-1; 0-374-19416-5

LC 2008-17921

This is a "brilliant and gutsy performance but a cryptic one. It expresses its meanings in hallucinated events that seem to vibrate on the page. At certain moments the book feels like a runaway subway car; you want it to slow down for you." Buffalo News

Wrede, Patricia C., 1953-

The Far West; Patricia C. Wrede. Scholastic Press 2012 378 p. $17.99

Grades: 7 8 9 10 11 12   **Fic**
1. Steampunk fiction 2. Twins 3. Fantasy fiction 4. Fantasy 5. Magic -- Fiction
ISBN 0545033446; 9780545033442

LC 2012288790

This young adult speampunk novel, by Patricia C. Wrede, concludes the "Frontier Magic" trilogy. "Eff is an unlucky thirteenth child . . . but also the seventh daughter

in her family. Her twin brother, Lan, is a powerful double seventh son. Her life at the edge of the Great Barrier Spell is different from anyone else's that she knows. . . . With Lan, William, Professor Torgeson, Wash, and Professor Ochiba, Eff finds that nothing on the wild frontier is as they expected." (Publisher's note)

The thirteenth child. Scholastic Press 2009 344p (Frontier magic) $16.99

Grades: 7 8 9 10 11 12   **Fic**
1. School stories 2. Fantasy fiction 3. Magic -- Fiction 4. Twins -- Fiction 5. Frontier and pioneer life -- Fiction
ISBN 978-0-545-03342-8; 0-545-03342-X

LC 2008-34048

Eighteen-year-old Eff must finally get over believing she is bad luck and accept that her special training in Aphrikan magic, and being the twin of the seventh son of a seventh son, give her extraordinary power to combat magical creatures that threaten settlements on the western frontier.

Wrede "creates a rich world where steam dragons seem as normal as bears, and a sympathetic character in Eff." Publ Wkly

Followed by Across the Great Barrier (2011)

Wright, Barbara

Crow; Barbara Wright. 1st ed. Random House 2012 297 p. (hardcover) $16.99; (lib. bdg.) $19.99; (ebook) $16.99

Grades: 9 10 11 12   **Fic**
1. Racism 2. African Americans -- Fiction 3. Historical fiction 4. Friendship -- Fiction 5. Family life -- Fiction 6. North Carolina -- Fiction 7. Race relations -- Fiction
ISBN 037586928X; 0375969284; 9780375869280; 9780375969287; 9780375982705

LC 2011014892

This historical novel by author Barbara Wright is set in the nineteenth century, when "Moses Thomas['s] . . . father, a reporter for an expanding African-American newspaper in Wilmington, NC, sets high expectations for . . . the general prosperity of his middle-class black community . . . An inflammatory article on the perceived threat to white womanhood provokes an equally incendiary response from Mr. Thomas' editor, and the issue becomes a flashpoint upon which the Wilmington election turns." (Bulletin of the Center for Children's Books)

Wright, Denis

Violence 101; a novel. G. P. Putnam's Sons 2010 213p $16.99

Grades: 8 9 10   **Fic**
1. Genius -- Fiction 2. Violence -- Fiction 3. New Zealand -- Fiction 4. Reformatories -- Fiction 5. Race relations -- Fiction
ISBN 978-0-399-25493-2; 0-399-25493-5

LC 2010-02851

First published 2007 in New Zealand

In a New Zealand reformatory, Hamish Graham, an extremely intelligent fourteen-year-old who believes in the compulsory study of violence, learns that it is not always the answer.

"Wright's novel is clever and biting, a tragedy of society's failure to deal with kids like Hamish and a satire of society's winking condemnations of violence. Hamish's actions can be revolting, despite his justifications, but he still draws empathy as a product of the environment at large. Hardly a comfortable book to read, but a gripping one." Publ Wkly

Wroblewski, David

★ The **story** of Edgar Sawtelle; a novel. Ecco 2008 566p hardcover o.p. pa $16.99

Grades: 9 10 11 12 Adult   **Fic**
1. Dogs -- Fiction 2. Homicide -- Fiction 3. Wisconsin -- Fiction 4. Speech disorders -- Fiction
ISBN 978-0-06-137422-7; 0-06-137422-9; 978-0-06-137423-4 pa; 0-06-137423-7 pa

"Set in rural nineteen-seventies Wisconsin, this loose retelling of Hamlet focusses on Edgar, a boy born mute and with a preternatural ability to commune with the dogs whose breeding and training is his family's business. Idyllic routine is threatened when Edgar's ne'er-do-well uncle comes to live with the family, and the menace persists even after his sudden departure. Soon afterward, Edgar's father dies of an apparent aneurysm; Edgar becomes convinced, but can't prove, that his uncle—who soon inserts himself back into the family—is to blame. . . . [The author] illustrates the relationship between man and canine (at times, from the dog's point of view) in a way that is both lyrical and unsentimental, and demonstrates an ability to create a coherent, captivating fictional world in which even supernatural elements feel entirely persuasive." New Yorker

Wunder, Wendy

★ The **museum** of intangible things; Wendy Wunder. Razorbill 2014 304 p. (hardback) $17.99

Grades: 8 9 10 11 12   **Fic**
1. Mental illness -- Fiction 2. Female friendship -- Fiction 3. Runaway teenagers -- Fiction 4. Manic-depressive illness -- Fiction 5. Runaways -- Fiction 6. Friendship -- Fiction 7. Best friends -- Fiction 8. Automobile travel -- Fiction
ISBN 1595145141; 9781595145147
                              LC 2013030169

In this book, by Wendy Wunder, "Hannah and Zoe haven't had much in their lives, but they've always had each other. So when Zoe tells Hannah she needs to get out of their down-and-out New Jersey town, they . . . head west. . . . As they chase storms and make new friends, Zoe tells Hannah she wants more for her. She wants her to live bigger, dream grander, aim higher. And so Zoe begins teaching Hannah all about life's intangible things." (Publisher's note)

"As Hannah and best friend Zoe (diagnosed bipolar) embark on a cross-country road trip, Zoe gives Hannah "intangible lessons" (e.g., Hannah learns insouciance when they overnight in an IKEA). When Zoe's irrationality gets scary, Hannah learns betrayal and, later, forgiveness. With each lesson, Hannah becomes more confident, building her own distinct identity. Meanwhile, Zoe is a complex character--intelligent, loyal, and funny." Horn Book

★ The **probability** of miracles. Razorbill 2011 360p $17.99

Grades: 8 9 10 11 12   **Fic**
1. Death -- Fiction 2. Maine -- Fiction 3. Cancer --

Fiction 4. Miracles -- Fiction
ISBN 978-1-59514-368-6; 1-59514-368-8

"Faced with death, one teen discovers life in this bittersweet debut. . . . Cynical and loner Campbell Cooper (an Italian-Samoan-American) gave up on magic after her parents divorced, her father died and she developed neuroblastoma. . . . Having exhausted Western medicine, her single mother suggests spending the summer after Cam's graduation in Promise, Maine, a hidden town . . . known to have mysterious healing powers. . . . Exploring both sides of Cam's heritage, the story unfolds through narration as beautiful as the sun's daily 'everlasting gobstopper descent behind the lighthouse.' Irreverent humor, quirky small-town charm and surprises along the way help readers brace themselves for the tearjerker ending." Kirkus

Wung-Sung, Jesper

The **last** execution; Jesper Wung-Sung; translation by Lindy Falk van Rooyen. Atheneum Books for Young Readers 2016 144 p. (hardcover) $17.99

Grades: 10 11 12   **Fic**
1. Denmark -- Fiction 2. Executions and executioners -- Fiction
ISBN 9781481429658; 9781481429665
                              LC 2015033461

This book, by Jesper Wung-Sung, is "based on the . . . true story of the last execution in Denmark's history. . . . Niels Nielson, a young peasant, was sentenced to death by beheading on the dubious charges of arson and murder. Does he have the right to live despite what he is accused of? That is the question the townsfolk ask as the countdown begins." (Publisher's note)

"This bleak Danish import imagines the last day of a real-life execution victim in 1853 Svendborg, Denmark. The observations of various townspeople--interspersed with the fifteen-year-old boy's own memories of poverty, rejection, loss, and finally rage--reveal the world that led the boy to his crime and his fate. Rich with symbolism, historical criticism, and contemporary resonance, this is an unflinching examination of capitol punishment." Horn Book

Wyatt, Melissa

Funny how things change. Farrar, Straus & Giroux 2009 196p $16.95

Grades: 9 10 11 12   **Fic**
1. Artists -- Fiction 2. Mountains -- Fiction 3. Country life -- Fiction 4. West Virginia -- Fiction
ISBN 978-0-374-30233-7; 0-374-30233-2
                              LC 2008-16190

Remy, a talented, seventeen-year-old auto mechanic, questions his decision to join his girlfriend when she starts college in Pennsylvania after a visiting artist helps him to realize what his family's home in a dying West Virginia mountain town means to him.

"Laconic but full of heart, smart, thoughtful and proudly working-class, Remy makes a fresh and immensely appealing hero." Kirkus

Wylie, Sarah

All these lives; Sarah Wylie. 1st ed. Margaret Ferguson Books/Farrar Straus Giroux 2012 248 p. (hardcover) $17.99

Grades: 9 10 11 12 **Fic**
1. Sisters -- Fiction 2. Leukemia -- Fiction 3. Teenagers
-- Suicide -- Fiction 4. Sick -- Fiction 5. Twins --
Fiction 6. Cancer -- Fiction 7. Family life -- Fiction 8.
Near-death experiences -- Fiction
ISBN 0374302081; 9780374302085; 9781429954952
LC 2011030779
This book tells the story of Dani. Ever "since surviving
a car crash and a chest infection as a child, 16-year-old Dani
has been told that she's a miracle" which she "interprets . . .
as evidence that she literally has nine lives. But Dani's twin,
Jena, is dying from leukemia, and Dani thinks her parents are
acting disturbingly normal under the circumstances. . . . She
persuades herself that by ridding herself of her extra 'lives,'
she can transfer them to her sister." (Publishers Weekly)

Wynne-Jones, Tim
★ **Blink** & Caution. Candlewick Press 2011
342p $16.99
Grades: 9 10 11 12 **Fic**
1. Crime -- Fiction 2. Guilt -- Fiction 3. Canada --
Fiction 4. Runaway teenagers -- Fiction
ISBN 978-0-7636-3983-9; 0-7636-3983-4
LC 2010-13563
"The short, punchy sentences Wynne-Jones fires like
buckshot; the joy, fear, and doubt that punctuate the teens'
every action. This is gritty, sure, but more than that, it's
smart, and earns every drop of its hopeful finish." Booklist

The **uninvited**. Candlewick Press 2009 351p
$16.99
Grades: 10 11 12 **Fic**
1. Canada -- Fiction 2. Vacations -- Fiction 3. Father-
daughter relationship -- Fiction
ISBN 978-0-7636-3984-6; 0-7636-3984-2
LC 2009-7520
After a disturbing freshman year at New York University, Mimi is happy to get away to her father's remote Canadian cottage only to discover a stranger living there who
has never heard of her or her father and who is convinced
that Mimi is responsible for leaving sinister tokens around
the property.
"This suspenseful and deftly crafted family drama will
appeal to older teens who are exploring their options beyond
high school." Voice Youth Advocates

Yancey, Rick
★ The **5th** Wave; Rick Yancey. G.P. Putnam's
Sons, an imprint of Penguin Group (USA) Inc. 2013
480 p. (hardcover) $18.99
Grades: 9 10 11 12 **Fic**
1. Science fiction 2. Extraterrestrial beings -- Fiction 3.
War -- Fiction 4. Survival -- Fiction
ISBN 0399162410; 9780399162411
LC 2012047622
In this post-apocalyptic novel, by Rick Yancey, "on a
lonely stretch of highway, Cassie runs from Them. The be-
ings who only look human, who roam the countryside killing
anyone they see. Who have scattered Earth's last survivors.
To stay alone is to stay alive, Cassie believes, until she meets
Evan Walker. Beguiling and mysterious, Evan Walker may

be Cassie's only hope for rescuing her brother--or even saving herself." (Publisher's note)
"Yancey makes a dramatic 180 from the intellectual
horror of his Monstrumologist books to open a gripping SF
trilogy about an Earth decimated by an alien invasion. The
author fully embraces the genre, while resisting its more
sensational tendencies... It's a book that targets a broad commercial audience, and Yancey's aim is every bit as good as
Cassie's." Pub Wkly

The **curse** of the Wendigo; [by] William James
Henry; edited by Rick Yancey. Simon & Schuster
Books for Young Readers 2010 424p il (Monstru-
mologist) $17.99; e-book $9.99
Grades: 9 10 11 12 **Fic**
1. Horror fiction 2. Orphans -- Fiction 3. Monsters
-- Fiction 4. Apprentices -- Fiction 5. Supernatural
-- Fiction
ISBN 978-1-4169-8450-4; 978-1-4169-8973-8 e-book
LC 2010-19233
Sequel to The monstrumologist (2009)
In 1888, twelve-year-old Will Henry chronicles his ap-
prenticeship with Dr. Warthrop, a New England scientist
who hunts and studies real-life monsters, as they discover
and attempt to destroy the Wendigo, a creature that starves
even as it gorges itself on human flesh.
This book "is as fast-paced, elegant, and, yes, gruesome
as its predecessor. . . . The development of the relationship
between hapless Will and the demanding monstrumologist is
the most rewarding aspect of the story." Publ Wkly
Followed by The Isle of Blood (2011)

The **final** descent; Rick Yancey. Simon & Schuster Books for Young Readers 2013 320 p. (Monstrumologist) (hardback) $18.99
Grades: 9 10 11 12 **Fic**
1. Monsters -- Fiction 2. Apprentices -- Fiction 3.
Horror stories 4. Orphans -- Fiction 5. Supernatural
-- Fiction
ISBN 144245153X; 9781442451537
LC 2013015811
In this final installment of Rick Yancey's Monstrumologist series, "Will Henry, now 16, often drunk and colder than
ever, helps Monstrumologist Pellinore Warthrop track down
the T. cerrejonensis, a giant, snakelike critter that poisons its
human prey then swallows them whole. At the same time,
the novel also fast-forwards decades later to 1911, when
Will returns to care for an elderly Warthrop and then re-
verts back to when he was first taken in by his employer."
(Kirkus Reviews)
"This fourth and final volume of the series (a blend of
gothic horror, cryptozoology, and Sherlockiana) features apprentice Will Henry in the throes of adolescent rebellion as
he seeks to escape the jealous, domineering monstrumologist Warthrop and wrest the affection of Lilly Bates away
from a rival suitor. Yancey has taken some considerable risks
here, ones that should thrill his ardent fans." (Horn Book)

The **infinite** sea; Rick Yancey. Putnam Publishing Group 2014 300 p. (5th wave) $18.99
Grades: 9 10 11 12 **Fic**
1. Science fiction 2. Apocalyptic fiction 3.

Extraterrestrial beings -- Fiction 4. War -- Fiction 5. Survival -- Fiction

ISBN 0399162429; 9780399162428

LC 2014022058

In this science fiction novel, by Rick Yancey, book 2 in the "5th Wave" series, "surviving the first four waves was nearly impossible. Now Cassie Sullivan finds herself in a new world, a world in which the fundamental trust that binds us together is gone. As the 5th Wave rolls across the landscape, Cassie, Ben, and Ringer are forced to confront the Others' ultimate goal: the extermination of the human race." (Publisher's note)

"Yancey's prose remains unimpeachable—every paragraph is laden with setting, theme, and emotion—and he uses it toward a series of horrifying set pieces, including a surgery scene that will have your pages sopping with sweat." Booklist

★ The **monstrumologist**; [by] William James Henry; edited by Rick Yancey. Simon & Schuster Books for Young Readers 2009 454p il $17.99; pa $9.99

Grades: 9 10 11 12   Fic

1. Orphans -- Fiction 2. Monsters -- Fiction 3. Apprentices -- Fiction 4. Supernatural -- Fiction

ISBN 978-1-4169-8448-1; 1-4169-8448-8; 978-1-4169-8449-8 pa; 1-4169-8449-6 pa

LC 2009-4562

ALA YALSA Printz Award Honor Book (2010)

In 1888, twelve-year-old Will Henry chronicles his apprenticeship with Dr. Warthrop, a scientist who hunts and studies real-life monsters, as they discover and attempt to destroy a pod of Anthropophagi.

"As the action moves from the dissecting table to the cemetery to an asylum to underground catacombs, Yancey keeps the shocks frequent and shrouded in a splattery miasma of blood, bone, pus, and maggots. . . . Yancey's prose is stentorian and wordy, but it weaves a world that possesses a Lovecraftian logic and hints at its own deeply satisfying mythos. . . . 'Snap to!' is Warthrop's continued demand of Will, but readers will need no such needling." Booklist

Other titles in this series include:

The curse of the wendigo (2010)

The Isle of Blood (2011)

Yansky, Brian

Alien invasion and other inconveniences. Candlewick Press 2010 227p $15.99

Grades: 9 10 11 12   Fic

1. Science fiction 2. Telepathy -- Fiction 3. Extraterrestrial beings -- Fiction

ISBN 978-0-7636-4384-3

LC 2009-49103

When a race of aliens quickly takes over the earth, leaving most people dead, high-schooler Jesse finds himself a slave to an inept alien leader—a situation that brightens as Jesse develops telepathic powers and attracts the attention of two beautiful girls.

"The story is action-packed, provocative, profound, and wickedly funny. Yansky takes on questions philosophical,

ecological, religious, moral, and social, and the satire is right on target." Horn Book Guide

Homicidal aliens and other disappointments; Brian Yansky. Candlewick Press 2013 336 p. $16.99

Grades: 9 10 11 12   Fic

1. Teenagers -- Fiction 2. Extraterrestrial beings -- Fiction

ISBN 0763659622; 9780763659622

LC 2013931461

"The reluctant hero from 'Alien Invasion and Other Inconveniences' is back in all his droll glory. . . . Now Jesse is revered as some sort of Chosen One all because he managed to kill one of the alien lords and escape. . . . But it's hard to argue with the multitude of new talents he is developing, including . . . killing aliens with his mind and grasping glimpses of alternate futures." (Publisher's note)

"Narrator Jesse (Alien Invasion and Other Inconveniences) continues to battle the lethal aliens who have taken control of Earth as thirty-million Sanginian colonists are about to arrive. Jesse finds that in addition to his telepathic abilities, he's now able to see glimpses of possible futures. The fast-paced action, realistically developed relationships, and dry, self-deprecating voice drive this readable and thought-provoking sequel." (Horn Book)

Yee, Lisa

Absolutely Maybe. Arthur A. Levine Books 2009 274p $16.99

Grades: 8 9 10 11 12   Fic

1. Fathers -- Fiction 2. Runaway teenagers -- Fiction 3. Los Angeles (Calif.) -- Fiction 4. Mother-daughter relationship -- Fiction

ISBN 978-0-439-83844-3; 0-439-83844-4

LC 2008-17787

When living with her mother, an alcoholic ex-beauty queen, becomes unbearable, almost seventeen-year-old Maybelline "Maybe" Chestnut runs away to California, where she finds work on a taco truck and tries to track down her birth father.

"The characters are complex and their friendships layered—they sweep readers up in their path." Publ Wkly

The **kidney** hypothetical, or, how to ruin your life in seven days; Lisa Yee. First edition Arthur A. Levine Books 2015 272 p. (hardcover: alk. paper) $17.99

Grades: 9 10 11 12   Fic

1. High school students -- Fiction 2. Dating (Social customs) -- Fiction 3. Schools -- Fiction 4. Brothers -- Fiction 5. Friendship -- Fiction 6. Family life -- Fiction 7. High schools -- Fiction

ISBN 0545230942; 0545230950; 9780545230940; 9780545230957

LC 2014005332

In this novel by Lisa Yee "Higgs Boson Bing has seven days left before his perfect high school career is completed. Then it's on to Harvard to fulfill the fantasy portrait of success that he and his parents have cultivated for the past four years. But something's not right. And when Higgs's girlfriend presents him with a seemingly innocent hypothetical question about whether or not he'd give her a kidney . . . the exposed fault lines reach straight down to the foundations of his life." (Publisher's note)

"With whip-smart writing, a fast-paced plot, plenty of humor, and just enough mystery to keep readers on edge, this is an emotional journey about breaking free of family, friends, and duty to discover what makes you happy." Booklist

Kidney hypothetical

How to ruin your life in seven days

Yolen, Jane

★ **Briar** Rose. Doherty Assocs. 1992 190p (Fairy tale series) hardcover o.p. pa $10.99

Grades: 8 9 10 11 12 Adult **Fic**
1. Fantasy fiction 2. Grandmothers -- Fiction 3. Jews -- Poland -- Fiction 4. Holocaust, 1933-1945 -- Fiction
ISBN 0-312-85135-9; 9780765382948 pa
LC 92-25456

"Yolen takes the story of Briar Rose (commonly known as Sleeping Beauty) and links it to the Holocaust. . . . Rebecca Berlin, a young woman who has grown up hearing her grandmother Gemma tell an unusual and frightening version of the Sleeping Beauty legend, realizes when Gemma dies that the fairy tale offers one of the very few clues she has to her grandmother's past. . . . By interpolating Gemma's vivid and imaginative story into the larger narrative, Yolen has created an engrossing novel." Publ Wkly

Curse of the Thirteenth Fey; the True Tale of Sleeping Beauty. Jane Yolen. Philomel Books 2012 290 p. $16.99

Grades: 6 7 8 9 10 **Fic**
1. Curses -- Fiction 2. Princesses 3. Family life 4. Fairy tales 5. Elves -- Fiction 6. Magic -- Fiction 7. Fairies -- Fiction 8. Prophecies -- Fiction 9. Family life -- Fiction
ISBN 0399256644; 9780399256646
LC 2011038847

In author Jane Yolen's book, "Gorse is the thirteenth . . . in a family of fairies tied to the evil king's land and made to do his bidding. . . . When accident-prone Gorse falls ill just as the family is bid to bless the new princess . . . [she] races to the castle with the last piece of magic the family has left. . . . But that is when accident, mayhem, and magic combine to drive Gorse's story into the unthinkable, threatening the baby, the kingdom, and all." (Publisher's note)

Except the queen; [by] Jane Yolen and Midori Snyder. Roc 2010 371p $23.95

Grades: 10 11 12 Adult **Fic**
1. Fantasy fiction 2. Fairies -- Fiction 3. Sisters -- Fiction
ISBN 978-0-451-46273-2; 0-451-46273-4
LC 2009-36063

Cast from the high court of the Fairy Queen, sisters Serena and Meteora must find a way to survive in the mortal realm of Earth. But when signs point to a rising power that threatens to tear asunder both fairy and human worlds, they realize that they were chosen to fight the menace because they were the only ones who could do what must be done.

"Unconventional narrative techniques and a full dose of magic and folklore give this urban fantasy a lyrical, mythic feel." Publ Wkly

Yoo, Paula

Good enough. HarperTeen 2008 322p $16.99; lib bdg $17.89

Grades: 7 8 9 10 **Fic**
1. Violinists -- Fiction 2. Korean Americans -- Fiction
ISBN 978-0-06-079085-1; 978-0-06-079086-8 lib bdg
LC 2007-02985

A Korean American teenager tries to please her parents by getting into an Ivy League college, but a new guy in school and her love of the violin tempt her in new directions.

"The frequent lists, . . . SAT questions, and even spam recipes are, like Patti's convincing narration, filled with laugh-out-loud lines, but it's the deeper questions about growing up with immigrant parents, confronting racism, and how best to find success and happiness that will stay with readers." Booklist

Yoon, Nicola

★ **Everything,** everything; Nicola Yoon. Delacorte Press 2015 320 p. (hardback) $18.99 **Fic**
1. Love stories 2. Allergy -- Fiction 3. Love -- Fiction 4. Friendship -- Fiction 5. Racially mixed people -- Fiction
ISBN 9780553496642
LC 2015002950

This young adult novel, by Nicola Yoon, tells "the story of Maddy, a girl who's literally allergic to the outside world, and Olly, the boy who moves in next door . . . and becomes the greatest risk she's ever taken. This . . . novel unfolds via vignettes, diary entries, illustrations, and more." (Publisher's note)

Young, Moira

Blood red road. Margaret K. McElderry Books 2011 512p (Dustlands trilogy) $17.99

Grades: 6 7 8 9 10 **Fic**
1. Science fiction 2. Twins -- Fiction 3. Orphans -- Fiction 4. Siblings -- Fiction 5. Kidnapping -- Fiction
ISBN 978-1-4424-2998-7; 1-4424-2998-4
LC 2011-03423

"When 18-year-old Saba's father is killed and her twin brother, Lugh, is kidnapped, she sets out to rescue him, along with their younger sister, Emmi, and Saba's intelligent raven, Nero. Their travels across the desert wasteland bring them to a violent city in which Saba is forced to fight for her life in an arena. When she escapes with the help of a group of women warriors, she and her new allies (including a handsome and infuriating male warrior named Jack) try to prevent Lugh from being sacrificed." (Publishers Weekly)

"Readers will . . . be riveted by the book's fast-paced mix of action and romance. It's a natural for Hunger Games fans." Publ Wkly

Young, Suzanne

A **need** so beautiful. Balzer + Bray 2011 267p $16.99; ebook $9.99

Grades: 8 9 10 11 12 **Fic**
1. Supernatural -- Fiction 2. Good and evil -- Fiction 3. Portland (Or.) -- Fiction
ISBN 978-0-06-200824-4; 0-06-200824-2; 978-0-06-208454-5 ebook; 0-06-208454-2 ebook
LC 2010040810

A compelling Need that Charlotte has felt all her life is growing stronger, forcing her to connect with people in crisis, but at the same time other changes are taking place and she is terrified by what Monroe, a doctor and family friend, says must happen next.

"Charlotte is an exceptionally likable character who demonstrates an extraordinary amount of personal growth as she learns to accept her fate. . . . A unique take on the age-old struggle of good vs. evil." SLJ

Yovanoff, Brenna

Fiendish; Brenna Yovanoff. Razorbill 2014 352 p. (hardback) $17.99

Grades: 9 10 11 12   Fic

1. Love -- Fiction 2. Magic -- Fiction 3. Supernatural -- Fiction

ISBN 1595146385; 9781595146380

LC 2013047610

In this book, by Brenna Yovanoff, "when Clementine was a child, dangerous and inexplicable things started happening in New South Bend. The townsfolk blamed the fiendish people out in the Willows and burned their homes to the ground. But magic kept Clementine alive, walled up in the cellar for ten years, until a boy named Fisher sets her free. Back in the world, Clementine sets out to discover what happened all those years ago. But the truth gets muddled in her dangerous attraction to Fisher." (Publisher's note)

"When Clementine, in a magical coma for years, is awakened, eerie things (grotesquely mutated animals, animated plants, uncanny weather) begin to happen. Clementine must sift through the mysteries of her childhood to figure out what's causing the wild magic. Yovanoff's world-building is sophisticated and precise. Powerful, haunting prose brings to life a world overflowing with wild magic, seething prejudice, and base fear." Horn Book

★ **Places** no one knows; Brenna Yovanoff. Delacorte Press 2016 384 p. (hc) $17.99

Grades: 9 10 11 12   Fic

1. School stories 2. Dreams -- Fiction 3. Sleep -- Fiction 4. Schools -- Fiction 5. High schools -- Fiction 6. Self-perception -- Fiction

ISBN 9780553522631; 9780553522648

LC 2015015299

In this novel, by Brenna Yovanoff, "Waverly Camdenmar spends her nights . . . [with] the tiny, nagging suspicion that there's more to life than student council and GPAs. Marshall Holt is a loser. He drinks on school nights and gets stoned in the park. . . . But then one night Waverly falls asleep and dreams herself into Marshall's bedroom. . . . In Waverly's dreams, the rules have changed. But in her days, she'll have to decide if it's worth losing everything for a boy who barely exists." (Publisher's note)

"There are two Waverly Camdenmars. One is the Waverly everyone sees: smart, driven, untouchable. The other is the Waverly who runs at night until her feet bleed, who spends hours meticulously analyzing her fellow students so she knows how to behave, and who, one night, dreams herself into the bedroom of Marshall Holt, a thoughtful slacker-stoner with a troubled home life who shouldn't even be on her radar. As her nighttime wanderings continue and their connection grows, Waverly must decide if he is something she wants in her waking life as well. . . . This is a

tightly woven, luminously written novel that captures the uncertain nature of high school and the difficult path of self-discovery." Booklist

★ The **replacement**. Razorbill 2010 343p $17.99

Grades: 9 10 11 12   Fic

1. Fantasy fiction 2. Death -- Fiction 3. Siblings -- Fiction 4. Supernatural -- Fiction 5. Missing children -- Fiction

ISBN 978-1-59514-337-2; 1-59514-337-8

LC 2010-36066

Sixteen-year-old Mackie Doyle knows that he replaced a human child when he was just an infant, and when a friend's sister disappears he goes against his family's and town's deliberate denial of the problem to confront the beings that dwell under the town, tampering with human lives.

"Yovanoff's spare but haunting prose creates an atmosphere shrouded in gloom and secrecy so that readers, like Mackie, must attempt to make sense of a situation ruled by chaos and fear. The ethical complications of the town's deal with the creatures of Mayhem are clearly presented but never overwrought, while Mackie's problematic relationship to the townspeople as both an outsider and a savior is poignantly explored." Bull Cent Child Books

Zadoff, Allen

★ **Boy** Nobody; a novel by Allen Zadoff. 1st ed. Little, Brown, and Co. 2013 352 p. (hardcover) $18

Grades: 9 10 11 12   Fic

1. Assassins -- Fiction 2. Undercover operations -- Fiction 3. Teenagers -- Conduct of life -- Fiction 4. Schools -- Fiction 5. High schools -- Fiction 6. Conduct of life -- Fiction 7. Interpersonal relations -- Fiction

ISBN 0316199680; 9780316199681

LC 2012029484

In this book by Allen Zadoff, the "unnamed 16-year-old protagonist lost his identity when he was kidnapped and his parents murdered. Forced into a grueling training program, the teen now gets sent on undercover missions, befriending the children of powerful targets, getting invited to their houses, and killing their parents. He never questions his orders or actions until he's given five days to infiltrate a ritzy private school and kill the mayor of New York City." (Publishers Weekly)

Food, girls, and other things I can't have. Egmont USA 2009 311p $16.99; lib bdg $19.99

Grades: 7 8 9 10   Fic

1. School stories 2. Obesity -- Fiction 3. Football -- Fiction 4. Popularity -- Fiction

ISBN 978-1-60684-004-7; 1-60684-004-5; 978-1-60684-051-1 lib bdg; 1-60684-051-7 lib bdg

LC 2009-16242

Fifteen-year-old Andrew Zansky, the second fattest student at his high school, joins the varsity football team to get the attention of a new girl on whom he has a crush.

"The author does not lead Andy down the expected path. When forced to make a decision, his choice is unique and the conclusion satisfying. . . . The possibly offensive locker room language is typical and lends credibility. More importantly, Andy's character is thoughtful and refreshing." SLJ

I am the mission; a novel. by Allen Zadoff. First edition Little, Brown and Co. 2014 432 p. (Unknown Assassin) (hardcover) $18

Grades: 9 10 11 12   **Fic**

  1. Adventure fiction 2. Assassins -- Fiction 3. Brainwashing -- Fiction

  ISBN 0316199699; 9780316199698; 9780316255042

                  LC 2013024561

In this young adult adventure novel by Allen Zadoff, part of The Unknown Assassin series, "Boy Nobody, haunted by the outcome of his last assignment, is given a new mission. . . . His objective: take out Eugene Moore, the owner of a military training and indoctrination camp for teenagers. . . . It sounds simple, but a previous operative couldn't do it. He lost the mission and is presumed dead. Boy Nobody is confident he can finish the job. Quickly." (Publisher's note)

"Zadoff has crafted another highly suspenseful, compulsively readable futuristic thriller with an agreeably intricate plot and a sympathetic—though often cold-blooded—protagonist." Booklist

Zail, Suzy

Playing for the commandant; Suzy Zail. Candlewick Press 2014 256 p. $16.99

Grades: 7 8 9 10 11 12   **Fic**

  1. Pianists -- Fiction 2. Holocaust, 1939-1945 -- Fiction 3. War stories 4. Historical fiction 5. Concentration camp inmates - Fiction

  ISBN 0763664030; 9780763664039

                  LC 2013955694

In this young adult novel by Suzy Zail, "Before, Hanna was going to be a famous concert pianist. She was going to wear her yellow dress to a dance. And she was going to dance with a boy. But then the Nazis came. Now it is up to Hanna to do all she can to keep her mother and sister alive, even if that means playing piano for the commandant and his guests." (Publisher's note)

"Zail's story is as gut-wrenching as any Holocaust tale . . . The haunting, matter-of-fact tone of Hanna's story will likely resonate with teens learning about the Holocaust." Booklist

Zailckas, Koren

Mother, mother; a novel. Koren Zailckas. Crown Publishers 2013 352 p. $24

Grades: 11 12 Adult   **Fic**

  1. Drug abuse -- Fiction 2. Dysfunctional families -- Fiction 3. Mother-child relationship -- Fiction 4. Mothers and daughters -- Fiction 5. Narcissists -- Family relationships -- Fiction

  ISBN 0385347235; 9780385347235

                  LC 2013010450

Alex Awards Winner (2014)

In this book, "Violet, the dysfunctional Hurst family's stoner middle child, cannot remember which family member slashed her 12-year-old brother Will the night she overdosed on some strange seeds. But her mother, Josephine, blames her, and has her committed to a psychiatric hospital. Violet has no idea who to turn to for help: her spineless, alcoholic

father, Douglas; her runaway older sister, Rose; or Will, the home-schooled mama's boy." (Publishers Weekly)

Zambrano, Mario Alberto

Loteria; A novel. by Mario Alberto Zambrano. HarperCollins 2013 288 p. $21.99

Grades: 9 10 11 12 Adult   **Fic**

  1. Family -- Fiction 2. Children of prisoners -- Fiction

  ISBN 0062268546; 9780062268549

In this novel by Mario Alberto Zambrano a girl "tells the story of her family's . . . demise using a deck of cards of the eponymous Latin American game of chance. With her older sister Estrella in the ICU and her father in jail, eleven-year-old Luz Castillo has been taken into the custody of the state. She retreats behind a wall of silence, writing in her journal and shuffling through a deck of loteria cards. Each of the cards' colorful images . . . sparks a random memory." (Publisher's note)

"An intriguing debut and an elegiac, miniature entry in the literature of Latin American diaspora." Pub Wkly

Zarr, Sara

★ **How** to save a life; Sara Zarr. Little, Brown 2011 341 p. $17.99

Grades: 6 7 8 9 10 11 12   **Fic**

  1. Adoption -- Fiction 2. Bereavement -- Fiction 3. Mother-daughter relationship -- Fiction 4. Colorado -- Fiction 5. Pregnancy -- Fiction 6. Family life -- Fiction

  ISBN 9780316036061

                  LC 2010045832

Told from their own viewpoints, seventeen-year-old Jill, in grief over the loss of her father, and Mandy, nearly nineteen, are thrown together when Jill's mother agrees to adopt Mandy's unborn child but nothing turns out as they had anticipated.

"Filled with so many frustrations, so many dilemmas needing reasonable solutions, and so much hope and faith in the midst of sadness, Zarr's novel is a rich tapestry of love and survival that will resonate with even the most cynical readers." Booklist

★ **The Lucy** variations; by Sara Zarr. 1st ed. Little, Brown and Co. 2013 320 p. (hardcover) $17.99

Grades: 7 8 9 10 11 12   **Fic**

  1. Pianists -- Fiction 2. Brothers and sisters -- Fiction 3. Ability -- Fiction 4. San Francisco (Calif.) -- Fiction 5. Family life -- California -- Fiction 6. Self-actualization (Psychology) -- Fiction

  ISBN 031620501X; 9780316205016

                  LC 2012029852

In this novel, by Sara Zarr, "Lucy Beck-Moreau once had a promising future as a concert pianist. . . . Now, at sixteen, it's over. A death, and a betrayal, led her to walk away. That leaves her talented ten-year-old brother, Gus, to shoulder the full weight of the Beck-Moreau family expectations. Then Gus gets a new piano teacher who is young, kind, and interested in helping Lucy rekindle her love of piano--on her own terms." (Publisher's note)

"The third-person narration focuses entirely on Lucy but allows readers enough distance to help them understand her behavior in ways Lucy cannot. Occasional flashbacks fill out the back story. The combination of sympathetic main character and unusual social and cultural world makes this satisfying coming-of-age story stand out." Kirkus

★ **Once** was lost. Little, Brown 2009 217p $16.99

Grades: 7 8 9 10   Fic

1. Clergy -- Fiction 2. Alcoholism -- Fiction 3. Kidnapping -- Fiction 4. Christian life -- Fiction

ISBN 978-0-316-03604-7; 0-316-03604-8

LC 2009-25187

As the tragedy of a missing girl unfolds in her small town, fifteen-year-old Samara, who feels emotionally abandoned by her parents, begins to question her faith.

"This multilayered exploration of the intersection of the spiritual life and imperfect people features suspense and packs an emotional wallop." SLJ

Roomies; Sara Zarr and Tara Altebrando. Little, Brown and Company 2014 288 p. $18

Grades: 9 10 11 12   Fic

1. Roommates -- Fiction 2. Teenage girls -- Fiction 3. Email -- Fiction 4. Friendship -- Fiction 5. Dating (Social customs) -- Fiction 6. Family life -- California -- Fiction 7. Family life -- New Jersey -- Fiction

ISBN 0316217492; 9780316217491

LC 2012048431

In this book, by Sara Zarr and Tara Altebrando, "Elizabeth receives her freshman-year roommate assignment at the beginning of summer [and] she shoots off an email to coordinate the basics. She can't wait to escape her New Jersey beach town, and her mom, and start life over in California. The first note to Lauren in San Francisco comes as a surprise; she had requested a single. . . . Soon the girls are emailing back and forth, sharing secrets even though they've never met." (Publisher's note)

"Jersey girl Elizabeth (EB) and San Franciscan Lauren, soon to be college roommates, correspond throughout the summer; chapters with alternating perspectives unwrap each girl's backstory, personality, and coming-to-terms with changes looming on the horizon. The premise will have mass appeal with teens who fantasize about their post-high-school futures, and the authors succeed in presenting two distinct and relatable narrative voices." (Horn Book)

Story of a girl; a novel. Little, Brown 2006 192p $16.99

Grades: 10 11 12   Fic

1. California -- Fiction 2. Family life -- Fiction

ISBN 978-0-316-01453-3; 0-316-01453-2

LC 2005-28467

Finalist for the National Book Award 2007

In the three years since her father caught her in the back seat of a car with an older boy, sixteen-year-old Deanna's life at home and school has been a nightmare, but while dreaming of escaping with her brother and his family, she discovers the power of forgiveness.

"This highly recommended novel will find a niche with older, more mature readers because of frank references to sex and some x-rated language." Voice Youth Advocates

★ **Sweethearts**. Little, Brown and Co. 2008 217p $16.99

Grades: 8 9 10 11 12   Fic

1. Love stories 2. School stories 3. Utah -- Fiction 4. Weight loss -- Fiction

ISBN 978-0-316-01455-7; 0-316-01455-9

LC 2007-41099

After losing her soul mate, Cameron, when they were nine, Jennifer, now seventeen, transformed herself from the unpopular fat girl into the beautiful and popular Jenna, but Cameron's unexpected return dredges up memories that cause both social and emotional turmoil.

"Zarr's writing is remarkable. . . . She conveys great delicacy of feeling and shades of meaning, and the realistic, moving ending will inspire excellent discussion." Booklist

Zeises, Lara M.

The **sweet** life of Stella Madison; [by] Lara Zeises. Delacorte Press 2009 230p $16.99; lib bdg $19.99

Grades: 9 10 11 12   Fic

1. Food -- Fiction 2. Journalism -- Fiction 3. Family life -- Fiction 4. Dating (Social customs) -- Fiction

ISBN 978-0-385-73146-1; 0-385-73146-9; 978-0-385-90178-9 lib bdg; 0-385-90178-X lib bdg

LC 2008-32024

Seventeen-year-old Stella struggles with the separation of her renowned chef parents, writing a food column for the local paper even though she is a junk food addict, and having a boyfriend but being attracted to another.

The author "has created a refreshing protagonist sure to captivate readers, who will enjoy following along as she learns about romance through food, and vice versa." SLJ

Zeitlin, Meredith

Freshman year & other unnatural disasters; Meredith Zeitlin. G.P. Putnam's Sons 2012 282 p. (hardcover) $16.99

Grades: 8 9 10 11 12   Fic

1. Humorous fiction 2. High school students -- Fiction 3. Schools -- Fiction 4. Friendship -- Fiction 5. High schools -- Fiction 6. New York (N.Y.) -- Fiction 7. Self-perception -- Fiction 8. Family life -- New York (State) -- New York -- Fiction

ISBN 0399254234; 9780399254239

LC 2011005690

This young adult novel, by Meredith Zeitlin, follows "Kelsey Finkelstein--fourteen and frustrated. Every time she tries to live up to her awesome potential, her plans are foiled. Kelsey wants to rebrand herself for high school to make the kind of mark she knows is her destiny. But just because Kelsey has a plan for greatness . . . it doesn't mean the rest of the world is in on it." (Publisher's note)

Zemser, Amy Bronwen

Dear Julia. Greenwillow Books 2008 327p $16.99; lib bdg $17.89

Grades: 7 8 9 10   Fic

1. Cooking -- Fiction 2. Contests -- Fiction 3. Feminism -- Fiction 4. Mother-daughter relationship

-- Fiction
ISBN 978-0-06-029458-8; 0-06-029458-2; 978-0-06-029459-5 lib bdg; 0-06-029459-0 lib bdg
LC 2008-3824

Shy sixteen-year-old Elaine has long dreamed of being the next Julia Child, to the dismay of her feminist mother, but when her first friend, the outrageous Lucida Sans, convinces Elaine to enter a cooking contest, anything could happen.

"Readers will laugh throughout, but Zemser never loses sight of Elaine's frailties and hopes." Publ Wkly

Zenter, Jeff

The **serpent** king; Jeff Zentner. Crown Books for Young Readers 2016 384 p. (hc) $17.99

Grades: 9 10 11 12   **Fic**
1. Bildungsromans 2. Teenagers -- Fiction 3. Friendship -- Fiction 4. Country life -- Fiction 5. Self-actualization (Psychology) -- Fiction
ISBN 9780553524024; 9780553524031
LC 2014044883

In this novel, by Jeff Zentner, "Dill has had to wrestle with vipers his whole life—at home, as the only son of a Pentecostal minister who urges him to handle poisonous rattlesnakes, and at school, where he faces down bullies who target him. . . . He and his fellow outcast friends must try to make it through their senior year of high school without letting the small-town culture destroy their creative spirits and sense of self." (Publisher's note)

"Characters, incidents, dialogue, the poverty of the rural South, enduring friendship, a desperate clinging to strange faiths, fear of the unknown, and an awareness of the courage it takes to survive, let alone thrive, are among this fine novel's strengths. Zentner writes with understanding and grace—a new voice to savor." Kirkus

Zettel, Sarah

Bad luck girl; Sarah Zettel. Random House Inc 2014 368 p. (The American fairy trilogy) (hardcover) $17.99

Grades: 7 8 9 10   **Fic**
1. Magic -- Fiction 2. Fairies -- Fiction 3. Chicago (Ill.) -- Fiction 4. Racially mixed people -- Fiction 5. Chicago (Ill.) -- History -- 20th century -- Fiction
ISBN 0375869409; 9780375869402; 9780375969409
LC 2013013855

In this book, by Sarah Zettel, "after rescuing her parents from the Seelie king at Hearst Castle, Callie is caught up in the war between the fairies of the Midnight Throne and the Sunlit Kingdoms. By accident, she discovers that fairies aren't the only magical creatures in the world. There's also Halfers, misfits that are half fairy and half other - laced with strange magic and big-city attitude. As the war heats up, Callie's world falls apart." (Publisher's note)

"Half-fairy, half-human Callie (Golden Girl; Dust Girl) has reunited with her family, thus starting a war between the two fairy kingdoms. Fleeing Los Angeles for Chicago, Callie realizes that to end the war she must stand and fight. Zettel brings the street life, locales, and culture of jazz-age Chicago into the imagery of her fantasy, packing the story with incident and adventure." Horn Book

Dust girl; Sarah Zettel. Random House 2012 292 p. (trade: alk. paper) $17.99

Grades: 6 7 8 9   **Fic**
1. Fairies -- Fiction 2. Voyages and travels -- Fiction 3. Father-daughter relationship -- Fiction 4. Magic -- Fiction
ISBN 9780375869389; 9780375873812; 9780375969386; 9780375983184
LC 2011043310

In this book, "a mixed-race girl in Dust Bowl Kansas discovers her long-lost father isn't just a black man: He's a fairy. . . . [A] strange man . . . tells Callie secrets of her never-met father. Soon Callie's walking the dusty roads with Jack, a ragged white kid. . . . Callie and Jack dodge fairy politics and dangers, from grasshopper people to enchanted food to magic movie theaters--but the conventional dangers are no less threatening." (Kirkus Reviews)

Golden girl; by Sarah Zettel. 1st ed. Random House Inc. 2013 308 p. (The American fairy trilogy) (hardcover) $17.99; (library) $20.99

Grades: 7 8 9 10   **Fic**
1. Fairies 2. Fantasy fiction 3. Voyages and travels 4. Magic -- Fiction
ISBN 0375869395; 9780375869396; 9780375969393
LC 2013006238

In this book, it's 1935, and Callie LeRoux has journeyed to Hollywood from Slow Run, Kan., in search of her white human mother and black fairy father. A fairy kidnap attempt is foiled by none other than the famous Renaissance man Paul Robeson, a human who seems impervious to fairy magic. . . . Callie just wants to find her parents and get the heck out of Dodge, but with a prophecy hanging over her head, it won't be easy." (Kirkus Reviews)

Palace of Spies; being a true, accurate, and complete account of the scandalous and wholly remarkable adventures of Margaret Preston Fitzroy... by Sarah Zettel. Harcourt, Houghton Mifflin Harcourt 2013 368 p. (Palace of spies) $16.99

Grades: 8 9 10   **Fic**
1. Spies -- Fiction 2. London (England) -- Fiction 3. Great Britain -- History -- 1714-1837 -- Fiction 4. Love -- Fiction 5. Orphans -- Fiction 6. Courts and courtiers -- Fiction 7. London (England) -- History -- 18th century -- Fiction 8. Great Britain -- History -- George I, 1714-1727 -- Fiction
ISBN 0544074114; 9780544074118
LC 2012046366

In author Sarah Zettel's book, "sixteen-year-old Peggy is a well-bred orphan who is coerced into posing as a lady in waiting at the palace of King George I. Life is grand, until Peggy starts to suspect that the girl she's impersonating might have been murdered. Unless Peggy can discover the truth, she might be doomed to the same terrible fate. But in a court of shadows and intrigue, anyone could be a spy--perhaps even the handsome young artist with whom Peggy is falling in love." (Publisher's note)

"In eighteenth-century London, destitute orphan Peggy Fitzroy agrees to impersonate the recently deceased spy Lady Francesca as maid of honor to Princess Caroline. With a war of succession, jilted love, and religious turmoil in the mix, Peggy must navigate intrigue and shady liaisons to un-cover the truth behind her predecessor's death. The feisty narrator and lush period details will garner fans for this new series." (Horn Book)

Other titles in this series are:
Dangerous Deceptions (2014)
The Assasin's Masque (2016)

Zevin, Gabrielle

All these things I've done. Farrar Straus Giroux 2011 354p $16.99

Grades: 8 9 10 11 12   **Fic**
1. Science fiction 2. Celebrities -- Fiction 3. Family life -- Fiction 4. New York (N.Y.) -- Fiction 5. Organized crime -- Fiction
ISBN 978-0-374-30210-8

LC 2010035873

In a future where chocolate and caffeine are contraband, teenage cellphone use is illegal, and water and paper are carefully rationed, sixteen-year-old Anya Balanchine finds herself thrust unwillingly into the spotlight as heir apparent to an important New York City crime family.

"Offering the excitement of a crime drama and the al-lure of forbidden romance, this introduction to a reluctant Godfather-in-the making will pique the interest of dystopia-hungry readers." Publ Wkly

Because it is my blood; Gabrielle Zevin. Farrar Straus Giroux 2012 350 p. $17.99

Grades: 7 8 9 10   **Fic**
1. Crime -- Fiction 2. Criminals -- Fiction 3. High school students -- Fiction 4. Science fiction 5. Mexico -- Fiction 6. Violence -- Fiction 7. Chocolate -- Fiction 8. Celebrities -- Fiction 9. New York (N.Y.) -- Fiction 10. Organized crime -- Fiction 11. Oaxaca de Juárez (Mexico) -- Fiction 12. Family life -- New York (State) -- New York -- Fiction
ISBN 0374380740; 9780374380748

LC 2011036991

In Gabrielle Zeven's book, "Anya Balanchine is deter-mined to follow the straight and narrow . . . since her re-lease from Liberty Children's Facility . . . Unfortunately, her criminal record is making it hard for her to do that. No high school wants her with a gun possession charge . . . But when old friends return demanding that certain debts be paid, Anya is thrown right back into the criminal world that she had been determined to escape." (Macmillan)

★ **Memoirs** of a teenage amnesiac. Farrar, Straus and Giroux 2007 271p $17; pa $8.99; eb-oook $40.00

Grades: 7 8 9 10   **Fic**
1. School stories 2. Amnesia -- Fiction 3. Friendship -- Fiction
ISBN 978-0-374-34946-2; 0-374-34946-0; 978-0-312-56128-4 pa; 0-312-56128-8 pa; 9781429956291

LC 2006-35287

After a nasty fall, Naomi realizes that she has no mem-ory of the last four years and finds herself reassessing every aspect of her life.

This is a "sensitive, joyful novel. . . . Pulled by the the heart-bruising love story, readers will pause to contemplate irresistible questions." Booklist

Zhang, Amy

Falling into place; by Amy Zhang. Greenwillow Books 2014 304 p. (hardback) $17.99

Grades: 9 10 11 12   **Fic**
1. Suicide -- Fiction 2. Teenagers -- Suicide 3. Youths' writings 4. Schools -- Fiction 5. High schools -- Fiction 6. Conduct of life -- Fiction 7. Emotional problems -- Fiction 8. Interpersonal relations -- Fiction
ISBN 0062295047; 9780062295040

LC 2014018247

In this young adult novel by Amy Zhang, "one cold fall day, high school junior Liz Emerson steers her car into a tree. . . . [This] nonlinear novel pieces together the short and devastating life of Meridian High's most popular junior girl. Mass, acceleration, momentum, force--Liz didn't under-stand it in physics, and even as her Mercedes hurtles toward the tree, she doesn't understand it now." (Publisher's note)

"Although the subject matter is heavy and there are a few easily brushed-off awkward moments, the breezy yet power-ful and exceptionally perceptive writing style, multifaceted characters, surprisingly hopeful ending, and pertinent con-temporary themes frame an engrossing, thought-provoking story that will be snapped up by readers." SLJ

This Is Where the World Ends; by Amy Zhang. Harpercollins Childrens Books 2016 304 p. il-lustrations $17.99

Grades: 9 10 11 12   **Fic**
1. Secrets -- Fiction 2. Friendship -- Fiction 3. Missing persons -- Fiction
ISBN 0062383043; 9780062383044

This book, by Amy Zhang, is "about best friends on a collision course with the real world. . . . Janie and Micah, Micah and Janie. That's how it's been ever since elemen-tary school, when Janie Vivien moved next door. Janie says Micah is everything she is not. . . . It's the perfect friend-ship—as long as no one finds out about it. But then Janie goes missing and everything Micah thought he knew about his best friend is colored with doubt." (Publisher's note)

"Edgy, taut, and compelling, this is a story of unrequited love, betrayal, and apocalyptic changes using lyrical lan-guage wrought with symbolism. Janie and Micah have been next-door neighbors and nighttime ninjas since childhood. Micah has long loved Janie from (not-so) afar while Janie remains elusive. Despite her steely exterior and manipula-tive ways, Janie loves Micah as much as he loves her, but she toys with him nonetheless. Similarities to John Green's Paper Towns (Dutton, 2008) end here. Micah wakes up at the hospital after a night of binge drinking; he vaguely re-calls a fire, but details are missing. Where is Janie? Why are the police questioning him? Events unfold through the alter-nating voices of Janie and Micah in nonlinear fashion until Janie's past and Micah's present collide. . . . The breadth of topics covered, figurative language employed, page-turning suspense, and spot-on delivery render this novel a must-have for high school libraries." SLJ

Zhang, Kat, 1991-

Once we were; the second book in the Hybrid chronicles. Kat Zhang. HarperTeen 2014 340 p. $17.99

Grades: 8 9 10 11 12 **Fic**
1. Science fiction 2. Sisters -- Fiction 3. Identity (Psychology) -- Fiction 4. Resistance to government -- Fiction 5. Identity -- Fiction 6. Government, Resistance to -- Fiction
ISBN 0062114905; 9780062114907; 9780062114914
LC 2013032811

In this sequel to "What's Left of Me," by Kat Zhang, "Eva and Addie struggle to share their body as they clash over romance and join the fight for hybrid freedom. . . . Addie and Eva escaped imprisonment at a horrific psychiatric hospital. Now they should be safe, living among an underground hybrid movement. But safety is starting to feel constricting. Faced with the possibility of being in hiding forever, the girls are eager to help bring about change—now." (Publisher's note)

"Because sisters Addie and Eva grew up hiding their hybrid nature, they're now learning-along with readers-some of the nuances of what it means for two souls to share one body...hang has a unique challenge: she must give each character two distinct personalities, which she skillfully manages. While this book lacks some of the freshness of What's Left of Me (HarperCollins, 2012), simply by virtue of being a sequel, the lovely, atmospheric storytelling is still very much present. Zhang has envisioned a complex, unique world and deftly brings it to life." (School Library Journal)

What's left of me. Harper 2012 343 p. $17.99
Grades: 8 9 10 11 12 **Fic**
1. Twins 2. Dystopian juvenile fiction 3. Science fiction
ISBN 0062114875; 9780062114877
LC 2012289047

This novel, by Kat Zhang, is the first book of the young adult science fiction "Hybrid Chronicles." "Eva and Addie started out the same way as everyone else--two souls woven together in one body, taking turns controlling their movements. . . . Finally Addie was pronounced healthy and Eva was declared gone. Except, she wasn't. . . . For the past three years, Eva has clung to the remnants of her life, . . . for a chance to smile, to twirl, to speak, Eva will do anything." (Publisher's note)

Zink, Michelle

Guardian of the Gate. Little, Brown 2010 340p $17.99
Grades: 7 8 9 10 **Fic**
1. Magic -- Fiction 2. Twins -- Fiction 3. Sisters -- Fiction 4. Supernatural -- Fiction 5. Good and evil -- Fiction
ISBN 978-0-316-03447-0; 0-316-03447-9
Sequel to: Prophecy of the sisters (2009)

In 1891 London, sixteen-year-old orphan Lia Milthorpe continues her quest to end an ancient prophecy requiring her to search for missing pages and human "keys" and develop her powers for an inevitable final confrontation with her twin sister Alice.

"An intense and captivating story that gives a whole new meaning to sibling rivalry." Voice Youth Advocates

★ **Prophecy** of the sisters. Little, Brown 2009 343p $17.99
Grades: 7 8 9 10 **Fic**
1. Twins -- Fiction 2. Sisters -- Fiction 3. Supernatural -- Fiction 4. Good and evil -- Fiction
ISBN 978-0-316-02742-7; 0-316-02742-1
LC 2008-45290

In late nineteenth-century New York state, wealthy sixteen-year-old twin sisters Lia and Alice Milthorpe find that they are on opposite sides of an ancient prophecy that has destroyed their parents and seeks to do even more harm.

"This arresting story takes readers to other planes of existence." Booklist
Followed by: Guardian of the gate (2010)

Zinn, Bridget

Poison; by Bridget Zinn. 1st ed. Disney/Hyperion Books 2013 276 p. (hardcover) $16.99
Grades: 7 8 9 10 11 12 **Fic**
1. Occult fiction 2. Fantasy fiction 3. Fantasy 4. Magic -- Fiction 5. Heroes -- Fiction 6. Princesses -- Fiction 7. Impersonation -- Fiction 8. Fugitives from justice -- Fiction
ISBN 1423139933; 9781423139935
LC 2012008693

In this novel, sixteen-year-old "Kyra is on the run. She may be one of the Kingdom of Mohr's most highly skilled potions masters, but she has also just tried—and failed—to poison Princess Ariana. And Kyra is determined to finish her mission even if it means killing her best friend. . . . In order to save her kingdom from a nefarious plot, Kyra will have to come to terms with all the gifts she possesses." (School Library Journal)

Zuckerman, Linda

A **taste** for rabbit. Arthur A. Levine Books 2007 310p $16.99
Grades: 7 8 9 10 **Fic**
1. Foxes -- Fiction 2. Animals -- Fiction 3. Rabbits -- Fiction 4. Resistance to government -- Fiction
ISBN 0-439-86977-3; 978-0-439-86977-5
LC 2007-7787

Quentin, a rabbit who lives in a walled compound run by a militaristic government, must join forces with Harry, a fox, to stop the sinister disappearances of outspoken and rebellious rabbit citizens.

"The blend of adventure, mystery and morality in this heroic tale of honor and friendship will appeal to middle-school fantasy fans." Publ Wkly

Zusak, Markus, 1975-

★ The **book** thief. Knopf 2006 552p il $16.95; lib bdg $18.99
Grades: 8 9 10 11 12 **Fic**
1. Death -- Fiction 2. Jews -- Germany -- Fiction 3. Books and reading -- Fiction 4. Holocaust, 1933-1945 -- Fiction 5. World War, 1939-1945 -- Fiction
ISBN 0-375-83100-2; 0-375-93100-7 lib bdg
LC 2005-08942

Michael L. Printz Award honor book, 2007

Trying to make sense of the horrors of World War II, Death relates the story of Liesel—a young German girl whose book-stealing and storytelling talents help sustain her family and the Jewish man they are hiding, as well as their neighbors.

"This hefty volume is an achievement—a challenging book in both length and subject, and best suited to sophisticated older readers." Publ Wkly

★ **I** am the messenger. Knopf 2005 357p hardcover o.p. pa $8.95

Grades: 9 10 11 12   **Fic**

1. Mystery fiction

ISBN 0-375-83099-5; 0-375-83667-5 pa

LC 2003-27388

Australian Children's Book Award for Older Readers

Michael L. Printz Award honor book, 2006

After capturing a bank robber, nineteen-year-old cab driver Ed Kennedy begins receiving mysterious messages that direct him to addresses where people need help, and he begins getting over his lifelong feeling of worthlessness. "Grades nine to twelve." (Bull Cent Child Books)

"Zusak's characters, styling, and conversations are believably unpretentious, well conceived, and appropriately raw. Together, these key elements fuse into an enigmatically dark, almost film-noir atmosphere where unknowingly lost Ed Kennedy stumbles onto a mystery—or series of mysteries—that could very well make or break his life." SLJ

S C STORY COLLECTIONS

21 proms; edited by David Levithan and Daniel Ehrenhaft. Scholastic 2007 289p pa $8.99

Grades: 9 10 11 12   **S C**

1. Short stories 2. School stories

ISBN 0-439-89029-2; 978-0-439-89029-8

LC 2007-297979

Short stories about going to the prom, when nothing ever goes as planned.

"The stories are witty, edgy, and unpredictable. 21 Proms is a definite must for all libraries and has something for every reader." Kliatt

Akpan, Uwem

Say you're one of them; [by] Uwem Akpan. Little, Brown and Company 2008 358p map hardcover o.p. pa $14.99

Grades: 11 12 Adult   **S C**

1. Short stories 2. Children -- Africa -- Fiction 3. Short stories -- By individual authors

ISBN 0-316-08637-1 pa; 0-316-11378-6; 978-0-316-08637-0 pa; 978-0-316-11378-6

LC 2008-11340

This is the author's first collection of short stories.

"Akpan's prose is beautiful and his stories are insightful and revealing, made even more harrowing because all the horror—and there is much—is seen through the eyes of children." Publ Wkly

Alfred Hitchcock's mystery magazine presents fifty years of crime and suspense; edited by Linda Landrigan. Pegasus 2006 560p pa $16.95

Grades: 11 12 Adult   **S C**

1. Short stories 2. Mystery fiction

ISBN 1-933648-03-1

"To commemorate its 50th anniversary, Alfred Hitchcock's Mystery Magazine staff-with input from its readers-selected 34 stories and arranged them chronologically here, starting with Jim Thompson's 'The Frightening Frammis' from February 1957 and ending with 'Voodoo' by Rhys Bowen from December 2004. . . . These are uniformly satisfying stories that have stood the test of time." Libr J

Almond, David, 1951-

Half a creature from the sea; A Life in Stories. David Almond; illustrated by Eleanor Taylor. Candlewick Press 2015 222 p. illustrations $16.99

Grades: 7 8 9 10   **SC**

1. Short stories -- Collections 2. England

ISBN 0763678775; 9780763678777

LC 2015931431

In this book, author David Almond "presents a beautiful collection of short fiction, interwoven with pieces that illuminate the inspiration behind the stories. May Malone is said to have a monster in her house, but what Norman finds there may just be the angel he needs. Joe Quinn's house is noisy with poltergeists, or could it be Davie's raging causing the disturbance? Fragile Annie learns the truth about herself in a photograph taken by a traveling man near the sea." (Publisher's note)

"Taylor's illustrations help add depth, as do the interstitial author's notes offering glimpses into each story's autobiographical roots and other inspirations. Likely to appeal to aspiring writers and fans of The Tightrope Walkers." Horn Book

Amnesty International

Free?: stories about human rights; [edited by] Amnesty International. Candlewick Press 2010 202p il $17.99; pa $8.99

Grades: 7 8 9 10   **S C**

1. Short stories 2. Freedom -- Fiction 3. Human rights -- Fiction

ISBN 978-0-7636-4703-2; 0-7636-4703-9; 978-0-7636-4926-5 pa; 0-7636-4926-0 pa

LC 2009-14720

An anthology of fourteen stories by young adult authors from around the world, on such themes as asylum, law, education, and faith, compiled in honor of the sixtieth anniversary of the Universal Declaration of Human Rights.

"Margaret Mahy writes about class with wit and intensity, as does Jamila Gavin, who sets the class war in India, where a young girl's family throws her out for resisting an arranged marriage. . . . David Almond explores school power plays in a story about a boy who says no to a popular bully. Hurricane Katrina is Rita Williams-Garcia's setting. Two contemporary Palestinian stories compare the current occupation with Native American experiences of oppression. . . . Sure to spark discussion and perhaps participation in Amnesty International." Booklist

Asimov, Isaac

★ **I,** robot; Bantam hardcover ed.; Bantam Books 2004 224p (Robot series) $24; pa $7.99

Grades: 7 8 9 10 11 12 Adult   S C

1. Short stories 2. Science fiction 3. Robots -- Fiction
ISBN 0-553-80370-0; 0-553-29438-5 pa

LC 2003-69139

First published 1950 by Gnome Press

"These loosely connected stories cover the career of Dr. Susan Calvin and United States Robots, the industry that she heads, from the time of the public's early distrust of these robots to its later dependency on them. This collection is an important introduction to a theme often found in science fiction: the encroachment of technology on our lives." Shapiro. Fic for Youth. 3d edition

The **beastly** bride; tales of the animal people. edited by Ellen Datlow & Terri Windling; introduction by Terri Windling; selected decorations by Charles Vess. Viking 2010 500p $19.99

Grades: 8 9 10 11 12   S C

1. Short stories 2. Supernatural -- Fiction
ISBN 978-0-670-01145-2; 0-670-01145-2

LC 2009-14317

A collection of stories and poems relating to animal transfiguration legends from around the world, retold and reimagined by various authors. Includes brief biographies, authors' notes, and suggestions for further reading

"The majority of these beastly tales make for fun, thoughtful, occasionally gripping, reading." Voice Youth Advocates

The **Best** American mystery stories of the century; Tony Hillerman, editor; Otto Penzler, series editor; with an introduction by Tony Hillerman. Houghton Mifflin 2000 813p hardcover o.p. pa $17.95

Grades: 11 12 Adult   S C

1. Short stories 2. Mystery fiction
ISBN 0-618-01267-2; 0-618-01271-0 pa

"This anthology is a cornerstone volume for any mystery library." Publ Wkly

Black, Holly, 1971-

The **poison** eaters and other stories. Big Mouth House 2010 212p $17.99

Grades: 9 10 11 12   S C

1. Short stories 2. Fantasy fiction
ISBN 978-1-931520-63-8; 1-931520-63-1

LC 2009051635

This is a collection of short stories by the author of Valiant (2005) and Ironside (2007). "Grades nine to twelve." (Bull Cent Child Books)

"For those with a penchant for dark, edgy, fantasy fiction, Holly Black . . . offers readers a collection of twelve stories. Ten tales have appeared in anthologies; two appear in print here for the first time. . . . Deftly blending both believable characters and realistic settings, Black serves up heady concoctions for those who like their fairy tales on the chilly side. The graphic nature of some of this collection's

stories make it best suited for fantasy fans in senior high school." Voice Youth Advocates

Block, Francesca Lia

The **rose** and the beast; fairy tales retold. HarperCollins Pubs. 2000 229p hardcover o.p. pa $6.99

Grades: 7 8 9 10   S C

1. Fairy tales 2. Short stories
ISBN 0-06-028129-4; 0-06-440745-4 pa

LC 00-22444

Nine classic fairy tales set in modern, magical landscapes and retold with a twist.

The author's "beautiful words turn modern-day Los Angeles into a fantastical world of fairies, angels, and charms. The context is very modern, with issues of drug addiction, rape, and suicide smoothly woven into the stories, which are infused with a palpable if not explicit eroticism." Booklist

Bradbury, Ray

The **illustrated** man. Avon Books 1997 275p $15.95

Grades: 9 10 11 12 Adult   S C

1. Short stories 2. Science fiction
ISBN 0-380-97384-7

LC 97-93228

First published 1951 by Doubleday; short stories originally published between 1948 and 1951

In this work "the stories are given a linking framework; they are all seen as magical tattoos becoming living stories, springing from the body of the protagonist." Sci Fic Ency

★ The **Martian** chronicles. Avon Books 1997 268p $15.95

Grades: 7 8 9 10   S C

1. Short stories 2. Science fiction
ISBN 0-380-97383-9

LC 96-95071

First published 1950 by Doubleday

This book's "closely interwoven short stories, linked by recurrent images and themes, tell of the repeated attempts by humans to colonize Mars, of the way they bring their old prejudices with them, and of the repeated, ambiguous meetings with the shape-changing Martians." Sci Fic Ency

Campoy, F. Isabel, 1946-

Yes! we are Latinos; by Alma Flor Ada and F. Isabel Campoy; illustrated by David Diaz. Charlesbridge 2013 96 p. ill. (reinforced) $18.95

Grades: 7 8 9 10   S C

1. Hispanic Americans -- Poetry 2. American poetry -- Latino authors 3. Short stories 4. Immigrants -- Fiction 5. Immigrants -- United States 6. Latin Americans -- United States 7. Emigration and immigration -- Fiction 8. Latin Americans -- Cultural assimilation 9. Latin Americans -- United States -- Fiction
ISBN 158089383X; 9781580893831

LC 2012027214

In this book, the authors "shape fictional portraits of 13 young people living in the U.S., who have diverse experiences and backgrounds but share a Latino heritage. The first-person narrative poems range from reflective to free-spirited, methodical to free-association. . . . Informative nonfictional interludes . . . address relevant subjects, including immigration, the challenges migrant workers face, and Cuba-U.S. history." (Publishers Weekly)

Includes bibliographical references and index

Card, Orson Scott

First meetings in the Enderverse. Tor Teen 2003 208p il $17.95; pa $6.99

Grades: 9 10 11 12   **S C**

1. Short stories 2. Science fiction

ISBN 0-7653-0873-8; 0-7653-4798-9 pa

LC 2003-55951

"Andrew 'Ender' Wiggins, a brilliant leader and tactician and destined to save Earth by destroying an entire alien civilization at the age of 12, was first introduced in Card's 'Ender's Game'. . . . That novella, plus three other stories (including one never before published) make up this . . . collection of tales, all dealing with first meetings that played significant roles in the life of Ender Wiggins. . . . All four stories use the future setting as a framework to explore various issues of religion, government control, population limits, education, and moral responsibility. Character, setting, plot—Card does them all right, and makes it look effortless. . . . For newcomers to Ender's universe and longtime fans, this book will hit the spot and whet the appetite for more." SLJ

Chambers, Aidan

The **kissing** game; short stories. Amulet Books 2011 216p $16.95

Grades: 9 10 11 12   **S C**

1. Short stories

ISBN 0-8109-9716-9; 978-0-8109-9716-5

LC 2010-32947

This is a collection of sixteen short stories by the author of Postcards from No Man's Land (1999) and This is All (2005). "Grades nine to twelve." (Bull Cent Child Books)

"This title offers sixteen wonderful short stories by an award-winning author. Only three tales are truly short stories—most are 'flash fiction.' These quick reads are meant to grab your attention quickly, tell your tale, and finish in just minutes. They are neat and seemingly simple stories, but they are thick with implication and have many possible meanings. . . . There is something for everyone—love, murder, fairy tales, adventure, science fiction, politics and more." Voice Youth Advocates

Chekhov, Anton Pavlovich

The **Russian** master and other stories; [by] Anton Chekhov; translated with an introduction and notes by Ronald Hingley. Oxford University Press 2008 233p (Oxford world's classics) pa $8.95

Grades: 9 10 11 12 Adult   **S C**

1. Short stories 2. Russia -- Fiction

ISBN 978-0-19-955487-4

LC 2009464906

A collection of eleven short stories written between 1892 and 1899.

Chopin, Kate

The **awakening** and selected stories; edited with an introduction by Sandra M. Gilbert. Penguin Books 2003 286p (Penguin classics) pa $8

Grades: 9 10 11 12   **S C**

1. Short stories

ISBN 0-14-243732-8

LC 2003-265744

In addition to the novel The awakening (1899) this volume also includes selected stories from Bayou folk (1894) and A night in Acadie (1897).

Cisneros, Sandra

★ **Woman** Hollering Creek and other stories. Random House 1991 165p hardcover o.p. pa $11.95

Grades: 11 12 Adult   **S C**

1. Short stories 2. Mexican Americans -- Fiction

ISBN 0-679-73856-8

LC 90-52930

"Unforgettable characters march through a satisfying collection of tales about Mexican-Americans who know the score and cling to the anchor of their culture." N Y Times Book Rev

Clarke, Arthur C.

★ The **collected** stories of Arthur C. Clarke. TOR Bks. 2001 966p hardcover o.p. pa $19.95

Grades: 11 12 Adult   **S C**

1. Short stories 2. Science fiction

ISBN 0-312-87821-4; 0-312-87860-5 pa

First published 2000 in the United Kingdom

"Although most of these stories date from between 1946 and 1970, seven earlier tales, rescued from what would now be called fanzines, extend coverage back to 1937, and a few snippets stretch it toward the present. At least two dozen stories bear titles that are household words among sf readers. . . . The stories demonstrate Clarke's dazzling and unique combination of command of the language, scientific and other kinds of erudition, and inimitable wit." Booklist

Cornered; 14 stories of bullying and defiance. [edited by] Rhoda Belleza. Running Press Teens 2012 383 p. $9.95

Grades: 7 8 9 10 11 12   **S C**

1. Short stories 2. School stories 3. Bullies -- Fiction

ISBN 9780762444281

LC 2011943133

This book is a "bully-themed anthology" of stories that focus "not only on teens who are targets of bullying, but also those who perpetrate it—and many . . . do both. Bullying [in the stories] takes many forms, including a teacher ridiculing students, a viral racist email and hazing on a soccer team. The contributors largely delve into bullies' behavior without resting on cliché . . . Most contributors also . . . observe that family dynamics can have as much impact as those at school." (Kirkus)

Crutcher, Chris

Angry management; three novellas. Greenwillow Books 2009 246p $16.99; lib bdg $17.89; pa $8.99

Grades: 9 10 11 12 S C
1. Short stories
ISBN 978-0-06-050247-8; 0-06-050247-9; 978-0-06-
050246-1 lib bdg; 0-06-050246-0 lib bdg; 978-0-06-
050248-5 pa; 0-06-050248-7 pa
LC 2008-52829
This is "a collection of three original and thematically
connected novellas for teens which introduces several new
characters and revisits some . . . Crutcher heroes." (Publisher's note) "Grades seven to ten." (Bull Cent Child Books)

"The stories are well-written, action packed, engrossing
and at times humorous. . . . A good introduction to Crutcher,
his latest book will certainly please current fans as well."
Voice Youth Advocates

Dahl, Roald
Skin and other stories. Viking 2000 212p
$15.99; pa $8.99
Grades: 7 8 9 10 S C
1. Short stories
ISBN 0-670-89184-3; 0-14-131034-0 pa
LC 99-58600
A collection of 13 of the author's short stories written for
adults. "Full of irony and unexpected twists, they smack of
the master's touch—every word carefully chosen, characters fully fleshed out in only a few pages, the sense of place
immediate." Booklist

Danticat, Edwidge
★ **Krik?** Krak! Vintage Books 1996 224p
(Vintage contemporaries) pa $12.95
Grades: 11 12 Adult S C
1. Short stories 2. Haiti -- Fiction 3. Haitian Americans
-- Fiction
ISBN 0-679-76657-X
LC 95-43449
First published 1995 by Soho Press
The author "touches upon life both in Haiti and in New
York's Haitian community, though we spend most of our
time in Port-au-Prince and the country town of Ville Rose.
The best of these stories humanize, particularize, give poi-
gnancy to the lives of people we may have come to think of
as faceless emblems of misery, poverty and brutality." N Y
Times Book Rev

Defy the dark; edited by Saundra Mitchell. Harper-
Teen 2013 496 p. (pbk bdgs) $9.99
Grades: 9 10 11 12 S C
1. Short stories 2. Shades and shadows 3. Light --
Fiction 4. Shadows -- Fiction
ISBN 006212353X; 9780062123534; 9780062123541
LC 2012029993
This short story collection, edited by Saundra Mitchell,
includes contributions from "sixteen established YA authors.
. . . Each story takes place either at night or in the dark. . . . In
Carrie Ryan's 'Almost Normal,' a group of teens witnesses
a zombie invasion from atop a roller coaster, and in Rachel
Hawkins's urban-legend-inspired 'Eyes in the Dark,' a teen
couple on a romantic interlude in the woods are hunted by
monsters." (School Library Journal)

"In this collection of seventeen original stories, wildly
varied aspects and interpretations of "dark" are explored.

The common thread is rather effective, even as the mix of
stories address everything from monsters to nightmares to
romance. Most thought-provoking here are the multiple un-
derstandings of the distinct quiet--and sometimes the horror-
-that can only be found in the dark." Horn Book

The **Del** Rey book of science fiction and fantasy; sixteen original works by speculative fiction's finest
voices. edited by Ellen Datlow. Del Rey Books
2008 400p pa $16
Grades: 11 12 Adult S C
1. Short stories 2. Fantasy fiction 3. Science fiction
ISBN 978-0-345-49632-4
LC 2008-4948
"This collection of cutting-edge writing has appeal to
older teens familiar with the demands of speculative fiction
at its best. The 16 pieces include tales of alien abduction
and war, murder, familial abuse, and alternate histories of
the world. . . . An anthology that's thought-provoking and
intellectually challenging." SLJ

Dozois, Gardner R.
Best of the best: 20 years of the Year's best sci-
ence fiction; [edited by] Gardner Dozois. St. Mar-
tin's Griffin 2005 672p hardcover o.p. pa $19.95
Grades: 9 10 11 12 S C
1. Short stories 2. Science fiction
ISBN 0-312-33655-1; 0-312-33656-X pa
LC 2004-51411
Dozois "collects 36 tales by some of the most notable au-
thors currently active in the genre, among them Gene Wolfe,
William Gibson, Connie Willis, Joe Haldeman and Tony
Daniel. Robert Silverberg provides a foreword." Publ Wkly

Enthralled; paranormal diversions. edited by Melissa Marr and Kelley Armstrong. HarperCollins
2011 452p $17.99; pa $9.99
Grades: 7 8 9 10 S C
1. Short stories 2. Supernatural -- Fiction 3. Voyages
and travels -- Fiction
ISBN 978-0-06-201579-2; 0-06-201579-6; 978-0-06-
201578-5 pa; 0-06-201578-8 pa
LC 2011019393
A collection of sixteen original short stories by writers
of paranormal tales, featuring journeys made by teens and
magical beings.

"These short stories are loosely connected by a very
openly interpreted journey motif. Psychics, genies, angels
and gargoyles join fairies and vampires to terrorize and romance their fellow characters. The diversity in authors allows for the sometimes-neglected horror implied in paranormal stories to be spotlighted. . . . This collection is ideal as a
sampler tray for paranormal readers looking to pick up new
authors to follow or to further explore the fictional worlds
they already know." Kirkus

Face relations; 11 stories about seeing beyond color. Simon & Schuster Books for Young Readers 2004 224p $17.95

Grades: 7 8 9 10   S C

1. Short stories 2. Race relations -- Fiction
ISBN 0-689-85637-7

"Contributed by familiar writers for young people, including Ellen Wittlinger, M. E. Kerr, Rita Williams-Garcia, Naomi Shihab Nye, and Jess Mowry, the stories ask challenging questions about what role race plays in family life, at school, in friendships, and in love. . . . This is a provocative collection." Booklist

Fear: 13 stories of suspense and horror; [selected by and with an] introduction by R.L. Stine. Dutton 2010 306p $16.99; pa $7.99

Grades: 7 8 9 10   S C

1. Short stories 2. Horror fiction
ISBN 978-0-525-42168-9; 0-525-42168-8; 978-0-14-241774-4 pa; 0-14-241774-2 pa

LC 2009-53284

"Thirteen highly suspenseful short stories. . . . [Stine] enlists some of the best in the business, such as Meg Cabot and F. Paul Wilson, Walter Sorrells and James Rollins, who offer plenty of heart-throbbing supernatural horror, crime suspense, shockers and sometimes a mixture of all three. . . . Fast-paced, shuddery-scary fun." Kirkus

Firebirds rising; an anthology of original science fiction and fantasy. edited by Sharyn November. Firebird 2006 530p hardcover o.p. pa $9.99

Grades: 7 8 9 10 11 12   S C

1. Short stories 2. Fantasy fiction 3. Science fiction
ISBN 0-14-240549-3; 978-0-14-240549-9; 0-14-240936-7 pa; 978-0-14-240936-7 pa

This is a collection of sixteen science fiction and fantasy stories.

"This anthology is a wonderful choice for any young adult collection." Voice Youth Advocates

Firebirds soaring; an anthology of original speculative fiction. [edited by Sharyn November; illustrated by Mike Dringenberg] Firebird 2009 574p il $19.99

Grades: 7 8 9 10 11 12   S C

1. Short stories 2. Fantasy fiction 3. Science fiction
ISBN 978-0-14-240552-9; 0-14-240552-3

LC 2008-29516

This anthology "contains 19 short stories by some of the top writers in this genre. . . . The selections vary in length, with some short stories, some novellas. Each work is introduced by an evocative illustration that beautifully sets the scene for the written work. The variety of styles and themes and a gathering together of so many talented writers in one work offer readers a banquet for the imagination. For fans of the genre, this is a must read." SLJ

First crossing; stories about teen immigrants. edited by Donald R. Gallo. Candlewick Press 2004 224p hardcover o.p. pa $8.99

Grades: 7 8 9 10   S C

1. Short stories 2. Immigrants -- Fiction
ISBN 0-7636-2249-4; 0-7636-3291-0 pa

LC 2003-65255

Ten short stories about teen immigrants by such authors as Pam Muñoz Ryan, Lensey Namioka, and David Lubar.

"Covering a wide range of cultural and economical backgrounds, these stories by 11 well-known authors touch on a variety of teen experiences, with enough attitude and heartfelt angst to speak to young adults anywhere." SLJ

Flake, Sharon G.

★ **Who** am I without him? short stories about girls and the boys in their lives. Jump at the Sun/Hyperion Books for Children 2004 168p $15.99; pa $7.99

Grades: 7 8 9 10   S C

1. Short stories 2. African Americans -- Fiction
ISBN 0-7868-0693-1; 1-4231-0383-1 pa

Ten short stories about African American teenage girls and their relationships with boys.

"Addressing issues and situations that many girls face in today's often complex society, this book is provocative and thought-provoking." SLJ

Gaiman, Neil

★ **Fragile** things; short fictions and wonders. William Morrow 2006 xxxi, 360p $26.95

Grades: 11 12 Adult   S C

1. Short stories 2. Horror fiction 3. Fantasy fiction
ISBN 978-0-06-051522-5; 0-06-051522-8

LC 2006-48135

"The stories are by turns horrifying and fanciful, often blending the two with a little sex, violence, and humor. . . . Gaiman skips along the edge of many adolescent fascinations—life, death, the living dead, and the occult—and teens with a taste for the weird will enjoy this book." SLJ

Geektastic; stories from the nerd herd. edited by Holly Black and Cecil Castellucci. Little Brown & Co. 2009 403p il $16.99

Grades: 7 8 9 10   S C

1. Short stories
ISBN 978-0-316-00809-9; 0-316-00809-5

LC 2009-455709

A collection of twenty-nine short stories about geeks.

"Although not all geekdoms are covered, topics include cosplay (dressing as characters), cons (conventions), SF television and movies, RPGs (roleplaying games), fantasy books, baton-twirling, astronomy, Rocky Horror, quiz bowl, and dinosaurs. Geek-themed comics by Hope Larson and Bryan Lee O'Malley separate the stories. . . . Although readers need not necessarily be geeks to appreciate this well-written collection, it will help. Buy for all the geeks in your library—including the librarian." Voice Youth Advocates

Green, John

Let it snow; three holiday romances. by John Green, Maureen Johnson, Lauren Myracle. Speak 2008 352p pa $9.99

Grades: 7 8 9 10 **S C**

1. Short stories 2. Christmas -- Fiction 3. Dating (Social customs) -- Fiction

ISBN 978-0-14-241214-5; 0-14-241214-7

LC 2008-25807

In three intertwining short stories, several high school couples experience the trials and tribulations along with the joys of romance during a Christmas Eve snowstorm in a small town.

"The premises for the stories are funny yet cringingly credible, the writing clever and sure-footed, and the outcomes are all lighthearted and cozily romantic." Bull Cent Child Books

Growing up Filipino II; more stories for young adults. collected and edited by Cecilia Manguerra Brainard. PALH 2010 257p $29.95; pa $21.95

Grades: 9 10 11 12 **S C**

1. Short stories 2. Philippines -- Fiction 3. Filipino Americans -- Fiction

ISBN 978-0-9719458-2-1; 978-0-9719458-3-8 pa

Sequel to Growing up Filipino (2003)

"This collection of 27 short stories, . . . reflects the impact of post-9/11 wartime sensibilities among Filipino writers living in the Philippines, the United States, and Canada. Although similar topics of family, memoir, and coming-of-age thread through both collections, the pieces are not grouped by theme, but nevertheless weave a constantly shifting tapestry of Filipino identity. The challenges and conflicts of unique ancestry and struggles for identity provide a rich background for modern urban realism. . . . There is plenty here to stimulate discussion and encourage an appreciation of Filipino writing and culture." SLJ

The **Hard** SF renaissance; edited by David G. Hartwell and Kathryn Cramer. TOR Bks. 2002 960p hardcover o.p. pa $23.95

Grades: 11 12 Adult **S C**

1. Short stories 2. Science fiction

ISBN 0-312-87635-1; 0-312-87636-X pa

"The 41 stories in this annotated anthology . . . [showcase] short fiction by veteran sf authors like Kim Stanley Robinson, Joe Haldeman, Bruce Sterling, Nancy Kress, Ben Bova and Arthur C. Clarke. . . . For libraries wanting a definitive collection of hard sf written since 1990, this is a priority purchase." Libr J

Hemingway, Ernest

★ The **complete** short stories of Ernest Hemingway; the Finca Vigia edition. Scribner 1987 650p hardcover o.p. pa $20

Grades: 11 12 Adult **S C**

1. Short stories

ISBN 0-684-84332-3

LC 87-12888

"To the 49 standard Short stories of Ernest Hemingway, this edition adds 14 from other books or magazines and seven never published before. . . . For all the repetition of previous collections and possible incompleteness despite the title, this volume is pure Hemingway in his most consistently satisfying format and, as such, belongs in most libraries." Booklist

Henry, O.

★ The **best** short stories of O. Henry; selected and with an introduction by Bennett A. Cerf, and Van H. Cartmell. Modern Lib. 1994 340p $22.95

Grades: 11 12 Adult **S C**

1. Short stories

ISBN 0-679-60122-8

First Modern Library edition published 1945

O. Henry "is best known for his observations on the diverse lives of everyday New Yorkers, 'the four million' neglected by other writers. He had a fine gift of humor and was adept at the ingenious depiction of ironic circumstances, in plots frequently dependent upon coincidence." Oxford Companion to Am Lit. 6th edition

Horowitz, Anthony

Bloody Horowitz. Philomel Books 2010 330p $12.99

Grades: 7 8 9 10 **S C**

1. Short stories 2. Horror fiction

ISBN 978-0-399-25451-2; 0-399-25451-X

LC 2009-44748

"These 12 stories are not for the squeamish as they include shudder-inducing scenes of burning flesh, dismembered bodies, electrocution, and death by squeezing in a massage chair. . . . Teens looking for gruesome tales won't be disappointed." SLJ

How beautiful the ordinary; twelve stories of identity. edited by Michael Cart. HarperTeen 2009 350p il $16.99

Grades: 9 10 11 12 **S C**

1. Short stories 2. Love -- Fiction 3. Sex role -- Fiction 4. Homosexuality -- Fiction

ISBN 978-0-06-115498-0; 0-06-115498-9

LC 2008-51769

Presents twelve stories by young adult authors, some presented in graphic or letter format, which explore themes of gender identity, love, and sexuality.

"This collection's refreshing perspective—that gay, lesbian, and transgendered lives simply are, as Cart states in the introduction, 'as wonderfully various, diverse, and gloriously complex as any other lives,' distinguishes it. Twelve acclaimed authors contribute stories ranging from sweet and nostalgic to lyrical and desperate, capturing the blissful/painful process of self-discovery. . . . This collection, with some detailed sexual descriptions, is sure to find its intended teen audience." SLJ

Hughes, Langston

★ **Short** stories of Langston Hughes; edited by Akiba Sullivan Harper; with an introduction by Arnold Rampersad. Hill & Wang 1996 299p hardcover o.p. pa $16

Grades: 11 12 Adult   **S C**
1. Short stories 2. African Americans -- Fiction
ISBN 0-8090-1603-6

LC 95-19554

"Dating from 1919 to 1963, these pieces vary in theme, covering life at sea, the trials and tribulations of a young pianist and her elderly white patron, a visiting writer's experience in Cuba, a young girl's winning an art scholarship but losing it when it's learned she is black, and an ambitious black preacher trying to gain fame by being nailed to a cross. If you crave good reading don't pass up this gem." Libr J

Hurston, Zora Neale

★ The **complete** stories; introduction by Henry Louis Gates, Jr. and Sieglinde Lemke. HarperCollins Pubs. 1995 xxiii, 305p hardcover o.p. pa $14.99
Grades: 11 12 Adult   **S C**
1. Short stories 2. African Americans -- Fiction
ISBN 0-06-016732-7; 0-06-135018-4 pa

LC 91-50438

This collection of Hurston's short fiction contains nineteen stories originally published between 1921 and 1951, arranged in the order in which they were published, and seven previously unpublished stories.

Includes bibliographical references

The **improbable** adventures of Sherlock Holmes; edited by John Joseph Adams; with assistance provided by David Barr Kirtley. Night Shade Books 2009 454p $15.95
Grades: 9 10 11 12 Adult   **S C**
1. Short stories 2. Mystery fiction 3. Great Britain -- Fiction 4. Holmes, Sherlock (Fictional character)
ISBN 978-1-59780-160-7

The editor's "goal was to highlight the best Sherlock Holmes stories of the last 30 years, emphasizing those that feature the fantastic. . . . This is a substantial collection that will entertain teen fans for hours, and may well seduce them to seek out the original." SLJ

Jackson, Shirley

★ The **lottery**; or, The adventures of James Harris. Farrar, Straus & Giroux 1949 306p hardcover o.p. pa $14
Grades: 11 12 Adult   **S C**
1. Short stories
ISBN 0-374-52953-1

The stories "in this collection seem to fall into three groups. There are the slight sketches, like genre paintings, dealing with episodes which are trivial in terms of plot but which by means of [the author's] precise, sensitive, and sharply focused style become luminous with meaning. . . . The second group comprises her social-problem sketches. . . . Her final group deals with fantasy, ranging from humorous whimsy to horrifying shock." Saturday Rev Lit

Kafka, Franz, 1883-1924

★ The **metamorphosis** and other stories; translated by Joachim Neugroschel. Scribner 1993 xxiii, 227p hardcover o.p. pa $13

Grades: 11 12 Adult   **S C**
1. Short stories
ISBN 0-684-19426-0; 0-684-80070-5 pa

LC 92-43912

This is a collection of thirty stories, some of which are quite short. The stories are arranged in order of their original publication dates.

King, Stephen, 1947-

Everything's eventual: 14 dark tales. Scribner 2002 459p $28
Grades: 11 12 Adult   **S C**
1. Short stories 2. Horror fiction
ISBN 0-7432-3515-0

LC 2002-17738

"Fourteen stories, most of them gems, featuring an array of literary approaches, plus an opinionated intro from King about the '(Almost) Lost Art' of the short story." Publ Wkly

Four past midnight. Viking 1990 763p hardcover o.p. pa $7.99
Grades: 11 12 Adult   **S C**
1. Short stories 2. Horror fiction
ISBN 0-451-17038-5 pa

LC 90-50046

This volume contains four novellas: The Langoliers; Secret window, secret garden; The library policeman; The sun dog.

This book "is hard to put down, truly chilling, and sure to be enjoyed by YA horror afficionados everywhere." SLJ

Night shift. Doubleday 1978 xxii, 336p hardcover o.p. pa $7.99
Grades: 11 12 Adult   **S C**
1. Short stories 2. Horror fiction
ISBN 0-385-12991-2; 0-307-74364-0 pa

LC 77-75146

The stories "all begin in our normal world, where everything is safe and warm. But in almost every instance, something slips, and we find ourselves in the nightmare world of the not-quite real. . . . Such stories require a willing suspension of disbelief, of course, but they also require an author who is an expert manipulator. . . . King is an expert." Best Sellers

★ **Skeleton** crew. Putnam 1985 512p hardcover o.p. pa $7.99
Grades: 11 12 Adult   **S C**
1. Short stories 2. Horror fiction
ISBN 0-451-16861-5 pa

LC 84-15947

This "collection of King's shorter work is a hefty sampler from all stages of his career, and demonstrates the range of his abilities. . . . There are several stories here that must rank among King's best." Publ Wkly

Kiss me deadly; 13 tales of paranormal love. edited by Trisha Telep. RP Teens 2010 430p pa $9.95
Grades: 7 8 9 10   **S C**
1. Love stories 2. Short stories 3. Supernatural --

Fiction
ISBN 978-0-7624-3949-2; 0-7624-3949-1
LC 2010-926067

A collection of short stories combining dark seduction and modern romance presents a variety of tales featuring the romantic lives of humans and werewolves, ghosts, fallen angels, zombies, and shape-shifters.

The stories "have varying lengths and tones, representing an impressive range of writing styles; it is likely that any fantasy reader will find at least one memorable story that speaks directly to his or her preferences." Bull Cent Child Books

Lanagan, Margo
Black juice. Eos 2005 201p $15.99; pa $5.99
Grades: 7 8 9 10 **S C**
1. Short stories
ISBN 0-06-074390-5; 0-06-074392-1 pa
LC 2004-8715

Michael L. Printz Award honor book, 2006

Provides glimpses of the dark side of civilization and the beauty of the human spirit through ten short stories that explore significant moments in people's lives, events leading to them, and their consequences.

"This book will satisfy readers hungry for intelligent, literary fantasies that effectively twist facets of our everyday world into something alien." SLJ

Yellowcake; stories. Margo Lanagan. Alfred A. Knopf 2013 240 p. (hardcover) $16.99; (library) $19.99
Grades: 9 10 11 12 **S C**
1. Short stories 2. Magic -- Fiction
ISBN 0375869204; 9780375869204; 9780375873355; 9780375969201; 9780375989315
LC 2012013139

This is a collection of ten short stories that "examine unexpected occurrences of magic in everyday lives." Some "of these literary fantasies are wholly original (a boy's mother prepares to ascend to a higher calling, circus oddities find someone else to stare at and speculate about, a shopping mall sheds its parasitic humans) and some are inspired by other tales (Passover and Exodus, Rapunzel, Charon and the River Styx)." (School Library Journal)

Le Guin, Ursula K.
Tales from Earthsea. Ace Books 2002 314p (The Earthsea cycle) rpt $16.99; pa $13.95
Grades: 11 12 Adult **S C**
1. Short stories 2. Fantasy fiction
ISBN 9780547851402 rpt; 0-441-00932-8
LC 2001-56673

First published 2001 by Harcourt

Five fantasy tales set on the archipelago of Earthsea with an essay on the people, languages, history and magic of the place.

"Inhabited by people no better or worse than ourselves, Earthsea is dominated by the practice of magic as precise as any science and as unpredictable in its social consequences. Since it is based entirely on language, Earthsea's magic serves as a metaphor for the writer's own sorcery. Yet despite Le Guin's strong bias toward the didactic there is no hint of by-the-numbers allegory here." N Y Times Book Rev

Legends: short novels by the masters of modern fantasy; edited by Robert Silverberg. TOR Bks. 1998 715p il hardcover o.p. pa $17.95
Grades: 11 12 Adult **S C**
1. Short stories 2. Fantasy fiction
ISBN 0-312-86787-5; 0-7653-0035-4 pa
LC 98-23593

"What is so noteworthy about this collection is the fact that all the selections are first rate and are well integrated into their universes." Booklist

Levithan, David
How they met, and other stories. Alfred A. Knopf 2008 244p $16.99; lib bdg $19.99
Grades: 9 10 11 12 **S C**
1. Love stories 2. Short stories
ISBN 978-0-375-84886-5; 978-0-375-94886-2 lib bdg
LC 2007-10586

This is a collection of eighteen stories describing the surprises, sacrifices, doubts, pain, and joy of falling in love.

"The author is a master of texture and detail. . . . Each richly imagined story will tap familiar veins of longing, memory, and anticipation." Bull Cent Child Books

Life on Mars: tales from the new frontier; an original science fiction anthology. edited by Jonathan Strahan. Viking 2011 333p $19.99
Grades: 7 8 9 10 **S C**
1. Short stories 2. Science fiction 3. Mars (Planet) -- Fiction
ISBN 978-0-670-01216-9; 0-670-01216-5
LC 2011-02998

"In this strong anthology, Strahan . . . collects stories by some of the most talented writers in science fiction. Ranging from the first Mars landing to the far future, they often make use of the most recent scientific data about the Red Planet. . . . Invoking some of the great authors of Martian tales, from Burroughs and Bradbury to Heinlein and Kim Stanley Robinson . . . , this anthology is sure to appeal to any teens who yearn to explore Earth's nearest neighbor." Publ Wkly

Link, Kelly
★ **Pretty** monsters; stories. decorations by Shaun Tan. Viking 2008 389p il $19.99; pa $9.99
Grades: 9 10 11 12 **S C**
1. Short stories 2. Horror fiction 3. Fantasy fiction 4. Science fiction
ISBN 978-0-670-01090-5; 0-670-01090-1; 978-0-14-241672-3 pa; 0-14-241672-X pa
LC 2008-33251

"Readers as yet unfamiliar with Link . . . will be excited to discover her singular voice in this collection of nine short stories, her first book for young adults. . . . [Subjects] range from absurd to mundane, all observed with equidistant irony. . . . The author mingles the grotesque and the ethereal to make magic on the page." Publ Wkly

★ The **Locus** awards; thirty years of the best in science fiction and fantasy. edited by Charles N.

Brown and Jonathan Strahan. Eos 2004 512p
pa $15.95
Grades: 9 10 11 12   **S C**
1. Short stories 2. Fantasy fiction 3. Science fiction
ISBN 0-06-059426-8

LC 2004-42054

"Whether readers are catching up on legendary science
fiction and fantasy, becoming reacquainted with old favorites, or grazing the field in hopes of discovering new ones,
this anthology delivers some of the finest science fiction and
fantasy ever written." SLJ

Love is hell; [by] Melissa Marr . . . [et al.] Harper-
Teen 2008 263p $16.99; pa $9.99
Grades: 7 8 9 10   **S C**
1. Love stories 2. Short stories 3. Supernatural --
Fiction
ISBN 978-0-06-144305-3; 0-06-144305-0; 978-0-06-
144304-6 pa; 0-06-144304-2 pa

LC 2007-49574

"Supernatural romance is the well-chosen theme of five
original stories by as many authors. . . . There's enough variety to round out the central theme, and consistently sup-
ple storytelling will lure readers through all five entries."
Publ Wkly

Marston, Elsa
★ **Santa** Claus in Baghdad and other stories
about teens in the Arab world. Indiana University
Press 2008 198p pa $15.95
Grades: 6 7 8 9 10   **S C**
1. Short stories 2. Middle East -- Fiction 3. Arab
countries -- Fiction
ISBN 978-0-253-22004-2; 0-253-22004-1

LC 2007-50768

A collection of eight stories, most previously published
in other anthologies, about what it is like to grow up in the
Middle East today.

"Marston, who has lived and visited the countries of
which she writes, offers a realistic portrait of the Middle
East that mixes possiblity and bleakness in equal measure."
Voice Youth Advocates

McKillip, Patricia A.
Harrowing the dragon. Ace Books 2005 310p
hardcover o.p. pa $14
Grades: 9 10 11 12   **S C**
1. Short stories 2. Fantasy fiction
ISBN 0-441-01360-0; 0-441-01443-7 pa

LC 2005-51311

"This collection of 13 stories by one of fantasy's most
elegant and luminescent writers brings together 25 years of
short fiction into one lyrical volume." Libr J

McKinley, Robin
Fire: tales of elemental spirits; [by] Robin
McKinley and Peter Dickinson. G. P. Putnam's Sons
2009 297p $19.99
Grades: 7 8 9 10   **S C**
1. Short stories 2. Fire -- Fiction 3. Mythical animals

-- Fiction
ISBN 978-0-399-25289-1; 0-399-25289-4

LC 2009-4730

"The settings of these five tales range from ancient to
modern, but they are all united by encounters with magical
creatures with an affinity for fire. . . . This collection of beautifully crafted tales will find a warm welcome from fans of
either author, as well as from fantasy readers in general." SLJ

Water: tales of elemental spirits; [by] Robin
McKinley, Peter Dickinson. Putnam 2002 266p
$18.99; pa $6.99
Grades: 7 8 9 10   **S C**
1. Short stories 2. Fantasy fiction 3. Mermaids and
mermen -- Fiction
ISBN 0-399-23796-8; 0-14-240244-3 pa

LC 2001-41642

"The masterfully written stories all feature distinct, richly detailed casts and settings . . . and focus as strongly on
action as on character. There's plenty here to excite, enthrall,
and move even the pickiest readers." SLJ

★ **Moccasin** thunder; American Indians stories for
today. edited by Lori Marie Carlson. HarperCollins 2005 156p $15.99
Grades: 7 8 9 10   **S C**
1. Short stories 2. Native Americans -- Fiction
ISBN 0-06-623957-5

LC 2004-22186

Presents ten short stories about contemporary Native
American teens by members of tribes of the United States
and Canada, including Louise Erdrich and Joseph Bruchac.

"This distinguished anthology offers powerful, beautifully written stories that are thoughtful and important for
teens to hear." SLJ

Molina-Gavilan, Yolanda
Cosmos latinos; an anthology of science fiction
from Latin America and Spain. translated, edited,
& with an introduction & notes by Andrea L. Bell
& Yolanda Molina-Gavilán. Wesleyan Univ. Press
2003 352p (Wesleyan early classics of science fiction series) hardcover o.p. pa $24.95
Grades: 11 12 Adult   **S C**
1. Short stories 2. Science fiction
ISBN 0-8195-6633-0; 0-8195-6634-9 pa

LC 2003-41182

This "is a survey of Spanish and Portuguese sf from
both sides of the Atlantic, most of it never before translated
into English. Coverage begins in the nineteenth century and
continues through the early years of the genre's definition
to include many more recent than older stories. . . . Many
stories exploit familiar sf territory—the technologically
advanced future, time travel and its repercussions, and so
on—but obscurer corners are visited, too, as in an alternate Crucifixion occurring on a far-distant world just being
explored by humans, and a recasting of the conquistadors
as spacefarers. A welcome expansion of the sf terrain for
Anglophones." Booklist

Includes bibliographical references

Monstrous affections; an anthology of beastly tales. edited by Kelly Link & Gavin J. Grant. Candlewick Press 2014 480 p. $22.99

Grades: 9 10 11 12   S C

1. Fantasy fiction 2. Short stories -- Collections 3. Monsters -- Fiction

ISBN 0763664731; 9780763664732

LC 2013953536

This speculative fiction collection, edited by Kelly Link and Gavin J. Grant, presents "a world where humans live side by side with monsters, from vampires both nostalgic and bumbling to an eight-legged alien who makes tea. Here you'll find mercurial forms that burrow into warm fat, spectral boy toys, a Maori force of nature, a landform that claims lives, and an architect of hell on earth." (Publisher's note)

"On the heels of their very successful short-story anthology, Steampunk!, editors Link and Grant turn to another currently popular theme: monsters, both familiar and strange, in all their various permutations. Like its predecessor, some fabulous talents--M. T. Anderson, Paolo Bacigalupi, Holly Black, Cassandra Clare, editor Link, and Patrick Ness--contribute to the appealing volume's welcome variety." Horn Book

Myers, Walter Dean, 1937-2014

★ **145th** Street; short stories. Delacorte Press 2000 151p hardcover o.p. pa $5.50

Grades: 7 8 9 10   S C

1. Short stories 2. African Americans -- Fiction 3. Harlem (New York, N.Y.) -- Fiction

ISBN 0-385-32137-6; 0-440-22916-2 pa

LC 99-36097

"These ten powerful stories create a vivid mosaic of life in the Harlem neighborhood of 145th Street. Memorable characters range from outgoing Big Joe, who decides to stage his own funeral party in Big Joe's funeral, to book-loving Monkeyman, who outsmarts the Tigros gang. . . . Beautifully told, Myers's stories offer an enticing collection for teens." Voice Youth Advocates

★ **What** they found; love on 145th street. Wendy Lamb Books 2007 243p $15.99; lib bdg $18.99

Grades: 8 9 10 11 12   S C

1. Short stories 2. Family life -- Fiction 3. African Americans -- Fiction 4. Harlem (New York, N.Y.) -- Fiction

ISBN 978-0-385-32138-9; 0-385-32138-4; 978-0-375-93709-5 lib bdg; 0-375-93709-9 lib bdg

LC 2007-7057

Companion volume to 145th street (2000)

Fifteen interrelated stories explore different aspects of love, such as a dying father's determination to help start a family business—a beauty salon—and the relationship of two teens who plan to remain celibate until they marry.

"Rich in both character and setting, these urban tales combine heartbreak and hope into a vivid tableau of a community. A priority purchase for all libraries, especially those in urban settings." SLJ

Na, An

No such thing as the real world; a short story collection. [by] An Na [et al.]; introduction by Jill Santopolo; [compiled by Laura Geringer and Jill Santopolo] HarperTeen 2009 246p $16.99

Grades: 8 9 10   S C

1. Short stories

ISBN 978-0-06-147058-5; 0-06-147058-9

LC 2008-22583

Six young adult authors present short stories featuring teens who have to face the "real world" for the first time.

"This unique collection will challenge students' intellect and have them questioning their own decision-making skills. A fine balance is straddled between sophisticated prose and authentic teen voices, uninhibited and peppered with profanity." SLJ

Nascimbene, Yan

The **creative** collection of American short stories; illustrated by Yan Nascimbene; introduction by Ray Bradbury. Creative Editions 2010 271p il $28.95

Grades: 9 10 11 12 Adult   S C

1. Short stories

ISBN 978-1-56846-202-8

LC 2008-41479

"This anthology is a great introduction to the short-story form. . . . The selections span more than 150 years of American writing and cover varied themes and settings. Ernest Hemingway, John Updike, Joyce Carol Oates, and Alice Walker are among the featured authors. Nascimbene's lovely watercolor illustrations complement each story." SLJ

Includes bibliographical references

★ The **Norton** book of science fiction; North American science fiction, 1960-1990. edited by Ursula K. Le Guin and Brian Attebery; Karen Joy Fowler, consultant. Norton 1993 869p hardcover o.p. pa $38.13

Grades: 11 12 Adult   S C

1. Short stories 2. Science fiction

ISBN 0-393-03546-8; 0-393-97241-0 pa

LC 93-16130

Damon Knight, Robert Silverberg, Connie Willis and Harlan Ellison are among the authors represented in this anthology of more than 60 stories.

A "compilation of intelligent and entertaining sf that belongs in virtually every fiction collection." Booklist

Nye, Naomi Shihab, 1952-

★ **There** is no long distance now; very short stories. Greenwillow Books 2011 201p $17.99

Grades: 7 8 9 10 11 12   S C

1. Short stories

ISBN 0-06-201965-1; 978-0-06-201965-3

LC 2010025559

"Very short stories offer glimpses into the everyday lives of young people. . . . As she does in her poetry, Nye achieves a perfect marriage of theme and structure in stories that reflect the moments, glimpses and epiphones of growing up." Kirkus

O'Brien, Tim

★ The **things** they carried; a work of fiction.
Houghton Mifflin Harcourt 2010 233p $24; pa
$14.95

Grades: 11 12 Adult   **S C**
1. Short stories 2. Vietnam War, 1961-1975 -- Fiction
ISBN 978-0-547-39117-5; 978-0-618-70641-9 pa
                                        LC 2010-292325
First published 1990
"This book may be selfconscious . . . but through its determination to treat these men with dignity and decency it
proves immensely affecting." Newsweek

O'Connor, Flannery

The **complete** stories. Farrar, Straus & Giroux
1971 555p hardcover o.p. pa $17

Grades: 11 12 Adult   **S C**
1. Short stories
ISBN 0-374-51536-0
This collection is "arranged in chronological order from
the story she wrote for her master's thesis at the University
of Iowa to 'Judgement Day.' . . . The stories here include
the original openings and other chapters of her two novels
'Wise Blood' and 'The Violent Bear It Away.'" N Y Times
Book Rev

Once upon a cuento; edited by Lyn Miller-Lachman.
Curbstone Press 2003 243p pa $15.95

Grades: 9 10 11 12   **S C**
1. Short stories 2. Hispanic Americans -- Fiction
ISBN 1-88068-499-3
                                        LC 2003-14667
"Fourteen Latino authors have contributed to this collection of 17 short stories." SLJ

Ortiz Cofer, Judith

An **island** like you; stories of the barrio. Puffin
Books 1996 165p $6.99; pa $6.99

Grades: 7 8 9 10 11 12   **S C**
1. Short stories 2. New Jersey -- Fiction 3. Puerto
Ricans -- Fiction
ISBN 9780545131339; 0-14-038068-X
                                        LC 96-23203
A collection of twelve stories about young people in Paterson New Jersey caught between their Puerto Rican heritage and their American surroundings.
"The combination of interweaving of characters, intensity of emotion, and deft control of language make this a
rewarding collection." Bull Cent Child Books

Outside rules; short stories about nonconformist
youth. edited, with an introduction by Claire Robson. Persea Books 2007 178p pa $9.95

Grades: 7 8 9 10   **S C**
1. Short stories
ISBN 0-89255-316-2; 978-0-89255-316-7
                                        LC 2006-22548
An anthology of fourteen short stories about youth who
do not quite fit in because they are too brainy, unathletic,
poor, the "wrong" religion, emotionally fragile, from non-

traditional families, not model-thin, or simply bent on following a unique path.
"The collection is broadly multicultural, and the stories
are consistently insightful, original, and discussion provoking in addition to being well written." Bull Cent Child Books

The **Oxford** book of gothic tales; edited by Chris
Baldick. Oxford University Press 2009 xxiii,
533p pa $19.95

Grades: 11 12 Adult   **S C**
1. Short stories 2. Horror fiction 3. Gothic romances
ISBN 978-0-19-956153-7
                                        LC 2009291584
First published 1992
This chronologically arranged anthology contains thirty-
seven stories dating from the 18th to 20th century. Among
the authors are Hawthorne, Poe, Stevenson, Hardy, Faulkner,
Welty, Borges, Angela Carter and Isabel Allende.
Includes bibliographical references

★ The **Oxford** book of short stories; chosen by V.S.
Pritchett. Oxford Univ. Press 1981 547p hardcover o.p. pa $19.95

Grades: 11 12 Adult   **S C**
1. Short stories
ISBN 0-19-214116-3; 0-19-958313-7 pa
                                        LC 81-156872
In addition to one of his own short stories, Pritchett has
selected 40 others, written in English during the 19th and
20th centuries. Most of the authors are English, Irish or
American and include Somerset Maugham, D. H. Lawrence,
Faulkner, Twain, and Eudora Welty.

Packer, ZZ

Drinking coffee elsewhere. Riverhead Bks.
2003 238p hardcover o.p. pa $14

Grades: 11 12 Adult   **S C**
1. Short stories 2. African Americans -- Fiction
ISBN 1-57322-378-6 pa; 1-57322-234-8
                                        LC 2002-73971
"The predominantly African American characters in
Packer's first collection of short fiction struggle to maintain their sense of self while they confront unexpected life
events." Booklist

Patrick, Denise Lewis

A **matter** of souls; Denise Lewis Patrick. Carolrhoda Lab 2014 186 p. (trade hard cover: alk.
paper) $16.95

Grades: 7 8 9 10 11 12   **S C**
1. American short stories 2. Race relations -- Fiction
3. Southern States -- Fiction 4. African Americans
-- History 5. Southern States -- History -- Fiction 6.
African Americans -- Southern States -- Fiction
ISBN 0761392807; 9780761392804
                                        LC 2013017597
This collection of short stories, by Denise Lewis Patrick, "considers the souls of black men and women across
centuries and continents. In each, she takes the measure of
their dignity, describes their dreams, and catalogs their fears.
Brutality, beauty, laughter, rage, and love all take their turns

in each story, but the final impression is of indomitable, luminous, and connected souls." (Publisher's note)

"Eight short stories with long memory cut to the quick—all the more as they could be true. Patrick's tales from the distant and not-so-distant past shed fresh light on interracial and intraracial conflicts that shape and often distort the realities of African-Americans. . . . The plots and characters change from one story to the next, but each one artfully tells a poignant truth without flinching. Shocking, informative and powerful, this volume offers spectacular literary snapshots of black history and culture." Kirkus

Peck, Richard

Past perfect, present tense: new and collected stories. Dial Bks. 2004 177p hardcover o.p. pa $6.99
Grades: 7 8 9 10 11 12   **S C**
1. Short stories
ISBN 0-8037-2998-7; 0-14-240537-X pa
LC 2003-10904

A collection of short stories, including two previously unpublished ones, that deal with the way things could be.

"The stories perfectly highlight Peck's range and expertise at characterization. Almost every one is a superb read-aloud. . . . This superior collection is a must for every library." SLJ

★ **Pick**-up game; a full day of full court. edited by Marc Aronson & Charles R. Smith Jr. Candlewick Press 2011 170p il $15.99; pbk. $6.99
Grades: 7 8 9 10   **S C**
1. Short stories 2. Basketball -- Fiction 3. New York (N.Y.) -- Fiction
ISBN 0-7636-4562-1; 978-0-7636-4562-5; 9780763660680

A series of short stories by such authors as Walter Dean Myers, Rita Williams-Garcia, and Joseph Bruchac, interspersed with poems and photographs, provides different perspectives on a game of streetball played one steamy July day at the West 4th Street court in New York City known as The Cage.

"This anthology squeaks out a win. . . . Sharp-elbow action alternates with an almost spiritual grace." Booklist

Poe, Edgar Allan

★ **Edgar** Allan Poe's tales of mystery and madness; illustrated by Gris Grimley. Atheneum Books for Young Readers 2004 135p il $17.95
Grades: 8 9 10 11 12   **S C**
1. Short stories 2. Horror fiction
ISBN 0-689-84837-4
LC 2003-10565

"With high-production values and gothic sensibilities thoroughly reflected in both text and art, this is an essential purchase for libraries. Adults can use it to lead young people to some great literature; readers will pluck it off the shelves themselves for creepy, entertaining fun." Booklist

Porter, Katherine Anne

★ **Pale** horse, pale rider: three short novels. Harcourt Brace Jovanovich 1990 208p $17

Grades: 11 12 Adult   **S C**
1. Short stories
ISBN 0-15-170755-3
LC 89-26886

First published 1939

"These three short novels include the title story, which concerns a young newspaperwoman in love with a soldier who dies in the 1918 influenza epidemic; 'Noon Wine,' the narrative of a shooting in the glare of a Texas midday; and 'Old Mortality,' a three-stage account of a Southern family that tries to believe its own myths about itself." Good Read

Prom nights from hell; [by] Meg Cabot . . . [et al.] HarperTeen 2007 304p $16.99; pa $9.99
Grades: 9 10 11 12   **S C**
1. Short stories 2. Horror fiction 3. School stories
ISBN 978-0-06-125310-2; 0-06-125310-3; 978-0-06-125309-6 pa; 0-06-125309-X pa
LC 2007-02986

"In this collection, five popular authors put a unique twist on prom. . . . Their prom nights involve demons, vampires, and the walking dead. . . . Although the stories are loosely tied to the theme, each author fills her tale with vastly different nightmarish characters and circumstances, making certain that there is something that will appeal to every reader." Voice Youth Advocates

Rice, David

Crazy loco; stories about growing up Chicano in southern Texas. Dial Books for Young Readers 2001 135p hardcover o.p. pa $6.99
Grades: 7 8 9 10 11 12   **S C**
1. Short stories 2. Texas -- Fiction 3. Mexican Americans -- Fiction
ISBN 0-8037-2598-1; 0-14-250056-9 pa
LC 00-59042

A collection of nine stories about Mexican American kids growing up in the Rio Grande Valley of southern Texas.

"Two great strengths of these stories are the pitch-perfect sense for the speech and thought patterns of teens and the vivid depiction of the daily lives of Mexican-Americans in Texas's Rio Grande Valley." SLJ

Robinson, Kim Stanley

The **Martians**. Bantam Bks. 1999 336p hardcover o.p. pa $7.50
Grades: 11 12 Adult   **S C**
1. Short stories 2. Science fiction
ISBN 0-553-80117-1; 0-553-57401-9 pa
LC 99-13115

Set in the universe of the author's Mars trilogy this volume includes vignettes, essays, fables, poems, and the following short stories: Michel in Antarctica; Exploring Fossil Canyon; Maya and Desmond; Four teleological trails; Coyote makes trouble; Michel in provence; Arthur Sternbach brings the curveball to Mars; Jackie on Zo; Keeping the flame; Big Man in love; Sexual dimorphism; What matters; Sax moments; A Martian romance; Purple Mars

"Also included is 'Green Mars,' a previously published novella about climbing Olympus Mons, the highest mountain in the solar system. . . . Some of the pieces here will be of interest only to those who have already read the trilogy, but the finest of the short fiction stands firmly on its own. As is the norm with Robinson's work, the stories are beautifully written, the characters are well developed and the author's passion for ecology manifests on every page." Publ Wkly

Salinger, J. D.

★ **Nine** stories. Little, Brown 1953 302p $24.95; pa $5.99

Grades: 11 12 Adult   **S C**

1. Short stories

ISBN 0-316-76956-8; 0-316-76950-9 pa

This collection "introduced various members of the Glass family who would dominate the remainder of Salinger's work. Critical response divided itself between high praise and cult worship. Most of the stories deal with precocious, troubled children, whose religious yearnings—often tilting toward the East—are in vivid contrast to the materialistic and spiritually empty world of their parents. The result was a perfect literary formula for the 1950s." Benet's Reader's Ency of Am Lit

Savit, Gavril

Anna and the Swallow Man; Gavriel Savit. Alfred A. Knopf 2016 240 p. illustrations $17.99

Grades: 9 10 11 12   **Fic**

1. Poland -- Fiction 2. Survival skills -- Fiction 3. World War, 1939-1945 -- Fiction 4. Survival -- Fiction 5. World War, 1939-1945 -- Poland -- Fiction 6. Poland -- History -- Occupation, 1939-1945 -- Fiction

ISBN 9780553513349; 9780553522068

LC 2014034472

This novel, by Gavriel Savit, is "set in Poland during the Second World War. . . . Anna Łania is just seven years old when the Germans take her father, a linguistics professor, during their purge of intellectuals in Poland. She's alone. And then Anna meets the Swallow Man. He is a mystery, strange and tall, a skilled deceiver with more than a little magic up his sleeve. And when the soldiers in the streets look at him, they see what he wants them to see." (Publisher's note)

"Full of sophisticated questions and advanced vocabulary, Savit's debut occasionally feels like an adult novel, but young readers with the patience for his gauzy pacing and oblique plot turns will be rewarded by a moving, thought-provoking story about coming-of-age in the midst of trauma." Booklist

Sedgwick, Marcus

★ The **ghosts** of heaven; Marcus Sedgwick. 1st American ed. Roaring Brook Press 2015 336 p. (hardback) $17.99

Grades: 9 10 11 12   **S C**

1. Science fiction 2. Space and time -- Fiction

ISBN 1626721254; 9781250073679; 9781626721258

LC 2014040471

Printz Award Honor Book (2016)

This collection of linked short stories, by Marcus Sedgwick, "range chronologically from the prehistoric past; to rural Britain at the end of the witch hunts in the eighteenth century; to the early twentieth century, at an insane asylum on Long Island; and finally to a spacecraft in deep space and the distant future." (Horn Book)

"What openly draws these stories together is a spiral and spinning symbolism that presents itself through vivid details, from the seemingly mundane to literary references. Individually they conform to conventions; together they defy expectations as they raise questions about humanity and its connections to the universe and one another." Kirkus

★ **Midwinterblood**; Marcus Sedgwick. Roaring Brook Press 2013 272 p. (hardcover) $17.99

Grades: 7 8 9 10 11 12   **S C**

1. Reincarnation -- Fiction 2. Islands 3. Love stories 4. Love -- Fiction 5. Islands -- Fiction 6. Scandinavia -- Fiction

ISBN 1596438002; 9781596438002

LC 2012013302

Printz Award Winner (2014)

Author Marcus Sedgwick presents seven stories about "an archaeologist who unearths a mysterious artifact, an airman who finds himself far from home, a painter, a ghost, a vampire, and a Viking." The stories "take place on the remote Scandinavian island of Blessed where a curiously powerful plant that resembles a dragon grows. . . . What secrets lurk beneath the surface of this idyllic countryside? And what might be powerful enough to break the cycle of midwinterblood?" (Publisher's note)

Shards and Ashes; edited by Melissa Marr and Kelley Armstrong; with additional stories by Veronica Roth, Kami Garcia, Margaret Stohl and more. Harpercollins Childrens Books 2013 x, 369 p.p (ebook) $7.99; (hardcover) $17.99

Grades: 7 8 9 10   **S C**

1. Science fiction 2. Dystopian fiction 3. Apocalyptic fiction

ISBN 9780062098474; 0062098462; 9780062098467

This book, edited by Melissa Marr and Kelley Armstrong, offers nine science fiction short stories. "The world is gone, destroyed by human, ecological, or supernatural causes. Survivors dodge chemical warfare and cruel gods; they travel the reaches of space and inhabit underground caverns. Their enemies are disease, corrupt corporations, and one another; their resources are few and their courage is tested." (Publisher's note)

★ **Shattered:** stories of children and war; edited by Jennifer Armstrong. Knopf 2002 166p hardcover o.p. pa $6.50

Grades: 7 8 9 10   **S C**

1. War stories 2. Short stories

ISBN 0-375-81112-5; 0-440-23765-3 pa

LC 2001-18609

"These selections will make teens cry, will make them angry, but most of all they will make them think." SLJ

Sideshow; ten original tales of freaks, illusionists, and other matters odd and magical. edited by

Deborah Noyes. Candlewick Press 2009 199p il $16.99

Grades: 7 8 9 10   **S C**

1. Short stories

ISBN 978-0-7636-3752-1; 0-7636-3752-1

LC 2008-37420

"This is a masterpiece of 10 short stories by world-class authors. Contributors include David Almond, Annette Curtis Klause, and Vivian Vande Velde. . . . Not all of the stories are traditional prose; several are graphic renditions, including Matt Phelan's masterfully drawn 'Jargo!' . . . Suspending disbelief, readers of this fantastic anthology may start investing in psychics and sleeping with the light on." SLJ

Singer, Isaac Bashevis

★ The **collected** stories of Isaac Bashevis Singer. Farrar, Straus & Giroux 1982 610p hardcover o.p. pa $20

Grades: 11 12 Adult   **S C**

1. Short stories 2. Jews -- Fiction

ISBN 0-374-12631-3; 0-374-51788-6 pa

Sixteen: stories about that sweet and bitter birthday; edited by Megan McCafferty. Three Rivers Press 2004 318p pa $10.95

Grades: 9 10 11 12   **S C**

1. Short stories

ISBN 1-4000-5270-X

LC 2003-27919

"Diverse as the teens the stories represent, this collection features Native Americans, teen mothers, queer boys and questioning girls, ancient Greeks, students abroad, and a teen author. . . . Adults wanting to relive their youth will get as much mileage out of the combined joy and misery of the protagonists as teens seeking assurance they are not alone at this bittersweet crossroads of life." Voice Youth Advocates

Spider Woman's granddaughters; traditional tales and contemporary writing by Native American women. edited and with an introduction by Paula Gunn Allen. Fawcett Columbine 1990 279p pa $15

Grades: 11 12 Adult   **S C**

1. Short stories 2. Native Americans -- Fiction

ISBN 0-449-90508-X

First published 1989 by Beacon Press

This is a collection of twenty-four stories by Native American women authors arranged in three thematic sections, 'The Warriors,' 'The Casualties,' and 'The Resistance.' The contributors include Marmon Silko, E. Pauline Johnson, Vickie L. Sears, Anna Lee Walters, Soge Track, LeAnne Howe and Louise Erdrich.

"Each of the stories in this collection, whether traditional or modern, expresses the urgency of survival—of not vanishing either individually or politically. And the quality of the stories is stunning." Women's Rev Books

Includes bibliographical references

Starry-eyed; 16 stories that steal the spotlight. edited by Ted Michael and Josh Pultz. Running Press Teens 2013 400 p. $9.95

Grades: 7 8 9 10 11 12   **S C**

1. Performing arts 2. Actors -- Fiction 3. Singers -- Fiction

ISBN 0762449497; 9780762449491

LC 2013940578

Editors Ted Michael and Josh Pultz present a "collection of fictional short stories [that] highlight the struggles, hopes, failures, and triumphs of young aspiring singers, dancers, actors, actresses, and performers. While these characters may feel out of place during their everyday lives, they are able to find a home onstage and in rehearsals. Woven throughout the anthology are personal anecdotes from several of today's most celebrated performers of stage, screen, and television." (Publisher's note)

★ **Steampunk!** an anthology of fantastically rich and strange stories. edited by Kelly Link and Gavin J. Grant. Candlewick Press 2011 432p pbk. $12.99

Grades: 8 9 10 11 12   **S C**

1. Short stories 2. Fantasy fiction

ISBN 0763657972; 9780763657970

LC 2010040742

In this collection of short stories edited by Kelly Link and Gavin J. Grant "fourteen [authors] of speculative fiction, including two graphic storytellers, embrace the [steampunk] genre's established themes and refashion them in surprising ways and settings as diverse as Appalachia, ancient Rome, future Australia, and alternate California." (Publisher's note)

"Veteran editors Link and Grant serve up a delicious mix of original stories from 14 skilled writers and artists. . . . Chockful of gear-driven automatons, looming dirigibles, and wildly implausible time machines, these often baroque, intensely anachronistic tales should please steampunks of all ages." Publ Wkly

Such a pretty face; short stories. edited by Ann Angel. Amulet Books 2007 267p $18.95

Grades: 9 10 11 12   **S C**

1. Short stories

ISBN 978-0-8109-1607-4; 0-8109-1607-X

LC 2006-23612

For this short story collection, the editor has "chosen stories reflecting the many definitions and ramifications of physical beauty. . . . This powerful, thought-provoking anthology will certainly find a place in public libraries. High school librarians are strongly urged to consider it for purchase, despite a few instances of profane language and several sexual references." Voice Youth Advocates

Taking aim; power and pain, teens and guns. edited by Michael Cart. HarperTeen 2015 368 p. illustrations (hardback) $17.99

Grades: 9 10 11 12   **SC**

1. Guns -- Fiction 2. Teenagers -- Fiction 3. Short stories -- Collections 4. Short stories 5. Firearms -- Fiction 6. Short stories, American

ISBN 9780062327352

LC 2015005621

In this collection of fiction, edited by Michael Cart, "[s]ixteen celebrated authors bring us raw, insightful stories that explore guns and teens. . . . From a boy whose low self-esteem is impacted when a gun comes into his possession to a student recalling a senseless tragedy that befell a favorite teacher, from a realistic look at hunting to a provocative look at a family that defies stereotypes, each emotional story stirs the debate to new levels." (Publisher's note)

"As a collection, this anthology functions less as an evaluation of whether guns are good or bad but, rather, as an incisive glimpse at how guns function, both symbolically and literally, in contemporary society. Sobering and thought-provoking." Booklist

Tan, Shaun

★ **Tales** from outer suburbia. Arthur A. Levine Books 2009 92p il $19.99

Grades: 7 8 9 10   **S C**

1. Short stories 2. Suburban life -- Fiction

ISBN 0-545-05587-3; 978-0-545-05587-1

LC 2008-13784

This is a collection of fifteen illustrated stories set in the Australian suburbs. "Grades five to ten." (Bull Cent Child Books)

"The term 'suburbia' may conjure visions of vast and generic sameness, but in his hypnotic collection of 15 short stories and meditations, Tan does for the sprawling landscape what he did for the metropolis in The Arrival . . . . Ideas and imagery both beautiful and disturbing will linger." Publ Wkly

Taylor, Laini

★ **Lips** touch; three times. illustrations by Jim Di Bartolo. Arthur A. Levine Books 2009 265p il $17.99

Grades: 8 9 10 11 12   **S C**

1. Short stories 2. Kissing -- Fiction 3. Supernatural -- Fiction

ISBN 978-0-545-05585-7; 0-545-05585-7

LC 2009-5458

These three stories about kissing feature elements of the supernatural. "Grades nine to twelve." (Bull Cent Child Books)

"Taylor offers a powerful trio of tales, each founded upon the consequences of a kiss. . . . Contemporary Kizzy, who so yearns to be a normal, popular teenager that she forgets the rules of her Old Country upbringing and is seduced by a goblin in disguise; Anamique, living in British colonial India, silenced forever due to a spell cast upon her at birth; and Esmé, who at 14 discovers she is host to another—non-human—being. . . . Each is, in vividly distinctive fashion, a mesmerizing love story that comes to a satisfying but never predictable conclusion. Di Bartolo's illustrations provide tantalizing visual preludes to each tale." Publ Wkly

Teeth; vampire tales. edited by Ellen Datlow & Terri Windling. HarperCollins 2011 xxvi, 452p $17.99; pa $9.99

Grades: 9 10 11 12   **S C**

1. Short stories 2. Horror fiction 3. Vampires -- Fiction

ISBN 978-0-06-193515-2; 0-06-193515-8; 978-0-06-193514-5 pa; 0-06-193514-X pa

A collection of nineteen short stories about vampires features tales from Cassandra Clare and Holly Black, Neil Gaiman, and Melissa Marr.

"Readers interested in vampires as something more than leading men will find plenty that's tragic or scary here, often leavened with a bit of (largely snarky) humor, and lots of thought-provoking material about life and death, friendship and loneliness. Great for diving in and out, . . . this collection might even win boys back to vampire lit." Kirkus

Things I'll never say; stories about our secret selves. Ann Angel. Candlewick Press 2015 320 p. $16.99

Grades: 10 11 12   **S C**

1. Secrets -- Fiction

ISBN 0763673072; 9780763673079

LC 2014944916

This book, by Ann Angel, "brings together some of today's most gifted [young adult] authors to explore, in a variety of genres, the nature of secrets: Do they make you stronger or weaker? Do they alter your world when revealed? Do they divide your life into what you'll tell and what you won't?" (Publisher's note)

"The balance and diversity that Angel has achieved here is lovely, and teens who pick this up will likely find a bit of herself or himself—or at least a friend—inside these pages. A collection to share widely." Booklist

Tolkien, J. R. R.

The **Silmarillion**; edited by Christopher Tolkien. 2nd ed; Houghton Mifflin 2001 xxiv, 365p il $28; pa $14

Grades: 9 10 11 12   **S C**

1. Short stories 2. Fantasy fiction

ISBN 0-618-13504-9; 0-618-12698-8 pa

LC 2001-16971

First published 1977

"Tolkien began writing these introductory legends in 1917 and, sporadically throughout his life, continued adding to them; his son Christopher has edited and compiled the various versions into a single cohesive work. Two brief tales, which outline the origin of the world and describe the gods who create and rule, precede the title story about the Silmarils—three brilliant, jewel-like creatures who are desired and fought over, setting up a clash between good and evil." Booklist

Tolstoy, Leo

Great short works of Leo Tolstoy; with an introduction by John Bayley; in the translations by Louise and Aylmer Maude. Harper & Row 1967 685p hardcover o.p. pa $15.95

Grades: 9 10 11 12   **S C**

1. Short stories 2. Russia -- Fiction

ISBN 0-06-058697-4 pa

Tomo; friendship through fiction: an anthology of Japan teen stories. edited by Holly Thompson;

cover and part-title illustrations by John Shelley. Stone Bridge Press 2012 383 p. (pbk.) $14.95

Grades: 7 8 9 10   **S C**

1. Japan -- Fiction 2. Short stories -- Collections 3. Teenagers 4. Friendship 5. Short stories

ISBN 1611720060; 9781611720068

LC 2011051530

This book of short stories, edited by Holly Thompson, is an "anthology of authors with direct or indirect Japanese 'heritage or experience.' The 36 tales (all but six of which are new) were gathered as contributions to the relief effort for victims of the 2011 earthquake and tsunami." The various entries focus on stories about Japanese and half-Japanese teenagers in a variety of genres, including historical fiction, contemporary teenage drama, and fantasy. Stories are indexed by plot themes, including friendship, ghosts, super-powers, and family relationships. (Kirkus)

Twain, Mark, 1835-1910

★ The **complete** short stories of Mark Twain; now collected for the first time. edited with an introduction by Charles Neider. Doubleday 1957 xxiv, 676p hardcover o.p. pa $6.95

Grades: 11 12 Adult   **S C**

1. Short stories

ISBN 0-553-21195-1 pa

"The sixty pieces which are here hospitably called short stories illustrate both the weaknesses and the strengths of Mark Twain as a writer of fiction." N Y Times Book Rev

A **Tyranny** of Petticoats; 15 Stories of Belles, Bank Robbers & Other Badass Girls. edited by Jessica Spotswood. Candlewick Press 2016 368 p. $17.99

Grades: 9 10 11 12   **S C**

1. Fantasy fiction 2. Adventure fiction 3. Heroes and heroines -- Fiction

ISBN 0763678481; 9780763678487

LC 2015942989

Editor Jessica Spotwood presents this short story collection "through history with American girls charting their own course. They are monsters and mediums, bodyguards and barkeeps, screenwriters and schoolteachers, heiresses and hobos. They're making their own way in often-hostile lands, using every weapon in their arsenals, facing down murderers and marriage proposals. And they all have a story to tell." (Publisher's note)

"There is range and balance in tone, voice, and approach, a challenge for anthologies. Placing the stories in historical order allows readers to move smoothly through, and a helpful author's note follows each selection. Readers of historical fiction and adventure need look no further." Kirkus

Under the moons of Mars; new adventures on Barsoom. edited by John Joseph Adams. Simon & Schuster Books for Young Readers 2012 xv, 352 p.p ill. (hardcover) $16.99

Grades: 6 7 8 9 10 11 12   **S C**

1. Science fiction 2. Adventure fiction 3. Short stories -- Collections 4. Short stories, American 5. Mars (Planet) -- Fiction 6. Science fiction, American

ISBN 9781442420304; 1442420294; 9781442420298; 9781442420311

LC 2011034391

This anthology, edited by John Joseph Adams, features several science fiction stories set in Edgar Rice Burroughs' Barsoom series. "Fans of all ages have marveled at the adventures of John Carter, an Earthman who suddenly finds himself in a strange new world. A century later, readers can enjoy this compilation of brand-new stories starring John Carter of Mars." (Publisher's note)

Unnatural creatures; stories. Neil Gaiman; [edited by] Rosemary Brosnan. 1st ed. HarperCollins 2013 480 p. ill. (hardcover) $17.99

Grades: 8 9 10 11 12   **S C**

1. Short stories 2. Fantasy fiction 3. Monsters -- Fiction

ISBN 0062236296; 9780062236296; 9780062236302

LC 2013933032

This fantasy-horror short story collection, compiled by Neil Gaiman and edited by Maria Dahvana Headley, "is a collection of short stories about the fantastical things that exist only in our minds. . . . The sixteen stories . . . range from the whimsical to the terrifying. The magical creatures range from werewolves to sunbirds to beings never before classified. E. Nesbit, Diana Wynne Jones, Gahan Wilson, and other literary luminaries contribute to the anthology." (Publisher's note)

Vande Velde, Vivian

Being dead; stories. Harcourt 2001 203p hardcover o.p. pa $6.95

Grades: 7 8 9 10   **S C**

1. Short stories 2. Horror fiction 3. Supernatural -- Fiction

ISBN 0-15-216320-4; 0-15-204912-6 pa

LC 00-12996

"Often humorous and sometimes evoking sympathy, this anthology will be enjoyed by lovers of mild horror as well as by those who like clever short stories." Voice Youth Advocates

Voices in first person; reflections on Latino identity. [edited by Lori Marie Carlson] Atheneum Books for Young Readers 2008 96p il $16.99

Grades: 6 7 8 9 10 11 12   **S C**

1. Short stories 2. American literature -- Hispanic American authors -- Collections

ISBN 978-1-4169-0635-3; 1-4169-0635-5

LC 2006-34161

A collection of brief fictional pieces about the experiences of Latinos in the United States, by such writers as Sandra Cisneros, Gary Soto, Oscar Hijuelos, and others.

"Carlson has drawn from both established and new writers, focusing on finding Latino voices that speak to contemporary readers. . . . This collection sparkles more than its predecessors because of its dynamic design, featuring black-and-white photographs and line illustrations incorporated with the text in a collage-like magazine layout." SLJ

Wallace, Rich

Losing is not an option: stories. Knopf 2003
127p hardcover o.p. pa $5.99

Grades: 7 8 9 10   S C

1. Short stories

ISBN 0-375-81351-9; 0-440-23844-7 pa

                      LC 2002-34036

Nine episodes in the life of a young man, from sneaking into his tenth football game in a row with his best friend in sixth grade to running his last high school race, the Pennsylvania state championships.

"Readers will nod with recognition as they follow this jock/poet/regular guy from the cusp of adolescence to the edge of adulthood." Horn Book Guide

Welcome to Bordertown; new stories and poems of
the Borderlands. edited by Holly Black and Ellen
Kushner; introduction by Terri Windling. Random House 2011 517p $19.99; lib bdg $22.99;
e-book $19.99

Grades: 7 8 9 10   S C

1. Short stories 2. Fantasy fiction 3. Poetry --
Collections 4. Supernatural -- Fiction

ISBN 978-0-375-86705-7; 0-375-86705-8; 978-0-375-
96705-4 lib bdg; 0-375-96705-2 lib bdg; 978-0-375-
89745-0 e-book

                      LC 2010-35558

This collection of short stories and poems focuses on Bordertown, "a city on the border between our human world and the elfin realm. Runaway teens come from both sides of the border to find adventure, to find themselves. Elves play in rock bands and race down the street on spell-powered motorbikes. Human kids recreate themselves in the squats and clubs and artists' studios of Soho." (Publisher's note)

"This is punk-rock, DIY fantasy, full of harsh reality and incandescent magic . . . Many of the stories echo with loss and discomfort; standouts include 'Crossings' by Janni Lee Simner, a chilling look at the difference between dreams and reality, and 'A Tangle of Green Men,' Charles De Lint's heartbreaking examination of love, loss and life. Poems and songs (from Patricia A. McKillip, Neil Gaiman and Jane Yolen, among others) balance the fiction. . . . A masterful anthology." Kirkus

Welty, Eudora

★ The **collected** stories of Eudora Welty. Harcourt Brace Jovanovich 1980 622p hardcover o.p.
pa $16

Grades: 11 12 Adult   S C

1. Short stories

ISBN 0-15-118994-3; 0-15-618921-6 pa

                      LC 80-7947

This volume contains four previously published collections: A curtain of green, and other stories; The wide net, and other stories; The golden apples and The bride of the Innisfallen, and other stories. Also included in this volume are two uncollected pieces: Where is the voice coming from? and The demonstrators.

White, Kiersten

And I darken; Kiersten White. Delacorte Press
2016 496 p. **Fic**

1. Princesses -- Fiction 2. Good and evil -- Fiction
3. Princesses -- Romania -- Transylvania -- Fiction 4.
Transylvania (Romania) -- History -- 15th century --
Fiction

ISBN 9780553522310; 9780553522327

                      LC 2015020681

"Ever since Lada Dragwlya and her brother, Radu, were wrenched from their homeland of Wallachia and abandoned by their father to be raised in the Ottoman courts, Lada has known that being ruthless is the key to survival, and when she meets Mehmed, the heir to the very empire that Lada has sworn to fight against, complications arise as Lada, Radu and Mehmed form a toxic triangle that strains the bonds of love and loyalty to the breaking point." (Publisher's note)

"The first in a trilogy from best-selling author White, this historical adventure set in the mid-15th century tells the story of Lada and Radu, the children of Vlad Dracul, prince of Wallachia (modern-day Romania). Shouldered with the inescapable curse of being female and the unrelenting burden of her beautiful, sensitive, and physically inept brother, Radu, Lada is perpetually spoiling for a fight. When her father tries to secure his throne by giving the children as hostages to the Ottoman Empire, Lada and Radu must find a way to survive and thrive in a world where no one cares if they live or die. . . . Highly recommended for all high school collections." SLJ

Wizards; edited by Jack Dann and Gardner Dozois.
Berkley Books 2007 400p hardcover o.p. pa
$16

Grades: 11 12 Adult   S C

1. Short stories 2. Fantasy fiction

ISBN 978-0-425-21518-0; 978-0-441-01588-7 pa

                      LC 2006-101534

"In this collection of first-published tales, wizards are the puppet masters of schemes ranging from the amusing to the diabolical. Contributors include such venerable masters as Jane Yolen, Peter S. Beagle, and Gene Wolfe as well as such relative newcomers as Andy Duncan and Jeffrey Ford. . . . A creative spectrum of tantalizing themes makes the volume versatile and compelling reading for all fantasy fans." Booklist

Working days: stories about teenagers and work;
edited by Anne Mazer. Persea Bks. 1997 207p
hardcover o.p. pa $9.95

Grades: 9 10 11 12   S C

1. Short stories 2. Work -- Fiction

ISBN 0-89255-223-9; 0-89255-224-7 pa

                      LC 96-50243

Fifteen stories relate the experiences of teenagers working for many different reasons in a variety of jobs. Lois Metzger, Victor Martinez, Norman Wong and Thylias Moss are among the contributors.

"This multicultural collection would fit any high school curriculum. Senior high school students and adults will identify with many of these protagonists while being challenged at the same time." ALAN

Wright, Richard
Uncle Tom's children; five long stories. Harper & Row 1938 xxx, 384p hardcover o.p. pa $13.95
Grades: 11 12 Adult   S C
1. Short stories 2. African Americans -- Fiction
ISBN 0-06-058714-8 pa
The stories in this collection deal with conflicts between whites and blacks in the South.

The **Year's** best dark fantasy & horror; edited by Paula Guran. 2010 ed.; Prime Books 2010 568p $19.95
Grades: 11 12 Adult   S C
1. Short stories 2. Horror fiction 3. Fantasy fiction
ISBN 978-1-60701-233-7

"Editor Guran has collected 39 thrilling and frightening horror stories published in 2009. . . . Fans of horror and dark fantasy. . . should welcome this collection with open arms." Booklist
Annual

AUTHOR, TITLE, AND SUBJECT INDEX

This index to the books in the Classified Collection includes author, title, and subject entries; added entries for publishers' series, illustrators, joint authors, and editors of works entered under title; and name and subject cross-references; all arranged in one alphabet.

The number or symbol in boldface type at the end of each entry refers to the Dewey Decimal Classification or to the Fiction (Fic) or Story Collection (S C) section where the main entry for the book will be found. Works classed in 92 will be found under the headings for the biographies' subject.

1,000 comic books you must read. Isabella, T. **741.5**
The **10** p.m. question. De Goldi, K. **Fic**
10-fold origami. Engel, P. **736**
The **100** best African American poems. **811**
100 essential American poems. **811**
100 essential modern poems. **821**
100 essential things you didn't know you didn't know. Barrow, J. D. **510**
100 great journeys. **910.2**
100 great monologues from the neo-classical theatre. **808.82**
100 great monologues from the Renaissance theatre. **822**
100 great poems of the twentieth century. **821**
100 heartbeats. Corwin, J. **333.95**
100 key documents in American democracy. **973**
100 most important science ideas. Henderson, M. **500**
100 sideways miles. Smith, A. **Fic**
1001 inventions that changed the world. **600**
1001 little fashion miracles. Jones, C. **646**
101 American English proverbs. Collis, H. **428**
101 great, ready-to-use book lists for teens. Keane, N. J. **028.5**
101 outstanding graphic novels. **741.5**
101 proverbs [series]
    Collis, H. 101 American English proverbs **428**
101 quantum questions. Ford, K. W. **530.1**
101 questions [series]
    Brynie, F. H. 101 questions about muscles to stretch your mind and flex your brain **612.7**
    Brynie, F. H. 101 questions about reproduction **612.6**
101 questions about muscles to stretch your mind and flex your brain. Brynie, F. H. **612.7**
101 questions about reproduction. Brynie, F. H. **612.6**
101 stories of the great ballets. Balanchine, G. **792.8**
102 minutes. Dwyer, J. **974.7**
1066: the year of the conquest. Howarth, D. A. **942.02**
1089 and all that. Acheson, D. J. **510**
10th grade. Weisberg, J. **Fic**
112 acting games. Levy, G. **792**

The **12** steps unplugged. R., J. **362.292**
12,000 miles in the nick of time. Jacobson, M. **910.4**
13 little blue envelopes. Johnson, M. **Fic**
130 projects to get you into filmmaking. Grove, E. **792.9**
14 minutes. Brant, J. **796.42**
145th Street. Myers, W. D. **S**
1491. Mann, C. C. **970.01**
15 short plays. McNally, T. **812**
150 great tech prep careers. **331.7**
17 & gone. Suma, N. R. **Fic**
172 hours on the moon. **Fic**
180 more. **811**
19 varieties of gazelle. Nye, N. S. **811**
1920S See Nineteen twenties
The **1950s.** Schwartz, R. A. **973.91**
The **1960s.** Maga, T. P. **973.923**
1960S See Nineteen sixties
The **1960s** cultural revolution. McWilliams, J. C. **973.92**
1968. Kaufman, M. T. **909.82**
1970S See Nineteen seventies
The **1980s.** Woodger, E. **973.92**
1980S See Nineteen eighties
The **1990s.** Schwartz, R. A. **909.82**
2010: the best men's stage monologues and scenes. **808.82**
2010: the best women's stage monologues and scenes. **808.82**
2011 scholarship handbook. College Entrance Examination Board **378.3**
2012 standard catalog of world coins, 1901-2000. Cuhaj, G. S. **737.4**
21. Santiago, W. **92**
21 proms. **S**
21st century science [series]
    New thinking about genetics **576.5**
    New thinking about pollution **628.5**
24 favorite one-act plays. **808.82**
37 things I love (in no particular order) Magoon, K. **Fic**
The **4** percent universe. Panek, R. **523.1**
4 plays. Inge, W. **812**
4-H guide to dog training and dog tricks. Rogers,

Abrams studio [series]

Micklewright, K. Drawing: mastering the language of visual expression **741.2**

Abrams, Amir

Hollywood High **Fic**

Abrams, Dennis

H.G. Wells **92**

The Treaty of Nanking **951**

Abrams, Floyd

Friend of the court **342**

Abrams, M. H.

A glossary of literary terms **803**

Abrams, Michael

Birdmen, batmen, and skyflyers **629.13**

Abramson, Jill

Obama **92**

ABRASIVES

See also Ceramics

ABRIDGMENTS

See also Literature

Absent. Williams, K. **Fic**

ABSENT MOTHERS -- FICTION

Howard, J. J. That time I joined the circus **Fic**

ABSENTEEISM (LABOR)

See also Hours of labor; Personnel management

Absolute zero and the conquest of cold. Shachtman, T. **536**

Absolutely Maybe. Yee, L. **Fic**

The **absolutely** true diary of a part-time Indian. Alexie, S. **Fic**

ABSTINENCE, SEXUAL *See* Sexual abstinence

ABSTRACT ART

See also Art

An **abundance** of Katherines. Green, J. **Fic**

Abuse And Violence Information For Teens. **362.76**

ABUSE OF ANIMALS *See* Animal welfare

ABUSE OF SUBSTANCES *See* Substance abuse

ABUSE, VERBAL *See* Invective

ABUSED CHILDREN *See* Child abuse

ABUSED WIVES *See* Abused women; Wife abuse

ABUSED WOMEN

Bickerstaff, L. Violence against women **362.88**

Simons, R. Gender danger **362.88**

Violence against women **362.83**

ABUSED WOMEN

See also Victims of crimes; Women

ABUSED WOMEN -- FICTION

Connor, L. The things you kiss goodbye **Fic**

Abusing over-the-counter drugs. Etingoff, K. **362.29**

ACADEMIC ACHIEVEMENT

Bain, K. What the best college students do **378.1**

Conley, D. T. College knowledge **378.1**

Gould, J. B. How to succeed in college (while really trying) **378.1**

Jones, J. B. The power of the media specialist to improve academic achievement and strengthen at-risk students **027.8**

Nichols, B. Improving student achievement **373.1**

Odden, A. R. Improving student learning when budgets are tight **371.2**

Zasloff, B. Hold fast to dreams **371.4**

ACADEMIC ACHIEVEMENT

See also Success

ACADEMIC ADVISING *See* Educational counseling

ACADEMIC DEGREES

See also Colleges and universities

ACADEMIC DISHONESTY *See* Cheating (Education)

ACADEMIC DISSERTATIONS *See* Dissertations

ACADEMIC FAILURE *See* Academic achievement

ACADEMIC FREEDOM

Reichman, H. Censorship and selection **025.2**

ACADEMIC FREEDOM

See also Intellectual freedom; Toleration

ACADEMIC LIBRARIES

See also Libraries

Growing schools **370.71**

ACADEMIC MAJORS *See* College majors

ACADEMIC WRITING -- HANDBOOKS, MANUALS, ETC

A manual for writers of research papers, theses, and dissertations **808.06**

ACADEMY AWARDS (MOTION PICTURES)

See also Motion pictures

Acceptance. Marcus, D. L. **378.1**

ACCESS TO HEALTH CARE

Kidder, T. Mountains beyond mountains **92**

ACCESS TO HEALTH CARE

See also Medical care

ACCESSIBILITY OF HEALTH SERVICES *See* Access to health care

Accessing the classics. Rosow, L. V. **011.6**

The **accident** season. Fowley-Doyle, M. **Fic**

ACCIDENT VICTIMS

Perl, L. Cruzan v. Missouri **344**

The **accidental** highwayman. Tripp, B. **Fic**

ACCIDENTS

Campbell, B. C. Disasters, accidents, and crises in American history **363.34**

Piven, J. The worst-case scenario survival handbook **613.6**

ACCIDENTS -- FICTION

Fowley-Doyle, M. The accident season **Fic**

Griffin, P. Burning blue **Fic**

McStay, M. Everything that makes you **Fic**

Minato, K. Confessions **Fic**

Oliver, L. Vanishing girls **Fic**

Perez, M. Dead is a killer tune **Fic**

Accidents of nature. Johnson, H. M. **Fic**

Reed, J. Living violet   **Fic**

AFRICAN AMERICAN TEENAGE GIRLS -- WASHINGTON (STATE) -- SEATTLE -- FICTION

Brockenbrough, M. The game of Love and Death   **Fic**

AFRICAN AMERICAN WOMEN

Bolden, T. Maritcha   92

Clinton, C. Harriet Tubman: the road to freedom   973.7

Dove, R. On the bus with Rosa Parks   811

Farrington, L. E. Creating their own image   709

Fleischner, J. Mrs. Lincoln and Mrs. Keckley   92

Honey, hush!   817

Hurston, Z. N. Their eyes were watching God   **Fic**

Schafer, D. L. Anna Madgigine Jai Kingsley   975.9

Stockett, K. The help   **Fic**

AFRICAN AMERICAN WOMEN

See also Black women; Women

AFRICAN AMERICAN WOMEN -- BIOGRAPHY

Mullenbach, C. Double victory   940.53

AFRICAN AMERICAN WOMEN -- CIVIL RIGHTS -- HISTORY -- 20TH CENTURY

Mullenbach, C. Double victory   940.53

AFRICAN AMERICAN WOMEN -- DICTIONARIES

Black women in America   920.003

AFRICAN AMERICAN WOMEN -- DRAMA

Shange, N. For colored girls who have considered suicide, when the rainbow is enuf   812

AFRICAN AMERICAN WOMEN -- EMPLOYMENT -- HISTORY -- 20TH CENTURY

Mullenbach, C. Double victory   940.53

AFRICAN AMERICAN WOMEN -- FICTION

Morrison, T. Beloved   **Fic**

AFRICAN AMERICAN WOMEN -- HEALTH AND HYGIENE

Fornay, A. Born beautiful   646.7

AFRICAN AMERICAN WOMEN -- HISTORY -- 20TH CENTURY

Mullenbach, C. Double victory   940.53

AFRICAN AMERICAN YOUNG MEN -- NEW YORK (STATE) -- NEW YORK -- BIOGRAPHY

Joseph, J. Panther baby   974.7

AFRICAN AMERICAN YOUTH

Levinson, C. Y. We've got a job   323.1

AFRICAN AMERICAN YOUTH

See also Youth

AFRICAN AMERICAN YOUTH -- ALABAMA -- BIRMINGHAM -- HISTORY -- 20TH CENTURY

Levinson, C. Y. We've got a job   323.1

AFRICAN AMERICAN YOUTH -- FICTION

Blythe, C. Revenge of a not-so-pretty girl   **Fic**

Volponi, P. The Final Four   **Fic**

AFRICAN AMERICANS

The African American almanac   305.8

African Americans and criminal justice   364.089

Africana: the encyclopedia of the African and African American experience   909

Du Bois, W. E. B. The souls of Black folk   305.8

Durham, D. A. Gabriel's story   **Fic**

Gates, H. L. The African-American century   305

Haley, A. Mama Flora's family   **Fic**

Hughes, L. Short stories of Langston Hughes   **S**

Hurston, Z. N. The complete stories   **S**

Hurston, Z. N. Novels and stories   813

Johnson, A. The first part last   **Fic**

Kidd, S. M. The secret life of bees   **Fic**

Lee, H. To kill a mockingbird   **Fic**

The Oxford W. E. B. Du Bois reader   305.896

Should America pay?   305.8

Southgate, M. The fall of Rome   **Fic**

Taylor, M. D. The land   **Fic**

Whitehead, C. Sag Harbor   **Fic**

Woodson, J. If you come softly   **Fic**

Wright, R. Uncle Tom's children   **S**

Wright, R. Works   818

AFRICAN AMERICANS

See also Blacks

AFRICAN AMERICANS -- BIBLIOGRAPHY

Neumann, C. E. Term paper resource guide to African American history   016

AFRICAN AMERICANS -- BIOGRAPHY

Haley, A. Roots   920

In the Shadow of Liberty   920

Shabazz, I. X   **Fic**

AFRICAN AMERICANS -- BIOGRAPHY

See also Blacks -- Biography

AFRICAN AMERICANS -- BIOGRAPHY -- DICTIONARIES

African American biographies   920.003

The African American national biography   920.003

Carey, C. W. African-American political leaders   920.003

Otfinoski, S. African Americans in the performing arts   920.003

Otfinoski, S. African Americans in the visual arts   920.003

AFRICAN AMERICANS -- BIOGRAPHY -- ENCYCLOPEDIAS

Bracks, L. African American almanac   973

AFRICAN AMERICANS -- BIOGRAPHY -- GRAPHIC NOVELS

Best shot in the West   978

AFRICAN AMERICANS -- BOOKS AND READING -- FICTION

No crystal stair   **Fic**

in motion pictures; Motion pictures

African Americans in science. Carey, C. W. **920.003**

AFRICAN AMERICANS IN TELEVISION BROADCASTING

See also Television broadcasting

African Americans in the military. Reef, C. **920.003**

AFRICAN AMERICANS IN THE MOTION PICTURE INDUSTRY

See also Blacks in the motion picture industry; Minorities in the motion picture industry; Motion picture industry

African Americans in the performing arts. Otfinoski, S. **920.003**

African Americans in the visual arts. Otfinoski, S. **920.003**

AFRICAN AMERICANS ON TELEVISION

See also Television

The African and Middle Eastern world, 600-1500. Pouwels, R. L. **956**

AFRICAN ART

See also Art

AFRICAN DIASPORA

Africana: the encyclopedia of the African and African American experience **909**

AFRICAN ELEPHANT -- EFFECT OF POACHING ON

Orenstein, R. Ivory, horn and blood **333.95**

AFRICAN LITERATURE

See also Literature

AFRICAN LITERATURE (ENGLISH)

See also Literature

AFRICAN LITERATURE -- ENCYCLOPEDIAS

Killam, G. D. Student encyclopedia of African literature **920**

AFRICAN LITERATURE -- HISTORY AND CRITICISM

Achebe, C. The education of a British-protected child **92**

African literature and its times **809**

Killam, G. D. Student encyclopedia of African literature **920**

African literature and its times. **809**

AFRICAN MUSIC

See also Music

AFRICAN MYTHOLOGY

Lynch, P. A. African mythology, A to Z **299.6**

AFRICAN MYTHOLOGY

See also Mythology

African mythology, A to Z. Lynch, P. A. **299.6**

AFRICAN NATIONAL CONGRESS

Mandela, N. Nelson Mandela speaks **968.06**

AFRICAN PEOPLES See Africans

AFRICAN POETRY -- COLLECTIONS

The Penguin book of modern African poetry **896**

The African slave trade. Davidson, B. **967**

African states and rulers. Stewart, J. **960**

African traditional religion. Lugira, A. M. **299.6**

African voices of the Atlantic slave trade. Bailey, A. C. **326**

African-American athletes. Aaseng, N. **920.003**

The African-American century. Gates, H. L. **305**

African-American experience [series]

Historic speeches of African Americans **815**

African-American poets. **811**

African-American political leaders. Carey, C. W. **920.003**

African-American writers. Sickels, A. **920**

African-American writers. Bader, P. **920.003**

Africana: the encyclopedia of the African and African American experience. **909**

AFRICANS

Alifirenka, C. I will always write back **305.235**

AFRICANS -- FICTION

Park, L. S. A long walk to water **Fic**

AFRICANS -- UNITED STATES -- FICTION

Griffin, P. The Orange Houses **Fic**

Afrika. Craig, C. **Fic**

AFRO-AMERICAN WOMEN IN LITERATURE

Gloria Naylor: critical perspectives past and present **813**

AFRO-AMERICANS See African Americans

After. Efaw, A. **Fic**

AFTER DINNER SPEECHES

See also Speeches

After hello. Mangum, L. **Fic**

After Jackie. Fussman, C. **796.357**

After the first death. Cormier, R. **Fic**

After the kiss. McVoy, T. E. **Fic**

After the snow. Crockett, S. D. **Fic**

AFTERLIFE See Future life

Afterlife with Archie. Aguirre-Sacasa, R. **741.5**

Afterlife with Archie [series]

Aguirre-Sacasa, R. Afterlife with Archie **741.5**

Aftermath of history [series]

Gay, K. The aftermath of the Chinese nationalist revolution **951.04**

Gay, K. The aftermath of the Russian Revolution **947.084**

Kallen, S. A. The aftermath of the Sandinista Revolution **972.85**

The aftermath of the Chinese nationalist revolution. Gay, K. **951.04**

The aftermath of the Russian Revolution. Gay, K. **947.084**

The aftermath of the Sandinista Revolution. Kallen, S. A. **972.85**

AFTERNOON TEAS

See also Cooking

Afterworlds. Westerfeld, S. **Fic**

AGE -- PHYSIOLOGICAL EFFECT See Aging

AGE AND EMPLOYMENT

See also Age; Employment

AGE DISCRIMINATION
>   *See also* Discrimination

The **age** of airpower. Van Creveld, M. L.   **358.4**

Age of Bronze. Shanower, E.   **741.5**

Age of bronze [series]

Shanower, E. Age of Bronze vol. 1: A Thousand Ships   **741.5**

Shanower, E. Age of Bronze: Sacrifice   **741.5**

Age of Bronze vol. 1: A Thousand Ships. Shanower, E.   **741.5**

Age of bronze volume 3A: Betrayal part one. Shanower, E.   **741.5**

Age of Bronze: Sacrifice. Shanower, E.   **741.5**

Age of consent.   **306.7**

The **age** of genius. Bradley, M. J.   **920**

AGEING *See* Aging

The Agency [series]

Lee, Y. S. The body at the tower   **Fic**

Lee, Y. S. A spy in the house   **Fic**

AGENT ORANGE -- FICTION

Lynch, C. Casualties of war   **Fic**

AGGREGATES *See* Set theory

AGGRESSIVE BEHAVIOR *See* Aggressiveness (Psychology)

AGGRESSIVENESS (PSYCHOLOGY)

Lorenz, K. On aggression   **152.4**

AGGRESSIVENESS (PSYCHOLOGY)
>   *See also* Human behavior; Psychology

AGGRESSIVENESS IN ADOLESCENCE -- CASE STUDIES

Vicious   **302.34**

AGGRESSIVENESS IN CHILDREN

Whitson, S. 8 keys to end bullying   **302.34**

The **agile** gene. Ridley, M.   **155.7**

Aging. Panno, J.   **612.6**

AGING
>   *See also* Age; Elderly; Gerontology; Longevity; Middle age; Old age

AGING

Panno, J. Aging   **612.6**

Agnes Quill. Roman, D.   **741.5**

AGNOSTICISM
>   *See also* Free thought; Religion

AGORAPHOBIA
>   *See also* Phobias

AGORAPHOBIA -- FICTION

De Goldi, K. The 10 p.m. question   **Fic**

Agosta, William C.

Thieves, deceivers, and killers   **577**

Agosto, Denise E.

(ed) Urban teens in the library   **027.62**

Agoston, Gabor

Encyclopedia of the Ottoman Empire   **956**

AGRICULTURAL BOTANY *See* Economic botany

AGRICULTURAL CHEMICALS

>   *See also* Agricultural chemistry; Chemicals

AGRICULTURAL CHEMISTRY
>   *See also* Chemistry

AGRICULTURAL CREDIT
>   *See also* Agriculture -- Economic aspects; Banks and banking; Credit

AGRICULTURAL ENGINEERING
>   *See also* Engineering

AGRICULTURAL INNOVATIONS
>   *See also* Technological innovations

AGRICULTURAL LABORERS

Hart, E. T. Barefoot heart   **973**

Haugen, B. Cesar Chavez   **92**

Stavans, I. Cesar Chavez   **92**

AGRICULTURAL MACHINERY
>   *See also* Machinery; Tools

AGRICULTURAL PRODUCTS *See* Farm produce

AGRICULTURE

Emerson, R. W. The portable Emerson   **818**

The Story of Seeds   **581.4**

AGRICULTURE
>   *See also* Life sciences

AGRICULTURE -- ECONOMIC ASPECTS
>   *See also* Economics

AGRICULTURE -- ENVIRONMENTAL ASPECTS

Green, J. Food and farming   **338.1**

AGRICULTURE -- RESEARCH
>   *See also* Research

AGRICULTURE -- SOCIETIES
>   *See also* Associations; Country life; Societies

AGRICULTURE -- STATISTICS
>   *See also* Statistics

AGRICULTURE -- STUDY AND TEACHING
>   *See also* Vocational education

AGRONOMY *See* Agriculture

Aguilar, David A.

Space encyclopedia   **523.1**

Aguilar-Moreno, Manuel

Handbook to life in the Aztec world   **972**

Aguirre, Ann

Enclave   **Fic**

Horde   **Fic**

Outpost   **Fic**

Aguirre-Sacasa, Roberto

Afterlife with Archie   **741.5**

Ahdieh, Renée

The wrath and the dawn   **Fic**

Ahmad, Dohra

Rotten English   **820**

AI (ARTIFICIAL INTELLIGENCE) *See* Artificial intelligence

AIDS. James, O.   **616.97**

AIDS (DISEASE)

Ashe, A. Days of grace   **796.342**

America discovered. Hayes, D. **917**
America in 1492. Josephy, A. M. **970.004**
America in the 1970s. Brill, M. T. **973.92**
America in Vietnam. **959.704**
America in world history. **973**
America's battle against terrorism. **973.931**
America's constitution. Amar, A. R. **342**
America's prisons: opposing viewpoints. **365**
America's role in the world. Margulies, P. **327**
America's vice presidents. Witcover, J. **352.23**
America's wetland. Knapp, B. **333.91**
America's women. Collins, G. **305.4**

AMERICA, CAPTAIN (FICTITIOUS CHARAC-
TER) -- COMIC BOOKS, STRIPS, ETC.
Gillen, K. Young Avengers **741.5**

American Academy of Religion
The HarperCollins dictionary of religion **200**

American ace. Nelson, M. **Fic**

AMERICAN ART
Bearden, R. A history of African-American art-
ists **709**
Heart to heart **811**

AMERICAN ART
See also Art

AMERICAN ARTIFICIAL SATELLITES
See also Artificial satellites

AMERICAN ARTISTS *See* Artists -- United States

AMERICAN AUTHORS
See also Authors

AMERICAN AUTHORS -- BIOGRAPHY
Don, K. Real courage **813**

AMERICAN BALLADS
See also American poetry

American Bar Association
The American Bar Association guide to workplace
law **344**
The American Bar Association guide to workplace
law. **344**

American Bird Conservancy
Lebbin, D. J. The American Bird Conservancy
guide to bird conservation **333.95**
The American Bird Conservancy guide to bird conservation. Lebbin, D. J. **333.95**

AMERICAN BISON *See* Bison

American born Chinese. **741.5**

American Canoe Association
Kayaking **797.1**

American chronicle. Gordon, L. G. **973.91**
American civil rights: primary sources. Des Chenes,
B. **323.1**
American Civil War. **973.7**

AMERICAN CIVIL WAR *See* United States --
History -- 1861-1865, Civil War

American Civil War. **973.7**

American Civil War reference library [series]
Hillstrom, K. American Civil War: biogra-

phies **973.7**
American Civil War: biographies. Hillstrom,
K. **973.7**

AMERICAN COLONIAL STYLE IN ARCHI-
TECTURE
See also Architecture

AMERICAN COOKING
Amason, J. This is why you're fat **394.1**
The Oxford encyclopedia of food and drink in
America **641.3**
Schlosser, E. Fast food nation **394.1**

AMERICAN COOKING
See also Cooking

AMERICAN COOKING -- HISTORY
Smith, M. D. History of American cooking **641.5**

American Council of Learned Societies
Concise dictionary of scientific biography **509**

American decades. **973.9**
American decades primary sources. **973.9**

American Diabetes Association
American Diabetes Association complete guide to
diabetes **616.4**
American Diabetes Association complete guide to
diabetes. American Diabetes Association **616.4**

AMERICAN DIARIES
See also American literature; Diaries

AMERICAN DRAMA
Critical survey of drama **809**

AMERICAN DRAMA
See also American literature; Drama

AMERICAN DRAMA -- 20TH CENTURY
Gurney, A. R. Love letters and two other plays: The
golden age and What I did last summer **812**

AMERICAN DRAMA -- AFRICAN AMERICAN
AUTHORS -- COLLECTIONS
Black theatre USA **812**

AMERICAN DRAMA -- COLLECTIONS
Great scenes from minority playwrights **812**
Millennium monologs **792**
Under 30 **812**
With their eyes **812**

AMERICAN DRAMA -- DICTIONARIES
Critical survey of drama **809**

AMERICAN DRAMA -- HISTORY AND CRITI-
CISM
Loos, P. A reader's guide to Lorraine Hansberry's A
raisin in the sun **812**

AMERICAN DRAMATISTS
See also American authors; Dramatists

AMERICAN DRAWING
See also Drawing

AMERICAN ECONOMIC ASSISTANCE *See*
American foreign aid

The American empire. **327**
American eras. **973.8**

AMERICAN ESPIONAGE

BIOGRAPHY -- TECHNIQUE *See* Biography as a literary form

BIOGRAPHY AS A LITERARY FORM

The autobiographer's handbook	**808**
Piercy, M. So you want to write	**808.3**

BIOGRAPHY AS A LITERARY FORM

See also Authorship; Literature

BIOGRAPHY, COLLECTIVE

Balchin, J. Science	**509**
Bradley, M. J. The age of genius	**920**
Bradley, M. J. The birth of mathematics	**510**
Bradley, M. J. The foundations of mathematics	**920**
Bradley, M. J. Mathematics frontiers	**920**
Bradley, M. J. Modern mathematics	**920**
Ellis, D. Children of war	**956.7**
Jocelyn, M. Scribbling women	**808.8**
Stone, T. L. Almost astronauts	**629.45**
What my father gave me	**920**
Windows into my world	**920**

BIOGRAPHY, INDIVIDUAL

Adler, D. A. Frederick Douglass	**92**
Armstrong, K. Muhammad	**297**
Ashe, A. Days of grace	**796.342**
Bailey, J. The lost German slave girl	**92**
Baker, D. The convert	**92**
Barakat, I. Tasting the sky	**92**
Barrowcliffe, M. The elfish gene	**92**
Berry, M. F. My face is black is true	**323**
Bolden, T. Maritcha	**92**
Bolden, T. W.E.B. Du Bois	**92**
Bortz, F. Beyond Jupiter	**92**
Brackett, V. Restless genius	**92**
Brady, P. Martha Washington	**92**
Brant, J. 14 minutes	**796.42**
Breslin, J. Branch Rickey	**92**
Brown, J. K. Amelia Earhart	**629.130**
Bryson, B. Shakespeare	**822.3**
Burgan, M. Nikola Tesla	**92**
Calcines, E. F. Leaving Glorytown	**92**
Campbell, P. J. Robert Cormier	**813**
Cetin, F. My grandmother	**92**
Christianson, G. E. Isaac Newton and the scientific revolution	**530**
Colman, P. Elizabeth Cady Stanton and Susan B. Anthony	**92**
Coltman, L. The real Fidel Castro	**92**
Cooper, M. L. Theodore Roosevelt	**92**
Cornwell, J. Seminary boy	**92**
Czisnik, M. Horatio Nelson	**92**
Dallek, R. Let every nation know	**92**
D'Amboise, J. I was a dancer	**92**
Danticat, E. Brother, I'm dying	**92**
Dash, J. A dangerous engine	**92**
Dawidoff, N. The crowd sounds happy	**92**
De la Bedoyere, C. No one loved gorillas more	**92**
Douglass, F. Autobiographies	**973.8**

Engle, M. The poet slave of Cuba: a biography of Juan Francisco Manzano	**92**
Feynman	**92**
Fleming, C. The Lincolns	**92**
Folklore, memoirs, and other writings	**398**
Forsyth, N. John Milton	**92**
Fradin, J. B. 5,000 miles to freedom	**326**
Fradin, J. B. Jane Addams	**92**
Frank, A. The diary of a young girl: the definitive edition	**92**
Fredston, J. A. Snowstruck	**551.3**
Freedman, R. Eleanor Roosevelt	**973.917**
Freedman, R. Franklin Delano Roosevelt	**973.917**
Freedman, R. The life and death of Crazy Horse	**978**
Gaustad, E. S. Roger Williams	**92**
Ghahramani, Z. My life as a traitor	**92**
Giblin, J. C. The rise and fall of Senator Joe McCarthy	**92**
Ginzberg, L. D. Elizabeth Cady Stanton	**92**
Goldstein, N. Jackie Ormes	**741.5**
González, R. Butterfly boy	**92**
Gorokhova, E. A mountain of crumbs	**92**
Greenberg, J. Andy Warhol	**92**
Hager, T. The alchemy of air	**92**
Hampton, W. Babe Ruth	**92**
Haney, E. L. Inside Delta Force	**356**
Hari, D. The translator	**92**
Heiligman, D. Charles and Emma	**92**
Hirsi Ali, A. Infidel	**92**
Hoose, P. Claudette Colvin	**92**
Hopping, L. J. Bone detective	**92**
Iyer, P. The open road	**92**
Jacobs, A. J. The year of living biblically	**220**
Jansen, H. Over a thousand hills I walk with you	**Fic**
Jiang Red scarf girl	**951.05**
Kamara, M. The bite of the mango	**92**
Katin, M. We are on our own	**741.5**
Keat, N. Alive in the killing fields	**92**
Kincaid, J. My brother	**813**
Kinzer, S. A thousand hills	**967.571**
Kluger, J. Splendid solution: Jonas Salk and the conquest of polio	**92**
Kohler, D. E. Rock 'n' roll soldier	**92**
Krakauer, J. Into the wild	**917.98**
Krauss, L. M. Quantum man	**92**
Kreidler, M. Four days to glory	**796.8**
Lee, H. Still life with rice	**973**
Lemasolai-Lekuton, J. Facing the lion	**967.62**
Lemon, A. Happy	**92**
Levy, A. The first emancipator	**92**
Li, C. N. The bitter sea	**92**
Longsworth, P. The world of Emily Dickinson	**811**
Lopez, S. The soloist	**92**
Maathai, W. Unbowed	**92**
Madden, K. Harper Lee	**92**

BOARD BOOKS FOR CHILDREN
See also Picture books for children

BOARD GAMES
Mayer, B. Libraries got game   025.2

BOARD GAMES
See also Games

BOARDING SCHOOLS *See* Private schools

BOARDING SCHOOLS -- FICTION
Acosta, M. Dark companion   Fic
Carriger, G. Curtsies & conspiracies   Fic
Carriger, G. Etiquette & espionage   Fic
Fishman, S. The well's end   Fic
Halpin, B. A really awesome mess   Fic
Hubbard, J. And we stay   Fic
Johnson, M. The madness underneath   Fic
Johnson, M. The shadow cabinet   Fic
Kindl, P. A school for brides   Fic
Laban, E. The Tragedy Paper   Fic
Maizel, R. Stolen nights   Fic
Miranda, M. Hysteria   Fic
Perkins, S. Isla and the happily ever after   Fic
Philpot, C. Even in paradise   Fic
Richmond, P. Always a catch   Fic
Rowell, R. Carry on   Fic
Southgate, M. The fall of Rome   Fic
Stand-off   Fic
Whitney, D. The rivals   Fic
Winger   Fic
Wolitzer, M. Belzhar   Fic
Wooding, C. Silver   Fic
Woon, Y. Life eternal   Fic

Boatner, Mark Mayo
The Civil War dictionary   973.7
Bob Dylan. Brown, D.   92
Bob Marley. Talamon, B.   92
Bob Miller's algebra for the clueless. Miller, R. 512
Bob Miller's clueless series
Miller, R. Bob Miller's algebra for the clueless 512
Bobbi Brown teenage beauty. Brown, B.   646.7
Bober, Natalie
Countdown to independence   973.3
Thomas Jefferson   92
Bobet, Leah
Above   Fic
An inheritance of ashes   Fic
Bobick, James E.
Balaban, N. E. The handy anatomy answer book   611
(ed) The handy science answer book   500
Bobrick, Benson
A passion for victory: the story of the Olympics in ancient and early modern times   796.4
Boburg, Shawn
Rhodes, J. E. Becoming Manny   92
Boccaccio, Giovanni, 1313-1375
About

Highet, G. The classical tradition   809
Bock, Caroline
LIE   Fic
Bodanis, David
E   530.1
Electric universe   537
Bodart, Joni Richards
Radical reads 2   028.5
Bodden, Valerie
Critical plant life   581.7
How to analyze the works of Frederick Douglass   973.7
Using the Internet   025.042
Bode, Carl
(ed) Emerson, R. W. The portable Emerson   818
Bodeen, S. A.
The Compound   Fic
The raft   Fic
Bodies in motion and at rest. Lynch, T.   113
Boduch, Jodie Lynn
(ed) Violence in the media   303.6
BODY *See* Human body
The **body** at the tower. Lee, Y. S.   Fic
Body brokers. Cheney, A.   617.9
BODY CARE *See* Hygiene
Body drama. Redd, N. A.   612
The **body** finder. Derting, K.   Fic
Body image.   306.4
BODY IMAGE
See also Human body; Mind and body; Personality; Self-perception
BODY IMAGE
Baish, V. Self-image and eating disorders   616.85
Body image   306.4
Graydon, S. In your face   391
Mills, J. E. Expectations for women   305.4
Zeilinger, J. A little f'd up   305.42
BODY IMAGE -- FICTION
Rainfield, C. Stained   Fic
BODY PIERCING
See also Personal appearance
BODY PIERCING -- ENCYCLOPEDIAS
DeMello, M. Encyclopedia of body adornment 391
Body piercing saved my life. Beaujon, A.   781.66
Body slammed! Villareal, R.   Fic
BODY SURFING *See* Surfing
BODY TEMPERATURE
See also Diagnosis; Physiology
BODY WEIGHT
See also Human body; Weight
BODY, HUMAN -- SOCIAL ASPECTS
DeMello, M. Encyclopedia of body adornment 391
BODYBUILDING
See also Exercise; Physical fitness
Weight lifting & strength building   613.7
BODYGUARDS -- FICTION

Micklos, J. Muhammad Ali **92**

BOXING -- FICTION

Dixon, J. Phoenix Island **Fic**

Friend, N. My life in black and white **Fic**

Lipsyte, R. The contender **Fic**

Sharenow, R. The Berlin Boxing Club **Fic**

Shea, J. A kid from Southie **Fic**

BOXING -- GRAPHIC NOVELS

Takahashi, R. One-pound gospel, vol. 1 **741.5**

The **boy** book. Lockhart, E. **Fic**

The **boy** from Ilysies. North, P. **Fic**

Boy in the black suit. Reynolds, J. **Fic**

The **boy** in the striped pajamas. Boyne, J. **Fic**

Boy meets boy. Levithan, D. **Fic**

Boy Nobody. Zadoff, A. **Fic**

The **boy** on the bridge. Standiford, N. **Fic**

The **boy** on the wooden box. Leyson, L. **92**

Boy proof. Castellucci, C. **Fic**

BOY SCOUTS -- COMIC BOOKS, STRIPS, ETC

Dawson, M. Troop 142 **741.5**

The boy Sherlock Holmes [series]

Peacock, S. Death in the air **Fic**

Peacock, S. The dragon turn **Fic**

Peacock, S. Eye of the crow **Fic**

Peacock, S. The secret fiend **Fic**

Peacock, S. Vanishing girl **Fic**

Boy toy. Lyga, B. **Fic**

Boy vs. girl. Robert, N. B. **Fic**

The **boy** who couldn't sleep and never had to. Pierson, D. C. **Fic**

The **boy** who fell out of the sky. Dornstein, K. **92**

The **boy** who harnessed the wind. Kamkwamba, W. **92**

Boy21. Quick, M. **Fic**

Boyce, Charles

Critical companion to William Shakespeare **822.3**

BOYCOTTS

See also Commerce; Consumers; Passive resistance

Boyd, Herb

(comp) Autobiography of a people **305.8**

Wright, S. Simeon's story **305.8**

Boyd, Maria

Will **Fic**

Boyer, Carl B.

A history of mathematics **510**

Boyer, Paul S.

(ed) The Oxford companion to United States history **973**

The **boyfriend** list. Lockhart, E. **Fic**

Boyle, Alan

The case for Pluto **523.4**

Boyle, Robert, 1627-1691

About

Baxter, R. Skeptical chemist **92**

Boynton, Robert S.

(ed) The New new journalism **071**

Boynton, Victoria

(ed) Encyclopedia of women's autobiography **920.003**

BOYS

See also Children

BOYS -- BOOKS AND READING

Sullivan, M. Serving boys through readers' advisory **028.5**

Welch, R. J. The guy-friendly YA library **027.62**

Zbaracki, M. D. Best books for boys **028.5**

BOYS -- FICTION

Ballard, J. G. Empire of the Sun **Fic**

Bradbury, R. Something wicked this way comes **Fic**

Foer, J. S. Extremely loud & incredibly close **Fic**

Grisham, J. The client **Fic**

Haddon, M. The curious incident of the dog in the night-time **Fic**

Hamill, P. Snow in August **Fic**

Harper, H. Letters to a young brother **170**

Heap House **Fic**

Ness, P. The knife of never letting go **Fic**

Slouka, M. Brewster **Fic**

Smith, A. 100 sideways miles **Fic**

Southgate, M. The fall of Rome **Fic**

Tucker, T. Over and under **Fic**

Whitehead, C. Sag Harbor **Fic**

Wray, J. Lowboy **Fic**

You hear me? **810**

BOYS -- HEALTH AND HYGIENE

Goldstein, M. A. Boys into men **613**

BOYS -- POETRY

Flake, S. G. You don't even know me **808.8**

BOYS -- POLITICAL ACTIVITY -- DENMARK -- BIOGRAPHY

Hoose, P. M. The boys who challenged Hitler **940.53**

BOYS -- PSYCHOLOGY -- FICTION

Quick, M. Boy21 **Fic**

Boys Don't Knit. Easton, T. S. **Fic**

Boys into men. Goldstein, M. A. **613**

The **boys** of the dark. Fisher, R. G. **365**

The **boys** of winter. Coffey, W. R. **796.962**

The **boys** who challenged Hitler. Hoose, P. M. **940.53**

The **boys'** crusade. Fussell, P. **940.54**

The **boys'** war. Murphy, J. **973.7**

BOYS, TEENAGE *See* Teenage boys

Boysen, Sarah Till

The smartest animals on the planet **591.5**

Braafladt, Keith

Technology and literacy **027.62**

Braasch, Gary

Earth under fire **363.7**

BRACHIOSAURUS

See also Dinosaurs

Year's celebrations   **394.26**

CHRISTMAS

    See also Christian holidays; Holidays

CHRISTMAS -- FICTION

My true love gave to me   **813**

CHRISTMAS -- WALES

Thomas, D. A child's Christmas in Wales   **828**

CHRISTMAS CARDS

    See also Greeting cards

CHRISTMAS COOKING

    See also Cooking

CHRISTMAS ENTERTAINMENTS

    See also Amusements; Christmas

A **Christmas** memory, One Christmas, & The Thanksgiving visitor. Capote, T.   **818**

CHRISTMAS MUSIC

    See also Music

CHRISTMAS STORIES *See* Christmas -- Fiction

CHRISTMAS TREE GROWING

    See also Forests and forestry

CHRISTMAS TREES

    See also Christmas decorations; Trees

Christopher Paolini. Bankston, J.   **92**

Christopher, Lucy

The killing woods   **Fic**

CHROMOSOMES

    See also Genetics; Heredity

CHRONIC DISEASES

Kaufman, M. Easy for you to say   **362.1**

CHRONIC DISEASES

    See also Diseases

CHRONIC FATIGUE SYNDROME

    See also Diseases

CHRONIC PAIN

    See also Chronic diseases; Pain

Chronicles of Faerie [series]

Melling, O. R. The book of dreams   **Fic**

Melling, O. R. The Hunter's Moon   **Fic**

Melling, O. R. The Light-Bearer's daughter   **Fic**

Melling, O. R. The Summer King   **Fic**

The Chronicles of Kazam [series]

Fforde, J. The Eye of Zoltar   **Fic**

Fforde, J. The last Dragonslayer   **Fic**

Fforde, J. The song of the Quarkbeast   **Fic**

The **chronological** encyclopedia of discoveries in space. Zimmerman, R.   **500.5**

CHRONOLOGY

    See also Astronomy; History; Time

The **Chronology** of American literature.   **810**

Chronology of the U.S. presidency.   **973.09**

A **chronology** of weather. Allaby, M.   **551.5**

CHRONOLOGY, HISTORICAL *See* Historical chronology

The Chrysalis Queen quartet [series]

McKenzie, N. Guinevere's gamble   **Fic**

McKenzie, N. Guinevere's gift   **Fic**

Chu, Miyoko

Songbird journeys   **598**

Chu, Wesley

The Lives of Tao   **Fic**

Chulito. Rice-Gonzalez, C.   **Fic**

Chupeco, Rin

The Girl from the Well   **Fic**

CHURCH

    See also Theology

CHURCH AND STATE

Mountjoy, S. Engel v. Vitale   **344**

CHURCH AND STATE

    See also Church; State, The

CHURCH AND STATE -- UNITED STATES

Judson, K. Religion and government   **296**

McIntosh, K. When religion & politics mix   **201**

CHURCH ARCHITECTURE

    See also Architecture

CHURCH ARCHITECTURE -- FICTION

Follett, K. The pillars of the earth   **Fic**

CHURCH BUILDINGS

King, R. Brunelleschi's dome   **726**

CHURCH BUILDINGS

    See also Buildings

CHURCH HISTORY

Bass, D. B. A people's history of Christianity   **270**

CHURCH OF JESUS CHRIST OF LATTER-DAY SAINTS

Book of Mormon The Book of Mormon   **289.3**

Bushman, C. L. Mormons in America   **289.3**

CHURCH SCHOOLS

    See also Private schools; Schools

CHURCH SCHOOLS -- FICTION

Blagden, S. Dear Life, You Suck   **Fic**

Church, Benjamin, 1639-1718

About

Philbrick, N. The Mayflower and the Pilgrims' New World   **973.2**

CHURCHES *See* Church buildings; Religious institutions

Chwast, Seymour

The odyssey   **741.5**

The **CIA** World Factbook 2014.   **028**

Cianciotto, Jason

(jt. auth) Cahill, S. LGBT youth in America's schools   **371.82**

Cicero, Marcus Tullius, 106-43 B.C.

About

Hamilton, E. The Roman way   **870**

Cid

The poem of the Cid   **861**

CIGARETTES

    See also Smoking; Tobacco

Ciment, James

(ed) Global social issues   **361**

(ed) Encyclopedia of conflicts since World War

Cobb, Cathy
The joy of chemistry — 540
Magick, mayhem, and mavericks — 541
Cobb, Geraldyn M., 1931-
About
Haynsworth, L. Amelia Earhart's daughters 629.13
Coben, Harlan, 1962-
Seconds away — Fic
Shelter — Fic
Cobley, Jason
Frankenstein — 741.5
Coburn, Broughton
Everest: mountain without mercy — 796.522
Cocaine. Chastain, Z. — 362.2
COCAINE
See also Narcotics
COCAINE
Chastain, Z. Cocaine — 362.2
Hecht, A. Cocaine and crack — 362.29
Cocaine and crack. Hecht, A. — 362.29
Cochise, Apache Chief, d. 1874
About
Brown, D. A. Bury my heart at Wounded Knee — 970.004
Cochran, Jacqueline, 1910?-1980
About
Haynsworth, L. Amelia Earhart's daughters 629.13
Cochrane, Kira
(ed) Journalistas — 808.8
Cocker, Mark
Rivers of blood, rivers of gold — 909
COCKROACHES
See also Insects
COCOA
Frydenborg, K. Chocolate — 338.7
COCOA
See also Beverages
COCOA TRADE -- HISTORY
Frydenborg, K. Chocolate — 338.7
COCOONS See Butterflies; Caterpillars; Moths; Silkworms
CODE DECIPHERING See Cryptography
CODE ENCIPHERING See Cryptography
Code name Pauline. — 940.54
Code name Verity. Wein, E. — Fic
Code of silence. Shoemaker, T. — Fic
Code talker. Nez, C. — 92
Code talker. Bruchac, J. — Fic
Code talkers and warriors. Holm, T. — 940.54
CODEPENDENCY
See also Abnormal psychology
CODES See Ciphers
Coe, Alexis
Alice and Freda Forever — 364.15
Coetzee, Frans
Coetzee, M. S. World War I — 940.3

Coetzee, Marilyn Shevin
World War I — 940.3
COFFEE
See also Beverages
COFFEE SHOPS See Restaurants
COFFEEHOUSES
See also Coffee industry; Restaurants
Coffey, Wayne R.
The boys of winter — 796.962
Coffin, Charles M.
(ed) Donne, J. The complete poetry and selected prose of John Donne — 821
COGNITION IN ADOLESCENCE
Siegel, D. J. Brainstorm — 155.5
COGNITION IN ANIMALS
Daisy to the Rescue — 590
Morell, V. Animal wise — 591.5
COGNITIVE STYLES
See also Intellect; Theory of knowledge
Cogwheels of the mind. Edwards, A. W. F. — 511.3
COHABITATION See Unmarried couples
Cohen Suarez, Ananda
Handbook to life in the Inca World — 985
Cohen, Andrew
Cox, B. Wonders of the universe — 523.1
Cohen, Harlan
The naked roommate — 378.1
Cohen, I. Bernard
The triumph of numbers — 519.5
Cohen, Joshua C.
Leverage — Fic
Cohen, Katherine
The truth about getting in — 378.1
Cohen, Leah Hager
Train go sorry — 371.9
Cohen, Lisa J.
The handy psychology answer book — 150
Cohen, Saul Bernard
(ed) The Columbia gazetteer of North America 917
(ed) The Columbia gazetteer of the world — 910.3
Cohen, Tish
Little black lies — Fic
Cohen, Walter
(ed) Shakespeare, W. The Norton Shakespeare — 822.3
Cohn, John M.
The complete library technology planner — 025
Cohn, Rachel
Cupcake — Fic
Gingerbread — Fic
Shrimp — Fic
Cohn, Roy, 1927-1986
About
Kushner, T. Angels in America — 812
COIFFURE See Hair
Coile, D. Caroline

COMMUNICABLE DISEASES -- TREATMENT
Murphy, J. Invincible microbe   **616.9**

COMMUNICATION -- FICTION
Trueman, T. Life happens next   **Fic**

COMMUNICATION AMONG ANIMALS *See*
Animal communication

COMMUNICATION IN MARRIAGE
See also Marriage

COMMUNICATION SYSTEMS, WIRELESS
See Wireless communication systems

Communications and broadcasting. Henderson,
H.   **384**

Communications and the arts. Wyckoff, C.   **331.7**

COMMUNISM
Pipes, R. Communism: a history   **335.4**
Stokes, G. The walls came tumbling down **947.085**

COMMUNISM
See also Collectivism; Political science; Totalitarianism

COMMUNISM -- CHINA
Jiang Red scarf girl   **951.05**
Shen, F. Gang of one   **92**

COMMUNISM -- UNITED STATES
Peery, N. Black radical   **92**

**COMMUNISM -- UNITED STATES -- HISTORY
-- 20TH CENTURY**
Aronson, M. Master of deceit   **363.25**

COMMUNISM AND LITERATURE
See also Communism; Literature

COMMUNISM AND RELIGION
See also Communism; Religion

Communism: a history. Pipes, R.   **335.4**

COMMUNIST COUNTRIES -- FICTION
Bass, K. Graffiti knight   **Fic**
Marsden, C. My Own Revolution   **Fic**

COMMUNIST LEADERS
Coltman, L. The real Fidel Castro   **92**
Cunningham, K. Joseph Stalin and the Soviet
Union   **92**
Gay, K. Mao Zedong's China   **951.05**
Markel, R. J. Fidel Castro's Cuba   **972.91**
Naden, C. J. Mao Zedong and the Chinese Revolu-
tion   **92**
Wade, R. A. The Bolshevik revolution and Russian
Civil War   **947.084**
Wyborny, S. Kim Jong Il   **92**

**COMMUNISTS -- UNITED STATES -- BIOGRA-
PHY**
Vapnek, L. Elizabeth Gurley Flynn   **92**

**COMMUNITIES -- UNITED STATES -- HIS-
TORY**
DiPiazza, F. D. Friend me!   **302.3**

COMMUNITIES, SPACE *See* Space colonies

COMMUNITY AND LIBRARIES *See* Libraries
and community

COMMUNITY AND SCHOOL

See also Community life

COMMUNITY CENTERS
See also Cities and towns -- Civic improvement; Community life; Community organization; Recreation; Social settlements

COMMUNITY CHESTS *See* Fund raising

The **community** college guide. Gonsher, D. **378.1**

COMMUNITY COLLEGES *See* Junior colleges

COMMUNITY DEVELOPMENT
See also Domestic economic assistance; Social change; Urban renewal

COMMUNITY EDUCATION -- AFRICA
Molloy, A. However Long the Night   **966.3**

COMMUNITY GARDENS
Smith, J. N. Growing a garden city   **635**

COMMUNITY HEALTH SERVICES
See also Community services; Public health

COMMUNITY LIFE
See also Associations

COMMUNITY LIFE -- FICTION
Berry, J. All the truth that's in me   **Fic**
Martinez, C. G. Pig Park   **Fic**

**COMMUNITY LIFE -- UNITED STATES -- HIS-
TORY**
DiPiazza, F. D. Friend me!   **302.3**

COMMUNITY ORGANIZATION
See also Community life; Social work

COMMUNITY-SUPPORTED AGRICULTURE
See also Agriculture; Food cooperatives

COMPACT CARS
See also Automobiles

COMPACT DISCS
See also Optical storage devices; Sound recordings

Compact research series
Bjornlund, L. Marijuana   **362.29**
Bjornlund, L. Oxycodone   **615**
Parks, P. J. Bath salts and other synthetic
drugs   **362.29**
Parks, P. J. Diet drugs   **615.7**
Parks, P. J. Methamphetamine   **362.29**

Compact research. Current issues [series]
Bjornlund, L. D. Teen smoking   **362.29**
Fredericks, C. Obesity   **616.3**
Friedman, L. S. Terrorist attacks   **363.32**
Parks, P. J. Drug legalization   **363.45**
Parks, P. J. Drunk driving   **363.1**
Parks, P. J. Video games   **794.8**
Robson, D. Disaster response   **363.34**

Compact research. Diseases and disorders [series]
Currie-McGhee, L. K. Drug addiction   **362.29**
Mooney, C. Mood disorders   **616.85**
Nakaya, A. C. ADHD   **618.92**
Parks, P. J. Down syndrome   **616.85**
Parks, P. J. Influenza   **616.2**
Parks, P. J. Learning disabilities   **371.9**

CONCEPTS
See also Perception

CONCERTS
See also Amusements; Music

Concise dictionary of scientific biography. American Council of Learned Societies **509**

Concise encyclopedia of Latin American literature. **860**

Concise guide to information literacy. Lanning, S. **020**

A **concise** history of Germany. Fulbrook, M. **943**

Concise history of science & invention. Goddard, J. **509**

Concise Oxford American thesaurus. **423**

Concise Oxford dictionary of quotations. **808.88**

Concise Oxford English dictionary. **423**

The **concise** Oxford Spanish dictionary. **463**

Concise rules of APA style. American Psychological Association **808**

CONCORD (MASS.) -- FICTION
Armistead, C. Being Henry David **Fic**

CONCORD (MASS.), BATTLE OF, 1775
See also Battles; United States -- History -- 1775-1783, Revolution -- Campaigns

CONCRETE CONSTRUCTION
See also Building

CONCRETE POETRY
See also Poetry

CONCUSSION, BRAIN *See* Brain -- Concussion

Condie, Ally

Crossed **Fic**

Matched **Fic**

Reached **Fic**

Condoleezza Rice. Rice, C. **92**

CONDORS -- FICTION
Hobbs, W. The maze **Fic**

Condra, Jill

(ed) The Greenwood encyclopedia of clothing through world history **391**

CONDUCT OF LIFE
Are athletes good role models? **306.4**

Brashares, A. The sisterhood of the traveling pants **Fic**

The Courage to be yourself **305.23**

Hafiz, D. The American Muslim teenager's handbook **297**

Harper, H. Letters to a young brother **170**

Hong, K. L. Life freaks me out **158**

Jacobs, L. F. The secrets of college success **378.1**

Moore, W. Discovering Wes Moore **975.2**

Palmer, P. Teen esteem **155.5**

Roberts, A. L. The thinking student's guide to college **378.1**

Shipp, J. The teen's guide to world domination **646.7**

Smith, A. D. Letters to a young artist **700**

Wolff, V. E. True believer **Fic**

CONDUCT OF LIFE
See also Ethics; Human behavior; Life skills

CONDUCT OF LIFE -- FICTION
Arntson, S. The wrap-up list **Fic**

Bick, I. J. The Sin eater's confession **Fic**

Brooks, K. The bunker diary **Fic**

Casanova, M. Frozen **Fic**

Mezrich, B. Bringing down the mouse **Fic**

This is the part where you laugh **Fic**

CONDUCTING
See also Music

Conducting action research to evaluate your school library. Sykes, J. A. **027.8**

CONDUCTORS (MUSIC)
Bernstein, B. Leonard Bernstein **92**

We'll understand it better by and by **782.25**

CONDUCTORS (MUSIC)
See also Musicians; Orchestra

Cones, Harold N.

Bryant, J. H. Dangerous crossings **998**

CONEY ISLAND (NEW YORK, N.Y.) -- HISTORY -- 19TH CENTURY -- FICTION
Milford, K. The Broken Lands **Fic**

CONFECTIONERY
See also Cooking

CONFEDERATE STATES OF AMERICA
Williams, D. Bitterly divided **973.7**

CONFEDERATE STATES OF AMERICA
See also United States -- History -- 1861-1865, Civil War

CONFEDERATE STATES OF AMERICA -- ARMY
Blount, R. Robert E. Lee **973.7**

Leonard, E. D. All the daring of the soldier **973.7**

McPherson, J. M. For cause and comrades **973.7**

Confessions. Minato, K. **Fic**

Confessions of the Sullivan sisters. Standiford, N. **Fic**

CONFIDENTIAL COMMUNICATIONS
See also Secrecy

CONFLICT MANAGEMENT
Lily, H. M. School violence and conflict resolution **371.7**

CONFLICT MANAGEMENT
See also Management; Negotiation; Problem solving; Social conflict

CONFLICT MANAGEMENT -- UNITED STATES
Lily, H. M. School violence and conflict resolution **371.7**

CONFLICT OF CULTURES *See* Culture conflict

CONFLICT OF GENERATIONS
See also Child-adult relationship; Interpersonal relations; Parent-child relationship; Social conflict

Dawson, Delilah S.
Servants of the storm **Fic**
Dawson, James
This Book Is Gay **306.76**
Dawson, Mike
Troop 142 **741.5**
DAY
   See also Chronology; Time
DAY CARE CENTERS
   See also Child care; Child welfare; Children
-- Institutional care
DAY DREAMS *See* Fantasy
Day of infamy. Lord, W. **940.54**
Day of tears. Lester, J. **Fic**
DAY OF THE DEAD
   See also Holidays
Day of the predator. Scarrow, A. **Fic**
The **day** we found the universe. Bartusiak, M. **520**
Day, Paul
Bacon, T. The ultimate guitar book **787.87**
Day, Sara
Women for change **920**
Day, Trevor
Genetics **576.5**
Day, Trevor
Oceans **551.46**
Daycare and diplomas. South Vista Education Center (Richfield, M. **306.874**
DAYS
   See also Calendars
Days of blood & starlight. Taylor, L. **Fic**
Days of grace. Ashe, A. **796.342**
Daytona 24 hours. O'Malley, J. J. **796.72**
The **DC** Comics encyclopedia. Beatty, S. **741.5**
DC COMICS GROUP
Beatty, S. The DC Comics encyclopedia **741.5**
The **DC** Comics guide to coloring and lettering comics. Chiarello, M. **741.5**
The **DC** comics guide to writing comics. O'Neil, D. **741.5**
De Fombelle, Timothée, 1973-
A prince without a kingdom **843**
Vango **Fic**
De Goldi, Kate
The 10 p.m. question **Fic**
De Gramont, Nina
Every little thing in the world **Fic**
De Heer, Margreet
Science, a discovery in comics **500**
De la Bedoyere, Camilla
Balancing work and play **155.9**
No one loved gorillas more **92**
Personal hygiene and sexual health **613**
De la Cruz, Melissa
Gates of Paradise **Fic**
Lost in time **Fic**

De la Cruz, Melissa
Blue bloods **Fic**
Masquerade **Fic**
Misguided angel **Fic**
Revelations **Fic**
The Van Alen legacy **Fic**
De la Peña, Matt
The living **Fic**
Mexican whiteboy **Fic**
De la Pena, Matt
Ball don't lie **Fic**
De la Peña, M. Mexican whiteboy **Fic**
We were here **Fic**
De Laszlo, Violet S.
(ed) Jung, C. G. The basic writings of C. G. Jung **150.19**
De Lint, Charles
The blue girl **Fic**
Dingo **Fic**
De Liz, Renae
Beagle, P. S. The last unicorn **741.5**
De Roy, Tui
Jones, M. Albatross **598**
De Vos, Gail
Storytelling for young adults **027.62**
Tales, rumors, and gossip **398**
What happens next? **398.2**
De Vosjoli, Philippe
The art of keeping snakes **639.3**
The **dead**. Higson, C. **Fic**
DEAD
Roach, M. Stiff **611**
DEAD
   See also Burial; Cremation; Death; Funeral rites and ceremonies; Obituaries
DEAD -- FICTION
Bow, E. Sorrow's knot **Fic**
Chupeco, R. The Girl from the Well **Fic**
Gaiman, N. The graveyard book graphic novel Volume 2 **741.5**
Lauren, C. Sublime **Fic**
Dead ends. Lange, E. J.
Dead girl in love. Singleton, L. J. **Fic**
The **Dead** Girls Detective Agency. Cox, S. **Fic**
The **dead** girls of Hysteria Hall. Alender, K. **Fic**
The **dead** I know. Gardner, S. **Fic**
Dead is [series]
Perez, M. Dead is just a dream **Fic**
Dead is a battlefield. Perez, M. **Fic**
Dead is a killer tune. Perez, M. **Fic**
Dead is just a dream. Perez, M. **Fic**
Dead rules. Russell, R. **Fic**
The **Dead** Sea scrolls Bible. **221**
Dead zones. **639.2**
The **dead-tossed** waves. Ryan, C. **Fic**
Deadly. Chibbaro, J. **Fic**

Famous last words **Fic**

The summer after you and me **Fic**

Dolamore, Jaclyn

Magic under glass **Fic**

Dole, Mayra L.

Down to the bone **Fic**

Dolin, Eric Jay

Leviathan **639.2**

DOLL FURNITURE

See also Miniature objects; Toys

Doller, Trish

The devil you know **Fic**

Something like normal **Fic**

DOLLHOUSES

See also Miniature objects; Toys

DOLLS

See also Toys

Dolnick, Edward

The rescue artist **364.1**

Domagk, Gerhard, 1895-1964

About

Hager, T. The demon under the microscope **615**

DOMESTIC ANIMALS

Rothman, J. Farm anatomy **630**

DOMESTIC ANIMALS

See also Animals

DOMESTIC ANIMALS -- FICTION

Watkins, S. What comes after **Fic**

DOMESTIC ARCHITECTURE

See also Architecture

DOMESTIC FICTION

Golden Boys **Fic**

DOMESTIC FICTION

See also Fiction

DOMESTIC FINANCE *See* Household budgets; Personal finance

DOMESTIC PRODUCT, GROSS *See* Gross domestic product

DOMESTIC RELATIONS

Abuse And Violence Information For Teens **362.76**

King, A. S. Everybody sees the ants **Fic**

Merullo, R. The talk-funny girl **Fic**

DOMESTIC RELATIONS

See also Interpersonal relations

DOMESTIC TERRORISM

See also Terrorism

DOMESTIC VIOLENCE

Abuse And Violence Information For Teens **362.76**

Domestic violence: opposing viewpoints **362.82**

Gordon, S. M. Beyond bruises **362.7**

DOMESTIC VIOLENCE

See also Violence

DOMESTIC VIOLENCE -- FICTION

Bilen, T. What she left behind **Fic**

Domestic violence: opposing viewpoints. **362.82**

DOMESTICATION *See* Domestic animals

DOMESTICS

Chibbaro, J. Deadly **Fic**

Garrison, M. Slaves who dared **920**

Slave narratives **305.5**

DOMINICAN AMERICANS

Alvarez, J. How the Garcia girls lost their accents **Fic**

Alvarez, J. Yo! **Fic**

Padilla Peralta Undocumented **92**

DOMINICAN AMERICANS -- FICTION

Díaz, J. The brief wondrous life of Oscar Wao

DOMINICAN REPUBLIC -- FICTION

Joseph, L. Flowers in the sky **Fic**

Don't eat this book. Spurlock, M. **614.5**

Don't even think about it. Mlynowski, S. **Fic**

Don't know much about mythology. Davis, K. C. **201**

Don't let go. Gagnon, M. **Fic**

Don't Look Now. Gagnon, M. **Fic**

Don't sit on the baby. Bondy, H. **649.1**

Don't steal copyrighted stuff! Gaines, A. **808**

Don't swallow your gum! Carroll, A. E. **612**

Don't turn around. Gagnon, M. **Fic**

Don, Katherine

Real courage **813**

Donald, Aida D.

Citizen soldier **92**

DONATION OF ORGANS, TISSUES, ETC. -- FICTION

Lynch, C. Pieces **Fic**

Donelson, Kenneth L.

Nilsen, A. P. Literature for today's young adults **028.5**

Donne, John

The complete poetry and selected prose of John Donne **821**

Donnelly, Jennifer

Revolution **Fic**

These shallow graves **Fic**

Donnelly, Jennifer

A northern light **Fic**

Revolution **Fic**

Donoghue, Emma

Room **Fic**

Donovan, Brian

Hard driving: the Wendell Scott story **92**

Don't cross your eyes-- they'll get stuck that way. Carroll, A. E. **610**

Dooley, Sarah

Livvie Owen lived here **Fic**

DOOR COUNTY (WIS.)

Anderson, J. L. The vanishing season **Fic**

The **door** in the moon. Fisher, C. **Fic**

The **door** of no return. Mussi, S. **Fic**

DOORS

See also Architecture -- Details; Buildings

Downham, Jenny
Unbecoming   **Fic**
Downham, Jenny
Before I die   **Fic**
You against me   **Fic**
Downie, N. A.
Vacuum bazookas, electric rainbow jelly, and 27
other Saturday science projects   **507.8**
Downing, David
Apartheid in South Africa   **968**
Downing, Douglas
Dictionary of computer and Internet terms   **004**
Downing, Thomas E.
Dow, K. The atlas of climate change   **551.6**
Downs, Todd
The bicycling guide to complete bicycle mainte-
nance & repair   **629.28**
Downsiders. Shusterman, N.   **Fic**
Dowswell, Paul
The Auslander   **Fic**
Doyle, Marissa
Courtship and curses   **Fic**
Doyle, Roddy, 1958-
A greyhound of a girl   **Fic**
Doyle, William
The Oxford history of the French Revolution **944.04**
Dozois, Gardner R.
Best of the best: 20 years of the Year's best science
fiction   **S**
(ed) Wizards   **S**
Dr. Bird's advice for sad poets. Roskos, E.   **Fic**
Dr. Frankenstein's daughters. Weyn, S.   **Fic**
Dr. Melissa Palmer's guide to hepatitis & liver dis-
ease. Palmer, M.   **616.3**
Dr. Radway's Sarsaparilla Resolvent. Kephart,
B.   **Fic**
Drabelle, Dennis
The great American railroad war   **385**
Dracula. Stoker, B.   **Fic**
Dracula, by Bram Stoker.   **823**
Dracula, Count (Fictional character)
About
Hill, W. The rising   **Fic**
DRAFT
Military draft: opposing viewpoints   **355.2**
DRAG CULTURE
See also Counter culture
The **dragon** turn. Peacock, S.   **Fic**
Dragon's Keep. Carey, J. L.   **Fic**
Dragon's kin. McCaffrey, A.   **Fic**
Dragonflight. McCaffrey, A.   **Fic**
Dragongirl. McCaffrey, T. J.   **Fic**
Dragonriders of Pern [series]
McCaffrey, A. Dragonflight   **Fic**
McCaffrey, T. J. Dragongirl   **Fic**
DRAGONS

McCaffrey, A. Dragonflight   **Fic**
Nigg, J. Wonder beasts   **398.24**
Weis, M. Mistress of dragons   **Fic**
DRAGONS
See also Animals -- Folklore; Folklore; Mon-
sters; Mythical animals
DRAGONS -- FICTION
Birch, C. Jamrach's menagerie   **Fic**
Carey, J. L. In the time of dragon moon   **Fic**
Fforde, J. The last Dragonslayer   **Fic**
Hahn, R. A creature of moonlight   **Fic**
Hartman, R. Seraphina   **Fic**
Hartman, R. Shadow scale   **Fic**
Hill, C. J. Slayers   **Fic**
Johnston, E. K. Prairie fire   **Fic**
Johnston, E. K. The story of Owen   **Fic**
Kagawa, J. Talon   **Fic**
DRAGONS IN ART
Eggleton, B. Dragons' domain   **743**
The **dragons** of Babel. Swanwick, M.   **Fic**
Dragons' domain. Eggleton, B.   **743**
Dragonwood. Stewart, A.   **Fic**
DRAINAGE
See also Agricultural engineering; Civil en-
gineering; Hydraulic engineering; Municipal
engineering; Reclamation of land; Sanitary
engineering
The Drake chronicles [series]
Harvey, A. Hearts at stake   **Fic**
Drake, Jane
Yes you can!   **361.2**
DRAMA
Critical survey of drama   **809**
Highet, G. The classical tradition   **809**
Patterson, M. The Oxford dictionary of plays **809**
DRAMA
See also Literature
DRAMA -- COLLECTIONS
24 favorite one-act plays   **808.82**
Actor's choice   **808.82**
Allen, L. Comedy scenes for student actors **808.82**
The Book of monologues for aspiring actors **808.82**
Cassady, M. The book of scenes for aspiring ac-
tors   **808.82**
Fierce & true   **812**
Great monologues for young actors   **808.82**
International plays for young audiences   **808.82**
Multicultural scenes for young actors   **808.82**
The Scenebook for actors   **808.82**
Scenes from classic plays, 468 B.C. to 1970
A.D.   **808.82**
Stevens, C. Sensational scenes for teens   **808.82**
The Ultimate audition book   **808.82**
DRAMA -- DICTIONARIES
Critical survey of drama   **809**
Griffiths, T. R. The Ivan R. Dee guide to plays and

DRESS *See* Clothing and dress

Dress your best. Kelly, C.   **391**

DRESSAGE *See* Horsemanship

Dressed. Landis, D. N.   **791.43**

The **dressmaker** of Khair Khana. Lemmon, G. T.   **92**

DRESSMAKERS

Fleischner, J. Mrs. Lincoln and Mrs. Keckley   **92**

Lemmon, G. T. The dressmaker of Khair Khana **92**

DRESSMAKING

Lemmon, G. T. The dressmaker of Khair Khana **92**

Smith, A. Sew step by step   **646.2**

DRESSMAKING

    See also Clothing and dress; Clothing industry

DREW, NANCY (FICTITIOUS CHARACTER)

Rehak, M. Girl sleuth   **813**

Drexler, K. Eric

Radical abundance   **303.48**

Dreyer, ZoAnn

Living with cancer   **362.1**

Dreyfus, Alfred, 1859-1935

    About

Tuchman, B. W. The proud tower   **909.82**

Drez, Ronald J.

Twenty-five yards of war   **940.53**

DRIED FOODS

    See also Food

Drifting toward love. Wright, K.   **306.76**

DRINKING AGE

    See also Age; Teenagers -- Alcohol use; Youth -- Alcohol use

DRINKING AND TEENAGERS *See* Teenagers -- Alcohol use

Drinking coffee elsewhere. Packer, Z.   **S**

DRINKING OF ALCOHOLIC BEVERAGES

Alcohol information for teens   **613.81**

DRINKING PROBLEM *See* Alcoholism; Drinking of alcoholic beverages

DRINKING WATER

Fagan, B. Elixir   **553.7**

Leahy, S. Your Water Footprint   **333.91**

DRINKING WATER

    See also Water; Water supply

DRINKS *See* Alcoholic beverages; Beverages; Liquors

Driskell, David C., 1931-

    About

McGee, J. L. David C. Driskell   **92**

Driver, Stephanie Schwartz

Understanding the Declaration of Independence   **973.3**

DRIVERS, AUTOMOBILE *See* Automobile drivers

DRIVING UNDER THE INFLUENCE OF ALCOHOL *See* Drunk driving

Drobna, Zoroslava

Wagner, E. Medieval costume, armour, and weapons   **399**

Drooker, Eric

Blood song   **741.5**

DROPOUTS

Stewart, G. B. Teenage dropouts   **373.12**

DROPOUTS

    See also Students; Youth

DROUGHTS

    See also Meteorology

The **drowned** cities. Bacigalupi, P.   **Fic**

Drowned City. Brown, D.   **363.34**

DRUG ABUSE

Adamec, C. A. Amphetamines and methamphetamine   **362.29**

Addiction: opposing viewpoints   **362.29**

Bjornlund, L. D. How dangerous are performance-enhancing drugs?   **362.29**

Bjornlund, L. Oxycodone   **615**

Burgess, M. Smack   **Fic**

Chastain, Z. Cocaine   **362.2**

Currie-McGhee, L. K. Drug addiction   **362.29**

Drug abuse sourcebook   **362.29**

Drug information for teens   **613.8**

Keegan, K. Chasing the high   **92**

Klosterman, L. The facts about drug dependence to treatment   **362.29**

Koertge, R. Stoner & Spaz   **Fic**

Kuhar, M. J. Drugs of abuse   **362.29**

Merino, N. Gateway drugs: opposing viewpoints   **362.29**

Mooney, C. Thinking critically   **362.29**

Nelson, S. Hallucinogens   **362.29**

Newton, D. E. Substance abuse   **362.29**

Parks, P. J. Drug legalization   **363.45**

Parks, P. J. Methamphetamine   **362.29**

Sanna, E. J. Marijuana   **362.29**

Sherman, J. Drug trafficking   **363.45**

Substance abuse, addiction, and treatment **362.29**

Teen drug abuse: opposing viewpoints   **362.29**

Walker, I. Addiction in America   **362.29**

Walker, I. Natural and everyday drugs   **362.29**

Walker, I. Painkillers   **362.29**

Walker, I. Sedatives and hypnotics   **362.29**

The war on drugs   **363.45**

DRUG ABUSE

    See also Social problems; Substance abuse

DRUG ABUSE -- ENCYCLOPEDIAS

Encyclopedia of drugs, alcohol & addictive behavior   **362.29**

DRUG ABUSE -- FICTION

Arcos, C. Out of reach   **Fic**

Brothers, M. Supergirl mixtapes   **Fic**

Zailckas, K. Mother, mother   **Fic**

Dynamic youth services through outcome-based planning and evaluation. Dresang, E. T. **025.1**

DYNAMICS

See also Mathematics; Mechanics

DYNAMITE

See also Explosives

DYSFUNCTIONAL FAMILIES

Brahmachari, S. Jasmine Skies **Fic**

Toten, T. The Unlikely Hero of Room 13B **Fic**

DYSFUNCTIONAL FAMILIES -- FICTION

Carter, C. Me, him, them, and it **Fic**

Elston, A. The rules for disappearing **Fic**

Griffin, N. The whole stupid way we are **Fic**

Herbach, G. Nothing special **Fic**

Konigsberg, B. The porcupine of truth **Fic**

McGarry, K. Dare You to **Fic**

Zailckas, K. Mother, mother **Fic**

DYSLEXIA

Schultz, P. My dyslexia **92**

DYSLEXIA -- FICTION

Chambers, A. Dying to know you **Fic**

Dyson, Marianne J.

Space and astronomy **520**

Dyson, Michael Eric

Come hell or high water **976.3**

Holler if you hear me: searching for Tupac Shakur **92**

DYSTOPIAN FICTION

Aguirre, A. Enclave **Fic**

Aguirre, A. Horde **Fic**

Allegiant **Fic**

Almond, D. The true tale of the monster Billy Dean **Fic**

Barry, M. Lexicon **Fic**

Bell, A. The reapers are the angels **Fic**

Brown, P. Golden Son **Fic**

Brown, P. Red Rising **Fic**

Bruchac, J. Killer of enemies **Fic**

Caine, R. Ink and bone **Fic**

Charbonneau, J. Graduation day **Fic**

Crossan, S. Breathe **Fic**

DeStefano, L. Fever **Fic**

Dos Santos, S. The culling **Fic**

Falls, K. Inhuman **Fic**

Gagnon, M. Don't let go **Fic**

Gagnon, M. Don't turn around **Fic**

Garner, E. Contaminated **Fic**

Garner, E. Mercy mode **Fic**

Hautman, P. The Klaatu terminus **Fic**

Healey, K. When we wake **Fic**

Isbell, T. The Prey **Fic**

Kinch, M. The fires of New SUN **Fic**

Kinch, M. The rebels of New SUN **Fic**

Kornher-Stace, N. Archivist wasp **Fic**

Lloyd-Jones, E. Illusive **Fic**

London, A. Guardian **Fic**

Lowry, L. Son **Fic**

Lu, M. Champion **Fic**

Lu, M. Prodigy **Fic**

MacHale, D. J. SYLO **Fic**

Maggot moon **Fic**

McCafferty, M. Thumped **Fic**

Mullin, M. Sunrise **Fic**

Myers, W. D. On a clear day **Fic**

Ness, P. More than this **Fic**

Ness, P. The knife of never letting go **Fic**

Okorafor, N. Who fears death **Fic**

Pearson, M. E. Fox forever **Fic**

Shards and Ashes **S**

Simmons, K. Three **Fic**

Terry, T. Fractured **Fic**

Unsworth, T. The one safe place **Fic**

Weaver, W. The survivors **Fic**

Williamson, J. Captives **Fic**

Zhang, K. What's left of me **Fic**

DYSTOPIAN FICTION

See also Fantasy fiction; Science fiction

DYSTOPIAN GRAPHIC NOVELS

Uglies **741.5**

DYSTOPIAS

Thomas, L. Quarantine 3: The Burnouts **Fic**

Woolston, B. Black helicopters **Fic**

DYSTOPIAS

See also Political science

E

E. Bodanis, D. **530.1**

E-MAIL

See also Data transmission systems; Telecommunication

E-MAIL REFERENCE SERVICES (LIBRARIES) See Electronic reference services (Libraries)

Eagle blue. D'Orso, M. **796.323**

Eagle, Adam Fortunate

Pipestone **92**

Eagle, MK

Answering teens' tough questions **027.62**

EAGLES

See also Birds; Birds of prey

EAR

Ear, nose, and throat **617.5**

Ear, nose, and throat. **617.5**

The **Ear,** the Eye, and the Arm. Farmer, N. **Fic**

Earhart, Amelia, 1897-1937

About

Brown, J. K. Amelia Earhart **629.130**

Winters, K. C. Amelia Earhart **92**

Earle, Liz

Skin care secrets **646.7**

Earls, Irene

Young musicians in world history **780.92**

EMERGENCIES *See* Accidents; Disasters; First aid

EMERGENCY MEDICINE

   See also Medicine

EMERGENCY PREPAREDNESS *See* Disaster relief

EMERGENCY RELIEF *See* Disaster relief

EMERGENCY SURVIVAL *See* Survival skills

Emerson, Ralph Waldo

   Collected poems & translations   **811**

   The portable Emerson   **818**

Emerson, Ralph Waldo, 1803-1882

         About

   Caravantes, P. Self-reliance: the story of Ralph Waldo Emerson   **92**

   A Historical guide to Ralph Waldo Emerson   **814**

   Ironside, F. Bloom's how to write about Ralph Waldo Emerson   **818**

   Wayne, T. K. Critical companion to Ralph Waldo Emerson   **818**

EMIGRANTS *See* Immigrants

EMIGRATION *See* Immigration and emigration

EMIGRATION AND IMMIGRATION

   Crossing into America   **810**

   Na, A. A step from heaven   **Fic**

EMIGRATION AND IMMIGRATION

   Andreu, M. E. The secret side of empty   **Fic**

EMIGRATION AND IMMIGRATION -- FICTION

   Campoy, F. I. Yes! we are Latinos   **S**

Emilie & the hollow world. Wells, M.   **Fic**

Emily Bronte's Wuthering Heights.   **823**

Emily Bronte's Wuthering Heights.   **823**

Emily Post prom and party etiquette. Senning, C. P.   **395**

Emily Post's Etiquette. Post, P.   **395**

EMINENT DOMAIN

   See also Constitutional law; Land use; Property

Eminent lives [series]

   Armstrong, K. Muhammad   **297**

   Bryson, B. Shakespeare   **822.3**

   Gottlieb, R. A. George Balanchine: the ballet maker   **92**

   Johnson, P. George Washington: the Founding Father   **92**

   Morris, E. Beethoven: the universal composer   **92**

Emmeluth, Donald

   Botulism   **616.9**

EMMY AWARDS

   See also Television broadcasting

Emond, Stephen

   Bright lights, dark nights   **Fic**

Emond, Stephen

   Happyface   **Fic**

Emotional intelligence. Goleman, D.   **152.4**

EMOTIONAL PROBLEMS

   Fusco, K. N. Tending to Grace   **Fic**

   Koertge, R. Margaux with an X   **Fic**

   McCormick, P. Cut   **Fic**

EMOTIONAL PROBLEMS -- FICTION

   Blagden, S. Dear Life, You Suck   **Fic**

   Carter, C. Me, him, them, and it   **Fic**

   Desir, C. Bleed like me   **Fic**

   Exit, pursued by a bear   **Fic**

   Gardner, S. The dead I know   **Fic**

   Halpin, B. A really awesome mess   **Fic**

   Hassan, M. Crash and Burn   **Fic**

   Hopkins, E. Smoke   **Fic**

   King, A. S. Reality Boy   **Fic**

   Luedeke, L. Smashed   **Fic**

   Mesrobian, C. Sex and violence   **Fic**

   Niven, J. All the bright places   **Fic**

   Price, N. Zoe letting go   **Fic**

   Schmidt, G. D. Orbiting Jupiter   **Fic**

   Walton, K. M. Empty   **Fic**

   Willey, M. Beetle Boy   **Fic**

   Wolitzer, M. Belzhar   **Fic**

   Zhang, A. Falling into place   **Fic**

EMOTIONAL PROBLEMS OF TEENAGERS

   Desir, C. Bleed like me   **Fic**

   Toten, T. The Unlikely Hero of Room 13B   **Fic**

EMOTIONAL STRESS *See* Stress (Psychology)

EMOTIONALLY DISTURBED CHILDREN

   Goleman, D. Emotional intelligence   **152.4**

EMOTIONALLY DISTURBED CHILDREN

   See also Exceptional children; Mentally ill

EMOTIONALLY DISTURBED CHILDREN -- FICTION

   Halpin, B. A really awesome mess   **Fic**

EMOTIONS

   Bender, A. The particular sadness of lemon cake   **Fic**

   Canfield, J. Chicken soup for the teenage soul [I-IV]   **158**

   Chicken soup for the teenage soul's the real deal **158**

   Goleman, D. Emotional intelligence   **152.4**

   Goleman, D. Social intelligence   **158**

EMOTIONS

   See also Psychology; Psychophysiology

EMOTIONS -- FICTION

   Niven, J. All the bright places   **Fic**

   Sutton, K. Some quiet place   **Fic**

EMOTIONS IN CHILDREN

   See also Child psychology; Emotions

EMPATHY

   See also Attitude (Psychology); Emotions; Social psychology

The emperor of any place. Wynne-Jones, T.

EMPERORS

   Bulfinch, T. Bulfinch's mythology   **398.2**

   Dray, S. Lily of the Nile   **Fic**

Encyclopedia of American Indian costume. Paterek, J. **391**

Encyclopedia of American Indian literature. **810**

Encyclopedia of American Indian wars, 1492-1890. Keenan, J. **970.004**

Encyclopedia of American literature. Facts on File, I. **810**

Encyclopedia of American poetry, the twentieth century. **811**

Encyclopedia of American religious history. Queen, E. L. **200.9**

Encyclopedia of ancient Egypt. Bunson, M. R. **932**

Encyclopedia of ancient Rome. Bunson, M. **937**

The encyclopedia of angels. Guiley, R. E. **200**

Encyclopedia of animal behavior. **591.5**

The encyclopedia of animals. **590**

Encyclopedia of aquarium & pond fish. Alderton, D. **639.34**

Encyclopedia of Asian-American literature. Oh, S. **810**

The encyclopedia of autism spectrum disorders. Turkington, C. **616.85**

Encyclopedia of biodiversity. Rice, S. A. **578.7**

Encyclopedia of body adornment. DeMello, M. **391**

Encyclopedia of British writers, 1800 to the present. **820**

Encyclopedia of Buddhism. Irons, E. A. **294.3**

Encyclopedia of careers and vocational guidance. J.G. Ferguson Publishing Company **331.7**

Encyclopedia of Catholicism. Flinn, F. K. **282**

Encyclopedia of chemistry. Rittner, D. **540**

Encyclopedia of Christianity. **230**

Encyclopedia of Christmas and New Year's celebrations. Gulevich, T. **394.26**

Encyclopedia of conflicts since World War II. **909.82**

The encyclopedia of crime scene investigation. Newton, M. **363.2**

Encyclopedia of drugs, alcohol & addictive behavior. **362.29**

The encyclopedia of early earth. Greenberg, I. **741.5**

The encyclopedia of Earth. Allaby, M. **910**

Encyclopedia of Earth and space science. **550**

Encyclopedia of earthquakes and volcanoes. Gates, A. E. **551.2**

Encyclopedia of electronic components. Platt, C. **621.381**

Encyclopedia of environmental issues. **363.7**

The encyclopedia of genetic disorders and birth defects. Wynbrandt, J. **616**

The encyclopedia of ghosts and spirits. Guiley, R. E. **133.1**

Encyclopedia of global resources. **333.7**

Encyclopedia of Greek and Roman mythology. Roman, L. **292**

The encyclopedia of hepatitis and other liver diseases. Chow, C. **616.3**

Encyclopedia of Hinduism. Jones, C. **294.5**

Encyclopedia of Hispanic-American literature. Ramirez, L. E. **810**

The encyclopedia of HIV and AIDS. Stratton, S. E. **362.196**

Encyclopedia of holidays and celebrations. **394.26**

Encyclopedia of human body systems. **612**

Encyclopedia of human evolution and prehistory. **599.93**

Encyclopedia of hurricanes, typhoons, and cyclones. Longshore, D. **551.55**

The encyclopedia of infectious diseases. Ashby, B. **616.9**

Encyclopedia of Islam. Campo, J. E. **297**

Encyclopedia of Islam in the United States. **297**

Encyclopedia of Judaism. Karesh, S. E. **296**

Encyclopedia of Latin America. **980**

Encyclopedia of Latin American history and culture. **980**

Encyclopedia of leadership. **658.4**

Encyclopedia of marine science. Nichols, C. R. **551.46**

Encyclopedia of mathematics. Tanton, J. S. **510**

Encyclopedia of medieval literature. Ruud, J. **809**

The encyclopedia of Middle East wars. **355**

Encyclopedia of Native American wars and warfare. **970.004**

Encyclopedia of native tribes of North America. Johnson, M. **970.004**

Encyclopedia of physical science. Gothard, L. Q. **500.2**

Encyclopedia of physics. Rosen, J. **530**

Encyclopedia of plague and pestilence. **614.4**

Encyclopedia of pollution. Gates, A. E. **363.7**

Encyclopedia of rap and hip-hop culture. Bynoe, Y. **782.42**

Encyclopedia of religion in America. **200.9**

Encyclopedia of religious rites, rituals, and festivals. **200**

Encyclopedia of revolutionary America. Gilje, P. A. **973.3**

The encyclopedia of schizophrenia and other psychotic disorders. Noll, R. **616.89**

Encyclopedia of science, technology, and ethics. **503**

The encyclopedia of sharks. Parker, S. **597**

The encyclopedia of skin and skin disorders. Turkington, C. **616.5**

Encyclopedia of society and culture in the medieval world. **909.07**

Encyclopedia of space and astronomy. Angelo, J. A. **520**

Encyclopedia of sports in America. **796**

The encyclopedia of survival techniques. Stilwell, A. **613.6**

Encyclopedia of terrorism. **363.32**

Encyclopedia of the age of the industrial revolution,

See also Game and game birds; Hunting

FALCONS

Tennant, A. On the wing   598

FALCONS -- FICTION

Whitman, E. Wildwing   Fic

Falkner, Brian

Brain Jack   Fic

The project   Fic

Fall for anything. Summers, C.   Fic

The **fall** of Rome. Southgate, M.   Fic

FALLACIES *See* Errors; Logic

Fallen angels. Myers, W. D.   Fic

Fallen Grace. Hooper, M.   Fic

The **fallen** man. Hillerman, T.   Fic

Falling. Wilhelm, D.   Fic

Falling hard.   811

Falling into place. Zhang, A.   Fic

FALLING STARS *See* Meteors

Falling to Earth. Worden, A.   92

Fallon, Michael

How to analyze the works of Andy Warhol   700

How to analyze the works of Georgia O'Keeffe   **759.13**

Fallon, Robert Thomas

A theatergoer's guide to Shakespeare   **822.3**

Fallout. Bond, G.   Fic

Falls, Kat

Inhuman   Fic

Falola, Toyin

Key events in African history   960

FALSE ACCUSATION

Faryon, C. J. Guilty of being weird   **364.152**

Lee, H. To kill a mockingbird   Fic

Richmond, M. No one you know   Fic

FALSE ACCUSATION -- FICTION

Grace, A. In too deep   Fic

Vango   Fic

False memory. Krokos, D.   Fic

FALSE MEMORY SYNDROME

See also Memory

FAME

Celebrity culture: opposing viewpoints   **306.4**

FAME -- FICTION

Barnes, J. Losers in space   Fic

Rudnick, P. Gorgeous   Fic

Shukert, R. Love me   Fic

Shukert, R. Starstruck   Fic

Familiar flowers of North America: eastern region.   **582.13**

Familiar flowers of North America: western region.   **582.13**

Familiar trees of North America: eastern region.   **582.16**

Familiar trees of North America: western region.   **582.16**

FAMILIES

Hidier, T. D. Bombay Blues   Fic

Schwartz, J. Oddly normal   **306.76**

Yee, L. The kidney hypothetical, or, how to ruin your life in seven days   Fic

FAMILIES -- ENGLAND

Burgess, M. The hit   Fic

Easton, T. S. Boys Don't Knit   Fic

Hardinge, F. Cuckoo Song   Fic

Pitcher, A. Ketchup clouds   Fic

FAMILIES -- FICTION

Allegiant   Fic

Amato, M. Get happy   Fic

Apelqvist, E. LGBTQ families   **306.87**

Block, F. L. Love in the time of global warming   Fic

Blumenthal, D. Mafia girl   Fic

Brown, J. R. No place to fall   Fic

Caine, R. Prince of Shadows   Fic

Casanova, M. Frozen   Fic

Davis, T. S. Happy families   Fic

Demetrios, H. Something real   Fic

Dessen, S. Saint Anything   Fic

FitzGerald, H. Deviant   Fic

Fowley-Doyle, M. The accident season   Fic

Frank, E. R. Dime   Fic

Friesner, E. Spirit's princess   Fic

Hemphill, S. Sisters of glass   Fic

Kephart, B. One thing stolen   Fic

Kim, D. K. Same difference   **741.5**

King, A. S. Everybody sees the ants   Fic

Knowles, J. See you at Harry's   Fic

LaCour, N. Everything leads to you   Fic

Littman, S. D. Backlash   Fic

Lockhart, E. We were liars   Fic

Matson, M. Second chance summer   Fic

Mazer, H. Somebody, please tell me who I am   Fic

Rosenfield, K. Inland   Fic

Roth, V. Insurgent   Fic

Sáenz, B. A. Aristotle and Dante discover the secrets of the universe   Fic

Tarttelin, A. Golden boy   Fic

Taub, M. Still star-crossed   Fic

Unbecoming   Fic

Zambrano, M. A. Loteria   Fic

FAMILIES -- INDIA

Brahmachari, S. Jasmine Skies   Fic

FAMILIES -- NEW JERSEY -- FICTION

Blume, J. Forever   Fic

FAMILIES -- PENNSYLVANIA

Alender, K. The dead girls of Hysteria Hall   Fic

FAMILIES -- TEXAS

The memory of light   Fic

FAMILIES -- UNITED STATES

Nutt, A. E. Becoming Nicole   **306.768**

FAMILIES OF DRUG ADDICTS -- FICTION

Arcos, C. Out of reach   Fic

FAMILY

FAMILY LIFE -- ILLINOIS -- CHICAGO -- FICTION

Martinez, C. G. Pig Park   **Fic**

Pauley, K. Cat Girl's day off   **Fic**

FAMILY LIFE -- ILLINOIS -- FICTION

Stone, T. I. Time between us   **Fic**

FAMILY LIFE -- INDIA -- FICTION

Whelan, G. All my noble dreams and then what happens   **Fic**

FAMILY LIFE -- IOWA -- FICTION

Kraus, D. Scowler   **Fic**

Smith, A. Grasshopper jungle   **Fic**

FAMILY LIFE -- ITALY -- FICTION

Beyer, K. The demon catchers of Milan   **Fic**

FAMILY LIFE -- JAPAN -- FICTION

Lowitz, L. Jet Black and the ninja wind   **Fic**

FAMILY LIFE -- KANSAS -- FICTION

Schantz, S. E. Fig   **Fic**

FAMILY LIFE -- LOUISIANA -- FICTION

Elston, A. The rules for disappearing   **Fic**

FAMILY LIFE -- MARYLAND -- FICTION

Moore, K. Neverwas   **Fic**

FAMILY LIFE -- MASSACHUSETTS -- FICTION

Thompson, H. The language inside   **Fic**

FAMILY LIFE -- MINNESOTA -- FICTION

Hattemer, K. The vigilante poets of Selwyn Academy   **Fic**

Rubens, M. Sons of the 613   **Fic**

FAMILY LIFE -- NEW JERSEY -- FICTION

Doktorski, J. S. The summer after you and me   **Fic**

Scott, K. This is so not happening   **Fic**

Zarr, S. Roomies   **Fic**

FAMILY LIFE -- NEW YORK (STATE) -- BROOKLYN -- FICTION

Reynolds, J. Boy in the black suit   **Fic**

When I was the greatest   **Fic**

FAMILY LIFE -- NEW YORK (STATE) -- FICTION

Castle, J. You look different in real life   **Fic**

Johnson, J. J. The theory of everything   **Fic**

Moore, C. The stalker chronicles   **Fic**

FAMILY LIFE -- NEW YORK (STATE) -- HARLEM -- FICTION

Manzano, S. The revolution of Evelyn Serrano   **Fic**

FAMILY LIFE -- NEW YORK (STATE) -- NEW YORK -- FICTION

Zeitlin, M. Freshman year & other unnatural disasters   **Fic**

Zevin, G. Because it is my blood   **Fic**

FAMILY LIFE -- PENNSYLVANIA -- FICTION

Andrews, J. Me & Earl & the dying girl   **Fic**

Matson, M. Second chance summer   **Fic**

FAMILY LIFE -- PENNSYLVANIA -- HERSHEY -- FICTION

Finneyfrock, K. The sweet revenge of Celia

Door   **Fic**

FAMILY LIFE -- RHODE ISLAND -- FICTION

Gray, C. Spellcaster   **Fic**

Gray, C. Steadfast   **Fic**

FAMILY LIFE -- TEXAS -- FICTION

The memory of light   **Fic**

FAMILY LIFE -- VIRGINIA -- FICTION

Lyne, J. H. Catch rider   **Fic**

FAMILY LIFE -- WASHINGTON (STATE) -- FICTION

Flores-Scott, P. Jumped in   **Fic**

Scott, M. Live through this   **Fic**

FAMILY LIFE -- WASHINGTON (STATE) -- SEATTLE -- FICTION

Trueman, T. Life happens next   **Fic**

FAMILY MEDICINE

    See also Medicine

FAMILY PLANNING *See* Birth control

FAMILY PLANNING -- HISTORY

Reproductive rights   **363.9**

FAMILY PLANNING ADVOCATES

Bausum, A. Denied, detained, deported   **325**

Notable women in the life sciences   **570.9**

FAMILY PROBLEMS

McCormick, P. Cut   **Fic**

Peters, J. A. Luna   **Fic**

Woodson, J. Miracle's boys   **Fic**

FAMILY PROBLEMS -- FICTION

Anderson, L. H. The impossible knife of memory   **Fic**

Armistead, C. Being Henry David   **Fic**

Beaufrand, M. J. The rise and fall of the Gallivanters   **Fic**

Bedford, M. Never ending   **Fic**

Bliss, B. No parking at the end times   **Fic**

Blythe, C. Revenge of a not-so-pretty girl   **Fic**

Brothers, M. Supergirl mixtapes   **Fic**

Brown, J. R. No place to fall   **Fic**

Burgis, S. Stolen magic   **Fic**

Carter, C. Me, him, them, and it   **Fic**

Castan, M. Fighting for Dontae   **Fic**

Chen, J. Return to me   **Fic**

Cremer, A. Invisibility   **Fic**

Crossan, S. One   **Fic**

Dessen, S. Saint Anything   **Fic**

Doller, T. Something like normal   **Fic**

Griffin, N. The whole stupid way we are   **Fic**

Hopkins, E. Rumble   **Fic**

Jaden, D. Never enough   **Fic**

Juby, S. The Truth Commission   **Fic**

Kehoe, S. W. The sound of letting go   **Fic**

Keplinger, K. A midsummer's nightmare   **Fic**

King, A. S. Ask the passengers   **Fic**

King, A. S. Reality Boy   **Fic**

Kirby, J. Golden   **Fic**

Knowles, J. See you at Harry's   **Fic**

Saint-Exupery, A. d. The little prince   **Fic**
Weis, M. Guardians of the lost   **Fic**
White, T. H. The once and future king   **Fic**
Wizards   **S**
Yolen, J. Briar Rose   **Fic**
Fantaskey, Beth
Buzz kill   **Fic**
Fantaskey, Beth
Jessica's guide to dating on the dark side   **Fic**
FANTASTIC FICTION *See* Fantasy fiction
FANTASTIC FOUR (FICTIONAL CHARACTERS)
Lee, S. Stan Lee's How to draw comics   **741.5**
Fantastic voyage. Asimov, I.   **Fic**
FANTASY
Fichtelberg, S. Encountering enchantment   **016**
Nix, G. Abhorsen   **Fic**
Nix, G. Lirael, daughter of the Clayr   **Fic**
Speaker-Yuan, M. Philip Pullman   **92**
Turner, M. W. The Queen of Attolia   **Fic**
FANTASY
    See also Dreams; Imagination
FANTASY FICTION
    See also Fiction
FANTASY FICTION -- AUTHORSHIP
Jones, D. W. Reflections   **823**
FANTASY FICTION -- BIBLIOGRAPHY
Fichtelberg, S. Encountering enchantment   **016**
Herald, D. T. Fluent in fantasy   **016**
Hollands, N. Read on . . . fantasy fiction   **016**
FANTASY FICTION -- HISTORY AND CRITICISM
Shippey, T. A. J.R.R. Tolkien   **828**
FANTASY FICTION
Brennan, S. R. Unspoken   **Fic**
Cameron, S. The dark unwinding   **Fic**
Carson, R. The crown of embers   **Fic**
Duane, D. So you want to be a wizard   **Fic**
Durst, S. B. Vessel   **Fic**
Fforde, J. The song of the Quarkbeast   **Fic**
Lanagan, M. The brides of Rollrock Island   **Fic**
McQuein, J. L. Arclight   **Fic**
Rutkoski, M. The winner's crime   **Fic**
Taylor, L. Days of blood & starlight   **Fic**
Wrede, P. C. The Far West   **Fic**
Zettel, S. Golden girl   **Fic**
Zinn, B. Poison   **Fic**
FANTASY FILMS
    See also Motion pictures
FANTASY GAMES
Barrowcliffe, M. The elfish gene   **92**
FANTASY GAMES
    See also Games; Role playing
FANTASY GAMES -- FICTION
Brezenoff, S. Guy in real life   **Fic**
FANTASY GRAPHIC NOVELS

Alanguilan, G. Elmer   **741.5**
Black, H. The Good Neighbors; book one: Kin   **741.5**
Clare, C. Clockwork angel   **Fic**
Crilley, M. Brody's ghost: book 1   **741.5**
Dunning, J. H. Salem Brownstone   **741.5**
Excalibur   **741.5**
Flight v2   **741.5**
Flight v3   **741.5**
Flight: Volume Four   **741.5**
Hartzell, A. Fox bunny funny   **741.5**
Henson, J. Jim Henson's tale of sand   **741.5**
Igarashi, D. Children of the sea, vol. 1   **741.5**
Inzana, R. Ichiro   **741.5**
Love, J. Bayou, volume one   **741.5**
Mashima, H. Fairy tail vol. 1   **741.5**
McCreery, C. Kill Shakespeare, vol. 1   **741.5**
Medley, L. Castle waiting   **741.5**
The Nameless City   **741.5**
Pope, P. Battling Boy   **741.5**
Siddell, T. Gunnerkrigg Court: orientation   **741.5**
Stevenson, N. Nimona   **741.5**
Tamaki, J. SuperMutant Magic Academy   **741.5**
Toboso, Y. Black butler, vol. 1   **741.5**
Wilson, G. W. Cairo   **741.5**
Yang, G. The eternal smile   **741.5**
Yolen, J. Foiled   **741.5**
FANTASY GRAPHIC NOVELS
    See also Graphic novels
FANTASY POETRY
    See also Poetry
FANTASY ROLE PLAYING GAMES *See* Fantasy games
FANTASY WRITERS
Anelli, M. Harry, a history   **823**
Bankston, J. Christopher Paolini   **92**
Brown, J. K. Ursula K. Le Guin   **92**
Fonstad, K. W. The atlas of Middle-earth   **823**
The girl who was on fire   **813**
Graphic Classics volume four: H. P. Lovecraft   **741.5**
J.R.R. Tolkien   **823**
J.R.R. Tolkien's The lord of the rings   **813**
Kirk, C. A. J.K. Rowling: a biography   **823**
Shippey, T. A. J.R.R. Tolkien   **828**
Speaker-Yuan, M. Philip Pullman   **92**
Tyson, E. S. Orson Scott Card   **813**
FANZINES
Rookie Yearbook Two   **305.23**
FAQ: teen life [series]
Broyles, J. Frequently asked questions about hate crimes   **364.15**
Worth, R. Frequently asked questions about teen fatherhood   **306.8**
Far far away. McNeal, T.   **Fic**
Far from home. Wendel, T.   **796.357**
Far from you. Sharpe, T.   **Fic**

Far from you. Schroeder, L. **Fic**

The **Far** West. Wrede, P. C. **Fic**

Farabee, Charles R.
National park ranger **363.6**

Faraday, Michael, 1791-1867
About
Guillen, M. Five equations that changed the world **530.1**
Malone, J. W. It doesn't take a rocket scientist **920**

Farah, Caesar E.
Islam: beliefs and observances **297**

Farewell to Manzanar. Houston, J. W. **940.53**

Fargnoli, A. Nicholas
Critical companion to James Joyce **823**
Critical companion to William Faulkner **813**

Farinango, Maria Virginia
The Queen of Water **Fic**

Farish, Terry
The good braider **Fic**

Farizan, Sara
If you could be mine **Fic**
Tell me again how a crush should feel **Fic**

Farm anatomy. Rothman, J. **630**

FARM LIFE
Rothman, J. **630**

FARM LIFE
See also Country life; Farmers

FARM LIFE -- FICTION
Bobet, L. An inheritance of ashes **Fic**

FARM LIFE -- GEORGIA -- FICTION
Coker, R. Chasing Jupiter **Fic**

FARM LIFE -- GRAPHIC NOVELS
Lemire, J. Essex County, Vol. 1: Tales from the Farm **741.5**

FARM LIFE -- IOWA -- FICTION
Kraus, D. Scowler **Fic**

FARM LIFE -- KANSAS -- FICTION
Schantz, S. E. Fig **Fic**

FARM LIFE -- MISCELLANEA
Rothman, J. Farm anatomy **630**

FARM LIFE -- NEBRASKA -- FICTION
Reed, A. Over you **Fic**

FARM LIFE -- OHIO -- FICTION
Wonders of the invisible world **Fic**

FARM LIFE -- PICTORIAL WORKS
Rothman, J. Farm anatomy **630**

FARM LIFE -- WISCONSIN -- FICTION
Bick, I. J. The Sin eater's confession **Fic**
Sutton, K. Some quiet place **Fic**

FARM MANAGEMENT
See also Farms; Management

FARM PRODUCE
Rothman, J. Farm anatomy **630**

FARM PRODUCE
See also Food; Raw materials

FARM PRODUCE -- MARKETING

See also Marketing; Prices

FARM TENANCY
See also Farms; Land tenure

Farmer, Lesley S. Johnson
Neal-Schuman technology management handbook for school library media centers **025.1**
Teen girls and technology **004**

Farmer, Nancy
The Ear, the Eye, and the Arm **Fic**
The house of the scorpion **Fic**
The lord of Opium **Fic**

Farmer, Paul, 1959-
About
Kidder, T. Mountains beyond mountains **92**

FARMERS
Berry, B. The ties that bind **920**
Lawrence, S. River house **92**
Nelson, M. The freedom business **811**
Philbrick, N. The Mayflower and the Pilgrims' New World **973.2**
Woodward, G. S. Pocahontas **92**

FARMERS
See also Agriculture

FARMERS -- FICTION
Peterfreund, D. For darkness shows the stars **Fic**

FARMING *See* Agriculture

FARMING, ORGANIC *See* Organic farming

FARMS -- FICTION
Teran, A. Ana of California **Fic**

Farnsworth, Philo T., 1906-1971
About
Horvitz, L. A. Eureka!: scientific breakthroughs that changed the world **509**

Farrand, John
Bull, J. L. The National Audubon Society field guide to North American birds, Eastern region **598**
Udvardy, M. D. F. National Audubon Society field guide to North American birds, Western region **598**

Farrar, Amy
ADHD **616.85**

Farrar, Christi Showman
(ed) Sears List of Subject Headings **025.43**

Farrell, Courtney
Green jobs **331.7**
The Gulf of Mexico oil spill **363.7**
Mental disorders **362.1**

Farrell, Jeanette
Invisible enemies **614.4**

Farrell, Mary Cronk
Pure grit **940.54**

Farrell, Susan Elizabeth
Critical companion to Kurt Vonnegut **813**
Critical companion to Tim O'Brien **813**

Farrey, Brian
With or without you **Fic**

FATHER-DAUGHTER RELATIONSHIP -- FICTION

Alpine, R. Canary	**Fic**
Amato, M. Get happy	**Fic**
Anderson, L. H. The impossible knife of memory	**Fic**
Bacigalupi, P. The doubt factory	**Fic**
Blumenthal, D. Mafia girl	**Fic**
Caletti, D. The last forever	**Fic**
Dessen, S. The moon and more	**Fic**
Doller, T. The devil you know	**Fic**
Donnelly, J. These shallow graves	**Fic**
The Forbidden Orchid	**Fic**
Friesner, E. Spirit's princess	**Fic**
Jensen, C. Skyscraping	**Fic**
Lake, N. Hostage Three	**Fic**
McQuerry, M. D. The Peculiars	**Fic**
Monninger, J. Whippoorwill	**Fic**
Rossetti, R. The girl with borrowed wings	**Fic**
Shepherd, M. Her Dark Curiosity	**Fic**
Shepherd, M. The madman's daughter	**Fic**
Treichel, E. A series of small maneuvers	**Fic**
Zettel, S. Dust girl	**Fic**

FATHER-SON RELATIONSHIP

Say, A. The Inker's Shadow	**741**

FATHER-SON RELATIONSHIP -- FICTION

Berk, J. Guy Langman, crime scene procrastinator	**Fic**
Gilbert, K. L. Conviction	**Fic**
Golden Boys	**Fic**
Green, S. Half wild	**Fic**
Lyga, B. Blood of my blood	**Fic**
Lyga, B. I hunt killers	**Fic**
McDonald, I. Be my enemy	**Fic**
Morpurgo, M. Listen to the Moon	**Fic**
Smelcer, J. Edge of nowhere	**Fic**
Villareal, R. Body slammed!	**Fic**
Willey, M. Beetle Boy	**Fic**
Wynne-Jones, T. The emperor of any place	

FATHER-SON RELATIONSHIP -- GRAPHIC NOVELS

TenNapel, D. Bad Island	**741.5**

FATHERS

See also Family; Men

FATHERS -- DEATH -- FICTION

Campbell, B. J. Once upon a river	**Fic**
Wroblewski, D. The story of Edgar Sawtelle	**Fic**

FATHERS -- FICTION

Bilen, T. What she left behind	**Fic**
Nelson, M. American ace	**Fic**
Resau, L. The jade notebook	**Fic**

FATHERS AND DAUGHTERS *See* Father-daughter relationship

FATHERS AND DAUGHTERS -- FICTION

Amato, M. Get happy	**Fic**
Anderson, L. H. The impossible knife of memory	**Fic**
Bacigalupi, P. The doubt factory	**Fic**
Bigelow, L. J. Starting from here	**Fic**
Dessen, S. The moon and more	**Fic**
Doller, T. The devil you know	**Fic**
Donnelly, J. These shallow graves	**Fic**
Falls, K. Inhuman	**Fic**
Fforde, J. The Eyre affair	**Fic**
Fishman, S. The well's end	**Fic**
Harrington, L. Alice Bliss	**Fic**
Jensen, C. Skyscraping	**Fic**
Kade, S. The rules	**Fic**
Keplinger, K. A midsummer's nightmare	**Fic**
King, A. S. Glory O'Brien's history of the future	**Fic**
Lake, N. Hostage Three	**Fic**
Lee, H. To kill a mockingbird	**Fic**
Monninger, J. Whippoorwill	**Fic**
North, P. Starglass	**Fic**
Oates, J. C. Freaky green eyes	**Fic**
Renn, D. Tokyo heist	**Fic**
Rosoff, M. Picture me gone	**Fic**
Rush, J. Altered	**Fic**
Shepherd, M. The madman's daughter	**Fic**
Treichel, E. A series of small maneuvers	**Fic**
Whipple, N. House of ivy and sorrow	**Fic**
Woodrell, D. Winter's bone	**Fic**

FATHERS AND SONS

Crowe, C. Mississippi trial, 1955	**Fic**
Foer, J. S. Extremely loud & incredibly close	**Fic**
Howrey, M. Blind sight	**Fic**
Smelcer, J. Edge of nowhere	**Fic**
Tucker, T. Over and under	**Fic**

FATHERS AND SONS *See* Father-son relationship

FATHERS AND SONS -- FICTION

Alexander, K. The crossover	**Fic**
Berk, J. Guy Langman, crime scene procrastinator	**Fic**
Bradbury, R. Something wicked this way comes	**Fic**
Character, driven	**Fic**
Emond, S. Bright lights, dark nights	**Fic**
Foer, J. S. Extremely loud & incredibly close	**Fic**
Gilbert, K. L. Conviction	**Fic**
Green, S. Half bad	**Fic**
Green, S. Half wild	**Fic**
Lyga, B. Blood of my blood	**Fic**
Lyga, B. I hunt killers	**Fic**
Nelson, M. American ace	**Fic**
Smith, A. 100 sideways miles	**Fic**
Villareal, R. Body slammed!	**Fic**
Wallace, S. N. Muckers	**Fic**

FATIGUE

See also Physiology

FATNESS *See* Obesity

Fattah, Hala Mundhir

A brief history of Iraq	**956.7**

Fattah, Moataz A.
(ed) Netzley, P. D. The Greenhaven encyclopedia of terrorism **363.32**

Faulkner, William, 1897-1962
About
Fargnoli, A. N. Critical companion to William Faulkner **813**
Weinstein, P. Becoming Faulkner **92**
William Faulkner **813**

The **fault** in our stars. Green, J. **Fic**

FAULTS (GEOLOGY)
See also Geology

FAUNA *See* Animals; Zoology

FAUNA FOUNDATION
Westoll, A. The chimps of Fauna Sanctuary **636.9**

Faurie, Bernadette
The horse riding & care handbook **636.1**

Faurot, Jeannette L.
(ed) Asian-Pacific folktales and legends **398.2**

Faust, Drew Gilpin
Mothers of invention **973.7**

Favor, Lesli J.
Weighing in **613.2**

Favorite folktales from around the world. **398.2**

Favorite Poem Project
Americans' favorite poems **808.81**

FAX TRANSMISSION
See also Data transmission systems; Telecommunication

Fayer, Steve
Hampton, H. Voices of freedom **323.1**

FEAR
King, S. The girl who loved Tom Gordon **Fic**

FEAR
See also Emotions

FEAR -- FICTION
Grant, M. Messenger of Fear **Fic**

FEAR IN CHILDREN
See also Child psychology; Fear

FEAR OF FOREIGNERS *See* Xenophobia

Fear of physics. Krauss, L. M. **530**

FEAR OF THE DARK
See also Fear; Fear in children

FEAR OF THE DARK -- GRAPHIC NOVELS
Gulledge, L. L. Will & whit **741.5**

Fear: 13 stories of suspense and horror. **S**

Fearless. Funke, C. **Fic**

FEAST DAYS *See* Religious holidays

Feathers. Hanson, T. **598**

FEATHERS
Hanson, T. Feathers **598**

Feaver, Peter
(jt. auth) Crossman, A. Getting the best out of college **378.1**

FECES
George, R. The big necessity **363.7**

FEDERAL BUDGET *See* Budget -- United States

FEDERAL COURTS *See* Courts -- United States

FEDERAL GOVERNMENT
See also Constitutional law; Political science; Republics

FEDERAL RESERVE BANKS
See also Banks and banking

FEDERAL SPENDING POLICY *See* United States -- Appropriations and expenditures

FEDERAL-STATE RELATIONS
See also Federal government; State governments

Federle, Tim
The great American whatever **Fic**

Feed. Anderson, M. T. **Fic**

Feedback. Wells, R. **Fic**

FEEDBACK (PSYCHOLOGY)
See also Psychology of learning

FEELING *See* Perception; Touch

FEELINGS *See* Emotions

Feelings, Tom
The middle passage **305.896**
Lester, J. To be a slave **326**

Fehlbaum, Beth
Big fat disaster **Fic**

Fehlbaum, Beth
Hope in Patience **Fic**

Feinberg, Barbara Silberdick
The Articles of Confederation **342**

Feingold, Russ
About
Profiles in courage for our time **920**

Feinman, Jay M.
Law 101 **340**

Feinstein, John
Foul trouble **Fic**

Feinstein, Michael
About
Feinstein, M. The Gershwins and me **782.421**

Feinstein, Stephen
Sexuality and teens **306.7**

Feldman, Jane
Lanier, S. Jefferson's children **973.4**

Feldman, Ruth Tenzer
Blue thread **Fic**

FELIDAE *See* Wild cats

Felin, M. Sindy
Touching snow **Fic**

FELINES *See* Cats

Felisbret, Eric
Graffiti New York **751.7**

Felix, Rebecca
Exploring caves **796.525**

Fell of dark. Downes, P. **Fic**

Fellow citizens. **352.23**

FELLOWSHIPS *See* Scholarships

FERAL CATS *See* Wild cats

Feral curse. Smith, C. L.   **Fic**

Feral nights. Smith, C. L.   **Fic**

The **Ferguson** guide to resumes and job hunting skills. Hinds, M. J.   **650.14**

Ferguson Publishing
The top 100   **331.7**

Ferguson Publishing
Food   **647.95**

Ferguson, Charles D.
Nuclear energy   **333.792**

Ferguson, Gary
Smith, D. W. Decade of the wolf   **599.77**

Ferguson, Olivia
(ed) Age of consent   **306.7**
(ed) Teen sex   **306.7**

Ferlinghetti, Lawrence
City lights pocket poets anthology   **808.81**
How to paint sunlight   **811**
These are my rivers   **811**

FERMENTATION
See also Chemical engineering; Chemistry; Microbiology

FERMENTED FOODS
See also Food

Fernandez Olmos, Margarite
U.S. Latino literature   **810**

FERNS
Parker, S. Ferns, mosses & other spore-producing plants   **587**

FERNS
See also Plants

Ferns, mosses & other spore-producing plants. Parker, S.   **587**

Ferrara, Miranda H.
(ed) Human diseases and conditions   **616**

Ferrari, Michelle
(comp) Reporting America at war   **070.4**

Ferrer, J. J.
The art of stone skipping and other fun old-time games   **790.1**

Ferrets. McKimmey, V.   **636.9**

FERRETS
McKimmey, V. Ferrets   **636.9**

Ferris, Julie
Ideas that changed the world   **609**

Ferro, Jeffrey
Prisons   **365**

Fershleiser, Rachel
(ed) I can't keep my own secrets   **808.8**
(ed) Not quite what I was planning   **920**

FERTILITY
See also Reproduction

FERTILITY CONTROL *See* Birth control

FERTILIZATION IN VITRO
Whitehouse, B. The match   **92**

FERTILIZATION IN VITRO
See also Genetic engineering; Reproduction

FERTILIZATION IN VITRO, HUMAN *See* Fertilization in vitro

FERTILIZATION OF PLANTS
See also Plant physiology; Plants

FERTILIZATION, TEST TUBE *See* Fertilization in vitro

FERTILIZERS
Hager, T. The alchemy of air   **92**

FERTILIZERS
See also Agricultural chemicals; Soils

FERTILIZERS AND MANURES *See* Fertilizers

FESTIVALS
Christianson, S. G. The international book of days   **394.26**
Encyclopedia of holidays and celebrations **394.26**
Holiday symbols and customs   **394.26**
Roy, C. Traditional festivals   **394.26**

FESTIVALS -- DICTIONARIES
Holidays, festivals, and celebrations of the world dictionary   **394.26**

FETAL ALCOHOL SYNDROME
See also Social problems

Fetal rights. Marzilli, A.   **342**

The **Fetch.** Whitcomb, L.   **Fic**

Fetching Dylan. Foster, S.   **636.7**

FETISHISM (SEXUAL BEHAVIOR)
See also Sex

Fetterolf, Monty L.
Cobb, C. The joy of chemistry   **540**

FETUS
Marzilli, A. Fetal rights   **342**

FETUS
See also Embryology; Reproduction

FEUDALISM
Gies, J. Life in a medieval castle   **940.2**

FEUDALISM
See also Land tenure; Medieval civilization

FEUDS *See* Vendetta

Feuereisen, Patti
Invisible girls   **362.7**

Fever. DeStefano, L.   **Fic**

Fever Crumb. Reeve, P.   **Fic**

Fever Crumb series
Reeve, P. Scrivener's moon   **Fic**

Fever, 1793. Anderson, L. H.   **Fic**

Feynman.   **92**

Feynman, Richard Phillips
The meaning of it all   **500**
Six easy pieces   **530**

Feynman, Richard Phillips, 1918-1988
About
Cropper, W. H. Great physicists   **530**
Feynman   **92**
Henderson, H. Richard Feynman   **92**

Fighting elites. Fredriksen, J. C.   **356**

Fighting for Dontae. Castan, M.   **Fic**

Fighting words [series]

   Ball, D. I.   Competing voices from native America   **970.004**

   Competing voices from World War II in Europe   **940.53**

Figueredo, Danilo H.

   A brief history of the Caribbean   **972.9**

FIGURE DRAWING

   Figure it out! human proportions   **741.5**

   Hart, C.   Human anatomy made amazingly easy   **743.4**

FIGURE DRAWING

   See also Artistic anatomy; Drawing

Figure it out! human proportions.   **741.5**

FIGURE PAINTING

   See also Artistic anatomy; Painting

FIGURES OF SPEECH

   See also Rhetoric; Symbolism

The **file** on Angelyn Stark. Atkins, C.   **Fic**

FILIPINO AMERICANS -- FICTION

   Arcos, C.   There will come a time   **Fic**

   Growing up Filipino II   **S**

Filipovic, Zlata

   (ed) Stolen voices   **920**

Fillmore, Millard, 1800-1874

        About

   Finkelman, P.   Millard Fillmore   **92**

FILM ADAPTATIONS

   See also Motion pictures

FILM CRITICISM

   See also Criticism

FILM DIRECTION *See* Motion pictures -- Production and direction

FILM FESTIVALS

   See also Festivals

FILM INDUSTRY (MOTION PICTURES) *See* Motion picture industry

FILM NOIR

   See also Motion pictures

FILM PRODUCTION *See* Motion pictures -- Production and direction

FILMMAKING *See* Motion pictures -- Production and direction

Filmmaking for teens. Lanier, T.   **791.43**

FILMS *See* Filmstrips; Motion pictures

FILMSTRIPS

   See also Audiovisual materials; Photography

The **final** days. Woodward, B.   **973.924**

The **final** descent. Yancey, R.   **Fic**

The **final** forest. Dietrich, W.   **333.75**

The **Final** Four. Volponi, P.   **Fic**

The **Final** Four.   **796.323**

Final harvest. Dickinson, E.   **811**

Final Jeopardy. Baker, S.   **006.3**

FINANCE

   See also Economics

FINANCE, HOUSEHOLD *See* Household budgets

FINANCE, PERSONAL

   Bostick, N.   Managing Money   **332**

   McGuire, K.   The teen money manual   **332.024**

   Mooney, C.   Smart savings and financial planning   **332.024**

FINANCE, PERSONAL *See* Personal finance

FINANCE, PERSONAL -- COMPUTER NETWORK RESOURCES

   Peterson, J. M.   Digital smarts   **332.024**

Financial aid for the disabled and their families, 2010-2012. Schlachter, G. A.   **378.3**

Financial aid smarts. McCormick, L.   **378.3**

FINANCIAL AID TO STUDENTS *See* Student aid

FINANCIAL CONSULTANTS

   Moying Li   Snow falling in spring   **92**

FINANCIAL CRASHES *See* Financial crises

FINANCIAL CRISES

   Bair, S.   The Bullies of Wall Street   **330.973**

   Connolly, S.   The stock market   **332.6**

   Lewis, M.   The big short   **330.9**

FINANCIAL INSTITUTIONS

   See also Associations

FINANCIAL PANICS *See* Financial crises

FINANCIAL PLANNING, PERSONAL *See* Personal finance

FINANCIERS

   Weyn, S.   Distant waves   **Fic**

FINANCIERS *See* Capitalists and financiers

Find me. Bernard, R.   **Fic**

Finding Audrey. Kinsella, S.   **Fic**

Finding Mr. Brightside. Clark, J.   **Fic**

Findling, John E.

   (ed) Events that changed America through the seventeenth century   **973.2**

   (ed) Events that changed the world through the sixteenth century   **909**

Fine, Sarah

   Of Metal and Wishes   **Fic**

Fine, Susan

   Bardin, M.   Zen in the art of the SAT   **378.1**

Fingeroth, Danny J.

   (ed) 101 outstanding graphic novels   **741.5**

FINGERPRINTS

   See also Anthropometry; Criminal investigation; Criminals -- Identification; Identification

Finishing school [series]

   Carriger, G.   Curtsies & conspiracies   **Fic**

Fink, Mark

   The summer I got a life   **Fic**

Finkelman, Paul

   (ed) Encyclopedia of the Harlem Renaissance **700**

   (ed) Encyclopedia of the new American nation **973**

1962 **811**

FIRST AID

The American Red Cross first aid and safety handbook **616.02**

FIRST AID

   See also Health self-care; Home accidents; Medicine; Nursing; Rescue work; Sick

The **first** civilizations to 500 BC. **930**

First contact. Kaufman, M. **576.8**

First crossing. **S**

First darling of the morning. Umrigar, T. N. **92**

First descent. Withers, P. **Fic**

The **first** emancipator. Levy, A. **92**

First freedoms. Haynes, C. C. **342**

FIRST GENERATION CHILDREN *See* Children of immigrants

First Girl Scout. Wadsworth, G. **92**

The **first** human. Gibbons, A. **599.93**

First humans. Stefoff, R. **599.93**

First ladies. Schneider, D. **920.003**

First ladies. Caroli, B. B. **920**

FIRST LOVES -- FICTION

   Half the world **Fic**

First meetings in the Enderverse. Card, O. S. **S**

The **first** part last. Johnson, A. **Fic**

The **first** part of King Henry the Fourth. Shakespeare, W. **822.3**

FIRST SEXUAL EXPERIENCES

   The V-word **306.7**

First shot. Sorrells, W. **Fic**

First steps series

   Marsh, D. Calligraphy **745.6**

First they killed my father. Ung, L. **959.6**

The **first** vertebrates. Holmes, T. **567**

The **First** World War. Gilbert, M. **940.3**

FIRST WORLD WAR *See* World War, 1914-1918

The **First** World War. Strachan, H. **940.3**

Fisanick, Christina

   (ed) Addiction: opposing viewpoints **362.29**

   (ed) Crime and criminals: opposing viewpoints **364**

   (ed) Debt: opposing viewpoints **332.024**

FISCAL POLICY -- UNITED STATES

Kramer, M. A people's guide to the federal budget **352.4**

Fischer, David Hackett

   Washington's crossing **973.3**

FISH *See* Fish as food; Fishes

FISH AS FOOD

   See also Cooking; Fishes; Food

FISH KILLS

   Dead zones **639.2**

Fisher, Catherine

   Incarceron **Fic**

   Sapphique **Fic**

Fisher, David

   Basic **355.5**

Fisher, David G.

   (ed) The solar system **523.2**

Fisher, Diana

   The art of rock painting **745.7**

Fisher, Jennifer Engel

   Price, J. Take control of Asperger's syndrome **616.85**

Fisher, Jerilyn

   (ed) Women in literature **809**

Fisher, Robin Gaby

   The boys of the dark **365**

FISHERIES *See* Commercial fishing

FISHERMEN

   Guterson, D. Snow falling on cedars **Fic**

   Kantner, S. Shopping for porcupine **92**

   Nelson, M. The freedom business **811**

FISHES

   Alderton, D. Encyclopedia of aquarium & pond fish **639.34**

   Boruchowitz, D. E. Mini aquariums **639.34**

   Pepperell, J. G. Fishes of the open ocean **597**

FISHES -- ECOLOGY

   See also Ecology

FISHES -- EFFECT OF WATER POLLUTION ON -- JUVENILE LITERATURE

   Dead zones **639.2**

FISHES -- ENCYCLOPEDIAS

   Alderton, D. Encyclopedia of aquarium & pond fish **639.34**

   Jennings, G. The new encyclopedia of the saltwater aquarium **639.34**

FISHES -- GEOGRAPHICAL DISTRIBUTION

   See also Biogeography

FISHES -- NORTH AMERICA

   Gilbert, C. R. National Audubon Society field guide to fishes, North America **597**

   Page, L. M. Peterson field guide to freshwater fishes of North America north of Mexico **597**

Fishes of the open ocean. Pepperell, J. G. **597**

FISHING

   Ellis, R. The empty ocean **577.7**

   Paulsen, G. Father water, Mother woods **799**

   Trailside (Television program) Fly fishing **799.1**

FISHING

   See also Sports

FISHING -- FICTION

   Swim that rock **Fic**

   Woolston, B. Catch & release **Fic**

FISHING INDUSTRY *See* Commercial fishing

FISHING, COMMERCIAL *See* Commercial fishing

Fishman, Charles

   The big thirst **333.91**

Fishman, Seth

   The well's end **Fic**

Fishman, Stephen

Horvitz, L. A. Eureka!: scientific breakthroughs that changed the world **509**

Fleming, Ann Marie
The Magical Life of Long Tack Sam **741.5**

Fleming, Candace
The family Romanov **947.08**
The Lincolns **92**
On the day I died **Fic**

Fleming, Fergus
Off the map **910.4**

Fleming, James Rodger
Fixing the sky **551.6**

Fleming, Louis B.
Yamazaki, J. N. Children of the atomic bomb **618.92**

Flesch, William
The Facts on File companion to British poetry, 19th century **821**

Flesh & bone. Maberry, J. **Fic**

Fletcher, Christine
Ten cents a dance **Fic**

Fletcher, Joann
Exploring the life, myth, and art of ancient Egypt **932**

Fletcher, Susan
Alphabet of dreams **Fic**

Flexibility & agility. **613.7**

A **flickering** light. Kirkpatrick, J. **Fic**

FLIES
See also Household pests; Insects; Pests

FLIGHT -- FICTION
Reeve, P. A Web of Air **Fic**

FLIGHT TO THE MOON See Space flight to the moon

Flight v2. **741.5**
Flight v3. **741.5**
Flight: Volume Four. **741.5**

FLIGHTS AROUND THE WORLD -- HISTORY -- 20TH CENTURYE
Brown, J. K. Amelia Earhart **629.130**

Flinn, Alex
Breaking point **Fic**
Breathing underwater **Fic**

Flinn, Frank K.
Encyclopedia of Catholicism **282**

Flip. Bedford, M. **Fic**

FLIPPED CLASSROOMS
See also Teaching

Flock. Delsol, W. **Fic**

FLOODS
See also Meteorology; Natural disasters; Rain; Water

FLOODS -- FICTION
Richards, J. Three rivers rising **Fic**

FLOODS -- MASSACHUSETTS -- BOSTON -- HISTORY -- 20TH CENTURY
Kops, D. The Great Molasses Flood **363.17**

FLOORS
See also Architecture -- Details; Buildings

FLORA See Botany; Plants

Floreen, Tim
Willful machines **Fic**

FLORENCE (ITALY) -- FICTION
Kephart, B. One thing stolen **Fic**

Flores-Scott, Patrick
Jumped in **Fic**

FLORIDA -- FICTION
Doller, T. The devil you know **Fic**
Gantos, J. The trouble in me **Fic**

The **Florida** manatee. Reep, R. L. **599.5**

Florio, James J.
About
Profiles in courage for our time **920**

FLORISTS
Diffenbaugh, V. The language of flowers **Fic**

FLOWER ARRANGEMENT
See also Decoration and ornament; Flowers; Table setting and decoration

FLOWER GARDENING
See also Gardening; Horticulture

FLOWERS
Burger, W. C. Flowers: how they changed the world **582.13**
Diffenbaugh, V. The language of flowers **Fic**

FLOWERS
See also Plants

FLOWERS -- DRYING
See also Plants -- Collection and preservation

FLOWERS -- FICTION
Hahn, R. A creature of moonlight **Fic**

Flowers for Algernon. Keyes, D. **Fic**

Flowers in the sky. Joseph, L. **Fic**

Flowers, Arthur
I see the promised land **92**

Flowers, Sarah
Evaluating teen services and programs **027.62**

Flowers, Sarah
Young adults deserve the best **027.62**

Flowers: how they changed the world. Burger, W. C. **582.13**

Floyd Patterson. Levy, A. H. **92**
Floyd Patterson. Stratton, W. K. **796.83**

Floyd, Samuel A.
The power of black music **780.89**

Flu. Cunningham, K. **614.5**

FLU See Influenza

Fluent in fantasy. Herald, D. T. **016**

FLUID MECHANICS
See also Mechanics

Fluke. **519.2**

FLY CASTING
Trailside (Television program) Fly fishing **799.1**

FLY CASTING

Andrews, J. Me & Earl & the dying girl **Fic**
Avery, T. My brother's shadow **Fic**
Benwell, S. The last leaves falling **Fic**
Betts, A. J. Zac and Mia **Fic**
Boyne, J. The boy in the striped pajamas **Fic**
Brothers, M. Weird Girl and What's His Name **813**
Brown, J. R. No place to fall **Fic**
Buzo, L. Love and other perishable items **Fic**
Calame, D. Call the shots **Fic**
Chambers, A. Dying to know you **Fic**
Cranse, P. All the major constellations **Fic**
Crossan, S. Breathe **Fic**
The darkest corners **Fic**
Deep sea **Fic**
Dinnison, K. You and me and him **Fic**
Dubosarsky, U. The golden day **Fic**
Elston, A. The rules for disappearing **Fic**
Farizan, S. Tell me again how a crush should feel **Fic**
Flores-Scott, P. Jumped in **Fic**
The Forgetting **Fic**
Gantos, J. The trouble in me **Fic**
Giles, G. Girls like us **Fic**
Griffin, N. The whole stupid way we are **Fic**
The Haters **Fic**
Hautman, P. What boys really want? **Fic**
Herbach, G. Nothing special **Fic**
Howe, J. The misfits **Fic**
Hubbard, J. Try not to breathe **Fic**
Johnston, E. K. Prairie fire **Fic**
Kinsella, S. Finding Audrey **Fic**
Knudsen, M. Evil librarian **Fic**
Konigsberg, B. The porcupine of truth **Fic**
LaCour, N. The Disenchantments **Fic**
Lieberman, L. Off pointe **Fic**
Littman, S. D. Backlash **Fic**
Lynch, C. Walking wounded **Fic**
Mangum, L. After hello **Fic**
Matson, M. Since you've been gone **Fic**
May, K. Kiki **Fic**
McCafferty, M. Sloppy firsts **813**
McCahan, E. Love and other foreign words **Fic**
McKay, S. E. Enemy territory **Fic**
The memory of light **Fic**
Moore, K. Amber House **Fic**
Moracho, C. Althea and Oliver **Fic**
Myers, W. D. Darius & Twig **Fic**
Myers, W. D. Invasion! **Fic**
Myracle, L. Yolo **Fic**
The Nameless City **741.5**
Niven, J. All the bright places **Fic**
Nowlin, L. If he had been with me **Fic**
Oates, J. C. Two or three things I forgot to tell you **Fic**
Oppel, K. Such wicked intent **Fic**
The passion of Dolssa **Fic**

Philpot, C. Even in paradise **Fic**
Pierson, D. C. The boy who couldn't sleep and never had to **Fic**
Quick, M. Boy21 **Fic**
Ryan, A. K. Spark **Fic**
Sáenz, B. A. Aristotle and Dante discover the secrets of the universe **Fic**
Salomon, P. A. All those broken angels **Fic**
Scelsa, K. Fans of the impossible life **Fic**
The serpent king **Fic**
Simone Upgrade U **Fic**
Smith, A. 100 sideways miles **Fic**
Solitaire **Fic**
Spears, K. Breakaway **Fic**
Stiefvater, M. Blue Lily, Lily Blue **Fic**
This is the part where you laugh **Fic**
This Is Where the World Ends **Fic**
This One Summer **741.5**
Tomo **S**
Truthwitch **Fic**
Vango **Fic**
Vasey, P. A troublesome boy **Fic**
Vaught, S. Freaks like us **Fic**
Vlahos, L. The Scar Boys **Fic**
Wallach, T. We all looked up **Fic**
Waters, D. Break my heart 1,000 times **Fic**
Whitman, S. The milk of birds **Fic**
Woolston, B. Catch & release **Fic**

FRIENDSHIP -- GRAPHIC NOVELS
Castellucci, C. Janes in love **741.5**
Castellucci, C. The Plain Janes **741.5**
Crilley, M. Miki Falls, Book One: Spring **741.5**
Gulledge, L. L. Page by Paige **741.5**
Lemire, J. Essex County, Vol. 1: Tales from the Farm **741.5**
Tamaki, M. Skim **741.5**
Weinstein, L. Girl stories **741.5**
Winick, J. Pedro & me **362.1**

FRIENDSHIP BETWEEN WOMEN *See* Female friendship

FRIENDSHIP IN WOMEN *See* Female friendship

Friesen, Katherine
(ed) God loves hair **Fic**

Friesner, Esther M.
Nobody's princess **Fic**
Sphinx's princess **Fic**
Sphinx's queen **Fic**
Threads and flames **Fic**

Froehner, Melissa Alberti
Palmer, P. Teen esteem **155.5**

FROGS
Beltz, E. Frogs: inside their remarkable world **597.8**
Elliott, L. The frogs and toads of North America **597.8**
Solway, A. Poison frogs and other amphibians **597.8**

1861-1865, Civil War -- Campaigns

GETTYSBURG (PA.), BATTLE OF, 1863 -- FICTION

Shaara, M. The killer angels   **Fic**

Getzinger, Donna

The Triangle Shirtwaist Factory fire   **974.7**

Gevinson, Tavi, 1996-

(ed) Rookie Yearbook Two   **305.23**

GEYSERS

> *See also* Geology; Geothermal resources; Physical geography; Water

Ghahramani, Zarah, 1981-

About

Ghahramani, Z. My life as a traitor   **92**

GHANA

Weatherly, M. Teens in Ghana   **966.7**

GHANA -- FICTION

Badoe, A. Between sisters   **Fic**

Mussi, S. The door of no return   **Fic**

Ghetto Brother.   **92**

The **ghost** and the goth. Kade, S.   **Fic**

The **ghost** map. Johnson, S.   **614.5**

GHOST STORIES

Alender, K. The dead girls of Hysteria Hall   **Fic**

Almond, D. Kit's wilderness   **Fic**

Armstrong, K. The awakening   **Fic**

Armstrong, K. The reckoning   **Fic**

Armstrong, K. The summoning   **Fic**

Bauer, J. Peeled   **Fic**

Block, F. L. Missing Angel Juan   **Fic**

Cypess, L. Nightspell   **Fic**

Dawson, D. S. Servants of the storm   **Fic**

De Lint, C. The blue girl   **Fic**

Dennard, S. Something strange and deadly   **Fic**

Fine, S. Of Metal and Wishes   **Fic**

Ford, M. The poisoned house   **Fic**

Gensler, S. The revenant   **Fic**

Griffin, A. Tighter   **Fic**

Hartnett, S. The ghost's child   **Fic**

Hawkins, R. Demonglass   **Fic**

Hudson, T. Hereafter   **Fic**

Hurley, T. Ghostgirl   **Fic**

Jackson, S. The haunting of Hill House   **Fic**

James, H. The turn of the screw   **Fic**

Jenkins, A. M. Beating heart   **Fic**

Johnson, M. The madness underneath   **Fic**

Johnson, M. The name of the star   **Fic**

Johnson, M. The shadow cabinet   **Fic**

Kade, S. The ghost and the goth   **Fic**

Kiernan, C. Into the grey   **Fic**

Kornher-Stace, N. Archivist wasp   **Fic**

Larbalestier, J. Razorhurst   **Fic**

Lauren, C. Sublime   **Fic**

Levithan, D. Marly's ghost   **Fic**

Pratchett, T. I shall wear midnight   **Fic**

Prose, F. The turning   **Fic**

Salomon, P. A. All those broken angels   **Fic**

Smith, S. The other side of dark   **Fic**

Smith-Ready, J. Shade   **Fic**

Smith-Ready, J. Shift   **Fic**

Whitcomb, L. A certain slant of light   **Fic**

Williams, K. Absent   **Fic**

GHOST STORIES

> *See also* Fantasy fiction; Horror fiction; Paranormal fiction

GHOST STORIES -- FICTION

Cox, S. The Dead Girls Detective Agency   **Fic**

Goelman, A. The path of names   **Fic**

Larbalestier, J. Razorhurst   **Fic**

GHOST TOWNS

Martinez, C. G. Pig Park   **Fic**

GHOST TOWNS

> *See also* Extinct cities

The **ghost's** child. Hartnett, S.   **Fic**

Ghostgirl. Hurley, T.   **Fic**

Ghosting. Pattou, E.   **Fic**

GHOSTS

Classic American ghost stories   **133.1**

Guiley, R. E. The encyclopedia of ghosts and spirits   **133.1**

GHOSTS

> *See also* Apparitions; Folklore; Spirits

GHOSTS -- ENCYCLOPEDIAS

Guiley, R. E. The encyclopedia of ghosts and spirits   **133.1**

GHOSTS -- FICTION

Alender, K. The dead girls of Hysteria Hall   **Fic**

Damico, G. Rogue   **Fic**

Doyle, R. A greyhound of a girl   **Fic**

Fleming, C. On the day I died   **Fic**

Johnson, M. The madness underneath   **Fic**

Johnson, M. The shadow cabinet   **Fic**

Kornher-Stace, N. Archivist wasp   **Fic**

Lauren, C. Sublime   **Fic**

McNamee, G. Beyond   **Fic**

McNeal, T. Far far away   **Fic**

Miller, K. How to lead a life of crime   **Fic**

Prose, F. The turning   **Fic**

Salomon, P. A. All those broken angels   **Fic**

The steep and thorny way   **Fic**

Waters, D. Break my heart 1,000 times   **Fic**

Westerfeld, S. Afterworlds   **Fic**

Winters, C. In the shadow of blackbirds   **Fic**

GHOSTS -- FICTION *See* Ghost stories

GHOSTS -- GRAPHIC NOVELS

Brosgol, V. Anya's ghost   **741.5**

Crilley, M. Brody's ghost: book 1   **741.5**

GHOSTS -- PSYCHOLOGICAL ASPECTS

Nuzum, E. Giving up the ghost   **133.109**

The **ghosts** of heaven. Sedgwick, M.   **S**

Ghosts of Tsavo. Caputo, P.   **599.75**

Ghosts of war. Smithson, R.   **956.7**

A thousand years of pirates	910.4

Gill, David Macinnis
Black hole sun — Fic
Invisible sun — Fic
Shadow on the sun — Fic
Soul enchilada — Fic

Gill, Sam D.
Native American religions — 299.7

Gillan, Jennifer
(ed) Growing up ethnic in America — 810
(ed) Unsettling America — 811

Gillan, Maria
(ed) Growing up ethnic in America — 810
(ed) Unsettling America — 811

Gillard, Arthur
(ed) Climate change — 363.7

Gillespie, Carmen
Critical companion to Alice Walker — 813
Critical companion to Toni Morrison — 813

Gillespie, Dizzy, 1917-1993
About
Boone, M. Dizzy Gillespie — 788.9

Gillespie, John Thomas, 1928-
Barr, C. Best books for high school readers — 011.6
Classic teenplots — 011.6

Gillespie, Kellie M.
Teen volunteer services in libraries — 021.2

Gillespie, Marcia Ann
Maya Angelou — 92

Gillespie, Michael Patrick
Fargnoli, A. N. Critical companion to James Joyce — 823

Gilliland, Ben
Rocket science for the rest of us — 520

Gillis, Peter B.
Beagle, P. S. The last unicorn — 741.5

Gilman, David
Blood sun — Fic
The devil's breath — Fic
Ice claw — Fic

Gilmore, Stephani
(ed) Golio, L. We Are the Youth — 306.768

Gilt. Longshore, K. — Fic

Gimpel, Diane
The transcontinental railroad — 385

Gingerbread. Cohn, R. — Fic

Ginn, Janel
(ed) Bilingual education — 370.117

Ginsberg, Allen
Collected poems, 1947-1997 — 811

Ginzberg, Lori D.
Elizabeth Cady Stanton — 92

Gioia, Dana
(ed) Twentieth-century American poetry — 811

Gioia, Ted
The history of jazz — 781.65

Gioseffi, Daniela
(ed) Women on war — 303.6

Giovanni, Nikki
(ed) The 100 best African American poems — 811
Blues — 811
Quilting the black-eyed pea — 811
The selected poems of Nikki Giovanni (1968-1995) — 811
(ed) Shimmy shimmy shimmy like my sister Kate — 811

Gipi
Notes for a war story — 741.5

The **girl** at midnight. Grey, M. — Fic
Girl at war. Nović, S. — Fic
Girl defective. — Fic
The **Girl** from Everywhere. — Fic
The **girl** from foreign. Shepard, S. — 92
The **Girl** from the Well. Chupeco, R. — Fic
The **girl** guide. Fonseca, C. — 646.7
Girl in the blue coat. — Fic
The **girl** in the mirror. Kearney, M. — Fic
The **girl** in the park. Fredericks, M. — Fic
Girl in translation. Kwok, J. — Fic
The **girl** is murder. Haines, K. M. — Fic
A **girl** named Digit. Monaghan, A. — Fic
A **girl** named Faithful Plum. Bernstein, R. — 792.802
A **girl** named Mister. Grimes, N. — Fic
The **girl** of fire and thorns. Carson, R. — Fic

GIRL SCOUTS
Wadsworth, G. First Girl Scout — 92

GIRL SCOUTS OF THE UNITED STATES OF AMERICA
Wadsworth, G. First Girl Scout — 92
Girl sleuth. Rehak, M. — 813
Girl stories. Weinstein, L. — 741.5
The **girl** who chased the moon. Allen, S. A. — Fic
The **Girl** Who Fell to Earth. Al-Maria, S. — 92
The **girl** who loved Tom Gordon. King, S. — Fic
The **girl** who was on fire. — 813
Girl with a pearl earring. Chevalier, T. — Fic
The **girl** with borrowed wings. Rossetti, R. — Fic
The **girl's** guide to rocking. Hopper, J. — 781.66
Girlbomb. Erlbaum, J. — 92

Girling, Richard
The Hunt for the Golden Mole — 591.68

GIRLS
Bender, A. The particular sadness of lemon cake — Fic
Campbell, B. J. Once upon a river — Fic
Chocolate for a teen's heart — 152.4
Cisneros, S. The house on Mango Street — Fic
DeWoskin, R. Big girl small — Fic
Fonseca, C. The girl guide — 646.7
Goldberg, M. Bee season — Fic
Golden, A. Memoirs of a geisha — Fic
Guene, F. Kiffe kiffe tomorrow — Fic

Brown, P. Golden Son **Fic**

Brown, P. Red Rising **Fic**

Charbonneau, J. Graduation day **Fic**

Charbonneau, J. Independent study **Fic**

Condie, A. Reached **Fic**

Dos Santos, S. The culling **Fic**

Graudin, R. Wolf by wolf **Fic**

Hill, C. J. Erasing time **Fic**

Johnson, A. D. The summer prince **Fic**

Lu, M. Prodigy **Fic**

Oliver, L. Requiem **Fic**

Pearson, M. E. Fox forever **Fic**

Peterfreund, D. Across a star-swept sea **Fic**

Simmons, K. Article 5 **Fic**

Zhang, K. Once we were **Fic**

GOVERNMENTAL INVESTIGATIONS

See also Administration of justice

GOVERNMENTAL INVESTIGATIONS -- UNITED STATES

Congress investigates **328**

GOVERNORS

Bailey, N. Female force **741.5**

Bausum, A. Unraveling freedom **940.3**

Brinkley, A. Franklin Delano Roosevelt **92**

Bruni, F. Ambling into history: the unlikely odyssey of George W. Bush **973.931**

Carter, J. An hour before daylight **973.926**

Cooper, M. L. Theodore Roosevelt **92**

DiSilvestro, R. L. Theodore Roosevelt in the Badlands **92**

Freedman, R. Franklin Delano Roosevelt **973.917**

Genovese, M. A. The Watergate crisis **973.924**

Gordon-Reed, A. Andrew Johnson **92**

Helfer, A. Ronald Reagan **741.5**

Kennedy, J. F. Profiles in courage **920**

Klein, J. The natural: the misunderstood presidency of Bill Clinton **973.929**

Lukes, B. L. Woodrow Wilson and the Progressive Era **92**

Profiles in courage for our time **920**

Renehan, E. J. The lion's pride: Theodore Roosevelt and his family in peace and war **92**

Robinson, G. By order of the president **940.53**

Schaller, M. Ronald Reagan **92**

GOVERNORS

See also State governments

GOVERNORS -- INDIANA -- BIOGRAPHY

Collins, G. William Henry Harrison **973.5**

Gowing, Lawrence

(ed) Biographical encyclopedia of artists **920.003**

GPS (NAVIGATION SYSTEM) *See* Global Positioning System

Grabowski, John

Television **621.388**

Grace. Scott, E. **Fic**

Grace, Amanda

In too deep **Fic**

Gracefully Grayson. Polonsky, A. **Fic**

Graceling. Cashore, K. **Fic**

GRADING AND MARKING (EDUCATION)

Strohmeyer, S. Smart girls get what they want **Fic**

GRADING AND MARKING (EDUCATION)

See also Educational tests and measurements

GRADING AND MARKING (STUDENTS) *See* Grading and marking (Education)

GRADUATE RECORD EXAMINATION

See also Colleges and universities -- Entrance examinations; Examinations

GRADUATION (SCHOOL) -- FICTION

Charbonneau, J. The Testing **Fic**

Graduation day. Charbonneau, J. **Fic**

Grady, Denise

Deadly invaders **614.4**

GRAFFITI

Ganz, N. Graffiti world **751**

GRAFFITI -- FICTION

Bass, K. Graffiti knight **Fic**

GRAFFITI -- NEW YORK (N.Y.) -- HISTORY

Felisbret, E. Graffiti New York **751.7**

Graffiti knight. Bass, K. **Fic**

Graffiti New York. Felisbret, E. **751.7**

Graffiti women. Ganz, N. **751.7**

Graffiti world. Ganz, N. **751**

GRAFT IN POLITICS *See* Political corruption

Graham, Martha

About

Freedman, R. Martha Graham, a dancer's life **792.8**

Grahame-Smith, Seth

(jt. auth) Austen, J. Pride and prejudice and zombies **Fic**

Grahl, Gary A.

About

Grahl, G. A. Skinny boy **92**

GRAIL

See also Folklore

GRAIL -- FICTION

Hemingway, A. The Greenstone grail **Fic**

Pyle, H. The story of the Grail and the passing of Arthur **398.2**

Grail prince. McKenzie, N. **Fic**

Grambo, Rebecca L.

Wolf: legend, enemy, icon **599.77**

GRAMMAR

See also Language and languages; Linguistics

Grammar Girl presents the ultimate writing guide for students. Fogarty, M. **428**

Grammar Girl's 101 words every high school graduate needs to know. Fogarty, M. **428**

Grammar the easy way

Barron's E-Z grammar **428**

GRAMMY AWARDS

See also Sound recordings

Castor, H. M. VIII   **Fic**

GREAT BRITAIN -- HISTORY -- HENRY VIII, 1509-1547 -- FICTION

Castor, H. M. VIII   **Fic**
Longshore, K. Brazen   **Fic**
Longshore, K. Gilt   **Fic**
Longshore, K. Tarnish   **Fic**

GREAT BRITAIN -- HISTORY -- STEPHEN, 1135-1154 -- FICTION

Follett, K. The pillars of the earth   **Fic**

GREAT BRITAIN -- HISTORY -- VICTORIA, 1837-1901 -- FICTION

Heap House   **Fic**

GREAT BRITAIN -- KINGS AND RULERS

Ashe, G. The discovery of King Arthur   **92**

GREAT BRITAIN -- KINGS AND RULERS

See also Kings and rulers

GREAT BRITAIN -- KINGS, QUEENS, RULERS, ETC. *See* Great Britain -- Kings and rulers

GREAT BRITAIN -- ROYAL NAVY

Czisnik, M. Horatio Nelson   **92**

GREAT BRITAIN -- SOCIAL LIFE AND CUSTOMS

Pool, D. What Jane Austen ate and Charles Dickens knew   **820**

The **great** Chicago fire. Owens, L. L.   **977.3**
The **great** circle. Philip, N.   **970.004**
Great comets. Burnham, R.   **523.6**
The **great** crash, 1929. Galbraith, J. K.   **338.5**
Great debates at the United Nations. Gorman, R. F.   **341.23**
The **Great** Depression. Burg, D. F.   **973.91**
The **Great** Depression and World War II, 1929 to 1949.   **973.91**

GREAT DEPRESSION, 1929-1939

Blumenthal, K. Six days in October   **332.64**
Burg, D. F. The Great Depression   **973.91**
Egan, T. The worst hard time   **978**
Galbraith, J. K. The great crash, 1929   **338.5**
The Great Depression and World War II, 1929 to 1949   **973.91**
Lifetimes: the Great War to the stock market crash: American history through biography and primary documents   **973.91**
McElvaine, R. S. The Depression and New Deal   **973.91**
Terkel, S. Hard times   **973.91**
Watkins, T. H. The hungry years   **973.91**

GREAT DEPRESSION, 1929-1939

See also Depressions; Economic conditions

GREAT DEPRESSION, 1929-1939 -- ENCYCLOPEDIAS

Encyclopedia of the Great Depression   **973.91**

GREAT DEPRESSION, 1929-1939 -- FICTION

Kennedy, W. Ironweed   **Fic**
The **great** dinosaur discoveries. Naish, D.   **567.9**

Great discoveries [series]

Krauss, L. M. Quantum man   **92**
Lemonick, M. D. The Georgian star   **92**
Reeves, R. A force of nature   **92**

Great discoveries in medicine.   **610.9**
Great displays for your library step by step. Phillips, S. P.   **021.7**

Great empires of the past [series]

Skelton, D. Empire of Alexander the Great   **938**

The **great** equations. Crease, R. P.   **509**
Great events from history, The 17th century, 1601-1700.   **909**
Great events from history, The 18th century, 1701-1800.   **909.7**
Great events from history, The 19th century, 1801-1900.   **909.81**
Great events from history, The ancient world, prehistory-476 C.E.   **930**
Great events from history, The Middle Ages, 477-1453.   **909.07**
Great events from history, The Renaissance & early modern era, 1454-1600.   **909**
Great events from history: The 20th century, 1901-1940.   **909.82**
Great events from history: The 20th century, 1941-1970.   **909.82**
Great events from history: The 20th century, 1971-2000.   **909.82**
Great expectations, by Charles Dickens.   **823**
Great Falls.   **Fic**
Great feuds in history. Evans, C.   **909**
Great feuds in medicine. Hellman, H.   **610**
Great feuds in science. Hellman, H.   **509**
The **great** fire. Murphy, J.   **977.3**
The **great** Gatsby. Fitzgerald, F. S.   **Fic**
The **great** Gatsby, by F. Scott Fitzgerald.   **813**

Great generals series

Frank, R. B. MacArthur   **92**
Woodworth, S. E. Sherman   **92**

Great Hispanic heritage [series]

Hasday, J. L. Ellen Ochoa   **92**
Sterngass, J. Jose Marti   **92**

Great interpersonal skills. Sommers, M. A.   **650.1**
Great lives from history, The 17th century, 1601-1700.   **920.003**
Great lives from history, The 18th century, 1701-1800. Great lives from history   **920.003**
Great lives from history, The 19th century, 1801-1900.   **920.003**
Great lives from history, The ancient world, prehistory-476 C.E.   **920.003**
Great lives from history, the Middle Ages, 477-1453.   **920.003**
Great lives from history, the Renaissance & early modern era, 1454-1600.   **920.003**
Great lives from history: the 20th century, 1901-

ment **613.2**

Smolin, L. A. Nutrition for sports and exercise **613.7**

GROTTOES *See* Caves

Groundbreaking scientific experiments, inventions, and discoveries of the 19th century. Windelspecht, M. **509**

Groundbreaking scientific experiments, inventions, and discoveries through the ages [series] Windelspecht, M. Groundbreaking scientific experiments, inventions, and discoveries of the 19th century **509**

Grounded. **Fic**

GROUNDS MAINTENANCE
    See also Gardening

GROUNDWATER
    See also Water

Groundwork guides [series]

Bales, K. Slavery today **306**

Caplan, G. L. The betrayal of Africa **960**

Forssberg, M. Sex for guys **306.7**

Laxer, J. Democracy **321.8**

Laxer, J. Oil **333.8**

Lorinc, J. Cities **307.7**

Nathan, D. Pornography **363.4**

Swift, R. Gangs **364.1**

Groundwork Guides [series]

Laxer, J. Empire **327**

GROUP DECISION MAKING
    See also Decision making

GROUP IDENTITY
    See also Identity (Psychology)

GROUP PROBLEM SOLVING
    See also Problem solving

GROUP RELATIONS TRAINING
    See also Interpersonal relations

GROUP THEORY
    See also Algebra; Mathematics; Number theory

GROUP VALUES *See* Social values

The **Grove** encyclopedia of classical art and architecture. **722**

The **Grove** encyclopedia of materials and techniques in art. **702.8**

Grove, Elliot

130 projects to get you into filmmaking **792.9**

Grove, S. E.

The glass sentence **Fic**

Grover, Jan

(ed) Food **363.8**

Grover, Sharon

Listening to learn **372.4**

Growing a garden city. Smith, J. N. **635**

Growing schools. **370.71**

Growing up ethnic in America. **810**

Growing up Filipino II. **S**

Growing up in slavery. **306**

Growing up in the care of strangers. **362.7**

Growing up Latino. **810**

GROWN-UP ABUSED CHILDREN *See* Adult child abuse victims

GROWTH
    See also Physiology

Gruber's complete SAT guide 2011. Gruber, G. R. **378.1**

Gruber, Gary R.

Gruber's complete SAT guide 2011 **378.1**

Grumet, Bridget Hall

Reconstruction era: primary sources **973.8**

Grun, Bernard

The timetables of history **902**

Grundy, Valerie

(ed) Correard The Oxford-Hachette French dictionary **443**

Grunfeld, A. Tom

Young, M. B. The Vietnam War: a history in documents **959.704**

Grunwald, Lisa

Women's letters **305.4**

GUANTANAMO BAY NAVAL BASE (CUBA) -- DETENTION CAMP -- FICTION

Perera, A. Guantanamo boy **Fic**

Guantanamo boy. Perera, A. **Fic**

The **guardian.** Sweeney, J. **Fic**

Guardian. London, A. **Fic**

GUARDIAN ANGELS -- FICTION

Brockenbrough, M. Devine intervention **Fic**

Guardian of the dead. Healey, K. **Fic**

Guardian of the Gate. Zink, M. **Fic**

Guardians of the lost. Weis, M. **Fic**

GUATEMALA -- FICTION

Brown, S. Caminar **Fic**

GUATEMALA -- HISTORY -- CIVIL WAR, 1960-1996 -- FICTION

Brown, S. Caminar **Fic**

Gubar, Susan

(comp) The Norton anthology of literature by women **820**

Guene, Faiza

Kiffe kiffe tomorrow **Fic**

Guerinot, Jim

Legends, icons & rebels **782.42**

GUERRILLA WARFARE

Fredriksen, J. C. Fighting elites **356**

GUERRILLA WARFARE
    See also Insurgency; Military art and science; Tactics; War

GUERRILLAS

Kinzer, S. A thousand hills **967.571**

Miller, C. C. Che Guevara **92**

See also Drama

Historical fiction. Johnson, S. L.   **016**

HISTORICAL FICTION

   See also Fiction

HISTORICAL FICTION

Baldwin, K. A School for Unusual Girls   **Fic**

Birch, C. Jamrach's menagerie   **Fic**

Boxers   **741.5**

Bray, L. The diviners   **Fic**

Cliff, T. Delilah Dirk and the Turkish Lieutenant   **741.5**

Cooper, M. The FitzOsbornes at war   **Fic**

Crichton, M. Pirate latitudes   **Fic**

Engle, M. The Lightning Dreamer   **Fic**

Feldman, R. T. Blue thread   **Fic**

The Forbidden Orchid   **Fic**

Gleason, C. The clockwork scarab   **Fic**

Gould, S. Cross my heart   **Fic**

Grove, S. E. The glass sentence   **Fic**

Hahn, M. D. Mister Death's blue-eyed girls   **Fic**

Hemphill, S. Hideous love   **Fic**

Hemphill, S. Sisters of glass   **Fic**

Higgins, J. Waiting for the queen   **Fic**

Johnson, S. L. Historical fiction   **016**

Johnson, S. L. Historical fiction II   **016**

Jones, E. The known world   **Fic**

Kidd, S. M. The invention of wings   **Fic**

Kirkpatrick, J. A flickering light   **Fic**

LaFevers, R. Grave mercy   **Fic**

Lennon, T. When love comes to town   **Fic**

Longshore, K. Gilt   **Fic**

Longshore, K. Tarnish   **Fic**

Lynch, J. N. My beautiful hippie   **Fic**

MacColl, M. Nobody's secret   **Fic**

Magoon, K. Fire in the streets   **Fic**

Manzano, S. The revolution of Evelyn Serrano   **Fic**

McKinney-Whitaker, C. The last sister   **Fic**

Meyer, L. A. Viva Jacquelina!   **Fic**

Moore, K. Neverwas   **Fic**

Morgenstern, E. The night circus   **Fic**

Perez, A. H. Out of darkness   **Fic**

Pratchett, T. Dodger   **Fic**

Preston, C. The scrapbook of Frankie Pratt   **Fic**

Preus, M. Shadow on the mountain   **Fic**

Reese, J. The strange case of Doctor Jekyll and Mademoiselle Odile   **Fic**

Ross, E. Belle epoque   **Fic**

Saints   **741.5**

Sanders, S. Rachel's secret   **Fic**

Sepetys, R. Out of the Easy   **Fic**

Shukert, R. Love me   **Fic**

The steep and thorny way   **Fic**

Strauss, V. Passion blue   **Fic**

Taub, M. Still star-crossed   **Fic**

Terry, C. L. Zero fade   **Fic**

Vango   **Fic**

Wallace, S. N. Muckers   **Fic**

Wein, E. Code name Verity   **Fic**

Wein, E. Rose under fire   **Fic**

Whelan, G. All my noble dreams and then what happens   **Fic**

Wilson, J. Victorio's war   **Fic**

Winters, C. In the shadow of blackbirds   **Fic**

Wright, B. Crow   **Fic**

HISTORICAL FICTION -- BIBLIOGRAPHY

Crew, H. S. Experiencing America's story through fiction   **813**

Historical fiction II. Johnson, S. L.   **016**

HISTORICAL FICTION, AMERICAN

Crew, H. S. Experiencing America's story through fiction   **813**

HISTORICAL FICTION, AMERICAN -- BIBLIOGRAPHY

Crew, H. S. Experiencing America's story through fiction   **813**

HISTORICAL GEOGRAPHY

   See also Geography; History

HISTORICAL GEOGRAPHY -- MAPS *See* Historical atlases

HISTORICAL GEOLOGY

   See also Geology

A **Historical** guide to Edgar Allan Poe.   **818**

A **Historical** guide to Ernest Hemingway.   **813**

A **Historical** guide to Henry David Thoreau.   **818**

A **Historical** guide to Nathaniel Hawthorne.   **813**

A **Historical** guide to Ralph Waldo Emerson.   **814**

A **Historical** guide to Walt Whitman.   **811**

Historical guides to American authors [series]

A Historical guide to Edgar Allan Poe   **818**

A Historical guide to Ernest Hemingway   **813**

A Historical guide to Henry David Thoreau   **818**

A Historical guide to Nathaniel Hawthorne   **813**

A Historical guide to Ralph Waldo Emerson   **814**

A Historical guide to Walt Whitman   **811**

Historical guides to controversial issues in America [series]

Black, B. Global warming   **363.7**

HISTORICAL NOVELS *See* Historical fiction

HISTORICAL REENACTMENTS

Wettersten, L. My faire lady   **Fic**

HISTORICAL REENACTMENTS

   See also History

HISTORICAL ROMANCES *See* Historical fiction

HISTORICAL SITES *See* Historic sites

Historical thesaurus of the Oxford English dictionary.   **423**

HISTORIOGRAPHERS *See* Historians

HISTORIOGRAPHY

   See also Authorship; History

HISTORY

Worldmark encyclopedia of the nations   **910.3**

HISTORY -- ATLASES *See* Historical atlases

HIV-POSITIVE CHILDREN -- BIOGRAPHY
Benjamin, A. Positive   362.196
HIV/AIDS. Cunningham, K.   616.97
The **hive** detectives. Burns, L. G.   638
HMONG (ASIAN PEOPLE)
    See also Indigenous peoples
HMONG AMERICANS -- MEDICINE
Fadiman, A. The spirit catches you and you fall down   306.4
Hoagstrom, Carl W.
(ed) Magill's encyclopedia of science: animal life   590
Hoare, Ben
Temperate grasslands   577.4
Hoban, Russell, 1925-2011
Soonchild   Fic
HOBBIES
    See also Amusements; Leisure; Recreation
The **hobbit.**   Fic
The **hobbit,** or, There and back again. Tolkien, J. R. R.   Fic
Hobbs, Hoyt
(jt. auth) Brier, B. Ancient Egypt   932.01
Hobbs, Will
Beardance   Fic
Bearstone   Fic
The maze   Fic
Hobby, Blake
(ed) Civil disobedience   809
(ed) Enslavement and emancipation   809
Hobby, Jeneen M.
(ed) Worldmark encyclopedia of the nations   910.3
Hobson, John Atkinson, 1858-1940
    About
Heilbroner, R. L. The worldly philosophers   330.1
Hochtritt, Lisa
(ed) Art and social justice education   372.5
Hockensmith, Steve
Pride and prejudice and zombies   Fic
Hockey. Vanderhoof, G.   796.962
HOCKEY
Coffey, W. R. The boys of winter   796.962
Vanderhoof, G. Hockey   796.962
Hocking, Amanda
Wake   Fic
Hodge, David
The complete idiot's guide to playing bass guitar   787.87
Hodge, Rosamund
Crimson bound   Fic
Cruel Beauty   Fic
Hodge, Russ
Evolution   576.8
Genetic engineering   660.6
Human genetics   599.93
The molecules of life   611

Hodge, Susie
How to survive modern art   709.04
Hodges, Flavia
Hanks, P. A dictionary of first names   929.4
Hodkin, Michelle
The evolution of Mara Dyer   Fic
Hodson, Sara S.
(jt. auth) Adam, P. Jack London, photographer   92
Hoekstra, Jonathan M.
The atlas of global conservation   333.95
Hoffer, Peter Charles
Hull, N. E. H. Roe v. Wade   344
Hoffman, Abbie
    About
McWilliams, J. C. The 1960s cultural revolution   973.92
Hoffman, Alice
Blue diary   Fic
Incantation   Fic
Hoffmann, Gretchen McCord
Copyright in cyberspace 2   346.04
Hoffmeister, Peter Brown
This is the part where you laugh   Fic
Hofstadter, Richard
America at 1750   973.2
Hogan, Lawrence D.
Shades of glory   796.357
Hogan, Linda
    About
Coltelli, L. Winged words: American Indian writers speak   897
Hogan, Walter
Humor in young adult literature   813
HOGS *See* Pigs
Hohn, Donovan
Moby-Duck   551.46
HOISTING MACHINERY
    See also Machinery
Holbrook, Sara
More than friends   811
Hold fast to dreams. Zasloff, B.   371.4
Hold me closer. Levithan, D.   Fic
Hold me closer, necromancer. McBride, L.   Fic
Hold still. LaCour, N.   Fic
Hold tight, don't let go. Wagner, L. R.   Fic
Holder, Nancy
Crusade   Fic
Hole in my life. Gantos, J.   813
The **hole** in the universe. Cole, K. C.   530.01
HOLIDAY COOKING
    See also Cooking
Holiday symbols and customs.   394.26
Holiday, Billie
Lady sings the blues   92
Holiday, Billie, 1915-1959
    About

Holiday, B. Lady sings the blues **92**

Weatherford, C. B. Becoming Billie Holiday **Fic**

HOLIDAYS

Christianson, S. G. The international book of days **394.26**

Encyclopedia of holidays and celebrations **394.26**

Holiday symbols and customs **394.26**

Webb, L. S. Holidays of the world cookbook for students **641.5**

HOLIDAYS -- DICTIONARIES

Holidays, festivals, and celebrations of the world dictionary **394.26**

HOLIDAYS -- FICTION

My true love gave to me **813**

Holidays of the world cookbook for students. Webb, L. S. **641.5**

Holidays, festivals, and celebrations of the world dictionary. **394.26**

HOLISTIC MEDICINE

See also Alternative medicine; Medicine

Holkeboer, Katherine Strand

Patterns for theatrical costumes **646.4**

Holland, Heather

(ed) GirlSpoken: from pen, brush & tongue **810**

Holland, Peter

(ed) Shakespeare, W. Much ado about nothing **822.3**

(ed) Shakespeare, W. Romeo and Juliet **822.3**

(ed) Shakespeare, W. The tempest **822.3**

Hollander, Barbara

Paying for college **378.3**

Hollander, Barbara Gottfried

The next big thing **004.068**

Hollander, John

(ed) American poetry: the nineteenth century **811**

Hollands, Neil

Read on . . . fantasy fiction **016**

Hollar, Sherman

(ed) Electronics **621.381**

(ed) Sound **534**

Holldobler, Bert

The leafcutter ants **595.7**

Hollen, Kathryn H.

The reproductive system **618**

Holler if you hear me: searching for Tupac Shakur. Dyson, M. E. **92**

Holley, Pam Spencer

(jt. auth) Bartel, J. Annotated book lists for every teen reader **028.5**

Holley, Pam Spencer

(jt. auth) Bartel, J. Annotated book lists for every teen reader **028.5**

(ed) Quick and popular reads for teens **028.5**

Hollingum, Ben

Maps and mapping the world **912**

Travel maps **912**

HOLLYWOOD (CALIF.) -- FICTION

Strasser, T. Famous **Fic**

HOLLYWOOD (LOS ANGELES, CALIF.) -- HISTORY -- 20TH CENTURY -- FICTION

Shukert, R. Love me **Fic**

Shukert, R. Starstruck **Fic**

Zettel, S. Golden girl **Fic**

Hollywood 101 [series]

Stevens, C. Sensational scenes for teens **808.82**

Hollywood High. Abrams, A. **Fic**

Holm, Tom

Code talkers and warriors **940.54**

Holman, James, 1786-1857

About

Roberts, J. A sense of the world **92**

Holmes, George

(ed) The Oxford history of Italy **945**

(ed) The Oxford history of medieval Europe **940.1**

Holmes, Hannah

The secret life of dust **551.51**

The well-dressed ape **612**

Holmes, Martha

(jt. auth) Barrington, R. Life **578.4**

HOLMES, SHERLOCK (FICTIONAL CHARACTER)

The improbable adventures of Sherlock Holmes **S**

King, L. R. The beekeeper's apprentice, or, on the segregation of the queen **Fic**

HOLMES, SHERLOCK (FICTITIOUS CHARACTER)

The improbable adventures of Sherlock Holmes **S**

King, L. R. The beekeeper's apprentice, or, on the segregation of the queen **Fic**

Wagner, E. J. The science of Sherlock Holmes **363.2**

Holmes, Thom

Early humans **599.93**

Evolution **576.8**

The first vertebrates **567**

Last of the dinosaurs **567.9**

Primates and human ancestors **569**

HOLOCAUST DENIAL

See also Holocaust, 1939-1945

HOLOCAUST SURVIVORS

Altman, L. J. Hidden teens, hidden lives **940.53**

Bitton-Jackson, L. I have lived a thousand years **940.53**

Kramer, C. Clara's war **92**

Leyson, L. The boy on the wooden box **92**

Wiesel, E. Night **92**

HOLOCAUST SURVIVORS

See also Holocaust, 1939-1945

HOLOCAUST SURVIVORS -- FICTION

Gleitzman, M. Now **Fic**

HOLOCAUST SURVIVORS -- GRAPHIC NOVELS

Spiegelman, A. MetaMaus **940.53**

The Holocaust through primary sources [series]

Byers, A.   Saving children from the Holocaust   **940.53**

Deem, J. M. Auschwitz   **940.53**

Deem, J. M. Kristallnacht   **940.53**

HOLOCAUST VICTIMS

Barnouw, D. The diary of Anne Frank: the critical edition   **92**

Dogar, S. Annexed   **Fic**

Frank, A. The diary of a young girl: the definitive edition   **92**

Jacobson, S. Anne Frank   **92**

HOLOCAUST, 1933-1945

Ackerman, D. The zookeeper's wife   **940.53**

Altman, L. J. Hidden teens, hidden lives   **940.53**

Ayer, E. H. Parallel journeys   **943.086**

Barnouw, D. The diary of Anne Frank: the critical edition   **92**

Bartoletti, S. C. Hitler Youth   **943.086**

Byers, A.   Saving children from the Holocaust   **940.53**

Deem, J. M. Auschwitz   **940.53**

Deem, J. M. Kristallnacht   **940.53**

Frank, A. The diary of a young girl: the definitive edition   **92**

Gies, M. Anne Frank remembered   **92**

Mara, W. Kristallnacht   **940.53**

Meltzer, M. Never to forget: the Jews of the Holocaust   **940.54**

HOLOCAUST, 1933-1945 *See* Holocaust, 1939-1945

HOLOCAUST, 1933-1945 -- FICTION

Dogar, S. Annexed   **Fic**

Gleitzman, M. Once   **Fic**

Sharenow, R. The Berlin Boxing Club   **Fic**

Yolen, J. Briar Rose   **Fic**

Zusak, M. The book thief   **Fic**

HOLOCAUST, 1933-1945 -- GRAPHIC NOVELS

Heuvel, E. A family secret   **741.5**

Jacobson, S. Anne Frank   **92**

Katin, M. We are on our own   **741.5**

Spiegelman, A. MetaMaus   **940.53**

Spiegelman, A. Maus   **940.53**

HOLOCAUST, 1933-1945 -- HISTORIOGRAPHY

Shermer, M. Denying history   **940.53**

HOLOCAUST, 1933-1945 -- PERSONAL NARRATIVES

Bitton-Jackson, L.   I have lived a thousand years   **940.53**

Kramer, C. Clara's war   **92**

Wiesel, E. Night   **92**

Witness   **940.53**

HOLOCAUST, 1939-1945

A bag of marbles   **940.53**

Bascomb, N. The Nazi hunters   **364.15**

Prins, M. Hidden like Anne Frank   **940.53**

Rappaport, D. Beyond courage   **940.53**

HOLOCAUST, 1939-1945

See also Antisemitism; Germany -- History -- 1933-1945; Jews -- Persecutions

HOLOCAUST, 1939-1945 -- FICTION

Boyne, J.   The boy in the striped pajamas

Keneally, T. Schindler's list   **Fic**

Macdonald, M. Odette's secrets   **Fic**

Yolen, J. Briar Rose   **Fic**

Zail, S. Playing for the commandant   **Fic**

HOLOCAUST, 1939-1945 -- PERSONAL NARRATIVES

See also Autobiographies

HOLOCAUST, JEWISH (1939-1945) *See* Holocaust, 1939-1945

HOLOCAUST, JEWISH (1939-1945) -- FICTION

HOLOCAUST, JEWISH (1939-1945) -- NETHERLANDS -- AMSTERDAM -- BIOGRAPHY

Anne Frank   **92**

HOLOCAUST, JEWISH (1939-1945) -- NETHERLANDS -- AMSTERDAM -- FICTION

Girl in the blue coat   **Fic**

HOLOCAUST, JEWISH (1939-1945) -- POLAND -- KRAKÓW -- PERSONAL NARRATIVES

Leyson, L. The boy on the wooden box   **92**

HOLOGRAPHY

See also Laser recording; Photography

Holschuh, Jodi

Nist, S. L. College rules!   **378.1**

Holt, David

Spiders in the hairdo   **398.2**

Holt, Leslie Edmonds

(jt. auth) Dresang, E. T. Dynamic youth services through outcome-based planning and evaluation   **025.1**

Holt, Michael F.

Franklin Pierce   **92**

Holtz, Thomas R.

Dinosaurs   **567.9**

Holub, Josef

An innocent soldier   **Fic**

The **Holy** Bible.   **220.5**

HOLY DAYS *See* Religious holidays

HOLY OFFICE *See* Inquisition

Holy people of the world.   **920.003**

HOLY ROMAN EMPIRE

Hinds, K. Everyday life in the Roman Empire **937**

HOLY SEE *See* Papacy; Popes

HOLY WAR (ISLAM) *See* Jihad

Holzer, Harold

(ed) The Lincoln mailbag   **973.7**

(ed) Lincoln, A. Abraham Lincoln the writer   **92**

HOME -- FICTION

Frost, H. Keesha's house   **Fic**

HOME ACCIDENTS

See also Accidents

HOME BIRTH

See also Childbirth

HOME CARE SERVICES

See also Medical care

HOME ECONOMICS

The experts' guide to 100 things everyone should know how to do **640**

Nakone, L. Organizing for your brain type **640**

HOME ECONOMICS -- ACCOUNTING *See* Household budgets

HOME EDUCATION *See* Correspondence schools and courses; Home schooling; Self-instruction

A **home** for Mr. Easter. Allen, B. A. **741.5**

Home front girl. Morrison, J. W. **977.3**

HOME INSTRUCTION *See* Home schooling

HOME LIFE *See* Family life

HOME SCHOOLING

Lerch, M. T. Serving homeschooled teens and their parents **027.6**

HOME SCHOOLING -- FICTION

Kephart, B. You are my only **Fic**

HOME TEACHING BY PARENTS *See* Home schooling

HOME VIDEO SYSTEMS

See also Television

HOME-BASED BUSINESS

See also Business; Self-employed; Small business

HOME-BASED EDUCATION *See* Home schooling

Homeland. Doctorow, C. **Fic**

HOMELESS

Lopez, S. The soloist **92**

Stringer, C. Sleepaway school **92**

HOMELESS *See* Homeless persons; Homelessness

Homeless bird. Whelan, G. **Fic**

HOMELESS PEOPLE *See* Homeless persons

HOMELESS PERSONS

Kennedy, W. Ironweed **Fic**

Lopez, S. The soloist **92**

Merino, N. Poverty and homelessness **362.5**

Padilla Peralta Undocumented **92**

HOMELESS PERSONS

See also Poor

HOMELESS PERSONS -- FICTION

Strasser, T. No place **Fic**

HOMELESS WOMEN -- FICTION

Hemingway, A. The Greenstone grail **Fic**

HOMELESSNESS

Strasser, T. No place **Fic**

HOMELESSNESS

See also Housing; Poverty; Social problems

HOMEMAKERS

Cetin, F. My grandmother **92**

Skloot, R. The immortal life of Henrietta Lacks **92**

Skloot, R. The immortal life of Henrietta Lacks **616**

Ung, L. Lucky child **92**

HOMEMAKING *See* Home economics

HOMEOPATHY

See also Alternative medicine; Pharmacy

Homer. **883**

Homer

Armitage, S. The odyssey **822**

The Iliad **883**

The Odyssey **883**

Odyssey The Odyssey **883**

Homer's The Iliad. **883**

Homer's The Odyssey. **883**

Homer's The Odyssey. **883**

Homer

Chwast, S. The odyssey **741.5**

Homeroom diaries. **Fic**

HOMESCHOOLING *See* Home schooling

HOMEWORK

See also Study skills

Homicidal aliens and other disappointments. Yansky, B. **Fic**

HOMICIDE

Bugliosi, V. Helter skelter **364.1**

Capote, T. In cold blood **364.1**

Mitchell, D. The Freedom Summer Murders **323.1**

HOMICIDE

See also Crime; Criminal law; Offenses against the person

HOMICIDE -- FICTION

Anderson, J. L. The vanishing season **Fic**

Bell, A. The reapers are the angels **Fic**

Ellen, L. Blind spot **Fic**

Giles, L. Fake ID **Fic**

Haas, A. Dangerous girls **Fic**

Hahn, M. D. Mister Death's blue-eyed girls **Fic**

Hopkins, E. Smoke **Fic**

Miranda, M. Hysteria **Fic**

Perez, M. Dead is just a dream **Fic**

Revis, B. A million suns **Fic**

Rosenfield, K. Amelia Anne is dead and gone **Fic**

Wasserman, R. The waking dark **Fic**

Waters, D. Break my heart 1,000 times **Fic**

HOMICIDE -- GRAPHIC NOVELS

Geary, R. The Lindbergh child **364.1**

Geary, R. The saga of the bloody Benders **364.152**

Geary, R. The terrible Axe-Man of New Orleans **364.152**

HOMICIDE TRIALS *See* Trials (Homicide)

HOMINIDS *See* Human origins

HOMINIDS, FOSSIL *See* Fossil hominids

HOMO SAPIENS *See* Human beings

HOMOSEXUAL MARRIAGE *See* Same-sex marriage

HOMOSEXUALITY

Mundy, L. Michelle   92
HOSPITAL LIBRARIES
   See also Libraries
HOSPITAL SHIPS
   See also Hospitals; Ships
Ford, M. T. Suicide notes   Fic
HOSPITALS
   See also Institutional care; Public health
HOSPITALS -- FICTION
Bryce, C. Anthem for Jackson Dawes   Fic
Frank, L. Two girls staring at the ceiling   Fic
Hutchinson, S. D. The five stages of Andrew Brawley   Fic
Lippert-Martin, K. Tabula rasa   Fic
HOSPITALS -- PERSONNEL MANAGEMENT
   See also Personnel management
HOSPITALS -- SANITATION
   See also Sanitation
Hosseini, Khaled
       About
The kite runner   813
Hosseini, Khaled, 1965-
The kite runner   Fic
Hostage Three. Lake, N.   Fic
HOSTAGES
   See also Terrorism
HOSTAGES -- FICTION
Bow, E. The Scorpion Rules   Fic
Fitzpatrick, B. Black ice   Fic
Lake, N. Hostage Three   Fic
Van Diepen, A. Takedown   Fic
Hostetler, John A.
Amish society   289.7
Hostetter, David
(ed) Congress investigates   328
Hot pink. Rubin, S. G.   92
The **hot** topic. Walker, G.   363.7
Hot topics [series]
Miller, D. A. Garbage and recycling   363.7
Hot X. McKellar, D.   512
The **hot** zone. Preston, R.   614.5
Hot, flat, and crowded. Friedman, T. L.   363.7
HOTEL EMPLOYEES
Rusesabagina, P. An ordinary man   92
HOTELS AND MOTELS -- FICTION
Johnson, M. Suite Scarlett   Fic
Hothouse. Lynch, C.   Fic
HOTLINES (TELEPHONE COUNSELING)
   See also Counseling; Information services; Social work
Houck, Colleen
Tiger's curse   Fic
Tiger's quest   Fic
Houdini, Harry, 1874-1926
       About
Lutes, J. Houdini: the handcuff king   741.5

Houdini: the handcuff king. Lutes, J.   741.5
Hough, Robert
Diego's Crossing   C
Houghton Mifflin Co.
The American Heritage dictionary of phrasal verbs   423
The American Heritage Spanish dictionary   463
The American Heritage student grammar dictionary   423
Houghton Mifflin Harcourt Publishing Co.
(comp) The American Heritage dictionary of the English language   423
Houle, Michelle M.
Modern British poetry, the world is never the same   821
An **hour** before daylight. Carter, J.   973.926
The **hour** of sunlight. Al Jundi, S.   92
Hourglass. McEntire, M.   Fic
Housden, Roger
(ed) Risking everything   808.81
HOUSE CLEANING
   See also Cleaning; Home economics; Household sanitation
HOUSE CONSTRUCTION
   See also Building; Domestic architecture
House of Dance. Kephart, B.   Fic
House of ivy and sorrow. Whipple, N.   Fic
House of purple cedar. Tingle, T.   Fic
House of Romanov
       About
Massie, R. K. The Romanovs   947.08
The **house** of the scorpion. Farmer, N.   Fic
The **house** of tomorrow. Bognanni, P.   Fic
The **house** on Mango Street. Cisneros, S.   Fic
HOUSE PLANTS
   See also Cultivated plants; Flower gardening; Plants; Window gardening
House, Callie, 1861-1928
       About
Berry, M. F. My face is black is true   323
The **House:** the history of the House of Representatives. Remini, R. V.   328
HOUSEHOLD BUDGETS
Bostick, N. Managing Money   332
HOUSEHOLD BUDGETS
   See also Cost and standard of living; Personal finance
HOUSEHOLD EMPLOYEES
   See also Home economics; Labor
HOUSEHOLD EMPLOYEES -- FICTION
Coats, J. A. The wicked and the just   Fic
Schlitz, L. A. The hired girl   Fic
HOUSEHOLD EMPLOYEES -- GRAPHIC NOVELS
Toboso, Y. Black butler, vol. 1   741.5
HOUSEHOLD EQUIPMENT AND SUPPLIES

Molloy, A. However Long the Night   **966.3**

HUMAN RIGHTS -- FICTION

McCormick, P. Never fall down   **Fic**

HUMAN RIGHTS -- POETRY

Fire in the soul   **808.81**

HUMAN RIGHTS ACTIVISTS

Carlin, J. Playing the enemy   **968.06**

Cetin, F. My grandmother   **92**

Gaines, A. Nelson Mandela and apartheid in world history   **968.06**

Mandela, N. Mandela   **968.06**

Menchu, R. I, Rigoberta Menchu   **92**

Salbi, Z. Between two worlds   **92**

Wiesel, E. Night   **92**

HUMAN RIGHTS WORKERS -- AFRICA

Molloy, A. However Long the Night   **966.3**

HUMAN SETTLEMENTS

   See also Human ecology; Human geography; Population; Sociology

HUMAN SEXUALITY *See* Sex

HUMAN SKIN COLOR -- FICTION

Sullivan, T. Golden boy   **Fic**

Human spaceflight. Angelo, J. A.   **629.45**

HUMAN SURVIVAL SKILLS *See* Survival skills

HUMAN TRAFFICKING

   See also Crimes against humanity; Sex crimes

HUMAN TRAFFICKING -- FICTION

Withers, P. Andreo's race   **Fic**

Human travel to the moon and Mars. Doeden, M.   **629.45**

HUMAN-ALIEN ENCOUNTERS -- FICTION

Lo, M. Inheritance   **Fic**

McDonald, I. Empress of the sun   **Fic**

Meyer, M. Cress   **Fic**

HUMAN-ANIMAL COMMUNICATION

Morell, V. Animal wise   **591.5**

HUMAN-ANIMAL COMMUNICATION -- FICTION

Pauley, K. Cat Girl's day off   **Fic**

HUMAN-ANIMAL RELATIONSHIPS

Bradshaw, J. Cat sense   **636.8**

Daisy to the Rescue   **590**

Montgomery, S. The good good pig   **636.4**

Morris, D. Monkey   **599**

Sexton, L. G. Bespotted   **636.72**

Stiefvater, M. Sinner   **Fic**

Weisman, A. The world without us   **304.2**

HUMAN-ANIMAL RELATIONSHIPS -- UNITED STATES

Bears in the backyard   **591.75**

HUMAN-PLANT RELATIONSHIPS

Weisman, A. The world without us   **304.2**

HUMANE TREATMENT OF ANIMALS *See* Animal welfare

HUMANISM

Rogers, C. R. A way of being   **150.19**

HUMANISM

   See also Culture; Literature; Philosophy

HUMANITARIAN ASSISTANCE *See* Humanitarian intervention

HUMANITARIAN ASSISTANCE, AMERICAN

Greitens, E. The Warrior's Heart   **92**

Mortenson, G. Stones into schools   **371.82**

HUMANITARIAN INTERVENTION

Mortenson, G. Stones into schools   **371.82**

HUMANITARIAN INTERVENTION

   See also Social action

HUMANITARIANS

The Eleanor Roosevelt encyclopedia   **973.917**

Freedman, R. Eleanor Roosevelt   **973.917**

Gibson, W. The miracle worker   **812**

Hayslip, L. L. When heaven and earth changed places   **92**

Herrmann, D. Helen Keller   **92**

Keating, A. M. Eleanor Roosevelt   **92**

Keller, H. Helen Keller: selected writings **92**

Keller, H. The story of my life   **92**

Keneally, T. Schindler's list   **Fic**

Miller, S. Miss Spitfire   **Fic**

Mortenson, G. Stones into schools   **371.82**

Rusesabagina, P. An ordinary man   **92**

HUMANITARIANS *See* Philanthropists

HUMANITARIANS -- BIOGRAPHY

Molloy, A. However Long the Night   **966.3**

HUMANITIES

   See also Humanism; Learning and scholarship

HUMANS IN SPACE *See* Space flight

Humans of New York. Stanton, B.   **974.7**

Humans of New York: stories.   **974.7**

Humans: an evolutionary history [series]

Stefoff, R. First humans   **599.93**

Stefoff, R. Ice age Neanderthals   **599.93**

Stefoff, R. Modern humans   **599.93**

Humes, Edward

Garbology   **628.4**

Humez, Alexander

On the dot   **411**

Humez, Nicholas

Humez, A. On the dot   **411**

HUMIDITY

   See also Meteorology; Weather

HUMOR *See* Wit and humor

Humor in young adult literature. Hogan, W.   **813**

HUMORISTS

   See also Wit and humor

HUMOROUS FICTION

Calame, D. Beat the band   **Fic**

Gantos, J. The trouble in me   **Fic**

The Haters   **Fic**

Pierson, D. C. Crap kingdom   **Fic**

Scieszka, J. Who done it?   **Fic**

Hurricane Katrina. **363.34**

HURRICANE KATRINA, 2005

Brown, D. Drowned City **363.34**

Dyson, M. E. Come hell or high water **976.3**

Hurricane Katrina **363.34**

Katrina: state of emergency **363.34**

Van Heerden, I. L. The storm **976.3**

Ward, J. Salvage the bones **Fic**

HURRICANE KATRINA, 2005

See also Hurricanes

HURRICANE KATRINA, 2005 -- FICTION

Woodson, J. Beneath a meth moon **Fic**

HURRICANE KATRINA, 2005 -- PERSONAL NARRATIVES

Voices rising **976.3**

Hurricane song. Volponi, P. **Fic**

HURRICANES

Emanuel, K. A. Divine wind **551.55**

Mooney, C. Storm world **363.7**

HURRICANES

See also Cyclones; Storms; Winds

HURRICANES -- ENCYCLOPEDIAS

Longshore, D. Encyclopedia of hurricanes, typhoons, and cyclones **551.55**

HURRICANES -- FICTION

This is the story of you **Fic**

Hurston, Zora Neale, 1891-1960

Folklore, memoirs, and other writings **398**

The complete stories **S**

Dust tracks on a road **92**

Novels and stories **813**

Their eyes were watching God **Fic**

Hurston, Zora Neale, 1891-1960

About

Hurston, Z. N. Dust tracks on a road **92**

Jones, S. L. Critical companion to Zora Neale Hurston **813**

Litwin, L. B. A reader's guide to Zora Neale Hurston's Their eyes were watching god **813**

Sapet, K. Rhythm and folklore **92**

Zora Neale Hurston **813**

Zora Neale Hurston's Their eyes were watching God **813**

Hurvitz, Mitchell M.

Karesh, S. E. Encyclopedia of Judaism **296**

Hurwin, Davida

Freaks and revelations **Fic**

Husain, Sarah

(ed) Voices of resistance **305.4**

HUSBAND ABUSE

See also Domestic violence

HUSBANDS

See also Family; Marriage; Married people; Men

Huser, Glen

Stitches **Fic**

Hush. Chayil, E. **Fic**

Hussein, Saddam

About

Schwartz, R. A. Encyclopedia of the Persian Gulf War **956.704**

Hussey, Tris

Create your own blog **006.7**

Hutchinson, S.

(ed) The encyclopedia of animals **590**

Oceans: a visual guide **551.46**

Hutchinson, Shaun David

The five stages of Andrew Brawley **Fic**

We are the ants **Fic**

HUTU (AFRICAN PEOPLE)

Hatzfeld, J. Machete season **967.571**

HUTU (AFRICAN PEOPLE) -- FICTION

Combres, E. Broken memory **Fic**

Huxley, Aldous

Brave new world revisited **303.3**

Brave new world: and, Brave new world revisited **828**

Huxley, Anthony Julian

Green inheritance **580**

HYBRID AUTOMOBILES

See also Automobiles

Hyde, Catherine Ryan

Jumpstart the world **Fic**

Hyde, Dayton O.

All the wild horses **599.66**

HYDRAULIC ENGINEERING

See also Civil engineering; Engineering; Fluid mechanics; Water power

HYDRAULIC MACHINERY

See also Machinery; Water power

HYDRAULIC STRUCTURES

See also Hydraulic engineering; Structural engineering

HYDRAULICS

See also Fluid mechanics; Liquids; Mechanics; Physics

HYDRODYNAMICS

See also Dynamics; Fluid mechanics; Hydraulic engineering; Hydraulics; Liquids; Mechanics

HYDROELECTRIC POWER PLANTS

Tabak, J. Wind and water **333.7**

HYDROGEN

See also Chemical elements

HYDROGEN AS FUEL

Tabak, J. Natural gas and hydrogen **333.8**

HYDROGEN BOMB

See also Bombs; Nuclear weapons

HYDROLOGY *See* Water

HYDROSTATICS

See also Fluid mechanics; Hydraulic engineering; Hydraulics; Hydrodynamics; Liquids; Mechanics; Physics; Statics

HYDROTHERAPY

See also Physical therapy; Therapeutics; Water

HYENAS

Ross, M. Predator   **599.7**

HYGIENE

George, R. The big necessity   **363.7**

HYGIENE

See also Medicine; Preventive medicine

HYGIENE -- HISTORY

Ashenburg, K. The dirt on clean   **391**

HYGIENE -- STUDY AND TEACHING *See* Health education

HYGIENE, SEXUAL *See* Sexual hygiene

HYGIENE, SOCIAL *See* Public health

Hyman, Jeremy S.

Jacobs, L. F. The secrets of college success   **378.1**

HYMN WRITERS

We'll understand it better by and by   **782.25**

Hynes, Maureen

(ed) God loves hair   **Fic**

Hynson, Colin

Cyber crime   **364.16**

Hypatia's heritage. Alic, M.   **509**

HYPERACTIVE CHILDREN

See also Children with disabilities

HYPERACTIVITY

See also Diseases

HYPERACTIVITY DISORDER *See* Attention deficit disorder

HYPERKINESIA *See* Attention deficit disorder; Hyperactivity

HYPERLINKS

See also Multimedia

HYPERSPACE *See* Fourth dimension

HYPERTEXT MARKUP LANGUAGE (DOCUMENT MARKUP LANGUAGE) *See* HTML (Document markup language)

HYPNOSIS *See* Hypnotism

HYPNOTISM

Rosen, M. Meditation and hypnosis   **154.7**

Stoker, B. Dracula   **Fic**

The **Hypo**. Van Sciver, N.   **92**

HYPOCHONDRIA -- FICTION

Raf, M. The symptoms of my insanity   **Fic**

Hysell, Shannon Graff

(ed) American reference books annual 2014, volume 45   **011**

Hyslop, Stephen G.

Atlas of the Civil War   **973.7**

Currie, R. The letter and the scroll   **220.9**

Hysteria. Miranda, M.   **Fic**

I

I am (not) the walrus. Briant, E.   **Fic**

I am a SEAL Team Six warrior. Wasdin, H. E.   **92**

I am J. Beam, C.   **Fic**

I am Malala. Lamb, C.   **92**

I am Mordred. Springer, N.   **Fic**

I am Morgan le Fay. Springer, N.   **Fic**

I Am Princess X.   **Fic**

I am Scout: the biography of Harper Lee. Shields, C. J.   **92**

I am the cheese. Cormier, R.   **Fic**

I am the darker brother.   **811**

I am the messenger. Zusak, M.   **Fic**

I am the mission. Zadoff, A.   **Fic**

I can't keep my own secrets.   **808.8**

I CHING

Brennan, J. H. The magical I ching   **299.5**

I crawl through it. King, A. S.   **Fic**

I did it without thinking. Hugel, B.   **155.5**

I Don't Live Here Anymore.   **833**

I don't want to be crazy. Schutz, S.   **92**

I feel a little jumpy around you.   **808.81**

I found it on the Internet. Harris, F. J.   **025.042**

I found it on the Internet. Harris, F. J.   **025.04**

I have lived a thousand years. Bitton-Jackson, L.   **940.53**

I heard God talking to me. Spires, E.   **811**

I hunt killers. Lyga, B.   **Fic**

I hunt killers [series]

Lyga, B. Blood of my blood   **Fic**

I just hope it's lethal.   **808.81**

I kissed a zombie, and I liked it. Selzer, A.   **Fic**

I know why the caged bird sings. Angelou, M.   **92**

I know why the caged bird sings, by Maya Angelou.   **818**

I never had it made. Robinson, J.   **92**

I never promised you a rose garden. Greenberg, J.   **Fic**

I see the promised land.   **92**

I shall wear midnight. Pratchett, T.   **Fic**

I swear. Davis, L.   **Fic**

I thought my father was God and other true tales from the National Story Project.   **810**

I want to be left behind. Peterson, B.   **92**

I was a dancer. D'Amboise, J.   **92**

I was here. Forman, G.   **Fic**

I will always write back. Alifirenka, C.   **305.235**

I write what I like. Biko, S.   **968.06**

I'll ask you three times, are you ok? Nye, N. S.   **92**

I'll give you the sun. Nelson, J.   **Fic**

I'm glad I did. Weil, C.   **Fic**

I, Rigoberta Menchu. Menchu, R.   **92**

I, robot. Asimov, I.   **S**

I.M. Pei. Rubalcaba, J.   **92**

Ibbitson, John

The Landing   **Fic**

Ibn al-Haytham. Steffens, B.   **92**

iBoy. Brooks, K.   **Fic**

IMMIGRANTS

See also Minorities

IMMIGRANTS -- FICTION

Walsh, A. A Long Way from Home   **Fic**

IMMIGRANTS -- GRAPHIC NOVELS

Kuper, P. The jungle   **741.5**

Novgorodoff, D. Slow storm   **741.5**

Tan, S. The arrival   **741.5**

IMMIGRANTS -- UNITED STATES

Bausum, A. Denied, detained, deported   **325**

Bergquist, J. M. Daily life in immigrant America, 1820-1870   **305.9**

Campoy, F. I. Yes! we are Latinos   **S**

Reyes, G. Madre and I   **92**

Scarpaci, V. The journey of the Italians in America   **305.8**

IMMIGRANTS -- UNITED STATES -- FICTION

Crowder, M. Audacity   **Fic**

Higgins, J. Waiting for the queen   **Fic**

Purcell, K. Trafficked   **Fic**

Volponi, P. The Final Four   **Fic**

IMMIGRANTS -- UNITED STATES -- HISTORY

This land is our land   **304.8**

IMMIGRANTS -- UNITED STATES -- SOCIAL CONDITIONS -- 21ST CENTURY

Iyer, D. We too sing America   **305.8**

Immigration.   **325**

IMMIGRATION AND EMIGRATION

Pagden, A. Peoples and empires   **909**

The **immortal** life of Henrietta Lacks. Skloot, R.   **616**

The **immortal** life of Henrietta Lacks. Skloot, R. **92**

The **immortal** rules. Kagawa, J.   **Fic**

IMMORTALITY

Westerfeld, S. The killing of worlds   **Fic**

IMMORTALITY

See also Eschatology; Soul; Theology

IMMORTALITY -- FICTION

Hemingway, A. The Greenstone grail   **Fic**

Sullivan, T. Shadowboxer   **Fic**

Immroth, Barbara Froling

(ed) Library services to youth of Hispanic heritage   **027.6**

Lukenbill, W. B. Health information in a changing world   **372**

IMMUNE SYSTEM

See also Anatomy; Physiology

IMMUNIZATION

See also Immunity; Public health

IMMUNOLOGY

See also Medicine

The impact of environmentalism [series]

Green, J. Food and farming   **338.1**

IMPEACHMENTS

See also Administration of justice

Imperial life in the emerald city. Chandrasekaran,

R.   **956.704**

IMPERIAL TRANS-ANTARCTIC EXPEDITION (1914-1917)

Alexander, C. The Endurance   **998**

Armstrong, J. Shipwreck at the bottom of the world   **919**

Imperial War Museum (London, England)

Moore, K. The Battle of Britain   **940.54**

Imperialism. Smith, B.   **325**

IMPERIALISM

See also Political science

IMPERIALISM

The American empire   **327**

Cocker, M. Rivers of blood, rivers of gold   **909**

Heilbroner, R. L. The worldly philosophers **330.1**

Industrialization and empire, 1783 to 1914   **330.9**

Kingsolver, B. The poisonwood Bible   **Fic**

Laxer, J. Empire   **327**

Smith, B. Imperialism   **325**

Westerfeld, S. The killing of worlds   **Fic**

IMPERIALISM -- GRAPHIC NOVELS

Schweizer, C. Crogan's march   **741.5**

IMPERSONATION -- FICTION

Zinn, B. Poison   **Fic**

The **importance** of being earnest and other plays. Wilde, O.   **822**

Impossible. Werlin, N.   **Fic**

The **impossible** knife of memory. Anderson, L. H.   **Fic**

The **impossible** rescue. Sandler, M. W.   **979.8**

IMPOSTORS

Massie, R. K. The Romanovs   **947.08**

IMPOSTORS AND IMPOSTURE

See also Crime; Criminals

IMPOTENCE

See also Diseases

Impressionism. Bingham, J.   **759.05**

IMPRESSIONISM (ART)

Bingham, J. Impressionism   **759.05**

Kallen, S. A. Claude Monet   **92**

IMPRESSIONISM (ART)

See also Art

Imprisoned. Sandler, M. W.   **940.53**

IMPRISONMENT *See* Prisons

IMPRISONMENT -- UNITED STATES

Schenwar, M. Locked down, locked out   **364.6**

The **improbable** adventures of Sherlock Holmes. **S**

The **improbable** theory of Ana and Zak. Katcher, B.   **Fic**

Improving student achievement. Nichols, B. **373.1**

Improving student learning when budgets are tight. Odden, A. R.   **371.2**

In a flash. Walters, E.   **Fic**

In cold blood. Capote, T.   **364.1**

In controversy [series]

Barbour, S. Is the world prepared for a deadly influ-

1947   **954.03**

**INDIA -- HISTORY -- AUTONOMY AND INDE-
PENDENCE MOVEMENTS**
Darraj, S. M. The Indian Independence Act of
1947   **954.03**

**INDIA -- HISTORY -- BRITISH OCCUPATION,
1765-1947 -- FICTION**
Whelan, G. All my noble dreams and then what
happens   **Fic**

INDIAN ART
    See also Art

INDIAN COOKING
    See also Cooking

INDIAN DRAMA
    See also Drama; Indian literature

INDIAN EPIC POETRY
    See also Epic poetry; Indian poetry

INDIAN FICTION
    See also Fiction; Indian literature
The **Indian** Independence Act of 1947. Darraj, S.
M.   **954.03**

INDIAN LANGUAGES
    See also Language and languages
Indian nations of North America. Treuer, A. **970.004**

INDIAN OCEAN
    See also Ocean

INDIAN PHILOSOPHY
    See also Philosophy

INDIAN POETRY
    See also Indian literature; Poetry

INDIANA -- FICTION
Niven, J. All the bright places   **Fic**

INDIANA -- POETRY
Crisler, C. L. Tough boy sonatas   **811**

INDIANAPOLIS (CRUISER)
Nelson, P. Left for dead   **940.54**

INDIANS OF NORTH AMERICA *See* Native
Americans; Native Americans -- North America;
Native Americans -- United States

INDIANS OF NORTH AMERICA -- ART *See*
Native American art

INDIANS OF NORTH AMERICA -- CHILDREN
See Native American children

INDIANS OF NORTH AMERICA -- COSTUME
See Native American costume

**INDIANS OF NORTH AMERICA -- LITERA-
TURE** *See* Native American literature

INDIANS OF NORTH AMERICA -- WOMEN
See Native American women

INDIC ART
Ram-Prasad, C. Exploring the life, myth, and art of
India   **954**

INDIC MYTHOLOGY
Ram-Prasad, C. Exploring the life, myth, and art of
India   **954**

INDIGENOUS PEOPLES

Cocker, M. Rivers of blood, rivers of gold   **909**

INDIGENOUS PEOPLES
    See also Ethnology

INDIGENOUS PEOPLES -- AMERICA *See* Native Americans

The **indigo** notebook. Resau, L.   **Fic**
The **indispensable** librarian.   **025.1**
Individual rights and the police.   **345**

INDIVIDUALISM
    See also Economics; Equality; Political sci-
ence; Sociology

INDIVIDUALITY
Fleischer, J. Rockin' the Boat   **920**

INDIVIDUALITY
    See also Consciousness; Psychology

INDIVIDUALITY -- FICTION
Patrick, C. The Originals   **Fic**
Tina's mouth   **741.5**
Indivisible.   **811**
IndiVisible.   **305.8**

INDOCTRINATION, FORCED *See* Brainwashing

INDONESIA -- FICTION
Meyer, L. A. The mark of the golden dragon   **Fic**

INDOOR AIR POLLUTION
    See also Air pollution

INDOOR GAMES
    See also Games

INDOOR GARDENING
    See also Gardening

INDUCED ABORTION *See* Abortion

INDUCTION COILS
    See also Electric apparatus and appliances

INDUSTRIAL ACCIDENTS
Kops, D. The Great Molasses Flood   **363.17**

INDUSTRIAL ACCIDENTS
    See also Accidents

**INDUSTRIAL ACCIDENTS -- MASSACHU-
SETTS -- BOSTON -- HISTORY -- 20TH
CENTURY**
Kops, D. The Great Molasses Flood   **363.17**

INDUSTRIAL ARBITRATION
    See also Industrial relations; Labor; Labor
disputes; Labor unions; Negotiation

INDUSTRIAL ARCHEOLOGY
    See also Archeology; Industries -- History

INDUSTRIAL ARTS
    See also Handicraft

INDUSTRIAL ARTS EDUCATION
Porterfield, D. Construction and trades   **331.7**

INDUSTRIAL ARTS EDUCATION
    See also Industrial arts; Vocational education

INDUSTRIAL BUILDINGS
    See also Buildings

**INDUSTRIAL BUILDINGS -- DESIGN AND
CONSTRUCTION**

See also Musicians

INSTRUMENTATION AND ORCHESTRATION
  See also Bands (Music); Composition (Music); Music; Orchestra

INSTRUMENTS, ASTRONOMICAL *See* Astronomical instruments

INSTRUMENTS, MUSICAL *See* Musical instruments

INSULTS *See* Invective

INSURANCE
  See also Estate planning; Finance; Personal finance

INSURANCE, SOCIAL *See* Social security

INSURGENCY -- FICTION
  Crossan, S. Breathe   **Fic**
  Dowswell, P. The Auslander   **Fic**
  Marillier, J. Raven flight   **Fic**
  Marillier, J. Shadowfell   **Fic**
  North, P. Starglass   **Fic**
  Scott, E. Grace   **Fic**
  Wein, E. Code name Verity   **Fic**
  Whelan, G. All my noble dreams and then what happens   **Fic**

Insurgent. Roth, V.   **Fic**

An integrated life of fitness [series]
  Hill, Z. B. Eating right & additional supplements for fitness   **612.3**
  Hill, Z. B. Exercise for physical & mental health   **612**
  James, S. Yoga & Pilates   **613.7**

INTEGRATED SCHOOLS *See* School integration

Integrating young adult literature through the common core standards. Ostenson, J. W.   **418**

INTEGRATION IN EDUCATION *See* School integration; Segregation in education

INTEGRATION, RACIAL *See* Race relations

INTELLECT
  Goleman, D. Emotional intelligence   **152.4**
  Goleman, D. Social intelligence   **158**
  Jolly, A. Lucy's legacy   **599.93**

INTELLECT
  See also Psychology

INTELLECTUAL FREEDOM
  Intellectual Freedom Manual   **025.2**
  Scales, P. R. Protecting intellectual freedom in your school library   **025.2**
  Selverstone, H. S. Encouraging and supporting student inquiry   **001.4**

INTELLECTUAL FREEDOM
  See also Freedom

Intellectual freedom front lines [series]
  Scales, P. R. Protecting intellectual freedom in your school library   **025.2**
Intellectual Freedom Manual.   **025.2**
Intellectual Freedom Manual.   **025.2**

INTELLECTUAL LIFE

The Britannica guide to theories and ideas that changed the modern world   **901**

INTELLECTUAL LIFE
  See also Culture

Intellectual property. Wherry, T. L.   **346.04**

INTELLECTUALS
  See also Persons; Social classes

INTELLIGENCE *See* Intellect

INTELLIGENCE AGENTS *See* Spies

INTELLIGENCE OF ANIMALS *See* Animal intelligence

INTELLIGENCE SERVICE
  See also Public administration; Research

INTELLIGENCE SERVICE -- FICTION
  Cormier, R. I am the cheese   **Fic**

INTELLIGENCE SERVICE -- UNITED STATES
  Weiner, T. Enemies   **363.25**
  Weiner, T. Legacy of ashes   **327.12**

INTELLIGENT BUILDINGS
  See also Buildings

INTEMPERANCE *See* Alcoholism; Temperance

Intensely Alice. Naylor, P. R.   **Fic**

INTERACTIVE MEDIA *See* Multimedia

INTERACTIVE MULTIMEDIA *See* Multimedia

INTERBEHAVIORIAL PSYCHOLOGY *See* Behaviorism

INTERCOLLEGIATE ATHLETICS *See* College sports

INTERCOMMUNICATION SYSTEMS
  See also Electronic apparatus and appliances; Telecommunication

INTERCULTURAL COMMUNICATION
  Fadiman, A. The spirit catches you and you fall down   **306.4**

INTERCULTURAL EDUCATION *See* Multicultural education

INTEREST (ECONOMICS)
  See also Banks and banking; Business mathematics; Capital; Finance; Loans

INTERGENERATIONAL RELATIONS -- FICTION
  Price, L. Starters   **Fic**

INTERIOR DESIGN
  See also Art; Decoration and ornament; Design; Home economics

INTERLIBRARY LOANS
  See also Library circulation; Library cooperation

INTERMARRIAGE
  See also Marriage

INTERMEDIATE SCHOOLS *See* Middle schools

INTERMEDIATE STATE *See* Eschatology; Future life

INTERNAL MIGRATION
  Harris, L. L. The great migration north, 1910-1970   **307.2**

Lemann, N. The promised land **973.9**

INTERNATIONAL ADOPTION

See also Adoption

INTERNATIONAL ARBITRATION

Allport, A. The Congress of Vienna **940.2**

INTERNATIONAL ARBITRATION

See also International cooperation; International law; International relations; International security; Treaties

The **international** book of days. Christianson, S. G. **394.26**

INTERNATIONAL COMPETITION

See also International relations; International trade

INTERNATIONAL COOPERATION

See also Cooperation; International law; International relations

INTERNATIONAL COPYRIGHT See Copyright

INTERNATIONAL ECONOMIC INTEGRATION

See also International economic relations; International finance

INTERNATIONAL ECONOMIC INTEGRATION -- CASE STUDIES

Goldstein, N. Globalization and free trade **382**

INTERNATIONAL ECONOMIC RELATIONS

Goldstein, N. Globalization and free trade **382**

INTERNATIONAL ECONOMIC RELATIONS

See also Economic policy; International relations

INTERNATIONAL MEDIATION See International arbitration

INTERNATIONAL ORGANIZATION

See also International relations; International security

International plays for young audiences. **808.82**

INTERNATIONAL POLICE

See also International cooperation; International organization; International relations; International security

INTERNATIONAL POLITICS See World politics

INTERNATIONAL RELATIONS

McPherson, S. S. Arctic thaw **333.79**

INTERNATIONAL RELATIONS -- ENCYCLOPEDIAS

Moore, J. A. Encyclopedia of the United Nations **341.23**

INTERNATIONAL SCIENCE AND ENGINEERING FAIR

Dutton, J. Science fair season **507.8**

INTERNATIONAL SECURITY

See also International relations

INTERNATIONAL SPACE STATION

Jones, C. Out of orbit **629.45**

INTERNATIONAL STANDARD BIBLIOGRAPHIC DESCRIPTION

See also Cataloging

INTERNATIONAL TRADE

See also Commerce; International economic relations

INTERNATIONALIZATION See Globalization

INTERNET

Crystal, D. Language and the internet **410**

Hafner, K. Where wizards stay up late **004**

Hoffmann, G. M. Copyright in cyberspace 2 **346.04**

Johnson, D. Learning right from wrong in the digital age **004.6**

Kling, A. A. Web 2.0 **006.7**

Parks, P. J. Online addiction **616.85**

INTERNET (COMPUTER NETWORK) See Internet

INTERNET -- DICTIONARIES

Downing, D. Dictionary of computer and Internet terms **004**

INTERNET -- FICTION

Doctorow, C. Pirate cinema **Fic**

INTERNET -- HOME SHOPPING SERVICES

See Internet marketing; Internet shopping

INTERNET -- LAW AND LEGISLATION

Marzilli, A. The Internet and crime **345**

Online pornography: opposing viewpoints **363.4**

Riley, G. B. Internet piracy **346**

INTERNET -- SAFETY MEASURES

Dingwell, H. The truth about Internet and online predators **004.6**

Hunter, N. Internet safety **005.8**

Johnson, D. Learning right from wrong in the digital age **004.6**

Mooney, C. Online predators **004.6**

Nakaya, A. C. Thinking critically **006.7**

INTERNET -- SECURITY MEASURES

January, B. Information Insecurity **323.44**

INTERNET -- SOCIAL ASPECTS

Rowell, R. Social media **302.23**

Schulman, N. In real life **302.3**

INTERNET -- VOCATIONAL GUIDANCE

Harmon, D. E. Careers in Internet security **005.8**

INTERNET ADDICTION -- POPULAR WORKS

Parks, P. J. Online addiction **616.85**

INTERNET ADDRESSES

See also Internet

INTERNET AND CHILDREN

Online pornography: opposing viewpoints **363.4**

INTERNET AND CHILDREN

See also Children

The **Internet** and crime. Marzilli, A. **345**

INTERNET AND TEENAGERS

See also Teenagers

INTERNET AUCTIONS

See also Auctions; Electronic commerce

INTERNET BANKING

Peterson, J. M. Digital smarts **332.024**

Weyn, S. Distant waves   **Fic**
Wright, O. How we invented the airplane   **92**

INVENTORS -- BIOGRAPHY
Helfand, L. They Changed the World   **609.2**
Yount, L. Nikola Tesla   **621.3**

INVENTORS -- FICTION
Bognanni, P. The house of tomorrow   **Fic**

**INVENTORS -- UNITED STATES -- BIOGRA-
PHY**
Blumenthal, K. Steve Jobs   **92**

**INVENTORS -- UNITED STATES -- BIOGRA-
PHY -- COMIC BOOKS, STRIPS, ETC.**
Helfand, L. They Changed the World   **609.2**

**INVENTORS -- UNITED STATES -- HISTORY
-- 20TH CENTURY**
Gertner, J. The idea factory   **384**

INVENTORY CONTROL
    See also Management; Retail trade

INVERTEBRATES
Alderton, D. Firefly encyclopedia of the vivari-
um   **639.3**
Attenborough, D. Life in the undergrowth   **592**
Naskrecki, P. The smaller majority   **591.7**

INVERTEBRATES
    See also Animals

INVERTEBRATES -- CONSERVATION
Fortey, R. Horseshoe crabs and velvet worms   **595**
Investigating depression and bipolar disorder.
Meisel, A.   **616.89**
Investigating diabetes. Ambrose, M.   **616.4**
Investigating diseases [series]
Ambrose, M. Investigating diabetes   **616.4**
Ambrose, M. Investigating eating disorders (an-
orexia, bulimia, and binge eating)   **616.85**
Ambrose, M. Investigating STDs (sexually trans-
mitted diseases)   **616.95**
Kelly, E. B. Investigating influenza and bird
flu   **616.2**
Kelly, E. B. Investigating tuberculosis and super-
bugs   **616.9**
Meisel, A. Investigating depression and bipolar
disorder   **616.89**
Investigating eating disorders (anorexia, bulimia,
and binge eating) Ambrose, M.   **616.85**
Investigating influenza and bird flu. Kelly, E.
B.   **616.2**
Investigating STDs (sexually transmitted diseases)
Ambrose, M.   **616.95**
Investigating tuberculosis and superbugs. Kelly, E.
B.   **616.9**

INVESTIGATIVE JOURNALISTS -- FICTION
Renn, D. Latitude zero   **Fic**

**INVESTIGATIVE REPORTING -- JUVENILE
FICTION**
Bond, G. Fallout   **Fic**

INVESTMENT AND SAVING *See* Saving and investment

INVESTMENTS
    See also Banks and banking; Capital; Finance
Invincible microbe. Murphy, J.   **616.9**
Invisibility. Cremer, A.   **Fic**

INVISIBILITY -- FICTION
Cremer, A. Invisibility   **Fic**
Invisible. Hautman, P.   **Fic**
Invisible enemies. Farrell, J.   **614.4**
Invisible giants.   **920**
Invisible girl. Stone, M. H.   **Fic**
Invisible girls. Feuereisen, P.   **362.7**
The invisible gorilla. Chabris, C.   **153.7**
The invisible kingdom. Ben-Barak, I.   **579**
Invisible sun. Gill, D. M.   **Fic**

INVISIBLE WEB -- STUDY AND TEACHING
Devine, J. Going beyond Google again   **025.042**

Inzana, Ryan
Ichiro   **741.5**

Ionesco, Eugene
Four plays   **842**
Rhinoceros, and other plays   **842**

IOWA -- FICTION
Adams, S. J. Sparks   **Fic**
Backes, M. M. The princesses of Iowa   **Fic**
Burd, N. The vast fields of ordinary   **Fic**
Kraus, D. Rotters   **Fic**
Kraus, D. Scowler   **Fic**
Smith, A. Grasshopper jungle   **Fic**
Woodson, J. Beneath a meth moon   **Fic**

IRAN
Moaveni, A. Lipstick jihad   **92**
Napoli, D. J. Beast   **Fic**

IRAN -- FICTION
Farizan, S. If you could be mine   **Fic**
Fletcher, S. Alphabet of dreams   **Fic**
Napoli, D. J. Beast   **Fic**

IRAN -- GRAPHIC NOVELS
Satrapi, M. The complete Persepolis   **741.5**

IRAN -- HISTORY -- 1941-1979
Wagner, H. L. The Iranian Revolution   **955**

IRAN -- HISTORY -- 1979-
Hakakian, R. Journey from the land of no   **92**
Nemat, M. Prisoner of Tehran   **92**

IRAN -- HISTORY -- 20TH CENTURY
Asayesh, G. Saffron sky   **92**

IRAN -- POLITICS AND GOVERNMENT
Moin, B. Khomeini   **92**
Nemat, M. Prisoner of Tehran   **92**
Wright, R. The last great revolution   **955.05**

IRAN -- SOCIAL CONDITIONS
Azam Zanganeh, L. My sister, guard your veil; my
brother guard, your eyes   **305**

IRAN -- SOCIAL CONDITIONS -- FICTION
Farizan, S. If you could be mine   **Fic**

JEWS -- ETHIOPIA -- FICTION
Oron, J. Cry of the giraffe   **Fic**
JEWS -- FICTION
Deep sea   **Fic**
North, P. Starglass   **Fic**
JEWS -- FOLKLORE
Yiddish folktales   **398.2**
JEWS -- FOLKLORE
    See also Folklore
JEWS -- FRANCE -- FICTION
A bag of marbles   **940.53**
Macdonald, M. Odette's secrets   **Fic**
JEWS -- GERMANY
Ayer, E. H. Parallel journeys   **943.086**
Deem, J. M. Kristallnacht   **940.53**
Mara, W. Kristallnacht   **940.53**
JEWS -- GERMANY -- FICTION
Blankman, A. Prisoner of night and fog   **Fic**
Sharenow, R. The Berlin Boxing Club   **Fic**
Zusak, M. The book thief   **Fic**
JEWS -- GRAPHIC NOVELS
Heuvel, E. A family secret   **741.5**
Sfar, J. The rabbi's cat   **741.5**
JEWS -- HISTORY
Goldstein, P. A convenient hatred   **305.892**
Rappaport, D. Beyond courage   **940.53**
Slavicek, L. C. The establishment of the state of Israel   **956.7**
JEWS -- HISTORY -- MAPS
A Historical atlas of the Jewish people   **909**
JEWS -- HUNGARY
Bitton-Jackson, L. I have lived a thousand years   **940.53**
JEWS -- HUNGARY -- FICTION
Wiseman, E. Puppet   **Fic**
JEWS -- INDIA
Shepard, S. The girl from foreign   **92**
JEWS -- LITERATURE *See* Hebrew literature; Jewish literature
JEWS -- NETHERLANDS
Barnouw, D. The diary of Anne Frank: the critical edition   **92**
Frank, A. The diary of a young girl: the definitive edition   **92**
JEWS -- NETHERLANDS -- AMSTERDAM -- BIOGRAPHY
Anne Frank   **92**
JEWS -- NETHERLANDS -- FICTION
Girl in the blue coat   **Fic**
JEWS -- NETHERLANDS -- GRAPHIC NOVELS
Jacobson, S. Anne Frank   **92**
JEWS -- NEW YORK (N.Y.)
Epstein, L. J. At the edge of a dream   **305.8**
Hamill, P. Snow in August   **Fic**
JEWS -- NEW YORK (N.Y.) -- FICTION

Chayil, E. Hush   **Fic**
JEWS -- PERSECUTIONS
Deem, J. M. Auschwitz   **940.53**
Deem, J. M. Kristallnacht   **940.53**
Keneally, T. Schindler's list   **Fic**
JEWS -- PERSECUTIONS
    See also Antisemitism; Persecution
JEWS -- PERSECUTIONS -- FICTION
Hoffman, A. Incantation   **Fic**
Oron, J. Cry of the giraffe   **Fic**
JEWS -- PERSECUTIONS -- HISTORY
Goldstein, P. A convenient hatred   **305.892**
JEWS -- POLAND
Ackerman, D. The zookeeper's wife   **940.53**
Kramer, C. Clara's war   **92**
Yolen, J. Briar Rose   **Fic**
JEWS -- POLAND -- FICTION
Gleitzman, M. Once   **Fic**
Sax, A. The war within these walls   **Fic**
Yolen, J. Briar Rose   **Fic**
JEWS -- POLAND -- NAREWKA -- BIOGRAPHY
Leyson, L. The boy on the wooden box   **92**
JEWS -- RELIGION *See* Judaism
JEWS -- RITES AND CEREMONIES *See* Judaism -- Customs and practices
JEWS -- RITUAL *See* Judaism -- Customs and practices; Judaism -- Liturgy
JEWS -- SOCIAL LIFE AND CUSTOMS
Schoem, D. College knowledge for the Jewish student   **378.1**
JEWS -- SWEDEN -- FICTION
Deep sea   **Fic**
JEWS -- UNITED STATES -- FICTION
Crowder, M. Audacity   **Fic**
Goelman, A. The path of names   **Fic**
JĪZAH (EGYPT) -- ANTIQUITIES
George, C. The pyramids of Giza   **932**
Jiang, Ji-li
             About
Jiang Red scarf girl   **951.05**
JIGSAW PUZZLES
    See also Puzzles
JIHAD
Esposito, J. L. Unholy war   **322.4**
JIHAD
    See also International relations; Islam
Jim Crow laws. Tischauser, L. V.   **342**
Jim Henson's tale of sand. Henson, J.   **741.5**
Jimenez, Francisco
Reaching out   **Fic**
Jinks, Catherine
Evil genius   **Fic**
Genius squad   **Fic**
The genius wars   **Fic**
Living hell   **Fic**

See also Animals; Forest animals

JUNGLE ECOLOGY

See also Ecology; Forest ecology

JUNGLES

See also Forests and forestry

JUNIOR COLLEGES

Gonsher, D. The community college guide   378.1

JUNIOR COLLEGES

See also Colleges and universities; Higher education

JUNIOR HIGH SCHOOL LIBRARIES *See* High school libraries

JUNIOR HIGH SCHOOLS

See also High schools; Public schools; Schools

JUNIOR HIGH SCHOOLS -- FICTION

Rubens, M. Sons of the 613   **Fic**

Juniors. Hemmings, K. H.   **Fic**

JUNK IN SPACE *See* Space debris

JUPITER (PLANET)

Chaple, G. F. Outer planets   **523.4**

JUPITER (PLANET)

See also Planets

Jurassic Park. Crichton, M.   **Fic**

JURISPRUDENCE, MEDICAL *See* Medical jurisprudence

JURISTS *See* Lawyers

Jurkowski, Odin L.

Technology and the school library   **027.8**

Jurmain, Suzanne

The secret of the yellow death   **614.5**

JURY

The right to a trial by jury   **345**

Just another hero. Draper, S. M.   **Fic**

Just listen. Dessen, S.   **Fic**

Just one day. Forman, G.   **Fic**

A **Just** response.   **973.931**

JUSTICE

See also Ethics; Law; Virtue

JUSTICE -- FICTION

Damico, G. Croak   **Fic**

JUSTICE LEAGUE (FICTIONAL CHARACTERS)

See also Fictional characters; Superheroes

JUSTICE, ADMINISTRATION OF *See* Administration of justice

JUSTICE, ADMINISTRATION OF -- UNITED STATES

Schenwar, M. Locked down, locked out   **364.6**

Juvenile arthritis. Rouba, K.   **618.92**

Juvenile court. Krygier, L.   **345**

JUVENILE COURTS

Jacobs, T. A.   They broke the law, you be the judge   **345**

Krygier, L. Juvenile court   **345**

Juvenile crime. Merino, N.   **364.36**

Juvenile crime and justice.   **364**

JUVENILE DELINQUENCY

Beaudoin, S. Wise Young Fool   **Fic**

Hubner, J. Last chance in Texas   **365**

Juvenile crime and justice   **364**

Krygier, L. Juvenile court   **345**

Kuklin, S. No choirboy   **364.66**

Merino, N. Juvenile crime   **364.36**

Mooney, C. Teen violence   **364.36**

Salzman, M. True notebooks   **371.9**

Should juveniles be tried as adults?   **345**

Watkins, S. Juvie   **Fic**

JUVENILE DELINQUENCY

See also Crime; Social problems

JUVENILE DELINQUENCY -- FICTION

Berry, N. The Notorious Pagan Jones   **Fic**

Dixon, J. Phoenix Island   **Fic**

Gantos, J. The trouble in me   **Fic**

Goodman, S. Kindness for weakness   **Fic**

Griffin, C. J. Nowhere to run   **Fic**

Suma, N. R. The walls around us   **Fic**

JUVENILE DETENTION HOMES -- FICTION

Beaudoin, S. Wise Young Fool   **Fic**

Jacobs, J. H. The twelve-fingered boy   **Fic**

Oakes, S. The sacred lies of Minnow Bly   **Fic**

Suma, N. R. The walls around us   **Fic**

JUVENILE PROSTITUTION

LLoyd, R. Girls like us   **92**

JUVENILE PROSTITUTION

See also Juvenile delinquency; Prostitution

JUVENILE PROSTITUTION -- FICTION

Frank, E. R. Dime   **Fic**

Leavitt, M. My book of life by Angel   **Fic**

Purcell, K. Trafficked   **Fic**

Juvie. Watkins, S.   **Fic**

The **Juvie** three. Korman, G.   **Fic**

K

The **K & W** guide to colleges for students with learning disabilities or attention deficit hyperactivity disorder. Kravets, M.   **378**

KABUL (AFGHANISTAN) -- FICTION

Hosseini, K. The kite runner   **Fic**

Kabul Beauty School. Rodriguez, D.   **305.4**

KABUL BEAUTY SCHOOL (AFGHANISTAN)

Rodriguez, D. Kabul Beauty School   **305.4**

Kade, Stacey

The ghost and the goth   **Fic**

The rules   **Fic**

Kafka.   **741.5**

Kafka, Franz, 1883-1924

The metamorphosis and other stories   **S**

Kagame, Paul

About

Kinzer, S. A thousand hills   **967.571**

Kagan, Neil

Kulik, Peter H.
(ed) Van Nostrand's scientific encyclopedia **503**

Kumar, Shiva
(ed) Witness **940.53**

Kummer, Patricia K.
North Korea **951.93**

KUNG FU
See also Martial arts

Kunitz, Stanley, 1905-2006
(comp) Blake, W. The essential Blake **821**
About
Fooling with words **808.1**

Kunzel, Bonnie Lendermon
Herald, D. T. Fluent in fantasy **016**
The teen-centered book club **027.62**

Kuper, Peter
The jungle **741.5**

Kurian, George Thomas
Timetables of world literature **809**

Kurlansky, Mark
Kurlansky, M. The world without fish **333.95**
The last fish tale **639.2**
Salt: a world history **553.6**

Kurson, Robert
Shadow divers **940.54**

Kurt Vonnegut. **813**

Kurt Vonnegut's Slaughterhouse-five. **813**

Kurtis, Bill
Garner, J. We interrupt this broadcast **070.1**

Kushner, Ellen
(ed) Welcome to Bordertown **S**

Kushner, Tony
Angels in America **812**

Kusky, Timothy M.
Encyclopedia of Earth and space science **550**
Climate change **551.6**
Earthquakes **551.2**
Tsunamis **551.46**

Kutch, Kristy Ann
Drawing and painting with colored pencil **741.2**

Kuznick, Peter J.
(jt. auth) Stone, O. The untold history of the United States **973.91**

KWANZAA
See also Holidays

Kwok, Jean
Girl in translation **Fic**

Kyle, Aryn
The god of animals **Fic**

Kyle-DeBose, Larryette
Harris, C. Charging the net **920**

L

L'Engle, Madeleine
A wrinkle in time **Fic**
A **la** carte. Davis, T. S. **Fic**

La Perdida. Abel, J. **741.5**
The **Lab.** Heath, J. **Fic**

Laban, Elizabeth
The Tragedy Paper **Fic**

Laberge, Monique
Biochemistry **612**

LaBlanc, Michael L.
(ed) Literature of developing nations for students **809**

LABOR
See also Economics; Social conditions; Sociology

LABOR (CHILDBIRTH) *See* Childbirth

LABOR -- ACCIDENTS *See* Industrial accidents

LABOR -- LAW AND LEGISLATION
The American Bar Association guide to workplace law **344**
Getzinger, D. The Triangle Shirtwaist Factory fire **974.7**

LABOR -- UNITED STATES
Ehrenreich, B. Nickel and dimed **305.5**
Reef, C. Working in America **305**

LABOR -- UNITED STATES -- DICTIONARIES
Murray, R. E. The lexicon of labor **331**

LABOR AND CAPITAL *See* Industrial relations

LABOR AND LABORING CLASSES *See* Labor; Labor movement; Working class

Labor and workplace issues in literature. Johnson, C. D. **810**

LABOR CONTRACT
See also Contracts; Industrial relations

LABOR DISPUTES
Tucker, T. Over and under **Fic**

LABOR DISPUTES
See also Industrial relations

LABOR DISPUTES -- FICTION
Tucker, T. Over and under **Fic**

LABOR ECONOMICS
See also Economics

LABOR LEADERS
Haugen, B. Cesar Chavez **92**
Miller, C. C. A. Philip Randolph and the African American labor movement **92**
Stavans, I. Cesar Chavez **92**
The **labor** movement. McNeese, T. **331.8**

LABOR MOVEMENT
Hillstrom, K. Workers unite! **331.8**
McNeese, T. The labor movement **331.8**

LABOR MOVEMENT
See also Social movements

LABOR MOVEMENT -- FICTION
Crowder, M. Audacity **Fic**

LABOR MOVEMENT -- TENNESSEE -- MEMPHIS -- HISTORY -- 20TH CENTURY
Bausum, A. Marching to the mountaintop **323.1**

LABOR ORGANIZATIONS *See* Labor unions

Long gone daddy. Hemphill, H.   Fic

LONG ISLAND (N.Y.) -- FICTION

Fitzgerald, F. S. The great Gatsby   Fic

Whitehead, C. Sag Harbor   Fic

LONG LIFE *See* Longevity

Long may she reign. White, E. E.   Fic

Long story short. Parkinson, S.   Fic

The **long** summer: how climate changed civilization.

Fagan, B. M.   **551.6**

Long Tack Sam

About

Fleming, A. M. The Magical Life of Long Tack

Sam   **741.5**

A **long** time coming. Thomas, E.   **324**

A **long** walk to water. Park, L. S.   Fic

A **Long** Way from Home. Walsh, A.   Fic

A **long** way gone. Beah, I.   **92**

Long, Richard A.

Gillespie, M. A. Maya Angelou   **92**

Long, Ruth Frances

The treachery of beautiful things   Fic

LONG-DISTANCE RUNNERS -- UNITED STATES -- BIOGRAPHY

Hillenbrand, L. Unbroken   **92**

LONG-TERM CARE FACILITIES

See also Hospitals; Medical care

LONGEVITY

Panno, J. Aging   **612.6**

LONGEVITY -- FICTION

Buckley-Archer, L. The many lives of John

Stone   Fic

Longfellow, Henry Wadsworth

Poems and other writings   **811**

Longitude. Sobel, D.   **526**

LONGITUDE

Raymo, C. Walking zero   **526**

Sobel, D. Longitude   **526**

LONGITUDE

See also Earth; Geodesy; Nautical astronomy

Longitudes and attitudes. Friedman, T. L. **973.931**

Longman, Jere

The girls of summer   **796.334**

Longshore, David

Encyclopedia of hurricanes, typhoons, and cy-

clones   **551.55**

Longshore, Katherine

Brazen   Fic

Gilt   Fic

Tarnish   Fic

Longshot. Allred, L.   **92**

Longsworth, Polly

The world of Emily Dickinson   **811**

Look me in the eye. Robison, J. E.   **92**

Looking for Alaska. Green, J.   Fic

Looks. George, M.   Fic

Looks Like Daylight. Ellis, D.   **970.1**

Loos, Pamela

(ed) Julius Caesar   **822.3**

A reader's guide to Lorraine Hansberry's A raisin in

the sun   **812**

Lopez, Adriana

(ed) Fifteen candles   **392**

Lopez, Steve

The soloist   **92**

The **lord** of Opium. Farmer, N.   Fic

The **lord** of the rings. Tolkien, J. R. R.   Fic

Lord Tophet. Frost, G.   Fic

Lord, Walter

Day of infamy   **940.54**

Lorenz, Konrad

On aggression   **152.4**

Lorimer Real Justice [series]

Faryon, C. J. Guilty of being weird   **364.152**

Lorinc, John

Cities   **307.7**

Lorraine Hansberry's A raisin in the sun.   **812**

LOS ANGELES (CALIF.) -- FICTION

Stiefvater, M. Sinner   Fic

Losers in space. Barnes, J.   Fic

Losing Faith. Jaden, D.   Fic

Losing is not an option: stories. Wallace, R.   S

Loss. Kessler, J.   Fic

LOSS (PSYCHOLOGY)

Fitzgerald, H. The grieving teen   **155.9**

Myers, E. When will I stop hurting?   **155.9**

LOSS (PSYCHOLOGY)

See also Psychology

LOSS (PSYCHOLOGY) -- FICTION

Clark, J. Finding Mr. Brightside   Fic

Robert, N. B. She wore red trainers   Fic

Sweeney, D. The minnow   **823**

Lost. Davies, J.   Fic

LOST AND FOUND POSSESSIONS -- FICTION

Huntley, A. The everafter   Fic

LOST ARCHITECTURE

See also Architecture

Lost boy, lost girl. Dau, J. B.   **962.4**

Lost city of the Incas. Bingham, H.   **985**

The **lost** conspiracy. Hardinge, F.   Fic

The **lost** crown. Miller, S.   Fic

The **lost** gate. Card, O. S.   Fic

The **lost** German slave girl. Bailey, J.   **92**

Lost Girl Found. Bassoff, L.   Fic

Lost history. Morgan, M. H.   **909**

Lost in a good book. Fforde, J.   Fic

Lost in time. De la Cruz, M.   Fic

Lost in Yonkers. Simon, N.   **812**

The **Lost** Marble Notebook of Forgotten Girl and

Random Boy. Jaskulka, M.   Fic

Lost mountain. Reece, E.   **622**

LOST TRIBES OF ISRAEL

See also Jews

Banghart, T. E. Shattered Veil	**Fic**	Kirby, J. Golden	**Fic**
Barrett, T. The Stepsister's Tale	**Fic**	Kiss me deadly	**S**
Bauman, B. A. Jersey Angel	**Fic**	Koja, K. Kissing the bee	**Fic**
Black, H. Black heart	**Fic**	Laban, E. The Tragedy Paper	**Fic**
Blankman, A. Prisoner of night and fog	**Fic**	LaFevers, R. Grave mercy	**Fic**
Bosworth, J. Struck	**Fic**	Lemire, J. Trillium	**741.5**
Briant, E. I am (not) the walrus	**Fic**	Levithan, D. Another day	**Fic**
Brockenbrough, M. The game of Love and Death	**Fic**	Levithan, D. Every day	**Fic**
Clare, C. Clockwork princess	**Fic**	Levithan, D. How they met, and other stories	**S**
Clark, J. Finding Mr. Brightside	**Fic**	Levithan, D. The lover's dictionary	**Fic**
Colasanti, S. Something like fate	**Fic**	Lo, M. Ash	**Fic**
Cole, K. Poison princess	**Fic**	Lo, M. Huntress	**Fic**
Connor, L. The things you kiss goodbye	**Fic**	Lo, M. Inheritance	**Fic**
Cooney, C. B. Janie face to face	**Fic**	Longshore, K. Brazen	**Fic**
Cornwell, B. Tides	**Fic**	Love is hell	**S**
Cross, J. Tempest	**Fic**	Madison, B. September Girls	**Fic**
Cypess, L. Death sworn	**Fic**	McCahan, E. Love and other foreign words	**Fic**
Derting, K. The last echo	**Fic**	McGarry, K. Dare You to	**Fic**
DeStefano, L. Sever	**Fic**	McGarry, K. Pushing the limits	**Fic**
Diffenbaugh, V. The language of flowers	**Fic**	McLemore The weight of feathers	**Fic**
Doller, T. Something like normal	**Fic**	Millay, K. The Sea of Tranquility	**Fic**
Emerald green	**Fic**	Miller, K. The eternal ones	**Fic**
Everything, everything	**Fic**	Mont, E. M. A breath of Eyre	**Fic**
Fichera, L. Hooked	**Fic**	Morgan, P. The beautiful and the cursed	**Fic**
Fiedler, L. Romeo's ex	**Fic**	Moskowitz, H. Gone, gone, gone	**Fic**
Fine, S. Of Metal and Wishes	**Fic**	My true love gave to me	**813**
Fink, M. The summer I got a life	**Fic**	Myracle, L. The infinite moment of us	**Fic**
Fitzpatrick, H. My life next door	**Fic**	Nelson, J. I'll give you the sun	**Fic**
Fitzpatrick, H. What I thought was true	**Fic**	Nowlin, L. If he had been with me	**Fic**
Flannery	**Fic**	Ockler, S. The Book of Broken Hearts	**Fic**
Forman, G. Just one day	**Fic**	Oppel, K. Such wicked intent	**Fic**
Garcia, K. Beautiful creatures	**Fic**	Parker, A. C. Gated	**Fic**
Garcia, K. Beautiful darkness	**Fic**	Perkins, S. Isla and the happily ever after	**Fic**
Georgia peaches and other forbidden fruit	**Fic**	Pratchett, T. Dodger	**Fic**
Golden, A. Memoirs of a geisha	**Fic**	Preston, C. The scrapbook of Frankie Pratt	**Fic**
Grant, K. M. Paradise red	**Fic**	Rabb, M. Kissing in America	**Fic**
Gratton, T. The blood keeper	**Fic**	Rebel of the sands	**Fic**
Gray, C. Spellcaster	**Fic**	Reed, J. Living violet	**Fic**
Green, J. The fault in our stars	**Fic**	Rennison, L. The taming of the tights	**Fic**
Griffin, P. Burning blue	**Fic**	Ross, E. Belle epoque	**Fic**
Hale, S. Book of a thousand days	**Fic**	Rothenberg, J. The catastrophic history of you & me	**Fic**
Hamilton, K. When the stars threw down their spears	**Fic**	Rowell, R. Eleanor & Park	**Fic**
Han, J. We'll always have summer	**Fic**	Rutkoski, M. The winner's crime	**Fic**
Haydu, C. A. OCD love story	**Fic**	Ryan, S. Empress of the world	**Fic**
Hemphill, S. Sisters of glass	**Fic**	Salisbury, M. The Sin Eater's daughter	**Fic**
Hodge, R. Cruel Beauty	**Fic**	Scheidt, E. L. Uses for boys	**Fic**
Hubbard, A. Ripple	**Fic**	Schindler, H. Playing hurt	**Fic**
If I Was Your Girl	**Fic**	Schreck, K. H. While he was away	**Fic**
Jaskulka, M. The Lost Marble Notebook of Forgotten Girl and Random Boy	**Fic**	Scott, K. This is so not happening	**Fic**
Kagawa, J. The immortal rules	**Fic**	Sedgwick, M. Midwinterblood	**S**
Kephart, B. One thing stolen	**Fic**	Selfors, S. Mad love	**Fic**
Kindl, P. Keeping the castle	**Fic**	Selfors, S. The sweetest spell	**Fic**
King, A. S. Ask the passengers	**Fic**	Shirvington, J. Entice	**Fic**
		Simone Upgrade U	**Fic**
		Smith, E. W. Back when you were easier to love	**Fic**

The **magicians.** Grossman, L.   **Fic**
MAGICIANS
  Fleming, A. M. The Magical Life of Long Tack
    Sam   **741.5**
  Lutes, J. Houdini: the handcuff king   **741.5**
  Stewart, M. Mary Stewart's Merlin trilogy   **Fic**
  Wizards   **S**
MAGICIANS -- FICTION
  Chima, C. W. The Crimson Crown   **Fic**
  Morgenstern, E. The night circus   **Fic**
MAGICIANS -- GRAPHIC NOVELS
  Dunning, J. H. Salem Brownstone   **741.5**
  Fleming, A. M. The Magical Life of Long Tack
    Sam   **741.5**
  Lutes, J. Houdini: the handcuff king   **741.5**
Magick, mayhem, and mavericks. Cobb, C.   **541**
Magida, Arthur J.
  (ed) How to be a perfect stranger   **203**
Magill's choice [series]
  American Indian biographies   **920.003**
  Ancient Greece   **938**
  Shakespeare   **822.3**
  Short story writers   **809**
Magill's encyclopedia of science.   **580**
Magill's encyclopedia of science: animal life.   **590**
Magill's medical guide.   **610.3**
Magill's survey of American literature.   **810**
Magill's survey of world literature.   **809**
Magill, Elizabeth
  (ed) College financing information for teens **378.3**
  (ed) Drug information for teens   **613.8**
  (ed) Pregnancy information for teens   **618.2**
Magistrale, Tony
  Student companion to Edgar Allan Poe   **813**
MAGNET SCHOOLS
  See also Public schools; School integration;
  Schools
MAGNETIC NEEDLE *See* Compass
MAGNETIC RESONANCE IMAGING
  See also Diagnosis
MAGNETISM
  Verschuur, G. L. Hidden attraction   **538**
MAGNETISM
  See also Physics
MAGNETS
  See also Magnetism
Magoc, Chris J.
  Environmental issues in American history   **333.7**
Magocsi, Paul R.
  Historical atlas of Central Europe   **911**
Magoon, Kekla
  37 things I love (in no particular order)   **Fic**
  Fire in the streets   **Fic**
  How it went down   **Fic**
  (jt. auth) Shabazz, I. X   **Fic**
Magoon, Kekla

The rock and the river   **Fic**
Maguire, Gregory, 1954-
  Egg & spoon   **Fic**
  Son of a witch   **Fic**
  Wicked   **Fic**
Mahabharata/Bhagavadgita
  Bhagavad Gita   **294.5**
Mahaffey, James A.
  Fusion   **621.48**
Mahony, Phillip
  (ed) From both sides now   **811**
Mahood, Kristine
  Booktalking with teens   **021.7**
  A passion for print   **027.62**
Mai, Larry L.
  The Cambridge Dictionary of human biology and
    evolution   **612**
MAIASAURA
  See also Dinosaurs
Maier, Pauline
  American scripture   **973.3**
MAIL-ORDER BUSINESS
  See also Business; Direct selling; Selling
Main Street & Babbitt. Lewis, S.   **813**
MAINE -- FICTION
  Blagden, S. Dear Life, You Suck   **Fic**
  Griffin, N. The whole stupid way we are   **Fic**
  Jacobson, J. The complete history of why I hate
    her   **Fic**
  King, S. Carrie   **Fic**
  Oliver, L. Delirium   **Fic**
  Oliver, L. Requiem   **Fic**
  Smith, J. E. This is what happy looks like   **Fic**
  Walker, B. F. Black boy/white school   **Fic**
  Wunder, W. The probability of miracles   **Fic**
MAINSTREAMING IN EDUCATION
  See also Children with disabilities; Educa-
  tion; Exceptional children
MAINTENANCE SERVICES EXECUTIVES
  St. John, W. Outcasts united   **796.334**
Mair, Victor H.
  (ed) The Shorter Columbia anthology of traditional
    Chinese literature   **895.1**
Mairowitz, David Zane
  Kafka   **741.5**
Maisie Dobbs. Winspear, J.   **Fic**
Maitre-Allain, Thierry
  Aquariums   **639.34**
Maizel, Rebecca
  Infinite days   **Fic**
  Stolen nights   **Fic**
Major. Balf, T.   **92**
Major battles and campaigns [series]
  Wood, W. J. Battles of the Revolutionary War,
    1775-1781   **973.3**
Major forms of world government [series]

See also Planets

The **Mercury** 13: the untold story of thirteen American women and the dream of space flight. Ackmann, M.   **629.45**

MERCY KILLING *See* Euthanasia

Mercy mode. Garner, E.   **Fic**

Meredith, Sheena
(jt. auth) Brewer, S. The pregnant body book **618.2**

Merino, Noel
Drug legalization   **363.45**
Gateway drugs: opposing viewpoints   **362.29**
Juvenile crime   **364.36**
Medical ethics   **174.2**
Poverty and homelessness   **362.5**
Smoking   **362.29**
U.S. military deployment   **355.4**
What rights should illegal immigrants have?   **342**

The **Merit** Birds. Powell, K.   **C**

MERLIN (LEGENDARY CHARACTER) -- FICTION
Bradley, M. Z. Priestess of Avalon   **Fic**
McKenzie, N. Guinevere's gamble   **Fic**
Stewart, M. Mary Stewart's Merlin trilogy   **Fic**

MERLIN (LEGENDARY CHARACTER) -- GRAPHIC NOVELS
Excalibur   **741.5**

MERMAIDS AND MERMEN
See also Mythical animals

MERMAIDS AND MERMEN -- FICTION
Madison, B. September Girls   **Fic**
Moskowitz, H. Teeth   **Fic**

MERMEN -- FICTION
Moskowitz, H. Teeth   **Fic**

Merrell, Billy
(ed) The Full spectrum   **306.76**
Talking in the dark   **811**

The **Merriam-Webster** dictionary of synonyms and antonyms.   **423**

Merriam-Webster Inc.
Merriam-Webster's collegiate dictionary   **423**
Merriam-Webster's collegiate thesaurus   **423**
Merriam-Webster's dictionary of English usage **428**

Merriam-Webster's collegiate dictionary. Merriam-Webster Inc.   **423**

Merriam-Webster's collegiate thesaurus. Merriam-Webster Inc.   **423**

Merriam-Webster's dictionary of English usage. Merriam-Webster Inc.   **428**

Merriam-Webster's geographical dictionary. **910.3**

Merriam-Webster's visual dictionary.   **423**

Merrick, Joseph Carey, 1862-1890
About
Pomerance, B. The Elephant Man   **822**

Merriman, John M.
(ed) Europe 1789 to 1914   **940.2**
(ed) Europe since 1914   **940.5**

Mersky, Roy M.
Leiter, R. A. Landmark Supreme Court cases   **347**

Merton, Thomas
(ed) Gandhi, M. Gandhi on non-violence   **322.4**

Mertz, Barbara
Temples, tombs, & hieroglyphs   **932**

Mertz, Leslie A.
The circulatory system   **616.1**

Merullo, Roland
The talk-funny girl   **Fic**

Merwin, John
Trailside (Television program) Fly fishing   **799.1**

Merzbach, Uta C.
(jt. auth) Boyer, C. B. A history of mathematics   **510**

Meshbesher, Wendy
(jt. auth) Hartman, E. What are the issues with genetic technology?   **660.6**

MESMERISM *See* Hypnotism

Mesrobian, Carrie
Cut both ways   **Fic**
Perfectly good white boy   **Fic**
Sex and violence   **Fic**

Messenger of Fear. Grant, M.   **Fic**
Messenger of truth. Winspear, J.   **Fic**

MESSINESS
See also Human behavior

METABOLIC DISORDERS
See also Diseases

METABOLISM
See also Biochemistry

METAFICTION
See also Fiction

METALLOGRAPHY
See also Metals

METALS
Halka, M. Metals and metalloids   **546**
Halka, M. Transition metals   **546**
Metals and metalloids. Halka, M.   **546**

METALWORKERS
Perl, L. Cruzan v. Missouri   **344**

METALWORKING MACHINERY
See also Machinery

MetaMaus. Spiegelman, A.   **940.53**
Metamorphoses. Ovid   **873**

METAMORPHOSIS
Stiefvater, M. Sinner   **Fic**

The **metamorphosis** and other stories. Kafka, F.   **S**
Metaphors dictionary.   **423**

METAPHYSICS
See also Philosophy

Metcalf, Gena
(ed) Obesity   **616.3**

Metcalf, Linda
How to say it to get into the college of your choice   **378.1**

See also Family; Women

MOTHERS -- FICTION

Fusco, K. N. Tending to Grace — Fic

Lewis, S. The secret ingredient — Fic

Lowry, L. Son — Fic

Stiefvater, M. Blue Lily, Lily Blue — Fic

MOTHERS AND DAUGHTERS -- FICTION

Arnold, D. Mosquitoland — Fic

Arnold, E. K. Infandous — Fic

Axelrod, K. The law of loving others — Fic

Blythe, C. Revenge of a not-so-pretty girl — Fic

Bosworth, J. Struck — Fic

Brothers, M. Supergirl mixtapes — Fic

Cohn, R. Gingerbread — Fic

Dorris, M. A yellow raft in blue water — Fic

Doyle, R. A greyhound of a girl — Fic

Farish, T. The good braider — Fic

Fixmer, E. Down from the mountain — Fic

Haddix, M. P. Full ride — Fic

Harrington, L. Alice Bliss — Fic

Howard, A. G. Unhinged — Fic

Howard, J. J. That time I joined the circus — Fic

Jones, L. Mister Pip — Fic

Kamata, S. Gadget Girl — Fic

Kirby, J. Golden — Fic

Kwok, J. Girl in translation — Fic

Lessing, D. M. The sweetest dream — Fic

Oates, J. C. Freaky green eyes — Fic

Reed, A. Over you — Fic

Resau, L. The jade notebook — Fic

Schantz, S. E. Fig — Fic

Sepetys, R. Out of the Easy — Fic

Simmons, K. Article 5 — Fic

Singleton, L. J. Dead girl in love — Fic

Stirling, T. When my heart was wicked — Fic

Unbecoming — Fic

Zailckas, K. Mother, mother — Fic

MOTHERS AND SONS

Donoghue, E. Room — Fic

Howrey, M. Blind sight — Fic

Maguire, G. Son of a witch — Fic

MOTHERS AND SONS *See* Mother-son relationship

Mothers of invention. Faust, D. G. — 973.7

MOTHS

See also Insects

MOTHS -- FICTION

Willey, M. A summer of silk moths — Fic

MOTION PICTURE ACTORS AND ACTRESSES *See* Actors

It's all your fault — Fic

MOTION PICTURE CAMERAS

See also Cameras; Cinematography

MOTION PICTURE CARTOONS *See* Animated films

MOTION PICTURE DIRECTION *See* Motion pictures -- Production and direction

MOTION PICTURE DIRECTORS

Eisner, W. Eisner/Miller: a one-on-one interview — **741**

Fallon, M. How to analyze the works of Andy Warhol — **700**

Greenberg, J. Andy Warhol — **92**

Hakakian, R. Journey from the land of no — **92**

Ragusa, K. The skin between us — **92**

Schein, E. Identical strangers — **92**

Shepard, S. The girl from foreign — **92**

MOTION PICTURE INDUSTRY

Dixon, W. W. A Short History of Film — **791.43**

Landis, D. N. Dressed — **791.43**

MOTION PICTURE INDUSTRY -- FICTION

LaCour, N. Everything leads to you — Fic

MOTION PICTURE PHOTOGRAPHY *See* Cinematography

MOTION PICTURE PRODUCERS AND DIRECTORS

See also Motion picture industry

MOTION PICTURE PRODUCERS AND DIRECTORS -- FICTION

Bruton, C. I Predict a Riot

MOTION PICTURE PRODUCTION *See* Motion pictures -- Production and direction

MOTION PICTURE SERIALS

See also Motion pictures

MOTION PICTURES

See also Audiovisual materials; Mass media; Performing arts

MOTION PICTURES -- BIOGRAPHY

See also Biography

MOTION PICTURES -- CATALOGS

Halsall, J. Visual media for teens — **016**

MOTION PICTURES -- CENSORSHIP

See also Censorship

MOTION PICTURES -- ETHICAL ASPECTS

See also Ethics

MOTION PICTURES -- FICTION

Castellucci, C. Boy proof — Fic

MOTION PICTURES -- HISTORY

Dixon, W. W. A Short History of Film — **791.43**

MOTION PICTURES -- PRODUCTION AND DIRECTION

Movie Making Course: Expanded and Updated for the Digital Generation — **791.4**

MOTION PICTURES -- PRODUCTION AND DIRECTION

See also Motion picture industry

MOTION PICTURES -- PRODUCTION AND DIRECTION -- FICTION

Doctorow, C. Pirate cinema — Fic

Pauley, K. Cat Girl's day off — Fic

MOTION PICTURES AND CHILDREN

MYSTERY FICTION

See also Fiction

MYSTERY FILMS

See also Motion pictures

MYSTERY GRAPHIC NOVELS

MYSTERY GRAPHIC NOVELS

See also Graphic novels

Mystery library [series]

MYSTERY STORIES *See* Mystery fiction

MYSTERY WRITERS

MYSTICISM

See also Spiritual life

MYSTICISM -- ISLAM

See also Islam

MYSTICISM -- JUDAISM

See also Medicine

NUCLEAR PHYSICS

Baxter, R. Ernest Rutherford and the birth of the atomic age   **530.092**

NUCLEAR PHYSICS

See also Physics

NUCLEAR PHYSICS -- HISTORY

Baxter, R. Ernest Rutherford and the birth of the atomic age   **530.092**

NUCLEAR POWER *See* Nuclear energy

NUCLEAR POWER PLANTS

Ferguson, C. D. Nuclear energy   **333.792**

NUCLEAR POWER PLANTS -- ACCIDENTS

Lusted, M. A. The Chernobyl Disaster   **363.1**

Lusted, M. A. The Three Mile Island nuclear disaster   **363.1**

NUCLEAR POWER PLANTS -- ENVIRON-MENTAL ASPECTS

See also Environment; Environmental health

NUCLEAR POWER PLANTS -- FIRES AND FIRE PREVENTION

See also Fire prevention; Fires

NUCLEAR PROPULSION

See also Nuclear energy

NUCLEAR REACTORS

Mahaffey, J. A. Fusion   **621.48**

NUCLEAR REACTORS

See also Nuclear energy; Nuclear engineering; Nuclear physics

NUCLEAR SUBMARINES

See also Nuclear propulsion; Submarines

NUCLEAR WARFARE

Sheinkin, S. Bomb   **623.4**

NUCLEAR WARFARE

See also War

NUCLEAR WARFARE -- FICTION

Shute, N. On the beach   **Fic**

NUCLEAR WEAPONS

Diehl, S. J. Nuclear weapons and nonproliferation   **355.8**

Sheinkin, S. Bomb   **623.4**

Nuclear weapons and nonproliferation. Diehl, S. J.   **355.8**

NUCLEIC ACIDS

Hodge, R. The molecules of life   **611**

NUCLEIC ACIDS

See also Biochemistry

NUMBER CONCEPT

Bellos, A. Here's looking at Euclid   **513**

Blastland, M. The numbers game   **510**

NUMBER CONCEPT

See also Apperception; Psychology

NUMBER GAMES

See also Arithmetic -- Study and teaching; Counting; Mathematical recreations

NUMBER SYSTEMS *See* Numbers

NUMBER THEORY

See also Algebra; Mathematics; Set theory

Numbers. Ward, R.   **Fic**

NUMBERS

Tabak, J. Numbers   **513**

Numbers [series]

Ward, R. Infinity   **Fic**

Numbers. Tabak, J.   **513**

The **numbers** game. Blastland, M.   **510**

NUMERATION *See* Numbers

NUMERICAL ANALYSIS

See also Mathematical analysis

NUMEROLOGY

See also Occultism; Symbolism of numbers

NUMISMATICS

See also Ancient history; Archeology; History

Numrich, Paul David

Mann, G. S. Buddhists, Hindus, and Sikhs in America   **294**

Nuñez Cabeza de Vaca, Alvar, 16th cent.

About

Childress, D. Barefoot conquistador   **92**

Nunn, Joan

Fashion in costume, 1200-2000   **391**

NUNS

Armstrong, K. The spiral staircase   **92**

Notable women in the life sciences   **570.9**

Slavicek, L. C. Mother Teresa   **92**

Spink, K. Mother Teresa   **92**

NUNS

See also Women

NUNS -- FICTION

Blagden, S. Dear Life, You Suck   **Fic**

Jarzab, A. The opposite of hallelujah   **Fic**

LaFevers, R. Mortal heart   **Fic**

Strauss, V. Passion blue   **Fic**

NUREMBERG TRIAL OF MAJOR GERMAN WAR CRIMINALS, 1945-1946

Jarrow, G. Robert H. Jackson   **92**

NURSE MIDWIVES *See* Midwives

NURSE PRACTITIONERS

See also Allied health personnel; Nurses

NURSERIES (HORTICULTURE)

See also Fruit culture; Gardening

NURSERY RHYMES

See also Children's poetry; Children's songs; Folklore

NURSERY SCHOOLS

See also Elementary education; Schools

NURSES

Farrell, M. C. Pure grit   **940.54**

Garrison, M. Slaves who dared   **920**

Oates, S. B. A woman of valor: Clara Barton and the Civil War   **92**

NURSES -- FICTION

Oh, Snap! Myers, W. D. **Fic**

Ohanian, Hans C.

Einstein's mistakes **530**

OHIO -- ANTIQUITIES

See also Antiquities

OHIO -- BIOGRAPHY

See also Biography

OHIO -- CHURCH HISTORY

See also Church history

OHIO -- CIVILIZATION

See also Civilization

OHIO -- CLIMATE

See also Climate

OHIO -- COMMERCE

See also Commerce

OHIO -- FICTION

Perkins-Valdez, D. Wench **Fic**

OHIO -- GAZETTEERS

See also Gazetteers

OHIO -- HISTORY -- 1787-1865 -- FICTION

Perkins-Valdez, D. Wench **Fic**

OHIO -- HISTORY -- 19TH CENTURY -- FICTION

McGinnis, M. A madness so discreet **Fic**

OHIO -- INTELLECTUAL LIFE

See also Intellectual life

OHIO -- MAPS

See also Maps

OHIO -- RACE RELATIONS

See also Race relations

OHIO -- RELIGION

See also Religion

OHIO -- STATISTICS

See also Statistics

Ohno, Apolo Anton

About

Uschan, M. V. Apolo Anton Ohno **796.91**

Oil. Gardner, T. **333.8**

OIL *See* Oils and fats; Petroleum

Oil. Laxer, J. **333.8**

OIL BURNERS

See also Heating; Petroleum as fuel

OIL FUEL *See* Petroleum as fuel

OIL INDUSTRY *See* Petroleum industry

Oil painting for the absolute beginner. Willenbrink, M. **751.45**

OIL POLLUTION OF WATER

See also Water pollution

OIL SPILLS

DeNapoli, D. The great penguin rescue **639.9**

OIL WELL DRILLING

See also Drilling and boring (Earth and rocks); Petroleum industry

OIL WELLS

See also Petroleum industry

Oima, Yoshitoki

A silent voice **741.5**

Oink. Whyman, M. **636.4**

Okabayashi, Kensuke

Manga for dummies **741.5**

Oketani, Shogo, 1958-

(jt. auth) Lowitz, L. Jet Black and the ninja wind **Fic**

Okey, Shannon

Knitgrrl **746.43**

OKLAHOMA -- FICTION

Tingle, T. House of purple cedar **Fic**

OKLAHOMA -- HISTORY -- LAND RUSH, 1893 -- FICTION

Tingle, T. House of purple cedar **Fic**

Oklahoma western biographies [series]

Remley, D. Kit Carson **92**

Wilkins, T. John Muir **333.7**

Okorafor, Nnedimma

The shadow speaker **Fic**

Okorafor, N. Who fears death **Fic**

OLD AGE -- FICTION

Blythe, C. Revenge of a not-so-pretty girl **Fic**

Fitzpatrick, H. What I thought was true **Fic**

Myers, W. D. Lockdown **Fic**

Sonnenblick, J. Notes from the midnight driver **Fic**

OLD NORSE LANGUAGE

See also Language and languages; Scandinavian languages

OLD NORSE LITERATURE

See also Literature; Medieval literature

Old school. Wolff, T. **Fic**

Old world and new. Kelly, K. **610**

Older, Daniel José

Shadowshaper **Fic**

Oldershaw, Cally

Firefly guide to gems **553.8**

Gems of the world **553.8**

The **oldest** rookie. Morris, J. **796**

Oldfield, Sara

Rainforest **578.7**

OLDUVAI GORGE (TANZANIA) -- ANTIQUITIES

Henderson, H. The Leakey family **599.909**

OLIGARCHY

See also Political science

Olive, M. Foster

Ecstasy **362.29**

Oliver, Charles M.

Critical companion to Ernest Hemingway **813**

Critical companion to Walt Whitman **811**

Oliver, Evelyn Dorothy

Lewis, J. R. The dream encyclopedia **154.6**

Oliver, Jana G.

The demon trapper's daughter **Fic**

Soul thief **Fic**

Oliver, Lauren

Dr. Melissa Palmer's guide to hepatitis & liver disease **616.3**

Palmer, Pat
Teen esteem **155.5**

Palmer, Robin
The Corner of Bitter and Sweet **Fic**

PALMISTRY
See also Divination; Fortune telling; Occultism

Palmowski, Jan
A dictionary of contemporary world history **909.82**

PALO ALTO (CALIF.) -- FICTION
Voorhees, C. Lucky fools **Fic**

PALSY See Parkinson's disease

Pampel, Fred C.
Tobacco industry and smoking **338.4**

PAMPHLETEERS
Aykroyd, C. Savage satire **92**
Collins, P. The trouble with Tom: the strange afterlife and times of Thomas Paine **92**
DeGategno, P. J. Critical companion to Jonathan Swift **828**
Highet, G. The classical tradition **809**
Jonathan Swift's Gulliver's travels **823**

PAMPHLETS -- DESIGN
See also Design

PAN AM FLIGHT 103 BOMBING INCIDENT, 1988
Dornstein, K. The boy who fell out of the sky **92**

PAN-AFRICANISM
See also Africa -- Politics and government

Panchyk, Richard
Charting the world **912**
The keys to American history **973**

PANCREAS -- CANCER
Casil, A. S. Pancreatic cancer **616.99**

Pancreatic cancer. Casil, A. S. **616.99**

Pandemonium. Oliver, L. **Fic**

Panek, Richard
The 4 percent universe **523.1**

Panic. Oliver, L. **Fic**

Panic. Draper, S. M. **Fic**

PANIC DISORDERS
Schutz, S. I don't want to be crazy **92**

PANIC DISORDERS
See also Abnormal psychology; Neuroses

PANICS (FINANCE) See Financial crises

Panno, Joseph
Aging **612.6**
Animal cloning **660.6**
Cancer **616.99**
The cell **571.6**
Gene therapy **615.8**
Stem cell research **616**
Viruses **579.2**

PANTHEISM

See also Philosophy; Religion

Pantheon fairy tale & folklore library [series]
Latin American folktales **398.2**
Yiddish folktales **398.2**

Panther baby. Joseph, J. **974.7**

Pantomime. Lam, L. **Fic**

PANTOMIMES
See also Acting; Amateur theater; Drama; Theater

Paolini, Christopher
Brisingr **Fic**
Eldest **Fic**
Eragon **Fic**
About
Bankston, J. Christopher Paolini **92**

PAPACY
See also Catholic Church; Church history

Papadakis, Alexandra
(ed) Stuppy, W. The bizarre and incredible world of plants **580**

Papademetriou, Lisa
Homeroom diaries **Fic**

Papagianni, Dimitra
(jt. auth) Morse, M. A. Neanderthals rediscovered **569.9**

PAPAL VISITS
See also Voyages and travels

PAPER
See also Fibers

Paper covers rock. Hubbard, J. **Fic**

PAPER CRAFTS
Hayakawa, H. Kirigami menagerie **736**
Perdana, J. Build your own paper robots **745.54**
Reeder, D. Papier-mache monsters **745.54**
Sowell, S. Paper cutting techniques for scrapbooks & cards **745.54**

PAPER CRAFTS
See also Handicraft

Paper cutting techniques for scrapbooks & cards. Sowell, S. **745.54**

Paper dance. Cruz, V. H. **811**

PAPER FOLDING See Origami; Paper crafts

PAPER MONEY
Friedberg, A. Paper money of the United States **769.5**

PAPER MONEY
See also Money

Paper money of the United States. Friedberg, A. **769.5**

PAPER SCULPTURE See Paper crafts

Paper towns. Green, J. **Fic**

PAPER WORK See Paper crafts

PAPIER-MÂCHÉ See Paper crafts

Papier-mache monsters. Reeder, D. **745.54**

PAPILLOMAVIRUSES
Parks, P. J. HPV

ings

PREHISTORY *See* Archeology; Fossil hominids; Prehistoric peoples

PREJUDICE *See* Prejudices

PREJUDICE-MOTIVATED CRIMES *See* Hate crimes

PREJUDICES

Goldstein, P. A convenient hatred   **305.892**

Griffin, J. H. Black like me   **305.8**

Guterson, D. Snow falling on cedars   **Fic**

It's not all black and white   **305.8**

Pitcher, A. My sister lives on the mantelpiece   **Fic**

Sanna, E. We shall all be free   **305.8**

Taylor, M. D. The land   **Fic**

PREJUDICES

    See also Attitude (Psychology); Emotions; Interpersonal relations

PREJUDICES -- FICTION

Coats, J. A. The wicked and the just   **Fic**

Walsh, A. A Long Way from Home   **Fic**

PREMENSTRUAL SYNDROME

    See also Menstruation

Premiere. Carlson, M.   **Fic**

PRENATAL CARE

    See also Pregnancy

PRENATAL DIAGNOSIS

    See also Diagnosis

Prentzas, G. S.

Careers as a paralegal and legal assistant   **340.023**

The Marshall Plan   **338.91**

PREPARATION GUIDES FOR EXAMINA-TIONS *See* Examinations -- Study guides

PREPARATORY SCHOOLS -- FICTION

Howe, K. Conversion   **Fic**

Konigsberg, B. Openly straight   **Fic**

Oates, J. C. Two or three things I forgot to tell you   **Fic**

Voorhees, C. Lucky fools   **Fic**

Walker, B. F. Black boy/white school   **Fic**

PREPARED CEREALS

    See also Breakfasts; Food

Preparing for college. Rooney, J. J.   **378.1**

PRESBYTERIAN CHURCH -- SERMONS

    See also Sermons

PRESCHOOL CHILDREN *See* Children

Prescott, Peter S.

(ed) The Norton book of American short stories **813**

PRESERVATION OF BOTANICAL SPECI-MENS *See* Plants -- Collection and preservation

PRESERVATION OF FORESTS *See* Forest conservation

PRESERVATION OF NATURAL RESOURCES *See* Conservation of natural resources

PRESERVATION OF NATURAL SCENERY *See* Landscape protection; Natural monuments; Nature conservation

PRESERVATION OF SPECIMENS *See* Taxidermy

PRESERVATION OF WILDLIFE *See* Wildlife conservation

The **presidency** A to Z.   **973.09**

The **President** Has Been Shot! Swanson, J. L.   **973.922**

President Kennedy has been shot. Trost, C.   **364.1**

The **President's** daughter. White, E. E.   **Fic**

PRESIDENTIAL ADVISERS

Genovese, M. A. The Watergate crisis   **973.924**

Rice, C. Condoleezza Rice   **92**

PRESIDENTIAL CAMPAIGNS -- UNITED STATES *See* Presidents -- United States -- Election

PRESIDENTIAL CANDIDATES

Aronson, M. Robert F. Kennedy   **92**

Bailey, N. Female force   **741.5**

Benson, H. RFK: a photographer's journal **973.923**

Boston globe Ted Kennedy   **92**

English, B. Last lion   **92**

Kennedy, J. F. Profiles in courage   **920**

Profiles in courage for our time   **920**

Sapet, K. Ted Kennedy   **92**

Thomas, E. A long time coming   **324**

PRESIDENTIAL CANDIDATES -- UNITED STATES

Schnall, M. What will it take to make a woman president?   **305.4**

PRESIDENTIAL CANDIDATES -- UNITED STATES -- BIOGRAPHY

Hillary Rodham Clinton   **92**

The **presidential** election process: opposing viewpoints.   **324.6**

Presidential elections 1789-2008. Congressional Quarterly, I.   **324.6**

Presidents. Hamilton, N. A.   **920.003**

PRESIDENTS

    See also Heads of state

PRESIDENTS

Abramson, J. Obama   **92**

Allen, R. M. Mr. Lincoln's High-Tech War **973.7**

Aretha, D. Jefferson Davis   **92**

Arnold, J. R. Robert Mugabe's Zimbabwe **968.91**

Bausum, A. Unraveling freedom   **940.3**

Bober, N. Thomas Jefferson   **92**

Brinkley, A. Franklin Delano Roosevelt   **92**

Bruni, F. Ambling into history: the unlikely odyssey of George W. Bush   **973.931**

Burner, D. John F. Kennedy and a new generation   **92**

Carlin, J. Playing the enemy   **968.06**

Carter, J. An hour before daylight   **973.926**

Coltman, L. The real Fidel Castro   **92**

Cooper, I. Jack   **973**

Cooper, M. L. Theodore Roosevelt   **92**

S. **Fic**
PRIDE AND VANITY
 See also Conduct of life; Sin
Priest, Cherie
 I Am Princess X **Fic**
Priestess of Avalon. Bradley, M. Z. **Fic**
Priestley, Joseph, 1733-1804
 About
 Horvitz, L. A. Eureka!: scientific breakthroughs
  that changed the world **509**
 Malone, J. W. It doesn't take a rocket scientist **920**
PRIESTS
 See also Clergy
PRIESTS -- FICTION
 Kiely, B. The gospel of winter **Fic**
 Vasey, P. A troublesome boy **Fic**
PRIMARIES
 See also Elections; Political conventions;
  Politics
**Primary documents in American history and con-
temporary issues** [series]
 Affirmative action **331.1**
Primary sourcebook series
 Hillstrom, K. The Cold War **909.82**
The **primate** family tree. Redmond, I. **599.8**
Primates. Ottaviani, J. **741.5**
PRIMATES
 See also Mammals
PRIMATES
 Holmes, T. Primates and human ancestors **569**
 Ottaviani, J. Primates **741.5**
 Primates of the world
 Redmond, I. The primate family tree **599.8**
PRIMATES -- BEHAVIOR
 Waal, F. d. Our inner ape **156**
PRIMATES -- BEHAVIOR
 See also Animal behavior
PRIMATES -- EVOLUTION
 Walter, C. Last ape standing **569.9**
Primates and human ancestors. Holmes, T. **569**
Primates of the world.
PRIMATOLOGISTS
 De la Bedoyere, C. No one loved gorillas more **92**
 Greene, M. Jane Goodall **92**
 Halloran, A. R. The song of the ape **599.885**
Prime [series]
 Gaines, A. Don't steal copyrighted stuff! **808**
 Mayer, R. H. When the children marched **323.1**
Prime baby. Yang, G. **741.5**
PRIME MINISTERS
 Arnold, J. R. Robert Mugabe's Zimbabwe **968.91**
 Fulbrook, M. A concise history of Germany **943**
 Wade, R. A. The Bolshevik revolution and Russian
  Civil War **947.084**
PRIME MINISTERS
 See also Cabinet officers; Executive power

Primiano, Jay
 Swim that rock **Fic**
Primitive mythology. Campbell, J. **201**
PRIMITIVE SOCIETIES
 See also Civilization; Ethnology
The **prince.** Machiavelli, N. **320.1**
The **Prince** of Mist. Ruiz Zafon, C. **Fic**
Prince of Shadows. Caine, R. **Fic**
Prince of stories. Wagner, H. **823**
A **prince** without a kingdom. De Fombelle, T. **843**
Prince, Liz
 About
 Prince, L. Tomboy **741.5**
PRINCES
 Donnelly, J. Revolution **Fic**
 Fulbrook, M. A concise history of Germany **943**
 Saint-Exupery, A. d. The little prince **Fic**
 Wade, R. A. The Bolshevik revolution and Russian
  Civil War **947.084**
 Whitcomb, L. The Fetch **Fic**
PRINCES -- FICTION
 Bardugo, L. Ruin and rising **Fic**
 Kontis, A. Enchanted **Fic**
 Nix, G. A confusion of princes **Fic**
PRINCES AND PRINCESSES *See* Princes; Prin-
cesses
PRINCESSES
 Jones, V. G. Pocahontas **92**
 Whitcomb, L. The Fetch **Fic**
 Woodward, G. S. Pocahontas **92**
PRINCESSES -- FICTION
 Aveyard, V. Red queen **Fic**
 Bow, E. The Scorpion Rules **Fic**
 Cokal, S. The Kingdom of little wounds **Fic**
 Lies, knives and girls in red dresses **Fic**
 Moriarty, J. The cracks in the kingdom **Fic**
 Tripp, B. The accidental highwayman **Fic**
 Winter **Fic**
 Yolen, J. Curse of the Thirteenth Fey **Fic**
**PRINCESSES -- ROMANIA -- TRANSYLVANIA
-- FICTION**
 And I darken **Fic**
The **princesses** of Iowa. Backes, M. M. **Fic**
The **Princeton** encyclopedia of birds. **598**
The **Princeton** encyclopedia of mammals. **599**
The **Princeton** field guide to dinosaurs. Paul, G.
S. **567.9**
Princeton field guides [series]
 Compagno, L. J. V. Sharks of the world **597**
 Kays, R. Mammals of North America **599**
 Paul, G. S. The Princeton field guide to dino-
  saurs **567.9**
Princeton Language Institute
 Roget's 21st century thesaurus in dictionary
  form **423**
Princeton Review series

Kuehn, S. Complicit **Fic**

Philpot, C. Even in paradise **Fic**

Rowell, R. Carry on **Fic**

Stand-off **Fic**

Stiefvater, M. The raven boys **Fic**

Vasey, P. A troublesome boy **Fic**

Walker, B. F. Black boy/white school **Fic**

Wells, R. Feedback **Fic**

Whitney, D. The rivals **Fic**

Wolitzer, M. Belzhar **Fic**

PRIVATEERING

See also International law; Naval art and science; Naval history; Pirates

Priwer, Shana

Ancient monuments **732**

Pro makeup. Spencer, K. **646.7**

Pro nail care. Toselli, L. **646.7**

PRO-ABORTION MOVEMENT See Pro-choice movement

PRO-CHOICE ACTIVISTS

Hull, N. E. H. Roe v. Wade **344**

PRO-CHOICE MOVEMENT

McBride, D. E. Abortion in the United States **363.46**

PRO-CHOICE MOVEMENT

See also Social movements

PRO-LIFE MOVEMENT

McBride, D. E. Abortion in the United States **363.46**

PRO-LIFE MOVEMENT

See also Social movements

PROBABILITIES

Rosenthal, J. Struck by lightning **519.2**

Tabak, J. Probability and statistics **519.2**

PROBABILITIES

See also Algebra; Logic; Mathematics; Statistics

Probability and statistics. Tabak, J. **519.2**

The **probability** of miracles. Wunder, W. **Fic**

PROBATION

Easton, T. S. Boys Don't Knit **Fic**

PROBATION

See also Corrections; Criminal law; Prisons; Punishment; Reformatories; Social case work

PROBIOTICS

See also Dietary supplements; Microorganisms

PROBLEM CHILDREN See Emotionally disturbed children

PROBLEM DRINKING See Alcoholism

PROBLEM SOLVING

Adam, J. A. Guesstimation **519.5**

Computing for ordinary mortals **004**

PROBLEM SOLVING

See also Psychology

PROCEDURE MANUALS

Gorman, M. Connecting young adults and libraries **027.62**

Miller, D. P. Crash course in teen services **027.62**

Stephens, C. G. Library 101 **027.8**

PROCUREMENT OF ORGANS, TISSUES, ETC.

Cheney, A. Body brokers **617.9**

Whitehouse, B. The match **92**

PRODIGAL SON (PARABLE)

See also Parables

Prodigy. Lu, M. **Fic**

PRODUCT RECALL

See also Consumer protection

PRODUCT SAFETY

See also Consumer protection

PRODUCTION See Economics; Industries

PRODUCTS, AGRICULTURAL See Farm produce

PRODUCTS, COMMERCIAL See Commercial products

PROFESSIONAL EDUCATION

See also Education; Higher education; Learning and scholarship

PROFESSIONAL ETHICS

See also Ethics

PROFESSIONAL SPORTS

See also Sports

PROFESSIONS

Careers **331.702**

Careers in biotechnology **660.6**

Careers in health care **610.73**

Gregory, M. G. The career chronicles **331.7**

McKenna, A. Nontraditional careers for women and men **331.702**

PROFESSIONS

See also Occupations; Self-employed

Professor Stewart's hoard of mathematical treasures. Stewart, I. **510**

The **professor's** daughter. Sfar, J. **741.5**

PROFESSORS See Educators; Teachers

Professors' guide [series]

Jacobs, L. F. The secrets of college success **378.1**

Profiles in courage. Kennedy, J. F. **920**

Profiles in courage for our time. **920**

Profiles in economics [series]

Rossig, W. Karl Marx **92**

Profiles in mathematics [series]

Corrigan, J. Alan Turing **92**

Profiles in science [series]

Baxter, R. Ernest Rutherford and the birth of the atomic age **530.092**

Baxter, R. Skeptical chemist **92**

Steffens, B. Ibn al-Haytham **92**

PROFIT

See also Business; Capital; Economics; Wealth

PROFIT SHARING

See also Commerce; Salaries, wages, etc.

PROTECTION OF ENVIRONMENT *See* Environmental protection

PROTECTION OF NATURAL SCENERY *See* Landscape protection; Natural monuments; Nature conservation

PROTECTION OF PLANTS *See* Plant conservation

PROTECTION OF WILDLIFE *See* Wildlife conservation

PROTEINS

Hodge, R. The molecules of life   **611**

PROTEINS

See also Biochemistry; Nutrition

PROTEST *See* Dissent

PROTEST MOVEMENTS

See also Social movements

PROTEST MOVEMENTS -- FICTION

Alexander, K. He said, she said   **Fic**

Doctorow, C. Pirate cinema   **Fic**

George, M. The difference between you and me **Fic**

Manzano, S. The revolution of Evelyn Serrano **Fic**

The **protest** singer. Wilkinson, A.   **92**

PROTESTANT CHURCHES

See also Christian sects; Church history; Protestantism

PROTESTANT REFORMATION *See* Reformation

Protestantism. Brown, S. F.   **280**

PROTESTANTISM

Brown, S. F. Protestantism   **280**

PROTESTANTISM

See also Christianity; Church history

Prothero, Stephen R.

Queen, E. L. Encyclopedia of American religious history   **200.9**

PROTONS

See also Atoms; Particles (Nuclear physics)

PROTOPLASM

See also Biology; Life (Biology)

Protopopescu, Orel Odinov

Liu Siyu A thousand peaks   **895.1**

PROTOZOA

See also Microorganisms

The **proud** tower. Tuchman, B. W.   **909.82**

Proulx, Annie, 1936-

About

Proulx, A. Bird cloud   **92**

PROVENCE (FRANCE) -- HISTORY -- 13TH CENTURY -- FICTION

The passion of Dolssa   **Fic**

PROVERBS

Collis, H. 101 American English proverbs   **428**

Cordry, H. V. The multicultural dictionary of proverbs   **082**

Oxford dictionary of phrase, saying, and quotation   **808.88**

PROVERBS

See also Folklore; Quotations

PROVIDENCE AND GOVERNMENT OF GOD

See also God

Provine, Robert R.

Laughter   **152.4**

Provoost, Anne

In the shadow of the ark   **Fic**

PRUNING

See also Forests and forestry; Fruit culture; Gardening; Trees

PRUSSIA

Salt to the sea   **Fic**

PSI (PARAPSYCHOLOGY) *See* Parapsychology

PSYCHE (GREEK DEITY)

See also Gods and goddesses

PSYCHIATRIC CARE *See* Mental health services

PSYCHIATRIC HOSPITALS

McCormick, P. Cut   **Fic**

PSYCHIATRIC HOSPITALS

See also Hospitals

PSYCHIATRIC HOSPITALS -- FICTION

Alender, K. The dead girls of Hysteria Hall   **Fic**

Jacobs, J. H. The Shibboleth   **Fic**

PSYCHIATRIC SERVICES *See* Mental health services

PSYCHIATRISTS

See also Psychologists

PSYCHIATRY

See also Medicine

PSYCHIC ABILITY -- FICTION

Bray, L. The diviners   **Fic**

Bray, L. Lair of dreams   **Fic**

Brockmann, S. Night sky   **Fic**

Derting, K. The last echo   **Fic**

The devil and Winnie Flynn   **Fic**

Garvey, A. Glass Heart   **Fic**

Moore, K. Amber House   **Fic**

Moore, K. Neverwas   **Fic**

Perez, M. Dead is just a dream   **Fic**

Smith, L. Sekret   **Fic**

Ward, R. Infinity   **Fic**

West, K. Split second   **Fic**

White, K. Perfect lies   **Fic**

Wonders of the invisible world   **Fic**

PSYCHIC PHENOMENA *See* Parapsychology

PSYCHIC TRAUMA -- FICTION

Exit, pursued by a bear   **Fic**

Rosenfield, K. Inland   **Fic**

PSYCHICAL RESEARCH *See* Parapsychology

PSYCHICS

See also Parapsychology; Persons

PSYCHICS -- FICTION

Albin, G. Crewel   **Fic**

Bray, L. Lair of dreams   **Fic**

Brockmann, S. Night sky   **Fic**

Rudman, P. S. The Babylonian theorem **510**

Pythagoras: pioneering mathematician and musical theorist of Ancient Greece. Karamanides, D. **92**

The **Pythagorean** theorem. Maor, E. **516.2**

PYTHON (COMPUTER LANGUAGE)

Teach your kids to code **005.13**

Q

QAIDA (ORGANIZATION)

Hillstrom, K. The September 11 terrorist attacks **973.931**

QAIDA (ORGANIZATION)

See also Terrorism

Qaiser, Annie

How to analyze the works of George Washington **973.4**

QUACKS AND QUACKERY

See also Impostors and imposture; Medicine; Swindlers and swindling

Quammen, David

(ed) Darwin, C. On the origin of species **576.8**

QUANTITY COOKING

See also Cooking

Quantum man. Krauss, L. M. **92**

QUANTUM MECHANICS *See* Quantum theory

QUANTUM THEORY

Cole, K. C. The hole in the universe **530.01**

Feynman, R. P. Six easy pieces **530**

Ford, K. W. 101 quantum questions **530.1**

Hakim, J. The story of science: Einstein adds a new dimension **509**

Hawking, S. W. The nature of space and time **530.1**

Hawking, S. W. The universe in a nutshell **530.1**

Hawking, S. The grand design **530.1**

Kakalios, J. The amazing story of quantum mechanics **530.1**

Orzel, C. How to teach physics to your dog **530.1**

Rigden, J. S. Einstein 1905 **530.1**

QUANTUM THEORY

See also Dynamics; Physics

QUANTUM THEORY -- GRAPHIC NOVELS

Ottaviani, J. Suspended in language **92**

Quarantine. Thomas, L. **Fic**

Quarantine. Thomas, L. **Fic**

QUARANTINE *See* Communicable diseases

QUARANTINE -- FICTION

Falls, K. Inhuman **Fic**

Thomas, L. Quarantine 3: The Burnouts **Fic**

QUARANTINE -- NEW YORK (STATE) -- NEW YORK -- HISTORY

Bartoletti, S. C. Terrible typhoid Mary **92**

Quarantine 3: The Burnouts. Thomas, L. **Fic**

QUARTZ

See also Crystals; Minerals

QUASARS

See also Astronomy; Radio astronomy

Quay, Sara E.

Westward expansion **978**

The **Queen** of Attolia. Turner, M. W. **Fic**

Queen of hearts. Brooks, M. **Fic**

The **Queen** of Water. Farinango, M. V. **Fic**

Queen, Edward L.

Encyclopedia of American religious history **200.9**

QUEENS

Dray, S. Lily of the Nile **Fic**

Friesner, E. M. Sphinx's princess **Fic**

Friesner, E. M. Sphinx's queen **Fic**

Klein, L. M. Cate of the Lost Colony **Fic**

Lever, E. Marie Antoinette **92**

Mertz, B. Temples, tombs, & hieroglyphs **932**

Meyer, C. Duchessina **Fic**

Nardo, D. Cleopatra **92**

Roller, D. W. Cleopatra **92**

Shecter, V. A. Cleopatra's moon **Fic**

Starkey, D. Six wives: the queens of Henry VIII **942.05**

QUEENS

See also Monarchy

QUEENS -- FICTION

Carson, R. The bitter kingdom **Fic**

Carson, R. The crown of embers **Fic**

Cashore, K. Bitterblue **Fic**

Chima, C. W. The Crimson Crown **Fic**

Cokal, S. The Kingdom of little wounds **Fic**

Salisbury, M. The Sin Eater's daughter **Fic**

The star-touched queen **Fic**

QUEER THEORY

See also Criticism

Quiñones-Hinojosa, Alfredo

About

Quiñones-Hinojosa, A. Becoming Dr. Q **92**

Quick and dirty tips [series]

Fogarty, M. Grammar Girl's 101 words every high school graduate needs to know **428**

QUICK AND EASY COOKING

See also Cooking

Quick and popular reads for teens. **028.5**

Quick cash for teens. Bielagus, P. G. **658.1**

Quick, Matthew

Boy21 **Fic**

Forgive me, Leonard Peacock **Fic**

Quicksand. **616.97**

QUILTING

Beyer, J. Quiltmaking by hand **746.46**

QUILTING

See also Needlework; Sewing

Quilting the black-eyed pea. Giovanni, N. **811**

Quiltmaking by hand. Beyer, J. **746.46**

QUILTS

Tobin, J. Hidden in plain view **973.7**

QUILTS -- DESIGN

See also Design

RAILROAD ACCIDENTS

See also Accidents; Disasters

RAILROAD ENGINEERING

See also Civil engineering; Engineering; Railroads

RAILROAD TRAVEL

See also Transportation; Travel; Voyages and travels

RAILROADS -- CALIFORNIA -- HISTORY -- 19TH CENTURY

Drabelle, D. The great American railroad war **385**

RAILROADS -- FICTION

Miéville, C. Railsea **Fic**

RAILROADS -- HISTORY

Gimpel, D. The transcontinental railroad **385**

RAILROADS -- STATISTICS

See also Statistics

RAILROADS -- UNITED STATES

Best shot in the West **978**

Railsea. Miéville, C. **Fic**

RAIN FOREST ANIMALS

Forsyth, A. Nature of the rainforest **577.3**

McAllister, I. The last wild wolves **599.77**

RAIN FOREST ECOLOGY

Forsyth, A. Nature of the rainforest **577.3**

Lowman, M. It's a jungle up there **92**

Lowman, M. Life in the treetops **577.34**

Moore, P. D. Tropical forests **577.3**

RAIN FOREST ECOLOGY

See also Ecology

RAIN FORESTS

Oldfield, S. Rainforest **578.7**

RAIN FORESTS

See also Forests and forestry

RAIN FORESTS -- FICTION

Gilman, D. Blood sun **Fic**

RAIN FORESTS -- PICTORIAL WORKS

Marent, T. Rainforest **578.7**

RAIN MAKING *See* Weather control

RAINBOW

See also Meteorology

Rainbow boys. Sanchez, A. **Fic**

Rainbow High. Sanchez, A. **Fic**

Rainbow road. Sanchez, A. **Fic**

Rainfield, Cheryl

Stained **Fic**

Rainforest. Oldfield, S. **578.7**

Rainforest. Marent, T. **578.7**

RAINFORESTS *See* Rain forests

Rainis, Kenneth G.

Cell and microbe science fair projects **571.6**

A guide to microlife **576**

A **raisin** in the sun. Hansberry, L. **812**

Rakove, Jack N.

(ed) The annotated U.S. Constitution and Declaration of Independence **342**

Raleigh, Walter Sir, 1552?-1618

About

Aronson, M. Sir Walter Ralegh and the quest for El Dorado **942.05**

Klein, L. M. Cate of the Lost Colony **Fic**

Ralph Bunche. Urquhart, B. E. **92**

Ralph Ellison. **813**

Ralph Ellison's Invisible man. **813**

Ralph Lauren. Mattern, J. **92**

Ralston, Aron

About

Ralston, A. Between a rock and a hard place **796.522**

Ram-Prasad, Chakravarthi

Exploring the life, myth, and art of India **954**

RAMADAN -- FICTION

Robert, N. B. Boy vs. girl **Fic**

The **Ramayana.** Narayan, R. K. **891**

The **Ramayana** and Hinduism. Ganeri, A. **294.5**

Ramazani, Jahan

(ed) The Norton anthology of modern and contemporary poetry **821**

Ramirez, Luz Elena

Encyclopedia of Hispanic-American literature **810**

Ramirez, Manny, 1972-

About

Rhodes, J. E. Becoming Manny **92**

Ramm, David

Rich, M. World authors, 2000-2005 **920.003**

Ramón y Cajal, Santiago, 1852-1934

About

Hellman, H. Great feuds in medicine **610**

Rapport, R. Nerve endings **612.8**

Rampersad, Arnold

Ashe, A. Days of grace **796.342**

(ed) The Oxford anthology of African-American poetry **811**

Ramses II, King of Egypt

About

Mertz, B. Temples, tombs, & hieroglyphs **932**

Ramsey, Dan

Teach yourself visually car care & maintenance **629.28**

Ramsey, Judy

Ramsey, D. Teach yourself visually car care & maintenance **629.28**

RANCH LIFE

DiSilvestro, R. L. Theodore Roosevelt in the Badlands **92**

Kyle, A. The god of animals **Fic**

RANCH LIFE

See also Farm life; Frontier and pioneer life

RANCH LIFE -- SPAIN -- FICTION

Kephart, B. Small damages **Fic**

RANCHERS

Craft, J. Our white boy **92**

RANCHES -- FICTION

Reporting America at war.   070.4

Reporting civil rights.   323.1

Reporting Vietnam.   070.4

Reporting World War II.   940.53

REPORTS -- PREPARATION *See* Report writing

Repossessed. Jenkins, A. M.   Fic

Representative American speeches.   815

REPRESENTATIVE GOVERNMENT AND REPRESENTATION
> *See also* Constitutional history; Constitutional law; Political science

REPRODUCTION
> Reproductive rights   363.9

REPRODUCTION
> *See also* Biology; Life (Biology); Physiology

REPRODUCTION -- TECHNOLOGICAL INNOVATIONS *See* Reproductive technology

REPRODUCTIVE BEHAVIOR *See* Sexual behavior in animals

REPRODUCTIVE ORGANS *See* Reproductive system

Reproductive rights.   363.9

Reproductive rights. Bringle, J.   613.9

Reproductive rights.   344

REPRODUCTIVE RIGHTS -- HISTORY
> Reproductive rights   363.9

The **reproductive** system. Krohmer, R. W.   618

REPRODUCTIVE SYSTEM
> *See also* Anatomy; Physiology; Sex -- Physiological aspects

REPRODUCTIVE SYSTEM
> Brewer, S. The pregnant body book   618.2
> Hollen, K. H. The reproductive system   618
> Krohmer, R. W. The reproductive system   618

The **reproductive** system. Hollen, K. H.   618

Reproductive technology. Zach, K. K.   618

REPRODUCTIVE TECHNOLOGY
> *See also* Biotechnology

REPRODUCTIVE TECHNOLOGY
> Green, R. M. Babies by design   176
> Zach, K. K. Reproductive technology   618

REPTILES
> Alderton, D. Firefly encyclopedia of the vivarium   639.3
> Attenborough, D. Life in cold blood   597.9
> Conant, R. A field guide to reptiles & amphibians   597.9
> Conant, R. Peterson first guide to reptiles and amphibians   597.9
> Ernst, C. H. Venomous reptiles of the United States, Canada, and northern Mexico   597.9
> Stebbins, R. C. A field guide to Western reptiles and amphibians   597.9

REPTILES
> *See also* Animals

REPTILES -- PHYSIOLOGY

> *See also* Physiology

REPUBLICAN PARTY (U.S.)
> *See also* Political parties

REPUBLICS
> *See also* Constitutional history; Constitutional law; Political science

Requiem. Oliver, L.   Fic

Resau, Laura
> (jt. auth) Farinango, M. V. The Queen of Water   Fic
> The indigo notebook   Fic
> The jade notebook   Fic
> Red glass   Fic
> The ruby notebook   Fic

Resch, John Phillips
> (ed) Americans at war   973

The **rescue** artist. Dolnick, E.   364.1

RESCUE DOGS
> *See also* Rescue work; Working dogs

RESCUE OF JEWS, 1939-1945 *See* World War, 1939-1945 -- Jews -- Rescue

Rescue warriors. Helvarg, D.   363.2

RESCUE WORK
> Helvarg, D. Rescue warriors   363.2
> Hurricane Katrina   363.34
> Sandler, M. W. The impossible rescue   979.8
> Van Tilburg, C. Mountain rescue doctor   616

RESCUE WORK -- FICTION
> Riggs, R. Library of souls   Fic

RESCUES
> Smith, B. The Stuff of Legend   741.5

RESEARCH -- METHODOLOGY
> MacLeod, D. How to find out anything   001.4

RESEARCH -- STUDY AND TEACHING
> The new digital scholar   808.02

RESEARCH AND DEVELOPMENT *See* Research

RESEARCH AND THE LIBRARY
> Selverstone, H. S. Encouraging and supporting student inquiry   001.4
> Volkman, J. D. Collaborative library research projects   025.5

Research for writing [series]
> Bodden, V. Using the Internet   025.042

A **research** guide for undergraduate students. Baker, N. L.   800

RESEARCH PAPER WRITING *See* Report writing

Research-based reading strategies in the library for adolescent learners. Bernadowski, C.   372.4

The **resistance.** Malley, G.   Fic

RESISTANCE TO DRUGS IN MICROORGANISMS *See* Drug resistance in microorganisms

RESISTANCE TO GOVERNMENT
> Civil disobedience   809
> Hoose, P. M. The boys who challenged Hitler   940.53

RUSSIA -- HISTORY -- 1905, REVOLUTION -- FICTION

Miller, S. The lost crown **Fic**

RUSSIA -- HISTORY -- 1917-1921, REVOLUTION

Fleming, C. The family Romanov **947.08**

RUSSIA -- HISTORY -- 1917-1991, SOVIET UNION -- FICTION

Smith, L. Sekret **Fic**

RUSSIA -- HISTORY -- NICHOLAS II, 1894-1917

Fleming, C. The family Romanov **947.08**

RUSSIA -- KINGS AND RULERS

Massie, R. K. The Romanovs **947.08**

Whitelaw, N. Catherine the Great and the Enlightenment in Russia **92**

RUSSIAN AMERICANS -- FICTION

Crowder, M. Audacity **Fic**

Kiem, E. Dancer, daughter, traitor, spy **Fic**

RUSSIAN LANGUAGE

See also Language and languages

RUSSIAN LITERATURE

See also Literature

RUSSIAN LITERATURE -- COLLECTIONS

The Portable nineteenth-century Russian reader **891.7**

The Portable twentieth-century Russian reader **891.7**

RUSSIAN LITERATURE -- DICTIONARIES

Handbook of Russian literature **891.7**

The **Russian** master and other stories. Chekhov, A. P. **S**

RUSSIAN ORTHODOX CHURCH

See also Christian sects; Orthodox Eastern Church

RUSSIAN REVOLUTION *See* Russia -- History -- 1917-1921, Revolution

RUSSIANS -- FICTION

Castellucci, C. Rose sees red **Fic**

RUSSIANS -- UNITED STATES

Solomon, A. The little bride **Fic**

Russo, Meredith

If I Was Your Girl **Fic**

Russon, Anne E.

Orangutans: wizards of the rainforest **599.8**

Russon, Penni

Breathe **Fic**

Rustin, Bayard, 1910-1987

About

Miller, C. C. No easy answers **92**

Ruth, Babe, 1895-1948

About

Hampton, W. Babe Ruth **92**

Ruth, Janice E.

Women of the suffrage movement **324.6**

Rutherford, Ernest, 1871-1937

About

Baxter, R. Ernest Rutherford and the birth of the atomic age **530.092**

Cropper, W. H. Great physicists **530**

Reeves, R. A force of nature **92**

Rutkoski, Marie

The shadow society **Fic**

The winner's crime **Fic**

Ruud, Jay

Critical companion to Dante **850**

Encyclopedia of medieval literature **809**

RWANDA

Hatzfeld, J. Machete season **967.571**

Kinzer, S. A thousand hills **967.571**

Nardo, D. The Rwandan genocide **967.571**

Rusesabagina, P. An ordinary man **92**

The Rwandan genocide **967.571**

RWANDA -- FICTION

Combres, E. Broken memory **Fic**

Jansen, H. Over a thousand hills I walk with you **Fic**

RWANDA -- GRAPHIC NOVELS

Stassen Deogratias **741.5**

RWANDA -- HISTORY

Nardo, D. The Rwandan genocide **967.571**

RWANDA -- HISTORY -- CIVIL WAR, 1994 -- PERSONAL NARRATIVES

Hatzfeld, J. Machete season **967.571**

Rusesabagina, P. An ordinary man **92**

RWANDA -- POLITICS AND GOVERNMENT

Gourevitch, P. We wish to inform you that tomorrow we will be killed with our families **967.571**

Kinzer, S. A thousand hills **967.571**

The **Rwandan** genocide. **967.571**

The **Rwandan** genocide. Nardo, D. **967.571**

Ryan White: my own story. White, R. **362.1**

Ryan, Amy Kathleen

Flame **Fic**

Glow **Fic**

Spark **Fic**

Zen & Xander undone **Fic**

Ryan, Carrie

The dark and hollow places **Fic**

The dead-tossed waves **Fic**

The Forest of Hands and Teeth **Fic**

Ryan, James D.

Jones, C. Encyclopedia of Hinduism **294.5**

Ryan, Margaret

Extraordinary oral presentations **808.5**

Ryan, Patrick

Gemini bites **Fic**

In Mike we trust **Fic**

Ryan, Sara

Empress of the world **Fic**

Ryan, Tom

Way to go **Fic**

Rybolt, Thomas R.

Adrift   **Fic**
  Herlong, M. The great wide sea   **Fic**
  Stevenson, R. A thousand shades of blue   **Fic**
Sailing the wine-dark sea. Cahill, T.   **909**
Sailor Moon.   **741.5**
SAILORS -- FICTION
  Birch, C. Jamrach's menagerie   **Fic**
SAILORS -- FICTION *See* Sea stories
SAILORS' LIFE *See* Sailors; Seafaring life
Saint Amant, Robert
  Computing for ordinary mortals   **004**
Saint Anything. Dessen, S.   **Fic**
SAINT BARTHOLOMEW'S DAY, MASSACRE OF, 1572
    See also France -- History -- 1328-1589, House of Valois; Huguenots; Massacres
Saint Iggy. Going, K. L.   **Fic**
SAINT KILDA (VIC.) -- FICTION
  Girl defective   **Fic**
SAINT PETERSBURG (RUSSIA)
  Anderson, M. T. Symphony for the city of the dead   **92**
SAINT PETERSBURG (RUSSIA) -- HISTORY -- 20TH CENTURY -- FICTION
  Standiford, N. The boy on the bridge   **Fic**
Saint-Exupery, Antoine de
  The little prince   **Fic**
Saints.   **741.5**
SAINTS
    See also Religious biography
SAINTS
  Bolt, R. A man for all seasons   **822**
  Bradley, M. Z. Priestess of Avalon   **Fic**
  Bury, J. B. Ireland's saint   **92**
  Ehrman, B. D. Peter, Paul, and Mary Magdalene   **225.9**
  Grimes, N. A girl named Mister   **Fic**
  Notable women in the life sciences   **570.9**
  Pernoud, R. Joan of Arc: her story   **92**
  Strathern, P. Thomas Aquinas in 90 minutes   **92**
Sakai, Stan
  Usagi Yojimbo, book one   **741.5**
  Usagi Yojimbo: Yokai   **741.5**
Sakora, Lea
  (ed) Is gun ownership a right?   **344**
SALADS
    See also Cooking
SALAMANDERS
    See also Amphibians
Salamone, Frank A.
  (ed) Encyclopedia of religious rites, rituals, and festivals   **200**
Salazar, Alberto
  (jt. auth) Brant, J. 14 minutes   **796.42**
Salazar, Alberto, 1958-
        About

Brant, J. 14 minutes   **796.42**
Salbi, Zainab
        About
  Salbi, Z. Between two worlds   **92**
Saldaña, René
  Saldaña, R. Dancing with the devil and other tales from beyond   **Fic**
Saldana, Rene
  A good long way   **Fic**
SALEM (MASS.) -- DRAMA
  Miller, A. The crucible   **812**
SALEM (MASS.) -- FICTION
  Hearn, J. The minister's daughter   **Fic**
  Hemphill, S. Wicked girls   **Fic**
SALEM (MASS.) -- HISTORY
  Aronson, M. Witch-hunt: mysteries of the Salem witch trials   **133.4**
  Goss, K. D. The Salem witch trials   **133.4**
Salem Brownstone. Dunning, J. H. **741.5**
The **Salem** witch trials. Goss, K. D. **133.4**
SALEM WITCH TRIALS
  Howe, K. Conversion   **Fic**
SALES AGENTS *See* Sales personnel
SALES MANAGEMENT
    See also Management; Marketing; Selling
SALES PERSONNEL
  Mozer, M. Careers as a commissioned sales representative   **658.85**
SALES PERSONNEL
    See also Retail trade
Sales, Leila
  Mostly good girls   **Fic**
  Past perfect   **Fic**
  This song will save your life   **Fic**
  Tonight the streets are ours   **Fic**
SALESMEN *See* Sales personnel
SALESWOMEN *See* Sales personnel
Salieri, Antonio, 1750-1825
        About
  Shaffer, P. Peter Shaffer's Amadeus   **822**
Salinger, J. D.
  The catcher in the rye   **Fic**
  Nine stories   **S**
Salisbury, Graham
  Eyes of the emperor   **Fic**
Salisbury, Joyce E.
  (ed) The Greenwood encyclopedia of daily life **390**
  (ed) The Greenwood encyclopedia of global medieval life and culture   **940.1**
Salisbury, Melinda
  The Sin Eater's daughter   **Fic**
SALK VACCINE *See* Poliomyelitis vaccine
Salk, Jonas, 1914-1995
        About
  Hellman, H. Great feuds in medicine   **610**
  Kluger, J. Splendid solution: Jonas Salk and the

Sayed, Kashua
Let it be morning — **Fic**
SAYINGS *See* Epigrams; Proverbs; Quotations
Sayler, Mary Harwell
The encyclopedia of the muscle and skeletal systems and disorders — **616.7**
Sayrafiezadeh, Saïd

About
Sayrafiezadeh, S. When skateboards will be free 92
Scagell, Robin
Stargazing with binoculars — **523.8**
Scales, Pat R.
Books under fire — **016.098**
Protecting intellectual freedom in your school library — **025.2**
SCANDALS
See also History
SCANDINAVIA -- FICTION
Sedgwick, M. Midwinterblood — **S**
SCANDINAVIAN LANGUAGES
See also Language and languages
SCANDINAVIAN LITERATURE
See also Literature
SCANDINAVIAN MYTHOLOGY *See* Norse mythology
The **Scar** Boys. Vlahos, L. — **Fic**
SCARABS -- FICTION
Gleason, C. The clockwork scarab — **Fic**
SCARCITY
Peacock, K. W. Food security — **338.1**
Scarecrow studies in young adult literature [series]
Aronson, M. Exploding the myths — **028.5**
Campbell, P. J. Campbell's scoop — **809**
Cart, M. The heart has its reasons — **813**
Glenn, W. J. Laurie Halse Anderson — **92**
Hogan, W. Humor in young adult literature — **813**
Molin, P. F. American Indian themes in young adult literature — **810**
Reed, A. J. S. Norma Fox Mazer — **813**
Tyson, E. S. Orson Scott Card — **813**
SCARECROWS
See also Plant conservation
SCARIFICATION (BODY MARKING)
DeMello, M. Encyclopedia of body adornment 391
Scarlet. Meyer, M. — **Fic**
Scarlett undercover. Latham, J. — **Fic**
Scarpaci, Vincenza
The journey of the Italians in America — **305.8**
Scarrow, Alex
Day of the predator — **Fic**
Scdoris, Rachael

About
Scdoris, R. No end in sight — **92**
Scelsa, Kate
Fans of the impossible life — **Fic**

The **Scenebook** for actors. — **808.82**
SCENERY *See* Landscape protection; Natural monuments; Views; Wilderness areas
Scenes from classic plays, 468 B.C. to 1970 A.D. — **808.82**
The **scent** of desire. Herz, R. S. — **152.1**
Scerri, Eric R.
The periodic table — **546.8**
Schaaf, Fred
The 50 best sights in astronomy and how to see them — **520**
Schaap, Jeremy
Triumph — **92**
Schaap, Phil
Marsalis, W. Jazz A-B-Z — **781.65**
Schacter, Daniel L.
The seven sins of memory — **153.1**
Schaefer, Emmett Robert
Thompson, C. White men challenging racism — **323**
Schafer, Daniel L.
Anna Madgigine Jai Kingsley — **975.9**
Schaffner, Ingrid
The essential Vincent van Gogh — **759.9**
Schall, Lucy
Genre talks for teens — **028.5**
Schaller, George B.
A naturalist and other beasts — **508**
Schaller, Michael
Ronald Reagan — **92**
Schantz, Sarah Elizabeth
Fig — **Fic**
Scharf, Caleb
Gravity's engines — **523.8**
Schechter, Abraham A.
Basic book repair methods — **025.7**
Scheeder, Louis
All the words on stage — **822.3**
Scheeren, William O.
Technology for the school librarian — **025.04**
Scheeres, Julia, 1967-

About
Scheeres, J. Jesus land — **92**
Scheibe, Lindsey
Riptide — **Fic**
Scheidt, Erica Lorraine
Uses for boys — **Fic**
Schein, Elyse

About
Schein, E. Identical strangers — **92**
Schenwar, Maya
Locked down, locked out — **364.6**
Schiaparelli, Elsa, 1890-1973

About
Rubin, S. G. Hot pink — **92**
Schier, Helga
The causes of school violence — **371.7**

SCHOOL PLAYS *See* Children's plays; College and school drama

SCHOOL PRINCIPALS *See* School superintendents and principals

SCHOOL PSYCHOLOGISTS

    See also Psychologists

School reform and the school library media specialist. Hughes-Hassell, S. **027.8**

SCHOOL REPORTS

    See also Report writing

School shootings. Hunnicutt, S. **371.7**

SCHOOL SHOOTINGS

    Cullen, D. Columbine **364.152**

SCHOOL SHOOTINGS

    See also Crime; School violence

SCHOOL SHOOTINGS -- FICTION

    Hassan, M. Crash and Burn **Fic**

    Quick, M. Forgive me, Leonard Peacock **Fic**

SCHOOL SHOPS

    See also Technical education

School spirits. Hawkins, R. **Fic**

SCHOOL SPORTS

    D'Orso, M. Eagle blue **796.323**

    Kreidler, M. Four days to glory **796.8**

SCHOOL SPORTS

    See also Sports; Student activities

SCHOOL SPORTS -- CORRUPT PRACTICES

    Devine, E. Press play **Fic**

SCHOOL SPORTS -- FICTION

    Barwin, S. Hardball **Fic**

    Fichera, L. Hooked **Fic**

SCHOOL STORIES

    21 proms **S**

    Abdel-Fattah, R. Does my head look big in this? **Fic**

    Abdel-Fattah, R. Ten things I hate about me **Fic**

    Abrahams, P. Reality check **Fic**

    Abrams, A. Hollywood High **Fic**

    Acosta, M. Dark companion **Fic**

    Albertalli, B. Simon vs. the Homo Sapiens agenda **Fic**

    Alender, K. Bad girls don't die **Fic**

    Alexie, S. The absolutely true diary of a part-time Indian **Fic**

    Anderson, K. D. Kiss & Make Up **Fic**

    Anderson, L. H. Prom **Fic**

    Anderson, L. H. Speak **Fic**

    Anderson, L. H. Twisted **Fic**

    Anhalt, A. Freefall **Fic**

    Archer, J. Through her eyes **Fic**

    Ashby, A. Zombie queen of Newbury High **Fic**

    Asher, J. The future of us **Fic**

    Asher, J. Thirteen reasons why **Fic**

    Away we go **Fic**

    Ayarbe, H. Compulsion **Fic**

    Badoe, A. Between sisters **Fic**

    Baer, M. Frost **Fic**

Baldwin, K. A School for Unusual Girls **Fic**

Baratz-Logsted, L. Crazy beautiful **Fic**

Barnes, J. Tales of the Madman Underground **Fic**

Bauer, J. Peeled **Fic**

Beaudoin, S. You killed Wesley Payne **Fic**

Bennett Wealer, S. Rival **Fic**

Benoit, C. You **Fic**

Benway, R. Also known as **Fic**

Berk, J. The dark days of Hamburger Halpin **Fic**

Bigelow, L. J. Starting from here **Fic**

Bjorkman, L. Miss Fortune Cookie **Fic**

Bjorkman, L. My invented life **Fic**

Bloor, E. A plague year **Fic**

Bond, G. Fallout **Fic**

Boyd, M. Will **Fic**

Brande, R. Evolution, me, & other freaks of nature **Fic**

Budhos, M. Ask me no questions **Fic**

Calame, D. Beat the band **Fic**

Carriger, G. Etiquette & espionage **Fic**

Castellucci, C. Rose sees red **Fic**

Castle, J. You look different in real life **Fic**

Chaltas, T. Because I am furniture **Fic**

Charlton-Trujillo, e. E. Fat Angie **Fic**

Chbosky, S. The perks of being a wallflower **Fic**

Chow, C. Bitter melon **Fic**

Coben, H. Shelter **Fic**

Cohen, J. C. Leverage **Fic**

Cohen, T. Little black lies **Fic**

Cohn, R. Shrimp **Fic**

Colasanti, S. So much closer **Fic**

Colasanti, S. Something like fate **Fic**

Conaghan, B. When Mr. Dog bites **Fic**

Cook, E. The education of Hailey Kendrick **Fic**

Cormier, R. Beyond the chocolate war **Fic**

Cormier, R. The chocolate war **Fic**

Cornered **S**

Corrigan, E. Accomplice **Fic**

Corrigan, E. Ordinary ghosts **Fic**

Coy, J. Crackback **Fic**

Crutcher, C. Period 8 **Fic**

Crutcher, C. Running loose **Fic**

Cummings, P. Blindsided **Fic**

De Goldi, K. The 10 p.m. question **Fic**

De Lint, C. The blue girl **Fic**

Delsol, W. Frost **Fic**

Delsol, W. Stork **Fic**

Derting, K. Desires of the dead **Fic**

Dessen, S. What happened to goodbye **Fic**

Dessen, S. Just listen **Fic**

Deuker, C. Gym candy **Fic**

Deuker, C. Painting the black **Fic**

Devine, E. Press play **Fic**

Dinnison, K. You and me and him **Fic**

Dooley, S. Livvie Owen lived here **Fic**

Draper, S. M. The Battle of Jericho **Fic**

death	**Fic**	Russell, R. Dead rules	**Fic**
McDonald, A. The anti-prom	**Fic**	Saldana, R. A good long way	**Fic**
McKissack, F. Shooting star	**Fic**	Sales, L. Mostly good girls	**Fic**
McMann, L. Fade	**Fic**	Sanchez, A. Getting it	**Fic**
McMann, L. Wake	**Fic**	Sanchez, A. Rainbow boys	**Fic**
McNish, C. Angel	**Fic**	Sanchez, A. Rainbow High	**Fic**
McVoy, T. E. After the kiss	**Fic**	Scelsa, K. Fans of the impossible life	**Fic**
Medina, M. Yaqui Delgado wants to kick your ass	**Fic**	Schindler, H. A blue so dark	**Fic**
		Schneider, R. The beginning of everything	**Fic**
Meminger, N. Shine, coconut moon	**Fic**	Schumacher, J. Black box	**Fic**
Mesrobian, C. Cut both ways	**Fic**	Schutt, C. All souls	**Fic**
Mesrobian, C. Sex and violence	**Fic**	Scott, E. Love you hate you miss you	**Fic**
Meyer, S. Eclipse	**Fic**	Scott, K. Geek magnet	**Fic**
Meyer, S. New moon	**Fic**	Scott, K. She's so dead to us	**Fic**
Meyer, S. Twilight	**Fic**	Seigel, A. Like the red panda	**Fic**
Miller, K. How to lead a life of crime	**Fic**	Shepard, J. Project X	**Fic**
Miranda, M. Hysteria	**Fic**	Shulman, M. Scrawl	**Fic**
Monaghan, A. A girl named Digit	**Fic**	Skovron, J. Misfit	**Fic**
A monster calls	**Fic**	Smith, H. T. A Sense of the Infinite	**Fic**
Moore, C. The stalker chronicles	**Fic**	Sones, S. What my girlfriend doesn't know	**Fic**
Moriarty, J. The year of secret assignments	**Fic**	Southgate, M. The fall of Rome	**Fic**
Myers, W. D. Game	**Fic**	St. James, J. Freak show	**Fic**
Myers, W. D. A star is born	**Fic**	Standiford, N. The boy on the bridge	**Fic**
Myracle, L. Ttyl	**Fic**	Stand-off	**Fic**
Myracle, L. Bliss	**Fic**	Staunton, T. Acting up	**Fic**
Nayeri, D. Another Faust	**Fic**	Stevenson, S. J. The Latte Rebellion	**Fic**
Neely, C. Unearthly	**Fic**	Stiefvater, M. Ballad	**Fic**
Nothing	**Fic**	Strasser, T. Give a boy a gun	**Fic**
Oates, J. C. Two or three things I forgot to tell you	**Fic**	Strasser, T. Wish you were dead	**Fic**
		Summers, C. Some girls are	**Fic**
Oliver, L. Before I fall	**Fic**	Sutton, K. Some quiet place	**Fic**
Ostow, M. So punk rock (and other ways to disappoint your mother)	**Fic**	Sweeney, J. The guardian	**Fic**
		Takoudes, G. When we wuz famous	**Fic**
Perez, A. H. Out of darkness	**Fic**	Tamaki, J. SuperMutant Magic Academy	**741.5**
Phillips, W. Fishtailing	**811**	Tayleur, K. Chasing boys	**Fic**
Philpot, C. Even in paradise	**Fic**	Terry, C. L. Zero fade	**Fic**
Pike, A. Illusions	**Fic**	Tharp, T. Knights of the hill country	**Fic**
Places no one knows	**Fic**	Tharp, T. The spectacular now	**Fic**
Polonsky, A. Gracefully Grayson	**Fic**	Thomas, R. Rats saw God	**Fic**
Portes, A. Anatomy of a misfit	**Fic**	Van de Ruit, J. Spud	**Fic**
Prom nights from hell	**S**	Van Draanen, W. The running dream	**Fic**
Quick, M. Forgive me, Leonard Peacock	**Fic**	Vande Velde, V. Remembering Raquel	**Fic**
Raf, M. The symptoms of my insanity	**Fic**	Vaught, S. Big fat manifesto	**Fic**
Randall, T. Dreams of the dead	**Fic**	Violi, J. Putting makeup on dead people	**Fic**
Rennison, L. The taming of the tights	**Fic**	Vivian, S. Not that kind of girl	**Fic**
Rex, A. Fat vampire	**Fic**	Volponi, P. The hand you're dealt	**Fic**
Rice-Gonzalez, C. Chulito	**Fic**	Voorhees, C. The brothers Torres	**Fic**
Rich, S. Elliot Allagash	**Fic**	Wallace, J. Out of shadows	**Fic**
Richards, N. D. Six months later	**Fic**	Wallace, R. One good punch	**Fic**
Roecker, L. The Liar Society	**Fic**	Walters, E. In a flash	**Fic**
Roecker, L. The lies that bind	**Fic**	Waltman, K. Next	**Fic**
Roecker, L. The third lie's the charm	**Fic**	Waltman, K. Slump	**Fic**
Rowell, R. Eleanor & Park	**Fic**	Warman, J. Breathless	**Fic**
Rowell, R. Fangirl	**Fic**	Warman, J. Where the truth lies	**Fic**
Ruby, L. Bad apple	**Fic**	Wasserman, R. Hacking Harvard	**Fic**
Ruditis, P. The four Dorothys	**Fic**	Waters, D. Generation dead	**Fic**

Scribbling women. Jocelyn, M. **808.8**

The **Scribner** encyclopedia of American lives. **920.003**

Scribner library of modern Europe [series]

Europe 1789 to 1914 **940.2**

Europe since 1914 **940.5**

Scribner science reference series

Life sciences before the twentieth century **570**

Life sciences in the twentieth century **509**

The Renaissance and the scientific revolution **509**

Scribner turning points library [series]

Tobacco in history and culture **394.1**

Scrivener's moon. Reeve, P. **Fic**

SCUBA DIVING

See also Deep diving; Water sports

Sculpting basics. Hessenberg, K. **731.4**

SCULPTORS

Hartt, F. Michelangelo Buonarroti **759**

Hirst, M. Michelangelo and his drawings **709**

Khan, Y. S. Enlightening the world **974.7**

King, R. Brunelleschi's dome **726**

Kirk, J. Kingdom under glass **92**

Somervill, B. A. Michelangelo **92**

Spires, E. I heard God talking to me **811**

SCULPTORS

See also Artists

SCULPTORS -- FICTION

Arnold, E. K. Infandous **Fic**

SCULPTURE

See also Art; Decoration and ornament

SCULPTURE -- POETRY

Spires, E. I heard God talking to me **811**

SCULPTURE -- TECHNIQUE

Hessenberg, K. Sculpting basics **731.4**

SEA ANIMALS See Marine animals

SEA BED See Ocean bottom

SEA FISHERIES See Commercial fishing

SEA LEVEL

Fagan, B. The attacking ocean **551.45**

SEA LEVEL -- HISTORY

Fagan, B. The attacking ocean **551.45**

SEA LIFE See Marine biology; Navies; Sailors; Seafaring life

SEA LIONS

Miller, D. Seals & sea lions **599.79**

Sea monsters. Everhart, M. J. **567.9**

The **Sea** of Tranquility. Millay, K. **Fic**

SEA POETRY

See also Poetry

SEA POLLUTION See Marine pollution

SEA SHELLS See Shells

SEA STORIES

Adrift **Fic**

Crichton, M. Pirate latitudes **Fic**

The Girl from Everywhere **Fic**

Golden, C. The sea wolves **Fic**

Meyer, L. A. The wake of the Lorelei Lee **Fic**

SEA STORIES

See also Adventure and adventurers; Adventure fiction; Fiction

SEA STORIES -- GRAPHIC NOVELS

Weing, D. Set to sea **741.5**

Sea turtles. Spotila, J. R. **597.92**

SEA TURTLES

Spotila, J. R. Sea turtles **597.92**

SEA WATER

See also Water

SEA WATER AQUARIUMS See Marine aquariums

SEA WAVES See Ocean waves

The **sea** wolves. Golden, C. **Fic**

SEA-SHORE See Seashore

Seabiscuit. Hillenbrand, L. **798.4**

SEABISCUIT (RACE HORSE)

Hillenbrand, L. Seabiscuit **798.4**

SEAFARING LIFE

Lavery, B. The conquest of the ocean **910.4**

SEAFARING LIFE

See also Adventure and adventurers; Manners and customs; Voyages and travels

SEAFARING LIFE -- FICTION

Frazier, A. Everlasting **Fic**

Meyer, L. A. Bloody Jack **Fic**

Meyer, L. A. In the belly of The Bloodhound **Fic**

Meyer, L. A. The mark of the golden dragon **Fic**

Meyer, L. A. Rapture of the deep **Fic**

Meyer, L. A. Under the Jolly Roger **Fic**

Meyer, L. A. Viva Jacquelina! **Fic**

Meyer, L. A. The wake of the Lorelei Lee **Fic**

SEAFARING LIFE -- GRAPHIC NOVELS

Weing, D. Set to sea **741.5**

SEAFOOD

See also Food; Marine resources

Seals & sea lions. Miller, D. **599.79**

SEALS (ANIMALS)

Miller, D. Seals & sea lions **599.79**

Williams, T. M. The odyssey of KP2 **599.79**

SEALS (ANIMALS)

See also Mammals; Marine mammals

SEALS (NUMISMATICS)

Shearer, B. F. State names, seals, flags, and symbols **929.9**

SEALS (NUMISMATICS)

See also Heraldry; History; Inscriptions; Numismatics

Seamon, Hollis

Somebody up there hates you **Fic**

Sean Griswold's head. Leavitt, L. **Fic**

Search and destroy. Hughes, D. **Fic**

SEARCH AND RESCUE OPERATIONS See Rescue work

SHOPPING CENTERS AND MALLS
    See also Commercial buildings; Retail trade
Shopping for porcupine. Kantner, S.   **92**
Shorebirds of North America, Europe, and Asia.
Chandler, R. J.   **598**
The **short** bus. Mooney, J.   **92**
SHORT FILMS
    See also Motion pictures
A **Short** History of Film. Dixon, W. W.   **791.43**
A **short** history of nearly everything. Bryson,
B.   **500**
A **short** history of philosophy. Solomon, R. C. **109**
A **short** history of the honey bee. Readicker-Hen-
derson, E.   **638**
A **short** history of the Korean War. Stokesbury, J.
L.   **951.9**
A **short** history of World War I. Stokesbury, J.
L.   **940.3**
Short Oxford history of Europe [series]
  The eighteenth century   **940.2**
  The nineteenth century   **940.2**
SHORT PLAYS *See* One act plays
SHORT STORIES
  21 proms   S
  Alexie, S. Ten little Indians   **813**
  Alfred Hitchcock's mystery magazine presents fifty
    years of crime and suspense   S
  Almond, D. Half a creature from the sea   **823.92**
  Am I blue?   **813**
  Amnesty International Free?: stories about human
    rights   S
  Asimov, I. I, robot   S
  The beastly bride   S
  The Best American mystery stories of the century S
  Black, H. The poison eaters and other stories   S
  Block, F. L. The rose and the beast   S
  Bradbury, R. The illustrated man   S
  Bradbury, R. The Martian chronicles   S
  Card, O. S. First meetings in the Enderverse   S
  A Century of great Western stories   **813**
  Chekhov, A. P. The Russian master and other sto-
    ries   S
  Chopin, K. The awakening and selected stories   S
  Cisneros, S. Woman Hollering Creek and other sto-
    ries   S
  Clarke, A. C. The collected stories of Arthur C.
    Clarke   S
  Coming of age in America   **813**
  Cornered   S
  Cosmos latinos   S
  Crane, S. Prose and poetry   **813**
  Crutcher, C. Angry management   S
  Dahl, R. Skin and other stories   S
  Danticat, E. Krik? Krak!   S
  Defy the dark   S
  The Del Rey book of science fiction and fantasy   S

Dozois, G. R. Best of the best: 20 years of the
  Year's best science fiction   S
Enthralled   S
Face relations   S
Fear: 13 stories of suspense and horror   S
Firebirds rising   S
Firebirds soaring   S
First crossing   S
Flake, S. G. You don't even know me   **808.8**
Fleming, C. On the day I died   **Fic**
Geektastic   S
Great short works of Leo Tolstoy   S
Green, J. Let it snow   S
Growing up ethnic in America   **810**
Growing up Filipino II   S
Growing up Latino   **810**
The Hard SF renaissance   S
Hemingway, E. The complete short stories of Er-
  nest Hemingway   S
Henry, O. The best short stories of O. Henry   S
Horowitz, A. Bloody Horowitz   S
How beautiful the ordinary   S
Hughes, L. Short stories of Langston Hughes   S
Hurston, Z. N. The complete stories   S
Hurston, Z. N. Novels and stories   **813**
The improbable adventures of Sherlock Holmes   S
Jackson, S. The lottery   S
Joyce, J. Dubliners   **823**
Kafka, F. The metamorphosis and other stories   S
Kim, D. K. Same difference   **741.5**
King, S. Everything's eventual: 14 dark tales   S
King, S. Four past midnight   S
King, S. Night shift   S
King, S. Skeleton crew   S
Kipling, R. Collected stories   **823**
Kiss me deadly   S
Lanagan, M. Yellowcake   S
Le Guin, U. K. Tales from Earthsea   S
Legends: short novels by the masters of modern
  fantasy   S
Life on Mars: tales from the new frontier   S
Link, K. Pretty monsters   S
The Locus awards   S
Love is hell   S
Marston, E. Santa Claus in Baghdad and other sto-
  ries about teens in the Arab world   S
McKillip, P. A. Harrowing the dragon   S
McKinley, R. Water: tales of elemental spirits   S
Moccasin thunder   S
Monstrous affections   S
Myers, W. D. 145th Street   S
Myers, W. D. What they found   S
Na, A. No such thing as the real world   S
Nascimbene, Y. The creative collection of Ameri-
  can short stories   S
Nix, G. To Hold the Bridge   **Fic**

Coltelli, L. Winged words: American Indian writers speak **897**

SILKWORMS

See also Beneficial insects; Insects; Moths

Sillett, Steve

About

Preston, R. The wild trees **577.3**

The **Silmarillion.** Tolkien, J. R. R. **S**

Silver. Wooding, C. **Fic**

SILVER

See also Chemical elements; Precious metals

The **Silver** Blade. Gardner, S. **Fic**

The **silver** kiss. Klause, A. C. **Fic**

SILVER MINES AND MINING

See also Mines and mineral resources

Silver phoenix. Pon, C. **Fic**

Silver, Eve

Rush **Fic**

Silver, H. Ward

(ed) The ARRL handbook for radio communication **2014**

Silver, Linda R.

Best Jewish books for children and teens **011.6**

Silver, Marc

My parent has cancer and it really sucks **616.99**

Silver, Maya

(jt. auth) Silver, M. My parent has cancer and it really sucks **616.99**

Silvera, Adam

More happy than not **Fic**

Silverberg, Robert

(ed) Legends: short novels by the masters of modern fantasy **S**

Silverstein, Shel

Where the sidewalk ends **811**

Silvey, Anita

The plant hunters **580.75**

Silvey, Anita

500 great books for teens **028.5**

Silvey, Craig

Jasper Jones **Fic**

Simeon's story. Wright, S. **305.8**

Simmons, Bill

The book of basketball **796.323**

Simmons, Kristen

Article 5 **Fic**

Three **Fic**

Simner, Janni Lee

Faerie after **Fic**

Thief eyes **Fic**

Simon vs. the Homo Sapiens agenda. Albertalli, B. **Fic**

Simon, Beth

About

Simon, R. Riding the bus with my sister **92**

Simon, Lizzie

About

Simon, L. Detour **616**

Simon, Neil

Brighton Beach memoirs **812**

The collected plays of Neil Simon **812**

Lost in Yonkers **812**

Simon, Rachel

Riding the bus with my sister **92**

Simon, Rachel, 1959-

About

Simon, R. Riding the bus with my sister **92**

Simone, Ni-Ni

(jt. auth) Abrams, A. Hollywood High **Fic**

Upgrade U **Fic**

Simons, Daniel

(jt. auth) Chabris, C. The invisible gorilla **153.7**

Simons, Rae

Gender danger **362.88**

Simple courage. Delaney, F. **910.4**

SIMPLE MACHINES

See also Machinery; Mechanical movements; Mechanics

SIMPLICITY

See also Conduct of life

Simply modern jewelry. Fox, D. **745.594**

Simpson, Carol

Copyright for schools **346**

Simpson, Colton

About

Simpson, C. Inside the Crips **364**

Simpson, D. P.

Cassell's Latin dictionary **473**

Simpson, William Kelly

(ed) The Literature of ancient Egypt **890**

Sims, Guy A.

Monster **741.5**

Simukka, Salla

As Red As Blood **Fic**

SIMULTANEITY (PHYSICS)

Fluke **519.2**

SIN

Fisher, C. Darkwater **Fic**

SIN

See also Ethics; Good and evil; Theology

The **Sin** eater's confession. Bick, I. J. **Fic**

The **Sin** Eater's daughter. Salisbury, M. **Fic**

SINAI CAMPAIGN, 1956

See also Egypt -- History; Israel-Arab conflicts

Since you've been gone. Matson, M. **Fic**

Sinclair, Evelyn

Ruth, J. E. Women of the suffrage movement **324.6**

Sinclair, Upton, 1878-1968

Adaptations

Kuper, P. The jungle **741.5**

Upton Sinclair's The jungle **813**

The **song** of the Quarkbeast. Fforde, J.   **Fic**
Song of the sparrow. Sandell, L. A.   **Fic**
Songbird journeys. Chu, M.   **598**
SONGS
> *See also* Poetry; Vocal music

Songs from this Earth on turtle's back.   **811**
SONGS, AFRICAN AMERICAN *See* African American music
Songwriter's market. Hatfield, G.   **782.42**
SONGWRITERS
The Beatles anthology   **782.421**
Kaufman, W. Woody Guthrie, American radical **92**
Lewis, J. P. Black cat bone   **811**
McWilliams, J. C. The 1960s cultural revolution   **973.92**
O'Keefe, S. Spin   **92**
Partridge, E. John Lennon   **92**
Roberts, J. The Beatles   **781.66**
Spitz, B. Yeah! yeah! yeah!   **920**
Wald, E. Escaping the delta   **92**
We'll understand it better by and by   **782.25**
Wilkinson, A. The protest singer   **92**
SONGWRITERS *See* Composers; Lyricists
SONGWRITERS AND SONGWRITING
Weil, C. I'm glad I did   **Fic**
Sonneborn, Liz
Carey, C. W. African-American political leaders   **920.003**
The end of apartheid in South Africa   **968.06**
The environmental movement   **333.72**
Harriet Beecher Stowe   **92**
Mark Twain   **92**
A to Z of American Indian women   **920.003**
Sonnenblick, Jordan
Notes from the midnight driver   **Fic**
The **sonnets**.   **821**
The **sonnets**. Mussari, M.   **822.3**
The **sonnets**. Shakespeare, W.   **821**
SONNETS
> *See also* Poetry

The **sonnets**.   **822.3**
Sonnets from the Portuguese. Browning, E. B. **821**
SONS
> *See also* Family; Men

SONS AND FATHERS *See* Father-son relationship
SONS AND MOTHERS *See* Mother-son relationship
The **sons** of liberty. Lagos, A.   **741.5**
The **sons** of liberty 2. Lagos, A.   **741.5**
Sons of the 613. Rubens, M.   **Fic**
Soo-Warr, Lavinia
Self-defense for women   **613.66**
Soonchild.   **Fic**
SOOTHSAYING *See* Divination
Sophie Scholl and the white rose. Dumbach, A. E.   **943.086**

Sophocles' Oedipus rex.   **882**
Sophocles' Oedipus rex.   **882**
SOPORIFICS *See* Narcotics
SORCERY *See* Magic; Occultism; Witchcraft
Sorenson, Georgia Jones
(ed) Encyclopedia of leadership   **658.4**
Soria, Gabriel
Abel, J. Life sucks   **741.5**
Sorrells, Walter
First shot   **Fic**
Whiteout   **Fic**
Sorrentino, Paul
Student companion to Stephen Crane   **813**
SORROW *See* Bereavement; Grief; Joy and sorrow
Sorrow's knot. Bow, E.   **Fic**
Soto, Gary
Novio boy   **812**
Partly cloudy   **811**
Sotomayor, Sonia, 1954-
> #### About

Sotomayor, S. My beloved world   **347.73**
SOUL
Roach, M. Spook   **133.9**
SOUL
> *See also* Future life; Human beings (Theology); Philosophy

SOUL -- FICTION
Brockenbrough, M. Devine intervention   **Fic**
Damico, G. Croak   **Fic**
Soul enchilada. Gill, D. M.   **Fic**
SOUL MUSIC -- HISTORY AND CRITICISM
Mendelson, A. A. American R & B   **781.644**
The **soul** of baseball. Posnanski, J.   **796.357**
Soul thief. Oliver, J.   **Fic**
Soulprint. Miranda, M.   **Fic**
SOULS -- FICTION
Moulton, C. A. Angelfire   **Fic**
The **souls** of Black folk. Du Bois, W. E. B.   **305.8**
Sound.   **534**
SOUND
The Britannica guide to sound and light   **534**
Sound   **534**
SOUND
> *See also* Physics; Pneumatics; Radiation

SOUND BOOKS
> *See also* Picture books for children; Toy and movable books

SOUND EFFECTS
> *See also* Sound

The **sound** of letting go. Kehoe, S. W.   **Fic**
SOUND RECORDING INDUSTRY -- UNITED STATES
Pinkney, A. D. Rhythm ride   **781.644**
SOUND RECORDINGS
Crews, K. D. Copyright law for librarians and edu-

Multicultural Spanish dictionary **463**

SPANISH LANGUAGE -- FICTION

Jones, P. Bridge **Fic**

SPANISH LANGUAGE -- STUDY AND TEACH-ING

Cracking the SAT Spanish Subject Test **460**

SPANISH LANGUAGE MATERIALS -- BILIN-GUAL

Saldaña, R. Dancing with the devil and other tales from beyond **Fic**

SPANISH LITERATURE

See also Literature; Romance literature

Spanish-American war. Golay, M. **973.8**

SPANISH-AMERICAN WAR, 1898

Golay, M. Spanish-American war **973.8**

Roosevelt, T. The Rough Riders **973.8**

SPANISH-AMERICAN WAR, 1898

See also Spain -- History; United States -- History -- 1865-1898; United States -- History -- 1898-1919

Spanking Shakespeare. Wizner, J. **Fic**

Spark. Ryan, A. K. **Fic**

Sparks. Adams, S. J. **Fic**

Spawforth, Antony

(ed) The Oxford classical dictionary **938**

Speak. Anderson, L. H. **Fic**

Speak a word for freedom. Gann, M. **326.8**

Speak truth to power. Kennedy, K. **920**

Speaker for the Dead. Card, O. S. **Fic**

Speaker's corner [series]

Iraq uncensored **956.7**

Speaker-Yuan, Margaret

Philip Pullman **92**

SPEAKING *See* Debates and debating; Lectures and lecturing; Preaching; Public speaking; Rhetoric; Speech; Voice

Speaking Out. **306.76**

SPEAR FISHING

See also Fishing

Spears, Kat

Breakaway **Fic**

Sway **Fic**

Spears, Richard A.

McGraw-Hill's American idioms dictionary **427**

McGraw-Hill's dictionary of American slang and colloquial expressions **427**

SPECIAL COLLECTIONS IN LIBRARIES *See* Libraries -- Special collections

SPECIAL EDUCATION -- FICTION

King, A. S. Reality Boy **Fic**

SPECIAL FORCES (MILITARY SCIENCE) -- UNITED STATES -- HISTORY

Fredriksen, J. C. Fighting elites **356**

SPECIAL LIBRARIES

See also Libraries

SPECIAL OLYMPICS

See also Olympic games; Sports for people with disabilities

Special siblings. McHugh, M. **362.4**

Specials. Westerfeld, S. **Fic**

SPECIE *See* Coins

SPECIES EXTINCTION *See* Extinction (Biology)

SPECIMENS, PRESERVATION OF *See* Plants -- Collection and preservation; Taxidermy; Zoological specimens -- Collection and preservation

The **spectacular** now. Tharp, T. **Fic**

SPECTERS *See* Apparitions; Ghosts

SPECTRUM ANALYSIS

See also Astronomy; Astrophysics; Chemistry; Optics; Radiation

SPEECH DISORDERS -- FICTION

Fusco, K. N. Tending to Grace **Fic**

Wroblewski, D. The story of Edgar Sawtelle **Fic**

SPEECH, FREEDOM OF *See* Freedom of speech

SPEECHES

Lend me your ears **808.85**

The Penguin book of twentieth-century speeches **808.85**

Speeches in world history **808.85**

Words that ring through time **808.85**

SPEECHES

See also Literature

Speeches in world history. **808.85**

SPEECHES, ADDRESSES, ETC. *See* Speeches

SPEECHES, ADDRESSES, ETC., AMERICAN *See* American speeches

Speechless. Harrington, H. **Fic**

SPEED (DRUG) *See* Methamphetamine

SPEED READING

See also Reading

SPEED SKATERS -- UNITED STATES

Uschan, M. V. Apolo Anton Ohno **796.91**

Speight, James G.

Lange's handbook of chemistry **540**

SPELEOLOGY *See* Caves

Spellcaster. Gray, C. **Fic**

Spellenberg, Richard

Familiar flowers of North America: eastern region **582.13**

Familiar flowers of North America: western region **582.13**

National Audubon Society field guide to North American wildflowers, western region **582.13**

SPELLERS

See also English language -- Spelling

SPELLING

Mary Elizabeth (Mary Elizabeth Miller) Painless spelling **372**

SPELLING BEES

See also Language and languages

SPELLING REFORM

See also Spelling

Spells. Pike, A.   **Fic**

SPELLS *See* Charms; Magic

Spence, Graham

   (jt. auth) Anthony, L. Babylon's ark   **590.73**

   (jt. auth) Anthony, L. The elephant whisperer   **599.67**

Spencer, Herbert, 1820-1903

About

   Durant, W. J. The story of philosophy   **109**

Spencer, Kit

   Pro makeup   **646.7**

Spengemann, William C.

   (ed) Hawthorne, N. The portable Hawthorne   **818**

Sphinx's princess. Friesner, E. M.   **Fic**

Sphinx's queen. Friesner, E. M.   **Fic**

SPICES

   See also Food

Spider Woman's granddaughters.   **S**

SPIDER-MAN (FICTIONAL CHARACTER)

   See also Fictional characters; Superheroes

Spider-Man (Fictional character)

About

   Kakalios, J. The Physics of Superheroes   **530**

   Lee, S. Stan Lee's How to draw comics   **741.5**

Spiders. Kelly, L.   **595.4**

Spiders. Dalton, S.   **595.4**

SPIDERS

   Dalton, S. Spiders   **595.4**

   Dourlot, S. Insect museum   **595.7**

   Eisner, T. Secret weapons   **595.7**

   Evans, A. V. National Wildlife Federation field guide to insects and spiders & related species of North America   **595.7**

   Kelly, L. Spiders   **595.4**

   Milne, L. J. The Audubon Society field guide to North American insects and spiders   **595.7**

   Stewart, A. Wicked bugs   **632**

SPIDERS -- NORTH AMERICA -- IDENTIFICATION

   Common spiders of North America   **595.4**

Spiders in the hairdo. Holt, D.   **398.2**

Spiegelman, Art, 1948-

   Spiegelman, A. MetaMaus   **940.53**

   In the shadow of no towers   **973.931**

   Maus   **940.53**

About

   Spiegelman, A. MetaMaus   **940.53**

Spiegelman, Vladek

About

   Spiegelman, A. Maus   **940.53**

Spieler, Matthew

   (jt. auth) Clift, E. Selecting a president   **324.6**

SPIES

   Meyer, L. A. Viva Jacquelina!   **Fic**

   Murphy, J. The real Benedict Arnold   **92**

   Phelps, M. W. Nathan Hale   **92**

   Philipson, I. J. Ethel Rosenberg   **92**

   Preus, M. Shadow on the mountain   **Fic**

   Sheinkin, S. The notorious Benedict Arnold   **92**

SPIES -- FICTION

   Smith, L. Sekret   **Fic**

   Three years and eight months   **Fic**

   Zettel, S. Palace of Spies   **Fic**

SPIES -- FRANCE -- BIOGRAPHY

   Caravantes, P. The many faces of Josephine Baker   **92**

The **spies** of Mississippi. Bowers, R.   **323.1**

Spike, John T.

   (ed) Mason, A. A history of Western art   **709**

Spillebeen, Geert

   Kipling's choice   **Fic**

Spilsbury, Louise

   (ed) Industrialization and empire, 1783 to 1914   **330.9**

   (ed) World wars and globalization, 1914 to 2010   **909.82**

Spin. O'Keefe, S.   **92**

SPINAL MUSCULAR ATROPHY -- PATIENTS

   Burcaw, S. Laughing at my nightmare   **92**

Spink, Kathryn

   Mother Teresa   **92**

SPINOSAURUS

   See also Dinosaurs

Spinoza, Benedictus de, 1632-1677

About

   Durant, W. J. The story of philosophy   **109**

The **spiral** staircase. Armstrong, K.   **92**

SPIRES

   See also Architecture; Church architecture

Spires, Elizabeth

   I heard God talking to me   **811**

SPIRIT *See* Soul

The **spirit** catches you and you fall down. Fadiman, A.   **306.4**

The **spirit** of Yellowstone. Meyer, J. L.   **978.7**

Spirit's princess. Friesner, E.   **Fic**

SPIRITISM *See* Spiritualism

SPIRITS

   See also Supernatural

SPIRITS -- FICTION

   Block, F. L. Teen spirit   **Fic**

   Boone, M. Compulsion   **Fic**

   Nix, G. To Hold the Bridge   **Fic**

SPIRITUAL GIFTS

   Albin, G. Crewel   **Fic**

SPIRITUAL HEALING

   See also Medicine -- Religious aspects; Spiritual gifts

SPIRITUAL LIFE

   Campbell, J. The power of myth   **201**

   Chopra, D. Fire in the heart   **204**

SPIRITUAL WARFARE -- FICTION

Gaiman, N. American gods   **Fic**

SPIRITUALISM

   See also Occultism; Supernatural

SPIRITUALISM -- FICTION

Jackson, S. The haunting of Hill House   **Fic**

Weyn, S. Distant waves   **Fic**

Winters, C. In the shadow of blackbirds   **Fic**

Spitz, Bob

Yeah! yeah! yeah!   **920**

Splat! Walters, E.   **Fic**

Splendid solution: Jonas Salk and the conquest of polio. Kluger, J.   **92**

The **Splendid** table's how to eat supper. Splendid table (Radio program)   **641.5**

SPLICING *See* Knots and splices

SPLICING OF GENES *See* Genetic engineering

Split. Avasthi, S.   **Fic**

SPLIT PERSONALITY *See* Multiple personality

Split second. West, K.   **Fic**

SPLIT-PAGE BOOKS

   See also Picture books for children; Toy and movable books

SPOILS SYSTEM *See* Political corruption

SPOKANE (WASH.) -- FICTION

Harmon, M. Under the bridge   **Fic**

The **Spoken** word revolution.   **811**

Spook. Roach, M.   **133.9**

Spoon River anthology. Masters, E. L.   **811**

Sport in the American West [series]

Craft, J. Our white boy   **92**

Sporting [series]

Ezra, M. Muhammad Ali   **92**

SPORTING EQUIPMENT *See* Sporting goods

SPORTING GOODS

Chetwynd, J. The secret history of balls   **796.3**

Sports. Gifford, C.   **796**

SPORTS

Gifford, C. Sports   **796**

The Lincoln Library of Sports Champions **920.003**

Musiker, L. H. The smart girl's guide to sports **796**

Nike is a goddess   **796**

Popular mechanics (Periodical) Why a curveball curves   **796**

Real sports reporting   **070.4**

Sports & fitness   **613.7**

Sports illustrated 2011 almanac   **796**

SPORTS

   See also Play; Recreation

Sports & fitness.   **613.7**

SPORTS -- CORRUPT PRACTICES

Mooney, C. Thinking critically   **362.29**

SPORTS -- ENCYCLOPEDIAS

Encyclopedia of sports in America   **796**

SPORTS -- EQUIPMENT AND SUPPLIES *See* Sporting goods

SPORTS -- GRAPHIC NOVELS

Inoue, T. Real, volume 1   **741.5**

SPORTS -- GRAPHIC NOVELS

   See also Graphic novels

SPORTS -- HISTORY

Chetwynd, J. The secret history of balls   **796.3**

SPORTS -- MEDICAL ASPECTS *See* Sports medicine

SPORTS -- PHYSIOLOGICAL ASPECTS

Epstein, D. The sports gene   **613.7**

SPORTS -- STATISTICS

   See also Statistics

SPORTS AND DRUGS *See* Athletes -- Drug use

SPORTS BETTING

O'Connor, H. M. Betting Game   **Fic**

SPORTS BROADCASTING *See* Radio broadcasting of sports; Television broadcasting of sports

SPORTS CARDS

   See also Sports

SPORTS CARS

   See also Automobiles

SPORTS DRAMA (FILMS)

   See also Motion pictures

SPORTS FOR PEOPLE WITH DISABILITIES

   See also People with disabilities

SPORTS FOR WOMEN

Sokolove, M. Y. Warrior girls   **796**

SPORTS FOR WOMEN

   See also Sports

Sports fundamentals series

Dearing, J. Volleyball fundamentals   **796.325**

Engh, D. Archery fundamentals   **799.3**

The **sports** gene. Epstein, D.   **613.7**

SPORTS HANDICAPPING *See* Sports betting

Sports illustrated 2011 almanac.   **796**

SPORTS IN TELEVISION *See* Television broadcasting of sports

SPORTS INJURIES

Sports injuries information for teens   **617.1**

SPORTS INJURIES -- FICTION

Lynch, C. Hit count   **Fic**

Sports injuries information for teens.   **617.1**

SPORTS MEDICINE

Everyday sports injuries   **617.1**

Sokolove, M. Y. Warrior girls   **796**

SPORTS MEDICINE

   See also Medical care; Medicine

SPORTS MEDICINE -- UNITED STATES

Fainaru, S. League of Denial   **617.1**

SPORTS RECORDS

   See also Sports

SPORTS SCANDALS *See* Sports -- Corrupt practices

The **sports** scholarships insider's guide. Wheeler, D.   **796**

SPORTS TEAMS

   See also Sports

Steps to success in watercolor   **751.42**

Swenson, May
Nature   **811**

A **swift** pure cry. Dowd, S.   **Fic**

Swift, Jonathan, 1667-1745
About
Aykroyd, C. Savage satire   **92**

DeGategno, P. J. Critical companion to Jonathan Swift   **828**

Highet, G. The classical tradition   **809**

Jonathan Swift's Gulliver's travels   **823**

Swift, Richard
Gangs   **364.1**

Swift, Sally
Splendid table (Radio program) The Splendid table's how to eat supper   **641.5**

Swim that rock.   **Fic**

Swim the fly. Calame, D.   **Fic**

SWIMMING
Hines, E. W. Fitness swimming   **613.7**

Swimming with piranhas at feeding time. Conniff, R.   **590**

SWIMMING/FICTION
Calame, D. Swim the fly   **Fic**

SWINDLERS AND SWINDLING
See also Crime; Criminals

SWINDLERS AND SWINDLING -- FICTION
Bliss, B. No parking at the end times   **Fic**

SWINE *See* Pigs

SWINE INFLUENZA
Parks, P. J. Influenza   **616.2**

Swissler, Becky
Winning lacrosse for girls   **796.34**

Switek, Brian
My beloved Brontosaurus   **567.91**

Written in stone   **576.8**

SWITZERLAND -- FICTION
García, C. Dreams of significant girls   **Fic**

Swofford, Anthony
Jarhead: a Marine's chronicle of the Gulf War and other battles   **956.704**

Swoon at your own risk. Salter, S.   **Fic**

The **sword** of Shannara. Brooks, T.   **Fic**

The **sword** of straw. Hemingway, A.   **Fic**

SWORDS
See also Weapons

SWORDS -- HISTORY
Reinhardt, H. The book of swords   **623.4**

Sybil exposed. Nathan, D.   **616.85**

SYDNEY (N.S.W.) -- HISTORY -- 20TH CENTU-RY -- FICTION
Larbalestier, J. Razorhurst   **Fic**

Sykes, Judith A.
Conducting action research to evaluate your school library   **027.8**

SYLO. MacHale, D. J.   **Fic**

Sylvia Plath.   **811**

Sylvia Plath. Reiff, R. H.   **92**

Sylvia Plath's The bell jar.   **813**

SYMBIOSIS
See also Biology; Ecology

SYMBOLIC LOGIC
Edwards, A. W. F. Cogwheels of the mind   **511.3**

Paulos, J. A. Once upon a number   **519.5**

SYMBOLIC LOGIC
See also Logic; Mathematics

SYMBOLISM
See also Art; Mythology

SYMBOLISM -- FICTION
Morrison, T. Beloved   **Fic**

SYMBOLISM IN ART
How to read a painting   **753**

SYMBOLISM IN LITERATURE
Highet, G. The classical tradition   **809**

SYMBOLISM IN LITERATURE
See also Literature; Symbolism

SYMBOLS *See* Signs and symbols

SYMBOLS, MATHEMATICAL *See* Mathematical notation

SYMPATHY
See also Conduct of life; Emotions

SYMPHONIES *See* Symphony

The **symphony.** Steinberg, M.   **784.2**

SYMPHONY
Steinberg, M. The symphony   **784.2**

Symphony for the city of the dead. Anderson, M. T.   **92**

SYMPTOMS *See* Diagnosis

The **symptoms** of my insanity. Raf, M.   **Fic**

SYNAGOGUES
See also Buildings; Religious institutions; Temples

Synar, Mike
About
Profiles in courage for our time   **920**

SYNCHRONIZED SWIMMING
See also Swimming

SYNESTHESIA -- FICTION
Anderson, R. J. Ultraviolet   **Fic**

SYNTHETIC DRUGS
Parks, P. J. Bath salts and other synthetic drugs   **362.29**

SYNTHETIC DRUGS OF ABUSE *See* Designer drugs

SYNTHETIC FABRICS
See also Fabrics; Synthetic products

SYNTHETIC FUELS
See also Fuel; Synthetic products

SYNTHETIC RUBBER
See also Plastics; Synthetic products

SYPHILIS
Uschan, M. V. Forty years of medical racism **174.2**

The **translator.** Hari, D. **92**

TRANSLATORS

Fooling with words **808.1**

Zenatti, V. When I was a soldier **92**

TRANSMISSION OF POWER *See* Electric lines; Electric power distribution; Power transmission

TRANSMUTATION (CHEMISTRY)

See also Atoms; Nuclear physics; Radioactivity

TRANSPLANTATION *See* Transplantation of organs, tissues, etc.

TRANSPLANTATION OF ORGANS, TISSUES, ETC.

Animal experimentation: opposing viewpoints **179**

Biomedical ethics: opposing viewpoints **174.2**

Foran, R. Organ transplants **617.9**

Picoult, J. My sister's keeper **Fic**

TRANSPLANTATION OF ORGANS, TISSUES, ETC. -- ETHICAL ASPECTS

See also Bioethics

TRANSPLANTATION OF ORGANS, TISSUES, ETC. -- FICTION

Cabot, M. Airhead **Fic**

Cabot, M. Being Nikki **Fic**

Cabot, M. Runaway **Fic**

Whaley, J. C. Noggin **Fic**

Wolfson, J. Cold hands, warm heart **Fic**

Transue, Emily R.

About

Transue, E. R. On call **92**

TRANSYLVANIA (ROMANIA) -- HISTORY -- 15TH CENTURY -- FICTION

And I darken **Fic**

Trapp, Robert

Discovering the world through debate **808.53**

TRAPPERS

Kantner, S. Shopping for porcupine **92**

Trashed. Backderf, D. **741.5**

Traugh, Susan M.

Vegetarianism **613.262**

Traumatic brain injury. Goldsmith, C. **617.4**

TRAUMATIC BRAIN INJURY

See also Brain -- Wounds and injuries

TRAVEL -- FICTION

Greenberg, I. The encyclopedia of early earth **741.5**

Hubbard, K. Wanderlove **Fic**

Rabb, M. Kissing in America **Fic**

Shusterman, N. UnSouled **Fic**

TRAVEL BOOKS *See* Voyages and travels; Voyages around the world

Travel maps. Hollingum, B. **912**

TRAVEL TRAILERS AND CAMPERS

See also Camping; Recreational vehicles

TRAVEL WRITING

See also Authorship

A **traveler's** guide to Mars. Hartmann, W. K. **523.4**

TRAVELERS

Belliveau, D. In the footsteps of Marco Polo **915**

Dornstein, K. The boy who fell out of the sky **92**

TRAVELERS

See also Voyages and travels

TRAVELING SALES PERSONNEL *See* Sales personnel

Traveling the freedom road. Osborne, L. B. **973.7**

TRAVELS *See* Voyages and travels

The **travels** of Marco Polo. Polo, M. **915**

The **treachery** of beautiful things. Long, R. F. **Fic**

Treanor, Nick

(ed) The Vietnam War **959.704**

TREASON

See also Crime; Political crimes and offenses; Subversive activities

TREASURE HUNT (GAME) -- FICTION

Walker, K. 7clues to winning you **Fic**

The **treasure** map of boys. Lockhart, E. **Fic**

A treasury of Victorian murder [series]

Geary, R. The murder of Abraham Lincoln **973.7**

Treasury of XXth century murder [series]

Geary, R. The Lindbergh child **364.1**

Geary, R. The terrible Axe-Man of New Orleans **364.152**

TREATIES

See also Diplomacy; International law; International relations

Treaties with American Indians. **342**

The **Treaty** of Nanking. Abrams, D. **951**

The **Treaty** of Versailles. **940.3**

TREATY OF VERSAILLES (1919)

The Treaty of Versailles **940.3**

Trebing, Katie, 2002-

About

Whitehouse, B. The match **92**

TREE HOUSES

See also Buildings

The **Tree** is older than you are. **860**

TREE PLANTING

See also Forests and forestry

TREES

Dirr, M. A. Dirr's encyclopedia of trees and shrubs **635.9**

TREES

See also Plants

TREES -- NORTH AMERICA

Familiar trees of North America: eastern region **582.16**

Familiar trees of North America: western region **582.16**

Sibley, D. The Sibley guide to trees **582.16**

TREES -- UNITED STATES

Plotnik, A. The urban tree book **582.16**

Trefil, James

Space atlas **520**

Barnouw, D. The diary of Anne Frank: the critical edition **92**

Frank, A. The diary of a young girl: the definitive edition **92**

Keneally, T. Schindler's list **Fic**

WORLD WAR, 1939-1945 -- JEWS
See also Jews

WORLD WAR, 1939-1945 -- JEWS -- DRAMA
Goodrich, F. The diary of Anne Frank **812**

WORLD WAR, 1939-1945 -- JEWS -- GRAPHIC NOVELS
Jacobson, S. Anne Frank **92**

WORLD WAR, 1939-1945 -- JEWS -- RESCUE
Leyson, L. The boy on the wooden box **92**
Rappaport, D. Beyond courage **940.53**

WORLD WAR, 1939-1945 -- JOURNALISTS
See also Journalists

WORLD WAR, 1939-1945
Langley, A. World War II **940.53**
Preus, M. Shadow on the mountain **Fic**
Sandler, M. W. Imprisoned **940.53**

WORLD WAR, 1939-1945 -- LITERATURE AND THE WAR
See also Literature

WORLD WAR, 1939-1945 -- MANPOWER
See also World War, 1939-1945 -- Economic aspects

WORLD WAR, 1939-1945 -- MAPS
See also Maps

WORLD WAR, 1939-1945 -- MEDICAL CARE
Farrell, M. C. Pure grit **940.54**

WORLD WAR, 1939-1945 -- MEDICAL CARE
See also Medical care

WORLD WAR, 1939-1945 -- MISSING IN ACTION
See also Missing in action; World War, 1939-1945 -- Prisoners and prisons

WORLD WAR, 1939-1945 -- MOTION PICTURES AND THE WAR
See also Motion pictures; War films

WORLD WAR, 1939-1945 -- NATIVE AMERICANS
Holm, T. Code talkers and warriors **940.54**
Nez, C. Code talker **92**

WORLD WAR, 1939-1945 -- NAVAL OPERATIONS
Ballard, R. D. Graveyards of the Pacific **940.54**
Nelson, P. Left for dead **940.54**

WORLD WAR, 1939-1945 -- NETHERLANDS -- PERSONAL NARRATIVES
Prins, M. Hidden like Anne Frank **940.53**

WORLD WAR, 1939-1945 -- PARTICIPATION, AFRICAN AMERICAN
Myers, W. D. Invasion! **Fic**

WORLD WAR, 1939-1945 -- PERSONAL NARRATIVES

Altman, L. J. Hidden teens, hidden lives **940.53**
Competing voices from World War II in Europe **940.53**
The good war **940.54**
Megellas, J. All the way to Berlin **940.54**
Nez, C. Code talker **92**
Samuel, W. W. E. The war of our childhood **940.53**

WORLD WAR, 1939-1945 -- PERSONAL NARRATIVES
See also Autobiographies; Biography

WORLD WAR, 1939-1945 -- PERSONAL NARRATIVES, AMERICAN
McMullan, J. Leaving China **92**

WORLD WAR, 1939-1945 -- POETRY
See also Historical poetry; War poetry

WORLD WAR, 1939-1945 -- POLAND -- FICTION
Anna and the Swallow Man **Fic**

WORLD WAR, 1939-1945 -- PRISONERS AND PRISONS
Farrell, M. C. Pure grit **940.54**
Hillenbrand, L. Unbroken **92**

WORLD WAR, 1939-1945 -- PRISONERS AND PRISONS
See also Concentration camps; Prisoners of war; Prisons

WORLD WAR, 1939-1945 -- PRISONERS AND PRISONS, GERMAN
Deem, J. M. The prisoners of Breendonk **940.53**

WORLD WAR, 1939-1945 -- PRISONERS AND PRISONS, GERMAN -- FICTION
Wein, E. Rose under fire **Fic**

WORLD WAR, 1939-1945 -- REFUGEES -- FICTION
Deep sea **Fic**

WORLD WAR, 1939-1945 -- REPARATIONS
See also Reconstruction (1939-1951); World War, 1939-1945 -- Economic aspects

WORLD WAR, 1939-1945 -- RESISTANCE MOVEMENTS *See* World War, 1939-1945 -- Underground movements

WORLD WAR, 1939-1945 -- SECRET SERVICE
Code name Pauline **940.54**

WORLD WAR, 1939-1945 -- SECRET SERVICE -- FRANCE
Caravantes, P. The many faces of Josephine Baker **92**

WORLD WAR, 1939-1945 -- SECRET SERVICE -- GREAT BRITAIN
Code name Pauline **940.54**
Sheinkin, S. Bomb **623.4**

WORLD WAR, 1939-1945 -- SECRET SERVICE -- SOVIET UNION
Sheinkin, S. Bomb **623.4**

WORLD WAR, 1939-1945 -- SOURCES
Competing voices from World War II in Eu-